THE COMMON LAW LIBRARY

Clerk & Lindsell on Torts

VOLUMES IN THE COMMON LAW LIBRARY

Arlidge, Eady & Smith on Contempt
Benjamin's Sale of Goods
Bowstead & Reynolds on Agency
Bullen & Leake & Jacob's Precedents of Pleadings
Charlesworth & Percy on Negligence
Chitty on Contracts
Clerk & Lindsell on Torts
Gatley on Libel and Slander
Goff & Jones, The Law of Restitution
Jackson & Powell on Professional Negligence
McGregor on Damages
Phipson on Evidence

THE COMMON LAW LIBRARY

CLERK & LINDSELL ON TORTS

TWENTY-THIRD EDITION

SWEET & MAXWELL

THOMSON REUTERS

Published in 2020 by Thomson Reuters, trading as Sweet & Maxwell.
Thomson Reuters is registered in England & Wales, Company number 1679046.
Registered Office and address for Service: 5 Canada Square, Canary Wharf, London E14 5AQ.

For further information on our products and services, visit *http://www.sweetandmaxwell.co.uk*.

Computerset by Sweet & Maxwell.
Printed and bound by CPI Group (UK) Ltd, Croydon, CR0 4YY.
No natural forests were destroyed to make this product; only farmed timber was used and replanted.
A CIP catalogue record of this book is available from the British Library.

ISBN (print): 978-0-414-07820-8

ISBN (e-book): 978-0-414-07822-2

ISBN (print and e-book): 978-0-414-07821-5

GENERAL EDITOR

MICHAEL A. JONES, B.A., LL.M., Ph.D.
Solicitor; Emeritus Professor of Law, University of Liverpool

CONSULTANT EDITOR

ANTHONY M. DUGDALE, B.A., B.C.L.
Emeritus Professor, Keele University

EDITORS

RODERICK BAGSHAW, B.C.L., M.A. (OXON.)
Fellow of Magdalen College, and Associate Professor of Law, University of Oxford

RICHARD A. BUCKLEY, M.A., D.Phil., D.C.L.
Of Lincoln's Inn, Barrister; Emeritus Professor of Law, University of Reading

HAZEL F. CARTY, M.A.
Of the Middle Temple, Barrister; Honorary Lecturer in Law, University of Manchester

KORIEH DUODU, B.A.
Of Lincoln's Inn, Barrister

PAULA GILIKER, B.A., M.A., B.C.L., Ph.D.
Professor of Comparative Law, University of Bristol

GWILYM HARBOTTLE, B.A.
Of Lincoln's Inn, Barrister

BEN LONGSTAFF, B.A.
Of Gray's Inn, Barrister

FELICITY MCMAHON, LL.B., LL.M.
Of the Middle Temple, Barrister

JOHN MURPHY, LL.B., LL.M.
Professor of Common Law, University of Lancaster

JENNY STEELE, B.A., LL.M.
Solicitor; Professor of Law, University of York

ANDREW TETTENBORN, M.A., LL.B.
Of Lincoln's Inn, Barrister; Professor of Private and Commercial Law, University of Swansea

First Edition	(1889)	J. F. Clerk and W. H. B. Lindsell
Second Edition	(1896)	" " " "
Third Edition	(1904)	Wyatt Paine
Fourth Edition	(1906)	" " " "
Fifth Edition	(1909)	" " " "
Sixth Edition	(1912)	" " " "
Seventh Edition	(1921)	" " " "
Eighth Edition	(1929)	W. A. Macfarlane and G. W. Wrangham
Ninth Edition	(1937)	Under the General Editorship of Harold Potter
Tenth Edition	(1947)	" " " "
Eleventh Edition	(1954)	Under the General Editorship of John Burke and Peter Allsop
Twelfth Edition	(1961)	General Editor: A. L. Armitage
Thirteenth Edition	(1969)	" " " "
Fourteenth Edition	(1975)	General Editor: Sir Arthur L. Armitage and R. W. M. Dias
Fifteenth Edition	(1982)	General Editor: R. W. M. Dias
Sixteenth Edition	(1989)	" " " "
Seventeenth Edition	(1995)	General Editor: Margaret R. Brazier
Second Impression	(1996)	" " " "
Third Impression	(1998)	" " " "
Eighteenth Edition	(2000)	General Editor: Anthony M. Dugdale
Second Impression	(2003)	" " " "
Nineteenth Edition	(2006)	General Editors: Anthony M. Dugdale and Michael A. Jones
Twentieth Edition	(2010)	General Editor: Michael A. Jones
Twenty-First Edition	(2014)	" " " "
Twenty-Second Edition	(2018)	" " " "
Twenty-Third Edition	(2020)	" " " "

PUBLISHER'S NOTE

In order to keep this work up to date and thus maintain its value to readers, this book will be supported by annual Cumulative Supplements.

PREFACE

We are pleased to present the 23rd edition of *Clerk & Lindsell*, which has as ever been fully and comprehensively updated. There has been only one small structural change for this edition, namely the suppression of the old Chapter 7 on Foreign Torts (and the consequent renumbering of the following chapters). We took the view that this was a highly specialised topic involving the complexities of private international law rather than substantive tort principles; it was becoming increasingly difficult to do justice to it, and we concluded that practitioners would be better served by specialist texts (see in particular *Dicey, Morris & Collins on the Conflict of Laws*, 15th edn (London: Sweet & Maxwell, 2012).

The editorial team has seen a few changes. Our sincere thanks go to Mark Simpson who has relinquished the position of Associate Editor, and to Bob Simpson for all his work on the Economic Torts since 2003; we extend a warm welcome to Roderick Bagshaw, who has taken over the latter. Last, but by no means least, we would like to extend our congratulations to Andrew Burrows who has left us after more than 30 years, following his elevation to the Supreme Court. We wish him well in his important new role, and hope he will continue to find this book of use there.

There has been surprisingly little legislation directly impacting on tort claims: most significant has been the seemingly technical but practically very significant increase in the discount rate for calculating future loss in personal injury actions from minus 0.75% to minus 0.25%). The political fallout from Brexit may have been momentous; by contrast, however, the immediate legal effect of the UK's formal departure from the EU on 31 January 2020 has been remarkably muted. Even the end of the transitional period on 31 December is likely to see little seismic change, the intention being for much EU law to be carried over either unaltered, or with very slight amendments, as retained EU legislation. Where possible, we have tried to use the lawyers' crystal ball to flag any relevant potential changes; but for obvious reasons we cannot guarantee that what we say will be absolutely correct.

If Brexit dominated the headlines in 2018 and 2019, the Coronavirus outbreak turned a great deal of life upside-down in 2020. Emergency legislation (the Coronavirus Act 2020 and innumerable sets of statutory regulations) granted extensive powers to restrict civil liberties on a temporary basis; modified some parts of mental health and mental capacity legislation; granted powers relating to potentially infectious persons; and empowered authorities to issue sweeping directions relating to events, gatherings, activities and premises. The legislation has only tangential relevance to tort actions, however; and given the variability of the restrictions and their (hopefully) temporary nature, we determined not to feature it in the text.

New legislation may have been thin on the ground; but tort decisions most certainly have not, with well over 30 from the Supreme Court alone in the three years since the last edition. Examples include *Robinson v Chief Constable of West Yorkshire* and *Poole BC v GN*. Here the court restated the importance of the distinction between acts and "pure" omissions in the context of negligence claims, and glossed yet again the relationship between the *Caparo* "tripartite test" for the existence of a duty of care and the courts' traditionally cautious approach in maintaining a strictly incremental approach to novel negligence claims. There have been two moderately important cases on the *Hedley Byrne* duty in the context of negligent misrepresentation (*Steel v NRAM Ltd* and *Playboy Club London Ltd v Banca Nazionale Del Lavoro SpA*); and two slightly difficult decisions on the correct approach to "loss of a chance" claims against solicitors (*Perry v Raleys Solicitors* and *Edwards v Hugh James Ford Simey*). Another decision, *Marex v Sevilleja*, enormously and welcomely simplified the law on duties of care owed to company shareholders, a matter of large practical importance.

Darnley v Croydon Health Services NHS Trust has meanwhile notably extended the scope of medical negligence in the context of Accident and Emergency departments; and still in the field of injury law *Dryden v Johnson Matthey Plc* returned to the vexed question of the meaning of "damage" for the purpose of personal injury claims. Two decisions on vicarious liability, *WM Morrison Supermarkets plc v Various Claimants* and *Barclays Bank plc v Various Claimants*, cut back what some saw as the over-extension of the doctrine through manipulation of the "close connection" test. Meanwhile, *Vedanta Resources plc v Lungowe* dealt with the politically very important question of the potential liability of a parent company in relation to the activities of its subsidiaries.

As regards less mainstream areas, there have been no fewer than three significant defamation cases in the Supreme Court. *Lachaux v Independent Print Ltd* gave some fairly substantial teeth to the requirement introduced by the Defamation Act 2013 that a claimant have suffered "serious harm" to reputation; *Serafin v Malkiewicz* did some fine-tuning on the s.4 public interest defence; and *Stocker v Stocker*, dealing with defamatory meaning, went some way towards protecting those who used strong words on social media sites. On personal liberty *R. (on the application of Jalloh) v Home Secretary* dealt with the relationship between false imprisonment and the concept of deprivation of liberty within art.5 of ECHR; and *R. (on the application of Hemmati) v Home Secretary* cut back the cases in which detention could be visited with mere nominal damages on the basis that the detention would have been lawful had the state gone the right way about it. *JSC BTA Bank v Khrapunov* provides important guidance on what constitutes "unlawful means" for the purposes of the tort of conspiracy. On damages, *Morris-Garner v One Step (Support) Ltd* clarified the approach to damages under Lord Cairns' Act, limited the availability of "*Wrotham Park* damages", kept them firmly within the camp of compensatory damages, and as a finishing touch rechristened them "negotiating damages".

We have endeavoured to state the law as at late April 2020, though a fair number of amendments have been possible at proof stage to flag later developments.

The Editors

August 2020

TABLE OF CONTENTS

TABLE OF CASES

Greenwell v Prison Commissioners (1951) 101 L.J. 486 CC 13-60
Greenwich Millennium Village Ltd v Essex Services Group Plc (formerly Essex Electrical Group Ltd); sub nom. HS Environment Services Ltd v DG Robson Mechanical Services Ltd [2014] EWCA Civ 960; [2014] 1 W.L.R. 3517; 156 Con. L.R. 1; [2014] 3 E.G.L.R. 111 4-31
Greenwood Tileries Ltd v Clapson [1937] 1 All E.R. 765 19-93
Greenwood v Bennett [1973] Q.B. 195; [1972] 3 W.L.R. 691; [1972] 3 All E.R. 586; [1972] R.T.R. 535; (1972) 116 S.J. 762 CA (Civ Div) 16-96, 16-102, 16-103
Greenwood, Re (1855) 24 L.J.Q.B. 148 14-123
Greer v Alstons Engineering Sales & Services Ltd [2003] UKPC 46; (2003) 147 S.J.L.B. 783 PC (Trin) 16-113, 16-114
Greers v Pearman and Corder (1922) 39 R.P.C. 406 .... 22-12, 22-15
Gregg v Scott [2005] UKHL 2; [2005] 2 A.C. 176; [2005] 2 W.L.R. 268; [2005] 4 All E.R. 812; [2005] P.I.Q.R. P24; [2005] Lloyd's Rep. Med. 130; (2005) 82 B.M.L.R. 52; (2005) 149 S.J.L.B. 145 .... 1-46, 2-26, 2-30, 2-89, 2-92, 2-93, 2-96, 2-97, 2-98, 2-99, 7-24, 7-97, 9-113, 9-114, 27-18
Gregory v Brunswick (1844) 6 M. & G. 953 21-47
Gregory v Derby (1839) 8 C. & P. 749 15-17
Gregory v Hill (1799) 8 T.R. 299 29-09
Gregory v Kelly [1978] R.T.R. 426 QBD 3-125, 7-223
Gregory v Piper (1829) 9 B.C. 591 6-38
Gregory v Portsmouth City Council [2000] 1 A.C. 419; [2000] 2 W.L.R. 306; [2000] 1 All E.R. 560; (2000) 2 L.G.L.R. 667; [2000] B.L.G.R. 203; [2000] Po. L.R. 3; (2000) 97(6) L.S.G. 36; (2000) 150 N.L.J. 131; (2000) 144 S.J.L.B. 82 HL .. 15-01, 15-02, 15-06, 15-09, 15-12, 15-64, 15-66, 15-68, 15-74, 21-85, 22-17
Gregory v Shepherds (A Firm) [2000] Lloyd's Rep. P.N. 724; [2000] P.N.L.R. 769; (2001) 81 P. & C.R. 10; [2000] 3 E.G.L.R. 49; [2000] 50 E.G. 100; [2000] E.G. 78 (C.S.); (2000) 97(26) L.S.G. 39; (2000) 97(28) L.S.G. 32; [2000] N.P.C. 69 CA (Civ Div) 9-20, 9-118, 9-164
Gregory v Tarlo (1964) 108 S.J. 219 9-170
Greig v Insole; World Series Cricket Pty v Insole [1978] 1 W.L.R. 302; [1978] 3 All E.R. 449; (1978) 122 S.J. 162 Ch D 23-17, 23-28, 23-30, 23-57, 28-04
Greyvensteyn v Hattingh [1911] A.C. 355 PC (Cape) 3-159, 29-24
Grice v Stourport Tennis, Hockey and Squash Club [1997] 9 C.L. 592; [1997] C.L.Y. 3859 .. 5-88, 6-22, 11-13
Grieves v FT Everard & Sons Ltd; Quinn v George Clark & Nem Ltd; Mears v RG Carter Ltd; Jackson v Brock Plc; Rothwell v Chemical & Insulating Co Ltd; Downey v Charles Evans Shopfitters Ltd; Storey v Clellands Shipbuilders Ltd; Topping v Benchtown Ltd (formerly Jones Bros (Preston) Ltd); Johnston v NEI International Combustion Ltd; Hindson v Pipe House Wharf (Swansea) Ltd [2007] UKHL 39; [2008] 1 A.C. 281; [2007] 3 W.L.R. 876; [2007] 4 All E.R. 1047; [2007] I.C.R. 1745; [2008] P.I.Q.R. P6; [2008] LS Law Medical 1; (2008) 99 B.M.L.R. 139; (2007) 104(42) L.S.G. 34; (2007) 157 N.L.J. 1542; (2007) 151 S.J.L.B. 1366 .... 1-29, 1-32, 2-68, 2-96, 7-05, 7-24, 7-97, 10-19, 12-04, 12-05, 12-37, 27-57
Griffin v Clwyd HA [2001] EWCA Civ 818; [2001] P.I.Q.R. P31 31-44
Griffin v Coleman (1859) 4 H. & N. 265 14-29
Griffin v Mersey Regional Ambulance Service [1998] P.I.Q.R. P34 CA (Civ Div) 3-89, 3-147, 7-165, 7-184, 7-212
Griffin v South West Water Services Ltd [1995] I.R.L.R. 15 Ch D 23-89
Griffin v UHY Hacker Young & Partners (A Firm) [2010] EWHC 146 (Ch); [2010] P.N.L.R. 20 .... 3-31, 9-15, 9-233
Griffin v US 500 F.2d 1059 (1974) 10-16
Griffith v Richard Clay & Sons Ltd [1912] 2 Ch. 291 CA 19-152, 27-133
Griffiths v Arch Engineering Co (Newport) Ltd [1968] 3 All E.R. 217 Assizes 10-38
Griffiths v British Coal Corp [2001] EWCA Civ 336; [2001] 1 W.L.R. 1493; [2001] P.I.Q.R. Q11; (2001) 60 B.M.L.R. 188 27-41
Griffiths v Brown; Griffiths v Lindsay [1999] P.I.Q.R. P131 QBD 3-89, 7-59
Griffiths v Chief Constable of Suffolk [2018] EWHC 2538 (QB); [2019] Med. L.R. 1; (2019) 168 B.M.L.R. 166 13-91
Griffiths v Commonwealth (1985) 72 F.L.R. 260 2-105
Griffiths v Earl of Dudley (1881-82) L.R. 9 Q.B.D. 357 QBD 27-90
Griffiths v Evans [1953] 1 W.L.R. 1424; [1953] 2 All E.R. 1364; (1953) 97 S.J. 812 CA 9-146
Griffiths v Gwynedd CC [2015] EWCA Civ 1440; [2016] R.T.R. 15 7-218

Khan v Commissioner of Police of the Metropolis [2008] EWCA Civ 723; (2008) 152(23) S.J.L.B. 31 18-35
Khan v Hussain [2019] CSOH 11; 2019 S.C. 322; 2019 S.L.T. 319; [2019] P.N.L.R. 14 .... 3-20, 3-31, 9-15
Khan v Meadows; sub nom. Khan v MNX, Meadows v Khan [2019] EWCA Civ 152; [2019] 4 W.L.R. 3; [2019] 4 W.L.R. 26; [2019] 2 All E.R. 607; [2019] P.I.Q.R. Q3; (2019) 167 B.M.L.R. 62 .... 2-139, 9-97, 9-115, 27-63
Khan v RM Falvey & Co; sub nom. Khan v Falvey [2002] EWCA Civ 400; [2002] Lloyd's Rep. P.N. 369; [2002] P.N.L.R. 28; (2002) 99(19) L.S.G. 30; (2002) 146 S.J.L.B. 108 9-168
Khashoggi v IPC Magazines Ltd [1986] 1 W.L.R. 1412; [1986] 3 All E.R. 577; (1986) 83 L.S.G. 3598; (1986) 136 N.L.J. 1111; (1986) 130 S.J. 862 CA (Civ Div) 21-77, 28-27
Khawam v Chellaram & Sons (Nig). *See* John Khalil Khawam & Co (t/a John Khalil Khawam) v K Chellaram & Sons (Nig) 24-145
Khodaparast v Shad [2000] 1 W.L.R. 618; [2000] 1 All E.R. 545; [2000] E.M.L.R. 265 CA (Civ Div) 15-09, 22-16, 22-17
Khorasandjian v Bush [1993] Q.B. 727; [1993] 3 W.L.R. 476; [1993] 3 All E.R. 669; [1993] 2 F.L.R. 66; (1993) 25 H.L.R. 392; [1993] Fam. Law 679; (1993) 137 S.J.L.B. 88 CA (Civ Div) 1-36, 14-18, 19-24, 19-63, 19-182, 23-74
Khuja v Times Newspapers Ltd. *See* PNM v Times Newspapers Ltd 26-49
Khyatt v Morgan [1962] N.Z.L.R. 791 19-85
Kiam v MGN Ltd [2002] EWCA Civ 43; [2003] Q.B. 281; [2002] 3 W.L.R. 1036; [2002] 2 All E.R. 219; [2002] E.M.L.R. 25; (2002) 99(11) L.S.G. 35 27-152
Kiam v Neil (No.2) [1996] E.M.L.R. 493 CA (Civ Div) 21-41
Kiddle v City Business Properties Ltd [1942] 1 K.B. 269 KBD 19-135, 19-137
Kidgill v Moor (1850) 9 C.B. 364 19-65
Kilgollan v William Cooke & Co [1956] 1 W.L.R. 527; [1956] 2 All E.R. 294; (1956) 100 S.J. 359 CA 12-58
Kilinc v Turkey (Application No 40145/98) unreported 7 June 2005 ECtHR 9-90
Killick v PricewaterhouseCoopers (No.1) [2001] 1 B.C.L.C. 65; [2001] Lloyd's Rep. P.N. 17; [2001] P.N.L.R. 1; [2001] W.T.L.R. 699 Ch D 3-142, 7-138, 9-41, 9-226
Kim v Oh [2013] NZHC 925; [2013] 2 N.Z.L.R. 825 9-151
Kimathi v Foreign and Commonwealth Office [2018] EWHC 1169 (QB) 31-24
Kimber v Press Association Ltd [1893] 1 Q.B. 65 CA 21-86, 21-131
Kimberly Clark Worldwide Inc v Procter & Gamble Ltd (No.1) [2000] F.S.R. 235; [2000] R.P.C. 422; (1999) 96(47) L.S.G. 32; (2000) 144 S.J.L.B. 9 CA (Civ Div) 24-137
Kimberly-Clark Ltd v Fort Sterling Ltd; sub nom. Kimberley Clark Ltd v Fort Sterling Ltd [1997] F.S.R. 877; (1997) 20(7) I.P.D. 20066 Ch D 25-17
Kinaston v Moor (1627) Cro. Car. 89 16-37
Kinch v Rosling [2009] EWHC 286 (QB) 17-49
Kine v Jolly. *See* Jolly v Kine 19-02, 19-147, 27-133
Kine v Sewell 150 E.R. 1157; (1838) 3 M. & W. 297 Ex Ct 21-115
King Features Syndicate Inc v O&M Kleeman Ltd [1941] A.C. 417; [1941] 2 All E.R. 403 HL 24-37
King v Bristow Helicopters Ltd; Morris v KLM Royal Dutch Airlines; sub nom. Hammond v Bristow Helicopters Ltd [2002] UKHL 7; [2002] 2 A.C. 628; [2002] 2 W.L.R. 578; [2002] 2 All E.R. 565; [2002] 1 All E.R. (Comm) 385; [2002] 1 Lloyd's Rep. 745; 2002 S.C. (H.L.) 59; 2002 S.L.T. 378; 2002 S.C.L.R. 499; [2002] C.L.C. 820; [2002] P.I.Q.R. P29; (2002) 99(13) L.S.G. 25; (2002) 146 S.J.L.B. 61; 2002 G.W.D. 9-274 7-223
King v Cole (1796) 6 T.R. 640 15-17
King v David Allen & Sons Billposting Ltd [1916] 2 A.C. 54 HL (UK-Irl) 18-57
King v Gardner (1980) 71 Cr. App. R. 13 DC 14-84
King v Gross (2008) 443 A.R. 214 .... 16-109, 16-111, 16-140
King v Grundon [2012] EWHC 2719 (QB) 21-241
King v Henderson [1898] A.C. 720 PC (Aus) 15-44
King v Hoare (1844) 13 M. & W. 494 30-14
King v Lewis; sub nom. Lewis v King [2004] EWCA Civ 1329; [2005] I.L.Pr. 16; [2005] E.M.L.R. 4; (2004) 148 S.J.L.B. 1248 21-05
King v Liverpool City Council [1986] 1 W.L.R. 890; [1986] 3 All E.R. 544; (1986) 18 H.L.R. 307; 84 L.G.R. 871; [1986] 1 E.G.L.R. 181; (1986) 278 E.G. 278; (1986) 83 L.S.G. 2492; (1986) 136 N.L.J. 334; (1986) 130 S.J. 505 CA (Civ Div) 7-68, 19-94
King v Patterson (1887) 83 L.T.J. 408 21-115

Moores v Sunbeam Products, Inc 425 F.Supp.2d 151 (Me 2003) 10-56

TABLE OF STATUTES

TABLE OF STATUTORY INSTRUMENTS

TABLE OF CIVIL PROCEDURE RULES

TABLE OF RULES OF THE SUPREME COURT

TABLE OF EUROPEAN SECONDARY LEGISLATION

REGULATIONS

DIRECTIVES

TABLE OF INTERNATIONAL TREATIES AND CONVENTIONS

CHAPTER 1

PRINCIPLES OF LIABILITY IN TORT

TABLE OF CONTENTS

Introduction This chapter has three functions. It considers the nature of tort liability and its relationship with other overlapping areas of substantive law. It considers the functions of tort law and the basis on which it develops with particular reference to the role of legislation and the balance between judicial and legislative tort law. It explains the framework of tort liability: the interests protected, the conduct sanctioned and the impact of the Human Rights Act. The aim is to enable any particular liability issue to be seen in the wider framework of liability and not just in relation to one particular tort, and to enable the user to navigate around the concepts of tort law. **1-01**

1. THE NATURE OF TORT LIABILITY

Civil wrong Torts are civil wrongs and according to Professor Birks[1] they are best viewed as "a distinct category of obligation-creating event within the fourfold classification of such events", the other categories being contracts, unjust enrichments and other events such as income generation giving rise to tax liability. What distinguishes civil wrongs is that, whilst in the other categories the nature of the **1-02**

[1] Birks, "The Concept of a Civil Wrong" in Owen (ed.), *Philosophical Foundations of Tort Law* (1995), p.51. See also Birks "Definition and Division" in Birks (ed.), *The Classification of Obligations* (1997).

causative event giving rise to the obligation also dictates the nature of the remedy,[2] wrongs "themselves dictate no fixed measure of response". Thus, a civil wrong can be defined simply as a "breach of a legal duty which affects the interests of an individual to a degree which the law regards as sufficient to allow that individual to complain on his or her own account rather than as a representative of society as a whole". As Birks notes, because this concept of a civil wrong is "broad and abstract, its explanatory power is weak". To explain why conduct should be regarded as a breach of such a duty, one has to consider "the policies and values underlying the recognition of the primary duty in question. It is there that economic efficiency has to contest the field with liberal autonomy and moral paternalism, for the primary duties lie on the frontiers of law, politics and philosophy." Rather than providing ready-made definitional answers to questions concerning the scope of the law of civil wrong, this approach provides a basis for understanding the nature of tortious liability and its relationship with other areas of law.

1-03 **Tort and contract** Winfield's classic definition of tort[3] focused on two key issues in distinguishing tort from contract. First, tortious duties are primarily fixed by law; contractual duties are based on the consent of the parties and the content of the duties are settled between those parties. Put slightly differently, contract is concerned with voluntary obligations and tort with involuntary obligations.[4] Secondly, tortious duties are owed to persons generally (in rem) whereas contractual duties are undertaken towards a specific person or persons (in personam). Winfield's distinction holds good for some torts: the duty not to commit a trespass is clearly imposed and defined by law, exists independently of the will of the parties, and is owed to all fellow members of society. But for the key tort of negligence it is problematic. The will of the defendant in undertaking, whether expressly or implicitly, responsibility for certain conduct may be crucial to the existence of a negligence duty.[5] That duty may be owed only to a specific individual or group, and not to persons generally.[6] Birks' broader approach to the concept of civil wrong recognises the conceptual overlap. He treats contract as distinct from tort only to the extent that the remedies may provide for enforcement of the primary obligation, the promise, for example by specific performance.[7] Burrows[8] similarly stresses the remedial distinction, contrasting the function of contract in fulfilling "the expectations engendered by a binding promise" which involves protecting the claimant's expectation interest by putting him "into as good a position as if the contract had been performed" with that of tort in compensating the claimant for

---

2 Thus, unjust enrichment dictates restitution, income results in taxation, and contracts may be enforced. Birks notes that to the extent that the law approaches contract through awarding compensation for the wrong of breach of contract, it "(i)n effect adds breach of contractual duty to the list of torts".

3 "Tortious liability arises from the breach of a duty primarily fixed by the law; such duty is towards persons generally and its breach is redressible by an action for unliquidated damages." Winfield, *Province of the Law of Tort* (1931), p.32.

4 See Atiyah, *The Rise and Fall of Freedom of Contract* (1979), p.408.

5 See the development of duties in relation to omissions and economic loss: paras 7-51 and 7-103.

6 *Caparo Industries Plc v Dickman* [1990] 2 A.C. 205, per Lord Bridge at 621; at 638, per Lord Oliver.

7 To the extent that it focuses on the secondary obligation to pay damages in respect of a breach, he regards the law as in effect adding "breach of contractual duty to the list of torts". Birks, "The Concept of a Civil Wrong" in Owen (ed.), *Philosophical Foundations of Tort Law* (1995), p.51.

8 Burrows, *Understanding the Law of Obligations* (1998), Ch.1.

"wrongful interference"[9] which involves protecting the claimant's status quo interest by putting him "into as good a position as if no wrong had occurred".[10] The justification for the distinction is that tort liability is imposed and hence, liability for failure to benefit would "represent too great an infringement of individual liberty", whereas there is no such objection to such liability where its basis is a voluntarily assumed obligation by which the defendant has chosen to restrict his freedom. Burrows argues that the distinction between voluntary and imposed obligations explains other differences, for example, punitive and restitutionary damages may be awarded for torts where liability is imposed, but not for contract where the obligation was voluntarily undertaken and should give rise to remedies which compensate rather than punish.

Secondary consequences In addition to the distinction relating to the measure and type of damages available, there are other *secondary* consequences of classifying an action as one in contract or tort. These will be analysed in the appropriate sections of this work. They include the following. There are persons, for example minors, who may be made liable in tort but are not liable in contract.[11] A different range of remedies, for example specific performance, rescission and rectification, are available in contract. The classic remedy in tort remains an award of unliquidated damages, though injunctions are regularly used, and in torts relating to intellectual property remedies such as an account of profits may be sought. Aside from the measure of damages, the most important consequences of distinctions between contract and tort now lie in the rules relating to limitation[12] and contributory negligence.[13] **1-04**

Interaction of tort and contract Principles of tort and contract interact in two situations. The first is where there is a contractual relationship between claimant and defendant but the claimant wishes to sue in tort in order to escape the narrower limitation principles in contract or to be able to make a claim going beyond what was agreed in the contract. In this situation, the courts will allow concurrent liability provided there is nothing in the contract which expressly or impliedly excludes liability in tort.[14] The second situation is where there is no contractual relationship between claimant and defendant but the damage arises out of the defendant's wrongful performance of a contract to which the claimant is not a party. Here, the doctrine of privity precludes a contractual action and the law of tort has **1-05**

---

[9] In an earlier article published in (1983) 99 L.Q.R. 217, Burrows had seen the function of tort as compensating wrongful harm. The switch to "wrongful interference" reflects the fact that wrongful harm could include that caused by breach of contract, and the fact that interference "neatly encapsulates the idea that in most areas of tort the defendant was a stranger to the [claimant] and the [claimant's] entitlement was for the defendant to remain a stranger rather than wrongly coming into contact with the [claimant]". Burrows, *Understanding the Law of Obligations* (1998), p.10.

[10] As Burrows notes, this argument is close to Stapleton's thesis that "the measure of damages in contract differs from that in tort in that the former is an 'entitled result' measure whereas the latter is a 'normal expectancies' measure". See, Stapleton "A New 'Seascape' for Obligations" in Birks (ed.), *The Classification of Obligations* (1997), pp.193–231; and also "The Normal Expectancies Measure in Tort Damages" (1997) 113 L.Q.R. 257.

[11] See para.5-54.

[12] See para.31-17.

[13] See para.3-76.

[14] See paras 7-128 to 7-133.

filled the gap by providing an action.[15] In the case of physical damage to the claimant, negligence liability has been imposed under the principle in *Donoghue v Stevenson*[16] and semi-strict liability has been imposed under the Consumer Protection Act 1987[17] and the Defective Premises Act 1972.[18] In the case of economic loss, there is more controversy concerning the extent to which tort should play a gap-filling role.

1-06 **Tort and equitable wrongs** The primary distinction between an action in tort and a claim for breach of trust is twofold according to Winfield.[19] The duty in the case of a trust is inevitably in personam, and not to persons generally, and compensation for breach of trust is assessed by reference to the loss to the trust property. It does not result in an award of unliquidated damages. While in certain contexts duties in tort may now be in personam and equitable remedies are available in tort, Winfield's definition continues to hold good in delimiting the ambit of trust. Claims in tort and for breach of trust may overlap where there has been a negligent or fraudulent breach of trust. In *Target Holdings Ltd v Redferns*[20] a claim for breach of trust in order to seek restoration of the trust property was made in a situation where it might not have been able to establish fraud against the defendant and a negligence claim might have failed on grounds of causation. In *Paragon Finance v Thakerar & Co (A Firm)*[21] breach of trust was claimed in order to take advantage of the statutory provision[22] that no period of limitation applies to a claim to recover trust property. In neither case was the tactic successful[23] and the courts are likely to be wary of allowing common law principles to be undermined by an inappropriate use of trust concepts.[24] The equitable wrongs of breach of fiduciary duty and breach of confidence are analogous to torts but differ in that their historical roots lie in the Court of Chancery rather than the common law courts. The main remedy for these wrongs is that of "equitable compensation" which seeks to put the claimant in as good a position as if no wrong had occurred. As Burrows has noted, the case law has been moving in the direction of removing distinctions between this remedy and compensatory damages for tort.[25] Birks has suggested that equitable wrongs should be considered alongside torts[26] and although, arguably, they cannot

15 The Contracts (Rights of Third Parties) Act 1999 now also modifies the privity principle: see para.3-145.

16 [1932] A.C. 562. See further para.7-15.

17 See para.10-45 onwards.

18 See para.11-85 onwards.

19 Winfield, *Province of the Law of Tort* (1931), Ch.6.

20 [1996] A.C. 421.

21 [1999] 1 All E.R. 400.

22 Limitation Act 1980 s.21.

23 In *Target* the House of Lords found that the loss was not attributable to the breach of trust, and in *Paragon* the Court of Appeal held there to be an arguable limitation defence in relation to constructive as opposed to express trusts on the ground that "any principled system of limitation should be based on the cause of action and not the remedy … [and] there is no case for distinguishing between an action for damages for fraud and its counterpart in equity merely because equity employs the formula of constructive trust to justify the exercise of the equitable jurisdiction": [1999] 1 All E.R. 400 at 414, per Millett LJ.

24 See the extra-judicial views of Millett LJ in "Equity's Place in the Law of Commerce" (1998) 114 L.Q.R. 214; and "Restitution and Constructive Trusts" 114 (1998) L.Q.R. 399.

25 See Burrows, *Understanding the Law of Obligations* (1998), p.14; referring to *Target Holdings Ltd v Redferns* [1996] A.C. 421; and *Swindle v Harrison* [1997] 4 All E.R. 705.

26 "Definition and Division" in Birks (ed.), *The Classification of Obligations* (1997).

be regarded as torts,[27] this work includes sections on both breach of fiduciary duty[28] and breach of confidence.[29]

Tort and restitution The development of the law of restitution is of enormous importance and a restitutionary claim may, on occasion, offer a more favourable remedy than that available in tort. Tort and restitution originally met in the doctrine of "waiver of tort". The claimant was deemed to have elected to forgo his remedy in tort in order to recover the moneys unlawfully accrued by the defendant. But as Burrows comments, waiver of tort is an inapt phrase[30] as the claimant is not forgoing his right to sue on the tort but rather, electing to pursue a restitutionary remedy for the tortious wrong rather than normal tortious damages. Restitution in this context[31] is concerned with liability to restore to the claimant what the defendant has gained as a result of the wrongdoing. Where the defendant's gain is more than the claimant's loss, the claimant may benefit from claiming restitutionary rather than tortious damages. The case law concerns the torts of trespass to land, wrongful interference with goods and nuisance. In addition the restitutionary remedy of account of profits is available for torts protecting intellectual property rights. 1-07

Tort and public law The extent to which the law of torts does and should operate to hold public authorities accountable for their dealings with private citizens is problematic. Public authorities enjoy no general immunity in tort nor are they subject to any separate system of law akin to *droit administratif* in France. A claimant injured by a negligently driven dustcart operated by a local authority, or injured in a medical accident in a NHS hospital, or libelled by a government official enjoys a remedy identical to that he could pursue were the defendant a purely private person. The difficulty arises where the alleged tortious conduct arises out of a public authority's conduct of its public obligations and the exercise of the statutory powers enjoyed to fulfil those obligations. Should public authorities be liable in tort for poor government, be it inadequate education for local children, inept inspection of building works or inequitable distribution of healthcare resources? Claims for breach of statutory duty have generally failed. Albeit local councils, prison governors and other public bodies may have been granted powers expressly designed to safeguard the welfare of those in their care, the judges have held that Parliament had no intention that a private right to claim compensation should ensue from such duties imposed on the relevant authorities. Claims based in negligence used to be rejected on the ground that no duty of care could be owed unless the authority had acted ultra vires but in *Barrett v Enfield LBC*[32] the House of Lords 1-08

27 Lord Denning has described breach of confidence liability as being based "not so much on property or on contract, but rather on the duty to be of good faith": *Fraser v Evans* [1969] Q.B. 349 at 361. There is some authority for the proposition that breach of confidence can constitute a tort: *A v B* [2002] EWCA Civ 337; [2003] Q.B. 195 at [4], per Lord Woolf; *Campbell v MGN Ltd* [2004] UKHL 22; [2004] 2 A.C. 457 at [14], per Lord Nicholls; *McKennitt v Ash* [2006] EWCA Civ 1714; [2008] Q.B. 73 at [8], per Buxton LJ.

28 See para. 9-22 onwards.

29 See Ch.26.

30 Burrows, *Law of Restitution* (1993), p.381.

31 There are two forms of restitution, that for unjust enrichment by subtraction and that for unjust enrichment by wrongdoing. The former is concerned with restoring what the defendant has taken at the expense of the claimant; the latter with restoring what the defendant has gained as a result of the wrong to the claimant. See further Burrows, *Law of Restitution*, 3rd edn (2010).

32 [2001] 2 A.C. 550 at 572 and 586, per Lords Slynn and Hutton.

expressed its preference for deciding such claims "by applying directly the common law concept of negligence rather than applying as a preliminary test the public law concept of *Wednesbury* unreasonableness to determine if the decision was outside the ambit of the discretion". However, the public service context remains an important factor in determining whether there has been a breach of duty.

1-09 The Human Rights Act 1998, which renders it unlawful for any public authority to act in a way which is incompatible with the European Convention on Human Rights (ECHR) and the potential for claims against the state for breach of EU law (so-called "eurotorts"), add to the potential areas of liability. Intentional or reckless unlawfulness can lead to liability under the developing tort of misfeasance in public office. Outside these areas of liability the mere fact that a public authority has acted unlawfully in public law terms does not give rise to a claim for damages, although it may be subject to judicial review. There has been concern that the present framework of law is both over-complex and inconsistent, and that it may unjustly deny compensation to victims of mere unlawful administration whilst over-compensating victims of negligent administration. Some would argue that the difficulties stem from attempting to use the private law principles of tort in a public law context and that the answer lies in replacing tort with a statutory framework to govern public law liability. However, the Law Commission's attempt to rationalise remedies in the context of administrative error by public authorities has not been received favourably. A proposal to introduce a differential liability regime requiring claimants bringing private law claims to demonstrate "serious fault" on the part of a public body where the activity engaged in was uniquely public in nature (a "truly public" test) has been rejected by consultees, and the Law Commission will not proceed with these proposals.[33] For the foreseeable future, reform in this area will have to rely on the incremental development of negligence and misfeasance liability along with the discretion inherent in applying the Human Rights Act and EU law.[34]

1-10 **Tort and crime** Little practical difficulty arises in distinguishing tort from criminal law. A tort action is instituted by an individual seeking redress for the wrong done to him. A criminal prosecution is normally instituted by the Crown or some other body expressly authorised by statute to bring criminal prosecutions for specific offences, for example agencies like the Medicines and Healthcare products Regulatory Agency or non-governmental organisations such as the RSPCA or NSPCC. Private prosecutions, although rare, remain possible. The purpose of the criminal law is to protect the public interest and punish wrongdoers. The purpose of tort is to vindicate the rights of the individual and compensate the victim for loss, injury or damage suffered by him, but the distinction in purpose between criminal law and tort is not, and never has been, entirely crystal-clear. The availability of exemplary damages in certain torts suggests an overtly, albeit limited, punitive function.[35] Tort and criminal law have always shared a deterrent function in relation to wrongdoing and the criminal courts are now empowered to order a convicted

---

33 Law Commission, *Administrative Redress: Public Bodies and the Citizen* (May 2010), Law Com. No.322.

34 See generally Ch.13.

35 See Law Commission, *Aggravated, Exemplary and Restitutionary Damages* (1997), Law Com. No.247; and the discussion of exemplary damages in *Kuddus v Chief Constable of Leicestershire Constabulary* [2001] UKHL 29; [2002] 2 A.C. 122.

person to pay compensation for any personal injury, loss or damage resulting from his offence or any other offence which is taken into consideration by the court in determining sentence. Such a compensation order may be made in addition to or instead of other punishments. Perhaps the most important feature of the relationship of tort and crime is that both serve to impose obligations of universal application designed to protect the good order of society.

2. THE FUNCTIONS AND DEVELOPMENT OF TORT LIABILITY

Functions of the law of torts As Professor Honoré[36] has suggested, there are two reasons why the state and courts make conduct tortious. From the claimant's perspective the purpose is "to define and give content to people's rights by providing them with a mechanism for protecting them and securing compensation if their rights are infringed". The compensatory role has tended to focus attention on the tort of negligence but the reference to rights is a reminder that tort law protects a wide range of interests against harmful conduct and that protection is not limited to compensation. Indeed, in many situations it is the publicity resulting from an action which may do most to protect rights. Tort law may serve an "ombudsman" function in this respect. **1-11**

Compensation or vindication of rights? The modern dominance of the tort of negligence, particularly in the context of personal injury claims, has tended to place emphasis on compensation as the primary function of the law torts. This has sometimes obscured its role in the vindication of the claimant's rights.[37] In *Ashley v Chief Constable of Sussex*[38] there was a difference of approach amongst their Lordships as to the function of the law of torts. A police officer shot dead the deceased in his home in the middle of the night during the course of an investigation into drug trafficking. The deceased had been standing naked in his bedroom and the police officer claimed that he had acted in self-defence.[39] The officer was prosecuted for murder but acquitted on the judge's direction. An inquest was opened, but adjourned pending the criminal investigation, and was not resumed. The deceased's family requested a public inquiry into the events that led to the shooting, but this was refused. The claimants were the father and the son of the deceased. They brought actions alleging assault and battery, false imprisonment, negligence and misfeasance in public office. The Chief Constable admitted negligence and false imprisonment, but denied the claim for assault and battery and misfeasance. He also agreed to pay damages in respect of the consequences of the negligence including, somewhat remarkably, aggravated damages. One of the issues before the House was whether the claimants should be permitted to have the action for assault and battery go to trial when the defendant had already agreed to provide full compensation. The majority held that the action should be allowed to proceed. For Lord Bingham it was "not the business of the court to monitor the motives of the parties in bring- **1-12**

---

36 Honoré, "The Morality of Tort Law" in Owen (ed.), *Philosophical Foundations of Tort Law* (1995), p.75.

37 See Witzleb and Carroll, "The role of vindication in torts damages" (2009) 17 Tort. L.R. 16; J. Varuhas, "The Concept of 'Vindication' in the Law of Torts: Rights, Interests and Damages" (2014) 34 O.J.L.S. 253.

38 [2008] UKHL 25; [2008] 1 A.C. 962.

39 See paras 3-148, 14-08 and 29-02 to 29-04 for discussion of that defence.

ing and resisting what is, on the face of it, a well-recognised claim in tort".[40] Similarly, for Lord Rodger, even assuming that one of the claimants' motives was to obtain a judicial finding about the circumstances in which the deceased was killed, that was not a reason for the court to stay their claims.[41] Lord Scott accepted that the purpose of awarding damages was not limited to compensation but could include a vindicatory purpose: "How is the deceased Mr Ashley's right not to be subjected to a violent and deadly attack to be vindicated if the claim for assault and battery, a claim that the Chief Constable has steadfastly and consistently disputed, is not allowed to proceed? Although the principal aim of an award of compensatory damages is to compensate the claimant for loss suffered, there is no reason in principle why an award of compensatory damages should not also fulfil a vindicatory purpose."[42] In contrast, Lord Neuberger considered that: "The desire for 'mere' vindication must be very rarely the sole private law ground on which a claim for a declaration is pursued or can even be justified"[43]; and for Lord Carswell "the civil courts exist to award compensation, not to conduct public inquiries. Nor is it their function to provide explanations ... the existence of a sanction by way of damages is the essential mark of a tort."[44] It is suggested that, on balance, the majority had the better of the argument here. Although an award of damages is the principal remedy in a tort claim, it would be simplistic to conclude that compensation is its only valid function. The vindication of the claimant's rights, a public acknowledgement that the claimant has suffered a wrong, may be just as important a social value for the law of tort to uphold.[45]

1-13 **Vindication of rights may not require vindicatory damages** Although the vindication of rights may protect important social values, there is a difference between saying that an award of damages can serve a vindicatory purpose and the claim that a special award of "vindicatory damages" should be made in circumstances where the claimant would otherwise be entitled only to nominal damages. In *Lumba v Secretary of State for the Home Department*[46] a majority of the Supreme Court held that claimants who had been falsely imprisoned by reason of the defendant's breach of public law principles, but who had suffered no loss because

---

[40] [2008] UKHL 25; [2008] 1 A.C. 962 at [4]. Contrast Lord Bingham's observations in *Watkins v Secretary of State for the Home Department* [2006] UKHL 17; [2006] 2 A.C. 395 at [9], in the context of an argument as to whether the tort of misfeasance in public office should, in some cases, be actionable without proof of damage: "it is correctly said that the primary role of the law of tort is to provide monetary compensation for those who have suffered material damage rather than to vindicate the rights of those who have not. If public officers behave with outrageous disregard for their legal duties, but without causing material damage, there are other and more appropriate ways of bringing them to book." But also compare Lord Walker's scepticism (at [69]–[72]) about whether the alternative remedies open to a claimant whose rights had been abused would provide an adequate remedy in the circumstances of that case (prison officers deliberately interfering with the claimant's constitutional right of access to the courts by opening correspondence with his legal advisers).

[41] [2008] UKHL 25; [2008] 1 A.C. 962 at [65]. So if the parties had a valid cause of action "justice is unlikely to be served by preventing them from advancing their cause of action on the ground that their motive for doing so is somehow improper": [2008] UKHL 25; [2008] 1 A.C. 962 at [70].

[42] [2008] UKHL 25; [2008] 1 A.C. 962 at [22].

[43] [2008] UKHL 25; [2008] 1 A.C. 962 at [111].

[44] [2008] UKHL 25; [2008] 1 A.C. 962 at [81].

[45] For example, in the case of parents suing following the death of a young child it seems entirely inappropriate to suggest that they are motivated to do so by the prospect of an award of £15,120 bereavement damages, plus funeral expenses, which will be the typical award in such a case.

[46] [2011] UKSC 12; [2012] 1 A.C. 245.

they would have been detained in any event if the defendant had complied with her public law duty, were entitled to nominal damages only.[47] Lord Dyson doubted whether vindicatory damages are ever justified as a remedy in tort (as opposed to a remedy for the infringement of a constitutional right where there is a written constitution, as in *Attorney General of Trinidad and Tobago v Ramanoop*[48]): "The implications of awarding vindicatory damages in the present case would be far reaching. Undesirable uncertainty would result. If they were awarded here, then they could in principle be awarded in any case involving a battery or false imprisonment by an arm of the state. Indeed, why limit it to such torts? And why limit it to torts committed by the state? I see no justification for letting such an unruly horse loose on our law."[49]

Deterrence From the defendant's perspective, Professor Honoré identified the function of tort law as being to "forbid or discourage" particular forms of conduct or "at a minimum, to warn those who indulge in it of the liability they may incur".[50] The deterrent effect as part of the purpose of potential tort liability is not often remarked upon by the courts, though in *Scout Association v Barnes* Jackson LJ noted that: "It is the function of the law of tort to deter negligent conduct and to compensate those who are the victims of such conduct."[51] More commonly, the notion of deterrence features as part of the assessment of the potential negative effects of imposing tort liability (e.g. as tending towards "defensive practice" on the part of certain public bodies if a duty of care in negligence was held to apply,[52] or as undermining socially desirable activities[53]). Professor Honoré notes that where strict liability is imposed, "the conduct is generally not wrongful in itself but the wrong consists in causing harm by engaging in certain types of risky activities". However, he argues that "[t]o justify the tort system, it is not enough to show that the state is entitled to take steps to minimise undesirable behaviour and to give individuals the power to protect their rights ... It must also be shown that some 1-14

47 Lord Walker, Lord Hope and Baroness Hale, dissenting on this point, would have awarded "vindicatory damages". See further *Bostridge v Oxleas NHS Foundation Trust* [2015] EWCA Civ 79; [2015] Med. L.R. 113; and *Parker v Chief Constable of Essex* [2018] EWCA Civ 2788; [2019] 1 W.L.R. 2238, applying *Lumba* and awarding nominal damages only in circumstances where, apart from a procedural error, the claimant would have been lawfully detained. Contrast *R. (on the application of Hemmati) v Secretary of State for the Home Department* [2019] UKSC 56; [2019] 3 W.L.R. 1156 where the policy under which the defendant detained the claimants was unlawful. It was "no answer to a claim for damages for unlawful imprisonment that the detention would have been lawful had the law been different", per Lord Kitchin at [112].

48 [2005] UKPC 15; [2006] 1 A.C. 328.

49 [2011] UKSC 12; [2012] 1 A.C. 245 at [101]; see also Lord Collins at [236]: "To make a separate award for vindicatory damages is to confuse the *purpose* of damages awards with the nature of the award. A declaration, or an award of nominal damages, may itself have a vindicatory purpose and effect. So too a conventional award of damages may serve a vindicatory purpose." The decision in *Lumba* is criticised in J. Varuhas, "The Concept of 'Vindication' in the Law of Torts: Rights, Interests and Damages" (2014) 34 O.J.L.S. 253, 279–282.

50 Whilst the compensatory function of tort could be achieved, to an extent, by state compensation schemes, the guidance function would, to an extent, be weakened by such a scheme for, as Honoré argues, it would "tend to undermine the sense of personal responsibility of some potential harmdoers": "The Morality of Tort Law" in Owen (ed.), *Philosophical Foundations of Tort Law* (1995), p.93.

51 [2010] EWCA Civ 1476 at [34]. Smith LJ agreed, at [36].

52 See para.7-24.

53 See paras 7-186 and 7-188 to 7-192.

principles of justice entitle the right-holders to sue the wrongdoers for compensation."[54] This justification can be found in a combination of the principles of corrective, distributive and retributive justice.

1-15 **Corrective justice** Honoré explains the principle of corrective justice in the following terms:

> "[I]t requires those who have without justification harmed others by their conduct to put the matter right. This they must do on the basis that the harm-doer and harm-sufferer are to be treated as equals, neither more deserving than the other. The one is therefore not entitled to become relatively better off by harming than the other. The balance must be restored."[55]

A sufficient causal link between the defendant's conduct and claimant's loss is required for corrective justice to justify compensation. Courts are reluctant to impose liability on defendants whose conduct may be peripheral to the harm for which a third party may be primarily responsible.[56] The most difficult borderline problems may arise where the decision of the claimant is a crucial factor in the causal chain.[57] A causal link is a *necessary* condition but as Honoré notes, it is not a *sufficient* condition. In particular, the requirement of fault on the part of the defendant may operate to limit "the pursuit of corrective justice".[58] The extent to which fault is a requirement of liability reflects the policy of the legislature and courts in relation to both the nature of the claimants right and the defendant's activity.

1-16 **Distributive justice** Honoré sees distributive justice as being concerned with the just distribution of burdens and losses, including risks, amongst members of a society. Thus, it may require "people to bear the risk of harming others by their conduct even where they are not at fault in doing so". Similarly, the vicarious liability of an employer can be justified on the ground that the employer has a degree of control over and stands to gain from his employees' activity and, hence, "must bear the risk that it will turn out to harm another".[59] In this way, distributive justice can be seen as supporting corrective justice, pointing to the situations in which correction would be justified. But it has been suggested that distributive justice may

---

54 Honoré, "The Morality of Tort Law" in Owen (ed.), *Philosophical Foundations of Tort Law* (1995), p.78.

55 Honoré, "The Morality of Tort Law" in Owen (ed.), *Philosophical Foundations of Tort Law* (1995), p.79. He notes that this view of corrective justice embodies a relational principle: "It can exist only when the harm-doer's wrong violates the harm-sufferer's right; the two cannot be dissociated."

56 See Stapleton "Duty of Care: Peripheral Parties and Alternative Opportunities for Deterrence" (1995) 111 L.Q.R. 301. Stapleton cites cases such as *Smith v Littlewoods Organisation Ltd* [1987] 1 A.C. 241. For an example in the context of nuisance liability, see *Hussain v Lancaster City Council* [2000] Q.B. 1.

57 Thus, in *Reeves v Commissioner of Police of the Metropolis* [2000] 1 A.C. 360, although both Lord Hoffmann for the majority and Lord Hobhouse dissenting, cited extracts from Hart and Honoré, *Causation in the Law*, they differed in their view as to whether the decision of the claimant to commit suicide was sufficiently autonomous to relieve the defendant of responsibility for his safety.

58 Honoré notes that other theorists would define corrective justice more narrowly as requiring compensation only if the person causing harm was at fault in doing so. Honoré's broader approach recognises that the value of corrective justice may underlie areas of strict liability.

59 Honoré, "The Morality of Tort Law" in Owen (ed.), *Philosophical Foundations of Tort Law* (1995), p.85.

also limit the application of corrective justice. In *McFarlane v Tayside Health Board*[60] the claimants were negligently advised that a vasectomy had rendered the husband infertile. Relying on that incorrect advice they ceased to take contraceptive precautions. As a consequence, a child was born. On grounds of distributive justice, Lords Steyn and Hope rejected their claim for the cost of bringing up the unwanted child.[61] Lord Steyn said:

> "It is possible to view the case simply from the perspective of corrective justice. On this approach the parents' claim must succeed. But one may also approach the case from the vantage point of distributive justice. It requires a focus on the just distribution of burdens and losses among members of a society. If the matter is approached in this way, it may become relevant to ask commuters on the Underground the following question: Should parents of an unwanted but healthy child be able to sue the doctor or hospital for compensation equivalent to the cost of bringing up the child for the years of his or her minority. I am firmly of the view that an overwhelming number of ordinary men and women would answer the question with an emphatic 'No'. And the reason for such a response would be an inarticulate premise as to what is morally acceptable and what is not. ... they will have in mind that many couples cannot have children and others have the sorrow and burden of looking after a disabled child. The realisation that compensation for financial loss in respect of upbringing a child would necessarily have to discriminate between rich and poor would surely appear unseemly to them."[62]

He concluded:

> "The truth is that tort law is a mosaic in which the principles of corrective and distributive justice are interwoven. And in situations of uncertainty and difficulty a choice sometimes has to be made between the two approaches."[63]

---

60 [2000] 2 A.C. 59.

61 Lords Clyde and, to some extent, Lord Slynn reached the same conclusion on grounds of proportionality or retributive justice. Lord Millett also reached the same conclusion on the more general ground of legal policy "which is to say our more or less inadequately expressed ideas of what justice demands", arguing that it was "morally offensive to regard a normal health baby as more trouble and expense than it is worth" and that it would be "subversive of the mores of society for parents to enjoy the advantages of parenthood while transferring to others the responsibilities which it entails".

62 [2000] 2 A.C. 59 at 82. In support of this approach, Lords Steyn and Hope cited Lord Hoffmann's speech in *Frost v Chief Constable of South Yorkshire Police* [1999] 2 A.C. 455, in which he held on grounds of distributive justice, that it was "wrong that policemen ... should have the right of compensation for psychiatric injury ... while the bereaved relatives are sent away with nothing".

63 [2000] 2 A.C. 59 at 83. See also Englard, *The Philosophy of Tort Law* (Dartmouth, 1993) p.56, where he adopts the theory of "complementarity" to explain the interaction of the two forms of justice in the legal context. Thus, he argues that the values "exercise a mutually restrictive influence" on any substantive issue. For example, the common corrective justice requirement of fault might be basically preserved but the court might relax the burden of proof by the use of presumptions to take account of the fact that the claimant might "encounter special difficulties in establishing fault, and on the other hand the defendant is in a position to spread the loss by insurance". On the other hand it is arguable that, when weighing the demands of distributive justice, if it is appropriate to take into account the defendant's ability to spread the loss through insurance one should also take into account the possibility that the claimant could have insured against the loss. Compare, e.g. the difference of view in the Court of Appeal on the relevance of a claimant's insurance position when considering an occupier's measured duty of care for a naturally occurring nuisance in *Lambert v Barratt Homes Ltd* [2010] EWCA Civ 681; [2010] B.L.R. 527; and *Vernon Knight Associates v Cornwall Council* [2013] EWCA Civ 950; [2013] B.L.R. 519; see para.7-183. See also *Renfrew Golf Club v Motocaddy Ltd* [2016] CSIH 57; 2016 S.C. 860 at [34], per Lord Carloway, commenting on the respective abilities of defendant and claimant to obtain insurance cover in a product liability case.

The difficulty with Lord Steyn's approach to distributive justice is twofold. First, his Lordship did not identify a single *principle* of distributive justice (and there are many different conceptions of distributive justice to choose from). The *policy* judgment underlying *McFarlane* is that the NHS should not have to be burdened with the financial cost of such claims when it has other calls on its resources, notwithstanding that the claimants have suffered financial loss as a result of negligence in their treatment.[64] Secondly, even if one could be confident that "commuters on the Underground" could articulate a conception of distributive justice, they will not in fact be asked their opinions. If one does not have to test one's intuition by actually asking people what they think, it is possible always to reach to a "just" outcome. As Hale LJ commented in *Parkinson v St James and Seacroft University Hospital NHS Trust*:

> "The traveller on the Underground is not here being invoked as a hypothetical reasonable man but as a moral arbiter. We all know that London commuters are not a representative sample of public opinion. We also know that the answer will crucially depend upon the question asked and the amount of relevant information and argument given to help answer it. The fact that so many eminent judges all over the world have wrestled with this problem and reached different conclusions might suggest that the considered response would be less emphatic and less unanimous."[65]

Appeals to distributive justice as a rhetorical device to support a policy judgment should only be made where the principles underpinning the court's conception of distributive justice have been fully articulated. Appeals to the views of the travelling public (whether on the Underground or the Clapham omnibus) are likely to founder on the simple riposte that the court is not actually going to ask them to express an opinion, and even if commuters were to be asked they are unlikely to speak with one voice (and the results of opinion polls are not normally regarded as principles of distributive justice).

1-17 The Court of Appeal has stated, correctly, that distributive justice has no role to play once liability has been established and the court is assessing the claimant's financial loss. At that point corrective justice should be the prevailing principle.[66]

1-18 **Risk and autonomy** In *Tomlinson v Congleton BC*[67] Lord Hoffmann considered one aspect of risk distribution, the relationship between the individual's freedom

---

In *Cox v Ministry of Justice* [2016] UKSC 10; [2016] A.C. 660 at [20], in the context of vicarious liability, Lord Reed noted that employers could be expected to have insured against their potential liability but that "employers insure themselves because they are liable: they are not liable because they have insured themselves".

64 That policy looks less defensible where the claimant has received treatment at a private clinic operating for profit, and covered by insurance, but in *ARB v IVF Hammersmith Ltd* [2018] EWCA Civ 2803; [2020] Q.B. 93 the Court of Appeal held that the legal policy issues that underpinned *McFarlane* also apply to breach of a strict contractual obligation (an application for permission to appeal was refused by the Supreme Court).

65 [2001] EWCA Civ 530; [2002] Q.B. 266 at [82]. In *Chester v Afshar* [2004] UKHL 41; [2005] 1 A.C. 134 at [83], Lord Hope remarked: "As I survey my fellow passengers … on the underground—such a variety in age, race, nationality and languages—I find it increasingly hard to persuade myself that any one view on anything other than the most basic issues can be said to be typical of them."

66 *Thompstone v Tameside and Glossop Acute Services NHS Trust* [2008] EWCA Civ 5; [2008] 1 W.L.R. 2207 at [47].

67 [2003] UKHL 47; [2004] 1 A.C. 46 at [45]–[47].

to take risk and the responsibility of others to limit such risks. Commenting on the responsibility of the occupier of land, he said:

> "I think it will be extremely rare for an occupier of land to be under a duty to prevent people from taking risks which are inherent in the activities they freely choose to undertake upon the land. If people want to climb mountains, go hang gliding or dive in lakes, that is their affair. ... the balance between risk on the one hand and individual autonomy on the other is not a matter of expert opinion. It is a judgment which the courts must make and which in England reflects the individualist values of the common law."

Underlying this, is a broader balance to be achieved by the law of tort, one expressed by Lord Steyn in *Gorringe v Calderdale MBC*[68]:

> "On the one hand the courts must not contribute to the creation of a society bent on litigation, which is premised on the illusion that for every misfortune there is a remedy. On the other hand, there are cases where the courts must recognise on principled grounds the compelling demands of corrective justice ... that wrongs should be remedied. Sometimes cases may not obviously fall in one category or the other. Truly difficult cases arise."

As part of the distributive justice equation, courts have to consider the balance of risk and responsibility at both an individual and a social level.

Retributive justice Whilst distributive justice compares the position of the claimant with that of other members of society, retributive justice compares the position of claimant and defendant. Honoré suggests that the retributive principle tempers that of corrective justice by requiring that defendants "should not to be exposed to disproportionately heavy losses".[69] In this context, loss spreading through insurance plays a key role. Indeed, it may remove any moral objection to strict liability. This does not mean that "loss spreading is an aim of the tort system as such, merely that some form of insurance is essential if a system of corrective justice is to operate fairly". It "serves to cushion losses which, whether the defendants are at fault or not, are out of scale with the gravity of their conduct". The notion of proportionality embodied in this principle of justice is pervasive. It influences both the imposition of liability[70] and, through principles of remoteness, its extent.[71] In *McFarlane v Tayside Health Board*[72] Lord Clyde rejected the cost of upbringing claim partly on this ground, saying: "reasonableness includes a consideration of the proportionality between the wrongdoing and the loss suffered thereby." He concluded that given the costs could include private education, the upbringing claim could be "wholly disproportionate to the doctor's culpability" and would not "accord with the idea of restitution".[73] The concern that the award of damages may be 1-19

---

68 [2004] UKHL 15; [2004] 1 W.L.R. 1057 at [2]. See also *Scout Association v Barnes* [2010] EWCA Civ 1476, per Jackson LJ at [34]: "It is not the function of the law of tort to eliminate every iota of risk or to stamp out socially desirable activities."

69 Honoré, "The Morality of Tort Law" in Owen (ed.), *Philosophical Foundations of Tort Law* (1995), p.89.

70 For example, concern about disproportionate liability is one reason for the reluctance of courts to impose duties in respect of psychiatric illness. See para. 7-69 onwards.

71 See para.2-144.

72 [2000] 2 A.C. 59 at 106.

73 Lord Slynn argued similarly that it would not be reasonable to impose such liability on the doctor as he "does not assume responsibility for those economic losses" and that if the client "wants to be able to recover such costs he or she must do so by an appropriate contract". However, it has

out of proportion to the defendant's culpability is problematic. The *damage* caused by a single act of negligence may be out of all proportion to the defendant's moral culpability, and yet once liability has been established, the defendant is liable to compensate the claimant in full. A moment's inattention by a motorist may lead to a catastrophic accident. A careless slip by an obstetrician may result in a child being born with severe brain damage. The financial consequences may run to millions of pounds. Nonetheless, it is axiomatic that corrective justice requires the court to ignore the disproportion between culpability and consequences, and award full compensation.[74]

1-20 **Justice, morality and policy** The speeches of Lords Millett and Steyn in *McFarlane v Tayside Health Board*[75] illustrate judicial thinking on the role of justice, morality and policy in the development of tort law. Lord Millett explained that "legal policy" was not the same as "public policy". It involved "a search for justice, and this demands that the dispute be resolved in a way which is fair and reasonable and accords with ordinary notions of what is fit and proper. It is also concerned to maintain the coherence of law and the avoidance of inappropriate distinctions if injustice is to be avoided in other cases."[76] Lord Steyn also stressed that he was not deciding the case on the "quicksands" of public policy but on principles of justice. Noting that distributive justice was a moral theory, he said:

> "It may be objected that the House must act like a court of law and not like a court of morals. That would only be partly right. The court must apply positive law. But judges' sense of the moral answer to a question, or the justice of the case, has been one of the great shaping forces of the common law. What may count in a situation of difficulty and uncertainty is not the subjective view of the judge but what he reasonably believes that the ordinary citizen would regard as right."[77]

His comment that "judges ought to strive to give the real reasons for their decision" rather than resorting to "unrealistic and formalistic propositions which mask the real reasons" suggests that the language of legal policy and justice should feature in hard cases.[78]

---

subsequently been held that the economic costs of raising a healthy child cannot be recovered even for breach of a strict contractual obligation: see *ARB v IVF Hammersmith Ltd* [2018] EWCA Civ 2803; [2020] Q.B. 93. In *McFarlane*, the House of Lords allowed the mother's claim for the discomfort and inconvenience of the unwanted pregnancy and childbirth. In its subsequent decision in *Rees v Darlington Memorial Hospital NHS Trust* [2003] UKHL 52; [2004] 1 A.C. 309 at [8] (see further paras 1-39 and 7-101) Lord Bingham, leading the majority, considered that the discomfort award did not give adequate recognition to the parents' loss and added a further conventional award of £15,000 to reflect the claimants' loss of autonomy. The majority Law Lords all regarded this as a modest award and concerns about disproportionate recovery were not raised.

74 See para.1-17.

75 [2000] 2 A.C. 59.

76 [2000] 2 A.C. 59 at 108.

77 As illustrations of the relevance of the moral dimension, Lord Steyn cited *Smith New Court Securities Ltd v Scrimgeour Vickers (Asset Management) Ltd* [1997] A.C. 254, in which he had stated that "as between the fraudster and the innocent party, moral considerations militate in favour of requiring the fraudster to bear the risk of misfortunes directly caused by the fraud"; and *Frost v Chief Constable of South Yorkshire Police* [1999] 2 A.C. 455, in which with Lord Hoffmann he had reasoned that "it would be morally unacceptable if the law denied a remedy to bereaved relatives but granted it to police officers who were on duty".

78 See the similar stress on articulating the reasons for decisions in the judgment of McHugh J in *Perre v Apand Pty Ltd* (1999) A.L.R. 606, and also his stress on the importance of predictability in the

The development of tort law In *Rees v Darlington Memorial Hospital NHS Trust*[79] Lords Steyn and Hope dissented from the majority view that a conventional award of £15,000 should be made for loss of autonomy. Lord Steyn said: 1-21

> "I regard the idea of a conventional award in the present case as contrary to principle. It is a novel procedure for judges to create such a remedy. There are limits to permissible creativity for judges. In my view the majority have strayed into forbidden territory. It is also a backdoor evasion of the legal policy enunciated in *McFarlane*'s case.[80] If such a rule is to be created it must be done by Parliament. ... It may well be that the Law Commissions and Parliament ought in any event, to consider the impact of the creation of a power to make a conventional award ... for the coherence of the legal system."

Lord Hope said:

> "The lack of any consistent or coherent ratio in support of the proposition in the speeches for the majority is disturbing. It underlines Lord Steyn's point that the examination of the issue at the oral hearing was cursory and unaccompanied by research."

Two separate issues are raised in these extracts. The first concerns the constitutional limit to the judges' role in developing tort law. To the extent that Lord Steyn is suggesting that novelty and a reversal of judicial policy are forbidden territory, it is considered, with respect, that this goes too far. Where what is in issue is the development of common law principles, it should be open to the highest court both to innovate and reappraise legal policy. The history of relying on Parliament is not entirely fruitful. For example, in 1982 in *McLoughlin v O'Brian*[81] Lord Wilberforce suggested that widening recovery for psychiatric illness should be left to Parliament. In 1998 the Law Commission duly reported to Parliament recommending such a widening, but in 2009 the government indicated that it was preferable to leave the courts to develop the law.[82] In the meantime the courts, led by the House of Lords, appear to have taken matters back into their own hands by taking a less restrictive approach. But the other concern raised by the two Lords is more weighty since it relates to the institutional competence of the judiciary to develop the law. It suggested that neither the coherence of the development (the use of a conventional award) nor its consequences had been properly argued or researched.[83] Ensuring coherence in a case law system which produces incremental growth is always going to be an issue but with a combination of articulated legal policy and 1-22

process of litigation without which "practitioners believe they cannot confidently advise what the law is" with the result that "the effectiveness of law as a social instrument is seriously diminished".

79 [2003] UKHL 52; [2004] 1 A.C. 309 at [46] and [74].

80 Where the House of Lords had refused to make an award for loss of autonomy and had held on distributive justice grounds that the parents had no entitlement to damages for the cost of bringing up the unwanted child.

81 [1983] 1 A.C. 410.

82 Ministry of Justice response to a Consultation on Damages, *The Law on Damages*, CP(R) 9/07, July 2009, p.51.

83 MacCormick, *Legal Reasoning and Legal Theory*, suggests that coherence and consequences are the two key factors to be considered by a judge when justifying a decision. The first asks whether the proposed decision will cohere with existing principles and authorities: the greater the inconsistency with the existing legal framework that will result from a proposed decision, the less likely it is to be adopted. The second concerns the broader consequences of the decision for potential litigants, the legal system and indeed the role of law in society. Will these consequences be acceptable in terms of justice or common sense?

an eye to the matrix of the tort,[84] i.e. the place of the development within the general scheme of the law, coherent development may be expected. In some circumstances, concern about lack of research into the consequences of a particular development could be met by advice from the Law Commission. The Commission's researched advice as to the assessment of non-pecuniary damages[85] provided the basis for a judicial change in the level of assessment. It may be that researched advice for the judiciary should be seen as being as much part of the Commission's role as that of making recommendations for the legislature.[86]

1-23 **The role of legislation** Intellectual property rights are protected partly by the tort of passing off but mainly by a framework of statutory protection. Aside from that area, legislation plays only a supplementary role in the substantive liability framework.[87] It has been used to clarify aspects of the common law as is the case with the Occupiers' Liability Acts of 1957 and 1984, the Torts (Interference with Goods) Act 1977, the Animals Act 1971, and the Defamation Acts 1996 and 2013. It has been used to extend the common law as with the Defective Premises Act 1972 and the Consumer Protection Act 1987 which was passed to comply with an EU Directive. Typically, these statutes are drafted at a level of generality which leaves key questions to judicial interpretation. Thus, the scope of the Occupiers' Liability Acts has been explored by the decision of the House of Lords in *Tomlinson v Congleton BC*[88] and that of the Animals Act by the judgment of the House in *Mirvahedy v Henley*.[89] Again, the scope of the Consumer Protection Act was widened beyond previous expectations by the judgment of Burton J in *A v National Blood Authority (No.1)*.[90] Such judgments interpret and apply the wording of the legislation but the reasoning process reflects the same policies as influence the development of common law liability. Such legislation cannot be seen in isolation from the broader framework and functions of tort law.

3. THE FRAMEWORK OF TORT LIABILITY

1-24 **Torts and tort** The traditional approach to tort law views it as comprising a series of discrete *torts* linked, as one commentator has put it, "more by marriage than by blood".[91] This approach has been inherited from the historical development of the law through the growth of different forms of action for different types of wrong. Each tort is seen as having its own characteristics in terms of the conduct it sanctions and the interest it protects. In the absence of overarching principles, each tort requires its own exposition. But the different tort actions do not function in

[84] Lord Steyn's phrase in *Three Rivers DC v Bank of England (No.3)* [2003] 2 A.C. 1 at 190.

[85] *Damages for Personal Injury: Non-Pecuniary Loss*, Law Commission Report No.257.

[86] In *Watkins v Secretary of State for the Home Department* [2006] UKHL 17; [2006] 2 A.C. 395 at [10], Lord Bingham said that the continuing work of the Law Commission on the liability of public bodies to compensate the wronged citizen, strengthened his view that the House of Lords should apply the existing law rather than seeking to extend its scope.

[87] In the remedial context, the Damages Act 1996 and the Fatal Accidents Act 1976 are significant and limitation periods are governed by the Limitation Act 1980.

[88] [2003] UKHL 47; [2004] 1 A.C. 46; see paras 7-185 and 11-32.

[89] [2003] UKHL 16; [2003] 2 A.C. 491; see para.20-08.

[90] [2001] 3 All E.R. 289.

[91] Cane, *The Anatomy of Tort Law* (1997), p.21. Cane rejects the traditional presentation of the law in favour of an analysis wholly based on the nature of the protected interests and the nature of the sanctioned conduct.

isolation. They must fit together to create the framework of liability. For the coherence of the law, the place of each tort has to be considered against the general scheme of the law of *tort*.[92] The scope and potential of any particular tort cannot be understood in isolation from others. For this reason, it is important to have an overview of the law of *tort*. This section seeks to provide this by analysing the interests protected and the conduct sanctioned by the law of tort. The final part of the section will consider the impact of the rights introduced by the Human Rights Act 1998 on the wrongs based framework of tort law.

Interests and conduct A wide range of interests are protected by tort law but not all interests are protected against all forms of conduct. Some are protected by the so-called strict liability torts against any conduct which causes harm to the interest; others are protected against unreasonable conduct and still others are protected against just intentional harming conduct. Many are protected at different levels against a mix of conduct by a mix of torts. The reason for this complex pattern is that tort law has to achieve a balance. As Cane explains: **1-25**

> "Because the imposition of tort liability on a person significantly impinges on that person's freedom of action and reduces their financial wealth, the law, to be fair, must strike a balance between the interests of victims and the interests of injurers. This it does by negatively limiting the definition of 'protected interests' and of 'sanctioned conduct' and protecting certain interests only from interference or damage resulting from certain types of sanctioned conduct. … Legal responsibility impinges on freedom to act … tort law balances freedom against responsibility."

An overview of tort law must look in both directions, at the importance of the victim's interest and the nature of the injurer's conduct.

(a) Interests protected by the law of torts

(i) Personal interests

Bodily integrity In *Parkinson v St James and Seacroft University Hospital NHS Trust*[93] Hale LJ citing this paragraph, said: **1-26**

> "The right to bodily integrity is the first and most important of the interests protected by the law of tort. … Included within that right are two others. One is the right to physical autonomy: to make one's own choices about what will happen to one's own body. Another is the right not to be subjected to bodily injury or harm. These interests are regarded as so important that redress is given both against intentional and negligent interference with them. In contrast, economic interests come very much lower in the list, and for obvious reasons … The object of much commercial activity is deliberately to harm the economic interests of competitors: only in very special situations, therefore, does the law recognise a liability to compensate those whose economic interests have been damaged."

The law of torts affords to mentally competent adults an absolute right of bodily integrity. Any deliberate touching of another, however trivial, constitutes a battery

---

92 See the comments of Lord Steyn in *Three Rivers DC v Bank of England* [2003] 2 A.C. 1 at 190: "The coherent *development* of the law requires the House to consider the place of the tort of misfeasance in public office against the general scheme of the law of tort."

93 [2001] EWCA Civ 530; [2002] Q.B. 266 at [56].

unless expressly or implicitly authorised by the claimant. From the recognition of this basic interest, protected by the ancient tort of trespass to the person, flows the body of principles protecting the citizen from unlawful seizure of his person and the foundation of the law relating to patient autonomy in medicine.[94]

1-27 **Personal liberty** As Hale LJ has said: "Loss of liberty is just as much an interference in bodily integrity as loss of a limb."[95] The tort of battery in protecting bodily integrity also serves to protect personal liberty. You cannot be touched against your will and so you cannot be forcibly dragged to gaol without lawful justification. However battery operates to vindicate the interests in *personal* freedom only where the violation takes the form of a direct contact with the person. Other torts must be called in aid to offer a more comprehensive protection of liberty. The threat of an immediate battery in order to constrain the claimant's liberty may constitute assault. Any conduct which confines the claimant within boundaries defined by the defendant constitutes the tort of false imprisonment. But the confinement must be complete; a partial restraint falls short of false imprisonment.[96] Other liberties such as freedom of speech, freedom to trade, and freedom of the press are defined not in terms of protected interests but negatively by reference to the circumstances in which the exercise of such freedoms are not wrongs against others. The citizen enjoys freedom of speech but only to the extent that he does not defame others. The landowner is free to enjoy his property, but only to the extent that his enjoyment does not result in the commission of the tort of nuisance.

1-28 **Physical security from injury** Battery, in protecting bodily integrity, clearly also protects physical safety and freedom from personal injury. Protection against personal injury, vindication of each individual's interest in health and physical well-being, are of prime importance in the law of torts. Thus in *Perrett v Collins*,[97] where a regulatory authority was held to owe a duty of care in respect of personal injury resulting from an air crash following its negligent safety inspection of the aircraft, Buxton LJ commented that "when one turns to the judgmental issues of justice, fairness and reasonableness the importance of the fact that what is put at risk is the [claimant's] body, and not just his goods, is ... deeply embedded in the law of negligence". Hobhouse LJ distinguished the refusal by the House of Lords in *Marc Rich & Co v Bishop Rock Marine Co Ltd*[98] to place a duty on a maritime inspection authority, on the ground that the loss in that case involved damage to property and not personal injury.

1-29 **Trivial injury** The protection of bodily integrity is not synonymous with protection from physiological changes to the body which produce no symptoms and have no measurable effect on the body. In *Rothwell v Chemical & Insulating Co*[99] the

94 See *F v West Berkshire HA* [1990] 2 A.C. 1, per Lord Goff. But there is no free-standing cause of action for interference with a patient's autonomy: *Shaw v Kovac* [2017] EWCA Civ 1028; [2017] 1 W.L.R. 4773 at [48].

95 *McLoughlin v Grovers (A Firm)* [2001] EWCA Civ 1743; [2002] Q.B. 1312 at 57.

96 *Bird v Jones* (1845) 7 Q.B. 742; see para.14-23.

97 [1998] 2 Lloyd's Rep. 255; [1999] P.N.L.R. 77.

98 [1996] A.C. 211.

99 [2007] UKHL 39; [2008] 1 A.C. 281. The Scottish Parliament legislated to reverse the effect of *Rothwell* in Scotland, providing that asbestos-related pleural plaques are personal injury which is not negligible and so constitute actionable harm for the purposes of a personal injuries claim (see

House of Lords concluded that symptomless pleural plaques developed by the claimants as a result of inhaling asbestos fibres did not constitute actionable damage; nor did they become actionable damage when combined with the anxiety of the claimants due to their knowledge of the risk of developing serious disease in the future as a result of their exposure to asbestos. Lord Hoffmann observed that:

> "… a claim in tort based on negligence is incomplete without proof of damage. Damage in this sense is an abstract concept of being worse off, physically or economically, so that compensation is an appropriate remedy. It does not mean simply a physical change, which is consistent with making one better, as in the case of a successful operation, or with being neutral, having no perceptible effect upon one's health or capability."[100]

Any personal injury must exceed a minimum threshold of severity in order to qualify as actionable damage. Thus, a "transient, trifling, self-limiting, reversible reaction to an irritant is not 'actionable injury' for the purposes of the law of tort."[101]

As a general rule, however, the law of tort places a high priority on security from physical harm. So important is the interest in physical safety that both at common law and, by means of legislation, strict liability has been imposed in certain circumstances. The common law tort of breach of statutory duty may give rise to strict liability where injuries are caused by breaches of health and safety legislation. The Animals Act 1971 and the Consumer Protection Act 1987 both impose a measure of strict liability for injuries caused by animals and defective products respectively. However, the importance attached to personal security has not led the courts to extend the rule in *Rylands v Fletcher* imposing strict liability for damage done by dangerous things escaping from land, to allow recovery for personal injury. In *Transco Plc v Stockport MBC*[102] Lord Hoffmann, after noting two early twentieth century cases in which damages for personal injury had been recovered under the rule, said: "But I think the point is now settled by two recent decisions of the House **1-30**

---

the Damages (Asbestos-Related Conditions) (Scotland) Act 2009 (2009 ASP 4)). In *AXA General Insurance Ltd v HM Advocate* [2011] UKSC 46; [2012] 1 A.C. 868 the Supreme Court held that the 2009 Act was not beyond the competence of the Scottish Parliament, nor was it subject to judicial review on the grounds of unreasonableness, irrationality and arbitrariness. The position is the same in Northern Ireland. See the Damages (Asbestos–related Conditions) Act (Northern Ireland) 2011; and *McCauley v Harland and Wolff Plc* [2015] NICA 28; [2016] N.I. 254 (holding that de minimis is not a defence, since that would subvert the purpose of the legislation, which was to reverse the effect of *Rothwell*).

[100] [2007] UKHL 39; [2008] 1 A.C. 281 at [7]. *Rothwell* should be contrasted with *Dryden v Johnson Matthey Plc* [2018] UKSC 18; [2019] A.C. 403, where employees became sensitised to platinum salts without developing any symptoms and would not develop symptoms unless they were further exposed to platinum salts. The Court of Appeal held that they had not suffered compensatable personal injury, and the financial loss they sustained as a result of no longer being able to work with platinum salts constituted pure economic loss which fell beyond the scope of the employers' duty. The Supreme Court disagreed. In *Rothwell* the pleural plaques were symptomless and had no effect on the claimants' ability to lead their lives or to work, whereas in *Dryden* the claimants' capacity for work had been impaired and they were therefore significantly worse off. This constituted actionable personal injury which was more than negligible (ibid. at [40]). *Dryden* is discussed by J. Huang, "Dryden v Johnson Matthey: the boundaries of actionable damage" (2019) 82 M.L.R. 737.

[101] *Saunderson v Sonae Industria (UK) Ltd* [2015] EWHC 2264 (QB) at [179] per Jay J. The medical evidence in this case distinguished between an irritant response to exposure to chemicals (which was regarded as minor) and an inflammatory response, though Jay J did not accept that this was an absolute distinction. If the degree of irritation was severe enough it could cross the line into actionable damage.

[102] [2003] UKHL 61; [2004] 2 A.C. 1 at [35].

of Lords: *Cambridge Water Co Ltd v Eastern Counties Leather Plc*,[103] which decided that *Rylands v Fletcher* is a special form of nuisance and *Hunter v Canary Wharf Ltd*[104] which decided that nuisance is a tort against land. It must, I think, follow that damages for personal injuries are not recoverable under the rule." To hold otherwise would have undermined the coherence of the law of tort by imposing strict liability for personal injuries but within the bounds set by torts developed to protect property interests.

1-31 **Psychiatric harm** The courts long ago accepted that health can be harmed by means other than overt physical attack or injury. Mental, as much as physical, health is protected by the law of torts. Conduct intended to shock and resulting in harm to the victim's mental or physical health was recognised as giving rise to liability in the late nineteenth century case of *Wilkinson v Downton*.[105] Negligent conduct which endangers the victim and thereby causes psychiatric harm is also recognised as giving rise to liability in just the same way as conduct causing physical injury.[106] However, the fear that liability for psychiatric harm to those who merely witness a shocking event will impose too great a burden on those such as motorists who may cause such an event, has led the courts to limit recovery to those who have a close emotional tie with those injured or endangered by the event.[107]

1-32 **Distress** As a general rule, torts that require proof of damage do not count "mere" distress or injury to feelings as compensatable loss. So with a claim in negligence for "pure" psychiatric harm (i.e. psychiatric harm that is not consequent on physical injury to the claimant) there can be no claim for emotional distress, anguish or grief[108] (as opposed to a recognised psychiatric condition) and with the tort of misfeasance in public office damage does not include "distress, injured feelings, distress or annoyance".[109] On the other hand, where the claimant suffers physical injury, the distress and anguish associated with coming to terms with the resulting disability or the knowledge that one's life expectancy has been reduced can be compensated as part of the overall award of damages for pain and suffering.[110] But anxiety at the risk of future harm is not, in itself, actionable injury, even when combined with symptomless physiological changes to the body[111]; and damages for fear of impending death are not recoverable by a victim's estate because "fear by itself, of whatever degree, is a normal human emotion for which no damages can be awarded".[112] With torts actionable per se, i.e. without proof of damage, dam-

[103] [1994] 2 A.C. 264.
[104] [1997] A.C. 655.
[105] [1897] 2 Q.B. 57.
[106] *Page v Smith* [1996] A.C. 155.
[107] See para.7-76 and note the Law Commission Report No.249 on *Liability for Psychiatric Illness* (1998).
[108] *McLoughlin v O'Brian* [1983] 1 A.C. 410 at 431, per Lord Bridge; *Alcock v Chief Constable of the South Yorkshire Police* [1992] 1 A.C. 310 at 409, per Lord Oliver. In *Hamilton-Jones v David & Snape (A Firm)* [2003] EWHC 3147 (Ch); [2004] 1 W.L.R. 924, Neuberger J considered that damages for distress at the loss of society of one's children were not recoverable in tort.
[109] *Watkins v Secretary of State for the Home Department* [2006] UKHL 17; [2006] 2 A.C. 395 at [7], per Lord Bingham.
[110] See para.27-56.
[111] *Rothwell v Chemical & Insulating Co* [2007] UKHL 39; [2008] 1 A.C. 281. See further para.7-97.
[112] *Hicks v Chief Constable of South Yorkshire Police* [1992] 2 All E.R. 65; [1992] P.I.Q.R. P433. See further para.7-96.

ages may be awarded to reflect injury to the claimant's feelings or distress, including in some instances aggravated damages[113]; and in limited circumstances damages for distress following negligent conduct may be available in contract,[114] or in bailment.[115] In the case of the deliberate infliction of distress, it is arguable that in principle a defendant *ought* to be held liable for the claimant's emotional reaction. The difficulty would be to identify when a defendant has set out intentionally to inflict distress, as opposed to merely behaving in a boorish or objectionable manner, and separating out cases where claimants are simply overly sensitive. Social interaction would become extremely limited if claimants "distressed" by perceived slights rushed to the courts for redress. In *Wainwright v Home Office*[116] Lord Hoffmann reserved his opinion on whether a single act intended to cause distress could give rise to liability at common law, commenting: "In workplaces all over the country, people constantly do and say things with the intention of causing distress and humiliation to others. This shows lack of consideration and appalling manners but I am not sure that the right way to deal with it is always by litigation." In the case of deliberate harassment statute provides for both criminal and civil liability. The Protection from Harassment Act 1997[117] imposes civil liability on a person who pursues a course of conduct which he ought to know amounts to harassment of another. The victim may be awarded damages for any anxiety caused by the harassment. This statutory liability is limited to a course of conduct, and so a single act intended to cause distress does not give rise to liability under the Act. One other statutory provision allows for damages for distress. The common law denied any claim for bereavement on the death of a loved one, but the Fatal Accidents Act 1976 s.1A provides statutory compensation for bereavement within narrow limits.[118] A claim for bereavement, fixed presently at a conventional sum of £15,120 (there is no enquiry into the severity of the claimant's grief), may be brought by a spouse of the deceased, or by the parents of an unmarried child under 18 years old. Disquiet at valuing a spouse's grief at £15,120 or denying any bereavement damages for the mother of a deceased 19-year-old child, or the child of deceased parents, illustrates the difficulty of allowing even limited compensation for distress.[119]

Family interests Interference with family rights was once protected by torts such as seduction and enticement. A man was regarded as having an interest in the practi- 1-33

113 See para.27-134.

114 See *Farley v Skinner* [2001] UKHL 49; [2002] 2 A.C. 732, in which the House of Lords held that damages in contract could be awarded for distress where a major object of the contract is to give "pleasure, relaxation or peace of mind", per Lord Steyn at [24]. There was no consideration whether the same principle would apply to a tortious claim where a major object of the relationship between the parties was to provide pleasure, relaxation or peace of mind for the claimant. See Jones and Morris "The Distressing Effects of Professional Incompetence" (2004) 20 P.N. 118.

115 *Yearworth v North Bristol NHS Trust* [2009] EWCA Civ 37; [2010] Q.B. 1 at [56]–[58].

116 [2003] UKHL 53; [2004] 2 A.C. 406 at [46].

117 See paras 14-19 to 14-22.

118 See para.27-93.

119 See, however, E. Descheemaeker, "Rationalising recovery for emotional harm in tort law" (2018) 134 L.Q.R. 602 who argues that "every wrong entitles the claimant to compensation for the ensuing emotional harm", notwithstanding "the unease that English law experiences towards moral loss or emotional harm". The author concedes that emotional distress on its own will not create a "wrong", but contends, inter alia, that once a wrong is established the damages award can reflect the claimant's emotional distress, even if the way an award of damages is expressed tends to conceal this.

cal services of his wife and children and in the sexual services of his wife. Such torts affirming an outdated conception of family relations have now been abolished. Attempts to protect parental rights more generally in tort have so far failed. In *Hamilton-Jones v David & Snape (A Firm)*[120] Neuberger J recognised that he was bound by the judgment of the Court of Appeal in *F v Wirral MBC*,[121] to hold that distress at the loss of society of one's child was not recoverable in tort. He commented that the *Wirral* judgment "unattractive though it may seem to many people", was carefully reasoned and represented the law. However, he did allow recovery in contract.[122] Perceived harms arising from modern methods of establishing a family will not necessarily be considered to be actionable. In *Yearworth v North Bristol NHS Trust*[123] the Court of Appeal held that the negligent destruction of the claimants' sperm which had been stored for possible future use in fertility treatment did not constitute "personal injury", though the Court accepted that the stored sperm was capable of being owned by the men who had provided it and that this could give rise to an action in bailment. And in *A v A Health and Social Services Trust*[124] the Court of Appeal in Northern Ireland held that the claimants, who had been born with a different skin colour from that of their parents as a result of negligence in the selection of gametes during the process of *in vitro* fertilisation carried out by the defendants, had not suffered compensatable damage. Although they may have suffered distress due to social prejudice the claimants could not point to "any physical or mental defect as a result of the process which led to their existence. As the judge correctly pointed out, they have no claim under the [Congenital Disabilities (Civil Liability) Act 1976] because they are healthy and normal children. Having a different skin colour from the majority of the surrounding population and their parents' cannot sensibly be regarded as damage or disability…".[125]

1-34 **Educational neglect and mental disability** In *Phelps v Hillingdon BC*[126] the House of Lords held that an education authority could be liable for the consequences of failure to diagnose a pupil's dyslexia and provide appropriate education. Lord Clyde said: "The loss claimed may be purely of an economic character. But the mental or psychological effects of negligent advice may in themselves be able to constitute a proper head of damages. Dyslexia is a condition which may become worse through the absence of an appropriate educational regime, and the frustration of an inappropriate regime may cause psychological stress and injury." In *Bracknell Forest BC v Adams*[127] the House of Lords was asked to determine the nature of the injury in such cases for the purpose of the limitation period. Giving the leading speech Lord Hoffmann confirmed that it constituted personal injury

[120] [2003] EWHC 3147 (Ch); [2004] 1 W.L.R 924.
[121] [1991] Fam. 69; [1991] 2 W.L.R. 1132.
[122] Solicitors were held liable for a mother's mental distress when the father removed children from the UK, the solicitors having negligently failed to request a renewal by the Passport Office of a restriction on issuing passports for the children.
[123] [2009] EWCA Civ 37; [2010] Q.B. 1.
[124] [2011] NICA 28; [2012] N.I. 77.
[125] [2011] NICA 28; [2012] N.I. 77 at [9]. The case is discussed by S. Sheldon, "Only skin deep? The harm of being born a different colour to one's parents" (2011) 19 Med. L. Rev. 657.
[126] [2001] 2 A.C. 619 at 670.
[127] [2004] UKHL 29; [2005] 1 A.C. 76; confirming *Robinson v St Helens MBC* [2002] EWCA Civ 1099; [2003] P.I.Q.R. P9.

rather than economic loss but put the point a little differently from Lord Clyde, saying:

> "Such a claim in a post-Cartesian world is for personal injury. … But on what basis can the lack of the ability to read and write be a personal injury? … Some mental disabilities are caused by irremediable defects in the brain circuitry. But the brain has the most remarkable capacity to compensate for defects by calling upon other parts of the circuitry. … It seems to me that Evans LJ [in the Court of Appeal in *X v Bedfordshire CC*] was quite right to draw the analogy with negligent failure to treat a physical injury which the defendant did not cause. … Treating the inability [to read and write] as an untreated injury … seems a sensible practical result."[128]

Reputation Reputation is extensively protected by the tort of defamation and to some extent by the tort of malicious falsehood.[129] The importance of an untarnished reputation and the esteem of the community is such that the onus of justifying any defamatory statement falls on the defendant, and liability for publication of a defamatory statement is strict. The importance of the interest was reflected in both the persistence of jury trial and the high levels of damages often awarded. However, legislation introduced a defence for non-intentional defamation (provided that an apology and some compensatory payment is made), and provided a non-jury summary procedure for minor cases. The courts have also sought to bring awards more into line with those made for personal injury.[130] More far-reaching reforms have been introduced by the Defamation Act 2013, including a higher threshold test for what constitutes actionable defamation and making jury trials the exception rather than the rule, in an attempt to provide greater protection to freedom of expression. Reputation exemplifies an interest where the interests of one individual can directly conflict with the interests of his peers. Freedom of speech, and a claimant's interest in his reputation, may have to be weighed in the balance. In *Derbyshire CC v Times Newspapers*[131] the House of Lords held that public authorities could not sue to protect their "governing" reputation. To allow such claims would infringe freedom of speech and inhibit proper criticism. The delicate balance between interest in reputation and other competing interests evolved within the tort of defamation prompted the New Zealand Court of Appeal to find that the interest in reputation should be exclusively protected by defamation and to reject any duty of care actionable in negligence in relation to reputation.[132] However, in *Spring v Guardian Assurance Plc*[133] the House of Lords held that the writer of a reference may owe a duty of care in negligence to the person who is the subject of the reference, so opening up the tort of negligence to a new role in the protection of reputation.[134] 1-35

128 [2004] UKHL 29; [2005] 1 A.C. 76 at [20]. Lord Hoffmann said that: "It would be drawing too fine a distinction to say that the neglect caused no injury because nothing could be done to repair the brain and the other parts of the brain which would have to be trained to compensate had never been injured."

129 See para.22-03.

130 See *John v MGN Ltd* [1997] Q.B. 586.

131 [1993] A.C. 534. See also *Reynolds v Times Newspapers* [2001] 2 A.C. 127.

132 *Bell-Booth Group v Att Gen* [1989] 3 N.L.Z.R. 148.

133 [1995] A.C. 296.

134 In contract, a former employee may also recover where his former employer's conduct in carrying on its business in a corrupt manner, has led to a stigma damaging his employment prospects: *Malik v Bank of Credit and Commerce International* [1998] A.C. 20. It is possible that stigma claims might also succeed in tort.

1-36 **Privacy** A number of torts indirectly protect privacy. Trespass to land and nuisance protect those with an interest in land from direct invasion and indirect interference as by taking photographs of activities on the land from outside its boundary. However, in *Hunter v Canary Wharf Ltd*[135] the House of Lords decided that nuisance protection was not available to those who had no legal interest in the land and hence, a child of the land owner would not be able to claim in respect of pestering telephone calls.[136] Defamation provides some protection as is illustrated by the case of *Tolley v Fry*[137] where the claimant was able to prevent the use of his image in the defendant's publicity on the grounds that it would give rise to defamation by innuendo. Malicious falsehood can also provide some protection as shown by *Kaye v Robertson*.[138] The claimant, a popular actor, suffered head injuries in a road accident and was recovering in an intensive care room in a hospital. A reporter from the defendant's newspaper defied the "keep out" signs on the door to the room, entered and purported to conduct an interview with the claimant. Because of his condition, the claimant could remember nothing but his agent, on discovering what had happened, sought an injunction to prevent publication of the purported interview. The Court of Appeal granted an injunction on the ground that the defendant was clearly proposing to commit the tort of malicious falsehood. The proposed publication was false in the sense that no real interview had taken place; it was malicious because the defendant knew it was untrue; and it would cause the claimant financial damage because it would have deprived him of his opportunity to sell his first interview after the accident. These were the three requirements for liability. But the court also held that the claimant had no claim for breach of privacy as such as there was no general tort of invasion of privacy.

1-37 **No tort of invasion of privacy** In *Wainwright v Home Office*,[139] the House of Lords confirmed that invasion of privacy did not of itself amount to a tort. The claimants' privacy had been invaded when they were strip-searched by prison officers prior to visiting a prisoner. The search had not been conducted in accordance with the relevant prison rules and hence, the defendant's conduct was not protected by statutory authority. One claimant had been touched during the search and successfully claimed damages under the tort of battery for the physical interference and resultant psychiatric injury.[140] The other claimant had not been touched and suffered only distress as a result of the experience. Her claim rested on an extension of the tort of trespass to cover the intentional causing of distress or the creation of a tort of invasion of privacy. The House of Lords rejected both suggestions. Lord Hoffmann gave the court's judgment in relation to the privacy argument. He noted that there were "a number of common law and statutory remedies of which it might be said that at least one of the underlying values they protect is a right of privacy. ... common law torts include trespass, nuisance, defamation and malicious falsehood; there is the equitable action for breach of confidence and statutory remedies under the Protection from Harassment Act 1997 and the Data Protec-

---

135 [1997] A.C. 655.

136 The Court of Appeal had previously allowed such a claim in *Khorasandjian v Bush* [1993] Q.B. 727 but this decision was overturned in *Hunter*.

137 [1931] A.C. 333.

138 [1991] F.S.R. 62.

139 [2003] UKHL 53; [2004] 2 A.C. 406.

140 The intimate nature of the touching resulted in the claimant suffering post-traumatic stress disorder. He was awarded £4,500 including £1,000 for aggravated damages by the trial judge.

tion Act 1998".[141] But he held that the common law should not elevate the underlying value into a principle of law itself. Rather it was preferable to develop particular tort actions to meet particular situations. That way detailed rules could be developed to balance privacy against other interests in the particular circumstances. In the absence of any evidence that the prison officers intended to cause the claimant distress, Lord Hoffmann considered that the situation did not justify developing any existing tort actions to provide a remedy. He also rejected the argument that the right for respect for private life under art.8 of the European Convention for the Protection of Human Rights required the common law to develop a general tort of invasion of privacy. Rather, the concern of the European court would be with whether English law provided an adequate remedy in specific cases where it considered there to have been an invasion of privacy. Subsequently, the European Court of Human Rights' concluded in *Wainwright v United Kingdom*[142] that the strip searches of prison visitors had failed to comply strictly with safeguards to protect the dignity of those searched constituted a breach of art.8, and, given the decision of the House of Lords, the lack of redress in the national courts meant there had also been a violation of art.13.

Privacy, breach of confidence, and misuse of private information In *Campbell v MGN*[143] Lady Hale cited *Wainwright* when finding there to be no new right of privacy, but Lord Nicholls also acknowledged that the protection of various aspects of privacy was a "fast developing area of the law" spurred by the enactment of the Human Rights Act. In that case the House of Lords held the defendants liable to the claimant, a fashion model, for publishing details of her narcotics treatment, including a photograph of her leaving a clinic, on the basis of an action for breach of confidence. In *Campbell* there was no previous relationship of confidence concerning the information and Lord Nicholls suggested that the essence of the modern action was better formulated as "misuse of private information". In *HRH Prince of Wales v Associated Newspapers*[144] Lord Phillips explained the law in the following terms: 1-38

> "The English court has recognised that it should, in so far as possible, develop the common law in such a way as to give effect to convention rights. [It] has been concerned to develop a law of privacy that provides protection of the rights to 'private and family life, his home and correspondence' recognised by art 8 of the convention. To this end, the courts have extended the law of confidentiality so as to protect art 8 rights in circumstances which do not involve a breach of a confidential relationship."

Where no breach of a confidential relationship was involved, the "balance between art 8 and art 10 rights will usually involve weighing the nature and consequences of the breach of privacy against the public interest, if any, in the disclosure of the private information".[145] Where, as with the publication of the personal diaries of the Prince of Wales, the information was obtained through breach of a confidential relationship: "a significant element to be weighed in the balance is the importance in a democratic society of upholding duties of confidence ... It is not enough to

[141] [2003] UKHL 53; [2004] 2 A.C. 406 at [18]. See now the Data Protection Act 2018.
[142] (2007) 44 E.H.R.R. 40.
[143] [2004] UKHL 22; [2004] A.C. 457 at [133] and [11] respectively. See para.26-37.
[144] [2006] EWCA Civ 1776; [2008] Ch. 57 at [25]–[26].
[145] [2006] EWCA Civ 1776; [2008] Ch. 57 at [65].

justify publication that the information in question is a matter of public interest."[146] It would seem that, whatever the judicial view as to the existence of a *tort* of privacy, it is clear that the courts have been fashioning a remedy for certain invasions of privacy by adapting the action for breach of confidence as viewed through the prism of art.8 of the Convention.[147] The courts have now reached the conclusion that a claim based on "misuse of private information" constitutes an actionable tort which is distinct from a claim in respect of breach of confidentiality.[148]

1-39 **Autonomy** In *Rees v Darlington Memorial Hospital NHS Trust*[149] a majority of a seven judge House of Lords recognised autonomy as an interest that could be protected by the law of tort. A sterilisation operation for which the defendant was responsible, was carried out negligently and its failure led to the claimant giving birth to an unwanted, but healthy child. Following its earlier decision in *McFarlane v Tayside Health Board*,[150] the House of Lords held that no damages could be awarded for the cost of bringing up such a child but the majority held that a conventional award of £15,000 should be made. Lord Bingham said that it "would not be intended to be compensatory … but … would afford some measure of recognition of the wrong done".[151] Lord Millett explained more fully that the award was "not for the birth of the child but for the denial of an important aspect of [the parents] personal autonomy, viz the right to limit the size of their family". He continued: "This is an important aspect of human dignity, which is increasingly being regarded as an important human right which should be protected by the law. The loss of this right is not an abstract or theoretical one. …the parents have lost the opportunity to live their lives in the way that they wished and planned to do. The loss of this opportunity, whether characterised as a right or a freedom, is a proper subject for compensation by way of damages."[152] The award is made without proof of financial loss. Dissenting, Lord Steyn argued that it was for Parliament to create such a novel remedy and that the "Law Commissions and Parliament ought in any event, to consider the impact of the creation of a power to make a conventional award … for the coherence of the tort system".[153] There may be other situations where autonomy could be recognised as an interest to be protected. In *Chester v Afshar*[154] Lord Steyn justified providing a remedy for a doctor's negligent failure to warn a patient of risks associated with surgery, on the basis of the need to "give due respect to the autonomy and dignity of each patient". However, he and the majority of the Lords chose to recognise this wrong by awarding the patient damages for the disability resulting from the surgery rather than for the loss of the op-

---

146 [2006] EWCA Civ 1776; [2008] Ch. 57 at [67].

147 See in particular *HRH Prince of Wales v Associated Newspapers* [2006] EWCA Civ 1776; [2008] Ch. 57; *McKennitt v Ash* [2006] EWCA Civ 1714; [2008] Q.B. 73 at [8]: " … the English courts have to proceed through the tort of breach of confidence, into which the jurisprudence of articles 8 and 10 has to be shoehorned"; *Murray v Express Newspapers Plc* [2008] EWCA Civ 446; [2009] Ch. 481.

148 *Vidal-Hall v Google Inc* [2015] EWCA Civ 311; [2016] Q.B. 1003 at [43] and [51]; endorsed by the Court of Appeal in *Gulati v MGN Ltd* [2015] EWCA Civ 1291; [2017] Q.B. 149 at [88]. See Ch.26.

149 [2003] UKHL 52; [2004] 1 A.C. 309.

150 [2000] 2 A.C. 59.

151 [2003] UKHL 52; [2004] 1 A.C. 309 at [8].

152 [2003] UKHL 52; [2004] 1 A.C. 309 at [123].

153 [2003] UKHL 52; [2004] 1 A.C. 309 at [46]. See also the similar views of Lord Hope at [77].

154 [2004] UKHL 41; [2005] 1 A.C. 134 at [18].

portunity to choose.[155] In *Rees*, autonomy was protected against negligent conduct but this raises the possibility that it might be protected against intentional conduct, for example, by the developing tort of misfeasance in a public office. However, there is no free-standing cause of action for interference with a claimant's autonomy. An action by a patient against a doctor for non-disclosure of the risks of treatment must be an action in negligence, albeit that the claim can be characterised as an interference with the patient's autonomous choices about whether to accept a particular medical treatment.[156]

(ii) Property interests

Possession The tort of trespass to land and the several chattel torts, in particular conversion, operate to protect interests in the possession of property, and the right to immediate possession thereof.[157] Consequently a claim in tort to assert such an interest will commonly raise questions of title to property. 1-40

Physical damage to property Just as from earliest times the writ of trespass protected interests in bodily integrity, so trespass to goods and land protected the integrity of property. In the context of negligence liability in *Murphy v Brentwood DC*[158] Lord Oliver said: "The infliction of physical injury to the person or property of another universally requires to be justified." Crucially, the statement that damages for physical damage to property are readily recoverable in the tort of negligence must be qualified in the sense that physical damage must be distinguished from pure economic loss. Physical damage, in the context of Lord Oliver's dictum, means actual tangible harm to the fabric of property, or to the land itself, caused by a factor external to the property. Defects in the property which simply render it less valuable, affect quality, but which do not affect safety, do not constitute physical damage. Where the allegation is, as it was in *Murphy*, that the negligence of the defendant had resulted in visible structural defects in the property itself, but no tangible damage to persons or separate property, the loss resulting from that damage must still normally be classified as economic loss. The loss is defined as the cost to the claimant of remedying the defect and the reduced value of the property he has acquired. Again, where physical damage is occasioned to property, only a person who enjoyed a proprietary interest in that property at the time that the relevant damage occurred can generally recover in negligence for the loss occasioned to him by that damage. Damage and destruction of property may well infringe the contractual rights and business expectations of others. Their loss will be classified as purely economic, and generally irrecoverable.[159] In those torts primarily concerned with protection of interests in real property, nuisance and *Rylands v Fletcher*, actual physical damage to the land, property erected on it, and, 1-41

---

155 It is not surprising that Lord Steyn did not consider a conventional award for loss of opportunity to choose given his view in *Rees*. Lord Hoffmann in his dissent did suggest that there was "a case for a modest solatium" but felt that the cost of litigation made the "law of torts an unsuitable vehicle for distributing the modest compensation which might be payable": [2004] UKHL 41; [2005] 1 A.C. 134 at [34]. However, claims for a modest solatium are likely to be less costly than those for a substantial disability award.

156 See *Shaw v Kovac* [2017] EWCA Civ 1028; [2017] 1 W.L.R. 4773 at [48].

157 See generally Chs 16 and 18.

158 [1991] 1 A.C. 398 at 487.

159 *Leigh & Sillivan Ltd v Aliakmon Shipping Co Ltd* [1986] A.C. 785; see generally at para.7-154.

it seems, goods stored on it will be recoverable. Where there is a continuing nuisance, a claim can be brought in respect of damage which originated prior to the claimant's acquisition of an interest in the property.[160]

1-42 **Enjoyment of property** The interest in enjoyment of land has long been protected by the tort of nuisance and by the closely related tort of *Rylands v Fletcher*.[161] The tort of nuisance is regarded as applying where the cause of the interference with the enjoyment of land is a continuing activity for which the defendant is responsible whereas the rule in *Rylands* applies where the interference has been caused by an isolated escape of something dangerous from the defendant's land. The tort of nuisance neatly illustrates the difficult process of balancing conflicting interests to ensure that the interest of one neighbour in the free and undisturbed enjoyment of his property does not violate the corresponding interest of adjoining neighbours.[162] Nuisance and *Rylands v Fletcher* derive "from a conception of mutual duties of adjoining or neighbouring landowners".[163] In *Cambridge Water Co v Eastern Counties Leather*[164] the House of Lords stressed the common elements of the two tort actions and in *Hunter v Canary Wharf*,[165] it stressed the proprietary nature of nuisance. Thus, an action in nuisance was only available to persons with an interest in the affected property and compensation for nuisance involving personal discomfort was to be measured by the resulting diminution of the value of the land and not by analogy with personal injury awards.

1-43 **Intangible property** Protection against physical damage to property, dispossession, and interference in the enjoyment of land sufficed for the forms of property interests common until the industrial and technological developments of the nineteenth and twentieth centuries. Intangible property such as trade reputation, copyright, patents and trade marks demands more subtle forms of protection. The law recognises and protects such property rights, but both their existence and vindication tend to depend on an amalgam of the principles of common law and equity, and increasingly on statute. To a large extent, statute now regulates the protection of patents, copyrights, registered trade marks and design, albeit the remedies to redress an infringement of those rights have tortious aspects. These are reviewed in Ch.24. The tort of conversion extends by fiction to protect a limited category of intangibles such as negotiable instruments but, it seems, will not be

---

160 *Delaware Mansions Ltd v Westminster City Council* [2001] UKHL 55; [2002] A.C. 321. See para.19-25.

161 The rights conferred by the law of nuisance arise by virtue of the general common law, and do not depend on the terms of any conveyance or transfer of the land: *Thornhill v Sita Metal Recycling Ltd* [2009] EWHC 2037 (QB); [2009] Env. L.R. 35 at [20], per HH Judge Seymour: "A nuisance is a wrong to the enjoyment, by a person in exclusive possession of the land affected, of that land. The right to complain of a nuisance is not a commodity to be bought or sold at whim. It is, in law, an incident of exclusive possession of land ... ".

162 This is sometimes referred to as the principle of "reasonable user", though this is not unproblematic (see *Coventry v Lawrence* [2014] UKSC 13; [2014] A.C. 822 at [179] per Lord Carnwath) and it only applies to intangible damage to the occupier's enjoyment of land. Where a nuisance causes physical damage there is no balancing exercise undertaken: *St Helens Smelting Co v Tipping* (1865) 11 H.L.C. 642; para.19-08.

163 *Read v Lyons* [1947] A.C. 156 at 173, per Lord Macmillan.

164 [1994] 2 A.C. 264.

165 [1997] A.C. 655.

extended further.[166] The tort of passing-off has developed to extend the protection afforded to trade reputation. Trade secrets continue to be protected initially by breach of confidence. Passing off and breach of confidence are examined in detail in Chs 25 and 26.

(iii) Economic interests

Pure economic loss "Pure economic loss" is the term used to describe an economic loss to the claimant which does not result from any physical damage to or interference with his person or tangible property. As Hobhouse LJ has observed, "in a competitive economic society the conduct of one person is always liable to have economic consequences for another and, in principle, economic activity does not have to have regard to the interests of others and is justifiable by the actor having regard to his own interests alone".[167] Hence, economic interests received limited protection. Pure economic loss will normally take two forms: wasted expenditure or loss of a gain, profits or profitability. The tort of deceit and the expanded tort of passing-off protect economic interests of both kinds where loss results from deliberate or reckless statements or conduct designed to induce the claimant to act against his interests, or to damage those interests with third parties. *Hedley Byrne v Heller*[168] allowed recovery of economic loss in negligence within the boundaries of a special relationship of a kind rendering it appropriate to require the defendant to safeguard the economic interests of the claimant. The outer limits of such special relationships, which will generally relate to wasted expenditure, are now set largely by *Caparo Industries Plc v Dickman*.[169] Loss of a potential gain, will, unless a consequence of physical damage, normally fall outside the ambit of torts. However, in *White v Jones*[170] the House of Lords confirmed that exceptionally the relationship between claimant and defendant can be such that responsibility for protecting the claimant's expectations properly rests with the defendant. Furthermore, a claimant who has been misled by a defendant into entering a particular transaction, may claim for the profits which would have been made had it entered an alternative transaction.[171] 1-44

Unfair competition The majority judgment in *Allen v Flood*[172] rejected the contention that the claimants enjoyed a "a legal right ... to pursue freely and without hindrance, interruption or molestation, the profession, trade or calling which he has adopted for his livelihood". They enjoyed at most a freedom to pursue their livelihood or business "conditioned by a precisely similar right in their fellow men". English law embraces the principle of free competition. Damage to business interests is actionable only if proved to be unlawful. Prior to *Allen v Flood* the 1-45

---

166 In *OBG Ltd v Allan* [2005] EWCA Civ 106; [2005] Q.B. 762 at [56], Peter Gibson LJ, with the agreement of Mance and Carnwath LJJ, on this point, said that there could be no conversion of a chose in action or contractual right. Despite the attraction of such a step, it was not open to the court to invent such a tort. This view was upheld by a bare majority of the House of Lords: [2007] UKHL 21; [2008] 1 A.C. 1. See para.16-36.

167 *Perrett v Collins* [1998] 2 Lloyd's Rep. 255; [1999] P.N.L.R. 77 at 84.

168 [1964] A.C. 465.

169 [1990] 2 A.C. 605.

170 [1995] 2 A.C. 207.

171 *East v Maurer* [1991] 1 W.L.R. 461, and see para.17-46.

172 [1898] A.C. 1.

discrete tort of inducing breach of contract had developed to prohibit competitors luring away key employees or business partners.[173] That tort's extension to interference with contracts, the development of the tort of intimidation,[174] and the evolution of what Lord Diplock described as the genus tort of unlawful interference with trade[175] has resulted in the law of torts playing a major role in restraint of unfair competition. Tort's role in regulating unfair competition was reviewed by the House of Lords in *OBG Ltd v Allen*.[176] Lord Hoffmann considered that the courts should be cautious in extending torts which were "designed only to enforce basic standards of civilised behaviour in economic competition".[177] Lord Nicholls took a wider view of the role of tort as being "to curb clearly excessive conduct" by providing "a remedy for intentional economic harm caused by unacceptable means".[178] Lord Walker, whilst supporting Lord Hoffmann's view, commented that neither approach was "likely to be the last word on this difficult and important area of the law".[179] The economic torts are analysed in detail in Ch.23.

(iv) Loss of chance

1-46 **Loss of chance** It has long been recognised that loss of a chance of avoiding a financial loss or making a financial gain is an interest recognised by the law of tort. The most common situation is where due to the negligence of a solicitor, a client has lost the chance of litigating and recovering compensation. So, if the client would have had a 25 per cent chance of recovering £100,000 in the lost litigation, it will be able to recover £25,000 against the negligent solicitor. The client does not have to prove on the balance of probabilities that it would have been successful in the litigation because the loss is recognised as being the chance. The same reasoning applies to the loss of a chance of insurance cover, tax saving, property sale and the successful outcome of a business negotiation.[180] Lord Hoffmann has said that in such cases, "the chance can itself plausibly be described as an item of property, like a lottery ticket".[181] In *Gregg v Scott*[182] a majority of the House of Lords concluded that, on the particular facts, loss of the chance of recovery from a medical condition would not be recognised as a protected interest. The defendant's negligence led to a nine-month delay in diagnosing the claimant's cancer. During that period the disease spread and the claimant's statistical chance of surviving reduced from 42 per cent to 25 per cent. The claimant sued for the loss of the 17 per cent chance of recovery. The majority of the Lords rejected this claim partly because of the difficulties of assessing the lost chance in medical cases[183] and partly because of the

---

173 See *Lumley v Gye* (1853) 2 El. & Bl. 216.
174 *Rookes v Barnard* [1964] A.C. 1129.
175 *Merkur Island Shipping Corp v Laughton* [1983] 2 A.C. 570 at 608.
176 [2007] UKHL 21; [2008] 1 A.C. 1.
177 [2007] UKHL 21; [2008] 1 A.C. 1 at [56].
178 [2007] UKHL 21; [2008] 1 A.C. 1 at [153].
179 [2007] UKHL 21; [2008] 1 A.C. 1 at [269].
180 See further paras 2-77, 9-113 and 27-14.
181 *Gregg v Scott* [2005] UKHL 2; [2005] 2 A.C. 176 at [83].
182 [2005] UKHL 2; [2005] 2 A.C. 176. See further para. 2-89 onwards.
183 Lord Phillips, [2005] UKHL 2; [2005] 2 A.C. 176 at [170], pointed to the difficulty of making deductions in an individual case on the basis of statistics. The claimant had defied the statistics by surviving the eight years from the misdiagnosis to the date of the Lords' judgment.

potentially radical impact on litigation[184] and for insurance companies and the National Health Service.[185] Their Lordships pointed out that the claimant was not left without a remedy because he could recover for the suffering and financial loss undoubtedly caused by the worsening of the disease due to the delay. These were recognised heads of loss. It should be noted that in assessing recognised heads of loss such as loss of income following disease or injury, the court will consider the chance of particular outcomes, e.g. whether but for the injury the claimant would have qualified as a teacher.[186] But this is part of the process of quantifying the loss resulting from damage to a recognised interest, i.e. personal injury caused by the defendant, and does not involve recognising loss of chance as the protected interest.

(v) Public interests

Public rights The primary function of the law of torts remains to protect private rights and private interests. There may however be circumstances in which an individual who can prove particular damage to himself from the violation of some public right may sue in tort. Public nuisance is a crime, but a person who has suffered actual damage over and above that inflicted on the public generally has a claim in tort. At its simplest, obstruction of the highway constitutes public nuisance and the individual who breaks his leg falling over the obstruction can recover in tort. Although these principles have the potential to limit the public right to use the highway, in its landmark decision, *DPP v Jones*,[187] the House of Lords held that a peaceful demonstration constituted reasonable user of the highway. The potential of public nuisance as a means of obtaining redress for and deterring undesirable public wrongs, such as environmental pollution, has been only partially explored.[188] **1-47**

Due process The tort of malicious prosecution historically protected the individual against abuse of the criminal process, albeit the interests vindicated thereby primarily concern liberty, property and reputation rather than due process itself.[189] The extension of liability to damage resulting from misuse of civil process **1-48**

---

[184] As Baroness Hale noted, [2005] UKHL 2; [2005] 2 A.C. 176 at [225], the "proportionate recovery effect must cut both ways". Litigants with less than a probable chance of recovery would get something but conversely, litigants with a probable but not certain chance of recovery would not get everything.

[185] See Lord Hoffmann, [2005] UKHL 2; [2005] 2 A.C. 176 at [90], where he argued that a step with such radical consequences should be left to Parliament. Contrast *Barker v Corus (UK) Plc* [2006] UKHL 20; [2006] 2 A.C. 572, where the House of Lords held that the claimant's damage, having contracted mesothelioma as a result of exposure to asbestos, consisted not of the mesothelioma itself, but of the risk or chance of contracting the disease following negligent exposure to asbestos by the defendant. This meant that an individual defendant who had exposed the claimant to asbestos was only liable to the extent that the period of exposure for which he was responsible contributed to the overall risk of the claimant contracting the disease. However, in *Durham v BAI (Run Off) Ltd* [2012] UKSC 14; [2012] 1 W.L.R. 867 the Supreme Court took a different view of the claimant's damage in such cases. The defendant's liability was not for the risk of developing the disease; rather the reality was that the defendant was being held responsible for the mesothelioma itself. For discussion of the relationship between *Barker v Corus* and *Gregg v Scott* see para.2-98.

[186] See for example *Doyle v Wallace* [1998] P.I.Q.R. Q146. In such a case the court will discount the earnings level of a teacher to take account of the chance that the claimant would not have qualified. See further para.27-14.

[187] [1999] 2 A.C. 240; [1999] 2 W.L.R. 625.

[188] See *AB v South West Water Services Ltd* [1993] Q.B. 705.

[189] See Ch.15.

and the emergent tort of misfeasance in public office[190] suggest tort does play a role in protecting the citizen against flagrant violation of due process. This does not extend to a general right to damages for maladministration.[191]

1-49 **Constitutional rights** In *Watkins v Secretary of State for the Home Department*[192] the Court of Appeal held that impeding access to a court by opening correspondence between a prisoner and his legal adviser could constitute the tort of misfeasance in public office, even in the absence of damage, relying on the old case of *Ashby v White*[193] where a misfeasance claim was upheld in relation to deprivation of the right to vote. This was on the basis that an infringement of such a "constitutional right" was so serious that it should be protected, even if there was no damage. However, the House of Lords reversed this decision,[194] taking the view that *Ashby v White* did not support the Court of Appeal's conclusions. One of the principal objections to the Court of Appeal's attempt to provide a special category of misfeasance in public office which would be actionable per se was the uncertainty, in a jurisdiction with an unwritten constitution, of identifying constitutional rights. Lord Rodger observed that: "The term 'constitutional right' works well enough, alongside equivalent terms, in the field of statutory interpretation. But, even if it were otherwise suitable, it is not sufficiently precise to define a class of rights whose abuse should give rise to a right of action in tort without proof of damage."[195]

1-50 **Damage and breach of statutory duty** A statute may well have, as one of its purposes, the protection of certain interests falling outside the routine classification of interests protected in tort or, arguably protecting a recognised interest against a broader range of wrongful conduct. That in itself is not enough. It must be established that Parliament intended to confer an individual right of action on a category of persons to whom the claimant belongs, not just that the statute was designed to benefit them in some general sense. So while the Prison Rules in part exist to protect prisoners, the House of Lords found that they were not intended to offer prisoners civil redress for any breach of the Rules.[196]

(b) Nature of the injurer's conduct

1-51 **Breach of duty** Winfield defined tortious liability as the breach of a duty primarily fixed by law. A violation of an interest protected by tort is unlawful because it is a breach of a duty owed by the defendant not to violate that interest of the claimant. Lord Denning in *Letang v Cooper*[197] held that intentional trespass was as

---

190 *Bourgoin SA v Ministry of Agriculture* [1986] Q.B. 716.

191 *R. v Knowsley MBC Ex p. Maguire* (1992) L.G.R. 653. See also *Sandhar v Department of Transport* [2004] EWCA Civ 1440; [2005] 1 W.L.R. 1632, where Brooke LJ at [57], expressed his regret that there was no means for compensating the claimant from public funds for losses resulting from what seemed to be maladministration.

192 [2004] EWCA Civ 966; [2005] Q.B. 883.

193 (1703) 1 E.R. 417.

194 [2006] UKHL 17; [2006] 2 A.C. 395.

195 [2006] UKHL 17; [2006] 2 A.C. 395 at [62]; see also per Lord Bingham at [26]: "the outcome in other than clear cases would necessarily be uncertain"; per Lord Carswell at [79]: "it would not be a readily workable expedient."

196 *R. v Deputy Governor of Parkhurst Prison Ex p. Hague* [1992] 1 A.C. 58.

197 [1965] 1 Q.B. 232.

much a breach of duty as negligent infliction of personal injury because all torts constituted a breach of a relevant duty. Conceptually, this analysis of tort as a progression of duties imposed by law to protect interests is attractive but it has little practical significance. Outside the tort of negligence, where proof of a duty and its breach is of primary importance, to say that commission of a tort requires that the claimant establishes a breach of duty says virtually nothing about what kind of wrongdoing the claimant must prove. Each tort has its own particular rules governing the conduct sufficient to engage liability. The details are explored in the succeeding chapters and this section undertakes only a very general survey of these kinds of wrongdoing on which liability in tort is based. It considers first, the relevance of damage; secondly, the significance of the key causal distinctions between direct and indirect damage and acts and omissions; and thirdly, the significance of the different types of fault recognised by the law of tort.

(i) Damage

Torts actionable per se In the majority of torts the claimant must establish that he suffered some actual damage, that the damage was in fact caused by the defendant's tortious conduct, and that the damage is not, in law, too remote. A small number of torts however do not require any proof of actual damage. They are actionable per se. The violation of the claimant's interest alone is sufficient to entitle him to a remedy in tort. The origin of the distinction between torts actionable on damage and those actionable without damage is historical. The action on the case regarded damage as the essence of the wrong. The writs of trespass did not.[198] The historical distinction between trespass and case may provide some explanation for the modern taxonomy of torts requiring proof of damage and torts actionable per se, but it hardly provides a principled rationale. So, for example, in *Watkins v Secretary of State for the Home Department*[199] Lord Carswell commented that: **1-52**

> "One might question, more generally, whether the law should continue to support a distinction between those actions in which proof of material damage is needed and those in which there is no such requirement. It might not unreasonably be said that any civil wrong should carry damages and that those who deliberately flout the law and deprive others of their rights by abusing their position should be liable to the victims of such acts."

However, his Lordship was not convinced that it would be appropriate for the House to take such a course, but if it were thought advisable to give the idea further consideration it should be done by the Law Commission "which would be well placed to consider in depth the issues and possible consequences of such a change in the law".[200] The most important modern instances of the torts actionable per se are the following. Each tort is fully dealt with in its appropriate chapter:

(1) Trespass to land, goods and the person remain actionable per se, although

[198] Note, however, Lord Walker's observation in *Watkins v Secretary of State for the Home Department* [2006] UKHL 17; [2006] 2 A.C. 395 at [74] pointing out that though the tort of libel (as did misfeasance in public office) developed from the action on the case, libel is actionable without proof of monetary loss, so that "ancient legal history" was not necessarily a good reason for maintaining the distinction between torts actionable per se and torts requiring proof of damage.

[199] [2006] UKHL 17; [2006] 2 A.C. 395 at [80].

[200] [2006] UKHL 17; [2006] 2 A.C. 395 at [81]–[82].

if it is still possible to found an action on a negligent trespass to the person it has been argued that damage must be proved in that instance.[201]

(2) In an action for nuisance alleging infringement of proprietary rights such as the rights of riparian owners, rights of light and rights of way, it is necessary only to show an appreciable infringement of the right and not that any tangible damage has been inflicted.[202]

(3) Libel is actionable per se.[203] Slander generally requires proof of damage but at common law certain kinds of slander are also actionable per se.[204]

(4) In a number of old cases relating to breach of duty by public officers, an action was held to lie on proof of breach of duty alone. In *Ashby v White*[205] the returning officer was found liable for refusing to accept the claimant's vote without proof of damage. The action on the case lay because the franchise was recognised as a legal right the infringement of which must be afforded a remedy.

1-53 **Constitutional rights, misfeasance and human rights** In *Watkins v Secretary of State for the Home Department*[206] the Court of Appeal, relying on *Ashby v White*,[207] held that where misfeasance in public office interferes with a "constitutional right", it was actionable per se and the court could award both nominal damages and, where appropriate, exemplary damages. Prison officers had interfered with the claimant's constitutional right to unimpeded access to a court by deliberately, and unlawfully, opening the claimant's correspondence with his legal advisers. The claimant had not suffered any "material damage" (meaning "financial loss or physical or mental injury", but excluding "distress, injured feelings, distress or annoyance"[208]). In the Court of Appeal Brooke LJ treated *Ashby* as turning on the constitutional right to vote rather than "as a case involving infringement of a franchise (being a property right)".[209] However, this analysis was rejected by the House of Lords.[210] Lord Rodger considered that *Ashby* did treat the right to vote as a property right[211]; and Lord Bingham, though conceding that "[w]e would now, of course, regard the right to vote as basic, fundamental or constitutional", pointed out that none of these expressions was used by Holt CJ in *Ashby v White*, and scarcely could have been, given the very limited franchise at that time. Thus, it was anachronistic to rely on *Ashby* for a proposition that it would not have been thought to support at the time. It was, said his Lordship, "entirely novel to treat the character of the right invaded as determinative, in the present context, of whether material damage need be proved".[212] Thus, there was no basis for the view that misfeasance in public office, when it involved breach of a constitutional right, should be action-

201 *Letang v Cooper* [1965] 1 Q.B. 232 at 240, 245.
202 *Nicholls v Ely Beet Sugar Factory Ltd* [1936] Ch. 343 at 383.
203 *Hayward v Hayward* (1887) 34 Ch. D. 198.
204 See para.21-47.
205 (1703) 2 Ld. Ray. 938. See further para.1-53.
206 [2004] EWCA Civ 966; [2005] Q.B. 883.
207 (1703) 2 Ld. Ray. 938.
208 *Watkins v Secretary of State for the Home Department* [2006] UKHL 17; [2006] 2 A.C. 395 at [7], per Lord Bingham.
209 [2004] EWCA Civ 966; [2005] Q.B. 883 at [48].
210 See in particular [2006] UKHL 17; [2006] 2 A.C. 395 at [13]–[14], and [25], per Lord Bingham; and at [49], per Lord Rodger to [57].
211 [2006] UKHL 17; [2006] 2 A.C. 395 at [55].
212 [2006] UKHL 17; [2006] 2 A.C. 395 at [25].

able per se.[213] The House of Lords did not consider that this left a claimant whose constitutional rights had been interfered with without any remedy. Judicial review, disciplinary proceedings, or even criminal prosecution might be appropriate.[214] Moreover, breach of a constitutional right could give rise to a claim under the Human Rights Act 1998. Lord Bingham noted that:

> "it may reasonably be inferred that Parliament intended infringements of the core human (and constitutional) rights protected by the Act to be remedied under it and not by development of parallel remedies … and if the evidence showed an egregious and deliberate abuse of power by a public officer one would expect the Strasbourg court to award compensation for non-pecuniary loss even though its practice is not to award exemplary damages."[215]

The existence of the remedy, combined with the uncertainty in identifying when a "constitutional right" had been interfered with, persuaded their Lordships that it would be wrong to create a new tort that was actionable per se.[216]

(ii) Causal distinctions

Direct act The historical distinction between trespass and case is of limited relevance when identifying the elements of wrongdoing.[217] Trespass lay only where a direct act on the part of the defendant resulted in unauthorised contact with the claimant's person, goods or land. Hitting a person or setting foot directly on his land were trespasses. Digging a hole into which he fell or working your own land so that the foundations of your neighbour's house subsided were not trespasses. If there was a sufficiently direct act, a trespass was committed and it mattered not whether that trespass was intentional or negligent. If the injury resulted from an indirect act causing damage the claimant had to resort to an action on the case. Much ink has been spilt in the debate about whether negligent trespass is still actionable as trespass. Lord Denning sought in *Letang v Cooper* to abolish once and for all distinctions between direct and consequential damage, between trespass and case, and establish a division between intentionally inflicted personal injuries (trespass) and unintentionally inflicted injury (negligence).[218] The better view is probably that a claimant may still sue for negligent trespass but will not be allowed to claim any advantage from the way in which he tries to describe his case.[219] Negligent trespass 1-54

---

213 See also para.1-49.

214 Though Lord Walker was sceptical about the value of these remedies for a prisoner in the claimant's position: [2006] UKHL 17; [2006] 2 A.C. 395 at [69].

215 [2006] UKHL 17; [2006] 2 A.C. 395 at [26] citing: *BB v United Kingdom* (2004) 39 E.H.R.R. 635 at [36]. On use of the Human Rights Act 1998 to protect constitutional rights, see also Rodger at [64] and Lord Walker at [73].

216 For discussion of what can amount to "damage" for the tort of misfeasance in public office see paras 13-139 to 13-142.

217 The 13th century writ of trespass required the defendant to have acted "with force and arms". By the mid-14th century the pressure to extend the scope of liability led to the development of a new trespass writ requiring the plaintiff to plead his special "case". The direct/indirect distinction between the old trespass writ and the new case writ did not emerge until the early 18th century. See further Baker, *An Introduction to English Legal History*, 5th edn (OUP, 2019).

218 [1965] 1 Q.B. 232 at 237.

219 See the eloquent judgment of Diplock LJ in *Letang v Cooper* [1965] 1 Q.B. 232. Thus, if the substance of the claim is based on the defendant's alleged negligence, the principles determining the defendant's liability will depend on the tort of negligence.

to land is still clearly actionable.[220] The more important consequence flowing from the distinction between trespass and case is that consequential damage, damage resulting only indirectly from the act of the defendant, can still never be actionable in trespass. Indirect damage to land falls within nuisance, not trespass to land. Personal injuries inflicted other than through the medium of a direct blow or collision give rise to liability only in negligence or, if inflicted intentionally, via the tort developing out of *Wilkinson v Downton*.[221]

1-55 **Acts and omissions** The action on the case and its modern heirs, in particular the torts of negligence and nuisance, gradually ensured that a claimant suffering consequential damage as a result of the defendant's tortious act was afforded an appropriate remedy. Liability in tort for the consequences of an omission to act remains problematic. The common law, unlike the civil law, has never imposed a duty to be a Good Samaritan.[222] Pushing a child into a pond constitutes battery. A local authority failing to fence a deep pool in a pleasure park may be liable in negligence if a child falls in and drowns. A stranger, unrelated to the child, may stand by with impunity and watch the child drown, even though he could have rescued the child with ease. He owes no duty to that child. Whatever the consequences, a failure to act is only actionable in tort if there is a prior duty to act to safeguard the relevant interest of the claimant. If a babysitter taking a child for a walk in the park fails to protect the child, she commits actionable negligence because, by assuming responsibility for the child, she subjects herself to a duty in tort. The circumstances sufficient to create a duty to act to protect others' interests have generated substantial case law in the tort of negligence. Very often liability for omission to act is closely related to the problem of liability for the acts of third parties. For example, the defendant's omission may have created the opportunity for another to inflict damage on the claimant and that other may be untraceable or just not worth suing. Negligence liability for omissions and for the conduct of third parties is fully explored in Chs 7 and 13.

1-56 It should be noted that liability for omissions is not solely an issue turning on the extent and scope of the duty of care in the tort of negligence. The Occupiers Liability Act 1957 imposes a duty to act to protect visitors to premises so that, for example, failure to repair a broken floorboard or to warn the visitor of the hazard will constitute a breach of the duty. The Occupiers Liability Act 1984 goes further, imposing a duty to act to protect uninvited entrants, persons whom the occupier would not voluntarily allow within their doors or on their land. In an action for breach of statutory duty the essence of the claim is often a failure to act; a failure to implement the measures required by statute to protect the claimants. In nuisance the substance of the action may well relate to an omission. For example, in *Leakey v National Trust*[223] an earthslide from a hill on the defendant's land threatened the claimant's adjoining property and had already caused some damage. The movement arose entirely from natural forces and not in any sense from the actions of the defendants, or the use to which they put their land. Nonetheless they were held liable in nuisance. They were subject to a duty to take positive action to protect adjoining landowners from damage ensuing from the state of their own property.

220 *League Against Cruel Sports Ltd v Scott* [1986] Q.B. 240; para.18-06.
221 See para.14-14.
222 See Lord Goff's comparison of the common and civil law in *Smith v Littlewoods Organisation Ltd* [1987] A.C. 241.
223 [1980] Q.B. 485.

In cases relating to public nuisance and the highway the common law comes close to imposing a mandatory obligation to act once a risk of injury or damage is or ought to be foreseeable.

(iii) Fault

Fault and responsibility The claimant's loss occasioned by the violation of his interest lies where it falls unless he can demonstrate that loss results from conduct on the part of the defendant which justifies the imposition of liability. This does not mean that every tort requires the same degree of moral culpability on the part of the defendant, or indeed any moral guilt at all. Within intentional torts, for example, battery and deceit, fault may well equate with moral guilt and be sufficient to engage criminal as well as tortious liability. Careless conduct giving rise to liability in negligence indicates fault in the form of disregard of the interests of others but the common law recognises no distinction between degrees of negligence. The drunken driver knocking over a child at 80mph in a built up area and the junior doctor falling on one occasion below standards of proper practice and harming a patient are both simply liable in the tort of negligence. 1-57

In torts said to be of strict liability, the justification rests on the defendant's responsibility for interfering with the protected interest, his engagement in an activity the outcome of which is interference with the interest.[224] In a product liability claim under the Consumer Protection Act 1987, it must be shown that the product causing injury was defective, and that responsibility for putting it into circulation rests with the defendant. In the tort of breach of statutory duty, breach of the relevant provision must be established and the claimant must show that his injury resulted from that breach and not solely from his own act.[225] In the tort of *Rylands v Fletcher* the escape of the dangerous substance must result from the accumulation on the defendant's land and not from the intervention of a third party. In the tort of nuisance there must be an unreasonable interference albeit one which results from a non-negligent miscalculation in the defendant's management of his business. The following paragraphs outline the four main categories of fault: intentional harm, intentional conduct, negligence and responsibility within the definition of a strict liability tort. 1-58

(1) Intentional harm

Motive as the basis of liability[226] The motive of causing harm will not generally give rise to liability in the absence of other unlawful conduct. There is no overarching principle of liability for ill-motivated and intentionally harmful acts. 1-59

[224] Honoré terms this "outcome responsibility": "The Morality of Tort Law" in Owen (ed.), *Philosophical Foundations of Tort Law* (1995), p.81. "Responsibility and Luck" (1988) 104 L.Q.R. 530 at 545. Cane has argued that this approach is too "agent orientated" and that the justification for strict liability is to be found in the interests of the victims: "Responsibility and Fault" in Cane and Gardner (eds), *Relating to Responsibility* (2001), p.109.

[225] *Boyle v Kodak Ltd* [1969] 1 W.L.R. 661.

[226] Previous editions have referred to an improper harmful motivation as "malice" but have noted that the term malice is also used to refer to an intended act as for example, in the case of a "malicious publication" which means simply an intended publication. It is for this reason that we have used the term "improperly intended harm" which more accurately describes the relevant fault.

In *Allen v Flood*[227] Lord Herschell declared that the "existence of a bad motive, in the case of an act which is not otherwise illegal, will not convert that act into a civil wrong". The classic illustration of this proposition is *Bradford v Pickles*.[228] There the defendant abstracted water running through undefined channels on his own land thus preventing that water reaching the claimant's adjoining reservoir. He did so out of spite, in revenge for the claimant's refusal to purchase his land at the price he demanded. In effect he set out to harm the claimant's business simply because it would not do as he wished. The House of Lords held no tort was committed. The claimant had no right to the water supply sufficient to render the defendant's actions on his own property unlawful. Motive was irrelevant: "No use of property which would be legal if due to a proper motive can become illegal because it is prompted by a motive which is improper or even malicious."[229] One exception to this general proposition is the tort of misfeasance in public office. In *Three Rivers DC v Bank of England (No.3)*[230] Lord Steyn explained that liability rested on the bad faith of the defendant in exercising a public power with the intention of injuring the claimant or with knowledge or recklessness as to probable injury to the claimant. The reason that the tort is an exception to the "no liability for bad motive" rule was that "in a legal system based on the rule of law executive or administrative power 'may be exercised only for the public good' and not for ulterior and improper purposes".[231] Improper motive is also a requirement of liability for the somewhat analogous torts of malicious prosecution where it is satisfied by the institution of proceedings for purposes other than the pursuit of justice; and for malicious falsehood where it is satisfied by knowledge of the falsity of the statement.

1-60 **Motive as a factor in liability** There are other situations where an improper motive may be a factor in establishing liability. In nuisance, conduct which might otherwise be regarded as tolerable will be regarded as an unreasonable interference if pursued with an improper or spiteful motive. So in *Christie v Davey*[232] the defendants retaliated to the claimant's playing of the piano, which they disliked, by banging on the party-wall with cooking pans. Their deliberate spite rendered the degree of noise they made unreasonable. Improper motive may also be relevant to establishing liability for conspiracy. In libel, a defence of honest opinion or qualified privilege will be defeated by malice in the sense of an improper motive. Harmful motivation may also be a reason for extending the scope of the interests protected by a tort. In *Wainwright v Home Office*[233] Lord Hoffmann said:

> "I do not resile from the proposition that the policy considerations which limit the heads of recoverable damage in negligence do not apply equally to torts of intention. If someone actually intends to cause harm by a wrongful act and does so, there is ordinarily no reason why he should not have to pay compensation. But I think that if you adopt such a principle,

---

227 [1898] A.C. 1 at 92. He went on to echo Lord Halsbury in *Bradford v Pickles* saying: "If it was a lawful act, however ill the motive might be, he had a right to do it. If it was an unlawful act, however good his motive might be, he had no right to do it."

228 [1895] A.C. 587.

229 [1895] A.C. 587 at 598, per Lord Halsbury.

230 [2003] 2 A.C. 1.

231 [2003] 2 A.C. 1 at 190.

232 [1893] 1 Ch. 316; see para.19-17.

233 [2003] UKHL 53; [2004] 2 A.C. 406 at [44]–[45]. Lord Hoffmann reserved his opinion on whether there should be liability for intentionally causing distress.

> you have to be very careful about what you mean by intend. … If … one is going to draw a principled distinction which justifies abandoning the rule that damages for mere distress are not recoverable, imputed intention will not do. The defendant must actually have acted in a way which he knew to be unjustifiable and either intended to cause harm or at least acted without caring whether he caused harm or not."

Lord Hoffmann's comments point to the essential distinction between intention to harm, where actual intention or at least recklessness must be shown, and weaker uses of intention in relation to the conduct in question where it may be acceptable to impute intention.[234]

Recklessness as to harm In *Three Rivers DC v Bank of England (No.3)*[235] Lord Steyn said: "reckless indifference to consequences is as blameworthy as deliberately seeking such consequences" and hence, the tort of misfeasance could be committed by conduct reckless as to harm as well as by conduct intended to harm. But Lord Steyn also held that recklessness in an objective sense was not sufficient. It was not enough to show that the defendant had failed to give any thought to the possibility of an objectively obvious risk.[236] Rather the defendant must act with a "state of mind of reckless indifference" in a subjective sense. Otherwise liability could "not be squared with a meaningful requirement of bad faith … which is the raison d'etre of the tort". Like intention, recklessness has a narrow meaning in relation to tort actions where motive is relevant. 1-61

(2) Intentional conduct

Intention and motive In several torts, particular conduct must be intended and the motive, harmful or otherwise, is irrelevant. In battery the claimant must establish that the defendant intentionally subjected him to a non-consensual contact. A surgeon, who without seeking her patient's consent, goes ahead and carries out a hysterectomy while performing a more minor operation to which the patient has agreed, may be liable in battery if there is no immediate necessity for more major surgery. She may have acted with a good motive, to promote what she judges to be the patient's best interests, but she intended the act which constitutes the violation 1-62

---

234 Lord Hoffmann criticised the actual decision in *Wilkinson v Downton* [1897] 2 Q.B. 57, on the ground that Wright J, by using a concept of imputed intention, had "watered down the concept as much as possible" and "clearly thought that the [claimant] should succeed whether the conduct of the defendant was intentional or negligent": [2003] UKHL 53; [2004] 2 A.C. 406 at [44]. The proper basis for the decision would have been genuine intention. See the similar reasoning of Lord Steyn in relation to recklessness in *Three Rivers*, para.1-61. See also *Rhodes v OPO* [2015] UKSC 32; [2016] A.C. 219 at [81] where the Supreme Court concluded that in a claim based on *Wilkinson v Downton* intention could not imputed to the defendant as a matter of law, though this does not prevent the court from inferring an intention as a matter of fact: "There are statements (and indeed actions) whose consequences or potential consequences are so obvious that the perpetrator cannot realistically say that those consequences were unintended", per Lord Neuberger, *Rhodes v OPO* [2015] UKSC 32; [2016] A.C. 219 at [112]. But recklessness is not sufficient to establish the required intention, which is *intention* to cause physical harm or severe mental or emotional distress. On the other hand, there is no requirement that the defendant intended to cause, or even foresaw, psychiatric harm: it is sufficient that he intended to cause the severe mental distress which in fact resulted in a recognisable psychiatric illness: *Rhodes v OPO* [2015] UKSC 32; [2016] A.C. 219 at [83] and [87]. Arguably, this is a form of "recklessness" with respect to causing psychiatric harm (as opposed to causing mental or emotional distress). See further para.14-16.

235 [2003] 2 A.C. 1 at 192.

236 This would suffice in criminal law under the approach in *R. v Caldwell* [1982] A.C. 341.

of the patient's interest in bodily integrity. No intention to cause physical injury is required, nor is any form of anger or ill-will.[237] But if the contact is accidental then the requisite intention is missing. Someone who is pushed against another commits no battery.[238]

1-63 **Conduct intended** The requisite conduct intended has to be identified in the context of the specific interest protected by the tort in question. Taking battery as an example the relevant interest is freedom from unauthorised contacts, however trivial. A simple intention to impose the contact suffices, coupled with an understanding that the contact exceeds what is acceptable. In the case of trespass to land, it is the conduct of entering the land which has to be intentional. If X deliberately and voluntarily crosses the boundary between his and the claimant's land he commits a trespass, albeit he is honestly mistaken as to where the boundary lies. He willed the act of entry in what proved to be a trespass.[239] But if the entry is accidental, as straying over a boundary in the dark, then the required intention is absent.[240] In the case of the economic torts the nature of what is intended will differ with the tort. In the case of procuring a breach of contract "an intention to cause a breach of contract is both necessary and sufficient", whereas with the tort of unlawful interference with economic interests the defendant must have intended to cause damage to the claimant.[241] Where the breach of contract was merely a foreseeable consequence of the defendant's acts the relevant intention will not be inferred.[242] The need to correctly identify the requisite intention in a particular tort is neatly illustrated by comparison of the torts of deceit and passing-off. In deceit the defendant must be shown to have made a false statement "knowingly" or "recklessly not caring whether it be true or false"[243] and intending that the claimant act on that statement to his detriment. An intent to deceive another must be proven.[244] The tort of passing-off complements deceit in protecting businesses from damage ensuing from false representations. It is committed whenever a trader conducts his business so as to mislead the public into believing his wares are those of the claimant and so by such, or analogous means, cashes in on the claimant's goodwill. No express intent to deceive the public need be proved. An intention to act in a manner likely to have that result suffices.[245]

1-64 **Objective intention and recklessness** In the context of torts requiring intentional conduct as opposed to intentional harm, there is less objection to employing a concept of imputed intention. Recklessness will generally be sufficient to establish liability.[246] So in deceit it is enough to show that the defendant has no belief in the

---

[237] *F v West Berkshire HA* [1990] 2 A.C. 1. See para.14-10.

[238] See para.14-04.

[239] *Basely v Clarkson* (1681) 3 Lev. 37; and see para.18-06.

[240] See para.18-07.

[241] *OBG Ltd v Allan* [2007] UKHL 21; [2008] 1 A.C. 1 at [8], per Lord Hoffmann. See paras 23-28 to 23-34, paras 23-79 to 23-81, and on intention in the tort of conspiracy see para.23-106.

[242] *OBG Ltd v Allan* [2007] UKHL 21; [2008] 1 A.C. 1 at [8], per Lord Hoffmann. See also at [62], per Lord Hoffmann and at [166], per Lord Nicholls.

[243] *Derry v Peek* (1889) L.R. 14 A.C. 337.

[244] Although this does not require evil motivation: *Ansbacher & Co Ltd v Binks Stern* [1998] P.N.L.R. 221. See para.17-20.

[245] *Spalding & Bros v AW Gamage Ltd* (1915) 84 L.J. Ch. 449. See para.25-19.

[246] See also the discussion of recklessness and imputed intention in *Rhodes v OPO* [2015] UKSC 32; [2016] A.C. 219, para.1-60 fn.234.

truth of the statement made, "not caring whether it was true or false".[247] Again, recklessness as to whether conduct will interfere with a contract may be regarded as supplying the necessary intentional element for the tort.[248]

Justification as a defence to intentional torts Motive, that is, the reason why the defendant acted as he did, while generally irrelevant to establishing prima facie liability will often be relevant to whether a defence is available to justify the defendant's act. Lawful arrest, self-defence, and emergency may justify trespass to the person. Powers of entry, search and seizure may justify trespass to land or goods. Inducing breach of contract may exceptionally be justified by the purpose for which the defendant acts, for example, preventing a state of affairs conducive to immorality.[249] The law recognises that violation of the claimant's interests can be justifiable on the grounds of a priority afforded to the interests of the defendant or the public interest. However where such interests operate to justify otherwise unlawful conduct the burden of proving justification, that why he did the act justifies doing it, lies on the defendant. 1-65

(3) Negligence

Negligence liability The primary importance of carelessness as the relevant fault engaging liability in tort naturally lies in the tort of negligence itself. The defendant will be liable in negligence if he falls below the standard of care demanded by the duty of care which he owes to the claimant. What constitutes that standard of care can be said to be the degree of care, competence and skill to be expected from a person engaging in the activity or function undertaken by the defendant. The starting point remains the definition of negligence given by Alderson B in *Blyth v Birmingham Waterworks Co*: "Negligence is the omission to do something which a reasonable man, guided upon those considerations which ordinarily regulate the conduct of human affairs, would do, or doing something which a prudent and reasonable man would not do."[250] What is reasonable is construed in the context in which the defendant acted. The surgeon must meet the standard of the reasonable surgeon. Unreasonable conduct must not uniformly be equated with carelessness in the popular sense. A failure to act reasonably may flow from a deliberate act or judgment, but one which in hindsight is shown to fall below the standard of conduct demanded of the defendant. A doctor can still be liable in negligence for a course of treatment on which in one sense he has carefully deliberated, because his judgment and or actions fail to measure up the standard required of his profession. 1-66

Objective standard of care The standard of care applied to the tort of negligence is objective. It does not depend on the defendant's subjective state of mind. The defendant must conform to the standards of the reasonable man even if by reason of psychiatric ill-health he is subjectively incapable of doing so.[251] Thus, although moral culpability and legal responsibility will often overlap, this is not always the case and in such cases liability in negligence comes close to a form of strict liability. 1-67

Negligence and other torts Negligence is not solely relevant to the tort of 1-68

---

[247] *Derry v Peek* (1889) L.R. 14 A.C. 337.

[248] See *Emerald Construction Ltd v Lowthian* [1966] 1 W.L.R. 691, and para.23-35.

[249] *Brimelow v Casson* [1924] 1 Ch. 302.

[250] (1856) 11 Exch. 781 at 784.

[251] *Dunnage v Randall* [2015] EWCA Civ 673; [2016] Q.B. 639, see para.7-169.

negligence itself. It may be that negligence constitutes the relevant fault, and/or breach of duty, in other torts too. The common duty of care imposed by statute on occupiers imports negligence as fault. In other contexts, the reasonableness of the defendant's conduct may be a relevant factor in determining liability under the relevant tort. In nuisance, careless management of the defendant's property may be the source of his liability to the claimant. So, for example, a failure to monitor and control noxious emissions from a factory according to accepted industry standards may give rise to liability in nuisance to adjoining occupiers.[252] There are instances where a defence to prima facie liability in a particular tort demands, in effect, proof of absence of negligence. Distributors of a libel may escape liability by establishing innocent publication under s.1 of the Defamation Act 1996 by showing that they took reasonable care in relation to the publication.[253] Liability under *Rylands v Fletcher* may be rebutted on proof that the escape resulted from the act of a third party whose presence and intervention the defendant could not reasonably have anticipated.[254] Again, the reasonableness of the defendant's effort to comply with a statutory duty may be relevant to the question of liability for the tort of breach of statutory duty.[255] Despite the relevance of reasonableness to nuisance, *Rylands v Fletcher*, defamation and breach of statutory duty, these torts are categorised as ones of strict liability.

(4) Strict liability

1-69 **Meaning of strict liability** There are a number of situations in which the defendant may be found liable for injury or damage in respect of conduct which cannot be shown to be either intentional or negligent. For example, the producer of an unsafe product is liable for injuries caused to a consumer under the Consumer Protection Act 1987. To establish liability the claimant need not prove that the event which caused his injury was either calculated by the defendant or resulted from any lack of care on his part. Within strict liability torts the claimant must establish that his injury resulted from the kind of conduct proscribed within the relevant tort. So in a products liability action under the Consumer Protection Act 1987 the consumer must prove that the product was defective, i.e. failed to meet the standard of safety "persons generally are entitled to expect". Such liability is generally styled strict liability and sometimes referred to as "absolute liability". The latter term is misleading as it suggests erroneously that where strict liability is engaged the defendant's liability is unchallengeable and that is rarely the case. Thus, there are a number of defences available to a defendant sued under the Consumer Protection Act 1987 which in effect allow him to plead that the injury was "not his fault". Strict liability is often not much more than a modified form of fault, albeit the relevant fault is far removed from real moral culpability. Strict liability must also be sharply distinguished from "no fault" compensation. Within a "no fault" scheme, such as the Accident Compensation Scheme in New Zealand or under the Vaccine Damage Payments Act 1979 in this country, all the claimant need prove is the occurrence of a prescribed injury and a causal link between that and a relevant event covered by the scheme. A better description of such provisions might be "no liability" schemes.

---

252 See para.19-31.
253 See para.21-175.
254 *Rickards v Lothian* [1913] A.C. 263.
255 See para.8-54.

Role of strict liability at common law The development of strict liability at common law has been haphazard and can be understood properly only within the context of each particular tort. Apart from the strict liability imposed on employers through the principle of vicarious liability[256] and explicable in terms of distributive justice,[257] the imposition of strict liability is rooted in the importance attached by the common law to the interest violated by the defendant. Interests in reputation receive a degree of strict liability protection through the tort of defamation. The defendant may be found liable for a defamatory statement albeit he neither intended to defame the claimant nor was negligent in so doing.[258] The primacy afforded to protection of property interests is illustrated by the tort of conversion where any dealing with another's goods in a manner constituting a denial of the latter's rights is tortious even though the defendant acted in good faith.[259] It is within the torts protecting interests in land that strict liability at common law appears most prevalent.[260] Liability in nuisance, particularly where the nuisance relates to the highway, can arise without proof of any intent or carelessness. The classic example of strict liability at common law is, of course, *Rylands v Fletcher*. The relationship of nuisance and liability under *Rylands v Fletcher* to that of negligence was clarified by two House of Lords decisions in the 1990s. 1-70

Nuisance, *Rylands v Fletcher* and negligence In *Cambridge Water Co v Eastern Counties Leather*,[261] Lord Goff stated that in both nuisance and under *Rylands v Fletcher*, reasonable foreseeability of the risk of harm being caused to the claimant's interest as a result of the defendant's activity was a requirement of liability. However, he regarded the *Rylands v Fletcher* principle as "one of strict liability in the sense that the defendant may be held liable notwithstanding that he has exercised all due care", and similarly noted that in the case of nuisance, "the fact that the defendant has taken all reasonable care will not of itself exonerate him from liability, the relevant control mechanism being found within the principle of reasonable user". Thus, there will be situations in which harm caused by the defendant may lead to liability in nuisance or *Rylands v Fletcher* but not liability in negligence. In *Hunter v Canary Wharf Ltd*[262] Lord Goff adopted Professor Newark's view that the essence of nuisance was that "it was a tort to land. Or to be more accurate it was a tort directed against the [claimant's] enjoyment of rights over land." Hence, a claimant who was personally affected but had no legal interest in the affected land could not claim in nuisance but only negligence or a tort based on intentional conduct. It followed that damages for nuisance were to be assessed on the basis of the diminution in the value of the land resulting from the interference. Thus, where land suffers from smoke from a neighbouring factory, the occupier may claim for the loss of amenity value in the land but if he suffers personal injury from 1-71

256 See Ch.6.

257 See para.1-16.

258 See *Hulton v Jones* [1910] A.C. 20. The apparent harshness of the rule in defamation is mitigated by the defences of justification, comment, qualified privilege and the procedure for offering amends in respect of unintentional defamation under the Defamation Act 1996.

259 See Ch.16.

260 Although trespass to land is normally classed as an intentional tort, the interpretation of "intention" in trespass to land as requiring no more than a deliberate and voluntary act, so that liability arises even where the defendant has no idea that he had intruded on another's property, means that, semantics apart, liability for trespass to land is strict in substance.

261 [1994] 2 A.C. 264 at 300–302.

262 [1997] A.C. 655 at 688.

inhaling the smoke "he may have a cause of action in negligence. But he does not have a cause in action in nuisance for his *personal* injury, nor for interference with his *personal* enjoyment."[263] Lord Goff noted the suggestion by Professor Gearty[264] that claims in respect of physical damage to the land should be excluded from private nuisance and left to negligence liability, but did not rule on the point. In *Transco Plc v Stockport MBC*[265] Lord Hoffmann, having noted that the rule in *Rylands v Fletcher* was a special form of nuisance, rejected an invitation to "kill off the rule" by absorbing it into the law of negligence, as being too radical a step and inconsistent with the judicial function.[266]

1-72 **Strict liability: statute** Strict liability derives from statute in three main instances:

(1) Legislation such as the Animals Act 1971 has been enacted to clarify, or on occasion modify,[267] strict liability as developed by the common law. The definition of the conduct giving rise to liability and of any defences available in the relevant tort are prescribed by the statute itself.
(2) A novel form of strict liability may derive from legislation. The implementation of the European Community Directive on Product Liability in the Consumer Protection Act 1987 creating strict liability for personal injury and, within limits, damage to private property, caused by defective products is of crucial importance.
(3) Liability may arise in the tort of breach of statutory duty when the claimant suffers injury as a consequence of a breach of a statutory obligation imposed on the defendant. Liability will arise only where on the true construction of the Act the intention of the legislature was to create a right of action "sounding in damages". Unfortunately statutes are generally silent as to parliamentary intent and it falls to the judges to interpret the legislative mind. Any trend towards a liberal inference of such intent to create a private law action for damages for breach of statutory duty, and so extend the potential ambit of strict liability in tort, was forcefully rejected by the House of Lords in *R. v Deputy Governor of Parkhurst Prison Ex p. Hague*.[268] The most common instance of strict liability derived from breach of a statutory duty has been in the context of employers' liability to employees in relation to breach of health and safety legislation.[269]

1-73 **Economic rationale for strict liability** Strict liability is sometimes criticised for breaking the link between a defendant's moral culpability and legal liability, though fault liability (typically in the form of an action in negligence) can also render the link between liability and culpability somewhat tenuous. For example, the objective standard of care in negligence means that a person can be held responsible for failing to achieve a standard of conduct that he was incapable of reaching, and the level of compensation payable will usually bear no relation either to the degree of fault or the defendant's means. But in any event it is rare for the person found to

263 [1997] A.C. 655 at 696, per Lord Lloyd.
264 "The Place of Private Nuisance in a Modern Law of Torts" [1989] C.L.J. 214.
265 [2003] UKHL 61; [2004] 2 A.C. 1 at [43].
266 In *Burnie Port Authority v General Jones Pty Ltd* (1994) 179 C.L.R. 520, the Australian High Court did decide to absorb liability under *Rylands v Fletcher* into the tort of negligence.
267 See, e.g. the Fires Prevention (Metropolis) Act 1774.
268 [1992] 1 A.C. 58.
269 First established in *Groves v Lord Wimborne* [1898] 2 Q.B. 402. See Ch.12.

be at fault to be the one who pays compensation. Liability insurance, particularly in the context of personal injuries, has effectively undermined the "moral" basis of fault liability. Moreover, fault liability places the burden of non-negligent harm on the victim rather than the person who caused the harm. As Bramwell B expressed the point in *Holmes v Mather*[270] people must put up with "such mischief as reasonable care on the part of others cannot avoid". Moreover, this was "for the convenience of mankind in carrying on the affairs of life". This view reflected the social and economic values of the 19th century. Economic liberalism and rugged individualism suggested that fault liability was a moral principle, and that it was unjust to hold a person responsible for causing harm that could not have been avoided by the exercise of reasonable care. But fault, as opposed to strict, liability also has the effect of transferring the risk of non-negligent harm from the person who created the risk to the person who suffered the harm. It is not entirely obvious why injured claimants, but not defendants, must bear the burden of non-negligently inflicted loss or injury. It is true that society as a whole derives economic benefits from certain activities, such as high-speed transport and manufacturing, with which substantial degrees of risk are associated. But if society as a whole benefits from such activities then it is arguably just that society as a whole should bear the cost, through the combination of strict liability and insurance, rather than placing a disproportionate burden on injured victims.

This view was clearly articulated by Lord Drummond Young in *Cairns v Northern Lighthouse Board*[271] commenting on the policy that underlies European Union legislation in the field of health and safety at work which is generally founded on the principle of strict liability: **1-74**

> "There are important economic reasons for taking such an approach, and indeed for making the protection afforded by such legislation applicable to all employees, whether or not they are employees of the person in breach of the legislation. The underlying economic theory is that the cost of workplace accidents is part of the cost of production of a good or service, and the most efficient way of absorbing that cost is by passing it to the ultimate consumer as part of the price of the product. In this way the cost can be insured against efficiently by the employer, with the premiums being reflected in the price. This is much more efficient than expecting employees to insure against the possible cost of injury through an accident at work; such a course would require a multiplicity of policies, and would not cater well for employees on short-term contracts, or who simply chose to spend their income on other things. Moreover, strict liability has a further advantage over fault-based liability in that it acts as an incentive to reduce the incidence of hazardous activities; the employer knows that if the risk of injury eventuates he will be liable, and thus he is encouraged to take steps to reduce the frequency with which the risk is incurred. Strict liability also encourages employers to do their utmost to ensure the least possible risk to employees' health and safety. These economic reasons can perhaps be supplemented by the moral argument that those who consume a good or service should pay a proper price for it, including the cost of compensating those injured in the production of the good or service in question. For all these reasons, strict liability has become the norm in European Union-inspired legislation governing health and safety at work."

This approach sees the injuries suffered by employees at work as part of the cost of production of the goods and services supplied by the employer to the public. Economic efficiency suggests that the cost of these injuries should be reflected in the price paid by customers for goods and services, otherwise either the price

[270] (1875) L.R. 10 Ex. 261 at 267.

[271] [2013] CSOH 22; 2013 S.L.T. 645 at [37]; see also at [38] and [43].

charged will be too low resulting in inefficient over-production or the employer will be "subsidised" in that not all of the costs of production will be met and profits will be too high. It is, perhaps, ironic then that the Enterprise and Regulatory Reform Act 2013, s.69 has abolished tort claims for breach of health and safety legislation, which has generally applied stricter forms of liability than negligence.[272] This has been justified on the basis that it is "unfair" to employers to hold them liable when they have exercised reasonable care for the safety of their employees. It ignores the Employers' Liability (Compulsory Insurance) Act 1969, which has been in force since 1 January 1972, requiring employers to insure against their potential liability to employees, which clearly undercuts the notion of "unfairness", and sweeps aside over a century of learning on employers' liability, restoring Baron Bramwell's social and economic values.

(c) Impact of the Human Rights Act 1998

1-75 **The effect of the Act** In *Re McKerr*,[273] Lord Hoffmann explained the effect of the Human Rights Act 1998:

> "Although people sometimes speak of the Convention [European Convention for the Protection of Human Rights] as having been incorporated into domestic law, that is a misleading metaphor. What the Act has done is to create domestic rights expressed in the same terms as those contained in the Convention. But they are domestic rights, not international rights. Their source is the statute, not the Convention. They are available against specific public authorities, not the United Kingdom as a state. And their meaning and application is a matter for domestic courts, not the court in Strasbourg."

1-76 **Vertical and horizontal impact** Section 6 of the Human Rights Act 1998 makes it unlawful for a public authority to act in a way which is incompatible with Convention rights, that is the rights in the European Convention for the Protection of Human Rights which are specified in s.1 of the 1998 Act.[274] The impact of this section on public authorities generally is considered in Ch.13.[275] It is often referred to as the "vertical impact". In this chapter, the concern is with the impact on the framework of tort liability as a whole, and this is often referred to as the "horizontal impact". Initially, it seemed that the vertical impact might have horizontal consequences as a result of the right to a hearing in art.6 of the Convention. Under s.6, courts are bound to give effect to this right because they come within the definition of public authorities. It is now clear that implementing the right to a hearing will not impact upon the wider substantive law because art.6 is now regarded as being concerned with the procedure of the law and not its substance. This interpretation of art.6 still left the possibility that the Act would have horizontal effect by encouraging the courts to develop new common law principles to give full effect to Convention rights and avoid the spectre of a claimant being able to recover under a Convention right but not under the law of tort. But it now seems clear that although the courts will be influenced by the Convention in the application of existing principles, they will not be pushed into developing tort law in this way and will be content, if necessary, to see the Convention rights filling any gap in the structure

---

[272] See para.12-02.

[273] [2004] UKHL 12; [2004] 1 W.L.R. 708 at [65].

[274] Those specified are arts 2–12 and 14 of the Convention, 1–3 of the First Protocol and 1–2 of the Sixth Protocol.

[275] See para.13-87 onwards.

of tort remedies. Furthermore, where existing tort actions overlap with Convention rights there is evidence that the courts are prepared to adopt some of the language and concepts of Convention jurisprudence. To that extent the Human Rights Act will continue to have a horizontal influence on the development of the common law of tort.[276]

Right to a hearing[277] Article 6 provides that: "In the determination of his civil rights and obligations everyone ... is entitled to a ... hearing." In *Z v UK*[278] the European Court of Human Rights recognised that the right to a hearing was concerned with procedural obstacles to a hearing and not situations where the substantive law precluded any basis for a hearing. In *Matthews v Ministry of Defence*[279] the House of Lords reviewed the nature of the distinction between procedural and substantive bars to an action. In this case, the claimant had sought a declaration of incompatibility between art.6 and the immunity from suit granted to the Crown by a certificate issued under s.10 of the Crown Proceedings Act 1947. The House of Lords dismissed this argument, making it clear that art.6 did not arise for consideration in that case, given that the immunity granted by s.10 meant that there was no substantive right of action in the first place. Lord Hoffmann said that the distinction between substance and procedure should not be drawn on the basis of formalistic comparison with the way the distinction is used in other areas of law, but with reference to the fundamental principles and purpose behind art.6. This was to protect the rule of law and the separation of powers. It was to prevent the executive intervening in a case, as a matter of arbitrary discretion, to instruct a court to dismiss an action.[280] The purpose of the certificate system giving immunity from tort action was not to give the government an arbitrary power to stop proceedings but to protect servicemen by ensuring that they received a pension. He took a similar view of the police immunity, saying: 1-77

> "a rule that people should not be entitled to compensation out of public funds for loss suffered on account of a failure of the police to take reasonable care in conducting a criminal investigation poses no threat to the rule of law ... It may or may not be fair as between victims of negligent police investigations and victims of road accidents but it is not a question of human rights ... These are questions of policy to be developed by the courts, subject if necessary to correction by democratic decision in Parliament. They raise issues of, amongst other things, fairness, but not of human rights."[281]

It is clear that the right to a hearing under art.6 will not put any pressure on the courts to develop substantive rights to actions in tort law.

---

276 "Section 3 of the Human Rights Act 1998 requires the court, so far as it is possible, to read and give effect to legislation in a manner which is compatible with the Convention rights. The English court has recognised that it should also, in so far as possible, develop the common law in such a way as to give effect to Convention rights. In this way horizontal effect is given to the Convention. This would seem to accord with the view of the European Court of Human Rights as to the duty of the court as a public authority: see *Von Hannover v Germany* (2004) 40 E.H.R.R. 1, paras 74 and 78, per Lord Phillips CJ in *Prince of Wales v Associated Newspapers* [2006] EWCA Civ 1776; [2008] Ch. 57 at [25].

277 See further para. 13-109 onwards.

278 [2001] 2 F.C.R. 246.

279 [2003] UKHL 4; [2003] 1 A.C. 1163.

280 [2003] UKHL 4; [2003] 1 A.C. 1163 at [29].

281 [2003] UKHL 4; [2003] 1 A.C. 1163 at [43].

1-78 **No new principles** In *Wainwright v Home Office*[282] the House of Lords was asked to develop a new tort of invasion of privacy in order to comply with the right to privacy contained in art.8 of the Convention. Giving the leading speech in the House of Lords, Lord Hoffmann rejected the suggestion with three arguments which are of general application. First, "the European Court is concerned only with whether English law provides an adequate remedy in a specific case in which it considers that there has been an invasion of privacy contrary to art.8". It did not require the adoption of "some high level principle of privacy". In other words, English law is free to continue the development of the law through a focus on wrongs and remedies and does not have to adopt rights-based principles. Secondly, he said that privacy was "an area which requires a detailed approach which can be achieved only by legislation rather than the broad brush of common law principle". Again, this points to the virtue of developing complex areas of law through detailed provision rather than general principle. Finally, he said that:

> "the coming into force of the 1998 Act weakens the argument for saying that a general tort of invasion of privacy is needed to fill gaps in the existing remedies. Sections 6 and 7 of the Act are in themselves substantial gap fillers: if it is indeed the case that a person's rights under art 8 have been infringed by a public authority, he will have a statutory remedy ... a finding that there was a breach of art 8 will only demonstrate that there was a gap in the English remedies for invasion of privacy which has since been filled by ss.6 and 7 of the 1998 Act. It does not require that the courts should provide an alternative remedy which distorts the principles of the common law."[283]

The gap-filling function ascribed to the Human Rights Act provided a further reason for holding to the pragmatic wrongs-based approach of tort law combined with detailed legislation where appropriate. Nonetheless, it is apparent that notwithstanding the rejection of an "over-arching tort of privacy"[284] the courts have continued to fashion a new form of tort (misuse of private information) based on the protection of some aspects of privacy, and in developing this new tort the courts have clearly drawn on the human rights jurisprudence.[285]

1-79 The "gap-filling" role of the Human Rights Act featured again in Lord Hoffmann's speech in *Marcic v Thames Water*[286] where the House of Lords held the defendant not liable in nuisance for failing to provide adequate sewerage because its conduct was regulated by the Director General of Water Services and it was his function, and not that of the court in a nuisance action, to order the construction of new sewers. If the Director failed in his duty, then, said Lord Hoffmann, the claimant would have a remedy under the Human Rights Act. The Act provided that fall-back remedy. It did not provide a primary right actionable through the tort of nuisance. Similarly, in *Watkins v Secretary of State for the Home Department*[287] the House of Lords refused to extend the tort of misfeasance in public office to protect constitutional rights in circumstances where the claimant had not suffered material damage, partly because it was considered that the Human Rights Act could be

---

282 [2003] UKHL 53; [2004] 2 A.C. 406 at [32] and [34].

283 In *Wainwright v UK* (2007) 44 E.H.R.R. 40 the European Court of Human Rights confirmed that, on the facts in *Wainwright* (involving strip searches of prison visitors), there had been a breach of art.8 of the Convention.

284 *Campbell v MGN Ltd* [2004] UKHL 22; [2004] 2 A.C. 457; [2004] 2 All E.R. 995 at [11], per Lord Nicholls, citing *Wainwright v Home Office* [2003] UKHL 53; [2004] A.C. 406.

285 See para.26-37 onwards.

286 [2003] UKHL 66; [2004] 2 A.C. 42 at [71].

287 [2006] UKHL 17; [2006] 2 A.C. 395; see para.1-53.

invoked to protect the citizen's constitutional rights in such cases. Lord Rodger said that: "In general, at least, where the matter is not already covered by the common law but falls within the scope of a Convention right, a claimant can be expected to invoke his remedy under the Human Rights Act rather than to seek to fashion a new common law right."[288]

Impact on existing principles The Human Rights Act has clearly had an impact on existing principles of liability. This has been most marked in the case of defamation where in several cases, including the landmark decision in *Reynolds v Times Newspapers Ltd*,[289] courts have considered the common law rules in the light of the convention right to free speech under art.10 and the jurisprudence of the European Court of Human Rights in applying that article. Similarly, the jurisprudence on the right to privacy under art.8 has influenced actions such as breach of confidence which protect privacy. In *Campbell v MGN*[290] Lord Hoffmann said that: **1-80**

> "What human rights law has done is to identify private information as something worth protecting as an aspect of human autonomy and dignity. ... The result of these developments has been a shift in the centre of gravity of the action for breach of confidence when it is used as a remedy for the unjustified publication of personal information. ... Instead of the cause of action being based on the duty of good faith applicable to confidential personal information and trade secrets alike, it focuses on the protection of human autonomy and dignity. ... [This] must influence the approach of the courts to the type of information which is regarded as entitled to protection."

Lord Hope doubted that the centre of gravity had shifted, as the task of the court was still to balance the public interests in maintaining confidentiality and favouring disclosure. Rather, "the language has changed following the 1998 Human Rights Act and we now talk about the right to respect for private life and the countervailing right to freedom of expression" and the Convention jurisprudence offered important guidance as to how these competing rights ought to be analysed.

D v East Berkshire Community Health NHS Trust[291] also illustrates a way in which the gap-filling role of Convention rights can shift the centre of gravity of a tort action. The House of Lords had previously held that local authority social services (and professionals such as social workers and psychiatrists) owed no duty of care when making a decision about whether or not to take a child into local authority care, for the policy reasons that potential liability resulting from any duty would have an adverse impact on the provision of services for the protection of children.[292] In *D v East Berkshire*, the Court of Appeal held that this decision could not survive the passage of the Human Rights Act 1998. In light of the jurisprudence emanating from the European Court of Human Rights it was no longer "legitimate to rule that, as a matter of law, no common law duty of care is owed to a child in relation to the investigation of suspected child abuse and the initiation and pursuit of care proceedings". The House of Lords accepted the logic of this argument, and held that doctors and social workers who suspect that a child has been the victim of abuse owe a duty to the child to exercise reasonable care in making judgments **1-81**

---

[288] [2006] UKHL 17; [2006] 2 A.C. 395 at [64], citing Lord Hoffmann in *Wainwright v Home Office* [2003] UKHL 53; [2004] 2 A.C. 406 at [33].
[289] [2001] 2 A.C. 127. See para.21-147.
[290] [2004] UKHL 22; [2004] 2 A.C. 457 at [50]–[52]. See further para. 26-37 onwards.
[291] [2003] EWCA Civ 1151; [2004] Q.B. 558; [2005] UKHL 23; [2005] 2 A.C. 373. See para.13-19.
[292] *X v Bedfordshire CC* [1995] 2 A.C. 633.

about the child's welfare,[293] though they also held that no duty of care was owed to the parents of a child suspected of being the victim of abuse because of the potential conflict between the interests of the child and those of the parents. In his dissenting speech on this latter issue, Lord Bingham pointed out that since the defendants would owe a Convention duty to the parents (under art.8) the defendants could still be faced with a potential "conflict of duties" owed to parents and child (though his Lordship considered that in practice this conflict was more apparent than real) and argued that unless the law of tort evolved to provide a remedy, the problem would be left to the Convention. He concluded: "I prefer evolution." Lord Rodger in the majority denying a common law duty, said that he reserved his "opinion as to whether it would be appropriate to modify the common law of negligence, rather than to found any action on the provisions of the Human Rights Act".[294]

1-82 *D v East Berkshire Community Health NHS Trust* represents, perhaps, the high water mark of the Human Rights Act being relied upon to modify existing tort principles, involving as it did a stark departure from what would otherwise have been binding House of Lords' authority. Subsequent decisions have tended to suggest that their Lordships are content to leave claimants to their Human Rights Act remedies rather than adapt the common law to fill a perceived gap. So in *Smith v Chief Constable of Sussex*[295] the claimant complained that the police had failed to act to prevent his former partner from attacking him, despite having been informed of previous attacks and death threats to the claimant. The Court of Appeal declined to strike out the claim as inconsistent with previous House of Lords authority.[296] Pill LJ commented that: "there is a strong case for developing the common law action for negligence in the light of Convention rights",[297] and considered that it was "unacceptable that a court, bound by section 6 of the 1998 Act, should judge a case such as the present by different standards depending on whether or not the claim is specifically brought under the Convention. The decision whether a duty of care exists in a particular situation should in a common law claim require a consideration of Article 2 rights."[298] The House of Lords[299] reversed the Court of Appeal, holding that no duty of care in negligence was owed by the police to the claimant. On the question of the interaction between the common law and Convention rights, Lord Bingham (again in a dissenting speech) agreed with the comments of Pill LJ and Rimer LJ in the Court of Appeal: although the existence of a Convention right could not call for the "instant manufacture of a corresponding common law right where none exists" nonetheless "one would be surprised if conduct which violated a fundamental right or freedom of the individual did not find a reflection in a body of law ordinarily as sensitive to human needs as the common law, and it is

---

293 [2005] UKHL 23; [2005] 2 A.C. 373.

294 [2005] UKHL 23; [2005] 2 A.C. 373 at [50] and [118].

295 [2008] EWCA Civ 39; [2008] P.I.Q.R. P12.

296 *Hill v Chief Constable of West Yorkshire* [1989] A.C. 53; and *Brooks v Commissioner of Police of the Metropolis* [2005] UKHL 24; [2005] 1 W.L.R. 1495.

297 [2008] EWCA Civ 39; [2008] P.I.Q.R. P12 at [53].

298 [2008] EWCA Civ 39; [2008] P.I.Q.R. P12 at [57]. See also per Rimer LJ at [45]: "where a common law duty covers the same ground as a Convention right, it should, so far as practicable, develop in harmony with it; if so, the common law may well require a re-visiting of the *Hill* policy considerations, at least in the context of cases raising considerations of the right to life. It appears to me odd that, in that particular context, our jurisprudence can apparently acknowledge two parallel, but potentially inconsistent, approaches to the same factual situation."

299 [2008] UKHL 50; [2009] 1 A.C. 225.

demonstrable that the common law in some areas has evolved in a direction signalled by the Convention".[300] On the other hand, Lord Hope considered that "the common law, with its own system of limitation periods and remedies, should be allowed to stand on its own feet side by side with the alternative remedy".[301] If there were gaps in the common law, they could be dealt with in domestic law under the Human Rights Act. Lord Brown also rejected the argument that, in a case such as *Smith*, the common law should develop "to reflect the Strasbourg jurisprudence". Given that the Human Rights Act provided for claims to be brought, it was "quite simply unnecessary now to develop the common law to provide a parallel cause of action".[302] Convention claims had "very different objectives from civil actions". Whereas civil actions were designed to compensate claimants for their losses, Convention claims were intended to uphold minimum human rights standards and to vindicate those rights.[303]

Similarly, in *Jain v Trent Strategic HA*[304] a health authority made an ex parte without notice application to a magistrate for the cancellation of the registration of the claimants' nursing home, which was granted. The statute which regulated nursing homes provided for a system of appeals, but the claimants' successful appeal was heard over four months after the order was made, by which time irrevocable damage had been done to the claimants' business. The appeal tribunal was scathing in their criticism of the conduct of the health authority. The House of Lords held that the health authority owed no duty of care in negligence to the claimants because the authority had exercised a statutory power the purpose of which was the protection of the residents of the home, whose interests were in potential conflict with those of the proprietors; moreover in judicial proceedings, a party does not owe a duty of care to the opposing party. Although the Human Rights Act 1998 did not apply (the events having occurred before the Act came into force), Lord Scott considered whether a remedy would have been available, and concluded that it probably would, on the basis of potential breaches of art.6 and art.1 of the First Protocol to the Convention. His Lordship then considered "whether this House should now, after the enactment of the 1998 Act, develop the duty of care so as to provide a common law tort remedy in cases such as this", but ultimately rejected 1-83

300 [2008] UKHL 50; [2009] 1 A.C. 225 at [58]; citing *D v East Berkshire Community NHS Trust*.

301 [2008] UKHL 50; [2009] 1 A.C. 225 at [82].

302 [2008] UKHL 50; [2009] 1 A.C. 225 at [136]. See also the comments of Lord Toulson in *Michael v Chief Constable of South Wales* [2015] UKSC 2; [2015] A.C. 1732 at [125] rejecting the claimant's argument that where there was a breach of Convention rights the common law should reflect that by providing an additional remedy in the tort of negligence. If there was no basis, applying orthodox common law principles, for a claimed duty of care then there was no rationale "for gold plating the claimant's Convention rights by providing compensation on a different basis from the claim under the Human Rights Act 1998".

303 [2008] UKHL 50; [2009] 1 A.C. 225 at [138]. The converse argument, that in considering claims under the ECHR the courts should take into account the policy issues that have resulted in a conclusion that no duty of care at common law was owed by the defendant and so hold that there has been no breach of Convention rights, was rejected by the majority of the Supreme Court in *Commissioner of Police of the Metropolis v DSD* [2018] UKSC 11; [2019] A.C. 196 (risk of defensive policing and the diversion of resources from police work to compensation claims not relevant to whether the police owe an operational duty under ECHR art.3 when investigating criminal offences). Lord Neuberger commented, at [97], that: "Just as the majority of this Court accepted in [*Michael v Chief Constable of South Wales* [2015] UKSC 2; [2015] A.C. 1732 at [123]–[128]] that the domestic tortious test for liability should not be widened to achieve consistency with the human rights test, so should the human rights test for liability not be narrowed to achieve consistency with the domestic, tortious test." See also per Lord Kerr at [68]. See further para.13-102.

304 [2009] UKHL 4; [2009] 1 A.C. 853.

this suggestion. Since, after 2 October 2000, art.6 and art.1 of the First Protocol had become part of domestic law, breaches of the Convention could be remedied under domestic law.[305] This left the claimants in *Jain* to pursue a remedy for breach of their Convention rights in the European Court of Human Rights. Conversely, just as the Convention should not normally be used to justify an expansion of common law liability, nor should it be employed to reduce existing common law protections. In *R. (on the application of Jalloh (formerly Jollah)) v Secretary of State for the Home Department*[306] the Supreme Court held that it would be a "retrograde step" to align the classic understanding of false imprisonment at common law with the Convention's much more nuanced concept of deprivation of liberty under art.5 which draws a distinction between the deprivation and the restriction of physical liberty. There was "no need for the common law to draw such a distinction and every reason for the common law to continue to protect those whom it has protected for centuries against unlawful imprisonment, whether by the State or private persons".[307]

1-84 Thus, the trend, notwithstanding the radical approach taken to developing the common law in line with Convention principles in *D v East Berkshire Community NHS Trust*, has been to treat Convention rights as offering a parallel remedy in cases where the common law and the Convention might otherwise appear to overlap. Perceived "gaps" in the common law will not necessarily be remedied by appeals to the Convention jurisprudence, and the Human Rights Act claim will be treated as closing the gap.[308] However, in practice, the approach of the European Court of Human Rights to the award of damages is very different from that of the common law, which tends to look to full compensation for the claimant's losses. In contrast, damages awards for breach of Convention rights are intended to acknowledge the infringement of the claimant's rights, without necessarily representing full compensation for the claimant's loss. That could leave claimants in a case such as *Jain v Trent Strategic HA* with significant losses to bear despite the vindication of their Convention rights.[309]

1-85 On the other hand, the Supreme Court has been willing to extend the range of potential claimants entitled to a remedy under the Convention in circumstances where the claimant would not have a tort remedy. In *Rabone v Pennine Care NHS Foundation Trust*,[310] the parents of an adult mental health patient who committed suicide were held to be entitled to damages for breach of art.2 by the defendant hospital (the hospital having been negligent in permitting the patient home leave when they knew of her suicidal state), although they did not qualify for an award of bereavement damages under s.1A of the Fatal Accidents Act 1976 because their daughter was an adult. Although technically the claimants in *Rabone* succeeded in obtaining a remedy for breach of their Convention rights, in reality this looks little different from a tort remedy dressed in Convention clothing. Indeed, Lord Mance

---

[305] [2009] UKHL 4; [2009] 1 A.C. 853 at [39], citing Lord Brown's comment in *Smith v Chief Constable of Sussex Police* [2008] UKHL 50; [2009] 1 A.C. 225 at [136]: " … it is quite simply unnecessary now to develop the common law to provide a parallel cause of action."

[306] [2020] UKSC 4; [2020] 2 W.L.R. 418.

[307] [2020] UKSC 4; [2020] 2 W.L.R. 418 at [33].

[308] See further The Hailsham Lecture 2009 delivered by Arden LJ, "Human Rights and Civil Wrongs: Tort Law under the Spotlight" [2010] P.L. 140.

[309] For discussion of tort and Convention damages awards see Steele, "Damages in tort and under the Human Rights Act: remedial or functional separation?" [2008] 67 C.L.J. 606; Varuhas, "A Tort-Based Approach to Damages under the Human Rights Act 1998" (2009) 72 M.L.R. 750.

[310] [2012] UKSC 2; [2012] 2 A.C. 72. See further paras 9-90, 9-105, 13-87, 13-89, and 13-92.

suggested that the European Court of Human Rights has, under the art.2 operational duty, begun to develop its own Convention rules of, "in effect, tortious responsibility".[311] As well as widening the range of potential claimants, *Rabone* extended the range of circumstances in which there might be a breach of the art.2 operational duty to cases involving "simple" negligence,[312] at least in situations where the victim could be categorised as vulnerable.[313] The line between tort rights and Convention rights is not easy to draw, and the boundary will probably continue to shift, as the courts' understanding of the relationship between the two bodies of law evolves.[314]

---

311 [2012] UKSC 2; [2012] 2 A.C. 72 at [121].

312 Though it is more difficult to establish a breach of the operational duty than simple negligence since the risk to the victim's life must be real and immediate, not merely foreseeable.

313 The Supreme Court rejected the suggestion that the patient must be formally detained before art.2 was engaged (thus departing from *Savage v South Essex Partnership NHS Foundation Trust* [2008] UKHL 74; [2009] 1 A.C. 681). *Rabone* was subsequently approved by the European Court of Human Rights in *Reynolds v United Kingdom* (2694/08) (2012) 55 E.H.R.R. 35.

314 See also *Smith v Ministry of Defence* [2013] UKSC 41; [2014] A.C. 52, discussed at paras 13-53, 13-54 and 13-93 on the inter-relationship between rights in tort and Convention rights.

CHAPTER 2

CAUSATION IN TORT: GENERAL PRINCIPLES

TABLE OF CONTENTS

1. INTRODUCTION

2-01 **General principles**[1] In the majority of torts the claimant must show that the defendant's wrongdoing caused him actual damage. In these torts, and indeed in torts actionable per se if substantial damages are sought, the claimant must establish that:

(1) the defendant's conduct did in fact result in the damage of which he complains; and
(2) the damage is not in law too remote a consequence of the defendant's wrongdoing.

Proof of causation is crucial to success in many actions in tort. Causation is thus relevant throughout the law of torts generally. In practice, many of the difficulties in proving factual causation surface in the tort of negligence. This is at least partly because claims for personal injuries are most commonly litigated in negligence, where the vagaries of human conduct, the presence of multiple tortfeasors, and the uncertain aetiology of disease[2] compound causal problems.

2-02 The term "causation" should be approached with caution. Judges tend to shy away from both scientific and philosophical formulae of causation,[3] preferring to adopt what is said to be a broad commonsense approach.[4] Although in many cases scientific evidence may be absolutely essential in deciding the causation question, the legal method is very different from the scientific method since the lawyer wants to know not simply what events or occurrences contributed to a particular outcome but whether the defendant should be held *liable* for that outcome. In the law of tort

1 See generally Hart and Honoré, *Causation in Law*, 2nd edn (1985); Williams [1961] C.L.J. 62; Fleming (1989) 68 Can. B. Rev. 661; (1991) 70 Can. B. Rev. 136; Stapleton (1988) 8 O.J.L.S. 111; Stauch (2001) 64 M.L.R. 191; Stapleton (2013) 129 L.Q.R. 39.

2 See Stapleton, *Disease and the Compensation Debate* (OUP, 1986), Ch.3. Judgments in negligence relating to such matters as the causation of industrial disease may well be relevant to analogous claims in product liability and nuisance where the claimant alleges that substances in a product, or pollutants emanating from the defendants' property, caused him to succumb to disease.

3 *Stapley v Gypsum Mines Ltd* [1953] A.C. 663 at 681 and 687; *The Wagon Mound (No.1)* [1961] A.C. 388 at 419.

4 *Admiralty Commissioners v SS Volute* [1922] 1 A.C. 129 at 145; *Jones v Livox Quarries Ltd* [1952] 2 Q.B. 608 at 616.

causes assume significance to the extent that they assist the court in deciding how to *attribute responsibility* for the claimant's damage. "The decision ... of the case must turn not simply on causation, but on responsibility."[5]

Factual causation and lost chances Factual causation is concerned with establishing the physical connection between the defendant's wrong and the claimant's damage. What evidence exists to link the defendant's wrongdoing to the damage, and is that sufficient to persuade the court that causation is established? Difficult questions requiring scientific evidence of cause and effect can arise in relation to factual causation, and the issue may depend heavily upon expert evidence. In some situations where there is scientific uncertainty about causal mechanisms, however, the courts may be persuaded to draw an inference that there must have been a causal connection between the defendant's wrong and the claimant's damage. Sometimes this is on the basis that the defendant's wrong made a material contribution to the damage, even where it is acknowledged that the contribution was not the sole or even the main cause of the harm.[6] Sometimes, the evidence points only to a material increase in the risk of harm to the claimant, but for essentially policy reasons the court nonetheless concludes that the causal link has been established.[7] An alternative approach to factual uncertainty is to adopt a probabilistic analysis by reference to the chance that the claimant had of avoiding the harm, and then award damages by reference to that chance of loss, rather than on an all or nothing basis. The claimant receives compensation which is reduced to reflect the chances, but may nonetheless be awarded damages even where the chance was less than 50 per cent (and so would not normally have succeeded where the courts apply the all or nothing approach based on proof of causation on the balance of probabilities).[8] However, as will be seen, the lost chance approach seems to be readily applied to cases involving pure financial loss, but there is considerable hesitancy about its role in relation to claims for personal injury. 2-03

Causation and the European Convention on Human Rights In *Van Colle v Chief Constable of the Hertfordshire Police*[9] the Court of Appeal held that where a claim is based on breach of art.2 of the European Convention on Human Rights the test for causation is not the same as that at common law but rather "whether the protective measures that were reasonably open [to the defendant] could have had a real prospect of altering the outcome and avoiding the death". On appeal to the House of Lords, only Lord Brown commented on this causation point, noting that Convention claims have "very different objectives from civil actions. Where civil actions are designed essentially to compensate claimants for their losses, Convention claims are intended rather to uphold minimum human rights standards and to vindicate those rights." This, said his Lordship, could "explain why a looser ap- 2-04

---

5 *M'Lean v Bell* (1932) 48 T.L.R. 467 at 469; and see *Weld-Blundell v Stephens* [1920] A.C. 956 at 986. See also the comment of Lord Hoffmann in *Environment Agency v Empress Car Co (Abertillery) Ltd* [1999] 2 A.C. 22 at 31, that "one cannot give a commonsense answer to a question of causation for the purpose of attributing responsibility under some rule without knowing the purpose and scope of the rule". For extensive discussion of the growing trend to approach questions of factual causation by reference to the scope of the defendant's duty see Stapleton, "Cause-in-Fact and the Scope of Liability for Consequences" (2003) 119 L.Q.R. 388.

6 See para.2-32.

7 See para.2-45.

8 See para.2-76.

9 [2007] EWCA Civ 325; [2007] 1 W.L.R. 1821 at [83].

proach to causation is adopted under the Convention than in English tort law. Whereas the latter requires the claimant to establish on the balance of probabilities that, but for the defendant's negligence, he would not have suffered his claimed loss … under the Convention it appears sufficient generally to establish merely that he lost a substantial chance of this."[10]

2-05 **Causation in law** Cases involving multiple causes, where the damage sustained by the claimant is the product of a number of events, only one of which is the defendant's wrongful conduct, give rise to particular problems. In these cases, the court is clearly faced with a choice as to which of several causes, including the defendant's actions, are to be treated as the operative or effective cause of the loss for the purpose of attributing legal responsibility. Sometimes there are two events, each of which was sufficient to have caused the claimant's damage. Sometimes, the defendant's conduct sets off a sequence of events, each one of which is a necessary link in the causal chain between the initial wrong and the claimant's damage, and the court has to determine whether any of the intervening events can be said to be so significant causally as to break the causal link, whether they are to be regarded as a novus actus interveniens. For example, where there have been two acts of negligence, say by the defendant causing personal injury to the claimant and in the subsequent medical treatment received by the claimant, it is not necessarily obvious that the second act of negligence excuses the defendant from responsibility for the ultimate consequences.[11] In these cases, typically there is no dispute or uncertainty as to what in fact happened to cause the claimant's damage; rather the question is which event will be treated as *the cause* for the purpose of attributing legal responsibility. The court clearly has to exercise a choice as to whether the defendant's wrongful conduct constituted the "legal cause" of the damage (hence "causation in law"). In this type of situation the courts often fall back on the pragmatic approach of the common law, and invoke judicial "common sense" as a guiding principle, though there are some underlying principles that can be teased out from the cases.

2-06 **Remoteness** Remoteness of damage, is not strictly speaking concerned with causation but with the limits of legal responsibility for damage which has undoubtedly been caused by the defendant.[12] Even where it is patent that the defendant's conduct caused the claimant's loss the question remains whether the defendant should be held responsible for all the consequences flowing from his wrongdoing. This tends to be more of an issue in the context of negligence and analogous torts

---

10 [2008] UKHL 50; [2009] 1 A.C. 225 at [138]; applied in *Savage v South Essex Partnership NHS Foundation Trust* [2010] EWHC 865 (QB); [2010] P.I.Q.R. P14; [2010] Med. L.R. 292.

11 See *Rahman v Arearose Ltd* [2001] Q.B. 351; and *Webb v Barclays Bank Plc and Portsmouth Hospitals NHS Trust* [2001] EWCA Civ 1141; [2002] P.I.Q.R. P8; paras 2-125 and 2-126.

12 This distinction between causation and remoteness is not one that is always drawn in the cases. This is partly due to the rather casual use of the word "remoteness", which is often employed to describe a causation problem, rather than being confined to setting the limits of actionability for damage admittedly caused by the defendant's wrong. Where there has been an intervening event, for example, the damage may be described as "too remote" a consequence. This is simply a way of saying that the defendant's conduct was not the effective cause of the damage. The word "remoteness" is being used here in a non-technical sense to mean far removed in causative effect from the original wrong. This use of language may also stem from the cases predating *The Wagon Mound (No.1)* [1961] A.C. 388, when it was believed that the test of remoteness in negligence was whether the consequences were the *direct* result of the defendant's wrong, as opposed to the *foreseeable* consequences. A test based on directness is effectively a *causation* test.

(such as nuisance) where questions of fault tend to cloud the issue. It is said that, since a defendant can only be held to be negligent where harm is foreseeable, because a reasonable man does not take precautions against unforeseeable consequences, it may not be fair or just to impose responsibility on the defendant for wholly unforeseeable consequences. For example, if as a result of D's carelessness one would have anticipated damage X, but in the circumstances damage X has not occurred, though damage Y has materialised, is it fair to hold D liable for damage Y? The problem tends not to arise so starkly with intentional torts, since the courts take the not unreasonable view that if the defendant inflicted damage intentionally he can hardly complain if the damage turns out to be not quite what he anticipated. Thus, most of the cases on remoteness of damage involve the tort of negligence and are concerned with the extent to which someone ought to be liable for consequences which he could not reasonably anticipate.[13] The policy of the law plays a significant role here, and though in theory the test of remoteness in fault-based torts (negligence, nuisance, some instances of breach of statutory duty) is foreseeability of the damage, this tends to be given a wide interpretation particularly in the case of personal injuries. This is not to suggest that policy has no role in determining factual causation. Causation is all too often not susceptible to exact scientific proof, and selection between causes is required. Once one is confronted with a choice, there are value judgments involved in making a selection.

The burden of proof The burden of proving causation rests with the claimant in almost all instances.[14] The claimant must adduce evidence that it is more likely than not that the wrongful conduct of the defendant in fact resulted in the damage of which he complains. On the other hand, there are occasions when the court is permitted to draw an inference that there must have been a causal link, taking a common-sense and pragmatic approach to the evidence, in circumstances where the evidence is somewhat equivocal.[15] So if the claimant proves that the defendant was in breach of duty and that damage occurred which was of a kind likely to have been caused by such a breach this may be enough for the court to infer that the damage was probably caused by the breach, even if the claimant is unable to prove positively the precise causal mechanism.[16] Sometimes the court may conclude for reasons of policy and fairness to claimants that conduct which increased the risk of damage to the claimant can be treated as equivalent to proof of the causal link.[17] These cases are the exception to the normal rule, however, that it is for a claimant to prove the causal link on the balance of probabilities.[18] Where scientific evidence is equivocal, the crucial issue from the claimant's point of view is whether the court 2-07

[13] See *The Wagon Mound (No.1)* [1961] A.C. 388.

[14] The burden of establishing the causal link is not less onerous in cases involving breach of statutory duty than in negligence: *Bonnington Castings Ltd v Wardlaw* [1956] A.C. 613 at 620, per Lord Reid.

[15] See para.2-32. Note that sometimes the defendant has an "evidentiary burden" which requires him to adduce evidence to rebut the inference that would otherwise be drawn, from the fact of his breach of duty and the claimant's damage, that there must have been a causal connection: see *J v North Lincolnshire CC* [2000] P.I.Q.R. P84 CA (eight-year-old child with global developmental delay injured in road traffic accident having wandered out of his school unnoticed).

[16] *Drake v Harbour* [2008] EWCA Civ 25; [2008] N.P.C. 11 at [28], per Toulson LJ. Longmore LJ commented, at [15], that in these circumstances the court should "be prepared to take a reasonably robust approach to causation". *Drake* was applied in *Vaile v Havering LBC* [2011] EWCA Civ 246; [2011] E.L.R. 274 at [32]. See also *Schembri v Marshall* [2020] EWCA Civ 358 at [52]–[53].

[17] See *Fairchild v Glenhaven Funeral Services Ltd* [2002] UKHL 22; [2003] 1 A.C. 32; para.2-53.

[18] It may be unwise to express the balance of probabilities in percentage terms since it carries the danger of "pseudo-mathematics": "the process is not scientific (although it may obviously include evalua-

will be prepared to draw an appropriate inference that there must have been some causal connection, since proof of causation often rests on the drawing of an inference of fact. In *Jones v Great Western Ry Co*[19] Lord Macmillan said:

> "The dividing line between conjecture and inference is often a very difficult one to draw. A conjecture may be plausible, but it is of no legal value, for its essence is that it is a mere guess. An inference in the legal sense, on the other hand, is a deduction from the evidence, and if it is a reasonable deduction it may have the validity of legal proof. The attribution of an occurrence to a cause is, I take it, always a matter of inference. The cogency of a legal inference of causation may vary in degree between practical certainty and reasonable probability. Where the coincidence of cause and effect is not a matter of actual observation there is necessarily a hiatus in the direct evidence, but this may be legitimately bridged by an inference from the facts actually observed and proved."

The burden of proof, is, ultimately, a burden of persuading the court to attribute legal responsibility for the claimant's damage to the defendant. If the judge is unable, on the evidence, to resolve the causation issue, but concludes simply that he is not persuaded that the claimant's symptoms were caused by the defendant's breach of duty, he is not required to go further and make a positive diagnosis of the cause of the claimant's symptoms. In these circumstances the action fails on the burden of proof.[20]

2-08 **Improbable theories and legitimate inferences** In *The Popi M*[21] the House of Lords held that a judge is not required to choose between two competing theories of causation, both of which he regards as extremely improbable, or one of which he regards as extremely improbable and the other as virtually impossible. In these circumstances, where all the facts are known, it is inappropriate to proceed on the basis of eliminating the impossible and concluding that the remaining explanation, however improbable, must be the cause. The appropriate conclusion is that the claimant has failed to discharge the burden of proof. However, such cases will be rare. In *Ide v ATB Sales Ltd; Lexus Financial Services (t/a Toyota Financial Services (UK) Plc v Russell*[22] Thomas LJ commented that:

> "In the vast majority of cases where the judge has before him the issue of causation of a particular event, the parties will put before the judges two or more competing explanations as to how the event occurred, which though they may be uncommon, are not improbable. In such cases, it is … a permissible and logical train of reasoning for a judge, having eliminated all of the causes of the loss but one, to ask himself whether, on the balance of probabilities, that one cause was the cause of the event. What is impermissible is for a judge to conclude in the case of a series of improbable causes that the least improbable or least unlikely is nonetheless the cause of the event."

But where there are only two competing causes, neither of which is improbable (even if they are uncommon events), then once one cause has been eliminated the

tion of scientific evidence) and to express the probability of some event having happened in percentage terms is illusory": *Nulty v Milton Keynes BC* [2013] EWCA Civ 15; [2013] 1 W.L.R. 1183 at [35] per Toulson LJ.

19 (1930) 47 T.L.R. 39 at 45.

20 *Davis and Docherty v Balfour Kilpatrick Ltd* [2002] EWCA Civ 736; applying *The Popi M* [1985] 1 W.L.R. 948; see para.2-08.

21 [1985] 1 W.L.R. 948.

22 [2008] EWCA Civ 424; [2008] P.I.Q.R. P13 at [4].

judge is entitled to conclude that the other was the probable cause of the damage.[23]

2. FACTUAL CAUSATION

(a) The "but for" test

The first step in establishing causation is to eliminate irrelevant causes, and this is the purpose of the "but for" test. The courts are concerned, not to identify all of the possible causes of a particular incident, but with the effective cause of the resulting damage in order to assign responsibility for that damage. The "but for" test asks: would the damage of which the claimant complains have occurred "but for" the negligence (or other wrongdoing) of the defendant? Or to put it more accurately, can the claimant adduce evidence to show that it is more likely than not, more than 50 per cent probable, that "but for" the defendant's wrongdoing the relevant damage would not have occurred. In other words, if the damage would have occurred in any event the defendant's conduct is not a "but for" cause. Thus, in *Barnett v Chelsea and Kensington Hospital Management Committee*,[24] the claimant's husband was sent home from a hospital casualty department after complaining of acute stomach pains and sickness. He died later that same day of what proved to be arsenic poisoning. The hospital admitted negligence in failing to treat the man promptly. His widow's claim under the Fatal Accidents Act nonetheless failed because of evidence that, even had he been treated promptly, he would still have died from the poison. There was no causal link between the defendants' negligence and the patient's death.[25] It is worth bearing in mind that the "but for" test functions as an exclusionary test, i.e. its purpose is to exclude from consideration irrelevant causes. The fact that the defendant's conduct is found to be a cause, applying the "but for" test, is not conclusive as to whether he should be held responsible in law since the function of the causal enquiry in law is to determine which causes have significance for the purpose of attributing legal responsibility. It is sometimes said that the law seeks the *causa causans* (effective factor) rather 2-09

---

23 [2008] EWCA Civ 424; [2008] P.I.Q.R. P13 at [19]–[20]. In *Nulty v Milton Keynes BC* [2013] EWCA Civ 15; [2013] 1 W.L.R. 1183 counsel argued that if there is a closed list of possible causes, and if one possibility is more likely than the other, by definition that has a greater probability than 50 per cent; and that if there is a closed list of more than two possible causes, the court should ascribe a probability factor to them individually in order to determine whether one had a probability figure greater than 50%. Toulson LJ rejected the argument: "It is not only over-formulaic but it is intrinsically unsound" (at [37]). There is no rule of law that if possible causes A and B are very much less likely than possible cause C then possible cause C becomes the probable cause. The question is: "on an overall assessment of the evidence (i.e. on a preponderance of the evidence) whether the case for believing that the suggested event happened is more compelling than the case for not reaching that belief" (at [37]; and see also [42]). See also *Graves v Brouwer* [2015] EWCA Civ 595; *Palmer v Nightingale (t/a Andover Pest Control)* [2016] EWHC 2800 (TCC); (2016) 170 Con. L.R. 19.

24 [1969] 1 Q.B. 428; *Metropolitan Ry Co v Jackson* (1877) 3 App. Cas. 193; *Wakelin v London and South Western Ry Co* (1886) 12 App. Cas. 41; *Fish v Kapur* [1948] 2 All E.R. 176.

25 See also *Robinson v Post Office* [1974] 1 W.L.R. 1176. The "but for" test will often operate to exclude the defendant's conduct as a cause of the claimant's harm: see, e.g. *The Empire Jamaica* [1957] A.C. 386; *BRS Ltd v AV Crutchley & Co Ltd* [1968] 1 All E.R. 811; *Leong Bee & Co v Ling Nam Rubber Works* [1970] 2 Lloyd's Rep. 247; *Hay v Dowty Mining Equipment Ltd* [1971] 3 All E.R. 1136; *Kay's Tutor v Ayrshire and Arran Health Board* [1987] 2 All E.R. 417 HL; *Allen v Ellis & Co* [1990] 11 E.G. 78; and see *Sumner v Port of London Authority and Southern Stevedores* [1974] 2 Lloyd's Rep. 92 (excluding claimant's contributory negligence on the "but for" test).

than the *causa sine qua non* (factor(s) without which damage could not have occurred).[26]

2-10 **"But for" test not always required: conversion** There are some circumstances, and some torts, where the "but for" test is not satisfied, but nonetheless the court considers it appropriate to attribute responsibility to the defendant's conduct.[27] In *Kuwait Airways Corp v Iraq Airways Co*[28] the claimants sought damages in respect of the loss of 10 airplanes taken by the Iraqi government following the invasion of Kuwait and subsequently handed over to the defendants for their use. The defendants argued that there was a general rule of liability in tort that the tortious act must have been at least a necessary condition of the damage, and that a claimant will fail if he cannot prove that the damage would not have happened but for the tort. On the facts, the claimants could not show that but for the defendants' tortious acts of conversion they would not have been kept out of possession of their airplanes, because the Iraqi government would have retained them or given them to some other state institution. The House of Lords held that the claimants did not have to satisfy the "but for" causation test in these circumstances. Lord Nicholls pointed out that in cases involving multiple wrongdoers:

> "the court may treat wrongful conduct as having sufficient causal connection with the loss for the purpose of attracting responsibility even though the simple 'but for' test is not satisfied. In so deciding the court is primarily making a value judgment on responsibility. In making this judgment the court will have regard to the purpose sought to be achieved by the relevant tort, as applied to the particular circumstances."[29]

Lord Hoffmann commented[30] that it would be an irrational system of tort liability which did not insist upon there being *some* causal connection between the tortious act and the damage, but there is:

> "no uniform causal requirement for liability in tort. Instead, there are varying causal requirements, depending upon the basis and purpose of liability. One cannot separate questions of liability from questions of causation. They are inextricably connected. One is never simply liable; one is always liable *for* something and the rules which determine what one is liable for are as much part of the substantive law as the rules which determine which acts give rise to liability."

In the case of conversion, a tort of strict liability, the causal requirements followed from the nature of the tort, which exists to protect proprietary or possessory rights in property, and is committed by an act inconsistent with those rights. It followed that it was irrelevant that if the defendants had not taken possession of the airplanes, someone else would have done so (i.e. the traditional "but for" test was not satisfied), and it was also irrelevant that, having taken possession, the defendants would have been prevented from restoring the aircraft (even if it had wished to do so) by circumstances beyond their control: "The liability is strict. Thus the causal questions are answered by reference to the nature of the liability."[31]

2-11 **"But for" test not always required: trespass** Where a tort is actionable per se,

---

26 *Holling v Yorkshire Traction Co Ltd* [1948] 2 All E.R. 662 at 664.
27 See the example at para.2-103 fn.365.
28 [2002] UKHL 19; [2002] 2 A.C. 883.
29 [2002] UKHL 19; [2002] 2 A.C. 883 at [74].
30 [2002] UKHL 19; [2002] 2 A.C. 883 at [127]–[128].
31 [2002] UKHL 19; [2002] 2 A.C. 883 at [129]. See further Cane (2002) 118 L.Q.R. 544.

such as trespass to the person, the claimant merely has to establish the requirements of the tort in order to establish liability and it is not a "defence" for a defendant to claim that he could have acted lawfully if in fact he had no lawful authority to do the act complained of. So, in the tort of false imprisonment where all that a claimant has to prove "is that he was directly and intentionally imprisoned by the defendant, whereupon the burden shifts to the defendant to show that there was lawful justification for doing so",[32] if the defendant acted unlawfully in detaining the claimant it is no defence for the defendant to prove that he could have lawfully detained the claimant. This so called "causation test" has no place in the tort of false imprisonment, since "the fact that a person could have been lawfully detained says nothing on the question whether he was lawfully detained."[33] On the other hand, the causation test is relevant if the claimant is seeking substantive, as opposed to nominal, damages.[34]

Two types of uncertainty The courts apply causation rules as part of the process of attributing responsibility for wrongful conduct. The first part of the process involves attempting to identify what happened as a matter of historical "fact". In a typical case of negligence, say a road traffic accident in which the defendant negligently drives his car onto the pavement striking and injuring the claimant, the causal inquiry is relatively straightforward. It is usually self-evident that the impact caused injury to the claimant, though there may be some dispute as to the extent of that injury, or whether particular injuries or disabilities are attributable to the defendant's breach of duty, or were, for example, pre-existing.[35] There are cases, however, where establishing the causal link between the defendant's wrong and the claimant's damage as a matter of "historical fact" is far from straightforward, either because: (1) the outcome of events depended upon hypothetical human actions; or (2) there is scientific uncertainty about the causal mechanism. In the first category of case the causal uncertainty derives from the fact that the "but for" test asks, essentially, whether the defendant's wrongful conduct made a difference to the outcome. Where the defendant's breach of duty involves an omission, particularly in the giving of advice or information, the outcome will often depend on what someone (the claimant, a third party, sometimes even the defendant) would have done had the defendant not omitted to perform the relevant duty. This necessarily involves asking a hypothetical question, after the event, as to how someone would have behaved if the circumstances had been different, a process that carries inherent uncertainty, not least because of the possibility that the evidence of the person in question (particularly a claimant or defendant) may be tempered by their knowledge of the actual outcome (i.e. the damage suffered by the claimant). In the second category of case, which almost invariably involve claims in respect of personal injuries, the scientific uncertainty is often simply a product of gaps in human knowledge about the aetiology of the particular medical condition, though this may be compounded in cases where there are multiple possible causes of the claimant's damage. This is typically problematic in two common forms of claim: 2-12

---

32 *Lumba v Secretary of State for the Home Department* [2011] UKSC 12; [2012] 1 A.C. 245 at [65], per Lord Dyson.

33 [2011] UKSC 12; [2012] 1 A.C. 245 at [239], per Lord Kerr.

34 See further para.15-139.

35 The classic example of this is a claim in respect of an injured back, where there is medical evidence, in the form of X-rays or MRI scans, that the claimant was already suffering from constitutional degenerative disease of the spine.

(a) claims relating to liability for disease, particularly industrial disease; and (b) claims where the scientific evidence suggests that the claimant's injury results from a combination of factors: "guilty" causes traceable to the defendants' fault, and, "innocent" causes unrelated to any wrongdoing on the part of the defendants. Often these types of claim will overlap. Cancers, deafness and other forms of disease and disability may well on occasion be thought to be caused by environmental factors, or poor employment practice, or medical negligence, but equally often have other unrelated causes. It may be argued that the condition has genetic origins, or results from environmental factors beyond the defendants' control, or is an inevitable result of the claimant's original disease. The quality of the expert scientific evidence is all important.[36] But even where the causal mechanism is reasonably well-understood in medical terms, so that it can be said of a *population* that, e.g. exposure to a particular toxin (such as tobacco smoke) will lead to an increase in the number of cases of a particular disease (such as lung cancer), it may be virtually impossible for an *individual* affected by exposure to the toxin to prove that his disease was caused by that exposure.[37]

(b) The uncertainty of hypothetical human conduct

(i) Claimant's hypothetical conduct

2-13 **Causation depends on claimant's conduct** The outcome of the "but for" test in *Barnett v Chelsea and Kensington Hospital Management Committee* depended upon expert evidence as to the consequences of arsenic poisoning and the effectiveness of an antidote. There are cases where the answer to the hypothetical question that the test poses ("what would have happened if there had not been a breach of duty by the defendant?") depends upon what a person would have done. In *McWilliams v Sir Williams Arrol & Co*,[38] a steel worker fell 70 feet to his death. The defendants were found to be in breach of statutory duty in failing to provide him with a safety harness, but the evidence established that the dead man had rarely if ever worn a safety harness even when one was provided. His widow's claim for breach of statutory duty failed. She could not show that "but for" the defendants' wrongdoing her husband's death would have been avoided, because the probability was that he would not have worn it.[39] On the other hand, in applying the "but for" test care must be taken to identify the precise scope of the duty imposed on the

36 See, e.g. *Reay v British Nuclear Fuels Plc* [1994] 5 Med. L.R. 1; *Wilsher v Essex AHA* [1988] A.C. 1074 HL.

37 "Observing that a small percentage of cases of cancer were probably caused by exposure to asbestos does not identify whether an individual is one of that group. And given the small size of the percentage, the observation does not, without more, support the drawing of an inference in a particular case": *Amaca Pty Ltd v Ellis* [2010] HCA 5; (2010) 263 A.L.R. 576 at [70] (where the issue was whether exposure to asbestos, as opposed to the deceased's smoking habit, caused his lung cancer). See further *Heneghan v Manchester Dry Docks Ltd* [2016] EWCA Civ 86; [2016] 1 W.L.R. 2036 at [8] and [9].

38 [1962] 1 W.L.R. 295 HL; and see *Wigley v British Vinegars Ltd* [1964] A.C. 307 HL (occupier's liability).

39 Lord Reid commented that it would not be right to draw such an inference too readily, because people do sometimes change their minds unexpectedly, but the evidence in this case was "overwhelming". In *Chief Constable of Hampshire v Taylor* [2013] EWCA Civ 496; [2013] I.C.R. 1150 at [19] Elias LJ (with whom Patten LJ agreed) suggested that where a defendant was found to have been in breach of the Personal Protective Equipment at Work Regulations 1992 the burden of proving that the claimant would not have used the protective equipment, if provided, lay with the defendant. His Lord-

defendant. It may be that the evidence does indeed show that the claimant would not, for example, have worn protective clothing or equipment even if it were provided. But if the defendant's duty is to take all reasonable care to enforce and/or supervise the use of protective equipment, the defendant will not avoid liability unless it can be shown that even had all reasonable steps been employed to ensure the claimant used the protective equipment, he would still have refused to do so or evaded those precautions.[40]

Negligent advice This type of causation question arises whenever the claimant's loss depends upon what the claimant would have done, hypothetically, if there had been no breach of duty by the defendant. Typically, this will occur in "advice" cases, where it is alleged that had the defendant not been negligent in the advice or information given (or not given) the claimant would have done something different, thereby avoiding the loss that has materialised. Thus, where an accountant supplies negligently audited accounts in reliance upon which the claimant purchases a company which proves to be worth less than anticipated, then even if the claimant is able to establish that the accountants owed him a duty of care, he must also prove that had the accounts been accurate he would not have proceeded with the purchase.[41] In claims against solicitors there will be a reasonably strong (though rebuttable) presumption that a client would have acted on the solicitors' advice.[42] 2-14

ship cited *McWilliams v Sir William Arrol* for this proposition (and the judgment of Longmore LJ in *Ali Ghaith v Indesit Company UK Ltd* [2012] EWCA Civ 642 at [23]). *Sed quaere*: the result in *McWilliams v Sir William Arrol* did not turn on the burden of proof, since there was overwhelming evidence that the deceased would probably not have used a safety belt, if supplied (see per Lord Devlin at 309). Viscount Kilmuir LC (with whom Lord Morris agreed) made it clear (at 299) that the burden of proving both breach of duty and causation lay with the claimant. Lord Reid considered (at 306) what amounts to proof *when there is no direct evidence* because the victim is deceased and so unable to give evidence. The starting point is to make certain assumptions: "If general practice or a regulation requires that some safety appliance shall be provided, one would assume that it is of some use, and that a reasonable man would use it. And one would assume that the injured man was a reasonable man. So the initial onus on the pursuer to connect the failure to provide the appliance with the accident would normally be discharged merely by proving the circumstances which led to the accident, and it is only where the evidence throws doubt on either of these assumptions that any difficulty would arise. Normally it would be left to the defender to adduce evidence, if he could, to displace these assumptions." Arguably in this situation, as with the principle of res ipsa loquitur (see para.7-207), there is an *evidential* burden on the defendant to adduce evidence which displaces the initial inference that the breach of duty caused or materially contributed to the injury. But if the defendant does that, and (as rarely occurs in practice) the probabilities are equal, the claim should fail on the basis that the claimant has not discharged the burden of proving causation.

40 *Nolan v Dental Manufacturing Co Ltd* [1958] 1 W.L.R. 936 CA; *Pape v Cumbria CC* [1992] 3 All E.R. 211 CA; *Bux v Slough Metals Ltd* [1973] 1 W.L.R. 1358 (employers liable for failing to instruct and supervise the claimant in the use of safety equipment).

41 See *JEB Fasteners Ltd v Marks Bloom & Co* [1983] 1 All E.R. 583.

42 See *Levicom International Holdings BV v Linklaters* [2010] EWCA Civ 494; [2010] P.N.L.R. 29, a case concerning negligent advice by a solicitor to a client about commencing proceedings where, at [284], Jacob LJ commented: "When a solicitor gives advice that his client has a strong case to start litigation rather than settle and the client then does just that, the normal inference is that the advice is causative. Of course the inference is rebuttable—it may be possible to show that the client would have gone ahead willy-nilly. But that was certainly not shown on the evidence here. The judge should have approached the case on the basis that the evidential burden had shifted to [the defendant] to prove that its advice was not causative." Stanley Burnton LJ observed, at [261], that: "one has to ask why a commercial company should seek expensive City solicitors' advice (and do so repeatedly) if they were not to act on it."

(ii) *Claimant's response to advice about risks of medical treatment*

2-15 **Negligent advice about the risks of medical treatment** Similarly, a patient who alleges that a doctor negligently failed to advise her about the risks of an operative procedure must prove that had she been informed about the risks she would have declined the treatment, thereby avoiding the risk that has now materialised.[43] This is a subjective test, i.e. it is a question of what *this claimant* would have done had the correct advice been given, not what a hypothetical reasonable claimant would have done.[44] In many cases resolution of the hypothetical question of what the claimant would have done had the defendant discharged his duty to advise about the risks, although dependent upon the credibility of evidence, is relatively straightforward. If the claimant would have proceeded with medical treatment even if given a warning, the defendant's breach of duty is not a cause of the damage (i.e. the physical harm which results from the materialisation of the non-disclosed risk). If, on the other hand, the claimant would never have accepted the treatment had she known about the risks the non-disclosure has caused the claimant's damage. The claimant would not have had that particular treatment and therefore the risk associated with the procedure would not have had an opportunity to materialise. There is, however, a third category of case where the claimant says that she would have postponed the decision, possibly in order to obtain further medical advice about the options, but she cannot in all honesty say what her ultimate decision would have been.[45] On one view, if the claimant would have undergone the procedure at some stage in the future, then she would have faced the same inherent risks associated

---

[43] See *Smith v Barking, Havering and Brentwood HA* (1988), [1994] 5 Med. L.R. 285; *McAllister v Lewisham and North Southwark HA* [1994] 5 Med. L.R. 343; *Lybert v Warrington HA* [1996] 7 Med. L.R. 71 CA; *Thompson v Blake-James* [1998] Lloyd's Rep. Med. 187 CA. There is no rule of law that a patient must give evidence personally about what would or would not have happened if she had been properly informed of the facts before making a decision: *Webb v Barclays Bank Plc and Portsmouth Hospitals NHS Trust* [2001] EWCA Civ 1141; [2002] P.I.Q.R. P8; [2001] Lloyd's Rep. Med. 500 at [42]. For more detailed discussion see M.A. Jones, *Medical Negligence*, 5th edn (Sweet & Maxwell, 2018), paras 7-081 to 7-114.

[44] cf. the Canadian approach in *Reibl v Hughes* (1980) 114 D.L.R. (3d) 1 Supreme Court of Canada, applying an objective test. The subjective test is, however, moderated by objective considerations which go to the credibility of the claimant's evidence that she would have done something different: see *Smith v Barking, Havering and Brentwood HA* (1988), [1994] 5 Med. L.R. 285. So, to say that the claimant would have acted rationally if given the appropriate advice is not to apply an objective "reasonable patient" test to causation, provided that there has been a scrupulous assessment of the claimant and her evidence and the judge has taken into account the personal and social considerations particular to the claimant: *Diamond v Royal Devon and Exeter NHS Foundation Trust* [2019] EWCA Civ 585; [2019] P.I.Q.R. P12 at [21]. If the evidence from the defendant doctor is that it is her practice not to disclose particular risks because if she did so most patients would choose to avoid the option that she considers to be the best, the claimant will have little difficulty in persuading the court that she would probably not have gone ahead with the option recommended by the doctor: see *Montgomery v Lanarkshire Health Board* [2015] UKSC 11; [2015] A.C. 1430 at [101]–[104].

[45] Though the court may be able to conclude, from other evidence, what the claimant would probably have done, ultimately: see, e.g. *McAllister v Lewisham and North Southwark HA* [1994] 5 Med. L.R. 343. There is a further factual variant where there are multiple risk factors, and the claimant is warned about some, but not all, of the risks. If, say, the evidence is that the claimant was informed about risk A but not about risk B, and risk A materialises but the claimant states that had he been informed about *both* risk A and B he would have declined the procedure and so avoided the risk that has materialised, does the claim succeed on causation? In *Wallace v Kam* [2013] HCA 19; (2013) 87 A.L.J.R. 648 the High Court of Australia held that in these circumstances the claim will fail. The fact that the claimant would have declined treatment had he been informed about the risk that has not materialised is irrelevant. This is because: "the policy that underlies requiring the exercise of reasonable care and skill in the giving of that warning is neither to protect that right to choose nor

with it, and so the defendant's negligent failure to inform her of those risks would have been of no causative effect. The alternative view is that the materialisation of a small random risk inherent in a particular medical treatment which produces injury to the claimant is the result of the particular time and circumstances in which the treatment was given (assuming that there is nothing which predisposes the particular patient to this risk), and therefore if treatment had been delayed to another occasion the probability is that the small inherent risk would not have materialised *on that occasion*, and so the materialisation of the risk is causally linked to the defendant's non-disclosure of the risk. In *Chester v Afshar*,[46] by a bare majority, the House of Lords held that the latter approach was correct.

The claimant had a history of back pain and was referred to the defendant surgeon, who told her that she needed surgery on her spine. The operation took place three days after the consultation. There was a 1–2 per cent risk that the operation would produce cauda equina syndrome, even if performed with reasonable care, which was not explained to the claimant. Though the operation was not carried out negligently, the claimant developed cauda equina syndrome. Had she been warned of the risks the claimant would not have consented to the surgery at that time but would have a sought a second or a third opinion. She could not say what her ultimate decision would have been. The judge found that it was improbable that any surgery she might eventually undergo would have been identical in circumstances to the operation she actually underwent. In a dissenting speech, Lord Hoffmann said that: "Where the breach of duty is a failure to warn of a risk, [the claimant] must prove that he would have taken the opportunity to avoid or reduce that risk. In the context of the present case, that means proving that she would not have had the operation."[47] Lord Bingham agreed with Lord Hoffmann that the claimant had not established "but for" causation, because she had not proved that 2-16

to protect the patient from exposure to all unacceptable risks. The underlying policy is rather to protect the patient from the occurrence of physical injury the risk of which is unacceptable to the patient. It is appropriate that the scope of liability for breach of the duty reflect that underlying policy" (at [36]). The position might have been different if there was a "risk of a single physical injury to which there are several contributing factors the combination of which operate to increase the risk of that physical injury occurring. To fail to warn the patient of one factor while informing the patient of another may in a particular case be to fail to warn the patient of the extent of the risk and thereby to expose the patient to a level of risk of the physical injury occurring that is unacceptable to the patient" (at [34], discussing the reasoning of Lord Caplan in *Moyes v Lothian Health Board* 1990 S.L.T. 444).

46 [2004] UKHL 41; [2005] 1 A.C. 134, applying the majority decision of the High Court of Australia in *Chappell v Hart* [1998] HCA 55; (1998) 156 A.L.R. 517; commented on by Cane (1999) 115 L.Q.R. 21. For comment on *Chester v Afshar* see Jones (2005) 13 Tort. L.R. 40; Stapleton, "Occam's Razor Reveals an Orthodox Basis for Chester v Afshar" (2006) 122 L.Q.R. 426; Maskrey and Edis, "Chester v Afshar and Gregg v Scott: Mixed Messages for Lawyers" [2005] J.P.I.L. 205.

47 [2004] UKHL 41 at [29]. His Lordship, at [31], described the claimant's argument that it was sufficient to show that she would not have had the operation at the time or by the surgeon that she did, even though the risk would have been the precisely same if she had had the operation at another time or by another surgeon as "about as logical as saying that if one had been told, on entering a casino, that the odds on No 7 coming up at roulette were only 1 in 37, one would have gone away and come back next week or gone to a different casino. The question is whether one would have taken the opportunity to avoid or reduce the risk, not whether one would have changed the scenario in some irrelevant detail." It is submitted, however, that this analogy is misleading because it makes the wrong comparison. A patient is seeking to avoid the adverse consequences of a risk materialising; the gambler is hoping that the risk (the chance) will materialise. Though it would be illogical for the gambler to say he would improve his chances of winning by going away and coming back next week or going to a different casino, that was not Miss Chester's complaint. The better analogy would be if two friends, A and B, were at a casino, and A asked B to place a £100 bet for him on No.7 at the

she would never have undergone the operation, which carried the same risk whenever it was performed, and the doctor's breach of duty had not increased the risk.

2-17 There are two problems with this approach. First it redefines the nature of the claimant's damage as "an increased exposure to the risk", rather than the physical consequences of the risk materialising. This is not how the courts treat successful claims for non-disclosure of risk. The claimant is compensated for the physical damage arising out of the materialisation of the risk. Moreover, if the damage consisted of an increased exposure to the risk then, on Lord Bingham's approach, a patient who was not informed about the risk and would never have gone ahead with treatment would be entitled to damages for having been exposed to the greater risk, even if the risk did not materialise.[48] Again, this is not how such cases are dealt with. Where the risk does not materialise there is no damage. Secondly, as the majority speeches in *Chester* indicate, a conclusion that in these circumstances there is no causal connection would undermine the very duty owed by the doctor. As Lord Hope put it:

> "the function of the law is to protect the patient's right to choose. If it is to fulfil that function it must ensure that the duty to inform is respected by the doctor. It will fail to do this if an appropriate remedy cannot be given if the duty is breached and the very risk that the patient should have been told about occurs and she suffers injury."[49]

This is an approach that Lord Hoffmann has taken on a number of other occasions. For example, in *Reeves v Commissioner of Police for the Metropolis* Lord Hoffmann said that where the law imposed a duty to guard against suicide attempts by a prisoner, "it would make nonsense of the existence of such a duty if the law were to hold that the occurrence of the very act which ought to have been prevented negatived causal connection between the breach of duty and the loss".[50] Lord Hope considered that to leave the patient who would find the decision about whether to accept medical treatment difficult without a remedy would render the duty useless. If the claim failed on grounds of causation it would render the duty:

> "a hollow one, stripped of all practical force and devoid of all content. It will have lost its ability to protect the patient and thus to fulfil the only purpose which brought it into existence. On policy grounds therefore I would hold that the test of causation is satisfied in this case. The injury was intimately involved with the duty to warn. The duty was owed

---

next spin of the wheel. Without consulting A, B decides to place the £100 bet on No.14 instead of No.7. B has not changed A's chances of winning. The chances of No.14 coming up are precisely the same as the chances of No.7 coming up. But if No.7 did come up, we would say that B's actions have *caused* A to lose the bet that he would otherwise have won. It makes no difference that, before the spin of the wheel, A had precisely the same chance of winning with No.14, nor that he would have precisely the same chance of winning (or losing) by placing another £100 bet on another spin of the wheel. Causation is a matter of historical fact, not future risk.

48 Lord Hoffmann considered, but then rejected, the possibility of a "modest solatium" in cases where the non-disclosure did not cause the patient any damage, on the basis that it would vindicate the patient's right to choose: [2004] UKHL 41 at [34].

49 [2004] UKHL 41 at [56].

50 [2000] 1 A.C. 360 at 367–368; see para.2-141. In *Chester* both Lord Hope and Lord Walker drew attention to Lord Hoffmann's previous analysis of causal problems in terms of the scope of a defendant's duty: see [2004] UKHL 41 at [84] and [91] respectively. Lord Walker referred also to *South Australia Asset Management Corp v York Montague Ltd* [1997] A.C. 191 at 212–213 (see para.2-186); and *Kuwait Airways Corp v Iraqi Airways Co (Nos 4 and 5)* [2002] UKHL 19; [2002] 2 A.C. 883 at 1091, 1106 (see para.2-10) where questions of causation were linked to the nature and purpose of the defendant's obligation.

by the doctor who performed the surgery that Miss Chester consented to. It was the product of the very risk that she should have been warned about when she gave her consent. So I would hold that it can be regarded as having been caused, in the legal sense, by the breach of that duty."[51]

2-18 Despite the majority speeches' reliance on the policy factors underlying the duty of care as a justification for concluding that causation was satisfied, it is clearly arguable that if the claimant's damage is considered to be the *physical consequences* of the materialisation of the risk, rather than simply being exposed to the risk, "but for" causation was readily established.[52] Lord Hoffmann's statement that "[w]here the breach of duty is a failure to warn of a risk, [the claimant] must prove that he would have taken the opportunity to avoid or reduce that risk" is only correct if the damage that forms the gist of the action is "exposure to risk". But, for example, a claim against an occupier of land in respect of a failure to warn of a danger on the property, with the result that the entrant suffers an injury caused by that danger, is not a claim for "exposure to risk"; it is a claim for the resulting physical injury, whether or not the occupier created or increased the risk. Similarly, a patient's claim in respect of non-disclosure of risk is for the *physical damage* attributable to the materialisation of the risk, not exposure to risk per se.[53] That is why if the risk does not materialise and no physical damage ensues there is no claim. In order to establish causation the *outcome* must be different, but the clear evidence in *Chester v Afshar* was that the outcome was different.[54] In other words, notwithstanding the resort to notions of fairness and policy by the majority, *Chester* could have been decided on the simple point that the claimant had established "but for" causation.

2-19 **Chester v Afshar limited to cases of negligent medical advice** The Court of Appeal has treated the majority ruling in *Chester v Afshar* as applying an exceptional rule to cases of negligent failure to warn patients about the risks of medical

---

51 [2004] UKHL 41 at [87]. Lord Walker agreed that such a claimant should not be without a remedy, "otherwise the surgeon's important duty would in many cases be drained of its content": [2004] UKHL 41 at [101]. See also, per Lord Steyn at [24] and [25].

52 Lord Hope observed, at [81], that: "The 'but for' test is easily satisfied ..."; and Lord Walker commented, at [94], that: "Bare 'but for' causation is powerfully reinforced by the fact that the misfortune which befell the claimant was the very misfortune which was the focus of the surgeon's duty to warn."

53 See *Wallace v Kam* [2013] HCA 19; (2013) 87 A.L.J.R. 648 at [9]: "However, consistent with the underlying purpose of the imposition of the duty to warn, the damage suffered by the patient that the common law makes compensable is not impairment of the patient's right to choose. Nor is the compensable damage exposure of the patient to an undisclosed risk. The compensable damage is, rather, limited to the occurrence and consequences of physical injury sustained by the patient as a result of the medical treatment that is carried out following the making by the patient of a choice to undergo the treatment" (citing this paragraph in the 20th edn, and M.A. Jones, *Medical Negligence*, 4th edn (London: Sweet & Maxwell 2008), para.7-072).

54 As Lord Steyn observed, [2004] UKHL 41 at [11]: "What is clear is that if she had agreed to surgery at a subsequent date, the risk attendant upon it would have been the same, i.e. 1%–2%. It is therefore improbable that she would have sustained neurological damage." See also *Wallace v Kam* [2013] HCA 19; (2013) 87 A.L.J.R. 648 at [20]: "The better analysis is that it is also a scenario in which a determination of factual causation should be made. Absent the negligent failure to warn, the treatment that in fact occurred would not have occurred when it did and the physical injury in fact sustained when the treatment occurred would not then have been sustained. The same treatment may well have occurred at some later time but (provided that the physical injury remained at all times a possible but improbable result of the treatment) the physical injury that was sustained when the treatment in fact occurred would not on the balance of probabilities have been sustained if the same treatment had occurred on some other occasion."

treatment.[55] For claims in respect to negligent advice by other professionals the traditional causation rules apply, and the claimant must normally demonstrate what advice should have been given, and that he would probably have acted on that advice thereby avoiding the loss. In *White v Paul Davidson & Taylor*[56] Arden LJ said that *Chester v Afshar* did not establish a new general rule on causation, but was an application of the principle in *Fairchild v Glenhaven Funeral Services Ltd*[57] that, in exceptional circumstances, rules of causation may be modified on policy grounds. The principle of informed consent to medical procedures had special importance in the law, but there were no particular policy reasons for departing from traditional principles of causation in an ordinary case of solicitors' negligence.[58] In *Beary v Pall Mall Investments (A Firm)*[59] Dyson LJ rejected a submission that *Chester v Afshar* should be applied generally in claims for negligent financial advice. *Chester* was exceptional and constituted a departure from established principles of causation, justified by the particular policy considerations involved in patients giving informed consent to medical treatment.

(iii) Claimant's response to misrepresentation and deceit

2-20 In the misrepresentation cases the defendant's representation may have been only one factor in the claimant's decision-making process about whether to enter a particular transaction. In *JEB Fasteners Ltd v Marks Bloom & Co*, Stephenson LJ said that the claimant's reliance on a negligent statement will constitute a cause of his loss "as long as a misrepresentation plays a real and substantial part, though not by itself a decisive part, in inducing the [claimant] to act".[60] In an action for deceit, however, the "but for" test does not apply. In *Downs v Chappell*,[61] the Court of Appeal held that, once it is proved that the claimant was in fact induced to act to his detriment by a material misrepresentation, the question of what the claimant would have done but for the fraudulent representation becomes irrelevant: "The judge was wrong to ask how [the claimants] would have acted if they had been told the truth. They were never told the truth. They were told lies in order to induce them to enter into the contract. The lies were material and successful."[62] There is clearly a strong element of policy in this approach in the context of actions for deceit (where, by definition, the defendant has been fraudulent), but somewhat surprisingly the same

---

55 *Chester v Afshar* does not apply to cases of negligent medical *treatment*: *Correia v University Hospital of North Staffordshire NHS Trust* [2017] EWCA Civ 356; [2017] Med. L.R. 292 (patient consented to three-stage operation, but surgeon negligently performed only the first two stages; it did not follow that the patient had not made an informed choice to have the surgery, and the injury was not "intimately linked" with the duty to warn). *Chester v Afshar* requires the claimant to prove that she would at least have deferred the treatment if she had been warned about the risk. It cannot apply where the court concludes, on the facts, that it is probable that even if warned about the risks the claimant would have proceeded with the operation as and when she did: *Duce v Worcestershire Acute Hospitals NHS Trust* [2018] EWCA Civ 1307; [2018] P.I.Q.R. P18 (a proposition for which, it might be thought, no Court of Appeal pronouncement was necessary).

56 [2004] EWCA Civ 1511; [2005] P.N.L.R. 15 at [40].

57 [2002] UKHL 22; [2003] 1 A.C. 32; see para.2-53.

58 [2004] EWCA Civ 1511 at [41]–[42].

59 [2005] EWCA Civ 415; [2005] P.N.L.R. 35 at [38].

60 [1983] 1 All E.R. 583 at 589.

61 [1997] 1 W.L.R. 426 at 433.

62 Cited with approval by Lord Clarke in *Hayward v Zurich Insurance Co Plc* [2016] UKSC 48; [2017] A.C. 142 at [38].

test was applied in *Downs v Chappell* to the second defendants who were guilty only of negligence.

In *Bristol and West Building Society v Mothew*,[63] the Court of Appeal considered itself bound by the decision in *Downs v Chappell* and accepted that, in an action for negligent misrepresentation, where the claimant proves that he relied on the defendant's incorrect advice or information, i.e. that he would not have acted as he did if he had not been given that advice or information, it is not necessary for him to go on to prove that he would not have acted as he did if he had been given proper advice or the correct information.[64] Millett LJ distinguished between the situation where the defendant has negligently given incorrect advice or incorrect information, where the "but for" test of causation appears not to apply, and the case where the claim is based on a failure to give appropriate advice or information. In the latter situation, the claimant must show what advice or information ought to have been given and prove (on a balance of probabilities) that if the missing advice or information had been given he would not have entered into the relevant transaction or would not have done so on disadvantageous terms.[65] This difference in approach appears to rest on a distinction between omissions and acts. If there is a complete failure to provide advice or information, in breach of duty, the claimant must prove what he would have done in the hypothetical situation of the advice or information having been given in order to establish a causal link between the negligence and the damage. If advice or information was provided, but it was incorrect, the claimant need only prove that he relied on it in fact, not that he would have acted differently had the advice or information been correct. The distinction between a failure to give advice and giving incorrect advice, though theoretically tenable, may be difficult to draw in practice.[66] The basic proposition is that the defendant's negligence should have caused the claimant's loss, and this will normally only be shown by demonstrating, on a balance of probabilities, that the outcome would have been different in the absence of negligence. It is not clear why this should be any different in cases of negligent misrepresentation, nor what advantage is brought by an excess of subtlety in classifying different types of negligence (acts and omissions) for the purpose of causation. Though the outcome is understandable in the context of fraud by a defendant, there is no obvious policy reason for adopting the same approach to causation in the case of defendants who have been merely careless. 2-21

---

[63] [1998] Ch. 1 at 11. *JEB Fasteners Ltd* was not cited or referred to in the judgments in *Mothew*. For a helpful analysis of *Bristol and West Building Society v Mothew see O'Sullivan* (2001) 17 P.N. 272.

[64] See, however, the comments of Hobhouse LJ in *Swindle v Harrison* [1997] 4 All E.R. 705 at 728 on this point, suggesting that *Downs v Chappell* did not bind the Court of Appeal in this manner.

[65] See also the explanation of Blackburne J in *Nationwide Building Society v Balmer Radmore (A Firm)* [1999] P.N.L.R. 606 at 656–658, distinguishing between the "what if" approach, which applies where the defendant failed to provide the claimant with information on which to decide upon a course of action where the issue is what course of action would the claimant have followed if the defendant had supplied the correct information, and the "but for" approach which asks what the claimant's position would have been but for the fraudulent supply of the incorrect information.

[66] In *White v Paul Davidson & Taylor* [2004] EWCA Civ 1511; [2005] P.N.L.R. 15 at [26] Ward LJ commented that: "It is perhaps much easier to state that there is a distinction between negligently failing to give proper advice and negligently giving incorrect advice than it is to identify any coherent basis on which the distinction is to be drawn. It seems to me that every case of giving incorrect advice necessarily involves failing to give proper advice." Thus it may be that what is missing from a solicitor's advice (the "omission" in the advice) makes the advice fall below the standard of reasonable care and in that situation it is a case of failing to give proper advice rather than giving incorrect advice, with the consequence that the claimant must establish causation by showing what advice ought to have been given, and proving that if it had been given he would have heeded it and thereby avoided the loss: [2004] EWCA Civ 1511; [2005] P.N.L.R. 15 at [29].

2-22 **Claimant's disbelief in truth of misrepresentation** If a claimant to whom a misrepresentation has been made does not believe the defendant's statement then it might be thought problematic for the claimant to allege that the misrepresentation was relied upon and that therefore this caused the loss by inducing the claimant to do or refrain from doing something. However, the argument that the claimants had not believed the defendant's fraudulent statements and therefore the misrepresentations had not caused loss was rejected by the Supreme Court in *Hayward v Zurich Insurance Co Plc*.[67] The defendant had brought a claim for personal injuries in which he had fraudulently exaggerated the effects of his injuries. The claimants were the insurers who settled the claim despite having strong suspicions that the injuries were exaggerated. Some time after the settlement the insurers were provided with evidence demonstrating that the defendant's claim was grossly exaggerated and they sought damages for deceit. The defendant argued that the insurers could not claim to have been induced to enter into the settlement by the misrepresentation if they had not believed it. The Supreme Court held that it was "not necessary, as a matter of law, to prove that the representee believed that the representation was true." Although the representee's state of mind could be relevant to the issue of inducement, in that there could be difficulty in establishing that he was induced to enter into the contract and that he has thereby suffered loss as a result, this is a question of fact. Belief is not an independent requirement. In order to establish the causal link it was only necessary for the claimant to "have been influenced by the misrepresentation". Nor was it necessary for the misrepresentation to have been the sole cause. On the facts of *Hayward* the crucial issue in entering into the settlement was not whether the insurers believed the defendant's misrepresentations but their assessment of the risk that the court might believe the defendant at a trial.[68] That was sufficient for the misrepresentation to have influenced their decision settle the case.

2-23 **Causation and the detection of fraud** The rule that the "but for" test does not apply in actions for deceit is based on the paradigm fact-situation where A makes a fraudulent statement to B, who believes the statement, even though he should not have done so if he had made proper enquiry. B was negligent, but A cannot say "you should not have believed me", nor can A's employer say "you should not have believed him". Where, however, a firm of auditors is engaged by a company to undertake an audit of the accounts, and an employee of the company makes a fraudulent statement which is believed by the auditors, the position is different. In this situation the auditors, B, were under a duty to A's employer to test the truthfulness of A's statements. Had B performed that duty with reasonable care, he would have realised the statements were false. B's loss (as a result of A's fraud) is his liability to A's employer for failure to perform that duty. B cannot then argue that the cause of that loss was A's fraud, for which the employer was vicariously liable.[69] Although a third party who was misled by A's false statements into entering into a

---

67 [2016] UKSC 48; [2017] A.C. 142.

68 [2016] UKSC 48; [2017] A.C. 142 at [19], [32] per Lord Clarke. Lord Toulson made the same point at [71]: "Mr Hayward's deceitful conduct was intended to influence the mind of the insurers, not necessarily by causing them to believe him, but by causing them to value his litigation claim more highly than it was worth if the true facts had been disclosed, because the value of a claim for insurers' purposes is that which the court is likely put on it."

69 *Barings Plc (In liquidation) v Coopers & Lybrand (A Firm)* [2003] EWHC 1319 (Ch); [2003] P.N.L.R. 34 at [732] and [733], per Evans-Lombe J.

transaction would be able to recover all losses flowing from that transaction, the auditors were not a "third party". They were in breach of a pre-existing duty, owed to A's employers, to guard against being misled by just such false statements, and it would make a nonsense of the auditors' duty to the company if the very act which ought reasonably to have been prevented gave rise to an equal and opposite counterclaim and so negatived the causal connection between the auditors' breach of duty and the client's loss.[70]

(iv) Defendant's hypothetical conduct

2-24 The causation problem is not limited to circumstances where the question is what the *claimant* would have done, in hypothetical circumstances, but also arises where there is a question as to what, hypothetically, the *defendant* would have done had she not been negligent. This is illustrated by *Bolitho v City and Hackney HA*,[71] in which the claimant, who was in hospital, suffered brain damage as a result of cardiac arrest caused by an obstruction of the bronchial air passages. The defendants admitted negligence because a doctor had not attended to the claimant in response to calls for assistance. The damage could have been avoided if the claimant had been seen by a doctor and "intubated", clearing the obstruction. The doctor who failed to respond said that had she attended she would not have intubated, and therefore the cardiac arrest and subsequent brain damage would have occurred in any event. There was evidence that a responsible body of professional opinion would have supported a decision not to intubate, although five medical experts for the claimant said that he should have been intubated, and it was agreed that this was the only course of action that would have prevented the damage. Lord Browne-Wilkinson said that in all cases the primary question is one of fact: did the wrongful act cause the injury? In cases where the breach of duty consists of an omission to do an act which ought to have been done (such as the failure of a doctor to attend the patient) the factual enquiry is necessarily hypothetical. The question is what would have happened if an event, which by definition did not occur, had occurred? The first question is: what would have happened—either the doctor would have intubated, had she attended, or she would not. The *Bolam* test,[72] by which standards of professional negligence are measured by reference to a responsible body of professional opinion, was not, and could not, be relevant to that question. The defendant doctor said that she would not have intubated, and therefore the claimant would in any event have sustained the brain damage. But she could not escape liability by proving that she would have failed to act as any reasonably competent doctor would have acted in the circumstances: "A defendant cannot escape liability by saying that the damage would have occurred in any event because he would have committed some other breach of duty thereafter."[73] Applying *Joyce v Wandsworth HA*,[74] Lord Browne-Wilkinson, concluded that there were two questions for the judge to decide on causation: (1) what would the doctor have

---

70 [2003] EWHC 1319 (Ch); [2003] P.N.L.R. 34 at [743]; applying *Reeves v Commissioner of Police for the Metropolis* [2000] 1 A.C. 360; see para.2-141.

71 [1998] A.C. 232 HL.

72 *Bolam v Friern Hospital Management Committee* [1957] 1 W.L.R. 582; see para.9-76.

73 per Lord Browne-Wilkinson at [1998] A.C. 232 at 240. See *Wright (A Child) v Cambridge Medical Group* [2011] EWCA Civ 669; [2013] Q.B. 312 at [56]–[61] per Lord Neuberger MR for discussion of the underlying rationale for this proposition. See para.2-127.

74 [1996] P.I.Q.R. P121.

done, or authorised to be done, if she had attended the claimant? and (2) if she would not have intubated, would that have been negligent? The *Bolam* test had no relevance to first question, but was central to the second.[75]

2-25 These are discrete questions. In the case of a negligent omission if the answer to (1) is that, on the facts, what the defendant would have done would probably have resulted in the damage to the claimant then the answer to (2) is irrelevant.[76] In *Gouldsmith v Mid Staffordshire General Hospitals NHS Trust*[77] the defendants were found to be in breach of duty in failing to refer the claimant patient to a specialist tertiary vascular unit. The central issue in the Court of Appeal was whether, if the claimant had been referred, surgery would have been carried out which could have saved some of the digits of her left hand from being amputated. There was no direct evidence as to which specialist centre the claimant would have been referred to, and therefore, unlike *Bolitho*, there was no direct evidence as to what the hypothetical specialist surgeon would have done. The evidence was that "most" specialist units would have operated, but nonetheless the judge held that the claim failed on causation because there was a minority of specialist units that would not have operated, and this minority view was *Bolam*-compliant (i.e. it would not have been negligent not to operate). A majority of the Court of Appeal held that the judge had only addressed the second causation question set out in *Bolitho*, namely would the failure to intervene have been negligent? There is, however, a prior question, i.e. what would have happened if the defendant had not been in breach of duty? If the claimant had been referred to a specialist vascular unit would the operation have been carried out? If the answer to that question was, probably, yes, then the second question "would it have been negligent not to operate?" did not arise.[78] The evidence that most specialist units would have operated was sufficient to establish, on the balance of probabilities, that had the claimant been referred it was probable that the surgery would have taken place.[79] On the other hand, if the defendants had produced evidence that, if they had not been in breach of duty, they would probably have referred the patient to a specialist centre that would not have operated the result on causation would have been different.

---

75 The *Bolam* test does not apply where what the judge is required to do is to make findings of fact. This is the case even where those findings of fact are subject to conflicting expert evidence. So if there is a dispute amongst expert witnesses about a question of fact (such as what was visible on a laboratory slide) the judge is entitled to prefer one group of experts over the other: *Penney, Palmer and Cannon v East Kent HA* [2000] Lloyd's Rep. Med. 41 at 46. This will frequently be the case on questions of causation. For example, where the issue is whether the claimant's medical condition would or would not have deteriorated with appropriate treatment, it is not simply a question of opting for the view of the majority of experts or of a reasonable body of medical opinion, since "that would be to import the well-known *Bolam* test into the issue of causation, where it has no proper place": *Cavanagh v Bristol and Weston HA* [1992] 3 Med. L.R. 49 at 56, per Macpherson J.

76 This is the case even though what the defendant *would* have done would have involved exercising greater care to avoid harm to the claimant than was reasonably required by what the defendant *should* have done: *Robbins v Bexley LBC* [2013] EWCA Civ 1233; [2014] B.L.R. 11 at [47]–[53], per Vos LJ and [69], per Aikens LJ (applying *Bolitho* to a case of damage to property by tree roots).

77 [2007] EWCA Civ 397; [2007] L.S. Law Med. 363.

78 [2007] EWCA Civ 397; [2007] L.S. Law Med. 363 at [29], per Pill LJ.

79 Maurice Kay LJ dissented on this point, on the basis that the claimant had to establish that she would have been referred to one of the specialist units which would have carried out the operation. Wilson LJ considered that this would place too heavy an evidential burden on the claimant in a case where the defendants had been found to be in breach of duty in failing to refer a patient, but had chosen to lead no evidence as to which particular specialist they would have referred the claimant to.

(v) *Third party's hypothetical conduct*

Where the question of what would have happened in hypothetical circumstances depends upon the actions of a third party, then a different approach is usually taken.[80] In *Allied Maples Group Ltd v Simmons & Simmons (A Firm)*,[81] the Court of Appeal held that in such cases, rather than take an "all or nothing" approach, on the balance of probabilities, the court should assess the chance that the third party would have acted in such a manner as would have avoided the harm sustained by the claimant. This chance can be assessed even where it is less than 50 per cent, and the claimant is then awarded damages on the basis of the value of the lost chance, rather than on a full liability basis.[82] 2-26

(c) Scientific uncertainty about causal mechanisms

Causation and industrial disease[83] The impossibility, in a significant number of claims for negligence and/or breach of statutory duty[84] in respect of industrial disease, of quantifying the exact proportion in which competing agents contributed to the onset of disease makes proof of causation particularly difficult. Once there is sufficient evidence that the "guilty" agent does cause the disease or disability to which the claimant has succumbed and that the greater the exposure to that agent the greater the risk of onset of disease, the claimant will not normally be required to do the impossible and demonstrate exactly why and how his condition arose.[85] However, in *Pickford v Imperial Chemical Industries Plc*,[86] the House of Lords held that where a claimant alleges that her condition has a physical cause she must go on to prove, on the balance of probabilities, that her injury was produced through a physical "route". The claimant alleged that she had developed a prescribed disease (PDA4, cramp of the hand or forearm due to repetitive movements) in the course of her employment as a secretary. There was conflicting medical evidence as to whether her condition was organic in nature, as a result of physical injury, or whether it was psychogenic (as the defendants contended). The trial judge dismissed the action, holding that the claimant had failed to establish that her condition was organic in nature or that it had been caused by her typing work. The Court of Appeal reversed the trial judge on the basis that he had misdirected himself that the onus was on the claimant to establish that the cause was organic. On appeal, the House of Lords held that the burden of proof was on the claimant to show that her condition had an organic cause, and ICI's failure to prove that the condition was psychogenic was simply one relevant factor in the decision as to whether the 2-27

---

80 In *Gregg v Scott* [2005] UKHL 2; [2005] 2 A.C. 176 at [82] Lord Hoffmann said that "[t]his apparently arbitrary distinction [between the rules applied to the actions of third parties and the actions of the claimant or defendant] obviously rests on grounds of policy", but his Lordship did not explain what that policy is.

81 [1995] 1 W.L.R. 1602; approved by the Supreme Court in *Perry v Raleys Solicitors* [2019] UKSC 5; [2020] A.C. 352.

82 See further at para.2-76.

83 For a scientific view of the problem see Coggon and Newman Taylor, "Causation and Attribution of Disease in Personal Injury Cases: A Scientific Perspective" [2009] J.P.I.L. 12.

84 In claims for breach of statutory duty, while clearly the burden proving causation remains with the claimant, evidence that the statutory duty was imposed to protect employees from the very kind of injury which ensued is relevant. See, e.g. *Nicholson v Atlas Steel Co Ltd* [1957] 1 W.L.R. 613; *Gardiner v Motherwell Machinery and Scrap Co* [1961] 1 W.L.R. 1424.

85 See para.2-32 onwards.

86 [1998] 1 W.L.R. 1189.

claimant's explanation of the cause should be accepted. Thus, the judge was correct to consider evidence other than the medical evidence and was entitled to conclude that the claimant had not satisfied the burden of proof.

2-28 These types of causation problem also tend to arise in medical negligence actions. In *Kay's Tutor v Ayrshire and Arran Health Board*,[87] the infant claimant contracted meningitis. In hospital he was given a massive overdose of penicillin which nearly killed him, but he recovered both from the toxic effects of the overdose and from meningitis. On recovery he was found to be profoundly deaf. Deafness is a recognised complication of meningitis. The hospital admitted negligence but denied liability for the deafness. No expert evidence linked overdoses of penicillin to such damage, but overdoses of such magnitude are almost unknown and previous recipients had died. The judge found for the claimant on causation on the basis that the effect of the overdose so weakened the claimant's system that he was much more likely to succumb to the complications of meningitis. Thus the defendants' negligence materially contributed to the claimant's injury. The House of Lords quashed his judgment for lack of any medical evidence that an overdose of penicillin increased the risk that meningitis would cause deafness: "… the paucity of such cases, none of which supports the suggested causal link, cannot of itself make good the lack of appropriate evidence."[88]

2-29 Thus, there are two stages to the process of establishing causation in cases of disease or adverse reactions to chemical agents, such as drugs. It must first be demonstrated, on the balance of probabilities, that the event which allegedly gave rise to the claimant's damage can ever cause that type of harm. It was on this basis that the claim in *Kay's Tutor v Ayrshire and Arran Health Board* failed, because there was no evidence that an overdose of penicillin can cause deafness.[89] Once it has been established that such an event can cause damage of that nature, the claimant must then prove that his particular damage was caused in this way. It is the second stage of the process that can present the greatest hurdle to claimants. In some cases, all the claimant will be able to point to is the statistical link between particular events or circumstances and the damage to individuals exposed to those events.

(i) Statistics and causation

2-30 Care has to be exercised when relying on statistics as a means of establishing causation. The court must look at the claimant's individual circumstances rather

---

[87] [1987] 2 All E.R. 417 HL. See also *Reay v British Nuclear Fuels Plc* [1994] 5 Med. L.R. 1 where the claimants were unable to prove that paternal pre-conception irradiation (radiation injury to the gonads resulting in mutation of spermatagonia) had caused the claimants' cancer.

[88] [1987] 2 All E.R. 417 HL at 421, per Lord Keith. See also *Dingley v Chief Constable of Strathclyde Police*, 2000 S.C. (HL) 77; (2000) 55 B.M.L.R. 1 HL—if there is insufficient evidence to establish whether as a general proposition multiple sclerosis can ever be triggered by trauma, the claimant will be unable to establish the specific issue that there was a connection between his injury in an accident and the subsequent onset of multiple sclerosis.

[89] See also *Loveday v Renton* [1990] 1 Med. L.R. 117 where the claimant failed to show, on a balance of probabilities, that pertussis vaccine could cause brain damage in young children, although it was "possible" that it did because the contrary could not be proved either. See also *Rothwell v Raes* (1990) 76 D.L.R. (4th) 280 where the Ontario Court of Appeal came to the same conclusion on pertussis vaccine. cf. *Best v Wellcome Foundation Ltd* [1993] 3 I.R. 421; [1994] 5 Med. L.R. 81 where the Supreme Court of Ireland held the defendants to have been negligent in distributing a *faulty* batch of pertussis vaccine, and an inference of causation was drawn from the temporal connection between the administration of the vaccine and the claimant's brain damage.

than at the general statistics. For example, in *Wardlaw v Farrar*[90] it was alleged that a general practitioner had been negligent in failing to diagnose a patient's pulmonary embolus and it was argued that the patient's chances of survival had been reduced by the delay in referring the patient to hospital for treatment. The evidence indicated that 85 per cent of patients diagnosed with a pulmonary embolus survive, but the patient did not respond to the usual beneficial effects of anti-coagulation therapy when she eventually received treatment in hospital, and subsequently died. Counsel argued that this fact should be ignored, since the issue had to be determined at the time of the negligent misdiagnosis. The Court of Appeal rejected the argument. In considering whether, on the balance of probabilities, the general practitioner's negligence had caused the death the court must take into account all relevant evidence, and the failure of anti-coagulant therapy to prevent the formation of a massive pulmonary embolism was a material piece of evidence. This pointed to the probability that the patient fell into the category of 15 per cent of patients who do not survive, despite treatment, for reasons that are not well-understood by medical science. Brooke LJ commented that:

> "While judges are of course entitled to place such weight on statistical evidence as is appropriate, they must not blind themselves to the effect of other evidence which might put a particular patient in a particular category, regardless of the general probabilities."[91]

On the other hand, care should be taken not to take the logic of this reasoning too far in the opposite direction. If the evidence is that, say, 80 per cent of patients survive with prompt treatment, but 20 per cent die even with prompt treatment, the fact that the patient died following delayed treatment does not establish that he probably fell into the 20 per cent category at the outset and therefore the delay did not contribute to the death. The assessment of causation would turn upon the detailed medical evidence, both as to the overall statistical chances of survival and the particular condition and circumstances of the patient.[92] To be a figure in a statistic does not, in itself, prove causation.[93] The difficulty of using statistics, which derive from trends in general populations, to prove what "probably" happened in a particular case is well recognised.[94] Moreover, analysis of the factual basis for draw-

---

90 [2003] EWCA Civ 1719; [2004] Lloyd's Rep. Med. 98; [2004] P.I.Q.R. P19.

91 [2003] EWCA Civ 1719; [2004] Lloyd's Rep. Med. 98; [2004] P.I.Q.R. P19 at [35].

92 This passage was cited with apparent approval in *Schembri v Marshall* [2020] EWCA Civ 358 at [44]. per McCombe LJ; see also at [46].

93 See the comments of Croom-Johnson LJ in *Hotson v East Berkshire AHA* [1987] A.C. 750 at 769: "If it is proved statistically that 25 per cent. of the population have a chance of recovery from a certain injury and 75 per cent. do not, it does not mean that someone who suffers that injury and who does not recover from it has lost a 25 per cent. chance. He may have lost nothing at all. What he has to do is prove that he was one of the 25 per cent. And that his loss was caused by the defendant's negligence. To be a figure in a statistic does not by itself give him a cause of action. If the plaintiff succeeds in proving that he was one of the 25 per cent. and that the defendants took away that chance, the logical result would be to award him 100 per cent. of his damages and not only a quarter …". See also the example of the two cab companies given by Lord Mackay in the House of Lords in *Hotson* [1987] A.C. 750 at 789.

94 See, e.g. *Gregg v Scott* [2005] UKHL 2; [2005] 2 A.C. 176 at [26]–[29], per Lord Nicholls. In *Sienkiewicz v Greif (UK) Ltd* [2011] UKSC 10; [2011] 2 A.C. 229 the Supreme Court was extremely cautious about the circumstances in which the use of epidemiological data to establish causation would be appropriate. Although epidemiological data may form an important element in the proof of causation, it had to be recognised that it deals with populations rather than individuals, and it would be inappropriate to reason from statistical data about causal effects within a population to a

ing appropriate conclusions from statistical evidence may be far from easy.[95] In some respects a test based on a balance of probability gives the standard proof a pseudo-scientific credibility. The notion that the event(s) in issue were more likely to have occurred than not, taking a balance of probability as 51:49, appears to confer on the decision-making process a degree of mathematical accuracy which simply is not available in most cases.[96] Proof of causation is almost invariably about a burden of persuasion, and sometimes statistics can be highly persuasive, when used appropriately.

2-31 **A mathematical approach to discrete causes?** In a case where the damage is not cumulative but is attributable to a single event, but it is not possible to identify which event, then a mathematical approach to determining the balance of probabilities may be applied. In *The Creutzfeldt-Jakob Disease Litigation, Groups A and C Plaintiffs*[97] the claimants had all developed Creutzfeldt-Jacob Disease (CJD) as a consequence of receiving human growth hormone (HGH) treatment contaminated with the CJD virus. The treatment, consisting of an injection, was given on a regular basis over a period of time. Although there was some uncertainty, the accepted scientific view was that the CJD was caused by a single injection or dose containing a sufficient titre of the CJD agent. There was no issue of a cumulative cause nor that some individuals are more susceptible to developing CJD. The defendants were found to have been in breach of duty from 1 July 1977 by failing to give appropriate information to clinicians treating the claimants about the risks of transmitting CJD. The claimants had received injections of HGH both before and after 1 July 1977, but it was not scientifically possible to identify whether they had received a contaminated dose before or after that date. The defendants were only liable if it could be proved that the claimants received the contaminated dose after that date. The claimants argued that if a victim received more doses after the cut-off date than before it then it was more likely than not that the contaminated dose was received after the cut-off date. By analogy, if a pack of cards was divided into two piles containing 27 and 25 cards respectively there is a higher probability that the pile of 27 cards contains the ace of spades. The defendants argued that this was a simplistic, mechanistic approach. There was a likelihood or possibility that a victim received a number of contaminated doses, although only one would prove fatal. If there were a number of potential aces of spades in the pack then the analogy of the pack of cards was inappropriate. Morland J rejected the defendants' argument that causation was only established if the preponderance of doses were given after the cut-off date, and that a preponderance should be substantial (possibly three-quarters or two-thirds). That argument, said his Lordship, would alter the civil standard of proof from the balance of probabilities to a standard of substantially

---

causal mechanism in an individual, unless there is something in the particular facts of the case which would enable the court to infer a causal link in relation to the individual claimant. But see C. McIvor, "Debunking Some Judicial Myths about Epidemiology and Its Relevance to UK Tort Law" (2013) 21 Med. L. Rev. 553 who argues that judicial caution is misplaced and that epidemiology is capable of providing a scientifically robust foundation for conclusions about causation in complex disease and medical negligence cases.

[95] See the speech of Lord Phillips in *Gregg v Scott* [2005] UKHL 2; [2005] 2 A.C. 176, discussed at para.2-95.

[96] See *Nulty v Milton Keynes BC* [2013] EWCA Civ 15; [2013] 1 W.L.R. 1183 at [35], per Toulson LJ, cited above para.2-07 fn.18.

[97] (1998) 54 B.M.L.R. 100.

probable or very probable. Thus, any straddler victim would succeed on causation if it was proved that he received the majority of doses after the cut-off date.

(ii) *Material contribution to the damage*

The difficulties facing claimants in proving causation in cases of industrial disease have persuaded the courts to relax the causal rules in some instances (normally where the difficulty of attributing causes is a product of scientific uncertainty). The claimant does not have to prove that the defendant's breach of duty was the sole, or even the main, cause of his damage provided he can demonstrate that it made a material contribution to the damage. The origin of this approach is the decision of the House of Lords in *Bonnington Castings Ltd v Wardlaw*[98] in which the claimant contracted pneumoconiosis from inhaling air which contained silica dust at his workplace. The main source of the dust was from pneumatic hammers for which the employers were not in breach of duty (the "innocent dust"). Some of the dust (the "guilty dust") came from swing grinders for which they were responsible by failing to maintain the dust-extraction equipment. There was no evidence as to the proportions of innocent dust and guilty dust inhaled by the claimant. Indeed, such evidence as there was indicated that much the greater proportion came from the innocent source. On the evidence the claimant could not prove "but for" causation, in the sense that it was more probable than not that had the dust-extraction equipment worked efficiently he would not have contracted the disease. Nonetheless, the House of Lords drew an inference of fact that the guilty dust was a contributory cause, holding the employers liable for the full extent of the loss. The claimant did not have to prove that the guilty dust was the sole or even the most substantial cause if he could show, on a balance of probabilities, the burden of proof remaining with the claimant, that the guilty dust had materially contributed to the disease. Anything which did not fall within the principle de minimis non curat lex would constitute a material contribution. *Bonnington Castings* is significant for two reasons. First, it was an express departure from the normal requirement to prove "but for" causation. Despite recovering damages in full in respect of the disease the claimant was not required to prove that the defendant's breach of duty caused the disease, merely that it contributed to its onset. Secondly, and perhaps more significantly, was the fact that their Lordships were willing to draw an *inference* that there must have been a material contribution in circumstances where the connection between the "guilty dust" and the claimant's medical condition was, in reality, little more than speculation.[99] 2-32

---

[98] [1956] A.C. 613. See S. Bailey, "Causation in negligence: what is a material contribution?" (2010) 30 L.S. 167 for extended discussion of *Bonnington Castings Ltd v Wardlaw*.

[99] Subsequently, in *Nicholson v Atlas Steel Foundry Engineering Co Ltd* [1957] 1 W.L.R. 613 on virtually identical facts, the House of Lords held the defendants liable for an employee's pneumoconiosis, even though, in the words of Viscount Simonds, it was "impossible even approximately to quantify" the respective contributions of guilty and innocent dust. See also *Clarkson v Modern Foundries Ltd* [1957] 1 W.L.R. 1210. Contrast *Amaca Pty Ltd v Ellis* [2010] HCA 5; (2010) 263 A.L.R. 576 where the High Court of Australia declined to apply the material contribution to damage approach in a case where the issue was whether the deceased's exposure to asbestos was a cause of his lung cancer, as opposed to the deceased's chronic smoking habit. The only evidence that the deceased's cancer was potentially caused by asbestos was epidemiological evidence, but this demonstrated that the relative risk due to smoking was much greater than the risk due to exposure to asbestos. The probability, on the evidence, was that it was the smoking and not the exposure to asbestos that caused

2-33 In *Bailey v The Ministry of Defence*[100] the claimant was a patient in hospital who sustained brain damage when, in a weakened physical state and so unable to react, she aspirated her own vomit and suffered cardiac arrest. The evidence indicated that the damage would probably not have occurred if the claimant was not in such a weakened state. There were two causes of her weakened state, pancreatitis (which was not attributable to the defendants' negligence) and a period of negligent care for which the defendants were responsible. The claimant could not prove "but for" causation because it was not possible to say, on the evidence, that in the absence of the pancreatitis she would nonetheless have been so weakened by the defendant's negligence that she would have been unable to respond naturally to her vomit and so have avoided the cardiac arrest and resulting brain damage. The claimant argued that the reason that she aspirated was her extreme weakness which was caused, or materially contributed to, by the defendant's negligence. The defendants argued that the case was governed by *Wilsher v Essex AHA*[101] and that adding a new risk to other risks which might also have caused harm was not proof of causation, even if the new risk arose from negligence. The Court of Appeal agreed with the trial judge's approach that there were two contributory causes of the claimant's weakness, the non-negligent cause and the negligent cause, and since each "contributed materially" to the overall weakness, and since the overall weakness caused the aspiration, causation was established. *Bonnington Castings v Wardlaw* was authority for the proposition that in a case involving cumulative causes, where the inadequacies of medical science mean that the relative potency of the causes cannot be established, a claimant merely has to establish that the defendant's breach of duty made a "material" contribution, which means something more than de minimis.[102] *Wilsher* was distinguished on the basis that it was not a case of causes cumulatively causing injury but a case where there were distinct causes which operated in a different way and might have caused the injury, where the claimant could

his lung cancer: "Questions of material contribution arise only if a connection between [the deceased's] inhaling asbestos and his developing cancer was established. Knowing that inhaling asbestos can cause cancer does not entail that in this case it probably did" (at [68]). In *Heneghan v Manchester Dry Docks Ltd* [2016] EWCA Civ 86; [2016] 1 W.L.R. 2036 the Court of Appeal agreed with the reasoning of the Court in *Amaca* that it is not possible to infer a material contribution to the claimant's damage from epidemiological evidence that exposure to asbestos can cause lung cancer. See also *Hanke v Resurfice Corp* [2007] 1 S.C.R. 333; [2007] 4 W.W.R. 1 at [19] where the Supreme Court of Canada did not accept that where there is more than one potential cause of an injury, the "material contribution" test must be used: "To accept this conclusion is to do away with the 'but for' test altogether, given that there is more than one potential cause in virtually all litigated cases of negligence."

100 [2008] EWCA Civ 883; [2009] 1 W.L.R. 1052. See Green (2009) 125 L.Q.R. 44; G. Turton (2009) 17 Med. L. Rev. 140.

101 See para.2-46.

102 Applying the interpretation of Lord Rodger in *Fairchild v Glenhaven* [2002] UKHL 22; [2003] 1 A.C. 32 at [129]. See further *Leigh v London Ambulance Service NHS Trust* [2014] EWHC 286 (QB); [2014] Med. L.R. 134 where *Bailey* was applied to a claim in respect of post-traumatic stress disorder and dissociative seizures attributed to the claimant being trapped between seats on a bus due to the dislocation of her knee. The defendants' admitted breach of duty resulted in a 17-minute delay in the arrival of an ambulance. Globe J concluded that it was a case where medical science could not establish the probability that "but for" the negligent delay, the PTSD would not have happened, but it was established that the contribution of the negligent delay was more than negligible, and so it made a material contribution to the development of the PTSD. In the case of asbestos-related industrial disease the defendant's contribution to the claimant's overall disability may be very small and still constitute a more than de minimis contribution: see *Carder v Secretary of State for Health* [2016] EWCA Civ 790; [2017] I.C.R. 392; and *Mayne v Atlas Stone Co Ltd* [2016] EWHC 1030 (QB); [2016] I.C.R. 957.

not establish which cause either "caused or contributed" to his injury.[103] On the evidence the claimant did not have to argue that the defendants' negligence had merely increased the *risk* of harm (as in *Wilsher*).[104]

In *Williams v The Bermuda Hospitals Board*[105] the Privy Council approved the application of *Bonnington Castings Ltd v Wardlaw* to a claim for clinical negligence where there had been a negligent delay in diagnosing and treating the claimant's ruptured appendix. The claimant developed complications after the surgery to remove his appendix. The sepsis from the ruptured appendix developed incrementally over a period of six hours, progressively causing myocardial ischaemia. Its development and effect on the heart and lungs was a single continuous process. The negligent period of the delay amounted to two hours and 20 minutes and therefore, said Lord Toulson, it was correct to infer on the balance of probabilities that the negligence had materially contributed to the process, and therefore materially contributed to the claimant's injury. For Lord Toulson the parallel of *Bonnington Castings* was "obvious". It was "immaterial whether the cumulative factors operate concurrently or successively". Commenting, obiter, on counsel's criticism of *Bailey v Ministry of Defence* Lord Toulson said that on the facts of *Bailey* the judge had been correct to hold the hospital liable for the consequences of the patient's aspiration of her vomit: 2-34

> "As to the parallel weakness of the claimant due to her pancreatitis, the case may be seen as an example of the well known principle that a tortfeasor takes his victim as he finds her. The Board does not share the view of the Court of Appeal that the case involved a departure from the 'but-for' test. The judge concluded that the totality of the claimant's weakened condition caused the harm. If so, 'but-for' causation was established. The fact that her vulnerability was heightened by her pancreatitis no more assisted the hospital's case than if she had an egg shell skull."[106]

Extent of defendant's contribution known—cumulative (divisible) harm Where it is possible to identify the extent of the contribution that the defendant's wrong made to the claimant's damage then the defendant is liable only to that extent, and no more. Thus, in *Thompson v Smiths Shiprepairers (North Shields) Ltd*[107] the claimant suffered progressive hearing impairment due to 2-35

---

103 [2008] EWCA Civ 883; [2009] 1 W.L.R. 1052 at [44].

104 See also *Boustead v North West Strategic HA (City Maternity Hospital Carlisle)* [2008] EWHC 2375 (QB); [2008] L.S. Law Med. 471—brain damaged baby with multiple possible causes that were found not to be competing, mutually exclusive, causes but causes which acted cumulatively. Mackay J, adopting a "robust and pragmatic approach to undisputed primary facts" (see para.2-46), applied *Bonnington Castings v Wardlaw*: since the causes were concurrent *cumulative* causes, the claimant had proved that the defendant's breach of duty had made a material contribution to his disabilities.

105 [2016] UKPC 4; [2016] A.C. 888; discussed by J. Stapleton and S. Steel, "Causes and contributions" (2016) 132 L.Q.R. 363; S. Green (2016) 32 P.N. 169.

106 [2016] UKPC 4; [2016] A.C. 888 at [47]. See also *John v Central Manchester and Manchester Children's University Hospitals NHS Foundation Trust* [2016] EWHC 407 (QB); [2016] 4 W.L.R. 54, Picken J holding that the material contribution to damage approach to causation can apply in cases of multiple causal factors (accidental head injury, negligent period of delay in operating on claimant, and non-negligent post-operative infection all contributed to claimant's cognitive and neuropsychological impairment; delay in operating had made a material contribution, applying *Bonnington Castings*, *Bailey* and *Williams*).

107 [1984] Q.B. 405; *Bowman v Harland and Wolff Plc* [1992] I.R.L.R. 349 at 359; *Dillon v Le Roux* [1994] 6 W.W.R. 280 at 300 BCCA, where the claimant had a pre-existing condition that was active and disabling prior to his admission to hospital, and the defendant doctor's negligence increased the damage to the claimant's heart.

industrial noise. The defendants were held liable only for that part of the deafness which occurred after the exposure to noise became a breach of duty. Although the claimant's deafness was probably entirely work-related, the defendants were not liable for that element of the deafness which occurred before they should have taken reasonable precautions to protect the claimant. At the point from which they were responsible, the claimant's hearing was already damaged, and therefore the defendants were liable only for the additional damage caused by the breach of duty.[108]

2-36 In *Holtby v Brigham Cowan (Hull) Ltd*,[109] the claimant, who worked as a marine fitter, was exposed to asbestos dust over a period of almost 40 years. For about half of that time he worked for the defendants, and for the remainder he worked for other employers doing the same sort of work in similar conditions. He developed asbestosis and sued the defendants, who were held to have been negligent and in breach of statutory duty. The judge held that the defendants were only liable for the damage they had caused, the evidence indicating that if the claimant had only been exposed to asbestos whilst working at the defendants' his condition would probably have been less severe. General damages were reduced by 25 per cent. The claimant appealed on the basis that once he established that the defendant's breach of duty materially contributed to his damage he was entitled to recover for the full extent of his loss, applying *Bonnington Castings Ltd v Wardlaw*.[110] Alternatively, he argued that once a claimant has proved that the defendant's conduct had made a material contribution to the damage the onus shifted to the defendant to prove that someone else was responsible for a specific part of the damage. The Court of Appeal rejected both arguments, upholding the judge's deduction of 25 per cent. Stuart-Smith LJ said that in both *Bonnington Castings* and *McGhee v National Coal Board*[111] the House of Lords had not considered the extent of the defendants' liability because it had not been argued that the defendants' were only liable to the extent of their material contribution—their case had been that they were not liable at all. The onus of proof remained with the claimant to show that the defendant's tortious conduct made a material contribution to the loss, but strictly speaking the defendants were liable only to the extent of that contribution.[112] If the point was never raised or argued by the defendant the claimant would succeed in full, as in *Bonnington Castings* and *McGhee*. But once it became an issue the burden of proof was the claimant's. Stuart-Smith LJ indicated that although strictly speaking the defendant did not have to plead that others were partly responsible, it was preferable for that to be done and for the question to be dealt with in evidence, otherwise

---

108 See para.2-104. Note that in assessing damages, the fact that the defendant's breach of duty has worsened an existing condition may lead to a higher assessment of the loss, since the consequences of the impairment may be greater. Thus, it is much worse to be totally deaf than half deaf, and the additional hearing loss (from half to totally deaf) causes greater damage than the initial hearing loss (from full hearing to half deaf). See, e.g. *Paris v Stepney BC* [1951] A.C. 367 (loss of an eye is significantly worse for a one-eyed man than a man with full eyesight).

109 [2000] I.C.R. 1086; [2000] 3 All E.R. 421 CA; see Owen (2000) 150 N.L.J. 1116; Owen [2000] J.P.I.L. 82; Gullifer (2001) 117 L.Q.R. 403; Caun [2003] J.P.I.L. 96; McCaul [2006] J.P.I.L. 6.

110 [1956] A.C. 613.

111 [1973] 1 W.L.R. 1 HL; see para.2-45.

112 Note, however, the observation of Lord Uist in *Wright v Stoddard International Plc and Novartis Grimsby Ltd* [2007] CSOH 173; 2008 Rep. L.R. 2 at [141] that the apportionment point was not argued in *Bonnington Castings* or *McGhee* "either because it was never even contemplated or because it was contemplated and considered to be a bad point". Rather the cases established that "where a pursuer proves that a single defender made a material contribution to his injury or illness, that defender is liable in full to the pursuer for causing the injury, and not just to the extent of his material contribution".

the defendant was at risk that he would be held liable for everything. Such cases, said his Lordship, should not be determined on the burden of proof, however; the question should be whether "at the end of the day and on consideration of all the evidence" the claimant had proved that the defendant was responsible for the whole or a quantifiable part of his disability. The difficulty of quantifying that part of the damage which is attributable to the defendant's negligence does not preclude a court from seeking to do so, even if this involves adopting a "broad brush" approach.[113] Thus, the court should not be astute to deny a claimant relief on the basis that he could not establish with demonstrable accuracy precisely what proportion of his injury was attributable to the defendant's tortious conduct.[114] Moreover, even where the defendant's contribution is so small that it would have made no discernible difference to the claimant's overall disability if it is possible to calculate the defendant's contribution the claimant is entitled to be compensated for that contribution.[115]

Prior to *Holtby* it had generally been assumed that once the claimant established a "material contribution to the damage" the defendant was liable for the full loss. After all, it is open to the defendant to join as third parties others whom he alleges are also responsible for the claimant's damage and to seek contribution from them under the Civil Liability (Contribution) Act 1978.[116] Of course, in those cases where it is perfectly clear that the defendant's tort contributed only part of the overall damage the defendant is liable only for that part which he caused, though this usually occurs in the context of discrete successive events, as where D1 damages C's car, and subsequently D2 causes further damage, D2 is liable only for the additional **2-37**

113 *Allen v British Rail Engineering* [2001] EWCA Civ 242; [2001] I.C.R. 942, which involved an action in respect of damage to the claimant's hands caused by the use of hand-held vibratory tools ("vibration white finger"). Damages were reduced to take account of the fact that, on the evidence, the exercise of reasonable care by the defendants would only have reduced the claimant's exposure by about half. The employer's liability was limited to the extent of the contribution which his tortious conduct made to the disability, even though the remaining damage was caused by the defendant's innocent conduct and the extent of the damage was aggravated by his tortious conduct. See also *Rugby Joinery UK Ltd v Whitfield* [2005] EWCA Civ 561; [2006] P.I.Q.R. Q2.

114 [2001] EWCA Civ 242; [2001] I.C.R. 942 at [20].

115 *Mayne v Atlas Stone Co Ltd* [2016] EWHC 1030 (QB); [2016] I.C.R. 957 (asbestos-induced diffuse pleural thickening contributed 5 per cent to deceased's overall disability (due to co-morbid medical conditions) of 70 per cent to 80 per cent; defendant's contribution to the total asbestos exposure was 8.16 per cent which amounted to 0.4 per cent of the overall disability; defendants held liable in respect of 0.4 per cent of the overall disability even though it would not have been perceptible to the deceased). See also *Carder v Secretary of State for Health* [2015] EWHC 2399 (QB) where Judge Gore QC rejected the defendant's argument that a 2.3 per cent contribution to the claimant's overall exposure to asbestos had made no addition to the claimant's symptoms or disability and so had not caused any actionable damage. The judge pointed out, at [35], that if there were two hypothetical claimants who had been exposed to exactly the same amount of asbestos fibres and developed asbestosis it "cannot be correct that the man who had 40 different and equal exposures contributing 2.5% each gets no compensation but the man who had, say, 10 equal exposures contributing 10% each recovers from all of them simply because, if that be the case, whereas 2.5% could not cause detectable symptoms 10% would". An appeal in *Carder* was dismissed: [2016] EWCA Civ 790; [2017] I.C.R. 392.

116 See para.4-13 onwards. See the dissenting (in part) judgment of Clarke LJ at [2000] 3 All E.R. 421 at 432. See also *Wright v Stoddard International Plc and Novartis Grimsby Ltd* [2007] CSOH 173; 2008 Rep. L.R. 2 at [147], per Lord Uist, declining to follow the approach taken by the Court of Appeal in *Holtby* in Scotland, partly because if the court had a non-statutory power to do what the Court of Appeal did in *Holtby*, there would have been no need for legislation providing for contribution between tortfeasors.

damage.[117] Cases of industrial disease are far less susceptible to such categorical determinations, as Stuart-Smith LJ recognised.[118] It was perhaps easier in *Holtby* than in many industrial disease cases since the evidence was that there was a linear progression of the disease depending on the amount of dust inhaled, and so it could be said that all the dust contributed to the final disability.[119] In such cases of cumulative harm where it is feasible, even if in a rough and ready fashion, to divide up the contribution made by different causes apportionment will be appropriate. But in cases where the damage is indivisible, resolving the causation issue will be more problematic. Moreover, it may be that "apportionment is not appropriate where it is not merely difficult but is impossible to allot particular loss to a particular cause".[120]

2-38 **Material contribution—indivisible harm** Where the damage sustained by the claimant is divisible the claimant can rely on *Bonnington Castings Ltd v Wardlaw* and the material contribution to the damage test for causation. This remains the case even if it is not possible, in practice, to apportion the damage caused by the defendant's breach of duty. However, where the damage is indivisible it is arguably inappropriate to apply the material contribution to the damage approach. In *B v Ministry of Defence*[121] the claimants were former service personnel who alleged that they had been exposed to excessive ionising radiation during atmospheric nuclear tests carried out by the British Government in the Pacific between 1952 and 1958, and as a result had, many years later, developed various forms of cancer. The Court of Appeal indicated that, though the test in *Bonnington Castings Ltd v Wardlaw* can be used where negligent and non–negligent causes have both contributed to the disease but it is not possible to apportion the harm caused, the claimant can only rely on a material contribution to the condition or disease "where the severity of the disease is related to the amount of exposure; further exposure to the noxious substance in question is capable of making the condition worse".[122] Since cancer is not a divisible condition (its severity does not depend on the extent of the exposure) the exposure to radiation had not made a material contribution to the disease, only to the risk that it might occur. With regard to cancer the claimants could not rely on *Bonnington Castings*, which applies:

> "only where the disease or condition is 'divisible' so that an increased dose of the harmful agent worsens the disease ... [In *Bonnington Castings* the] tort did not increase the risk

[117] *Performance Cars Ltd v Abraham* [1962] 1 Q.B. 33.

[118] "The question of quantification may be difficult and the court only has to do the best it can using its common sense ... Cases of this sort, where the disease manifests itself many years after the exposure, present great problems, because much of the detail is inevitably lost ... But ... the court must do the best it can to achieve justice, not only to the claimant but the defendant, and among defendants": per Stuart-Smith LJ in *Holtby v Brigham Cowan (Hull) Ltd* [2000] 3 All E.R. 421 at 429.

[119] In which case, logically, the defendants should have been liable for only 50 per cent of the loss, rather than the 75 per cent assessed by the judge (given the period of time the claimant had worked for the defendants). Stuart-Smith LJ explained this as the judge "erring on the side of generosity" to the claimant.

[120] *John v Central Manchester and Manchester Children's University Hospitals NHS Foundation Trust* [2016] EWHC 407 (QB); [2016] 4 W.L.R. 54 at [99] per Picken J, distinguishing *Holtby* as a case where it was not impossible but "merely difficult to work out what damage had been caused by particular factors". The impossibility of attributing causes is not the same as the impossibility of making a precise apportionment.

[121] [2010] EWCA Civ 1317; (2011) 117 B.M.L.R. 101, Smith LJ giving the judgment of the Court.

[122] [2010] EWCA Civ 1317; (2011) 117 B.M.L.R. 101 at [134] (and [149] where the Court of Appeal accepted the defendants' submissions on this issue).

> of harm; it increased the actual harm. Similarly in [*Bailey v Ministry of Defence*[123]], the tort (a failure of medical care) increased the claimant's physical weakness. She would have been quite weak in any event as the result of a condition she had developed naturally. No one could say how great a contribution each had made to the overall weakness save that each was material. It was the overall weakness which led to the claimant's failure to protect her airway when she vomited with the result that she inhaled her vomit and suffered a cardiac arrest and brain damage. In those cases, the pneumoconiosis and the weakness were divisible conditions. Cancer is an indivisible condition; one either gets it or one does not. The condition is not worse because one has been exposed to a greater or smaller amount of the causative agent."[124]

Smith LJ expressed a similar view, obiter, *Dickins v O2 Plc*[125] in the context of claims for psychiatric harm, on the apparent assumption that psychiatric conditions are indivisible or not "dose-related".

Apportionment and discrete events *Holtby v Brigham Cowan (Hull) Ltd* and *Allen v British Rail Engineering* involved conditions in which there was a cumulative cause operating over a period of time. In *Environment Agency v Ellis*[126] the defendant argued that a similar approach should be applied to discrete accidents. The claimant had symptomless pre-existing degenerative changes in his spine, which would probably have started to produce symptoms in about 10 years. He suffered an injury to his back in June 1998 which was attributable to the negligence of his employers. He suffered a further injury to his back at work in May 1999 which was treated as not being the responsibility of his employers (a claim in respect of that accident having been struck out on a limitation point). In April 2000 the claimant fell down a flight of stairs at home because his back gave way, causing a serious injury to his right knee, following which he was no longer able to work. On the basis that the back problem was causative of the fall, the defendants argued that there were three causes of the claimant's loss and that there should be an apportionment between each of them: (i) the pre-existing spinal degeneration; (ii) the June 1998 accident; and (iii) the May 1999 accident. They attributed 70 per cent to the pre-existing degeneration, 20 per cent to the June 1998 accident, and 10 per cent to the May 1999 accident. The Court of Appeal held that pre-existing spinal degeneration was not causally relevant, except when it came to the assessment of damages.[127] The defendants' alternative argument was that, if the spinal degeneration was not relevant, there should be an apportionment of two-thirds to the June 1998 accident and one-third to the May 1999 accident. The Court of Appeal also rejected this argument. May LJ explained the basic position: 2-39

> "It is a commonplace that, if a passenger is injured in a collision between two motor vehicles when each driver's negligence was a material contributing cause of the collision and therefore the injury, the passenger can recover the full amount of his loss from either of the drivers, provided that he does not recover in total more than the full amount of the loss. The two drivers are left to sort out the appropriate contribution between each

123 See para.2-33.

124 [2010] EWCA Civ 1317; (2011) 117 B.M.L.R. 101 at [150]. The decision of the Court of Appeal was affirmed by the Supreme Court on a different (limitation) point: [2012] UKSC 9; [2013] 1 A.C. 78. See also *Heneghan v Manchester Dry Docks Ltd* [2016] EWCA Civ 86; [2016] 1 W.L.R. 2036 at [46]–[47] per Lord Dyson MR.

125 [2008] EWCA Civ 1144; [2009] I.R.L.R. 58. See para.2-43.

126 [2008] EWCA Civ 1117; [2009] P.I.Q.R. P5; [2009] L.S. Law Med. 70.

127 See para.2-173.

> other under the Civil Liability (Contribution) Act 1978. This is a common illustration of how uncontentious law treats the necessary causation element of the tort of negligence."[128]

On this basis the 1999 accident, "if it had any causative effect, would no more reduce Mr Ellis' damages than would the negligence of a second driver when the injured passenger claimed his full loss against a negligent first driver".[129] A claimant who satisfied the "but for" test does not have to prove that the negligence was the only or chronologically the last cause of his injuries. The defendants had not argued that the 1999 accident was a full blown intervening event, but merely a "contributory intervening factor". But, said his Lordship, there is:

> "no free-standing principle which would give apportioning effect to a *contributory* intervening event. The expression appears to have overtones of contributory negligence which is not in point in the present appeal. The single question therefore is whether this case is one where exceptionally the *Holtby* and *Allen* principles should apply."[130]

May LJ concluded that they should not. *Holtby* and *Allen* should be limited to industrial disease or injury cases where there had been successive exposure to harm by a number of agencies, where the effect of the harm was divisible, and where it was unjust for an individual defendant to bear the whole of the loss. They do not apply to "single accident" cases, and the accident of April 2000 was, essentially, a single indivisible event.[131]

2-40 **Material contribution to psychiatric damage** In *Page v Smith (No.2)*,[132] the claimant had suffered for several years from chronic fatigue syndrome. At a time when the disease appeared to be in remission he was involved in a minor collision with a motor vehicle negligently driven by the defendant and, soon afterwards, he suffered an acute recrudescence of chronic fatigue syndrome. Evidence that stress materially contributed to that disease, together with the juxtaposition of the accident and the claimant's renewed illness, were held to be sufficient to establish that the defendant's negligence materially contributed to the claimant's illness, notwithstanding that the claimant's reaction to the accident was "not necessarily proportional to the trauma". In cases involving traumatic events which precipitate a psychiatric reaction (typically, the traditional "nervous shock" cases producing "post-traumatic stress disorder") the temporal sequence generally makes it easier

---

128 [2008] EWCA Civ 1117; [2009] P.I.Q.R. P5 at [1].

129 [2008] EWCA Civ 1117; [2009] P.I.Q.R. P5 at [37].

130 [2008] EWCA Civ 1117; [2009] P.I.Q.R. P5 at [38].

131 [2008] EWCA Civ 1117; [2009] P.I.Q.R. P5 at [39].

132 [1996] 1 W.L.R. 855 CA. In *Simmons v British Steel* [2004] UKHL 20; 2004 S.C. (HL) 94; [2004] I.C.R. 585 the claimant sustained a minor head injury in an accident at work for which his employers were held responsible. He subsequently suffered an exacerbation of a pre-existing skin condition (psoriasis) and went on to develop a personality change and severe depression. The House of Lords held that the claimant was entitled to damages for the psoriasis and the depression on the basis that they were produced in part by the claimant's anger at the happening of the accident. Although part of the claimant's anger was attributable to his perception of the way he had been treated by his employers after the accident, there was sufficient causal connection between the anger at the happening of the accident itself and the psoriasis and the depression that it could be concluded there had been a material contribution those conditions. See also *Vernon v Bosley (No.1)* [1997] 1 All E.R. 577 applying this approach to psychiatric damage; *Farrell v Merton, Sutton and Wandsworth HA* (2000) 57 B.M.L.R. 158.

to persuade the court to draw an inference that there must be a causal link between the defendant's negligence and the claimant's psychiatric state.[133]

In cases involving allegations of occupational stress, however, where an employee alleges that the employer's negligent system of work has so overstressed him that he has suffered permanent psychiatric damage, the causal link is more difficult to establish. In *Hatton v Sutherland*[134] the Court of Appeal said that there are no occupations which are inherently dangerous to mental health since it is not the job, but the interaction between the individual and the job which causes the harm. All occupations involve some element of stress and it can be difficult to anticipate which employees are foreseeably likely to succumb. Moreover, there are many other stressful factors in ordinary life which can affect an individual employee's mental health (e.g. illness, divorce, bereavement) and can contribute to mental breakdown. The claimant must demonstrate that the psychiatric illness is not due simply to stress at work but that it was the employer's specific breach of duty that caused the damage. Thus: "Where there are several different possible causes, as will often be the case with stress related illness of any kind, the claimant may have difficulty proving that the employer's fault was one of them."[135] In other words, proof of a psychiatric condition together with a "stressful" working environment is not sufficient to establish a causal link, though the employee does not have to prove that the employer's breach of duty was the sole cause, merely that it made a material contribution to his mental illness.[136] 2-41

On the other hand, the statement that a claimant only has to establish that the breach of duty made a material contribution to his mental illness is possibly more problematic than in cases of physical harm. It is arguable that, in the light of the Court of Appeal decision *Holtby v Brigham & Cowan (Hull) Ltd*,[137] where it is possible to identify the extent of the contribution made by the defendant's negligence to the claimant's psychiatric damage, then the defendant is only liable to that extent. This view was canvassed in *Hatton v Sutherland*[138] although there was recognition that it could give rise to some difficult factual questions in differentiating between multiple possible causes (and even co-morbid psychiatric states). In *Barber v Somerset CC*[139] Lord Walker approved the exposition and commentary by the Court of Appeal in *Hatton v Sutherland* as a valuable contribution to the develop- 2-42

133 See, e.g. *Donachie v The Chief Constable of the Greater Manchester Police* [2004] EWCA Civ 405; *The Times*, 6 May 2004, where the Court of Appeal approved the application of *Bonnington* to a case of physical injury (stroke) brought on by increased stress due to an unforeseeable psychiatric reaction.

134 [2002] EWCA Civ 76; [2002] I.C.R. 613; [2002] 2 All E.R. 1. See further para.12-37.

135 [2002] EWCA Civ 76; [2002] I.C.R. 613 at [35]. See *Cross v Highlands and Islands Enterprise*, 2001 S.C.L.R. 547; [2001] I.R.L.R. 336 (Court of Session, OH), where the pursuer failed to prove that the cause of his illness was work-related. See also *Pratley v Surrey CC* [2003] EWCA Civ 1067; [2004] P.I.Q.R. P17, where the Court of Appeal distinguished between the risk to an employee of psychiatric harm from having too heavy a workload in the future, and the risk due to the employee's reaction to a specific event when he perceived that the employers were not taking his concerns seriously. In *MacLennan v Hartford Europe Ltd* [2012] EWHC 346 (QB) the claimant unable to establish any causal link between workplace stress and chronic fatigue syndrome; nor that her condition ought reasonably to have been foreseen by her employer, not least because, as a human resources manager, the claimant was aware of the need to inform her employer about stress and any perceived risks to her health but had not done so.

136 [2002] EWCA Civ 76; [2002] I.C.R. 613, applying *Bonnington Castings Ltd v Wardlaw*.

137 [2000] I.C.R. 1086; [2000] 3 All E.R. 421; see at para.2-36.

138 See *Hatton v Sutherland* [2002] EWCA Civ 76; [2002] I.C.R. 613; [2002] 2 All E.R. 1 at [36]–[41]; and *Rahman v Arearose Ltd* [2001] Q.B. 351; para.2-125.

139 [2004] UKHL 13; [2004] 1 W.L.R. 1089; [2004] 2 All E.R. 385 at [63].

ment of the law, though not having heard argument on the section dealing with apportionment and quantification of damage thought it better to "express no view on those topics".

2-43 In *Dickins v O2 Plc*[140] the Court of Appeal doubted whether apportionment was appropriate in a case of psychiatric harm, specifically questioning the approach taken by Hale LJ in *Hatton v Sutherland*. This was on the basis that psychiatric harm is an "indivisible injury" to which the material contribution test can be applied. As Smith LJ expressed the point: "if in one breath the judge holds that all that can be said about the effect of the tort is that it made an unspecified material contribution, it is illogical for him, in the next breath, to attempt to assess the percentage effect of the tort as a basis for apportionment of the whole of the damages."[141] Apportionment was usually carried out only in cases where the injury is divisible, where the seriousness of the medical condition is "dose-related". In that situation the tort has caused only part of the overall injury, and in assessing damages the pragmatic course may be to assess damages for the whole loss and then apportion the loss between the tortious and the non-tortious causes. Such an approach would work, said Smith LJ, in cases such as dust exposure, noise-induced deafness and hand/arm vibration syndrome, but it was questionable whether it could apply to a case of psychiatric injury where there were multiple causes of the breakdown:

> "I respectfully wish (*obiter*) to express my doubts as to the correctness of Hale LJ's approach to apportionment. My provisional view (given without the benefit of argument) is that, in a case which has had to be decided on the basis that the tort has made a material contribution but it is not scientifically possible to say how much that contribution is (apart from the assessment that it was more than *de minimis*) and where the injury to which that has lead is indivisible, it will be inappropriate simply to apportion the damages across the board. It may well be appropriate to bear in mind that the claimant was psychiatrically vulnerable and might have suffered a breakdown at some time in the future even without the tort. There may then be a reduction in some heads of damage for future risks of non-tortious loss. But my provisional view is that there should not be any rule that the judge should apportion the damages across the board merely because one non-tortious cause has been in play."[142]

This view rests on the notion that psychiatric illness is an "indivisible harm", though given the medical uncertainty as to the causal mechanisms involved in most psychiatric illness (with, possibly, post-traumatic stress disorder being the exception) this looks more like a layperson's assumption than medical truth.[143] It may be that for some psychiatric conditions the medical uncertainty is such that it is not possible to say that the defendant's breach of duty has contributed to the illness, as opposed to contributing to the risk of developing the illness. If so, a causal analysis

[140] [2008] EWCA Civ 1144; [2009] I.R.L.R. 58.

[141] [2008] EWCA Civ 1144; [2009] I.R.L.R. 58 at [43].

[142] [2008] EWCA Civ 1144; [2009] I.R.L.R. 58 at [46]. See also per Sedley LJ at [53]. See also *B v Ministry of Defence* [2010] EWCA Civ 1317; (2011) 117 B.M.L.R. 101, para.2-38.

[143] Psychiatric conditions are often considered by the medical profession to be multi-factorial in their aetiology, i.e. there is often no one single cause. Indeed, in some instances it may be meaningless to think of the relationship between different factors and the patient's psychiatric state as a simple "cause and effect" mechanism.

based on the decision of the House of Lords in *Fairchild v Glenhaven Funeral Services Ltd*[144] may be more appropriate.

These issues were considered again in *BAE Systems (Operations) Ltd v Konczak*.[145] Underhill LJ noted that the difference between the view expressed in *Hatton v Sutherland* and that of Smith LJ in *Dickins* was that Smith LJ appeared to suggest that psychiatric harm could never be divisible, whereas in *Hatton* the court had said that where there were multiple extrinsic causes, a "sensible attempt" should be made to apportion the harm between what is and is not attributable to the defendant's wrong. *Hatton* recognised that there may be cases where the harm was "truly indivisible" and that in such cases apportionment would be wrong, but there may be some cases where the harm would be divisible.[146] Whether it is possible to make a "sensible attempt" to apportion the damage will depend on the facts and the medical evidence.[147] Although the guidance given on apportionment in *Hatton* had been obiter, if there were differences between the views expressed in *Hatton* and *Dickins*, *Hatton* should be followed.[148] The tribunal or court should: 2-44

> "try to identify a rational basis on which the harm suffered can be apportioned between a part caused by the employer's wrong and a part which is not so caused. I would emphasise, because the distinction is easily overlooked, that the exercise is concerned not with the divisibility of the causative contribution but with the divisibility of the harm. In other words, the question is whether the tribunal can identify, however broadly, a particular part of the suffering which is due to the wrong; not whether it can assess the degree to which the wrong caused the harm."[149]

Moreover, if the claimant had a pre-existing mental disorder or vulnerability to psychiatric harm the court should take that into account in the assessment of damages by discounting the award to reflect the risk that the claimant would have developed the mental health condition in the future in any event, just as it would if the claimant had a vulnerability to developing a physical condition in the future. This principle applies whenever the claimant had a predisposition to develop the mental health problem in the future, whether the psychiatric harm is divisible or not (i.e. it is quite separate from the process of deciding whether the harm is capable of being apportioned for the purpose of determining causation).

(iii) Material contribution to the risk of damage

In *McGhee v National Coal Board*,[150] the claimant contracted dermatitis from the presence of brick dust on sweaty skin. Some exposure to brick dust was an inevitable result of working in brick kilns in respect of which there was no breach of duty by his employers. But his employers negligently failed to provide washing facilities at the site so that the claimant cycled home coated with abrasive brick dust. Medical evidence established that brick dust caused the dermatitis but it was impos- 2-45

[144] [2002] UKHL 22; [2003] 1 A.C. 32. See para.2-53.

[145] [2017] EWCA Civ 1188; [2018] I.C.R. 1. For further discussion of *BAE Systems (Operations) Ltd v Konczak* see S. Bailey, "Apportionment and psychiatric injury" (2018) 34 P.N. 42.

[146] [2017] EWCA Civ 1188; [2018] I.C.R. 1, per Underhill LJ at [67].

[147] *Rahman v Arearose Ltd* [2001] Q.B. 351 provides an example where the medical evidence did distinguish between different causes of different aspects of the claimant's mental state: see para.2-125.

[148] [2017] EWCA Civ 1188; [2018] I.C.R. 1 at [70] and [92], per Underhill and Irwin LJJ respectively.

[149] [2017] EWCA Civ 1188; [2018] I.C.R. 1 at [71], per Underhill LJ.

[150] [1973] 1 W.L.R. 1 HL.

sible to prove whether it was the additional "guilty" exposure to dust which triggered dermatitis in this claimant or whether he would have developed the disease in any event as a result of the "innocent" exposure during the normal working day. At best it could be said that the failure to provide washing facilities materially increased the risk of the claimant contracting dermatitis. The House of Lords held the defendants liable on the basis that it was sufficient for a claimant to show that the defendants' breach of duty made the risk of injury more probable even though it was uncertain whether it was the actual cause. A majority of their Lordships treated a "material increase in the risk" as equivalent to a material contribution to the damage. Lord Simon, for example, said that "a failure to take steps which would bring about a material reduction of the risk involves, in this type of case, a substantial contribution to the injury".[151] Lord Wilberforce explicitly recognised that this process involves overcoming an "evidential gap" by drawing an inference of fact which, strictly speaking, the evidence does not support (as was done in *Bonnington Castings*), and, moreover, that this fictional inference was drawn for policy reasons.[152]

2-46 The view of Lord Wilberforce that, for policy reasons, the burden of proof should effectively be reversed in such a case was criticised by the House of Lords in *Wilsher v Essex AHA*.[153] The infant claimant, a premature baby, on two occasions received excess oxygen as a result of negligence by junior doctors in monitoring oxygen levels in his blood. He developed retrolental fibroplasia (RLF) rendering him almost blind. The expert evidence suggested that excess oxygen could have toxic effects on the retina, but RLF also occurs in premature babies who do not receive oxygen, and a causal link exists between RLF and at least four other conditions common in very premature babies. The trial judge relied in effect on Lord Wilberforce's judgment in *McGhee*[154] and held it was for the defendants to prove that the claimant's condition did not result from excess oxygen. The Court of Appeal rejected the suggestion that the burden of proof should be reversed, but by a majority relied on *McGhee* to conclude that as there was evidence that excess oxygen could cause RLF, even allowing for the impact of the other "innocent" causative agents, a court could properly infer that excess oxygen (the "guilty" agent) made a material contribution to the claimant's injury. The House of Lords disagreed, relying heavily on the dissenting judgment of Sir Nicolas Browne-Wilkinson VC who had observed that: "A failure to take preventive measures against one out of five possible causes is no evidence as to which of those five caused the injury."[155] In *McGhee* there was no doubt that brick dust caused the dermatitis, and sound evidence that the longer the abrasive brick dust adhered to the skin, the more likely it was that dermatitis would develop. In *Wilsher* it had not been proven that excess oxygen, rather than some different agent such as intraventricular haemorrhage,

---

[151] [1973] 1 W.L.R. 1 HL at 8, per Lord Simon. See also per Lords Reid and Salmon at 6 and 12–13, respectively.

[152] [1973] 1 W.L.R. 1 HL at 7: "in the absence of proof that the culpable condition had in the result no effect, the employers should be liable for an injury, squarely within the risk they created and that they, not the pursuer, should suffer the consequences of the impossibility, foreseeably inherent in the nature of his injury, of segregating the precise consequence of their fault."

[153] [1988] A.C. 1074 HL.

[154] And on his own earlier judgment in *Clark v MacLennan* [1983] 1 All E.R. 416.

[155] [1987] Q.B. 730 at 779. In *Fairchild v Glenhaven Funeral Services Ltd* [2002] UKHL 22; [2003] 1 A.C. 32 at [69] Lord Hoffmann took the view that there were policy questions at stake in *Wilsher*, such as the potential burden of increased liability upon the NHS. These policy issues were not explicitly addressed in *Wilsher*.

caused or contributed to the claimant's RLF. Nor had it been proven that excess oxygen was likely to increase the risk that any of the other "innocent" agents would trigger RLF. *McGhee* did not permit a court simply to infer that where there was a "guilty" and an "innocent" explanation of the claimant's damage the "guilty" explanation should be preferred. Lord Bridge said of *McGhee* that that judgment propounded no new principle of law but simply exemplified a robust and pragmatic approach to the undisputed primary facts of the case:

> "where the layman is told by the doctors that the longer brick dust remains on the body, the greater the risk of dermatitis, although the doctors cannot identify the process of causation scientifically, there seems nothing irrational in drawing the inference as a matter of common sense that the consecutive periods when brick dust remained on the body probably contributed cumulatively to the causation of dermatitis."[156]

Lord Bridge's view that *McGhee* did not establish a principle of law, but was simply concerned with the circumstances in which it is legitimate to draw an inference that causation has been established in fact, was subsequently rejected by the House of Lords in *Fairchild v Glenhaven Funeral Services Ltd*.[157] Although in *Fairchild* it was said that *Wilsher* was still correct on its facts, their Lordships considered that there can be some circumstances where, for reasons of justice and fairness a claimant should be permitted to succeed on causation even though the "but for" test was not satisfied.

The effect of Wilsher The effect of *Wilsher* was that where the defendant's breach of duty increases an *existing* risk factor the court could (choosing to take a robust and pragmatic view of the evidence, if necessary) infer that there must have been some material contribution to the claimant's damage (i.e. the court may rely on *McGhee* in order to apply *Bonnington Castings*). Where, however, the defendant's breach of duty merely adds a new, discrete, risk factor to the existing risk factor(s) it is not legitimate to infer that it was the "guilty" risk factor which probably caused the damage.[158] This proposition is still correct after *Fairchild*. **2-47**

Defendant's negligence more than doubles existing risk Although *Wilsher* makes it clear that where there is more than one discrete risk factor, one of which was created by the defendant's breach of duty, the claimant cannot rely on *McGhee* to establish causation, if the breach of duty more than doubles the existing risk the **2-48**

[156] [1988] A.C. 1074 at 1088.

[157] [2002] UKHL 22; [2003] 1 A.C. 32. See para.2-53.

[158] This statement must be read in the context of the facts in *Wilsher* itself, however. There may be cases where, although there were existing risk factors, the evidence about the effect of the risk created by the defendant is so overwhelming that the conclusion that it probably materially contributed to the claimant's damage is almost inevitable. Thus, if hypothetically, the evidence in *Wilsher* was that the four existing risk factors, although present, only rarely produced RLF, whereas there was scientific evidence pointing to a very high correlation between excess oxygen and RLF, it would be legitimate to draw the conclusion that it was probable that the oxygen did in fact cause the RLF. That would be the common sense conclusion for both the layman and the judge. See *John v Central Manchester and Manchester Children's University Hospitals NHS Foundation Trust* [2016] EWHC 407 (QB); [2016] 4 W.L.R. 54 at [95]–[97], per Picken J making this point and confirming that the material contribution to damage test is not confined to "single agency" cases and can apply "just as much to multiple factor cases as it does to 'single agency' cases". The existence of other, non-negligent factors which may have caused or contributed to the damage *may* prevent the court from inferring that the negligent factor was a contributing cause, but this will depend on the strength of the evidence overall.

claimant does not have to rely on *McGhee*. In *Novartis Grimsby Ltd v Cookson*[159] the claimant developed cancer of the bladder (a non-divisible form of damage). He was a smoker and had been exposed to a toxic agent (aromatic amines) at work, both of which are known risk factors for bladder cancer. However, the evidence indicated that the risk associated with aromatic amines was 70 per cent of the total risk. The Court of Appeal held that the claimant had established "but for" causation because the risk attributable to the occupational exposure to the toxic agent more than doubled the risk associated with smoking. There was no need to consider whether the negligent exposure materially contributed to the harm or materially contributed to the risk of developing the harm.[160] Smith LJ observed that: "The natural inference to draw from the finding of fact that the occupational exposure was 70 per cent of the total is that, if it had not been for the occupational exposure, the respondent would not have developed bladder cancer. In terms of risk, if occupational exposure more than doubles the risk due to smoking, it must, as a matter of logic, be probable that the disease was caused by the former."[161]

2-49 In *Sienkiewicz v Greif (UK) Ltd*[162] Lord Phillips agreed with Smith LJ's proposition: "as a matter of logic, if a defendant is responsible for a tortious exposure that has more than doubled the risk of the victim's disease, it follows on the balance of probability that he has caused the disease." However, where *Fairchild v Glenhaven Funeral Services Ltd*[163] applies to determine causation it is not appropriate to apply such a statistical approach, and accordingly the claimant cannot be *required* to prove that the defendant's breach of duty had more than doubled the risk. Lord Phillips said that where two agents have operated cumulatively and simultaneously in causing the onset of a disease there was "no scope for the application of the 'doubles the risk' test". In that situation *Bonnington Castings v Wardlaw*[164] would apply, with the consequence that where the disease was indivisible (as with lung cancer) a defendant who had tortiously contributed to the cause of the disease would be liable in full; and where the disease was divisible (as with asbestosis) the tortfeasor would be liable for the share of the disease for which he

---

159 [2007] EWCA Civ 1261.

160 In other words the line of authority from *Bonnington Castings* to *Fairchild v Glenhaven Funeral Services Ltd* (see paras 2-53 to 2-73) is irrelevant in these circumstances.

161 [2007] EWCA Civ 1261 at [74]. See also *Jones v Secretary of State for Energy and Climate Change* [2012] EWHC 2936 (QB) where Swift J used a "doubling of the risk" approach to the determination of causation of both lung and bladder cancers where the claimants had been exposed to carcinogenic fumes and dust. See further *Heneghan v Manchester Dry Docks Ltd* [2016] EWCA Civ 86; [2016] 1 W.L.R. 2036 at [8], per Lord Dyson MR, where epidemiological evidence showed a more than doubling of the risk that it was asbestos rather than smoking which caused the deceased's lung cancer. This provided the answer to the "what" question, i.e. what toxin probably caused the lung cancer? It was not sufficient, however, to answer the "who" question, which arises in a multiple contributor case, where the issue is which contributor's asbestos caused the claimant's indivisible damage, i.e. lung cancer? In order to attribute causation to each of the multiple tortfeasors the court had to rely on *Fairchild v Glenhaven Funeral Services Ltd* [2002] UKHL 22; [2003] 1 A.C. 32 (para.2-53). *Heneghan* is discussed by R. Geraghty [2016] J.P.I.L. C83. See also *Magill v Panel Systems (DB Ltd)* [2017] EWHC 1517 (QB); [2017] Med. L.R. 440—deceased was due to have heart surgery, but was diagnosed with mesothelioma attributable to defendants' negligence and the surgery was postponed; he died from a heart attack; the failure to have surgery doubled the risk of death; defendants were held liable for the death on basis that they had caused or contributed to an indivisible injury, i.e. a heart arrhythmia, which caused the death.

162 [2011] UKSC 10; [2011] 2 A.C. 229 at [78].

163 [2002] UKHL 22; [2003] 1 A.C. 32; see para.2-53.

164 [1956] A.C. 613; see para.2-32.

was responsible.[165] On the other hand:

> "Where the initiation of the disease is dose related, and there have been consecutive exposures to an agent or agents that cause the disease, one innocent and one tortious, the position will depend upon which exposure came first in time. Where it was the tortious exposure, it is axiomatic that this will have contributed to causing the disease, even if it is not the sole cause. Where the innocent exposure came first, there may be an issue as to whether this was sufficient to trigger the disease or whether the subsequent, tortious, exposure contributed to the cause. I can see no reason in principle why the 'doubles the risk' test should not be applied in such circumstances, but the court must be astute to see that the epidemiological evidence provides a really sound basis for determining the statistical probability of the cause or causes of the disease."[166]

Finally, where there were competing alternative (as opposed to cumulative) potential causes of a disease or injury there was no reason in principle why epidemiological evidence should not be used to show that one of the causes was more than twice as likely as all the others put together to have caused the disease or injury.[167]

There must be some evidence to link the defendant's breach of duty to the claimant's harm, other than the simple assertion that it increased the general risk of harm, before an inference that it must have made a material contribution can be drawn. In *Tahir v Haringey HA*,[168] the claimant alleged that the delay in providing medical treatment rendered his condition worse than it would otherwise have been, on the basis that, in general terms, delay in operating in his type of case increases the neurological deficit and impairs the prospect of recovery. The Court of Appeal held that where there has been negligence resulting in delayed medical treatment it was not sufficient for the claimant to show that there was a material increase in the risk or that delay *can* cause damage. He has to go further and prove that damage was *actually* caused by the delay. In the absence of findings of fact that identify or quantify the additional harm, it was not appropriate for a judge to adopt a proportionate approach by quantifying the total disability and then asking what proportion of that disability is attributable to the delay.[169] **2-50**

---

165 [2011] UKSC 10; [2011] 2 A.C. 229 at [90].

166 [2011] UKSC 10; [2011] 2 A.C. 229 at [91].

167 [2011] UKSC 10; [2011] 2 A.C. 229 at [93]. But the "doubling of risk" test should be used with caution. In *Williams v The Bermuda Hospitals Board* [2016] UKPC 4; [2016] A.C. 888 at [48] Lord Toulson said that: "If it is a known fact that a particular type of act (or omission) is likely to have a particular effect, proof that the defendant was responsible for such an act (or omission) and that the claimant had what is the usual effect will be powerful evidence from which to infer causation, without necessarily requiring a detailed scientific explanation for the link. But inferring causation from proof of heightened risk is never an exercise to apply mechanistically. A doubled tiny risk will still be very small."

168 [1998] Lloyd's Rep. Med. 104. See also *Hardaker v Newcastle HA & the Chief Constable of Northumbria* [2001] Lloyd's Rep. Med. 512 at [69].

169 See also *Brown v Lewisham and North Southwark HA* [1999] Lloyd's Rep. Med. 110 CA. It is reasonable to draw a common sense inference that an increased risk of harm must have made a material contribution to the damage where there is some evidence which supports such an inference. Where there were no objective signs or symptoms of any aggravation or worsening of the claimant's condition following an allegedly negligently undertaken journey (between two hospitals) it was not reasonable to draw an inference that the journey contributed to a deterioration. See further *Thompson v Bradford* [2005] EWCA Civ 1439; [2006] Lloyd's Rep. Med. 95; following *Brown v Lewisham and North Southwark HA*. cf. *Athey v Leonati* [1997] 1 W.W.R. 97, where the Supreme Court of Canada held that the defendant's negligence, which the trial judge had concluded was no more than

(iv) *Multiple tortfeasors and contribution to the risk*

(1) The problem

2-51 The possibility that the claimant's damage has been caused by more than one potential defendant (and that the claimant has also been contributorily negligent) is not uncommon. A judge must reach a conclusion on liability and should not dismiss the possibility that both (or all) parties are responsible unless he can decide which of them is solely responsible.[170] Where there is no evidence to indicate the real proportion in which each party contributed to the relevant damage, responsibility will normally be assigned equally.[171] In *Fitzgerald v Lane*, the claimant stepped onto a pelican crossing without looking. He was hit by a car driven by D1, thrown up on to the bonnet of the car and back on to the road where he was struck by a car driven by D2. All three parties were found to have acted negligently. The claimant suffered severe injuries including damage to his neck resulting in partial tetraplegia. It could not be established whether the act of D1 alone, or the combined impact of D1 and D2, caused the crucial injury. The Court of Appeal[172] found both D1 and D2 liable on the ground that the negligence of both of them had materially increased the risk of the relevant injury. On appeal to the House of Lords[173] concerning apportionment of damages only, it was held that the appropriate reduction to reflect the degree of the claimant's contributory negligence should be ascertained before apportioning liability between the tortfeasors.

2-52 More difficult still are cases where the evidence is that either A or B must have caused the relevant injury, and one or the other must be solely to blame, but the claimant simply cannot prove which. In *Cook v Lewis*,[174] A and B were out shooting. Both fired in the direction of C who was injured but his injury resulted from a single bullet. He could not prove from which gun the bullet came. The Canadian Supreme Court suggested that if two defendants were found negligent in circumstances where the claimant was unable to prove which of them caused his injury, the onus of disproving liability is thrown on each of the defendants. If both fail to disprove causation, both will be found liable.[175] In a case where either A or B is responsible for the damage but the claimant cannot prove which, if A and B are both employed

---

a 25 per cent contributory factor to the claimant's injury, constituted a material contribution to the damage and held the defendant liable for the full loss.

170 *Bray v Palmer* [1953] 1 W.L.R. 1455.

171 *Baker v Market Harborough Industrial Co-operative Society Ltd* [1953] 1 W.L.R. 1472; *France v Parkinson* [1954] 1 W.L.R. 581; *WM Wood (Haulage) Ltd v Redpath* [1967] 2 Q.B. 520; *The Tojo Maru* [1968] 1 Lloyd's Rep. 365; *Howard v Bemrose* [1973] R.T.R. 32 CA; cf. *Knight v Fellick* [1977] R.T.R. 316 where the Court of Appeal suggested that *Baker v Market Harborough Industrial Co-operative Society Ltd* should be confined to the particular circumstances of that case, and concluded that the fact that there was a collision between two vehicles and that there is no explanation, is not necessarily a basis for inferring that there was negligence. See *Nettleship v Weston* [1971] 2 Q.B. 691 at 702–703 for discussion of the respective responsibilities of a learner driver and her driving instructor.

172 [1987] Q.B. 781 CA.

173 [1989] A.C. 328 HL.

174 [1951] S.C.R. 830; and see *Summers v Tice* (1948) 119 P. (2d) 1; *Oliver v Mills* (1926) 144 Missouri 852. Note also the development of "market share" liability in products litigation in *Sindell v Abbott Laboratories* (1980) 607 P. (2d) 924; see generally Fleming in (1989) 68 Can. Bar Rev. 661; and (1991) 70 Can. Bar Rev. 137.

175 Of course, a defendant in this position will normally be faced with same problems of proof as the claimant, and so reversing the burden of proof effectively places responsibility on the defendants. One argument supporting this approach is that it is the combined effect of the defendants' actions

by the same employer, the latter will be vicariously liable come what may, and the claimant is not required to identify the responsible individual tortfeasor.[176]

(2) Fairchild v Glenhaven Funeral Services

The problem created by the existence of multiple possible defendants combined with gaps in scientific knowledge about the aetiology of a particular disease was graphically illustrated in *Fairchild v Glenhaven Funeral Services Ltd*,[177] which involved three combined appeals where workers had developed mesothelioma following exposure to asbestos at work. They had all worked for a number of employers and at a number of sites where they had negligently been exposed to asbestos fibres. Mesothelioma is a form of cancer which is invariably fatal, with death usually occurring within two years of its appearance. The disease can be latent for up to 40 years, but may develop within 10 years. The precise mechanics of the aetiology of the disease are unknown, but the vast majority of cases of mesothelioma result from exposure to asbestos. In the UK 50 or 60 people develop mesothelioma each year where there has been no history of exposure to asbestos dust, in contrast to 1,500 where there is a history of exposure to asbestos. Thus, the overwhelming probability was that the employees' mesothelioma was caused by their occupational exposure to asbestos. The problem, however, was that on the current level of scientific knowledge about the disease the claimants could not identify which employer was responsible because, unlike asbestosis which is also caused by exposure to asbestos dust, mesothelioma is not a "cumulative disease". With asbestosis there is a minimum dose of asbestos below which there is no risk that asbestosis will develop, and above that minimum dose the severity of the condition, if it develops, increases in relation to the total dose of asbestos inhaled. In the case of a cumulative disease, where the severity of the condition is related to the period of exposure, each negligent employer is responsible for a proportionate part of the damage.[178] In contrast, mesothelioma arises when one of the mesothelial cells in the pleura of the lung is damaged and undergoes malignant transformation, the tumour developing from the single malignant cell. The *risk* that mesothelioma will occur increases in relation to the total dose of asbestos received, but the severity of the condition and the resulting disability do not vary with the dose. It may be caused by a single fibre, a few fibres, or many fibres. Further exposure to asbestos once the malignancy has developed does not exacerbate the condition. The problem for a claimant that this creates was explained by Lord Bingham: 2-53

> "So if C is employed successively by A and B and is exposed to asbestos dust and fibres during each employment and develops a mesothelioma, the very strong probability is that this will have been caused by inhalation of asbestos dust containing fibres. But C could have inhaled a single fibre giving rise to his condition during employment by A, in which

which has prevented the claimant from proving which of them caused his damage, and therefore it is only fair and just that the burden of proof be placed upon the defendants rather than the innocent claimant: see *Cook v Lewis* [1951] S.C.R. 830 at 832–833.

176 *Cassidy v Minister of Health* [1951] 2 K.B. 343.

177 [2002] UKHL 22; [2003] 1 A.C. 32. For discussion of *Fairchild* see Stapleton (2002) 10 Torts L.J. 276; Weir [2002] C.L.J. 519; Morgan (2003) 66 M.L.R. 277; and Coley [2003] J.P.I.L. 15. And see more generally Stapleton (2003) 119 L.Q.R. 388. For discussion of some of the insurance implications of *Fairchild* see Merkin (2004) 120 L.Q.R. 233.

178 See *Holtby v Brigham & Cowan (Hull) Ltd* [2000] I.C.R. 1086; [2000] 3 All E.R. 421 CA; para.2-36.

case his exposure by B will have had no effect on his condition; or he could have inhaled a single fibre giving rise to his condition during his employment by B, in which case his exposure by A will have had no effect on his condition; or he could have inhaled fibres during his employment by A and B which together gave rise to his condition; but medical science cannot support the suggestion that any of these possibilities is to be regarded as more probable than any other. There is no way of identifying, even on a balance of probabilities, the source of the fibre or fibres which initiated the genetic process which culminated in the malignant tumour."[179]

2-54 The House of Lords reversed the decision of the Court of Appeal that the claimants had failed to establish causation because they could not prove on a balance of probabilities that the "guilty" fibres were the result of any particular defendant's breach of duty. Their Lordships held that, in the special circumstances of this type of case, there should be a relaxation of the normal rule that a claimant must prove that but for the defendant's breach of duty he would not have suffered the damage, applying *McGhee v National Coal Board*. Following a review of how courts in many other jurisdictions have approached this type of problem, Lord Bingham noted that most jurisdictions would afford a remedy to the claimant, whether by treating an increase in risk as equivalent to a material contribution to the damage, or by placing the burden of proof on the defendant, or by enlarging the ordinary approach to tortfeasors acting in concert, or on more general grounds influenced by policy considerations.[180] The possible injustice of imposing liability on a defendant who has not been proved to have caused the claimants' damage had to be weighed against the injustice to claimants.[181]

2-55 Contrary to the view expressed by Lord Bridge in *Wilsher v Essex AHA*,[182] the decision of the House of Lords in *McGhee v National Coal Board*[183] did not rest upon a "robust and pragmatic" approach to the drawing of an inference of fact.[184] Rather, *McGhee* decided a question of law which was "whether, on the facts of the case as found, a pursuer who could not show that the defender's breach had probably caused the damage of which he complained could nonetheless succeed".[185] The ratio of *McGhee*, said Lord Bingham, was "that in the circumstances no distinction was to be drawn between making a material contribution to causing the disease

---

179 [2002] UKHL 22 at [7]. Of course, the problem is compounded if there are more than two negligent defendants.

180 [2002] UKHL 22 at [32].

181 Lord Bingham said, [2002] UKHL 22 at [33]: " … there is a strong policy argument in favour of compensating those who have suffered grave harm, at the expense of their employers who owed them a duty to protect them against that very harm and failed to do so, when the harm can only have been caused by breach of that duty and when science does not permit the victim accurately to attribute, as between several employers, the precise responsibility for the harm he has suffered. I am of opinion that such injustice as may be involved in imposing liability on a duty-breaking employer in these circumstances is heavily outweighed by the injustice of denying redress to a victim." See also Lord Nicholls at [36]: "these appeals should be allowed. Any other outcome would be deeply offensive to instinctive notions of what justice requires and fairness demands." Lord Hoffmann considered, at [63], that: "it would be both inconsistent with the policy of the law imposing the duty and morally wrong for your Lordships to impose causal requirements which exclude liability."

182 [1988] A.C. 1074 at 1088.

183 [1973] 1 W.L.R. 1.

184 See per Lord Bingham [2002] UKHL 22; [2003] 1 A.C. 32 at [22]; Lord Nicholls at [45]; Lord Hoffmann at [70]; Lord Rodger at [142], [144] and [150]; cf. the speech of Lord Hutton.

185 [2002] UKHL 22; [2003] 1 A.C. 32 at [21], per Lord Bingham.

and materially increasing the risk of the pursuer contracting it".[186] This was not, said Lord Hoffmann, because the burden of proof was reversed.[187] It would be artificial to treat the employer as having a burden of proof in a case in which *ex hypothesi* the state of medical knowledge is such that the burden cannot be discharged. Nor was materially increasing the risk equivalent to materially contributing to the damage, because that was precisely what the expert witnesses were not prepared to say in *McGhee*. Thus, what their Lordships meant in *McGhee* was that, "in the particular circumstances, a breach of duty which materially increased the risk should be treated *as if* it had materially contributed to the disease". *Wilsher*, however, was correctly decided on its facts.[188] It was one thing, said Lord Bingham, "to treat an increase of risk as equivalent to the making of a material contribution where a single noxious agent is involved, but quite another where any one of a number of noxious agents may equally probably have caused the damage".

(3) Applying Fairchild

Limits to Fairchild Without caution, *Fairchild* could be interpreted as creating a general principle that whenever a claimant has difficulty in establishing causation, and a defendant's breach of duty has increased the risk of harm to the claimant, the rules of "but for" causation should be relaxed. The problem with such an approach is that, in the context of negligence at least, a defendant is held to be in breach of duty precisely because his conduct has unreasonably increased the risk of harm to the claimant. But proof of breach of duty is not proof of causation, and the principle will not apply merely because the claimant has difficulty in discharging the burden of proof.[189] What then are the limits of the *Fairchild/McGhee* principle? Lord Bingham specified six conditions: 2-56

> "(1) C was employed at different times and for differing periods by both A and B, and (2) A and B were both subject to a duty to take reasonable care or to take all practicable measures to prevent C inhaling asbestos dust because of the known risk that asbestos dust (if inhaled) might cause a mesothelioma, and (3) both A and B were in breach of that duty in relation to C during the periods of C's employment by each of them with the result that during both periods C inhaled excessive quantities of asbestos dust, and (4) C is found to be suffering from a mesothelioma, and (5) any cause of C's mesothelioma other than the inhalation of asbestos dust at work can be effectively discounted, but (6) C cannot (because of the current limits of human science) prove, on the balance of probabilities, that his mesothelioma was the result of his inhaling asbestos dust during his employ-

---

186 [2002] UKHL 22; [2003] 1 A.C. 32.

187 [2002] UKHL 22; [2003] 1 A.C. 32 at [65].

188 [2002] UKHL 22; [2003] 1 A.C. 32 at [22], per Lord Bingham; at [70], per Lord Hoffmann; at [118], per Lord Hutton; at [149], per Lord Rodger.

189 [2002] UKHL 22; [2003] 1 A.C. 32 at [43], per Lord Nicholls. See also *Clough v First Choice Holidays and Flights Ltd* [2006] EWCA Civ 15; [2006] P.I.Q.R. P22; [2006] N.P.C. 8 (ordinary accident in which claimant slipped and fell; *Fairchild* did not apply). Note also that, conversely, proof of causation is not proof of breach of duty. So where a claimant has been exposed to asbestos in a number of employments, although the *Fairchild* principle may assist in establishing causation against an individual defendant, the fact that the claimant has developed mesothelioma does not, of itself, give rise to an inference that that defendant was also in breach of duty: *Brett v Reading University* [2007] EWCA Civ 88 at [21] and [24]. For the test of breach of duty in a case of mesothelioma see *Williams v University of Birmingham* [2011] EWCA Civ 1242; [2012] P.I.Q.R P4 at [40]; *Bussey v 00654701 Ltd (formerly Anglia Heating Ltd)* [2018] EWCA Civ 243; [2018] I.C.R. 1242; para.13-32.

ment by A or during his employment by B or during his employment by A and B taken together."[190]

If each of these conditions is satisfied (and in "no other case") then his Lordship considered that it was "just and in accordance with common sense" to treat the conduct of A and B in exposing C to a risk to which he should not have been exposed as making a material contribution to the contracting by C of a condition against which it was the duty of A and B to protect him.[191] This conclusion followed even if either A or B was not before the court.

2-57 Lord Hoffmann also limited the principle to circumstances in which there was a duty specifically intended to protect *employees* against being unnecessarily exposed to the risk of (among other things) a particular disease and it is proved that the greater the exposure *to asbestos*, the greater the risk of contracting that disease.[192] Where medical science could not prove whose asbestos was more likely than not to have produced the cell mutation which caused the disease, "a rule requiring proof of a link between the defendant's asbestos and the claimant's disease would, with the arbitrary exception of single-employer cases, empty the duty of content" with the result that the duty could not effectively exist.[193] In those circumstances "it would be both inconsistent with the policy of the law imposing the duty and morally wrong for your Lordships to impose causal requirements which exclude liability".[194]

2-58 Lord Rodger suggested that certain conditions were necessary, but may not always be sufficient, for applying the principle. These conditions are clearly at a higher level of generality than those indicated by Lord Bingham or Lord Hoffmann: (1) the principle applies where the claimant has proved all that he possibly can, but the causal link could only ever be established by scientific investigation and the current state of the relevant science leaves it uncertain exactly how the injury was caused; (2) the defendant's conduct must not only have created a material risk of injury to a class of persons but have created a material risk of injury to the claimant himself; (3) the defendant's conduct must have been capable of causing the claimant's injury; (4) the claimant's injury must have been caused by the eventuation of the kind of risk created by the defendant's wrongdoing; it does not apply where the claimant has merely proved that his injury could have been caused by a number of different events, only one of which is the eventuation of the risk created by the defendant's wrongful act or omission (as in *Wilsher*); (5) the claimant must prove that his injury was caused, if not by exactly the same agency as was involved in the defendant's wrongdoing, at least by an agency that operated in substantially the same way (e.g. where a workman suffered injury from exposure to dusts coming from two sources, the dusts being particles of different substances each of which could have caused his injury in the same way); (6) the principle applies where the other possible source of the claimant's injury is a similar wrongful act or omission of another person, but it can also apply where, as in *McGhee*, the

---

190 [2002] UKHL 22; [2003] 1 A.C. 32 at [2].
191 [2002] UKHL 22; [2003] 1 A.C. 32 at [34].
192 [2002] UKHL 22; [2003] 1 A.C. 32 at [61].
193 [2002] UKHL 22; [2003] 1 A.C. 32 at [62]. Though the duty to take reasonable steps not to expose individuals to asbestos would still apply to cases of asbestosis, so that the fact that some claimants who developed mesothelioma could not prove causation would not necessarily "empty the duty of content": see Stapleton (2002) 10 Torts L.J. 276 at 296; and Morgan (2003) 66 M.L.R. 277, 282.
194 [2002] UKHL 22; [2003] 1 A.C. 32 at [63].

other possible source of the injury is a similar, but lawful, act or omission of the same defendant.[195]

Although both Lord Bingham and Lord Hoffmann emphasised that the *Fairchild* principle should be limited to the specific conditions that they laid down, it is difficult to see how, or indeed why, it should be so severely restricted. For example, there is no obvious reason to limit *Fairchild* to the relationship between employer and employee, still less to the specifics of mesothelioma caused by exposure to asbestos.[196] In this respect Lord Rodger's conditions probably reflect a more principled approach. In any event, both Lord Bingham and Lord Hoffmann acknowledged that the principle could be developed to apply in new situations. As Lord Nicholls expressed it: "Policy questions will loom large when a court has to decide whether the difficulties of proof confronting the [claimant] justify taking this exceptional course. It is impossible to be more specific."[197] 2-59

Different noxious agents An issue that was unresolved in *Fairchild* was whether it applies where there are multiple tortfeasors and they add to the risk of damage caused by *different* noxious agents, but by the same, or broadly the same, mechanism.[198] It is questionable whether the point of distinction between *Wilsher* and *Fairchild* (or *McGhee*) is that there was only one type of noxious agent in *Fairchild* but several in *Wilsher*. For example, what if C in *Fairchild* had been exposed to asbestos dust by employer A but to a different cancer-producing agent by employer B? Assume that both agents are capable of producing mesothelioma, but it is not possible to identify which agent caused the cancer. Does C fall within *Wilsher* or *Fairchild*? If the relaxation of the causal test was limited, as Lord Bingham limited it, to exposure to asbestos dust, then the claim fails, applying *Wilsher*. The injustice that *Fairchild* seeks to address is not, however, specifically limited to a particular noxious agent. This is apparent from their Lordships' survey of the jurisprudence from other jurisdictions, which reveal a similar conceptual problem arising in very different factual circumstances, the most obvious being the "hunting cases" where the claimant is simultaneously shot by two or more negligent hunters but cannot identify which one shot him.[199] There is no need to limit the relaxation of the "but for" test to cases specifically involving the inhalation of asbestos. In *Fairchild* Lord Hoffmann had some difficulty seeing why it should make any difference of principle if a claimant had been "exposed to two different agents—asbestos dust and some other dust—both of which created a material risk 2-60

[195] In *Sanderson v Hull* [2008] EWCA Civ 1211; [2009] P.I.Q.R. P7 at [48] and [50] Smith LJ thought that Lord Rodger's sixth condition had now disappeared, though, with that caveat, regarded his conditions as a "useful guide to the scope of" *Fairchild*.

[196] In *Sanderson v Hull* [2008] EWCA Civ 1211; [2009] P.I.Q.R. P7 at [42] and [45] Smith LJ considered that Lord Bingham's conditions were not intended to exclude the application of *Fairchild* to other conditions and circumstances, and Lord Hoffmann had not intended to limit it to cases of mesothelioma. In *Heneghan v Manchester Dry Docks Ltd* [2016] EWCA Civ 86; [2016] 1 W.L.R. 2036 at [48] it was accepted that *Fairchild* applied to lung cancer caused by exposure to asbestos. See also the comments of Lord Hodge (with whom Lord Mance, Lord Clarke and Lord Carnwath agreed) in *International Energy Group Ltd v Zurich Insurance Plc UK* [2015] UKSC 33; [2016] A.C. 509 at [98] and [109] that *Fairchild* is not confined to mesothelioma.

[197] [2002] UKHL 22; [2003] 1 A.C. 32 at [43].

[198] According to Lord Bingham, no, but according to Lord Hoffmann and Lord Rodger, possibly yes. For further discussion see Stapleton (2002) 10 Torts L.J. 276, 294–298.

[199] In this situation courts have usually reversed the burden of proof: see *Cook v Lewis* [1951] S.C.R. 830 (Supreme Court of Canada); para.2-52; *Summers v Tice*, 199 P.2d 1 (1948) (Supreme Court of California).

of the same cancer and it was equally impossible to say which had caused the fatal cell mutation".[200] However, in *Barker v Corus*[201] he considered that his own view in *Fairchild* had been wrong, at least in so far as it focused on different types of dust. The true distinction related to the *causal mechanism*, rather than the specific causal agent. Thus, for Lord Hoffmann it is an essential condition for the operation of the "*Fairchild* exception" that:

> "the impossibility of proving that the defendant caused the damage arises out of the existence of another potential causative agent which operated in the same way. It may have been different in some causally irrelevant respect, as in Lord Rodger's example of the different kinds of dust, but the mechanism by which it caused the damage, whatever it was, must have been the same. So, for example, I do not think that the exception applies when the claimant suffers lung cancer which may have been caused by exposure to asbestos or some other carcinogenic matter but may also have been caused by smoking and it cannot be proved which is more likely to have been the causative agent."[202]

Similarly, although Lord Scott regarded different types of asbestos as constituting a single agent, his Lordship considered that if the outcome might have been produced by one of a number of different agents and the guilty agent could not be identified (as in *Wilsher*) the "*Fairchild* exception" did not apply.[203]

2-61 In *Novartis Grimsby Ltd v Cookson*[204] the claimant developed bladder cancer having been exposed to two different noxious agents: (i) cigarette smoke; and (ii) aromatic amines at work. Although the claim succeeded on causation on the basis that the risk of developing bladder cancer from exposure to aromatic amines was more than double the risk from smoking,[205] Smith LJ commented on Lord Hoffmann's observations in *Barker v Corus*:

> "Although Lord Hoffmann was there saying that the exception would not apply where one causative agent was occupational and the other was smoking, he plainly had in mind that the two agents would act on the body in a different way. In the present case, the evidence was that the amines in cigarette smoke act on the body in the same way as the amines in the occupational exposure. It seems to me that it is highly arguable that the mesothelioma exception [i.e. the principle in *Fairchild*] should apply to bladder cancer and that it would be sufficient if a claimant were to prove that the occupational exposure had made a material contribution to the risk of him developing the disease."[206]

Thus, the crucial point of distinction between *Wilsher* and *Fairchild* is not that there are different noxious agents, but the causal mechanism by which those noxious agents cause the harm. If the causal mechanism is the same then *Fairchild* will apply, but if the causal mechanism is different *Wilsher* will apply.

---

200 [2002] UKHL 22; [2003] 1 A.C. 32 at [72]; such a distinction was "not ... a principled distinction".
201 [2006] UKHL 20; [2006] 2 A.C. 572.
202 [2006] UKHL 20; [2006] 2 A.C. 572 at [24]. See also *Amaca Pty Ltd v Ellis* [2010] HCA 5; (2010) 263 A.L.R. 576 where the High Court of Australia applied the traditional "but for" causation test where the issue was whether exposure to asbestos, as opposed to the deceased's smoking habit, had caused his lung cancer.
203 [2006] UKHL 20; [2006] 2 A.C. 572 at [64].
204 [2007] EWCA Civ 1261.
205 See para.2-48.
206 [2007] EWCA Civ 1261 at [72]. It may be that in *Barker* Lord Hoffmann had simply assumed that the causal mechanism for the production of lung cancer "caused by smoking" is different from the causal mechanism where lung cancer is the result of exposure to asbestos or "some other carcinogenic matter". But this, presumably, would be a matter for medical evidence.

Scientific uncertainty The *Fairchild* principle can only be used to deal with scientific uncertainty. It cannot be invoked just because proving the causal link is difficult and depends on the court making primary findings of fact. In *Sanderson v Hull*[207] the claimant contracted campylobacter enteritis whilst working for the defendants plucking turkeys. The only means by which she could have contracted this infection was by the bacterium entering her body by her mouth, which probably occurred when she inadvertently touched her mouth with her hands. The defendants were held to have been in breach of duty in failing to warn the claimant of the risks of contracting the infection, and advising her as to the precautions she should take. There were various possible ways in she could have picked up the infection on her hands, some of which could have been a consequence of the defendants' breach of duty and others of which would not. The judge held that causation had been established because the breach of duty had materially increased the risk of the claimant contracting the infection. However, the Court of Appeal held that the claimant was not entitled to rely on *Fairchild* to establish causation. *Fairchild* could only be relied on where "there was some other exposure which could have been a potential cause of the injury and … it was *scientifically* impossible for her to show which exposure caused the injury".[208] Merely proving that the breach of duty increased the risk of the claimant contracting the infection was not enough. The difficulty of proof that the claimant had, said Smith LJ, stemmed from the judge's failure to make adequate findings of fact. The cause of the infection was known: the claimant transferred some bacteria from her hands to her mouth. The question was how that had happened, and had the method of transfer resulted from the defendants' breach of duty. The judge could have made appropriate findings of fact, on the balance of probabilities, that would have enabled a decision to be made on the basis of "but for" causation. 2-62

Similarly, *Fairchild* has no application to an ordinary case of personal injury consequent on an individual, specific occasion of negligence for which a single party was responsible. In this situation the court must apply the ordinary "but for" test, on the balance of probabilities.[209] Nor can *Fairchild* be employed to overcome scientific uncertainty in circumstances where the claimant has not suffered actionable injury.[210] 2-63

Effect of non-tortious exposures In *Barker v Corus (UK) Plc*[211] B had been exposed to asbestos during three material periods. The first two exposures were as a result of breaches of duty by his employers. The third exposure was while B was working as a self-employed plasterer when he had failed to take reasonable care to avoid asbestos. One issue was whether *Fairchild* could apply where there was a 2-64

---

207 [2008] EWCA Civ 1211; [2009] P.I.Q.R. P7.

208 [2008] EWCA Civ 1211; [2009] P.I.Q.R. P7 at [52], emphasis added.

209 *Clough v First Choice Holidays and Flights Ltd* [2006] EWCA Civ 15; [2006] P.I.Q.R. P22; [2006] N.P.C. 8. In *Sanderson v Hull* [2008] EWCA Civ 1211; [2009] P.I.Q.R. P7 at [31] Smith LJ commented that if any principle is to be derived from *Clough* it is that the "*Fairchild* exception" will not apply to a personal injury claim arising from a single incident. However, see the doubts about this proposition expressed by Burrows, "Uncertainty about Uncertainty: Damages for Loss of a Chance" [2008] J.P.I.L. 31 at 40.

210 *Saunderson v Sonae Industria (UK) Ltd* [2015] EWHC 2264 (QB) at [183], where Jay J commented that it was "conceptually and legally incoherent" to argue that exposure to a smoke flume containing irritant chemicals had increased the risk of the claimants suffering personal injuries when the issue before the court was whether the claimants had suffered any actionable harm at all.

211 [2006] UKHL 20; [2006] 2 A.C. 572.

period of exposure to asbestos for which there was no culpable defendant (either because there was a period of exposure for which the claimant was himself culpable, or there was a period of exposure for which no-one was culpable). The House of Lords was unanimous that for the "*Fairchild* exception" to apply it was not necessary to prove that all the exposures to a toxic agent were tortious. Indeed, that had been the position in *McGhee v National Coal Board* (where the defendant was responsible for both tortious and non-tortious periods of exposure to brick dust), which their Lordships had approved in *Fairchild*. As Lord Hoffmann put it in *Barker v Corus*: "once one accepts that the exception can operate even though not all the potential causes of damage were tortious, there is no logic in requiring that a non-tortious source of risk should have been created by someone who was also a tortfeasor."[212] It followed that it was:

> "irrelevant whether the other exposure was tortious or non-tortious, by natural causes or human agency or by the claimant himself. These distinctions may be relevant to whether and to whom responsibility can also be attributed, but from the point of view of satisfying the requirement of a sufficient causal link between the defendant's conduct and the claimant's injury, they should not matter."[213]

This view was endorsed by the Supreme Court in *Sienkiewicz v Greif (UK) Ltd*,[214] in which there were two conjoined appeals (*Sienkiewicz v Greif* and *Willmore v Knowsley MBC*) where individuals had developed mesothelioma having been exposed to asbestos by only one defendant, but where the evidence indicated that they had also been exposed to asbestos as a result of the background environmental risk. The defendants argued that in such circumstances the *Fairchild* principle did not apply and the claimant had to prove causation on the basis that the defendants' tortious exposure of the deceased to asbestos had "more than doubled the risk" of developing mesothelioma from the background environmental risk. Neither claimant could do this, since in *Sienkiewicz* the evidence was that the tortious exposure had increased the risk attributable to the non-tortious environmental exposure by 18 per cent and in *Willmore* there was no evidence as to the precise increase in the risk. The Supreme Court rejected the defendants' argument. The claimants' problems in proving causation arose from the same "rock of uncertainty" that had been identified by Lord Bingham in *Fairchild*, and the same policy considerations applied.[215] There was no justification for distinguishing cases involving multiple tortious exposures from cases of a single tortious exposure by applying a "doubles the risk" test of causation in the case asbestos-induced mesothelioma.

(4) Joint liability for the damage or several liability for the risk of damage?

2-65 **Joint or several liability** The decision to relax the usual rules of causation in

[212] [2006] UKHL 20; [2006] 2 A.C. 572 at [16].

[213] [2006] UKHL 20; [2006] 2 A.C. 572 at [17]. See also at [58]–[59], per Lord Scott; and at [99], per Lord Rodger (though note his Lordship's reservation at [100]–[101] in the rare situation where the victim himself was solely responsible for a material exposure to asbestos dust); and at [117], per Lord Walker.

[214] [2011] UKSC 10; [2011] 2 A.C. 229, discussed by J. Stapleton, "Factual causation, mesothelioma and statistical validity" (2012) 128 L.Q.R. 221; S. Steel and D. Ibbetson, "More grief on uncertain causation in tort" [2011] C.L.J. 451.

[215] [2011] UKSC 10; [2011] 2 A.C. 229 at [142], per Lord Rodger; see also per Lord Phillips at [103].

Fairchild was explicitly based on considerations of justice and fairness to claimants, faced with an impossible task of proving causation applying the traditional "but for" test. In *Barker v Corus (UK) Plc*[216] the defendants argued that *Fairchild* could produce an unfair result for defendants in a case of asbestos-induced mesothelioma since, not only would a defendant be held liable when he might not have caused the disease (though a defendant, as much as a claimant, could not prove this one way or the other), but he would also be held liable in full for the consequences of the claimant's disease. A solvent or insured defendant could be held liable for the whole loss if he was unable to obtain contribution under the Civil Liability (Contribution) Act 1978 from an insolvent, uninsured defendant. The House of Lords accepted that this could produce unfairness to defendants and in a radical re-interpretation of *Fairchild* redefined the nature of the damage for which the defendants were to be held responsible, effectively reducing an individual defendant's responsibility to several liability for the risk created by his breach of duty. Given that, where the *Fairchild* principle applies, the creation of a material risk of mesothelioma is sufficient to establish causation, and therefore liability, the damage that the defendant should be regarded as having caused, said their Lordships, was *the creation of the risk or chance of contracting mesothelioma*, and not the mesothelioma itself. Thus, a defendant would be liable to the extent that he added to the risk. As Lord Hoffmann put it:

> "Consistency of approach would suggest that if the basis of liability is the wrongful creation of a risk or chance of causing the disease, the damage which the defendant should be regarded as having caused is the creation of such a risk or chance. If that is the right way to characterise the damage, then it does not matter that the disease as such would be indivisible damage. Chances are infinitely divisible and different people can be separately responsible to a greater or lesser degree for the chances of an event happening."[217]

On this approach the claimant was not entitled to full compensation for the mesothelioma against an individual defendant, only compensation for the defendant's contribution to *the risk* of contracting mesothelioma, which it was assumed (for want of a better method) was to be calculated as a percentage of the damages that would be awarded on a full liability basis for causing mesothelioma, discounted to reflect the defendant's contribution to the overall risk.[218] Moreover, there would normally be no issue of contribution by other defendants or contributory negligence by the claimant, because a "defendant is liable for the risk of disease which he himself has created and not for the risks created by others, whether they are defendants, persons not before the court or the claimant himself".[219] The "damage" they have caused (exposure of the claimant to risk) is not the same. There

216 [2006] UKHL 20; [2006] 2 A.C. 572. See Kramer, "Smoothing the Rough Justice of the Fairchild Principle" (2006) 122 L.Q.R. 547; Khoury, "Causation and Risk in the Highest Courts of Canada, England and France" (2008) 124 L.Q.R. 103.

217 [2006] UKHL 20; [2006] 2 A.C. 572 at [35].

218 [2006] UKHL 20; [2006] 2 A.C. 572 at [48], per Lord Hoffmann; and at [62], per Lord Scott.

219 [2006] UKHL 20; [2006] 2 A.C. 572 at [47], per Lord Hoffmann; see also at [63], per Lord Scott and at [118], per Lord Walker. Contrast Lord Rodger's powerful dissenting speech on the question of apportionment, complaining that the majority were "not so much reinterpreting as rewriting the key decisions in *McGhee* … and *Fairchild*" (at [71]). The majority were not just on a mission to tidy up the reasoning in *McGhee* and *Fairchild*, but were "spontaneously embarking upon this adventure of redefining the nature of the damage suffered by the victims" in order to enable defendants to be made severally liable for a share of the damages, rather than being jointly liable for the whole of the damages (at [86]). Several liability transferred the risk of the insolvency of potential defend-

would be several, rather than joint, liability for discrete periods of exposure. It would be possible, of course, for two defendants to have been negligent with respect to the same period of exposure (for example, an occupier of premises and the employer of an employee working on those premises), in which case a contribution claim would be appropriate. By the same token, it would be possible for a claimant to have been contributorily negligent in a period of exposure for which a defendant was responsible, e.g. by failing to take reasonable precautions against inhalation of asbestos dust. But if the claimant were to be negligent with respect to his own safety during a period of self-employment, that would not fall to be taken into account as reducing the damages payable by a defendant who negligently exposed the claimant to risk during a different period. The claimant's negligence would not have contributed to the same damage for which the defendant was responsible.[220]

2-66 **Compensation Act 2006 s.3—asbestos-induced mesothelioma** Following *Barker v Corus (UK) Plc*, an amendment to the Compensation Bill was rapidly introduced to re-establish the principle that defendants are jointly and severally liable for the mesothelioma caused by asbestos exposure itself, and not simply their respective contribution to the risk of contracting mesothelioma. The Compensation Act 2006 s.3 provides that where a "responsible person" (the defendant) has negligently or in breach of statutory duty caused or permitted another person (the victim) to be exposed to asbestos, and the victim has contracted mesothelioma as a result of the exposure, and it is not possible to determine with certainty whether it was that exposure or another exposure which caused the victim to become ill, and the defendant is liable in tort by virtue of the exposure, in connection with damage caused to the victim by the disease (whether by reason of having materially increased a risk or for any other reason), the defendant shall be liable in respect of the whole of the damage caused to the victim by the disease, and that liability is jointly and severally with any other responsible person.[221] The defendant's joint and several liability is irrespective of whether the victim was also exposed to asbestos:

(i) other than by the defendant, whether or not in circumstances in which another person has a liability in tort; or
(ii) by the defendant in circumstances in which he has no liability in tort.

In other words, the defendant will be jointly and severally liable in a situation such as *Fairchild* itself, where all the other defendants were also liable in tort to the claimant, and where the victim has also been exposed to asbestos non-negligently by another person (as considered in *Barker v Corus*). Although s.3(2) is not explicit on the point, the wording ("whether or not in circumstances in which another person

---

ants from solvent defendants and their insurers to claimants, who as a result would have to bring actions against multiple defendants, and seek to recover damages in respect of that defendant's overall contribution to the risk: "As a result, claimants will often end up with only a small proportion of the damages which would normally be payable for their loss. The desirability of the courts, rather than Parliament, throwing this lifeline to wrongdoers and their insurers at the expense of claimants is not obvious to me" (at [90]).

220 Though note Lord Rodger's and Lord Walker's reservations, [2006] UKHL 20; [2006] 2 A.C. 572 at [95] and [116] respectively, about whether no duty would be owed by the owner or occupier of a building to a labour-only subcontractor, even though technically the worker is self-employed.

221 s.16(3) of the Compensation Act 2006 provides that s.3 shall be treated as having always had effect, but it does not apply to a claim which has been settled or legal proceedings which have been determined before 3 May 2006 (s.16(4)).

has liability in tort") is such that the defendant could be liable where the victim himself was also responsible for a period of exposure to asbestos (where, for example, he was self-employed for a period and failed to exercise reasonable care for his own safety, as was assumed to be the case in *Barker v Corus* itself). The victim owes no duty of care to himself and so is not liable to himself in tort in respect of his own carelessness. The defendant will also be jointly and severally liable in circumstances where part of the victim's exposure is attributable to non-negligent conduct by the defendant (as where the defendant has taken reasonable precautions in respect of part of the claimant's exposure, or where part of the victim's exposure pre-dated the time from which the risks of asbestos exposure became known, so that the defendant was not in breach of duty in respect of that particular period of exposure).

Section 3(3) of the Act provides for a defendant to claim contribution from another responsible person, and for a finding of contributory negligence. Section 3(4) provides that in determining the extent of the contributions of different responsible persons a court shall have regard to the relative lengths of the periods of exposure for which each was responsible (though a different basis of apportionment can be agreed by the defendants or applied by the court if there is a more appropriate basis for doing so in a particular case).[222] Contributory negligence could take the form of an employee failing to take appropriate precautions for his own safety during a period of negligent exposure by an employer, but it is arguable that a claimant who has failed to exercise reasonable care for his own safety by exposing himself to asbestos during a different period could also be found to be contributorily negligent (e.g. during a period of self-employment or in a domestic setting, for example if he pulled down an old shed in his garden which had been lined with asbestos boards[223]). **2-67**

Effect of the Compensation Act 2006 s.3 In *Sienkiewicz v Greif (UK) Ltd*[224] the Supreme Court held that s.3 of the Compensation Act 2006 had not changed the rules on causation. All that the section did was hold that, in the case of asbestos-induced mesothelioma, if the common law reached the conclusion that liability was established applying whatever test of causation was the correct test at common law, the defendant would be jointly and severally liable for the damage and not simply severally liable for contributing to the risk of damage. In other words, s.3 did not change the basis on which causation was to be established (which was a matter for the common law), but created a special rule of joint liability in mesothelioma cases once causation was established.[225] Lord Rodger commented that: "Section 3 was not concerned with prescribing the basis for defendants being held responsible for claimants' mesothelioma. Rather, its purpose was to reverse the decision of the House of Lords in *Barker*."[226] Moreover, the Act only applies in the very specific context of mesothelioma and exposure to asbestos. The general principle of common law established by *Barker v Corus* remained applicable to other forms of **2-68**

---

222 For discussion of the process of apportionment of responsibility between defendants in a case of asbestos exposure causing mesothelioma see *Russell v London Fire & Emergency Planning Authority* [2005] EWHC 581 (QB).

223 See Lord Rodger's speech in *Barker v Corus* [2006] UKHL 20; [2006] 2 A.C. 572 at [94].

224 [2011] UKSC 10; [2011] 2 A.C. 229.

225 [2011] UKSC 10; [2011] 2 A.C. 229 at [70], per Lord Phillips.

226 [2011] UKSC 10; [2011] 2 A.C. 229 at [131].

personal injury, such as the dermatitis sustained by the claimant in *McGhee v National Coal Board*.[227] Section 3 provides no assistance to a future Mr McGhee.

2-69 **Claims under the Fatal Accidents Act 1976** Although the majority of their Lordships in *Barker v Corus* appear to have assumed that redefining the claimant's damage as the defendant's contribution to the risk of harm made no difference to a claim under the Fatal Accidents Act 1976,[228] not least because two of the claimants in the litigation before the House had died, it is not obvious that this approach fits well with the wording of the Act. Section 1(1) provides that:

> "If death is caused by any wrongful act, neglect or default which is such as would (if death had not ensued) have entitled the person injured to maintain an action and recover damages in respect thereof, the person who would have been liable if death had not ensued shall be liable to an action for damages, notwithstanding the death of the person injured."

In *Barker v Corus*, however, the defendants were not held liable for the wrongful act of contributing to the deceased's mesothelioma, which is what killed the deceased, but for contributing to the risk of contracting mesothelioma. The majority approach is expressly that the individual defendants had *not* caused the death, merely contributed to the risk of death. But as Lord Rodger pointed out:

> "By any reckoning, death brought on by mesothelioma is indivisible, indeed the classically indivisible injury. Viscount Dunedin once said scornfully of a hypothetical case where two dogs had worried a sheep to death, 'Would we then have to hold that each dog had half killed the sheep ... ?': *Arneil v Paterson* [1931] A.C. 560, 565. It is similarly unthinkable that the law would hold that, vis à vis the claimant, defendant A one-fifth killed the victim of mesothelioma, defendant B one-quarter killed him, defendant C forty per cent killed him and so forth."[229]

A dependant claiming under the Fatal Accidents Act has always been required to prove that *the death* was *caused* by the defendant's wrongful act, and if she establishes causation she is entitled to damages in full in respect of her loss of dependency, assessed in accordance with well-established principles under ss.3 and 4 of the Act, subject only to reduction for contributory negligence. There is no provision in the Act allowing for proportionate liability as between claimants and defendant (though defendants can claim contribution from other defendants under the Civil Liability (Contribution) Act 1978). Logically, in a case such as *Barker v Corus*, either the dependants recover in full for their loss of dependency, applying normal principles, on the basis that their Lordships did not purport, and indeed had no power, to amend the Fatal Accidents Act, or the dependants have no claim at all under the Act, on the basis that the damage for which the defendant is held responsible did not cause the death. This issue was not addressed in the majority speeches in *Barker v Corus*, and though the Compensation Act 2006 s.3 now reduces the practical import in the context of asbestos-related mesothelioma, it remains potentially problematic in any other comparable situation of industrial disease resulting in the death of the employee where there are multiple tortfeasors.

---

227 [1973] 1 W.L.R. 1. Thus, in *Heneghan v Manchester Dry Docks Ltd* [2016] EWCA Civ 86; [2016] 1 W.L.R. 2036, where the deceased's lung cancer was caused by exposure to asbestos and the defendants were responsible for 35.2 per cent of the whole exposure, the claimant recovered 35.2 per cent of the damages that would have been awarded on a full liability basis.

228 See, e.g. [2006] UKHL 20; [2006] 2 A.C. 572 at [63], per Lord Scott.

229 [2006] UKHL 20; [2006] 2 A.C. 572 at [69].

Restoring an "orthodox" interpretation of Fairchild? In *Durham v BAI (Run Off) Ltd*[230] the Supreme Court had to revisit the question of the combined effect of *Fairchild v Glenhaven Funeral Services Ltd* and *Barker v Corus UK Ltd*. The issue was whether employers' liability insurance policies responded to claims by former employees against their former employers in respect of negligent exposure to asbestos when the employees developed mesothelioma many years later. The answer to that question depended, in part, on whether the wording of the relevant insurance policies covered a situation where the exposure to asbestos occurred during the period of insurance but the injury to the employees manifested itself many years after the period of insurance, applying the principles of insurance law. However, the answer also depended on the correct approach to causation in the claims by the employees against their former employers. If *Barker v Corus* had the effect that an employer was only liable to the extent that his negligence contributed to the risk that the employee would develop mesothelioma, and was not liable for causing the mesothelioma itself, then the insurance policies would not respond to the claims. If, on the other hand, the effect of *Fairchild* was that, for reasons of policy, the common law was prepared to accept a weak, or broad, view of the causal requirements in the case of asbestos-induced mesothelioma, but the defendant was nonetheless to be regarded as having *caused the mesothelioma* (as opposed to having contributed to *the risk* of the employee developing mesothelioma) the insurance policies would respond to the claims. 2-70

Lord Mance JSC (with whom Lord Kerr, Lord Clarke and Lord Dyson JJSC agreed) considered that the distinction said to have been drawn in *Barker* between materially contributing to increasing the risk of a disease and causing that disease was "elusive", and it was "over-simple" to describe the legal responsibility established in *Fairchild* and *Barker* as being liability "for the risk".[231] If the cause of action were simply for the risk created by exposing someone to asbestos: 2-71

> "then the risk would be the injury; damages would be recoverable for every exposure, without proof by the claimant of any (other) injury at all. That is emphatically not the law … The cause of action exists because the defendant has previously exposed the victim to asbestos, because that exposure *may* have led to the mesothelioma, not because it did, and because mesothelioma has been suffered by the victim… . The actual development of mesothelioma is an essential element of the cause of action. In ordinary language, the cause of action is 'for' or 'in respect of' the mesothelioma, and in ordinary language a defendant who exposes a victim of mesothelioma to asbestos is, under the rule in *Fairchild* and *Barker*, held responsible 'for' and 'in respect of' both that exposure and the mesothelioma."[232]

Lord Mance concluded that "for the purposes of the insurances" liability for mesothelioma following exposure to asbestos during an insurance period involved a "weak" or "broad" causal link sufficient for the disease to be regarded as "caused" within the insurance period. It was not accurate to treat the employer's liability as being either solely or strictly for the risk. The reality was that the "employer is be-

230 [2012] UKSC 14; [2012] 1 W.L.R. 867 (also known as "the Trigger litigation"); N. McBride and S. Steel, "The 'trigger' litigation" (2012) 28 P.N. 285; G. Meggitt, "The 'rock of uncertainty'—mesothelioma, insurers and the courts" [2013] J.B.L. 563.

231 [2012] UKSC 14; [2012] 1 W.L.R. 867 at [66].

232 [2012] UKSC 14; [2012] 1 W.L.R. 867 at [65].

ing held responsible for the mesothelioma".[233] For the purposes of the policies, said his Lordship, the negligent exposure of an employee to asbestos could:

> "properly be described as having a sufficient causal link or being sufficiently causally connected with subsequently arising mesothelioma for the policies to respond. The concept of a disease being 'caused' during the policy period must be interpreted sufficiently flexibly to embrace the role assigned to exposure by the rule in *Fairchild* and *Barker*."[234]

Lord Clarke, who clearly had reservations as to whether *Barker* was correctly decided,[235] took the view that the injury was the mesothelioma, not the risk of developing mesothelioma, but that "by creating the risk of mesothelioma in the future, the employer is *deemed to have caused* the mesothelioma, if it should develop in the future".[236]

2-72 **Effect of Durham v BAI (Run Off) Ltd** On one view, it was arguable that *Durham v BAI (Run Off) Ltd* had effectively overruled *Barker* on the issue of the nature of the damage for which the employer is responsible, without expressly doing so. That was certainly the interpretation of the Court of Appeal in *International Energy Group Ltd v Zurich Insurance Plc UK*[237] where Toulson LJ said that the decision in *Barker* "has become past history". Lord Mance's judgment in *Durham v BAI (Run Off) Ltd* was "entirely consistent with Lord Rodger's dissenting judgment in *Barker* and indeed their approach was fundamentally identical".[238] This meant that under *Fairchild* the damage in respect of which a victim might sue was his contraction of mesothelioma and the wrongful exposure to asbestos in the course of his employment met the causal requirements for him to be entitled to hold the employer responsible in law for his illness.[239] Aikens LJ said that it was clear from the majority judgments in *Durham* that the "mesothelioma itself is the damage and it is that damage which is the 'gist' of the cause of action of the employee against the employer. Or put the other way, the essence of the cause of action is not that the employee has been tortiously exposed to the risk of mesothelioma".[240] Maurice Kay LJ agreed with both judgments. However, when *International Energy Group Ltd v Zurich Insurance Plc UK*[241] reached the Supreme Court their Lordships were unanimously of the view that *Durham* had not changed the common law position and that *Barker* still applied (subject to s.3 of the Compensation Act 2006) where a claimant is suing his employer.

2-73 The decision in *Durham v BAI (Run Off) Ltd* was important in establishing that employers' liability insurance policies responded to claims for asbestos-induced mesothelioma. If it had not done so then in many instances employers would have had no effective insurance cover and employees would have had no effective claim against an insolvent employer. In that case, s.3 of the Compensation Act 2006 would have been an irrelevance. However, their Lordships said in *International Energy Group Ltd v Zurich Insurance Plc UK* that there had been no challenge to the cor-

233 [2012] UKSC 14; [2012] 1 W.L.R. 867 at [73].
234 [2012] UKSC 14; [2012] 1 W.L.R. 867 at [74].
235 [2012] UKSC 14; [2012] 1 W.L.R. 867 at [83].
236 [2012] UKSC 14; [2012] 1 W.L.R. 867 at [85], emphasis added.
237 [2013] EWCA Civ 39; [2013] 3 All E.R. 395 at [13].
238 [2013] EWCA Civ 39; [2013] 3 All E.R. 395 at [23].
239 [2013] EWCA Civ 39; [2013] 3 All E.R. 395 at [28].
240 [2013] EWCA Civ 39; [2013] 3 All E.R. 395 at [48].
241 [2015] UKSC 33; [2016] A.C. 509; discussed by J. Fulbrook [2015] J.P.I.L. C188; J. Morgan (2015) C.L.J. 74 395; S. Green (2016) 132 L.Q.R. 25.

rectness of *Barker* in *Durham*. Lord Mance said that in *Durham* the court had accepted that within the "*Fairchild* enclave" it was necessary to adopt a "weak" notion of causation, in order to protect victims of mesothelioma and then held that this weak notion of causation carries through into an insurance context.[242] Neither the Compensation Act 2006 nor *Durham* was inconsistent with or undermined the decision in *Barker* which therefore remains as part of the common law.[243]

(5) Conclusions

There was much initial uncertainty as to how and when a claimant could rely on a material increase in risk in order to establish causation. Where the *McGhee/Fairchild* principle applies then a material increase in the risk of harm to the claimant can be treated *as if* it were a material contribution to the damage. The difficulty has been to identify precisely when the relevant conditions are satisfied. Professor Stapleton[244] identified a number of factors that *cannot* be freestanding requirements for the *McGhee/Fairchild* principle to apply: 2-74

- that the defendant was solely responsible for all the sources of risk to the victim (true in *McGhee*, but not *Fairchild*);
- that all tortfeasors are before the court (all three claimants in *Fairchild* had been exposed to asbestos by parties not before the court);
- that the defendant was the claimant's employer (the claims in *Fairchild* also involved actions against occupiers);
- that the defendant was solely responsible for all the tortious sources of risk to the victim (true in *McGhee*, but not *Fairchild*);
- that there was more than one tortfeasor responsible for tortious exposures (true in *Fairchild*, but not in *McGhee*);
- that the defendant's tortious conduct consisted of a failure to ameliorate a situation that the defendant had earlier created innocently (true in *McGhee*, but not *Fairchild*).

There are a number of propositions concerning the effect and application of *Fairchild* that can now be advanced: 2-75

(1) *McGhee v National Coal Board* remains good law. It did not involve either reversing the burden of proof or the drawing of an inference of fact, based on a robust and pragmatic view of the evidence, to overcome an evidential gap; it established a principle of law.

(2) *Wilsher v Essex AHA* is also good law, and so where there are "innocent" possible causes of the claimant's damage, and the defendant adds another "guilty" possible cause, the increase in overall risk cannot be equated with a material contribution to the damage (as in *Wilsher*, approved in *Fairchild*). Thus, *McGhee/Fairchild* applies where there are multiple tortfeasors, but not where there are multiple different causes. The crucial issue is not the nature of the causal factor (such as different types of asbestos dust) but the nature of the causal mechanism.

---

[242] [2015] UKSC 33; [2016] A.C. 509 at [49].

[243] [2015] UKSC 33; [2016] A.C. 509 at [31]. The common law position was relevant in *International Energy Group Ltd v Zurich Insurance* because, although it involved asbestos-induced mesothelioma, the appeal was from Guernsey where s.3 of the Compensation Act 2006 does not apply.

[244] (2002) 10 Torts L.J. 276, 292.

(3) Where there are multiple tortfeasors and they all add to the risk of damage caused by the *same* noxious agent then the principle applies (since that was the decision in *Fairchild* itself). Following *Fairchild* it had been unclear whether the principle applies where there are multiple tortfeasors and they add to the risk of damage caused by *different* noxious agents, but by the same, or broadly the same, mechanism.[245] *Barker v Corus* established that *Fairchild* can apply in this situation provided that the increased risk can be attributed the same causal mechanism.[246]

(4) *Fairchild* had also left open the question whether the principle applies where there is a single tortfeasor and he adds to the risk of damage caused by the *same* noxious agent, where there is another party who also contributes to the risk by the same mechanism, but that party is "innocent", i.e. not in breach of duty. Logically this seemed to fall within *McGhee* (where there were periods of "innocent" and "guilty" exposure by the single defendant). *Barker v Corus* makes it clear that it is irrelevant that there were periods of "innocent" exposure by a third party; the principle can still apply. Moreover, *Sienkiewicz v Greif (UK) Ltd*[247] confirms that *Fairchild* will also apply even though other periods of exposure were not attributable to any individual but were "environmental".

(5) Similarly *Barker v Corus* held that the principle in *Fairchild* applies even though a claimant who has developed mesothelioma had been exposed to asbestos dust during a period of self-employment, as well as during periods of employment. The claimant does not have to establish that he was an "innocent" victim of a breach of duty by others.

(6) The exposure to the risk of harm must be "not insignificant",[248] or the breach of duty must have "contributed substantially to the risk" that the claimant would contract the disease.[249] Their Lordships did not indicate what a *substantial* contribution meant, perhaps not surprisingly given that on any view of the facts in *Fairchild* the defendants' contribution clearly was substantial. Other cases may arise, however, where the only solvent or traceable defendant exposed the claimant to the risk for a relatively short period, where the issue will be important. It will be recalled that in *Bonnington Castings Ltd v Wardlaw* the House of Lords held that anything that did not fall within the principle de minimis non curat lex would constitute a material contribution to the claimant's damage, and it would seem that a similar test is appropriate where the breach of duty contributes to the *risk of* damage.[250] In *Sienkiewicz v Greif (UK) Ltd*[251] the Supreme Court rejected

[245] According to Lord Bingham, no, but according to Lord Hoffmann and Lord Rodger, possibly yes. See Stapleton (2002) 10 Torts L.J. 276, 294–298.

[246] e.g. different types of asbestos dust, having the same mechanism for producing mesothelioma; or aromatic amines contained material used in the production of dyestuffs and amines in cigarette smoke: *Novartis Grimsby Ltd v Cookson* [2007] EWCA Civ 1261.

[247] [2011] UKSC 10; [2011] 2 A.C. 229.

[248] [2002] UKHL 22 at [42], per Lord Nicholls.

[249] [2002] UKHL 22 at [47], per Lord Hoffmann.

[250] In *Cox v Rolls Royce Industrial Power (India) Ltd* [2007] EWCA Civ 1189 at [21] the Court of Appeal accepted that, in a case of mesothelioma, exposure of the deceased to significant levels of asbestos dust "for at least a week" would be more than de minimis. In *Athey v Leonati* [1997] 1 W.W.R. 97 the Supreme Court of Canada held that the defendant's negligence, which the trial judge had concluded was no more than a 25 per cent contributory factor to the claimant's injury, constituted

the defendants' argument that in order to constitute a *material* increase in the risk it must be shown that the defendant's tortious exposure of the claimant had more than doubled the environmental, non-tortious risk. An increase in risk of developing mesothelioma as a result of exposure to asbestos of 18 per cent over the background risk constituted a material increase in the risk. If the exposure was de minimis then it would not constitute a material increase in the risk. However, Lord Phillips doubted whether it was possible to define, in quantitative terms, what amounts to de minimis for this purpose. This was a question for the judge on the particular facts of each case.[252]

(7) Following *Fairchild* the claimant was entitled to full compensation from the negligent defendant, with no question of apportioning the loss.[253] However, *Barker* held that a defendant is only liable to the extent that he contributed to the risk of the condition developing (measured, crudely, by reference to the defendant's contribution to the overall period of exposure). The Compensation Act 2006 s.3 changed this in the case of asbestos-induced mesothelioma (but no other condition), so that the defendant is liable in full for the consequences of the mesothelioma.[254] For any other condition, where the *Fairchild* principle applies, the loss is in effect apportioned by reference to the extent to which the defendant contributed to the risk.

(8) A defendant is entitled to seek contribution against any other defendant liable in respect of the "same damage" under the Civil Liability (Contribution) Act 1978. However, since *Barker v Corus* states that where *Fairchild* applies defendants are liable only to the extent that they contributed to the risk, if they are responsible for different periods of exposure they will not be liable for the "same damage" and therefore a contribution claim under the Civil Liability (Contribution) Act will not be possible. If the defendants were responsible for the same period of exposure (e.g. an occupier of premises and the employer of the claimant working on those premises) a contribution claim under the 1978 Act will be appropriate, since the defendants have contributed to the same risk. In the case of asbestos-induced mesothelioma defendants are liable for the full consequences of the mesothelioma and are entitled to seek contribution from other defendants.[255]

(9) It has been accepted that the *Fairchild* principle could be extended to other factual circumstances in future cases, but only with considerable caution, and it has now been held to apply to asbestos-induced lung cancer.[256] Given the discussion in the speeches in *Fairchild* of cases at some remove from the precise facts of asbestos-induced mesothelioma, such as the "hunting

---

a material contribution to the damage.

251 [2011] UKSC 10; [2011] 2 A.C. 229.

252 [2011] UKSC 10; [2011] 2 A.C. 229 at [108].

253 cf. *Holtby v Brigham Cowan (Hull) Ltd* [2000] I.C.R. 1086; [2000] 3 All E.R. 421 CA, para.2-36, where the claimant was suffering from asbestosis.

254 See para.2-66. See A. McKenna [2016] J.P.I.L. 114 arguing that s.3 of the Compensation Act 2006 needs amendment to include lung cancer.

255 Compensation Act 2006 s.3; para.2-66.

256 *Heneghan v Manchester Dry Docks Ltd* [2016] EWCA Civ 86; [2016] 1 W.L.R. 2036.

cases" (as in *Cook v Lewis*[257]) it appeared that if a similar case were to arise, the principle would, logically, be extended to cover that situation. However, the Court of Appeal has subsequently held that *Fairchild* does not apply to ordinary cases of personal injury consequent on an individual, specific occasion of negligence.[258] Whether the facts of a case such as *Cook v Lewis* can be considered an ordinary case of personal injury remains to be seen. In *B v Ministry of Defence*[259] the Court of Appeal said that there was "no foreseeable possibility that the Supreme Court would be willing to extend the *Fairchild* exception so as to cover conditions … which have multiple potential causes some of which have not even been identified". The inroad into the normal rules of causation made by *Fairchild* applied "only to cases where the cause of the condition is known. It does not apply where the cause is unknown".[260]

(10) On one view, there is no reason why the *Fairchild* principle should be confined to *scientific* uncertainty about causation. In *Fitzgerald v Lane*[261] the Court of Appeal applied *McGhee* to a case involving three discrete possible causes of injury, namely three distinct impacts in a road traffic accident involving a pedestrian and two vehicles. This case suggested that *McGhee* was not limited to factual uncertainties due to gaps in medical knowledge about the cause of injuries or diseases, but could apply to other types of factual uncertainty.[262] However, in *Sanderson v Hull*[263] the Court of Appeal indicated that it can only be invoked to overcome problems of scientific uncertainty. It cannot be used just because proving causation is difficult given the known facts.

(11) The view taken by the House of Lords in *Barker v Corus* of the *Fairchild* principle, that a defendant is held liable only to the extent that his breach of duty contributes to the risk of harm, rather than the harm itself, creates a potential problem for its application in Fatal Accidents Act 1976 cases (despite the fact that two of the claimants in *Barker* had died). This is because of the inconsistency between the rule that a claimant under the Act must prove that *the death* was caused by the defendant's wrongful act and *Barker v Corus* which provides that the defendant is liable for contributing to *the risk* of the deceased contracting mesothelioma rather than for causing the mesothelioma itself (and the subsequent death). This is not an issue in an asbestos-induced mesothelioma case because of the effect of s.3 of the Compensation Act 2006, although it is potentially relevant to any other fatal disease (e.g. other forms of cancer) to which *Fairchild* can apply.

(12) Finally, it is worth remembering that in a case where the defendant's

---

257 [1951] S.C.R. 830; see para.2-52.

258 *Clough v First Choice Holidays and Flights Ltd* [2006] EWCA Civ 15; [2006] P.I.Q.R. P22; [2006] N.P.C. 8; *Sanderson v Hull* [2008] EWCA Civ 1211; [2009] P.I.Q.R. P7 at [31], per Smith LJ.

259 [2010] EWCA Civ 1317; (2011) 117 B.M.L.R. 101 at [154].

260 In the Supreme Court, Lord Phillips PSC agreed that there was no foreseeable possibility of the Supreme Court extending the principle in *Fairchild*: *B v Ministry of Defence* [2012] UKSC 9; [2013] 1 A.C. 78 at [158]. See also, per Lord Brown JSC at [75].

261 [1987] Q.B. 781.

262 In *Fairchild* [2002] UKHL 22 at [170] Lord Rodger, without deciding the issue, was inclined to the view that in *Fitzgerald v Lane* the Court of Appeal had been correct to apply *McGhee*.

263 [2008] EWCA Civ 1211; [2009] P.I.Q.R. P7.

negligence has more than doubled the existing risk of developing a condition, such as cancer, by the same causal mechanism, the claimant does not have to rely on *Fairchild* in order to establish causation because the "but for" test is satisfied.[264]

3. Loss of a Chance

Proof, on the balance of probabilities, of a causal link between the defendant's wrong and the claimant's damage normally entitles the claimant to recover damages in full from the defendant (subject to any reduction for contributory negligence). No account is taken of the strength or weakness of the proof, once the balance is tipped in the claimant's favour. There is no discounting of the damages award to reflect the degree to which the court was convinced of the causal link. By the same token, if the claimant fails to persuade the court of the causal link, the claim will fail, regardless of how close the claimant came to overcoming the balance of probabilities. So it matters not whether the court considered that there was a 40 per cent probability or zero probability that there was a causal link. The claim still fails. An alternative approach to problems of causal uncertainty is to deal with them on the basis of "proportionate loss", and assess the claimant's chance of obtaining a benefit or avoiding a loss.[265] In this situation the claimant's damage is effectively recategorised as the *chance* of obtaining a benefit or avoiding a loss, rather than the loss itself. Damages are then awarded as a proportion of the damages that would have been awarded for the full loss. They are discounted to reflect the chance of avoiding the loss or securing the benefit. Although this approach has been adopted in respect of claims for financial loss against certain categories of professional, attempts to persuade the House of Lords to take a similar approach to cases involving personal injury, where negligent medical treatment has led to a delay in treatment have, so far, been less successful.[266] Accordingly, the cases are discussed under two discrete headings: (a) loss of a chance of financial benefit; and (b) loss of a chance of a better medical outcome. **2-76**

(a) Loss of a chance of financial benefit

It has long been established that a claimant is entitled to claim in contract in respect of a lost chance of obtaining a benefit,[267] and for many years it has been possible to frame an action for loss of a chance against a solicitor where, as a result of the solicitor's negligence, the client has lost the opportunity to bring proceedings (e.g. because the limitation period has been allowed to expire). The client, in an action against the solicitor, does not have to prove that he would have won the original litigation, merely that he has lost "some right of value, some chose in action of reality and substance".[268] Damages are then discounted to reflect his chances of suc- **2-77**

---

264 *Novartis Grimsby Ltd v Cookson* [2007] EWCA Civ 1261. And in a case of asbestos-induced mesothelioma the claimant cannot be *required* to prove that the defendant's negligence has more than doubled the existing risk of developing mesothelioma: *Sienkiewicz v Greif (UK) Ltd* [2011] UKSC 10; [2011] 2 A.C. 229.

265 See Neuberger, "Loss of a Chance and Causation" (2008) 24 P.N. 206.

266 See para.2-86.

267 *Chaplin v Hicks* [1911] 2 K.B. 786—lost opportunity to win a beauty contest.

268 *Kitchen v Royal Air Force Association* [1958] 1 W.L.R. 563 at 576.

cess in the original action.[269] This applies notwithstanding that the claimant's chance of success in the original action is put at less than 50 per cent.[270]

2-78 The leading case on this issue in the context of solicitors' negligence is *Allied Maples Group Ltd v Simmons & Simmons (A Firm)*.[271] The claimants purchased a number of businesses and commercial properties from a rival company, G. After completion of the purchase it became apparent that one of the companies had onerous liabilities for which the claimants were responsible, and the claimants were unable to reclaim this from G under the terms of the sale. The trial judge held that the defendants, who were the claimants' solicitors for the purchase, had been negligent in failing to warn about a potentially open-ended liability and that if they had known of this risk the claimants would have taken steps to obtain a warranty from G or protect themselves in some other way. The Court of Appeal held that where the claimant's loss depends on the hypothetical action of a third party (in this case G), either in addition to action by the claimant or independently of such action, the claimant need only prove that there was a substantial chance that the third party would have acted to eliminate any loss to the claimant.

2-79 Stuart-Smith LJ said[272] that the classification of the causation issue into "all or nothing" on the balance of probabilities or the quantification of the "loss of a chance" depends upon whether the negligence consists in some positive act or misfeasance, or an omission or nonfeasance:

(1) In the case of a positive act of misfeasance the question of causation is one of historical fact, which once established on the balance of probability is taken as true. The claimant recovers damages in full. Quantifying the claimant's loss, however, may depend upon uncertain future events, such as the degree to which the claimant's medical condition will deteriorate or improve, whether he would have continued to earn at the same rate etc. These issues are dealt with on the basis of an assessment of the risk, often expressed in percentage terms, that the event will or will not occur.

(2) Where the defendant's negligence consists of an omission, e.g. to provide proper equipment, or to give proper instructions or advice, causation depends, not upon a question of historical fact, but on the answer to the hypothetical question, what would the claimant have done if the equipment had been provided or the instruction or advice given. This will be a matter of inference to be determined from all the circumstances. The claimant's own evidence that he would have acted to obtain the benefit or avoid the risk, while important, may not be believed by the judge, especially if there is compelling evidence that he would not.[273] Although the question is a hypothetical one, the claimant must prove on the balance of probability that he would have taken action to obtain the benefit or avoid the risk, and as with positive acts of misfeasance, if he does establish that, there is

---

[269] For example, if due to negligence, a solicitor loses an action on behalf of the claimant against a negligent motorist worth, say, £10,000, and there was a 70 per cent chance of winning that claim, the claimant receives as damages from the solicitor 70 per cent of the value of the claim against the motorist, i.e. £7,000. If he only had a 30 per cent chance of a successful claim against the motorist, he recovers £3,000 from the solicitor.

[270] See, e.g. *Corfield v DS Bosher & Co* [1992] 1 E.G.L.R. 163, where damages were awarded on the basis that the claimant had a one third chance of success.

[271] [1995] 1 W.L.R. 1602.

[272] [1995] 1 W.L.R. 1602 at 1609–1611.

[273] As, e.g. in *McWilliams v Sir William Arrol & Co Ltd* [1962] 1 W.L.R. 295.

no discount of the damages simply because the balance is only just tipped in his favour.

(3) Where, as in *Allied Maples* itself, the claimant's loss depends on the hypothetical action of an independent third party, either in addition to action by the claimant, or independently of it, the claimant does not have to prove on the balance of probability that the third party *would* have acted so as to confer the benefit or avoid the risk to the claimant. The claimant succeeds if he shows that he had a substantial chance, as opposed to a speculative one, that he would have been successful in negotiating total or partial protection, the evaluation of the chance being a question of quantification of damages. There was "no difference in principle between the chance of gaining a benefit and the chance of avoiding a liability". Nor does it depend upon the claimant proving that the chance of success was over 50 per cent. Provided the chance is substantial it may be less than 50 per cent.

Allied Maples has frequently been followed[274] and in *Perry v Raleys Solicitors*[275] the Supreme Court approved the "sensible, fair and practicable dividing line" laid down in *Allied Maples*. In an action for professional negligence, where the question whether the client would have been better off depends upon what the client would have done upon receipt of competent advice, this must be proved by the claimant on the balance of probabilities. Where the claimed beneficial outcome depends upon what others would have done, the court must adopt the loss of chance approach.[276] The defendants had failed to advise the client to make a claim for a "services award" under a compensation scheme for former miners who had **2-80**

[274] See, e.g. *Stovold v Barlows* [1996] P.N.L.R. 91; *First Interstate Bank of California v Cohen Arnold & Co* [1996] P.N.L.R. 17; *Motor Crown Petroleum Ltd v SJ Berwin & Co (A Firm)* [2000] Lloyd's Rep. P.N. 438; *Charles v Hugh James Jones & Jenkins (A Firm)* [2000] 1 W.L.R. 1278 CA; *Perkin v Lupton Fawcett (A Firm)* [2008] EWCA Civ 418; [2008] P.N.L.R. 30 (claimants succeeded in respect of 20 per cent chance of being better off financially); *Wellesley Partners LLP v Withers LLP* [2015] EWCA Civ 1146; [2016] Ch. 529; *McGill v Sports and Entertainment Media Group* [2016] EWCA Civ 1063; [2017] 1 W.L.R. 989. See further paras 9-168 and 9-169; and for detailed discussion see *Jackson & Powell on Professional Liability*, 8th edn (London: Sweet & Maxwell, 2017), para.11–268 onwards. It is possible, though the matter remains unresolved, that in a claim by a disappointed beneficiary in a "negligent will" case (see para.9-122) the question of what the deceased testator would have done had there been no breach of duty should be assessed on the basis of a lost chance, rather than the balance of probabilities (treating the testator as a third party in the action between the disappointed beneficiary and the negligent solicitor): *Feltham v Freer Bouskell* [2013] EWHC 1952 (Ch); [2014] P.N.L.R. 2 at [96]–[112].

[275] [2019] UKSC 5; [2020] A.C. 352 at [21]. *Perry* is discussed by J. Bates, "'Honestly, what are the chances?!' Causation and quantification of a claim for the loss of a chance in professional negligence claims where the claimant's honesty is in dispute" (2019) 35 P.N. 191.

[276] [2019] UKSC 5; [2020] A.C. 352 at [20]. The claimant does not have an option to choose whether to base a claim on a lost chance or to prove a claim on a balance of probabilities: *Assetco Plc v Grant Thornton UK LLP* [2019] EWHC 150 (Comm); [2019] Bus. L.R. 2291 at [406]–[415], per Bryan J. Of course, on a particular set of facts the evidence may be that the chance of the third party acting in a particular way was almost certain, such that in assessing the claimant's chance of obtaining a benefit or avoiding a loss the chance will be virtually 100 per cent and there will be no reduction of the damages award (ibid. at [416]). Alternatively, the chance of a successful outcome may be almost zero, with the result that it is assessed as merely speculative, not substantial, so that causation will not be proved, as e.g. in *Mount v Barker Austin (A Firm)* [1998] P.N.L.R. 493; and *Hatswell v Goldbergs (A Firm)* [2001] EWCA Civ 2084; [2002] Lloyd's Rep. P.N. 359. See also *Hanif v Middleweeks* [2000] Lloyd's Rep. P.N. 920 at [14], per Mance LJ: "the court only assesses prospects and awards damages on a percentage basis—unless it is overwhelmingly clear on the material before the court that the claimant was almost bound to succeed or had, conversely, only a negligible prospect of success, in which case the court may move to a 100% or nil award".

developed vibration white finger. The services award was intended to compensate for tasks that the claimant was no longer able to perform, due to his medical condition, such as gardening and DIY. In the action against the solicitors for the lost opportunity to claim for a services award, the trial judge concluded that the claimant had given dishonest evidence about his ability to perform the tasks, and held that he had not proved that he would have made an honest claim, if competently advised. The Court of Appeal held, inter alia, that the judge had been in error in conducting a trial within a trial on the causation issue as to whether the claimant would have brought an honest claim if competently advised. The issue, said the Court, was if the claimant had made a services claim, what would have been his chances of success? The Supreme Court disagreed. The taking of some positive step by the client is an essential, though not necessarily sufficient, element in the chain of causation, and the client is best placed to assist the court with that question. This should be dealt with on the balance of probabilities. If the client proves, even on the narrowest balance, that he would have brought the claim, there is no discount in the value of the claim to take account of the substantial possibility that he might not have brought the claim. Conversely, if he fails to prove on the balance of probabilities that he would have initiated the action the client gets nothing. There was no reason in principle or in justice why either party to the professional negligence proceedings should be deprived of the full benefit of an adversarial trial of that issue.[277] The mere fact that in determining the issue of what the claimant would have done involves consideration of facts that would have been relevant to the underlying claim is not a good reason not to subject them to the forensic rigour of a trial.[278] Moreover, the claimant had to prove that, properly advised, his claim for a services award would have been an honest claim. Given that the loss of "nuisance value" claims cannot be the subject of an action in negligence against professional advisors,[279] "then so, a fortiori, must dishonest claims".[280]

2-81 **Assessing the chance of success** Where the original claim was struck out because a fair trial of the issues was no longer possible as a result of delay by the solicitors, the judge should not attempt to try the original claim in the action against the negligent solicitors, but should make a realistic assessment of the claimant's prospects of success in the original claim.[281] In *Mount v Barker Austin (A Firm)*[282] Simon Brown LJ set out four principles governing this type of claim: (1) the claim-

---

277 [2019] UKSC 5; [2020] A.C. 352 at [22]–[24].

278 [2019] UKSC 5; [2020] A.C. 352 at [24], [37] and [41]. On the other hand, where the question is one which turns on the assessment of a lost chance, rather than upon proof on the balance of probabilities, it is generally inappropriate to conduct a trial within a trial: ibid. at [31].

279 *Kitchen v Royal Air Force Association* [1958] 1 W.L.R. 563 at 575.

280 [2019] UKSC 5; [2020] A.C. 352 at [26]. The court "simply has no business rewarding dishonest claimants": ibid. at [27].

281 *Sharif v Garrett & Co (A Firm)* [2001] EWCA Civ 1269; [2002] 1 W.L.R. 3118 at [18]–[22]. The Supreme Court did not disagree with this proposition in *Perry v Raleys Solicitors* [2019] UKSC 5; [2020] A.C. 352 at [38]. Lord Briggs simply pointed out that in *Sharif* the client had already started his claim, which was struck out for want of prosecution, and did not need to prove anything about what he would have done, on the balance of probabilities. This will be the situation in any case where proceedings have already been issued and the claim has been lost through a negligent procedural error or delay by the claimant's solicitors: [2019] UKSC 5; [2020] A.C. 352 at [33]. See also *Sharpe v Addison* [2003] EWCA Civ 1189; [2004] P.N.L.R. 23 and *Pearson v Sanders Witherspoon* [2000] P.N.L.R. 110 at 126–135 CA for discussion of how the court should assess the lost chance of successful litigation. For discussion of how to approach the assessment where there are multiple contingencies, each with its own probability see *Langford v Hebran* [2001] EWCA Civ 361; [2001]

ant has the legal burden of proving that he had a real and substantial rather than a negligible prospect of success; (2) the defendants have an evidential burden to show that despite having acted for the claimant in the litigation and charged for their services, that litigation was of no value, that burden being heavier in a case where the solicitors have failed to advise the client of the hopelessness of his prospects; (3) if it is more difficult now for the court to assess the strength of the claimant's original case than it would have been at the time of the original action this should not count against the claimant, but rather against the negligent solicitor; (4) when assessing the claimant's chances of success the court should tend towards a generous assessment, given that it was the defendant's negligence which lost the claimant the opportunity of succeeding in full or in fuller measure.[283] Clearly, the court must be satisfied that the claimant has lost something of value. An action which was bound to fail or had no substantial prospect of success and was merely speculative was not something of value. It is only if the claim passes that test that the court should evaluate in percentage terms the full value of the lost claim.[284]

In *Dixon v Clement Jones Solicitors (A Firm)*[285] the Court of Appeal said that in assessing the chance of success the court's job is not to find what the original decision in the underlying litigation would have been if that litigation had been fought out, but to assess the claimant's prospects of success. Thus, where the outcome in the underlying litigation would have depended on what the claimant would have done, hypothetically, if she had received appropriate information or advice from the original defendant, the claimant does not have to prove that causation issue on a balance of probabilities in order to show that the original claim had some prospects of success.[286] She merely has to prove that the original action had some value which was not negligible. The causation issue in the original action is merely one of a number of issues that are relevant to the prospect of success (which could include the prospects of settling the claim, as well as succeeding at a trial).[287] However, in **2-82**

P.I.Q.R. Q13; *Assetco Plc v Grant Thornton UK LLP* [2019] EWHC 150 (Comm); [2019] Bus. L.R. 2291 at [418]–[449], per Bryan J.

282 [1998] P.N.L.R. 493 at 510–511; apparently approved by the Supreme Court in *Perry v Raleys Solicitors* [2019] UKSC 5; [2020] A.C. 352 at [34], though *Perry* was not concerned with assessing the value of the lost chance, except to say that the loss of what would have been a dishonest claim involves no loss at all.

283 In *Phillips & Co v Whatley* [2007] UKPC 28; [2007] P.N.L.R. 27 at [45] the Privy Council confirmed that where there is doubt in assessing the lost chance, the court should err in favour of the claimant, since it is the defendant's negligence that has created the uncertainty.

284 *Hatswell v Goldbergs (A Firm)* [2001] EWCA Civ 2084; [2002] Lloyd's Rep. P.N. 359 at [48], per Sir Murray Stuart-Smith (claimant's action in negligence against a firm of solicitors in respect of allowing a claim for medical negligence to become statute barred under the Limitation Act 1980 held to have no value, because the medical negligence claim was bound to fail). On the other hand, a decision that the claim was bound to fail does raise the question of what the solicitors were doing running the litigation in the first place. In *Dixon v Clement Jones Solicitors (A Firm)* [2004] EWCA Civ 1005; [2005] P.N.L.R. 6 at [30] Rix LJ described Hatswell as a "rare case" where the loss of the underlying litigation was worthless. In *Mount v Barker Austin (A Firm)* [1998] P.N.L.R. 493 the defendants also managed to prove that the original litigation had been bound to fail. For discussion of different ways of calculating lost chances see Evans, "Lies, damn lies and loss of a chance" (2006) 22 P.N. 99.

285 [2004] EWCA Civ 1005; [2005] P.N.L.R. 6 at [27], per Rix LJ.

286 [2004] EWCA Civ 1005; [2005] P.N.L.R. 6 at [42].

287 Rix LJ at [31] and [41] distinguished between cases where the claim against negligent solicitors is based on the loss of litigation due to the original action being struck out (as in *Dixon*) and cases involving loss of a transaction (as in *Allied Maples*), where the claimant would have to prove what she would have done, hypothetically, on a balance of probabilities.

Perry v Raleys Solicitors,[288] Lord Briggs clearly had some reservations about this reasoning, since it appears to proceed on the basis that the claimant only had to prove what she would have done in the underlying litigation (where the issue was whether she would have entered a financially disastrous transaction had she been given competent advice by her accountants) on the basis of the chances of her entering the transaction rather than the balance of probabilities:

> "A rigid application of the *Allied Maples* test, namely whether the fact in issue was something that the claimant rather than a third party would have done, might lead to the opposite conclusion."

2-83 **Assessing the chance of success in light of subsequent events** Where new evidence becomes available or events occur after the date of the notional trial which would have changed the court's approach to the claim or the assessment of the damage, the issue arises as to whether the court should take this into account or whether it should proceed to make an assessment of the claimant's prospects on the basis of the information that would have been available at the date of the notional trial. In *Dudarec v Andrews*[289] liability was admitted in the initial claim against a negligent motorist for an accident in 1982, but there was an outstanding issue as to whether the claimant had failed to mitigate his loss by refusing to undergo surgery for a medical condition that was then believed to affect the claimant. The claim against the motorist was struck out in 1996 for want of prosecution, and in the subsequent action against the claimant's negligent solicitors the question of the claimant's alleged failure to mitigate arose in assessing the loss. However, in 2004, following further medical investigations, it was discovered that the claimant did not have the medical condition, and there was no need for surgery to correct it. The Court of Appeal held that, in assessing the loss in the action against the solicitors, where evidence becomes available for the first time after the date of the notional original trial, the facts as they had turned out should be taken into account.[290] The position may be different, however, if evidence emerges of an entirely new matter which could not possibly have been discovered at the date of the notional trial. The situation may depend on the circumstances. So, if a claimant had died of unrelated causes between the date of the notional trial and the assessment of damages, this should be taken into account because otherwise the claimant's estate would receive an unjustified windfall.[291]

2-84 This issue was considered again in *Edwards v Hugh James Ford Simey (A Firm)*[292] where the Court of Appeal emphasised that the question is what has the claimant lost as at the date of the original trial or settlement (applying the principles set out in *Mount v Barker Austin (A Firm)*[293]). The court should not simply assess "the strength of the case as at the date of the professional negligence trial, asking the claimant what he can now prove, on the basis of expert evidence which would

---

288 [2019] UKSC 5; [2020] A.C. 352 at [40].

289 [2006] EWCA Civ 256; [2006] 1 W.L.R. 3002.

290 Applying *Charles v Hugh James Jones & Jenkins (A Firm)* [2000] 1 W.L.R. 1278.

291 [2006] EWCA Civ 256; [2006] 1 W.L.R. 3002 at [64], per Smith LJ. On this point see *Whitehead v Hibbert Pownall & Newton* [2008] EWCA Civ 285; [2009] 1 W.L.R. 549 (action against solicitors in respect of negligent conduct of claim against hospital for damages for "wrongful birth" relating to the cost to the mother of raising a disabled child limited to the period between the child's birth and the mother's later death by suicide).

292 [2018] EWCA Civ 1299; [2018] P.N.L.R. 30.

293 [1998] P.N.L.R. 493; see para.2-81.

not have been in existence had the original matter proceeded with competent representation".[294] Only in exceptional cases should the court take into account after-coming evidence. In both *Dudarec v Andrews*[295] and *Charles v Hugh James Jones & Jenkins*[296] the relevant after-coming evidence would and should have been available at the notional trial date, had the litigation been competently conducted. What would constitute exceptional circumstances in which after-coming evidence should be taken into account? There:

> "is no established threshold over which a party must step before such an after-coming event, which could not and would not have been known, should alter the outcome ... [But] there must be a requirement for a significant or serious scale to the consequences of the supervening event, before it should be permitted to establish an exception to the normal principle".[297]

An example would be the subsequent death of the claimant where the original claim included future losses, such as loss of earnings. In *Edwards v Hugh James Ford Simey* itself, where the after-coming evidence would not have been available at the notional date of settlement, the evidence had an element of uncertainty, and the value of the claim was relatively small, the case did not fall within the exception. The Supreme Court dismissed the defendants' appeal without expressing a concluded view on the admissibility of subsequently acquired evidence in a professional negligence claim.[298] It was sufficient to find that a subsequent medical report relied on by the defendant solicitors was not relevant to the action for the loss of an opportunity to claim an award under a Department for Trade and Industry compensation scheme for miners who had developed vibration white finger. The scheme was a "rough and ready" method of providing compensation based on tariffs for particular levels of severity of the condition. The claimant was not making a claim in a conventional personal injuries action and the defendants were not entitled to construct a counterfactual based on evidence that would not have been used under the compensation scheme.

Claims in contract and tort At one time there was some debate as to whether claims in respect of lost chances were limited to actions in contract. In *Allied Maples* Stuart-Smith LJ cited both *Chaplin v Hicks* and *Kitchen v Royal Air Force Association*, which both involved claims in contract, and of course the disappointed clients in *Allied Maples* itself clearly had a contractual relationship with the negligent solicitors.[299] But his Lordship also relied upon a dictum of Lord Lowry in *Spring v Guardian Assurance Plc*,[300] a case involving a negligent employment 2-85

294 [2018] EWCA Civ 1299; [2018] P.N.L.R. 30 at [69].
295 [2006] EWCA Civ 256; [2006] 1 W.L.R. 3002.
296 [2000] 1 W.L.R. 1278.
297 [2018] EWCA Civ 1299; [2018] P.N.L.R. 30 at [73].
298 [2019] UKSC 54; [2019] 1 W.L.R. 6549.
299 Albeit that the solicitor-client relationship is characterised as giving rise to concurrent liabilities in contract and tort.
300 [1995] 2 A.C. 296 at 327: "Once the duty of care is held to exist and the defendants' negligence is proved, the [claimant] only has to how that by reason of that negligence he has lost a reasonable chance of employment (which would have to be evaluated) and has thereby sustained loss ... He does not have to prove that, but for the negligent reference, [the third party] *would* have employed him." (Original emphasis.)

reference about a former employee, which is undoubtedly a tort case,[301] and *First Interstate Bank of California v Cohen Arnold & Co* was a claim for the tort of negligent misrepresentation.[302] It would seem that the categorisation of a claim as one for breach of contract or breach of a tortious duty makes no difference to the question of whether it can be dealt with on the basis of the loss of a chance.

(b) Loss of a chance of a better medical outcome

2-86 The "but for" test creates particular problems for claimants in actions for medical negligence where the alleged negligence consists of a missed or delayed diagnosis. A patient attending a doctor or hospital usually does so because they already have a medical problem following injury or the onset of disease. If, as a result of negligence, the correct diagnosis is not made then the condition may deteriorate or fail to improve. Can the deterioration be attributed to the negligence? Applying the "but for" test, if appropriate treatment would have made a difference then the omission to treat has caused the deterioration, but this is determined on the balance of probabilities. So the answer to this question depends on the patient's prospects of successful treatment at the time when the correct diagnosis should have been made. If the patient had a better than 50:50 chance of an improved medical outcome with prompt treatment the failure to treat has caused the deterioration, but if the patient had a less than 50:50 chance it did not. On this approach, whenever a patient with a less than even chance of successful treatment attends a doctor, negligent diagnosis or delay in implementing treatment will not give rise to a claim because the action will always fail on causation. This has led some judges to adopt an alternative analysis in which the nature of the claimant's damage is redefined in terms of the lost opportunity of a better medical outcome, or "loss of a chance" of avoiding the adverse medical outcome. The claimant is then compensated for the loss of that chance, with damages being discounted to reflect the percentage chance of avoiding the outcome that the claimant has lost.

2-87 In *Hotson v East Berkshire AHA*,[303] the claimant fell and injured his hip. The defendants' negligence resulted in a delay in treatment and he ultimately developed avascular necrosis of the hip joint. The medical evidence was that, even had he received prompt and proper treatment, there was a 75 per cent likelihood that avascular necrosis would still have ensued from the original traumatic injury. Simon Brown J awarded the claimant compensation for the "lost" 25 per cent chance of avoiding avascular necrosis.[304] The House of Lords reversed his judgment and that of the Court of Appeal. Their Lordships held that the trial judge's finding of fact showed that it was more likely than not (75:25) that avascular necrosis itself was an inherent complication of the original injury, and so the claimant had failed to prove causation. Had the claimant proved that the "chance" of avascular necrosis resulting from the negligent delay in treatment was estimated as 51:49 he would have recovered full compensation for the consequences of his disability. In other words, this was not a "lost chance" case, it was an all or nothing case—either the fall or the misdiagnosis caused the disability, and on the balance of probabilities it

---

301 See further the decision of the House of Lords in *Davies v Taylor* [1974] A.C. 207, also relied upon by Stuart-Smith and Hobhouse LJJ.

302 See also *J Sainsbury Plc v Broadway Malyan (A Firm), (Ernest Green Partnership Ltd, Third Party)* [1999] P.N.L.R. 286 at 322–329; and *Doyle v Wallace* [1998] P.I.Q.R. Q146.

303 [1987] A.C. 750 CA and HL. See Stapleton (1988) 8 O.J.L.S. 111; (1988) 104 L.Q.R. 389.

304 [1985] 1 W.L.R. 1036.

was the fall. The valuation of a "lost chance" would only arise once causation had been established.[305]

Hotson left two questions unanswered. First, what, if any, was the relationship between the situation in *Hotson* and *McGhee v National Coal Board*.[306] In *McGhee*, the claimant could arguably show no more than a "lost chance": that had washing facilities been provided he would not have contracted dermatitis. In *Hotson* Lord Mackay distinguished *McGhee*. The precise aetiology of Mr McGhee's disease could not be evaluated. In *Hotson*, the expert evidence concluded positively that avascular necrosis was more likely than not to have arisen from the "innocent" cause (the fall). He suggested that in *McGhee* it was reasonable to infer causation because: **2-88**

> "Although no precise figures could be given in that case … one might, for example, say that it was established that of 100 people working under the same conditions as the pursuer and without facilities for washing at the end of the shift, 70 contracted dermatitis: of 100 people working in the same conditions as the pursuer when washing facilities were provided … 30 contracted dermatitis."[307]

Secondly, on appropriate facts could a claim for "loss of a chance" ever be actionable in tort? Their Lordships expressly left open the question of whether loss of a chance of an improved medical outcome, or of avoiding the relevant loss or damage, was ever recoverable in tort.[308] Given that loss of a chance can be actionable in contract,[309] it seemed that claimants in tort were at a distinct disadvantage for no obvious reason.[310] Subsequently, the Court of Appeal decision in *Allied Maples Group Ltd v Simmons & Simmons* appeared to highlight the disparity in the courts' approach to claims against professionals in respect of financial loss, where a loss of chance may be actionable, and claims in the context of medical negligence where *Hotson* seemed to bar such actions. The decision of the House of Lords in *Fairchild v Glenhaven Funeral Services Ltd*[311] to ease the burden of proof for a claimant faced with otherwise insuperable problems in overcoming the "but for" test, again raised the question of whether requiring claimants in all medical negligence cases to prove their loss on the balance of probabilities was appropriate. If it would be unjust, or

---

305 But as Stapleton (1988) 104 L.Q.R. 389 at 393 points out, this failed to address the essence of the claimant's argument, which was whether a claim formulated as a loss of a chance was acceptable at all. If the nature of the damage could be redefined as the loss of a chance of a successful outcome, rather than the outcome itself (the disability), then on a traditional causation test the defendants' negligence clearly did cause the damage (i.e. the chance was lost). Logically, the question of whether the negligence caused the damage is an issue that can only be dealt with after the nature of the damage has been defined.

306 [1973] 1 W.L.R. 1; see para.2-45.

307 [1987] A.C. 750 at 786. Note though the figures Lord Mackay uses. If it were shown that only 49 contracted dermatitis where washing facilities were absent, would the claim fail as in *Hotson*? Claimants seem to benefit from inexactitude in these cases.

308 [1987] A.C. 750 at 786 at 789 and 793. The Canadian Supreme Court followed *Hotson* in *Laferrière v Lawson* (1991) 78 D.L.R. (4th) 609. For the position in Australia, see *Malec v JC Hutton Proprietary Ltd* (1990) 169 C.L.R. 638; *Poseidon Ltd v Adelaide Petroleum NL* (1994) 68 A.L.J.R. 313. See further para.9-113.

309 *Chaplin v Hicks* [1911] 2 K.B. 786, CA; *Kitchen v Royal Air Forces Association* [1958] 1 W.L.R. 563 CA.

310 This had been one factor in the Court of Appeal's approach to the matter in *Hotson*. The objection was that there was no sense in a distinction which allowed damages to be recovered from a private doctor but not against a NHS doctor: see [1987] A.C. 750 at 760 and 768, per Sir John Donaldson MR and Croom-Johnson LJ respectively.

311 [2002] UKHL 22; [2003] 1 A.C. 32, see para.2-53.

unfair, or "morally wrong"[312] to impose a test of causation which would inevitably preclude liability in *Fairchild* why did the same notions of morality or justice not apply—were the victims of medical negligence entitled to a different brand of justice and morality from the victims of industrial disease?

2-89 **Gregg v Scott** These issues were central to the decision of the House of Lords in *Gregg v Scott*.[313] Due to the negligence of his general practitioner, there was a nine-month delay in the claimant receiving treatment for cancer, and this significantly reduced his chances of survival[314] from 42 per cent to 25 per cent.[315] The trial judge, applying *Hotson*, dismissed the claim on the basis that the claimant would probably not have been cured in any event. In the Court of Appeal the claimant advanced two arguments. First (the "quantification argument"), that the delay in diagnosis had caused physical damage because the claimant's tumour had grown in size causing pain and suffering, and the treatment was more drastic with greater side-effects than would have been the case if it had occurred sooner. If the claimant had suffered physical damage he was entitled to compensation for his reduced life expectancy as a matter of assessment of quantum of damage (where future contingencies are measured on the basis of their chances of occurring). Secondly (the "loss of chance argument"), the case was factually different from *Hotson*, so that *Hotson* did not preclude a claim based on a reduced prospect of survival; but even if *Hotson* did apply the decision of the House of Lords in *Fairchild* permitted the court to depart from it. By a majority the Court of Appeal dismissed the claimant's appeal[316] and by a 3:2 majority the House of Lords also rejected the claim. Unfortunately, there were almost as many opinions as there were judges as to the correct resolution of this problem.[317] Despite the majority decision of their Lordships it remains arguable that in some circumstances a missed diagnosis could give rise to a claim based on a lost chance of a better medical outcome.

---

312 See the quotations at para.2-54 fn.181. Compare the comments of Sir John Donaldson MR in the Court of Appeal in *Hotson v East Berkshire AHA* [1987] A.C. 750 at 759–760: "As a matter of common sense, it is unjust that there should be no liability for failure to treat a patient, simply because the chances of a successful cure by that treatment were less than 50%. Nor, by the same token, can it be just that if the chances of a successful cure only marginally exceed 50%, the doctor or his employer should be liable to the same extent as if the treatment could be guaranteed to cure. If this is the law, it is high time that it was changed ...".

313 [2005] UKHL 2; [2005] 2 A.C. 176. For comment see: Stapleton, "Loss of the chance of cure from cancer" (2005) 68 M.L.R. 996; Peel, "Loss of a Chance in Medical Negligence" (2005) 121 L.Q.R. 364; Reid, "Gregg v Scott and lost chances" (2005) 21 P.N. 78; Maskrey and Edis, "Chester v Afshar and Gregg v Scott: Mixed Messages for Lawyers" [2005] J.P.I.L. 205; Lord Hoffmann, who was one of the judges in *Gregg v Scott*, has expressed his extra-judicial views at (2005) 121 L.Q.R. 592, 600–601.

314 Defined by the medical experts as survival for 10 years from the date of first treatment.

315 This highly simplified version of the facts was apparently accepted, or assumed to be correct, by all of their Lordships except Lord Phillips, who took a radically different approach to the proof of the relevant facts. See para.2-95.

316 [2002] EWCA Civ 1471; [2003] Lloyd's Rep. Med. 105 (Latham LJ dissenting).

317 Including significant differences in the Court of Appeal. For comment on the Court of Appeal decision see E. Peel, "'Loss of a Chance' Revisited: Gregg v Scott" (2003) 66 M.L.R. 623; M.A. Jones, "Another Lost Opportunity?" (2003) 19 P.N. 542.

(i) *The quantification argument*

2-90 The argument that the delay in treatment had resulted in physical damage, namely the growth of the tumour, and that the claimant's reduced life expectancy could be dealt with simply as a matter of quantifying his loss was rejected by the majority of their Lordships, though for Lord Hoffmann this was on the basis that it had not been proved that the claimant's likely premature death would be attributable the growth of the tumour.[318] Lord Nicholls regarded the argument as superficially attractive, but, without expressly rejecting the argument, considered that it did not get to the heart of the problem.[319] Lord Hope seemed to take a different view of the facts and considered that "it was proved on a balance of probabilities that the tumour spread because of the delay in treatment, that this was a physical injury which was caused by the doctor's negligence and that this gave [the claimant] a cause of action for the pain and suffering that was caused by that injury and all its other adverse consequences".[320] Lord Phillips appears to have agreed with Lord Hope that where a doctor's negligence caused the spread of a patient's cancer the patient can recover for the effect that the spread of the cancer had on his life expectancy, commenting that that "conclusion is not, as a matter of principle, in any way at odds with the current law".[321] However, Lord Phillips considered that it had not been proven on the facts that the defendant's negligent delay had actually reduced the claimant's life expectancy.

2-91 On the other hand, even if it was not demonstrated that the growth of the tumour had reduced the claimant's life expectancy, there could be an award of damages to reflect the fact that the delay could have resulted in more intrusive treatment, and more pain, suffering and distress than would have been experienced had treatment commenced promptly.[322] Of course, this would have to be proved on a balance of probabilities.

---

318 [2005] UKHL 2; [2005] 2 A.C. 176 at [68]. Baroness Hale apparently took a similar view, on the basis that there was no finding of fact by the trial judge that the delay in treatment caused the "upstaging" (i.e. the growth) of the tumour (at [202]).

319 [2005] UKHL 2; [2005] 2 A.C. 176 at [58].

320 [2005] UKHL 2; [2005] 2 A.C. 176 at [96]. His Lordship added, at [117]: "The fact that there was a physical injury has been proved on a balance of probabilities. So too has the fact that, in addition to pain and suffering, it caused a reduction in the prospects of a successful outcome. I would hold that, where these factors are present, the way is open for losses which are consequential on the physical injury to be claimed too.... I see the reduction in the prospects of a successful outcome as one element among several in the claim for which there is a single cause—the enlargement of the tumour. This was a physical injury ...". See also at [121].

321 [2005] UKHL 2; [2005] 2 A.C. 176 at [187]; see also at [191].

322 [2005] UKHL 2; [2005] 2 A.C. 176 at [191]. Baroness Hale said, at [206], that:

> "The defendant is liable for any *extra* pain, suffering, loss of amenity, financial loss and loss of expectation of life which may have resulted from the delay. If, without the delay, the claimant would have achieved a longer gap before more radical treatment became necessary, then he should be entitled to damages to reflect the acceleration in his suffering. If the pain and suffering he would have suffered anyway was made worse by the anguish of knowing that his disease could have been detected earlier, then he should be compensated for that."

It would appear that counsel for the claimant did not pursue this aspect of the claim. The physical, psychological and financial consequences of delayed diagnosis arising from the need for more intrusive or aggressive treatment have always been recoverable: see M.A. Jones, *Medical Negligence*, 5th edn (London: Sweet & Maxwell, 2018), paras 5-129 and 5-130; and *Laferrière v Lawson* (1991) 78 D.L.R. (4th) 609 (Supreme Court of Canada).

(ii) The loss of chance argument

2-92 The loss of chance argument was that the defendant's negligence had reduced the claimant's chances of survival from 42 per cent to 25 per cent; this reduction of prospects was something of value and the claimant was entitled to be compensated for that loss.[323] Despite the majority view refusing the appeal, the effect of the ruling of the House of Lords in *Gregg v Scott* on the loss of chance argument is equivocal. Lord Nicholls was strongly supportive of it, and Lord Hope agreed with Lord Nicholls, whilst also accepting the quantification argument. Lord Hoffmann rejected the loss of chance approach, as did Baroness Hale, though she did consider that in some cases there could be a modest claim in respect of "lost years". Lord Phillips agreed that, on the facts, Mr Gregg's appeal should be dismissed, but considered that in certain cases "there may be a case for permitting a recovery of damages that is proportionate to the increase in the chance of the adverse outcome".[324]

2-93 For Lord Nicholls, the loss of a 45 per cent prospect of recovery was just as much a real loss for a patient as the loss of a 55 per cent prospect of recovery. It would be "irrational and indefensible" to deny any remedy to a patient with a 45 per cent chance of recovery whose prospects of recovery were reduced to nil by a negligent diagnosis.[325] It would also render the doctor's duty "empty of content". The purpose of a doctor's duty was "to promote the patients' *prospects* of recovery by exercising due skill and care in diagnosing and treating the patient's condition".[326] If negligent diagnosis or treatment diminished the patient's prospects of recovery, a law which did "not recognise this as a wrong calling for redress would be seriously deficient today".[327] Drawing the comparison with claims in respect of loss of a chance of financial benefit, his Lordship considered that since loss of a financial

323 The trial judge had calculated the value of the lost chance as 20 per cent of the damages that would have been awarded for the loss of the certainty of a cure: [2005] UKHL 2; [2005] 2 A.C. 176 at [164].

324 [2005] UKHL 2; [2005] 2 A.C. 176 at [190].

325 [2005] UKHL 2; [2005] 2 A.C. 176 at [3]. Lord Nicholls was well aware of the inherent problem of using statistics to prove what may or may not have happened in a particular case: see his comments at [28]. Despite this it would not be acceptable to reject all statistical evidence out of hand, particularly where the reason why the actual outcome for the individual claimant is not known is that the defendant's negligence has prevented that outcome from becoming known: at [32].

326 [2005] UKHL 2; [2005] 2 A.C. 176 at [24] (original emphasis).

327 [2005] UKHL 2; [2005] 2 A.C. 176 at [25]. Later, Lord Nicholls commented, at [43], that if a patient's prospects of recovery were to be treated as non-existent whenever they fell short of 50 per cent, the law would "deserve to be likened to the proverbial ass". See also the comments of the Court of Appeal in *Coudert Brothers v Normans Bay Ltd* [2004] EWCA Civ 215; *The Times,* 24 March 2004 at [32] and [68], per Waller LJ and Laws LJ respectively, expressing concern at the outcome of the Court of Appeal decision in *Gregg v Scott*. In *Gavalas v Singh* [2001] VSCA 23; [2001] 3 V.R. 404 the Victoria Court of Appeal held that a claimant who had lost the chance of making a full recovery because of a negligent delay in diagnosing a brain tumour was entitled to damages for future loss of earnings and the additional cost of future medical treatment attributable to that lost chance. Callaway JA said, at 409, that: "No advanced system of law could now deny recovery where late diagnosis, in breach of duty to the patient, appreciably reduces the prospects of success of an operation." However, in *Tabet v Gett* [2010] HCA 12; (2010) 265 A.L.R. 227, the High Court of Australia has unanimously ruled that damages for loss of a chance of a better medical outcome should not be awarded. Hayne and Bell JJ, at [69] said: "the language of loss of chance should not be permitted to obscure the need to identify whether a plaintiff has proved that the defendant's negligence was more probably than not a cause of damage (in the sense of detrimental difference). The language of possibilities (language that underlies the notion of loss of chance) should not be permitted to obscure the need to consider whether the possible adverse outcome has in fact come home, or will more probably than not do so."

opportunity or chance will give rise to a claim against a negligent professional adviser, justice required that loss of a chance should also constitute actionable damage where what is lost is the chance of health or even life itself.[328] For Lord Nicholls this view was also supported by the decision of the House of Lords in *Fairchild v Glenhaven Funeral Services Ltd*, which provided an illustration of the court being prepared to adapt the rules of causation "so as to leap an evidentiary gap when overall fairness plainly so requires".[329]

Lord Hoffmann took the view that for events in the past the law assumes that there is no inherent uncertainty about what happened, nor about whether something which happened in the past will cause something to happen in the future: "Everything is determined by causality. What we lack is knowledge and the law deals with lack of knowledge by the concept of the burden of proof."[330] The progress of the claimant's cancer was not random, but was governed by laws of causality, and an inability to establish that the delay in diagnosis and treatment reduced the claimant's expectation of life could not be remedied by treating the outcome as having been indeterminate.[331] This assumption that past events are determinate (and therefore to be decided upon on an all or nothing basis) is, of course, precisely that: an assumption. His Lordship acknowledged that there are exceptions to this rule, including the relaxation of the "but for" test applied in *Fairchild v Glenhaven Funeral Services Ltd*[332] and the loss of chance approach applied in *Allied Maples Group Ltd v Simmons & Simmons (A Firm)*[333] where the outcome depends on the actions of a third party. He did not, however, attempt to explain the policy basis for these exceptions, other than the suggestion that to extend the *Fairchild* principle, without identifying any control mechanisms to limit its application, would amount to a legislative act and have "enormous consequences" for insurance companies and the National Health Service.[334] Baroness Hale agreed that reformulating claims on the basis of loss of a chance would have major consequences. Almost any claim for loss of an outcome could be reformulated as a claim for loss of a chance of that outcome. And if claimants could recover proportionate damages where the chance was less than 50 per cent, why could defendants not argue that where a claimant has proved his loss on the balance of probabilities, their liability should be limited to the extent that the claimant has proved his loss beyond the 50 per cent hurdle? This form of proportionate liability would increase the complexity of ordinary personal injury claims, and cause "more problems ... than the policy benefits are worth".[335] **2-94**

Lord Phillips undertook a lengthy analysis of the facts, and the statistics which **2-95**

---

328 [2005] UKHL 2; [2005] 2 A.C. 176 Lord Hope agreed, at [121], that a patient who was already suffering from illness at the date of the doctor's negligence from which he had at that date significant prospects of recovery should have a cause of action for the reduction in those prospects.

329 [2005] UKHL 2; [2005] 2 A.C. 176 at [31].

330 [2005] UKHL 2; [2005] 2 A.C. 176 at [79].

331 [2005] UKHL 2; [2005] 2 A.C. 176 at [80].

332 [2002] UKHL 22; [2003] 1 A.C. 32; see para.2-53.

333 [1995] 1 W.L.R. 1602; see para.2-78.

334 [2005] UKHL 2; [2005] 2 A.C. 176 at [90]; cf. the reaction of Lord Nicholls at [52]–[56] to the possibility that a ruling in favour of the claimant would increase the financial burden on the NHS or lead to "defensive medicine".

335 [2005] UKHL 2; [2005] 2 A.C. 176 at [225]. Baroness Hale also noted, at [218], the anomalous distinction between the position of solicitors and doctors sued on the basis of a loss of chance: "So why should my solicitor be liable for negligently depriving me of the chance of winning my action, even if I never had a better than evens chance of success, when my doctor is not liable for negligently depriving me of the chance of getting better, even if I never had a better than evens

formed the basis of the findings of fact, and concluded that counsel and the Court of Appeal had misunderstood both the effect of the evidence and the findings made by the trial judge.[336] The view that the claimant's chances of survival had fallen from 42 per cent to 25 per cent was "fallacious".[337] The statistics were based on an assumption that the cohort that made up the statistical model used by the expert witnesses consisted of patients with the same stage of disease as the claimant, but that assumption was questionable, on the evidence. The fact that the claimant had survived to the date of the trial (some five years after treatment had commenced), and indeed to the date of the appeal hearing in the House of Lords (some eight years after treatment had commenced), suggested that applying a statistical approach to an individual's progress was highly problematic. If the claimant was in the minority of patients who survived, it was difficult to say that the negligence of the defendant had deprived him of the prospect of surviving. In other words, Mr Gregg's survival itself tended to disprove the causal connection between the delayed diagnosis and his "lost chance" of surviving, since as time went on it was becoming increasingly apparent that he had not lost this chance at all: "The closer that Mr Gregg comes to being a survivor the smaller is the likelihood that the delay in commencing his treatment has had any effect on his expectation of life."[338] Thus, for Lord Phillips the facts had changed between the date of trial and the appeal hearing. The likelihood was that the defendant's negligence had not prevented the claimant's cure, but had made that cure more painful.

(iii) *Loss of a chance of a better medical outcome after Gregg v Scott*

2-96 Notwithstanding the rejection of the claimant's appeal, it remains arguable that, on the right facts, a claim based on loss of chance could succeed in a medical negligence action. Lord Nicholls and Lord Hope were in favour of the loss of chance argument, but in a limited set of circumstances. Lord Nicholls distinguished the situation in *Gregg v Scott* from the factual situation in *Hotson v East Berkshire AHA*. Medical negligence cases could be divided into two categories, depending upon whether the patient's condition at the time of the negligence does or does not give rise to significant medical uncertainty as to what the outcome would have been in the absence of negligence. The patient's actual condition at the time of the negligence will often be determinative. *Hotson* fell into the category where there was no significant uncertainty about what would have happened to the claimant's hip. The medical evidence was that, on a balance of probabilities (75:25), at the time of the negligent diagnosis, the hip was already doomed to develop a permanent disability. *Gregg v Scott* fell into the other category: "Identifying Mr Gregg's condition when he first visited Dr. Scott did not provide an answer to the crucial question of what would have happened if there had been no negligence. There was

chance of getting better? Is this another example of the law being kinder to the medical profession than to other professionals?" Baroness Hale did not answer this question, other than to observe, somewhat cryptically, at [220], that: "There is not much difference between the money one expected to have and the money one expected to have a chance of having: it is all money. There is a difference between the leg one ought to have and the chance of keeping a leg which one ought to have." It is unclear why these differences should mean that the solicitor is held liable but the doctor is not.

336 [2005] UKHL 2; [2005] 2 A.C. 176 at [126].

337 [2005] UKHL 2; [2005] 2 A.C. 176 at [147].

338 [2005] UKHL 2; [2005] 2 A.C. 176 at [169]. See also *Bulled v McClure* [2006] EWHC 2444 (QB) where it was arguable that the claimant's prospects of survival had increased by the date of the trial to more than 50 per cent (though the claimant also failed to establish breach of duty).

considerable medical uncertainty about what the outcome would have been had Mr Gregg received appropriate treatment nine months earlier."[339] As with the economic "loss of chance" cases, Lord Nicholls considered that Mr Gregg's prospects of recovery, expressed in percentage terms of the likelihood, represented the medical reality of his position so far as medical knowledge was concerned. The law should be slow to disregard medical reality in the context of a legal duty whose very aim was to protect medical reality, given that the doctor's duty was to maximise the patient's prospects of recovery, whether those prospects were good or poor.[340] Lord Hope also distinguished the position in *Hotson*, because the fundamental question of fact to be answered in *Hotson* related to a point in time before the negligent failure to treat began, and therefore was to be treated as a matter of past fact. In *Gregg* the injury which affected the claimant's prospects of recovery (the enlargement of the tumour) still lay in the future when he was seen by the doctor.[341] His Lordship also distinguished *Gregg* from a claim for compensation for a disease from which the claimant does not presently suffer, and with which it is probable that he will never be afflicted (e.g. where the claimant has been exposed to a toxic agent which could produce illness in the future). The claim that there is an increased risk of contracting the disease would be regarded as too speculative.[342]

Despite upholding the judge's conclusion on the facts, Lord Phillips also appeared to contemplate that, in an appropriate case, a claim for loss of a chance could be appropriate. His Lordship could "envisage the application of this approach once the adverse outcome, which the exercise of due care might have averted, has occurred. I find it less easy to see the basis on which the claim is established where the adverse outcome is still prospective".[343] The factual complications of *Gregg*, and the fact that Mr Gregg was still alive, meant that the case was "not a suitable vehicle for introducing into the law of clinical negligence the right to recover damages for the loss of a chance of a cure. Awarding damages for the reduction of the prospect of a cure, when the long term result of treatment is still uncertain, is not a satisfactory exercise. Where medical treatment has resulted in an adverse outcome and negligence has increased the chance of that outcome, *there may be a case for permitting a recovery of damages that is proportionate to the increase in the chance of the adverse outcome*."[344] It would seem that for Lord Phillips it was not so much 2-97

339 [2005] UKHL 2; [2005] 2 A.C. 176 at [38], per Lord Nicholls.

340 [2005] UKHL 2; [2005] 2 A.C. 176 at [42].

341 [2005] UKHL 2; [2005] 2 A.C. 176 at [109].

342 [2005] UKHL 2; [2005] 2 A.C. 176 at [118]. Thus, there would be no claim for proportionate damages based on the risk that the disease itself might materialise. Where, as a result of the defendant's negligence, there is a risk that at some point in the future the claimant will suffer physical injury and death, and the claimant foreseeably develops a psychiatric condition as a result of this knowledge there will be a claim in respect of the psychiatric reaction: *CJD Litigation: Group B Plaintiffs v Medical Research Council* (1997), [2000] Lloyd's Rep. Med. 161; (1997) 41 B.M.L.R. 157. See O'Sullivan, "Liability for Fear of the onset of future Medical Conditions" (1999) 15 P.N. 96. cf. *Rothwell v Chemical & Insulating Co Ltd* [2007] UKHL 39; [2008] 1 A.C. 281; para.7-97 (no liability for claimant's psychiatric reaction to knowledge that he has been exposed to asbestos and that therefore there is a risk that he may develop cancer and die; such a psychiatric reaction was not foreseeable in an individual of reasonable fortitude).

343 [2005] UKHL 2; [2005] 2 A.C. 176 at [188].

344 [2005] UKHL 2; [2005] 2 A.C. 176 at [190] (emphasis added). See also Lord Neuberger's extra-judicial comments on *Gregg v Scott*, "Loss of a Chance and Causation" (2008) 24 P.N. 212: "The questions which should have been asked were: what was the claimant's life expectancy without the treatment, and by how much would that expectancy have been increased if he had had the treatment.

the principle of awarding damages for loss of chance that concerned him, but the problem of identifying whether the claimant had actually lost anything.

2-98 It will be recalled that in *Barker v Corus (UK) Plc*[345] the House of Lords held that claims to compensation in a case such as *Fairchild v Glenhaven Funeral Services Ltd*[346] are based on the defendants' respective contributions to the *risk* of developing harm, and not the harm itself. The defendants were liable in proportion to the "chance" that their breach of duty had caused the claimants' mesothelioma. Lord Hoffmann said that the reason why the majority in *Gregg v Scott* had concluded that Mr. Gregg could not claim that the damage he suffered was the increased chance of a premature death which had been caused by the delay in diagnosis was *not* because "there was some conceptual objection to treating the diminution in the chances of a favourable outcome or (putting the same thing in a different way) the increase in the risk of an unfavourable outcome as actionable damage", but rather that "the adoption of such a rule in *Gregg v Scott* would in effect have extended the *Fairchild* exception to all cases of medical negligence, if not beyond, and would have been inconsistent with *Wilsher*".[347] However, in reality there were two factual differences between *Barker v Corus* and *Gregg v Scott*. First, the damage which the defendant's breach of duty had contributed to the risk of occurring had materialised in *Barker* (as in *Fairchild*), whereas Mr. Gregg was still alive and so the risk of the damage materialising remained prospective. Secondly, in *Gregg v Scott* the breach of duty consisted of an omission to take steps to reduce the risk of the harm eventuating, whereas in *Barker* (and *Fairchild*) the defendants' breach of duty created/added to the risk of the claimants developing mesothelioma. The second distinction is irrelevant, since it is a distinction between an omission and a positive act, and in the context of the doctor-patient relationship an omission to act to prevent harm can be just as culpable as positively causing harm. The first distinction would exclude Mr. Gregg from a claim for loss of a chance (just as Lord Phillips' analysis did). But if Mr. Gregg had died before the appeal hearing in the House of Lords, it would be difficult to point to a meaningful distinction between *Gregg v Scott* and *Barker v Corus*. The fact that the cancer that created a risk of premature death was an "innocent" cause and that the delayed diagnosis which increased that risk of premature death was a "guilty" cause is irrelevant, since it is clear that

---

Your life expectancy is the age which you have a 50% prospect of reaching: you have a less than 50% chance of living any longer and a better than 50% chance of living to any earlier date. So, if the claimant's life expectancy was 43, but would have been 47 if he had had the treatment, one can say that, on the balance of probabilities, he lost 4 years of life. He would have had a 50% chance of living to 47 but, as it is, he only has a 50% chance of living to 43." Lord Neuberger suggested that if the claimant had put his case in this way, "it may well be that at least one of the three in the majority, possibly Lord Hoffmann or Baroness Hale, would have changed sides". In *Wright (A Child) v Cambridge Medical Group* [2011] EWCA Civ 669; [2013] Q.B. 312 at [80]–[84] Lord Neuberger MR returned to the issue, pointing out that *Gregg v Scott* (unlike *Wright*) did not turn upon what a third party would hypothetically have done but for the defendant's negligence (which was the basis of the Court of Appeal's approach in *Allied Maples Group Ltd v Simmons & Simmons* [1995] 1 W.L.R. 1602). Nonetheless, although the reasoning of the House of Lords in *Gregg* did "not conclusively shut out, as a matter of strict logic, this court from applying a loss of a chance approach in this case" his Lordship considered that the Court of Appeal should not expand the loss of a chance doctrine into the realm of clinical negligence, though "the question would be appropriate for reconsideration by the Supreme Court" (at [84]). See also per Elias LJ at [93].

345 [2006] UKHL 20; [2006] 2 A.C. 572.

346 [2002] UKHL 22; [2003] 1 A.C. 32 (claimant develops mesothelioma due to exposure to asbestos but due to scientific uncertainty it is impossible to identify which of the defendants is responsible).

347 [2006] UKHL 20; [2006] 2 A.C. 572 at [39].

Fairchild can apply where there are both innocent and guilty causes.[348] Lord Hoffmann's observation that *Fairchild* is a narrow exception to the usual rules of establishing causation may be true, but it does not explain why *Gregg v Scott* is not also an exception. The distinction is entirely pragmatic, i.e. to avoid creating a wider range of potentially successful claims for medical negligence, whereas the purpose of adopting a causation test based on a defendant's proportionate contribution to the risk of developing mesothelioma in *Barker v Corus* was precisely the opposite (i.e. it was designed to reduce defendants' potential liability in a case where the *Fairchild* principle applied).[349]

Conclusion On this basis, it is arguable that a claimant in a medical negligence action could claim for loss of a chance of a better medical outcome where: (1) there was significant medical uncertainty about the outcome at the time of the alleged negligence (Lord Nicholls); (2) the injury which affected the claimant's prospects lay in the future at the time of the alleged negligence[350] (Lord Hope); and (3) the outcome is known (Lord Phillips).[351] In some respects, and notwithstanding their Lordships' approval of the outcome of *Gregg v Scott* in *Barker v Corus*, it is arguable that *Barker* supports this view. It has been held at first instance, however, that a claim based on loss of a chance is not appropriate in the context of an action in respect of a defective product under s.3 of the Consumer Protection Act 1987.[352] **2-99**

4. CAUSATION IN LAW

Factual causation is an explanatory inquiry—how in fact did the damage occur? The normal rule is that the defendant's wrongdoing must be shown to be a necessary condition for the occurrence of the claimant's damage, though that rule **2-100**

---

348 See para.2-64.

349 See also Burrows, "Uncertainty about Uncertainty: Damages for Loss of a Chance" [2008] J.P.I.L. 31 who also argues that *Gregg v Scott* involves unexpressed policy concerns to limit claims against medical professionals; and that the "control" mechanisms in *Barker* for limiting claims for loss of chance are: (1) that the damage should have actually materialised; and (2) that the damage must be caused by a single causative agent (as opposed to a multiple causative agent such as occurred in *Wilsher v Essex* [1988] A.C. 1074). Professor Burrows concludes (rightly, it is suggested) that *Gregg v Scott* is a single causative agent case. On this view, if Mr. Gregg had died there would be no material difference between *Gregg v Scott* and *Barker v Corus* (where the mesothelioma had materialised).

350 Query whether this is effectively the same condition as (1)?

351 Baroness Hale also seemed to contemplate, at [207], that a modest claim for reduction of life expectancy could arise where the delay in starting treatment had shortened the claimant's life expectancy compared to patients in the claimant's position who received prompt treatment, even if with prompt treatment the patient would probably have died. This involves comparing the median life expectancy of that population of patients and considering to what extent the delayed diagnosis has reduced the claimant's life expectancy. On this basis the claimant would be entitled to compensation for that shortening of his (already inevitably shortened) life. Lord Neuberger has supported this approach, extra-judicially: "Implications of Tort Law decisions", Address to Northern Ireland Personal Injury Bar's Inaugural Conference, 13 May 2017, para.17 (available at *www.supremecourt.uk/docs/speech-170513.pdf* [Accessed 1 April 2020]). His Lordship also considered that *Gregg v Scott* may be capable of being explained by reference to "the principle that if you ask a silly question you get a silly answer", pointing out that there was no logical ground for basing the claim on ten years' survival other than that the expert medical evidence was that patients are deemed to be "cured" once they have been in remission for ten years. If a different period was used ("why ten and not five or twenty?") the survival statistics would probably have been different, possibly leading to a different legal outcome.

352 *A v The National Blood Authority* [2001] 3 All E.R. 289 at [176]–[180], per Burton J.

(the "but for" test) is sometimes relaxed to enable a claimant to overcome the causation hurdle when it might otherwise seem unjust to require the claimant to prove the impossible. The outcome of the explanatory inquiry may, but will not necessarily, indicate where *responsibility* for causing the damage should be attributed. Sometimes it is apparent that the defendant's wrongdoing was a necessary condition, but there were also other events without which the damage would not have occurred. The court may then have to make a choice as to whether the defendant's wrongdoing is to be treated as having causative relevance, or whether the other causes, without which the damage would also not have occurred, effectively supersede the causative potency of the defendant's wrongdoing.[353] Although there are occasions when policy judgments have to made in respect factual causation, the selection of which of several causes is to be treated as the cause in law of the damage patently involves policy judgments about attributing responsibility. Common sense may be said to be the starting point,[354] but as Lord Hoffmann has pointed out "one cannot give a commonsense answer to a question of causation for the purpose of attributing responsibility under some rule without knowing the purpose and scope of the rule",[355] and "the purpose and scope of the rule" inevitably involves an element of policy judgment. Ultimately, the court has to determine what damage the defendant should be held responsible for. In *Rahman v Arearose Ltd*[356] Laws LJ commented that:

> "Once it is recognised that the first principle is that every tortfeasor should compensate the injured claimant in respect of that loss and damage for which he should justly be held responsible, the metaphysics of causation can be kept in their proper place: of themselves they offered in any event no hope of a solution of the problems which confront the courts in this and other areas. The law has dug no deeper in the philosophical thickets of causation than to distinguish between a *causa sine qua non* and a *causa causans*. The latter is an empty tautology. The former proves everything, and therefore nothing: if A kills B by stabbing him, the birth of either of them 30 years before is as much a *causa sine qua non* of the death as is the wielding of the knife. So the law makes appeal to the notion of a proximate cause; but how proximate does it have to be? As a concept, it tells one nothing. So in all these cases the real question is, what is the damage for which the defendant under consideration should be held responsible."

2-101 **Selection of the predominant cause** Although it is not necessary for the court to alight upon a single event as the sole legal cause, where a combination of causes produces the claimant's damage there is a tendency to attempt to select the predominant cause or causes. In *Stapley v Gypsum Mines*,[357] Lord Reid observed that:

> "One may find that as a matter of history several people have been at fault and that if any one of them had acted properly the accident would not have happened, but that does not mean that the accident must be regarded as having been caused by the faults of all of them. One must discriminate between those faults which must be discarded as being too remote

353 "Two causes may both be necessary preconditions of a particular result—damage to X—yet the one may, if the facts justify that conclusion, be treated as the real, substantial, direct or effective cause, and the other dismissed as at best a causa sine qua non and ignored for the purposes of legal liability": *Stapley v Gypsum Mines Ltd* [1953] A.C. 663 at 687, per Lord Asquith.

354 *Cork v Kirby MacLean Ltd* [1952] 2 All E.R. 402 at 407; *Yorkshire Dale Steamship Co Ltd v Minister of War Transport* [1942] A.C. 691 at 706, per Lord Wright.

355 *Environment Agency v Empress Car Co (Abertillery) Ltd* [1999] 2 A.C. 22 at 31.

356 [2001] Q.B. 351 at [32]–[33].

357 [1953] A.C. 663 at 681. See also *Norris v William Moss & Sons Ltd* [1954] 1 W.L.R. 346 at 351.

> and those which must not. Sometimes it is proper to discard all but one and to regard that one as the sole cause, but in other cases it is proper to regard two or more as having jointly caused the accident. I doubt whether any test can be applied generally."

In *Stapley*, two miners, neither senior to his colleague, were instructed to bring down a dangerous part of the roof where they were working. Both men understood that they were not to resume work until this was done. The attempt was unsuccessful and the two men nonetheless jointly decided to resume work. The roof did fall and the claimant's husband was killed. The trial judge held both men caused the accident entitling the dead man's widow to 50 per cent of full compensation. The Court of Appeal reversed his judgment finding the deceased was substantially responsible for his own demise. The House of Lords, by a bare majority, restored the trial judge's finding on causation. The dead man, they concluded, would not have gone ahead with the dangerous enterprise of resuming work beneath the unsafe roof without the support and co-operation of his workmate. Their Lordships disagreed with the trial judge on apportionment though, finding the deceased 80 per cent to blame and his companion 20 per cent only. Similar reasoning on causation in the case of a joint enterprise was applied by the House of Lords in *Imperial Chemical Industries Ltd v Shatwell*.[358] Once again their Lordships ultimately found that the fatal accident would not have happened without the agreement of the deceased's fellow-worker. However, while confirming *Stapley* on causation, in *Shatwell* the action failed on the basis of a successful defence of volenti non fit injuria.[359]

In *Stapley* and *Shatwell* judgments concerning the "responsible" causes of the relevant injury rested largely on common-sense analysis of the events leading up to the crucial accident.[360] Did the disputed cause have any significant effect? Was the conduct of the person for whom the defendants were vicariously liable such that **2-102**

---

358 [1965] A.C. 656 at 670–671, 679–680, 685 and 690–691.

359 See para.3-129.

360 "The interpretation to be applied does not involve any metaphysical or scientific view of causation. Most results are brought about by a combination of causes, and the search for 'the cause' involves a selection of the governing explanation in each case", per Viscount Simon LC in *Yorkshire Dale Steamship Co Ltd v Minister of War Transport* [1942] A.C. 691 at 698. See also *Galoo Ltd v Bright Grahame Murray* [1994] 1 W.L.R. 1360 at 1374, where the claimants alleged that the defendants had been negligent in auditing the accounts of a company. The accounts failed to show that the company was insolvent as a result of which the company continued to trade and thereby incurred trading losses. Glidewell LJ held that in deciding whether the defendant's breach of duty was the effective or dominant cause of the claimant's loss, as opposed to merely providing the occasion for the loss, the court should make a common sense judgment (applying the approach of the High Court of Australia in *March v E & MH Stramare Pty Ltd* (1991) 99 A.L.R. 423). Continuing to trade may or may not lead to losses, depending upon whether the company traded profitably or not, and, on a common-sense basis, the defendant's negligence could not be said to have caused the claimant's trading losses. cf. *Young v Purdy* [1997] P.N.L.R. 130, 138 where Leggatt LJ said that he found the test of judicial common sense in *Galoo* "an unsure guide in seeking to ascertain whether a particular breach of duty of care which results in loss is to be regarded in law as having caused it". See further *Sasea Finance Ltd v KPMG* [2000] 1 All E.R. 676 at 683 where the Court of Appeal distinguished *Galoo* on the facts, on the basis that where accountants had a duty to inform the claimants of major fraud on the company being perpetrated by a senior employee the failure to give a warning could be a cause of the continuing losses rather than merely providing the opportunity for those losses to arise. In *Saddington v Colleys Professional Services*, (1995) [1999] Lloyd's Rep. P.N. 140 CA an overvaluation of a property resulting in a mortgage advance did not cause a loss to the borrower when the money was invested in a business which subsequently failed. It merely provided the opportunity for the loss to occur. *Saddington* was applied in *Moore v Zerfahs* [1999] Lloyd's Rep. P.N. 144 CA.

it was proper to find him responsible for the injury to his colleague? Clearly in answering that second question an element of policy enters the equation. That element of policy may on occasion be expressed much more overtly. In *Rouse v Squires*,[361] it was held that the prior negligence of a lorry driver who skidded and obstructed the motorway continued to be an operative cause, and contributed to a subsequent accident when another driver failed to see the obstruction in dark, frosty conditions, and skidded, killing the claimant. Cairns LJ[362] suggested that:

> "If a driver so negligently manages his vehicle as to cause it to obstruct the highway and constitute a danger to other road users, including those who are driving too fast or not keeping a proper lookout, but not those who deliberately or recklessly drive into the obstruction, then the first driver's negligence may be held to have contributed to the causation of an accident of which the immediate cause was the negligent driving of the vehicle which because of the presence of the obstruction collides with it or with some other vehicle or some other person."

In *Wright v Lodge*,[363] the Court of Appeal relied on that dictum to exculpate the claimant from responsibility for her own carelessness in not pushing her car off the nearside of a dual carriageway after a breakdown. The defendant's subsequent reckless driving was found to be the substantive cause of the ensuing collision. As a matter of policy, it seems, deliberate or reckless conduct may eclipse an act of prior negligence, albeit "but for" that prior negligence the relevant damage would not have occurred.[364]

(a) Successive sufficient causes

2-103 Where there are two simultaneous, independent events, each of which would have been sufficient to cause the damage, the "but for" test produces the patently absurd conclusion that neither was a cause.[365] The only sensible solution here is to say that both caused the damage.[366] Where the two events are separated in time, the simple answer is that the first event should be treated as the cause. This is normally the case where both events are tortious, but where one of the events is not a tort a different rule applies.

---

361 [1973] 1 Q.B. 889; cf. *Knightley v Johns* [1982] 1 W.L.R. 349, where a subsequent act of negligence by a police officer was held to break the causal link between the claimant's damage and the initial negligence of a motorist.

362 [1973] 1 Q.B. 889 at 898.

363 [1993] 4 All E.R. 299.

364 Complex situations can arise where vehicles or vessels are involved in successive collisions. Each case is largely particular to its own facts but see generally *Fitzgerald v Lane* [1987] Q.B. 781 CA; [1989] A.C. 328 HL; *Miraflores (Owners) v George Livanos (Owners)* [1967] 1 A.C. 826; *The Calliope* [1970] P. 172; *The San Onofre* [1922] P. 243; *SS Singleton Abbey v SS Paludina* [1927] A.C. 16.

365 The classic illustration is that of two fires started simultaneously by A and B, each of which spreads to C's house. But for A's act, would the house have been destroyed? Yes, because B's fire would have destroyed it. Therefore A's fire is not a "but for" cause. But the same reasoning applies to B's fire, and therefore one can show that B's fire was not a "but for" cause.

366 See *Kuwait Airways Corp v Iraq Airways Co* [2002] UKHL 19; [2002] 2 A.C. 883 at [74], per Lord Nicholls: "In this type of case, involving multiple wrongdoers, the court may treat wrongful conduct as having sufficient causal connection with the loss for the purpose of attracting responsibility even though the simple 'but for' test is not satisfied. In so deciding the court is primarily making a value judgment on responsibility."

(i) Successive torts

In *Performance Cars Ltd v Abraham*,[367] D1 collided with the claimants' car causing damage which required that the whole of the lower part of the bodywork be resprayed. Before this could be done D2 collided with the car in such a way that, had there been no earlier collision, the whole of the lower part of the bodywork would have to be resprayed. Judgment against D1 remained unsatisfied so the claimants sought to recover the whole cost of the respray from D2. It was held this was not recoverable. D2 was only responsible for the additional damage inflicted on an already damaged vehicle. The need for a total respray arose not from the act of D2, but from the antecedent and independent act of D1. This conclusion reflects a wider principle that, normally, a defendant "must take his victim as he finds him". The principle may work to the claimant's advantage in some cases,[368] but it can also work to a defendant's advantage, so that where a tortfeasor damages an already damaged item of property or injures a claimant who is already disabled, he is only liable for the *additional damage* that he has caused. **2-104**

In *Baker v Willoughby*,[369] the defendant negligently damaged the claimant's leg in a road traffic accident, significantly affecting his mobility. Before the case came to court the claimant was shot in the same leg in a robbery and the leg had to be amputated. The defendant argued that his responsibility was limited to the loss caused by the original injury up to the date of the robbery—the amputation submerged or obliterated the original injury. The loss occasioned thereafter derived from the loss of the leg altogether and that was the responsibility of the robbers. The House of Lords held that the defendant was liable for all the consequences of the original injury, as if the second incident had never occurred. To find otherwise would be an injustice to the claimant for (even if the robbers could be sued) they would be held liable only for the additional damage inflicted on an already damaged leg (applying *Performance Cars Ltd v Abraham*). After the shooting the claimant would have gone uncompensated for the difference between a "sound" and a "damaged" leg,[370] i.e. that part of his disability caused by the initial accident. The House of Lords considered that he should not be allowed to fall between two tortfeasors. In this type of situation the "but for" test does not assist because it demonstrates that from the date of the shooting neither tortfeasor caused the loss. But for the negligence of the motorist would Mr Baker have sustained a loss due to a damaged leg after the shooting? The answer is yes, because the leg would have been damaged by the shooting, and therefore the initial negligence is not a "but for" cause after the shooting. Similarly, but for the shooting would Mr Baker have continued to have a damaged leg? The answer is also yes, because absent the robbery the leg would still have been damaged as a result of the accident, and therefore the shooting is also not a "but for" cause of the disability which already existed when he was shot (though clearly it did cause the additional damage). A test which produces the conclusion that neither tortfeasor caused the harm cannot be of any assistance in a situation where simple common sense indicates that one or both of them should be responsible.[371] Applying a causation test to two consecutive torts, the initial tortfeasor continues to be responsible for any ongoing damage or dis- **2-105**

---

[367] [1962] 1 Q.B. 33.
[368] See para.2-170.
[369] [1970] A.C. 467; see McGregor (1970) 22 M.L.R. 378; Strachan (1970) 33 M.L.R. 386.
[370] [1970] A.C. 467 at 492–495.
[371] An alternative solution to this problem is that adopted by the Court of Appeal in *Baker v Wil-*

ability attributable to his tort, and the second tortfeasor is responsible only for the additional damage caused by the second tort.

(ii) Supervening non-tortious events

2-106 Where the subsequent supervening event is non-tortious the courts apply a different test. If the supervening event is a sufficient cause, i.e. it would have been sufficient in itself to cause the loss, the causative effect of the initial tort is treated as spent or obliterated. In *Carslogie SS Co Ltd v Royal Norwegian Government*[372] the defendant's vessel negligently inflicted substantial damage on the claimant's ship. Temporary repairs restored the ship to seaworthiness and she set sail for the US. The voyage to the US would not have taken place "but for" the original collision. Crossing the Atlantic, a heavy storm inflicted further damage to the ship. On reaching the US the damage caused by the collision was repaired at the same time as the storm damage. The total time for the repairs was 51 days. The collision damage alone would have taken 10 days. The House of Lords held that the claimant could not claim for the loss of use of the vessel for the 10 days attributable to the collision damage because the ship was in any event out of use at that time for the storm damage repairs. The defendants were not liable for the storm damage either, because this damage "was not in any sense a consequence of the collision, and must be treated as a supervening event occurring in the course of a normal voyage". The original collision was clearly a "but for" cause of the storm damage, in the sense that had the collision not occurred, the ship would not have been on the particular voyage in which the storm damage occurred. But the tort was merely part of the history of events that placed the ship in that place at that time, and this in itself is not a "cause" of harm that arises from some independent mechanism.[373] The storm damage was not within the risk created by the defendants' negligence.[374]

2-107 **Vicissitudes of life** In *Jobling v Associated Dairies Ltd*,[375] the facts were similar to *Baker v Willoughby*, except that the second supervening event was non-tortious. The House of Lords came to the same conclusion as in *Carslogie SS*, applying a "vicissitudes of life" test, rather than a causation test. The claimant suffered a back injury at work in 1973 for which his employers admitted liability. In 1976, the claimant succumbed to myelopathy, a condition rendering him totally unfit for work and unrelated to his original injury. The defendants were held liable only for the incapacity suffered by the claimant from 1973 to 1976 when supervening illness rendered him unable to work at all. This result was justified on the basis

---

loughby, namely that the second tortfeasor is liable for the whole loss, having caused the claimant to "lose" his right of action against the original wrongdoer. See *Griffiths v Commonwealth* (1985) 72 F.L.R. 260 at 273; and for comment on *Griffiths*, see Hudson (1987) 38 N.I.L.Q. 190.

372 [1952] A.C. 292.

373 There are many "but for" causes of damage that are treated as having no legal significance. So, if the pedestrian run down by a negligent motorist on a zebra crossing had not chosen to cross the road at that point, at that time, the accident would not have happened, just as it would not have happened if the pedestrian had decided to stay in bed all day. The pedestrian's decision to get out of bed that morning, or to cross the road on the zebra crossing, is not legally relevant, but simply part of the history events.

374 Contrast the position where collision damage rendered the ship more susceptible to storm damage, if a storm should occur. In that situation, the tortfeasor may be responsible for the additional damage attributable to the ship's susceptibility to damage. See, e.g. *Wieland v Cyril Lord Carpets Ltd* [1969] 3 All E.R. 1006.

375 [1982] A.C. 794; see Evans (1982) 45 M.L.R. 329; Hervey (1981) 97 L.Q.R. 210.

that when assessing damages for future loss of earnings the award is discounted to reflect the possibility that other contingencies might, in any event, have reduced the claimant's earning capacity or working life. A subsequent illness is one of these "vicissitudes of life", and, applying the principle that the court will not speculate about future events when the facts are known, the illness must be taken into account. The defendant should not be held responsible for a loss which, in any event, would have overtaken the claimant. The subsequent imprisonment of the claimant due to the commission of a criminal offence by the claimant is also a vicissitude of life that should not be disregarded when considering the effects of the tort on the claimant's earning capacity. Thus, the claimant's loss of earning capacity during his imprisonment will be attributed to his incarceration rather than the tort.[376]

Their Lordships in *Jobling* were critical of *Baker v Willoughby*, but much of the criticism was unjustified. For example, Lords Wilberforce and Edmund-Davies suggested that if the claimant had received an award from the Criminal Injuries Compensation Board in respect of the shooting he would have been over-compensated. But since at that time the CICB assessed an award on a similar basis to an award of damages in tort any award would have taken account of the claimant's existing disability, so there would have been no double compensation. Lord Wilberforce observed that the interaction of damages awards and the social security system meant that there was no means of knowing whether the claimant in *Jobling* would be over-compensated if he were awarded damages for the period after 1976 or under-compensated if left to his benefit. This, unfortunately, is true of most other personal injury actions; it is not the basis of a distinction between the two cases. *Jobling v Associated Dairies* cannot be satisfactorily reconciled with *Baker v Willoughby*. Lords Russell[377] and Keith[378] distinguished between successive torts and tortious injury followed by the onset of disease, and in practical terms it would seem that *Baker v Willoughby* will apply where the supervening event is a tort, but that *Jobling v Associated Dairies Ltd* will apply where it is non-tortious. Looking at *Jobling* in terms of causation, there is little logical justification for the outcome. If the injury caused the claimant's partial disability, the illness could only have *caused* the additional loss, just as the tortfeasor who shot Mr Baker could only have *caused* the additional disability. Hypothetically, if Mr Baker had not injured his leg in the road traffic accident, and had then been shot, the whole of his disability would have been caused by the amputation as a result of the shooting. But we know that this is a hypothetical situation, and that what actually happened was that the first tortfeasor (Mr Willoughby) caused the initial disability, and the second tortfeasor (the robber) added to that disability. In terms of *causation*, precisely the same argument applied to Mr Jobling. The difference was that in *Jobling* their Lordships approached the problem as a question of quantum, and in assessing an award of damages for future loss the court will take into account the possibility of subsequent illness or disability unrelated to the tort.[379] 2-108

Conclusion The net result of the cases involving supervening events is that where 2-109

---

[376] See *Gray v Thames Trains Ltd* [2009] UKHL 33; [2009] 1 A.C. 1339, discussed at paras 3-17 to 3-19.

[377] [1982] A.C. 794 at 810.

[378] [1982] A.C. 794 at 815; but see Lord Bridge's rejection of the successive torts explanation at 819–821; and see Lord Edmund-Davies at 807.

[379] In *Rahman v Arearose Ltd* [2001] Q.B. 351 at [32]–[33], Laws LJ commented that: "Although the reasoning in *Jobling*'s case involved the raising of some judicial eyebrows as to the approach taken by the House in *Baker*'s case, with great respect I see no inconsistency whatever between the two cases." Note that where there is dispute about whether the second event is tortious, the court will be faced with the problem of deciding whether *Baker v Willoughby* or *Jobling v Associated Dairies*

there are successive sufficient causes of damage where both events are tortious, causal responsibility will be attributed to the first tort, but where one event is tortious and the other is non-tortious causal responsibility will be attributed to the non-tortious event, no matter in what order the events occur. If the first event is non-tortious, the tortfeasor is responsible only for the additional damage that the tort caused, and if the second event is non-tortious and would have caused the same loss as the tort, then applying *Carslogie SS Co Ltd v Royal Norwegian Government* and *Jobling v Associated Dairies* the non-tortious event is treated as supervening the damage caused by the tort.

(b) Intervening acts

2-110 **Definition** Where the defendant's conduct forms part of a sequence of events leading to harm to the claimant, and the act of another person, without which the damage would not have occurred, intervenes between the defendant's wrongful conduct and the damage, the court has to decide whether the defendant remains responsible or whether the act constitutes a novus actus interveniens, i.e. whether it can be regarded as breaking the causal connection between the wrong and the damage. The defendant's conduct may have satisfied the "but for" test, in the sense that without his wrongful conduct the damage would not have occurred. But this, in itself, is not determinative of whether he should be held responsible where other causally relevant events have played a role. Thus, in the majority of cases where a plea of novus actus succeeds, there will have been a prior finding that the original wrongdoing does indeed satisfy the "but for" test of factual causation. It is *a* cause of the damage. On grounds of equity and policy, the court then proceeds to find that in the light of subsequent events, the defendant should not be held answerable for consequences beyond his control.[380] A novus actus may take three forms:

(i) some natural event independent of any human agency;
(ii) an act (or omission) by a third party;
(iii) the conduct of the claimant himself.

Whatever its form the novus actus must constitute an event of such impact that it "obliterates" the wrongdoing of the defendant. There is no concept of an "intervening *contributory* event", i.e. an event that does not fully break the causal link between the "but for" cause and the damage, but merely contributes to the damage. If the second event is considered to be an intervening act, so breaking the causal link between the first event and the damage, then the first event is not regarded as a cause of the damage at all. But if the second event does not break the causal link, the first event remains a cause of damage for which the tortfeasor is fully responsible. There is no basis for apportioning the loss between the two events (subject to the tortfeasor's potential claim for contribution under the Civil Liability (Contribution) Act 1978 against another tortfeasor).[381]

2-111 Often the courts have to resort to metaphor and, again, "common sense". Did the

---

Ltd applies. Where the court is assessing damages for future loss of earnings and there is a chance that, had the claimant remained at work, he would have been the victim of a further tort which would have ended his career the damages should be discounted to reflect that chance (i.e. *Jobling* applies): *Heil v Rankin* [2001] P.I.Q.R. Q3 CA (claimant a police officer suffering from post-traumatic stress disorder).

380 See *Rouse v Squires* [1973] 1 Q.B. 889 at 898; *Wright v Lodge* [1993] 4 All E.R. 299 CA.

381 *Environment Agency v Ellis* [2008] EWCA Civ 1117; [2009] P.I.Q.R. P5; [2009] L.S. Law Med. 70;

intervening event "isolate", or "insulate" or "eclipse" the defendant's conduct so that it was merely the occasion of the harm rather than the cause of it? Was the intervening act "no mere conduit pipe through which consequences flow from [defendant to claimant], no mere part of a transmission gear set in motion by [the defendant]"?[382] The proliferation of expressions indicates that there is no simple test, and though common sense may point the way, the language of causation tends to obscure the evaluative nature of the decisions that the courts must inevitably make. There are two broad approaches, causation and fault. The causation approach asks whether the intervening act was reasonable in the circumstances, though in this context "reasonable" tends to refer to the voluntariness of the act, not whether it was careless. The more voluntary the act the less reasonable it is, and the more potent its causative effect. But even deliberate actions may be "involuntary", for example, where a person is forced to make a response to a situation brought about by the defendant's negligence. Careless behaviour is generally less potent causally than a deliberate act. The fault approach turns on the foreseeability of the intervention. Deliberate, and even criminal conduct, does not always amount to a novus actus, in circumstances where it was foreseeable. But this, in turn, will depend upon the nature of the defendant's duty. If the defendant was under a duty to prevent the very intervention that occurred he cannot complain that that intervention broke the causal link, since that would render the duty ineffective.[383] The conceptual link between causation and the duty of care can also work in the defendant's favour, so that the claim may fail where the scope of the defendant's duty does not extend to the particular form of loss sustained by the claimant. In such a case the claim will fail, not because of an intervening act, but rather because the damage does not fall within the losses contemplated by the defendant's duty. For example, in *Calvert v William Hill Credit Ltd*[384] the Court of Appeal distinguished *Reeves v Commissioner of Police for the Metropolis*[385] (where the causation issue was whether the deceased's suicide broke the chain of causation between the suicide and the breach of duty by the police). *Calvert* was not a case where the claimant's deliberate conduct (in continuing to gamble with the defendants after the defendants had undertaken to prevent him from gambling with them on the telephone for a period of six months) broke the chain of causation. Rather, the scope of the defendants' duty did not extend to preventing him from gambling in other ways, and in quantifying his loss the court could not ignore other gambling losses which the claimant would probably have sustained but for their breach of duty: "The law not only prescribes the appropriate causal connection, but also the scope of the duty and the scope of the loss which the causal connection links."

(i) *Acts of nature*

Act of nature Relatively rarely, an intervening natural event may operate to eclipse the defendant's wrongdoing as the effective cause of the damage suffered **2-112**

see para.2-39.

382 *Weld-Blundell v Stephens* [1920] A.C. 956 at 986, per Lord Sumner.

383 See *Reeves v Commissioner of Police for the Metropolis* [2000] 1 A.C. 360 at 367–368, per Lord Hoffmann.

384 [2008] EWCA Civ 1427; [2009] Ch. 330 at [48]; see para.2-188 fn.609.

385 [2000] 1 A.C. 360.

by the claimant.[386] In torts of strict liability, in particular *Rylands v Fletcher*, a natural novus actus may operate to relieve the defendant of liability.[387] In *Nichols v Marsland*,[388] extraordinary rainfall, unprecedented in that area, caused ornamental lakes to burst their embankments and flood adjoining land. It was held a defence of act of God applied.[389] Arguably, the defence of act of God is simply novus actus under another name.

2-113 The fact that a natural event was unforeseeable is not necessarily a basis for concluding that it constituted a novus actus interveniens. In *Humber Oil Terminal Trustee Ltd v Owners of the Ship "Sivand"; The Sivand*,[390] the *Sivand* negligently damaged the claimant's harbour installations. The claimant engaged contractors to carry out the repairs on standard terms, which provided for additional payment to the contractor if physical conditions were encountered which could not have been reasonably foreseen by an experienced contractor, adding to the cost of carrying out the repairs. The contractors lost a barge when the sea bed under one of the barge's legs collapsed. The contractors recovered this additional cost from the claimants under the terms of the contract, and the claimants then sought to recover that cost from the owners of the *Sivand*. The defendants argued that the unforeseen condition of the sea bed constituted an intervening event that broke the chain of causation between their admitted negligence and the additional loss sustained by the claimants. The Court of Appeal held that the defendants were liable for the additional sum. Although the collapse of the sea bed was unforeseeable it did not have the effect of breaking the chain of causation, unless it affected the claimant's duty to mitigate the loss. Since the claimant had acted entirely reasonably in engaging the contractors on standard terms they had not failed to mitigate their loss.

(ii) Intervening conduct of a third party

2-114 No precise or consistent test can be offered to define when the intervening conduct of a third party will constitute a novus actus interveniens sufficient to relieve the defendant of liability for his original wrongdoing. The question of the effect of a novus actus "can only be answered on a consideration of all the circumstances and, in particular, the quality of that later act or event".[391] Four issues need to be addressed. Was the intervening conduct of the third party such as to render the original wrongdoing merely a part of the history of events? Was the third party's conduct either deliberate or wholly unreasonable? Was the intervention foreseeable? Is the conduct of the third party wholly independent of the defendant, i.e. does the defendant owe the claimant any responsibility for the conduct of

---

386 See the discussion of *Carslogie SS Co Ltd v Royal Norwegian Government* [1952] A.C. 292, at para.2-106.

387 See para.19-93.

388 (1876) 2 Ex. D. 1; *Nichols v Marsland* has been much criticised on its facts but the principle seems sound; see para.19-93.

389 Act of God refers to events caused by the forces of nature "which no human foresight can provide against, and of which human prudence is not bound to recognise the possibility": *Tennent v Earl of Glasgow* (1864) 2 M. (HL) 22 at 26, per Lord Westbury.

390 [1998] 2 Lloyd's Rep. 97 CA.

391 *Hogan v Bentinck West Hartley Collieries (Owners) Ltd* [1949] 1 All E.R. 588 at 593, per Lord Simonds.

that intervening third party? In practice, in most cases of novus actus more than one of the above issues will have to be considered together.[392]

The impact of the intervening conduct In *The Oropesa*,[393] a collision occurred between the *Oropesa* and the *Manchester Regiment* caused by the negligent navigation of the *Oropesa*. The *Manchester Regiment* was badly damaged and her captain set out in a lifeboat to consult the captain of the *Oropesa* about salvaging his ship. The lifeboat capsized in heavy seas causing loss of life. The personal representatives of one of the drowned sailors sued the owners of the *Oropesa* in respect of his death. The defendants contended that the drowning resulted, not from the original negligence of the *Oropesa*, but from the decision of the captain of the *Manchester Regiment* to put to sea in the lifeboat. It was held that the action of the captain of the *Manchester Regiment* did not constitute a novus actus. His decision to put to sea might not be readily foreseeable, but was a reasonable response to the danger into which the *Oropesa* had catapulted his ship and his crew. The loss of the lifeboat and its men remained a consequence properly attributable to the initial wrongdoing. The captain's act did not eclipse that wrongdoing; it was not "ultroneous, something unwarrantable, a new cause which disturbs the sequence of events, something which can be described as either unreasonable or extraneous or extrinsic".[394] 2-115

Compare *The Oropesa* with *Knightley v Johns*.[395] The first defendant's admitted negligence caused the blockage of a tunnel. After considerable confusion, the second defendant, a police inspector, took charge. He did not immediately close the tunnel which should have been standard practice after such an accident. He later instructed the claimant, a police motorcyclist, to ride the wrong way back through the tunnel, against the traffic, to ensure that the tunnel was closed. While doing so, the claimant was hit and injured by the third defendant who was driving too fast into the tunnel. The Court of Appeal set aside a judgment for the claimant against the first defendant. The sequence of events subsequent to the original negligence eclipsed the defendant's wrongdoing: "too much happened here, too much went wrong, the chapter of accidents was too long and varied to impose on the first defendant liability."[396] 2-116

Deliberate or unreasonable conduct It may well be easier to establish a novus actus when the intervention of the third party is deliberate and intended. In 2-117

[392] This paragraph was considered at length by Aikens LJ in *Chubb Fire Ltd v Vicar of Spalding* [2010] EWCA Civ 981; [2010] 2 C.L.C. 277 at [68]–[73], a case where vandals had set off a fire extinguisher in a church, and the suppliers of the fire extinguisher had allegedly failed to advise the church about the respective cost of cleaning up the resultant mess associated with different types of extinguisher. His Lordship concluded that the problem of intervening acts is now considered in terms of whether it is "fair" to hold the defendants responsible: "the ultimate question is: what is the extent of the loss for which a defendant ought fairly or reasonably or justly to be held liable" (at [64]). The answer, on the facts, was that it was unfair to hold the suppliers of the fire extinguisher liable for the actions of the vandals. Arden and Longmore LJJ agreed that the action should fail on the basis that the church had not proved that it would have chosen a different option even if the correct advice had been given, but expressed no view on the question of intervening acts.

[393] [1943] P. 32; cf. *The Empire Squire* (1943) 169 L.T. 252.

[394] [1943] P. 32 at 39.

[395] [1982] 1 W.L.R. 349.

[396] [1982] 1 W.L.R. 349 at 367.

Dominion Natural Gas Ltd v Collins and Perkins,[397] Lord Dunedin said the defendants will not be liable "if the proximate cause of the accident is not the negligence of the defendant but the conscious act of another's volition". Lord Sumner in *Weld-Blundell v Stephens*[398] said: "In general even though A is in fault, he is not responsible for injury to C which B, a stranger to him, deliberately chooses to do. Though A may have given the occasion for B's mischievous activity, B then becomes a new and independent cause ... he insulates A from C." So if A commits a battery resulting in the claimant's admission to hospital, and then the claimant is subsequently assaulted by a hospital porter, A is not responsible for those subsequent injuries.[399] If the defendant accumulates non-natural substances on his property so as to fall within the rule in *Rylands v Fletcher*, he will not be liable if a complete stranger breaks into his property and engineers the escape of those substances.[400] However, the key word is stranger. The deliberate act may be shown to be that of a third party for whom in the circumstances the defendant bears responsibility.

2-118 The more unreasonable the conduct of the third party, the more likely that conduct is to constitute a novus actus. A defendant creating an obstruction on the road likely to trigger further accidents may normally expect to bear responsibility for the further consequences of his initial negligence. If a subsequent collision is caused by outright recklessness,[401] or total bungling by those involved in dealing with the first incident, the chain of causation may be broken.[402] However, this should not be taken to suggest that only deliberate or wholly unreasonable conduct can constitute novus actus. The intervention need not even be unlawful per se.[403] It is simply that the more flagrant and overwhelming the intervention the more likely it is to amount to a novus actus. The most that can be said is that deliberate interventions are more likely to break the chain of causation than negligent acts, negligent conduct is more likely to constitute a novus actus than non-negligent conduct, and positive acts are more likely to operate as novus actus than omissions.[404]

2-119 Even a criminal act by a third party will not necessarily constitute an intervening act,[405] though in these circumstances the issue will tend to shade into a ques-

---

397 [1909] A.C. 640 at 646.

398 [1920] A.C. 956 at 986.

399 Though there are some circumstances where negligence by A creates a greater foreseeable risk of further negligence by B than otherwise would be the case, e.g. where a doctor negligently records incorrect details in a patient's medical record it is foreseeable that later another doctor may negligently rely upon the accuracy of the record, in which case A may be partly responsible for the damage caused by B's negligence: see *Price v Milawski* (1977) 82 D.L.R. (3d) 130 Ontario CA; see also *Reeves v Carthy* [1984] I.R. 348 Supreme Court of Ireland; *Prendergast v Sam & Dee Ltd* [1989] 1 Med. L.R. 36 CA, a pharmacist's negligence in misreading a doctor's prescription, and supplying a patient with the wrong drug, did not break the chain of causation from the doctor's initial negligence in writing an illegible prescription.

400 e.g. *Perry v Kendricks Transport Co Ltd* [1956] 1 W.L.R. 85 CA.

401 *Wright v Lodge* [1993] 4 All E.R. 299; see para.2-102.

402 *Knightley v Johns* [1982] 1 W.L.R. 349; see para.2-116.

403 *SS Singleton Abbey v SS Paludina* [1927] A.C. 16 at 28.

404 *Knightley v Johns* [1982] 1 W.L.R. 349 at 365. See *Clarke v Crew* (1999) 149 N.L.J. 899 CA, for an example of negligent conduct that did not break the chain of causation (negligence by the prison service was foreseeable by the police when the police negligently gave the prison the wrong date of arrest, with the result that the claimant was detained longer than he should have been).

405 See *Marshall v Rubypoint Ltd* (1997) 29 H.L.R. 850 CA, where a landlord was found liable to his tenant in respect of a burglary, resulting in personal injuries and stolen property, since the state of the front door to the premises was found to be a substantial cause of the burglary.

tion of the nature of the defendant's duty.[406] *Environment Agency v Empress Car Co (Abertillery) Ltd*[407] concerned criminal liability for "causing" polluting matter to enter controlled waters contrary to the Water Resources Act 1991 s.85(1), where it was the act of an unknown person who had opened the tap of a diesel oil tank. Lord Hoffmann commented that:

> "These examples show that one cannot give a commonsense answer to a question of causation for the purpose of attributing responsibility under some rule without knowing the purpose and scope of the rule. Does the rule impose a duty which requires one to guard against, or makes one responsible for, the deliberate acts of third persons? If so, it will be correct to say, when loss is caused by the act of such a third person, that it was caused by the breach of duty … Before answering questions about causation, it is therefore first necessary to identify the scope of the relevant rule. This is not a question of common sense fact; it is a question of law. In *Stansbie v Troman*,[408] the law imposed a duty which included having to take precautions against burglars. Therefore breach of that duty caused the loss of the property stolen."[409]

Foreseeability of intervening conduct The foreseeability of the third party's intervening conduct is clearly relevant, but not conclusive to questions of novus actus. In *Knightley v Johns*,[410] the fact that the first defendant would not readily have contemplated such a string of foolish errors by the police called to deal with the obstruction created by his negligence was significant in concluding that there had been a novus actus. But the unforeseeability of events does not necessarily render intervening conduct a novus actus. In *The Oropesa*,[411] the captain's conduct in putting to sea was not readily foreseeable. In *Philco Radio and Television Corp of Great Britain Ltd v J Spurling Ltd*,[412] the defendants negligently delivered parcels of flammable film scrap to the claimant's premises. A typist touched one of the parcels with a lighted cigarette to pass the time by making a "small innocuous bonfire" having no idea that the substance was violently inflammable or explosive. The defendants were held liable for the explosion which seriously damaged the claimant's premises. Her act, although almost certainly unforeseeable, was not a novus actus. It was not so unreasonable, or of such overwhelming impact, as to obliterate the risk created by the defendants' original negligence.[413] 2-120

The mere fact that the intervening conduct was unforeseeable is not sufficient to render it a novus actus and nor does the mere foreseeability of the intervention impose liability for such conduct. In *Quinn v Burch Brothers (Builders) Ltd*,[414] Salmon LJ summed up the role of foreseeability: "the foreseeability test is a handmaiden of the law, it is by no means a maid-of-all-work. To my mind it cannot serve as the true criterion when the question is, how was the damage caused? It may be a useful guide, but it is by no means the true criterion." Suggestions by 2-121

406 See para.2-122.
407 [1999] 2 A.C. 22 HL.
408 [1948] 2 K.B. 48; see para.7-61.
409 [1999] 2 A.C. 22 at 31.
410 [1982] 1 W.L.R. 349 at 365–366.
411 [1943] P. 32; see para.2-115.
412 [1949] 2 All E.R. 882. Note the doubts expressed on the facts of the case by Jenkins LJ at 888.
413 Note that for the purpose of remoteness of damage the defendant does not have to foresee the precise manner in which the damage was caused where the accident is simply a variant on the foreseeable: see *Hughes v Lord Advocate* [1963] A.C. 837, at para.2-160.
414 [1966] 2 Q.B. 370 at 394.

Lord Reid in *Dorset Yacht Co v Home Office*[415] that the true test of novus actus was not whether the relevant intervention was "a mere foreseeable possibility" but was it "very likely or probable" should also be discounted. If intervening conduct is foreseeable, it is less likely to constitute a novus actus than unforeseeable conduct. The more likely the intervention the less likely it is to break the chain of causation. Foreseeability of any degree is not conclusive. The true question is whether the defendant should properly bear responsibility for the third party's intervention.

2-122 **Responsibility for the intervening party—the defendant's duty** When the original wrongdoing of the defendant provides an opportunity for separate and subsequent wrongdoing, the courts must determine whether the defendant can fairly be held responsible for the full consequences of the risk he created. The question is often essentially one of policy. In *Lamb v Camden LBC*,[416] the defendants carelessly broke a water-main outside the claimant's house. Escaping water undermined the foundations and caused subsidence making the house temporarily uninhabitable. Squatters moved into the house causing £30,000 worth of damage. The defendants were liable for the flood damage, but not for the damage caused by the squatters albeit they knew squatting was rife in that part of London. That was a risk against which the claimant could have insured, or taken more efforts to protect herself. The defendants had no right to enter and secure the building. Lord Denning consequently held that as a matter of policy the subsequent damage was too remote.[417] Watkin LJ[418] said: "I have the instinctive feeling that squatters' damage is too remote … although on the primary facts I, too, would regard the damage or something like it as reasonably foreseeable in these times." It is clear that judges are struggling to find appropriate principles when they have to resort to judicial instinct. The problem that *Lamb v Camden* produced was as much a product of the manner in which it was argued. The defendants were clearly responsible for the flood damage and therefore it was conceded that they owed a duty of care to the claimant. The question of liability for the damage caused by the squatters was then argued as question of "remoteness of damage" (not even as one of causation). It is submitted that *Lamb* was really a case concerned with the extent of the defendants' duty—or as Lord Denning put it: "who's responsibility was it to keep the squatters out?"[419] In *Perl v Camden LBC*,[420] on broadly similar facts the action was dealt with, and dismissed, in terms of the defendants' duty, although Oliver LJ suggested that "the question of the existence of duty and that of whether damage brought about by the act of a third party is too remote are simply two facets of the same problem."[421]

2-123 **Intervention by irresponsible third party** Intervening conduct by a third party

---

415 [1970] A.C. 1004 at 1030; criticised in *Smith v Littlewoods Organisation Ltd* [1987] A.C. 241 at 260–261; and in *Lamb v Camden LBC* [1981] Q.B. 625 at 644.

416 [1981] Q.B. 625 CA.

417 [1981] Q.B. 625 at 637; and see per Oliver LJ at 644.

418 [1981] Q.B. 625 at 647.

419 It does not follow, of course, that simply because a defendant owes a duty of care in the tort of negligence to avoid damage A, that he also owes a duty to avoid damage B so that the question of compensation for B has to be treated as an issue of remoteness of damage in the context of the claim for A. See, e.g. *Spartan Steel & Alloys Ltd v Martin & Co (Contractors) Ltd* [1973] 1 Q.B. 27 in the context of claims for pure economic loss.

420 [1984] Q.B. 342.

421 [1984] Q.B. 342 at 348. For discussion of some of the problems created by treating duty and remoteness as merely interchangeable mechanisms for dealing with the same issue see Kidner (1989) 9 L.S.

not responsible, or not fully responsible, for his actions will be much less likely to constitute a novus actus.[422] An act of a child is much less likely than an act of an adult to break the chain of causation, albeit the child may have acted deliberately and voluntarily. So where a mischievous boy started up a car[423] and when children stampeded a horse[424] there was no finding of novus actus interveniens. Similarly intervention by animals will not generally amount to a novus actus.[425]

Intervening medical treatment A problem arises when it is alleged that the effective cause of the claimant's injury was not the original wrongdoing but either inept or ill-advised medical treatment, or a refusal by the claimant to undergo effective and available medical treatment.[426] In *Hogan v Bentinck West Hartley Collieries (Owners) Ltd*,[427] a miner injured his thumb at work. He suffered from a congenital defect, an additional top joint to that thumb. Initial treatment failed to relieve his pain and part of the thumb including the "false" thumb was amputated leaving him able to do only light work. Evidence suggested that amputation, while a proper treatment for the congenital defect, was not the appropriate treatment for the injury to the thumb. The question which went to the House of Lords was whether the man's incapacity resulted from the original injury or the operation. By a majority of three to two it was held that the inappropriate treatment operated as a novus actus. Lord Reid dissented forcefully. He reluctantly accepted prior authority that intervening medical treatment could constitute a novus actus, but argued that only "grave lack of skill and care" could do so, and even then, only where it was abundantly clear that appropriate treatment would have averted the disability of which the claimant complains.[428] It is submitted that Lord Reid was correct, and that only medical treatment so grossly negligent as to be a completely inappropriate response to the injury inflicted by the defendant should operate to break the chain of causation.[429] 2-124

In *Rahman v Arearose Ltd*[430] the claimant was seriously assaulted by two black youths, causing an injury to his right eye. His employers were held liable in negligence for failing to take reasonable care to reduce the risk of such assaults. Subsequently, as a result of the negligence of a surgeon who conducted a bone graft, 2-125

1. The principles governing liability in negligence for the conduct of third parties are discussed at paras 7-60 to 7-68.

422 *Weld-Blundell v Stephens* [1920] A.C. 956 at 985.

423 *Martin v Stanborough* (1924) 41 T.L.R. 1.

424 *Haynes v Harwood* [1935] 1 K.B. 146; and see *Shiffman v Order of St John* (1936) 80 S.J. 341. In this situation the tendency is for the court to conclude that it was part and parcel of the defendant's duty to take care to prevent the very intervention that has occurred.

425 *Arneil v Paterson* [1931] A.C. 560; unless of such overwhelming impact as to constitute the equivalent of a supervening natural event, for example, D negligently leaves open a farmyard gate and a tiger escaped from the zoo gets into the yard and mauls the farmer.

426 For the claimant's refusal of medical treatment see para.2-135.

427 [1949] 1 All E.R. 588. The case involved a claim against his employers under the Workmen's Compensation Act 1925.

428 [1949] 1 All E.R. 588 at 607–608.

429 This proposition was approved by the Court of Appeal in *Webb v Barclays Bank plc and Portsmouth Hospitals NHS Trust* [2001] EWCA Civ 1141; [2002] P.I.Q.R. P8; [2001] Lloyd's Rep. Med. 500 at [55]. See further *Conley v Strain* [1988] I.R. 628; see also *Thompson v Toorenburgh* (1975) 50 D.L.R. (3d) 717, at para.2-128. In *Mitchell v Rahman* (2002) 209 D.L.R. (4th) 621 (Man. CA) it was held that negligent misdiagnosis of a dislocated shoulder following a road traffic accident broke the causal link between the accident and the permanent disability which the claimant developed, applying *Hogan v Bentinck West Hartley Collieries Ltd*.

430 [2001] Q.B. 351.

he was rendered blind in the right eye. In addition to the physical injuries, the claimant developed severe psychiatric consequences, including post-traumatic stress disorder, a severe depressive disorder, a specific phobia of Afro-Caribbean people, and enduring personality change. The psychiatric reaction was partly due to the assault and partly due to the loss of his eye, and the psychiatric evidence indicated that the post-traumatic stress disorder was due to the loss of the eye; the phobia was due to the assault and subsequent events; and the personality change was due to the synergistic interaction between the depression and the post-traumatic stress disorder. The Court of Appeal held that a second act of negligence did not necessarily break the causal link between an initial act of negligence and the subsequent damage. Laws LJ commented that:

> "it does not seem to me to be established as a rule of law that later negligence always extinguishes the causative potency of an earlier tort. Nor should it be. The law is that every tortfeasor should compensate the injured claimant in respect of that loss and damage for which he should justly be held responsible. To make that principle good, it is important that the elusive conception of causation should not be frozen into constricting rules. It is true that the idea of a supervening cause—*novus actus interveniens*—is generally deployed in cases where it is suggested that the first tortfeasor should bear responsibility for the effects of the second tort, and this is not such a case: [counsel for the hospital] accepts that the second defendants are solely responsible for the loss of the eye. However the spirit of *novus actus* rattles its chains at the suggestion that the first defendants should bear some responsibility, given that this is not a case of concurrent torts, for the continuing effects of the claimant's psychological damage after the loss of vision in the right eye."[431]

Nonetheless, once one had left behind:

> "the dogmas of *novus actus* and eggshell skulls, there is nothing in the way of a sensible finding that while the second defendants obviously (and exclusively) caused the right-eye blindness, thereafter each tort had its part to play in the claimant's suffering."[432]

2-126 Similarly, in *Webb v Barclays Bank Plc and Portsmouth Hospitals NHS Trust*[433] the claimant injured an already vulnerable knee in a fall at work for which her employers were responsible. The Court of Appeal held that the subsequent negligence of a surgeon in advising the claimant to undergo an above the knee amputation of her leg "did not eclipse the original wrongdoing". The employers were held liable for all the damage attributable to the fall, and 25 per cent of the damage attributable to the amputation. Thus, if the claimant acts reasonably in seeking or accepting treatment, negligence in carrying out the treatment is not necessarily a novus actus interveniens relieving the first tortfeasor from liability for the claimant's subsequent condition. The original injury can be regarded as carrying some risk that medical treatment might be negligently given.

---

431 [2001] Q.B. 351 at [29].

432 [2001] Q.B. 351 at [34]. For criticism of the court's approach in *Rahman v Arearose Ltd see Weir* [2001] C.L.J. 237.

433 [2001] EWCA Civ 1141; [2002] P.I.Q.R. P8; [2001] Lloyd's Rep. Med. 500. If subsequent medical negligence does not necessarily break the causal link, it will be even more difficult to establish a break in the chain of causation where the later medical treatment is not negligent: see *Horton v Evans* [2006] EWHC 2808 (QB); [2007] P.N.L.R. 17 (pharmacist who negligently failed to check the dosage of a prescription with the prescribing doctor held liable for the patient's adverse drug reaction, although another doctor had subsequently repeated the prescription relying only on the information on the label of the medication bottle and what he was told by the patient).

Hypothetical "intervening" medical treatment In *Wright (A Child) v Cambridge Medical Group*[434] a general practitioner negligently delayed referring the claimant to hospital by two days, and following negligent treatment by the hospital the patient developed a permanent disability in the hip. The general practitioner argued that the delay had not caused the loss because with appropriate treatment at the hospital the disability would have been avoided. The trial judge proceeded on the basis that even if the claimant had been referred promptly by the general practitioner it was probable that the hospital would have treated the claimant negligently on that hypothetical occasion also, so that the delay in referral had not caused the disability. The Court of Appeal held that, on the facts, the judge was not entitled to draw the inference that the hospital would probably have been negligent whenever the claimant had been referred.[435] However, Lord Neuberger MR went further, holding that this inference was not open to the judge as a matter of law. His Lordship derived this proposition from consideration of the statement of Lord Browne-Wilkinson in *Bolitho v City and Hackney Health Authority*[436] that a defendant cannot escape liability by saying that the damage would have occurred in any event because he would have committed some other breach of duty thereafter. Lord Neuberger MR suggested that one reason why this proposition is correct is that: **2-127**

> "by committing the breach of duty, the doctor has prevented the patient from the opportunity of being treated appropriately, and had the patient had that opportunity, she would have had a claim for the same damage against the doctor for the very negligence upon which the doctor is relying to avoid liability. In other words, if a negligent doctor contends that the damage would have occurred anyway, because he would have committed a subsequent act of negligence, the patient can say that, if that argument is correct, it gets the doctor nowhere: as a result of his breach of duty, the doctor has deprived her of the right to claim for damages for the subsequent (if notional) act of negligence."[437]

The same reasoning applied where the hypothetical negligence was not that of the defendant, but of a third party such as a hospital, so that:

> "in a case where a doctor has negligently failed to refer his patient to a hospital, and, as a consequence, she has lost the opportunity to be treated as she should have been by a hospital, the doctor cannot escape liability by establishing that the hospital would have negligently failed to treat the patient appropriately, even if he had promptly referred her. Even if the doctor established this, it would not enable him to escape liability, because, by negligently failing to refer the patient promptly, he deprived her of the opportunity to be treated properly by the hospital, and, if they had not treated her properly, that op-

434 [2011] EWCA Civ 669; [2013] Q.B. 312.

435 The claimant was admitted to hospital on a Friday. If she had been admitted on the preceding Wednesday (when she should have been referred) it was probable that she would have been seen by different doctors, including a consultant, and there was a "powerful case" for thinking that her treatment would have been significantly better (per Lord Neuberger MR at [72]; see also per Elias LJ at [91] and Smith LJ at [124]). The hospital was not involved in the litigation, which was a matter of some "regret and surprise" to Lord Neuberger MR (at [86]). On the face of it the trial judge's inference was pretty startling. It amounted to a finding that the hospital (or at least the paediatric unit to which the claimant was referred) was so incompetently run that it was always more likely than not to treat a patient negligently.

436 [1998] A.C. 232 at 240; para.2-24.

437 [2011] EWCA Civ 669; [2013] Q.B. 312 at [58].

portunity would be reflected by the fact that she would have been able to recover damages from them".[438]

Nor could it be said that the hospital's negligence had broken the chain of causation. The hospital's failure to treat the claimant properly "was not such an egregious event, in terms of the degree or unusualness of the negligence, or the period of time for which it lasted, to defeat or destroy the causative link between the defendants' negligence and the claimant's injury".[439]

2-128 **Intervening omissions** A dictum of Goff LJ in *Muirhead v Industrial Tank Specialities Ltd*[440] suggests that where the intervening conduct consists of a negligent failure to prevent damage caused by the defendant's wrong it may not constitute a novus actus,[441] although his Lordship did qualify this by adding that a negligent omission had no causative effect unless it was "a wholly independent cause of the damage, i.e. a novus actus interveniens". This approach was taken in the Canadian case of *Thompson v Toorenburgh*[442] where it was said that the failure to provide an actus interveniens which would have saved an accident victim's life was not the same as committing an actus interveniens that caused her death. The defendant who caused the initial accident was held liable for the death, despite the inadequacy of the medical treatment provided by the hospital.[443]

---

438 [2011] EWCA Civ 669; [2013] Q.B. 312 at [61]. See also per Elias LJ at [98]. This rationale, that the doctor cannot rely on the hypothetical later negligence of the hospital as excusing his own negligence, because the doctor has deprived the patient of the opportunity to sue the hospital is criticised by N. McBride and S. Steel, "Suing for the loss of a right to sue: why Wright is wrong" (2012) 28 P.N. 27.

439 [2011] EWCA Civ 669; [2013] Q.B. 312 at [37], per Lord Neuberger MR. Smith LJ thought that the case was "very close to the line", but agreed that the permanent damage to the hip suffered by the claimant was not too remote from the delay in referring her to hospital, the crucial point being that the delay shortened the period available to the hospital to provide effective treatment and increased the risk that the claimant would suffer permanent harm by reducing the margin of error available to the hospital. In those circumstances the general practitioner's breach of duty had an ongoing effect on events which was not completely wiped out by the hospital's failure to act correctly (at [131]–[132]). Elias LJ accepted that the concept of novus actus interveniens did not apply because it was foreseeable that the hospital doctors could be negligent from time to time; nor was the hospital's negligence so gross or egregious as to be treated as breaking the chain of causation (at [111]). However, Elias LJ dissented as to the outcome on the basis that the claimant's permanent disability did not fall within the scope of the general practitioner's duty (at [111]–[112]), sed quaere. For comment on *Wright* see N. McBride and S. Steel, "Suing for the loss of a right to sue: why Wright is wrong" (2012) 28 P.N. 27; J. McQuater [2011] J.P.I.L. C172; K. Amirthalingam, "Causation and the medical duty to refer" (2012) 128 L.Q.R. 208.

440 [1986] Q.B. 507 at 533.

441 cf. the distinction drawn between omissions and acts in *Knightley v Johns* [1982] 1 W.L.R. 349.

442 (1975) 50 D.L.R. (3d) 717 (British Columbia CA). Robertson JA said, at 721, that: "Mrs. Thompson would almost certainly have recovered if proper treatment had been applied speedily; the doctors failed to apply that treatment and so failed to save her life, but they did not cause her death. They failed to provide an *actus interveniens* that would have saved her life, but that is not the same as committing an *actus interveniens* that caused her death." Note, however, that the court was careful to avoid categorising the medical treatment as negligent, although on the facts it is difficult to see how the treatment could have been reasonable.

443 cf. *Commonwealth of Australia v Martin* (1985) 59 A.L.R. 439 (Fed. Ct of Australia) where M was injured in a road traffic accident and death was inevitable without proper corrective surgery. The medical treatment was performed negligently and M died four days later. It was held that both the negligent motorist and the negligent doctor had caused the death, and it was not necessary to show that the doctor's negligence constituted a novus actus interveniens before he could be held responsible.

(iii) *Intervening conduct of the claimant*

When the conduct of the claimant exacerbates or adds to the injuries of which he complains, that conduct will generally result in a reduction of his damages on grounds of contributory negligence, or failure in his duty to mitigate damage.[444] However it may be that the conduct of the claimant is so wholly unreasonable and/or of such overwhelming impact that that conduct eclipses the defendant's wrongdoing and constitutes a novus actus. His own conduct is found to be the effective cause of his injury.[445] In *McKew v Holland & Hannen & Cubitts (Scotland) Ltd*,[446] the claimant suffered an injury to his leg caused by the defendant's negligence. The injured leg tended to give way under him. Some days after the accident he went to inspect a flat and on leaving descended a steep stair with no handrail, ahead of his family, and holding a child by the hand. He lost control of his leg, fell and fractured his ankle. The House of Lords held that his folly in exposing himself to the danger posed by the staircase made his own conduct the sole cause of his subsequent injury. The courts will not be eager to find a claimant's response to injury, or her subsequent conduct unreasonable.[447] If a claimant, weakened by an initial injury, and exercising ordinary prudence in everyday life, suffers subsequent injury the defendant will normally be liable for that injury. In *Wieland v Cyril Lord Carpets Ltd*,[448] the defendants' negligence had resulted in neck injuries forcing the claimant to wear a surgical collar. This meant that she could not use her bifocal spectacles with her usual skill and she tripped and fell. The defendants were held liable for the further injuries caused by the fall. Such injuries were still within the risk created by the defendants rather than a result of danger to which she had deliberately or unreasonably exposed herself. **2-129**

Similarly, in *Spencer v Wincanton Holdings Ltd*[449] the claimant suffered an accident at work for which his employers were responsible. Three years later this resulted in him having an above the knee amputation of the right leg. The defendants did not dispute that they were responsible for the consequences of the amputation. Eight months later, whilst putting petrol in his car without using a prosthesis or his walking sticks the claimant fell and suffered further injury that resulted in him becoming wheelchair dependent. The question was whether the employers were responsible for the additional injuries sustained in the fall. The Court of Appeal held that the claimant's conduct did not constitute a novus actus interveniens and that the employers were responsible, though damages were reduced by one third for the claimant's contributory negligence. Sedley LJ had some difficulty with the approach adopted by Lord Reid in *McKew v Holland & Hannen & Cubitts (Scotland) Ltd*[450] where it was suggested that: "if the injured man acts unreasonably he cannot hold the defender liable for injury caused by his own unreasonable conduct. His unreasonable conduct is novus actus interveniens. The chain of causation has been broken and what follows must be regarded as caused **2-130**

---

444 See para.3-58.

445 In *Pitts v Hunt* [1991] 1 Q.B. 24 at 51, Beldam LJ noted that a 100 per cent reduction for contributory negligence was illogical. Such a finding necessarily implies that the claimant was solely responsible for the damage of which he complains.

446 [1969] 3 All E.R. 1621 HL; and see *The Flying Fish* (1865) 34 L.J.P.M.A. 113; *Rushton v Turner Bros* [1960] 1 W.L.R. 96; *The Pacific Concord* [1961] 1 W.L.R. 873.

447 See *Emeh v Kensington, Chelsea and Westminster AHA* [1985] Q.B. 1012.

448 [1969] 3 All E.R. 1006.

449 [2009] EWCA Civ 1404; [2010] P.I.Q.R. P8.

450 [1969] 3 All E.R. 1621 at 1623.

by his own conduct and not by the defender's fault or the disability caused by it." As Sedley LJ put it: "The difficulty with which this formulation presents trial courts is that 'unreasonable' is a protean adjective. Its nuances run from irrationality to simple incaution or unwisdom. It is helpful to locate its correct position on the scale of meanings by recalling that its purpose in this context is to determine the point at which the law regards a consequence as too remote."[451] His Lordship preferred a formulation based on "fairness".[452] Although fairness might be no more precise than reasonableness, what it did suggest was that:

> "a succession of consequences which in fact and in logic is infinite will be halted by the law when it becomes unfair to let it continue. In relation to tortious liability for personal injury, this point is reached when (though not only when) the claimant suffers a further injury which, while it would not have happened without the initial injury, has been in substance brought about by the claimant and not the tortfeasor."[453]

2-131 In the 19th edition of this text it was suggested that "for the claimant's subsequent conduct to be regarded as a novus actus interveniens it should be such as can be characterised as reckless or deliberate" and that "unreasonable conduct can be dealt with by a finding of contributory negligence." However, in *Spencer v Wincanton Holdings Ltd* the Court of Appeal did not accept that this formulation provided a helpful test. Sedley LJ was "uneasy about the importation of a formula ('recklessly or deliberately') from the field of criminal law, where recklessness is commonly equated with intent. Intent has no obvious bearing on contributory fault: an intentional act may be anything from a fault-free act to a novus actus interveniens, and between those poles anything from an act of gross recklessness to one of forgivable inadvertence."[454] Aikens LJ considered that: "The line between a set of facts which results in a finding of contributory negligence and a set of facts which results in a finding that the 'unreasonable conduct' of the claimant constitutes a novus actus interveniens is not, in my view, capable of precise definition. ... [E]ach case will depend on the facts and ... the court will have to apply a value judgment to the facts as found."[455] Mr Spencer's decision to attempt to put petrol in his car without using a prosthesis or his walking sticks could, of course, be variously described as

---

451 [2009] EWCA Civ 1404; [2010] P.I.Q.R. P8 at [11].

452 Citing Lord Bingham in *Corr v IBC Vehicles Ltd* [2008] UKHL 13; [2008] 1 A.C. 884 at [15]; see para.2-140.

453 [2009] EWCA Civ 1404; [2010] P.I.Q.R. P8 at [15]. See also *Dalling v R J Heale & Co Ltd* [2011] EWCA Civ 365 where the defendants' negligence resulted in a head injury to the claimant producing "executive dysfunction", which reduced his ability to control his excessive drinking. More than three years after the original accident the claimant fell whilst drunk and sustained a further head injury. The tort had impaired the claimant's ability to control his alcohol consumption so that the act of getting drunk was not a free and voluntary act. The Court of Appeal held that it was fair to hold the defendants partially responsible for the injuries attributable to the fall whilst the claimant was drunk. cf. *Smith v Youth Justice Board for England and Wales* [2010] EWCA Civ 99 where it was held that a custody officer at a secure training centre who was involved, with two other officers, in the death of a 15-year-old boy from the excessive use of force in applying a restraint technique could not claim damages against her employers in respect of post-traumatic stress disorder. Responsibility for the boy's death, and its effect on the claimant's mental health, lay with the claimant (along with the other officers): "It would be rightly regarded as unjust if she were to recover damages for its effect on her" (at [36] per Sedley LJ). The claim thus failed on the ground of causation. Sedley LJ (repeating the views he had expressed in *Spencer v Wincanton Holdings Ltd*) held that the causal effects of an event will come to an end "when it becomes unfair to let it continue".

454 [2009] EWCA Civ 1404; [2010] P.I.Q.R. P8 at [19].

455 Commenting on this in *Clay v TUI UK Ltd* [2018] EWCA Civ 1177; [2018] 4 All E.R. 672 at [28] Hamblen LJ said that: "Various considerations may, however, commonly be relevant. In a case

"intentional", "deliberate", "unreasonable", "negligent" or (as Sedley LJ put it) a "misjudgment". Arguably, none of these terms provides much assistance in deciding whether it was "fair" to hold the defendants responsible for the consequences of his fall. On the other hand, the way in which the court chooses to characterise the claimant's conduct, the value judgment that is brought to bear on the issue, is not unimportant in reaching a conclusion.[456] On this basis, it is suggested that where a defendant has been negligent and the claimant has also been negligent (or has made a "misjudgment") the power to apportion damages for contributory negligence provides a better solution in reaching a "fair" outcome than finding that the claimant's mistake breaks the chain of causation.[457]

For example, in *March v E & MH Stramare Pty Ltd*,[458] the defendant parked a truck across the centre line of a six-lane street, partially blocking the offside lane in each direction. The claimant motorist, who was intoxicated at the time, was injured when he collided with the stationary truck. The Supreme Court of South Australia held that the defendant's negligence did not cause the injuries, the negligence of the claimant being the "real cause". The High Court of Australia allowed the claimant's appeal on the basis that the defendant owed a duty of care to all road users, "including the inattentive and those whose faculties were impaired by alcohol". The claimant's negligence did not take him outside the class of persons 2-132

---

involving intervening conduct, these may include: (1) The extent to which the conduct was reasonably foreseeable in general, the more foreseeable it is, the less likely it is to be a novus actus interveniens. (2) The degree of unreasonableness of the conduct in general, the more unreasonable the conduct, the more likely it is to be a novus actus interveniens and a number of cases have stressed the need for a high degree of unreasonableness. (3) The extent to which it was voluntary and independent conduct in general, the more deliberate the act, the more informed it is and the greater the free choice involved, the more likely it is to be a novus actus interveniens." Contrasting the case with *Sayers v Harlow Urban DC* [1958] 1 W.L.R. 623, where the claimant, trapped in a public lavatory due to a faulty lock, was injured in attempting to escape from the toilet cubicle, Hamblen LJ observed, at [35], that in *Sayers* the court "considered it to be a case where the inconvenience was great and the danger slight; hence no novus actus interveniens. On the judge's findings, the present case was one of some inconvenience and the danger obvious and life threatening; hence a novus actus interveniens". The claimant in *Clay*, trapped on a balcony outside his hotel room due to a faulty lock, had attempted to climb to the balcony of an adjoining room and fell from the second storey. The Court of Appeal, Moylan LJ dissenting, upheld the judge's conclusion that the claimant's conduct was so unreasonable as to constitute a novus actus interveniens.

[456] So, e.g. it is hardly surprising when a court holds that the defendant is not responsible for a claimant's voluntary, deliberate and informed decision to use heroin. In *Wilson v Coulson* [2002] P.I.Q.R. P22 QBD, the claimant alleged that brain damage sustained in a road traffic accident, for which the defendant was responsible, had produced a personality change, which led to him becoming addicted to heroin. Harrison J held that the defendant was not liable for further brain damage caused by a heroin overdose, because the claimant's decision to use heroin was voluntary, deliberate and informed, and he had not lost the capacity or the power to say no: "He was the author of his own misfortune and what followed was caused by his own conduct". cf. *Dalling v R J Heale & Co Ltd* [2011] EWCA Civ 365, para.2-130 fn.453.

[457] See Millner (1971) 22 N.I.L.Q. 168, 176–179, commenting on *McKew v Holland & Hannen & Cubitts (Scotland) Ltd* [1969] 3 All E.R. 1621; *Sayers v Harlow Urban DC* [1958] 1 W.L.R. 623. In *Spencer v Wincanton Holdings Ltd* [2009] EWCA Civ 1404; [2010] P.I.Q.R. P8 at [22] it was pointed out that contributory negligence had not been pleaded in *McKew*. In *Hicks v Young* [2015] EWHC 1144 (QB) at [44] Edis J came to the conclusion that, applying the test of fairness, novus actus interveniens should be applied differently in the tort of negligence as compared to trespass to the person on precisely the same facts (claimant's unreasonable actions did not break the chain of causation in negligence, resulting instead in a finding of contributory negligence, although the same unreasonable actions constituted novus actus interveniens in trespass to the person, where the defence of contributory negligence does not apply).

[458] (1991) 99 A.L.R. 423.

to whom the defendant owed a duty of care—on the contrary, the claimant's "intoxication and associated carelessness took him within the class of inattentive drivers to whom the truck represented the greatest hazard".[459] Once it was accepted that the defendant owed a duty to take reasonable precautions against negligent conduct by others, he could not assert that the circumstances which gave rise to a breach of that duty constituted a novus actus interveniens. The claimant was held 70 per cent contributorily negligent.

2-133 **Emergency or dilemma** Conduct, whether on the part of a third party or the claimant himself, will not constitute a novus actus where it is a panic or reflex reaction to a position of immediate danger created by the defendant's wrongdoing. So in *Scott v Shepherd*,[460] the intervention of bystanders who tossed away the lighted squib thrown by the defendant did not exculpate him from liability to the claimant who was ultimately injured by that squib. In *Brandon v Osborne Garrett Co Ltd*,[461] a skylight crashed into the roof of a shop where the claimant was standing with her husband. She instinctively clutched her husband and tried to pull him out of danger. The defendants were liable for the injury occasioned to her by straining her leg.

2-134 **Rescuers** On analogous principles a deliberate act of rescue will virtually never constitute a novus actus.[462] The defendant will not be allowed to absolve himself for responsibility for the consequences of a danger which he had created. Rescue may be an act of "conscious volition" but it is a normal, reasonable and definable response to another's plight. "The cry of distress is a summons for relief."[463]

2-135 **Refusal of medical treatment** Where a claimant refuses medical treatment which would alleviate his condition or prevent it from deteriorating the question of whether this can break the causal link may arise. A claimant has an obligation to mitigate his loss, which may include seeking suitable medical treatment, except where there is a substantial risk of further injury or the outcome is uncertain.[464] Mitigation is a principle applied to the assessment of damages, but this stage will not be reached if the refusal of recommended treatment is categorised as an intervening act. It could be argued that a patient's refusal to accept medical treatment on, say, religious grounds does not break the chain of causation, since it represents a failure (even if an "unreasonable" failure) to intervene to prevent the

---

459 (1991) 99 A.L.R. 423 at 434, per Deane J. cf. *Dymond v Pearce* [1972] 1 Q.B. 496—a motor cyclist collided with a lorry parked on highway in such a way as to constitute a public nuisance, but the Court of Appeal held that the negligence of the motor cyclist was the sole cause of the accident; *Wills v TF Martin (Roof Contractors)* [1972] 1 Lloyd's Rep. 541—motorist who collided with a skip that was obstructing the road, because he was not looking where he was going, was the sole cause of the accident; cf. *Drury v Camden LBC* [1972] R.T.R. 391—claimant collided with an unlit skip on a road during the hours of darkness; claimant and defendant held equally responsible.

460 (1773) 3 Wils. 403; *Howard v Bergin* [1925] Ir. R. 110.

461 [1924] 1 K.B. 548.

462 Unless the reaction of the rescuer is so grossly foolish and disproportionate to the danger as in effect to be a "sham" rescue; see *Cutler v United Dairies (London) Ltd* [1933] 2 K.B. 297 explained in *Haynes v Harwood* [1935] 1 K.B. 146; and see *Crossley v Rawlinson* [1982] 1 W.L.R. 369, but query whether this case, in which the defendant was held not liable for injuries sustained by the claimant when running to a fire on the defendant's vehicle, is correctly decided; cf. *Bridge v Jo* [1999] 3 W.W.R. 167.

463 *Wagner v International Ry Co* (1921) 232 N.Y. Rep. 176. Liability to rescuers is discussed at para.7-34.

464 See para.27-09.

damage caused by the defendant.[465] Moreover, if negligent medical treatment by health professionals does not necessarily break the causal link,[466] then maybe an unreasonable refusal by a claimant to accept medical treatment does not break the causal link. In the criminal law it has been held that a patient's refusal to undergo a blood transfusion on religious grounds did not break the chain of causation between a criminal assault and the patient's death, resulting in a charge of manslaughter.[467] This approach is clearly based on policy considerations appropriate to the criminal law. In *R. v Blaue*[468] Lawton LJ suggested that where the victim brought a civil claim the concept of foreseeability could operate in the wrongdoer's favour, presumably by breaking the chain of causation. But a decision to refuse medical treatment would not necessarily be categorised as "unreasonable", even under the civil law, because it is considered to be reasonable to conduct one's life according to a religious faith, even though those specific beliefs are not widely accepted within society. Ultimately, this issue turns upon the courts' assessment of who should bear the burden of the claimant's religious beliefs.[469]

Failed sterilisation cases In *Emeh v Kensington, Chelsea and Westminster AHA*,[470] the claimant underwent sterilisation. Despite this she conceived again, but did not appreciate that she was, or could be, pregnant until well into the second trimester of pregnancy. She refused to have an abortion, albeit an abortion could have been lawfully performed. The trial judge held that she could not recover for the cost of bringing up her child because her refusal to terminate the pregnancy was unreasonable, and became the sole, effective cause of the birth of the child. The Court of Appeal overturned this judgment. Abortion at over 18 weeks into pregnancy is attended by trauma and risk. Slade LJ argued that, save in the most exceptional circumstances, a choice to refuse termination of pregnancy could not be regarded as unreasonable.[471] Where the defendant has created the claimant's dilemma, he should rarely be allowed to claim that the claimant acted unreasonably in deciding how to respond to that dilemma. In *McFarlane v Tayside Health* 2-136

465 By analogy with the position where a third party fails to intervene: see para.2-128.
466 See paras 2-125 and 2-126.
467 *R. v Blaue* [1975] 1 W.L.R. 1411 at 1415, per Lawton LJ: "It does not lie in the mouth of the assailant to say that his victim's religious beliefs which inhibited him from accepting certain kinds of treatment were unreasonable. The question for decision is what caused her death. The answer is the stab wound. The fact that the victim refused to stop this end coming about did not break the causal connection between the act and the death." See also *R. v Malcherek* [1981] 1 W.L.R. 690; *R. v Cheshire* (1991) 93 Cr. App. R. 251; *R. v Dear* [1996] Crim. L.R. 595.
468 *R. v Blaue* [1975] 1 W.L.R. 1411 at 1415.
469 See also *Hobbs v Robertson* (2004) 243 D.L.R. (4th) 700 (British Columbia SC)—surgeon not liable for death of a patient due to blood loss when the patient had signed a document releasing the surgeon and hospital from "any responsibility whatsoever" for complications arising from the patient's refusal to accept blood. The death was due to the patient's refusal to accept blood, rather than the surgeon's negligence in creating the circumstances in which a blood transfusion, which would have saved her life, became necessary.
470 [1985] Q.B. 1012 CA.
471 [1985] Q.B. 1012 at 1023. It is difficult to imagine what could possibly constitute such "exceptional circumstances". Purchas LJ appeared to suggest that where the sole motivation for the refusal to terminate the pregnancy was "commercial", in that the claimant continued the pregnancy merely to increase the damages that would be awarded in the action for the failed sterilisation, that would be a factor to be considered in deciding whether the chain of causation had been broken. It is highly unlikely that such a plea could be established by a defendant.

Board,[472] the House of Lords emphatically confirmed that the failure to undergo a termination of pregnancy or the failure to give the child up for adoption following birth did not break the chain of causation between a negligently performed sterilisation operation or negligent advice as to the success of the sterilisation procedure and the birth, although their Lordships did limit the potential damages awarded in such actions on other grounds.[473]

2-137 Where, following a failed sterilisation operation, a claimant knew that she was not sterile, and nonetheless proceeded to have sexual intercourse without taking contraceptive measures, this does break the chain of causation between the negligent performance of the surgery and the subsequent birth of a child. Although the defence of volenti non fit injuria did not apply in these circumstances because the claimant's acceptance of the risk must occur either before or at the same time as the negligent act or omission, the claimant's decision constituted a novus actus interveniens.[474]

2-138 In *Parkinson v St James and Seacroft University Hospital NHS Trust*[475] the Court of Appeal held that *McFarlane* did not apply where the child was born disabled. The parents of a disabled child born following a negligently performed sterilisation operation were entitled to the additional costs of raising that child (i.e. those costs over and above the costs of raising a healthy child, not the full costs of maintenance). Brooke LJ emphasised, however, that if the child's disabilities were brought about between conception and birth "by some ultroneous cause", the negligent surgeon should not, without more, be held liable for the economic consequences of the child's disabilities.[476] The fact that the child's disabilities were not present at birth will not necessarily break the causal link. Thus, in *Groom v Selby*[477] there was a negligent failure to conduct a pregnancy test with the result that the claimant was unaware that she was pregnant until 15 weeks. Had she been informed sooner she would have undergone a termination of the pregnancy. The

472 [2000] 2 A.C. 59 at 74, 81, 97, 105, 112–113.

473 Claims based on the cost of the child's upbringing were ruled out, although the mother is entitled to damages for the pain, suffering and inconvenience of pregnancy and childbirth. See further at paras 7-98 to 7-102.

474 *Sabri-Tabrizi v Lothian Health Board*, 1998 S.C. 373; (1998) 43 B.M.L.R. 190. cf. *Pidgeon v Doncaster HA* [2002] Lloyd's Rep. Med. 130 (county court) where the judge distinguished *Sabri-Tabrizi v Lothian Health Board* and *McKew v Holland & Hannen & Cubitts (Scotland) Ltd* (see para.2-129). The claimant was negligently advised in 1988 that a smear test for cervical cancer was normal, when it showed pre-cancerous abnormalities. A further test in 1997 resulted in a diagnosis of cervical cancer. In the intervening period the claimant had been spoken to on no less than seven occasions about the need to have smear test, and had received four letters from the defendants' cervical cancer screening programme about the need to have a smear test. The claimant had not undergone the test because she found it painful and embarrassing, although she was aware that she could develop cervical cancer. It was held that the claimant's failure to undergo a smear test did not break the causal link between the original negligence and the development of cancer. The difference between this and the cases of *Sabri-Tabrizi* and *McKew* was that in those cases the claimants knew about their particular condition (not being sterile and weakness in the leg), whereas the claimant did not know of her condition, and had been reassured by the reported result of the 1988 test. There was "an important difference between a claimant indulging in behaviour against a background of known vulnerability, whether it be weakness of the leg or ability to conceive, and a claimant failing to take steps which may well reveal a condition, if in fact present, having previously been reassured that it was not present" (at [23]). The claimant may have been unwise or unreasonable, but her failure was not "so utterly unreasonable" as to break the chain of causation. She was, however, assessed to be two-thirds contributorily negligent.

475 [2001] EWCA Civ 530; [2002] Q.B. 266.

476 [2001] EWCA Civ 530; [2002] Q.B. 266 at [53].

477 [2001] EWCA Civ 1522; [2002] Lloyd's Rep. Med. 1.

child was born apparently healthy, but quite by chance, the child developed meningitis within three to four weeks of the birth as a result of an infection which was probably contracted during the course of the birth. The Court of Appeal rejected the defendant's argument that this was an intervening cause. The child's condition was a rare, but a natural and foreseeable consequence of childbirth. The fact that it was mere chance that the child happened to have a disability or that the disability developed after the birth was irrelevant. It is arguable, on the other hand, that disabilities due to an infection arising after the perinatal period would break the causal link. The risk of disablement to an otherwise healthy child is one of the vicissitudes of life.

Both *Parkinson* and *Groom v Selby* were distinguished by the Court of Appeal in *Khan v Meadows*.[478] The claimant consulted the defendant doctor for advice about whether she carried the gene for haemophilia. Following a blood test the claimant was given advice that led her to believe that any child she had would not have haemophilia. Subsequently she conceived and gave birth to a son who had both haemophilia and autism. In a "wrongful birth" claim for the additional costs associated with haemophilia and autism, the defendant accepted that but for causation was established since if the claimant had known that she was at risk of having a child with haemophilia she would have had tests conducted during the pregnancy and would have had a termination of the pregnancy. The defendant also accepted that she was liable for the additional costs associated with the condition of haemophilia, but argued that she was not liable for the costs associated with the child's autism. The Court of Appeal agreed that, given the claimant's specific enquiry about the haemophilia gene, the scope of the defendant's duty was limited to the consequences of negligent advice about haemophilia (applying the *SAAMCO*[479] test). The risk of autism is a risk that exists with every pregnancy; it is not a risk that increases if the child has haemophilia. The risk to the claimant of having a child with autism was not increased by the defendant's advice. The scope of the defendant's duty was to advise in relation to haemophilia in order to provide the claimant with an opportunity to avoid the risk of having a child with haemophilia. It was not to protect her from all the risks associated with pregnancy and continuing with the pregnancy.[480] 2-139

Claimant's suicide The significance of suicide (or attempted suicide) by the claimant crops up in two different contexts. The first is where the claimant suffers injury as a consequence of the defendant's breach of duty and then goes on to attempt suicide, allegedly as a result of the original injury which may have produced psychiatric sequelae (such as depression) predisposing the claimant to make the suicide attempt. The second situation is where the claimant was known to be suicidal and the defendant, by reason of the particular relationship with the claimant, was under a duty to exercise reasonable care to prevent the suicide attempt. 2-140

---

478 [2019] EWCA Civ 152; [2019] 4 W.L.R. 26; J. McQuater [2019] J.P.I.L. C6.

479 *South Australia Asset Management Corp v York Montague Ltd* [1997] A.C. 191; see para.2-186.

480 *Parkinson* and *Groom v Selby* were different because: "In each the doctor had undertaken the task of protecting a patient from an unwanted pregnancy, in *Groom* the pregnancy itself, in Parkinson the continuation of the pregnancy. In both, the disability arose from genetic causes or foreseeable events during the course of the pregnancy which were not due to a new intervening cause": [2019] EWCA Civ 152; [2019] 4 W.L.R. 26 at [11].

Corr v IBC Vehicles Ltd[481] falls into the first category. The deceased suffered an accident at work and subsequently developed depression. Some six years after the accident he committed suicide. The deceased's widow brought a claim against his employers. The deceased's depression was admitted to have been a foreseeable consequence of the defendants' negligence, and the evidence was that suicide is a not uncommon consequence of severe depression. It was held that the suicide did not break the chain of causation between the employers' negligence and the consequences of the suicide. Lord Bingham accepted that the deceased was not insane, but neither was he fully responsible for his actions. Depression, possibly very severe depression, was a foreseeable consequence of the defendants' breach of duty,[482] but in any event the claimant did not have to demonstrate that suicide itself was foreseeable, on the basis that "a tortfeasor who reasonably foresees the occurrence of some damage need not foresee the precise form which the damage may take".[483] If, said Lord Bingham, the victim of a tort took a voluntary, informed decision as an adult of sound mind, making and giving effect to a personal decision about his own future, that could break the chain of causation. But on the facts of *Corr v IBC Vehicles* the suicide was:

> "not a voluntary, informed decision taken by him as an adult of sound mind making and giving effect to a personal decision about his future. It was the response of a man suffering from a severely depressive illness which impaired his capacity to make reasoned and informed judgments about his future, such illness being, as is accepted, a consequence of the employer's tort. It is in no way unfair to hold the employer responsible for this dire consequence of its breach of duty, although it could well be thought unfair to the victim not to do so."[484]

The more unsound the mind of the victim the less likely it is that his suicide will be seen as a novus actus interveniens. Lord Scott considered that causation was established on the basis that the defendant must take his victim as he finds him, including his psychiatric condition brought about as a result of the physical injuries caused by the employers' breach of duty.[485]

2-141 *Reeves v Commissioner of Police for the Metropolis*[486] provides an example of the second category of case, where the defendant was under a duty to exercise reasonable care to prevent the suicide attempt. The deceased hanged himself in a police cell. The defendants were aware that he was a suicide risk, but the flap on the cell door had been left down allowing the deceased to tie his shirt through the

---

[481] [2008] UKHL 13; [2008] 1 A.C. 884.

[482] [2008] UKHL 13; [2008] 1 A.C. 884 at [13]: "a reasonable employer would … have recognised the possibility not only of acute depression but also of such depression culminating in a way in which, in a significant minority of cases, it unhappily does." Lord Neuberger commented, at [56], that: "It is notorious that severely depressed people not infrequently try to kill themselves: indeed, the evidence before us suggests that the chances are higher than 10%. While I would not attribute to a reasonable defendant … the knowledge that the likelihood of suicide attempts among severe depressives is higher than 10%, I would expect him to appreciate that there was a substantial risk of a suicide attempt by someone who suffers from severe depression, and that suicide attempts often succeed."

[483] [2008] UKHL 13; [2008] 1 A.C. 884; applying *Hughes v Lord Advocate* [1963] A.C. 837.

[484] [2008] UKHL 13; [2008] 1 A.C. 884 at [16].

[485] [2008] UKHL 13; [2008] 1 A.C. 884 at [29]. In *Pigney v Pointers Transport Services Ltd* [1957] 1 W.L.R. 1121 the same conclusion has been reached even though, at the time, suicide was still a criminal offence. *Pigney* was not referred to by their Lordships in *Corr v IBC Vehicles Ltd*.

[486] [2000] 1 A.C. 360. See also *Kirkham v Chief Constable of Greater Manchester Police* [1990] 2 Q.B. 283 CA.

spy hole in the door and hang himself. There was no evidence that the deceased had been diagnosed as suffering from any specific mental disorder. The defendants conceded that a duty of care was owed to the prisoner, but denied liability on the basis that his own act of suicide constituted a novus actus, breaking the causal link.[487] The House of Lords held that the suicide did not constitute a novus actus. The damage arose from breach of a duty to prevent just such an act and thus did not obliterate the defendants' wrongdoing. It was not a new act, but the very harm that the defendants were under a duty to try to prevent. Lord Hoffmann commented that in cases where the law imposes a duty to guard against loss caused by the free, deliberate and informed act of a human being, "it would make nonsense of the existence of such a duty if the law were to hold that the occurrence of the very act which ought to have been prevented negatived causal connection between the breach of duty and the loss".[488] Though a duty to protect a person of full understanding from causing harm to himself was very rare, once it was admitted that this was such a rare case in which such a duty was owed, it was self-contradictory to say that the breach could not have been a cause of the harm because the victim caused it to himself.[489]

(iv) *Intervening conduct of the defendant*

A defendant cannot rely on his own subsequent negligence so as to break the causal connection between his original act of negligence and the claimant's loss. This proposition ought to be self-evident, and indeed is reflected in the comment of Lord Browne-Wilkinson in *Bolitho v City and Hackney HA*[490] that: "A defendant cannot escape liability by saying that the damage would have occurred in any event because he would have committed some other breach of duty thereafter." In *Coudert Brothers v Normans Bay Ltd*[491] there were two discrete allegations of negligence against the defendant firm of solicitors. The defendants argued that the second act of negligence broke the causal link between the first act of negligence and the claimants' loss, whilst also contending that the claimants could not rely on the second act of negligence as founding their claim because that was statute-barred. The Court of Appeal rejected the argument on the ground that there is a principle of public policy that a person should not be entitled to rely on his own wrong in order to secure a benefit. Laws LJ also considered that the result was "consonant with modern ideas of causation now being developed in the cases. Authority supports the proposition that the resolution of causation issues, certainly **2-142**

[487] An argument that the defence of ex turpi causa non oritur actio applied was not pursued on appeal to the House of Lords. Similarly, it was accepted by the defendant that a claim that the deceased was volenti was subsumed within the argument about causation. If the argument on causation failed so would the allegation of volenti.

[488] [2000] 1 A.C. 360 at 367–368.

[489] [2000] 1 A.C. 360 at 368. On the duty of care owed by the police and prison authorities to prisoners who are foreseeably at risk of committing suicide see also: *Orange v Chief Constable of West Yorkshire Police* [2001] EWCA Civ 611; [2002] Q.B. 347; *Keenan v UK (Application No.27229/95)* (2001) 33 E.H.R.R. 38; (2001) 10 B.H.R.C. 319, where the European Court of Human Rights held that inadequate medical treatment and a lack of effective monitoring of a prisoner who was an identified suicide risk could constitute a breach of art.3 of the European Convention for the Protection of Human Rights. See also *McGlinchey v UK* [2003] Lloyd's Rep. Med. 264; (2003) 72 B.M.L.R. 168. There is no duty on prison authorities to treat every prisoner as a potential suicide risk: *Smiley v Home Office* [2004] EWHC 240 (QB).

[490] [1998] A.C. 232 at 240.

[491] [2004] EWCA Civ 215; *The Times*, 24 March 2004.

in the law of tort, is by no means merely a fact-finding exercise; in many instances it is an evaluative judgment, concerned to establish the extent to which a defendant should justly be held responsible for what has befallen the claimant."[492]

2-143 **Intervening disciplinary proceedings** Where, following an accident at work, an employee has been disciplined, demoted and suffered a loss of earnings, but his employers subsequently settle a claim in respect of the employee's injuries on the basis that they are liable for a proportion of the damage (the employee being contributorily negligent), the admission of liability is inconsistent with the argument that the loss of earnings was entirely attributable to the disciplinary proceedings, and not the employer's breach of duty. Thus, in *Casey v Morane Ltd*[493] the claimant was entitled to recover the loss of earnings caused by his demotion, subject to a deduction of 15 per cent in respect of his contributory negligence. Mance LJ suggested that, ordinarily, where an employee was justifiably disciplined after an accident, following an objective review of his conduct, and lost income as a result, "the law would be likely to select as the relevant cause of that loss his own conduct and nothing else, and that this would be so even though another person's negligence also contributed to the occurrence of the accident".[494] This would still be the case even if the other negligent party was also disciplined. The court drew an analogy with a road traffic accident caused by the negligence of two drivers where, following a prosecution, the claimant is disqualified from driving and loses income as a result. The loss of income would be due to the independent decision of the court having adjudicated on the claimant's own conduct, and therefore the loss of earnings would be attributable to the claimant's conduct and not the other driver's negligence.[495] With respect, there is a difference between a court imposing a penalty for criminal conduct which results in financial loss to the claimant, which would rightly be treated as an intervening cause, and the potential defendant to a tort action imposing a financial penalty following disciplinary proceedings. The decision of the court is an intervening event of an independent "third party", whereas the decision of the employer to institute disciplinary proceedings is the subsequent conduct of the defendant himself. In conducting disciplinary proceedings the employer is far more likely to concentrate on the employee's culpability than his own (as would appear to have occurred in *Casey v Morane Ltd* itself). Clearly, if the claimant is wholly responsible for his own inappropriate conduct leading to the accident and is then disciplined, the resulting loss of earnings can be attributed to the claimant's conduct rather than the defendants' breach of duty. But if the claimant is wholly responsible for the accident the claim for injuries and loss resulting from the accident would in any event fail on grounds of causation. Whether the employer has taken disciplinary proceedings would be irrelevant to the causation issue. Moreover, the fact that an employer has disciplined an employee is clearly not binding on a court in assessing the respective responsibilities of employer and employee for the consequences of an industrial accident. In *Casey v Morane Ltd* the apportionment of responsibility was agreed between the parties, but even if the apportionment was contested, it must remain a question of fact for the court whether the loss of earnings is partly attributable to the employer's breach of duty, otherwise employers might be tempted to discipline careless employees in order to avoid

492 [2004] EWCA Civ 215 at [64].
493 [2001] I.C.R. 316 CA.
494 [2001] I.C.R. 316 CA at [27]. See also at [37], per Peter Gibson LJ.
495 [2001] I.C.R. 316 CA at [28], per Mance LJ and at [37], per Peter Gibson LJ.

compensation claims, and thereby avoid the consequences of their own carelessness.

5. Remoteness of Damage

The concept of remoteness of damage is not truly concerned with questions of causation, although where remoteness is based on a test of "direct consequences" it can make some sense to think of remoteness in terms of causation. The function of a test of remoteness is to set an outer limit to the damage for which the defendant will be held responsible. The possible consequences of any human conduct are potentially endless. The defendant's wrongdoing may trigger a series of events stretching well beyond one's normal expectations of possible consequences. The law does not, however, impose indefinite liability. A line must be drawn to confine the responsibility of the defendant to those consequences of his wrongdoing which it is proper for him to shoulder.[496] Thus, even when it is quite clear that the defendant's wrong *caused* the damage, it may be said that the damage was too remote if it is not of the same type as would normally be anticipated in similar circumstances, or if it occurred in an unusual way. Remoteness of damage places limits on the defendant's responsibility, and in the context of the tort of negligence there is a significant overlap between the concepts of remoteness of damage and duty of care, which is also concerned with setting out the boundaries of liability for careless conduct. **2-144**

Questions of remoteness tend to arise most commonly in actions for negligence and torts involving a significant element of fault (such as nuisance), and most of the cases in the following sections of this chapter arise from claims in negligence. Should the defendant be held responsible where objectively he has acted carelessly, but the resulting damage is more extensive, or of a different type, or occurred in a different manner from that which could normally be anticipated? In a system of fault liability, holding a person liable for the unpredictable or freakish consequences of his negligence may seem unfair because of a sense of disproportion between the fault and the damage. **2-145**

(a) Remoteness and torts other than negligence

(i) Torts where questions of remoteness do not arise

There are a number of torts where the question of remoteness of damage is simply not relevant because the specific requirements of the tort lay down all the conditions for liability. Once those conditions are satisfied the court considers that it is reasonable to hold the defendant fully responsible for all the consequences. For example, in defamation the concept of remoteness of damage does not feature at all. The requirements for establishing liability in defamation are sufficiently stringent that once the elements of the tort are established, and it is clear that there are no defences, damage to the claimant (in the form of injury to reputation) is generally presumed to have occurred and it is deemed to be reasonable that the claimant should be fully compensated for that damage. Similarly, remoteness is rarely relevant in actions for breach of statutory duty because as part of establishing the defendant's liability the claimant must show that the damage he suffered **2-146**

---

496 *Liesbosch Dredger v SS Edison* [1933] A.C. 449 at 460.

falls within the ambit of the statute, namely that it was of the type that the statute was intended to prevent and that the claimant belonged to the category of persons that the statute was intended to protect.[497] If this is proved then there is little scope for a defendant to argue that he should not be held responsible because he could not have anticipated that particular damage or the damage occurred in some bizarre or freakish manner which it would not be reasonable to expect him to be responsible for.

(ii) Remoteness and trespass to the person

2-147 The test of remoteness in trespass to the person is directness of the consequence, not foreseeability of the damage. This stems from the historical development of the writ of trespass, the two most prominent features of which were that trespass was actionable per se, i.e. without proof of damage, and that the interference with the claimant had to be a direct result of the defendant's act. Indirect or consequential harm was the subject of an action for "trespass on the case" later referred to as an action on the case, or simply "case". The traditional example of the distinction between direct and indirect harm is that of a log thrown onto the highway. If the log strikes someone the injury is direct and trespass would lie, but if it simply lies in the road and obstructs the highway and someone trips over it, the injury is indirect and the claimant would have to sue in case, and prove damage. In the modern cases, remoteness of damage is rarely an issue in trespass to the person, probably because trespass is now seen as a tort of intention (although the defendant's intention relates to an intention to do the act which amounts to trespass; there is no requirement that the defendant intended to harm the claimant[498]).

2-148 However, the remoteness issue was relevant in *Hicks v Young*[499] where the defendant was held liable in both negligence and trespass to the person (for false imprisonment) and the claimant had been found contributorily negligent. A taxi driver, believing that his passenger was not going to pay the fare, drove off with the passenger in the back of the taxi and the passenger jumped out of the moving vehicle, sustaining injury as a consequence. Were the personal injuries sustained in the escape attempt a direct result of the false imprisonment? Edis J held that they were not: in order to satisfy the test of directness the claimant's injuries "must be the consequence of a reasonable and necessary act intended to bring the unlawful imprisonment to an end". Given that the claimant had been found contributorily negligent in the negligence action, he had not acted reasonably in making the escape attempt and the injuries he sustained were therefore too remote for the purposes of a claim in trespass to the person.[500]

---

497 See *Gorris v Scott* (1874) L.R. 9 Ex. 125.

498 *Wilson v Pringle* [1987] Q.B. 237 CA at 249: "It is the act and not the injury which must be intentional. An intention to injure is not essential to an action for trespass to the person."

499 [2015] EWHC 1144 (QB).

500 Edis J reached this conclusion because of the view he took of the overall fairness of the case, namely that defendant and claimant were equally responsible for the claimant's injuries. Contributory negligence is not a defence to an action for trespass to the person (see *Co–operative Group (CWS) Ltd v Pritchard* [2011] EWCA Civ 329; [2012] Q.B. 320; para.3-68), and so a finding that the injuries were the direct result of the false imprisonment would have rendered the defendant liable for the full loss. The claimant was awarded £250 damages for the false imprisonment before he jumped out of the taxi.

(iii) Remoteness and torts of strict liability

It is perfectly possible to combine a liability rule based on causation, strict liability, with a remoteness rule based on foreseeability of the damage.[501] In *Cambridge Water Co Ltd v Eastern Counties Leather Plc*[502] the House of Lords held that although the rule in *Rylands v Fletcher* involves strict liability, in the sense that the defendant may be held liable notwithstanding that he has exercised all reasonable care to prevent the escape of a dangerous thing from his land, nonetheless foreseeability of damage of the relevant type was a prerequisite of liability.[503] This may at first sight seem paradoxical. The act or event triggering breach of the strict duty may itself have been unforeseeable. In *Cambridge Water* the defendants' wrongdoing derived from their non-natural use of land, the bulk storage of toxic chemicals. They were liable for the escape of the chemicals regardless of whether they could have foreseen or prevented that escape, but their liability was limited to the type of consequences a reasonable person might have contemplated when accumulating toxic chemicals on his land. In some instances liability may be truly strict, and the defendant held liable for all the consequences whether foreseeable or not. For example, the Animals Act 1971 s.2(1) provides that the keeper of an animal belonging to a dangerous species is liable for "any damage" caused by that animal (subject to the defences provided for in the Act). So the keeper of a dangerous animal is liable for any damage, even if it is not caused by the characteristic of the animal that renders it dangerous (e.g. if an escaped tiger trips up a pedestrian in the street the keeper is liable for the injuries caused by the fall). **2-149**

In practice, the remoteness rules for the relatively few torts that involve true strict liability tend to be specific to the individual torts, and there is little in the way of general guidance. This is not surprising if the point of remoteness rules is to set a limit on the proper extent of a defendant's liability, since the proper extent of a defendant's liability will be something to be judged in the context of the underlying policy objectives of the specific tort. Indeed, it is possible for a tort to have two distinct remoteness rules, depending upon the nature of the conduct that gives rise to breach of the relevant obligation. In *Kuwait Airways Corp v Iraq Airways Co*[504] the House of Lords held that the test of remoteness in the tort of wrongful interference with goods could be either foreseeability or directness of consequence depending on the nature of the defendant's conduct. Lord Nicholls pointed out that the tort of conversion can be committed innocently, and for a person "who can prove he acted in the genuine belief the goods were his" the test should be foreseeability—the defendant is liable for the losses the true owner can be expected to have suffered as a result of the defendant's misappropriation of the claimant's goods. Where, however, the defendant has knowingly converted the claimant's goods he acts dishonestly, and there was no good reason why the remoteness test of "directly and naturally" applied in cases of deceit should not apply in such cases.[505] **2-150**

---

501 In *Galashiels Car Co Ltd v Millar* [1949] A.C. 275 the defendants were found liable in breach of statutory duty, albeit they had no reason to believe that their lift, which crashed and killed a workman, was in anything other than perfect working order. But, given the breach of a truly strict statutory duty, the kind of damage which occurred, injury and death, was just the kind of damage to be expected.

502 [1994] 2 A.C. 264 at 302.

503 [1994] 2 A.C. 264 at 306.

504 [2002] UKHL 19; [2002] 2 A.C. 883.

505 [2002] UKHL 19; [2002] 2 A.C. 883 at [103]–[104]. See also at [169], per Lord Hope.

(iv) Remoteness and intended consequences

2-151 "The intention to injure the [claimant] disposes of any question of remoteness."[506] Consequences intended by the defendant will never be too remote.[507] So in actions for deceit all the damage directly attributable to the defendant's fraud is recoverable, regardless of whether or not such damage was reasonably foreseeable.[508] The loss does not have to be foreseeable.[509] Nor, it is suggested, is there authority to support any restriction of liability to foreseeable kinds of damage alone in any of the intentional torts.[510] Liability in such torts extends to all the consequences which can be linked to the tortious conduct, provided those consequences are properly attributable as a matter of causation to the defendant's conduct and not to some novus actus interveniens.

2-152 Where the defendant is reckless as to, in the sense of indifferent to, the consequences of his act, the consequences will be treated as intended. In *Scott v Shepherd*,[511] the defendant threw a lighted firework into the marketplace. It fell close to A, who in alarm flung it away from his stall so that it landed on B's stall, who similarly acted on a reflex throwing the firework away from him so that it ultimately hit and injured the claimant. The defendant was held liable. He acted in reckless disregard of the consequences of his conduct, and the intervening conduct of A and B, in the agony of the moment, was an obvious result of his original fault. Where the defendant acts deliberately committing an intentional tort, and the consequence is one he should have anticipated, his is liable for all such consequences whether he willed them or not. He is presumed to intend consequences he should have had regard to.[512]

---

506 *Quinn v Leathem* [1901] A.C. 495 at 537.

507 In the case of a fraudulent representation, there is a rebuttable presumption that the representor intended the representee to rely on it: *Pan Atlantic Insurance Co Ltd v Pine Top Insurance Co Ltd* [1995] 1 A.C. 501 at 542; *Barton v County NatWest Ltd* [1999] Lloyd's Rep. Banking 408 at 421.

508 *Smith New Court Securities Ltd v Citibank NA* [1997] A.C. 254, HL; *Doyle v Olby (Ironmongers) Ltd* [1969] 2 Q.B. 158; *Shelley v Paddock* [1980] Q.B. 348; *Swindle v Harrison* [1997] 4 All E.R. 705; see para.17-50; and see *Langridge v Levy* (1873) 2 M. & W. 519. Moreover, the test of *causation* in deceit is highly favourable to claimants: see *Downs v Chappell* [1997] 1 W.L.R. 426 CA; see further the discussion of the correct approach to causation in actions for deceit by Evans-Lombe J in *Barings Plc (In Liquidation) v Coopers & Lybrand (A Firm)* [2002] EWHC 461 (Ch); [2002] P.N.L.R. 39 at [124]–[148]. Note also that damages for breach of s.2(1) of the Misrepresentation Act 1967 are measured on the same basis as that for the tort of deceit rather than negligence, and so include unforeseeable losses: *Royscot Trust Ltd v Rogerson* [1991] 2 Q.B. 297. *Komercni Banka AS v Stone and Rolls Ltd* [2002] EWHC 2263 (Comm); [2003] 1 Lloyd's Rep. 383—not all benefits to the claimant arising from a defendant's deceit fall to be deducted from the claimant's loss. The question is whether the benefit arose out of the complex of obligations and benefits which were intrinsic to the venture or transaction.

509 Nor does the defence of contributory negligence apply. The defendant who intends to mislead the claimant cannot argue that if the claimant had exercised greater care he would not have been taken in by the defendant's fraud. See para.3-73.

510 See *Wilson v Pringle* [1987] Q.B. 237; see para.14-07.

511 (1773) 2 W.Bl. 892; see also *Adams v Kelly* (1824) Ry. & M. 157.

512 *Wilkinson v Downton* [1897] 2 Q.B. 57. On the interpretation of "imputed intention" in *Wilkinson v Downton*, see now the decisions of the House of Lords in *Wainwright v Home Office* [2003] UKHL 53; [2004] 2 A.C. 406; and the Supreme Court in *Rhodes v OPO* [2015] UKSC 32; [2016] A.C. 219, discussed at para.14-16. For cases concerning intended consequences in nuisance see *Betterton's Case* (1695) Holt 538; *Lyons v Gulliver* [1914] 1 Ch. 631; *Dwyer v Mansfield* [1946] K.B. 437; and regarding unlawful detention on grounds of insanity see *Harnett v Bond* [1925] A.C. 669; *Everett v Griffiths* [1921] 1 A.C. 631; *Harnett v Fisher* [1927] 1 K.B. 402.

(b) Remoteness and liability in negligence for physical damage

Remoteness and negligence In practice the vast majority of cases that involve issues of remoteness of damage arise in claims for negligence where, almost by definition, the damage to the claimant was unintended. Given that a defendant found to be in breach of a duty of care must be taken to have foreseen some form of damage to the claimant, the remoteness test is concerned with the outer limits of a defendant's responsibility for causing damage where that damage has occurred in an unusual or unexpected way, or is of a type different from that which the claimant ought reasonably to have foreseen as part and parcel of being held to be in breach of duty. If damage X was foreseeable, but damage X has not occurred, though damage Y has materialised as a result of the defendant's negligence, is it appropriate to hold the defendant responsible for damage Y? Fault liability is based on the premise that it is fair and reasonable to require a defendant to compensate for damage that he can reasonably foresee was likely to arise as a consequence of his failure to heed, and take precautions against, an unreasonable risk. But does fault liability require compensation where, even though the defendant has taken an unreasonable risk, the consequences were entirely unanticipated? How far should the defendant's responsibility for the safety of others extend? There are two broad approaches to this question. The first takes the view that a defendant is responsible for all the direct consequences of his negligence, no matter how unusual or unexpected. This is essentially a causation test. The second holds that a person is responsible only for consequences that could reasonably have been anticipated. Although, in theory, it is now accepted that foreseeability is the correct test, in practice decisions about what it is that must be foreseen, combined with the principle that a defendant must "take his victim as he finds him" mean that the limits of actionability lie somewhere between these two approaches. The remaining paragraphs of this chapter are concerned with the remoteness test applied to the tort of negligence, though, as will be seen, the same principles apply to public nuisance.[513] 2-153

(i) *Foreseeability and directness*

Re Polemis In *Re Polemis and Furness, Withy & Co Ltd*[514] the Court of Appeal concluded that a negligent defendant should be liable for all the direct consequences attributable to his negligence. The claimants' ship was destroyed by fire caused by the negligence of the servants of the charterers. A plank, which had been carelessly placed as part of a platform at the forward end of the hatchway, was dislodged and fell into the hold. Unknown to all parties, the hold happened to be full of petrol vapour, which was ignited by a spark struck by the falling plank, and the entire ship was destroyed by fire. The charterers were held liable for the loss of the whole ship. Scrutton LJ said: 2-154

> "Once the act is negligent, the fact that its exact operation was not foreseen is immaterial … In the present case it was negligent in discharging cargo to knock down the planks of the temporary staging, for they might easily cause some damage either to workmen,

[513] See para.2-159. And as a consequence of *Cambridge Water Co Ltd v Eastern Counties Leather Plc* [1994] 2 A.C. 264 the same rules would seem to apply to private nuisance and claims based on *Rylands v Fletcher*.

[514] [1921] 3 K.B. 560.

> cargo or the ship. The fact that they did directly produce an unexpected result does not relieve the person who was negligent from the damage which his negligent act directly caused."[515]

Bankes LJ said that given the damage was a direct result of the negligence "the anticipations of the person whose negligent act has produced the damage appear to me to be irrelevant". On this view foreseeability "goes to culpability, not to compensation".[516]

2-155 There are two possible interpretations of the *Polemis* decision. The first is that as long as some damage, however slight, of a particular kind was foreseeable to the person or property of the claimant, he can recover for the full extent of it, though neither the extent nor precise manner of its incidence was foreseeable. The decision merely indicates that what is signified by "kind" of damage is simply the broad categories of physical damage to property and (in the light of later cases) to the person. On this interpretation, the point of significance is that damage to the ship, whether by denting the hold or by fire remains damage to property.[517] The second possible interpretation is that suggested by the quoted dictum of Scrutton LJ, namely, that once the defendant's conduct was foreseeably likely to injure anyone, he is liable for all "direct" consequences, even for an unforeseeable kind of damage.

2-156 **The Wagon Mound** In *Overseas Tankship (UK) Ltd v Morts Docks Engineering Co Ltd*,[518] known as *Wagon Mound (No.1)*, the defendants negligently allowed a quantity of furnace oil to spill into the sea. This oil spread over the water and came to lie beneath the claimants' wharf, fouling their slipways and halting repair work on two other ships. The claimants continued welding operations and it appears that a fragment of molten metal set the oil ablaze, despite it having a very high flashpoint, damaging the claimants' wharf. The claimants sued the defendants in negligence and nuisance, but only the negligence issue was pressed. Some damage to the claimant's wharf, in the form of fouling of the slipways, was reasonably foreseeable as the result of the spillage, but that fire was found to be unforeseeable because scientific opinion at the time was that the oil, lying as it was in a thin film over cool water, was unlikely to ignite. The Privy Council accepted the "direct consequences" interpretation of *Polemis* and declared that case to be wrongly decided. Viscount Simonds explained the basis of their decision as follows:

> "It does not seem consonant with current ideas of justice or morality that, for an act of negligence, however slight or venial, which results in some trivial foreseeable damage, the actor should be liable for all the consequences, however unforeseeable and however grave, so long as they can be said to be 'direct'. It is a principle of civil liberty ... that a man must be considered to be responsible for the probable consequences of his act. To demand more of him is too harsh a rule, to demand less is to ignore that civilised order requires the observance of a minimum standard of behaviour."[519]

The essential factor in determining liability was whether the damage is of such a

---

515 [1921] 3 K.B. 560 at 577.

516 *Weld-Blundell v Stephens* [1920] A.C. 956 at 984, per Lord Sumner.

517 This interpretation is justified by the findings of fact in the case by the arbitrators, namely, "That the causing of the spark could not reasonably have been anticipated from the falling of the board, though some damage to the ship might reasonably have been anticipated": [1921] 3 K.B. 560 at 563. For full discussion see Dias [1962] C.L.J. 151.

518 [1961] A.C. 388.

519 [1961] A.C. 388 at 422-423. Viscount Simonds went on (at 425) to castigate Lord Sumner's dictum in *Weld-Blundell v Stephens* [1920] A.C. 956 at 984, that foreseeability "goes to culpability, not to

kind as the reasonable man should have foreseen. Damage to the wharf by fire was a different kind of damage from that caused by fouling, and as the fire was unforeseeable, the defendants were not liable in negligence. For Viscount Simonds:

> "It is not the act but the consequences on which tortious liability is founded. Just as … there is no such thing as negligence in the air, so there is no such thing as liability in the air. … [T]he only liability that is in question is the liability for damage by fire. It is vain to isolate the liability from its context and to say that [the defendant] is or is not liable, and then to ask for what damage he is liable. For his liability is in respect of that damage and no other. If, as admittedly it is, [the defendant's] liability (culpability) depends on the reasonable foreseeability of the consequent damage, how is that to be determined except by the foreseeability of the damage which in fact happened—the damage in suit? And, if that damage is unforeseeable so as to displace liability at large, how can the liability be restored so as to make compensation payable?"[520]

Despite being of only persuasive authority, the *Wagon Mound (No.1)* has been followed by subsequent English courts. The test of remoteness in the tort of negligence is that the defendant is liable only for damage of a kind which a reasonable man should have foreseen. If the very kind of damage that was foreseeable occurs, the defendant is liable for the full extent of that damage, albeit he might well not have expected damage of that extent or degree.[521] There is, however, no requirement that the defendant foresee the precise manner in which the damage occurred, provided that it is within the general range of the risk created by his negligence.[522] **2-157**

The moral basis of the test, as enunciated by Viscount Simonds, has not been fully accepted. As for the justice of the matter, it should be remembered that the extent of *foreseeable* damage rarely corresponds with the degree of a defendant's fault, and the measure of damages, even for damage of the same physical extent, will vary from case to case. Thus, a foreseeability test can lead to dire consequences from a venial act of negligence. Moreover, Viscount Simonds' emphasis on fairness for defendants may overlook the question of what is fair for claimants. If a choice has to be made as to where the loss should lie, then as between an innocent claimant and a defendant who *ex hypothesi* is guilty of wrongful conduct it is not obviously unfair to make the defendant responsible. Where hard choices have to be made the criterion of fairness merely begs the question: to whom should the court be fair? Considerations of this kind have undoubtedly influenced courts in their application of the foreseeability test to physical damage: little foreseeability of the kind of damage has been required; a broad categorisation has generally been applied to the kind of damage that must be foreseen; foreseeability of the extent of the damage has not been required; the so-called "eggshell skull" rule has been reaffirmed. The effect has been that though the courts apply a foreseeability test, in practice it does not look so different from the test propounded in *Polemis*. **2-158**

Level of foreseeability In *Wagon Mound (No.2)*,[523] arising out of the same events, the Privy Council reached a different conclusion as to the foreseeability of fire. In *Wagon Mound (No.1)*, the claim had been brought by the owners of the wharf whereas in *Wagon Mound (No.2)*, it was brought by owners of the ships damaged **2-159**

---

compensation" as "fundamentally false".

520 [1961] A.C. 388 at 425.

521 See para.2-168.

522 See para.2-161.

523 [1967] 1 A.C. 617.

by the fire. The judge found that there was a minimal risk of fire, but held that this was so slight as to be negligible and hence, following the requirement in *Wagon Mound (No.1)* that damage had to be reasonably foreseeable, he dismissed the claims in negligence. He went on to hold that the claimants succeeded in nuisance because foreseeability was not necessary to liability in nuisance.[524] The Privy Council reversed this decision, holding that:

(a) foreseeability is the appropriate test of remoteness in public nuisance; but
(b) since a slight risk of fire had been found to be foreseeable, the defendants were liable in negligence after all.

The difference in result between the two cases was based on a significant difference in the findings of fact. In the first it had been found that fire damage was not foreseeable at all. In the second, the trial judge found that a slight risk of fire was foreseeable, but the possibility was so remote he felt entitled to ignore it. The Privy Council stressed the point that here there was some foreseeability of the kind of damage, namely fire, however remote the possibility may have been.[525] Thus, once it is established that the damage sustained by the claimant was foreseeable, the *likelihood* that it would have occurred is irrelevant. In *The Heron II*,[526] for example, Lord Upjohn said that "the tortfeasor is liable for any damage which he can reasonably foresee may happen as a result of the breach however unlikely it may be, unless it can be brushed aside as far-fetched". The degree of likelihood that a particular result will ensue relates to the question whether or not the defendant's conduct was careless in the light of that likelihood[527]; it is not relevant to the kind of damage to be expected from the carelessness.

(ii) Manner of the occurrence

2-160 **Precise accident need not be foreseeable** The fact that the damage occurred in an unforeseeable way does not necessarily mean that it was not foreseeable.[528] In *Hughes v Lord Advocate*[529] employees of the Post Office in breach of their duty left a manhole in the road uncovered. A canvas tent was erected over it and lighted paraffin lamps were placed round it. The claimant, a child, picked up a lamp and with the aid of a ladder clambered down into the manhole. In the course of his reascent the lamp was knocked back into the hole. Through an unusual combination of circumstances an explosion occurred and the claimant was burned. The majority of the judges in the Scottish Court of Session, Inner House, held against the claimant on the ground that, even though it might have been foreseeable that he would be burned by the overturning of the lamp, it was not foreseeable that he would be burned by an explosion sparked off by the overturned lamp. The House

---

524 [1963] 1 Lloyd's Rep. 402.

525 [1967] 1 A.C. 617 at 641. Perhaps the reason why the claimants in the *Wagon Mound (No.1)* chose not to stress even a slight foreseeability of fire may be that, had they done so, they would have been met by a plea of contributory negligence in deciding to resume welding operations in the face of that risk. If the risk was foreseeable to the defendants it should have been foreseeable to the claimants, and at that time contributory negligence was a complete defence in New South Wales.

526 [1969] 1 A.C. 350 at 422.

527 See para.7-176.

528 The precise concatenation of events need not be anticipated if the harm is within the general range of what is reasonably foreseeable: *Stewart v West African Terminals Ltd* [1964] 2 Lloyd's Rep. 371 at 375.

529 [1963] A.C. 837.

of Lords unanimously rejected the distinction and held that as long as it was foreseeable that the claimant might be burned by the lamp, it was immaterial that neither the extent of his injury nor the precise chain of events leading to it was foreseeable. Lord Pearce commented that: "to demand too great precision in the test of foreseeability would be unfair to [claimants] since the facets of misadventure are innumerable."[530]

Accident within scope of foreseeable risk If the kind of accident which occurred falls within the scope of the foreseeable risk created by the defendant's negligence it will not be too remote. In *Jolley v Sutton LBC*[531] the House of Lords took a broad approach towards this issue. The defendants admitted negligence in failing to remove from its land an upturned boat with rotten planking. The claimant, aged 14, was injured when he jacked up the boat and crawled underneath. The Court of Appeal found the defendants not liable on the ground that the only foreseeable risk was to "children who were drawn to the boat climbing upon it and being injured by the rotten planking giving way beneath them."[532] The House of Lords reversed the decision, upholding the view of the trial judge that the foreseeable risk was that children would "meddle with the boat at the risk of some physical injury". As the actual accident and resulting injury fell within this description, the defendant was held liable. Lord Hoffmann emphasised that what had to be foreseen was "not the precise injury which occurred but injury of a given description." Since the defendants had conceded that there was a foreseeable risk that children would be attracted to the boat and might suffer minor injuries, the wider risk of more serious injury fell within the scope of the defendants' duty of care. It "would have cost the defendant no more trouble to avoid the injury which happened than he should in any case have taken".[533] Lord Steyn commented that there was no suggestion in Viscount Simonds' speech in *The Wagon Mound (No.1)* that "the *precise* manner of which the injury occurred ... had to be foreseeable".[534] The point is illustrated by the *Trecarrell*[535] where the defendants were held liable for a fire caused by one of their employees dropping a drum of inflammable liquid which was ignited by a short circuit in an electric cable that had been severed by the falling drum. 2-161

The broad approach taken to the description of the foreseeable risk by the House of Lords in *Jolley* throws doubt on two other much criticised decisions. In *Doughty* 2-162

530 [1963] A.C. 837 at 853. See also *Wisniewski v Central Manchester HA* [1998] Lloyd's Rep. Med. 223 CA—the defendants liable in respect of hypoxia suffered by the claimant infant during the course of his birth when the defendants' negligence created a risk of oxygen starvation in the womb, though the actual mechanism by which the claimant sustained the hypoxia was an unforeseen rare event (strangulation as a result of a knot in the umbilical cord). In *Spencer v Wincanton Holdings Ltd* [2009] EWCA Civ 1404; [2010] P.I.Q.R. P8 the claimant sustained a relatively minor accident to his knee which through complications resulted, three years later, in an above the knee amputation. Eight months after the amputation the claimant fell and sustained further injuries which rendered him wheelchair dependent. The Court of Appeal rejected the defendants' argument that this was damage of a kind which was not reasonably foreseeable. The consequences that had to be foreseen were not to be narrowly defined. The "kind of consequence" in question was personal injury and the damage resulting from it. If personal injury and its consequences, i.e. amputation, were foreseeable at the time of the initial accident, it followed that personal injury resulting from that amputation was also a consequence that was reasonably foreseeable at the time of the initial accident.

531 [2000] 1 W.L.R. 1082.

532 [1998] 1 W.L.R. 1546 at 1555, per Roch LJ.

533 [2000] 1 W.L.R. 1082 at 1093.

534 [2000] 1 W.L.R. 1082 at 1090.

535 [1973] 1 Lloyd's Rep. 402.

v Turner Manufacturing Co Ltd[536] an asbestos cement cover was negligently dropped into very hot, molten liquid by a workman employed by the defendants. The cover slid in obliquely from a height of only a few inches and so caused no splash. A minute or two later chemical changes inside the asbestos due to the high temperature, brought about an eruption of the liquid. The claimant, another employee, who happened to be on the spot delivering a message, was burned. The possibility of an eruption occurring in this way was unknown at the time. The Court of Appeal, following *Wagon Mound (No.1)* and distinguishing *Hughes*, held that the claimant was not entitled to recover. The language of the court suggests that a distinction has to be drawn between burning by a splash and by an eruption of molten liquid and it seems to imply that even if injury by splashing had been foreseeable, the claimant would not have recovered because he was injured by an unforeseeable eruption. The decision might be justified on the ground that a splashing and a subsequent eruption were two different kinds of accident[537] and as the eruption was unforeseeable, it was too remote. However, as in *Jolley*, it would have cost the defendant no more trouble to avoid the injury which happened, i.e. that caused by the eruption, than it should in any case have taken to avoid the possibility of injury by splashing. Hence, it is arguable that the court should have adopted a description of the foreseeable injury broad enough to encompass that caused by the eruption. In *Att Gen v Hartwell*[538] Lord Nicholls questioned whether *Doughty* "would commend itself today" in the light of *Hughes* and *Jolley*. The second case is *Crossley v Rawlinson*[539] in which the claimant, whilst running towards a burning vehicle with a fire extinguisher, tripped in a concealed hole and was injured. In holding that the defendant, whose negligence had resulted in the need to rescue, was not liable the court seemed to draw a distinction between injuries caused in the rescue attempt itself and those caused on the way to the attempt. It might be argued that the kind of accident was unforeseeable, but following *Jolley*, it is arguable that the accident was within the risk created by the negligence.

(iii) Type of damage

2-163 The damage will be too remote if it is not of the same "kind" or "type" as the foreseeable damage. The problem is to know what constitutes the same type of damage, although there tends to be some overlap between this issue and the question of how, precisely, the damage occurred.[540] It would have been possible for the courts to take a broad view of the classification of damage, dividing it into personal injury, property damage and financial loss. Although this categorisation has not been formally adopted, in practice the courts have reached the point where this is virtually the position (though in the case of financial loss, the recoverable damage is very much linked to the scope of the defendant's duty of care).

---

536 [1964] 1 Q.B. 518.

537 Indeed, the danger from splashing had exhausted itself by the time the eruption occurred. So whatever danger might have been created by the original act this had ceased to be operative when the injury was sustained.

538 [2004] UKPC 12; [2004] 1 W.L.R. 1273 at [29].

539 [1982] 1 W.L.R. 369.

540 "Sometimes, depending on the circumstances, personal injury as a type of damage may need to be broken down further, distinguishing between personal injury arising from one particular cause and personal injury arising from another. A defendant may be regarded as owing a duty of care in respect of one but not the other": *Att Gen v Hartwell* [2004] UKPC 12; [2004] 1 W.L.R. 1273 at [28], per Lord Nicholls.

The answer depends on the question The decision as to whether a particular type of harm is foreseeable often depends on how the court chooses to frame the question. In *Hughes v Lord Advocate* the claimant suffered burns due to an unforeseeable explosion. The question asked by the House of Lords was whether burning was foreseeable, to which the answer was yes, because it was foreseeable that a paraffin lamp might overturn and burn the claimant. If, however, the question had been was burning by an explosion foreseeable, the answer would have been negative.[541] *Hughes* suggests that the courts should take a broad approach to categorising the "kind of damage" in a personal injury context.[542] In the case of an occupational disease, foreseeability of the risk of injury of the same type is sufficient. The defendant does not have to foresee the precise disease that the employee is likely to contract. Thus, if it was known that exposure to asbestos dust could produce lung disease (such as asbestosis) it is irrelevant that the causal link between asbestos and mesothelioma was not established until a later date.[543] **2-164**

Similarly, in *Muirhead v Industrial Tank Specialities Ltd*[544] the question was whether the manufacturers of pumps used to circulate the water at a commercial fish farm were responsible for the destruction of the claimants' stock of lobsters when the pumps cut out, with the result that the system for oxygenating the water failed. The trial judge had found that the manufacturers could not have foreseen the physical damage, namely the killing of the stock of lobsters, partly because of evidence as to the speed with which a tankful of lobsters would die in such circumstances. On appeal, Goff LJ considered that the judge had not asked the correct question. The real question was whether damage of the relevant *type* was reasonably foreseeable, "i.e. physical harm to fish stored in a tank at a fish farm by reason of failure of the circulation and oxygenation pumps ...".[545] On that basis, the manufacturers were liable for the loss of the lobsters because they knew that their pumps were being sold to fish farms, and should have realised that they were being used for circulation and oxygenation of water in tanks where fish were kept, so they could foresee that if the pumps failed, "physical harm to the fish was liable to occur". **2-165**

---

541 Contrast *Doughty v Turner Manufacturing Co Ltd* where the question asked by the Court of Appeal was whether burning *as a result of* a chemical eruption was foreseeable (answer: no), rather than "was burning foreseeable?" (answer: yes).

542 Such an approach was taken at first instance in *Bradford v Robinson Rentals Ltd* [1967] 1 W.L.R. 337. The claimant suffered frostbite as a result of being sent by his employer on a journey in a van not equipped with a heater. Rees J held that although the consequences of prolonged exposure to cold would be commonly thought to include colds, chilblains or even pneumonia, "frostbite which is admittedly unusual is nevertheless of the type and kind of injury which was reasonably foreseeable": [1967] 1 W.L.R. 337 at 344. A much narrower categorisation was employed in *Tremain v Pike* [1969] 1 W.L.R. 1556, in which the claimant, a herdsman employed by the defendants, contracted a rare disease, which was the result of coming into contact with rats' urine. He alleged that the defendants had been negligent in allowing rats to infest the farm buildings. They were held not liable on the ground that they had not been negligent. Payne J added however that even though injury through rat-bites or even illness through food contamination was foreseeable, this unforeseeable rare disease was a "different kind" of injury. It seems likely, however, that this narrow approach would not survive the reasoning in *Jolley v Sutton LBC* [2000] 1 W.L.R. 1082, see para.2-161.

543 *Jeromson v Shell Tankers (UK) Ltd* [2001] EWCA Civ 101; [2001] I.C.R. 1223. In a case of occupational deafness the fact that the foreseeable risk was of harm caused over a period of time rather than the traumatic injury that the claimant had sustained was "neither here nor there": *Royal Opera House Covent Garden Foundation v Goldscheider* [2019] EWCA Civ 711; [2020] I.C.R. 1 at [46]; applying *Hughes v Lord Advocate*.

544 [1986] Q.B. 507.

545 [1986] Q.B. 507 at 532.

2-166 **Personal injury—physical harm and psychiatric harm** It was formerly the view that there was a difference in kind between physical injury and psychiatric injury, but in *Page v Smith*[546] the House of Lords held that if physical injury to the claimant was foreseeable the defendant was liable for any psychiatric damage which the claimant sustained as a result of the defendant's negligence, even though physical injury did not in the event occur and the psychiatric damage was itself unforeseeable. Lord Lloyd said that there was no justification for regarding physical and psychiatric injury as different "kinds" of injury: "Once it is established that the defendant is under a duty of care to avoid causing personal injury to the [claimant] it matters not whether the injury in fact sustained is physical, psychiatric or both."[547] The implication of this, though not discussed in the House of Lords, is that the courts will increasingly approach the determination of the *type of damage* with a very broad brush, possibly going so far as to treat all forms of personal injury as foreseeable as a result of the occurrence of any foreseeable form of personal injury. If there is to be no distinction between *physical* injury and *psychiatric* injury (and the claimant can recover for unforeseeable psychiatric injury, provided some unrelated physical injury is foreseeable), there is little obvious justification for distinguishing between *different types of physical injury*, at least in the case of personal injuries. It might be said that, strictly speaking, *Page v Smith* was a case concerning the existence of a duty of care, rather than remoteness of damage, and that it should be confined to the duty question. But this would be to take too rigid an approach to the categories of duty and remoteness, and to ignore the frequent references in the majority speeches to notions that are normally to be found when dealing with questions of remoteness of damage (such as "the defendant must take his victim as he finds him").[548] On the other hand, in *R. v Croydon HA*,[549] a case concerning a missed diagnosis following an X-ray, Kennedy LJ did not accept that *Page v Smith* had extended the boundaries of foreseeability in this manner (though there was no analysis of the speeches in *Page v Smith* and his Lordship did not attempt to explain why the case did not have this effect).

2-167 **Damage to property** With regard to property damage, the *Wagon Mound (No.1)*[550] establishes that there is a difference in kind between fire and pollution damage. Its disapproval of *Polemis*[551] also suggests that there is a difference between damage by impact and damage by fire. This appears to be a more restrictive approach than that taken in relation to personal injury. Cases in which the issue has been relevant are comparatively few. In *Vacwell Engineering Co Ltd v BDH*

546 [1996] 1 A.C. 155. See also *Simmons v British Steel* [2004] UKHL 20; 2004 S.C. (HL) 94; [2004] I.C.R. 585.

547 [1996] 1 A.C. 155 at 190. In *Corr v IBC Vehicles Ltd* [2006] EWCA Civ 331; [2007] Q.B. 46 at [67] Sedley LJ commented that "[t]he law of negligence no longer draws any distinction, for purposes of foreseeability and causation, between physical and psychological injury".

548 Note, however, that for the purpose of establishing breach of duty in the context of a claim for psychiatric harm arising from occupational stress the court will distinguish between different types of foreseeable risk of psychiatric harm: see *Pratley v Surrey CC* [2003] EWCA Civ 1067; [2004] P.I.Q.R. P17, where the Court of Appeal, distinguished between the foreseeable risk of psychiatric injury resulting from a continuing work overload in the future, and the unforeseeable risk of collapse in the short-term arising from disappointment of the employee's "cherished idea" for meeting long-term problems.

549 [1998] P.I.Q.R. Q26 CA at 32–33.

550 [1961] A.C. 388.

551 [1921] 3 K.B. 560.

Chemicals Ltd,[552] in which a chemical came into contact with water and the reaction led to an explosion of unforeseeable violence causing extensive damage, Rees J said: "It would also be foreseeable that some damage to property would or might result. In my judgment the explosion and the type of damage being foreseeable, it matters not in the law that the magnitude of the former and the extent of the latter were not." This suggests that the type of damage in question here was "some damage to property", indicating a wide interpretation of the type of harm.[553]

(iv) Extent of the damage

Unforeseeable extent of damage irrelevant If the type of harm and the manner of its occurrence were foreseeable it is irrelevant that the physical extent of the damage was unforeseeable. In *Hughes v Lord Advocate*, Lord Reid said: "No doubt it was not to be expected that the injuries would be as serious as those which the appellant in fact sustained. But a defender is liable, although the damage may be a good deal greater in extent than was foreseeable."[554] This rule applies to psychiatric harm as much as it does to physical injuries, irrespective of any predisposition in the claimant which, unknown to the defendant, increases the likelihood of more extensive damage.[555] The same principle also applies to property damage. In *Vacwell Engineering Co Ltd v BDH Chemicals Ltd*[556] it was known that a particular chemical manufactured and supplied by the defendants was liable to react with water, but on this particular occasion there was a violent explosion which caused extensive damage to the premises. A minor explosion was foreseeable, but an explosion of the magnitude which did occur was not foreseeable. Nonetheless, the defendants were held liable for the full extent of the damage.[557] **2-168**

Nonfeasance The rule that a defendant is liable even for the unforeseeable extent of physical damage does not apply to a case of nonfeasance where the defendant has done nothing to create the danger. It is exceptional for there to be a duty to act positively, though such a duty does arise where the defendant is responsible for abating a naturally occurring nuisance. In *Holbeck Hall Hotel v Scarborough BC*,[558] the Court of Appeal held that in a case of nonfeasance it would not be just and reasonable to impose liability for damage which, though of the same type as that which was foreseeable, was vastly more extensive than that which was foreseen or could have been foreseen without extensive geological investigation. In such **2-169**

---

552 [1971] 1 Q.B. 88 at 110 (emphasis added).

553 See also *Muirhead v Industrial Tank Specialities Ltd* [1986] Q.B. 507, para.2-128, where "physical harm to the fish" was the categorisation of the type of damage.

554 [1963] A.C. 837 at 845.

555 *Page v Smith* [1996] 1 A.C. 155; *Brice v Brown* [1984] 1 All E.R. 997.

556 [1971] 1 Q.B. 88 (the appeal was settled and damages varied, but the remoteness point was unchallenged: [1971] 1 Q.B. 111 CA).

557 Rees J said "the explosion and the type of damage being foreseeable, it matters not in the law that the magnitude of the former and extent of the latter were not": [1971] 1 Q.B. 88 at 110. See also *Parsons v Uttley, Ingham & Co Ltd* [1978] Q.B. 791, where the Court of Appeal held that, provided injury to property was foreseeable (in this case a mild illness of pigs), the defendants were liable for their death through an unforeseeably serious disease. The defendants negligently failed to leave open the ventilator of a hopper, which they installed for the claimants, with the result that nuts stored in it became mouldy. When fed with these nuts the claimants' pigs developed a serious illness from which a large number died. This was a case in contract, but the court treated the rules of remoteness in tort and contract on this point as being the same.

558 [2000] Q.B. 836.

circumstances the scope of the defendants' duty may be limited to warning the claimants of such risk as they were aware of or ought to have foreseen and sharing such information as they had about the problem. Thus the subjective duty upon an occupier to abate a naturally occurring nuisance is limited not merely by the occupier's ability to abate the nuisance but by its foreseeable extent.

(v) *Eggshell skulls*

2-170 **The "eggshell skull" rule** Long before *Wagon Mound*, it was an established doctrine that a defendant has to take his victim as he finds him, which means that if it was reasonable to foresee some injury, however slight, to the claimant, assuming him to be a normal person, then the defendant is answerable for the full extent of the injury which the claimant may sustain owing to some peculiar susceptibility. The rule applies only when the claimant's pre-existing hypersensitivity is triggered into inflicting the injury complained of, or an existing injury is aggravated by the defendant's act. Where the injury itself pre-exists and was not caused by the defendant, it is not attributable to him.[559] So, too, if the aggravation of the claimant's damage is merely accelerated and not caused by the defendant's action, the latter is not liable in respect of it.[560] The clear example of the hypersensitivity type of case is that of persons suffering from haemophilia[561] or "egg-shell" skulls. Mackinnon LJ said that "one who is guilty of negligence to another must put up with idiosyncrasies of his victim that increase the likelihood or extent of damage to him: it is no answer to a claim for a fractured skull that its owner had an unusually fragile one".[562]

2-171 The eggshell skull rule overlaps, but is not coextensive with, the general principle that the extent of the harm need not be foreseeable. Where the claimant's predisposition simply exacerbates the otherwise foreseeable type of harm, then it is little more than the mechanism by which that principle comes into effect. Conversely, the general principle can apply in the absence of any predisposition or weakness in the claimant. However, it is arguable that the eggshell skull rule goes beyond the proposition that the physical extent of the damage does not have to be foreseeable.

2-172 In *Smith v Leech Brain & Co Ltd*[563] a workman suffered a burn on his lip when a fleck of molten metal splashed onto it. His employers were at fault in not having provided him with a proper shield. The burn healed, but due to a premalignant condition the burn triggered a cancerous growth leading eventually to the workman's death. It was proved that he had a predisposition to cancer, but this condition might never have become malignant were it not for the burn. Lord Parker CJ, having stated that the *Wagon Mound (No.1)*[564] had not changed the rule that a tortfeasor must take his victim as he finds him, held the defendants liable for the death:

---

559 *Jobling v Associated Dairies* [1982] A.C. 794.

560 *Cutler v Vauxhall Motors Ltd* [1971] 1 Q.B. 418.

561 *Bishop v Arts & Letters Club of Toronto* (1978) 83 D.L.R. (3d) 107.

562 *Owens v Liverpool Corp* [1939] 1 K.B. 394 at 400–401.

563 [1962] 2 Q.B. 405. For an unusual example of the eggshell skull rule see *Singh v Aitken* [1998] P.I.Q.R. Q37 (county court)—defendants' negligence resulted in the death of S, who at the time of his death had an outstanding claim for damages for personal injuries against another tortfeasor. His death reduced the value of that claim substantially. Defendants held liable to compensate for the reduction in value of S's claim against the first tortfeasor. The defendants had to take S as they found him, namely a man with an unanswerable claim to a large sum, which was lost as a result of their negligence.

564 [1961] A.C. 388.

> "The test is not whether these employers could reasonably have foreseen that a burn would cause cancer and that he would die. The question is whether these employers could reasonably foresee the type of injury he suffered, namely, the burn. What, in the particular case, is the amount of damage which he suffers as a result of that burn, depends upon the characteristics and constitution of the victim."[565]

Lord Parker classified the type of injury as "the burn". The "type" of injury that caused the death, triggered off by the burn, was cancer. A burn would seem to be a different type of harm from cancer. Only if the harm is categorised broadly as "personal injury" could the damage be regarded as merely greater in extent than the foreseeable damage. The eggshell skull rule contains a strong element of policy, particularly in the case of personal injuries. As Professor Fleming put it: "human bodies are too fragile and life too precarious to permit a defendant nicely to calculate how much injury he might inflict."[566]

"Crumbling skulls" In *Environment Agency v Ellis*[567] the claimant had symptomless, pre-existing degenerative changes in his spine, which, on the medical evidence, would probably have started to produce symptoms in about ten years. He suffered an injury to his back in June 1998 which was attributable to the negligence of his employers, and in April 2000 the claimant fell down a flight of stairs at home because his back gave way, causing a serious injury to his right knee. He was no longer able to work. The defendants argued, inter alia, that there were multiple causes of the claimant's loss, and that 70 per cent of the loss should be attributed to the pre-existing degeneration. The Court of Appeal rejected the argument on the evidence, but also as a matter of principle. May LJ said that: **2-173**

> "the pre-existing spinal degeneration was a condition which affected Mr Ellis, not an event for which somebody (including Mr Ellis himself if he were careless) might or might not be responsible. It was not a cause in the sense that careless driving or negligent or non-negligent exposure to vibration may be a cause of damage. On the contrary, it was a condition akin to that which underlies the so called eggshell skull principle—see *Smith v Leech Brain* [1962] 2 Q.B. 405 at 414 and *Page v Smith* [1996] A.C. 155 at 182, 189."[568]

Of course, the assessment of the claimant's damages takes into account the probability that his back would have deteriorated progressively, the damages being calculated on the basis that accident brought forward the deterioration of the claimant's spine by 10 years (and so the causative effect of the tort expires after 10 years). The Canadian courts refer to such cases as "crumbling skull" cases. In *Athey v Leonati*[569] the Supreme Court of Canada observed that: "As long as a defendant is *part* of the cause of an injury, the defendant is liable, even though his act alone was not enough to create the injury. There is no basis for a reduction of liability because of the existence of other preconditions: defendants remain liable for all

565 [1961] A.C. 388 at 415. See also *Warren v Scruttons Ltd* [1962] 1 Lloyd's Rep. 497—injury to claimant's finger, resulting in a blood infection, producing a deterioration in the sight of one of his eyes due to an existing predisposition to developing ulcers in the eye. Defendants held liable for the damage to the eye.

566 J.G. Fleming, *The Law of Torts*, 9th edn (LBC Information Services, 1998), p.235.

567 [2008] EWCA Civ 1117; [2009] P.I.Q.R. P5; [2009] L.S. Law Med. 70.

568 [2008] EWCA Civ 1117; [2009] P.I.Q.R. P5; [2009] L.S. Law Med. 70 at [36].

569 [1997] 1 W.W.R. 97 at 103.

injuries caused or contributed to by their negligence." But the defendant is not responsible for the debilitating effects of the claimant's pre-existing condition which he would have experienced in any event. The defendant is liable only for any additional damage.

2-174 **Medical complications** The eggshell skull rule applies to complications from medical treatment the need for which has arisen from an injury caused by the defendant. Thus, in *Robinson v Post Office*[570] the claimant was injured as a result of the defendant's negligence. He was given an anti-tetanus injection by his doctor, but nine days later he suffered a serious allergic reaction to the injection. The Court of Appeal held the defendants liable for this injury, stating that a person who could reasonably foresee that the victim of his negligence may require medical treatment is liable for the consequences of the treatment "although he could not reasonably foresee those consequences or that they could be serious". In this situation it would seem that there is no question of the type of consequence having to be foreseeable, provided the need for treatment is foreseeable.

2-175 **Psychiatric harm** Claims in respect of psychiatric damage are also consistent with this principle. If physical injury was foreseeable to the claimant then it is irrelevant that psychiatric harm was unforeseeable, and irrelevant that physical injury did not occur.[571] The claimant is entitled to compensation for his psychiatric harm, no matter how extensive, and no matter that it was the product of a constitutional predisposition to developing a psychiatric condition. In cases where the claimant was not exposed to the risk of physical harm, but developed a psychiatric condition as a result of what he or she observed (and so is regarded as a "secondary victim"), the claimant must demonstrate (inter alia) that psychiatric harm was foreseeable in a person of "ordinary fortitude".[572] So, if the claimant is particularly sensitive to developing a psychiatric condition, there will be no liability (in the form of a ruling that the defendant owed no duty of care) unless the circumstances are such that a person who is not over-sensitive to developing a psychiatric condition would have done so. But once that point has been reached the defendant is liable for the full extent of the psychiatric harm, even if this is exacerbated by the claimant's particular sensitivity.[573]

2-176 **Psychiatric harm following physical injury** It is not uncommon for a claimant to develop a major psychiatric condition following a relatively minor physical injury. Provided that a causal connection (medically) can be demonstrated between the physical injury and the psychiatric condition, the defendant is liable in full for the psychiatric consequences, no matter how unforeseeable. For example, in *Shorey v PT Ltd*[574] the High Court of Australia held that the claimant was entitled to recover for the consequences of a conversion disorder which resulted in paraplegia, although there was no organic cause of the paraplegia, where the defendant's negligence had resulted in the claimant suffering a fall. The physical effects of the fall were probably resolved within about 12 months, but the fall was held to be the

---

570 [1974] 1 W.L.R. 1176.
571 See *Page v Smith* [1996] 1 A.C. 155; para.2-166.
572 See para.7-75.
573 *Page v Smith* [1996] 1 A.C. 155; *Brice v Brown* [1984] 1 All E.R. 997.
574 [2003] HCA 27; (2003) 197 A.L.R. 410.

cause of the conversion disorder, because it was the trigger or "sentinel event".[575] Similarly, in *Simmons v British Steel*[576] the claimant suffered a head injury at work which produced some minor physical symptoms for a few weeks. He experienced an exacerbation of a pre-existing skin condition, and developed a personality change resulting in a severe depressive illness. The House of Lords held that a causal connection could be established between the anger the claimant experienced following the accident and his psychiatric reaction. Given that he was a "primary victim" (he had actually sustained physical injury, unlike the claimant in *Page v Smith*) it was not necessary to demonstrate that his psychiatric reaction was foreseeable and the defendants had to take their victim as they found him.

Sensitive property Where the unexpected magnitude of the damage is caused by the unexpected sensitivity of the *property* damaged, it is submitted that here too the defendant should be liable for the full extent. To distinguish between personal injury and property damage in respect of hypersensitivity would be unacceptable. First, there is no hint of such a distinction in *Wagon Mound (No.1)*, and the majority of cases have applied its principle without alluding to any difference in the law. Secondly, to distinguish between personal and property damage seems anomalous and might conceivably lead to absurdity. Suppose that the defendant inflicts a laceration on a horse, which happens to be haemophilic and bleeds to death. There is no justification in principle for saying that he is liable for the full extent of the injury to a human being, but not to an animal. Thirdly, the principle that a defendant should only be liable to the foreseeable extent of property damage would lead to the practical difficulty of estimating what this would have been when it has been swallowed up in the larger unforeseeable damage. Suppose that a defendant drops a lighted cigarette on a carpet. The foreseeable extent of the burn would be no more than a small hole. If, through some unexpected combination of circumstances, the entire carpet is destroyed, how is the foreseeable extent to be measured? Damages for this would have to be awarded on the basis of a guess, not proven facts. On the other hand, there is a risk that applying the eggshell skull rule to property damage could effectively destroy the distinction drawn by the Privy Council in the *Wagon Mound (No.1)*. For example, if a ship with a hold full of petrol vapour could be regarded as sensitive property having a "predisposition" to explode if it sustained an impact, and impact damage was a foreseeable consequence of the defendant's negligence, a decision that the defendant was liable for the full extent of the resulting damage by explosion would seem to resurrect *Re Polemis*. 2-177

(vi) Claimant's impecuniosity

In *Liesbosch Dredger v SS Edison*[577] the claimants' dredger was sunk due to the defendants' negligence. The claimants were under contract to complete a piece of 2-178

---

575 Kirby J observed, [2003] HCA 27; (2003) 197 A.L.R. 410 at [44], that: "The principle of law is that a negligent defendant must take its victim as it finds her and must pay damages accordingly. It is not to the point to complain that the injury, in the form of the fall, was trivial in itself and that it would be unfair to burden the [defendants] with the obligation to bear costs consequent upon the fact that the [claimant] was peculiarly susceptible to developing bizarre symptoms inherent in a conversion disorder. If such symptoms were genuine and a consequence of the subject trauma, the apparent disproportion between cause and effect is not an exculpation for the negligent party. It does not render the damage 'unforeseeable' or otherwise outside the scope of the damages that may be recovered."

576 [2004] UKHL 20; 2004 S.C. (HL) 94; [2004] I.C.R. 585.

577 [1933] A.C. 449.

work for which they needed a dredger, but they could not afford to purchase a new vessel and so hired a substitute dredger at an exorbitant rate. The substitute dredger was also more expensive to work than the *Liesbosch*. This made the performance of their contractual obligations much more expensive. The House of Lords held that they were not entitled to claim this additional expense because it was not an immediate consequence of the negligence, but was the result of their own want of means which was an "extraneous matter". The defendant did not have to take the claimant as he found him with respect to his impecuniosity. The question that *The Liesbosch* raised was: if a defendant has to take his victim as he finds him should he happen to have an eggshell skull, why did the same rule not apply to the claimant's impecuniosity? After all, a defendant has to take the claimant as he finds him with respect to his earning capacity. If the defendant causes injury to a high earner, he has to compensate him in full for the loss of earnings. Lord Wright's explanation was that the claimants' "financial disability" was not the same as a physical weakness, where the extent of the *physical* damage may be greater as a consequence of that weakness. Nor was it equivalent to an interference with the claimant's profit-earning capacity (where he was a high earner) because the claimants' impecuniosity was "extrinsic".[578]

2-179 The *Liesbosch* had frequently been distinguished. Thus, it was not applied where a decision to defer repairs on a property was based on "commercial prudence" rather than mere impecuniosity[579]; where the claimant's impecuniosity was not the sole cause of the financial loss[580]; and where there was only one head of damage, the cost of repair, whereas in the *Liesbosch* the cost of hiring the replacement dredger was a separate head of damage from the cost of its replacement.[581]

2-180 **Claimant's impecuniosity may be relevant where foreseeable** In *Lagden v O'Connor*[582] the House of Lords held that the rule in the *Liesbosch* that a defendant is not responsible for damage attributable to the claimant's impecuniosity could no longer be regarded as good law. It was not necessary to say that the *Liesbosch* case was wrongly decided. But the law had "moved on" and the correct test today is whether the loss was reasonably foreseeable. Lord Hope said that:

> "The wrongdoer must take his victim as he finds him … This rule applies to the economic state of the victim in the same way as it applies to his physical and mental vulnerability. It requires the wrongdoer to bear the consequences if it was reasonably foreseeable that the injured party would have to borrow money or incur some other kind of expenditure to mitigate his damages."[583]

The effect is that the defendant must take the claimant as he finds him, not only with

---

578 [1933] A.C. 449 at 461. It is not clear, however, why the claimant's lack of resources to purchase a replacement profit-earning chattel is any more "extrinsic" than his capacity (or indeed his lack of capacity) to earn an high income from his labour.

579 *Dodd Properties (Kent) Ltd v Canterbury City Council* [1980] 1 W.L.R. 433.

580 *Mattocks v Mann* [1993] R.T.R. 13.

581 *Alcoa Minerals of Jamaica Ltd v Broderick* [2002] 1 A.C. 371.

582 [2003] UKHL 64; [2004] 1 A.C. 1067.

583 [2003] UKHL 64; [2004] 1 A.C. 1067 at [61]. Lord Nicholls commented, at [6], that it was not acceptable that a financially well-placed claimant would be able to hire a replacement vehicle, and obtain re-imbursement from the defendant's insurers, but an impecunious claimant would not. *Lagden* was applied in *Haxton v Philips Electronics UK Ltd* [2014] EWCA Civ 4; [2014] 1 W.L.R. 2721 (widow whose life expectancy had been reduced by defendant's negligence entitled to recover the diminution in the value of her existing claim for loss of dependency under the Fatal Accidents Act 1976 arising out of the death of her husband; it was "reasonably foreseeable that a curtailment

respect to his physical constitution but also with respect to his means. In practical terms this means that a motorist whose vehicle is off the road for repairs as a result of damage caused by a negligent defendant is entitled to enter into a credit hire agreement for the purpose of hiring an alternative vehicle while the vehicle is off the road and recover the additional cost of credit from the defendant (in practice the defendant's insurers), provided the claimant's impecuniosity is such that he would have been unable to obtain a replacement vehicle had he not used a credit hire company.[584]

Consequential loss: unusually high profits A second difficulty in *The Liesbosch*[585] concerns profit-earning capacity. It is well known that a person may recover damages for the impairment of his profit-earning capacity. It follows, therefore, that a defendant will have to pay more if he injures a highly paid specialist than if he injures a tramp.[586] Lord Wright apparently accepted this rule as applicable only to the impairment of one's *personal* profit-earning capacity as distinct from the impairment of the profit-earning capacity of one's tools. The latter was also rejected without explanation as being "extrinsic". However, compensation was awarded in the *Liesbosch* for the loss on the contract for the period between the sinking of the dredger and the time when a substitute could reasonably have been available. Lord Wright justified this on the basis that "the measure of damages in such cases is the value of the ship to her owner as a going concern at the time and place of the loss".[587] In other words, it is reasonable to foresee that by damaging the dredger her owners would incur some loss at least "in respect of the delay and prejudice caused to them in carrying out the works entrusted to them".[588] In later cases it has been held that a reasonable loss of profits can be recovered in such situations.[589] What is not recoverable is any unusually high profits that the claimant anticipated making. This limitation on the "full extent" rule may be justified in the light of the remoteness rule applying to claims in contract for such losses. Unusually high profits would only be recoverable in contract if they had been notified to the defendant so as to bring them within his contemplation. To allow wider recovery of such losses in tort might be seen as undermining contract principles. 2-181

(c) Remoteness and liability in negligence for pure economic loss

(i) Conceptual issues

Relationship between remoteness and duty In the tort of negligence there is clearly a relationship between the remoteness of damage and the nature and scope of the defendant's duty of care. Since remoteness is concerned with setting the outer limits of the defendant's responsibility in circumstances where the damage has occurred in unusual or unanticipated ways, it makes no sense to attempt to identify 2-182

of life may lead to a diminution in the value of a litigation claim and if a claimant has such a claim, the wrongdoer must take the victim as he finds him", per Elias LJ at [23]).

584 See *Stevens v Equity Syndicate Management Ltd* [2015] EWCA Civ 93; [2015] 4 All E.R. 458 (claimant entitled only to the basic hire rate, not the costs of any additional services received under the credit hire agreement); *McBride v UK Insurance Ltd* [2017] EWCA Civ 144; [2017] R.T.R. 27.

585 [1933] A.C. 449.

586 cf. per Scrutton LJ in *The Arpad* [1934] P. 189 at 202.

587 [1933] A.C. 449 at 464.

588 [1933] A.C. 449 at 465.

589 *The Soya* [1956] 1 W.L.R. 714; *The Naxos* [1972] 1 Lloyd's Rep. 149.

those limits without also addressing the question of what consequences the duty of care imposed upon the defendant was designed to avoid. There is no such thing as a "duty in the air" to act carefully[590] only a duty to avoid inflicting damage carelessly (in certain defined situations). In cases involving physical damage to the claimant or the claimant's property it is, on the whole, easier to identify the limits of liability for the purpose of remoteness by reference to the limitations of cause and effect and the laws of physics, and generally, there will be a duty of care not to inflict physical harm by some positive conduct. There is, however, no general duty of care not to inflict pure economic loss on others[591] and in seeking to establish the limits of liability by reference to the concept of remoteness it is difficult even to begin the process without considering the scope of the defendant's duty to protect the claimant from pure economic loss.[592] Duty and remoteness are, in this context, two sides of the same coin.

2-183 **Relationship of contract and tort actions** The normal basis for recovery of pure economic loss is an action in contract. The remoteness test for contract is based on the kind of loss that the defendant could reasonably contemplate as a consequence of his breach. In *The Heron II*,[593] Lords Reid and Pearce stated that the "contemplation" test in contract required a greater degree of probability than the foresight test in tort. Types of economic loss are also categorised more narrowly than types of physical damage as is illustrated by the leading case of *Victoria Laundry (Windsor) Ltd v Newman Industries Ltd*.[594] The defendants failed to deliver a boiler to a laundry. If it had been delivered on time, the laundry would have been able to complete exceptionally profitable government contracts. The Court of Appeal held that the defendants could only contemplate normal loss of profits resulting from their failure to deliver and that therefore the exceptional losses were too remote and irrecoverable.

2-184 **Concurrent liability in contract and tort** In *Wellesley Partners LLP v Withers LLP*[595] the Court of Appeal held that in the case of concurrent liability in contract and tort the contractual test for remoteness of damage should be applied. In the case of concurrent liability the tortious liability normally arises because one party has assumed a responsibility towards another, and it would be anomalous if the party pursuing the remedy in tort were able to assert that the other party had assumed

---

590 *The Wagon Mound* [1961] A.C. 388 at 425, per Viscount Simonds.

591 See para.7-103.

592 See the discussion of *South Australia Asset Management Corp v York Montague Ltd* [1997] A.C. 191 at para.2-186. Note, however, that there is an increasing tendency of courts to approach cases involving physical damage to the claimant in terms of the scope of the defendant's duty. See, e.g. *R. v Croydon HA* [1998] P.I.Q.R. Q26, where the Court of Appeal limited the damages payable for the birth of a child in respect of a negligent examination of a chest X-ray as part of a pre-employment medical examination which failed to spot a significant abnormality in the claimant, because the scope of the duty of care owed by the radiologist who examined the X-ray did not extend to the claimant's private life and her decision to become pregnant.

593 [1969] 1 A.C. 350 at 386 and 413. Lord Reid and Lord Pearce justified the narrower contemplation test in contract, on the basis that whilst in a contractual relationship, the claimant would have an opportunity of notifying the defendant of any unusual losses he might suffer in the event of breach and hence it was reasonable to limit recovery for non-notified losses to those which were objectively likely, in the normal tort case involving strangers, notification would not be possible and hence it was only reasonable to allow a wider category of loss to be recovered through the foresight test.

594 [1949] 2 K.B. 528.

595 [2015] EWCA Civ 1146; [2016] Ch. 529.

responsibility for a wider range of damage than he would be taken to have assumed under the contract.[596] Floyd LJ observed that since the parties contract on the basis that liability will be confined to damage of the kind which is in their reasonable contemplation, it made no sense for the existence of a concurrent duty in tort to upset this agreement, particularly since the tortious duty arises out of the same assumption of responsibility as exists under the contract.[597]

Loss arising out of defendant's contract with a third party It is also strongly arguable that where the tortious claim for economic loss arises from the defendant's breach of a contract with a third party, the narrower contractual test of remoteness should apply. In the High Court of Australia this approach was taken by McHugh J in *Kenny & Good Pty Ltd v MGICA (1992) Ltd*.[598] The claimant insured a loan made by a bank on the security of property valued for the bank by the defendant. The defendant negligently overvalued the property and when the borrower defaulted, the insurer suffered loss in having to indemnify the bank. The issue was whether the defendant was liable for just the amount of his overvaluation or for the full amount of the loss which included an element caused by a recession in property prices. McHugh J held that the contract principles of remoteness should apply where the claimant is "a free rider on the contract" as in such a case "the defendant's duty to the [claimant] arises out of the defendant's assumption of responsibility". Applying this principle to the ordinary valuation, he concluded that as a true valuation should take into account market falls which could be reasonably contemplated, the difference between the overvaluation and the true value would incorporate the market falls which could be contemplated and were not too remote. Market falls which would not have been taken into account in a true valuation were beyond reasonable contemplation and losses due to such falls should not be borne by the defendant as they were too remote.[599] 2-185

SAAMCO and the scope of the duty In *South Australia Asset Management Corp v York Montague Ltd*[600] (generally known as "*SAAMCO*"), the House of Lords also considered the extent of a valuer's liability for a negligent overvaluation where some of the claimant's loss was the result of a subsequent fall in the property market. Valuers provided negligent valuations of property which were used as security for loans. When the borrowers subsequently defaulted the value of the property proved to be inadequate to cover the loan. In the period between the making of the loans and enforcing the security the property market had collapsed, with the result that the lenders' losses were significantly greater than simply the difference between the negligent valuations and the true valuations that should have been 2-186

---

596 [2015] EWCA Civ 1146; [2016] Ch. 529 at [68], per Floyd LJ.

597 [2015] EWCA Civ 1146; [2016] Ch. 529 at [80]; see also Roth J at [157]. *Wellesley Partners LLP v Withers LLP* was applied in *Wright v Lewis Silkin LLP* [2016] EWCA Civ 1308; [2017] P.N.L.R. 16; and *Agouman v Leigh Day (A Firm)* [2016] EWHC 1324 (QB); [2016] P.N.L.R. 32.

598 [1999] HCA 2; (1999) 63 A.L.R. 611; [2000] Lloyd's Rep. P.N. 25 at 34. See the similar view of the Canadian Supreme Court in *BDC Ltd v Hofstrand Farms Ltd* (1986) 26 D.L.R. (4th) 1; and *British Columbia Hydro v BG Checo International Ltd* (1993) 99 D.L.R. (4th) 577 (SCC).

599 On the particular facts he found the valuer liable for the full loss because the report "was essentially concerned with the safety of a loan investment". It warranted that 65 per cent of the valuation "could safely be lent on the property" and represented that "the property would have sufficient value to enable a lender to recover that sum and interest at any time during the next five years".

600 [1997] A.C. 191 (also cited as *Banque Bruxelles Lambert SA v Eagle Star Insurance Co* [1997] A.C. 191).

made. The lenders' claimed the full loss, including the losses attributable to the fall in market value, on the basis either that had they known the true value they would not have lent the money at all (and therefore would not have been exposed to the risk of the fall in the property market), or that they would have lent much smaller amounts, so that the value of the property would still have been sufficient to provide security even allowing for the fall in the market. Giving the leading speech, Lord Hoffmann considered that whether the claim was brought in tort or contract, the answer depended upon the scope of the valuer's duty. A defendant should only be liable for the kind of loss which fell within the scope of its duty of care. A valuer engaged to provide a valuation of property was providing information upon which a lender could base a decision, taking into account a number of other matters, as to whether to advance a loan secured on the property to a borrower. The valuer was not advising the lender whether to advance the loan. Their Lordships distinguished between *providing information* for the purpose of enabling someone else to decide upon a course of action and a duty to *advise* someone as to what course of action he should take. In the case of advice the adviser must take reasonable care to consider all the potential consequences of that course of conduct, and if he is negligent he will be responsible for all the foreseeable loss which is a consequence of that course of action, but if the duty is only to supply information he must take reasonable care to see that the information is correct, and if he is negligent he will be responsible for the foreseeable consequences of the information being wrong:

> "Rules which make the wrongdoer liable for all the consequences of his wrongful conduct are exceptional and need to be justified by some special policy. Normally the law limits liability to those consequences which are attributable to that which made the act wrongful. In the case of liability in negligence for providing inaccurate information, this would mean liability for the consequences of the information being inaccurate."[601]

Applied to a valuer who overvalues property as security for a loan, the usual consequence of the information being wrong "is that the lender makes an advance which he thinks is secured to a correspondingly greater extent".[602] In other words, the lender has lost security to the amount of the overvaluation. Its losses falling within this amount are recoverable as being within the scope of the duty. Losses going beyond this amount fall outside the scope of the duty and are not recoverable. The court should take into account only the difference between the negligent valuation and the correct valuation at the time of the valuation, and not the fall in market value of the property in the interim even if, had the borrower known the true value

---

601 [1997] A.C. 191 at 213, per Lord Hoffmann. See also *Hughes-Holland v BPE Solicitors* (also known as *Gabriel v Little*) [2017] UKSC 21; [2018] A.C. 599 at para.2-192; discussing and applying *South Australia Asset Management Corp v York Montague Ltd*. Where the defendant has been fraudulent then the whole risk of loss, including the risk of falls in the market, will be imposed upon the defendant: ibid. On the distinction between an "informer" and an "adviser" see *Dugdale* (1996) 12 P.N. 71 at 75; and generally on *SAAMCO*, Stapleton (1997) 113 L.Q.R. 1. Lord Hoffmann subsequently conceded that the restriction on the valuer's liability in *SAAMCO* was not best described by some limitation on the scope of his duty. In "Causation" (2005) 121 L.Q.R. 592 at 596 Lord Hoffmann said: "The scope of the duty of care is to take reasonable care to get the valuation right. It has nothing to do with the extent of the consequences for which the valuer is liable. When one considers what causal relationship is required, one is really speaking about extent of the liability and not about the scope of the duty. Professor Stapleton is right. I shall try to mend my language in future. But I will say this. There is a close link between the nature of the duty and the extent of liability for breach of that duty." See further Kinsky, "*SAAMCO* 10 years on: causation and scope of duty in professional negligence cases" (2006) 22 P.N. 86.

602 [1997] A.C. 191 at 213 at 219.

of Lords unanimously rejected the distinction and held that as long as it was foreseeable that the claimant might be burned by the lamp, it was immaterial that neither the extent of his injury nor the precise chain of events leading to it was foreseeable. Lord Pearce commented that: "to demand too great precision in the test of foreseeability would be unfair to [claimants] since the facets of misadventure are innumerable."[530]

Accident within scope of foreseeable risk If the kind of accident which occurred falls within the scope of the foreseeable risk created by the defendant's negligence it will not be too remote. In *Jolley v Sutton LBC*[531] the House of Lords took a broad approach towards this issue. The defendants admitted negligence in failing to remove from its land an upturned boat with rotten planking. The claimant, aged 14, was injured when he jacked up the boat and crawled underneath. The Court of Appeal found the defendants not liable on the ground that the only foreseeable risk was to "children who were drawn to the boat climbing upon it and being injured by the rotten planking giving way beneath them."[532] The House of Lords reversed the decision, upholding the view of the trial judge that the foreseeable risk was that children would "meddle with the boat at the risk of some physical injury". As the actual accident and resulting injury fell within this description, the defendant was held liable. Lord Hoffmann emphasised that what had to be foreseen was "not the precise injury which occurred but injury of a given description." Since the defendants had conceded that there was a foreseeable risk that children would be attracted to the boat and might suffer minor injuries, the wider risk of more serious injury fell within the scope of the defendants' duty of care. It "would have cost the defendant no more trouble to avoid the injury which happened than he should in any case have taken".[533] Lord Steyn commented that there was no suggestion in Viscount Simonds' speech in *The Wagon Mound (No.1)* that "the *precise* manner of which the injury occurred ... had to be foreseeable".[534] The point is illustrated by the *Trecarrell*[535] where the defendants were held liable for a fire caused by one of their employees dropping a drum of inflammable liquid which was ignited by a short circuit in an electric cable that had been severed by the falling drum. 2-161

The broad approach taken to the description of the foreseeable risk by the House of Lords in *Jolley* throws doubt on two other much criticised decisions. In *Doughty* 2-162

530 [1963] A.C. 837 at 853. See also *Wisniewski v Central Manchester HA* [1998] Lloyd's Rep. Med. 223 CA—the defendants liable in respect of hypoxia suffered by the claimant infant during the course of his birth when the defendants' negligence created a risk of oxygen starvation in the womb, though the actual mechanism by which the claimant sustained the hypoxia was an unforeseen rare event (strangulation as a result of a knot in the umbilical cord). In *Spencer v Wincanton Holdings Ltd* [2009] EWCA Civ 1404; [2010] P.I.Q.R. P8 the claimant sustained a relatively minor accident ... which through complications resulted, three years later, in an above the knee amputation. ... after the amputation the claimant fell and sustained further injuries which rendered ... The Court of Appeal rejected the defendants' argument that this was dam... foreseeable. The consequences that had to be foreseen were ... consequence" in question was personal injury and the dam... consequences, i.e. amputation, were foreseeable at ... resulting from that amputation was ... initial accident.

v Turner Manufacturing Co Ltd[536] an asbestos cement cover was negligently dropped into very hot, molten liquid by a workman employed by the defendants. The cover slid in obliquely from a height of only a few inches and so caused no splash. A minute or two later chemical changes inside the asbestos due to the high temperature, brought about an eruption of the liquid. The claimant, another employee, who happened to be on the spot delivering a message, was burned. The possibility of an eruption occurring in this way was unknown at the time. The Court of Appeal, following *Wagon Mound (No.1)* and distinguishing *Hughes*, held that the claimant was not entitled to recover. The language of the court suggests that a distinction has to be drawn between burning by a splash and by an eruption of molten liquid and it seems to imply that even if injury by splashing had been foreseeable, the claimant would not have recovered because he was injured by an unforeseeable eruption. The decision might be justified on the ground that a splashing and a subsequent eruption were two different kinds of accident[537] and as the eruption was unforeseeable, it was too remote. However, as in *Jolley*, it would have cost the defendant no more trouble to avoid the injury which happened, i.e. that caused by the eruption, than it should in any case have taken to avoid the possibility of injury by splashing. Hence, it is arguable that the court should have adopted a description of the foreseeable injury broad enough to encompass that caused by the eruption. In *Att Gen v Hartwell*[538] Lord Nicholls questioned whether *Doughty* "would commend itself today" in the light of *Hughes* and *Jolley*. The second case is *Crossley v Rawlinson*[539] in which the claimant, whilst running towards a burning vehicle with a fire extinguisher, tripped in a concealed hole and was injured. In holding that the defendant, whose negligence had resulted in the need to rescue, was not liable the court seemed to draw a distinction between injuries caused in the rescue attempt itself and those caused on the way to the attempt. It might be argued that the kind of accident was unforeseeable, but following *Jolley*, it is arguable that the accident was within the risk created by the negligence.

(iii) *Type of damage*

2-163 The damage will be too remote if it is not of the same "kind" or "type" as the foreseeable damage. The problem is to know what constitutes the same type of damage, although there tends to be some overlap between this issue and the question of how, precisely, the damage occurred.[540] It would have been possible for the courts to take a broad view of the classification of damage, dividing it into personal injury, property damage and financial loss. Although this categorisation has not been formally adopted, in practice the courts have reached the point where this is virtually the position (though in the case of financial loss, the recoverable damage is very much linked to the scope of the defendant's duty of care).

---

536 *[1964]* 1 Q.B. 518.

537 Indeed, the danger from splashing had exhausted itself by … whatever danger might have been created by the ori… the injury was sustained.

538 [2004] UKPC 12; [2004] 1 W.L.R. …

539 [1982] 1 W.L.R. 369.

540 "Sometimes, de… broken …

of the property, he would never have advanced the loan.

Remoteness and the scope of the duty Lord Hoffmann did not refer to remoteness in *SAAMCO*, although in a subsequent decision he stated that "It was not suggested that the possibility of a fall in the market was unforeseeable".[603] However, Lord Hobhouse has commented that whilst the scope of the duty is a distinct legal concept, it is analogous to the concept of remoteness.[604] It is arguable that the scope of duty test should be seen as the key element in the application of the remoteness principle to pure economic loss. What the defendant can reasonably contemplate as a consequence of his breach must depend upon the scope or purpose of his duty. If the risk of the particular kind of damage fell outside the purpose of the defendant's duty, then however foreseeable that risk in general terms, it would not fall within the reasonable contemplation of the defendant. Whether the scope of the duty is seen as an independent test or as the key element in the concept of remoteness, it has had a major impact in limiting tortious liability for pure economic loss.[605] 2-187

(ii) *Impact of SAAMCO*

Non-recoverable economic loss As an illustration of the scope of duty principle, Lord Hoffmann referred to *Banque Keyser Ullman SA v Skandia UK Insurance Co Ltd*.[606] The defendant underwriter had failed to warn lending banks that due to the fraud of their insurance brokers, their credit insurance policies were not fully underwritten. The House of Lords held the defendant not liable for losses suffered by the banks due to the fraud of the borrower which fell within an exception to the insurance policies. Lord Hoffmann said of the case: "The failure to inform lenders of the broker's fraud induced them to think that valid policies were in place. But even if this had been true, the loss would still have happened. The insurers would still have been able to repudiate the policies under the fraud exception." The loss resulted from the fraud exclusion in the policy and that was not within the risk created by the alleged negligence. The subsequent decision of Laddie J in *BCCI v Price Waterhouse (No.4)*[607] illustrates the potential of the principle to exclude recovery of economic loss. Laddie J struck out the claimants' claims for billions of US dollars lost through investments, loans and guarantees over the four-year period 2-188

---

603 *Nykredit Mortgage Bank Plc v Edward Erdman Group Ltd* [1997] 1 W.L.R. 1627 at 1639.

604 *Platform Home Loans v Oyston Shipways Ltd* [2000] 2 A.C. 190 at 208. He noted that in the *Wagon Mound* which restated the remoteness principle for negligence "it is the scope of the tort which determines the extent of the remedy to which the injured party is entitled": ibid. at 209. In *Cossey v Lonnkvist* [2000] Lloyd's Rep. P.N. 885 at 888, Evans LJ followed the view of Lord Hobhouse and treated the *SAAMCO* rule as analogous to remoteness.

605 See further the discussion of the interrelationship between remoteness and the scope of the duty by Roth J in *Wellesley Partners LLP v Withers LLP* [2015] EWCA Civ 1146; [2016] Ch. 529 at [153]–[155]. In the illustrative cases in the following paragraphs there has been a contractual relationship between claimant and defendant but the courts have not distinguished between contractual and tortious claims for failure to take reasonable care.

606 [1991] 2 A.C. 249.

607 [1999] B.C.C. 351. See also *Bristol & West Building Society v Fancy Jackson* [1997] 4 All E.R. 582, where Chadwick J applied the principle to hold that the losses resulting from a borrower's default were not attributable to the defendant solicitor negligently informing the claimant, a lender, that he had investigated title when returns from a title search had yet to be received. Chadwick J accepted that the negligence had caused the loan to be made but held that no loss was attributable to the negligence. If the solicitor had correctly secured a clear search, the losses due to default would still have occurred. This was clear from the fact that it transpired that there were no defects in the title.

subsequent to an allegedly negligent audit conducted by the defendants. The claimants argued that if the audit had been properly conducted and the massive lack of internal control of the business had been reported, it would have ceased the loss-making activities. Citing *SAAMCO* Laddie J held that as the auditors "were not asked to advise on what investments or loans to make or guarantees to assume, such losses were not attributable to their alleged breach of duty". Similarly, in *Andrews v Barnett Waddingham LLP (A Firm)*[608] the defendant consulting actuaries were held negligent in the advice given to a client about the application of the Policyholders Protection Act 1975. The client would not have purchased a with-profits annuity from Equitable Life Assurance had he known the true position, but the loss he sustained was attributable to the subsequent downturn in the investment performance of Equitable Life, not the effect of the operation of the Policyholders Protection Act 1975 (since Equitable Life was not insolvent, and the statute was therefore not relevant). The Court of Appeal, applying *SAAMCO*, held that the defendants were not liable for the loss, since it did not fall within the scope of the defendants' duty. The negligence related to the protection afforded to a client if the insurer were to become insolvent, but the loss was attributable to a downturn in investment performance.[609]

2-189 **Recoverable economic loss** In *Rubenstein v HSBC Bank Plc*[610] the defendant bank had advised the claimant to invest in a particular investment fund on the basis that it was equivalent to, and so as safe as, a cash deposit. The claimant lost a substantial sum following the collapse of Lehman Brothers in September 2008 which resulted in a loss of confidence in the financial markets, and a consequent reduction in the value of the fund. The judge held that the claimant's financial loss was too remote, because the unprecedented financial turmoil which surrounded the collapse of Lehman Brothers was not reasonably foreseeable by the defendants. The Court of Appeal disagreed. Relating the scope of the defendants' duty to the issue of remoteness of the damage, Rix LJ observed that the claimant had been misled into thinking that the investment was the same as cash. It was difficult, therefore,

608 [2006] EWCA Civ 93; [2006] P.N.L.R. 24.

609 If the claimant had pleaded and proved that the defendants had been negligent in the decision to recommend the Equitable Life with-profits annuity, as opposed to an annuity with a fixed five per cent annual increase or an increase linked to RPI, the position may have been different. See *Rubenstein v HSBC Bank Plc* [2011] EWHC 2304 (QB); [2012] P.N.L.R. 7 at [106], per Judge Havelock-Allan QC; distinguishing *Andrews v Barnett Waddingham LLP (a firm)* on precisely this point (reversed on appeal, but not affecting this issue: [2012] EWCA Civ 1184; [2013] P.N.L.R. 9). See also *Calvert v William Hill Credit Ltd* [2008] EWCA Civ 1427; [2009] Ch. 330 where the defendants had assumed responsibility to the claimant to exclude him from telephone gambling with them for six months, but the scope of the defendants' duty of care did not extend to preventing him from gambling with them in other ways or with other bookmakers, and the quantification of his loss could not ignore other gambling losses which the claimant would probably have sustained but for the defendants' breach of duty: "The law not only prescribes the appropriate causal connection, but also the scope of the duty and the scope of the loss which the causal connection links" (at [48]). To similar effect is *Haugesund Kommune v Depfa ACS Bank* [2011] EWCA Civ 33; [2011] 3 All E.R. 655 where the defendant solicitors were in breach of duty in failing to advise a lender that swap transactions entered into with Norwegian municipalities were invalid. The Court of Appeal held that, notwithstanding that the lender would not have entered into the transactions had it been informed of their invalidity, the lender was not entitled to recover from the solicitors losses attributable to the creditworthiness or impecuniosity of the municipalities or to the lender's inability to enforce a judgment against the municipalities because such losses fell outside the scope of the solicitors' duty, which was limited to advising on the validity of the transactions.

610 [2012] EWCA Civ 1184; [2013] P.N.L.R. 9.

to argue that the loss was too remote given that it arose from the very factor that made the investment unsuitable in the first place, namely its inherent susceptibility to risk from market movements. The insolvency of Lehman Brothers may have been unforeseeable, but the claimant was not invested in Lehman Brothers. It was the collapse in the value of the market securities in which the claimant's money had been invested which caused the loss, "but such a loss was both foreseeable and foreseen".[611] But in any event, the claimant had been advised that the investment into which he had put his money was the same as a cash deposit, which it was not: "It was the bank's duty to protect Mr Rubenstein from exposure to market forces when he made clear that he wanted an investment which was without any risk ... It is wrong in such a context to say that when the risk from exposure to market forces arises, the bank is free of responsibility because the incidence of market loss was unexpected."[612]

Distinction between advice and information In *SAAMCO*,[613] Lord Hoffmann distinguished the position of a professional whose duty it was to advise whether or not a course of action should be taken, from one whose duty is simply to provide information. An adviser "must take reasonable care to consider all the potential consequences of that course of action. If he is negligent, he will therefore be responsible for all the foreseeable loss which is a consequence of that course of action being taken." The difficulty of distinguishing between information and advice is illustrated by the decision in *Aneco Reinsurance Underwriting Ltd v Johnson & Higgins Ltd*.[614] The defendant insurance brokers were negligent in failing to disclose material risks to a reinsurer, with the result that the reinsurers were able to avoid the reinsurance contract with the claimant reinsurers. Had the defendants disclosed the risks it would have become apparent that reinsurance cover was not available in the market on any terms for the particular risks, and therefore the claimants would not have agreed to enter into the contract of insurance at all. The claimants suffered a loss of $30m on the insured risk. The reinsurance contract had provided cover for $10m of this risk. At first instance Cresswell J applied *SAAMCO* and awarded damages of $10m as being the amount of cover the brokers had failed to secure. On appeal, the House of Lords held the defendants liable for the full loss of $30m on the basis that if the brokers had discharged their duty of care the claimants would have been alerted to the non-availability of any reinsurance, and they would not have taken the main risk and suffered the full loss of $30m. Their Lordships considered that the defendants had undertaken to *advise* about the transaction, not merely to provide information.[615] 2-190

In *SAAMCO* the lender's assessment of the risk was only partly influenced by the 2-191

---

611 [2012] EWCA Civ 1184; [2013] P.N.L.R. 9 at [117].

612 [2012] EWCA Civ 1184; [2013] P.N.L.R. 9 at [118].

613 [1997] A.C. 191 at 214.

614 [2001] UKHL 51; [2002] 1 Lloyd's Rep. 157. Contrast *Intervention Board for Agricultural Produce v Leidig* [2000] Lloyd's Rep. P.N. 144, where the defendant was found to be informing rather than advising.

615 "The key to the giving of advice is that the information is either accompanied by a comment or value judgment on the relevance of that information to the client's investment decision, or is itself the product of a process of selection involving a value judgment so that the information will tend to influence the decision of the recipient. In both these scenarios the information acquires the character of a recommendation": *Rubenstein v HSBC Bank Plc* [2011] EWHC 2304 (QB); [2012] P.N.L.R. 7 at [81], per Judge Havelock-Allan QC (the decision was reversed on appeal, but the issue of whether the defendants had given the claimant advice rather than information was not contested in the appeal: [2012] EWCA Civ 1184; [2013] P.N.L.R. 9).

value of the security it was expecting to obtain,[616] whereas in *Aneco Reinsurance* the judgment about the market assessment of the reinsurance risks was central to the claimants' decision to undertake those risks. Their Lordships indicated that the *SAAMCO* principle creates a sub-rule that valuers are not generally liable for all the foreseeable consequences of their negligence, but only for the consequences of the valuation being wrong. This sub-rule is an exception to the more general rule that professionals are normally liable for the foreseeable consequences of their negligence. *SAAMCO*, said Lord Lloyd, is "an example of a special class of case—typically that of a valuer, but not confined to valuers—where a scope of the defendant's duty is confined to the giving of specific information".[617]

2-192 In *Hughes-Holland v BPE Solicitors*[618] Lord Sumption had reservations about drawing accurate distinctions between giving advice and passing on information. Confusion had arisen because of:

> "the descriptive inadequacy of these labels. On the face of it they are neither distinct nor mutually exclusive categories. Information given by a professional man to his client is usually a specific form of advice, and most advice will involve conveying information. Neither label really corresponds to the contents of the bottle."

Cases will fall into the "information" category where a professional adviser contributes a limited part of the material on which the client relies in deciding whether to enter into a transaction, but there are other considerations, and the assessment of the commercial merits of the transaction is exclusively a matter for the client.[619] In such cases the defendant's responsibility does not extend to the decision itself even where the material which the defendant supplied is known to be critical to the decision to enter into the transaction. The fact that the information provided was critical to the claimant's decision did not itself turn it into an "advice" case, otherwise the defendant would become the underwriter of the financial fortunes of the whole transaction by assuming a duty of care in relation to only one element of someone else's decision. Lord Sumption added that, in classifying the material as information or advice, every case was likely to depend on the range of matters for which the defendant assumed responsibility and no more exact rule

---

[616] Other factors included, e.g. the value of the borrower's covenant to repay the loan, and the lender's own policy on the percentage of the value of the security it was prepared to lend, which in turn would be affected by its own judgment as to the commercial risk involved and the expected return which was reflected in the interest rate charged to the borrower.

[617] [2001] UKHL 51; [2002] 1 Lloyd's Rep. 157 at [13]. Contrast *Lloyds Bank Plc v Burd Pearse (A Firm)* [2001] EWCA Civ 366; [2001] Lloyd's Rep. P.N. 452 where it was held that in a conveyancing transaction the failure of solicitors to draw to the lender's attention matters, such as restrictive covenants, which might affect the value of the property being taken as security for a loan constituted the provision of information rather than advice; and therefore their liability was limited to the difference in the value of the property with and without the restrictive covenants as at the date of the conveyance. Where subsequent events demonstrate that the claimant has suffered no loss the court should take that into account: *Bacciottini v Gotelee & Goldsmith (A Firm)* [2016] EWCA Civ 170; [2016] 4 W.L.R. 98 (planning restriction on property restricting its residential use; after purchase planning restriction removed at cost of £250; claim against negligent solicitors for £100,000 [i.e. difference between value of the property with and without the restriction at the date of purchase] rejected; claimants awarded £250, the cost of removing the restriction).

[618] *Hughes-Holland v BPE Solicitors* (also known as *Gabriel v Little*) [2017] UKSC 21; [2018] A.C. 599 at [39].

[619] [2017] UKSC 21; [2018] A.C. 599 at [41].

could be stated.[620] *Aneco Reinsurance* was not authority for any general proposition of law beyond the particular factual context of that case.

In *Manchester Building Society v Grant Thornton LLP*,[621] commenting on Lord Sumption's judgment in *Hughes-Holland v BPE Solicitors*, Hamblen LJ held that the trial judge had been wrong to approach the issue of liability on the basis of an assumption of responsibility by the defendants rather than considering whether it was an "advice" or "information" case. This was because: **2-193**

> "determining whether it is an 'advice' or 'information' case involves a decision as to assumption of responsibility. If it is an 'advice' case, as defined by Lord Sumption, then the defendant will have assumed responsibility for the decision to enter into the transaction; if it is an 'information' case, then the defendant will only have assumed responsibility for the consequences of the advice or information being wrong. In accordance with the guidance provided by the authorities and, in particular, *Hughes-Holland*, this issue is to be addressed by considering whether it is an 'advice' case or an 'information' case, rather than by asking an open-ended question as to the extent of assumption of responsibility."[622]

While it was correct that the defendant auditors had given negligent accounting advice about the correct accounting treatment of long-term interest rate swaps they were not involved in the claimants' decision to enter into the swaps. The defendants had given advice but "what matters is not whether advice is given, but the purpose and effect of the advice given. In order to be an 'advice' case, the advice needs to involve responsibility for 'guiding the whole decision making process', which [the defendants'] accounting advice manifestly did not."[623]

---

620 [2017] UKSC 21; [2018] A.C. 599 at [44]. On the facts of *Hughes-Holland v BPE Solicitors*, where the defendant solicitors had drawn up a loan facility agreement and charge over a property for the claimant, the solicitors had not assumed responsibility for the claimant's decision to lend money for the purpose of a property development scheme. They were unaware of the nature of the proposed development, its likely cost, the financial capacity of the borrower to fund it without the loan or the value of the property in its developed or undeveloped state. Their negligence had the effect of confirming one of a number of factors in the lender's assessment of the viability of the project, but even if that assumption had been correct the lender would still have lost the money because the project was not commercially viable.

621 [2019] EWCA Civ 40; [2019] 1 W.L.R. 4610.

622 [2019] EWCA Civ 40; [2019] 1 W.L.R. 4610 at [58].

623 [2019] EWCA Civ 40; [2019] 1 W.L.R. 4610 at [64].

CHAPTER 3

GENERAL DEFENCES

TABLE OF CONTENTS

1. Introduction

3-01 **Scope of the chapter** When a claimant fails to establish the primary elements of the particular tort of which he complains, his action necessarily fails. He may however succeed in proving that prima facie a tort has been committed, only to be met with a defence by virtue of which the defendant argues that he is exculpated from liability in all the circumstances. A number of defences are peculiar to the particular tort in question. For example, publication of a defamatory statement may be excused on the ground of privilege. Such specific defences are dealt with later in the context of the particular tort. Other defences are much more general, applying, if not to all, then to many torts. The very term "defence" must be approached with some caution. A defendant in a claim in negligence who successfully rebuts the claimant's arguments that he owed him a duty of care has "defended" the action against him, but he does so not on the basis of a general defence which justifies or excuses his conduct, but by showing no prima facie liability ever attached to him. This chapter is concerned with true defences the effect of which is to justify or excuse conduct which would otherwise be tortious. Unfortunately, the line between a failure to establish prima facie liability and a successful plea of a general defence is not always clear. Logically, if the defendant argues that a novus actus interveniens breaks the chain of causation, he denies that prima facie liability for his conduct has been proven. He does not offer justification or excuse for his conduct. Novus actus is properly a question of causation.[1] Yet sometimes it appears to be treated as a defence, and, when novus actus appears in its guise of act of God that nearly always seems to be the case. There is also an overlap between the defence of ex turpi causa and the duty of care in the tort of negligence. Generally, a claimant's wrongdoing is the basis of a defence, and is treated as such by the courts. But sometimes the court considers that illegal activity of the claimant is such that no duty of care should be owed in the circumstances, with the result that there is no tort to which the defence can apply. The policy underlying the denial of the claim remains the same, but the conceptual tool used to reach that result is different. On the whole, it is submitted that it is better to treat the claimant's wrongdoing as the basis of a general defence, since it could be a relevant issue in torts other than

[1] See para.2-110.

negligence where the concept of duty of care plays no role, and therefore would not be available as a means of dealing with egregious conduct by the claimant.

This chapter will examine general defences in tort in five groups:

(1) the claimant's wrongdoing;
(2) contributory negligence;
(3) consent or assumption of the risk of damage by the claimant;
(4) exclusion of liability; and
(5) miscellaneous defences authorising or excusing the conduct of the defendant.

2. CLAIMANT'S WRONGDOING (EX TURPI CAUSA)[2]

Claimant's wrongdoing not a defence per se Liability in tort involves the commission of a legal wrong by the defendant, and generally this requires some culpable conduct on the part of the defendant. Torts imposing strict liability are comparatively rare. At the very least there will usually be some element of fault or carelessness by the defendant, but of course the defendant's conduct can range from inadvertent carelessness up to very serious criminal offences. Such egregious behaviour is not limited to defendants, and the question arises as to what the position should be where a claimant has engaged in serious wrongful behaviour. Although the law can never completely mirror moral values there is undoubtedly a connection between legal rules and moral judgments.[3] If in some instances moral condemnation of the defendant influences the shape of legal rules (as, for example, in relation to remoteness of damage in the tort of deceit) at what point should moral condemnation of the claimant lead to the conclusion that it would be wrong to compensate the claimant? The dilemma confronting the courts where the claimant has engaged in wrongful conduct was expressed by Bingham LJ in *Saunders v Edwards*: 3-02

> "On the one hand, it is unacceptable that any court of law should aid or lend its authority to a party seeking to pursue or enforce an object or agreement which the law prohibits. On the other hand, it is unacceptable that the court should, on the first indication of unlawfulness affecting any aspect of a transaction, draw up its skirts and refuse all assistance to the [claimant], no matter how serious his loss or how disproportionate his loss to the unlawfulness of his conduct. ... on the whole the courts have tended to adopt a pragmatic approach to these problems, seeking, where possible, to see that genuine wrongs are righted, so long as the court does not thereby promote or countenance a nefarious object or bargain which it is bound to condemn."[4]

Not all wrongful conduct by a claimant will affect his entitlement to a remedy. The mere fact that the claimant was engaged in reprehensible or criminal conduct is not

---

[2] No cause of action arises from illegal or flagrantly immoral acts: ex turpi causa non oritur actio. The Latin tag expresses the broad principle of this defence though it is also referred to simply as the "illegality defence" (see the Law Commission report *The Illegality Defence*, Law Com. No.320, March 2010). In this chapter the terms ex turpi causa and the illegality defence are used interchangeably.

[3] See, e.g. the speech of Lord Steyn in *Smith New Court Securities Ltd v Citibank NA* [1997] A.C. 254 at 280: "The law and morality are inextricably interwoven. To a large extent the law is simply formulated and declared morality."

[4] [1987] 1 W.L.R. 1116 at 1134; see also the comments of Evans LJ in *Revill v Newbery* [1996] Q.B. 567 at 579.

necessarily a basis for dismissing his claim.[5] For example, evidence that the claimant was well over the legal blood alcohol limit whilst driving when a road traffic accident caused entirely by the negligence of the defendant occurred will not bar the claimant's remedy in tort. The illegality, or immorality, of the claimant's own actions must be regarded as both serious and related to the events from which the claim to a remedy arises. Thus, Lord Asquith has suggested that if one burglar picks the pocket of another on their way to the scene of the intended crime, the aggrieved burglar may still sue in tort.[6] And where the claimant's act is the very thing that the defendant was under a duty to exercise reasonable care to prevent the claimant's wrongdoing will not necessarily bar his claim.[7] Moreover, there may also be competing public policy interests which outweigh the policy that wrongdoers should not benefit from their criminal conduct.[8]

3-03 **Ex turpi causa non oritur actio** It is a well-established maxim in contract that a claimant cannot found his claim on an illegal act or agreement.[9] Formerly, the rule applied where the claimant had to rely on the illegality in order to assert his claim,[10] but the Supreme Court has now introduced a broader approach than simply reliance on the illegality.[11] Where a claimant's success in tort depends on establishing a contract, and that contract is tainted by illegality, the claim in tort may also fail.[12] At its simplest it is a matter of public policy that a claimant is not permitted to ground a claim on illegality.[13]

---

5 "[T]he fact that a [claimant] was engaged in an illegal activity which brought about his injury does not automatically bring it about that his claim for damages for personal injury … must be dismissed": *Pitts v Hunt* [1991] 1 Q.B. 24 at 53. In *Cross v Kirkby*, *The Times,* 5 April 2000, Judge LJ commented: "The claimant must be acting unlawfully. But the claim is not doomed to failure merely because the claimant can accurately be described as a wrongdoer whose injuries stemmed from or had their origin in his own criminal conduct. If that represented the single comprehensive test, taken to its logical conclusion, it would mean that the concept of outlawry had been revived."

6 *National Coal Board v England* [1954] A.C. 403 at 428-429.

7 *Reeves v Commissioner of Police of the Metropolis* [1999] Q.B. 169 CA—suicide of a prisoner where the defendants were under a duty to exercise reasonable care to warn the prison authorities that he was a known suicide risk. In these circumstances the defence of volenti non fit injuria does not apply either, although contributory negligence may be relevant: *Reeves v Commissioner of Police of the Metropolis* [2000] 1 A.C. 360 HL. See also *Singularis Holdings Ltd (In Liquidation) v Daiwa Capital Markets Europe Ltd* [2019] UKSC 50; [2019] 3 W.L.R. 997—bank's breach of duty to client company in failing to identify fraudulent conduct of client's director was the very thing that the duty was intended to prevent.

8 See, e.g. paras 3-52 and 3-53.

9 See *Chitty on Contracts*, 33rd edn (London: Sweet & Maxwell, 2018), Ch.16.

10 *Tinsley v Milligan* [1994] 1 A.C. 340 HL.

11 See *Patel v Mirza* [2016] UKSC 42; [2017] A.C. 467; see paras 3-25 to 3-28.

12 *Taylor v Chester* (1869) L.R. 4 Q.B. 309; though see *Saunders v Edwards* [1987] 1 W.L.R. 1116 (claimant recovered damages for fraud even though the contract on which it was based contained a false valuation to escape stamp duty).

13 An analogous principle applies where, though it is clear there is no principle of public policy preventing the claimant maintaining a cause of action, public policy may prevent the recovery of part of the damages sought: ex turpi causa non oritur damnum. See *Hewison v Meridian Shipping Pte Ltd* [2002] EWCA Civ 1821; [2003] I.C.R. 766; [2003] P.I.Q.R. P17 at [28], per Clarke LJ.

(a) Conceptual foundation of ex turpi causa[14]

There has been some confusion in the cases as to when and why the courts will accept that the claimant's wrongful conduct should bar his action for damages in tort.[15] Even the use of the Latin tag, ex turpi causa, has been disputed.[16] There is no doubt that a defence of "illegality" can be pleaded in tort. In *Clunis v Camden and Islington HA*[17] the Court of Appeal expressly rejected a submission that at common law it is limited to actions in contract. This view was unequivocally confirmed by the House of Lords in *Gray v Thames Trains Ltd*.[18] In *Kirkham v Chief Constable of Greater Manchester Police*[19] it was said that the defence was not limited to cases where the claimant's conduct was criminal, but extended in principle to other reprehensible or grossly immoral conduct, in circumstances where it would not be proper to afford the claimant a remedy for his injury.[20] Thus, the term "illegality" does not convey the full potential range of the defence. The burden of proving the defence rests with the defendant.[21] **3-04**

A problem which has troubled the courts has been a lack of clarity as to conceptual foundation of ex turpi causa.[22] Indeed, just about the only thing on which there has been judicial agreement is that the law on the illegality defence in tort is **3-05**

---

14 The Law Commission Consultation Paper, *The Illegality Defence in Tort*, No.160 (2001), provisionally proposed that the common law defence of illegality should be replaced with a structured discretion to bar a claim when the claim arises from or is connected to an illegal act on the part of the claimant. The Commission subsequently concluded that legislative reform was not appropriate in the context of tort actions, but that the courts should be more explicit about the policy justifications for applying the illegality defence: *The Illegality Defence*, Law Com. No.320, March 2010.

15 The Court of Appeal has held that ex turpi causa does not apply to a claim for breach of a Convention right under the European Convention on Human Rights: *Al Hassan-Daniel v Revenue and Customs Commissioners* [2010] EWCA Civ 1443; [2011] Q.B. 866.

16 In *Pitts v Hunt* [1991] 1 Q.B. 24 at 57, Dillon LJ questioned "whether or not the defence is correctly called *ex turpi causa*".

17 [1998] Q.B. 978. See also *Hewison v Meridian Shipping Pte Ltd* [2002] EWCA Civ 1821; [2003] I.C.R. 766; [2003] P.I.Q.R. P17 at [54], per Ward LJ.

18 [2009] UKHL 33; [2009] 1 A.C. 1339.

19 [1990] 2 Q.B. 283 at 291.

20 Although there are no cases in the English law of tort where the claim has been defeated by the claimant's immorality. Given the plurality of modern conceptions of morality it is difficult to think of cases where this could arise in the absence of conduct which is also unlawful. In *Patel v Mirza* [2016] UKSC 42; [2017] A.C. 467 at [120] Lord Toulson said that the defence may possibly apply to "certain aspects of public morality, the boundaries of which have never been made entirely clear". See also *Les Laboratoires Servier v Apotex Inc* [2014] UKSC 55; [2015] A.C. 430 at [25], per Lord Sumption on the categories of non-criminal conduct that might be covered by ex turpi causa (see para.3-35 fn.114). The defence has been held not to apply to suicide, whether or not the claimant is of sound mind. See *Kirkham v Chief Constable of Greater Manchester Police* [1990] 2 Q.B. 283; and *Reeves v Commissioner of Police of the Metropolis* [1999] Q.B. 169 CA.

21 *Reeves v Commissioner of Police for the Metropolis* [1999] Q.B. 169 at 186, per Buxton LJ. This assumes, however, that ex turpi causa is a *defence*. Lord Sumption, in particular, has taken the view that ex turpi causa, though described as a defence, is in reality "a rule of judicial abstention", and that the public interest may require the court to take the point of its own motion: *Les Laboratoires Servier v Apotex Inc* [2014] UKSC 55; [2015] A.C. 430 at [23]; *Jetivia SA v Bilta (UK) Ltd* [2015] UKSC 23; [2016] A.C. 1 at [62] and [100]; and *Patel v Mirza* [2016] UKSC 42; [2017] A.C. 467 at [262]. See also on this point *Al Hassan-Daniel v Revenue and Customs Commissioners* [2010] EWCA Civ 1443; [2011] Q.B. 866 at [9]; *O v Ministry of Defence; West v Ministry of Defence* [2006] EWHC 19 (QB) at [11]; *Lexi Holdings Plc v DTZ Debenham Tie Leugn Ltd* [2010] EWHC 2290 (Ch) at [11]. On the other hand there are frequent references in the cases to the "defence" of ex turpi causa or illegality, and for convenience this is how it will be referred to here.

22 "The search for principle is elusive": *Hewison v Meridian Shipping Pte Ltd* [2002] EWCA Civ 1821; [2003] I.C.R. 766; [2003] P.I.Q.R. P17 at [56], per Ward LJ. See also per Tuckey LJ at [49].

a mess.[23] There have been various theories as to when the defence should apply: (i) when it is impossible for the court to determine the standard of care; (ii) when awarding damages to the claimant would be an affront to the public conscience; (iii) where the claimant has to rely on his own illegality in order to assert his claim; and (iv) when awarding damages to the claimant would undermine the integrity of the legal system. There is also potential for some overlap with other conceptual tools used by the courts, such as the duty of care in the tort of negligence, where the claimant's illegal conduct may lead the court to conclude that the defendant did not owe a duty of care to the claimant in the circumstances.

3-06 One of the difficulties in developing a coherent approach to the defence of illegality has been its potential to provide a defence to various causes of action, involving claims in contract, property, tort or unjust enrichment, and in a wide variety of circumstances. A test that works in one context may be unsuited to being applied in another. For example, the issues at stake in a contract action relating to real property may be completely different from the issues in a tort action in respect of personal injuries. Another problem has been judicial disagreement at the highest level as to whether the illegality defence should rest on a tight, rule-based approach or whether a wide range of factors should be taken into account by the court.[24] This has made it extremely difficult to identify a single test for applying the defence; indeed it may be that following the decision of the Supreme Court in *Patel v Mirza*[25] there is no "test" as such, but rather a broad approach which takes into account the different circumstances of each case.

(i) "Impossible" to set a standard of care

3-07 On one view, the defence applied in circumstances where it was "impossible" for the court to determine an appropriate standard of care, in which case the conclusion would be that no duty of care was owed by the defendant to the claimant.[26] Although this approach had support at the highest level in Australia[27] it produced real difficulties in its application (when could it be said that it was "impossible" for the court to set a standard of care; how did the defence operate in the context of torts where there is no standard or duty of care as such, for example in trespass to the

[23] "The case law is notoriously untidy", per Lord Toulson in *Les Laboratoires Servier v Apotex Inc* [2014] UKSC 55; [2015] A.C. 430 at [57]; "a large body of inconsistent authority which rarely rises to the level of general principle", per Lord Sumption, [2014] UKSC 55; [2015] A.C. 430 at [14]; "a perplexing mass of inconsistent case-law", per Lord Sumption in *Jetivia SA v Bilta (UK) Ltd* [2015] UKSC 23; [2016] A.C. 1 at [62]; "a generalised statement of the conceptual basis for the doctrine ... has always proved elusive", per Lord Hughes in *Hounga v Allen* [2014] UKSC 47; [2014] 1 W.L.R. 2889 at [54]; "The application of the defence of illegality to claims in tort is highly problematic", per Lord Wilson in [2014] UKSC 47; [2014] 1 W.L.R. 2889 at [25]; the law on the topic is "in some disarray", per Lord Neuberger in *Patel v Mirza* [2016] UKSC 42; [2017] A.C. 467 at [164]; "the law of illegality has been a mess", per Lord Sumption [2016] UKSC 42; [2017] A.C. 467 at [265].

[24] See *Hounga v Allen* [2014] UKSC 47; [2014] 1 W.L.R. 2889; *Les Laboratoires Servier v Apotex Inc* [2014] UKSC 55; [2015] A.C. 430; *Jetivia SA v Bilta (UK) Ltd* [2015] UKSC 23; [2016] A.C. 1; and *Patel v Mirza* [2016] UKSC 42; [2017] A.C. 467.

[25] [2016] UKSC 42; [2017] A.C. 467; see paras 3-25 to 3-27.

[26] See *Pitts v Hunt* [1991] 1 Q.B. 24.

[27] *Jackson v Harrison* (1978) 19 A.L.R. 129; *Gala v Preston* (1991) 100 A.L.R. 29.

person?). This prompted the High Court of Australia to reverse its approach,[28] and the test has never received widespread support in the English courts.[29]

(ii) Affront to the public conscience

3-08 Another approach was that the defence should apply in circumstances where it would be an "affront to the public conscience" to grant the relief which the claimant sought because the courts would thereby appear to assist or encourage the claimant in illegal conduct or to encourage others in similar acts.[30] Compensating criminals for damage sustained in the course of committing a crime would tend to bring the law into disrepute. However, in *Tinsley v Milligan*[31] the House of Lords criticised the affront to the public conscience test on the basis that it left too much discretion in the hands of the judges to determine the appropriate degree of moral turpitude in the claimant's conduct before deciding whether the defence applies. Lord Browne-Wilkinson said that the consequences of being a party to an illegal transaction could not depend on "such an imponderable factor as the extent to which the public conscience would be affronted by recognising rights created by illegal transactions".[32]

(iii) Claimant's reliance on his own illegality

3-09 In *Tinsley v Milligan*[33] the defendant claimed an equitable interest in property purchased with funds from both claimant and defendant, though the property had been vested in the sole name of the claimant with the object of defrauding the Department of Social Security. The House of Lords held that the defendant was entitled to recover her equitable interest in the property provided that she was not forced to plead or rely on the illegality, even if it emerged that the title on which she relied was acquired in the course of carrying through an illegal transaction. Lord Goff was particularly critical of the "so-called public conscience test" on the ground that it was little different from saying that the court has a broad discretion whether to grant or refuse relief. The objection was that in cases of this nature (where the issue was whether equitable property rights could be acquired as a result of an il-

---

28 *Miller v Miller* [2011] HCA 9; (2011) 275 A.L.R. 611 at [54]: "Setting a norm of behaviour as between criminals may be difficult, but it is not impossible." The issue was whether the court *should* set a standard of care in the particular case, and this was a question of policy.

29 The most prominent authority being *Pitts v Hunt* [1991] 1 Q.B. 24. An alternative view was that the claimant's criminal conduct was such that in the circumstances no duty of care was owed, irrespective of how "difficult" it might be to set a *standard* of care: see *Vellino v Chief Constable of the Greater Manchester Police* [2001] EWCA Civ 1249; [2002] 1 W.L.R. 218 at para.3-29; *Ashton v Turner* [1981] Q.B. 137.

30 See *Euro-Diam Ltd v Bathurst* [1990] 1 Q.B. 1 at 35; *Thackwell v Barclays Bank Plc* [1986] 1 All E.R. 676; *Saunders v Edwards* [1987] 1 W.L.R. 1116; *Kirkham v Chief Constable of the Greater Manchester Police* [1990] 2 Q.B. 283 at 291; *Howard v Shirlstar Container Transport Ltd* [1990] 1 W.L.R. 1292. It followed that where there was no affront to the public conscience ex turpi causa did not apply: *Reeves v Commissioner of Police of the Metropolis* [1999] Q.B. 169 (suicide of deceased, who was a known suicide risk, in police custody where police owed a duty of care to prevent suicide; Buxton LJ commented, at 185, that if "it shocks the conscience of the ordinary citizen" that a suicide should recover damages, why were the defendants under a duty of care to take steps to prevent the suicide?)

31 [1994] 1 A.C. 340.

32 [1994] 1 A.C. 340 at 369.

33 [1994] 1 A.C. 340.

legal transaction) the position had long been governed by a system of rules, rather than discretion.

3-10 It is certainly possible to fit some tort claims into this approach. For example, in *Clunis v Camden & Islington HA*[34] the claimant, a man with a history of mental disorder and seriously violent behaviour, killed a stranger in a sudden and unprovoked attack three months after his discharge from hospital where he had been detained under the Mental Health Act 1983. He was charged with murder, but a plea of manslaughter on the ground of diminished responsibility was accepted by the prosecution and he was ordered to be detained indefinitely in a special hospital. He sued the health authority for negligence in failing to provide after care, alleging that with proper treatment he would not have committed the crime and therefore would not have been convicted and detained following a conviction. The Court of Appeal held that the claim was barred because the claimant had to rely on his commission of the offence as the basis for his claim, and therefore the ex turpi causa defence applied. The public policy that the court will not lend its aid to a litigant who relies on his own criminal or immoral act was not confined to a particular cause of action:

> "In our view the [claimant's] claim does arise out of and depend upon proof of his commission of a criminal offence. But whether a claim brought is founded in contract or in tort, public policy only requires the court to deny its assistance to a [claimant] seeking to enforce a cause of action if he was implicated in the illegality and in putting his case forward he seeks to rely upon the illegal acts."[35]

This policy would only apply, however, to cases in which the claimant was presumed to have known that he was doing an unlawful act.[36]

3-11 The problem with the "claimant's reliance on his own illegality" test in tort actions is that though it "fits" some tort scenarios, the range of potential circumstances in which illegality may be an issue is extremely wide. In a case involving a contract or a transfer of property there is a specific transaction (tainted by illegality) which the claimant may or may not have to rely upon in order to assert his claim. In tort, whilst there are some cases of this nature (often involving fraud or where, as in *Clunis*, the claimant is seeking compensation for the consequences of a criminal offence), in the typical personal injuries case it is not clear what aspect of the "transaction" or event the claimant would be "relying" upon in bringing his claim. Is the claimant injured in a road traffic accident which occurred during the course of making his escape from a burglary relying on the fact that he and his co-thief (now defendant) were engaged in criminal activity or the fact that the defendant failed to exercise reasonable care in driving a vehicle?[37] It may be true that the defendant would not have been driving in that manner had it not been for the attempt to escape, but that is merely the reason for the negligent driving it is not something

---

34 [1998] Q.B. 978.

35 [1998] Q.B. 978 at 987; applied in *Henderson v Dorset Healthcare University NHS Foundation Trust* [2018] EWCA Civ 1841; [2018] 3 W.L.R. 1651 on very similar facts; *O v Ministry of Defence, West v Ministry of Defence* [2006] EWHC 19 (QB). See also *Hunter Area Health Service v Presland* [2005] NSWCA 33; (2005) 63 N.S.W.L.R. 22, where a majority of the Court of Appeal of New South Wales reached a similar conclusion to *Clunis* on similar facts (although the claimant had been found not guilty by reason of insanity rather than guilty of manslaughter due to diminished responsibility, as occurred in *Clunis*).

36 Applying *Adamson v Jarvis* (1827) 4 Bing. 66 at 72-73; *Burrows v Rhodes* [1899] 1 Q.B. 816. On the question of the claimant's mental state, see further para.3-46.

37 Consider *Ashton v Turner* [1981] Q.B. 137.

that the claimant has to rely upon in order to show that the defendant was driving carelessly. The same is true in the case of a burglar who falls through defective flooring in premises that he is in the process of burgling. He may be a trespasser engaged in criminal activity, but he does not have to *rely* on that fact in order to assert that he was injured due to negligent maintenance of the premises[38] (whereas the burglar blown up by his incompetent colleague in the process of "blowing the safe", probably does have to rely on his own criminal acts). True, the occupier may point out that if the claimant had not been engaged in burgling the premises he would not have fallen, but it is his presence on the premises, combined with their defective condition, which is the cause of his injury, not his purpose or motive for being there. It would be an odd result if an action against his fellow thief for negligence in carrying out the burglary would be barred by ex turpi causa, but the claim against the occupier for the defective floor would not.[39]

"Reliance on illegality" confined to property cases In *Gray v Thames Trains Ltd*[40] Lord Hoffmann regarded the approach adopted in *Tinsley v Milligan* as specific to cases of involving rights in property. The claimant in *Gray* suffered minor physical injuries and post-traumatic stress disorder as a result of the defendant's negligence. He subsequently attacked and killed a third party and was convicted of manslaughter on the basis of diminished responsibility (due to his impaired mental health following the accident) resulting in his incarceration. The claimant argued that his claim for loss of earnings was founded upon the defendants' act of negligence in causing psychiatric harm to him and not on the unlawful killing. He did not have to "rely" on the illegality to establish his claim. Lord Hoffmann commented (at [30]): 3-12

> "That of course is true; if the defendants had not been negligent, or the damage had no connection with the train crash which could be described as causal, the claim would not have got past the starting post. But that is not the point; in this kind of case, the question is whether recovery is excluded because the immediate cause of the damage was the act of manslaughter, which resulted in the sentence of the court."

The claimant also argued that for ex turpi causa to apply it had to be shown that he had had to plead his own unlawful act. Lord Hoffmann was dismissive. The pleadings had nothing to do with the issue:

> "I did not find any of this discussion very helpful. The maxim *ex turpi causa* expresses not so much a principle as a policy. Furthermore, that policy is not based upon a single justification but on a group of reasons, which vary in different situations."[41]

It followed that where the questions of fairness and policy were different, the content of the rule would be different. This suggested that where a claimant has to rely on his own illegal act ex turpi causa could be invoked to defeat the claim, but that this is merely a *sufficient* and not a *necessary* criterion for the defence to apply.

---

38 cf. *Revill v Newbery* [1996] Q.B. 567.

39 Though see *McCracken v Smith* [2015] EWCA Civ 380; [2015] P.I.Q.R. P19 where the Court of Appeal considered that a party to a joint enterprise of deliberately riding a trail bike dangerously would be caught by the ex turpi defence in a negligence action against his "partner in crime", but the defence did not apply to a claim against a third party motorist who had been negligent in contributing to the cause of a crash between the bike and his vehicle.

40 [2009] UKHL 33; [2009] 1 A.C. 1339 at [30]; see para.3-17.

41 [2009] UKHL 33; [2009] 1 A.C. 1339 at [30].

3-13 **"Reliance on illegality" no longer the test** In *Patel v Mirza*[42] a majority of the Supreme Court considered that a test based on the claimant having to rely on the illegality depended on a procedural question of whether the claimant had to plead the illegal act, which was arbitrary. In *Nelson v Nelson* the High Court of Australia had unanimously rejected the reliance test, with McHugh J observing that:

> "The [reliance] rule has no regard to the legal and equitable rights of the parties, the merits of the case, the effect of the transaction in undermining the policy of the relevant legislation or the question whether the sanctions imposed by the legislation sufficiently protect the purpose of the legislation. Regard is had only to the procedural issue; and it is that issue and not the policy of the legislation or the merits of the parties which determines the outcome. Basing the grant of legal remedies on an essentially procedural criterion which has nothing to do with the equitable positions of the parties or the policy of the legislation is unsatisfactory, particularly when implementing a doctrine which is founded on public policy."[43]

Taking a similar view in *Patel v Mirza*, the Supreme concluded that the reliance test as set out in *Tinsley v Milligan* should no longer apply.

(iv) The integrity of the legal system

3-14 A fourth rationale advanced for the ex turpi causa defence is that it is concerned with maintaining the integrity of the legal system. Over 200 years ago in *Holman v Johnson*[44] Lord Mansfield CJ expressed the broad view of public policy that: "No court will lend its aid to a man who founds his cause of action upon an immoral or an illegal act." Although this statement can be seen as underpinning the "affront to the public conscience" test it is arguable that the true rationale is that the *courts* cannot be seen to aid a claimant who, while seeking to enforce his own rights, is at one and the same time prepared to flout the rights of others. A court seen to be aiding the claimant whilst ignoring the claimant's own illegality could well bring the administration of justice into disrepute, undermining the integrity of the legal system. In *Hall v Hebert*[45] the Supreme Court of Canada adopted this approach, though the Court took a rather narrow view of when the integrity of the legal system was at stake. McLachlin J, delivering the majority judgment, said that:

> "to allow recovery in these cases would be to allow recovery for what is illegal. It would put the courts in the position of saying that the same conduct is both legal, in the sense of being capable of rectification by the court, and illegal. It would, in short, introduce an inconsistency in the law. It is particularly important in this context that we bear in mind that the law must aspire to be a unified institution, the parts of which—contract, tort, the criminal law—must be in essential harmony. For the courts to punish conduct with the one hand while rewarding it with the other, would be to 'create an intolerable fissure in the law's conceptually seamless web': Weinrib, 'Illegality as a Tort Defence' (1976) 26 UTLJ 28, 42. We thus see that the concern, put at its most fundamental, is with the integrity of the legal system."

---

[42] [2016] UKSC 42; [2017] A.C. 467; see paras 3-25 to 3-27.
[43] (1995) 184 C.L.R. 538, 609.
[44] (1775) 1 Cowp. 341 at 343.
[45] [1993] 4 W.W.R. 113; (1993) 101 D.L.R. (4th) 129 at 165.

In *Miller v Miller*[46] the High Court of Australia suggested that the correct approach to the illegality defence is to ask: 3-15

"would it be incongruous for the law to proscribe the plaintiff's conduct and yet allow recovery in negligence for damage suffered in the course, or as a result, of that unlawful conduct? Other questions, such as whether denial of liability will deter wrongdoers or advantage some at the expense of others, are neither helpful nor relevant. And likewise, resort to notions of moral outrage or judicial indignation serves only to mask the proper identification of what is said to produce the response and why the response could be warranted."

The High Court considered that in the case of a statutory offence the court should consider whether an award of damages would be inconsistent with the purposes of the statute.[47] In the case of the offence of illegally taking and using a motor vehicle, one of the purposes of proscribing the conduct was because of its association with reckless and dangerous driving (it was not simply a crime against property). The court concluded that the statutory purpose of a law proscribing dangerous or reckless driving was not consistent with one offender owing a co-offender a duty to take reasonable care: "The inconsistency or incongruity arises regardless of whether reckless or dangerous driving eventuates. It arises from the recognition that the purpose of the statute is to deter and punish using a vehicle in circumstances that often lead to reckless and dangerous driving."[48]

The issue then becomes: when does compensating a claimant undermine the integrity of the legal system, appear to be incongruous, or create the impression of condoning the claimant's illegal conduct? In *Hall v Hebert* the majority view was that the integrity of legal system was only likely to be threatened in two situations: (1) where an award of damages would effectively allow a person to profit from illegal or wrongful conduct; or (2) would permit an evasion or rebate of a penalty prescribed by the criminal law. To permit recovery in such cases, said the Supreme Court of Canada, would be to allow recovery for what is illegal, and the court would be placed in the position of saying that the same conduct is both legal, in the sense of being capable of rectification by the court, and illegal. On this basis there was no room for ex turpi causa to operate in tort to deny damages for personal injuries because compensation for injuries could not be said to be the *profit* from an illegal act. The award of damages merely restored the claimant to his previous, non-injured condition. On the other hand, English law has continued to apply ex turpi causa to some claims involving personal injury, though the notion of preserving the integrity of the legal system is considered to be a useful filter through which to rationalise the concept.[49] 3-16

Some of these issues were addressed by the House of Lords in *Gray v Thames* 3-17

---

46 [2011] HCA 9; (2011) 275 A.L.R. 611 at [16].

47 [2011] HCA 9; (2011) 275 A.L.R. 611 at [74].

48 [2011] HCA 9; (2011) 275 A.L.R. 611 at [101]. A similar idea seems to underlie the view that ex turpi causa applies when awarding compensation would create the appearance that the court was condoning a claimant's unlawful conduct. In *Cross v Kirkby*, *The Times*, 5 April 2000 Beldam LJ said that: "the principle applies when the claimant's claim is so closely connected or inextricably bound up with his own criminal or illegal conduct that the court could not permit him to recover without appearing to condone that conduct." In *Hewison v Meridian Shipping Pte Ltd* [2002] EWCA Civ 1821; [2003] I.C.R. 766; [2003] P.I.Q.R. P17 at [74] Ward LJ observed that "the need not to appear to condone the illegality continues to be a relevant factor".

49 So, e.g. in *Hounga v Allen* [2014] UKSC 47; [2014] 1 W.L.R. 2889 at [44] Lord Wilson commented that: "Concern to preserve the integrity of the legal system is a helpful rationale of the aspect

Trains Ltd.[50] The claimant was a passenger on a train involved in a serious crash. He sustained minor physical injuries but developed post-traumatic stress disorder, with a significant personality change. Almost two years after the accident he stabbed a stranger to death, following a "road rage" incident, and pleaded guilty to manslaughter on the grounds of diminished responsibility. He was ordered to be detained in a secure hospital under s.37 of the Mental Health Act 1983. The defendants accepted that they were liable in principle for the claimant's losses, including loss of earnings before the killing, but denied responsibility in respect of loss of earnings after the killing on the basis of ex turpi causa. The claimant did not claim damages for the consequences of being detained in a mental hospital (a claim that would have been rejected on the authority of *Clunis v Camden and Islington HA*), but claimed to be entitled to the loss of earnings attributable his developing PTSD, including the loss of earnings after the date of the killing. The House of Lords concluded that there was undoubtedly a causal link between the claimant's criminal offence and the claim for loss of earnings (reversing the decision of the Court of Appeal that there had been no "inextricable link" between the offence and the lost earnings). Causation was clear and it was "hard to think of a more inextricable link."[51] Although it was true, said Lord Hoffmann, that if the claimant had not committed manslaughter his earning capacity would have been impaired in any event by the PTSD caused by the defendants' negligence, the court should not disregard subsequent events[52]; and so in assessing damages for the consequences of the PTSD on his earning capacity the fact that the claimant would have been unable to earn anything after his arrest should not be ignored.[53]

3-18 **The wide form and the narrow form** In *Gray v Thames Trains Ltd* Lord Hoffmann identified two forms of the ex turpi causa rule of public policy:

> "In its wider form, it is that you cannot recover compensation for loss which you have suffered in consequence of your own criminal act. In its narrower and more specific form, it is that you cannot recover for damage which flows from loss of liberty, a fine or other punishment lawfully imposed upon you in consequence of your own unlawful act. In such a case it is the law which, as a matter of penal policy, causes the damage and it would be inconsistent for the law to require you to be compensated for that damage."[54]

His Lordship considered that the distinction between the two forms was significant because there is a justification for the narrow rule which does not necessarily apply to the wide version of the rule, namely the inconsistency that would arise between the criminal law and the law of tort if the claimant were to receive compensation for the consequences of a sentence imposed by the criminal law.[55] This form of "inconsistency" is very much in tune with the concept of maintain-

---

of policy which founds the defence even if the instance given by McLachlin J [in *Hall v Hebert*] of where that concern is in issue may best be taken as an example of it rather than as the only conceivable instance of it."

50 [2009] UKHL 33; [2009] 1 A.C. 1339.

51 [2009] UKHL 33; [2009] 1 A.C. 1339 at [48].

52 Applying *Jobling v Associated Dairies Ltd* [1982] A.C. 794; see para.2-107.

53 See also per Lord Brown, [2009] UKHL 33; [2009] 1 A.C. 1339 at [95] and [96].

54 [2009] UKHL 33; [2009] 1 A.C. 1339 at [29] and [32].

55 Citing the decisions of the Supreme Court of Canada in *British Columbia v Zastowny* [2008] SCC 4; [2008] 1 S.C.R. 27; and the New South Wales Court of Appeal in *State Rail Authority of New South Wales v Wiegold* (1991) 25 N.S.W.L.R. 500 at 514 where Samuels JA said: "If the law of negligence were to say, in effect, that the offender was not responsible for his actions and should

ing the "integrity of the legal system", but it is narrower in its focus, which is on the inconsistency of compensating for *the penalty* imposed by the criminal court. It is not as wide as the rationale that awarding compensation would appear to condone the claimant's unlawful conduct, and for that to apply a defendant would have to invoke the wide version of the rule.

On the facts of *Gray*, Lord Hoffmann said that the narrow form of the rule (that a claimant cannot receive compensation for the consequences of a sentence imposed by the criminal law) was sufficient to dispose of the claimant's loss of earnings claim (and any claim for general damages for his detention, conviction and damage to reputation). But a claim for an indemnity against any claims which might be brought by dependants of the person he had killed, and a claim for general damages for feelings of guilt and remorse consequent upon the killing, were not a consequence of the sentence of the criminal court. These claims fell within the wide form of the rule. This differs from the narrow version in that: (i) it cannot be justified on the basis of inconsistency, but "has to be justified on the ground that it is offensive to public notions of the fair distribution of resources that a claimant should be compensated (usually out of public funds) for the consequences of his own criminal conduct"; and (ii) the wide rule raises problems of causation which do not arise with the narrow rule.[56] The difficulty was to distinguish cases where the rule applied from those where the injury was a consequence of the claimant's unlawful act only in the sense that it would not have happened if he had not been committing an unlawful act. The distinction drawn by Lord Hoffmann rested on the ordinary principles applied to distinguish between causing something and merely providing the occasion for someone else to cause something. Although the terms "inextricably linked" and "integral part" could be found in the cases, it would be better, said his Lordship, to avoid such metaphors and treat the question as simply one of causation: 3-19

> "Can one say that, although the damage would not have happened but for the tortious conduct of the defendant, it was caused by the criminal act of the claimant? (*Vellino v Chief Constable of the Greater Manchester Police* [2002] 1 WLR 218). Or is the position that although the damage would not have happened without the criminal act of the claimant, it was caused by the tortious act of the defendant? (*Revill v Newbery* [1996] QB 567)."[57]

In *Gray*, the claimant's liability to compensate the dependants of the person he had killed was an immediate "inextricable" consequence of his having intentionally killed him, and the same was true of his feelings of guilt and remorse. Thus, the wide form of the rule applied and the claimant was not entitled to damages in respect of those heads of damage.

Following *Gray*, it is clear that the narrow form of ex turpi causa is based on a concern to protect the integrity of the legal system. If an award of damages would effectively constitute compensation for or reimbursement of the penalty applied by a criminal court (whether a fine or imprisonment) then the claim arises ex turpi 3-20

be compensated by the tortfeasor, it would set the determination of the criminal court at nought. It would generate the sort of clash between civil and criminal law that is apt to bring the law into disrepute." See also per Lord Rodger and Lord Brown in *Gray v Thames Trains Ltd* [2009] UKHL 33; [2009] 1 A.C. 1339 at [77]–[82] and [93] respectively.

56 [2009] UKHL 33; [2009] 1 A.C. 1339 at [51].

57 [2009] UKHL 33; [2009] 1 A.C. 1339 at [54]; see also the comments of Lord Rodger at [74] concerning the term "inextricably linked".

causa.[58] The wide form, said Lord Hoffmann, has to be justified on the ground that it is "offensive to public notions of the fair distribution of resources that a claimant should be compensated (usually out of public funds) for the consequences of his own criminal conduct". This does not look that dissimilar from the notion that ex turpi will apply where an award of damages would be "affront to the public conscience". It does not confer an open-ended discretion on the court to refuse to award damages (which was a criticism of the "affront to the public conscience" approach), because it is combined with a causation test. The claimant cannot recover for a loss "suffered in consequence of [his] own criminal act". The court will have to decide (in cases where an award of damages would be offensive to public notions of the fair distribution of resources) whether the claimant's loss was caused by his illegal conduct or merely provided the occasion for someone else to cause the loss. This is not necessarily a simple task, as the case law on causation and intervening acts demonstrates.[59]

3-21 If the claimant is seeking to profit from illegal or wrongful conduct then, as suggested by the Supreme Court of Canada in *Hall v Hebert*, an award of damages would undermine the integrity of the legal system. This would fall within the wide version of ex turpi causa identified by Lord Hoffmann in *Gray v Thames Trains Ltd*, but the wide version goes well beyond this.[60] As with cases where the claimant has to *rely* on his own illegal conduct, if the claimant is seeking to profit from his own wrongdoing the action will be ex turpi causa but, again, it is suggested that these are *sufficient* not *necessary* criteria for the defence to apply.[61]

(v) The integrity of the legal system: rules or judicial discretion?

3-22 **Reliance test rejected** Despite the ruling in *Gray* the question of the correct approach to the illegality defence continued to occupy the Supreme Court in no less than four cases over a period of two years.[62] There was agreement that ex turpi causa is based on public policy, and that that policy is concerned with protecting the integrity of the legal system. However, there was a significant difference of opinion as to the scope of the defence and how it should be applied. The question was whether, once ex turpi causa is engaged, it should apply as a rigid rule of law removing any discretion from the court, or whether the court is required to look at the wider picture and weigh competing policy matters that would point to imposing liability on the defendant notwithstanding the claimant's turpitude.

3-23 Lord Sumption was strongly in favour of the former approach,[63] insisting that *Tinsley v Milligan* was binding authority and that it had rejected the idea that ex

---

[58] This narrow form also applies to penalties imposed by a statutory regulatory body: *Khan v Hussain* [2019] CSOH 11; 2019 S.C. 322; 2019 S.L.T. 319.

[59] See para.2-110.

[60] And, unlike *Hall v Hebert*, does not preclude ex turpi causa applying to a claim for personal injuries. The High Court of Australia has also accepted that the defence can apply to claims for personal injuries: *Miller v Miller* [2011] HCA 9; (2011) 275 A.L.R. 611.

[61] See further the discussion of his Lordship's approach to the wide version of ex turpi causa at para.3-19.

[62] *Hounga v Allen* [2014] UKSC 47; [2014] 1 W.L.R. 2889; *Les Laboratoires Servier v Apotex Inc* [2014] UKSC 55; [2015] A.C. 430; *Jetivia SA v Bilta (UK) Ltd* [2015] UKSC 23; [2016] A.C. 1; and *Patel v Mirza* [2016] UKSC 42; [2017] A.C. 467. See N. Strauss, "Ex turpi causa oritur actio?" (2016) 132 L.Q.R. 236.

[63] *Les Laboratoires Servier v Apotex Inc* [2014] UKSC 55; [2015] A.C. 430 at [13]; *Jetivia SA v Bilta (UK) Ltd* [2015] UKSC 23; [2016] A.C. 1 at [62]; *Patel v Mirza* [2016] UKSC 42; [2017] A.C. 467 at [261]–[265].

turpi causa involved an exercise of discretion by the court. The majority in *Tinsley*, said Lord Sumption, had favoured the reliance test which was not discretionary in nature; nor did it involve achieving proportionality between the claimant's misconduct and his loss. Nor did the two "tests" established by Lord Hoffmann in *Gray v Thames Trains Ltd* (the "wide" form and the "narrow" form) leave any scope for the exercise of discretion. The narrow form operated automatically once it was clear that the loss claimed was a penalty imposed by a criminal court or the necessary consequence of the sentence. The wider form was simply a question of causation.[64] For Lord Sumption the illegality defence arises in the public interest, irrespective of the interests or rights of the parties, and the public interest may require the court to take the point of its own motion, contrary to the normal rules of adversarial litigation.

In *Jetivia SA v Bilta (UK) Ltd*[65] Lords Toulson and Hodge said that if the reliance test meant that ex turpi can only apply when the claimant has to plead the illegality as part of the claim, its effect would be procedural not substantive, and the law would be in an unsatisfactory state. They pointed out that in *Hounga v Allen*[66] Lord Wilson had concluded that the importance of preserving the integrity of the legal system did not outweigh the prominent strain of current public policy against human trafficking and in favour of the protection of its victims. Whereas Lord Sumption took the view that the illegality defence does not depend on a judicial value judgment about the balance of the equities, for Lords Toulson and Hodge *Hounga v Allen* involved a statement of principle that a weighing of competing policy objectives was not only permitted but required in some cases (and this must necessarily involve a judgment about the competing equities).[67] 3-24

These differing views were evident in *Patel v Mirza*.[68] The claimant paid £620,000 to the defendant under an illegal agreement between them to use the money for the purpose of "insider dealing". However, the insider information from a third party was not forthcoming, so the money was never used to place a bet on the movement of a company's share price. The defendant refused to hand the money back to the claimant who then brought a claim for breach of contract and unjust enrichment. The defendant's argument that because the contract was tainted by illegality[69] and therefore ex turpi causa applied to the claimant's action was unanimously rejected by the Supreme Court. There was no unanimity, however, as to the correct approach to the illegality defence. A nine judge Court divided sharply, yet again, on the correct basis underpinning the application ex turpi causa, with the majority taking the view that a range of factors should be taken into account, while the minority considered that this would confer too much discretion on the courts, requiring value judgments to be made about the respective claims of the public interest and those of the parties. 3-25

64 "Neither the narrower nor the wider rule depended on the court's assessment of the significance of the illegality, the proportionality of its application or the merits of the particular case": *Les Laboratoires Servier v Apotex Inc* [2014] UKSC 55; [2015] A.C. 430 at [19].

65 [2015] UKSC 23; [2016] A.C. 1.

66 [2014] UKSC 47; [2014] 1 W.L.R. 2889; see para.3-52.

67 [2015] UKSC 23; [2016] A.C. 1 at [173].

68 [2016] UKSC 42; [2017] A.C. 467. For discussion see J. Goudkamp, "The end of an era? Illegality in private law in the Supreme Court" (2017) 133 L.Q.R. 14; E. Lim, "Ex Turpi Causa: Reformation not Revolution" (2017) 80 M.L.R. 927; and S. Green and A. Bogg (eds), *Illegality after Patel v Mirza* (2018) Hart Publishing.

69 It amounted to a conspiracy to commit the offence of insider dealing under s.52 of the Criminal Justice Act 1993.

3-26 Lord Sumption (with whom Lords Mance and Clarke agreed) noted that the implications of the claimant's illegal conduct are not in all respects the same in the law of tort as in they are other branches of law, but at the most fundamental level of policy the law's internal coherence requires that contract, tort and criminal law should be in harmony. Civil courts could not coherently give effect to legal rights founded on criminal acts which are contrary to the state's public law.[70] But, for Lord Sumption, a test which sought to balance a range of factors was "unprincipled" because ex turpi causa was designed to vindicate the public interest as against the interests and legal rights of the parties, and therefore it could not "depend on an evaluation of the equities as between the parties or the proportionality of its impact upon the claimant".[71] If the application of the illegality principle was to depend on the court's view of how illegal the illegality was or how much it mattered to the parties, there would be no principle to guide the evaluation "other than the judge's gut instinct". Lord Toulson's approach, requiring a weighing of the policy factors involved and the nature and circumstances of the claimant's illegal conduct was, said Lord Sumption, too vague, conferred too much discretion on the court, and would lead to "complexity, uncertainty, arbitrariness and lack of transparency".[72]

3-27 Lord Toulson (with whom Lady Hale, and Lords Kerr, Wilson, Hodge and Neuberger agreed) noted that in *Gray v Thames Trains* Lord Hoffmann had said that ex turpi causa constituted a policy based on a group of reasons, which vary in different situations. The courts had therefore evolved varying rules to deal with different situations. Because questions of fairness and policy were different in different cases and led to different rules, one could not simply extrapolate rules applicable to one situation and apply them to another.[73] An approach based on rules, plus exceptions to those rules, had never produced a satisfactory position, because:

> "there are so many variables, for example, in seriousness of the illegality, the knowledge and intentions of the parties, the centrality of the illegality, the effect of denying the defence and the sanctions which the law already imposes. To reach the best result in terms of policy, the judges need to have the flexibility to consider and weigh a range of factors in the light of the facts of the particular case before them."[74]

There were two policy reasons underpinning illegality as a defence to a civil claim. One was that a person should not be allowed to profit from his own wrongdoing. The other, linked, consideration was that "the law should be coherent and not self-defeating, condoning illegality by giving with the left hand what it takes with the right hand."[75] For the majority, determining whether allowing a claim tainted by illegality was contrary to the public interest, because it would be harmful to the integrity of the legal system, required that the court should:

(a) consider the underlying purpose of the prohibition which has been transgressed and whether that purpose will be enhanced by denial of the claim;

[70] [2016] UKSC 42; [2017] A.C. 467 at [230]–[233].
[71] [2016] UKSC 42; [2017] A.C. 467 at [262].
[72] [2016] UKSC 42; [2017] A.C. 467 at [265].
[73] [2016] UKSC 42; [2017] A.C. 467 at [29].
[74] [2016] UKSC 42; [2017] A.C. 467 at [92].
[75] [2016] UKSC 42; [2017] A.C. 467 at [99].

(b) consider any other relevant public policies which may be rendered ineffective or less effective by denial of the claim[76]; and
(c) consider whether denial of the claim would be a proportionate response to the illegality, bearing in mind that punishment is a matter for the criminal courts.[77]

Various factors could be relevant to whether it would be disproportionate to refuse relief to which the claimant would otherwise be entitled, but there was no definitive list because of the infinite variety of cases. Potentially relevant factors included: "the seriousness of the conduct, its centrality to the contract, whether it was intentional and whether there was marked disparity in the parties' respective culpability."[78]

The consequence of this analysis for the majority in *Patel* was that *Tinsley v Milligan* should no longer be followed. A requirement that the claimant had to rely on the illegal contract or plead its illegality before the defence applied made "the question whether the court will refuse its assistance to the claimant to enforce his title to his property depend on a procedural question and it has led to uncertain case law about what constitutes reliance".[79] Moreover, although *Patel v Mirza* was a case in contract and unjust enrichment, there was no suggestion in the majority judgments that the same approach should not be applied to tort actions. In *Henderson v Dorset Healthcare University NHS Foundation Trust* the Court of Appeal confirmed that *Patel* is not confined to contract cases.[80] 3-28

(vi) Relationship to duty of care in negligence

There are some cases where the courts refuse to impose a duty of care in negligence because of the claimant's illegal conduct. In *Vellino v Chief Constable* 3-29

[76] *Hounga v Allen* [2014] UKSC 47; [2014] 1 W.L.R. 2889; and *R. (Best) v Chief Land Registrar* [2015] EWCA Civ 17; [2016] Q.B. 23 were said to be illustrations of cases in which there were countervailing public interest considerations ([2016] UKSC 42; [2017] A.C. 467 at [103]).

[77] [2016] UKSC 42; [2017] A.C. 467 at [101] and [120].

[78] [2016] UKSC 42; [2017] A.C. 467 at [107]. Lord Neuberger acknowledged, at [173], that where a judge has to take into account various factors and decide how much weight to give each of them the difference between judgment and discretion was "in practice pretty slight."

[79] [2016] UKSC 42; [2017] A.C. 467 at [110]–[111]. In response to the argument of the minority in *Patel v Mirza* that Lord Toulson's approach confers too much discretion on the court and will lead to uncertainty Lord Kerr said that since the preservation of the integrity of the legal system is *par excellence* a public policy consideration "the taking into account of countervailing policy considerations, in order to decide whether to give effect to it in a particular instance, is the only logical way to proceed" ([2016] UKSC 42; [2017] A.C. 467 at [129]). His Lordship added that: "Certainty or predictability of outcome may be a laudable aim for those who seek the law's resolution of genuine, honest disputes. It is not a premium to which those engaged in disreputable conduct can claim automatic entitlement" ([2016] UKSC 42; [2017] A.C. 467 at [137]).

[80] [2018] EWCA Civ 1841; [2018] 3 W.L.R. 1651; [2019] P.I.Q.R. P3 at [81]. See also *XX v Whittington Hospital NHS Trust* [2018] EWCA Civ 2832; [2019] 3 W.L.R. 107 at [65], per McCombe LJ (though note that in the Supreme Court *Patel v Mirza* and the illegality defence were said to be irrelevant to the outcome in *XX v Whittington* [2020] UKSC 14; [2020] 2 W.L.R. 972 at [40], per Lady Hale, and at [59], per Lord Carnwath). See further *Gujra v Roath* [2018] EWHC 854 (QB); [2018] 1 W.L.R. 3208 at [25] where Martin Spencer J said that: "it seems to me that Lord Toulson was, in *Patel*, laying down a test that was intended to cover all cases where the common law doctrine of illegality is pleaded as a defence to a civil claim." In that case, the defence was applied to a claim for malicious prosecution.

of the Greater Manchester Police[81] the claimant was injured when he jumped from a second floor window to evade arrest by the police. He alleged that the police were under a duty of care not negligently to let him escape once they had arrested him. It is clear that the police must come under some duty of care to persons they have arrested, since the fact of detention prevents a prisoner from avoiding certain dangers (e.g. if a prisoner fell ill, the police would undoubtedly have a duty to seek medical treatment for him). Similarly, it is well established that the police may owe a duty of care to a prisoner known to be suicidal to take reasonable precautions to prevent suicide attempts.[82] However, by a majority, in *Vellino* the Court of Appeal held there was no duty of care owed to a prisoner who was attempting to escape from custody. Schiemann LJ commented that: "To suggest that the police owe a criminal the duty to prevent the criminal from escaping, and that the criminal who hurts himself while escaping can sue the police for the breach of that duty, seems to me self-evidently absurd."[83] The claimant was the author of his own misfortune and by breaking away from an officer arresting him he was committing a criminal offence. His Lordship accepted that there was an overlap between the considerations which had to be taken into account in determining whether a duty of care existed and whether the defence of ex turpi causa applied, but based his decision on the absence of a duty of care rather than the defence. Sir Murray Stuart-Smith agreed that:

> "if the facts are such that the maxim *ex turpi causa non oritur actio* is applicable, it does not matter whether the correct legal analysis is that the defendants owed no duty of care, because the third limb of the test in *Caparo Industries plc v Dickman* [1990] 2 A.C. 605, namely that it is just fair and reasonable to impose a duty of care, is not satisfied, or that the maxim affords a freestanding reason for holding that the cause of action does not arise or cannot be pursued."[84]

3-30 *Vellino* followed and applied *Sacco v Chief Constable of the South Wales Constabulary*,[85] where the Court of Appeal held that the police were not liable to a prisoner who, while being transported in the back of a police van, kicked open the rear doors of the van in an attempt to escape and was injured when he fell out of the vehicle. In *Sacco* Schiemann LJ said:

> "Second, he was engaged in a criminal act, namely attempting to escape from lawful custody. As a matter of legal policy, I see no reason to permit a man to recover damages against the police if he hurts himself as part of that illegal enterprise. The basis of such recovery must be either an allegation of a breach of a duty owed to him not to let him escape, or of a duty owed to him to take care that he does not hurt himself if he tries to escape. I see no reason to create such duties owed to him. It is common ground that the policy of the law is not to permit one criminal to recover damages from a fellow criminal who fails to take care of him whilst they are both engaged on a criminal enterprise. The reason for that rule is not the law's tenderness towards the criminal defendant, but the law's unwillingness to afford a criminal [claimant] a remedy in such circumstances. I see no reason why that unwillingness should be any the less because the defendant is a policeman and not engaged in any crime."

---

[81] [2001] EWCA Civ 1249; [2002] 1 W.L.R. 218.

[82] As was conceded in *Reeves v Commissioner of Police for the Metropolis* [2000] 1 A.C. 360; and see *Orange v Chief Constable of West Yorkshire Police* [2001] EWCA Civ 611; [2002] Q.B. 347.

[83] [2001] EWCA Civ 1249; [2002] 1 W.L.R. 218 at [19]. *Vellino* was approved by Lord Hoffmann in *Gray v Thames Trains Ltd* [2009] UKHL 33; [2009] 1 A.C. 1339 at [53].

[84] [2001] EWCA Civ 1249; [2002] 1 W.L.R. 218 at [62].

[85] unreported 15 May 1998.

Sedley LJ dissented in *Vellino*, concluding that arresting officers owe a prisoner a duty not to afford both a temptation to escape and an opportunity of doing so when there is a known risk that the prisoner will do himself real harm, even if much of the blame for hurting himself will ultimately come to rest on the prisoner himself. The power to apportion responsibility under the Law Reform (Contributory Negligence) Act 1945 "afforded a far more appropriate tool for doing justice than the blunt instrument of turpitude. In many cases, classically where both parties have been involved in a single criminal enterprise, the outcome would be the same."[86] But this argument proves too much, since it is an argument for abolishing all tort defences except contributory negligence. Moreover, it is not necessarily correct to suggest that in the case of a joint criminal enterprise the result would be the same, since it is not appropriate to apportion 100 per cent contributory fault to a claimant.[87] The argument that the claimant is 100 per cent at fault for damage is an argument that, as a question of causation, he is wholly responsible for his own injuries, which is not that different from Schiemann LJ's view that the claimant was the author of his own misfortune. Nor is it clear why a claimant engaged in a joint criminal enterprise should be regarded as wholly responsible for his own injuries when he sues his fellow criminal, but not when he sues the police.

(b) Applying ex turpi causa

Notwithstanding the greater clarity as to the rationale of the ex turpi causa defence following the decisions of the House of Lords in *Gray v Thames Trains Ltd*[88] and the Supreme Court in *Patel v Mirza*[89] it remains the case that some degree of caution is appropriate in attempting to state how the ex turpi causa defence will be applied in practice. There was no criticism of *Gray* in *Patel v Mirza*,[90] and so the narrow and wide form of ex turpi causa set out in *Gray* will, presumably, continue to be relevant. If the claimant's loss falls within the narrow form, as an attempt to compensate for or mitigate a penalty applied by a criminal court, or, it would seem, a penalty imposed by a regulatory body,[91] then it will necessarily be caught by the defence[92]; though the narrow form only applies to losses flowing from 3-31

86 [2001] EWCA Civ 1249; [2002] 1 W.L.R. 218 at [55].

87 See para.3-58 fn.199. Sedley LJ did not explain in what way the outcome would be the same.

88 [2009] UKHL 33; [2009] 1 A.C. 1339.

89 [2016] UKSC 42; [2017] A.C. 467, see paras 3-25 to 3-27.

90 "It is impossible to discern in the majority judgments in *Patel* any suggestion that *Clunis or Gray* were wrongly decided or to discern that they cannot stand with the reasoning in *Patel*": *Henderson v Dorset Healthcare University NHS Foundation Trust* [2018] EWCA Civ 1841; [2018] 3 W.L.R. 1651 at [88].

91 *Khan v Hussain* [2019] CSOH 11; 2019 S.C. 322; 2019 S.L.T. 319 (pursuer not entitled to maintain action in contract and negligence against accountant for losses attributable to sanctions imposed on him by the Financial Services Authority, since this was a consequence of his own dishonest conduct rather than him acting on professional advice).

92 However, note that the narrow rule applies to a penalty judged to have been imposed for the personal fault of the claimant. So where the conviction itself does not carry any personal fault, as may be the case with a strict liability offence, the rationale of the narrow rule does not apply: *Griffin v UHY Hacker Young & Partners (A Firm)* [2010] EWHC 146 (Ch); [2010] P.N.L.R. 20 (claimant, who had been a director of a company that had gone into insolvent liquidation, had been convicted of the strict liability offence under the Insolvency Act 1986 s.216(3) of becoming a director of another company using a trade name of the liquidated company without obtaining leave of the court, a conviction that he attributed to his ignorance of the rule as a result of negligent advice given by the defendants).

the sentence imposed, and not to other losses attributable to the conviction.[93] If the claimant's loss potentially falls within the wide form of the defence ("you cannot recover compensation for loss which you have suffered in consequence of your own criminal act") then, according to Lord Hoffmann, the defence can apply where it is "offensive to public notions of the fair distribution of resources that a claimant should be compensated (usually out of public funds) for the consequences of his own criminal conduct", and there is a causal link between the illegality and the claimant's damage.[94] The terms "inextricably linked" and "integral part" can be found in earlier cases but the issue, said Lord Hoffmann, was simply one of causation.

3-32 However, even if there is a causal connection between the claimant's loss and the criminal activity the court must be satisfied that it would be "offensive to public notions of the fair distribution of resources" to allow the claimant to be compensated for the consequences of his criminal conduct. *Patel v Mirza* indicates that in reaching a judgment on this issue the court should take into account: (a) the underlying purpose of the prohibition which has been transgressed and whether that purpose will be enhanced by denial of the claim; (b) any other relevant public policies which may be rendered ineffective or less effective by denial of the claim; and (c) whether denial of the claim would be a proportionate response to the illegality.[95] Lord Toulson did not set out a prescriptive list of potentially relevant factors for considering whether it would be disproportionate to refuse a remedy to the claimant, but they included the seriousness of the offence, its centrality to the contract,[96] whether it was intentional and whether there was a marked disparity in the parties' respective culpability. There was no guidance as to the respective weights to be given to each of these factors, which are matters to be assessed by the trial judge.[97] Cases pre-dating *Gray v Thames Trains Ltd* and particularly *Patel v Mirza* discussed

---

[93] *Griffin v UHY Hacker Young & Partners (A Firm)* [2010] EWHC 146 (Ch); [2010] P.N.L.R. 20.

[94] "Can one say that, although the damage would not have happened but for the tortious conduct of the defendant, it was caused by the criminal act of the claimant? … Or is the position that although the damage would not have happened without the criminal act of the claimant, it was caused by the tortious act of the defendant?": [2009] UKHL 33; [2009] 1 A.C. 1339 at [54].

[95] [2016] UKSC 42; [2017] A.C. 467 at [101] and [120]. His Lordship considered that "that trio of necessary considerations can be found in the case law": ibid. at [101]. See also *Singularis Holdings Ltd (In Liquidation) v Daiwa Capital Markets Europe Ltd* [2019] UKSC 50; [2019] 3 W.L.R. 997 (applying ex turpi causa would undermine the "carefully calibrated" duty owed by the defendant bank to a client to protect the client from just the sort of misappropriation of its funds as had occurred, and would not be a proportionate response). See further *Stoffel & Co v Grondona* [2018] EWCA Civ 2031; [2018] P.N.L.R. 36 where the Court of Appeal applied Lord Toulson's three factors in a claim against a firm of solicitors for negligence in failing to register the claimant's title to property. The claimant had participated in a mortgage fraud with a third party in order to obtain loan funds from a lender for the benefit of the third party, but this illegality was not a reason to bar her claim against the negligent solicitors. There was "no public interest in allowing negligent conveyancing solicitors …, who are not party to, and know nothing about, the illegality, to avoid their professional obligations simply because of the happenstance that two of the clients for whom they act are involved in making misrepresentations to the mortgagee financier" but there was "a genuine public interest in ensuring that clients who use the services of solicitors are entitled to seek civil remedies for negligence/breach of contract" in circumstances where the client was not seeking to profit from the mortgage fraud (at [37]–[38], per Gloster LJ). It would have been entirely disproportionate to deny the claim (at [39]).

[96] In tort cases where there is no contract this may be interpreted as the centrality of the criminal behaviour to the claimant's loss, which may possibly be just another way of specifying the importance of the causal link.

[97] In *Singularis Holdings Ltd (In Official Liquidation) v Daiwa Capital Markets Europe Ltd* [2018] EWCA Civ 84; [2018] 1 W.L.R. 2777 at [65] Sir Geoffrey Vos C said that an appellate court should

below should be considered in the context of these decisions of the House of Lords and Supreme Court.[98]

(i) *Seriousness of the claimant's conduct*

It is not possible to state with any confidence how reprehensible the claimant's conduct must be. The courts tend to approach this as a question of fact, though clearly it is linked to the underlying policy of the defence of ex turpi causa that an award of damages should not bring the legal process into disrepute. Thus, the more serious the offence the more likely it is that the defence will apply,[99] though this is not automatically the case because of the "proportionality" requirement—the seriousness of the defendant's conduct may outweigh that of the claimant.[100] In *Hewison v Meridian Shipping Pte Ltd*[101] Ward LJ commented that: "There is no doubt in my judgment that the claimant's conduct must be shown to be so clearly reprehensible as to justify the condemnation of the court. ... Where to draw the line between what is serious and what is trivial is not always easy." **3-33**

It is clear that the seriousness of the claimant's offence was an important factor in both *Clunis*,[102] and *Gray*.[103] In *Murphy v Culhane*,[104] a widow sued in respect of her husband's death in the course of a violent affray. Lord Denning ruled that consideration be given to a defence of ex turpi as well as to questions of volenti and **3-34**

---

not interfere in a trial judge's application of the test in *Patel v Mirza* "merely because it would have taken a different view had it been undertaking the evaluation. ... an appellate court should only interfere if the first instance judge has proceeded on an erroneous legal basis, taken into account matters that were legally irrelevant, or failed to take into account matters that were legally relevant". However, the Supreme Court had reservations about this approach, since an appellate court is as well placed to evaluate the arguments as the trial judge: [2019] UKSC 50; [2019] 3 W.L.R. 997 at [21].

98 At this point it may be worth recalling Lord Hoffmann's observation in *Gray v Thames Trains Ltd* [2009] UKHL 33; [2009] 1 A.C. 1339 at [30] that the policy underpinning ex turpi causa "is not based upon a single justification but on a group of reasons, which vary in different situations." This suggests that the factors relevant to the outcome will carry different weights depending on the context in which the issue arises.

99 In *Vellino v Chief Constable of the Greater Manchester Police* [2001] EWCA Civ 1249; [2002] 1 W.L.R. 218 at [70] Sir Murray Stuart-Smith said that: "In the case of criminal conduct this has to be sufficiently serious to merit the application of the principle. Generally speaking a crime punishable with imprisonment could be expected to qualify. If the offence is criminal but relatively trivial, it is in any event difficult to see how it could be integral to the claim." See also *Joyce v O'Brien* [2013] EWCA Civ 546; [2014] 1 W.L.R. 70 at [51]–[52], per Elias LJ, para.3-44.

100 See *Standard Chartered Bank v Pakistan National Shipping Corp (No.2)* [2000] Lloyd's Rep. 218 at 230, per Evans LJ where there was a weighing of the claimant's deceitful conduct against the fraud of the defendants: "The conduct of SCB was not so egregious, though potentially unlawful, and its share of responsibility for its own loss was not so weighty that the court should refuse to entertain the claim."

101 [2002] EWCA Civ 1821; [2003] I.C.R. 766; [2003] P.I.Q.R. P17 at [71].

102 [1998] Q.B. 978.

103 See also *Worrall v British Railways Board* Unreported 1999 CA, where the claimant alleged that an accident caused by the defendant's negligence brought about personality changes which led him to commit two serious criminal offences, and he claimed damages for the losses flowing from his imprisonment. The Court of Appeal, applying *Clunis*, held that public policy meant that the court should not assist a claimant who pleads and relies on his own criminal conduct to establish his claim. He was fully responsible for his actions (and had not claimed otherwise in the criminal proceedings—his defence had been an alibi, and he had not relied on any psychiatric evidence). See further *Wilson v Coulson* [2002] P.I.Q.R. P22; para.2-131 fn.456.

104 [1977] Q.B. 94.

contributory negligence. In *Pitts v Hunt*,[105] the claimant was seriously injured in a motorcycle accident. He was a pillion passenger on a motor cycle involved in a collision which killed the rider. Both he and the rider had been drinking heavily prior to the accident. The claimant knew that the rider was uninsured and did not hold a licence. He had actively and forcefully encouraged the rider to drive in a reckless and dangerous manner. The Court of Appeal unanimously held that the claimant's own criminal conduct precluded him from recovering damages from the deceased rider's estate. *Pitts v Hunt* is not authority for the proposition that driving a vehicle whilst uninsured, or having drunk excessive amounts of alcohol, or driving or encouraging someone to drive recklessly will necessarily give rise to the defence of ex turpi causa. It was the combination of all of these factors that persuaded the court, whatever the theoretical basis for the defence, that the claimant's action should not succeed. Anti-competitive acts in breach of the Competition Act 1998 are of sufficiently serious turpitude to engage ex turpi causa, with the result that a party to such an agreement cannot claim damages for loss caused by being a party to that illegal agreement[106]; an attempted civil law bribe (intending to induce a breach of fiduciary duty) could be sufficient to engage the principle of ex turpi causa[107]; and an allegation of tax evasion may possibly give rise to the defence.[108] The misuse of illegal drugs is sufficiently serious to engage the illegality defence[109] as is making off without paying a taxi fare, contrary to s.3 of the Theft Act 1968 (an offence punishable by up to two years' imprisonment)[110]; and participating in a joint criminal enterprise with the rider of a bike to ride the bike dangerously (an offence also punishable by up to two years' imprisonment).[111]

3-35 The potential severity of the sentence for a criminal offence is not in itself an indication that the defence will apply. In *Wallett v Vickers*[112] it was held that ex turpi causa did not apply where a motorist had been driving his vehicle dangerously (punishable by up to two years' imprisonment), lost control, crashed and was killed. He had been driving alongside the defendant's vehicle on a dual carriageway at up to twice the speed limit, with each driver trying to get to the point where the road narrowed to a single lane ahead of the other. The defendant was convicted of dangerous driving and sentenced to six months' imprisonment. Males J concluded that there was no criminal joint enterprise, which required an intention to assist or encourage the commission of the crime:

"In the absence of a criminal joint enterprise between the claimant and the defendant,

---

105 [1991] 1 Q.B. 24.

106 *Safeway Stores Ltd v Twigger* [2010] EWCA Civ 1472; [2011] 2 All E.R. 841.

107 *Nayyar v Denton Wilde Sapte* [2009] EWHC 3218 (QB); [2010] P.N.L.R. 15 (an appeal on a different point was refused: *Nayyar v Denton Wilde Sapte* [2010] EWCA Civ 815). Though bribery will not necessarily mean that a claim should be refused, at least in circumstances where it is alleged that all the parties have engaged in dishonesty: see *Bank St Petersburg PJSC v Arkhangelsky* [2020] EWCA Civ 408; [2020] 4 W.L.R. 55 at [91].

108 *K/S Lincoln v CB Richard Ellis Hotels Ltd* [2009] EWHC 2344 (TCC); [2010] P.N.L.R. 5.

109 *B v Chief Constable of X* [2015] EWHC 13 (QB); [2015] I.R.L.R. 284.

110 *Beaumont v Ferrer* [2016] EWCA Civ 768; [2017] P.I.Q.R. P1.

111 *McCracken v Smith* [2015] EWCA Civ 380; [2015] P.I.Q.R. P19; but where the claimant pillion passenger did not encourage or assist the rider to ride dangerously there is no criminal joint enterprise, and mere foreseeability of dangerous riding is not enough: *Clark v Farley* [2018] EWHC 1007 (QB); [2018] P.I.Q.R. P15. Engaging in a conspiracy to defraud an insurance company by setting fire to vehicles at the owner's instigation is not a "minor transgression": *Gujra v Roath* [2018] EWHC 854 (QB); [2018] 1 W.L.R. 3208 at [30].

112 [2018] EWHC 3088 (QB); [2019] P.I.Q.R. P6.

dangerous driving by the claimant will not bar a claim pursuant to the ex turpi causa principle."[113]

Infringement of a foreign patent does not cross the threshold of "turpitude"; only criminal acts and quasi-criminal acts would sufficiently engage the public interest.[114]

Immoral conduct In *Kirkham v Chief Constable of Greater Manchester Police*,[115] the Court of Appeal considered that, exceptionally, conduct other than criminal conduct could give rise to a defence of ex turpi. A prisoner committed suicide in prison. The police knew that he had previously attempted suicide and remained a suicide risk, but failed to pass that information on to the prison authorities. It was held that suicide was not an affront the public conscience at least where there was medical evidence that the suicide was "not in full possession of his mind". Farquharson LJ said that the position might be different where the victim was wholly sane. Subsequently, in *Reeves v Commissioner of Police for the Metropolis*,[116] the Court of Appeal held that when the deceased had committed suicide in circumstances where the defendant was in breach of his duty of care to prevent such self-harm, the suicide did not give rise to a defence of ex turpi, irrespective of the deceased's state of mind. The defendant's duty of care was owed because there was a foreseeable risk of suicide by the deceased, not because of his state of mind. Given modern public attitudes to suicide, and the fact that it has not been a criminal offence since 1961, it could not be said to be an affront to the public conscience to allow a claim based on suicide where the defendant was in breach of a duty to protect the deceased from harming himself. In *Hegarty v Shine*,[117] the claimant contracted a venereal disease from her lover. Her claim in battery (on the basis that she had not given a valid consent to sexual intercourse) was rejected, partly on the grounds that no cause of action should be founded on flagrant sexual immorality. It would seem unlikely that today extra-marital intercourse would be regarded as so shocking as to justify depriving the claimant of a remedy for conduct which would otherwise amount to an actionable wrong. Thus, notwithstanding the Court of Appeal's assertion in *Kirkham* that grossly immoral (as opposed to unlawful) conduct could justify refusing a remedy, there are no modern cases where this has occurred and it is difficult to think of circumstances which might be regarded as so serious that the ex turpi defence should apply. 3-36

113 [2018] EWHC 3088 (QB); [2019] P.I.Q.R. P6 at [43]; applying *McCracken v Smith* [2015] EWCA Civ 380; [2015] P.I.Q.R. P19. In passing, Males J noted, at [38], that careless driving is at the low end of the spectrum of turpitude: "careless driving is a criminal offence but nobody would suggest that careless driving by the claimant prevents the recovery of damages (reduced as appropriate on account of contributory negligence) in a road traffic case where both drivers are partly to blame. In such a case the recovery of damages does not offend public notions of the fair distribution of resources and poses no threat to the integrity of the law."

114 *Les Laboratoires Servier v Apotex Inc* [2014] UKSC 55; [2015] A.C. 430. Lord Sumption, at [25], identified as examples of acts which would engage the ex turpi causa defence: cases of dishonesty or corruption; some anomalous categories of misconduct such as prostitution (which without being criminal was contrary to public policy); and the infringement of statutory rules enacted for the protection of the public interest and attracting civil sanctions of a penal character, such as competition law. Torts (other than those involving dishonesty), breaches of contract, statutory and other civil wrongs offended interests which are essentially private, not public, did not engage ex turpi causa.

115 [1990] 2 Q.B. 283 at 291.

116 [1999] Q.B. 169 CA.

117 (1878) 14 Cox C.C. 145.

(ii) *Causal connection with the claimant's loss*

3-37 However reprehensible the claimant's own wrongdoing, a plea of ex turpi will only succeed if the claimant's conduct has a sufficient causal connection with the injury of which he complains.[118] The "connection" of the illegality with the claimant's injury is essentially a causation test which, since the decision of the House of Lords in *Gray v Thames Trains*, is increasingly treated by the courts as the crucial factor.[119] In *Delaney v Pickett*[120] the Court of Appeal held that a claim by a passenger injured by the negligent driving of the defendant was not defeated by ex turpi causa, notwithstanding that it was probable that both defendant and claimant were in possession of cannabis with intent to supply it at the time of the accident. The criminal behaviour was not causally linked to the claimant's damage. As Ward LJ put it:

> "Here the crucial question is whether, on the one hand, the criminal activity merely gave occasion for the tortious act of the defendant to be committed or whether, even though the accident would never have happened had they not made the journey, which at some point involved their obtaining and/or transporting drugs with the intention to supply, or on the other hand whether the immediate cause of the claimant's damage was the negligent driving. The answer to that question is in my judgment quite clear. Viewed as a matter of causation, the damage suffered by the claimant was not caused by his or their criminal activity. It was caused by the tortious act of the defendant in the negligent way in which he drove his motor car. In those circumstances the illegal acts are incidental and the claimant is entitled to recover his loss."[121]

---

[118] Hence Lord Asquith's comment that a burglar whose pocket is picked by another burglar on their way to the scene of the intended crime could sue the thief: *National Coal Board v England* [1954] A.C. 403 at 428-429. There is essentially no causal connection between the theft and the criminal enterprise upon which they are engaged. See also *Saunders v Edwards* [1987] 1 W.L.R. 1116 (no causal connection between claimant's agreement with defendant to undervalue property for the purpose of evading tax and defendant's fraudulent misrepresentation to claimant inducing claimant to purchase the property); *Sweetman v Nathan* [2003] EWCA Civ 1115; [2004] P.N.L.R. 7 (claimant's fraud against a bank in relation to a property transaction did not preclude a claim for negligence against the firm of solicitors acting for him in the transaction; the fact that the loss may not have occurred but for the claimant's deceit of the bank was irrelevant); *Churchill Car Insurance v Kelly* [2006] EWHC 18 (QB); [2007] R.T.R. 26 (no causal connection between claimant driving a vehicle unlawfully displaying a stolen tax disc and accident caused by the defendant's negligent driving); *McLaughlin v Morrison* [2013] CSOH 163; 2014 S.L.T. 111 at [42] (injuries caused by defender's decision to drive her vehicle deliberately at the pursuer, not the pursuer's alleged criminal involvement in attacking a building); *McCracken v Smith* [2015] EWCA Civ 380; [2015] P.I.Q.R. P19 (no causal connection between claimant passenger's joint criminal enterprise with the rider of a trail bike to ride it dangerously and the negligence of a motorist in contributing to the cause of a crash between the bike and his vehicle, though the claimant was contributorily negligent; Clarke LJ, at [87], observed that: "If the position were otherwise, any driver whose road traffic offence constituted turpitude, but who was only partially to blame, would fail to recover from anyone else whose negligence caused the accident.").

[119] Note, however, the criticism by Lord Sumption of the test of an "inextricable link" between the illegality and the loss in *Patel v Mirza* [2016] UKSC 42; [2017] A.C. 467 at [240], though this was a dissenting judgment.

[120] [2011] EWCA Civ 1532; [2012] 1 W.L.R. 2149.

[121] [2011] EWCA Civ 1532; [2012] 1 W.L.R. 2149 at [37]. See also per Tomlinson LJ at [73]: "there was no relevant nexus between the illegality upon which the claimant was engaged and the tortious conduct of [the defendant] which gave rise to his injuries". cf. *Smith v Stratton* [2015] EWCA Civ 1413 where the occupants of a vehicle had been dealing drugs and the claimant passenger was injured in an accident during an attempt to escape the pursuit of a police vehicle. The use of the car was integral to the supply of drugs because it facilitated the sale of drugs and provided a means of rapid

Delaney can be constrasted with *Joyce v O'Brien*[122] in which the claimant was injured when he fell from the rear of a van being driven by the defendant. The parties had jointly stolen a set of ladders from a house and the ladders were too long to fit into the van with the rear doors closed, so the claimant was standing on the rear footplate holding onto the ladders and the van when he lost his grip. The Court of Appeal held that the claim was barred by ex turpi causa. Elias LJ (with whom Rafferty and Ryder LJJ agreed) indicated that the same causation principle should apply whether thc criminal is acting alone or as part of a joint enterprise. The additional feature in a joint enterprise claim is that: **3-38**

> "the claimant may be denied recovery not merely where the injury results directly from his own criminal conduct, but also where it results from the action of a joint participator carried on in furtherance of the joint enterprise. In certain cases the injury will still be treated as having been caused by the claimant even though the direct cause of the injury was his co-defendant."[123]

For this purpose the injury would be caused by, rather than occasioned by, the criminal activity of the claimant where the joint criminal illegality affects the standard of care which the claimant is reasonably entitled to expect from his partner in crime.[124] It was also linked to questions of foreseeability:

> "where the character of the joint criminal enterprise is such that it is foreseeable that a party or parties may be subject to unusual or increased risks of harm as a consequence of the activities of the parties in pursuance of their criminal objectives, and the risk materialises, the injury can properly be said to be caused by the criminal act of the claimant even if it results from the negligent or intentional act of another party to the illegal enterprise. I do not suggest that this necessarily exhausts situations where the ex turpi principle applies in joint enterprise cases, but I would expect it to cater for the overwhelming majority of cases."[125]

On the facts of *Joyce* the claimant's own carelessness in taking the risk he did as part of his criminal offending was a cause of, and not merely the occasion of, his injury. The accident was precisely the kind of accident which could have been

escape if escape was called for; ex turpi causa applied. Similarly, in *Blake v Croasdale* [2018] EWHC 1919 (QB); [2019] R.T.R. 8 ex turpi was applied where a vehicle being used to facilitate the supply of drugs crashed, having been driven at speed to escape from the police.

122 [2013] EWCA Civ 546; [2014] 1 W.L.R. 70.

123 [2013] EWCA Civ 546; [2014] 1 W.L.R. 70 at [27].

124 [2013] EWCA Civ 546; [2014] 1 W.L.R. 70 at [28]. This, said his Lordship, was consistent with the result in *Ashton v Turner* [1981] Q.B. 137; and *Pitts v Hunt* [1991] 1 Q.B. 24, but focused on causation rather than duty, so re-casting cases suggesting that when ex turpi causa applies to a joint criminal enterprise case no duty of care is owed to give effect to Lord Hoffmann's causation principle in *Gray v Thames Trains Ltd*. In *Ashton* the claimant and defendant were drunken burglars making their get-away from the scene of the crime in the defendant's car. The claimant was injured as a result of the defendant's reckless driving. His claim was dismissed as contrary to public policy on the basis that the defendant did not owe his passenger a duty of care in the circumstances. In *Pitts* the claimant's conduct in encouraging the defendant to drive recklessly, knowing that he had drunk an excessive amount of alcohol, was directly linked as a matter of causation to the resulting accident which caused the claimant's injuries.

125 [2013] EWCA Civ 546; [2014] 1 W.L.R. 70 at [29], per Elias LJ. Query, however, how the foreseeability of the risk determines the question of which conduct (defendant's or claimant's) *caused* the damage (as opposed to the parties' relative *culpability* for the damage).

foreseen as the result of the need to make a quick getaway even if the defendant had not been driving so dangerously.[126]

3-39 **Defendant's reaction to provocation disproportionate** In a case of trespass to the person, if the defendant's reaction to provocation by the claimant is so disproportionate that the defence of self-defence does not apply there would have to be a very clear justification to dismiss the claim against him on other grounds. Although in a joint crime of violence where two parties are fighting unlawfully the foreseeable consequences of the confrontation would not found a claim, where the claimant sustains injuries because the defendant has voluntarily committed a different kind of serious crime against him the claimant's conduct "does not in law cause that injury for the purpose of the particular rule of causation applicable to this defence. … To hold otherwise would be go to behind another important principle of the law which is that those who commit crime are responsible for their own actions."[127]

3-40 **Where claimant cannot lawfully take advantage of lost opportunity** Where the claimant has an action for negligence and a particular head of damage involves a lost opportunity of avoiding a loss or of making a gain the head of damage will be irrecoverable if the claimant could not lawfully have taken advantage of opportunity allegedly lost.[128] The loss is not causally linked to the defendant's breach of duty because even in the absence of the breach the claimant could not lawfully have avoided it.

(iii) Proportionality

3-41 **Proportionality between claimant's and defendant's conduct** The degree and culpability of the claimant's criminality has in some cases been weighed against the conduct of the defendant. Evidence of some degree of participation in crime will not result in denial of a remedy where the defendant's conduct is by far the more culpable.[129] Breaking the skull of an assailant who struck the first blow will be

---

126 [2013] EWCA Civ 546; [2014] 1 W.L.R. 70 at [46]. See also *Beaumont v Ferrer* [2016] EWCA Civ 768; [2017] P.I.Q.R. P1 where the claimants sustained injury by jumping from a moving taxi with the intention of avoiding the fare. The Court of Appeal held that the claimants' injuries were caused by their own criminal acts of making off without payment.

127 *Flint v Tittensor* [2015] EWHC 466 (QB); [2015] 1 W.L.R. 4370 at [55], per Edis J.

128 So in *Rance v Mid-Downs HA* [1991] 1 Q.B. 587 the claimant alleged that as a result of the defendants' negligence a foetal abnormality was not detected during the course of a pregnancy, and she was therefore deprived of the opportunity of terminating the pregnancy. Due to the length of the gestation, however, an abortion on the ground of serious foetal handicap would not have been lawful under the Abortion Act 1967 (as it then stood). Brooke J held that on the facts there had been no negligence, but that in any event on the ground of public policy the court would not award compensation in circumstances where the claimant could not have turned her lost opportunity to value without breaking the law. In *Briody v St Helens and Knowsley AHA* [2001] EWCA Civ 1010; [2002] Q.B. 856 it was held that a claim for damages in respect of rendering the claimant infertile could not include the cost of procedures connected with surrogate motherhood if those procedures would be in breach of the Surrogacy Arrangements Act 1985. However, in *XX v Whittington Hospital NHS Trust* [2020] UKSC 14; [2020] 2 W.L.R. 972 a majority of the Supreme Court concluded that due to changes in the law and in social values, public policy no longer supported this proposition. The claimant was entitled to recover the reasonable costs of entering commercial surrogacy arrangements in California, even though commercial surrogacy remains unlawful in the UK.

129 *Burrows v Rhodes* [1899] 1 Q.B. 816; *Shelley v Paddock* [1980] Q.B. 348; *Saunders v Edwards*

unlikely to result in a successful plea of ex turpi.[130] The requirement for some element of proportionality between the claimant's wrongdoing and the defendant's conduct featured prominently in *Revill v Newbery*.[131] The 76-year-old defendant was sleeping in a shed on his allotment in order to protect his property from burglars and, on hearing the claimant attempting to break in, fired a shotgun through a small hole in the door without being able to see whether he was likely to hit anyone, injuring the claimant. The Court of Appeal held that the defendant was in breach of his duty of care to the claimant (in firing blind at body level rather than not at all or upwards as a warning shot) and could not rely on ex turpi because he had employed excessive force out of all proportion to the claimant's conduct (the claimant's damages were reduced by two-thirds for contributory negligence). The case is notable for two particular features. First, the concern expressed by the Court of Appeal that the fact that the claimant was a burglar should not mean that he effectively became an "outlaw", beyond the protection of the civil law.[132] Of course, it is not strictly correct to suggest that the burglar becomes an "outlaw" since he is entitled to the full protection of the criminal law if the occupier, in seeking to defend his property or person, exceeds acceptable limits. The defendant in *Revill* was prosecuted on charges of wounding under the criminal law, and was acquitted by a jury. This highlights the second feature of the case, namely the public sympathy which was expressed for the defendant, and indeed the sense of public outrage (at least in the popular press) that the defendant should have to compensate a burglar for his injuries.[133] If liability for negligence rests upon moral judgments as to who ought reasonably to be compensated for the losses associated with social activity then it may be that, in this context, the law is out of step with public perceptions of right

[1987] 1 W.L.R. 1116.

130 *Lane v Holloway* [1968] 1 Q.B. 379 (elderly man provoked a fight with a younger neighbour who then violently battered him). cf. *Cross v Kirkby, The Times*, 5 April 2000 CA, where the defendant struck the claimant on the head with a baseball bat, having been attacked by the claimant with the bat. In the circumstances, the defendant's response was held not to have been out of proportion to the initial attack. *Lane v Holloway* was different because the defendant's response to a trivial blow was completely out of proportion. In *Flint v Tittensor* [2015] EWHC 466 (QB); [2015] 1 W.L.R. 4370 at [53] Edis J compared the seriousness of the claimant's misconduct with the seriousness of the defendant's misconduct as part of the assessment of whether the claimant's loss was causally linked to his wrongdoing (applying the causation test from *Gray v Thames Trains Ltd*): "It is necessary to do this in order to decide whether, for the purposes of the causation rule applicable to this public policy defence, the one caused the other. The cases about 'proportionality' being irrelevant are not cases which concern two people using unlawful force against each other, but about persons injured in the course of committing crime by the negligence of others." A disproportionate reaction by the defendant to provocation by the claimant, in effect, breaks the causal link.

131 [1996] Q.B. 567.

132 "[B]y enacting section 1 of the [Occupiers' Liability Act 1984], Parliament has decided that an occupier cannot treat a burglar as an outlaw and has defined the scope of the duty owed to him": [1996] Q.B. 567 at 577, per Neill LJ Evans LJ commented, at 579, that applying ex turpi would mean that a trespasser who was also a criminal was effectively an outlaw, who was debarred by the law from recovering compensation for any injury which he might sustain. cf. the suggestion of Lord Denning MR in *Cummings v Grainger* [1977] Q.B. 397 at 406 that ex turpi causa might bar a claim by a burglar bitten by a guard dog, and, in particular, his obiter remarks in *Murphy v Culhane* [1977] Q.B. 94 at 98 to the effect that ex turpi would apply if a burglar was shot by a householder subsequently convicted of manslaughter; cf. *Bigcharles v Merkel* [1973] 1 W.W.R. 324, where the defence did not apply against a burglar of commercial premises who was shot dead, though he was held 75% contributorily negligent.

133 There was subsequently a public collection for the defendant which paid the damages (some £4,100) awarded in favour of the claimant.

and wrong.[134] It is true that the effect of the defence is that the claimant recovers nothing, and that this can sometimes seem a harsh conclusion, but this is no less true of the defence of volenti non fit injuria, which is still applied today, and can be applied to far less egregious conduct on the part of the claimant.[135]

3-42 There are a number of problems with this form of the proportionality requirement. First, in the context of the debate undertaken in *Revill* it appears to introduce the notion of the reasonableness of the *defendant's* conduct, which is clearly relevant to the defence of self-defence. Self-defence is a defence to the intentional tort of trespass to the person, but it is not relevant to a claim in negligence which was the basis of the claimant's action in *Revill*. In comparing the *negligence* of the defendant with the *intentional* wrongdoing of the claimant, it is arguable that the Court of Appeal got this assessment wrong on the facts of *Revill*,[136] since the defendant was actually acquitted of the offence of wounding.[137] More importantly, it is questionable to what extent the defendant's conduct is relevant to the defence of ex turpi causa at all. If the defence is based on the public policy that a claimant should not be permitted to recover damages where it would bring the law into disrepute, the focus should be on the *claimant's* conduct, not the defendant's.[138] Taking into account the relative conduct of defendant and claimant creates the real possibility that in one case the defence will succeed (where the defendant is comparatively "innocent") and in another the defence will fail (where the defendant is also seriously culpable) where the claimants' conduct is identical. It seems odd to further a public policy of not permitting claimants guilty of serious criminal offences to recover damages for injuries sustained during the course of committing those offences, by considering whether the defendant's conduct was more serious.

3-43 In *Hewison v Meridian Shipping Pte Ltd*[139] Ward LJ said that the measure of disproportion is "between the claimant's conduct and the seriousness of the loss he will incur if his claim is not allowed. This test of proportionality is not quite the same as judging whether the claimant's wrongdoing is disproportionate to the defendant's wrongdoing."[140] The relevance of the defendant's conduct was expressly questioned by the Court of Appeal in *Cross v Kirkby*.[141] The claimant, who was involved in disrupting a hunt, armed himself with a baseball bat and struck the

---

[134] Consider, in an entirely different context, the comment of Lord Millett in *McFarlane v Tayside Health Board* [2000] 2 A.C. 59 at 111: "There is something distasteful, if not morally offensive, in treating the birth of a normal, healthy child as a matter for compensation." Query where, on the scale of moral offensiveness, compensating burglars for injuries sustained during the course of their criminal activity falls.

[135] Compare *McGinley or Titchener v British Railways Board* [1983] 1 W.L.R. 1427, where a trespasser crossing a railway line was held to be volenti to the risk of negligence by the railway company. It is not clear why the policy of the law should seek to bar a remedy to a claimant who, essentially, takes a stupid risk in crossing a railway line, whilst permitting a burglar, who takes a deliberate risk, to maintain an action.

[136] See Weir [1996] C.L.J. 182 for cogent criticism.

[137] Note that *Lane v Holloway* [1968] 1 Q.B. 379, where the question of the proportionality of the defendant's response was first considered, involved battery by both claimant and defendant.

[138] See *Vellino v Chief Constable of the Greater Manchester Police* [2001] EWCA Civ 1249; [2002] 1 W.L.R. 218 at [70] where Sir Murray Stuart-Smith said that: "The principle is one of public policy; it is not for the benefit of the defendant. Since if the principle applies, the cause of action does not arise, the defendant's conduct is irrelevant. There is no question of proportionality between the conduct of the claimant and defendant."

[139] [2002] EWCA Civ 1821; [2003] I.C.R. 766; [2003] P.I.Q.R. P17.

[140] [2002] EWCA Civ 1821; [2003] I.C.R. 766; [2003] P.I.Q.R. P17 at [72].

[141] *The Times*, 5 April 2000 CA.

defendant with it. The defendant wrested the bat from the claimant and struck him a single blow to the head, fracturing his skull. The Court of Appeal held that the defendant had acted in self-defence, and that the claimant's action was barred on the ground that his injuries arose from his own unlawful acts.[142] Beldam LJ said that although the ex turpi defence was frequently raised by the defendant it was not for his benefit. The question was not whether the defendant was precluded from relying on the defence of ex turpi causa because he used disproportionate and unlawful force; the question was whether the claimant was precluded from recovering because of his illegal and criminal conduct. The rule was not for the benefit of the defendant, but because the court will not lend its aid to the claimant.

Proportionality between claimant's turpitude and claimant's loss Arguably the concept of proportionality is relevant, in the sense that the court should look at the seriousness of the claimant's wrongdoing in deciding whether it is appropriate to compensate him for damage sustained in the course of that wrongdoing. Thus, in *Hounga v Allen*[143] Lord Hughes suugested that: "although the relative turpitude of claimant and defendant is not the test, the extent of the claimant's turpitude may be relevant to determining whether there is a sufficiently close connection between the illegal act and the claim." Minor offences can readily be disregarded,[144] but there comes a point at which the courts should not entertain the claims to compensation of those injured whilst engaged in serious criminal activity—at least, to do so risks bringing the legal system into disrepute. The difficulty is to draw the line between "minor" and "serious" offences. In *Joyce v O'Brien*,[145] in response to the claimant's argument that a principle of proportionality should apply and that it would not be offensive to the public to permit recovery where the criminal offence was of a relatively trivial nature, Elias LJ accepted that there should be some flexibility in the operation of ex turpi causa: 3-44

> "The doctrine will not apply, for example, to minor traffic offences. I suspect that in most joint criminal liability cases at least, the nature and characteristics of the principal offence will in practice determine which acts of a co-conspirator will attract the application of the ex turpi doctrine, and for relatively trivial offences the range of such acts is likely to be very limited. Nonetheless, I recognise that there may be a problem in determining in certain cases whether the offence attracts the application of the doctrine or not."[146]

However, on the facts of *Joyce*, Elias LJ concluded that wherever the precise line was to be drawn, the theft of the ladders fell clearly on the side applying ex turpi causa. It was not merely an imprisonable offence but carried a seven year maximum sentence, and moreover it was not a strict liability offence which could be committed without any real moral culpability.[147]

In *Patel v Mirza* Lord Toulson had indicated that the issue was "whether denial 3-45

142 *Revill* was distinguished on the ground that: (1) the Occupiers' Liability Act 1984 effectively provides that an occupier cannot treat a burglar as an "outlaw", and if Revill's claim had been barred it would have been tantamount to treating him as an outlaw; (2) the discharge of a shotgun towards a burglar who had shown no intention of violence towards the defendant could not be said to be an integral part or a necessarily direct consequence of the burglary.

143 [2014] UKSC 47; [2014] 1 W.L.R. 2889 at [58] (emphasis added).

144 And, arguably, mere "immoral" conduct should not form part of the assessment at all.

145 [2013] EWCA Civ 546; [2014] 1 W.L.R. 70; see para.3-38.

146 [2013] EWCA Civ 546; [2014] 1 W.L.R. 70 at [51].

147 [2013] EWCA Civ 546; [2014] 1 W.L.R. 70 at [52]. See also *McCracken v Smith* [2015] EWCA Civ

of the claim would be a proportionate response to the illegality, bearing in mind that punishment is a matter for the criminal courts",[148] which on one view suggests some comparison between the *extent* of the claimant's loss and the seriousness of the offence (given that in sentencing offenders the criminal law seeks to balance punishment with the seriousness of the offence). This could produce the odd result that where a claimant has suffered serious injury the outcome might be different from that where he had sustained minor injury. But none of the cases pre-dating *Patel* have taken this view. The issue of proportionality has been seen as linked to the seriousness of the claimant's criminal conduct rather than the seriousness of the damage sustained (and so the value of any damages that would be lost if ex turpi causa is applied). Thus, ex turpi causa may apply more extensive "punishment" (by refusing an award of damages) than would be considered appropriate in the context of a criminal offence.

(iv) Relevance of the claimant's mental state

3-46 In *Clunis v Camden & Islington HA*,[149] counsel for the claimant had argued that the correct approach was the "affront to the public conscience" test and that the defence should not apply where the claimant's degree of responsibility was diminished by virtue of mental disorder. This argument is consistent with the line taken by the Court of Appeal in *Kirkham v Chief Constable of Greater Manchester Police*[150] where it was held that awarding damages following a suicide would not affront the public conscience, where there was medical evidence that the suicide was "not in full possession of his mind".[151] It was held in *Clunis* that because the claimant had been convicted of a serious criminal offence, public policy would preclude the court from entertaining his claim "unless it could be said that he did not know the nature and quality of his act or that what he was doing was wrong".[152] His responsibility for the killing was reduced by his mental disorder, but his mental state did not justify a verdict of not guilty by reason of insanity. Diminished

380; [2015] P.I.Q.R. P19—joint criminal enterprise to ride a trail bike dangerously sufficiently serious to engage the ex turpi defence, given that the offence was punishable on conviction on indictment by up to two years' imprisonment: "On no view is it a trivial offence" (per Richards LJ [43]). Clarke LJ commented, at [86]: "It may be that the dividing line should be between those offences which are, and those which are not, punishable by imprisonment. Or it may be that the criterion is simply whether the public interest requires the doctrine to apply to a crime of the category in question."

148 [2016] UKSC 42; [2017] A.C. 467 at [101] and [120]. See also *Gujra v Roath* [2018] EWHC 854 (QB); [2018] 1 W.L.R. 3208 at [30] where Martin Spencer J considered that the loss of damages claimed in an action for malicious prosecution (in respect of being remanded in custody for a few weeks and then being electronically tagged for a few months) was not "in any way disproportionate to the unlawfulness of the claimant's conduct in associating himself with a serious attempted fraud upon an insurance company". See further *Stoffel & Co v Grondona* [2018] EWCA Civ 2031; [2018] P.N.L.R. 36 at [39] where Gloster LJ set out a list of factors taken into account in concluding that, on the facts of that case, it would be "entirely disproportionate" to deny a claim against negligent solicitors for failing to register the claimant's title to property where the claimant had participated in a mortgage fraud. There was no risk that enforcement of the claim would undermine the integrity of the justice system.

149 [1998] Q.B. 978.

150 [1990] 2 Q.B. 283.

151 [1990] 2 Q.B. 283 at 291, per Lloyd LJ. Farquharson LJ said, at 296, that an action could hardly be said to be grounded in immorality where "grave mental instability" on the part of the victim has been proved, although "the position may well be different where the victim is wholly sane".

152 [1998] Q.B. 978 at 989.

responsibility did not remove liability for his criminal act, and therefore he had to be taken to have known what he was doing and that it was wrong. Public policy must not allow the law of tort to be an "instrument to enforce obligations alleged to arise out of the claimant's own criminal act". This makes a great deal hang on the distinction between the criminal law defence of diminished responsibility and the defence of insanity, with an apparent presumption that mentally disordered offenders who have some awareness of their condition and some "responsibility" for their conduct, however impaired their reasoning might be, will be caught by the public policy defence of ex turpi causa non oritur actio.[153] In *Reeves v Commissioner of Police of the Metropolis*, however, the Court of Appeal held that the ex turpi causa defence should not apply to a suicide *whether or not the claimant was of sound mind*.[154] There was no distinction in this respect between persons suffering from a mental illness and persons who were not, since the claimant recovers damages, not because of his mental state, but because he is a suicide risk and has not received the care that he should have. To this extent, *Reeves* was a conscious departure from *Kirkham*, though it does seem to be at odds with *Clunis* on the question of the claimant's mental state.[155] Possibly, suicide and self-harm by the claimant is a special case, where the claimant's mental state is irrelevant, but in cases where the claimant is seeking compensation for the legal consequences of the harm that he has inflicted on others, it must be demonstrated that he was simply not responsible for his actions, even though those actions have had legal repercussions (such as his detention under the Mental Health Act 1983).

In *Gray v Thames Trains Ltd*[156] Lord Hoffmann, having set out the narrow and the wide forms of ex turpi causa, dealt with the causation issue of the wide form of the rule as it applied to the facts in *Gray*,[157] but did not address the question of whether it was "offensive to public notions of the fair distribution of resources that a claimant should be compensated … for the consequences of his own criminal conduct" or what factors would be taken into account in applying this. Perhaps his Lordship considered that manslaughter on the grounds of diminished responsibility so obviously fell within this formulation that it did not require elaboration. Certainly, he considered that the sentence imposed by a criminal court must be assumed to be what the criminal court regarded as appropriate to reflect the personal responsibility for the crime he has committed.[158] Lord Phillips was less dogmatic on this issue. There could be extreme circumstances, said his Lordship, (though *Gray* was not such a case) where a claimant has been ordered to be detained under s.37 of the Mental Health Act 1983 where the offending behaviour has played no part in the decision to impose the hospital order, and in this situation it was strongly **3-47**

153 The difference between *Kirkham* and *Clunis* is striking. Applying *Kirkham* the illegality defence only applies where it can be said that the claimant was "wholly sane", whereas according to *Clunis* the defence applies unless the claimant is wholly insane, provided, of course, the claim is essentially based on his illegal act.

154 [1999] Q.B. 169 at 185 per Buxton LJ: "If it shocks the conscience of the ordinary citizen that a suicide could recover, why is it the duty of the police, not merely as public officers but in the private law of negligence, to take reasonable steps to prevent suicide? … Here, the alleged turpitudinous act is the very thing that the defendant had a duty to try to prevent, imposed by a law of negligence which itself appeals to public conscience or at least to public notions of reasonableness."

155 Judgment in *Reeves* was handed down on 10 November 1997 and in *Clunis* on 5 December 1997. Neither judgment refers to the other.

156 [2009] UKHL 33; [2009] 1 A.C. 1339.

157 See para.3-18.

158 [2009] UKHL 33; [2009] 1 A.C. 1339 at [41].

arguable that "the hospital order should be treated as being a consequence of the defendant's mental condition and not of the defendant's criminal act. In that event the public policy defence of ex turpi causa would not apply".[159] More problematic would be where there is a need to detain the defendant both for his own treatment and the protection of the public, but the sentencing judge makes it clear that the defendant does not bear significant personal responsibility for his offence. His Lordship reserved his position on whether ex turpi causa would apply in that situation.[160]

(v) *Illegality in the context of the employment relationship*

3-48 In *Hewison v Meridian Shipping Pte Ltd*[161] the claimant was employed as a crane operator on a ship, and suffered serious injuries in an accident on board a vessel for which his employers were responsible. At the time of the accident he was 35 years old, and brought a claim for damages including loss of future earnings up to age 62. The claimant was epileptic, having had a total of three seizures between the ages of 17 and 19. He had not had any seizures since then, and took medication for his epilepsy daily. As a result of the accident he had another seizure, and his epilepsy was eventually discovered by the employers. The chances of him having a seizure before age 62, in the absence of the accident were put at 20 per cent. The defendants accepted that they were liable for the accident, but challenged the claimant's entitlement to an award of damages for loss of future earnings because the claimant had lied to them about his medical condition when he applied for the job, and subsequently when completing medical questionnaires. If the employers had known about his epilepsy they would not have employed him at sea, due to the hazardous nature of the work and the risk both to the claimant and others. It was argued for the defendants, and accepted by the Court of Appeal, that the claimant had committed the criminal offence of obtaining a pecuniary advantage by deception contrary to the Theft Act 1968 s.16.[162] By a majority, the Court of Appeal held that it was contrary to public policy to award damages for the loss of future earnings because the claimant's continued employment would have required him to continue to deceive his employers by fraudulently representing that he did not suffer from epilepsy. It was accepted that it was not a case where the maxim ex turpi causa non oritur actio applied, because there was no principle of public policy which prevented the claimant from pursuing his cause of action for damages; rather the issue was whether he was barred from recovering part of the loss. As Clarke LJ put it:

> "The principle can perhaps be stated as a variation of the maxim so that it reads *ex turpi causa non oritur damnum*, where the *damnum* is the loss which would have been recovered but for the relevant illegal or immoral act. A classic example is the principle that a person who makes his living from burglary cannot have damages assessed on the basis of what he would have earned from burglary but for the defendant's negligence."[163]

3-49 It would not be sufficient to bar the claimant's entitlement to damages that he had been party to some collateral or insignificant illegality or unlawful act.[164] For Clarke LJ, the claimant's unlawful act was neither collateral nor insignificant. The decep-

---

159 [2009] UKHL 33; [2009] 1 A.C. 1339 at [15].
160 See also, per Lord Rodger at [83] and Lord Brown at [103].
161 [2002] EWCA Civ 1821; [2003] I.C.R. 766; [2003] P.I.Q.R. P17.
162 See now the Fraud Act 2006.
163 [2002] EWCA Civ 1821 at [28].
164 [2002] EWCA Civ 1821 at [36] and [43], per Clarke LJ.

tion struck at the root of the employment contract under which he earned remuneration, and it was not insignificant because of the risks potentially involved to others if a seafarer should have the misfortune to have a seizure while working. Tuckey LJ favoured a broad test, namely: was the claim or the relevant part of it based substantially (and not therefore collaterally or insignificantly) on an unlawful act? "Such a broad test has the merit of simplicity. It does not involve the judge having to make very specific and difficult value judgments about precisely how serious the misconduct is or whether it would result in imprisonment or whether the claimant's loss is disproportionate to his misconduct."[165] Ward LJ, dissenting, preferred a more structured approach which involved considering the answers to five questions:

(1) Was the action founded on illegality?
(2) Is the claim closely connected or inextricably bound up with the claimant's own criminal conduct?
(3) Was this serious misconduct?
(4) Was the claimant's loss disproportionate to his misconduct?
(5) Could the court condone his conduct?

Applying those criteria Ward LJ would have concluded that the claim for future loss of earnings should not have been barred on grounds of policy, though there should have been a 20 per cent. discount to allow for the possibility that the seizures would have occurred again before the claimant's retirement. The approach of the majority could theoretically mean that any employee who has engaged in conduct that could potentially lead to his dismissal (making exaggerated and untruthful statements in a curriculum vitae when applying for a job, for example) might find his claim for future loss of earnings barred on the basis that he had committed a criminal offence and his expectation of future earnings depended upon the continuing deception of his employer (whether the employer was the defendant or not).

In *Major v Ministry of Defence*[166] the claimant had also told a lie, about her psychiatric history, in order to obtain employment with the RAF, and was dismissed three and a half years later when this was discovered. The claimant's psychiatric problems stemmed from an accident that occurred when she was aged 13 on a visit to a Royal Marines base. The Court of Appeal distinguished *Hewison* on the basis that in *Hewison* the claimant had obtained his employment by deception (a lie about his medical condition) and his entitlement to future earnings in that job depended upon a continuing deception, but the injury for which Miss Major was claiming compensation occurred before she obtained her employment,[167] or alternatively she was put in the position of being unable to work by the defendants' tort, and the fact that in order to gain employment (co-incidentally, as it happened, with the defendants) she would have to behave deceitfully was a matter that she was entitled complain of in respect of the defendants' tort.[168] 3-50

Collateral illegality Cases arising in the employment context involving so-called "collateral illegality", such as attempts to defraud the Inland Revenue by either withholding or falsely declaring tax and national insurance contributions, will 3-51

165 [2002] EWCA Civ 1821 at [51].
166 [2003] EWCA Civ 1433; (2003) 147 S.J.L.B. 1206.
167 [2003] EWCA Civ 1433 at [18], per Chadwick LJ.
168 [2003] EWCA Civ 1433 at [12], per Buxton J.

usually not fall within the ex turpi defence. In *Hall v Woolston Hall Leisure Ltd*[169] the Court of Appeal held that an employee's acquiescence in the employer's failure to deduct tax and national insurance contributions from wages, did not bar the employee from bringing a complaint of sex discrimination (a statutory tort) against the employer. The complaint of sex discrimination was not so closely bound up or linked with the unlawful conduct that the court would be seen to be condoning unlawful conduct by the employee. Mance LJ commented that:

> "While the underlying test therefore remains one of public policy, the test evolved in this court for its application in a tortious context thus requires an inextricable link between the facts giving rise to the claim and the illegality, before any question arises of the court refusing relief on the grounds of illegality. In practice, as is evident, it requires quite extreme circumstances before the test will exclude a tort claim."[170]

In *Vakante v Addey and Stanhope School*,[171] on the other hand, the Court of Appeal held that a claimant who illegally obtained work when barred from doing so, while his application for asylum was under consideration, could not maintain a claim for the statutory tort of race discrimination. He was entirely responsible for the illegality of his employment contract, which was obtained by fraud. He could not then complain about acts of discrimination if they consisted of the allegedly discriminatory manner of operating the illegal contract, since the operation of the contract was inextricably linked with the illegal conduct and to permit him to recover compensation for discrimination would appear to condone his illegal conduct.[172]

3-52 In *Hounga v Allen*[173] the Supreme Court ruled unanimously that the claimant's action against her employer for the statutory tort of unlawful discrimination was not caught by the ex turpi defence, notwithstanding that she had been working illegally, having entered the UK on a six-month visitor's visa. Lord Wilson considered that, on the facts, if the claimant had not been a victim of human trafficking by the defendant employer, the circumstances were so close to it that the distinction did not matter. His Lordship concluded that there was not an inextricable link between the claimant's illegal contract of employment and the defendant's acts of race discrimination. There were also countervailing issues of public policy, given that the claimant was a victim of human trafficking: "The public policy in support

---

169 [2001] 1 W.L.R. 225.

170 [2001] 1 W.L.R. 225 at [79]. In *Newman v Folkes and Dunlop Tyres Ltd* [2002] P.I.Q.R. Q2, QBD, it was held that where earnings are from a lawful source, collateral illegality in the performance of the contract, such as the deliberate failure to pay tax or national insurance contributions, does not preclude a claimant recovering in respect of lost earnings; see also *Finnis v Caulfield (t/a James Car Hire)* [2002] EWHC 3223 (QB), distinguishing between dishonesty in the actual receipt of income and subsequent dishonesty in failing to declare income for tax purposes. The receipt of income itself, unlike benefit fraud, does not involve a criminal act, and provided the calculation of a claimant's lost earnings was net of the tax that should have been paid, the court was not condoning the fraud on the Inland Revenue by making an award of damages; cf. *Hunter v Butler* [1996] R.T.R. 396 CA—the deceased's earnings were obtained from "moonlighting", whereby he did not disclose his earnings while drawing social security benefits at the full rate, and the Court of Appeal held that his widow was not entitled to claim for loss of dependency under the Fatal Accidents Act 1976.

171 [2004] EWCA Civ 1065; [2005] I.C.R. 231.

172 The Court distinguished *Hall* on the basis that the claimant in *Hall* was aware of the employer's illegal performance of her employment contract but was not herself participating in the illegality.

173 [2014] UKSC 47; [2014] 1 W.L.R. 2889. *Hounga* is commented on by J. Goudkamp and M. Zou, "The defence of illegality in tort law: beyond judicial redemption?" (2015) 74 C.L.J. 13; J. Fisher, "The ex turpi causa principle in Hounga and Servier" (2015) 78 M.L.R. 854.

of the application of that defence, to the extent that it exists at all, should give way to the public policy to which its application is an affront."[174] Lord Hughes accepted that there was not a sufficiently close connection between the illegality and the tort to bar the claim: the immigration offences committed by the claimant merely provided the setting or context in which the tort was committed. On the other hand, a claim for damages for breach of the contract of employment (or, by statutory extension, for unfair dismissal), would have been different since such a claim would depend on a lawfully enforceable contract of employment whereas the claimant's whole employment was illegal.

(vi) Property rights

It may be that actions concerned with the exercise of rights over property are in a different category from claims based on the infliction of loss. Thus, the fact that property has been acquired illegally does not confer a common law power on the police to confiscate that property by refusing to return it. In the absence of a statutory power to confiscate the property[175] the police must return cash belonging to the claimant which is believed to be the proceeds of drug trafficking[176] and must return a stolen vehicle to the thief if there is no one with a better title to the vehicle.[177] The courts' concern is to avoid establishing a mechanism of non-statutory expropriation by means of a defence to a civil claim where property had been seized from persons who were not subsequently convicted of a criminal offence. Similarly, the fact that a trespasser in adverse possession of real property may be committing a criminal offence does not prevent the acquisition of title to the land because there are competing public policy interests at stake, namely that title to land should not be left uncertain in the face of long possession to which there has been no adverse reaction.[178] These are examples of the need for certainty in rights of property overriding otherwise legitimate policy concerns in the law of torts. **3-53**

---

174 [2014] UKSC 47; [2014] 1 W.L.R. 2889 at [52].

175 On which see the Proceeds of Crime Act 2002. In *Sharma v Top Brands Ltd* [2015] EWCA Civ 1140; [2017] 1 All E.R. 854 at [48] Etherton C commented that the Proceeds of Crime Act 2002 "provides no clear steer for the scope and application of the common law principle of ex turpi causa non oritur actio in a civil action for negligence and breach of duty".

176 *Webb v Chief Constable of Merseyside Police* [2000] Q.B. 427 CA.

177 *Costello v Chief Constable of Derbyshire Constabulary* [2001] EWCA Civ 381; [2001] 1 W.L.R. 1437; *Gough v Chief Constable of West Midlands* [2004] EWCA Civ 206; *The Times*, 4 March 2004; see Getzler (2001) 117 L.Q.R. 565, commenting on *Costello*.

178 See *R. (on the application of Best) v Chief Land Registrar* [2015] EWCA Civ 17; [2016] Q.B. 23 where the Court of Appeal held that a trespasser could apply to be the registered proprietor even though part of the period of adverse possession involved the commission of a criminal offence (since the coming into force of s.144(1) of the Legal Aid, Sentencing and Punishment of Offenders Act 2012 which criminalised squatting in a residential building having entered it as a trespasser where the trespasser is living or intending to live in the building). In *Rashid v Nasrullah* [2018] EWCA Civ 2685; [2020] Ch. 37 at [69] Lewison LJ commented that *Patel v Mirza* [2016] UKSC 42; [2017] A.C. 467 was not a warrant for the rewriting of history. The Supreme Court in *Patel* had approved the balance struck in *Best*. Applying the doctrine of illegality on the facts of *Rashid* (the defendant was registered as the proprietor of the claimant's land following a fraud perpetrated by the defendant's father and the defendant had been in adverse possession for over 20 years) would undermine the law of adverse possession and the law of limitation more generally (at [75]). King LJ and Peter Jackson LJ agreed (at [83]) that "the scope for the doctrine of illegality is greatly reduced by the fact that the whole point of limitation is to limit the time for bringing claims, including good claims". The "careful statutory framework" of the Limitation Act 1980 would "in almost every case incorporate all the considerations mentioned in *Patel v Mirza*".

(vii) Trespassers

3-54 The Animals Act 1971 s.5(3), provides a defence to a claim under the Act by a trespasser in respect of damage inflicted by a dangerous animal kept on premises other than for the reasonable protection of persons or property.[179] Beyond this very specific defence, evidence that the claimant was a trespasser on the defendant's land when the tort was committed is unlikely to operate as a complete answer to liability in tort. The Occupiers' Liability Act 1984 imposes a duty of care to trespassers in certain limited circumstances.[180] When the Act does not apply, the judgment in *British Railways Board v Herrington*[181] still has effect—imposing a "common duty of humanity" to trespassers. In *Westwood v Post Office*,[182] the defendants, in breach of their statutory duty, failed to maintain a trap-door in the floor of a motor-room in a safe condition. A notice on the door of the room barred entry to unauthorised persons. The deceased used the room without authorisation to gain access to the roof, fell through the trap-door and was killed. The House of Lords held the defendants liable to his estate. The fact he was a trespasser in the room was irrelevant and did not bar a claim. The relevant statute applied to the whole of the premises, including the motor-room, for the protection of the workforce. The judgment of the Court of Appeal in *Revill v Newbery*[183] makes it clear that evidence that the claimant was a trespasser, even a trespasser intent on burglary, will not necessarily give rise to the defence of ex turpi causa, but other defences to trespass may be relevant, depending upon the circumstances.[184]

(viii) Relationship to other defences

3-55 **Ex turpi, volenti and contributory negligence** There will be many instances where a plea of ex turpi may overlap with the defences of volenti and/or contributory negligence. In *Murphy v Culhane*,[185] where the claimant's husband had voluntarily participated in a violent affray, the Court of Appeal ruled that the facts raised issues of ex turpi, volenti and contributory negligence. It might equally well be argued that his own criminal conduct should bar him from a remedy, or that he assumed the risk of injury, or that his own fault contributed to his injuries. Conduct insufficiently grave or connected with the ultimate injury to give rise to a successful defence of ex turpi may still constitute contributory negligence. So if X punches Y with his fist and Y responds by stabbing him, a plea of ex turpi may fail but X's damages nonetheless be reduced on the grounds of his contributory fault.[186]

---

179 See para.29-21.
180 See para.11-64.
181 [1972] A.C. 877.
182 [1974] A.C. 1.
183 [1996] Q.B. 567.
184 See paras 29-05 and 29-06.
185 [1977] Q.B. 94; and see *Cummings v Granger* [1977] Q.B. 397 at 406.
186 *Barnes v Nayer, The Times,* 19 December 1986 CA. In *Revill v Newbery* [1996] Q.B. 567, a burglar's damages were reduced by two thirds for contributory negligence; and in *Reeves v Commissioner of Police for the Metropolis* [2000] 1 A.C. 360, where the suicide victim was of sound mind, the claimant's damages were reduced by one half. See also *McCracken v Smith* [2015] EWCA Civ 380; [2015] P.I.Q.R. P19, para.3-37 fn.118 (no causal connection between claimant's criminal actions and defendant motorist's negligence for the purposes of the ex turpi causa defence, but claimant was found contributorily negligent, which requires a causal connection between the claimant's damage and his own negligent conduct: see para.3-60).

(ix) Fraudulent claims

The fact that, during the course of litigation, a claimant has made fraudulent claims in respect of particular heads of loss does not prevent him from succeeding in respect of other heads of loss which were clearly proved, though the fraudulent exaggeration of a claim is an abuse of process and the court has jurisdiction to strike out such a claim at any stage of proceedings.[187] The power to strike out should only be exercised where it is just and proportionate to do so, and after a trial it will be exercised only in very exceptional circumstances. The court may also set aside a compromise agreement where the amount of the settlement has been based on the claimant's fraudulent representations as to the severity of his injuries.[188] The Criminal Justice and Courts Act 2015 s.57 provides that where the claimant has been "fundamentally dishonest" in a claim for damages for personal injuries the court *must* dismiss the claim entirely unless the court is satisfied that the claimant would suffer substantial injustice.[189] The Act does not define "fundamentally dishonest", though the Explanatory Notes to the Bill referred to gross exaggeration of the claim or collusion in a fraudulent claim brought by another person in connection with the same incident or series of incidents.[190] The intention of s.57 is to reverse *Summers v Fairclough Homes Ltd* by creating a presumption that a fraudulent claim or a fraudulent head of claim will result in the whole claim being struck out, though the court retains a discretion not to do so if the claimant would suffer "substantial injustice". **3-56**

---

187 *Summers v Fairclough Homes Ltd* [2012] UKSC 26; [2012] 1 W.L.R. 2004.

188 See *Hayward v Zurich Insurance Co Plc* [2016] UKSC 48; [2017] A.C. 142; see para.2-22 for consideration of the causation issues where a defendant's insurer suspects that the claim is fraudulent but nonetheless settles the claim for substantial damages. Note that a fraudulent claim may result in an award of exemplary damages in the tort of deceit against the persons responsible for the fraud: *Hassan v Cooper* [2015] EWHC 540 (QB); [2015] R.T.R. 26; *Axa Insurance UK Plc v Financial Claims Solutions Ltd* [2018] EWCA Civ 1330; [2019] R.T.R. 1. Fraudulent claims can also lead to proceedings for contempt of court: *Zurich Insurance Plc v Romaine* [2019] EWCA Civ 851; [2019] 1 W.L.R. 5224; *Aviva Insurance Ltd v Kovacic* [2017] EWHC 2772 (QB); *Aviva Insurance Ltd v Nazir* [2018] EWHC 1296 (QB); *Calderdale and Huddersfield NHS Foundation Trust v Atwal* [2018] EWHC 961 (QB); (2018) 162 B.M.L.R. 169. This includes contempt committed by dishonest lawyers or expert witnesses: *Liverpool Victoria Insurance Co Ltd v Khan* [2018] EWHC 2581 (QB); and [2019] EWCA Civ 392; [2019] 1 W.L.R. 3833 (on the question of appropriate sentence).

189 This includes dishonesty by the claimant in relation to a related claim by another person in connection with the same incident giving rise to the claimant's primary claim. See further B. Dixon, "Fundamental Dishonesty and the Criminal Justice and Courts Act 2015" [2015] J.P.I.L. 108; B. Dixon and J. McQuater, "Fundamental Dishonesty: Guidance for Practitioners" [2016] J.P.I.L. 121; J. McQuater, "Fundamental dishonesty: review and update" [2019] J.P.I.L. 261.

190 For consideration of the meaning of the term "fundamentally dishonest" see *London Organising Committee of the Olympic and Paralympic Games (In Liquidation) v Sinfield* [2018] EWHC 51 (QB); [2018] P.I.Q.R. P8; *Razumas v Ministry of Justice* [2018] EWHC 215 (QB); [2018] P.I.Q.R. P10; *Molodi v Cambridge Vibration Maintenance Service* [2018] EWHC 1288 (QB); [2018] R.T.R. 25; *Pinkus v Direct Line* [2018] EWHC 1671 (QB); [2018] P.I.Q.R. P20; *Patel v Arriva Midlands Ltd* [2019] EWHC 1216 (QB); [2019] 1 W.L.R. 6598 (claimant's conduct dishonest by the objective standard of ordinary decent people, applying the criminal law standard set out in *Ivey v Genting Casinos UK Ltd (t/a Crockfords Club)* [2017] UKSC 67; [2018] A.C. 391); and *Howlett v Davies* [2017] EWCA Civ 1696; [2018] 1 W.L.R. 948 (where the issue was addressed in the context of CPR r.44.16).

(x) Illegality affecting a particular head of loss

3-57 The claimant's illegality may relate to a particular head of damages rather than the whole claim, in which case the correct approach is to deny compensation for that particular form of loss.[191] For example, *AB v Royal Devon and Exeter NHS Foundation Trust*[192] involved an assessment of damages where the claimant lacked capacity to manage a large lump sum award, and the issue was whether the award should include any of the costs associated with the claimant's incapacity. The incapacity was to a complex combination of the claimant's personality disorder, his impulsive personality, a mild head injury and the effects of historic illegal drug abuse. Irwin J held that in the year following the award of damages the claimant would face particularly difficult and complex decisions about managing the award and he would lack capacity even if he managed to stay free from serious drug abuse. In that period the lack of capacity was not directly caused by or "inextricably bound up with" any illegal acts, and so he was entitled to the additional costs associated with his incapacity. After that period, however, the claimant would face more manageable decisions and if he was incapable of making those decisions it would be because he had reverted to the abuse of illegal drugs. Thus, no award for the costs associated with the incapacity should be made for the period after one year.[193]

3. CONTRIBUTORY NEGLIGENCE[194]

(a) Fault of the claimant

3-58 Where it is found that the sole, effective cause of the relevant damage is the claimant's own conduct he recovers nothing because he fails to establish causation.[195] At common law where some fault on the part of the claimant contributed to the damage of which he complains, that contributory negligence operated as a complete defence.[196] Section 1(1) of the Law Reform (Contributory Negligence) Act 1945 removed the complete bar on claims and provided for apportionment of the loss:

> "Where any person suffers damage as the result partly of his own fault and partly of the fault[197] of any other person or persons, a claim in respect of that damage[198] shall not be defeated by reason of the fault of the person suffering the damage, but the damages

[191] *Burns v Edman* [1970] 2 Q.B. 541 (no claim for loss of dependency under the Fatal Accidents Act where the deceased's earnings out of which the dependants' were supported were attributable entirely to proceeds of crime); *Hunter v Butler* [1996] R.T.R. 396 (to similar effect where deceased's earnings were the proceeds of "moonlighting", i.e. drawing social security benefits whilst also working and failing to declare the earnings). See also *Hewison v Meridian Shipping Pte Ltd* [2002] EWCA Civ 1821; [2003] I.C.R. 766; [2003] P.I.Q.R. P17; para.3-48.

[192] [2016] EWHC 1024 (QB).

[193] Applying Lord Hoffmann's wide form of *ex turpi causa* in *Gray v Thames Trains Ltd* [2009] UKHL 33; [2009] 1 A.C. 1339, para.3-17 onwards.

[194] See Williams, *Joint Torts and Contributory Negligence* (1951); Kidner (1991) 11 L.S. 1. See also para.7-171.

[195] See *McKew v Holland & Hannen & Cubitts (Scotland) Ltd* [1969] 3 All E.R. 1621, HL; and see para.2-129.

[196] *Butterfield v Forrester* (1809) 11 East 60, per Ellenborough CJ.

[197] Defined in s.4 as "negligence—breach of statutory duty or other act or omission which gives rise to liability in tort or would, apart from this Act, give rise to the defence of contributory negligence".

[198] Defined in s.4 as including loss of life and personal injury and thus probably including any loss for which damages can be awarded in tort; but see *Drinkwater v Kimber* [1951] 2 All E.R. 713 CA.

recoverable in respect thereof shall be reduced to such extent as the court thinks just and equitable having regard to the claimant's share in the responsibility for the damage ..."

Thus evidence that the claimant's own negligence contributed to the damage in question will result in an apportionment of damages according to the degree of fault on either side. It would seem to follow that any finding that the claimant's damages should be reduced by 100 per cent is illogical, as such a result necessarily indicates that the claimant's fault alone is the effective cause of his injury.[199] Section 1 does not come into operation unless the court is satisfied that there is fault on the part of both parties which has caused damage. It is then expressly provided that the action shall not be defeated by reason of the fault of the person suffering the damage, but a finding that he is entirely responsible for the damage effectively defeats his claim. Thus, where the Act applies, i.e. where the fault of both claimant and defendant have contributed to the damage, the court *must* make an apportionment, which it will fail to do by assessing the claimant's contribution as 100 per cent.[200] Where the court is inclined to the view that a finding of 100 per cent contributory negligence would be appropriate it is probably better to treat the problem as a question of causation—in such circumstances the claimant's conduct

---

199 *Pitts v Hunt* [1991] 1 Q.B. 24 at 50, per Beldam LJ. There are cases where 100 per cent reduction has been made. See *McMullen v NCB* [1982] I.C.R. 148; *Jayes v IMI (Kynoch) Ltd* [1985] I.C.R. 155, where the Court of Appeal were prepared to apply 100 per cent contributory negligence in a case of breach of statutory duty in circumstances where the statutory intention was clearly to protect the workman from his own carelessness. The comments of the Court of Appeal in *Pitts v Hunt* were made without any reference to *Jayes v IMI (Kynoch) Ltd*. In *Reeves v Commissioner of Police for the Metropolis* [1999] Q.B. 169 at 195, Morritt LJ in a dissenting judgment, was prepared to follow *Jayes* in preference to *Pitts v Hunt*. The House of Lords' decision in *Reeves* [2000] 1 A.C. 360 does not address the question of whether it is logically possible to find that the defendant's negligence had some causal effect (in order to establish liability) but that the claimant's fault constituted 100 per cent responsibility for the resulting damage. Lord Hoffmann, at 371-372, discussed the trial judge's finding of 100 per cent contributory negligence (which Morritt LJ, dissenting, would also have applied in the Court of Appeal) without suggesting that it was never possible to make such an apportionment. Rather Lord Hoffmann's view was that in a case involving a suicide in police custody, a finding of 100 per cent contributory negligence would give no weight at all to the policy of the law in imposing a duty of care upon the police to try to prevent such suicides attempts. In *Anderson v Newham College of Further Education* [2002] EWCA Civ 505; [2003] I.C.R. 212 a two-judge Court of Appeal suggested that the decision in *Jayes v IMI (Kynoch) Ltd* had been reached per incuriam, since the decision of the House of Lords in *Boyle v Kodak Ltd* [1969] 1 W.L.R. 661 was not cited. Sedley LJ commented at [19]: "... *Jayes* should, in my respectful view, not be followed by judges of first instance and should not be relied upon by advocates in argument. The relevant principles are straightforward. Whether the claim is in negligence or for breach of statutory duty, if the evidence, once it has been appraised as the law requires, shows the entire fault to lie with the claimant there is no liability on the defendant. If not, then the court will consider to what extent, if any, the claimant's share in the responsibility for the damage makes it just and equitable to reduce his damages. ... If there is liability, contributory negligence can reduce its monetary quantification, but it cannot legally or logically nullify it." See also *Brumder v Motornet Service and Repairs Ltd* [2013] EWCA Civ 195; [2013] 1 W.L.R. 2783 at [4], where it was conceded that a finding of 100% contributory negligence was wrong in principle.

200 See also *Wynbergen v Hoyts Corp Pty Ltd* (1997) 149 A.L.J.R. 25 in which the High Court of Australia employed this rationale to support the conclusion that it was not open to the court to make a finding that the claimant was 100 per cent contributorily negligent. The argument for 100 per cent deduction could be that both the fault of the defendant and the claimant contributed to the *damage*, but *responsibility* for the purpose of apportioning *damages* was entirely the claimant's. Query, however, whether this is simply another way of saying that the defendant's fault did not contribute to the loss.

was the sole cause, breaking the chain of causation between the defendant's negligence and the damage.[201]

(b) Contribution to damage

3-59 The defence of contributory negligence is available whenever the claimant's own negligence contributes to the damage of which he complains. It is not limited to cases where the claimant's fault contributes to the occurrence inflicting that damage.[202] Contributory negligence is thus relevant, even where the defendant is solely responsible for the incident in which the claimant suffers injury, if the negligence of the claimant contributes to the extent or nature of his ensuing injuries.[203] In *Froom v Butcher*,[204] the claimant suffered facial injuries in a road accident caused entirely by the negligence of the defendant. He was not wearing a seat-belt and the impact of the collision threw him against the windscreen. His damages were reduced on the ground that his own contributory negligence in failing to wear a seat-belt was a partial cause of the injury. Had he suffered injury of a different nature, for example, burns when the collision caused an explosion, no reduction in damages would have been made. His own fault, failing to wear a seat-belt, would have been irrelevant to the injury in question.[205] Any contributory negligence on the part of the claimant, however imprudent his behaviour, must be shown to be a cause of the relevant damage.

3-60 **Causation and contributory negligence** Causation is crucial in a plea of contributory negligence. Lord Atkin summed up the position as follows[206]:

> "If the [claimant] were negligent but his negligence was not a cause operating to produce the damage there would be no defence. I find it impossible to divorce any theory of contributory negligence from the concept of causation."

So if the claimant's own carelessness is in effect either not a cause of his injury or of trivial import, there is no contributory negligence. The complexity of attempting to select the predominant cause or causes of damage has already been addressed in Ch.2.[207] In the context of contributory negligence, the judges have made frequent pleas for a common-sense approach: "The question of contributory negligence must be dealt with somewhat broadly and on commonsense grounds as a jury would probably deal with it."[208] When the common law rule that contributory negligence constituted a complete defence applied, the courts tended to seek to avoid a finding of contributory negligence where the claimant's blameworthi-

---

201 See paras 2-129 to 2-132.

202 *Craze v Meyer-Dumore Battlers' Equipment Co Ltd* [1936] 2 All E.R. 1150 at 1151.

203 *Capps v Miller* [1989] 1 W.L.R. 839 CA (the trial judge who made no reduction for a motorcyclist's failure to secure his helmet fell into the error of focusing on responsibility for the occurrence rather than the injury).

204 [1976] Q.B. 286; and see *O'Connell v Jackson* [1972] 1 Q.B. 270 (motorcyclist suffered head injuries while not wearing helmet).

205 As in *Lertora v Finzi* [1973] R.T.R. 161 (even if the claimant had worn a safety-belt his injuries would not have been reduced); *Stanton v Collinson* [2010] EWCA Civ 81; [2010] R.T.R. 26 (the court should avoid intensive inquiry into fine degrees of contributory negligence).

206 *Caswell v Powell Duffryn Associated Collieries Ltd* [1940] A.C. 152 at 165.

207 See paras 2-101 and 2-102.

208 *The Volute* [1922] 1 A.C. 129 at 144, per Lord Birkenhead; *Stapley v Gypsum Mines Ltd* [1953] A.C. 663 at 681.

ness was significantly less than that of the defendant. The "last opportunity" rule played the largest part in the judicial effort to mitigate the effect of the common law rule on contributory negligence.

"Last opportunity" as a test of causation *Davies v Mann*[209] best illustrates the "last opportunity" test. The claimant left his ass tethered on the highway causing an obstruction. The defendant driving his wagon much too fast drove into the animal and killed it. It was uncertain whether the defendant ever saw the ass. Had he used proper care he could have avoided injury to the beast. It was held that, notwithstanding his own carelessness, the claimant's action succeeded because the defendant could easily have avoided the consequences of the claimant's prior negligence. From *Davies v Mann* derived the "rule that when both parties are careless, the party which has the last opportunity of avoiding the results of the other's carelessness alone is liable".[210] The Law Reform (Contributory Negligence) Act 1945[211] renders the "last opportunity" test otiose,[212] since it enables the court to apportion responsibility equitably between the parties. The court does not have to strain to find some basis for concluding that the claimant was blameless in order to avoid the unfair conclusion that even a small degree of fault on the part of the claimant could defeat the claim against a possibly more culpable defendant.[213] The question of whether the defendant had the final opportunity to avoid inflicting injury, had he not been careless, is now relevant only in the following contexts: 3-61

(1) Where the facts establish, for example in cases like *Davies v Mann* of obstruction on the highway, that the subsequent negligence of the defendant eclipses the prior negligence of the claimant, and therefore the defendant's negligence is the sole cause of the damage.[214]
(2) Once contributory negligence is established, the question of who had the last opportunity to avoid inflicting the damage may be relevant in settling the comparative blameworthiness of each party.[215]

But where the claimant's negligence is found as a fact to be an operating cause of the relevant injury, that negligence should not be discounted altogether.[216]

Proving causation in contributory negligence In implementing the 1945 Act the courts have established the following principles when assessing the causative effect of the claimant's fault: 3-62

(1) In determining whether the claimant's fault contributed to his injury the

209 (1842) 10 M. & W. 546.

210 See *The Boy Andrew* [1948] A.C. 140 at 148-149. The last opportunity meant last *clear* opportunity: *The Volute* [1922] 1 A.C. 129 at 145.

211 The Maritime Conventions Act 1911 had earlier provided for apportionment in the case of collisions at sea.

212 It has been said that the rule of last opportunity is dead: *Jones v Livox Quarries Ltd* [1952] 2 Q.B. 608 at 615.

213 See *Stapley v Gypsum Mines Ltd* [1953] A.C. 663 at 677; *Davies v Swan Motor Co (Swansea) Ltd* [1949] 2 K.B. 291 at 318, per Evershed LJ.

214 *Davies v Swan Motor Co (Swansea) Ltd* [1949] 2 K.B. 291 at 323, per Denning LJ. The principles applicable should be the same as those applied to multiple tortfeasors: see *Wright v Lodge* [1993] 4 All E.R. 299 CA; para.2-102.

215 See *Cakebread v Hopping Bros (Whetstone) Ltd* [1947] K.B. 641.

216 See *Capps v Miller* [1989] 1 W.L.R. 839 CA.

same rules should apply as when deciding whether the defendant caused those injuries. The basic rules of factual causation should not differ.[217]

(2) It is irrelevant whether the operative fault of the claimant is prior, or subsequent, to the wrongdoing of the defendant.[218]

(3) Broad common sense should be used to judge cause and effect on the facts of each particular case.[219]

(4) Foreseeability of the precise manner of injury is not relevant.[220]

3-63 In *Jones v Livox Quarries Ltd*,[221] the claimant was riding down a slope on the back of the defendants' vehicle driven by a workmate. He had been forbidden to do so. Another vehicle of the defendants was negligently driven into the back of the vehicle on which the claimant was perched. He suffered crush injuries. He might have expected his folly to result in injury if he fell off the back of the vehicle, but would probably not have contemplated what did ensue. Nonetheless he was held to be contributorily negligent. His own carelessness exposed him, not just to the risk of falling off the vehicle, but also of the crush injury which did occur. Had he been shot by a careless sportsman while perched on the vehicle, his negligence would not have been contributory, simply part of the history of events.[222] *The Volute*[223] provides a further example of causation in contributory negligence. The vessel, *The Volute*, the convoy leader, changed course without signalling, endangering *The Radstock*, which negligently put on full steam ahead. It was held that the subsequent error on the part of *The Radstock* contributed to the ensuing collision and apportionment under the Maritime Conventions Act 1911 was ordered. The collision would not have occurred "but for" the combination of errors. It mattered not that there was no "strictly synchronous negligence".

3-64 **Lifestyle choices and the causal link** In *St George v Home Office*[224] the claimant, who was 29, had been abusing alcohol and drugs since the age of 16. He suffered serious brain damage following an epileptic seizure, having fallen from an upper bunk while in prison and suffered a head injury which exacerbated the effects of the seizure. The prison authorities were aware that he was an intravenous heroin user, that he drank alcohol heavily and that he had been having fits. MacKay J held that he was contributorily negligent, reducing the award of damages by 15 per cent, on the basis that he was at fault:

> "in relation to the choices he had made in his life prior to the events of this night. That fault has caused or contributed to the dreadful injuries in this way, not because they have put him in prison, but because he was knowingly risking injury to his health by doing what he was doing, even if he did not know how it would happen. This is so as much as if he

---

217 See *Jones v Livox Quarries Ltd* [1952] 2 Q.B. 608; *Davies v Swan Motor Co (Swansea) Ltd* [1949] 2 K.B. 291.

218 *The Volute* [1922] 1 A.C. 129 HL, decided under the Maritime Conventions Act 1911.

219 *The Volute* [1922] 1 A.C. 129 HL at 144; *Stapley v Gypsum Mines Ltd* [1953] A.C. 663; *Marvin Sigurdson v British Columbia Electric Railway Co Ltd* [1953] A.C. 291 at 299 PC.

220 *Jones v Livox Quarries Ltd* [1952] 2 Q.B. 608.

221 *Jones v Livox Quarries Ltd* [1952] 2 Q.B. 608.

222 *Jones v Livox Quarries Ltd* [1952] 2 Q.B. 608 at 616; see also the example given by Singleton LJ at 612: a man seated on an unsafe wall would not be contributorily negligent if injured when a car drove into the wall.

223 [1922] 1 A.C. 129 HL. For an example of subsequent carelessness by a workman constituting negligence see *Ross v Associated Portland Cement Manufacturers Ltd* [1964] 1 W.L.R. 768.

224 [2008] EWCA Civ 1068; [2009] 1 W.L.R. 1670.

> had wandered abroad in a drug-induced state of intoxication and walked into the path of a negligently driven car."[225]

This takes a sweeping approach to the nature of contributory fault. Many individuals "knowingly risk injury to their health" from lifestyle choices, such as drinking alcohol, overeating, or even engaging in risky activities such as mountaineering or sky-diving. On this view, any subsequent negligence, e.g. by a doctor failing to make a correct diagnosis or treating the condition inappropriately, would be subject to a contributory negligence defence as a result of the individual having engaged in an activity that involved "knowingly risking injury to his health". The Court of Appeal reversed the ruling on contributory negligence. Dyson LJ accepted that the judge was entitled to hold that the claimant was at fault in becoming addicted to drugs and alcohol, and to infer that the claimant must have known that the abuse of drugs and alcohol on the scale necessary to lead to addiction was dangerous to his health. Moreover, it was also correct that but for the addiction, the claimant would not have suffered a withdrawal seizure and would not have fallen from the top bunk and suffered the head injury: "In that sense his injury was the result partly of his addiction. But in my view the addiction was not a potent cause of the injury."[226] The injury triggered by the fall "was too remote in time, place and circumstance and was not sufficiently connected with the negligence of the prison staff or, to use Lord Birkenhead's words,[227] was not sufficiently 'mixed up with the state of things brought about' by the prison staff on 3 November to be properly regarded as a cause of the injury".[228] The claimant's addiction was simply part of the history which had produced his medical and psychological conditions when he was admitted to prison.[229] Dyson LJ rejected the analogy with a person in a drug-induced state of intoxication walking into the path of a negligently driven car. The closer analogy was: "with the case of a claimant who seeks medical treatment for a condition from which he is suffering as a result of his own fault and sustains injury as a result of negligent treatment. Examples of such a condition are lung cancer caused by smoking or cirrhosis of the liver caused by excessive consumption of alcohol."[230] In such a case the claimant's fault in smoking or consuming excessive alcohol was "not a potent cause of the injury suffered as a result of the negligent medical treatment. The fault is not sufficiently closely connected with the defendant's negligence." Rather, it was simply part of the claimant's history.[231]

---

225 [2007] EWHC 2774 (QB) at [58].
226 [2008] EWCA Civ 1068; [2009] 1 W.L.R. 1670 at [51].
227 In *The Volute* [1922] 1 A.C. 129 at 144.
228 [2008] EWCA Civ 1068; [2009] 1 W.L.R. 1670 at [56].
229 [2008] EWCA Civ 1068; [2009] 1 W.L.R. 1670 at [56]; citing Denning LJ in *Jones v Livox Quarries Ltd* [1952] 2 Q.B. 608 at 616.
230 [2008] EWCA Civ 1068; [2009] 1 W.L.R. 1670 at [58].
231 [2008] EWCA Civ 1068; [2009] 1 W.L.R. 1670 at [58]. See also *Calvert v William Hill Credit Ltd* [2008] EWCA Civ 1427; [2009] Ch. 330 at [70]—the fact that the claimant was a pathological gambler due to lifestyle choices made before the defendant bookmakers undertook a duty to prevent him from gambling with them on the telephone for a period of six months was not a basis for a finding of contributory negligence. The defendant's duty arose because the claimant, acknowledging that he was a problem gambler, had sought the defendants' assistance. A reduction of damages for contributory negligence would negate the duty of care. On the other hand, a finding of contributory negligence would have been appropriate if the claimant had continued to gamble despite periods of clarity when he could have taken steps to deal with his habit, though not from the point at which he became a severe pathological gambler who had completely lost control of his gambling. The claim

(c) Scope of contributory negligence

3-65 Contributory negligence is most often invoked as a defence in actions in the tort of negligence. Prior to the 1945 Act, the defence was available in actions for nuisance on the highway,[232] and breach of statutory duty.[233] Authority for its more general application to other torts was slight. The fact that contributory negligence operated as a complete defence at common law provoked doubts about its applicability to torts of intentional wrongdoing.[234] The introduction of apportionment of damages triggered both a greater willingness by defendants to plead contributory negligence in torts other than negligence and a greater readiness by the judiciary to allow such pleas. The Act authorises apportionment where the claimant suffers damage "as the result partly of his own fault and partly of the fault" of another. Fault is defined as "negligence, breach of statutory duty or other act or omission which gives rise to liability in tort or would, apart from this Act, give rise to the defence of contributory negligence". It has been suggested that this definition should be read as applying the first limb of the definition to the defendant and the whole to the conduct of the claimant.[235] Thus, in theory a defence of contributory negligence would be available to any action in tort (save where expressly excluded by statute) and in any other case where at common law such a defence defeated the claimant's claim.

3-66 **Breach of statutory duty** The defence of contributory negligence is available in an action for breach of statutory duty.[236] Such a defence was recognised at common law and apportionment is now available under the 1945 Act. Where the relevant legislation is designed expressly to protect the safety of employees care must be taken not to classify every "risky act due to familiarity with the work or some inattention resulting from noise or strain" as contributory negligence.[237] Breach of statutory duty on the part of the employee himself, as much as any carelessness, may amount to contributory negligence on his part.[238]

3-67 **Nuisance** There is ample and unequivocal authority that contributory negligence operates as a defence to a nuisance on the highway.[239] It has tended to be assumed that the defence is available generally in both public and private nuisance but there is no clear authority to this effect.

3-68 **Intentional injury to the person** Prior to the decision of the Court of Appeal in

failed on other grounds; see para.2-111.

[232] *Butterfield v Forrester* (1809) 11 East 60.

[233] *Caswell v Powell Duffryn Associated Collieries Ltd* [1940] A.C. 152.

[234] *Quinn v Leathem* [1901] A.C. 495 at 537.

[235] *Forsikringsaktieselskapet Vesta v Butcher* [1989] A.C. 852 at 862, per O'Connor LJ. See also the discussion of the meaning of the word "fault" in s.1(1) of the 1945 Act in *Standard Chartered Bank v Pakistan National Shipping Corp (No.4)* [2001] Q.B. 167, particularly in the judgment of Ward LJ.

[236] *Caswell v Powell Duffryn Associated Collieries Ltd* [1940] A.C. 152; and see para.8-64.

[237] *Staveley Iron and Chemical Co Ltd v Jones* [1956] A.C. 627 at 648; *Toole v Bolton MBC* [2002] EWCA Civ 588 at [14].

[238] *Boyle v Kodak Ltd* [1969] 1 W.L.R. 661. If it is found that the employee's own breach of duty constitutes the sole cause of his injury his claim must still fail altogether: *Ginty v Belmont Building Supplies Ltd* [1959] 1 All E.R. 414.

[239] *Butterfield v Forrester* (1809) 11 East 60; *Trevett v Lee* [1955] 1 W.L.R. 113 at 122.

Co-operative Group (CWS) Ltd v Pritchard[240] it had been thought that the balance of authority supported the view that contributory negligence was available as a defence to a claim of trespass to the person.[241] However, in *Pritchard* it was held that contributory negligence could not be relied upon in an action for trespass to the person (specifically battery or assault). This was on the basis that the analysis of the meaning of the word "fault" in Law Reform (Contributory Negligence) Act 1945 undertaken by the House of Lords in *Standard Chartered Bank v Pakistan National Shipping Corp (No.2)*[242] and *Reeves v Commissioner of Police for the Metropolis*[243] meant that, as applied to a claimant, fault could only be taken into account if his conduct gave rise to a defence of "contributory negligence" at common law before the passing of the Act.[244] Since there was no case before the Act which held that contributory negligence constituted a defence to assault and battery the Act could not be relied on to reduce a claimant's damages for assault and battery. Aikens LJ concluded that:

> "Insofar as there are cases since the 1945 Act that suggest that the Act can be used to reduce damages awarded for the torts of assault or battery in a case where it is found that the claimant was 'contributorily negligent' they are unsatisfactory and cannot stand with statements of principle made in two subsequent House of Lords decisions. ... [T]he 1945 Act cannot, in principle, be used to reduce damages in cases where claims are based on assault and battery, despite the remarks in such cases as *Lane v Holloway* and *Murphy v Culhane*, which I would say are not binding on this court. Moreover, it seems to me that such a conclusion is in keeping with the purpose of the 1945 Act, as set out in section 1(1), which was to relieve claimants whose actions would previously have failed, not to reduce the damages which would have previously have been awarded to claimants."[245]

Smith LJ agreed with the analysis, whilst expressing the view that it was regrettable that the court could not apportion damages where the claimant has, by his misconduct, contributed to the occurrence of the incident. However, a change in the law would require the intervention of Parliament.

Intentional self-harm by claimant It is also now clear that "fault" within the 1945 Act extends to intentional acts on the *part of the claimant* in those rare cases where the defendant has a duty to prevent deliberate self-harm by the claimant. Thus, in *Reeves v Commissioner of Police for the Metropolis*[246] the House of Lords held that the suicide of the deceased could give rise to a defence of contributory negligence in a claim by his dependants under the Fatal Accidents Act 1976. The deceased killed himself while in police custody after having been identified as a "suicide risk". Their Lordships held that suicide did not constitute a novus actus interveniens where self-harm was the very kind of harm which the defendants owed a duty to prevent. But where the deceased was of sound mind at the time he killed 3-69

[240] [2011] EWCA Civ 329; [2012] Q.B. 320; applied in *McAleer v Chief Constable of the PSNI* [2014] NIQB 53. For discussion see J. Goudkamp, "Contributory negligence and trespass to the person" (2011) 127 L.Q.R. 519. See also *Hicks v Young* [2015] EWHC 1144 (QB) (contributory negligence not a defence to tort of false imprisonment); *R. (on the application of Diop) v Secretary of State for the Home Department* [2018] EWHC 3420 (Admin); [2019] A.C.D. 30 (to same effect).

[241] See the 20th edition of this Work, para.3-54, and the cases cited there.

[242] [2002] UKHL 43; [2003] 1 A.C. 959.

[243] [2000] 1 A.C. 360.

[244] See the discussion of this point at para.3-74.

[245] [2011] EWCA Civ 329; [2012] Q.B. 320 at [62].

[246] [2000] 1 A.C. 360.

himself he bore at least partial responsibility for his death, which was the result of the combination of the failure of the police to protect him from himself and his own deliberate decision to end his life.[247] If this were not the case, then the strange result would be that damages could be reduced where the claimant was careless but not where he deliberately caused harm to himself. In *Reeves*, damages were reduced by 50 per cent. It may be that where the deceased is of unsound mind his suicide would not give rise to a reduction in damages for contributory negligence, by analogy with the position of young children who are not of full understanding.[248]

3-70 *Reeves* concerned self-harm where the defendant was, unusually, under a duty of care to prevent the self-harm. In some cases the defendant may be responsible for a claimant's self-harm, even though he was not under a duty to prevent it, simply because it is regarded as a consequence of other injuries for which the defendant is responsible. In *Corr v IBC Vehicles Ltd*[249] the deceased committed suicide having developed clinical depression after an accident at work. The House of Lords were divided as to whether contributory negligence should apply. Lord Bingham and Lord Walker considered that it was inappropriate to attach any blame to Mr. Corr given that his judgment was impaired by the severe depression brought about by the defendants' negligence.[250] Lord Scott accepted that the deceased's suicidal tendencies had been caused by the employers' negligence, but "he was not an automaton. He remained an autonomous individual who retained the power of choice. The evidence that clinical depression leads often to suicidal tendencies and that between 1 in 10 and 1 in 6 persons succumb to those tendencies is evidence also that between 9 in 10 and 5 in 6 persons do not."[251] His Lordship would have reduced the damages by 20 per cent. Lord Mance and Lord Neuberger considered that contributory negligence could apply in principle to such a case, but that no deduction should be made because the issue had not been dealt with in detail at any stage of the proceedings. Lord Mance commented:

> "a conclusion that a person suffering from depressive illness has no responsibility at all for his or her own suicide, and is in effect acting as an automaton, may be open to question in law, at least when the person's capacity to make a reasoned and informed judg-

---

247 As Lord Hoffmann observed, [2000] 1 A.C. 360 at 370, this situation is only likely to arise in the rare case where the defendant owes a duty to take reasonable care to prevent the claimant from deliberately injuring himself. Normally, the deliberate infliction of damage upon himself would have the effect of breaking the causal link between the defendant's breach of duty and the resulting damage. Such a duty is not owed where there is no foreseeable risk of suicide by the prisoner: *Orange v Chief Constable of West Yorkshire Police* [2001] EWCA Civ 611; [2002] Q.B. 347. There is no duty on prison authorities to treat every prisoner as a potential suicide risk: *Smiley v Home Office* [2004] EWHC 240 (QB).

248 [2000] 1 A.C. 360 at 372, per Lord Hoffmann. Or it may be that "a mentally ill patient could only be held to the degree of care permitted by his diminished capacity", at 385, per Lord Hope. The question of the suicide's precise mental state could give rise to some nice questions of fact, sometimes on rather scant evidence. See, e.g. Lord Hoffmann's "unease" at the finding that the prisoner in *Reeves* was of sound mind, at 372. See also *Calvert v William Hill Credit Ltd* [2008] EWCA Civ 1427; [2009] Ch. 330 at [71] where, in an action for negligence by a pathological gambler against a firm of bookmakers, the Court of Appeal appeared to suggest that contributory negligence would not apply to a severe pathological gambler who had lost control of his gambling, as opposed to one who was merely suffering an impairment of control.

249 [2008] UKHL 13; [2008] 1 A.C. 884.

250 Contrast the position when it is a defendant whose mental state is impaired: see *Dunnage v Randall* [2015] EWCA Civ 673; [2016] Q.B. 639, para.7-169 (defendant with florid paranoid schizophrenia, suffering from delusions, required to come up to the standard of the objectively reasonable man).

251 [2008] UKHL 13; [2008] 1 A.C. 884 at [31].

ment is described as 'impaired' rather than eliminated ... It may be right, not only to consider more closely with the benefit of expert evidence what is involved in 'impairment' but also, as Lord Hope suggested in *Reeves* at p.385A, to identify differing degrees of impairment and responsibility. It may also be relevant if other factors were also operating on the claimant, independently of the accident and the consequent depression—for example, impending exposure of lack of probity, financial ruin or matrimonial breakdown."[252]

Strict liability torts Section 6(4) of the Consumer Protection Act 1987 provides for a defence of contributory negligence in a "strict" product liability claim under that Act. Section 10 of the Animals Act 1971 expressly permits a defence of contributory negligence to a claim under that Act.[253] There is some authority to suggest contributory negligence is available to a claim under the rule in *Rylands v Fletcher*.[254] It is unclear though whether this firmly establishes the availability of contributory negligence in that tort or is better explained on the basis that on the evidence it was the claimant, rather than the defendant, who was responsible for the relevant escape. On the other hand, since the rule in *Rylands v Fletcher* has been explained to be a species of liability in nuisance,[255] if contributory negligence is a defence to nuisance there is no obvious reason why it should not apply to actions under *Rylands v Fletcher*. 3-71

Contributory negligence excluded The Torts (Interference with Goods) Act 1977 s.11(1)[256] expressly excludes the defence of contributory negligence, providing bluntly: "Contributory negligence is no defence in proceedings founded on conversion, or on intentional trespass to goods." 3-72

Contributory negligence and the tort of deceit Authority prior to the 1945 Act firmly established that a defence of contributory negligence was not available in an action for deceit,[257] and, despite the liberal and enabling language of s.4, it has been confirmed that contributory negligence cannot be pleaded in deceit, since where the defendant intended that the claimant should rely on his statement to the claimant's detriment, it is not open to him to argue that the loss could have been avoided if the claimant had taken more care to avoid being duped by the defendant.[258] 3-73

Contributory deceit not a defence to an action in deceit The question of *contributory deceit* by the claimant is not specifically covered by the Act, but the same principle applies where the defendant is liable in the tort of deceit. In *Standard Chartered Bank v Pakistan National Shipping Corp (No.4)* the claimants had been 3-74

252 [2008] UKHL 13; [2008] 1 A.C. 884 at [51]. See also, per Lord Neuberger at [64]–[69] for discussion of the relationship between the deceased's mental state and contributory negligence.

253 See para.20-16.

254 *PMG v Liverpool Corp* [1923] A.C. 587; *Dunn v Birmingham Canal Navigation Co* (1872) L.R. 7 Q.B. 244.

255 *Cambridge Water Co Ltd v Eastern Counties Leather Plc* [1994] 2 A.C. 264.

256 See para.16-130.

257 *Central Ry Co of Venezuela v Kisch* (1867) L.R. 2 H.L. 99 at 120.

258 *Alliance and Leicester Building Society v Edgestop Ltd* [1993] 1 W.L.R. 1462; *Nationwide Building Society v Thimbleby & Co* [1999] P.N.L.R. 733. Similarly, in *Corporacion Nacional del Cobre de Chile v Sogemin Metals Ltd* [1997] 1 W.L.R. 1396 it was held that a party who had conspired to bribe the claimant's employees could not plead the claimant's own lack of diligence as a means of reducing the damages payable. However, the claimant remains under a duty to take reasonable steps to mitigate his loss: *Smith New Court Securities Ltd v Citibank NA* [1997] A.C. 254 HL.

induced to make a payment by the defendants' fraudulent misrepresentation, though they would not have made the payment if they had not mistakenly thought that they could obtain reimbursement from the third party (which they attempted to do by misrepresenting the true position to that third party). They sued the defendants in deceit. It was held that the Law Reform (Contributory Negligence) Act 1945 could not be relied upon by a defendant found liable in deceit where the claimant's own conduct amounted to an attempted deceit of a third party. In the Court of Appeal[259] Ward LJ accepted that deceit by a claimant can constitute contributory "fault" on the part of the claimant.[260] However, the question remained whether apart from the Act, the claimant's negligence and/or attempted deception would have given rise to the defence of contributory negligence at common law. The common law applied a causation test, namely whether the claimant's negligence could be said to have contributed to his loss (if so, the contributory negligence was a complete defence, the fact that the defendant's negligence also contributed to the loss being irrelevant). However, the common law applied special rules of causation to the tort of deceit. So long as the defendant's fraudulent misrepresentation was *a* cause of the loss suffered by the claimant, the claimant recovered in full even though there were other factors causing the claimant's loss. Thus, the defendant's deceit is treated as the sole cause of the loss, and the defendant thus failed to establish that the claimant was a person who "suffers damage as the result partly of his own fault".[261] The House of Lords affirmed the decision of the Court of Appeal.[262] Lord Hoffmann observed that, the definition of "fault" in the 1945 Act is divided into two limbs, one of which is applicable to defendants and the other to claimants. In the case of a defendant, fault means "negligence, breach of statutory duty or other act or omission" which gives rise to a liability in tort. In the case of a claimant, it means "negligence, breach of statutory duty or other act or omission" which gives rise (at common law) to a defence of contributory negligence. It followed that conduct by a claimant could not be "fault" within the meaning of the Act unless it gave rise to a defence of contributory negligence at common law. This was in accordance with the purpose of the Act, which was to relieve claimants whose actions would previously have failed, not to reduce the damages which previously would have been awarded against defendants.[263] So where the claimant relied on the defendants' fraudulent representation, in that he would not have parted with his money if he had known the representation was false, it is irrelevant that he held some other negligent or irrational belief about another matter and, but for that belief, would not have parted with his money either. As a matter of policy the law simply ignores the claimants' other reasons for making the payment because it "would not seem just that a fraudulent defendant's liability should be reduced on the grounds that, for whatever

[259] [2001] Q.B. 167.

[260] Relying on *Reeves v Commissioner of Police for the Metropolis* [2000] 1 A.C. 360 HL, that "fault" can include intentional acts by the claimant, as well as negligence.

[261] [2001] Q.B. 167 at [115] and [121], per Ward LJ. This interpretation of the Act was reinforced by Ward LJ's perspective on the policy issues that the defendant's fraudulent conduct raised: "Commercial fraud must be condemned. It can only be properly condemned by an award of the whole of the damage which the defendants intended to cause. Highwaymen in commerce forfeit the right to just and equitable treatment." [2001] Q.B. 167 at [126].

[262] *Standard Chartered Bank v Pakistan National Shipping Corp (Nos 2 & 4)* [2002] UKHL 43; [2003] 1 A.C. 959.

[263] [2002] UKHL 43; [2003] 1 A.C. 959 at [12].

reason, the victim should not have made the payment which the defendant successfully induced him to make".[264]

Contributory negligence and fiduciary duties The Act does not apply to actions based on breach of fiduciary duty, and general equitable principles should not be used to achieve the same outcome since a claim based on breach of fiduciary duty can only succeed where the defendant has acted intentionally and it is inappropriate to reduce damages for a deliberate wrong simply because the claimant has been careless.[265] 3-75

Contributory negligence and contract At common law the defence of contributory negligence was not available in contract,[266] and nothing in the 1945 Act expressly extends contributory negligence to actions for breach of contract. Difficulty arises, however, when there is concurrent liability in contract and tort. If the claimant elects to sue in contract, is the defendant debarred from pleading contributory negligence? In *Forsikringsaktieselskapet Vesta v Butcher*,[267] Hobhouse J identified three categories of case involving a breach of contract: 3-76

(1) where liability does not depend on negligence but arises from breach of a strict contractual duty;
(2) where liability arises from breach of a contractual obligation which is expressed in terms of exercising reasonable care, but does not correspond to a common law duty of care which would exist independently of the contract; and
(3) where the defendant's negligent breach of contract would have given rise to liability in the tort of negligence independently of the existence of the contract.

In a category (3) case, damages could be reduced for the claimant's contributory negligence.[268] The only relevance of the contract in this situation was whether it had varied or redefined the tortious relationship by excluding apportionment. The Court of Appeal[269] upheld this analysis, agreeing that in a category (3) case the Act applies. It would not be right, said O'Connor LJ, that in a case of concurrent liability in contract and tort (e.g. employers' liability cases) the claimant should be able to avoid the apportionment of damages by pleading his case in contract rather than tort. Thus, a private patient suing her doctor or a client claiming damages for his solicitor's negligence cannot improve their position by framing the claim in

264 [2002] UKHL 43; [2003] 1 A.C. 959 at [16], per Lord Hoffmann.

265 *Nationwide Building Society v Balmer Radmore (A Firm)* [1999] P.N.L.R. 606 Ch D.

266 *Basildon DC v JE Lesser (Properties) Ltd* [1985] Q.B. 839; *AB Marintrans v Comet Shipping Co Ltd* [1985] 1 W.L.R. 1270.

267 [1986] 2 All E.R. 488 at 508.

268 Following the decision of the Court of Appeal in *Sayers v Harlow Urban DC* [1958] 1 W.L.R. 623.

269 [1989] A.C. 852. See also *Barclays Bank Plc v Fairclough Building Ltd (No.2)* [1995] I.R.L.R. 605 (industrial cleaners who had taken on the potentially hazardous job of cleaning an asbestos roof were held to owe a concurrent duty of care in the tort of negligence, and therefore it was a category (3) case where the Act could be applied). cf. *Astley v Austrust Ltd* [1999] HCA 6; (1999) 161 A.L.R. 155, where the High Court of Australia held that contributory negligence applies only to actions in tort, not contract. In cases of concurrent liability in contract and tort a claimant was entitled to sue in either contract or tort or both, and therefore could avoid the effect of the apportionment legislation by suing in contract only.

contract.[270] However, contributory negligence continues to be unavailable where the relevant breach is of a strict contractual duty (category (1)),[271] although apportionment can sometimes be achieved in some contractual actions by resorting to principles of causation.[272] Even where the claim relates to breach of a duty to exercise reasonable care, if that duty arises solely from the contract with no parallel duty of care in tort (category (2)), contributory negligence remains unavailable.[273]

3-77 In *Gran Gelato Ltd v Richcliff (Group) Ltd*,[274] Sir Donald Nicholls V-C held that where liability under s.2(1) of the Misrepresentation Act 1967 was concurrent with liability in the tort of negligence the defence of contributory negligence applied.[275] The Law Commission has proposed legislation to permit the more general availability of a defence of contributory negligence in claims for breach of contract.[276]

3-78 **Duty unnecessary in contributory negligence** Contributory negligence does not mean that the claimant commits a breach of duty towards the defendant,[277] although it includes such a case; it means that the claimant failed to use reasonable care for his own safety and so contributed to his own damage:

> "When contributory negligence is set up as a defence, its existence does not depend on any duty owed by the injured party to the party sued, and all that is necessary to establish such a defence is to prove … that the injured party did not in his own interest take reasonable care of himself and contributed, by his want of care, to his own injury. For when contributory negligence is set up as a shield against the obligation to satisfy the whole of the [claimant's] claim, the principle involved is that, where a man is part author of his own injury, he cannot call on the other party to compensate him in full."[278]

If in fact the claimant has caused damage to the defendant by a breach of duty, the

---

[270] *UCB Bank Plc v Hepherd Winstanley & Pugh (A Firm)* [1999] Lloyd's Rep. P.N. 963 CA (breach of the implied term that they would carry out a retainer with the skill and care of a reasonably competent solicitor is the same as liability in the tort of negligence independently of any contract; accordingly, it is a category (3) case to which the Act can apply); *Bristol & West Building Society v Fancy and Jackson (A Firm)* [1997] 4 All E.R. 582; *Omega Trust Co Ltd v Wright Son & Pepper (No.2)* [1998] P.N.L.R. 337. Similarly, valuers providing valuations of property for the purpose of a mortgage security can plead contributory negligence in a claim by the lender in respect of negligent overvaluation: *UCB Bank Plc v David J Pinder Plc* [1998] P.N.L.R. 398.

[271] See *Barclays Bank Plc v Fairclough Building Ltd* [1995] Q.B. 214 CA.

[272] See *Tennant Radiant Heat Ltd v Warrington Development Corp* [1988] 11 E.G. 71; cf. *Raflatac Ltd v Eade* [1999] 1 Lloyd's Rep. 506 at 510. Normally, use of causation principles in contract will result in the claim failing entirely: see *Lambert v Lewis* [1982] A.C. 225, where a retailer sold a defective towing hitch and the buyer continued to use it after it was obviously broken, causing an accident; the dealer was not liable to indemnify the buyer because the accident was caused not by the breach of contract but the buyer's own carelessness.

[273] *Raflatac Ltd v Eade* [1999] 1 Lloyd's Rep. 506.

[274] [1992] Ch. 560.

[275] This view was accepted (obiter) as correct by the Court of Appeal in *Taberna Europe CDO II Plc v Selskabet (formerly Roskilde Bank A/S) (In Bankruptcy)* [2016] EWCA Civ 1262; [2017] Q.B. 633 at [52], applying observations of Lord Hoffmann in *Standard Chartered Bank v Pakistan National Shipping Corp (Nos 2 & 4)* [2002] UKHL 43; [2003] 1 A.C. 959 at [16]–[17].

[276] *Contributory Negligence as a Defence in Contract*, Law Com. Report No.219 (1993).

[277] *Ellerman Lines Ltd v H & G Grayson Ltd* [1919] 2 K.B. 514 at 535; and [1920] A.C. 466 at 477; *Lewis v Denye* [1939] 1 K.B. 540 at 554; *Davies v Swan Motor Co (Swansea) Ltd* [1949] 2 K.B. 291 at 309; *Jones v Livox Quarries Ltd* [1952] 2 Q.B. 608 at 615; *Staveley Iron and Chemical Co Ltd v Jones* [1956] A.C. 627 at 648.

[278] *Nance v British Columbia Electric Ry* [1951] A.C. 601 at 611, per Viscount Simon.

defendant will counterclaim in respect of this. A counterclaim being a cross-action, the claimant is the defendant in the counterclaim.

(d) The standard of care

The standard of care in contributory negligence is what is reasonable in the circumstances, which in most cases corresponds to the standard of care in the tort of negligence.[279] Although contributory negligence does not depend on a breach of duty to the defendant, it does depend on foreseeability. Just as carelessness in ordinary actions in negligence requires foreseeability of harm to others, so contributory negligence requires foreseeability of harm to oneself. A person is guilty of contributory negligence whenever he ought reasonably to have foreseen that, if he did not act prudently, he might suffer injury, and he must take into account the possibility of others being careless.[280] The standard of reasonable care is normally objective[281]; and the care which the claimant should take is to avoid accidents of the general class as opposed to the particular accident.[282] The fact that the claimant acts under a public duty does not absolve him from the need to take care.[283] To be at fault the claimant must have had some reasonable freedom to choose to avoid incurring the risk that was partly responsible for his injury, but an addiction to tobacco will not necessarily prevent a finding of contributory negligence.[284] **3-79**

Breach of statutory duty Where the defendant is in breach of a statutory duty, the standard by which the claimant's contributory negligence is judged is sometimes less exacting than that used for ordinary negligence. This is commonly the case in actions by employees against their employers.[285] Lord Tucker put it this way: **3-80**

> "This is not so illogical as may appear at first sight when it is remembered that contributory negligence is not founded on breach of duty, although it generally involves a breach of duty, and that in Factory Act cases the purpose of imposing the absolute obligation is to protect the workmen against those very acts of inattention which are sometimes relied upon as constituting contributory negligence so that too strict a standard would defeat the object of the statute."[286]

The Court of Appeal has also cautioned against undermining the object of statu-

---

279 *AC Billings & Sons Ltd v Riden* [1958] A.C. 240. See para.7-171.

280 per Denning LJ in *Jones v Livox Quarries Ltd* [1952] 2 Q.B. 608 at 615.

281 For claimant's low intelligence, see *Baxter v Woolcombers* (1963) 17 S.J. 533.

282 *Samways v Westgate Engineers* (1962) 106 S.J. 937.

283 *Hambley v Shepley* (1967) 63 D.L.R. (2d) 94.

284 *Badger v Ministry of Defence* [2005] EWHC 2941 (QB); [2006] 3 All E.R. 173 at [46], per Stanley Burnton J. The claimant had continued to smoke cigarettes, knowing that this created a risk of damaging his health. His damages were reduced by 20 per cent for contributory negligence in a claim in respect of lung cancer caused by the defendants' negligent exposure of the claimant to asbestos: "A reasonably prudent man, warned that there is a substantial risk that smoking will seriously damage his health, would stop smoking" (at [48]). See also *Horsley v Cascade Insulation Services Ltd* [2009] EWHC 2945 (QB).

285 See para.12-91 onwards.

286 *Staveley Iron and Chemical Co Ltd v Jones* [1956] A.C. 627 at 648; approving *Flower v Ebbw Vale Steel, Iron and Coal Co Ltd* [1934] 2 K.B. 132 at 140; and *Caswell v Powell Duffryn Associated Collieries Ltd* [1940] A.C. 152 at 166. See also *Lewis v Denye* [1940] A.C. 921 at 931; *Wraith v Flexile Metal Co Ltd* [1943] 1 K.B. 240; *Gallagher v Dorman Long Co Ltd* [1947] 2 All E.R. 38; *Carr v Mercantile Produce Co Ltd* [1949] 2 K.B. 601 at 608; *Smith v Chesterfield and District Co-operative Soc Ltd* [1953] 1 W.L.R. 370; *Harrison v Metropolitan-Vickers Electrical Co Ltd* [1954] 1 W.L.R. 324 at 328; *John Summers & Sons Ltd v Frost* [1955] A.C. 740 at 754, 773 and 777-778; *Field v EE Jeavons & Co Ltd* [1965] 1 W.L.R. 996; *Smith (formerly Westwood) v NCB* [1967] 1

tory provisions by too readily making findings of contributory negligence.[287] The claimant's conduct must be judged in the context of the circumstances of his work and in the light of the defendant's statutory responsibility for his welfare. In some circumstances the risk may be so great that the employer has a duty to issue an absolute prohibition against using a dangerous method of working.[288] A difference may also exist in nuisance.[289] These instances lend support to the statement that "the reasonable defendant is not allowed to have lapses, but the reasonable [claimant] is".[290] This means that claimants are sometimes judged by less exacting standards than defendants, which in turn suggests that apportionment of responsibility will vary according to the nature of the claimant's wrongdoing. In *Quintas v National Smelting Co Ltd*,[291] the trial court held the defendants liable for breach of statutory duty, but not for common law negligence, and held that the claimant was 75 per cent responsible. The Court of Appeal held them liable for common law negligence, but not for breach of statutory duty and considered that, on this basis, the claimant was only 50 per cent responsible. Sellers LJ said:

> "The nature and extent of the defendants' duty is, in my view, highly important in assessing the effect of the breach or failure of duty on the happening of the accident giving rise to the [claimant's] claim and on the conduct of the [claimant]. There is an interaction of factors, acts and omissions to be considered."[292]

3-81 **Anticipating danger** A reasonable claimant must not expect that others will always observe due care in their conduct. "A prudent man will guard against the possible negligence of others, when experience shows such negligence to be

W.L.R. 871; *Ryan v Manbre Sugars* (1970) 114 S.J. 454. For the type of accident against which it is necessary to protect a workman who is concentrating on his task, see *McArdle v Andmac Roofing Co* [1967] 1 W.L.R. 356. Failure by an employee to keep a look out will not amount to contributory negligence if he is entitled to assume that his fellow-workmen will not move the machinery which caused the accident: *Wright v R Thomas and Baldwins* (1966) 1 K.I.R. 327; *Kansara v Osram (GEC) Ltd* [1967] 3 All E.R. 230. Contributory negligence is not a defence where, even if the employee had taken the precautions suggested by the defendant employer, the defendant would still have been in breach of statutory duty: *Toole v Bolton MBC* [2002] EWCA Civ 588—employee failed to wear gloves provided by the employer, but the gloves would probably not have prevented the injury even if used.

287 "Where there has been such a breach of statutory duty by the employer ... it is important to ensure that the statutory requirement placed on the employer is not emasculated by too great a willingness on the part of the courts to find that the employee has been guilty of contributory negligence. It is very easy for a judge with the advantage of hindsight to identify some act on the part of the employee which would have avoided the accident occurring. That in itself does not demonstrate negligence on the part of the employee ... . To impose too strict a standard of care on the workman would defeat the object of the statutory requirement": per Keene LJ in *Cooper v Carillion Plc* [2003] EWCA Civ 1811 at [13]; *Mullard v Ben Line Steamers Ltd* [1970] 1 W.L.R. 1414; cf. *Jayes v IMI (Kynoch) Ltd* [1985] I.C.R. 155, where the Court of Appeal made a finding of 100 per cent contributory negligence in a case of breach of statutory duty, even though the intention of the statute was to protect a workman from his own folly. See, however, the discussion of *Jayes v IMI (Kynoch) Ltd* at para.3-58 fn.199.

288 *King v Smith* [1995] I.C.R. 339 (window cleaner standing on the exterior sill of a second floor window, with no means of attaching a safety harness; window cleaner 30 per cent responsible, employer 70 per cent on the basis of a failure to provide an adequate warning).

289 *Trevett v Lee* [1955] 1 W.L.R. 113 at 122, per Lord Evershed MR, sed quaere.

290 Williams, *Joint Torts and Contributory Negligence* (1951), p.353; but see also p.358.

291 [1961] 1 W.L.R. 401. See also *Mullard v Ben Line Steamers Ltd* [1970] 1 W.L.R. 1414; *Bux v Slough Metals Ltd* [1973] 1 W.L.R. 1358.

292 [1961] 1 W.L.R. 401 at 408.

common."[293] Normally, a claimant should, for his own protection, keep his eyes open and take proper precautions to guard against the occurrence of an accident. However, where he has been thrown off his guard by the conduct of the defendant, and reasonably induced to believe that he may proceed with safety, a lesser degree of care and circumspection may be required of him.[294] This simply reflects the requirement to exercise reasonable care *in all the circumstances*.

Contributory negligence of children Conduct on the part of a child which contributes to an accident will not necessarily be judged in the same light as similar conduct by an adult. What is negligence in an adult is not necessarily negligence in a child. The exercise of "ordinary care must mean that degree of care which may reasonably be expected of a person in the [claimant's] situation",[295] which in the case of a very young child could be nil.[296] So in *Gardner v Grace*,[297] where a child, aged three-and-a-half years, ran out into a road and was knocked over by the defendant's cart, it was held that the defence of contributory negligence did not apply. In *Yachuk v Oliver Blais Co Ltd*,[298] a boy of nine went with his brother, aged seven, to a petrol station and obtained petrol by falsely representing that it was wanted for his mother's car which was "stuck down the street". He then made a torch with it to use in a game and, on lighting the torch, the petrol caught fire and the boy was burned. The Privy Council held that there was no contributory negligence on the ground that the boy did not know that petrol was likely to burst into flame if heat were brought near it. 3-82

In considering whether a child has taken reasonable care for his own safety regard must be had to the age of the child, the circumstances of the case and the knowledge by the particular child of the dangers to which the defendant's negligence has exposed him. In *Gough v Thorne*,[299] Lord Denning MR said that a very young child cannot be guilty of contributory negligence; an older child may be, but it depends 3-83

---

293 per Lord Du Parcq in *Grant v Sun Shipping Co* [1948] A.C. 549 at 567.

294 *Pressley v Burnett*, 1914 S.C. 874; per Lord Cairns in *North Eastern Ry v Wanless* (1874) L.R. 7 H.L. 12 at 15; *Mercer v SE & C Railway's Managing Committee* [1922] 2 K.B. 549; per Lords Cairns and Selbourne in *Dublin, Wicklow and Wexford Ry v Slattery* (1878) 3 App. Cas. 1155 at 1165 and 1193; per Lord Esher in *Smith v South Eastern Ry* [1896] 1 Q.B. 178 at 183; *Bridges v North London Ry* (1873-74) L.R. 7 H.L. 213; *Praeger v Bristol and Exeter Ry* (1871) 24 L.T. 105; *Struthers v British Railways Board* (1969) 119 N.L.J. 249.

295 per Lord Denman in *Lynch v Nurdin* (1841) 1 Q.B. 29 at 113; *Pearson v Coleman Bros* [1948] 2 K.B. 359; *Gough v Thorne* [1966] 1 W.L.R. 1387; *French v Sunshine Holiday Camp (Hayling Island)* (1963) 107 S.J. 595; *Whitehouse v Fearnley* (1964) 47 D.L.R. (2d) 472; *Spiers v Gorman* [1966] N.Z.L.R. 897; *Jones v Lawrence* [1969] 3 All E.R. 267; *Minter v D & H Contractors (Cambridge)*, *The Times*, 30 June 1983; *Ducharme v Davies* [1984] 1 W.W.R. 699 (three-year-old infant not capable of negligence). In the pre-1945 cases judges may have denied contributory negligence in order to ensure the child received a remedy at all, whereas today in similar circumstances they may apportion responsibility.

296 The Occupiers' Liability Act 1957 s.2(3)(a), warns expressly that "an occupier must be prepared for children to be less careful than adults". The *Royal Commission on Civil Liability and Compensation for Personal Injury*, Cmnd.7054 (1978), Vol. I, para.1077 recommended that where a child is under 12 contributory negligence should not be pleadable.

297 (1858) 1 F. & F. 359; *Lay v Midland Ry* (1874-75) 34 L.T. 30; and see *Lynch v Nurdin* (1841) 1 Q.B. 29 (child aged seven-and-a-half not contributorily negligent when he mischievously climbed on to the defendant's cart). *Lynch v Nurdin* "has been treated in subsequent cases as sound law", per A. L. Smith LJ in *Harrold v Watney* [1898] 2 Q.B. 320 at 322; and "remains an authority on the question of contributory negligence of children", per Slesser LJ in *Liddle v Yorkshire (North Riding) CC* [1934] 2 K.B. 101 at 129; *Creed v McGeoch Sons Ltd* [1955] 1 W.L.R. 1005.

298 [1949] A.C. 386.

299 [1966] 1 W.L.R. 1387; *Gardner v Grace* (1858) 1 F. & F. 359 (contributory negligence does not ap-

on the circumstances. A judge should only find a child guilty of contributory negligence if he or she is of such an age as reasonably to be expected to take precautions for his or her own safety. This is not an entirely subjective test, because the question is whether an "ordinary child" of the claimant's age could be expected to have done any more than the claimant, and an ordinary child is neither a "paragon of prudence" nor "scatter-brained".[300] Theoretically, there is no age below which, as a matter of law, it can be said that a child cannot be guilty of contributory negligence, but in practice it is unreasonable to exact a high standard.[301] On the other hand, with older children there may be no good reason to apply a different standard from that applied to an adult.[302]

3-84 **Contributory negligence of disabled persons** Ordinarily, the standard of care expected of a defendant is based on the assumption that others possess normal faculties,[303] but when it is known that a person to whom the duty is owed has some physical disability, for example only one eye,[304] a higher standard of care is required of the defendant. It is a different question, however, whether, assuming there is a breach of duty, the claimant's physical or mental disability can be taken into account in deciding whether there has been contributory negligence on his part. On principle, it would seem that when it has to be decided whether a person has taken reasonable care for his own safety, "reasonable" must have reference to his individual circumstances and infirmities. Although a motor vehicle is being driven negligently, an active man might get out of the way and avoid an accident, but if

---

ply to an infant "of tender age", in this case 3¼ years).

300 [1966] 1 W.L.R. 1387 at 1391, per Salmon LJ. See also *Mullin v Richards* [1998] 1 W.L.R. 1304 where the Court of Appeal held that the standard of care to be applied to a *defendant* 15-year-old schoolgirl was whether an "ordinarily prudent and reasonable 15-year-old schoolgirl" would have appreciated the risk of harm to the claimant (applying the decision of the High Court of Australia in *McHale v Watson* (1966) 115 C.L.R. 199).

301 The decision in *McKinnell v White*, 1971 S.L.T. 61 in which a child aged five, who was hit by a car on running across a road, was held equally to blame with the driver, looks particularly harsh; *Morales v Eccleston* [1991] R.T.R. 151 CA (11-year-old boy held to be 75 per cent contributorily negligent when he was injured after he ran out on to a busy road without looking); *Paramasivan v Wicks* [2013] EWCA Civ 262 (13-year-old boy held 75 per cent contributorily negligent when he ran into the road without looking); *Jackson v Murray* [2015] UKSC 5; [2015] 2 All E.R. 805 (13-year-old 50 per cent contributorily negligent in crossing a rural road from behind a school minibus without looking); *Ellis v Kelly* [2018] EWHC 2031 (QB); [2018] 4 W.L.R. 124 (no finding of contributory negligence against an eight-year-old child who ran into the road—it was a case of "momentary misjudgment" by the child set against reckless conduct on the part of the defendant motorist. Yip J considered that a finding of contributory negligence against an eight-year-old is uncommon; contrast *AB v Main* [2015] EWHC 3183 (QB), which Yip J appeared to accept was an "outlier"). See L. Macfarlane, "Rethinking childhood contributory negligence: 'blame', 'fault'—but what about children's rights?" 2018 Jur. Rev. 75, contrasting the courts' approach to children's contributory negligence with the rights-based approach applied to determining children's interests in other areas of the law.

302 *Phethean-Hubble v Coles* [2012] EWCA Civ 349; [2012] R.T.R. 31 (16-year-old cyclist who turned from the pavement into the road in front of defendant's car held to be 50 per cent contributorily negligent; the judge had not been justified in reducing an initial assessment of 50 per cent contributory negligence to 33 per cent by reason of the claimant's age). One study has found, perhaps counter-intuitively, that in practice children falling within the 10–19 years age range were more likely to have a finding of contributory negligence made against them than adults: J. Goudkamp and D. Nolan "Contributory Negligence in the Twenty-First Century: An Empirical Study of First Instance Decisions" (2016) 79 M.L.R. 575. See further J. Goudkamp and D. Nolan, "Contributory Negligence in the Court of Appeal: An Empirical Study" (2017) 37 L.S. 437.

303 per Lord Wright in *Bourhill v Young* [1943] A.C. 92 at 109.

304 *Paris v Stepney BC* [1951] A.C. 367. Totally blind: *Haley v London Electricity Board* [1965] A.C. 778; cf. *Pritchard v PO* [1950] W.N. 310.

an elderly person cannot do so and is run down he was not, even under the old law, prevented from recovering.[305] It would seem that his damages should not be reduced, provided he exercised such care as was reasonable having regard to his age and physical condition.[306] In *Spearman v Royal United Bath Hospitals NHS Foundation Trust*,[307] it was held that a claimant who had had a prior brain injury that had produced a change of personality and a strong phobia of hospitals, and also suffered from Type 1 diabetes which resulted in frequent hypoglycaemic attacks, during which he became single-minded and stubborn, had not been contributorily negligent when, in attempting to leave a hospital he climbed five flights of stairs to the roof and fell from the roof. He had a history of acting unpredictably, without regard for his own safety, and was suffering from the effects of a hypoglycaemic attack which could also result in a patient acting unpredictably, irrationally and out of character. Martin Spencer J commented that:

> "Just as a young child is not guilty of contributory negligence in running out into a road where the child is so young as not to appreciate the danger of so doing, so too where a person's state of mind is such that, whether temporarily or permanently, they do not appreciate that they are putting themselves in danger and it cannot be said that they should have so appreciated. Otherwise, that would be to penalise a person for being ill or of unsound mind, and the law does not do that."[308]

The question of the standard to be applied to a disabled claimant was considered by the Western Australia Court of Appeal in *Town of Port Hedland v Hodder (No.2)*,[309] but there was marked judicial disagreement as to the correct approach. The claimant, who was blind, deaf, intellectually disabled and suffered from cerebral palsy, dived into the shallow end of a swimming pool, struck his head on the bottom and was rendered quadriplegic. The pool had diving blocks at the shallow end which the trial judge found were an "invitation" to dive or jump. Martin CJ, in the minority on this point, suggested that there was no logic or justice in a system of law which took a subjective view of the claimant when it came to causation (given that a tortfeasor must take the victim as he is found) and assessing compensation, but proceeded on an entirely hypothetical and unreal basis to assess the question of whether the claimant has failed to take reasonable care for his or her own safety. "The harshness, injustice and unfairness" of an objective approach which ignored the claimant's various disabilities was manifest: "It assumes a miracle of biblical proportions and requires the court to assess the question of contributory negligence in some parallel universe in which the blind can see, 3-85

---

305 *Daly v Liverpool Corp* [1939] 2 All E.R. 142, 143, per Stable J: "I cannot believe that the law is quite so absurd as to say that, if a pedestrian happens to be old and slow and a little stupid, and does not possess the skill of the hypothetical pedestrian, he or she can only walk about his or her native country at his or her own risk." See also *M'Kibbin v Glasgow Corp*, 1920 S.C. 590.

306 Contrast the standard of care applied to defendants with disabilities: see *Dunnage v Randall* [2015] EWCA Civ 673; [2016] Q.B. 639, para.7-169.

307 [2017] EWHC 3027 (QB); [2018] Med. L.R. 244.

308 [2017] EWHC 3027 (QB); [2018] Med. L.R. 244 at [74]. Contrast *Bright v Bourn* [2018] EWHC 1948 (QB), where a claimant who had suffered a brain injury and a stroke, and was unable to live on his own, was held to have been contributorily negligent when struck by a motorcycle while crossing the road. The judge cited *Dunnage v Randall* [2015] EWCA Civ 673; [2016] Q.B. 639 for the proposition that "a duty to take reasonable care for his own safety" was "not, in the circumstances of this case, reduced or any way diminished because of his disability" (at [21]). Despite the brain injury the claimant "was very independent, able to go out on his own and travelled widely on his own".

309 [2012] WASCA 212.

the deaf can hear, the lame can walk or even run, and the cognitively impaired are somehow restored to full functionality."[310] McLure P considered that the claimant had not been contributorily negligent, applying an objective standard[311]; whereas Murphy JA would have upheld the trial judge's assessment of 10 per cent contributory negligence.

3-86 **Contributory negligence in traffic cases** Contributory negligence, as much as negligence itself, must be judged according to the circumstances of each case. The rejection of "rules of law" defining contributory negligence, in favour of a flexible assessment of the particular facts in issue, is well illustrated by numerous traffic cases. It was once the "rule" that a person who collides with an unlit vehicle at night must be contributorily negligent, since he must either have been going too fast or not keeping a proper look-out. Subsequent judgments have firmly rejected any such "rule" in favour of an assessment of the facts of each case.[312]

3-87 **Collisions with pedestrians** The relative destructive power of motor vehicles in comparison to human bodies tends to lead the court to take the view that a greater burden of care lies with the negligent motorist than a negligent pedestrian. In *Eagle v Chambers*[313] the Court of Appeal reduced a finding of 60 per cent contributory negligence to 40 per cent in a case where the claimant, aged 17, who was in an emotional state, had been walking unsteadily along the white line in the middle of a dual carriageway at night. Hale LJ commented that:

> "There is a qualitative difference between a finding of 60% contribution and a finding of 40% which is not so apparent in the quantitative difference between 40% and 20%. It is rare indeed for a pedestrian to be found more responsible than a driver unless the pedestrian has suddenly moved into the path of an oncoming vehicle. That is not this case. The court 'has consistently imposed upon the drivers of cars a high burden to reflect the fact that the car is potentially a dangerous weapon': Latham LJ in *Lunt v Khelifa* [2002] EWCA Civ 801, at [20]."[314]

---

310 [2012] WASCA 212 at [156].

311 [2012] WASCA 212 at [292]: "With the exception of children, the issue of negligent breach at common law by both a plaintiff and a defendant involves a judgment that the person ought to have behaved differently, not that they were capable of doing so."

312 See para.7-209 onwards.

313 [2003] EWCA Civ 1107; [2004] R.T.R. 9.

314 [2003] EWCA Civ 1107; [2004] R.T.R. 9 at [16]. In *Lunt v Khelifa* the Court of Appeal had upheld a finding of 30% contributory negligence in the case of a drunken pedestrian who stepped out in front of an oncoming vehicle. In *Jackson v Murray* [2015] UKSC 5; [2015] 2 All E.R. 805, [26], [38], and [50] the Supreme Court approved the approach taken in *Eagle v Chambers* to the assessment of contributory negligence in cases involving collisions between pedestrians and motor vehicles. See also *Sabir v Osei-Kwabena* [2015] EWCA Civ 1213; [2016] P.I.Q.R. Q4, applying *Jackson v Murray* and *Eagle v Chambers* in emphasising the higher causative potency of a motor vehicle in comparison to a pedestrian who steps in front of an approaching vehicle (claimant assessed as 25 per cent contributorily negligent). On the other hand, foolhardy behaviour by pedestrians is likely to result in higher assessments of contributory negligence: *Belka v Prosperini* [2011] EWCA Civ 623 (pedestrian's contributory negligence assessed at two-thirds where he took take a deliberate risk in running across the road in front of a vehicle which had the right of way); *Lightfoot v Go-Ahead Group Plc* [2011] EWHC 89 (QB); [2011] R.T.R. 27 (40 per cent reduction for contributory negligence in the case of a drunken pedestrian on the road). See further D. Dyal, "Contributory negligence in pedestrian road traffic accidents" [2018] J.P.I.L. 23.

Bailey v Geddes[315] appeared to prescribe that the driver of a vehicle who collides with a pedestrian on a pedestrian crossing cannot plead contributory negligence. Any such "rule" has now been distinguished to the point of extinction. Thus, it did not apply when a pedestrian stepped in front of a vehicle so unexpectedly that it was too late for the driver to do anything[316]; nor when a pedestrian stepped off the pavement on to the crossing, since it must be limited to collisions with pedestrians while they are actually on the crossing.[317] A pedestrian is not on the crossing if he steps off an island in the centre of the road, for each half of the road must be treated as a separate crossing.[318] On the other hand, a driver must approach a crossing prepared for ill-advised actions on the part of pedestrians, especially if his view of the crossing is obscured.[319] 3-88

Traffic lights It has also been held that the driver of a vehicle who crosses a junction controlled by lights with the lights in his favour is not negligent if he collides with another vehicle which has entered the crossing against the lights.[320] This, too, cannot be regarded as laying down a rule of law, as in a subsequent case, where a driver acted within his rights in continuing, although the lights changed from green to amber just as he approached them, and collided with another vehicle which had entered the crossing with the lights in its favour, it was held that both drivers were at fault.[321] Similarly, in *Griffin v Mersey Regional Ambulance*,[322] a motorist who crossed a junction on a green light and collided with an ambulance crossing against a red light was held 60 per cent contributorily negligent. What all these diverse cases demonstrate is that decisions on facts should never be elevated to rules of law. 3-89

Seat-belts and crash-helmets When the failure of the claimant to wear a seat-belt or a crash-helmet contributes to the injuries which he suffers as a result of a collision, he will normally be held contributorily negligent. Thus in *Froom v Butcher*,[323] the claimant sustained head injuries when he was thrown against the windscreen by the impact of the collision. He was not wearing a seat-belt and was 3-90

---

315 [1938] 1 K.B. 156.

316 *Knight v Sampson* [1938] 3 All E.R. 309.

317 *Chisholm v LPTB* [1939] 1 K.B. 426.

318 *Wilkinson v Chetham-Strode* [1940] 2 K.B. 310.

319 *Upson v LPTB* [1949] A.C. 155; *Kayser v LPTB* [1950] 1 All E.R. 231; *Hurt v Murphy* [1971] R.T.R. 186 (collision with a pedestrian not on a crossing); *Williams v Needham* [1972] R.T.R. 387 (pedestrian who stepped into the road without looking held two-thirds to blame); *Mulligan v Holmes; Yorkshire Bank v Holmes* [1971] R.T.R. 179 (pedestrians on a crossing marked with studs when the green light favoured traffic, held 20 per cent to blame); *Rehill v Rider Holdings Ltd* [2012] EWCA Civ 628; [2013] R.T.R. 5 (pedestrian who stepped onto a Pelican crossing against the red light, and into the path of a bus, held 50 per cent contributorily negligent); *Adams v Gibson* [2016] EWHC 3209 (QB) (inebriated pedestrian who stepped into road close to, but not on, a crossing held one-third to blame).

320 *Joseph Eva Ltd v Reeves* [1938] 2 K.B. 393; *Knight v Wiper Supply Services* (1965) 109 S.J. 358.

321 *Godsmark v Knight Bros (Brighton), The Times,* 12 May 1960; approved in *Radburn v Kemp* [1971] 1 W.L.R. 1502; cf. *Lang v London Transport Executive* [1959] 1 W.L.R. 1168; *Sudds v Hanscombe* [1971] R.T.R. 212.

322 [1998] P.I.Q.R. P34 CA; *Purdue v Devon Fire and Rescue Service* [2002] EWCA Civ 1538—motorist who collided with a fire engine while crossing a junction when the lights were green in his favour held to be 20 per cent contributorily negligent. See also *Craggy v Chief Constable of Cleveland Police* [2009] EWCA Civ 1128 where a collision at a junction controlled by traffic lights was between two emergency vehicles attending different emergencies.

323 [1976] Q.B. 286 CA. *Gleeson v Court* [2007] EWHC 2397 (QB); [2008] R.T.R. 10 (claimant agreed to travel in the boot of the defendant's car and was thrown out of the car following a collision due to defendant's negligence; claimant's contributory negligence held to be equivalent to failing to wear

found to be contributorily negligent. In *O'Connell v Jackson*,[324] the claimant sustained severe head injuries when he was knocked off his motorcycle. Those injuries would have been less severe had he been wearing a crash-helmet and his damages were reduced by 15 per cent. The personal opinion of the claimant on the efficiency and safety of seat-belts will be disregarded, since the standard is objective. A reasonable person should protect him/herself in modern traffic by taking such a precaution. Moreover, it is now a criminal offence to fail to wear a seat-belt.[325] It is only likely to be considered reasonable not to wear a seat-belt if the claimant suffers from a medical condition making it more dangerous to wear the belt than risk the consequences of not doing so. In *MacKay v Borthwick*,[326] the claimant was held not to be contributorily negligent in failing to wear a seat-belt on a short journey as she suffered from a hiatus hernia on which the belt would have pressed. In *Condon v Condon*,[327] it was held that if a claimant could establish by medical evidence that she suffered from a true phobia concerning seat-belts, her failure to wear a seat-belt would not amount to contributory negligence. It is difficult to envisage circumstances in which it would be reasonable not to wear a crash-helmet.[328]

3-91 Whenever failure to wear a seat-belt or crash-helmet is pleaded as contributory negligence, it must be shown that had the claimant taken the relevant precaution his injuries would indeed have been reduced. In *Froom v Butcher*,[329] the Court of Appeal gave guidance on apportionment in seat-belt cases. Damages should be reduced by 25 per cent if the injury would have been prevented altogether by use of a belt; if the injury would have been less severe, but there would still have been some injury the reduction should be 15 per cent; but if the injuries would have been the same even with the use of a belt there should be no reduction.[330] In *Traynor v*

---

a seat-belt).

324 [1972] 1 Q.B. 270; see also *Capps v Miller* [1989] 1 W.L.R. 839 where the claimant was held contributorily negligent in failing to fasten his crash helmet securely. For discussion of the position of cyclists who fail to wear helmets see Fulbrook, "Cycle Helmets and Contributory Negligence" [2004] J.P.I.L. 171. In *Smith v Finch* [2009] EWHC 53 (QB) it was held that the failure of a bicyclist to wear a helmet could constitute contributory negligence even though there is no legal compulsion for cyclists to wear safety helmets (though there was no finding contributory negligence on the facts).

325 Road Traffic Act 1988 s.14 (see also s.15). The cases all relate to front seat belts; but since it is a criminal offence to fail to wear a back seat-belt where a belt is fitted, such a failure may also constitute contributory negligence.

326 1982 S.L.T. 265 (Outer House).

327 [1978] R.T.R. 483.

328 A difficulty arises in the context of followers of the Sikh religion who are exempt from road traffic regulations requiring motorcyclists to wear helmets (Road Traffic Act 1988, s.16(2)). Such a person might argue Parliament had found it "reasonable" for him to prefer his faith to considerations of safety. Query, however, whether it is reasonable to expect the defendant to pay for the consequences of the claimant's religious beliefs.

329 [1976] Q.B. 286. In *Gawler v Raettig* [2007] EWHC 373 (QB) Gray J stated that Lord Denning's observations in *Froom v Butcher* on apportionment in seat-belt cases did not constitute mere suggestion or guidance; rather the indicated percentages for the reduction of damages were binding.

330 In *J (A Child) v Wilkins* [2001] R.T.R. 19; [2001] P.I.Q.R. P12 the Court of Appeal held that the same principles of apportionment as apply to contributory negligence should also apply to a case involving contribution under the Civil Liability (Contribution) Act 1978 when there was a failure to wear a seat-belt. The claimant was a two-year-old child who was held on her mother's knee in the front passenger seat of a car being driven by her aunt. The defendant negligently collided with the car, causing serious injuries to the claimant which could have been wholly avoided if she had been restrained in an approved child seat. The defendant joined the claimant's mother and aunt as CPR

Donovan,[331] a plea of contributory negligence failed on evidence that, even had the claimant worn a belt, her injuries would have been just as severe, albeit of a different nature. It appears though that in apportioning damage the courts are not required to consider exactly what injury the claimant would have sustained had he worn a belt.[332]

Drunken drivers A passenger who accepts a lift in a vehicle driven by a person whom he knows to be drunk is likely to be found contributorily negligent if he suffers injury in an accident caused at least in part by the driver's impaired capacity to drive carefully.[333] When the claimant has accompanied the defendant on a prolonged drinking bout, knowing full well that the defendant will be going to drive, he is still contributorily negligent albeit his own capacity to judge the reasonableness of his conduct is similarly impaired.[334] But where there is no evidence that the defendant was acting in a way which would indicate that he was unable to drive safely, the claimant passenger will not necessarily be held contributorily negligent simply by failing to question the defendant driver as to how much alcohol he has consumed.[335] 3-92

Contributory negligence in an emergency or dilemma Where the conduct of the defendant has placed the claimant in personal peril he may be found to have taken reasonable care for his own safety in the "agony of the moment" albeit hindsight shows that he would have been safe had he acted differently. Provided that he acted reasonably in the emergency or dilemma created by the defendant's wrongdoing, his conduct will not amount to contributory negligence.[336] 3-93

Contributory negligence in rescue cases Contributory negligence is also 3-94

Pt 20 defendants. The Court of Appeal upheld the judge's assessment that liability should be apportioned 75 per cent to the defendant and 25 per cent to the Pt 20 defendants, applying the approach adopted in *Froom v Butcher*. See also *Hughes v Williams* [2013] EWCA Civ 455; [2013] P.I.Q.R. P17 (mother negligent in restraining three-year-old child on a booster seat, for which the child did not meet the height or age criteria, rather than a forward facing child seat with a 5-point harness; mother held liable to 25 per cent contribution under the Civil Liability (Contribution) Act 1978). See also *EMS (A Minor) v ES* [2018] NIQB 36.

331 [1978] C.L.Y. 2612; *Lertora v Finzi* [1973] R.T.R. 161; *Smith v Finch* [2009] EWHC 53 (QB) (no finding of contributory negligence because the failure of a cyclist to wear a helmet made no difference since the injuries would not have been reduced or prevented by wearing a helmet); *Stanton v Collinson* [2010] EWCA Civ 81; [2010] R.T.R. 26 (the court should avoid intensive inquiry into fine degrees of contributory negligence).

332 *Patience v Andrews* [1983] R.T.R. 447.

333 *Owens v Brimmell* [1977] Q.B. 859 (20 per cent reduction); *Donelan v Donelan and General Accident Fire and Life Assurance* [1993] P.I.Q.R. P205 (75 per cent reduction where defendant drove claimant's car at the claimant's instigation and the claimant knew that the defendant was both an inexperienced driver and drunk. Logically the defendant must establish that it was inebriation, rather than some other cause, which caused the relevant accident or causation is not proven in respect of the passenger's contributory negligence.)

334 [1977] Q.B. 859; and see *Pitts v Hunt* [1991] 1 Q.B. 24; *Joslyn v Berryman* [2003] HCA 34; (2003) 198 A.L.R. 137.

335 *Booth v White* [2003] EWCA Civ 1708; (2003) 147 S.J.L.B. 1367—claimant knew that the defendant had been drinking, but had not paid much attention to how much alcohol the defendant, who was subsequently found to be almost two times over the legal limit of alcohol consumption, had consumed.

336 *Jones v Boyce* (1816) 1 Stark. 493; *Clayards v Dethick* (1848) 12 Q.B. 439; *The City of Lincoln* (1889) 15 P. & D. 15; *Sayers v Harlow Urban DC* [1958] 1 W.L.R. 623. For full discussion, see para.7-165.

potentially relevant in "rescue" cases. If, in a situation of peril created by the defendant's wrongdoing, a brave person rushes in to the rescue, he will not be prevented from recovering fully in respect of any damage he sustains.[337] Here, too, while making due allowance for the urgency and lack of time for deliberation, the rescuer must still act reasonably, or he may be met with a charge of contributory negligence.[338] The question of what risks a rescuer can reasonably take in an attempt to save life or limb should not be judged too critically.[339] In *Tolley v Carr*[340] the claimant was attempting to move a vehicle that had come to a halt in the outside lane of a motorway when he was struck by two other vehicles, suffering serious injuries. Hickinbottom J rejected the defendants' contention that the claimant had been contributorily negligent. Applying the "generous approach of the common law to those who imperil themselves in order to save others from risks arising from the negligence of others", Hickinbottom J noted that: "The law appreciates that a rescuer may act—and may feel impelled to act—under the pressures of the moment, where delay may be considered vital to the safety of those he is considering protecting from risk. It is not appropriate to subject a rescuer's actions, or his subjective view of the risks involved to himself and/or to others, to fine scrutiny in the court room."[341]

(e) Doctrine of identification

3-95 It is possible for an action in negligence to be met by a charge of contributory negligence, not of the claimant himself, but of a third party. The principal cases where a claimant will be identified in this way with the contributory negligence of another are those of vicarious liability, dependants suing under the Fatal Accidents Act 1976 and a child suing under the Congenital Disabilities (Civil Liability) Act 1976.[342] If an employer's property has been entrusted to an employee and is damaged through the combined negligence of the employee and a third party, the employer's action against the third party can be met by an allegation of contributory negligence by the employee.[343] Dependants suing under the Fatal Accidents Act 1976 are statutorily identified with the contributory negligence of the deceased by virtue of s.5.[344] A child born disabled as a result of a pre-natal occurrence is identi-

---

[337] *Brandon v Osborne, Garrett Co* [1924] 1 K.B. 548; and see para.2-134 and para.7-34.

[338] See, e.g. *Harrison v British Railways Board* [1981] 3 All E.R. 679.

[339] See, e.g. *Watt v Hertfordshire CC* [1954] 1 W.L.R. 835 on the risks that a *defendant* is reasonably entitled to take in order to save life and limb.

[340] [2010] EWHC 2191 (QB); [2011] R.T.R. 7.

[341] [2010] EWHC 2191 (QB); [2011] R.T.R. 7 at [23]. Moreover, "exceptional bravery is not the same as foolhardiness", ibid. at [47]. See also the Social Action, Responsibility and Heroism Act 2015 s.4, which provides that in considering whether a person was negligent the court must have regard to "whether the alleged negligence or breach of statutory duty occurred when the person was acting heroically by intervening in an emergency to assist an individual in danger." See para.7-192. Although directed principally at defendants, there is nothing in the Act which precludes its application to claimants where issues of contributory negligence arise.

[342] For other possible cases and for full discussion generally, see Williams, *Joint Torts and Contributory Negligence* (1951), Chs 17 and 18.

[343] *Chaplin v Hawes* (1828) 3 C. & P. 554; *Carberry v Davies* [1968] 1 W.L.R. 1003. An employee not being vicariously liable for his employer is not identified with his negligence: *Drew v Western SMT*, 1947 S.C. 222.

[344] If the dependant's own negligence combines with that of the deceased and the defendant in bringing the death about, it is doubtful whether the dependant's claim will always be reduced according to the deceased's share in the blame, even if the dependant had been more to blame than the deceased.

fied with the contributory negligence of the parent by virtue of the Congenital Disabilities (Civil Liability) Act 1976 s.1(7).[345]

The tendency of the law has been to move away from identification rather than towards it. Thus, a person is no longer identified with a carrier[346]; nor with his bailee[347]; nor is a child in the charge of an adult identified with the latter's negligence[348]; nor is a husband or wife identified with the negligence of the other spouse,[349] unless in the particular case he or she was acting as the employee of the other.[350] **3-96**

The issue of identification at common law arose, but was not resolved, in *Gorham v British Telecommunications Plc*.[351] The claimants were the spouse and children of the deceased who was a customer of an insurance company which gave negligent advice to the deceased about pensions and life cover. The Court of Appeal held that, by analogy with the wills cases,[352] the insurance company owed a duty of care to the customer's dependant spouse and children where it was clear that he intended to create a benefit for them on his death. It was found that in relation to part of the loss the deceased himself had been negligent in failing to take steps to remedy the situation brought about by the defendants' negligence. Pill and Schiemann LJJ held that this broke the causal link between the defendants' negligence and the relevant financial loss, and neither considered it appropriate to comment on the question of contributory negligence. Sir Murray Stuart-Smith, dissented on the causation issue, and then considered whether the deceased's contributory negligence should be taken into account to reduce the claimants' award of damages. The Law Reform (Contributory Negligence) Act 1945 s.1(1) provides that the damages "... shall be reduced to such extent as the court thinks just and equitable having regard to *the claimant's share* in the responsibility for the damage" (emphasis added). Read literally this would appear to preclude reducing the claimants' award in *Gorham*, since it was not their negligence which contributed to the loss. Sir Murray Stuart-Smith suggested that this problem could be overcome because it was acknowledged in *White v Jones* that the court was fashioning a remedy to meet an apparent injustice. The duty of care owed to the beneficiaries in *White* was said to be subject to any contractual terms between the testator and the solicitor to which the dependants were not party, which might exclude or restrict the solicitor's liability to the testator. There was, said his Lordship, no reason why the same principle should not apply to contributory negligence on the part of the testator, and in *Gorham* on the part of the deceased customer. Fashioning a remedy to meet the justice of the case also required justice for the defendants which would be achieved by reducing the award of damages to the dependants to reflect the deceased's negligence. It remains to be **3-97**

This point might have arisen in *Dawrant v Nutt* [1961] 1 W.L.R. 253, but it was not considered. If the deceased had not been negligent, but his death was the result of the negligence of the defendant and the dependant, it seems beyond doubt that the latter's damages will be reduced in proportion to his default: *Mulholland v McCrea* [1961] N.I. 135; but an innocent dependant is not identified with a negligent dependant: *Dodds v Dodds* [1978] Q.B. 543.

345 For possible wider implications of this provision see para.5-58.

346 *The Bernina* (1888) 13 App. Cas. 1.

347 *France v Parkinson* [1954] 1 W.L.R. 581; *Wellwood v Alexander King Ltd* [1921] 2 Ir. R. 274.

348 *Oliver v Birmingham and Midland Omnibus Co Ltd* [1933] 1 K.B. 35; *Ducharme v Davies* [1984] 1 W.W.R. 699.

349 *Mallett v Dunn* [1949] 2 K.B. 180; *Drinkwater v Kimber* [1952] 2 Q.B. 281.

350 *Lampert v Eastern National Omnibus Co Ltd* [1954] 1 W.L.R. 1047; *Berrill v Road Haulage Exec* [1952] 2 Lloyd's Rep. 490.

351 [2000] 1 W.L.R. 2129.

352 See *White v Jones* [1995] 2 A.C. 207.

seen whether, in a case where the customer's negligence is not regarded as being so potent as to break the causal link, a court would adopt Sir Murray Stuart-Smith's approach or apply the literal wording of the 1945 Act.[353]

(f) Proof of contributory negligence

3-98 The burden of proving contributory negligence by the claimant rests on the defendant,[354] but this may be inferred from the claimant's own evidence,[355] or on a balance of probabilities from the facts.[356] As Tasker Watkins J said: "In such cases, as in every other case where contributory negligence is alleged, the burden of proving on the balance of probabilities that a [claimant] has contributed to the cause of damage suffered lies on he who alleged it, namely the defendant."[357] The claimant's knowledge of a danger is not of itself evidence of contributory negligence,[358] though it may be relevant in other ways.[359] If the defendant does plead contributory negligence the court is under no obligation to take it into account.[360]

(g) Apportionment

3-99 Where the Law Reform (Contributory Negligence) Act 1945 applies, s.1(1) directs the court to reduce the claimant's damages "to such extent as the court thinks just and equitable having regard to the claimant's share in the responsibility for the damage". The court cannot refuse to reduce the award because it is just and equitable to do so,[361] but where one of the parties is less than 10 per cent responsible no apportionment should normally be made.[362] If there are two accidents and the first contributed causally to the second, there will be a sub-apportionment of that

---

353 For discussion of some of the complexities of attributing the negligence of third parties to a claimant for the purpose of contributory negligence in the professional negligence context see H. Evans, "Attribution and professional negligence" (2003) 19 P.N. 470.

354 *Wakelin v L & SW Ry* (1886) 12 App. Cas. 41 at 47; *Flower v Ebbw Vale Steel, Iron and Coal Co Ltd* [1936] A.C. 206 at 221; *Heranger (Owners) v S.S. Diamond (Owners)* [1939] A.C. 94 at 104; *Booth v White* [2003] EWCA Civ 1708; (2003) 147 S.J.L.B. 1367.

355 *Sharpe v S Ry* [1925] 2 K.B. 311; *Baker v Longhurst & Sons Ltd* [1933] 2 K.B. 461 at 468; *Kerry v Keighley Electrical Engineering Co Ltd* [1940] 3 All E.R. 399.

356 *Gibby v E Grinstead Gas and Water Co* [1944] 1 All E.R. 358; *Caswell v Powell Duffryn Associated Collieries Ltd* [1940] A.C. 152 at 169; *Chapman v Copeland* (1966) 116 N.L.J. 810. See also para.7-201 onwards.

357 *Owens v Brimmell* [1977] Q.B. 859 at 864. On the need for the defendant to prove that the claimant's injury could have been avoided or reduced, see *Barker v Murdoch*, 1977 S.L.T. 75 (Outer House); *Roberts v Sparks* [1977] C.L.Y. 2643; *Condon v Condon* [1978] R.T.R. 483.

358 *Hesketh v Liverpool Corp* [1940] 4 All E.R. 429.

359 *Slater v Clay Cross Co Ltd* [1956] 2 Q.B. 264; cf. *Dawrant v Nutt* [1961] 1 W.L.R. 253. See also *Bill v Short Bros and Harland* [1963] N.I. 1.

360 *Taylor v Simon Carves*, 1957 S.L.T. 23 Sh. Ct; *Fookes v Slaytor* [1978] 1 W.L.R. 1293; followed in *Christie v Bridgestone Australia Pty* (1984) 33 S.A.S.R. 377. See also Lord Asquith's comment in 69 L.Q.R. 317 that he had tried unsuccessfully to persuade counsel to plead contributory negligence in *Dann v Hamilton* [1939] 1 K.B. 509. See also *William J Judge v William Reape* [1968] I.R. 226.

361 *Boothman v British Northrop Ltd* (1972) 13 K.I.R. 112.

362 *Johnson v Tennant Bros Ltd* Unreported 1954 CA; though this rule may be questioned, at least where the claimant is in breach of a statutory duty: *Capps v Miller* [1989] 1 W.L.R. 839 at 848–849. In *Sahib Foods Ltd v Paskin Kyriakides Sands (A Firm)* [2003] EWCA Civ 1832; [2004] P.N.L.R. 22 at [69] the Court of Appeal observed that "it is open to the court to conclude that the share of a claimant's responsibility is so small by reference to that of the defendant that it would not be just and equitable to reduce the damages at all".

part of the subsequent damage which is attributable to the first accident.[363] In *Fitzgerald v Lane*,[364] the claimant was a pedestrian who was injured in a road traffic accident involving two negligent motorists. The trial judge found that all three parties were equally blameworthy, and made an award of two thirds of the full loss against each of the defendants. The House of Lords held that this was an error of law. The judge had elided the question of contributory negligence with contribution between tortfeasors under the Civil Liability (Contribution) Act 1978. The assessment of the claimant's share of responsibility for the damage should be made by comparing his conduct with the totality of the defendants' negligence, not with the extent to which each defendant's conduct contributed to the damage. Thus, the percentage reduction of the claimant's damages will be the same against each defendant. Any differences in the respective responsibilities of the defendants should be dealt with in contribution proceedings between the defendants after the issue of contributory negligence between the claimant and the defendants has been decided.

The discretion implicit in a test based on what is "just and equitable" allows the court to take an ad hoc approach to apportionment, treating the issue as essentially a question of fact. The court's disapproval of the claimant's conduct may be reflected in a large reduction for contributory negligence.[365] Where a particular type of accident is common it may be sensible to have guidelines for the appropriate deduction in order to produce both a reasonable level of consistency and certainty.[366] It is not simply a case of assessing the comparative blameworthiness of the parties, but of their respective "responsibility for the damage". So, for example, in the case of breach of strict statutory duty the defendant may not have been particularly careless, but may still bear a substantial responsibility for the damage.[367] In assessing the respective responsibilities of the parties the court should take into account the scope of the defendant's duty and the extent to which that duty involved tak- **3-100**

---

363 *The Calliope* [1970] P. 172.

364 [1989] 1 A.C. 328.

365 See *Barrett v Ministry of Defence* [1995] 1 W.L.R. 1217 CA where a naval airman died when he fell unconscious and choked to death on his own vomit, having consumed a large amount of extremely cheap alcohol supplied at a Norwegian naval base. The defendants had assumed a duty of care as to how he was treated once he fell unconscious. Damages were reduced by two thirds for the deceased's contributory negligence. See also *Jebson v Ministry of Defence* [2000] 1 W.L.R. 2055 (soldier injured when, in a drunken state, he fell off an army truck after a night out organised by the defendants held 75 per cent contributorily negligent).

366 See, e.g. *Froom v Butcher* [1976] Q.B. 286, para.3-91 in the context of the failure of passengers in a vehicle to wear a seat-belt. The fact that a standard reduction for contributory negligence of 25 per cent can apply to the failure to wear a seatbelt, and a reduction of 20 per cent will normally apply to accepting a lift from a drunken driver (*Owens v Brimmell* [1977] Q.B. 859, para.3-92) does not mean that a claimant who both accepted a lift from a drunken driver and failed to wear a seatbelt will be subject to a 45 per cent deduction for contributory negligence: *Best v Smyth* [2010] EWHC 1541 (QB)—maximum reduction of 30 per cent on the facts. See also *Clark v Farley* [2018] EWHC 1007 (QB); [2018] P.I.Q.R. P15 at [77], per Yip J: "the correct approach is to look at relative blameworthiness and causative potency as a whole, rather than assessing elements of contributory negligence separately and adding the percentages together." For an argument there should be more fixed apportionment rules see J. Goudkamp, "Apportionment of damages for contributory negligence: a fixed or discretionary approach?" (2015) 35 L.S. 621.

367 per Lord Hoffmann in *Reeves v Commissioner of Police for the Metropolis* [2000] 1 A.C. 360 at 371: " ... what section 1 requires the court to apportion is not merely degrees of carelessness but 'responsibility' and ... an assessment of responsibility must take into account the policy of the rule, such as the Factories Acts, by which liability is imposed. A person may be responsible although he has not been careless at all, as in the case of breach of an absolute statutory duty. And he may have been careless without being responsible, as in the case of 'acts of inattention' by workmen."

ing precautions against the claimant's own negligence. That should then be weighed against the question of whether the claimant's fault was causative of the damage and "if it was, what the relative blameworthiness and causative potency of the parties' respective faults were".[368]

3-101 **Role of appellate court** In *Jackson v Murray*[369] the Supreme Court reviewed the principles to be applied to an assessment of apportionment in cases of contributory negligence and the circumstances in which an appellate court can overturn an assessment. Lord Reed observed that:

> "It is not possible for a court to arrive at an apportionment which is demonstrably correct. The problem is not merely that the factors which the court is required to consider are incapable of precise measurement. More fundamentally, the blameworthiness of the pursuer and the defender are incommensurable. The defender has acted in breach of a duty (not necessarily a duty of care) which was owed to the pursuer; the pursuer, on the other hand, has acted with a want of regard for her own interests. The word 'fault' in section 1(1), as applied to 'the person suffering the damage' on the one hand, and the 'other person or persons' on the other hand, is therefore being used in two different senses. The court is not comparing like with like."[370]

The court has to weigh both the causative potency of the conduct of the defendant and claimant as well as their respective blameworthiness. This is a rough and ready exercise which can produce a range of legitimate views as to what is just and equitable.[371] It follows that an appellate court should not lightly interfere with an apportionment fixed by the judge of first instance. The question was:

> "whether the court below went wrong. In the absence of an identifiable error, such as an error of law, or the taking into account of an irrelevant matter, or the failure to take account of a relevant matter, it is only a difference of view as to the apportionment of responsibility which exceeds the ambit of reasonable disagreement that warrants the conclusion that the court below has gone wrong. In other words, in the absence of an identifiable error, the appellate court must be satisfied that the apportionment made by the court below was not one which was reasonably open to it."[372]

A wide difference of view as to the apportionment which is just and equitable could nonetheless justify the conclusion that the court below has gone wrong. An apportionment should not be changed merely because the appellate court disagreed as to the precise figure, but it can be altered if it was "outside the range of reasonable determinations". On the facts (a 13-year-old girl stepped out from behind a minibus into the path of the defendant motorist who was travelling too fast in the

---

[368] *Sahib Foods Ltd v Paskin Kyriakides Sands (A Firm)* [2003] EWCA Civ 1832; [2004] P.N.L.R. 22 at [66]—fire started as a result of claimants' negligence, but the rapid spread of the fire was the result of failing to install fire-resistant panels, which was attributable both to the defendant architects' negligence and the claimants' negligence in giving the defendants incorrect information as to the activities that would be carried out in the area. Claimants held responsible for the immediate fire damage, and two-thirds responsible for the spread of the fire. See also *St George v Home Office* [2008] EWCA Civ 1068; [2009] 1 W.L.R. 1670; para.3-64 (claimant's pre-accident lifestyle choices in becoming addicted to drugs and alcohol not of sufficient causative potency, looking at the comparative blameworthiness of the parties, to make it just and equitable to reduce damages for contributory negligence); and *Blackmore v Department for Communities and Local Government* [2017] EWCA Civ 1136; [2018] Q.B. 471.

[369] [2015] UKSC 5; [2015] 2 All E.R. 805; discussed by Tavares [2015] J.P.I.L. C152.

[370] [2015] UKSC 5; [2015] 2 All E.R. 805 at [27].

[371] [2015] UKSC 5; [2015] 2 All E.R. 805 at [28].

[372] [2015] UKSC 5; [2015] 2 All E.R. 805 at [35].

circumstances) a majority of the Supreme Court considered that responsibility should be apportioned equally and this justified departing from the Extra Division's assessment that the claimant was 70 per cent responsible (the trial judge having made an assessment of 90 per cent contributory negligence). This does not necessarily mean that a difference of 20 per cent in the assessment will justify the appellate court in substituting a different apportionment. Lord Reed considered that the "view that parties are equally responsible for the damage suffered by the pursuer is substantially different from the view that one party is much more responsible than the other. Such a wide difference of view exceeds the ambit of reasonable disagreement, and warrants the conclusion that the court below has gone wrong".[373]

Apportionment in cases of economic loss Initially, when liability for negligent misstatement under *Hedley Byrne & Co Ltd v Heller & Partners Ltd*[374] was considered to be based on the concept of reasonable reliance by the claimant on the defendant's statement, there was some speculation that contributory negligence might not be relevant at all in such cases, since if the claimant had acted with a sufficient lack of care to be characterised as negligent for the purpose of contributory negligence how could it be said that he placed reasonable reliance on the defendant's misstatement? If his reliance was not reasonable then no duty of care would arise, so that the issue of contributory negligence became otiose. Now, liability under *Hedley Byrne* is understood to be based on the concept of a voluntary undertaking of responsibility by the defendant, and there have been a number of cases, mostly involving professional liability,[375] where the claimant has been found contributorily negligent. In the case of significant negligence by the claimant there is also the possibility that the claim may fail entirely on the basis that the defendant's breach of duty did not cause the loss.[376] In the case of physical damage the question of apportionment is, on the whole, relatively straightforward, but a claimant's contribution to financial loss can be more complicated: 3-102

> "It tends to be clear whether a [claimant] has contributed to his own physical injury. The causation and nature of economic loss is more complex with the result that the [claimant's] conduct may be regarded as contributing to some but not all aspects of the loss. Again, whilst it is clearly negligent for a [claimant] to take a risk with his own physical safety, it may be perfectly sensible for him to run the risk of economic loss in the hope of making a profit."[377]

Nonetheless, the courts should apply an objective standard of care to the claimant's conduct in this situation—the claimant should not be permitted to argue that as a "reasonable businessman" the risk of loss on a particular transaction was offset by the prospects of profit on other transactions, and therefore he was not negligent in entering into a risky transaction, since this places the whole risk of loss upon the negligent defendant.[378]

[373] [2015] UKSC 5; [2015] 2 All E.R. 805 at [44]. There was a "qualitative difference between a finding of 60% contribution and a finding of 40% which was not so apparent in the quantitative difference between 40% and 20%": ibid. at [38], citing Hale LJ in *Eagle v Chambers*; see the quotation at para.3-87.

[374] [1964] A.C. 465.

[375] See paras 9-175, 9-206, 9-271.

[376] See *Strover v Harrington* [1988] 1 Ch. 390.

[377] Dugdale (1999) 62 M.L.R. 281; commenting on the decision of the Court of Appeal in *Platform Home Loans v Oyston Shipways Ltd* [1998] Ch. 466.

[378] See para.7-171.

3-103 **Apportionment and the SAAMCO "cap"** Most of the cases concerning contributory negligence in cases of economic loss have arisen from the losses sustained by lenders following the collapse of the property market in the early 1990s. Lenders sought to shift much of this loss to negligent valuers and solicitors, who in turn argued that the lenders were also contributorily negligent in a variety of ways, such as failing to make proper enquiries as to the borrower's ability to service the loan[379]; failure to give proper instructions[380]; failing to query large discrepancies in valuations by different valuers of the same property[381]; failing to apply their own procedures to check material facts and lending an imprudently high percentage of property valuation.[382] When assessing damages in respect of a negligent valuation the House of Lords has held that the lender's loss is measured by the difference between the negligent valuation and the correct valuation at the time of the valuation, and should not take into account falls in the market value of the property, on the basis that the valuer's duty of care is normally limited to providing information upon which the lender will make a decision, and does not extend to advising the lender as to whether he should make the loan.[383] The effect of this, in some cases, is to "cap" the lender's actual loss, restricting it to a maximum of the difference between the "correct" valuation and the negligent valuation. In *Platform Home Loans Ltd v Oyston Shipways Ltd*,[384] the question was how contributory negligence should be dealt with where the claimant's damages are limited by the *SAAMCO* cap. The claimants had been negligent in both failing to check information provided by the borrower and imprudently lending 70 per cent of the value of the property without ensuring adequate security for the loan. The trial judge made an overall assessment of 20 per cent contributory negligence, without apportioning that percentage between the two instances of contributory negligence (though on appeal it was accepted by the claimants that the failure to check the borrower's loan application contributed 5 per cent). The claimants' actual loss was £611,748, but the *SAAMCO* cap reduced this to £500,000 (the difference between the correct and the negligent valuation). The issue on appeal to the House of Lords was whether the 20 per cent contributory negligence should be deducted

379 *Mortgage Corp Plc v Halifax (SW) Ltd (No.2)* [1999] Lloyd's Rep. P.N. 159; *Barclays Bank Plc v Christie Owen & Davies Ltd (t/a Christie & Co)* [2016] EWHC 2351 (Ch); [2017] P.N.L.R. 8, where the lender had disregarded the dishonest use of a previous loan to the borrower by the borrower's directors because it considered that it could still make money out of its relationship with the customer.

380 *Housing Loan Corporation Plc v William H Brown Ltd* [1999] Lloyd's Rep. P.N. 185 CA.

381 *Cavendish Funding Ltd v Henry Spencer Sons Ltd* [1998] P.N.L.R. 122 CA.

382 *Platform Home Loans Ltd v Oyston Shipways Ltd* [2000] 2 A.C. 190. There is no necessary reason why a lender's share of responsibility should be limited to a share of the amount of the imprudent excess lending. The excess lending may be the immediate reason for the additional loss, but without the excess lending it may be that there would have been no transaction and no loss at all. Thus, it may be appropriate to arrive at a share of the overall loss which the lender should be required to bear: *Arab Bank Plc v John D Wood Commercial Ltd* [2000] 1 W.L.R. 857; [2000] Lloyd's Rep. P.N. 173 at 204, [109], per Mance LJ.

383 *South Australia Asset Management Corp v York Montague Ltd* [1997] A.C. 191 HL (also cited as *Banque Bruxelles Lambert SA v Eagle Star Insurance Co Ltd* [1997] A.C. 191, and referred to as the *SAAMCO* litigation); *Nykredit Mortgage Bank Plc v Edward Erdman Group Ltd (No.2)* [1997] 1 W.L.R. 1627. See paras 2-186 to 2-191.

384 [2000] 2 A.C. 190; Howarth (2000) 8 Tort. L.R. 85.

from the actual loss of £611,748 (producing a damages award of £489,398) or whether it should be deducted from the capped sum of £500,000 (producing a damages award of £400,000).[385] Their Lordships, reversing the Court of Appeal, held that the percentage for contributory negligence should be deducted from the claimant's actual loss (described as the "basic loss") before the *SAAMCO* cap is applied. Thus, the 20 per cent deduction for contributory negligence was taken from the sum of £611,748, producing an award of £489,398. Since this sum was below the cap of £500,000, the claimants recovered £489,398. If the cap had been, say, £450,000 then that would have been the limit of the defendant's liability. As Lord Hobhouse emphasised, the *SAAMCO* cap is not concerned with causation. It does not ask what loss was actually caused by the defendant's negligence, rather, it limits the damages payable to that loss falling within the scope of the defendant's duty of care. The claimant must, of course, still prove that the actual damage sustained was caused by the defendant's negligence. If the actual damage is less than the cap, the claimant recovers in full. If it exceeds the cap, the damages are limited to the cap. Apportionment under s.1 of the Law Reform (Contributory Negligence) Act 1945 is concerned with the claimant's share of responsibility for the *actual damage* sustained (the "basic loss"),[386] taking into account both causation and fault. The artificial *SAAMCO* cap only comes into play after that calculation has been made.[387]

4. Consent and Assumption of Risk

(a) Consent

Consent and liability "One who has invited or assented to an act being done towards him cannot, when he suffers from it, complain of it as a wrong."[388] Consent, on the part of the claimant, negativing liability in tort may take two forms: 3-104

(1) The claimant may authorise the doing of the act which would otherwise constitute an invasion of his interest. For example, a landowner invites archaeologists to dig on his land or a patient consents to surgery. It is arguable that those who engage in contact sports also impliedly authorise those contacts which are a legitimate part of the game (e.g. a footballer implicitly agrees to any legitimate tackle in the course of the game).

(2) The claimant may consent to assume the risk of a tort being committed (e.g.

[385] The claimants' alternative argument that contributory negligence should be confined to the negligence attributable to the failure to check the loan application form, on the basis that their imprudent lending policy related to matters outside the scope of the duty of care owed by the valuers and was therefore not relevant to the loss caused by the valuer's breach of duty, was rejected both by the Court of Appeal and the House of Lords.

[386] [2000] 2 A.C. 190 at 212. Lord Hobhouse's approach is based on the wording of s.1(1) of the Act; see para.3-58. The same approach is taken where damages are limited by a contractual cap, i.e. the deduction for contributory negligence is made before the cap is applied: *Natixis SA v Marex Financial Ltd* [2019] EWHC 3163 (Comm).

[387] Producing the apparently odd conclusion that the claimants, having been found 20 per cent contributorily negligent, received only £10,600 (or 2.1 per cent) less than they would have received if they had not been negligent (in the absence of contributory negligence they would have received £500,000, the cap). The situation might be different where the lender's contributory negligence has contributed directly to the valuer's over-valuation; then the deduction for contributory negligence might be applied to the amount of the overvaluation as well as the overall loss: [2000] 2 A.C. 190 at 215, per Lord Millett. For further discussion see Dugdale (1999) 15 P.N. 164; and Murdoch "Client negligence: a lost cause?" (2004) 20 P.N. 97.

[388] *Smith v Baker* [1891] A.C. 325 at 300, per Lord Herschell.

a passenger on a drunken spree in a light aircraft assumes the risk of disaster).[389]

The classic term volenti non fit injuria ("no wrong is done to one who consents") is sometimes used to cover both types of case, but its application in negligence and related torts is problematic. There is a distinction between the intentional torts where it is appropriate to talk in terms of the defence of consent, and negligence where volenti non fit injuria is more appropriate. For example, a claimant can consent to an invasion of his personal integrity through, say, participation in a contact sport, but he does not thereby agree to accept the risk of negligently inflicted damage during the course of the game. A patient can consent to surgery, but she does not thereby assume the risk of the operation being performed negligently. The requirements for a successful plea of volenti non fit injuria are significantly more stringent[390] than, for example, a simple consent to physical contact (whether socially, or in a sporting or medical context).

3-105 **Consent and the intentional torts** The interest protected in many of the intentional torts consists of a right of control, of an individual's person, liberty, goods or land.[391] If the claimant invites a kiss or steps into a helicopter he cannot complain of battery or false imprisonment. In trespass to the person it has been said that the onus is on the claimant to prove the absence of consent,[392] because physical contact with another is only tortious if imposed against a person's will. This appears to be inconsistent, however, with the weight of authority which regards consent as a defence,[393] and as a general rule the burden of proving a discrete defence rests with the defendant. Moreover, it is submitted that on principle the presumption should be that a person does object to physical contact unless it is consented to. Conceptually, within the intentional torts few difficulties arise.

---

389 See *Morris v Murray* [1991] 2 Q.B. 6 CA; para.3-119.

390 See para.3-108.

391 It may be more usual in the case of consent to entry on land to speak of giving leave or licence to enter; see para.18-32. In *Arthur v Anker* [1997] Q.B. 564, the Court of Appeal held that the trespass to goods inherent in wheel-clamping could, in appropriate conditions, be justified by a defence of consent or volenti. Where a motorist parked his vehicle on clearly marked private land in defiance of a notice indicating that unauthorised vehicles would be clamped, he was found voluntarily to have accepted both the risk that his vehicle would be clamped and the risk that it would not be released unless he paid a reasonable charge. An exorbitant charge or delay in releasing the vehicle after the motorist had indicated a willingness to pay would exceed the boundaries of any implied consent and render further detention of the vehicle tortious. In *Vine v Waltham Forest LBC* [2000] 1 W.L.R. 2383 the Court of Appeal held that a wheel-clamper must prove that the car driver saw and understood the significance of a notice warning that parked cars would be clamped. Note that the Protection of Freedoms Act 2012 s.54 makes wheel-clamping a criminal offence in some circumstances, and the express or implied consent to the wheel-clamping of a person entitled to remove the vehicle does not render the wheel-clamping lawful for the purposes of the offence.

392 *Freeman v Home Office (No.2)* [1984] Q.B. 524 at 539.

393 See *Collins v Wilcock* [1984] 1 W.L.R. 1172 at 1177 where Goff LJ referred to consent as a defence; see also *R. v Brown* [1994] 1 A.C. 212 at 246–247; *T v T* [1988] Fam. 52 at 66; *Wilson v Pringle* [1987] Q.B. 237 at 252, per Croom-Johnson LJ; *Re F (Mental Patient: Sterilisation)* [1990] 2 A.C. 1 at 29, per Neill LJ. It would seem that consent is regarded as a defence in both Canada (*Hambly v Shepley* (1967) 63 D.L.R. (2d) 94 at 95, Ontario CA; *Reibl v Hughes* (1980) 114 D.L.R. (3d) 1 at 9, Supreme Court of Canada) and Australia (*Secretary, Department of Health and Community Services v JWB* (1992) 106 A.L.R. 385 at 453, per McHugh J, High Court of Australia). In *Ashley v Chief Constable of Sussex* [2006] EWCA Civ 1085; [2007] 1 W.L.R. 398 at [31] Sir Anthony Clarke MR commented that it is "open to debate whether McCowan J's conclusion [in *Freeman v Home Office (No.2)*] on burden of proof is correct", though whatever the position in the context of consent, the burden of proving self-defence was the defendant's.

Consent, if present, negatives liability. What must be established is that it was a consent freely given[394] and applied to the conduct of which the claimant now complains.[395]

Consent and medical procedures Surgery and any other medical procedure involving physical contact with the patient constitutes a battery unless authorised by the patient or justifiable on grounds of lawful necessity. Consent and medical treatment is dealt with in Ch.9.[396] The patient's consent only authorises the relevant "touching" by the doctor; it does not relieve him of his duty of care in negligence. In particular while consent may insulate the doctor from a claim in trespass to the person,[397] he may still be held negligent if he fails to give the patient adequate advice about whether or not to agree to that specific procedure.[398] 3-106

Consent and crime When a tortious act is simultaneously criminal, questions may arise about the effect of any consent to the crime. The House of Lords in *R. v Brown*[399] has confirmed that the victim's consent cannot constitute a good defence in criminal proceedings where an assault: (a) results in bodily harm which is more than merely trifling or transient; and (b) is not justified by some "good reason". Mutual sexual gratification among adult sadomasochists does not come within the category of "good reason". Surgical operations and lawful contact sports are given as examples of occasions where ascertainable bodily harm is justifiable; but does it follow that if for the purposes of the criminal law, the victim's consent is irrelevant, that is also the case in tort? Could one sado-masochist subsequently sue another in battery? Could a patient who voluntarily participated in an unlawful operation[400] later sue the surgeon? There is no clear authority on the point. *Murphy v Culhane*[401] suggests a participant in a criminal affray may nonetheless be answered with a plea of volenti. Perhaps the correct answer lies in the relationship between the defences of volenti and ex turpi causa. There is no obvious reason why the criminality of the defendant's conduct should prevent him relying on the consent of the claimant as a defence.[402] The question is whether as a matter of public policy 3-107

---

394 Submission is not the same as consent, and so an apparent consent is not genuine where it has been overridden by psychological coercion: *London Borough of Haringey v FZO* [2020] EWCA Civ 180; [2020] E.L.R. 232 at [126]–[129], per McCombe LJ (apparent consent to sexual relationship not true consent in law where derived from grooming and abuse when claimant was a minor).

395 The proper boundaries of consent and the intentional torts to the person are explored at paras 14-93 to 14-99.

396 See paras 9-53 to 9-72.

397 *Chatterton v Gerson* [1981] Q.B. 432. Provided that the consent obtained relates to the particular procedure performed. For example, does consent to the administration of a general anaesthetic constitute consent to an epidural anaesthetic? See *Davis v Barking, Havering and Brentwood HA* [1993] 4 Med. L.R. 85.

398 *Montgomery v Lanarkshire Health Board* [2015] UKSC 11; [2015] A.C. 1430; see paras 7-199 and 9-86. See also para.2-15 onwards for the causation issues that arise in these cases.

399 [1994] 1 A.C. 212; *R. v Coney* (1882) 8 Q.B.D. 534; *Bravery v Bravery* [1954] 1 W.L.R. 1169; *R. v Donovan* [1934] 2 K.B. 498. *R. v Brown* was distinguished in *R. v Wilson* [1997] Q.B. 47. See also Law Commission Consultation Paper No.139, *Consent in the Criminal Law* (1995).

400 e.g. if a kidney were sold contrary to the Human Tissue Act 2004 s.32 or 33.

401 [1977] Q.B. 94.

402 Providing that the defendant's conduct does not exceed the ambit of the consent given by the claimant so that in a fist fight the defendant's blow is not out of all proportion to the claimant's assault.

the claimant who chose to participate in criminal conduct should be allowed to make a claim in tort at all.[403]

(b) Volenti non fit injuria

3-108 **The meaning of volenti** Volenti non fit injuria is a voluntary agreement by the claimant to absolve the defendant from the legal consequences of an unreasonable risk of harm created by the defendant, where the claimant has full knowledge of both the nature and extent of the risk.[404] When it applies it is a complete defence; the claimant recovers nothing. On this basis there are at least three requirements for the defence to apply:

(1) agreement by the claimant to absolve the defendant from legal responsibility for his conduct;
(2) this agreement must be voluntary, not due to compulsion by the defendant or external circumstances; and
(3) the claimant should have full knowledge of the nature and extent of the risk it is alleged that he has assumed.

A strict insistence on these requirements would mean that the defence should rarely succeed, and indeed it is invoked less frequently than it once was, partly because the Law Reform (Contributory Negligence) Act 1945 allows the court to achieve what is arguably a fairer outcome by apportioning responsibility in cases of contributory negligence (and there can be a significant overlap between conduct that might be classified as volenti and contributory negligence). The decline of volenti is also partly attributable to changing social values and the perception that conduct which in a previous age would have fallen under the umbrella of a robust doctrine of individual responsibility is not necessarily undertaken voluntarily.[405]

3-109 **Assuming the risk of injury?** The volenti defence is sometimes referred to as "voluntary assumption of risk" though this phrase can lead to some conceptual confusion in those situations where the law effectively places the risk of harm on the individual who sustains it. For example, a spectator at a sporting event who is injured when the ball is knocked out of the playing area into the crowd will not normally be entitled to claim damages for negligence, but this will be because there was no negligence on the part of the player, i.e. no breach of a duty of care (e.g. in the case of a batsmen at cricket who hits a six).[406] It has been said that in this situation the spectator has "assumed the risk of injury", presumably by voluntarily be-

---

403 See para.3-02 onwards.

404 "If the defendants desire to succeed on the ground that the maxim *volenti non fit injuria* is applicable, they must obtain a finding that the claimant freely and voluntarily, with full knowledge of the nature and extent of the risk he ran, impliedly agreed to incur it": *Letang v Ottawa Electric Ry Co* [1926] A.C. 725 at 731.

405 In the 19th century volenti non fit injuria, together with contributory negligence and the doctrine of "common employment" formed the "unholy trinity" of defences, which all but prevented any claim by employees for injuries sustained at work. In *Smith v Baker* [1891] A.C. 325, the House of Lords finally recognised that a worker who remained in his job despite being aware of unsafe working practices did not necessarily do so voluntarily when the options were to work or starve.

406 See, e.g. *Wooldridge v Sumner* [1963] 2 Q.B. 43 in which a spectator was injured when a horse crashed through a rope barrier during a show-jumping competition. Diplock LJ rejected a plea of volenti. "Consent" on the part of the spectator was irrelevant. Nonetheless, the action failed because the defendant was not negligent. His duty was to abide by the rules of the competition and not to exhibit flagrant disregard for the safety of spectators.

ing present at the game. This is an inappropriate use of the term assumption of risk. The defendant is not liable in this situation because he was not negligent, and the claimant has "assumed the risk" only in the sense that the law deems that everyone "assumes" the risk of non-negligently inflicted injury. The harm lies where it falls. One might as well say that by going on to a public road members of the public assume the risk of not being entitled to recover damages for injuries which cannot be proved to have been caused by someone else's negligence. But this is simply a way of saying that there is no liability without fault and that life occasionally involves a risk of injury. For example, in *Tomlinson v Congleton BC*[407] the House of Lords held that a local authority was not liable for the claimant's injuries when he dived into shallow water at the edge of a lake and struck his head on the bottom. The authority had prohibited swimming in the lake and put up notices warning of the danger. Although the defence of volenti was not raised, their Lordships stressed that in considering what precautions it was reasonable for an occupier to take under the Occupiers' Liability Acts 1957 and 1984, the court should have regard to the ordinary risks of life which individuals could be expected to encounter as result of their own activities. So, Lord Hoffmann commented that "it will be extremely rare for an occupier of land to be under a duty to prevent people from taking risks which are inherent in the activities they freely choose to undertake upon the land. If people want to climb mountains, go hang gliding, or swim or dive in ponds or lakes, that is their affair."[408] In *Geary v Wetherspoon Plc*[409] the claimant fell whilst attempting to slide down a banister. Coulson J concluded that she had voluntarily assumed the risk because she "freely chose to do something which she knew to be dangerous. … She knew that sliding down the banisters was not permitted, but she chose to do it anyway. She was therefore the author of her own misfortune. The defendant owed no duty to protect her from such an obvious and inherent risk. She made a genuine and informed choice and the risk that she chose to run materialised with tragic consequences."[410]

(i) Claimant's agreement

Further conceptual confusion stems from the notion of the claimant's *agreement* to accept the risk, which can be express or implied and has been held to be possible both before the relevant act of negligence and after the defendant's negligence has occurred. Apart from the difficulty of deciding, on any given set of facts, whether an implied agreement can be inferred from the claimant's conduct before the act of negligence (where at least there must have been some sort of interaction between claimant and defendant), finding an implied agreement to absolve the defendant from the legal consequences of his negligence after the negligent conduct has occurred is highly problematic. This tends to be done in circumstances where the negligence has created a risk of harm, and the claimant, **3-110**

---

407 [2003] UKHL 47; [2004] 1 A.C. 46.

408 [2003] UKHL 47; [2004] 1 A.C. 46 at [45]. On the other hand, where an occupier is in breach of a mandatory requirement of the criminal law the approach adopted in *Tomlinson* may not apply, possibly on the basis that there is no genuine and informed choice to run the risk by the claimant or on the basis that there should not have been an available choice, given the requirements of the criminal law: *James v White Lion Hotel* [2020] P.I.Q.R. P10 at [97].

409 [2011] EWHC 1506 (QB); [2011] N.P.C. 60.

410 [2011] EWHC 1506 (QB); [2011] N.P.C. 60 at [46]. See also *Schuller v S.J. Webb Nominees Pty Ltd* [2015] SASCFC 162; (2015) 124 S.A.S.R. 152 (drunken customer in a bar who fell whilst dancing on a chair held to have assumed the risk of injury).

realising that there is a risk, nonetheless proceeds to encounter that risk, suffering injury as result. Two problems arise. First, it is very likely that the "implied agreement" is simply a legal fiction.[411] Whereas it may be reasonable to infer an implied agreement between the parties where there is some course of dealing between them, as for example if they have been on a drinking spree and then jointly engaged in a dangerous activity,[412] there is no obvious basis for suggesting that a person who merely encounters and then proceeds to run a particular risk has thereby agreed to waive any claim against the person who negligently created that risk. Secondly, it is unclear why the court would want to invoke such a fiction, when there are other, arguably more logical, conceptual tools available to deal with such cases. Someone who takes an unreasonable risk is guilty of negligence, just as someone who creates an unreasonable risk is guilty of negligence. In those circumstances, apportioning the damages for contributory negligence may be the appropriate response, or in an extreme case it may be held that the claimant's negligence constitutes a novus actus interveniens, breaking the causal link.[413]

3-111 **Agreement to waive the claim** Some of these difficulties stem from different conceptions of the volenti defence, by different judges. In *Nettleship v Weston*,[414] Lord Denning expressed the doctrine as operating as follows:

> "Now that contributory negligence is not a complete defence, but only a ground for reducing the damages, the defence of *volenti non fit injuria* has been closely considered and in consequence, it has been severely limited. Knowledge of the risk of injury is not enough. Nor is a willingness to take the risk of injury. Nothing will suffice short of an agreement to waive any claim for negligence. *The [claimant] must agree, expressly or impliedly to waive any claim for any injury that may befall him due to the lack of reasonable care by the defendant*."

On this approach there must be an agreement of some kind, express or implied, *before* the relevant act of negligence by the defendant occurs. The claimant's decision to run a known risk which has already been created by the defendant's negligence could not constitute volenti. Similarly, in *Wooldridge v Sumner*[415] Diplock LJ said that: "The consent that is relevant is not consent to risk of injury but consent to the lack of reasonable care that may produce that risk." The claimant could not have agreed to run the risk that the defendant might be negligent because the claimant would only play his part after the defendant had been negligent.[416] In *Nettleship v Weston*, itself the defendant was a learner-driver receiving instruction from the claimant, a friend. He had specifically asked about her

---

411 See Jaffey [1985] C.L.J. 87 at 91.

412 See, e.g. *Morris v Murray* [1991] 2 Q.B. 6.

413 See para.2-110. Note that there are also other conceptual tools which the court can invoke to express the idea that an individual should take responsibility for his or her own actions, where the claimant is effectively the author of his own misfortune. See, e.g. *Barrett v Ministry of Defence* [1995] 1 W.L.R. 1217 where the Court of Appeal held that the defendants did not owe a duty of care to prevent a naval airman from consuming an excessive amount of alcohol, since it was fair, just and reasonable for the law to leave a responsible adult to assume responsibility for his own actions in consuming alcoholic drink.

414 [1971] 2 Q.B. 691 at 701 (emphasis added).

415 [1963] 2 Q.B. 43 at 69.

416 [1963] 2 Q.B. 43 at 69–70. Note also Diplock LJ's eminently logical comment that "if the consent precedes the act of negligence, the [claimant] cannot at that time have full knowledge of the extent as well as the nature of the risk which he will run". The claimant in *Wooldridge* was a photographer at a horse show who was knocked over when a horse being ridden in a competition got out of control.

insurance cover. In her third lesson the defendant's negligence resulted in an accident injuring the claimant's knee. Her plea of volenti failed. There was no evidence that the defendant had agreed to waive any right of action or to absolve the claimant from legal responsibility for her conduct, indeed quite the contrary since the claimant had enquired about the defendant's insurance cover before getting into the car. However, Lord Denning suggested that had the claimant been a professional instructor the result might well have been different, on the basis that, even if there was no express contract between the parties, it might in those circumstances be reasonable to infer an agreement that the professional would assume the risk of his pupil's inexperience, absolve her from responsibility and carry his own insurance cover.[417] It is not clear, however, why professional driving instructors should be deemed to accept a risk of injury from the inexperienced motorist, any more than any other road user who "knows" that at least some drivers are inexperienced, drunk, incompetent etc. On what evidence would this deemed agreement be based, and what social policy would it serve to exclude a particular category of claimants merely on the basis of their profession?[418]

Express and implied antecedent agreement For volenti to apply in the case of an antecedent "agreement", there must at least be some sort of relationship between the parties. A stranger could not be deemed to have agreed to run the risk merely because he knows that the defendant has a propensity to act negligently.[419] Even where there is such a relationship, the claimant's mere knowledge that the defendant is likely to act negligently is not sufficient to imply an agreement.[420] Where the agreement is express, whether as a contractual term or by notice,[421] then it is operating as an exclusion of liability which should fall within s.2 of the Unfair Contract Terms Act 1977 or s.57, 62 or 65 of the Consumer Rights Act 2015.[422] The courts have been willing to derive an implied agreement that the defendant shall not be liable for future negligence, from the parties' conduct, usually in cases involving either excessive consumption of alcohol or criminal behaviour, and sometimes both.[423] There is, however, a curious problem with the notion that the parties can impliedly agree to achieve a result when statute bars express agreement to achieve the very same result. If an express contract term or notice is subject to the Unfair Contract Terms Act 1977 or the Consumer Rights Act 2015 then why should an implied agreement avoid the Act?[424] 3-112

"Agreement" after the defendant's breach of duty Volenti, explained in terms 3-113

---

417 [1971] 2 Q.B. 691 at 702.

418 See now the Road Traffic Act 1988 s.149; para.3-125. On the other hand, see *Imperial Chemical Insurance v Shatwell* [1965] A.C. 656; para.3-129, where it was arguable that there was a relationship between the parties in which they effectively, though no doubt without thinking about the legal implications, agreed to run a risk together.

419 See the example of Mellish LJ in *Woodley v Metropolitan District Ry Co* (1877) 2 Ex. D. 384 at 394.

420 Thus, the fact that a passenger in a vehicle driven by the defendant knows that the defendant has driven negligently in the past does not make him volens to future acts of negligence by the driver: *Morris v Murray* [1991] 2 Q.B. 6 at 13.

421 See, e.g. *Bennett v Tugwell* [1971] 2 Q.B. 267; *Arthur v Anker* [1997] Q.B. 564 CA.

422 See *Johnstone v Bloomsbury HA* [1992] 1 Q.B. 333, where the Court of Appeal accepted the possibility that a contractual term which expressly raised the defence of volenti might fall within s.2(1) of the Unfair Contract Terms Act 1977.

423 See *Morris v Murray* [1991] 2 Q.B. 6; *Ashton v Turner* [1981] Q.B. 137; *Pitts v Hunt* [1991] 1 Q.B. 24, where the Court of Appeal would have applied volenti but for the effect of the Road Traffic Act 1988 s.149.

424 In *Pitts v Hunt* [1991] 1 Q.B. 24, the Court of Appeal held that the Road Traffic Act 1988 s.149 bar-

of an implied agreement to absolve the defendant of responsibility for a breach of duty, relies all too often on an artificial construction of such an agreement with hindsight. The workmen in *Shatwell* probably gave no thought to such matters, though they knew that there was a serious risk of physical injury and the process of identifying an implied agreement between them at least had some basis in fact. The mere fact that the claimant clearly appreciated the risk and was willing to take it should not in itself be a basis for inferring an agreement.[425] Indeed, in *Wooldridge v Sumner*,[426] Diplock LJ went so far as to say that in the absence of an express contract volenti has no application to negligence simpliciter.[427] If it is difficult to establish volenti from an implied antecedent agreement, it should be virtually impossible to establish where the defendant's negligence has already created a dangerous state of affairs and the claimant has simply proceeded to encounter the risk, at least if the defence is based on agreement. There are, however, some cases which suggest that volenti applies where the claimant merely encounters an existing danger created by the defendant's negligence in circumstances where there was no direct communication between the parties,[428] a view which appears to be supported by certain statutory provisions.[429] The fact that the claimant was aware of and nonetheless ran the risk should not, of itself, be sufficient to establish volenti, particularly where it is reasonable for him to do so.[430] Knowledge of a risk is not consent. The problem remains, however, that if the claimant has acted unreasonably in taking a known risk, why is his conduct not merely contributory negligence? A defendant who takes an unreasonable risk is simply negligent, so why not a claimant? And how is the distinction to be drawn between claimants who are negligent and those who are volenti?

3-114 **Another approach?** There is a suggestion in some of the cases that volenti may operate in a different manner by limiting the scope of the defendant's duty of care.[431] Thus, in *Nettleship v Weston*[432] Salmon LJ, in a dissenting judgment, suggested that a passenger who accepted a lift in a vehicle knowing the driver to be too drunk to drive safely could not expect the driver to drive other than dangerously. Since the

ring reliance on the volenti defence in the case of road traffic accidents applied to all forms of volenti, express and implied.

425 *Lynch v Ministry of Defence* [1983] N.I. 216 at 237; *Waldick v Malcolm* (1991) 83 D.L.R. (4th) 114 (Supreme Court of Canada)—volenti requires not merely knowledge of the physical risk but consent to the legal risk, i.e. a waiver of legal rights that may arise from the harm that is being risked.

426 [1963] 2 Q.B. 43 at 69.

427 See, however, an explanation of this comment in *Morris v Murray* [1991] 2 Q.B. 6 at 13–14 and 22–23.

428 See, e.g. *Titchener v British Railways Board* [1983] 1 W.L.R. 1427; *Dann v Hamilton* [1939] 1 K.B. 509 at 517.

429 Such as the Occupiers' Liability Act 1957 s.2(5), the Unfair Contract Terms Act 1977 s.2(3), and the Consumer Rights Act 2015 s.65(2), which assume that volenti is available in circumstances not amounting to an agreement, since other subsections deal with the case of agreement between the parties, namely s.2(1) of the Occupiers' Liability Act 1957, s.2(1) (2) of the Unfair Contract Terms Act 1977, and ss.57(1), 62(1) and 65(1) of the Consumer Rights Act 2015; see Jaffey [1985] C.L.J. 87, 93–95.

430 See, e.g. *Clayards v Dethick* (1848) 12 Q.B. 439.

431 See the 17th edn of this work, para.3-44.

432 [1971] 2 Q.B. 691. In *Cook v Cook* (1968) 68 A.L.R. 353 the High Court of Australia applied a lower standard of care where a passenger knew that the driver was a learner, But *Cook v Cook* has now been overruled in *Imbree v McNeilly* [2008] HCA 40; (2008) 236 C.L.R. 510; (2008) 248 A.L.R. 647 (the standard of care to be expected of an inexperienced learner driver is the same as that owed by any other person driving a motor vehicle, namely to take reasonable care to avoid injury to others).

duty of care springs from the relationship between claimant and defendant, the very nature of the relationship created precludes any duty on the part of the driver to drive with ordinary care. In *Morris v Murray*,[433] Fox LJ doubted whether in practice the gap between the concept of implied waiver of claim and the "no duty" approach was "a very wide one".[434] In that case the Court of Appeal declined to enter into theoretical debate on the nature of volenti and suggested that whichever approach is applied the criteria for judging whether the claimant is volenti and so fails in his claim are the same. Although this may simply be a matter of using different language or analysis to achieve the same result, it is submitted that it is preferable to keep the conceptual analysis both clear and consistent. A defendant who undertakes a task which creates the risk of physical injury to others will normally be held to owe a duty to exercise reasonable care not to inflict that harm. The duty derives from the defendant's conduct in undertaking to perform the task which carries a foreseeable risk of harm. It does not derive from what the potential victims may or may not do. Their conduct will be reflected in the defences available to an action. It is simply not helpful to conceive of a duty of care which varies according to the claimant's reaction to the risk created by an *ex hypothesi* negligent defendant.

(ii) Agreement must be voluntary

The claimant: **3-115**

> "cannot be said to be truly 'willing' unless he is in a position to choose freely, and freedom of choice predicates, not only full knowledge of the circumstances on which the exercise of choice is conditional, so that he may be able to choose wisely, but the absence of any feeling of constraint so that nothing shall interfere with the freedom of his will."[435]

If the relationship between the claimant and defendant is such that doubt must exist as to whether the claimant can truly voluntarily decide whether or not to assume a risk of danger created by the defendant, volenti cannot apply. So where a workman was instructed to take out a temperamental horse and only reluctantly agreed to do so, he was found not to be volens to injuries sustained when the horse threw him off the cart.[436] He had no real chance to say no, for to do so might have risked his job. The absence of real choice in most instances means that only very exceptionally will volenti be available to an employer against an employee.[437] The element of compulsion need not come from the defendant, and so an employee who has been instructed by his employer to enter the defendant's premises is not volens to the risks he encounters there.[438]

The requirement that the choice be real also means that the claimant must have the requisite mental capacity to make a choice. In *Kirkham v Chief Constable for Greater Manchester Police*,[439] the deceased's husband, who was mentally ill and had made previous attempts at suicide, committed suicide in prison. The police were **3-116**

---

433 [1991] 2 Q.B. 6.

434 [1991] 2 Q.B. 6 at 15; and see *Condon v Basi* [1985] 1 W.L.R. 866 at 868.

435 *Bowater v Rowley Regis BC* [1944] K.B. 476 at 479, per Scott LJ; *Imperial Chemical Industries v Shatwell* [1965] A.C. 656 at 681–682, per Lord Hodson.

436 *Bowater v Rowley Regis BC* [1944] K.B. 476.

437 See further at para.3-126.

438 *Burnett v British Waterways Board* [1973] 1 W.L.R. 700.

439 [1990] 2 Q.B. 283.

found to be negligent in not passing on crucial information about the man's mental disturbance to the prison authorities. They pleaded volenti. The Court of Appeal held that, while an act of suicide or attempted suicide by a person of sound mind might constitute the defence of volenti, this would not be the case where someone's judgment was impaired by mental illness because he was deprived of the ability to make a real choice.[440] It does not follow, however, that a person who does have the capacity to choose will be held to be volenti. *Reeves v Commissioner of Police for the Metropolis*[441] also involved the suicide of a prisoner who was a known suicide risk, but he was not found to be mentally ill. The House of Lords held that the defence of volenti did not apply where the claimant's act is the very thing that the defendant was under a duty to take reasonable precautions to prevent, irrespective of the suicide's mental state. The duty of care arose because the deceased was incarcerated and was a known suicide risk, not because of his mental state, and so it would be strange to draw a distinction between different mental states when applying the volenti defence. Moreover, if the suicide of a sane person exempted the police from liability that could be achieved by holding that there was no duty of care owed to a sane person in such circumstances. To say that there is a duty and then to hold that there was no liability because the very act that the duty was intended to prevent results in the defence of volenti was effectively the same as saying that there was no duty, and yet the defendant conceded that he owed a duty of care in the circumstances. Thus, the distinction drawn in *Kirkham* between a claimant of sound and unsound mind was irrelevant. Once the court concluded, or the defendant conceded (as in *Reeves*), that the defendant was under a duty of care to take reasonable steps to prevent a suicide attempt the volenti defence could not apply.

(iii) Claimant's knowledge

3-117 **Knowledge of danger** Obviously, if it is alleged that the claimant bore responsibility for his own injuries, it must be shown that he was fully aware of the relevant danger and consequent risk.[442] Knowledge of danger on the part of the claimant will sometimes absolve the defendant from liability without resort to volenti, or at any rate any notion of volenti based on an agreement to waive liability. For example, under the Occupiers' Liability Act 1957 a warning of a danger on the premises sufficient to enable the visitor to be reasonably safe discharges the occupier's common duty of care.[443] This is not because the visitor exempts the occupier from responsibility towards him, or voluntarily accepts the risk, but because the occupier has fulfilled his duty to him by measures sufficient to protect him from injury during his visit. Moreover, there is no duty to warn an adult of an obvious risk of which any adult would be aware in circumstances where he is free to take

---

[440] See also the discussion of the relevance of the deceased's mental state in *Corr v IBC Vehicles Ltd* [2006] EWCA Civ 331; [2007] Q.B. 46, where the deceased committed suicide, having developed clinical depression after an accident at work. The House of Lords affirmed the decision of the Court of Appeal in *Corr*: [2008] UKHL 13; [2008] 1 A.C. 884. Only Lord Bingham's speech touched upon the volenti defence, which was rejected as having "no independent validity" given that the deceased's suicide was not something to which he had "consented voluntarily and with his eyes open but an act performed because of the psychological condition which the employer's breach of duty had induced" (at [18]).

[441] [2000] 1 A.C. 360 HL.

[442] *Letang v Ottawa Ry* [1926] A.C. 725 at 731; *ICI Ltd v Shatwell* [1965] A.C. 656.

[443] See paras 11-40 to 11-41; and see *Gledhill v Liverpool Abattoir Utility Co Ltd* [1957] 1 W.L.R. 1028; *Hurley v Dyke* [1979] R.T.R. 265.

appropriate precautions for his own safety.[444] In this situation there tends to be an overlap of the language of breach of duty and volenti, though strictly if the defendant is not in breach of duty there is no need for a defence of volenti.

Knowledge must be full and complete The general rule in volenti requires that the defendant demonstrate that the claimant had full knowledge of the nature and extent of the risk which he is alleged to have assumed.[445] It is not enough to show danger was apparent or that in a general sense the claimant was aware of the risk. In *Sterner v Lawson*,[446] the defendant loaned his powerful motorcycle to the 17-year-old claimant. He gave the youth only brief instructions about how to handle the machine. The claimant's inexperience led to an accident in which he suffered injury. The Supreme Court of British Columbia rejected the defendant's plea of volenti, holding that the claimant was not aware of the precise dangers of the machine, only generally aware that he was embarking on a risky exercise. He was found 50 per cent contributorily negligent. 3-118

Objective or subjective knowledge? A difficult question arises where, objectively, the claimant ought to have been fully aware of the risks he ran, but on a subjective test the particular claimant was not so aware. In *Morris v Murray*,[447] the claimant agreed to go on a pleasure flight with a friend who had to his knowledge consumed the equivalent of 17 whiskies that afternoon. The claimant had also been drinking heavily. Any sober person would have been fully aware of the danger of the enterprise, but in the Court of Appeal the question arose as to whether the claimant's intoxication was so great that he could not be said to be aware of the nature and extent of the risk of going on a flight with a drunken pilot. Stocker LJ said[448] that he would not go so far as to say that the test was objective, rather the question was whether there was evidence that the claimant was so intoxicated that he was incapable of appreciating the nature of the risk and did not in fact appreciate it, and so did not consent to it. The court unanimously found that, on the particular facts, the claimant was aware of the risk. Even in his drunken state, the claimant should have appreciated the extreme danger. Commenting upon the claimant's statement in evidence that if he had been sober he would not have gone on the flight, Fox LJ said: 3-119

---

444 *Ratcliff v McConnell* [1999] 1 W.L.R. 670 CA (no liability to an adult trespasser who dived into the shallow end of a swimming pool at night); *Staples v West Dorset DC* (1995) 93 L.G.R. 536 (no liability to claimant who slipped on a sea wall covered in algae and visibly slippery); *Darby v National Trust* [2001] EWCA Civ 189; [2001] P.I.Q.R. P27 (no liability to a visitor who drowned while swimming in a pond where the risks were "perfectly obvious"); *Tomlinson v Congleton BC* [2003] UKHL 47; [2004] 1 A.C. 46 (no liability to claimant injured when diving into a shallow lake despite signs warning against the risk). Thus: "A duty to protect against obvious risks or self-inflicted harm exists only in cases in which there is no genuine and informed choice, or in the case of employees, or some lack of capacity, such as the inability of children to recognise danger …": [2003] UKHL 47 at [46], per Lord Hoffmann. See also *Donoghue v Folkestone Properties Ltd* [2003] EWCA Civ 231; [2003] Q.B. 1008; *Rhind v Astbury Water Park Ltd* [2004] EWCA Civ 756; [2004] N.P.C. 95; *Evans v Kosmar Villa Holidays Plc* [2007] EWCA Civ 1003; [2008] 1 W.L.R. 297; *Poppleton v Trustees of the Portsmouth Youth Activities Committee* [2008] EWCA Civ 646; [2009] P.I.Q.R. P1; *Maylin v Dacorum Sports Trust (t/a XC Sportspace)* [2017] EWHC 378 (QB); *Geary v Wetherspoon Plc* [2011] EWHC 1506 (QB); [2011] N.P.C. 60 (claimant who fell whilst attempting to slide down a banister had voluntarily assumed the risk).

445 See *Dann v Hamilton* [1939] 1 K.B. 509 at 518.

446 [1977] 5 W.W.R. 628.

447 [1991] 2 Q.B. 6 CA.

448 [1991] 2 Q.B. 6 CA at 29.

"That is no doubt so but it does not establish that he was in fact incapable of understanding what he was doing that afternoon. If he was capable of understanding what he was doing, then the fact is that he knowingly and willingly embarked on a flight with a drunken pilot."[449]

This leaves open the possibility that, if on the particular facts, the claimant can demonstrate that she was not capable, subjectively, of understanding the risk the volenti defence will fail, incidentally creating the paradox that Stocker LJ identified that the more intoxicated the claimant is, the more likely it is that he was incapable of appreciating the risk, so defeating the volenti defence.

3-120 Thus, it is arguable that constructive knowledge will not suffice for volenti. Where the claimant did not know, but ought reasonably to have known, of the risk he is not volens, though this could be relevant to contributory negligence.[450] The Animals Act 1971 s.5(2) allows for a defence of volenti as did the common law. A claimant whose illiteracy prevented him appreciating the warning "beware of the dog" was not barred from recovery at common law when he entered premises unaware and was attacked by the dog.[451] On the other hand, in *Cummings v Granger*[452] a woman who well knew that the defendant's yard was policed by a savage Alsatian was found to be volenti.

3-121 **Volenti not scienti** Even full and complete knowledge of danger is not of itself enough to sustain a plea of volens. The maxim is volenti not scienti non fit injuria.[453] In *Bowater v Rowley Regis Corp*,[454] the claimant was fully aware of the danger posed by the temperamental horse. He knew that if he did take the horse out he risked injury. He was not volens because he did not consent that that risk should be his responsibility alone. A plea of volens requires evidence the claimant agreed, or understood, that the defendant was absolved from responsibility to protect his (the claimant's) interest.

(iv) Statutory defence of consent

3-122 Where statute expressly imposes a duty sounding in tort the Act may also provide specific defences, one of which can be consent. Thus, the Animals Act 1971 imposes strict liability for damage caused by an animal belonging to a dangerous species and, in some situations, damage caused by an animal belonging to a non-dangerous species. Section 5(2) provides that: "A person is not liable under section 2 of this Act for any damage suffered by a person who has voluntarily accepted the risk thereof." In *Cummings v Granger*[455] Ormrod LJ suggested that these words should be given their ordinary English meaning and not be complicated by the "old, long history of the doctrine of volenti. That doctrine was developed in

---

449 [1991] 2 Q.B. 6 CA at 16.

450 *Dixon v King* [1975] 2 N.Z.L.R. 357.

451 *Sarch v Blackburn* (1830) 4 C. & P. 297.

452 [1977] Q.B. 397; and see para.20-16 and para.29-21.

453 *Smith v Baker* [1891] A.C. 325; *Thomas v Quatermaine* (1887) 18 Q.B.D. 685 at 696, per Bowen LJ; *Wooldridge v Sumner* [1963] 2 Q.B. 43 at 69–70, per Diplock LJ; *Nettleship v Weston* [1971] 2 Q.B. 691 at 701, per Lord Denning MR; cf. Congenital Disabilities (Civil Liability) Act 1976 s.1(4), providing that the parents' knowledge of the risk of disability due to an occurrence which occurred prior to conception defeats the child's claim.

454 [1944] K.B. 476 CA; see para.3-111.

455 [1977] Q.B. 397 at 408, and see para.20-16 and para.29-21.

quite different conditions. It has nothing to do with strict liability; and I would not like to see that defence whittled down by too fine distinctions as to what 'voluntarily accepted the risk' means." This might indicate that a statutory defence of "consent" is somehow different from volenti at common law, and that the strict requirements of volenti do not apply to a statutory defence of consent. There are some statutes, however, where the legislation expressly preserves the common law defence.[456]

(v) *Vehicle accidents*

Drunken drivers In *Dann v Hamilton*,[457] the claimant accepted a lift in a car with a driver whom she knew to be drunk. She suffered injuries in a collision caused by the driver's negligence. The defendant's plea of volenti failed. Asquith J doubted whether volenti could ever apply where the consent of the claimant was relied on to absolve the defendant of liability for a subsequent act of negligence. He would have restricted the maxim to cases "where a dangerous physical condition has been brought about by the negligence of the defendant, and, after it has arisen, the [claimant], fully appreciating its dangerous character, elects to assume the risk thereof".[458] The ratio of *Dann v Hamilton* is more limited in scope. He found that in that case "the [claimant], by embarking in the car … with knowledge that through drink the driver had materially reduced his capacity for driving safely, did not impliedly consent to, or absolve the driver from liability for any subsequent negligence on his part whereby she might suffer harm".[459] Asquith J did suggest that the result might be different in cases of extreme inebriation, where the drunkenness of the driver was so extreme and so glaring that accepting a lift was equivalent to "engaging in an intrinsically and obviously dangerous occupation, intermeddling with an unexploded bomb or walking on the edge of an unfenced cliff".[460] But from 1939 to 1990, the general assumption in England[461] was that knowledge that the defendant was drunk might lead to a plea of contributory negligence[462] but would not constitute the defence of volenti. 3-123

Doubt was first cast on *Dann v Hamilton* in *Pitts v Hunt*.[463] The claimant was a pillion passenger on a motorcycle ridden by the defendant. After hours of drinking together the claimant egged the defendant on to a "reckless, irresponsible and idiotic" journey ending in a disastrous accident. The Court of Appeal held that, were it not for the fact that s.148(3) of the Road Traffic Act 1972 (predecessor to s.149 of the 1988 Act) barred such a plea, they would have regarded the claimant's claim as defeated by volenti. A defence of volenti based on knowledge of the defendant's 3-124

---

456 See the Occupiers' Liability Act 1957 s.2(5) and the Occupiers' Liability Act 1984 s.1(6) which provide that no duty is owed to entrants in respect of "risks willingly accepted" by the entrant, with the question whether the risk was so accepted to be decided on "the same principles as in other cases in which one person owes a duty of care to another".

457 [1939] 1 K.B. 509; and see *Ashton v Turner* [1981] Q.B. 137.

458 [1939] 1 K.B. 509 at 517.

459 [1939] 1 K.B. 509 at 518; approved in *Slater v Clay Cross Co Ltd* [1956] 2 Q.B. 264 CA; and *Nettleship v Weston* [1971] 2 Q.B. 691 CA.

460 [1939] 1 K.B. 509 at 518

461 Though not in other common law jurisdictions, see in particular *Insurance Commissioners v Joyce* (1948) 77 C.L.R. 39; *Roggenkame v Bennett* (1950) 80 C.L.R. 292; *Car and General Insurance Co v Seymour and Moloney* (1956) 2 D.L.R. (2d) 265.

462 See *Owens v Brimmell* [1977] Q.B. 859; *Donelan v Donelan and General Accident Fire and Life Assurance* [1993] P.I.Q.R. P205.

463 [1991] 1 Q.B. 24 CA.

inebriation finally succeeded in *Morris v Murray*.[464] The claimant and defendant spent the afternoon drinking heavily, and the claimant then accepted the offer of a ride in the defendant's light aircraft. Soon after take-off the plane crashed and the defendant was killed. The claimant's action against the deceased's estate failed on the basis of the volenti defence. The claimant freely participated in a course of action which he must have known was fraught with danger. The deceased's state was such that he was in effect incapable of exercising any normal care.[465] Knowledge that a defendant has been drinking is not, as such, enough to absolve him from a normal duty of care. Knowledge that he is so drunk that he cannot even attempt to exercise care is quite different. A person with such knowledge who co-operates in an enterprise likely to result in disaster may well be defeated by a plea of volenti, except where the Road Traffic Act 1988 s.149 applies.

3-125 **Road Traffic Act** Inebriation causing a road traffic accident cannot today give rise to a plea of volenti. Section 149 of the Road Traffic Act 1988[466] provides that where a person uses a motor vehicle in circumstances in which liability insurance is required[467] (this includes liability to passengers):

> "any antecedent agreement or understanding between them (whether intended to be legally binding or not) shall be of no effect so far as it purports or might be held—
>
> (a) to negative or restrict any such liability of the user in respect of persons carried in or upon the vehicle as is required by section 145 of this Act to be covered by a policy of insurance, or
>
> (b) to impose any conditions with respect to the enforcement of any such liability of the user."

In addition, s.149(3) provides that "the fact that a person so carried has willingly accepted as his the risk of negligence on the part of the user shall not be treated as negativing any such liability of the user". The effect of s.149 is that in no circumstances involving the use of a motor vehicle on a public road can it now be held that a passenger in or on the vehicle assumed any risk of injury arising out of his presence in or on the vehicle.[468] However, conduct which could otherwise constitute volenti may still amount to contributory negligence, or as in *Pitts v Hunt* give rise to the defence of ex turpi causa.

(vi) Work accidents

3-126 The volenti defence is now rarely applied to a claim of personal injury by an employee against his employer. In *Bowater v Rowley Regis BC*, Goddard LJ said that:

---

464 [1991] 2 Q.B. 6.

465 [1991] 2 Q.B. 6 at 17, per Fox LJ: "It seems to me, however, that the wild irresponsibility of the venture is such that the law should not intervene to award damages and should leave the loss where it falls. Flying is intrinsically dangerous and flying with a drunken pilot is great folly. The situation is very different from what has arisen in the motoring cases."

466 See also the Public Passenger Vehicles Act 1981 s.29 prohibiting the exclusion of a carrier's liability for personal injury or death to a passenger in a public service vehicle.

467 Liability insurance is required where a person uses a motor vehicle "on a road or other public place": Road Traffic Act 1988 s.143.

468 *Pitts v Hunt* [1991] 1 Q.B. 24; *Gregory v Kelly* [1978] R.T.R. 426; *Winnik v Dick* 1984 S.L.T. 185. *Ashton v Turner* [1981] Q.B. 137, in which it had been held that the predecessor to s.149 (the Road Traffic Act 1972 s.148(3)) did not apply to cases of implied agreement, was disapproved on this point by the Court of Appeal in *Pitts v Hunt*.

"The maxim *volenti non fit injuria* is one which in the case of master and servant is to be applied with extreme caution. Indeed, I would say that it can hardly ever be applicable where the act to which the servant is said to be *volens* arises out of his ordinary duty, unless the work for which he is employed is one in which danger is necessarily involved."[469]

In *Smith v Baker*,[470] the claimant was employed by the defendants to drill holes in a rock cutting near a crane, which was being used for the purpose of raising stones. The crane was periodically swung around with stones over the claimant's head without warning. The claimant was aware of the danger arising from the practice of omitting to give warning, and had worked this way for some months when a stone fell and injured him. The House of Lords held that the mere fact the claimant remained in the defendants' service with knowledge of the dangerous practice did not as a matter of law preclude him from recovering, and that it was a question for the jury whether he had contracted to take the risk of accidents upon himself. The claimant in *Smith v Baker* may have "voluntarily" subjected himself to the inherent danger of his work, but he had not accepted the additional risk created by his employers' negligence in omitting effective warnings to their staff. A person may be said to "consent" to the risks inherent in a dangerous occupation, but this is not a case of volenti.[471] Some jobs involve risks which the exercise of reasonable care by the employer cannot avoid. If one of these risks materialises the employer is not liable, not because the employee is volenti but because there is no breach of duty by the employer. Thus, "a horse breaker must take the risk of being thrown or injured by a restive or unbroken horse. It is an ordinary risk of his employment".[472] So, exceptional circumstances apart, if a horse breaker is injured by the horse he is trying to break, he will be unable to establish negligence on the part of his employer. The employer will have no reason to invoke volenti by way of defence. If, on the other hand, the injury is attributable to the negligence of the employer, for example if it is due to a defective piece of equipment in respect of which the employer is under a non-delegable duty, then the defence of volenti non fit injuria will be of no avail. Though the employee has agreed to take the risks of injury inherent in his occupation which cannot be avoided by the exercise of reasonable care, he has not agreed to take the risks attributable to the negligence of his employer.

A further difficulty in relation to employees is the extent to which any undertaking or agreement to assume the risk of his employers' negligence is truly voluntary. **3-127**
Employees may, in effect, feel that they must agree or be dismissed.[473] Particularly,

---

469 [1944] K.B. 476 at 480; cf. at 479, per Scott LJ; *Williams v Port of Liverpool Stevedoring Co Ltd* [1956] 1 W.L.R. 551; *Staveley Iron and Chemical Co Ltd v Jones* [1956] A.C. 627; *ICI Ltd v Shatwell* [1965] A.C. 656; *O'Reilly v National Rail and Tramways Appliances Ltd* [1966] 1 All E.R. 499; *Hugh v NCB*, 1972 S.C. 252.

470 [1891] A.C. 325; applied in *Harris v Brights Asphalt Contractors* [1953] 1 Q.B. 617. See also *Baker v James* [1921] 2 K.B. 674; *Bowater v Rowley Regis BC* [1944] K.B. 476; *Burnett v British Waterways Board* [1973] 1 W.L.R. 700 (to which the Unfair Contract Terms Act 1977 s.2(1) or the Consumer Rights Act 2015, s.65(1) would apply now).

471 *Taylor v Sims* (1942) 58 T.L.R. 339 (considered in *Christmas v General Cleaning Contractors* [1952] K.B. 141 at 148, per Denning LJ ([1953] A.C. 180 HL); *Cilia v James* [1954] 1 W.L.R. 721; *Wilson v Tyneside Window Cleaning Co* [1958] 2 Q.B. 110); and see *Garcia v Harland and Wolff Ltd* [1943] K.B. 731; and cf. *Watt v Hertfordshire CC* [1954] 1 W.L.R. 835.

472 *Bowater v Rowley Regis BC* [1944] K.B. 476 at 481, per Goddard LJ.

473 *Bowater v Rowley Regis BC* [1944] K.B. 476.

if a source of danger comes into existence after the claimant enters employment, the question arises of whether the employee should be faced with the choice of accepting the danger without compensation or quitting the job.[474] However, where an employer has done all he can to minimise a risk to an employee but it is not possible to eliminate the risk completely, the employee cannot sue her employer for, in effect, not dismissing her. In *Withers v Perry Chain Co Ltd*,[475] the claimant was susceptible to dermatitis. Her employer provided protective clothing and found work for her entailing the minimal possible risk. Nonetheless, she succumbed to the complaint. The action failed, not because the claimant agreed to waive any claim, but because her employer was not in the circumstances negligent.

3-128 **Volenti and breach of statutory duty** In a number of cases involving employers the question will also arise of whether volenti can ever be a good defence to an action for breach of statutory duty. It has been suggested that it cannot. Lord Normand suggested that once a common law duty became a statutory duty, that had "the effect in a civil action of depriving the infringer of the benefit of the plea of *volenti non fit injuria*".[476] The argument is that once statute has enjoined a pattern of behaviour as a duty, no individual can absolve another from having to obey it. Thus, as a matter of public policy volenti cannot erase the duty or breach of it.[477]

3-129 In *ICI Ltd v Shatwell*,[478] the House of Lords created a limited exception to this rule, the effect of which appears to be that, although a person cannot by consent dispense with a statutory duty, such consent can nevertheless amount to a waiver of a right of action in certain circumstances. An employer of the consenting party may then reap the benefit of such waiver provided it does not contravene public policy. In this case two shot-firers of equal rank, A and B, collaborated in a method of work which they both knew to be dangerous and contrary to statutory regulations imposed on them personally, when carrying out an electrical circuit test in the open without taking cover. A charge exploded, injuring both. A sued his employers on account of B's breach of statutory duty. It was accepted on all sides that the employers were not to blame in any way, even technically, since on the wording of the provision the duty was laid on the shot-firers personally. Any liability of the employers could only be vicarious. They were held not liable. Lord Pearce said that the volenti defence should be available where the employer was not himself in breach of statutory duty and was not vicariously in breach of statutory duty through the fault of an employee whose commands the claimant was bound to obey, and where the claimant assented to and took part in the breaking of the statutory duty. The reasoning seems to be that A could not by his consent absolve B from his statutory duty,[479] but A had thereby deprived himself of his right to sue B, and his

---

474 *Clarke v Holmes* (1862) 7 H. & N. 937; *Yarmouth v France* (1887) 19 Q.B.D. 647; *London Graving Dock v Horton* [1951] A.C. 737 at 746.

475 [1961] 1 W.L.R. 1314 CA. See also *Henderson v Wakefield Shirt Co Ltd* [1997] P.I.Q.R. P413—if there are no reasonable changes that can be made to the system of work when an employee develops work-related symptoms, a reasonable employer does not have to offer a wholly different job to the employee. cf. *Coxall v Goodyear Great Britain Ltd* [2002] EWCA Civ 1010; [2003] 1 W.L.R. 536.

476 *Alford v NCB* [1952] 1 All E.R. 754 at 757.

477 *Baddeley v Earl Granville* (1887) 19 Q.B.D. 423; *Wheeler v New Merton Board Mills Ltd* [1933] 2 K.B. 669; *ICI Ltd v Shatwell* [1965] A.C. 656 at 678, per Viscount Radcliffe.

478 [1965] A.C. 656; followed in *O'Reilly v National Rail and Tramway Appliances Ltd* [1966] 1 All E.R. 499; *Bolt v W Moss Sons* (1966) 110 S.J. 385.

479 So Upjohn LJ in the Court of Appeal said: "If as a matter of principle the employee cannot contract

employers were given the vicarious benefit on non-actionability. As Lord Pearce put it: "it was an implied term [of the men's agreement] (to the benefit of which the employers are vicariously entitled) that [the claimant] would not sue [the deceased] for any injury that he might suffer if an accident occurred".[480] The position seems to be that:

(1) Where a statutory duty is imposed on the employer, he is normally liable for its breach, regardless of consent.

(2) Where it is imposed on the employer, but the breach is committed by a wilfully disobedient employee, Lord Reid in *Shatwell* left the point open.[481] It is submitted that the employer should continue to be liable because such a duty is personal and non-delegable, and the employer is not being held liable vicariously, but personally for a breach of his primary duty. Secondly, to allow the employer to escape from liability would be to defeat the object of the statute.[482]

(3) Where the duty is on the employee alone, the *Shatwell* decision bars one employee, who consents to its breach by another employee on whom it is laid, from suing the employer, provided that public policy is not infringed.

Shatwell illustrates the exceptional circumstances in which volenti may be pleaded against an employee. There was no evidence of any coercion by the employer, or of one junior employee by his superior. They collaborated freely and defied their employers' orders. As Lord Reid put it "there is a world of difference between two fellow servants collaborating carelessly, so that the acts of both contribute to cause injury to one of them, and two fellow servants combining to disobey an order deliberately, though they know the risk involved".[483] *Shatwell* was followed in *Hugh v NCB*,[484] where the claimant, in company with other mine workers, jumped off a moving train in breach of regulations and was knocked over in the rush and injured by the train. The defendants had done all they could to bring the regulations to the notice of their employees and to instruct them in the risk, and they also had a system of policing the mine shaft to try to prevent such behaviour. They were held not liable on the ground of volenti. This implies that the pursuer was deemed to have waived his right of action, although a preferable ground might have been the principle in *Ginty v Belmont Building Supplies Ltd*,[485] which refuses an action where the defendant's breach of statutory duty is coterminous with the claimant's own act. **3-130**

out of the benefit of the statutory duty owed to him by his employers, I cannot see any logical reason why one employee should be allowed to contract out of a statutory duty owed to him by a fellow employee." (Quoted in (1964) 27 M.L.R. 735). The regulations have since been altered so as to lay the duty directly on employers; the *Shatwell* decision cannot now be followed.

480 [1965] A.C. 656 at 688; see also Lord Donovan at 693.

481 [1965] A.C. 656 at 673.

482 Except perhaps where the breach of duty is so technical that it may be ignored: *Bolt v W Moss Sons* (1966) 110 S.J. 385; cf. *O'Reilly v National Rail and Tramway Appliances Ltd* [1966] 1 All E.R. 499. For non-delegable duties, see para.6-67 onwards.

483 [1965] A.C. 656 at 672.

484 1972 S.C. 252.

485 [1959] 1 All E.R. 414; see also *Boyle v Kodak* [1969] 1 W.L.R. 661; *McMullen v NCB* [1982] I.C.R. 148. See further *Brumder v Motornet Service and Repairs Ltd* [2013] EWCA Civ 195; [2013] 1 W.L.R. 2783, considered at para.12-90.

(vii) Rescuers

3-131 If a defendant through his breach of duty puts another person or his property in peril it is no answer to an action against him by a rescuer injured through a reasonable attempt at rescue to say that he was volens or contributorily negligent.[486] "Danger invites rescue", said Cardozo J. "The cry of distress is the summons to relief. The law does not ignore these reactions of the mind in tracing conduct to its consequences."[487] The rescuer who has intervened to save another from death or injury acts under compulsion of a legal, social or moral duty and therefore the defendant cannot be heard to say that his actions were voluntary even though he acts with full knowledge of the danger. In *Haynes v Harwood*,[488] a policeman ran out of the police station to stop a runaway horse and was injured. The Court of Appeal held that volenti did not apply. Although in this case there was some suggestion that a policeman owes a special duty to avert a risk to the public, such as a runaway horse in a public street, Greer LJ adopted the American law, as expressed by Professor Goodhart.[489] Where, however, the emergency has passed by the time the claimant intervenes and no one is in danger the claimant may be held to be volenti.[490]

(viii) Sport

3-132 In cases involving injury to spectators or competitors at sporting events the courts sometimes speak in terms of assumption of risk. In *Wooldridge v Sumner*,[491] for example, Diplock LJ said that a "person attending a game or competition takes the risk of any damage caused to him by any act of a participant done in the course of and for the purposes of the game or competition". This is not an application of volenti non fit injuria. It is correct that in a sport which necessarily involves some physical contact the players can be taken impliedly to consent to those contacts which occur within the ordinary performance of the game. But this consent negatives what would otherwise be a battery for those contacts that can reasonably be expected to occur in the course of the game,[492] and so competitors "assume the risk

486 With regard to contributory negligence, see para.3-94. More fully on rescue, see para.7-34.

487 *Wagner v International Railroad*, 232 N.Y. 176 at 180 (1921).

488 [1935] 1 K.B. 146; *Baker v TE Hopkins & Son Ltd* [1959] 1 W.L.R. 966; *Vinnyey v Star Paper Mills Ltd* [1965] 1 All E.R. 175; and as to risks which may be undertaken to save life, cf. *Watt v Hertfordshire CC* [1954] 1 W.L.R. 835. In *Hambley v Shepley* (1967) 63 D.L.R. (2d) 94, a policeman, who blocked with his own car the path of an escaping motorist and was injured, was held entitled to recover. See also *Morgan v Aylen* [1942] 1 All E.R. 489; *Brandon v Osborne, Garrett Co* [1924] 1 K.B. 548—a sudden emergency may render the act of rescue more or less a reflex action, as in the case of the wife, who clutched her husband to save him from falling glass, and injured herself. On the other hand: "If a rescuer acts with a wanton disregard of his own safety it might be that in some circumstances it might be held that an injury to him was not the result of the negligence that caused the situation of danger": *Baker v TE Hopkins & Sons Ltd* [1959] 1 W.L.R. 966 at 977, per Morris LJ.

489 [1935] 1 K.B. 146 at 157; following (1935) 5 C.L.J. 192; (1948) 64 L.Q.R. 36.

490 See *Cutler v United Dairies Ltd* [1933] 2 K.B. 297 where the claimant went to the assistance of the driver of a horse which had run away into a field, but there was no immediate danger. The case is criticised by Williams, *Joint Torts and Contributory Negligence*, p.306. *Jones v Wabigwan* (1968) 1 D.L.R. (3d) 40 is another case where the defendant's negligence was exhausted before the claimant's intervention.

491 [1963] 2 Q.B. 43 at 68. See also *Hall v Brooklands Auto Racing Club* [1933] 1 K.B. 205 at 214.

492 See, e.g. *Dann v Hamilton* [1939] 1 K.B. 509 at 516.

of injury" from such contacts in the absence of negligence.[493] This is no more than saying that in the absence of a battery there is no liability for non-negligently inflicted injury, and in this sense everyone assumes the risk of accidental injury when liability depends on the proof of negligence. It is not, however, consent to negligence by other competitors. Thus, in *Smoldon v Whitworth*,[494] a case in which a colts rugby player sued the referee in negligence for failing to control the manner in which the players were scrummaging, the Court of Appeal stated that:

> "The [claimant] had of course consented to the ordinary incidents of a game of rugby football of the kind in which he was taking part. Given, however, that the rules were framed for the protection of him and other players in the same position, he cannot possibly be said to have consented to a breach of duty on the part of the official whose duty it was to apply the rules and ensure as far as possible that they were observed."

Similarly, spectators do not assume the risk of negligence simply by being present at the event. For the purposes of volenti the relevant consent "is not consent to the risk of injury but consent to the lack of reasonable care that may produce that risk".[495] In *Murray v Harringay Arena Ltd*,[496] a six-year-old boy was injured when a puck at an ice-hockey match was hit out of the rink and landed among the **3-133**

---

[493] "In a sport which inevitably involves the risk of some physical contact, the participants are taken impliedly to consent to those contacts which can reasonably be expected to occur in the course of the game, and to assume the risk of injury from such contacts. Thus, for example, in the context of a fight with fists, ordinarily neither party has a cause of action for any injury suffered during the fight", per Dyson LJ in *Blake v Galloway* [2004] EWCA Civ 814; [2004] 1 W.L.R. 2844 at [21]. This principle applies both to formal sports and games, and informal "horseplay" where the game was conducted in accordance with tacitly agreed understandings that were objectively ascertainable. So where the claimant was struck in the eye by a piece of bark chipping in the course of good-natured horseplay involving the throwing of twigs and pieces of bark "the claimant must be taken to have impliedly consented to the risk of a blow on any part of his body, provided that the offending missile was thrown more or less in accordance with the tacit understandings or conventions of the game", [2004] EWCA Civ 814; [2004] 1 W.L.R. 2844 at [24].

[494] [1997] P.I.Q.R. P133 at 147. See also *Watson v British Boxing Board of Control* [2001] Q.B. 1134 CA, where the claimant was a professional boxer who sustained a sub-dural haemorrhage in a fight, and claimed that the defendants had been negligent in failing to provide appropriate medical assistance during a fight. The Court of Appeal held that although he had consented to the risk of an injury such as he received at his opponent's hands, he had not, by agreeing to fight under the defendant's rules, accepted any risk which flowed from those rules not having been as carefully worked out as they should have been. See also *Wattleworth v Goodwood Road Racing Co Ltd* [2004] EWHC 140 (QB); [2004] P.I.Q.R. P25 at [174] where Davis J stated that a driver in a motor race accepts the inherent risks of motor racing, but does not consent to negligence by those responsible for the safety of the circuit (though on the facts there was no breach of duty). *Watson* is discussed by George, "Negligent Rule-Making in the Court of Appeal" (2002) 65 M.L.R. 106. See generally Yeo, "Accepted Inherent Risks Among Sporting Participants" (2001) 9 Tort. L.R. 114.

[495] *Wooldridge v Sumner* [1963] 2 Q.B. 43 at 69, per Diplock LJ. Sometimes the language of consent and assumption of risk is used in order to "justify" an apparently lower standard of care in the context of sporting events. Thus, in *Hall v Brooklands Auto-Racing Club* [1933] 1 K.B. 205 at 214, Scrutton LJ said that: "What is *reasonable care* would depend on the perils which might reasonably be expected to occur, and the extent to which the *ordinary spectator might be expected to appreciate and take the risk of such perils*", [emphasis added] cited by Diplock LJ in *Wooldridge v Sumner* at 66–67, where the standard of care expected of a competitor was said to be "reckless disregard of a spectator's safety". It is submitted, however, that such a test is inappropriate. The test remains reasonable care in all the circumstances, which allows for errors in the heat of the moment: see *Condon v Basi* [1985] 1 W.L.R. 866; *Caldwell v Maguire and Fitzgerald* [2001] EWCA Civ 1054; [2002] P.I.Q.R. P6; para.7-166.

[496] [1951] 2 K.B. 529. See also *Browning v Odyssey Trust Co Ltd* [2014] NIQB 39 (no negligence by the occupiers of an ice hockey arena when a spectator was hit by a puck during the warm-up before a match).

spectators. The Court of Appeal held that the defendants were not liable, but this was on the basis that there had been no negligence. A small boy could not be said to have agreed to assume the risk and/or waive a right to claim. On the other hand, a spectator's knowledge that a particular sporting event involves an element of risk does not mean that he is aware of, and has thereby consented to, negligence by the organisers in respect of the safety arrangements.[497]

(ix) Volenti and contributory negligence

3-134 Not infrequently the defence of volenti arises in conjunction with a defence of contributory negligence and it is not always easy to distinguish between them. One distinction, which has become apparent, is that contributory negligence is and always has been a defence to a breach of statutory duty, while volenti is not a defence except within the narrow limits of *Shatwell*.[498] This reflects the basic difference between them. No one can absolve another from a statutory obligation by consenting to a breach of it, whereas a person's contributory negligence in bringing upon himself some injury resulting from a breach of statutory obligation does not absolve the wrongdoer from his obligation but only affects his own claim to damages. Secondly, there is usually a greater degree of deliberation involved in the defence of volenti than in contributory negligence. The gist of the latter is that the claimant did not think as he should have done.[499] Thirdly, contributory negligence operates to reduce damages according to the degree of fault; volenti is a total defence.[500] Because it is possible to dispense a more finely adjusted justice between parties by apportioning damages, courts tend to interpret situations in terms of contributory negligence rather than volenti,[501] with the result that the distinction between them has become blurred and volenti has been relegated to the background. "Now that contributory negligence is not a complete defence, but only a ground for reducing damages", said Lord Denning MR, "the defence of *volenti non fit injuria* has been closely considered and, in consequence, it has been severely limited".[502] Nonetheless, as *Morris v Murray*[503] demonstrates, volenti survives to bar a claim where it is clear that the source of the claimant's harm is his voluntary and wholehearted participation in an obviously dangerous enterprise.

5. Exclusion of Liability

3-135 **At common law** At common law a defendant could employ three primary means to exclude or limit liability in tort. He could enter into an express contract excluding or limiting liability; he could give notice that the claimant entered on to his land subject to his agreeing to exempt the defendant from liability in respect of his occupation of that land[504]; or he could issue a disclaimer making it clear that he

---

497 *White v Blackmore* [1972] 2 Q.B. 651.
498 [1965] A.C. 656.
499 See Lord Reid, [1965] A.C. 656 at 672.
500 See generally Williams, *Joint Torts and Contributory Negligence* (1951), pp.295–340.
501 See, e.g. the remark of Lord Porter in *Stapley v Gypsum Mines Ltd* [1953] A.C. 663 at 677. See also *McMath v Rimmer Bros (Liverpool) Ltd* [1962] 1 W.L.R. 1; *ICI Ltd v Shatwell* [1965] A.C. 656 at 672, per Lord Reid; and at 686, per Lord Pearce.
502 *Nettleship v Weston* [1971] 2 Q.B. 691 at 701.
503 [1991] 2 Q.B. 6.
504 *Ashdown v Samuel Williams & Sons Ltd* [1957] 1 Q.B. 409; *White v Blackmore* [1972] 2 Q.B. 651.

undertook no responsibility for information or advice offered to the claimant.[505] The Unfair Contract Terms Act 1977 and the Consumer Rights Act 2015 radically restrict defendants' freedom to opt out of tortious liability in all three cases.[506] The 1977 Act had to be read in conjunction with the Unfair Terms in Consumer Contracts Regulations 1999,[507] which ran in parallel to the 1977 Act, implementing rather more extensive controls of contract terms where such terms had not been individually negotiated between a seller or a supplier and a consumer. The Consumer Rights Act 2015 has created new statutory controls over consumer contracts, including restrictions on a defendant's right to exclude liability by means of a contract term or notice, and has replaced the Unfair Terms in Consumer Contracts Regulations 1999. Attempts to exclude duties in tort by contract or by notice are now governed by different statutory regimes depending on the status of the claimant (consumer or non-consumer) and the status of the defendant (trader/business or private individual).[508]

(a) Unfair Contract Terms Act 1977

By virtue of s.1(3), the Unfair Contract Terms Act 1977 applies only to "business liability", that is liability for breaches of obligations or duties arising: **3-136**

"(a) from things done or to be done by a person in the course of a business[509] (whether his own business or another's); or

(b) from the occupation of premises used for the business purposes of the occupier."

Section 2(1) of the Act provides:

"A person cannot by reference to any contract term or to a notice given to persons generally or to particular persons exclude or restrict his liability for death or personal injury resulting from negligence."

---

505 As in *Hedley Byrne & Co v Heller & Partners* [1964] A.C. 465.

506 Note that there is also an argument that in the context of liability imposed by statute a defendant cannot exclude liability under the statute, unless the statute expressly permits him to do so. If Parliament has imposed the obligation on the defendant it is not open to him to exclude that duty either by notice or by persuading the claimant to excuse him. For example, the Occupiers' Liability Act 1957 s.2(1) permits an occupier to "restrict, modify or exclude his duty to any visitor or visitors by agreement or otherwise" in so far as he is free to do so (the most significant restriction on his freedom to do so being the Unfair Contract Terms Act 1977 and the Consumer Rights Act 2015 in relation to occupation of premises for business purposes). In contrast, the Occupiers' Liability Act 1984 contains no provision permitting an occupier to exclude a duty arising under that Act, and it is arguable that it is simply not possible for the occupier to exclude the obligation by notice or otherwise, although the Act (s.1(6)) does preserve the defence of volenti non fit injuria. See further paras 11-74 to 11-76.

507 SI 1999/2083.

508 Note that other statutory provisions may permit the exclusion of liability for negligence in the context of the specific service covered by the statute. See, e.g. the Electricity Act 1989 s.21; on which see *AE Beckett & Sons (Lyndons) Ltd v Midlands Electricity Plc* [2001] 1 W.L.R. 281 CA (s.21 permits terms which restrict liability in respect of economic loss caused by the interruption or variation of the supply of electricity, but not the negligent installation of electrical equipment).

509 "Business" is not comprehensively defined in the Act. Section 14 merely provides that business "includes a profession and the activities of any government department or local or public authority". Arguably any activity that is not within the remit of private domestic life should be covered. The issue is not whether the activity is "commercial" in the sense of being designed to make a profit, but whether it takes place in the public sphere. Thus, charitable bodies, educational institutions and even religious institutions ought to fall within the Act. cf. para.11-53 for a more tentative view.

The Consumer Rights Act 2015 amends s.2 to provide that it does not apply to a consumer contract or a consumer notice[510] (which are now governed by ss.62 and 65 of the Consumer Rights Act 2015), so by default the Unfair Contract Terms Act 1977 applies to non-consumer contracts and notices, provided the defendant is acting in the course of a business. Negligence includes breach of any obligation arising from an express or implied term of a contract to take reasonable care or exercise reasonable skill in the performance of the contract; any common law duty to take reasonable care or exercise reasonable skill (but not any stricter duty); and the common duty of care imposed by the Occupiers' Liability Act 1957 and the Occupiers' Liability Act (Northern Ireland) 1957.[511] The 1977 Act thus makes it clear that, for example, employers cannot exempt themselves from their duty of care to their workforce.[512] Similarly, commercial enterprises cannot by notice exclude their duty to their visitors who are not consumers in respect of personal injuries, although private households can theoretically do so.[513]

3-137 In respect of damage other than death or personal injury, s.2(2) of the 1977 Act goes on to provide that:

> "a person cannot so exclude or restrict his liability for negligence except in so far as the term or notice satisfies the requirement of reasonableness."

Any attempt to exclude or limit liability is thus subject to judicial scrutiny. Guidelines as to what constitutes "reasonableness" are provided in s.11 of the 1977 Act and were elaborated in *Smith v Eric S Bush*.[514] The essence of the exercise is to ascertain whether it is fair to allow the defendant to opt out of liability to the claimant, and the strength of the parties' respective bargaining power is crucial.

3-138 **Disclaimers** The decision of the House of Lords in *Smith v Eric S Bush*[515] confirmed that the 1977 Act applies, not simply when the relevant contract term or notice seeks to exclude an existing duty of care, but also where a disclaimer purports to operate to prevent any duty of care arising. Section 11(3) provides that "the requirement of reasonableness under this Act is that it should be fair and reasonable to allow reliance [on the disclaimer] having regard to all the circumstances obtaining when the liability arose or (but for this notice) would have arisen". Section 13(1) goes on to provide:

> "To the extent that this Part of this Act prevents the exclusion or restriction of any liability it also prevents—
>
> (a) making the liability or its enforcement subject to restrictive or onerous conditions;
> (b) excluding or restricting any right or remedy in respect of the liability, or subjecting a person to any prejudice in consequence of his pursuing any such right or remedy;

---

510 Unfair Contract Terms Act 1977 s.2(4). See para.3-141 for definitions of these terms.

511 Unfair Contract Terms Act 1977 s.1(1). See para.11-53. Note that there is no reference to the obligations imposed by the Occupiers' Liability Act 1984.

512 See *Johnstone v Bloomsbury HA* [1992] 1 Q.B. 333 CA. Note Sch.1 para.4 providing that s.2(1) and (2) of the 1977 Act do not extend to contracts of employment except in favour of the employee. Contracts of employment are not consumer contracts for the purposes of Pt 2 ("Unfair Terms") of the Consumer Rights Act 2015: s.61(5) of the 2015 Act.

513 What constitutes occupation for business purposes is discussed more fully at para.11-55.

514 [1990] 1 A.C. 831 (though the claimant in this case would now be regarded as a "consumer"). See para.3-139; see further at para.7-139.

515 [1990] 1 A.C. 831.

(c) excluding or restricting rules of evidence or procedure;

and (to that extent) sections 2, 6 and 7 also prevent excluding or restricting liability by reference to terms and notices which exclude or restrict the relevant obligation or duty."

In *Smith v Eric S Bush*, the defendant surveyors argued that their express warning to the claimant purchasers that they undertook no duty of care to them, as opposed to their client building societies, operated to prevent any duty to the claimants ever arising. Their Lordships found that the cumulative effect of ss.11(3) and 13(1) renders the 1977 Act applicable whenever the relationship of the parties is such that "but for" a purported disclaimer of liability a duty of care would be found. Any variety of disclaimer must satisfy the requirements of reasonableness.

The reasonableness test Section 11(1) provides that in determining the reasonableness of the exclusionary term the question is whether it was fair and reasonable having regard to the circumstances which were, or ought reasonably to have been, known to or in the contemplation of the parties when the contract was made.[516] In *Smith v Eric S Bush*, Lord Griffiths identified a number of factors which were relevant: Were the parties of equal bargaining power? In the case of advice, would it have been reasonably practicable to obtain the advice from an alternative source taking into account considerations of cost and time? How difficult is the task being undertaken for which liability is being excluded? What are the practical consequences, taking into account the sums of money at stake and the ability of the parties to bear the loss involved, particularly in the light of the existence of liability insurance?[517] In *Omega Trust Co Ltd v Wright Son & Pepper*[518] the Court of Appeal accepted that it was reasonable for valuers to rely on a clause in a valuation report stating that it was for the private and confidential use of their client and should not be relied upon by third parties for any use whatsoever without the express written authority of the valuers. The defendants' client, Omega, had, unknown to the defendants, passed the report to the second claimants who had advanced a loan to a third party against the security of the property valued in the defendants' report. The claimants suffered loss when the third party defaulted on the loan, and the property, which had been negligently overvalued, was insufficient to cover the debt. The crucial distinction between this case and *Smith v Eric S Bush* was that it was a commercial setting rather than a domestic householder purchasing his home (which would now be governed by the Consumer Rights Act 2015). The parties were of equal bargaining power and it would have been easy for the second claimants to obtain their own independent advice or ask the defendants if they could rely on the valuation. The defendants were entitled to know who their clients were and to whom their duty was owed.[519] 3-139

---

[516] See also Sch.2 to the Act.

[517] [1990] 1 A.C. 831 at 858–859. See also s.11(4).

[518] [1997] P.N.L.R. 424.

[519] See also *McCullagh v Lane Fox and Partners Ltd* [1996] 18 E.G. 104 where the Court of Appeal held that it was not unfair or unreasonable to allow an estate agent to rely on a standard disclaimer contained in particulars of sale to the effect that "none of the statements contained in these particulars as to this property are to be relied on as statements or representations of fact"; *Governor and Company of the Bank of Scotland v Fuller Peiser*, 2002 S.C.L.R. 255; [2002] P.N.L.R. 13 where the lender relied on a valuation report prepared by the defendant for the purchaser of a hotel. It was reasonable to allow the defendant to rely on a clause excluding liability to anyone other than the purchaser client because the lender was a large commercial organisation and the transaction was

3-140 **The 1977 Act and volenti** Section 2(3) of the 1977 Act provides that: "Where a contract term or notice purports to exclude or restrict liability for negligence a person's agreement to or awareness of it is not of itself to be taken as indicating his voluntary acceptance of any risk."[520] Section 2(3) prevents a defendant evading the operation of the 1977 Act by pleading a contractual exclusion of liability as conclusive evidence of volenti. In *Johnstone v Bloomsbury HA*,[521] a junior hospital doctor brought an action against his employing health authority alleging breach of the latter's duty to take reasonable care of his health and safety by requiring him to work excessive hours. Refusing to strike out the claimant's claim, the Court of Appeal opined that a clause in the contract of employment empowering the defendant to require the claimant to work such hours could only constitute a plea of volenti or an attempt to restrict the ambit of the employer's duty of care. If the latter was the true construction, the clause might well fall foul of s.2(1) of the 1977 Act. Section 2(3) provokes two difficulties well illustrated by *Johnstone v Bloomsbury HA*:

(1) If the defendants in such a case plead volenti, i.e. that the claimant assumed the risk of injury to health inherent in the hours junior doctors work, how do they demonstrate voluntary acceptance of that risk, separate and independent from the agreement embodied in the contract? Will volenti depend on evidence that the claimant took some sort of separate initiative to assume the risk in question?

(2) If volenti depends in any case on agreement to waive a breach of duty, the paradox comes about that formal contractual agreements are regulated by the 1977 Act but informal implicit agreements are not. Can Dr Johnstone's employers argue that while they cannot exclude liability via Dr Johnstone's explicit contract, his conduct in arriving at work as a junior doctor implicitly waives any claim arising out of the rigours of the job? The answer to this question should be "no"[522] on the basis that an employee's acquiescence with what are effectively unsafe working practices should not be treated as evidence of volenti, a point acknowledged by the House of Lords over a hundred years ago.[523]

---

entirely commercial in nature; *Taberna Europe CDO II Plc v Selskabet (formerly Roskilde Bank A/S) (In Bankruptcy)* [2016] EWCA Civ 1262; [2017] Q.B. 633 at [26], per Moore-Bick LJ: "parties to commercial contracts are entitled to determine for themselves the terms on which they will do business" (investors who relied on an "investor presentation" on defendants' website bound by a disclaimer of liability for the statements contained in it); *Barclays Bank Plc v Grant Thornton UK LLP* [2015] EWHC 320 (Comm); [2015] 1 C.L.C. 180 (disclaimer in two non-statutory audit reports reasonable; claimants were "sophisticated business parties … able to protect their own interests and do not require the protection of the 1977 Act in the same way as small companies or consumers", per Cooke J at [91]). Contrast *Hirtenstein v Hill Dickinson LLP* [2014] EWHC 2711 (Comm) at [173]–[180] Leggatt J (firm of solicitors not entitled to rely on limitation of liability clause in contract of retainer with a client because, although the client "was an experienced and capable businessman, well able to look after his own interests", the solicitors had failed to draw the client's attention to the clause, in breach of the Solicitor's Code of Conduct 2007).

520 A similar provision is to be found in the Consumer Rights Act 2015 s.65(2).

521 [1992] 1 Q.B. 333 CA.

522 Though see the remarks of Leggatt LJ who said that the employer's duty to exercise reasonable care for the health of employees could not be used to override an express term of the contract of employment as to the number of hours to be worked per week, even if the hours were excessive and injured the claimant's health: "Those who cannot stand the heat should stay out of the kitchen."

523 See *Smith v Baker* [1891] A.C. 325.

(b) Consumer Rights Act 2015

Part 2 of the Consumer Rights Act 2015 regulates unfair terms in consumer contracts and consumer notices. A consumer contract is a contract between a trader and a consumer, but does not include a contract of employment or apprenticeship.[524] A trader is "a person acting for purposes relating to that person's trade, business, craft or profession, whether acting personally or through another person acting in the trader's name or on the trader's behalf",[525] and a consumer is "an individual acting for purposes that are wholly or mainly outside that individual's trade, business, craft or profession".[526] A consumer notice is a notice that relates to rights or obligations as between a trader and a consumer or purports to exclude or restrict a trader's liability to a consumer, and includes an announcement, whether or not in writing, and any other communication or purported communication.[527] Section 62 provides that neither an unfair term of a consumer contract nor an unfair consumer notice is binding on the consumer. A term or notice is unfair if, contrary to the requirement of good faith, it causes a significant imbalance in the parties' rights and obligations under the contract to the detriment of the consumer.[528] These provisions are, in broad terms, the equivalent of s.2(2) of the Unfair Contract Terms Act 1977 which subject contract terms and notices seeking to exclude or restrict liability for damage other than death or personal injury caused by negligence to a test of reasonableness. Section 65 is, in broad terms, the equivalent of s.2(1) of the 1977 Act. Section 65(1) provides that "a trader cannot by a term of a consumer contract or by a consumer notice exclude or restrict liability for death or personal injury resulting from negligence". So, for example, a doctor cannot exclude liability for negligence causing personal injury or death to a patient in any circumstances. A business will be unable to exclude liability in negligence to visitors for death or personal injury by posting a notice purporting to exclude that liability.[529] If the visitor is a consumer then s.65(1) will invalidate the notice, and if the visitor is not a **3-141**

[524] Consumer Rights Act 2015 s.61(1)–(3).

[525] Consumer Rights Act 2015 s.2(2). "Business" includes the activities of any government department or local or public authority: s.2(7).

[526] Consumer Rights Act 2015 s.2(3).

[527] Consumer Rights Act 2015 s.61(4),(7),(8). It does not include a notice relating to rights, obligations or liabilities as between an employer and an employee: s.61(5).

[528] Consumer Rights Act 2015 s.62(4) and (6). Schedule 2, with s.63(1), of the Act contains an indicative and non-exhaustive list of terms of consumer contracts that may be regarded as unfair. In addition, s.49(1) implies a term into every consumer contract to supply a service that the trader must perform the service with reasonable care and skill (the equivalent of s.13 of the Supply of Goods and Services Act 1982 for non-consumer contracts), and s.57(1) provides that any term of the contract which purports to exclude the trader's liability for breach of the obligation to perform the service with reasonable care and skill is not binding on the consumer. See further paras 9-06 and 9-39.

[529] As with the Unfair Contract Terms Act 1977 "negligence" covers a contractual or tortious duty to take reasonable care or exercise reasonable skill, and the common duty of care imposed by the Occupiers' Liability Act 1957 and the Occupiers' Liability Act (Northern Ireland) 1957, but not the obligations imposed by the Occupiers' Liability Act 1984. Schedule 2 to the Consumer Rights Act 2015 provides, inter alia, that a contract term which has the object or effect of excluding or limiting the trader's liability in the event of the death of or personal injury to the consumer resulting from an act or omission of the trader may be regarded as unfair (and therefore not binding on the consumer under s.62(1)). Given that s.65(1) prevents the exclusion or restriction of liability for death or personal injury resulting from *negligence*, this provision leaves it open for the court to declare terms restricting or excluding liability for breach of a stricter obligation than negligence to be non-binding where the consumer has suffered personal injuries or death.

consumer then s.2(1) of the 1977 Act will apply. As with the 1977 Act, a defendant cannot rely on an exclusionary contract term or notice to invoke the volenti defence. Section 65(2) provides that where a term of a consumer contract, or a consumer notice, purports to exclude or restrict a trader's liability for negligence, a person is not to be taken to have voluntarily accepted any risk merely because the person agreed to or knew about the term or notice. Although the precise wording of the Unfair Contract Terms Act and the Consumer Rights Act 2015 differs in places,[530] it is thought that with regard to attempts to exclude liability the effect of the legislation is similar. In practice, the exclusion of liability to consumers is regulated by the 2015 Act, and the exclusion of liability to non-consumers continues to be regulated by the 1977 Act.

(c) Exclusions and third parties

3-142 Even when persons are entitled to limit their liability, those with whom they subcontract cannot as a general rule avail themselves of any contractual limitation of liability between the contracting parties.[531] Similarly, where a contract between A and B limits the liability of B with regard to A's goods, and the contract between B and a carrier, C, with regard to the same goods limits the liability of C to B, C cannot avail himself of either limitation in an action against him by A for negligence. He is not party to the contract between A and B, and A is not party to the contract between him and B.[532] A partial exception to this has been introduced by the Judicial Committee of the Privy Council, which has held that where it can be shown that a carrier contracted on behalf of a stevedore, the latter may then avail himself of an exemption agreed on between the shipper and the carrier.[533] A contract was, in effect, implied between the owner of the goods and the stevedore engaged by the carrier to unload the cargo. That solution was subsequently described in *Southern Water Co v Carey*[534] as "uncomfortably artificial". In that case subcontractors were sued for negligence in the design and supply of equipment for a sewerage scheme. The main contract exempted both main and sub-contractors from liability in respect of such defects. The judge held that the existence of the exemption clause in that main contract (to which the subcontractors were not party) negatived any duty of care in tort.[535] This decision reflects a general trend, at least in "commercial" as opposed to "consumer" cases, which has been to give effect to the

[530] The most obvious difference being the wording applied by s.62(4) and (6) of the 2015 Act to unfair terms or notices ("if, contrary to the requirement of good faith, it causes a significant imbalance in the parties' rights and obligations ... to the detriment of the consumer") as opposed to the wording of s.2(2) of the 1977 Act ("cannot so exclude or restrict his liability for negligence except in so far as the term or notice satisfies the requirement of reasonableness").

[531] *Midland Silicones Ltd v Scruttons Ltd* [1962] A.C. 446. Though see para.3-145.

[532] *Lee Cooper Ltd v CH Jeakins & Sons Ltd* [1967] 2 Q.B. 1; *Morris v CW Martin & Sons Ltd* [1966] 1 Q.B. 716 (on which see *Garnham, Harris and Elton Ltd v AW Ellis (Transport) Ltd* [1967] 1 W.L.R. 940; *Moukataff v BOAC* [1967] 1 Lloyd's Rep. 396); *Genys v Matthews* [1966] 1 W.L.R. 758; *Gillette Industries v WH Martin* [1966] 1 Lloyd's Rep. 57; *Gilchrist Watt and Sanderson Pty Ltd v York Products Pty Ltd* [1970] 1 W.L.R. 1262.

[533] *New Zealand Shipping Co Ltd v Satterthwaite & Co Ltd* [1975] A.C. 154; *Port Jackson Stevedoring Pty Ltd v Salmond Spraggon (Australia) Pty Ltd (The New York Star)* [1981] 1 W.L.R. 138.

[534] [1985] 2 All E.R. 1077.

[535] cf. the dissenting speech of Lord Brandon of Oakbrook in *Leigh & Sillavan Ltd v Aliakmon Shipping Co Ltd* [1986] A.C. 785. His Lordship could not find "any convincing legal basis for qualifying a duty of care owed by A to B by reference to a contract to which A is, but B is not, a party". It is arguable, however, that the existence of the exemption clause is relevant either to the question of

contractual structure by which the parties defined the nature of their relationship.[536] So if the parties are in a contractual chain with no direct contractual relationship, the possible existence of exemption clauses which might be unenforceable against a claimant suing in tort (due to the absence of privity) has been held to be a good reason for denying the existence of a duty of care.[537]

Third parties and physical damage Allowing contractual exclusion clauses to take effect between parties who are not in a relationship of privity of contract through the mechanism of denying the existence of a duty of care makes sense in the context of claims for pure economic loss. It is less obviously an appropriate mechanism in the case of physical damage to property or person. However, in *Norwich City Council v Harvey*[538] the Court of Appeal allowed a defendant subcontractor to take the benefit of a clause in a main contract between the main contractor and a building owner which provided that the building owner should continue to bear the risk of loss by fire. The building was damaged by a fire caused by the subcontractor's negligence. The Court of Appeal relied on the provisions of the main contract, to which the subcontractor was not privy, to hold that no duty of care was owed by the subcontractor to the building-owner. The lack of privity did not prevent the subcontractor from "relying on the clear basis on which all the parties contracted in relation to damage to the employer's building caused by fire".[539] It is difficult to reconcile this decision with traditional reasoning on contractual limitation of liability and third parties. It is one thing to say that the contractual structure, including exemption clauses, is such that it is not just and reasonable to impose a duty of care in respect of pure economic loss, given that the parties have chosen not to enter into a direct contractual relationship. It is quite another, however, to dismiss the strictures of privity of contract in order to exclude a duty of care which, in the absence of any contract, would quite clearly have been owed to the claimant, when, presumably, the parties have also chosen to structure their relationship so as to avoid direct contractual obligations and immunities. 3-143

Norwich City Council v Harvey was distinguished by the House of Lords in *British Telecommunications Plc v James Thomson & Sons (Engineers) Ltd*,[540] in which the pursuer entered into a construction contract with the main contractor under which "nominated subcontractors" were expressly entitled to cover under a policy of insurance against the risk of fire to be taken out by the pursuer, or were entitled to waiver of any right of subrogation by the insurers. The main contractor entered into a contract with the defender on the same terms as those applying between the pursuer and the main contractor. The defender was not a nominated subcontractor, and therefore was a "domestic contractor" for the purposes of the provisions of the 3-144

---

the proximity of the relationship between the parties or the question of whether it is just, fair or reasonable to impose a duty of care. See *Pacific Associates Inc v Baxter* [1990] 1 Q.B. 993 at 1022–1023, per Purchas LJ and the discussion of this issue by Neuberger J in *Killick v Pricewaterhouse-Coopers* [2001] P.N.L.R. 1; [2001] Lloyd's Rep. P.N. 17 at 21–24. See also para.7-141.

[536] See, e.g. Greater *Nottingham Co-operative Society Ltd v Cementation Piling and Foundations Ltd* [1989] Q.B. 71; *Saipem SpA and Conoco (UK) Ltd v Dredging VO2 BV and Geosite Surveys Ltd (The "Voltex Hollandia") (No.2)* [1993] 2 Lloyd's Rep. 315 at 322. In the context of consumer transactions, compare *Smith v Eric S Bush* [1990] 1 A.C. 831.

[537] *Simaan General Contracting Co v Pilkington Glass Ltd (No.2)* [1988] Q.B. 758 at 782–783 and 785–786.

[538] [1989] 1 W.L.R. 828.

[539] [1989] 1 W.L.R. 828 at 837, per May LJ.

[540] [1999] 1 W.L.R. 9.

main contract. There was a fire causing damage to the premises which was alleged to be the result of negligence by the defender's employees. The defender argued that in the light of the insurance provisions in the main contract it was not just, fair or reasonable to impose a duty of care upon them owed to the pursuer. The difficulty with this argument, as Lord Morison pointed out in a strong dissenting judgment in the Court of Session,[541] is that it tends to confuse the effect of the contractual provisions on the contractual rights and obligations of the parties with their effect on the general duty in tort to take reasonable care. His Lordship considered that the strong presumption, in the case of physical damage negligently caused by the defendant, that the *Donoghue v Stevenson* duty of care should apply was not displaced by a contract to which the defenders were not a party, placing the risk of fire damage on the pursuer. In the House of Lords it was accepted that it was proper to take account of the contractual provisions in determining the question of whether it was just, fair or reasonable to impose a duty of care, but if one must take account of the contract then it was proper to take account of all the terms of the contract. More specifically, the distinction drawn in the contract between the position of a nominated subcontractor and a domestic subcontractor meant that the former were entitled to the protection of the main contract, whereas the latter were not. The insurance premium would have been set taking into account this allocation of risk.[542]

3-145 **Contracts (Rights of Third Parties) Act 1999** This Act radically changed the traditional rules on privity of contract.[543] It permits a person who is not a party to a contract (a "third party") to enforce a term of the contract in his own right if (a) the contract expressly provides that he may; or (b) the term purports to confer a benefit on him (unless the parties did not intend the term to be enforceable by the third party).[544] The third party must be expressly identified in the contract by name, as a member of a class or as answering a particular description, but need not be in existence when the contract is entered into[545]; and the third party can only enforce a term of a contract in accordance with any other relevant terms of the contract.[546] The third party is entitled to any remedy that would have been available to him in an action for breach of contract if he had been a party to the contract, including the same rules relating to damages,[547] injunctions and specific performance. Where a contract term excludes or limits liability the third party is entitled to rely on the exclusion or limitation,[548] provided that he could have done so had he been party to the

---

541 See (1996) 82 B.L.R. 1.

542 Lord Mackay, with whom all of their Lordships agreed, disposed of the case on this narrow point. The wider question of whether the principle established by *Norwich City Council v Harvey* was correct was not addressed.

543 The Act is based on the Law Commission Report, *Privity of Contract: Contracts for the Benefit of Third Parties*, Law Com. No.242 (1999). For comment see: MacMillan (2000) 63 M.L.R. 721; Roe (2000) 63 M.L.R. 887; Burrows [2000] L.M.C.L.Q. 540; Andrews [2001] C.L.J. 352; Stevens (2004) 120 L.Q.R. 292.

544 Contracts (Rights of Third Parties) Act 1999 s.1(1) and (2).

545 Contracts (Rights of Third Parties) Act 1999 s.1(3).

546 Contracts (Rights of Third Parties) Act 1999 s.1(4).

547 s.5 prevents a defendant being doubly liable for the same loss, where the promisee has recovered damages in respect of the third party's loss, and the third party then brings a claim against the defendant.

548 Contracts (Rights of Third Parties) Act 1999 s.1(6).

contract.[549] The Act does not change the position at common law—any remedy available under the Act is in addition to the parties' common law rights.[550] On the other hand, s.7(2) provides that s.2(2) of the Unfair Contract Terms Act 1977 (which subjects the exclusion of liability for negligence to a reasonableness test in the case of "business liability") does not apply where the negligence consists of the breach of an obligation arising from a term of a contract and the person seeking to enforce that obligation is a third party acting in reliance on s.1 of the 1999 Act.

6. MISCELLANEOUS DEFENCES

(a) Necessity

There is a somewhat vague principle of necessity which robs the defendant's intentional acts of culpability, a defence which seems to be allied to that of the remedy of "self-defence".[551] Both are linked by the common requirement of reasonableness. So far as they exist, they only represent "lawful justification and excuse" for what would otherwise be a tortious invasion of another person's rights. The main differences between necessity and self-defence are, first, that the latter presupposes some kind of attack against the person acting in defence, which necessity does not; and, secondly, that in cases of self-defence it would usually be the case that the claimant is in the wrong himself. A convenient nomenclature might be to speak of self-preservation in cases of necessity, and self-defence in the other. Nothing however turns on the terminology. 3-146

The defendant must not have been at fault in creating the crisis in which he claims to have acted under necessity.[552] This is illustrated by *Rigby v Chief Constable of Northampton*,[553] which also draws a distinction in the application of the defence. The police fired a canister of CS gas into the claimant's shop to flush out a dangerous psychopath without having fire-fighting equipment to hand, and the shop was burnt out. It was held that necessity was a defence to a claim in trespass, since the police had not been negligent in creating the emergency; but they were liable in negligence for firing the canister without waiting for the fire-fighting equipment to arrive. In other words, necessity is a defence to an action in trespass if there is no negligence in creating the emergency that prompted the intrusion, but necessity does not excuse negligence in the performance of the intrusion. It must follow that necessity can never be a defence to an action in negligence. 3-147

Protecting persons and property The test of necessity is the same with regard 3-148

---

549 Contracts (Rights of Third Parties) Act 1999 s.3(6).

550 Contracts (Rights of Third Parties) Act 1999 s.7(1).

551 See Williams (1953) 6 C.L.P. 216; and for "agency of necessity", see *Sachs v Miklos* [1948] 2 K.B. 23; *Munro v Willmott* [1949] 1 K.B. 295; cf. *Newark* (1954) 17 M.L.R. 580 at 581; (1956) 19 M.L.R. 320 at 321 arguing that there should not be a defence of necessity in a civil action, for although there may be moral justification for causing damage to the claimant in order to avoid greater harm to the defendant or others, that is no justification for placing the cost of that action upon the innocent claimant.

552 *Southport Corp v Esso Petroleum Co Ltd* [1954] 2 Q.B. 182 at 194 and 198 CA; [1956] A.C. 218 at 242 HL. Where an emergency vehicle (fire brigade, ambulance or police) passes through a red traffic light the defence of necessity does not apply, but the situation is now covered by the Traffic Signs Regulations and General Directions 2016 (SI 2016/362) Sch.14 Pt 1 para.5 which provides that the vehicle must not proceed in such a manner or at such a time as to endanger any person: see *Griffin v Mersey Regional Ambulance* [1998] P.I.Q.R. P34. This does not absolve motorists passing through a green light from exercising reasonable care.

553 [1985] 1 W.L.R. 1242.

to persons and property, namely that the act was reasonably necessary to prevent harm to a third party, or to the claimant, or to the defendant himself. With regard to third parties, the relation between the defendant and the third party will be relevant, for example whether he is acting in preservation of his family or a stranger. The action taken may result in injury to the person or the property of another, but the test of reasonableness will require more justification for the former than for the latter. As Devlin J said: "The safety of human lives belongs to a different scale of values from the safety of property. The two are beyond comparison and the necessity for saving life has at all times been considered a proper ground for inflicting such damage as may be necessary upon another's property."[554] Acts in protection of a third person's property are less likely to fall within the defence today than in the past. The older attitude is seen in *Cope v Sharpe (No.2)*[555] where it was held that the defendant was justified in trespassing onto the claimant's land to prevent a fire from spreading to land over which the defendant's master enjoyed shooting rights on the basis that there was a real and imminent danger.[556] In *Workman v Cowper*,[557] the defendant was prosecuted for shooting a dog because of an alleged threat to sheep. On appeal, it was held that the test was the same whether the shooting was done in defence of one's own property or that to another, but that on the facts the danger had not been sufficiently real or imminent. In *Ashley v Chief Constable of Sussex*[558] the Court of Appeal suggested that *Cope v Sharpe (No.2)* is authority for the proposition that in the case of defence of property it is not sufficient for the defence to apply for the defendant reasonably to believe that there was a danger to property; there must in fact be such a danger to property. This was in distinction to the defence of self-defence (and, presumably, defence of a third party from personal injury or death) where it is sufficient for the defendant to prove that he reasonably (albeit mistakenly) thought that it was necessary to defend himself against attack or an imminent risk of attack, and that the force he used was reasonable. This approach to the defence of self-defence was upheld by the House of Lords.[559] However, two of their Lordships (Lord Scott and Lord Rodger), though expressly leaving the point open, considered that it was strongly arguable that, in the context of civil actions, an honest and reasonable (though mistaken) belief in a state of facts that would otherwise justify the defendant's actions was not sufficient, and that a defendant would have to go on to prove that the facts actually existed.[560]

3-149 The common law defence of "defence of property" may provide a defence to the offence of aggravated trespass under the Criminal Justice and Public Order Act 1994 s.68, but in order for the defence to apply the use of reasonable force must be in order to defend property from actual or imminent damage which constituted

---

554 *Southport Corp v Esso Petroleum Co Ltd* [1953] 3 W.L.R. 773 at 779; on appeal [1956] A.C. 218 at 235 HL.

555 [1912] 1 K.B. 496.

556 In *Ashley v Chief Constable of Sussex* [2006] EWCA Civ 1085; [2007] 1 W.L.R. 398 at [201] Arden LJ, commenting on *Cope v Sharpe (No.2)* said that it was clear that "real" could not mean real in the sense of a danger that actually materialised. Rather: "It means 'real' in the sense that the risk is realistic, not without substance, in the light of what was then known." The fact that it subsequently turned out that there was no danger to property would make no difference to the defence.

557 [1961] 2 Q.B. 143.

558 [2006] EWCA Civ 1085; [2007] 1 W.L.R. 398 at [41] and [78].

559 [2008] UKHL 25; [2008] 1 A.C. 962.

560 cf. Lord Carswell, [2008] UKHL 25; [2008] 1 A.C. 962 at [76], who rejected the view that the defendant has to prove more than an honest and reasonable belief in facts justifying his conduct, commenting that in so far as *Cope v Sharpe (No.2)* [1912] 1 K.B. 496; and *Cresswell v Sirl* [1948] 1 K.B. 241 may be said to support a different conclusion they were not correct.

or could constitute an unlawful or criminal act. The sowing of genetically modified maize seed was not unlawful, even if the seed might blow onto neighbouring land, and therefore the defendants could not rely on the defence.[561]

Acting in the public interest Acting in the public interest used to be another case of necessity, for example pulling down property in time of war, but nowadays even the power of the Crown to act in this way is severely circumscribed.[562] Action on behalf of the "common weal", apart from the necessities of war, is illustrated by *Dewey v White*[563] where, as a result of a fire, a stack of chimneys was in danger of falling onto the highway. To avoid this happening some firemen threw it down and damaged a third party's house. They were held not liable. Today, in the light of the availability of public services to deal with this type of emergency, it may not be necessary for an individual to resort to such action. Lord Denning MR took a stern line when the Court of Appeal rejected the plea of necessity by defendants who occupied the claimant's vacant house for the benefit of homeless families. "Necessity", he said: **3-150**

> "would open a door which no man could shut … The plea would be an excuse for all sorts of wrongdoing. So the courts must, for the sake of law and order, take a firm stand. They must refuse to admit the plea of necessity to the hungry and the homeless; and trust that their distress will be relieved by the charitable and the good."[564]

Prevention of crime A more important instance of action in the public interest is prevention of crime.[565] Section 3 of the Criminal Law Act 1967 gives any member of the public the right to use "such force as is reasonable in the prevention of crime". This draws no distinction between acting on behalf of one's family or on behalf of strangers, nor does the provision make clear the relation between the right under it and the common law right of self-defence. It seems that they overlap, the common law right being wider in that it applies even when no crime is being committed.[566] **3-151**

Prevention of breach of the peace The powers of the police to prevent a breach of the peace may, in extreme circumstances, justify interference with the rights of citizens acting lawfully on the basis that it is necessary *in extremis* to do so. In *Austin v Commissioner of Police of the Metropolis*[567] it was held that the police had acted lawfully in cordoning off Oxford Circus and detaining over a thousand people for a period of some seven hours even though the police could not reasonably have believed that everyone inside the cordon was intent on committing a breach of the peace (indeed they knew that some were peaceful protestors and that others were entirely innocent bystanders caught up in the police cordon). Both the Court of Ap- **3-152**

---

561 *DPP v Bayer* [2003] EWHC 2567 (Admin); [2004] 1 W.L.R. 2856.

562 Y.B. 21 Hen. VII, f. 27b; Dyer, f. 36b; *Att Gen v De Keyser's Royal Hotel* [1920] A.C. 508; *Burmah Oil Co Ltd v Lord Advocate* [1965] A.C. 75 (reversed by the War Damage Act 1965); *Nissan v Att Gen* [1968] 1 Q.B. 286; see also para.5-15 onwards.

563 (1827) M. & M. 56; cf. *Ward v London CC* [1938] 2 All E.R. 341; *Wood v Richards* [1977] R.T.R. 201.

564 *Southwark LBC v Williams* [1971] 1 Ch. 734 at 744. In *Monsanto Plc v Tilly* [2000] Env. L.R. 313, the Court of Appeal held that campaigners against genetically modified crops were not entitled to rely on the defence of necessity in response to a claim for trespass to land (involving the pulling up of the crops) undertaken as part of a publicity campaign against such crops.

565 *Hambley v Shepley* (1967) 67 D.L.R. (2d) 94.

566 See para.14-52.

567 [2007] EWCA Civ 989; [2008] Q.B. 660; affirmed at [2009] UKHL 5; [2009] 1 A.C. 564.

peal and the House of Lords accepted that this defence can apply only in truly exceptional circumstances.[568]

3-153 **Acting in the claimant's interest** The defence of necessity is most often invoked to justify action taken to protect the claimant himself. If a patient is brought into hospital unconscious, the defence of necessity justifies treatment immediately required to save his life or prevent irreversible damage to health.[569] The House of Lords in *F v West Berkshire HA*[570] has held that where a patient is incapable of authorising treatment because of mental incapacity the defence of necessity applies to authorise treatment. Doctors may lawfully do whatever responsible medical opinion deems to be in the best interests of the patient.[571] Nor is the defence of necessity limited in such cases to doctors and/or other health professionals. A person discovering someone unconscious in the street or finding a mentally handicapped person sick or in danger is equally justified in doing whatever is necessary to protect their welfare.[572] In *R. v Bournewood Community and Mental Health Services NHS Trust Ex p. L*[573] the House of Lords held that necessity may justify detaining a mentally incapacitated person for his own safety and welfare. Subsequently in *HL v United Kingdom*[574] the European Court of Human Rights held that L's detention contravened arts 5(1) and 5(4) of the European Convention on Human Rights. Although L was of unsound mind (he suffered from autism) and had not resisted his detention, the common law defence of necessity did not provide a set of procedural rules and there was no provision for review of L's detention (unlike detention under the Mental Health Act 1983) so that it could not be shown that L's detention was not arbitrary. The Mental Capacity Act 2005 establishes a statutory regime providing for the welfare and care of individuals who lack the capacity to

568 See the propositions set out by the Court of Appeal: [2007] EWCA Civ 989; [2008] Q.B. 660 at [35]. Argument in the House of Lords took a different course, and counsel conceded that if there was no breach of the claimants' rights under art.5 of the ECHR there would be no false imprisonment at common law: [2009] UKHL 5; [2009] 1 A.C. 564. Sed quaere: see para.14-64. Of course, if there was no false imprisonment at common law there was no need for a defence of necessity. In *Austin v United Kingdom* (39692/09) (2012) 55 E.H.R.R. 14 the European Court of Human Rights held that there had been no breach of art.5(1); see para.13-103.

569 *Wilson v Pringle* [1987] Q.B. 237 at 252.

570 [1990] 2 A.C. 1.

571 Responsible medical opinion is determined by the *Bolam* test, i.e. the treatment is necessary if a responsible body of professional opinion agree that it was in the best interests of the patient to have that treatment: see *Bolam v Friern Hospital Management Committee* [1957] 1 W.L.R. 582. This would be the case even if another responsible body of professional opinion disagreed. This is a remarkably wide test of necessity, since it effectively grants the medical profession the ability to decide for itself what the limits of this defence should be, and means that incapacitated patients have the right to be protected only from negligent treatment, not controversial treatment. See further Jones (1989) 5 P.N. 178. For this reason the Court of Appeal has held that where the question of appropriate medical treatment comes before a court for decision, while there may be a number of different options which could be lawful in any particular case (since there can be more than one responsible practice), logically there is only one best option, and the court must choose that option in making decisions in the patient's best interests rather than leaving the doctors to choose from the lawful options: *Re S (Adult Patient: Sterilisation)* [2001] Fam. 15 CA.

572 [1990] 2 A.C. 1 at 76.

573 [1999] A.C. 458 HL. The question of whether a third party's interests should ever be considered in a case concerned with the best interests of an incapacitated patient has been left open by the Court of Appeal: *R-B (A Patient) v Official Solicitor* [2000] Lloyd's Rep. Med. 87.

574 (45508/99) (2005) 40 E.H.R.R. 32; 17 B.H.R.C. 418.

make decisions for themselves.[575] The Act reflects, in many respects, the common law position, but effectively replaces the common law rules.

3-154 The principle of necessity in the case of medical treatment is limited to instances where the claimant's own wishes cannot be discerned and it is assumed that he would wish to be treated. In *Re T (Adult: Refusal of Medical Treatment)*[576] the Court of Appeal held that a competent adult has an absolute right to refuse medical treatment, even if in so doing he risks death. Where a conflict arises between the individual's right of self-determination and society's interest in preserving life, the former prevails. There must, however, be unequivocal evidence that the individual has exercised that right freely and in full knowledge of the consequences of his decision to refuse treatment. In cases of doubt, the doubt should be resolved in favour of the preservation of life.[577] The fundamental principle remains however that society cannot impose society's concept of the claimant's interests on a claimant who has clearly articulated his own interests. *Leigh v Gladstone*,[578] holding that necessity justified the force-feeding of a prisoner, is no longer good law.[579] Moreover, where a patient, whilst competent, has made it clear that he does not wish to have a particular treatment a doctor is not justified in relying upon the principle of necessity, once the patient becomes incompetent, to provide that treatment in the belief that it is in the patient's best interests.[580] A refusal of consent, given in advance of the circumstances in which it was to take effect should be observed provided it remains the wish of the patient.[581] The termination of invasive treatment is not unlawful in these circumstances; rather it is unlawful to continue to treat a patient who has expressed a clear and competent wish not to be treated, and the advent of the Human Rights Act 1998 does not support an alternative view. Thus, a mentally competent patient being kept alive by a respirator is entitled to demand that the respirator be removed even if this will inevitably result in her death.[582] The Mental Capacity Act preserves the principle of respecting a patient's "advance decision" to refuse medical treatment whilst competent.[583]

3-155 **Protecting the foetus** It is not lawful to impose non-consensual medical treat-

---

575 The scheme was amended by the Mental Capacity (Amendment) Act 2019. See para.14-124 onwards for discussion.

576 [1993] Fam. 95 CA; see para.9-57. See also *Airdale NHS Trust v Bland* [1993] A.C. 789 at 857, 864, 882 and 891, per Lords Keith, Goff, Browne-Wilkinson and Mustill respectively. See also *Re AK (adult Patient) (Medical Treatment: Consent)* [2001] 1 F.L.R. 129—a competent adult patient's refusal to consent to medical treatment must be observed, even where death may result.

577 *Re T (Adult: Refusal of Treatment)* [1993] Fam. 95 at 103; *St George's Healthcare NHS Trust v S* [1999] Fam. 26 at 63 CA: "if there is reason to doubt the reliability of the advance directive (for example it may sensibly be thought not to apply to the circumstances which have arisen), then an application for a declaration may be made."

578 (1906) 26 T.L.R. 139; see para.14-82.

579 *Secretary of State for the Home Department v Robb* [1995] Fam. 127. Where, however, the prisoner is not competent necessity may justify force-feeding: *R. v Collins and Ashworth Hospital Authority Ex p. Brady* [2000] Lloyd's Rep. Med. 355; (2001) 58 B.M.L.R. 173.

580 *Malette v Shulman* (1990) 67 D.L.R. (4th) 321, Ontario CA; approved by Butler-Sloss LJ in *Re T (Adult: Refusal of Medical Treatment)* [1993] Fam. 95 CA. See also *Re C (Adult: Refusal of Medical Treatment)* [1994] 1 W.L.R. 290.

581 *Airedale NHS Trust v Bland* [1993] A.C. 789 at 857, per Lord Keith, and 864, per Lord Goff, who added that: "in such circumstances especial care may be necessary to ensure that the prior refusal of consent is still properly to be regarded as applicable in the circumstances which have subsequently occurred."

582 *Re B (Adult: Refusal of Medical Treatment)* [2002] EWHC 429 (Fam); [2002] 2 All E.R. 449.

583 Mental Capacity Act 2005 ss.24–26. See further paras 14-126 and 9-61 to 9-62.

ment upon a competent patient who is refusing consent, even if the consequences of that refusal might be death or serious injury. In *Re T (Adult: Refusal of Medical Treatment)*[584] Lord Donaldson left open the possibility that an exception might apply to justify imposing non-consensual treatment on a competent woman in order to save a viable foetus. In *Re S (Adult: Refusal of Medical Treatment)*[585] Sir Stephen Brown P granted a declaration that it would be lawful to perform a Caesarean section operation on a competent 30-year-old woman who had refused consent to the operation, because it was "in the vital interests" of the patient and her unborn child. This decision was widely criticised in that it appeared to contradict the clear dicta of their Lordships in *Airedale NHS Trust v Bland* that a competent patient is entitled to refuse treatment for any reason, even if death is the likely result.[586] In two subsequent Court of Appeal decisions it has been re-affirmed that a competent woman who is refusing treatment cannot be compelled to accept treatment in order to protect the interests, or indeed the life, of the foetus. In *Re MB (Medical Treatment)*[587] the Court of Appeal held that on the facts the patient was not competent because she was refusing to consent to a Caesarean section because of a needle phobia, but nonetheless stated, obiter, that a competent patient had an absolute right to refuse to consent to medical treatment for any reason, rational or irrational, or for no reason at all, even where that decision might lead to his or her death; and that the court had no jurisdiction to take into account the interests of an unborn child at risk from a competent mother's refusal of consent to medical intervention. In *St. George's Healthcare NHS Trust v S*,[588] the Court of Appeal held, this time as the ratio of the case, that there was no jurisdiction to compel a competent woman to undergo medical treatment without her consent to protect the interests of the foetus. Until birth, the foetus had no interests which could be asserted against its mother.[589]

(b) Self-defence

3-156 A form of justifiable action in the interest of the defendant is self-defence, which implies some kind of attack on him, usually by the claimant who is in the wrong himself. A defendant is entitled to act reasonably in defence of himself, his property or third parties. The force used must not be greater than was needed to repel the attack, or what the situation required.[590] In *Lane v Holloway*,[591] the defendant was held liable for a savage blow out of all proportion to the provocation. But a person attacked by a prize-fighter does not have to adhere to the Queensberry rules in his defence,[592] and if he is threatened with an assault he does not necessarily have to

584 [1993] Fam. 95.

585 [1993] Fam. 123.

586 [1993] A.C. 789. The decision also appeared to conflict with established law on the legal status of the foetus, namely that a foetus has no legal personality until it is born and cannot, while a foetus, be made a ward of court: *Paton v British Pregnancy Advisory Service* [1979] Q.B. 276; *C v S* [1988] Q.B. 135; *Re F (In Utero)* [1988] 2 Fam. 122.

587 [1997] 2 F.L.R. 426.

588 [1999] Fam. 26.

589 *Re S (Adult: Refusal of Medical Treatment)* is effectively overruled.

590 "A man cannot justify a maim for every assault; as if A strike B, B cannot justify drawing his sword and cutting off his hand; but it must be such an assault whereby in probability his life may be in danger", *Cook v Beal* (1697) 1 Ld Raym. 176; *Cockcroft v Smith* (1705) 11 Mod. 43.

591 [1968] 1 Q.B. 379. For the effect of provocation, see *Barnes v Nayer, The Times,* 19 December 1986. But see also *Att Gen's Reference (No.2 of 1983)* [1984] Q.B. 456.

592 *Turner v Metro-Goldwyn-Mayer Pictures Ltd* [1950] 1 All E.R. 449 at 471.

wait for the other to give the first blow, because then it might be too late.[593] In *Cross v Kirkby*[594] the claimant struck the defendant with a baseball bat and, following a struggle, the defendant wrested the bat from the claimant and struck him a single blow to the head, fracturing his skull. The Court of Appeal held that the defendant had acted in self-defence. Medical evidence that the force of the blow was greater than average was not a basis for overlooking the wider question of whether the defendant had done what he honestly thought necessary for his own defence in the anguish of the moment. This is not to suggest that the defence is subjective. The claimant is entitled to use only reasonable force. But the reasonableness of the force must inevitably depend on the circumstances, and the defendant's honest belief about the circumstances which he faced will be relevant to that assessment. In *Cross v Kirkby* Judge LJ commented that:

> "When acting in self-defence … the victim of violence … genuinely believing (and here with every reason) that the violence would be likely to continue until brought to an end, he could not be expected, and the law does not require him to measure the violence to be deployed with mathematical precision."

Of course, if the defendant did not honestly believe that the force used was necessary in his defence, the use of force would probably not be considered to be reasonable. The crucial point is that, the court should look at the situation as it presented itself to the defendant at the time, not with the benefit of hindsight in the calm atmosphere of the courtroom.[595] Unlike the criminal law, where the defence of self-defence can succeed on the basis of the defendant's honest (though unreasonable) belief as to the relevant facts, the civil law requires not only an honest, but a reasonably held, belief by the defendant that he was about to be attacked.[596]

Self-defence and injury to third parties What would be the position if the defendant injured a bystander when defending himself against an attack? Self-defence cannot avail against the bystander, who was not attacking. In the early common law, when liability was strict, subject only to specific defences, the defendant was liable. Self-defence would have been a defence against the attacker had he been injured, but not against the bystander.[597] Today liability for personal injury is based on fault, so the defence might be absence of fault as long as the act in self-defence was itself reasonable, i.e. the defence of inevitable accident,[598] or possibly necessity. 3-157

593 *Beckford v The Queen* [1988] A.C. 130 at 144.

594 *The Times,* 5 April 2000 CA.

595 So "the court must have regard to all the circumstances of the case, including the fact that the action may have to be taken in the heat of the moment": *Ashley v Chief Constable of Sussex* [2006] EWCA Civ 1085; [2007] 1 W.L.R. 398 at [82], per Sir Anthony Clarke MR; see also per Auld LJ at [173].

596 *Ashley v Chief Constable of Sussex* [2008] UKHL 25; [2008] 1 A.C. 962; affirming [2006] EWCA Civ 1085; [2007] 1 W.L.R. 398. The burden of proof lies with the defendant. *Ashley* was applied in *Davis v Commissioner of Police of the Metropolis* [2016] EWHC 38 (QB). For consideration of what constitutes reasonable force in the context of the criminal law see the Criminal Justice and Immigration Act 2008 s.76 (as amended); and for interpretation of s.76 in "householder cases" see *R. (on the application of Collins) v Secretary of State for Justice* [2016] EWHC 33 (Admin); [2016] Q.B. 862.

597 Brian CJ in *The Case of Thorns* (1466) Y.B. 6 Ed. 4, f. 7 pl. 18; *Lambert v Bessey* (1681) T. Ray. 421 at 423.

598 See para.3-172.

In *Scott v Shepherd*,[599] the defendant threw a lighted squib into a crowded marketplace. It landed on the stall of X, who to save himself and his goods, threw it aside. It fell on the stall of Y, who to save his goods, did the same; and the squib exploded in the claimant's face. The defendant was held liable to the claimant; but two judges said, obiter, that X and Y would not have been liable because they acted "under a compulsive necessity for their own safety and self-preservation". In *Mohmed v Barnes*,[600] Turner J noted that *Scott* had been decided long before the emergence of the tort of negligence in its modern form, and that caution should be exercised in applying the dicta in *Scott* as though the law has stood still. Where the claimant was an innocent bystander and it was not the defendant's intention to inflict harm, the availability of a remedy should be gauged by the application of the usual tests for breach of duty and causation in negligence. The use of descriptive terms such as "self-defence" or "emergency" was apt to mislead by implying that some special and different test of liability should be applied:

> "The better modern view is that the stallholders X and Y in *Scott* would have escaped liability because their conduct was objectively reasonable, without the need to demonstrate a 'compulsive necessity for their own safety and self-preservation'."[601]

If a defendant was acting in circumstances involving elements of self-defence or emergency these were factors to be taken into account in the overall judgment as to what courses of action were objectively reasonable at the time.

3-158 **Defence of property** When defending property against trespassers reasonable force may be used to prevent them from entering, or to expel them if they have entered.[602] The defendant must be in possession of the property in order to avail himself of the defence.[603] It may be reasonable to take more drastic measures to protect property when one is absent than when one is present[604]; but it is unlawful to set traps, such as spring guns, which are likely to cause death or serious injury.[605] Where an animal is used to protect property the Animals Act 1971 s.5(3)(b) provides that its keeper will not be liable to a trespasser if keeping the animal for that purpose was reasonable.[606] When property is attacked by dogs the common law rule is that a person may kill an attacking dog in order to repel the attack, or to prevent a renewed attack, if killing is the only practical means of protecting his own property and is reasonably necessary in all the circumstances.[607] The defendant must be entitled to protect the property. Section 9 of the Animals Act 1971 provides a defence to an action for killing or injuring a dog if it is proved that the defendant

---

599 (1772) 2 Wm. Bl. 892.
600 [2019] EWHC 87 (QB) at [22].
601 [2019] EWHC 87 (QB) at [23].
602 See para.29-06 onwards.
603 *Holmes v Bagge* (1853) 1 El. & Bl. 782.
604 *Deane v Clayton* (1817) 7 Taunt. 489 at 521.
605 *Bird v Holbrook* (1828) 4 Bing. 628; Offences against the Person Act 1861 s.31.
606 *Cummings v Grainger* [1977] Q.B. 397. The keeping of guard dogs is governed by the Guard Dogs Act 1975, passed after the event that gave rise to *Cummings v Grainger*, so it did not apply. This Act only creates a criminal offence, but breach of it may be evidence that it was unreasonable to keep the animal within s.5(3) of the Animals Act: [1977] Q.B. 397 at 406, per Lord Denning MR.
607 *Cresswell v Sirl* [1948] 1 K.B. 241; *Hamps v Darby* [1948] 2 K.B. 311; *Goodway v Becher* (1951) 115 J.P. 435; *Workman v Cowper* [1961] 2 Q.B. 143. For consideration of different approaches to the meaning of "reasonably necessary" see *Ashley v Chief Constable of Sussex* [2006] EWCA Civ 1085; [2007] 1 W.L.R. 398; affirmed [2008] UKHL 25; [2008] 1 A.C. 962; at para.3-148.

"acted for the protection of livestock", and the livestock or the land on which it was situated belongs to the defendant or to any person under whose express or implied authority he is acting. The defendant must notify the police within 48 hours of the incident. The defence will not apply if the circumstances are such that the keeper of the dog would not have been liable for the dog killing or injuring the livestock by virtue of s.5(4).[608] A person will only be regarded as acting for the protection of livestock if: (a) the dog is worrying or is about to worry the livestock and there are no other reasonable means of ending or preventing the worrying; or (b) the dog has been worrying livestock, has not left the vicinity and is not under the control of any person and there are no practicable means of ascertaining to whom it belongs.[609] A reasonable belief that these conditions were satisfied is sufficient for the purpose of the defence.[610]

Defence against common dangers When danger to property is threatened by what is sometimes called the "common enemy" (fire or flood), the law is that as long as the danger is still approaching, it may be diverted away from the defendant's property, even onto another's property.[611] Once it has come on the defendant's land, he may not then get rid of it to the detriment of another.[612] Duress, short of physical compulsion, is no defence.[613] Nor can the sacrifice of an innocent party be justified to maximise the chances of the defendant's survival.[614] **3-159**

(c) Authorisation

Authorised acts Acts may be authorised by the common law or by statute. In the case of the former, the right depends on decided cases and means no more than the absence of a duty-situation prohibiting the activity on grounds of policy, i.e. that there is no duty not to do it. The existence of a private right is the result of some specific grant and needs proof, whereas the existence of a general right will be judicially noticed as a matter of law. **3-160**

Superior orders are no defence. If one person commands another to commit a tort they are both answerable as joint tortfeasors. To this there is a limited exception, known as "act of state", when authorisation or subsequent ratification by the Crown of an act, otherwise tortious, against a foreigner on foreign soil, is a defence to the person who executes the order.[615] **3-161**

Statutory authority The circumstances in which a breach of statutory duty may give rise to an action at common law, and when a failure to exercise a statutory **3-162**

[608] i.e. where "the livestock was killed or injured on land on to which it had strayed and either the dog belonged to the occupier or its presence on the land was authorised by the occupier."

[609] Animals Act 1971 s.9(3).

[610] Animals Act 1971 s.9(4).

[611] *Greyvenstein v Hattingh* [1911] A.C. 355 (locusts); *Gerrard v Crowe* [1921] 1 A.C. 395 (water); *Home Brewery Co Ltd v Williams Davis & Co (Leicester) Ltd* [1987] Q.B. 339.

[612] *Whalley v The Lancashire & Yorkshire Ry Co* (1884) 13 Q.B.D. 131.

[613] *Gilbert v Stone* (1647) Style Aleyn 35; *Smith v Stone* (1647) Style 65; *Weaver v Ward* (1616) Hob. 134; *Gibbons v Pepper* (1695) 1 Ld. Ray 38.

[614] *R. v Dudley and Stevens* (1884) 14 Q.B.D. 273 (eating the cabin-boy!).

[615] *Buron v Denman* (1848) 2 Ex. 167. The defence does not avail against a foreigner on British soil: *Johnstone v Pedlar* [1921] 2 A.C. 262; nor against a British subject even on foreign soil: *Walker v Baird* [1892] A.C. 491, though some doubt was expressed in *Att Gen v Nissan* [1970] A.C. 179.

power may amount to a breach of duty are dealt with elsewhere.[616] Statutes operate differently when they provide exemptions from liability. In all cases the overriding rule is that the precise effect of a given provision depends on its wording. Thus, in *Karuppan Bhoomidas v Port of Singapore Authority*[617] the Privy Council construed a bye-law of the Singapore Harbour Board that "the board undertakes no responsibility as stevedores" as not excluding its vicarious liability for the negligence of its employees.

3-163 A more difficult question is to what extent statutory authority is a defence to an action in respect of damage occasioned in exercising a statutory power. The first and overriding consideration is that in order for statutory authority to succeed as a defence, the defendant must have acted without negligence, on the ground that a statute would never authorise negligence. The leading case is *Geddis v Proprietors of the Bann Reservoir*.[618] The defendants had statutory authority to maintain a reservoir and to cleanse the channel of a river. They negligently failed to keep the latter clean and it overflowed, causing damage to the claimant. They were held liable on the basis that they were not authorised to discharge their functions negligently.

3-164 In *Tate & Lyle Industries Ltd v Greater London Council*,[619] the defendant council had statutory authority to execute certain works in the river Thames. These caused silting, which interfered with access to the claimants' jetties. It was shown that the defendants could have adopted a different design for their works, which would have minimised the interference. The House of Lords held that because of this, statutory authority was no defence to liability in public nuisance. (They were held not liable in negligence for a different reason.)

3-165 **Power and nuisance**[620] Apart from express provision or necessary implication, a statute does not authorise the creation of a nuisance.[621] "Necessary implication" is judged according to the facts of each case. In *Allen v Gulf Oil Refining Ltd*,[622] the defendants acquired power by private Act of Parliament to construct an oil refinery, but not specifically to operate it. The House of Lords held, by a majority, that in so far as the operation of a refinery entailed smell, noise, vibrations and such like as well as some alteration of the environment and impairment of amenities, Parliament must be deemed to have authorised these.[623] On the other hand private rights are important and interference with them will not be justified if the defendant has a choice as to how he exercises his powers, whether in a way that causes a nuisance or not. It is the right of others, not his own convenience, that will be decisive. So, a rate-aided fever hospital, authorised as such by statute, could not be built so as

616 See Chs 8 and 13.

617 [1978] 1 W.L.R. 189.

618 (1878) 3 App. Cas. 430.

619 [1983] 2 A.C. 509.

620 See para.19-87 onwards.

621 *Hammersmith Ry v Brand* (1869) L.R. 4 H.L. 171; *London, Brighton etc Ry v Truman* (1885) 11 App. Cas. 45; *Buley v BRB* [1975] C.L.Y. 2458.

622 [1981] A.C. 1001; reversing the Court of Appeal [1980] Q.B. 156, where Lord Denning MR had suggested that just as there is a presumption against compulsory acquisition of property without compensation, so also there should be a presumption against compulsory infliction of damage without compensation.

623 As Lord Diplock commented: "Parliament can hardly be supposed to have intended the refinery to be nothing more than a visual adornment to the landscape in an area of natural beauty."

to become a nuisance to adjoining occupiers,[624] nor could locomotives be run so as to constitute a nuisance under a statute authorising a railway but not the running of locomotives.[625] Similarly, a statute authorising tramways did not authorise setting up stables for horses (at that time necessarily incidental) in a place where they constituted a nuisance,[626] and a highway authority was liable for failing to remove an abandoned tram track that was a nuisance and had become vested in the authority.[627]

Even where the particular act is authorised, the incidental commission of a nuisance in the course of or following performance will involve liability unless it was a necessary consequence of that act.[628] It was said in *Dunne v North Western Gas Board*[629] that a person acting under a mandatory statutory obligation (e.g. to maintain a supply of water, electricity or gas) does not incur liability under *Rylands v Fletcher*[630] or in nuisance (whether or not the statute contains a saving clause retaining liability for nuisance) provided that what is done was expressly required to be done, or is reasonably incidental to it, and that it is done without negligence. Where there is a statutory power, but no nuisance clause, the position is the same. But where there is a power with a nuisance clause the undertakers are liable for nuisance even if they are not negligent. **3-166**

There has been a discernible tendency for the courts to interpret "necessary implication" and "reasonably incidental" in the light of social utility. If the interference is very small in comparison with the public advantage to be derived from the activity complained of it has sometimes been held that the statutory authority is a sufficient justification.[631] **3-167**

Power and Rylands v Fletcher The statute may expressly or by necessary implication give relief from liability under the rule in *Rylands v Fletcher*,[632] though in this case liability may still be incurred through negligence if this is proved.[633] If it does not give such relief, liability may be incurred under this head,[634] although it **3-168**

---

624 *Metropolitan Asylum District v Hill* (1881) 6 App. Cas. 193; cf. *Att Gen v Nottingham Corp* [1904] 1 Ch. 673; *City of La Portage la Prairie v BC Pea Growers* (1965) 54 D.L.R. (2d) 503.

625 *Jones v Festiniog Ry* (1868) L.R. 3 Q.B. 733; cf. *Vaughan v Taff Vale Ry* (1860) 5 H. & N. 679.

626 *Rapier v London Tramways* [1893] 2 Ch. 588.

627 *Simon v Islington BC* [1943] K.B. 188.

628 *Dell v Chesham Urban DC* [1921] 3 K.B. 427; cf. *Kennedy v The Queen* (1970) 13 D.L.R. (3d) 442; *Provender Millers v Southampton CC* [1940] Ch. 131; *Pride of Derby Angling Association v British Celanese* [1953] Ch. 149; *Smeaton v Ilford Corp* [1954] Ch. 450.

629 [1964] 2 Q.B. 806; and see now *Department of Transport v NW Water Authority* [1984] A.C. 336.

630 (1868) L.R. 3 H.L. 330.

631 e.g. *Edgington v Swindon BC* [1939] 1 K.B. 86; *Oakes v Minister of War Transport* (1944) 60 T.L.R. 319; *Ching Garage Ltd v Chingford Corp* [1961] 1 W.L.R. 470; *Att Gen of New Zealand v Lower Hutt Corp* [1964] A.C. 1469 (not a case of nuisance, but the Privy Council held that a power to provide "pure water" was not abused by adding fluoride, since this was conducive to the better dental health of the community).

632 See para.19-91. See *North-Western Utilities etc v London Guarantee etc Co* [1936] A.C. 108 at 120; *Smeaton v Ilford Corp* [1954] Ch. 450 at 478; *Dunne v North Western Gas Board* [1964] 2 Q.B. 806; cf. *Pearson v North Western Gas Board* [1968] 2 All E.R. 669 at 672; *Allen v Gulf Oil Refining Ltd* [1981] A.C. 1001.

633 *Green v Chelsea Waterworks* (1894) 70 L.T. 547; *Hardaker v Idle DC* [1896] 1 Q.B. 335.

634 *Jones v Festiniog Ry* (1868) L.R. 3 Q.B. 733; *Charing Cross Electricity Co v London Hydraulic Co* [1914] 3 K.B. 772.

has been suggested obiter that a local authority in exercising statutory powers is outside the scope of the rule in *Rylands v Fletcher*.[635]

3-169 **Power and trespass** Likewise, a statutory power must be exercised in such a way that it does not effect a trespass, unless the exact right entitles a trespass to be committed. Thus, a statutory power to arrest without warrant will not be extended to cover any interference with the person not expressly authorised, notwithstanding that the police act in good faith.[636] However, if a discretion to requisition land is sufficiently widely stated, the court will not interfere where the power has been exercised in good faith.[637]

(d) Mistake

3-170 Mistake may lead the defendant into liability which he did not, and sometimes could not, reasonably anticipate. However, mistake of law will not excuse, nor, speaking generally, will mistake of fact. So, to deal with the goods of one person under the honest and even reasonable[638] mistake that they belong to someone else is a conversion.[639] To mow the grass of a neighbour under the mistaken notion that it is one's own is a trespass.[640] So, also, to publish a libel to a person under the mistaken belief that he is privileged to receive the communication would still be actionable,[641] as would a publication under the belief that no such person as the claimant in fact existed[642] (subject to the protection afforded by ss.2–4 of the Defamation Act 1996, and that afforded to innocent disseminators of a libel).[643] Belief in the truth of the statement is no defence in defamation.

3-171 Nevertheless, wherever wrongful motive, or reasonableness is a condition of liability, then a bona fide mistake of fact may have the effect of negativing liability (although strictly, a mistake as to a matter which is a condition of liability is not a true "defence"; rather the requirements for liability have not been met). So, an involuntary bailee may return chattels to a person under the mistaken belief that he is the bailor[644] provided that he has acted reasonably. From the earliest times a bona fide belief in the truth of a statement was a defence in slander of title,[645] and also a defence in deceit. The whole question that will arise will be whether the necessary intention or negligence can be said to be present.

---

635 *Pride of Derby etc v British Celanese* [1953] Ch. 149 at 189, per Denning LJ; but cf. at 176, per Sir Raymond Evershed MR; and *Smeaton v Ilford Corp* [1954] Ch. 450 at 478.

636 *Christie v Leachinsky* [1947] A.C. 573; and para.14-65 onwards. But see the tendency with regard to seizure of goods in cases like *Elias v Pasmore* [1934] 2 K.B. 164; and *Chic Fashions (West Wales) Ltd v Jones* [1968] 2 Q.B. 299. The Police and Criminal Evidence Act 1984 s.26(1) abrogates earlier statutory provisions specifically giving the police the power to arrest without warrant. This does not apply, however, to statutes conferring a general power of arrest, so that a police officer acting under such a statutory power is entitled to arrest without a warrant: *Gapper v Chief Constable of the Avon and Somerset Constabulary* [2000] 1 Q.B. 29 CA.

637 *Carltona Ltd v Commissioners of Works* [1943] 2 All E.R. 560.

638 See *Consolidated Co v Curtis* [1892] 1 Q.B. 495.

639 *Hollins v Fowler* (1875) L.R. 7 H.L. 757.

640 *Basely v Clarkson* (1682) 3 Lev. 37.

641 See para.21-64.

642 *Hulton & Co v Jones* [1910] A.C. 20; para.21-10.

643 See Ch.21.

644 *Elvin and Powell v Plummer Roddis* (1933) 50 T.L.R. 158; see para.16-80.

645 *Gerard v Dickenson* (1590) 4 Co. Rep. 18a.

(e) Inevitable accident

Difficulties have arisen in the past in actions of trespass over "inevitable accident", that is, an accident "not avoidable by any such precaution as a reasonable man, doing such an act then and there, could be expected to take".[646] In actions other than trespass there was little difficulty, for whenever liability involved proof of fault as part of the prima facie case, the fact that the occurrence was an "inevitable accident" negatived fault which meant that there was no liability to which a defence could apply. The defence of inevitable accident is no more than another way of pleading "no prima facie case of fault". On the other hand, if liability is strict, i.e. does not rest on fault, inevitable accident is no defence because a plea of "no fault" is irrelevant. In such cases nothing less than act of God will excuse, even though some defences seem tantamount to saying "no fault".[647] The difficulties occurred in the early forms of trespass where it was possible to establish a prima facie case without proof of fault. The onus was then on the defendant to prove innocence, so inevitable accident was truly a defence to liability arising without proof of fault.[648] Later trespass was modified into liability dependent on proof of fault as part of the prima facie case.[649] At least in actions of trespass to the person and to goods, whether occurring on or off the highway, the claimant must prove intention or negligence as part of his case, so that in this respect there is now no difference between an action alleging trespass and an action alleging a negligent injury. Inevitable accident has thus become equivalent to saying "no prima facie case" here too, save in those cases where a prima facie case can be made out by the mere fact of some occurrence (res ipsa loquitur). A plea of inevitable accident then functions as a form of defence in that the defendant is required to adduce some evidence which might explain how the accident could have happened without fault on his part, although, strictly, the burden of proof remains with the claimant throughout.[650] **3-172**

Taking all reasonable care has been held not to be a defence in certain forms of nuisance where the nuisance was the act of the defendant,[651] and apparently in some cases even where it is not.[652] This is because liability depends, not so much on the wrongdoing of the defendant, as on the event, namely, an unreasonable interference with the claimant's use or enjoyment of land or of some right in respect of it. If there is unreasonable interference, then the fact that the defendant has taken all **3-173**

---

646 Pollock, *Torts*, 15th edn, p.97; cf. *Fowler v Lanning* [1959] 1 Q.B. 426; *Bell Telephone Co of Canada v The Ship Mar-Tirenno* (1974) 52 D.L.R. (3d) 702.

647 On the other hand, true examples of strict liability in tort are difficult to find these days. The rule in *Rylands v Fletcher*, is now subject to foreseeability of the damage and this must mean that the old defence of Act of God is subsumed within the foreseeability requirement: see *Cambridge Water Co Ltd v Eastern Counties Leather Plc* [1994] 2 A.C. 264.

648 "The distinction is seen at once in pleading. In trespass the defendant must plead inevitable accident ... In negligence he need only plead a denial", per Devlin J in *Southport Corp v Esso Petroleum Co Ltd* [1953] 3 W.L.R. 773 at 781.

649 *Holmes v Mather* (1875) L.R. 10 Ex. 261; *Stanley v Powell* [1891] 1 Q.B. 86; *NCB v Evans* [1951] 2 K.B. 861; *Fowler v Lanning* [1959] 1 Q.B. 426; *Beals v Hayward* [1960] N.Z.L.R. 131; *Letang v Cooper* [1965] 1 Q.B. 232. cf. *Bell Can v Cope (Sarnia)* (1980) 11 C.C.L.T. 170, where the Ontario High Court accepted that trespass is now founded on fault, but added that once direct damage to the claimant or his goods was shown, the onus of disproving fault was on the defendant. For the role of inevitable accident in negligence, see Bing (1977) 1 M.L.J. 6.

650 *Ng Chun Pui v Lee Chuen Tat* [1988] R.T.R. 298 PC.

651 *Rapier v London Tramways Co* [1893] 2 Ch. 588 at 599.

652 *Tarry v Ashton* (1876) 1 Q.B.D. 314; *Wringe v Cohen* [1940] 1 K.B. 229; *Sedleigh-Denfield v O'Callaghan* [1940] A.C. 880; see para.19-189.

reasonable care is no defence. Equally, taking all reasonable care to avoid the publication of a defamatory statement, as distinct from avoidance of the publication of a statement at all, is no defence at common law.[653] Thus, inevitable accident cannot be said to be a general principle for exemption from liability. The "defence" only amounts to a traverse either: (1) of the voluntariness of the act or omission of the defendant on which the action depends; or (2) of the intention or carelessness necessary to render such act or omission actionable.[654]

(f) Limitation

3-174 No one should remain under threat of being sued indefinitely. Accordingly, time-limits are imposed within which claimants must issue their actions and these limits vary with different kinds of action. This complex topic will be dealt with in a later chapter.[655]

(g) Personal immunity

3-175 There are some other general exemptions from liability. There are exemptions from liability enjoyed by certain types of individuals, for example judicial officers.[656] These are really not concerned with the nature of tortious liability, but with immunity conferred by the law upon certain persons, and they are left for consideration elsewhere. It is only necessary to remark that it is not an immunity for a particular kind of tort (though in practice only certain torts are likely to be affected), but for a particular kind of person. From these must be distinguished situations where there is liability, but the wrongdoer is protected from action, for example diplomats.[657]

---

653 *Hulton & Co v Jones* [1910] A.C. 20; *Cassidy v Daily Mirror Newspapers* [1929] 2 K.B. 331; *Newstead v London Express Newspapers Ltd* [1940] 1 K.B. 377. A protection against damages was introduced by s.4 of the Defamation Act 1952, now replaced by ss.2–4 of the Defamation Act 1996: see para.21-182 onwards. Where the defendant only disseminates the libel, see *Weldon v Times Book Co* (1911) 28 T.L.R. 143; *Bottomley v Woolworth & Co* (1932) 48 T.L.R. 521; and para.21-175.

654 Although within the meaning of insurance policies words such as "accidental bodily injury" are held to include negligent acts: *Marcel Beller v Hayden* [1978] Q.B. 694 (considering *Gray v Barr* [1971] 2 Q.B. 554).

655 See Ch.31.

656 See para.5-101 and following.

657 *Dickinson v Dell Solar* [1930] 1 K.B. 376 (insurance company liable though the diplomat himself could not be sued); see also *Zoernsch v Waldock* [1964] 1 W.L.R. 675. Liability of a surety: *Magdalena Steam Navigation Co v Martin* (1859) 2 E. & E. 95 at 115.

Chapter 4

JOINT LIABILITY AND CONTRIBUTION

Table of Contents

1. Introduction

Scope of chapter This chapter considers the ascription and extinction of liability of multiple defendants where more one than person is responsible for the totality of the loss or damage suffered by the claimant in a tort action. Central to the chapter is the juristic distinction to be drawn between joint and several tortfeasors. 4-01

2. Joint and Several Torts

Joint and several torts Where damage is caused as the result of torts committed by two or more tortfeasors, the tortfeasors may be: (1) joint tortfeasors (for example, where D1 and D2 are each responsible for a joint, tortious venture which injures C); (2) several tortfeasors causing the same damage; or (3) several tortfeasors causing different damage. If one of a number of joint tortfeasors, or of several tortfeasors causing the same damage, is sued alone, he is liable for the whole damage, though he did but a small part of it.[1] In the case of several tortfeasors causing different damage, on the other hand, each is liable only for the damage which he has caused.[2] 4-02

Definition of joint tortfeasors Who, then, are joint tortfeasors? One way of answering the question is to see whether the cause of action against each tortfeasor is the same. If the same evidence would support an action against each, they are joint tortfeasors.[3] They will be jointly liable for a tort which they both commit or for the commission of which they are both responsible, but not where each is independently responsible for a separate tort and the two torts combine to produce the same damage.[4] Nor will there be joint tortfeasance where A and B are acting 4-03

---

1 *Clark v Newsam* (1847) 1 Ex. 131 at 140; *Damiens v Modern Society Ltd* (1910) 27 T.L.R. 164. He may be entitled to contribution from the other tortfeasors: see para.4-13 onwards.

2 See para.4-07.

3 *Brunsden v Humphrey* (1884) 14 Q.B.D. 141 at 147, per Bowen LJ.

4 See, e.g. *The Koursk* [1924] P. 140 where the owners of two ships, the Koursk and the Clan Chisholm, were independently negligent causing a collision between those two ships to occur so that the Clan Chisholm would subsequently collide with a third ship, the Itria.

jointly in a potentially tortious manner, but A alone causes injury to the claimant. Thus, where two drivers are racing one another at excessive speeds, and only one driver crashes (thereby causing injury to his passenger), the other driver—though also having driven recklessly—cannot be treated as a joint tortfeasor.[5]

4-04 Thus, the agent who commits a tort on behalf of his principal and the principal himself are joint tortfeasors; so are the employee who commits a tort in the course of his employment and his employer (even if the employer became insolvent before the time of the trial[6]); so are an independent contractor who commits a tort and his employer, in those cases in which the employer is liable for his independent contractor.[7] Equally, a parent company and its subsidiary may be regarded as joint tortfeasors in respect of loss or injury suffered by employees of the subsidiary *so long as* a supervisory duty is borne by the parent company.[8] But the mere fact that a parent company appoints a director of the subsidiary who holds responsibility for health and safety matters in that company is not enough to attach liability to the parent company. He would need to be acting not just as a director of the subsidiary, but also on behalf of the parent in order for this to be the case.[9] Finally, a company director and the company itself may be regarded as joint tortfeasors where the director "is sufficiently bound up in [the company's] acts" to make him personally liable.[10] This will certainly occur where the wrongful acts complained of arise from a director's participation in a manner that goes beyond the mere exercise of his power of control through the constitutional organs of the company. An example is where he facilitates the breach of a design right with a view to enabling a breach of that right to occur.[11] Apart from these instances, concerted action is required. Where one person instigates another to commit a tort[12] they are joint tortfeasors;

---

5 *Davis v Catto* [2011] CSIH 85; 2012 Rep. L.R. 40.

6 *Catanzano v Studio London Ltd* UKEAT/0487/11/DM (7 March 2012).

7 See, e.g. *Clark v Hosier Dickson Ltd* [2003] EWCA Civ 1467. For further instances in which an employer will be liable for the torts of an independent contractor, see para.6-65 onwards.

8 *Chandler v Cape Plc* [2012] EWCA Civ 525; [2012] 1 W.L.R. 3111. As Arden LJ explained, at [80]: "[T]his case demonstrates that in appropriate circumstances the law may impose on a parent company responsibility for the health and safety of its subsidiary's employees. Those circumstances include a situation where, as in this case, (1) the business of the parent and subsidiary are in a relevant respect the same; (2) the parent has, or ought to have, superior knowledge on some relevant aspect of health and safety in the particular industry; (3) the subsidiary's system of work is unsafe as the parent company knew, or ought to have known; and (4) the parent knew or ought to have foreseen that the subsidiary or its employees would rely on its using that superior knowledge for the employees' protection." Contrast *AAA v Unilever Plc* [2018] EWCA Civ 1532; [2018] B.C.C. 959: parent company owed no duty of care to those affected by acts or omissions of its subsidiary which had been responsible for its own decision-making and had not sought advice from the parent company. See also para.12-08 onwards.

9 *Thompson v Renwick Group Plc* [2014] EWCA Civ 635; [2014] P.I.Q.R. P18 at [25], per Tomlinson LJ. It is a question, then, of the level of control and supervision the parent has exercised over the subsidiary: *Lungowe v Vedanta Resources Plc* [2019] UKSC 20; [2019] 2 W.L.R. 1051 at [49].

10 *Koninklijke Philips Electronics NV v Princo Digital Disc GmbH* [2003] EWHC 2588 (Pat); [2004] 2 B.C.L.C. 5. See also *Contex Drouzhba v Wiseman* [2006] EWHC 2708 (QB); [2007] 1 B.C.L.C. 758; and *Global Crossing Ltd v Global Crossing Ltd* [2006] EWHC 2043 (Ch) where it was held that even where a company is dormant when the action is brought, a director and anyone else personally bound up in the commission of a tort (such as the company secretary who helped incorporate the defendant company in this passing off case) will be joint tortfeasors.

11 *Societa Esplosivi Industriali SpA v Ordnance Technologies (UK) Ltd (formerly SEI (UK) Ltd)* [2007] EWHC 2875 (Ch); [2008] 2 All E.R. 622 at [103], per Lindsay J.

12 *Brooke v Bool* [1928] 2 K.B. 578; *MCA Records Inc v Charly Records Ltd (No.5)* [2001] EWCA Civ 1441; [2002] E.M.L.R. 1; *White v Withers LLP* [2009] EWCA Civ 1122; [2010] 1 F.L.R. 859.

so are persons whose respective shares in the commission of a tort are done in furtherance of a common design.[13] However, it is important to appreciate that although mere facilitation of the commission of a tort will not suffice, a sufficient common design may nonetheless be held to exist where D1 makes a more than de minimis contribution to the commission of a tort by D2. The Supreme Court in *Fish & Fish Ltd v Sea Shepherd UK*[14] found that while a common design would normally be expressly communicated between the principal and the accessory, it could be inferred. The assistance, however, had to be more than de minimis or trivial. Lord Neuberger advised that "once the assistance is shown to be *more than trivial*, the proper way of reflecting the defendant's relatively unimportant contribution to the tort is through the court's power to apportion liability, and then order contribution, as between the defendant and the primary tortfeasor".[15] For this reason, any case of unlawful means conspiracy could be explained in terms of joint tortfeasance where the unlawful means used constitute the commission of a tort. However, since the unlawful means in this tort can also include other wrongs, such as the commission of a common law crime,[16] it cannot be said that unlawful means conspiracy is an otiose cause of action.[17] "All persons in trespass who aid or counsel, direct, or join, are joint trespassers."[18] Similarly, according to the decision of Mackay J in *Daniels v Commissioner of Police for the Metropolis*,[19] there may be joint tortfeasance under the Protection from Harassment Act 1997 where the harassment on at least two occasions has been perpetrated by more than one person, each acting on separate occasions, in furtherance of some joint design. And anyone complicit in the commission of a deceit may likewise be regarded as a joint-tortfeasor so long as there is a common design.[20] However, an alleged joint tortfeasor cannot have actively co-operated to bring about the relevant act of the primary tortfeasor if he (the alleged joint tortfeasor) did not know about that act.[21]

Equally, mere similarity of design on the part of independent actors, causing independent damage, is not enough; there must be concerted action towards a common end.[22] A person who only facilitated (as opposed to procured) a tort would not **4-05**

---

13 This statement of the law was approved in *The Koursk* [1924] P. 140 at 151, 156 and 159; and see *Brooke v Bool* [1928] 2 K.B. 578 at 585; *Mahesan v Malaysia Government Officers' Co-operative Housing Society Ltd* [1978] A.C. 374; *MCA Records Inc v Charly Records Ltd (No.5)* [2001] EWCA Civ 1441; [2002] E.M.L.R. 1.

14 [2015] UKSC 10; [2015] A.C. 1229 (Lords Sumption and Mance dissenting on the question of whether the charity's assistance could properly be regarded as de minimis and not from a difference about legal principles). Applied in *Glaxo Wellcome UK Ltd (t/a Allen & Hanburys) v Sandoz Ltd* [2017] EWCA Civ 227; [2017] F.S.R. 32. The Supreme Court also advised that there was no formula for determining whether that had happened and establishing liability was so fact-sensitive that it would be unwise for a court to produce such a formula. For a recent application, see *Red Bull GmbH v Big Horn UK Ltd* [2020] EWHC 124 (Ch); [2020] E.T.M.R. 27.

15 [2015] UKSC 10; [2015] A.C. 1229 at [57] (emphasis added).

16 See *Customs and Excise Commissioners v Total Network SL* [2008] UKHL 19; [2008] 1 A.C. 1174. (The common law crime involved was that of cheating the Inland Revenue.)

17 cf. Stevens, *Torts and Rights* (Oxford: OUP, 2006), p.249.

18 *Petrie v Lamont* (1842) Car. Marsh. 93 at 96, per Tindal CJ.

19 [2006] EWHC 1622 (QB).

20 *Dadourian Group International Inc v Simms* [2009] EWCA Civ 169; [2009] 1 Lloyd's Rep. 601.

21 *National Guild of Removers and Storers Ltd v Luckes* [2017] EWHC 3176 (IPEC).

22 The decision of Lord Ellenborough in *Hume v Oldacre* (1816) 1 Stark. 352, that where a huntsman rode after his hounds over the claimant's land he was liable for the whole damage done by those following him, on the ground that the parties were co-trespassers, can hardly be supported on that ground. See also *Cook v Lewis* [1952] 1 D.L.R. 1 (two men hunting together held, by Supreme Court

be liable as a joint tortfeasor.[23] Still less will persons be joint tortfeasors when there is not even similarity of design, but independent wrongful acts accidentally resulting in one form of damage.[24] So, for example, the parent or guardian of a child whose personal negligence enables the child to commit a tort may be liable as well as the child for the resulting damage, but not as a joint tortfeasor.[25] On the other hand, there will be joint tortfeasance where the completion of the tort requires distinct acts on the part of both tortfeasors. An example is that of reutilising material in which the claimant has database rights. In such a case the actual infringement committed by D1 (i.e. that of copying the database material) is combined with the independent act of another party, D2, who makes use of the copied information. So, where a German company (D1) copied information from the internet in which the claimant (based in the UK) had database rights, and the German company then worked in tandem with a UK-based company (D2) to make that information available in the UK via an alternative internet source from that controlled by the claimant, D1 and D2 could be regarded as joint tortfeasors.[26]

4-06 Torts of all kinds may be joint, and in this respect libel and slander[27] form no exception.[28] If, however, the publication is on an occasion of qualified privilege or amounts to honest opinion, only those who published with malice will be liable[29] and so the mere fact of joint publication does not necessarily make all the publishers joint tortfeasors. Where a particular state of mind is required for liability in tort, two or more persons will not be joint tortfeasors even in respect of a common tort unless, at the time, they had the required state of mind in common.[30]

4-07 **Several tortfeasors causing different damage** Where two or more tortfeasors cause different damage to the same claimant, the causes of action against each tortfeasor are entirely distinct from one another and the claimant can recover from each tortfeasor only that part of his damage for which the particular tortfeasor is

---

of Canada, not to be joint tortfeasors); *League Against Cruel Sports Ltd v Scott* [1986] Q.B. 240; *Intel Corp v General Investment Corp (No.2)* [1991] R.P.C. 235 Patents Court. The law on joint tortfeasors is the same whether or not the alleged common design is between two individuals or a parent company and its subsidiary.

23 *Generics (UK) Ltd v H Lundbeck A/S* [2006] EWCA Civ 1261; *CBS v Amstrad* [1988] A.C. 1013.

24 *The Koursk* [1924] P. 140 at 156.

25 *Bebee v Sales* (1916) 32 T.L.R. 413; *Newton v Edgerley* [1959] 1 W.L.R. 1031. cf. *Donaldson v McNiven* [1952] 2 All E.R. 691; *Gorely v Codd* [1967] 1 W.L.R. 19.

26 *Football Dataco Ltd v Sportradar GmbH* [2010] EWHC 2911 (Ch); [2011] F.S.R. 10. (The Court of Appeal allowed the defendants' appeal in part, but not affecting this point: [2011] EWCA Civ 330; [2011] 1 W.L.R. 3044).

27 If slanderers act in concert, or if an employee utters a slander within the scope of his employment, there will be a joint tort. But the mere utterance of the same slanderous words by two or more people will not make them joint tortfeasors: *Chamberlaine v Willmore* (1621) Palm. 131. They may, however, be joined in the same action as defendants: see *Thomas v Moore* [1918] 1 K.B. 555.

28 See, e.g. *Veliu v Mazrekaj* [2006] EWHC 1710 (QB); [2007] 1 W.L.R. 495 at [14], per Eady J.

29 *Egger v Viscount Chelmsford* [1965] 1 Q.B. 248; see para.21-206 onwards. The defence of honest opinion is now stated in s.3 Defamation Act 2013. The defence is defeated if the claimant shows that the defendant did not hold the opinion: s.3(5)

30 *Gardiner v Moore* [1969] 1 Q.B. 55 at 91, per Thesiger J. Where the same damage is inflicted on the claimant but the acts do not fall within one of the categories of joint torts, then the defendants will be "several concurrent tortfeasors": see, e.g. *Drinkwater v Kimber* [1952] 2 Q.B. 281.

responsible.[31] In the absence of evidence to apportion the damages, they will be apportioned equally between the tortfeasors.[32]

Formerly the distinction between joint tortfeasors and several tortfeasors causing the same damage had great importance because where there was a joint tort there could only be one action and one judgment for the whole amount of the damages to which the claimant was entitled. In the case of several tortfeasors, on the other hand, each tortfeasor was responsible for a separate tort and successive actions could be brought against them even though the damage suffered by the claimant was one and indivisible. Now, by virtue of s.3 of the Civil Liability (Contribution) Act 1978[33] a judgment recovered against any person liable in respect of the same damage is no bar to an action, or to the continuance of an action, against any other person jointly liable in respect of the same damage.[34] Successive actions against joint tortfeasors and others jointly or severally liable to the claimant are subject to the safeguard against a multiplicity of actions that whenever more than one action is brought by the claimant in respect of the same damage the claimant will not be entitled to costs unless the court is of the opinion that there was reasonable ground for bringing the action. Although successive actions against tortfeasors are permissible, whether they are joint tortfeasors or several tortfeasors causing the same damage, they may of course be made defendants in the same action,[35] in which case only one judgment for a single sum may be given against all defendants.[36] It is even open to a potential defendant whom the claimant does not propose to join as a co-defendant to request (under CPR r.19.4(2)) that he or she should be joined as a co-defendant; and the court even has a discretion under CPR r.19.2(2) to join such a party of its own motion. In *Coal Mining Contractors v Davies*,[37] X sought to be made a co-defendant with Y fearful that, first, Y would not put up a proper defence to the action and that, secondly, X would later be made liable to Y in contribution proceedings. Y resisted this application as did the claimant. The Court of Appeal therefore had to consider whether it ought, in this case, to make X a co-defendant. In the course of their deliberations, their Lordships set out the various factors that were relevant to the exercise of their discretion. They said that they must bear in mind the following: (1) X's reason for wishing to be joined (in this case, the fear that X would be disadvantaged by allowing Y to conduct the defence alone); (2) the claimants' reason for wishing to exclude X from the proceedings (in this case, the danger that the proceedings would become needlessly protracted and thus prohibitively expensive); (3) the interest of Y in conducting the defence alone (in the present case, a concern about costs). In this case, the interests 4-08

31 *Performance Cars Ltd v Abraham* [1962] 1 Q.B. 33; *Holtby v Brigham Cowan (Hull) Ltd* [2000] 3 All E.R. 421.

32 *Bank View Mill v Nelson Corp* [1942] 2 All E.R. 477 at 483; reversed on other grounds [1943] 1 K.B. 337.

33 See para.4-12 of the 19th edition of this work, for problems concerning torts committed before the 1978 Act came into force but not sued upon until after that date.

34 A satisfied judgment against one tortfeasor remains a bar to action against the other tortfeasors, joint or several, in respect of the same damage save in the case of a foreign judgment: *Kohnke v Karger* [1951] 2 K.B. 670.

35 CPR r.7.3.

36 *Sir John Heydon's Case* (1612) 11 Co. Rep. 59; *Egger v Viscount Chelmsford* [1965] 1 Q.B. 248; *Broome v Cassell & Co Ltd* [1972] A.C. 1027.

37 [2006] EWCA Civ 1360; [2007] 1 W.L.R. 3232.

of the claimants and Y held sway given that, as Waller LJ put it, Y would "fight liability properly".[38]

4-09 The freedom for claimants to bring successive actions in respect of the same damage against different defendants appears now to be in the process of being curtailed by the courts. Multiplicity of actions is being discouraged[39] and claimants would be well-advised to sue all potential defendants in a single action. In *Morris v Wentworth-Stanley*,[40] the Court of Appeal explained that the purpose of s.3 of the 1978 Act was to remove the common law defence of "release by judgment" in its entirety, so that judgment against one of two or more persons jointly liable for the same debt or damage should not in itself be a bar to an action against those others who were liable but not party to the judgment. It was not intended to remove the rule that release of one person jointly liable for the debt operated to release all others jointly liable by accord and satisfaction (in the absence of a reservation by the claimant of a right to maintain the claim against the other joint debtors). Section 3 did not detract from the general proposition that it was plainly desirable that all persons who are to be sued should be sued at the same time and in the same proceedings where such a course is reasonably practicable. If this is not done, then the rule on issue estoppel in *Henderson v Henderson*[41] could be invoked to render a second action an abuse of process.

4-10 The only remaining consequence of the distinction between joint tortfeasors and several tortfeasors causing the same damage was that release of one joint tortfeasor whether under seal or by way of accord and satisfaction[42] releases all the others,[43] and this is not strictly the case with several tortfeasors. Moreover, a mere covenant not to sue one joint tortfeasor does not have this effect,[44] and in the past courts have been reluctant to construe an agreement with one tortfeasor as a release rather than a covenant not to sue.[45] On the other hand, the decision of the House of Lords in *Jameson v Central Electricity Generating Board*[46] has created potential problems for the unwary claimant who accepts a settlement from one several tortfeasor. There, J brought a claim against his former employer (BE) for personal injuries (malignant mesothelioma) due to exposure to asbestos. He reached a settlement with BE "in full and final settlement and satisfaction" of his claim. J died before the money was paid over, and therefore it fell into his estate and was inherited by his widow. After his death, his executors brought an action under the Fatal Accidents Act 1976 on behalf of his widow for her loss of dependency against the CEGB, at whose premises J had carried out work for BE. The basis of the claim for damages was the same exposure of J to asbestos, with similar allegations of negligence and breach of statutory duty. CEGB then joined BE as a third party. The

---

38 [2006] EWCA Civ 1360; [2007] 1 W.L.R. 3232 at [21].

39 See, e.g. *Talbot v Berkshire CC* [1994] Q.B. 290; and *Wain v F Sherwood and Sons Transport Ltd* [1999] P.I.Q.R. P159.

40 [1999] Q.B. 1004.

41 (1843) 3 Hare 100. For issue estoppel, see para.30-24. It is not an abuse of process for D1 to fail to claim contribution against D2 when both are sued by C, and subsequently to bring contribution proceedings against D2: *Sweetman v Shepherd* [2000] C.P. Rep. 56 CA.

42 See *Gardiner v Moore* [1969] 1 Q.B. 55 at 92.

43 *Thurman v Wild* (1840) 11 A. & E. 453; *Cutler v McPhail* [1962] 2 Q.B. 292.

44 *Apley Estates Co Ltd v de Bernales* [1947] Ch. 217; *Gardiner v Moore* [1969] 1 Q.B. 55.

45 *Bryanston Finance Ltd v De Vries* [1975] Q.B. 703. Lord Denning MR seemed prepared to discard such a distinction, as being "an arid and technical distinction without any merits": [1975] Q.B. 703 at 723.

46 [2000] 1 A.C. 455.

Court of Appeal held that the claimants were entitled to maintain the action under the Fatal Accidents Act 1976, and that CEGB were entitled to contribution from BE under the Civil Liability (Contribution) Act 1978 on the basis that their respective liabilities were "in respect of the same damage", namely the alleged wrong that caused injury and death to J.[47] On appeal to the House of Lords, the question of whether CEGB were entitled to claim contribution against BE was not pursued, but was assumed to be correct by Lord Hope. The issue was whether the claimants were entitled to maintain the Fatal Accidents Act claim against CEGB, the answer to which depended upon whether the liability of concurrent (i.e. several) tortfeasors for the same harm is discharged by a settlement which has been entered into with one of them.[48] In order for the claimants to succeed under the Fatal Accidents Act, the deceased must have been entitled to maintain an action in respect of the wrong causing the death immediately before his death.[49] The difficulty which the majority of the House of Lords (Lord Lloyd dissenting) sought to address was that J's widow had inherited the £80,000 paid by BE to J's estate under the settlement. She had also been awarded £142,000 against CEGB as the agreed sum for the loss of her dependency under the Fatal Accidents Act, but s.4 of that Act provides that any benefits accruing to the dependant from the estate of the deceased, including sums received as compensation for the injuries, are to be disregarded. Thus, if the Court of Appeal's decision stood, she would receive "double" compensation, whereas BE would be liable to a claim for contribution under the Civil Liability (Contribution) Act 1978 from CEGB, notwithstanding the settlement reached with J before his death. On the other hand, the claimant contended that the settlement that J reached with BE was less than the full value of the claim, and the claimant should be able to make up the shortfall by claiming against the other tortfeasor.

Lord Hope said that the basic rule is that damages are compensatory, and that a claimant cannot recover more than the amount of his loss.[50] The question, then, was whether the agreement between J and one concurrent tortfeasor had "satisfied" his claim for damages, because if it had not, then it would not extinguish J's widow's claim against the other concurrent tortfeasor. This was to be tested by looking at the terms of the agreement and comparing it with what had been claimed. The intention of the parties is to be found in the wording of the settlement. If it is not expressed to be in full and final satisfaction, or if the claimant specifically reserves the right to maintain a claim against other concurrent tortfeasors, it should not have the effect of extinguishing those claims. The question, said Lord Hope, is not whether the claimant has received the full value of his claim but whether the sum which he has received in settlement of it was intended to be in full satisfaction of the tort.[51] This takes effect from the date of the settlement, not the date when pay- 4-11

47 See para.4-22 for the meaning of "the same damage".

48 It was not a case of accord and satisfaction which would have extinguished the liability of joint tortfeasors. The normal rule has been that a release from liability granted to a joint tortfeasor will release the others, whereas a release of one of several concurrent tortfeasors will not—CEGB and BE were concurrent, rather than joint, tortfeasors.

49 Fatal Accidents Act 1976 s.1. In *Pickett v British Rail Engineering Ltd* [1980] A.C. 136, the House of Lords assumed that where the deceased had sued the defendant to a judgment or settled his claim while still alive, the dependants could not sue under the 1976 Act.

50 [2000] 1 A.C. 455 at 471.

51 This approach has since been followed in *Heaton v AXA Equity Law Life Assurance Society Plc* [2002] UKHL 15; [2002] 2 A.C. 329. In explaining *Jameson*, their Lordships held that where a claim is compromised, it need not necessarily be in full and final satisfaction for all the damage claimed,

ment is made under the settlement (subject to the proviso that if payment is not made the agreement becomes void ab initio).

4-12 The consequence of the majority ruling of the House of Lords in *Jameson* is that claimants should be advised when accepting a settlement expressly to reserve their rights to maintain an action against any other concurrent tortfeasors.[52] If this had been done in *Jameson* then the element of "double recovery" that their Lordships were anxious to avoid would still have occurred. This, as Lord Lloyd pointed out in his strong dissenting speech, is a consequence of the effect of s.4 of the Fatal Accidents Act 1976, which provides that in a claim under the Act for loss of dependency any benefit accruing to the dependants from the deceased's estate is to be ignored. Thus, this is an explicit result of a deliberate policy choice taken by Parliament. Similarly, the fact that BE might have been subject to a claim for contribution by CEGB, notwithstanding that BE had already made a "full and final settlement" with J is also the result of the wording of the Civil Liability (Contribution) Act 1978 as interpreted by the courts; a view upheld by the Court of Appeal in *Jameson* and not appealed to their Lordships' House.

3. Contribution

4-13 **Contribution and indemnity between joint tortfeasors** At common law the general rule for both joint tortfeasors, and several tortfeasors causing the same damage was that there could be no award of contribution or indemnity between them in the absence of an express or implied agreement which was not itself void on public policy grounds.[53] Now, however, s.1(1) of the 1978 Act extends the right to contribution beyond tortfeasors alone and provides that: "… any person liable in respect of any damage suffered by another person may recover contribution from any other person liable in respect of the same damage (whether jointly with him or otherwise)".[54] The words in parentheses can have special significance in the context of the tort of inducing breach of contract, for while the parties cannot be joint tortfeasors (because the contract breaker can only be liable for breach of contract in the absence of any conspiracy), the two parties are nonetheless jointly responsible for causing the same damage.[55]

4-14 **Who may claim contribution?** Any person liable to another whether in tort, contract, breach of trust or otherwise,[56] may now recover contribution from any

but might instead be a lesser sum agreed for tactical reasons. In such a case a claimant is not precluded from making a further claim against a concurrent tortfeasor. In order to establish the full value of a claim, the terms of the settlement agreement and their context will be the primary point of reference. In the present case, the agreement in question did not represent the full measure of H's loss, nor had the separate claims against the third party been part of the compromise.

52 See, e.g. *Rawlinson v North Essex HA* [2000] Lloyd's Rep. Med. 54—settlement of claim against a pharmaceutical company barred a subsequent claim against the hospital in respect of damage attributable to the use of the drug myodil in the performance of a myelogram.

53 *Merryweather v Nixon* (1799) 8 T.R. 186.

54 The Civil Liability (Contribution) Act 1978 is applied automatically to all proceedings for contribution brought in England and Wales, irrespective of any choice of law rules: see *Roberts v Soldiers, Sailors, Airmen and Families Association* [2019] EWHC 1104 (QB); [2020] Q.B. 310; affirmed at [2020] EWCA Civ 926.

55 See, e.g. *Thames Valley Housing Association Ltd v Elegant Homes (Guernsey) Ltd* [2011] EWHC 1288 (Ch); [2011] N.P.C. 54.

56 Civil Liability (Contribution) Act 1978 s.6(1).

other person liable in respect of the same damage, regardless of the basis of the latter's liability.[57] Liability in respect of any damage means liability which has been or could be established in an action brought in England and Wales, even though the rules of private international law require the application of foreign law to determine any issue in dispute.[58] But a foreign judgment, it seems, gives no right to seek contribution from others liable in respect of the same damage. By s.1(2), even if, on the date when a claim for contribution is made, the claimant has ceased to be liable in respect of the damage in question—for example, if he has discharged his liability by payment or by compromise or the period of limitation has expired—he is still entitled to contribution providing that he was liable in respect of the relevant damage at the time when he was ordered to make the payment in respect of which contribution is sought, or when he made or agreed to make the payment. If D1 is sued for negligence in respect of personal injuries within three years of the damage being caused, he may recover contribution from D2 even if when he makes his claim three years have elapsed and the injured person could no longer sue D2.[59] But if D1 and D2 are jointly or concurrently liable for a tort created by virtue of anti-discrimination legislation, claims in respect of contribution are almost certainly only justiciable in the ordinary courts since an employment tribunal does not have jurisdiction to determine such matters.[60]

Effect of exclusion and limitation clauses One particular complication that might arise in this context centres on the effect of an exclusion clause that purports to exclude liability on the part of one of the tortfeasors. The leading case is *Co-operative Retail Services Ltd v Taylor Young Partnership Ltd*.[61] There, a firm of architects and a firm of consulting engineers were being sued in respect of fire dam- **4-15**

---

[57] The right to claim contribution (which may be a payment in kind: *Baker & Davies Plc v Leslie Wilks* [2005] EWHC 1179 (TCC); [2005] 3 All E.R. 603) passes on the defendant's death to his personal representatives whether or not his liability had been established/admitted before his death: *Ronex Ltd v John Laing Construction Ltd* [1983] Q.B. 398. The defence of ex turpi causa non oritur actio cannot be relied upon in an answer to a claim for contribution under the 1978 Act: *K v P* [1993] Ch. 140, per Ferris J. The reason is that this would be inconsistent with the scheme of the Act: *Patel v Mirza* [2016] UKSC 42; [2017] A.C. 476 at [244], per Lord Sumption. Section 6(1) of the Act is "deliberately wide" and should not be subjected to a condition precedent which is not to be found in the Act. Moreover, the Act gives the court ample power to fix the amount of contribution at a level, including zero, which takes into account all the factors which are relevant to ex turpi causa non oritur actio.

[58] Civil Liability (Contribution) Act 1978 s.1(6). See also *RA Lister Co Ltd v EG Thomson (Shipping) Ltd* [1987] 1 W.L.R. 1614; *Virgo S.S. Co SA v Skaarup Shipping Corp (The Kapetan Georgis)* [1988] 1 Lloyd's Rep. 352, per Hirst J: "nothing in the 1978 Act limits its scope to liabilities incurred in England and Wales."

[59] But D1 must bring his claim within two years of being ordered, agreeing to make or making a payment in respect of the damage: Limitation Act 1980 s.10. Note that where D1's agreement to settle requires embodiment in a consent order before the agreement becomes effective, there is authority that the two-year period runs from the date on which the consent order is made rather than the earlier date on which the agreement is reached: *Knight v Rochdale Healthcare NHS Trust* [2003] EWHC 1831 (QB); [2004] 1 W.L.R. 371. For the treatment of Pt 36 offers, see *Chief Constable of Hampshire v Southampton City Council* [2014] EWCA Civ 1541; [2015] P.I.Q.R. P5 (distinguishing Knight). A voluntary interim payment does not trigger the start of the two-year period for commencing contribution proceedings: *Spire Healthcare Ltd v Brooke* [2016] EWHC 2828 (QB); [2017] 1 W.L.R. 1177. Nor does an agreement in principle "subject to contract": *RG Carter Building Ltd v Kier Business Services Ltd* [2018] EWHC 729 (TCC); [2018] 1 W.L.R. 4598.

[60] *Beresford v Sovereign House Estates Ltd* [2012] I.C.R. D9 (EAT) at [12] per Underhill J.

[61] [2002] UKHL 17; [2002] 1 W.L.R. 1419.

age caused in the course of constructing new headquarters for the claimant. The architects and consulting engineers sought a contribution from two further parties, the main contractor and/or the electrical sub-contractor, alleging that the fire, if negligently caused, was the responsibility of all four parties. Upholding the decision of the Court of Appeal, it was held by the House of Lords that no contribution could be sought from either the main contractor or the electrical sub-contractor because of the existence of express terms in the main contract and sub-contract which excluded the main contractor and the electrical sub-contractor from liability for fire damage, this damage being covered by a joint names insurance policy which was taken out by the main contractor on behalf of all those engaged in the construction. Crucially, the joint names insurance policy taken out by the main contractor provided for the costs of reinstatement work whatever the cause of the fire. As such, any liability on the part of the contractor and electrical sub-contractor to the claimant lay only in respect of other damage making s.1(1) inapplicable for there was no possibility of the contribution claim being made "in respect of the same damage".

4-16 Notwithstanding the foregoing, it has been decided that rather different considerations apply where one co-defendant is liable for deceit and thus unable to take advantage of a limitation or exclusion clause. In *Nationwide Building Society v Dunlop Haywards (DHL) Ltd and Cobbetts (A Firm)*,[62] D1 was liable to the claimant for the tort of deceit, while D2 (D1's solicitors) had negligently failed to identify that deceit and in turn notify the claimants of it. The totality of the loss suffered by the claimants was held to be approximately £13.2 million, but that figure had to be reduced to £6.6 million by virtue of the claimants' 50 per cent contributory negligence. The question that then arose was whether D2's limitation of liability clause (placing the limit at £5 million) was to be given effect, or whether the full £6.6 million was to be divided between D1 and D2. In alighting upon the latter figure, Clarke J held that although "there is something to be said for the view that a defendant who has a limitation clause should not be in a worse position than he would have been if both defendants had a similar clause" it was nonetheless the case "that it would be inconsistent with the scheme of the Act if, as part of the process of determining what is a just and equitable contribution, I was to proceed on the basis that the amount to be proportioned is to be reduced by the effect of *one defendant's* limitation clause".[63] Ultimately, in other words, the judge was unprepared to allow D1 the benefit of a limitation clause which, by virtue of his fraud, he could never have relied on had the limitation clause been his own.

4-17 **Contribution in respect of settlement** Section 1(4) of the Civil Liability (Contribution) Act 1978 seeks to discourage unnecessary litigation by enabling a party to a settlement to recover contribution from others liable with him in respect of the damage for which he has agreed to compensate the person suffering damage. The section provides that a person may recover contribution if he has made or agreed to make any payment:

> "… in bona fide settlement or compromise of any claim made against him in respect of any damage (including a payment into court which has been accepted) … without regard to whether or not he himself is or ever was liable in respect of the damage, provided,

---

[62] [2009] EWHC 254 (Comm); [2010] 1 W.L.R. 258.

[63] [2009] EWHC 254 (Comm); [2010] 1 W.L.R. 258 at [75] (emphasis added).

however, that he would have been liable assuming that the factual basis of the claim against him could be established."[64]

The requirement that the settlement or compromise be bona fide seems aimed at excluding collusive settlements but is insufficient to exclude the injudicious or unreasonable settlement to which the party from whom contribution is sought would not have agreed. On the other hand, it has been held that the imposition of such an agreement on a third party can be justified even though the third party played no part in formulating its terms. For where such a settlement or agreement has been approved by the court, the agreement acquires a status beyond merely a private agreement between the first and second parties to the litigation. Rather, in having been approved by the court in the exercise of its procedural powers, it would lie with any properly interested third party to invite the court to re-examine the terms of the agreement.[65] Furthermore, contribution can only be sought, of course, from persons liable for the damage. To safeguard the rights of the person from whom contribution is sought, while the person seeking contribution need not prove that he was liable on the facts, it must be shown that if the factual basis of the claim could be established, then in law the person seeking contribution was liable for the damage. Where proceedings have begun, the person seeking contribution can establish liability on the basis of the facts set out in the statement of claim.[66] In other cases, the factual basis of the claim may have to depend on the facts as he understood, or ought to have understood them, to be and the question in such a case of the bona fide nature of the settlement becomes crucial.

What is recoverable? Section 1 of the Civil Liability (Contribution) Act 1978 is concerned with liability not quantum, so a person from whom contribution is sought is entitled to argue that certain heads of loss were irrecoverable in law by the claimant from the defendant (notwithstanding that such heads of loss were included as part of a settlement between claimant and defendant), and therefore could not form part of the sum in respect of which the defendant was entitled to claim contribution.[67] Similarly, D1 is not entitled to claim contribution from D2 in respect of parts of a settlement which are excessive, because they have been overstated by the claimant. The absence of a right to contribution here is justified on the basis that a contribution under the Act is only available in respect of sums which the claimant was entitled to claim from D1 in law. As such, where it is impossible to quantify a "just and equitable share of the loss", and thus a clear amount that D1 is entitled to claim by way of contribution, no claim for contribution will be available.[68] More contentious is whether sums paid to the claimant in a settlement for the claimant's costs should be recoverable in contribution proceedings. Although it is hard to think of costs as part of "the same damage", the Court of Appeal has suggested that "the 1978 Act enables the party claiming contribution to **4-18**

64 *Arab Monetary Fund v Hashim (No.8)* (1994) 6 Admin. L.R. 348.

65 *AB v British Coal Corp* [2004] EWHC 1372 (QB).

66 See, e.g. *WH Newson Holdings Ltd v IMI Plc* [2016] EWCA Civ 773; [2017] Ch. 27, notably [52]–[62]: s.1(4) gives the defendant in the main proceedings the benefit of an assumption that the factual basis pleaded in the statement of claim could be established against it.

67 *J Sainsbury Plc v Broadway Malyan (A Firm), (Ernest Green Partnership Ltd, Third Party)* [1999] P.N.L.R. 286.

68 *Abbey National Bank Plc v Matthews & Son* [2003] EWHC 925 (Ch); [2003] 1 W.L.R. 2042.

recover a contribution towards a payment made in respect of the injured party's costs".[69]

4-19 **Liability to contribution after settlement with claimant** It is made clear in s.1(4) that release of one joint wrongdoer, while it may still bar an action against others jointly liable, will not bar a claim for contribution.[70] But if a person settles the matter of his liability with the claimant by means of a release or otherwise, can he then be sued for contribution by some other person liable, jointly or otherwise, in respect of the same damage? The Act provides no express answer. In *Jameson v Central Electricity Generating Board*,[71] the Court of Appeal held that the answer was "yes", and though this particular matter was not appealed to the House of Lords, Lord Hope assumed the proposition to be correct. However, the decision of their Lordships in *Jameson* means that where there is a settlement in full and final satisfaction of C's claim against D1 (irrespective of whether this is discounted from its full "value" for litigation risk or otherwise) this operates as a bar to a claim by C against D2, so that D2 will have no liability to pay damages to C for which he is likely to seek contribution from D1.[72] *McGill v Sports and Entertainment Media Group* clarified that the *Jameson* principle is not confined to concurrent tortfeasors: "the true question which has to be answered is whether, by settling the earlier action, the claimant has fixed the full measure of his loss, so that he has no remaining loss to recover from anybody else. The answer to this question depends on the proper construction of the compromise agreement, placed in its factual and legal context."[73] On the other hand, *Heaton v Axa Equity & Law Life Assurance Society Plc*[74] makes it clear that if, for tactical reasons, the settlement is not in full and final satisfaction, or if C reserves his right to claim against other tortfeasors, D1 remains open to a contribution claim from D2 when C either sues D2 to judgment or settles his claim with D2.

4-20 **From whom may contribution be claimed?** Contribution is recoverable from any person liable in respect of the same damage as the party seeking contribution.[75] A person who would not be liable in an action brought against him by the claimant will therefore generally not be liable in a claim for contribution.[76] An exception to the rule that contribution may only be claimed from someone himself li-

---

[69] *Parkman Consulting Engineers v Cumbrian Industrials Ltd* [2001] EWCA Civ 1621; [2002] B.L.R. 64 at [123], per Henry LJ; *Mouchel Ltd v Van Oord (UK) Ltd* [2011] EWHC 1516 (TCC); [2011] B.L.R. 492. cf. *J Sainsbury Plc v Broadway Malyan (A Firm), (Ernest Green Partnership Ltd, Third Party)* [1999] P.N.L.R. 286.

[70] See, e.g. *Stott v West Yorkshire Car Co Ltd* [1971] 2 Q.B. 651; *BRB (Residuary) Ltd v Connex South Eastern Ltd (formerly South Eastern Train Co Ltd)* [2008] EWHC 1172; [2008] 1 W.L.R. 2867.

[71] [1998] Q.B. 323; [2000] 1 A.C. 455 HL.

[72] See, e.g. *Vanden Recycling Ltd v Kras Recycling BV* [2017] EWCA Civ 354; [2017] C.P. Rep. 33: satisfaction of the consent judgment against one tortfeasor in full and final settlement of the claims against it would bar claims against the concurrent tortfeasors for the same damage. Satisfaction of a settlement agreement as opposed to a judgment will only have this effect if the sum agreed and paid was intended to fix the full measure of the claimant's loss.

[73] [2016] EWCA Civ 1063; [2017] 1 W.L.R. 989 at [91], per Henderson J.

[74] [2002] UKHL 15; [2002] 2 A.C. 329. The question of whether any particular settlement is full and final so as to "wipe the slate clean" will be a question of fact to be answered by close scrutiny of the terms of the settlement in question: *Cape & Dalgleish v Fitzgerald* [2002] UKHL 16; [2003] 1 C.L.C. 65. See also *Dowdall v William Kenyon & Sons Ltd* [2014] EWHC 2822 (QB).

[75] Civil Liability (Contribution) Act 1978 s.1(1).

[76] See, e.g. *Knapp v Railway Executive* [1949] 2 All E.R. 508.

able to the claimant is contained in s.1(3) of the Civil Liability (Contribution) Act 1978, which provides:

> "A person shall be liable to make contribution … notwithstanding that he has ceased to be liable in respect of the damage in question since the time when the damage occurred, unless he ceased to be liable by virtue of the expiry of a period of limitation or prescription which extinguished the right on which the claim against him in respect of the damage was based."

Liability to make contribution remains even if a person has ceased to be liable to the claimant by virtue of the expiry of a period of limitation, unless a period of limitation or prescription has extinguished the right on which the action against him was based. This proviso has only a limited remit: most periods of limitation in tort merely bar the remedy, not the right.[77] Thus, in an ordinary tort action, the fact that D2 would not be liable to C because C's limitation period has expired does not prevent D1 bringing a contribution claim against D2. Similarly, in *Logan v Uttlesford DC*[78] the Court of Appeal held that where D2 has settled C's claim against him (and has therefore ceased to be liable to C by reason of the settlement) D2 may still be liable to make a contribution to D1. The claim for contribution fell literally within the scope of s.1(3) and remained valid. In *Jameson v Central Electricity Generating Board*, the Court of Appeal endorsed this approach.[79]

There is a problem reconciling s.1(3) with ss.1(5) and 6 of the Act. Section 1(5) provides that a judgment given in any action brought in any part of the United Kingdom by or on behalf of the person who suffered the relevant damage shall be conclusive in the proceedings for contribution as to any issue determined by that judgment in favour of the person from whom contribution is sought. The Law Commission's Draft Bill expressly limited this bar to a claim for contribution to a judgment resting on a determination of the merits of the claim and not on the fact that the claim was statute-barred.[80] Whether s.1(5) can be interpreted to exclude judgments resting only on a successful plea of limitation,[81] or some other issue not going to the merits—for example, dismissal for want of prosecution[82]—remains to be seen. At the very least, it has been held that s.1(5) should be construed so as not to bar an appeal.[83] Section 6(1) of the Civil Liability (Contribution) Act 1978 clearly refers to a person who "is liable in respect of any damage". A person previously held not liable by the courts would appear to be outside the literal terms of the provisions made for contribution by the Act. Alternatively, it could be argued that s.1(5) must be read subject to s.1(3), and any issue determined by a judgment in favour 4-21

---

77 Thus in an action for conversion the owner's right to the chattel is extinguished by the expiry of the limitation period. See generally paras 31-30 and 31-32.

78 (1986) 136 N.L.J. 541. See also *RA Lister Ltd v Thomson Shipping* [1987] 1 W.L.R. 1614, per Hobhouse J.

79 [1998] Q.B. 323; [2000] 1 A.C. 455 HL. The point was not pursued on appeal to the House of Lords, but was assumed to be correct.

80 *Law Commission Report No.79*, Draft Bill, cl.3(7). And see *Hart v Hall and Pickles Ltd* [1969] 1 Q.B. 405.

81 *Nottingham HA v Nottingham City Council* [1988] 1 W.L.R. 903 at 911–912.

82 See *Hart v Pickles Ltd* [1969] 1 Q.B. 405. See also *RA Lister Ltd v Thomson Shipping* [1987] 1 W.L.R. 1614 at 1623, per Hobhouse J (obiter): "dismissal of … proceedings against the charterers for want of prosecution … would not have amounted to a determination of the merits" in favour of D2.

83 *Moy v Pettman Smith (A Firm)* [2005] UKHL 7; [2005] 1 W.L.R. 581.

of the person against whom contribution is sought interpreted as subject to the proviso contained in s.1(3).[84]

4-22 **"Same damage"** By s.1(1) of the Civil Liability (Contribution) Act 1978 contribution is recoverable from any person liable in respect of the same damage as the party seeking contribution. At one time, the courts gave a broad interpretation to this phrase so as to include substantially or materially similar damage.[85] But in *Royal Brompton Hospital NHS Trust v Hammond (No.3)*[86] the House of Lords overruled this approach stating that the words "liable in respect of the same damage" were to receive their ordinary and natural meaning. In that case, contractors were responsible for delayed construction work per se, whereas a firm of architects (by issuing certain extension certificates) were liable for the claimant losing the opportunity to sue the contractors for that delay. The contractors and the architects were not, therefore, responsible for the same damage. Equally, in another case in which the first defendant's conversion of property merely provided the opportunity for the second defendant to convert that self-same property at a later date, the damage associated with each separate conversion could not be regarded as the same damage. This is because "each conversion amounts to a separate wrong" and "the damage for each conversion falls ... to be assessed having regard to the value of the goods in the open market at the time and in the place at which the conversion occurs".[87] Similarly, where D1 undervalued a commercial property on behalf of a building society and D2 later defaulted in making repayments of the mortgage advanced by the building society on that property, D1 and D2 were not responsible for the "same damage". The losses associated with D1's undervaluation were not the same as the loss caused by D2's non-payment of a debt.[88]

4-23 **"Same damage" may entail distinguishing damages from restitution** The restrictive approach to the interpretation of "same damage" begun in the *Royal Brompton Hospital NHS Trust* case was continued at first instance in *Niru Battery Manufacturing Co v Milestone Trading Ltd (No.2)*.[89] In that case a claimant had successfully sued the first defendants in negligence in respect of a false certificate they had produced that had caused the claimants mistakenly to transfer $5.8 million to the second defendants who, in turn, released the money to a third party with whom

[84] But the wording of s.1(5) makes it awkward to exclude other judgments based on a technicality in favour of the person against whom contribution is sought unless "any issue" in s.1(5) is robustly limited to issues of merit alone, excluding all other issues.

[85] *Friends Provident Life Office v Hillier, Parker, May and Rowden* [1997] Q.B. 85.

[86] [2002] UKHL 14; [2002] 1 W.L.R. 1397. Contrast, however, the approach taken by the New Zealand Supreme Court in *Hotchin v New Zealand Guardian Trust Co Ltd* [2016] NZSC 24; [2016] N.Z.L.R. 906, noted by Stace (2017) 133 L.Q.R. 20.

[87] *VFS Financial Services (UK) Ltd v Euro Auctions (UK) Ltd* [2007] EWHC 1492 (QB) at [126], per Judge Richard Seymour QC.

[88] *Howkins & Harrison v Tyler* [2001] P.N.L.R. 27; [2001] Lloyd's Rep. P.N. 1 CA. See also *Dingles Building (NI) Ltd v Brooks* [2003] P.N.L.R. 8 (loss caused by a failure to obtain a contract for C was not the same as depriving C of the chance to obtain seven necessary signatures on that contract); *Webb v Barclays Bank Plc* [2001] EWCA Civ 1141; [2002] P.I.Q.R. P8; [2001] Lloyd's Rep. Med. 500 (D2's negligent medical advice that compounds the problems caused to C by D1 does amount to a contribution to the "same damage"); *Cohen v Davies* [2006] EWHC 768 (Ch); [2006] P.N.L.R. 33 (D2's negligent advice possibly contributed to depletion of company assets when it should have been wound up). cf. *Luke v Kingsley Smith* [2003] EWHC 1559 (QB); [2004] P.N.L.R. 12.

[89] [2003] EWHC 1032 (Comm); [2003] 2 All E.R. (Comm) 365. See in similar vein *Jubilee Motor Policies Syndicate 1231 at Lloyd's v Volvo Truck & Bus (Southern) Ltd* [2010] EWHC 3641 (QB).

the money was eventually lost. Subsequently, however, the first defendants sought a contribution from the second defendants either under s.1 of the 1978 Act, or by virtue of the equitable remedy of subrogation. In relation to the 1978 Act point, Moore-Bick J held the statute to be inapplicable since the first and second defendants were not liable in respect of the "same damage". His reasoning was that the action in tort against the first defendants (for the negligently produced certificate) was distinguishable from the action brought against the second defendants since this was for *restitutionary damages* (based on their unjust enrichment at the expense of the claimants).[90] On appeal, the suggestion that a compensatory claim and a restitutionary claim should be treated as different forms of damage was cast in doubt in so far as Clarke LJ stated that: "on the question of whether a claim for restitution is a claim for 'compensation', I do not think that it would be appropriate for me to express my own view"[91] while Sedley LJ agreed with Moore-Bick J that "a claim in restitution is axiomatically not a claim in damages".[92]

The uncertainty arising from the decision in *Niru Battery* was effectively resolved by the Court of Appeal in *Charter Plc v City Index Ltd*.[93] There, Carnwath LJ held that even though a claim for knowing receipt (as arose in that case) might generally be described as restitutionary, that did not preclude it being treated as an action concerned with recovering compensation for the purposes of the 1978 Act. He said: "In ordinary language (adopting a wide view of the 1978 Act) City Index's liability ... can properly be referred to as liability to 'compensate'."[94] All that remains to be seen, then—assuming a case with the appropriate facts arises—is whether a freestanding restitutionary claim, which is not contingent upon some prior tort or breach of trust, will be treated as different damage, thus excluding the application of the 1978 Act. It is submitted that the weight of authority is in favour of such a distinction. 4-24

"Same damage" entails distinguishing damage caused negligently and fraudulently In *Nationwide Building Society v Dunlop Haywards (DHL) Ltd and Cobbetts (A Firm)*,[95] D1 fraudulently overstated the value of property used as security for a bank loan. D2 (D1's solicitors) negligently failed to notice the gross overvaluation. Given the different remoteness tests that apply in deceit and negligence there arose a question of what amounted to the "same damage" in respect of which D1 and D2 were jointly liable. A second question was whether the defendants could invoke the defence of contributory negligence, for while this defence can be used in negligence, it cannot be used in deceit. A final question turned on the significance of the negligence/deceit dichotomy for the purposes of calculating D1's and D2's respective contributions. 4-25

In relation to the first question, Clarke J held that "the same damage" for present 4-26

---

[90] Notwithstanding this finding, Moore-Bick J did state (at [56]) that a recovery could be sought by way of the equitable remedy of subrogation on the basis that, had the second defendants never paid the claimants' monies to a third party, neither the first nor the second defendants would have incurred any liability. The Court of Appeal confirmed this: [2004] EWCA Civ 487; [2004] 2 All E.R. (Comm) 289.

[91] [2004] EWCA Civ 487; [2004] 2 All E.R. (Comm) 289 at [78]. Butler-Sloss LJ concurred with this judgment in a single sentence.

[92] [2004] EWCA Civ 487; [2004] 2 All E.R. (Comm) 289 at [83].

[93] [2007] EWCA Civ 1382; [2008] Ch. 313.

[94] [2007] EWCA Civ 1382; [2008] Ch. 313 at [32].

[95] [2009] EWHC 254 (Comm); [2010] 1 W.L.R. 258.

purposes meant only those losses for which the liability of D1 and D2 overlapped. (So, for example, the claimant's loss of opportunity to lend the money elsewhere could not be taken into account in assessing D2's liability as such loss would be too remote for the purposes of a negligence action). With regard to the second question, the judge held that the contributory negligence defence could be invoked (even though it was not strictly available to D1 on account of D1's fraud). Bearing in mind the Law Reform (Contributory Negligence) Act 1945 provides that the court must apply justice and equity to matters of contributory negligence, Clarke J said it would be "neither just nor equitable that the amount of contribution which [the solicitors] ... are to be ordered to make should be assessed by treating the damage for which both defendants are responsible as the totality of the claimant's loss, ignoring contributory negligence ... To do so would be to visit on [them] ... the approach taken by the Court, partly for reasons of deterrence, against fraudsters, when [D2] are innocent of any fraud".[96] On the third question concerning the parties' respective shares of liability, Clarke J held that "the relative proportions should be 80 per cent/20 per cent [since] ... [t]he moral blameworthiness of [D1] and the causative potency of the fraud ... are very much greater than that of D2".[97]

4-27 Equally, in *Birse Construction v Haiste Ltd*[98] the claimants designed and constructed a reservoir for Anglian Water Authority, retaining the defendants as consulting engineers. AWA employed N as their construction engineer, to issue all necessary certificates. The reservoir was defective. Under the settlement of the claim brought by AWA against the claimants, the claimants agreed to build a new reservoir at their own expense. The claimants brought a claim to recover this financial loss against the defendants and the defendants claimed contribution from N. The issue was whether the liability of N to AWA was liability in respect of the same damage as the defendants, within s.1(1) of the 1978 Act. The Court of Appeal held that the loss suffered by AWA in not having a properly working reservoir at the time that they had expected, and the loss sustained by the claimants in having to construct another reservoir at their own expense, and the damages the defendant might have to pay to the claimants (or for which N might be liable to AWA) were not "the same damage" within the meaning of s.1(1).

4-28 **Procedure**[99] The right to contribution accrues when the defendant is held liable in respect of the damage, or when he agrees to make a payment in compensation for that damage and no action to recover contribution may be brought more than two years after the date on which the right to contribution accrues.[100] But questions of contribution between parties joined as co-defendants can be disposed of at the end of the proceedings in which judgment is given against them, even if separate proceedings for contribution have not been instituted.[101] Contribution proceedings between defendants can also continue after the claimant's claim has been settled as

96 [2009] EWHC 254 (Comm); [2010] 1 W.L.R. 258 at [71].
97 [2009] EWHC 254 (Comm); [2010] 1 W.L.R. 258 at [77].
98 [1996] 1 W.L.R. 675.
99 See CPR Pt 20.
100 Limitation Act 1980 s.10. The period may be extended where the person seeking contribution is under a disability or is the victim of fraud, concealment or mistake: s.10(5).
101 *Croston v Vaughan* [1938] 1 K.B. 540; *Bell v Holmes* [1956] 1 W.L.R. 1359. cf. *Wilkinson v Rea* [1941] 1 K.B. 688 at 703–704; *Oertli v EJ Bowman (London) Ltd* [1956] R.P.C. 341.

if they had been brought by a separate action and there is no need for fresh proceedings to be started.[102]

4. APPORTIONMENT

Apportionment of damages Section 2(1) of the Civil Liability (Contribution) Act 1978 provides that the amount of the contribution recoverable from any person "shall be such as may be found by the court[103] to be just and equitable having regard to the extent of that person's responsibility for the damage in question". The court may order contribution amounting to a complete indemnity or exempt a person altogether from liability to make contribution.[104] So wide is this discretion that the court may even decline to allow a party from whom a contribution is sought to be joined to the action where it forms the view that "no court would think it just and reasonable that [the party in question] should be ordered to make a contribution".[105] In one case in which a police officer had sexually harassed a woman he was interviewing and his Chief Constable disciplined him fully upon learning of the facts, the Chief Constable was held to be entitled to claim a full indemnity from the offending officer after being held vicariously liable for his tort—there is no policy reason why this should not occur.[106] But, by s.2(3), where the amount of damages which could have been awarded against the person from whom contribution is sought in an action by the person suffering the relevant damage was subject to a limit imposed by statute, or an agreement made before the damage occurred,[107] or to any reduction in respect of the contributory negligence of the person bringing the action,[108] then the contribution ordered cannot be a greater amount than that limited or reduced amount. In other words, a defendant cannot be required to pay more by way of contribution than he would have been liable to pay to the claimant. So, where D1 pays in full for the totality of C's losses (which may comprise several different heads of loss), D1 may only seek a contribution from D2 in respect of those heads of loss for which D2 was partly responsible.[109] Furthermore, in *Fitzgerald v* 4-29

---

102 *Stott v West Yorkshire Car Co Ltd* [1971] 2 Q.B. 651; not following *Calvert v Pick* [1954] 1 W.L.R. 456.

103 An arbitrator, under the terms of a standard form arbitration agreement, has the power to make an award of contribution under the Act: *Wealands v CLC Contractors Ltd, Key Scaffolding Ltd, Third Parties* [1999] 2 Lloyd's Rep. 739.

104 Civil Liability (Contribution) Act 1978 s.2(2). See *Saipem SpA and Conoco (UK) Ltd v Dredging VO2 BV and Geosite Surveys Ltd* [1993] 2 Lloyd's Rep. 315; *Re-Source America International Ltd v Platt Site Services Ltd* [2004] EWCA Civ 665; [2004] N.P.C. 89 at [53], per Tuckey LJ; *Dawson v Bell* [2016] EWCA Civ 96; [2016] 2 B.C.L.C. 59.

105 *African Strategic Investment (Holdings) Ltd v Main* [2011] EWHC 2223 (Ch) at [47], per Bernard Livesey QC.

106 *KD v Chief Constable of Hampshire* [2005] EWHC 2550 (QB). See also *Mohidin v Commissioner of Police of the Metropolis* [2016] EWHC 105 (QB); [2016] 1 Costs L.R. 71.

107 But when "business liability" is in issue such agreements are now invalid where the person suffering damage as a result of negligence suffers personal injuries, and in other cases of negligence must be proved to be reasonable: Unfair Contract Terms Act 1977 s.2. The Consumer Rights Act 2015 provides (from 1 October 2015) rather different treatment to consumers—agreements involving consumers will need to satisfy the requirement of good faith if they are effectively to exclude liability for negligence causing damage other than death or personal injury: ss.62 and 65.

108 See also s.2(3)(c) of the Civil Liability (Contribution) Act 1978, which extends s.2(3) to any corresponding limit or reduction under foreign law when foreign law determines the rights of the parties.

109 *Ball v Banner* [2000] Lloyd's Rep. P.N. 569 (reversed on other grounds: *Ball v Banner*, unreported 30 June 2000 CA).

Lane,[110] the House of Lords stressed that apportionment of liability in a case of contributory negligence between the claimant and defendants should be kept separate from the apportionment of contribution between the defendants inter se.[111] Any deduction from the award of damages for the claimant's contributory negligence should take place before the question of contribution between defendants is addressed.[112]

4-30 There was some initial controversy as to the proper basis of apportionment but in *Downs v Chappell*[113] Hobhouse LJ clarified that: "[i]t is just and equitable to take into account both the seriousness of the respective parties' faults and their causative relevance. A more serious fault having less causative impact on the plaintiff's damage may represent an equivalent responsibility to a less serious fault which had a greater causative impact."[114] By contrast, where the causative potency of both parties' acts is equal, but the moral blameworthiness of one party's conduct is significantly greater than that of the other, the court will probably depart from an equal division of the damages.[115] The apportionment of damages is substantially a matter for the discretion of the trial judge and an appellate court will revise his award only in very exceptional circumstances.[116] On the other hand, the trial judge must not take into account the fact that one of the parties held, or had the potential to hold, liability insurance to cover the loss in question when deciding what is a just and equitable apportionment of the damages.[117] Moreover, if there have been previous proceedings arising out of the same accident, as where the defendant claiming contribution from a third party had previously brought proceedings (as claimant)

---

110 [1989] 1 A.C. 328.

111 Where there are concurrent tortious and contractual duties to exercise reasonable care, contributory negligence can be raised as a defence to a claim for breach of that duty, unless the contract specifically provided against this: *Forsikringsaktieselskapet Vesta v Butcher* [1989] A.C. 852. Contributory negligence is not a defence to a claim for damages founded on breach of a strict contractual obligation: *Barclays Bank Plc v Fairclough Building Ltd* [1995] Q.B. 214. Nor is it a defence where the contractual duty, though expressed in terms of exercising reasonable care, does not correspond to a common law duty of care in tort. The effect of this in the context of contribution claims is significant. For example, if the retailer of a faulty electric blanket is sued for injuries caused to the claimant, injuries to which the claimant's own negligence substantially contributed, he will be ordered to pay the full amount of damages to the claimant on the basis of breach of a strict contractual duty as to quality. However, in proceedings for contribution from the manufacturer, the retailer will only recover as a maximum the amount reduced to take account of the claimant's contributory negligence (the manufacturer's liability to the claimant being in the tort of negligence), even if in the circumstances the responsibility for the injuries is virtually entirely that of the manufacturer.

112 This approach was adopted in *Nationwide Building Society v Dunlop Haywards (DHL) Ltd and Cobbetts (A Firm)* [2009] EWHC 254 (Comm); [2010] 1 W.L.R. 258.

113 [1997] 1 W.L.R. 426. In similar vein see *Madden v Quirke* [1989] 1 W.L.R. 702; *West London Pipeline & Storage Ltd v Total UK Ltd* [2008] EWHC 1296 (Comm); [2008] Lloyd's Rep. I.R. 688. See also *Brian Warwicker Partnership Plc v HOK International Ltd* [2005] EWCA Civ 962; [2006] P.N.L.R. 5, where it was said that non-causative factors that also involve a breach of duty are relevant considerations.

114 [1997] 1 W.L.R. 426 at 445.

115 *Furmedge v Chester-Le-Street DC* [2011] EWHC 1226 (QB).

116 See, e.g. the unwillingness of the Court of Appeal to disturb the apportionment judged appropriate by the trial judge in *West v Wilkinson* [2008] EWCA Civ 1005. cf. *Andrews v Initial Cleaning Services Ltd* [2000] I.C.R. 166, where the Court of Appeal reversed the trial judge's apportionment. Responsibility as between the claimant's employers and the occupiers of premises on which she was injured lay substantially with the employers.

117 *West London Pipeline and Storage Ltd v Total UK Ltd* [2008] EWHC 1296; [2008] Lloyd's Rep. I.R. 688.

against the third party (as defendant) and both had been held equally to blame, the principle of res judicata[118] may operate so as to prevent the third party from denying that he was equally to blame with the defendant.[119] Where this is so, the trial judge must apportion the damages between them equally. Another circumstance in which the discretion of the trial judge will be circumscribed is where the parties have themselves agreed a figure before trial that represents the loss caused by one of the co-defendants.[120] Finally, there will be some scope for the exercise of discretion in those rare cases where there is dual vicarious liability, even though such liability does not require fault on the part of either employer. Nevertheless, where D1 and D2 are both vicariously liable for the tort of a shared employee, it may be just and equitable to divide responsibility equally between them where the tortfeasor had been so much a part of the work, business or organisation of both defendants that it is fair to make both answer for his acts.[121]

5. INDEMNITY

Contractual indemnity or contribution in respect of liability for tort It not infrequently happens that a contract between two persons enables one of them to recover from the other an indemnity or contribution—or damages for breach of contract equivalent to indemnity or contribution—in the event that he becomes liable to a third party in tort. This may arise where there is a contract of insurance properly so called, or as an incident of some other contract such as, typically, a contract for the hire of plant or equipment. In *Spalding v Tarmac Civil Engineering Ltd*,[122] an accident was caused by the driver of an excavator which had been hired, together with its driver, by the first defendants from the second defendants. Both defendants were liable to the claimant: the first defendants for breach of regulations made under the Factories Act 1961 and the second defendants, vicariously, for the negligence of the driver who had remained their servant. The contract of hire contained a clause providing that the second defendants should alone be responsible for all claims arising in connection with the operation of the excavator by the driver. The House of Lords held that the first defendants were therefore entitled to be indemnified by the second defendants. Similarly, in *Sims v Foster Wheeler Ltd*[123] where one of two tortfeasors had been required to bear 25 per cent of the damages recovered by the claimant, it was held that he was entitled to recover an equivalent sum from his sub-contractor by way of damages for breach of contract.[124] The contract under which the alleged right to indemnity or contribu- 4-31

118 See para.30-24.

119 *Bell v Holmes* [1956] 1 W.L.R. 1359. See also *Marginson v Blackburn CC* [1939] 2 K.B. 426.

120 *Moy v Pettman Smith* [2003] EWCA Civ 467; [2003] P.N.L.R. 31 (a decision on the allocation of costs between the defendants; subsequently the House of Lords held that one of the two defendants had not been negligent: [2005] UKHL 7; [2005] 1 W.L.R. 581).

121 *Viasystems Ltd v Thermal Transfer (Northern) Ltd* [2005] EWCA Civ 1151; [2006] Q.B. 510; *Various Claimants v Catholic Child Welfare Society* [2012] UKSC 56; [2013] 2 A.C. 1.

122 [1967] 1 W.L.R. 1508; *Driver v William Willett (Contractors) Ltd* [1969] 1 All E.R. 665; *Gillespie Brothers & Co Ltd v Roy Bowles Transport Ltd* [1973] Q.B. 400. As to when the cause of action under a contract of indemnity arises, see *RH Green and Silley Weir Ltd v BRB* [1985] 1 W.L.R. 570.

123 [1966] 1 W.L.R. 769 (decision under the Law Reform (Married Women and Tortfeasors) Act 1935). See also *Wright v Tyne Improvement Commissioners* [1968] 1 W.L.R. 336. cf. *Hadley v Droitwich Construction Co Ltd* [1968] 1 W.L.R. 37.

124 In *Thompson v T Lohan (Plant Hire) Ltd* [1987] 1 W.L.R. 649, the plant hire contract provided that the hirer was to be liable for the negligence of the owner's employee while operating the plant. Held,

tion arises must be shown to grant such a right in respect of the very circumstances in which the claimant suffered loss. Yet if such clauses are intended, effectively, to exonerate the plant owner from negligence liability, the usual contra proferentem approach to interpreting the exculpatory contractual term will be adopted. So, in one case involving plant/operator hire, the contract stipulated that the hirer was to indemnify the plant owner in respect of "all claims by any person whatsoever for injury to person or property caused by, or in connection with, the use of the plant during the hire period". The operator was injured by virtue of negligence on the part of the owner and no such indemnity could be claimed. If the owners intended to exonerate themselves from their own negligence, then they had to bring their intentions to the notice of prospective hirers in very specific terms.[125] In contrast, in *Greenwich Millennium Village Ltd v Essex Services Group Plc (formerly Essex Electrical Group Ltd)*,[126] an agreement to "indemnify H against any liability arising out of any breach of their agreement or any act, default or negligence" did operate in respect of workmanship defects that led to flooding in a block of flats even though H should have detected the defects on inspection. The Court of Appeal found that in construing an indemnity clause, the court had to have regard to the commercial context of the contract. In the case of a construction contract, a failure by the indemnitee to spot defects perpetrated by its contractor should not ordinarily defeat the operation of an indemnity clause, even if that clause failed expressly to encompass damage caused by the negligence of the indemnitee. It would largely defeat the commercial purpose of the contractual chain if "failure to notice" prevented the indemnity clause from operating.

4-32 In *Lambert v Lewis*,[127] a trailer became detached from the Land Rover towing it and slewed across the road injuring the claimants and killing two other members of the family. The accident was caused partly by the faulty design of the coupling which attached the trailer to the Land Rover and partly by the negligence of the driver of the Land Rover who continued to use the coupling after he had become aware that it was damaged. The owner was ordered to pay 25 per cent of the total award of the damages. In third party proceedings he sought to recover his loss from the retailer of the defective coupling on the grounds that the latter was in breach of implied warranties that the coupling was reasonably fit for its purpose and that it was of merchantable quality. The House of Lords held that no contractual indemnity in respect of damages payable to a third party could arise where the essence of the claimant's liability was his own negligent failure to take some precaution unless the other contracting party had warranted that any such precaution was unnecessary[128]; and no such warranty had been given or could be implied.

4-33 The retailers' fourth party proceedings against the manufacturers to recover any damages which they might be ordered to pay to the owner of the Land Rover thus did not fall to be decided by the House of Lords. But Lord Diplock commented that dismissal of their appeal should not be taken as approval of the view that economic

---

that this was not an exclusion clause, in that it did not purport to exclude liability to a person injured by the employee's negligence, therefore it was not invalidated by s.2(1) of the Unfair Contract Terms Act 1977. cf. *Phillips Products Ltd v Hyland* [1987] 1 W.L.R. 659 which treated an identical "transfer" clause as an unreasonable exclusion of liability under s.2(2).

125 *Jose v MacSalvors Plant Hire Ltd* [2009] EWCA Civ 1329; [2010] T.C.L.R. 2 at [17]–[18] per Ward LJ.

126 [2014] EWCA Civ 960; [2014] 1 W.L.R. 3517.

127 [1982] A.C. 225.

128 Approving *Hadley v Droitwich Construction Co Ltd* [1968] 1 W.L.R. 37 at 43, per Winn LJ.

loss suffered by a distributor in the chain between manufacturer and ultimate consumer—which consisted of liability to pay damages and arose from the defective state of the goods put into circulation by the manufacturer—was necessarily not recoverable under the *Donoghue v Stevenson* principle. This view was supported by Hirst J in *The Kapetan Georgis*.[129]

The principle of these cases precedes any statutory introduction of rights to contribution.[130] The Civil Liability (Contribution) Act 1978 s.7(3) provides that the right to recover contribution under the Act supersedes any right, other than an express contractual right, to recover contribution otherwise than under the Act. But the Act does not affect any express or implied contractual or other right to indemnity, or any express contractual provision regulating or excluding contribution. The effect of this section is to replace the common law on contribution between persons liable for the same damage by the provisions of the statute. It does not affect the right of a tortfeasor to enforce an indemnity from a fellow tortfeasor as in *Spalding v Tarmac Civil Engineering Ltd*. Nor is a tortfeasor's right to recover damages for breach of contract, as distinct from contribution, removed. Thus the principles illustrated in *Sims v Foster Wheeler Ltd* and *Lambert v Lewis* remain intact. The Act does not render enforceable any agreement for indemnity not enforceable had it not been passed. Express promises of indemnity which are void at common law are, therefore, still void even though, probably, contribution or perhaps an indemnity can now be awarded under the Act against one tortfeasor in favour of another notwithstanding that an express, but void, promise of indemnity had been given. On the other hand, this approach will not be taken where there exists a valid indemnity agreement within an insurance contract which the defendant is unable to invoke because he fails to meet the conditions set out in the insurance agreement.[131] The apportionment of damages between tortfeasors under the Act may, however, lead to a result different from that produced by the application of a contract existing between them, and it therefore remains necessary to determine whether a contractual right to indemnity or contribution can be enforced even where the parties to it are tortfeasors liable in respect of the same damage. **4-34**

The law on this matter is not entirely free from doubt, but it is submitted that a contractual indemnity against liability in respect of an unintentional tort, whether arising under a contract of insurance properly so called or not, is always valid even if the tort also amounts to a criminal offence. The decisive factor is whether or not the act giving rise to liability is a deliberate wrongful act, not whether it happens to be criminal as well as tortious. In *Spalding v Tarmac Civil Engineering Ltd*, noth- **4-35**

---

129 *Virgo S.S. Co SA v Skaarup Shipping Corp* [1988] 1 Lloyd's Rep. 352. While acknowledging the general rule that negligently inflicted pure economic loss is not recoverable, Hirst J asserted that where the relevant claim for economic loss was part of a chain which originates in a claim for physical damage, the general rule may not apply.

130 Note that in *Lambert v Lewis*, the Civil Liability (Contribution) Act 1978 would not have helped the retailers, had they been ordered to pay an indemnity, because they and the manufacturers would not be liable for the same damage to the same claimant. The retailers would have been liable to the owner of the vehicle to indemnify him in respect of the loss caused by their breach of contract. The manufacturers were liable to the people physically injured as a result of the defective design of the coupling.

131 In *United Marine Aggregates Ltd v GM Welding & Engineering Ltd* [2012] EWHC 779 (TCC) D had failed to remove from an area in which welding work had been conducted all combustible material as required by the "Burning and Welding Warranty" contained in D's insurance contract. As such, D was unable to rely on the contractual indemnity contained in the insurance contract (reversed on appeal in relation only to the question of recoverable costs: [2013] EWCA Civ 516).

ing was made of the fact that the first defendants, being liable for breach of statutory duty, were also guilty of a criminal offence,[132] and in two cases insured motorists were held entitled to indemnity under their insurance policies notwithstanding that their negligence had been such as to amount to the crime of manslaughter.[133] Similarly, an indemnity against liability for defamation was held good where the publisher reasonably supposed the matter published not to be defamatory,[134] but not where he knew that it was defamatory.[135] Where the indemnity agreement is between an employee and employer, the critical question will be whether the crime could be said to be committed in a misguided discharge of the employee's contractual duties. In *Coulson v News Group Newspapers Ltd*,[136] a newspaper editor sought to rely on an indemnity agreement with his employer in order to claim back the costs of defending criminal proceedings based on the editor's illicit payments to police officers and unlawful interception of private communications. It was held that he could do so. The Court of Appeal distinguished between criminal charges arising out of the allegedly criminal manner in which he had done his job as editor, and criminal charges associated with an act that had nothing whatever to do with the performance of his job. Their Lordships gave as an example of the former, the publication of material alleged to be in contempt of court. According to McCombe LJ, such criminal charges should be seen as "the very occupational hazards of editorship" and precisely the kind of thing for which the indemnity exists.[137]

4-36 A possible problem here is Denning J's judgment in *Askey v Golden Wine Co Ltd*[138] suggesting criminality (in this case founded on gross negligence) rather than intentionality is the key. Public policy, he held, requires that no right of indemnity or contribution or damages should be enforced in respect of expenses which a person incurs by reason of being compelled to make reparation for his own crime.[139] It is submitted, however, that while a person should not generally be entitled to an indemnity against a fine or other penal consequence of his criminal offence,[140] public policy is better served by allowing an indemnity against civil liability to be enforced unless the act of the person claiming the indemnity is both deliberate and manifestly unlawful or, at least, unless the facts making it unlawful were known to

[132] If they had been prosecuted the first defendant might have been able to escape conviction under the provisions of the Factories Act 1961 s.161, but the matter was not considered.

[133] *Tinline v White Cross Insurance Association Ltd* [1921] 3 K.B. 327; *James v British General Insurance Co Ltd* [1927] 2 K.B. 311 (both cases decided before motor insurance became compulsory). See, however, the observations on these cases of Scrutton and Greer LJJ in *Haseldine v Hosken* [1933] 1 K.B. 822 at 833 (solicitor's indemnity policy void in so far as it purported to indemnify him against the consequences of entering into a champertous agreement).

[134] *Daily Mirror Newspapers Ltd v Exclusive News Agency* (1937) 81 S.J. 924.

[135] *Smith v Clinton* (1908) 99 L.T. 840. The Defamation Act 1952 s.11 provides that such an indemnity shall be unlawful only if the person indemnified knows that the proposed publication is defamatory.

[136] [2012] EWCA Civ 1547; [2013] I.R.L.R. 116.

[137] [2012] EWCA Civ 1547; [2013] I.R.L.R. 116 at [48].

[138] (1948) 64 T.L.R. 379. cf. *Strongman (1945) Ltd v Sincock* [1955] 2 Q.B. 525.

[139] Denning J relied on *Beresford v Royal Insurance Co Ltd* [1938] A.C. 586, a case of an intentional criminal offence (suicide).

[140] See *Gray v Thames Trains Ltd* [2009] UKHL 33; [2009] 1 A.C. 1339; and *Patel v Mirza* [2016] UKSC 42; [2017] A.C. 467. Occasionally an indemnity even against the penal consequences of an act has been upheld: *Cointat v Myham* [1913] 2 K.B. 220 (reversed on other grounds, 84 L.J.K.B. 2253). cf. *Colburne v Patmore* (1834) 1 C.M. & R. 73; and *Leslie v Reliable Advertising and Addressing Agency Ltd* [1915] 1 K.B. 652.

him even if he did not appreciate its illegality.[141] Certainly, a right to indemnity exists when a person is induced by fraud to perform an act which is apparently lawful but proves to be unlawful by reason of facts unknown to the person claiming indemnity, and the same is true when such an act is procured or authorised by another.[142] Equally, if one of two joint tortfeasors agrees to indemnify the other *after* the criminal event giving rise to civil liability, the agreement can be treated as valid, for the relevant rule of public policy applies only to indemnity agreements that are made *prior* to the commission of the criminal-cum-tortious act in question.[143]

Indemnity: employer and employee Where an employee commits a tort in the course of his employment, he and his employer are joint tortfeasors and, accordingly, if the employer meets the claimant's claim for damages he is entitled to claim contribution from the employee under the Act of 1978.[144] In *Lister v Romford Ice and Cold Storage Co Ltd*,[145] however, the House of Lords held by a majority that, independently of statute, the employers of a lorry driver for whose negligence they had been held liable were entitled to claim damages from the driver, equivalent to an indemnity, on the basis of a breach by the driver of an implied term in his contract of employment to the effect that he would exercise reasonable care in the performance of his duties. The decision in *Lister v Romford Ice and Cold Storage Co Ltd* does not apply where the employer had himself or by other employees been guilty of negligence, and in such a case the employer's only remedy is under the Act of 1978.[146] It has also been held that the decision does not apply where the employee, though acting in the course of his employment, is not actually carrying out the duties for which he was employed.[147] On the other hand, it is irrelevant that the employer is covered against liability by a policy of insurance and that the action, though in his name, is brought by the insurers exercising their right of subrogation.[148] 4-37

The implications of *Lister v Romford Ice and Cold Storage Co Ltd* for industrial relations led, ultimately, to employers' liability insurers entering into an agreement whereby they would not institute claims against employees of insured employers in respect of the death or injury of fellow employees unless the weight of evidence indicated either collusion or wilful misconduct.[149] The agreement seems to have operated satisfactorily, but it did not cover the facts of *Morris v Ford Motor Co Ltd*[150] where a problem very similar to that raised in *Lister v Romford Ice and Cold Storage Co Ltd* came before the Court of Appeal. In *Morris*, the claim- 4-38

141 *Burrows v Rhodes* [1899] 1 Q.B. 816 at 829, per Kennedy J (where the fact that the act might have been criminal was held to be irrelevant).

142 *Adamson v Jarvis* (1827) 4 Bing. 66; *Dugdale v Lovering* (1875) L.R. 10 C. & P. 196; *Sheffield Corp v Barclay* [1905] A.C. 392.

143 *Mulcaire v News Group Newspapers Ltd* [2011] EWHC 3469 (Ch); [2012] Ch. 435 at [43]–[45], per Sir Andrew Morritt C.

144 See paras 4-13 to 4-28.

145 [1957] A.C. 555; *Semtex Ltd v Gladstone* [1954] 1 W.L.R. 945.

146 *Jones v Manchester Corp* [1952] 2 Q.B. 852.

147 *Harvey v RG O'Dell (Galway, Third Party)* [1958] 2 Q.B. 78, where, however, the employer was awarded contribution amounting to 100 per cent under the Law Reform (Married Women and Tortfeasors) Act 1935.

148 *Lister v Romford Ice and Cold Storage Co Ltd* [1957] A.C. 555 at 572, per Viscount Simonds.

149 For the terms of the agreement see *Morris v Ford Motor Co Ltd* [1973] Q.B. 792 at 799, per Lord Denning MR.

150 [1973] Q.B. 792.

ant, who was employed by a firm of cleaners, was injured while working at the factory of the defendants as a result of the negligence of their employee. He recovered damages from Ford who were themselves reimbursed by the cleaners under an indemnity clause contained in their contract with the cleaners, and the cleaners then claimed to be subrogated to Ford's right of action against the negligent employee. The Court of Appeal held by a majority that the claim failed. In Lord Denning MR's view, the doctrine of subrogation depended upon the principles of equity. In the circumstances it would be unjust to make the servant personally liable, and therefore no right of subrogation existed. Alternatively, his Lordship considered, if the right of subrogation depended on implied contract, then the contract of indemnity contained no appropriate implied term.[151] James LJ, concurring in the result, preferred the view that the right of subrogation is inherent in every contract of indemnity[152] unless there is a term, express or implied, to the contrary. In the light of the inter-departmental committee's report of the agreement between insurers, and of evidence that Ford had adopted a policy renouncing their entitlement to sue their employees for negligence, his Lordship held that the contract of indemnity contained such an implied term. As he pointed out, the contract between the cleaners and Ford was operative in an industrial setting in which subrogation of the cleaners to the rights and remedies of Ford against Ford's employees would be unacceptable and unrealistic.[153]

4-39 The decision of the majority in *Morris v Ford Motor Co Ltd* seems to be one dictated rather by practical necessity than by legal principle and it is difficult to reconcile the decision with that in *Lister v Romford Ice and Cold Storage Co Ltd* itself. For there, too, the action was brought under a right of subrogation and the setting was similarly industrial. In practice, however, *Lister* is virtually a dead letter as a result of the agreement between insurers and, in refusing to extend that case to a situation not actually covered by the agreement, the Court of Appeal has done little more than recognise the realities of accident litigation in an industrial setting.[154]

4-40 **Indemnity: mesothelioma cases** Two particular problems concerning indemnity are apt to arise in mesothelioma cases. The first occurs where the claimant was tortiously exposed to asbestos during the currency of a third party insurance contract held by the employer, but the disease does not become manifest until many years later by which time the defendant employer has changed insurer. The second problem centres on cases where the inhalation of the relevant asbestos dust occurs over a long period of time, only part of which was covered by the policy on the basis of which the employer now seeks to claim an indemnity. In both cases, the relevant insurer may seek to deny liability to pay all or part of any indemnity sought. In *Durham v BAI (Run Off) Ltd*,[155] the insurance policy in question made the insurer liable to indemnify the employer in respect of illness contracted or sustained by an employee during the currency of the policy. However, the mesothelioma in this case

---

151 [1973] Q.B. 792 at 800–802. See also *The Yasin* [1979] 2 Lloyd's Rep. 45.

152 [1973] Q.B. 792 at 812. With this part of his Lordship's judgment, Stamp LJ was in agreement: [1973] Q.B. 792 at 804.

153 [1973] Q.B. 792 at 814–815. See also *The Yasin* [1979] 2 Lloyd's Rep. 45.

154 In *Bell v Alliance Medical Ltd* [2015] CSOH 34; 2015 S.C.L.R. 676, Lord Boyd commented, however, that although some of the considerations that underpin the rule in *Lister v Romford Ice and Cold Storage Co Ltd* [1957] A.C. 555 may now be seen as outmoded, the ratio remains good law in England and Wales and Scotland.

155 [2012] UKSC 14; [2012] 1 W.L.R. 867.

did not manifest itself, nor was it actionable, until after the relevant insurance contract had ceased. Nonetheless, Lord Mance JSC held that "for the purposes of the insurances, liability for mesothelioma following upon exposure to asbestos created during an insurance period involves a sufficient 'weak' or 'broad' causal link for the disease to be regarded as 'caused' within the insurance period".[156] On this footing, the insurer was held liable to pay the indemnity.

In *Zurich Insurance Plc UK Branch v International Energy Group Ltd*,[157] by contrast, the insurance policy in question had only been in place for part of the period during which the relevant employee had been tortiously exposed to asbestos dust. The insurer argued that it was unfair that it should be expected to pay a full indemnity when it had only been paid an insurance premium for six of the 27 years during which there had been tortious exposure. The Supreme Court allowed Zurich's appeal, holding unanimously that where, as here, the claim was brought in Guernsey (where the Compensation Act 2006 has not been enacted) the common law rule of proportionate recovery, established in *Barker v Corus UK Ltd*,[158] continued to apply. On this basis, an employer's liability insurer would only be liable for a pro rata part of the employer's liability to the victim. However, by a majority of four to three, the court concluded that, had the position in Guernsey been as in the UK under the Compensation Act 2006, Zurich would have been liable in the first instance to meet in full the loss in respect of which IEG paid compensation, but would, in respect of the 21 years not covered by the insurance cover, have equitable rights to contribution pro rata from any other co-insurer able to contribute and, in respect of any period where there was no such insurer, from IEG itself as a self-insurer.[159] **4-41**

---

156 [2012] UKSC 14; [2012] 1 W.L.R. 867 at [73].

157 [2015] UKSC 33; [2016] A.C. 509 (allowing appeal in part against [2013] EWCA Civ 39; [2013] 3 All E.R. 395). For critical commentary, see R. Merkin, "Insurance and Reinsurance in the *Fairchild* Enclave" (2016) 36 L.S. 302.

158 [2006] UKHL 20; [2006] 2 A.C. 572. See also *Heneghan v Manchester Dry Docks Ltd* [2016] EWCA Civ 86; [2016] 1 W.L.R. 2036 (proportionate rule still applies to non-mesothelioma cases).

159 On the operation on the broad equitable approach, see *RSA Insurance Plc v Assicurazioni Generali Spa* [2018] EWHC 1237 (QB); [2019] 1 All E.R. (Comm) 115. For the impact on reinsurers, see *Equitas Insurance Ltd v Municipal Mutual Insurance Ltd* [2019] EWCA Civ 718; [2020] Q.B. 418.

39 [2012] UKSC 14 at [74] per Lord Mance.

40 [2015] UKSC 33; [2016] A.C. 509, following appeal in Guernsey: [2013] EWCA Civ 39; [2013] 3 W.L.R. 1474. For a critical commentary see [illegible] "Insurance and [illegible]" (2016) [illegible].

42 [illegible]

Chapter 5

CAPACITY AND PARTIES

Table of Contents

1. Introduction

Scope of chapter Prima facie, all persons are entitled to sue and are liable to be sued in tort actions. The various exceptions to this general rule are considered in this chapter. **5-01**

2. THE CROWN

5-02 **Immunity at common law** At common law, there was no right of action against the Crown. As it was said that "the King can do no wrong",[1] petitions of right would not lie for torts. The actual wrongdoer, acting on behalf of the Crown, did not enjoy this immunity, but while he personally could be sued, his superior officers could not, since he was not their servant, but, like them, the servant of the Crown.[2] In practice, however, the Treasury would pay ex gratia compensation in appropriate cases. Such a system was inadequate at a time when the Crown had become the largest employer, contractor and occupier of property in the country and the need for change was manifest.

(a) Crown Proceedings Act 1947

5-03 **Crown immunity in tort** Complete Crown immunity was brought to an end by the Crown Proceedings Act 1947. Section 2(1) provides that:

> "Subject to the provisions of this Act, the Crown shall be subject to all those liabilities in tort to which, if it were a private person of full age and capacity, it would be subject—
> (a) in respect of torts committed by its servants or agents;
> (b) in respect of any breach of those duties which a person owes to his servants or agents at common law by reason of being their employer; and
> (c) in respect of any breach of the duties attaching at common law to the ownership, occupation, possession or control of property."

Section 2(2) provides that where the Crown is bound by a statutory duty which is binding also upon persons other than the Crown and its officers, it shall be subject to the same liabilities (if any) for breach of that duty as it would be if it were a private person. Torts or breaches of duty committed abroad give rise to a cause of action against the Crown[3] only if the tort or breach of duty is committed by the UK Government and not by Her Majesty's Government in another of her jurisdictions.[4] Proceedings are brought against the appropriate government department and if none of the authorised government departments are appropriate, the Attorney General may be made the defendant.[5] On the other hand, where tortious liability cannot be established personally on the part of, say, a Secretary of State or prison governor, there is no point pursuing an alternative remedy against the Crown (as a "public authority" liable for the acts or omissions of any servant, agent or other person or entity empowered to exercise public functions) for breach of a Convention right under ss.6–8 of the Human Rights Act 1998. In *Morgan v Ministry of Justice* Supperstone J made it clear that no such action would lie. In such circumstances, he explained, "the Crown cannot be the only public authority, and therefore there must be some limit on the circumstances in which proceedings can be brought against

---

1 Hale P.C., Vol.1, p.43.

2 *Bainbridge v Postmaster General* [1906] 1 K.B. 178.

3 *Tito v Waddell* [1977] Ch. 106 at 252–256.

4 Crown Proceedings Act 1947 s.40(2)(b); *Mutasa v Att Gen* [1980] Q.B. 114. The Crown can only be sued pursuant to the Crown Proceedings Act 1947: see *Trawnik v Lennox* [1985] 1 W.L.R. 532. Third party proceedings against the Crown are civil proceedings against the Crown within CPR r.66. The trial of those proceedings should, therefore, be heard in London: *St Martins Property Investments v Philips Electronics (UK)* [1995] Ch. 73.

5 Crown Proceedings Act 1947 s.17.

the Crown as opposed to some other public authority".[6] Section 40(1) makes it clear that the Act does not authorise proceedings in tort to be brought against the Sovereign in a private capacity.

Torts "committed by servants or agents" By s.2(1)(a), the Crown is made vicariously liable also for torts committed by its employees in the course of their employment, and for the torts of its independent contractors if committed in circumstances which would render a private employer liable.[7] A proviso adds that the Crown shall not be liable unless the act or omission in question would, apart from the Act, have given rise to a cause of action in tort against "the servant or agent". So, for example, where servants of the Crown did not act in the knowledge that their acts were illegal—as is required for the tort of misfeasance in public office—there could be no vicarious liability for this tort on the part of the Crown.[8] The proviso also preserves such defences as act of state[9] and the exercise of statutory or prerogative powers.[10] **5-04**

The Crown may be liable for the tortious act of its employee which is ultra vires the statute creating the powers under which the act is purported to be done, just as the Crown may be liable for the negligent exercise by its employees of such powers.[11] **5-05**

The liability of the Crown for the torts of its officers (i.e. Ministers and other employees) is limited to those cases where the officer is appointed directly or indirectly by the Crown and is (normally) paid wholly out of the Consolidated Fund, or its equivalent.[12] This excludes the police and other public officers who are appointed or paid by local or other public authorities.[13] A public corporation is not a Crown employee merely because it is under the control of a government department.[14] Section 2(3) states that where functions are conferred by the law directly on an officer of the Crown, he is regarded for the purpose of the section as if he were acting under the Crown's instructions. Section 2(4) gives the Crown the benefit of any statute regulating or limiting the liability of a government department or Crown officer. **5-06**

---

6 [2010] EWHC 2248 (QB) at [52].

7 The word "agent" in s.2(1)(a) includes an independent contractor employed by the Crown (s.38(2)), but the Crown is not subject to any greater liabilities in respect of acts or omissions of its independent contractors than it would be if it were a private person: s.40(2)(d). For an example of Crown liability for an independent contractor: see *Darling v Att Gen* [1950] 2 All E.R. 793. Note also the increased willingness of the courts to find non-delegable duties: *GB v Home Office* [2015] EWHC 819 (QB). *GB v Home Office* was not followed, however, in *Razumas v Ministry of Justice* [2018] EWHC 215 (QB); [2018] P.I.Q.R. P10 due to its entirely different legislative backdrop.

8 *Chagos Islanders v Att Gen* [2004] EWCA Civ 997. See also paras 13-132 to 13-147.

9 See paras 5-16 to 5-18.

10 See para.5-15.

11 See, e.g. *X v Bedfordshire CC* [1995] 2 A.C. 633; *Phelps v Hillingdon London BC* [2000] 2 A.C. 619; and *Barrett v Enfield LBC* [2001] 2 A.C. 550. See also Ch.13.

12 Crown Proceedings Act 1947 s.2(6).

13 See *Fisher v Corp of Oldham* [1930] 2 K.B. 364; *Lewis v Cattle* [1938] 2 K.B. 454 (police constables); *Stanbury v Exeter Corp* [1905] 2 K.B. 838 (agricultural inspector). By the Police Act 1996 s.88 (see para.6-18) a chief officer of police is liable for torts committed by constables under his direction and control.

14 *Tamlin v Hannaford* [1950] 1 K.B. 18; *Glasgow Corp v Central Land Board*, 1956 S.C. (HL) 1.

5-07 **Scope of the Act** Section 2(1)(b) of the Act makes the Crown liable for breach of the common law duty owed by an employer to his employees.[15] Under s.2(1)(c), certain other liabilities attaching to the ownership, occupation, possession or control of property at common law continue to apply to the Crown such as liability in nuisance and under the rule in *Rylands v Fletcher*.[16] Section 2(2) renders the Crown liable for breach of statutory duty, provided the duty binds persons other than the Crown as well as the Crown itself, and provided that breach of duty renders those others liable in tort.[17] This proviso was included in order to prevent the creation of a new branch of the law of tort by converting constitutional and administrative law into a collection of duties owed to individuals. It must still be shown that the Crown is bound by the statute in question, either expressly[18] or by necessary implication.[19] Subject to the reservation of certain statutory rights, s.3 provides for proceedings against the Crown for infringement, by a Crown "servant or agent", with the authority of the Crown, of a patent, registered trade mark or the right in a registered design, design right or copyright.[20] The position of the Crown in respect of ships, docks, harbours and canals owned or occupied by the Crown is broadly assimilated to that of a private person so that, for example, the provisions governing limitation of liability contained in the Merchant Shipping Act 1995 apply in cases involving ships belonging to the Crown.[21] Salvage claims may be brought by or against the Crown,[22] but no proceedings in rem may be commenced against any of HM ships or other property.[23]

(b) Armed forces

5-08 **Armed forces exemption** It was provided by s.10(1) that no act or omission by a member of the armed forces on duty shall subject either him or the Crown to liability in tort for causing the death or injury of another member of the armed forces who "at the time when that thing was suffered" was also on duty or who, though not on duty, was on any service property, provided that the Secretary of State for Social Services certified that the suffering of the injury or death would be treated as attributable to service for the purposes of entitlement to the award of a pension under the Royal Warrant. Further, by s.10(2) no action lay against the Crown, or against the officer of the Crown actually responsible, for injury or death suffered by a member of the armed forces where "that thing suffered by him" was in consequence of the condition of service property, provided that the Secretary of State certified as above.[24]

---

15 For full discussion of these duties, see Ch.12.

16 (1866) L.R. 1 Ex. 265; (1868) L.R. 3 H.L. 330.

17 This includes liability under both the Occupiers' Liability Act 1957 and the Occupiers' Liability Act 1984.

18 e.g. the Factories Act 1961 s.173.

19 *Cooper v Hawkins* [1904] 2 K.B. 164; *Bombay Province v Bombay Municipal Corp* [1947] A.C. 58; *R. (on the application of Black) v Secretary of State for Justice* [2017] UKSC 81; [2018] A.C. 215 (Crown not bound by the prohibition on smoking in public places in the Health Act 2006 Pt 1 Ch.1).

20 See also Patents Act 1977 s.129.

21 Merchant Shipping Act 1995 s.192.

22 Merchant Shipping Act 1995 s.230.

23 Crown Proceedings Act 1947 s.29.

24 This provision is unaffected by the Occupiers' Liability Act 1957. See s.6 of that Act. *Adams v War Office* [1955] 1 W.L.R. 1116 made it clear that s.10 applied, provided the Minister so certified. It was not necessary that under the terms of the Royal Warrant an award should actually be payable.

In *Pearce v Secretary of State for Defence*,[25] the House of Lords held that reference to "that thing suffered" in both s.10(1) and (2) was not a reference to the tortfeasor's act or omission but instead a reference to the casualty or other event caused and from which the personal injury or death resulted. Thus, in *Pearce*, alleged negligence by scientists, during nuclear testing, led to soldiers being exposed to radiation. The thing suffered by the soldier was the exposure to radiation, i.e. a consequence of the nature or condition of the land, rather than the negligent acts of the scientists (unconnected with the condition of the land).[26] But this focus on the exposure to radiation, rather than on any given act of negligence, may well spawn problems of evidence for the purposes of the operation of the Limitation Act 1980. For example, in *B v Ministry of Defence*[27]—a case in which soldiers had been exposed to radiation by virtue of MoD thermonuclear testing in the South Pacific in the 1950s—the question of when the soldiers could be deemed to have acquired the requisite knowledge for the purposes of the 1980 Act was only finally resolved by the Supreme Court.[28] **5-09**

In *Quinn v Ministry of Defence*,[29] the claimant, during his service in the Royal Navy, had stripped asbestos insulation from boilers and pipes, which had caused, among other things, mesothelioma. He argued that the removal of the asbestos had been done under an unsafe system of work, and that the Crown was in breach of a duty in tort to provide a safe system of work. The Court of Appeal, applying *Pearce v Secretary of State for Defence*, held that the Crown had immunity by virtue of s.10(2) of the Crown Proceedings Act 1947. The claimant's injuries were a consequence of "the nature or condition" of the ships on which he served, not of an unsafe system of work. Moreover, it was impossible to accept that Parliament intended that the Crown should be immune from claims in respect of death or personal injury suffered by a member of the armed forces in consequence of the nature or condition of the land, premises, ship, aircraft or vehicles, but should not be immune if the cause of the injury was an act or omission on the part of Crown servants which caused the land or equipment to be dangerous or resulted in the injured member of the armed forces not being protected from the danger.[30] In *Derry v Ministry of Defence*,[31] the claimant, a soldier, alleged that a military doctor had been negligent in failing to diagnose cancer. He brought an action against the **5-10**

---

25 [1988] A.C. 755; overruling *Bell v Secretary of State for Defence* [1986] 1 Q.B. 322.

26 However, it was held that although the liability of the Atomic Energy Authority (whose employees were negligent) had been transferred by the Atomic Energy Authority (Weapons Group) Act 1973, the 1973 Act should not be interpreted as conferring on the Secretary of State the right to rely on s.10 of the 1947 Act.

27 [2012] UKSC 9; [2013] 1 A.C. 78.

28 The claims had originally been issued in 2005, on the basis of the soldiers' suspicion that they had tortiously been exposed to radiation. The claimants argued, however, that it was not until 2007, when they received an expert's report confirming the likelihood that their illness was attributable to radiation exposure, that they gained the requisite knowledge for the purposes of s.14 of the Limitation Act 1980. The Supreme Court ruled that, although it was not logically impossible to issue a claim without *sufficient knowledge* for the purposes of s.14, on the facts of this case, the claimants did in fact possess the requisite knowledge more than three years before the issue of proceedings.

29 [1998] P.I.Q.R. P387.

30 The court also concluded, both on existing authority and as a matter of public policy, that no contract of employment exists between members of the armed forces and the Crown. The position may be different in the case of a civil servant: see *R. v Lord Chancellor's Department Ex p. Nangle* [1991] I.C.R. 743.

31 [1999] P.I.Q.R. P204.

Ministry of Defence for personal injury and loss of life expectancy, arguing that the Ministry could not rely on the immunity contained in the Crown Proceedings Act 1947 s.10 where there was a negligent failure to diagnose a pre-existing medical condition. The Court of Appeal held that the immunity applied. The "thing suffered" for the purpose of s.10(1) was the misdiagnosis, which occurred on each occasion that he was examined at the military hospital, when he was on Crown land, and therefore fell within that subsection.

5-11 **Repeal of armed forces' exemption** The decisions in *Pearce*, *Quinn* and *Derry* all concerned events which occurred before the repeal of s.10 of the Crown Proceedings Act 1947 by s.1 of the Crown Proceedings (Armed Forces) Act 1987.[32] The repeal of s.10 was not retrospective. It ceased to have effect "except in relation to anything suffered by a person in consequence of an act or omission committed before the date on which this Act is passed",[33] i.e. 15 May 1987. By s.2 of the 1987 Act this repeal is subject to the (limited) power of the Secretary of State to revive the effect of s.10 for the "purpose of any warlike operations in any part of the world outside the United Kingdom". The existing system of benefits for servicemen, payable in cases of death or personal injury, regardless of fault, was maintained.[34]

5-12 In relation to the fact that s.10 of the Crown Proceedings Act continues to apply in respect of death and personal injury suffered prior to 15 May 1987, it is noteworthy that in *Matthews v Ministry of Defence*[35] the House of Lords rejected the argument that s.10 was incompatible with the right to a fair trial enshrined in art.6(1) of the European Convention on Human Rights (which was given effect under English Law by virtue of the Human Rights Act 1998). According to their Lordships, s.10 governed only a *substantive* right. It thus followed that the *procedural* right to a fair and public court hearing afforded by art.6 was unaffected. As such, the serviceman in this case, whose illness was attributable to the asbestos with which he had come into contact during his pre-1987 service, had no cause of action.[36]

5-13 **Armed forces' duty of care** In *Mulcahy v Ministry of Defence*,[37] the claimant was a soldier in the Gulf War who was injured by a fellow soldier. The claimant alleged that the Ministry of Defence was vicariously liable for negligence. The Secretary of State had not acted to reintroduce the s.10 immunity, so the question was whether there was a duty of care owed at common law. The Court of Appeal held that a serviceman owes no duty of care to fellow servicemen in battle conditions since it is not fair, just or reasonable to impose a duty of care on a soldier in respect of his conduct towards a fellow soldier when engaging the enemy during hostilities. Nor was there an obligation on the Ministry to maintain a safe system of work in battle situations. The position might have been different if the injury had not been incurred during "battle conditions". The Supreme Court has now made

[32] On the Crown Proceedings (Armed Forces) Act 1987, see Boyd [1989] P.L. 237.

[33] s.1. See, e.g. *Wood v Ministry of Defence* [2011] EWCA Civ 792 at [3].

[34] See, however, *R. v Ministry of Defence Ex p. Walker* [1999] 1 W.L.R. 1209; affirmed [2000] 1 W.L.R. 806 on the Criminal Injuries (Overseas) Scheme, which provides compensation for members of the armed forces who are the victims of crimes of violence abroad.

[35] [2003] UKHL 4; [2003] 1 A.C. 1163.

[36] On the construction of art.6, see further para.1-74.

[37] [1996] Q.B. 732.

clear that an action based on breach of art.2 of the European Convention on Human Rights may be available where a soldier's life is placed in extreme jeopardy otherwise than in "battle conditions".[38] Furthermore, it has been held by the Supreme Court in *Smith v Ministry of Defence*[39] that art.2 applies extra–territorially so long as the state exercises control and authority over the soldier in question. Their Lordships also made clear in that case that the common law duty to provide safe equipment and a safe system of work applies outside battle conditions[40]; and that such conditions are to be judged as a question of fact.[41]

(c) Judicial and prerogative powers

Judicial acts Section 2(5) excludes proceedings against the Crown for acts done by any person "while discharging or purporting to discharge any responsibilities of a judicial nature vested in him or any responsibilities which he has in connection with the execution of the judicial process".[42] The phrase "execution of the judicial process" receives a wide interpretation so that the purely administrative errors of a Registrar will also be caught.[43] The exception may well also extend to Crown employees such as members of administrative tribunals and inspectors at public inquiries carrying out duties which, at least for the purpose of conferring absolute privilege in defamation proceedings, have been classified as judicial.[44] *Mazhar v Lord Chancellor*[45] confirmed that the Human Rights Act 1998 had not modified the constitutional principle of judicial immunity. Likewise, the Crown was not to be held vicariously liable for the acts of the judiciary. 5-14

Prerogative and statutory powers Section 11 expressly reserves the right of the Crown to exercise with impunity all its prerogative[46] and statutory powers, and in particular the powers exercisable, whether in peace or war, for the purpose of defence of the realm and training of the armed forces. This should not be understood as meaning, however, that the Crown incurs no liability to pay compensation for 5-15

---

38 *R. (on the application of Smith) v Oxfordshire Assistant Deputy Coroner* [2010] UKSC 29; [2011] 1 A.C. 1. On the question whether any British soldier on active service overseas is within the jurisdiction of the UK for the purposes of the European Convention on Human Rights, see now *Smith v Ministry of Defence* [2013] UKSC 41; [2014] A.C. 52 and the discussion at paras 13-88 and 13-93.

39 [2013] UKSC 41; [2014] A.C. 52 at [46] per Lord Hope JSC (Lord Walker, Baroness Hale and Lord Kerr JJSC agreed). For further discussion of this case see paras 13-09, 13-53, 13-54, 13-88, and 13-93.

40 [2013] UKSC 41; [2014] A.C. 52 at [94]–[98].

41 [2013] UKSC 41; [2014] A.C. 52 at [96].

42 For a full discussion of judicial acts, see paras 5-101 to 5-120. In *Begraj v Secretary of State for Justice* [2015] EWHC 250 (QB), the court noted that the purpose of s.9(3) of the Human Rights Act 1998 was to preserve the s.2(5) of the Crown Proceedings Act 1947 position in the context of human rights damages claims. Where, therefore, a judge would benefit from judicial immunity in respect of a particular act, the state would equally not be liable under s.9(3) of the Human Rights Act 1998 (at [20]).

43 *Quinland v Governor of Belmarsh Prison* [2002] EWCA Civ 174; [2003] Q.B. 306.

44 *Jones v Department of Employment* [1989] Q.B. 1 (a social security adjudicating officer does not perform judicial duties).

45 [2019] EWCA Civ 1558; [2020] 2 W.L.R. 541.

46 The Admiralty or a Secretary of State may issue a certificate to the effect that the act or omission in question was necessary for such purpose, and this is conclusive (though it may still remain for the court to decide whether the alleged prerogative power exists).

loss caused by the exercise of prerogative powers.[47] On the contrary, there is a general rule that where the Crown takes property in the exercise of the prerogative, it must pay for it.[48] A common law exception exists so far as actual battle damage is concerned,[49] and now, by the War Damage Act 1965,[50] there is no liability in respect of damage to, or destruction of, property caused by acts lawfully done by, or on the authority of, the Crown during, or in contemplation of the outbreak of, a war in which the Sovereign was, or is, engaged.

(d) Acts of state

5-16 **Acts of state** It has always been the general rule that employees of the Crown are personally liable for torts committed by them. An exception to this rule exists, however, in the case of acts of state. Not only is the immunity of the Crown itself preserved by the Crown Proceedings Act[51] for acts of state, so, too, are the employees of the Crown immune.

5-17 An act of state has been defined as "an act of the Executive as a matter of policy performed in the course of its relations with another state, including its relations with the subjects of that state, unless they are temporarily within the allegiance of the Crown".[52] An injury inflicted upon a foreigner, therefore, elsewhere than in British territory, if done by the authority of (or ratified by) the Crown, cannot give rise to a cause of action either against the Crown or against the person who caused the injury.[53] But the authority of, or ratification by, the Crown is probably no defence to an action by a British citizen even if outside British territory.[54] Equally, it is of no avail in any case where the wrongful act was committed in British territory.[55] For these purposes, British territory does not include territory abroad over which British troops have acquired de facto control. As Underhill J explained in one case in which the British Army had gained control of certain territory within Iraq: "[t]here is no rule at common law that the fact that British forces in the course of their operations abroad may on a temporary basis gain de facto control of a particular location brings that location within the jurisdiction of the Crown or of the English courts."[56]

5-18 In *Rahmatullah v Ministry of Defence*,[57] the Supreme Court reviewed the defence

---

47 *Att Gen v De Keyser's Royal Hotel* [1920] A.C. 508; *Burmah Oil Co Ltd v Lord Advocate* [1965] A.C. 75.

48 *Nissan v Att Gen* [1970] A.C. 179 at 227–228, per Lord Pearce.

49 *Burmah Oil Co Ltd v Lord Advocate* [1965] A.C. 75 at 102–103 and 110–111, per Lord Reid; at 162–163, per Lord Pearce; at 169–170, per Lord Upjohn.

50 s.1(1). The Act is retrospective and reversed *Burmah Oil Co Ltd v Lord Advocate* [1965] A.C. 75, in its result.

51 See para.5-03.

52 Collier, "Act of State as a Defence against a British Subject" [1968] C.L.J. 102. The defence dates from *Buron v Denman* (1848) 2 Ex. 167; 154 E.R. 327.

53 *Feather v The Queen* (1856) 6 B. & S. 257 at 296, per Cockburn CJ. See also *Buron v Denman* (1848) 2 Exch. 167. For the converse case see *Carr v Francis Times & Co* [1902] A.C. 176.

54 *Nissan v Att Gen* [1970] A.C. 179 at 213, per Lord Reid. See also *Amalgamated Metal Trading Ltd v DTI, The Times,* 21 March 1989. Perhaps the right view is that there can be no such thing as an act of state between the Crown and its subjects: Collier, op. cit., at 111.

55 *Johnstone v Pedlar* [1921] 2 A.C. 262 at 272, per Lord Finlay; *Commercial and Estates Co of Egypt v Board of Trade* [1925] 1 K.B. 271 at 290 and 297.

56 *Al Jedda v Secretary of State for Defence* [2009] EWHC 397 (QB) at [84]; affirmed [2010] EWCA Civ 758; [2011] Q.B. 773.

57 [2017] UKSC 1; [2017] A.C. 649 (allowing appeal against [2015] EWCA Civ 843).

of Crown act of state and held that the claims in tort would be barred if they related to acts which were: sovereign acts by their nature (that is, inherently governmental in nature), committed abroad, with the prior authority or subsequent ratification of the Crown, and in the conduct of foreign relations of the Crown.[58] The class of acts must be so closely connected to that policy to be necessary in pursuing it.[59] In this case, the claimants alleged that they had been wrongfully detained or mistreated by UK and US troops during conflicts in Iraq and Afghanistan. The Supreme Court held that the doctrine extended at least to the conduct of military operations which were themselves lawful in international law,[60] but would not apply to torture or maltreatment in that such acts are not inherently governmental. It would also not generally apply to the expropriation of property.[61] On the assumed facts, therefore, the doctrine of Crown act of state would apply. In that Crown act of state would only arise when there were overriding reasons of public policy not to apply foreign tort law, it did not conflict with art.6 ECHR. The English doctrine of act of state will in any event not operate to preclude the courts from hearing proceedings between private litigants simply because those proceedings would incidentally raise questions as to the acts of foreign sovereign powers. The doctrine is also not a defence to claims made under the Human Rights Act 1998.[62] Any further extension of the defence of act of state is unlikely.[63]

(e) Other acts

Statutes amending the law of torts In many cases it is clear that statutes passed with the intention of amending the law of torts apply to proceedings under the Crown Proceedings Act. Thus, the Law Reform (Personal Injuries) Act 1948, the Occupiers' Liability Acts 1957 and 1984, the Congenital Disabilities (Civil Liability) Act 1976, the Civil Liability (Contribution) Act 1978, and the Limitation Act 1980 all bind the Crown, while the Crown Proceedings Act itself provides that the provisions relating to contributory negligence contained in the Law Reform (Contributory Negligence) Act 1945 apply to the Crown.[64] Similar provisions contained in the Merchant Shipping Act 1995 also bind the Crown and its ships.[65] And it is equally clear that the Crown is bound by the Human Rights Act 1998.[66] 5-19

---

58 In principle an act can only be a Crown act of state if it has been authorised, or ratified, by a government policy or decision which is a lawful exercise of the Crown's powers as a matter of English domestic law: *Alseran v Ministry of Defence* [2017] EWHC 3289 (QB)); [2019] Q.B. 1251. See also Smith, "Acts of state in Belhaj and Rahmatullah" (2018) 134 L.Q.R. 20.

59 Lady Hale (with whom Lord Wilson and Lord Hughes agreed) [2017] UKSC 1; [2017] A.C. 649 at [37].

60 This is not, however, the same as saying that the acts themselves were necessarily authorised in international law: Lady Hale [2017] UKSC 1; [2017] A.C. 649 at [37].

61 But see Lord Sumption [2017] UKSC 1; [2017] A.C. 649 at [94].

62 Lady Hale (with whom Lord Wilson and Lord Hughes agreed) in *Rahmatullah* [2017] UKSC 1; [2017] A.C. 649 at [14]. See, e.g. *Mohammed v Secretary of State for Defence* [2017] UKSC 2; [2017] A.C. 821.

63 For the distinction between Crown act of state and foreign act of state, see Lord Mance in *Rahmatullah* [2017] UKSC 1; A.C. 649 at [50]–[52] and Lord Sumption at [89]. For foreign act of state and its relationship with state immunity, see now *Belhaj v Straw* [2017] UKSC 3; [2017] A.C. 964.

64 s.4(2) and (3). Section 4(2) was repealed by the Civil Liability (Contribution) Act 1978 and replaced by s.5 of that Act.

65 Merchant Shipping Act 1995 ss.187 and 192.

66 Human Rights Act 1998 s.22(5).

There is some doubt whether the Defamation Acts 1952, 1996 and 2013, which make no mention of the Crown, bind the Crown by necessary implication.

5-20 A further unanswered question is whether the Crown is bound by the Fatal Accidents Act 1976 and the Law Reform (Miscellaneous Provisions) Act 1934, so far as those Acts enable actions to be brought on behalf of the estates of deceased persons. Section 32 of the Crown Proceedings Act provides that no proceedings by or against the Crown shall abate or be affected by the demise of the Crown and actions against the Crown can therefore be brought or continued after the death of the Sovereign independently of that part of s.1 of the 1934 Act which provides for the survival of causes of action against the estates of deceased persons. No provision is made, however, for the converse case where a person dies possessed of a cause of action against the Crown,[67] and there seems to be no reported decision on the point.

5-21 The policy of the Crown Proceedings Act seems clearly to require that in the kind of case under consideration the same rules should apply as where the defendant is a private person, and the argument can be made that, under s.2(1) of the Act itself, the Crown is in general to be treated "as if it were a private person of full age and capacity" (though the Sovereign cannot be sued in a personal capacity). Moreover, the Limitation Act 1980, which does bind the Crown,[68] amends the provisions of, inter alia, the 1934 Act and the Fatal Accidents Act.[69] On the other hand, it is provided by s.40(2)(f) of the Crown Proceedings Act that, save as otherwise provided by the Act, nothing in the Act shall "affect ... any presumption relating to the extent to which the Crown is bound by any Act of Parliament". The point remains open, but it is submitted that the better view is that the Acts do bind the Crown.[70] Although it was the general position at common law, it would be quite bizarre in modern circumstances if a claimant could maintain an action against the Crown for, say, breach of the Occupiers' Liability Act 1957, if he were injured, but his estate and dependants could not sue if he died.

5-22 **Foreign judgments** The State Immunity Act 1978 provides that English courts shall recognise judgments given against the UK in any other state party to the European Convention on State Immunity.[71] Such judgments are conclusive between the parties in all proceedings arising from the same cause of action in the following circumstances. The judgment must be final and result from proceedings in which the Crown was not entitled to immunity by virtue of foreign rules corresponding to those embodied in the State Immunity Act itself.[72] The court need not recognise any judgment where to do so would be manifestly contrary to public policy, or where the judgment resulted from proceedings which were procedurally unfair or inadequate. The Act also contains provisions to deal with concurrent actions against the Crown here and abroad and to govern choice of jurisdiction and choice of law in actions against the Crown.[73]

67 But s.10 of the Crown Proceedings Act had appeared to assume that the Fatal Accidents Acts 1846 and 1959 (now repealed and replaced by the Fatal Accidents Act 1976), and the Law Reform (Miscellaneous Provisions) Act 1934 did bind the Crown.

68 Limitation Act 1980 s.37.

69 Limitation Act 1980 ss.11, 12 and 13.

70 On this whole question, see Williams, *Crown Proceedings*, pp.55–58.

71 State Immunity Act 1978 ss.18, 19.

72 State Immunity Act 1978 s.18(1), (2).

73 State Immunity Act 1978 s.19.

The Civil Jurisdiction and Judgments Act 1982 s.31, provides for the recognition and enforcement of overseas judgments against states other than the UK in certain circumstances. However, before such recognition and enforcement can occur, two conditions must be satisfied. The first is that "the normal conditions for recognition and enforcement of judgments are fulfilled". The second is that "the foreign State would not have been immune if the foreign proceedings had been brought in the United Kingdom".[74] 5-23

3. Postal Services

Legislative background The relevant law in connection with the tortious liability of postal service providers is now contained in the Postal Services Act 2000. The general position is governed by s.90 of that Act which provides immunity in tort for a "universal service provider" in respect of "anything done or omitted to be done in relation to any postal packet in the course of transmission by post". By s.90(2) the immunity extends to any "officer, servant, employee, agent or subcontractor of the operator". The term "universal service provider" is defined in s.65 of the Postal Services Act 2011 in terms of any postal operator so designated by OFCOM under s.35 of that Act. 5-24

Limitation of liability Leaving aside the general position, it is further provided that limited liability may be imposed in connection with inland packages sent by registered post. However, for such liability to be imposed, two conditions must be met. First, under s.91(1), the universal service provider must subscribe to a special scheme provided for by s.89 of the Postal Services Act 2000. Secondly, by s.91(2), the loss or damage must be due to "any wrongful act of, or any neglect or default by, an officer, servant, employee, agent or sub-contractor of the postal operator while performing or purporting to perform in that capacity his functions in relation to the receipt, conveyance, delivery or other dealing with the packet". 5-25

Section 92 of the Postal Services Act 2000 sets out those entitled to sue and the limits of liability. In relation to the former matter, s.92(1) makes it clear that it is normally only the sender or the addressee of a packet who may sue. However, s.92(3) grants the court a general discretion to allow some third party to sue on behalf of either the sender or the addressee where the sender or addressee is either unable or unwilling to enforce his or her own reliefs or remedies. In either case, s.92(4) makes it clear that where the loss is not that of the sender or addressee, the money or property recovered is to be held on trust for any person who would, but for s.92, have been entitled to sue for such losses. 5-26

Under s.92(5) of the 2000 Act, liability is limited either to the market value of the packet or, in a case governed by a s.89 scheme, to the maximum amount specified under the terms of the scheme. The Act is not prescriptive as to the terms of a s.89 scheme. Rather, it is left to each particular universal service provider, at its own election, to enter into such a scheme setting out the cost of services, the limits of liability and other terms and conditions which are applicable to the services concerned. 5-27

---

74 *NML Capital Ltd v Argentina* [2011] UKSC 31; [2011] 2 A.C. 495 at [118], per Lord Collins (with whom Lord Walker agreed), interpreting Civil Jurisdiction and Judgments Act 1982 s.31(1)(a); (4). The same conclusion was reached by Lord Phillips (at [54]). See also *Ben-Rafael v Iran* [2015] EWHC 3203 (QB); *Heiser's Estate v Iran* [2019] EWHC 2074 (QB).

4. FOREIGN STATES AND AMBASSADORS

(a) Foreign states

5-28 **State Immunity Act 1978** The once controversial common law in this area has now been replaced by the State Immunity Act 1978. That Act seeks to restrict the immunity of foreign states from the jurisdiction of United Kingdom courts where the essence of the action against the state relates to commercial transactions undertaken by that state, or to a wrong committed in the UK in circumstances that make it appropriate for the obligations of the foreign government to be determined by UK courts.[75] In *Benkharbouche v Secretary of State for Foreign and Commonwealth Affairs*,[76] Lord Sumption examined the historical background to state immunity, noting that the progressive adoption of a restrictive doctrine of state immunity over the last 70 years had been due to the growing significance of state trading organisations in international trade. Importantly, individual states within the US do not constitute states for the purposes of the State Immunity Act. Rather, they are to be regarded as mere "constituent territories" within the federal state of the US.[77] To a large extent the Act embodies the provisions of the European Convention on State Immunity of 1972. It also enabled the Government to ratify the Brussels Convention of 1926[78] relating to state-owned vessels.[79]

5-29 **Heads of state** Section 20 of the Act provides that, subject to any necessary modifications, the Diplomatic Privileges Act 1964 applies to heads of state, members of their family forming part of their household and their "private servants" as it applies to heads of diplomatic missions, their families and "servants".[80] This section reiterates the personal immunity of foreign heads of state[81] and clarifies the position regarding their families and attendants.

5-30 **Immunity in tort**[82] Section 1 of the State Immunity Act 1978 continues the general immunity of foreign states from the jurisdiction of UK courts (although this immunity will not justify a striking out if the state is merely a co-defendant, since the court may need to analyse the case in depth in order to establish the liability of

---

75 It is clear that the state immunity principle is not inconsistent with the right to a fair trial contained in art.6 of the European Convention on Human Rights: see *McElhinney v Ireland* (31253/96) (2002) 34 E.H.R.R. 13.

76 [2017] UKSC 62; [2019] A.C. 777 at [51]–[52]. The case itself held that there would only be state immunity in an employment claim if the claim arose from an inherently sovereign act.

77 *Pocket Kings Ltd v Safenames Ltd* [2009] EWHC 2529 (Ch); [2010] Ch. 438.

78 International Convention for the Unification of Certain Rules relating to the Immunity of State-owned Vessels (Cmd.5672) and Protocol (Cmd.5763).

79 See *Hispano Americana Mercantil SA v Central Bank of Nigeria* [1979] 2 Lloyd's Rep. 277.

80 See paras 5-39 to 5-42. On the immunity of an ex-head of state for acts of torture see: *R. v Bow Street Metropolitan Stipendiary Magistrate Ex p. Pinochet Ugarte (No.3)* [2000] 1 A.C. 147; *Harb v Aziz* [2015] EWCA Civ 481; [2016] Ch. 308 (no state immunity for the estate of deceased head of state in respect of private acts done whilst head of state).

81 See *Bank of Credit and Commerce International (Overseas) Ltd (In Liquidation) v Price Waterhouse (No.1)* [1997] 4 All E.R. 108.

82 See s.16 for matters excluded from Pt I of the Act, and see also s.8 regarding a state's liability as a member of a company, unincorporated body or partnership. Proceedings in relation to armed forces of a state while present in the UK are excluded from the ambit of the 1978 Act by s.16(2). For immunity under the common law, see *Littrell v Government of the United States of America (No.2)* [1995] 1 W.L.R. 82. See also paras 5-43 to 5-45.

the other, non-immune defendant(s)[83]). By s.14(2) of the Act, this immunity is extended to any "separate entity" (such as a state official). But the immunity is only conferred so long as the separate entity is performing an official function of state. Perhaps oddly, this even embraces acts of state that contravene peremptory norms of international law (such as the prohibition on torture).[84] When the state is entitled to immunity from suit the court must give effect to that immunity even if the state fails to put in an appearance.[85] States are no longer immune from actions in respect of death, personal injury,[86] damage to or loss of property caused by an act or omission in the UK.[87] So far as actions for defamation are concerned, these remain firmly within the scope of state immunity,[88] as do some actions for pure financial loss unrelated to any physical damage. But if the financial loss results from a tort arising from a commercial transaction, immunity from suit is removed by s.3 of the Act. Furthermore, "commercial transaction" is widely defined to include not only contracts and loan arrangements but any other transaction or activity, whether of a commercial, industrial, financial, professional or other similar character, into which a state enters or in which it engages other than in the exercise of sovereign authority.[89] This last phrase is undefined by the Act and provides a possible loophole for states seeking to avoid restrictions on their immunity from suit.[90]

Immovable property Actions relating to any interest of foreign states in immovable property in the UK or arising from any obligation attached to the ownership, possession or use of immovable property in the UK are exempted by s.6 from the **5-31**

83 *Tajik Aluminium Plant v Ermatov (No.4)* [2006] EWHC 2374 (Comm).

84 *Jones v Ministry of the Interior for the Kingdom of Saudi Arabia* [2006] UKHL 26; [2007] 1 A.C. 270 [compliant with art.6(1) ECHR: *Jones v United Kingdom (34356/06)* (2014) 59 E.H.R.R. 1]; *Al Attiya v Al Thani* [2016] EWHC 212 (QB).

85 State Immunity Act 1978 s.1(2).

86 See *Ogelegbanwei v Nigeria* [2016] EWHC 8 (QB). For these purposes, it has been held that personal injury can be construed so as to include psychiatric illness "if, but only if, it was consequent on a physical injury in the sense of some damage to the body as opposed to the mind": *Nigeria v Ogbonna* [2012] 1 W.L.R. 139 at [14], per Underhill J (EAT).

87 State Immunity Act 1978 s.5. This section will not apply when the action relates to the operation of a ship, or the carriage of cargo, or passengers on a ship owned by a state party to the Brussels I regulation, or to the carriage of cargo owned by a state party to that regulation on any other ship. An employee of a foreign state suffering death or personal injury as the result of an act or omission in the UK may as a result of s.5 have a cause of action against the state in the UK if the injury results from a breach of the state's common law duties as an employer even if he was within the classes of person restricted from suit against that state as respects proceedings arising out of the contract of employment: see s.4.

88 *Grovit v De Nederlandsche Bank* [2005] EWHC 2944 (QB); [2006] 1 W.L.R. 3323; affirmed at [2007] EWCA Civ 953; [2008] 1 W.L.R. 51. It was also held in this case that: (1) Council Regulation 44/2001 has to be read subject to the international law of state immunity; and (2) while the ECtHR had accepted that conferring state immunity interfered with art.6 rights, it was nonetheless a permissible interference given that granting the defence of state immunity fulfilled the legitimate aim of complying with international law.

89 State Immunity Act 1978 s.3(3). See *Alcom Ltd v Republic of Colombia* [1984] 1 A.C. 580; and *Amalgamated Metal Trading Ltd v DTI*, *The Times*, 21 March 1989.

90 In *Kuwait v Iraqi Airways Co* [1995] 1 W.L.R. 1147 Lord Goff held (at 1160) that: "…the ultimate test of what constitutes an act *jure imperii* [in respect of which a foreign sovereign may claim immunity] is whether the act in question is of its own character a governmental act, as opposed to an act which any private citizen can perform". In *Kuwait Airways Corp v Iraqi Airways Corp (No.11)* [2003] EWHC 31(Comm); [2003] 1 Lloyd's Rep. 448 the painting of wrongfully retained, requisitioned aircraft was held to be a governmental act.

general immunity conferred by s.1.[91] Consequently, foreign states are now subject to the Occupiers' Liability Acts and all common law duties incumbent on those owning, possessing or using land in the UK. However, there is an exception contained in s.16(1)(b). This preserves immunity in respect of property used for the purposes of the mission in "proceedings concerning a state's title to or its possession of property".[92] The Court of Appeal in *Intpro Properties (UK) Ltd v Sauvel*[93] held that the private residences of diplomats, other than the head of a mission, were not property used for the purposes of a diplomatic mission. Section 16(1)(b) of the State Immunity Act contemplated only premises used predominantly for the professional diplomatic purposes of the mission. The fulfilment of occasional social obligations of an official nature at the home of a junior diplomat is insufficient to bring that home within the scope of the subsection. The court also considered the relationship between s.6(1) and s.16(1)(b) of the Act. No immunity attached to proceedings which related solely to the use of immovable property by the mission and did not raise any issue of title or right to possession, even where the property was used for the purposes of the mission. Therefore, claims under the Occupiers' Liability Acts and actions relating to breach of any common law duties arising from the occupation of land and premises may be brought against a foreign state even where the property in question is used for the purposes of the state's diplomatic mission.

5-32 **Intellectual property and ships** Immunity from proceedings relating to infringement of patents, trade marks and similar rights is removed by s.7 in so far as those rights are registered or protected in the UK. Section 10 applies to Admiralty proceedings and other claims which could be made the subject of Admiralty proceedings. States are not immune to actions in rem against a state-owned ship or actions in personam to enforce a claim in connection with such a ship where, at the time when the cause of action arose, the ship was in use, or was intended to be used for commercial purposes. Similar provisions cover actions relating to a ship's cargo. When an action in rem is brought against one state-owned vessel to enforce a claim against another the state may still claim immunity from proceedings unless both ships are used or intended for use for commercial purposes.[94]

5-33 **Definition of state** The Act applies to any foreign or commonwealth state other than the UK and references to states include the head of state in his public capacity, the government of the state, and any department of government.[95] But a separate

[91] A court may also entertain proceedings against persons other than states, notwithstanding that the proceedings relate to property in the possession of a state or in which a state claims an interest, if the state would not have been immune had the proceedings been brought directly against the state, or if the claim of an interest in the property is unsupported by prima facie evidence: s.6(4). Property for the purposes of s.6(4) would appear to include movable as well as immovable property. See also s.6(2), (3).

[92] The Diplomatic and Consular Premises Act 1987 provides a procedure whereby the Secretary of State must consent to land being diplomatic or consular premises, unless the land was accepted as such immediately before s.1 came into operation (1 January 1988).

[93] [1983] 2 W.L.R. 908.

[94] State Immunity Act 1978 s.10(3).

[95] s.14. Under s.21 any question as to whether a country is a state is to be resolved by a certificate from the Secretary of State, while s.15 confers power on Her Majesty by Order in Council to restrict or extend the immunities granted to any state. A certificate issued under s.21 can only be challenged in court if it is not a genuine certificate, or if it appears on its face to be ultra vires. The accuracy of

entity with independent legal personality is excluded from the definition of state for the purpose of the Act and granted immunity only when: (1) the proceedings against it relate to anything done by it in the exercise of sovereign authority; and (2) the circumstances are such that a state would have been immune.[96] So a government news agency with independent legal existence sued for libel will fail in a plea of immunity unless it can prove that it acted in the exercise of sovereign authority. Its everyday publications are excluded from the scope of immunity; and commercial agencies, even when they may be able to satisfy the test of sovereign authority, must also show that a state if sued would be immune in respect of the transactions in dispute.[97] On the other hand, the property of a state's central bank or other monetary authority is not to be regarded as used or intended for use for commercial purposes.[98]

In *Kuwait v Iraqi Airways Co*,[99] the main issue for the House of Lords was whether the seizure and subsequent use of Kuwaiti aircraft by Iraqi Airways Company (a separate entity distinct from the organs of government of the State of Iraq) was covered by immunity under s.14(2) of the 1978 Act. To show this, IAC had to prove that the proceedings against it related to something done by it in the exercise of sovereign authority and that the circumstances were such that a state would have been immune. It was held that the initial seizure was covered by the immunity, as acts done in the exercise of sovereign authority. The seizure was essentially a governmental act. However, the retention and use of the aircraft after the Iraqi Government passed legislation purportedly vesting the property in IAC did not constitute acts done in the exercise of sovereign authority. 5-34

Procedural and remedial immunity Proceedings against states must be initiated and conducted in the manner provided for by s.12[100] of the Act, and s.13 confers wide privileges on states in respect of refusal to grant disclosure of documents, and exempts states from certain remedies generally available in English courts. Briefly, foreign states are immune from the remedy by injunction, or any execution against state property movable or immovable save with their consent, and save in respect of property in use or intended for use for commercial purposes. 5-35

A state's immunity from specific remedies does not confer immunity against a claim for damages where damages are available as an alternative or additional 5-36

the statements contained in the certificate is not subject to judicial review: *Koo Golden East Mongolia v Bank of Nova Scotia* [2007] EWCA Civ 1443; [2008] Q.B. 717; *Grovit v De Nederlandsche Bank* [2007] EWCA Civ 953; [2008] 1 W.L.R. 51.

96 State Immunity Act 1978 s.14(2).

97 See *Krajina v Tass Agency* [1949] 2 All E.R. 274; *Baccus SRL v Servicio Nacional Del Trigo* [1957] 1 Q.B. 438.

98 State Immunity Act 1978 s.14(4). This section confers wider privileges on state banks than they may have enjoyed at common law: see *Hispano Americana Mercantil SA v Central Bank of Nigeria* [1979] 2 Lloyd's Rep. 277.

99 [1995] 1 W.L.R. 1147.

100 See *Westminster CC v Government of the Islamic Republic of Iran* [1986] 1 W.L.R. 979, per Peter Gibson J; *PCL v Y* [2015] EWHC 68 (Comm); [2015] 1 W.L.R. 3948. Note that service of proceedings on a state under the State Immunity Act 1978 s.12(1) can only be served at the Ministry of Foreign Affairs in the country concerned: *Kuwait v Iraqi Airways Co* [1995] 1 W.L.R. 1147. Section 12 does not, however, preclude the court from dispensing with service in exceptional circumstances: *Qatar National Bank (QPSC) v Government of Eritrea* [2019] EWHC 1601 (Ch). On the scope of s.12, see *General Dynamics UK Ltd v Libya* [2019] EWCA Civ 1110; [2019] 1 W.L.R. 6137.

remedy in that class of claim. Thus, the immunity of the Republic of France from any order compelling her to permit the landlord entry on to premises devised to her did not thereby preclude an award of damages for loss suffered as a result of breaches of covenants reserving to the landlord rights of entry.[101] *Alcom Ltd v Republic of Colombia*[102] concerned the current bank account of the Republic of Colombia's diplomatic mission, used for defraying the expenses of running the mission. The question was whether the court had jurisdiction in garnishee proceedings to order the attachment of the whole or part of the account to satisfy the judgment obtained against the state by the claimant. The House of Lords held that only if the judgment creditor could show evidence that the account was employed by the foreign state solely for being drawn on to settle liabilities incurred in commercial transactions could it be brought within the exception in s.13(4) of the Act, permitting enforcement of judgment against property used for commercial purposes.[103] The certificate of the head of mission that the property was not used for commercial purposes was sufficient evidence unless the contrary was proved. These privileges extend to separate entities where they submit to the jurisdiction in cases where they would be entitled to immunity.[104]

5-37 **Submission to the jurisdiction** Finally, a state immune under the Act may choose to submit to the jurisdiction of a UK court and in doing so waive immunity in respect of those proceedings. Section 2 provides that a state may submit to the jurisdiction expressly after the proceedings have arisen, or by a prior written agreement.[105] States will be deemed to have submitted where the state itself instituted proceedings or took any step in the proceedings[106] save to claim immunity[107] or protect an interest in property when the state would have been entitled to immunity had the proceedings been brought against the state.[108] Submission extends to any appeal but only to counterclaims if they arise out of the same legal relationship or facts of the claim.[109]

5-38 **Foreign states as claimants** In *Mbasogo v Logo Ltd (No.1)*,[110] the facts were as follows. The President of Equatorial Guinea together with the Republic of Equatorial Guinea appealed against a first instance decision to strike out their claims for damages arising out of an attempted coup d'état. The President and the Republic

---

[101] *Intpro Properties (UK) Ltd v Sauvel* [1983] 2 W.L.R. 908.
[102] [1984] A.C. 580.
[103] On the meaning of "in use for commercial purposes", see *SerVaas Inc v Rafidain Bank* [2012] UKSC 40; [2013] 1 A.C. 595.
[104] State Immunity Act 1978 s.14(3).
[105] The prior agreement now sufficient must be an agreement to submit to the jurisdiction. A choice of law clause in an agreement selecting the law of the UK as the proper law of the agreement is not enough: s.2(2). See also *Ahmed v Saudi Arabia* [1996] I.C.R. 25.
[106] State Immunity Act 1978 s.2(3).
[107] *Kuwait Airways Corp v Iraqi Airways Co* [1995] 1 Lloyd's Rep. 25.
[108] State Immunity Act 1978 s.2(4). See also s.2(5) regarding a state acting unaware of facts entitling it to immunity.
[109] State Immunity Act 1978 s.2(6). Further, s.2(7) designates the head of a state's diplomatic mission as having authority to make the submission. By s.13(3), however, such submission does not of itself imply any submission to the enforcement jurisdiction of the courts. Separate consent to that is needed. On the question of who can waive immunity under s.2(7), see *Arab Republic of Egypt v Gamal-Eldin* [1996] I.C.R. 13 EAT; *Malaysian Industrial Development Authority v Jeyasingham* [1998] I.C.R. 307 EAT.
[110] [2006] EWCA Civ 1370; [2007] Q.B. 846.

argued that the respondents had planned a coup designed to overthrow the government of Equatorial Guinea. Although the coup failed, the government argued that the respondents' actions had caused the government serious financial loss in the shape of the cost of investigating, detaining and prosecuting the conspirators, as well as the costs of increased security. The first instance judge struck out the government's claim for damages and (together with the President whose claim rested on different grounds), the government appealed arguing that its claim was an entirely conventional conspiracy claim. Adopting the approach that it would be wrong for the English courts to lend their assistance to the assertion of sovereign authority by one state in the territory of another, the Court of Appeal considered the critical question to be whether the government was asserting a claim which, by its nature, involved the assertion of a sovereign right. It went on to find that the claim pleaded in this case arose as a direct result of the various decisions taken by the government to protect the state and citizens of Equatorial Guinea in response to the conspiracy. These, the Court of Appeal held, were losses that could only be suffered by the governing body of the state since the defence of a state and its subjects was a paradigm function of government. As such, the government's claim for special damages failed on the basis that the claim fell beyond the competence of the English court.

(b) Ambassadors

Ambassadors The law governing diplomatic immunity is contained in the Diplomatic Privileges Act 1964[111] which gives the force of law to the Vienna Convention on Diplomatic Relations of 1961, as set out in Sch.1 to the Act. The immunity granted is from suit and not from liability.[112] Thus, if proceedings are begun at a stage when the defendant is no longer protected by his diplomatic status, and do not relate to his performance of functions as a member of the diplomatic mission, no immunity exists.[113] 5-39

Immunity Immunity depends on mutual agreement so no immunity is conferred by reason of diplomatic status unless the representative of the foreign country in question has been accepted or received by this country.[114] Subject to this, diplomatic 5-40

[111] See s.1. See also *Empson v Smith* [1966] 1 Q.B. 426; International Organisations Act 1981; Commonwealth Secretariat Act 1966; Consular Relations Act 1968. Individuals carrying out inspections for international arms control purposes have similar immunities: Arms Control and Disarmament (Privileges and Immunities) Act 1988 s.1; Arms Control and Disarmament (Inspections) Act 1991 s.5; Chemical Weapons Act 1996 s.27; Landmines Act 1998 s.15; Nuclear Explosions (Prohibition and Inspections) Act 1998 s.8 (not yet in force).

[112] *Dickinson v Del Solar* [1930] 1 K.B. 376 (insurance company liable even though diplomat defendant could not be sued).

[113] *Empson v Smith* [1966] 1 Q.B. 426; *Shaw v Shaw* [1979] Fam. 62.

[114] *R. v Governor of Pentonville Prison Ex p. Teja* [1971] 2 Q.B. 274. If a question arises of whether a person is entitled to immunity under the Act, a certificate issued by or under the authority of the Secretary of State stating any fact is conclusive of that fact: Diplomatic Privileges Act 1964, s.4: *R. v Governor of Pentonville Prison Ex p. Osman (No.2)* [1989] C.O.D. 446. The conclusion to be drawn from the facts is now a question for the court. cf. *Engelke v Musmann* [1928] A.C. 433. See also *R. v Lambeth Justices Ex p. Yusufu* [1985] Crim. L.R. 510; *Mohamed v Breish* [2019] EWHC 306 (Comm); affirmed [2020] EWCA Civ 637; and *Al Attiya v Al Thani* [2016] EWHC 212 (QB): FCO certificate provides conclusive evidence of the facts despite an absence of evidence that the defendant had ever undertaken any function as a diplomatic agent in the UK since November 2013.

agents—i.e. the head of a mission and the members of its staff having diplomatic rank—are immune from civil jurisdiction except in three specific cases.[115] Members of the administrative and technical staff of a mission are similarly immune, except that their immunity does not extend to acts performed outside the course of their duties, and members of the service staff are immune in respect of acts performed in the course of their duties.[116] Private servants of members of a mission may enjoy immunity to the extent that may be specified by Order in Council.[117] Members of the families forming part of the households of diplomatic agents and of members of the administrative and technical staff of a mission enjoy immunities equivalent to those enjoyed by the heads of their families.[118] The scope of the immunity is different, however, if the person claiming immunity is a British national, in which case a diplomatic agent is immune only in respect of official acts performed in the exercise of his functions, and other members of the mission are entitled to immunity only to the extent that may be provided by Order in Council.[119] The scope of the immunity may also be reduced by Order in Council with respect to a particular mission if it appears that the country sending that mission affords to members of the UK mission in its territory immunities less extensive than those provided by the Act and Convention.[120] If the member of the mission, or the private servant of such a member, who is a British national, is also a citizen of a Commonwealth country or the Republic of Ireland, then he is entitled to the privileges and immunities to which he would have been entitled had he not been a British national.[121]

5-41 **Duration of immunity** Immunity is enjoyed from the moment the person entitled to it enters the UK on proceeding to take up his post or, if he is already in the UK, from the moment that his appointment is notified to the Secretary of State.[122] On the cessation of his functions, a person's immunity expires[123] when he leaves the

---

115 Convention art.31(1). The exceptions are: (a) an action relating to private immovable property not held on behalf of the sending state for the purposes of the mission (the private residences of diplomats other than the head of a mission do not constitute premises held on behalf of the sending state for the purposes of the mission: *Intpro Properties (UK) Ltd v Sauvel* [1983] 2 W.L.R. 908); (b) an action relating to succession in which the diplomatic agent is involved as executor, administrator, heir or legatee as a private person and not on behalf of the sending state; (c) an action relating to any professional or commercial activity exercised by the diplomatic agent outside his official functions (See now *Reyes v Al-Malki* [2017] UKSC 61; [2019] A.C. 735). The immunity conferred by the Commonwealth Secretariat Act 1966 upon the Secretariat itself and upon certain members of its staff does not extend to actions for damage caused by motor vehicles. See the Schedule to the Act, paras 1 and 6, and cf. para.5.

116 Convention art.37(2), (3). *B (A Child) (Care Proceedings: Diplomatic Immunity), Re* [2002] EWHC 1751 (Fam); [2003] Fam. 16. As to who qualifies as a member of the mission, see *Arab Republic of Egypt v Gamal-Eldin* [1996] I.C.R. 13; *Ahmed v Saudi Arabia* [1996] I.C.R. 25.

117 Convention art.37(4); Diplomatic Privileges Act 1964 s.2(6).

118 Convention art.37(1), (2).

119 Convention art.38(1), (2); Diplomatic Privileges Act 1964 s.2(6).

120 Diplomatic Privileges Act 1964 s.3.

121 Diplomatic Privileges (British Nationals) Order 1999 (SI 1999/670).

122 Convention art.39. A defendant in an action who only becomes entitled to immunity after the writ has been issued and validly served upon him may nevertheless have the proceedings stayed; and an unconditional appearance entered before he became entitled to immunity does not constitute a waiver of immunity, for at that date there was no immunity to be waived: *Ghosh v D'Rozario* [1963] 1 Q.B. 106.

123 See *Shaw v Shaw* [1979] Fam. 62 (when an action is begun against a defendant at a time when he is entitled to diplomatic immunity and he later applies to have the proceedings struck out on the

country (or upon the expiry of a reasonable time to allow him to do so[124]). If a member of a mission dies, his family continue to enjoy immunity until the expiry of a reasonable time in which to leave the country.

Waiver of immunity The immunity of any person may be waived by the sending state, but the waiver must be express.[125] If, however, a person entitled to immunity initiates proceedings he is precluded from invoking his immunity in respect of any counterclaim directly connected with thc principal claim.[126] Separate waiver is required before execution may be levied on any judgment[127] and in any case execution cannot be levied against a diplomatic agent except in one of the three specific cases referred to above and provided the measures concerned can be taken without infringing the inviolability of his person or of his residence.[128] Note that by s.2(3) a waiver by the head of the mission of any state (or any person for the time being performing his functions) is deemed to be a waiver by that state. 5-42

5. VISITING FORCES

Visiting forces The State Immunity Act 1978 does not apply to proceedings relating to anything done by, or in relation to, the armed forces of a state while in the UK. Their liability continues to be governed by the Visiting Forces Act 1952.[129] Exemptions, privileges and immunities subsisting in respect of various enactments[130] by virtue of the rule of law with respect to the application of enactments to the Crown are extended to the visiting forces[131] of countries to which the Visiting Forces Act 1952 applies,[132] and to property held or used for the purposes of such forces, as if they were part of the home forces.[133] Similarly, the provisions of certain other enactments which confer specific exemptions, immunities or privileges on the home forces are also extended to visiting forces.[134] 5-43

By s.9(1) of the Visiting Forces Act, the Secretary of State for Defence may make arrangements whereby claims in respect of acts or omissions of members of visiting forces will be satisfied by the payment by the Minister of such amounts as may 5-44

---

grounds of his immunity, the relevant date for deciding the issue of immunity from suit is when his application to strike out comes before the court). On the residual immunity for acts performed in the exercise of the diplomat's official functions as a member of the mission under art.39(2), see *Reyes v Al-Malki* [2017] UKSC 61; [2019] A.C. 735.

124 What constitutes a reasonable period is a matter for the court to determine in the context of interstate diplomatic relations: *A Local Authority v X* [2018] EWHC 874 (Fam); [2019] Fam. 313.

125 Convention art.32(1)(2). *A Company v Republic of X* [1990] 2 Lloyd's Rep. 520, per Saville J. A sovereign state is not bound by an inter partes agreement to waive diplomatic privileges over property unless it gives an undertaking of consent to the court itself.

126 Convention art.32(3).

127 Convention art.32(4).

128 Convention art.31(3).

129 State Immunity Act 1978 s.16(2).

130 For these enactments see Visiting Forces and International Headquarters (Application of Law) Order 1999 (SI 1999/1736).

131 For definition see Visiting Forces Act 1952 s.12(1). See also International Headquarters and Defence Organisations Act 1964, which applies provisions similar to those in the Visiting Forces Act 1952 to certain international headquarters and defence organisations.

132 These include the Commonwealth countries, certain former colonies, the US and many European countries.

133 Visiting Forces Act 1952 s.8(2); SI 1999/1736.

134 SI 1999/1736.

be adjudged by any UK court, or agreed between the claimant and the Minister. While s.9 does not provide for the Secretary of State to defend proceedings for a claim, s.9A[135] now enables the Secretary of State, if a sending state requests it, to transfer any liability in tort in respect of a relevant claim to the Ministry of Defence. This was introduced under the Armed Forces Act 2011 to bring the UK in line with other NATO states and remove the difficulty that if the Secretary of State did not succeed in settling the claim and the matter had to be decided by the courts, the sending state would have to act for itself, not necessarily an easy task bearing in mind that it would find itself in unfamiliar proceedings.

5-45 In *Holland v Lampen-Wolfe*,[136] the claimant was a US citizen teaching at a military base in the UK operated by the US Government. She brought a defamation action against another US citizen employed by the US Department of Defense. The Court of Appeal held that state immunity did not arise under the State Immunity Act 1978, because s.16(2) excluded from the Act things done by or in relation to the armed forces of a foreign state while present in the UK, and although the claimant was not a member of the armed forces the defendant's conduct was clearly something done by the armed forces. Immunity at common law applied, however, since the provision of education to armed forces posted away from their own country was a normal and necessary part of the overall activity of maintaining those forces in a foreign country.[137]

6. BANKRUPTS

5-46 **Bankrupt as defendant** By s.382(1) and (4) of the Insolvency Act 1986 a bankruptcy debt is defined as a debt[138] or liability (including liability in tort) to which the bankrupt is subject at the commencement of the bankruptcy or to which he may become subject after the commencement of the bankruptcy by reason of any obligation incurred before the commencement of the bankruptcy. By s.382(2) the bankrupt shall be deemed to become subject to liability in tort by reason of an obligation incurred at the time when the cause of action accrued. Torts committed after the bankruptcy are not bankruptcy debts, and presumably the bankrupt remains personally liable. Any torts committed before the bankruptcy are now bankruptcy debts.[139] If it is a debt provable in the bankruptcy,[140] s.285(3) denies a remedy against the property or person of the bankrupt. It remains to be seen what tortious claims will become provable debts.[141]

5-47 **Bankrupt as claimant?** Where a tort is committed against the person or property of a bankrupt the question arises whether it is the bankrupt himself who can sue or whether the cause of action is vested in his trustee. It is clear that if the act

135 In force from 6 April 2013.
136 [1999] 1 W.L.R. 188.
137 Affirmed [2000] 1 W.L.R. 1573 HL.
138 "Debt" is defined in s.382(3).
139 According to *T & N Ltd, Re* [2005] EWHC 2870 (Ch); [2006] 1 W.L.R. 1728, a wrongful exposure to asbestos that has not given rise to any material damage (in the shape of a diagnosable asbestos related disease) by the time of the bankruptcy, does not count as a tort for these purposes.
140 See s.412 and Sch.9 and rules made thereunder.
141 Deceit will certainly suffice: *Vekaria v Jackson* [2009] EWHC 1514 (Ch). See also s.281 of the Insolvency Act 1986 (effect of discharge) now moved to Ch.1A (from 6 April 2016); in particular s.281(5) and (6) and rules made thereunder: *Heath v Tang* [1993] 1 W.L.R. 1421.

complained of causes damage only to property belonging to the bankrupt at the date of the bankruptcy, it is the trustee alone who can sue, for the damage has diminished the value of the bankrupt's estate divisible among the creditors.[142] But the trustee can, if he wishes, validly assign the cause of action back to the bankrupt with the result that the action may be maintained by the bankrupt alone and in his own name.[143] It is also clear that if the damage is purely personal to the bankrupt himself, as in cases of slander[144] and, presumably, personal injuries, then it is the bankrupt alone who can sue,[145] subject, of course, to any available defences.

Although there is no authority that confirms this, it seems that a bankrupt may, in certain circumstances, be able to invoke the tort of negligence to sue for purely economic losses (so far as such losses are recoverable under that tort). The matter was considered in *Smeaton v Equifax Plc*.[146] In that case, the respondent was a bankrupt who had had a bankruptcy order against him rescinded in May 2002. The appellant, a credit reference agency, had not been notified of its rescission and it did not amend its records concerning the respondent. In July 2006 the respondent had his application for a business loan declined on the basis of "adverse data" on his credit file. The respondent then brought an action against the appellant alleging, inter alia, that his inability to secure the loan had resulted in a loss of projected profits for his new company. The respondent sought to base his claim on an assumed responsibility owed to all those whose personal data the appellant held. On the facts, the Court of Appeal held that no duty was owed. However, what was *not* ruled out was the notion that a bankrupt might *in principle* succeed in a negligence action for pure economic loss.[147] **5-48**

In some cases the act complained of may be such as to cause damage to property and also damage of a personal nature. If, as a result, there are two causes of action, the one in respect of damage to property and the other in respect of personal damage, as for instance where a vehicle which the bankrupt is driving is run into and both vehicle and driver are damaged,[148] then the trustee may sue for the one and the bankrupt for the other. The same may be true even where there is a single cause of action: the cause of action may be split. In so far as it relates to damage to property it will pass to the trustee and in so far as it relates to personal damage it will remain with the bankrupt.[149] Thus, in cases of trespass to land or goods, where the manner of the trespass is such as to cause personal annoyance to the bankrupt, a right of action remains in him in respect of that damage though, semble, the trustee **5-49**

---

142 *Beckham v Drake* (1849) 2 H.L.C. 579.

143 *Ramsey v Hartley* [1977] 1 W.L.R. 686; *Weddell v JA Pearce Major* [1988] Ch. 1.

144 *Ex p. Vine, Re Wilson* (1878) 8 Ch. D. 364.

145 It is an open question whether a cause of action under the Fatal Accidents Act 1976 passes to the trustee of a bankrupt executor or dependant. It has been held in New Zealand that it does not: *Richter, Re* [1929] N.Z.L.R. 364.

146 [2013] EWCA Civ 108; [2013] 2 All E.R. 959.

147 Consider also *Sebry v Companies House* [2015] EWHC 115 (QB); [2016] 1 W.L.R. 2499 (Registrar of Companies had a common law duty of care, when entering a winding-up order on the companies register, to take reasonable care to ensure that the order was not registered against the wrong company).

148 *Brunsden v Humphrey* (1884) 14 Q.B.D. 141. See, however, *Talbot v Berkshire CC* [1994] Q.B. 290 and *Wain v F Sherwood and Sons Transport Ltd* [1999] P.I.Q.R. P159, where the Court of Appeal suggested that *Brunsden v Humphrey* might well have been decided differently if *Henderson v Henderson* (1843) 3 Hare 100, applying the doctrine of res judicata, had been cited.

149 *Wilson v United Counties Bank* [1920] A.C. 102. See, however, *Wenlock v Moloney* (1967) 111 S.J. 437.

alone can sue for physical damage to the property itself.[150] The trustee and the bankrupt can bring separate actions to recover their appropriate damages, or they can join as claimants in one action, in which case the damages will be separately assessed.[151] In *Ord v Upton*[152] the Court of Appeal held that where a bankrupt brought an action for personal injuries in respect of both loss of earnings and pain and suffering, the cause of action vested in the trustee despite the bankrupt's right to recover personal damages. Furthermore, any personal damages recovered for pain and suffering were to be held on a constructive trust for the bankrupt by the trustee.[153]

5-50 **Liability insurance** At common law, if a tortfeasor who was insured against liability became bankrupt, the moneys payable to him as indemnity under the policy of insurance formed part of his estate and were available for distribution among his creditors.[154] Until 1 August 2016, s.1 of the Third Parties (Rights against Insurers) Act 1930 provided that on the bankruptcy (or in the case of a company, the liquidation) of an insured tortfeasor, the bankrupt's rights against the insurer under the policy were transferred to, and vested in, the claimant. This avoids the general creditors taking a share of the compensation at the expense of the victim. On this basis, the claimant simply stood in the bankrupt's shoes so far as the insurer is concerned. Accordingly, he had no direct right of action against the insurer until the liability to him of the bankrupt had been established and its amount ascertained, if necessary by an action against the bankrupt personally.[155] In *Bradley v Eagle Star Insurance Co Ltd*,[156] an insured company had been wound up and dissolved before the existence and extent of its liability had been established. The House of Lords held that in these circumstances no right of indemnity could be transferred to and vested in the appellant under s.1(1) of the Act. The third party could not rely on the Act to sue the insurers direct. In the absence of even a nominal defendant the claimant could not assert that the "true defendant" was the insurer.

5-51 With the coming into force of the Third Parties (Rights against Insurers) Act 2010,[157] s.1(3) now permits the claimant to bring proceedings to enforce the rights

[150] *Brewer v Dew* (1843) 11 M. & W. 625; *Rogers v Spence* (1844) 13 M. & W. 571; *Rose v Buckett* [1901] 2 K.B. 449. Twin losses may also be caused by negligence that results in the claimant's bankruptcy. These are: (i) economic loss (in the shape of loss of future earnings that would have accrued but for the bankruptcy); and (ii) loss of status and reputation (synonymous with bankruptcy). In such cases, the former loss vests in the trustee while the latter, being of a personal nature, vests in the bankrupt: *Mulkerrins v Pricewaterhouse Coopers* [2003] UKHL 41; [2003] 1 W.L.R. 1937.

[151] *Wilson v United Counties Bank* [1920] A.C. 102.

[152] [2000] Ch. 352. See also *Hayes v Butters* [2014] EWHC 4557 (Ch); [2015] Ch. 495.

[153] [2000] Ch. 352 at 370, per Aldous LJ.

[154] *Harrington Motor Co Ltd, Re* [1928] Ch. 105.

[155] *Post Office v Norwich Union Fire Insurance Society Ltd* [1967] 2 Q.B. 363. The reason is that under an indemnity policy an insured has no right of action against his insurer until his own liability to the injured person has been established. There is no duty for the insurers to give information to a third party until liability has been established by action, arbitration or agreement: *Woolwich Building Society v Taylor* [1995] 1 B.C.L.C. 132; see also *Nigel Upchurch Associates v Aldridge Estates Investment Co Ltd* [1993] 1 Lloyd's Rep. 535. Where the insured is a company in liquidation the leave of the court must be obtained before proceedings are begun (Insolvency Act 1986 s.130(2)).

[156] [1989] 2 A.C. 957.

[157] The Third Parties (Rights against Insurers) Act 2010 gives effect, with minor modifications, to the recommendations set out in the Law Commission and the Scottish Law Commission's 2001 joint report *Third Parties—Rights against Insurers* (Law Com No.272; Scot Law Com No.184) which was accepted by the Government in 2002. For transition provisions, see Third Parties (Rights against

against the insurer without having established the bankrupt's liability, although the claimant cannot enforce those rights without having established that liability.[158] Where the insured person is a dissolved body corporate, s.6A now permits the claimant to recover damages from an insurer of that company without needing to restore the company to the register as a preliminary step.[159] This addresses the problem highlighted by *Bradley v Eagle Star Insurance* and avoids the need for a claimant to bring preliminary proceedings against the insured.[160] Section 2 of the Act provides a new mechanism to enable a third party to bring proceedings against an insurer without first establishing the fact and amount of the insured's liability.[161] On this basis, the claimant need only issue one set of proceedings against the insurer and may ask the court to make declarations both on the insured's liability to the claimant and the insurer's liability under the policy. If, in an action by the bankrupt, the insurer would have had a defence according to the terms of the policy, that defence will prevail against the injured person.[162] The 2010 Act s.10 also specifically establishes a right of set-off in respect of a liability the insured has to the insurer under the contract of insurance.[163] The action against the insurers, pursuant to the Act, must be commenced within the ordinary limitation period (i.e. proceedings have to be issued within six years of the cause of action arising, not the date of the bankruptcy).[164] Section 12 does provide, however, that if the claimant has issued proceedings against the insured in time, the claimant will not be time-barred from issuing fresh proceedings against the insurer for a declaration under s.2(2)(a).

Insurers) Act 2010 Sch.3(3). The Act does not apply to reinsurance liabilities: see s.15.

158 On the operation of s.1 of the Third Parties (Rights against Insurers) Act 2010 and the transitional provisions, see *Redman v Zurich Insurance Plc* [2017] EWHC 1919 (QB); [2018] 1 W.L.R. 280. Schedule 3 to the 2010 Act expressly made it clear that the 1930 Act continued to apply where, before 1 August 2016, someone had become insolvent for the purposes of the 2010 Act and had incurred a liability against which they were insured. As liability was incurred when damage was caused, not when a claimant had established a right to compensation, in this case the 1930 Act applied. The transitional provisions did not provide for the 2010 regime to be applied retrospectively, so as to run in parallel with the regime under the 1930 Act.

159 Inserted by the Third Parties (Rights Against Insurers) Regulations 2016 (SI 2016/570). Note also the Third Parties (Rights Against Insurers) Act 2010 (Consequential Amendment of Companies Act 2006) Regulations 2018 (SI 2018/1162) which deals with a situation where the company has been dissolved many years before the claim is made and an application to restore the company to the register is out of time under s.1030(4) of the Companies Act 2006. By enabling the insurer to restore the company to the register, it facilitates the instigation of proceedings against other potential co-defendants in personal injury actions, e.g. asbestos claims.

160 The new procedure removes the need to restore a dissolved company to the register of companies solely for the purpose of bringing an action against the company in order to establish the insured company's liability to the claimant so that the claimant could rely on the Third Parties (Rights against Insurers) Act in order to claim against the insurer.

161 The operation of s.2 of the Third Parties (Rights against Insurers) Act 2010 was explained in *BAE Systems Pension Funds Trustees Ltd v Royal & Sun Alliance Insurance Plc* [2017] EWHC 2082 (TCC); [2018] 1 W.L.R 1165. An employment tribunal is a "court" within the meaning of the 2010 Act s.2(6): *Watson v Hemingway Design Ltd, EAT*, 16 December 2019 (under appeal).

162 *Farrell v Federated Employers Insurance Association Ltd* [1970] 1 W.L.R. 1400; *Firma C-Trade SA v Newcastle Protection and Indemnity Association* [1991] 2 A.C. 1.

163 Note, however, the uncertainty highlighted in *International Energy Group Ltd v Zurich Insurance Plc* [2015] UKSC 33; [2016] A.C. 509 at [92]–[97].

164 *Lefevre v White* [1990] 1 Lloyd's Rep. 569.

7. CHILDREN

5-52 **Age of majority** By the Family Law Reform Act 1969 a person attains full age on reaching the age of 18. And, by s.105 of the Children Act 1989, a person is to be regarded as a "child" until he or she attains that age.[165]

5-53 **Liability of children** There is no defence of minority as such known to the law of tort and, save that a child must have a litigation friend to conduct proceedings on his behalf,[166] a child may be sued in tort as if he were of full age.[167] However, by analogy with the cases concerning contributory negligence of young children[168] the age of a child defendant is relevant in torts involving negligence, intention or malice. In *Mullin v Richards*,[169] the Court of Appeal held that the test for negligence was not whether the actions of the defendant were such as an ordinarily prudent and reasonable adult in the defendant's situation would have realised they created a risk of injury, but whether an ordinarily prudent and reasonable child of the defendant's age, in the defendant's situation, would have appreciated the risk. Accordingly a 15-year-old schoolgirl was not liable when, playing at fencing with plastic rulers with a classmate, one of the rulers broke and a piece of plastic entered the claimant's eye.

5-54 **Liability of child where tort connected with contract** A child cannot be sued in tort if the tort action is in effect a means of enforcing a contract that does not bind him. Thus in *R Leslie Ltd v Sheill*,[170] the defendant, a child, had fraudulently acquired a loan from the claimant by representing that he was of full age and thus in possession of the relevant contractual capacity to enter into such an agreement. In an action framed in the tort of deceit, the court held him not liable: to have found otherwise would have been merely a roundabout way of giving effect to the contractual loan. An interesting but, as yet, unanswered question is whether there may be any liability in negligence on the part of a child where the law would recognise concurrent contractual and tortious duties. Certainly, a child can be held liable in tort where, although arising out of a contract in the sense that but for the contract there would have been no opportunity for the tort, it is in fact independent of the contract. Thus, where a minor (lacking contractual capacity) hired a horse and loaned it to a friend who jumped it contrary to a contractual stipulation that the horse should not be jumped, the minor was held liable for trespass.[171] The question whether in such cases the wrongful act is in mere excess of, or entirely outside, the contract is one of degree.[172]

5-55 **Child bailee**[173] A bailment is usually accompanied by a contract, either express or implied by law, to restore the goods upon the determination of the bailment. This is not, however, essential. There may be a complete bailment without a contract.

---

165 The term "child" is also adopted throughout the Civil Procedure Rules: see CPR rr.2.3 and 21.1(2).

166 CPR r.21.2.

167 See, e.g. *Gorely v Codd* [1967] 1 W.L.R. 19. With regard to trespass, however, see now *Wilson v Pringle* [1987] Q.B. 237.

168 Generally, see para.3-82. See *McHale v Watson* (1966) 115 C.L.R. 199 H. Ct of Aus.

169 [1998] 1 W.L.R. 1304. See further para.7-170.

170 [1914] 3 K.B. 607.

171 *Burnard v Haggis* (1863) 14 C.B. (N.S.) 45 at 53.

172 cf. *Walley v Holt* (1876) 35 L.T. 631; *Fawcett v Smethurst* (1914) 84 L.J.K.B. 473.

173 See also Ch.16 (interference with goods).

Goods may be delivered on a condition or trust not amounting to a contract, so as to create a special property in the bailee, while leaving the general property in the bailor.[174] The minority of such a bailee would not affect his rights and liabilities in tort. He could bring an action, whilst his special property lasted, against any person who deprived him of the goods.[175] On the determination of the bailment by effluxion of time, or by some act on his part so inconsistent with the condition of the bailment as to entitle the bailor to treat it as determined,[176] the whole property in the goods would revert to the bailor, who could sue him for conversion if the goods were not restored.[177]

Contract procured by fraud of child Where goods are delivered to a child in pursuance of a contract of sale, the position is different. The property in the goods may pass to him even though the contract was obtained by his fraud, and the seller has then no remedy by way of an action for conversion or deceit, for that would be in substance a means of enforcing the contract to pay the price.[178] A child who procures a contract by a fraudulent representation that he is of age is not liable either on the contract or for the tort of deceit.[179] He is, however, subject to an equitable obligation to restore any property which can be traced to his possession if obtained by such a fraud. He will be compelled to restore his ill-gotten gains, or to release the party deceived from obligations or acts in law induced by the fraud. But this obligation is very limited. If there is no possibility of restoring the very thing obtained by the fraud there is no remedy. For any remedy would amount to the enforcement of a void contract.[180] Restitution stops where repayment begins.[181] In addition, by s.3 of the Minors' Contracts Act 1987, if a contract is unenforceable against the defendant because he was a child at the time the contract was made the court may require the defendant "if it is just and equitable to do so" to transfer to the claimant any property acquired by the defendant under the contract or any property representing it. Though the equitable relief, just discussed, is preserved, statutory relief is more general and not limited to cases where the child is guilty of fraud. 5-56

Liability of parent A parent is not, as such, liable for the torts of his child.[182] If, however, the circumstances are such as to bring into existence the relationship of employer and employee between parent and child, and a tort is committed by the child in the course of his employment, or if the parent has himself been guilty of negligence, then he will be liable.[183] 5-57

174 See *R. v McDonald* (1885) 15 Q.B.D. 323 (child hirer of furniture, no valid contract of hire, but if child sells the furniture, he is guilty of larceny).
175 (1885) 15 Q.B.D. 323 at 325.
176 e.g. a pledging of the goods by the child.
177 *Mills v Graham* (1804) B. & P. 1 N.R. 140.
178 *Leslie v Sheill* [1914] 3 K.B. 607.
179 *Leslie v Sheill* [1914] 3 K.B. 607.
180 *Leslie v Sheill* [1914] 3 K.B. 607 (limiting *Stocks v Wilson* [1913] 2 K.B. 235).
181 *Leslie v Sheill* [1914] 3 K.B. 607 at 618, per Lord Sumner.
182 *North v Wood* [1914] 1 K.B. 629; *Gorely v Codd* [1967] 1 W.L.R. 19.
183 *Bebee v Sales* (1916) 32 T.L.R. 413; *Carmarthenshire County Council v Lewis* [1955] A.C. 549. See also para.7-235.

5-58 **Pre-natal injuries** The Congenital Disabilities (Civil Liability) Act 1976[184] governs this area of law in respect of births on or after 22 July 1976. The Act confers a right of action on a child who is born alive[185] and disabled in respect of the disability,[186] if it is caused by an occurrence which affected either parent's ability to have a normal healthy child, or affected the mother during pregnancy, or affected the mother or child in the course of its birth, causing disabilities which would not otherwise have been present.[187] A defendant is liable to the child if he is or would, if sued in time, have been liable in tort to the parent. Yet it is no answer that the parent has suffered no actionable injury.[188] Thus, the child's action is derivative, in that it depends on a tortious duty owed to the parent. This formulation of duty to the child as deriving from a tort against the parent leaves certain questions for interpretation by the courts. If the defendant negligently injures either parent in his or her reproductive capacity, or the mother in pregnancy, in such a way as to inflict no apparent damage, can there in fact be a breach of duty to the parent unless the duty of care owed to avoid causing him physical injury is extended to include taking care not to subject him or her to the risk of later producing a disabled child? It seems clear that a child damaged by a drug taken by its mother during pregnancy, for example, can sue the manufacturer even though the mother did not suffer any harm, if there was a breach of a duty of care owed to the mother. But if there was no breach of duty to the mother—for example, if the drug was intended to and did have therapeutic effects for her—it is difficult to see how there could be any claim by the child injured by the drug. This reflects the policy of the Act in maintaining the priority of the mother's interests over those of the foetus. Thus, in a situation of medical "conflict" between the interests of the mother and the child, there is no legal conflict. A proper discharge of the doctor's duty of care to the mother prevents a duty to the foetus from arising. The child's mother is expressly excluded from liability to her child,[189] except that by virtue of s.2 she owes a duty of care towards her unborn child when driving a motor vehicle when she knows or ought reasonably to know herself to be pregnant. The child's father enjoys no such immunity.

5-59 **Defences** The defendant is not liable in respect of pre-conception injuries if either or both parents knew of the risk of the child being born disabled unless the child's

---

184 See also para.9-92 and note, too, the state compensation scheme introduced by the Vaccine Damage Payment Act 1979.

185 "Alive" is defined as having a life separate from its mother: Congenital Disabilities (Civil Liability) Act 1976 s.4(2)(a).

186 Disability means "being born with any deformity, disease or abnormality, including predisposition (whether or not susceptible of immediate prognosis) to physical or mental defect in the future": Congenital Disabilities (Civil Liability) Act 1976 s.4(1). But note Murphy (1994) 10 P.N. 94 who argues that there is a distinction between being injured or damaged and suffering a "disability". Note also the negligent selection of gametes which results in a child being born with a different skin colour from its parents is not born "disabled": *A v A Health and Social Services Trust* [2011] NICA 28; [2012] N.I. 77.

187 Congenital Disabilities (Civil Liability) Act 1976 s.1(1) and (2). No damages, however, can be recovered in respect of lost earnings in a case where the child's lifespan has been shortened by the injuries inflicted during childbirth: *Whipps Cross University NHS Trust v Khazar Iqbal* [2007] EWCA Civ 1190; [2008] P.I.Q.R. P9.

188 Congenital Disabilities (Civil Liability) Act 1976 s.1(3).

189 See s.1(1).

father is the defendant and he alone was aware of the relevant risk.[190] Damages payable to the child will be reduced if it is shown that the affected parent shared responsibility for the child being born disabled, to the extent that the court thinks just and equitable having regard to the extent of the parent's responsibility.[191] A defendant who advised or treated the parent in a professional capacity is not liable if he acted reasonably on received professional opinion of the time.[192] The damages payable must compensate the child for the disability with which it was born and all the ensuing consequences of that disability.[193] The child's cause of action accrues at its birth; however, time will not run against the child under the Limitation Act 1980 until he reaches majority.[194] Section 3 of the Act provides separate rules in respect of children injured pre-conceptually, or pre-natally, by occurrences involving nuclear matter or the emission of ionising radiation.

Section 1A effectively extends the provisions of s.1 of the Act to children born disabled as a result of damage to an embryo or to gametes in the course of infertility treatment, by the placing in a woman of an embryo, or of sperm and eggs or of artificial insemination. Where the disability results from an act or omission in the course of the selection, or the keeping or use outside the body of the embryo carried by the woman or of the gametes used to bring about the creation of the embryo, and a person is answerable under the section to the child in respect of the act or omission, the child's disabilities are to be regarded as damage resulting from the wrongful act of that person. A person is answerable under s.1A if he was, or would if sued in due time have been, liable in tort to one or both of the parents, and it is no answer that the parent suffered no actionable injury. 5-60

"Wrongful life" An action under s.1 of the Act is limited to "disabilities which would not otherwise have been present".[195] This wording excludes so-called "wrongful life" actions. But it is arguable that under the wording of s.1A the negligent *selection* of an embryo for implantation or of the gametes[196] does give rise to a wrongful life claim, since the child's argument is that had the defendant chosen the embryo carefully, or properly screened the gametes, its existence would not have 5-61

---

190 Congenital Disabilities (Civil Liability) Act 1976 s.1(4). Query, however, how great the risk of conceiving a disabled child must be before the defence applies. Section 1(6) provides that liability to the child can be excluded or limited by a contract term excluding liability to the parent(s), but liability for death or personal injury caused by negligence cannot be excluded by virtue of the Consumer Rights Act 2015 s.65 (bar on exclusion or restriction of negligence liability for consumers). See para.3-135 onwards.

191 Congenital Disabilities (Civil Liability) Act 1976 s.1(7); except where the mother causes the damage in the course of driving a motor vehicle: s.2. The use of the word "responsibility" rather than "fault" in this section has led some writers to speculate whether damages to the child might be reduced not only where the affected parent contributes to the occurrence affecting his or her ability to have normal children, but where their later conduct can be said to be responsible for the birth of the disabled child.

192 Congenital Disabilities (Civil Liability) Act 1976 s.1(5). Nor is he liable simply because he departed from received professional opinion.

193 Congenital Disabilities (Civil Liability) Act 1976 s.4(3). To avoid the problem of how the measure of damages can be assessed, bearing in mind that the normal rule is to place the claimant as far as possible in the same position as if the tort had never been committed, s.4(3) also provides that liability is to be deemed to be liability for personal injuries sustained by the child immediately after its birth.

194 Limitation Act 1980 s.28(1).

195 Congenital Disabilities (Civil Liability) Act 1976 s.1(2)(b).

196 e.g. the negligent screening of a sperm donor for HIV.

been brought about, because a different embryo would have been implanted or different gametes would have been used, with the result that this *particular* child would not have been created. This inconsistency in the Act appears to have gone unnoticed by Parliament.

8. Persons of Unsound Mind

5-62 **Liability of persons of unsound mind** There is limited authority on the liability in tort of persons of unsound mind. It is suggested that they are liable to the same extent as persons of sound mind, provided that the torts are committed by them while in that condition of mind which is essential to liability for all defendants. In its absence, it would appear that there is no voluntary act at all. In cases where liability depends on some specific state of mind[197] insanity may be strong evidence to show that the necessary element is lacking, and may therefore constitute a good defence. To actions for trespass,[198] conversion, defamation[199] and others in which the only intent necessary to establish liability is the intent to do the physical act complained of, insanity will presumably be no defence, unless it is of such an extreme character as to deprive its victim of all power of deliberate choice.[200] In *Morriss v Marsden*,[201] the claimant was held entitled to damages for a violent assault and battery on the ground that the defendant's act was voluntary, and that he knew the nature and quality of his act though not that it was wrong. The rules in *McNaghten's* case[202] do not necessarily provide the correct test for determining responsibility in tort.[203]

5-63 **Negligence liability**[204] In *Dunnage v Randall*,[205] the Court of Appeal held that there was no principle which required the law to excuse a person suffering from a mental disorder from liability in negligence. Only defendants whose medical incapacity had the effect of entirely eliminating any fault or responsibility could be excused. A defendant who was merely impaired by medical problems, whether physical or mental, could not escape liability if his actions, however irrational, caused injury by failing to exercise reasonable care. In the case itself, the appellant had suffered extremely serious burns when trying to assist his uncle who had set himself on fire with petrol. The uncle was subsequently diagnosed as having suf-

---

197 e.g. malicious prosecution; libel on a privileged occasion.

198 But see *Beals v Hayward* [1960] N.Z.L.R. 131.

199 In *Emmens v Pottle* (1885) 16 Q.B.D. 354 at 356, Lord Esher MR said that a lunatic's liability for a libel depended upon whether he was sane enough to know what he was doing. cf. also *Hanbury v Hanbury* (1892) 8 T.L.R. 559 at 560. It might be thought from these dicta that a lunatic would only be liable if he knew what he was publishing was a libel; but it is submitted that that would be inconsistent with *Hulton v Jones* [1910] A.C. 20.

200 In *Weaver v Ward* (1616) Hob. 134, it is said without qualification that "if a lunatic hurt a man he shall answer in trespass", but this proposition would appear too wide. In *Krom v Schoonmaker* (1848) 3 Barb. 647, it was decided in the Supreme Court of the United States that an action of false imprisonment lay against a lunatic who in his capacity of justice of the peace caused the claimant to be wrongfully imprisoned; but it is presumed that the extent of the insanity in that case was not great. See also *Beals v Hayward* [1960] N.Z.L.R. 131.

201 [1952] 1 All E.R. 925.

202 (1843) 10 Cl. & Fin. 200.

203 *Morriss v Marsden* [1952] 1 All E.R. 925.

204 See further para.7-169.

205 [2015] EWCA Civ 673; [2016] Q.B. 639.

fered from florid paranoid schizophrenia. Nevertheless, the Court applied the objective standard of care test. The uncle's mind, although deluded, had directed his actions. His disease did not excuse him from needing to take the care of a reasonable man.[206] Equally, in *Roberts v Ramsbottom*,[207] the defendant suffered a stroke just before getting into his car. In the course of his journey he negligently injured the claimant and was held to be in breach of his duty of care. The objective standard meant that "[t]he driver will be able to escape liability if his actions at the relevant timc were wholly beyond his control ... But if he retained some control, albeit imperfect control, and his driving, judged objectively, was below the required standard, he remains liable."[208]

In *Mansfield v Weetabix Ltd*,[209] the Court of Appeal held that a driver who becomes unable to control a vehicle will not be liable for damage caused by his loss of control if he is unaware of the disabling condition from which he is suffering, whether the disabling event is sudden or gradual. On this point, said the court, *Roberts v Ramsbottom* had been wrongly decided, though the decision in *Roberts* could still be supported on the alternative ground that the defendant continued to drive when he was unfit to do so, and when he should have been aware of his unfitness. The defendant will be liable if he knew that he was susceptible to periods of unfitness to drive[210] or if he ought to have known that he was subject to a condition rendering him unfit to drive.[211] Arden LJ distinguished *Mansfield* in *Dunnage*. *Mansfield* decided that a driver who gets into his car mentally and physically fit for the journey but then has an unforeseen episode which causes him to lose control of the vehicle is not guilty of negligence—he was acting with due care when he started to drive. In contrast, the uncle in *Dunnage* was not in control of machinery of which he unforeseeably lost control nor was he ever in possession of the petrol can or lighter with which he set himself on fire "in circumstances when he had performed his duty of care".[212] It was irrelevant that neither party had suggested that he should have known that he was susceptible to this form of attack. This seems an attempt to reduce *Mansfield* to its facts and reassert the objective approach. As Arden LJ later stated: 5-64

> "The objective standard of care reflects the policy of the law. It is not a question of the law discriminating unfairly against people with physical or mental illness ... There will be hard cases, as this case may be one, where a person does not know what action to take to avoid injury to others. However, his liability is no doubt treated in law as the price for being able to move freely within society despite his schizophrenia."[213]

Capacity to sue of persons of unsound mind Normally no special rules apply to the bringing of actions by persons of unsound mind except that a person who (by reason of mental disorder within the meaning of the Mental Health Act 1983[214]) is 5-65

206 See *White v White* [1950] P. 39 at 49, 57–59, per Denning LJ, cited in *Dunnage v Randall*.
207 [1980] 1 W.L.R. 823.
208 [1980] 1 W.L.R. 823 at 832, per Neill J.
209 [1997] P.I.Q.R. P526.
210 *Hill v Baxter* [1958] 1 Q.B. 277.
211 *Waugh v James K Allan Ltd* [1964] 2 Lloyd's Rep. 1; *C v Burcombe* [2003] C.L.Y. 3030; *Green v Haynes* [2014] EWHC 4297 (QB).
212 [2015] EWCA Civ 673 at [147]. The other judges did not comment on this. For criticism of this reasoning, see Goudkamp and Ihuoma (2016) 32 P.N. 137, 138–140.
213 [2015] EWCA Civ 673 at [153].
214 Mental Health Act 1983 s.1(2), where mental disorder is defined as "any disorder or disability of

incapable of managing his affairs, must have a litigation friend to conduct proceedings on his behalf.[215] No action in respect of acts done in pursuance of the Mental Health Act, however, may be brought without the leave of the High Court.[216] Time will not run under the Limitation Act 1980 until the claimant ceases to be under the disability, provided that he was under a disability when the cause of action accrued.[217] Where X commits a tort against Y causing Y to suffer unsoundness of mind, and Y thereafter commits a crime against Z (as a result of his diminished mental capacities) for which Y is convicted and subsequently detained in hospital, a question arises as to whether Y can pursue an action for damages against X. In *Gray v Thames Trains*,[218] the House of Lords held that the defence of ex turpi causa can be invoked to defeat any claims based on (i) the fact that Y was sentenced by a criminal court (and therefore lost earnings because of his conviction); or (ii) losses that were simply a consequence of his crime (rather than the sentence), such as damages payable to Z (or Z's dependants) as a result of the wrong done to Z. However, if the claimant is so profoundly mentally disturbed that he or she is completely unable to appreciate the unlawful nature of his act (and thus immune from conviction), or if he or she does not have the mental capacity to make a real choice, the defence of ex turpi cannot be raised.[219]

9. HUSBAND AND WIFE

5-66 **Law Reform (Married Women and Tortfeasors) Act 1935** At common law a married woman could neither sue nor be sued unless her husband was joined with her as claimant or defendant. Now, under s.1 of the Law Reform (Married Women and Tortfeasors) Act 1935 a married woman may sue or be sued in all respects as if she were a *femme sole* and is made subject to the law relating to bankruptcy and to the enforcement of judgments and orders. Furthermore, by s.3 it is provided that a husband shall not, by reason only of his being her husband, be liable in respect of any tort committed by his wife. That said, a husband and wife may be liable for the tort of conspiracy, and one spouse may be sued alone for the resulting damage despite the immunity granted to spouses in respect of criminal conspiracies.[220]

5-67 **Actions between husband and wife** Under the Law Reform (Husband and Wife) Act 1962,[221] both parties to a marriage have a right of action in tort against the other as if they were not married.[222]

---

the mind; and 'mentally disordered' shall be construed accordingly".

215 CPR r.21.2. See *S(FG) (Mental Health Patient), Re* [1973] 1 W.L.R. 178.

216 Mental Health Act 1983 s.139(2). In *Winch v Jones* [1986] Q.B. 296, the Court of Appeal held that the correct test for leave to sue is whether on the material before the court the complaint appears to deserve fuller investigation, not whether the applicant has a prima facie case; cf. *James v London Borough of Havering* (1992) 15 B.M.L.R. 1. See further para.14-116.

217 Limitation Act 1980 s.28(1). See generally para.31-21.

218 [2009] UKHL 33; [2009] 1 A.C. 1339.

219 In *Gray v Thames Trains* [2009] UKHL 33; [2009] 1 A.C. 1339, Lord Hoffmann adverted (at [27]) to the fact that the PTSD from which C was suffering diminished, but did not extinguish, his criminal responsibility. For discussion of the scope of this exception, see *Henderson v Dorset Healthcare University NHS Foundation Trust* [2018] EWCA Civ 1841; [2018] 3 W.L.R. 1651 (under appeal). See also paras 3-31 to 3-32.

220 *Midland Bank Trust Co Ltd v Green (No.3)* [1982] Ch. 529.

221 s.1(1). *McLeod v McLeod* (1963) 113 L.J. 420 (County Court).

222 The old rule that the court could stay proceedings if it appeared either that no substantial benefit

10. ASSIGNEES

Assignees A right of action for damages in respect of a tort was at one time thought to be incapable of assignment on public policy grounds.[223] Although the extent to which causes of action in tort can be assigned is still less than fully settled, the Court of Appeal introduced some measure of clarification in *Simpson v Norfolk and Norwich University Hospital NHS Trust*.[224] The appellant argued that a bare cause of action for personal injuries inflicted by virtue of the defendant's negligence was incapable of assignment. There, in deciding the case, the Court of Appeal stipulated as follows. First, a right to recover compensation for personal injury could not be assigned so long as it was an essentially personal chose in action. But as Moore-Bick LJ pointed out, "the obligation to pay compensation, which arises by operation of law, is not one that is personal in the sense that it depends upon the identity of the claimant".[225] As such it could be regarded as a chose in action—a species of property within the meaning of s.136 of the Law of Property Act 1925—and therefore assignable. Secondly, and by way of a caveat, his Lordship added that, on public policy grounds, the law would not recognise the assignment of a right to litigate if the person acquiring that right lacked sufficient interest, or if the assignment was only taken in order to enable the assignee to make a profit out of the litigation.[226] Unfortunately, the Court of Appeal failed to offer absolute clarity here when it observed that perceptions of what is in the public interest change over time, thus rendering it uncertain just when an assignment would be considered void for reasons of public policy. And in the very same paragraph of its judgment, the Court of Appeal also pointed out that it was not possible to state definitively what will amount to a sufficient interest in order to render the assignment valid.[227] **5-68**

An assignment which is intended to promote litigation in exchange for a share of the proceeds may be described as champertous. It is illegal and void.[228] Similarly, assignments that amount to maintenance (i.e. those that amount to stirring up litigation by giving aid to a party to bring an action with no just cause or excuse) are also regarded as contrary to public policy. Where, however, the assignee has an appropriate interest in the litigation the same public policy considerations may not apply.[229] In *Camdex International Ltd v Bank of Zambia (No.1)*,[230] for instance, Hobhouse LJ noted that what was objectionable was trafficking in litigation where the party **5-69**

---

would accrue to either party from the continuation of the proceedings or that the question in issue could be more conveniently disposed of under the Married Women's Property Act 1882 was abolished by the Civil Procedure (Modification of Enactments) Order 1998 (SI 1998/2940) para.4. See, however, CPR r.12.10(a)(ii) in the case of an application for default judgment.

223 *Defries v Milne* [1913] 1 Ch. 98. A claim for statutory compensation in respect of damage caused by the lawful exercise of statutory powers, as under the Land Clauses Consolidation Act 1845 s.68, is not a claim for damages for a wrongful act and so is assignable: *Dawson v Great Northern and City Ry* [1905] 1 K.B. 260.

224 [2011] EWCA Civ 1149; [2012] Q.B. 640.

225 [2011] EWCA Civ 1149; [2012] Q.B. 640 at [9].

226 [2011] EWCA Civ 1149; [2012] Q.B. 640 at [24].

227 [2011] EWCA Civ 1149; [2012] Q.B. 640 at [24].

228 *Laurent v Sale* [1963] 1 W.L.R. 829. This is not affected by the abolition of criminal and civil liability for maintenance under the Criminal Law Act 1967 ss.13(1), 14(1) and s.14(2). See generally *Trendtex Trading v Credit Suisse* [1982] A.C. 679.

229 *Camdex International Ltd v Bank of Zambia (No.1)* [1998] Q.B. 22.

230 [1998] Q.B. 22.

ultimately litigating could show no legitimate interest in the action. On the other hand, he also noted the modern tendency to recognise less specific interests so as to justify the support of the litigation of another and to reduce the modern-day significance of champerty and maintenance.[231]

5-70 Indeed, in *Trendtex Trading Corp v Credit Suisse*, Lord Roskill said that though it was still a fundamental principle of our law that you cannot assign a bare right to litigate:

> "an assignee who can show that he has a genuine commercial interest in the enforcement of the claim of another and to that extent takes an assignment of that claim to himself is entitled to enforce that assignment unless by the terms of that assignment he falls foul of our law of champerty."[232]

Thus, the court should look at the "totality of the transaction". If the assignment is of a property right or interest and the cause of action is ancillary to that right or interest, or if the assignee has a genuine commercial interest in taking and enforcing it for his own benefit, there seems to be no policy reason to prevent such an assignment. Although *Trendtex* was an assignment of an action arising out of contract, it is arguable that, unless an arbitrary line is to be drawn between tort and contract, the notion of "genuine commercial interest" could be carried over into assignments of tort actions so that, for example, an assignment to a bank of the assignor's claim for damages for negligent misstatement inducing a contract which the bank has financed would be valid.[233] On this basis, the assignment of causes of action which are essentially personal in nature such as claims for defamation, false imprisonment or personal injuries would still not be permitted.

5-71 **Assignment of property** An assignment of property is clearly not invalidated by the rule of public policy merely because the property is the subject of litigation, or because it cannot be recovered without litigation.[234] It follows that an assignment of the damages to be recovered in an action in tort is good, for it is an assignment not of a bare cause of action, but of property, namely, the fruits of an action as and when recovered.[235] If the assignment is effected in accordance with the requirements of s.136 of the Law of Property Act 1925, the assignee can sue in his own name.[236]

5-72 **Exceptions and non-assignability** There are three exceptions to the general rule that rights of action in tort are not assignable: first, a chose in action may be assigned to the Crown[237]; secondly, rights of action of any kind which pass to a trustee

---

[231] An assignment by a limited company to a majority shareholder of the right to pursue an action in the name of the company is not invalid as contrary to public policy on the basis that it was made with the intention of enabling the assignee to obtain legal aid or avoid an order for security for costs in the litigation, at least where the assignor has a continued interest in the fruits of the litigation; nor does it make any difference that the assignee has the right to pursue the action in the name of the assignor: *Norglen Ltd v Reeds Rains Prudential Ltd; Circuit Systems Ltd (In Liquidation) v Zuken-Redac (UK) Ltd* [1999] 2 A.C. 1.

[232] [1982] A.C. 679 at 703.

[233] See *Investors Compensation Scheme Ltd v West Bromwich Building Society* [1997] P.N.L.R. 541.

[234] *Dawson v Great Northern and City Ry* [1905] 1 K.B. 260 at 271.

[235] *Glegg v Bromley* [1912] 3 K.B. 474.

[236] *Compania Colombiana de Seguros v Pacific Steam Navigation Co* [1965] 1 Q.B. 101.

[237] Co. Litt. 232b, Hargrave and Butler's note.

in bankruptcy (including rights of action for torts to the debtor's property) are assignable by the trustee to a stranger,[238] or back to the bankrupt himself (who will then be able to sue alone and in his own name[239]); thirdly, where an insurer has paid under an indemnity policy the loss sustained by the assured, he is subrogated to the latter's rights even though those rights are in tort.[240] In each case, though, the assignment must take place before the assignee can bring the action in question; for an attempt to do so *before* the assignment occurs will be an abuse of process.[241]

Transfers of undertakings Where there is a transfer of an undertaking within the meaning of the Transfer of Undertakings (Protection of Employment) Regulations 2006 (SI 2006/246) then on the transfer of an employee's contract of employment as part of the transfer of that undertaking, liability to pay the employee compensation for personal injuries sustained as a result of the transferor's negligence or breach of statutory duty passes to the new employer.[242] Similarly, where the transferor had effected an employer's liability insurance policy, the right to indemnity under the policy in respect of liability to an employee also transfers to the new employer under the Regulations.[243] **5-73**

11. Corporations

Capacity to sue A corporation can sue for any tort in the same way as an individual,[244] except that some torts such as assault and false imprisonment cannot, by their nature, be committed against a corporation. The right of action vests in the corporation, not its members. Thus, if a shareholder suffers a loss in the value of his shareholding due to a tort committed against the company, it is the company, not the shareholder who can recover.[245] A corporation can sue for the malicious presentation of a winding-up petition,[246] inducing breach of contract[247] and for **5-74**

---

238 *Seear v Lawson* (1880) 15 Ch. D. 426; *Guy v Churchill* (1888) 40 Ch. D. 481. The distinction between the right of an assignee to sue in his own name and his right to sue in the name of the assignor may be very material: see *Western Bank of Scotland v Addie* (1867) L.R. 1 Sc. & Div. 145 at 166.

239 *Ramsey v Hartley* [1977] 1 W.L.R. 686. In *Stein v Blake* [1996] A.C. 243, A and B had mutual claims against each other. When A became bankrupt the question arose whether his claim against B continued to exist so that A's trustee could assign it to a third party, or whether the effect of s.323 of the Insolvency Act 1986 extinguished the claims of A and B and substituted a claim for the net balance owing after setting off one against the other. The House of Lords held that the bankruptcy extinguished the claims as separate choses in action and replaced them by a claim for the net balance owing after setting one off against the other. If the set-off was in the bankrupt's favour, this could be assigned to the bankrupt before the net balance had been ascertained by the taking of an account between himself and the other party.

240 *King v Victoria Insurance Co* [1896] A.C. 250; *Compania Colombiana de Seguros v Pacific Steam Navigation Co* [1965] 1 Q.B. 101.

241 *Pickthall v Hill Dickinson LLP* [2009] EWCA Civ 543; [2009] P.N.L.R. 31.

242 *Bernadone v Pall Mall Services Group* [2000] 3 All E.R. 544.

243 *Bernadone v Pall Mall Services Group* [2000] 3 All E.R. 544 (but note that the decision was made in relation to the former regulations: i.e. the Transfer of Undertakings (Protection of Employment) Regulations 1981 (SI 1981/1794)).

244 And a company in appropriate circumstances can sue directors of the company for conspiracy to cause damage to the company: *Belmont Finance Corp Ltd v Williams Furniture Ltd* [1979] Ch. 250; *Bilta (UK) Ltd (In Liquidation) v Nazir* [2015] UKSC 23; [2016] A.C. 1.

245 *Johnson v Gore Wood & Co (No.1)* [2002] 2 A.C. 1.

246 *Quartz Hill Consolidated Gold Mining Co v Eyre* (1883) 11 Q.B.D. 674.

247 *Mainstream Properties Ltd v Young* [2007] UKHL 21; [2008] 1 A.C. 1.

defamation, provided that the defamatory matter is published about the corporation in the way of its business.[248] Thus, slanderous words describing the sole owner of a company as a "bloody crook" and someone in respect of whom "I have to count my fingers after shaking hands with him" have been regarded as only applicable to an individual.[249] On the other hand, if the words used make it clear that if, as a result of the director's conduct, the company is not to be trusted in the conduct of its financial affairs, then the company's trading reputation will have been defamed, and an action by the company may be brought quite apart from any personal action brought by the director.[250] A company's reputation can also be injured by a libel (although the injury must sound in money[251]); and an action for malicious falsehood can also be maintained so long as the words used make reference to the particular corporate claimant.[252]

5-75 **Liability to be sued** It was formerly thought that a corporation, being a fictitious person, could not be liable where liability involved some specific state of mind.[253] It is now well settled, however, that it can, and accordingly a corporation may be sued for wrongs involving harassment,[254] fraud or malice.[255] So far as the tort of harassment is concerned, it does not matter that the repeated act in question is not obviously under the direction of a senior figure within the company. In *Ferguson v British Gas*[256] where the appellant company was seeking to strike out an action brought by a former customer under the Protection from Harassment Act 1997, the claimant had repeatedly been sent threats of possible legal action and demands for payment by the company that were groundless (given that she had changed energy supplier and no longer had any liability towards British Gas). A central plank of the appellant's argument was that the correspondence in question had been generated automatically by a computer and thus could not be associated with the mind of someone sufficiently senior within the company to be treated as the active mind of the company. In refusing to accept this argument, Jacob LJ said:

> "One simply does not know whether what happened to Ms Ferguson is an extraordinary one-off case, or whether there are so many similar cases that senior management must

[248] *Metropolitan Saloon Omnibus Co v Hawkins* (1859) 4 H. & N. 87; *South Hetton Coal Co v North Eastern News Association* [1894] 1 Q.B. 133. The damage to a corporation's trading reputation will not meet the required statutory threshold of "'serious harm' unless it has caused or is likely to cause the body serious financial loss": Defamation Act 2013 s.1(2).

[249] *Shendish Manor Ltd v Coleman* [2001] EWCA Civ 913. Followed in *Undre v Harrow LBC* [2016] EWHC 931 (QB); [2017] E.M.L.R. 3.

[250] *Applause Store Productions Ltd v Raphael* [2008] EWHC 1781 (QB); [2008] Info. T.L.R. 318.

[251] *Lewis v Daily Telegraph Ltd* [1964] A.C. 234 at 262, per Lord Reid—see now the "serious financial loss" requirement under Defamation Act 2013 s.1(2). Defamation reflecting solely on individuals within the corporation, however, is not actionable by the corporation.

[252] *Marathon Mutual Ltd v Waters* [2009] EWHC 1931 (QB); [2010] E.M.L.R. 3.

[253] e.g. *Stevens v Midland Counties Ry* (1854) 10 Ex. 352; *Abrath v North Eastern Ry* (1886) 11 App. Cas. 247 at 250, per Lord Bramwell.

[254] *Majrowski v Guy's and St Thomas' NHS Trust* [2006] UKHL 34; [2007] 1 A.C. 224.

[255] *Barwick v English Joint Stock Bank* (1867) L.R. 2 Ex. 259; *Citizens' Life Ass Co v Brown* [1904] A.C. 423; *Glasgow Corp v Lorimer* [1911] A.C. 209. In the case of actions for fraudulent misrepresentation as to the credit of a third party, by s.6 of the Lord Tenterden's Act 1828 no such action lies against a "person", unless the representation is in writing signed by him. A corporation is a person within the section: *Hirst v West Riding Union Banking Co* [1901] 2 K.B. 560; *Banbury v Bank of Montreal* [1918] A.C. 626. See para.17-55.

[256] [2009] EWCA Civ 46; [2010] 1 W.L.R. 785.

know about it but are prepared to tolerate the position because it brings in the money. And even if liability can be avoided on that basis, there is the real potential for liability on the 'ought to know' basis [of section 1 of the Act]."[257]

Ultra vires It may happen that the tort for which the corporation is sued is committed in the course of an activity which is beyond the powers of the corporation. Such cases are governed by s.39 of the Companies Act 2006. This provides that: "[t]he validity of an act done by a company shall not be called into question on the ground of lack of capacity by reason of anything in the company's constitution". Section 40(1) reads: "In favour of a person dealing with a company in good faith, the power of the directors to bind the company, or authorise others to do so, is deemed to be free of any limitation under the company's constitution". **5-76**

Liability for torts of corporators The commission of a tort by one of the corporators will not necessarily render the corporation liable: their liability and that of their corporation are in the alternative. They cannot both be liable,[258] unless in the particular case the corporators are in the position of agents. Thus, if the corporators, acting in their corporate capacity in a matter within the scope of their corporate powers, under a bona fide mistake of fact, order an act to be done which turns out to be tortious, the corporation will be liable and the corporators will not.[259] But the fact that they purport to act in their corporate capacity will not conclude the question against the corporation. The wrongful act may be so wilful and malicious as to make it the personal tort of the corporators.[260] **5-77**

Liability to corporators As a general rule, a corporation is liable to its own corporators for the torts of its agents to the same extent as it is liable to strangers. It is, of course, no defence to an action against a company for damages for personal injuries to plead that the claimant was a shareholder.[261] **5-78**

Liability of directors of limited company[262] The directors of a limited company cannot be held liable for the torts of the employees of the company, unless they ordered and procured the acts to be done, merely by reason of their position as directors. On the other hand, a company and its directors may be conspirators.[263] Also, if there are facts from which it may be inferred that the relationship of principal and agent has been established between the directors and the company, they may be liable, but the mere fact that they are the sole directors and shareholders is not sufficient.[264] **5-79**

In *C Evans Ltd v Spritebrand Ltd*,[265] the Court of Appeal held that where it was **5-80**

---

257 [2009] EWCA Civ 46; [2010] 1 W.L.R. 785 at [28].

258 *Harman v Tappenden* (1801) 1 East. 555; *Mill v Hawker* (1874) L.R. 9 Ex. 309; ibid. in Ex. Ch. (1875) L.R. 10 Ex. 92.

259 *Mill v Hawker* (1874) L.R. 9 Ex. 309 at 322, per Kelly CB.

260 See, e.g. *R. v Watson* (1788) 2 T.R. 199.

261 Companies Act 2006 s.655.

262 For discussion of a director's duties to the company see the Law Commission Report, *Company Directors: Regulating Conflicts of Interest and Formulating a Statement of Duties*, No.261 (1999) Cm 4436.

263 *Mancetter Developments Ltd v Garmanson Ltd* [1986] Q.B. 1212.

264 *Rainham Chemical Works v Belvedere Fish Guano Co* [1921] 2 A.C. 465; *Performing Right Soc v Ciryl Syndicate* [1924] 1 K.B. 1.

265 [1985] 1 W.L.R. 317.

sought to make a company director liable for the tortious act of a company employee or agent, the extent of his personal involvement in the company's tort had to be carefully examined. If the director had authorised, directed and procured the acts complained of, it was not an essential condition of his liability that he knew, or was reckless as to whether, the acts authorised were tortious unless the primary tortfeasor's state of mind, or knowledge, was an essential ingredient of the tort alleged. Aldous J, reviewing this decision in *PLG Research Ltd v Ardon International Ltd*,[266] concluded: "a director will not be liable unless his involvement would be such as to render him liable as a joint tortfeasor if the company had not existed". A person who only facilitated (as opposed to procured) a tort would not be liable as a joint tortfeasor. But if he facilitates the commission of a tort *with a view* to committing that tort in a way that goes beyond the legitimate exercise of his power of control through the constitutional organs of the company, the director may be liable as a joint tortfeasor. What is critical in such a case is the presence of a "common design" that the company's tortious acts should take place.[267]

5-81 It has been said that where a director is the only person through whom, at the relevant time, the company was able to fulfil its obligations, he will be personally liable for breach of any duty owed to the claimant when the performance of that duty necessarily depended on him and him alone.[268] In *Williams v Natural Life Health Foods Ltd*,[269] however, the director of a company was not held personally liable for negligent misstatements. In order to fix a director with personal liability it had to be shown that he had assumed personal responsibility for the negligent misstatements made on behalf of the company. The test is objective. The fact that the director owned and controlled the company and that the claimants were given a brochure linking the performance of the company with that of the director were not sufficient to constitute an assumption of personal responsibility by the director to the claimants for misleading advice given by the company. There had been no personal dealings between the claimants and the director which might have indicated an assumption of personal liability.

5-82 In cases of deceit, however, things are different. In *Standard Chartered Bank v Pakistan National Shipping Corp (No.2)*,[270] a company director wrote a letter in which false representations were made on company notepaper. Notwithstanding the fact that the representation had all the appearance of being made on behalf of the company, their Lordships were adamant that the director could not escape personal liability. The approach in *Williams v Natural Life Health Foods* was distinguished on the basis that in that case the action had been for negligent misrepresentation. As Lord Hoffmann explained:

> "[*Williams* involved] an action for damages for negligent misrepresentation [and] in such a case liability depended upon an assumption of responsibility by the defendant … just

---

[266] [1993] F.S.R. 197.

[267] *Societa Esplosivi Industriali SpA v Ordnance Technologies (UK) Ltd* [2007] EWHC 2875 (Ch); [2008] 2 All E.R. 622 at [76], per Lindsay J. See also para.4-04.

[268] *Fairline Shipping Corp v Adamson* [1975] Q.B. 180. As to joint liability of company and directors see *Wah Tat Bank Ltd v Chan Cheng Kum* [1975] A.C. 507.

[269] [1998] 1 W.L.R. 830. See also para.7-107.

[270] [2002] UKHL 43; [2003] 1 A.C. 959. Applied in *Inter Export LLC v Townley* [2017] EWHC 530 (Ch): company director liable in deceit for the value of a consignment of oil after the supplier had relied upon various misrepresentations she had made about the company's ability to pay for the oil (affirmed [2018] EWCA Civ 2068).

> as an agent can contract on behalf of another without incurring personal liability, so an agent can assume responsibility on behalf of another ... without assuming personal responsibility ... [But] [t]his reasoning cannot in my opinion apply to liability for fraud. No one can escape liability for his fraud by saying, 'I wish to make it clear that I am committing this fraud on behalf of someone else and I am not to be personally liable'."[271]

In the wake of this decision, it was arguably unclear which of negligent and fraudulent misrepresentations attracted the application of a special rule. However, in the light of both *Contex Drouzhba Ltd v Wiseman*[272] and *Renault UK Ltd v Fleetpro Technical Services*,[273] it has since become clear that it is cases of fraud that attract the special treatment. And it has elsewhere been held that the *Williams* principle is a rule of general application in tort.[274] That said, the objective test associated with determining whether a company director has assumed a personal responsibility is by no means an easy one to apply. Each case will turn on its own facts, for, as Walker J noted in *Macquarie Internationale Investments Ltd v Glencore UK Ltd*, there is a "lack of any principled or practical basis for distinguishing between assuming tortious responsibility in the course of acting as a director and doing so when not in the course of so acting".[275]

One point of discussion has been whether, where the personal liability in deceit of a sole director (who embodies the mind and will of the company) has been established, the courts should treat the company's liability as primary rather than vicarious even though the director's wrongdoing constitutes fraud. The courts will not usually attribute fraud to a company on the basis that "it is contrary to common sense and justice to attribute to a principal knowledge of something that his agent would be anxious to conceal from him".[276] The courts have made it clear that there is no principle of law that in any proceedings where the company is suing a third party for breach of a duty owed to it by that third party, the fraudulent conduct of a director will automatically be attributed to the company if it is a one-man company.[277] Indeed, where the fraudulent conduct of a director causes loss, not only to some third party, but also to the company itself, there is Supreme Court authority that the courts are unwilling to attribute the fraudulent conduct to the company which will be treated in law as a victim in its own right.[278] *Singularis Holdings Ltd (in liquidation) v Daiwa Capital Markets Europe Ltd*[279] confirms that the courts will be guided by the factual context and the purpose for which the question of attribution is relevant. On the facts of this case, the context in which the defendant bank's breach of its duty of care to the company had arisen and the purpose of the duty led the Supreme Court to find that it would have been wrong to attribute the fraud 5-83

---

271 [2002] UKHL 43; [2003] 1 A.C. 959 at [21]–[22]. Lords Mustill, Slynn, Hobhouse and Rodger all concurred.

272 [2007] EWCA Civ 1201; [2008] B.C.C. 301.

273 [2007] EWHC 2541 (QB); [2008] Bus. L.R. D17.

274 See, e.g. *Koninklijke Philips Electronics NV v Princo Digital Disc GmbH* [2003] EWHC 2588 (Pat); [2004] 2 B.C.L.C. 50 (patent infringement).

275 [2008] EWHC 1716 (Comm); [2008] 2 B.C.L.C. 565 at [63].

276 *Meridian Global Funds Management Asia Ltd v Securities Commission* [1995] 2 A.C. 500 at 511.

277 Any indication to the contrary in *Stone & Rolls Ltd v Moore Stephens* [2009] UKHL 39; [2009] 1 A.C. 1391 should now be regarded as laid to rest in *Singularis Holdings Ltd (in liquidation) v Daiwa Capital Markets Europe Ltd* [2019] UKSC 50; [2019] 3 W.L.R. 997 at [34].

278 *Bilta (UK) Ltd v Nazir (No.2)* [2015] UKSC 23; [2016] A.C. 1.

279 [2019] UKSC 50; [2019] 3 W.L.R. 997 (dismissing appeal from [2018] EWCA Civ 84).

perpetrated by the director to the company, even if (as sole shareholder) he could be regarded as its directing mind and will.

5-84 **Liability of parent companies** If a parent company can be shown to be in breach of a personal duty owed to employees of a subsidiary company, that parent company may be held liable for a breach of that duty, even if the subsidiary company has ceased to exist. So, where a parent company was under an ongoing duty to provide health and safety advice to the employees of its subsidiary, the fact that its subsidiary had ceased to trade did not absolve the parent company of its joint and several liability towards the former employees.[280] The scope of *Chandler v Cape Plc*[281] is being tested in a number of cases.[282]

12. UNINCORPORATED ASSOCIATIONS AND TRADE UNIONS

5-85 **Unincorporated associations** An unincorporated association can only sue or be sued by means of a representative action under CPR r.19.6.[283] This rule provides that:

> "Where more than one person has the same interest in a claim (a) the claim may be begun; or (b) the court may order that the claim be continued, by or against one or more of the persons who have the same interest as representatives of any other persons who have that interest."

The rule is prima facie applicable to actions to establish a right against a fund, rather than to actions to enforce a personal liability[284]; and the Court of Appeal, in refusing to make the chairman, secretary and vice-chairman of an unincorporated association the representatives of the association in an action for a libel in the association's magazine, expressed a doubt whether the rule should ever be applied to tort actions.[285] It has been held, however, in an action against a member's club,[286] that in an appropriate case the court will make such an order in an action for tort, provided that the members whose names appear on the claim are persons who can fairly be taken to represent the body of club members, and that they and all the other club members have a common interest in resisting the claim.[287]

---

[280] *Chandler v Cape Plc* [2012] EWCA Civ 525; [2012] 1 W.L.R. 3111. For the limitations on when a parent company will owe such a duty, see *Thompson v Renwick Group Plc* [2014] EWCA Civ 635; [2015] B.C.C. 855; and *AAA v Unilever Plc* [2018] EWCA Civ 1532; [2018] B.C.C. 959; and paras 4-04 and 12-08.

[281] [2012] EWCA Civ 525; [2012] 1 W.L.R. 3111.

[282] See, most recently, *His Royal Highness Okpabi v Royal Dutch Shell Plc* [2018] EWCA Civ 191; [2018] B.C.C. 668; *AAA v Unilever Plc* [2018] EWCA Civ 1532; [2018] B.C.C. 959; and *Lungowe v Vedanta Resources Plc* [2019] UKSC 20; [2019] 2 W.L.R. 1051. These cases are discussed in more detail at paras 12-09 to 12-11.

[283] Except in cases where statutes creating certain bodies are interpreted as imposing liability to be sued in their collective name: see para.5-90, regarding trade unions and see Friendly Societies Act 1974 s.103; *Longdon-Griffiths v Smith* [1951] 1 K.B. 295. The Friendly Societies Act 1992 now covers the establishment of incorporated, registered Friendly Societies. A representative action is clearly not necessary when suing an individual or individuals, rather than the whole body of members: see *Brown v Lewis* (1896) 12 T.L.R. 455.

[284] *Hardie and Lane v Chiltern* [1928] 1 K.B. 663.

[285] *Mercantile Marine Assoc v Toms* [1916] 2 K.B. 243; *Longdon-Griffiths v Smith* [1951] 1 K.B. 295.

[286] *Campbell v Thompson* [1953] 1 Q.B. 445.

[287] For application of this rule, see *Astellas Pharma v Stop Huntingdon Animal Cruelty* [2011] EWCA

CPR r.19.6 allows representative orders to be made to enable members of an unincorporated association to sue. In *Prudential Assurance Co Ltd v Newman Industries*,[288] Vinelott J stated that a representative action could be brought by a claimant on behalf of himself and all other members of a class where each member had a separate cause of action in tort provided three conditions were satisfied: 5-86

(i) that the relief claimed in the representative action would not confer a right of action on a member of the club which that member could not have asserted in a separate action;
(ii) that there was an "interest" shared by all members of the claim represented; and
(iii) that it was for the benefit of the class that the claimant be permitted to sue in a representative action.[289]

Claims by members against the association The members of the committee of a member's club will not, normally, owe any duty of care towards the members of the club. This anomalous immunity derives from the law of unincorporated associations by which the club has no separate legal identity from that of its members, so that technically a member suing the club by means of an action against the club's committee as representatives of the members is, in law, suing herself. Thus in *Robertson v Ridley*,[290] the Court of Appeal held that a club was not liable to its members in respect of injuries caused by reason of the condition of the club's premises, although the result would have been different if the rules of the club had expressly provided for such liability. However, May LJ stressed that very clear words would be necessary to impose such a duty and that a provision in the rules that the chairman and secretary were responsible in law for the conduct of the club was insufficient to render them liable to the club's members in respect of the injuries. It may be, however, that an officer of the club, such as the steward, is personally liable for negligence to a member. If appointed by the committee to be responsible for the premises he is in truth appointed by all the members operating through the committee, and so is the agent of each member to do reasonably carefully all the things he is appointed to do. In that way he comes to owe a duty to each of the members to take reasonable care and to carry out his duties without negligence.[291] 5-87

The unfairness of the consequences of *Robertson v Ridley* is patent. It places form over substance. While it is theoretically correct to say that a member of an unincorporated members club is in the same legal relationship as all other members 5-88

Civ 752; (2011) 155(26) S.J.L.B. 27. In *United Kingdom NIREX Ltd v Barton*, *The Times*, 14 October 1986, Henry J held that where there was an apparent conflict of interest amongst members of an unincorporated association, it would be inappropriate to proceed against selected members as representative of the whole.

288 [1981] Ch. 229.

289 Although Vinelott J contended that in a representative action, there was no jurisdiction to award damages, this statement appears to go too far. An inquiry as to damages was directed in *EMI Records v Riley* [1981] 1 W.L.R. 923 (a representative action for infringement of copyright), and see the discussion of this area in *Irish Shipping Ltd v Commercial Union Assurance Co Plc* [1991] 2 Q.B. 206. See also *Artistic Upholstery Ltd v Art Forma (Furniture) Ltd* [1999] 4 All E.R. 277 (an unincorporated association can, through its members, own goodwill which can found an action for passing off).

290 [1989] 1 W.L.R. 872; *Shore v Ministry of Works* [1950] 2 All E.R. 228.

291 *Prole v Allen* (1950) 209 L.T. 183. The members of the Court of Appeal in *Robertson v Ridley* disagreed as to the correctness of the decision in *Prole v Allen*.

to each other, and therefore would technically be suing herself, there is a world of difference between the situation of the average householder, who could be expected to maintain his own premises in a reasonable state of repair and would have no-one to blame if he was injured as a consequence of his own failure to do so, and a single member of a club, with possibly several hundred other members, who is not realistically in a position to undertake repairs to the premises. Later cases, possibly recognising the anomaly, have tended to deny the existence of a complete immunity. In *Owen v Northampton BC*,[292] Ralph Gibson LJ indicated that *Robertson v Ridley* was not authority for a blanket immunity, based merely upon their joint membership, for members of a club against claims by another member of the club. It was held that a member of a club or officer of a club, when performing a task on behalf of other members, who thereby becomes aware of a risk of injury, could owe them a duty to inform them of that risk. In *Hibernian Dance Club v Murray*,[293] Hutchison LJ said that there was a strong arguable basis for joining committee members in a representative capacity in a personal injuries claim based on occupiers' liability against an unincorporated club. It was open to the claimant to contend that the committee members were the agents of the members in relation to the occupation of the premises and the employment of staff and the exercise of reasonable care to visitors to the premises. In *Grice v Stourport Tennis, Hockey and Squash Club*,[294] the Court of Appeal held that in determining the potential liability of the club officers, membership of the club, though not itself giving rise to a duty of care, did not provide immunity where a duty otherwise arises. In deciding whether a duty of care arose, the court may look to the rules of the club.

5-89 **Co-operative and community benefit societies** By contrast to the situation with unincorporated members' clubs, co-operative and community benefit societies (Bencoms) registered under s.3 of the Co-operative and Community Benefit Societies Act 2014[295] do owe a duty to members under the Occupiers' Liability Act 1957, to see that the premises are reasonably safe for use and occupation by the members.[296] The effect of registration under the Act is that there comes into existence a separate legal person, the body corporate, in which is vested the buildings and land occupied by the club. The society may sue and be sued by its registered name. A member injured as a result of defects in the state of the premises can then sue the club in its own name.

5-90 **Trade unions: capacity** Sections 10 and 12(2) of the Trade Union and Labour Relations (Consolidation) Act 1992, while providing that a trade union[297] shall not be, or be treated as if it were, a body corporate, also provide that a trade union shall be capable of suing and of being sued in its own name and that any judgment

292 (1992) 156 L.G. Rev. 23.

293 [1997] P.I.Q.R. P46 at 55.

294 [1997] 9 C.L. 592.

295 This replaced, on 1 August 2014, s.3 of the Industrial and Provident Societies Act 1965. The new Act consolidates and replaces existing legislation governing all such societies and, notably, replaces the old term "industrial and provident society" with the terms "community benefit society" and "co-operative society". Registration rules are issued by the Financial Conduct Authority. Industrial and provident societies registered before 1 August 2014 will now be called "registered societies".

296 *Gesner v Wallingford and District Labour Party Supporters' Association Club Ltd, The Times,* 2 June 1994.

297 For the current definition of a trade union, see Trade Union and Labour Relations (Consolidation) Act 1992 s.1.

against a trade union shall be enforceable against any property held in trust for the union as if it were a body corporate.[298] Trade unions still attract immunity from liability for certain of the economic torts during a trade dispute, but they must comply with a wide range of provisions to do so, particularly provisions on secret ballots prior to the authorisation, endorsement or any call to industrial action.[299]

Trade unions: tort liability Trade unions have been, at various times, both fully liable in tort and almost completely immune from tort actions.[300] The current position is governed by s.20 of the Trade Union and Labour Relations (Consolidation) Act 1992, which sets out the test[301] for the liability of a trade union for certain proceedings in tort. These proceedings concern the economic torts of inducing breach of contract and intimidation.[302] Any such acts will be deemed to be done by the union if, and only if, the relevant acts were "authorised or endorsed" by the trade union. However, there is also a set of procedural requirements that must be met. These include giving the employer notice of the intention to put a strike ballot to union members and a requirement that the employer be told how many of its workforce are union members likely to be affected.[303] Any failure to comply with these procedural requirements may ground an application by the employer for an interim injunction restraining the union from undertaking the proposed industrial action.[304] Section 20(2) lists the trade union committees or personnel capable of authorising or endorsing industrial action.[305] In certain circumstances, the union may be able to repudiate the authorisation or endorsement, but the repudiation rules are complex.[306] What is plain, however, is that a failure to repudiate the authorisation or endorsement of clear, tortious conduct on the part of union members may justify an interim injunction against the defendant union in order to restrain any further unlawful and intimidating industrial action.[307] On the other hand, where the conduct in question is not clearly tortious, and it seems likely that the defendant union will be able to establish a trade dispute defence, an interim injunction will not be granted.[308] **5-91**

Section 22 of the Trade Union and Labour Relations (Consolidation) Act 1992 sets limits on the amount of damages payable by a trade union. Such limits do not apply to actions for negligence, nuisance or breach of duty resulting in personal injury or for breach of duty in connection with the ownership, occupation, possession, control or use of property, or proceedings brought by virtue of Pt I of the Consumer Protection Act 1987. Section 23 of the 1992 Act protects certain funds **5-92**

298 Similar provisions apply to an unincorporated employers' association: ss.127–130.

299 See Pt V of Trade Union and Labour Relations (Consolidation) Act 1992 and ss.17–22 of the Trade Union Reform and Employment Rights Act 1993. The acts must be in contemplation or furtherance of a trade dispute: see discussion in Ch.23.

300 For detailed discussion see para.23-130 onwards.

301 Derived from s.13(1) of the Trade Union and Labour Relations Act 1974; s.15 of the Employment Act 1982; s.6 of the Employment Act 1990.

302 See Ch.23 for full discussion (including consideration of the continuing vitality of the latter).

303 Trade Union and Labour Relations (Consolidation) Act 1992 s.226A.

304 *Metroline Travel Ltd v Unite* [2012] EWHC 1778 (QB); [2012] I.R.L.R. 749; *British Airways Plc v British Airline Pilots' Association* [2019] EWCA Civ 1663; [2020] I.R.L.R. 43.

305 Section 20(5) provides that liability on the part of the union under the prescribed conditions does not affect the liability of any individual.

306 Trade Union and Labour Relations (Consolidation) Act 1992 s.21.

307 *Gate Gourmet London Ltd v Transport and General Workers Union* [2005] EWHC 1889 (QB); [2005] I.R.L.R. 881.

308 *Balfour Beatty Engineering Services Ltd v Unite* [2012] EWHC 267 (QB); [2012] I.C.R. 822.

of both trade unions and employers' associations against enforcement of any award of damages.

5-93 **Defamation** A trade union can no longer maintain an action for defamation, unless it is a special register body, because s.10(1) of the 1992 Act operates to deprive trade unions of the necessary personality capable of suffering defamation.[309] On the other hand, it has been mooted obiter that there may be a variant tort—namely, "business defamation"—which is animated by the fact that defamatory claims made about the union have the capacity to "adversely affect the union's ability to keep its members or attract new ones or to maintain a convincing attitude towards employers".[310] That the tort would be a variant of the traditional tort of defamation was thought explicable in terms of the fact that it neither reflects on the claimant's character or personal qualities (as would an ordinary claim for defamation), nor requires proof of malice (as would the tort of malicious falsehood).[311]

5-94 **Vicarious liability** As for vicarious liability for other torts—for example, negligence[312] and nuisance—apparently ordinary common law principles apply (whether or not the tort was committed in furtherance of a trade dispute). Exactly how vicarious liability principles apply to a trade union is unclear, especially in the case of non-employees, such as shop stewards. In *Heatons Transport v Transport and General Workers' Union*,[313] the House of Lords found, on the facts of the case, "general implied authority" ("emanating from the bottom", i.e. the members) for the shop stewards to take the unofficial action that they had undertaken. Although Lord Wilberforce was careful to restrict the decision in the *Heatons* case to vicarious liability under the now defunct Industrial Relations Act 1971 and its concept of "unfair industrial practices", Scott J in *Thomas v National Union of Mineworkers (South Wales Area)*[314] established vicarious liability by applying the principle of the *Heatons* case, namely: "was the servant or agent acting on behalf of, and within the scope of the authority conferred by, the master or principal."

5-95 The vicarious liability principle also applies in relation to other unincorporated associations. Thus, it has been held that an unincorporated association of lay brothers may be liable on this basis for the torts committed by brothers who perform teaching duties at a school. However, for such vicarious liability to be imposed, two hurdles have to be crossed. First, it must be shown that the relationship between the defendant association and the brother actually perpetrating abuse is sufficiently akin to that of employer and employee. Secondly, it must also be shown that the defendants had placed the abuser in such a position not merely that the abuser could carry

---

309 *Electrical, Electronic, Telecommunication and Plumbing Union v Times Newspapers Ltd* [1980] Q.B. 585.

310 See *Thornton v Telegraph Media Group Ltd* [2010] EWHC 1414 (QB); [2011] 1 W.L.R. 1985 at [37] (quoting Lord Keith in *Derbyshire CC v Times Newspapers Ltd* [1993] A.C. 534 at 547).

311 See, generally, Gatley on *Libel and Slander*, 12th edn, (London: Sweet & Maxwell 2014) at [8.24].

312 A trade union owes a duty of care to use reasonable skill and care in advising or acting for a member in an employment dispute, though once the union engages solicitors to act on behalf of the member that duty ceases and any failings in the advice rendered is the responsibility of the solicitors: see *Friend v Institution of Professional Managers Specialists* [1999] I.R.L.R. 173.

313 [1972] I.C.R. 308. *Heatons* was applied in *Unite the Union v Nailard* [2017] I.C.R. 121 (EAT) in relation to a claim that the union was vicariously liable for the sexual harassment of the claimant by elected branch officials. Affirmed on appeal: [2018] EWCA Civ 1203; [2019] I.C.R. 28.

314 [1985] I.C.R. 886.

on the business of the defendant, but also in a manner which created or significantly increased the risk that the victim would suffer abuse.[315]

13. Partners

Partners are jointly and severally liable to any persons not themselves partners for the torts of any one of them acting in the ordinary course of the business of the firm, or with the authority of his co-partners.[316] The question of whether any given act has been done in the ordinary course of business is one of fact. Depending on the circumstances, even fraudulent conduct may sometimes be treated as having been done in this way.[317] But if X has several businesses, and Y is a partner in only one or some of them, any fraudulent representation made by X under the auspices of a business venture that he runs alone will not result in liability on Y's part if Y is ignorant of, and in no way sanctions or agrees with the making of, the fraudulent representation. In such circumstances, the fact that X's fraudulent misrepresentation stated that Y was his partner will not suffice to bring Y within s.14 of the Partnership Act 1890 (which extends liability to a person "who knowingly suffers himself to be represented, as a partner in a particular firm").[318] Unless it is "inappropriate", partners must sue and be sued in the name of their firm.[319] And although the Protection from Harassment Act 1997 makes reference to a person pursuing a course of conduct that amounts to harassment, it has been held that it is perfectly appropriate to regard a partnership as "a person" for the purposes of this statute.[320] In addition to statutory vicarious liability, a partner may have a primary, personal liability. Of course, the partners may also be vicariously liable on ordinary common law principles.[321] However, where someone is a mere "salaried partner" with no stake in the equity of the partnership, he will not be liable unless the claimant has relied upon a representation that he is a partner proper who can be taken to authorise the work of his "fellow" partners.[322] **5-96**

Not always will the defendant partnership hold itself out as being a partnership. In such a case the court is entitled to infer the existence of a partnership from an agreement, express or implied, that the persons concerned intend to carry on a busi- **5-97**

---

315 *Catholic Child Welfare Society v The Institute of the Brothers of the Christian Schools* [2012] UKSC 56; [2013] 2 A.C. 1. See also *A v Trustees of the Watchtower Bible and Tract Society* [2015] EWHC 1722 (QB). For non-abuse cases see *Wm Morrison Supermarkets Plc v Various Claimants* [2020] UKSC 12; [2020] 2 W.L.R. 941. See further paras 6-01 to 6-03.

316 Partnership Act 1890 ss.10 and 12. See *Hamlyn v Houston* [1903] 1 K.B. 81; but note *Meekins v Henson* [1964] 1 Q.B. 472 for the distinction between vicarious liability arising under s.10 and primary, personal liability of individual partners. See further *Flynn v Robin Thompson & Partners (A Firm)* (2000) 97(6) L.S.G. 36 in which Thorpe LJ queried whether the boundaries of s.10 were co-terminous with the vicarious liability of an employer for the misconduct of employees. Nonetheless, an assault carried out by a partner of a firm on an opponent bringing an action against the firm constitutes such extraordinary conduct as to fall outside s.10. An incoming partner cannot be liable as a principal for the earlier negligent acts of a co-partner, since by definition such acts cannot have been done on his behalf: *HF Pension Scheme Trustee Ltd v Ellison* [1999] P.N.L.R. 894.

317 *Dubai Aluminium Co Ltd v Salaam* [2002] UKHL 48; [2003] 2 A.C. 366. See also *Northampton Regional Livestock Centre Co Ltd v Cowling* [2015] EWCA Civ 651; [2016] P.N.L.R. 5.

318 *UCB Home Loans Corp Ltd v Soni* [2013] EWCA Civ 62.

319 CPR Pt 7 PD 5A.

320 *Iqbal v Dean Manson Solicitors* [2011] EWCA Civ 123; [2011] I.R.L.R. 428.

321 e.g. *Lloyd v Grace Smith & Co Ltd* [1912] A.C. 716.

322 *Nationwide Building Society v Lewis* [1998] Ch. 482.

ness in common.[323] Thus, in *Grant v Langley*,[324] despite "an almost total lack of the paperwork which is normally retained for accounting purposes in businesses keeping proper books" the court was nonetheless prepared to infer a partnership based on the fact that the defendants were carrying on a family business together with a view to profit. As such, the normal principles of joint and several liability could be invoked to attach liability to two brothers in the family partnership after their (senior partner) father had been made bankrupt two years prior to the issue of the writ.

5-98 From time to time, partnerships—such as those formed by solicitors—may merge or otherwise reconstitute themselves (for example, as limited liability partnerships). In such cases, the newly constituted partnership will not generally bear an ongoing commitment or duty to keep under review all previous advice proffered by the earlier partnership if at the time of the merger or reconstitution, the retainer was complete. As Akenhead J explained in *Shepherd Construction v Pinsent Masons LLP*:

> "There is something commercially and professionally worrying if professional people are held responsible for reviewing all previous advice or indeed services provided. There is a difference to be drawn between a specific retainer or commission which imposes a continuing duty on a professional to keep earlier advice or services under review and some sort of obligation which requires the professional to review and revise previous advice given, or services provided, on commissions or retainers which are complete."[325]

14. Joint Claimants

5-99 **Joint claimants in tort** Under the Civil Procedure Rules a single claim form (formerly a writ) can be used to start all claims which can be conveniently disposed of in the same proceedings.[326] This includes claimants who are jointly entitled to a remedy. All persons jointly entitled to a remedy should normally be made parties and any one of them who does not consent to being joined as a claimant must be made a defendant.[327]

5-100 In the case of libels committed against a member of a firm, there may well be a double injury: one to the reputation of the individual member,[328] and another to the reputation of the firm.[329] For each, distinct actions will lie. And presumably the individual member, after recovering in an action for the injury to himself personally, may sue alone in a second action for the damage to the firm in respect of his interest in it. The same principle applies to a company and the person controlling the company.[330]

---

323 Partnership Act 1890 s.1.

324 Unreported 5 April 2001.

325 [2012] EWHC 43 (TCC); [2012] B.L.R. 213 at [31].

326 CPR r.7.3.

327 CPR r.19.2. The court may order a person to be added as a new party if it is desirable to add the new party so that the court can resolve all the matters in dispute in the proceedings, or there is an issue involving the new party and an existing party which is connected to the matters in dispute: CPR r.19.2(2). For discussion of the position where multiple claimants have claims in respect of wrongful interference with goods see paras 16-82 and following.

328 *Harrison v Bevington* (1838) 8 C. & P. 708.

329 *Forster v Lawson* (1826) 3 Bing. 452.

330 *Lewis v Daily Telegraph* [1963] 1 Q.B. 340; affirmed [1964] A.C. 234.

15. JUDICIAL ACTS

(a) General

Judicial and ministerial acts Officers of courts of justice act either judicially or ministerially. A judicial act is one which involves the exercise of a discretion, in which something has to be heard and decided. A ministerial act is one which the law points out as required to be done under the circumstances, without leaving any choice of alternative courses. Every purely formal step in a legal process, and everything which is necessary to carry into execution what has been judicially decided, is ministerial. However, it is not always easy to distinguish between the two classes of acts. Where an application was made to a magistrate to issue a distress warrant against a defaulting ratepayer he had jurisdiction to inquire whether the rate had been duly made and published, whether it had been paid or otherwise satisfied,[331] and whether the alleged defaulter was exempted from rateability.[332] But if satisfied on these points, he was bound to issue his warrant, and could not deal with any question of the validity of the rate itself. The issuing of the warrant, therefore, was a ministerial act, though the preliminary inquiry constituted a judicial act. On this analogy, it was sought in *Linford v Fitzroy*[333] to recover damages against a magistrate in an action for unreasonably refusing to grant bail in a case of misdemeanour; and it was contended that, although the magistrate might have a judicial discretion as to the sufficiency of the bail tendered, once this preliminary condition was satisfied his duty became simply ministerial.[334] The court held, however, that the duty could not be thus divided, and must be treated as entirely judicial.[335] 5-101

Judicial acts Responsibility in respect of judicial acts depends not upon the particular office which a person holds, but upon the function performed on the occasion in question.[336] So, a disciplinary tribunal can be characterised as acting judicially,[337] as can certain acts of subordinate officers of courts of justice, even though many of their duties are purely ministerial. Conversely, magistrates who are the judges of courts of summary jurisdiction, also have certain ministerial functions.[338] Either way, even where a function is not characterised as judicial there may be a duty on the officer to act fairly and impartially so as to comply with the 5-102

331 *Kershaw, Leese Co v Stockport Overseers* [1923] 2 K.B. 129.
332 *Whenman v Clark* [1916] 1 K.B. 94; *Shillito v Hinchliffe* [1922] 2 K.B. 236.
333 (1849) 13 Q.B. 240.
334 See now Bail Act 1976 s.4 and Sch.1, as amended.
335 For the distinction between a judicial and ministerial act, see *Garnett v Ferrand* (1827) 6 B. & C. 611; *Ward v Freeman* (1852) 2 Ir. C.L.R. 460; *Scremby Corn Rents, Re* [1960] 1 W.L.R. 1227.
336 See *Everett v Griffiths* [1921] 1 A.C. 631 at 682–683; *Doswell v Impey* (1823) 1 B. C. 163. For liability for judicial acts under s.9 of the Human Rights Act 1998, see *W v Ministry of Justice* [2015] EWCA Civ 742; [2016] Q.B. 676; and *Mazhar v Lord Chancellor* [2019] EWCA Civ 1558; [2020] 2 W.L.R. 541. Note also proposed reforms under the Human Rights Act 1998 (Remedial) Order (SI 2019 Draft).
337 *Baxendale-Walker v Middleton* [2011] EWHC 998 (QB).
338 See, e.g. *R. v Cornwall Quarter Sessions Ex p. Kerley* [1956] 1 W.L.R. 906 (a justice condemning food under the Food and Drugs Act 1938 s.10 was not sitting as a court of summary jurisdiction, but acting in an executive capacity).

right to a fair trial under art.6 of the European Convention on Human Rights.[339] Failure to act fairly may give rise to an application for judicial review.[340]

5-103 **Different kinds of courts** In considering the responsibility for judicial acts it is necessary to bear in mind, first, the distinction between courts of record and courts not of record, and, secondly, the distinction between the Supreme Court and courts of limited jurisdiction.[341] Courts of record include the Supreme as well as various inferior courts: the essential feature is that their proceedings can be proved only by their own official record, and that their judges possess the power to punish for contempt of court. Judges not of record—and magistrates' courts are not of record—have no judicial power in respect of contempt as such, though they may direct the removal of persons disturbing their proceedings. It should be noted that under provisions contained in ss.31–35 of the Courts Act 2003, magistrates continue to enjoy greater protection from suit than other judges of limited jurisdiction.

5-104 **Abuse and absence of jurisdiction distinguished** If an act purporting to be judicial is alleged to be a legal wrong, the claimant may seek to establish his case in one of two ways: first, on the ground that, although the act was within the scope of the authority given by law, it was not an honest exercise of that authority; secondly, on the ground that the act in question was not a judicial act at all, but a pure tort committed under the colour of judicial authority. In other words, the cause of action may be either an abuse of jurisdiction or an absence of jurisdiction. However, a mere allegation that a decision reached was *fundamentally* wrong provides no basis for an action in tort.[342]

5-105 **Abuse of jurisdiction** No action lies in respect of any mere abuse of jurisdiction of a court of record[343] since it is thought less evil that corrupt or malicious judges should be protected, than that honest judges should be exposed to the risk of frivolous and vexatious proceedings. With respect to courts not of record, the position is less clear.[344] Yet there seems to be no reason of principle for distinguishing in this context between courts of record and courts not of record; and it is submitted that both should be entitled to equal protection.[345]

5-106 **Absence of jurisdiction** If a judicial person acts outside the limits of his jurisdiction, the question arises whether he can be liable for those acts and their consequences as a private individual might be. In principle, any judge who acts

---

339 *R. (on the application of D'Costa) v Secretary of State for Constitutional Affairs* [2006] EWHC 465 (Admin). But note that in this case, Ouseley J refused to be drawn on the question of whether District Probate Registrars held a form of judicial office.

340 *R. v Birmingham City Justices Ex p. Chris Foreign Foods (Wholesalers Ltd)* [1970] 1 W.L.R. 1428.

341 See *Sirros v Moore* [1975] Q.B. 118; *Re McC* [1985] A.C. 528.

342 *Hinds v Liverpool County Court* [2008] EWHC 665 (QB); [2008] 2 F.L.R. 63.

343 Crown Proceedings Act 1947 s.2(5). See also *Sirros v Moore* [1975] Q.B. 118; *Hinds v Liverpool CC* [2008] EWHC 665 (QB); [2008] 2 F.L.R. 63; *Pius v Chief Land Registrar* [2013] EWHC 2216 (Ch).

344 Sections 31–35 of the Courts Act 2003 give statutory protection to magistrates. But doubt exists as to whether an action on the case for abuse of jurisdiction survives elsewhere: see *Re McC* [1985] A.C. 528 at 540–541 (in relation to the equivalent provisions under the Justices of the Peace Act 1979).

345 See *Sirros v Moore* [1975] Q.B. 118.

without jurisdiction may be liable in tort for his act.[346] A distinction has to be made between judges of the Supreme Court and judges of limited jurisdiction. A judge of the Supreme Court is the sole arbiter of what matters fall within his jurisdiction and thus can never be said to exceed his authority unless he acts without any colour or show of right[347]: he "is absolutely immune from personal civil liability in respect of any judicial act which he does in his capacity as a judge of that court".[348] The lawfulness of proceedings in an inferior court is open to inquiry and review by the Supreme Court.[349] Authority prior to 1975 established that a judge of limited jurisdiction might be liable in tort if found to have acted beyond his jurisdiction.[350]

In *Sirros v Moore*,[351] Lord Denning MR attempted to abolish any distinction in respect of the scope of the immunity afforded to judges of the Supreme Court and judges of limited jurisdiction. In modern conditions, Lord Denning contended (with the support of Ormrod LJ): "as a matter of principle the judges of superior courts have no greater claim to immunity than the judges of the lower courts."[352] Any judge who knowingly acts without jurisdiction should be liable for his act. Any judge, including a magistrate, who acted in the honest belief that his acts were within his jurisdiction should be immune from civil liability. In *Re McC*[353] the House of Lords again reviewed the authorities on the liability of judges of limited jurisdiction. Their Lordships concluded that in so far as Lord Denning MR's judgment in *Sirros v Moore* sought to equate the immunity from suit of those purporting to exercise the limited jurisdiction of inferior courts (including magistrates) with that of judges of the Supreme Court it must be rejected.[354] The judgments in *Re McC* confirmed that the original provisions of the Justices of the Peace Act 1979 preserved a right of action against magistrates although Lord Templeman suggested that the continued liability of magistrates should be subject to review by Parliament. His proposal was acted on in s.108 of the Courts and Legal Services Act 1990 which amended the Justices of the Peace Act 1979 to extend the statutory protection of magistrates. This extended protection is now to be found in the Courts Act 2003.[355] **5-107**

But what of other courts of limited jurisdiction? In *Re McC* no concluded opinion was expressed on the liability of other judges of limited jurisdiction. The majority judgment in *Sirros v Moore*, in so far as it relates to judges of limited jurisdiction other than magistrates, was not expressly overruled. But Lord Bridge expressed the opinion that the distinction between superior and inferior courts in relation to the immunity of judges acting beyond their jurisdiction "is so deeply rooted in our law that it certainly cannot be eradicated by the Court of Appeal and probably not by your Lordships' House".[356] It must, therefore, be assumed that judges of limited jurisdiction remain liable in certain circumstances for acts beyond their jurisdiction. **5-108**

346 *Re McC* [1985] A.C. 528 at 540; *Sirros v Moore* [1975] Q.B. 118 at 139.

347 For example, a judge describing a jury's verdict in favour of an acquittal as "perverse" then proceeding to pass sentence: see per Lord Bridge in *Re McC* [1985] A.C. 528 at 540.

348 *Sirros v Moore* [1975] Q.B. 118 at 140.

349 By way of application for judicial review: see the Senior Courts Act 1981 s.31. As to the hybrid status of the Crown Court see *Re McC* [1985] A.C. 528 at 550.

350 *Houlden v Smith* (1850) 14 Q.B. 841; *Willis v MacLachlan* (1876) 1 Ex. D. 376.

351 [1975] Q.B. 118. Note the comments of Lord Woolf M.R. in *Warren v Warren* [1997] Q.B. 488.

352 [1975] Q.B. 118 at 136.

353 [1985] A.C. 528.

354 [1985] A.C. 528 at 541–542, per Lord Bridge.

355 Discussed fully at paras 5-121 to 5-124.

356 [1985] A.C. 528 at 550.

(b) Error of law

5-109 **Wrongly assumed jurisdiction** Jurisdiction may be wrongly assumed through error of law or fact. With regard to error of law, a distinction is sometimes made between absence of jurisdiction and excess of jurisdiction. If on the facts before him a judge has no competence to deal with the matter at all, yet he proceeds to do so, he acts without jurisdiction.[357] But if, having authority to deal with it on one footing, he deals with it on another, he acts in excess of jurisdiction.[358] An excess of jurisdiction is simply an absence of jurisdiction as to part of the proceedings.

5-110 **Entire absence of jurisdiction** There may be an entire absence of jurisdiction from the very nature of the case dealt with, or from the fact that the necessary conditions precedent have not been complied with. A defect of jurisdiction may, however, be cured by appearance[359] unless the appearance was under protest.[360] The parties cannot by consent confer on the court a jurisdiction that it does not have. Thus, where an order made by the justices recited that the wife's allegation of cruelty had not been proved but that the husband had consented to the order being made, the order was bad on its face for want of jurisdiction.[361] There was equally a want of jurisdiction in *R. v Waltham JJ Ex p. Solanke*.[362] In that case, the claimant had been imprisoned by magistrates for breach of a High Court order that the magistrates mistakenly believed had been properly registered in the magistrates' court. Due to an oversight, the order had in fact never been so registered. The claimant served his term of imprisonment but later sought a judicial review in which it was conceded that, since the High Court order had not been properly registered, the justices had no jurisdiction to act in the matter. The justices did not contest liability in false imprisonment.

5-111 **Excess of jurisdiction** The problem of excess of jurisdiction arises most frequently where the court has jurisdiction to entertain the matter, but deals with it in an unauthorised manner. So if a person is put on trial for one offence and convicted of another, or if he is convicted of one offence and punished for another, the conviction in one case and the punishment in the other are altogether bad,[363] and acts resulting from the orders may be tortious.[364] In *Davis v Capper*,[365] a magistrate who remanded a prisoner for an unreasonable length of time was liable to an action for false imprisonment because his power was to remand only for a reasonable time. The magistrates in both *Re McC*[366] and *R. v Manchester City Magistrates' Court Ex p. Davies*[367] acted in excess of jurisdiction and were liable. The juvenile panel in *Re McC* had jurisdiction to sentence the claimant, but in imposing a custodial sentence without meeting the conditions laid down in art.15(1) of the

357 As in *R. v Waltham JJ Ex p. Solanke* [1986] Q.B. 479; affirmed [1986] Q.B. 983.
358 As in *R. v Manchester City Magistrates' Court Ex p. Davies* [1988] 1 W.L.R. 667; affirmed [1989] Q.B. 631.
359 *R. v Hughes* (1879) 4 Q.B.D. 614; *R. v Brentford JJ Ex p. Catlin* [1975] Q.B. 455.
360 *Dixon v Wells* (1890) 25 Q.B.D. 249.
361 *O'Connor v Isaacs* [1956] 2 Q.B. 288.
362 [1986] Q.B. 479; affirmed [1986] Q.B. 983.
363 *R. v Brickhall* (1864) 33 L.J.M.C. 156. See also *Moore v Wilson* (1903) 5 F. (Jus.) 88.
364 See *Prickett v Gratrex* (1846) 8 Q.B. 1020; *Leary v Patrick* (1850) 15 Q.B. 266.
365 (1829) 10 B. & C. 28 (and see Magistrates' Courts Act 1980 ss.128, 128A and 129).
366 [1985] A.C. 528.
367 [1988] 1 W.L.R. 667; affirmed [1989] Q.B. 631.

Treatment of Offenders (Northern Ireland) Order 1976 they exceeded that jurisdiction. And in the latter case, the Manchester justices were authorised by s.102 of the General Rate Act 1967 to commit rate defaulters to gaol. Their failure to address themselves to the question of whether that default was due to wilful refusal or culpable neglect, as required by s.103 of the 1967 Act as a condition precedent to committal, took them outside that original jurisdiction to hear and determine the matter of the default. Note that magistrates would now in similar circumstances be protected from suit unless bad faith were proved against them.[368]

Mere irregularity does not destroy jurisdiction Irregularity of procedure alone does not create a defect in jurisdiction. Such an irregularity based on an error of law may be sufficient to quash any conviction or determination of the judge of limited jurisdiction, and in appropriate cases found an application for judicial review, without necessarily founding an action against the judge for any consequent trespass to the person or goods. In *Re McC*[369] Lord Bridge made it clear that the then new test of excess of jurisdiction in *Anisminic v Foreign Compensation Commission*[370] has no application to the issue of the liability of judges of limited jurisdiction. He opined that "once justices have duly entered upon the summary trial of a matter within their jurisdiction, only something quite exceptional occurring in the course of their proceeding to a determination can oust their jurisdiction so as to deprive them of protection for a subsequent trespass".[371] On the assumption that all judges of limited jurisdiction, other than magistrates, remain liable for acts in excess of jurisdiction, his words are presumably generally applicable but offer little assistance to distinguish excess of jurisdiction from mere irregularity. Where, albeit enjoying jurisdiction to embark on the matter before him, a judge of limited jurisdiction is required to establish a condition precedent before imposing a particular type of sentence, failure to meet that condition will result in an excess of jurisdiction. Thus imposing a prison sentence without, as demanded by the relevant legislation, informing the accused of his right to legal aid,[372] or establishing the necessary causal connection between default in paying rates and culpable neglect[373] resulted in liability for false imprisonment. But if the judge has in fact jurisdiction to imprison the claimant, it seems that even "hopeless" irregularity in achieving that end will not deprive him of jurisdiction.[374] 5-112

Fundamental irregularity Where the judge of limited jurisdiction has jurisdiction over the offence and the offender, and his jurisdiction to detain the offender or order seizure of his goods is not dependent on any condition precedent, it is undecided whether there may be such gross and fundamental irregularities of procedure which will give rise to a defect in jurisdiction. Failure by a presiding 5-113

---

368 See para.5-122.

369 [1985] A.C. 528.

370 [1969] 2 A.C. 147.

371 [1985] A.C. 528 at 546.

372 *Re McC* [1985] A.C. 528 at 546.

373 *R. v Manchester City Magistrates' Court Ex p. Davies* [1988] 1 W.L.R. 667; affirmed [1989] Q.B. 631.

374 *Re McC* [1985] A.C. 528 at 551 and 558. Note that where a person was believed, and who believed himself, to have the necessary judicial authority he will be regarded in law as possessing such authority de facto: *Coppard v HM Customs and Excise Commissioners* [2003] EWCA Civ 511; [2003] Q.B. 1428, where the statutory power to authorise a circuit judge to sit as a judge of the Queen's Bench Division had not been exercised through an oversight.

magistrate to consult his brethren was held not to destroy their jurisdiction.[375] In *Bott v Ackroyd*,[376] magistrates both convicted and imposed a penalty and costs: the conviction and warrant were drawn up and signed by them leaving a blank for the amount of costs which was afterwards filled in by the clerk. An action against the magistrates in respect of proceedings taken under the warrant failed. They acted irregularly but not so as to deprive themselves of jurisdiction. Nevertheless, a "gross and obvious irregularity of procedure"—such as one magistrate absenting himself from the hearing and relying on hearsay from his colleague—or a fundamental breach of the rules of natural justice—such as refusing to allow the defendant to give his evidence—may be sufficient to destroy the jurisdiction of the court.[377] It is submitted that the irregularity must be such as to strike at the very root of the judicial process rendering the trial little more than a "sham".

(c) Error of fact

5-114 **Error of fact** It may be a question of fact whether jurisdiction exists or not, and this question may arise in respect of the very issue that is to be decided by the court, or in respect of some subordinate or collateral matter. Of course, in one sense, no person in a judicial position is entitled to make an order which the facts do not justify, but, if the judge's jurisdiction were made to depend on the correctness of inferences, the result would be that in all cases the judge would be liable for a mere erroneous exercise of judgment. The true test, therefore, assuming that whatever has been alleged is true, is whether there exists jurisdiction to deal with it.[378] The decision of any court on a matter which by law it is appointed to decide is conclusive, except in so far as an appeal may lie. So, if the judge of an inferior court has come to such a decision, a superior court cannot reopen the question in any action brought against that judge.[379] It makes no difference if the inferior court has acted without legal evidence, or adopted an irregular procedure,[380] unless the irregularity is so gross and obvious as to destroy that court's jurisdiction.[381]

5-115 **Error of fact of collateral matter** The objection to the jurisdiction may arise not on the main issue but on some collateral point which may be brought to the attention of the court. Thus, it may be alleged that the matters in question arose outside the local limits within which the court has authority, or that there is a dispute of title which will oust its jurisdiction. In such cases the court has, before proceeding further, to decide this preliminary question. Its decision on this matter is not final, as is a decision on the merits, but will be reviewed in the superior court on an application for judicial review.[382] The inferior court cannot give itself jurisdiction by

---

375 *Penney v Slade* (1939) 5 Bing. N.C. 319.

376 (1859) 28 L.J.M.C. 207. See also *Ratt v Parkinson* (1851) 20 L.J.M.C. 208; *Mitchell v Foster* (1850) 12 A. & E. 472.

377 *Re McC* [1985] A.C. 528 at 546–547, per Lord Bridge.

378 Per curiam, *Cave v Mountain* (1840) 1 M. & G. 257. See also *Ashcroft v Bourne* (1832) 3 B. & Ad. 684; *Lowther v Earl of Radnor* (1806) 8 East 113.

379 *Kemp v Neville* (1861) 10 C.B. (N.S.) 523; *Brittain v Kinnaird* (1819) 1 B. & B. 432.

380 *Cave v Mountain* (1840) 1 M. & G. 257; *Kemp v Neville* (1861) 10 C.B. (N.S.) 523.

381 *Re McC* [1985] A.C. 528 at 546–547.

382 *Thompson v Ingham* (1850) 14 Q.B. 710; per curiam, *Bunbury v Fuller* (1853) 9 Ex. 111. The case of *R. v Dayman* (1857) 7 E. & B. 672, illustrates the difficulty which sometimes arises in determining whether a decision is on the merits or on a collateral point.

an erroneous finding of facts.[383] But a tribunal may be entrusted by the legislature with jurisdiction to determine whether the preliminary state of facts exists, as well as the jurisdiction; and on finding that it does exist, to proceed further or do something more.[384]

(d) Knowledge

Knowledge of absence of jurisdiction A judge of a court of limited jurisdiction, other than a magistrate prior to 1990, was never liable unless he had "knowledge or means of knowledge of which he ought to have availed himself of that which constitutes the defect of jurisdiction".[385] He is always supposed to know the law and therefore it was no defence to plead that he acted wrongly through mistake of law.[386] Where the judge acted outside his jurisdiction because of a mistake of fact, the evidence before him must have been such as to lead any reasonable man to the conclusion that there was an absence of jurisdiction.[387] In *Sirros v Moore*,[388] Buckley LJ stated that any judge, including a judge of the Supreme Court, who acts without jurisdiction should be liable if he acted on the basis of a mistake of law or due to careless ignorance or disregard of the relevant facts that found his jurisdiction. **5-116**

If prima facie it appears that jurisdiction has been assumed through a mistake of law, it is for the defendant to prove, if he can, that the mistake was in truth one of fact. In *Houlden v Smith*,[389] the defendant was a county court judge, and judgment had been given in one of his courts against the claimant, who resided at Cambridge, out of the jurisdiction. The court declined to assume in the absence of evidence that the mistake was one of fact, as to the claimant's real residence, and not of law, as to the extent of the jurisdiction.[390] **5-117**

(e) Remedies

Remedy for act done without jurisdiction If a judicial person is liable at all for acting without jurisdiction, the ordinary remedy is trespass for any invasion of **5-118**

---

383 It was said in *Brown v Cocking* (1868) L.R. 3 Q.B. 672 that the superior court has no jurisdiction to interpose where the inferior court has decided, on conflicting evidence, a question of jurisdiction. It seems, however, in such cases rather a rule of convenience that the court which had not had the witnesses before it should accept the finding of the court which has, just as the Court of Appeal may refuse under the circumstances to overrule a judge of first instance. The superior court cannot lose its jurisdiction to inquire into facts simply because such inquiry will be difficult: *Elston v Rose* (1868) L.R. 4 Q.B. 4. cf. *Sammy-Joe v GPO Mount Pleasant Office* [1967] 1 W.L.R. 370.

384 *R. v Special Commissioners* (1888) 21 Q.B.D. 313; *R. v Swansea Commissioners* [1925] 2 K.B. 250.

385 *Calder v Halket* (1839) 3 Moo P.C. 28 at 77, per Parke B; *Palmer v Crone* [1927] 1 K.B. 804 (referred to with apparent approval in *Sammy-Joe v GPO Mount Pleasant Office* [1967] 1 W.L.R. 370).

386 *Houlden v Smith* (1850) 14 Q.B. 841. In the old case of *Hammond v Howell* (1677) 2 Mod. 218, the defendant was the Recorder of London, and he had fined and imprisoned the claimant for misconduct as a juror in returning a wrong verdict. The court held that the action did not lie because the defendant had general jurisdiction to punish misconduct in jurors, although he took an erroneous view of what was such misconduct. The mistake here was one of law, but in the very issue to be decided and not in a collateral matter.

387 *Pike v Carter* (1825) 3 Bing. 78; *Polley v Fordham (No.2)* (1904) 91 L.T. 525. See also *Calder v Halket* (1839) 3 Moo P.C. 28; and *Carratt v Morley* (1841) 1 Q.B. 18 as to whether the claimant had to prove absence of reasonable and probable belief by the judge that he acted within his jurisdiction.

388 [1975] Q.B. 118 at 141.

389 (1850) 14 Q.B. 841.

390 See also *M'Creadie v Thomson* (1907) S.C. 1176.

person or property which may have been committed by the officers or agents of the law in obedience to the unauthorised decision.[391] The mere fact that the party against whom an order had been made has been put to expense in getting it quashed does not appear to be of itself a cause of action.[392] If an order is partly within the jurisdiction and partly without, the person making it is not answerable for what is done in carrying it into effect, provided that the bad part has not been acted upon.[393]

5-119 **Proceedings authorising conduct** It is a general rule that the proceedings of any court, which are regular on the face of them and which have not been subsequently set aside or quashed, are a sufficient justification for an act done in pursuance of their authority.[394] If, however, the setting forth of such proceedings discloses any fatal defect, then, being a mere nullity, they are not available as a defence.[395]

5-120 **Liability of judicial officer for manner of execution** A judicial person is answerable only for the strict consequences of any order or judgment which he may give; and he has no general responsibility for the manner in which the ministerial officer of the court executes its process. Even where special bailiffs are appointed, their mistake or misconduct does not affect him, if such appointment is according to the ordinary practice of the court.[396]

16. STATUTORY PROTECTION OF JUSTICES

5-121 **Courts Act 2003** Section 31(1) of the Courts Act 2003 affords immunity to a justice of the peace in respect of anything he does or omits to do "(a) in the execution of his duty as a justice of the peace, and (b) in relation to a matter within his jurisdiction". This was extended, until 5 April 2020, to justices' clerks (and assistant clerks) exercising by virtue of an enactment the function of a justice of the peace. From 6 April 2020, following the removal of the justices' clerk role from the statute, the section will be amended to exclude reference to these roles.[397]

5-122 Section 32 of the Courts Act 2003 sets out the limited circumstances in which justices, and until 5 April 2020 their (assistant) clerks, may be sued. It does so, however, in terms that might be interpreted as providing further immunity for acts done in good faith beyond the jurisdiction of the justice. The causes of action created are thus limited to the acts or omissions of justices that are (a) in the purported exercise of their duties (but not actually within their jurisdiction); and (b) done in bad faith.

5-123 **Limitation of actions** The ordinary periods of limitation apply to actions against justices. Even though convictions and orders must be quashed before an action can

[391] See *O'Connor v Isaacs* [1956] 2 Q.B. 288. See also, however, the observations of Blackburn J in *Pease v Chaytor* (1861) 1 B. & S. 658 at 674, with reference to jurisdiction assumed on a mistake of fact.

[392] *Sommerville v Mirehouse* (1860) 1 B. & S. 652. This seems to be the ground on which the decision of Hill J in this case proceeded.

[393] *Barton v Bricknell* (1850) 13 Q.B. 393.

[394] *Basten v Carew* (1825) 3 B.C. 649; *Brittain v Kinnaird* (1819) 1 B. & B. 432.

[395] *Crepps v Durden* (1777) 2 Cowp. 640; *Mitchell v Foster* (1840) 12 A. & E. 472. Formerly the record might be demurred to, though not traversed.

[396] *Tunno v Morris* (1835) 2 C.M. & R. 298. cf. *Bradley v Carr* (1841) 3 M. & G. 221.

[397] See Courts and Tribunals (Judiciary and Functions of Staff) Act 2018 Sch.1(1) para.27. In order to broaden the role of these lawyers to provide leadership across all jurisdictions, the Government is removing this role, but not function, from statute.

be brought for false imprisonment consequent on the conviction or order, the cause of action accrues, and time starts to run at the date of imprisonment and not at the date of the subsequent quashing of the conviction or order.[398]

Indemnity Section 35(3) of the Courts Act 2003 provides that the Lord Chancellor must indemnify a justice of the peace (and until 5 April 2020, justices' clerk or assistant clerk)[399] in respect of (a) indemnifiable amounts which relate to criminal matters, unless it is proved, in respect of the matters giving rise to the proceedings or claim, that he acted in bad faith; and (b) other indemnifiable amounts if, in respect of the matters giving rise to the proceedings or claim, he acted reasonably and in good faith. "Indemnifiable amounts" include damages awarded against him and certain costs (s.34 of the 2003 Act prohibits an order for costs in some circumstances). By s.35(4) the Lord Chancellor may indemnify a justice of the peace (and justices' clerk or assistant clerk until 5 April 2020) in respect of other indemnifiable amounts unless it is proved, in respect of the matters giving rise to the proceedings or claim, that he acted in bad faith. 5-124

17. MINISTERIAL ACTS

Ministerial acts A ministerial act may consist either in the carrying out of some formal step of procedure or in the execution of the orders and judgment of a court of justice. No liability is incurred by an official who simply forwards the process of the court in the ordinary course of business, without exercising any judgment of his own in the matter. It is nothing to him that the process itself is ill-founded or illegal. If a magistrate backs a warrant to be executed within his jurisdiction which has been illegally issued in the first instance, the remedy (if any) for the person arrested under such warrant is not against the magistrate who backed it but against the magistrate by whom it was issued.[400] In *Dews v Riley*,[401] the judge of a county court made an invalid order of commitment. The defendant, as clerk of the court, made out a warrant in pursuance of the order under which the claimant was arrested. It was held that the defendant was not liable inasmuch as he was, in accordance with his duty, simply putting into form an order of his superior officer, which he had no power to review. Consequently the issue of the warrant was not his act but that of the judge. Where, however, the judges of an inferior court, having jurisdiction to order payment of a debt in instalments, and (upon proof of default in payment) to award imprisonment, made an order for payment by instalments "or execution to issue", and left it to their clerk to issue execution subsequently on proof of default without further intervention of the court, it was held that the clerk in so doing was not acting ministerially. He was taking upon himself an unauthorised judicial function, and was held liable for the consequences.[402] 5-125

Failure to carry out step of procedure It would seem that any official who wrongfully neglects to carry out any step of procedure which a party is entitled to require of him is liable to the person so aggrieved for any damage which may be 5-126

398 *O'Connor v Isaacs* [1956] 2 Q.B. 288.
399 Courts and Tribunals (Judiciary and Functions of Staff) Act 2018 Sch.1(1) para.30(3).
400 *Clark v Woods* (1848) 2 Ex. 395.
401 (1851) 11 C.B. 434. See also *Demer v Cook* (1903) 88 L.T. 629.
402 *Andrews v Marris* (1841) 1 Q.B. 3.

proved to have resulted. In the Irish case of *Ward v Freeman*,[403] where a county court judge was sued for refusing to receive notice of appeal in an action pending before him, the court, while divided in opinion on the question of whether the reception of the notice was a ministerial act, were agreed that, assuming it to be such, an action would lie.[404]

18. Constables

5-127 **Torts by constables** Section 88 of the Police Act 1996 provides that the chief officer of police for a police area is liable in respect of any unlawful conduct of constables under his direction and control in the performance or purported performance of their functions in like manner as a master is liable in respect of torts committed by his servants in the course of their employment.[405] Somewhat controversially—since vicarious liability is generally understood to involve liability without fault—this statutory vicarious liability of a Chief Constable has been held to extend to the payment of exemplary damages.[406] Section 88 does not, however, prevent, restrict nor otherwise constrain the ability of the Commissioner to obtain a contribution or indemnity from an officer or officers whose misconduct had led to his having to deal with a claim for which he was responsible under the Act.[407] In addition, s.88(6) extends the Chief Constable's liability to an international joint investigation team formed under the leadership of a constable who is a member of a police force, and renders the chief officer of police vicariously liable for any unlawful conduct, in the performance or purported performance of his functions as such, of any member of that team who is neither a constable nor an employee of the police authority. Any damages or costs awarded against the chief officer are to be paid out of the police fund as is any settlement of a claim approved by the local policing body.[408] Furthermore, the local policing body has a discretion to pay any damages or costs awarded against, or sum in settlement of a claim against, any member of a force maintained by them.[409]

5-128 So far as individual constables are concerned, an important series of police powers are set out in the Police and Criminal Evidence Act 1984 and the Criminal Justice and Public Order Act 1994. These relate, broadly, to the power of constables to arrest and detain persons suspected of criminal offences, to search persons and enter premises, and to seize property. Constables' common law powers in respect of breaches of the peace are unaffected by the 1984 Act. Whether acting under their common law powers or their statutory powers, constables acquire immunity in tort from what would otherwise constitute a battery, a trespass or a false

---

403 (1852) 3 Ir. C.L.R. 460.

404 See also per Lord Mansfield CJ in *Douglas v Yallop* (1759) 2 Bur. 722; cf. *Robinson v Gell* (1852) 12 C.B. 191.

405 In *Weir v Bettison (Sued as Chief Constable of Merseyside)* [2003] EWCA Civ 111; [2003] I.C.R. 708 a Chief Constable was held liable for the acts of an off-duty policeman who assaulted the claimant in a borrowed police van in which the constable made it clear to the claimant that he was a police officer. See also para.6-18.

406 *Rowlands v Chief Constable of Merseyside* [2006] EWCA Civ 1773; [2007] 1 W.L.R. 1065. See also para.6-18.

407 *Mohidin v Commissioner of Police of the Metropolis* [2016] EWHC 105 (QB); [2016] 1 Costs L.R. 71. As Lord Lloyd-Jones commented in *James-Bowen v Commissioner of Police of the Metropolis* [2018] UKSC 40; [2018] I.C.R. 1353 at [31], the possibility of such a claim is not fanciful, at least in cases where deliberate misconduct is alleged.

408 Police Act 1996 s.88(2).

409 Police Act 1996 s.88(4).

imprisonment.[410] Furthermore, nothing in the Act affects a police constable's ability to invoke a common law defence, such as self-defence in the context of an alleged battery.[411] Where the powers in the statute are exceeded, however, no immunity may be claimed. In such cases, the offending officer may well be required to indemnify the Chief Constable in respect of his vicarious liability towards the claimant. [412] On the other hand, it may take a good deal to exceed one's powers given that the House of Lords has held that, in relation to the defence of self-defence, an officer will be entitled to act in self-defence if he mistakenly but reasonably and honestly thought that his acts were necessary to defend himself against attack or an imminent risk of attack.[413]

Protection of constable by warrant At one time persons executing the warrants of justices were exposed to a double danger. If the warrant was issued without jurisdiction it was a nullity, and they could not plead its protection for any interference with the person or property of others. If it was issued with jurisdiction, they were still liable for anything they did which was not covered by its authority. They were thus endangered not only by their own mistakes, but by the mistakes of the justices. This situation was remedied by the Constables' Protection Act 1750 s.6. The object of this statute is that a constable who has obeyed a warrant may be protected,[414] and yet a party who has suffered a wrong may be under no difficulty as to his remedy. On inspection of the warrant the injured party can see whether it directed the act of which he complains. (Notably, a constable is not required to inform a man when he is actually arrested whether the arrest is by virtue of a warrant or otherwise.[415]) If the warrant did direct the act, the claimant has no remedy against the constable, but may possibly sue the justice. If it did not, then the constable is liable.[416] More recently, the court in *Khan v Chief Constable of West Midlands*[417] examined the application of s.6 of the Constables' Protection Act 1750 in relation to a claim for damage to property caused during a search of premises under a magistrate's warrant. The court ruled that what was done during the search was reasonably calculated to achieve the purpose of the warrant and so there was nothing to undermine the protection of the 1750 Act. The section does not apply where the cause of action is against the constable in respect of something which the warrant did not authorise.[418] There are thus two issues that arise in connection with warrants: first, whether a valid warrant was properly executed; and secondly whether the warrant had the scope to confer the authority claimed by the constable. 5-129

410 For full discussion of these statutory and common law powers, see para.14-65 onwards.

411 See, e.g. *Ashley v Chief Constable of Sussex* [2008] UKHL 25; [2008] 1 A.C. 962.

412 *KD v Chief Constable of Hampshire* [2005] EWHC 2550 (QB).

413 *Ashley v Chief Constable of Sussex* [2008] UKHL 25; [2008] 1 A.C. 962.

414 Although the warrant protects the constable, a person who maliciously and without reasonable cause instituted the process which induced the court to order the arrest may be liable in damages to the person arrested: *Roy v Prior* [1971] A.C. 470.

415 *R. v Kulynycz* [1971] 1 Q.B. 367.

416 In *Mouncher v Chief Constable of South Wales* [2016] EWHC 1367 (QB) at [453], Wyn Williams J accepted that the quashing of the warrant is a necessary pre-requisite to the bringing of a civil action under s.6.

417 [2017] EWHC 2185 (QB).

418 *Hoye v Bush* (1840) 1 Man. & G. 775.

5-130 **Wrongful execution of warrant** A constable may be liable to an action of trespass or other tort though he believes himself to be acting under the authority of a warrant.[419] The following situations must be considered:

(a) He may not be the person to whom the warrant is directed, though this will not matter if he is acting within his police area.[420]

(b) He may have executed it on the wrong person or the wrong property. However honestly mistaken, a constable cannot be justified if he arrests A by virtue of a warrant directed against B; or if he takes C's goods under a distress against D.[421] But where a constable enters under a search warrant he may now be entitled to seize goods constituting evidence of crime generally by virtue of the general power of seizure under s.19 of the Police and Criminal Evidence Act 1984.

(c) He may have executed it at the wrong time.[422] As a rule, warrants may be executed at any hour of the day; but in relation to search warrants it is the usual and proper course to direct that the search shall only take place in the daytime.[423]

(d) He may have failed to give due notice of the grounds on which he claims to effect the apprehension.[424]

(e) He may not have had the warrant with him at the time of the alleged wrongful act. He who seeks to execute a warrant ought to be in a position to produce it, if demanded.[425] This does not apply, however, to a warrant to arrest a person charged with an offence: in such a case, the officer would have the necessary grounds for an arrest without a warrant.[426]

(f) He may have executed the warrant improperly by breaking open an outer door, and if so, not merely the breaking of the door, but the subsequent arrest, will be an unlawful act. The general rule is that the outer door of the party's own house may be forced if necessary to execute any process to which the Crown is a party, but not otherwise.[427] Thus, the substantial distinction is between civil and criminal process. Under the latter head would appear to fall all warrants of apprehension on a criminal charge, and all warrants of commitments on conviction, even though the alternative of a fine is given. But if a penalty simply is imposed in the first instance, and imprisonment subsequently ordered, not as an alternative, but in order to enforce payment in default of sufficient distress, this, it would appear, is a

[419] Thomas [1962] Crim. L.R. 597.

[420] Magistrates' Courts Act 1980 s.125(2).

[421] *Hoye v Bush* (1840) 1 Man. & G. 775; *Kay v Grover* (1831) 7 Bing. 312.

[422] As regards place, there is no longer any difficulty as a warrant issued by a justice of the peace may be executed anywhere in England and Wales: Magistrates' Courts Act 1980 s.125(2).

[423] *Hale*, Vol.2, p.113.

[424] *Mackalley's Case* (1611) 9 Rep. 65 at 68; *Christie v Leachinsky* [1947] A.C. 573.

[425] *Galliard v Laxton* (1862) 2 B. & S. 363; *R. v Purdy* [1975] Q.B. 288 (warrant need not be actually on the person of the constable providing that it is in his possession in the sense of being under his control and available to be produced as part and parcel of the arrest); *De Costa Small v Kirkpatrick* (1979) 68 Cr. App. R. 186 (not enough that constable knew the warrant was at a nearby police station).

[426] See Police and Criminal Evidence Act 1984 s.24(2).

[427] Quaere must permission be first sought and refused before force is used save where the arrest could in any case be effected without a warrant or in cases of serious crime: see *Swales v Cox* [1981] Q.B. 849. See also *Ex p. Henry, Re Von Weissenfeld* (1892) 36 S.J. 276, where a bankrupt had failed to attend his public examination.

process which is civil in its nature, and therefore enforceable under the limitations applicable to civil process. It would seem to follow that on a distraint for a fine or penalty the outer door cannot be broken.[428] That said, in some cases certain statutes *do* confer the power of forcible entry; thus force may be used to enter premises specified in a warrant for the purposes of assessing the risk posed by a sex offender under the Sexual Offences Act 2003.[429]

(g) He may at the time of the arrest or seizure have been guilty of an assault, or subsequently thereto may have improperly confined his prisoner or otherwise acted in an unauthorised manner[430]; but this will probably not make him a trespasser ab initio.[431] Indeed, it has been held that an officer may use reasonable and necessary steps to detain the occupants of a house in the course of the execution of a search warrant so as to nullify any action in trespass or false imprisonment.[432]

(h) He may, in executing a distress warrant, have exposed himself to liability to an action for excessive distress, against which the Constables Protection Act 1750 s.6, will afford him no protection.[433]

(i) He may, in executing a warrant to search premises, have searched persons found thereon, this being unlawful unless the warrant expressly included the search of persons.[434]

(j) Section 16 of the Police and Criminal Evidence Act 1984 enacts detailed rules for the execution of search warrants.[435]

Scope of justices' warrants The execution of magistrates' warrants is now regulated by statute.[436] Magistrates may direct warrants for the apprehension of persons charged with offences, whether indictable or punishable on summary conviction, to any constable by name or by description of his office, or to any particular constable and all other constables within their jurisdiction, or generally to all constables within their jurisdiction.[437] Any such warrant may be executed in any county or place in England or Wales, either by the person to whom the warrant was originally directed, or by any constable of the county or place in which the arrest takes place.[438] **5-131**

---

428 See *R. v Myers* (1786) 1 T.R. 265.

429 s.96B. This is compliant with art.8 ECHR: *M v Chief Constable of Hampshire* [2014] EWCA Civ 1651; [2015] 1 W.L.R. 1176.

430 e.g. by seizing an excessive number of documents: see *Bell v Chief Constable of Greater Manchester* [2005] EWCA Civ 902 (obiter).

431 See *Smith v Egginton* (1837) 7 A. & E. 167; *Wiltshire v Barrett* [1966] 1 Q.B. 312 at 323.

432 *Connor v Chief Constable of Merseyside* [2006] EWCA Civ 1549; [2007] H.R.L.R. 6 (detention of claimants in a police car during a warranted search for firearms was reasonable on the facts of this case).

433 *Sturch v Clarke* (1832) 4 B. & Ad. 113.

434 *Herman King v R.* [1969] 1 A.C. 304. See para.18-64 onwards.

435 See para.18-64 onwards.

436 Magistrates' Courts Act 1980. A warrant holds good though the justice by whom it is issued dies or ceases to hold office: s.124.

437 Magistrates' Courts Act 1980 s.125.

438 Magistrates' Courts Act 1980 s.125(2). Warrants that need to be executed in Scotland or Northern Ireland can be executed there by virtue of s.136 of the Criminal Justice and Public Order Act 1994.

5-132 **Scope of default warrants** Warrants may be issued for the apprehension of defaulting witnesses.[439] Section 76 of the Magistrates' Courts Act 1980 provides that magistrates may issue a warrant to commit to prison for default in paying a civil debt in certain circumstances. Such warrants, if issued in England or Wales, may be similarly executed in any county or place in England or Wales,[440] but in other cases the common law rule appears to apply, and the constable unless addressed by name cannot act outside the limits of his constablewick.

5-133 **Other protection** Although he makes a mistake in the execution of a warrant which will deprive him of the right to arrest under it, a constable may nevertheless be protected by his general authority as an officer of the peace. Thus, if he arrests the wrong man under a warrant, he will still be protected if he reasonably suspected the person whom he actually took into custody to be guilty of an offence for which he was liable to be arrested.[441] And even if he makes a mistake in the execution of a warrant, and is therefore liable for wrongful arrest, he will be entitled to the protection of the Constables Protection Act 1750 in respect of a subsequent detention of the person apprehended, if the warrant directed such detention.[442]

5-134 **Miscellaneous officers** By statute, numerous officials may enter and inspect premises and in some cases seize goods and documents. Certain powers are limited to constables. The vast majority are exercisable by duly authorised officials of the body whose duty it is to exercise the functions set out in the empowering statute. The officer may be required to give notice of his intention to enter premises to the occupier, though certain statutes authorise entry at all reasonable times.[443] The power may extend to vehicles.[444] It is almost invariably an offence to obstruct such an officer in the execution of his duty.[445] If the officer fails to obtain entry but can satisfy a magistrate that he has reasonable grounds for entry under the relevant statute then the magistrate can in some cases issue a warrant authorising the use of force.[446]

---

439 Magistrates' Court Act 1980 s.97.

440 Magistrates' Courts Act 1980 s.125(2).

441 See *Hoye v Bush* (1840) 1 Man. & G. 775. See also *R. v Kulynycz* [1971] 1 Q.B. 367.

442 s.6; *Horsfield v Brown* [1932] 1 K.B. 355.

443 See, e.g. Consumer Rights Act 2015 s.77 and Sch.5 para.23; replacing Consumer Protection from Unfair Trading Regulations 2008 (SI 2008/1277) reg.21 from 1 October 2015.

444 e.g. Medicines Act 1968 s.111.

445 See Control of Pollution Act 1974 s.92(6). But if the official has not got proper authorisation for his entry he is a trespasser and it is no offence to attempt to deter his entry by reasonable force: *Brunner v Williams* (1975) 73 L.G.R. 266.

446 e.g. Medicines Act 1968 s.111; Mines and Quarries (Tips) Act 1969 s.13; Consumer Rights Act 2015 s.77 and Sch.5 paras 32 to 33. But see the Health and Safety at Work etc Act 1974 s.20.

Chapter 6

VICARIOUS LIABILITY

Table of Contents

1. Introduction

Scope of chapter A person is liable not only for torts committed by himself,[1] but also, classically for those torts he has authorised or subsequently ratified. Authorising a tort involves instigating or procuring another to commit a tort. While this classical understanding of vicarious liability tends to relate simply to the commission of a common law tort by an employee, it is now clear that vicarious liability is neither limited to the commission of common law torts, nor the commission of torts by those who are employees in the strict sense. According to Lord Phillips JSC in *Various Claimants v Catholic Child Welfare Society*,[2] the question of whether D2 can be held liable for the torts of D1 involves a two-stage test. The first stage entails considering "the relationship of D1 and D2 to see whether it is one that is capable of giving rise to vicarious liability".[3] And in the background, here, is the "policy objective underlying vicarious liability … to ensure, in so far as it is fair, just and reasonable, that liability for tortious wrong is borne by a defendant with the means 6-01

[1] But note that liability may result from negligence in the selection of his servants: *Williams v Curzon Syndicate* (1919) 35 T.L.R. 475; *Adams (Durham) v Trust Houses* [1960] 1 Lloyd's Rep. 380.
[2] [2012] UKSC 56; [2013] 2 A.C. 1.
[3] [2012] UKSC 56; [2013] 2 A.C. 1 at [21].

to compensate the victim".[4] The question of whether it is fair, just and reasonable to impose such liability was said by Lord Phillips to be illuminated by reference to five considerations, namely (at [35]):

> "(i) the employer is more likely to have the means to compensate the victim than the employee and can be expected to have insured against that liability; (ii) the tort will have been committed as a result of activity being taken by the employee on behalf of the employer; (iii) the employee's activity is likely to be part of the business activity of the employer; (iv) the employer, by employing the employee to carry on the activity will have created the risk of the tort committed by the employee; (v) the employee will, to a greater or lesser degree, have been under the control of the employer."

6-02 The second stage of the test requires there to be a sufficient "connection that links the relationship between D1 and D2 and the act or omission of D1".[5] This matter is to be determined by asking "whether the workman was working on behalf of an enterprise or on his own behalf and, if the former, how central the workman's activities were to the enterprise and whether these activities were integrated into the organisational structure of the enterprise".[6] In this connection, the relationship between D1 and D2 need not be one of employer–employee in the strict sense. Accordingly, vicarious liability can be imposed where there is a relationship that is merely "akin to that between an employer and an employee".[7] Equally, the vicarious liability principle is not confined to D1's commission of a tort in the strict sense. In *Majrowski v Guy's and St Thomas' NHS Trust*[8] the House of Lords held that the doctrine can be invoked in connection with equitable wrongs and breaches of statutory obligations (so long as those statutory breaches are capable of grounding an award of damages).[9]

6-03 Ratification[10] of a tort involves, in effect, its subsequent authorisation. The act of authorisation or ratification renders the tort the act of the authoriser or ratifier,[11] so that he or she becomes vicariously liable. In addition, vicarious liability can also be imposed in respect of acts that have been neither authorised nor ratified if, according to the rather vague test laid down by the House of Lords in *Lister v Hesley Hall Ltd*, the employee's tort was "so closely connected with his employment that it would be fair and just to hold the [employer] vicariously liable".[12] Finally, there are circumstances in which the torts of an independent contractor may produce liability on the part of an employer: this occurs on the basis of the latter's breach of a non-delegable duty of care.[13]

---

4 [2012] UKSC 56; [2013] 2 A.C. 1 at [34].
5 [2012] UKSC 56; [2013] 2 A.C. 1 at [21].
6 [2012] UKSC 56; [2013] 2 A.C. 1 at [49].
7 [2012] UKSC 56; [2013] 2 A.C. 1 at [47]. See further para.6-35.
8 [2006] UKHL 34; [2007] 1 W.L.R. 398.
9 [2006] UKHL 34; [2007] 1 W.L.R. 398 at [10] and [57], per Lords Nicholls and Hope respectively.
10 As to ratification, see para.6-90.
11 Where the principal is a statutory corporation, and the act is one altogether outside the corporation's powers.
12 [2001] UKHL 22; [2002] 1 A.C. 215 at [28], per Lord Millett.
13 e.g. an employer may be liable directly to an employee for failure to supply a safe system of work, a situation involving only two parties (see, e.g. *General Cleaning Contractors Ltd v Christmas* [1953] A.C. 180). By contrast, and by definition, cases of vicarious liability always involve three parties.

Employees and independent contractors The two most important classes of person for whose torts another person may ultimately be liable are employees and independent contractors. Yet on Supreme Court authority, vicarious liability cannot be imposed upon an employer in relation to the torts committed by an independent contractor because, despite the significant changes that have occurred in this area of law in recent years, "[t]here is nothing … to suggest that the classic distinction between employment and relationships akin or analogous to employment, on the one hand, and the relationship with an independent contractor, on the other hand, has been eroded".[14] The so-called "classic distinction" is said to be justified on the basis that an employee, engaged under a contract of employment, works principally for the benefit of his employer, whereas an independent contractor is "carrying on business on his own account".[15] Both classes consist of persons employed to do work, and for practical purposes it will typically be the case that if the worker is not an employee he is an independent contractor. Traditionally, the distinction between them was taken to lie in the different amounts of control exercisable by the employer, particularly control over the manner in which the work was to be done.[16] Yet as Lady Hale pointed out in *Barclays Bank Plc v Various Claimants*, control "does not have the significance which once it did … [given that] [i]n today's world an employer is likely to be able to tell an employee what to do but not (at least always) how to do it".[17] Added to this is the fact that the use made of the distinction between employees and independent contractors for other purposes,[18] has revealed the deficiencies of this control test as a criterion of general validity. **6-04**

Normally, for vicarious liability to arise,[19] the alleged employee must have been employed to work for the employer as opposed to having been asked, or even ordered, to perform a gratuitous service in a context quite different from that usually understood by the term employment. The schoolboy distributing the mid-morning milk to fellow-pupils does so as a pupil obeying his teacher and the school is not vicariously liable for his negligence, but only liable if it is in breach of its own duty to make reasonably safe arrangements for the performance of that task and supervise the boy with care.[20] Similarly, a local authority is not vicariously liable for foster parents' negligence which causes injury to a child boarded out with them.[21] **6-05**

---

14 *Barclays Bank Plc v Various Claimants* [2020] UKSC 13; [2020] 2 W.L.R. 960 at [24], per Lady Hale.

15 *Barclays Bank Plc v Various Claimants* [2020] UKSC 13; [2020] 2 W.L.R. 960 at [27], per Lady Hale.

16 The notion of an independent contractor would seem to include a solicitor, yet it has been held that where a solicitor of a judgment creditor negligently directed the sheriff to take the goods of the wrong person in execution, the client was liable for the act of the solicitor: *Jarmain v Hooper* (1843) 6 M. & G. 827. This rule, though anomalous, is settled law: *Wilson v Tumman* (1843) 6 M. & G. 236, per Tindal CJ; *Chetty v Marikar* [1931] A.C. 77 PC. On the other hand, the rule will not be extended to acts beyond the scope of the solicitor's authority: *Smith v Keal* (1882) 9 Q.B.D. 340; *Hewitt v Spiers* (1896) 13 T.L.R. 64.

17 [2020] UKSC 13; [2020] 2 W.L.R. 960 at [20].

18 e.g. to decide if a worker is an employee and, therefore, capable of benefiting from the rights now contained in the Employment Rights Act 1996.

19 For exceptions see para. 6-35.

20 *Watkins v Birmingham City Council* (1976) 126 N.L.J. 442.

21 *S v Walsall MBC* [1985] 1 W.L.R. 1150.

2. LIABILITY FOR EMPLOYEES

(a) Relationship of employer and employee

6-06 **Relationship of employer and employee** A number of different tests to identify an employer/employee relationship have been suggested by the courts. Although important features of the relationship suggested in the cases as tests for determining whether the parties are employer and employee are considered below, the decision in each individual case will ultimately turn on the view taken by the court of the relationship between the parties considered as a whole.[22]

6-07 **Relevance of parties' intention** In interpreting the nature of the contract, the actual intention of the parties, though relevant,[23] is not conclusive. In *Ferguson v Dawson & Partners (Contractors) Ltd*,[24] for example, almost the only express term of the contract between the labourer and the defendant construction company was the defendants' direction that the work was to be classed as self-employed. The Court of Appeal concluded that, viewed holistically, the relationship was one of employer/employee. The expressed intention of the defendant was a mere device to gain tax and national insurance advantages. The same result will follow, even where the worker has actively sought independent contractor status.[25] On the other hand, the intention of the parties is likely to be highly relevant where there are conflicting indications of the nature of the contractual relationship. For example, in *Massey v Crown Life Insurance*,[26] the worker had previously worked for the company both as an employee and under a general agency agreement. At his instigation, a new agreement was drawn up whereby he continued to perform the same managerial duties as before, but he was now labelled self-employed. It was held that the agreement itself was the best source from which to discover the true legal status of the worker: in this case independent contractor rather than employee.[27]

6-08 In *Lee Ting Sang v Chung Chi-Keung*[28] the Privy Council held that the nature of "the relationship has to be determined by an investigation and evaluation of the factual circumstances in which the work is performed, [and] that the question of whether or not the work was performed in the capacity of an employee or as an independent contractor is to be regarded by the appellate court as a question of fact to be determined by the trial court".[29] Various methods of distinguishing between an employee and an independent contractor have been advanced by the courts. Yet, with the extension of vicarious liability to relationships "akin to" a contract of employment in recent years, their importance has declined. Nonetheless, they are

---

22 See, e.g. *Sellers Arenascene Ltd v Connolly (No.2)* [2001] EWCA Civ 184; [2001] I.C.R. 760.

23 Peter Gibson LJ in *Express Echo Publications Ltd v Tanton* [1999] I.R.L.R. 367 said (at 370): "one starts with the common intention of the parties that [the appellant] should not be an employee".

24 *Ferguson v Dawson & Partners (Contractors) Ltd* [1976] 1 W.L.R. 1213 at 1222 and 1230.

25 *Young and Woods Ltd v West* [1980] I.R.L.R. 201.

26 [1978] 1 W.L.R. 676. See also *BSM (1257) Ltd v Secretary of State for Social Services* [1978] I.C.R. 894. In *Young and Woods Ltd v West*, above, Stephenson LJ stressed that the important aspects of the *Massey* case were that there had been a deliberate change in the basis of the employment and that ambiguity was present, given the unusual nature of the work in question.

27 In similar vein, see *Calder v H Kitson Vickers & Sons (Engineers) Ltd* [1988] I.C.R. 232.

28 [1990] 2 A.C. 374.

29 [1990] A.C. 374 at 414, per Lord Griffiths. See also *Carmichael v National Power Plc* [1999] 1 W.L.R. 2042.

still worth noting since the ability to show that the immediate tortfeasor is an employee places beyond doubt the question of whether the relationship is sufficient to attract the application of the vicarious liability principle.

(i) Control test

Control Lord Thankerton in *Short v J & W Henderson Ltd*[30] stated that there were four indicia of a contract of service, namely: (a) the master's power of selection; (b) the payment of remuneration; (c) the master's right to control the method of doing the work; and (d) the master's right of suspension or dismissal.. From among these, the classic test for distinguishing an employee from an independent contractor is (c), the control test. Even today, this test is sometimes referred to. And even though the control that the employer has over the method of working is not conclusive as regards the question of whether there is a contract of service, it may well be enough to show that the relationship is one that is "akin to" a contract of employment (and therefore capable of animating the vicarious liability principle).[31] **6-09**

The issue of control relates not merely to whether the employer dictates the method of working but also whether he controls the hours of work. In *WHPT Housing Association Ltd v Secretary of State for Social Services*[32] an architect was engaged on what was termed a "freelance basis" to work for the appellants at an hourly rate. Despite a high degree of supervision and control over his method of work, and notwithstanding his almost total integration into the business, he was held to be an independent contractor. The fact that he retained sole control over his hours of service weighed heavily with the court.[33] **6-10**

Limitations of the control test The limitations of the control test were most forcibly brought out in a series of cases concerning negligent hospital treatment. But even in the case of persons with no professional qualifications, it is often unrealistic to hold that the employer has any effective control. Recognising this, Lord Phillips has set out a much more limited conception of the control test in the modern era. In his view, "the significance of control today is that the employer can direct what the employee does, not how he does it".[34] However, in *Armes v Nottinghamshire CC*,[35] where the Supreme Court decided that a local authority was vicariously liable for the abusive way in which a foster child had been treated by his foster parents, it was held to be significant that the local authority exercised a **6-11**

---

30 (1946) 62 T.L.R. 427 at 429; *Mersey Docks and Harbour Board v Coggins and Griffith (Liverpool) Ltd* [1947] A.C. 1 at 17, per Lord Porter.

31 *Levitt v Euro Building and Maintenance Contractors Ltd* [2019] EWHC 2926 (QB) at [38].

32 [1981] I.C.R. 737. And see *Wickens v Champion Employment* [1984] I.C.R. 365. cf. *Nethermere (St Neots) Ltd v Taverna* [1984] I.C.R. 612.

33 But note, if the worker is directly under the personal control or supervision of his employer, the prima facie inference is that he is engaged as an employee and not as a contractor: *Smith v Martin* [1911] 2 K.B. 775.

34 *Various Claimants v Catholic Child Welfare Society* [2012] UKSC 56; [2013] 2 A.C. 1 at [36]. It has also been hinted that the absence of control in this watered-down sense may be fatal to the attempt by C to rely on D's vicarious liability: *Cox v Ministry of Justice* [2016] UKSC 10; [2016] A.C. 660 at [22]; *Kafagi v JBW Group Ltd* [2018] EWCA Civ 1157. Equally, the complete absence of integration into D's enterprise (the third of Lord Phillips' criteria concerning fairness in the Catholic Child Welfare Society case (see para.6-01)) might also be fatal to the imposition of vicarious liability: *Davis v Fessey* unreported 5 April 2018 QBD at [17].

35 [2017] UKSC 60; [2018] A.C. 355.

significant degree of control over both what the foster parents did and how they did it. It was held that other factors were important, as well, viz: the fact that (i) the torts were committed in the course of an activity carried out for the benefit of the local authority; (ii) the placement of children with foster parents created a relationship of authority and trust which rendered the children particularly vulnerable to abuse; (iii) the local authority's powers of approval, inspection, supervision and removal did not have any parallel in ordinary family life; and (iv) local authorities could more easily compensate the victims of abuse.[36]

(ii) The organisation test

6-12 **The "organisation" test** The limitations of the control test prompted the development of other tests for the existence of an employment relationship. In *Stevenson, Jordan and Harrison Ltd v Macdonald*,[37] Denning LJ suggested the so-called "organisation" or "integration" test:

> "One feature which seems to run through the instances is that, under a contract of service, a man is employed as part of the business, and his work is done as an integral part of the business; whereas under a contract for services, his work, although done for the business, is not integrated into it but is only accessory to it."

This involves asking whether the worker was part of the employer's organisation; was his work co-ordinated by the employer, so that the employer controlled the "where" and "when", rather than the "how"? This approach, however, has been judicially noted to suffer from flaws of its own.[38]

(iii) Multiple test

6-13 **The "multiple" test** The more modern approach is to abandon the idea of a single test and to take a "multiple factor" approach. In the speech of Lord Wright in *Montreal v Montreal Locomotive Works Ltd*[39] the following factors were suggested as important in assessing the economic reality: control, ownership of the tools, chance of profit and risk of loss. MacKenna J found this analysis useful in *Ready Mixed Concrete (South East) Ltd v Minister of Pensions and National Insurance*.[40] And in *Market Investigations Ltd v Minister of Social Security*,[41] it was said that additional factors include such matters as whether the man performing the services provides his own equipment, whether he hires his own helpers, what degree of financial risk he takes, what degree of responsibility for investment and management he has, and whether and how far he has an opportunity of profiting from sound management in the performance of his task.[42] That approach was approved by the

---

36 [2017] UKSC 60; [2018] A.C. 355 at [59]–[73] (applying the five factors set out in the *Catholic Child Welfare Society* case (see para.6-01)).

37 [1952] 1 T.L.R. 101 at 111; *Bank voor Handel en Scheepvaart NV v Slatford* [1953] 1 Q.B. 248 at 295.

38 *Ready Mixed Concrete (South East) Ltd v Minister of Pensions and National Insurance* [1968] 2 Q.B. 497 at 524.

39 [1947] D.L.R. 161 at 169.

40 [1968] 2 Q.B. 497. See also *Kapfunde v Abbey National Plc* [1999] I.C.R. 1.

41 [1969] 2 Q.B. 173.

42 *Market Investigations Ltd v Minister of Social Security* [1969] 2 Q.B. 173 at 185, per Cooke J.

Privy Council in *Lee Ting Sang v Chung Chi-Keung*,[43] but since a relationship "akin to" a contract of employment can now suffice to attract the application of the vicarious liability principle, it is probable that this lower threshold will negate the need for an elaborate examination of all of these matters in any given case.

No universal test Ultimately, there is no single test that determines the existence of an employer/employee relationship. But since vicarious liability is no longer contingent upon there being a contract of employment in the strict sense, the absence of any such universal test is now of limited practical significance. 6-14

The issue of mutuality In employment law cases where the issue of the status of a worker has arisen within the context of rights now contained in the Employment Rights Act 1996, the courts have stressed the need for "mutuality" in order for the relationship to be that of employer/employee.[44] This involves an essential core of mutual obligations: to be ready to work and to pay for that work.[45] If the worker has the choice whether or not to work for a given period, the contract would seem to lack "mutuality".[46] Equally, where workers are engaged on an "ad hoc and casual basis" with no obligation on the employer to provide work and no obligation on the worker to accept work, the requirement of mutuality is not satisfied.[47] 6-15

Compulsory employment It does not affect the existence of the relationship that the employer is not allowed by law to do the work for himself, but is compelled to employ an agent of a particular class to do it for him, provided the employer is allowed the power of controlling and dismissing the agent, and provided the class from which the agent is to be taken is sufficiently large to give the employer a practical power of selection.[48] But where the class is so limited that the employer has practically no power of selection he is not responsible for the negligence of the person employed. It was on this ground that at common law the master of a ship was in general not liable for the negligence of a pilot employed by him in a compulsory pilotage district.[49] 6-16

Superior employees and delegated power of control The fact that a head employee may select and dismiss under-employees does not make them his 6-17

---

43 [1990] 2 A.C. 374.

44 The need for mutuality was stressed in *Clark v Oxfordshire HA* [1998] I.R.L.R. 125; and *Carmichael v National Power Plc* [1999] 1 W.L.R. 2042.

45 The Court of Appeal in *Clark v Oxfordshire HA* [1998] I.R.L.R. 125 accepted that an obligation to work as required and an obligation on the other party to pay a retainer during such periods when no work was not offered would be likely to suffice.

46 *O'Kelly v Trusthouse Forte Plc* [1984] Q.B. 90. One way round this requirement for those workers who are most likely to be affected (i.e. casual workers and homeworkers) is to show that in practice they tend to work on a regular basis. Thus the Court of Appeal accepted that there was an "umbrella" or "global" contractual obligation to continue to work and to provide work in *Nethermere (St Neots) Ltd v Taverna* [1984] I.C.R. 612.

47 *Stevedoring and Haulage Services Ltd v Fuller* [2001] EWCA Civ 651; [2001] I.R.L.R. 627.

48 See, e.g. *Martin v Temperley* (1843) 4 Q.B. 298.

49 *The Halley* (1868) L.R. 2 P.C. 193 at 201. By s.16 of the Pilotage Act 1987 the owner and master are liable for such negligence in waters to which that Act extends. Note, too, that in *Oceangas (Gibraltar) Ltd v Port of London Authority* [1993] 2 Lloyd's Rep. 292, the Port of London Authority was not vicariously liable for the torts of pilots they supplied. See also *Esso Petroleum Co v Hall Russell Co* [1989] A.C. 643.

employees.[50] Equally, "superior public officers are not responsible for the negligence or misconduct of inferior officers in their several departments, though the superior officers appointed them and had the power of dismissing them".[51] The inferiors are firmly employees of the Crown. Where officials are appointed under statutory authority by a public authority, whether they are properly regarded as employees depends upon the construction of the particular statute.[52]

(b) Particular types of employment

6-18 **Police** A police officer is neither an employee of the Crown[53] nor of the police authority.[54] Yet under the Police Act 1996, the chief officer of police for any police area is made liable "in respect of any unlawful conduct of constables under his direction and control in the performance or purported performance of their functions in like manner as a master is liable in respect of any unlawful conduct of his servants in the course of their employment and accordingly shall, in the case of a tort, be treated for all purposes as a joint tortfeasor".[55] And although the statute goes on to state that the chief officer is to be treated as a joint tortfeasor for all purposes, the idea of joint tortfeasance is somewhat difficult to square with the decision in *Rowlands v Chief Constable of Merseyside*[56] in which the respondent Chief Constable was singled out as the sole defendant in order to help justify the making of a sizeable award of exemplary damages against him in respect of the assault, false imprisonment and malicious prosecution of the appellant by two of his police officers. As to the perceived basis for an award of exemplary damages, Moore-Bick LJ (who delivered a judgment on behalf of the entire Court of Appeal) identified two factors. The first was the need properly to reflect "the jury's 'vigorous disapproval' of the conduct of the police force as an institution"[57]; while the second was that "only by this means [i.e. awarding exemplary damages] can awards of an adequate amount be made against those who bear public responsibility for the conduct of the officers concerned".[58] And so long as one accepts that seeking to mark substantially the jury's disapproval of the police force as a whole might *indirectly* serve to fulfil one of the goals of punitive damages—that is, to prompt an employer to take measures to reduce the prospect of future such incidents—then the Chief Constable's vicarious liability for exemplary damages can be justified even though, conventionally, vicarious liability is understood to entail li-

---

50 *Stone v Cartwright* (1759) 6 T.R. 411. So, too, with agents employed by directors of a company: *Weir v Bell* (1878) 3 Ex. D. 238.

51 *Tobin v The Queen* (1864) 16 C.B. (N.S.) 310 at 351, per Erle CJ.

52 See *Stanbury v Exeter Corp* [1905] 2 K.B. 838; *Metropolitan Meat Industry Board v Sheedy* [1927] A.C. 899.

53 See para.5-06.

54 *Fisher v Oldham Corp* [1930] 2 K.B. 364.

55 s.88 of the Police Act 1996. In relation to the performance, or purported performance, of an officer's functions, this provision is to be interpreted in line with the common law approach to vicarious liability, namely, by asking whether the tort committed was sufficiently closely connected with the tortfeasor's position as a police officer: *Allen v Chief Constable of Hampshire* [2013] EWCA Civ 967 at [30], per Gross LJ. See also *Weir v Bettison (sued as Chief Constable of Merseyside)* [2003] EWCA Civ 111; [2003] I.C.R. 708.

56 [2006] EWCA Civ 1773; [2007] 1 W.L.R. 1065.

57 [2006] EWCA Civ 1773; [2007] 1 W.L.R. 1065 at [42].

58 [2006] EWCA Civ 1773; [2007] 1 W.L.R. 1065 at [47].

ability regardless of fault on the part of the employer.[59] What is more difficult to justify, given that the statute expressly makes the Chief Constable a joint tortfeasor "for all purposes", is the way in which Moore-Bick LJ felt able to treat the Chief Constable as the sole defendant in the case,[60] thus enabling him to side-step the rule propounded in *Broome v Cassell & Co Ltd* that awards of exemplary damages in respect of *joint torts* should be based on the lowest figure for which any of the co-defendants could be made liable.[61] Notwithstanding these points, it is at least clear that damages and costs awarded against a chief officer under this section are to be paid out of the police fund,[62] as are any sums required to settle a claim against him if the settlement is approved by the local policing body.[63] In the case of a police cadet, it is the chief officer of a police force that will be vicariously liable.[64]

Hospital medical staff and other professionals[65] It is well established that hospital authorities can be held vicariously liable for the negligence of members of their medical staff, whether professionally qualified or not. Such professionally qualified persons as radiographers,[66] house surgeons,[67] full-time assistant medical officers[68] and staff anaesthetists[69] have all been held to be employees of the hospital authority for the purposes of this doctrine. Indeed, any member of the full-time staff of a hospital should be regarded as the employee of the hospital authority.[70] **6-19**

Visiting consultants and surgeons, on the other hand, have been said not to be the employees of the hospital authority.[71] However, since the tendency has been to treat the question of the hospital authority's liability as raising issues of primary, as well as vicarious, liability, the matter is of little importance: the hospital authority is itself under a duty to its patients; and it does not discharge this duty simply by delegating its performance to someone else, regardless of whether the delegation is to an employee or an independent contractor.[72] As such, it makes no difference whether or not a visiting consultant is a servant.[73] There is some support for this view in *Wilsher v Essex AHA*.[74] And it is an important issue given the liability implica- **6-20**

---

59 For a general justification of exemplary damages within the context of vicarious liability, see Law Commission Report No.247, paras 5.209–5.230. And for specific justification on the economic ground that it assists in prompting employers to deter similar conduct in the future, see Law Commission Report No.247 at paras 5.219–5.221. As a matter of English law, however, the question of a fault-free employer being made liable for exemplary damages remains open: see *Kuddus v Chief Constable of Leicestershire Constabulary* [2001] UKHL 29; [2002] 2 A.C. 122 at [47].

60 [2006] EWCA Civ 1773; [2007] 1 W.L.R. 1065 at [40].

61 See [1972] A.C. 1027 at 1063, per Lord Hailsham.

62 Police Act 1996 s.88(2)(a).

63 Police Act 1996 s.88(2)(b).

64 For discussion see *Wiltshire Police Authority v Wynn* [1981] Q.B. 95. Now s.28(3) of the Police Act 1996.

65 See generally, C. Beuerman, "Do Hospitals Owe a So-Called 'Non-Delegable' Duty to Their Patients? (2018) 26 Med. L. Rev. 1.

66 *Gold v Essex CC* [1942] 2 K.B. 293; see further para.9-102.

67 *Collins v Hertfordshire CC* [1947] K.B. 598; *Cassidy v Ministry of Health* [1951] 2 K.B. 343.

68 *Cassidy v Ministry of Health* [1951] 2 K.B. 343.

69 *Roe v Minister of Health* [1954] 2 Q.B. 66.

70 *Cassidy v Ministry of Health* [1951] 2 K.B. 343 at 362, per Denning LJ.

71 *Collins v Hertfordshire CC* [1947] K.B. 598 at 619–620, per Hilbery J.

72 *Gold v Essex CC* [1942] 2 K.B. 293 at 301, per Lord Greene MR; at 309, per Goddard LJ; *Cassidy v Ministry of Health* [1951] 2 K.B. 343 at 362–365, per Denning LJ.

73 *M v Calderdale and Kirklees HA* [1998] Lloyd's Law Rep. Med. 157.

74 [1987] Q.B. 730 (the Court of Appeal decision was overturned by the House of Lords on the issue

tions in an age where the NHS is making increasing use of agency staff and private clinics (and deputising services in the case of GPs).[75] Note also that by s.3 of the National Health Service Act 2006, clinical commissioning groups are under a duty to provide, inter alia, "medical, dental, ophthalmic, nursing and ambulance services", and that, also, it was held in relation to the corresponding provision in the National Health Service Act 1977 that this duty is also not one that can be discharged merely by the appointment of competent doctors and nurses.[76]

6-21 **Professionals** The idea that vicarious liability may be imposed in respect of the acts of professionals was endorsed by the House of Lords in *Phelps v Hillingdon LBC* where, in relation to the potential vicarious liability of an education authority in respect of the acts and omissions of its professional employees, Lord Slynn said:

> "I accept that, as was said in *X (minors) v Bedfordshire County Council* [1995] 2 A.C. 633, there may be cases where to recognise such a vicarious liability on the part of the authority may so interfere with the performance of the local education authority's duties that it would be wrong to recognise any liability on the part of the authority. It must, however, be for the local authority to establish that: it is not to be presumed and I anticipate that the circumstances where it could be established would be exceptional."[77]

It has since been added that this potential vicarious liability of a local education authority is not confined to the acts of educational psychologists and teachers—the two classes of employees considered in *Phelps*. Rather, it may also be extended to the acts or omissions of an education officer performing the statutory functions of a local education authority.[78]

6-22 **Club servants** Whether the relationship of employer and employee exists between the members of an ordinary members' club and the club servants has seemingly never been decided. The position is probably that the members, as such, cannot be regarded as responsible for the acts of the club employees, though there may be circumstances which would make them responsible. The feature which distinguishes clubs from other societies is that: "no member as such becomes liable to pay to the funds of the society or to anyone else any money beyond the subscription required by the rules."[79] Accordingly, "[i]f liabilities are to be fastened on any of their members, it must be by reason of the acts of those members themselves, or by reason of the acts of their agents; and the agency must be made out by the person who relies on it, for none is implied by the mere fact of association".[80] It may therefore be that for any act of negligence by the employee the committee would be liable, for they are not only members of the club but are

---

of causation: [1988] A.C. 1074). But see also *Bull v Devon HA* [1993] 4 Med. L.R. 117; *Kondis v State Transport Authority* (1984) 55 A.L.R. 225.

75 See *Bull v Devon HA* [1993] 4 Med. L.R. 117; *M v Calderdale HA* [1998] Lloyd's Med. Rep. 157 (though note the criticism of *M v Calderdale* in *A (A Child) v Ministry of Defence* [2004] EWCA Civ 641; [2004] Q.B. 183 at [52], per Lord Phillips MR).

76 *Razzel v Snowball* [1954] 1 W.L.R. 1382.

77 [2001] 2 A.C. 619 at 653.

78 *Carty v London Borough of Croydon* [2005] EWCA Civ 19; [2005] 1 W.L.R. 2312. See also para.13-10.

79 *Wise v Perpetual Trustee Co* [1903] A.C. 139 at 149.

80 *London Association for Protection of Trade v Greenlands* [1916] 2 A.C. 15 at 39, per Lord Parker.

also for some purposes its representatives. In *Brown v Lewis*,[81] where the committee of a football club employed an incompetent person to repair a stand and in consequence of his negligence a spectator was injured, the members of the committee were held liable, but only because they had the duty of providing the stand and had employed an incompetent person to carry out the duty. They were held liable for their own personal negligence. It might be, however, that in some cases the committee would be liable as employers quite apart from any personal negligence.[82] In any given case, the court may look to appointments made by the club and the club rules in order to determine whether vicarious liability exists.[83] Proprietary clubs pose no difficulty, for the club servants are clearly the employees of the proprietor.

Borrowed employees If A lends his employee to B for a job and the employee causes damage in the course of doing that job, the question may arise whether the person vicariously liable for the damage is the general employer or the temporary employer. This is a question of fact in each case[84]; and the facts of one case cannot govern another. They are only useful so far as similarity of facts can help guide a decision. The whole problem was considered in *Mersey Docks and Harbour Board v Coggins and Griffith*.[85] In that case, a harbour authority lent a mobile crane to a firm of stevedores for loading a ship, providing a craneman who was employed and paid and liable to be dismissed by that authority, though the general hiring conditions stipulated that cranemen so provided should be the employees of the hirers. The craneman injured a third person by driving the crane negligently. The injured person sued the harbour authority and the stevedores. The House of Lords held that the harbour authority, as general permanent employer, was liable, not having discharged the heavy burden of proof so as to shift to the stevedores its prima facie responsibility for the negligence of the craneman, who, in the manner of his driving, was exercising the discretion it had invested in him. It was further held that the question of whether the employer was responsible for his negligence was not determined by any agreement between the harbour authority and the stevedores.[86] **6-23**

This case establishes that no single, conclusive test can be laid down. "Who is paymaster; who can dismiss, how long the alternative service lasts; what machinery is employed; have all to be kept in mind."[87] All of their Lordships agreed, however, that the most important issue is which of the two employers, the general or the temporary, has the right to control the employee's method of working,[88] and they thus applied the same test to this question as to the established question of whether **6-24**

---

81 (1896) 12 T.L.R. 455.

82 See para.5-87, especially the discussion of *Robertson v Ridley* [1989] 1 W.L.R. 872. And see *102 Social Club and Institute Ltd v Bickerton* [1977] I.C.R. 911 at 917–919.

83 *Grice v Stourport Tennis, Hockey and Squash Club* [1997] C.L.Y. 3859. cf. the position in Scots Law: *Carmichael v Bearsden and District Rifle & Pistol Club*, 2000 S.L.T. 49.

84 *M'Cartan v Belfast Harbour Commissioners* [1911] 2 I.R. 143.

85 [1947] A.C. 1.

86 [1947] A.C. 1 at 14, per Lord Macmillan. See also *Chowdhary v Gillot* [1947] 2 All E.R. 541. cf. *Denham v Midland Employers Mutual Assurance Ltd* [1955] 2 Q.B. 437. Questions arising between the general and the temporary employers are governed by the contract between them.

87 [1947] A.C. 1 at 17, per Lord Porter.

88 [1947] A.C. 1 at 12, per Viscount Simon; at 14, per Lord Macmillan; at 17, per Lord Porter; at 20, per Lord Simonds; at 21–22, per Lord Uthwatt. And see *Karuppan Bhoomidas v Port of Singapore Authority* [1978] 1 W.L.R. 189; cf. *Cross v Redpath Dorman Long (Contracting) Ltd* [1978] I.C.R. 730.

a worker is a servant or an independent contractor. The limitations of this control test have already been mentioned.[89]

6-25 **Dual vicarious liability** In cases where the courts are simply unable to decide which of employer A or employer B should be held vicariously liable, they may impose dual vicarious liability as was done by the Court of Appeal in *Viasystems (Tyneside) Ltd v Thermal Transfer (Northern) Ltd*.[90] In that case, the question that arose was whether a fitter's mate supplied on a labour-only basis by employer A to temporary employer B would render A or B vicariously liable in respect of any torts committed by the mate. On the basis that both employers had sufficient control of the mate to prevent his negligence, the Court of Appeal held them both vicariously liable for the flooding he negligently caused.[91] The Supreme Court has since confirmed this dual vicarious liability device and made clear that the critical test is whether the employee "is so much a part of the work, business or organisation of both employers that it is just to make both employers answer for his negligence".[92]

6-26 The finding that an employee may be equally integrated into both employers' organisations has an important implication. This is that, since vicarious liability does not require fault to be shown on the part of an employer, it follows, as was pointed out in *Viasystems*, that dual vicarious liability will typically be shared equally between the two employers.[93]

6-27 **Agency workers** In *McMeechan v Secretary of State for Employment*,[94] the Court of Appeal held that a temporary worker can be an employee of an employment agency in respect of a particular assignment, even if he is not an employee under their general terms of engagement. Such a contract might even be implied from not only the documentary evidence, but also from what was said and done, at the time of the engagement.[95] On the other hand, a contract of employment with an agency will not exist in every case. In *Montgomery v Johnson Underwood*,[96] for instance, the employment agency only paid the worker on the basis of time sheets approved by the client company and the agency had also terminated the assignment at the request of the client company. The Court of Appeal held that, in these circumstances, the worker was not the employee of the agency. *McMeechan* was distinguished on the basis that, in that case, there were review/grievance procedures as between the agency and the worker.[97] Also, where the agency worker has acted contrary to the Equality Act 2010, a court will have to assess whether the worker in question acted as an employee or agent of the agency and whether the agency took all reasonable steps to prevent the worker from committing the act in question or anything of that description.[98]

---

89 See para.6-11.

90 [2005] EWCA Civ 1151; [2006] Q.B. 510; [2005] 4 All E.R. 1181.

91 [2005] EWCA Civ 1151 at [16].

92 *Various Claimants v Catholic Child Welfare Society* [2012] UKSC 56; [2013] 2 A.C. 1.

93 [2005] EWCA Civ 1151; [2006] Q.B. 510 at [52] and [85], per May and Rix LJJ.

94 [1997] I.R.L.R. 353.

95 *Franks v Reuters Ltd* [2003] EWCA Civ 417; [2003] I.C.R. 116.

96 [2001] I.R.L.R. 7 (EAT).

97 *Montgomery* was applied in *Dacas v Brook Street Bureau (UK) Ltd* [2004] EWCA Civ 217; [2004] I.C.R. 1437 where the agency had neither day-to-day control over the tasks performed by the worker nor any general obligation to find work for her.

98 See Equality Act 2010 s.109(4); *Mahood v Irish Centre Housing Ltd* [2011] Eq. L.R. 586 (EAT),

3. LIABILITY OF THE EMPLOYER

Liability of employer for torts of employee[99] Where the relationship of employer and employee exists, the employer is liable for the torts of the employee that are committed in the course of the employee's employment. The nature of the tort is immaterial and the employer is liable even where liability depends upon a specific state of mind and his own state of mind is innocent.[100] However, in order for the employer to be liable, it is not enough, merely, that the tort was committed by his employee. The wrong must have occurred in the course of the employee's employment, or have been closely connected with the acts the employee was engaged to perform.[101] Where the wrong does so occur, and the question of the employer's liability in contribution proceedings arises, the decision of the House of Lords in *Dubai Aluminium Co Ltd v Salaam*[102] becomes relevant. It was held there that the moral innocence of the employer is irrelevant; he should be treated as standing in the employee's shoes. The issue in that case was whether a firm of solicitors was vicariously liable for a partner's alleged dishonest assistance in a breach of trust under s.10 of the Partnership Act 1890. It was held that "wrongful acts" were not confined to common law torts and in fact extended to this equitable wrong. Applying *Lister v Hesley Hall Ltd*,[103] Lord Millett asserted that the best approach was to ask whether the wrongful conduct was so clearly connected with the acts that the partner was authorised to do that "for the purpose of the liability of the firm or the employer to third parties, the wrongful conduct may fairly and properly be regarded as done by the partner while acting in the ordinary course of the firm's business or the employee's employment".[104] 6-28

(a) Course of employment

Close connection test The question whether a wrongful act is within the course of employment is a mixed question of fact and law,[105] and no simple test is appropriate to cover all cases.[106] The hitherto most frequently adopted test was that 6-29

but applying the equivalent provision in the now repealed Race Relations Act 1976.

[99] The vicarious liability of employers for acts of sex or race discrimination under the relevant statutes would appear to be wider than under the common law: see *Jones v Tower Boot Co* [1997] I.C.R. 254. Furthermore, it was noted in *Livesey v Parker Merchanting Ltd* [2004] WL 229098 (EAT) that the House of Lords had clarified in *Lister v Hesley Hall Ltd* [2001] UKHL 22; [2002] 1 A.C. 215 that in considering the issue of vicarious liability under common law principles the court should not be drawn into a comparison with the approach taken to similar statutory concepts such as that contained in s.109 of the Equality Act 2010.

[100] So, e.g. in *Adams v Law Society* [2012] EWHC 980 (QB), Foskett J recognised the possibility of an institution being held vicariously liable in respect of an employee's misfeasance in a public office.

[101] *Dubai Aluminium Co Ltd v Salaam* [2002] UKHL 48; [2003] 2 A.C. 366; *Credit Lyonnais Nederland NV (now known as Generale Bank Nederland NV) v Export Credits Guarantee Department* [2000] 1 A.C. 486.

[102] *Dubai Aluminium Co Ltd v Salaam* [2002] UKHL 48; [2003] 2 A.C. 366.

[103] [2001] UKHL 22; [2002] 1 A.C. 215.

[104] Applied in *JJ Coughlan Ltd v Ruparelia* [2003] EWCA Civ 1057; [2004] P.N.L.R. 4.

[105] In *HSBC Bank Plc v 5th Avenue Partners Ltd* [2009] EWCA Civ 296; [2009] 1 C.L.C. 503, Etherton LJ held (at [56]) that, ultimately, the decision as to whether there is vicarious liability "is a conclusion of law, based on primary facts, rather than a simple question of fact".

[106] Not only are there the two major tests considered below but also a separate test applicable to cases of deceit. As Lord Keith explained in *Armagas Ltd v Mundogas SA* [1986] A.C. 717 at 780: "[d]ishonest conduct perpetrated with no intention of benefiting the employer but solely with that

propounded by Salmond, namely, that a wrongful act is deemed to be done in the course of the employment (at 763):

> "if it is either (1) a wrongful act authorised by the master, or (2) a wrongful and unauthorised mode of doing some act authorised by the master. It is clear that the master is responsible for acts actually authorised by him: for liability would exist in this case, even if the relation between the parties was merely one of agency, and not one of service at all. But a master, as opposed to the employer of an independent contractor, is liable even for acts which he has not authorised, provided they are so connected with acts which he has authorised that they may rightly be regarded as modes—although improper modes—of doing them."

Adopting this test, the courts historically sought to distinguish between those acts of an employee which constitute an improper mode of carrying out his duties and those acts which fall outside the scope of his employment. However, in the light of *Lister v Hesley Hall Ltd*,[107] that test is now inadequate in cases involving an employee's intentional wrongdoing. In *Lister*, the issue for the House of Lords was whether the employers of a warden of a school boarding house could be vicariously liable for the acts of sexual abuse perpetrated by that warden on boys in his care. Their Lordships held that the Salmond test was unhelpful in cases involving intentional wrongdoing, particularly where the employee sets out to benefit himself. Instead, they looked to the close connection between the acts in question and the nature of the employment. As Lord Steyn put it, the test for whether an employee has acted in the course of his employment was whether the tort was "so closely connected with his employment that it would be fair and just to hold the [employer] vicariously liable".[108] Applying this test to the facts of *Lister* it was held that, rather than the employment merely furnishing an opportunity to commit the sexual abuse, the connection between the employment and the torts was very strong. Lord Steyn observed: "the reality was that the County Council were responsible for the care of the vulnerable children and employed [the warden] … to carry out that duty on its behalf. And the sexual abuse took place while the employee was engaged in duties at the very time and place demanded by his employment."[109] Thus, he concluded, the sexual abuse was "inextricably interwoven with the carrying out by the warden of his duties".[110]

6-30 In similar vein, the Court of Appeal held in *Gravil v Carroll*[111] that a punch thrown by the defendant club's player in the mêlée that followed the final whistle

---

of procuring a personal gain or advantage to the employee is governed, in the field of vicarious liability, by a set of principles and a line of authority of peculiar application." In such cases the court must enquire whether the claimant was justified in relying on the false statement made by the employee. But note that no such question of reasonable reliance is to be posed in cases of negligent misstatement: *HSBC Bank Plc v 5th Avenue Partners Ltd* [2009] EWCA Civ 296; [2009] 1 C.L.C. 503.

107 [2001] UKHL 22; [2002] 1 A.C. 215.

108 [2001] UKHL 22; [2002] 1 A.C. 215 at [28]. Lord Millett also held, at [70], that the critical issue was "the closeness of the connection between the employee's duties and his wrongdoing". For a declaration that this will involve an evaluative judgment on the part of the first instance judge that the Court of Appeal should be loathe to disturb, see *Haringey LBC v FZO* [2020] EWCA Civ 180; [2020] E.L.R. 232 at [153].

109 [2001] UKHL 22; [2002] 1 A.C. 215 at [25].

110 [2001] UKHL 22; [2002] 1 A.C. 215 at [28]. See also *B v Nugent Care Society* [2009] EWCA Civ 827; [2010] 1 W.L.R. 516.

111 [2008] EWCA Civ 689; [2008] I.C.R. 1222.

in a professional rugby match could be regarded as a sufficiently ordinary incident of a rugby match to engage the defendant's vicarious liability.[112] Likewise, a managing director who assaulted an employee at a private drinking session that followed a work's party, triggered the vicarious liability of the company for whom both he and the assaulted employee worked, given that he had attended the post-party drinking session in his capacity as managing director.[113] Furthermore, there can plausibly be said to be a close enough connection between the rape of one member of the armed forces by another such member *even though the latter* perpetrated the rape after a social event and at a military base that was not his usual place of work. The fact that he received remuneration specifically connected to his being temporarily at that base, the fact that he was still subject to orders while there, and the fact that he would not have had access to the claimant but for his temporarily being stationed there all combined to suggest that the close connection test could well be satisfied.[114] Where, however, an employee returns to his place of work, while drunk, in order to assault a fellow employee who is working a night shift, there will not be a sufficiently close connection for vicarious liability to be imposed: this would be "an independent venture of [the employee's] own, separate and distinct from [his] employment as a Senior Health Assistant at a care home".[115] Equally, unlike teachers, there is not a strong enough connection between a person being engaged as a kitchen porter at a school and his assaulting a pupil.[116]

More broadly, *Lister* gives rise to considerable confusion. As Lord Nicholls accepted in the later case of *Dubai Aluminium Co Ltd v Salaam*, the close connection test tells us nothing about what type or degree of connection is necessary. As **6-31**
he put it: "[t]his lack of precision is inevitable, given the infinite range of circumstances where the issue arises ... Essentially the court makes an evaluative judgment in each case, having regard to all the circumstances and, importantly, having regard also to the assistance provided by previous court decisions."[117] But that said, the the Supreme Court did proffer some clarification of the circumstances in *Mohamud v Wm Morrison Supermarkets Ltd*.[118] In that case, the claimant went into the kiosk at a petrol station owned by the defendant supermarkets to see if it was possible to get something printed from a USB stick. The defendant's employee refused the request using racially offensive language. The claimant was ordered to leave the premises and the employee followed the claimant across the forecourt to his car before physically attacking him. The Supreme Court held that the defendant could be held liable on the basis of the close connection test. Two matters were declared to be relevant when deciding whether the close connection test has been

---

112 [2008] EWCA Civ 689; [2008] I.C.R. 1222 at [23].

113 *Bellman v Northampton Recruitment Ltd* [2018] EWCA Civ 2214; [2019] I.C.R. 459.

114 *TPKN v Ministry of Defence* [2019] EWHC 1488 (QB). (Note: the case did not definitively decide that the close connection test *was satisfied*. It was an appeal against a previous decision in which the claim had been struck out. It was held merely that the first court had erred in striking out that claim.)

115 *Weddall v Barchester Healthcare Ltd* [2012] EWCA Civ 25; [2012] I.R.L.R. 307 at [45], per Pill LJ; cf. *Wallbank v Wallbank Fox Designs Ltd* [2012] EWCA Civ 25; [2012] I.R.L.R. 307.

116 *EXE v Governors of the Royal Naval School* [2020] EWHC 596 (QB).

117 [2002] UKHL 48; [2003] 2 A.C. 366 at [26]. Despite this reference to the value of previous case law decided under the Salmond test, there is now a significant body of case law applying the close connection test. Whichever test is applied, the process of establishing vicarious liability is not one that is susceptible to being dealt with by summary process: *Cercato-Gouveia v Kyprianou* [2001] EWCA Civ 1887.

118 [2016] UKSC 11; [2016] A.C. 677.

satisfied. "The first question is what functions or 'field of activities' have been entrusted by the employer to the employee", or in other words, "what was the nature of his job"?[119] The second question is whether "there was a sufficient connection between the position in which he [the employee] was employed and his wrongful conduct to make it right for the employer to be held liable under the principle [of vicarious liability]".[120] This approach was emphatically preferred to the notion that there could realistically be a precise "measure [of] the closeness of connection, as it were, on a scale of 1 to 10".[121] In the instant case, their Lordships noted, first, that the employee's job included attending to customers and answering enquiries. They then held that what occurred was an unbroken chain of events in which the attack was intimately bound up with the employee's demand that the claimant should leave the defendant's premises. Accordingly, it was appropriate to identify a sufficiently close connection here between the employee's position and his tortious conduct.[122]

6-32 An example of the uncertainty at play can be observed in *Maga v Birmingham Roman Catholic Archdiocese Trustees*,[123] a case one step removed from the facts of *Lister v Hesley Hall*. In *Maga*, the claimant (who suffered from learning difficulties) brought a claim against a Roman Catholic archdiocese in respect of the sexual abuse he suffered as a child at the hands of a Roman Catholic priest employed by the archdiocese. The claimant was not himself a Catholic but he had met the priest in the course of the latter's youth work at such events as church discos which were open to all young people. He had also done various odd jobs for the priest, including some in the presbytery where part of the sexual abuse occurred. The Court of Appeal held the archdiocese vicariously liable even though the claimant was not a Catholic parishioner and had nothing especially to do with the Church. The priest's special responsibility for youth work, and the development of his relationship with the claimant via the work done for him by the claimant (which gave the priest an opportunity to be alone with him), both arose from his employment by the archdiocese as a priest. As such, the acts of sexual abuse were held to be sufficiently closely connected to his employment by the archdiocese and the latter could be held vicariously liable.

6-33 Another case in which all the circumstances of the case made it fair and just to conclude that the tort committed had a sufficiently close connection with the employment contract was *Brink's Global Services Inc v Igrox Ltd*.[124] There, an employee, engaged to fumigate containers prior to their being shipped, returned after work to one such container and stole several silver bars that were never recovered. Nonetheless, Moore-Bick LJ (at [30]) noted that by virtue of his job, the thief, Renwick, "was authorised to enter the secure compound where the container was stored and ... allowed to enter the container and thus have access to its contents". Accordingly, it was held that there was a "sufficiently close connection between Renwick's theft of the silver and the purpose of his employment to make it fair and just that Igrox [his employer] should be held vicariously liable".[125] In the

---

119 [2016] UKSC 11; [2016] A.C. 677 at [44], per Lord Toulson JSC (with whom all the other members of the court agreed).
120 [2016] UKSC 11; [2016] A.C. 677 at [45].
121 [2016] UKSC 11; [2016] A.C. 677 at [45].
122 [2016] UKSC 11; [2016] A.C. 677 at [47].
123 [2010] EWCA Civ 256; [2010] 1 W.L.R. 1441.
124 [2010] EWCA Civ 1207; [2011] I.R.L.R. 343.
125 [2010] EWCA Civ 1207; [2011] I.R.L.R. 343 at [30].

light of this decision, it is somewhat easier to see how certain earlier cases—such as *Morris v CW Martin and Sons Ltd*[126] and *Lloyd v Grace Smith & Co Ltd*[127] (which have widely been thought to turn upon the defendant's breach of a non–delegable duty of care)[128]—came to be presented in *Lister* as involving vicarious liability. On the other hand, the courts ought not to speculate about whether an employee is working late when he commits a tort on or near works premises after usual working hours have finished. The mere fact that someone is still wearing their work clothes is not conclusive evidence that they were still at work.[129] Indeed, as the Supreme Court stated via a single speech delivered by Lord Reed in *WM Morrison Supermarkets Plc v Various Claimants*, "the close connection test is not merely a question of timing or causation" (in the sense that, but for X having the particular job, he would never have been able to commit the tort in question).[130] Rather, it is to be "decided by orthodox common law reasoning … based on the application to the case before the court of the principle set out by Lord Nicholls at para 23 of *Dubai Aluminium*, in the light of the guidance to be derived from decided cases".[131] (In the passage referred to, Lord Nicholls opined that: "the wrongful conduct must be so closely connected with acts the … [tortfeasor] was authorised to do that, for the purpose of the liability of the firm or the employer to third parties … [it would be right to regard his or her conduct as done] … while acting in the ordinary course of the firm's business or the employee's employment".[132]) Accordingly, in the *Morrison's* case itself, it was held that the defendants were not vicariously liable for the misuse of private information by one of its employees (a data controller) who had used a personal computer at home to disseminate via the internet a great deal of personal information concerning many other fellow employees. Crucially, his "disclosure of the data on the internet did not form part of … [his] functions or field of activities … it was not an act which he was authorised to do".[133] The fact that, but for his job as a data controller he would not have obtained access to all the data was not conclusive of the question of a close connection. Rather, as Lord Reed was at pains to point out, it was clear that he: "was not engaged in furthering his employer's business when he committed the wrongdoing in question. On the contrary, he was pursuing a personal vendetta".[134] For this reason, his "wrongful conduct was not so closely connected with acts which he was authorised to do that … it can fairly and properly be regarded as done by him while acting in the ordinary course of his employment".[135]

Broad approach In similar claimant-friendly vein to *Lister* is the decision in *Kooragang Investment Pty Ltd v Richardson and Wrench Ltd*[136] where it was held that in establishing a particular employee's "course of employment", the court 6-34

[126] [1966] 1 Q.B. 716.
[127] [1912] A.C. 716.
[128] In the light of such confusion, Lord Nicholls deliberately left these two cases to one side in *Dubai Aluminium*: see [2002] UKHL 48; [2003] 2 A.C. 366 at [27]–[28].
[129] *Fletcher v Chancery Supplies Ltd* [2016] EWCA Civ 1112.
[130] [2020] UKSC 12; [2020] 2 W.L.R. 941 at [26].
[131] *WM Morrison Supermarkets plc v Various Claimants* [2020] UKSC 12; [2020] 2 W.L.R. 941 at [26].
[132] *Dubai Aluminium Co Ltd v Salaam* [2002] UKHL 48; [2003] 2 A.C. 366 at [23].
[133] *WM Morrison Supermarkets Plc v Various Claimants* [2020] UKSC 12; [2020] 2 W.L.R. 941 at [31].
[134] *WM Morrison Supermarkets Plc v Various Claimants* [2020] UKSC 12; [2020] 2 W.L.R. 941 at [47].
[135] *WM Morrison Supermarkets Plc v Various Claimants* [2020] UKSC 12; [2020] 2 W.L.R. 941 at [47].
[136] [1982] A.C. 462 at 471.

should not dissect the employee's tasks into component parts but should ask in a general sense: "what was the job at which he was engaged for his employer?"[137] Indeed, the idea that the courts should look more broadly to the question of whether what the employee was doing was in the furtherance of the employer's interests was made clear in the *Dubai Aluminium* case.[138] However, it is not vital that the employee's conduct be for the benefit of his employer. For even when the employee's conduct is not of benefit to the employer, this "does not mean that his conduct was not within the nature of his job viewed broadly and that there was not sufficient connection between the position in which he was employed and his wrongful conduct to make it right for [an employer] … to be held liable".[139]

6-35 **Relationship akin to employment** The most recent type of extension of the vicarious liability principle has occurred in cases in which the immediate tortfeasor can be said to be in a relationship with the defendant which is "akin to employment". So, for example, the relationship between a Roman Catholic priest and a bishop is regarded as close enough in character to an employer–employee relationship so as to make it fair and just that the diocese should be held vicariously liable in respect of acts of child abuse perpetrated by the priest.[140] The same is true of the relationship between lay brothers of the Catholic Church and the particular religious, unincorporated association to which they belong.[141] That the work arrangements between prisoners and the prison authorities for whom they perform remunerated tasks can also be held to fall within the present extension to the vicarious liability principle was confirmed by the Supreme Court in *Cox v Ministry of Justice*.[142] Their Lordships confirmed that, although the relationship in issue could be distinguished from a true contract of employment on the basis that it was not one voluntarily entered into, it was nonetheless sufficiently akin to an employment contract for vicarious liability to be imposed. As Lord Reed JSC explained, the fact that the prison service was obliged by statute to provide useful work for inmates was "not incompatible with the imposition of vicarious liability".[143] Equally, the present relationship was held not to be fundamentally different from an employer/employee relationship in so far as the prison service was a *not* a business whose primary purpose was to make a profit. It was enough, said Lord Reed JSC, that the tortfeasor was engaged in furthering the defendant's interests in a broad sense, regardless of whether those interests are commercial in nature.[144] There may even be vicarious liability imposed upon an organsiation for whom the wrongdoer works without pay, so long as the tasks that the worker undertakes are sufficiently a part of the organisation's business activities.[145] Where, however, an agent makes unauthorised use of a facility that has only been made available to him by virtue of his being the agent of the defendant, and he does so

---

137 See *Ilkiw v Samuels* [1963] W.L.R. 991 at 1004 (a case concerning a prohibition); *McPherson v Devon AHA* [1986] 7 C.L. 3.

138 [2002] UKHL 48; [2003] 2 A.C. 366.

139 *Group Seven Ltd v Notable Services LLP* [2019] EWCA Civ 614; [2019] 3 W.L.R. 1011 at [153].

140 *JGE v English Province of Our Lady of Charity* [2012] EWCA Civ 938; [2013] Q.B. 722.

141 *Various Claimants v Catholic Child Welfare Society* [2012] UKSC 56; [2013] 2 A.C. 1 at [47], per Lord Phillips JSC.

142 [2016] UKSC 10; [2016] A.C. 660.

143 [2016] UKSC 10; [2016] A.C. 660 at [38].

144 [2016] UKSC 10; [2016] A.C. 660 at [30].

145 *DSN v Blackpool Football Club Ltd* [2020] EWHC 595 (QB) at [159]–[162], per Griffiths J.

for entirely personal reasons, there will be no vicarious liability on the part of the defendant. In such circumstances, the agent may be said to have engaged in an enterprise that is recognisably distinct from that of the defendant and as such will not have met the test applied at the second stage of the vicarious liability enquiry[146] "[t]o describe … [the agent's] activity as in any sense an integral part of the business activities of … [the defendant] would be a complete distortion of the true position or facts".[147] Similarly, there was no vicarious liability for the negligence of a locum GP who caused harm to a patient by negligently advising her to stop taking conventional medicine for her pre-existing mental health problems and instead find healing through God.[148] The locum's indoctrination of the claimant was no part of the business activity of the surgery that engaged him. Whereas the surgery was in the business of providing medical assistance, the relevant activities of the doctor which caused the claimant's suffering were religious, not medical, in nature. Accordingly, it could not be said that, by engaging the locum, the owners of the surgery had created or enhanced the risk of the tort's commission; and the case could be distinguished from the activity of the warden in *Lister*. Whereas the warden in *Lister* had been endowed with particular pastoral duties towards the children he abused (the abuse being closely connected with his exercise of those pastoral duties), the locum was not engaged to evangelise or indoctrinate anyone.[149]

In relation to the third aspect of the appeal in *Cox*—premised on what had been said in a previous case[150] about vicarious liability only ever being imposed where it is fair, just and reasonable to do so—their Lordships were unpersuaded by the Ministry's contention that it would not be fair, just and reasonable to impose vicarious liability in the prison context. They took the view that the prospect of fraudulent claims arising out of alleged torts committed by prisoners against one another was a risk of entirely quotidian proportions against which the courts are sufficiently experienced in guarding.[151] There was, therefore, no especial risk that the recognition of vicarious liability in this context would lead to an undesirable drain on scarce public resources. In any event, their Lordships were clear that it is plainly fair, just and reasonable to hold the prison service "liable to compensate a victim of negligence … whether the negligent member of the team is a civilian or a prisoner".[152] More generally, the question of whether it is fair, just and reasonable to impose vicarious liability in a situation where the relationship in issue is alleged to be one that is "akin to an employment contract", is to be judged in the light of the five policy factors identified by Lord Phillips in the *Christian Brothers* case.[153] But, crucially, these five factors do not determine the question of whether the relationship can be regarded as one that is "akin to an employment contract". That is a prior question, governed by "the detailed features of the relationship".[154] The **6-36**

[146] *Frederick v Positive Solutions (Financial Services) Ltd* [2018] EWCA Civ 431. On the first and second stages of the vicarious liability enquiry, see para.6-01.

[147] [2018] EWCA Civ 431 at [67].

[148] *Brayshaw v Partners of Apsley Surgery* [2018] EWHC 3286 (QB); [2019] 2 All E.R. 997.

[149] [2018] EWHC 3286 (QB); [2019] 2 All E.R. 997 at [68].

[150] *Various Claimants v Catholic Child Welfare Society* [2012] UKSC 56; [2013] 2 A.C. 1.

[151] [2016] UKSC 10; [2016] A.C. 660 at [44].

[152] [2016] UKSC 10; [2016] A.C. 660 at [42]. See also *Armes v Nottinghamshire County Council* [2017] UKSC 60; [2018] A.C. 355, holding a local authority vicariously liable for abuse of children by foster parents, the authority having placed the children with the foster parents.

[153] For details, see para.6-01.

[154] *Barclays Bank Plc v Various Claimants* [2020] UKSC 13; [2020] 2 W.L.R. 960 at [18], per Lady

five policy factors illuminate only the subsequent matter of whether it is fair to impose vicarious liability in the context of a relationship that has already been judged to be "akin to an employment contract".

6-37 **Houseparents** While it might be possible to impose vicarious liability for sexual abuse perpetrated by a "houseparent" working in a children's home (using the *Lister* close connection test), no such liability can be imposed in relation to sexual abuse perpetrated by the houseparent's son in the absence of his discharging any of the functions actually expected of his parents.[155] Where he does not do this, there will be nothing to suggest that his relationship to the children's home is one that is akin to employment.

(b) Examples of the modern broad approach

6-38 **Prohibited conduct** The broad approach to the imposition of vicarious liability outlined in paras 6-34 to 6-37, is particularly apparent in cases where the employer has given the employee instructions which prohibit certain acts. Whether those instructions will prevent the acts in question from being within the course of the employee's employment depends upon whether they merely prohibit a particular mode of carrying out the employment, or whether they restrict the class of acts which the employee is employed to perform. In *CPR v Lockhart*,[156] an employee was authorised to use his own car on outside jobs, provided it was covered by insurance. The Privy Council held that his employers, despite this stipulation, were liable for the damage he caused when he drove an uninsured car for the purposes of his work. In *LCC v Cattermoles (Garages) Ltd*,[157] the duties of a garage hand, forbidden to drive vehicles, did involve moving vehicles by manhandling. His employers were held liable for damage caused by his negligence while driving such a vehicle when he had been instructed to move it so as to stop it obstructing access to the defendants' petrol pumps.

6-39 An especially tricky case in relation to prohibitions on certain forms of conduct is *Gravil v Carroll*.[158] In that case, a professional rugby player's contract of employment specifically prohibited him from physically assaulting an opponent. It also provided, however, that the club could be vicariously liable for the "acts or omissions of the player during the employment". Taking the two provisions together, the Court of Appeal concluded that the prohibition on assaulting opponents did not mean that the punch that was thrown by one of the defendant's players was necessarily outside the player's contract of employment. Rather, according to their Lordships, since "the contract expressly contemplates that the club may be vicariously liable for the acts of the player" this could "only be on the basis that the act might be committed in the course of the employment".[159]

6-40 Cases where drivers had been forbidden to give lifts to unauthorised persons have

Hale.

155 *EL v Children's Society* [2012] EWHC 365 (QB). See also *XVW v Gravesend Grammar School for Girls* [2012] EWHC 575; [2012] E.L.R. 417.

156 [1942] A.C. 591. See also *Gregory v Piper* (1829) 9 B. & C. 591; *Limpus v London General Omnibus Co* (1862) 1 H. & C. 862; *Performing Right Society v Mitchell Booker* [1924] 1 K.B. 762.

157 [1953] 1 W.L.R. 97; *Spencer v Curtis Bros* (1962) 102 S.J. 390; *Ilkiw v Samuels* [1963] W.L.R. 991.

158 [2008] EWCA Civ 689; [2008] I.C.R. 1222.

159 [2008] EWCA Civ 689; [2008] I.C.R. 1222 at [24].

also proved problematic.[160] In *Twine v Bean's Express*,[161] the Court of Appeal held that the employer was not liable to a hitchhiker who had been given a lift by their employee, contrary to express prohibition. The best explanation of this decision must be that giving the lift was "an act of a class which [the driver] was not employed to perform at all".[162] However, in *Rose v Plenty*,[163] a milkman who deliberately defied an order not to employ children to help on the rounds did not go outside the sphere of his employment in allowing the 13-year-old claimant to assist him. The milkman was still performing the duties for which he was employed, albeit breaching an instruction not to take on any unauthorised passengers. He merely continued his job of delivering milk in an unauthorised manner. Had he taken the boy up on his float for a lift to school the result would have been quite different.[164] Of course, a driver, although acting outside the course of his employment in giving a prohibited lift, could still be acting within the course of his employment in relation to, for example, another road user harmed through his negligence.

So it can be seen that the effect of any prohibition placed by the employer on his servants will depend on analysis of the nature of the servant's duties and the prohibition, and what actual breach of the prohibition is committed by the servant. The key question is always whether the employee's conduct was outside the range of duties which he or she was employed to undertake. **6-41**

Surrounding circumstances To determine whether a wrongful act is done by an employee in the course of his employment, all the surrounding circumstances must be taken into account and not merely the particular act that leads to the damage. Thus in *Century Insurance Co v Northern Ireland Road Transport Board*,[165] the driver of a petrol tanker was delivering petrol to a garage, and while the petrol was flowing from his vehicle into an underground tank he lit a cigarette, carelessly throwing away the burning match. The ensuing explosion caused considerable damage. Although the act of lighting a cigarette was in itself unconnected with the driver's employment, considered in conjunction with the delivery of petrol it was seen to amount to negligence in the course of his employment. **6-42**

In *Ilkiw v Samuels*,[166] a lorry driver, despite being forbidden to do so, allowed a workman to move his lorry a short distance inside a warehouse without having made any inquiry as to the workman's competence as a driver. The workman was quite incompetent and negligently caused an injury to the claimant. The defendants, who were the employers of the lorry driver but not of the workman, were held liable on the ground that the driver had been negligent in allowing the workman to drive given that, notwithstanding the prohibition, the driver was employed not only to drive but also to be in charge of the lorry in all circumstances while on duty.[167] **6-43**

160 See *Twine v Bean's Express* (1946) 175 L.T. 131 at 132; cf. *Young v Edward Box & Co* [1951] 1 T.L.R. 789.
161 (1946) 52 T.L.R. 458.
162 (1946) 52 T.L.R. 458 at 459.
163 [1976] 1 W.L.R. 141 at 150.
164 Herein lies an important distinction between *Rose v Plenty* and *Twine v Bean's Express*.
165 [1942] A.C. 509.
166 [1963] 1 W.L.R. 991; *Ricketts v Thomas Tilling Ltd* [1915] 1 K.B. 644. See also *Marsh v Moores* [1949] 2 K.B. 208.
167 [1963] 1 W.L.R. 991 at 998, per Wilmer LJ; at 1002, per Danckwerts LJ. cf. the different reasoning of Diplock LJ at 1003 and 1006.

In *Kay v ITW Ltd*,[168] the employee was a fork-lift truck driver who was also authorised to drive a small van. On finding a five-ton lorry (not belonging to his employer) blocking the entrance to the warehouse to which he needed to gain access, he moved the lorry. The Court of Appeal held that he had acted in the course of his employment since he was seeking to remove an obstruction which prevented him from fulfilling his task of returning the fork-lift truck. But the case comes close to the dividing line between, on the one hand, acts which constitute a wrong (or even a stupid) mode of doing an authorised act and, on the other, acts which involve doing something which the employee has no business at all to be doing. It is certainly not the law that the employer is liable whenever the wrongful act was done by the employee in the belief that it would advance his employer's business.[169] On the other hand, "the line should be drawn fairly high in favour of the innocent sufferer injured by the act of somebody who was employed by the defendant employer and who was seeking to further that employer's interests".[170]

6-44 **Acts incidental to the employment** An act done by an employee will not necessarily be excluded from the course of the employee's employment merely because it is not an act which the employee is actually employed to perform. Provided that it is reasonably incidental to the employment, the employer will remain responsible.[171] Employees arriving at their place of work to start work will generally be regarded as within their course of employment from when they arrive until they leave providing they neither arrive unreasonably early nor leave unreasonably late.[172] Also, an employee on his way between his home and his place of work (or vice versa) will not ordinarily be in the course of employment.[173] However, where the only feasible means of transport for the claimant to reach his place of employment was to accept a lift in a Land Rover sent by the employing company to collect him, the claimant was held to be in the course of his employment during that journey.[174] And when an employee is required as part of his duties to drive a colleague around the country in order for them to do their jobs as salesmen, it is an act reasonably incidental to the employment of the driver that he will take his colleague home.[175]

6-45 **Place of work** On occasion, the particular circumstances may be so closely connected with the performance of the job that the travel may be classified as reasonably incidental to the employment. So, an employee travelling between two places of work will normally be acting within the course of his employment. In *Smith v*

---

168 [1968] 1 Q.B. 140.

169 [1968] 1 Q.B. 140 at 154, per Sellers LJ. But see *Rose v Plenty* [1976] 1 W.L.R. 141, per Lord Denning MR.

170 *Kay v ITW Ltd* [1968] 1 Q.B. 140 at 156. See also *Stone v Taffe* [1974] 1 W.L.R. 1575.

171 *Whatman v Pearson* (1868) L.R. 3 C. & P. 422; *Ruddiman v Smith* (1889) 60 L.T. 708; *Harvey v RG O'Dell, Galway (Third Party)* [1958] 2 Q.B. 78; cf. *Crook v Derbyshire Stone* [1956] 1 W.L.R. 432; *Hilton v Thomas Burton (Rhodes)* [1961] 1 W.L.R. 705. And see *Nelson v Raphael* [1979] R.T.R. 437.

172 *Compton v McClure* [1975] I.C.R. 378; *R. v National Insurance Comp Ex p. East* [1976] I.C.R. 206.

173 See *Vandyke v Fender* [1970] 2 Q.B. 292; cf. *Smith v Stages* [1989] A.C. 928; *Buckley's Stores Ltd v National Employers Mutual General Insurance Association Ltd* [1978] Ir. R. 351.

174 *Paterson v Costain Press (Overseas)* [1979] 2 Lloyd's Rep. 204.

175 *Elleanor v Cavendish Woodhouse Ltd and Comerford* [1973] 1 Lloyd's Rep. 313; cf. *R. v Industrial Benefits Tribunal Ex p. Fieldhouse* (1974) 17 K.I.R. 63 at 65.

Stages,[176] an employee who had been working away from his normal place of employment negligently caused an accident while driving home in his own car. He had been travelling home in order that he could start work at his ordinary place of employment later in the week. The employer knew he was using his own car, and the travelling day was paid as a working day so that the employers were entitled to direct how the employee should act during that day. The employer was held vicariously liable. Again, should the employment entail travelling between bases, the employee may be acting within the course of his employment if he actually travels directly to and from his home to such bases rather than going via his main base.[177] By contrast, an employer was held not liable when his employee was guilty of negligence while cycling home to lunch even though he had had permission to use the bicycle for that purpose.[178] Nor, in a rather different context, was a policeman representing his police force in a football match within the scope of his employment.[179] But where an off-duty soldier is injured in dangerous recreational activity that has negligently been sanctioned by a superior officer, that officer—by virtue of the fact that hierarchy and military discipline continue to be important even during periods of recreation—will trigger the vicarious liability of the Ministry of Defence.[180]

Deviations from employer's business Deviations from the task to be performed, for the employee's own purposes, may still be within the course of employment. It is a question of degree: at some point the deviation may be such that it can be regarded as a separate activity and the prospect of vicarious liability will cease to exist. A totally unauthorised journey by a driver, on business of his own, will take him out of the course of his employment.[181] Yet, as the court in *Storey v Ashton*[182] made clear, the extent—both spatial and temporal—of the detour is relevant. So the court contrasted "merely going a roundabout way home" with starting "an entirely new journey". The purpose of the deviation will also be important. In *A & W Hemphill Ltd v Williams*,[183] the employer was held vicariously liable by the House of Lords even though their employee driver had substantially deviated from his authorised route. As the deviation was at the request of the defendant's passengers, the court held that the driver was not on a "frolic of his own"[184] and was still undertaking the employer's business, namely the transport of passengers. 6-46

Employee acting on his own initiative An employee acting on his own initiative (rather than his employer's) may be acting within the course of his employment. This will be the case where the employer either expressly or by implication has 6-47

176 [1989] A.C. 928. cf. *Nottingham v Aldridge* [1971] 2 Q.B. 739 (where the occupants of the car were travelling in unpaid time and were not on duty but merely returning to duty after a weekend off).

177 *Nancollas v Insurance Officer* [1985] 1 All E.R. 833. See [1985] 1 All E.R. 833 at 840 for relevant factors, highlighted by Sir John Donaldson MR.

178 *Highbid v Hammett* (1932) 49 T.L.R. 104. However, with regard to travelling during working hours, cf. *Harvey v O'Dell* [1958] 2 Q.B. 78; *Smith v Stages* [1989] A.C. 928 at 951, per Lord Lowry (suggesting that this case "primarily exemplifies incidental deviation or interruption").

179 *R. v National Insurance Comp Ex p. Michael* [1977] 1 W.L.R. 109.

180 *Ministry of Defence v Radclyffe* [2009] EWCA Civ 635.

181 *Mitchell v Crassweller* (1853) 13 C.B. 237.

182 *Storey v Ashton* (1869) L.R. 4 Q.B. 476 at 480; *Whatman v Pearson* (1868) L.R. 3 C. & P. 422; *A & W Hemphill Ltd v Williams* [1966] 2 Lloyd's Rep. 101.

183 [1966] 2 Lloyd's Rep. 101.

184 *Joel v Morison* (1834) 6 C. & P. 501 at 503.

given the employee a discretion which he must exercise in the course of his employment. The employer will be liable for a wrongful exercise of such discretion. So, where D2 has given D1 actual authority to negotiate with a claimant on his behalf, and has expressly authorised D1 to do whatever he considers necessary to secure a loan from the claimant, D2 will be vicariously liable for any actionable misrepresentation made by D1 to the claimant which results in loss to the latter.[185] All employees are deemed to have a discretion to act for the protection of the employer's property. Thus in *Poland v Parr*,[186] an off-duty employee gave a boy a cuff on the neck when he thought the boy was stealing sugar from his employer's cart. The boy fell and injured his leg and the employers were held liable, even though the employee was not employed to look after the sugar. The act complained of must, however, be such that it is reasonably necessary for the protection of the employer's property, or at least it must be such that it would have been reasonably necessary had the circumstances in fact been as the employee supposed them to be. An employee has no discretion in the course of his employment to punish or to give into custody one whom he supposes to have made an attempt upon his employer's property and so, if he acts after all danger to the property is over, or where no danger could be supposed to exist, his act will not be done in the course of his employment.[187]

6-48 The facts of a particular case may show that in the circumstances the employee has been vested with a discretion to act in other ways. If this is so, the honest exercise of the discretion will be within the course of employment.[188] Thus, for example, in *Smith v North Metropolitan Tramways Co*,[189] the claimant was a passenger in a crowded tram and said to the conductor that he would pay his fare as soon as he could get his hand in his pocket, whereupon the conductor pushed him off the tram so that he fell and suffered injury. It was held that the defendants were liable.[190]

6-49 In these cases, as in the cases concerned with the protection of property, the employer will not be liable unless the exigency is in fact such—or at least is reasonably supposed by the employee to be such—as would justify the employee in exercising his discretion.[191] Furthermore, it must be established in each case that the employer has, expressly or impliedly, given his employee a discretion which the employee purports to exercise. This is a question of fact,[192] but it seems that an employee cannot have, in the course of his employment, a discretion to do acts of

---

[185] *Khakshouri v Jimenez* [2017] EWHC 3392 (QB) at [124]–[125], per Green J.

[186] *Poland v Parr* [1927] 1 K.B. 366; cf. *Rees v Thomas* [1899] 1 Q.B. 1015; *Lowe v Pearson* [1899] 1 Q.B. 261; *Jones v Tarr* [1926] 1 K.B. 25 (cases decided under the Workmen's Compensation Acts).

[187] See, e.g. *Allen v London and SW Ry* (1870) L.R. 6 Q.B. 65 at 72, per Lush J; *Hanson v Walker* [1901] 1 K.B. 390.

[188] The point was made by Willes J in *Bayley v MS & L Ry* (1873) L.R. 7 C. & P. 415 at 420. See also *Ewbank v Nutting* (1849) 7 C.B. 797; *Giles v Taff Vale Ry* (1853) 2 E. & B. 822; *Goff v Great Northern Ry* (1861) 3 El. & El. 673; *Moore v Metropolitan Ry* (1872) L.R. 7 Q.B. 36; *Owners of Apollo v Port Talbot Co* [1891] A.C. 499; *Lowe v Great Northern Ry* (1893) 62 L.J.Q.B. 524; *Lambert v Great Eastern Ry* [1909] 2 K.B. 776.

[189] (1891) 55 J.P. 630. cf. *Keppel Bus Co Ltd v Sa'ad bin Ahmad* [1974] 1 W.L.R. 1082.

[190] See also *Furlong v S London Tramways* (1884) C. & E. 316; *Whittaker v LCC* [1915] 2 K.B. 676; *Percy v Glasgow Corp* [1922] 2 A.C. 299.

[191] *Walker v SE Ry* (1870) L.R. 5 C. & P. 640; *Gwilliam v Twist* [1895] 2 Q.B. 84. cf. *Harris v Fiat Motors* (1907) 23 T.L.R. 504.

[192] The time, place and opportunity of consulting the master before acting are material circumstances to be considered: *Bank of New South Wales v Owston* (1879) 4 App. Cas. 270 at 289.

a class which the employer himself could not lawfully do.[193] The employer is liable for the wrongful exercise by his employee of a discretion vested in the employee, but he is not liable where no discretion exists.[194] If tasks have been delegated to an employee or agent in very general terms, then that delegation necessarily implies the grant of a discretion to determine how the tasks may best be completed.[195]

Assault by employee Many of thc cases dealt with in the previous paragraph were cases of assault and, in cases in which the interests of the employer are the motivation for such assaults, the correct approach is to consider the discretion, if any, which is vested in the employee. In other cases, such as those involving acts of vengeance, spite or sexual exploitation, it is submitted that the more likely approach will now be to use the "close connection test" promulgated in *Lister v Hesley Hall Ltd*.[196] **6-50**

An odd case in this context, however, is *Weir v Bettison (sued as Chief Constable of Merseyside)*.[197] There, an off-duty policeman had borrowed a marked police van without permission in order to help his girlfriend move home. During the course of unloading the van, he had engaged in an argument with the claimant whom he alleged had been rifling through his girlfriend's belongings which were in the process of being transferred to her flat. The policeman manhandled the claimant into the van and there assaulted him. He had indicated to the claimant that he was a police officer and told him that he was proposing to take him to the police station. It was held that the policeman had been acting in his capacity as a constable. During the assault he had been apparently exercising his authority as a constable and the force used was not so excessive as to take him beyond the performance of his functions as a police officer. As such, the Chief Constable was held vicariously liable under s.88(1) of the Police Act 1996. **6-51**

Damage to goods bailed to the employer An employer will be liable if goods bailed to him are negligently damaged by her employee, acting in the course of his employment. The employer may still be liable even though the employee, when he damaged the goods, was, as in *Aitchison v Page Motors Ltd*, using them for private purposes.[198] However, it is submitted that the better understanding of cases of this kind—such as *Morris v CW Martin & Sons Ltd*[199]—is that the employee's tort has put the employer in breach of a non-delegable duty of care (even though in *Lister v Hesley Hall Ltd* Lord Steyn was of the view that there was no such special rule in bailment cases[200]). **6-52**

In one case, the defendant's employee had been sent simply to collect the claimant's car from the repairers, but he used it for his own purposes. When an accident occurred in which the car was destroyed, it was held that the employee had **6-53**

---

[193] See *Charleston v London Tramways Co* (1888) 4 T.L.R. 629.

[194] *Forsyth v Manchester Corp* (1913) 107 L.T. 600. See also *Houghton v Pilkington* [1912] 3 K.B. 308.

[195] *Nelson v Raphael* [1979] R.T.R. 437.

[196] [2001] UKHL 22; [2002] 1 A.C. 215 at [28], per Lord Millett. See para.6-29.

[197] [2003] EWCA Civ 111; [2003] I.C.R. 708.

[198] (1935) 154 L.T. 128. See also the moot case discussed by Lord Denning MR in *Morris v CW Martin & Sons Ltd* [1966] 1 Q.B. 716 at 724–725.

[199] [1966] 1 Q.B. 716.

[200] [2001] UKHL 22; [2002] 1 A.C. 215 at [22].

been negligent within the course of his employment.[201] But if a passer-by had been injured in the accident, it is likely that the court would have found him to have been on a "frolic of his own". Thus an employee may be acting within the course of his employment qua one person, and outside it qua another. In *Morris v CW Martin & Sons Ltd*,[202] Lord Denning MR expressed the view that this sort of result was confusing and should be got rid of. He thought that the only way to do this was by reference to the duty imposed by the law upon the employer personally. The defendants in a case such as *Aitchison* would owe the owner of the car the non-delegable duty of a bailee for reward. The bailee would be put in breach of this duty by the negligence of an employee to whom custody of the car had been entrusted; but the employer would owe no such duty to a passer-by injured in the accident and for this reason would not be liable to him. This is, no doubt, an acceptable explanation of the result in *Aitchison*. For it is clear that, in some cases, a defendant's duty may be broken through the wrongful act of another, whether employee or agent.[203]

6-54 **Employee's theft** It was formerly thought that an employer could not be liable for a theft committed by his employee on the ground that the act of stealing must necessarily be an act outside the course of his employment.[204] However, theft by an employee, to whom the goods had been entrusted, has been interpreted to be an improper mode of performing what he was employed to do. This is the explanation of the decision of the Court of Appeal in *Morris v CW Martin & Sons Ltd*[205] favoured by their Lordships in *Lister v Hesley Hall*. In *Morris*, the employee's theft of the claimant's fur coat amounted to the dishonest performance of that which he had been employed to do. It is submitted that, mindful of the interpretation of *Morris* adopted in *Lister v Hesley Hall*, in cases of theft by an employee the first sensible question to ask is whether or not the stolen goods had been put in the custody of the employee by his employer. If they had, then the theft will have been committed by the employee in the course of his employment and, unless there is something in the contract of bailment to the contrary,[206] the employer will be vicariously liable.[207] If they were not so entrusted to the employee, then the employer will not be vicariously liable for the theft, though he may be liable for a breach of a personal duty of care owed to the bailor. The decision of the Court of Appeal in *Morris v CW Martin & Sons Ltd* was approved by the Privy Council in *Port Swettenham Authority v TW Wu & Co*.[208] Note, however, that in such cases the goods concerned must in some way have been entrusted to the employee for the employer to be liable. The

201 *Aitchison v Page Motors Ltd* (1935) 154 L.T. 128.

202 [1966] 1 Q.B. 716 at 725.

203 See para.6-65 et seq.

204 *Cheshire v Bailey* [1905] 1 K.B. 237. cf. *Abraham v Bullock* (1902) 86 L.T. 796.

205 [1966] 1 Q.B. 716; *Mendelssohn v Normand Ltd* [1970] 1 Q.B. 177.

206 In *John Carter (Fine Worsteds) Ltd v Hanson Haulage (Leeds) Ltd* [1965] 2 Q.B. 495 it seems to have been accepted that a bailee's liability for theft by his servant, if any, would be vicarious: [1965] 2 Q.B. 495 at 524–525, per Davies LJ; at 533, per Russell LJ. cf. *Mendelssohn v Normand Ltd* [1970] 1 Q.B. 177.

207 *Giblin v McMullen* (1868) L.R. 2 P.C. 317, a case of gratuitous bailment, may prove something of a stumbling block to this view, but in that case no argument that the bailee was vicariously liable was presented. And *Giblin v McMullen* was gravely doubted as good authority in *Port Swettenham Authority v TW Wu & Co* [1979] A.C. 580.

208 [1979] A.C. 580.

mere fact that the employment provided the opportunity for the theft will not be sufficient.[209]

Fraud of employee In *Armagas Ltd v Mundogas (The Ocean Frost)*[210] the House of Lords endorsed a line of authority indicating that vicarious liability for fraud is governed by "a set of principles and a line of authority of peculiar application" so that "it is unnecessary to consider the development of the basis of vicarious liability in relation to torts such as negligence or trespass, which have followed a somewhat different line".[211] And this remains the case notwithstanding the considerable development this area of the law has otherwise undergone in recent years.[212] The principal will still be vicariously liable "if, but only if, the deceitful conduct of the agent was within his or her actual or ostensible authority".[213] Of its very nature, fraud involves the deception of the victim and by that deception his persuasion to part with his property or do some other act to his own detriment and to the benefit of the person practising the fraud. For this reason the decision whether an employee committed fraud in the course of his employment can only be made after the authority, actual or ostensible, with which the employee is clothed has been ascertained. Thus in *Uxbridge Permanent Benefit Building Society v Pickard*,[214] a case of fraud committed by a solicitor's clerk, counsel for the defendant solicitor argued that the case should be treated as analogous to those cases in which an employee had been held to be on a "frolic of his own", but the argument was rejected.[215] The liability of an employer for fraud committed by his employee, though part of the law of employer and employee, has, in fact, a close connection with the law of principal and agent in contract, for there, too, the liability of the principal depends upon the authority, actual or ostensible, with which the agent is clothed. 6-55

An especially thorny problem in relation to fraud centres on the question of whether a company can be held vicariously liable for the fraudulent acts committed by a director. The law in this area has undergone a process of refinement in recent years and the leading case is now *Bilta (UK) Ltd (in liquidation) v Nazir*.[216] The first thing that the Supreme Court did in that case was to confine the previous leading authority—*Stone & Rolls Ltd v Moore Stephens*[217]—to its own particular facts. Lords Toulson and Hodge JJSC proffered a joint speech declaring, "*Stone & Rolls* should be regarded as a case which has no majority ratio decidendi. It stands as authority for the point which it decided, namely that on the facts of that case no claim lay against the auditors, but nothing more."[218] Having cleared the ground for a fresh approach in this context, their Lordships then went on to state that the ques- 6-56

209 See *Heasmans (A Firm) v Clarity Cleaning Co Ltd* [1987] I.C.R. 949; *Irving v Post Office* [1987] I.R.L.R. 289.

210 [1986] A.C. 717.

211 [1986] A.C. 717 at 780.

212 See para.6-01.

213 *Winter v Hockley Mint Ltd* [2018] EWCA Civ 2480; [2019] 1 W.L.R. 1617 at [48].

214 [1939] 2 K.B. 248.

215 [1939] 2 K.B. 248 at 254.

216 [2015] UKSC 23; [2016] A.C. 1.

217 [2009] UKHL 39; [2009] 1 A.C. 1391.

218 [2015] UKSC 23; [2016] A.C. 1 at [154]. The Supreme Court not only reiterated but also amplified the dissatisfaction with *Stone & Rolls* expressed in *Bilta* such that, now, it seems reasonable to regard the former as having been effectively overruled. It was certainly said that "*Stone & Rolls* can finally be laid to rest": [2019] UKSC 50; [2019] 3 W.L.R. 997 at [34]. See further para.9-16.

tion of whether the knowledge of a director could be attributed to a company was a context-dependent one. They identified three different types of case in which the question of attribution of knowledge may occur:

> "It is helpful in the civil sphere, to consider the attribution of knowledge to a company in three different contexts, namely (i) when a third party is pursuing a claim against the company arising from the misconduct of a director, employee or agent, (ii) when the company is pursuing a claim against a director or an employee for breach of duty or breach of contract, and (iii) when the company is pursuing a claim against a third party."[219]

Their Lordships then explained that attribution of the acts and the state of a director's mind would not necessarily occur. In the first type of case, they said, the question of attribution will depend on whether the company's liability is direct or merely vicarious. If the liability is direct, the wrongful conduct of the director can be attributed to the company under the normal rules of agency. If, however, the liability of the company is merely vicarious, the company is held responsible for the agent's acts but is not itself deemed to be a wrongdoer. There is no attribution of a director's acts and state of mind. Accordingly, in a case where the company has successfully been sued by a victim of a director's fraud, and the company subsequently seeks to sue a third party which was negligent in not detecting and preventing that fraud, there will not generally be a basis for invoking the illegality defence against the company attempting thereby to recoup the damages it had to pay the fraud victim. The exception that was made in *Stone & Rolls* of one-man-company cases—where the director was regarded as inseparable from the company of which he was the directing mind and will—has now been rejected in *Singularis Holdings Ltd (In Liquidation) v Daiwa Capital Markets Europe Ltd*. In that case, the Supreme Court, wholeheartedly endorsed the view of the judge at first instance that, in such cases, there is no principle of law that, where the company is suing a third party in tort, the fraudulent conduct of the sole director will be attributed automatically to the company.[220]

6-57 In the second type of case, where the company is seeking to sue a director because he has, in breach of a fiduciary duty owed to the company, defrauded that company, the illegality defence will not normally be available. The reason given in *Bilta* was that, if the defence were generally available in such circumstances, the director's duty not to defraud the company would be an empty or worthless one. As Toulson and Hodge JJSC put it, it would be "absurd to attribute knowledge to the company and so defeat its claim"[221] every time a director defrauded the company. On the other hand, their Lordships did not lay down a blanket rule in this respect. The most important exception they alluded to involved a company which specifically ratifies a director's breach of duty. In such circumstances, they held, it would in fact be appropriate to attribute the director's acts and knowledge to the company so as to support the illegality defence.[222]

6-58 In the third type of case—i.e. where a company claims against a third party—the question of whether a director's act or state of mind can be attributed to the company will depend on the nature of the claim. If the claim is against an insur-

[219] [2015] UKSC 23; [2016] A.C. 1 at [204].
[220] [2019] UKSC 50; [2019] 3 W.L.R. 997 at [34].
[221] [2015] UKSC 23; [2016] A.C. 1 at [206]. Lord Mance JSC offered a very similar analysis in this regard: [2015] UKSC 23; [2016] A.C. 1 at [42].
[222] [2015] UKSC 23; [2016] A.C. 1 at [206].

ance company, then the usual rules of attribution found in the law of agency will apply so as to give rise to the defence. Where, however, the claim is against a third party who has acted as an accessory to a director's breach of duty, no such attribution will be available since, "there is no good policy reason to attribute to the company the act or the state of mind of the director who was in breach of his fiduciary duty".[223] Although his reasoning was not quite identical, Lord Mance JSC also stressed the fact that the availability of the illegality defence was context-dependent where directorial fraud was in issue.[224] Lord Neuberger PSC (with whom Lords Clarke and Carnwath JJSC concurred) not only expressed his agreement with Lord Mance's analysis in this respect, but also said that, "whether or not it is appropriate to attribute an action by, or a state of mind of, a company director or agent to the company ... must depend on the nature and factual context of the claim in question".[225] Although some matters concerning the illegality defence remain shrouded in doubt following *Bilta*, it cannot now be doubted that its availability must be handled very differently in the context of: (1) claims brought by a company against its own directors for having defrauded the company, and (2) claims in which the company is suing a third party.

The decision in *Barwick v English Joint Stock Bank*[226] first established the possibility of vicarious liability for fraud committed by employees who are not directors of the company, and in *Lloyd v Grace, Smith & Co*[227] a solicitor was held liable for the fraud of his managing clerk who induced a client to transfer property to him and then dishonestly disposed of the property for his own benefit. The case was decided on the ground that the claimant was invited by the firm of solicitors to deal with their managing clerk, who was in fact held out as authorised to transact the claimant's business on behalf of the firm. In such cases, the court is not entitled to expect a fraud victim to make enquiries about the legitimacy of a transaction even if there are reasonable grounds for suspicion. All that matters is that the defendant's employee had actual or ostensible authority to act in the way that he did and that the claimant was defrauded.[228] **6-59**

The principle to be derived from *Lloyd* is that the employer will be liable if the fraudulent conduct of the employee falls within the scope of the employee's authority, actual or ostensible.[229] This was reaffirmed by the House of Lords in *The Ocean Frost*.[230] Lord Keith asserted that "the essential feature for creating liability in the employer is that the party contracting with the fraudulent servant should have altered his position to his detriment in reliance on the belief that the servant's activities were within his authority, or, to put it another way, part of his job".[231] Such authority may be either actual or ostensible, but as Lord Keith noted, cases of **6-60**

---

223 [2015] UKSC 23; [2016] A.C. 1 at [207].

224 [2015] UKSC 23; [2016] A.C. 1 at [43]–[45].

225 [2015] UKSC 23; [2016] A.C. 1 at [9].

226 (1867) L.R. 2 Ex. 259.

227 [1912] A.C. 716.

228 *Quinn v CC Automotive Group Ltd* [2010] EWCA Civ 1412; [2011] 2 All E.R. (Comm) 584 at [27] per Gross LJ.

229 Although the claimant in *Lloyd v Grace, Smith & Co* was a client of the defendants and so in a contractual relationship with them, this fact was immaterial: *Uxbridge Permanent Benefit Building Society v Pickard* [1939] 2 K.B. 248. For a full discussion of ostensible authority in a case of contract: see *Freeman and Lockyer v Buckhurst Park Properties (Mangal) Ltd* [1946] 2 Q.B. 480.

230 [1986] A.C. 717. See also *Credit Lyonnais Nederland NV v Export Credits Guarantee Department* [2000] 1 A.C. 486.

231 [1986] A.C. 717 at 781.

ostensible specific authority, rather than ostensible general authority, would be rare and unusual. Certainly, an employee cannot confer authority upon himself simply by representing that he has it. The employer must, by words or conduct, have induced the impaired party's belief that the employee was acting within his authority.

6-61 Of course, the claimant must show that he in fact relied upon the actual or ostensible authority with which he alleges the employer had clothed his employee. In *Kooragang Investment Property Ltd v Richardson and Wrench Ltd*,[232] the respondents instructed one of their employees, a valuer, not to act for a particular group of companies, in which he had a financial interest. Nevertheless, he prepared certain valuations on the strength of which that group was lent money by the appellants. He had stamped the valuations with the respondents' corporate name but his name did not appear on the valuations submitted to the appellants. It was held that as the appellants had no knowledge that the valuations were prepared by an employee of the respondents, they did not act on any ostensible authority delegated to the employee. The liability of the respondents, therefore, depended on the actual authority delegated to the employee. This had been effectively limited by the prohibition against preparing valuations for that particular group.

6-62 **Injuries caused by fellow servant and "horseplay" cases**[233] An employee who injures his colleague through acts of "horseplay" will only render his employer vicariously liable if those acts of horseplay or the particular practical joke are deemed to be in the course of his employment. So in *Aldred v Nacanco*,[234] where an employee in the staff washroom pushed a washbasin that was known to be unsteady against her colleague, the claimant, causing personal injuries, the Court of Appeal held that this was a deliberate act which had nothing to do with her employment. On the other hand, an employer could be personally liable for a breach of his primary duty of care if, for example, he failed to prevent habitual horseplay that undermined a safe system of work.[235]

6-63 **Nature of employer's liability** Earlier controversy whether an employer is held liable for damage done by his employee in the course of his employment because the employee has committed a tort or because he himself has broken some duty which he personally owes to the claimant has now been resolved in favour of the first view. The two views may be called respectively "servant's tort" view, and "master's tort" view. Decisions indicating that the "master's tort" approach represents the correct analysis of the nature of an employer's liability may not have been expressly overruled, but in the face of two decisions of the House of Lords[236]

---

232 [1982] A.C. 462.

233 The doctrine of common employment was abolished by the Law Reform (Personal Injuries) Act 1948. But the fact that the injured claimant was in common employment with the defendant's servant may still be relevant when deciding the effect of a prohibition on the scope of employment of the servant inflicting injury (*Stone v Taffe* [1975] 1 W.L.R. 1575) and also in relation to a defence of volenti (*ICI v Shatwell* [1965] A.C. 656). See further para.3-108 onwards.

234 [1987] I.R.L.R. 292. The court cited with approval Salmond's classic definition of vicarious liability and disapproved of its reformulation by Conyer J in *Harrison v Michelin Tyre Co Ltd* [1985] 1 All E.R. 918, where it was held that a momentary act of foolish horseplay did not take an employee out of the scope of his employment.

235 See *Hudson v Ridge Manufacturing Co Ltd* [1957] 2 Q.B. 348.

236 *Stavely Iron and Chemical Co v Jones* [1956] A.C. 627; *Imperial Chemical Industries Ltd v Shatwell*

endorsing, albeit not strictly necessarily, the "servant's tort" view of employer's liability, these decisions are now of marginal relevance. The position today, despite some contrary authority, would appear to be that the employer's liability is based on a requirement of public policy that the master be responsible for wrongs done by his servants in the course of their employment.[237] But even if the "servant's tort" approach to an employer's liability is established, there may still be occasions on which it can be found that the master himself owed a duty to the claimant and that that duty was broken by the act of an employee.[238] The employer in such circumstances is of course liable, but liability is primary not vicarious.[239]

Employee's breach of statutory duty The "master's tort"/"servant's tort" debate comes to the fore when a statutory duty imposed directly and solely on an employee is broken by the employee without his being guilty of common law negligence. Only if the "servant's tort" approach is accepted can the employer be liable. In *Majrowski v Guy's and St Thomas' NHS Trust*[240] the House of Lords explained that an employer can be vicariously liable in such circumstances. According to Lord Nicholls: "[u]nless the statute expressly or impliedly indicates otherwise, the principle of vicarious liability is applicable where an employee commits a breach of a statutory obligation sounding in damages while acting in the course of his employment."[241] Lords Hope and Brown used very similar words to make the same point in their speeches,[242] while Baroness Hale and Lord Carswell both concurred. On the other hand, their Lordships also stressed that this proposition was merely a general one and that it would be a matter of statutory interpretation in relation to any given statute to determine whether it was appropriate *in any particular case* to impose vicarious liability on the employer. Since then, it has also been held that although liability under the Protection from Harassment Act 1997 turns on a guilty mind of sorts, this provides no bar to the imposition of vicarious liability on a corporate or unincorporated body.[243] Nor is it an objection that the statute imposes liability on *a person* since corporate and unincorporated bodies fall within the definition of the "person" in the Interpretation Act 1978 for civil liability purposes.[244] The fact that the relevant statute speaks in terms of an employee's rights (rather than the duty of his or her fellow employee) constitutes no obstacle.[245] 6-64

[1965] A.C. 656. And the "servant's tort" view is adopted in the Crown Proceedings Act 1947 s.2(1) and the Police Act 1996 s.88(1).

237 *Rose v Plenty* [1976] 1 W.L.R. 141 at 144 and 147; *Riddick v Thames Board Mills Ltd* [1977] Q.B. 881 at 894, per Lord Denning MR. Note also *Imperial Chemical Industries Ltd v Shatwell* [1965] A.C. 656 where the House of Lords held the master not to be liable since the servant whose tortious act caused the claimant's injury could himself have relied on the defence of volenti non fit injuria. And see *Stavely Iron Chemical Co v Jones* [1956] A.C. 627; cf. *WB Anderson & Sons Ltd v Rhodes* [1967] 2 All E.R. 850.

238 This was expressly recognised by their Lordships in *ICI v Shatwell* [1965] A.C. 656.

239 See further paras. 12-04 onwards.

240 [2006] UKHL 34; [2007] 1 W.L.R. 398.

241 [2006] UKHL 34; [2007] 1 W.L.R. 398 at [17]. The duty not to pursue a course of conduct that amounts to harassment under the Protection from Harassment Act 1997 can certainly be treated in this way: see *Iqbal v Dean Manson Solicitors* [2011] EWCA Civ 123; [2011] I.R.L.R. 428 at [63], per Rix LJ.

242 [2006] UKHL 34; [2007] 1 W.L.R. 398 at [57] and [81] respectively.

243 *Iqbal v Dean Manson Solicitors* [2011] EWCA Civ 123; [2011] I.R.L.R. 428 at [63], per Rix LJ.

244 *Iqbal v Dean Manson Solicitors* [2011] EWCA Civ 123; [2011] I.R.L.R. 428 at [63], per Rix LJ.

245 *Timis v Osipov* [2018] EWCA Civ 2321; [2019] I.C.R. 655.

4. Independent Contractors

(a) General

6-65 **Introduction** If the employer has employed an independent contractor to do work for him, the rule is that the employer is not responsible for any tort committed by that contractor in the course of the execution of the work. This longstanding principle of the common law was reasserted forcefully by a unanimous Supreme Court in *Barclays Bank Plc v Various Claimants*.[246] In that case, Barclays had engaged a doctor to provide medical assessments of certain existing employees as well as a number of potential employees. The assessments formed part of the bank's recruitment and employment procedures. Strictly speaking, the doctor was engaged as an independent contractor. Various claimants alleged that the doctor had assaulted them sexually in the course of the medical assessments and the question for the court was whether the bank could be held vicariously liable for those assaults. In a speech delivered by Lady Hale, with which all the other members of the court agreed, it was held that the Bank could not be held liable on this basis. According to her Ladyship, although the law in relation to vicarious liability had undergone considerable development in the previous few years, it still stopped short of allowing an employer to be held vicariously liable for the torts committed by his independent contractors. In her words, the law maintained "the classic distinction between employment and relationships akin or analogous to employment, on the one hand, and the relationship with an independent contractor, on the other".[247]

6-66 The employees of a contractor, whilst acting as such, stand in the same position as their employer. But the employer of the contractor is not automatically liable for the torts committed by the contractor's employees.[248] Of course, even though the damage complained of may have been caused by the wrongful act or omission of an independent contractor or his employee, it may also be attributable to the negligence or other personal fault of the employer. If, for example, he has negligently selected an incompetent contractor, or if he has employed an insufficient number of men,[249] or has himself so interfered with the manner of carrying out the work that damage results,[250] he will himself have committed a tort for which he can be held liable. Also, if the employer has authorised or ratified the independent contractor's tort, then on normal principles he will be jointly liable for that tort.[251]

6-67 **Exceptions to the general rule: non-delegable duties** To the general rule that an employer is not liable for the negligence of an independent contractor there are certain apparent exceptions. They are not, however, true exceptions because the employer's liability is dependent upon a finding that the employer is, himself, in breach of some duty which he personally owes to the claimant. If the circumstances

---

[246] [2020] UKSC 13; [2020] 2 W.L.R. 960.

[247] *Barclays Bank Plc v Various Claimants* [2020] UKSC 13; [2020] 2 W.L.R. 960 at [24], per Lady Hale.

[248] *Milligan v Wedge* (1840) 12 A. & E. 737; *Salsbury v Woodland* [1970] 1 Q.B. 324; *D & F Estates Ltd v Church Commissioners for England* [1989] A.C. 177. The position might, of course, be affected by contract: see, e.g. *National Trust v Haden Young* (1994) 72 B.L.R. 1.

[249] *Pinn v Rew* (1916) 32 T.L.R. 451.

[250] *McLaughlin v Pryor* (1842) 4 M. & G. 48; *Burgess v Gray* (1845) 1 C.B. 578.

[251] See, e.g. *Ellis v Sheffield Gas Consumer's Co* (1853) 2 E. & B. 767.

are such that the law imposes a strict duty upon the employer, then he cannot discharge his duty by delegating performance of the work in question to an independent contractor. If, therefore, the duty is not fulfilled, the employer is liable even though the immediate cause of the damage is the contractor's wrongful act or omission. The contractor, by his acts, puts the employer in breach of a personal duty. Such duties are often described as "non-delegable" and may arise either by statute or at common law.[252] For present purposes, they are to be contrasted with the ordinary duty to take reasonable care which can be discharged by the employment of a contractor reasonably supposed by the employer to be competent.[253] Often, indeed, a non-delegable duty will be a strict duty.[254] At the very least, the non-delegable duty is "a duty not merely to take care, but a duty to provide that care is taken",[255] so that, if care is not taken, the duty is broken.

(b) Statutory non-delegable duties

Statutory duties Where a statute requires a person to do a particular act, and an independent contractor employed by him fails to do that act, he cannot escape liability by pleading that the fault was not his, but was that of his independent contractor.[256] Statutes creating non-delegable duties of this kind are extremely numerous, and it is a question of construction whether any given statute imposes such a duty upon the defendant.[257] For instance, on its proper construction, the Immigration (Places of Detention) Direction 1996 did not impose a non-delegable duty of care upon the Home Office in relation to the claimant in *Quaquah v Group 4 Securities Co (No.2)*.[258] The Home Office had discharged its own duty by using all reasonable care in selecting the private company that had been chosen to run a detention centre and whose employees were the immediate tortfeasors. **6-68**

Where a statute confers on a person a power to carry out certain works, the statute may, expressly or by implication, impose upon that person a tortious duty to take reasonable care in the exercise of the power.[259] This duty, it seems, is non-delegable.[260] So where certain Ministries, acting under statutory powers, caused a trial bore-hole to be made upon the claimant's land, and the independent contractor employed for the work negligently left a pile of timber unfenced in the claimant's field, whereby the claimant's horse was injured, it was held that the Ministries were liable.[261] Nonetheless, it is important to construe the statute carefully in order to determine the extent of the duty owed in the exercise of the statu- **6-69**

---

252 For an attempt to explain such duties see Murphy, "Juridical Foundations of Common Law Non-Delegable Duties" in Neyers et al (eds), *Emerging Issues in Tort Law* (2007).

253 See *Aiken v Stewart Wrightson Members' Agency Ltd* [1995] 1 W.L.R. 1281 (cf. the contractual duty owed in that case).

254 But not always: see, e.g. *Rivers v Cutting* [1982] 1 W.L.R. 1146. See also, Murphy (2007) 30 U.N.S.W.L.J. 86.

255 per Langton J in *The Pass of Ballater* [1942] P. 112 at 117.

256 See, e.g. *Gray v Pullen* (1864) 5 B. & S. 970; *Robinson v Beaconsfield RDC* [1911] 2 Ch. 188. cf. *Hyams v Webster* (1867) L.R. 2 Q.B. 264.

257 *Whitby v Burt, Boulton and Hayward Ltd* [1947] K.B. 918; *Hosking v De Havilland Aircraft Co Ltd* (1949) 83 Ll. L. Rep. 11.

258 [2001] 7 C.L. 523.

259 *Fisher v Ruislip-Northwood Urban DC* [1945] 1 K.B. 584, where the earlier cases are reviewed.

260 *Hardaker v Idle DC* [1896] 1 Q.B. 335; *Darling v Att Gen* (1950) 210 L.T. 189.

261 *Darling v Att Gen* (1950) 210 L.T. 189.

tory power. In *Rivers v Cutting*,[262] a police officer, acting under the power contained in reg.4 of the Removal and Disposal of Vehicle Regulations 1968 to remove or arrange for the removal of a vehicle, arranged for the claimant's vehicle to be removed by a local garage. The claimant sued the chief constable for the negligence of the garage in the removal. It was held that the regulation conferred on the police two distinct powers: the power to remove, and the power to arrange for the removal of, the vehicle. In exercising this latter power, the police officer owed a duty of care in the choice of an independent contractor to do the work. But that was the full extent of the duty.

(c) Common law non-delegable duties

6-70 **Common law duties** If a non-delegable duty is found to exist at common law, then the employer of an independent contractor is as much liable for its breach as if the duty had been created by statute. A particular difficulty that has beset this area of law is that of knowing when such a duty exists at common law.[263] In the past, it has been impossible to state general principles with any degree of confidence since the English courts have generally failed to identify or adhere to any such principles. That said, a telling feature of the leading cases on non-delegable duties is the fact that there is nearly always an *affirmative duty* for which the defendant has assumed responsibility.[264] This aspect of the cases was certainly stressed in the now leading case of *Woodland v Swimming Teachers Association*.[265] There, the Supreme Court was faced with a case in which the claimant had suffered severe brain injury during a school swimming lesson held at a local authority swimming pool. The lesson in question was organised and provided by an independent contractor. In relation to the action against the local education authority, the claimant alleged breach of a non-delegable duty. In finding for the claimant, the Supreme Court offered the following guidance on the imposition of non-delegable duties to exercise reasonable care. Specifically side-lining those cases concerning highways and hazards (considered below), Lord Sumption—with whom Lords Clarke, Toulson and Wilson agreed—opined as follows:

> "[T]he remaining cases are characterised by the following defining features: (1) The claimant is a patient or a child, or for some other reason is especially vulnerable or dependent on the protection of the defendant against the risk of injury … (2) There is an antecedent relationship between the claimant and the defendant, independent of the negligent act or omission itself, (i) which places the claimant in the actual custody, charge or care of the defendant, and (ii) from which it is possible to impute to the defendant the assumption of a positive duty to protect the claimant from harm, and not just a duty to refrain from conduct which will foreseeably damage the claimant … (3) The claimant has no control over how the defendant chooses to perform those obligations, i.e. whether personally or through employees or through third parties. (4) The defendant has delegated to a third party some function which is an integral part of the positive duty which he has assumed towards the claimant; and the third party is exercising, for the purpose of the function thus delegated to him, the defendant's custody or care of the claimant and the element of

---

262 [1982] 1 W.L.R. 1146.

263 For an attempt to explain such duties see Murphy, "Juridical Foundations of Common Law Non-Delegable Duties" in Neyers et al (eds), *Emerging Issues in Tort Law* (2007).

264 For endorsement of the assumption of responsibility criterion, see *S v Lothian Health Board* [2009] CSOH 97; 2009 S.L.T. 689.

265 [2013] UKSC 66; [2014] A.C. 537.

control that goes with it. (5) The third party has been negligent not in some collateral respect but in the performance of the very function assumed by the defendant and delegated by the defendant to him."[266]

Mindful of the emphasis in *Woodland* on the presence of especial claimant vulnerability or dependency in typical non-delegable duty cases, Coulson J in *GB v Home Office*[267] held that a non-delegable duty is owed by the Home Office to immigration detainees in respect of the provision of medical care while being held in an immigration removal centre. He noted the vulnerability of such persons and held there to be "a positive duty to protect GB from harm" which included a duty to provide medical care.[268] By contrast, despite the admitted vulnerability of children in local authority care, the Court of Appeal in *NA v Nottinghamshire County Council*[269] did not feel that it was appropriate to regard a local authority as having been in breach of a non-delegable duty to take reasonable steps to protect a young girl in its care from harm when she was abused at the hands of foster parents with whom the defendant authority had placed her. According to Tomlinson LJ, "[i]n order to be non-delegable a duty must relate to a function which the purported delegator … has assumed for itself a duty to perform".[270] On appeal, the Supreme Court agreed that a local authority does not come under a non-delegable duty owed to children placed with foster parents in respect of the day to day care that those children receive.[271] Such a duty would create a potential conflict between the local authority's duty towards a child under s.18 of the Child Care Act 1980 and the authority's interests in avoiding exposure to liability.[272] A non-delegable duty would also (inappropriately) amount to a form of state insurance for the actions of the child's family members.[273]

Nuisance[274] Apart from cases involving a withdrawal of support (dealt with in the next paragraph), liability for nuisances caused by independent contractors is not terribly straightforward. *Spicer v Smee*[275] suggests that the general rule is that the occupier will be liable in nuisance for the act of his independent contractor. However, *Matania v National Provincial Bank Ltd*[276] supports the contrary view, namely, that liability for the act of the independent contractor depends on whether the work entails an inherent risk of creating a nuisance. In *Matania*, the claimant occupied the second and third floors of a building, and the defendants, who occupied the first floor, employed independent contractors to carry out certain alterations. In the 6-71

266 [2013] UKSC 66; [2014] A.C. 537 at [23]. In a separate judgment, Baroness Hale also signalled (at [38]) her approval of this five-point summary of the law.
267 [2015] EWHC 819 (QB).
268 [2015] EWHC 819 (QB) at [28]–[34].
269 [2015] EWCA Civ 1139; [2016] Q.B. 739.
270 [2015] EWCA Civ 1139; [2016] Q.B. 739 at [25]. Similarly, although the Ministry of Justice owes prison inmates a non-delegable duty to arrange the provision of healthcare, that duty does not extend to the actual delivery of such care since delivering "[h]ealthcare is not … part of the prison institution's mainstream (or essential) function": *Razumas v Ministry of Justice* [2018] EWHC 215 (QB); [2018] P.I.Q.R. P10 at [151], per Cockerill J.
271 *Armes v Nottinghamshire County Council* [2017] UKSC 60; [2018] A.C. 355 at [48].
272 *Armes v Nottinghamshire County Council* [2017] UKSC 60; [2018] A.C. 355 at [45].
273 Note, however, that the Supreme Court did come to the conclusion that the local authority could be vicariously liable for the abuse of children placed in the care of foster parents. See para.6-11.
274 See para.19-72.
275 [1946] 1 All E.R. 489.
276 [1936] 2 All E.R. 633.

course of the work, the contractors caused a nuisance to the claimant by reason of the noise and dust produced by their operations, and it was held that the defendants were liable. Slesser LJ stated that "if the act done is one which in its very nature involves a special danger of nuisance being complained of, then the employer of the contractor will be responsible if there is a failure to take the necessary precautions that the nuisance shall not arise".[277] It is submitted that this is the correct approach.[278]

6-72 **Withdrawal of support from neighbouring land** In *Bower v Peate*,[279] the parties were owners of two adjoining houses. The claimant was entitled to support from the defendant's land. The defendant employed an independent contractor to pull down his house and rebuild it. The contractor used insufficient supports on the claimant's house and it was consequently damaged. The decision was that where one of two adjoining houses is entitled to support from the other or from the soil underlying it, the owner of the servient tenement, if desirous of rebuilding his house and of excavating the foundations for that purpose, cannot escape responsibility for the consequences of thereby withdrawing the support to which the adjoining house is entitled, by entrusting the task of excavation and rebuilding to an independent contractor. That decision was followed by the House of Lords in *Dalton v Angus*,[280] and the same principle was applied in *Hughes v Percival*,[281] to what was also a case of withdrawal of support. In *Alcock v Wraith*,[282] the defendants were liable for damage caused to their neighbour's property when negligent re-roofing work was undertaken on the defendants' property by an independent contractor.[283]

6-73 **Operations on the highway**[284] Where a person causes operations to be undertaken on the highway, which may cause danger to persons using that highway, he is liable for damage resulting from the negligence of an independent contractor in carrying out those operations.[285] On this principle, a local authority was held liable where its contractor, employed to make up a highway, negligently left a heap of soil in the road, unlighted and unprotected, with the result that the claimant was injured.[286] The same principle applies to places other than the highway where the

277 [1936] 2 All E.R. 633 at 646.

278 See also *Alcock v Wraith* [1991] 59 B.L.R. 16; *Johnson (t/a Johnson Butchers) v BJW Property Developments Ltd* [2002] EWHC 1131 (TCC); [2002] 3 All E.R. 574.

279 (1876) 1 Q.B.D. 321.

280 (1881) 6 App. Cas. 740 at 829. Note that in *Stoneman v Lyons* [1975] 133 C.L.R. 550, *Dalton v Angus* was relied upon, but the absence of any easement of support was fatal to the claim.

281 (1882–83) L.R. 8 App. Cas. 443. The case of removal of support afforded by a party-wall to a modern house seems to stand on the same footing as the removal of support afforded by soil to an ancient one. cf. *Richards v Rose* (1854) 9 Exch. 218 at 221 (mines).

282 [1991] 59 B.L.R. 16.

283 In similar vein see *Johnson (t/a Johnson Butchers) v BJW Property Developments Ltd* [2002] EWHC 1131 (TCC); [2002] 3 All E.R. 574; and *Willmott Dixon Construction Ltd v Robert West Consulting Ltd* [2016] EWHC 3291 (TCC); [2017] P.N.L.R. 17.

284 See further para.19-186.

285 *Penny v Wimbledon Urban DC* [1898] 2 Q.B. 212 at 217; affirmed [1899] 2 Q.B. 72.

286 *Penny v Wimbledon Urban DC* [1898] 2 Q.B. 212. See also *Tarry v Ashton* (1876) 1 Q.B.D. 314 (heavy lamp projecting over public pavement); *Holliday v National Telephone Co* [1899] 2 Q.B. 329 (unguarded molten solder on highway); *Daniel v Rickett, Cockerell & Co Ltd* [1938] 2 K.B. 322 (open cellar flap in pavement).

public may lawfully pass, such as the platform of a railway station,[287] and on a navigable river.[288]

No such non-delegable duty attaches to a person who is simply using the highway for passing and repassing,[289] and there is no special category of case covering acts done near a highway in circumstances in which, if due care is not taken, injury to passers-by on the highway may be caused. In *Salsbury v Woodland*,[290] for example, the Court of Appeal refused to expand the category of work done on the highway to include work done near the highway. **6-74**

The rule in Rylands v Fletcher[291] A person who brings and keeps upon his land something which is likely to do damage if it escapes does so at his peril[292] and consequently he cannot excuse himself for the escape on the basis that he had employed a competent contractor to place and confine the matter in the position from which it escaped. In fact, the escape in *Rylands v Fletcher* itself was caused by the negligence of the independent contractor employed to build the reservoir on the defendant's land, and the defendant's duty in that case was clearly non-delegable.[293] **6-75**

Escape of fire[294] An occupier is liable for the escape of fire which is due to the negligence of his independent contractor.[295] In *Black v Christchurch Finance Co*,[296] where the defendants had employed an independent contractor to burn scrub on their land, and the fire had spread to the adjoining land of the claimant, Lord Shand began by saying that "a proprietor who executes such an operation is bound to use all reasonable precautions to prevent the fire extending to his neighbour's property". He then added that "if he authorises another to act for him he is bound, not only to stipulate that such precautions shall be taken, but also to see that these are observed, otherwise he will be responsible for the consequences".[297] So in *Balfour v Barty-King*,[298] the defendants were liable when independent contractors, employed to thaw out a frozen pipe in the loft of the defendant's house, negligently used a blowlamp **6-76**

---

287 *Pickard v Smith* (1861) 10 C.B. (N.S.) 470.

288 *The Snark* [1900] P. 105.

289 The owner of a motor vehicle is thus not liable for an accident caused by the unroadworthiness of the vehicle if this was due not to his own negligence but to that of an independent contractor: *Phillips v Britannia Hygienic Laundry Co* [1923] 1 K.B. 539; affirmed [1923] 2 K.B. 832; *Stennett v Hancock* [1939] 2 All E.R. 578.

290 [1970] 1 Q.B. 324.

291 (1866) L.R. 1 Ex. 265; affirmed (1868) L.R. 3 H.L. As to the modern scope of this rule see Murphy (2004) 24 O.J.L.S. 643.

292 Though certain defences are open to him. See paras 19-44 et seq.

293 See also *Tarry v Ashton* (1876) 1 Q.B.D. 314 at 319, per Blackburn J. cf. *Blake v Woolf* [1898] 2 Q.B. 426; *Johnson (t/a Johnson Butchers) v BJW Property Developments Ltd* [2002] EWCA 1131 (TCC); [2002] 3 All E.R. 574.

294 See further paras 19-155 to 19-167.

295 *Johnson (t/a Johnson Butchers) v BJW Property Developments Ltd* [2002] EWHC 1131 (TCC); [2002] 3 All E.R. 574. Note also the Fires Prevention (Metropolis) Act 1774. But note, too, that there is a conflict of views about whether this Act applies to fires intentionally lit which spread accidentally (see paras 19-157 and 19-159).

296 [1894] A.C. 48.

297 [1894] A.C. 48 at 54. And see *H & N Emanuel Ltd v GLC* [1971] 2 All E.R. 835 at 841. cf. *Eriksen v Clifton* [1963] N.Z.L.R. 705, where a proposed independent contractor lit the fire before he was authorised to do so and even before any contract with the proprietor had come into existence.

298 [1957] 1 Q.B. 496.

in proximity to inflammable material and thereby caused a fire which spread to and damaged the claimant's house next door. Indeed, "the occupier is liable for the escape of fire which is due to the negligence of anyone other than a stranger" and an independent contractor is not a stranger for this purpose.[299]

6-77 **Extra hazardous activities** In many of the cases cited above, emphasis was placed upon the dangerous nature of the defendant's undertaking and in *Honeywill and Stein Ltd v Larkin Bros Ltd* Slesser LJ, delivering the judgment of the Court of Appeal, enunciated a general principle of liability in respect of "extra-hazardous or dangerous operations". He said:

> "Even of these, it may be predicted that if carefully and skilfully performed, no harm will follow; as instances of such operations may be given those of removing support from adjoining houses, doing dangerous work on the highway, or creating fire or explosion: hence it may be said, in one sense, that such operations, because they are inherently dangerous, and hence are done at the principal employer's peril."[300]

Since *Honeywill* was decided, however, the principle concerning extra-hazardous activities has been curtailed significantly. In *Bottomley v Todmorden Cricket Club*,[301] Brooke LJ noted the fact that, in modern circumstances, the House of Lords might prefer to avoid the subtleties associated with the language of "extra-hazardous activities" and elect instead to follow the view of Mason J in the High Court of Australia in *Stevens v Brodribb Sawmilling Co Pty Ltd*, namely, that "the traditional common law response to the creation of a special danger is not to impose strict liability but to impose a higher standard of care in the performance of an existing duty."[302] Just a few years later, in *Biffa Waste Services Ltd v Maschinenfabrik Ernst Hese GmbH*, Stanley Burnton LJ said, "this [appeal] court is not free to make as robust a decision as that of the High Court of Australia, but in our judgment, the doctrine enunciated in *Honeywill* is so unsatisfactory that its application should be kept as narrow as possible. It should be applied only to activities that are exceptionally dangerous whatever precautions are taken."[303]

6-78 **Bailment** Whether or not a contractual bailee is liable for loss or damage to the goods caused by his independent contractor is in principle dependent upon the terms of the contract of bailment itself, but in the absence of an express term to the contrary he will generally be liable. In *Riverstone Meat Co Pty Ltd v Lancashire Shipping Co Ltd*,[304] the claimant's goods were damaged while on board the defendant's ship by reason of the unseaworthiness of the ship, and it was proved that this was due solely to the negligence of an employee of an independent firm of ship-repairers who had been employed by the defendants before the voyage. The defendants' duty under the bill of lading contract was only "to exercise due

[299] *H & N Emanuel Ltd v GLC* [1971] 2 All E.R. 835 at 839.
[300] [1934] 1 K.B. 191 at 200.
[301] [2003] EWCA Civ 1575; [2001] P.I.Q.R. P 18.
[302] (1986) 160 C.L.R. 16 at 30.
[303] [2008] EWCA Civ 1257; [2009] Q.B. 725 at [78]. For further endorsement of this restrictive approach, see *Willmott Dixon Construction Ltd v Robert West Consulting Ltd* [2016] EWHC 3291 (TCC); [2017] P.N.L.R. 17 at [14]: "no non-delegable duty can now be said to arise from this alleged exception unless the works are exceptionally or unusually dangerous".
[304] [1961] A.C. 807. cf. *Leesh River Tea Co Ltd v British India Steam Navigation Co Ltd* [1967] 2 Q.B. 250.

diligence" to make the ship seaworthy,[305] but nevertheless the House of Lords held that they were liable.[306] Even if there is no direct contractual relationship between bailor and bailee, it is submitted that the bailee's duty is "non-delegable" so long as the bailment is for reward,[307] and perhaps even if it is gratuitous.[308]

Occupiers' liability[309] The Occupiers' Liability Act 1957 provides[310]: **6-79**

> "Where damage is caused to a visitor[311] by a danger due to the faulty execution of any work of construction, maintenance or repair by an independent contractor employed by the occupier, the occupier is not to be treated without more as answerable for the danger if in all the circumstances he had acted reasonably in entrusting the work to an independent contractor and had taken such steps (if any) as he reasonably ought in order to satisfy himself that the contractor was competent and that the work had been properly done."[312]

A distinction must presumably be drawn, however, between negligent work that leaves the premises unsafe and injury arising directly from the negligent nature of the work actually being performed on the occupier's premises by the subcontractor. In *Knight v Fox*[313] the defendant (himself a contractor) was not liable where he employed a subcontractor to build a bridge over a railway, and the subcontractor's workmen improperly caused a pole of the scaffolding to project over the footway, whereby the claimant fell over the pole in the dark and was injured. There seems no reason on principle why, if the defendant had been an occupier rather than a contractor, he would have been liable for the negligence of the subcontractor.

Employer's common law duty to employee[314] Notwithstanding the non-delegable duty owed by an employer to his employee established in *Wilson's and Clyde Coal Co v English*,[315] the House of Lords held in *Davie v New Merton Board Mills Ltd*[316] that employers were not liable in respect of an injury suffered by their employee in consequence of the negligence of the manufacturer of a standard tool which they had bought from reputable suppliers and which the claimant had been using in the course of his work. The result of the case, so far as it relates to injuries caused by defective equipment, has since been reversed by the Employers' Liability (Defective Equipment) Act 1969.[317] That Act provides that where an employee suffers personal injury in the course of his employment in consequence of a defect in equipment[318] provided by his employer for the purposes of the **6-80**

305 Australian Carriage of Goods by Sea Act 1924 s.5 and Sch. (the Hague Rules) art.III, r.1.

306 cf. *W Angliss & Co (Australia) Pty Ltd v PO Steam Navigation Co* [1927] 2 K.B. 456, where the negligence was that of the shipbuilder.

307 This seems to follow from the reasoning in *Morris v CW Martin & Sons Ltd* [1966] 1 Q.B. 716.

308 *Morris v CW Martin & Sons Ltd* [1966] 1 Q.B. 716 at 725, per Lord Denning MR. And see *Port Swettenham Authority v TW Wu and Co* [1979] A.C. 580.

309 See further para. 11-02 onwards.

310 Occupiers' Liability Act 1957 s.2(4)(b). See para.11-57.

311 i.e. an invitee or licensee: Occupiers' Liability Act 1957 s.1(2).

312 And see *Ferguson v Welsh* [1987] 1 W.L.R. 1553.

313 (1850) 5 Exch. 721. cf. *Hodgson v British Arc Welding Co Ltd* [1946] K.B. 302.

314 See further Ch.12.

315 [1938] A.C. 57.

316 [1959] A.C. 604; *Mason v Williams and Williams Ltd* [1955] 1 W.L.R. 549. Cf. *Riverstone Meat Co Pty Ltd v Lancashire Shipping Co Ltd* [1961] A.C. 807.

317 See para.12-18.

318 See *Coltman v Bibby Tankers Ltd (The Derbyshire)* [1988] A.C. 276: a ship can be equipment.

employer's business, and the defect is attributable to the fault of a third party, the injury shall be deemed to be attributable to the negligence of the employer. Notwithstanding the 1969 Act, *Davie* continues to cast some doubt on the extent of the employer's duty at common law. It is submitted that the best explanation of the case is contained in *Sumner v William Henderson & Sons Ltd.*[319] There, the claimant's wife, an employee of the defendants, was killed in a fire which broke out on their premises. On a special case, Phillimore J held that if the fire had been due to the negligence of the manufacturer of an electric cable which the defendants had purchased and which was being installed at the time, then the defendants would not be liable; but if the fire had been due to the negligence of independent contractors engaged in the installation of the cable on the defendant's premises, then the defendants would have been liable. His Lordship considered that the ratio of *Davie* was that the employers had not delegated their duty to the manufacturers of the tool: in purchasing the tool from a reputable supplier they had discharged it. Although the Court of Appeal subsequently set aside the judgment of Phillimore J on procedural grounds[320] the validity of his reasoning has not been impugned and it therefore seems that, despite *Davie*, the employer's common law duty may still be generally described as non-delegable.[321] The employer must answer for the negligence of anyone doing work on his behalf which affects the safety of his employees. On the other hand, where the negligent third party is working on behalf of some other employer, the employer of the claimant will not be liable for that negligence. In *McGarvey v Eve NCI Ltd*[322] the claimant, who was employed by A, was injured when he was instructed to use an unsuitable set of ladders supplied by B (to whom A's company was subcontracted). A had instructed the claimant to follow directions issued by B but had also failed to provide the claimant with proper safety instruction. In the result, the Court of Appeal held A two thirds liable and B one third liable in respect of the claimant's injuries.

6-81 The House of Lords in *McDermid v Nash Dredging*[323] reviewed the law in this area. There, the claimant was employed by the defendants working on a tug in a Swedish fjord. He was instructed to go and work as a deckhand on another tug owned by a separate company within the same group as the defendants. As a result of the negligence of the master of the tug on which he was working, the claimant lost his leg. It was held that the employer had a non-delegable duty to take reasonable care to provide a "safe system of work". The employer could not escape liability if the duty, having been delegated, was not then properly performed. Although a system had been developed which might have been safe, it was not operated at the time of the accident and, therefore, the duty was not performed. The defendants were accordingly liable. Whether the employer has complied with his non-delegable duty is to be determined by assessing all the circumstances of the case. In *Cook v Square D Ltd*[324] the claimant was assigned by his employer, the defendant, to a company in Saudi Arabia. He was injured due to the unsafe condi-

---

319 [1964] 1 Q.B. 450.

320 [1963] 1 W.L.R. 823.

321 Note that this non-delegable duty also extends to a Chief Constable (subject to policy considerations): *Mullaney v Chief Constable of West Midlands* [2001] EWCA Civ 700.

322 [2002] EWCA Civ 374.

323 [1987] A.C. 906. Note *Nicol v Allyacht Spares Pty* (1987) 163 C.L.R. 611 HC of Australia: if unsafe system of work devised by injured employee, employee still able to complain, though contributory negligence will reduce the size of the award.

324 [1992] P.I.Q.R. P33.

tion of the Saudi premises. It was held that the defendant had complied with his non-delegable duty of care: he was not responsible for the daily events on the premises some 8,000 miles away; the occupiers and main contractors were well-known international companies. There can also be circumstances in which, in addition to the breach of the employer's non-delegable duty of care, there is a breach on the part of the person to whom the employee has been assigned.[325]

(d) Casual or collateral negligence

Casual or collateral negligence Even though the employer is under a non-delegable duty, he will not be liable for damage negligently caused by his independent contractor if the contractor's negligence is what is called "casual or collateral", for the contractor's collateral negligence does not place the employer in breach of his non-delegable duty. So in *Padbury v Holliday and Greenwood Ltd*,[326] the defendants employed a subcontractor to put metallic casements into the windows of a house which the defendants were building. While one of the casements was being fixed, the man employed in fixing it placed an iron tool on the window-sill. The wind blew the window on to it, and it was knocked off the sill and injured the claimant who was a passer-by in the street. Although the defendants' duty was, it is submitted, non-delegable[327] they were held not liable as the injury was the result of collateral negligence.[328] **6-82**

It is submitted that negligence is collateral if it does not arise in the doing of the very act the contractor was employed to perform. As was pointed out in *Penny v Wimbledon Urban DC*[329] where the contractor had left a heap of soil in the roadway unlighted and unprotected: if, for example, a pickaxe had been left in the roadway by one of the contractor's servants it would have been casual or collateral negligence only.[330] In *Holliday v National Telephone Co*,[331] the defendants were laying telephone wires under a street and employed a plumber to make certain connections. The plumber dipped a blowlamp into molten solder, causing an explosion which injured the claimant. The Divisional Court[332] treated this as a case of collateral negligence but the Court of Appeal reversed their decision on the ground that it was negligence in the very act the plumber was employed to perform.[333] **6-83**

5. LOAN OF CHATTEL

Background In this special category of case, a defendant may be vicariously liable when he lends his chattel (usually his car)[334] to another and that other, by his negligence in the use of the chattel, causes injury to the claimant. Some commenta- **6-84**

[325] *McGarvey v Eve NCI Ltd* [2002] EWCA Civ 374.

[326] (1912) 28 T.L.R. 494; *Pearson v Cox* (1877) L.R. 2 C.P. 369. cf. *Salsbury v Woodland* [1970] 1 Q.B. 324 at 348, per Sachs LJ.

[327] See para.6-67

[328] (1912) 28 T.L.R. 494 at 495.

[329] [1899] 2 Q.B. 72 at 76.

[330] So also, it is submitted, would it have been collateral negligence if the contractor's servant had been driving negligently on his way to or from the place of work.

[331] [1899] 2 Q.B. 392; cf. *Reedie v L & NW Ry* (1849) 4 Exch. 244.

[332] [1899] 1 Q.B. 221.

[333] [1899] 2 Q.B. 392 at 400, per A. L. Smith LJ; *Darling v Att Gen* (1950) 210 L.T. 189.

[334] The doctrine has been applied to a boat: *The Thelma* [1953] 2 Lloyd's Rep. 613. However, it is unlikely to apply to all chattels.

tors regard this category of vicarious liability as depending on principles of agency, while others hold that the relationship between the defendant and the actual tortfeasor falls within the principles of the law of vicarious liability proper. It is submitted that it is best to view this category as sui generis.

6-85 **Essentials of liability** To be liable, the defendant must retain both a right to control the use of the chattel and must have an interest in the purpose for which it is being used. Thus in *Ormrod v Crosville Motor Services Ltd*,[335] A, the owner of a car, requested B to drive it to Monte Carlo where, it was intended, they would meet and go on holiday in the car together. While still in England, B negligently caused an accident, and for this A was held liable. Originally, it seems, the right to control (which is one of the conditions of liability and which, probably, provides its theoretical basis) was strictly construed. Thus, in the earlier cases involving vehicles, it was stressed that the owner retained the right of control, even though he had entrusted the driving to someone else, where the owner had remained present in the vehicle.[336] In *Parker v Miller*,[337] however, the owner was liable notwithstanding that he was not present.

6-86 On the other hand, even though he retains the right to control in this attenuated sense, the owner will not be liable unless he also has an interest in the use being made of his chattel. Lord Wilberforce stated in *Morgans v Launchbury*: "it must be shown that the driver was using it for the owner's purposes, under delegation of a task or duty."[338] Thus in *Nelson v Raphael*,[339] where the seller of a car asked a friend to hand the car over to the buyer, it was held that the friend acted as the seller's agent when demonstrating the controls to the buyer.[340] By contrast, in *Hewitt v Bonvin*,[341] the defendant lent his car to his son exclusively for the son's personal use and it was held that, because the defendant had no interest in the purposes for which the journey in question was undertaken, he was not liable for the son's negligent driving of the car.[342]

6-87 In *Launchbury v Morgans*,[343] a majority of the Court of Appeal sought to expand the principles described above in such a way as to come close to holding that the

---

335 [1953] 1 W.L.R. 1120. For other cases, see *The Trust Co Ltd v De Silva* [1956] 1 W.L.R. 376; *Carberry v Davies* [1968] 1 W.L.R. 1103; *Vandyke v Fender* [1970] 2 Q.B. 292 at 303, per Lord Denning MR; and at 307, per Sachs LJ.

336 *Wheatley v Patrick* (1837) 2 M. & W. 650; *Samson v Aitchison* [1912] A.C. 844.

337 (1926) 42 T.L.R. 408. See also *Ormrod v Crosville Motor Services Ltd* [1953] 1 W.L.R. 112. cf. *Chowdhary v Gillot* [1947] 2 All E.R. 541 where, although the owner was actually present in the car he had given up his right to control it because the car had already been delivered to a garage for repair and the garage was in possession of it as bailee. See also *Samson v Aitchison* [1912] A.C. 844 at 849, per Lord Atkinson, approving a statement of the trial judge; *Norton v Canadian Pacific Steamships Ltd* [1961] 1 W.L.R. 1057.

338 [1973] A.C. 127 at 135.

339 [1979] R.T.R. 437.

340 See in similar vein *John Laing Construction v Ince* [2001] C.L.Y. 4543. It may well be that mere ownership will suffice to secure the liability of the owner of the chattel: *Barnard v Sully* (1931) 47 T.L.R. 557. cf. *Rambarran v Gurracharran* [1970] 1 W.L.R. 556, where the presumption was rebutted. See also *Nottingham v Aldridge* [1971] 2 Q.B. 739, where a car was used by an employee for driving himself and a fellow employee to work. This was done with the employer's authority and he paid a mileage allowance, but the car was not his and he was accordingly not liable.

341 [1940] 1 K.B. 188; *Britt v Galmoye* (1928) 44 T.L.R. 294; *Norton v Canadian Pacific Steamships Ltd* [1961] 1 W.L.R. 1057; cf. *Carberry v Davies* [1968] 1 W.L.R. 1103.

342 See also *Klein v Calouri* [1971] 1 W.L.R. 619.

343 [1971] 2 Q.B. 245; [1973] A.C. 127.

owner of a motor vehicle is liable for the negligence of anyone, or at least of any member of his family, who drives it with his permission. This view was, however, rejected by the House of Lords which reaffirmed the law as stated above.[344] Further, the interest that the owner must have in the purposes for which the vehicle is borrowed must be specific and identifiable. In *Norwood v Navan*,[345] a husband was not liable when his wife merely used his car to go on a shopping expedition with friends even though he knew that she often took the car and in the course of her journey she did some general shopping for the family. The greater part of the journey was clearly for her own purposes. It may be that ownership of the car is not as such necessary; the right of possession may well suffice.

6. Principal and Agent

Principal and agent Both employees and independent contractors may be classified as "agents", for they are both persons who do work for another. The question arises, however, whether there are rules of law peculiar to "agents" which are not included in the preceding paragraphs. In two classes of case the word "agent" is commonly used: namely, cases where the owner of a vehicle gets a friend to drive it for him,[346] and cases of vicarious liability for fraud.[347] In the former class of case the word "agent" is used because the word "employee" does not, in the context, accord with ordinary usage. 6-88

Cases of vicarious liability for fraud require slightly more extended treatment. As has been shown, the principles in this class of case are not the same as those generally applicable in cases of employer and employee. The test of liability is authority, actual or ostensible, not course of employment.[348] The analogy with contractual liability for agents is a close one and it is for this reason that in cases of fraud the word "agent" is used, even though the fraud is that of an employee acting in the course of his employment. 6-89

7. Ratification of Torts

Ratification of torts An act done for another, though unauthorised by him, becomes his act if he subsequently ratifies it.[349] Thus in *Carter v St Mary Abbot's* 6-90

---

344 A number of their Lordships agreed that the law may be in need of change but held that this could only come via legislation: [1973] A.C. 127.

345 [1981] R.T.R. 457.

346 See paras 6-84 to 6-87.

347 See paras 6–55 to 6-61.

348 See paras 6-55 et seq. See *Navarro v Moregrand Ltd* [1951] 2 T.L.R. 674 at 680. The existence of a contract of service is, of course, evidence of authority, but authority may be proved otherwise than by proof of employment as a servant.

349 *Wilson v Tumman* (1843) 6 M. & G. 236 at 242, per Tindal CJ. This decision was cited in *Keighley, Maxsted & Co v Durant* [1901] A.C. 240 at 246, per Lord Macnaghten; and at 254 per Lord Davey. Whether, in order to allow of a ratification, the doer of the act must show by express words or conduct at the time that he is acting on behalf of the person who subsequently ratifies is not clear in tort, though the statement of the law by Tindal CJ in *Wilson v Tumman*, "not assuming to act for himself but for such other person", applies to tort as well as contract. The probability is that the law is the same both for contract and tort as part of the law of agency in this respect. In contract he must act for the other: *Keighley, Maxsted & Co v Durant* [1901] A.C. 240; see as to tort, [1901] A.C. 240 at 260, per Lord Robertson.

Vestry,[350] the defendants caused a warrant to be issued by a justice directing the levy of a sum due from a debtor by distress and sale of his goods, and the brokers seized goods belonging to the claimant and let by him to the debtor's wife. The defendants, having learnt from the claimant what had occurred, replied to his letter saying that they were at a loss to understand his threat of proceedings, and would accept service of any process he might issue. It was held that there was evidence of ratification of the seizure and that the defendants were liable.[351]

6-91 **Evidence of ratification** "Ratification must be evidenced by clear adoptive acts, which must be accompanied by full knowledge of all the essential facts",[352] and there can be no ratification unless the party on whose behalf the acts complained of were done "ratified the acts of the agents with knowledge that they did them not according to authority, or unless he meant to take upon himself, without inquiry, the risk of any irregularity which they might have committed, and to adopt all their acts".[353] Therefore where, in an action of trespass against a landlord, it appeared that he gave a broker a warrant to distrain for rent and the broker took away and sold a fixture and paid the proceeds to the defendant, who received them without inquiry, but without knowledge that anything irregular had been done, it was held that the receipt of the proceeds did not amount to ratification.[354] Also, where a railway company's inspector arrested a passenger on a charge of travelling without a ticket and took him before a magistrate, the mere fact of the company's attorney appearing to support the charge was, in the absence of any evidence that he or the company knew that the inspector had proceeded by arrest instead of summons as he should have done, held to be no evidence of ratification by the company of the arrest.[355] In a later case under similar circumstances it was held, on the contention that the company had ratified their inspector's action, that (a) there could be no ratification unless the original act was in some sense done on behalf, and for the benefit, of the company; and (b) the mere fact that the attorney of the company had appeared to prosecute without relevant evidence was not alone sufficient evidence of ratification.[356] The fact that a party, who is sued for trespass committed by one purporting to act on his behalf, has offered a compromise is no evidence of ratification.[357]

6-92 **Relation back** Where a person ratifies the act of one who though without authority professed to act as his agent, such ratification will usually relate back to the time

---

350 (1900) 64 J.P. 548; *Whitehead v Taylor* (1837) 10 A. & E. 210.

351 Aliter, if the seizure is by the sheriff himself or his officers and the process is valid though the wrong goods are seized, for the sheriff acts on behalf of the court: *Wilson v Tumman* (1843) 6 M. & G. 236; *Morris v Salberg* (1889) 22 Q.B.D. 614.

352 per Lord Atkinson in *Eastern Construction Co v National Trust Co* [1914] A.C. 197 at 213.

353 *Freeman v Rosher* (1849) 13 Q.B. 780 at 798, per Tindal CJ. See also the curious case of *Lamont v Duggle* [1953] C.P.L. 491.

354 *Freeman v Rosher* (1849) 13 Q.B. 780; *Haselar v Lemoyne* (1858) 5 C.B. (N.S.) 530. It must be assumed that in these cases there was no notice to the defendant of the illegality before the action was brought, for it could hardly be contended that the act of retaining the proceeds after notice was not a ratification, even though the original receipt was innocent. Cf. *Becker v Riebold* (1913) 30 T.L.R. 142 (keeping goods illegally seized with knowledge of the illegality is evidence of ratification).

355 *Eastern Counties Ry v Broom* (1851) 6 Exch. 314.

356 *Walker v South Eastern Ry* (1870) L.R. 5 C. & P. 640 at 643.

357 *Roe v Birkenhead etc Ry* (1851) 7 Exch. 36. As to evidence of ratification, cf. *Haselar v Lemoyne* (1858) 5 C.B. (N.S.) 530; *Carter v St Mary Abbot's Vestry* (1900) 64 J.P. 548.

of the act done, so that if the act was one which, though unlawful if done without the authority of the principal, might have been lawfully done with such authority, the effect of ratification will be to divest the claimant of the cause of action which until then he had against the professed agent. Where one professes to distrain as bailiff for another "it is sufficient for the defendant in his cognisance to say generally 'as bailiff of J.S.' without showing his authority, and a subsequent agreement by J.S. to the distress amounts to an authority as much as if he had previously directed the defendant to distrain".[358] And this holds good equally where the principal be a subject or the Crown.[359] Similarly, ratification by the claimant of the act of a professed agent may deprive the defendant of a vested defence. Thus if one person without authority issues a writ on behalf of another in order to prevent the operation of a Statute of Limitations, and that other ratifies his act after the time limited by the statute has expired, the effect will be to divest the defendant of the defence under the statute, which was open to him until the ratification.[360]

8. LIMITATIONS ON LIABILITY

Exemplary damages The issue of whether exemplary damages are available where the liability of the defendant is vicarious was debated by the House of Lords in *Kuddus v Chief Constable of Leicestershire*.[361] Although in general terms their Lordships were prepared to countenance a more expansive role for exemplary damages in that case, Lord Scott believed that, as a matter of principle, exemplary damages should not be available in a vicarious liability claim. Since then, however, such damages have been awarded on a vicarious liability basis in *Rowlands v Chief Constable of Merseyside*.[362] However, that case involved the vicarious liability of a chief constable under s.88 of the Police Act 1996 (rather than common law vicarious liability) and a significant basis for the decision was the desire to mark the jury's "vigorous disapproval of the conduct of the police force as an institution".[363] It remains to be seen, therefore, whether this decision will provide the basis for the courts' more general move away from what was said in *Kuddus* about the principled basis for refusing exemplary damages in the context of vicarious liability. 6-93

Limitation of actions[364] At one time, it was thought that intentional torts could not be regarded as falling within s.11 of the Limitation Act 1980. In *A v Hoare*,[365] however, the House of Lords held that the s.11 expression "negligence, nuisance or breach of duty" had been intended to cover cases of trespass to the person and that, therefore, s.33 of that Act could be invoked to disapply the usual limitation 6-94

---

[358] *Potter v North* (1669) 1 Wms. Saund. 347(c), n.4. See also *Hull v Pickersgill* (1819) 1 Brod. & B. 282; *Whitehead v Taylor* (1839) 10 A. & E. 210.

[359] *Buron v Denman* (1848) 2 Exch. 167; *Secretary of State for India v Kamachee Boye Sahaba* (1859) 13 Moo P.C. 22.

[360] See *Shaw, Savill and Albion Co v Timaru Harbour Board* (1890) 15 App. Cas. 429, where a colonial court, having held that ratification of notice of action after the time for giving it had expired was too late, the Privy Council, after hearing an appeal against that decision, proceeded to hear a cross-appeal upon the merits, which would have been unnecessary had they thought the appeal to be ill-founded.

[361] [2001] UKHL 29; [2002] 2 A.C. 122.

[362] [2006] EWCA Civ 1773; [2007] 1 W.L.R. 1065. See further para.6-18.

[363] [2006] EWCA Civ 1773; [2007] 1 W.L.R. 1065 at [42].

[364] See further Ch.31.

[365] [2008] UKHL 6; [2008] 1 A.C. 844.

period. Furthermore, since some of the conjoined appeals in *A v Hoare* were based on the vicarious liability of local authorities for sexual assault committed by teachers whom they had employed, it can be said with confidence that the facility to extend the limitation period in respect of intentional torts can be invoked even where the defendant is only liable by virtue of vicarious liability.

Chapter 7

NEGLIGENCE

Table of Contents

1. THE TORT OF NEGLIGENCE

7-01 **The nature of negligence liability** Negligence is recognised as a separate tort but unlike other torts, negligence is not limited to the protection of a particular kind of interest. Rather, negligence liability is based on the conduct of the defendant and may be imposed in respect of a wide range of interests[1] damaged by that conduct. Hence, it may overlap with narrower torts which protect just one particular interest. The area of overlap is greatest with the stricter liability torts which require lesser culpability. Any interest protected by such a tort is also likely to fall within the scope of negligence liability. Thus a negligent interference with enjoyment of land may give rise to both liability in negligence and nuisance[2] or under *Rylands v Fletcher*.[3] Negligent failure to maintain safety standards by an employer may give rise to both liability for negligence and for the tort breach of statutory duty.[4] Negligent harm to reputation may give rise to both liability for negligence where it occurs within a special relationship causing economic loss,[5] and for defamation which provides wide protection irrespective of fault but subject to a web of defences designed to protect freedom of speech.

7-02 There is less overlap with the intentional torts which require greater culpability than negligence. It is true that whenever an interest is protected by the tort of negligence, it is likely that it will also be protected by an intentional tort. Thus, pecuniary damage caused by a careless false statement falls under negligence; but if caused by an intentional false statement liability is in deceit. But there are two reasons why the overlap is more limited. First, it may be inappropriate to classify intentional conduct as being careless. For example, it can hardly be said that an intentionally false statement has also been made carelessly. But this is not always the case: an intentional touching which constitutes a trespass might also be the result of a careless decision by the defendant and give rise to liability in both negligence and trespass.[6] Secondly, there are interests which do not merit protection by negligence and are protected only by the intentional torts. Thus, whilst there is liability for intentional interference with a person's trading relationships under the so-called economic torts, there is no liability for negligent interference with such

---

1 The tort of negligence protects interests in physical and mental health, reputation, property interests, economic relationships and public rights. For a full analysis of the interests protected by the law of torts generally, see paras 1-26 to 1-50.

2 *Goldman v Hargrave* [1967] 1 A.C. 645. Commenting on *Goldman* in *Delaware Mansions Ltd v Westminster City Council* [2001] UKHL 55; [2002] 1 A.C. 321 at [31] Lord Cooke said: "The label nuisance or negligence is treated as of no real significance. In this field … the concern of the common law lies in working out the fair and just content and incidents of a neighbour's duty rather than affixing a label and inferring the extent of the duty from it."

3 See para.19-44 onwards.

4 See Ch.8.

5 *Spring v Guardian Assurance Plc* [1995] 2 A.C. 296.

6 This overlap has given rise to some problems. In *Letang v Cooper* [1965] 1 Q.B. 232 at 239, Lord Denning suggested that a careless application of force to another would be actionable only in negligence with trespass being confined to intentional conduct. The better view is that a claimant may still sue for negligent trespass but will not be able to claim any advantage from framing his case in trespass. See para.1-54. But even if Lord Denning's view were to be accepted, overlaps would remain. Thus, a surgeon failing to inform a patient "in broad terms of the nature of the procedure intended" would be liable in both battery (because in such circumstances any consent by the patient would be vitiated) and negligence. See paras 9-60 and 9-85. There is no difference, for the purpose of the Limitation Act 1980, between actions in battery and negligence: *A v Hoare* [2008] UKHL 6; [2008] 1 A.C. 844.

interests. Negligence liability would impose too great a restriction on free competition. Malicious prosecution falls into the same category. There is no equivalent negligence liability for bringing a "careless" prosecution.

Negligence liability may also overlap with non-tortious grounds of liability under contractual, equitable or public law principles.[7] This potential overlap may give rise to difficulties where negligence principles point in a different direction from those of other grounds of liability. On occasion, the courts have found it necessary to limit the scope of negligence liability by reference to the other non-tortious principles in order to maintain the coherence of the law.[8] Subject to these qualifications, negligence liability has the potential to apply in a wide range of situations to protect a wide range of interests. It is this potential which has led the courts to develop a complex series of requirements controlling the scope of liability. 7-03

Requirements of the tort of negligence There are four requirements, namely: 7-04

(1) The existence in law of a duty of care situation, i.e. one in which the law attaches liability to carelessness. There has to be recognition by law that the careless infliction of the kind of damage in question on the class of person to which the claimant belongs by the class of person to which the defendant belongs is actionable.
(2) Breach of the duty of care by the defendant, i.e. that there was a failure to measure up to the standard set by law.
(3) A causal connection between the defendant's careless conduct and the damage.
(4) That the particular kind of damage to the particular claimant is not so unforeseeable as to be too remote.

When these four requirements are satisfied, the defendant is liable in negligence. Only then is it relevant to consider the assessment of damages, i.e. the compensation for the damage for which the defendant is responsible. There is no magic in the order as set out, nor should it be supposed that courts proceed from points (1) to (4) in sequence. In this text, causation and remoteness are considered in a separate chapter as the principles are relevant to other forms of tort liability. This chapter considers first, the duty requirement and secondly, the issue of breach.

Requirement for actionable damage Damage is the gist of the tort of negligence. Without damage there is no tort. Negligence does not impose a duty to act carefully; it is a duty not to inflict damage carelessly.[9] But the damage that has been caused must be recognised by the court as "actionable damage". Damage in this sense is "an abstract concept of being worse off, physically or economically, so that compensation is an appropriate remedy."[10] In the context of personal injury, actionable damage does not mean simply a physiological change. The damage must have some perceptible effect on the claimant's health or capability. Thus, symptomless pleural plaques on the lungs developed as a result of inhaling asbestos fibres do not constitute actionable damage; nor does this become actionable damage when combined with the anxiety of the claimants due to their knowledge of the risk of 7-05

7 For explanation of the overlap and distinctions, see paras 1-03 to 1-08.

8 See *Downsview Nominees Ltd v First City Corp Ltd* [1993] A.C. 295.

9 See the quotation from Viscount Simonds speech in *Overseas Tankship (UK) Ltd v Morts Dock & Engineering Co Ltd (The Wagon Mound)* [1961] AC 388 at 425, at para.2-156.

10 *Rothwell v Chemical & Insulating Co* [2007] UKHL 39; [2008] 1 A.C. 281 at [7].

developing serious disease in the future as a result of their exposure to asbestos.[11] On the other hand, if the claimant's otherwise symptomless condition requires the claimant to avoid situations likely to bring on symptoms and this impacts on the claimant's ability to work this does constitute actionable harm. In *Dryden v Johnson Matthey Plc*[12] employees had been sensitised to platinum salts but had not developed any symptoms and would not develop symptoms unless they were further exposed to platinum salts. This had financial consequences for them because they were no longer able to work with platinum salts. The Court of Appeal had held that the employees had not suffered compensatable personal injury because their financial loss constituted pure economic loss which did not fall within the scope of an employers' duty of care for the health and safety of employees.[13] However, the Supreme Court took the view that the sensitisation to platinum salts did constitute actionable personal injury because the claimants' bodily capacity for work had been impaired and they were significantly worse off. This distinguished the case from *Rothwell v Chemical & Insulating Co* where the pleural plaques were "nothing more than a marker of exposure to asbestos dust, being symptomless in themselves and not leading to or contributing to any condition which would produce symptoms, even if the sufferer were to be exposed to further asbestos dust" whereas the sensitisation of the claimants to platinum salts in *Dryden* constituted "a change to their physiological make-up which means that further exposure now carries with it the risk of an allergic reaction, and for that reason they must change their everyday lives so as to avoid such exposure."[14] The loss of part of their capacity to work was a loss of bodily function.[15]

7-06 The harm must also exceed a minimum threshold of severity in order to qualify as actionable damage. Thus, a "transient, trifling, self-limiting, reversible reaction to an irritant is not 'actionable injury' for the purposes of the law of tort."[16]

2. DUTY OF CARE

(a) The nature of the duty concept

7-07 **Duty** The tort of negligence is committed when the damage is sustained. The period of limitation begins to run from the date of that damage.[17] The duty in negligence, therefore, is not simply a duty not to act carelessly; it is a duty not to inflict damage carelessly. Since damage is the gist of the action, what is meant by "duty of care situation" is that it has to be shown that the courts recognise as action-

11 *Rothwell v Chemical & Insulating Co* [2007] UKHL 39; [2008] 1 A.C. 281. See also *A v A Health and Social Services Trust* [2011] NICA 28; [2012] N.I. 77 (claimants born with a different skin colour from that of their parents due to negligence in the selection of gametes for in vitro fertilisation had not suffered actionable damage: "Having a different skin colour from the majority of the surrounding population and their parents' cannot sensibly be regarded as damage or disability…" at [9]).

12 [2018] UKSC 18; [2019] A.C. 403; discussed by J. Huang, "Dryden v Johnson Matthey: the boundaries of actionable damage" (2019) 82 M.L.R. 737.

13 *Greenway v Johnson Matthey Plc* [2016] EWCA Civ 408; [2016] 1 W.L.R. 4487.

14 [2018] UKSC 18; [2019] A.C. 403 at [47], per Lady Black.

15 Although there was a clear financial consequence linked to working capacity in *Dryden* the principle ought also to apply outside the work context, so that if, for example, the claimant had been sensitised to another substance that had a significant impact on daily life, e.g. restricting the claimant's leisure activities, that too should be treated as actionable bodily harm.

16 *Saunderson v Sonae Industria (UK) Ltd* [2015] EWHC 2264 (QB) at [179], per Jay J.

17 Determining the date on which damage occurs may give rise to difficulty: see para.31-10 onwards.

able the careless infliction of the kind of damage of which the claimant complains,[18] on the type of person to which he belongs, and by the type of person to which the defendant belongs. It is a preliminary consideration whether liability is even *capable* of attaching to the defendant in the given type of situation. In the words of Lord Wright:

> "It is essential in English law that the duty should be established: the mere fact that a man is injured by another's act gives in itself no cause of action: if the act is deliberate, the party injured will have no claim in law even though the injury is intentional so long as the other party is merely exercising a legal right: if the act involves a lack of due care, again no case of actionable negligence will arise unless the duty to be careful exists."[19]

The list of situations giving rise to a duty of care is not fixed. As Lord Macmillan famously said: "The grounds of action may be as various and manifold as human errancy; and the conception of legal responsibility may develop in adaptation to altering social conditions and standards. The criterion of judgment must adjust and adapt itself to the changing circumstances of life. The categories of negligence are never closed".[20] Parliament or the courts can create new duty situations. Duty is a dynamic concept.

Notional duty It is important to distinguish the question whether a notional duty of care exists from the narrower questions of whether a factual duty is owed to the claimant and whether the kind of damage is too remote. A notional duty applies to a general class of relationship and damage. Hence, the key question is whether, in relation to all factual situations within that class, a notional duty exists. However powerful the arguments in favour of a duty on the particular facts of the claimant's case, they may be outweighed by counter arguments relating to the general class of relationship within which that case falls to be assessed.[21] As Lord Browne-Wilkinson has said, with reference to the public interest aspect of the duty test: **7-08**

> "In English law the decision as to whether it is fair, just and reasonable to impose a liability in negligence on a particular class of would-be defendants depends on weighing in the balance the total detriment to the public interest in all cases from holding such class liable in negligence against the total loss to all would-be claimants if they are not to have a cause of action in respect of the loss they have individually suffered … . The decision does not depend on weighing the balance between the extent of the damage to the claimant and the damage to the public in each particular case."[22]

The point is well illustrated by *Ancell v McDermott*, where Beldam LJ said in relation to the duty of police officers to warn of road hazards:

> "The question is not whether the police officers in the circumstances found to obtain in this particular case owed a duty to the [claimants], but whether in any circumstances of

[18] "[T]he bare question whether a defendant owes a claimant a duty of care, without defining the scope of the duty with reference to the injury or loss for which the claimant claims damages, is conceptually questionable": *Rice v Secretary of State for Trade and Industry* [2007] EWCA Civ 289; [2007] I.C.R. 1469 at [6], per May LJ.

[19] *Grant v Australian Knitting Mills Ltd* [1936] A.C. 85 at 103.

[20] *Donoghue v Stevenson* [1932] A.C. 562 at 619.

[21] Thus, in *Palmer v Tees HA* [1999] Lloyd's Rep. Med. 351 at 356, Stuart-Smith LJ rejected the argument that the scope of the notional duty could be extended "simply because the facts of a given case are particularly horrifying or heart-rending".

[22] *Barrett v Enfield LBC* [2001] 2 A.C. 550 at 559.

> the kind pleaded, a police constable owes a duty to other drivers to protect them from, or warn them against, hazards created by others on the road."[23]

Noting that such a notional duty would include "the constable on the beat who failed to notice a danger on the pavement" and "the officer who misinterpreted a breathalyser" as well as the particular case involving the officer who failed to take action upon noticing a serious oil spillage on the road, Beldam LJ concluded that no notional duty could be imposed in relation to that class of activities. Clearly the level of generality at which the notional duty is pitched is crucial.[24] The wider the scope of the alleged notional duty, the more difficult it will be to justify liability in all the situations falling within it. The narrower the scope of the duty, the easier it will be to justify liability in all situations falling within its scope. But to define the duty narrowly, it must be possible to draw defensible lines between those situations that fall within the duty and those outside its scope.[25]

7-09 **Factual duty** Once a notional duty of a given scope has been accepted, then the question is whether the particular claimant comes within the scope of that duty so as to render the damage actionable at his suit. The question becomes one of factual duty. Thus, in *Bourhill v Young*[26] it was accepted that the defendant motorcyclist owed a notional duty of care to those within the foreseeable area of risk caused by his driving but it was held that, on the particular facts, he did not owe a duty to the particular claimant, a bystander, who suffered unforeseeable psychiatric harm as a result of witnessing the accident. The fact that the motorcyclist would have owed a duty of care to the driver of a car involved in the accident was irrelevant. As Lord Wright said, "if the [claimant] has a cause of action it is because of a wrong to herself. She cannot build on a wrong to someone else."[27]

7-10 **Duty to class of claimant** As a general rule it is not necessary that the claimant should have been within the defendant's contemplation as an identified individual. It is sufficient if he falls within the class of persons who might foreseeably suffer the particular loss to which the duty relates. In the case of the duty relating to simple physical injury, that will mean those who are within the area of foreseeable injury

---

23 [1993] 4 All E.R. 355 at 359.

24 See *Alexandrou v Oxford* [1993] 4 All E.R. 328 in which the narrow question was whether the police owed a duty of care to the owner of an intruder alarm which, when activated, made an automatic 999 call to the police station. The trial judge concluded that a duty was owed to the class of owners of intruder alarms connected to police stations but in the Court of Appeal, Glidewell LJ held that the judge had defined the class too narrowly and that if the police came under a duty to this claimant, it must follow that they would be under a similar duty to any person who informs them, whether by 999 call or in some other way, of any crime against himself or his property. The notional duty question had to be answered at that level of generality and, on that basis, no notional duty was owed.

25 In the words of May J in *Topp v London Country Bus South West Ltd* [1993] 3 All E.R. 448 at 460, the task of the court is "to be alive to the consequences of a decision that one particular set of facts gives rise to a duty of care and to consider carefully whether there is a line to be drawn beyond which a duty is not recognised and, if so, where to draw the line".

26 [1943] A.C. 92. An instructive American case is *Palsgraf v Long Island Railroad*, 248 N.Y. 339 (1928), where an employee of the defendants knocked a package out of the hands of a passenger at a railway station. Unknown to them the package contained fireworks, which exploded, and the concussion overturned a weighing machine on to the claimant some way down the platform. The claimant failed because it was not reasonably foreseeable that the dropping of a package in those circumstances would have inflicted any injury on a person situated where the claimant was.

27 [1943] A.C. 92 at 108.

when the danger materialises. In *Farrugia v Great Western Ry Co*[28] the defendant company had loaded their lorry with too large a container. When the lorry was driven under a bridge the container was thrown off and injured the claimant who happened to be running behind the lorry with a view to clambering on board. The Court of Appeal, rejecting the defendants' contention that they could not have anticipated the claimant's presence there at that moment, held them liable. Lord Greene MR said:

> "I cannot see, on any ground of principle or common sense, why a distinction should be made between the [claimant] running in the road to get on the lorry and a foot passenger lawfully crossing the road immediately behind the lorry. I should have thought the duty was a duty to take care vis-à-vis anyone—not this [claimant] as such, but anyone—the general class of person who, at the moment when the danger materialised, might happen to be in the near neighbourhood."[29]

Again, in *Haley v London Electricity Board*[30] it was sufficient for the blind claimant to show that those undertaking pavement works should foresee risks to blind pedestrians.

Class of claimant and scope of duty In the case of other forms of injury and loss, the class may be more tightly limited by the scope of the notional duty.[31] In cases where damage has been caused by a third party such as *Home Office v Dorset Yacht Co Ltd*,[32] the foreseeable class is limited to those likely to be affected by the defendant's failure to control the third party.[33] In cases where psychiatric injury has been caused, the notional duty is limited by a number of requirements and hence, at the level of factual duty, the question is whether the claimant comes within a class satisfying those requirements. In cases where economic loss has been suffered following reliance on the defendant's statement, the notional duty is restricted to those to whom the defendant assumed a responsibility and the question will be whether the claimant comes within this class. These qualifications to the foreseeability criterion are not exceptions to a general rule but simply reflect the fact that the question to be asked at the level of factual duty is determined by the scope of the notional duty. **7-11**

Notional duty and remoteness Even if a notional duty exists and a factual duty is owed to the class within which the claimant comes, there will be no liability unless the kind of damage suffered is a foreseeable consequence of the breach of the **7-12**

---

28 [1947] 2 All E.R. 565; see also *Buckland v Guildford Gas Light and Coke Co* [1949] 1 K.B. 410; *Carmarthenshire CC v Lewis* [1955] A.C. 549; *Videan v BTC* [1963] 2 Q.B. 650 at 675–676, 683.

29 [1947] 2 All E.R. 565 at 567.

30 [1965] A.C. 778.

31 Though unusual circumstances may *extend* the scope of the defendant's duty. So, although a caterer would normally owe no duty to warn guests at a function that the food supplied may contain eggs because a person who is allergic to eggs can generally be expected to look after his own interests, if the function is a Sikh wedding where it is known that, for religious reasons, the food should not contain eggs so that a guest with an egg allergy would have felt quite safe in eating it without further inquiry, the caterer's duty may extend to giving such a warning: *Bhamra v Dubb (t/a Lucky Caterers)* [2010] EWCA Civ 13. However, query why the caterer's contractual duty to avoid offending religious sensitivities changes the nature of his duty in tort; cf. *Darby v National Trust* [2001] EWCA Civ 189; [2001] P.I.Q.R. P27 (breach of duty to warn visitors about risk of contracting infection from swimming in a pond, but defendant not liable for swimmer's death from drowning).

32 [1970] A.C. 1004.

33 See paras 7-60 and 13-70.

notional duty. Thus, in the first *Wagon Mound* case[34] the foreseeable damage from spilling a quantity of furnace oil into the waters of a harbour was held to be pollution, not fire. Because such damage was a foreseeable risk and easily preventable, the defendant's conduct was careless. It would have been actionable by a person suffering pollution damage. But the claimants' property was damaged by fire and this was damage of a different kind from pollution. The fire was too remote a kind of damage. Issues of remoteness are inter-linked with those of causation and both are analysed in Ch.2. The point to be made here is that whilst foreseeability plays a role in both the test for notional duty and remoteness, the role is different as is the function of the concepts. In the case of notional duty, foreseeability of harm is just one of the criteria used to determine whether a notional duty should be owed and it is applied in relation to the general type of conduct for which the defendant is responsible. The question is whether the level of risk created by that type of conduct is such as to justify a general duty of care in relation to it. In the case of remoteness, foreseeability of the kind of harm is the sole test and it is applied in the light of the particular breach of duty for which the defendant was responsible. The question is whether the kind of damage was fairly within the risk created by the defendant.[35]

7-13 **Notional duty and causation** Even if both the claimant and the kind of damage are foreseeable, there may still be a further question, namely whether the defendant should be held causally responsible for the manner in which the damage was caused. The question of causation cannot be divorced from that of duty. The policy underlying the duty may influence the application of causation principles.[36] Further, in cases where the damage was a direct result of the conduct of a third party and only indirectly the consequence of the defendant's conduct, courts may analyse the problem at either the level of notional duty or by reference to the principles of causal responsibility, and the two issues may merge.[37] In one sense this is inconsequential as much the same criteria are used under both heads. However, it is suggested that notional duty is the appropriate concept to use when the question is whether the general causal pattern could give rise to a duty, whereas causation is appropriate when the question is whether liability is justified on the particular facts of the case. This distinction may be illustrated by contrasting two 1993 decisions of the Court of Appeal. The duty approach was taken in *Topp v London Country Bus*.[38] The issue was whether the owner of a minibus left with its ignition keys and unlocked outside a pub for nine hours, was liable to the victim of an accident in which it was involved after it had been stolen. May J, whose judgment was endorsed by the Court of Appeal, placed primary weight on the general nature of the relationship rather than the particular facts. He concluded that it would not be reasonable to impose a duty on the public generally to secure their vehicles to prevent them being stolen by criminals and used to cause damage to third parties.

---

34 [1961] A.C. 388.

35 See para.2-153 onwards.

36 See for example *Chester v Afshar* [2004] UKHL 41; [2005] 1 A.C. 134, where the importance attached to the duty to warn a patient of the risks of surgery led the House of Lords to apply the principles of causation so as to provide the patient with a remedy. See further para.2-16.

37 See, e.g. *Lamb v Camden LBC* [1981] Q.B. 625. See further para.2-122.

38 [1993] 3 All E.R. 448 (QBD) and 464 (CA); [1993] 1 W.L.R. 976.

In *Wright v Lodge*[39] a causation analysis was adopted. The question was whether the driver of a car who failed to move her car to the hard shoulder after breaking down in the slow lane of a dual carriage way, was liable to a motorist on the opposite side of the carriage way who was struck by a lorry which had gone out of control and crossed the central reservation after hitting the stationary car. The Court of Appeal concluded that the reckless speed at which the lorry was being driven was such as to "exclude (the car driver's) conduct as being causative of the subsequent accident".[40]

(b) The test for notional duty

The neighbour principle The modern search for a general test capable of determining whether a notional duty should exist in any given type of relationship begins with the celebrated judgment of Lord Atkin in *Donoghue v Stevenson*.[41] After noting that the courts had hitherto been "concerned with the particular relations which came before them in actual litigation" and had found it sufficient simply "to say whether the duty exists in those circumstances", he went on to suggest that "There must be, and is, some general conception of relations giving rise to a duty of care, of which the particular cases found in the books are but instances". He formulated the general conception in these words: 7-14

> "The rule that you are to love your neighbour becomes in law, you must not injure your neighbour; and the lawyer's question, who is my neighbour? receives a restricted reply. You must take reasonable care to avoid acts or omissions which you can reasonably foresee would be likely to injure your neighbour. Who, then, in law is my neighbour? The answer seems to be—persons who are so closely and directly affected by my act that I ought reasonably to have them in contemplation as being so affected when I am directing my mind to the acts or omissions which are called in question."[42]

As Lord Atkin explained, there were two elements in this formulation. The first was the test of reasonable foresight. A duty would exist only where injury was reasonably foreseeable. The second was the proximity requirement, namely that the duty was limited to "persons so closely and directly affected" by the defendant's act that they should be in his contemplation. As Lord Atkin noted, this concept of proximity was wider than that of physical closeness. It turned on the closeness of the relationship. The significance of the foreseeability test and the proximity requirement was apparent from their application in *Donoghue* itself.

Donoghue v Stevenson A bottle of ginger beer, sold by a manufacturer to a retailer and by him to a purchaser, was consumed by the claimant, a friend of the purchaser to whom it had been given and who thus had no contractual relationship with anyone. The claimant alleged she suffered illness as a result of the contamination of the beer by a decomposing snail in the bottle. With no contractual remedy available, she sued the manufacturer in tort. A preliminary point of law as to whether the manufacturer was even capable of being liable to her was referred to the House of Lords, which by a bare majority ruled in the affirmative, and referred 7-15

39 [1993] 4 All E.R. 299.
40 [1993] 4 All E.R. 299 at 307, per Parker LJ. Woolf and Staughton LJJ considered the case solely in terms of a break in the chain of causation.
41 [1932] A.C. 562.
42 [1932] A.C. 562 at 580.

the case back for decision.[43] Lord Atkin's conclusion on the duty issue was as follows (at 599):

> "... a manufacturer of products which he sells in such a form as to show that he intends them to reach the ultimate consumer in the form in which they left him, with no reasonable possibility of intermediate examination, and with the knowledge that the absence of reasonable care in the preparation or putting up of the products will result in injury to the consumer's life or property, owes a duty to the consumer to take that reasonable care."

The requirement that the manufacturer know of the danger to the consumer stemmed from an application of the reasonable foresight test; and the requirement that he intend the products to reach the consumer "in the form in which they left him, with no reasonable possibility of intermediate examination" stemmed from an application of the proximity test. Taken together, knowledge and the absence of possible intermediate examination defined the scope of the notional duty applicable to manufacturer-consumer relationships.[44]

7-16 **Developing a universal test** Lord Atkin's foreseeability and proximity test was clearly intended to be of general application, capable of assisting courts in determining the scope of the notional duty in relation to all kinds of acts and omissions. But it was only the means by which the ratio of *Donoghue* was determined and not the ratio itself. That was confined to the liability of a manufacturer of goods towards ultimate consumers. Hence, courts were not bound to apply the Atkin test and for some years remained reluctant to utilise it, particularly in the face of prior authority denying the existence of a notional duty of care. The key change of attitude came with the House of Lords' decision in *Dorset Yacht Co Ltd v Home Office*[45] where the test was used to support the conclusion that prison officers owed a notional duty of care in respect of the custody of prisoners to owners of near-by property likely to be damaged if the prisoners escaped. The likelihood that the property would be damaged meant that the owners were "closely and directly affected" by the officers' conduct and hence the requirement of proximity was satisfied. The Atkin test was given strong endorsement, particularly by Lord Reid:

> "the well-known passage in Lord Atkin's speech should I think be regarded as a statement of principle. It is not to be treated as if it were a statutory definition. It will require qualification in new circumstances. But I think that the time has come when we can and should say that it ought to apply unless there is some justification or valid explanation for its exclusion."[46]

7-17 **Fairness and the three stage test** After a period during which the courts had

---

43 Owing to the death of one of the parties, the suit was settled so that there was in fact no decision as to whether there had been a snail in the ginger beer. The story of the case is recounted by McBryde in Burns (ed.), *Donoghue v Stevenson and the Modern Law of Negligence* (1991).

44 Over subsequent years the scope of the notional duty applicable to manufacturers has been extended by interpreting the term "reasonable possibility" of intermediate inspection to mean "reasonable *probability*". See para.10-08 onwards.

45 [1970] A.C. 1004. In *Anns v Merton LBC* [1978] A.C. 728 at 757, Lord Wilberforce observed that " ... it may well be that full recognition of the impact of *Donoghue v Stevenson* ... came only with the decision of this house in *Home Office v Dorset Yacht Co*".

46 *Dorset Yacht Co Ltd v Home Office* [1970] A.C. 1004 at 1027; See also Lord Pearson at 1054 and Lord Morris at 1034. Lord Diplock was more cautious, saying at 1060:

> "Used as a guide to the characteristics which will be found to exist in conduct and relationships which give rise to a legal duty of care this aphorism marks a milestone in the modern development of the law of negligence. But misused as a universal it is manifestly false."

debated both the relationship of foreseeability and proximity and the relevance of policy considerations,[47] the outcome was summarised by Lord Bridge in *Caparo Industries Plc v Dickman*[48]:

> "What emerges is that, in addition to the foreseeability of damage, necessary ingredients in any situation giving rise to a duty of care are that there should exist between the party owing the duty and the party to whom it is owed a relationship characterised by the law as one of 'proximity' or 'neighbourhood' and that the situation should be one in which the court considers it fair, just and reasonable that the law should impose a duty of a given scope on the one party for the benefit of the other."[49]

This passage has been cited in numerous subsequent decisions.[50] It has come to be known as the three stage, or tripartite, test encompassing: (1) foreseeability of harm to the claimant; (2) proximity of relationship between claimant and defendant; and (3) whether imposing a duty would be fair, just and reasonable. Commenting on the role of the three criteria in *Caparo*, Lord Oliver said:

> "… it is difficult to resist the conclusion that what have been treated as three separate requirements are, at least in most cases, in fact merely facets of the same thing, for in some cases the degree of foreseeability is such that it is from that alone the requisite proximity can be deduced, whilst in others the absence of the essential relationship can most rationally be attributed simply to the court's view that it would not be fair and reasonable to hold the defendant responsible."[51]

The criteria can be viewed as overlapping.[52] It has been said that "the two headings (proximity and justice) are no more than two labels under which the court examines the pros and cons of imposing liability in negligence in a particular type of case".[53] To an extent, this is true of whatever formula is used to determine duty. As Sir Robin Cooke has observed:

> "Ultimately the exercise can only be a balancing one and the important object is that all relevant factors be weighed. There is no escape from the truth that, whatever formula be used, the outcome in a grey area case has to be determined by judicial judgment. Formulae can help organise thinking but they cannot provide answers."[54]

The last point is significant, for although the factors which are relevant to one

---

47 The debate centred on the so-called "two-stage test" of Lord Wilberforce in *Anns v Merton LBC* [1978] A.C. 728 at 751–752, a case concerning local authority liability for an omission. However, the test seemed to equate proximity with contemplation or foreseeability. The lack of a proximity requirement in the sense of a "close and direct relationship" led to criticism of the Wilberforce test and its eventual replacement by a "three stage test" in *Caparo*.

48 [1990] 2 A.C. 605 at 617 to 618.

49 Lord Oliver also referred to this three stage, foreseeability, proximity, justice and reasonableness test, [1990] 2 A.C. 605 at 633, and Lord Jauncey at 658 cited Lord Griffiths' speech in *Smith v Eric S Bush* [1990] 1 A.C. 831 at 865, as authority for "the three criteria … foreseeability of damage, proximity of relationship and reasonableness".

50 See for example in the House of Lords: *Spring v Guardian Assurance Plc* [1995] 2 A.C. 296 at 333, per Lord Slynn; *Marc Rich & Co v Bishop Rock Marine* [1996] A.C. 211 at 235, per Lord Steyn.

51 [1990] 2 A.C. 605 at 618.

52 "These considerations inevitably shade into each other": *Elguzouli-Daf v Commissioner of Police of the Metropolis* [1995] Q.B. 335 at 349, per Steyn LJ.

53 *White v Jones* [1995] 2 A.C. 207 at 221, per Nicholls V-C; *Caparo Industries Plc v Dickman* [1990] 2 A.C. 605 at 628, per Lord Roskill: "… they are but labels descriptive of the very different factual situations which can exist in particular cases and … must be carefully examined … before it can be pragmatically determined whether a duty of care exists …".

54 *South Pacific Manufacturing Co Ltd v New Zealand Security Consultants & Investigations Ltd*

criterion may also be relevant to another, the criteria help organise thinking because they direct the court to the different questions with reference to which the balancing exercise is conducted.[55]

7-18 **Three stage test applies to "novel" cases only** In *Robinson v Chief Constable of West Yorkshire*[56] Lord Reed said that the proposition that *Caparo* had established a test that applies to all claims in negligence, and that as a result the court will only impose a duty of care where it considers it fair, just and reasonable to do so, was mistaken.[57] *Caparo* had repudiated the idea that there is a single test which can be applied in all cases. Novel cases should be considered using the incremental approach.[58] Where claims are not novel, but fall within an existing category of duty, *Caparo* is not relevant and the court simply has to apply established principles to the particular circumstances of the case. It is not appropriate in such cases for the court to resort to what it considers to be fair, just and reasonable, discarding established principles, in order to achieve a result that the court thinks better fits the broader merits. Such an approach would be "a recipe for inconsistency and uncertainty." In a novel case the court has to exercise judgment when deciding whether a new duty of care should be imposed, and it is the exercise of this judgment that involves consideration of what is "fair, just and reasonable".[59]

7-19 Lord Reed returned to this theme in *Poole BC v GN*,[60] stating that *Caparo* was "widely misunderstood as establishing a general tripartite test" which was little more than the discredited *Anns* two stage test[61] with the addition of a requirement that the imposition of a duty of care should also be fair, just and reasonable. This led to the courts weighing questions of public policy which they were "not well equipped to conduct in a convincing fashion".[62] *Caparo* had not imposed a universal tripartite test for the existence of a duty of care, but "recommended an incremental approach to novel situations, based on the use of established categories of liability as guides, by analogy, to the existence and scope of a duty of care in cases which fall outside them."[63] The courts had, apparently, been confused by and misunderstood the effect of *Caparo*, particularly in the context of the liabilities of public authorities in negligence, until clarification was provided by the Supreme Court in

---

[1992] 2 N.Z.L.R. 282 at 294. As Lord Pearce put it in *Hedley Byrne & Co Ltd v Heller & Partners Ltd* [1964] A.C. 465 at 536, the answer "depends ultimately on the courts' assessment of the demands of society for protection from the carelessness of others".

55 In *Perre v Apand Pty Ltd* (1999) 164 A.L.R. 606 at 684, Kirby J noted the value of the labels in the threefold test in helping to "steer the mind through the task in hand" by providing the "headings to which considerations may be assigned".

56 [2018] UKSC 4; [2018] A.C. 736 at [21]–[29]. See further paras 13-42 to 13-44.

57 Citing *Michael v Chief Constable of South Wales Police* [2015] UKSC 2; [2015] A.C. 1732 at [106] where Lord Toulson observed that in *Caparo* Lord Bridge had emphasised that "the concepts both of 'proximity' and 'fairness' were not susceptible of any definition which would make them useful as practical tests, but were little more than labels to attach to features of situations which the law recognised as giving rise to a duty of care. Paradoxically, this passage in Lord Bridge's speech has sometimes come to be treated as a blueprint for deciding cases, despite the pains which the author took to make clear that it was not intended to be any such thing."

58 See para.7-27.

59 [2018] UKSC 4; [2018] A.C. 736 at [27], per Lord Reed.

60 [2019] UKSC 25; [2019] 2 W.L.R. 1478; see further para.13-03.

61 *Anns v Merton LBC* [1978] A.C. 728; see fn.47 above.

62 [2019] UKSC 25; [2019] 2 W.L.R. 1478 at [30].

63 [2019] UKSC 25; [2019] 2 W.L.R. 1478 at [64].

Michael v Chief Constable of South Wales Police[64] and *Robinson*. It followed that the reasoning in cases in the intervening period had in some cases, and to varying degrees, been superseded by later developments.[65] In applying this incremental approach care has to be taken to identify the correct category of liability to which the case is most closely analogous. So in both *Robinson* and *Poole BC* the lower courts had failed to spot that the outcome in each case depended on the long-established distinction between liability for acts and non-liability for omissions, or as Lord Reed preferred to express this category the distinction between causing harm and failing to prevent harm (or failing to confer a benefit).[66]

Foreseeability and proximity The criterion of reasonable foreseeability focuses on the knowledge that someone in the defendant's position would be expected to possess. The greater the awareness of the potential for harm, the more likely it is that this criterion will be satisfied. If the risk of harm is far-fetched, a duty will not arise. Proximity focuses on the broader relationship between the parties. In a much cited passage of his judgment in *Sutherland Shire Council v Heyman*,[67] Deane J described the requirement as follows: **7-20**

> "It involves the notion of nearness or closeness and embraces physical proximity (in the sense of space and time) between the person or property of the claimant and the person or property of the defendant, circumstantial proximity such as an overriding relationship … of professional man and client and what might (perhaps loosely) be referred to as causal proximity in the sense of the closeness or directness of the causal connection or relationship between the particular course of conduct and the loss or injury sustained. It may reflect an assumption by one party of a responsibility to take care to avoid or prevent injury, loss or damage to the person or property of another or reliance by one party upon such care being taken where the other party ought to have known of such reliance. Both the identity and relative importance of the factors which are determinative of an issue of proximity are likely to vary in different categories of case."

Thus proximity may consist of various forms of closeness—physical, circumstantial, causal or assumed. It involves considering the relationship from the perspective of both the defendant and the claimant.[68] At root, it will reflect "a balancing of the claimant's moral claim to compensation for avoidable harm and the defendant's moral claim to be protected from an undue burden of legal responsibility".[69] As such it will inevitably overlap with considerations of justice between the parties.[70]

---

64 [2015] UKSC 2; [2015] A.C. 1732.

65 *Poole BC v GN* [2019] UKSC 25; [2019] 2 W.L.R. 1478 at [34].

66 *Robinson* involved a positive act of negligence by the police, giving rise to a duty of care (see para.7-25), whereas *Poole BC* involved an omission to confer a benefit by protecting the claimants from their neighbours, in respect of which the local authority owed no duty of care.

67 (1985) 60 A.L.R. 1 at 55–56.

68 As Neill LJ has said: "the question 'who is my neighbour?' prompts the response, 'Consider first those who would consider you to be their neighbour'": *McNaughton Papers Group v Hicks Anderson* [1991] 2 Q.B. 113 at 126.

69 per Richardson J in *South Pacific Manufacturing Co Ltd v New Zealand Security Consultants & Investigations Ltd* [1992] 2 N.Z.L.R. 282 at 306.

70 Thus, they will often be considered together: see for example, Swinton-Thomas LJ in *Perrett v Collins* [1999] P.N.L.R. 77 at 100.

7-21 **Fairness, justice and reasonableness** Justice and reasonableness is a test of "ordinary reason and common sense".[71] It has been said that, in itself, "the expression means little more than that the court should only impose a duty of care if it considers it right to do so".[72] As such it encompasses a wide range of considerations. At its narrowest, it focuses on justice and fairness as between the parties. At a broader level, it will consider the reasonableness of a duty from the perspective of legal policy, focusing on the operation of the legal system and its principles. At a still wider but more controversial level, it may take account of the social and public policy implications of imposing a duty. It is probably this broader approach to the question of whether to impose a duty of care that the Supreme Court was seeking to curb, at least below appellate level, in *Poole BC v GN*,[73] indicating that "in the ordinary run of cases, courts should apply established principles of law, rather than basing their decisions on their assessment of the requirements of public policy".

7-22 **Justice** As Bingham MR said in *X (Minors) v Bedfordshire CC*,[74] "the rule of public policy which has first claim on the loyalty of the law [is] that wrongs should be remedied". Again, in *McFarlane v Tayside Health Board*[75] Lord Steyn referred to the significance of corrective justice which "requires somebody who has harmed another without justification to indemnify the other". However, he noted that this principle might have to be balanced against that of distributive justice calling for a just distribution of burdens and losses. In the same case Lord Clyde rejected the parents' claim for the cost of bringing up an unwanted child on the grounds that "reasonableness includes a consideration of the proportionality between the wrongdoing and the loss suffered thereby" and that such a loss would be "wholly disproportionate to the doctor's culpability" and would not "accord with the idea of restitution".[76] Similar considerations have led the courts to restrict liability for psychiatric illness.[77] In other situations, the need to provide an effective remedy has been found to outweigh the burden placed upon the defendant by the imposition of a duty.[78] Assessing the burden may involve considering the relative exposure to risk of the class of claimant and defendant concerned and the availability of protection

---

71 per Saville J in *Minories Finance Ltd v Arthur Young (A Firm)* [1989] 2 All E.R. 105 at 110. The origin of the requirement is the speech of Lord Radcliffe in *Davis Contractors Ltd v Fareham Urban DC* [1956] A.C. 696 at 728, in which he referred to the court as "the spokesman of the fair and reasonable man". In *Home Office v Dorset Yacht Co Ltd* [1970] A.C. 1004 at 1039, Lord Morris cited Lord Radcliffe when suggesting that fairness and reasonableness were relevant to the imposition of a duty of care.

72 *Glaister v Appleby-in-Westmorland Town Council* [2009] EWCA Civ 1325; [2010] P.I.Q.R. P6 at [58], per Toulson LJ.

73 [2019] UKSC 25; [2019] 2 W.L.R. 1478 at [64].

74 [1995] 2 A.C. 633 at 662. He added that the remedy of compensation was "usually the best the law can do" and accepted that imposition of a duty could make a "contribution to the maintenance of high standards". These general propositions were endorsed by Lord Browne-Wilkinson in *Bedfordshire* [1995] 2 A.C. 633 at 749 and by Lord Slynn in *Barrett v Enfield LBC* [2001] 2 A.C. 550 at 568. See also the endorsement of righting wrongs as "one of the most basic aspirations of the law" by Lord Steyn in *Chester v Afshar* [2004] UKHL 41; [2005] 1 A.C. 134 at [25].

75 [2000] 2 A.C. 59 at 82.

76 [2000] 2 A.C. 59 at 106. But note that a small but negligent error by a motorist may result in liability for large damages, and courts have not been concerned about proportionality in this context.

77 See paras 7-69 onwards, particularly from para.7-75.

78 See Lord Woolf in *Spring v Guardian Assurance Plc* [1995] 2 A.C. 296 at 352 (employer owes duty of care to employee in respect of an inaccurate employment reference).

through insurance[79] or contractual arrangements.[80] Thus, in *Donoghue v Stevenson* the fact that but for negligence liability the consumer who was not also the purchaser would be left with no remedy at all, was a key factor in justifying the duty.[81]

Legal policy The reasonableness of a duty from the broader perspective of the operation and coherence of the law will also be relevant. Thus, courts may consider the so-called floodgates argument, i.e. that if a duty is to be imposed on the facts of the particular case, it will have to be imposed in a wide range of similar situations with the result that the burden of liability on the class of defendant may be considered to be disproportionate to the conduct involved. Courts will also be reluctant to impose a duty which may give rise to indeterminate liability, that is, where the number and nature of claims resulting from breach of the proposed duty cannot be realistically calculated. This is a particular problem where negligence has a "ripple effect", for example, where economic loss "ripples" down a chain of parties[82] or where the impact of a shocking accident "ripples" out from relatives of the victim to friends, rescuers and mere witnesses. The overall framework of the legal system may also be relevant on the ground that it would not be just and reasonable to impose negligence liability if the rights and duties of the parties have been clearly defined by equity,[83] statute[84] or other tort actions. The wider interests of the legal system may include concerns about the evidentiary difficulties following imposition of a duty, for example, in relation to psychiatric harm[85] and the appropriateness of a tort law remedy.[86] At the broadest level, perceptions of community attitudes and goals may also be relevant.[87] Thus, in two leading cases, Lord Steyn purported to consider the likely views of commuters on the Underground when 7-23

79 See the explanation of the duty imposed on the surveyor in *Smith v Bush* [1990] 1 A.C. 831 and the lack of duty on the accountant in *Caparo* [1990] 2 A.C. 605 given by Hoffmann J in *Morgan Crucible v Hill Samuel* [1991] Ch. 295 at 302:

> "The typical (house purchaser) is a person of modest means and making the most expensive purchase of his or her life. He is very unlikely to be insured against the manifestation of inherent defects. The surveyor can protect himself relatively easily by insurance. The take-over bidder, on the other hand, is an entrepreneur taking high risks for high reward and while some accountants may be able to take out sufficient insurance, others may not. Furthermore, the take-over bidder is a limited liability company and the accountants are individuals for whom, save in so far as they are covered by insurance, liability would mean personal ruin."

80 See, e.g. Ralph Gibson LJ in *Pacific Associates Inc v Baxter* [1990] 1 Q.B. 993 at 1032 (imposition of duty of care would cut across and be inconsistent with the structure of contractual relationship entered into by the parties).

81 Leading illustrations of this argument leading to the imposition of a duty, are provided by *White v Jones* [1995] 2 A.C. 207; and *Spring v Guardian Assurance Plc* [1995] 2 A.C. 296.

82 See Stapleton, "Duty of Care and Economic Loss" (1991) 107 L.Q.R. 249, 255.

83 *Downsview Nominees Ltd v First City Corp Ltd* [1993] A.C. 295 at 316 per Lord Templeman.

84 *Deloitte Haskins & Sells v National Mutual Life* [1993] A.C. 774.

85 See Lord Wilberforce in *McLoughlin v O'Brian* [1983] 1 A.C. 410 at 421; and Lord Steyn in *White v Chief Constable of South Yorkshire Police* [1999] 2 A.C. 455 at 493.

86 See for example, Lord Hoffmann's concern in *Wainwright v Home Office* [2003] UKHL 53; [2004] 2 A.C. 406 at [45], about the appropriateness of tort litigation as a means of dealing with distress caused by workplace behaviour; and in *Chester v Afshar* [2004] UKHL 41; [2005] 1 A.C. 134 at [34] about its suitability as a vehicle for distributing modest compensation to patients not properly warned of the risks of treatment.

87 See, e.g. the reference by Lord Templeman to the fact that "the public are exhorted to purchase their homes and cannot find houses to rent" when arguing in *Smith v Eric S Bush* [1990] 1 A.C. 831 at 854, that it was "not fair and reasonable for building societies and valuers to agree together to impose on purchasers the risk of loss arising as a result of carelessness on the part of valuers".

seeking answers to what might be a morally acceptable legal policy,[88] though this was clearly a rhetorical device intended to elicit support for his view.[89] The existence of statutory regulation may be taken as evidence of community values and "may encourage the court to hold that certain interests warrant protection"[90] but in other situations it may be taken as evidence that the claimant is so adequately protected that a further common law remedy would not be just and reasonable.[91] Statutory regulation may also be seen as setting the remedial limits beyond which the common law should not go.[92]

7-24 **Public policy** More general considerations of the "public good" have been invoked by the courts. Thus a duty has been denied on the grounds that it would lead to defensive decision making in policing,[93] social services,[94] social housing,[95]

---

88 *White v Chief Constable of South Yorkshire Police* [1999] 2 A.C. 455 at 493; *McFarlane v Tayside Health Board* [2000] 2 A.C. 59 at 82. This approach is not always applicable: in *Chester v Afshar* [2004] UKHL 41; [2005] 1 A.C. 134, Lord Steyn made no reference to the underground passenger and at [83], Lord Hope remarked: "As I survey my fellow passengers ... on the underground—such a variety in age, race, nationality and languages—I find it increasingly hard to persuade myself that any one view on anything other than the most basic issues can be said to be typical of them."

89 There was no suggestion that his Lordship was actually going to conduct a survey of commuters' views on the issues.

90 per Cooke P in *South Pacific Manufacturing Co Ltd v New Zealand Security Consultants and Investigations Ltd* [1992] 2 N.Z.L.R. 282 at 298.

91 *Jones v Department of Employment* [1989] Q.B. 1 CA (common law duty of care inconsistent with statutory procedures for appealing decisions about social security benefits); applied in *Murdoch v Department for Work and Pensions* [2010] EWHC 1988 (QB).

92 See for example the view of Lord Mackay LC in *Murphy v Brentwood DC* [1991] 1 A.C. 398 at 472:

> "it is relevant to take into account that parliament has made provisions in the Defective Premises Act 1972 imposing on builders and others undertaking work in the provision of dwellings obligations relating to the quality of their work. For this House in its judicial capacity to create a large new area of responsibility on local authorities in respect of defective buildings would in my opinion not be a proper exercise of judicial power."

93 *Hill v Chief Constable of West Yorkshire* [1989] A.C. 53; *Smith v Chief Constable of Sussex Police* [2008] UKHL 50; [2009] 1 A.C. 225. In *Robinson v Chief Constable of West Yorkshire* [2018] UKSC 4; [2018] A.C. 736 at [112] Lord Hughes acknowledged that "the danger of defensive policing lacks hard evidence" but nonetheless considered that the risk of defensive practice was inevitable, since "we see the consequences of defensive behaviour daily in the actions of a great many public authorities. I do not see that it can seriously be doubted that the threat of litigation frequently influences the behaviour of both public and private bodies and individuals." Of course, whether the threat of litigation influences potential defendants to exercise reasonable care (as it should) or produces an over-reaction is another matter. See also the difference of view expressed in *Michael v Chief Constable of South Wales* [2015] UKSC 2; [2015] A.C. 1732 as to whether imposing a duty of care on the police would lead to defensive practices between Lord Toulson (at [121]–[122]) and Lord Kerr (at [179], who considered that it was arguable that the risk of litigation improves professional standards). Note that arguments about the risk of defensive practice arising from imposing liability on the police in respect of the manner in which they investigate criminal offences do not apply to claims based on art.3 of the ECHR: *Commissioner of Police of the Metropolis v DSD* [2018] UKSC 11; [2019] A.C. 196 at [71], per Lord Kerr: "Carrying out police investigations efficiently should not give rise to a diversion of resources. On the contrary, it should lead to more effective investigation of crime, the enhancement of standards and the saving of resources. There is no reason to suppose that the existence of a right under article 3 to call to account egregious errors on the part of the police in the investigation of serious crime would do other than act as an incentive to avoid those errors and to deter, indeed eliminate, the making of such grievous mistakes." See also per Lord Neuberger at [97]; cf. Lord Hughes (dissenting). For a critique of the resort to "policy" without supporting evidence to justify the conclusion see Smith (2009) 125 L.Q.R. 215.

94 *X v Bedfordshire CC* [1995] 2 A.C. 633.

regulatory activity[96] or inhibit the work of advocates.[97] But assessments of public policy can change as is shown by the conclusion that the policy reasons supporting social service[98] or advocates immunity[99] are no longer applicable. On occasion, broader consequential arguments are invoked[100] but judges are rightly hesitant to pursue such arguments when they have neither the full information nor the basis on which to evaluate the information that is presented. In *McLoughlin v O'Brian*[101] Lord Scarman commented that considerations of social, economic and financial policy, "are not such as to be capable of being handled within the limits of the forensic process". In *Spring v Guardian Assurance Plc*[102] Lord Lowry warned against the use of speculative policy reasons, commenting that "public policy should be invoked only in clear cases in which the potential harm to the public is incontestable, ... whether the anticipated harm to the public will be likely to occur must be determined on tangible grounds instead of on mere generalities and ... the burden of proof lies on those who assert that the court should not enforce a liability which prima facie exists." Thus, in *Capital and Counties Plc v Hampshire CC*[103] Stuart-Smith LJ dismissed a range of consequential arguments against the liability of the fire brigades as unsubstantiated, and in *Rothwell v Chemical & Insulating Co*[104] Lord Hoffmann, whilst agreeing with the decision of the Court of Appeal to reject claims for anxiety caused by harmless pleural plaques, rejected the policy reasons given by the Court on the ground that they were "consequentialist in nature" and "speculative".[105] In *Barrett v Enfield LBC*,[106] the House of Lords was equally dismissive of the "policy" argument that imposition of a duty might lead to

---

95 A duty of care on a social landlord to warn tenants about the risk of violence from another tenant "would deter social landlords from intervening to reduce the incidence of anti-social behaviour": *Mitchell v Glasgow City Council* [2009] UKHL 11; [2009] 1 A.C. 874 at [28], per Lord Hope; see also per Baroness Hale at [77]. See Mullender (2009) 125 L.Q.R. 384.

96 *Yuen Kun-Yeu v Att Gen of Hong Kong* [1988] A.C. 175; *Harris v Evans* [1998] 1 W.L.R. 1285.

97 *Rondel v Worsley* [1969] 1 A.C. 191.

98 *D v East Berkshire NHS Trust* [2003] EWCA Civ 1151; [2004] Q.B. 558; affirmed [2005] UKHL 23; [2005] 2 A.C. 373; and approved in *Poole BC v GN* [2019] UKSC 25; [2019] 2 W.L.R. 1478 at [75], [83]. See para.13-19.

99 *Arthur JS Hall & Co v Simons* [2002] 1 A.C. 615. See also *Jones v Kaney* [2011] UKSC 13; [2011] 2 A.C. 398, holding that the immunity that formerly applied to expert witnesses in respect of claims for negligence should be abolished (see paras 9-42 and 13-49); *Smith v Ministry of Defence* [2013] UKSC 41; [2014] A.C. 52 narrowing the scope of "combat immunity" (see para.13-53).

100 See for example Lord Keith's assertion in *Rowling v Takaro Properties Ltd* [1988] A.C. 473 at 502, that imposing a duty of care on local authorities in relation to building inspection might lead inspectors to increase "unnecessarily, the requisite depth of foundations, thereby imposing a very substantial and unnecessary financial burden on members of the community". In *Gregg v Scott* [2005] UKHL 2; [2005] 2 A.C. 176 at [90], Lord Hoffmann invoked the financial consequences to the NHS as a reason for rejecting the loss of chance claim, whilst Lord Nicholls at [54], argued that it was for Parliament to introduce legislation if it felt that the financial consequences were not acceptable.

101 [1983] 1 A.C. 410 at 430.

102 [1995] 2 A.C. 296 at 326.

103 [1997] Q.B. 1004 at 1044. The arguments included the fear that imposition of a duty would open the floodgates of litigation, distract fire brigades from fire-fighting, lead to massive claims against the taxpayer and have an adverse effect on insurance practice. The court did restrict the scope of the duty owed by fire brigades but on grounds of proximity rather than policy and fairness. See para.13-46.

104 [2007] UKHL 39; [2008] 1 A.C. 281 at [17]. See also per Lord Hope at [50]. See further para.7-97.

105 The Court of Appeal [2006] EWCA Civ 27; [2006] 4 All E.R. 1161 had cited the stress of medical litigation on the claimants and the disproportionate costs of such litigation as reasons for rejecting the claims.

106 [2001] 2 A.C. 550 at 568 and 589, per Lords Slynn and Hutton. See also the rejection of the "defensive practice" argument by Lord Nicholls in *Gregg v Scott* [2005] UKHL 2; [2005] 2 A.C.

defensive conduct or diversion of resources to record keeping or self-justification. In the Australian High Court, McHugh J has warned against basing a duty on assumptions that insurance may be readily available and that consequently a duty would have the effect of "loss spreading".[107] However, where imposition of a duty would undermine an established insurance framework, then it will be a legitimate consideration.[108]

7-25 **Public policy and existing categories of duty** Appeals to "justice" or "legal policy" or broader issues of "public policy" might all be considered to fall under the third limb of the *Caparo* "tripartite test" for duty of care, namely whether imposition of a duty would be "fair, just and reasonable". On the other hand, it is also arguable that justice and legal policy could just as readily be addressed as part of the enquiry about the foreseeability of harm to the claimant and the relationship of proximity between the parties. Wider policy concerns about the social and economic consequences of imposing or not imposing a duty of care clearly do come within the third limb, but defendants cannot invoke these concerns in order to avoid liability in categories of case where the courts have already decided that a duty of care should be imposed. In *Robinson v Chief Constable of West Yorkshire*[109] Lord Reed emphasised that where there is an existing category of duty, as where liability would arise at common law for a positive act of negligence by a private individual, concerns about public policy cannot override that liability simply because the defendant is performing a statutory function (an obvious example of this would be driving a motor vehicle on a public road). The true question, said his Lordship, is whether, properly construed, the statute excludes the liability which would otherwise arise. In *Robinson* the police had been negligent in knocking over a 76-year-old frail lady in the street whilst attempting to arrest a suspected offender, which constituted a positive act of negligence for which there was no "immunity" in the form of an absence of a duty of care, such as where the claimant's injury is caused by a third party whom the police have failed to apprehend (which would constitute an omission to act). A private individual who had negligently knocked the claimant over causing injury would have owed a duty of care, and there was no reason why the police would not come under a similar duty (though the question of what constitutes a breach of that duty might be more nuanced, given that the police have to take into account the risk of a suspect resisting arrest). As noted above, when drawing analogies with existing categories of liability it will be important to identify the correct category of case.[110]

7-26 In *Perrett v Collins*[111] Hobhouse LJ stressed that where a case fell within the established categories of liability, "a defendant should not be allowed to seek to

176 at [55]–[56]; and by Lord Lloyd-Jones in *Darnley v Croydon Health Services NHS Trust* [2018] UKSC 50; [2019] A.C. 831 at [22].

107 *Perre v Apand Pty Ltd* (1999) 164 A.L.R. 606 at 640. He said that these considerations "do not assist but rather impede the relevant inquiry". See further *Lambert v Barratt Homes Ltd* [2010] EWCA Civ 681; [2010] B.L.R. 527; and *Vernon Knight Associates v Cornwall Council* [2013] EWCA Civ 950; [2013] B.L.R. 519 (para.7-183) where there was a marked difference of opinion as to the relevance of the insurance position of the parties when considering an occupier's "measured duty of care" in respect of naturally occurring hazards.

108 See *Marc Rich & Co v Bishop Rock Marine Co Ltd* [1996] 1 A.C. 211, where Lord Steyn rejected a duty partly on the ground that it would undermine the existing insurance practice which was based on the Hague Rules.

109 [2018] UKSC 4; [2018] A.C. 736 at [41]. See further paras 13-42 to 13-44.

110 See para.7-19.

111 [1999] P.N.L.R. 77. In *Robinson v Chief Constable of West Yorkshire* [2018] UKSC 4; [2018] A.C.

escape from liability by appealing to some vaguer concept of justice or fairness" as the previous authorities "have by necessary implication held that it is just, fair and reasonable that the claimant should recover". In *Perrett* the claimant had suffered personal injury in the crash of an aircraft which the defendant had negligently certified as being in airworthy condition. Hobhouse LJ considered that as the case fell within the recognised category of liability for personal injury, the only question was whether there was sufficient foreseeability and proximity. This latter requirement was satisfied by the fact that the defendant had an involvement in the activity which gave him a "measure of control over and responsibility for a situation, which if dangerous, will be liable to injure the claimant". He concluded: "Once this proximity exists, it ceases to be material what form the unreasonable conduct takes. The distinction between negligent misstatement and other forms of careless conduct ceases to be legally relevant." Thus, the fact that the negligence of the defendant:

> "did not involve the direct infliction of physical damage did not exclude the existence of a duty of care … The highest that the point could be put is that where the conduct would amount to a direct invasion … a special justification is required to negative liability. But where on general principle in the context of foreseeable risk of personal injury, a duty of care exists, lack of directness, unless it destroys the causative link, provides the defendant with no answer."[112]

Incrementalism In his speech in *Caparo*, Lord Bridge observed that the criteria for duty of care were "not susceptible of any such precise definition as would be necessary to give them utility as practical tests, but amount in effect to little more than convenient labels to attach to the features of different specific situations which the law recognises pragmatically as giving rise to a duty of care of a given scope." The law attached greater significance to the more traditional categorisation of distinct recognisable situations as guides to the existence, the scope and the limits of the varied duties of care which the law imposes.[113] In *Reeman v Department of Transport* Phillips LJ explained the essence of incrementalism thus: 7-27

> "When confronted with a novel situation the court does not … consider these matters [foreseeability, proximity and fairness] in isolation. It does so by comparison with established categories of negligence to see whether the facts amount to no more than a small extension of a situation already covered by authority, or whether a finding of the existence of a duty of care would effect a significant extension to the law of negligence. Only in exceptional cases will the court accept that the interests of justice justify such an extension."[114]

The greater the step forward required to impose liability, the more courts will need

736 at [26] Lord Reed expressly endorsed the approach of Hobhouse LJ.

112 [1999] P.N.L.R. 77 at 91. See also *Watson v British Boxing Board of Control Ltd* [2001] Q.B. 1134; and *Wattleworth v Goodwood Road Racing Co Ltd* [2004] EWHC 140 (QB); [2004] P.I.Q.R. P25 imposing a duty of care on organisations responsible for safety arrangements at sporting events in respect of personal injuries sustained by participants in the sport; see further para.13-59.

113 *Caparo Industries Plc v Dickman* [1990] 2 A.C. 605 at 618. Lord Bridge referred to the wisdom of the dictum of Brennan J in *Sutherland Shire Council v Heyman* (1985) 60 A.L.R. 1 at 43–44: "It is preferable, in my view, that the law should develop novel categories of negligence incrementally and by analogy with established categories, rather than by a massive extension of a prima facie duty of care restrained only by indefinable 'considerations which ought to negative, or to reduce or limit the scope of the duty or the class of person to whom it is owed.'"

114 [1997] P.N.L.R. 618 at 625.

to evaluate the consequences and be assured that it is what justice requires. He went on to cite as an example of such an exceptional case, *White v Jones*,[115] where a majority of the House of Lords recognised that a solicitor could be liable to an intended beneficiary of his client's will. Lord Goff was prepared to impose a duty going beyond the accepted principles and limits because there was no other way to produce practical justice for the beneficiary and because in the 15 years since Megarry J had taken this step at first instance, it appeared that such liability had created no problems in practice. The importance of taking an incremental approach to decisions about novel negligence claims which go beyond the existing categories of duty was emphasised by Lord Reed in both *Robinson v Chief Constable of West Yorkshire*[116] and *Poole BC v GN*.[117] The third limb of the "tripartite test" (whether the imposition of a duty of care would be fair, just and reasonable) forms part of the assessment of whether such an incremental step ought to be taken in a novel case. But "in the ordinary run of cases, courts should apply established principles of law, rather than basing their decisions on their assessment of the requirements of public policy."[118]

7-28 Incrementalism is not a panacea.[119] There is little to be gained by substituting one label for another label. As Lord Bingham observed in *Commissioners of Customs and Excise v Barclays Bank Plc*[120]:

> "the incremental test is of little value as a test in itself, and is only helpful when used in combination with a test or principle which identifies the legally significant features of a situation. The closer the facts of the case in issue to those of a case in which a duty of care has been held to exist, the readier a court will be … to find that there has been an assumption of responsibility or that the proximity and policy conditions of the threefold test are satisfied. The converse is also true."

Whichever approach is taken, the aim must be to balance adherence to general principles with the flexibility demanded by a pragmatic approach and, in so doing, provide sufficient predictability for the law to remain effective.

7-29 **Conclusion** In *Caparo Industries Plc v Dickman* Lord Roskill commented that: "there is no simple formula or touchstone to which recourse can be had in order to provide in every case a ready answer to the questions whether, given certain facts, the law will or will not impose liability for negligence or in cases where such liability can be shown to exist, determine the extent of that liability."[121] Whether it be Lord Atkin's "neighbour principle" or Lord Bridge's "tripartite test" or even simple "incrementalism" they are all expressed at too abstract a level to be of practical use. The flesh can be put on the bones of the duty of care only by looking to

---

115 [1995] 2 A.C. 287.

116 [2018] UKSC 4; [2018] A.C. 736 at [21], [27].

117 [2019] UKSC 25; [2019] 2 W.L.R. 1478 at [64]; see para.7-19.

118 [2019] UKSC 25; [2019] 2 W.L.R. 1478 at [64].

119 "I fully agree that in deciding whether or not there is a duty of care in a new situation the Courts should decide gradually, step by step and by analogy with previous cases.… But the label 'incremental' solves few problems": *South Pacific Manufacturing Co Ltd v New Zealand Security Consultants & Investigations Ltd* [1992] 2 N.Z.L.R. 282 at 295 per Cooke P.

120 [2006] UKHL 28; [2007] 1 A.C. 181 at [7]. See also *Islington LBC v UCL Hospital NHS Trust* [2005] EWCA Civ 596; [2006] P.I.Q.R. P9 at [27] where Buxton LJ suggested that incrementalism was a "check or guide to the application of the *Caparo* tests; and that, in particular, if a claimant could demonstrate that his case did no more than incrementally extend an already recognised head of liability, that was a good indication that his claim met the *Caparo* requirements".

121 [1990] 2 A.C. 605 at 628.

the broad categories of cases to see how the principles have been applied in specific fact-situations.

As a general rule, as Lord Reed explained in *Robinson v Chief Constable of West Yorkshire*[122] and *Poole BC v GN*,[123] where a defendant has by some positive act of carelessness caused physical damage, either to persons or to property, a duty of care will be owed to the injured person or the owner of the damaged property. The careless infliction of foreseeable damage on another or their property is usually itself sufficient to create a relationship of "proximity" between the injured claimant and the negligent defendant. The problem areas relate primarily to non-physical harm, such as purely economic loss or psychiatric harm, liability for omissions (which in this context is a term of art), and where it is considered that the particular status of either the claimant or the defendant should be taken into account. This does not necessarily mean that no duty of care will be owed, but the circumstances in which a duty is owed may be more restrictive. In these cases there is likely to be a close focus on the nature of any *antecedent relationship* between the claimant and defendant, or the relationship between the parties and a third party through, or by reason of, whom the damage to the claimant has occurred. **7-30**

The following sections of this chapter consider the rules applied to the duty of care in relation to: **7-31**

(1) the status of the parties (paras 7-32 to 7-50);
(2) omissions (paras 7-51 to 7-68);
(3) psychiatric injury (paras 7-69 to 7-97);
(4) loss of autonomy on the birth of an unwanted child (paras 7-98 to 7-102); and
(5) economic loss (paras 7-103 to 7-156).

Those developed to limit public service liability are considered in Ch.13, and the duties owed in relation to professional services, defective products, the occupation of premises, and the liability of employers to employees are considered in detail in Chs 9, 10, 11, and 12 respectively.

(c) Claimant's status

Foetus and congenital disability claims For many years it was uncertain whether a foetus had sufficient status to be owed a duty of care. In respect of births after 21 July 1976, the Congenital Disabilities (Civil Liability) Act 1976 now settles the law. It grants a right of action to a child who is born alive but disabled[124] because of an occurrence which affected either parent's ability to have a normal child or affected the mother during pregnancy, or affected the mother or child in the course of its birth.[125] **7-32**

Wrongful life claims A different kind of moral problem arises where it is claimed **7-33**

---

[122] [2018] UKSC 4; [2018] A.C. 736 at [41].

[123] [2019] UKSC 25; [2019] 2 W.L.R. 1478.

[124] Being born with a different skin colour from that of one's parents as a result of negligence in the selection of gametes during a process of in vitro fertilisation does not constitute a disability: *A v A Health and Social Services Trust* [2011] NICA 28; [2012] N.I. 77 (discussed by S. Sheldon, "Only skin deep? The harm of being born a different colour to one's parents" (2011) 19 Med. L. Rev. 657).

[125] For detail see paras 5-58 and 10-82 to 10-85. The common law position was settled by *Burton v Islington HA* [1993] Q.B. 204, where after survey of Commonwealth and US decisions, Dillon LJ held that there was a duty to take care not to cause damage to a newly born child through injuries inflicted whilst the child was *en ventre sa mere*. The Act replaces any common law right in respect

that the defendant was negligent not in causing the pre-natal injuries but in failing to prevent the birth of an injured child. A child brought a common law claim on this basis in *McKay v Essex AHA*.[126] The child was born with severe disabilities caused not by anyone's negligence but because of its mother having contracted rubella. It was alleged that the defendant doctor had negligently failed to detect the illness and advise the mother of the desirability of an abortion. The child claimed that the doctor owed it a duty of care to advise its mother about the possibility of an abortion and that as a result of the doctor's alleged negligence, it had been born to a "wrongful life" of suffering. The Court of Appeal rejected the claim on the ground that it would be contrary to public policy as a violation of the sanctity of human life. Nor can a child bring a "wrongful life" claim under the Congenital Disabilities (Civil Liability) Act because actions are limited to "disabilities which would not otherwise have been present" but for the negligence.[127] However, the mother may be able to claim for loss of the freedom to choose not to give birth.[128]

7-34 **Rescuers** Where the defendant has negligently created a situation endangering life or property, he may be liable to a claimant who suffers injury as a direct result of attempting rescue. It was at one time considered that no duty was owed in such a situation for the simple reason that the injured person volunteered to run the risk of the rescue. The direct cause of his injury was said to be his own decision and not the defendant's conduct. Attitudes changed with the decision of Cardozo J in *Wagner v International Ry Co*[129] in which he stated:

> "Danger invites rescue. The cry of distress is the summons to relief. The law does not ignore these reactions of the mind in tracing conduct to its consequences. It recognises them as normal. It places their efforts within the range of the natural and probable. The wrong that imperils life is a wrong to the imperilled victim; it is a wrong also to his rescuer."

The Court of Appeal first accepted a duty of care to rescuers in *Haynes v Harwood*[130] where the defendant left his horse unattended in a street with some children nearby, one of whom threw a stone at the horse causing it to bolt. The claimant, a policeman, endeavoured to stop it and was injured. It was held that a duty was owed as the act of the child was foreseeable and so too was the claimant's rescue attempt. The existence of the duty was confirmed by the Court of Appeal in *Baker v TE*

---

of births after 21 July 1976 and the common law is irrelevant for all but the most exceptional case where the limitation period from a pre-1976 birth has not yet expired.

126 [1982] Q.B. 1166; see para.9-94.

127 s.1(2)(a) and (b). See also *Criminal Injuries Compensation Authority v First-tier Tribunal (Social Entitlement Chamber)* [2017] EWCA Civ 139; [2017] 4 W.L.R. 60 (child born with genetic disorder as a result of the incestuous rape of his mother not entitled to award of criminal injuries compensation). The Court of Appeal in *McKay* considered that the 1976 Act governed all claims in respect of births occurring after its commencement and hence, that wrongful life claims could not be brought as they were not within the terms of the statute. Note, however, that s.1A of the 1976 Act does provide for a "wrongful life" claim in the case of the negligent selection of an embryo or gametes during *in vitro* fertilisation: see para.5-61. But the negligence must result in actionable damage, which does not include being born with a different skin colour from one's parents: *A v A Health and Social Services Trust* [2011] NICA 28; [2012] N.I. 77.

128 This is a claim for loss of autonomy and is discussed below at para.7-101.

129 (1921) 133 NE 437; 232 NY 176 at 180.

130 [1935] 1 K.B. 146.

Hopkins & Son Ltd[131] where the defendants' defective system of work led to an accumulation of lethal gas inside a well which overpowered two workers. A doctor attempted to rescue them and he, too, succumbed. Citing the dictum of Cardozo J, the Court held that in so far as the doctor's action was a reasonable attempt at rescue, his estate could recover.

Nature of duty owed to rescuer The duty to a rescuer is independent of any duty to the party rescued. Thus, a defendant may owe a duty to the rescuer even though he owes no duty to the victim. In *Videan v British Transport Commission*[132] the party originally endangered and injured by the defendant's negligent driving of a train, was a trespasser and unable to recover because the court held that although the presence of lawful visitors on the railway line was foreseeable, that of trespassers was not. Nevertheless, the rescuer was owed a duty as it was foreseeable that someone would be endangered by the negligent driving and hence, injury to a potential rescuer such as the claimant, a station master, was also foreseeable.[133] Again, a defendant who negligently imperils himself can be liable to a rescuer for damage sustained in a rescue attempt although clearly the defendant owes himself no duty to preserve his own safety.[134] Indeed, there is no need for there to be anyone in actual danger, provided it is foreseeable that a rescuer could reasonably perceive there to be a danger.[135] A rescuer may also be owed a duty by someone who has unsuccessfully attempted an earlier rescue where that rescue attempt placed the victim in a position of increased danger.[136] Similarly, he may be owed a duty by the organiser of the rescue attempt. In exceptional circumstances, the negligence of the rescue organiser may break the chain of causation from the original negligence creating the danger. Thus, in *McFarlane v EE Caledonia*[137] Stuart-Smith LJ stated that if the captain of the vessel attempting to rescue survivors of the Piper Alpha oil rig fire had "negligently and in breach of his duty taken the vessel into a position of danger where those on board were injured, this would be a *novus actus interveniens* for which the defendants [operators of the oil rig] would not be liable". However, he also noted that in the case of a catastrophic emergency, "those in charge of rescue vessels may not be able to judge to a nicety exactly how near it is safe to bring their vessels". An error of judgment in organising an emergency rescue will rarely amount to negligence. 7-35

Foreseeability of rescue The rescuer can only recover where the rescue attempt is reasonably foreseeable. The policeman in *Haynes* and the doctor in *Baker* could both be said to have a professional responsibility to assist the public, but where hu- 7-36

131 [1959] 1 W.L.R. 966.

132 [1963] 2 Q.B. 650 at 669, 675–676 and 682–683.

133 It follows that it is immaterial that the injury to the rescuer is not of the same kind as that incurred by the person rescued. In *Chadwick v British Railways Board* [1967] 1 W.L.R. 912, a railway collision occurred through the admitted fault of the defendants. The claimant, who lived nearby, went to the rescue of the passengers who had been wounded and killed. He suffered psychiatric harm as a result of his experience, and it was held that he could recover. However, it is questionable whether this claimant would now succeed, following the decision of the House of Lords in *White v Chief Constable of the South Yorkshire Police* [1999] 2 A.C. 455, unless he was actually exposed to the risk of physical injury during the rescue and so qualified as a "primary victim". See para.7-71.

134 *Harrison v British Railways Board* [1981] 3 All E.R. 679 at 685, Boreham J argued that the proposition followed "almost inevitably" from *Videan*.

135 *Ould v Butler's Wharf Ltd* [1953] 2 Lloyd's Rep. 44.

136 See *Horsley v MacLaren* [1971] 2 Lloyd's Rep. 410, Sup. Ct of Canada.

137 [1994] 2 All E.R. 1.

man life is endangered it is reasonable to foresee others attempting rescue. A parent is likely to attempt to rescue an endangered child.[138] In the case of a disaster, it may be reasonably foreseeable that ordinary members of the public may attempt rescue. Thus, in *Chadwick v British Railways Board*[139] where a railway collision occurred through the admitted fault of the defendants, the claimant, who lived nearby and went to the rescue of injured passengers, was able to recover for the psychiatric harm suffered as a result of his experience. Where property is endangered by fire, it is reasonably foreseeable that firemen will attempt rescue. In *Ogwo v Taylor*[140] the defendant, who carelessly started a fire in his own house, was held liable to a fire officer who was injured while helping to put it out. The defendant owed the same duty of care to a fire officer fighting a fire as was owed to any other visitor, although he could reasonably expect a fire officer to exercise the ordinary skills of the profession. The House of Lords rejected the "fireman's rule" accepted in some US jurisdictions under which it is said that "the fireman cannot complain of negligence in the creation of the very occasion for his engagement".[141] A more difficult question is whether it may be reasonably foreseeable that a "non-professional" will attempt to rescue endangered property. In the Canadian case of *Hutterley v Imperial Oil & Calder*[142] a person was able recover in respect of injuries sustained in rescuing his own property. Furthermore, in *Hyett v Great Western Ry*[143] a person was able to recover for injuries sustained in attempting to rescue his employer's property. The Court of Appeal stated that in such situations regard should be had to the relationship of the rescuer to the property in peril and the degree of danger. There may be some situations where a rescue attempt is not reasonably foreseeable. The most obvious example is where the danger itself has passed.[144]

7-37 **Careless rescue** If the method of rescue chosen is itself unreasonable then there will be a reduction of damages for contributory negligence. In *Harrison v British*

---

[138] per Slesser LJ in *Cutler v United Dairies Ltd* [1933] 2 K.B. 297 at 306; *Videan v BTC* [1963] 2 Q.B. 650. An unusual example is to be found in a Canadian case, *Urbanski v Patel* (1978) 84 D.L.R. (3d) 650, where a doctor negligently removed a patient's kidney instead of an ovarian cyst, and the patient nearly died because it was her misfortune to have had only one kidney. Her father donated one of his kidneys to save her life, and was entitled to recover.

[139] [1967] 1 W.L.R. 912.

[140] [1988] A.C. 431.

[141] per Weintraub CJ in *Krauth v Geller* (1960) 157 A.2d 129 at 130, Supreme Court of New Jersey. According to Lord Bridge "the American fireman's rule has no place in English law" [1988] A.C. 431 at 449. In *White v Chief Constable of South Yorkshire Police* [1999] 2 A.C. 455 at 471, Lord Goff confirmed that the "fireman's rule" had no application where members of the rescue services suffered psychiatric illness but also suggested that a professional rescuer "by reason of his training and experience [may] be expected to have more resilience in the face of tragic events ... than an ordinary member of the public possesses". See also *Wembridge Claimants v Winter* [2013] EWHC 2331 (QB), para.12-07, where Irwin J rejected the argument that the fire service should have an immunity from claims by their employees. See also para.11-39.

[142] (1956) 3 D.L.R. (2d) 719.

[143] [1948] 1 K.B. 345. See also *Merrington v Ironbridge Metal Works Ltd* [1952] 2 All E.R. 1101; *Russell v McCabe* [1962] N.Z.L.R. 393. The principle has been applied to sailors, who go to the help of another ship in distress, see *The Gusty* [1940] P. 159.

[144] See *Cutler v United Dairies (London) Ltd* [1933] 2 K.B. 297. See also *Schlink v Blackburn* (1993) 109 D.L.R. (4th) 331, where the British Columbia Court of Appeal held that a motorist who caused an accident could not foresee that a "near relative of (the other party to the accident) on learning of the accident would panic and rush ... to reach the accident scene" and injure his foot in so doing. The court stressed that this was not a "rescue" case as there was no evidence any danger to the parties to the accident.

Railways Board[145] the guard injured in attempting to rescue a passenger trying to board a moving train, was found to be 20 per cent contributorily negligent because he had tried to grab the passenger rather than following rules and applying the hand brake. However, as Boreham J said in that case, there "is a feeling of distaste about finding a rescuer guilty of contributory negligence. It can rarely be appropriate to do so."[146] If the careless conduct of the rescuer is such that the type of accident causing his injury is unforeseeable, then damage may be regarded as too remote.[147] This principle was invoked by the judge in *Crossley v Rawlinson*,[148] where the claimant, running with a fire extinguisher to put out a fire in a lorry, tripped up and fell. It was held that as the particular manner in which the rescuer was injured was unforeseeable, there was no liability even though the rescue attempt itself was foreseeable. The decision has been criticised on the ground that this type of accident was entirely foreseeable, given that the rescuer was acting in the heat of the moment. The injured or endangered victim will have no claim against a careless rescuer unless the rescue attempt has added to the injury or danger.[149]

Wrongdoers Where a claimant's own wrongdoing is intimately connected with his negligence claim against the defendant, he may be denied recovery on the basis of the defence of illegality which is also referred to as the maxim ex turpi causa no oritur actio. But the illegality of the claimant's conduct may also be a reason for denying a duty in the first place thus obviating the need to plead it as a defence. In *Vellino v Chief Constable of the Greater Manchester Police*[150] the claimant was injured when he jumped from a second floor window to evade arrest by the police. He alleged that the police were under a duty of care not negligently to let him escape once they had arrested him. The Court of Appeal held there was no duty of care owed to a prisoner who was attempting to escape from custody. Schiemann LJ commented that: "To suggest that the police owe a criminal the duty to prevent the criminal from escaping, and that the criminal who hurts himself while escaping can sue the police for the breach of that duty, seems to me self-evidently absurd."[151] The claimant was the author of his own misfortune and by breaking away from an officer arresting him he was committing a criminal offence. His Lordship accepted that there was an overlap between the considerations which had to be taken into account in determining whether a duty of care existed and whether the defence of ex turpi causa applied, but based his decision on the absence of a duty of care rather than the defence. Sir Murray Stuart-Smith agreed that: 7-38

> "if the facts are such that the maxim *ex turpi causa non oritur actio* is applicable, it does not matter whether the correct legal analysis is that the defendants owed no duty of care, because the third limb of the test in *Caparo Industries*, namely that it is just fair and

145 [1981] 3 All E.R. 679. See also *Jeffrey v Commodore Cabaret Ltd* (1995) 128 D.L.R. (4th) 535, where the Canadian Supreme Court held that the claimant who attempted to stop a fight in a bar following the failure of the defendant owner to intervene, should recover damages but subject to a reduction of 50 per cent for contributory negligence.

146 See, e.g. *Tolley v Carr* [2010] EWHC 2191 (QB); [2011] R.T.R. 7, para.3-94, where Hickinbottom J was unwilling to subject a rescuer's actions to the fine scrutiny of hindsight. See also the Social Action, Responsibility and Heroism Act 2015 s.4, below para.7-192.

147 See further para.2-153.

148 [1982] 1 W.L.R. 369.

149 This follows from the principle that there is no liability for pure omissions and is discussed further at para.7-54. See also the Social Action, Responsibility and Heroism Act 2015 s.4, para.7-192.

150 [2001] EWCA Civ 1249; [2002] 1 W.L.R. 218.

151 [2001] EWCA Civ 1249; [2002] 1 W.L.R. 218 at [19].

reasonable to impose a duty of care, is not satisfied, or that the maxim affords a freestanding reason for holding that the cause of action does not arise or cannot be pursued."[152]

As most of the case law treats illegality as a defence rather than a bar to duty, it is discussed in detail in Ch.3 rather than here.[153]

7-39 **Suicide** Where the claimant's injury is due to his suicide or attempted suicide, public policy issues also arise. One situation in which a defendant's negligence may be held responsible for the injury is where he has responsibility for the claimant, ought to be aware of his suicidal tendency and negligently fails to take precautions to protect the claimant from himself. Hospital, prison or police authorities are potentially within this category. The question whether any potential duty is displaced on public policy grounds or by the fact that the injuries resulted from the claimant's own decision came before the Court of Appeal in *Kirkham v Chief Constable of Greater Manchester Police*.[154] The case concerned a detainee whom the police knew to have suicidal tendencies. The police negligently failed to inform the prison authorities of this when the detainee was remanded to their custody. It was found that but for this negligence, the detainee's suicide would have been prevented. The police argued that there was no liability on three grounds: that there was no duty to protect a person from the risk of injury created by himself, that the deceased's voluntary act of suicide gave rise to the defence of consent or volenti non fit injuria, and thirdly, that a claim arising out of a suicide was barred by public policy.[155] On the first ground the Court of Appeal held that there was a duty on a person having custody of another to take all reasonable steps to prevent harm to that other. The volenti defence was rejected on the ground that as the deceased was clinically depressed, his decision was not truly volens. Finally, the Court held that public policy did not preclude a claim since the Suicide Act 1961 had done more than abolish the crime of suicide. In the words of Lloyd LJ, it was "symptomatic of a change in the public attitude to suicide generally. It is no longer regarded with the same abhorrence as it once was".[156] In *Reeves v Commissioner of Police of the Metropolis*[157] the House of Lords held that where a detainee was of sound mind when he committed suicide, the damages could be reduced on the grounds of contributory negligence.[158]

7-40 A second situation is where the claimant suffers injury due to the defendant's negligence, for example, in a road accident, and the result of the injury is to make

---

[152] [2001] EWCA Civ 1249; [2002] 1 W.L.R. 218 at [62].

[153] See para.3-02 onwards.

[154] [1990] 2 Q.B. 283.

[155] In *Hyde v Tameside HA, The Times*, 16 April 1981; (1986) 2 P.N. 26 Lord Denning stated obiter that no duty should arise in relation to attempted suicide as: "By his act, in self-inflicting serious injury, [the claimant] has made himself a burden on the community … The policy of [the] law should be to discourage these actions."

[156] [1990] 2 Q.B. 283 at 291.

[157] [2000] 1 A.C. 360. Note that in some cases of suicide art.2 of the European Convention on Human Rights will be engaged such that the relatives of the deceased may be entitled to damages from a public authority (such as the NHS) where there has been a culpable failure to prevent the suicide. See *Savage v South Essex Partnership NHS Trust* [2008] UKHL 74; [2009] 1 A.C. 681 (mental patient detained in hospital under the Mental Health Act 1983); *Rabone v Pennine Care NHS Trust* [2012] UKSC 2; [2012] 2 A.C. 72 (voluntary mental patient in hospital); and *Reynolds v United Kingdom* (2694/08) (2012) 55 E.H.R.R. 35, discussed at paras 9-90, 9-105, 13-87, 13-89, 13-91 and 13-92.

[158] See further para.3-46.

him suicidal. In this situation there is no doubt that the defendant owes a duty of care and the question is whether the suicide breaks the causal link between the defendant's negligence and the consequences of the death. In *Corr v IBC Vehicles Ltd*[159] the House of Lords held the defendant employer liable for the suicide of an employee which flowed from a psychiatric illness which had been caused by a work accident which had been caused by the employer's negligence. In theory it is possible for the chain of causation to be broken if the deceased took a voluntary, informed decision to take his own life, but in practice if the deceased was suffering from a psychiatric condition as a result of the initial injury it will probably difficult for the defendant to demonstrate this.[160]

(d) Defendant's status

Exercise of a property right The exercise of a property right may confer a protected status on a defendant. In *Stephens v Anglian Water Authority*[161] it was alleged that the defendant had negligently extracted water from its land with the result that it caused the collapse of the claimant's neighbouring property. The Court of Appeal held that the defendant owed the claimant no duty of care as he had an unqualified right to extract water from his land "regardless of the consequences, whether physical or pecuniary, to his neighbour".[162] This followed from the nineteenth century case of *Bradford Corp v Pickles*[163] in which the House of Lords had held that a landowner had no right to the flow of water from a neighbour's land and hence the latter was entitled to interfere with that flow as he wished. However, a landowner does owe a neighbouring owner a duty of care to avoid foreseeable damage to his land, for example, by not providing adequate support for the neighbouring land.[164] Extraction of water by a defendant leading to deprivation of support for the claimant's land may result in liability.[165] It is questionable whether the distinction between the unlimited right to extract water and the duty to provide subjacent strata support can be justified but it appears that only the House of Lords or legislation can alter the position.[166] 7-41

Occupier's exclusions A second instance of protected status is provided by the case of *Ashdown v Samuel Williams & Sons Ltd*.[167] The defendant, an occupier of land, put up a notice stating that those who entered the land did so at their own risk. The Court of Appeal held that the notice was sufficient to exclude the negligence liability to a visitor which would otherwise have arisen. It did not matter that the visitor had not actually agreed to the terms of the notice. The court reasoned that 7-42

159 [2008] UKHL 13; [2008] 1 A.C. 884. cf. *White v Lidl UK GmbH* [2005] EWHC 871 (QB)—deceased committed suicide six months after sustaining minor physical injuries as a result of defendant's negligence; defendant not liable to deceased's widow for his psychiatric reaction to the suicide, which had not been reasonably foreseeable even with hindsight.

160 See further para.2-140.

161 [1987] 1 W.L.R. 1381.

162 [1987] 1 W.L.R. 1381 at 1387, per Slade LJ.

163 [1895] A.C. 587.

164 See *Holbeck Hall Hotel v Scarborough BC* [2000] Q.B. 836.

165 See *Lotus Ltd v British Soda Ltd* [1972] Ch. 123, where a landowner was able to bring an action against a neighbour whose activity in liquefying rock salt beneath his land and extracting it in the form of brine, deprived the former's land of support and caused the collapse of his buildings.

166 In *Stephens v Anglian Water Authority* [1987] 1 W.L.R. 1381 at 1397 Slade LJ disclaimed responsibility, saying: "Whether or not this state of the law is satisfactory is not for us to say."

167 [1957] 1 Q.B. 409.

as the occupier had a right to exclude visitors altogether from his land and would owe no duty to them if they entered as trespassers, he also had a right to exclude them unless they were taken to have agreed to the notice.[168] This protected status was subsequently recognised in the Occupiers' Liability Act 1957.[169] It has been qualified by the prohibition on excluding business liability for personal injuries contained in the Unfair Contract Terms Act 1977 and the Consumer Rights Act 2015,[170] and its common law justification must now be questionable in view of *British Railways Board v Herrington*[171] in which the House of Lords recognised that an occupier did owe a modified duty to a trespasser.[172]

7-43 **Vendors and lessors of premises** In 1906 in *Cavalier v Pope*[173] the House of Lords held that a landlord who had carelessly allowed his premises to get into a dangerous state of disrepair, owed no duty of care to the tenant's wife injured by the collapse of a floor. The court held that the only duty was that owed to the tenant himself under the tenancy contract. In *Bottomley v Bannister*[174] the Court of Appeal extended the "contract only" approach to a vendor who had negligently created the danger when building the house. He was held immune from any duty in tort to the purchaser and his wife who were injured as a result of the defective construction. *Bottomley* was decided shortly before *Donoghue v Stevenson*. In the light of the neighbour principle established by *Donoghue*, the Court of Appeal subsequently held that the immunity did not apply to one who negligently built a house but was not its vendor,[175] and then doubted that the immunity applied to a builder/vendor.[176] Finally, in *Rimmer v Liverpool City Council*,[177] the Court of Appeal decided that *Bottomley* was no longer good law. In *Rimmer* a landlord was held liable in tort to a tenant injured as a result of a defect in the design and construction for which the landlord had been responsible. The common law position is paralleled by s.3 of the Defective Premises Act which contains a statutory abolition of the builder/vendor and builder/lessor immunity for all disposals of property after 1973. However, the immunity of the "bare landlord or vendor", i.e. one who is not also the builder, remains unaffected by the overruling of *Bottomley*[178] and is merely qualified rather than abolished by the provisions of the Defective Premises Act.[179] Thus, under the current law one who sells or lets premises will not be under a com-

---

168 See para.11-46 onwards.

169 s.2(1) provides: "An occupier of premises owes … the common duty of care to all his visitors, except in so far as he is free to and does … exclude his duty … by agreement or otherwise" (emphasis added).

170 See paras 11-52 to 11-55, and para.3-141.

171 [1972] A.C. 877.

172 See para.11-65 onwards.

173 [1906] A.C. 428. See para.11-84.

174 [1932] 1 K.B. 458.

175 *Sharpe v Sweeting & Son Ltd* [1963] 1 W.L.R. 665.

176 In *Dutton v Bognor Regis Urban DC* [1972] 1 Q.B. 373, both Lord Denning and Sachs LJ treated *Bottomley* as having been superseded by *Donoghue*, but as *Dutton* concerned the liability of a local authority their views were obiter.

177 [1985] Q.B. 1.

178 At common law the immunity remains, for as Stephenson LJ stated in *Rimmer*, the authority of *Cavalier v Pope* which established the immunity was "too deeply entrenched in our law for any court below the highest to disturb or destroy it".

179 s.3 of the Defective Premises Act has no effect on the bare landlord or vendor as it only applies to those doing work on premises. Section 4 places a duty on landlords to take care to see that persons using the premises are reasonably safe from injury or damage to their property, but it only applies where the landlord has an obligation to repair and does not apply to vendors. See further paras 11-85

mon law duty to take care to protect or warn the occupiers or users of the premises against dangers of which he is aware unless he was responsible for creating the danger through his design or construction, or has undertaken a repair obligation. It is difficult to justify this immunity on the ground that the remedy against the bare vendor/landlord should be limited to contract for whilst this argument remains attractive in the context of pure economic loss,[180] it was rejected in the context of physical damage by *Donoghue*. It is suggested that *Cavalier v Pope* should be overruled at the next opportunity.[181]

Litigants A litigant does not owe a duty of care to another litigant regarding the manner in which the litigation is conducted.[182] The safeguards against impropriety in the conduct of litigation are to be found in the rules and procedures of the court rather than the law of tort.[183] Though a litigant must not wilfully or recklessly mislead the court, they are not required to ensure that only the best evidence is relied upon or to check the evidence relied upon by their opponents. Such a duty would result in all litigation becoming unnecessarily lengthy and additionally expensive.[184] **7-44**

Provision of public services Those who provide public services may owe no duty of care either because the nature of the public service means that there is insufficient proximity or that it would not be fair, just and reasonable to impose a duty; or the issue concerned is regarded as non-justiciable, i.e. a matter of social or economic policy not capable of being evaluated by a court. In particular, judges and witnesses in judicial proceedings and the police in their role of investigating and suppressing crime are regarded as owing no duty of care. The scope of these rules is considered in detail in Ch.9 on Professional Liability and Ch.13 on Public Service Liability.[185] **7-45**

Conflicts of interest There may be situations where a defendant's primary duty to a third party may preclude a duty of care to the claimant. Thus, in *Kapfunde v Abbey National Plc*[186] the Court of Appeal held that a doctor engaged by a company to assess the medical questionnaires of potential employees, owed no duty of care to those who had completed the questionnaire. Similarly, in *Briscoe v Lubrizol Ltd*[187] underwriters of a company's health care scheme were held to owe no duty of care to an employee when assessing the validity of his claim to benefits from the scheme. In both cases the loss claimed was purely economic and the reasoning might be thought less likely to apply where the claim relates to physical harm. **7-46**

to 11-87.

180 See para.7-128.

181 For now, however, it remains: see *Boldack v East Lindsey DC* (1999) 31 H.L.R. 41 CA; *Drysdale v Hedges* [2012] EWHC 4131 (QB); [2012] 3 E.G.L.R. 105; *Essex CC v Davies* [2019] EWHC 3443 (QB); [2020] P.I.Q.R. P7.

182 *Customs and Excise Commissioners v Barclays Bank Plc* [2006] UKHL 28; [2007] 1 A.C. 181 at [18], per Lord Bingham; *The Commissioners for Her Majesty's Revenue and Customs v Charles (t/a Boston Computer Group Europe)* [2019] EWCA Civ 2176; [2020] S.T.C. 158.

183 *Business Computers International Ltd v Registrar of Companies* [1988] Ch. 229.

184 *The Commissioners for Her Majesty's Revenue and Customs v Charles (t/a Boston Computer Group Europe)* [2019] EWCA Civ 2176; [2020] S.T.C. 158 at [42]–[43].

185 See para.9-40 onwards and paras 13-49 and 13-55.

186 [1999] I.C.R. 1; [1999] Lloyd's Rep. Med. 48. See also *R. v Croydon HA* [1998] Lloyd's Rep. Med. 44.

187 [2000] I.C.R. 694; [2000] P.I.Q.R. P39.

However, in *R. v Croydon HA*[188] the Court of Appeal doubted whether a company doctor who failed to notice a potentially dangerous condition when examining a prospective employee, was under any duty of care to warn the person of the danger; and in *X (Minors) v Bedfordshire CC*[189] Lord Browne-Wilkinson said that a doctor instructed by an insurance company to examine an applicant for life insurance "does not by examining the applicant, come under any general duty of medical care to the applicant. He is under a duty not to damage the applicant in the course of the examination: but beyond that his duties are owed to the insurance company and not the applicant."[190]

7-47 The Court of Appeal in *Phelps v Hillingdon LBC*[191] applied the same reasoning to deny a duty on the part of an educational psychologist but the House of Lords[192] reversed this decision, concluding that the fact that the psychologist owed a duty to the employing authority was no reason for holding that no duty was owed to the child being assessed. In *D v East Berkshire NHS Trust*[193] the Court of Appeal, following *Phelps*, held that the defendant could be vicariously liable for the alleged negligence of its doctors when making a diagnosis of non-accidental injury to a child. A duty could be owed by the doctor to the child when making such a diagnosis or recommending that the child should be taken into care.[194] This conclusion was accepted by the House of Lords. However, it was held that no duty was owed to the parents of a child who was suspected to be the victim of abuse because the child's interests were in potential conflict with the interests of the parents if the professionals involved in the investigation were to owe a duty both to the victim of suspected abuse and the suspected perpetrator of that abuse.[195] The appropriate level of protection for a parent suspected of abusing his child was that the clinical

---

188 [1998] Lloyd's Rep. Med. 44.

189 [1995] 2 A.C. 633.

190 [1995] 2 A.C. 633 at 752.

191 [1999] 1 W.L.R. 500.

192 [2001] 2 A.C. 619. If the no duty reasoning had been upheld, it is difficult to see how any employed professional could owe a duty to a client/patient. See further para.13-15.

193 [2003] EWCA Civ 1151; [2004] Q.B. 558; affirmed [2005] UKHL 23; [2005] 2 A.C. 373. See further para.13-19.

194 Effectively departing from the view of the House of Lords in *X (Minors) v Bedfordshire CC*. A suggestion by the Court of Appeal in *CN v Poole BC* [2017] EWCA Civ 2185; [2018] 2 W.L.R. 1693 that the decision in *D v East Berkshire NHS Trust* was inconsistent with later decisions of the House of Lords and Supreme Court, and had been impliedly overruled, was firmly rejected by the Supreme Court in *Poole BC v GN* [2019] UKSC 25; [2019] 2 W.L.R. 1478. Thus, medical professionals and social workers do owe a duty of care to children when making decisions about their welfare (at least where the decision is to intervene to remove a child into care, as opposed to a decision not to intervene, which may be categorised as an omission unless there has been an assumption of responsibility by the defendant: see para.13-20). In *Poole BC v GN* itself it was held that a local authority did not owe a duty of care arising out of the authority's responsibilities under the Children Act 1989 to the claimant children in respect of harassment and abuse by neighbours, since this constituted an omission and there had been no assumption of responsibility to the children by the local authority (see paras 13-21, 13-71 and 13-72).

195 Note, however, *Merthyr Tydfil CBC v C* [2010] EWHC 62 (QB); [2010] P.I.Q.R. P9, where Hickinbottom J, whilst accepting that a local authority does not owe a duty of care to those who are suspected of abusing a child, concluded that there is no general principle that where a local authority owe a duty of care to a child, it cannot as a matter of law at the same time owe a duty of care to the parents of that child. The fact that there was "some conceivable potential for such a conflict in the future is insufficient to make an authority immune from a suit in negligence at that hands of a parent" (at [36]). (The claimant's action against the local authority was in respect of psychiatric harm that she suffered due to the alleged failure of the local authority properly to investigate her concerns that her children had been abused by an older child). It may be that the decision in *Merthyr Tydfil*

and other investigations had to be conducted in good faith. Lord Nicholls said that:

> "A doctor is obliged to act in the best interests of his patient. In these cases the child is his patient. The doctor is charged with the protection of the child, not with the protection of the parent. The best interests of a child and his parent normally march hand-in-hand. But when considering whether something does not feel 'quite right', a doctor must be able to act single-mindedly in the interests of the child. He ought not to have at the back of his mind an awareness that if his doubts about intentional injury or sexual abuse prove unfounded he may be exposed to claims by a distressed parent."[196]

In *Jain v Trent Strategic HA*[197] it was held that a public authority exercising a statutory power, the purpose of which was the protection of the residents of a nursing home, owed no duty of care to the owners of the home as to the manner in which it exercised that power. The authority might owe a duty to the residents but could not also owe a duty to the proprietors, whose interests could conflict with those of the residents (applying *D v East Berkshire Community Health NHS Trust*).[198] Similarly, an employer does not owe a duty to employees to defend a civil action brought against the employer, based on vicarious liability for the alleged misconduct of those employees, in a manner that protects the employees from economic or reputational harm. The interests of the employer and the employees are fundamentally different. In *James-Bowen v Commissioner of Police of the Metropolis*[199] the Supreme Court held that the employees' interests were in protecting their reputation and the potential financial consequences of an adverse outcome, whereas the employer's interests involved weighing a number of factors: the prospects of successfully defending the action (involving an assessment of the reliability and verac- **7-48**

CBC v C turned on its "quite exceptional facts": *F-D v Children and Family Court Advisory Service* [2014] EWHC 1619 (QB); [2015] 1 F.C.R. 98 (CAFCASS did not owe a duty of care to the parent of a child when giving advice to the court about a child's welfare due to potential conflict with the statutory duty imposed on CAFCASS).

196 [2005] UKHL 23; [2005] 2 A.C. 373 at [85]; see also per Lord Rodger at [110] and Lord Brown at [129]. cf. Lord Bingham's dissenting speech at [37] arguing that the potential conflict of duties was more apparent than real. See also *West Bromwich Albion FC Ltd v El-Safty* [2006] EWCA Civ 1299; [2007] P.I.Q.R. P7; [2007] L.S. Law Med. 50 at [25] where (in a claim by a professional football club against a doctor in respect of its financial loss arising out of the negligent treatment of one of its players) Rix LJ considered that there was a potential conflict of interest between the club and the player: "the danger of a conflict of interest between a sports employer and a sportsman, all the more important where the sportsman may think that his principal interest is tied up in his soonest possible availability to his employer, must loom large. It militates against implying a contract with the employer rather than with the patient, or with the employer as well as with the patient."

197 [2009] UKHL 4; [2009] 1 A.C. 853. See also *Desmond v Chief Constable of Nottinghamshire* [2011] EWCA Civ 3; [2011] 1 F.L.R. 1361 where the Court of Appeal held that no duty of care is owed by the police to a person applying for an enhanced criminal record certificate, even though errors in the information provided affected the claimant's ability to obtain employment, partly on the basis that if such a duty were held to exist "there would be a plain conflict between the … putative duty to [the claimant] and the statutory purpose of protecting vulnerable young people" (at [49]). See further *C v T Borough Council* [2014] EWHC 2482 (QB); [2015] E.L.R. 1 (no duty owed when providing information to the police for the purpose of an enhanced criminal record certificate); *Jowhari v NHS England* [2014] EWHC 4197 (QB) (no duty owed to dentist arising out of removal from a dental performers list since statutory scheme was designed to protect the public from unsuitable dentists and a private law duty owed to the dentist would conflict with the statutory scheme).

198 See further para.13-51. In a rather different context, see *Hilton v Barker Booth & Eastwood* [2005] UKHL 8; [2005] 1 W.L.R. 567, where the House of Lords held a solicitor under a duty to disclose to a client relevant but confidential information about another client. In effect, the solicitor had to break its duty to one or other client and should not have got itself into that position. See paras 9-131, 9-153 and 9-156.

199 [2018] UKSC 40; [2018] 1 W.L.R. 4021.

ity of the employees), the importance attached to successfully defending the claim, what resources should be devoted to its defence, and whether the cost and effort of defending the claim was justified. In addition, the Commissioner of Police, as a holder of public office, has a public duty to act as she considers appropriate in the interests of the police service, and this duty was totally inconsistent with her owing a duty of care to protect the reputational interests of her employees in such circumstances.[200]

7-49 **Status as an employee** There is an argument for treating the defendant's status as an employee as a reason for denying a duty to third parties in respect of negligence in the course of employment. In the Canadian Supreme Court decision in *London Drugs*[201] La Forest J held that it was unfair for an employee to owe a duty of care to his employer's client in respect of careless conduct which damaged the client's property.[202] The employee would normally lack the resources to meet the claim and the opportunity to decline the risk of liability. Compensation for the client could be ensured by holding the employer to be directly rather than vicariously liable. Although his colleagues considered that such a change to the accepted notion that the employee is personally liable was too radical, there are stronger arguments for applying such reasoning to economic loss where the duty may be based on an assumption of responsibility by the defendant.[203] However, in *Merrett v Babb*,[204] the Court of Appeal relied on *Phelps v Hillingdon LBC*[205] in concluding that an employed surveyor could owe a duty of care to a client of his employer.

7-50 **General tort immunities** Several categories of persons are not liable in tort, either absolutely or subject to qualification, but since their legal positions concern all torts they are discussed in appropriate places elsewhere. They include the Crown, foreign sovereigns and states and diplomatic representatives, visiting forces, minors (but only where action in tort would be an indirect way of circumventing their immunity in contract), corporations with regard to ultra vires acts, trade unions and other unincorporated associations. The detail is explained in Ch.5 on Capacity.

(e) Omissions[206]

7-51 **The principle** In *Smith v Littlewoods Organisation Ltd*[207] Lord Goff stated the fundamental principle that "the common law does not impose liability for what are

---

[200] In addition, Lord Lloyd-Jones noted that a duty owed to the employees would inevitably inhibit the conduct of the defence, and would also be "inconsistent with the important legal policy which encourages the settlement of civil claims and seeks to promote out of court settlement. The resulting risk of exposure to consequential claims would, in many situations, operate as a powerful disincentive to settlement": [2018] UKSC 40; [2018] 1 W.L.R. 4021 at [35]–[36].

[201] *London Drugs Ltd v Kuehne & Nagel International Ltd* (1992) 97 D.L.R. (4th) 261.

[202] La Forest J argued that the immunity should not extend to "non-contractual liability", e.g. where an employee in the course of employment negligently caused a road accident injuring a stranger. Here the stranger's only means access to the firm's liability insurance policy would be through showing that the employee was personally liable and the employer was vicariously liable.

[203] See further para.7-136.

[204] [2001] EWCA Civ 214; [2001] Q.B. 1174.

[205] [1999] 1 W.L.R. 500.

[206] On the distinction between omissions and acts, see para.1-55. See generally S. Steel, "Rationalising omissions liability in negligence" (2019) 135 L.Q.R. 484.

[207] [1987] A.C. 241 at 247.

called pure omissions". As authority he cited the speech of Lord Diplock in *Home Office v Dorset Yacht Co Ltd*[208]:

> "The parable of the good Samaritan which was evoked by Lord Atkin in *Donoghue v Stevenson* illustrates, in the conduct of the priest and Levite who passed by on the other side, an omission which was likely to have as its reasonable and probable consequence damage to the health of the victim of the thieves, but for which the priest and Levite would have incurred no civil liability in English Law. Examples could be multiplied … you need not warn (your neighbour) of a risk of physical danger to which he is about to expose himself …; you may watch your neighbour's goods being ruined by a thunderstorm though the slightest effort on your part could protect them from the rain …"[209]

The difference between acts and omissions involves a distinction between the infliction of harm by the defendant through some positive action and allowing harm to occur to the claimant by failing to prevent it (the harm being caused through some other agency). In *Poole BC v GN*[210] Lord Reed preferred to express this as "a distinction between causing harm (making things worse) and failing to confer a benefit (not making things better) … partly because the former language better conveys the rationale of the distinction drawn in the authorities, and partly because the distinction between acts and omissions seems to be found difficult to apply."

The principle only applies to pure omissions. A person who creates a danger, however blamelessly, may come under a consequential duty to take precautions to prevent injury resulting. Thus, a motorist who has to leave his vehicle unlit, may be under a duty to warn other motorists of the obstruction.[211] A manufacturer aware of a dangerous feature in its product may be under a duty to warn users[212] and this may apply where the dangerous defect is discovered subsequent to the sale of the product.[213] It was said that "a manufacturer who realises that omitting to warn customers about something which might result in injury to them must take reasonable steps to attempt to warn them, however lacking in negligence he may have been when the goods were sold". In such cases, the omission is not considered in isolation but as part of the activity as a whole. It is simply the element which makes the activity negligent. The whole activity amounts to a "misfeasance". The pure omission principle applies only where the failure to act can be viewed in isolation from other aspects of the defendant's activity and classed as "nonfeasance". Thus, a negligent failure by the police to apprehend an offender, with the result that he goes on to commit further offences, injuring the claimant, constitutes an omission for which the police will not be responsible, but negligence in the course of arrest- 7-52

208 [1970] A.C. 1004 at 1060.

209 In similar vein Viscount Dilhorne said that a person would not be liable if "he fails to warn a person nearby whom he sees about to step off the pavement into the path of an oncoming vehicle or if he fails to rescue a child in difficulties in a pond": [1970] A.C. 1004 at 1027.

210 [2019] UKSC 25; [2019] 2 W.L.R. 1478 at [28].

211 *Lee v Lever* [1974] R.T.R. 35. See para.7-216.

212 *Vacwell Engineering Co Ltd v BDH Chemicals Ltd* [1971] 1 Q.B. 111.

213 *E Hobbs Farms Ltd v Baxendale Chemical Co Ltd* [1992] 1 Lloyd's Rep. 54 at 65, per Deputy Judge Ogden QC: "a manufacturer who realises that omitting to warn customers about something which might result in injury to them must take reasonable steps to attempt to warn them, however lacking in negligence he may have been when the goods were sold." There, a product advertised as "self-extinguishing" caused extensive fire damage to a customer. The manufacturer was held liable in negligence for failing to correct its advertising once it became clear that the product might not be "self-extinguishing". See further para.10-32.

ing a suspect with the result that police officers cause injury to the claimant constitutes a positive act falling into an existing category of the duty of care.[214]

7-53 **Justification** The basis of the principle lies in the priority given by the common law to the autonomy of the individual and, hence, the reluctance to require an individual to act as if he or she were "my brother's keeper". In *Stovin v Wise*[215] Lord Hoffmann elaborated in the following terms:

> "One can put the matter in political moral or economic terms. In political terms it is less of an invasion of an individual's freedom for the law to require him to consider the safety of others in his actions than to impose upon him a duty to rescue or protect. A moral version of this point may be called the 'Why pick on me?' argument. A duty to prevent harm to others or to render assistance to a person in danger or distress may apply to a large and indeterminate class of people who happen to be able to do something. Why should one be held liable rather than another? In economic terms the efficient allocation of resources usually requires an activity should bear its own costs ... But there is no similar justification for requiring a person who is not doing anything to spend money on behalf of someone else ... . So there must be some special reason why he should have to put his hand in his pocket."

Lord Goff recognised that the repugnance of some extreme applications of the principle to "modern thinking" might eventually lead to its reconsideration by the courts.[216] However, the general principle remains and a duty to take affirmative action in the interests of another will be imposed only where there is a special reason.

7-54 **No general duty to rescue** One consequence of the "pure omission" rule is that, in the absence of a special reason, neither a private individual nor a public service owes a duty of care to respond to an emergency by attempting a rescue. As Stuart-Smith LJ explained in *Capital and Counties Plc v Hampshire CC*[217]:

> "... a doctor who happened to witness a road accident will very likely go to the assistance of anyone injured, but he is not under any legal obligation to do so (save in certain limited circumstances) ... if he volunteers assistance, his only duty as a matter of law is not to make the victim's condition worse."[218]

---

214 *Robinson v Chief Constable of West Yorkshire* [2018] UKSC 4; [2018] A.C. 736. See also *Rigby v Chief Constable of Northamptonshire* [1985] 1 W.L.R. 1242 for another example of a "positive" act causing damage by the police during the course of attempting to apprehend an offender for which there could be responsibility. Note that it may be difficult to determine whether a particular case involves a positive act or an omission, in which case it will be inappropriate to strike out an action as disclosing no reasonable cause of action; rather it is better to reach a conclusion after a trial to determine the facts: *Chief Constable of Essex v Transport Arendonk BvBa* [2020] EWHC 212 (QB); [2020] R.T.R. 22.

215 [1996] A.C. 923 at 943–944. In *Commissioners of Customs and Excise v Barclays Bank Plc* [2006] UKHL 28; [2007] 1 A.C. 181, Lord Hoffmann applied his reasoning in *Stovin* to support his conclusion that a common law duty of care to act positively could not be derived from a court order imposed on a defendant any more than it could from a statutory duty imposed on a defendant. For fuller consideration of the case see para.7-111.

216 [1987] A.C. 241 at 271. Lord Goff also cited the comment of Fleming, *The Law of Torts*, 6th edn (1983), p.138 that the omission principle provoked an "invidious comparison with affirmative duties of good-neighbourliness in most countries outside the common law orbit".

217 [1997] Q.B. 1004 at 1035.

218 Contrast *Kent v Griffiths, Roberts and London Ambulance Service* [2001] Q.B. 36, where the ambulance service was held to owe a duty to exercise reasonable care in effecting a "rescue" based on its undertaking to respond to the emergency call. Note that in *Woods v Lowns* (1995) 36

The leading authority is *East Suffolk Rivers Catchment Board v Kent*.[219] The claimant's land was flooded by sea-water and the defendant Board, although under no duty to repair the breach in the sea wall, did undertake such repairs but so negligently that the land remained flooded for much longer than it would had the repair been efficient. The House of Lords held that the Board was not liable because its neglect did not inflict any more damage than would a total omission. *Capital and Counties* illustrates the crucial distinction between an ineffective rescue and a damaging rescue, i.e. one that makes the claimant's position worse. The Court of Appeal held the fire service liable in respect of an incident where it had negligently turned off the claimant's sprinkler system with the result that the fire spread more than it would have done had the fire service not intervened.[220] However, there was no liability for incidents where the service failed to fully extinguish the fire before leaving the premises with the result that it revived and destroyed the premises. There was no difference between simply failing to turn up to effect a "rescue" and turning up but negligently failing to carry out the "rescue", unless the claimant's position was worsened as a result.[221] By the same token, if the defendant was not under a duty to exercise reasonable care to prevent a third party causing physical injury to the claimant, then, in the absence of a special relationship or an undertaking of responsibility, the defendant will not owe a duty to protect the claimant from the economic consequences of that physical damage.[222]

Damaging rescues[223] Some difficulty concerns what can be regarded as conduct making the situation worse. This problem is illustrated by *OLL v Secretary of State for Transport*[224] where the coastguard not only misdirected their own lifeboat but also the Royal Navy helicopter. As a result there was a delay in reaching children whose canoeing trip had got into difficulties. It was argued that the misdirection to the Royal Navy was analogous to the turning off of the sprinkler in *Capital and Counties*, it made the situation worse than it would have been. May J rejected the argument on the ground that "Misdirecting other rescuers does not of itself inflict direct physical injury" and liability could not be imposed "by assessing a level of intervention which falls short of intervention which results in positive injury directly 7-55

N.S.W.L.R. 344; [1996] Aus. Torts Rep. 81–376, it was held that a doctor could owe a duty of care to respond properly to a request to provide medical assistance to someone collapsing close by his surgery. The court stressed the relevance of physical proximity, the fact that the request was made in a professional context, i.e. when the doctor was at his place of practice, and that failure to respond to an emergency was regarded as professional misconduct. In the UK, general practitioners owe a duty to every patient accepted onto their NHS list whether as a permanent patient or temporary resident. See further para.9-50.

219 [1941] A.C. 74.

220 Stuart-Smith LJ suggested that the analogous situation in the *East Suffolk* case would have arisen had "the [claimant] constructed a temporary wall which contained the floodwater to a relatively small area, and the defendants then came upon the land to repair the main wall and negligently destroyed the temporary wall so that the area of flooding increased before the repairs were completed" [1997] Q.B. 1004 at 1034.

221 Applied in *AJ Allan (Blairnyle) Ltd v Strathclyde Fire Board* [2016] CSIH 3; 2016 S.C. 304; *Mackay v Scottish Fire & Rescue Service* [2015] CSOH 55; 2015 S.L.T. 342.

222 *Glaister v Appleby-in-Westmorland Town Council* [2009] EWCA Civ 1325; [2010] P.I.Q.R. P6—local authority owed no duty to claimant, who had been injured by a loose horse at a fair, to see that appropriate liability insurance was taken out to cover the potential liability of a third party for such injuries (the third party owner of the horse being untraceable).

223 See generally J. Fulbrook, "Rescuers and the Concept of a 'Negligent Rescue'" [2013] J.P.I.L. 81.

224 [1997] 3 All E.R. 897.

inflicted".[225] The logical extension of this view would be that the coastguard would not have been liable if it had advised the Royal Navy to abandon its rescue attempt in the negligently mistaken belief that its own rescue had succeeded. It is arguable that in this situation the defendant has negligently deterred or prevented someone else from rescuing an accident victim and has thereby made the victim's position worse, not simply failed to make it better.[226]

7-56 **Special reasons for affirmative duty** Three situations may be identified which, in effect, represent exceptions to the "pure omissions" rule: First, where there is a special relationship between the parties which entitles one party to rely on affirmative action being taken by the other. Secondly, where there is a specific assumption of responsibility by one party to act affirmatively to benefit the other. Thirdly, where one party must bear a specific responsibility for protecting the other from harm caused by third parties.

(i) Special relationship

7-57 **Protective relationships** There are a number of relationships where the responsibility of one party for the care of the other is recognised as giving rise to an affirmative duty to prevent harm. Thus, the occupier of land owes a duty to a visitor to "take such care as is reasonable to see that the visitor is reasonably safe in using the premises"[227] and this may require taking positive steps to control natural danger on the land. In *Goldman v Hargrave*[228] the Privy Council held that the occupier may be liable to neighbouring occupiers for failing to control a natural danger on his land. In that case a tree on the defendant's land caught fire. The defendant cut down the tree but failed to extinguish the fire. A wind revived the fire which spread to the claimant's property. Lord Wilberforce said that the law now recognised an occupier's duty as one of "a more positive character than merely to abstain from creating, or adding to, a source of danger" and held that there was "a general duty on occupiers in relation to hazards occurring on their land, whether natural or man-made".[229] Again, an employer owes an affirmative duty to take care to prevent harm to his employees[230] as does a carrier to a passenger,[231] a parent or school to a child,[232]

---

225 [1997] 3 All E.R. 897 at 908.

226 See *Kent v Griffiths* [2001] Q.B. 36 where the ambulance service were held to owe a duty of care having undertaken to attend a patient on receiving an emergency phone call; if they had declined to accept the call the patient's general practitioner would have driven the patient to the hospital Accident & Emergency department sooner and the patient would have received prompt treatment.

227 Occupiers' Liability Act 1957 s.2(1). See para.11-24.

228 [1967] 1 A.C. 645.

229 [1967] 1 A.C. 645 at 657. The *Goldman* principle that the occupier owes a positive duty to act to protect neighbours from natural dangers, has been accepted by the Court of Appeal in *Leakey v National Trust* [1980] Q.B. 485. In both cases the court suggested that the occupier's resources could be taken into account in determining whether the duty had been broken. See para.7-181. In *Holbeck Hall Hotel v Scarborough BC* [2000] Q.B. 836, the Court of Appeal held that given the duty imposed liability for nonfeasance, it was not just and reasonable for the duty to extend to damage which was greater in extent than anything that was foreseeable. See para.2-169.

230 See for example *Charlton v Forest Ink Printing Co Ltd* [1980] I.R.L.R. 331 (duty to take precautions against attacks on employees). In the case of the military the protective employment relationship may extend to events occurring while off-duty because rank and military discipline can remain relevant: *Ministry of Defence v Radclyffe* [2009] EWCA Civ 635.

231 See for example *Horsley v MacLaren* [1971] 2 Lloyd's Rep. 410, Supreme Court of Canada: owner of ship under a duty of care to save a passenger who falls overboard. See also Merchant Shipping

a custodial authority to a detainee,[233] the management of a nightclub to a customer in respect of an assault by another customer,[234] a hotel to a guest in respect of an assault by a third party,[235] and, arguably, health professionals to members of a patient's family where the patient has a genetic condition that could also affect those family members.[236] The basis of the duty in these situations was said by Beldam LJ in *Barrett v Ministry of Defence*,[237] to be "reliance express or implied in the relationship which the party to whom the duty is owed is entitled to place on the other party to make provision for his safety." In *Barrett* the Court of Appeal held that the Ministry owed no duty of care to prevent off-duty servicemen consuming too much alcohol at the mess bar. There was no entitled reliance as it was "reasonable for the law to leave a responsible adult to assume responsibility for his own actions in consuming alcoholic drink".[238]

Act 1995 s.92 (duty of ship to assist the other in case of collision) and s.93 (duty to assist aircraft in distress). But there is no duty to warn passengers of hazards likely to be encountered after the journey has been completed merely because they are close to the passenger's destination: *Fernquest v City & County of Swansea* [2011] EWCA Civ 1712 (defendants aware of icy pavement close to a bus stop, but not liable for failing to warn passenger who slipped on the ice after he had alighted from a bus).

232 See *Surtees v Kingston-upon-Thames BC* [1991] 2 F.L.R. 559 at 584 (parent). *Barnes v Hampshire CC* [1969] 1 W.L.R. 1563; (school); *Smoldon v Whitworth* [1997] P.I.Q.R. P133 (referee of juniors rugby match). But the duty to the child may not extend to protecting the child's financial interests, at least where the preservation of the family unit is at stake: *VL (A Child) v Oxfordshire CC* [2010] EWHC 2091 (QB); [2010] P.I.Q.R. P20. See also *XA v YA* [2010] EWHC 1983 (QB); [2011] P.I.Q.R. P1—the court should be slow to find a parent in breach of a duty of care owed to their children, particularly where such a duty could only have been discharged by the break-up of the family. See para.7-224 onwards.

233 *Ellis v Home Office* [1953] 2 Q.B. 135.

234 *Everett v Comojo (UK) Ltd (t/a Metropolitan)* [2011] EWCA Civ 13; [2012] 1 W.L.R. 150.

235 *Al-Najar v Cumberland Hotel (London) Ltd* [2019] EWHC 1593 (QB); [2019] 1 W.L.R. 5953 at [187], per Dingemans J; applying *Everett v Comojo (UK) Ltd (t/a Metropolitan)* [2011] EWCA Civ 13. Dingemans J considered that the hotel had assumed a duty to take reasonable care to protect guests because it invited them to come and stay at the hotel.

236 *ABC v St George's Healthcare NHS Foundation Trust* [2017] EWCA Civ 336; [2017] P.I.Q.R. P15; sed quaere, and contrast *Smith v University of Leicester NHS Trust* [2016] EWHC 817 (QB). See further *ABC v St George's Healthcare NHS Trust* [2020] EWHC 455 (QB) (no breach of duty or causation, on the facts).

237 [1995] 1 W.L.R. 1217 at 1224.

238 Beldam LJ distinguished the Canadian decisions in *Crocker v Sundance Northwest Resorts Ltd* (1988) 51 D.L.R. (4th) 321; and *Jordan House Ltd v Menow* (1973) 38 D.L.R. (3d) 105, where the supplier of alcohol was held under a duty to prevent harm to a customer from excessive alcohol consumption, as being based on additional factors. In *Crocker* it was the fact that the defendant had supplied him with equipment to participate in a ski race knowing that he was drunk; in *Jordan House* it was the fact that there was an invitee/invitor relationship between the defendant and his habitual customer whom he evicted knowing that he was unsteady and would have to cross a busy road. In *CAL No.14 Pty Ltd v Motor Accidents Insurance Board* [2009] HCA 47; (2009) 239 C.L.R. 390; (2009) 260 A.L.R. 606 the High Court of Australia held that the proprietor and licensee of licensed premises owed no general duty of care at common law to customers requiring them to monitor and minimise the service of alcohol or to protect customers from the consequences of the alcohol they choose to consume. The High Court found the decision of the Supreme Court of Canada in *Jordan House* to be "unconvincing". See also *Schuller v S.J. Webb Nominees Pty Ltd* [2015] SASCFC 162, applying *CAL No.14 Pty Ltd v Motor Accidents Insurance Board*, holding that the owners of a motel did not owe a duty of care to a drunken customer who injured herself when she fell from a chair upon which she had been dancing, despite repeated requests from the bar staff to get down. See generally, Fulbrook, "Alcohol and Third Parties—'Dram Shop Liability' and Beyond" [2007] J.P.I.L. 220.

7-58 **Public services**[239] It is clear that the general provision of a public service is unlikely to give rise to such entitled reliance on the part of any member of the public as to justify an affirmative duty being imposed on the service. In *Stovin v Wise* the claimant's road accident was partially caused by the lack of visibility resulting from an obstruction which the highway authority had failed to remove. Lord Hoffmann rejected the argument that the authority owed an affirmative duty based on the "general reliance" placed on it by the public, saying that:

> "The foundation for the doctrine of general reliance is missing in this case, because we are not concerned with provision of a uniform identifiable benefit or service. Every hazardous … junction is different and requires a separate decision as to whether anything should be done to improve it."[240]

(ii) *Specific assumption of responsibility*

7-59 **Assumption of responsibility** Where a defendant assumes responsibility to a claimant to perform a service and fails to do so, he can be liable for the loss suffered by the claimant in relying upon that undertaking. Thus, in *Welsh v Chief Constable of the Merseyside Police*[241] and *Swinney v Chief Constable of the Northumbria Police*[242] it was held that where the prosecution or police service had given an undertaking to take some action, it could owe an affirmative duty to take reasonable care to honour the undertaking. Again, a gratuitous insurance agent who had undertaken to act for a car owner was held liable for failing to warn him that his policy had been cancelled.[243] In *Calvert v William Hill Credit Ltd*[244] the Court of Appeal held that the defendants had assumed a responsibility to the claimant to exclude the claimant from telephone gambling with them for six months, although the scope of the defendants' duty of care did not extend to preventing him from gambling with them in other ways or with other bookmakers. The undertaking may be implied from the defendant's conduct. Thus, in *Barrett v Ministry of Defence*[245] the Court of Appeal, having held that there was no duty to prevent the victim (an off-duty airman) drinking excessive alcohol, accepted the defendant's concession

---

239 See further para.13-62 onwards.
240 [1996] A.C. 923 at 957.
241 [1993] 1 All E.R. 692.
242 [1997] Q.B. 464; see para.13-40; cf. *Desmond v Chief Constable of Nottinghamshire* [2011] EWCA Civ 3; [2011] 1 F.L.R. 1361—no duty of care owed by the police to a person applying for an enhanced criminal record certificate, even though errors in the information provided affected the claimant's ability to obtain employment. There was no assumption of responsibility by the police beyond that required by the proper performance of the statutory duty to provide a certificate. See also *C v T Borough Council* [2014] EWHC 2482 (QB); [2015] E.L.R. 1; *CLG v Chief Constable of Merseyside* [2015] EWCA Civ 836. See para.13-41.
243 *Bromley LBC v Ellis* [1971] 1 Lloyd's Rep. 97 CA.
244 [2008] EWCA Civ 1427; [2009] Ch. 330. See further para.2-111. Cf. *The Ritz Hotel Casino Ltd v Al-Daher* [2014] EWHC 2847 (QB); [2015] 4 All E.R. 222 (no duty on casino to restrain defendant from using or extending her credit facility with the casino, given her "almost unimaginable wealth", the probability that the defendant was not addicted to gambling, and that there was nothing that should have alerted the casino that the defendant was out of control with her gambling).
245 [1995] 1 W.L.R. 1217. See also *Jebson v Ministry of Defence* [2000] 1 W.L.R. 2055, where the Court of Appeal held the defendant vicariously liable for injuries to the claimant suffered as a result falling out of a lorry at the end of a night of drinking organised by the company commander. By taking responsibility for the organisation and transport of the group, the commander had impliedly undertaken a duty of care to the claimant. Contrast *Griffiths v Brown* [1999] P.I.Q.R. P131, where a taxi driver's duty to a drunk passenger was held to be limited to setting him down safely and did not extend to ensuring that he could then get home safely.

that once the victim had collapsed and his colleagues had taken him to his room, it had assumed a responsibility for him and because medical assistance was not summoned, it had fallen short of the standard reasonably to be expected.[246] A more difficult issue arises where the defendant's conduct has simply lulled the claimant into abstaining from taking steps for his own protection. Courts are most likely to impose a duty in this situation where physical security is in issue. Thus a railway has been held liable for failing to lock an access to a line crossing with the result that a pedestrian crossed and was hit by a train. The railway was under no general duty to lock the access but its practice of keeping it locked when a train was passing induced the public to believe that it was safe to cross when the access was unlocked.[247] Determining whether a rescue service has assumed a responsibility to a victim has given rise to some difficulties and is discussed in Ch.13.

(iii) *Specific responsibility for protection from third parties*

Basis of liability In *Smith v Littlewoods Organisation Ltd*[248] Lords Mackay and Goff, who gave the leading judgments, agreed that there was no general duty to prevent a third party from causing damage to another but disagreed as to the reason and the basis of exceptions to the general rule. Lord Mackay argued that the reason lay in the difficulty of predicting whether a third party would cause damage as a result of the defendant's neglect. For this reason the general principle of reasonable foreseeability would not be easy to satisfy. It would only be reasonable to foresee such third party intervention where it was probable. Lord Goff disagreed, considering that the reason for the limited duty was not the unpredictability of human conduct but the more fundamental reluctance of the common law to "impose liability for what are called pure omissions", taken along with "the general perception that we ought not to be held responsible in law for the deliberate wrongdoing of others".[249] Exceptions to this general position had to be based not on "generalised principle" but on special circumstances giving rise to "narrower but still identifiable principles". Lord Goff identified four such circumstances: 7-60

(a) where there is a special relationship between defendant and claimant based on an assumption of responsibility by the defendant;
(b) where there is a special relationship between the defendant and the third party based on control by the defendant;
(c) where the defendant is responsible for a state of danger which may be exploited by a third party; and

[246] See also *Ministry of Defence v Radclyffe* [2009] EWCA Civ 635 where the Court of Appeal held that an officer's presence at an off-duty swimming party gave rise to an assumption of responsibility to junior ranks to prevent them from taking undue risks: "They asked him if they might jump. The very fact that they asked predicates reliance sufficient for a duty of care and their assumption that he had authority to order them not to jump. That authority derived from his rank and the fact of his and their military employment. His authority was no doubt more circumscribed than if they had all been on duty. The fact that they were off duty did not mean that the military relationship became irrelevant": per Sir Anthony May P at [21]; cf. *Geary v Wetherspoon Plc* [2011] EWHC 1506 (QB); [2011] N.P.C. 60—occupiers of premises had not assumed any specific responsibility to a customer who chose to slide down a banister and fell off; nor was there any evidence of specific reliance by the claimant on the defendant. The position might have been different "if the defendant had been organising banister-sliding competitions" (per Coulson J at [60]).

[247] *Mercer v South Eastern & Chatham Ry Companies' Managing Committee* [1922] 2 K.B. 549.

[248] [1987] A.C. 241.

[249] [1987] A.C. 241 at 271.

(d) where the defendant is responsible for property which may be used by third party to cause damage.

It is suggested that the approach of Lord Goff is to be preferred for two reasons. First, as he noted,[250] in some cases a duty had been imposed on the basis of an assumption of responsibility where the third party intervention was not foreseeable as likely and, conversely, no duty had been imposed in cases where it was foreseeable, for example, on occupiers to prevent third parties from entering their property. Lord Goff concluded that "the problem in these cases could (not) be solved simply through the mechanism of foreseeability".[251] Secondly, since foreseeability was applied to this third party damage situation in the leading 1960s decision of *Dorset Yacht*,[252] the approach of the courts to questions of imposing a duty has become more sophisticated with the use of proximity and justice as criteria and the recognition that close attention has to be paid to the particular type of relationship involved.

7-61 **Assumption of responsibility to claimant** Lord Goff cited *Stansbie v Troman*[253] as an illustration of an assumption of responsibility by a defendant leading to liability for damage directly caused by a third party. A decorator, left alone to work in a house, was asked to lock the premises if he left. He failed to do so and was held liable for the damage caused by a thief who entered during his absence. The case was decided in contract but Lord Goff commented that "such responsibility might well be held to exist in other cases where there is no contract, as for example where a person left alone in a house has entered as a licensee of the occupier". In *Swinney v Chief Constable of the Northumbria Police*[254] the Court of Appeal refused to strike out a claim by a police informant in respect of personal injuries caused by third parties as a result of the police negligently allowing the informant's name to become known to the criminal fraternity. It was arguable that the police had assumed a responsibility of confidentiality to the claimant. In the welfare context, in *W v Essex CC*[255] the Court of Appeal held that by analogy with cases such as *Swinney*, a local authority "assumed a responsibility for the accuracy of its positive assurances [about the character of a foster child] to the [fostering] parents" and hence, could be liable for injuries inflicted by the foster child on

---

[250] [1987] A.C. 241 at 279.

[251] [1987] A.C. 241 at 279.

[252] *Home Office v Dorset Yacht Co Ltd* [1970] A.C. 1004.

[253] [1948] 2 K.B. 48.

[254] [1997] Q.B. 464. Note that at the trial, Jackson J held that although a duty was owed, there had been no breach: *Swinney v Chief Constable of Northumbria Police* (1999) 11 Admin. L.R. 811; *The Times* 25 May 1999. Although the police may undertake responsibility for the physical safety of an informant, the relationship does not mean that they have undertaken responsibility to protect the informant from pure economic loss: *An Informer v Chief Constable* [2012] EWCA Civ 197; [2013] Q.B. 579. See also *PBD v Chief Constable of Greater Manchester* [2013] EWHC 3559 (QB) (no duty of care owed to a person about to be charged with a criminal offence for negligently revealing his true identity to former criminal associates with the result that he had to enter the witness protection programme); *CLG v Chief Constable of Merseyside* [2015] EWCA Civ 836 (allegation that police had carelessly disclosed the address of witnesses of a shooting incident to the defendants in the resulting criminal trial; no duty of care owed to witnesses, distinguishing Swinney on the basis that there had been no assumption of responsibility by the police; claimants had contacted the police following the shooting incident and gave routine statements; address was not disclosed to the police on a confidential basis). See further para.13-40.

[255] [1999] Fam. 90. This aspect of the case was not raised in the House of Lords [2001] 2 A.C. 592.

the parents' other children; and in *Barrett v Enfield LBC*[256] the House of Lords held that a council could be found to have assumed parental responsibility to a child in care and to be liable to the child for harm done by inappropriate foster parents. *Swinney*, *Essex* and *Barrett* concern public services and are discussed further in Ch.13.[257]

Assumption of responsibility by public authorities Such cases are extremely fact-sensitive, but as a general rule it will be rare for a public authority to be found to have assumed responsibility to a claimant to protect them from harm caused by a third party. In *Smith v Chief Constable of Sussex Police*[258] the claimant complained that the police had failed to act to prevent his former partner from attacking him, despite having been informed of previous attacks and death threats to the claimant. The House of Lords held that no duty of care in negligence was owed by the police to the claimant.[259] The same conclusion was reached by the Supreme Court in *Michael v Chief Constable of South Wales*[260] where a majority of the justices held that the police did not owe a duty of care to a woman killed by her ex-partner when she had made an earlier 999 phone call to the police complaining that her ex-partner had assaulted her and had threatened to kill her. There had been no assumption of responsibility to the deceased arising from what had been said to her when she phoned the emergency number requesting assistance.[261] Similarly, in *Mitchell v Glasgow City Council*[262] the House of Lords held that a social landlord did not owe a duty of care to a tenant to warn him that another tenant, about whom he had 7-62

---

256 [2001] 2 A.C. 550. But where the claim is in respect of pure economic loss (an alleged failure to apply for criminal injuries compensation on behalf of a minor) a local authority exercising parental responsibilities will not necessarily owe the child a duty of care: *VL (A Child) v Oxfordshire CC* [2010] EWHC 2091 (QB); [2010] P.I.Q.R. P20.

257 See paras 13-40, 13-27 and 13-14 respectively.

258 [2008] UKHL 50; [2009] 1 A.C. 225; see para.13-35; Burton, "Failing to Protect: Victims' Rights and Police Liability" (2009) 72 M.L.R. 283.

259 Applying *Hill v Chief Constable of West Yorkshire* [1989] A.C. 53; and *Brooks v Commissioner of Police of the Metropolis* [2005] UKHL 24; [2005] 1 W.L.R. 1495. See also *Rathband v Chief Constable of Northumbria* [2016] EWHC 181 (QB), discussed at para.13-45. On the liability of the police generally see paras 13-31 to 13-45. Contrast *Robinson v Chief Constable of West Yorkshire* [2018] UKSC 4; [2018] A.C. 736 where the claimant's injury was caused by a positive act of negligence by the police, rather than an omission to prevent harm to the claimant by a third party. See paras 7-25 and 13-42.

260 [2015] UKSC 2; [2015] A.C. 1732; see paras 13-37 and 13-38.

261 [2015] UKSC 2; [2015] A.C. 1732 at [138], per Lord Toulson, distinguishing Kent v Griffiths [2001] Q.B. 36 on the basis that the call handler in that case gave misleading assurances that an ambulance would be arriving shortly. Though as Lord Kerr noted in a dissenting judgment, at [165], the possibility that the police could be found to have undertaken responsibility to someone who called for emergency assistance, depending on what the call handler happened to say to the caller, creates the risk of arbitrary distinctions being drawn. So, e.g. in *Sherratt v Chief Constable of Greater Manchester* [2018] EWHC 1746 (QB); [2019] P.I.Q.R. P1 it was held that the police had assumed responsibility to the deceased (who committed suicide) on the basis of the information given by the call handler to the deceased's mother when she telephoned 999 to express her concerns about her daughter's mental state. The call handler gave specific assurances that police officers would be dispatched as a priority to the daughter's house to check on her wellbeing and that, if necessary, the police would arrange for her daughter's transfer to hospital. The clear assurance to the mother, combined with detrimental reliance by the mother on that assurance, distinguished the case from *Michael v Chief Constable of South Wales* (given the lack of assurances in *Michael*). The circumstances, said King J, were closer to *Kent v Griffiths* where a general practitioner and the claimant's husband had relied on assurances that an ambulance would arrive promptly.

262 [2009] UKHL 11; [2009] 1 A.C. 874. See further paras 13-64, 13-70, 13-72 and 13-94 for comment on *Mitchell*.

made a number of complaints, had threatened to kill him.[263] And in *Poole BC v GN*[264] the Supreme Court concluded that a local authority did not owe a duty of care arising out of the authority's responsibilities under the Children Act 1989 to the claimant children in respect of harassment and abuse by neighbours. Lord Reed accepted that public authorities could be subject to the same common law duties as private individuals if they had created the source of the danger or had assumed a responsibility to protect the claimant from harm, unless such a duty would be inconsistent with the legislation from which their duties or powers are derived, but public authorities do not owe a duty of care at common law merely because they have statutory powers or duties, even if, by exercising their statutory functions, they could prevent a person from suffering harm.[265] This was a case where it was alleged that the local authority had failed to provide a benefit to the claimant, by protecting him from harm inflicted by third parties, and on the pleaded facts they had not assumed a responsibility to do so.

7-63 On the other hand, there are some situations where it can be said that a public authority has expressly assumed responsibility to provide assistance. For example, an Accident and Emergency department of a NHS hospital holds itself out to the public as willing to accept patients for treatment following accidental injury or in emergency situations, and so will be taken to owe a duty of care to those presenting themselves for treatment.[266] This duty applies to the actions of healthcare professionals and, in some circumstances, the actions of non-medical staff. In *Darnley v Croydon Health Services NHS Trust*[267] the Supreme Court held that the duty applied to an Accident and Emergency department receptionist who, it was alleged, had given the claimant incorrect information about how long he would have to wait

---

[263] Lord Hope commented that: "as a general rule, … a duty to warn another person that he is at risk of loss, injury or damage as the result of the criminal act of a third party will arise only where the person who is said to be under that duty has by his words or conduct assumed responsibility for the safety of the person who is at risk": [2009] UKHL 11; [2009] 1 A.C. 874 at [29]. See also *Thomson v Scottish Ministers* [2013] CSIH 63; 2013 S.C. 628—no duty of care owed by the Prison Service to a member of the public killed by a prisoner on short term leave, where the risk to the general public, even if grave, was not enough to satisfy the requirement of proximity; there had to be a special risk of harm to the claimant greater than that to which the general public were exposed; *Furnell v Flaherty* [2013] EWHC 377 (QB)—no duty owed by local authority or Health Protection Agency to defendant to notify outbreak of E.coli at defendant's petting farm, or to take steps to limit visitors' exposure to infection; mere knowledge on the part of the local authority or Health Protection Agency fell far short of giving rise to an assumption of responsibility.

[264] [2019] UKSC 25; [2019] 2 W.L.R. 1478. See further paras 13-21, 13-71 and 13-72.

[265] [2019] UKSC 25; [2019] 2 W.L.R. 1478 at [65]. In *X v Hounslow LBC* [2009] EWCA Civ 286; [2010] H.L.R. 4 at [60] the Court of Appeal had commented that: "a public authority will not be held to have assumed a common law duty merely by doing what the statute requires or what it has power to do under a statute, at any rate unless the duty arises out of the relationship created as a result, such as in Lord Hoffmann's example of the doctor patient relationship". However, in *Poole BC v GN* [2019] UKSC 25; [2019] 2 W.L.R. 1478 at [72] Lord Reed noted that, though the correctness of the decision itself was not in question, "the dicta should not be understood as meaning that an assumption of responsibility can never arise out of the performance of statutory functions."

[266] *Barnett v Chelsea and Kensington Hospital Management Committee* [1969] 1 Q.B. 428. In *Poole BC v GN* [2019] UKSC 25; [2019] 2 W.L.R. 1478 at [80] Lord Reed observed that "… a public body which offers a service to the public often assumes a responsibility to those using the service. The assumption of responsibility is an undertaking that reasonable care will be taken, either express or more commonly implied, usually from the reasonable foreseeability of reliance on the exercise of such care. Thus, whether operated privately or under statutory powers, a hospital undertakes to exercise reasonable care in the medical treatment of its patients."

[267] [2018] UKSC 50; [2019] A.C. 831; C. Purshouse, "The impatient patient and the unreceptive receptionist: Darnley v Croydon Health Services NHS Trust" (2019) 27 Med. L. Rev. 318.

to be seen by the medical staff, as a result of which he left the hospital and subsequently suffered a serious deterioration in his medical condition. Once he had presented himself to the receptionist, provided any requested information and been booked in, the claimant was accepted into the system and entered into a relationship of patient and healthcare provider with the defendants. The standard of care expected of non-medical staff may be different from that applied to healthcare professionals, depending on the circumstances, but in the context of providing misleading information to a patient it was not appropriate to distinguish between medical and non-medical staff.[268]

There may also be situations where the claimant is in a particularly close relationship with a public authority, such that no express assumption of responsibility is required to establish a duty of care. In *Selwood v Durham CC*[269] the Court of Appeal held that it was at least arguable that two NHS Trusts had assumed responsibility to a social worker employed by a local authority who was attacked and seriously injured by a mental health patient. The social worker worked closely with the two NHS Trusts to provide integrated health and social care. The working relationship between the three defendants (the Trusts and the local authority) was set out in a lengthy policy document governing working arrangements. The patient was known to have a history of violent behaviour and posed a risk of harm to others. Employees of the Trusts became aware that he had expressed his intention to kill the claimant if he saw her, but the claimant was not warned. Smith LJ considered that it was possible to infer an assumption of responsibility from the circumstances, and in particular the close working relationship, "to do what was reasonable in the circumstances to reduce or avoid any foreseeable risk of harm to which an employee of a co-signatory was exposed in the course of their joint operations".[270] Given that the defendants, in their capacity as employers, would owe a duty of care to their employees, it was not a big step to suggest that they could owe a duty of care in respect of the actions of a third party to someone in the claimant's position, since "the force of some of the policy considerations which render a wider duty undesirable is much less than if the duty is said to be owed to the world at large".[271] 7-64

Control over third party In *Carmarthenshire CC v Lewis*,[272] the House of Lords held an education authority liable for injuries to a motorist who swerved to avoid a four-year-old child who ran onto the road after escaping from the nursery school run by the authority. The age of the child and the proximity of the school to the road meant that failure by the authority to exercise proper control over the child would clearly endanger others and hence, a duty was owed by the authority. A similar duty 7-65

---

[268] "The respondent had charged its non-medically qualified staff with the role of being the first point of contact with persons seeking medical assistance and, as a result, with the responsibility for providing accurate information as to its availability": [2018] UKSC 50; [2019] A.C. 831 at [17], per Lord Lloyd-Jones. His Lordship considered that this was an established category of duty of care, by analogy with the decision of the Court of Appeal in *Kent v Griffiths, Roberts and London Ambulance Service* [2001] Q.B. 36: "In both cases, as a result of the provision of inaccurate information by non-medically qualified staff, there was a delay in the provision of urgently required medical attention with the result that serious physical injury was suffered" (at [20]).

[269] [2012] EWCA Civ 979; [2012] P.I.Q.R. P20.

[270] [2012] EWCA Civ 979; [2012] P.I.Q.R. P20 at [52].

[271] [2012] EWCA Civ 979; [2012] P.I.Q.R. P20 at [53].

[272] [1955] A.C. 549.

to exercise control is owed by parents of a child.[273] In some circumstances a doctor may be held responsible for the conduct of a patient. In the Canadian case of *Pittman Estate v Bain*[274] a doctor was held liable to the wife of a patient for failing to warn the patient that he was HIV positive, with the result that his wife also contracted HIV. In this kind of case, liability is based not so much on control as on the knowledge that the third party may be a potential danger to others coupled with the power to take reasonable steps to reduce the risk. In *Pittman* the victim was known to the doctor and the steps involved warning the patient. It is suggested that English courts would also impose a duty in such a situation.[275] In *Tarasoff v Regents of the University of California*,[276] the Supreme Court of California held a psychiatrist under a duty to a person named by his patient as his intended victim, either to control the conduct of the patient to prevent him from causing harm, or at least to warn of his dangerous propensities. In *Palmer v Tees HA*[277] the Court of Appeal, after noting that in America the *Tarasoff* duty was limited to identified potential victims, held that no similar duty would be owed where the defendant knew its patient was a danger to children but not any particular, identified child. The control exercised by the police and prison authorities over detainees may also give rise to liability in some circumstances, and this is discussed in Ch.13.[278] That exercised by regulatory authorities is less likely to give rise to liability, because such public services are often regarded as acting for public rather than private benefit. Again, the detail is discussed in Ch.13.

7-66 **Responsibility for danger** The third situation identified by Lord Goff in *Smith v Littlewoods Organisation Ltd*[279] as giving rise to a duty is where the defendant "negligently causes or permits to be created a source of danger, and it is reasonably foreseeable that third parties may interfere with it and, sparking off the danger, thereby cause damage to persons in the position of the [claimant]". He cited as an example of such a case, *Haynes v Harwood*[280] where the defendant's employee was responsible for creating a source of danger by leaving a horse-drawn van unattended in a busy street, the danger was sparked off by a mischievous child throwing a stone at the horses causing them to bolt and the defendant was held liable for the resulting injuries. Lord Goff held that the principle had no application to the facts of *Smith*, as "the empty cinema could (not) be properly described as an unusual

273 See the frequently cited dictum of Dixon J in *Smith v Leurs* (1970) C.L.R. 256: "It appears now to be incumbent on a parent who maintains control over a young child to take reasonable care so as to exercise that control as to avoid conduct on his part exposing the person or property of others to unreasonable damage." See further para.7-229.

274 (1994) 112 D.L.R. (4th) 257.

275 More borderline would be cases where the victim was not known to the doctor: see *Spillane v Wasserman* (1992) 13 C.C.L.T. (2d) 267, where doctors responsible for treating a patient's epilepsy were held liable to the victim of a road accident caused by his having an epileptic fit whilst driving a heavy truck on the ground that they had not warned him not to drive such vehicles and had not reported his condition to the vehicle registration authorities; and the similar decision in *Freese v Lemmon* (1973) 210 N.W.2d 576, Supreme Court of Iowa. See further: M.A. Jones, *Medical Negligence*, 5th edn (2018), paras 2-147 to 2-153 and 2-156.

276 (1976) 551 P.2d 334.

277 [1999] Lloyd's Rep. Med. 351.

278 See para.13-60.

279 [1987] A.C. 241 at 272.

280 [1935] 1 K.B. 146. He gave a further example of a person who stored a large quantity of fireworks in an unlocked shed when it was foreseeable that mischievous boys might trespass into the shed and set off the fireworks. See also *Holian v United Grain Growers Ltd* (1980) 112 D.L.R. (3d) 611, where there was theft of a poisonous chemical by young children.

danger in the nature of a fire hazard". Indeed, Lord Goff stressed that liability under this principle would be very rare for otherwise the ordinary householders could "be held liable for acting in a socially acceptable manner".[281] This restrictive approach was confirmed in *Topp v London Country Bus Ltd*.[282] The defendant had carelessly left a minibus unlocked, with keys in the ignition, outside a pub for some nine hours until it was stolen by a third party who, minutes later, negligently drove the bus into the claimant. May J held that although it was foreseeable that the bus might be stolen and the thief might injure other road users, there could be no liability under the danger principle as a "parked minibus is no more a source of danger than every other vehicle on the road".[283]

Responsibility for vehicle drivers If the vehicle owner creates a special danger, e.g. by negligently causing an obstruction of the highway, then as Cairns LJ held in *Rouse v Squires*,[284] he may be liable for the damage caused by those who carelessly drive into the obstruction. The careless driving of the third party converts or "sparks" the dangerous obstruction into the damage.[285] The suggestion of Goff LJ in his judgment in *P Perl (Exporters) Ltd v Camden LBC*[286] that the defendant might be liable where "he hands over a car to be driven by a person who is drunk or plainly incompetent, who then runs over the claimant" illustrates another situation which may fall within this danger category. Canadian courts have gone further, imposing liability on the "commercial or social host" who serves alcohol to custom- **7-67**

---

281 Lord Goff noted that "there are nowadays many things which might be described as possible sources of fire if interfered with by third parties, ranging from matches to firelighters to electric irons and gas cookers and even oil-fired central heating systems". Leaving these commonplaces of modern life unprotected from third party intervention could not give rise to liability.

282 [1993] 1 W.L.R 926 CA.

283 [1993] 3 All E.R. 448 at 459; affirmed by the Court of Appeal: [1993] 1 W.L.R 926; [1993] 3 All E.R. 464. May J suggested that a duty might have been improperly conceded in *Hayman v London Transport Executive* [1982] CA transcript 74, where a bus company was found liable for damage caused by a stolen bus following previous complaints of buses being stolen. He distinguished *Hayman* as decided on its own special facts. The rejection of *Hayman* and policy reasons given for denying a duty, the lack of inherent danger and the unfairness of holding motorists liable for the damage done by their stolen cars, suggest that even a high degree of foreseeability of theft would be insufficient to ground a duty. See further *Rankin (Rankin's Garage & Sales) v J.J.* 2018 SCC 19; (2018) 422 D.L.R. (4th) 317, where a majority of the Supreme Court of Canada reached the same outcome as *Topp v London Country Bus Ltd*, but on the basis that the theft of an unlocked vehicle, with keys left in the ashtray, by two youths was unforeseeable. In the absence of an evidentiary basis the risk of theft in general did not necessarily include the risk of theft by minors (who were more likely to drive a stolen vehicle in a dangerous manner). Sed quaere. See J. Goudkamp and J. Plunkett, "The foreseeability element of the duty of care" (2019) 135 L.Q.R. 521, 524 who comment that the finding that the risk of theft by minors leading to bodily injury was not foreseeable was "highly contestable" and bordered on being "palpably wrong".

284 [1973] Q.B. 889 at 899. See also the similar decision of the High Court of Australia in *March v E & MH Stramare Pty Ltd* (1991) 99 A.L.R. 423. See para.2-132 for discussion of this decision.

285 However, although creating a dangerous obstruction gives rise to a notional duty situation, the decision in *Wright v Lodge* [1993] 4 All E.R. 299; [1993] R.T.R. 299 establishes that the particular damage which results may be too remote if the driving of the third party was reckless rather than simply negligent. See further para.2-102.

286 [1984] Q.B. 342 at 359, citing *Ontario Hospital Services Commission v Borsoski* (1974) 54 D.L.R. (3d) 339. In *Smith v Littlewoods Organisation Ltd* [1987] A.C. 241 at 272, Lord Goff treated this example as falling within the category of a special relationship of defendant and third party. Arguably, it should be regarded as falling within his third category where the defendant negligently creates a source of danger.

ers or guests who then attempt to drive home drunk and cause an accident.[287] On the other hand, the High Court of Australia has held that there is no general duty of care owed by a proprietor or licensee of licensed premises to customers to monitor and minimise the service of alcohol or to protect customers from the consequences of the alcohol they choose to consume.[288] It seems unlikely that English courts would be prepared to follow the Canadian lead in the case of social hosts, as it would involve shifting part of the burden of liability from the insured motorist to the uninsured host, and even in the case of the commercial sale of alcohol the primary responsibility must remain with the individual who chooses to consume it.[289]

7-68 **Responsibility for property** The final category of duty identified by Lord Goff was where the occupier of property knows or has the means of knowing that the conduct of a third party on his property is endangering neighbouring property. As an example he cited *Thomas Graham & Co Ltd v Church of Scotland General Trustees*[290] where the occupiers of a disused church who knew that vandals had repeatedly entered and lit fires were held liable for damage to neighbouring property caused by a fire spreading from the church. In *Smith v Littlewoods Organisation Ltd*[291] neighbouring property was also damaged by fire spreading from the defendant's property after vandals had entered, but Lord Goff held that there was no liability under the property principle because they had no means of knowing of the fire risk created by third parties on their property. If the defendants had been warned by the police or others that children were continuing to enter the premises, then the position might have been different. Lord Goff stressed that reasonable foreseeability that third parties might enter and endanger neighbouring property was insufficient to ground a duty to take care to prevent third parties from entering. Such an approach would "impose an unreasonable burden on ordinary householders and an unreasonable curb on the enjoyment of their property".[292] He reaffirmed his own decision in *P Perl (Exporters) Ltd v Camden LBC*,[293] that the occupiers of property insufficiently secured to prevent entry by intruders were not liable for damage to

287 See for example: *Mayfield Investments Ltd v Stewart* (1995) 121 D.L.R. (4th) 222, in which the Supreme Court of Canada held that the defendant restaurant owner who served drinks to a group of four customers did owe a duty of care to the claimant who was subsequently injured on the highway as a result of drunken driving of one of the group. However, the defendant was not liable as it was reasonable for him to assume that one of the two non-drinkers in the group would have driven the group's car. See also *Wince v Ball* (1996) 136 D.L.R. (4th) 104, where it was held that a social host would only be liable if it could be shown that he had contributed in some way to the drunk driving by a guest. Simply allowing a teenage drinking party would not result in liability being imposed on the parents for any resultant drunk driving accidents. See further Boivin, "Social host liability in Canada" (2004) Tort. L.R. 164; and Hamad "The intoxicated pedestrian" (2005) 13 Tort. L.R. 14; Fulbrook, "Alcohol and Third Parties—'Dram Shop Liability' and Beyond" [2007] J.P.I.L. 220.

288 *CAL No.14 Pty Ltd v Motor Accidents Insurance Board* [2009] HCA 47; (2009) 239 C.L.R. 390; (2009) 260 A.L.R. 606; applied in *Schuller v S.J. Webb Nominees Pty Ltd* [2015] SASCFC 162.

289 In *Munro v Porthkerry Park Holiday Estates*, *The Times*, 9 March 1984 Beldam J thought that in some circumstances a licensee's duty of care might extend to refusing to serve a customer with alcohol, though on the facts there was no evidence that the customer was incapable through drink.

290 1982 S.L.T. 26.

291 [1987] A.C. 241.

292 [1987] A.C. 241 at 280. Lord Goff pointed to the injustice of the old lady who leaves the ground floor window open for her cat or the elderly gentleman who leaves his French windows open whilst he weeds at the bottom of the garden, being held liable for the actions of a thief who enters their house and uses it as access to neighbouring property.

293 [1984] Q.B. 342.

neighbouring property done by intruders entering via the unsecured property. Similarly, he approved the decision in *King v Liverpool City Council*[294] in which it was held that an owner of property was not liable for damage to neighbouring property caused by a water leak resulting from a vandal entering the owner's property and damaging the plumbing. He concluded (at 279):

> "The practical effect is that it is the owner of the damaged premises (or in the vast majority of cases, his insurers) who is left with a worthless claim against the vandal, rather than the occupier of the property which the vandal entered (or his insurers), a conclusion which I find less objectionable than one which may throw an unreasonable burden on ordinary householders."

(f) Psychiatric injury and distress

Psychiatric injury A claimant can recover in respect of a recognised psychiatric illness[295] suffered as a result of his own physical injury or imperilment or as a result of the physical injury or imperilment of another caused by the defendant. Any recognised psychiatric illness will suffice. There has been recovery for morbid depression,[296] hysterical personality disorder,[297] post-traumatic stress disorder,[298] pathological grief disorder[299] and chronic fatigue syndrome.[300] In the case of illness suffered as a result of the trauma of being endangered or physically injured, the claimant is referred to as a "primary victim" and will recover provided that *physical injury* was reasonably foreseeable as a result the defendant's negligence. It is possible that a claimant who was in some other way a direct participant in the incident may also be treated as a primary victim and be able to recover if *psychiatric illness* was foreseeable, even if they were not in danger of physical injury. In the case of illness suffered solely as a result of the injury or endangerment of another, **7-69**

[294] [1986] 1 W.L.R. 890. On the same ground he also approved of the decision in *Lamb v Camden London Borough* [1981] Q.B. 625 that the local authority whose negligence had damaged the claimant's house with the result that it had to be left vacant for repairs, was not liable for further damage done by vandals.

[295] *McLoughlin v O'Brian* [1983] 1 A.C. 410 at 431, per Lord Bridge; *Alcock v Chief Constable of the South Yorkshire Police* [1992] 1 A.C. 310 at 409, per Lord Oliver. This excludes ordinary grief, distress or any other normal human emotion. In *Saadati v Moorhead* 2017 SCC 28; (2017) 409 D.L.R. (4th) 395 the Supreme Court of Canada held that, in Canadian law, there was no requirement that a claimant seeking to establish liability for mental injury was required to prove, by expert evidence, that he was suffering from a condition that would be diagnosed as a psychiatric illness by the medical profession. The claimant did not have to prove that he was suffering from a particular psychiatric illness to which the medical profession had attached a "label"; it was sufficient that the defendant could have foreseen mental injury. There was no necessary relationship between reasonably foreseeable mental injury and a diagnostic classification scheme. Moreover, said the Supreme Court, there should be no difference between claims for mental injury and claims for physical injury, and there was no requirement for claimants alleging physical injury to show that their condition carried a particular classificatory label. *Saadati* is discussed by M. McInnes, "Negligent infliction of mental harm in the Supreme Court of Canada" (2018) 134 L.Q.R. 1. For concern about using the shifting diagnostic criteria for psychiatric conditions in the legal context see J. Ahuja, "Liability for psychological and psychiatric harm: the road to recovery" (2015) 23 Med. L. Rev. 27 at 39–40; and R. Orr, "Speaking with different voices: the problems with English law and psychiatric injury" (2016) 36 L.S. 547.

[296] *Hinz v Berry* [1970] 2 Q.B. 40.

[297] *Brice v Brown* [1984] 1 All E.R. 997.

[298] The illness in question in *White v Chief Constable of the South Yorkshire Police* [1999] 2 A.C. 455. The claim failed on other grounds.

[299] *Vernon v Bosley (No.1)* [1997] 1 All E.R. 577.

[300] *Page v Smith* [1996] A.C. 155.

the claimant is referred to as a "secondary victim" and recovery is subject to a number of policy restrictions. In addition, there are a number of special cases where illness results from factors other than personal injury or imperilment. The result is a "patchwork quilt of distinctions which are quite difficult to justify".[301] The whole area of law was reviewed in 1998 by the Law Commission[302] which recommended reform of the law by both legislation and the courts. Since the report there has been no legislation but the courts seem to have adopted a more flexible approach to the distinction between primary and secondary victims and a less restrictive approach to recovery by secondary victims. In the light of this, legislative reform seems unnecessary.[303]

(i) Primary victims

7-70 **The foreseeability test** The law relating to primary victims was developed by the House of Lords in *Page v Smith*.[304] In *Page* the claimant was involved in a relatively minor road accident caused by the defendant's negligent driving. Although not physically injured, he suffered from a severe reoccurrence of chronic fatigue syndrome brought on by the shock of the accident. Influenced by the hindsight knowledge that no physical injury had resulted, the Court of Appeal found that it was not reasonably foreseeable that a person of reasonable fortitude would suffer psychiatric illness as a result of such an accident and on that ground, held that no duty of care was owed to the claimant in respect of his illness. A majority of the House of Lords reversed this decision on the ground that in the case of a primary victim foreseeability of physical injury alone was sufficient to enable the claimant to recover in respect of psychiatric illness.[305] Lord Lloyd, giving the leading speech, said that there was no justification for treating physical and psychiatric injury as different kinds of injury.[306] Thus, he argued that the fortuitous absence of actual physical injury could not mean that a different test, that is of foreseeability of psychiatric illness, had to be applied.[307] Applying the "eggshell skull" rule that the defendant must take his victim as he finds him,[308] he also concluded that "in the case of a primary victim it is [not] appropriate to ask whether he is a person of 'ordinary

---

301 *White v Chief Constable of the South Yorkshire Police* [1999] 2 A.C. 455 at 500, per Lord Steyn.

302 *Liability for Psychiatric Illness*, Law Com. No.249.

303 In its Response to a Consultation on Damages the Ministry of Justice concluded that: "The arguments in this complex and sensitive area are finely balanced. On balance the Government continues to take the view that it is preferable for the courts to have the flexibility to continue to develop the law rather than attempt to impose a statutory solution": *The Law on Damages*, CP(R) 9/07, July 2009, p.51.

304 [1996] A.C. 155. The division of claimants into "primary" victims and "secondary" victims was first made in Lord Oliver's speech in *Alcock v Chief Constable of South Yorkshire* [1992] 1 A.C. 310. This was initially a descriptive rather than a prescriptive categorisation.

305 The Court of Appeal followed *Page* in *Giblett v Murray*, *The Times* 25 May 1999, in which the claimant who was involved in a road accident was able to recover in respect of an unforeseeable resulting psychiatric conditions which rendered her incapable of sexual relations.

306 See further para.2-166.

307 [1996] A.C. 155 at 187. He developed the point saying:

> "Why should it make any difference that the physical illness that the [claimant] undoubtedly suffered as a result of the accident operated through the medium of the mind, or of the nervous system, without physical injury? If he had suffered a heart attack, it cannot be doubted that he would have recovered damages for pain and suffering, even though he suffered no broken bones. It would have been no answer that he had a weak heart."

308 Lord Lloyd cited *Malcolm v Broadhurst* [1970] 3 All E.R. 508, for this proposition. However, there

phlegm"'[309] and hindsight had no part to play in considering whether a duty was owed. The approach of Lord Lloyd was criticised by the Law Commission as giving more favourable treatment to those fearing for their own safety than for the safety of others and suggesting that "physical injury is more worthy of legal support than psychiatric illness".[310] Nevertheless, in the absence of criticism of the decision from practitioners or the judiciary, the Commission did not recommend its reversal.[311] Subsequently the House of Lords has applied Page in *British Steel Plc v Simmons*[312] where the claimant suffered minor physical injuries in an accident caused by his employer's negligence and then suffered a severe depressive illness caused either by the accident itself or by his frustration and anger following the accident. Lord Rodger, whose speech was endorsed by the House, said that following *Page* the defendants were liable even if the depressive illness was not foreseeable and that it made no difference whether the illness sprang from the accident or the claimant's anger at the happening of the accident because either way, it had been caused by the accident.[313]

Definition of primary victim In *Alcock v Chief Constable of South Yorkshire Police*[314] Lord Oliver introduced the concept of the "primary victim" to apply to those cases "in which the claimant was involved, either mediately or immediately, as a participant" and included in that category the so-called rescue cases which established that a duty was owed "not only to those threatened ... by his [the defendant's] careless acts but also to those who, as a result, are induced to go to their rescue and suffer injury in so doing". In *Page* Lord Lloyd seemed to take a narrower view of the concept, describing the claimant in that case as a primary victim because: "He was himself directly involved in the accident, and well within the range of foreseeable physical injury."[315] The Law Commission rejected this narrower approach, saying: "It should not be a condition of a rescuer's entitlement to **7-71**

are likely to be many more "eggshell personalities" that there are "eggshell skulls" and it is questionable whether a rule developed with physical injury in mind should be applied to psychiatric injury.

309 [1996] A.C. 155 at 189. It follows that there is "no requirement for a primary victim who brings a claim for 'pure' psychiatric injury to show that the injury was caused by shock": *YAH v Medway NHS Foundation Trust* [2018] EWHC 2964 (QB); [2019] 1 W.L.R. 1413, per Whipple J at [34].

310 Para.5.47. The Commission also noted fears that the lack of any requirement to prove foreseeability of psychiatric illness in the case of primary victims, would "risk 'opening the floodgates' of litigation". Lord Lloyd's approach was criticised on more technical grounds by Lord Goff in his dissenting speech in *White v Chief Constable of the South Yorkshire Police* [1999] 2 A.C. 455 at 475, as being contrary to authority, inconsistent with the principle that the kind of damage suffered should be foreseeable, and misunderstanding the eggshell skull rule which Lord Goff considered to be only applicable once liability had been established, for example, on the basis of some physical damage.

311 The Commission did recommend that courts be "encouraged to consider abandoning attaching practical consequences to whether the claimant may be described as a primary or secondary victim": para.5.53.

312 [2004] UKHL 20; [2004] I.C.R. 585; [2004] P.I.Q.R. P33.

313 [2004] UKHL 20; [2004] I.C.R. 585; [2004] P.I.Q.R. P33 at [55] and [56]. See also *Donachie v Chief Constable of the Greater Manchester Police* [2004] EWCA Civ 405; *The Times*, 6 May 2004: Police officer physically endangered because of negligently run surveillance operation; extreme stress of operation led to a clinical psychiatric state; psychiatric injury not foreseeable but Chief Constable found liable; and *A v Essex CC* [2003] EWCA Civ 1848; [2004] 1 W.L.R. 1881: adopting parents foreseeably at risk of physical injury from violent child; psychiatric injury not foreseeable but adoption authority held liable. See further para.13-27.

314 [1992] 1 A.C. 310 at 407 and 409.

315 [1996] A.C. 155 at 184.

recover damages for psychiatric illness that he or she is in physical danger."[316] However, in *White v Chief Constable of South Yorkshire Police*[317] the majority, led by Lord Steyn, accepted Lord Lloyd's reference to "the range of foreseeable" injury as setting the limit to the category. This was significant in the case because the claimants were police officers who had rescued the Hillsborough victims but had not themselves been within the range of foreseeable physical injury. The majority concluded that they were not primary victims and their claim failed as they could not satisfy the requirements of recovery as secondary victims.[318] Following this approach, a rescuer would only fall into the primary victim category if he was exposed to physical danger. Lord Steyn explained the recovery of the rescuer in *Chadwick v British Transport Commission*[319] on this ground. There, the claimant had suffered psychiatric illness after entering a wrecked railway carriage to help the injured but there was an element of personal danger as "there was clearly a risk that the carriage might collapse".[320] Lord Goff dissented on the ground that the police officers' role as rescuers and as employees[321] with no choice but to become involved in the events, qualified them as primary victims within the approach adopted by Lord Oliver. Later case law suggests that the courts may be prepared to take a more flexible approach to the category of primary victim.[322] A possible compromise between the majority and minority view in *White*, might be to accept the narrow "endangerment" requirement as a justification for allowing recovery where illness was not foreseeable but to recognise "participation" as a justification for allowing recovery where illness was foreseeable but the remaining requirements for secondary victim recovery were not met.

7-72 **Rescuers** The basis on which a rescuer may recover as a primary victim was clarified by *Cullin v London Fire & Civil Defence Authority*.[323] The claimants were firefighters who suffered psychiatric illness following attendance at fires where fellow firefighters were killed. The defendant sought to strike out the claims on two related grounds; first, that the particular event, e.g. the collapse of a wall, which had lead to the deaths of their colleagues had not endangered the claimants; and secondly, that their illness had not been caused by fear for their own safety. The Court of Appeal refused to strike out the claims. Swinton Thomas LJ doubted the first ground, suggesting that the "relevant event" should be identified in the light of the totality of the evidence and that the defendant's argument placed it "within too narrow a compass".[324] He rejected the second ground as contrary to Lord Steyn's statement in *White* that: "In order to recover compensation for pure psychiatric harm as a rescuer it is not necessary to establish that his psychiatric condition was caused

316 para.7.3. Ironically, in the light of *White*, it concluded: "We would confidently expect that, in so far as there is any confusion on this issue, it will soon be dispelled by the courts and we do not think that legislation is necessary".

317 [1999] 2 A.C. 455.

318 As Lord Steyn admitted, underlying the rejection of the claim was the feeling that to allow the claim of the police officers would sit "uneasily with the denial of the claims of the relatives ... in *Alcock* ..." and might "perplex the man on the Underground" [1999] 2 A.C. 455 at 495.

319 [1967] 1 W.L.R. 912.

320 [1999] 2 A.C. 455 at 499. Nevertheless, Lord Steyn noted that Waller J had decided the case not on the basis of the element of personal danger but rather on the basis of the horrific nature of the whole experience.

321 In which category he included quasi-employees such as police officers.

322 See para.7-74.

323 [1999] P.I.Q.R. P314.

324 [1999] P.I.Q.R. P314 at P319.

by the perception of the physical danger."[325] One issue left open by *White* is whether to qualify as a primary victim the rescuer must be within the range of physical risk or whether it is sufficient for him to reasonably believe that this is the case. In *McFarlane v EE Caledonia Ltd*[326] Stuart-Smith LJ considered that a rescuer believing himself to be in danger should recover.[327] However, in another case stemming from rescue attempts following the Piper Alpha disaster, *Hegarty v EE Caledonia*,[328] Brooke LJ said that once it had been found that the rescue vessel had never been in danger, it was almost inevitable that the claimant's fear for his life should be found to be irrational. It should be noted that in *White*, Lord Steyn concluded that the claimant must "satisfy the threshold requirement that he objectively exposed himself to danger or reasonably believed that he was doing so".[329] This suggests that a perception of danger as well as actual danger might suffice.[330]

Participation Lord Oliver in *Alcock*[331] included within the primary victim category "cases where the negligent act of the defendant has put the [claimant] in the position of being, or thinking that he is about to be or has been, the involuntary cause of another's death or injury and the illness stems from the shock to the [claimant] of the consciousness of this supposed fact". The leading example of recovery in this category is *Dooley v Cammell Laird*[332] where a crane driver suffered psychiatric illness after seeing a defective rope on his crane snap thereby causing the crane to drop its load into the hold of a ship where he knew his fellow employees were working. Although no one was injured he feared for their safety. In *Hunter v British Coal Corp*[333] a majority of the Court of Appeal refused to extend the *Dooley* principle to a situation where the employee thought he was the cause of a fatal accident to a fellow worker but only managed to reach the scene of the accident 15 minutes after the event. Brooke LJ considered that "[t]he law requires 7-73

325 [1999] 2 A.C. 455 at 499. In other words, exposure to risk of physical injury is a *threshold* test for qualifying as a primary victim; it is not a *causation* test for the psychiatric harm.

326 [1994] 2 All E.R. 1.

327 On the facts, the claimant failed as it could not be said that the defendants ought reasonably to have foreseen that a person of ordinary fortitude in his position would suffer from psychiatric illness: [1994] 2 All E.R. 1 at 11–12.

328 [1997] 2 Lloyd's Rep. 259 at 271.

329 [1999] 2 A.C. 455 at 499. In *Monk v PC Harrington Ltd* [2008] EWHC 1879 (QB); [2009] P.I.Q.R. P3 the claimant developed post-traumatic stress disorder following an accident at work in which a platform fell 60 feet hitting two workers below, killing one and injuring the other. The claimant was foreman at the site. He heard about the accident immediately and attended the scene to assist the two injured workers. It was held that the claimant was a "rescuer" because he gave assistance which was not "trivial or peripheral" (applying a dictum of Lord Griffiths in *White v Chief Constable of South Yorkshire Police* [1999] 2 A.C. 455 at 465) but he was not a primary victim because he was not exposed to danger and did not reasonably believe himself to be in danger in going to the assistance of two workers (or if he did have such a belief it was not a reasonable one).

330 See further the discussion in the Law Commission Report, *Liability for Psychiatric Illness*, Law Com. No.249 (1998) at paras 2.16–2.18.

331 [1992] 1 A.C. 310 at 408.

332 [1951] 1 Lloyd's Rep. 271. See also *Galt v British Railways Board* (1983) 133 N.L.J. 870, where a train driver came upon two workmen as he rounded a bend, and being unable to stop, feared he had killed them; and *Wigg v British Railways Board*, *The Times*, 4 February 1986, where a train driver came upon the body of a dead person who had been struck by the door of the train he had been driving. There was recovery in both cases. Contrast *Robertson & Rough v Forth Road Bridge Junior Board*, 1996 S.L.T. 263, where recovery was denied on the ground that the workers who had seen their colleague blown off the bridge, did not believe they had been the cause of the accident.

333 [1999] Q.B. 140.

a greater degree of physical and temporal proximity ... before [the claimant] could properly be treated as a direct or primary victim".[334]

7-74 However, the Law Commission[335] concluded that as "the floodgates objection does not apply in relation to involuntary participants, there would appear to be no reason to restrict their current rights of recovery" and later case law shows the court taking a wider view of the category of primary victim based around direct involvement in the incident. In *W v Essex CC*[336] Lord Slynn, considering the case of psychiatric injury suffered by parents as a result of feeling responsible for unwittingly introducing an abuser to their children, commented that "the categorisation of those claiming to be included as primary ... victims is not ... finally closed" and that there was nothing in the cases which "conclusively" showed that these parents were "prevented from being primary victims". In *Farrell v Avon HA*,[337] Bursell J, following the views expressed in *Essex*, treated the claimant, who suffered psychiatric illness as a result of being told negligently and wrongly that his new born baby had died, as a primary victim. He was physically involved in the incident and this justified his treatment as a primary victim.[338] In *McLoughlin v Jones*,[339] Hale LJ regarded the claimant who allegedly suffered psychiatric illness as a result of imprisonment following the alleged negligence of the defendant solicitor, as a primary victim. The significance of treating the claimant as a primary victim in these cases was the avoidance of the policy restrictions imposed by earlier case law upon recovery by secondary victims.

(ii) *Secondary victims*

7-75 **Reasonably foreseeable psychiatric illness** In *Alcock v Chief Constable of South Yorkshire Police*[340] Lord Oliver described a secondary victim as one who "was no more than the passive and unwilling witness of injury caused to others". In the case of such victims, the starting point is whether psychiatric illness to the claimant was a reasonably foreseeable consequence of the defendant's negligence. Thus in *Hambrook v Stokes*[341] it was held that a claim could be brought on behalf of a mother who had seen a lorry careering out of control from the direction in which she had just left her children, as the defendant should have anticipated that someone in her position might be so terrified for her children that she suffered illness. In

334 [1999] Q.B. 140 at 154. Hobhouse LJ dissented on the ground that the employee's participation in the event justified his categorisation as a primary victim. See also *Monk v PC Harrington Ltd* [2008] EWHC 1879 (QB); [2009] P.I.Q.R. P3 where the claimant believed that he was responsible for an accident in which a platform fell onto two workers because he had supervised the erection of the platform, but on the evidence his belief was not reasonable and therefore he did not qualify as a primary victim as an "unwilling participant" in the event. An unreasonable belief that the claimant had caused the accident was not a reasonably foreseeable consequence of the defendants' negligence.

335 *Liability for Psychiatric Illness*, Law Com. No.249, paras 7.5–7.8.

336 [2001] 2 A.C. 592.

337 [2001] Lloyd's Rep. Med. 458.

338 See also *AB v Tameside and Glossop HA* [1997] P.N.L.R. 140; [1997] 8 Med. L.R. 91 where Brooke LJ was prepared to impose liability on a health authority for communicating accurate but distressing information in a careless manner resulting in psychiatric illness to the recipient of the information; and *Allin v City and Hackney HA* [1996] 7 Med. L.R. 167, where the defendants were found liable for inaccurately telling a patient who had just given birth that her baby had died. In neither case was the primary victim issue discussed.

339 [2001] EWCA Civ 1743; [2002] Q.B. 1312.

340 [1992] 1 A.C. 310 at 407.

341 [1925] 1 K.B. 141.

contrast, in *Bourhill v Young*,[342] the House of Lords rejected the claim of a bystander who heard but did not see an accident, on the ground that the defendant could not have reasonably foreseen that a person in the claimant's position would suffer shock as a result of his negligent driving. Unless the defendant has special knowledge to the contrary, the test will be applied on the basis that the claimant has a "normal standard of susceptibility" to psychiatric illness.[343] Once the claimant has established that it was reasonably foreseeable that a person of normal susceptibility would suffer some psychiatric illness, the normal "eggshell skull" rule applies so that the susceptible claimant may recover for the full extent of the illness.[344] The test is applied with hindsight, in the light of all that has happened[345] and the facts known to the defendant at the time.[346] In the view of the Law Commission, this means that "one should assess whether the psychiatric illness is reasonably foreseeable on the assumption that the defendant knows what has happened to the immediate victim".[347] The Commission supported this approach to the foreseeability of the psychiatric illness but considered that hindsight should not apply to the injury or imperilment itself. Thus, where the claimant's psychiatric illness was a result of an accident injuring another, the claimant would not recover if that accident could not have been reasonably foreseen by the defendant. The fact that the illness was foreseeable in the light of the accident, would not be relevant. Although expert evidence may be relevant, the test is for the judge to apply "relying on his own opinion of the operation of cause and effect in psychiatric medicine".[348]

---

342 [1943] A.C. 92.

343 [1943] A.C. 92 at 110, per Lord Wright. Lord Porter at 117 referred to a person of "customary phlegm". The Law Commission, *Liability for Psychiatric Illness* Law Com. No.249, para.5.26, suggested that this test be interpreted as "meaning nothing more than that, in deciding whether psychiatric illness was reasonably foreseeable (and analogously to reasonable foreseeability in physical injury cases), one can take into account the robustness of the population at large to psychiatric illness". Note that in *McLoughlin v Jones* [2001] EWCA Civ 1743; [2002] Q.B. 1312 at [46], Brooke LJ held that where there was a contractual relationship between the parties, the test of foreseeability was: "damages can only be recovered if it is foreseeable that psychiatric illness would have been suffered by the claimant, given all those features of his personal life and disposition of which the defendants were aware". He held that the trial judge had been wrong to strike out the claim on the basis of the "person of reasonable fortitude test".

344 *Brice v Brown* [1984] 1 All E.R. 997. Damages may be reduced to take account of the fact that the claimant might at some point have suffered the illness in any event: *Page v Smith (No.2)* [1996] 1 W.L.R. 855 at 857.

345 *McLoughlin v O'Brian* [1983] 1 A.C. 410 at 420, per Lord Wilberforce; at 432, per Lord Bridge.

346 In *Farrell v Avon HA* [2001] Lloyd's Rep. Med. 458 at 472, Bursell J said: "[E]ven if the court's decision is made ex post facto, logic dictates that foreseeability depends on the facts known to the defendant at the relevant time." The case concerned an unmarried father who suffered psychiatric illness as a result of being told negligently and wrongly by the defendant's medical staff that his new born baby had died.

347 *Liability for Psychiatric Illness* Law Com. No.249, para.5.17. The Commission illustrated the point with the example of a mother who suffers psychiatric illness as a result of thinking about a potential accident which might have injured her son but which in fact was avoided. In such a case, the courts should assess the foreseeability of her illness on the basis that she is aware that the accident did not actually happen.

348 *McLoughlin v O'Brian* [1983] 1 A.C. 410 at 432, per Lord Bridge. Note, however, that causal mechanisms are not well-understood in the case of psychiatric medicine. The American Psychiatric Association's *Diagnostic and Statistical Manual of Mental Disorders*, 5th edn (2013) (DSM-V) identifies the causal mechanism for only one psychiatric condition, post-traumatic stress disorder. The Manual is meant to be a diagnostic guide, rather than a basis for attributing causal relationships. It has been widely criticised as medicalising normal human experiences. See J. Ahuja, "Liability for psychological and psychiatric harm: the road to recovery" (2015) 23 Med. L. Rev. 27 at 39–40,

7-76 **Policy restrictions** In addition to the requirement of reasonable foreseeability of psychiatric illness, claims by secondary victims are subject to special restrictions on policy grounds. In *White v Chief Constable of the South Yorkshire Police*[349] Lord Steyn identified four features of claims for psychiatric harm which together explained the restrictive approach to duty developed by the courts:

> "Firstly, there is the complexity of drawing the line between acute grief [for which damages are irrecoverable] and psychiatric harm ... . In order to establish psychiatric harm expert evidence is required ... . It is a costly and time consuming business ... it would have implications for the administration of justice. Secondly, there is the effect of the expansion of the availability of compensation on potential claimants who have witnessed gruesome events ... . The litigation is sometimes an unconscious disincentive to rehabilitation. [Thirdly,] the abolition of the special rules governing the recovery of damages for psychiatric harm would increase the class of persons who can recover damages in tort ... . [I]n cases of pure psychiatric harm there is potentially a wide class of [claimants] involved. Fourthly, the imposition of liability for pure psychiatric harm in a wide range of situations may result in a burden of liability on defendants which may be disproportionate to tortious conduct involving perhaps momentary lapses of concentration, e.g. in a motor car accident."[350]

In the case of primary victims, Lord Steyn considered that the requirement of physical injury or imperilment sufficiently restricted the category of potential claimants. The problem lay with secondary victims, victims of what he termed "pure psychiatric harm". Here, there was "wide scope for potential liability ... illustrated by the rather unique events of Hillsborough but also accidents involving trains, coaches and buses, and the everyday occurrence of serious collisions of vehicles all of which may result in gruesome scenes" and by the "paradigm case ... [of the] workman who witnessed a tragic accident to an employee". In his view, these considerations justified the three requirements for recovery established by the first Hillsborough decision, *Alcock v Chief Constable of the South Yorkshire Police*,[351] namely: "(i) that [the claimant] had a close tie of love and affection with the person killed, injured or imperilled; (ii) that he was close to the incident in time and space; (iii) that he directly perceived the incident rather than, for example, hearing about it from a third person."[352] To these three must be added a fourth, also established by *Alcock*, namely, that the illness was induced by a sudden shocking event. Finally, particular problems are raised by situations where the defendant was the immediate victim.

---

reporting some of the criticisms of DSM V; and R. Orr, "Speaking with different voices: the problems with English law and psychiatric injury" (2016) 36 L.S. 547, esp. at 557–559.

349 [1999] 2 A.C. 455 at 493.

350 The Law Commission Report on *Liability for Psychiatric Illness* (Law Com. No.249) para.6.7, was convinced only by the argument that the widening concept of psychiatric illness might lead to a flood of claims if the floodgates, that is the policy restrictions on duty, were removed to allow claims based on pure foreseeability.

351 [1992] 1 A.C. 310 at 406, per Lord Ackner.

352 [1999] 2 A.C. 455 at 496. The three requirements originate in the judgment of Tobriner J in *Dillon v Legg* (1968) 68 Cal.2d 728. In *McLoughlin v O'Brian* [1983] 1 A.C. 410, whilst Lord Bridge cited this judgment and the three requirements in the context of applying the test of foreseeability, Lord Wilberforce supported by Lord Edmund-Davies, treated them as contributing not to an evaluation of the degree of foreseeability, but as being necessary on policy grounds to limit the scope of the duty. In *Alcock v Chief Constable of South Yorkshire* [1992] 1 A.C. 310, the House of Lords unanimously endorsed the view of Lord Wilberforce.

Close tie of love and affection In *McLoughlin v O'Brian*[353] Lord Wilberforce contrasted the closest of family ties between parent and child or husband and wife, with that of the ordinary bystander and said that whilst the law recognised the claims of the closest category, it denied those of the bystander and would need to consider very carefully cases where the tie was less than in the closest category. In *Alcock v Chief Constable of the South Yorkshire Police*[354] the House of Lords took a more flexible approach to the relationship requirement. Lord Keith said: 7-77

> "I think it sufficient that reasonable foreseeability be the guide … . The kinds of relationships which may involve close ties of love and affection are numerous … It is reasonably foreseeable that those bound by them may in certain circumstances be at real risk of psychiatric illness if the loved one is injured or put in peril."[355]

Lord Ackner suggested that the difference between the parental or spousal relationship referred to by Lord Wilberforce and other relationships, was that in the case of the former there was a rebuttable presumption that "the love and affection normally associated with persons in those relationships is such that the defendant ought reasonably to contemplate that they may be so closely and directly affected by his conduct as to suffer shock resulting in psychiatric illness", whilst in the case of "more remote relatives and, a fortiori, friends" it could reasonably be expected that they would not suffer illness from the shock and hence they would have to prove that their relationship was so close as to be comparable to that of a parental or spousal relationship.[356] On the facts, the Lords denied recovery to a claimant who had witnessed the accident in which his two brothers were killed, on the ground that he had produced no evidence of a close tie of love and affection with his brothers and no presumption was to be made in the case of siblings.[357] The Law Commission recommended a legislative extension of the category of relationships covered by the presumption to include siblings and cohabitants[358] and it is suggested that notwithstanding the *Alcock* decision, it is open to the courts to adopt this recommendation.

Bystanders The requirement of a close tie means that mere bystanders cannot 7-78

353 [1983] 1 A.C. 410 at 422.

354 [1992] 1 A.C. 310.

355 [1992] 1 A.C. 310 at 397.

356 [1992] 1 A.C. 310 at 403. Lord Keith also spoke of the relationship having "to be proved by a [claimant], though no doubt being capable of being presumed in appropriate cases".

357 Contrast *Shorter v Surrey and Sussex Healthcare NHS Trust* [2015] EWHC 614 (QB); (2015) 144 B.M.L.R. 136 where the defendants conceded that a relationship between sisters which, on the evidence, was almost like mother and daughter was sufficiently close and loving to satisfy this element of the test for a "secondary" victim. In *RE (A Minor) v Calderdale and Huddersfield NHS Foundation Trust* [2017] EWHC 824 (QB); [2017] Med. L.R. 390 at [48], the defendants conceded that a grandmother who was present at the traumatic birth of her grandchild was in a sufficiently close relationship. See also *King v Philcox* [2015] HCA 19; (2015) 320 A.L.R. 398 where the High Court of Australia held that at common law a motorist could owe a duty of care to the brother of a passenger killed in an accident caused by the motorist's negligence, where the brother did not witness the accident but came upon the aftermath (the action failed due to statutory restrictions on the category of claimants where the claimant was not present at the accident itself).

358 *Liability for Psychiatric Illness*, Law Com. No.249, para.6.27. In proposing this limited extension of the presumption, the Commission sought to balance the desire to avoid distressing cross-examination as to "love and affection" with the danger of including categories where there was no close tie. The stepparent-stepchild relationship was excluded from the presumption as such relationships "vary enormously", and the relationship of claimant and victim who she treated as her child was also excluded on the ground that it was best left to the evidence.

recover. In *Alcock* Lords Ackner and Oliver suggested a possible exception to this position where there were "circumstances of such horror as would be likely to traumatise even the most phlegmatic spectator".[359] However, in *McFarlane v EE Caledonia Ltd*[360] where the claimant had witnessed the most horrific fire on the Piper Alpha oil rig, Stuart-Smith LJ refused to find a duty arguing that to do so would raise theoretical and practical problems: theoretical, because to extend the duty to bystanders would mean basing it simply upon foreseeability and this would run counter to "the whole basis of the decision in *Alcock*'s case (which was) that the test of proximity is not simply reasonable foreseeability"; practical problems, because it would be difficult to limit what should be regarded as horrific, as "reactions to horrific events are entirely subjective; who is to say that it is more horrific to see a petrol tanker advancing out of control on a school ... than to see a child run over on a pedestrian crossing". The Law Commission[361] also considered that an exception for "particularly horrific" incidents would be problematic if not unworkable, but concluded that it should be left to judicial development to extend recovery to bystanders if it was felt that the policy objections had been overcome.

7-79 **Employees** The Court of Appeal in *White*[362] held for the claimants with Rose LJ in part basing the liability of the defendant to its police officers taking part in the Hillsborough rescue on the proposition that an "employee may ... recover against his employer for ... psychiatric injury caused in the course of his employment by the employer's negligence". When this decision was reversed by the House of Lords,[363] Lord Steyn expressly rejected the notion that the employer/employee relationship was a special case. He said:

> "It is a non sequitur to say that because an employer is under a duty to an employee not to cause him physical injury, the employer should as a necessary consequence of that duty (of which there is no breach) be under a duty not to cause the employee psychiatric injury. The rules to be applied when an employee brings an action against his employer for harm suffered at his workplace are the rules of tort. One is therefore thrown back to the ordinary rules of the law of tort which contain restrictions on the recovery of compensation for psychiatric harm."[364]

Thus, to recover an employee has to establish that he is an endangered or participating primary victim or that he is a secondary victim with a close tie to the person injured or imperilled. If the employee satisfies either of those requirements, he may recover.[365] Lord Hoffmann in *White*[366] expressly rejected the so-called "fireman's rule" under which an employee such as a fireman or policeman whose job may

359 [1992] 1 A.C. 310 at 403, per Lord Ackner who gave the illustration of witnessing a "petrol tanker careering out of control into a school in session and bursting into flames" and at 416, per Lord Oliver.

360 [1994] 2 All E.R. 1 at 14. See also *Robertson v Forth Road Bridge Joint Board*, 1996 S.L.T. 263, where it was held that an employer owed no duty to an employee who witnesses the horror of seeing a fellow worker being swept off the bridge.

361 *Liability for Psychiatric Illness*, Law Com. No.249, paras 7.11–7.15.

362 Reported as *Frost v Chief Constable of the South Yorkshire Police* [1998] Q.B. 254.

363 [1999] 2 A.C. 455 at 497.

364 Where the psychiatric harm has resulted from occupational stress rather than a shocking event, the employer/employee relationship is the basis of the liability rules developed by the courts. See paras 7-91 and 12-37 onwards.

365 See also *French v Sussex CC* [2006] EWCA Civ 312 where the claimant police officers suffered stress and psychiatric illness as a result of criminal and disciplinary charges which followed a police operation in which a suspect had been fatally shot. The claimants, who had not seen the shooting, alleged that the defendant was negligent in failing to give proper instructions to those involved in

require him to participate in dangerous incidents, is disqualified from claiming on the basis that he accepts psychiatric illness as a risk of the job.

Physical and temporal proximity In *McLoughlin v O'Brian*[367] Lord Wilberforce stated that: "As regards proximity to the accident, it is obvious that this must be close in both time and space. It is after all, the fact and consequence of the defendant's negligence that must be proved to have caused the 'nervous shock'." In *McLoughlin* the claimant did not witness the accident which injured her family but she saw them in hospital two hours later. Lord Wilberforce held that the duty should extend to situations such as this where the claimant had suffered shock on "direct perception of some of the events which go to make up the accident as an entire event, and this includes … the immediate aftermath".[368] But the immediate aftermath that causes the shock must form part of "the accident as an entire event". Lord Wilberforce noted that the victims in *McLoughlin* "were in the same condition (in the hospital), covered with oil and mud, and distraught with pain" as they would have been at the scene of the accident itself. In *Alcock*, Lord Jauncey concluded that relatives who had not witnessed the death of the victim but identified the body in the mortuary some nine or more hours later were not within the immediate aftermath. He distinguished *McLoughlin* on the grounds that a longer period of time had elapsed since the accident and the fact that the visits to the mortuary "were not made for the purpose of giving comfort to the victim but purely for the purpose of identification". Whilst commenting that "to essay any comprehensive definition (of the immediate aftermath) would be a fruitless exercise", his speech clearly indicates that to form part of the accident as an entire event, the experience must be sufficiently related in both time[369] and nature[370] to the original accident. Of the two factors it is suggested that it is the nature of the experience which is crucial. The longer the time lapse between accident and witness the more likely it is that what is witnessed will differ in nature from the experience of the original accident. The Law Commission[371] drew attention to *Taylorson v Shieldness Produce Ltd*[372] in which the claimant saw his son in hospital 10 hours after his accident and was 7-80

the operation. The Court of Appeal struck out the claims. This was psychiatric injury as a remote consequence of an untoward event caused by a failure of the defendant to give proper instruction to officers as to how they should carry out their duties. But if officers who had witnessed the shooting would have no claim (applying *White*) the claimants could not succeed either.

366 [1999] 2 A.C. 455 at 511.

367 [1983] 1 A.C. 410.

368 [1983] 1 A.C. 410 at 422; citing *Benson v Lee* [1972] V.R. 879, in which a mother recovered when although being in her home 100 yards away from the accident, she suffered shock after being informed of it and running out to the scene. See also *Vernon v Bosley (No.1)* [1997] 1 All E.R. 577; [1997] R.T.R 1; [1997] P.I.Q.R. P255; in which the claimant watched the police attempts to recover from the river the car in which his daughters had drowned and was held to be sufficiently proximate.

369 In *McLoughlin* Lord Wilberforce suggested that the majority of the Australian High Court in *Chester v Waverley Municipal Council* (1939) 62 C.L.R. 1, were correct to hold that the discovery of a child's body floating in a trench after a prolonged search, fell outside the "immediate aftermath". A clearer example is perhaps *Rhodes v Canadian National Ry* (1990) 75 D.L.R. (4th) 248, where the claimant did not see the wreckage of the train crash in which her son died until eight days after the disaster. Her claim was rejected on the ground that her psychiatric illness was not caused by "fright, terror or horror". Note that in *Hunter v British Coal Corp* [1999] Q.B. 140, the claimant was unable to recover because he had not witnessed the incident and had been prevented from seeing the aftermath.

370 In *Jaensch v Coffey* (1984) 54 A.L.R. 417 at 462, Deane J said that "the 'immediate aftermath' extended to the hospital to which the victim was taken and persisted for so long as he remained in the state produced by the accident up to and including the immediate post-accident treatment".

371 *Liability for Psychiatric Illness*, Law Com. No.249, paras 6.12–6.15.

held to be insufficiently proximate in time. It considered the proximity requirement as exemplified by this decision to be too restrictive and recommended legislative abolition of the requirement.[373] The subsequent Court of Appeal decision in *Galli-Atkinson v Seghal*[374] adopted a less restrictive approach. Reversing the lower court decision, Latham LJ leading the court, held that a mother who saw her daughter's badly injured body in the mortuary two hours after the fatal car accident, was within the immediate aftermath which extended from "the moment of the accident until the moment [the mother] left the mortuary". Unlike the mortuary visit in Alcock, this visit "was not merely to identify the body. It was to complete the story."[375]

7-81 **Proximity to which event?** In most instances it is likely that the event that causes injury to the victim will be relatively close in time and space to the occurrence of the injury itself, often almost instantaneous. But in some cases there may be a delay between the initial accident and the physical consequences of the accident to the accident victim. The question then arises as to which event, the initial accident or the later occurrence of injury, a secondary victim must witness in order to satisfy the requirements of physical and temporal proximity. In *Taylor v A Novo (UK) Ltd*[376] the Court of Appeal held that in order to qualify as a secondary victim the claimant must witness the original accident or its immediate aftermath. The claimant's mother was injured at work when a stack of racking boards was negligently tipped over on top of her. Three weeks later she suddenly and unexpectedly collapsed and died at home as a result of deep vein thrombosis and pulmonary emboli, which had been caused by the accident at work. The claimant did not witness the accident at work, but she did witness her mother's death and developed post-traumatic stress disorder. The defendants conceded that the claimant satisfied all the criteria to qualify as a secondary victim, with the exception of the requirement that she be present at the scene of the accident which caused the death or its immediate aftermath. The Court of Appeal rejected the claimant's argument that the relevant "event" to which she must be proximate in time and space was not the initial accident but her mother's collapse and death caused by the accident. Lord Dyson MR did not accept that there were two events; there was a single accident or event which had two consequences, the first of which was injury to the claimant's mother's head and arm, and the second, three weeks later, was her death. To allow the claimant

372 [1994] P.I.Q.R. P329.

373 In *Coates v Government Insurance Office of New South Wales* (1995) 36 N.S.W.L.R. 1, Kirby P. suggested that proximity to the accident should not be a requirement and said that "... the law should recognise that it is as much the direct emotional involvement of a person in an accident, as his or her physical presence at or near the scene or directly in its aftermath, that is pertinent to nature of the injury suffered". In *Tame v New South Wales* [2002] HCA 35; (2002) 191 A.L.R. 449 parents recovered for psychiatric harm suffered as a result of what they were told about their son's death; and similarly in *Gifford v Strang Patrick Stevedoring Pty Ltd* [2003] HCA 33; (2003) 198 A.L.R. 100 children recovered damages after developing psychiatric illness as a result of being told about their father's death. For commentary on *Tame*, see Trindade (2003) 119 L.Q.R. 204; and on *Gifford* see Handford (2003) 11 Tort. L.R. 127. See also *W v Essex CC* [2001] 2 A.C. 592, where Lord Slynn considered that parents suffering from shock on learning of the sexual abuse of their children four weeks after the events might still come within a flexible concept of the immediate aftermath.

374 [2003] EWCA Civ 697; [2003] Lloyd's Rep. Med. 285.

375 [2003] EWCA Civ 697; [2003] Lloyd's Rep. Med. 285 at [26].

376 [2013] EWCA Civ 194; [2014] Q.B. 150.

to recover as a secondary victim in such circumstances "would be to go too far".[377] If the claimant's argument were accepted, said his Lordship, she would be able to succeed even if her mother's death had occurred months and possibly years after the accident. On the other hand if her mother had died in the accident and the claimant had not witnessed the accident but had come on the scene shortly *after* the immediate aftermath she would not have qualified as a secondary victim: "The idea that Ms Taylor could recover in the first situation but not in the others would strike the ordinary reasonable person as unreasonable and indeed incomprehensible. In this area of the law, the perception of the ordinary reasonable person matters. That is because where the boundaries of proximity are drawn in this difficult area should, so far as possible, reflect what the ordinary reasonable person would regard as acceptable."[378] For policy reasons the right of action of secondary victims was subject to strict control mechanisms, and "any further substantial extension ... should only be done by Parliament". For Lord Dyson, the paradigm secondary victim case is one involving an accident which (i) more or less immediately causes injury or death to a primary victim; and (ii) is witnessed by the claimant: "In such a case, the relevant event is the accident. It is not a later consequence of the accident."[379]

Means of perception In *McLoughlin*[380] Lord Wilberforce said "the shock must come through sight or hearing of the event or its immediate aftermath". He specifically left for later consideration whether some equivalent of sight or hearing, e.g. simultaneous television, would suffice. In *Alcock*, only two of the claimants had directly witnessed the event at the football ground where the victims were crushed to death. The remaining claimants had either watched the events on television or been informed of them by third parties. However, the television pictures did not show pictures of suffering by recognisable individuals. They merely informed the claimants of the disaster in the same way as would the radio or a third party. Whilst conceding that the pictures would give rise to feelings of the deepest anxiety and distress, the House of Lords concluded that they were no more shocking than information from a third party. No duty was owed because the trauma did not arise from the original impact of the transmitted image.[381] This is not because shock to the claimant in such circumstances is not foreseeable. In *Ravenscroft v Rederiaktiebolaget Transatlantic*[382] it was clearly established that the claimant's shock as a consequence of being told about the horrific circumstance of a relative's death was **7-82**

[377] [2013] EWCA Civ 194; [2014] Q.B. 150 at [29].

[378] [2013] EWCA Civ 194; [2014] Q.B. 150 at [30].

[379] [2013] EWCA Civ 194; [2014] Q.B. 150 at [32]. *Taylor v A Novo (UK) Ltd* was applied in *RS v Criminal Injuries Compensation Authority* [2013] EWCA Civ 1040; [2014] 1 W.L.R. 1313; and *Paul v Royal Wolverhampton NHS Trust* [2019] EWHC 2893 (QB); [2020] P.I.Q.R. P5 (deceased's daughters witnessed his death from a heart attack some 14 months after alleged clinical negligence; witnessing the death was not the relevant event for the purpose of establishing the temporal and physical proximity required by *Alcock*).

[380] [1983] 1 A.C. 410 at 422.

[381] Note that both Lord Ackner and Oliver considered that there might be circumstances where the television pictures might have a sufficient direct impact to create the proximity necessary for a duty: [1992] 1 A.C. 310 at 405 and 417.

[382] [1991] 3 All E.R. 73. Ward J held that the defendant owed a duty to a mother who was told about the death of her son shortly after the fatal accident but did not see his body or suffering. He cited psychiatric evidence to the effect that there was a "real risk that (a mother may suffer psychiatric illness) even though she is not present at the accident, does not then and there or at the aftermath see or hear what has taken place but only learns about it later". See also *Palmer v Tees HA* [1999]

a real risk. It is because the defendant is regarded as responsible for the horrific events themselves and not for the distribution of information about the events. Lord Keith in *Alcock* doubted the finding of liability in *Ravenscroft* precisely because the cause of the psychiatric illness was the news of the death and not the witnessing of the death.[383] The Law Commission criticised this requirement, citing *Taylor v Somerset HA*[384] as an example of its unduly restrictive effect.[385] In *Taylor* the claimant's husband died of a heart attack in hospital and the claimant saw the body about 40 minutes after the death. Her claim failed on the ground that she had not directly perceived the immediate aftermath: being told of her husband's death was not sufficient and her visit to the mortuary to confirm his death went to the fact of death rather than the circumstances in which it was brought about.[386] The Commission recommended legislative abolition of the requirement and as noted in the previous paragraph, it remains open to the courts to implement this recommendation.

7-83 **Sudden shock** In *Alcock*[387] Lord Ackner said that what was required was "the sudden appreciation by sight or sound of a horrifying event, which violently agitates the mind". Lord Keith required "a sudden assault on the nervous system" and Lord Oliver a "sudden and unexpected shock to the nervous system". Both considered that the television pictures of the Hillsborough disaster would have given rise to grave concern rather than shock. Provided part of the cause of the psychiatric illness is the shocking experience, the claimant may recover even if there are other causes such as an abnormal grief reaction. Thus in *Vernon v Bosley (No.1)*,[388] the claimant was able to recover although it was impossible to distinguish between the aspects of his illness attributable to the experience at the scene of the road ac-

---

Lloyd's Rep. Med. 351 at 360, in which Stuart-Smith LJ rejecting claims by parents of a murdered child who saw her body a day after its discovery, said: "I cannot accept that what happens in the imagination is the same thing as the sudden appreciation by sight or sound of the horrifying event."

383 [1992] 1 A.C. 310 at 398. Similar doubts were expressed by Lord Ackner and Lord Oliver at 401 at 418. *Ravenscroft* was subsequently reversed by the Court of Appeal in the light of the doubts expressed by their Lordships: [1992] 2 All E.R. 470 (Note).

384 [1993] 4 Med. L.R. 34.

385 *Liability for Psychiatric Illness*, Law Com. No.249, para.6.12.

386 See also *Young v MacVean* [2015] CSIH 70; 2016 S.C. 135, where the pursuer had walked past the scene of an accident and formed the view that someone must have died. She came to the gradual realisation over a fairly short period of time that her son had been killed in the accident, subsequently confirmed by the police, and later she identified her dead son at the mortuary. The Inner House of the Court of Session held that she did not qualify as a "secondary" victim because the events did not involve the sudden appreciation by direct sight or sound of a horrifying event or of the immediate aftermath. Her psychiatric illness was not the result of direct perception of the distressing event. Contrast *Galli-Atkinson v Seghal* [2003] EWCA Civ 697; [2003] Lloyd's Rep. Med. 285, where the claimant had been told of her daughter's death by police at the scene of the accident and had seen the body two hours later in the mortuary, the Court of Appeal rejected the finding of the lower court that the shock had been caused merely by being told of the death. The telling formed part of the overall immediate aftermath which included the visit to the mortuary. The visit to the mortuary was part of the story and not simply for identification.

387 [1992] 1 A.C. 310 at 401, per Lord Ackner, at 398, per Lord Keith and at 411, per Lord Oliver. See Brennan J in *Jaensch v Coffey* (1984) 155 C.L.R. 549 at 565:

> "A [claimant] may recover only if the psychiatric illness is the result of physical injury negligently inflicted on him by the defendant or it is induced by 'shock'. Psychiatric illness caused in other ways attracts no damages, though it is reasonably foreseeable that psychiatric illness might be a consequence of the defendant's carelessness."

Hence, there would be no recovery for "the spouse who has been worn down by caring for a tortiously injured husband … and who suffers psychiatric illness as a result".

388 [1997] 1 All E.R. 577.

cident in which his children died and those which were symptoms of an abnormal grief reaction.[389] The shock may still be regarded as resulting from a sudden appreciation even if the event is protracted. In *North Glamorgan NHS Trust v Walters*[390] the defendant negligently failed to diagnose the claimant's baby as suffering from acute hepatitis. The event was a 36 hour period beginning with the claimant who was sharing a hospital room with her baby being wakened by the baby having an epileptic fit, going through a period when misdiagnosis delayed treatment for brain damage, and ending with her being told that the brain damage was severe and agreeing to termination of the baby's life support. The Court of Appeal regarded this as a single horrifying event in which "there was an inexorable progression from the moment when the fit causing the brain damage occurred as a result of the failure of the hospital properly to diagnose and then treat the baby [to] the dreadful climax when the child died in her arms. It is a seamless tale" as a result of which the mother "reeled under successive blows [to her nervous system]".[391] If no aspect of the illness is attributable to a shocking experience, it seems that recovery will be denied. Thus, in *Taylorson v Shieldness Produce Ltd*[392] the claimants saw their son only after treatment following the accident and although spending two days with him in intensive care until the life support was switched off, were unable to recover as their illness could not be attributed to one shocking event. However, the Law Commission regarded the "shock-induced" requirement as vague, having no psychiatric meaning, and unjustly discriminating against those inflicted with psychiatric illness developing over a period of time, such as depression, and it recommended that the requirement be abolished by legislation.[393] The *Walters* decision suggested that the courts were moving towards the same view.

However, in later cases involving allegations of medical negligence the courts have insisted on a "shocking" event occurring over a relatively short time. Events that are prolonged over hours or days are unlikely to satisfy the requirement. The event must be something that would be recognised as "horrifying" by a person of **7-84**

---

389 Evans LJ distinguished as raising a question of remoteness, the decision in *Calascoine v Dixon* (1993) 19 B.M.L.R. 97, where recovery was denied in respect of illness caused by grief but triggered by events subsequent to the incident such as the acquittal of the defendant on a charge of causing death by dangerous driving. The claimant in *Calascoine* did recover for those elements of her illness attributable to the shock of the incident itself.

390 [2002] EWCA Civ 1792; [2003] P.I.Q.R. P16. Contrast *Sion v Hampstead HA* [1994] 5 Med. L.R. 170, where on similar facts the Court of Appeal rejected the claim on the grounds that the claimant's medical report made no reference to shock. *Walters* seems to reflect the development of a less restrictive approach by the courts.

391 [2002] EWCA Civ 1792; [2003] P.I.Q.R. P16 at [35] and [45], per Ward LJ.

392 [1994] P.I.Q.R. P329. See also *Sion v Hampstead HA* [1994] 5 Med. L.R. 170, where the claimant was unable to recover from a hospital alleged to have negligently treated his son as the illness resulted from watching his son slowly deteriorate and die rather than from a shocking incident.

393 *Liability for Psychiatric Illness*, Law Com. No.249, paras 5.28–5.34. In *Tame v New South Wales* [2002] HCA 35; (2002) 191 A.L.R. 449 the High Court of Australia abandoned the sudden shock requirement: per Gleeson CJ at [18], Gaudron J at [66], Gummow J at [206] and Kirby J at [213]. See also *Wicks v State Rail Authority of New South Wales* [2010] HCA 22; (2010) 241 C.L.R. 60 where, in the context of statutory rules limiting recovery for "mental harm" to certain claimants who "witnessed, at the scene, a person being killed, injured or put in peril", the High Court of Australia held that this was not necessarily limited to an event that may be measured in minutes. So, in a claim by two police officers who assisted at the scene of a rail disaster for several hours, the High Court held that the perils to which living passengers were subjected as a result of the defendants' negligence did not end when the carriages came to rest: "A person is put in peril when put at risk; the person remains in peril ... until the person ceases to be at risk" (at [50]), which was when they had been rescued by being taken to a place of safety.

ordinary susceptibility and this must be judged by objective standards.[394] In *Shorter v Surrey and Sussex Healthcare NHS Trust*[395] the negligence (a failure to diagnose a subarachnoid haemorrhage) had started a week before it became apparent and the consequences started to manifest themselves. The claimant's sister suffered a further bleed in the brain which, some hours later, resulted in her death. The claimant saw her sister twice at the hospital. On the first occasion her sister's condition was fluctuating, she did not have obvious injuries and did not appear to be in any obvious or immediate danger. On the second occasion, some nine hours or so later, she was on a life support machine. There had been four phone conversations about her sister's deteriorating condition in the interim, and before the claimant saw her on the life support machine her brother-in-law had told her that they had "lost her". Swift J said that when the claimant saw her sister on the life support machine it was not "a sudden or unexpected shock", and concluded that the facts did not amount to a "seamless single horrifying event", but were a series of events over a period of time which gave rise to an accumulation of gradual assaults on the claimant's mind. She did not qualify as a "secondary" victim.

7-85 Similarly, in *Liverpool Women's Hospital NHS Foundation Trust v Ronayne*[396] the claimant's wife developed severe, life-threatening, peritonitis following negligently performed surgery. She was admitted to hospital as an emergency and the claimant saw his wife before she was taken into the operating theatre for an emergency operation, hooked up to various machines, monitors and drips. The following day he saw his wife again in her post-operative condition, unconscious, connected to a ventilator, being given intravenous antibiotic. The claimant's wife ultimately made a full recovery over a period of weeks. The claimant alleged that he suffered post-traumatic stress disorder from what he had witnessed. The Court of Appeal reversed the trial judge's finding that these circumstances, which spanned a period of 36 hours, constituted a single shocking event. The facts were not comparable to *North Glamorgan NHS Trust v Walters*. There was, said Tomlinson LJ, "a series of events over a period of time. There was no 'inexorable progression' and the claimant's perception of what he saw on the two critical occasions was in each case conditioned or informed by the information which he had received in advance and by way of preparation".[397] The sequence of events was far from seamless, and there was no sudden appreciation of an event. Rather, there was a series of events which gave rise to an accumulation of gradual assaults on the claimant's mind.[398] What the claimant witnessed was not horrifying by objective standards. Though "both alarming and distressing" it was not exceptional.[399]

---

394 *Shorter v Surrey and Sussex Healthcare NHS Trust* [2015] EWHC 614 (QB); (2015) 144 B.M.L.R. 136 at [214] per Swift J, approved by Tomlinson LJ in In *Liverpool Women's Hospital NHS Foundation Trust v Ronayne* [2015] EWCA Civ 588; [2015] P.I.Q.R. P20 at [13].

395 [2015] EWHC 614 (QB); (2015) 144 B.M.L.R. 136.

396 [2015] EWCA Civ 588; [2015] P.I.Q.R. P20.

397 [2015] EWCA Civ 588; [2015] P.I.Q.R. P20 at [36].

398 [2015] EWCA Civ 588; [2015] P.I.Q.R. P20 at [40].

399 *Ronayne* was applied in *Owers v Medway NHS Foundation Trust* [2015] EWHC 2363 (QB); [2015] Med. L.R. 561 where a husband had witnessed the effects of his wife suffering a stroke which the defendants had negligently failed to diagnose and treat. Stewart J concluded that although the events were "very distressing" they were not "horrifying" or "wholly exceptional" by objective standards and by reference to persons of ordinary susceptibility. See also *Wild v Southend University Hospital NHS Foundation Trust* [2014] EWHC 4053 (QB); [2016] P.I.Q.R. P3 where it was held that a father present in the delivery room when it was discovered that the baby had already died in utero had not witnessed a horrific event leading to death or serious injury and so was not a "secondary" victim.

Immediate victim as defendant A further policy restriction on recovery by secondary victims was referred to by Lord Oliver in *Alcock*,[400] namely whether a duty would be owed where the negligent defendant was the immediate victim, e.g. the case of "the mother who suffers shock and psychiatric injury through witnessing the death of her son when he negligently walks in front of an oncoming motor car". Lord Oliver left the question open but suggested that the courts would be likely to follow the view of Deane J in *Jaensch v Coffey*[401] that a duty should be excluded on grounds of policy.[402] The Law Commission evaluated this suggestion. Against the restriction was the argument that there is no such bar where the defendant's self-inflicted injury results in the claimant's physical injury, for example where the claimant has been injured in the course of rescuing the defendant. The most persuasive argument in favour of the restriction was that otherwise there would, in effect, be a duty on individuals to look after themselves, simply in order to protect others from the likely psychiatric effects of an accident and that this would place an undesirably restrictive burden on one's self-determination. In *Greatorex v Greatorex*[403] Cazalet J accepted the self-determination argument. The claimant was a fireman who attended a car crash where the victim who was to blame for the crash, turned out to be his own son. The claimant suffered post-traumatic stress and sued his son (effectively suing his son's motor insurers). Following *White*, his claim as a primary victim failed as he was never in any danger and although he satisfied all the *Alcock* requirements for secondary victim recovery, he failed because imposing a duty on his son to avoid self-inflicted injury would limit the son's right to self-determination. With only this first instance decision the matter is not settled. The Law Commission had recommended that the law should adopt a compromise position under which there should be no general restriction, but "courts should have the scope to decide not to impose a duty of care where satisfied that its imposition would not be just and reasonable because the defendant chose to cause his or her own death, injury or imperilment".[404] It is certainly arguable that it is only just and 7-86

To similar effect are: *Less v Hussain* [2012] EWHC 3513 (QB); [2013] Med. L.R. 383; and *Wells v University Hospital Southampton NHS Foundation Trust* [2015] EWHC 2376 (QB); [2015] Med. L.R. 477 at [86] (obiter). Contrast *RE (A Minor) v Calderdale and Huddersfield NHS Foundation Trust* [2017] EWHC 824 (QB); [2017] Med. L.R. 390 where during the delivery the child became "stuck" due to shoulder dystocia, which one of the defendants' expert witnesses described as "one of the most frightening of medical emergencies". Goss J held (at [47] and [48]) that both the mother and the child's grandmother (who was present throughout) had experienced a sudden, shocking event "that was exceptional in nature and horrifying as judged by objective standards and by reference to persons of ordinary susceptibility". The judge (at [40]) considered that, in any event, the mother qualified as a "primary" victim on the basis that the baby's head "had crowned but her body remained in the birth canal. At this point she was not a separate legal entity from her mother and, in law, they are to be treated as one." See also *YAH v Medway NHS Foundation Trust* [2018] EWHC 2964 (QB); [2019] 1 W.L.R. 1413, per Whipple J at [22]: "settled law" that a "mother is a primary victim in so far as she suffers personal injury consequent on negligence which occurs before the baby is born". Nor does the mother cease to be a primary victim at the moment the child is born: "The fact that the claimant's psychiatric damage became manifest later in time, after [the baby] was born, does not change the claimant's status" (at [24]); and *Zeromska-Smith v United Lincolnshire Hospitals NHS Trust* [2019] EWHC 980 (QB) at [96].

400 [1992] 1 A.C. 310 at 418.

401 (1984) 155 C.L.R. 549 at 604.

402 The analogy of the rescue cases would suggest that a duty should be owed in such a circumstance. See para.7-35.

403 [2000] 1 W.L.R. 1970. See also *Homsi v Homsi* [2016] VSC 354.

404 *Liability for Psychiatric Illness*, Law Com. No.249, paras 5.34–5.43. The decision in *Greatorex* could

reasonable for those who engage in very dangerous activities to take out insurance against the potential psychiatric as well as physical consequences to others.[405]

7-87 **Immediate victim owed no duty** A related issue arises where the immediate victim was owed no duty of care by the defendant. The Law Commission gave two examples of this situation. In the first, the victim is owed no duty because his injury was sustained while pursuing a criminal activity. In this situation the Commission suggested that it might still not be inconsistent with public policy to impose a duty of care in respect of psychiatric illness suffered by the loved one of that immediate victim. The principle established in the rescue case of *Videan v British Transport Commission*,[406] that the duty to the relative may be regarded as independent of the existence of any duty to the immediate victim, supports this view. In the second situation, the victim is owed no duty because the defendant has simply failed to warn the victim of a danger and would not normally owe a duty in respect of that omission. Here, the Commission suggested that "on the same reasoning (that there is no general duty to act for the benefit of another) the defendant should not normally owe a duty of care to a loved one who suffered psychiatric illness consequent on the immediate victim/s injury". In the light of these two contrasting examples, the Commission recommended that the courts should have a discretion as to whether to impose a duty or not in such situations.[407]

7-88 **Contributory negligence of immediate victim** A further question is whether contributory negligence of the immediate victim should be imputed to the secondary victim so as to justify a reduction in damages awarded for the illness. This issue has not been considered by English courts. In *Alcock v Chief Constable of the South Yorkshire Police*[408] Lord Oliver commented that:

> "[i]f the primary victim is himself 75% responsible for the accident, it would be a curious and wholly unfair situation if the [claimant] were entitled to recover damages for his traumatic injury from the person responsible only in a minor degree whilst he in turn remained unable to recover any contribution from the person primarily responsible since the latter's negligence vis-à-vis the [claimant] would not even have been tortious."

But his concern was the suggestion that a negligent immediate victim could not be a defendant and, hence, could not be subject to a contribution claim.[409] He was not suggesting that the primary victim's contributory negligence should be imputed to the secondary victim. The Law Commission considered that to reduce the claimant's damages in line with the contributory negligence of the immediate victim was not

---

lead to a significant anomaly where the accident victim's injuries were partially contributed to by the negligence of another defendant, who, presumably, would be liable for the claimant's psychiatric harm. If in *Greatorex* the son's injuries had been produced by a combination of his own negligence and that of another motorist, the father might be able to claim against the third party while having no claim against his own son with the result that the third party would be liable for the full damages with no contribution claim against the son.

405 See Teff, "*Liability for psychiatric injury*" (1998) 61 M.L.R 849 at 855; and Mullany and Handford, *Tort Liability for Psychiatric Damage* (1993), pp.215–220.

406 [1963] 2 Q.B. 650. See para.7-35.

407 Paras 6.36 to 6.41.

408 [1992] 1 A.C. 310 at 418.

409 See para.7-86; and Mullany and Handford, *Tort Liability for Psychiatric Damage* (1993), pp.253–254.

attractive as "it would be contrary to the underlying principle that the defendant owes a separate duty of care directly to the claimant".[410]

(iii) Psychiatric illness resulting from factors other than personal injury or imperilment

Illness as a result of damage or danger to property In *Attia v British Gas*,[411] the Court of Appeal held as a preliminary issue that damages could be recovered in respect of psychiatric illness resulting from the claimant witnessing the destruction of her property. There, it was alleged that the defendant had negligently allowed a fire to destroy the claimant's home and she had suffered psychiatric illness as a result of witnessing the blaze upon her return to the home. There were no personal injuries to anyone else and the claimant had not been at risk of physical injury. The court considered that if such illness was a foreseeable consequence of witnessing the events, then the illness would not be regarded as unforeseeable as a matter of law. It was a question of fact, depending on the medical evidence.[412] Bingham LJ cited other possible examples such as where "the scholar's life's work of research were destroyed before his eyes as a result of the defendant's careless conduct". He considered that it would not be fair to exclude such situations from the scope of a duty on policy grounds. *Owens v Liverpool Corp*,[413] in which relatives of a deceased recovered for psychiatric illness suffered as a result of seeing the defendant crash into the hearse and overturn the coffin, may also be regarded as an example of liability stemming from property damage. However, basing liability on mere foreseeability would appear to allow for wider recovery in the case of witnessing property damage than in the case of psychiatric illness stemming from witnessing injury to other persons where the *Alcock* limitations apply. As the Law Commission observed, "it seems to give a higher value to property than to human life".[414] 7-89

In *Yearworth v North Bristol NHS Trust*[415] the Court of Appeal touched upon, but did not resolve, the question whether a claimant who develops a recognised psychiatric condition as a result of learning that sperm which had been stored for possible future use in fertility treatment had been negligently destroyed by the defendants. The court noted that in *Attia v British Gas* the claimant had actually 7-90

---

410 para.5.39.

411 [1988] Q.B. 304.

412 Note, however, that since the defendants undoubtedly owed the claimant a duty of care not to burn her house down, the question of liability for psychiatric injury was treated as a matter of remoteness of damage rather than duty. It is questionable whether it is appropriate to permit recovery for a head of loss (psychiatric damage) where the duty of care was doubtful simply because there was another head of loss (damage to property) where a duty of care was clearly owed.

413 [1939] 1 K.B. 394. The possibility of liability for distress at the death of a favourite pet cat or dog was also mooted. In *Alcock v Chief Constable of South Yorkshire* [1992] 1 A.C. 310 at 412 Lord Oliver noted that *Owens v Liverpool Corp* had been disapproved by three members of the House of Lords in *Bourhill v Young* [1942] A.C. 100.

414 Para.7.27. The Commission made no recommendation in relation to this form of liability, concluding at para.7.30 that "[o]nly if the common law were to reach an unsatisfactory position, would legislative reform become expedient". The problem with *Attia* is that recovery for psychiatric illness is treated as parasitic on the duty not to negligently damage the property. But just because there is a duty not to cause physical damage to property, it does not follow that there has to be a duty in relation to other forms of loss such as psychiatric illness which are the foreseeable consequence of the damage.

415 [2009] EWCA Civ 37; [2010] Q.B. 1 at [55].

observed the destruction of her home, but that the claimants in *Yearworth* had only learned of the destruction of their sperm after the event, and queried whether this distinction was appropriate (while noting that it simply reflects the distinction applied to the recovery of foreseeable psychiatric harm by a secondary victim as a result of personal injury to another). The issue did not have to be resolved because the court concluded that the stored sperm was capable of being owned by the men who had provided it and that this could give rise to an action in bailment.[416]

7-91 **Occupational stress** In *Walker v Northumberland CC*[417] Colman J held that a social worker was entitled to damages for a second nervous breakdown caused by stress at work. Liability was based on the duty of the employer to provide his employee with a reasonably safe system of work and although that duty had been developed in cases involving physical injury, Colman J saw no logical reason why the risk of psychiatric injury should be excluded from the scope of that duty. In *Hatton v Sutherland*[418] Hale LJ approved *Walker* and held that the key question was whether a harmful reaction to the pressures of the workplace was reasonably foreseeable in the individual employee concerned. Crucially, she suggested that unless "he knows of some particular problem or vulnerability, an employer is entitled to assume that his employee is up to the normal pressures of the job". However, in *Barber v Somerset CC*[419] the House of Lords stressed that the onus remained on the employer to give positive thought for the welfare of its workers. Thus, it is not always the employee who is in the best position to decide whether to continue working and the onus does not necessarily fall on the stressed employee to decide to take a period of sick leave and to seek medical help. As Smith LJ pointed out in *Dickins v O2 Plc*:

> "If that were the law, it would be impossible for any claimant ever to establish liability for illness due to stress at work; the responsibility for his health and for continuing at work in the face of signs of excessive stress would lie only on the claimant himself. That is not the law, as cases such as *Hatton* and *Barber* have made clear. There may be cases in which the employee is able to make appropriate decisions but the judge was quite entitled to take the view that, after the respondent had told [the defendants] about the condition she was in, some responsibility passed to the employer."[420]

7-92 In the absence of knowledge of the employee's vulnerability, there may still be liability if the employee is exposed to a traumatic event at work and the employer fails to provide appropriate counselling. In *Melville v The Home Office*[421] the claimant had helped to cut down a prisoner who had committed suicide by hanging.

416 See para.16-41.
417 [1995] 1 All E.R. 737; [1995] I.C.R. 702.
418 [2002] EWCA Civ 76; [2002] 2 All E.R. 1; [2002] P.I.Q.R. P21.
419 [2004] UKHL 13; [2004] 1 W.L.R. 1089. See further para.12-37.
420 [2008] EWCA Civ 1144; [2009] I.R.L.R. 58 at [34]. Nonetheless, claims for occupational stress often fail on the basis either that the employee's psychiatric reaction was unforeseeable (and the employer was entitled to take what the employee said at face value) or on the basis that there was no causal connection between any breach of duty and the psychiatric illness. See, e.g. *Olulana v Southwark LBC* [2014] EWHC 2707 (QB); *Daniel v Secretary of State for the Department of Health* [2014] EWHC 2578 (QB); *Easton v B&Q Plc* [2015] EWHC 880 (QB).
421 Decided as one of the co-joined appeals in *Hartman v South Essex Mental Health and Community Care NHS Trust* [2005] EWCA Civ 6; [2005] I.C.R. 782. Compare *Pratt v Scottish Ministers* [2013] CSIH 17; 2013 S.L.T. 590 on an alleged failure to provide counselling services following an incident where the claimant prison officer ingested blood from a prisoner known to be a drug addict. The claim for psychiatric harm (attributable to the claimant's morbid fear of blood-borne disease fuelled

Contrary to its own procedures, the Home Office failed to offer the claimant counselling. The claimant recovered in respect of his resulting psychiatric illness even though there had been no indication before the incident that he was likely to suffer from stress.

Psychiatric harm following disciplinary proceedings In *French v Sussex CC*[422] the Court of Appeal held that where employees suffered stress and consequent psychiatric illness as a result of criminal and disciplinary charges which followed an allegedly negligently organised police operation this was not, and was not analogous to, a "stress at work" case. The employees had to satisfy the *Alcock* criteria for psychiatric illness following a traumatic event (which they could not do). On the other hand, in *Yapp v Foreign and Commonwealth Office*[423] the Court of Appeal accepted that the approach adopted in the stress at work cases (and the analysis developed by Hale LJ in *Hatton v Sutherland*) could be applied to a one-off event such as the unfair imposition of a disciplinary sanction by the employer.[424] However, it would not usually be foreseeable that even seriously unfair disciplinary action would lead the employee to develop a psychiatric illness (as opposed to distress and anger) unless there were signs, of which the employer was or should have been aware, of some pre-existing vulnerability to psychiatric harm. It would be exceptional that an apparently robust employee, with no history of any psychiatric ill-health, would develop a depressive illness as a result even of a very serious setback at work and the employer would be entitled to assume that an employee is of "reasonable fortitude" in the absence of actual or constructive knowledge to the contrary.[425] 7-93

Assumption of responsibility In *Leach v Chief Constable of Gloucestershire Constabulary*[426] the Court of Appeal refused to strike out a negligence claim against the police by the claimant, a voluntary worker who, as an "appropriate adult", attended the traumatic interview of a mentally disordered suspect. The claimant suffered psychiatric illness as a result of the experience. The court held that although the police owed no duty of care to protect such volunteers from psychological harm, they could owe a duty to provide counselling services for such volunteers. Henry LJ based the decision on the ground that the relationship between the volunteer and the police satisfied the proximity test just as much as would that between employee and employer. Pill LJ rested his decision on the assumption of responsibility by the police to the volunteer and the justice of imposing a duty in these circumstances. 7-94

---

by abnormal or irrational beliefs) failed on both breach of duty and causation, with the Inner House of the Court of Session also doubting whether the prison service owed the claimant a duty of care in circumstances where there was no evidence that the defendants considered, or ought to have considered, that the low-level emotional support that they could have offered would have been effective to prevent the claimant developing psychiatric illness.

422 [2006] EWCA Civ 312.

423 [2014] EWCA Civ 1512; [2015] I.R.L.R. 112.

424 Applying *Croft v Broadstairs & St Peter's Town Council* [2003] EWCA Civ 676.

425 See also *Coventry University v Mian* [2014] EWCA Civ 1275; [2014] E.L.R. 455; [2014] Med. L.R. 502 (employer not in breach of duty because, in the circumstances, instituting disciplinary procedures was within the range of reasonable responses by an employer); *Piepenbrock v The London School of Economics and Political Science* [2018] EWHC 2572 (QB); [2018] E.L.R. 596 (claimant's psychiatric reaction to defendants' handling of complaint against the claimant not reasonably foreseeable); *K v Chief Constable of the Police Service of Scotland* [2020] CSIH 18; 2020 S.L.T. 503

426 [1999] 1 W.L.R. 1421.

The liability in *McLoughlin v Jones*[427] of a solicitor to his client for the psychiatric illness resulting from the negligent handling of the client's case, can similarly be explained on this basis. It is suggested that such a duty might arise from other relationships such as patient and psychiatrist.[428] In *Butchart v The Home Office*[429] Latham LJ, giving the judgment of the Court of Appeal, cited *McLoughlin v Jones* when refusing to strike out the claim of a prisoner who alleged that he had suffered psychiatric illness as a result of witnessing the suicide of a cell mate who was known to be a suicide risk. The claimant alleged that it was known that he was vulnerable to psychiatric harm. Latham LJ considered that the claim was not a "nervous shock" case. Rather the real question was "whether or not the relationship between the appellant and the respondent gave rise to a duty of care which encompassed a duty to take reasonable steps to avoid psychiatric harm".[430] His Lordship concluded that, given the relationship between vulnerable prisoner and gaoler, if the pleaded facts were established, it was "inevitable that the duty of care which the appellant owed to the respondent included a duty to take reasonable steps to minimise the risk of psychiatric harm".[431]

7-95 **Psychiatric illness as a result of distressing news** In *AB v Tameside and Glossop HA*,[432] Brooke LJ was prepared to impose liability on a health authority for communicating accurate but distressing information in a careless manner resulting in psychiatric illness to the recipient of the information. The claimants alleged they suffered psychiatric illness as a result of receiving a letter from the authority informing them that they had been treated by someone subsequently discovered to have been HIV positive. They claimed that the authority should have arranged for their general practitioners to tell them face to face and the failure to do this had increased their shock and distress. The Court of Appeal found that the use of the letter was not unreasonable or negligent and, hence, there was no liability on the facts. Again, in *Farrell v Avon HA*,[433] a hospital authority was held to owe a duty to the claimant who suffered psychiatric illness as a result of being told negligently and wrongly by hospital staff that his new born baby had died.

---

427 [2001] EWCA Civ 1743; [2002] Q.B. 1312.

428 See *X (Minors) v Bedfordshire CC* [1995] 2 A.C. 633 at 666. It was claimed that a child had suffered psychiatric damage as a result of the allegedly negligent decision by the defendant psychiatrist that it should be taken from its mother and placed in local authority care. The defendant argued that the claim should fail as Lord Ackner had stated in *Alcock* that recovery for nervous shock had "yet to include psychiatric illness caused by the accumulation over a period of time of more gradual assaults on the nervous system". Bingham MR dismissed this argument saying that: "It would be little short of absurd if the child were held to be disentitled to claim damages for injury of the very type which the psychiatrist should have been exercising care to try and prevent." The claim failed on other grounds (but see now *Poole BC v GN* [2019] UKSC 25; [2019] 2 W.L.R. 1478 at [74] indicating that the correct approach in a case such as *X (Minors) v Bedfordshire CC* is to consider whether the defendant is alleged to have harmed the claimant, or one in which the defendant is alleged to have failed to provide a benefit to the claimant by protecting him from harm).

429 [2006] EWCA Civ 239; [2006] 1 W.L.R. 1155.

430 [2006] EWCA Civ 239; [2006] 1 W.L.R. 1155 at [17].

431 [2006] EWCA Civ 239; [2006] 1 W.L.R. 1155 at [20].

432 [1997] P.N.L.R. 140; [1997] 8 Med. L.R. 91, though note that counsel for the defendants conceded that a duty of care was owed in this situation. See also *Allin v City and Hackney HA* [1996] 7 Med. L.R. 167, where the defendants were found liable for negligently telling a patient who had just given birth that her baby had died. For full discussion of the Commonwealth authorities, see Mullany and Handford, *Tort Liability for Psychiatric Damage* (1993), pp.183–191.

433 [2001] Lloyd's Rep. Med. 458.

(iv) Distress

Distress A claimant can recover damages for distress resulting from a physical injury to himself caused by the defendant's negligence[434] but not for simple distress suffered through fear of injury to himself. Thus in *Hicks v Chief Constable of Yorkshire Police*[435] Lord Bridge said "those trapped in the crush at Hillsborough who were fortunate enough to escape without injury have no claim in respect of the distress they suffered in what must have been a truly terrifying experience". Nor can a person recover for distress suffered as the result of injury to someone else caused by the defendant's negligence.[436] Thus in *Kralj v McGrath*[437] where the negligence of the defendant obstetrician resulted in the claimant suffering great pain and losing her baby shortly after birth, Woolf J awarded damages for distress but said: "I emphasise that in considering what is the appropriate figure to award to Mrs Kralj I will look at the consequences to her of what was done and not award any damages merely for the fact that, like any mother, she naturally suffered grief as a result of the death of Daniel (the baby)."[438] Similarly, in *RK and MK v Oldham NHS Trust*,[439] Simon J dismissed a claim by parents for emotional distress suffered as a result of their child being taken into care on the basis of the defendant's allegedly negligent diagnosis of child abuse, saying that: "In English Law no damages are awarded unless either there is physical harm or there is a recognisable psychiatric disorder … . Emotional responses to unpleasant experiences of even the most serious type do not found a claim for damages." Again, in *Hamilton-Jones v David & Snape (A Firm)*,[440] Neuberger J considered that such damages would be irrecoverable in tort albeit in the context of distress at the loss of society of one's children. The principle was affirmed by the House of Lords *Wainwright v Home Office*[441] where the issue left undecided was whether the same policy considerations precluded recovery for distress where the defendant's conduct was intentional rather 7-96

---

434 Under the heading of "Pain and Suffering". See further para.27-56.

435 [1992] 2 All E.R. 65; [1992] P.I.Q.R. P433. The House of Lords rejected claims in respect of the fear of impending death suffered by victims of the Hillsborough stadium disaster. See also *Reilly and Reilly v Merseyside RHA* [1995] 6 Med. L.R. 246 CA, in which it was held by the Court of Appeal that the claimants who had suffered panic and worry when trapped in a hospital lift for 20 minutes, could not recover because there was no evidence of psychiatric damage or physical injury to them. Mann LJ cited *Hicks* and stated that fear was a normal human emotion for which there was no recovery.

436 *Hinz v Berry* [1970] 2 Q.B. 40. Per Lord Wilberforce in *McLoughlin v O'Brian* [1983] 1 A.C. 410, 418: "Damages cannot at common law, be awarded for grief or sorrow". See also *Kirkham v Boughey* [1958] 2 Q.B. 338, where a husband, whose wife had been severely injured in a road accident as a result of the defendant's negligence, failed to recover damages for a reduction in his earnings due to his having, because of anxiety for his wife, declined to resume more remunerative employment abroad.

437 [1986] 1 All E.R. 54.

438 [1986] 1 All E.R. 54 at 62. See also *Buckley v Farrow & Buckley* [1997] P.I.Q.R. Q78 CA, where Simon Brown LJ stated that it was "plain beyond argument that an infant child, deprived of his mother's care as a result of her being tortiously injured, cannot recover damages against the tortfeasor". The mother may recover for her loss of ability to provide the care: *Lowe v Guise* [2002] EWCA Civ 197; [2002] Q.B. 1369. In the case of a death the Fatal Accidents Act 1976 s.1A provides for a fixed sum as damages for bereavement to the surviving spouse or to the parents of an unmarried minor child. See further para.27-93.

439 [2003] Lloyd's Rep. Med. 1. However, the European Court of Human Rights found that there had been a breach of the parent's art.8 rights on the particular facts: *MAK v United Kingdom* (45901/05) [2010] 2 F.L.R. 451; (2010) 51 E.H.R.R. 14.

440 [2003] EWHC 3147 (Ch); [2004] 1 W.L.R. 924.

441 [2003] UKHL 53; [2004] 2 A.C. 406.

than merely negligent. Aside from the possibility of recovery for distress where the conduct is intentional, it is clear that there may be recovery in contract where the purpose of the contract is to protect the claimant from distress.[442] The only possibility of recovery under the tort of negligence would be where the purpose of the duty was to prevent the kind of distress which occurred.

7-97 **Disease anxiety** A claimant can recover for anxiety caused by a physical condition for which the defendant's negligence is responsible. In *Gregg v Scott*[443] members of the House of Lords whilst holding that the claimant could not recover for the reduction in his chance of recovery from cancer caused by the defendant's negligent failure to diagnose, did suggest that he could recover for the anguish of knowing that the disease could have been detected earlier.[444] However, where the negligence has not caused any physical damage, anxiety attributable to the knowledge that there is risk that the claimant may develop a physical condition in the future is not actionable. In *Rothwell v Chemical & Insulating Co*[445] the House of Lords rejected claims against a negligent employer by six employees who developed anxiety as a result of developing pleural plaques following exposure to asbestos, and one employee who had developed a depressive illness as a result of his anxiety. Pleural plaques involve physiological change to the lungs but they are symptomless, and represent a "marker" that the individual has been exposed to asbestos. Exposure to asbestos gives rise to a risk that the individual may develop asbestosis or mesothelioma (a terminal cancer) in the future, but pleural plaques produce no symptoms affecting an individual's health. Their Lordships held that the symptomless plaques were not compensatable damage[446] and could not become damage by aggregation with the risk which they evidenced or the anxiety which that risk caused. Their Lordships also rejected the claim of the employee who had developed a psychiatric illness on the ground that it was not reasonably foreseeable that the creation of a risk of an asbestos related disease would cause psychiatric illness to a person of reasonable fortitude.[447] They distinguished *CJD Litigation:*

---

[442] See *Farley v Skinner* [2001] UKHL 49; [2002] 2 A.C. 732: recovery against a surveyor for negligent failing to inform a client of the likelihood of disturbance by aircraft noise. The client was distressed as a result of the noise. See Jones and Morris "The Distressing Effects of Professional Incompetence" (2004) 20 P.N. 118.

[443] [2005] UKHL 2; [2005] 2 A.C. 176. See further para.2-89.

[444] Baroness Hale at [206]; Lord Phillips at [191]; Lord Hope (who would have allowed recovery for the lost chance as well) at [123].

[445] [2007] UKHL 39; [2008] 1 A.C. 281; Leczykiewicz (2008) 124 L.Q.R. 548.

[446] The Scottish Parliament has legislated to reverse the effect of *Rothwell* in Scotland, providing that asbestos-related pleural plaques are personal injury which is not negligible and so constitute actionable harm for the purposes of a personal injuries claim (see the Damages (Asbestos-Related Conditions) (Scotland) Act 2009 (2009 ASP 4)). In *AXA General Insurance Ltd v HM Advocate* [2011] UKSC 46; [2012] 1 A.C. 868 the Supreme Court held that the 2009 Act was not beyond the competence of the Scottish Parliament, nor was it subject to judicial review on the grounds of unreasonableness, irrationality and arbitrariness. The position is the same in Northern Ireland. See the Damages (Asbestos-related Conditions) Act (Northern Ireland) 2011; and *McCauley v Harland and Wolff Plc* [2015] NICA 28; [2016] N.I. 254.

[447] Distinguishing *Page v Smith* [1996] A.C. 155, where the claimant, having been exposed to the risk of foreseeable physical harm which did not eventuate was held to be entitled to damages for unforeseeable psychiatric harm which did eventuate. The difference was said to be that in *Page* the claimant's psychiatric condition was characterised as a reaction to an immediate or sudden, alarming event, whereas in *Rothwell* the employee's psychiatric illness had been caused by apprehension that the event may occur *in the future*. Since the creation of such a risk was not in itself actionable,

Group B Plaintiffs v Medical Research Council[448] where damages were awarded to claimants who had developed a recognised psychiatric condition (not merely anxiety) from contemplating the risk that they would develop a fatal medical condition in the future as a result of the defendants' negligence on the basis that in that case there was a clear finding that the psychiatric harm was foreseeable (and had actually been foreseen by the defendants).

(g) Unwanted childbirth and loss of autonomy

No duty in respect of cost of unwanted child In *McFarlane v Tayside Health Board*[449] the House of Lords held that where medical negligence resulted in an unwanted pregnancy and birth of a healthy child, the mother was entitled to recover damages for the pain and distress suffered during pregnancy and birth and for the financial loss associated with the pregnancy but the parents were not entitled to recover damages for the cost of rearing the child. For a number of reasons, the Lords concluded that it would not be fair, just and reasonable to impose a duty in relation to such economic loss. Lords Steyn and Clyde both considered that to award compensation for the high cost of upbringing would be disproportionate to the nature of the wrongdoing. Lord Millett reflected the views of several members of the House when he said that: 7-98

> "the law must take the birth of a normal healthy baby to be a blessing not a detriment. In truth it is a mixed blessing … [b]ut society itself must regard the balance as beneficial. It would be repugnant to its own sense of values to do otherwise. It is morally offensive to regard a normal, healthy baby as more trouble and expense than it is worth."[450]

Claims in respect of a disabled child In *Parkinson v St James and Seacroft University Hospital NHS Trust*[451] a surgeon for whom the defendant was responsible, negligently performed a sterilisation with the result that the patient became pregnant again. The child was born with an autistic disorder. Following *McFarlane*, the Court of Appeal held that the parents could not recover the normal costs of bringing up the child but by a majority held that the additional costs attributable to the disability could be recovered. Giving the leading judgment, Hale LJ justified recovery of the additional costs on the ground that whilst there was a rough equilibrium of cost and benefit[452] in the case of a healthy but unwanted child, this was not the case with a disabled child. In *Rees v Darlington Memorial* 7-99

---

it would be an unwarranted extension of the principle in *Page v Smith* to apply it to psychiatric illness caused by apprehension of the possibility of an unfavourable event which had not actually happened.

448 [2000] Lloyd's Rep. Med. 161.

449 [2000] 2 A.C. 59.

450 [2000] 2 A.C. 59 at 114. Lord Slynn said, at 76, that if a client wanted to be able to recover the costs of raising a healthy child he or she must do so "by an appropriate contract"; but in *Rees v Darlington Memorial Hospital NHS Trust* [2003] UKHL 52; [2004] 1 A.C. 309 at [133] Lord Scott considered that the "same result must be reached whether the claimant was a private patient or an NHS patient", i.e. whether the claim was brought in contract or tort. In *ARB v IVF Hammersmith Ltd* [2018] EWCA Civ 2803; [2020] Q.B. 93 the Court of Appeal confirmed that whether the action was based in tort or on breach of a strict contractual obligation, the same policy objections to awarding compensation for the costs of raising a healthy child applied.

451 [2001] EWCA Civ 530; [2002] Q.B. 266.

452 As from the pleasure of a child's company, pride in his achievements, the hope of reciprocity of family feelings and the passing on of one's genes. However, this attempt to explain *McFarlane* as a case of a "deemed equilibrium" where the burdens of parenthood were deemed to be cancelled out by

Hospital[453] the claimant was a woman with very poor eyesight who had been advised to have a sterilisation to avoid the possibility of having a child as she would only be able to look after it by purchasing extra help. The defendant was responsible for the negligent failure of the sterilisation and the birth of the healthy, unwanted child. The claimant sued for the extra expense in bringing up the child caused by her own disability. In the House of Lords, three Law Lords would have allowed the claim but the majority of four Law Lords rejected the claim as contrary to the principle established in *McFarlane* in respect of a healthy child. *Parkinson* was not overruled, though some doubt was cast on its status.[454] Lord Scott, while expressly leaving the question of the correctness of *Parkinson* open, commented that: "a distinction may need to be drawn between a case where the avoidance of the birth of a child with a disability is the very reason why the parents sought medical treatment to avoid contraception and a case where the medical treatment was sought simply to avoid contraception."[455] His Lordship did not address the question of what the position might be if the parent(s) had mixed motives for seeking to avoid the birth of a child, which is probably not an uncommon situation particularly with an older mother where the risk of foetal disability is significantly increased. Lord Millett, on the other hand, refused to "distinguish between the various motives which the parties might have for desiring to avoid a pregnancy".[456]

7-100 In *Farraj v King's Healthcare NHS Trust*,[457] on a preliminary issue, Swift J applied the *Caparo* three stage test to hold that a private laboratory which had cultured foetal cells for DNA analysis by King's, owed a duty of care to the claimants who had retained King's to screen for a severe hereditary blood disease. Relying on the culture, King's subsequently informed the claimants that their foetus did not have the disease. The claimants brought an action for damages when it was discovered that the child had the disease. Swift J noted that *Rees* had "cast considerable doubt" on the decision in *Parkinson*, but concluded that "for the present, the decision in *Parkinson* represents the law".[458]

7-101 **Claim for loss of parents' autonomy** Although the majority in *Rees* applied *McFarlane* and rejected the claim for the disability costs, they did award the parents a conventional sum of £15,000 for "denial of an important aspect of [her] personal autonomy, viz the right to limit the size of [her] family".[459] According to Lord Millett, this sum is to be awarded "without proof of financial loss" and will not be

---

the benefits was said to be wrong in *Rees v Darlington Memorial Hospital* [2003] UKHL 52; [2004] 1 A.C. 309 at [28], per Lord Steyn; [59], per Lord Hope; [94], per Lord Hutton; and [111], per Lord Millett.

453 [2003] UKHL 52; [2004] 1 A.C. 309. See further para.9-97.

454 Lords Steyn, Hope and Hutton (at [35], [57] and [91] respectively) considered that the decision in *Parkinson* was correct. Lord Bingham doubted whether it was correct (at [9]). Lord Nicholls did not expressly refer to *Parkinson*, but the implication of his speech is that it is wrong (at [18]). Lord Millett expressly left the correctness of *Parkinson* open (at [112]).

455 [2003] UKHL 52; [2004] 1 A.C. 309 at [145]. In *Rees* the surgeon knew that the sterilisation was wanted in order to avoid the costs associated with the woman's disability. The line between surgery to avoid the costs associated with a disabled child and to avoid the costs associated with parental disability, is hard to draw.

456 [2003] UKHL 52; [2004] 1 A.C. 309 at [112].

457 [2006] EWHC 1228 (QB); [2006] P.I.Q.R. P29.

458 [2006] EWHC 1228 (QB); [2006] P.I.Q.R. P29 at [39]. Subsequently, the Court of Appeal held that though the laboratory had been in breach of duty, the hospital had not: *Farraj v King's Healthcare NHS Trust* [2009] EWCA Civ 1203; [2010] 1 W.L.R. 2139.

459 Lord Millett's explanation at [2003] UKHL 52; [2004] 1 A.C. 309 at [123]. Lord Millett had been

"susceptible of increase or decrease by reference to the circumstances of the particular case".[460] The House of Lords in *McFarlane* had not taken up a similar suggestion and for that reason the minority Law Lords in *Rees* considered the autonomy award to be contrary to the policy in *McFarlane* and an example of creativity on a controversial issue which should have been left to the legislature. Despite these misgivings, it is clear that the loss of autonomy claim can be brought in any case where negligence has led to the birth of an unwanted child, whether healthy or disabled.

Loss of autonomy claims In *Rees* Lord Millett described autonomy as "an important aspect of human dignity which is increasingly being regarded as an important human right which should be protected by law".[461] There may be other situations where the purpose of a duty of care could be seen as the protection of the claimant's autonomy. For example, the doctor's duty of care to warn a patient of risks associated with a treatment has as its purpose the protection of the patient's right to choose. In *Chester v Afshar*[462] Lord Steyn justified providing a remedy for a doctor's failure to warn on the basis of the need to give "due respect to the autonomy and dignity of each patient".[463] In *Chester* the majority of the House of Lords gave effect to the patient's right to autonomy by adopting a somewhat controversial approach to causation to enable the patient to claim compensation for the physical damage resulting from the risk of which she was not warned.[464] An alternative approach would have been recognition of the importance of the right to autonomy with a conventional award along the lines of that given in *Rees*.[465] However, in *Shaw v Kovac*[466] the Court of Appeal held that there is no free-standing cause of action for interference with a claimant's autonomy. An action by a patient against a doctor for non-disclosure of the risks of treatment will be an action in negligence, which requires proof of damage over and above an interference with autonomy per se.[467] 7-102

in the minority in *McFarlane* in suggesting such an award.

460 [2003] UKHL 52; [2004] 1 A.C. 309 at [125].

461 [2003] UKHL 52; [2004] 1 A.C. 309 at [123].

462 [2004] UKHL 41; [2005] 1 A.C. 134.

463 [2004] UKHL 41; [2005] 1 A.C. 134 at [18]. He quoted Dworkin's explanation in *Life's Dominion* (1993), p.224:

> "The value of autonomy derives from the capacity it protects: the capacity to express one's own character—values, commitments, convictions, and critical as well as experiential interests—in the life one leads. Recognising an individual right of autonomy makes self-creation possible. It allows each of us to be responsible for the shaping of our lives according to our own coherent or incoherent—but in any case, distinctive—personality. It allows us to lead our own lives rather than being led along them."

464 See para.2-16 onwards for a full analysis of the causation argument in *Chester*.

465 Dissenting in *Chester* [2004] UKHL 41; [2005] 1 A.C. 134, Lord Hoffmann mooted the idea of "a modest solatium" (at [34]) and Lord Bingham pointed to the problem of "reinforcing the right by providing for the payment of potentially very large damages" as compensation for the unwarned risk (at [9]). Lord Steyn, giving the leading majority speech, was perhaps unlikely to have argued for a conventional solatium because in *Rees* he had described such a conventional award as "contrary to principle" and a matter for Parliament and the Law Commissions to consider: [2003] UKHL 52; [2004] 1 A.C. 309 at [46]. See para.1-39.

466 [2017] EWCA Civ 1028; [2017] 1 W.L.R. 4773 at [48].

467 See paras 7-199 and 7-200.

(h) Financial loss resulting from reliance or dependence

7-103 One person's negligent conduct may cause financial loss to another unrelated to any physical damage where that other is dependent upon that person's services for his financial well being or relies on that person's statements when making financial decisions. Such a loss is referred to as a "pure" financial or economic loss as it is not the consequence of physical damage to the person's body or property. Three features distinguish such loss from loss resulting from physical damage. First, whilst the links between negligence and physical damage depend largely on the laws of nature and necessarily limit the type of relationship giving rise to a claim, those between negligence and pure financial loss are primarily human in creation and can form a complex web through which financial losses can ripple out from the one negligent act. Secondly, because the economic relationships are frequently created rather than imposed, the participants in the web have a greater opportunity to use contracts[468] to determine the level of risk to be taken and the degree of protection from loss required. Furthermore, in some situations legislation provides a framework for relationships in which risk, protection and responsibility are already balanced. Thirdly, as Hobhouse LJ has observed, "in a competitive economic society the conduct of one person is always liable to have economic consequences for another and, in principle, economic activity does not have to have regard to the interests of others and is justifiable by the actor having regard to his own interests alone".[469] Furthermore, as McHugh J has noted, "pure economic losses frequently result in mere transfers of wealth. The claimant's loss is the defendant's or a third party's gain [whereas] harm to a person or property ordinarily involves a new loss to social wealth".[470] These features have led the courts to take a more restrictive approach to the imposition of a duty of care in relation to pure financial loss than in relation to physical damage. A special relationship between the parties is required to justify a duty. The starting point for any analysis of the required relationship is the decision of the House of Lords in *Hedley Byrne & Co Ltd v Heller & Partners Ltd*.[471]

(i) The need for a special relationship

7-104 **Hedley Byrne** The decision of the House of Lords in *Hedley Byrne* established that a person who made a negligent statement could owe a duty of care to a person who suffered financial loss through reliance upon the statement. The claimants were advertising agents who were placing contracts on behalf of a client on terms that they, the claimants, were to be personally liable should the client default. In order to safeguard themselves the claimants, acting through their bankers, obtained a credit reference from defendants who were the client's bankers. The reference was given without charge and was favourable, although it was stated to be given "without responsibility". The claimants relied on this reply, which was mislead-

---

468 In *Miller v United States Steel Corp* (1990) 902 F.2d 573 at 574, Posner J, speaking of the term "economic loss", said: "It would be better to call it 'commercial loss', not only because personal injuries are economic losses too … but also and more important, because tort law is a superfluous and inapt tool for resolving such purely commercial disputes. We have a body of law designed for such disputes. It is called contract law." McHugh and Gummow JJ in *Perre v Apand Pty Ltd* (1999) 164 A.L.R. 606, both cited this dictum with approval.

469 *Perrett v Collins* [1999] P.N.L.R. 77 at 84. *Perre v Apand Pty Ltd* (1999) 164 A.L.R. 606.

470 *Perre v Apand Pty Ltd* (1999) 164 A.L.R. 606 at 623.

471 [1964] A.C. 465.

ing, and suffered loss as a result when the client became insolvent. The House of Lords held that the defendants would have owed a duty of care had they not included a clear indication in their reply that they were not undertaking any duty of care. On the question when such a duty of care would be owed, the House of Lords said that this would be so whenever there was a "special relationship" between claimant and defendant.

Extension of the principle The *Hedley Byrne* principle was extended to omissions by *Midland Bank Trust Co Ltd v Hett, Stubbs and Kemp*[472] in which Oliver J held that a solicitor's failure to protect an option by registering it could be actionable by the client in tort on the basis of the *Hedley Byrne* principle. In *Henderson v Merrett Syndicates Ltd*[473] Lord Goff approved *Midland Bank* and extended the principle to cases of negligent performance of a service. Agents who had managed the affairs of Lloyd's Names were held to owe a duty of care to such persons in relation to economic losses whether or not they had been in a direct contractual relationship with them. Lord Goff referred to the speeches of Lords Devlin and Morris in *Hedley Byrne*, saying that they "show that the principle extends beyond the provision of information and advice to include the performance of other services".[474] The Court of Appeal followed this reasoning in *Barclays Bank Plc v Fairclough Building Ltd*[475] when it held that a subcontractor, responsible for the negligent cleaning of a roof, owed a duty of care in tort not to cause economic loss to its immediate employer, another subcontractor in the contractual chain. Although the *Hedley Byrne* decision was concerned with negligent misstatements, it is now clear that its principle governs all situations in which financial loss has been caused by reliance or dependence on another's negligent conduct. 7-105

Special relationship In *Hedley Byrne* Lord Reid explained that the familiar *Donoghue v Stevenson* test for duty of care was not an adequate control where the loss resulted from negligent words rather than acts because words could be spread and thereby have a wider impact.[476] All the Law Lords agreed that a duty in this context could only be imposed if there was a special relationship between the parties but they explained the nature of that relationship in differing terms. Lord Reid stated it would arise where: 7-106

> "the party seeking the information and advice was trusting the other to exercise such a degree of care as the circumstances required, where it was reasonable for him to do that and where the other gave the information or advice when he knew or ought to have known that the inquirer was relying on him."[477]

Lord Morris gave a more consensual emphasis, suggesting that the giver of the information must "undertake to apply his skill for the benefit of the claimant".[478] Lord Devlin focused on assumption of responsibility, saying:

> "... the categories of special relationships, which may give rise to a duty to take care ...

---

472 [1979] Ch. 384.

473 [1995] 2 A.C. 145.

474 [1995] 2 A.C. 145 at 180.

475 (1995) 76 B.L.R. 1.

476 The House of Lords seemed more concerned about the fact that the loss was caused by words than by the fact that the loss was financial in nature. See further Stapleton (1991) 107 L.Q.R. 249.

477 [1964] A.C. 465 at 534.

478 [1964] A.C. 465 at 502.

are not limited to contractual relationships or to relationships of fiduciary duty, but also include relationships which … are 'equivalent to contract' that is, where there is an assumption of responsibility in circumstances in which, but for the absence of consideration, there would be a contract."[479]

7-107 **Assumption of responsibility** In *Henderson v Merrett Syndicates Ltd*[480] Lord Goff identified the governing principle of *Hedley Byrne* as being assumption of responsibility by the defendant along with reliance by the claimant. He said (at 180) that from the speeches in *Hedley Byrne*:

"we can derive some understanding of the breadth of the principle underlying the case. We can see that it rests upon a relationship between the parties, which may be general or specific to the particular transaction, and which may or may not be contractual in nature. All of their Lordships spoke in terms of one party having assumed or undertaken a responsibility towards the other. On this point, Lord Devlin spoke in particularly clear terms … Further, Lord Morris spoke of that party being possessed of a 'special skill' which he undertakes 'to apply for the assistance of another who relies upon such skill'."

Lord Goff noted that the concept of assumption of responsibility:

"provides its own explanation why there is no problem in cases of this kind about liability for pure economic loss; for if a person assumes responsibility to another in respect of certain services, there is no reason why he should not be liable in damages in respect of economic loss which flows from the negligent performance of those services."[481]

In *Williams v Natural Life Health Foods Ltd*,[482] Lord Steyn said that "there was no better rationalisation for the relevant head of tort liability than assumption of responsibility [because] the backcloth against which the *Hedley Byrne* case was decided" was that of "the restricted conception of contract in English law, resulting from the combined effect of the principles of consideration and privity of contract" which meant that "the law of tort, as the general law, has to fulfil an essentially gap-filling role". The facts that support an assumption of responsibility and tort liability in English law would often support contractual liability in other European law systems. Again, in *Smith v Bush*,[483] Lords Templeman and Jauncey identified the assumption of responsibility by the defendant to the claimant as the criterion for determining whether such a relationship existed. In *Smith* the claimant sued a firm of surveyors in respect of a negligent house valuation report which the firm had prepared on the instructions of the building society which was proposing to grant a mortgage to the claimant to finance her purchase of the house. The claimant had paid a valuation fee to the building society and was provided with a

---

479 [1964] A.C. 465 at 528.

480 [1995] 2 A.C. 145. He cited the speech of Lord Devlin and that of Lord Morris where he said "it should now be regarded as settled that if someone possessed of a special skill undertakes to apply that skill for the assistance of another person who relies on such skill, a duty of care will arise", but noted that: "All their Lordships spoke in terms of one party having assumed or undertaken a responsibility towards the other." See also Lord Goff's speech in *Spring v Guardian Assurance Plc* [1995] 2 A.C. 296, where he stated that: "All the members of the Appellate Committee in [*Hedley Byrne*] spoke in terms of the principle resting upon an assumption or undertaking of responsibility by the defendant towards the [claimant], coupled with a reliance by the [claimant] on the exercise by the defendant of due care and skill." As *Hedley Byrne* had not been argued by counsel as a basis of liability in *Spring*, Lord Goff conceded that his analysis in that case was of "limited authority".

481 [1995] 2 A.C. 145 at 181.

482 [1998] 1 W.L.R. 830 at 837.

483 [1990] 1 A.C. 831.

copy of the report by the society. Relying on the report, she purchased the house and subsequently discovered that because the report had not identified a defect in the house she was put to extra expense. The surveyor was held to owe the purchaser a duty of care. After citing Lord Devlin's reference to assumption of responsibility, Lord Templeman concluded that:

> "the relationship between the valuer and the purchaser is 'akin to contract'. The valuer knows that the consideration which he receives derives from the purchaser and is passed on by the mortgagee, and the valuer knows that the valuation will determine whether or not the purchaser buys the house."[484]

Objective test of assumption of responsibility In *Hedley Byrne* Lord Devlin referred to the necessary assumption of responsibility as not being imposed by the law but undertaken voluntarily.[485] However, in *Henderson*[486] Lord Goff said that "an objective test will be applied when asking the question whether responsibility should be held to have been assumed by the defendant to the claimant". Lord Steyn amplified the point in *Williams v Natural Life Foods Ltd*[487] saying: 7-108

> "The touchstone of liability is not the state of mind of the defendant. An objective test means that the primary focus must be on things said or done by the defendant or on his behalf in his dealings with the claimant. Obviously, the impact of what the defendant says or does must be judged in the light of the relevant contextual scene. Subject to this qualification, the primary focus must be on exchanges … which cross the line between the defendant and the [claimant]."

In *Electra Private Equity Partners v KPMG Peat Marwick*[488] the Court of Appeal, applying Lord Steyn's dictum, reversed the decision of Carnwath J to strike out an action against the defendants precisely because the judge had imposed too stringent a test when requiring evidence of *conscious* assumption of responsibility by the defendants. In *Commissioners of Customs & Excise v Barclays Bank*[489] Lord Bingham agreed that "the assumption of responsibility test is to be applied objectively … and is not answered by consideration of what the defendant thought or intended". But as Lord Bingham noted, this creates a problem, in that:

> "the further this test is removed from the actions and intentions of the actual defendant, and the more notional the assumption of responsibility becomes, the less difference there is between this test and the threefold test."[490]

On the other hand, in *White v Jones*[491] Lord Browne-Wilkinson explained that the concept required the defendant to assume responsibility for performing the task but not for legal liability to the claimant: "If the responsibility for the task is assumed by the defendant he thereby creates a special relationship between himself and the

---

484 [1990] 1 A.C. 831 at 846.

485 [1964] A.C. 465 at 529.

486 [1995] 2 A.C. 145 at 181.

487 [1998] 1 W.L.R. 830 at 835.

488 [1999] Lloyd's Rep. P.N. 670.

489 [2006] UKHL 28; [2007] 1 A.C. 181 at [5], citing Lord Slynn's statement in *Phelps v Hillingdon LBC* [2001] 2 A.C. 619 at 654 that assumption of responsibility "means simply that the law recognises that there is a duty of care. It is not so much that responsibility is assumed as that it is recognised or imposed by the law".

490 [2006] UKHL 28; [2007] 1 A.C. 181.

491 [1995] 2 A.C. 207 at 273.

[claimant] in relation to which the law (not the defendant) attaches a duty to carry out carefully the task so assumed."[492] The usefulness of terms such as "assumption of responsibility" is open to question. As Lord Hoffmann explained in *Commissioners of Customs & Excise v Barclays Bank*:

> "There is a tendency, which has been remarked upon by many judges, for phrases like 'proximate', 'fair, just and reasonable' and 'assumption of responsibility' to be used as slogans rather than practical guides to whether a duty should exist or not. These phrases are often illuminating but discrimination is needed to identify the factual situations in which they provide useful guidance."[493]

7-109 **Three stage test**[494] The three stage test of foreseeability, proximity, and fairness, justice and reasonableness introduced by the House of Lords in *Caparo Industries v Dickman*[495] provided a more sophisticated test for duty than its *Donoghue* precursor and was used in *Caparo* to reject the argument that an auditor owed a duty of care to a shareholder who relied on the audit report when making a further investment and suffered loss when it transpired that the audit report had negligently endorsed an overvaluation of the company. Lord Bridge stated that, assuming there was sufficient proximity between the auditor and the shareholder, the scope of the auditor's duty could not extend to investment decisions taken by shareholders or others. Lord Oliver similarly considered that it would not be reasonable to extend the auditor's duty in such a way because the purpose of the audit report was to provide "those entitled to receive the report with information to enable them to exercise those powers which their respective proprietary interests confer on them [e.g. to vote at company meetings] and not for the purposes of individual speculation with a view to profit". Both Law Lords criticised the assumption of responsibility test as not helping identify the key factors in a case.[496] Other judges in the 1990s took a similar view and it could be said that the "fairness and justice" limb of the three stage approach gave courts a more direct opportunity to focus on the policy issues. Thus, in the 1994 House of Lords decision in *Spring v Guardian Assurance Plc*[497] where the majority of the Lords held that an employer owed a duty of care to an ex-employee when preparing an employment reference and could be liable for economic loss suffered as a result of his failure to secure employment because of a negligently inaccurate reference, Lords Woolf and Slynn cited the policies of increasing openness in the employment relationship and the importance of protecting an individual's right to earn his livelihood whilst in dissent Lord Keith

---

492 He commented that some of the judicial criticism of the concept (for which see para.7-109) as unhelpful would not have been made if the words had been understood as referring to an assumption or responsibility for the task rather than of legal liability to the claimant for its careful performance. However, query what it means to say that the defendant "assumed responsibility for the task". Presumably, a motorist "assumes responsibility" for the task driving a motor car by getting into it and driving, but that is not why he owes a duty of care to other road users. All competent "actors" assume responsibility in some sense for their actions by "acting", but this says nothing about the circumstances in which they will be held to owe a duty of care.

493 [2006] UKHL 28; [2007] 1 A.C. 181 at [35].

494 See para.7-17 above.

495 [1990] 2 A.C. 605.

496 [1990] 2 A.C. 605 at 637, per Lord Oliver: "It tells us nothing about the circumstances from which such attribution arises." See Lord Bridge at 623.

497 [1995] 2 A.C. 296.

considered that a duty would undermine the defence of qualified privilege applicable in defamation and inhibit the giving of full and fair references.[498]

Multi-test approach Both the tests of assumption of responsibility and proximity and fairness have their strengths. Assumption of responsibility points to the analogy with contract and fairness allows broader policy factors to be considered. Rather than regarding the tests as rivals, the most helpful approach may be that taken by Sir Brian Neill in *BCCI (Overseas) Ltd v Price Waterhouse (No.2)*.[499] After explaining that "the search for a principle or test has followed three separate but parallel paths" (the threefold test stated by Lord Griffiths in *Smith v Bush*; the assumption of responsibility test; and the incremental approach recognised by Lord Bridge in *Caparo*), he commented that: 7-110

> "The fact that all these approaches have been used and approved by the House of Lords in recent years suggests:
>
> (a) that it may be useful to look at any new set of facts by using each of the three approaches in turn …
>
> (b) that if the facts are properly analysed and the policy considerations correctly evaluated the several approaches will yield the same result."

This analysis sees the different approaches as mutually supportive rather than exclusive in their application.[500] Each may be used to check the provisional conclusion reached by application of the other approaches.

The House of Lords applied this multi-test approach in *Commissioners of Customs and Excise v Barclays Bank Plc*.[501] The claimant had obtained a freezing injunction in respect of accounts held by a debtor at the defendant bank. It argued that the defendant owed it a duty of care not to allow payments out of those accounts. The House of Lords held that no duty of care in respect of the freezing order was owed by the bank to the Commissioners. There was no assumption of responsibility because the bank had no choice but to comply with the order[502] and an assumption is normally generated by "something which the defendant has 7-111

498 An example of the range of policy arguments that may be considered relevant in an economic loss case is provided by the judgment of McHugh J in the High Court of Australia decision in *Esanda Finance Corp v Peat Marwick Hungerfords* (1997) 142 A.L.R. 750; [2000] Lloyd's Rep. P.N. 684. He justified holding that auditors owed no duty of care to creditors relying on the audit report on a number of policy grounds including fear that wider liability would reduce the supply of auditing services because the insurance cost would reduce the number of firms offering services and the quality of such services would be reduced because of cost cutting measures necessary to meet the insurance bill.

499 [1998] P.N.L.R. 564 at 583.

500 For examples of this cross-checking approach, see Owen J in *Heritage Joinery v Krasner* [1999] P.N.L.R. 906 at 917; *McFarlane v Tayside Health Board* [2000] 2 A.C. 59 at 83, where Lord Slynn considered the nature of the assumption of responsibility by the defendant when coming to the conclusion that it would not be fair, just and reasonable for him to bear the economic losses claimed; *HSBC Bank Plc v 5th Avenue Partners Ltd* [2009] EWCA Civ 296; [2009] 1 C.L.C. 503; *Playboy Club London Ltd v Banca Nazionale Del Lavoro SpA* [2016] EWCA Civ 457; [2016] 1 W.L.R. 3169 at [17] (affirmed on appeal: [2018] UKSC 43; [2018] 1 W.L.R. 4041; see para.7-113); and *Seddon v Driver and Vehicle Licensing Agency* [2019] EWCA Civ 14; [2019] 1 W.L.R. 4593 at [56]–[87] (no duty of care owed to prospective purchaser of a motor vehicle by the DVLA as to the accuracy of the information contained in the vehicle registration document).

501 [2006] UKHL 28; [2007] 1 A.C. 181; Gee (2006) 122 L.Q.R. 535.

502 [2006] UKHL 28; [2007] 1 A.C. 181 at [14], per Lord Bingham.

decided to do".[503] Furthermore, in Lord Bingham's view, the claim failed the policy/fairness stage of the threefold test. He gave[504] a number of grounds for reaching this conclusion: the freezing order regime made sense on the basis that the only duty owed by the bank was to the court; it would be anomalous if an action in negligence lay against the bank "who had allowed the horse to escape from the stable" but not against the target of the order, the opposing litigant "the owner who rode it out"; imposing a duty would be a radical innovation with implications, e.g. in the case of a witness summons where economic loss was a foreseeable consequence of breach; the bank's potential exposure which it would have no opportunity to resist, might be for a few millions as here or very much more. Lord Hoffmann drew attention to the fact that the claim sought to impose liability for an omission and argued that just as a common law duty of care to act cannot be derived from a statutory duty, "[l]ikewise, you cannot derive one from an order of the court".[505] Lord Mance said that it was:

> "difficult in any meaningful sense to speak of the bank as having voluntarily assumed responsibility even for the task in relation to which it was allegedly negligent, let alone responsibility towards the Commissioners for the task. In a very general sense any bank, indeed anyone carrying on any activity during the course of which they might have cause to hold the monies or possessions of another, might be said to accept the risk that a third party might obtain a freezing order in respect of such monies or possessions. But that is to assign to the concept of voluntary assumption of responsibility so wide a meaning as to deprive it of effective utility."[506]

7-112 **Emphasis** What the judgments in *Barclays Bank* illustrate is that the further away the parties are from a relationship akin to contract the less likely it is that the subjective tenor of the assumption of responsibility test will be particularly helpful and the more likely it is that the analysis will commence with a consideration of the threefold test. Thus, in cases of negligent performance of services as opposed to statements and even more so in the case of negligent performance of public services[507] or negligent failure to perform services (as was the case in *Barclays*

---

503 [2006] UKHL 28; [2007] 1 A.C. 181 at [38], per Lord Hoffmann.

504 [2006] UKHL 28; [2007] 1 A.C. 181 at [17]–[21].

505 [2006] UKHL 28; [2007] 1 A.C. 181 at [39]; citing *Gorringe v Calderdale MBC* [2004] UKHL 15; [2004] 1 W.L.R. 1057. See also *St John Poulton's Trustee in Bankruptcy v Ministry of Justice* [2010] EWCA Civ 392; [2011] Ch. 1 where it was held that there was no common law duty on a court to send a notice of a bankruptcy petition, with a request that it be registered in the register of pending actions, to the Chief Land Registrar, in breach of the statutory duty imposed by the Insolvency Rules 1986 r.6.13. The defendant's only obligation to do anything at all arose out of the statutory provision, and in the absence of a claim for breach of statutory duty there was no basis for a claim in negligence (applying *Gorringe v Calderdale MBC* [2004] UKHL 15; [2004] 1 W.L.R. 1057; and *Customs and Excise Commissioners v Barclays Bank Plc* [2006] UKHL 28; [2007] 1 A.C. 181). See also *Smeaton v Equifax Plc* [2013] EWCA Civ 108; [2013] 2 All E.R. 959 applying similar reasoning in rejecting an argument for a duty of care to be owed by credit reference agencies to members of the public. Contrast *Sebry v Companies House* [2015] EWHC 115 (QB); [2016] 1 W.L.R. 2499; distinguishing *John Poulton's Trustee in Bankruptcy v Ministry of Justice* on the basis that that case involved a pure omission whereas *Sebry* involved a positive act of entering of false information into the Register of Companies. See para.7-116.

506 [2006] UKHL 28; [2007] 1 A.C. 181; Gee (2006) 122 L.Q.R. 535 at [94].

507 In *Reeman v Department of Transport* [1997] P.N.L.R. 618 at 637, a case concerned with the Department's liability for economic loss flowing from an inaccurate ship's certificate, Peter Gibson LJ doubted that assumption of responsibility was the appropriate approach where there was no situation equivalent to contract.

Bank) the threefold test will predominate, but it may still be helpful to consider whether the defendant can be taken to have assumed a responsibility. Conversely, in a case where the relationship of the parties is akin to contract, the assumption of responsibility approach may be dominant for the reason suggested by Lord Steyn in *Williams*, namely, that where the tortious duty is being asked to fill the gap left by the contractual doctrines of consideration and privity, it is natural to focus on the bilateral relationship of responsibility and reliance. But this should not preclude the court from checking its conclusion by considering the fairness and justice of the duty or by examining analogous duty situations to ensure that the imposition of a duty would be an incremental rather than a radical step. Under both tests, a court is likely to consider three factors: the purpose of the statement or service; the knowledge of the defendant; and the reasonableness of the reliance or dependence of the claimant.[508] As with the two tests, these factors will often be mutually supportive of a conclusion: the clearer the purpose, the more the knowledge, the more the reliance is likely to be reasonable; and vice versa.

(ii) *Relevant factors*

(1) The purpose of the statement or service

Purpose of statement Where the statement is provided in response to the claimant's request, its purpose may be identified from the nature of the request. In other cases, the purpose may be clear from instructions given to the professional by a third party. Thus in *Hedley Byrne*, where the bank responded to a request to supply information about its customer's creditworthiness, it was clear that the purpose was to enable the person to whom it was directed, i.e. a client of the requesting bank, to advance credit to the customer. But where the existence of the person who will actually rely on the statement is unknown to the defendant, then the defendant will not have the relevant knowledge of the purpose of the transaction, and so will not assume responsibility to that unknown person. In *Banca Nazionale del Lavoro SPA v Playboy Club London Ltd*[509] a bank responded to a request for a credit reference on a customer made by a casino's agent. The bank had **7-113**

---

[508] A more complex and much cited formulation was given by Neill LJ in *James McNaughton Paper Group Ltd v Hicks Anderson & Co* [1991] 2 Q.B. 113 at 125, where he identified six factors:

(1) the purpose for which the statement was made;
(2) the purpose for which the statement was communicated;
(3) the relationship between the adviser, the advisee and any relevant third party;
(4) the size of any class to which the advisee belongs;
(5) the state of knowledge of the adviser;
(6) reliance by the advisee.

Again, in *Reeman v Department of Transport* [1997] P.N.L.R. 618 at 639, Lord Bingham provided another piece of much cited guidance in relation to statements saying that they must be:

> "[claimant]-specific; that is it must be given to the actual [claimant] or a member of an [identifiable] group to which the [claimant] belongs. Secondly, the statement must be purpose-specific: the statement must be made for the very purpose for which the actual [claimant] has used it. Thirdly, the statement must be transaction-specific: the statement must be made with reference to the very transaction into which the [claimant] has entered in reliance upon it."

Both formulations can be adapted for services with the concept of dependence substituted for that of reliance.

[509] [2018] UKSC 43; [2018] 1 W.L.R. 4041.

no knowledge of the casino, an arrangement designed to preserve the confidentiality of the casino's customers. When the casino sued the bank in respect of the negligent reference the Supreme Court held that no duty of care had arisen between bank and casino. Lord Sumption said that it was fundamental to such a duty that the defendant is assuming a responsibility to an identifiable (although not necessarily identified) person or group of persons. The representor "must not only know that the statement is likely to be communicated to and relied upon by [the claimant]. It must also be part of the statement's known purpose that it should be communicated and relied upon by [the claimant], if the representor is to be taken to assume responsibility to [the claimant]."[510] There was no evidence that the bank knew that its reference would be communicated to or relied upon by anyone other than the agent.

7-114 In other cases, the context of the professional's retainer will identify the purpose of the statement. Thus, in *Caparo*[511] the House of Lords held that in its statutory context, the purpose of an audit report was restricted to enabling shareholders to exercise their proprietary interests in the management of the company and did not extend to enabling shareholders or anyone else to make informed investment decisions. It followed that no duty was owed to shareholders or investors suffering investment losses as a result of relying on a negligent audit report. Similarly in the absence of special knowledge, auditors owe a duty neither to creditors who rely on the audit report when advancing credit[512] nor to guarantors relying on the report in deciding whether to continue with a guarantee on behalf of the company.[513] However, where auditors give audit-related advice to directors or shareholders of the client the purpose of that information may be sufficiently clear to give rise to a duty to the recipients.[514] The circumstances of the communication may indicate the purpose. In *Peach Publishing Ltd v Slater & Co*[515] it was held that accountants owed no duty of care to purchasers of their client who had relied on the accountants' statement that the management accounts were "essentially reliable, subject to not having been audited" which was communicated to both them and the client at the acquisition meeting prior to the purchase. The circumstances of the meeting led to the conclusion that the purpose for which the statement was communicated was to indicate to the client that it might give a qualified warranty as to the accounts. The accountants were present at the meeting as adviser to the client and not as an independent expert "on whom those on both sides of the transaction might be

---

510 [2018] UKSC 43; [2018] 1 W.L.R. 4041 at [11]. Lord Mance pointed out, at [25], that had the representation been made, expressly or impliedly, for the benefit of an unnamed (rather than an entirely undisclosed) principal or client of the agent, the case would have paralleled *Hedley Byrne & Co Ltd v Heller & Partners Ltd* and the claim should then have succeeded.

511 [1990] 2 A.C. 605.

512 *Al-Saudi Bank v Clarke Pixley (A Firm)* [1990] Ch. 313; *Esanda Finance Corp v Peat Marwick Hungerfords* (1997) 142 A.L.R. 750; [2000] Lloyd's Rep. P.N. 684. Similarly, an actuary producing a report on a client's pension fund does not owe a duty of care to a third party who relied on that report when purchasing the client even though the actuary was aware that its report had been passed to the third party: *Precis (521) v William Mercer Ltd* [2005] EWCA Civ 114; [2005] P.N.L.R. 28. See also *Man Nutzfahrzeuge AG v Freightliner Ltd* [2007] EWCA Civ 910; [2008] P.N.L.R. 6.

513 *Ikumene v Leong* (1993) 9 P.N. 181.

514 Thus in *Coulthard v Neville Russell* [1998] P.N.L.R. 276, *Siddell v Smith Cooper & Partners* [1999] P.N.L.R. 511, and *The Law Society v KPMG Peat Marwick* [2000] 1 W.L.R. 1921; [2000] P.N.L.R. 831, the Court of Appeal refused to strike out claims brought by directors, shareholders, and the Law Society, respectively. See further paras 9-225 to 9-228.

515 [1998] P.N.L.R. 364.

expected to rely". The purpose may not always be clear as is illustrated by the difference of opinion in relation to the listing particulars and prospectuses issued in connection with the sale of shares or other securities.[516] Where, however, "a company actively invites potential investors to make use of information originally produced for a different purpose, it can hardly complain if they do so".[517]

The purpose of advice or information is significant in other contexts such as surveying and valuing. In *Reeman v Department of Transport*[518] the claimant purchased a fishing boat relying on a seaworthiness certificate issued by the defendant following a survey. The survey was negligently inaccurate. When this was discovered the certificate was revoked and the claimant, being unable to use the boat, suffered economic loss. Citing *Caparo*, the court rejected the claim on the ground that the purpose of the certificate was to promote safety at sea and not to enable purchasers to make sound investments.[519] More difficult is the case of *Beaumont v Humberts*[520] where a house purchaser suffered loss when the insurance taken out in reliance on a valuation proved inadequate to cover the cost of reinstatement following a fire. The majority held that there was a duty but the dissenting judgment holding that the valuer could not reasonably contemplate that his reinstatement valuation would be relied on by the mortgagor when insuring the property seems more in line with the *Caparo* focus on the purpose of a statement. 7-115

Purpose of service The purpose of a service may indicate that the provider assumes a responsibility to those intended to benefit from it. In *Ministry of Housing and Local Government v Sharp*[521] the defendant, who was responsible for the local land charges registry, negligently issued a certificate on a piece of land which failed to specify the charge held over the land by the claimant. A prospective purchaser bought the land in reliance upon the clear certificate and under the provisions of the registration scheme, this meant that the claimant's charge was unenforceable. The Court of Appeal held the defendant liable to the claimant for the value of the lost charge. Lord Denning justified the decision on the ground that "[t]he very object of the registration system is to *secure* [the incumbrancer, i.e. the claimant] against loss. The system breaks down utterly if he is left to bear the loss himself".[522] Similarly, in *Sebry v Companies House*[523] it was held that the Registrar 7-116

---

516 Contrast *Al Nakib Investments (Jersey) Ltd v Longcroft* [1990] 1 W.L.R. 1390, where it was held that the purpose of the prospectus was to guide those subscribing to shares and not those purchasing on the market, with *Possfund Custodian Trustees v Diamond* [1996] 1 W.L.R. 1351, where it was suggested that changes in the legislation governing the issue of securities meant that listing particulars and prospectuses should now be regarded as intended to protect "after market" purchases.

517 *Taberna Europe CDO II Plc v Selskabet (formerly Roskilde Bank A/S) (In Bankruptcy)* [2016] EWCA Civ 1262; [2017] Q.B. 633 at [11], per Moore-Bick LJ ("investor presentation" placed on defendants' website intended to be relied upon by potential investors for the purpose of deciding whether to invest in its subordinated securities; however, no duty of care because defendants were entitled to rely on a disclaimer in the document).

518 [1997] P.N.L.R. 618.

519 See also *Seddon v Driver and Vehicle Licensing Agency* [2019] EWCA Civ 14; [2019] 1 W.L.R. 4593, applying *Reeman* (no duty of care owed by DVLA to a prospective purchaser of a motor vehicle as to the accuracy of the information contained in the vehicle registration document).

520 [1990] 2 E.G.L.R. 166.

521 [1970] 2 Q.B. 223. The loss was caused not by the claimant relying on any statement of the defendant but simply by the failure of the defendant's registration service.

522 cf. *Santander UK Plc v Keeper of the Registers of Scotland* [2013] CSOH 24; 2013 S.L.T. 362—the land registry in Scotland were not liable in negligence for losses sustained by a lender when a borrower fraudulently persuaded the land registry to accept a discharge of the borrower's mortgage,

of Companies owed a duty of care to a company on the register which was not in liquidation but which was wrongly recorded as having been wound up by order of the court. This required reasonable care in recording the information accurately on the register, though there was no obligation to check the accuracy of information supplied by third parties. Drawing an analogy with *Ministry of Housing and Local Government v Sharp*, Edis J concluded that where the Registrar alters the status of a company on the Register by recording a winding up order against it he assumes a responsibility to that company, given that the company has no opportunity to protest that the entry is mistaken.[524]

7-117 The purpose of the service was also an element in the House of Lords' decision in *White v Jones* that a solicitor retained by a testator owed a duty of care to the intended beneficiary of the will. Lord Browne-Wilkinson stated that "the solicitor by accepting the instructions has entered upon, and therefore assumed responsibility for, the task of procuring the execution of a skilfully drawn will knowing that the beneficiary is wholly dependent upon his careful carrying out or his function".[525] As in the case of statements, questions arise as to the purpose of a service. An example is provided by the Court of Appeal decision in *Carr-Glynn v Frearsons (A Firm)*[526] where it was held that a solicitor's duty of care to an intended beneficiary extended to serving a notice of severance of the joint tenancy over the bequeathed property. The fact that the testator's estate would also have a claim against the solicitor did not bar the claim of the intended beneficiary. Chadwick LJ explained that:

> "the key ... is to recognise that ... the duties owed by the solicitors are limited by reference to the kind of loss from which they must take care to save harmless the persons to whom those duties were owed.... The loss from which the testator and his estate are to be saved harmless is the loss which those interested in the estate ... will suffer if effect is not given to the testator's testamentary intentions.... The duty owed ... to the specific

---

with the result that a later lender took priority on sale of the mortgaged property. It was not fair just and reasonable to impose a duty of care on the land registry (distinguishing *Ministry of Housing and Local Government v Sharp*). A large commercial banking enterprise takes a number of commercial risks when making a decision to lend money, one of which is as to the honesty of their customer. If a duty of care were imposed on the land registry, then it would be the public purse that would bear the loss and not the commercial enterprise that initially assumed the risk (per Lord Boyd at [107]).

523 [2015] EWHC 115 (QB); [2016] 1 W.L.R. 2499. See also *Schubert Murphy v The Law Society* [2017] EWCA Civ 1295; [2017] 4 W.L.R. 200 (arguable that the Law Society could owe a duty of care if it negligently listed a fraudster as a solicitor on the official Roll of solicitors published on its website because solicitors and members of the public relied on the accuracy of the Roll).

524 "Effectively, the system places a degree of trust ... in the Registrar's staff to ensure that it does not damage companies which have no way of defending themselves against errors": [2015] EWHC 115 (QB); [2016] 1 W.L.R. 2499 at [111].

525 [1995] 2 A.C. 207 at 275. The *White* principle was applied in *Gorham v British Telecommunications Plc* [2000] 1 W.L.R. 2129, to impose a duty on a pension adviser to the dependants of its client, and both *White* and *Gorham* were followed in *Dean v Allin & Watts (A Firm)* [2001] EWCA Civ 758; [2001] 2 Lloyd's Rep. 249; [2001] P.N.L.R. 39, to impose a duty on a solicitor to a party on the other side of his client's transaction. However, it will be rare for a solicitor to be found to have assumed responsibility to a party on the other side of an arms' length transaction. Reliance by the other party in such circumstances "is presumptively inappropriate", given that it will not normally be reasonable for the other party to rely on what the solicitor said and it would be unusual for the solicitor reasonably to foresee such reliance: *Steel v NRAM Ltd (formerly NRAM Plc)* [2018] UKSC 13; [2018] 1 W.L.R. 1190 at [32], per Lord Wilson. For detailed discussion of the will and related cases, see paras 9-122 to 9-128.

526 [1999] Ch. 326 at 337.

> legatee … is, also, a duty to take care to ensure that effect was given to the testator's testamentary intentions."

Hence, the claims of the estate and the legatee could be regarded as complementary. Both followed from the purpose of the service.

The purpose of the service may also point in the opposite direction leading to the conclusion that no duty of care should be owed. In *Clarke v Bruce Lance & Co*[527] it was claimed that a solicitor retained by a client in relation to the grant of a fixed price option over his property to a third party, also owed a duty to the devisee of that property under the client's will to advise the client that the grant would adversely affect the devisee's interest. The Court of Appeal rejected the claim on a number of grounds including the fact the granting of the option did not have as its object the benefit of the claimant devisee and that "in no way can it be said that [the solicitor's] contemplation of the [claimant] in relation to the grant of the option, was 'actual, nominate and direct"'. Similarly, *West Bromwich Albion FC Ltd v El-Safty*[528] illustrates the importance of the purpose of the service, whichever test for duty is used. The claimant referred one of its professional footballers to the defendant surgeon for treatment. The defendant's negligent treatment resulted in the footballer being unable to play again.[529] The claimant sued for over three million pounds as representing the loss of the value of the footballer's contract. It was held that there was no contract between the claimant and defendant and hence, the claim had to rest on a duty of care in tort. The Court of Appeal held that the defendant owed no duty of care to the claimant in respect of its financial loss. Rix LJ found that there was no proximity as "the dominant relationship is that of the doctor and his patient, and the dominant context is that of the [patient's] health, not his employer's financial security".[530] There was no assumption of responsibility to advise the club as the immediate interest was medical, not financial, and it would not have been just to impose liability for financial loss because: **7-118**

> "if WBA had wanted [the defendant's] advice for the purposes of its own interests, it could have made that plain to him. He would then have been in a position where he could choose to charge for that advice and the risks involved in giving it and/or disclaiming liability."[531]

527 [1988] 1 W.L.R. 881.

528 [2006] EWCA Civ 1299; [2007] P.I.Q.R. P7; [2007] L.S. Law Med. 50. See also *Harrison v Technical Sign Co Ltd* [2013] EWCA Civ 1569; [2014] P.N.L.R. 15—surveyor owed no duty to a tenant or to members of the public when asked by the tenant to inspect an awning over the tenant's shop front for damage because the surveyor was acting as an agent of the landlord of the property, and the request from the tenant was one of complaint; the surveyor was not asked to advise the tenant or to inspect the shop front on its behalf. In *Seddon v Driver and Vehicle Licensing Agency* [2019] EWCA Civ 14; [2019] 1 W.L.R. 4593 at [66] the Court of Appeal noted that motor vehicle registration documents are provided by the DVLA for the statutory purpose of collecting tax and ensuring vehicles operating on the roads are registered, not "for the private purpose of informing the commercial decisions of those who may choose to purchase registered vehicles."

529 The footballer successfully claimed damages for loss of earnings from the defendant: *Appleton v El Safty* [2007] EWHC 631.

530 [2006] EWCA Civ 1299; [2007] P.I.Q.R. P7 at [60]. The Court placed some reliance on *Islington LBC v UCL Hospital NHS Trust* [2005] EWCA Civ 596; [2006] P.I.Q.R. P9.

531 [2006] EWCA Civ 1299; [2007] P.I.Q.R. P7 at [63]. The Court of Appeal were also influenced by their take on what they considered the insurance position of the parties should have been. Rix LJ commented that: "… if it is permissible in such a context to think of where insurance for such liabilities naturally lie, I would think that whereas insurance against liability to patients for the consequences of negligent medical advice or treatment would naturally lie with treating doctors, insurance against financial loss arising from the ill-health of employees, even where that is increased

(2) Knowledge of the defendant

7-119 **Knowledge of the particular use** Although a statement has been provided for a client for one purpose, the defendant's knowledge that it is being used by a third party for another purpose may be sufficient to give rise to a duty. Thus, in *Smith v Eric S Bush*[532] the House of Lords held that a surveyor who prepared a valuation for a building society to enable it to meet its statutory duty in relation to loans, owed a duty of care to a purchaser to whom the valuation was passed and who relied on it as an indication of the value of the property to be purchased. The Lords stressed both the surveyor's knowledge that the purchaser would probably rely on his report and the fact that the purchaser had paid the society a sum to defray the surveyor's fee, when coming to the conclusion that the surveyor had assumed responsibility to the purchaser.[533] It is clear that the imposition of a duty depends on the defendant knowing as opposed to merely foreseeing, that specific interests of the claimant are at issue. Knowledge of the particular type of transaction was a key issue in *Galoo Ltd v Bright Grahame Murray*.[534] It was held that accountants could owe a duty of care to the purchaser of shares in the client as they knew that the price at which the shares were to be sold was to be calculated by reference to the company's net profits as shown in the accounts which the defendants were producing. However, other claims for losses resulting from subsequent additional purchases of shares and loans advanced to the company were struck out on the grounds that the accountants were not alleged to have known that their work would be relied upon for these transactions. In *Royal Bank of Scotland Ltd v Bannerman Johnstone Maclay*[535] it was emphasised that it is knowledge and not intention that is relevant. There, a bank brought a claim against auditors for the bank's lending losses incurred in reliance on the audit report. Lord Gill noted that it is sufficient in some circumstances that the provider of the information or advice knows that it will be passed to a third party recipient for a specific purpose and that the recipient is likely to rely on it for that purpose:

> "No doubt an express intention on the part of the provider of the information or advice that the third party will rely upon it will more strongly support the existence of proximity. In some cases it may be essential; but I cannot see why the desiderative element implicit in that intention should be essential in every case. If it were, it would follow, I think, that where the provider of information or advice expressly intended that it should not be relied on by any third party recipient, he would not incur liability. That is not the law. Such an intention could not prevail against the actual or presumed knowledge of the provider that the information or advice was likely to be relied on by the third party."[536]

---

or exacerbated by third parties, naturally lies with their employers" (at [63]). See also, per Mummery LJ (at [84]).

532 [1990] 1 A.C. 831.

533 See also *Morgan Crucible Co Plc v Hill Samuel Bank Ltd* [1991] Ch. 295, where the Court of Appeal concluded that those responsible for issuing defence documents on behalf of a company to its own shareholders advising rejection of a take-over bid, could owe a duty of care to the take-over bidder. It was arguable that the defendants "must have known and indeed intended" that the claimant would rely on the documents when increasing their bid.

534 [1994] 1 W.L.R. 1360.

535 [2005] CSIH 39; 2005 1 S.C. 437; [2005] P.N.L.R. 43 at [49]–[50].

536 See also *BCCI (Overseas) v Price Waterhouse (No.2)* [1998] P.N.L.R. 564 at 588, where Sir Brian Neill said liability depends "not on intention but on the actual or presumed knowledge of the adviser".

On the other hand, the defendant's knowledge of the claimant's particular use does not necessarily make it reasonable for the claimant to rely on the information, especially where the defendant has clearly disclaimed responsibility, the claimant did not seek an express assumption of responsibility from the defendant, and the disclaimer was reasonable as between two sophisticated commercial parties.[537]

Knowledge of reliance Knowledge that the advisee will rely on the statement without obtaining independent advice will also be relevant. In *James McNaughton Paper Group Ltd v Hicks Anderson & Co*[538] the defendant accountants had shown the draft accounts of their client to the claimants who were proposing a takeover of the client. The defendants were held to owe no duty of care as they had no knowledge that the claimants would rely on accounts marked "draft" or on their oral statements about the accounts "*without any further inquiry or advice* for the purpose of reaching a concluded agreement with [the client]".[539] The same principles apply where the defendant has provided a service. The case for imposing a duty will be strongest where the defendant knows that his service is likely to impact directly upon the claimant without there being any independent check on the quality of that service. Thus, in the case of a building employer suffering loss as a result of the negligent work of a subcontractor or local authority inspector, one reason for the reluctance to impose a duty on the negligent defendant has been that the employer will be likely to have engaged his own professionals to check on the quality of the work.[540] **7-120**

Where the information is within the claimant's knowledge or where the information provided by the defendant could have readily been checked by the claimant it will neither be reasonable for the claimant to have relied on the information, nor foreseeable to the defendant that the claimant would rely on the information. In *Steel v NRAM Ltd (formerly NRAM Plc)*[541] the defendant was a solicitor, acting for a borrower, who carelessly drew up documents releasing all the properties on which **7-121**

---

[537] *Barclays Bank Plc v Grant Thornton UK LLP* [2015] EWHC 320 (Comm); [2015] 1 C.L.C. 180.

[538] [1991] 2 Q.B. 113.

[539] [1991] 2 Q.B. 113 at 145, Neill LJ's emphasis. Similarly, in *Scullion v Bank of Scotland Plc* [2011] EWCA Civ 693; [2011] 1 W.L.R. 3212 the Court of Appeal held that a valuer preparing a valuation report for a mortgagee did not owe a duty of care to the purchaser for a buy-to let transaction. That was a commercial transaction (in contrast with *Smith v Eric S Bush* [1990] 1 A.C. 831 where the purchaser was buying his own home) and a valuer was entitled to conclude that the purchaser was commercially astute and more likely to obtain, and afford, an independent valuation or survey. See also *McCullagh v Lane Fox & Partners* [1996] P.N.L.R. 205, where it was held that an estate agent owed no duty of care to a prospective purchaser of a property in respect of a statement about the area of the plot as he was entitled to assume that his statements would be independently checked by the purchaser or his advisers. *McCullagh* was distinguished in *Duncan Investments Ltd v Underwoods* [1997] P.N.L.R. 521 at 538, on the ground that the estate agent advising a purchaser as to the resale price of property "ought to have realised, that he was, and was to be, the only source of advice". The defendant's appeal in *Duncan* was allowed but only in relation to damages and not liability: [1998] P.N.L.R. 754.

[540] See for example, *Investors in Industry Ltd v South Bedfordshire DC* [1986] Q.B. 1034 at 1062, per Slade LJ. See also *Patchett v Swimming Pool & Allied Trades Association Ltd* [2009] EWCA Civ 717; [2010] 2 All E.R. (Comm) 138—no assumption of responsibility from statements made on trade association's website because potential customers were advised to obtain an information pack which would have revealed that a swimming pool installer with whom the claimants had entered into a contract, but who had become insolvent, was only an affiliate member of the trade association, and so was not subject to the same vetting as a full member and was not subject to the trade association's bond and warranty scheme.

[541] [2018] UKSC 13; [2018] 1 W.L.R 1190.

the loan was secured instead of the intended partial release. The lender executed the release, with the consequence that they had no security over the properties when the borrower became insolvent, and then sued the solicitor in negligence for the loss of the money loaned to the borrower. The Supreme Court held that there had been no assumption of responsibility by the solicitor to the lender. It was not reasonable for the lender to have relied on the solicitor's representations and it was not reasonably foreseeable to the solicitor that the lender would so rely since it had failed to check the accuracy of the representations. Any prudent bank taking basic precautions would have checked the accuracy of the representations by reference to its file or by asking for further clarification. Thus, Lord Wilson commented:

> "a commercial lender about to implement an agreement with its borrower referable to its security does not act reasonably if it proceeds upon no more than a description of its terms put forward by or on behalf of the borrower. The lender knows the terms of the agreement and indeed, as in this case, is likely to have evolved and proposed them. ... No authority has been cited to the court, nor discovered by me in preparing this judgment, in which it has been held that there was an assumption of responsibility for a careless misrepresentation about a fact wholly within the knowledge of the representee. The explanation is, no doubt, that in such circumstances it is not reasonable for the representee to rely on the representation without checking its accuracy and that it is, by contrast, reasonable for the representor not to foresee that he would do so."[542]

7-122 On the other hand, where to the defendant's knowledge the claimant is relying on the defendant's representations about his own beliefs and intentions, there is no requirement for the claimant to make further independent inquiry. So in *HSBC Bank Plc v 5th Avenue Partners Ltd*[543] the Court of Appeal held that there was no need for the claimants to seek advice on the truthfulness and reliability of HSBC's representations because "being representations about HSBC's own intentions and beliefs, [they] were uniquely within the knowledge of, and could only be verified by, HSBC itself. They were not verifiable by some independent expert."[544]

7-123 **Subsequent knowledge** In *McCullagh v Lane Fox & Partners Ltd*[545] the Court of Appeal considered whether a duty could arise when at the time the erroneous statement was made, the defendant would have expected the claimant to have made independent inquiries but subsequently discovered that he would be relying without making such inquiries. The defendant estate agent had negligently misstated the size of the property the claimant wished to purchase but only realised on the following day that the claimant would be exchanging contracts without having his own survey. The majority of the Court of Appeal considered that no duty was owed when the defendant misstated the area as "at that time he would have been entitled reasonably to take the view that his statement would be independently checked and would not be relied upon". They further doubted whether a duty would arise when he subsequently discovered the reliance, as it was "doubtful whether a mere failure to correct an innocent misrepresentation can give rise to liability in tort unless either (a) the representor assumed responsibility for its truth at the time when the

---

542 [2018] UKSC 13; [2018] 1 W.L.R. 1190 at [38].

543 [2009] EWCA Civ 296; [2009] 1 C.L.C. 503.

544 [2009] EWCA Civ 296; [2009] 1 C.L.C. 503 at [51]; distinguishing *James McNaughton Paper Group Ltd v Hicks Anderson & Co.*

545 [1996] P.N.L.R. 205.

representation was originally made, or (b) the representor subsequently became aware that it was untrue and was likely to be acted upon, before it was in fact acted upon by the representee".[546] Where knowledge of the purpose for which a statement is to be used or of the recipient who will be relying upon it, has been acquired subsequent to the making of that statement then it is suggested, by analogy with *McCullagh*, that no duty will arise. The representor did not assume responsibility for the statement at the time it was made and subsequent knowledge of recipient and purpose cannot justify imposing responsibility. If, after acquiring subsequent knowledge of the recipient, the purpose or the intention to rely without further investigation, the representor confirms the statement to the recipient, that confirmation may amount to a fresh assumption of responsibility sufficient to found a duty.[547] And in some circumstances, such as pre-contract negotiations, a representation made with a view to inducing the recipient to enter the contract may be considered to be a continuing representation as to the accuracy of the facts contained in the representation, such that the representor assumes responsibility to the person entering into the contract in reliance on it, even though the identity of that person has changed (to the representor's knowledge) in the interim.[548]

Knowledge of the class to which the advisee belongs The defendant may know of the claimant only as a member of a class of persons likely to be relying on his work.[549] The larger the class of persons the more difficult it may be to infer that a duty of care was owed to the individuals within it. Knowledge that a client intended to show audited accounts to its creditors to support existing or further borrowings is unlikely to lead to a duty to members of the creditor class as the resulting liability would be indeterminate.[550] On the other hand, in *Aiken v Stewart Wrightson Members' Agency Ltd*[551] it was held that Lloyds managing agents owed a duty of care when placing run-off reinsurance policies to Names who joined the particular syndicates after the policy had been effected although the identity of these individuals would not have been known at the time that the policy was effected. Part of the purpose of taking such policies was to benefit incoming members. Similar reasoning would suggest that a solicitor who was negligent in advising on a will would owe a duty to beneficiaries who were unidentified by name in the will. Where the defendant's lack of knowledge of the claimant's identity is not counterbalanced by clear knowledge that the purpose of his work was to benefit the claimant as a **7-124**

---

546 [1996] P.N.L.R. 205 at 242, per Sir Christopher Slade.

547 See *Lowe Lippmann Figdor & Franck v AGC (Advances) Ltd* [1992] 2 V.R. 671 Supreme Court of Victoria, where Brooking J denied a duty in a case where an auditor was informed subsequent to its work, that a copy of its report would be sent to a creditor. He commented that if there was liability in such a case:

> "the auditor would face the danger of being sued by all sorts of third persons if, on the day before the report was signed, the company informed him of its intention to broadcast the audited reports by distributing them to all those with whom it had or hoped to have business dealings."

548 See *Cramaso LLP v Ogilvie-Grant* [2014] UKSC 9; [2014] A.C. 1093, para.7-131.

549 If the defendant is unaware of the existence of the claimant, even as an unidentified member of an identifiable class, then he will not have the required knowledge for a duty of care to arise: see *Banca Nazionale del Lavoro SPA v Playboy Club London Ltd* [2018] UKSC 43; [2018] 1 W.L.R. 4041; see further para.7-113.

550 See the judgment of Millet J in *Al-Saudi Banque v Clarke Pixley (A Firm)* [1990] Ch. 313 at 337. As McHugh J pointed out in *Perre v Apand Pty Ltd* (1999) 164 A.L.R. 606 at 633, it is the indeterminancy of claimants rather than the number which is the main concern.

551 [1995] 1 W.L.R. 1281.

member of a limited class of persons, no duty will arise. Thus, in *Preston v Torfaen BC*[552] it was held that a soil engineer who investigated an in-filled site prior to a house being constructed upon it owed no duty of care to a subsequent purchaser of the house. The claimant was not identified at the time of the work, other than as a member of a general class of potential purchasers.

(3) Reasonable reliance or dependence

7-125 **Reasonable reliance or dependence** The test is one of reasonable reliance or dependence, because in some cases there is no factual reliance by the claimant on the defendant. In cases of negligent statements the claimant's loss is usually caused by his factual reliance upon the statement but this is not always the case. In *Spring v Guardian Assurance Plc*[553] the claimant had lost his job as a result of a negligently prepared reference sent by the defendant, his ex-employer to his new employer. The House of Lords held that the employment relationship justified reasonable reliance by the claimant on the defendant.[554] But to distinguish this type of situation from one where the claimant actually relies on the statement, it may be preferable to describe the claimant as reasonably depending on his employer to take care in giving the reference.[555] This is all the more the case with negligent services. In *White*

---

552 (1993) 36 Con. L.R. 48.

553 [1995] 2 A.C. 296.

554 Lord Goff said at [1995] 2 A.C. 296 at 319:

> "The provision of such references is a service regularly provided by employers to their employees; ... Furthermore, when such a reference is provided by an employer, it is plain that the employee relies on him to exercise due skill and care in the preparation of the reference before making it available to the third party."

Ministry of Housing v Sharp [1970] 2 Q.B. 223 is another example of loss caused to a claimant by a third party relying on the negligent statement.

555 The danger in using the term "reasonable reliance" in relation to a fact situation like that in *Spring* is apparent from the dissent of Lord Keith on the ground that the claimant had not factually relied on the defendant's statement. In *Gatt v Barclays Bank Plc* [2013] EWHC 2 (QB) at [34]–[35], Judge Moloney QC was prepared to apply *Spring* to the provision of information by a bank to a credit reference agency, the duty being owed not solely to the customer about whom the reference was provided, but also the spouse of that customer where she was a joint account holder and co-director of a family business that was dependent on her husband's credit. The judge noted "the importance of credit rating in the modern world and the analogies (more than just semantic) between job references and credit references". The action failed on the facts. In *Durkin v DSG Retail Ltd* [2014] UKSC 21; [2014] 1 W.L.R. 1148 a bank that had provided credit for a consumer transaction (the purchase by the claimant of a computer) conceded that it was under a duty of care not to make untrue statements about the claimant to credit reference agencies. The Supreme Court held that it was in breach of that duty by notifying the credit reference agencies that the claimant had defaulted on the credit agreement without first checking the claimant's assertion that the contract of sale had been rescinded. On the other hand, a credit reference agency does not owe a duty of care in negligence to members of the public about whom it collects data: *Smeaton v Equifax Plc* [2013] EWCA Civ 108; [2013] 2 All E.R. 959 (credit reference agency's responsibilities governed by the Data Protection Act 1998 (see now the Data Protection Act 2018) and the Consumer Credit Act 1974; there was no scope for imposing a co-extensive duty in tort). Similarly, there is no duty of care owed by the police to a person applying for an enhanced criminal record certificate, even though errors in the information provided affect the claimant's ability to obtain employment: *Desmond v Chief Constable of Nottinghamshire* [2011] EWCA Civ 3; [2011] 1 F.L.R. 1361. There was no assumption of responsibility by the police beyond that required by the proper performance of the statutory duty to provide a certificate, and there was no sufficient relationship between the police and the claimant (distinguishing *Spring*). See further para.13-41.

v Jones[556] members of the House of Lords struggled to analyse the relationship of the claimant, a disappointed beneficiary, and the defendant solicitor in terms of reliance. Lord Nolan described the relationship as one of "implicit" reliance and in the earlier case of *Ross v Caunters*[557] Megarry V-C had termed it "passive reliance". Lord Browne-Wilkinson in *White*, admitted that there was no personal reliance but justified a duty on the ground that "society as a whole does rely on solicitors to carry out their will-making functions carefully".[558] Again, it may be helpful to describe this as a relationship of reasonable dependence to distinguish it from a situation of actual reliance. Whether the relationship is termed reliance or dependence, the key question is whether it was reasonable for the claimant to rely or depend on the defendant to take care. Clearly, where the defendant expressly assumes a responsibility towards the claimant it will be reasonable for the claimant to trust the defendant to exercise care. In the absence of an express undertaking, a number of other factors will be relevant to the reasonableness question: the dependence and vulnerability of the claimant, the availability of independent advice, the contractual context and opportunity to secure contractual safeguards, the authority and status of the defendant, and the informal context in which the advice is given.

Dependence and vulnerability In the leading Australian High Court decision of **7-126** *Perre v Apand Pty Ltd*[559] McHugh J suggested that "reliance and assumption of responsibility are merely indicators of the claimant's vulnerability to harm from the defendant's conduct" and that it is "the concept of vulnerability rather than these evidentiary factors which is the most relevant criterion for determining whether a duty of care exists". He argued that in a case such as *White*, vulnerability could rest on the defendant's control of the claimant's right, interest or expectation and the court may be spared the necessity of finding some element of reliance. This attractive analysis formed part of a broader thesis that the reasons for "upholding or denying a duty in particular cases should be regarded as the principles to be applied in determining whether a duty exists in cases within that category".[560] The contrast of two House of Lords' decisions illustrates the point. In *Smith v Bush*[561] a surveyor was held to owe a duty to a house purchaser to whom the third party lender had passed his report. The purchaser was not independent of the third party, rather she had paid a valuation fee to that third party out of which the surveyor had been paid.

---

556 [1995] 2 A.C. 207.

557 [1980] Ch. 297.

558 [1995] 2 A.C. 207 at 276. See also *Sebry v Companies House* [2015] EWHC 115 (QB); [2016] 1 W.L.R. 2499, where a company went into liquidation as a result of an incorrect entry made by the Registrar of Companies in the companies register stating that it was the subject of a winding up order, with the result that it was no longer able to obtain credit. Edis J drew an analogy with *White v Jones* in concluding that the Registrar owed a duty of care to the company. The company had not relied on the statement, but had suffered injury because other people relied on it. The beneficiaries under the will in *White v Jones* had no way of protecting themselves against the loss of a gift. Similarly, the "Company had no way of protecting itself against harm resulting from the promulgation of a false statement that it was in liquidation" (at [91]).

559 (1999) 164 A.L.R. 606 at 639.

560 McHugh J identified indeterminancy of liability, autonomy of the individual, the claimant's vulnerability to risk and the defendant's knowledge of that risk as being the four principles relevant to the duty question and around which the law should be structured. Kirby J in *Perre* argued that these were no more than criteria for "giving content to the universal requirement of undertaking the policy analysis required by the third stage of the *Caparo* approach".

561 [1990] 1 A.C. 831.

The purchaser was not in a position to make any necessary judgments herself. She had already paid for a valuation and it would be unreasonable to expect her to pay for a second, independent valuation.[562] It was unlikely that she would be able to obtain insurance against the inherent defects which should have been revealed by the survey. By contrast, in *Caparo Industries Plc v Dickman*[563] the take-over bidder who had received the audit report as a shareholder was independent, an "entrepreneur taking high risks for high reward",[564] and well able to make any necessary judgments itself. No duty was owed. Another obvious example of vulnerability and dependence is provided by *Gorham v British Telecommunications Plc*[565] where the Court of Appeal followed *White v Jones* when imposing a duty on a pension adviser to the dependants of its client.

7-127 **Availability of independent advice** In *McNaughton Papers Group Ltd v Hicks Anderson & Co (A Firm)* Neill LJ observed that "[i]n business transactions conducted at arms' length it may sometimes be difficult for an advisee to prove that he was entitled to act on a statement without taking any independent advice".[566] On the facts, he found that it was to be anticipated that the claimant, an experienced businessman, "would have access to and would consult with his own accountancy advisers". He was not entitled to rely on the draft accounts prepared by the defendants when purchasing the defendants' client. Similar conclusions have been reached where the claimant has relied on informal or qualified[567] statements of accountants when purchasing the client. Conversely, the more formal the context in which the advice is given[568] or the more it is cast in the form of an assurance,[569] the more the recipient may be entitled to rely rather than having to verify.

7-128 **Contractual context** The contractual context may also be relevant to whether it is reasonable to impose a duty. In *Henderson v Merrett Syndicates Ltd*[570] the House of Lords held that Lloyd's managing agents owed a duty of care to Names for whom they indirectly acted, the Names' direct contracts being with member's agents who, in turn, retained the managing agents. The relationship was such that the Names were reasonably entitled to rely on the managing agents. Lord Goff noted (at 195–196) that the case was:

---

562 Contrast the position where the purchase is of a buy-to let property by a purchaser who is effectively making a commercial investment decision: *Scullion v Bank of Scotland Plc* [2011] EWCA Civ 693; [2011] 1 W.L.R. 3212 (no duty owed by valuer to purchaser in respect of report provided to mortgagee). See also *Seddon v Driver and Vehicle Licensing Agency* [2019] EWCA Civ 14; [2019] 1 W.L.R. 4593 (no duty owed by DVLA to purchaser of "historic vehicle" as to the accuracy of information contained in the vehicle registration document; the claimant "could have arranged for his own expert inspection of the vehicle. The substantial price he was paying for the vehicle [£250,000] called for all precautions to be taken", at [81](5) per Hamblen LJ).

563 [1990] 2 A.C. 605.

564 per Hoffmann J in *Morgan Crucible v Hill Samuel* [1991] Ch. 295 at 302, when drawing the distinction between *Smith* and *Caparo* in terms of the fairness and justice of the relationship.

565 [2000] 1 W.L.R. 2129.

566 [1991] 2 Q.B. 113 at 126.

567 *Peach Publishing Ltd v Slater & Co* [1998] P.N.L.R. 364.

568 See for example, *ADT v Binder Hamlyn* [1996] B.C.C. 808, where the statements were made by the accountants at a meeting arranged specifically for the purchasers to satisfy themselves before proceeding.

569 See for example the assurance given by the defendant solicitors in *Allied Finance and Investments Ltd v Haddow & Co* [1983] N.Z.L.R. 22 NZCA.

570 [1995] 2 A.C. 145 at 195.

"most unusual; in many cases in which a contractual chain comparable to the present case is constructed it may well prove to be inconsistent with an assumption of responsibility which has the effect of short-cutting the contractual structure so put in place by the parties.... [for example, under] the ordinary building contract, [where] the main contractor sub-contracts with sub-contractors or suppliers (often nominated by the building owner) ... it will not ordinarily be open to the building owner to sue the sub-contractor or supplier direct under the *Hedley Byrne* principle."

This suggests that the earlier Lords' decision in *Junior Books Ltd v Veitchi Co Ltd*[571] where a nominated subcontractor responsible for negligently laying defective flooring was held liable to the building owner for the economic loss resulting from having to replace the flooring, should be regarded as exceptional. It might be justifiable on the ground that the subcontractor was nominated for its special skill on which the employer was reasonably entitled to rely. In *Robinson v PE Jones (Contractors) Ltd*[572] Jackson LJ summarised Lord Goff's analysis of the relationship between contractual and tortious duties in the following terms:

"(i) When A assumes responsibility to B in the *Hedley Byrne* sense, A comes under a tortious duty to B, which may extend to protecting B against economic loss.
(ii) The existence of a contract between A and B does not prevent such a duty from arising.
(iii) In contracts of professional retainer, there is commonly an assumption of responsibility which generates a duty of care to protect the client against economic loss."

However, an ordinary building contract does not, in itself, give rise to an assumption of responsibility between the builder and the building owner, and (in the absence of physical injury to the owner or some other property) their relationship will be governed by the terms of the contract rather than the law of tort. Stanley Burnton LJ added:

"In my judgment, it must now be regarded as settled law that the builder/vendor of a building does not by reason of his contract to construct or to complete the building assume any liability in the tort of negligence in relation to defects in the building giving rise to purely economic loss. The same applies to a builder who is not the vendor, and to the seller or manufacturer of a chattel. The decision of the House of Lords in *Anns v Merton LBC*, like its earlier decision in *Junior Books Ltd v Veitchi Co. Ltd* [1983] 1 A.C. 520, must now be regarded as aberrant, indeed as heretical."[573]

An example of a contractual context inconsistent with a tortious duty is provided by *Pacific Associates Inc v Baxter*.[574] The claimants were contractors engaged in dredging work under the supervision of the defendant engineer who was retained by the employer. The claimants' contract with the employer contained clauses providing that the engineer would not be personally liable for acts under the contract and for the arbitration of disputes between the contractor and employer. The contractor claimed that the geological information in the tender document issued by the engineer had under-estimated the amount of hard materials to be dredged and that the engineer had acted negligently in rejecting the contractor's claims for extra **7-129**

571 [1983] 1 A.C. 520.
572 [2011] EWCA Civ 9; [2012] Q.B. 44 at [80].
573 [2011] EWCA Civ 9; [2012] Q.B. 44 at [80] at [92].
574 [1990] 1 Q.B. 993; *Galliford Try Infrastructure Ltd (Formerly Morrison Construction Ltd) v Mott MacDonald Ltd* [2008] EWHC 1570 (TCC); [2009] P.N.L.R. 9.

payment for removal of unforeseen hard materials. The contractor recovered some of its alleged loss from the employer following an arbitration settlement and then sought to recover the balance through a negligence action against the employer. The Court of Appeal held that it would not be reasonable to impose a *Hedley Byrne* duty because it would "cut across and be inconsistent with the structure of relationships created by the contracts, into which the parties had entered".[575]

7-130 In *Riyad Bank v Ahli United Bank (UK) Plc*[576] the Court of Appeal considered the significance of the contractual context and, in particular, Lord Goff's comment in *Henderson v Merrett Syndicates Ltd* (at 195) that "in many cases ... a contractual chain ... may well prove to be inconsistent with an assumption of responsibility which has the effect of ... short-circuiting the contractual structure so put in place by the parties ... [for example under] the ordinary building contract". In *Riyad*, it had been arranged that a Sharia-compliant investment fund established by a Saudi bank, would receive investment advice from the defendant, a Kuwaiti bank. To avoid the adverse marketing impact of being directly advised by a Kuwaiti bank, it was decided that the advice should be supplied via a contract between the two banks and then via a contract between the Saudi bank and its separately established fund. The Court of Appeal rejected the argument of the Kuwaiti bank that the contractual structure was inconsistent with it owing any tortious duty directly to the fund. Longmore LJ suggested that Lord Goff was "simply not considering cases such as the present where direct and substantial contact has occurred between parties who are subsequently separated by a contractual chain".[577] Buxton LJ also noted the direct dealings between the parties and stressed the differences between "an ad hoc contractual arrangement such as we are concerned with and the formalised and multi-party structure of a building contract".[578]

7-131 **Pre-contract representations** Where a person has been induced to enter into a contract after a misrepresentation has been made to him by another party to the contract,[579] and has suffered loss as a result, s.2(1) of the Misrepresentation Act 1967 provides a remedy if the person making the misrepresentation would be liable in damages had the misrepresentation been made fraudulently, notwithstanding that the misrepresentation was not made fraudulently. The Act creates a statutory tort which is more advantageous to claimants than an action in negligence, since there is no question whether a duty of care exists and the defendant bears the burden of proving that he had reasonable grounds to believe and did believe up to the time

---

575 The difficulty of determining whether the contractual structure is inconsistent with a tortious duty is illustrated by the contrasting decision of the Canadian Supreme Court in *Edgeworth Constructions Ltd v ND Lea & Associates Ltd* (1993) 107 D.L.R. (4th) 169. In *RM Turton & Co Ltd v Kerslake & Partners* [2000] Lloyd's Rep. P.N. 967, the majority of the New Zealand Court of Appeal followed *Pacific Associates* and distinguished *Edgeworth* as resting on its particular contractual context. In *Mirant-Asia Pacific Ltd v Oapil* [2005] EWCA Civ 1585; [2006] B.L.R. 187, it was held that a consultant engineer owed a duty to its employer and not to a third party involved in the project.

576 [2006] EWCA Civ 780; [2006] 2 Lloyd's Rep. 292; [2007] P.N.L.R. 1.

577 [2006] EWCA Civ 780; [2006] 2 Lloyd's Rep. 292; [2007] P.N.L.R. 1 at [30].

578 [2006] EWCA Civ 780; [2006] 2 Lloyd's Rep. 292; [2007] P.N.L.R. 1 at [137].

579 The Act only applies where as a result of the misrepresentation the representee enters into a contract with the representor and the representee's loss arises as a result of entering into that contract. It does not apply where A is induced to enter into a contract with B as a result of a misrepresentation made by C (assuming that C is not acting as B's agent): *Taberna Europe CDO II Plc v Selskabet (formerly Roskilde Bank A/S) (In Bankruptcy)* [2016] EWCA Civ 1262; [2017] Q.B. 633 at [43]–[44], [47], per Moore-Bick LJ (obiter).

the contract was made that the facts represented were true.[580] But if for some reason the Act does not apply the claimant may be owed a *Hedley Byrne* duty in negligence where he has relied on a representation made during the course of pre-contract negotiations.[581] In some cases a pre-contract representation may be regarded as a continuing representation as to the accuracy of what is asserted, in circumstances where the defendant has assumed responsibility to the claimant. In *Cramaso LLP v Ogilvie-Grant*[582] the defendants made representations to E as to the estimated grouse population of a grouse moor with a view to persuading E to take a lease of the moor. E decided to proceed and instructed his solicitors to conclude the transaction in the name of a limited liability partnership formed for the specific purpose of taking the tenancy. After the lease had been granted it was discovered that the grouse population was significantly smaller than had been represented.[583] The defendants argued that at the date that the representation was made Cramaso LLP did not exist so there was no one other than E who could reasonably have been foreseen as relying on the representation, and accordingly there was no proximity between the claimant and the defendants. The Supreme Court held that a pre-contractual representation could, in some circumstances give rise to a continuing responsibility of the representor as to its accuracy where there is an interval of time between the making of the representation and the conclusion of a contract in reliance upon it. The issue then was whether the representation, and responsibility for its accuracy, continued after the identity of the contracting party had changed. The Supreme Court accepted that it was possible for a representation to have continuing effect even though the parties to the contract were not the original representor and representee, where the inference from the parties' conduct was that they had proceeded with the negotiation and conclusion of the contract on the basis of the continued accuracy of the representation. That gave rise to a further inference "that the risk of harm being suffered as a result of reliance upon it, in the event that it was inaccurate, continued to be foreseeable. In such circumstances, the representor may be taken to have assumed responsibility for the accuracy of the representation towards the contracting party who relied upon it, even though that person was not the original representee."[584] On the facts, the representation as to the grouse population had a continuing effect which created a continuing responsibility of the defendants for its accuracy and "the change in the identity of the prospective

---

580 See para.17-02.

581 *Esso Petroleum Co. Ltd v Mardon* [1976] Q.B. 801, where the facts pre-dated the passing of the Misrepresentation Act 1967.

582 [2014] UKSC 9; [2014] A.C. 1093.

583 The facts were not dissimilar to those of *Esso Petroleum Co. Ltd v Mardon*, where the issue was the throughput of petrol at a petrol station: see para.7-135 fn.595.

584 [2014] UKSC 9; [2014] A.C. 1093 at [26], per Lord Reed JSC. His Lordship drew an analogy with *Briess v Woolley* [1954] A.C. 333 (see para.17-18) in which a fraudulent misrepresentation was made in the course of pre-contractual discussions by a shareholder in a company. Later, he was authorised by the other shareholders to continue negotiations as their agent, and subsequently a contract was concluded. The shareholders were held liable to the other party to the contract, notwithstanding that the representation had been made by the shareholder before he began to negotiate on their behalf. It made no difference in *Cramaso LLP v Ogilvie-Grant* that the claim was in negligence (a claim of fraud having been rejected on the facts at first instance), nor that in *Briess v Woolley* the representation had been made by someone who later became the agent of the defendants whereas in *Cramaso* the representation was made to someone who later became the agent of the claimant ([2014] UKSC 9; [2014] A.C. 1093 at [28]–[29]; see also per Lord Toulson JSC at [58]–[64]).

contracting party did not affect the continuing nature of the representation, or the respondents' continuing responsibility for its accuracy".[585]

7-132 **Contractual warranties** It is worth keeping in mind that, apart from any claim in negligence, the contract may give rise to obligations entirely distinct from an obligation to exercise reasonable care, as where the defendant is found to have given a warranty. For example, in *Platform Funding Ltd v Bank of Scotland Plc*[586] a surveyor valuing a property for the purposes of a mortgage was misled by a fraudster into valuing the wrong property. The Court of Appeal held that the effect of the valuation certificate given by the surveyor was that he had guaranteed that he had actually valued the property referred to in the certificate, and he was therefore liable for the lender's loss (the fraudulent borrower having defaulted on the loan) without proof of fault.

7-133 **Scope of contract between parties** The scope of any contract between defendant and claimant may also be relevant. In *Tai Hing Cotton Mill Ltd v Liu Chong Hing Bank Ltd*[587] the Privy Council refused to impose on a customer a tortious duty to his bank which would have been more extensive than his contractual duty. Although Lord Goff in *Henderson* rejected the wider dicta of Lord Scarman in *Tai Hing* to the effect that there could never be a tortious duty between contracting parties, he seemed to accept that the decision could be justified on the ground that the proposed tortious duty was more extensive than the duties imposed by the contract.[588] In *J Nunes Diamonds Ltd v Dominion Electric Protection Co*[589] the Canadian Supreme Court seems to have applied somewhat similar reasoning. After entering into a contract with the claimant, the defendants negligently stated that the burglar alarm system which they had hired to the claimant was foolproof. The hiring contract expressly stated that no warranties were given as to the operation of the system. The court held the defendants not liable on the ground that to allow the claim would amount to varying the contract from one of hire to one of insurance. However, it should be noted that in *Nunes Diamonds* the statement was directly inconsistent with the terms of the contract. Where this is not the case, it may be argued that there is no inconsistency in imposing a duty in relation to a statement going beyond the express scope of the contract. In *Holt v Payne Skivington (A Firm)*[590] Hirst LJ stated the position as follows:

"In our opinion, there is no reason in principle why a *Hedley Byrne* type duty of care can-

---

585 [2014] UKSC 9; [2014] A.C. 1093 at [30]. Lord Toulson JSC commented, at [57], that a "a matter of general principle, a representation made during contractual negotiations for the purpose of inducing a contract will ordinarily be regarded as continuing until the contract is actually concluded because it will generally be reasonable for the representee to continue to rely on it", though there may be exceptions, e.g. where there had been a material change of circumstances which would make the representation irrelevant.

586 [2008] EWCA Civ 930; [2009] Q.B. 426.

587 [1986] A.C. 80.

588 [1995] 2 A.C. 145 at 186. See also Lord Bridge in *Scally v Southern Health and Social Services Board* [1992] 1 A.C. 294 at 303: "If a duty of the kind in question was not inherent in the contractual relationship, I do not see how it could possibly be derived from the tort of negligence." It is also of note that Lord Woolf in *Spring v Guardian Assurance Plc* [1995] 2 A.C. 296 at 353, cited Lord Bridge and was concerned to show that the tortious duty owed by an employer when giving a reference was no wider than that which could be implied as a term of the employment contract.

589 (1972) 26 D.L.R. (3d) 699.

590 [1996] P.N.L.R. 179 at 195.

not arise in an overall set of circumstances where, by reference to certain limited aspects of those circumstances, the same parties enter into a contractual relationship involving more limited obligations than those imposed by the duty of care in tort. In such circumstances the duty of care in tort and the duties imposed by the contract will be concurrent but not coextensive."

On the facts, no more extensive duty in tort was found to exist.

Opportunity to secure contractual safeguards In *Peach Publishing Ltd v Slater & Co*[591] one reason for denying a duty where the claimant had purchased a company relying on accounts prepared by the defendant, was the fact that the claimant had safeguarded its position by taking a contractual warranty from the company relating to the accounts. The claimant's reliance on the warranty further suggested that it was not entitled to rely on the accountants' oral assurance. The availability of contractual safeguards is particularly relevant in the construction context. Thus, in *Pacific Associates Inc v Baxter* one reason for holding that an engineer did not owe a duty of care to a contractor suffering economic loss as a result of his decisions was that the contractor was safeguarded by the terms of its contract with the employer.[592] However, despite the existence of contractual safeguards, other factors such as the skill or authority of the defendant may entitle the claimant to reasonably rely on the defendant's service or statement.[593] **7-134**

Authority and skill of defendant In *Mutual Life & Citizens' Assurance Co Ltd v Evatt*[594] a majority of the Privy Council held that a *Hedley Byrne* duty could only apply where the defendant carries on the business of giving the kind of advice that is sought, or claims to possess considerable skill and competence in it. Hence, no duty could be imposed on an insurance company in respect of advice it gave on investment matters. Lords Reid and Morris dissented on the ground that the question was simply whether the advice was given on a business occasion, or in the course of the defendant's business. This dissenting opinion was preferred by the Court of Appeal in *Esso Petroleum Co Ltd v Mardon*.[595] In *Spring v Guardian Assurance*[596] Lord Goff, noting the non-binding effect of *Mutual Life* and the "formidable dissenting opinion" of Lords Reid and Morris, stated that the refer- **7-135**

591 [1998] P.N.L.R. 364.

592 See also *Seddon v Driver and Vehicle Licensing Agency* [2019] EWCA Civ 14; [2019] 1 W.L.R. 4593 where the Court of Appeal concluded that the DVLA did not owe a duty of care to the purchaser of a "historic vehicle" as to the accuracy of information contained in the vehicle registration document because the purchaser could have stipulated for contractual warranties by the vendor and/or he could have arranged for his own expert inspection of the vehicle.

593 Thus *Junior Books Ltd v Veitchi Co Ltd* [1983] 1 A.C. 520, in which a nominated subcontractor was held to owe a tortious duty to the nominating employer which cut across the normal contractual chain of liability, might be justified on the basis that the subcontractor was nominated for its special skill on which the employer was entitled to place direct reliance.

594 [1971] A.C. 793. The majority opinion in *Evatt's* case was disapproved by Gibbs CJ and Mason J in the High Court of Australia in *Shaddock v Parramatta City Council* (1981) 55 A.L.J.R. 713. See also its rejection by the New Zealand Court of Appeal in *Meates v Att Gen* [1983] N.Z.L.R. 308; and the Canadian Supreme Court in *Hodgkins v Hydro-Electric Commission of Nepean* (1975) 60 D.L.R. (3d) 1.

595 [1976] Q.B. 801. In the course of negotiations for a lease of a petrol station, the claimants made a careless, false statement to the defendant about how much petrol it was likely to sell. The defendant took the lease; later, when sued for the rent, he counterclaimed in respect of the misstatement. It was held that there was a special relationship giving rise to a duty of care and it did not matter that the claimant was not in the business of giving advice of that sort.

596 [1995] 2 A.C. 296 at 320.

ence to special skill in *Hedley Byrne* had "to be understood in a broad sense, certainly broad enough to embrace special knowledge" and that this could include situations where the "defendant has access to information and fails to exercise due care ... in drawing on that source of information". Thus, he concluded that the principle was applicable to an employer preparing a reference in respect of an employee. Although the inflexible view of *Mutual Life* has been rejected, it remains the case that a claimant is much more likely to be able to show that he is entitled to depend on a service or statement where the work is undertaken by a person who is exercising a special skill in a business context. This is particularly the case when the information being given relates to matters which are within the exclusive preserve of the defendant. Thus, in *Smith v Eric S Bush*[597] Lord Griffiths commented: "the valuer is discharging the duties of a professional man ... . The essence of the case against him is that he as a professional man realised that the purchaser was relying on him to exercise proper skill and judgment in his profession." Conversely, a duty is unlikely to be owed where a professional is giving advice clearly outside the scope of his expertise. Thus, in *Stevens v Bermondsey and Southwark Group Hospital Management Committee*[598] a hospital casualty officer who erroneously told the claimant that nothing much was wrong with him, was held to owe no duty in respect of the economic loss the claimant suffered when settling his personal injury claim for a small sum in reliance on that statement. Paull J considered that the doctor's duty was limited to the medical sphere and, in the absence of special circumstances, did not extend to matters of legal liability.[599]

7-136 **Status of defendant** A particular problem arises in relation to professional employees. In *Edgeworth Constructions Ltd v ND Lea & Associates Ltd*[600] La Forest J in the Supreme Court of Canada, argued that although the employer, an engineering firm, owed a *Hedley Byrne* duty to a contractor to which faulty tender specifications had been issued, the individual engineer responsible for issuing the faulty information did not owe a duty. This was because the recipient "could not reasonably rely for indemnification on the individual engineers". To do so "it would have to show that it was relying on the particular expertise of an individual engineer without regard to the corporate character of the engineering firm". In *Williams v Natural Life Health Foods Ltd*[601] Lord Steyn regarded the view of La Forest J in *Edgeworth* as being "consistent with English law" and adopting his emphasis on the need for *reasonable* reliance rather than merely reliance in fact, held that the claimants who were customers of a company could not have reasonably looked to the defendant director of the company for indemnification against loss. However,

597 [1990] 1 A.C. 831 at 865.
598 (1963) 107 S.J. 478.
599 cf. *Hughes v Lloyds Bank Plc* [1998] P.I.Q.R. P98 where the claimant had asked for a letter from her general practitioner for the express purpose of settling her claim against a negligent motorist and alleged that the doctor had negligently provided misleading information as to her prognosis, as a result of which she settled her action against the motorist for less than it was worth. The Court of Appeal held that the general practitioner owed the claimant a duty to take reasonable care to describe her condition accurately and make, so far as possible, a reliable prognosis.
600 (1993) 107 D.L.R. (4th) 169. See also *London Drugs Ltd v Kuehne & Nagel Ltd* (1992) 97 D.L.R. (4th) 261. La Forest J commented that in the case of professional employees it was not enough for the claimant to show that it had relied on the employee's reputation. It had to show that it had relied on his "pocket-book"; and *Trevor Ivory v Anderson* [1992] 2 N.Z.L.R. 31, in which the director of a one-man consultancy firm was held not to owe a *Hedley Byrne* duty to a client of the firm to which he had given advice.
601 [1998] 1 W.L.R. 830. See further para.5-81.

in *Phelps v Hillingdon LBC*,[602] the House of Lords held that an educational psychologist employed by a local authority could owe a duty of care to a child who had been referred to the psychologist. The damage in *Phelps* was categorised as "personal injury" but in *Merrett v Babb*[603] the Court of Appeal relied on *Phelps* in concluding that an employed surveyor could owe a duty of care in respect of economic loss to a client of his employer despite the absence of personal dealings between the parties. Aldous LJ dissented on the basis of *Williams* but the majority in *Merrett* distinguished *Williams* as being concerned with the status of directors and not employees. The point remains open for the House of Lords to consider and it is suggested that the status of the defendant as an employee should be a factor to be taken into account in considering whether a claimant's reliance on that individual is reasonable.

Informal or social context Where the advice is given informally it is unlikely to be sufficiently authoritative to entitle reliance. An oral answer to a planning enquiry,[604] information given by an auditor in an informal and half-remembered conversation,[605] an off the cuff response to a business inquiry[606] or statements which are merely sales talk,[607] are unlikely to give rise to liability. Similarly, where the relationship between the parties is social it may not be reasonable for the claimant to rely on the defendant being legally accountable. For this reason, in *Spring v Guardian Assurance Plc*[608] Lords Slynn and Woolf doubted whether a reference provided by a social acquaintance would give rise to liability under the *Hedley Byrne* principle. However, in *Chaudhry v Prabhakar*[609] liability was imposed in a social relationship. The defendant, who advised a friend on the purchase of a car, conceded that he was under a *Hedley Byrne* duty to the friend and argued unsuccessfully that the standard to be expected was subjective rather than objective. May LJ doubted (at 38) whether the concession on duty was correct arguing that to impose such a duty would "make social relations and responsibilities between friends unnecessarily hazardous". However, Stuart-Smith LJ seemed to suggest that **7-137**

602 [2001] 2 A.C. 619.

603 [2001] EWCA Civ 214; [2001] Q.B. 1174. See also *Yazhou Travel Investment Co Ltd v Bateson Starr (A Firm)* [2005] P.N.L.R. 31 (HC, Hong Kong). See para.9-17. In *Hart Investments Ltd v Fidler* [2007] EWHC 1058 (TCC); [2007] P.N.L.R. 26, Roger Stewart QC followed *Merrett v Babb* in holding that an engineer owed a personal tortious duty of care to developers on the ground that the relationship was close and there was an understanding that the engineer's professional indemnity insurance would be available to the claimants.

604 *Tidman v Reading BC* [1994] 3 P.L.R. 72; [1994] N.P.C. 136.

605 *Electra v KPMG Peat Marwick* [1998] P.N.L.R. 135; reversed on other grounds [1999] Lloyd's Rep. P.N. 670.

606 See *Howard Marine and Dredging Co v A Ogden & Sons (Excavations) Ltd* [1978] Q.B. 574, where the majority of the Court of Appeal concluded that a company chartering barges was not under a duty when one of their employees misrepresented the capacity of a barge in an oral, off the cuff response to an inquiry. Lord Denning MR said that no duty was owed where "the opinion, information or advice is given in circumstances in which it appears that it is unconsidered and it would not be reasonable for the recipient to act upon it without taking further steps to check it". Shaw LJ dissented on this point, arguing that the subject-matter of the inquiry was so important and the effort required to give a correct answer so minimal that the defendant was under a duty. See also *Fashion Brokers Ltd v Clarke Hayes (A Firm)* [2000] P.N.L.R. 473; [2000] Lloyd's Rep. P.N. 398, where a telephone response to a planning enquiry by a local authority employee did not give rise to a duty.

607 The reason why the estate agent in *Shields v Broderick* (1984) 8 DLR (4th) 96, was held not liable for telling a purchaser not to worry about selling his own home before making an unconditional offer to buy, as his own home "would sell very easily".

608 [1995] 2 A.C. 296 at 337, 345.

609 [1989] 1 W.L.R. 29.

the duty would have existed in the absence of the concession, arguing that the principal-agent relationship between the parties indicated that "the occasion is not a purely social one, but to use Lord Reid's expression, is in a business connection".[610] It is submitted that the view of May LJ should be followed. It would be unfair to impose a duty where the relationship is social in origin, unless there is clear evidence that the person is assuming legal responsibility for the advice he gives.[611]

(iii) Disclaimers[612]

7-138 **Effect of disclaimers** A disclaimer of liability in respect of a statement or service may be sufficient to preclude a finding of assumption of responsibility and reasonable reliance. This was the case in *Hedley Byrne* itself where the credit reference provided by the defendant bank was stated to be given without responsibility and as a result the bank was held to owe no duty. In *McCullagh v Lane Fox & Partners Ltd*[613] Hobhouse LJ explained that a disclaimer was not to be construed narrowly in the same way as an exclusion clause, rather the court should "treat the existence of the disclaimer as one of the facts relevant to answering the question whether there had been an assumption of responsibility by the defendants for the relevant statement. This question must be answered objectively by reference to what the reasonable person in the position of [the claimant] would have understood at the time he finally relied upon the representation." The estate agent's disclaimer in the case was contained in the particulars of the property and provided that "all statements contained in these particulars are made without responsibility". Hobhouse LJ criticised the approach of the trial judge in treating this disclaimer as if it were a contractual exclusion and construing it narrowly so as not to apply to the oral misrepresentation of the agent. Rather, he concluded that "the mere fact that [the employee] when showing [the claimant] around the property, gave the same information [as had been in the written particulars] orally would not lead a reasonable person to conclude that the defendants were thereby choosing to assume responsibility for the statement which they said in the particulars they were not assuming responsibility for".[614] However, the wording must be sufficient to cover the

---

610 However, the principal-agent relationship was itself conceded by the defendant. Stocker LJ whilst basing his decision on the concession, commented (at 36) that: "The first question … is whether any duty of care is owed … where the relationship of the parties is such that no voluntary assumption of legal responsibility was intended or can properly be imputed and where the giving of the advice was motivated solely out of friendship. Thus, in my view, in the absence of other factors giving rise to such a duty, the giving of advice sought in the context of family, domestic or social relationships will not in itself give rise to any duty in respect of such advice."

611 As occurred in *Burgess v Lejonvarn* [2017] EWCA Civ 254; [2017] P.N.L.R. 25 (architect who agreed to help friends with a garden landscape project had undertaken responsibility and, though not under a duty to provide professional services (in the absence of a contract), she owed a duty of care in respect of the services she actually provided; she had provided the services in the expectation that this would lead to paid work. At a subsequent trial it was found that there had been no breach of duty by the architect: *Burgess v Lejonvarn* [2018] EWHC 3166 (TCC); (2018) 181 Con. L.R. 204). This same policy is applied in contractual actions. See *Balfour v Balfour* [1919] 2 K.B. 571. A party to a social or family arrangement will not be held liable in contract unless there is positive evidence that the party intended to enter into a contractual relationship.

612 See further para.3-135 onwards and paras 9-36 to 9-39 and 9-181 to 9-184.

613 [1996] P.N.L.R. 205 at 237.

614 [1996] P.N.L.R. 205 at 237.

conduct of the defendant[615] and to disclaim responsibility. In *Henderson v Merrett Syndicates Ltd*[616] wording which provided that Lloyd's agents had absolute discretion as to the acceptance of risks on behalf of Names, was held to be insufficient. Lord Goff said that "in the present case the words ... should [have been] directed towards the scope of the agents' authority" to be effective. An exclusion or limitation of liability clause in a contract between the defendant and its contractual employer may also be held to affect or limit the defendant's liability to a third party claimant arising from performance of its contractual duties.[617] On the other hand, in *Precis (521) v William Mercer Ltd*[618] Arden LJ stated, obiter, that a disclaimer attached to a valuer's report by the client when passing it on to the claimant third party, could not be relevant to whether the valuer had assumed a responsibility to the third party because the valuer was unaware of the disclaimer.

Statutory control of disclaimers[619] Disclaimers are subject to the provisions of the Unfair Contract Terms Act 1977 and the Consumer Rights Act 2015.[620] The Consumer Rights Act governs unfair terms in consumer contracts and unfair consumer notices,[621] and the Unfair Contract Terms Act applies to "business liability" in the context of non-consumer transactions.[622] Under both statutes it is not possible to exclude liability for personal injury or death resulting from negligence.[623] Disclaimers in relation to other forms of damage are subject to statutory control. Under the Consumer Rights Act 2015 s.62 an unfair term of a consumer contract or an unfair consumer notice is not binding on the consumer, and a term or notice is unfair if contrary to the requirement of good faith, it causes a significant imbalance in the parties' rights and obligations to the detriment of the consumer.[624] Under the Unfair Contract Terms Act 1977 s.2(2) a person cannot in the course of his business "exclude or restrict his liability for negligence except in so far as the term or notice satisfies the requirement of reasonableness".[625] In applying the test under s.2(2), the courts have regard to the nature of the relationship between the parties. **7-139**

615 See for example, *Duncan Investments Ltd v Underwoods (A Firm)* [1998] P.N.L.R. 754, in which the Court of Appeal held that a clause disclaiming an estate agent's responsibility for representations made on behalf of the vendor could not apply to advice given on its own behalf.

616 [1995] 2 A.C. 145 at 183.

617 See *Killick v PriceWaterhouseCoopers* [2001] P.N.L.R. 1.

618 [2005] EWCA Civ 114; [2005] P.N.L.R. 28 at [26].

619 See further para.3-135 onwards and paras 9-37 to 9-39.

620 *Smith v Eric S Bush* [1990] 1 A.C. 831 HL, decided that disclaimers fell within s.13(1) of the Unfair Contract Terms Act 1977 which provides that to the extent to which s.2 prevents the exclusion or restriction of liability, it also prevents "excluding or restricting liability by reference to terms or notices which restrict the relevant obligation or duty".

621 See para.3-141 for definitions.

622 See para.3-136.

623 Unfair Contract Terms Act 1977 s.2(1); Consumer Rights Act 2015 s.65(1).

624 The Act contains an indicative and non-exhaustive list of terms of consumer contracts that may be regarded as unfair: Consumer Rights Act 2015 s.63(1), and Pt 1 of Sch.2.

625 With regard to a contract term the Unfair Contract Terms Act 1977 s.11(1) provides that the requirement of reasonableness is that the term shall have been "a fair and reasonable one to allow to be included having regard to the circumstances which were, or ought reasonably to have been, known to or in the contemplation of the parties when the contract was made"; and s.11(3) applies to a non-contractual notice, providing that reasonableness means that "it should be fair and reasonable to allow reliance on it, having regard to all the circumstances obtaining when liability arose or (but for the notice) would have arisen".

In *Smith v Eric S Bush*[626] the surveyor's disclaimer of responsibility for the valuation passed on by the lender to the purchaser was regarded as unreasonable and ineffective. Lord Griffiths stressed four factors: the claimant's lack of bargaining power; the unreasonableness of expecting the claimant to seek a private valuation given that he would then be paying twice for the same service; the elementary level of skill required in compiling a valuation report which needs to note only observable defects; and finally, the fact that "denying the surveyor the right to exclude liability would distribute the risk of his negligence amongst all house purchasers through an increase in his fees to cover insurance" whereas otherwise "the whole risk would fall on the one unfortunate purchaser".[627] By contrast, the disclaimer in *McCullagh v Lane Fox & Partners Ltd*[628] was regarded as reasonable as the prospective purchaser could be expected to verify the particulars of the property himself.

7-140 The purpose and scope of the disclaimer will also be relevant. In *Omega Trust Co Ltd v Wright Son & Pepper*[629] a disclaimer in a property valuation for a commercial lender which stated that it was not to be relied on by third parties, was held to be reasonable as against another lender who joined the client in making a loan on the security of the property. Henry LJ said:

> "It seems to me that this professional valuer, valuing expensive properties in a commercial context, was entitled to know who his client was and to whom his duty was owed. He was entitled … to refuse to assume liability to any unknown lender, indeed, I would go further and say that he is entitled to refuse to assume liability to any known lender to whom he had not agreed. He was entitled to increase the fee … as a term of permitting the second lender to rely on the valuation because … potentially it can be more expensive to be sued by two lenders rather than one."[630]

Before the Consumer Rights Act 2015, s.2(2) of the Unfair Contract Terms Act 1977 applied to consumer and commercial contracts alike, but in assessing whether a disclaimer satisfied the test of reasonableness the courts took the view that the more commercial the relationship between the parties, the more likely it would be that a disclaimer would satisfy the test of reasonableness.[631] Thus, a disclaimer in an engineer's report to a contractor[632] or an accountant's report to an investor[633] would be more likely to be effective. Indeed, the disclaimer which was effective in deny-

---

[626] [1990] 1 A.C. 831 (the claimant in this case would now be regarded as a "consumer" and so the Consumer Rights Act 2015 would apply).

[627] [1990] 1 A.C. 831 at 857. See further para.9-182.

[628] [1996] P.N.L.R. 205 at 239.

[629] [1997] P.N.L.R. 424.

[630] [1997] P.N.L.R. 424 at 430–431.

[631] See *The Governor and Company of the Bank of Scotland v Fuller Peiser* [2002] P.N.L.R 13; 2002 S.L.T. 574, where a disclaimer of third party liability in a survey report was held reasonable given that the third party pursuer was a commercial bank engaged in a commercial transaction; *Barclays Bank Plc v Grant Thornton UK LLP* [2015] EWHC 320 (Comm); [2015] 1 C.L.C. 180 at [91] per Cooke J: disclaimer in a non-statutory audit report held to be reasonable in a case where "sophisticated business parties are able to protect their own interests and do not require the protection of the 1977 Act in the same way as small companies or consumers".

[632] Analogous to the disclaimer in the contractor-employer contract in *Pacific Associates Inc v Baxter* [1990] 1 Q.B. 993. This disclaimer pre-dated the Unfair Contract Terms Act and hence the issue did not arise but the tenor of the judgments suggests that it would have been regarded as reasonable. In *Galliford Try Infrastructure Ltd (Formerly Morrison Construction Ltd) v Mott MacDonald Ltd* [2008] EWHC 1570 (TCC); [2009] P.N.L.R. 9 at [333], Akenhead J did not consider that the Unfair Contract Terms Act 1977 applied to disclaimers in specifications for a building contract (see para.7-142), but if it had been necessary to decide whether the disclaimers were fair and reasonable would

ing the duty in *Hedley Byrne* might well be held reasonable for the purpose of the Act.[634]

Disclaimers and duty In *Smith v Eric S Bush*[635] Lord Griffiths expressed the view that the court should determine whether a duty would have existed "but for" the disclaimer before considering whether the disclaimer was reasonable. This approach was based on the reference in the Unfair Contract Terms Act to the "exclusion of the relevant duty" which seemed to suggest that the existence of the duty should be established before the exclusion was considered. However, in *First National Commercial Bank Plc v Loxleys*[636] Nourse LJ said that since the observations of Lord Griffiths in *Smith*: "the law has moved on, or perhaps back, since then, in particular through the decision of the House of Lords in *Henderson v Merrett Syndicates* ... which has rehabilitated the 'assumption of responsibility' concept". He concluded: "In this uncertain state of the law I cannot be confident that the duty of care issue can be decided as a discrete point. It is at least possible that the existence or not of such a duty will be held to depend partly on the effect of the disclaimer."[637] As many of the factors which are relevant to the assumption of responsibility and reasonable reliance necessary to establish a duty are also relevant to whether the disclaimer is reasonable, this would seem the better approach. Indeed, in *Royal Bank of Scotland Ltd v Bannerman Johnstone Maclay*,[638] the failure to make use of the opportunity to disclaim was regarded as potentially supporting an assumption of responsibility based on knowledge of the claimant's intended use.[639] 7-141

In *Galliford Try Infrastructure Ltd (Formerly Morrison Construction Ltd) v Mott MacDonald Ltd*[640] a design and build contractor retained by a building development company brought an action in negligence against consulting engineers retained by a wholly owned subsidiary of the building development company. Although there had been negotiations about establishing a contractual relationship between the claimants and the consulting engineers, this was not implemented. The project was completed late, and the claimants alleged that their losses due to delay 7-142

---

have concluded they were because: (a) both parties were large sophisticated commercial organisations, with access to in-house legal expertise; each was on an equal footing; (b) such disclaimers were relatively common amongst consulting engineers; (c) their wording was clear and there was no good reason why the claimants should not have known of them; and (d) compliance with the disclaimers was not impracticable.

633 e.g. in a situation such as the take-over bid in *Morgan Crucible v Hill Samuel* [1991] Ch. 295 or an auditor's non-statutory audit report to a company relied upon by a lender: *Barclays Bank Plc v Grant Thornton UK LLP* [2015] EWHC 320 (Comm); [2015] 1 C.L.C. 180.

634 See, e.g. *Robinson v PE Jones (Contractors) Ltd* [2011] EWCA Civ 9; [2012] Q.B. 44 where the Court of Appeal upheld the trial judge's conclusion that clauses in a building contract limiting the building owner's remedies against a builder to a claim under the NHBC agreement (thereby excluding any liability in negligence) satisfied the test of reasonableness in the Unfair Contract Terms Act 1977, given the benefits which the purchaser obtained under the NHBC agreement.

635 [1990] 1 A.C. 831 at 857.

636 [1997] P.N.L.R. 211 at 214.

637 [1997] P.N.L.R. 211 at 215.

638 [2005] CSIH 39; 2005 1 S.C. 437; [2005] P.N.L.R. 43 at [63].

639 The fact that an auditor's disclaimer of responsibility in relation to an audit report is void in a claim by the company against the auditor (as a result of what was the Companies Act 1985 s.310; see now Companies Act 2006 s.532) is irrelevant in relation to a claim by a third party against the auditor, and there is nothing in the Act to prevent an auditor disclaiming liability to a third party: [2005] CSIH 39; 2005 1 S.C. 437; [2005] P.N.L.R. 43 at [64].

640 [2008] EWHC 1570 (TCC); [2009] P.N.L.R. 9.

were attributable to their reliance on the consulting engineers' negligent advice in relation to the design of the project. The specification for the project included disclaimers of responsibility by the defendants to "any person other than the person by whom it was commissioned". In holding that the defendants owed no duty of care to claimants Akenhead J commented that the disclaimers were "pointers" towards there being no duty of care: "They acted as a kind of warning to [the claimants] not to rely upon material produced by [the defendants] either on the drawings or specifications themselves or to any change to or amplification of them. The fact that [the claimants] may not have paid any attention to them is immaterial; that was its risk."[641] The disclaimers were not exclusion clauses, but were "simply aspects of the factual background from which the court determines whether a duty of care arises". They were a reminder to the claimants not to rely upon what it itself had not commissioned.[642]

7-143 **Prominence of the disclaimer** In *Taberna Europe CDO II Plc v Selskabet (formerly Roskilde Bank A/S) (In Bankruptcy)*[643] the claimants, who were professional investors, complained that a disclaimer was tucked away, in small print, at the back of a document on which they had relied (an "investor presentation" on the defendants' website). The Court of Appeal held that this was irrelevant to whether the disclaimer should take effect because it was intended to be read by experienced professional investors, who were aware that it was necessary to read a document of that kind in its entirety. Moore-Bick LJ noted that "there has been an increasing willingness in recent years to recognise that parties to commercial contracts are entitled to determine for themselves the terms on which they will do business."[644] The defendants were entitled to include in the investor presentation a disclaimer of liability for the statements contained in it.

(i) Financial loss resulting from the acquisition of defective property

7-144 **Dangerous defects** A person who unknowingly acquires a product or building which is defective will suffer economic loss in repairing or replacing it when the defect is discovered. For a period it was considered that where such defects endangered the acquirer or his property, the loss could be regarded as a form of physical damage and the acquirer could claim against anyone whose negligence was responsible under the simple *Donoghue v Stevenson* principle without having to establish the assumption of responsibility required for recovery of economic loss. This treatment of dangerous defects as equivalent to physical damage began with the Court of Appeal decision in *Dutton v Bognor Regis Urban DC*.[645] The claimant had bought a house that had been built on a disused rubbish tip and which after the purchase began to show signs of cracking and settlement. The local authority was held liable to the claimant for negligently approving the inadequate foundations constructed by the builder. Lord Denning MR classified the loss as physical

641 [2008] EWHC 1570 (TCC); [2009] P.N.L.R. 9 at [330].
642 See [2008] EWHC 1570 (TCC); [2009] P.N.L.R. 9 at [331]–[332].
643 [2016] EWCA Civ 1262; [2017] Q.B. 633 at [16].
644 [2016] EWCA Civ 1262; [2017] Q.B. 633 at [26].
645 [1972] 1 Q.B. 373.

damage[646] and, applying *Donoghue v Stevenson*, held that as loss was foreseeable and there was no possibility of intermediate inspection once the foundations were covered up, e.g. by a surveyor, there was sufficient proximity to support a duty. He justified classifying the loss as physical, as otherwise "it would mean that, if the inspector negligently passes the house as properly built and it collapses and injures a person, the council are liable; but, if the owner discovers the defect in time to repair it—and he does repair it—the council are not liable. That is an impossible distinction. They are liable in either case." This approach was approved by the House of Lords in *Anns v Merton LBC*[647] and widely applied. However, in the 1980s judicial and academic disquiet developed as the consequences in terms of widespread claims against local authorities rather than the more blameworthy builders, became apparent. The House of Lords finally rejected the *Dutton* classification of defects in *D & F Estates Ltd v Church Commissioners*.[648] The defendants were builders who built a block of flats with defective plasterwork; the claimants, later occupiers of one of the flats, sued the defendants for the damage to flooring caused by falling plaster and for the cost of having the plastering re-done. The House of Lords allowed the first claim but rejected the second. In distinguishing the claims, Lord Bridge said:

> "If the hidden defect in the chattel is the cause of personal injury or of damage to property other than the chattel itself, the manufacturer is liable. But if the hidden defect is discovered before any such damage is caused, there is no longer any room for the application of the *Donoghue v Stevenson* principle. The chattel is now defective in quality, but is no longer dangerous. It may be valueless or it may be capable of economic repair.... If the same principle applies in the field of real property to the liability of the builder of a permanent structure which is dangerously defective, that liability can only arise if the defect remains hidden until the defective structure causes personal injury or damage to property other than the structure itself. If the defect is discovered before any damage is done, the loss sustained by the owner of the structure, who has to repair or demolish it to avoid a potential source of danger to third parties, would seem to be purely economic."[649]

Dangerous defects and economic loss[650] In *Murphy v Brentwood DC*[651] the House of Lords applied the same reasoning to overrule *Dutton* and *Anns* and hold that a local authority owed no duty to a purchaser of a house with defective foundations which had been negligently approved by the authority. The loss was categorised as purely economic and recoverable only under the *Hedley Byrne* principle where there was a special relationship between the parties. Lord Keith cited *Junior Books Ltd v Veitchi Co Ltd*[652] as an example of liability under that principle. In *Junior Books* nominated subcontractors whose negligent work had **7-145**

---

646 [1972] 1 Q.B. 373 at 396, per Lord Denning MR, at 403–404, per Sachs LJ.
647 [1978] A.C. 728.
648 [1989] A.C. 177.
649 [1989] A.C. 177 at 206.
650 See further paras 9-211 and 9-212.
651 [1991] 1 A.C. 398. On the same day the House of Lords gave judgment in *Department of Environment v Thomas Bates & Son Ltd* [1991] 1 A.C. 499, in which it was held that following *Murphy*, a builder owed no duty to the tenant of a building in respect of the cost of strengthening pillars which due to the builder's negligence, were not strong enough to support the potential design load of the building. For application of the principles to architects, see para.9-211.
652 [1983] 1 A.C. 520. Similarly, he cited *Pirelli General Cable Works Ltd v Oscar Faber & Partners (A Firm)* [1983] 2 A.C. 1. In *Abbott v Will Gannon & Smith Ltd* [2005] EWCA Civ 198; [2005] P.N.L.R. 30, the Court of Appeal held that for the purpose of deciding when the limitation period started to run, the decision in *Pirelli* that it was on the occurrence of physical damage occurring

resulted in defects in a factory floor were held to owe a duty of care to the building owner in respect of the repair costs. In the light of Lord Goff's view in *Henderson v Merrett Syndicates*[653] that the ordinary relationship of building owner and his nominated subcontractor does not embody an assumption of responsibility giving rise to a duty under the *Hedley Byrne* principle, it may be more appropriate to justify *Junior Books* on the ground that the subcontractors were nominated for their special skill in floor work and that element of skill gave rise to the necessary assumption of responsibility and concomitant reliance.

7-146 In *Robinson v PE Jones (Contractors) Ltd*[654] the Court of Appeal emphasised that beyond the realm of a professional's relationship with a client, it is highly unlikely that a contract will create concurrent liability in tort. Jackson LJ noted that the relationship between the manufacturer of a product or the builder of a building and the immediate client is primarily governed by the contract between those two parties: "Absent any assumption of responsibility, there do not spring up between the parties duties of care co-extensive with their contractual obligations. The law of tort imposes a different and more limited duty upon the manufacturer or builder. That more limited duty is to take reasonable care to protect the client against suffering personal injury or damage to other property."[655] There was nothing in the facts of the case to suggest that the builder had assumed responsibility in the *Hedley Byrne* sense. It involved a normal building contract for the construction of a house to an agreed specification. The contract provided warranties of quality and set out the purchaser's remedies in the event of a breach of warranty. It was not a professional relationship where the claimant was paying for advice or for the preparation of reports or plans on which the claimant would act.[656]

7-147 Although neither *D & F Estates Ltd* nor *Murphy* dealt with the position of others involved in the construction of buildings such as fabricators, architects and consulting engineers, it is clear that these must be treated in the same way as builders.[657] As Lord Bridge's speech in *Murphy* made clear, the same reasoning ap-

(para.31-10), remained good law despite the treatment of such damage as economic loss in the subsequent House of Lords decision in *Murphy*. Note that in *Bank of East Asia Ltd v Tsien Wui Marble Factory* (1999) 2 HK C.F.A. 349, the Hong Kong Final Court of Appeal reached a similar conclusion but Lord Nicholls dissented arguing that the damage had to be classified as economic. However, such economic loss would normally occur when the physical defects became patent and affected the economic value of the premises.

653 [1995] 2 A.C. 145 at 195.

654 [2011] EWCA Civ 9; [2012] Q.B. 44.

655 [2011] EWCA Civ 9; [2012] Q.B. 44 at [68].

656 [2011] EWCA Civ 9; [2012] Q.B. 44 at [83]. See also the comments of Stanley Burnton LJ at [92] (quoted at para.7-128).

657 The *Murphy* reasoning has been applied at first instance to an architect in *Lancashire and Cheshire Association of Baptist Churches Inc v Howard & Seddon Partnership* [1993] 3 All E.R. 467; and to an architect and engineer in *Wessex Regional HA v HLM Design* (1994) 10 Cons. L.J. 165. See also *Hart Investments Ltd v Fidler* [2007] EWHC 1058 (TCC); [2007] P.N.L.R. 26, in which the collapse of building frontage due to defective design was classed as economic loss but the designer was held liable on the basis of his close relationship with the claimants who were developing the building. In *Payne v John Setchell Ltd* [2002] P.N.L.R. 7 at 176, HH Judge Humphrey Lloyd QC after extensive consideration of the authorities held that there was nothing in the speeches in *Murphy* "which on their Lordships' reasoning justifies a distinction being made between the 'designer' and the 'builder', nor is there any operational, practical or social reason to do so". Hence a structural engineer did not owe a tort duty to his contractual client in respect of the allegedly negligent design of foundations which it was claimed led to the eventual subsidence of the client's house.

plies to products and both Lord Keith[658] and Lord Oliver[659] criticised the view that the user of a dangerously defective product could recover repair costs.[660] In *Nitrigin Eireann Teoranta v Inco Alloys Ltd*[661] May J applied the reasoning to hold that the manufacturer of pipes was not liable in tort to the purchaser for the cost of repairing cracks allegedly due to negligent manufacture. The cracking was "damage to the pipe itself constituting a defect of quality resulting in economic loss irrecoverable in negligence".[662] In *Rivtow Marine Ltd v Washington Iron Works*[663] the Canadian Supreme Court held that the user of a product (a logging crane) could recover the loss sustained due to the manufacturer's negligent delay in warning of defects which resulted in the crane having to be repaired during what would have been the most profitable period of its use. However, it is difficult to justify this decision in terms of assumption of responsibility and in *Hamble Fisheries Ltd v Gardner and Sons Ltd*[664] the Court of Appeal held that the *Rivtow* principle was not recognised in English Law and, hence, a shipowner could not recover loss of profit during the period of repairs to the ship's engine which were necessitated by its negligent design for which the defendant was responsible.

Damage to other property and the complex structure theory[665] The House of Lords in *D & F Estates v Church Commissioners*[666] drew a distinction between damage to other property, for which a negligent builder was liable, and damage to the actual premises he had built, for which he was not. Lord Bridge said that it was arguable that: 7-148

> "in the case of complex structures, as indeed possibly in the case of complex chattels, one element of the structure should be regarded … as distinct from another element, so that damage to one part of the structure caused by a hidden defect in another part may qualify to be treated as damage to 'other property'."[667]

He explained the principle further in *Murphy v Brentwood DC*:

> "A critical distinction must be drawn between some part of a complex structure which is said to be a 'danger' only because it does not perform its proper function in sustaining the other parts and some distinct item incorporated in the structure which positively malfunctions so as to inflict positive damage on the structure in which it is incorporated. Thus, if a defective central heating boiler explodes and damages a house … I see no reason to doubt that the owner of the house, if he can prove that the damage was due to the negligence of the boiler manufacturer … can recover damages in tort on *Donoghue v Stevenson* principles. But the position in law is entirely different where, by reason of the inadequacy of the foundations of the building to support the weight of the superstructure,

[658] [1991] 1 A.C. 398 at 469.

[659] [1991] 1 A.C. 398 at 488.

[660] The view of Laskin and Hall JJ giving the minority judgment in *Rivtow Marine Ltd v Washington Iron Works* [1974] S.C.R. 1189 at 1220.

[661] [1992] 1 W.L.R. 498.

[662] The repair was ineffective and the pipe ruptured causing an explosion which disabled the rest of the claimant's plant. May J held that as on the assumed facts the claimant's conduct in repairing the pipe had been reasonable, it was entitled to claim in respect of the explosion damage.

[663] [1974] S.C.R. 1189.

[664] [1999] 2 Lloyd's Rep. 1. See para.10-19.

[665] See further paras 10-21 to 10-24 in relation to products.

[666] [1989] A.C. 177.

[667] [1989] A.C. 177 at 207.

differential settlement and consequent cracking occurs. Here, once the first cracks appear, the structure as a whole is seen to be defective."[668]

It is not the complexity of the structure which is crucial but the functional distinctness of the item causing the damage. The same point applies to products. In *Aswan Engineering Establishment Co v Lupdine Ltd*[669] it had been argued that the packaging of a product, e.g. its carton, could be regarded as a separate item from the product itself so as to give rise to liability if the defective condition of the packaging damaged the product. Nicholls LJ rejected this argument as pressing "the extent of *Donoghue v Stevenson* unacceptably far".[670] Where subsequent to the claimant's acquisition of the building or product it is damaged by work done to it, e.g. alteration,[671] or packaging, simple *Donoghue* liability may result.

7-149 The issue of what constitutes "other property" can involve nice questions of fact, particularly in the context of a construction project with multiple contractors. In *Linklaters Business Services (formerly Hackwood Services Co) v Sir Robert McAlpine Ltd*[672] sub-contractors fitted insulation material to steel pipework used for air conditioning. It was alleged that defects in the fitting of the insulation allowed water and air to penetrate the insulated pipework with the result that the steel rusted and corroded. The sub-contractors applied to strike out the contractors' claim for contribution on the basis that the sub-contractors owed no duty of care to the building owners (the lessees who had undertaken substantial renovation work to the building). The issue was whether the insulated steel pipework was one "thing" or, given that the pipework was part of an installation in an overall building, whether it was to be considered simply as an indivisible part of the whole building. Akenhead J, on the assumption that the corrosion and rusting was classified as physical damage to the steel pipework, refused to strike out the claim. This was an

---

668 [1991] 1 A.C. 398 at 478. Lord Keith (at 470) endorsed this view. In *Payne v John Setchell Ltd* [2002] P.N.L.R. 7 at 183, HH Judge Humphrey Lloyd QC held that in the light of Lord Bridge's comments, the "complex structure theory exception is no longer tenable". But it was applied by an Official Referee, Mr Recorder Jackson QC, in *Jacobs v Moreton & Partners* (1994) 72 B.L.R 92, to hold that the constructors of a defective raft foundation could owe a duty to a subsequent purchaser of a house built on the raft which had to be demolished because of the raft defects. The Referee noted that the raft had been inserted under an already built house and had been constructed by persons who had no responsibility for the house construction. In *Murphy* [1991] 1 A.C. 398 at 475 Lord Bridge had suggested, obiter, a further exception to the non-recoverability of repair costs where: "a building stands so close to the boundary of the building owner's land that after discovery of the dangerous defect it remains a potential source of injury to persons or property on neighbouring land or on the highway, the building owner ought, in principle, to be entitled to recover in tort from the negligent builder the cost of obviating the danger, whether by repair or by demolition, so far as that cost is necessarily incurred in order to protect himself from potential liability to third parties." Lord Bridge did not explain the rationale for distinguishing between the cost of avoiding the risk of harm to persons on the property (non-recoverable) as opposed to the cost of avoiding the risk of harm to persons adjacent to the property (possibly recoverable), though it may be that the former can be avoided simply by excluding persons from the property whereas the latter cannot be avoided except by repair or demolition. But in *Thomas v Taylor Wimpey Developments Ltd* [2019] EWHC 1134 (TCC); [2019] P.N.L.R. 26 Judge Keyser QC, after careful analysis, concluded that Lord Bridge's qualification does not represent the law, and that there is no exception to the general rule established by *D & F Estates v Church Commissioners* and *Murphy v Brentwood DC* for properties where the defect creates a risk of harm on neighbouring land or the highway.

669 [1987] 1 W.L.R. 1. See further para.10-24.

670 [1987] 1 W.L.R. 1 at 29. Lloyd LJ was "provisionally" more sympathetic to the argument: [1987] 1 W.L.R. 1 at 21.

671 See for example *Lindenberg v Joe Canning* (1993) 9 Cons. L.J. 43.

672 [2010] EWHC 1145 (TCC); [2010] B.L.R. 537.

area of developing jurisprudence and there were too many factual uncertainties for summary judgment or for a striking out. His Lordship noted that *Murphy v Brentwood DC* and *D & F Estates v Church Commissioners*:

> "do not specifically address the extent of any duty of care owed by a sub-contractor or supplier who provides an element of or within the building being constructed or developed, save that it is clear that the duty of care does not extend to cover the cost of replacement or repair, or the loss, of the element itself … . What has not been explored and examined in any great detail is the extent of the duty of care owed by those in the position of sub-contractors … and suppliers whose carelessness in and about providing the work, materials, services or equipment which are incorporated into a building or structure causes consequential damage to other elements of the building. The scope of this duty and where the dividing lines are remain to be explored jurisprudentially and in practice."[673]

On the other hand, in *Broster v Galliard Docklands Ltd*[674] Akenhead J was less circumspect in holding that builders who had designed and constructed a row of six terraced houses for the first defendant were not liable for damage to the properties. The claimants had purchased the houses from the first defendant. The houses had a common roof, and in a very high wind the roof lifted and fell back damaging both the roof and the houses, allegedly because the roof joists had not been strapped to the walls. The builders argued that they were not liable to the purchasers because the damage to the roof and walls was damage to "the thing itself". Akenhead J, applying Lord Bridge's statement of principle in *Murphy v Brentwood DC*, agreed:

> "It would be wholly artificial to argue that the segment of the roof over each individual terraced unit was to be considered as separate from the whole roof or indeed that the roof as a whole was to be considered as separate from the walls of the units below. It follows that there is damage 'to the thing itself'. Put another way, the duty of care does not extend to protect the owners of the property from damage to the roof itself or to the units below caused by the dislodgement of the roof. The House of Lords in the context of negligence has repeatedly warned against an artificial sub-division of a building, no matter how large, into constituent elements and, whether or not the 'complex structure' theory still has a material part to play in the law of negligence relating to buildings and structures, it does not extend to a case such as this."[675]

Statutory consequences The reclassification of dangerous defects as a form of economic loss in *D & F Estates Ltd* and *Murphy* reduced the significance of s.3 of the Latent Damage Act 1986 whilst increasing that of s.1 of the Defective Premises Act 1972. Section 3 was passed to deal with a limitation problem, namely that damage to property might not be discovered until after the owner of the property at the time the damage had occurred, had sold the property to another. Under the normal rules the owner at the time of the occurrence of the damage could have a cause of action if owed a duty but the subsequent owner who discovered the damage would not, because no property of his was damaged during his ownership. To overcome this, s.3 provided that where the owner at the time of damage had a cause of action but did not know of the damage, a fresh cause of action accrued to the subsequent purchaser on the date he acquired the property. Thus, if a builder's 7-150

---

673 [2010] EWHC 1145 (TCC); [2010] B.L.R. 537 at [27]. This point was not resolved on appeal, though the Court of Appeal commented that they were "issues which may require the attention of the Supreme Court in due course": *Southern Insulation (Medway) Ltd v How Engineering Services Ltd* [2010] EWCA Civ 999 at [10].

674 [2011] EWHC 1722 (TCC); [2011] P.N.L.R. 34.

675 [2011] EWHC 1722 (TCC); [2011] P.N.L.R. 34 at [16].

negligence resulted in defective foundations causing subsidence and giving the first owner a cause of action, a second owner would also have a cause of action if the damage caused by the subsidence did not become apparent until after his purchase. This section was based on the premise that the owner at the time the damage occurred would normally be owed a duty under *Dutton* and *Anns* principles. Under *D & F* and *Murphy* such a duty will not normally arise and hence, the situations in which a subsequent owner is likely to be able to take advantage of s.3 are likely to be rare.[676]

7-151 **Defective Premises Act 1972** Section 1 of the Defective Premises Act 1972 provides that a "person taking on work for or in connection with the provision of a dwelling-house" owes a duty to "see that the work which he takes on is done in a workmanlike or, as the case may be, professional manner, with proper materials and so that as regards that work the dwelling will be fit for habitation when completed". This section was of limited significance as the limitation period is six years from the date of completion and as many cases of subsidence etc do not become apparent until after that time, a common law action under *Anns* was often a more significant remedy.[677] The overruling of *Anns* refocused attention on the scope of s.1. It applies only to dwelling-houses; purchasers of commercial premises are limited to their rights at common law.[678] Nor does the duty apply to improvements to an existing dwelling-house,[679] though it can apply to the conversion of a property from, say, commercial use to a dwelling-house, and where the work constitutes the provision of a new dwelling where the "identity" of the property has been changed.[680] The duty is owed by builders and others, e.g. architects[681] and developers, in respect of both new construction and improvements, but it does not apply to an approved inspector performing statutory functions to ensure compliance with building regulations.[682] It is owed both to the person commissioning the work, and to "any person who acquires an interest, whether legal or equitable, in the dwell-

---

676 See, e.g. *Broster v Galliard Docklands Ltd* [2011] EWHC 1722 (TCC); [2011] P.N.L.R. 34 at [20]–[22].

677 *Payne v John Setchell Ltd* [2002] P.N.L.R. 7 illustrates a situation in which subsequent acquirers of homes could have recovered under the Act against an engineer allegedly responsible for negligent design of the foundations but for the claim being barred by the six-year period from completion.

678 A dwelling is "the place where a person or household lives to the exclusion of members of another household" and so in a block of flats the individual apartments constitute separate dwellings: *Rendlesham Estates Plc v Barr Ltd* [2014] EWHC 3968 (TCC); [2015] 1 W.L.R. 3663 at [43], per Edwards-Stuart J. It followed that the common parts of the building were not part of a dwelling, though work on the structural and common parts of a block of flats constitutes work that is "carried out in connection with the provision of each apartment in the block" ([2014] EWHC 3968 (TCC); [2015] 1 W.L.R. 3663 at [47]). Quaere where a building is partly a dwelling-house and partly commercial, e.g. where a businessman has a house built which includes an office. It is suggested that provided a substantial proportion of the building is for residential use it will be covered.

679 *Jenson v Faux* [2011] EWCA Civ 423; [2011] 1 W.L.R. 3038.

680 The extent and cost of the works is not decisive in determining whether the identity of the property has changed: "There may be cases in which a small amount of work might be needed to create a separate one-floor dwelling which would thus fall within s.1 of the 1972 Act; but there can be very extensive works to a house or dwelling which will not make it a dwelling whose identity is 'wholly different' from before": *Jenson v Faux* [2011] EWCA Civ 423; [2011] 1 W.L.R. 3038 at [18], per Longmore LJ.

681 *Thompson v Clive Alexander & Partners* (1993) 59 Build. L.R. 77.

682 *Lessees and Management Company of Herons Court v Heronslea Ltd* [2019] EWCA Civ 1423; [2019] 1 W.L.R. 5849.

ing"[683]; thus including not only subsequent purchasers and mortgagees, but apparently anyone, such as a cohabitee, who by contribution to the purchase price or otherwise gains an interest in it. The person undertaking the work is liable not only for what he himself does but also for the work of independent subcontractors employed by him.[684] The duty under s.1 applies to failure to carry out remedial work[685] as well as carrying out work badly but in either case the claimant can only claim in respect of defects which render the premises unfit for habitation.[686] Defects in quality which do not affect the property's fitness for habitation are not covered.[687]

(j) Financial loss following damage to another's property

The exclusionary rule The general rule has been that no duty is owed by a defendant who negligently damages property belonging to a third party, to a claimant who suffers loss because of a dependence upon that property or its owner. The leading authority is the 1875 case of *Cattle v Stockton Waterworks Co*[688] where the claimant suffered economic loss in performing a contract with a third party as a result of damage to that party's property. The defendant's negligence led to the saturation of an embankment on the third party's land and made it more difficult for the claimant to complete his contract with the third party to tunnel through the embankment. As a result, the claimant failed to make as much profit as would otherwise have been the case and sued the defendant for that loss of profit. Blackburn J held that such loss was irrecoverable on the ground that no property of the claimant was damaged. The rule was affirmed by the Privy Council and House of Lords respectively in *Candlewood Navigation Corp Ltd v Mitsui OSK Lines Ltd*[689] and *Leigh & Sillavan Ltd v Aliakmon Shipping Co*.[690] In *Candlewood* the Privy Council held that a time charterer of a vessel could not sue for the profit it would have made during the period that the vessel was under repair following a collision caused by the defendant's negligence. In the *Aliakmon* case, the claimant had agreed to buy a cargo to be shipped on the defendant's vessel. Because of poor 7-152

683 s.1(1)(b).

684 Assuming he is in the business of undertaking such work; s.1(4).

685 *Andrews v Schooling* [1991] 1 W.L.R. 783. On an interlocutory application the Court of Appeal held that developers of a flat were in principle liable to the purchaser for failing to take adequate steps to exclude damp from it.

686 As to the meaning of "unfit for habitation" see *Bole v Huntsbuild Ltd* [2009] EWCA Civ 1146; (2009) 127 Con. L.R. 154; *Thompson v Clive Alexander & Partners* (1993) 59 B.L.R. 77; and especially *Rendlesham Estates Plc v Barr Ltd* [2014] EWHC 3968 (TCC); [2015] 1 W.L.R. 3663 at [60]–[83] where Edwards-Stuart J undertook an extensive discussion of the meaning of the term "fit for habitation". In *Harrison v Shepherd Homes Ltd* [2011] EWHC 1811 (TCC); (2011) 27 Const. LJ 709 Ramsey J held that the s.1(1) duty is a single duty, so that the obligation to complete the work in a workmanlike manner and with proper materials is to be measured by reference to whether the dwelling is "fit for habitation"; they are not three distinct duties (applying *Alexander v Mercouris* [1979] 1 W.L.R. 1270, CA). Significant defects in the foundations of the properties in question were "properly matters which could be said to give rise to a lack of fitness for habitation": [2011] EWHC 1811 (TCC) at [164]. (An appeal on the assessment of damages only was dismissed: [2012] EWCA Civ 904; [2012] 3 E.G.L.R. 83).

687 "The mischief at which the Act is directed is the construction of dwellings that are not fit for habitation: it was not intended to compensate owners for the loss of a bargain": *Rendlesham Estates Plc v Barr Ltd* [2014] EWHC 3968 (TCC); [2015] 1 W.L.R. 3663 at [78] Edwards-Stuart J.

688 (1875) L.R. 10 Q.B. 453.

689 [1986] A.C. 1.

690 [1986] A.C. 785. The practical effect of this decision has been mitigated by the Carriage of Goods by Sea Act 1992. See further para.7-156.

stowage, the cargo was damaged. At the time of the damage the claimant was neither the owner nor possessor of the cargo but under the terms of the purchase contract, it had assumed the risk of damage to the cargo. The House of Lords held that as the property was owned by a third party at the time it was damaged, the claimant had no claim. The problem in both cases was that the claimant had no proprietary interest in the damaged property but only a contractual interest which resulted in economic loss as a consequence of the damage. However, where the claimant has a beneficial interest in trust property damaged by the defendant's negligence the exclusionary rule does not apply and, by joining the legal owner of the property to the proceedings, he can recover his foreseeable economic loss consequential on the physical damage to the trust property.[691]

7-153 A different illustration of the general rule is provided by *Spartan Steel & Alloys Ltd v Martin*[692] where the claimant had to shut down its manufacturing operations due to a power cut caused by the defendants negligently cutting the supply line owned by a third party electricity supplier. The Court of Appeal held that the claimant was entitled to recover the profits that were lost due to its own property being damaged by the power cut (a "melt" that had to be removed from an electric arc furnace) because these losses were the result of physical damage to the claimant's property. This is not regarded as pure economic loss, but economic loss consequent on physical damage.[693] The claimant was unable to recover the lost profit on four other melts that would have been processed in the period when the power supply was cut. This constituted pure economic loss, unrelated to any physical damage to

---

691 *Colour Quest Ltd v Total Downstream UK Plc* [2010] EWCA Civ 180; [2011] Q.B. 86, where the Court of Appeal held that a duty of care was owed to a beneficial owner of property just as much as to a legal owner of property and the beneficial owner can recover the extra expenditure to which he was put or the loss of profit consequent on the physical damage. Provided the legal owner could be joined in the proceedings, it was irrelevant that the beneficial owner was not in possession of the property (distinguishing *Leigh & Sillavan Ltd v Aliakmon Shipping Co*).

692 [1973] Q.B. 27; see also *Electrochrome Ltd v Welsh Plastics Ltd* [1968] 2 All E.R. 205; *SCM (UK) Ltd v WJ Whittall Ltd* [1971] 1 Q.B. 337.

693 Although claims for financial loss flowing from damage to the claimant's property are not considered to be pure economic loss, and so are normally recoverable, not all financial losses fit neatly into this categorisation. In *Network Rail Infrastructure Ltd v Conarken Group Ltd* [2011] EWCA Civ 644; [2012] 1 All E.R. (Comm) 692 the defendants negligently damaged a bridge belonging to the claimants who were required to pay certain sums to train operating companies as a result of delays to rail services whilst repairs were carried out. The payments were made under the terms of a complex contract between the claimants and the train operating companies, and were intended to compensate the train operating companies for, inter alia, the immediate and future loss of revenue due to delays in the rail service. The Court of Appeal held that the claimants were entitled to recover the contractual payments, even though under the contractual formula part of the sum was not directly related to lost income but included, e.g. sums related to incentive payments and estimates of lost future income. Pill LJ, although agreeing with the outcome, clearly had some reservations. It was: "too simplistic in circumstances such as the present to say that because a kind of loss, financial loss, is reasonably foreseeable to one who causes physical damage, all financial loss agreed between the victim and a third party is reasonably foreseeable. Had there been no such contract, analysis of the headings under which the alleged loss is claimed, and the manner in which it is calculated, would be necessary. The existence of the contract does not, in my judgment, remove the need for such analysis" (at [78]). Moore-Bick LJ took the view that the terms of the contract were similar to liquidated damages provisions commonly found in commercial contracts. The way in which the payments had been calculated was irrelevant: all that mattered was that they represented a genuine and reasonable attempt to assess the damage caused to the train operating companies. Jackson LJ considered that the loss of revenue was plainly foreseeable and the action "should be characterised as a simple claim for loss of income consequent upon damage to revenue earning property. This is a well-established category of recoverable economic loss" (at [150]). See further *Network Rail Infrastructure Ltd v Handy* [2015] EWHC 1175 (TCC).

the claimant's property. In *Spartan Steel* the claimant's operations were dependent upon the property owned by the third party. Such dependence may arise where there is no contract. In *Weller v Foot & Mouth Disease Research Institute*[694] the claimants, two firms of cattle auctioneers, were unable to recover from the defendants the profits lost owing to the closure of the markets following an outbreak of foot and mouth disease allegedly caused by the defendants' negligence in allowing the escape of a strain of foot and mouth virus. The virus damaged the cattle owned by third parties and the claimants' business was dependent upon the ability of those third parties to bring their cattle to market.[695] In *D Pride & Partners (A Firm) v Institute for Animal Health*[696] Tugendhat J considered whether claims by farmers for "loss of condition" of livestock (the animals were older, and either bigger and fatter or thinner, but in either case less valuable) as a result of restrictions on the movement of livestock during an outbreak of foot and mouth disease were claims for physical damage. It was arguable, said Tugendhat J, that the claimant farmers who alleged that their pigs had gone to the abattoir oversized had a real prospect of succeeding in the contention that that was physical damage, and so of recovering the loss of profit consequential upon that, but not any other economic loss. However, the farmers were not members of an identifiable class, and there was no means of distinguishing them from others who had suffered loss as a result of the outbreak (such as livestock auctioneers or livestock transporters). Thus, the claims of most of the farmers were subject to the "exclusionary rule" that they were not entitled to claim in respect of indirect economic loss, and the others could not establish that a duty of care was owed to them in respect of "indirect physical loss" because they were not members of an ascertainable class to whom a duty of care would be owed.

The rationale of the no-recovery rule The reasons given by the courts for the no-recovery rule fall under the heads of both proximity and fairness. In *Cattle* the court was primarily concerned with the possibility of indeterminate liability should a duty be recognised. Blackburn J in *Cattle* suggested that but for the no-recovery rule there might be claims for loss of wages by the workmen affected by physical damage to their place of employment and he endorsed the view that the courts should redress "only the proximate and direct consequences of wrongful acts". A similar consideration influenced Lord Denning in *Spartan Steel*. He commented that "[i]f claims for economic loss were permitted for this particular hazard (a power cut) there would be no end of claims. Some might be genuine, but many might be inflated or even false." To allow all claims for such economic loss would lead to unacceptable indeterminacy because of the ripple effects caused by contracts and expectations. Proximity requires some special relationship between the defendant and the person suffering relational economic loss, one which goes beyond mere contractual or non-contractual dependence on the damaged property. However, 7-154

694 [1966] 1 Q.B. 569.

695 The leading US case of *State of Louisiana v M/V "Testbank"* (1985) 752 F. 2d 1019, provides another illustration of non-contractual relational loss. Two vessels had collided in the Mississippi River Gulf. Toxic chemicals were lost overboard and caused the closure of the outlet to navigation and fishing for 20 days. Forty claims were brought by fishers, marine operators, cargo terminal operators and restaurant owners. The Fifth Circuit Appeals Court affirmed the dismissal of all the claims except those of the commercial fishers which were justified on the ground that "fishermen possess a proprietary interest in fish in waters they normally harvest sufficient to allow recovery for their loss". Note that US Admiralty law does allow "contractual" relational loss in the *Candlewood* situation.

696 [2009] EWHC 685 (QB); [2009] N.P.C. 56.

there are some "no recovery" situations where proximity and indeterminancy would not be a problem. The *Aliakmon* is such a case. Shippers are aware that damage to the cargo may cause economic loss to the buyer who bears the risk under a c & f contract. The relationship is close and direct and the recognition of a duty to such a purchaser would not open the floodgates to unlimited liability to an indefinite number of other persons whose contractual rights were adversely affected. Nevertheless, Lord Brandon, giving the leading judgment in the *Aliakmon*, argued that any detraction from the general rule of non-recovery "would lead to attempts to have it permitted in a variety of other particular cases, and the result would be that certainty ... would be seriously undermined. Yet certainty of the law is of the utmost importance ... in commercial matters".[697] He went on to counter the suggestion that denying liability was depriving the buyer of a fair remedy, with the argument that the lack of remedy was the buyer's fault for failing to include in the sale contract a provision requiring the seller to assign its rights to the buyer or exercise them on the buyer's behalf.[698]

7-155 **Exceptional recovery** In *Caltex Oil (Australia) Pty v The Dredge "Willemstad"*[699] the High Court of Australia allowed recovery where the oil supply to the claimant's refinery was cut because the defendant damaged the supply pipeline which was not owned by the claimant. Although the ratio decidendi was not entirely clear, what seems to have influenced the High Court most was the fact that the damage to the claimant's refinery was specifically foreseeable.[700] In *Canadian National Ry Co v Norsk Pacific S.S. Co*[701] the Supreme Court of Canada developed an exception based on the notion of "joint venture".[702] The defendant negligently damaged a railway bridge owned by a third party with the result that the claimant had to reroute its trains and suffered economic loss as a consequence. Giving the leading judgment, McLachlin J held that the close connection between claimant and the bridge (it was the predominant user of the bridge which was an integral part of its railway system and it supplied inspection and consulting services for the bridge) brought the situation within the joint venture category and justified a finding of proximity.[703] She rejected the policy (or fairness) argument that the claimant should have insured or protected itself by the terms of its contract with the bridge owner arguing that little weight should be given to these factors as against that of the moral

---

697 [1986] A.C. 785 at 817.

698 See the similar argument of Lord Denning in *Spartan Steel* [1973] Q.B. 27, that it was open to the claimant to protect itself by, in that case, installing a stand-by generator or taking out insurance against a power cut.

699 (1976) 136 C.L.R. 529.

700 (1976) 136 C.L.R. 529 at 555–556, per Gibbs J; at 577–578, per Stephen J; at 593, per Mason J.

701 (1992) 91 D.L.R. (4th) 289.

702 The House of Lords had used the notion of joint venture in the shipping case of *Morrison S.S. Co v Greystoke Castle* [1947] A.C. 265, but the case had been regarded as turning on the principles of maritime law rather than establishing any general principle.

703 The exceptional nature of the Norsk decision was illustrated by the subsequent Canadian decision in *Bow Valley Husky Ltd v Saint John Shipbuilding* (1997) 153 D.L.R. (4th) 385. The defendants' negligence led to a fire on a third party's oil rig which the claimant was using for drilling. The claimant was contractually bound to pay rental to the third party during the period whilst the rig was out of action due to the fire damage. The claimant argued that it was engaged in a joint venture with the rig owner and was entitled to recover under the principle in *Norsk*. The Supreme Court rejected the claim partly on the basis that the third party and the claimant had already allocated risks in the contract. In her judgment, McLachlin J was concerned that further exceptions should not be "assiduously" pursued as "what is required is a clear rule predicting when recovery is available".

culpability of the defendant.[704] In *Perre v Apand Pty Ltd*[705] the Australian High Court cautiously expanded the scope of exceptional recovery. The defendant negligently supplied diseased potato seed to a grower who produced a diseased crop. This resulted in a quarantine being imposed on all growers within a 20 kilometre radius of the outbreak. The claimants fell within the quarantine and suffered losses both as growers and processors. McHugh J considered that the law in this area "should be developed incrementally by reference to the reasons why the material facts in analogous cases did or did not found a duty".[706] He identified the key reasons in pure economic loss cases as being indeterminancy, autonomy, vulnerability and knowledge. In *Perre*, there was little risk of indeterminancy[707]; the autonomy of the defendant was already limited by its liability for the physical damage; the claimant was vulnerable as there was nothing it could do by way of contract to protect itself; and the defendant knew of the risks of supplying diseased seed. Hence, a duty should be imposed. The current willingness of the English appellate courts to articulate policy reasoning rather than to rely on bright lines excluding liability, suggests that the incremental approach in *Perre* might be followed.[708] It should also be noted that an action in nuisance for the continuing impact of interference which commenced prior to the claimant's acquisition of the property, is not precluded by this rule.[709]

Statutory exception for latent damage Although the general rule remains that only the owner of goods can sue for damage to them, a statutory exception was introduced by s.3 of the Latent Damage Act 1986.[710] This provides that where property has been damaged so as to give rise to a cause of action, but has then been acquired by another before the damage was discoverable, the acquirer will have a cause in action against the person whose negligence damaged that property. This provision was intended to give a cause of action to purchasers of buildings which were subject to latent damage at the time of purchase. Its significance has been considerably reduced now that latent problems such as subsidence are regarded as 7-156

[704] La Forest J gave a powerful dissenting judgment arguing that the claimant's preponderant usage of the bridge etc "did not justify a finding of common adventure" and endorsing the view of Lord Keith that the exception should be confined to the shipping context. Although McLachlin J may have been right to criticise the insurance and contractual protection arguments as unrealistic, there is no doubt that the judgment of La Forest J reflects what has been the approach of the English courts.

[705] (1999) 164 A.L.R. 606.

[706] (1999) 164 A.L.R. 606 at 630.

[707] McHugh J did not consider the processors of potatoes to be an ascertainable class and dissented in respect of the claimants' claim for its processing losses.

[708] In *D Pride & Partners (A Firm) v Institute for Animal Health* [2009] EWHC 685 (QB); [2009] N.P.C. 56 at [125]–[126] Tugendhat J noted this sentence from the 19th edition of this work, but distinguished *Perre* on the basis that the class of potential claimants was very much greater than the class of potential claimants in *Perre*.

[709] *Delaware Mansions Ltd v Westminster City Council* [2001] UKHL 55; [2002] 1 A.C. 321.

[710] The section provides that where:

"(a) a cause of action ('the original cause of action') has accrued to any person in respect of negligence to which damage to any property in which he has an interest is attributable … and

(b) another person acquires an interest in that property after the date on which the original cause of action accrued but before the material facts about the damage have become known to any person who, at the time when he first has knowledge of those facts, has any interest in the property;

a fresh cause of action in respect of that negligence shall accrue to that other person on the date on which he acquires his interest in the property."

defects in the building rather than damage to it and, as a result, unlikely to give rise to any cause of action at all. But the words of this section seem wide enough to cover the situation in the *Aliakmon* case, provided only (as is likely to be the case) the buyer did not, when becoming owner of the goods, know that they had been damaged so as to give rise to liability on the part of the defendant. It should also be noted that the Carriage of Goods by Sea Act 1992 mitigates the practical effect of the *Aliakmon* decision.[711]

3. BREACH OF DUTY

(a) Introduction

7-157 **Reasonableness** A defendant will be regarded as in breach of a duty of care if his conduct falls below the standard required by the law. The standard normally set is that of a reasonable and prudent man. In the often cited words of Baron Alderson:

> "Negligence is the omission to do something which a reasonable man, guided upon those considerations which ordinarily regulate the conduct of human affairs, would do; or doing something which a prudent and reasonable man would not do."[712]

The key notion of reasonableness provides the law with a flexible test, capable of being adapted to the circumstances of each case. For example, a motorist should drive with reasonable care, but the speed at which it would be reasonable for him to travel when driving through a crowded town is slower than along an open and deserted country road.[713] The behaviour of individuals and the circumstances giving rise to harm are so variable that a flexible test of this nature is essential. Consequently the courts resist attempts to crystallise the required standard into a series of more definite, discrete rules. Decisions in individual cases as to what amounts to reasonable or unreasonable conduct are regarded as useful guides but no more.[714] Although appellate courts accept the findings of specific facts by trial courts, they hold themselves free to substitute their own inference as to whether or not those facts constitute carelessness. This is perhaps why so many reported cases tend to be cited on the question whether particular conduct should be treated as careless. This tendency has been deplored. The House of Lords in *Qualcast (Wolverhampton) Ltd v Haynes*[715] emphasised the undesirability of attempting to reduce to rules of law the question whether or not reasonable care has been taken.[716]

---

711 The Act provides that for the claimant to acquire the seller's rights against the carrier, it is sufficient for him to have become the lawful holder of the bill of lading.

712 *Blyth v Birmingham Waterworks* (1856) 11 Ex. 781 at 784; see also per Lord Macmillan in *Glasgow Corp v Muir* [1943] A.C. 448 at 457; per Lord Reid in *London Graving Dock v Horton* [1951] A.C. 737 at 785.

713 The failure to act reasonably in any given set of circumstances gives rise to degrees of culpability varying from serious inattention to momentary lapse. These differences in the moral, rather than in the legal, attitude towards such shortcomings are reflected in phrases such as "gross negligence"; "ordinary negligence" and "slight negligence". In law there are no degrees of negligence, and "gross negligence is ordinary negligence with a vituperative epithet", per Rolfe B in *Wilson v Brett* (1843) 12 L.J. Ex. 264. "Generally speaking in civil cases 'gross' negligence has no more effect that negligence without an opprobrious epithet", per Lord Wright in *Caswell v Powell Duffryn Associated Collieries Ltd* [1940] A.C. 152 at 175.

714 *Qualcast (Wolverhampton) Ltd v Haynes* [1959] A.C. 743.

715 [1959] A.C. 743, especially, per Lord Keith at 755, and Lord Somervell at 757–758.

716 In *Foskett v Mistry* [1984] R.T.R. 1, the Court of Appeal stressed that in running down cases li-

Standard and duty The standard of care required in particular circumstance is sometimes formulated in terms of a particular duty, e.g. the motorist is under a duty to give a turn signal. Such formulations may be regarded as helpful in a descriptive way. But this use of duty terminology is misleading. The standard of care required is what would be reasonable in the circumstances. The point is illustrated by *N v Agrawal*[717] where Stuart-Smith LJ, rejecting the first instance finding that a prosecution expert owed a duty to attend court and was liable for the psychiatric injury to the alleged victim of the crime stemming from his failure to attend and the consequent collapse of the case, said: 7-158

> "In my judgment an attempt to formulate a duty of care in this way is wholly misconceived. If a duty of care exists at all it is a duty to take reasonable care to prevent the [claimant] from suffering injury of the type in question, in this case psychiatric injury. A failure to give evidence could be a breach of such a duty; but it is not the duty itself. Thus a motorist owes a duty to take care not to injure other road users or damage their property. He does not owe a duty to take care to blow his horn; his failure to do so when proper care requires that he should, may amount to a breach of the duty of care."[718]

To express the standard in terms of a duty is to confuse two distinct questions. The duty question is concerned with the general nature of the relationship between the parties and asks whether there should be a duty of care in that kind of relationship. The scope of any duty may be described by reference to the circumstances of the relationship. Thus the relationship between the parties may justify a duty of care to prevent harm being caused by third parties and the restricted nature of that duty of care will tend to suggest that what is reasonably required should not place an onerous burden on the defendant. However, the specific level of care required, e.g. whether a warning should have been given, will depend on the particular circumstances of the case. Both duty and standard turn on reasonableness but in the case of duty, the question is whether the nature of the relationship reasonably requires that care be taken; whilst in the case of standard, the question is what conduct is reasonably required in the particular circumstances.

The criteria of reasonableness The level of care that will be reasonably required in any particular circumstance is the product of three sets of criteria each of which contains tensions and requires a balancing exercise. The first is that of objectivity. In principle, the standard of care expected of the reasonable person is objective and does not take into account the weaknesses or inexperience of the particular defendant. But this may mean that an individual may be liable for failing to live up to a standard which he cannot meet.[719] Consequently, objectivity may be tempered by basing the standard on what might be expected objectively from an "inexperienced" group, or by accommodating the special circumstances of the case, e.g. an emergency, within the objective test, or by varying the objective requirement in the light of the special relationship between the parties. The second criterion involves a balancing of costs and benefits, asking whether it is reasonable for the defendant 7-159

ability depends on the failure to take reasonable care in particular situations and that authorities should seldom be cited on this.

717 [1999] P.N.L.R. 939.

718 [1999] P.N.L.R. 939 at 943.

719 So where the defendant has held himself out as competent in a particular field of expertise he will be held to the objective standards of that field: see e.g. *Wright v Troy Lucas and Co* [2019] EWHC 1098 (QB) (defendant, a sole trader in a litigation firm who had a law degree but no legal qualifications, held to the standard of skill of a legal professional in a firm of solicitors).

to bear the cost of a particular form of precautionary conduct in the light of the level of protection and benefit it will confer on the claimant and others. This test can only be applied in a fairly crude way and hence the courts have considerable discretion as to the weight to be given to different factors. The third criterion is that of common practice and expectations. Courts will be influenced by the evidence of common practice of those engaged in the activity in question but this must sometimes be balanced against what are conceived to be the reasonable expectations of those who may be affected by the activity. The growth of liability insurance has raised expectations in relation to activities such as driving, but moral considerations, e.g. as to the need to prove fault may still be influential. The result of these tensions, is that different standards apply in different situations.

(b) The criteria of reasonableness

(i) Objectivity

7-160 **Test related to activity not actor** The objective standard required by the law is one which relates to the type of activity in which the defendant is engaged rather than to the category of actor to which the defendant belongs. The significance of this distinction is illustrated by the Court of Appeal decision in *Wilsher v Essex AHA*.[720] A trainee hospital doctor had made a mistake when undertaking specialist work in a special care baby unit to which he was attached. On his behalf it was argued that no more could be expected of him than could be reasonably required of a person having his formal qualifications and practical experience. Giving the judgment for the majority,[721] Mustill LJ rejected this argument saying:

> "… this notion of a duty tailored to the actor, rather than to the act which he elects to perform, has no place in the law of tort … . I prefer [the proposition which] relates the duty of care not to the individual, but to the post which he occupies … . In a case such as the present, the standard is not just that of the averagely competent and well informed junior houseman … but of such a person who fills a post in a unit offering a highly specialised service."[722]

Mustill LJ supported this principle on the ground that:

> "it would be a false step to subordinate the legitimate expectation of the patient that he will receive from each person concerned with his care a degree of skill appropriate to the task which he undertakes, to an understandable wish to minimise the psychological and financial pressures on hard-pressed young doctors."

Browne-Wilkinson V-C dissented on the issue, arguing that the activity standard would result in liability without any personal fault and hence, that the objective standard had to be based on the actor's qualifications and experience.

---

720 [1987] Q.B. 730. (The standard of care to be applied was not in issue on appeal to the House of Lords: [1988] A.C. 1074.) See further para.9-73.

721 Glidewell LJ agreed that the "law required the trainee to be judged by the same standard as his more experienced colleagues". But with Mustill LJ, he found that the trainee had acted with reasonable care as he had sought the advice of his expert superior, he had satisfied the test and it was his superior who was held to be negligent.

722 [1987] Q.B. 730 at 750–751. See also *FB v Princess Alexandra Hospital NHS Trust* [2017] EWCA Civ 334; [2017] P.I.Q.R. P17 (senior house officer in hospital Accident & Emergency department held to the same standard as a consultant doctor in taking a history. History taking was "a basic skill which hospital doctors at all levels are expected to possess", per Jackson LJ at [64]).

Policy justification Basing the objective standard on the activity rather than the actor gives the reasonable expectations of the claimant priority over those of the defendant. This policy is most evident in cases where the activity affects the safety of the general public and where, as a consequence, it is likely that those undertaking the activity will be insured. The point is well illustrated by *Nettleship v Weston*.[723] The defendant was a learner-driver who crashed into a lamp post injuring her instructor who was a front seat passenger. At first instance, she was held not liable on the ground that she had been doing her best to control the car. Giving the leading judgment in the Court of Appeal, Lord Denning found her liable, commenting that: **7-161**

> "The learner driver may be doing his best, but his incompetent best is not good enough. He must drive in as good a manner as a driver of skill, experience and care, who is sound in mind and limb, who makes no errors of judgment, has good eyesight and hearing, and is free from any infirmity…. The high standard thus imposed by the judges is, I believe, largely the result of the policy of the Road Traffic Acts. Parliament requires every driver to be insured against third party risks…. we are, in this branch of the law, moving away from the concept: 'No liability without fault'. We are beginning to apply the test: 'On whom should the risk fall?' Morally the learner driver is not at fault; but legally she is liable to be because she is insured and the risk should fall on her."[724]

Special relationships In *Nettleship v Weston*, Salmon LJ dissented, arguing that the special relationship between the learner and the instructor made the "learner's lack of skill and experience a highly relevant circumstance", with the result that the learner would not be liable "if an accident occurs as a result of some mistake which any prudent beginner doing his best can be expected to make".[725] This view was based on the judgment of Dixon J in the High Court of Australia decision in *The Insurance Commissioner v Joyce*.[726] In *Cook v Cook*,[727] the High Court affirmed its view on facts similar to those in *Nettleship*, stating that in the case of the relationship of pupil and instructor the standard of care was that reasonably expected of an unqualified and inexperienced driver. However, *Cook v Cook* has subsequently been overruled by the High Court of Australia in *Imbree v McNeilly*[728] where it was held that the standard of care to be expected of an inexperienced learner driver is the same as that owed by any other person driving a motor vehicle, namely to take reasonable care to avoid injury to others, thus bringing Australian law into line with English law on this issue, which has been unchallenged since the majority decision in *Nettleship v Weston*. **7-162**

On the other hand, where the relationship has given the defendant greater than average *knowledge* of the risk, then as a reasonable man he should take precautions against it.[729] So in *Baker v Quantum Clothing Group*[730] the House of Lords held that a judge was entitled to conclude that employers who had greater **7-163**

---

723 [1971] 2 Q.B. 691.

724 [1971] 2 Q.B. 691 at 699–700.

725 On the facts Salmon LJ concluded that because the learner had assured her instructor that he would be covered by her insurance in the event of an accident, she had accepted responsibility for any injuries caused by a "failure to exercise the ordinary driver's standards of reasonable care".

726 (1948) 77 C.L.R. 39 at 56.

727 (1968) 68 A.L.R. 353.

728 [2008] HCA 40; (2008) 236 C.L.R. 510; (2008) 248 A.L.R. 647.

729 *Stokes v Guest, Keen & Nettlefold (Bolts & Nuts) Ltd* [1968] 1 W.L.R. 1776 at 1783, per Swanwick J.

730 [2011] UKSC 17; [2011] 1 W.L.R. 1003.

knowledge than the average employer of the risks to employees of exposure to noise at work between 85dB(A)lepd and 90dB(A)lepd could be in breach of their duty, even though the knowledge of the average employer was based on a government Code of Practice on occupational exposure to noise levels (and recommended that noise should not exceed 90dB(A)lepd). Larger employers had the resources to look beyond the Code of Practice and reach their own conclusions about the nature and extent of the risks posed to their employees and "their appreciation that the Code limit was no longer acceptable was sufficient to found liability."[731] Thus, the defendant's subjective level of *knowledge* can raise but not lower the standard of care. However, a subjective level of *skill* is irrelevant: the particularly skilled defendant only has to conform to the standard to be expected of the reasonably skilled person in the relevant situation.

7-164 **Categorisation of activity** Although the particular relationship between the parties will not be regarded as directly relevant to the standard of care required, it may influence the categorisation of the activity against which an objective assessment is to be made. Thus in *Philips v Whiteley*[732] where a jeweller had performed a defective ear piercing, the fact that the claimant knew she was being treated by a simple jeweller was a key factor in persuading the court that the defendant had only to conform to the standards of jewellers rather than those to be expected if the activity were to be conducted by a surgeon. In other situations the courts may use the categorisation of the activity to shift the balance between the parties. Fleming comments that the law "has dealt rather leniently with the 'little man', conscious ... of his lack of liability insurance".[733] Thus, a householder repairing a door has been required to conform to the standards of a reasonable carpenter rather than a reasonable professional,[734] and a volunteer first aider has been required to conform to the standard of volunteers rather than professionals.[735] Reluctance to place excessive demands on the public services may also be relevant to categorisation. In *Knight v Home Office*[736] Pill J, after noting the limited resources available for the public service, held that the standard of care required of a prison hospital caring for a mentally ill detainee could not be judged "by the standard appropriate to a psychiatric hospital outside prison".[737]

7-165 **Acting in an emergency** Where the defendant's conduct has occurred in the course of responding to an emergency this will be regarded as relevant to the objective standard of care required. All that is necessary in such a circumstance is that

---

731 [2011] UKSC 17; [2011] 1 W.L.R. 1003 at [104], per Lord Dyson. Though note Lord Mance's view (at [25]) that this appears to penalise employers "who have a safety department and medical officers and take noise more seriously than the ordinary reasonable employer" since they are held liable, while others are not. In his Lordship's opinion that was "appropriate if extra resources or diligence lead to relevant fresh knowledge. But here they have led simply to the formation or inception of a different view to that generally accepted about what precautions to take. In such a case, the effect of the judge's approach is not to blame employers 'for not ploughing a lone furrow'; rather, it positively blames them for ploughing a lone furrow but not doing so deeply enough."

732 [1938] 1 All E.R. 566.

733 *The Law of Torts*, 9th edn (1998), p.124.

734 *Wells v Cooper* [1958] 2 Q.B. 265.

735 *Cattley v St John Ambulance Brigade* (1990) unreported. See Griffiths (1990) 6 P.N. 48.

736 [1990] 3 All E.R. 237.

737 But note that *Knight* was distinguished in *Brooks v Home Office* [1999] 2 F.L.R. 33 where Garland J held that a pregnant prisoner on remand was entitled to the same standard of antenatal care as if she were at liberty, subject to the practical constraints of having to be escorted to hospital.

the conduct should not have been unreasonable, taking the exigencies of the particular situation into account.[738] Thus in *Ng Chun Pui v Lee Chuen Tat*[739] the Privy Council held that the driver of a coach, who had braked, swerved and skidded when another car had cut in front of him without warning, had acted reasonably in the emergency. Hospital, police and fire services may all be faced with emergency situations. In the hospital context it has been said that "full allowance must be made for the fact that certain aspects of treatment may have to be carried out in ... battle conditions".[740] But some emergencies can be anticipated and planned for, especially in a professional context, and it may be negligent to fail to make appropriate arrangements to deal with an emergency.[741] Chasing a suspected criminal may count as an emergency situation. So in *Marshall v Osmond*[742] the claimant, a suspect, was injured when a police car drew up alongside the car from which he was starting to run away. It was held that in such circumstances the police action should not be judged by the same standard of care as would apply when there is time for reflection. But the extent to which the emergency justifies the risk taken will be a matter of degree. It may not absolve an emergency vehicle driver of responsibility for going through red traffic lights,[743] and the speed at which an emergency vehicle may travel when responding to an emergency must take account of the prevailing road conditions.[744] Again, in *Rigby v Chief Constable of Northamptonshire*[745] the police fired a canister of CS gas into the claimant's shop to flush out a dangerous psychopath. The shop caught fire. The police were found

---

738 This is sometimes referred to as the rule in *The Bywell Castle* (1879) 4 P. & D. 219. It used to be thought that the principle was limited to fear of personal injury, not danger to property; but this is not so. See, per Lord Sumner in *S.S. Singleton Abbey v S.S. Paludina* [1927] A.C. 16 at 28.

739 [1988] R.T.R. 298 PC. See also *Parkinson v Liverpool Corp* [1950] 1 All E.R. 367, where the driver of a bus braked suddenly to avoid a dog which appeared suddenly in front of him and a passenger was thrown to the floor of the bus. The driver was held to have acted reasonably in the emergency. *Parkinson* was applied in a similar set of circumstances in *Wooller v LTB* [1976] R.T.R. 206.

740 *Wilsher v Essex AHA* [1987] Q.B. 730 at 749, per Mustill LJ who continued: "An emergency may overburden the available resources, and, if an individual is forced by circumstances to do too many things at once, the fact that he does one of them incorrectly should not lightly be taken as negligence." On the facts of the case, he held this consideration to be irrelevant as there was no evidence that the defendant's "attention had been distracted" or that they had "to take a difficult decision on the spur of the moment". See also *Darnley v Croydon Health Services NHS Trust* [2018] UKSC 50; [2019] A.C. 831 at [22], per Lord Lloyd-Jones: "It is undoubtedly the fact that Hospital A&E departments operate in very difficult circumstances and under colossal pressure. This is a consideration which may well prove highly influential in many cases when assessing whether there has been a negligent breach of duty."

741 See *Bull v Devon AHA* [1993] 4 Med. L.R. 117 CA (inadequate system for calling consultant obstetrician to emergency delivery). But this may depend on how rare the foreseeable emergency is and the resources available to deal with it: *Garcia v St Mary's NHS Trust* [2006] EWHC 2314 (QB) at [95]–[96].

742 [1983] Q.B. 1034; cf. *Henry v Chief Constable of Thames Valley* [2010] EWCA Civ 5; [2010] R.T.R. 14—reasonable for police officer to use his vehicle as a means of impeding a suspect's escape but in the circumstances (claimant was dismounting from his motorcycle at his home) not in such a manner as would create any foreseeable risk of injury. In some circumstances, e.g. where a dangerous suspect was at large, a police officer might be justified in using a car as a trap or barrier even if that created a risk of injuring the suspect.

743 See *Griffin v Mersey Regional Ambulance* [1998] P.I.Q.R. P34. See para.7-184.

744 *Armsden v Kent Police* [2009] EWCA Civ 631; [2009] R.T.R. 31 (speed of police vehicle using flashing blue warning light, but not its siren, excessive when approaching a junction round a bend); *Smith v Chief Constable of Nottinghamshire Police* [2012] EWCA Civ 161; [2012] R.T.R. 23 (police vehicle responding to an emergency, with flashing blue lights, being driven at 40–50mph in a busy town centre on a Friday night hit pedestrian in the middle of the road; police driver found negligent).

745 [1985] 1 W.L.R. 1242.

to be negligent in not having fire-fighting equipment to hand when there was a substantial risk of fire. Where the situation allows time for reflection but still presents a dilemma, the courts may still make allowances.[746] It is arguable that although a person's failings are not ordinarily taken into account in determining the reasonableness of conduct, the contrary should be the case where such a person is placed in an emergency, which is not of his making. Any judgment on the reasonableness of his reaction should take account of his limitations.

7-166 **Sporting activity—participants** It is recognised that the participant in a game or competition is in a somewhat analogous position to one faced with an emergency in that he may have to take a decision in the heat of the moment. In *Wilks v Cheltenham Cycle Club*[747] the Court of Appeal measured the defendant's conduct in a motor-cycle scramble race against the standard of a reasonable competitor and held him not to have been negligent in losing control, leaving the course and hitting a spectator. In *Caldwell v Maguire and Fitzgerald*[748] the Court of Appeal upheld the dismissal of a claim by a jockey that he had been injured in a race incident due to the careless riding of the defendants who had been found guilty of careless riding by the Jockey Club. The Court approved the view of the trial judge that *in practice*, given the circumstances, the threshold for liability was high. There would be no liability for errors of judgment, oversights or lapses of which any participant might be guilty in the context of a fast-moving contest. It was not possible to characterise momentary carelessness as negligence. The Jockey Club's finding of careless riding was relevant but not determinative of negligence. Again, in *Condon v Basi*[749] the Court of Appeal held that the fact that the defendant's tackle which broke the claimant's leg in a football match, was a foul and a breach of the rules of the game did not of itself make it negligent. However, applying a test of reasonableness in the sporting circumstances of the case, the court held the defendant to be in breach. The same approach, requiring a high degree of carelessness for liability, is also applied to informal play involving vigorous physical activity within conventions.[750] In *Harrison v Vincent*[751] the Court of Appeal took the view that where the error of judgment is made in preparation for competition rather than "in the flurry and excitement of the sport", no special allowance need be made for the

---

746 An example is *The Ketch Frances v The Highland Loch* [1912] A.C. 312. Very shortly before the Highland Loch was due to be launched, the Frances fouled her anchor in the path of the launching. Preparations for launching having already been made, it would have been dangerous to workmen and property to have left the Highland Loch as she was. In the circumstances the defendants decided to proceed with the launching and so run the risk of colliding with the Frances. A collision did result with extensive damage to the Frances. It was held that the defendants were not liable as they had acted reasonably in the dilemma.

747 [1971] 1 W.L.R. 668.

748 [2001] EWCA Civ 1054; [2002] P.I.Q.R. P6. See McArdle and James "Are you experienced? 'Playing cultures', sporting rules and personal injury litigation after Caldwell v Maguire" (2005) 13 Tort. L.R. 193.

749 [1985] 1 W.L.R. 866. See also *McCracken v Melbourne Storm Rugby League Club* [2007] NSWCA 353; [2007] Aust. Torts Reports 81–925, where the Appeal Court held two professional rugby league players liable to another injured in a tackle. Crucial to the finding was evidence of the intention to harm the opponent and the fact that the defendants pleaded guilty in the sport's disciplinary proceedings.

750 *Blake v Galloway* [2004] EWCA Civ 814; [2004] 1 W.L.R. 2844: 15-year-old boys playing a game of throwing bark chippings at each other. Defendant not liable when his throw accidentally caught claimant in the eye.

751 [1982] R.T.R. 8.

sporting circumstance. In that case the negligent error consisted of a failure to maintain a motor-cycle combination prior to the race.[752]

Organisers of sporting activity and officials The organisers of a sporting event or game will owe a duty of care to the participants,[753] as will the officials responsible for controlling the game and applying the rules. In *Smoldon v Whitworth & Nolan*[754] a referee of a colts rugby match was held in breach of his duty to control the match so as to ensure that the players were not exposed to unnecessary risk of injury from collapsing scrums and to have particular regard to the fact that some of the players (including the injured claimant) were under the age of 18. The standard of care required will be adjusted to the circumstances.[755] It is arguable that the standard to be expected of an official in charge of a sporting event will vary with the level of that event.[756] The organisers of a sporting event owe a duty to exercise reasonable care in assessing the risks to which it is reasonable to expose the participants, having regard to the social utility that comes from participation in the sport and the recognition that most forms of sporting activity involve some risk of injury: "Enjoyable competitive activities are an important and beneficial part of the life of the very many people who are fit enough to participate in them … . such activities are almost never risk-free … . a balance has to be struck between the level of risk involved and the benefits the activity confers on the participants and thereby on society generally."[757] The difficulty of coming to an appropriate assessment of the balance between the benefits and the risks of the activity is illustrated by the decision in 7-167

752 See also *Phee v Gordon* [2013] CSIH 18; 2013 S.C. 379; 2013 S.L.T. 439—an amateur golfer does not act in the heat of competition in deciding to play a shot when other golfers are in the vicinity; cf. *McMahon v Dear* [2014] CSOH 100; 2014 S.L.T. 823 (golfer in a competition not in breach of duty when his ball struck an official "ball watcher" who was not visible to the golfer when he played his shot; the danger of being hit was a risk incidental to the competition, which the pursuer accepted when undertaking the task of officiating).

753 See *Watson v British Boxing Board of Control Ltd* [2001] Q.B. 1134.

754 [1997] P.I.Q.R. P133. Lord Bingham CJ held that the claimant was not *volens* to the risk of injury, having consented to the ordinary incidents of the game and not to a breach of duty by the official whose duty it was to apply the rules of the game. See para.3-132 for discussion of the defence of consent in relation to sport.

755 "The level of care required is that which is appropriate in all the circumstances, and the circumstances are of crucial importance. Full account must be taken of the factual context in which a referee exercises his functions, and he could not be properly held liable for errors of judgment, oversights or lapses of which any referee might be guilty in the context of a fast-moving and vigorous contest. The threshold of liability is a high one. It will not easily be crossed.": *Smoldon v Whitworth & Nolan* [1997] P.I.Q.R. P133 at P139.

756 In *Vowles v Evans* [2003] EWCA Civ 318; [2003] 1 W.L.R. 1607, Lord Phillips MR commented that: "There is scope for argument as to the extent to which the degree of skill to be expected of a referee depends upon the grade of the referee or of the match." On the facts the argument was not relevant as the referee was qualified and the allegations of breach did not involve any higher standard than the basic competence appropriate to the qualification. The Court of Appeal's confirmation that the referee was not in breach in *Allport v Wilbraham* [2004] EWCA Civ 1668 illustrates the difficulty of establishing liability where there is conflicting evidence from opposing teams.

757 *Uren v Corporate Leisure (UK) Ltd* [2010] EWHC 46 (QB); [2010] N.P.C. 7 at [59], per Field J In *Browning v Odyssey Trust Co Ltd* [2014] NIQB 39 the occupiers of an ice hockey arena were held not to have been negligent when a spectator was hit by a puck during the warm-up before a match. Gillen J commented, at [32], that "the risks were no different from those which exist in a number of other sporting arenas including field hockey, football, cricket, rugby or golf. Such risks are amongst the jolts and jogs to be expected of sporting life." See also *Tomlinson v Congleton BC* [2003] UKHL 47; [2004] 1 A.C. 46, para.7-185.

Uren v Corporate Leisure (UK) Ltd,[758] where the Court of Appeal, though agreeing with Field J's statement of principle, questioned whether the judge had reached the correct balance between the level of risk and the social utility of the game that the claimant had been participating in. Although such judgments were "very much a matter for the trial judge", the Court of Appeal considered that Field J had taken an incorrect approach to the assessment of the degree of risk of serious injury (the risk of spinal injury from diving head-first into a shallow pool of water); if the risk assessment was flawed that threw into question whether the appropriate balance between the degree of risk and the social value of the game had been reached.[759] The position will be different where the accident was wholly unforeseeable.[760]

7-168 **Disability** In an often cited dictum Lord Macmillan said that the test of reasonableness "eliminates the personal equation and is independent of the idiosyncrasies of the particular person whose conduct is in question".[761] This applies to such matters as temperament, intellect, education and the general state of mind of the defendant. Thus, in *Barnet v Chelsea and Kensington Hospital Management Committee*,[762] a doctor who failed to examine a patient because he was suffering from fatigue and feeling unwell, was held to have been negligent. The application of the principle to physical and mental disability is more problematic. In *Roberts v Ramsbottom*[763] Neill J applied the dictum to a case where a driver crashed into the claimant after suffering a stroke and becoming incapable of controlling his car with care. Neill J accepted that the driver was unaware of his unfitness to drive and was not morally to blame for continuing to drive, but held he would escape the application of the normal reasonableness criterion only where "his actions at the relevant time were wholly beyond his control". However, in *Mansfield v Weetabix Ltd*[764] the Court of Appeal refused to impose liability where a lorry had crashed into the claimant's shop as a result of the driver suffering from hypoglycaemia. Leggat LJ held that "the standard of care that [the driver] was obliged to show … was that

---

758 [2011] EWCA Civ 66; [2011] I.C.R. D11.

759 At the re-trial the defendants were held liable on the basis that the risk assessment that they had carried out was inadequate in failing to take into account the potential severity of the injury, even though the likelihood of it occurring was small; the risk could have been eliminated by banning head-first diving, without significantly detracting from its social value: *Uren v Corporate Leisure (UK) Ltd* [2013] EWHC 353 (QB) (Foskett J considered that a warning to participants of the dangers of diving would have been sufficient, but accepted the expert evidence that banning it was the appropriate response to the risk: at [204]–[208]). See also *Phee v Gordon* [2013] CSIH 18; 2013 S.C. 379; 2013 S.L.T. 439 (golf club jointly liable with a golfer for injury to the claimant caused by a stray golf ball because the club had not undertaken a risk assessment and had failed to place warning signs (club held 80 per cent responsible and golfer 20 per cent); *Sutton v Syston Rugby Football Club Ltd* [2011] EWCA Civ 1182 (rugby club under duty to inspect pitch for foreign objects at a reasonable walking pace before a game or training session; claim failed on causation); *Corbett v Cumbria Kart Racing Club* [2013] EWHC 1362 (QB); [2013] L.L.R. 671 (organisers of a motorcycle and sidecar race negligent in arrangement of safety barriers in that an ambulance was parked too close to the barriers; claimant left the track at speed, went through the barriers and collided with the ambulance). For discussion of the position of sports coaches see N. Partington, "Professional liability of amateurs: the context of sports coaching" [2015] J.P.I.L. 232.

760 *Blair-Ford v CRS Adventures Ltd* [2012] EWHC 2360 (QB) (freak accident during "welly-wanging" event was not reasonably foreseeable and therefore, despite a "dynamic risk assessment" having been carried out, no steps were required to modify the method of throwing the welly, nor was there any need to provide specific warnings to the claimant).

761 See *Glasgow Corp v Muir* [1943] A.C. 448 at 457.

762 [1969] 1 Q.B. 428.

763 [1980] 1 W.L.R. 823. See further paras 5-63 to 5-64.

764 [1998] 1 W.L.R. 1263 at 1268.

which is to be expected of a reasonably competent driver unaware that he is or may be suffering from a condition which impairs his ability to drive". *Roberts* was distinguished on the ground that there the driver had "continued to drive when he was unfit to do so and when he should have been aware of his unfitness".[765] A similar approach, sensitive to a defendant's incapacity, has been adopted by Scots,[766] Canadian[767] and American[768] courts. The same sensitivity should be shown to those suffering from permanent physical disabilities such as deafness or blindness. Such a person can only have reasonable freedom to participate in the ordinary activities of life if allowance is made for his condition. The general public will be adequately protected by requiring the disabled person to recognise the limitations of his condition. As Fleming suggests "a reasonable blind person would refrain from driving a car, but may venture unattended into the street even at the risk of thereby occasionally impeding traffic".[769]

In *Dunnage v Randall*[770] the claimant suffered serious burns when he attempted, unsuccessfully, to prevent the defendant, his uncle, from setting light to himself. The defendant was suffering from delusions due to florid paranoid schizophrenia and had doused himself in petrol. The Court of Appeal held that the defendant was in breach of duty. The suggestion, taken from the medical evidence, that the nature of the defendant's actions was such that they were involuntary or irrational was irrelevant to his liability. It was only if it could be said that there was no act at all by the defendant (such as being in a state of automatism or sleepwalking) that he could escape liability. Rafferty LJ stressed that: **7-169**

"Unless a defendant can establish that his condition entirely eliminates responsibility—I avoid use of 'fault' so as to emphasise my point—he remains vulnerable to liability if he does not meet the objective standard of care. It is the entirety of the elimination which drives this conclusion, and once that entirety is eroded or diminished, he is fixed with the standard."[771]

Although, as Arden LJ expressed it, the defendant was "driven by his delusions", the objective standard of care reflects the policy of the law that everyone should owe the same duty of care for the protection of innocent victims.[772] There was, said the Court, no difference between mental and physical disability, though

[765] Neill J gave ([1998] 1 W.L.R. 1263 at 1268 at 1266–1267) this as an alternative ground for the decision in *Roberts*. See also *Green v Haynes* [2014] EWHC 4297 (QB) (defendant in breach of duty when he ought to have been aware that he was unfit to drive a vehicle or, alternatively, drove in a manner which prevented him from taking reasonable precautions if his condition deteriorated).

[766] *Waugh v James K Allan Ltd*, 1964 S.L.T. 173, where the accident occurred as a result of the driver suddenly, and without warning, suffering a coronary thrombosis. The Lord Ordinary accepted a defence of inevitable accident and rejected the pursuer's claim. Subsequent appeals to the Inner House of the Court of Session and the House of Lords were unsuccessful.

[767] *Att Gen of Canada v Connolly* (1989) 64 D.L.R. (4th) 84. It was held that it would not be just to apply the strict approach in *Ramsbottom* where the defendant's mental state was such that he was not capable of foreseeing harm resulting from his act.

[768] *Breunig v American Family Insurance Co* (1970) 173 N.W.2d 619.

[769] *The Law of Torts*, 9th edn (1998), p.125.

[770] [2015] EWCA Civ 673; [2016] Q.B. 639. For comment see Spencer [2015] J.P.I.L. C200; J. Goudkamp and M. Ihuoma "A tour of the tort of negligence" (2016) 32 P.N. 137.

[771] [2015] EWCA Civ 673; [2016] Q.B. 639 at [114]. See also Vos LJ at [131]: "only defendants whose attack or medical incapacity has the effect of entirely eliminating any fault or responsibility for the injury can be excused. ... The actions of a defendant, who is merely impaired by medical problems, whether physical or mental, cannot escape liability if he causes injury by failing to exercise reasonable care."

[772] Vos LJ noted, [2015] EWCA Civ 673; [2016] Q.B. 639 at [130], that: "The courts have consist-

it would seem that in practice it may be easier to establish a sudden onset of physical disability such as an unforeseeable heart attack (or the rare form of hypoglycaemia that occurred in *Mansfield v Weetabix Ltd*) when driving a motor vehicle, such that the defendant had no control of his actions at all, than it would be to prove that a mentally disordered defendant had no control over his actions whatsoever. The defendant in *Dunnage v Randall* was aware of what he was doing, even if he was "driven by his delusions" and was unable to appreciate that it was wrong.

7-170 **Age** In the context of the standard of care applicable to a boy of 12, Kitto J in *McHale v Watson*[773] stated the principle as follows:

> "The standard of care being objective, it is no answer for (a child), any more than it is for an adult to say that the harm he caused was due to his being abnormally slow-witted, quick tempered, absent minded or inexperienced. But it does not follow that he cannot rely in his defence upon a limitation on the capacity for foresight or prudence, not as being personal to himself, but as being a characteristic of humanity at his stage of development and in that sense normal."

The boy's conduct in throwing a sharp rod which ricocheted off a post and hit a girl, was held not to be negligent when judged against the standard of an ordinary boy of that age and maturity. The approach taken in *McHale* was followed by the Court of Appeal in *Mullin v Richards*,[774] where Hutchison LJ stated that the test was "not whether the actions of the defendant were such as an ordinarily prudent and reasonable adult in the defendant's situation would have realised gave rise to a risk of injury [but] whether an ordinarily prudent and reasonable 15-year-old schoolgirl in the defendant's position would have realised as much".[775] In *Orchard v Lee*[776] a 13-year-old boy playing tag in an area of school where he was permitted to play, and not breaking any school rules, was held not liable for a collision with the claimant who was a lunchtime supervisor. Waller LJ commented that: "for a child to be held culpable the conduct must be careless to a very high degree and where a child of 13 is partaking in a game within a play area, not breaking any rules, and is not acting to any significant degree beyond the norms of that game, he or she will not be held culpable."[777] In part, the concession to children may be based on a disinclination to allow actions which may well be fruitless. In part, it may be encouraged by

---

ently and correctly rejected the notion that the standard of care should be adjusted to take account of personal characteristics of the defendant. The single exception in respect of the liability of children should not, I think, be extended." Contrast the position of a claimant with a mental disability where the allegation is that there was contributory negligence: *Spearman v Royal United Bath Hospitals NHS Foundation Trust* [2017] EWHC 3027 (QB); [2018] Med. L.R. 244. See para.3-84.

773 (1966) 115 C.L.R. 199 at 213.

774 [1998] 1 W.L.R. 1304 at 1308.

775 The 15-year-old's conduct in injuring her friend when play-fencing with rulers was found not to be negligent. See also *Staley v Suffolk CC and Dean Mason* (1985) unreported, where it was held that a 12-year-old was negligent in hurling a ball at another boy and hitting the claimant by mistake. The principle that a child is not expected to take the same degree of care as an adult is well recognised where the child is a claimant, both in relation to the degree of care for the child required from an adult, see *Latham v Johnson* [1913] 1 K.B. 398 at 416; and in relation to contributory negligence, see *Yachuk v Oliver Blais Co Ltd* [1949] A.C. 386.

776 [2009] EWCA Civ 295; [2009] P.I.Q.R. P16.

777 [2009] EWCA Civ 295; [2009] P.I.Q.R. P16 at [11]. His Lordship added, at [19], that: "13 year old boys will be 13 year old boys who will play tag. They will run backwards and they will taunt each other. If that is what they are doing and they are not breaking any rules they should not be held liable in negligence. Parents and schools are there to control children and it would be a retrograde step to visit liability on a 13-year-old for simply playing a game in the area where he was allowed to do

the fact that the public are to some extent safeguarded against the lower standard applicable to children by the care expected of those supervising children[778] and the principle accepted by American courts that where children are engaged in activities normally only undertaken by adults, e.g. driving, they will be judged by the normal adult standards.[779] It seems unlikely that an analogous concession from the adult standard will be made for the elderly. The elderly are more likely than children to participate in adult activities such as driving, and less likely to be supervised. In *Roberts v Ramsbottom*[780] Neill J regarded the age of the 73-year-old driver as irrelevant.

Contributory negligence[781] In principle the same objective standard should be applied when considering whether a claimant has failed to take reasonable care of his own interests so as to justify a reduction of damages for contributory negligence. If, objectively the conduct poses substantial risks of damage, it should not be relevant that a claimant subjectively considered those risks to be worth running for the benefits to be gained. To adopt a subjective standard towards the conduct of the claimant would impose a disproportionate risk upon the defendant. For example, where a claimant makes risky loans calculating that loss on any particular loan will be offset by gains on other loans, its conduct may still be regarded as negligent in relation to the loss-making loan. If it brought an action against, say, a valuer whose negligence led to the security for the loan being inadequate, its damages would be reduced in respect of its contributory negligence.[782] However, where the defendant's negligence poses an emergency or dilemma for the claimant, it will be proper to apply subjective criteria. Thus, the age or incapacity of the claimant should be taken into account when considering whether he has acted with adequate care for his own interests. Whilst it may be sound policy to expect the elderly to take an objective level of care to avoid causing accidents, it would be unfair to expect them to take such a level of care to avoid a risk created by the defendant's negligence. Rather, the defendant must take his victim as he finds him.[783] **7-171**

(ii) Balancing cost and benefit

The relevant factors Balancing cost and benefit involves a number of factors. Assessing the benefit of a particular precaution will involve considering the degree of likelihood that the harm will occur but for the precaution and the severity of that harm. On the cost side of the equation, the expense of the precaution and the general utility of the activity which may be lost if precautions have to be taken, both need to be considered. **7-172**

Likelihood of harm The pattern of a reasonable person's behaviour is determined with reference to the likelihood of harm *before* and irrespective of its occurrence. No harm may occur and hence there may be no tort, yet the conduct may still be condemned as careless. If, for example, a motorist cuts into a stream of traffic from **7-173**

---

so."

[778] See para.7-229.

[779] *Terre Haute First National Bank v Stewart* (1984) 455 N.E.2d 262.

[780] [1980] 1 W.L.R. 823.

[781] See further para.3-58.

[782] See *Platform Home Loans Ltd v Oyston Shipways Ltd* [2000] 2 A.C. 190.

[783] See para.2-170. For this reason the contributory negligence of a child should not be judged in the same light as that of an adult: see para.3-82.

a side-street without warning or slackening of speed, his conduct is careless even though he avoids a collision. This is because of the likelihood of hitting someone. Negligence presupposes unreasonable behaviour in the face of the foreseeable likelihood that harm may occur.

7-174 **Knowledge at the time of the occurrence** The likelihood of harm is gauged with reference to the state of knowledge which could be attributed to the defendant at the time of the occurrence. In *Roe v Minister of Health*[784] disinfectant, in which ampoules of anaesthetic were stored, had seeped into the ampoules through invisible cracks. The possibility that this might occur was not generally known at the time of the incident, which occurred in 1947. The claimants, who received spinal injections of the anaesthetic, became paralysed. The hospital authorities were held not liable because the risk to the claimants was not reasonably foreseeable at that date. "We must not look at the 1947 accident with 1954 spectacles" said Denning LJ.[785] In *Roe* the conduct in question was that of doctors and it was judged according to what reasonable doctors would have foreseen in 1947. In other cases the technical evidence may be less clear as is evident from the conflicting outcomes of *The Wagon Mound*[786] in which the fire damage was held to be unforeseeable, and *The Wagon Mound (No.2)*,[787] in which in relation to the same occurrence, it was held that a small but significant risk of the same fire damage was foreseeable.[788] Further difficulty may arise where the views of the layman and expert as to likelihood differ. Suppose that the defendant is a layman and that a reasonable layman would foresee a particular kind of harm as likely to result, will special scientific knowledge to the contrary be relied on to hold him not liable, even though this is disproved by the event? If he is held not liable, it would be contrary to the principle that a criterion of foreseeability is the defendant's standard of knowledge. Conversely, will specialised knowledge be relied on to hold a layman liable for damage which a reasonable layman would not have foreseen? *Graham v Co-operative Wholesale Society Ltd*[789] suggests that it will not. The test seems to be the actual or constructive knowledge which a reasonable and prudent defendant would have had if he consulted such literature or made such inquiries as were reasonably expected of him.[790]

7-175 **Known vulnerability of potential victims** The likelihood of harm will also depend on any vulnerability of potential victims of which the defendant knew, or should have known. For example, children are known to be less aware of threats

---

784 [1954] 2 Q.B. 66. See also *Graham v Co-operative Wholesale Society Ltd* [1957] 1 W.L.R. 511; *Richards v Highway Ironfounders (West Bromwich) Ltd* [1957] 1 W.L.R. 781; *Doughty v Turner Manufacturing Co Ltd* [1964] 1 Q.B. 518.

785 [1954] 2 Q.B. 66 at 84. See also *Glasgow Corp v Muir* [1943] A.C. 448 at 454, per Lord Thankerton:

> "The court must be careful to place itself in the position of the person charged with the duty and to consider what he or she should have reasonably anticipated as a natural and probable consequence of neglect, and not to give undue weight to the fact that a distressing accident has happened, or that witnesses are prone to express regret, ex post facto, that they did not take some step which it is now realised would definitely have prevented the accident."

786 [1961] A.C. 38.

787 [1967] 1 A.C. 617.

788 For an explanation see Dias [1967] C.L.J. 62.

789 [1957] 1 W.L.R. 511.

790 *Wright v Dunlop Rubber Co* (1973) 13 K.I.R. 255; *Wallhead v Ruston and Hornsby* (1973) 14 K.I.R. 285.

to their safety. Hence, if the defendant is felling a tree while children are watching him, it is not enough for him to warn them to go away before the tree falls; he should take more active steps to see that they are out of the way, for children are attracted by such operations and are too young to appreciate danger.[791] In *Haley v London Electricity Board*[792] the defendants were held liable to a blind man who had fallen into an excavation in the pavement. A long-handled hammer, which had been placed slantwise across the pavement in front of it, was an adequate guard for persons with sight, but inadequate for the needs of blind persons. The House of Lords held that these should have been taken into account, since it is reasonably foreseeable that blind persons will pass along pavements.[793] On the other hand, it is not reasonable to expect that blind persons will cross a road without being accompanied or without any indication of their disability. Therefore, "a blind or deaf man who crosses the traffic on a busy street cannot complain if he is run over by a careful driver who does not know and could not be expected to observe and guard against the man's infirmity".[794] In such a case, the amount of care a driver must take is that required towards non-disabled persons unless he knows or ought to know of the disability of those likely to be endangered by his driving. Where a defendant has failed to take reasonable care in relation to a class of vulnerable potential victims, it does not follow that he will be liable for injuries to a victim who was not vulnerable because in such a case the victim may not be able to establish that the negligence caused the injury.[795]

Degree of likelihood of harm What is relevant is the degree of likelihood that **7-176**

---

[791] *Mourton v Poulter* [1930] 2 K.B. 183. But see also *Stevens v Blaenau Gwent CBC* [2004] EWCA Civ 715; [2004] H.L.R. 54: Defendant had not installed first floor window locks in its rental premises on the ground that the danger of children being trapped by fire without a window escape route outweighed the danger of the falling out of a window, the injury which occurred to the claimant. Whilst accepting this general decision was justifiable, the trial judge found the defendant negligent on the ground it had not responded to a request for locks from the claimant's mother following an incident in which the claimant had almost fallen out. The Court of Appeal reversed the finding on the ground that the defendant was entitled to assume appropriate vigilance on the part of the mother to prevent the child getting to the window. See also *Adams v Rhymney Valley DC* [2001] P.N.L.R. 4.

[792] [1965] A.C. 778. See also *Pollock v Cahill* [2015] EWHC 2260 (QB) (blind visitor fell from a second floor window; occupier in breach of duty for leaving the window open and failing to warn the visitor).

[793] Statistics were quoted to show that large numbers of unaccompanied blind persons walk daily in the street and that, therefore, the electricity authority should have anticipated their presence on pavements. See also *Lips v Older* [2004] EWHC 1686 (QB); [2005] P.I.Q.R. P14—landlord's failure to provide handrail to guard against a drop beside the path to the front door held negligent, since it was readily foreseeable that any of his tenants (largely students) and especially the claimant with a known drink problem, "would return to the premises in drink".

[794] per Lord Wright in *Bourhill v Young* [1943] A.C. 92 at 109.

[795] *Davies v Wyre Forest DC* [1998] P.I.Q.R. P58. Alton J in holding the design and supervision of a leisure pool to be negligent, commented:

> "There was some discussion as to whether that duty of care [for the claimant's safety when using the pool] is variable, and it must be right that how one performs a particular duty must depend upon the class of persons, for example, young, old, fit, disabled and the like, who one might reasonably anticipate will use the facility. If one anticipates a range of persons would use that facility then ... surely the defendant must design to accommodate the safety of the broadest class of anticipated visitor. That is not, however, to say that if a fit, able person should have been in a position to safely negotiate a particular feature, he is entitled to succeed because an unfit or disabled person would not. In such circumstances a claimant would not be able to prove negligence as causative of his injury."

harm may occur. In Lord Dunedin's words: "People must guard against reasonable probabilities, but they are not bound to guard against fantastic possibilities."[796] The point is well illustrated by contrasting the cricketing cases of *Bolton v Stone*[797] and *Miller v Jackson*.[798] In *Bolton* the claimant was hit by a ball driven from the defendant's cricket ground on to a quiet road. The evidence was that balls had been hit out of the ground on perhaps six occasions in 30 years. The risk of harm was foreseeable but the chances were small. The House of Lords held that the defendants were not liable for continuing to play cricket as it was reasonable to ignore such a small risk.[799] In *Miller* by contrast, balls were hit out of the ground eight or nine times a season and had damaged the claimant's property on a number of occasions. The Court of Appeal held that the risk of damage was so great that the defendants were negligent each time the ball was hit out of the ground and caused damage. It should be noted that *Bolton* is not authority for the view that it is always reasonable to disregard a low likelihood. The other factors in the balance, e.g. the severity of the harm and the cost of precautions, must also be taken into account.

7-177 **Severity of the harm** The degree of care also depends on the magnitude of the consequences that are likely to ensue. As Lord Macmillan said: "Those who engage in operations inherently dangerous must take precautions which are not required of persons engaged in the ordinary routine of daily life."[800] The more serious the consequences, the greater the degree of care which has to be shown. Thus, if gas is brought in containers onto a ship in the course of construction, the degree of care required from those who brought it is to be measured by the danger involved.[801] In *Paris v Stepney BC*[802] a one-eyed man, employed as a garage hand, was using a hammer to loosen a bolt when he was struck in his remaining eye by a chip from the bolt, and he became totally blind. It was held that the amount of care which should have been exercised by his employer in providing safety equipment was greater in his case than in the case of a two-eyed man doing similar work on the principle that "the more serious the damage which will happen if an accident occurs, the more thorough are the precautions which an employer must take".[803] This principle can work in the defendant's favour, so that where the severity of the harm that can reasonably be foreseen is relatively minor, less will be expected by way of precautions against the risk.[804]

7-178 **Cost of precautions** The cost and practicability of overcoming a risk are matters which can properly be taken into consideration in deciding whether reason-

796 *Fardon v Harcourt-Rivington* (1932) 146 L.T. 391 at 392.
797 [1951] A.C. 850.
798 [1977] Q.B. 966.
799 Lord Radcliffe commented that the level of likelihood was such that a reasonable man would neither have increased the height of the fences around the ground nor stopped playing on the ground. See also *Whippey v Jones* [2009] EWCA Civ 452; (2009) 159 N.L.J. 598—foreseeability of the *possibility* of injury when letting a dog off the leash in a park insufficient to establish breach of duty when the dog was not known to jump up at people (applying *Bolton v Stone*); see para.20-27; and *Addis v Campbell* [2011] EWCA Civ 906 (applying *Whippey v Jones*).
800 *Glasgow Corp v Muir* [1943] A.C. 448 at 456.
801 *Beckett v Newalls Insulation Co Ltd* [1953] 1 W.L.R. 8.
802 [1951] A.C. 367. This case was followed in *Porteous v NCB*, 1967 S.L.T. 117 (Court of Session), another instance of a one-eyed workman. See also *Pentney v Anglian Water Authority* [1983] I.C.R. 464.
803 [1951] A.C. 367 at 385, per Lord Morton.
804 See *Perry v Harris* [2008] EWCA Civ 907; [2009] 1 W.L.R. 19; para.7-226.

able care has been used or not. "In every case of a foreseeable risk, it is a matter of balancing the risk against the measures necessary to eliminate it."[805] In *Latimer v AEC Ltd*[806] the floor of a factory became slippery with water and oil owing to a flood caused by a heavy rainfall. The occupiers took such steps as they could to overcome this, but were not able to overcome it entirely. A workman slipped on the floor and was injured, but it was held that the occupiers, having done all they reasonably could, were not bound to go to the extreme length of closing the factory until the floor became normal.[807] Again, in *B (A Child) v London Borough of Camden*[808] the defendants were held not negligent in failing to lag central heating pipes against which a nine-month-old baby had become trapped with resulting burns. The cost of protection would have been substantial, the risk of such accidents was slight, and the primary responsibility for protecting the child rested with the parents. In *Keown v Coventry Healthcare NHS Trust*[809] Longmore LJ said, obiter, that there were two reasons why it would not be reasonable to expect the NHS Trust to provide protection from the risk of falling from a normal fire escape. The first was that: "the resources of a Trust are much more sensibly utilised in the treatment and care of patients … rather than catering for the contingency that children will climb where they know they should not go". The second was that: "if the courts say such protection should be afforded … it is more likely that what will happen will be what happened in this case. The Trust has now built a perimeter fence around the entire site … the hospital ground is becoming like a fortress. The amenity which local people had of passing through the grounds … and which children had of harmlessly playing in the grounds has now been lost."

Conversely where the cost of the precautions is minimal, the defendant may be expected to guard against small risks. Thus in *The Wagon Mound (No.2)*[810] the precaution which would have eliminated the small risk of oil being discharged from the defendant's ship catching fire on the surface of the water, was simple and cheap. It was merely the closing of a valve to prevent the discharge. Finding the defendant liable, the Privy Council commented that a reasonable man would not ignore such a small risk "if action to eliminate it presented no difficulty, involved no disadvantage and required no expense".[811] **7-179**

Lack of resources The general principle is that the actual resources available to **7-180**

---

805 per Denning LJ in *Latimer v AEC Ltd* [1952] 2 Q.B. 701 at 711 (affirmed [1953] A.C. 643); per Lord Reid in *The Wagon Mound (No.2)* [1967] 1 A.C. 617 at 642–643. See *Nilsson v Redditch BC* [1995] P.I.Q.R. P199, in which an appeal against liability was allowed because the trial judge had failed to consider the issues of practicability and cost.

806 [1953] A.C. 643. See also *Aiken v Port of London Authority* [1962] 1 Lloyd's Rep. 30, where the cost of preventive measures was held to outweigh the risk.

807 This case might be compared with *Johnson v Rea* [1961] 1 W.L.R. 1400, where soda ash, while being loaded onto a ship from a shed, seeped to the floor, making it slippery. The claimant, who was delivering chemicals for loading, was asked by the stevedores responsible for the loading to carry them through the shed, but he was warned that the floor was slippery. He fell and suffered injury. It was held by the Court of Appeal that the defendants were negligent and that the claimant was not. The defendants had created a danger and had taken no steps to protect the claimant. Mere warning was not enough.

808 [2001] P.I.Q.R. P9.

809 [2006] EWCA Civ 39; [2006] 1 W.L.R. 953 at [17].

810 [1967] 1 A.C. 617.

811 [1967] 1 A.C. 617 at 642. See also *Haley v London Electricity Board* [1965] A.C. 778, where the House of Lords expressly referred to the simple precautions that would have been required to prevent blind pedestrians falling into a hole, and to the fact that the authority had the necessary resources.

a defendant are not relevant when assessing whether reasonable care has been taken. The provider of services or products must ensure that sufficient resources are available for reasonable care to be taken. Thus, an architect who departs from normal safety levels in order to bring the design of a building within the limited budget allowed by the client, will be liable to anyone injured as a result of the inadequate safety provision.[812] The architect has a choice: he can refuse the commission unless it is adequately funded. The principle applies equally to non-commercial suppliers of services. In *PQ v Australian Red Cross Society*[813] the court firmly rejected the notion that the standard to be expected of the Red Cross in testing blood donations for the AIDS virus should be determined in the light of the financial constraints of the charity. The charity has a choice. If it lacks adequate resources, it should choose not to provide the service. However, in the context of the liability of public services and of occupiers in relation to naturally occurring hazards, the defendant's lack of choice may justify taking into account his actual resources. The position of public services is discussed in Ch.13.[814]

7-181 **Occupiers' resources when dealing with natural hazards** An occupier owes an affirmative duty of care to prevent a natural hazard arising on his land from harming others,[815] but his lack of choice in the matter has led courts to take account of his actual resources. In *Goldman v Hargrave*[816] where the Privy Council held that the occupier owed a duty to neighbouring property owners to take care in extinguishing a fire which had started naturally on his land, Lord Wilberforce said:

> "The law must take account of the fact that the occupier on whom the duty is cast has, ex hypothesi, had this hazard thrust upon him through no seeking or fault of his own. His interest, and his resources, whether physical or material, may be of a very modest character either in relation to the magnitude of the hazard, or as compared with those of his threatened neighbour. A rule which required of him in such unsought circumstances in his neighbour's interest a physical effort of which he is not capable, or an excessive expenditure of money, would be unenforceable or unjust ... The standard ought to be to require of the occupier what it is reasonable to expect of him in his individual circumstances.... the owner of a small property where a hazard arises which threatens a neighbour with substantial interests should not have to do as much as one with larger interests of his own at stake and greater resources to protect them ..."

In *Leakey v National Trust*[817] it was emphasised that this approach entailed a broad and not a detailed assessment of the defendant's capacity to find money. It is suggested that despite Lord Wilberforce's reference to individual circumstances, it is the resources to be expected of the particular class of occupier, e.g. of a small property, rather than the resources of the particular individual which should be taken into account.

---

812 *Voli v Inglewood Shire Council* (1963) 110 C.L.R. 74.
813 [1992] 1 V.R. 19. See (1992) 108 L.Q.R. 8.
814 See para.13-81.
815 See para.7-57.
816 [1967] 1 A.C. 645 at 633. In *British Railways Board v Herrington* [1972] A.C. 877 the House of Lords similarly held that the occupier's resources should be taken into account when determining whether he had satisfied the duty of common humanity owed to a trespasser. That duty has now been superseded by the duty contained in the Occupiers' Liability Act 1984. See paras 11-63 and 11-68.
817 [1980] Q.B. 485 at 526 per Megaw LJ.

This modified standard of care is known as a "measured duty of care"[818] but setting the scope of the duty is not without difficulty.[819] In *Holbeck Hall Hotel v Scarborough BC*[820] Stuart-Smith LJ suggested that the third limb of the *Caparo* test,[821] namely whether it would be fair, just and reasonable to impose a duty or the extent of the duty claimed, could be called in aid. The claimants' hotel was situated on a cliff overlooking the sea and the land between the hotel and the sea was occupied by the defendant local authority. Due to natural erosion the cliff was inherently unstable and there had been at least two landslips on the authority's land. Following a further, much larger, landslip the hotel was undermined and had to be demolished. The Court of Appeal held that it was not fair, just or reasonable to impose liability on the local authority. Although the risk of landslips was foreseeable the defendants did not have knowledge, either actual or presumed, that there was a serious risk of a major landslip. This could only have been discovered by an expensive investigation of the underlying geology. In those circumstances the scope of the defendants' measured duty of care was limited to warning neighbours of such risk as they were aware of or ought to have foreseen and sharing such information as they had acquired relating to it.[822] **7-182**

In *Lambert v Barratt Homes Ltd*[823] the Court of Appeal stated that in considering what it is reasonable for the individual occupier to do to satisfy the measured duty of care the court must consider all the circumstances, including the claimants' right to recover the cost of remedial works from another defendant and the likelihood that the claimants were insured against damage to their properties by flooding. A local authority had sold a parcel of land to a developer who built houses on the land and in doing so blocked part of a drainage ditch and drain. Water accumulated on land retained by the local authority and occasionally flooded the claimants' properties. The Court of Appeal noted that a local authority could be expected to have access to funds far in excess of those available to the individual claimants, but the resources of the local authority were not the only issue: "it is well known that most local authorities are under a degree of financial pressure. Moreover their resources are held for public purposes and are not generally available for the benefit of private citizens."[824] The fact that the claimants had a right to recover the whole of the cost of the remedial work from the developer was "a powerful factor" to be taken into account when determining the scope of authority's duty of care and it was accordingly not fair, just or reasonable to impose on the authority a duty to carry out and pay for any part of the work. The authority's duty was limited to a duty to co-operate in a solution which involved the construction of suitable drain- **7-183**

---

818 The phrase used by Lord Wilberforce in *Goldman v Hargrave* [1967] 1 A.C. 645 at 662.

819 "In considering the scope of the measured duty of care, the courts are still in relatively uncharted waters": *Holbeck Hall Hotel v Scarborough BC* [2000] Q.B. 836 at [49] per Stuart-Smith LJ.

820 [2000] Q.B. 836 at [51]. See also para.2-169.

821 See paras 7-17 onwards. Although *Caparo* is concerned with the question of whether a duty of care should be imposed and the standard of care is concerned with whether there has been a breach of that duty, in this context the two issues are inextricably linked (through the mechanism of setting the scope of the duty).

822 [2000] Q.B. 836 at [54]. See also *Coope v Ward* [2015] EWCA Civ 30; [2015] 1 W.L.R. 4081 (collapse of wall between claimants' and defendants' properties which had provided support for the claimants' land; defendants' measured duty of care was limited to allowing the claimants access to their land in order to enable works to be carried out; unreasonable to impose on the defendants a liability to contribute to the cost of the construction of a wall which was entirely on the claimants' land from which the defendants would derive no benefit). See further para.19-23.

823 [2010] EWCA Civ 681; [2010] B.L.R. 527.

824 [2010] EWCA Civ 681; [2010] B.L.R. 527 at [22].

age and a catch pit on their retained land. In reaching this conclusion the Court also considered that the insurance position was a factor that could be taken into account: "The likelihood is that as householders the residents were insured against damage to their properties by flooding and when considering their ability to carry out and bear the cost of the work required to safeguard those properties we see no reason to ignore the possibility of their obtaining the necessary funds from their insurers".[825] On the other hand, in *Vernon Knight Associates v Cornwall Council*[826] both Jackson LJ and Sir Stanley Burnton doubted whether the availability of insurance was a relevant consideration.[827] Jackson LJ suggested that the test for the content of the measured duty required the court must have regard to all the circumstances, including the extent of the foreseeable risk, the available preventive measures, the costs of such measures and the resources of both parties (though disregarding the insurance position). Of course, as a general rule, a local authority will have greater resources than a private individual, but that is not a factor that, *per se*, will tip the balance against a local authority: "Where the defendant is a public authority with substantial resources, the court must take into account the competing demands on those resources and the public purposes for which they are held. It may not be fair, just or reasonable to require a public authority to expend those resources on infrastructure works in order to protect a few individuals against a modest risk of property damage."[828] In *Vernon* the claimant's property was flooded on two occasions because a system of drains, gullies and a catchpit installed in the adjacent road by the local authority to deal with the known problem of flooding was blocked. The authority had a system for checking the drains for blockages during periods of heavy rain, but the system was not implemented on the two occasions in question. The Court of Appeal concluded that the judge had not applied too high a standard in holding the local authority liable for the flood damage. There was no good reason (such as lack of resources or other more urgent work) why the system failed on those two occasions. The heavy rainfall had occurred during normal working hours but the local authority employees had continued dealing with routine maintenance work. This differed from *Lambert* in that, there, the remedial work would have involved expensive infrastructure works.

7-184 **The utility of the activity** The degree of risk should also be balanced against the end to be achieved by the activity in question, including its importance and social utility. In *Ward v London CC*[829] the driver of a fire-engine, in hurrying to a fire, ignored the stop-light at a light-controlled crossing and collided with the claimant's car, which was proceeding with the lights in its favour. The authority responsible for the fire service was held liable. In this case the need to put out fires quickly had

---

825 [2010] EWCA Civ 681; [2010] B.L.R. 527. The Court noted, however, that it was "not necessary to reach any final conclusion on the question in this case".

826 [2013] EWCA Civ 950; [2013] B.L.R. 519.

827 [2013] EWCA Civ 950; [2013] B.L.R. 519 at [47] and [70]. Sir Stanley Burnton commented: "The availability of insurance is not normally relevant to a duty in tort. I can think of no case in which a claim in tort has been rejected on the ground that it is a subrogated claim.… I cannot think that it would be appropriate for the Court to have to inquire as to the insurance market in any case in which the question [of the extent of the measured duty] arises."

828 [2013] EWCA Civ 950; [2013] B.L.R. 519 at [49].

829 [1938] 2 All E.R. 341. For another example of the liability of an emergency service crossing junction lights at red, see *Griffin v Mersey Regional Ambulance* [1998] P.I.Q.R. P34; *Armsden v Kent Police* [2009] EWCA Civ 631; [2009] R.T.R. 31 on the duty of the driver of a police vehicle using flashing blue warning light, but not its siren, to exercise reasonable care.

to be balanced against the risk of disobeying the rules of the road. Underlying the judgment there seems to be the feeling that where there exists a highly efficient and well-organised fire-fighting service, there is no need for any individual fire-engine driver to incur risks like this.[830] In *Daborn v Bath Tramways Motor Co Ltd*[831] the question for decision was whether in wartime the driver of an ambulance, which had a left-hand drive, was negligent in turning into an offside lane without a signal. It was held that there was no negligence in the light of: "the necessity in time of national emergency of employing all transport resources which were available, the inherent limitations and incapacities of this particular form of transport" and the need to "balance the risk against the consequences of not assuming that risk".[832] These considerations were adopted in *Watt v Hertfordshire CC*,[833] where Denning LJ said: "It is well settled that in measuring due care you must balance the risk against the measures to eliminate the risk. To that proposition there ought to be added this: you must balance the risk against the end to be achieved."[834] In a different context in *Thompson v Home Office*[835] the governor of a young offenders' institution was held not in breach of duty in allowing inmates to have razors one of which was used to attack the claimant, as the risk had to be weighed against the utility of trusting the inmates thereby assisting in their rehabilitation.

The utility of freedom to take risks In *Tomlinson v Congleton BC*[836] Lord Hoffmann stressed utility both in the sense of the social benefit which would be lost if precautions were taken but also in the sense of the importance of preserving individual freedom of choice even if that means taking risks. The defendant was the occupier of a park with a lake and sandy beaches formed from a disused sand quarry. Signs on the beach said: "Dangerous Water No Swimming". Tomlinson dived into shallow water and broke his back. The Court of Appeal had held the defendant in breach of duty for failing to replace the sandy beaches with reeds to physically prevent anyone from getting into the water. The House of Lords reversed this decision. Giving the leading speech, Lord Hoffmann said that the risk of injury had to be balanced not just against the cost of the required precautions but also the social value of the activities which would thereby be prevented and the freedom of people to decide for themselves whether to take risks. On the question of social value, he said: "The majority of people who went to the beaches to sunbathe, paddle and play were enjoying themselves in a way which gave them pleasure and caused no risk to themselves or anyone else. This must be something to be taken into account in deciding whether it was reasonable to expect the council to destroy the beaches."[837] On the question of free will, he said: 7-185

> "it will be extremely rare for an occupier of land to be under a duty to prevent people from taking risks which are inherent in the activities they freely choose to undertake upon the

---

830 [1938] 2 All E.R. 341. See the remarks of Charles J at 343.

831 [1946] 2 All E.R. 333.

832 [1946] 2 All E.R. 333 at 336.

833 [1954] 1 W.L.R. 835 at 838 (fire service justified in taking additional risk in transporting a heavy lifting jack to the scene of an accident where a woman was trapped under a lorry).

834 See the similar comments of Coleman J in *Walker v Northumberland CC* [1995] I.C.R. 702; [1995] 1 All E.R. 737. For the standard of care expected of an employer in preventing employee stress see para.12-40.

835 [2001] EWCA Civ 331.

836 [2003] UKHL 47; [2004] 1 A.C. 46.

837 [2003] UKHL 47; [2004] 1 A.C. 46 at [42].

land. If people want to climb mountains, go hang gliding or swim or dive in ponds or lakes, that is their affair. Of course the landowner may for his own reasons wish to prohibit such activities. He may think that they are a danger or inconvenience to himself or others … . But the law does not require him to do so."[838]

In the light of these balancing factors, he decided that there was no breach of duty. Although the case concerns the standard of care expected under the Occupiers' Liability Act 1984, Lord Hoffmann's observations are of general application.[839]

7-186 **Balancing risk and utility** In *Scout Association v Barnes*[840] the Court of Appeal held that the failure of a judge to refer to Lord Hoffmann's analysis in *Tomlinson v Congleton BC* of the balancing exercise that has to be performed does not necessarily mean that there is an error of law, provided that the judge actually undertakes an assessment of balance between the social value of the activity giving rise to the risk and the cost of preventative measures. The defendants were found to be in breach of duty in respect of injury to a 13-year-old scout sustained when playing a game in which boys rushed to the centre of a hall to compete for possession of blocks when the lights were turned off. The judge considered that playing the game in the dark added to the risk of injury, but the only value it added was to increase the excitement of the game. Smith LJ accepted that scouting activities have social value and will often properly include an element of risk, but that could not mean that any scouting activity, however risky, is acceptable just because scouting is a good thing: "the law of tort must not interfere with activities just because they carry some risk. Of course, the law of tort must not stamp out socially desirable activities. But whether the social benefit of an activity is such that the degree of risk it entails is acceptable is a question of fact, degree and judgment, which must be decided on

838 [2003] UKHL 47; [2004] 1 A.C. 46 at [45]. See also *Poppleton v Trustees of the Portsmouth Youth Activities Committee* [2008] EWCA Civ 646; [2009] P.I.Q.R. P1—no duty to train or supervise an adult engaging in "bouldering" at the defendants' indoor climbing premises: "If the law required training or supervision in this case, it would equally be required for a multitude of other commonplace leisure activities which nevertheless carry with them a degree of obvious inherent risk—as for instance bathing in the sea" (at [20], per May LJ) (applied in *Maylin v Dacorum Sports Trust (t/a XC Sportspace)* [2017] EWHC 378 (QB), another case of a fall from height whilst bouldering); *Risk v Rose Bruford College* [2013] EWHC 3869 (QB); [2014] E.L.R. 157—no duty owed by defendant to 21-year-old student who dived head first into a shallow inflatable pool at an event organised by the Student Union on the defendants' premises. *Poppleton* was distinguished in *Pinchbeck v Craggy Island Ltd* [2012] EWHC 2745 (QB) where the defendants had assumed responsibility for the safety of the claimant who was injured in a fall whilst "bouldering", and so they were under a duty to provide appropriate supervision and instruction. Where the claimant's free will is circumscribed, as in the employer-employee relationship, the defendant may have a greater responsibility: *Ministry of Defence v Radclyffe* [2009] EWCA Civ 635 at [22]—defendants liable for injury to claimant, a lieutenant in the Irish Guards, who jumped off a bridge 65 feet above a river whilst off duty; claimant had jumped off the same bridge the day before, having been urged to do so by a more senior officer because it would have been "bad form" not to do so, and it was necessary for the officers to show that they were as brave as the men (who had requested permission from the senior officer to make the jump). And where the claimant should not have had a choice because of a mandatory requirement of the criminal law imposed upon the defendant to take precautions against the relevant risk then the principle in *Tomlinson* may not apply: *James v White Lion Hotel* [2020] P.I.Q.R. P10 (QBD) at [97] ("the exercise of ordinar[y] reasonable care, requires compliance with a specific safety requirement of the criminal law"—deceased held 60 per cent contributorily negligent having fallen from a bedroom window with a dangerously low sill).

839 In relation to Occupiers' Liability, see para.11-32. His observations are also relevant to the defence of volenti: see the discussion at para.3-109.

840 [2010] EWCA Civ 1476.

an individual basis and not by a broad brush approach."[841] By a majority, the Court held that the judge was correct in concluding that the additional risk created by turning off the lights was not justified by the additional excitement for the participants in the game.[842] *Scout Association v Barnes* illustrates the difficulty of drawing a balance between the social value of an activity and the risk it creates. It can be contrasted with *Cole v Davis-Gilbert*[843] where the claimant fell and broke her leg due to a hole in a village green, which had been dug for the maypole at the annual village fête organised by the Royal British Legion. The Court of Appeal allowed the appeal of the Legion against the finding of the trial judge that was in breach of its duty of care to the claimant by failing to take reasonable steps to ensure that the hole was adequately filled in. The court concluded that the accident was caused not by inadequate infilling of the hole but by removal of the infill, perhaps by children. Baker LJ commented:

> "Accidents happen, and sometimes they are what can be described as pure accidents in the sense that the victim cannot recover damages for the resulting injury because fault cannot be established. If the law were to set a higher standard of care than that which is reasonable in cases such as the present, the consequences would quickly become inhibited. There would be no fêtes, no maypole dancing and none of the activities that have come to be associated with the English village green for fear of what might conceivably go wrong."[844]

In *Watt v Hertfordshire CC* and *Daborn v Bath Tramways Motor Co Ltd* the utility was related to the effective performance of the rescue and emergency services, and the saving of life or limb may justify taking considerable risk.[845] On the other hand, where the risk of injury is low, less significant utilities may be taken into account. Thus, in *Bolton v Stone*[846] the utility of playing cricket as a sport was held to outweigh the remote possibility of a ball being hit out of that particular cricket-field. If, however, the likelihood of injury is high, the social utility of playing sport will be outweighed. In *Hilder v Associated Portland Cement Manufacturers Ltd*[847] the defendants habitually allowed boys to play football on a piece of ground owned by them and adjoining the highway. The ground was bounded only by a low wall. A ball was kicked out of the ground, and it hit and killed a passing motorcyclist. The defendants were held liable because the likelihood of balls being kicked out **7-187**

---

841 [2010] EWCA Civ 1476 at [49].

842 Ward LJ, though clearly hesitant about the outcome (see [2010] EWCA Civ 1476 at [50]) agreed with Smith LJ that the judge had engaged "in the *Tomlinson* task of balancing the social value of the activity giving rise to the risk and the cost of the preventative measures: more fun playing in the dark but more risk; less fun and less risk playing with the lights on. Is the benefit of added fun worth the added risk? He decided it was not worth it" (at [59]). Jackson LJ dissented on the basis that he could not see how the increased risks from turning off the lights outweighed the social benefits of the activity.

843 [2007] EWCA Civ 396.

844 [2007] EWCA Civ 396 at [36].

845 See para.7-184; cf. the taking of risks in a commercial context: "If this accident had occurred in a commercial enterprise without any emergency there could be no doubt that the servant would succeed. But the commercial end to make profit is very different from the human end to save life or limb", per Denning LJ in *Watt v Hertfordshire CC* [1954] 1 W.L.R. 835 at 838.

846 [1951] A.C. 850. See also *Uren v Corporate Leisure (UK) Ltd* [2011] EWCA Civ 66; [2011] I.C.R. D11 and the analysis of Foskett J in *Uren v Corporate Leisure (UK) Ltd* [2013] EWHC 353 (QB) on the balance to be drawn between the degree of risk of injury and the social utility of a game (para.7-167).

847 [1961] 1 W.L.R. 1434. See also *Miller v Jackson* [1977] Q.B. 966, where cricket balls landed fairly often in the claimants' gardens and the Court of Appeal held the defendant club liable in negligence.

of that ground was great, and this outweighed the desirability of keeping children off the streets.

7-188 **The Compensation Act 2006** Despite the decision of the House of Lords in *Tomlinson v Congleton BC* firmly restating the balance to be drawn between the responsibility of potential defendants to exercise care for others and the responsibility of individuals who wish to take risks for the consequences of their own actions, Parliament considered it appropriate to intervene. Section 1 of the Compensation Act 2006 provides that:

> "A Court considering a claim in negligence or breach of statutory duty may, in determining whether the defendant should have taken particular steps to meet a standard of care (whether by taking precautions against a risk or otherwise) have regard to whether a requirement to take those steps might—
> (a) prevent a desirable activity from being undertaken at all, to a particular extent or in a particular way, or
> (b) discourage persons from undertaking functions in connection with a desirable activity."

The Act provides no definition of what constitutes a "desirable activity" and though on one view this should be treated as the same as the "social utility" wording of Lord Hoffmann's test in *Tomlinson*, there is an argument that it is potentially wider than "social utility".[848] The problem with the section is that if a court would have reached a conclusion that the defendant had taken such an unreasonable risk that he should be held to be in breach of duty at common law it is difficult to see why it should come to a different conclusion on the basis that a finding that this particular defendant was negligent might prevent or discourage others from undertaking a desirable activity. If the defendant has taken an "unreasonable" risk which has caused harm to another person, how can taking into account the possibility that others might be discouraged from undertaking functions in connection with a desirable activity somehow make the risk taken by the defendant "reasonable"? It may well be desirable not to discourage socially beneficial activities, but it can hardly be desirable to encourage those engaged in otherwise beneficial activities to act negligently and injure others.

7-189 In *Hopps v Mott MacDonald Ltd*[849] Christopher Clarke J said that he took into account the Compensation Act 2006 s.1, when considering whether civilian contractors in Iraq and the Ministry of Defence had been in breach of duty in transporting the claimant around Basra in a standard production Land Rover, rather than an armoured vehicle. The vehicle was blown up by an improvised explosive device. In deciding whether particular steps, such as confining the claimant to the airport until armoured vehicles were available for transport, should have been taken the

[848] This was the view of House of Commons Constitutional Affairs Committee in its report on the Bill: HC 754–1, para.68.

[849] [2009] EWHC 1881 (QB) at [93]. See also *Humphrey v Aegis Defence Services Ltd* [2014] EWHC 989 (QB) (defendants justified in employing interpreters who were not as physically fit as other employees engaged as private defence contractors in Iraq, even though this increased the risk of injury to others, because interpreters were a "scarce commodity" and the defendants were engaged in the socially valuable activity of reconstruction work which would be prevented without interpreters; Compensation Act 2006 s.1 applied, although it "add[ed] nothing to *Tomlinson*" (at [112])). The Court of Appeal dismissed the claimant's appeal without referring to the Compensation Act 2006: [2016] EWCA Civ 11; [2017] 1 W.L.R. 2937.

court was entitled to have regard to whether such steps would prevent "the desirable activity of reconstruction of a shattered infrastructure after a war in a territory occupied by HM forces, particularly when failure to expedite that work would carry with it risks to the safety of coalition forces and civilian contractors in Iraq as a whole". It is not clear how this assessment of the balance of risks differed from the common law's approach in determining whether there has been a breach of duty. In *Uren v Corporate Leisure (UK) Ltd*[850] the Court of Appeal accepted that s.1 of the Compensation Act 2006 added nothing to the common law which "at least since *Tomlinson v Congleton Borough Council*, if not before" has required the court to take into account the matters set out in the section. Although s.1 purports to enable the courts to shift the balance of the assessment of negligence towards defendants, the reality is that it has not made any substantive change to the way in which the courts have, for many years, determined whether a defendant is in breach of duty.[851]

The Social Action, Responsibility and Heroism Act 2015[852] Having attempted to alter the courts' approach to the determination of breach of duty in the Compensation Act 2006, apparently without much success, Parliament has again intervened through the Social Action, Responsibility and Heroism Act 2015. By s.1 the Act (which extends to England and Wales) applies "when a court, in considering a claim that a person was negligent or in breach of statutory duty, is determining the steps that the person was required to take to meet a standard of care". Section 2 provides that the court "must have regard to whether the alleged negligence or breach of statutory duty occurred when the person was acting for the benefit of society or any of its members." The term "acting for the benefit of society" is not defined but presumably covers a wide range of activities. There is no obvious reason to limit it to the actions of, say, voluntary organisations raising funds for charitable purposes or hospitals treating patients. A vehicle delivering goods to a supermarket is, in a broad sense, "acting for the benefit of society" since it is arguable that without the **7-190**

850 [2011] EWCA Civ 66; [2011] I.C.R. D11 at [13]. See also *Scout Association v Barnes* [2010] EWCA Civ 1476, per Jackson LJ at [34]: "It is not the function of the law of tort to eliminate every iota of risk or to stamp out socially desirable activities … This principle is now enshrined in s.1 of the Compensation Act 2006. That provision was not in force at the time of the claimant's accident. However, the principle has always been part of the common law." The courts tend to regard sporting endeavours as "desirable activity". In *Sutton v Syston Rugby Football Club Ltd* [2011] EWCA Civ 1182 at [13] Longmore LJ commented that it was "important that neither the game's professional organisation nor the law should lay down standards that are too difficult for ordinary coaches and match organisers to meet. Games of rugby are, after all, no more than games and, as such are obviously desirable activities within the meaning of section 1 of the Compensation Act 2006." However, this does not resolve the issue of the degree of risk of harm that it is justifiable to accept in pursuing such desirable activities, whether sporting or otherwise.

851 Herbert "The Compensation Act 2006" [2006] J.P.I.L. 337 at 338 comments: "A cynical observer might sum it up thus: s.1 provides nothing new, to address a problem that doesn't actually exist. It merely 'codifies' existing law …". Williams was equally dismissive, commenting that s.1 "looks like a strongly media-driven phoney solution to a phoney problem": Williams, "Politics, the Media and Refining the Notion of Fault: Section 1 of the Compensation Act 2006" [2006] J.P.I.L. 347 at 352–353. Indeed, it has been suggested that the government itself did not regard s.1 as constituting any change to the existing law: A. Morris, "Spiralling or Stabilising? The Compensation Culture and Our Propensity to Claim Damages for Personal Injury" (2007) 70 M.L.R. 349, 368.

852 The Act applies where the act or omission giving rise to the claim occurs on or after 13 April 2015: Social Action, Responsibility and Heroism Act 2015 (Commencement and Transitional Provision) Regulations 2015 (SI 2015/808) art.3.

distribution of food across the country "society" would soon descend into anarchy. Even the commercial provision of leisure activities could be said to be "acting for the benefit of society or … its members". On a broad interpretation, the only defendants who would not fall within s.2 are those engaged in positively anti-social activities (such as criminals) and private individuals acting for their own purposes (such as a private motorist wanting to get from A to B). Having identified that the defendant's conduct falls within s.2, the court must then "have regard" to the fact that the breach of duty occurred when the person was acting for the benefit of society or its members. It does not specify what the court must then do, having taken into account the defendant's benevolent intentions: how much weight should the court attach to social benefit when considering whether the defendant has taken an unreasonable risk of harm to others? Given that the courts already take into account the utility of the defendant's activity when determining whether he has taken an unreasonable risk it is difficult to see what s.2 adds to the common law.

7-191 Section 3 provides that the "court must have regard to whether the person, in carrying out the activity in the course of which the alleged negligence or breach of statutory duty occurred, demonstrated a predominantly responsible approach towards protecting the safety or other interests of others". When considering whether a defendant was in breach of duty the issue is whether the act(s) or omission(s) which caused the claimant's damage fell below the standard of reasonable care in the circumstances. It is not, and never has been, whether a defendant is "predominantly" or generally careful. There is no such thing as an "average" standard of care whereby a failure to exercise reasonable care on one occasion can somehow be compensated for by the defendant's otherwise careful or even exemplary conduct. A lifetime of careful driving does not excuse the one occasion when a motorist carelessly drove into a pedestrian crossing the road. A glittering professional career does not exculpate the surgeon who on a single occasion makes a negligent mistake resulting in the death of the patient. Most people are careful about the safety of others most of the time, and so can probably be said to demonstrate "a predominantly responsible approach towards protecting the safety or other interests of others". However, it is difficult to see how that can excuse a negligent defendant merely because he has only occasionally failed to exercise reasonable care.

7-192 Finally, s.4 states that the "court must have regard to whether the alleged negligence or breach of statutory duty occurred when the person was acting heroically by intervening in an emergency to assist an individual in danger". This is something the courts already do, and have done for many years. The duty in negligence is to take reasonable care "in all the circumstances", and the circumstances allow for the possibility that a defendant may have had to make a judgment call in the heat of the moment during the course of an emergency.[853] The courts are careful not to apply unrealistic standards, with the benefit of hindsight, in the calm and measured atmosphere of the courtroom.[854] It is possible that Parliament had in mind claims against the emergency services. Claims against the police, the fire brigade and the coastguard for negligent rescue attempts will not arise in

---

853 See para.7-165.

854 See, e.g. *Tolley v Carr* [2010] EWHC 2191 (QB); [2011] R.T.R. 7, para.3-94, where the judge rejected a plea of contributory negligence against a claimant who acted as a rescuer. *Harrison v British Railways Board* [1981] 3 All E.R. 679, para.7-37, is a rare example of a finding of contributory negligence against a rescuer injured in the course of an attempted rescue.

any event unless the defendant has made the claimant's position worse than it already was, since there is no general obligation to effect a rescue.[855] But even where the duty arises, the standard of care applied takes account of the difficulty of effecting the rescue and the urgency of the situation. Moreover, it is debatable whether the emergency services would be considered to be acting "heroically", as opposed to simply doing their job. It is difficult to avoid the conclusion that the Social Action, Responsibility and Heroism Act 2015, much like s.1 of the Compensation Act 2006, has a merely symbolic function and makes no substantive change to the law.[856]

Cost/benefit analysis In *Cekan v Haines*,[857] a leading Australian appellate judge, Kirby P., argued that the courts would need to give "further detailed attention in the future to the economic theory which supports arguments about what reasonable care requires". To illustrate, he referred to the case of *United States v Carroll Towing Co*[858] in which Learned Hand J propounded his well-known formulation of the negligence standard. This requires the judge to measure three things: the probability of an accident occurring (P); the magnitude of the loss if it occurs (L); and the burden or cost of taking precautions that would avert it (B). The product of the first two, the probability and loss, is the benefit to be gained from taking the precautions. If the benefit exceeds the cost of the precautions, the failure to take those precautions amounts to negligence.[859] There are a number of problems with this approach. It is difficult to provide a court with the relevant data of costs and benefits.[860] Economic theorists argue that a far more sophisticated formula than that put forward by Hand J is required to achieve the most efficient outcome.[861] In the light of these problems, the most that can be hoped for is that an appreciation of cost/benefit analysis will provide the courts with "a valuable aid to clear thinking about the factors that are relevant to a judgement of negligence".[862] Moreover, fairness between the parties should be the overriding criterion; fairness from the perspective of the claimant's reasonable expectations as much as from the cost/benefit stance of the defendant. The fair and reasonable man should reflect the community's values as much as those of the calculating utilitarian.[863] These values will 7-193

---

855 See paras 7-54 and 7-55. The ambulance service does have a duty to respond to an emergency call, since once the call has been accepted they have undertaken responsibility: *Kent v Griffiths, Roberts and London Ambulance Service* [2001] Q.B. 36.

856 For critique see R. Mulheron, "Legislating Dangerously: Bad Samaritans, Good Society, and the Heroism Act 2015" (2017) 80 M.L.R. 88.

857 (1990) 21 N.S.W.L.R. 296. He also commented that one of the "chief defects of the law of negligence" was its failure "develop more than a general notion of the economic consequences of asserting the requirements of reasonable care".

858 (1947) 159 F.2nd 169.

859 In formula terms, where PL > B there is negligence, but if the benefit (PL) is less than the costs (B), i.e. PL > B, there is no negligence.

860 Thus in *Cekan* there was no evidence as to the benefits of the proposed precautions in terms of an estimated avoidance of injuries, and Kirby P could only assert that the costs of the precaution would be "self-evidently most substantial". But note that the Learned Hand formulation was applied by the New Zealand Court of Appeal in *Wilson & Horton v Att Gen* [1997] 2 N.Z.L.R. 513 CA.

861 The result of attempts to refine the Hand formula has been described by one critic as "economic stalemate". See Englard, *The Philosophy of Tort Law* (1993), p.42.

862 Posner J in *US Fidelity & Guaranty Co v Jadranska Slobodna Plovidba*, 638 F.2d 1022 at 1026 (1982).

863 As Hoffmann J said in the context of determining duty in *Morgan Crucible v Hill Samuel* [1991] Ch. 295 at 303, "(the courts) should be more concerned with what appears to be fair and reason-

be reflected in both the common practice of those engaged in an activity and the expectations of those affected by it.

(iii) Common practice and expectations

7-194 **Common practice** Failure to adopt common practice in relation to a safety precaution is strong evidence of carelessness for it suggests that the defendant did not do what others in the community considered to be reasonable. However, the failure to conform to a common practice is not necessarily conclusive of negligence.[864] Conversely, conformity with common practice is prima facie evidence that the proper standard of care is being taken.[865] Thus, in *Thompson v Smiths Shiprepairers (North Shields) Ltd*[866] it was held that where there had long been a general practice of inaction with regard to the possibility of deafness through industrial noise, the defendants were only liable for failure to take steps once there was awareness of the danger and protective equipment had become available. For this purpose 1963 was adopted as the operative date, and the claimants were held not to be entitled to damages for impairment of hearing sustained before 1963. In exceptional situations the court may still find that a person who has conformed to a common practice, has acted carelessly because the practice itself gives rise to unreasonable risks. Thus, in *Lloyds Bank Ltd v Savory & Co*[867] the fact that the bank had followed the practice adopted by all other banking concerns did not absolve them from liability. In *Cavanagh v Ulster Weaving Co Ltd*,[868] the House of Lords held that the adoption of a general practice did not absolve the employers from a charge of negligence in the way in which they had provided a "safe" system of work.

7-195 **Common practice: complying with Codes of Practice** Codes of practice issued by professional or governmental bodies may constitute good evidence of what constitutes reasonable care, since they often represent current professional or expert opinion as to what is desirable in order to avoid accidental harm. In *Barber v Somerset CC*[869] the failure of the defendants' managers to follow the published guide on Managing Occupational Stress was a major reason for the finding of negligence. Similarly, a failure to follow the British Standards has been held to amount to negligence since they reflected the consensus of practical experience.[870] But Codes of Practice and professional guidance are not conclusive either way: the

---

able than with wider utilitarian calculations". His comment is equally applicable to the standard of care issues.

864 *Brown v Rolls-Royce Ltd* [1960] 1 W.L.R. 210, especially per Lord Keith at 214, and Lord Denning at 216.

865 *Stokes v Guest, Keen and Nettlefold (Bolts and Nuts) Ltd* [1968] 1 W.L.R. 1776 at 1783. See also per Lord Normand in *Paris v Stepney BC* [1951] A.C. 367 at 382.

866 [1984] Q.B. 405. See further para.12-29.

867 [1933] A.C. 201.

868 [1960] A.C. 145.

869 [2004] UKHL 13; [2004] 1 W.L.R. 1089.

870 *Ward v The Ritz Hotel (London) Ltd* [1992] P.I.Q.R. P315. See also *Seymour v Ockwell* [2005] EWHC 1137 (QB); [2005] P.N.L.R 39 at [77]—regulations governing financial advisers were strong evidence as to what is expected of a competent financial advisor in most situations; *Horton v Evans* [2006] EWHC 2808 (QB); [2007] P.N.L.R. 17 at [41], per Keith J: the requirement of the Royal Pharmaceutical Society's Code of Practice for each prescription to be professionally assessed by a pharmacist "mirrored pharmacists' obligations under the common law".

failure to follow them may be held not to constitute negligence and, conversely, complying with a Code may not absolve the defendant. So in *Green v Building Scene Ltd*[871] the Court of Appeal held that although a failure to comply with Building Regulations or the British Standards Institution's recommendations about the safety of a staircase was evidence which the court should take into account, it was not conclusive.[872] On the other hand, in *Baker v Quantum Clothing Group*[873] the Supreme Court held that a government Code of Practice issued in 1972 on occupational exposure to noise levels between 85dB(A)lepd and 90dB(A)lepd set the standard for the reasonable and prudent employer without specialist knowledge until the late 1980s, so that the "average" employer was not in breach of duty in following the guidance. However, the Code did not provide an excuse to large employers with actual knowledge of the risks of exposure to noise levels between 85dB(A)lepd and 90dB(A)lepd, since they had come to the conclusion that the 90dB limit was no longer acceptable.[874]

Professional standards: the Bolam test Evaluation of conduct against common practice is of particular importance in the context of professional liability where it is referred to as the *Bolam* test after the case of *Bolam v Friern Hospital Management Committee*[875] in which McNair J gave the classic exposition of the test, in that case in relation to doctors: 7-196

> "[A doctor] is not guilty of negligence if he has acted in accordance with a practice accepted as proper by a responsible body of medical men skill in that particular art ... Putting it the other way around, a man is not negligent, if he is acting in accordance with such a practice merely because there is a body of opinion which takes a contrary view."

In *Maynard v West Midlands Regional HA*[876] the House of Lords applied the *Bolam* test to hold that doctors who followed a more invasive diagnostic procedure rather than opting for a less invasive alternative, were not liable for the damaging

871 [1994] P.I.Q.R. P259.

872 Distinguishing *Ward v The Ritz Hotel (London) Ltd* on the basis that in *Ward* ignoring the British Standards requirements created a dangerous trap for the visitor, whereas in *Green* the failure to apply British Standards did not create a trap for anyone. See also *Johnson v Bingley* [1997] P.N.L.R. 392, where it was held that a solicitor's breach of the Guide to Professional Conduct was not per se proof of negligence. The *Guide* was proper and accepted practice for solicitors, but negligence was a legal concept, and neither the Law Society nor any other body could, by issuing rules or codes of conduct, alter the law.

873 [2011] UKSC 17; [2011] 1 W.L.R. 1003.

874 Lord Dyson commented, [2011] UKSC 17; [2011] 1 W.L.R. 1003 at [101], that: "There is no rule of law that a relevant code of practice or other official or regulatory instrument necessarily sets the standard of care for the purpose of the tort of negligence. The classic statements by Swanwick J in *Stokes* and Mustill J in *Thompson v Smiths Shiprepairers (North Shields) Ltd* [1984] Q.B. 405 ... remain good law. What they say about the relevance of the reasonable and prudent employer following a 'recognised and general practice' applies equally to following a code of practice which sets out practice that is officially required or recommended. Thus to follow a relevant code of practice or regulatory instrument will often afford a defence to a claim in negligence. But there are circumstances where it does not do so. For example, it may be shown that the code of practice or regulatory instrument is compromised because the standards that it requires have been lowered as a result of heavy lobbying by interested parties; or because it covers a field in which apathy and fatalism has prevailed amongst workers, trade unions, employers and legislators ...; or because the instrument has failed to keep abreast of the latest technology and scientific understanding."

875 [1957] 1 W.L.R. 582 at 587.

876 [1984] 1 W.L.R. 634.

consequences as the more invasive procedure was an accepted practice. Lord Scarman said: "in the realm of diagnosis and treatment, negligence is not established by preferring one respectable body of opinion to another."[877] The test is one of quality not quantity: the practice of a small number of specialists can form a responsible body of opinion.[878] The test does not require the professional to evaluate the choice between different practices: so long as an accepted practice is chosen.[879] It is applicable to all professions[880] but does not apply where the professional is making a judgment based on common sense rather than professional skill.[881] The test only applies to the practice adopted by the professional. It does not apply to issues of fact such as the condition of the patient[882] or the causation of damage.[883] If there are two expert views on such matters, the judge has to determine which is correct whereas if there are two expert approaches as to how a professional should respond to the factual situation, then the judge does not have to decide which was correct but whether the professional acted reasonably in following one of the approaches.[884]

7-197 **Logical scrutiny of practice: the Bolitho test** It is open to the court to hold an accepted professional practice to be negligent and thus, to provide no protection to the professional who has followed it. In *Edward Wong Finance Co Ltd v Johnson, Stokes and Master*[885] the Privy Council held a Hong Kong conveyancing practice involving risk to the client to be negligent despite its widespread adoption by the profession and approval by the local professional body.[886] More often, courts will also consider whether a general practice posed an unreasonable risk on the particular

---

877 [1984] 1 W.L.R. 634 at 636.

878 *De Freitas v O'Brien* [1995] 6 Med. L.R. 108.

879 *Adams v Rhymney Valley DC* [2001] P.N.L.R. 4. The defendant chose an accepted key lock design for windows without considering the alternative button lock design which, unlike the key lock, would have enabled the claimant's children to escape a house fire. The defendant was not in breach of duty because a competent designer could have used the key design. See also *Stevens v Blaenau Gwent CBC* [2004] EWCA Civ 715; [2004] H.L.R. 54; para.7-175 fn.791 where the defendant was not negligent for deciding not to provide window locks and a child fell out of an unlocked window.

880 For detail see Ch.9 where the test is discussed in relation to the medical, legal, surveying, construction and finance professions.

881 *JD Williams & Co Ltd v Michael Hyde & Associates Ltd* [2001] P.N.L.R. 8: architect held negligent in failing to require further investigation of the possibility that a gas powered heating system would discolour fabrics to be stored in the building being designed. Ward LJ held Bolam inapplicable on the ground that no special architectural skills were required in this judgment.

882 *Penney Palmer & Cannon v East Kent HA* [2000] Med. L.R. 41, where Lord Woolf MR held that *Bolam* had no application to the factual question of what the claimants' smear tests showed. Three expert witnesses would have considered the smear slides to be normal and two would have considered them abnormal. Lord Woolf MR upheld the decision of the trial judge that the slides showed abnormality. The question then was whether a reasonable professional would treat the abnormality as too minor to merit further investigation and intervention. *Bolam* would be relevant to this question. The Court of Appeal upheld the trial finding of negligence.

883 *Loveday v Renton* [1990] 1 Med. L.R. 117.

884 See *D v South Tyneside Health Care NHS Trust* [2003] EWCA Civ 878; [2004] P.I.Q.R. P12.

885 [1984] A.C. 296.

886 In such cases, it seems that the court is not influenced by any moral criticism of the defendant's conduct but by the view that the risks are best borne by those providing the service and able to spread the loss through insurance. See the comments of Hoffmann LJ, "The reasonableness of lawyers' lapses" (1994) 10 P.N. 6. Commenting on the conveyancing cases, he said:

> "The underlying truth seems to be that judges regard conveyancing as an activity which should give a result to the client. The solicitor is insured and it seems only fair that the risk of the mistake should be borne by the underwriters rather than the client."

facts of the case. In *Patel v Daybells (A Firm)*[887] the Court of Appeal held that a conveyancing practice similar to that condemned in *Wong* was not negligent in the particular factual context of the case. The House of Lords cited *Wong* in the key decision of *Bolitho v City and Hackney HA*.[888] One issue in *Bolitho* was whether a registrar would have been acting negligently had she failed to intubate a child suffering from severe breathing difficulties.[889] The expert evidence for the defendant and claimant established that there were two schools of thought: one would intubate and one would not. Applying the *Bolam* test, the judge held that failure to intubate could not be negligent. The claimant appealed on the ground that the non-intubation practice had to be ignored as it could not be logically justified. The House of Lords accepted the need for logical justification but found that the defendants' expert evidence was not illogical and hence, there was no breach. Lord Browne-Wilkinson said (at 242) that the *Bolam* test required the court to be:

> "satisfied that the exponents of the body of medical opinion relied upon can demonstrate that such opinion has a logical basis. In particular, in cases involving the weighing of risks against benefits, the judge before accepting a body of opinion as being responsible, reasonable or respectable, will need to be satisfied that, in forming their view, the experts have reached a defensible conclusion on the matter."

The logical scrutiny required by *Bolitho* has subsequently been applied to hold a particular medical decision to be negligent.[890] But, by the same token, where the views of expert witnesses supportive of the defendant do stand up to logical analysis the inevitable conclusion will be that the defendant was not in breach of duty.[891] The need for logical scrutiny of working practices applies just as much to other professional contexts. Auditor and valuation cases in particular, have tended to involve the trial courts in an exhaustive examination of the practice adopted by the defendant.[892] Even reliance on a leading textbook will not provide a defence if the view adopted in the book cannot be justified.[893]

Public expectations In a broad sense the development of third party liability insurance has undoubtedly had an effect on public expectations as to safety standards. Lord Denning recognised its relevance in motoring cases, commenting **7-198**

887 [2001] EWCA Civ 1229; [2002] P.N.L.R. 6.

888 [1998] A.C. 232. See para.9-77

889 The question was asked as a hypothetical because, due to negligence, the doctor had failed to attend the child. The defence argument was that this negligent failure to attend did not cause the brain damage which resulted from the breathing difficulty because, even if she had attended, the registrar would have taken no further action by way of intubation, to relieve the breathing. Hence, the question was whether such a failure to intubate would itself have been negligent, since the defendant could not avoid a finding of causation by saying that had she not failed to attend she would have done or omitted to do something which was itself negligent.

890 See, e.g. *Marriott v West Midlands AHA* [1999] Lloyd's Rep. Med. 23; *Taaffe v East of England Ambulance Service NHS Trust* [2012] EWHC 1335 (QB); (2012) 128 B.M.L.R. 71 at [68]–[70].

891 *Carter v Ministry of Justice* [2010] EWCA Civ 694 at [22].

892 See for example *Barings Plc v Coopers & Lybrand (No.7)* [2003] EWHC 1319 (Ch); [2003] P.N.L.R. 34 (auditor) and *Goldstein v Levy Gee (A Firm)* [2003] EWHC 1574 (Ch); [2003] P.N.L.R. 35 (valuer).

893 See *Dean v Allin & Watts* [2001] EWCA Civ 758; [2001] 2 Lloyd's Rep. 249; [2001] P.N.L.R. 39, where Lightman J held that following the view expressed in *Snell's Equity* and Cheshire & Burn's *Real Property* did not provide a defence when any reasonably competent lawyer practising in property would have realised that there was uncertainty on the point.

that "we are, in this branch of the law, moving away from the concept: 'No liability without fault.' We are beginning to apply the test: 'On whom should the risk fall?' Morally the learner driver is not at fault; but legally she is liable to be because she is insured and the risk should fall on her."[894] The presence of liability insurance clearly influences expectations in motoring, professional[895] and employers' liability cases.[896] On the other hand, the House of Lords has also warned against raising public expectations as to safety and risk too far. Thus, in *Tomlinson v Congleton BC*[897] Lord Hoffmann stressed that the public should not expect all risk to be eliminated and in a very different context in *Phelps v Hillingdon LBC*,[898] Lord Nicholls said that poor quality teaching should not be equated with negligence.

7-199 **Common practice, expectations and risk warnings to patients** One area in which the tension between common practice and public expectations has been clear is that of the standard of care required of a doctor warning a patient of the risks associated with a proposed treatment.[899] In *Sidaway v Bethlem Royal Hospital Governors*[900] the House of Lords held that the *Bolam* test applied in this situation and the question was whether the doctor had followed a reasonable medical practice. If that was the case, there would be no liability even if a reasonable patient would have wished to have been more fully informed. However, some thirty years after *Sidaway*, in *Montgomery v Lanarkshire Health Board*[901] the Supreme Court concluded that the *Bolam* test was no longer appropriate. The pursuer, who was pregnant, was diabetic and of small stature. She was not informed that the risk of shoulder dystocia occurring during a vaginal delivery of the baby was 9–10 per cent in diabetic patients, nor that there was also a small risk of serious injury to the child (brachial plexus injury 0.2 per cent, and prolonged hypoxia resulting in cerebral palsy or death less than 0.1 per cent). The consultant considered that these risks were low but that if she told diabetic patients about them they would all opt for an elective Caesarean section, which was not in their interests. During the course of the delivery shoulder dystocia occurred and the baby suffered both a brachial plexus injury and brain damage. The Supreme Court unanimously held that the *Bolam* test should no longer apply in this situation. There had been important changes in the doctor-patient relationship since *Sidaway*. Patients were more widely regarded as persons holding rights, rather than passive recipients of the care of the medical profession, and were often treated as consumers exercising choices. Patients had much greater access to information about symptoms, investigations, treatment op-

---

894 *Nettleship v Weston* [1971] 2 Q.B. 691 at 700. He applied similar reasoning in *Dutton v Bognor Regis Urban DC* [1972] 1 Q.B. 373 at 397, saying: "In short, we look at the relationship of the parties: and then say, as a matter of policy, on whom the loss should fall."

895 See the extra-judicial comments of Hoffmann LJ in (1994) 10 P.N. 6.

896 Although there are dangers in resolving liability questions by reference to the underlying insurance position of the parties: see, e.g. the comments of Jane Stapleton, "Tort, Insurance and Ideology" (1995) 58 M.L.R. 820 at 843.

897 [2003] UKHL 47; [2004] 1 A.C. 46. See para.7-185. See also *Scout Association v Barnes* [2010] EWCA Civ 1476 at [34] per Jackson LJ: "It is not the function of the law of tort to eliminate every iota of risk or to stamp out socially desirable activities".

898 [2001] 2 A.C. 619.

899 See further para.9-86.

900 [1985] A.C. 871.

901 [2015] UKSC 11; [2015] A.C. 1430; discussed by R. Heywood and J. Miola, "The changing face of pre-operative medical disclosure: placing the patient at the heart of the matter" (2017) 133 L.Q.R. 296.

tions and risks. The idea that patients were uninformed and unable to understand medical matters was now manifestly untenable. Moreover, changes in medical practice, through guidance issued by the General Medical Council, meant that doctors were more likely to disclose information and reach consensual decisions with patients about treatment options. Medical paternalism was no longer an appropriate model of the doctor-patient relationship:

> "An adult person of sound mind is entitled to decide which, if any, of the available forms of treatment to undergo, and her consent must be obtained before treatment interfering with her bodily integrity is undertaken. The doctor is therefore under a duty to take reasonable care to ensure that the patient is aware of any material risks involved in any recommended treatment, and of any reasonable alternative or variant treatments. The test of materiality is whether, in the circumstances of the particular case, a reasonable person in the patient's position would be likely to attach significance to the risk, or the doctor is or should reasonably be aware that the particular patient would be likely to attach significance to it."[902]

This is the "prudent patient" test of information disclosure adopted in Canada and **7-200** Australia[903] which puts the court in the position of deciding what a prudent patient would have wanted to know about a proposed treatment, rather than leaving it to the medical profession to decide what the patient should be told.[904] Alternatively, even if the objective "reasonable patient" would not have attached significance to the risk, if the doctor knew or ought to have known that the individual patient would attach significance to the risk it will be a breach of duty to fail to disclose it. This more subjective element of the test allows for differences in the patient's circumstances from those of the hypothetical reasonable patient, though in practice it may more frequently be an issue where the patient manifests concern through asking questions about risks or alternative treatments.[905] In applying the test, the assessment of what constitutes a "material risk" does not depend simply on percentages or the magnitude of the risk. The court should also take into account the nature of the risk, the potential effects on the life of the patient, the importance to the patient of the potential benefits of the treatment, the alternative treatments available, and the risks involved in those alternatives.[906] The information must also be

---

902 [2015] UKSC 11; [2015] A.C. 1430 at [87].

903 *Reibl v Hughes* (1980) 114 D.L.R. (3d) 1 (SCC); *Rogers v Whitaker* (1992) 175 C.L.R. 479 (HCA).

904 [2015] UKSC 11; [2015] A.C. 1430 at [83]: "Responsibility for determining the nature and extent of a person's rights rests with the courts, not with the medical professions."

905 There are two exceptions to the prudent patient test: (1) information may be withheld if the doctor reasonably considers that disclosure would be seriously detrimental to the patient's health (but this is a limited exception and should not be used to subvert the general principle, preventing the patient from making an informed choice because the doctor considers that the patient will make a choice contrary to her best interests: [2015] UKSC 11; [2015] A.C. 1430 at [91]); (2) circumstances of necessity, e.g. where the patient is unconscious or otherwise unable to make a decision.

906 [2015] UKSC 11; [2015] A.C. 1430 at [89]. On the facts of *Montgomery* the Supreme Court concluded that the pursuer should have been informed of the risks of proceeding to a vaginal delivery and that there should have been a discussion about the alternative of Caesarean section. The contrast between the risks of the two forms of delivery was "stark". The therapeutic exception did not apply, though the consultant obstetrician considered that it was not generally in the maternal interest to have a Caesarean section. The doctor's duty was to explain to the patient why she considered one of the available treatment options to be medically preferable to the others, whilst taking care to see that the patient was aware of the considerations for and against each option ([2015] UKSC 11; [2015] A.C. 1430 at [95]). *Montgomery* was applied in *Webster v Burton Hospitals NHS Foundation Trust* [2017] EWCA Civ 62; [2017] Med. L.R. 113; *Thefaut v Johnston* [2017] EWHC 497 (QB); [2017]

presented to the patient in a comprehensible manner. *Montgomery* involves a two-stage test: (1) what risks associated with an operation were or should have been known to the medical professional in question; (2) were the risks material?[907] The second limb is a matter for the court, but the first falls within the expertise of medical professionals. If the risk was not known the question of its materiality does not arise: "a clinician is not required to warn of a risk of which he cannot reasonably be taken to be aware".[908]

(c) Proof of carelessness

7-201 **Burden of proof** The onus of proof, on the balance of probabilities,[909] that the defendant has been careless falls upon the claimant.[910] If the claimant's evidence is equally consistent with the presence or absence of negligence in the defendant, his action will fail.[911] Thus in *Pickford v Imperial Chemical Industries Plc*,[912] the claimant's claim in respect of repetitive strain injury failed. It was held that the onus was on the claimant to prove that her condition had been caused by repetitive movements whilst typing. Whilst the defendant employer's failure to prove an alternative explanation was a factor to be taken into account in deciding whether the claimant had discharged the onus, it was not decisive as it still left open the question of

---

Med. L.R. 319; *KR v Lanarkshire Health Board* [2016] CSOH 133; *Gallardo v Imperial College Healthcare NHS Trust* [2017] EWHC 3147 (QB); [2018] P.I.Q.R. P6 (failure to inform about outcome of surgery, prognosis, and the follow-up care and treatment options); *Hassell v Hillingdon Hospitals NHS Foundation Trust* [2018] EWHC 164 (QB); (2018) 162 B.M.L.R. 120 (claimant not told about risk of paralysis as a result of spinal cord injury and not advised about conservative treatment options); *Mills v Oxford University Hospitals NHS Trust* [2019] EWHC 936 (QB); (2019) 170 B.M.L.R. 100 (claimant not informed about alternative surgical technique and the comparative risks and benefits); *Mordel v Royal Berkshire NHS Foundation Trust* [2019] EWHC 2591 (QB) (inadequate system for checking patient understood the essential elements and purpose of an ultrasound scan for Down's syndrome). In *Ollosson v Lee* [2019] EWHC 784 (QB); [2019] Med. L.R. 287 at [156] Stewart J held that it was not necessary to inform a patient of the percentage risk of chronic scrotal pain following a vasectomy; it was sufficient for the surgeon to describe it as a "small" risk: "the word 'small' is clearly an everyday word which encompasses and satisfactorily conveys the level of risk involved" (sed quaere).

[907] *Duce v Worcestershire Acute Hospitals NHS Trust* [2018] EWCA Civ 1307; [2018] P.I.Q.R. P18.

[908] [2018] EWCA Civ 1307; [2018] P.I.Q.R. P18 at [43].

[909] *Bonnington Castings Ltd v Wardlaw* [1956] A.C. 613; *Brown v Rolls-Royce Ltd* [1960] 1 W.L.R. 210 at 215–216.

[910] Hence at the close of the claimant's case, the defendant is entitled to submit that there is no case for him to answer.

[911] per Lord Macmillan in *Jones v Great Western Ry* (1930) 47 T.L.R. 39 at 45; *Wright v Callwood* [1950] 2 K.B. 515; *Gardiner v Motherwell Machinery and Scrap Co* [1961] 1 W.L.R. 1424; *Knight v Fellick* [1977] R.T.R. 316.

[912] [1998] 1 W.L.R. 1189; [1998] I.C.R. 673; discussed in more detail at para.2-27. See also *Brett v University of Reading* [2007] EWCA Civ 88, where the Court of Appeal stressed that it was for the claimant to establish that the employer had failed to take care rather than for the employer to establish that it had taken any necessary precautions. On the other hand, where the defendant is under a duty to measure noise levels in the workplace and negligently fails to do so the court will look more benevolently on the claimant's evidence that the noise levels were excessive: *Keefe v Isle of Man Steam Packet Co Ltd* [2010] EWCA Civ 683 at [19] per Longmore LJ, noting that "a defendant who has, in breach of duty, made it difficult or impossible for a claimant to adduce relevant evidence must run the risk of adverse factual findings". See also *MacKenzie v Alcoa Manufacturing (GB) Ltd* [2019] EWCA Civ 2110; [2020] P.I.Q.R. P6 for discussion of when it is appropriate to draw adverse inferences.

what caused the injury.[913] In one circumstance the burden of proof is reversed. Under s.11 of the Civil Evidence Act 1968, proof that a person has been convicted of an offence shall be taken as proof that he committed the offence unless the contrary is proved. If the conviction is relevant to the facts in issue, s.11 means that the defendant will have to disprove negligence. Thus, in *Wauchope v Mordecai*[914] where the claimant suffered injury when the defendant opened the door of his car as he approached on his bicycle and the defendant was convicted for this, the Court of Appeal reversed the trial judge's finding that the claimant had failed to prove negligence.[915]

Inference of carelessness The question in every case is, what is the reasonable inference from the known facts? Thus, in *Carroll v Fearon*[916] it was held that negligence on the part of a manufacturer of a tyre having a lethal defect which led to tread strip and an accident was established by evidence of a defective manufacturing process without any requirement to identify a responsible individual or act of negligence. It was inferred from the fact that if the process had worked as intended, the defect should not have been present. Courts approach matters of inference on a common sense basis and where the evidence relating to negligence is particularly within the control of the defendant, little affirmative evidence may be required from the claimant to establish a prima facie case which it will then be for the defendant to rebut.[917] The failure of the defendant to give evidence, may be regarded as strengthening the claimant's case.[918] 7-202

Res ipsa loquitur A further circumstance in which the court may infer carelessness on the part of the defendant is where the claimant can show that the nature of the accident suggests both negligence and the defendant's responsibility. Drawing the inference in such a circumstance is often described as an application of res ipsa loquitur. However, it is important to note that this label represents a rule of evidence and states no principle of law.[919] As Morris LJ said: "This convenient and succinct formula possesses no magic qualities: nor has it any added virtue, other than that of brevity, merely because it is expressed in Latin."[920] It is only a convenient label 7-203

---

913 It is different where there is evidence that two parties are at fault but the court is unable to decide which is more to blame. In such a situation the court will infer that both are equally to blame: *Baker v Market Harborough Industrial Co-operative Society Ltd* [1953] 1 W.L.R. 1472.

914 [1970] 1 W.L.R. 317.

915 The trial judge had been unaware that s.11 had come into force.

916 [1998] P.I.Q.R. P416. See further para.10-26.

917 In *Snell v Farrell* (1990) 72 D.L.R. (4th) 289, Sopinka J stressed that the judge as trier of fact, is entitled to draw inferences from the evidence and does not have to approach issues from the narrow viewpoint of an expert witness. Hence, he was entitled to take into account the fact that in many medical negligence cases the facts would lie particularly within the knowledge of the defendant and in these circumstances little affirmative evidence on the part of the claimant would justify drawing an inference of causation in the absence of evidence to the contrary. Although these comments were made in the context of proof of causation, it is suggested that they are equally applicable to proof of negligence.

918 *Wisniewski v Central Manchester HA* [1998] P.I.Q.R. P324, where Brooke LJ held that the trial judge was entitled to treat the doctor's failure to give evidence "in the face of a charge that his negligence had been causative, as strengthening the [claimant's] case on causation".

919 Thus, it is not necessary for res ipsa loquitur to be specifically pleaded: *Bennett v Chemical Construction (GB) Ltd* [1971] 1 W.L.R. 1571.

920 *Roe v Minister of Health* [1954] 2 Q.B. 66 at 87; cf. per Evershed MR in *Moore v Fox & Sons* [1956] 1 Q.B. 596 at 607.

to apply to a set of circumstances in which a claimant proves a case so as to call for a rebuttal from the defendant, without having to allege and prove any specific act or omission on the part of the defendant. He merely proves a result, not any particular act or omission producing the result. Res ipsa loquitur, which stems from the judgment of Erle CJ in *Scott v London and St Katherine Docks*,[921] applies where (1) the occurrence is such that it would not have happened without negligence, and (2) the thing that inflicted the damage was under the sole management and control of the defendant, or of someone for whom he is responsible or whom he has a right to control. If these two conditions are satisfied it follows, on a balance of probability, that the defendant, or the person for whom he is responsible, must have been negligent. There is, however, a further negative condition: (3) there must be no evidence as to why or how the occurrence took place. If there is, then appeal to res ipsa loquitur is inappropriate for the question of the defendant's negligence must be determined on that evidence.

7-204 **Occurrence cannot normally happen without negligence** Common experience suggests that in the absence of negligence, bales of sugar do not usually fall from hoists,[922] barrels do not fall from warehouse windows,[923] cranes do not collapse,[924] trains do not collide,[925] aircraft do not usually crash,[926] and stones are not found in buns.[927] In these situations courts have inferred that negligence has been the cause of the accident. A classic illustration is *Bennett v Chemical Construction (GB) Ltd*[928] in which two heavy panels fell upon the claimant workman and the defendants called no evidence. Although the judge was unable to say precisely how they came to fall, he concluded that they could only have done so because of the negligence of those working on the panels and his view was upheld by the Court of Appeal. As both the safety and reliability of machines and the training of operators has improved, the courts have become less hesitant in concluding that an accident is so unusual that it is probably the result of fault on the part of those responsible for maintaining or operating the machine. Thus, where a car veers on to the pavement hitting a pedestrian[929] or into the opposite lane hitting another vehicle,[930] or skids,[931] the inference of negligence is likely to arise. In the medical context,[932] courts have been prepared to hold that leaving swabs in the patient's body after an operation is sufficient to give rise to the inference.[933] Even the failure of the treatment itself has been considered sufficient. In *Cassidy v Ministry of*

---

921 (1865) 3 H. & C. 596 at 601.

922 *Scott v London Dock Co* (1865) 3 H. & C. 596.

923 *Byrne v Boadle* (1863) 2 H. & C. 722.

924 *Swan v Salisbury Constructions* [1966] 1 W.L.R. 204.

925 *Skinner v LB & SC Ry* (1850) 5 Exch. 787.

926 *George v Eagle Air Services Ltd* [2009] UKPC 21; [2009] 1 W.L.R. 2133.

927 *Chapronière v Mason* (1905) 21 T.L.R. 633.

928 [1971] 1 W.L.R. 1571.

929 *Ellor v Selfridge & Co Ltd* (1930) 46 T.L.R. 236; *Widdowson v Newgate Meat Corp* [1998] P.I.Q.R. P138.

930 *Davis v Bunn* (1936) 56 C.L.R. 246.

931 *Richley v Faull (Richley, Third Party)* [1965] 1 W.L.R. 1454. Though where the vehicle skidded on black ice which could not reasonably have been foreseen the inference of negligence may be rebutted: *Smith v Fordyce* [2013] EWCA Civ 320.

932 See further para.9-106.

933 *Mahon v Osborne* [1939] 2 K.B. 14.

Health,[934] Denning LJ, in applying res ipsa, put the claimant's argument in these terms: "I went into hospital to be cured of two stiff fingers. I have come out with four stiff fingers and my hand is useless. That should not happen if due care had been used. Explain it if you can." However, in *Delaney v Southmead Hospital Authority*[935] the Court of Appeal in holding that the application of res ipsa loquitur to an anaesthesia incident was rebutted by evidence that common practice had been followed, commented that it was doubtful if the maxim was of much help in medical negligence cases as medical science was not so precise as to anticipate the precise risk of carrying out routine procedures. There was always room for the wholly unexpected result to occur even when the correct procedure was followed. There are areas of conduct where experience suggests that losses can occur randomly. Thus in *Stafford v Conti Commodity Services Ltd*[936] it was held that losses on the commodity market did not lead to an inference of negligence against the brokers responsible for managing the dealings.

Sole management and control To establish the defendant's responsibility it is necessary to show that the damage has been caused by something under the sole management and control of the defendant or someone for whom he is responsible or whom he has a right to control.[937] The defendant's control need only exist at the time of the hypothetical negligence, e.g. manufacturing the product, rather than the time of the accident or injury. But where the product could have been interfered with between manufacture and accident, the claimant must establish "at least the improbability of such interference having caused the relevant defect".[938] Where the defendant is responsible for all the staff who might have been in control at the relevant time, res ipsa loquitur will apply even if it is impossible to say which particular individual was responsible.[939] But when a thing or operation is under the control of two persons not in law responsible for each other, whether the maxim res ipsa loquitur applies to either person is doubtful.[940] Where the claimant himself was in charge of the thing that did the harm and had seen nothing amiss with it, the maxim obviously cannot apply.[941] **7-205**

Cause of occurrence unknown to claimant Res ipsa loquitur has no application when the cause of the occurrence is known. This is because there is then no need to do more than to decide whether on these facts negligence on the part of the defendant has been proved or not. When a bus left the road and fell down an embankment, the cause of the accident being a burst tyre due to an impact fracture **7-206**

934 [1951] 2 K.B. 343 at 365.

935 (1992) 26 B.M.L.R. 111; [1995] 6 Med. L.R. 355. See also *Ratcliffe v Plymouth HA* [1998] Lloyd's Rep. Med. 162 at 172, per Brooke LJ and para.9-106. See also M.A. Jones, *Medical Negligence*, 5th edn (2018), paras 3-161 and 3-168.

936 [1981] 1 All E.R. 691.

937 *Wing v London General Omnibus Co* [1909] 2 K.B. 652 at 663; reversing into a parked car is not ipso facto careless: *Hume v Ingleby* [1975] R.T.R. 502.

938 per Megaw LJ in *Lloyde v West Midlands Gas Board* [1971] 1 W.L.R. 749 at 756. It was held that res ipsa loquitur could not apply to a gas explosion caused by the disintegration of a gas meter supplied by the defendant, as the claimant had not shown that third party interference was improbable.

939 *Cassidy v Ministry of Health* [1951] 2 K.B. 343.

940 In *Roe v Minister of Health* [1954] 1 W.L.R. 128 at 133, McNair J decided that it did not apply, but in the Court of Appeal ([1954] 2 Q.B. 66 at 82), Denning LJ disagreed with this opinion and said that each person could be called on for an explanation.

941 *Hardy v Thames and General Lighterage* [1967] 1 Lloyd's Rep. 228.

which does not necessarily leave any visible marks on the outer tyre, it was held that res ipsa did not apply, but that the bus company were negligent in not having a proper system of tyre inspection.[942] Where the defendant does give evidence relating to the possible cause of the damage and level of precaution taken, the court may still conclude that the evidence provides an insufficient explanation to displace the inference of negligence. In *Henderson v Jenkins & Sons*[943] a failure of brakes occurred on a lorry because of leakage of oil fluid through a corroded hole in a tube. The owners of the lorry showed that generally accepted procedures for servicing had been followed and suggested that a latent defect might have led to the corrosion. The House of Lords, nevertheless, held that the inference of negligence had not been displaced. Lord Pearson noted that the degree of corrosion suggested an abnormal cause, e.g. carrying salt fish or cattle, and the owners had failed to show evidence that the lorry had not been used in such an unusual way.[944]

7-207 **Procedural effect of res ipsa loquitur** One view of the effect of res ipsa loquitur is that it simply raises an inference of negligence which requires the defendant to provide a reasonable explanation of how the accident could have occurred without his negligence. On this view, the defendant does not have to prove on the balance of probabilities that his explanation is the correct one. If it is equally as plausible as that of the claimant, the claimant will fail as he bears the burden of proof.[945] The alternative view is that res ipsa reverses the burden of proof so that if the defendant shows that his explanation is equally plausible but not more so, then he will lose. Lords Reid and Donovan supported this view in *Henderson*'s case.[946] However, in *Ng Chun Pui v Lee Chuen Tat*[947] the Privy Council stated that the burden of proof does not shift to the defendant. A coach veered across the carriageway, crossed the central reservation and collided with a bus coming in the opposite direction. The claimant called no evidence, and the court held that these facts by themselves would have justified an inference of negligence. The defendants, however, gave the explanation that an unidentified car had suddenly cut across their coach, whose driver braked immediately and then skidded. In the light of this evidence the Privy Council held that there could be no inference of negligence, since the driver's reaction in the emergency was not negligent. Thus if the defendant provides an equally

---

942 *Barkway v South Wales Transport Co* [1950] A.C. 185. Similarly, when a cricket ball was driven out of the ground by a batsman and injured a pedestrian on the highway, it was held that as the cause of the injury was known, res ipsa did not apply: *Bolton v Stone* [1951] A.C. 850. See too, Evershed MR in *Moore v R Fox & Sons* [1956] 1 Q.B. 596 at 614; quoted with approval by Edmund Davies LJ in *Wilks v Cheltenham Home Guard Motor Cycle and Light Car Club* [1971] 1 W.L.R. 668 at 674.

943 [1970] A.C. 282.

944 [1970] A.C. 282 at 303.

945 See *The Kite* [1933] P. 154.

946 [1970] A.C. 282. A similar view seemed to have been taken by the Court of Appeal in *Ward v Tesco Stores Ltd* [1976] 1 W.L.R. 810. However, in *Hall v Holker Estate Co Ltd* [2008] EWCA Civ 1422; [2008] N.P.C. 143 at [33] Sir Mark Potter P commented that: "The judgments in *Ward v Tesco* do not of course relieve the claimant of the overall burden of proof. He must show that the occurrence of the accident is *prima facie* evidence of a lack of care on the part of the defendant in failing to provide or implement a system designed to protect the claimant from risk of accident or injury. In such circumstances, as made clear by Lawton LJ …: 'Such burden of proof as there is on defendants … is evidential, not probative.'"

947 [1988] R.T.R. 298. It was said that "the so-called doctrine of *res ipsa loquitur* … is no more than the use of a Latin maxim to describe the state of the evidence from which it is proper to draw an inference of negligence".

plausible explanation, this will redress the balance of probability, if it has tilted against him, and the claimant will be back where he started, namely, having to establish his case by positive evidence which he is unlikely to be able to do. On the other hand, the defendant cannot hope to redress the balance in this way merely by putting up theoretical possibilities; his assertion must have some colour of probability about it.[948] Proof by the defendant that there was a system in place to deal with the particular hazard (such as spillages in a restaurant or shop) may not be sufficient to discharge the evidential burden when there is no direct evidence as to how long the liquid had been on the floor.[949]

(d) Particular instances of breach

Many common instances of breach are dealt with in chapters specific to the type of activity. Breach by professionals is covered in Ch.9; that of manufacturers in Ch.10; of occupiers in Ch.11; of employers in Ch.12; and of public services in Ch.13. Negligence resulting in damage to goods is a form of interference with goods under the provisions of the Torts (Interference with Goods) Act 1977 and is considered further in Ch.16. This structure enables comparisons to be drawn between negligence liability based on carelessness and other forms of liability relating to the specific type of activity. However, breach in relation to road accidents, the liability of carriers, and breach in relation to care for children, are treated in this section. **7-208**

(i) Road accidents

General principles Road users owe a duty of care to fellow users and will be liable in negligence if breach of that duty causes damage. UK law has not followed the example of other European jurisdictions where an element of strict liability has been introduced for road accidents. The mere fact that a collision has occurred will not justify imposing liability in the absence of evidence of negligence.[950] However, the existence of compulsory third party insurance[951] has encouraged the courts to insist on a high level of care being exercised. It underlies the rule that a learner or **7-209**

---

[948] This passage was cited and applied in *Widdowson v Newgate Meat Corp* [1998] P.I.Q.R. P138, where the Court of Appeal applied the maxim to a driver who provided no explanation for having collided with a pedestrian. See also *Moore v R Fox & Sons* [1956] 1 Q.B. 596 at 607; *Colvilles Ltd v Devine* [1969] 1 W.L.R. 475.

[949] *Dawkins v Carnival Plc (t/a P&O Cruises)* [2011] EWCA Civ 1237; [2012] 1 Lloyd's Rep. 1 (the existence of a system to clean up spillages did not in itself give rise to the inference that the spillage must have occurred a very short time before the claimant fell, in circumstances where there were many employees who could have given evidence but did not do so). See also *Ward v Tesco Stores Ltd* [1976] 1 W.L.R. 810 (yoghurt); and *Hassan v Gill* [2012] EWCA Civ 1291; [2013] P.I.Q.R. P1 (grape) where shopkeepers were held liable for slips by customers in the absence of evidence about the system for dealing with spillages, and in particular the length of time that the spillage had been present. Contrast *Lougheed v On The Beach Ltd* [2014] EWCA Civ 1538 at [32], per Tomlinson LJ distinguishing *Dawkins v Carnival Plc* and *Ward v Tesco Stores Ltd*: "Not everything which is foreseeable is likely. There was here no evidence that slipping at this place was a known likely risk, with sufficient frequency of occurrence that it required a system to remove it, so that an accident could be inferred to be the result of the absence of a system which ought to have been in place or a failure in the operation of the system."

[950] *Knight v Fellick* [1977] R.T.R. 316; *Ng Chun Pui v Lee Chuen Tat* [1988] R.T.R. 298.

[951] Dating from the Road Traffic Act 1930.

inexperienced driver is expected to measure up to the standard of the experienced,[952] and the rule that the defendant must take his victim as he finds him and will, for example, be held liable for unforeseeable psychiatric harm arising from an accident.[953] Again, failure to anticipate carelessness on the part of others is regarded as careless in itself.[954] In a well-known passage, Lord Uthwatt said:

> "[I] dissent from the view that drivers are 'entitled to drive on the assumption that other users of the road, whether drivers or pedestrians, will behave with reasonable care.' It is common experience that many do not. A driver is not, of course, bound to anticipate folly in all its forms, but he is not entitled to put out of consideration the teachings of experience as to the form those follies commonly take."[955]

On the other hand, that does not mean a road user is negligent in failing to anticipate all foreseeable possibilities.[956] Establishing breach in road accident cases is largely a matter for common sense rather than expert opinion. In *Liddell v Middleton*[957] the Court of Appeal noted it was the exception rather than the rule for expert witnesses to be required in such cases: expert evidence should be confined to matters outside the knowledge and experience of the layperson.[958]

7-210 **Highway Code** The starting point for a common-sense approach to fault is the Highway Code. The Road Traffic Act 1988 s.38(7) provides that failure to observe a provision of the Code may be relied on to establish liability. But the Code is only guidance[959] and failure to comply with the Code will not necessarily mean that the defendant has been negligent[960] and conversely, compliance with the Code will not necessarily absolve the defendant.[961] The particular circumstances rather than the

---

952 *Nettleship v Weston* [1971] 2 Q.B. 691.

953 *Page v Smith* [1996] 1 A.C. 190. See para.7-70.

954 *Lang v LTE* [1959] 1 W.L.R. 1168; *Foskett v Mistry* [1984] R.T.R. 1.

955 *London Passenger Transport Board v Upson* [1949] A.C. 155 at 173.

956 See, e.g. *Burridge v Airwork Ltd* [2004] EWCA Civ 459, where the Court of Appeal held that a cyclist was not contributorily negligent in failing to anticipate that the driver of a vehicle which had stopped on the hard shoulder would, without warning, open his door into the face of the cyclist. It would have been putting the standard too high to require a cyclist to give all stationary vehicles a wide berth. In *Scott v Gavigan* [2016] EWCA Civ 544 the Court of Appeal held that it was not foreseeable to the rider of a moped that a drunken pedestrian would run into the path of the moped when he was only 10 metres away. The action of the claimant was "an egregious folly". As Christopher Clarke LJ put it (at [17]): "In one sense any sort of foolishness is foreseeable. As is well known, some people do silly or absurd things; or deliberately take risks. The question is, however, whether what happened was the sort of thing that, in the applicable circumstances, this defendant, acting reasonably, ought to have foreseen."

957 [1996] P.I.Q.R. P36.

958 But where an expert is used the judge cannot reject the expert evidence on the basis merely that it does not accord with his own experience of driving a motor vehicle: *Smith v Hammond* [2010] EWCA Civ 725; [2010] R.T.R. 30 (judge entitled to reject expert evidence, but must give reasons).

959 In *Croston v Vaughan* [1938] 1 K.B. 540 at 551–552, Greer LJ said: "The Highway Code is not binding as a statutory regulation; it is only something which may be regarded as information and advice to drivers."

960 In *Rosser v Lindsay, The Times,* 25 February 1999, CA, it was held that the Highway Code requirement for frequent use of mirrors was not a prescriptive rule for drivers on a construction site but merely a useful guide, and so the trial judge was entitled to treat the claimant's argument based on the Code as a "counsel of perfection" and not an application of reasonable care; *Goad v Butcher* [2011] EWCA Civ 158—failure to observe the Highway Code might be evidence of negligence but whether such a failure actually constitutes negligence depends on the facts of the case.

961 *White v Broadbent and British Road Services* [1958] Crim. L.R. 129. Similarly, it has been held that

general guidance of the Code may be the determining factor.[962] Perhaps the most important general provision of the Code is as to the rule of the road under which drivers approaching each other must go to the left in order to pass. If a collision occurs on the driver's wrong side of the road, i.e. the right side, it will place a burden on that driver to show why it was reasonable for him to depart from the rule of the road. The driver who uses the wrong side of the road is bound to exercise more care and keep a better look-out to avoid a collision than would be requisite if he were to confine himself to the proper side.[963] Aside from these generalisations, the most helpful guidance as to what may constitute breach can be provided by examining the case law concerning some major causes of accidents: speed, road junctions, and pedestrians and animals.

Speed The speed at which a vehicle should be driven must be reasonable in the circumstances.[964] The general rule is that the vehicle should be driven at a speed which enables the driver to stop within the limits of his vision, particularly having regard to the weather and the state of the road.[965] In *Armstrong v Cottrell*[966] the Court of Appeal stated that where the driver had seen the claimant child hovering at the edge of the road and intent on crossing it was incumbent upon the driver to reduce speed to a degree sufficient to avoid an accident and to sound the horn to warn of likely danger. Again, if a driver sees a pedestrian in time to avoid a collision but does not slow thinking that the pedestrian has time to move away, he will be liable if owing to age or infirmity the pedestrian does not move.[967] Clearly, to exceed a speed limit is evidence of negligence but it may not amount to negligence where it gives rise to no significant risk of an accident.[968] The police may be liable for an accident caused by speeding in pursuit of a criminal, if care proportionate to the speed has not been shown.[969] Although it has been held that a driver is under no duty to give warning of his intention to slow down,[970] the driver of a following vehicle at a safe distance cannot be blamed if the vehicle ahead stops so suddenly as to give 7-211

a driver who crossed a junction on a green light was liable for hitting a cyclist who had not cleared the junction before the lights changed against him: *Radburn v Kemp* [1971] 1 W.L.R. 1502.

962 *Rae v Friel*, 1992 S.C.C.R. 688; 1993 S.L.T. 791: driving whist using a mobile phone, Highway Code a relevant circumstance but not conclusive; *Cavin v Kinnaird*, 1994 S.L.T. 111: stopping distances in the Code could not be relied upon in place of evidence; *Soils Ltd v Bromwich* [1998] C.L.Y. 1380: signalling on approach to junction not necessarily bound by Code but by circumstances.

963 *Day v Smith* (1983) 133 N.L.J. 726.

964 Thus, in *McLeod v Receiver of Metropolitan Police* [1971] Crim. L.R. 364, a police car, driven at 70 mph in answer to an emergency call, collided with another car. The police driver was held to blame, not for fast driving, but for driving at such a speed that he lost control. In *Langley v Dray and MT Motor Policies at Lloyds* [1998] P.I.Q.R. P314 CA, it was held that a joy rider, speeding to escape a pursuing police car, was liable for the personal injuries suffered by the police driver when the police car skidded and crashed.

965 *Harvey v Road Haulage Executive* [1952] 1 K.B. 120; *Hill-Venning v Beszant* [1950] 2 All E.R. 1151. The dictum of Scrutton LJ in *Baker v Longhurst & Sons Ltd* [1933] 2 K.B. 461, 468, that a motorist at night who fails to stop within the limits of his vision must necessarily be negligent, has been repeatedly declared not to lay down a rule of law. See *Morris v Luton Corp* [1946] 1 K.B. 114. See generally the Highway Code.

966 [1993] P.I.Q.R. P109.

967 *Daly v Liverpool Corp* [1939] 2 All E.R. 142.

968 *Saleem v Drake* [1993] P.I.Q.R. P129. Contrast *Armstrong v Cottrell* [1993] P.I.Q.R. P109.

969 See for example, *Cox v Dixon* (1984) 134 N.L.J. 236: unmarked police car speeding in pursuit at 60 mph in 30 mph zone held liable for collision with motorist turning on to road; *Armsden v Kent Police* [2009] EWCA Civ 631; [2009] R.T.R. 31.

970 *Jungnickel v Laing* (1966) 111 S.J. 19.

him no chance of avoiding a collision.[971] A sudden braking may raise an inference of negligence in the absence of an explanation from the driver.[972]

7-212 **Road junctions** Joining a main road from a minor road is potentially hazardous and frequently both parties to a collision will be held liable. In *Worsfield v Howe*[973] the driver's vision of the main road he wished to join was obscured by a stationary tanker, so he inched forward to get in front of the tanker when he was hit by the claimant motorcyclist who was overtaking the tanker. The Court of Appeal held both claimant and defendant equally to blame for the accident. The driver may be excused in such circumstances if signalled to move forward by another driver[974] but this will not always be the case. In *Garston Warehousing Co Ltd v OF Smart (Liverpool) Ltd*[975] the claimant who was waiting to emerge from a side road onto a main road, was signalled to emerge by the driver of a bus, which had halted on the main road. As he emerged very slowly, the defendant drove past the bus notwithstanding signals from the bus driver, and collided with the claimant. The defendant was held two-thirds to blame and the claimant one-third. Light controlled crossings provide for clearer identification of who is to blame as a vehicle should not proceed beyond the stop-line while the signal is at red.[976] But a driver should anticipate that others may cross against the lights, e.g. when they are changing.[977] A driver of an emergency vehicle may treat a red signal as a "Give Way" sign but may be liable for not proceeding with care,[978] whilst a driver crossing on green and colliding with such an emergency vehicle may be held contributory negligent.[979] Similarly, a police driver crossing lights at red whilst in pursuit of suspected criminals may be held liable for a resulting collision.[980] If it is obvious that the lights are not functioning, both drivers may be to blame for proceeding without caution.[981]

---

971 *Croston v Vaughan* [1938] 1 K.B. 540. The driver of a following vehicle may be negligent if he keeps so close and that he cannot pull up in time if the vehicle ahead stops suddenly: *Thompson v Speeding* [1973] R.T.R. 312. The question is always one of fact: *Scott v Warren* [1974] R.T.R. 104.

972 *Elizabeth v MIB* [1981] R.T.R. 405. See also *Ng Chun Pui v Lee Chuen Tat* [1988] R.T.R. 298, where the Privy Council held that driver's explanation was sufficient to prevent any inference of negligence arising. See para.7-207.

973 [1980] 1 W.L.R. 1175.

974 See *Clarke v Winchurch* [1969] 1 W.L.R. 69.

975 [1977] R.T.R. 377.

976 *Ryan v Smith* [1967] 2 Q.B. 893; *Hopwood Homes v Kennerdine* [1975] R.T.R. 82.

977 *Radburn v Kemp* [1971] 1 W.L.R. 1502.

978 In *Craggy v Chief Constable of Cleveland Police* [2009] EWCA Civ 1128 a fire engine with lights flashing and siren on entered a junction against a red light and there was a collision with a police car, also with lights and siren on, which had a green light in its favour. The Court of Appeal held that the judge had placed an unreasonably high burden on the driver of the police car in holding him one third responsible, given that the chance of two emergency vehicles entering the junction at the same time was remote. The accident was wholly the fault of the driver of the fire engine.

979 *Griffin v Mersey Regional Ambulance* [1998] P.I.Q.R. P34.

980 In *DPP v Harris* [1995] R.T.R. 100, the defendant police officer in pursuit of a car containing individuals thought likely to commit an armed robbery collided with a car after proceeding through a red light. The defendant had stopped to check if it was safe and then carried on. It was held that the defence of necessity was not open to the defendant as the situations where a police car could pass through a red light were laid down in reg.34 of the Traffic Signs Regulations and General Directions 1981 (see now the Traffic Signs Regulations and General Directions 2016 (SI 2016/362) Sch.14 Pt 1 para.5). See also *Armsden v Kent Police* [2009] EWCA Civ 631; [2009] R.T.R. 31 on the duty of the driver of police vehicle using a flashing blue warning light, but not its siren, attending an emergency.

981 *Ramoo s/o Erulapan v Soo Swee* [1971] 1 W.L.R. 1014; *Smithers v H & M Transport (Oxford)* (1983) 133 N.L.J. 558.

At uncontrolled crossings a motorist should generally give way to vehicles coming from the right[982] and should give way when crossing onto a major road.[983] But it is still the business of persons driving on the main road to approach a crossing with caution.[984] Hence, it may be negligent to try to overtake when approaching a road junction, but much depends upon the particular circumstances.[985] Thus in *Joliffe v Hay*[986] the claimant intended to turn right and was struck by the defendant. The court held that as the claimant had only checked his rear view once he had failed to maintain a proper lookout and was guilty of a lack of reasonable care. Liability of the defendant was assessed at only 70 per cent as a consequence.

Pedestrian crossings It is the duty of a person driving over a pedestrian crossing at the entrance to a street to drive slowly and with caution.[987] If the crossing is an uncontrolled crossing within the meaning of the Traffic Signs Regulations and General Directions 2016,[988] the driver must give precedence to foot-passengers on the crossing.[989] But a pedestrian himself will be held wholly or in part responsible for the collision if he steps off the footpath onto the crossing so as to give the driver of the vehicle no reasonable chance of avoiding him.[990] Indeed, a pedestrian who started crossing a road when it was clear, has been held partly to blame for not looking again while crossing.[991] So too has a pedestrian who walked on to a pelican 7-213

[982] As Sellers LJ has said, "It is a well-recognised and conventional practice, rather than a rule … that the vehicle which has the other on its right-hand side is the give-way vehicle. It may not be established as obligatory but it is a very salutary guiding rule." *McIntyre v Coles* [1966] 1 W.L.R. 831 at 834.

[983] In *Wadsworth v Gillespie* [1978] C.L.Y. 2534, the defendant, who was approaching an intersection with a major road, looked twice at a motorcyclist approaching from her right. Seeing that the latter's indicator was signalling a left turn, i.e. into the minor road, she moved into the major road and was run into by the motor-cyclist. The latter had accidentally knocked his indicator and was unaware that it was flashing a left turn. The court held him one-third to blame and the defendant two-thirds, since she should have made sure that he was indeed turning left before moving into the main road.

[984] *Lang v London Transport Executive* [1959] 1 W.L.R. 1168; *Truscott v McLaren* [1982] R.T.R. 34.

[985] *Worsfold v Howe* [1980] 1 W.L.R. 1175.

[986] 1991 S.L.T. 151.

[987] Thus in *Shephard v H West & Son* (1962) 106 S.J. 817, where a pedestrian crossed the road in front of a bus, which had halted at traffic lights, just as the lights changed from red to amber and was run into by a lorry, which was endeavouring to get in front of the bus before it moved off, it was held that the lorry driver had been negligent in not having waited until the bus was halfway across the crossing before overtaking. The pedestrian was held not to have been negligent.

[988] SI 2016/362 Sch.14 Pt 5 para.7(1): "Every pedestrian who is on the carriageway within the limits of a Zebra crossing, which is not for the time being controlled by a constable in uniform or traffic warden, before any part of a vehicle has entered those limits has precedence within those limits over that vehicle and the driver must accord such precedence to any such pedestrian."

[989] *Kozimor v Adey* (1962) 106 S.J. 431; Criminal law: *Hughes v Hall* [1960] 1 W.L.R. 733; a cyclist pushing a cycle is a "foot passenger": *Crank v Brooks* [1980] R.T.R. 441.

[990] *Clifford v Drymond* [1976] R.T.R. 134. See also *Kozimor v Adey* (1962) 106 S.J. 431; and *Maynard v Rogers* (1970) 114 S.J. 320, in both of which the pedestrians were held more to blame. cf. *Mulligan v Holmes* [1971] R.T.R. 179, where two pedestrians were crossing a road at a crossing marked with studs and when the lights were green in favour of the traffic. The defendant, driving negligently, hit them. They were held 20 per cent to blame. In *Williams v Needham* [1972] R.T.R. 387 the driver of a vehicle noticed a pedestrian waiting to cross. He assumed that she would look before doing so and gave no warning. She did cross without looking and was run over. The driver was held one-third to blame.

[991] *Hurt v Murphy* [1971] R.T.R. 186. See also *Liddell v Middleton* [1996] P.I.Q.R. P36.

crossing when the lights were showing green for traffic and red for pedestrians[992] and similarly a pedestrian attempting to cross a busy dual carriageway when a footbridge was available.[993] In *Tremayne v Hill*[994] Court of Appeal held that a pedestrian does not have to cross a road only at a pedestrian crossing and that, provided he takes reasonable care, he may cross where he likes. He may also assume that other road users will act lawfully in observing lights and road signs.

7-214 **Pedestrian accidents** The driver will sometimes escape liability even though the pedestrian runs in front of the car from the other side of the road. In *Ebanks v Collins and Motor Insurance Bureau*[995] the claimant, a six-year-old child, leaving a sweet shop, ran from between parked cars colliding with the defendant's car. The Court of Appeal rejected the child's claim, holding that nothing showed the defendant was driving at an inappropriate speed and the fact that he was unable to stop in time, even given the fact that he was on the other side of the road, did not mean that in every case of this type the driver should have been able to avoid a collision. There was nothing to find the defendant to be at fault. If a pedestrian is hit by a vehicle mounting the pavement, this is prima facie evidence of negligence,[996] and this will be so even if the immediate cause is a skid for which the driver can offer no reasonable explanation.[997] It is not necessarily negligent for a pedestrian to walk along the nearside of a country road[998] and if a pedestrian walking along the road way is hit from behind, that may be evidence of driver negligence.[999] Pedestrians may also be held liable for negligently causing accidents. Thus, in *Barry v MacDonald*[1000] a pedestrian stepped into the path of an oncoming scooter with the result that the rider was killed. The pedestrian was held liable. The circumstances in which an injured pedestrian may be found to be guilty of contributory negligence are discussed in Ch.3.[1001]

---

992 *Fitzgerald v Lane* [1987] Q.B. 781. The pedestrian was hit by two motorists who were both driving too fast and failing to keep a proper look out. Decision affirmed by the House of Lords [1989] A.C. 328, on the basis that the pedestrian's claim against the two drivers should be reduced to 50 per cent on account of his contributory negligence. That reduced sum was apportioned equally between the drivers.

993 *Connaire v McGuire* [1994] C.L.Y. 3343.

994 [1987] R.T.R. 131.

995 [1994] C.L.Y. 3401.

996 *Ellor v Selfridge* (1930) 46 T.L.R. 236; see also *Watson v Thomas S Whitney & Co Ltd* [1966] 1 W.L.R. 57 (vehicle overlapping pavement).

997 *Liffen v Watson* [1940] 1 K.B. 556. A violent and unexplained skid may well imply negligence: *Richley v Faull (Richley, Third Party)* [1965] 1 W.L.R. 1454. But a skid on unforeseeable black ice will rebut an inference of negligence: *Smith v Fordyce* [2013] EWCA Civ 320.

998 *Parkinson v Parkinson* (Note) [1973] R.T.R. 193; followed in *Kerley v Downes* [1973] R.T.R. 188; *Probert v Moore* [2012] EWHC 2324 (QB).

999 *Page v Richards*, reported in *Tart v Chitty* [1933] 2 K.B. 453. See also *Powell v Phillips* [1972] 3 All E.R. 864, where a pedestrian, who stepped off the pavement because it was covered with snow and was struck from behind by a car, and despite the fact that she acted in breach of the Highway Code, the Court of Appeal held that this raised no presumption of negligence by her. Contrast *Widdowson v Newgate Meat Corp* [1998] P.I.Q.R. P138 CA, where the Court of Appeal based liability on the maxim res ipsa loquitur in circumstances in which the defendant driver provided no explanation for having collided with the claimant pedestrian.

1000 (1966) 110 S.J. 56; *Green v Hills* (1969) 113 S.J. 385; *The Times*, 22 April 1969. See also the statement of Viscount Simon in *Nance v British Columbia Electric Ry* [1951] A.C. 601 at 611: "When a man steps from the kerb into the roadway, he owes a duty to traffic which is approaching him with risk of collision to exercise due care."

1001 See paras 3-87 and 3-88. See also D. Dyal, "Contributory negligence in pedestrian road traffic accidents" [2018] J.P.I.L. 23.

Animals Liability for animals is fully analysed in Ch.20 but it should be noted here that road accidents are frequently caused by a negligent failure to control an animal. In the case of a horse the main danger is that the rider will lose control when the horse is frightened by an overtaking car. If damage results, the rider may have to explain why control was lost to rebut an inference of negligence[1002] and the overtaking driver may have to show that he gave the horse sufficient berth.[1003] *Mirhavedy v Henley*[1004] illustrates the scope of strict liability under the "known characteristic" provision of the Animals Act 1971 for horses causing an accident by escaping on to the road and a preference for placing liability on the horse owner rather than leaving an injured motorist without a remedy. Liability for dogs which escape and cause accidents can also rest on knowledge of an escaping characteristic but can also rest on simple negligence. In *Gomberg v Smith*[1005] the defendant was held to be negligent in walking his dog without a lead alongside a road in a built-up area. The dog ran across the road and collided with the claimant's vehicle causing it damage. 7-215

Dangers on the road A person who negligently creates a danger on the road will be liable for any resulting accident. Thus, a local authority which planted trees adjacent to the road and failed to cut them back was held liable when a branch broke a bus window and injured a passenger,[1006] but where the defendant's tree fell on the road causing an accident and there was nothing to indicate this was likely to happen, there was no liability.[1007] Construction work on the road can lead to liability, so where a local authority put in a drainage pipe and reinstated the surface, it was held liable for negligently failing to discover that the surface had subsided. The successful claimant was thrown off his cycle by the uneven road surface.[1008] Even the marker studs in the middle of the road can constitute a danger if they become loose and so a highway authority has been held liable for injury to a cyclist knocked over by a loose stud.[1009] The authority's failure to take reasonable care to maintain the road led to its liability. In *Levine v Morris*[1010] an authority was held liable for positioning the leg of a road sign so close to the edge of the carriageway as to endanger road users.[1011] In *Cassin v Bexley LBC*[1012] the police and the council had 7-216

1002 *Haimes v Watson* [1981] R.T.R. 90.

1003 *Carryfast Ltd v Hack* [1981] R.T.R. 464. See also *Stoddart v Perucca* [2011] EWCA Civ 290—motorist collided with a horse, the rider having attempted to cross a road at a trot without looking; motorist held 50 per cent responsible for the collision, even though the rider was considered to be significantly more at fault, taking into account the fact that the motorist was driving a car.

1004 [2003] UKHL 16; [2003] 2 A.C. 491. See para.20-08.

1005 [1963] 1 Q.B. 25.

1006 *Hale v Hants and Dorset Motor Service Ltd* [1947] 2 All E.R. 628.

1007 *Caminer v Northern and London Investment Trust* [1951] A.C. 88.

1008 *Newsome v Darton Urban DC* [1938] 3 All E.R. 93.

1009 *Skilton v Epsom Urban DC* [1937] 1 K.B. 112.

1010 [1970] 1 W.L.R. 71.

1011 See also *Bird v Pearce & Somerset CC (Third Party)* [1978] R.T.R. 290 where a highway authority was held to owe motorists a duty of care not to create dangers by obliterating markings, though in *Gorringe v Calderdale MBC* [2004] UKHL 15; [2004] 1 W.L.R. 1057 some doubt was cast on the correctness of the decision in *Bird v Pearce*. See further *Foulds v Devon CC* [2015] EWHC 40 (QB) (inspection and maintenance of railings by the local authority with a view to protecting pedestrians from falling down a drop onto a road below, did not amount to an undertaking of responsibility by the authority to a cyclist who crashed into the railings and fell over the drop. The railings were not intended to act as a crash barrier).

1012 (1999) 1 L.G.L.R. 810; [1999] B.L.G.R. 694.

an agreement that the council would clear the road of bollards which might be used as missiles in a protest march. The council removed the bollards before the march and the claimant, a motorcyclist hit one of the plinths left behind. The council argued that it had discharged its duty to take reasonable care by doing as the police requested. The Court of Appeal held that the authority had a duty to keep the road safe until it was closed, that they had a duty not to remove the bollards until that occurred and as it had not ensured this it had failed in its duty and so was liable. The House of Lords' decision in *Stovin v Wise*[1013] established that there is no liability for an omission to remove a dangerous obstruction adjacent to a highway but where the authority has created the danger the position is different. In *Kane v New Forest DC*,[1014] *Stovin* was distinguished on the ground that the defendant planning authority in *Kane* had created the source of danger since it had required the construction of the footpath and knew that the sightlines to the road made it dangerous to use. Private individuals may also be liable. Leaving a vehicle without lights in a dark road may be evidence of negligence.[1015] Parking on a bend may also be negligent.

7-217 **Responsibility of the highway authority for road maintenance** The Highways Act 1980 s.41(1), imposes on "[t]he authority who are for the time being the highway authority for a highway maintainable at the public expense ... a duty ... to maintain the highway".[1016] In *Mills v Barnsley Metropolitan Borough Council*[1017] Steyn LJ, commenting on the s.41 duty, said that:

> "In order for a plaintiff to succeed against a highway authority in a claim for personal injury for failing to maintain or repair the highway, the plaintiff must prove that:
>
> (a) the highway was in such a condition that it was dangerous to traffic or pedestrians

[1013] [1996] A.C. 923. Applied in *Sumner v Colborne* [2018] EWCA Civ 1006; [2019] Q.B. 430 (no duty in respect of vegetation on land adjacent to the highway which obstructed visibility of road users, distinguishing *Yetkin v Newham LBC* [2010] EWCA Civ 776; [2011] Q.B. 827 where the defendants had planted vegetation on the central reservation of a highway).

[1014] [2001] EWCA Civ 878; [2002] 1 W.L.R. 312. See also *Yetkin v Newham LBC* [2010] EWCA Civ 776; [2011] Q.B. 827—planting shrubbery in a central reservation such as to obscure the view of pedestrians attempting to cross the road created a foreseeable danger to users of the highway, and it did not have to be established that the authority had created a "trap".

[1015] per Edmund Davies J in *Parish v Judd* [1960] 1 W.L.R. 867 at 870–871. It was held to be plain and obvious negligence to leave a lorry on the wrong side of the road at night with its lights on: *Chisman v Electromation (Export) Ltd* (1969) 6 K.I.R. 456; *Watson v Heslop* [1971] R.T.R. 308. In *Wagner v Grant* [2016] CSIH 34; 2016 S.L.T. 699 the driver of a large milk tanker that was "lit up better than a Christmas tree" was held to have been negligent in obstructing both lanes of the road while reversing into a farm entrance, though the motorcycle rider who rode into it was held to have been 60 per cent contributorily negligent. A motorist, who has to leave his vehicle unlit, may be negligent if he fails to display a warning sign, but this does not absolve other drivers. See *Lee v Lever* [1974] R.T.R. 35. A vehicle parked on the highway in a manner that creates a dangerous obstruction may also constitute a public nuisance: *Dymond v Pearce* [1972] 1 Q.B. 496 CA (though on the facts the collision with the lorry on this case was held to be entirely due to the fault of the motorcyclist who ran into the back of the lorry).

[1016] The duty was originally imposed on highway authorities by s.44(1) of the Highways Act 1959 but that Act maintained the former exemption of liability for non-repair and hence the authority could only be sued for misfeasance, e.g. obstruction of the highway. The exemption for non-repair was removed by s.1(1) of the Highways (Miscellaneous Provisions) Act 1961. For the meaning of "a highway maintainable at the public expense" see the Highways Act 1980 s.36; and *Barlow v Wigan Council* [2020] EWCA Civ 696.

[1017] [1992] P.I.Q.R. P291 at P292–P293.

in the sense that, in the ordinary course of human affairs, danger may reasonably have been anticipated from its continued use by the public;

(b) the dangerous condition was created by the failure to maintain or repair the highway; and

(c) the injury or damage resulted from such a failure."

The test of dangerousness is one of "reasonable foresight of harm to users of the highway" but the courts "should not impose unreasonably high standards, otherwise scarce resources would be diverted from situations where maintenance and repair of the highways is more urgently needed."[1018]

In addition to other defences that might be available, s.58(1) provides that a highway authority can escape liability by proving "that the authority had taken such care as in all the circumstances was reasonably required to secure that the part of the highway to which the action relates was not dangerous for traffic".[1019] Section 58(2) provides that the circumstances the court must to take into account include: **7-218**

(a) the character of the highway and the traffic reasonably expected to use it;
(b) the standard of maintenance appropriate to such a highway;
(c) the state of repair which a reasonable person would expect;
(d) the knowledge which the highway authority had, or should reasonably have had, of the dangerous condition in question; and
(e) the kind of warning notices that had been displayed pending repair.

It also provides that it is no defence:

> "to prove that the highway authority had arranged for a competent person to carry out or supervise the maintenance of the part of the highway to which the action relates unless it is also proved that the authority had given him proper instructions with regard to the maintenance of the highway and that he had carried out the instructions."

Section 58 requires an objective judgment based on the risk to users of the highway, and does not take account of the highway authority's resources.[1020] This is because:

> "The obligation to maintain highways in a structural condition which makes them free from foreseeable danger to traffic using the road in the ordinary way is an unqualified obligation of highway authorities of long standing. If Parliament had wanted to weaken that fundamental obligation, now contained in section 41, it would have done so. Section 58 had a different purpose. Section 58 was designed simply to afford a defence to a claim for damages brought against a highway authority which was able to demonstrate that it had done all that was reasonably necessary to make the road safe for users, not an

---

1018 [1992] P.I.Q.R. P291 at P294 and P295.

1019 In *Griffiths v Liverpool Corp* [1967] 1 Q.B. 374 Diplock LJ explained that under s.58(2) the defendant bears the burden of proving that reasonable care was taken, whilst for negligence liability it is the claimant who must prove lack of care. On the facts, the lack of skilled tradesmen available to the authority was not regarded as relevant as the authority had failed to prove that a labourer would not have detected and been able to deal with the dangerous pavement flagstones. Note also *Roe v Sheffield City Council* [2003] EWCA Civ 1; [2004] Q.B. 653 which concerned an action for injury to a road user arising from disrepair of tramlines in the highway causing a vehicle to skid. The claim was for breach of s.28 of the Tramways Act 1870 which involved the same duty as that imposed on a highway authority by the Highways Act 1980 s.41. The defendants were held liable. Pill LJ at [61] said that the standard of maintenance is measured by considerations of safety.

1020 *Wilkinson v York City Council* [2011] EWCA Civ 207; *Crawley v Barnsley MBC* [2017] EWCA Civ 36; [2017] 1 W.L.R. 2329.

authority which decided that it was preferable to allocate its resources in other directions because other needs were more pressing than doing what was reasonably required to make the roads safe."[1021]

7-219 **Scope of the duty** Under the legislation the authority may be liable to a road user who has "suffered physical injury to person or property while using the highway when it was in a dangerous condition due to want of repair and maintenance". In *Wentworth v Wiltshire CC*[1022] the Court of Appeal held that the reference to "dangerous for traffic" in the statutory defence, meant that the liability did not extend to a person suffering purely economic loss or to a person suffering loss in his capacity as an adjoining landowner rather than as a user of the highway.[1023] In *Goodes v East Sussex CC*[1024] the House of Lords held that the statutory duty to maintain the highway did not require the highway authority to keep it free from ice, but this ruling was overturned by s.111 of the Railways and Transport Safety Act 2003 which inserted s.41(1A) into the Highways Act 1980. This provides that an authority is "under a duty to ensure, so far as is reasonably practicable, that safe passage along a highway is not endangered by snow or ice".[1025] The duty under s.41(1) has been held to apply to drainage,[1026] but it does not extend to a duty to remove surface-lying material, obstructions or spillages, whether or not they result in danger to road users.[1027] The s.41 duty is not limited to a duty not to create a "trap" into which the user of a highway has been enticed, nor is it owed only to reasonably careful, prudent road users.[1028] In *Stovin v Wise*[1029] it was held that the duty did not extend to work on land not forming part of the highway and hence, there was no statutory liability for failing to remove a high bank on land adjacent to the highway which

---

1021 *Wilkinson v York City Council* [2011] EWCA Civ 207 at [35] per Toulson LJ. A code of practice, Well-Maintained Highways, gives guidance to highway authorities as to the frequency of inspection for dangers and identifies categories of defect by seriousness and suggested urgency of repair. A code of practice is not determinative of whether there has been a breach of s.41, or whether a defence under s.58 has been established, but it can be evidence of good practice: see *AC v Devon CC* [2013] EWCA Civ 418; [2014] R.T.R. 1; [2013] P.I.Q.R. P19; *Griffiths v Gwynedd CC* [2015] EWCA Civ 1440; [2016] R.T.R. 15; *Crawley v Barnsley MBC* [2017] EWCA Civ 36; [2017] 1 W.L.R. 2329.

1022 [1993] Q.B. 654.

1023 The claimant farmer had claimed a financial loss of £77,000 resulting from the inability of the Milk Marketing Board to collect milk from his farm because the access road was too dangerous for its tankers to use. The claim was brought under the identical provisions of the 1959 and 1961 legislation and failed on the ground that it was for pure economic loss suffered in the capacity of adjoining occupier rather than user of the road.

1024 [2000] 1 W.L.R. 1356.

1025 The "reasonably practicable" provision focuses attention on the whether the authority's gritting policy was realistic and achievable and whether it was properly implemented.

1026 See *Thoburn v Northumberland CC* (1999) 1 L.G.L.R. 819.

1027 *Valentine v Transport for London* [2010] EWCA Civ 1358; [2011] P.I.Q.R. P7 where it was held that there was no duty in respect of an accident caused by gravel/loose debris on the highway, applying *Goodes v East Sussex CC* [2000] 1 W.L.R. 1356. The fact that s.41(1A) had extended the duty to the removal of snow and ice (thus reversing the conclusion on the specific facts of *Goodes*) merely served to emphasise the general rule that a highway authority is not under a duty to remove other surface material such as spillages of oil, landslips, mud or the accumulation of grit. In *Rollinson v Dudley MBC* [2015] EWHC 3330 (QB); [2016] P.I.Q.R. P6 Haddon-Cave J held that the s.41 duty does not extend to an obligation to remove moss from the surface of a road. The contrary suggestion was "absurd". On the other hand, where an accidental spillage of concrete has hardened and bonded to the surface of the road the concrete has become part of the fabric of the road sufficient to bring it within s.41: *Thomas v Warwickshire CC* [2011] EWHC 772 (QB) at [74].

1028 *Yetkin v Newham LBC* [2010] EWCA Civ 776; [2011] Q.B. 827.

1029 [1996] A.C. 923.

was creating a dangerous situation by limiting visibility.[1030] Again, in *Gorringe v Calderdale MBC*[1031] the House of Lords held that the duty to maintain under s.41 was concerned with repair and did not extend to installation of warning signs and that the general duty to improve road safety under s.39 could not give rise to a specific duty to an individual to install such signs.

(ii) The liability of carriers

Transport of passengers Those responsible for transport must take reasonable care in relation to the condition of the vehicle and the safety of goods and passengers. Liability as to the condition of the vehicle depends on the character in which the passenger enters the vehicle, whether as a "lawful visitor" or a trespasser. A duty of care may be owed to a lawful visitor under the Occupiers' Liability Act 1957[1032] or at common law. There will be no liability for latent defects, undiscoverable on reasonable examination, but there is a duty to inspect and test the vehicles periodically and to repair the defects which a reasonable examination should have revealed.[1033] A similar duty of care extends to the property of passengers.[1034] A non-delegable duty of reasonable care may result from an appropriate undertaking to the passenger.[1035] The power of carriers to limit or exclude their liability by contract or notice has been curtailed by the Unfair Contract Terms Act 1977,[1036] the Consumer Rights Act 2015[1037] and the Road Traffic Act 1988.[1038] With regard to a trespasser, liability under the Occupiers' Liability Act 1984 depends, amongst other things, on the occupier's knowledge.[1039] 7-220

Railways Those responsible for the operation of the service, the rolling stock, 7-221

1030 cf. where by some positive act the highway authority creates a danger on the highway by limiting visibility: *Yetkin v Newham LBC* [2010] EWCA Civ 776; [2011] Q.B. 827 (planting shrubs in a central reservation which obscured the view of pedestrians attempting to cross the road; highway authority held liable).

1031 [2004] UKHL 15; [2004] 1 W.L.R. 1057. See also *Thompson v Hampshire CC* [2004] EWCA Civ 1016; [2005] B.L.G.R. 467—no responsibility under s.41 for a highway's layout, as opposed to the state of repair of the structure; but the highway can include the verge: *West Sussex CC v Russell* [2010] EWCA Civ 71; [2010] R.T.R. 19—highway authority responsible for accident when wheel of claimant's vehicle ran into a "drop-off" between the carriageway and the verge of between 6 and 12 inches.

1032 s.1(3) provides that the Act applies to a person having control of a vehicle (see para.11-07) but in so far as the injury stems from the careless driving of the vehicle, it would seem to result from breach of an activity duty which is governed by the common law: see further paras 11-03 and 11-04.

1033 *Readhead v Midland Ry* (1869) L.R. 4 Q.B. 379. The standard of care is illustrated by *Henderson v HE Jenkins & Sons* [1970] A.C. 282, for discussion of which see para.7-206.

1034 *Houghland v RR Low (Luxury Coaches) Ltd* [1962] 1 Q.B. 694; *Mannix v NM Paterson & Sons* [1965] 2 Lloyd's Rep. 108.

1035 *Rogers v Night Riders (A Firm)* [1983] R.T.R. 324: here all that the defendant did was to put customers in touch with independent drivers of vehicles.

1036 See also para.3-136.

1037 See para.3-141.

1038 s.149(3). See *Pitts v Hunt* [1991] 1 Q.B. 24, in which the Court of Appeal held that s.148(3) applied to exclude any defence of volenti which would otherwise be available to a driver. Note also the Public Passenger Vehicles Act 1981 s.29 rendering void any provision in a contract for the conveyance of a passenger in a public service vehicle that attempts to negative or restrict liability to the passenger for personal injury or death.

1039 See para.11-65. When a driver of a lorry is forbidden to give a lift to anyone not employed by the lorry owners and does so in breach of his orders, the person so carried may have no right of action against the lorry owners if he is injured by the negligent driving of the driver: *Conway v George Wimpey & Co Ltd* [1951] 2 K.B. 266; but see *Rose v Plenty* [1976] 1 W.L.R. 141, in which the track and signalling, "shall use care and diligence so that no accident shall happen".[1040] The standard of care is that of a reasonably careful and skilful person or body of persons carrying on such an undertaking. The collision of two trains is evidence of negligence,[1041] so is driving a train into buffers,[1042] driving one so as to cause it to leave the rails,[1043] stopping the train with a jerk[1044] and starting without warning.[1045] Care must be taken to prevent platforms[1046] and carriages[1047] being so overcrowded that injury results.[1048] Reasonable care must be taken to see that the doors are properly shut before the train starts.[1049] If the door comes open when the train is in motion, this may be evidence of negligence on the part of the railway operator.[1050] The platforms at which passengers have to board or alight from trains should be reasonably safe for the purpose.[1051] In respect of pedestrians on the track, the Court of Appeal has held that the circumstances make the standard of reasonable care different from that of a driver on the road[1052]; but the driver should nonetheless take reasonable care to watch the track ahead to avoid persons who might be in peril.[1053] In *Thames Trains Ltd v Health & Safety Executive*,[1054] Morland J dismissed the Executive's application to strike out the claims of victims of the Ladbroke Grove rail crash. He held that it could be reasonably argued that the Executive should be made liable not for failing to use statutory powers involving expenditure of money, but for failing negligently to use, as the public would expect, their statutory powers through the Railway Inspectorate in carrying out routine duties of inspection and supervision. The decision was upheld on appeal.[1055]

---

vehicle owner was held vicariously liable on the ground that the lift was given to further the employer's business. See further para.6-40. The passenger would in any case have a right of action against the driver.

1040 per Bramwell B in *Wright v Midland Ry* (1873) L.R. 8 Ex. 137 at 140.

1041 *Ayles v South Eastern Ry* (1868) L.R. 3 Ex. 146.

1042 *Burke v Manchester Sheffield & Lincolnshire Ry* (1870) 22 L.T. 442.

1043 *Dawson v Manchester Sheffield & Lincolnshire Ry* (1862) 5 L.T. 682.

1044 *Angus v London, Tilbury and Southend Ry* (1906) 22 T.L.R. 222.

1045 *Caterson v Commissioner for Railways* (1972) 128 C.L.R. 99.

1046 *Hogan v South Eastern Ry* (1873) 28 L.T. 271.

1047 per Lord Blackburn in *Metropolitan Ry v Jackson* (1877) 3 App. Cas. 193 at 209.

1048 But generally there is no liability to a passenger who is injured while in the train by his fellow passengers, e.g. by being rushed off his feet by other passengers hurrying out of the compartment: *Machen v Lancashire & Yorkshire Ry* (1919) 88 L.J.K.B. 371.

1049 *Brookes v London Passenger Transport Board* [1947] 1 All E.R. 506 (door in underground left open, a passenger fell out when the train started and recovered damages).

1050 *Gee v Metropolitan Ry* (1873) L.R. 8 Q.B. 161. Note that in *Easson v London & North Eastern Ry* [1944] K.B. 421, where an offside door of an express corridor train came open, it was held that this did not give rise to even a prima facie case of negligence on the ground that such doors are not under the continuous control of the railway authority during the journey. This would seem to be of no application to trains where door locking is electronically controlled.

1051 The platform and approaches must be reasonably safe: *Bloomstein v Ry Executive* [1952] 2 All E.R. 418; *Stowell v Ry Executive* [1949] 2 K.B. 519. But there is no liability if the railway authority takes reasonable care either to remove the source of danger: *Tomlinson v Ry Executive* [1953] 1 All E.R. 1; or gives reasonable warning to enable passengers to avoid it: *Blackman v Ry Executive* [1954] 1 W.L.R. 220.

1052 per Morris LJ in *Trznadel v British Transport Commission* [1957] 1 W.L.R. 1002 at 1006.

1053 *Conway v BTC* (1962) 106 S.J. 78; *Geddes v British Railways Board* (1968) 4 K.I.R. 373.

1054 [2002] EWHC 1415 (QB); [2003] P.I.Q.R. P14.

1055 [2003] EWCA Civ 720; (2003) 147 S.J.L.B. 661.

Road transport The principles of common law negligence set out above in relation to railways apply also to road transport.[1056] A mechanical failure may be evidence of negligence.[1057] Negligent driving may also lead to liability.[1058] In driving a vehicle, the driver is negligent if he stops or starts with a jerk,[1059] but a bus driver has been held not to be negligent in moving off before all the passengers were seated.[1060] There is much case law concerned with the standard of care of a conductor.[1061] Applied to modern conditions, it suggests that the person responsible for the transport should take reasonable care to warn his passengers of any dangers[1062] and prevent them from acting negligently.[1063] A passenger is negligent if he attempts to board or to leave the vehicle when it is in motion.[1064] A motorist has been held to be negligent for not encouraging a passenger to wear a seat belt[1065]; and the Court of Appeal has ruled that failure to wear a seat belt will normally amount to contributory negligence in the passenger,[1066] subject to a causal connection being established between such failure and the injury.[1067] **7-222**

Ships and aircraft Similar considerations to those above apply to the carriage of passengers and their luggage by sea, although the liability of the shipowner is regulated by contract and statute.[1068] This apart, reasonable care must be taken to **7-223**

1056 For the carriage of international goods, see Carriage of Goods by Road Act 1965 (as amended); on which see *Ulster-Swift Ltd v Taunton Meat Haulage Ltd* [1977] 1 W.L.R. 625.

1057 A sudden failure of brakes on a lorry owing to corrosion of a brake pipe was held to imply negligence in the owners, who had to show that their vehicle could not have come into contact with a corrosive substance, or, if it had, that the precautions they had taken were all that could reasonably be required of them: *Henderson v Henry E Jenkins & Sons* [1970] A.C. 282.

1058 Thus, it is evidence of negligence if a sudden swerve causes injury to a passenger: *Western Scottish Motor Traction Co Ltd v Fernie* [1943] 2 All E.R. 742. But contrast *Parkinson v Liverpool Corp* [1950] 1 All E.R. 360, where it was held not negligent for the driver of a bus, driving with due care, to apply his brakes suddenly to avoid a dog even though it causes a passenger, who had stood up in order to alight, to fall and injure himself; cf. *Sutherland v Glasgow Corporation*, 1949 S.C. 563, 572, per Lord Jamieson: "The driver's first duty is to his passengers and in ordinary circumstances he is not justified in taking action to avoid a dog or other small animal if thereby he is subjecting his passengers to the risk of injury".

1059 *Geeves v London General Omnibus Co Ltd* (1901) 17 T.L.R. 249.

1060 *Mauro v Romania and City of Winnipeg* [1988] W.W.R. 684; *Fletcher v United Counties Omnibus Co Ltd* [1998] P.I.Q.R. P154 CA; cf. *Steel v McGill's Bus Service Ltd* [2015] CSOH 5; 2015 S.C.L.R. 617, where a bus driver was held to be negligent in failing to ensure that an elderly and unsteady passenger was seated before moving off causing her to lose her balance and fall.

1061 See for example *Davies v Liverpool Corp* [1949] 2 All E.R. 175.

1062 *Prescott v Lancashire United Transport Co* [1953] 1 W.L.R. 232. But there is no duty to warn of dangers encountered by a passenger after alighting from the vehicle: *Fernquest v City & County of Swansea* [2011] EWCA Civ 1712.

1063 *Curley v Mannion* [1965] I.R. 543.

1064 *McSherry v Glasgow Corp*, 1917 S.C. 156.

1065 *Pasternak v Poulton* [1973] 1 W.L.R. 476, approved in *Froom v Butcher* [1976] Q.B. 286. Wearing a seat-belt is compulsory: Motor Vehicles (Wearing of Seat Belts) Regulations 1993, SI 1993/176; and a driver who does not ensure that a child under the age of 14 is wearing a seat-belt, if there is one available, commits an offence: Road Traffic Act 1988 s.15. Also the operator of a bus in which any of the passenger seats are equipped with seat belts must take all reasonable steps to ensure that passengers are notified that they are required to wear a seat belt: Road Traffic Act 1988 s.15B (subject to the exception in s.15B(6) for buses used to provide a local service).

1066 *Froom v Butcher* [1976] Q.B. 286.

1067 *Owens v Brimmell* [1977] Q.B. 859; see also *Gregory v Kelly* [1978] R.T.R. 426.

1068 The Merchant Shipping Act 1995 lays down an extensive regime governing carriage of passengers by sea and gives force to the provisions of the Convention relating to the Carriage of Passengers and their Luggage by Sea and the Convention on Limitation of Liability for Maritime Claims 1976.

make the cabins safe,[1069] to provide suitable accommodation for luggage,[1070] and to warn passengers against the slippery condition of the deck.[1071] In the case of aircraft, the Civil Aviation Act 1982 s.76 imposes strict liability for damage caused to person or property on land or water,[1072] and the Carriage by Air Act 1961[1073] gave effect to the Warsaw Convention 1929 and its amendment in the Montreal Convention 1999 imposing on the carrier liability for damage without proof of negligence, in the event of a passenger suffering death, wounding or other bodily injury[1074] while on board the aircraft or boarding or disembarking. There is no common law right of action in respect of claims falling under the 1961 Act. Specialist texts should be consulted in relation to claims concerning ships and aircraft.

(iii) Care for children

7-224 **Parental duty to child** In *Surtees v Kingston-Upon-Thames BC*[1075] an adult claimant brought a negligence claim against her former foster parents and the local authority responsible for her placement in respect of foot injuries sustained through immersion in hot water when she was two years old. She alleged that while left unattended she must have placed her foot in a basin of hot water whilst her foster parents alleged that she had turned on the hot tap herself. The Court of Appeal held that a parental duty of care did not arise automatically but only where there was sufficient foreseeability of the injury. On the facts, it found that the foster mother did owe a duty as she had control over the claimant but by a majority it also found that she was not in breach of the duty as the injury was too remote to be attributed to her fault. Browne-Wilkinson VC refused to characterise as negligent "the care which ordinary, loving and careful mothers are able to give to individual children, given the rough and tumble of modern life" and said that the court "should be wary in its approach to holding parents in breach of a duty of care owed to their children".[1076] This observation was cited with approval by Lord Hutton in *Barrett v Enfield LBC*[1077] where the House of Lords considered that a local authority might owe a duty in relation to psychiatric problems caused to a child in its care by alleg-

---

1069 *Jones v Oceanic Steam Navigation Co* [1924] 2 K.B. 730.

1070 *Upperton v Union-Castle Co* (1902) 19 T.L.R. 687.

1071 *Beaumont-Thomas v Blue Star Line Ltd* [1939] 3 All E.R. 127.

1072 Though note that s.76(1) excludes liability for trespass or nuisance by reason only of the flight of an aircraft over any property at a reasonable height. On this see *Peires v Bickerton's Aerodromes Ltd* [2017] EWCA Civ 273; [2017] 1 W.L.R. 2865.

1073 As amended by the Carriage by Air Acts (Implementation of the Montreal Convention 1999) Order 2002 (SI 2002/263).

1074 The Convention does not cover psychiatric injury where there is no bodily injury (such as brain damage) to a passenger: *King v Bristow Helicopters Ltd* [2002] UKHL 7; [2002] 2 A.C. 628. In *Deep Vein Thrombosis, Re* [2005] UKHL 72; [2006] 1 A.C. 495, it was held that the onset of deep vein thrombosis was not capable of being an "accident" within the requirements of art.17 of the Warsaw Convention which needed to be an event or happening which was unexpected or unusual and external to the passenger. On the meaning of "accident" under the Montreal Convention see: *Barclay v British Airways Plc* [2008] EWCA Civ 1419; [2010] Q.B. 187; *Labbadia v Alitalia (Societa Aerea Italiana SpA)* [2019] EWHC 2103 (Admin); [2019] 2 Lloyd's Rep. 273.

1075 [1991] 2 F.L.R. 559; [1992] P.I.Q.R. P101.

1076 [1991] 2 F.L.R. 559 at 583; [1992] P.I.Q.R. P101. Beldam LJ dissented, arguing that it required only momentary thought to remove the child from the vicinity of the tap. See also the comments of Baroness Hale on *Surtees* in *Woodland v Essex County Council* [2013] UKSC 66; [2014] A.C. 537 at [41] agreeing with Beldam LJ. See also *S v Walsall MBC* [1985] 1 W.L.R. 1150, where at first instance, foster parents were held liable for foot burns to a two-year-old, on the basis of res ipsa loquitur.

1077 [2001] 2 A.C. 550.

edly negligent placements with unsuitable foster parents. In distinguishing the position of parents, Lord Hutton cited Browne-Wilkinson VC and said "it would be wholly inappropriate that a child should be permitted to sue his parents for decisions made by them in respect of his upbringing which could be shown to be wrong" as there were "very real public policy considerations to be taken into account if the conflicts inherent in legal proceedings are to be brought into family relationships".[1078] Lord Slynn commented that "the court should be slow to hold that a child can sue its parents for negligent decisions in its upbringing".[1079]

Similar policy issues arise where a third party alleges that a parent has been negligent in supervising a child. This is most likely to arise in the context of road traffic accidents where a child has run into the road and been struck by a vehicle. If the child is too young to be found contributorily negligent, the defendant motorist may seek contribution from the parent under the Civil Liability (Contribution) Act 1978 on the basis that the parent did not provide appropriate supervision and so was negligent in allowing the child to run into traffic. In *Ellis v Kelly*,[1080] Yip J rejected an argument that either the child or the parent must be negligent if a child runs into the road in circumstances where an older child or adult would be held contributorily negligent. The responsibility of the child and the parent should be considered separately by reference to the appropriate standard of care.[1081] Moreover, there could be serious implications of finding parents liable in such circumstances: "Parents are not reasonably able to secure insurance to guard against the risk of claims arising out of their parenting generally. … In a case in which the parent owns assets such as the family home, the family may face fears that action will be taken to enforce against the property. The potential to interfere with family life, including the rights of siblings, is significant."[1082] Routinely joining parents in such litigation would also create a risk of encouraging an over-cautious approach, "interfering with parents' assessments of when it is appropriate to allow children some freedom to foster growth and independence."[1083] It followed, said Yip J, that caution should be exercised by courts considering claims against parents in such cases. **7-225**

[1078] [2001] 2 A.C. 550 at 587. The position of the local authority was distinguishable as it employed trained staff to advise it in relation to the care of children. See also *Woodland v Essex County Council* [2013] UKSC 66; [2014] A.C. 537 at [25] and [41], distinguishing the position of parents and a school, in that the school can be subject to a non-delegable duty of care involving greater responsibility for the safety of children than that of parents.

[1079] [2001] 2 A.C. 550 at 573. See also *Rhodes v OPO* [2015] UKSC 32; [2016] A.C. 219 at [94] per Lord Neuberger. In *XA v YA* [2010] EWHC 1983 (QB); [2011] P.I.Q.R. P1 Thirlwall J stated, obiter, that it was not fair, just and reasonable to impose a duty of care on a mother to protect a child of the family from physical assault by the child's father where the only means of discharging the duty would have been to break up the family unit by one means or another. The mother had also been the victim of domestic violence and was in a vulnerable psychological state. Thirlwall J doubted "that the imposition of a common law duty of care would improve the lives of children within the home" and considered that it was "undesirable for the ordinary civil courts to have to judge, retrospectively, the decisions of a mother about how best to ensure a secure upbringing for her children in the context of a claim for damages for negligence" (at [143]).

[1080] [2018] EWHC 2031 (QB); [2018] 4 W.L.R. 124.

[1081] [2018] EWHC 2031 (QB); [2018] 4 W.L.R. 124 at [72]. On the evidence, holding the child's mother responsible would "impose far too high a standard on an ordinary parent making ordinary decisions in the course of parenting as to how to keep her child reasonably safe while gradually being allowed more responsibilities and freedoms" (at [71]).

[1082] [2018] EWHC 2031 (QB); [2018] 4 W.L.R. 124 at [77].

[1083] [2018] EWHC 2031 (QB); [2018] 4 W.L.R. 124 at [78].

7-226 **The standard of care** In *Perry v Harris*[1084] the defendants hired a bouncy castle for their children's 10th birthday party. The claimant was an 11-year-old child using the bouncy castle who was accidentally struck on the head by the foot of 15-year-old boy who did a somersault. The claimant suffered a depressed skull fracture with serious and permanent consequences. At first instance the defendants were held liable in negligence for failing adequately to supervise the children playing on the bouncy castle, although one of the defendants had maintained fairly constant supervision, and the accident had happened during a brief moment when she had been distracted by another child. The Court of Appeal reversed this finding, taking the view that the judge had applied too stringent a test for breach of duty:

> "There is a dearth of case precedent that deals with the duty of care owed by parents to their own or other children when they are playing together. It is impossible to preclude all risk that, when playing together, children may injure themselves or each other, and minor injuries must be commonplace. It is quite impractical for parents to keep children under constant surveillance or even supervision and it would not be in the public interest for the law to impose a duty upon them to do so. Some circumstances or activities may, however, involve an unacceptable risk to children unless they are subject to supervision, or even constant surveillance. Adults who expose children to such circumstances or activities are likely to be held responsible for ensuring that they are subject to such supervision or surveillance as they know, or ought to know, is necessary to restrict the risk to an acceptable level."[1085]

The test for the standard of care was "that which a reasonably careful parent would show for her own children".[1086] It was not reasonably foreseeable that boisterous play on the bouncy castle would involve a significant risk of serious harm, and therefore the standard of care required was that appropriate to protect children from a foreseeable risk of physical harm that fell short of serious injury. This standard did not require uninterrupted supervision of the children using the bouncy castle. A reasonably careful parent would have acted in the same way as the defendant.

7-227 Duty and breach are most likely to arise where the child is travelling in a car driven by a parent who will have insurance cover for liability to the child. Thus a parent should take reasonable steps to see that a child passenger wears a seat-belt or is secured in an appropriate child seat.[1087] A similar policy is reflected in s.2 of the Congenital Disabilities (Civil Liability) Act 1976 which provides an exception to the general immunity of the mother under the Act where her negligent driving of a car results in injury to her unborn child.

7-228 **Commonwealth case law** Commonwealth case law also suggests that the parental protective duty is not automatic but only arises where justified by the

---

[1084] [2008] EWCA Civ 907; [2009] 1 W.L.R. 19. See also *Cockbill v Riley* [2013] EWHC 656 (QB) (householder not liable for injuries sustained when 16-year-old belly-flopped or dived into a paddling pool at a party).

[1085] [2008] EWCA Civ 907; [2009] 1 W.L.R. 19 at [34].

[1086] [2008] EWCA Civ 907; [2009] 1 W.L.R. 19 at [37].

[1087] See *J (A Child) v Wilkins* [2001] R.T.R. 19; [2001] P.I.Q.R. P12; and *Hughes v Williams* [2013] EWCA Civ 455; [2013] P.I.Q.R. P17, both of which involved claims for contribution under the Civil Liability (Contribution) Act 1978 against parents. It is a criminal offence for a driver not to ensure that a child passenger below the age of 14 is wearing a seat-belt if there is one available: Road Traffic Act 1988 s.15.

particular circumstances. In *McCallion v Dodd*[1088] a four-year-old child was hit by the defendant motorist when walking in the dark along the roadside with its parents. The defendant claimed a contribution from the father alleging that he was in breach of his duty to his child. The majority of the New Zealand Court of Appeal held that a duty would only arise where a parent had assumed a responsibility to the child and that on the facts, the father did owe a duty and was in breach. In *Hahn v Conley*[1089] the majority of the High Court of Australia followed the approach in *McCallion*. There, a three-year-old was knocked down by the defendant motorist as she crossed the road to see her grandfather who was standing on the other side. The defendant claimed a contribution from the grandfather alleging that he was in breach of his duty to the claimant in failing to stop her crossing the road. In the majority dismissing the claim, Barwick and McTiernan JJ held that the grandfather was not under a duty to take such positive action and Windeyer J found that there was a duty but no breach. Again, in *Arnold v Teno*[1090] where a child was hit by the defendant driver when she ran into the road from behind an ice cream van, the Supreme Court of Canada held that a mother who instructed her children how to cross roads and of the danger of dashing out from behind or in front of ice cream vans, was not in breach in failing to do more to prevent the accident.

Responsibility to third parties for damage done by child There is no general duty arising simply from parenthood to prevent a child from causing damage to third parties and a parent is not vicariously liable for his child.[1091] Rather, any duty must be based on the particular responsibility of the parent for the kind of damage caused by the child. The most obvious basis of responsibility arises where the parent has given a child a dangerous object or allowed him to use it. In *Newton v Edgerley*[1092] a father of a 12-year-old child who allowed him to buy a shotgun was held liable to another child accidentally shot with the gun. The father should have forbidden the use of the gun or carefully instructed the child as to its safe use.[1093] The harmful potential of the object is one factor to be considered. In the leading case of *Smith v Leurs*[1094] parents were held not liable for an eye injury caused by their son's use of a catapult. They knew he had such a device but had taken reasonable care in warning him about the dangers and receiving his assurance that he would 7-229

1088 [1966] N.Z.L.R. 710.

1089 (1971) 126 C.L.R. 276.

1090 (1978) 83 D.L.R. (3d) 609.

1091 *Moon v Towers* (1860) 8 C.B. (N.S.) 611; 141 E.R. 1306. See *B v Arkin* (1996) 138 D.L.R. (4th) 309. No vicarious liability for child shoplifting. Liability only for negligent failure to control child.

1092 [1959] 1 W.L.R. 1031.

1093 See also *Edwards v Smith* [1941] 1 D.L.R. 736, where the father was held liable despite having instructed his son not to use a gun without supervision. He should have taken positive steps to ensure that the child was not able to use it unsupervised; and *Curmi v McLennan* [1994] 1 V.R. 513, where a father was held liable for a gun injury caused when he allowed his son and friends to stay unsupervised in a boathouse where he kept a loaded gun.

1094 (1945) 70 C.L.R. 256. See also *Donaldson v McNiven* [1952] 2 All E.R. 691, where a father was held not liable for injury caused by his son's airgun as the son had promised to use it only in the cellar. Lord Goddard CJ said that the father "cannot be watching his son all day and every day, nor is there any obligation on him to do so". Compare *Beebee v Sales* (1916) 32 T.L.R. 413, where a father was held liable for an eye injury caused by his 15-year-old son's use of an airgun but primarily on the ground that he permitted his son to use it after being warned of his son's dangerous conduct by a neighbour whose window had been broken by a pellet from the airgun.

only use it against the house wall. Again, in *Ricketts v Erith BC*[1095] a shopkeeper was not liable for selling a child a bow and arrow which was subsequently used to injure the claimant. The same result is likely to have applied to the parent, although the case is problematic as the judge emphasised that the boy was "intelligent and bright-looking". Whilst it is clear that the age of the child is relevant,[1096] his presumed temperament can hardly be so. If the parent knows that the child has an aggressive temperament, then that should be relevant to the degree of care required.[1097] In *Hatfield v Pearson*[1098] a Canadian appeal court rejected the notion that a father had to lock away a rifle on the ground that one could impute a mischievous nature to all boys of his son's age and that therefore, instructing his son never to use the rifle was insufficient. The court held that such a duty would only arise where the child had previously shown an unusual propensity to meddle.

7-230 **School responsibility** A teacher is expected to show such care towards a child under his charge as would be exercised by a reasonably careful parent,[1099] taking into account the conditions of school life as distinct from home life,[1100] the number of children in the class[1101] and the nature of those children.[1102] A teacher cannot be expected to insure children against injury from ordinary play in the playground[1103] or, indeed, the classroom.[1104] Failure to supervise with the result that a young child "escapes" from school may lead to liability for resulting injuries to the child[1105] but it must be remembered that "a balance has to be struck between security and preventing a school being turned into a fortress" and that "whatever precautions are taken there is always a risk particularly if a child is determined to act in a way which

1095 [1943] 2 All E.R. 629.

1096 See for example, *North v Wood* [1914] 1 K.B. 629, where a father was held not liable for damage done by his 17-year-old daughter's dog as she was considered old enough to exercise control over the dog.

1097 Starke J in *Smith v Leurs* (1970) C.L.R. 256 at 260, did say that "young boys despite the mischievous tendencies, cannot be classed as wild animals", but where there is knowledge of a child's unusual characteristic the analogy of knowledge based liability for domestic animals may be applicable.

1098 (1957) 6 D.L.R. (2d) 593.

1099 *Ricketts v Erith BC* [1943] 2 All E.R. 629; *Prince v Gregory* [1959] 1 W.L.R. 177. On the other hand, there has to be some recognition that a teacher is not in an identical situation to that of a parent in a domestic setting: see T. Petts, "Visualising a parent with a very large family: the liability of teachers for accidents at school" [2017] J.P.I.L. 13.

1100 *Lyes v Middlesex CC* (1962) 61 L.G.R. 443; applied in *Jacques v Oxfordshire CC* (1967) 66 L.G.R. 440.

1101 *Somerset CC v Kingscott* [1975] 1 W.L.R. 283.

1102 For the duty of local authority towards deaf and dumb children, see *Ellis v Sayers Confectioners* (1963) 61 L.G.R. 299.

1103 See *Ward v Hertfordshire CC* [1970] 1 W.L.R. 356, in which Lord Denning rejected the claim of the "charming little boy" who had hit his head against the playground wall, on the ground that: "it is impossible so to supervise them that they never fall down and hurt themselves". But a school has a duty to provide appropriate supervision in the playground during breaks: see *Palmer v Cornwall CC* [2009] EWCA Civ 456; [2009] E.L.R. 314, where it was held that one dinner lady to supervise 300 pupils during a lunch break at school was inadequate and clearly negligent.

1104 See *Mullin v Richards* [1998] 1 W.L.R. 1304, CA, where the teacher was held not liable at first instance for failing to prevent the classroom "ruler fencing" which led to injury to one of the schoolgirls involved.

1105 *Barnes (An Infant) v Hampshire CC* [1969] 1 W.L.R. 1563; *Jenney v North Lincolnshire CC* [2000] B.L.G.R. 269; [2000] P.I.Q.R. P84. In *Jenney* the defendant was held in breach of duty as it could not show a non-negligent explanation for the presence of the child on a road during school hours. The degree of supervision was adequate but there was no system for securing all the exits.

breaks the rules designed to protect him or her".[1106] School premises must be kept in proper repair and a pupil injured by the defective condition of the playground,[1107] of a classroom door,[1108] or from snow on the chapel steps[1109] may therefore recover damages for his injuries. Reasonable steps should be taken to protect pupils from the dangers of practical work.[1110]

School's non-delegable duty The responsibility of a school authority does not necessarily end at the school gate. In *Woodland v Essex County Council*[1111] the 10-year old claimant suffered severe injuries in the course of a swimming lesson arranged by the school but provided and supervised by a third party. The Supreme Court held that the school owed a non-delegable duty with respect to the safety of its pupils and though performance of the school's educational functions can be delegated to others, responsibility for negligence in carrying out those functions cannot.[1112] Since schools exercise control over pupils, who are both vulnerable and highly dependent on the observance of proper standards of care by those in control, when a school delegates control to someone else it is reasonable that the school should be answerable for the careful exercise of that control. This applies only where an independent contractor is performing functions which the school has assumed a duty to perform, generally in school hours and on school premises (or at other times or places where the school may carry out its educational functions). The school would not owe a non-delegable duty in relation to matters that it is not their duty to perform, for example where independent contractors provide extra-curricular activities outside school hours, such as school trips in the holidays[1113]; nor for the negligence of those to whom no control over the child has been delegated, such as bus drivers or the theatres, zoos or museums to which children may be taken by school staff in school hours. In applying this to the claim in *Woodland* itself Lord Sumption noted that: 7-231

> "The swimming lessons were an integral part of the school's teaching function. They did not occur on school premises, but they occurred in school hours in a place where the school chose to carry out this part of its functions. The teaching and the supervisory functions of the school, and the control of the child that went with them, were delegated by the school … The alleged negligence occurred in the course of the very functions which the school assumed an obligation to perform and delegated to its contractors. It must follow that if the latter were negligent in performing those functions and the child was injured as a result, the educational authority is in breach of duty."[1114]

Playing and bullying It is the duty of the school to supervise children in the 7-232

1106 *Nwabudike v London Borough of Southwark* [1997] E.L.R. 35.

1107 *Ching v Surrey CC* [1910] 1 K.B. 736.

1108 *Morris v Caernarvon CC* [1910] 1 K.B. 840.

1109 *Woodward v Hastings Corp* [1945] K.B. 174.

1110 e.g. unfenced machinery: *Butt v Inner London Education Authority* (1968) 66 L.G.R. 379.

1111 [2013] UKSC 66; [2014] A.C. 537.

1112 The relevant characteristics of the relationships which may give rise to such a non-delegable duty were set out by Lord Sumption [2013] UKSC 66; [2014] A.C. 537 at [23]. See para.6-70.

1113 See e.g. *XVW v Gravesend Grammar Schools for Girls* [2012] EWHC 575 (QB); [2012] E.L.R. 417 (school not liable for rape of claimant pupils by a local man on a school trip to Belize).

1114 [2013] UKSC 66; [2014] A.C. 537 at [26]. The Supreme Court acknowledged that this places a greater responsibility on a school or education authority than would apply to parents: see per Lord Sumption at [25](6) and per Baroness Hale at [41]. Part of the rationale for the imposition of a non-delegable duty was that this was a reasonable response to the modern trend of public authorities to "outsource" their services, and that in the past education authorities would have been vicariously liable to claimants injured in this way (ibid. at [25](4) and [40]). At the trial on liability both the playground but supervision before school[1115] or as the children leave school may not be required. In *Wilson v The Governors of the Sacred Heart Roman Catholic School*,[1116] it was held that the school was not negligent in failing to supervise the departure of pupils to the school gate at the end of the day in the same way as the dinner break would have been supervised. Hirst LJ said:

> "the very short period in which the pupils moved from the school building to the gate at the other end of the playground is quite different [from the dinner break period in the playground]. Moreover, and to my mind most importantly, there was no evidence that supervision at that juncture, as contrasted with the lunch break, is standard procedure, as it surely would be if it was a reasonable requirement."

In *Kearn-Price v Kent CC*,[1117] Dyson LJ, giving the judgment of the Court of Appeal, distinguished *Wilson* when holding the defendant liable for a playground injury in the pre-school period caused by a leather football. The use of such footballs had been banned by the school and a pre-school spot check would not have imposed an undue burden on the school. These circumstances and the limited evidence of school practice distinguished the case from *Wilson*. In *Bradford-Smart v West Sussex CC*[1118] the Court of Appeal held that a school could be liable to a bullied pupil for failing to use its disciplinary powers to prevent the conduct and that the duty could extend to bullying outside the school premises as where a teacher saw one pupil attacking another outside the school gates. On the facts, it held that taking into account the magnitude of the risk, the extent of the harm, and the practicality and likely effectiveness of steps, there was no breach of duty. There had been no evidence of an adverse effect on the claimant's educational performance and professional opinion would be agreed that enough had been done.

7-233 **Sports supervision** Misuse of gymnasium equipment may lead to liability[1119] and common practice may be no defence if risks remain. In *Cassidy v City of Manchester*[1120] a 13-year-old playing goalkeeper in an indoor hockey game was injured when she tripped on the leg of a bench being used as the goal. The teacher's evidence was that the positioning of the bench had been adopted in his teaching training college and by other local schools. It was conceded that it was not universal practice, but the education authority argued, by analogy with medical cases, that it had followed a "respected body of opinion in the gymnastic field which recognised the propriety of such practice". Hutchison LJ upheld the finding of liability by the trial judge, commenting that the picture would have been different if the practice had been universal. He also rejected the claim that the girl had been contributorily negligent, saying what she did was "the sort of thing that an enthusiastic child may do in the heat of a game of hockey". Failure adequately to supervise contact sports

swimming teacher and the lifeguard were held to have been negligent in failing to identify that the claimant was in difficulties in the swimming pool: *Woodland v Maxwell* [2015] EWHC 273 (QB).

1115 *Mays v Essex CC*, *The Times*, 11 October 1975 (no duty to supervise play on a frosty patch before school started).

1116 [1998] P.I.Q.R. P145; *Webster v Ridgeway Foundation School* [2010] EWHC 157 (QB); [2010] E.L.R. 694—no duty to prevent an assault which took place on school premises after school.

1117 [2002] EWCA Civ 1539; [2003] P.I.Q.R. P11.

1118 [2002] EWCA Civ 7; [2002] 1 F.C.R. 425. See also Elvin, "The Liability of Schools for Bullying" [2002] C.L.J. 255.

1119 *Fowles v Bedfordshire CC* [1995] P.I.Q.R. P380 where lack of supervision and mispositioning of a safety mat led to injury and liability.

1120 unreported 12 July 1995.

such as rugby may also give rise to liability.[1121] The same is true of potentially dangerous activities such as swimming.[1122] However, there are limits to what can be expected of a school. In *Chittock v Woodbridge School*[1123] it was held that issuing a reprimand to a school student who had skied off piste contrary to instructions was within the reasonable range of responses for the teacher to have adopted. Failure to prevent the student skiing or requiring him to ski subject to supervision did not amount to negligence. The school was not liable for a subsequent injury to the student caused by his careless skiing. In any case, supervision would not have prevented the second accident. The Court of Appeal has held that a school's responsibility to its pupils does not extend to taking out insurance on their behalf against sporting injuries, nor to advising their parents to take out such insurance.[1124] Where facilities or activities are offered to adults, a school may expect more foresight of risk to be shown.[1125]

Educational development In *Phelps v Hillingdon LBC*[1126] the House of Lords held that an educational psychologist employed by a local authority could owe a duty of care to a child who had been referred to the psychologist. The reduction of a child's level of achievement as a result of failure to diagnose dyslexia and to take appropriate action, was regarded as a form of "personal injury".[1127] Lord Nicholls said that the duty would extend to teachers of all pupils and not just those with special educational needs, and he was "not persuaded by fears" that resources would be diverted from teaching to litigation or that schools would focus on defensive record keeping. Rather the courts would weed out hopeless claims and ensure the door was not open to claims based on poor quality teaching. Lord Clyde similarly argued that "[a]ny fear of a flood of claims may be countered by the consideration that in order to get off the ground the claimant must be able to demonstrate that the standard of care fell short of that set by the *Bolam* test" which would allow for different approaches to teaching method and practice.[1128] In *Robinson v St Helens* 7-234

1121 *Smoldon v Whitworth* [1997] P.I.Q.R. P133. See para.7-167.

1122 *O'Shea v Royal Borough of Kingston on Thames* [1995] P.I.Q.R. P208 (local authority pool but the principle is the same: prohibition of diving was the only safe system).

1123 [2002] EWCA Civ 915; [2003] P.I.Q.R. P6. See also *Hammsersley-Gonsalves v Redcar and Cleveland BC* [2012] EWCA Civ 1135; [2012] E.L.R. 431 (claimant pupil struck by golf club swung by another pupil; teacher could not be expected to see every action of each of 22 boys and so held not negligent in supervising the group); *Porter v Barking & Dagenham LBC, The Times,* 9 April 1990 (QBD) (allowing two 14-year-old boys to practise putting the shot unsupervised not negligent); *Murray v McCullough* [2016] NIQB 52 (school discharged its duty of care to 15-year-old pupil who suffered dental injuries when hit in the mouth by a hockey stick by highly recommending the use of a mouth guard; no obligation to make the wearing of mouth guards mandatory); *Pook v Rossall School* [2018] EWHC 522 (QB); [2018] E.L.R. 402 (no breach of duty in allowing ten-year-old child to run from changing rooms to hockey pitch).

1124 *Van Oppen v Trustees of the Bedford Charity* [1990] 1 W.L.R. 235.

1125 In *Comer v St Patrick's RC School* (1997) unreported, Buxton LJ rejected a claim by a parent injured in a fathers' day race, saying: "It was not reasonably foreseeable that in these circumstances any adult in the situation in which this race took place would so run as to expose himself to injury."

1126 [2001] 2 A.C. 619. See paras 13-15 and 13-30.

1127 As to the nature of the injury, see further para.1-34.

1128 It follows that a claim that a student failed to reach an appropriate level of educational achievement due to negligent teaching requires expert evidence as to responsible educational practice in order to apply the *Bolam* test: *Abramova v Oxford Institute of Legal Practice* [2011] EWHC 613 (QB); [2011] E.L.R. 385.

MBC[1129] the Court of Appeal followed the House of Lords in holding that the psychological harm following a misdiagnosis of dyslexia was classed as a personal injury. Brooke LJ stated that a claimant was entitled to recover for psychological harm falling short of a recognisable psychiatric injury as such harm was the "kind of damage which the duty exists to prevent".

7-235 **School's liability to third parties** In the leading case of *Carmarthenshire CC v Lewis*[1130] a child of four at a nursery school was left unattended, so that he left the classroom and got onto the highway, with the result that the driver of a lorry swerved to avoid the child, struck a telegraph post and was killed. The school was held liable to the estate of the driver. Lord Goddard said that the applicable standard of care was that of the "careful parent".[1131]

7-236 **Local authority responsibility for harm inflicted by foster parents** In *NA v Nottinghamshire CC*[1132] the Court of Appeal held that a non-delegable duty was not owed by a local authority in respect of intentional harm inflicted by a foster parent on a child placed with foster parents by the authority, though the Court differed in their reasons. Tomlinson LJ considered that fostering was not a function which was an integral part of the positive duty assumed by the local authority because a local authority cannot itself provide foster care, but only arrange for it to be provided by others; by arranging the foster placement the local authority discharged rather than delegated its duty to provide accommodation and maintenance for the child. Burnett LJ accepted that the local authority was "under a duty to care for the child – to promote its welfare and to protect it from harm", but this was not an unqualified duty; it had to be qualified by "reasonable practicability". The English cases concerning non-delegable duties were all concerned with negligence, not claims for assault, and if the claim could not succeed applying the principles of vicarious liability for assault (a claim based on vicarious liability had been rejected) it was difficult to imagine circumstances in which the court would go on to fix a defendant with liability for breach of a non-delegable duty not to assault the claimant. Black LJ was less convinced that the deliberate nature of the foster parents' conduct should be decisive, since the question turned on the nature of the local authority's duty. It might extend to a duty not to assault the child (reflecting a parent's duty not to assault the child), and that duty not to assault the child would be the duty entrusted to the foster parents by the local authority. However, to impose a non-delegable duty on a local authority would be unreasonably burdensome and contrary to the interests of other children in care. It would be likely to result in more of the local authorities' scarce resources being employed in an attempt to ensure that nothing went wrong and would lead to defensive practice in relation to the placement of children. The judge had been correct to conclude that the imposition of a non-delegable duty would not be fair, just and reasonable. On Appeal, the Supreme Court agreed that a local authority does not come under a non-delegable duty in respect of the abuse of children placed with foster parents.[1133] A non-delegable duty would risk creating a conflict between the local authority's duty towards children under the Child

[1129] [2002] EWCA Civ 1099; [2003] P.I.Q.R. P9 at [36].
[1130] [1955] A.C. 549.
[1131] [1955] A.C. 549 at 561.
[1132] [2015] EWCA Civ 1139; [2016] Q.B. 739; S. Tofaris, "Vicarious Liability and Non-Delegable Duty for Child Abuse in Foster Care: A Step Too Far?" (2016) 79 M.L.R. 884.
[1133] *Armes v Nottinghamshire County Council* [2017] UKSC 60; [2018] A.C. 355; although the Supreme

Care Act 1980 and the authority's interests in avoiding potential liability, and would also, in effect, constitute a form of state insurance for the actions of the child's family members.

Court went on to hold that the local authority could be vicariously liable for the abuse of children placed in the care of foster parents; see para.6-11.

CHAPTER 8

BREACH OF STATUTORY DUTY

TABLE OF CONTENTS

1. INTRODUCTION

General principles[1] Legislation covers most aspects of social and economic activity, regulating relationships between private individuals and between private individuals and public bodies. Almost all public bodies rely upon a legislative framework authorising their activities, creating both the power to act and, in many cases, duties to act in the discharge of public functions. Sometimes the activities of public bodies correspond broadly to those of private individuals (for example, in the provision of health care through the National Health Service) but many have no direct counterpart in private law. This will tend to be the case where the public body is engaged in a "regulatory" function with a view to protecting the public, or sections of the public, from harm (in its broadest sense). Often, it may be very obvious that a failure to discharge a statutory duty could cause damage to someone, but it does not follow that they are entitled to claim damages at common law for such a breach of duty. A person who has suffered damage as a result of the breach of a statutory duty *may* have an action in tort, classified by Lord Browne-Wilkinson in *X (Minors) v Bedfordshire CC*[2] as an "action for breach of statutory duty 8-01

[1] See, generally, Stanton, Skidmore, Harris and Wright, *Statutory Torts* (London: Sweet & Maxwell, 2003); Buckley, "Liability in Tort for Breach of Statutory Duty" (1984) 100 L.Q.R. 204; K. Stanton, "New Forms of the Tort of Breach of Statutory Duty" (2004) 120 L.Q.R. 324.

[2] [1995] 2 A.C. 633.

simpliciter". In English law this is a specific common law action which is distinct from the tort of negligence, even where the negligence action is based on a common law duty of care arising either from the imposition of a statutory duty or from the performance of it. The careless performance of a statutory duty does not in itself give rise to any cause of action in the absence of either a right of action for "breach of statutory duty simpliciter" or a common law duty of care in negligence. The question, then, is when will breach of a statute give rise to an action for damages at common law?

8-02 **Parliamentary intention** Some statutes are expressly designed to create new civil remedies,[3] and others are intended to modify or clarify existing common law rights of action.[4] Equally, there are some statutes which create criminal sanctions but which state expressly that they do not confer any civil remedy[5]; and some may create both criminal and civil remedies.[6] Unfortunately, most legislation fails to give any express guidance as to whether an action for damages is available for its breach, and then the courts have to decide what Parliament intended. Determining Parliament's intention when it has pointedly declined to express one is something of a haphazard process. The courts look to the construction of the statute, relying upon a number of "presumptions" for guidance, but in practice there are so many conflicting presumptions, with variable weightings, that it can be extremely difficult to predict how the courts will respond to a particular statute.[7]

8-03 One particular area, industrial safety legislation, has tended to dominate the action for breach of statutory duty.[8] Indeed, it has been suggested that when it concerns industrial welfare, penal legislation results in absolute liability in tort, and in all other cases it is ignored.[9] This statement was an admitted oversimplification, both as to the type of legislation which is treated as actionable and the standard of liability, but even today it is not an unreasonable working hypothesis. On the whole, if the statute prescribes a safety standard which more or less corresponds to a common law duty it will be easier to infer an action, although there are exceptions both ways. But where a statute imposes general administrative functions on public bodies and involves the exercise of broad administrative discretion following subjective judgments the courts are unlikely to find that Parliament intended to create a private law right of action for breach of the statutory duty.[10]

---

3 e.g. the Fatal Accidents Acts (consolidated in the Fatal Accidents Act 1976); Misrepresentation Act 1967; Nuclear Installations Act 1965.

4 e.g. Occupiers' Liability Acts 1957 and 1984.

5 e.g. Guard Dogs Act 1975; Safety of Sports Grounds Act 1975.

6 e.g. Protection from Harassment Act 1997.

7 "You might as well toss a coin to decide it", per Lord Denning MR in *Ex p. Island Records Ltd* [1978] Ch. 122 at 135. "In effect the judge can do what he likes, and then select one of the conflicting principles stated by his predecessors in order to justify his decision" in Williams, "The Effect of Penal Legislation in the Law of Tort" (1960) 23 M.L.R. 233 at 246. In *Todd v Adams and Chope (t/a Trelawney Fishing Co) (The Margaretha Maria)* [2002] EWCA Civ 509; [2002] 2 Lloyd's Rep. 293 at [15], Neuberger J described the last three sentences of this paragraph as "regrettably, correct".

8 The exceptionally long incubation periods of some industrial diseases can sometimes require the courts to construe legislative provisions which have long since ceased to be in force: see e.g. *McDonald v National Grid* [2014] UKSC 53; [2015] A.C. 1128 (considering the Factory and Workshop Act 1901, the Asbestos Industry Regulations 1931 and the Factories Act 1937).

9 Williams, "The Effect of Penal Legislation in the Law of Tort" (1960) 23 M.L.R. 233 at 246.

10 *X (Minors) v Bedfordshire CC* [1995] 2 A.C. 633 at 732; *O'Rourke v Camden LBC* [1998] A.C. 188 HL.

Essentials of the action Much of this chapter is taken up with determining when breach of a statutory standard gives rise to an action in private law for breach of statutory duty. The construction of each statute turns ultimately on its particular wording and it is difficult to formulate principles of general application. It is possible here only to give broad guidelines as to how the courts are likely to react to particular types of legislation. Once the question of whether the statute is ever actionable in private law has been determined, there are four further issues that must be considered: **8-04**

(1) The claimant must show that the damage he suffered falls within the ambit of the statute, namely that it was of the type that the legislation was intended to prevent and that the claimant belonged to the category of persons that the statute was intended to protect. It is not sufficient simply that the loss would not have occurred if the defendant had complied with the terms of the statute. This rule performs a function similar to that of remoteness of damage.
(2) It must be proved that the statutory duty was breached. The standard of liability varies considerably with the wording of the statute, ranging from liability in negligence to strict liability.
(3) As with other torts, the claimant must prove that the breach of statutory duty caused his loss, which he will fail to do if the damage would have occurred in any event.
(4) Finally, there is the question whether there are any defences available to the action.[11]

2. CATEGORISING BREACHES OF STATUTORY DUTY

Distinguish public law actions In *X (Minors) v Bedfordshire CC*,[12] Lord Browne-Wilkinson, having pointed to the obvious distinction between actions for damages based on a private law cause of action and actions in public law to enforce the performance of a statutory duty, now brought by way of judicial review, observed that private law claims could be classified into four categories: **8-05**

(a) actions for breach of statutory duty simpliciter (i.e. irrespective of carelessness);
(b) actions based solely on the careless performance of a statutory duty in the absence of any other common law right of action;
(c) actions based on a common law duty of care arising either from the imposition of the statutory duty or from the performance of it; and
(d) misfeasance in public office.[13]

Breach of statutory duty simpliciter Category (a) is the subject of this chapter. The basic proposition is that, in the ordinary case, a breach of statutory duty does not, by itself, give rise to any private law cause of action. Such a cause of action can arise if it can be shown, as a matter of construction of the statute, that the "statutory duty was imposed for the protection of a limited class of the public and that Parliament intended to confer on members of that class a private right of action for **8-06**

---

[11] In *Fytche v Wincanton Logistics Plc* [2003] EWCA Civ 874; [2003] I.C.R. 1582; [2004] 4 All E.R. 221 at [17], Waller LJ commented that he had found the guidelines in this paragraph helpful.
[12] [1995] 2 A.C. 633.
[13] See para.13-132 onwards. for discussion of the tort of misfeasance in public office.

breach of the duty".[14] There is no general rule by which one can determine the intention of Parliament, but there are a number of "indicators". Thus, if the statute provides no other remedy for its breach and the parliamentary intention to protect a limited class is shown, this indicates that there may be a private action, since otherwise there would be no means of enforcing the protection that the legislation was intended to grant. Where the statute does provide an alternative remedy to enforce the relevant duty that will normally indicate that the statutory right was designed to be enforceable by those means and not by private right of action. However, the mere existence of some other remedy is not necessarily decisive. It may still be possible to show that on the true construction of the Act the protected class was intended by Parliament to have a private remedy.[15] On the other hand, statutory provisions establishing a regulatory system or a scheme of social welfare for the benefit of the public at large have not been held to give rise to a private law right of action for damages for breach of statutory duty:

> "Although regulatory or welfare legislation affecting a particular area of activity does in fact provide protection to those individuals particularly affected by that activity, the legislation is not to be treated as being passed for the benefit of those individuals but for the benefit of society in general."[16]

8-07 **Careless performance of a statutory duty** Category (b) cases do not give rise to any independent private law claim. Thus, the careless performance of a statutory duty does not in itself give rise to any cause of action in the absence of either a right of action for breach of statutory duty simpliciter (category (a)) or a common law duty of care in negligence (category (c)). Where a statute authorises the carrying out of an activity which would necessarily involve the commission of a private law wrong, such as private nuisance, the statute provides a defence to a claim based on that common law wrong on the ground that if Parliament has authorised the activity and the nuisance is an unavoidable consequence of that activity Parliament must also have authorised the nuisance.[17] On the other hand, unless there is express provision in the statute, if the activity has been carried on negligently so as to cause a nuisance the defendant will be responsible, and the defence of statutory authority will not apply. Thus, the careless exercise of a statutory power or duty will negate a defence of statutory authorisation to an existing common law right of action, but where there is no freestanding common law right of action the negligent exercise of the power or duty will not, of itself, create one.[18]

8-08 **Common law duty of care** Category (c) consists of actions based on a common law duty of care in the tort of negligence arising either from the imposition of the

---

14 [1995] 2 A.C. 633 at 731.

15 [1995] 2 A.C. 633 at 731. For example, where statutory duties are imposed on employers for the protection of employees; see para.8-17; or where the statutory duty is concerned with the safety of the highway for the protection of road users: *Roe v Sheffield City Council* [2003] EWCA Civ 1; [2004] Q.B. 653.

16 [1995] 2 A.C. 633 at 731–732.

17 *Allen v Gulf Oil Refining Ltd* [1981] A.C. 1001; *Geddis v Proprietors of the Bann Reservoir* (1878) 3 App. Cas. 430 at 455. See para.19-87.

18 See the summary of Lord Browne-Wilkinson in *X (Minors) v Bedfordshire CC* [1995] 2 A.C. 633 at 732–733. See also, per Lord Jauncey at 728–729: "Thus careless performance of an authorised act rather than amounting to breach of a new duty simply removes a defence to a common law right of action."

statutory duty or from its performance.[19] The claim alleges either that a statutory duty gives rise to a common law duty of care or that in the course of carrying out a statutory duty the defendant has brought about such a relationship between himself and the claimant that a duty of care arises at common law.[20] Alternatively, irrespective of the position of the statutory body, it is claimed that the authority's servant was under a duty of care to the claimant in the course of carrying out the authority's statutory function, for which the authority is vicariously liable. In this situation, either the claim must be based on an existing situation where a common law duty of care in negligence has been held to exist or the claimant must establish that it is appropriate, applying the *Caparo* tripartite test,[21] to establish a new duty of care. As a general proposition, a common law duty of care cannot be superimposed on a statutory duty if the observance of the common law duty of care would be inconsistent with, or have a tendency to discourage, the due performance of the statutory duty.[22]

In *Gorringe v Calderdale MBC*[23] Lord Hoffmann, speaking of the relationship between statutory duties and common law negligence, indicated that it would be "unusual if the mere existence of the statutory duty could generate a common law duty of care",[24] and found it "difficult to imagine a case in which a common law duty can be founded simply upon the failure (however irrational) to provide some benefit which a public authority has power (or a public law duty) to provide".[25] Lord Scott went further, observing that "if a statutory duty does not give rise to a private right to sue for breach, the duty cannot create a duty of care that would not have been owed at common law if the statute were not there".[26] Lord Hoffmann was clear, however, that these comments were limited to situations in which an attempt is made to impose on a public authority a common law duty to act, based **8-09**

---

19 For detailed discussion see Ch.13. See also Bailey, "Public authority liability in negligence: the continued search for coherence" (2006) 26 L.S. 154.

20 [1995] 2 A.C. 633 at 735.

21 *Caparo Industries Plc v Dickman* [1990] 2 A.C. 605. See paras 7-17 onwards.

22 [1995] 2 A.C. 633 at 739. See also *Jain v Trent Strategic HA* [2009] UKHL 4; [2009] 1 A.C. 853; [2009] 1 All E.R. 957 and para.8-39.

23 [2004] UKHL 15; [2004] 1 W.L.R. 1057.

24 [2004] UKHL 15; [2004] 1 W.L.R. 1057 at [23].

25 [2004] UKHL 15; [2004] 1 W.L.R. 1057 at [32]. This would be a "category (b) case"; see para.8-07. In *Godden v Kent and Medway Strategic HA* [2004] EWHC 1629 (QB); [2004] Lloyd's Rep. Med. 521 the claimants argued that the defendant health authority owed a common law duty of care to take steps to protect them from a general practitioner who had been convicted of a number of indecent assaults on patients, arising from the National Health Service Act 1977 s.29. This section conferred authority to make arrangements for the provision of general medical services in a particular locality. The claimants accepted that it did not create an action for breach of statutory duty "simpliciter" (category (a), above). Gray J struck out the claim as disclosing no reasonable cause of action, since s.29 did not provide that the defendants were responsible for the provision of medical services in their locality (which was the responsibility of medical practitioners); rather it was concerned with the structure and administration of the NHS [in other words, it was a category (b) case]. However, his Lordship refused to strike out an allegation that a common law duty of care owed to patients at risk of abuse from the general practitioner arose from the knowledge that employees of the health authority had acquired of his actions (for which the health authority could be vicariously liable), since there was nothing in the Act which could be said to have excluded the existence of such a duty of care [in other words this was a category (c) claim].

26 [2004] UKHL 15; [2004] 1 W.L.R. 1057 at [71]. See also *X v Hounslow LBC* [2009] EWCA Civ 286; [2009] 2 F.L.R. 262; [2009] N.P.C. 63 (no duty owed by local authority to vulnerable adults abused by third parties); *Sandford v London Borough of Waltham Forest* [2008] EWHC 1106 (QB); [2008] B.L.G.R. 816 (no duty of care to supply disability aids or equipment to claimant since this was simply an attempt to enforce the performance of the local authority's statutory duty).

solely on the existence of a broad public law duty. In cases where public authorities have actually done acts or entered into relationships or undertaken responsibilities which give rise to a common law duty of care:

> "the fact that the public authority acted pursuant to a statutory power or public duty does not necessarily negative the existence of a duty. A hospital trust provides medical treatment pursuant to the public law duty in the National Health Service Act 1977, but the existence of its common law duty is based simply upon its acceptance of a professional relationship with the patient no different from that which would be accepted by a doctor in private practice. The duty rests upon a solid, orthodox common law foundation and the question is not whether it is created by the statute but whether the terms of the statute (for example, in requiring a particular thing to be done or conferring a discretion) are sufficient to exclude it."[27]

In truth, this looks very much like the distinction between acts and omissions that underpins a significant body of the law of negligence.[28] The argument seems to be that a broad, public law duty (a "target duty") cannot supply the wherewithal upon which to build the relevant relationship between claimant and defendant in order to establish a duty of care in negligence. Thus failure by a water company to comply with its statutory obligation under s.106 of the Water Industry Act 1991 to allow access to its sewers does not give rise to a claim for common law nuisance.[29]

8-10 **Relationship between the parties** If, however, there are other features of the relationship between the parties to which the tort of negligence would, in the absence of the statutory duty, attach significance in deciding whether a duty of care should be owed, the existence of the statute will not preclude a conclusion that a duty of care should be imposed, unless there is something in the statute to exclude or limit such a duty.[30] In *Rice v Secretary of State for Trade and Industry; Thompson v Secretary of State for Trade and Industry*[31] the claimants were registered dock workers who worked at Liverpool docks between 1955 and 1967. Under a statutory scheme derived from the Dock Workers (Regulation of Employment) Act 1946 s.1 and operated by the National Dock Labour Board (NDLB) registered dock workers would turn up for work in the morning and if there was work available would be allocated to a registered employer. When a dock worker was not working for a registered employer he was in the employment of NDLB. The claimants had worked for a registered employer unloading asbestos in hessian sacks, with virtually no precautions taken for their safety. They had both developed asbestos-related disease. The issue was whether the NDLB owed a duty of care in respect of the health and safety of the claimants (the registered employer no longer being in existence and their insurers being unidentifiable). The Court of Appeal held that NDLB did owe a duty of care to the workers. The imposition of a duty of care was

---

27 [2004] UKHL 15; [2004] 1 W.L.R. 1057 at [38].

28 See, e.g. *Stovin v Wise* [1996] A.C. 923, and paras 7-51 onwards. See also *Furnell v Flaherty* [2013] EWHC 377 (QB) in which a negligence claim against a public health regulator for allegedly failing to take a proactive role in events surrounding an E.Coli outbreak at a visitor attraction was struck out.

29 See *Dwr Cymru Cyfyngedig (Welsh Water) v Barratt Homes Ltd* [2013] EWCA Civ 233; [2013] 1 W.L.R. 3486. The claimants' only remedy is to seek an order compelling performance of the public law duty: see *Barratt Homes Ltd v Dwr Cymru Cyfyngedig (Welsh Water)* [2009] UKSC 13; [2010] 1 All E.R. 965 (decided in earlier proceedings between the same parties).

30 See, per Lord Steyn in *Gorringe v Calderdale MBC* [2004] UKHL 15; [2004] 1 W.L.R. 1057 at [3].

31 [2007] EWCA Civ 289; [2007] I.C.R. 1469; [2007] P.I.Q.R. P23.

consistent with the policy of the statute. It was not a broad target power or duty directed at the public at large. It was a specific duty to protect individual employees against a known serious risk to their health. Thus, although the principles in *Stovin v Wise* and *Gorringe* applied, NDLB would have undertaken an equivalent common law duty if they had been a private organisation in an equivalent relationship with the dock workers and performing and undertaking equivalent functions. Although the relationships were highly unusual, *Rice* can therefore be explained as a case where the statutory obligations provided the context for the relationship between the parties, and it was the nature of that relationship, rather than the statutory duties themselves, that gave rise to the duty of care.[32] Similarly, in *Smith v The Ministry of Defence*[33] the Supreme Court held, by a majority, that the well-established common law duty of care owed by an employer to his employee enabled negligence actions to proceed against the Ministry of Defence in respect of service personnel killed or injured in Iraq due to the provision of allegedly defective equipment or inadequate training.

3. Is the Breach Actionable?

Express provision Simply because the damage suffered by the claimant appears to fall within the terms of the statute, it does not necessarily follow that an action for breach of statutory duty simpliciter will lie. If, of course, the statute in question or some other statute[34] expressly provides that a civil remedy does[35] or does not[36] lie for breach of the duty there is less difficulty. On the other hand, even where the statute expressly provides for a civil remedy for its breach there can still be questions as to the extent of its application.[37] For example, in *Merlin v British Nuclear Fuels Plc*,[38] it was held that the term "damage to property" in s.7(1) of the Nuclear Installations Act 1965 meant physical damage to tangible property and did not extend to economic loss. Contamination by ionising radiation which did not damage the fabric of the property but increased the risk of injury to the health of occupants in the future, and reduced the value of the property, was not actionable. *Merlin* was distinguished by the Court of Appeal in *Blue Circle Industries Plc v* 8-11

32 See [2007] EWCA Civ 289; [2007] I.C.R. 1469; [2007] P.I.Q.R. P23 at [42], per May LJ (with whom Keene and Smith LJJ agreed). The issues of breach of duty and causation in this case were dealt with subsequently in *Rice (Executrix) v Secretary of State for Business Enterprise and Regulatory Reform* [2008] EWHC 3216 (QB).

33 [2013] UKSC 41; [2014] 1 A.C. 52. See further paras 13-53 to 13-54.

34 s.71 of the Health and Safety at Work Act 1974 provided for civil liability for breach of the Building Regulations, now repealed and replaced by s.38 of the Building Act 1984 but still not in force. It has been suggested that there is liability for breach of the Building Regulations even without s.38: *Anns v London Borough of Merton* [1978] A.C. 728 at 759, per Lord Wilberforce. cf. *Peabody Donation Fund (Governors) v Sir Lindsay Parkinson & Co Ltd* [1985] A.C. 210 HL.

35 For examples of express provisions in a statute that a civil remedy will lie for a breach of the duty created see: Nuclear Installations Act 1965 s.12 and the Nuclear Installations Act 1969; Gas Act 1965 s.14(1); Health and Safety at Work Act 1974 s.47(2); Highways Act 1980 s.41; Consumer Protection Act 1987 s.41; Water Resources Act 1991 s.48A (added by the Water Act 2003 s.24). The Protection from Harassment Act 1997 expressly creates both a criminal offence and a civil remedy for breach of the Act.

36 e.g. Health and Safety at Work Act 1974 s.47(1)(a), which negatives civil liability for breach of ss.2–8 of the Act.

37 In addition to showing that the statute imposes a liability to civil action the claimant must of course show that this liability attaches to the particular defendant sued: see *Smith v George Wimpey & Co Ltd* [1972] 2 Q.B. 329.

38 [1990] 2 Q.B. 557.

Ministry of Defence,[39] where it was held that contamination of land by radioactive material constitutes physical damage to the land, even though the consequence was economic in that the property was worth less and expenditure was incurred in removing the contaminated top soil. The extensive cleansing operations and restrictions on the use of the land was sufficient to demonstrate physical damage and thus enable the claimants to recover for the consequent diminution in the value of their property.[40] In *No.1 West India Quay (Residential) Ltd v East Tower Apartments Ltd*[41] the Court of Appeal drew attention to the reasoning underlying the legislative provision in s.4 of the Landlord and Tenant Act 1988 that: "A claim that a person has broken any duty under this Act may be made the subject of civil proceedings in like manner as any other claim in tort for breach of statutory duty." By adding a remedy which was not available at common law a less draconian and more precise approach to relief for breach of the Act was afforded to the court.[42]

8-12 **Statute is silent** Frequently, however, the statute is either silent as to any remedy or merely prescribes a criminal penalty. It is at this point that the presumptions or "indicators"[43] have to be relied upon, though they provide a rather uncertain guide. The initial, working, presumption appears to be that there is no civil remedy for breach of the statute. Some indicators point in favour of Parliament having intended to create a private law action; more seem to point away from such a conclusion.[44] The difficulty in applying the indicators is compounded by the fact that there is no explicit weighting of the indicators, though as a general proposition where the damage is physical, particularly personal injuries, the claimant is on stronger ground than where the damage is economic loss[45]; and where the claim is against a public

---

39 [1999] Ch. 289 CA.

40 See also the Highways Act 1980 s.41, which imposes a duty on highway authorities to maintain the highway (subject to the defence in s.58 for the highway authority to prove that it exercised reasonable care) and s.41(1A) (inserted by the Railways and Transport Safety Act 2003 s.111) which provides that "a highway authority are under a duty to ensure, so far as is reasonably practicable, that safe passage along a highway is not endangered by snow or ice" (reversing *Goodes v East Sussex CC* [2000] 1 W.L.R. 1356). The duty to maintain the highway under s.41 does not include a duty to provide appropriate warning signs of hazards on the highway, since this does not involve repair of the physical or structural condition of the highway or render it more or less passable for ordinary traffic: *Gorringe v Calderdale MBC* [2004] UKHL 15; [2004] 1 W.L.R. 1057. See also *Valentine v Transport for London* [2010] EWCA Civ 1358; [2011] P.I.Q.R. P7; cf. *Wilkinson v York City Council* [2011] EWCA Civ 207. The expression "maintain and keep in good condition and repair" in s.28 of the Tramways Act 1870 involves the same duty as that imposed on a highway authority by the Highways Act 1980 s.41. This is an absolute duty, but it does not require perfection. The standard of maintenance is measured by considerations of safety: *Roe v Sheffield City Council* [2003] EWCA Civ 1; [2004] Q.B. 653, per Pill LJ at [61] and [62] (cf. Sedley LJ at [91]–[96]). The duty applies to a dangerous accumulation of water on the surface of the highway, caused by a longstanding blockage of the highway drainage system: *Mott MacDonald Ltd v Department of Transport* [2006] EWCA Civ 1089; [2006] 1 W.L.R. 3356. cf. *Ali v City of Bradford* [2010] EWCA Civ 1282; [2012] 1 W.L.R. 161 (no civil action for breach of statutory duty against a highway authority for failing to prevent obstruction of the highway contrary to the Highways Act 1980 s.130(3)).

41 [2018] EWCA Civ 250; [2018] 1 W.L.R. 5682.

42 See, per Lewison LJ in [2018] EWCA Civ 250; [2018] 1 W.L.R. 5682 at [21].

43 *X v Bedfordshire CC* [1995] 2 A.C. 633 at 731, per Lord Browne-Wilkinson. See also *Dwr Cymru Cyfyngedig (Welsh Water) v Barratt Homes Ltd* [2013] EWCA Civ 233; [2013] 1 W.L.R. 3486 in which the various presumptions or "indicators" were considered by the Court of Appeal.

44 See, e.g. *Digicel v Cable & Wireless* [2010] EWHC 774 (Ch). See also *Claimants in the Royal Mail Group Litigation v Royal Mail Group Ltd* [2020] EWHC 97 (Ch).

45 See, e.g. *Morshead Mansions Ltd v Di Marco* [2014] EWCA Civ 96; [2014] 1 W.L.R. 1799 (no ac-

authority, especially in respect of the failure to perform some regulatory function, the claimant's prospects of success are low.

The "narrow" construction test A common law action for breach of statutory duty arises only when the claimant can establish that Parliament intended that breach of the relevant statutory duty should be actionable by an individual harmed by that breach. At one time the courts adopted a liberal approach to the imposition of civil liability for breach of a statutory duty.[46] This has been replaced by the "construction approach" whereby the court seeks to construe the legislation in order to find the intention of Parliament.[47] In *Ex p. Island Records*,[48] a majority of the Court of Appeal suggested that interference with a private right as a result of a criminal act would justify a civil action by the injured individual. That view was firmly rejected, however, by the House of Lords in *Lonrho Ltd v Shell Petroleum Co Ltd (No.2)*.[49] Lonrho sought compensation from the defendants, their competitors in the oil trade, alleging that they had suffered heavy losses because they complied with Orders in Council prohibiting trade with the illegal regime in Southern Rhodesia, while the defendants flagrantly flouted those sanctions orders. Lord Diplock, with whom the rest of the House concurred, expressly rejected the broad principle of liability expounded by Lord Denning in *Ex p. Island Records*. He reasserted the general rule[50] for liability for violation of a statute that: **8-13**

> "… where an Act creates an obligation, and enforces the performance in a specified manner … that performance cannot be enforced in any other manner. … Where the only manner of enforcing performance for which the Act provides is prosecution for the criminal offence of failure to perform the statutory prohibition for which the Act provides, there are two classes of exception to this general rule."[51]

The first exception is "where on the true construction of the Act it is apparent that the obligation or prohibition was imposed for the benefit or protection of a particular class of individuals, as in the case of the Factories Acts and similar legislation".[52] The second arises "where the statute creates a public right" (that is, a right to be enjoyed by all those of Her Majesty's subjects who wish to avail themselves of it) and a particular member of the public suffers what Brett J in *Benjamin v Storr*[53] described as "particular direct and substantial" damage "other and different from that which was common to all the rest of the public".[54] The Orders in Council prohibiting trade with Rhodesia were designed to bring down the illegal regime, and

tion for breach of statutory duty for contravention of s.21 and s.22 of the Landlord and Tenant Act 1985 which imposes an obligation to provide tenants with details of service charges).

46 *Couch v Steel* (1854) 3 E. & B. 402 at 415; *Groves v Lord Wimborne* [1898] 2 Q.B. 402 at 407, where A.L. Smith LJ said that proof that there had been a breach of the defendant's statutory duty, and that the claimant had thereby been injured would prima facie establish the claimant's cause of action; *Monk v Warbey* [1935] 1 K.B. 75 at 81, per Greer LJ.

47 "The only rule which in all circumstances is valid is that the answer must depend on a consideration of the whole Act and the circumstances, including the pre-existing law, in which it was enacted", per Lord Simonds in *Cutler v Wandsworth Stadium Ltd* [1949] A.C. 398 at 407.

48 [1978] Ch. 122 at 139.

49 [1982] A.C. 173.

50 *Doe d. Bishop of Rochester v Bridges* (1831) 1 B. & Ad. 847 at 859.

51 [1982] A.C. 173 at 185. See also *Brown v InnovatorOne Plc* [2012] EWHC 1321 at [1273].

52 See [1982] A.C. 173 at 185.

53 (1874) L.R. 9 C. & P. 400 at 407.

54 [1982] A.C. 173 at 186. As to the applicability of Lord Diplock's second exception see Stanton, Skidmore, Harris and Wright, *Statutory Torts* (2003), paras 2.024–2.025.

not to benefit or protect traders such as Lonrho. Lonrho could bring themselves into neither exception so as to escape the general rule that violation of a statute per se is not actionable at the suit of an individual.[55]

(a) Duty imposed for the protection of a particular class of individuals[56]

8-14 **Protection of a limited class of the public** The fact that a statutory provision was designed to protect a particular class of individuals may, but not necessarily will, lead to the conclusion that breach of the duty gives rise to a common law action for damages.[57] In some instances the existence of an action for breach of statutory duty is clear and longstanding. Thus, industrial safety legislation designed to protect workers from injury at work has long been treated as conferring a common law action.[58] On the other hand, legislation creating administrative mechanisms for the protection of children at risk of neglect or abuse, though clearly intended to protect a particular class of the public, does not confer such an action.[59] Similarly, s.117 of the Mental Health Act 1983, which imposes a duty to provide after-care services for patients discharged from mental hospitals, while undoubtedly designed to promote the social welfare of such individuals does not give rise to an action for breach of statutory duty.[60] The claimant must establish that Parliament intended that

---

55 *Ex p. Island Records* was an action for an injunction whereas *Lonrho Ltd v Shell Petroleum Co Ltd* was a claim for damages, but in *RCA Corp v Pollard* [1983] Ch. 135 the Court of Appeal confirmed that the wide statement of principle in *Ex p. Island Records* was no longer correct, whether the claim was for damages or an injunction.

56 See Stanton, Skidmore, Harris and Wright, *Statutory Torts*, (2003), paras 2.019–2.023.

57 In *Trustee in Bankruptcy of St John Poulton's Trustee in Bankruptcy v Ministry of Justice* [2010] EWCA Civ 392; [2011] Ch. 1 the Court of Appeal held that the Insolvency Rules 1986 r.6.13, intended to protect creditors in an insolvency, cannot give rise to an action for breach of statutory duty in the event of failure by a court to comply with a requirement in the Rules to notify the Chief Land Registrar of the filing of a petition against the bankrupt.

58 See para.8-17.

59 *X (Minors) v Bedfordshire CC* [1995] 2 A.C. 633. Though see now *Z v UK* [2001] 2 F.L.R. 612; [2001] 2 F.C.R. 246 (ECtHR) granting compensation to the claimants in *X (Minors) v Bedfordshire CC* for breach of art.3 of the European Convention for the Protection of Human Rights. The failure of a social services authority to intervene to prevent serious, long-term neglect and abuse of children amounted to inhuman and degrading treatment within the meaning of art.3. The UK was also found to have been in breach of art.13 of the Convention in that the applicants did not have available to them an appropriate means of determining their allegations that the authority had failed to protect them from inhuman or degrading treatment or the possibility of obtaining an appropriate award of compensation for the damage suffered as a consequence. On *Z v UK* see Gearty (2002) 65 M.L.R. 87; Davies (2001) 117 L.Q.R. 521. Note that if similar facts to *X (Minors) v Bedfordshire CC* were to recur, the children would now be owed a duty of care in the tort of negligence: *JD v East Berkshire Community Health NHS Trust* [2005] UKHL 23; [2005] 2 A.C. 373; affirming the Court of Appeal decision ([2003] EWCA Civ 1151; [2004] Q.B. 558) to depart from *X (Minors) v Bedfordshire CC* on this point.

60 *Clunis v Camden and Islington HA* [1998] Q.B. 978 CA. The wording of the section fell short of the "exceptionally clear statutory language" required by Lord Browne-Wilkinson in *X v Bedfordshire CC* in order to create a claim for breach of statutory duty arising out of social welfare legislation. cf. *AK v Central and North West London Mental Health NHS Trust* [2008] EWHC 1217 (QB); [2008] P.I.Q.R. P19; [2008] L.S. Law Med. 428. In *Richards v Worcestershire County Council* [2017] EWCA Civ 1998; [2018] Med. L.R. 131 at [80] Jackson LJ expressed agreement, obiter, with the proposition in *Clunis v Camden and Islington HA* that inadequate after-care services, contrary to s.117 of the Mental Health Act 1983, do not give rise to an action for damages for breach of statutory duty.

the statute should confer a private law right of action "sounding in damages".[61] In *R. v Deputy Governor of Parkhurst Prison Ex p. Hague*,[62] the House of Lords reiterated that the primary question in relation to an action for breach of statutory duty is always whether the legislature intended to create a civil remedy for aggrieved individuals:

> "The fact that a particular provision was intended to protect certain individuals is not of itself sufficient to create a private law right of action upon them, something more is required to show that the legislature intended such conferment."[63]

So the fact that one of the purposes of the Prison Rules is to protect the welfare of prisoners was insufficient to create a right to sue for breach of those rules relating to the discipline and segregation of prisoners. Similarly, the fact that the safety provisions in Ch.II of Pt V of the Merchant Shipping Act 1995 and the Fishing Vessel (Safety Provisions) Rules 1975[64] were enacted for the protection of those who go to sea in fishing vessels does not create a right of action in damages for their breach.[65] In *Cullen v Chief Constable of the Royal Ulster Constabulary*[66] Lord Millett considered that the right of detained persons to consult in private with a solicitor, and to be informed of the reasons for delaying access to a solicitor, contained in s.15 of the Northern Ireland (Temporary Provisions) Act 1987 and s.58 of the Police and Criminal Evidence Act 1984 was not for the protection of a limited class. It was a:

> "quasi-constitutional right of fundamental importance in a free society—indeed its existence may be said to be one of the tests of a free society—and like *habeas corpus* and the right to a fair trial it is available to everyone. It is for the benefit of the public at large. We can all of us, the innocent as well as the guilty, sleep more securely in our beds for the knowledge that we cannot be detained at any moment at the hands of the state and denied access to a lawyer."[67]

This dictum must however now be read, along with the majority decision of the House of Lords in the case itself to the effect that breach of a detained person's right to consult a solicitor does not give right to an action for damages for breach of statutory duty, alongside the unanimous decision of a seven member Supreme Court that the failure of Scottish criminal law to afford such a right to detained persons constituted a breach of art.6 of the European Convention on Human Rights.[68]

General public as a particular class What was left unclear in *Lonrho* itself was 8-15

---

61 *Pickering v Liverpool Daily Post and Echo Newspapers Ltd* [1991] 2 A.C. 370.

62 [1992] 1 A.C. 58 HL.

63 [1992] 1 A.C. 58 at 170–171, per Lord Jauncey.

64 SI 1975/330. See now the Fishing Vessels (Codes of Practice) Regulations 2017 (SI 2017/943).

65 *Todd v Adams and Chope (t/a Trelawney Fishing Co) (The Margaretha Maria)* [2002] EWCA Civ 509; [2002] 2 Lloyd's Rep. 293.

66 [2003] UKHL 39; [2003] 1 W.L.R. 1763.

67 [2003] UKHL 39; [2003] 1 W.L.R. 1763 at [67]. Unfortunately, the facts of *Cullen* demonstrated precisely the opposite of this assertion. Mr Cullen was detained at the hands of the state and denied access to a lawyer, and then denied compensation for this breach of the law. Query how easily any of us should sleep, whether guilty or innocent. cf. the dissenting speeches of Lord Bingham and Lord Steyn taking the view that s.15 protected the rights of a limited and specific class, i.e. detained persons.

68 See *Cadder v HM Advocate* [2010] UKSC 43; [2010] 1 W.L.R. 2601.

the status of Atkin LJ's dictum in *Phillips v Britannia Hygienic Laundry Co.*[69] Denying that in order for to sue for breach of statutory duty an aggrieved claimant had to bring himself within some sub-class of the community, he said:

> "The duty may be of such paramount importance that it is owed to all the public. It would be strange if a less important duty, which is owed to a section of the public may be enforced by an action while a more important duty owed to the public at large cannot. The right of action does not depend on whether a statutory commandment or prohibition is pronounced for the benefit of the public, or for the benefit of a class. It may be conferred on anyone who can bring himself within the benefit of the Act, including one who cannot be otherwise specified than as a person using the highway."

It would seem that after the judgment in *Lonrho* a duty owed to the public to promote the general welfare of society or to pursue some other governmental aim is not actionable at the suit of an injured individual, unless he establishes special damage as a result of the defendant's breach of a public right. Atkin LJ's example, by contrast, established exceptionally that a class as wide and general as users of the highway can constitute a sufficient particular class of individuals to satisfy Lord Diplock's first exception, albeit all members of the public are potentially members of that class.[70] In *X v Bedfordshire CC*,[71] Lord Browne-Wilkinson appeared to endorse the view that only a limited class of the public can benefit from a private law right of action for breach of statutory duty. He did not, however, consider the judgment of Atkin LJ in *Phillips v Britannia Hygienic Laundry*. Notwithstanding the criticism which has been levelled at that judgment,[72] it is submitted that Atkin LJ's criticism of the notion of benefit of a specific class as a condition for liability in damages for breach of statutory duty retains much persuasive force. It is an inherently vague notion which seems to be giving effect to two objectives which would benefit from more explicit recognition and discussion. The first is the importance of limiting claimants to those within the risk of the danger envisaged by the statute,[73] and the second is that of protecting statutory undertakers from huge potential liabilities.[74]

8-16 The key question is always whether Parliament intended to confer private law rights. Once there is sufficient evidence that Parliament intended the relevant duty to be enforceable by private action, it is suggested that it does not matter whether

---

[69] [1923] 2 K.B. 832 at 841.

[70] As in *Monk v Warbey* [1935] 1 K.B. 75 CA. See also *Roe v Sheffield City Council* [2003] EWCA Civ 1; [2004] Q.B. 653, where the Court of Appeal held that a private law cause of action for injury to a road user arises from breach of the Tramways Act 1870 ss.25 and 28, which provide that tramways laid in the highway shall be laid and maintained in such a way that the rail is on a level with the surface of the road, and provide for the maintenance and repair of the highway in the immediate vicinity of the tramway (the road between the rails and 18 inches either side of the rails). Pill LJ commented, at [49], that the situation was much more akin to the statutes imposing duties on employers with respect to the safety of their employees than to schemes of social welfare considered in *X (Minors) v Bedfordshire CC* [1995] 2 A.C. 633.

[71] [1995] 2 A.C. 633.

[72] See, e.g. per Lord Rodger in *Morrison Sports Ltd v Scottish Power Plc* [2010] UKSC 37; [2010] 1 W.L.R. 1934 at [39].

[73] The decision of the Supreme Court in *Morrison Sports Ltd v Scottish Power Plc* (previous note) can probably be explained on this ground: the claimants sought to recover the cost of weatherproofing a building which had become exposed as a result of the demolition of a neighbouring building following a fire caused by the defendants' alleged breach of the Electricity Supply Regulations 1988. But the loss would not appear to have been within the risk of the kind of harm envisaged by the Regulations (cf. *Gorris v Scott* (1874) L.R. 9 Exch. 125).

[74] See Buckley, "Liability in Tort for Breach of Statutory Duty" (1984) 100 L.Q.R. 204, 210–214.

the class of persons protected by the statute embraces the public at large,[75] or a smaller designated category of individuals.[76] Thus, in *Monk v Warbey*[77] the defendant allowed an uninsured driver to drive his car contrary to the Road Traffic Act 1930 s.35. The driver negligently injured the claimant, but the claimant's judgment against the driver remained unsatisfied. The defendant vehicle owner was held liable to compensate the claimant, even though his breach of statutory duty did not cause the claimant's injury, it merely prevented him from recovering damages from the driver.[78] Further examples of successful actions include: an education authority was liable to a child injured through breach of their statutory duty to maintain the school premises[79]; lock owners were liable to a person suffering loss through their failure to repair the lock as required by statute[80]; a farmer whose land was flooded was able to recover damages from the local authority who were responsible by statute for maintaining the drains[81]; a person recovered damages who lost the benefit of a local land charge through the registrar's breach of his duties under the Land Charges Act 1925.[82]

Industrial safety legislation It has long been established that breach of legislation intended to promote industrial safety can give rise to an action for breach of statutory duty by an injured worker, notwithstanding that such legislation usually prescribes criminal law sanctions for its breach.[83] Workers clearly constitute a class of the public that the legislation was intended to protect from personal injury, and industrial safety legislation has been the one area where the courts have consist- 8-17

75 *Monk v Warbey* [1935] 1 K.B. 75 CA; *Phillips v Britannia Hygienic Laundry Co* [1923] 2 K.B. 832 at 841, per Atkin LJ; *Roe v Sheffield City Council* [2003] EWCA Civ 1; [2004] Q.B. 653 at [49]—"road users" a sufficiently specific class of the public.

76 But see to the contrary effect: *Clegg, Parkinson & Co v Earby Gas Co* [1896] 1 Q.B. 592 at 595; *Att Gen v St Ives RDC* [1990] 1 Q.B. 312 at 324.

77 [1935] 1 K.B. 75. cf. *Phillips v Britannia Hygienic Laundry Co Ltd* [1923] 2 K.B. 832, where the Court of Appeal held that breach of the construction and use regulations which govern the condition of motor cars on the highway did not give rise to a civil action, on the basis that a common law action for negligence was sufficient remedy for an accident caused by the dangerous condition of a vehicle.

78 The benefit of the principle in *Monk v Warbey* is confined to third parties who have themselves suffered death, personal injury, or damage to property. In *Bretton v Hancock* [2005] EWCA Civ 404; [2005] R.T.R. 22; [2006] P.I.Q.R. P1 B was a passenger in her own car, which she had permitted an uninsured driver to drive. She was injured in an accident caused partly by the driver of her car and partly by the driver of the other car involved. The latter sought, in reliance on *Monk v Warbey*, to recover from B a sum respecting the other driver's irrecoverable contribution to the damages to which B was entitled. The Court of Appeal held that B was not liable: the *Monk v Warbey* principle does not extend to "the liability of one tortfeasor to contribute with another tortfeasor" (per Rix LJ at [47]).

79 *Ching v Surrey CC* [1910] 1 K.B. 736 (on which see the comment of Sir Thomas Bingham MR in *E (A Minor) v Dorset CC* [1995] 2 A.C. 633 at 698). An action will lie for breach of s.10 of the Education Act 1944: *Reffell v Surrey CC* [1964] 1 W.L.R. 358; but not breach of s.8 of that Act: *Keating v Bromley LBC* [1995] 2 A.C. 633; *Phelps v Hillingdon LBC* [2001] 2 A.C. 619 HL.

80 *Blundy Clark v LNE Ry* [1931] 2 K.B. 334; see also *Guilfoyle v Port of London Authority* [1932] 1 K.B. 336 (swing bridge).

81 *Att Gen v St Ives RDC* [1990] 1 Q.B. 312.

82 *Ministry of Housing and Local Government v Sharp* [1970] 2 Q.B. 223.

83 e.g. *Groves v Lord Wimborne* [1898] 2 Q.B. 402 (statutory duty to fence machinery); *Black v Fife Coal Co* [1912] A.C. 149 (mines regulations); *Kininmonth v William France, Fenwick & Co* (1949) 82 Ll. L. Rep. 768 (dock regulations); *Knapp v Railway Executive* [1949] 2 All E.R. 508 (duty to put gates on level crossings).

ently allowed common law actions for breach of statutory duty.[84] Over the years, employers' liability claims have almost invariably been based on the twin actions of negligence and breach of statutory duty, with the latter often having distinct advantages over a claim in negligence.[85] Nevertheless it cannot be assumed that the statutory duty claim will always be more favourable than the common law. In finding for the defendants in *Baker v Quantum Clothing Group*[86] the Supreme Court held, by a 3 to 2 majority, that the extent of liability for injury to hearing by noise was no greater under s.29(1) of the Factories Act 1961 than in common law negligence. Lord Dyson said: "there is no principle of law that a statutory obligation cannot be interpreted as being co–terminous with a common law duty".[87] Since, however, the two dissentients (Lords Kerr and Clarke) would have construed s.29(1) as imposing a stricter duty than the common law,[88] the observations of the majority on the relationship between industrial safety legislation and the common law of negligence should perhaps be approached with caution when other statutory provisions fall to be construed.

(b) Significance of the remedy provided by the statute

8-18 **No remedy provided by the statute** It has been suggested that when a statute creates a duty, but imposes no penalty, civil or criminal, for its breach, a presumption arises that a person injured thereby will be able to sue in tort for breach of statutory duty.[89] If "the statute provides no other remedy for its breach and the Parliamentary intention to protect a limited class is shown, that indicates that there may be a private right of action since otherwise there is no method of securing the protection the statute was intended to confer".[90] If such a presumption exists it tends to be given little weight. The House of Lords made it clear in *R. v Deputy Governor of Parkhurst Prison Ex p. Hague*[91] that the mere fact that no sanction is prescribed for breach of a statutory provision designed to protect particular individuals, does not necessarily mean that a private right of action will be available. Counsel for the appellant had argued that in the absence of any remedy prescribed in the Prison Rules relating to discipline and segregation of prisoners, a right of action for breach of those Rules must arise. Their Lordships disagreed. In every instance, whether or

---

84 The scope for such claims has, however, been reduced by the Enterprise and Regulatory Reform Act 2013 s.69 which amends the Health and Safety at Work etc. Act 1974 s.47 to *reverse* a former presumption in that section in favour of civil liability for breach of health and safety legislation. See paras 12-02 and 12-46.

85 See generally Ch.12. The standard of care prescribed by the statute may be stricter than in negligence, and the defence of volenti non fit injuria is not available to an action for breach of statutory duty, except in rare circumstances. On the other hand, an action in negligence may apply where the statute is silent. For example, if the statute prescribes a safety precaution to be adopted by a worker, reasonable care on the part of the employer may require him to take reasonable steps to see that the worker has complied with the statute: see *Bux v Slough Metals Ltd* [1973] 1 W.L.R. 1358 CA.

86 [2011] UKSC 17; [2011] 1 W.L.R. 1003.

87 [2011] UKSC 17; [2011] 1 W.L.R. 1003 at [127].

88 See especially per Lord Clarke in [2011] UKSC 17; [2011] 1 W.L.R. 1003 at [191] onwards. See also the reversed decision of the Court of Appeal: [2009] EWCA Civ 499; [2009] PIQR P19.

89 "For otherwise the statute would be but a pious aspiration", see *Cutler v Wandsworth Stadium Ltd* [1949] A.C. 398 at 407, per Lord Simonds. cf. Buckley (1984) 100 L.Q.R. 204 at 217–20 who argues that, far from justifying a civil action, this type of legislation should not give rise to any liability because it will usually consist of administrative instructions to public bodies which have to exercise a wide discretion. On the question of discretion conferred on public authorities see para.8-31.

90 *X v Bedfordshire CC* [1995] 2 A.C. 633 at 731, per Lord Browne-Wilkinson.

91 [1992] 1 A.C. 58.

not any alternative remedy is provided in the statute, evidence must be advanced that Parliament intended that aggrieved individuals should be able to sue for damages. The objects of the relevant provision must be scrutinised:

> "The Prison Act 1952 is designed to deal with the administration of prisons and the management and control of prisoners. It covers such wide-ranging matters as central administration, prison officers, confinement and treatment of prisoners, release of prisoners on licence […]. Its objects are far removed from those of legislation such as the Factories and Coal Mines Acts whose prime concern is to protect the health and safety of persons who work therein."[92]

The House of Lords held unanimously that no private law claim lay in respect of breach of r.43 or any analogous Prison Rule relating to segregation of prisoners or discipline in prisons. Lord Jauncey considered that breach of the Prison Rules could never give rise to private rights,[93] because Parliament did not intend to empower the Home Secretary to confer rights to sue for compensation on prisoners. However, Lord Bridge suggested[94] that those rules concerned with industrial safety in prison workshops could give rise to a claim for breach of statutory duty, on the basis that such rules were closely analogous to statutory provisions designed to protect the health and safety of employees.

Similarly, in *Olotu v Home Office*,[95] the Court of Appeal held that the failure of the Crown Prosecution Service to comply with the prescribed time-limit for remand in custody laid down in the Prosecution of Offences (Custody Time Limits) Regulations did not give rise to an action for breach of statutory duty on the part of the claimant who remained in custody for 81 days beyond the 112 days maximum period allowed by the Regulations. The intention of the Regulations was to achieve greater expedition in the prosecution of offences and to ensure that accused persons did "… not languish in prison for excessive periods awaiting trial". The claimant clearly belonged to the class of persons that the Regulations were intended to protect. However, the Court of Appeal found that neither Parliament nor the Secretary of State would have envisaged circumstances where both the Crown Prosecution Service failed to comply with its duty under the Regulations and the person on remand failed to apply for immediate bail as she was entitled to do on the expiry of the 112 days. Thus, there would be no consideration of, or intention to create, a private law right to claim for damages in such a case.[96] The proposition that the absence of a remedy in the statute creates a presumption in favour of an action in tort for breach of statutory duty is further weakened by *St John Poulton's Trustee in Bankruptcy v Ministry of Justice*.[97] In this case the Court of Appeal held that the Insolvency Rules 1986 r.6.13, intended to protect creditors in an insolvency, do not give rise to an action for breach of statutory duty in the event of **8-19**

---

92 [1992] 1 A.C. 58 at 171.

93 [1992] 1 A.C. 58 at 171. No action for breach of statutory duty founded on a breach of the Prison Rules 1964 (see now the Prison Rules 1999 (SI 1999/728)) has yet succeeded: see *Becker v Home Office* [1972] 2 Q.B. 407 CA; *Williams v Home Office (No.2)* [1981] 1 All E.R. 1211; appeal dismissed on procedural grounds [1982] 2 All E.R. 564 CA.

94 [1992] 1 A.C. 58 at 171 at 160.

95 [1997] 1 W.L.R. 328.

96 Of course, the claimant had an alternative remedy in *Olotu*. See also *R. v Governor of Brockhill Prison Ex p. Evans (No.2)* [1999] Q.B. 1043 CA; affirmed [2001] 2 A.C. 19 HL—remedy of false imprisonment for prisoner detained beyond release date; *Clarke v Crew* (1999) 149 N.L.J. 899 CA—remedy in the tort of negligence for detaining a prisoner beyond the period authorised by the court.

97 [2010] EWCA Civ 392; [2011] Ch. 1.

failure by a court to comply with the requirement in the Rules to notify the Chief Land Registrar of the filing of a petition against the bankrupt, notwithstanding the absence of any sanction for breach of the Rules. The duty rested upon court officials and the absence of a sanction was therefore of little relevance since "Court officers and staff have, it may be assumed, every reason to carry out their duties efficiently, and no reason to fail to do so".[98]

8-20 **Some other remedy provided by the statute** If the statute imposes a penalty for its breach but is silent regarding a civil remedy, one has "to consider the scope and purpose of the statute and in particular for whose benefit it is intended".[99] In *Lonrho v Shell Petroleum Co Ltd (No.2)*,[100] Lord Diplock unequivocally reasserted the "general rule" that where a statute creates an obligation and enforces performance in a specified manner "that performance cannot be enforced in any other manner". Where the only manner of performance provided for by the statute is the criminal process there are two exceptions to that general rule:

(i) where "on the true construction of the Act it is apparent that the obligation or prohibition was imposed for the benefit of a particular class of individuals";
(ii) when a statute creates a public right and an individual member of the public suffers "'particular direct and substantial damage' other and different from that which was common to all the rest of the public".[101]

The application of Lord Diplock's first exception is theoretically unproblematic. Can it be established that the purpose of the relevant statutory provision was primarily to protect the interests of a defined class of the general public, be they, say, workmen or recording artists?[102] This makes the exception appear to be more simple to apply than it is, since the crucial issue is identifying the statutory purpose, or parliamentary intention, in circumstances where the existence of a criminal sanction would tend to point against a civil remedy and there is little guidance as to when or how a contrary conclusion will be reached.

8-21 Lord Diplock's second exception is more difficult to interpret.[103] He gives as an example the case of *Boyce v Paddington BC*,[104] a judgment relating to breach by the defendant of legislation relating to open spaces. The special damage accruing to the claimant from the loss of light caused to him by the erection of a hoarding entitled him to sue for the interference with his private right without joining the Attorney General in the action. The concept of special or particular damage is taken from cases of public nuisance, a criminal offence which can give rise to a private law action for damages where the claimant suffers particular damage over and above that suffered by members of the public generally.[105] It is unclear precisely when this exception will apply in the context of breach of statutory duty, since it is

---

98 [2010] EWCA Civ 392; [2011] Ch. 1 at [104], per Pill LJ; see also, per Lloyd LJ at [42].
99 *Black v Fife Coal Co Ltd* [1912] A.C. 149 at 165; *Atkinson v Newcastle etc Waterworks Co* (1877) 2 Ex. D. 441; *Cutler v Wandsworth Stadium Ltd* [1949] A.C. 398 at 408 and 413. See also Williams (1960) 23 M.L.R. 233.
100 [1982] A.C. 173 HL; *RCA v Pollard* [1983] Ch. 135 CA.
101 [1982] A.C. 173 HL; *RCA v Pollard* [1983] Ch. 135 CA at 185–186.
102 *Rickless v United Artists Corp* [1988] 1 Q.B. 40 CA.
103 See Stanton, Skidmore, Harris and Wright, *Statutory Torts* (2003), para.2.024, who comment that: "No action has been successfully based on these words since they were uttered."
104 [1923] 1 Ch. 109.
105 See para.19-181 onwards.

arguable that a member of the public who has suffered actual loss as a result of a criminal offence has suffered particular damage, but their Lordships in *Lonrho* explicitly rejected the "broad" interpretation of breach of statutory duty: being the victim of a statutory offence does not necessarily create a private law action for breach of the statute.[106] The question to which no answer has yet emerged, then, is precisely when will the claimant's loss constitute particular damage?

Consider the statute as a whole In *Issa v Hackney LBC*,[107] the Court of Appeal emphasised that in looking at the alternative remedies provided by the statute for an alleged breach of statutory duty the court must look at the statute as a whole. It was held that breach of s.94(2) of the Public Health Act 1936, making it a criminal offence to commit a statutory nuisance, did not give rise to a civil remedy for breach of statutory duty. The Act had to be read as a whole and construed as at the date of its enactment. **8-22**

Inadequate remedy The courts have sometimes looked to the substance of the remedy provided by the statute in order to assess its adequacy. If it is considered in reality to provide an ineffective remedy it may be disregarded. Thus, in *Groves v Lord Wimborne*,[108] an employee succeeded in an action against his employer for breach of statutory duty to fence dangerous parts of machinery. The legislation provided for a fine for breach of up to £100, all or part of which could be applied for the benefit of the injured person, but this was at the discretion of the Secretary of State. The fact that the employee might not receive any benefit, that the fine was a criminal sanction which would be assessed by reference to the nature of the offence rather than the severity of the injury, and the £100 limit, all pointed to the interpretation that Parliament had not intended to take away the common law remedy that the Factories Acts had prima facie conferred on injured workmen.[109] Similarly, in *Reffell v Surrey CC*[110] it was held that a pupil at a local authority school, who was cut by a thin pane of glass, could maintain an action for breach of the Education Act 1944. Referring to the "strong presumption" that an action would lie where the statute provides no penalty for the breach, Veale J said that this applied to the case because the remedy under the Act was an application for mandamus. On the other hand, in *Olotu v Home Office*,[111] the Court of Appeal considered that the statutory right to apply for release on bail or habeas corpus and mandamus justified denying a private law action for damages to a claimant who had been remanded in custody for an excessive period in breach of the Prosecution of Offences Act 1985 and the custody regulations made under it.[112] It would seem that the inadequacy of the remedy is rarely regarded as significant these days. Thus, in **8-23**

---

106 See para.8-13.

107 [1997] 1 W.L.R. 956.

108 [1898] 2 Q.B. 402.

109 See also *Morrison Sports Ltd v Scottish Power Plc* [2007] CSOH 131; 2007 S.L.T. 1103 at [35], per Lord Wheatley (remedy provided by statute [a fine at level 5 of the standard scale] for breaches of the Electricity Supply Regulations 1988 reg.17, reg.24 and reg.25 (SI 1988/1057) was "patently inadequate" having regard to the potential interest of the claimants whose property was damaged in a fire attributable to the breaches). Lord Wheatley's decision on this point was subsequently affirmed by the inner House: see [2009] CSIH 92; 2010 S.L.T. 243 at [47], but reversed by the Supreme Court: [2010] UKSC 37; [2010] 1 W.L.R. 1934.

110 [1964] 1 W.L.R. 358.

111 [1997] 1 W.L.R. 328.

112 See also *R. v Governor of Brockhill Prison Ex p. Evans (No.2)* [1999] Q.B. 1043 CA; affirmed [2001] 2 A.C. 19 HL; and *Clarke v Crew* (1999) 149 N.L.J. 899 CA, fn.96 above.

Clunis v Camden and Islington HA,[113] the Court of Appeal said that the primary means of enforcing s.117 of the Mental Health Act 1983, which creates a duty to provide after-care for a psychiatric patient who has been detained under the Act and then released, was by way of complaint to the Secretary of State. The difficulty for a psychiatric patient deprived of after-care is that, by the nature of his medical condition, he may be in no state to appreciate the need to complain.

8-24 In *Cullen v Chief Constable of the Royal Ulster Constabulary*[114] the House of Lords was divided on the question of whether judicial review was an effective remedy for persons detained by the police. The claimant was detained in custody under the Prevention of Terrorism (Temporary Provisions) Act 1989, and was denied the right to consult in private with a solicitor, and to be informed of the reasons for delaying his access to a solicitor, in breach of s.15 of the Northern Ireland (Temporary Provisions) Act 1987.[115] The Police and Criminal Evidence Act 1984 s.58 confers similar rights in respect of detention for non-terrorist offences. The question was whether this breach gave rise to a civil action for damages. By a bare majority[116] the House of Lords held that it did not on the ground that judicial review would be "a much more effective remedy for a claimant to seek than the bringing of an action for nominal damages months or years after the period of detention has ended."[117] But the view of the minority that judicial review would fail to provide an adequate remedy,[118] may be said to be reinforced by the subsequent decision of the Supreme Court in *Cadder v HM Advocate*[119] that the failure of Scottish criminal law to afford a right to detained persons to consult a solicitor constituted a breach of art.6 of the European Convention on Human Rights.

8-25 **Alternative remedies** In determining whether Parliament intended to benefit a class by conferring a right to sue for damages for breach of duty, the court will look at the alternative remedies available to the claimant. Is there a criminal sanction sufficient to enforce the relevant duty and protect the claimant? Could the claimant seek compensation in contract or in another tort? A person contravening the Merchandise Marks Acts 1887 to 1953 was not liable in private law under the Acts to a rival trader,[120] and a landlord was not liable to his tenant whom he harassed contrary to what is now the Protection from Eviction Act 1977 s.1.[121] A purchaser of a vehicle with defective brakes had no right of action against the seller for his breach of the Road Traffic Act,[122] and a driver had no action for breach of statu-

---

113 [1998] Q.B. 978. cf. *AK v Central and North West London Mental Health NHS Trust* [2008] EWHC 1217 (QB); [2008] P.I.Q.R. P19; [2008] L.S. Law Med. 428.

114 [2003] UKHL 39; [2003] 1 W.L.R. 1763.

115 See now the Terrorism Act 2000 Sch.8 paras 7 and 8.

116 Lords Hutton, Millett and Rodger.

117 [2003] UKHL 39; [2003] 1 W.L.R. 1763 at [39].

118 See [2003] UKHL 39; [2003] 1 W.L.R. 1763 at [20], per Lord Bingham and Lord Steyn: "In our respectful view the majority has also failed to give sufficient weight to two factors. First, there are plainly formidable practical problems in a detainee applying for judicial review when he has been denied access to a solicitor. Secondly, in any event, it is not easy to know whether one has an arguable case for judicial review unless reasons have been given. If there are adequate answers to these points, we are not aware of them."

119 [2010] UKSC 43; [2010] 1 W.L.R. 2601.

120 *Bollinger v Costa Brava Wine Co Ltd* [1960] Ch. 262 at 287. The Merchandise Marks Acts were repealed and replaced by the Trade Descriptions Act 1968 s.41(2), Sch.2.

121 *McCall v Abelesz* [1976] Q.B. 585 CA.

122 *Badham v Lambs Ltd* [1946] K.B. 45 (a decision on s.8(1) of the Act of 1934; see now Road Traf-

tory duty against a motorist who illegally parked on a clearway.[123] The complex scheme of different remedies for breach of the listing rules made under s.74 of the Financial Services and Markets Act 2000 has been held to be inconsistent with the existence of "a cause of action at the suit of a private person".[124] Moreover, if the alternative remedy would normally be adequate but, due to exceptional circumstances, was not available in the case in question, it may still negate a claim in tort for breach of statutory duty.[125] However, the owner of a car who allows it to be driven by an uninsured driver, contrary to the Road Traffic Act 1988 s.143, is liable to be sued by a person whom the driver negligently injures[126]; and a cause of action will lie for breach of the Pedestrian Crossings Regulations.[127] Where the statute is designed to protect physical safety,[128] there is a greater willingness to interpret the statute as conferring a right of action, despite the existence of a penalty. Industrial safety legislation furnishes plentiful examples: an employee can recover for breach of the statutory duty to fence dangerous machinery[129] and a miner for injury caused through breach of mines regulations[130]; but non-industrial penal legislation is less readily construed as conferring a private law right to damages for its breach.[131]

The availability of an alternative common law remedy has never been a decisive consideration. The existence of an action in negligence for breach of an employer's non-delegable duty did not preclude the employee's action for breach of statutory duty established by *Groves v Lord Wimborne*.[132] Conversely, the absence of a common law remedy has not necessarily persuaded the courts to allow an action for breach of a statute. In *Issa v Hackney LBC*,[133] the defendant local authority was convicted for its failure as landlord to abate conditions in their property injuring the **8-26**

fic Act 1988 s.41A).

123 *Coote v Stone* [1971] 1 W.L.R. 279. The courts seem generally unwilling to infer actions for breach of duties imposed by the Road Traffic Acts. *Monk v Warbey* [1935] 1 K.B. 75; and *LPTB v Upson* [1949] A.C. 155 are rather exceptional.

124 See *Hall v Cable and Wireless Plc* [2009] EWHC 1793 (Comm); [2010] 1 B.C.L.C. 95 at [16], per Teare J. See also *Brown v InnovatorOne Plc* [2012] EWHC 1321.

125 See *Francis v London Borough of Southwark* [2011] EWCA Civ 1418; [2012] H.L.R.16 (no damages for wrongful denial of the right to buy a council house under the Housing Act 1985 s.118: the Act provided its own remedies but these did not avail the claimant due, inter alia, to the subsequent demolition of the house).

126 *Monk v Warbey* [1935] 1 K.B. 75 (a decision on the Act of 1930); *Martin v Deane* [1971] 2 Q.B. 208; cf. *Daniels v Vaux* [1938] 2 K.B. 203; *Bretton v Hancock* [2005] EWCA Civ 404; [2005] R.T.R. 22. Car-owners are not statutorily required to insure against the *Monk v Warbey* obligation *itself*: see *Sahin v Havard* [2016] EWCA Civ 1202; [2017] 1 W.L.R. 1853 (claimant unable to sue *insurer* of car-owner to recover the value of a judgment against the latter for damage caused by an uninsured driver whom she permitted to drive the car).

127 *London Passenger Transport Board v Upson* [1949] A.C. 155 (a decision on the regulations of 1941). See now the Traffic Signs Regulations and General Directions 2016, SI 2016/362.

128 Contrast *Cutler v Wandsworth Stadium* [1949] A.C. 398 where the duty was to provide space on a dog-racing track for bookmaking and the House of Lords held that no action lay on the part of a bookmaker; and *Watt v Kesteven CC* [1955] 1 Q.B. 408 CA (duty to make schools available).

129 *Groves v Lord Wimborne* [1898] 2 Q.B. 402; cf. *Carroll v Andrew Barclay & Sons Ltd* [1948] A.C. 477; and *Biddle v Truvox Engineering Co* [1952] 1 K.B. 101. Note, however, that an employee does not always fall within the scope of the protective legislation: see paras 8-51 and 8-53.

130 *Black v Fife Coal Co* [1912] A.C. 149; *National Coal Board v England* [1954] A.C. 403 (shot-firing regulations).

131 See, however, *London Passenger Transport Board v Upson* [1949] A.C. 155; *Monk v Warbey* [1935] 1 K.B. 75; and *Scott v Green & Sons* [1969] 1 W.L.R. 301 CA (Highways Act 1959 s.154(5)).

132 [1898] 2 Q.B. 402.

133 [1997] 1 W.L.R. 956.

child claimants' health. In construing the statute, the Court of Appeal held that the vast majority of victims of a statutory nuisance under the Act would enjoy alternative civil remedies against their private sector landlords. Parliament would not have intended to create a civil remedy, which would necessarily have been available to all victims of statutory nuisance, solely to assist the small minority who lacked such alternative remedies.

8-27 In *M (A Minor) v Newham LBC*,[134] Staughton LJ considered that a whole range of extra-judicial remedies (such as complaint to one's Member of Parliament, the National Society for the Prevention of Cruelty to Children, the local government ombudsman or the "sanction" of severe criticism in the press or a public enquiry when an error is made) were relevant when considering the means of enforcing child protection legislation. His Lordship made no attempt to assess the effectiveness of these remedies. In both *TP and KM v UK*[135] and *Z v UK*[136] (in which the unsuccessful claimants in *M v Newham LBC* and *X (Minors) v Bedfordshire CC*[137] respectively claimed for a breach of their human rights) the European Court of Human Rights concluded that the UK was in breach of art.13 of the European Convention for the Protection of Human Rights in that there was a failure to provide an appropriate remedy for the breaches of art.8 and art.3, respectively, that the Court found proved. This does not, in itself, indicate that Staughton LJ's comments are misplaced, since his Lordship was considering the common law action for breach of statutory duty, whereas the European Court of Human Rights was considering remedies for breach of the European Convention. Nonetheless, it does emphasise the importance of considering the effectiveness of administrative remedies when the claimant is seeking compensation for personal injuries. By the same token, in *Phelps v Hillingdon LBC*[138] (in the context of an action in negligence against an education authority) Lord Clyde commented that:

> "even if there are alternative procedures by which some form of redress might be obtained, such as resort to judicial review, or to an ombudsman, or the adoption of such statutory procedures as are open to parents, which might achieve some correction of the situation for the future, it may only be through a claim for damages at common law that compensation for the damage done to the child may be secured for the past as well as the future."

8-28 In *Richardson v Pitt-Stanley*,[139] the Court of Appeal held, by a majority, that no action in damages for breach of statutory duty lay for breach of s.1 of the Employers' Liability (Compulsory Insurance) Act 1969 against either the employer-company or any director who in breach of s.1 connived at or facilitated a failure to insure under the Act. The claimant had been awarded damages in respect of an accident at work against the defendants, his employers. The defendant company however had gone into liquidation and failed to insure against liability to the claimant as required by the 1969 Act. Distinguishing *Monk v Warbey*,[140] the Court of Appeal found that no civil cause of action for breach of the analogous provisions of the 1969 Act arose, largely because alternative remedies available to the claimant

---

[134] [1995] 2 A.C. 633 at 671.
[135] [2001] 2 F.L.R. 549.
[136] [2001] 2 F.L.R. 612; [2001] 2 F.C.R. 246.
[137] [1995] 2 A.C. 633.
[138] [2001] 2 A.C. 619 at 672.
[139] [1995] Q.B. 123.
[140] [1935] 1 K.B. 75, where an action was held to lie for breach of the duty to insure imposed by the Road Traffic Act.

at common law and the imposition of substantial criminal penalties militated against the imposition of civil liability under the Act. This decision appears to run contrary to the policy of the Employers' Liability (Compulsory Insurance) Act 1969, which is to protect the financial position of injured employees bringing actions against their employers. Nevertheless in *Campbell v Peter Gordon Joiners Ltd*[141] the Supreme Court, on appeal from the Inner House of the Court of Session, chose to uphold the authority of *Richardson v Pitt-Stanley* on similar facts. The pursuer suffered a serious personal injury whilst an employee of an insolvent company of which the defender had been sole director. However, the failure of the company to insure, contrary to the Act, meant that the pursuer would be unable to obtain the damages to which he would become entitled if he succeeded in establishing liability for the accident in subsequent proceedings. By a bare majority a five-member Supreme Court held that the pursuer's claim would fail. In so holding the Court upheld the decision of the Court of Session which that court had reached by a 2–1 majority. The judgment of Lord Carnwath, with whom Lord Mance and Lord Reed agreed, expressed the view of the majority. They considered a close examination of the actual wording of the statute to be the correct approach and referred[142] (albeit without formally accepting) to doubts which have occasionally been expressed about the continued applicability of long-established presumptions and guidelines relating to the imposition of liability for the breach of statutory duty, including that in favour of employees injured in breach of industrial safety legislation.[143] Lord Toulson and Lady Hale, in forcefully expressed dissenting judgments in favour of the pursuer's claim, emphasised the continued importance of those guidelines which "have stood the test of time" and should "continue to be the law unless and until the Supreme Court makes a conscious decision otherwise".[144]

Administrative remedies In determining whether or not Parliament intended to confer private law rights on a person aggrieved by breach of a statutory duty, proper regard must also be paid to any administrative appeals process or complaints procedure created for the enforcement of that duty.[145] In relation to the protection of children at risk,[146] and provision for the education of children with special needs,[147] the Court of Appeal found that elaborate measures existed in the relevant Acts for remedying any default. Ample provision was made for redress of grievances, making it highly unlikely any private law right was envisaged. This approach was upheld by the House of Lords. Commenting on the legislative framework of the Education Act 1981, Lord Browne-Wilkinson said that it involved the parents of the child at every stage of the decision-making process and gives them rights of appeal against the authority's decisions: **8-29**

"I have never previously come across a statutory procedure which provided for such close

141 [2016] UKSC 38; [2016] A.C. 1513.
142 See [2016] UKSC 38; [2016] A.C. 1513 at [11]–[12].
143 See, e.g. Lord Diplock in *Lonrho Ltd v Shell Petroleum Co Ltd (No 2)* [1982] A.C. 173 at 185.
144 See, per Lord Toulson in [2016] UKSC 38; [2016] A.C. 1513 at [41]–[42].
145 See *Robinson v Workington Corp* [1897] 1 Q.B. 619 CA; *Wyatt v Hillingdon LBC* (1978) 76 L.G.R. 627 CA. See also *Neil Martin Ltd v Revenue and Customs Commissioners* [2007] EWCA Civ 1041; [2008] Bus. L.R. 663 (right of appeal under s.561(9) of the Income Tax and Corporation Taxes Act 1988 indicated that no right of action for damages was intended for breach of the duty under s.561(2) of the same statute to issue a tax certificate).
146 *M v Newham London BC* [1995] 2 A.C. 633 CA at 671 and 679.
147 *E v Dorset CC* [1995] 2 A.C. 633 CA at 701.

involvement of those who would be affected by a decision in the making of that decision or which conferred more generous rights of appeal. To suggest that Parliament intended, in addition, to confer a right to sue for damages is impossible."[148]

8-30 **Public law remedies** When the duty imposed on a public authority necessarily requires the exercise of the authority's discretion, any action for breach of that statutory duty may have to proceed by way of an application for judicial review, rather than an action in tort. The House of Lords held in *O'Reilly v Mackman*[149] that as a general principle challenges to decisions of a public authority on the grounds that the authority contravened public law principles, for example, acted ultra vires, must proceed by way of CPR Pt 54.[150] In *Cocks v Thanet DC*,[151] the claimant started an action for breach of the statutory duty imposed by the Housing (Homeless Persons) Act 1977. The defendants had refused to house him permanently on the grounds that they considered him to be intentionally homeless. His action in tort was struck out as an abuse of process. Their Lordships held that to establish breach of statutory duty the claimant must first prove that the decision holding him to be intentionally homeless was ultra vires. He must proceed by way of an application for judicial review and his claim for damages, if the court found in his favour, could be annexed to that application. The requirement for leave to apply for judicial review and the short time-limit for such applications place persons seeking compensation for breach of statutory duties incorporating a discretionary element at a substantial procedural disadvantage. In *O'Rourke v Camden LBC*,[152] the House of Lords held that a housing authority's duty to provide temporary accommodation to homeless persons under s.63(1) of the Housing Act 1985, although framed in objective terms, does not confer any private law right to sue for damages. Part III of the Housing Act 1985 (see now Pt VII of the Housing Act 1996), was part of scheme of social welfare providing housing assistance to individuals for the benefit of society in general which required in its implementation an element of subjective judgment on the part of the housing authority indicative of a public law function, and had been intended by Parliament to be enforceable solely by way of judicial review, not an action for breach of statutory duty.[153]

(c) Actions against public authorities

8-31 The more general the duty cast of a public authority, the less likely it is that a private right of action will be found to lie. Hence it has been held that no action lies

---

[148] *X v Bedfordshire CC* [1995] 2 A.C. 633 HL at 769. See also *Phelps v Hillingdon LBC* [2001] 2 A.C. 619 HL; para.8-38.

[149] [1983] 2 A.C. 237 HL.

[150] Formerly RSC Ord.53.

[151] [1983] 2 A.C. 286 HL.

[152] [1998] A.C. 188.

[153] In *Calveley v Chief Constable of Merseyside* [1989] 1 A.C. 1228, the House of Lords held that the obligation imposed by the Police (Discipline) Regulations 1985 to give notice to a police officer under investigation as soon as is practicable of the matters alleged against him did not give rise to an action for damages for breach of statutory duty if not performed. The remedy if an officer was prejudiced by a failure to give notice was by way of judicial review. See also *Cullen v Chief Constable of the Royal Ulster Constabulary* [2003] UKHL 39; [2003] 1 W.L.R. 1763; para.8-44, where a majority of the House of Lords held that a person detained in custody who was denied access to a lawyer would have a remedy by way of judicial review. See further *Jones v Department of Employment* [1989] 1 Q.B. 1 at 22 and 25, per Glidewell and Slade LJJ denying the existence of a duty of care in negligence where the decisions of a social security adjudication officer were subject to a statutory right of appeal.

against the Minister of Education for breach of his duty "to promote the education of the people of England and Wales"[154] and actions in public law against the Minister of Health for failing to provide an efficient and comprehensive health service have failed.[155] Similarly, a provision requiring an authority to act "effectively, efficiently and economically" has been held to be incapable of giving rise to an action for breach of statutory duty.[156] The claimant must generally establish a defined and specific duty owed to him personally, rather than a "political" duty owed to society at large, but even specific duties will not necessarily give rise to action.[157] A duty to publish information to the whole world is unlikely to give rise to an action for damages for breach of statutory duty for economic loss, in view of the enormous number of potential claimants.[158]

The status of public law remedies now tends to be seen as part of the wider question of whether it is ever appropriate to bring claims for breach of statutory duty against public authorities when they are exercising discretionary regulatory functions. In many respects this parallels the debate that has taken place in the context of claims for breach of a common law duty of care where the damage has allegedly occurred as a result of a public authority's failure properly to carry out its public functions.[159] That debate, in addition to analysing the proximity of relationship between the parties, has tended to invoke wide policy issues, such as the impact on the defendants' resources, the risk of defensive practices, or the potential to cut across the statutory functions. Those policy factors are equally applicable to actions for breach of statutory duty, though there still tends to be an emphasis on determining the "intention of Parliament" through an analysis of the statutory wording and the broad context of the legislation. At this point the provision of alternative administrative remedies may be emphasised, together with the discretionary nature of the authority's duties (which will often depend upon the exercise of judgment as to whether particular conditions are satisfied) and the fact that the legislation is a wide measure designed to promote the public welfare rather than the private law claims of individuals adversely affected by a failure properly to implement it. **8-32**

X v Bedfordshire CC[160] is symptomatic of a general trend against finding that a private law remedy lies against public authorities charged with the protection of the public welfare. Lord Browne-Wilkinson suggested that only exceptionally will "… **8-33**

[154] *Watt v Kesteven CC* [1955] 1 Q.B. 408.

[155] *R. v Secretary of State for Social Services Ex p. Hincks* (1979) 123 S.J. 436; affirmed (1980) 1 B.M.L.R. 93 CA. On the question of enforcing rights to medical treatment under the National Health Service Act 1977 (now the National Health Service Act 2006), see also *R. v Central Birmingham HA Ex p. Walker* (1987) 3 B.M.L.R. 32, CA; *R. v Central Birmingham HA Ex p. Collier* unreported 1988 CA; *R. v Cambridge HA Ex p. B.* [1995] 1 W.L.R. 898 CA. See further *Danns v Department of Health* [1998] P.I.Q.R. P226 CA —no duty under s.2 of the Ministry of Health Act 1919 to disseminate information to the general public about the known failure rates of vasectomy.

[156] See *Human Fertilisation and Embryology Authority v ARGC Ltd* [2016] EWHC 460 (QB) (per Foskett J considering s.8ZA of the Human Fertilisation and Embryology Act 1990).

[157] In *Trustee in Bankruptcy of St John Poulton's Trustee in Bankruptcy v Ministry of Justice* [2010] EWCA Civ 392; [2011] Ch. 1 the Court of Appeal held that a specific duty on a court to comply with straightforward notification requirements imposed by the Insolvency Rules 1986 r.6.13 could not give rise to an action in favour of creditors adversely affected by breach of the duty. See also para.8-19.

[158] See *Sebry v Companies House* [2015] EWHC 115 (QB); [2016] 1 W.L.R. 2499 at [106], per Edis J in respect of an error in the statutory Companies Register (on the particular facts the defendants were, however, liable for common law negligence).

[159] See Bailey, "Public authority liability in negligence: the continued search for coherence" (2006) 26 L.S. 154.

[160] [1995] 2 A.C. 633.

an administrative system designed to promote the social welfare of the community" give rise to private rights enforceable by an action for breach of statutory duty. This is partly because enforcement by the civil law is seen as unlikely to be Parliament's choice of an effective means of enforcing public protection measures. More significant, perhaps, is the courts' perception of the economic consequences of the potentially large number of cases against public authorities that might ensue, both in terms of the impact upon a local authority's resources and its consequent effect on the ability of the authority to carry out its statutory functions.[161] This was certainly expressed to be an important factor in denying that social services authorities owed a common law duty of care in the tort of negligence, and cannot have been far from their Lordships minds when addressing the issue of breach of statutory duty. Notwithstanding the fact that the child protection legislation (the Children and Young Persons Act 1969, the Child Care Act 1980, and the Children Act 1989) was clearly for the protection of a limited class, namely children at risk, and that until 1991 the legislation contained only limited machinery for enforcing those statutory duties, the House of Lords held that a social services authority were not liable for breach of statutory duty in respect of the manner in which they conducted an investigation or made a decision whether or not to remove a child into care. The legislation established an administrative system designed to promote the social welfare of the community. The judgments to be made were of "peculiar sensitivity", involving striking a difficult balance between protecting a child from the risk of harm and harm created by disrupting the relationship between the child and its parents in being removed into care. Decisions would often have to be taken on the basis of inadequate and disputed facts. All the statutory provisions were dependent upon the subjective judgment of the local authority. Lord Browne-Wilkinson doubted whether a claim for breach of statutory duty could ever arise where the relevant duty was dependent on the defendant first having formed a subjective belief. The language and structure of the legislation was inconsistent with any intention to create private law rights. In such a context it required exceptionally clear statutory language to show a parliamentary intention that social services authorities should be liable in damages for an erroneous judgment.[162] Accordingly, it was impossible to treat such duties as being more than public law duties. In *Poole BC v GN*[163] the Supreme Court held that without more, such as an assumption of responsibility in the specific case, the provisions of the Children Act 1989 are not capable of generating a common law duty of care on social workers to protect children from abuse by third parties wholly unrelated to the children's own families.

8-34 **A human rights perspective** It may be that, with hindsight, some of the policy concerns expressed by Lord Browne-Wilkinson in *X (Minors) v Bedfordshire CC* come to be viewed as overstated, particularly when viewed from a human rights perspective. The unsuccessful claimants in *M v Newham LBC* and *X (Minors) v Bedfordshire CC* took a complaint to the European Court of Human Rights. In the case *M v Newham* it was held that the failure of the social services authority properly to involve the child's mother in the investigation of alleged sexual abuse of her child (with the consequence that the child was unnecessarily taken into local authority care) constituted a breach of art.8 of the European Convention for the

[161] See the comments of Lord Bridge in *Murphy v Brentwood DC* [1991] 1 A.C. 398 at 482, in the context of a negligence action.

[162] [1995] 2 A.C. 633 at 747.

[163] [2019] UKSC 25; [2019] 2 W.L.R. 1478.

Protection of Human Rights, the right to respect for family life.[164] The local authority had refused to disclose to the mother a video of an interview with the child. If this had been done it would have been apparent to the mother that the local authority had failed to identify the abuser, and had mistakenly identified her partner as the abuser. The refusal to disclose the video denied the mother adequate involvement in the decision-making process concerning the care of her daughter, and this constituted a breach of art.8. There was also a breach of art.13 which guarantees a right to an effective remedy, since neither the mother nor her daughter had the possibility of obtaining an enforceable award for compensation for the damage suffered due to breach of art.8.

In the case of *X (Minors) v Bedfordshire CC* the European Court of Human Rights found that the failure of the social services authority to intervene to prevent serious, long-term neglect and abuse of children constituted inhuman and degrading treatment and found the UK to be in breach of art.3 of the Convention.[165] As in *TP and KM v UK* the UK was also found to have been in breach of art.13 of the Convention in that the applicants did not have available to them an appropriate means of determining their allegations that the authority had failed to protect them from inhuman or degrading treatment or the possibility of obtaining an appropriate award of compensation for the damage suffered as a consequence. In both cases the court awarded substantial compensation. It was emphasised that the abuse in *Z v UK* was both serious and had been occurring for some considerable time, and it seems likely, therefore, that not all failures to intervene to protect children at risk of harm will meet the requirements of "inhuman and degrading treatment" under art.3. Subsequently, in *JD v East Berkshire Community Health NHS Trust*[166] the Court of Appeal held that *X (Minors) v Bedfordshire CC; M (A Minor) v Newham London BC* could not survive the Human Rights Act 1998. Accordingly, it was no longer "legitimate to rule that, as a matter of law, no common law duty of care is owed to a child in relation to the investigation of suspected child abuse and the initiation and pursuit of care proceedings".[167] Although it was possible that there could be factual situations where it was not fair, just or reasonable to impose a duty of care each case would fall to be determined on its individual facts. This remarkable decision (effectively the Court of Appeal overruled the House of Lords' decision in *X v Bedfordshire* on the basis of the human rights jurisprudence) was upheld by the House of Lords,[168] who also agreed with the Court of Appeal's conclusion that, though a duty of care could be owed to the child when making such a decision, no such duty was owed to the parents or the person suspected of abuse. **8-35**

In *Phelps v Hillingdon LBC*[169] a seven judge House of Lords held that policy factors, such as those canvassed in *X (Minors) v Bedfordshire CC*, should not be conclusive against the possibility of a common law duty of care in negligence owed by an educational psychologist or a teacher when making an assessment of a pupil's educational needs. Clearly, there is no authority for the proposition that such claims **8-36**

164 *TP and KM v UK* [2001] 2 F.L.R. 549.

165 *Z v UK* [2001] 2 F.L.R. 612; [2001] 2 F.C.R. 246. For discussion of *Z v UK* see Gearty (2002) 65 M.L.R. 87; Davies (2001) 117 L.Q.R. 521.

166 [2003] EWCA Civ 1151; [2004] Q.B. 558.

167 [2003] EWCA Civ 1151; [2004] Q.B. 558 at [84]. See also *Poole BC v GN* [2019] UKSC 25; [2019] 2 W.L.R. 1478 in which the Supreme Court confirmed that the decision of the Court of Appeal in *JD v East Berkshire Community Health NHS Trust* remained good law despite doubts expressed by the Court of Appeal itself in the *Poole* case (see [2017] EWCA Civ 2185; [2018] 2 W.L.R. 1693).

168 [2005] UKHL 23; [2005] 2 A.C. 373.

169 [2001] 2 A.C. 619.

will in future give rise to an action for breach of statutory duty. Indeed, *Phelps* is clear authority that there is no private law action for breach of statutory duty based on breach of the Education Acts 1944 or 1981 in respect of the failure to provide suitable education for an individual pupil.[170] On the other hand an action based in common law negligence, arising out of the public authority's performance of its statutory duties, or a claim based on a breach of the European Convention for the Protection of Human Rights, though not necessarily coterminous with breach of a statutory provision, might go a significant way towards filling the gap for claimants.

8-37 **Claims against education authorities** In *Keating v Bromley LBC*,[171] the claimant brought an action against the education authority arguing that the authority's failure to provide any or any appropriate education for children with special educational needs, in breach of the Education Acts 1944 and 1981, gave rise to a claim for damages. Once again, their Lordships accepted that children having special educational needs formed a class of persons for whose benefit the relevant legislation was enacted. However, nothing in the legislation demonstrated a Parliamentary intention to give that class a right of action in damages for breach of statutory duty. As was the case in the child abuse claims, no duty could arise unless a series of judgments were first made by the education authority. Moreover, an elaborate system for consultation and appeals clearly indicated that the system provided adequate remedies for any grievance on the part of the parents. "To suggest that Parliament intended, in addition, to confer a right to sue for damages is impossible."

8-38 This approach to an action for breach of statutory duty was confirmed by the House of Lords in *Phelps v Hillingdon LBC*,[172] where it was held that there was no action for breach of statutory duty for a failure to identify, diagnose and treat the special educational needs of a pupil, namely the claimant's learning difficulties and/or dyslexia, in breach of the Education Acts 1944 and 1981 or the Education (Special Needs) Regulations 1983.[173] Lord Slynn said that although the duties were intended to benefit a particular group, mainly children with special educational needs, the Act was essentially providing a general structure for all children who fall within its provisions.[174] The general nature of the duties imposed on local authorities in the context of a national system of education and the remedies available by way of appeal and judicial review indicated that Parliament did not intend to create a statutory remedy by way of damages. Much of the Act was concerned with conferring discretionary powers or administrative duties in an area of social welfare where normally damages have not been awarded when there has been a failure to perform a statutory duty. On the other hand, their Lordships refused to strike out as disclosing no reasonable cause of action claims that an educational psychologist or teacher owed a duty of care in the tort of negligence to a pupil to exercise reasonable care when making an educational assessment of that pupil for the purpose of determining future educational provision for the child.

---

170 See para.8-38.

171 [1995] 2 A.C. 633. In the House of Lords this case was heard with two other "education cases" (*E (A Minor) v Dorset CC* and *Christmas v Hampshire CC* in which the actions were based upon a common law duty of care in negligence) together with the "abuse cases" (*X v Bedfordshire CC* and *M v Newham LBC*).

172 [2001] 2 A.C. 619; applied in *Carty v Croydon LBC* [2005] EWCA Civ 19; [2005] 1 W.L.R. 2312.

173 SI 1983/29.

174 [2001] 2 A.C. 619 at 652.

Negligence actions against public authorities A similar line of reasoning to that of *X v Bedfordshire CC* can be seen in other cases where the action against a public body is framed in negligence (as it was also in both the abuse cases and the education cases in *X v Bedfordshire*). Thus, in *Jain v Trent Strategic HA*[175] the House of Lords held that a public authority exercising a statutory power, the purpose of which was the protection of the residents of a nursing home, owed no duty of care to the owners of the home as to the manner in which it exercised that power because of the potential conflict of interest between interests of the residents and those of the proprietors.[176] Lord Scott said: 8-39

> "… where action is taken by a State authority under statutory powers designed for the benefit or protection of a particular class of persons, a tortious duty of care will not be held to be owed by the State authority to others whose interests may be adversely affected by an exercise of the statutory power. The reason is that the imposition of such a duty would or might inhibit the exercise of the statutory powers and be potentially adverse to the interests of the class of persons the powers were designed to benefit or protect, thereby putting at risk the achievement of their statutory purpose."[177]

Similarly, in *Harris v Evans*,[178] it was held that an inspector of the Health and Safety Executive did not owe a duty of care to the owner of a business when making recommendations as to whether a particular activity should be authorised under the Health and Safety at Work etc. Act 1974. The statute was concerned with public safety, and it was implicit in the statutory regime that enforcement decisions could have adverse economic consequences for a business enterprise. The legislation provided a suitable appeals mechanism, and moreover, the imposition of a duty of care would probably have a detrimental effect on the system created in the interests of public safety by producing an unduly cautious and defensive approach by inspectors to the use of their enforcement powers under the Act.[179]

Of course, the mere fact that the relationship between the parties arises out of the exercise of statutory functions by a public authority is not necessarily a reason for immunity in a case which would otherwise fall within common law principles for the existence of a duty of care. In *Welton v North Cornwall DC*[180] the Court of Appeal held that a local authority could be liable for negligent misstatement where an environmental health officer negligently required the owner of premises to undertake unnecessary works to secure compliance with the Food Safety Act 1990, 8-40

175 [2009] UKHL 4; [2009] 1 A.C. 853; [2009] 1 All E.R. 957.

176 See also *Jowhari v NHS England* [2014] EWHC 4197 (QB) (National Health Service does not owe a common law duty of care to a dentist who suffers economic loss as a result of his being wrongly excluded from a statutory list of dentists entitled to practise NHS dentistry within a particular locality).

177 [2009] UKHL 4; [2009] 1 A.C. 853; [2009] 1 All E.R. 957 at [28]. See also the comments of Lord Rodger in *Mitchell v Glasgow City Council* [2009] UKHL 11; [2009] 1 A.C. 874 at [62] (no duty of care requiring a social landlord, in the exercise of its statutory power to do so, to institute possession proceedings to evict a disruptive tenant in order to protect other tenants).

178 [1998] 1 W.L.R. 1285 CA.

179 See also *Lam v Brennan and Borough of Torbay* [1997] P.I.Q.R. P488 (power to grant or refuse planning permission under the Town and Country Planning Act 1971 s.29, did not give rise to a common law duty of care: planning authorities have to consider a range of factors and adverse effects upon some members of the public may be unavoidable).

180 [1997] 1 W.L.R. 570. See also *T (A Minor) v Surrey CC* [1994] 4 All E.R. 577, where a local authority which negligently advised a parent that there was no reason why a child should not be placed with a particular child-minder was held liable for negligent misstatement when the child suffered injury in the child-minder's care.

causing the owner to incur substantial unnecessary expenditure.[181] Similarly, the House of Lords has accepted that it is arguable that a social services authority could owe a duty of care in negligence to children who were not in its care when making decisions about the foster placement of a child with the claimants' family, when that child was known to have committed sexual abuse on younger children in the past.[182] And although highway authorities are not liable merely for omitting to exercise a statutory power so as to protect road users from the consequences of their own carelessness,[183] this principle will not protect such an authority from liability for common law negligence where it creates a new source of danger by planting shrubs which obscure visibility.[184]

8-41 In *Phelps v Hillingdon LBC*[185] the House of Lords confirmed that the fact that acts which are claimed to be negligent are carried out within the ambit of a statutory discretion is not in itself a reason why it should be held that no claim for negligence can be brought in respect of them. Thus, a local education authority could be vicariously liable for the negligence of an educational psychologist or teacher when making an educational assessment of a child, notwithstanding that the breach of duty occurred in the course of the performance of a statutory duty and that a breach of the authority's duty under the Education Acts 1944 and 1981 did not give rise to a claim for breach of statutory duty. Lord Slynn commented that:

> "it is only where what is done has involved the weighing of competing public interests or has been dictated by considerations on which Parliament could not have intended that the courts would substitute their views for the views of ministers or officials that the courts will hold that the issue is non-justiciable on the ground that the decision was made in the exercise of a statutory discretion."[186]

Moreover:

> "If a duty of care would exist where advice was given other than pursuant to the exercise of statutory powers, such duty of care is not excluded because the advice is given pursuant to the exercise of statutory powers. This is particularly important where other remedies laid down by the statute (e.g. an appeals review procedure) do not in themselves provide sufficient redress for loss which has already been caused."[187]

There may be cases, said Lord Slynn, where such liability on the part of the educa-

---

181 See also *Neil Martin Ltd v Revenue and Customs Commissioners* [2007] EWCA Civ 1041; [2008] Bus. L.R. 663 in which the Court of Appeal held (see per Chadwick LJ at [73]) that an Inland Revenue employee who mistakenly assumed a non-existent authority to make an application on behalf of a taxpayer (instead of the application which the taxpayer wished to make), and to complete a statutory declaration in support of that unauthorised application, could owe the taxpayer a common law duty of care (rendering his employers, the Inland Revenue, vicariously liable for his negligence).

182 *W v Essex CC* [2001] 2 A.C. 592. See also *Barrett v Enfield LBC* [2001] 2 A.C. 550, where the House of Lords refused to strike out a claimant's action in negligence against the local authority in respect of decisions taken about his upbringing after he had been taken into care. Although the decision to take a child into care in the exercise of a statutory power was not justiciable, it did not follow that having taken the child into care the authority could not owe a duty of care in respect of what was or was not done in relation to the child, once in care. See further *S v Gloucestershire CC* [2001] Fam. 313 CA.

183 See *Gorringe v Calderdale MBC* [2004] UKHL15; [2004] 1 W.L.R. 1057. See also para.8-09.

184 See *Yetkin v Newham LBC* [2010] EWCA Civ 776; [2011] Q.B. 827. cf. *Sumner v Colborne and Denbighshire CC* [2018] EWCA Civ 1006; [2019] Q.B. 430.

185 [2001] 2 A.C. 619; applying *Barrett v Enfield LBC* [2001] 2 A.C. 550.

186 [2001] 2 A.C. 619 at 653.

187 [2001] 2 A.C. 619 at 653.

tion authority may interfere with the performance of the local education authority's duties so that it would be wrong to recognise any liability on the part of the authority. But this was for the local authority to establish; it would not be presumed, and the circumstances where it could be established would be "exceptional". The proposition that where acts claimed to be negligent are carried out within the ambit of a statutory discretion that is not in itself a reason why no claim for negligence can be brought in respect of them was also applied, in unusual circumstances, in *Connor v Surrey CC*.[188] The claimant headmistress brought a claim for stress at work against her employer, the local education authority. She suffered a nervous breakdown following unjust allegations of racism made against her by present and former members of the school's governing body. She claimed successfully that the defendants should have used their statutory discretion to dissolve the governing body, which had become dysfunctional, and replace it with an interim executive board. The Court of Appeal rejected the contention that the authority's discretion whether or not to exercise its power in this way was not justiciable. The court emphasised that the claim was based on the common law duty of care owed by an employer to its employee, it was not a case in which an attempt was being made to derive the duty of care from the statute itself. Furthermore, on the facts of the case there was no conflict between the defendants' public and private law duties. From both perspectives the chaotic state of the governance of the school had called for intervention by the authority.

(d) Other factors in determining whether the breach is actionable

The courts have occasionally been influenced against allowing an action for breach of statutory duty by the prospect of the extensive liability that the defendant would face, who would thereby find himself in the position of the claimant's insurer. Thus, the Court of Appeal was unwilling to hold Newcastle Waterworks liable for fire damage which might have been prevented had they maintained the pressure of water in their pipes which a statute required.[189] Similarly, it has been held that the duty placed by s.13 of the Fire Services Act 1947 (now s.38 of the Fire and Rescue Services Act 2004) on the fire brigade to take all reasonable measures to ensure that there was an adequate supply of water for fire fighting, did not create a private law action, but was merely part of the fire brigade's administrative duties to procure water for fire fighting.[190] There is no rule against recovery of economic loss in an action for breach of statutory duty. Where the claimant can establish, as was the case in *Rickless v United Artists Corp*,[191] that the purpose of the statute was to safeguard his financial interests an action will lie.[192] On the other **8-42**

---

188 [2010] EWCA Civ 286; [2011] Q.B. 429.

189 *Atkinson v Newcastle etc Waterworks Co* (1877) L.R. 2 Ex. D. 441.

190 *Capital and Counties Plc v Hampshire CC* [1997] Q.B. 1004 CA. Nor is there any duty of care in the tort of negligence, either to respond to an emergency call or to fight a fire competently, unless the negligence causes additional damage over and above that which would have been caused had they not intervened; cf. *Kent v London Ambulance Service* [2001] Q.B. 36 CA, on the common law duty of care of the ambulance service once a call for assistance is received and accepted.

191 [1988] 1 Q.B. 40.

192 But cf. *Trustee in Bankruptcy of St John Poulton's Trustee in Bankruptcy v Ministry of Justice* [2010] EWCA Civ 392; [2011] Ch. 1 (creditors in an insolvency unable to recover losses caused by failure of county court staff to comply with a statutory duty relating to registration of the petition). See also para.8-19.

hand, it would seem that following the trend in negligence[193] the courts will be cautious about inferring such an intention.[194] In particular where the essence of the complaint is that the defendant's violation of statute has made the claimant's business less profitable,[195] compelling evidence will be required to prove that the statute was designed to protect the claimant's profitability.

(e) Kind of damage sustained by the claimant

8-43 The alleged breach of statutory duty must give rise to the kind of damage generally remediable in tort. In *Pickering v Liverpool Daily Post and Echo Newspapers Ltd*,[196] the House of Lords found that the unauthorised publication of information concerning the claimant in breach of the Mental Health Tribunal Rules, though adverse to the patient's interests, did not give rise to a claim for breach of statutory duty. Such a violation of privacy was not a loss or injury of a kind for which the law awards damages. The breach of the statute must result in personal injury, damage to property or recognised economic loss. It will become apparent that in general the courts are much more ready to infer a right of action for breach of statutory provisions designed to ensure personal safety, particularly of employees. They are cautious about inferring the existence of such an action where the harm suffered is economic loss.[197]

8-44 In *Cullen v Chief Constable of the Royal Ulster Constabulary*[198] a majority of the House of Lords considered that there could be no action for breach of statutory duty in respect of the failure to permit a person detained in custody to have access to a solicitor or to give reasons for this (in breach of s.15 of the Northern Ireland (Temporary Provisions) Act 1987 or the parallel provision in s.58 of the Police and Criminal Evidence Act 1984 relating to non-terrorist offences) where the claimant had suffered no harm as a consequence. Lord Hutton said that "harm" meant "some substantial detriment or distress which calls for an award of damages to compensate

---

[193] *Wentworth v Wiltshire CC* [1993] Q.B. 654 CA; and see *Scally v Southern Health and Social Services Board* [1992] A.C. 294.

[194] "In my opinion, the court will more readily construe a statutory provision so as to provide a civil cause of action where the provision relates to the safety and health of a class of persons rather than where they have merely suffered economic loss", per Stuart Smith LJ in *Richardson v Pitt-Stanley* [1995] Q.B. 123 at 132. The irony of this remark is that the claimant was seeking to recover from the directors of his employer the financial loss attributable to the fact that a judgment debt against the employer in respect of the claimant's claim for personal injuries remained unsatisfied because the employer was uninsured.

[195] *RCA v Pollard* [1983] Ch. 135.

[196] [1991] 2 A.C. 370 HL.

[197] See *R. v Deputy Governor of Parkhurst Prison Ex p. Hague* [1992] 1 A.C. 58 at 160-161, per Lord Bridge. See also *Greenway v Johnson Matthey Plc* [2014] EWHC 3957 (QB); [2015] P.I.Q.R. P10 at [34], per Jay J (aff'd [2016] EWCA Civ 408; [2016] 1 W.L.R. 4487): "interests of an economic nature" not normally included in the concept of "welfare" in the Health and Safety at Work etc Act 1974). The decision of the Court of Appeal in *Greenway v Johnson Matthey Plc* (affirming Jay J) was subsequently reversed by the Supreme Court, but without affecting the point in the text, i.e. the Court held that, correctly interpreted, the facts indicated that the claimants had suffered physical damage (so the question of the irrecoverability of economic loss in breach of statutory duty and negligence did not arise): see *Dryden v Johnson Matthey Plc* [2018] UKSC 18; [2019] A.C 403. Note the availability of actions for economic loss occasioned by violation of European Union legislation: see para.8-46.

[198] [2003] UKHL 39; [2003] 1 W.L.R. 1763.

him for that harm".[199] There should be no award of nominal damages "where, not only did the appellant suffer no personal injury, injury to property or economic loss, but there was no evidence of any harm sustained by him and where judicial review would have afforded an effective and speedy remedy".[200] Lord Millett also emphasised that the breach of s.15 was "made in good faith" and "had no adverse consequences of any kind, neither prolonging his detention nor prejudicing the conduct of his defence and rendering his trial unfair, and causing him neither financial loss nor physical harm or mental distress".[201] This leaves unanswered the question of what the position would be if there were evidence that the claimant did suffer damage in such a situation. Lord Hutton acknowledged that the *Royal Commission on Criminal Procedure*[202] considered that a person who suffered substantial inconvenience, distress or other disadvantage as a result of a breach of such a right should be able to obtain damages[203]; and Lord Millett commented that "denial of the right by itself (that is to say where it does not cause or prolong unlawful detention) is incapable of causing loss or injury of a kind for which the law normally awards damages",[204] suggesting by implication that if such a breach did cause or prolong unlawful detention then an action might lie.[205] As Lords Bingham and Steyn pointed out in their joint dissenting speech, Lord Hutton's view that there should be no award of damages unless there has been harm as he sought to define it "weakens significantly the reasoning in principle of the majority". In their Lordships' view the fact that breach of the duty to allow access to a solicitor was not likely to lead to personal injury, damage to property or economic loss pointed to the "natural and obvious solution" that the breach should be actionable per se.[206] The status of the majority decision in *Cullen's* case may also be said to have been undermined by the unanimous decision of a seven member Supreme Court that the failure of Scottish criminal law to afford a right to detained persons to consult a solicitor constituted a breach of art.6 of the European Convention on Human Rights.[207]

(f) Secondary legislation

A difficult question arises when an alleged breach of statutory duty consists of a breach of regulations made under an Act of Parliament.[208] Does the enabling Act empower the Minister to make regulations conferring private rights of action? In *R. v Deputy Governor of Parkhurst Prison Ex p. Hague*, Lord Jauncey[209] held that s.47 of the Prison Act 1952, empowering the Home Secretary to make and amend **8-45**

199 [2003] UKHL 39; [2003] 1 W.L.R. 1763 at [33].

200 [2003] UKHL 39; [2003] 1 W.L.R. 1763 at [42], per Lord Hutton.

201 [2003] UKHL 39; [2003] 1 W.L.R. 1763 at [59].

202 (1981), Cmnd.8092.

203 [2003] UKHL 39 at [44].

204 [2003] UKHL 39 at [69].

205 Though query whether the detention would have to be independently "unlawful", or whether a breach of s.15 or s.58 which prolonged the detention, would itself make the detention unlawful.

206 [2003] UKHL 39 at [19].

207 See *Cadder v HM Advocate* [2010] UKSC 43; [2010] 1 W.L.R. 2601. See also para.8-14.

208 See *Refell v Surrey CC* [1964] 1 W.L.R. 358; *London Passenger Transport Board v Upson* [1949] A.C. 155; *Phillips v Britannia Hygiene Laundry Co* [1923] 2 K.B. 832.

209 [1992] 1 A.C. 58 at 171. See also *Olotu v Home Office* [1997] 1 W.L.R. 328 at 339, where Mummery LJ doubted that Parliament intended to authorise the Secretary of State to confer a private law right of action when making regulations as to custody time limits under the Prosecution of Offences Act 1985.

the Prison Rules, conferred no power on him to make regulations granting private rights to prisoners. Lord Bridge, however suggested that breach of those Rules pertaining to the employment, and health and safety, of prisoners in prison workshops might well give rise to a private right of action. Both agreed that the scope of the legislative intent in granting the relevant rule-making power must be considered. It would seem that a claim for breach of statutory duty can be founded on secondary legislation, but only if it is clear that Parliament in enacting the primary legislation authorised the Minister to create private rights for the benefit of individual claimants.[210] Where the statute enables the Minister to create rules concerning the safety of a particular class of claimants through secondary legislation, but empowers the Minister to exempt certain categories of potential defendant from the rules, this will tend to indicate that there was no intention to impose civil liability for breach of those rules.[211]

(g) Breach of European Union law[212]

8-46 Where provisions of European Union laws were held to be directly applicable in Member States, prior to the departure of the UK from the European Union, the question arose whether an individual suffering loss or harm as a consequence of violation of those provisions had a remedy in tort in England. In *Garden Cottage Foods v Milk Marketing Board*,[213] the claimant's case was that he had suffered financial loss as a consequence of violation of what was then art.86 of the EEC Treaty which prohibits abuse of a dominant trading position. Article 86 had earlier been held by the European Court of Justice to create direct rights in respect of the individuals concerned, which national courts must protect.[214] Consequently Lord Diplock categorised a breach of the duty imposed by art.86 not to abuse a dominant position as a breach of a statutory duty imposed not only for the purpose of promoting the general economic prosperity of the Common Market but also for the benefit of private individuals to whom loss or damage was caused by a breach of that duty:

> "If this categorisation be correct, and I can see none other that would be capable of giving rise to a civil cause of action in English private law on the part of a private individual who sustained loss or damage by reason of the breach of a directly applicable provision of the EEC Treaty, the nature of the cause of action cannot, in my view, be affected by the fact that the legislative provision by which the duty is imposed takes the negative form of a prohibition of particular kinds of conduct rather than the positive form of an obligation to do particular acts."[215]

---

210 cf. *Trustee in Bankruptcy of St John Poulton's Trustee in Bankruptcy v Ministry of Justice* [2010] EWCA Civ 392; [2011] Ch. 1 (Insolvency Act 1986 s.412 did not authorise creation by the Insolvency Rules 1986 r.6.13 of private rights for the benefit of creditors). See also para.8-19.

211 *Todd v Adams and Chope (t/a Trelawney Fishing Co) (The Margaretha Maria)* [2002] EWCA Civ 509; [2002] 2 Lloyd's Rep. 293 at [25], per Neuberger J—no action in respect of breach of safety regulations in relation to fishing vessels under the Merchant Shipping Act 1995 s.121, and the Fishing Vessel (Safety Provisions) Rules 1975 (SI 1975/330), because it would be strange if two identical vessels had accidents caused by the same defects but in one case there was no claim because the vessel had been exempted from the rules.

212 See Stanton, Skidmore, Harris and Wright, *Statutory Torts* (2003), Ch.6.

213 [1984] A.C. 130 HL.

214 *Belgische Radio en Televisie v SV SABAM* Case 127/73, [1974] E.C.R. 51.

215 [1984] A.C. 130 at 141.

In *Francovich v Italian Republic*,[216] the European Court of Justice held that an individual was entitled to damages for the failure of a Member State properly to implement EU legislation, and later cases made it clear that the entitlement included other types of breaches of EU law. In *R. v Secretary of State for Transport Ex p. Factortame Ltd (No.4)*,[217] it was held that European Community law confers a right to damages when three conditions are satisfied: **8-47**

(1) the rule of Community law breached was intended to confer rights on individuals;
(2) the breach was sufficiently serious[218];
(3) there is a direct causal link between the breach and the damage sustained.[219]

It seems to be clear that the right to damages is properly categorised as an action for breach of statutory duty.[220] Nevertheless, the three conditions evidently differ from the somewhat haphazard common law "rules" on breach of statutory duty. Moreover, if statutory regulations are introduced to implement a European Union Directive, it does not follow that a claimant can fortuitously take advantage of the common law "rules" in an action for breach of the regulations, instead of the relevant criteria of European Union law, where those criteria happen to be less favourable to his claim than the common law approach.[221]

Following the departure of the UK from the European Union the question arises as to whether the common law "rules", or the European approach, will now govern claims for damages based on breach of retained EU law. The European Union (Withdrawal) Act 2018, however, provides as follows in s.6 (as amended by the European Union (Withdrawal Agreement) Act 2020): **8-48**

> "(3) Any question as to the validity, meaning or effect of any retained EU law is to be decided, so far as that law is unmodified on or after IP completion day and so far as they are relevant to it—
>
> (a) in accordance with any retained case law and any retained general principles of EU law ..."

Section 6(3)(4) goes on to provide expressly that the Supreme Court is not bound by retained EU case law, and s.6(5A) that other courts will not be bound by it according to delegated legislation, to be made under the Act, identifying the courts or tribunals which will enjoy this freedom. It would therefore appear that the "European" approach to breach of statutory duty will apply to claims based on

216 (C-6 and 9/90) [1993] 2 C.M.L.R. 66.

217 [1996] Q.B. 404 at 499 ECJ.

218 As to what constitutes a serious breach, see *R. v HM Treasury Ex p. British Telecommunications Plc* [1996] Q.B. 615; *Dillenkofer v Federal Republic of Germany* [1997] Q.B. 259 ECJ; *R. v Secretary of State for Transport Ex p. Factortame Ltd (No.5)* [2000] 1 A.C. 524 HL; *Byrne v Motor Insurers Bureau* [2008] EWCA Civ 574; [2009] Q.B. 66; *Test Claimants in the Franked Investment Group Litigation v Inland Revenue Commissioners* [2010] EWCA Civ 103; [2010] S.T.C. 1251; [2010] B.T.C. 265; reversed in part at [2012] UKSC 19; [2012] 2 A.C. 337; *Delaney v Secretary of State for Transport* [2015] EWCA Civ 172; [2015] 1 W.L.R. 5177.

219 For an unsuccessful attempt to obtain damages for breach of the three conditions see *AB v Home Office* [2012] EWHC 226; [2012] 4 All E.R. 276 in which the claimant sought compensation for alleged breach of an EC Directive (the "Citizens Directive") relating to residence. For a successful attempt see *Barco De Vapor BV v Thanet DC* [2014] EWHC 490 (Ch); [2015] Bus. L.R. 593.

220 See *Secretary of State for Transport v Arriva Rail East Midlands Ltd* [2019] EWCA Civ 2259; [2020] P. & C.R. 17 at [72].

221 See *EnergySolutions EU Ltd v Nuclear Decommissioning Authority* [2017] UKSC 34; [2017] 1 W.L.R. 1373.

retained EU law, unless and until a court which is empowered to do so, decides otherwise in the context of the particular claim before it.

(h) Proposals for reform

8-49 The tests which the courts purport to use to determine whether a statute carries civil liability for its breach largely conflict with one another. "In effect the judge can do what he likes, and then select one of the conflicting principles stated by his predecessors in order to justify his decision."[222] Various proposals have been made to clarify the position. Professor Glanville Williams argued for a theory of "concretisation". Where a statutory duty overlaps with an existing common law duty—for example, where parts of the Road Traffic Acts and regulations made under it cover the same ground as the common law liability of a negligent motorist—breach of the statutory duty should automatically involve civil liability within the area of overlap, because it "concretises" the standard of care at common law. Outside this area, civil liability ought to be imposed only where there are clear indications in the statute that it is intended.[223] In 1969, the Law Commission examined the question and made a more radical proposal, recommending the enactment of a general statutory presumption in favour of actionability in the absence of an express provision to the contrary.[224] This recommendation was not acted upon, however, and 30 years later the Commission proposed in a consultation paper that the action for breach of statutory duty should be abolished and replaced by an entirely new, wider, remedy enabling individuals to obtain financial redress from public bodies if those bodies had been "seriously at fault".[225] In its final report following the consultation, however, the Commission dropped the proposal for the new remedy, from which it followed that the suggestion that the existing remedy of breach of statutory duty should be abolished was also not proceeded with.[226] Within individual Acts of Parliament there can perhaps be discerned a trend for Parliament to be more ready either expressly to exclude any action for breach of statutory duty[227] or in certain cases expressly to grant a private law remedy.[228] A prominent example of a statutory provision expressly designed to create new civil remedies is the Financial Services and Markets Act 2000 s.138D(2).[229] This provides that contravention of a defined type of delegated legislation promulgated by the Financial Conduct Authority "is actionable at the suit of a private person who suffers loss as a result of the contravention subject to the defences and other incidents applying to actions for breach of statutory duty". In *Rubenstein v HSBC Bank Plc*[230] an investor who had been mis-sold an inappropriate product by the defendant bank was awarded substantial damages for, inter alia, breach of statutory duty pursuant

---

222 Williams, "The Effect of Penal Legislation in the Law of Tort" (1960) 23 M.L.R. 233 at 246.
223 Williams, "The Effect of Penal Legislation in the Law of Tort" (1960) 23 M.L.R. 233 at 246.
224 See Law Com. No.21 (Scots Law Com. No.11), *The Interpretation of Statutes*, para.38 and Appendix A(4).
225 See *Law Com. CP 187* (2008) at paras 4.95 to 4.105.
226 See *Administrative Redress: Public Bodies and the Citizen*, Law Com No.232 paras 3.73 and 3.74.
227 See Consumer Protection Act 1987 s.41.
228 e.g. Trade Union and Labour Relations (Consolidation) Act 1992 s.145; Local Government Act 1988 s.17.
229 Substituted by the Financial Services Act 2012 s.21.
230 [2012] EWCA Civ 1184; [2013] 1 All E.R. (Comm) 915.

to this section. The provision is a good illustration of the beneficial simplification which express statements of parliamentary intention can facilitate.

4. Damage within the Ambit of the Statute

Injury not contemplated by the statute Non-compliance with a statutory duty cannot be actionable unless the injury was of the type which the statute was passed to prevent.[231] If a statute requires something to be done with a view to avoiding one particular type of damage, then, if non-compliance with the statute results in another form of damage, no action will lie, on the basis that the damage which occurred was not within the statute. Each case turns upon the interpretation of the statute, and this factor makes it difficult to formulate any more precise principle. The harm may not be within the ambit of the statute either: 8-50

(a) because the claimant does not come within the particular category of persons contemplated; or
(b) because the type of damage was not that which the statute was intended to guard against.

For example, in *Wentworth v Wiltshire CC*,[232] it was found that the statutory duty to maintain the highway was imposed on local authorities to protect users of the highway from personal injury. Breach of that duty did not give rise to a claim for economic loss. Similarly, in *Polestar Jowetts Ltd v Komori UK Ltd*[233] it was held that health and safety regulations made under the Health and Safety at Work etc. Act 1974 were for the purpose of protecting individuals from personal injury, not for that of protecting employers from damage to property or financial loss.

Claimant not contemplated by the statute A statute may impose a duty towards persons generally, in which case no question can arise of whether the claimant is within the class protected.[234] But more usually a statute is passed in favour of a limited class, such as employees, and they alone will have a possible cause of action. Thus, a fireman who was electrocuted while fighting a fire in a factory had no cause of action for the breach of regulations involved, as these had been made for the benefit of "persons employed".[235] Similarly a building contractor was not normally[236] liable under the Construction (Working Places) Regulations 1966 to the 8-51

[231] "When seeking to articulate what constitutes actionable harm, it is necessary to have regard to the object and scope of the statutory duty imposed": per Marcus Smith J in *Britned Development Ltd v ABB* [2018] EWHC 2616 (Ch); [2019] Bus. L.R. 718 at [427].

[232] [1993] Q.B. 654 CA. See also *Stovin v Wise* [1994] 1 W.L.R. 1124 at 1129–1130, where the Court of Appeal held that the statutory duty to maintain the highway does not extend to work on land not forming part of the highway, and therefore there was no breach of duty for failing to remove an obstruction to visibility on land adjoining the highway. For liability in negligence, see [1996] A.C. 923 HL.

[233] [2006] EWCA Civ 536; [2006] 1 W.L.R. 2472.

[234] e.g. *Monk v Warbey* [1935] K.B. 75 (duty imposed by the Road Traffic Acts to insure vehicles was imposed for the benefit of all road users).

[235] *Hartley v Mayoh & Co* [1954] 1 Q.B. 383; *Knapp v Railway Executive* [1949] 2 All E.R. 508 (duty to keep level crossing gates in the proper position was to protect the public using the road, not the train driver); *Ndri v Moorfields Eye Hospital NHS Trust* [2006] EWHC 3652 (QB) (the Control of Substances Hazardous to Health Regulations 1999 do not apply to a patient treated in hospital to whom a substance is administered); cf. *Canadian Pacific Steamships Ltd v Bryers* [1958] A.C. 485.

[236] However, he may have been so liable: (a) where reg.3(1)(b) of either set of regulations applied:

employee of a subcontractor,[237] nor was he normally liable under the Construction (General Provisions) Regulations 1961 for injury to a labour-only subcontractor working on "the lump".[238] The expression "any person" in s.29 of the Factories Act 1961 comprehended all those who entered a factory to work for the purposes of the factory, and accordingly, a window cleaner who was employed as an independent contractor by the factory owner was within the ambit of the duty imposed by the section.[239] Similarly, the expression "every person employed ... on the premises" in s.14(1) of that Act included a person who at the relevant time, was acting outside the scope of his employment[240] and s.16 of the Offices, Shops and Railway Premises Act 1963, which required all floors "to be of sound construction and properly maintained", protected an employee who went where he had no business to be.[241] Breach of a duty "not to do anything likely to endanger the safety or health of himself or other persons on or near the installation" is not actionable by the claimant if the breach did not actually endanger the claimant's health, even though the breach caused the death and serious injury of others.[242]

8-52 Section 2 of the Dramatic and Musical Performers' Protection Act 1958 made it a criminal offence to make unauthorised recordings of dramatic and musical performances without the performers' consent.[243] "Bootlegged" recordings result in financial losses both to performers themselves and to the recording companies authorised by performers to make bona fide recordings. The Court of Appeal held in *Rickless v United Artists Corp*[244] that performers constituted a class of persons intended to be protected by the Act. Thus when a film was made consisting of an unauthorised use of clips from old Peter Sellers films his widow recovered damages for breach of statutory duty. On the other hand, the claimants in *RCA Corp v*

Donaghey v Boulton & Paul Ltd [1968] A.C. 1; and (b) where the contract of services was a mere sham: *Ferguson v Dawson* [1976] 1 W.L.R. 1213. See Mordsley (1975) 38 M.L.R. 504.

237 *Smith v George Wimpey & Co Ltd* [1972] 2 Q.B. 329; approving *Bunker v Charles Brand & Son Ltd* [1969] 2 Q.B. 480; and *Taylor v Sayers* [1971] 1 W.L.R. 561. Nor was he generally liable under the Construction (Working Places) Regulations 1966 to the independent contractor himself: *Clare v Whittaker & Son* [1976] I.C.R. 1. (The 1966 Regulations were revoked by the Construction (Health, Safety and Welfare) Regulations 1996 (SI 1996/1592); see now the Construction (Design and Management) Regulations 2015 (SI 2015/51).

238 *Jones v Minton Construction Ltd* (1973) 15 K.I.R. 309. However, in *Ferguson v John Dawson & Partners* [1976] 1 W.L.R. 1213, noted (1977) 40 M.L.R. 479, the Court of Appeal, by a majority, held a man working "on the lump" to be an employee rather than an independent contractor. On the liability of independent contractors on building sites under the Construction (Lifting Operations) Regulations 1961, see *Williams v West Wales Plant Hire Co Ltd* [1984] 1 W.L.R. 1311. See now Lifting Operations and Lifting Equipment Regulations 1998 (SI 1998/2307) and the Manual Handling Operations Regulations 1992 (SI 1992/2793).

239 *Wigley v British Vinegars Ltd* [1964] A.C. 307 HL; cf. *Canadian Pacific Steamships Ltd v Bryers* [1958] A.C. 485 (Shipbuilding Regulations 1931 reg.10); and *Mace v R & H Green etc Ltd* [1959] 2 Q.B. 14 (Docks Regulations 1934 reg.11(1)). Note that the Factories Act 1961 s.29 was repealed by the Workplace (Health, Safety and Welfare) Regulations 1992 (SI 1992/3004).

240 *Uddin v Associated Portland Cement Manufacturers Ltd* [1965] 2 Q.B. 15 CA (a decision on s.14(1) of the Act of 1937) followed in *Allen v Aeroplane and Motor Aluminium Castings Ltd* [1965] 1 W.L.R. 1244 and in *Westwood v Post Office* [1974] A.C. 1.

241 *Westwood v Post Office* [1974] A.C. 1; Hepple [1973] C.L.J. 211.

242 *McFarlane v Wilkinson* [1997] 2 Lloyd's Rep. 259 CA, where the claimant suffered psychiatric damage as result of witnessing the *Piper Alpha* disaster, but was never actually in physical danger (Offshore Installations (Operational Safety Health and Welfare) Regulations 1976 reg.32(3)(a)).

243 See now Copyright, Designs and Patents Act 1988.

244 [1988] 1 Q.B. 40.

Pollard[245] were recording companies who sought to restrain the sale of bootlegged recordings, arguing that even if an individual damaged by a breach of statutory duty not intended nor designed to protect his interests could not claim damages for his loss, it was still open to the court to grant an injunction to protect his interests. The Court of Appeal held that recording companies were not persons contemplated by the Dramatic and Musical Performers' Protection Act 1958, nor was the Act designed to protect their business and commercial interests.

Type of damage outside scope of the Act Usually a statutory duty is imposed to prevent some particular form of harm, either to the community at large or to a class of the community. Thus, in order to succeed it must be shown that the damage suffered was within the scope of the contemplated injury. In *Gorris v Scott*,[246] it was held that no action lay for sheep washed overboard when carried as deck cargo without proper pens, in contravention of a statute which was intended to prevent the spread of contagious disease and not to safeguard cargo from the perils of the sea. Similarly, the claimant could not recover damages from a water company which had failed to maintain a certain pressure of water in their pipes when his house was destroyed by fire[247]; nor could the claimant recover for damage suffered from purchasing diseased pigs which had been sent to market in contravention of a regulation designed to avoid infection of cattle.[248] In *Fytche v Wincanton Logistics Plc*[249] the House of Lords held that the requirement for employers to provide steel capped safety boots is for the protection of employees against the risk of injury from falling weights or contact with hard or sharp objects, not to protect against the risk of frostbite. The whole language and scope of the statute must be considered carefully to discover whether or not there was an intention to grant a remedy.[250] Thus, a miner recovered for breach of the requirement that "the roof and sides of every travelling road … shall be made secure",[251] being injured when a bogie in which he was riding was derailed upon striking a stone which had fallen from the roof, although the primary object of the provision was to prevent direct impact from a fall.[252] The requirement that the claimant's damage must fall within the scope of the statute is analogous to the rules of remoteness of damage in the tort 8-53

245 [1983] Ch. 135; *CBS Songs Ltd v Amstrad Consumer Electronics Plc* [1988] 1 Ch. 612 CA; affirmed [1988] A.C. 1013 HL.

246 (1874) L.R. 9 Ex. 125.

247 *Atkinson v Newcastle etc Waterworks Co* (1877) 2 Ex. D. 441, where a penalty of £10 was held to be the only sanction against a waterworks company that had failed to maintain sufficient water pressure; cf. *Dawson & Co v Bingley Urban DC* [1911] 2 K.B. 149 CA, where the relevant legislation contained no remedy for its breach. See also *Read v Croydon Corp* [1938] 4 All E.R. 631, where it was held that breach of a different section of the Waterworks Clauses Act 1847 requiring the supply of pure and wholesome water was actionable despite provision for a penalty; *Bowden v South West Water Services Ltd* [1998] Env. L.R. 445 QBD—the provisions of the Water Industry Act 1991 and the Water Resources Act 1991 are actionable in public law only.

248 *Ward v Hobbs* (1878) 4 App. Cas. 13. See also *Vallance v Falle* (1884) 13 Q.B.D. 109; *Hemmings v Stoke Poges Golf Club* [1920] 1 K.B. 720.

249 [2004] UKHL 31; [2004] 4 All E.R. 221; [2004] I.C.R. 975 (considering the effect of the Personal Protective Equipment at Work Regulations 1992 (SI 1992/2966), reg.7). See further paras 12-59 and 12-60.

250 *Atkinson v Newcastle etc Waterworks Co* (1877) 2 Ex. D. 441; *Phillips v Britannia Hygienic Laundry Co Ltd* [1923] 2 K.B. 832; *Clarke and Wife v Brims* [1947] K.B. 497.

251 Coal Mines Act 1911 s.49.

252 *Grant v National Coal Board* [1956] A.C. 649. See also *Gatehouse v John Summers & Sons Ltd* [1953] 1 W.L.R. 742 (Electricity Regulations 1908); but cf. *Evans v Sanderson Bros and Newbould* (1968) 4 K.I.R. 115 CA; *Dooley v Cammell Laird & Co* [1951] 1 Lloyd's Rep. 271 (Shipbuilding Regulations 1931).

of negligence, which provide that the damage must be of the type that was reasonably foreseeable.[253] But if the damage is of the type that the statute was meant to prevent then, as with negligence, it is irrelevant that the precise manner in which it occurred was not foreseen.[254]

5. The Standard of Liability

8-54 **"Statutory negligence"** In *Lochgelly Iron & Coal Co Ltd v M'Mullan*,[255] the House of Lords came close to equating an action for breach of statutory duty with an action in negligence. Lord Atkin said that all that was necessary to show "is a duty to take care to avoid injuring; and if the particular care to be taken is prescribed by statute, and the duty to the injured person to take the care is likewise imposed by statute, and the breach is proved, all the essentials of negligence are present".[256] Negligence did not depend on the court agreeing with the legislature that the precaution ought to have been taken, because the "very object of the legislation is to put that particular precaution beyond controversy". On this approach breach of a statutory duty constitutes negligence per se, but it applies only to legislation which is designed to prevent a particular mischief in respect of which the defendant is already under a duty at common law.[257] Failure to meet the prescribed statutory standard is then treated as unreasonable conduct amounting to negligence, because a reasonable man would not ignore precautions required by statute, and the defendant cannot claim that the harm was unforeseeable because the legislature has already anticipated it. The statutory standard "crystallises" the question of what constitutes carelessness. On the other hand, where legislation does not deal with circumstances in which there is an existing common law duty, then, unless expressly stated, breach of the statute would not give rise to an action, because the damages may greatly exceed the penalty considered appropriate by the legislature.

8-55 The advantage of the negligence per se rule, it is said, is that it avoids the search for a fictional parliamentary intention. But in practice it creates a presumptive parliamentary intent that when a statute fits the rule (i.e. covers the same ground as an existing common law rule) breach will give rise to civil liability. An alternative approach is that breach of the statute is not conclusive as to liability, but provides prima facie evidence of negligence. On this version it is open to the defendant to argue that in spite of his contravention of the statute, nonetheless he acted reasonably in the circumstances and therefore should not be liable in negligence. This approach was adopted by the Supreme Court of Canada in *The*

---

253 See para.2-153 onwards.

254 *Donaghey v Boulton & Paul Ltd* [1968] A.C. 1 at 26, per Lord Reid:

> "It is one thing to say that if the damage suffered is of a kind totally different from that which it is the object of the regulation to prevent, there is no civil liability. But it is quite a different thing to say that civil liability is excluded because the damage, though precisely of the kind which the regulation was designed to prevent, happened in a way not contemplated by the maker of the regulation."

See also per Lord Guest at 34: "The precise way in which the accident happened is not material if the accident which happened was the type of accident against which the regulation was designed"; citing *Hughes v Lord Advocate* [1963] A.C. 837; see para.2-160.

255 [1934] A.C. 1.

256 [1934] A.C. 1 at 9.

257 Williams (1960) 23 M.L.R. 233 at 252.

Queen in Right of Canada v Saskatchewan Wheat Pool,[258] essentially in order to avoid the imposition of strict liability, though strict liability in the case of industrial safety legislation was regarded as an exception.[259] On this basis, the action for breach of statutory duty is not an independent tort, but merely an evidentiary principle of the tort of negligence.[260]

Relationship to the tort of negligence Despite the comments of the House of Lords in *Lochgelly Iron etc Co v M'Mullan*,[261] this view has not taken hold in English law. Liability for breach of statutory duty is in reality sui generis and independent of any other form of tortious liability. Thus, breach of statutory duty has not been limited to circumstances in which a common law duty of care already existed.[262] Lord Wright made it clear that the action is not for "negligence in the strict or ordinary sense"[263] but "belongs to the category often described as that of cases of strict or absolute liability".[264] The two actions can overlap, but failure by the claimant to establish breach of a relevant statute does not necessarily prevent a successful claim in negligence. Indeed, statutory duties may be instrumental in suggesting to the courts what additional precautions a reasonable man would take. So if regulations require an employer to supply goggles to his workmen, reasonable care may require him to encourage their use.[265] Often the statutory obligation will extend beyond the requirements of reasonable care, and in many cases there would be little advantage to the claimant if it did not. How far breach of statutory duty involves strict or absolute liability depends, however, on what is meant by strict or absolute liability. The issue generally arises in one of two ways. 8-56

Standard of care In the first type of case, the defendant argues as follows: 8-57

> "Of course I knew or had reason to know that I was not complying with the letter of the statute; but it would have been impracticable, unwise or unnecessary to do so."

As judges do not like litigants to call the law an ass, this argument usually fails; to the extent that it does, liability for breach of statutory duty is indeed "strict" or "absolute". Thus where the Factories Act provided that "every dangerous part of any machinery ... shall be securely fenced", in *John Summers & Sons Ltd v Frost*[266] a factory owner was held liable for an injury caused by the unfenced part of a grind-

---

[258] (1983) 143 D.L.R. (3d) 9. See Rogers [1984] C.L.J. 23.

[259] A blanket objection to strict liability seems misplaced, at least without some consideration of the respective policy objectives of fault and strict liability. See Matthews (1984) 4 O.J.L.S. 429 at 431.

[260] The converse proposition also applies in Canadian law. Mere compliance with a standard laid down by statute does not necessarily provide a defence to an action in negligence: *Ryan v Victoria* (1999) 168 D.L.R. (4th) 513 (SCC).

[261] [1934] A.C. 1.

[262] See *Monk v Warbey* [1935] 1 K.B. 75; *Warder v Cooper* [1970] Ch. 495.

[263] *London Passenger Transport Board v Upson* [1949] A.C. 155 at 168.

[264] *Caswell v Powell Duffryn Associated Collieries Ltd* [1940] A.C. 152 at 177.

[265] *Bux v Slough Metals Ltd* [1973] 1 W.L.R. 1358 CA; Barrett (1974) 37 M.L.R. 577. The obligation on employers to see that employees use protective equipment is now contained in regulations. See the Personal Protective Equipment at Work Regulations 1992 (SI 1992/2966) reg.10(1): "Every employer shall take all reasonable steps to ensure that any personal protective equipment provided to his employees by virtue of reg.4(1) is properly used."

[266] [1955] A.C. 740. The fence must provide "complete protection against contact": per Lord Morton at 757. See also *Pearce v Stanley Bridges Ltd* [1965] 1 W.L.R. 931 CA; *Dexter v Tenby Electrical Accessories* [1991] Crim. L.R. 839; *MacMillan v Wimpey Offshore Engineers and Constructors*, 1991 S.L.T. 515. But contrast the approach in *Mizra v Ford Motor Co* [1981] I.C.R. 757 CA.

ing wheel, even though it would have been impossible to use the machine if the dangerous part was indeed securely fenced. Many statutory duties, however, have a built-in escape-route for the situation where strict compliance would be foolish or impracticable, and this prevents strict liability in the present sense arising. Thus the Factories Act 1961 s.29(1), created an obligation to provide and maintain safe means of access "so far as reasonably practicable",[267] and the Mines and Quarries Act 1954 s.157, provided a defence if it "was impracticable to avoid or prevent the contravention".[268] Sometimes, the courts find an escape-route in an ambiguous phrase. Thus, although the Mines and Quarries Act 1954 s.48(1), provided that "it shall be the duty of the manager to take ... such steps by way of ... supporting the roof and sides of the road ... as may be necessary for keeping the road ... secure", the House of Lords construed this as imposing a duty which was not absolute. It did not render a manager liable if he obtained all the information which the section required him to obtain and then acted in the light of this with due care and skill,[269] though he remained under an obligation "to take steps to prevent the emergence of foreseeable insecurity".[270] Nor did it require him to prop up that part of the coal-face which it was the whole object of the exercise to bring down.[271] Similarly, even though the Factories Act 1961 s.28(1), required that "all floors ... shall be of sound construction and properly maintained", no liability was incurred when a workman slipped on a floor which owing to transient and exceptional circumstances was wet and oily, for it was a question of degree whether such temporary inefficiency constituted a breach of the duty[272]; and a duty to provide "suitable goggles" has been held not to require the provision of perfect goggles.[273]

8-58 In the second type of case, the defendant says: "neither I nor my servants or

---

[267] But a claimant who alleged a breach of s.29(1) did not have to prove that it would have been reasonably practicable for his employer to provide and maintain safe means of access, as the onus is on the employer to establish that it was not reasonably practicable to make it any safer: *Nimmo v Alexander Cowan & Sons Ltd* [1968] A.C. 107 HL. The "reasonably practicable" qualification contained in s.28(1) has been held to mean that all reasonable means must be taken: *Braham v J Lyons & Co* [1962] 1 W.L.R. 1048 CA. See also *Dorman Long (Steel) Ltd v Bell* [1964] 1 W.L.R. 333 HL. For the interpretation of similar words in s.29(2), see *Thompson v Bowaters United Kingdom Paper Co Ltd* [1975] K.I.L.R. 47, and in s.63(1), see *Cartwright v GKN Sankey Ltd* (1973) 14 K.I.R. 349 CA; *Wallhead v Rushton & Hornsby Ltd* (1973) 14 K.I.R. 285. Note that the Workplace (Health, Safety and Welfare) Regulations 1992 (SI 1992/3004), repeal the Factories Act 1961 s.29.

[268] The meaning of "impracticable" in s.157 was considered in *Sanderson v National Coal Board* [1961] 2 Q.B. 244 CA; and *Jayne v National Coal Board* [1963] 2 All E.R. 220. If a defendant wishes to rely on such a defence, he must expressly plead it: *Bowes v Sedgefield DC* [1981] I.C.R. 234 CA. As to the distinction between "impracticable" and "not reasonably practicable"; see *Sanders v FH Lloyd & Co Ltd* [1982] I.C.R. 360; *Hammond v NCB* [1984] 1 W.L.R. 1218.

[269] *Brown v National Coal Board* [1962] A.C. 574 HL. See Fridman (1969) 32 M.L.R. 174; cf. *O'Hara v National Coal Board*, 1973 S.L.T. (Notes) 25; *Aitken v National Coal Board*, 1973 S.L.T. (Notes) 48.

[270] *John G Stein & Co Ltd v O'Hanlon* [1965] A.C. 890 HL. See also *Brazier v Skipton Rock Co Ltd* [1962] 1 W.L.R. 471; *Tomlinson v Beckermet Mining Co Ltd* [1964] 1 W.L.R. 1043 CA; *Beiscak v National Coal Board* [1965] 1 W.L.R. 518; *Soar v National Coal Board* [1965] 1 W.L.R. 886 CA; *Sanderson v Millom Hematite etc Co Ltd* [1967] 3 All E.R. 1050; *Venn v National Coal Board* [1967] 2 Q.B. 557; *Robson v National Coal Board* [1968] 3 All E.R. 159.

[271] *Gough v National Coal Board* [1959] A.C. 698; *Anderson v National Coal Board*, 1970 S.C. 42.

[272] *Latimer v AEC Ltd* [1953] A.C. 643. Nevertheless, even temporary lack of safety could sometimes have given rise to liability under s.29(1): *Cox v HCB Angus Ltd* [1981] I.C.R. 683; *Johnston v Caddies Wainwright Ltd* [1983] I.C.R. 407.

[273] *Daniels v Ford Motor Co* [1955] 1 W.L.R. 76 CA; *Bux v Slough Metals* [1973] 1 W.L.R. 1358 CA; cf. *Rogers v George Blair & Co* (1971) 11 K.I.R. 391 CA. In *Gerrard v Staffordshire Potteries* [1995]

agents knew or could reasonably have known that the statute had not been complied with." Here the defendant is not saying that compliance with the law would have been unreasonable, but rather that he made reasonable efforts to comply with it. Whereas this line of argument occasionally fails, the courts are often sympathetic towards it; and in this sense, liability for breach of statutory duty is not routinely "strict" or "absolute". Thus, there was no liability for breach of a statutory duty to supply pure water unless the supplier ought to have realised the risk of pollution.[274] When a cellar flap collapsed under a pedestrian, the occupier was not liable under the Highways Act 1959 s.154, which imposed on him a duty to keep it in good condition, because the reason for its collapse was that a lorry had mounted the pavement and cracked it only a few minutes before the accident, and no reasonable occupier could have discovered it or done anything about it in the interval.[275] Indeed, some cases assert a general principle that liability for breach of statutory duty is not strict in this sense.[276] Nevertheless, strict liability in this sense has sometimes been imposed. Where the Factories Act 1961 s.22(1), said that "every hoist or lift shall be of good mechanical construction ... and shall be properly maintained", a mechanical breakdown was held to establish liability, although it could not be explained and was impossible to foresee.[277] Ultimately, the exact nature of the duty will at all times depend upon the precise wording of the statute in question. There are no principles of universal validity.

A decision that in given circumstances the defendant is in breach of his statutory duty may depend on whether he is being prosecuted with a view to punishment, or sued by a claimant seeking compensation. As the law stands, however, the answer is supposed to be the same whether the proceedings are civil or criminal. However, the Health and Safety at Work Act 1974 s.15(6)(b), empowers the Secretary of State to create defences available to a person prosecuted for breach of Health and Safety Regulations; but s.47(3) further provides that such defences shall not be available in civil proceedings unless the defence is expressed to apply to civil as well as to criminal proceedings. **8-59**

I.C.R. 502 CA, it was held that where there was a "reasonably foreseeable risk of injury to the eyes of any person engaged in the work from particles or fragments thrown off", then once there was objective evidence that such a risk existed, the employer was subject to an absolute duty under the Protection of Eyes Regulations 1974 to provide eye protection. The obligation on employers (and the self-employed) to provide suitable personal protective equipment is now contained in the Personal Protective Equipment at Work Regulations 1992 (SI 1992/2966) reg.4. In order to be "suitable", the equipment must, inter alia, be effective to prevent or adequately control the risk or risks involved without increasing overall risk "so far as is practicable".

274 *Read v Croydon Corp* [1938] 4 All E.R. 631.

275 *Scott v Green & Sons Ltd* [1969] 1 W.L.R. 301 CA. For other cases where liability was held less than strict, see *Ministry of Housing and Local Government v Sharp* [1970] 2 Q.B. 223 (Land Charges Act 1925 s.17(2)); and *Rippingale Farms Ltd v Black Sluice Internal Drainage Board* [1963] 1 W.L.R. 1347 (Black Sluice Drainage Act 1765 s.44).

276 *Read v Croydon Corp* [1938] 4 All E.R. 631 at 651; *Hammond v St Pancras Vestry* (1874) L.R. 9 C. & P. 316.

277 *Galashiels Gas Co Ltd v O'Donnell* [1949] A.C. 275.

6. CAUSATION

8-60 **Damage** In most cases, a statute will not give rise to a cause of action unless its breach has caused damage to the claimant, though occasionally a statute has been construed to make a breach actionable per se.[278]

8-61 **Causation** Where, as usual, damage is required, the claimant must show on the balance of probabilities[279] that the damage was caused, both in fact and as a matter of law, by the defendant's breach of duty. There is no principle of law differentiating proof of factual causation in breach of statutory duty from the test applicable in negligence. Nor is the burden of proof different in principle.[280]

8-62 **Intervening acts** Even where the claimant can show causation in fact, the court may still reject the defendant's breach of statutory duty as the legal cause of the damage in favour of some other more important factual cause, with which the defendant's breach of statutory duty interacted. Thus, if the court sees as the main cause of the accident a deliberate act of folly by an employee, the employer is not liable.[281] By the same token, a deliberate act of folly by a fellow employee may break the causal link between an employer's breach of statutory duty and the claimant's damage.[282] On the other hand a reasonable act by an employee, albeit with hindsight a dangerous act, as where the employee tried to remove an obstruction from a walkway,[283] will not break the chain of causation.

7. DEFENCES

8-63 **Volenti non fit injuria** The question of whether volenti non fit injuria can ever be a defence to an action for breach of statutory duty has usually arisen in the context of claims by employees against their employers for injuries suffered during their employment, and accordingly the issue is dealt with in more detail in

---

278 See *Ashby v White* (1703) 2 Ld. Raym. 938 at 954 and 955 on the statutory right to vote (but actions for damages are now precluded by the Representation of the People Act 1985); *Simmonds v Newport etc Coal Co Ltd* [1921] 1 K.B. 616 at 631 CA.

279 *Bonnington Castings Ltd v Wardlaw* [1956] A.C. 613. "'Post hoc, ergo propter hoc' is a fallacy in respect of a breach of a statutory regulation": *Quinn v Cameron and Robertson Ltd* [1958] A.C. 9 at 23, per Viscount Simonds. See also *Nicholson v Atlas Steel etc Co Ltd* [1957] 1 W.L.R. 613 HL; *Clarke v ER Wright & Son* [1957] 1 W.L.R. 1191 CA; *Clarkson v Modern Foundries Ltd* [1957] 1 W.L.R. 1210; *Corn v Weir's (Glass) Ltd* [1960] 1 W.L.R. 577 CA; *Williams v Harland and Wolff Ltd* [1963] 2 Lloyd's Rep. 16. A contribution is material unless the maxim de minimis non curat lex can be applied to it: *Quinn v Cameron and Robertson Ltd* [1958] A.C. 9 at 23, per Viscount Simonds. Note, however, that where the extent of the defendant's contribution to the damage is known, he is liable only to that extent: *Holtby v Brigham & Cowan (Hull) Ltd* [2000] 3 All E.R. 421 CA. See paras 2-36 to 2-37.

280 For discussion of factual causation see para.2-09 onwards.

281 *Rushton v Turner Brothers Asbestos Co Ltd* [1960] 1 W.L.R. 96; *Horne v Lec Refrigeration Ltd* [1965] 2 All E.R. 898. An employee who fails to prove a breach of statutory duty may nevertheless succeed in establishing a breach of his employer's common law duty: see, e.g. *Nolan v Dental Manufacturing Co Ltd* [1958] 1 W.L.R. 936; *Bux v Slough Metals* [1973] 1 W.L.R. 1358; *Jayes v IMI (Kynoch)* [1985] I.C.R. 155 CA.

282 *Horton v Taplin Contracts Ltd* [2002] EWCA Civ 1604; [2003] I.C.R. 179 (where a fellow employee deliberately overturned a scaffolding tower on which the claimant was standing).

283 *McGovern v British Steel Corp* [1988] I.C.R. 608 CA.

Ch.12.[284] As a matter of principle it would seem that where Parliament has imposed a duty on the defendant, then unless expressly permitted to rely on the defence,[285] it should not be open to the defendant to neglect the relevant precautions and then argue that the claimant has accepted the risk of harm. It has been said that any agreement to contract out of a statutory duty is void,[286] and so it could be argued that where the volenti defence rests upon *agreement* between the parties it should not apply. However, in some cases volenti has been held to apply where the claimant, knowing of the defendant's breach of duty, has nonetheless proceeded to encounter the risk.[287] It would be distinctly odd, however, for the courts to distinguish between different forms of the volenti defence in order to determine whether it should apply to an action for breach of statutory duty. Either Parliament's will can be subverted by the parties or it cannot. In any event, there are other techniques available to the courts where they consider that the claimant's conduct is such that the defendant should not be held responsible. For example, the claimant might have some difficulty in establishing that the breach *caused* his loss, in circumstances where, otherwise, he would normally be regarded as having assumed the risk.[288]

Contributory negligence Contributory negligence was a complete defence at common law, even where the statute imposed an absolute duty,[289] and since the Law Reform (Contributory Negligence) Act 1945, the court has had power to apportion responsibility and award the claimant reduced damages.[290] The degree of carelessness which amounts to contributory negligence varies with the circumstances.[291] In the context of breach of statutory duty, the issue has most frequently arisen in employers' liability actions, and in that context the standard of care required of the claimant is sometimes lower than that applied to defendants in an ordinary negligence action.[292] In *Caswell v Powell Duffryn Associated Collieries Ltd*,[293] the House of Lords held that in the case of a workman in a factory or mine due regard must be paid to the conditions in which he works, "to the long hours and fatigue, to the slackening of attention which naturally comes from constant repetition of the same operation, to the noise and confusion ... to his preoccupation in what he is actually doing at the cost perhaps of some inattention to his own safety".[294] Thus, where the claimant was guilty of a momentary error in entering a dark compartment without a torch, the Court of Appeal refused to judge him **8-64**

[284] See para.12-88. See also paras 3-128 to 3-130.

[285] As, for example, in the Occupiers' Liability Act 1957 s.2(5) and the Occupiers' Liability Act 1984 s.1(6).

[286] *Baddeley v Earl Granville* (1887) 19 Q.B.D. 423 at 426, per Wills J.

[287] See para.3-110.

[288] For example, where he engages in a deliberate act of folly: *Rushton v Turner Bros Asbestos Co Ltd* [1960] 1 W.L.R. 96.

[289] *Caswell v Powell Duffryn Associated Collieries Ltd* [1940] A.C. 152; *Lewis v Denye* [1940] A.C. 921; *Smith v A Baveystock & Co Ltd* [1945] 1 All E.R. 531 CA.

[290] See para.3-58 onwards.

[291] See *Cakebread v Hopping Bros (Whetstone) Ltd* [1947] K.B. 641 CA; *Barcock v Brighton Corp* [1949] 1 K.B. 339; *Hopwood v Rolls-Royce* (1947) 176 L.T. 514 at 520, per Lord Greene MR.

[292] See paras 3-80 and 12-91.

[293] [1940] A.C. 152.

[294] [1940] A.C. 152 at 178 and 179, per Lord Wright. See also, per Lord Atkin at 166. See also the comment of Keene LJ in *Cooper v Carillion Plc* [2003] EWCA Civ 1811 at [13], cited at para.3-80 fn.287. Contrast the position where the accident did not arise out of momentary inattention by the employee: where "a risk has been consciously accepted by an employee, it seems to me that different considerations may arise. That is particularly so where the employee is skilled and the precaution in question is neither esoteric nor one which he could not take himself", per Latham LJ in

harshly, and found him only one third to blame for the accident.[295] A measure of carelessness in such circumstances will therefore be ignored in an action by the employee; but, on the other hand, if the facts are that the operative and effective cause of the accident was a deliberate act of folly by the employee, his claim will fail altogether on grounds of causation.[296] Where a statutory duty is imposed on an employee for his own protection, breach of this duty may constitute contributory negligence, though his breach will not fall within the principle ex turpi causa non oritur actio.[297]

8-65 **Delegation of duty** In view of the general principle that where a duty is cast upon a person he cannot escape the responsibility for seeing it performed by delegating it to a contractor,[298] it is clear that if a statutory duty is broken it will be no defence that an independent contractor was employed, unless upon a true construction of the statute delegation can be regarded as a fulfilment of the obligation.[299] But the question of whether it is a defence to show that performance of the tasks required for fulfilment of a statutory duty laid on the employer was delegated by the employer to the claimant himself has received different answers from the courts. At one stage they were prepared to recognise such a defence,[300] though with strict limitations[301]; but the view which seems now to have prevailed is that delegation of performance of the duty to the claimant is not in itself a defence, although it may give rise to the defence that the defendant's breach of statutory duty is co-

---

Sherlock v Chester City Council [2004] EWCA Civ 201 at [32], where the Court of Appeal held the employee 60 per cent contributorily negligent.

295 *Mullard v Ben Line Steamers Ltd* [1970] 1 W.L.R. 1414 CA; applying dicta in *Staveley Iron and Chemical Co Ltd v Jones* [1956] A.C. 627 at 648; and in *Quintas v National Smelting Co Ltd* [1961] 1 W.L.R. 401 CA at 408. See also *Cooper v Carillion Plc* [2003] EWCA Civ 1811 at [13], per Keene LJ; *McGuiness v Key Markets* (1973) 13 K.I.R. 249 CA; *Geddes v United Wires*, 1973 S.L.T. (Notes) 50; *Payne v Peter Bennie* (1973) 14 K.I.R. 395.

296 *Rushton v Turner Brothers Asbestos Co Ltd* [1960] 1 W.L.R. 96.

297 *National Coal Board v England* [1954] A.C. 403; *Progress and Properties Ltd v Craft* (1976) 12 A.L.R. 59 (High Court of Australia). See para.3-02 onwards.

298 *Dalton v Angus* (1881) 6 App. Cas. 740 at 829.

299 *Gray v Pullen* (1864) 5 B. & S. 970; *Hole v Sittingbourne etc Ry* (1861) 6 H. & N. 488. The principle was also applied in *Mulready v JH and W Bell Ltd* [1953] 2 Q.B. 117 CA; but in *Donaghey v Boulton and Paul Ltd* [1968] A.C. 1, the House of Lords disapproved the reasoning of the Court of Appeal in that case, pointing out that performance of the duty had not in fact been delegated by the defendants, as they had remained in effective charge of the work.

300 *Smith v Baveystock & Co Ltd* [1945] 1 All E.R. 531 CA; *Gallagher v Dorman Long & Co Ltd* [1947] 2 All E.R. 38; *Barcock v Brighton Corp* [1949] 1 K.B. 339; *Beal v E Gomme Ltd* (1949) 65 T.L.R. 543; *Johnson v Croggan & Co Ltd* [1954] 1 W.L.R. 195 (where the claimant was also under a statutory duty to comply with the requirements of the regulations concerned).

301 The employer must have made it clear to his employee that he was doing more than merely giving instructions as to the method of carrying out the work: *Manwaring v Billington* [1952] 2 All E.R. 747 CA.

extensive with that of the claimant.[302] This is an issue that tends to arise in the context of employers' liability actions and it is dealt with in Ch.12.[303]

Act of God and inevitable accident It will depend on the exact wording of the statute whether these defences are available.[304] It is quite possible for the duty to be framed so as to preclude a defence of act of God[305] and inevitable accident, in the sense that the exercise of reasonable care will not be a defence to an absolute duty.[306] On the other hand, in the absence of clear words there will apparently be no liability for damage where there is an absence of any human agency, as where a ship which had been abandoned by her crew was blown against harbour piers.[307] **8-66**

302 "The important and fundamental question … is not whether there was a delegation, but simply the usual question: whose fault was it?" *Ginty v Belmont Building Supplies Ltd* [1959] 1 All E.R. 414 at 423 and 424. This statement was approved by the Court of Appeal in *McMath v Rimmer Bros (Liverpool) Ltd* [1962] 1 W.L.R. 1; and *Boyle v Kodak Ltd* [1969] 1 W.L.R. 661; and by the House of Lords in *Ross v Associated Portland Cement Manufacturers Ltd* [1964] 1 W.L.R. 768—subject to the reservation that "fault" in this context is not necessarily equivalent to blameworthiness; rather, it is a question of causation. See also *Brumder v Motornet Service and Repairs Ltd* [2013] EWCA Civ 195; [2013] 1 W.L.R. 2783.

303 See para.12-89.

304 *Witham Outfall Board v Boston Corp* (1937) 156 L.T. 756 at 760.

305 *GW Ry v SS Mostyn* [1928] A.C. 57 at 74, 93 and 104; *Makin v LNE Ry* [1943] K.B. 467.

306 As where damage was caused by the manoeuvres of a vessel which were made necessary by the action of another vessel: *GW Ry v SS Mostyn* [1928] A.C. 57.

307 *River Wear Commissioners v Adamson* (1877) 2 App. Cas. 743; as explained in *GW Ry v SS Mostyn* [1928] A.C. 57.

30 See para.12-[illegible].

31 [illegible] (1971) [illegible] at 790.

32 Cf. [illegible] [1926] [illegible] at 70 and 104; [illegible] [1942] K.B. 467.

CHAPTER 9

PROFESSIONAL LIABILITY

TABLE OF CONTENTS

1. GENERAL CONSIDERATIONS[1]

(a) Professional liability in general

Professions There is no conclusive definition of a profession.[2] In 1919 Scrutton LJ suggested the following guidelines, which are adopted for the purpose of this chapter: **9-01**

> "[A] 'profession' in the present use of language involves the idea of an occupation requiring either purely intellectual skill, or manual skill controlled, as in painting or sculpture, or surgery, by the intellectual skill of the operator, as distinguished from an occupation which is substantially the production or sale or arrangements for sale of commodities."[3]

Of those occupations falling within this broad definition we concentrate on those professions which have generated significant case law in England involving questions of professional negligence and related liabilities: in particular, medical practitioners, lawyers, surveyors, architects, consulting engineers and financial professionals, such as accountants or insurance brokers. The concentration here will be on legal liability: it should be noted, however, that other forms of dispute resolution are of increasing importance in this field.[4]

---

1 See, generally, *Jackson & Powell on Professional Liability*, 8th edn (2017).

2 See *Jackson & Powell on Professional Liability*, 8th edn (2017), para.1-003.

3 *Commissioners of Inland Revenue v Maxse* [1919] 1 K.B. 647, 657 (definition of "profession" in taxing statute).

4 For example, NHS Resolution, previously the NHS Litigation Authority, operates a mediation scheme dating from 2016 to deal with clinical negligence cases, with the NHS paying the costs of unrepresented claimants. (The scheme is statutory in Wales under the NHS Redress (Wales) Measure 2008). Again, the Professional Negligence Bar Association and others administer an adjudication scheme which since mid-2016 has been available for all non-medical professional negligence cases. See H. Vernon, "NHS Resolution—25 Years On" [2019] J.P.I.L. 283; and M. Ahmed, "A novel alternative dispute resolution procedure for professional negligence claims" (2019) 35 P.N. 54.

9-02 **Professional liability** In principle, the rules governing a professional person's liability for negligence are no different from those governing the liability of anyone else who undertakes a specific task and professes some special skill in carrying out that task. As Tindal CJ put it in 1838[5]:

> "Every person who enters into a learned profession undertakes to bring to the exercise of it a reasonable degree of care and skill. He does not undertake, if he is an attorney, that at all events you shall gain your case, nor does a surgeon undertake that he will perform a cure, nor does he undertake to use the highest possible degree of care and skill."

The nature and functions of the traditional professions have, however, resulted in certain significant distinctions in the application of basic tort rules to professionals. These distinctions have both restricted liability in some contexts and extended it in others.

9-03 First, as Tindal CJ remarked, professionals are rarely deemed to guarantee results; solicitors do not undertake to win cases in any event, nor doctors to cure their patients come what may.[6] Secondly, the law takes account of the large degree of self-regulation traditionally permitted to professionals. Courts are thus unwilling to make a finding of negligence in the absence of expert evidence of what would have been proper conduct.[7] Furthermore, of even greater importance is the principle enunciated by McNair J in *Bolam v Friern Hospital Management Committee*,[8] concerning doctors but undoubtedly applying to professionals generally.[9] A doctor acting in accordance with a practice accepted as proper by a responsible body of medical opinion was (he said) not to be regarded as negligent "merely because there is a body of opinion which would take a contrary view". However, its significance should not be overrated. Judges are today increasingly prepared to scrutinise the general practices of professions and prevent them being prayed in aid if not satisfied that they represent a body of "responsible" opinion.[10] Furthermore, its limits

---

5 *Lanphier v Phipos* (1838) 8 C. & P. 475; cf. *Guilmet v Campbell*, 188 N.W.2d 601 (1971) (guarantee by physician of success: damages awarded); and *Thake v Maurice* [1986] Q.B. 644 (similar guarantee found by judge at first instance and one of the appellate judges, though eventually rejected).

6 Apart from *Lampier v Phipos*, above, see e.g. *Greaves & Co v Baynham Meikle* [1975] 1 W.L.R. 1095, 1100 (Lord Denning MR); *Thake v Maurice* [1986] Q.B. 644, 686 (Nourse LJ); *Platform Funding Ltd v Bank of Scotland Plc* [2008] EWCA Civ 930; [2009] Q.B. 426 at [15] (Moore-Bick LJ). So too they are not readily held to guarantee the competence of independent third parties: see the architects' case of *Midlothian Council v Bracewell Stirling Architects* [2018] CSIH 21; 2018 S.C.L.R. 606; [2018] P.N.L.R. 25.

7 See, e.g. *Pantelli Associates Ltd v Corporate City Developments Number Two Ltd* [2010] EWHC 3189 (TCC); [2011] P.N.L.R. 12; *Caribbean Steel Co Ltd v Price Waterhouse* [2013] UKPC 18; [2013] 4 All E.R. 338; *Wattret v Thomas Sands Consulting Ltd* [2015] EWHC 3455 (TCC); [2016] P.N.L.R. 15. But the rule is not immutable: *ACD (Landscape Architects) Ltd v Overall* [2012] EWHC 100 (TCC); [2012] P.N.L.R. 19 at [16] (Mann J). Indeed, it has been held in England not to apply to most cases of lawyers' negligence, apparently on the basis that judges know about legal practice: *Bown v Gould & Swayne* [1996] P.N.L.R. 130. On the general admissibility of expert evidence in professional negligence cases, see *Devon Commercial Property Ltd v Barnett* [2019] EWHC 700 (Ch) at [117]–[123].

8 [1957] 1 W.L.R. 582, 587–588.

9 See *Gold v Haringey HA* [1988] Q.B. 481, 488-489 (Lloyd LJ); also *Nye Saunders & Partners (a firm) v Bristow* (1987) 37 B.L.R. 97, 103 (Stephen Brown LJ). Indeed, even university academics have benefited from it (!): *Siddiqui v University of Oxford* [2016] EWHC 3150 (QB).

10 See in particular *Bolitho v City & Hackney Health Authority* [1998] A.C. 232, 241–243 (Lord Browne-Wilkinson); also *G & K Ladenbau v Crawley & de Reya* [1978] 1 W.L.R. 266, 282 (Mocatta J). In addition, note *Brown v Gould & Swayne* [1996] P.N.L.R. 130, 136–137, where Millett LJ sug-

must be borne in mind. For one thing, its effects are largely concerned with considered responses to known problems: in so far as the negligence alleged is failure to foresee a problem at all, the fact that a large number of professionals did not think of it either is of limited significance.[11] So too, it now seems that advice about the risks inherent in a particular course of action may not be subject to the rule.[12] Yet again, while affording a considerable margin of appreciation to professionals, the law does not entitle a professional to exoneration on the ground only that his mistake was a mere "error of judgment". On the contrary: unless such an error falls within the boundaries of current and accepted practice, liability will follow.[13] Thirdly, the trust placed by a client in a professional person will often give rise to certain other obligations apart from a duty of care: for example, an obligation of confidentiality, or a fiduciary obligation affecting property entrusted by the client to the professional.[14]

(b) Duties of care to clients, patients and others

Physical damage and economic loss As with the rest of the law of tort, there is generally less difficulty in establishing liability for professional negligence resulting in physical damage to persons or property than for negligence resulting in economic loss alone, especially where the victim is someone other than the defendant's client.[15] Thus an architect who designs a house with a structural defect will in general be liable if it falls down and injures someone (whether his own client, a purchaser of the house, or a mere passer-by), or for that matter damages property such as a car.[16] By contrast, he will not normally be liable to a subsequent owner of the building for the cost of stopping it from collapsing, or of repairing it when it has.[17] On the other hand, this is not to say that a professional can never be 9-04

gested that today questions of acceptable conveyancing practice should be regarded as largely questions of law.

[11] *199 Knightsbridge Development Ltd v WSP UK Ltd* [2014] EWHC 43 (TCC) (failure by designer of water system, in common with most other such designers, to foresee particular problem in high-rise buildings: negligence found).

[12] This was made clear in the context of medical treatment in *Montgomery v Lanarkshire Health Board* [2015] UKSC 11; [2015] A.C. 1430. Although that decision was based largely on the value of a patient's right to bodily self-determination, the same principle has been applied, with less justification, to advice as to risk given by solicitors (*Baird v Hastings* [2015] NICA 22) and financial advisers (*O'Hare v Coutts & Co* [2016] EWHC 2224 (QB)). It seems a fair inference that it now applies to professional liability generally: see, on the subject as a whole, R. Jackson, "The professions: power, privilege and legal liability" (2015) 31 P.N. 122.

[13] "The test is the standard of the ordinary skilled man exercising or professing to have that special skill" (Lord Edmund-Davies in *Whitehouse v Jordan* [1981] 1 W.L.R. 246, 258). It follows that if a surgeon fails to measure up to that standard in any respect ("clinical judgment" or otherwise), he has been negligent.

[14] See para.9-21 onwards.

[15] Where the victim is the client, professionals in general owe concurrent duties to their clients in both contract and tort, whether the consequences take the form of physical injury (as with doctors) or mere monetary loss (as with solicitors or stockbrokers). See para.9-06 for details.

[16] See, e.g. *Clay v AJ Crump & Sons Ltd* [1964] 1 Q.B. 533; and *Rimmer v Liverpool City Council* [1985] Q.B. 1 (personal injury); *Pearson Education Ltd v Charter Partnership Ltd* [2007] EWCA Civ 130; [2007] B.L.R. 324 (property damage).

[17] Implicit in *Department of the Environment v Thomas Bates & Sons Ltd* [1991] 1 A.C. 499 (builder not liable in such circumstances); cf. *Murphy v Brentwood DC* [1991] 1 A.C. 398. Such damage counts as economic loss for these purposes: see *Sutherland Shire Council v Heyman* (1985) 157 C.L.R. 424, 503–505 (Deane J); cited with approval by Lord Keith in *Murphy v Brentwood DC* [1991] 1 A.C. 398, 467.

liable for economic loss to third parties. On the contrary, there is, for example, clear authority holding solicitors,[18] surveyors,[19] accountants[20] and financial advisers[21] liable in such circumstances. The point of distinction, it is submitted, is that these cases depend on a specific finding of a special relationship between the parties, or something like it, sufficient to create the necessary degree of proximity[22]: in the absence of such a finding, there will be no duty of care.[23]

9-05 **Clients and patients: statements and advice** Negligent statements on the part of any professional must be considered with some care. Where there is a contract for professional services between professional and client, negligent advice given in the course of that relationship is likely to give rise to tortious liability.[24] Nevertheless, in all cases the scope of any alleged duty owed to the client or patient must be analysed. For example, if a professional passes on information or advice emanating from a third party it may well be that he acts merely as a conduit, accepting no personal responsibility for it[25]; on the other hand, circumstances may indicate that he is adopting it as his own and thereby accepting a responsibility to take care.[26] Again, if a statement is made or advice is given gratuitously, the claimant must generally show that it was made or given in circumstances in which it was reasonable to rely on that statement or advice, such as in the context of a professional relationship.[27] Whether a duty is owed will always depend on the social context of the advice which the professional elects to give. Thus casual statements, such as where a doctor or solicitor gives an informal opinion at a dinner-party, are extremely unlikely to result in liability.[28]

9-06 **Clients and patients: concurrent liability in contract and tort** Most professional services in England, other than medical treatment within the NHS, are provided pursuant to a contract between the professional and the client. Since s.13 of the Supply of Goods and Services Act 1982,[29] like the common law, implies a

---

[18] *Ross v Caunters* [1980] Ch. 297; *White v Jones* [1995] 2 A.C. 207 (would-be beneficiary of will negligently drawn or not drawn at all); cf. *Al-Kandari v JR Brown & Co* [1988] Q.B. 665.

[19] *Yianni v Edwin Evans* [1982] Q.B. 438; *Smith v Eric S. Bush* [1990] 1 A.C. 831 (valuer acting for mortgagee owes duty to mortgagor who buys sub-standard house as a result).

[20] *JEB Fasteners Ltd v Marks Bloom & Co* [1981] 3 All E.R. 289 (the claim failed on causation, upheld on appeal: [1983] 1 All E.R. 583).

[21] *Gorham v British Telecommunications Plc* [2000] 1 W.L.R. 2129.

[22] As in *Caparo Industries plc v Dickman* [1990] 2 A.C. 605 (auditors of company not liable to predator: though cf. *JEB Fasteners Ltd v Marks Bloom & Co* [1981] 3 All E.R. 289).

[23] *White v Jones* [1995] 2 A.C. 207, 255 (Lord Goff); *Customs & Excise Commissioners v Barclays Bank Plc* [2006] UKHL 28; [2007] 1 A.C. 181 at [73] (Lord Walker).

[24] *Henderson v Merrett Syndicates Ltd* [1995] 2 A.C. 145.

[25] *Partridge v Barclays Bank Plc* [2013–2015] Gib. L.R. 325 (bank passing on property valuation).

[26] *Webster v Liddington* [2014] EWCA Civ 560; [2014] P.N.L.R. 26 (doctor distributing brochure re patient rejuvenation remedy).

[27] As in, e.g. *Hedley Byrne & Co Ltd v Heller & Partners Ltd* [1964] A.C. 465. A more recent instance is *Burgess v Lejonvarn* [2017] EWCA Civ 254; [2017] P.N.L.R. 25 (free advice to homeowner by architect at start of project: project later abandoned).

[28] See *Fish v Kelly* (1864) 17 C.B.N.S. 194, where Byles J said an attorney would not be liable for advice provided to a casual acquaintance on a train; also *Mohr v Cleaver* [1986] W.A.R. 67, 72 where Burt CJ said pithily that liability would not arise from an "off-the-cuff or kerbstone opinion". It is true that in *Chaudhry v Prabhakar* [1989] 1 W.L.R. 29 a non-professional who advised negligently on the purchase of a car was held liable: but that was hardly a case of mere casual advice. See para.7-137.

[29] Or, in the case of services provided to a consumer, s.49 of the Consumer Rights Act 2015.

term that services supplied in the course of a business will be rendered with reasonable care and skill, it follows that professional negligence will normally constitute a breach of contract. Nevertheless it is now clear that this does not bar concurrent liability in tort: a matter of some little importance, since while in some situations a claimant may be better off suing in contract,[30] in others the existence of a duty in tort may have considerable advantages for him, for example in terms of limitation.[31] Earlier authority having been mixed,[32] the matter of concurrent liability was put beyond doubt in 1994 by the House of Lords in *Henderson v Merrett Syndicates Ltd*.[33] Certain Names at Lloyd's sued their underwriting agents, with whom they were in contractual relation, for negligence. An issue of limitation arose,[34] and the Names alleged the agents were concurrently liable in tort so as to have the benefit of a longer period of limitation. Lord Goff, delivering the leading judgment, held that the Names could sue in tort, and that the existence of a contractual relationship was no objection. As a matter of principle, he said:

> "it is difficult to see why concurrent remedies in tort and contract, if available against the medical profession, should not also be available against members of other professions, whatever form the relevant damage may take."[35]

Since *Henderson*, it has been accepted that any professional is prima facie liable to his client in both contract and tort.

However, while there may be procedural advantages to suing in tort, as regards substantive liability any duty in tort is likely (save in very exceptional circumstances[36]) to be co-extensive with, and certainly no more generous than, any contractual duty.[37] Moreover, this principle applies not only to the extent of any duty **9-07**

[30] For instance, A may contract for services as an undisclosed principal of B, allowing B to sue for negligence for his own benefit. But this is not available in tort, for example under *Hedley Byrne & Co Ltd v Heller & Partners Ltd* [1964] A.C. 465. See *Playboy Club London Ltd v Banca Nazionale del Lavoro SpA* [2018] UKSC 43; [2018] 1 W.L.R. 4041.

[31] In particular, because (i) time runs in contract from the time of breach, but in the tort of negligence from the time when damage is suffered, which may be a good deal later (the point at issue in *Midland Bank v Hett, Stubbs & Kemp* [1979] Ch. 384; and *Henderson v Merrett Syndicates Ltd* [1995] 2 A.C. 145); and (ii) a contract claimant cannot claim the benefit of the "latent damage" provision in s.14A of the Limitation Act 1980 (see *Iron Trades Mutual Insurance Ltd v Buckenham* [1990] 1 All E.R. 808; approved in *Société Commerciale de Réassurance v ERAS Ltd* [1992] 2 All E.R. 82).

[32] Until the 1970s, it was generally thought that while liability for physical damage or personal injury was concurrent (e.g. *Edwards v Mallan* [1908] 1 K.B. 1002), liability for economic loss lay only in contract (see *Bagot v Stevens Scanlon & Co Ltd* [1966] 1 Q.B. 197). However, following *Hedley Byrne & Co Ltd v Heller & Partners Ltd* [1964] A.C. 465 a series of decisions had accepted the possibility of concurrent liability (see e.g. *Midland Bank Trust Co Ltd v Hett, Stubbs & Kemp* [1979] Ch. 384; *Ross v Caunters* [1980] 1 Ch. 297, 308; and *Nitrigin Eireann Teoranta v Inco Alloys* [1992] 1 W.L.R. 498, 503).

[33] [1995] 2 A.C. 145. Followed in the Commonwealth generally: see *Astley v Austrust Ltd* (1999) 197 C.L.R. 1; *Central Trust Co v Rafuse* [1986] 2 S.C.R. 147; *Riddell v Porteous* [1999] 1 N.Z.L.R. 9.

[34] i.e. proceedings had been started within six years of loss suffered, but not of the acts alleged to have constituted negligence.

[35] [1995] 2 A.C. 145, 190. See too *Equitas Ltd v Walsham Bros & Co Ltd* [2013] EWHC 3264 (Comm): [2014] P.N.L.R. 8 at [41]–[52] (Males J).

[36] For example, *Holt v Payne Skillington* [1996] P.N.L.R. 179 (surveyors retained to advise purchasers, but not on planning matters; when surveyors chose to give free advice on planning point, duty of care owed in tort but not contract). In the event the claim failed for lack of proof of negligence.

[37] *Tai Hing Cotton Mills Ltd v Liu Chong Hing Bank Ltd* [1986] 1 A.C. 80, 107 ("Their Lordships do

but also to the measure of any damages recoverable,[38] and (importantly) any question of remoteness of damage.[39]

9-08 **Clients, patients and personal representatives** Where a client (or patient) dies before an action is brought, issues may arise as to the right to sue of personal representatives or those entitled under the estate. Essentially the position is as follows. First, if it is alleged that the professional's negligence actually caused the death of the client, the personal representatives may sue under the Fatal Accidents Act 1976 for the benefit of any dependants, and in addition may recover for the estate any loss or damage suffered by the client before his death under the Law Reform (Miscellaneous Provisions) Act 1934. Secondly, in any case of a deceased client, the benefit of any liability of the professional to the client incurred before the latter's death[40] will pass to the estate under the Law Reform (Miscellaneous Provisions) Act 1934. This may on occasion include not only losses suffered by the client during his life, but also on occasion losses to the estate itself. Thus in *Otter v Church, Adams, Tatham & Co*[41] a solicitor who negligently failed to advise his client to disentail land while alive was liable to the estate when the land passed to a reversioner. There is some argument as to whether the estate ought in such cases to be limited to the sum that could have been recovered by the client in his lifetime, but it is suggested that the better position is that it is not: hence where solicitors negligently failed to arrange term life assurance for a client in his lifetime, they were liable to the estate for the value of the would-be payout.[42] However, two important limitations must be noted. First, there will be no liability if the duty broken was one whose scope excluded an obligation to guard against potential losses to the estate.[43] Secondly, the 1934 Act applies only where the deceased had a cause of action

---

not … accept that the parties' mutual obligations in tort can be any greater than those to be found expressly or by necessary implication in their contract."); also *Freemont (Denbigh) Ltd v Knight Frank LLP* [2014] EWHC 3347 (Ch); [2015] P.N.L.R. 4 [148]–[149].

38 See the *Canadian decision in BG Checo International Ltd v British Columbia Hydro & Power Authority* [1993] 1 S.C.R. 12, 37–38.

39 A point finally settled in the solicitors' negligence case of *Wellesley Partners LLP v Withers LLP* [2015] EWCA Civ 1146; [2016] Ch. 529. See A. Taylor, "Whither remoteness? Wellesley Partners LLP v Withers LLP" (2016) 79 M.L.R. 678; A. Tettenborn, "Professional liability and remoteness: contract v tort" (2016) 32 P.N. 68. This reflected a general previous belief: see e.g. *Tai Hing Cotton Mills Ltd v Liu Chong Hing Bank Ltd* [1986] 1 A.C. 80, 107 ("Their Lordships do not … accept that the parties' mutual obligations in tort can be any greater than those to be found expressly or by necessary implication in their contract"); and cf. *BG Checo International Ltd v British Columbia Hydro & Power Authority* [1993] 1 S.C.R. 12, 37–38 (where concurrent liability, damages principles should be the same).

40 But a duty of care or retainer does not pass *in abstracto*: *Reader v Molesworths Bright Clegg* [2007] EWCA Civ 169; [2007] 1 W.L.R. 1082 (duty to advise client when alive does not comport duty to estate to advise it after death).

41 [1953] Ch. 280.

42 See *McLellan v Fletcher* (1987) 3 P.N. 202 (*contra*, though, *Lynne v Gordon Doctors & Walton (A Firm)* (1991) 135 S.J.L.B. 29). *Otter v Church, Adams, Tatham & Co* [1953] Ch. 280 seems a similar case: it is difficult to see any loss suffered by the client while alive. The point may well be significant with regard to advice by a solicitor or accountant on inheritance tax, which ipso facto does not affect the client's lifetime wealth.

43 See *Carr-Glyn v Frearsons* [1999] Ch. 326 (failure to advise testator to sever joint tenancy: no duty in respect of diminution in value of estate, but only to beneficiaries under will); and see also *Corbett v Bond Pearce* [2001] EWCA Civ 531; [2001] 3 All E.R. 769 (will invalidly executed: solicitors settle claim by would-be legatees: no further liability for estate's costs incurred in probate litigation, since this would merely create windfall gain for those taking in default).

already vested in him when he died. Where the professional's liability was in contract this will normally be the case[44]; but since a tort action for negligence arises only when loss is suffered, it follows that where a solicitor's negligence is actionable only in tort and causes loss only to the client's estate, the Act cannot be used.[45] Thirdly, the above two methods are, it seems, exhaustive of the rights of the estate. It has sometimes been argued that even if the estate cannot sue under the 1934 or 1976 Acts it might be able to allege a discrete duty of care in tort owed to it as an estate: but the courts have not been receptive to such claims.[46]

Duties to third parties: physical damage Liability in contract is normally limited to the client or patient. Under the Contracts (Rights of Third Parties) Act 1999 it is entirely possible for the professional to undertake an additional contractual duty to some other person.[47] But, it is suggested, such a duty is unlikely to be inferred without very clear words or convincing implication.[48] By contrast, liability in tort contains no such inbuilt limitation, and in a suitable case a professional's liability in tort may extend to third parties suffering damage as a result of his negligence. In particular, when a professional ought reasonably to foresee that in providing a service for his client or patient, he may place other persons at risk of direct physical harm, he will generally[49] owe those third parties a duty of care. Architects and engineers whose negligent design of a building endangers the client, his visitors, and casual bystanders may similarly be liable for ensuing injuries, whoever happens to be the victim.[50] It is easy to imagine an analogous situation with a doctor. Were he, for instance, negligently to send home a patient with a seriously **9-09**

---

44 Since breach of contract is actionable *per se*, at least for nominal damages.

45 See *Daniels v Thompson* [2004] EWCA Civ 307; [2004] P.N.L.R. 33 (negligent inheritance tax advice to client seven years before death; since claim in contract statute-barred, no claim by estate under 1934 Act).

46 See *Daniels v Thompson* [2004] EWCA Civ 307; [2004] P.N.L.R. 33 at [45]–[54], followed (admittedly with some reluctance) in *Rind v Theodore Goddard (A Firm)* [2008] EWHC 459 (Ch); [2008] P.N.L.R. 24. See too the Scots decision in *Steven (Ex'or of Thomson) v Hewats* [2013] CSOH 60; [2013] P.N.L.R. 23 (solicitors bungle estate duty scheme: no claim by executor acting as such, following doubts expressed earlier in *Mathews v Hunter & Robertson Ltd* [2008] CSOH 88; 2008 S.L.T. 634; [2008] P.N.L.R. 35).

47 See, e.g. *Crowson v HSBC Insurance Brokers Ltd* [2010] Lloyd's Rep. I.R. 441 (refusal to strike out third-party claim under 1999 Act against insurance broker with regard to D&O cover). This may become relevant elsewhere too, for example if a practice should become established whereby vendors of real property regularly obtain surveyors' reports for the use of potential purchasers.

48 This is particularly true in areas such as medicine, where there might otherwise arise an awkward conflict of duties: see *Bot v Barnick* [2018] EWHC 3132 (QB) (private hospital owed no contractual duty to patient's partner). See too the Australian decision in *Harriton v Stephens* (2004) 59 N.S.W.L.R. 694, a court denied "wrongful life" recovery to a child as a third party beneficiary of the doctor's contractual duty to its mother under the equivalent Australian rule. (The case was appealed on other grounds to the High Court of Australia: see *Harriton v Stephens* [2006] HCA 15; (2006) 80 A.L.J.R. 791.) In practice advisers often draft their terms of service so as specifically to exclude the effect of the 1999 Act.

49 But not invariably: see, e.g. *Sutradhar v Natural Environment Research Council* [2006] UKHL 33; [2006] 4 All E.R. 490; [2006] P.N.L.R. 36 (government-sponsored report on purity of Bangladeshi aquifers for water management purposes: no liability to citizens allegedly poisoned by contaminant in those aquifers). (Lord Nicholls at [36] in the same case comfortingly said that the same would apply to the author of a supposedly authoritative legal textbook!)

50 *Clay v AJ Crump & Sons Ltd* [1964] 1 Q.B. 533 (passer-by); *Rimmer v Liverpool City Council* [1985] Q.B. 1 (tenant's child); *Indigo Mist Pty Ltd v Palmer* [2012] NSWCA 239 (employee). But the mere fact of inspection for some unconnected purpose will not give rise to any such duty to passers-by: see *Harrison v Technical Sign Co Ltd* [2013] EWCA Civ 1569; [2014] P.N.L.R. 15.

infectious disease, it is suggested that the courts would have little difficulty in holding the doctor liable.[51]

9-10 Matters are less straightforward, however, where the alleged negligence amounts to simple omission to take steps to protect the third party from injury. Here there is normally no liability. So, for example, health professionals in diagnosing illness generally owe a duty to the patient, but not to others such as relatives.[52] Again, there is no case in England[53] making a professional liable for failing to inform the authorities that a client may amount to a public danger; for example where a doctor or solicitor knows that his client is mentally ill and making threats against an ex-girlfriend, or is an alcoholic who regularly drives when drunk, or is HIV positive but continues to indulge in unprotected intercourse. Thus in *Palmer v Tees NHS Trust*[54] an unstable out-patient attached to the defendant hospital brutalised and murdered a little girl. Her estate sued the hospital for failing to confine, supervise or otherwise control the patient concerned; but the hospital was held to have owed her no duty of care in the circumstances.[55]

9-11 However, while this is the default position, liability may sometimes attach in cases of obvious and drastic danger. In *ABC v St George's Healthcare NHS Trust*[56] the Court of Appeal refused to strike out a claim against a hospital for failing to break medical confidence and warn a family member about a serious inherited disease affecting a patient. Again, professional obligations may possibly affect the matter of duty here. Thus professional regulation increasingly allows, and sometimes even requires, client or patient confidentiality to be overridden in cases of severe danger; and where it is there is no obvious reason not to impose liability.[57]

9-12 **Duties to third parties: economic loss**[58] In respect of economic loss, liability to third parties will be imposed only in a limited range of circumstances. Foreseeability of financial loss to a person other than the client is not of itself enough, for a number of reasons. Where the complaint is that a professional has provided substandard service, the claim to compensation of a third party who neither employed nor paid him is a great deal weaker than that of the client himself. The professional may well not have intended to provide any assurance at all to those

---

51 cf. *Evans v Liverpool Corporation* [1906] 1 K.B. 160, para.9-51.

52 In *Child & Family Agency v A* [2018] IEHC 112, for example, Twomey J in the Irish High Court declined to order a breach of medical confidentiality to allow disclosure of the HIV status of a man to his girlfriend.

53 But see in the US context, *Tarasoff v Regents of the University of California*, 551 P. 2d 334 (1976); *Semler v Psychiatrics Institute of Washington*, 538 F. 2d 121 (1976); and *Durtlinger v Artiles*, 673 P. 2d 86 (1983); also the Canadian decision in *Brown v University of Alberta Hospital* (1997) 145 D.L.R. (4th) 63.

54 [1998] Lloyd's Law Rep. Med. 447; [2000] P.N.L.R. 87.

55 Note, however, that if the victim were another inmate it must be arguable, since *Rabone v Pennine Care NHS Foundation Trust* [2012] UKSC 2; [2012] 2 A.C. 72; and *Reynolds v United Kingdom* (2012) 55 E.H.R.R. 35, that there would be a claim for the infringement of the right to life under art.2 of the ECHR.

56 [2017] EWCA Civ 336; [2017] P.I.Q.R. P15. Also in *Child & Family Agency v A* [2018] IEHC 112, referred to above, Twomey J at [4] expressed the test as being one whether "on the balance of probabilities, the failure to breach patient confidentiality creates a significant risk of death or very serious harm to an innocent third party."

57 For example, the GMC imposes a professional duty on doctors to inform the DVLA of incapacitated drivers who insist on continuing behind the wheel: see its publication *Confidentiality: reporting concerns about patients to the DVLA or the DVA*. If such a failure were to result in a severe accident, the imposition of liability cannot be excluded.

58 See S. Hedley, "Goodbye Privity, Hello Contorts" [1995] C.L.J. 27.

other than his clients. Again, the interests of the client and the third party may well be opposed or inconsistent: and, in certain cases, there may be perceived dangers of potential double liability, or of open-ended liability. The exact principles on which duties to third parties are founded are by no means clear. They differ from profession to profession, and for details the reader is referred to more specific coverage below. Certain general principles may be suggested, however.

(a) There must be a fairly close degree of proximity between the parties.[59]
(b) There will generally not be liability to an indeterminate class of persons, or in respect of an indeterminate class of transactions.[60]
(c) Where a professional undertakes to provide advice or information for a client knowing that the client intends to use that information or advice to induce a third party to act in a manner which will be to his detriment if the professional is negligent, the professional may, unless the circumstances make it clear that he accepts liability only to the client,[61] owe a duty to the third party.[62] The key question will often[63] be whether the third party can reasonably, and may foreseeably,[64] rely on the advice or information provided by the professional.[65]
(d) There will generally be no duty imposed where the duty owed to the client would conflict with the suggested duty to the third party,[66] or where there

---

59 A feature repeatedly stressed in discussing the extent of liability. See, e.g. *Ross v Caunters* [1980] Ch. 297, 308 (Megarry VC); *White v Jones* [1995] 2 A.C. 207, 269 (Lord Goff), 271 (Lord Browne-Wilkinson); *Clarke v Bruce Lance & Co* [1988] 1 W.L.R. 881, 888 (Balcombe LJ); *Caparo Industries Plc v Dickman* [1990] 2 A.C. 605, 621 (Lord Bridge), 658 (Lord Jauncey); *Seymour v Ockwell* [2005] EWHC 1137 (QB); [2005] P.N.L.R. 39 at [126].

60 Thus in relation to statements, the House of Lords in *Caparo Industries Plc v Dickman* [1991] 2 A.C. said that in general a duty would be owed only if the defendant knew that (i) his statement would foreseeably reach the claimant or a class of which he was a member; and (ii) it was intended to be used and relied on in respect of the particular transactions in which the claimant in fact used it. So while shareholders were a foreseeable class of claimants, auditors' reports were not sent to them in order for them to make up their mind about whether they wanted to take over the company. See also *Al Nakib Investments v Longcroft* [1990] 1 W.L.R. 1390; and also the shipping cases of *The Morning Watch* [1990] 1 Lloyd's Rep. 547; and *The Nicholas H.* [1994] 1 Lloyd's Rep. 492, dealing with the liabilities of classification societies.

61 As happened, for example, in *BDW Trading Ltd v Integral Geotechnique (Wales) Ltd* [2018] EWHC 1915 (TCC); [2018] P.N.L.R. 34 (report stated to be for benefit of client only, with limited exception in case of a formal assignment of its benefit: held, no liability to third parties in other circumstances where exception inapplicable).

62 *JEB Fasteners Ltd v Marks Bloom & Co* [1981] 3 All E.R. 289 (upheld on appeal on the causation issue: [1983] 1 All E.R. 583). See too *Royal Bank of Scotland plc v Bannerman Johnstone Maclay* [2005] CSIH 39; 2005 S.C. 437; [2005] P.N.L.R. 43.

63 But not invariably. In *White v Jones* [1995] 2 A.C. 207 a disappointed legatee recovered from negligent solicitors despite the lack of any reliance. But the House of Lords realised that this was a somewhat unusual situation.

64 See *Ta Ho Ma Pty Ltd v Allen* (1999) 47 N.S.W.L.R. 1 (mortgagee's claim against valuer fails since reliance unforeseeable).

65 See, e.g. *Raja v Austin Gray* [2002] EWCA Civ 1965; [2003] Lloyd's Rep. P.N. 126 (valuer employed by receiver who undervalues property to be sold by the latter owes no direct duty to property owner: lack of reliance an important feature).

66 *Clarke v Bruce Lance & Co, above* at 370; *Connolly-Martin v Davis* [1999] P.N.L.R 826; *Huxford v Stoy, Hayward and Co* (1989) 5 B.C.C. 421; *Kamahap Investments v Chu's Central Market* (1989) 64 D.L.R. (4th) 167. But this is not so, of course, if the defendant professed to be acting for both parties concerned: see *Mortgage Express v Bowerman (No 2)* [1996] 2 All E.R. 836 (solicitor acting for mortgagor and mortgagee obtained suspicious information from mortgagor; liable for failing to pass on to mortgagee).

is a chain of contractual relationships between the professional and his client, and the client and the third party, which would be subverted by the imposition of a direct duty in tort.[67]

(e) Where the object of the duty undertaken to the client is to confer a benefit on the third party, a duty may be owed concurrently to that person so as to allow him to recover for loss of any expected benefit,[68] but this is not invariable. The tendency is to limit such recovery to cases where, if unable to sue the professional, the third party could not recover against anyone and would thus be left without a remedy.[69] Where there would be double liability, the third party claimant will almost invariably fail.[70]

(f) There is, in general, no duty to persons other than clients in respect of breaches of professional duties affecting the quality (as against the safety) of goods or buildings.[71]

9-13 **Duties of care and assignment** The benefit of a duty of care owed by a professional is not infrequently assigned to someone else as a means of creating a de facto duty to third parties. A common instance is where a property developer assigns the benefit of his arrangements with an architect or other adviser to a subsequent owner or developer.[72] Such assignments are on principle valid,[73] unless the professional specifically stipulated against assignment[74]; the assignee is in essence allowed the same measure of recovery as the assignor would have had had there been no assignment[75] (but no more[76]).

---

67 See *Henderson v Merrett Syndicates Ltd* [1995] 2 A.C. 145, 534 (Lord Goff).

68 *Ross v Caunters* [1980] Ch. 297; *White v Jones* [1995] 2 A.C. 207; *Richards v Hughes* [2004] EWCA Civ 266; [2004] P.N.L.R. 35 (accountants allegedly botched school fees tax saving scheme: CA refused to strike out claim by children whose fees were to be paid, though sceptical as to prospects of success). cf. *Al-Kandari v Brown (J.R.) and Co* [1987] Q.B. 514; *Arbuthnott v Fagan & Feltrim Underwriting Agencies Ltd*, *The Times*, 26 July 1994. Note that where professional advice is provided to X, the courts will not allow Y to sue in tort under the rule in *Hedley Byrne & Co Ltd v Heller & Partners Ltd* [1964] A.C. 465 on the basis that he was acting as X's undisclosed principal: see *Playboy Club London Ltd v Banca Nazionale del Lavoro SpA* [2018] UKSC 43; [2018] 1 W.L.R. 4041, criticised in J. Grower and O. Sherman, "Equivalent to contract? Confronting the nature of the duty arising under Hedley Byrne v Heller" (2019) 135 L.Q.R. 177.

69 Compare *White v Jones* [1995] 2 A.C. 207 (solicitor liable to disappointed legatee, since no other remedy for claimant) with *Raja v Austin Gray* [2002] EWCA Civ 1965; [2003] Lloyd's Rep. P.N. 126 (receiver liable to owner for sale at undervalue: hence no need for additional liability of valuer who undervalued property). See too *Mortensen v Laing* [1992] 2 N.Z.L.R. 282 (insurance assessor owes no duty to insured, who has adequate remedy against insurer).

70 See, e.g. *Carr-Glyn v Frearsons* [1999] Ch. 326 (*White v Jones* duty owed to legatee only because of finding that estate could not have sued in own name); and cf. *Corbett v Bond Pearce* [2001] EWCA Civ 531; [2001] 3 All E.R. 769.

71 See *Dept of the Environment v Thomas Bates & Sons Ltd* [1991] 1 A.C. 499; and *Murphy v Brentwood DC* [1991] 1 A.C. 398 (realty); cf. *Simaan General Contracting v Pilkington Glass Ltd (No.2)* [1988] Q.B. 758 (personalty).

72 Sometimes specific provision is made for this. In such a case this is likely to be regarded as exhaustive, such that if the formal process of assignment is omitted the third party will automatically have no claim: see *BDW Trading Ltd v Integral Geotechnique (Wales) Ltd* [2018] EWHC 1915 (TCC); [2018] P.N.L.R. 34.

73 *Offer-Hoar v Larkstore Ltd* [2006] EWCA Civ 1079; [2006] 1 W.L.R. 2926.

74 *Linden Gardens Trust Ltd v Lenesta Sludge Disposal Ltd* [1994] 1 A.C. 85; and see too *Alfred McAlpine Construction Ltd v Panatown Ltd* [2001] 1 A.C. 518.

75 *Offer-Hoar v Larkstore Ltd* [2006] EWCA Civ 1079; [2006] 1 W.L.R. 2926; *Pegasus Management Holdings SCA v Ernst & Young (A Firm)* [2012] EWHC 738 (Ch); [2012] P.N.L.R. 24; *Equitas Ltd v Walsham Bros & Co Ltd* [2013] EWHC 3264 (Comm); [2014] P.N.L.R. 8; *Walker Group Construc-*

Duties to clients and others: the impact of company law In respect of a given transaction a professional may be in breach of duty both to a company and to a shareholder in that company. Examples include where accountants negligently advise a company and its shareholders about a deal with a third party, or where lawyers carelessly advise a businessman who operates through a company he partly owns.[77] Under the company law rule in *Foss v Harbottle*,[78] the decision whether and on what terms the company should sue to recover its loss is the company's, acting if necessary through a general meeting: the shareholder cannot bring proceedings in his own right. In *Prudential Assurance Co Ltd v Newman Industries Ltd (No 2)*[79] the Court of Appeal held, further, that even if the shareholder was owed a separate duty of care by the relevant professional—there a firm of accountants—he could not recover damages reckoned by a depreciation in his shareholding or on loss of shareholder benefits such as dividends or capital distributions, since this would amount to circumventing the rule in *Foss v Harbottle*. This restriction was approved by the House of Lords in the solicitors' negligence case of *Johnson v Gore Wood*,[80] and remains good law today. It was once thought, following suggestions by Lord Millett in *Johnson v Gore Wood*,[81] that this represented a more general principle. In particular, it was thought to bar claims by shareholders of any losses suffered by them owing to a wrong done to the relevant company, and indeed to extend to claims by creditors whose chances of payment had been diminished.[82] However, in 2020 in *Sevilleja v Marex Financial Ltd*[83] the Supreme Court trenchantly discountenanced any extension of the bar beyond claims by a shareholder to recover for a loss in the value of his shareholding or lost distributions caused by a wrong to the company. In all other cases, subject to any restrictions on double recovery, the fact that the company might also have sued the defendant is out of account. 9-14

Duties of care: illegality There is no doubt that a professional may be liable for negligently failing to prevent a client from being illegally defrauded by employees,[84] 9-15

tions Pty Ltd v Tzaneros Investments Pty Ltd [2017] NSWCA 27; (2017) 94 N.S.W.L.R. 108.

76 See *Dawson v Great Northern & City Railway Co* [1905] 1 K.B. 260; and *Equitas Ltd v Walsham Bros & Co Ltd* [2013] EWHC 3264 (Comm); [2014] P.N.L.R. 8 at [132] (Males J).

77 As in e.g. *Prudential Assurance Co Ltd v Newman Industries Ltd (No 2)* [1982] Ch. 204; and *Johnson v Gore Wood & Co* [2002] 2 A.C. 1.

78 (1843) 2 Hare 461.

79 [1982] Ch. 204; see esp at 224, and also *Sevilleja v Marex Financial Ltd* [2020] UKSC 31; [2020] 3 W.L.R. 255 at [37].

80 [2002] 2 A.C. 1.

81 See [2002] 2 A.C. 1 at 66.

82 See e.g. *Perry v Day* [2004] EWHC 3372 (Ch); [2005] 2 B.C.L.C. 405; *Gardner v Parker* [2004] EWCA Civ 781; [2004] 2 B.C.L.C. 554; *Breeze v Norfolk Chief Constable* [2018] EWHC 485 (QB); [2018] 2 B.C.L.C. 638 at [24]–[25].

83 [2020] UKSC 31; [2020] 3 W.L.R. 255. This case concerned a claim that a wrong done to a company had prejudiced a creditor's chance of recovery; the creditor was nevertheless allowed to proceed against the wrongdoer. A minority would have reversed *Prudential Assurance Co Ltd v Newman Industries Ltd (No 2)* [1982] Ch. 204 itself, but that view did not prevail.

84 See, e.g. *Barings Plc v Coopers & Lybrand (No 7)* [2003] EWHC 1319 (Ch); [2003] P.N.L.R. 34 (accountants); *Singularis Holdings Ltd (In Official Liquidation) (A Company Incorporated in the Cayman Islands) v Daiwa Capital Markets Europe Ltd* [2019] UKSC 50; [2019] 3 W.L.R. 997 (stockbrokers).

or even from inadvertently falling foul of the criminal law.[85] But issues of illegality may nevertheless affect liability. In particular, relief may be refused to a claimant guilty of conscious illegality. Thus it is clear that there can be no recovery against a negligent professional in respect of a criminal penalty imposed on the claimant for knowing wrongdoing.[86] Again, a client of an accountant has been held disentitled to sue for negligence in connection with a transaction intended all along to be combined with a substantial tax fraud.[87] On the other hand, in any case where illegality is pleaded the court must take into account the underlying purpose of the prohibition transgressed and other relevant public policies, and must keep in mind the need to invoke illegality with a due sense of proportionality.[88] Thus in *Stoffel & Co v Grondona*[89] a negligence claim by a buyer against conveyancing solicitors was held not barred by fact that claimant had been "fronting" for a different party in fraud of her mortgage lender.

9-16 Some difficulty was in the past caused by the case where a fraudster who was in control of a company misappropriated its assets and the company, having been put into liquidation by its creditors, then sought to to sue its erstwhile professional advisers for negligently failing to prevent the fraud concerned. It was once thought that no claim lay, on the basis that the fraudster's machinations had to be attributed to the company itself, a proposition apparently accepted by the House of Lords in 2009 in *Stone & Rolls Ltd (in liquidation) v Moore Stephens (A Firm)*.[90] But this solution, although it had something to be said for it,[91] at least where there were no innocent shareholders,[92] has now been effectively rejected. Doubt was

---

85 See, e.g. the solicitors' case of *Robinson v Ness & Co (A Firm)* [2017] EWHC 2305 (planning laws); the accounting cases of *Coulthard v Neville Russell* [1998] P.N.L.R. 276 (technical company assistance in purchasing own shares); and *Griffin v UHY Hacker Young & Partners* [2010] EWHC 146 (Ch); [2010] P.N.L.R. 20 (breach of "phoenix" provisions of Companies Acts); and also *Osman v J Ralph Moss Ltd* [1970] 1 Lloyd's Rep. 313 (insurance brokers liable for negligently leaving motorist uncovered so that he was fined).

86 See *Henderson v Dorset Healthcare University NHS Foundation Trust* [2018] EWCA Civ 1841; [2018] 3 W.L.R. 1651 (medical liability); and *Day v Womble Bond Dickinson (UK) LLP* [2020] EWCA Civ 447; [2020] P.N.L.R. 19 (solicitors' negligence). Both cases relied on the earlier *Gray v Thames Trains Ltd* [2009] UKHL 33; [2009] 1 A.C. 1339, to the same effect. So too with professional sanctions: *Khan v Hussain* [2019] CSOH 11; 2019 S.C. 322; [2019] P.N.L.R. 14.

87 See the Irish decision in *English v O'Driscoll* [2016] IEHC 584; [2017] P.N.L.R. 9. It is suggested that this result would apply in England even since the narrowing of the illegality defence in *Patel v Mirza* [2016] UKSC 42; [2017] A.C. 467. This is certainly suggested by the Scots case of *Khan v Hussain* [2019] CSOH 11; 2019 S.C. 322; [2019] P.N.L.R. 14 (financial adviser told lies about income, allegedly on advice of accountant that this was acceptable: no recovery from accountant when fined heavily by regulator).

88 See generally *Patel v Mirza* [2016] UKSC 42; [2017] A.C. 467.

89 [2018] EWCA Civ 2031; [2018] P.N.L.R. 36.

90 [2009] UKHL 39; [2009] 1 A.C. 1391. The effective claimant, of course, was the victim of the fraud, a bank relieved of some $100 million, who had put the company into liquidation and then persuaded the liquidator to sue for its benefit. For an approving note, see P. Watts, "Audit Contracts and Turpitude" (2010) 126 L.Q.R. 14; for a less approving one, E. Ferran, "Corporate Attribution and the Directing Mind and Will" (2011) 127 L.Q.R. 239.

91 Since its effect was indirectly to impose a duty of care on financial advisers to protect third parties from being defrauded by their client, a duty which might well not have been imposed directly on orthodox tort principles.

92 That it should be limited to such cases was it seems accepted: see *Stone & Rolls* [2009] UKHL 39; [2009] 1 A.C. 1391 at [28] (Lord Phillips). Admittedly it was left open in *Jetivia SA v Bilta (UK) Ltd* [2014] UKSC 23; [2016] A.C. 1 at [29]; but the position seems logical.

thrown on *Stone & Rolls* in a 2014 Supreme Court case,[93] and in 2019 it was effectively overruled in *Singularis Holdings Ltd v Daiwa Capital Markets Europe Ltd*.[94] There, a company defrauded of most of its assets by its controller as a result of a breach of duty by the brokers controlling them successfully recovered damages from the latter. Any suggestion that the fraud of the controller should be attributed to the company so as to bar the claim was roundly discountenanced.

Duty of care: personal liability of employed professional Most actions for negligence on the part of an employed professional are brought against the latter's employer: he probably has the deeper pocket, and in addition is more likely to be covered by insurance. But if this is not possible (for example, where the employer is uninsured and bankrupt or the employee acted outside the scope of his employment), how far is it possible to sue the employee personally? There is little doubt on the matter when the employed professional causes physical damage or injury in the course of his employment: he is himself a tortfeasor and can be sued accordingly.[95] With economic loss, such as that arising from negligent advice, the point is more difficult. As a general rule, the courts have been disinclined to make an employee personally liable under the rule in *Hedley Byrne & Co Ltd v Heller & Partners Ltd*[96] saying that normally such a person is not to be regarded as accepting responsibility for what he says.[97] Thus in *Bradford & Bingley Plc v Hayes*[98] mortgage lenders sued a surveyor and his employers for negligence in misvaluing property: the employers were held liable, but the employee was not. But the rule is not absolute. In *Merrett v Babb*,[99] an employed valuer who negligently overvalued a house was held personally liable to the client, the partnership which employed him having become bankrupt and failed to maintain professional indemnity cover. The only relevant differences between this case and *Bradford*[100] seem to be that (a) the employer there was a limited company (and hence there was a need to preserve the separation between the corporation and those associated with it), whereas here the employer was unincorporated; and (b) that the client in *Bradford* was a business and in *Merrett* an individual. It is suggested that this 9-17

[93] It was referred to in *Jetivia SA v Bilta (UK) Ltd* [2014] UKSC 23; [2016] A.C. 1 at [30] as a case to be put "on one side in a pile and marked 'not to be looked at again'". Similarly, the Ontario Court of Appeal found it of "limited assistance" in *Livent Inc. v Deloitte & Touche*, 2016 ONCA 11; (2016) 393 DLR (4th) 1. It is also worth noting, more generally, that in *Patel v Mirza* [2016] UKSC 42; [2017] A.C. 467 the Supreme Court, while not commenting directly on *Stone & Rolls*, emphasised the need to tailor the application of the ex turpi causa maxim to those cases where public policy genuinely demands the dismissal of a suit.

[94] [2019] UKSC 50; [2019] 3 W.L.R. 997.

[95] e.g. *Fairline Shipping Corp. v Adamson* [1975] Q.B. 180 (storage company director negligently fails to keep goods refrigerated: liable for spoilage).

[96] [1964] A.C. 465.

[97] On which see the general discussion in *Williams v Natural Life Health Foods Ltd* [1998] 1 W.L.R. 830 (company controller and director not personally liable for allegedly negligent advice given by him on behalf of employer).

[98] Unreported 25 July 2001. See too *Summit Advances Ltd v Bush* [2015] EWHC 665 (QB); [2015] P.N.L.R. 18.

[99] [2001] EWCA Civ 214; [2001] Q.B. 1174.

[100] Which, perhaps oddly, did not refer to *Merrett*.

distinction is difficult to defend,[101] and that in practice *Merrett v Babb* is likely to be limited to cases on identical or very similar facts.[102]

(c) Negligence vs stricter liability

9-18 **Professional services: liability presumptively only for negligence** Whether the claimant sues in tort or contract, the professional's duty in respect of his services is generally limited to the exercise of care and skill. Thus a doctor does not undertake that treatment will be successful, but only that he will carry it out with proper care[103]; an architect certifying building work gives no guarantee against defects that no skill could uncover[104]; and while a solicitor for a mortgage lender undertakes to show a high degree of care to prevent monies falling into the hands of fraudsters, he gives no absolute guarantee that they will not.[105]

9-19 **Professional services: exceptional cases of strict liability** Nevertheless, the above statement is only partly true. There are at least three circumstances in which the professional may be subject to a stricter liability. First, it is perfectly possible, though rather unlikely, for a professional person to guarantee results by an express term in his contract.[106] Secondly, some duties are in their nature strict. A professional is, for example, generally bound to carry out the work he has accepted instructions to do: he will hence be liable if he does not do it, even without negligence.[107] Duties to pay money, or account for monies received on a client's account, are, not surprisingly, similarly treated.[108] Thirdly, stricter liability may be imposed by statute. For instance, where goods are supplied in the course of render-

---

[101] As rightly pointed out by Colman J in *BP Plc v Aon Ltd* [2006] EWHC 424 (Comm); [2006] Lloyd's Rep. I.R. 577 at [80].

[102] The court was sceptical of personal claims in *Devine v McAteer* [2008] NI Ch 7; [2008] P.N.L.R. 31. See too the judgment of Colman J in *BP Plc v Aon Ltd* [2006] EWHC 424 (Comm); [2006] Lloyd's Rep. I.R. 577 at [80]; the Scots decision in *Milne v Gray* [2008] CSOH 84; 2008 S.C.L.R. 558; [2008] P.N.L.R. 34; and the suggestion of Hildyard J in *Challinor v Juliet Bellis & Co* [2013] EWHC 347 (Ch) at [719]–[742] (reversed on different grounds at [2015] EWCA Civ 59; [2016] W.T.L.R. 43) that personal liability of an employed person for negligent advice was very much the exception rather than the rule. But note the Hong Kong decision in *Yazhou Travel Investment Co Ltd v Bateson Starr* [2004] 1 HKLRD 969; [2005] P.N.L.R. 31 (although non-liability was the rule, personal nature of solicitor-client relationship meant a contrary inference readily available in such cases (as it was there)).

[103] e.g. *Lanphier v Phipos* (1838) 8 C. & P. 475; *Thake v Maurice* [1986] Q.B. 644; *Eyre v Measday* [1986] 1 All E.R. 488 (no promise about effectiveness of sterilisation: hence no liability when failed despite care taken).

[104] *Dhamija v Sunningdale Joineries Ltd* [2010] EWHC 2396 (TCC); [2011] P.N.L.R. 9.

[105] *Nationwide Building Society v Davisons Solicitors* [2012] EWCA Civ 1626; [2013] P.N.L.R. 12, especially at [51]–[58] (Morritt C).

[106] As in the Michigan decision in *Guilmet v Campbell*, 188 N.W.2d 601 (1971), where such a promise by a doctor was indeed established and damages awarded. A British example is *Mortgage Corporation Ltd v Mitchells Roberton*, 1997 S.L.T. 1305 (contractual promise by solicitors not to release loan monies unless and until valid real security in place). But promises of unconditional success, unsurprisingly, are not lightly inferred: see, e.g. *Thake v Maurice* [1986] Q.B. 644 (promise of medical success alleged, but not found on the facts); and *Martin v JRC Commercial Mortgages Plc* [2012] EWCA Civ 63; [2012] P.N.L.R. 18 (no promise by mortgage broker to obtain mortgage in any event, it being inherently unlikely that an absolute guarantee of results was ever intended).

[107] A neat example is *Platform Funding Ltd v Bank of Scotland Plc* [2008] EWCA Civ 930; [2009] Q.B. 426 (surveyor liable when reported on different house from that referred to in instructions, even though mistake due to fraud of third party and he was entirely blameless).

[108] *Equitas Ltd v Walsham Bros & Co Ltd* [2013] EWHC 3264 (Comm); [2014] P.N.L.R. 8 at [49] (Males J).

ing a service, the supplier is strictly liable for defects in the same way as a seller.[109] Thus a pharmacist dispensing drugs on a private prescription is liable if, through no fault of his own, the drug is defective; a doctor injecting a private patient with a contaminated vaccine is responsible for the state of the vaccine[110]; and an architect providing materials under a "design and build" contract will be strictly liable for the condition of those materials. Again, the effect of the Consumer Protection Act 1987 is that the professional person will be liable for any defect in goods he himself produces,[111] and in respect of other goods will be liable as a supplier unless he identifies the person who supplied him with the goods.[112] This may be of some significance in medical malpractice claims.[113]

Professional services: liability for the fault of independent contractors Presumptively a professional person, like most other defendants, is vicariously liable for the negligence of his employees, but not for that of independent contractors.[114] Nevertheless, in certain cases professional liability may comprise not only vicarious responsibility for employees, but in addition a non-delegable duty to see that care is taken by anyone to whom a task is delegated, including independent contractors. Such liability may occasionally arise by statute[115]: but it may also arise at common law, in at least two situations. One is where a professional person acts as agent for a client, as for example in the case of an insurance broker or underwriting agent. Here the prima facie rule is that he is liable for the negligence of any sub-agent employed by him to carry out his functions, even if not himself at fault.[116] Secondly, such liability may also arise where (i) the claimant is in some way vulnerable or dependent vis-à-vis the defendant; (ii) there is some existing relationship between claimant and defendant[117] carrying with it a duty to provide a service to and in addition care for, and take positive steps to protect, the claimant; 9-20

---

[109] See Supply of Goods and Services Act 1982 ss.3–5 (in the case of non-commercial buyers, the Consumer Rights Act 2015 ss.9–11). For an interesting case on the borderline, see *Ter Neuzen v Korn* (1995) 127 D.L.R. (4th) 577 (arranging for supply of semen does not count as supply of goods so as to attract strict liability, but involves only a duty to show due diligence).

[110] See A. Bell, "The Doctor and the Supply of Goods and Services Act" [1984] L.S. 175.

[111] Section 2(2). For details of the Act, see para.10-45 onwards. See too M. Brazier and E. Cave, *Medicine, Patients and the Law*, 6th edn (2016), Ch 10.

[112] Section 2(3).

[113] For an example, see the decision of the ECJ on the Product Liability Directive in *Veedfald v Århus Amtskommune* [2003] 1 C.M.L.R. 41 (hospital strictly liable under product liability law for condition of cleansing fluid for transplanted organs). See also, however, the German decision on the Directive in *KG (Berlin)*, 03.04.2014, Az. 20 U 253/12 (doctor who modifies artificial hip not a "producer"). Generally, see M. Brazier and E. Cave, *Medicine, Patients and the Law*, 6th edn (2016), Ch.10; and M. Powers & A. Barton, *Clinical Negligence*, 5th edn (2015), Ch.13.

[114] e.g. *Gregory v Shepherds* [2000] P.N.L.R. 769 (English solicitor not liable for negligence of Spanish lawyer in handling Spanish conveyancing transaction); *Phelps v Stewarts (A Firm)* [2007] EWHC 1561 (Ch); [2007] P.N.L.R. 32 (solicitors not liable for fault of negligent tax consultant engaged by them). See also *A (A Child) v Ministry of Defence* [2004] EWCA Civ 641; [2005] Q.B. 183 (no liability in Army medical service for subcontracted hospital); and generally Ch.6; and *Barclays Bank Plc v Various Claimants* [2020] UKSC 13; [2020] 2 W.L.R. 960.

[115] Architects, for example, may be liable for the negligence of independent contractors engaged by them in so far as they are involved in the construction or renovation of dwelling-houses: see Defective Premises Act 1972 s.1(1) and para.7-151.

[116] See, e.g. *Henderson v Merrett Syndicates Ltd* [1995] 2 A.C. 145 (members' agent at Lloyd's of London held to have undertaken responsibility for negligence of sub-agents employed by him); *Coolee Ltd v Wing Heath & Co* (1930) 38 Ll.L. Rep. 188 (insurance broker employing sub-broker); *Simmons v Rose* (1862) 31 Beav. 1 (country solicitor employing London agent).

[117] For example, hospital and patient, or school and pupil.

(iii) the duty to take care is delegated to someone over whom the claimant has no power of choice; and (iv) the negligence of the party actually at fault takes place directly in the course of providing the service delegated to that person.[118] In practice this means that hospitals and similar organisations who undertake to provide (rather than merely arrange for) medical care are likely to find themselves liable for the negligence of anyone whose services they make use of in order to provide that care.[119] So too[120] will prison authorities subcontracting the treatment of inmates.[121] It remains to be seen whether the courts will widen the idea of vulnerability and dependence still further so as to cover (for example) lawyers or stockbrokers who employ agents to look after a client's interests on a continuing basis.

(d) Liability as trustee

9-21 **Professional holding property as trustee** In many cases where a professional handles money or property on behalf of others, he becomes a trustee of it, either because required to do so by law (as in the case of client funds held by solicitors, stockbrokers and insurance brokers[122]) or because of ad hoc arrangements (notably in conveyancing transactions[123]). If such a trust arises, then his duty is to employ the funds strictly in accordance with his authority: any disbursement of them other than in accordance with the terms of the trust[124] is a breach of trust. For this the trustee is in general strictly liable without proof of fault[125] (and, importantly, without

118 *Woodland v Swimming Teachers Association* [2013] UKSC 66; [2014] A.C. 537 at [23] (Lord Sumption). In that case a school was held liable for the negligence of an independently-employed lifeguard at a school swimming event. See para.6-70 and para.7-231.

119 See *Cassidy v Ministry of Health* [1951] 2 K.B. 343, 362–363 (Denning LJ); *Roe v Minister of Health* [1954] 2 Q.B. 66, 81–82 (Denning LJ); *X (Minors) v Bedfordshire County Council* [1995] 2 A.C. 633, 740 (Lord Browne-Wilkinson); approved by Lord Sumption in *Woodland v Swimming Teachers Association* [2013] UKSC 66; [2014] A.C. 537 at [23]. See generally para.9-102 onwards.

120 *A (A Child) v Ministry of Defence* [2004] EWCA Civ 641; [2005] Q.B. 183; to the contrary, was disapproved by Lord Sumption in *Woodland v Swimming Teachers Association* [2013] UKSC 66; [2014] A.C. 537 at [23]–[24].

121 *GB v Home Office* [2015] EWHC 819 (QB).

122 Solicitors: see the SRA Accounts Rules 2017, made by the Solicitors Regulation Authority under the Solicitors Act 1974. Insurance brokers: see the CASS 5 rules, made under the Financial Services and Markets Act 2000 by the Financial Services Authority (now the Financial Conduct Authority). Stockbrokers: CASS 8, from the same source.

123 For example, in a mortgage transaction solicitors regularly hold the mortgage funds on trust for the lender pending disbursement. In an ordinary property sale they may or may not hold the completion monies on trust for the purchaser before completion: compare *Purrunsing v A'Court & Co* [2016] EWHC 789 (Ch); [2016] 4 W.L.R. 81; and *P&P Property Ltd v Owen White & Catlin LLP* [2018] EWCA Civ 1082; [2019] Ch. 273.

124 But note that the terms of any trust are likely to be far from coterminous with the general obligations of the professional. It is thus entirely possible for the professional to be in breach of retainer but not in breach of trust, as where a solicitor for a lender fails to reveal relevant information to the lender before disbursing mortgage monies. Here his only liability is in negligence. See *Bristol & West Building Society v Mothew* [1998] Ch. 1, 24 (Millett LJ); *Target Holdings Ltd v Redferns* [1996] A.C. 421, 436 (Lord Browne-Wilkinson); *AIB Group (UK) Plc v Mark Redler & Co Solicitors* [2013] EWCA Civ 45; [2013] P.N.L.R. 19 at [13] (Patten LJ); also *Gabriel v Little* [2013] EWCA Civ 1513 (a point not raised on appeal in *BPE Solicitors v Hughes-Holland* [2017] UKSC 21; [2018] A.C. 599).

125 See *Target Holdings Ltd v Redferns* [1996] A.C. 421. So there is automatic breach of trust where solicitors part with mortgage lenders' monies against either a bogus solicitors' undertaking engineered by fraudsters (*Lloyds TSB Bank Plc v Markandan & Uddin* [2012] EWCA Civ 65; [2012] 2 All E.R. 884) or a forged transfer (*Nationwide Building Society v Davisons Solicitors* [2012]

the possibility of reduction of liability for contributory negligence[126]), his duty being not so much to compensate for the beneficiary's net loss, as with damages in contract or tort,[127] as to put the beneficiary in the position he would have occupied had the terms of the trust been observed.[128] However, even where such strict liability exists it may be possible for the defendant to claim the protection of s.61 of the Trustee Act 1925, which gives the court a discretion to exonerate a trustee from liability if he has acted honestly and reasonably, and ought fairly to be excused for his breach of trust.[129]

(e) Liability for breach of fiduciary duty

Liability for breach of fiduciary duty[130] Quite apart from liability in contract and tort, or for breach of trust, a professional may also owe concurrent equitable duties to his client known as fiduciary duties. These duties may add significantly to his liabilities, and therefore some reference must be made to them. 9-22

(i) Fiduciary duties generally

Incidence of fiduciary duties The paradigm fiduciary is, of course, the trustee himself.[131] To some extent, fiduciary duties imposed on those who are not strictly trustees, including professionals, exist because their position is to a greater or lesser extent analogous to that of the trustee. Nevertheless, any attempt to list who is, and who is not, a fiduciary in the professional context is probably a vain one. A fiduciary, as Millett LJ has observed, "is not subject to fiduciary obligations because he 9-23

EWCA Civ 1626; [2013] P.N.L.R. 12). Conversely the same may apply to solicitors paying property purchase monies to fraudsters: e.g. *Purrunsing v A'Court & Co* [2016] EWHC 789 (Ch); [2016] 4 W.L.R. 81; and *P & P Property Ltd v Owen White & Catlin Ltd* [2018] EWCA Civ 1082; [2019] Ch. 273. Note that the new Law Society Code for Completion, effective 1 May 2019, allows solicitors held liable here to pass on the bill to the seller's solicitors by providing for the latter to warrant that they are acting for the true owners of the property to be sold.

126 Whether under the Law Reform (Contributory Negligence) Act 1945 or under s.61 of the Trustee Act 1925: see *Lloyds TSB Bank Plc v Markandan & Uddin (A Firm)* [2012] EWCA Civ 65; [2012] 2 All E.R. 884.

127 "[T]he common law rules of remoteness of damage and causation do not apply" (Lord Browne-Wilkinson in *Target Holdings Ltd v Redferns* [1996] A.C. 421, 434); *AIB Group (UK) Plc v Mark Redler & Co Solicitors* [2013] EWCA Civ 45; [2013] P.N.L.R. 19 at [47] (Patten LJ).

128 See, e.g. *Target Holdings Ltd v Redferns* [1996] A.C. 421, 434–435 (Lord Browne-Wilkinson); *AIB Group (UK) Plc v Mark Redler & Co* [2014] UKSC 58; [2015] A.C. 1503. In such cases some care may have to be taken, in the absence of express agreement as to the terms of any trust, in determining whom the monies are actually held in trust for. See, e.g. *Bellis v Challinor* [2015] EWCA Civ 59; [2016] W.T.L.R. 43 (monies paid into solicitor's client account disbursed to fraudsters: no claim by payers, since on the facts the trust was in favour of the fraudsters from the beginning); also *Chang v Mishcon de Reya* [2015] EWHC 164 (Ch) (similar).

129 A point first made by Rimer J in *Lloyds TSB Bank Plc v Markandan & Uddin (A Firm)* [2012] EWCA Civ 65; [2012] 2 All E.R. 884 at [61]; for an example see see *Nationwide Building Society v Davisons Solicitors* [2012] EWCA Civ 1626; [2013] P.N.L.R. 12 (solicitors entirely innocently duped into releasing loan monies to bogus solicitors in league with fraudsters). But s.61 sets a high hurdle and most such applications fail: for a recent instance see *Purrunsing v A'Court & Co* [2016] EWHC 789 (Ch); [2016] 4 W.L.R. 81 (solicitor duped into acting for fraudster in property transaction too credulous when faced with evasive answers). On the application of s.61 to professionals such as solicitors, see generally M. Haley, "Section 61 of the Trustee Act 1925: a judicious breach of trust?" [2017] C.L.J. 537, 557 et seq.

130 *Jackson & Powell on Professional Liability*, 8th edn (2017), para.2–140 onwards. See too P. Turner, "Measuring equitable compensation for breach of fiduciary duty" [2014] C.L.J. 257.

131 *Keech v Sandford* (1726) Sel. Cas. Ch. 61; *Price v Blakemore* (1843) 6 Beav. 507.

is a fiduciary; it is because he is subject to them that he is a fiduciary".[132] It is preferable to rationalise the incidence of fiduciary obligations by reference to the nature of the fiduciary's relationship with others.[133] Broadly speaking, while the precise content of individual fiduciary relationships can vary widely,[134] a fiduciary relationship is imposed by law[135] in any case where the professional owes an exclusive loyalty to his principal's interests, and must put these above all others, including his own.[136] Thus although the classic fiduciary may be the trustee, closely followed by the company director,[137] it seems clear that nearly all professionals can, at least in some contexts, find themselves liable to fiduciary obligations. A professional may, for example, hold monies in such a way as to make his position analogous to that of a trustee: if he then wrongly pays out those monies, this may be characterised as a breach of fiduciary duty.[138] Again, since agents owe well-established fiduciary duties,[139] it follows that parallel obligations are owed by insurance brokers[140] and stockbrokers.[141] Yet again, it is beyond doubt that solicitors are subject to extensive fiduciary liabilities.[142] Accountants too owe at least some such duties,[143] as do surveyors acting on behalf of clients.[144] It has been said peremptorily that medical practitioners are not fiduciaries[145]; nevertheless, whether they are necessarily incapable of owing fiduciary duties of any kind is less certain.[146] In

132 *Bristol & West Building Society v Mothew* [1988] Ch. 1, 18 (borrowing from P. Finn, *Fiduciary Obligations*, p.2).

133 J. Shepherd, "Towards a Unifying Concept of Fiduciary Relationships" (1981) 97 L.Q.R. 51; see also *Hospital Products v United States Surgical Corporation* (1984) 156 C.L.R. 41, 97 (Mason J); *White v Jones* [1995] 2 A.C. 206, 271 (Lord Browne-Wilkinson); *Brewer v Iqbal* [2019] EWHC 182 (Ch); [2019] P.N.L.R. 15 at [36]–[42].

134 *Henderson v Merrett Syndicates Ltd* [1995] 2 A.C. 145, 206 (Lord Browne-Wilkinson).

135 It is suggested that fiduciary duties are essentially imposed by law rather than by agreement, though they can where necessary be modified by the parties: see P. Finn, "The Fiduciary Principle", in T.G. Youdan (ed.), *Equity, Fiduciaries and Trusts*.

136 See *Bristol & West Building Society v Mothew* [1998] Ch. 1, 18 (Millett LJ); *Breen v Williams* (1996) 70 A.L.J.R. 772, 793–799 (Gaudron and McHugh JJ), 782 (Dawson and Toohey JJ), 808 (Gummow J). See also P. Finn, The Fiduciary Principle, in T. Youdan (ed.), *Equity, Fiduciaries and Trusts*; D. Hayton, Fiduciaries in Context: An Overview, in P. Birks (ed.), *Privacy and Loyalty*, Ch. 11; R. Austin, Moulding the Content of Fiduciary Duties, in A. Oakley (ed.), *Trends in Contemporary Trust Law*, Ch.7. The rationale appears to be that such allegiance on the part of the fiduciary counterbalances the principal's inherent vulnerability to abuse in such relationships: see *Hospital Products Ltd v United States Surgical Corporation* (1984) 156 C.L.R. 41, 68.

137 *Regal (Hastings) Ltd v Gulliver* [1976] 2 A.C. 134.

138 e.g. *Bristol & West Building Society v May, May & Merrimans* [1996] 2 All E.R. 801. Inadvertent wrongdoing will, however, generally not suffice: see *Bristol & West Building Society v Mothew* [1998] Ch. 1; and *Birmingham Midshires Building Society v Infields* (1999) 66 Con. L.R. 20.

139 *Boston Deep Sea Fishing and Ice Co v Ansell* (1888) 39 Ch. D. 389.

140 *Jackson & Powell on Professional Liability*, 8th edn (2017), para.16–014; and see, e.g. *North & South Trust Co v Berkeley* [1971] 1 W.L.R. 470 (brokers acting for insured and also for loss-adjusters).

141 e.g. *Armstrong v Jackson* [1917] 2 K.B. 822.

142 e.g. *Boardman v Phipps* [1967] 2 A.C. 46; *Islamic Republic of Iran v Denby* [1987] 1 Lloyd's Rep. 367.

143 e.g. when advising on proposed litigation: *Bolkiah (Prince Jefri) v K.P.M.G.* [1999] 2 A.C. 222.

144 e.g. *Satnam Ltd v Dunlop Heywood* [1999] 3 All E.R. 652.

145 *Sidaway v Bethlem Royal Hospital* [1985] A.C. 871, 884 (Lord Scarman).

146 Imagine, for example, that a doctor was bribed to prescribe a particular pill to his patient; or referred him to a clinic for no better reason than that he owned a half interest in the clinic. It would seem peculiar if the patient had no remedy. In Canada the idea of physicians as fiduciaries is well-developed: e.g., *Norberg v Wynrib* (1992) 92 D.L.R. (4th) 449 (doctor liable for demanding—and getting—sexual favours); *McInerney v MacDonald* [1992] 2 S.C.R. 138 (patient's right to information).

certain cases the employees of fiduciaries may owe their own personal duties of loyalty over and above those owed by the employers themselves.[147] On the other hand, it seems clear that there must be an element of conscious action of some kind which conflicts with the principal's interests[148]; a person cannot be in breach of fiduciary duty through mere inadvertence, however negligent.[149]

Fiduciary duties: content Fiduciary obligations typically cluster around two general duties[150] on the part of the fiduciary: not to bend his position to his own or to a third party's advantage, and not, in any matter within the scope of his service,[151] to have a personal interest or an inconsistent engagement with a third party, unless freely and with full information consented to by his principal or authorised by law.[152] Although this is not an exhaustive list,[153] and the obligations vary very much according to the context, the chief heads of duty are listed below. 9-24

The rule against personal interest or gain Equity's proscriptions on personal gain by fiduciaries are broad and highly significant to professional malpractice. For obvious reasons, bribes[154] and secret commissions[155] are prohibited. But the proscription goes much further, and in principle covers all unauthorised gains.[156] In 9-25

---

147 See, e.g. *JD Wetherspoon Plc v Van De Berg & Co Ltd* [2007] EWHC 1044 (Ch); [2007] P.N.L.R. 28 (employees of property search consultancy potentially personally liable to clients for diverting secret profits to their own friends).

148 "The nature of the obligation determines the nature of the breach. The various obligations of a fiduciary merely reflect different aspects of his core duties of loyalty and fidelity. Breach of fiduciary obligation, therefore, connotes disloyalty or infidelity. Mere incompetence is not enough. A servant who loyally does his incompetent best for his master is not unfaithful and is not guilty of a breach of fiduciary duty." See *Bristol & West Building Society v Mothew* [1998] Ch. 1, 18 (Millett LJ). For an example of such a conscious breach, see *Nationwide Building Society v Richard Grosse & Co* [1999] Lloyd's Rep. P.N. 348 (certification by solicitors to lender of loan despite knowledge of collusive back-to-back sale).

149 *Bristol & West Building Society v Mothew* [1998] Ch. 1 (solicitor acting for lender and borrower failed to tell lender that borrower had given second charge: liability for negligence at common law, but not for breach of fiduciary duty in equity). See too *Leeds & Holbeck Building Society v Arthur & Cole (A Firm)* [2002] P.N.L.R. 4. For criticism of this approach see S. Elliott (1999) 12(1) T.L.I. 74; J.D. Heydon, "The negligent fiduciary" (1995) 111 L.Q.R. 1.

150 A third duty sometimes referred to is a duty in equity to take care in and about the conduct of the principal's business: e.g. *Nocton v Lord Ashburton* [1914] A.C. 932. But even if such a duty exists, breach of it is not regarded as a breach of fiduciary duty: see *Bristol & West Building Society v Mothew* [1998] Ch. 1, 17; and cf. *Permanent Building Society v Wheeler* (1994) 14 A.C.S.R. 109, 157 (Ipp J.). Since duties of care of this type will almost invariably be paralleled by a duty at common law, they are of no real importance in the professional context.

151 Note that service here may include a past relationship: *Longstaff v Birtles* [2001] EWCA Civ 1219; [2002] 1 W.L.R. 470.

152 P. Finn, The Fiduciary Principle, in T.G. Youdan (ed.), *Equity, Fiduciaries and Trusts*.

153 For example, a professional fiduciary may also owe a duty, when exercising a discretion, not to fail to take account of relevant matters (see *Brewer v Iqbal* [2019] EWHC 182 (Ch); [2019] P.N.L.R. 15 at [44]–[48], dealing with an administrator's duty in determining whether to sell assets and in what circumstances). But they are the most important in the context of professional liability.

154 For a case of bribe-taking in a professional context see *Islamic Republic of Iran Shipping Lines v Denby* [1987] 1 Lloyd's Rep. 367 (solicitors).

155 e.g. *Imperial Mercantile Credit Association v Coleman* (1873) L.R. 6 H. L. 189 (stockbroker); *Andrews v Ramsay & Co* [1903] 2 K.B. 635 (estate agent). More recently, see *McWilliam v Norton Finance (UK) Ltd* [2015] EWCA Civ 186; [2015] P.N.L.R. 22.

156 Though the terms of the relationship may modify this. An insurance broker, as an agent, owes fiduciary duties to his client, the assured: yet in most cases he is perfectly properly paid by the insurer.

Boardman v Phipps,[157] the defendant fiduciary was a solicitor to a trust which had a minority shareholding in a private company. Some of the trustees prevailed on him to acquire a majority shareholding in his own name. The company's fortunes improved: hence both trust and defendant profited. The House of Lords, by a majority, made the defendant account to the trust in respect of his profit, even though what the defendant had done had not harmed the trust but rather benefited it.[158] The rule requiring disgorgement was absolute, not dependent on knowing wrongdoing or bad faith,[159] and could be disapplied only if there was strong evidence that the fiduciary's gain had been made with the "full knowledge and assent" of the principal.[160] Similarly, a professional must not act in a situation where his own interests conflict with his duty to give his undivided loyalty to the client.[161]

9-26 **The rule against self-dealing** A trustee must not, exercising his power as such, cause the trust to sell trust property to himself or buy it from him: if he does, he commits a breach of duty and the transaction is voidable without reference to whether it was in good faith or otherwise fair.[162] Other fiduciaries are similarly bound. This head of liability does not often arise in connection with professional liability, but it may: for example, where a stockbroker instructed to buy shares for a client instead transfers his own shares to that client.[163]

9-27 **Transactions with fiduciaries: the fair dealing rule** A trustee may have dealings with his beneficiaries, but if he does they must be fair and the beneficiary must be fully informed: if not, the trustee is in breach of duty and the transaction voidable.[164] This form of fiduciary liability, which can apply to other fiduciaries as well,[165] can be significant in the professional context. Thus solicitors have been held guilty of breach of fiduciary duty when making a loan to a client without making it clear that they stood to make undisclosed profits from it,[166] and for entering into a hotel business in partnership with a client without disclosing the full facts so as to enable the clients to make a properly informed decision.[167]

---

157 [1967] 2 A.C. 46.

158 It is highly arguable that this strict position on unauthorised profiteering by fiduciaries is inappropriate in the modern era; see Jones (1968) 84 L.Q.R. 472; P. Finn, *Fiduciary Obligations*, 130–168; and *Murad v Al-Saraj* [2005] EWCA Civ 959; [2005] W.T.L.R. 1573 at [82], [201] (Arden and Jonathan Parker LJJ).

159 cf. *Keech v Sandford* (1726) Sel. Cas. Ch. 61.

160 *Boardman v Phipps* [1967] 2 A.C. 46, 105 (Lord Hodson).

161 *Longstaff v Birtles* [2001] EWCA Civ 1219; [2002] 1 W.L.R. 470 (advice to buy into partnership in which solicitors held interest); see too *Day v Mead* [1987] 2 N.Z.L.R. 443. The person owed this duty may, for obvious reasons, include those closely connected with the client, such as the shareholders in a private company: *Ratiu v Conway* [2005] EWCA Civ 1302; [2006] 1 All E.R. 571.

162 See *Ex p. James* (1803) 8 Ves. 337; *Campbell v Walker* (1800) 5 Ves. 678; *Holder v Holder* [1968] Ch. 353 CA; *Re Thompson's Settlement, Thompson v Thompson* [1986] Ch. 99; B. McPherson, "Self-Dealing Trustees", in A. Oakley (ed.), *Trends in Contemporary Trust Law* (1997, OUP).

163 *Armstrong v Jackson* [1917] 2 K.B. 822.

164 The so-called "fair dealing" rule: *Coles v Trecothick* (1804) 9 Ves. 234. See *Thompson v Eastwood* (1877) 2 A.C. 215; *Demerara Bauxite Ltd v Hubbard* [1923] A.C. 673. But note that the remedy of rescission is in the discretion of the court: *Johnson v EBS Pensioner Trustees Ltd* [2002] EWCA Civ 164; [2002] Lloyd's Rep. P.N. 309.

165 See, e.g. *Lewis v Hillman* (1852) 3 H.L.C. 607; *Moody v Cox* [1917] 2 Ch. 71, 79–80 (Lord Cozens-Hardy MR) (solicitors).

166 *Swindle v Harrison* [1997] 4 All E.R. 705.

167 *Longstaff v Birtles* [2001] EWCA Civ 1219; [2002] 1 W.L.R. 470; noted A. Sprince (2002) 18 P.N. 96.

Conflict of interest[168] Apart from proscribing self-interested activity on the part of the fiduciary, equity also seeks to ensure that he acts in his principal's best interests by denying him the opportunity to act in anyone else's, be that his own or a third party's, where these will or may conflict with those of the beneficiary. In the professional setting, the so-called "double employment rule" prima facie prohibits any professional from acting for a second client or anyone else whose interests might conflict with those of his primary client.[169] It also prevents a professional who has acted for one party later acting for another party whose interests are opposed to those of the first client, despite the fact that he is technically no longer subject to fiduciary duties, unless there is no possibility of misuse of information obtained while acting for the first client.[170] 9-28

However, the law has to recognise that it is often commercially convenient for a professional fiduciary to accept an otherwise inconsistent engagement. For example, in a small and simple conveyancing transaction it may well be cost-effective for the same firm of solicitors to act for mortgagor and mortgagee, or vendor and purchaser. To this end, it is now clear that a professional may accept otherwise inconsistent engagements if he has secured the informed consent of both clients,[171] with all material facts disclosed.[172] Indeed, the law has gone further and on occasion implied consent to act for those whose interests might conflict.[173] Further, it should be noted that where such consent is present, it may incidentally affect the content of the fiduciary duty itself.[174] 9-29

(ii) *Remedies for breach of fiduciary duty*

Generally Where a breach of fiduciary duty by a professional is proved, the relevant remedies are effectively three: (a) an injunction to prevent a continuing breach; (b) disgorgement of gains wrongfully made; and (c) compensation for any 9-30

---

168 C. Hollander & S. Salzedo, *Conflicts of Interest*, 5th edn (2016).

169 *Fullwood v Hurley* [1928] 1 K.B. 498; cf. *Moody v Cox* [1917] 2 Ch. 71. See too *JD Wetherspoon Plc v Van De Berg & Co. Ltd* [2007] EWHC 1044 (Ch); [2007] P.N.L.R. 28 (property finders liable to clients for secretly giving information to third parties allowing them to buy, and profit from, sites of interest to clients).

170 e.g. *Bolkiah (Prince Jefri) v KPMG* [1999] 2 A.C. 222 (accountants): see also *A Lloyd's Syndicate v X* [2011] EWHC 2487 (Comm); [2012] 1 Lloyd's Rep. 123 (expert witness, though no conflict on the facts). In practice this is the context in which the conflict of interest question most often arises.

171 *Clark Boyce v Mouat* [1994] 1 A.C. 428; S. Fennell (1994) 10 P.N. 22. The position is different in Canada, where a professional is unable to accept inconsistent engagements simply by obtaining the parties' consent to do so, and where, as a result, allegations that the fiduciary has been unable to resist acting in that way are frequently framed as breach of fiduciary duty: see, for example, *Davey v Woolley, Hames, Dale & Dingwall* (1982) 133 D.L.R. (3d) 647.

172 *Moody v Cox* [1917] 2 Ch. 71; *Fullwood v Hurley* [1928] 1 K.B. 498, 502 (Scrutton LJ). Note, however, that the facts that need to be disclosed are only those relevant to the decision whether to allow the fiduciary to act for the other side. There is no need to advise as to the wisdom of the transaction as a whole: *Clark Boyce v Mouat* [1994] 1 A.C. 428.

173 *Kelly v Cooper* [1993] 1 A.C. 205 (real estate agent can properly act for sellers of neighbouring tropical beach hideaways, even though vendors effectively in competition with each other, since well-known that such agents regularly acted for numerous clients).

174 *Kelly v Cooper* [1993] 1 A.C. 205, above (where estate agent properly acting for competing sellers A and B, no duty to pass on to A information received in confidence from B); see too *Medsted Associates Ltd v Canaccord Genuity Wealth (International) Ltd* [2019] EWCA Civ 83; [2019] 1 W.L.R. 4481 (effect of knowledge of client that fiduciary remunerated by other party, though not at what level).

loss suffered. Little more need be said of (a),[175] but (b) and (c) deserve brief coverage.

9-31 **Disgorgement of profits** A fiduciary professional is under a general equitable liability to disgorge any profits or gains made in breach of duty.[176] The fact that he acted in good faith, or with no intent to benefit at the expense of the claimant, or that the claimant might not have been able to make the profit, is irrelevant.[177] Moreover, such profits or gains will be held on constructive trust for the beneficiary-client[178]: it follows that if the fiduciary still has them the beneficiary can take them ahead of general creditors, and also that he can follow them in so far as they have been used to purchase other assets.[179]

9-32 **Compensation** Where a professional's breach of fiduciary duty causes loss to his beneficiary, the latter has a right to equitable compensation. However, it should be noted that the essence of breach of fiduciary duty is disloyalty: from which it follows that before he can be liable for breach of fiduciary duty, some conscious and intentional breach of his obligation has to be shown.[180] Mere negligent failure to advise, or pass on relevant information, is not enough.[181] The measure of recovery is, in most cases, similar (though not necessarily identical) to that in contract and tort.[182] Indeed, in most cases of actions against professional fiduciaries by their clients the fiduciary duties outlined above can equally be regarded as implied contractual duties. Thus the claimant must prove that but for the breach of fiduci-

---

175 It arises most commonly in cases of alleged conflict of interest, as in *Bolkiah (Prince Jefri) v KPMG* [1999] 2 A.C. 222 (accountants); and *Ball v Druces & Attlee* [2002] P.N.L.R. 23 (solicitors).

176 In a few cases, such as where the fiduciary is also an agent, there is a parallel liability at common law: e.g. *Boston Deep Sea Fishing and Ice Co v Ansell* (1888) 39 Ch. D. 389. Little in practice turns on this, save possibly with regard to limitation and the award of interest.

177 *Boardman v Phipps* [1967] 2 A.C. 46. For examples see *Ball v Druces & Attlee (No.2)* [2004] EWHC 1402; [2004] P.N.L.R. 39 (though there the claim failed for other reasons); *Chirnside v Fay (No.2)* [2007] 1 N.Z.L.R. 433; [2007] P.N.L.R. 6; *Seymour v Ockwell* [2005] EWHC 1137; [2005] P.N.L.R. 39.

178 *FHR European Ventures LLP v Cedar Capital Partners LLC* [2014] UKSC 45; [2015] A.C. 250.

179 See *FHR European Ventures LLP v Cedar Capital Partners LLC* [2014] UKSC 45; [2015] A.C. 250; also *Daraydan Holdings Ltd v Solland International Ltd* [2004] EWHC 622 (Ch); [2005] Ch. 119; and *Att-Gen for Hong Kong v Reid* [1994] 1 A.C. 324.

180 "The nature of the obligation determines the nature of the breach. The various obligations of a fiduciary merely reflect different aspects of his core duties of loyalty and fidelity. Breach of fiduciary obligation, therefore, connotes disloyalty or infidelity. Mere incompetence is not enough. A servant who loyally does his incompetent best for his master is not unfaithful and is not guilty of a breach of fiduciary duty." See *Bristol & West Building Society v Mothew* [1998] Ch. 1, 18 (Millett LJ). For an example of such a conscious breach, see *Nationwide Building Society v Richard Grosse & Co* [1999] Lloyd's Rep. P.N. 348 (certification by solicitors to lender of loan despite knowledge of collusive back-to-back sale).

181 *Bristol & West Building Society v Mothew* [1998] Ch. 1 (solicitor acting for lender and borrower failed to tell lender that borrower had given second charge: liability for negligence at common law, but not for breach of fiduciary duty in equity). See too *Leeds & Holbeck Building Society v Arthur & Cole (A Firm)* [2002] P.N.L.R. 4. For criticism of this approach see S. Elliott, "Fiduciary liability for client mortgage frauds" (1999) 13 T.L.I. 74; J.D. Heydon, "The negligent fiduciary" (1995) 111 L.Q.R. 1.

182 It was once thought that there were limitation advantages in suing for breach of fiduciary duty rather than at common law: but in *Companhia de Sequros Imperio v Heath (REBX) Ltd* [2001] 1 W.L.R. 112 the Court of Appeal held that the provisions of the Limitation Act 1980 relating to claims in contract and tort would apply by analogy to claims for breach of fiduciary duty, even if dishonesty were established.

ary duty, he would not have suffered the loss he did.[183] Thus if a solicitor fails to make a relevant disclosure in breach of his fiduciary duty when dealing with his client, the client can recover compensation if, but only if, he can show that he would not otherwise have acted as he did had full disclosure been made.[184] But there may be an exception where the breach of fiduciary duty is not only deliberate but dishonest, allowing the claimant to recover the entire loss suffered as a result of the transaction entered into with or through the fiduciary.[185] Where liability for breach of fiduciary duty is established, it now seems clear that contributory negligence by the claimant is irrelevant.[186]

(f) Breach of confidence[187]

The duty of confidence The second crucial area in which equity operates in relation to professional liability is in relation to duties of confidentiality.[188] Breach of confidence by a professional is generally treated as serious professional misconduct and in addition will normally be actionable at the instance of the aggrieved client or patient. A duty of confidence may often be implied into the professional's contract for his services, but there is no doubt that it may equally arise quite independently of contract.[189] Whatever its source, in order for it to be invoked, the normal rule is that there must be evidence that the information is confidential in nature, and that it has been entrusted to the defendant[190] by the claimant on terms that it is to be kept confidential.[191] Thus, personal information entrusted by clients and patients to lawyers,[192] estate agents[193] and medical practitioners[194] gives rise to an implied professional obligation of confidentiality, including a right to damages **9-33**

183 *Swindle v Harrison* [1997] 4 All E.R. 705, 717 (Evans LJ); *Nationwide Building Society v Balmer Radmore* [1999] P.N.L.R. 606, 670–671 (Blackburne J.). On causation generally in breach of fiduciary duty cases, see J.D. Heydon, "Causal Relationships Between a Fiduciary's Default and the Principal's Loss" (1994) 110 L.Q.R. 328.

184 *Swindle v Harrison* [1997] 4 All E.R. 705; see too *Nationwide Building Society v Balmer Radmore* [1999] P.N.L.R. 606. The rule is the same where a professional is guilty of simple breach of trust: *Target Holdings Ltd v Redferns* [1996] 1 A.C. 421.

185 *Nationwide Building Society v Balmer Radmore* [1999] P.N.L.R. 606, 669 (Blackburne J): see too the slightly puzzling Privy Council decision in *Brickenden v London Loan & Savings Co* [1934] 3 D.L.R. 465.

186 *Nationwide Building Society v Balmer Radmore* [1999] P.N.L.R. 606, 673–677; see A. Dugdale (1999) 15 P.N. 164.

187 See Ch.26.

188 See generally F. Gurry, *Breach of Confidence* (2nd edn, 2012); and L. Bently & B. Sherman, Intellectual Property, 4th edn (2014), Chs 44-46.

189 See *Seager v Copydex Ltd* [1967] 1 W.L.R. 923.

190 Or otherwise reached the defendant in the course of working for the claimant: for example, where a solicitor gathers information from third parties for the purpose of litigation being conducted by the claimant.

191 It is now clear that information may be confidential, and hence subject to duties of non-disclosure, even though it has not been entrusted to anyone at all: see *Campbell v MGN Ltd* [2004] UKHL 22; [2004] 2 A.C. 457. But this is not likely in practice to affect questions of professional malpractice.

192 e.g. *Ashburton (Lord) v Pape* [1913] 2 Ch. 469; *Parry-Jones v Law Society* [1969] 1 Ch. 1, 7, 9. See too P. Matthews, "Breach of Confidence and Legal Privilege" (1984) 1 L.S. 77.

193 See, e.g. *Walsh v Shanahan* [2013] EWCA Civ 411; [2013] 2 P. & C.R. DG7.

194 *Wyatt v Wilson* (1820) unreported but referred to in *Prince Albert v Strange* (1849) 41 E.R. 1171 at 1179; *Hunter v Mann* [1974] 1 Q.B. 767, 772; *X. v Y.* [1988] 2 All E.R. 648. See J. Loughrey, "Medical Information, Confidentiality, and a Child's Right to Privacy" (2003) 23 L.S. 510.

in the event of breach.[195] Knowledge of clients' finances subjects accountants to duties of confidentiality, as do any trade secrets entrusted to architects and engineers.[196] There is authority in Canada that liability for breach of this obligation may be triggered by mere negligence; hence a doctor was held liable for culpably allowing his patient's embarrassing medical records to get into the wrong hands.[197] Where a professional is bound by a duty of confidentiality, it follows a fortiori that he cannot be liable to his client for failing to pass on confidential information which he could not have disclosed without that client's consent.[198]

9-34 The duty of confidence is not, of course, absolute. It may be excluded by agreement.[199] More importantly, disclosure may be justified in the public interest,[200] or where there is a statutory duty to disclose information,[201] or on order of the court (only lawyers being protected by privilege against disclosure in England).[202]

9-35 The courts will, however, define public interest fairly narrowly, weighing the primary public interest in maintaining confidentiality against the merits of access to particular information. Thus disclosure of the identities of two doctors found to be HIV positive,[203] and of information of the adverse effects of a pregnancy testing device after the product had been withdrawn,[204] were both held not to be justified. So too it has been held that speculation of wrongdoing without an apparently solid basis in fact, and information merely suppletive of what authorities

---

[195] e.g. *Cornelius v De Taranto* [2001] EWCA Civ 1511; (2001) 68 B.M.L.R. 62 (improper disclosure by psychiatrist); *Walsh v Shanahan* [2013] EWCA Civ 411; [2013] 2 P. & C.R. DG7 (ditto by estate agent).

[196] See *Coco v A.N. Clark (Engineers) Ltd* [1969] R.P.C. 41; *Dunford & Elliot v Johnson* [1978] F.S.R. 143 at 148.

[197] *Peters-Brown v Regina District Health Board* [1997] 1 W.W.R. 638.

[198] See *Marsh v Sofaer* [2003] EWHC 3334 (Ch); [2004] P.N.L.R. 24 (solicitor who discovered in the course of litigation that client impaired not liable for failing to pass this information to other solicitors who acted for the same client in subsequent criminal proceedings).

[199] See, e.g. *Mortgage Express Ltd v Sawali* [2010] EWHC 3054 (Ch); [2011] P.N.L.R. 11 (solicitors acting for purchasers and mortgage lenders: purchasers' common-form authorisation to share files with lenders: no right to object to disclosure to lenders in course of litigation by latter).

[200] The jurisprudence on what amounts to a "public interest" defence is enormous. See, e.g. *Initial Services v Putterill* [1968] 1 Q.B. 396; *Fraser v Evans* [1969] 1 Q.B. 349; *Lion Laboratories Ltd v Evans* [1985] Q.B. 526. Professional standards laid down by the appropriate bodies may of course be relevant here: see, e.g. the Accounting Standards laid down by the Financial Reporting Council, or the guidance for doctors from the GMC on matters such as the reporting of patients who insist on driving while incapacitated. See too *ABC v St George's Healthcare NHS Trust* [2017] EWCA Civ 336; [2017] P.I.Q.R. P15 (refusal to strike out claim against hospital for failing to break medical confidence and warn family member about inherited disease); also *Child & Family Agency v A* [2018] IEHC 112, where Twomey J in the Irish High Court thought it might be justifiable to order a breach of medical confidentiality to allow disclosure of the HIV status of a man to his girlfriend (though on the facts he declined to do so).

[201] e.g. the Proceeds of Crime Act 2002 s.330 (duty to report suspicions of money laundering, matters of particular relevance to lawyers and accountants); and the Public Health (Control of Disease) Act 1984 ss.13, 45C, 45F and 45P and SI 2010/659 (duty of doctors to pass on details of those suffering from notifiable diseases or other conditions threatening public health). But a mere request from authorities will not normally do, even where those authorities could if they wished have obtained a court order for disclosure: see *Saab v Dangate Consulting Ltd* [2019] EWHC 1558 (Comm); [2019] P.N.L.R. 29.

[202] See P. Matthews, "Breach of Confidence and Legal Privilege" (1984) 1 L.S. 77. And see *Robertson v Canadian Imperial Bank of Commerce* [1994] 1 W.L.R. 1493; and *Saab v Dangate Consulting Ltd* [2019] EWHC 1558 (Comm); [2019] P.N.L.R. 29 at [210]–[218] (Cockerill J).

[203] *X v Y* [1988] 2 All E.R. 648.

[204] *Schering Chemicals Ltd v Falkman Ltd* [1982] Q.B. 1.

already know, will not suffice.[205] In contrast, in *W v Egdell*[206] a consultant psychiatrist engaged by a prisoner to report on his suitability for parole was held justified in sending a report on his patient to the Home Office. The report suggested that the prisoner could not be safely released, and, the court held, the interest in protecting the public clearly outweighed any argument in favour of confidentiality. In similar vein, the Canadian Supreme Court has stated that medical confidentiality may be displaced where there is a clear risk of serious and imminent harm to a specific person or closely-defined group of possible victims.[207] It is not necessary to demonstrate that there has been wrongdoing on the part of the client or patient to justify a breach of confidence,[208] but the onus is on the defendant to establish that the conduct of the claimant, or the public policy arguments in favour of disclosure, are such that the duty of confidence should exceptionally be displaced.[209] It is possible that there might even be a common law duty to break confidence, for example where a patient is known to be suffering from a genetically-transmissible disease and there is a clear danger that unless warning is given his grandchildren may be born affected by it.[210]

(g) Professional liability: exclusion of duty

Excluding professional liability[211] At common law anyone, including a professional, can by agreement exclude or limit any liability he would otherwise be under in contract or tort. Provided the agreement covers the relevant events,[212] and subject to the public policy rule preventing exclusion or limitation of liability for a person's own fraud or deliberate wrongdoing,[213] it is entirely valid. By statute, he may **9-36**

---

205 See the private investigators' case of *Saab v Dangate Consulting Ltd* [2019] EWHC 1558 (Comm); [2019] P.N.L.R. 29.

206 [1990] Ch. 359. This is in accordance with the demands of ECHR art.8: *Z v Finland* (1998) 25 E.H.R.R. 371.

207 See *Smith v Jones* (1999) 169 D.L.R. (4th) 385 (patient unburdens himself to psychiatrist about disconcerting sado-masochistic fantasies concerning prostitutes: medical confidence displaced to allow psychiatrist to tell authorities); also *Child & Family Agency v A* [2018] IEHC 112, above. Indeed, in the European context this exception may be mandated by art.10 of the European Convention on Human Rights: see *Juppala v Finland* [2009] 1 F.L.R. 617 (infringement of art.10 to make discloser of suspicions of child abuse liable to defamation proceedings).

208 *Lion Laboratories Ltd v Evans* [1985] Q.B. 526, 550 (Griffiths LJ); *Attorney-General v Guardian Newspapers Ltd (No.2)* [1990] 1 A.C. 109, 268–269 (Lord Griffiths).

209 *X v Y* [1988] 2 All E.R. 648.

210 *ABC v St George's Healthcare NHS Foundation Trust* [2017] EWCA Civ 336; [2017] P.I.Q.R. P15 (refusal to strike out such a claim as unarguable): on which, see R. Gilbar, "It's Arrived! Relational Autonomy Comes to Court: ABC v St George's Healthcare NHS Trust" (2018) 26 Med. L. Rev. 125. Compare, however, *C v Cairns* [2003] Lloyd's Rep. Med. 90, exonerating a doctor for having failed in 1975 to pass on to the police suspicions of sexual interference with a child.

211 A. Arnull, "Professional Advisers and Limitations on Liability" (2003) 19 P.N. 494.

212 The interpretation of the clause can be a matter of some complexity: see, e.g. *University of Keele v Price Waterhouse* [2004] EWCA Civ 583; [2004] P.N.L.R. 43 (clause held not to cover liability in question). Note that as between commercially sophisticated parties, the previous tendency of judges to construe clauses against the person seeking to exclude liability is much reduced, with the emphasis lying now on a businesslike reading of the clause concerned. See the consulting engineers' case of *Persimmon Homes Ltd v Ove Arup & Partners Ltd* [2017] EWCA Civ 373; [2017] P.N.L.R. 29 at [56]–[59] (Jackson LJ); also G. McMeel, "The Impact of Exemption Clauses and Disclaimers: Construction, Contractual Estoppel and Public Policy", in A. Dyson, J. Goudkamp & F. Wilmot-Smith (eds), *Defences in Contract* (Oxford: Hart, 2017), p.234.

213 See *Pearson & Son Ltd v Dublin Corp'n* [1907] A.C. 351; and *HIH Casualty Ltd v Chase Manhat-*

equally exclude the liability of third parties, such as his own servants and agents.[214] Similar rules apply to agreements excluding liability for breach of trust.[215] Such clauses are not uncommon in standard forms, especially in respect of limitation of liability.[216] Professional regulators, on the other hand, may disapprove of such conduct and take steps to prevent it.[217] More importantly, statute now considerably restricts professionals' freedom of contract. In some cases this is done with specific reference to a single profession. Thus s.60(5) of the Solicitors Act 1974 renders void any provision in a "contentious business agreement"[218] with a solicitor purporting to exclude liability for negligence to a non-corporate, non-business client. The Companies Act 2006 severely restricts the powers of auditors engaged to carry out a statutory audit from excluding liability for negligence or breach of duty.[219] Furthermore, there also seem now to be binding limits on exclusions by professionals, such as insurance brokers or stockbrokers, regulated by the Financial Conduct Authority.[220]

9-37 **General statutory limitations on exclusion: commercial cases** The provisions of the Unfair Contract Terms Act 1977 are relevant to questions of exclusion of liability with regard to commercial claimants. In particular, s.2(2) provides that in the case of loss or damage caused by negligence (other than personal injury[221]) any exclusion or restriction of liability (including liability in tort to a third party[222]) is

---

tan Bank [2003] UKHL 6; [2003] 2 Lloyd's Rep. 61 at [16] (Lord Bingham). But there is no bar on exclusion of liability for deliberate wrongdoing by employees for whom one is vicariously liable: *Frans Maas (UK) Ltd v Samsung Electronics (UK) Ltd* [2004] EWHC 1502 (Comm); [2004] 2 Lloyd's Rep. 251. Nor is there any bar, such as appears in some civil law systems, on the exclusion of liability for gross negligence.

214 Contracts (Rights of Third Parties) Act 1999 s.1(6). See para.3-145.

215 See *Armitage v Nurse* [1998] Ch. 241; and *Spread Trustee Co Ltd v Hutcheson* [2011] UKPC 13; [2012] 2 A.C. 194. Again there can be no exoneration for deliberate personal wrongdoing: *Armitage v Nurse* [1998] Ch. 241, 253 (Millett LJ).

216 For example, both the commercial and domestic versions of the 2018 RIBA architect's Professional Services Contract contain in cll.7.2 and 7.3 a limitation to the amount of professional indemnity insurance carried by the architect, and a "net contribution" clause limiting recovery to the proportion of damages the architect would have had to pay if all others liable had been sued. Again, accountancy firms not infrequently insert caps on liability in their letters of engagement to clients.

217 For example, the Solicitors Regulation Authority by para.2.07 of the Solicitors' Code of Conduct prohibits total exclusions of liability but will countenance limitation of liability to a sum no less that the compulsory indemnity insurance carried by solicitors (currently £2 million). Rules made under the Financial Services and Markets Act 2000, s.137A, generally prohibit unreasonable exclusion by financial advisers, stockbrokers and others regulated by the Financial Conduct Authority of any duty with regard to retail clients: see the FCA *Conduct of Business Sourcebook*, para.2.1.3.

218 Defined by s.59(1).

219 Section 532 generally forbids exclusion. Note, however, that under the following sections limitations are exceptionally allowed if (a) agreed from year to year; (b) approved or ratified by ordinary resolution; and (c) not such as to reduce the auditor's liability more than is fair and reasonable. These provisions pre-empt the Unfair Contract Terms Act 1977 (s.534(3)(b)(i)).

220 Since the *Conduct of Business Sourcebook* prohibits unreasonable exclusions (para.2.1.3); and by s.137D(2) of the Financial Services and Markets Act 2000 breach of regulations made under it, including those in the Sourcebook, may be actionable as a breach of statutory duty.

221 Personal injury liability cannot be excluded at all: s.2(1). This is of limited relevance to commercial claimants, but could theoretically protect a sole trader. In this connection, note that the Act has no effect on an indemnity clause whereby they can recover any damages paid from someone else in the contractual chain other than the victim himself is enforceable: *Thompson v T Lohan (Plant Hire)* [1987] 1 W.L.R. 649.

222 *Smith v Eric S Bush (A Firm)* [1990] 1 A.C. 831. The Act does not affect contractual liability to a

ineffective except in so far as it satisfies the "requirement of reasonableness".[223] Reasonableness is defined by s.11 of the Act[224]; and the onus of proving that an exclusion of liability is reasonable rests on the person seeking to rely on it.[225] For these purposes, moreover, it seems no distinction is drawn in the context of negligent advice between excluding liability and declining to accept responsibility in the first place: despite suggestions that liability for negligent misstatement arises from an explicit or implicit assumption of responsibility,[226] both types of clause have been held by the House of Lords[227] to be tantamount to exclusion clauses and hence subject to the control of the Act.[228]

In practice, however, it seems that where the client is a business with the resources to look after its own interests, exclusions or limitations of liability are likely to be looked on with indulgence,[229] and that it will take a good deal to persuade a court to strike them down as unreasonable.[230] **9-38**

---

third party under the Contracts (Rights of Third parties) Act 1999.

[223] See too s.3 of the Misrepresentation Act 1967, subjecting to a requirement of reasonableness any negation of liability for misrepresentation.

[224] See s.11(1) (term to be "a fair and reasonable one to be included having regard to the circumstances which were, or ought reasonably to have been, known to or in the contemplation of the parties when the contract was made.").

[225] s.11(5). See, e.g. *Simpson v Harwood Hutton (A Firm)* [2008] EWHC 1376 (QB) (estate agents' limitation clause automatically struck down because no evidence led in support).

[226] See *Hedley Byrne & Co Ltd v Heller & Partners Ltd* [1964] A.C. 465, 529 (Lord Diplock).

[227] *Harris v Wyre Forest District Council* [1990] 1 A.C. 831 (a case decided with *Smith v Eric S. Bush*, below). This was a consumer case, to which at the time the 1977 Act, rather than the Consumer Rights Act 2015, applied; but the reasoning is equally relevant to commercial claims.

[228] What mattered was, it was said, was simply whether liability would have arisen but for the clause, however the latter was drafted: see, especially Lord Griffiths at 857, Lord Templeman at 847–848 and Lord Jauncey at 872–873. See too *Avrora Fine Arts Investment Ltd v Christie, Manson & Woods Ltd* [2012] EWHC 2198 (Ch); [2012] P.N.L.R. 35; *Barclays Bank Plc v Grant Thornton UK LLP* [2015] EWHC 320 (Comm); [2015] 1 C.L.C. 180; also cf. *Springwell Navigation Corp v JP Morgan Chase Bank* [2010] EWCA Civ 1221; [2010] 2 C.L.C. 705 at [181] (denial that any representation or warranty being made does not immunise term from control under s.3 Misrepresentation Act 1967). See generally E. Macdonald, "Exception clauses: exclusionary or definitional?" (2012) 29 J.C.L. 47; L. Ho and T. Mathias, "Basis clauses and the Unfair Contract Terms Act 1977" (2014) 130 L.Q.R. 377.

[229] In *Dennard v PricewaterhouseCoopers LLP* [2010] EWHC 812 (Ch) the same tendency was confirmed in the professional field, where Vos J (obiter) had no doubt that accountants should be allowed to limit their liability to £1 million in the case of a negligent valuation of business assets. Even if there was an element of inequality between the parties, the claimants were, he said, at [226], capable of protecting their own interests and were "not to be regarded as innocents abroad". See too *Barclays Bank Plc v Grant Thornton UK LLP* [2015] EWHC 320 (Comm); [2015] 1 C.L.C. 180; [55]–[91] (Cooke J). This reflects the general approach towards the 1977 Act: see the (non-professional) cases of *Watford Electronics Ltd v Sanderson* [2001] EWCA Civ 317; [2001] 1 All E.R. (Comm) 696; and *Frans Maas (UK) Ltd v Samsung Electronics (UK) Ltd* [2004] EWHC 1502 (Comm); [2004] 2 Lloyd's Rep. 251. On the other hand, compare *Ampleforth Abbey Trust v Turner & Townsend Project Management Ltd* [2012] EWHC 2137 (TCC); (2012) 144 Con. L.R. 115, striking down as unreasonable a curious clause requiring a project manager to insure liability to £10 million but then limiting its liability to the amount of its fees.

[230] One case may well be where a professional rule or code of practice forbids the exclusion concerned. This is regarded as a strong indication of unreasonableness: see *Hirtenstein v Hill Dickinson LLP* [2014] EWHC 2711 (Comm) at [179] (£3 million limitation of solicitor's liability not prominent enough in the context of the relevant code of practice).

9-39 **General statutory limitations on exclusion: consumer cases** The Consumer Rights Act 2015[231] provides for general controls over professionals' exclusion or limitation of liability to consumers.[232] Liability for negligently-caused death or personal injury cannot be excluded or limited at all.[233] Other liability in tort for negligence[234] can be, but only if the exclusion[235] is not "unfair"[236]: that is, not one which, "contrary to the requirement of good faith, ... causes a significant imbalance in the parties' rights and obligations under the contract to the detriment of the consumer".[237] Contractual liabilities to take care, on the other hand, cannot be excluded,[238] nor yet prevented from arising by a provision limiting any assumption of responsibility.[239] Liability for breach can, however, be restricted, provided that the restriction is not "unfair" within the above definition and that the consumer remains entitled to recover at least the price paid.[240] With regard to other liabilities, such as those based on breach of trust or fiduciary duty, terms or notices which would exclude or limit them will once again be valid only if not "unfair" in the sense referred to earlier in this paragraph.[241]

(h) Immunities from suit

(i) Arbitral immunity

9-40 **Arbitrators and the like** By statute, an arbitrator is immune from suit in respect of anything done in good faith in the course of the arbitration.[242] This would clearly preclude any action for professional negligence. At common law prior to 1974, a

---

231 Replacing for these purposes the Unfair Contract Terms Act 1977, which is now limited to non-consumer cases, but continues to apply to consumer cases in respect of events before 1 October 2015.

232 A consumer is defined for these purposes as an individual acting wholly or mainly outside his trade, business, craft or profession: s.2.

233 See s.65.

234 Which, it seems, includes liability to third parties: see s.61(4), referring merely to a notice purporting to "exclude or restrict a trader's liability to a consumer", or which "relates to rights or obligations as between a trader and a consumer". There is no need for the consumer to be a client of, or have a contract with, the trader.

235 It does not seem to matter whether the term excludes a duty or prevents it arising by limiting any assumption of responsibility: all that is required is that the term (or notice) "relates to rights or obligations as between a trader and a consumer" (s.61(4)(a)). So the reasoning in *Harris v Wyre Forest DC* [1990] 1 A.C. 831, above, para.9-37, will continue to apply under the 2015 Act.

236 See s.62(1).

237 See s.62(4). For the interpretation of this generally, see *Chitty on Contracts* (33rd edn, 2019), para.38-390 onwards). In the specific context of a consumer professional negligence claim, see the decision in *West v Ian Finlay & Associates* [2014] EWCA Civ 316; [2014] B.L.R. 324 (limitation of architects' liability not over-restrictive, since clearly expressed and not the result of great inequality of bargaining power)(a case decided under the previous Unfair Terms in Consumer Contracts Regulations 1999 reg.5(1)). This is a change from the previous law, which under the Unfair Contract Terms 1977 merely required such terms to be fair and reasonable. Whether cases decided under the previous law would be decided the same way today remains to be seen. *Smith v Eric S. Bush* [1990] 1 A.C. 831, disapplying a lender's surveyor's exclusion of liability to an average house-buyer, probably would be. It may be open to question, however, whether the distinction between average and well-heeled house-buyers exemplified by cases such as *McCullagh v Lane Fox & Partners Ltd* [1996] P.N.L.R. 205, with exclusion of liability vis-à-vis the latter permitted, will be carried over to the new regime.

238 See s.57(1). See too s.57(4).

239 See s.57(5) (putting the decision in *Harris v Wyre Forest DC* [1990] 1 A.C. 831 into statutory form).

240 See s.57(3).

241 See s.62.

242 Arbitration Act 1996, s.29(1).

broadly analogous rule applied to anyone else engaged to exercise professional skill to determine a matter in dispute.[243] The House of Lords, however, in *Sutcliffe v Thackrah*[244] and *Arenson v Arenson*,[245] severely restricted the applicability of the common-law professional immunity from suit attaching to decision-makers. Lord Simon of Glaisdale in *Arenson v Arenson* discussed the public policy argument for generous immunities for decision makers[246]:

> "[T]he journey starts at the wrong place and ends at the wrong place. It starts with the immunity conferred on an arbitrator for reasons of public policy. But in my judgment this is a secondary and subordinate consideration of public policy. There is a primary and anterior consideration of public policy, which should be the starting point. This is that, where there is a duty to act with care with regard to another person and there is breach of such duty causing damage to that other person, public policy in general demands that such damage should be made good to the party to whom the duty is owed by the person owing the duty. There may be a supervening and secondary public policy which demands nevertheless, immunity from suit in the particular circumstances."

Such considerations have been found to justify the continuing immunities of judges,[247] and it seems of anyone who genuinely has a matter submitted to him where there is "a formulated dispute between at least two parties which his decision is required to resolve".[248]

Beyond those categories, it is doubtful whether any further quasi-arbitral immunities still exist. In particular, no immunity now attaches to a professional person simply because his task is to determine a question in issue between two parties, nor because in so doing he must act fairly and impartially. Thus in *Sutcliffe v Thackrah*[249] an architect charged with issuing interim certificates entitling builders to claim payment was held not immune to suit by the building owner for negligence: his function was in no sense judicial or arbitral. Nor are auditors immune where they undertake to value shares in order to establish a "fair value" for their sale by the claimant[250]; nor yet experts appointed to determine a revised rent in accordance with a rent review clause[251]; nor, it seems, mediators.[252] 9-41

243 e.g. *Chambers v Goldthorpe* [1901] 1 K.B. 624; *Finnegan v Allen* [1943] K.B. 425. The reason was a perceived unfairness in such a person being liable to be "shot at from both sides": *Arenson v Arenson* [1977] A.C. 405, 418 (Lord Simon).

244 [1974] A.C. 727.

245 [1977] A.C. 405.

246 [1977] A.C. 405 at 419.

247 See above, para.5-101 onwards; and see R. Brazier, "Judicial Immunity and the Independence of the Judiciary" [1976] P.L. 397.

248 *Arenson v Arenson* [1977] A.C. 405, 424 (Lord Simon). But even here, see the comments of Lord Kilbrandon, [1977] A.C. 405 at 431, and of Lords Salmon and Fraser, [1977] A.C. 405, at 440, 442. Essentially the defendant's function must involve something in the nature of the presentation of the parties' respective cases and the evidence of witnesses: *Palacath Ltd v Flanagan* [1985] 2 All E.R. 161, 165–166.

249 [1974] A.C. 727. The liability of expert certifiers etc, following this case, is the reason for the courts' general refusal to set aside expert determinations on the ground of mistake: see *Jones v Sherwood Computer Services Ltd* [1992] 1 W.L.R. 277.

250 *Arenson v Arenson* [1977] A.C. 405. See too *N. v C.* [1998] 1 F.L.R. 63 (valuer appointed by court to appraise house the subject of a financial provision order not covered by arbitrator's immunity, though the claim failed on other grounds).

251 *Palacath Ltd v Flanagan* [1985] 2 All E.R. 161. See too *Killick v PriceWaterhouseCoopers* [2001] P.N.L.R. 1 (accountants valuing shares pursuant to "market value buy-out" provision owe duty to both parties, whether or not appointed by them).

(ii) *Witness immunity and collateral attack on previous decisions*

9-42 **Testimony and connected matters** Witnesses of fact cannot be sued for negligence in respect of what they say in court,[253] nor yet for acts or omissions closely connected with such testimony, such as preparation or collection of evidence[254] (though in the latter case the immunity does not extend to the deliberate fabrication of false testimony designed to deceive the court[255]). The position of expert witnesses, however, is less straightforward. If not instructed by the litigant who later seeks to sue them, they enjoy the same immunity as witnesses of fact from actions in negligence or otherwise.[256] If instructed by the litigant, in contrast, it was held by the majority of the Supreme Court in *Jones v Kaney*,[257] reversing a long line of previous authority,[258] that there was no reason why they should not on principle owe a duty of care to those on whose behalf they agreed to testify. Thus the court refused to strike out a claim by a personal injury claimant that his medical expert had negligently allowed herself to be browbeaten by an opposing expert into damaging and unjustified admissions, with the result that the settlement he obtained had been much reduced. The immunity from suit of someone appointed and paid to advance a client's interests was (it was said) anomalous[259]; the lack of it would

---

[252] Antipodean authority so suggests: see *Tapoohi v Lewenberg (No. 2)* [2003] VSC 410; and *McCosh v Williams* [2003] NZCA 192; and also A. Koo, "Exploring mediator liability in negligence" (2016) 45 C.L.W.R. 165.

[253] See, e.g. *Watson v McEwan* [1905] A.C. 480 (evidence of allegedly confidential matters); *N v Agrawal* [1999] P.N.L.R. 939 (immunity where witness absented herself from trial altogether); *Jones v Kaney* [2011] UKSC 13; [2011] 2 A.C. 398 at [65] (Lord Phillips); *A v Chief Constable of Hampshire* [2012] EWHC 1517 (QB). The basis is the absolute privilege of the witness: see *R v Skinner* (1772) Lofft 55, 56 ("Neither party, witness, counsel, jury or judge, can be put to answer civilly, or criminally, for words spoken in office."—Lord Mansfield); and *Taylor v Serious Fraud Office* [1999] 2 A.C. 177, 208 (Lord Hoffmann).

[254] See *Evans v London Hospital Medical College* [1981] 1 W.L.R. 184 (alleged negligence in handling samples used as evidence); *Darker v Chief Constable of the West Midlands Police* [2001] A.C. 435, 463–465 (Lord Hutton); *Smart v Forensic Science Service Ltd* [2013] EWCA Civ 783; [2013] P.N.L.R. 32 at [26] (Moses LJ).

[255] See *Darker v Chief Constable of the West Midlands Police* [2001] A.C. 435; *Smart v Forensic Science Service Ltd* [2013] EWCA Civ 783; [2013] P.N.L.R. 32.

[256] *Jones v Kaney* [2011] UKSC 13; [2011] 2 A.C. 398 at [72]–[73] (Lord Collins); *Baxendale-Walker v Middleton* [2011] EWHC 998 (QB) at [128] (Supperstone J). Presumably this means that a court-appointed expert continues to be immune, as in *O'K (E) v K (D)* [2001] 1 I.R. 636 (plaintiff's marriage declared null on basis of expressed opinion of court-appointed psychiatrist as to her mental state when marriage celebrated: no action against psychiatrist). On the other hand, expert witnesses are subject to a duty to the court, and may be subjected to third-party costs orders for the benefit of opposing parties under s.51(1) of the Senior Courts Act 1981, even in the case of mere negligence. See *Phillips v Symes (No 2)* [2004] EWHC 2330 (Ch); [2005] 1 W.L.R. 2043; *A Local Authority v Trimega Laboratories Ltd* [2013] EWCC 6 (Fam); [2014] P.N.L.R. 7; and N. Andrews, "Liability of expert witnesses for wasted costs in civil proceedings" [2005] C.L.J. 566.

[257] [2011] UKSC 13; [2011] 2 A.C. 398. See too *Ridgeland Properties Ltd v Bristol City Council* [2011] EWCA Civ 649; [2011] R.V.R. 232 at [47] (Sullivan LJ); K. Hughes [2011] C.L.J. 516; and S. Carr & H. Evans, "The Removal of Immunity for Expert Witnesses" (2011) 27 P.N. 128. *Jones v Kaney* seems to have had a cautious welcome in some parts of the Commonwealth: see e.g. *EBR Holdings Ltd (In Liq) v McLaren Guise Associates Ltd* [2016] NZCA 622; [2017] 3 N.Z.L.R. 589, refusing to strike out such a claim. But it has not as yet been accepted in Australia.

[258] On which see generally *Stanton v Callaghan* [2000] 1 Q.B. 75 (upholding the immunity of an expert engineer called by a litigant: overruled in *Jones v Kaney*).

[259] See [2011] UKSC 13; [2011] 2 A.C. 398 at [57] (Lord Phillips) and [110] (Lord Dyson).

not discourage potential expert witnesses from testifying[260] or being properly frank in doing so[261]; nor was potential liability inconsistent with the expert's duty to the court.[262] By way of exception, however, it was suggested that in order to prevent the use of civil proceedings for negligence as a collateral attack on a criminal conviction, such proceedings should be barred unless and until the original conviction had been overturned.[263]

Given that immunity no longer exists for the giving or preparation of expert evidence, a fortiori none exists as to preliminary investigation with a view to possible future testimony.[264] So in *Palmer v Durnford Ford*[265] an engineer reporting on a mechanical defect in a lorry with a view to possible litigation was held not immune; and in *D v East Berkshire Community NHS Trust*[266] the view was expressed that investigations to determine whether child abuse might have occurred were not covered by any immunity even though care proceedings might be likely in the event that they proved positive.[267] 9-43

Collateral attack Proceedings against any professional are liable to be struck out if they involve a collateral attack on the decision of a court of competent jurisdiction. This is mainly important in the criminal context, in which (for example) an action against a solicitor may be struck out where it amounts in effect to a collateral attempt to impugn the result of prior criminal proceedings.[268] So too with prior civil proceedings: there may be an impermissible collateral attack if the action aims to upset a previous unimpeachable finding of fact,[269] or if it trenches on court proceedings privilege, as with a suit against a court-appointed expert charged with the valuation of property the subject of matrimonial proceedings.[270] Nevertheless the doctrine is not as strictly applied in this case, since the bypassing of appeal as a means of redress is not as serious a problem.[271] Only if the proceedings are "manifestly unfair" to the defendant, or there is some other compelling public policy, will a strike-out be appropriate;[272] and even here it may be more apposite 9-44

260 [2011] UKSC 13; [2011] 2 A.C. 398 at [56], [83], [110] (Lords Phillips, Collins and Dyson).
261 [2011] UKSC 13; [2011] 2 A.C. 398 at [56], [83], [94], [118] (Lords Phillips, Collins, Kerr and Dyson).
262 [2011] UKSC 13; [2011] 2 A.C. 398 at [46]–[50] and [120] (Lords Phillips and Dyson).
263 [2011] UKSC 13; [2011] 2 A.C. 398 at [60] (Lord Phillips).
264 *D v East Berkshire Community NHS Trust* [2003] EWCA Civ 1151; [2004] Q.B. 558, 597 at [116] (Lord Phillips MR); following *Darker v Chief Constable of the West Midlands Police* [2001] 1 A.C. 435, 448. Lord Phillips in *D v East Berkshire* admitted the distinction could be a very fine one: see [2003] EWCA Civ 1151; [2004] Q.B. 558.
265 [1992] Q.B. 483.
266 [2003] EWCA Civ 1151; [2004] Q.B. 558 (appealed on another point, [2005] UKHL 23; [2005] 2 A.C. 373).
267 Lord Phillips doubted an earlier holding to the contrary in *X (Minors) v Bedfordshire County Council* [1995] 2 A.C. 633, 775, being of the view that it could not stand with dicta of Lord Hope in the later *Darker v Chief Constable of the West Midlands Police* [2001] 1 A.C. 435, 448.
268 e.g. *Somasundaram v M. Julius Melchior & Co* [1988] 1 W.L.R. 1394; *Smith v Linskills (A Firm)* [1996] 1 W.L.R. 763. See also *Hall (Arthur JS) & Co v Simons* [2002] 1 A.C. 615.
269 As in *Laing v Taylor Walton (A Firm)* [2007] EWCA Civ 1146; [2008] P.N.L.R. 11.
270 e.g. *N v C* [1997] 1 F.L.R. 63.
271 See, e.g. *Feakins v Burstow* [2005] EWHC 1931 (QB); [2006] P.N.L.R. 6 at [77]; also *Nesbitt v Gateshead Citizen's Advice Bureau* [2007] EWCA Civ 249; [2007] P.N.L.R. 24.
272 *Nesbitt v Gateshead Citizen's Advice Bureau* [2007] EWCA Civ 249; [2007] P.N.L.R. 24 at [24] (Smith LJ).

to invoke the doctrine of abuse of process as a means of preventing re-argument of matters which were, or should have been, raised in previous proceedings.[273]

(iii) Public policy

9-45 **Decisions with a public interest implication**[274] Professionals may be immune from suit where their functions involve a careful weighing up of delicate and confidential matters and action in the public interest rather than that of any individual.[275] This has arisen in particular in respect of advice leading to decisions on the welfare of the young. The starting point is *X v Bedfordshire County Council*,[276] where a local authority educational psychologist allegedly failed to assess properly the question whether the claimant had suffered child abuse and thus did not take steps to prevent that abuse recurring. In another case heard at the same time, a local authority psychiatrist was alleged to have negligently diagnosed abuse by the claimant's mother, with traumatic results for the family. In yet another, a child alleged negligence by local authority professionals in assessing its educational needs. It was held by the House of Lords that it was not "fair, just and reasonable" that a duty of care should be owed in any of these situations, given the need to take such decisions as much in the public interest as in the interest of any individual.

9-46 However, the wide immunity there suggested by the House of Lords has since largely disappeared as a result of subsequent cases. In *Barrett v Enfield LBC*[277] the House declined to strike out a claim arising out of decisions taken in respect of a child already in the care of a local authority who alleged that he had suffered trauma and injury as a result of its incompetence. The Court of Appeal in *S v Gloucestershire County Council*[278] acted similarly on a claim arising out of alleged failure by a local authority to supervise foster parents with whom it boarded a child: and in *Phelps v Hillingdon Borough Council*[279] the House of Lords effectively declined to follow the *Bedfordshire* case when it allowed a child to sue an education authority for negligence in deciding what its educational requirements were.

9-47 Significantly, the decisions in *Barrett* and *Gloucestershire* were reached with one eye on the European Convention on Human Rights.[280] The matter was further complicated when the European Court determined that the decisions in *X v Bedfordshire County Council* had themselves violated the children's rights under

---

[273] See para.9-136.

[274] See below, para.13-08 onwards, and note that it may be preferable to describe the situation as one of an absence of a duty of care rather than an immunity: see para.13-56.

[275] A straightforward example is *Jain v Trent Strategic Health Authority* [2009] UKHL 4; [2009] 1 A.C. 853 (no action for negligence against authority taking steps to shut care home, allegedly without checking its facts properly: no duty of care owed in the circumstances). It is worth noting, however, that Lord Scott at [11]–[18] pointed out that, had the events occurred after the Human Rights Act 1998 came into force, the First Protocol to the ECHR might have been highly relevant. See further para.1-83.

[276] [1995] 2 A.C. 633. See too *H v Norfolk CC* [1997] 1 F.L.R. 384.

[277] [2001] 2 A.C. 550.

[278] [2001] Fam. 313 (alleged abuse by foster-father).

[279] [2001] 2 A.C. 619.

[280] See [2001] 2 A.C. 550, 558 onwards; and [2001] Fam. 313, 339 et seq. respectively. The stress then was on art.6, guaranteeing the "day in court". But the matter was complicated because the decision of the ECtHR in *Osman v United Kingdom* (1998) 29 E.H.R.R. 245, which informed both decisions, was itself later heavily qualified by the same court in *Z v United Kingdom* (2001) 34 E.H.R.R. 97.

art.3[281] (in the case of failure to prevent abuse) and art.8[282] (in the case of children unnecessarily and negligently removed into care). In *D v East Berkshire Community NHS Trust*[283] the Court of Appeal took the hint, and held that as a result of the Human Rights Act 1998 the *Bedfordshire* case should no longer be followed. They thus decided that, even in cases of decisions whether or not to take a child into care, the immunity no longer applied to actions by the children. On the other hand, it should be noted that the immunity adumbrated in the *Bedfordshire* case continues to apply to proceedings by those other than the children involved, a point now confirmed by the House of Lords. In *East Berkshire* three claimants were not children, but parents. As a result of allegedly negligent investigations by paediatricians and others into injuries suffered by their children, they had been suspected of child abuse and separated from their offspring; only later were they exonerated and reunited. They sued the authorities employing the investigators for the resulting trauma, but failed in the Court of Appeal.[284] This was on the basis that it was necessary to make decisions on the basis of the welfare of the children as a paramount consideration, and that the imposition of a duty to parents would unacceptably cut across that necessity, given that their interests might well be diametrically opposed to that of their children. The parents appealed to the House of Lords, but the House by a majority[285] upheld the Court of Appeal's decision on this point.[286]

2. MEDICINE AND ALLIED PROFESSIONS[287]

(a) Duties in general

Liability of medical practitioners and hospitals to patients A medical practitioner may be liable[288] to his patient either in contract[289] or in tort.[290] Once a person has been accepted as a patient, the medical practitioner must exercise reasonable care and skill in his treatment of that patient. Any negligent error in carrying out treatment, or omission to provide adequate treatment, will be actionable if it has 9-48

[281] Which prohibits inhuman or degrading treatment. In this context cf. *Z v United Kingdom* (2001) 34 E.H.R.R. 97.

[282] Which guarantees family life from unjustified incursions. In this context cf. *TP & KM v United Kingdom* (2001) 34 E.H.R.R. 42.

[283] [2003] EWCA Civ 1151; [2004] Q.B. 558. See too *AD v Bury Metropolitan Borough Council* [2006] EWCA Civ 1; [2006] 1 W.L.R. 917; *L v Pembrokeshire County Council* [2007] EWCA Civ 446; [2007] 1 W.L.R. 2991; and an earlier decision in the Privy Council, *B v Att-Gen of New Zealand* [2003] UKPC 61; [2003] 4 All E.R. 833.

[284] *D v East Berkshire Community NHS Trust* [2003] EWCA Civ 1151; [2004] Q.B. 558, 591 at [86].

[285] Lord Bingham dissenting.

[286] *D v East Berkshire Community NHS Trust* [2005] UKHL 23; [2005] 2 A.C. 373.

[287] See generally M.A. Jones, *Medical Negligence*, 5th edn (2018); M. Brazier and E. Cave, *Medicine, Patients and the Law*, 6th edn (2016); *Jackson & Powell on Professional Liability*, 8th edn (2017), Ch.13; M. Simpson (ed.) *Professional Negligence and Liability*, Ch.14.

[288] The NHS Redress Act 2006, born out of hope rather than experience, provides for the possibility of securing patient compensation without recourse to litigation. But the scheme it envisaged was never activated, and probably never will be. However, a broadly similar redress scheme was introduced in Wales under devolved powers, and this has been brought into effect: see NHS Redress (Wales) Measure 2008, in effect from 1 April 2011. On these provisions see E. Cave, "Redress in the NHS" (2011) 27 P.N. 136. The Medical Protection Society in 2017 launched an initiative to limit traditional medical liability in a number of ways, with a view to saving costs: see Medical Protection Society, *Clinical negligence costs: striking a balance* (2017).

[289] *de la Giroday v Brough* (1997) 33 B.C.L.R. (3d) 171.

[290] A point established for at least 175 years: see *Gladwell v Steggal* (1839) 5 Bing. N.C. 733.

caused injury to the patient. Hospital authorities and thus their staff similarly owe a duty to any patient admitted for treatment, including a patient presenting himself at a casualty unit[291]; and a general practitioner owes a duty to every patient accepted onto his NHS list, whether permanent or temporary. Failure to attend such a patient will be actionable on proof that any reasonably competent general practitioner would have recognised that attendance was necessary.[292] Whenever a medical practitioner elects to provide treatment to someone who is not his patient, he is liable if he fails to exercise proper care and skill and as a result the claimant's position is made worse.

9-49 Most cases of medical malpractice concern clinical matters: but a medical practitioner may also be liable for non-climical wrongs, for example where he causes a patient to suffer mental health problems by over-zealous and wholly inappropriate religious proselytism.[293]

9-50 **Liability for refusal to provide treatment** A doctor in private practice is not, it is suggested, liable for refusal to provide treatment to a person not his patient: liabilities for pure omission are not generally countenanced.[294] There is some authority, however, that this does not necessarily apply to a doctor within the NHS, at least in cases where his contract with the NHS requires emergency attendance.[295] With regard to health authorities, decisions not to provide treatment are subject to judicial review for unlawfulness[296] (though reasonable decisions based on clinical judgment[297] or the need to distribute finite resources[298] will not be readily impugned). It might well be, however, that there is also a positive duty to take reasonable steps to provide it, such that a failure to do so through incompetence would give rise to liability in tort.[299] In the event that a patient dies as a result of a failure to provide obviously necessary treatment otherwise generally available, it is also very argu-

---

291 e.g. *Barnett v Chelsea & Kensington HMC* [1969] 1 Q.B. 428 (patient sent home from casualty by doctor who negligently failed to spot symptoms of arsenical poisoning. The action failed, but for other reasons). See too *Darnley v Croydon Health Services NHS Trust* [2018] UKSC 50; [2019] A.C. 831.

292 *Edler v Greenwich and Deptford HMC*, *The Times*, 7 March 1953; *Kavanagh v Abrahamson* (1964) 108 S.J. 320. The *Bolam* test applies here, so only if no reasonable doctor would have refused to attend will the doctor be liable: see *Morrison v Forsyth* [1995] 6 Med. L.R. 6.

293 As in *Brayshaw v Partners of Apsley Surgery* [2018] EWHC 3286 (QB); [2019] 2 All E.R. 997.

294 *Capital & Counties Plc v Hampshire County Council* [1997] Q.B. 1004, 1035 (Stuart-Smith LJ).

295 See the old case of *Barnes v Crabtree*, *The Times*, 1 and 2 November 1955; cf. the Australian decision in *Lowns v Woods* [1996] Aust Tort Reps 81-376; and M. Brazier and E. Cave, *Medicine, Patients and the Law*, 6th edn (2016), para.7-200. This seems consistent with analogous authority elsewhere: e.g. *Kent v Griffiths* [2001] Q.B. 36 (at least some duty in ambulance service to respond with due expedition).

296 e.g. *R v North West Lancashire Health Authority, ex p. A* [2000] 1 W.L.R. 977; *R (Rogers) v Swindon NHS Primary Care Trust* [2006] EWCA Civ 392; [2006] 1 W.L.R. 2649.

297 *Re R (a minor)(wardship: medical treatment)* [1991] 4 All E.R. 177, 187.

298 e.g. *R v Central Birmingham HA, ex p. Walker* (1987) 3 B.M.L.R. 32; *R v Central Birmingham HA, ex p. Collier* (Unreported, Court of Appeal, 6 Jan 1988). This judicial holding back is, it has been held, consistent with art.8 of the ECHR: see *R (Condliff) v North Staffordshire Primary Care Trust* [2011] EWCA Civ 910; [2012] 1 All E.R. 689.

299 In *Barnett v Chelsea & Kensington HMC* [1969] 1 Q.B. 428, 435, Nield J clearly suggested that a hospital casualty department would not be liable if it closed its doors and refused to see anyone. But in *Kent v Griffiths* [2001] Q.B. 36 it was held that ambulance crews owed at least some duty to arrive with due expedition, and it would seem difficult to distinguish the position of health authorities.

able that the state's liability under art.2 of the European Convention on Human Rights might be engaged.[300]

Liability to those other than patients[301] There is no reason why a doctor should not be liable in tort to someone other than his patient if the requirements of foreseeability and proximity are satisfied. Thus in *Evans v Liverpool Corporation*[302] a hospital prematurely discharged a small boy with scarlet fever. The child went home and infected his family. The hospital escaped liability, but only on the basis that no negligence could be attributed to it.[303] Similarly, in *McFarlane v Tayside Health Board*[304] it was not disputed that where a hospital negligently advised that a father's vasectomy had been effective, it could be liable to the mother for the pangs of unnecessary childbirth. In addition, there is no reason why there should not be liability for psychiatric injuries to non-patients caused by various forms of medical malpractice, for example where a mother sees her baby suffering from the gruesome results of medical negligence a short time before.[305] However, the general rules applicable to such injuries[306] apply equally here, notably the requirement that the claim arise from witnessing a particular traumatic incident.[307] In practice this greatly reduces the scope for such claims in the medical context. **9-51**

However, the limits of such liability need to be noted. For one thing, it seems difficult to make a medical practitioner liable for a pure omission under this head. Thus although there is some authority that a doctor or medical authority that knows a **9-52**

[300] cf. *Rabone v Pennine Care NHS Foundation Trust* [2012] UKSC 2; [2012] 2 A.C. 72; also more recently the decision of the ECtHR in *Fernandes v Portugal* (2018) 66 E.H.R.R. 28, accepting at [201] that where failure to provide treatment resulted from a "systemic or structural dysfunction" there might be a breach of art.2. On the latter see K. Dierkes, "Prevention of suicide duties for voluntarily hospitalised patients" [2019] E.H.R.L. Rev. 327.

[301] R. Mulheron, *Medical Negligence: Non-Patient and Third Party Claims* (2010, Ashgate).

[302] [1906] 1 K.B. 160. This head of liability could be significant where, for example, negligent non-diagnosis of a STD causes the patient to infect his wife.

[303] Having employed an apparently competent doctor as an independent contractor.

[304] [2000] 2 A.C. 59; overruling *Emeh v Kensington & Chelsea & Westminster AHA* [1985] Q.B. 1012 on this point: see too *Kealey v Berezowski* (1996) 30 O.R. (3d) 37. Note that the case was pointedly not followed by the High Court of Australia: *Cattanach v Melchior* [2003] HCA 38; (2003) 215 C.L.R. 1. New Brunswick similarly allows claims for upbringing costs: *Stockford v Johnston* (2008) 335 N.B.R. (2d) 74.

[305] As in *YAH v Medway NHS Foundation Trust* [2018] EWHC 2964 (QB); [2019] 1 W.L.R. 1413. See too *Farrell v Avon HA* [2001] Lloyd's Rep. Med. 458 (father has claim for psychiatric injury as primary victim on being falsely told baby dead and given wrong deceased infant to cuddle); *Froggatt v Chesterfield & North Derbyshire Royal Hospital NHS Trust* [2002] All E.R. (D) 218 (Dec) (unnecessary mastectomy: husband and son recover for psychiatric injury caused as a result); also *North Glamorgan NHS Trust v Walters* [2002] EWCA Civ 1792; [2003] P.I.Q.R. P16. Note that where a baby is injured in the womb and the mother suffers psychiatric injury there and then the mother can sue as a primary victim since the baby is not yet a separate person at time of the negligence: *RE (a child) v Calderdale and Huddersfield NHS Foundation Trust* [2017] EWHC 824 (QB); (2017) 156 B.M.L.R. 204.

[306] See para.7-69 onwards.

[307] *Liverpool Women's Hospital NHS Foundation Trust v Ronayne* [2015] EWCA Civ 588; [2015] P.I.Q.R. P20; *Shorter v Surrey & Sussex Healthcare NHS Trust* [2015] EWHC 614 (QB); (2015) 144 B.M.L.R. 136; *Owers v Medway NHS Foundation Trust* [2015] EWHC 2363 (QB); [2015] Med. L.R. 561. In addition there must it seems be a fairly close proximity in time between the alleged negligence and the claimant's traumatic experience: see *Paul v Wolverhampton Health Authority* [2019] EWHC 2893; [2020] P.I.Q.R. P5 (no claim by daughters who witnessed father's death 14 months after alleged failure to diagnose heart condition). For criticism of this position, see A. Burrows & J. Burrows, "A Shocking Requirement in The Law on Negligence Liability for Psychiatric Illness" (2016) 24 Med. L. Rev. 278.

patient is dangerous owes a duty to take steps to restrain or otherwise prevent him from causing harm to a third party,[308] and that a health authority may have to take steps to test family members for inherited diseases where it knows from having treated a patient that they are likely to be suffering from them,[309] the courts have stopped short of saying that a doctor in diagnosing a patient owes a general duty to third parties who might be affected by the diagnosis.[310] Secondly, any duty tends to be limited to protecting third parties from actual illness or injury. With other losses, although it is certainly possible that there may be a duty,[311] in practice it is unlikely. Thus where an applicant for a job is required to be examined by his prospective employer's company doctor and the latter negligently reports him seriously unhealthy, it has been held that no duty of care is owed: the mere fact that negligence may foreseeably harm the applicant is insufficient to allow the court to infer an undertaking of responsibility towards him.[312] And similarly, where a consultant examining an injured footballer allegedly misdiagnosed his injuries and thereby unnecessarily deprived his club of his highly profitable services, it was held that no duty was owed to the club.[313]

(b) Consent to treatment[314]

9-53 **Capacity to consent** On principle, anyone aged 16 or over[315] has capacity to consent to medical treatment,[316] and anyone over 18 to refuse it,[317] save—importantly—where there is some illness or other condition depriving the person concerned of the power to make or communicate a decision. This raises the question: what level of mental capacity is required to make a person competent to decide? At common law, there was a strong presumption in favour of capacity. A person did not lack capacity to consent (or refuse consent) simply because he suffered from some degree of mental handicap or mental disorder. Provided he could

---

[308] A possibility apparently accepted in Australia (*Hunter & New England Local Health District v McKenna* [2014] HCA 44; (2014) 314 A.L.R. 505 at [31]. But there may be strong countervailing arguments in a particular case, notably the need strictly to circumscribe powers to constrain a patient against his will, which may make it appropriate to deny a duty. That was held to be the case in Hunter itself.

[309] *ABC v St George's Healthcare NHS Trust* [2017] EWCA Civ 336; [2017] P.I.Q.R. P15 (omission by father's doctor to inform daughter that father had Huntington's disease, allegedly resulting in possible defects in daughter's own child: strikeout refused). See also R. Gilbar, "It's Arrived! Relational Autonomy Comes to Court: ABC v St George's Healthcare NHS Trust" (2018) 26 Med. L. Rev. 125.

[310] *Smith v University of Leicester NHS Trust* [2016] EWHC 817 (QB) (late diagnosis of congenital disease: no duty owed to family of patient, even though latter would have been invited to be tested as a result of timeous diagnosis).

[311] e.g. if an employee wishing to move jobs requires a clean bill of health from his existing company doctor and the latter negligently misreports the state of his health: cf. *Spring v Guardian Assurance Plc* [1995] 2 A.C. 296.

[312] *Kapfunde v Abbey National Plc* [1998] I.R.L.R. 583.

[313] *West Bromwich Albion Football Club Ltd v El-Safty* [2006] EWCA Civ 1299; [2007] P.I.Q.R. P7 (criticised, J. O'Sullivan, "Negligent medical advice and financial loss: 'sick as a parrot'?" [2007] C.L.J. 14). See too *Bot v Barnick* [2018] EWHC 3132 (QB) (no liability to partner of patient for incautious remarks on patient's sanity which allegedly caused relationship problems).

[314] M.A. Jones, *Medical Negligence* (5th edn), Ch.6; L. Skene, "When Can Doctors Treat Patients Who Cannot or Will Not Consent?" (1997) 23 Monash L.R. 77.

[315] For those under 16, see below, para.9-63.

[316] Family Law Reform Act 1969 s.8. Strictly speaking this does not exclude the power of a parent or the court to override a lack of consent: see para.9-64.

[317] For refusal of consent by minors aged between 16 and 18, see para.9-64.

understand "the nature, purpose and implications of treatment"[318] he remained competent.[319]

9-54 The matter is now governed, however, by the Mental Capacity Act 2005.[320] Besides reiterating the common law presumption of capacity,[321] this sets a statutory definition of an incompetent patient for the purpose of deciding when consent may be dispensed with: he must be "unable to make a decision for himself in relation to the matter because of an impairment of, or a disturbance in the functioning of, the mind or brain".[322] Such inability is further defined as incapacity (a) to understand the information relevant to a decision[323]; (b) to retain that information; (c) to use or weigh that information as part of the decision-making process; or (d) to communicate his decision (whether by talking, using sign language or any other means).[324] But it is specifically provided that a person is not to be treated as unable to make a decision merely because he makes an unwise one.[325] What is required, it has been said,[326] is a broad, general understanding of the kind expected from the population at large, rather than a comprehension of every last piece of relevant information[327]: furthermore, mere indecision, avoidance or vacillation are not as such tantamount to incapacity.[328] The 2005 Act merely states that certain persons are *not* competent to make a decision: it does not say expressly that those outside this category *are* competent. It has been held accordingly that even if a person is not incompetent within the Act (for example because there is no mental impairment), the courts' jurisdiction at common law[329] to intervene where consent is not genuine and unconstrained remains.[330]

---

318 *Re C (Adult: Refusal of Medical Treatment)* [1994] 1 W.L.R. 290, 294–295.

319 A straightforward example was *Re C (Adult: Refusal of Medical Treatment)* [1994] 1 W.L.R. 290 (injunction against amputation of schizophrenic's leg when patient refused, even though the result would be death from gangrene). See too *Re T* [1998] 1 F.L.R. 48 (disturbed, but not incapacitated, 25-year-old competent to refuse kidney dialysis).

320 In force from 1 April 2007.

321 See s.1(2).

322 Mental Capacity Act 2005 s.2(1). The mere fact that there is such a disturbance is thus not enough: it has to be shown that by reason of it, the patient is unable to make a decision for himself. See, e.g. *Heart of England NHS Foundation Trust v JB* [2014] EWHC 342 (COP); (2014) 137 B.M.L.R. 232.

323 Including the reasonably foreseeable consequences of that decision: s.3(3).

324 Section 3(1).

325 Section 1(4).

326 *Heart of England NHS Foundation Trust v JB* [2014] EWHC 342 (COP); (2014) 137 B.M.L.R. 232 at [26] (Peter Jackson J). So too, a fortiori, a large degree of eccentricity: see *Kings College Hospital NHS Foundation Trust v C* [2015] EWCOP 80; [2016] C.O.P.L.R. 50 (woman with personality disorder and a colourful past life and failed suicide attempt behind her refused dialysis despite clear indications of death in 10 days: held, competent to do so).

327 See too *Re Z* [2016] EWCOP 4 (woman with Asperger's syndrome and borderline learning disability: still competent to decide on residence).

328 *Heart of England NHS Foundation Trust v JB* [2014] EWHC 342 (COP); (2014) 137 B.M.L.R. 232 at [26] (Peter Jackson J). So too, a fortiori, a large degree of eccentricity: see *Kings College Hospital NHS Foundation Trust v C* [2015] EWCOP 80; [2016] C.O.P.L.R. 50 (woman with personality disorder and a colourful past life and failed suicide attempt behind her refused dialysis despite clear indications of death in ten days: held, competent to do so).

329 See, e.g. *Re T (Adult: Refusal of Treatment)* [1993] Fam. 95; *Re SA (Vulnerable Adult with Capacity: Marriage)* [2006] 1 F.L.R. 867.

330 *Re L (Vulnerable Adults with Capacity: Court's Jurisdiction)* [2012] EWCA Civ 253; [2013] Fam. 1.

(i) Adults

9-55 **Adults not suffering incapacity: refusal of consent** Any medical treatment involving physical contact with the patient's body is prima facie a battery unless the patient has expressly or implicitly consented to that contact[331] and has not withdrawn that consent[332] (unless the treatment is otherwise justified by some specific common law or statutory power[333]). It is no answer to a competent patient's claim in battery that the doctor believed that he was acting in the patient's best interests, or even that he in fact did so. The point was trenchantly affirmed by the Court of Appeal in *R v St George's Healthcare Trust, ex p. S*[334] A pregnant mother who refused medical attention, having been told that if she had her child at home both she and it would probably die, was forcibly hospitalised and treated. Save where the hospital was protected under the terms of the Mental Health Act 1983, the mother was held entitled to damages.[335] It was the paramount right of this individual to decide for herself whether or not to accept medical treatment, even where refusal of treatment risked death itself.[336] It has been said, however, that the court's power to override a patient's wishes may revive if the patient later loses capacity: for example, if a woman refuses a Caesarian operation but hours later loses all rationality in the agony of the complicated childbirth she had previously opted for.[337]

9-56 Where there is potential doubt about a person's ability to consent, Butler-Sloss P. in *Re B (Consent to Treatment: Capacity)*[338] laid down certain guidelines for those involved. A patient was presumed to have the mental capacity to make decisions to refuse treatment: if the matter was unclear, the matter had to be resolved as soon as possible by normal medical procedures, during which time the patient had to be fully informed of the steps being taken and given such treatment as was in his best interests.[339] If all appropriate steps to resolve the matter failed, the hospital should

331 The consent given must be to the actual procedure performed, so that a doctor who injected a patient in her left arm despite her express wish to have the injection in her right arm was found liable in trespass: *Allan v New Mount Sinai Hospital* (1980) 109 D.L.R. (3d) 635.

332 *Connolly v Croydon Health Services NHS Trust* [2015] EWHC 1339 (QB) (there was, however, no effective withdrawal on the facts).

333 For example, a warrant may be issued by a magistrate to allow non-consensual testing and hospitalisation (though not treatment) of a person thought to be carrying infectious or public-health-critical diseases: Public Health (Control of Disease) Act 1984 ss.45A–45O.

334 [1999] Fam. 26. See too *Re T (Adult: Refusal of Medical Treatment)* [1993] Fam. 95, 102; *Airedale NHS Trust v Bland* [1993] A.C. 789, 864; *Re AK (Medical Treatment) (Consent)* [2001] 1 F.L.R. 129 (motor neurone disease sufferer).

335 See too *Re B (Consent to Treatment: Capacity)* [2002] EWHC 429 (Fam); [2002] 2 All E.R. 449 (treatment given to paralysed but lucid patient despite unequivocal refusal: hospital summarily required to discontinue it, and £100 damages awarded for past treatment); also *Malette v Shulman* (1990) 76 D.L.R. (4th) 321.

336 See too *Secretary of State for the Home Department v Robb* [1995] Fam. 127 (no right to force-feed prisoner determined to starve himself to death). *Leigh v Gladstone* (1909) 26 T.L.R. 169, to the contrary, is clearly no longer good law.

337 *Guys & St Thomas' NHS Foundation Trust v R* [2020] EWCOP 4; (2020) 173 B.M.L.R. 80 at [57]–[63] (Hayden J). This, with respect, seems dangerous. In so far as the loss of the ability to decide stems from the very same affliction the patient has declined treatment for, it seriously devalues the right to decline treatment.

338 [2002] EWHC 429 (Fam); [2002] 2 All E.R. 449.

339 It seems to follow that if there is a reasonable doubt about ability to consent, at common law it is lawful *pro tempore* forcibly to treat a patient who does not want to be treated and is in fact perfectly lucid.

not hesitate to apply to the court or consult the Official Solicitor.[340] It should be noted that under the Mental Capacity Act 2005, there is a general authorisation of treatment to preserve life while an application to the court is pending.[341]

On the other hand, a refusal of treatment, even by one otherwise competent, must be clear, voluntary and unambiguous in order to be effective. The courts have arrogated to themselves a power to disregard, in the name of promoting autonomy, even an apparently unequivocal refusal which they regard as resulting from incomplete information, irrational phobia or outside pressure. Thus in *Re T (Adult: Refusal of Medical Treatment)*[342] a pregnant woman was grievously injured in an accident and hospitalised, in acute pain and heavily medicated. The hospital wished to deliver her child by Caesarean section. After some time alone with her mother, a devout Jehovah's Witness, she refused to agree to a blood transfusion, and signed a form confirming this refusal. The child was eventually stillborn, and T became unconscious. Without a blood transfusion she was likely to die. The Court of Appeal upheld the grant of a declaration authorising doctors to administer it, on the basis that T's decision to refuse the treatment had arguably been (1) made at a time when T, under medication, had not been able to weigh up the issues[343]; (2) not entirely free because of the influence of the mother; and (3) based on inadequate information, since T had never been fully informed about its consequences, in particular the availability and efficacy of substitutes for blood products.[344] Again, in *Re MB*[345] the Court of Appeal upheld an order for treatment by injection despite the patient's refusal, on being satisfied that the refusal was due to nothing more than an irrational phobia of needles. In *Re T*, Lord Donaldson MR summed up the law thus[346]: **9-57**

> "Society's interest is in upholding the concept that all human life is sacred and that it should be preserved if at all possible. It is well established that in the ultimate the right of the individual is paramount. ... In case of doubt [however] that doubt falls to be resolved in favour of the preservation of life, for if the individual is to override the public interest he must do so in clear terms."

Moreover, it is clear that the jurisdiction just referred to survives the enactment of the Mental Capacity Act 2005, at least in so far as the subject's inability to make

---

340 [2002] EWHC 429 (Fam); [2002] 2 All E.R. 449 at [100]. See too *St George's Healthcare NHS Trust v S* [1999] Fam. 26, 63 (Judge LJ).

341 See s.6(6), (7).

342 [1993] Fam. 95. This power survives the enactment of the Mental Capacity Act 2005: see *Re L (Vulnerable Adults with Capacity: Court's Jurisdiction)* [2012] EWCA Civ 253; [2013] Fam. 1.

343 Under the Mental Capacity Act 2005 this might factor have been sufficient to negative competence in any case: see s.2(2), making it clear that inability to make a decision due to a temporary disturbance of the brain—including, presumably one due to medication—may suffice.

344 Quaere, however, how far this goes. Could a hospital, by refusing to provide the information necessary to allow a patient to make an informed decision, thereafter justify forcible treatment in the patient's best interests on the basis that the latter's refusal was not properly informed? Surely not. Also, presumably it must be open to a patient to waive the need for information, by saying something like "I do not care if there is something I do not know about: I still refuse consent."

345 [1997] 2 F.L.R. 426. With respect, this is somewhat tendentious. If a patient has a right irrationally to refuse treatment, why should the presence of a morbid or irrational phobia make any difference?

346 [1993] Fam. 95 at 112; endorsed in *Airedale NHS Trust v Bland* [1993] A.C. 789 at 864; and exploding the theory derived from *Leigh v Gladstone* (1909) 26 T.L.R. 169 that "medical necessity" justified life-saving treatment quite regardless of the patient's wishes. In *Secretary of State for the Home Department v Robb* [1995] Fam. 127 it was duly confirmed that prison authorities had no right to force-feed a prisoner even if it was in the latter's best interests to do so.

an autonomous choice is due not to a malfunctioning of the brain but to some other factor such as religious fanaticism or the overbearing influence of a third party.[347]

9-58 **Consent: the interests of the viable foetus** What if a woman's refusal of treatment will necessarily impact on an unborn child? In *Re S (Adult: Surgical Treatment)*[348] a declaration was granted at first instance authorising the forcible performance of a Caesarean section on a mother-to-be, on the basis that however competent she might have been to refuse treatment for herself, the unborn child had rights of its own which she could not override. But subordinating a pregnant woman's right of self-determination to the welfare of the unborn child runs contrary to the established principle of the common law denying legal personality to the foetus,[349] and in *Re MB*[350] the Court of Appeal clearly discountenanced the idea that the interests of an unborn child could be relevant in such cases. It follows that the reasoning in *Re S* must now be taken as having been discredited, and that the only consent that matters is the mother's.

9-59 **No indication as to wishes of patient** What of a patient who is unconscious and where doctors have no information as to his wishes about treatment? At common law, in such a situation any treatment immediately necessary to safeguard life or health was justified on grounds of necessity,[351] and the same principle applied to a patient who was conscious but unable to communicate: doctors were entitled to provide treatment in the patient's best interests.[352] The matter is now covered by the Mental Capacity Act 2005, which provides much the same result with regard to those over 16.[353] Where a person is unable to understand or weigh relevant information, or communicate a decision, owing to impairment of, or a disturbance in the functioning of, the mind or brain[354] (a phrase which pretty clearly includes unconsciousness), then under s.5(2) any treatment is justified if reasonably believed to be in that person's best interests.[355] A number of safeguards apply. The doctor must take into account whether the patient will regain capacity,[356] and if so when[357];

---

347 *Re L (Vulnerable Adults with Capacity: Court's Jurisdiction) (No 2)* [2012] EWCA Civ 253; [2013] Fam. 1 at [53]–[69] (McFarlane LJ); also *Re SA (Vulnerable Adult with Capacity: Marriage)* [2006] 1 F.L.R. 867 at [76]–[77] (Munby J). Neither case concerned medical treatment: but both are in point.

348 [1993] Fam. 123;R. Scott, "The pregnant woman and the Good Samaritan: can a woman have a duty to undergo a Caesarean section?" (2000) 20 O.J.L.S. 407. See also *Re T* [1993] Fam. 95, 102–103 (Lord Donaldson MR).

349 See, e.g. *Re F (In Utero)* [1988] Fam. 122 (wardship jurisdiction not applicable to foetus).

350 [1997] 2 F.L.R. 426. See too *Guys & St Thomas' NHS Foundation Trust v R* [2020] EWCOP 4; (2020) 173 B.M.L.R. 80 at [49]–[55] (Hayden J); and *Winnipeg Child & Family Services v G* (1997) 152 D.L.R. (4th) 193, to the same effect.

351 *Re F (Mental Patient: Sterilisation)* [1990] 2 A.C. 1; cf. *Wilson v Pringle* [1987] Q.B. 237, 252.

352 *R v Bournewood NHS Trust Ex p. L* [1999] A.C. 458, 485, 489 (Lord Goff) (autistic but conscious patient).

353 But subject to further safeguards. This takes account of the decision of the ECtHR in *HL v United Kingdom* (2005) 40 E.H.R.R. 32, in which the lack of such safeguards was held to render the decision in *R v Bournewood NHS Trust Ex p. L* [1999] A.C. 458, above, a contravention of the right to liberty under art.5 of the ECHR.

354 See Mental Capacity Act 2005 s.2(1).

355 For an analysis of "best interests", see H. Taylor, "What are 'Best Interests'? A Critical evaluation of 'Best Interests' Decision-Making in Clinical Practice" (2016) 24 Med. L. Rev. 176.

356 Section 4(3)(a).

357 Section 4(3)(b).

try to encourage the patient to participate in the decision[358]; consider his past wishes, beliefs and values, if known[359]; and consider the views of anyone the patient wishes to be consulted, and anyone else caring for the person or interested in his welfare.[360] In addition, treatment is justified only where the person providing reasonably believes it is necessary to prevent harm to the patient,[361] and where that treatment is in fact a proportionate response.[362] It should be noted that the defence under s.5 applies not only where the patient is in fact incapable, but where the doctor reasonably believes him to be so.[363] In addition, the 2005 Act gives the court jurisdiction to make a declaration as to the lawfulness or otherwise of treatment.[364] While an application to the court is pending, there is a general authorisation of treatment to preserve life.[365]

Adults: what amounts to consent[366] Sufficient information must be given to the patient about the proposed treatment to enable him to give a valid consent to what is to be done to him.[367] If no explanation has in fact been made, the alleged consent by the patient is in form only and not a real and valid consent.[368] But providing that the patient has been informed in broad terms of the nature of the procedure intended, and gives consent, that consent is real[369]; in particular, it will not be vitiated by a failure to warn of possible risks and side-effects inherent in the treatment proposed (though in such a case the doctor may be liable in negligence).[370] It seems that consent obtained by fraud or the withholding of information in bad faith will vitiate consent and make the administration of the treatment a battery, at least where the deception goes as to the nature of the treatment or the necessity for it.[371] It is suggested, however, that elsewhere the better position is that if the patient **9-60**

358 Section 4(4).

359 Section 4(5). Presumably this means that it would be hard, though not necessarily impossible, to justify administering a blood transfusion to a known Jehovah's Witness under the Act.

360 Section 4(6).

361 Section 6(2).

362 Section 6(3).

363 See s.5(1).

364 Section 15.

365 See s.6(6), (7).

366 M.A. Jones, *Medical Negligence* (2018), 5th edn, para.6-033 onwards.

367 Standard NHS consent forms state that the effect and nature of the treatment has been explained to the patient (though if they have not, it is hard to see the mere statement having much effect).

368 *Chatterton v Gerson* [1981] Q.B. 432, 443. But presumably a patient can dispense with the need for full information by making it clear that he consents in any event.

369 *Chatterton v Gerson* [1981] Q.B. 432, 443, above. See too *Hills v Potter* [1984] 1 W.L.R. 641, 653 (Hirst J); *Sidaway v Bethlem Royal Hospital* [1985] A.C. 871; *Brushett v Cowan* (1990) 69 D.L.R. (4th) 743 (consent given to muscle biopsy deemed to be a general consent to investigate what was wrong with the patient, and hence to include a bone biopsy). What constitutes the "nature" of treatment may be problematic. A patient who agreed to be vaccinated against rubella recovered damages in trespass when the syringe also contained a contraceptive drug: *Potts v North West RHA*, unreported, see *The Guardian*, 23 July 1983. And see T. Feng, "Failure of Medical Advice: Trespass Or Negligence" (1987) 7 L.S. 149.

370 See *Sidaway v Bethlem Royal Hospital* [1985] A.C. 871; *Re Creutzfeldt-Jakob Disease Litigation (No.1)* (2000) 54 B.M.L.R. 1. cf. *Freeman v Home Office* [1984] Q.B. 524, 555–556; and generally G. Robertson, "Informed Consent to Medical Treatment" (1981) 97 L.Q.R. 102.

371 See *Chatterton v Gerson* [1981] Q.B. 432, 443; *Sidaway v Royal Bethlem Hospital* [1984] Q.B. 498, 511 (decision upheld, [1985] A.C. 871). Straightforward examples are *Appleton v Garrett* [1997] 8 Med. L.R. 75 (dentist civilly liable for battery when he gave unnecessary treatment as part of a scheme to defraud the NHS); *R v Tabassum* [2000] Lloyd's Rep. Med. 404 (bogus breast examination in fact for defendant's own amusement; no valid consent to touching of breasts in circumstances); and the Australian decision in *Dean v Phung* [2012] NSWCA 223. See M.A. Jones,

understood the nature of the treatment the proper cause of action is in negligence rather than battery.[372]

9-61 **Advance directives**[373] At common law, it seems that if a person issued an advance directive refusing consent to medical treatment which, properly construed, was to apply even where that person was in no state to consent (e.g. through unconsciousness or medical sedation), that directive had to be respected.[374] The matter is now governed, however, by the Mental Capacity Act 2005. Under s.26(1) any advance decision refusing treatment of a particular type must be respected, and liability will be incurred for disobeying it, subject to a number of safeguards. In the case of life-saving treatment, the directive must be in writing, signed and witnessed.[375] And in all cases it must have been made when the patient was over 18 and had capacity[376]; and the patient must lack capacity at the time of the proposed treatment.[377] The directive must not have been withdrawn,[378] and no act must have been done which is clearly inconsistent with the advance directive remaining the patient's fixed decision.[379] The directive must cover the relevant circumstances,[380] and will not be regarded as covering life-sustaining treatment unless it explicitly says so.[381] In addition, it will not be binding if there are reasonable grounds for believing that unanticipated circumstances now exist which would have affected the patient's decision had he anticipated them.[382] The court is given explicit jurisdiction to grant a declaration as to whether or not an advance directive is in force, and if it is whether it covers a given treatment.[383] A direction which does not satisfy these requirements will be taken into account by a court in deciding what is in a patient's best interests, but accorded relatively little weight.[384]

9-62 Three safeguards exist for the doctor. First, he does not incur liability for carrying out or continuing treatment unless, at the time, he is satisfied that an advance directive exists which is valid and applicable to the treatment.[385] Secondly, he is protected from liability for the consequences of withholding or withdrawing treatment if, at the time, he reasonably believes that a directive exists which is valid and

Medical Negligence, 5th edn (2018), para.6-067.

372 See *R v Richardson* [1999] Q.B. 444 (dentist treated patients while disqualified: although patients would not have agreed had they known true facts, conviction for assault quashed).

373 See generally A. Maclean, "Advance Directives and the Rocky Waters" [2008] Med. L. Rev. 7; also M.A. Jones, *Medical Negligence*, 5th edn (2018), para.6-026 onwards.

374 *Airedale NHS Trust v Bland* [1993] A.C. 789, 857 (Lord Keith), 864 (Lord Goff); *Re T (Adult: refusal of Medical Treatment)* [1993] Fam. 95. So too in Canada: *Malette v Shulman* (1990) 67 D.L.R. (4th) 321 (unconscious Jehovah's Witness carrying card prohibiting blood transfusion: assault, and substantial damages therefor, when transfused nonetheless).

375 Mental Capacity Act 2005 s.25(6).

376 Mental Capacity Act 2005 s.24(1).

377 Section 25(3).

378 Section 25(2)(a).

379 Section 25(2)(c).

380 Section 25(4)(a), (b).

381 Section 25(5). For a case where this was so, and the court had no compunction in ordering its following, see *NHS Cumbria CCG v Rushton* [2018] EWCOP 41; (2018) 168 B.M.L.R. 43.

382 Section 25(4)(c).

383 Section 26(4).

384 *W v M* [2011] EWHC 2443 (Fam); [2012] 1 W.L.R. 1653 at [6] (Baker J); see too *NHS Cumbria CCG v Rushton* [2018] EWCOP 41; (2018) 168 B.M.L.R. 43 at [25] (Hayden J).

385 Section 26(2). In the event of doubt such treatment should be given: *A Local Authority v E* [2012] EWHC 1639 (CoP); (2012) 127 B.M.L.R. 133.

applicable to the treatment.[386] And thirdly, he is permitted to give life-sustaining treatment or do any act he reasonably believes to be necessary to prevent a serious deterioration in the patient's condition while an application to the court is pending.[387] In practice, one suspects that doctors and hospitals will be inclined to seek the advice of the court in the majority of cases.

(ii) Children

9-63 **Older children: consent to treatment**[388] Section 8 of the Family Law Reform Act 1969 provides that a minor over the age of 16 can give an effective consent to any surgical, medical or dental treatment[389] without his parents' or guardians' concurrence. In addition, the powers under the Mental Capacity Act 2005 apply to minors over this age.[390] What of children under 16? In *Gillick v West Norfolk and Wisbech AHA*[391] the applicant sought a declaration that any medical treatment, and in particular contraceptive treatment, of a child under 16 (save in emergency) was unlawful unless authorised by parental consent. The House of Lords rejected her claim, holding (by a majority of four to one)[392] that a child under 16 can give a valid consent to treatment generally, providing that he has attained the necessary degree of maturity, intelligence and understanding to comprehend the nature of the treatment proposed. Parental rights to authorise treatment of their children derived from parental responsibilities to care for their child and were not in substitution for the child's right to make his own decision as and when he reached "a sufficient understanding and intelligence to be capable of making up his own mind on the matter".[393] By a majority of three to two[394] the House of Lords further held that a child under 16, who had attained that sufficient understanding, could give a valid consent to contraceptive[395] and/or abortion treatment. What mattered in each instance was whether the child was competent to make a judgment for himself. If he was, the "*Gillick* competent" child[396] could authorise his own treatment and so insulate the doctor from liability in battery.

9-64 **Older children: refusal of treatment**[397] A child over 16 (by s.8 of the Family Law Reform Act 1969) and a *Gillick*-competent child under 16 (by virtue of *Gil-*

386 Section 26(3).
387 Section 26(5).
388 M.A. Jones, *Medical Negligence*, 5th edn (2018), para.6–193 onwards.
389 "Treatment" does not include participation in clinical research or to donation of blood or tissue: *Re R (A Minor) (Wardship: Medical Treatment)* [1992] Fam. 11. Such "non-treatment" decisions are governed by the principles in *Gillick v West Norfolk and Wisbech AHA*, below.
390 See Mental Capacity Act 2005 s.2(5) (Act not to apply to those under 16).
391 [1986] A.C. 112.
392 Lord Brandon rested his judgment solely on the question of whether providing contraceptive advice or treatment constituted aiding or abetting unlawful sexual intercourse with a girl under 16, and thus did not address the general issue of capacity to consent to medical treatment.
393 [1986] A.C. 112 at 186 (Lord Scarman).
394 Lord Templeman, who agreed with the majority on the general issue of capacity, expressed the opinion ([1986] A.C. 112 at 201) that no girl under 16 enjoyed the necessary level of maturity to consent on her own behalf to contraceptive treatment.
395 Lord Fraser ([1986] A.C. 112 at 174) set out guidelines to be followed by medical staff offering contraception to young girls.
396 For what amounts to "Gillick competence", see too *Re L* [1998] 2 F.L.R. 810.
397 S. Gilmore and J. Herring, "'No' is the Hardest Word: Consent and Children's Autonomy" (2011) 23 C.F.L.Q. 3; and E. Cave and J. Walbank, "Minors' capacity to refuse treatment" (2012) 20 Med. L. Rev. 423.

lick, above) can consent to treatment even if their parents wish them not to have it. But do they have a converse right to refuse treatment if their parents (or the court) wish them to undergo it? Two judgments of the Court of Appeal make it clear that the answer is no, at least as regards the court's power to authorise the treatment. In *Re R (A Minor) (Wardship: Medical Treatment)*[398] a 15-year-old girl suffering from a degree of mental disorder refused to continue taking anti-psychotic medication. The Court of Appeal found that, despite being nearly 16, her mental disorder, especially her fluctuating mental state, meant that she was not *Gillick*-competent. However they also held that, even if she were so competent, the court in the exercise of its wardship jurisdiction could overrule her refusal of treatment. Thus authority to authorise treatment on behalf of the child survived side by side with the *Gillick*-competent child's authority to act for himself. In *Re W (A Minor) (Medical Treatment)*[399] the Court of Appeal endorsed this result. W, 16 and anorexic, was refusing effective treatment for her condition. Their Lordships held that s.8 of the Family Law Reform Act 1969 merely empowered a minor of 16 to authorise treatment independently of his parents; it did not displace the concurrent curial power to authorise treatment. Nonetheless a purported refusal of treatment by a person under 18 must be given due weight by doctors seeking to ascertain the best interests of their young patient. Doctors, furthermore, cannot be compelled to act on a parental demand for treatment.[400] In *South Glamorgan County Council v W & B*[401] the principles in *Re R* and *Re W* were relied on to authorise medical examinations under the Children Act 1989 despite the grant in that Act[402] of an express statutory right to refuse to submit to such examinations. Douglas Brown J held that a court could still order a non-consensual examination under its inherent jurisdiction preserved by s.100 of that Act, "in an appropriate case, where other remedies under the Children Act have been used and exhausted and found not to bring about the desired result [the court] can resort to other remedies".

9-65 Can a parent in the exercise of parental power authorise treatment of a child over 16, or *Gillick*-competent child under that age, against the latter's will in the absence of a court order? In *Re R (A Minor) (Wardship: Medical Treatment)*[403] Lord Donaldson MR gave a positive answer: if, he said, a *Gillick*-competent child declined or refused consent, "consent can be given by someone else who has parental rights or responsibilities".[404] This has never been discountenanced in so many words: it may now, however, be open to some doubt.[405]

9-66 **Younger children** In the case of younger children who clearly have not yet

398 [1992] Fam. 11.

399 [1993] Fam. 64; and see *Re KW and H (Minors) (Medical Treatment)* [1993] 1 F.L.R. 854; *Re E (Minor) (Wardship: Medical Treatment)* [1993] 1 F.L.R. 386. It seems that, where life is at stake, a combination of the value traditionally placed by the law on human life and also art.2 of the ECHR means that a refusal of treatment will rarely, if ever, be upheld. See *An NHS Foundation Hospital v P* [2014] EWHC 1650 (Fam) (lucid patient very nearly 18, having taken suicidal overdose, knowingly resolutely and coherently refused treatment: order for forcible therapy made).

400 See *Re J. (A Minor) (Wardship: Medical Treatment)* [1993] Fam. 15.

401 [1993] 1 F.L.R. 574.

402 See ss.38(6), 43(8), 44(7).

403 [1992] Fam. 11.

404 [1992] Fam. 11, 24. See too *Re E (A Minor) (Medical Treatment)* [1991] 2 F.L.R. 585 (though there the child was handicapped).

405 A counter-argument is that if Lord Donaldson is right, a parent can authorise a child otherwise furnished with discretion to be forcibly restrained for the purpose of treatment for his own good. But in *Re D (a child) (residence order: deprivation of liberty)* [2019] UKSC 42; [2019] 1 W.L.R. 5403 the Supreme Court denied that a parent could authorise detention of a non-*Gillick*-competent child;

reached the level of maturity and understanding to consent to treatment on their own behalf (i.e. *Gillick*-incompetent children), parental consent authorises any treatment clearly for the benefit of the child, and thus protects the doctor from a claim in battery.[406] Parents do not however have a converse right to veto treatment. In cases of emergency, abandonment or neglect it is clear that doctors can lawfully act to safeguard a child's life or health without parental agreement on the basis of necessity.[407] Furthermore, even where parents honestly believe that they are acting in the child's best interests, their judgment may be overruled by the court. So in *Re B (A Minor) (Wardship: Medical Treatment)*[408] parents of a Downs syndrome baby refused consent to an operation necessary to save her life believing it would be kinder to let her die. The Court of Appeal ordered that surgery go ahead; it was not for parents—or courts—to say a child should die unless the quality of life confronting that child was "demonstrably awful".[409] On a similar principle, where parents refuse blood transfusions for religious reasons so as to endanger the child's life, an order is almost certain to be made to disregard the parental veto.[410] Conversely, while parents' wishes that a child be given a chance to live are in account and likely to be given great weight, they too are not conclusive if, on the whole, it is in the child's best interests that further treatment be withheld.[411]

Nor do parents enjoy an absolute right to determine what treatment a child receives. *In Re D (Wardship: Sterilisation)*[412] Heilbron J refused to endorse a mother's decision that her 11-year-old handicapped daughter be sterilised, holding that the girl's mental disability was not so profound that she would never be able to decide such matters for herself. Subsequently in *Re B (A Minor) (Wardship:* **9-67**

and Lady Black at [72] and [88] suggested that the parental power of constraint ended with the attainment of the age of discretion. The continuation of a parental power to authorise forcible treatment of a child that was *Gillick*-competent would seem to sit ill with this result.

406 Quaere whether it extends to authorising the detention of a child: the point was pointedly left open by Lady Black in *Re D (a child) (residence order: deprivation of liberty)* [2019] UKSC 42; [2019] 1 W.L.R. 5403 at [90], though the judgment of Lady Hale (with whom Lady Arden agreed) at [50] in the same case suggests a positive answer.

407 *Gillick v West Norfolk AHA* [1986] A.C. 112 at 189 (Lord Scarman) and 205 (Lord Templeman). And see too the even more extreme *Re A (Children) (Conjoined Twins: Surgical Separation)* [2001] Fam. 147 (necessity justifies surgical separation of Siamese twins even though death of one certain to result).

408 [1981] 1 W.L.R. 1421.

409 As was held to be the case in *Re C (A Minor) (Wardship: Medical Treatment)* [1990] Fam. 26; *Re J (A Minor) (Wardship: Medical Treatment)* [1991] Fam. 33. On the other hand, this is not an absolute rule: see *Re T (A Minor)(Wardship: Medical Treatment)* [1997] 1 W.L.R. 242, where a mother's decision to refuse consent to a liver transplant for a baby was upheld in exceptional circumstances. See too *X (Baby) v An NHS Trust* [2012] EWHC 2188 (Fam); (2012) 127 B.M.L.R. 188.

410 See, for example, *Re O (A Minor) (Medical Treatment)* [1993] 2 F.L.R. 149.

411 *Portsmouth NHS Trust v Wyatt* [2004] EWHC 2247 (Fam); [2005] 1 F.L.R. 21. See too two tragic cases of very young children in a close to vegetative state through irreversible brain damage: *Great Ormond Street Hospital for Children NHS Foundation Trust v Yates* [2017] EWCA Civ 410; [2018] 4 W.L.R. 5, especially at [112], a case that received massive media publicity as the "Charlie Gard case"; and *Re E (A Child)* [2018] EWCA Civ 550; [2019] 1 W.L.R. 594. In both orders were made authorising withdrawal of treatment. Note that in *Gard v United Kingdom* (2017) 65 E.H.R.R. SE9; (2017) 157 B.M.L.R. 59 (a follow-on from Yates, above), the position in English law with regard withdrawal of life support from a seriously ill baby was held in to be accordance with art.8 of the ECHR. Generally note E. Cave, "Who Knows Best (Interests)? The Case of Charlie Gard" (2018) 26 Med. L. Rev. 500; and the rather critical C. Auckland & I. Goold, "Parental Rights, Best Interests and Significant Harms: Who Should Have the Final Say over a Child's Medical Care?" [2019] C.L.J. 287.

412 [1976] Fam. 185.

Sterilisation),[413] the House of Lords, while authorising the sterilisation of a much more severely handicapped 17-year-old, suggested that such radical and irreversible treatment required judicial sanction and could not be authorised by parent or guardian alone.[414] Parents may consent to unequivocally beneficial treatment,[415] but where the "best interests"[416] of a child are disputed,[417] medical practitioners may be well advised to seek the opinion of the court to ensure no battery is committed against the child.[418]

(iii) Persons suffering from mental incapacity

9-68 **Generally** A distinction has to be drawn here according to whether the claimant was or was not liable to be detained under the Mental Health Act 1983.[419]

9-69 **Non-detainable mentally incapacitated patients** At common law,[420] a mentally incapacitated person over the age of 18 could not validly consent to, or refuse, treatment. Nor could his relatives consent on his behalf, or for that matter the court[421] (though there could be a declaration as to lawfulness on the basis that medical treatment was in the patient's best interests[422] if carried out to save life or prevent deterioration in physical or mental health).[423] Today, however, the matter is governed by the Mental Capacity Act 2005,[424] providing as follows. Where a person

413 [1988] A.C. 199 HL.

414 "In my opinion sterilisation of a girl under 18 should only be carried out with the leave of a High Court Judge. A doctor performing a sterilisation operation with the consent of the parents might still be liable in criminal, civil or professional proceedings" (Lord Templeman at [1988] A.C. 199, 205). There will also today be a need to take into account art.8 of the ECHR: cf. *An NHS Trust v DE* [2013] EWHC 2562 (Fam); (2013) 133 B.M.L.R. 123.

415 So where a gynaecological operation needed to preserve a mentally handicapped child's physical health would have the inevitable result of rendering her infertile there was no requirement to invoke the wardship jurisdiction. Parental consent is sufficient to authorise a therapeutic procedure; *Re E (A Minor) (Medical Treatment)* [1991] 2 F.L.R. 585.

416 It will always be easier to define therapeutic procedures as in the child's best interests; see *Re E*, above; but the interests of a child are not limited to interests in physical health; see *S v S* [1972] A.C. 24 at 27 (blood tests to establish paternity). But "best interests" must relate to that individual child's welfare so, for example, eugenic grounds can never justify sterilisation of a minor; see *Re M (A Minor) (Wardship: Sterilisation)* [1988] 2 F.L.R. 497.

417 See, for example, *Re B (Wardship: Abortion)* [1991] 2 F.L.R. 426 (authorising abortion for a 12-year-old girl against her mother's wishes).

418 Applications to resolve disputes relating to medical treatment of minors can be made now via an application for a "specific issue" or "prohibited steps" order under s.8 of the Children Act 1989. Alternatively an application may be made via s.100 preserving the inherent jurisdiction: see C. Gilham, "The Dilemma of Parental Choice" (1993) 143 New L.J. 1219.

419 Effectively the former category comprises those detained in hospital under one or more of the powers in Pt II of the 1983 Act, or on leave from such a hospital under s.17.

420 The common law position remains relevant for events before 1 October 2007 (when the relevant provisions of the Mental Capacity Act 2005 came into force), and after that date for any matters not pre-empted by the 2005 Act.

421 Since the disappearance of the former *parens patriae* jurisdiction of the High Court: see *Re F (Mental Patient: Sterilisation)* [1990] 2 A.C. 1, 59 onwards. Lord Bridge in *Re F* lamented the lack of a specific jurisdiction to consent for the patient: ibid. at 52.

422 Including an interim declaration: see *NHS Trust v T (adult patient: refusal of medical treatment)* [2004] EWHC 1279 (Fam); [2005] 1 All E.R. 387, applying CPR 25.1(1)(b).

423 See *Re F (Mental Patient: Sterilisation)* [1990] 2 A.C. 1, especially at 55 (Lord Brandon). See too *Airedale NHS Trust v Bland* [1993] A.C. 789.

424 An Act based largely on Law Commission Report No.231, *Mental Incapacity* (1995). See O. Ward,

lacks capacity to decide,[425] then under s.5(2) any treatment is justified if reasonably believed by the person giving it to be in that person's best interests,[426] . a term that may include not only self-regarding matters but also where appropriate the promotion of the interests of others or the community.[427] A number of safeguards apply. The doctor[428] must try to encourage the patient to participate in the decision[429]; consider his past wishes, beliefs and values, if known[430]; and furthermore consider the views of anyone the patient wishes to be consulted, and those of anyone else caring for him or interested in his welfare.[431] In addition, forcible treatment is justified only where the person providing it reasonably believes it is necessary to prevent harm to the patient,[432] and where that treatment is in fact a proportionate response.[433] It should be noted that the defence under s.5 applies not only where the patient is in fact incapable, but where the doctor reasonably believes him to be so.[434] Where a patient lacks decision-making capacity, it should be noted that there is no absolute requirement to obtain a court order to administer treatment in a patient's best interests, even if the inevitable outcome is the death of the patient.[435]

In addition, the court now has an explicit statutory jurisdiction to make a declaration as to whether a patient has or lacks capacity in respect of a decision or class of decisions,[436] and where he does not have that power as to the lawfulness or **9-70**

"The Mental Capacity Act 2005" [2005] N.I.L.Q. 275; J. Coggon, "Ignoring the Moral and Intellectual Shape of the Law after Bland: The Unintended Side-Effect of a Sorry Compromise" (2007) 27 L.S. 110. It has been in force since 1 October 2007. A Code of Practice as to the application of the Act is issued by the Ministry of Justice pursuant to ss.42 and 43, the current version dating from 2015. Consultation began for a further revision in 2019.

425 i.e. where he cannot understand or weigh relevant information, or communicate a decision, owing to impairment of, or a disturbance in the functioning of, the mind or brain: 2005 Act s.2(1). Partial understanding may still be consistent with a lack of overall capacity: see the blood transfusion case of *Manchester University NHS Foundation Trust v DE* [2019] EWCOP 19; (2019) 170 B.M.L.R. 187. An important feature of the legislation is that a person may well have capacity to take some decisions but not others: see *Masterman-Lister v Jewell* [2002] EWCA Civ 1889; [2003] 1 W.L.R. 1511; and *Re W (medical treatment: anorexia)* [2016] EWCOP 13; (2016) 151 B.M.L.R. 220.

426 A concept which, it should be noted, does not encompass anything motivated by a desire to bring about the patient's death: s.4(5). On this see J. Coggon, "Ignoring the Moral and Intellectual Shape of the Law after Bland: The Unintended Side-Effect of a Sorry Compromise" (2007) 27 L.S. 110.

427 See *Home Secretary v Skripal* [2018] EWCOP 6; [2018] Med. L.R. 276 (taking of blood sample from unconscious victim of alleged poison attack by foreign agents for purposes of analysis to determine origin of poison).

428 Or, mutatis mutandis, any other medical personnel involved.

429 Section 4(4).

430 Section 4(6). Presumably this means that it would be hard, though not necessarily impossible, to justify administering a blood transfusion to a known Jehovah's Witness.

431 Section 4(7). Failure to do this may render an action unlawful and possibly trigger a breach of the patient's right to private and family life under art.8 of the ECHR: *Winspear v City Hospitals Sunderland NHS Foundation Trust* [2015] EWHC 3250 (QB); [2016] Q.B. 691.

432 Section 6(2).

433 Section 6(3).

434 See s.5(1). The point was confirmed in *An NHS Trust v Y* [2018] UKSC 46; [2019] A.C. 978 at [92].

435 This was confirmed by the Supreme Court in *An NHS Trust v Y* [2018] UKSC 46; [2019] A.C. 978, rebuffing a challenge based on art.2 of the ECHR. Earlier authorities had suggested that at common law such approval might be necessary: e.g. Airedale NHS Trust v Bland [1993] A.C. 789 at 859, 873, 875, 885.

436 Including future decisions. In suitable cases the court has jurisdiction to make a prospective declaration under s.15: see *Guys & St Thomas' NHS Foundation Trust v R* [2020] EWCOP 4; (2020) 173 B.M.L.R. 80.

otherwise of treatment in his own best interests.[437] This is a power which will normally be exercised in favour of treatment,[438] though obviously not invariably so.[439] In addition there is a power to make a decision on behalf of the patient[440] or appoint a person (known as a "deputy") to decide on his behalf.[441] Pending an application to the court, there is a general immunity in respect of treatment to preserve the patient's life.[442]

9-71 Where a person is already in a hospital or care home, there is an additional power in the administration of the organisation to detain that person and provide compulsory treatment to sustain life or prevent serious deterioration pending a court order,[443] unless a valid advance direction or other authorised decision to refuse treatment is in force.[444] From a date in 2020, these arrangements fall to be replaced with a more general administrative power vested (subject to safeguards) in hospitals and care homes where a person is, and in other cases in a local authority, to authorise deprivation of liberty where this is in the patient's best interests or necessary to prevent harm.[445]

9-72 **Patients liable to be detained under the Mental Health Act 1983** At common law no distinction was drawn between compulsorily detained mental patients and others of unsound mind.[446] The provisions of the Mental Capacity Act 2005, however, now apply to patients liable to be detained under the Mental Health Act 1983 as to other patients lacking capacity,[447] save for treatment for mental illness.[448] Treatment for mental illness, by contrast, is governed largely by the 1983 Act s.63

---

437 See s.15. Note, however, that the intervention of the court, while it may be helpful, is not strictly necessary as a matter of law: *An NHS Trust v Y* [2018] UKSC 46; [2019] A.C. 978.

438 See *Aintree University Hospitals NHS Foundation Trust v James* [2013] UKSC 67; [2014] A.C. 591 (only appropriate not to allow treatment if ineffective and of no benefit at all); also the earlier *DH NHS Foundation Trust v PS* [2010] EWHC 1217 (Fam); [2010] 2 F.L.R. 1236, on which R. Mullender, "Involuntary medical treatment, incapacity, and respect" (2011) 127 L.Q.R. 167; and also *W v M* [2011] EWHC 2443 (CoP); [2012] 1 W.L.R. 1653.

439 See *A NHS Foundation Trust v X* [2014] EWCOP 35; (2014) 140 B.M.L.R. 41 (anorexic and alcohol-dependent patient who maintained habits despite repeated force-feeding in hospital: although highest regard due to the preservation of life, declaration granted that in the circumstances, lawful not to force-feed). Provided that a suitable legal framework is provided, a court jurisdiction to authorise non-treatment is likely to survive a challenge under art.2 of the ECHR. See the decisions of the ECtHR in *Lambert v France* (2016) 62 E.H.R.R. 2; (2015) 145 B.M.L.R. 28; and *Gard v United Kingdom* (2017) 65 E.H.R.R. SE9; (2017) 157 B.M.L.R. 59; and also the subsequent English decision in *An NHS Trust v Y* [2018] UKSC 46; [2019] A.C. 978.

440 See ss.16(1)(a), 17(1)(d). There was no such power at common law: *Re F (Mental Patient: Sterilisation)* [1990] 2 A.C. 1, 59 onwards.

441 Section 16(2)(b). It would seem that the "treatment" to which the deputy must consent does not include the withdrawal of life-support: see *Aintree University Hospitals NHS Foundation Trust v James* [2013] UKSC 67; [2014] A.C. 591 at [18]–[19] (Lady Hale) (though contra in Canada, it would seem: see *Rasouli (Litigation Guardian) v Sunnybrook Health Sciences Centre* [2013] SCC 53; (2013) 364 D.L.R. (4th) 195).

442 See s.6(6), (7).

443 Mental Capacity Act 2005 s.4A (in force from 1 April 2009). In certain cases, however, such detention may fall foul of art.5 or art.8 of the ECHR, as in *Hillingdon LBC v Neary* [2011] EWHC 1377 (CoP); [2011] 4 All E.R. 584 (detention of autistic patient in support unit without proper regard to whether better off there, or to his own clearly-expressed desire to be at home).

444 Mental Capacity Act 2005 Sch.A1 para.12(1)(f).

445 See s.4A of the 2005 Act (as inserted by the Mental Capacity (Amendment) Act 2019) and Sch.AA1, which will replace Sch.A1. On the 2019 Act, cf. N. Pearce, "Mental Capacity (Amendment) Bill" [2018] Fam. Law 1230.

446 *T v T* [1988] Fam. 52.

447 Section 28. An example of a case where a declaration of capacity was made in respect of a

of which essentially dispenses with the requirement for consent to treatment for mental disorder (i.e. psychiatric treatment[449]).

(c) What amounts to medical negligence

(i) In general

What amounts to medical negligence: general[450] To amount to medical negligence, any alleged error in diagnosis and/or treatment must be shown to derive from a failure to attain the required degree of skill and competence of a reasonable practitioner.[451] This question falls to be answered, of course, in the light of the practitioner's specialisation[452] and also the seniority of the post that he holds.[453] Thus a general practitioner is not expected to attain the standard of a consultant obstetrician when delivering a baby. However if he elects to practise obstetrics he must attain the skill of a general practitioner undertaking obstetric care of his own patients,[454] and in all cases general practitioners and other doctors must exercise care in determining when to refer a patient for a consultant's or other second opinion.[455] In determining the standard of competence to be achieved, the normal negligence rule applies that no allowance is made for inexperience or personal lack of competence.[456] A practitioner faced with a matter beyond his competence must refer **9-73**

compulsorily detained patient is Hayden J's decision in *Guys & St Thomas' NHS Foundation Trust v R* [2020] EWCOP 4; (2020) 173 B.M.L.R. 80.

448 Though in practice one suspects that the majority of patients detained for psychiatric treatment will fall within the definition in s.2 of the Mental Capacity Act 2005 of those "unable to make a decision for himself in relation to the matter because of an impairment of, or a disturbance in the functioning of, the mind or brain." For the relation between the 1983 and 2005 Acts, see *An NHS Trust v A* [2013] EWHC 2442 (COP); [2014] Fam. 161.

449 Including force-feeding, at least where ancillary to psychiatric treatment: *B v Croydon Health Authority* [1995] 1 F.L.R. 470. See too *Barker v Havering & Brentwood NHS Trust* [1999] Lloyd's Rep. Med. 101 ("treatment" includes assessment). This is generally regarded as consistent with the ECHR: *R (N) v M* [2002] EWCA Civ 1789; [2003] 1 W.L.R. 562. See generally para.14-100 onwards.

450 For a comprehensive discussion on the extensive case law on medical negligence see M.A. Jones, *Medical Negligence* (5th edn, 2018), Ch.3; *Jackson & Powell on Professional Liability*, 8th edn (2017), Ch.13.

451 "The test is the standard of the ordinary skilled man exercising and professing to have that special skill. A man need not profess the highest expert skill, it is well established law that it is sufficient if he exercises the ordinary skill of a competent man exercising that particular art." See *Bolam v Friern HMC* [1957] 1 W.L.R. 582, 586 (McNair J). This was approved by the Privy Council in *Chin Keow v Government of Malaysia* [1967] 1 W.L.R. 813; and by the House of Lords in *Whitehouse v Jordan* [1981] 1 W.L.R. 246. See too *Maynard v West Midlands RHA* [1984] 1 W.L.R. 634; and *Sidaway v Bethlem Royal Hospital* [1985] A.C. 871. On the other hand, there may be a tendency to avoid over-strict standards where this might discourage innovative or adventurous treatment: cf. the cautious approach in the New Zealand decision in *Ellis v Counties Manukau District Health Board* [2007] 1 N.Z.L.R. 196.

452 *Maynard v West Midlands RHA* [1984] 1 W.L.R. 634, 638 (Lord Scarman); cf. *Shakoor v Kang Situ* [2001] 1 W.L.R. 410 (Chinese traditional healing).

453 *Wilsher v Essex AHA* [1987] Q.B. 730, 751 (Mustill LJ) (reversed on a different point at [1988] A.C. 1074). See too *FB v Princess Alexandra Hospital NHS Trust* [2017] EWCA Civ 334; [2017] P.I.Q.R. P17 at [57]–[60] (Jackson LJ: standard reckoned by post held or then being fulfilled, e.g. in the case of "acting up"). See also *Dowson v Lane* [2020] EWHC 642 (QB). Note that his Lordship left it open whether a higher duty might be owed in contract: see [61]–[62].

454 *Hucks v Cole, The Times,* 9 May 1968; [1993] 4 Med. L.R. 393.

455 *Payne v St Helier Group HMC* [1952] C.L.Y. 2442.

456 *Wilsher v Essex Area Health Authority* [1987] Q.B. 730: reversed on another point [1988] A.C. 1074.

the patient to a consultant or other expert[457]; by doing so he will discharge his duty.[458] Similarly, all hospitals are on principle judged by the same standard: a prisoner, for example, is entitled to the same standard of care in a prison hospital (subject to those constraints necessitated by his incarceration itself) as any other patient.[459] In *Wilsher*, Mustill LJ left open the question of whether the standard of care might be affected by "battle conditions".[460] It is now clear, however, that this is a very relevant factor, and a doctor should not be harshly judged when faced with a life-threatening condition where immediate measures are required.[461]

9-74 **Hindsight** Professional practice must be judged in the context of proper practice at the time of the alleged negligence. Where a practice has been shown to be attended by risk the question is whether at the time of the accident that risk should have been known and guarded against by a practitioner in that speciality. The equipment and resources[462] available to the practitioner must be assessed. As Denning LJ put it in a 1954 case concerning events some time previously, "We must not look at a 1947 accident with 1954 spectacles."[463]

9-75 **Effect of departure from accepted practice** The fact that a practitioner departed from accepted current practice or from some official standard is evidence, but not conclusive evidence, of negligence on his part. Lord Clyde in the Scots decision in *Hunter v Hanley*[464] put it thus:

> "[I]n regard to allegations of deviation from ordinary professional practice such a deviation is not necessarily evidence of negligence. Indeed it would be disastrous if this were so, for all inducement to progress in medical science would then be destroyed. Even a substantial deviation from normal practice may be warranted by the particular circumstances. To establish liability by a doctor where deviation from normal practice is alleged, three facts require to be established. First of all it must be proved that there is a usual and normal practice; secondly it must be proved that the defendant has not adopted that practice; and thirdly (and this is of crucial importance) it must be established that the course the doctor adopted is one which no professional man would have taken if he had been acting with ordinary care."

See also *Djemal v Bexley HA* [1995] 6 Med. L.R. 269 and *FB v Princess Alexandra Hospital NHS Trust* [2017] EWCA Civ 334; [2017] P.I.Q.R. P17 at [59] (Jackson LJ). The same goes for any other incapacity personal to the practitioner, such as his own illness: *Nickolls v Ministry of Health, The Times*, 4 February 1955 CA.

457 *Payne v St Helier Group HMC* [1952] C.L.Y. 2992. See also *Poole v Morgan* [1987] 3 W.W.R. 217 (newly trained ophthalmologist liable for not referring complicated case to consultant).

458 *Wilsher v Essex AHA* [1987] Q.B. 730, 774 (Glidewell LJ).

459 *Brooks v Home Office* [1999] 2 F.L.R. 33. Pill J's contrary suggestion in *Knight v Home Office* [1990] 3 All E.R. 237, 243 now seems discredited.

460 See [1987] Q.B. 730, 749.

461 *Vernon v Bloomsbury HA* [1995] 6 Med. L.R. 297 (not negligent considerably to exceed recommended dose of gentamicin in emergency brought on by endocarditis); *Mulholland v Medway NHS Foundation Trust* [2015] EWHC 268 (QB); (2015) 144 B.M.L.R. 50 (busy hospital doctor entitled to rely on advice from A&E team without carrying out exhaustive analysis of his own). cf. *Hardaker v Newcastle HA* [2002] Lloyd's Rep. Med. 512 (re duty owed by the police as surrogate providers of emergency medical attention).

462 *Whiteford v Hunter* (1950) 94 S.J. 758 (mistaken diagnosis could have been avoided with a cystoscope: but since at the time cystoscopes not generally available, not negligent).

463 *Roe v Minister of Health* [1954] 2 K.B. 66 at 84. See also *E v Australian Red Cross Society* (1991) 99 A.L.R. 601 (HIV infection from blood transfusion in 1984: no negligence, given the then limited state of knowledge about HIV).

464 1955 S.C. 200, 206.

So in *Clark v MacLennan*[465] the claimant suffered from stress incontinence after childbirth. Within six weeks after the birth the defendant operated to repair weakness in her bladder muscles, but the repair broke down. Normal practice was to delay surgery for at least three months; and in the absence of any satisfactory explanation for departing from it the defendant was held liable in negligence. Again, in *Richards v Swansea NHS Trust*[466] delayed birth by Caesarian section led to severe disablement. Field J inferred negligence from the fact that the time taken to carry out the operation had been twice that provided in official guidelines. However, a suggestion in *Clark* that the burden actually shifts to the defendant to disprove negligence on proof of deviation from normal practice[467] was later roundly disapproved by the House of Lords,[468] which reiterated that it is for the claimant to prove negligence. The rule is merely that, in the absence of an appropriate explanation for a deviation from normal practice, that burden of proof will often be satisfied.

Negligence: the Bolam test and professional practice[469] The standard of care demanded of medical practitioners is that required of any professional person. However, the vital decision in *Bolam v Friern H.M.C.*[470] makes it clear that, in determining whether a defendant has fallen below the required standard of care, great regard must be shown to responsible medical opinion, and to the fact that reasonable doctors may differ. As McNair J put it, a practitioner who acts in conformity with an accepted current practice is not negligent "merely because there is a body of opinion which would take a contrary view".[471] The point is neatly illustrated by *Maynard v West Midlands Regional Health Authority*.[472] The defendants subjected the claimant to a diagnostic procedure, mediastinoscopy. This carried a risk of damage to the vocal chords, which unfortunately materialised. Having heard experts on both sides, the trial judge held for the claimant. His judgment was overruled in the Court of Appeal and the House of Lords. As Lord Scarman said, "a judge's 'preference' for one body of distinguished professional opinion to another also professionally distinguished is not sufficient to establish negligence in a 9-76

465 [1983] 1 All E.R. 416.

466 [2007] EWHC 487 (QB); (2007) 96 B.M.L.R. 180. But the departure must be relatively substantial: see *Darnley v Croydon Health Services NHS Trust* [2017] EWCA Civ 151; [2017] Med. L.R. 245 (15-minute officially-recommended A&E waiting time extensible at least to 30 minutes without a finding of negligence) (the case was appealed on other grounds at [2018] UKSC 50; [2019] A.C. 831). The importance of guidelines and protocols in this connection is touched on in M. Brazier and E. Cave, *Medicine, Patients & the Law*, 6th edn (2016) para.7.11.

467 See [1983] 1 All E.R. 416, 427.

468 See *Wilsher v Essex AHA* [1988] A.C. 1074.

469 M.A. Jones, "The Bolam Test and the Responsible Expert" (1999) 7 Tort L.R. 226.

470 [1957] 1 W.L.R. 582. This is fairly universally accepted in the common law world; for example, in Ireland see the similar (though not absolutely identical) *Dunne v National Maternity Hospital* [1989] I.R. 91, 109. In *Hii Chii Kok v Ooi Peng Jin London Lucien*[2017] SGCA 38; (2017) 162 B.M.L.R. 28 at [79]–[83], Sundaresh Menon CJ in the Singapore Court of Appeal resisted an invitation to move away from it on the basis that it was too favourable to the medical profession.

471 *Bolam v Friern HMC* [1957] 1 W.L.R. 582, 587–588. This statement formed part of a jury direction in a case where the administration of ECT had disastrous side-effects. The jury took the hint and found for the defendants.

472 [1984] 1 W.L.R. 582. Other examples are legion. See, e.g. *Hughes v Waltham Forest AHA* [1991] 2 Med.L.R. 155; *Rance v Mid-Downs HA* [1991] 1 Q.B. 587; and *Buxton v Abertawe Bro Morgannwg University Local Health Board* [2010] EWHC 1187 (QB); (2010) 115 B.M.L.R. 62; *Baker v Cambridgeshire and Peterborough NHS Foundation Trust* [2015] EWHC 609 (QB), [2], [29] (application of *Bolam* test to psychiatrist). Note also *D v South Tyneside NHS Trust* [2003] EWCA Civ 878; [2004] P.I.Q.R. P12 (choice of healthcare trust not to observe disturbed patient hourly is within *Bolam* and hence no liability for self-harm that such observation would have prevented).

practitioner".[473] Again, in *Whitehouse v Jordan*[474] the allegation was that the defendant persisted too long in an attempt to deliver a baby by use of forceps and should have proceeded more speedily to Caesarean section. Despite damning evidence from expert witnesses of the dangers of pulling so many times with forceps, the House of Lords reversed the judge's finding of negligence. The defendant's equally eminent experts had testified that they would have followed the practice. It followed that the claimant failed the *Bolam* test. As with individual practitioners, so with organisations: a general hospital policy will not generally be held to amount to negligence if supported by a respectable, if minority, body of opinion.[475] The practical result is that proving fault in a doctor on the basis of his choice of a particular technique or method can be very difficult. Since even a relatively small body of supportive medical opinion may be effective to satisfy the *Bolam* test,[476] the claimant effectively has to show that no body of respectable medical opinion would have supported what the doctor did.

9-77 Nevertheless, the limitations on *Bolam* must be borne in mind. It applies only to professional decisions whether or not to use a certain form of treatment, and not to simple cases of carelessness or inadvertence, such as misreading the result of a cervical smear test.[477] Nor does it apply to matters not involving professional judgment, such as poor managerial organisation.[478] Moreover, judges are now more willing to scrutinise the medical opinion in accordance with which the defendant acted. In *Bolitho v City and Hackney HA*,[479] Lord Browne-Wilkinson emphasised that a doctor was not entitled to be exonerated merely because some other doctors would have acted as he did. The practice relied on had to be respectable, responsible and reasonable; it had to have a logical basis[480]; and where it involved weighing

---

[473] See [1984] 1 W.L.R. 582, 587–588. See too *Lane v Worcestershire Acute Hospitals NHS Trust* [2017] EWHC 1900 (QB) (priority between two urgent treatments, both necessary; not for judge to select). But note *Smith v Tunbridge Wells HA* [1994] 5 Med. L.R. 334.

[474] [1981] 1 W.L.R. 246; see M. Brazier and E. Cave, *Medicine Patients & The Law*, 6th edn (2016), paras 8.13 to 8.14.

[475] *Cowley v Cheshire & Merseyside Strategic HA* [2007] EWHC 48 (QB); (2007) 94 B.M.L.R. 29 (hospital policy of denying certain drugs to pregnant women until onset of labour professionally defensible, and hence not negligent).

[476] *De Freitas v O'Brien* [1995] 6 Med. L.R. 108 (11 spinal surgeons). See too *Sharpe v Southend HA* [1997] 8 Med. L.R. 299, where Cresswell J emphasised that a medical expert testifying as to his preferred practice should indicate as a matter of course whether he thought a responsible body of medical opinion might disagree with him.

[477] *Penney v East Kent HA* [2000] Lloyd's Rep. Med. 41 at [27]. For such matters the rule is that the test must not be ruled negative unless the tester is absolutely confident that this is the case: see the same case at first instance (*Penney v East Kent HA* [1999] Lloyd's Rep. Med. 123, 127) and the Irish decision in *Morrissey v Health Service Executive* [2020] IESC 6; [2020] P.N.L.R. 17.

[478] See *Collins v Mid-Western Health Board* [2000] 1 I.R. 154 (failure by hospital to have proper admissions procedures, however widespread, cannot be equated to a medical practice followed by specialists in a particular field). See too *Hamed v Mills* [2015] EWHC 298 (QB) (*Bolam* not applicable to football club doctor employed to check health of employees).

[479] [1998] A.C. 232; also *C v North Cumbria University Hospitals NHS Trust* [2014] EWHC 61 (QB); [2014] Med. L.R. 189 at [23]–[25] (Green J). See generally R. Mulheron, "Trumping Bolam: a critical legal analysis of Bolitho's 'gloss'" [2010] C.L.J. 609. See too *E v Australian Red Cross Society* (1991) 99 A.L.R. 601 (warning against too ready acceptance of common medical practice).

[480] cf. *Taaffe v East of England Ambulance Service NHS Trust* [2012] EWHC 1335 (QB); (2012) 128 B.M.L.R. 71 (failure by paramedics to infer cardiac problems from chest pains not defensible under *Bolam*); also *C v North Cumbria University Hospitals NHS Trust* [2014] EWHC 61 (QB); [2014] Med. L.R. 189 at [25] (expert report that did not reflect evidence given or true facts of case may not be logical); and *Lane v Worcestershire Acute Hospitals NHS trust* [2017] EWHC 1900 (QB) at [12]–

comparative risks, it had to be shown that those advocating it had directed their minds to the relevant matters and reached a defensible conclusion.[481]

Moreover, there is a major qualification to the *Bolam* principle with regard to medical advice, where in order to protect a patient's rights to personal autonomy a stricter test than *Bolam* is now accepted. This development, stemming from the Supreme Court's decision in *Montgomery v Lanarkshire Health Board*[482] and which very substantially reduces the practical significance of *Bolam* in the medical context,[483] is dealt with below at para.9-86. **9-78**

(ii) Diagnosis[484]

Negligence in diagnosis A practitioner must take care to diagnose accurately; so it is negligent to send home a person showing clear symptoms of poisoning,[485] or to dismiss the victim of a serious attack with a few painkillers.[486] A wrong diagnosis, however, is of itself no evidence of negligence.[487] It must be established that the practitioner either omitted to carry out an examination or test which the symptoms indicated as necessary,[488] or the patient's history should have prompted, or that he reached a conclusion which no reasonably competent doctor would have arrived at.[489] Nevertheless, in some cases any reasonable doctor will be on notice of possible problems. Thus failure to diagnose fractures after a serious accident will be clear evidence of negligence,[490] as will omission to test for angina in the case of a patient exhibiting symptoms clearly indicative of it.[491] **9-79**

Practitioners must be prepared to reassess diagnoses where appropriate,[492] and must not jump to over-hasty conclusions.[493] But where diagnosis is disputed, the claimant is likely to fail absent evidence that the practitioner omitted to take a **9-80**

---

[19]; and *Bradfield-Kay v Cope* [2020] EWHC 1351 (QB).

481 See [1998] A.C. 232, 241 et seq. For cases where the proffered body of medical opinion was rejected, see *Newell v Goldberg* [1995] 6 Med. L.R. 371; *Marriott v West Midlands RHA* [1999] Lloyd's Rep. Med. 23.

482 [2015] UKSC 11; [2015] A.C. 1430. See too *Healy v Buckley* [2015] IECA 251.

483 Since a large proportion of medical negligence cases involve negligent advice or failure to advise in some form.

484 M.A. Jones, *Medical Negligence*, 5th edn (2018), paras 4–010 to 4–050.

485 *Barnett v Chelsea & Kensington HMC* [1969] 1 Q.B. 428 (where, however, the claim failed on causation grounds).

486 *Shaw v Stead* [2019] EWHC 520 (QB); (2019) 170 B.M.L.R. 174.

487 *Hunter v Hanley*, 1955 S.C. 200, 206; and see M. Brazier and E. Cave, *Medicine, Patients & the Law*, 6th edn (2016) para.7.12.

488 For example, failure to check for serious head injury following an accident (*Marriott v West Midlands RHA* [1999] Lloyd's Rep. Med. 23) or to diagnose manic depression and take suitable steps (see *Mahmood v Siggins* [1996] 7 Med. L.R. 76, holding the doctor liable for the patient's subsequent suicide). But cf. *Doy (A Child) v Gunn* [2013] EWCA Civ 547; [2013] Med. L.R. 327 (no breach of duty not to test child showing bacteraemia and symptoms of colic in case meningitis might be present).

489 cf. *Schanczl v Singh* [1988] 2 W.W.R. 465.

490 *Newton v Newton's Model Laundry Ltd, The Times,* 3 November 1959 (doctor failed to diagnose a broken knee-cap after serious fall).

491 See the Scottish decision in *Brown v Craig Nevis Surgery* [2018] CSOH 84; cf. *Langley v Campbell, The Times,* 6 November 1975 (malarial symptoms in person recently returned from tropics) and also the decision of the Supreme Court of Ireland in *Collins v Mid-Western Health Board* [2000] 1 I.R. 154 (failure to spot potential seriousness of respiratory problems: patient later died from brain haemorrhage).

492 *Dale v Munthali* (1978) D.L.R. (3d) 388.

493 *Hess v Erwyn Bissell* (1988) 45 D.L.R. (4th) 621.

course of action that a competent colleague would have seen as required.[494] So too, if the alleged negligence is that a painful, risky or invasive investigation should,[495] or should not[496] have been performed, negligence is unlikely to be established if the defendant's decision is supported by reputable experts. It should be noted, however, that the duty to diagnose symptoms and act on them may be limited by the circumstances in which the examination is carried out. Thus where a company doctor examining a prospective employee failed to notice a condition that would make childbirth hazardous, the Court of Appeal strongly doubted whether he owed her any duty to apprise her of that condition[497]; furthermore, it seems that a doctor treating a patient for one condition prima facie owes no duty to spot other, unrelated, symptoms.[498]

(iii) Treatment and prescribing

9-81 **Negligence in planning treatment and prescribing** In determining what drugs to prescribe or what treatment to plan for a patient, the practitioner must on principle decide on clinical grounds: the fact that a patient is insistent on receiving a given treatment will not, without more, absolve him.[499] Again, a doctor will be negligent if he fails to check the patient's history and to be alert to potential drug reactions. A clinic which failed to inquire of the deceased whether she had an allergy to penicillin and injected her with that drug was held liable for her death an hour after the injection.[500] But a very slight risk may legitimately be disregarded.[501] Where several doctors are involved with one patient, failure to communicate where necessary with each other will be negligent.[502] So, too, will a doctor who, having treated someone, fails to give him adequate information in terms of instructions to return for further treatment or attend another hospital.[503]

9-82 Where a practitioner is prescribing drugs, an erroneous overdose will normally

---

[494] *Crivon v Barnet Group HMC, The Times,* 19 November 1958; *Pudney v Union-Castle Mail Steamship Co Ltd* [1953] 1 Lloyd's Rep. 73.

[495] *Whiteford v Hunter* [1950] W.N. 553.

[496] *Maynard v West Midlands RHA* [1984] 1 W.L.R. 634.

[497] *R v Croydon HA* [1998] Lloyd's Rep. Med. 44; cf. the criminal law decision in *R. v Rose* [2017] EWCA Crim 1168; [2018] Q.B. 328 (optometrist failing to spot obvious signs of deadly hydrocephalus not guilty of manslaughter).

[498] See *Brown v Lewisham & Southwark HA* [1999] Lloyd's Rep. Med. 110, 118. Sed quaere whether this will always apply. If a doctor while treating his patient failed to notice patent indications of an obvious life-threatening condition requiring immediate treatment, would he really escape liability were he not even to warn the patient about it? cf. the approach of the Canadian court in *Brown v University of Alberta Hospital* (1997) 145 D.L.R. (4th) 63 (doctor examining child or vulnerable patient under duty to pass on indications of possible abuse to the authorities).

[499] *Holdsworth v Luton and Dunstable University Hospital NHS Foundation Trust* [2016] EWHC 3347 (QB); (2017) 154 B.M.L.R. 172 at [38]. Presumably, however, there must come a point where a patient's claim is barred: namely, if he insists on treatment having received full information, including knowledge of the doctor's view that that treatment is useless or clinically unsound.

[500] *Chin Keow v Government of Malaysia* [1967] 1 W.L.R. 813. See too *Hanson v Airedale NHS Trust* [2003] 3 C.L. 390 (where patient known to be heavy smoker complained of chest pains, duty to expedite checks for heart trouble).

[501] *Pearce v United Bristol Healthcare* [1999] P.I.Q.R. P53 (0.1–0.2 per cent risk of stillbirth could be disregarded).

[502] *Hucks v Cole* (1968) [1993] 4 Med. L.R. 393.

[503] *Joyce v Wandsworth HA* [1996] 7 Med. L.R. 1. See too *Hamed v Mills* [2015] EWHC 298 (QB) (doctor examining footballer for employing club failed to pass on vital recommendations for tests for possible heart trouble to club's own physician, instead certifying player on balance fit to play).

be held to be negligent.[504] Decisions as to whether to prescribe a given drug must of course be taken on the basis of the doctor's own clinical judgment. A doctor is not liable for failing to prescribe a drug merely because the patient wants it and is prepared to pay, even if with hindsight it appears that the drug would in fact have done some good.[505]

Errors in treatment To give rise to recovery, an injury resulting from the treatment or surgery undertaken by the medical practitioner must be shown to be the result of (1) an error on the part of the defendant rather than the materialisation of a risk inherent in the treatment[506]; and (2) an error which a reasonably competent medical practitioner would have avoided.[507] A negligent error may be a failure to observe a routine precaution,[508] or a mechanical error,[509] or an error in clinical judgment in the management of the patient.[510] It may relate not only to the original treatment, but also to failure to keep proper notes[511] or provide proper aftercare,[512] or to deal with complications subsequent to treatment or surgery,[513] or for that matter any other breach of the duty owed by the doctor.[514] On the other hand, in deciding whether negligence has been shown, the difficulty of surgery, and any evidence that the surgery had to be completed speedily, will be taken into account.[515] **9-83**

A common example of negligence based on the failure to take proper precautions relates to the leaving of surgical materials in the body.[516] Indeed, in such a case a finding of negligence is virtually inevitable.[517] Equally, failure to check anaesthetic equipment before use,[518] or using the wrong anaesthetic,[519] will almost always be negligent. A technical error in the course of administering an injection is clearly capable of being negligent, but the courts allow for the difficulties inherent even in routine procedures such as injections. That the needle broke is not conclusive **9-84**

---

504 *Dwyer v Roderick, The Times,* 12 November 1983 CA. See J. Finch, "A Costly Oversight for Pharmacists" (1982) 132 New L.J. 176. So also where the doctor prescribed the correct dose, but wrote the prescription so badly that the pharmacist misread it: *Prendergast v Sam & Dee* [1989] 1 Med. L.R. 36.

505 *Rhodes v Spokes* [1996] 7 Med. L.R. 135.

506 *Ashcroft v Mersey RHA* [1983] 2 All E.R. 245; affirmed on appeal [1985] 2 All E.R. 96.

507 *Whitehouse v Jordan* [1981] 1 W.L.R. 246.

508 e.g. *Urry v Bierer, The Times,* 15 July 1955 (not using tapes on swabs).

509 *Gonda v Kerbel* (1982) 24 C.C.L. 7 (clumsy sigmoidoscopy perforating claimant's bowel).

510 *Whitehouse v Jordan* [1981] 1 W.L.R. 246.

511 *Telles v South West Strategic HA* [2008] EWHC 292 (QB). And to have them readily to hand: *Lorraine v Wirral University Teaching Hospital NHS Trust* [2008] LS Law Med. 573.

512 e.g. *Joyce v Wandsworth HA* [1996] 7 Med. L.R. 1 (failure to warn patient to obtain advice if symptoms recurred). See too *Morris v Winsbury-White* [1937] 4 All E.R. 494.

513 *Morris v Winsbury-White* [1937] 4 All E.R. 494.

514 cf. *L v Robinson* [2000] 3 N.Z.L.R. 499 (doctor who improperly inveigled patient into sexual relationship liable in negligence).

515 *Voller v Portsmouth Corporation* (1947) 203 L.T.J. 264. The same goes for other professionals: see *Darnley v Croydon Health Services NHS Trust* [2018] UKSC 50; [2019] A.C. 831 at [22] (constant pressure on A&E departments likely to be highly influential in assessing whether fault shown).

516 e.g. surgical gauze (*Dryden v Surrey CC* [1936] 2 All E.R. 535); drainage tubes (*Hocking v Bell* [1948] W.N. 21); or swabs (*Urry v Bierer, The Times,* 15 July 1955).

517 *Urry v Bierer, The Times,* 15 July 1955. The surgeon may also be liable, since he is bound properly to direct his helpers: *Mahon v Osborne* [1939] 2 K.B. 14.

518 See M. Brazier and E. Cave, *Medicine Patients & The Law*, 6th edn (2016), para.7.13; and cf. the criminal case of *R. v Adomako* [1995] 1 A.C. 171 (manslaughter conviction upheld for negligent mishandling of anaesthetic equipment).

519 cf. *Collins v Hertfordshire CC* [1947] K.B. 598; and *Jones v Manchester Corporation* [1952] 2 Q.B. 852.

evidence of negligence[520]; needles may break for a number of reasons. By contrast, injecting the patient in the wrong area will generally be negligent.[521] Accidental injury to unrelated tissue in surgery is again not necessarily negligent[522]; it must be shown that any competent surgeon could have avoided inflicting that injury.

(iv) Failure to inform

9-85 **Negligent failure to inform**[523] Even though the patient may have sufficiently consented to treatment to prevent an action in battery, there remains a vital duty in the law of negligence[524] to take reasonable steps[525] to inform the patient on the inherent risks and side-effects of that treatment,[526] and of possible alternatives that may be available.[527] This duty to inform extends to both therapeutic and non-therapeutic treatments,[528] and to effects other than specifically clinical ones.[529] Where there are a number of different treatments available, it may extend to telling the patient about the comparative risks involved.[530] Such a duty may in suitable cases be owed not only to the patient but also to a third party.[531]

9-86 It was long assumed that the *Bolam* test referred to above applied to this duty as to any other[532]: provided that the practitioner followed respectable practice in decid-

---

520 *Brazier v Ministry of Defence* [1965] 1 Lloyd's Rep. 26; *Hunter v Hanley*, 1955 S.C. 200.

521 *Caldeira v Gray* [1936] 1 All E.R. 540.

522 *Ashcroft v Mersey RHA* [1985] 2 All E.R. 96; *White v Westminster Hospital, The Times,* 26 October 1961; *Chubey v Ahsan* (1977) 71 D.L.R. (3d) 550.

523 M.A. Jones, *Medical Negligence*, 5th edn (2018), paras.4–052 to 4–074 and Ch.7.

524 Indeed, this duty goes a good deal further, since whereas battery on principle lies only in respect of surgery or other invasive treatments, the duty to warn is equally applicable to all forms of treatment, including oral drug therapy. See M. Brazier, "Patient Autonomy and Consent to Treatment: the Role of the Law?" (1987) 7 L.S. 169, 179–180.

525 But only these. As a Californian judge pithily put it, "the patient's interest in information does not extend to a lengthy polysyllabic discourse on all possible complications. A mini-course in medical science is not required." (*Cobbs v Grant*, 502 P.2d 1, 11 (1972)). Moreover, for obvious reasons, the urgency of treatment may curtail any duty to inform that does exist: *Monument v Baker* (2007) 55 S.R. (NSW) 22.

526 *Chatterton v Gerson* [1981] Q.B. 432, 443 (Bristow J); *Pearce v United Bristol Healthcare NHS Trust* [1999] P.I.Q.R. P53, P59 (Mummery LJ); *Chester v Afshar* [2004] UKHL 41; [2005] 1 A.C. 134 at [16]–[17] (Lord Bingham).

527 See *Williamson v East London & City HA* [1998] 1 Lloyd's Rep. Med. 6; *Van Mol v Ashmore* (1997) 168 D.L.R. (4th) 637.

528 *Gold v Haringey HA* [1988] Q.B. 481 (failure to warn of risk of failure inherent in sterilisation operation).

529 *Williamson v East London & City HA* [1998] 1 Lloyd's Rep. Med. 6 (failure to tell patient of alternatives to mastectomy: patient recovers £20,000 for trauma over lost breast).

530 *Birch v UC London Hospital NHS Foundation Trust* [2008] EWHC 2237 (QB); (2008) 104 B.M.L.R. 168; also *Haughian v Payne* (1987) 37 D.L.R. (4th) 624 and *Cory v Bass* [2012] ABCA 136; (2012) 522 A.R. 220. See R.Heywood [2009] C.L.J. 30. In California this duty has been held, it is suggested rightly, to extend to explaining the comparative risks of treatment and no treatment at all: *Truman v Thomas*, 611 P. 2d 902 (1980).

531 e.g. *Thompson v Bradford* [2004] EWHC 2424 (QB) (inadequate warning to parents concerning possible effects of anti-polio injection on infant) (reversed on the issue of causation, [2005] EWCA Civ 1439; [2006] Lloyd's Rep. Med. 95); *Howarth v Adey* [1996] 2 V.R. 535 (duty to warn of problems inherent in risky obstetric procedure owed not only to mother but to child, who in the event was born with cerebral palsy). *Montgomery v Lanarkshire Health Board* [2015] UKSC 11; [2015] A.C. 1430, referred to below, is another such case.

532 Indeed, it applies "to every aspect of the duty of care owed by a doctor to his patient in the exercise of his healing functions as respects that patient:"—Lord Diplock in *Sidaway v Bethlem Royal Hospital* [1985] A.C. 871, 893–894.

ing on the information to be given, he was protected.[533] But in 2015 the Supreme Court in *Montgomery v Lanarkshire Health Board*,[534] following the lead of several other common law jurisdictions,[535] departed from earlier House of Lords authority[536] and took the view that such an approach was inappropriate in respect of a duty whose raison d'être was the protection of a patient's personal autonomy and right to self-determination. Under the view taken by a majority of the court,[537] while the determination of whether an appreciable risk exists remains subject to the *Bolam* test,[538] as does the decision on how to deal with it,[539] the duty on doctors as regards information is now simply one to take reasonable care to ensure that a patient is aware of all material risks inherent in a given treatment.[540] This is a matter for the court to determine. It should be noted, however, that *Montgomery* only applies where injury is actually suffered. The mere fact of failure to inform the patient properly is not of itself actionable.[541]

The relevant test is whether a reasonable person in the patient's position[542] would be likely to attach significance to the risk,[543] since only thus can the patient's right to autonomy be given effect.[544] Unless the patient makes it clear that he does not wish to discuss the matter and wants to consent in any case, he must be apprised of any material risks involved in any recommended treatment and of any reason- **9-87**

---

533 See *Sidaway v Bethlem Royal Hospital* [1985] A.C. 871; and *Blyth v Bloomsbury AHA* (1987) [1993] 4 Med. L.R. 151 CA. There was some justification for this: an over-propensity to warn may be self-defeating, as observed by Lord Templeman in *Sidaway* ([1985] A.C. 871, 904); and in R. Heywood, "Excessive Risk Disclosure: the Effects of the Law on Medical Practice" (2005) 7 Med. Law Int. 93.

534 [2015] UKSC 11; [2015] A.C. 1430. See too *Healy v Buckley* [2015] IECA 251; *Hii Chii Kok v Ooi Peng Jin London Lucien* [2017] SGCA 38; (2017) 162 B.M.L.R. 28. On the issue generally see R. Heywood & J. Miola, "The changing face of pre-operative medical disclosure: placing the patient at the heart of the matter" (2017) 133 L.Q.R. 296.

535 Notably Australia (*Rogers v Whittaker* (1992) 110 C.L.R. 625), Canada (*Reibl v Hughes* (1980) 114 D.L.R. (3d) 1) and Ireland (*Fitzpatrick v White* [2007] IESC 51; [2008] 3 I.R. 551).

536 i.e. *Sidaway v Bethlem Royal Hospital* [1985] A.C. 871, above.

537 Lord Neuberger PSC and Lords Kerr, Clarke, Wilson, Reed and Hodge.

538 *Duce v Worcestershire Acute Hospitals NHS Trust* [2018] EWCA Civ 1307; [2018] P.I.Q.R. P18, especially at [42]–[44].

539 See the Scottish decision in *Taylor v Dailly Health Centre* [2018] CSOH 91; 2018 S.L.T. 1324.

540 [2015] UKSC 11; [2015] A.C. 1430 at [82]. See C.P. McGrath, "'Trust me, I'm a patient . . .': disclosure standards and the patient's right to decide" [2015] C.L.J. 211; R. Heywood, "R.I.P. Sidaway: patient-oriented disclosure - a standard worth waiting for?" (2015) 23 Med. L. Rev. 455.

541 A point put beyond doubt by the CA in *Shaw v Kovac* [2017] EWCA Civ 1028; [2017] 1 W.L.R. 4773; and also in the Singapore decision in *ACB v Thomson Medical Pte Ltd* [2017] SGCA 20; [2017] 1 S.L.R. 918. Similarly it is always open to a defendant to plead that the claimant would have opted for the relevant procedure in any case: e.g. *Diamond v Royal Devon & Exeter NHS Foundation Trust* [2019] EWCA Civ 585; [2019] P.I.Q.R. P12.

542 Unless the practitioner knows, or should know, that this specific patient attaches significance to it: in that case the matter has to be disclosed (see [2015] UKSC 11; [2015] A.C. 1430 at [87]). The characteristics of the actual patient may be of some little importance, for example where it is known that he attaches importance to a given sport or pastime: *Thefaut v Johnston* [2017] EWHC 497 (QB); [2017] Med. L.R. 319 at [56] (Green J).

543 [2015] UKSC 11; [2015] A.C. 1430 at [87]–[88]. The likelihood of the risk eventuating, and its severity, are of course highly relevant here: see *Hii Chii Kok v Ooi Peng Jin London Lucien* [2017] SGCA 38; (2017) 162 B.M.L.R. 28 at [140]. It follows that genuinely negligible risks can still be ignored: see *Tasmin v Barts Health NHS Trust* [2015] EWHC 3135 (QB) (tiny risks inherent in foetal blood sampling); and also *A v East Kent Hospital University NHS Foundation Trust* [2015] EWHC 1038 (QB); [2015] Med. L.R. 262 at [84].

544 [2015] UKSC 11; [2015] A.C. 1430 at [75]–[81]. See too at [108] (Lady Hale). For discussion see J. Laing, "Delivering informed consent post-*Montgomery*: Implications for medical practice and provessionalism" (2017) 33 P.N. 128.

able alternative or variant treatments.[545] In deciding whether an alternative treatment is reasonable, it seems that the *Bolam* criterion applies: but in advising of the risks associated with such treatments, *Montgomery* rules.[546] The only qualifications are these: (i) a doctor may withhold information seriously detrimental to the patient's health[547]; and (ii) the requirement does not apply in circumstances of necessity, for example where an unconscious patient requires urgent treatment.[548] To satisfy the *Montgomery* requirements, any information given must be comprehensible and such as to enable a patient to make an informed decision[549]; a blizzard of technicality followed by a formulaic signature on a consent form is not enough.[550]

9-88 The principle in *Montgomery*, moreover, applies not only to therapy proper but to all medical advice, so that it covers (for example) advice whether to continue with labour or submit to a Caesarian birth.[551] No doubt it also covers warnings as to the risks inherent in medical experimentation.[552] Indeed, despite the lack of any potential interference with the patient's autonomy in deciding whether to submit to treatment, it now seems that it will be applied to all cases turning on advice or the lack of it. Thus in *Spencer v Hillingdon Hospital NHS Trust*[553] it was equally held to apply to failure to advise post-operative treatment; and in *Webster v Burton Hospitals NHS Foundation Trust*[554] the Court of Appeal applied *Montgomery* rather than *Bolam* to a failure to advise early inducement in a troublesome pregnancy. Furthermore, it has been held that a patient's rejection of an offer of treatment must equally be informed: so a mother who declined a Down's syndrome test recovered damages when her child proved to be afflicted, on the basis that she had merely been asked about whether she wished the test and not simultaneously supplied with further information about its benefits.[555] Indeed, these developments seem to indicate that in many medical contexts, *Montgomery* is increasingly becoming the rule and *Bolam* the exception.

---

545 [2015] UKSC 11; [2015] A.C. 1430 at [87].

546 See the carefully-argued Scottish decision in *AH v Greater Glasgow Health Board* [2018] CSOH 57; 2018 S.L.T. 535 at [43]–[45] (Lord Boyd); also *Mills v Oxford University Hospitals NHS Trust* [2019] EWHC 936 (QB); (2019) 170 B.M.L.R. 100 (where the point was admitted).

547 [2015] UKSC 11; [2015] A.C. 1430 at [88]. On this see E. Cave, "The ill-informed: Consent to medical treatments and the thrapeutic exception" (2017) 46 C.L.W.R. 140.

548 [2015] UKSC 11; [2015] A.C. 1430 at [88].

549 Thus a fairly informal oral warning of "small" risk of testicular pain following vasectomy was held sufficient, despite the lack of further detail: see *Ollosson v Lee* [2019] EWHC 784 (QB); [2019] Med. L.R. 287. If the information is broadly correct, the presence of a minor inaccuracy is not fatal: *Connolly v Croydon Health Services NHS Trust* [2015] EWHC 1339 (QB).

550 [2015] UKSC 11; [2015] A.C. 1430 at [90]; see too *Thefaut v Johnston* [2017] EWHC 497 (QB); [2017] Med. L.R. 319 at [59] (Green J).

551 *Tasmin v Barts Health NHS Trust* [2015] EWHC 3135 (QB).

552 So held in Canada: *Halushka v University of Saskatchewan* (1965) 53 D.L.R. (2d) 436.

553 *Spencer v Hillingdon Hostpital NHS Trust* [2015] EWHC 1058 (QB): see esp. at [32]. See too *Gallardo v Imperial College Healthcare NHS Trust* [2017] EWHC 3147 (QB); [2018] P.I.Q.R. P6.

554 [2017] EWCA Civ 62; [2017] Med. L.R. 113. See also *Hii Chii Kok v Ooi Peng Jin London Lucien* [2017] SGCA 38; (2017) 162 B.M.L.R. 28 at [121].

555 *Mordel v Royal Berkshire NHS Foundation Trust* [2019] EWHC 2591 (QB). With respect, the potential burden placed on defendants by this case, to give full information about treatments declined as well as those accepted, seems somewhat heavy.

(d) Medical negligence: particular issues

(i) Self-harm

No general duty to guard against self-harm A competent and non-vulnerable adult has the right, if he so wishes, to risk harm to himself or take his own life. It follows that doctors and hospitals generally owe no duty to protect a patient from deliberate self-harm. This was the case at common law,[556] and in *Savage v South Essex Partnership NHS Trust*[557] it was accepted that art.2 of the European Convention on Human Rights, protecting the right to life, made no difference. 9-89

Self-harm: vulnerable victims Whatever the position with a sane and unconstrained adult, it is clear that where a person is particularly vulnerable, as with a child, prisoner or mental patient, matters are different and there may here be a duty of care.[558] This applies to medical professionals as to any other defendant.[559] Moreover, human rights jurisprudence makes it clear that in such cases art.2[560] and possibly art.8[561] of the Convention are engaged. In *Savage v South Essex Partnership NHS Foundation Trust*[562] the House of Lords accordingly held potentially liable a mental hospital which failed to take steps to prevent the suicide of a detained mental patient. If, they said, a hospital either failed to take general measures to guard against suicide by mental patients, or knowing of a particular risk of suicide failed to take reasonable steps to stop it, they would be liable.[563] In the later *Rabone v Pennine Care NHS Foundation Trust*[564] the Supreme Court set its seal on this development by applying it to an informal, non-detained patient negligently allowed leave in the course of which she hanged herself. The principle, it was said, applied not simply to those under state constraint, but to anyone "especially vulnerable by reason of their physical or mental condition".[565] It follows from this that 9-90

---

556 For a straightforward example, see the decision of the High Court of Australia in the non-medical case of *CAL No 14 Pty Ltd v Motor Accidents Insurance Board* [2009] HCA 47; (2009) 260 A.L.R. 606 (drunk patron leaves bar on motorcycle and is killed: no duty on landlord to stop him).

557 [2008] UKHL 74; [2009] 1 A.C. 681, especially at [12] (Lord Scott) and [25] (Lord Rodger].

558 *Reeves v Metropolitan Police Comm'r* [2000] 1 A.C. 360 (duty to guard against suicide by prisoner).

559 e.g. *Baker v Cambridgeshire and Peterborough NHS Foundation Trust* [2015] EWHC 609 (QB) at [27] (indication by GP of possible suicidal tendencies in person with bipolar affective disorder: duty in psychiatrist to whom referred to take steps). This is also implicit in cases such as *Rabone v Pennine Care NHS Foundation Trust* [2012] UKSC 2; [2012] 2 A.C. 72.

560 e.g. *Keenan v UK* (2001) 33 E.H.R.R. 913; cf. *Kilinĉ v Turkey* (Application No 40145/98) (unreported) ECtHR, 7 June 2005.

561 e.g. *K v Central & North West London Mental Health NHS Trust* [2008] EWHC 1217 (QB); [2008] P.I.Q.R. P19 at [73]. The argument is that an unsuccessful suicide attempt or other self-harm may compromise a person's later private life.

562 [2008] UKHL 74; [2009] 1 A.C. 681.

563 Strictly speaking, *Savage* was a claim not at common law but for damages for breach of art.2 of the Convention. But it is suggested that the same result would follow at common law.

564 [2012] UKSC 2; [2012] 2 A.C. 72. This development was approved wholeheartedly by the ECtHR in *Reynolds v United Kingdom* (2012) 55 E.H.R.R. 35.

565 [2012] UKSC 2; [2012] 2 A.C. 72 at [22] (Lord Dyson). This again was decided under s.8 of the Human Rights Act 1998, the claimants being the suicide's parents, who were barred from claiming under domestic law by the limited provisions of the Fatal Accidents Act 1976 as to who could claim for wrongful death. See generally A. Tettenborn, "Wrongful Death, Human Rights and the Fatal Accidents Act" (2012) 128 L.Q.R. 327.

health professionals dealing with vulnerable patients, be they in prison hospitals,[566] mental hospitals or possibly even in the hands of ordinary doctors or other professionals,[567] will owe this limited duty to prevent actual or attempted suicide. There is nevertheless a crumb of comfort for them here. In a suitable case where the patient retains a degree of autonomy, a deduction for contributory negligence will be appropriate,[568] as it is elsewhere where suicide is made the subject of a wrongful death claim.[569]

(ii) *Antenatal injuries*

9-91 **Antenatal injuries** For a long time it was unclear whether a child could sue at common law for injuries inflicted *in utero*; it was, however, finally established in 1992 that it could.[570] But the point is now moot. Today the matter is governed by the Congenital Disabilities (Civil Liability) Act 1976,[571] which replaces any liability at common law,[572] and imposes liability for antenatal injuries, but only in carefully defined circumstances.

9-92 **The Congenital Disabilities (Civil Liability) Act 1976[573]** Under the 1976 Act, a child born alive[574] and suffering from injuries as a result of an occurrence which affected (1) either parent in his or her ability to have healthy children; or (2) the mother in the course of her pregnancy; or (3) either mother or child in the course of labour, has an action against any person responsible for that occurrence, provided that that person would have been liable in tort[575] to the affected parent had the latter been injured. Thus a doctor who negligently prescribed a drug causing deformities in a foetus would be liable to the child if and when born. Section 1A of the Act[576] extends its effects to IVF babies, and in addition creates a statutory liability to the child in respect of negligence in the care or treatment of embryos or gametes outside the body which lead to its being born disabled.[577] Section 1(5) of the 1976 Act expressly enacts the *Bolam* test in the context of actions for antenatal injury:

"The defendant is not answerable to the child, for anything he did or omitted to do when

566 cf. *Nyang v G4S Care & Justice Services Ltd* [2013] EWHC 3946 (QB) (person detained pending deportation: accepted, duty to prevent self-harm).

567 See *PPX v Aulakh* [2019] EWHC 717 (QB), where a GP in charge of a troubled patient was regarded as being under a duty to refer him to a crisis mental health team if he had given indications of a present suicidal intention (which on the facts he had not).

568 In *PPX v Aulakh* [2019] EWHC 717 (QB), above, it was held that if liability had been established a 25 per cent reduction would have been appropriate.

569 See generally *Corr v IBC Vehicles Ltd* [2008] UKHL 13; [2008] 1 A.C. 884; see para.3-70.

570 *Burton v Islington HA* [1993] Q.B. 204. See too *X & Y v Pal* (1991) 23 N.S.W.L.R. 26, where it was said that a common law duty was owed to children conceived after negligent failure to diagnose a condition in the mother that could harm them, such as congenital syphilis.

571 See too para.5-58.

572 Section 4(5).

573 See M. Brazier and E. Cave, *Medicine, Patients and the Law*, 6th edn (2016), paras.11.13 onwards.

574 The mother will have an action herself if the child is stillborn or she miscarries as a result of medical negligence, and she suffers injury as a result.

575 Including strict product liability under Consumer Protection Act 1987: see s.6(3) of that Act. But the Act does not apply, apparently, in contract, e.g. if the only claim lies under ss.9–10 of the Consumer Rights Act 2015.

576 Inserted by the Human Fertilisation and Embryology Act 1990.

577 Hence creating something similar to an action for "wrongful life", denied elsewhere: for mention of the anomaly, see R. Scott, "Reconsidering 'wrongful life' in England after thirty years: legislative mistakes and unjustifiable anomalies" [2013] C.L.J. 115.

responsible in a professional capacity for treating and advising the parent, if he took reasonable care having due regard to the then received professional opinion applicable to the particular class of case; but this does not mean that he is so liable only because he departed from received opinion."[578]

For the purposes of contributory negligence, the unborn child is identified with the affected parent; so damages payable to it may be reduced where that parent shares responsibility for its being born disabled.[579]

Evidence establishing negligence in the treatment of the affected parent will normally be sufficient to meet the pre-condition of liability in tort to that parent, but two sets of circumstances pose difficulties. First, the requirement that the defendant be liable in tort to the parent can cause problems. Suppose that an obstetrician knows that a baby is in distress and likely to be damaged if he fails to intervene by forceps or Caesarean section. He will be negligent if he fails to advise the mother of what is needed. But if despite his efforts the mother refuses consent to intervention and the child is born damaged, the child has no action against the obstetrician or his mother. The mother is immune from suit under the Act[580]; and the obstetrician has committed no tort against her.[581] Secondly, no liability arises out of events taking place before conception where either parent was aware of the risk of a baby being born defective as a result. So where a doctor prescribes a drug to a woman with a warning that it may be teratogenic, he will not be liable if she subsequently conceives a child which is indeed born deformed.[582] 9-93

Antenatal injury and "wrongful life"[583] A medical practitioner is liable to a child when his negligence causes the child to be born disabled: for instance, where he botches a difficult birth. But he is not liable to the child where as a result of negligence he fails to detect disabilities which, if known to the mother, would have caused her to terminate her pregnancy. In *McKay v Essex Area Health Authority*[584] the claimant child was severely damaged by rubella contracted by her mother in the early months of pregnancy. It was alleged that the defendants' negligence was responsible for the mother being told, wrongly, that tests for the disease were negative. Had she known that she had rubella she would have had an abortion. The Court of Appeal held that neither at common law[585] nor under the 1976 Act[586] could 9-94

[578] Quaere whether this section, which specifically refers to "advice", precludes the application to cases of antenatal injury in England and Wales of the principle in *Montgomery v Lanarkshire Health Board* [2015] UKSC 11; [2015] A.C. 1430, where the issue was precisely one of negligent advice to the pregnant mother before the birth. The issue did not arise in *Montgomery*, an appeal from Scotland where the 1976 Act does not apply.

[579] Section 1(7). Refusing to terminate the pregnancy by agreeing to an abortion is not, however, sharing responsibility for the child being born disabled: *Emeh v Kensington and Chelsea and Westminster AHA* [1985] Q.B. 1012.

[580] See s.1; except where her negligent driving of a vehicle causes injury to the unborn child: s.2.

[581] He cannot compel the mother to submit to intervention: see *Re F (In Utero)* [1988] Fam. 122.

[582] Section 1(4). The position is probably the same at common law in any case: *Paxton v Ramji* (2008) 299 D.L.R. (4th) 614; *Bovingdon v Hergott* (2008) 290 D.L.R. (4th) 126.

[583] M.A. Jones, *Medical Negligence*, 5th edn (2018), para.2–140 onwards; A. Morris & S. Saintier, "To be or not to be? Wrongful Life and Misconceptions" (2003) 11 Med. L. Rev. 167; R. Scott, "Reconsidering "wrongful life" in England after thirty years: legislative mistakes and unjustifiable anomalies" [2013] C.L.J. 115.

[584] [1982] Q.B. 1166.

[585] [1982] Q.B. 1166 at 1176 and 1182. A Canadian court has reached the same conclusion (*Lacroix (Guardian) v Dominique* (2001) 202 D.L.R. (4th) 121), as has the High Court of Australia, by a

such an action for "wrongful life" be maintained in England.[587] To succeed in a claim under the 1976 Act, a child must establish that but for the negligence of the defendant he would have been born without the relevant disability.

(iii) Failed sterilisation

9-95 **Failed sterilisation** Where a medical practitioner carries out a sterilisation[588] negligently, so that the surgery is unsuccessful[589] and the claimant gives birth to an unplanned child, the claimant can on principle recover. There will be little difficulty in establishing that a practitioner is liable for negligence in carrying out a sterilisation or vasectomy if he is careless in carrying out the surgery itself. In *Thake v Maurice*[590] it was held that failure to warn the claimant of the risk that nature might reverse the vasectomy carried out by the defendant was negligent. Had he and his wife been aware of this risk she would have recognised her pregnancy at an earlier stage when it was still possible to have an abortion.[591] However, failure to warn of the failure rate of male or female sterilisation does not import a term into a contract between the practitioner and the patient that the former guarantees the success of his treatment,[592] nor does it normally constitute an actionable negligent misrepresentation.[593] Where an action is brought in respect of a failed sterilisation, a refusal by the mother of an offer to terminate the pregnancy is not a *novus actus interveniens* making the mother and not the doctor responsible for the child's birth.[594] On the other hand, other matters may well break the chain of causation, for example continued indulgence in unprotected intercourse after knowledge that the operation may have failed.[595]

9-96 **Failed sterilisation: limitations on recovery** There is no doubt that the victim of a failed sterilisation can recover in respect of the trauma of childbirth and any loss of earnings resulting from the process of parturition.[596] However, beyond this recovery is severely circumscribed. In particular it has been held that, at least where

---

majority (*Harriton v Stephens* [2006] HCA 15; (2006) 80 A.L.J.R. 791, noted K. Warner (2007) 123 L.Q.R. 209). Some US jurisdictions, by contrast, disagree: see e.g. *Curlender v Bio-Science Laboratories* 165 Cal. Rptr. 477 (1980); and *Turpin v Sortini*, 31 Cal 3d 220 (1982); and J. Skolnik, "Compensating a California Wrongful Life Plaintiff for General Damages" (2003) 36 Loy. L.A. L. Rev. 1677.

[586] [1982] Q.B. 1166 at 1181.

[587] The precise boundaries of "wrongful life," however, may be difficult. If a botched abortion causes a child to be born disabled, is the child's action one for "wrongful life" (no liability) or obstetric injury (liability)? A Canadian court had said the latter: *Cherry v Borsman* (1992) 94 D.L.R. (4th) 487.

[588] The same principles apply to unsuccessful abortion: *Scuriaga v Powell* (1979) 123 S.J. 406.

[589] Including the case where the practitioner fails to notice that the patient is already pregnant: *Crouchman v Cleveland Medical Laboratories Ltd*, unreported 9 July 1997.

[590] [1986] Q.B. 644; cf. *Lybert v Warrington HA* [1996] 7 Med. L.R. 72; and *Gold v Haringey HA* [1988] Q.B. 481, where a similar action failed, but only because at that time there was a respectable body of medical opinion which would not have given such a warning.

[591] A claimant who had conscientious objections to abortion thus could not recover, for she would be unable to prove damage resulting from the defendant's negligence.

[592] *Thake v Maurice* [1986] Q.B. 644; *Eyre v Measday* [1986] 1 All E.R. 488.

[593] *Eyre v Measday* [1986] 1 All E.R. 488.

[594] *Emeh v Kensington & Chelsea & Westminster AHA* [1985] Q.B. 1012; *Fredette v Wiebe* (1989) 29 D.L.R. (4th) 534.

[595] *Sabri-Tabrizi v Lothian Health Board*, 1998 S.L.T. 607.

[596] See *Thake v Maurice* [1986] Q.B. 644; *Udale v Bloomsbury HA* [1983] 1 W.L.R. 1098; *Allan v*

the child is born healthy, there can be no damages reflecting the cost to the wronged parent in raising it. In the Scots case of *McFarlane v Tayside Health Board*[597] an unwanted child was born as a result of the defenders' incorrect advice that a vasectomy they had carried out had been effective. The House of Lords held that the costs of bringing up the child were not recoverable, the majority[598] on the basis that this was an economic loss in respect of which it was not fair, just and reasonable to subject the defenders to any duty of care. In addition, two of their Lordships[599] held that in any case this loss should be irrecoverable on the basis that it fell to be offset by the benefits of bringing up a healthy child,[600] however imponderable those might be. It should be noted that this restriction seems to be based on an overriding public policy: hence it applies to claims in contract as much as to those in tort.[601]

However, after *McFarlane* there were a number of developments. In *Parkinson v St James & Seacroft University NHS Trust*[602] the Court of Appeal distinguished *McFarlane* and held that where the child was born disabled there could be a claim for the extra costs incurred over and above normal child-rearing expenses. After this, the matter came again before a seven-judge House of Lords in *Rees v Darlington Memorial Hospital NHS Trust*,[603] where the issue was whether *McFarlane* (which was controversial[604]) should be departed from, and if not whether it applied to claims by a parent who was herself disabled. The House was unanimous in upholding *McFarlane* and declining to give damages for child-rearing expenses; and a bare majority[605] decided that it made no difference that the parent was disabled. However, the majority also put a gloss on the *McFarlane* bar and decided that where it applied there should nevertheless be a conventional award **9-97**

Greater Glasgow Health Board, 1998 S.L.T. 580. These cases were accepted as correct by the House of Lords in *McFarlane v Tayside Health Board* [2000] 2 A.C. 59. In *Whitehead v Searle* [2007] EWHC 1060 (QB) at [94]–[97] (appealed on other grounds at [2008] EWCA Civ 285; [2009] 1 W.L.R. 549), Griffith Williams J discussed whether the father might have a claim, for example for gratuitous care provided. And in *Schumann v Veale Wasbrough* [2013] EWHC 3730 (QB); [2014] P.N.L.R. 14 at [68] Dingemans J thought such a claim probably did lie (the point did not arise on appeal: [2015] EWCA Civ 441; [2015] P.N.L.R. 25). But this seems difficult, given that no duty was owed to the child itself.

597 [2000] 2 A.C. 59, overruling *Emeh v Kensington & Chelsea & Westminster AHA* [1985] Q.B. 1012 on this point. Note that *McFarlane* was pointedly not followed by the High Court of Australia: *Cattanach v Melchior* [2003] HCA 38; (2003) 215 C.L.R. 1.

598 Lords Slynn, Steyn and Hope.

599 Lords Millett and Hope.

600 But see the scepticism on this point in the Australian decision in *Cattanach v Melchior* [2003] HCA 38; (2003) 215 C.L.R. 1.

601 *ARB v IVF Hammersmith Ltd* [2018] EWCA Civ 2803; [2020] Q.B. 93. Lord Steyn had specifically left this point open in *McFarlane* (see [2000] 2 A.C. 59, 76), as had Lords Slynn (at 76) and Clyde (at 99).

602 [2001] EWCA Civ 530; [2002] Q.B. 266. Lord Steyn had left this issue undecided in *McFarlane*: see [2000] 2 A.C. 59, 84.

603 [2003] UKHL 52; [2004] 1 A.C. 309 (criticised, V. Chico, "Wrongful Conception; Policy, Inconsistency and the Conventional Award" (2007) 8 Med. Law Int. 139; and C. Purshouse, "Liability for lost autonomy in negligence: Undermining the coherence of tort law?" (2015) 22 Torts L.J. 226).

604 It has been rejected in Singapore: see *ACB v Thomson Medical Pte Ltd* [2017] SGCA 38 (on which, K. Amirthalingam, "Reproductive negligence: unwanted child or unwanted parenthood?" (2018) 134 L.Q.R. 15), though here damages were awarded on a different basis. The point has been left open in New Zealand: see *J v Accident Compensation Corporation* [2017] NZCA 441; [2017] 3 N.Z.L.R. 804 at [39]–[41].

605 Lords Bingham, Nicholls, Millett and Scott.

of £15,000 to mark the wrong done to the parents.[606] What was not finally decided was whether an award could still be made for the extra costs of bringing up a disabled child,[607] but the better position[608] seems to be that it can.[609] Such awards have been made, both in England and in the Commonwealth.[610]

(iv) Liability of other medical and quasi-medical professionals

9-98 **Nursing staff**[611] Nursing staff, as well as medical practitioners, owe a duty of care to the patients in their care, though there are few decided cases on the matter. Nevertheless, the principle relating to the liability of doctors applies equally to nurses.[612] The nurse must thus attain the standard of competence and skill to be expected from a person holding their post.[613] The more skilled the job undertaken by the nurse, the higher the standard of care expected. Very often, the nurse's duty is in practice discharged by bringing any concerns in relation to a patient to the attention of the medical practitioner caring for the patient. A nurse who fails to take note and act on instructions given her by the attending medical practitioner will be liable for any consequent injury to the patient. Thus a nurse who, in breach of instructions, continued treatment with streptomycin after the course should have finished was found liable in negligence.[614] But, in deciding whether a nurse has acted negligently, account is taken of the pressurised environment in which they often work. A busy triage nurse, it has been said, cannot be expected to engage in an exercise in exhaustive diagnosis.[615]

---

606 Following a suggestion put out by Lord Millett in *McFarlane*: [2000] 2 A.C. 59, 114. See too para.7-98 onwards. But this artificial measure is not available where the unwanted child is stillborn: see *Less v Hussain* [2012] EWHC 3513 (QB); (2013) 130 B.M.L.R. 51.

607 Logically it could be argued that such a claim would be anomalous. Having decided over 20 years ago that the disabled child cannot itself sue for "wrongful birth" (see *McKay v Essex AHA* [1982] Q.B. 1116), it would be somewhat curious if the law were now to admit a claim for damages of a similar sort through the medium of an action by the parents for the extra costs of upbringing.

608 On the basis that the three dissentients in *Rees* (Lords Steyn, Hope and Hutton) regarded *Parkinson* as correct. Of the majority, Lords Bingham and Nicholls thought no claim should lie. But Lord Millett left the point open, as did Lord Scott: though the latter thought a distinction might have to be drawn between cases where the failed sterilisation was with a view to preventing the birth of a disabled child and those where it was not. Thus only two out of seven Law Lords clearly disapproved of *Parkinson*, and even then what they said was obiter.

609 Such is generally accepted in the profession. For instance, in *Farraj v King's Healthcare NHS Trust* [2008] EWHC 2468 (QB) at [2] (appealed on other grounds: [2009] EWCA Civ 1203; [2010] 1 W.L.R. 2139); in *P v Taunton & Somerset NHS Trust* [2009] EWHC 1965 (QB); [2009] LS Law Medical 598; (2009) 110 B.M.L.R. 164 at [7]; and in *Meadows v Khan* [2019] EWCA Civ 152; [2019] 4 W.L.R. 26 the ability to recover for such extra costs was admitted. It was decided in Meadows, however, that the only relevant disability was that in respect of which negligence had been shown. So where a doctor failed to spot a haemophilia gene and as it happened a child was born with both haemophilia and autism, the mother recovered in respect of the former but not the latter. The autism was, said the court, outside the scope of any duty owed by the doctor.

610 A claim for the costs of raising a disabled child was allowed by the Canadian Supreme Court in *Krangle (Guardian ad litem) v Brisco* [2002] 1 S.C.R. 205; and seems to have been permitted in England in *McGuinn v Lewisham & Greenwich NHS Trust* [2017] EWHC 88 (QB).

611 D. Kloss, "Demarcation in medical practice: the extended role of the nurse" (1988) 4 P.N. 41.

612 Including the *Bolam* principle: *Crammond v Medway NHS Foundation Trust* [2015] EWHC 3540 (QB).

613 e.g. *Mahon v Osborne* [1939] 2 K.B. 14 (failure to remove swabs); *Voller v Portsmouth Corporation* (1947) 203 L.T.(Jo). 264 (allowing equipment to become contaminated).

614 *Smith v Brighton & Lewes HMC*, *The Times*, 2 May 1958.

615 *Mulholland v Medway NHS Foundation Trust* [2015] EWHC 268 (QB); (2015) 144 B.M.L.R. 50

Dentists There are few reported cases relating to the liability of dentists.[616] Indeed, where a patient is treated by an NHS dentist he has no contract with the dentist, nor do dentists maintain lists of patients analogous to those operated by general practitioners. It is submitted, however, that dentists, even in the NHS, are subject to the same principles in relation to the tort of negligence as are their medical colleagues.[617] Where a dentist supplies materials to a patient, such as dentures or possibly material for fillings, he may be strictly liable for any defect in those materials. This is certainly the case in contract (i.e. where the patient is a private patient), since a person supplying materials in the course of a contract for services impliedly warrants that they are of satisfactory quality.[618] In tort he could conceivably be liable under the Consumer Protection Act 1987[619] as a "manufacturer" of fitments which he himself made. 9-99

Pharmacists The standard of care demanded of pharmacists is high, reflecting their status and their position as having the "last opportunity" to safeguard a patient from a dangerous drug. A pharmacist does not discharge his duty of care by dispensing as written the prescription presented to him. He should recognise and check with the issuing doctor a prescription where a dangerous dosage of a drug is prescribed.[620] It is not necessarily an excuse if the pharmacist dispenses erroneously a drug dangerous to the patient because he was misled by the doctor's bad handwriting; it may well be that he should have realised that the prescription as he read it was inappropriate for the patient.[621] The pharmacist has no contract with the patient, and hence no contractual liability, when he dispenses a NHS prescription.[622] When he dispenses a private prescription, however, the ordinary rules as to sale and supply of goods[623] apply; hence the drug or appliance supplied must be of satisfactory quality and fit for its purpose. Furthermore, as a result of the Consumer Protection Act 1987,[624] a pharmacist supplying drugs on an NHS prescription may also be liable under that Act for any defect in the drug unless and until he names the person who supplied it to him, or even as a producer if he concocts it himself. 9-100

Other allied professions Similar principles to those relating to the liability of medical practitioners govern that of other allied professions too, such as physiotherapists,[625] ambulance crews and paramedics,[626] A&E receptionists[627] and 9-101

---

at [86]–[90] (Green J). See too *Crammond v Medway NHS Foundation Trust* [2015] EWHC 3540 (QB).

616 *Lock v Scantlebury, The Times,* 25 July 1963; and *Fish v Kapur* [1948] 2 All E.R. 176 are rare examples. See too *C (A Child) v Ramdoo*, unreported, Oxford County Court, 10 February 2012 (£1,400 general damages for removal of wrong tooth).

617 Thus it has been held that a dentist has the same duty to warn of possible problems as a doctor: *Keuper v McMullin* (1987) 30 D.L.R. (4th) 408.

618 Consumer Rights Act 2015 ss.8, 9; *Samuels v Davis* [1943] 1 K.B. 526.

619 On which see Ch.10; also M.A. Jones, *Medical Negligence*, 5th edn (2018), Ch 10.

620 *Horton v Evans* [2006] EWHC 2808 (QB); [2007] P.N.L.R. 17.

621 *Prendergast v Sam & Dee* [1989] 1 Med. L.R. 36 CA (the doctor with the illegible handwriting was held jointly liable).

622 *Pfizer v Ministry of Health* [1965] A.C. 512; *Appleby v Sleep* [1968] 1 W.L.R. 948.

623 See the Consumer Rights Act 2015 ss.9-14; cf. A. Bell, "The Doctor and the Supply of Goods and Services Act 1982" (1984) 4 L.S. 175.

624 See Ch.10 below.

625 *Clarke v Adams* (1950) 94 S.J. 599.

626 *Taaffe v East of England Ambulance Service NHS Trust* [2012] EWHC 1335 (QB); (2012) 128

others.[628] Thus in *X (Minors) v Bedfordshire CC*[629] a local authority educational psychologist allegedly provided misleading advice to parents over their children's schooling. The House of Lords declined to strike out a claim in negligence by the children; and in *D v East Berkshire Community NHS Trust*[630] the Court of Appeal held that medical and other experts employed by a local authority owed a duty of care to children in respect of decisions about whether or not they should be taken into care.[631] However, it must be remembered that considerations of public policy may well impinge here to a greater extent than elsewhere.[632] Thus in *D v East Berkshire Community NHS Trust*[633] it was held that local authority experts advising on whether children should be (or not be) taken into care owed a duty to the children, but not to the parents: recognition of a duty to the latter, it was pointed out, would cut across the principle that such decisions had to be taken in the interests of the children concerned and no-one else.

(e) Liability of hospitals, health authorities and other bodies[634]

9-102 **Vicarious liability for medical negligence**[635] There is now[636] no doubt that hospitals, health authorities and other bodies (such as prisons or detention centres) employing professional medical staff are vicariously liable for any negligence shown by them in the course of their employment.[637] It matters not whether the individual responsible for a patient's injuries is a nurse, a physiotherapist, senior consultant, or any other employee[638]; provided that person is indeed employed and acted within the scope of his employment, the defendant is vicariously liable for his tort. This rule, moreover, applies not only to employees properly so called, but

B.M.L.R. 71; *Hayes v South East Coast Ambulance Service NHS Foundation Trust* [2015] EWHC 18 (QB); *Welds v Yorkshire Ambulance Service NHS Trust* [2016] EWHC 3325 (QB); (2016) 155 B.M.L.R. 101.

627 *Darnley v Croydon Health Services NHS Trust* [2018] UKSC 50; [2019] A.C. 831 (A&E receptionists expected to act as an averagely competent and well-informed person performing the function of a receptionist at a department providing emergency medical care: liable when, owing to receptionist's alleged overestimate of waiting time, the patient left prematurely and suffered complications as a result). See C. Purshouse, "The Impatient Patient and the Unreceptive Receptionist" (2019) 27 Med. L. Rev. 318.

628 e.g. police administering emergency aid (see *Hardaker v Newcastle HA* [2002] Lloyd's Rep. Med. 512), and specialist laboratories to whom hospitals send samples to analyse (*Farraj v King's Healthcare NHS Trust* [2009] EWCA Civ 1203; [2010] 1 W.L.R. 2139; and cf. *Morrissey v Health Service Executive* [2020] IESC 6; [2020] P.N.L.R. 17).

629 [1995] 2 A.C. 633. For another case concerning psychiatrists, see *Landau v Werner* (1961) 105 S.J. 1008.

630 [2003] EWCA Civ 1151; [2004] Q.B. 558; appealed on another point at [2005] UKHL 23; [2005] 2 A.C. 373.

631 Similarly, *S v Gloucestershire County Council* [2001] Fam. 313 had earlier held that such experts were liable for failing to look after children already in council care.

632 See para.9-45.

633 [2005] UKHL 23; [2005] 2 A.C. 373. See para.9-47.

634 M.A. Jones, *Medical Negligence* (5th edn), Ch.9.

635 For vicarious liability generally, see Ch.6.

636 It was not always so: see e.g. *Hillyer v St Bartholomew's Hospital* [1909] 2 K.B. 820; and O. Kahn-Freund, "Servants and Independent Contractors" (1951) 14 M.L.R. 504.

637 *Gold v Essex CC* [1942] 2 K.B. 293; *Cassidy v Ministry of Health* [1951] 2 K.B. 343; *Roe v Minister of Health* [1954] 2 Q.B. 66.

638 e.g. someone in charge of communication with patients. cf. *AB v Tameside HA* [1997] P.N.L.R. 140 (alleged insensitive communication of possible danger from AIDS-contaminated doctor leading to psychiatric injury: duty of care conceded, though action failed on the facts).

to those in an analogous position. An example might arise where a hospital was run by a religious order and the negligence was that of a member of the order rather than a physician employed by it.[639] However, not everyone involved in patient care falls necessarily to be treated as an employee of the hospital or health authority. In the absence of a relationship closely akin to employment as described above, there is no general vicarious liability in hospitals or similar organisations for independent contractors.[640] Again, a fortiori a private patient may well[641] have selected the consultant to care for him, contracted directly with that consultant for the necessary treatment or surgery, and then contracted separately with the hospital or clinic for nursing and ancillary care. In such a case there can be no vicarious liability for any negligence of his.

Medical negligence: employer's liability for own fault[642] Apart from any question of vicarious liability, a hospital, health authority or other organisation responsible for providing care may also be directly liable to a claimant on the basis of some personal fault committed by it, without the necessity to show personal negligence in any employee.[643] Such liability can take a number of forms. First, it may be liable for failing to supervise those under its control or jurisdiction and where necessary to take steps to discipline or dismiss them for misconduct.[644] Secondly, an organisation may be under a duty to provide treatment, and liable for failure to do so.[645] Thirdly, a defendant may be liable for organisational faults,[646] for example failure to have sufficient equipment on hand to deal with emergencies, adequate co-ordination, or adequate arrangements for diagnosis of patients arriving in casualty.[647] But in this case, at least as regards publicly-funded hospitals, the courts will pay some regard to budgetary constraints: for example, in so far as the allocation of resources raises legitimate issues of political or administrative **9-103**

639 cf. *Various Claimants v Catholic Child Welfare Society* [2012] UKSC 56; [2013] 2 A.C. 1 (brutalisation by teacher in similar position). On this basis a dental practice was held vicariously liable by a county court for the negligence of a dentist it regularly used but technically employed on a freelance basis for tax reasons: *Ramdhean v Agedo* 2020 WL 00620352 (Leeds Cty Ct, 28 January 2020).

640 See *Farraj v King's Healthcare Trust* [2009] EWCA Civ 1203; [2010] 1 W.L.R. 2139; and *Morrissey v Health Service Executive* [2020] IESC 6; [2020] P.N.L.R. 17 at [12.1]–[12.20] (no vicarious liability for negligence of independent testers of samples). Note, however, that there may be such liability on the more limited basis adumbrated in *Woodland v Swimming Teachers Association* [2013] UKSC 66; [2014] A.C. 537; see para.9-104 below.

641 Though not invariably. Some large private hospitals may well supply the services of senior "in-house" staff to those patients who have not chosen to employ their own outside specialists. For their negligence they will no doubt be vicariously liable in the ordinary way.

642 M.A. Jones, *Medical Negligence*, 5th edn (2018), paras 9-027 to 9-062. But this must be read with care in the light of the decision in *Woodland v Swimming Teachers Association* [2013] UKSC 66; [2014] A.C. 537, below.

643 See *Wilsher v Essex AHA* [1987] 1 Q.B. 730, 747, per Mustill LJ (possibility that health authority "owed a duty to ensure that the special baby care unit functioned according to the standard reasonably expected of such a unit. This approach would not require any consideration of the extent to which the individual doctors measured up to the standards demanded of them as individuals, but would focus attention on the performance of the unit as a whole."), and also at 778 (Browne-Wilkinson LJ).

644 *Godden v Kent & Medway SHA* [2004] EWHC 1629 (QB); [2004] Lloyd's Rep. Med. 521 (refusal to strike out claim for negligence in failing to proceed against GP with known propensity to improper actions against patients).

645 e.g. prisons. See *Steele v Home Office* [2010] EWCA Civ 724; (2010) 115 B.M.L.R. 218 (denial of access to dentist for seven months).

646 Accepted in, e.g. *Robertson v Nottingham HA* [1997] 8 Med. L.R. 1.

647 e.g. *Collins v Mid-Western Health Board* [2000] 1 I.R. 154.

decision-making, it may not be negligent not to have particular equipment available.[648]

9-104 **Medical negligence: liability for independent contractors** A series of judgments from the 1950s onwards, in England[649] and elsewhere,[650] suggested that since the central function of a hospital or health authority was to ensure the provision of healthcare to patients, it ought to be directly liable to those patients for any negligence in the performance of that function, without reference to whether the person actually responsible for the negligence was an employee or an independent contractor. These suggestions were emphatically endorsed as correct by the Supreme Court in *Woodland v Swimming Teachers Association*,[651] where it was said that such direct liability was appropriate where (as in the case of a patient) the claimant was dependent on the care or protection of the defendant, there was some antecedent relationship between the parties, and the person at fault had been negligent in the performance of the function assumed by the defendant and delegated to him.[652] It should be emphasised, however, that liability of this kind is limited to negligence in the actual provision of healthcare to patients,[653] and also applies only to organisations that actually undertake the provision of healthcare rather than merely arranging incidentally for its provision by someone else.[654] Nor,

---

648 *Ball v Wirral HA* [2003] Lloyd's Rep. Med. 165 (hospital had only four ventilators and none was made available to a baby who needed one: no negligence in the health authority merely because it did not have more at its disposal).

649 Notably *Cassidy v Ministry of Health* [1951] 2 K.B. 343, 360–362 (Denning LJ's minority judgment); *Roe v Minister of Health* [1954] 2 Q.B. 66, 82 (ditto); *X (Minors) v Bedfordshire County Council* [1995] 2 A.C. 633, 740 (Lord Browne-Wilkinson); *Robertson v Nottingham HA* [1997] 8 Med. L.R. 1, 13 (Brooke LJ); also *M v Calderdale HA* [1998] Lloyd's Rep. Med. 157.

650 See *Commonwealth v Introvigne* (1982) 150 C.L.R. 258, 270, 275 (Gibbs and Murphy LJJ); also *Ellis v Wallsend District Hospital* (1989) 17 N.S.W.L.R. 553 (though cf. the Canadian *Yepremian v Scarborough General Hospital* (1980) 110 D.L.R. (3d) 513).

651 [2013] UKSC 66; [2014] A.C. 537. The case did not concern medical negligence, but this does not affect its authority.

652 See [2013] UKSC 66; [2014] A.C. 537 at [22]–[23] (Lord Sumption); also [34]–[38] (Baroness Hale). For a discussion of the application of these principles to medical negligence see P. Giliker, "Non-delegable duties and institutional liability for the negligence of hospital staff: fair, just and reasonable?" (2017) 33 P.N. 109; but for a sceptical view of Lord Sumption's dicta, note C. Beuermann, "Do Hospitals Owe a So-Called 'Non-Delegable' Duty of Care to Their Patients?" (2018) 26 Med. L. Rev. 1. A county court has duly found that a dental practice owes a non-delegable duty in respect of a dentist who provided services to it as an independent contractor: see *Ramdhean v Agedo* 2020 WL 00620352 (Leeds Cty Ct, 28 January 2020).

653 See Lord Sumption at [2013] UKSC 66; [2014] A.C. 537 at [24]; approving *Farraj v King's Healthcare NHS Trust* [2009] EWCA Civ 1203; [2010] 1 W.L.R. 2139 (hospital not liable for negligence of independent analytical laboratory). For a case where the claimant was a patient and succeeded, see the Irish decision in *Morrissey v Health Service Executive* [2020] IESC 6; [2020] P.N.L.R. 17.

654 [2013] UKSC 66; [2014] A.C. 537 at [19]; approving the result in *A v Ministry of Defence* [2004] EWCA Civ 641; [2005] Q.B. 183 (Ministry not liable for negligence of hospital subcontracted to treat Service families). But the line can be difficult to draw. In so far as prisons and similar institutions undertake, or are required, to provide healthcare to inmates, they are liable for the fault of independent contractors to whom they delegate: *GB v Home Office* [2015] EWHC 819 (QB). However, this is generally not the case today; and as a result prisons are not, it seems, liable for the negligence of independent medical personnel or organisations entrusted by them with prisoner healthcare. See *Razumas v Ministry of Justice* [2018] EWHC 215 (QB); [2018] P.I.Q.R. P10; following the earlier *Morgan v Ministry of Justice* [2010] EWHC 2248 (QB) and distinguishing *GB v Home Office*, above.

it is submitted, does it apply to negligence on the part of a consultant or physician specifically chosen by the patient.[655]

Hospitals and health authorities: negligence and the Human Rights Act 1998. In addition to common law negligence, in certain limited circumstances s.8 of the Human Rights Act 1998 may provide an alternative direct cause of action against a hospital for what is effectively professional negligence, based on either art.2 of the Convention (the right to life)[656] or possibly art.8 (the right to a private life).[657] This will, it seems, be true where (a) the hospital is administered by a body that counts as a public authority; and (b) that patient was in a vulnerable position,[658] for example as a child or mental patient. In such a case it was held by the House of Lords in *Savage v South Essex Partnership NHS Foundation Trust*,[659] and again by the Supreme Court in *Rabone v Pennine Care NHS Foundation Trust*,[660] that art.2 might be engaged if either there had been a systemic failure to guard against a patient's death, or alternatively the hospital had had knowledge of a particular threat and had failed to take proper steps to counter it.[661] 9-105

(f) Medical negligence: the proof of fault

Generally A patient alleging negligence against a medical practitioner has, as we have seen, to prove (1) that his mishap results from an error; and (2) that that error is one that a reasonably skilled and careful practitioner would not have made. It is therefore normally crucial to establish how the mishap occurred, and to produce expert evidence that any error made was a negligent error. In certain cases, however, the claimant may be able to invoke res ipsa loquitur.[662] An inference of negligence will arise against a medical practitioner when an accident occurs which in the ordinary course of things does not happen if the practitioner has exercised reason- 9-106

---

[655] See Lord Sumption at [2013] UKSC 66; [2014] A.C. 537 at [23], limiting liability to cases where the claimant had no substantial say in the selection of the subcontractor. See too *Ellis v Wallsend District Hospital* (1989) 17 N.S.W.L.R. 553.

[656] e.g. if a disturbed patient commits suicide. There is an important point here: under the ECtHR jurisprudence the class of relatives who can complain under art.2 is wide and fairly indeterminate, and goes well beyond those who can sue under the Fatal Accidents Act 1976. This was essentially why the claim in *Rabone v Pennine Care NHS Foundation Trust* [2012] UKSC 2; [2012] 2 A.C. 72, where the claimants were parents of an adult suicide disenfranchised under the 1976 Act, was brought under the Human Rights Act 1998 and not at common law.

[657] On the basis that (for example) attempted self-harm may compromise the patient's subsequent private life. This possibility was mentioned in *K v Central & North West London Mental Health NHS Trust* [2008] EWHC 1217 (QB); [2008] P.I.Q.R. P19 at [73].

[658] For an ordinary patient it seems clear that art.2 is not engaged by mere medical negligence, though possibly it might be in the case of systemic administrative failings. See *Savage v South Essex Partnership NHS Foundation Trust* [2008] UKHL 74; [2009] 1 A.C. 681 at [8]–[11] (Lord Scott) and [91] (Baroness Hale, citing *Powell v United Kingdom* (2000) 30 E.H.R.R. CD362).

[659] [2008] UKHL 74; [2009] 1 A.C. 681 (detained mental patient absconded and threw herself under train: no strikeout of s.8 claim).

[660] [2012] UKSC 2; [2012] 2 A.C. 72. The difference between *Savage* and *Rabone* was that the former case involved a detained patient and the latter a voluntary one, a distinction stated by the Supreme Court in *Rabone* to be irrelevant. See too *Reynolds v United Kingdom* (2012) 55 E.H.R.R. 35 (ECtHR holds UK in breach of art.2 when mental patient fell through inadequately-secured window).

[661] In *Savage v South Essex Partnership NHS Foundation Trust* [2008] UKHL 74; [2009] 1 A.C. 681 it had been said that gross negligence was necessary to engage the state's liability under art.2, but in *Reynolds v United Kingdom* (2012) 55 E.H.R.R. 35 the ECtHR seemingly said that this was too restrictive.

[662] See para.7-203 onwards.

able care and skill.[663] Thus in *Saunders v Leeds Western Health Authority*[664] a cardiac arrest in the course of surgery was held to give rise to an inference of negligence; and it has been said that a swab left in the patient's body would be similarly treated.[665] However, to establish that the occurrence itself is evidence of negligence it must be demonstrated that it is an occurrence which, generally, should not happen. So dislocating the lower jaw in an operation to remove teeth was found to be of itself "by no means proof of negligence"[666]; and evidence that even in a small number of cases what has gone wrong goes wrong despite due care can prevent the application of res ipsa loquitur.[667] Furthermore, the facts must point to negligence on the part of the person sued or his servants; though when the patient is a NHS patient, evidence that any one of the staff employed by the hospital authority has been negligent will establish a prima facie case against the authority.[668] In practice, it is fair to say, it is likely that res ipsa loquitur will be fairly limited in the medical context,[669] and that it will apply rarely, if ever, where the negligence alleged lies in the choice of procedure to be followed.[670]

9-107 Even if res ipsa loquitur applies, the burden of proof of negligence does not as such shift from the claimant.[671] Once an explanation consistent with the exercise of due care is advanced to explain a medical mishap, the issue becomes whether in the light of that explanation, the claimant's injury was more likely than not to have ensued from an absence of care and skill.[672] An attempt in *Clark v MacLennan*[673] by Peter Pain J to develop a much broader doctrine of inference of medical negligence, switching the onus of proof of negligence to the defendant on proof of deviation from normal practice, and the onus of proof of causation on evidence of an injury which normal practice was designed to prevent, was firmly discountenanced by the House of Lords in *Wilsher v Essex Area Health Authority*.[674]

---

663 *Mahon v Osborne* [1939] 2 K.B. 14.
664 (1985) 129 S.J. 225
665 *Mahon v Osborne* [1939] 2 K.B. 14, 50. See too *Cassidy v Ministry of Health* [1951] 2 K.B. 343 (operation for Dupuytren's contraction; hand later found to be paralysed; held, mishap itself constituted evidence of negligence).
666 *Lock v Scantlebury, The Times,* 25 July 1963; *Fish v Kapur* [1948] 2 All E.R. 171.
667 See *Considine v Camp Hill Hospital* (1982) 133 D.L.R. (3d) 11.
668 *Cassidy v Ministry of Health* [1951] 2 K.B. 343. Where a patient is treated privately and cannot pinpoint whether it is the consultant engaged by him or the staff employed by the hospital or clinic who are responsible for the mishap, his action will it seems fail because he cannot prove which defendant is negligent; but cf. *Roe v Ministry of Health* [1954] 2 Q.B. 66, 82 and para.9-103.
669 See *Hussain v King Edward VII Hospital* [2012] EWHC 3441 (QB) at [11]–[12] (Eady J) (appeal dismissed, [2013] EWCA Civ 1863; (2014) 136 B.M.L.R. 54); *Thomas v Curley* [2013] EWCA Civ 117; [2013] Med. L.R. 141 at [10] (Lloyd-Jones LJ).
670 See *Ratcliffe v Plymouth HA* [1998] Lloyd's Rep. Med. 162, 172 (Brooke LJ); cf. *Delaney v Southmead HA* [1995] 6 Med. L.R. 355 and para.7-204.
671 See *Ng Chun Pui v Lee Chuen Tat* [1988] R.T.R. 298 (not a medical negligence case, but still applicable here).
672 *Roe v Minister of Health* [1954] 2 Q.B. 66; *Brazier v Minister of Defence* [1965] 1 Lloyd's Rep. 26.
673 [1983] 1 All E.R. 416.
674 [1988] A.C. 1074.

(g) Medical negligence: causation[675]

(i) General rule

Causation can be difficult to prove in the medical negligence context: nevertheless, with a few exceptions[676] the ordinary rules on causation apply here as elsewhere.[677] It remains for the claimant to establish[678] that the defendants' negligence caused, or at the very least materially contributed to, his injuries. So, for example, in *Barnett v Chelsea & Kensington HMC*[679] a hospital negligently failed to diagnose arsenical poisoning in a patient on arrival and sent him home, whereupon he died. But since it was clear on the evidence that he would still have died even if the poisoning had been diagnosed on arrival, the hospital escaped liability. So too, where a patient is already suffering from some ailment and further negligence ensues causing the same type of ailment, the defendant is liable only to the extent of the exacerbation.[680] 9-108

Causation: several possible causes It is enough on principle that negligence materially contributes to the claimant's injury: the fact that some other cause may have done so as well will not as such prevent the claimant recovering, and recovering in full.[681] However, this situation must be distinguished from the case where injury could have been caused (in the sense of contributed to) by one only of two or more discrete causes, only one of which involved negligence. In such a situation, the claimant will fail if he cannot positively show that the latter was indeed the cause. Thus in *Wilsher v Essex Area Health Authority*[682] a very premature baby was given excess oxygen. He succumbed to an incurable condition of the retina 9-109

675 M.A. Jones, *Medical Negligence*, 5th edn (2018), paras.5-001 to 5-166; also Ch.2.

676 Notably the decision in *Chester v Afshar* [2004] UKHL 41; [2005] 1 A.C. 354, above, para.2-15 onwards.

677 *Wilsher v Essex AHA* [1988] A.C. 1074.

678 The question of what is meant by "establish" raises scientific issues beyond the scope of this book. It is sometimes the practice for claimants when to lead epidemiological or similar evidence that, had proper procedures been followed, the relative risk of what in fact happened would have been reduced below 0.5. This is controversial, particularly in the light of remarks in *Sienkiewicz v Grief (UK) Ltd* [2011] UKSC 10; [2011] 2 A.C. 229; but the practice remains. See *Rich v Hull & East Yorkshire Hospitals NHS Trust* [2015] EWHC 3395 (QB); [2016] Med. L.R. 33 at [142]–[143] (Jay J). For a sceptical approach to the use of statistics, see *Hague v Dalzell* [2016] EWHC 2753 (QB).

679 [1969] 1 Q.B. 428. See too *Holt v Edge* [2007] EWCA Civ 602; (2007) 98 B.M.L.R. 74; *Wootton v J Docter Ltd* [2008] EWCA Civ 1361; [2009] LS Law Med. 63 (wrong, though fairly similar, contraceptive negligently dispensed by mistake: patient became pregnant: no claim in absence of proof that difference in pills contributed to conception); *McCoy v East Midlands Strategic Health Authority* [2011] EWHC 38 (QB); (2011) 118 B.M.L.R. 107 (failure by doctor to notice that CTG trace might indicate possibility of hypoxia and order a retest: but since retest concerned would have done no better, no liability).

680 *Reaney v University Hospital of North Staffordshire NHS Trust* [2015] EWCA Civ 1119; [2016] P.I.Q.R. Q3 (hospital negligently caused pressure sores to be suffered by already incapacitated patient who, as it was, required continuous care).

681 *Williams v Bermuda Hospitals Board* [2016] UKPC 4; [2016] A.C. 888 (existing abdominal sepsis negligently prolonged owing to medical malpractice: sepsis being indivisible, the patient recovered). See too *Bailey v Ministry of Defence* [2008] EWCA Civ 883; [2009] 1 W.L.R. 1052; (2008) 103 B.M.L.R. 134; *Rich v Hull & East Yorkshire Hospitals NHS Trust* [2015] EWHC 3395 (QB); [2016] Med. L.R. 33 at [198]–[212] (Jay J); and *John v Central Manchester NHS Foundation Trust* [2016] EWHC 407 (QB); [2016] 4 W.L.R. 54. See M. Stauch, "'Material Contribution' as a Response to Causal Uncertainty: Time for a Rethink" [2009] C.L.J. 27.

682 [1988] A.C. 1074 (followed in *Rothwell v Raes* (1990) 76 D.L.R. (4th) 280). See too *Kay v Ayrshire*

causing near blindness which, on the evidence, might have resulted from the excess oxygen or any one or more of four other causes. Peter Pain J held that where defendants negligently failed to take precautions, and the very damage that those precautions were designed to guard against occurred, the burden moved to the defendant to prove that the damage did not result from his breach of duty. The House of Lords forcefully disagreed. The onus of proving causation had rested on the claimant throughout; the judge having misdirected himself at first instance, the claim had to be reheard.

9-110 *Wilsher* remains the general rule. However, there seems to be one qualification, arising from a combination of the (non-medical) causation cases of *McGhee v National Coal Board*[683] and *Fairchild v Glenhaven Funeral Services Ltd.*[684] In *McGhee* the pursuer contracted dermatitis from contact with brick dust while working for the defenders, who were held to have been negligent in not providing proper washing facilities. But it was unclear whether the dermatitis was caused by the absence of washing facilities alone, or by the unavoidable levels of ambient brick dust during the working day (for which the defendants were not responsible). Nevertheless the defenders were held liable to the claimant. It is certainly possible to find distinctions between *Wilsher* and *McGhee*.[685] But significantly, a further principle was suggested to exist in *McGhee*: namely that, where a claimant had been injured as a result of a state of affairs and the defendant's negligence had been such as to bring about that state of affairs, then the defendant was liable unless he positively disproved any connection between his fault and the damage suffered.[686] After some doubts,[687] these suggestions were at least partly approved by the House of Lords in *Fairchild v Glenhaven Funeral Services Ltd.*[688] In cases where it was clear what state of affairs had caused the injury, but unclear who had brought about that state of affairs,[689] the burden of proof was indeed on the defendant to exculpate himself if he could.[690] If he could not do so, he would be liable, though possibly only to the extent that his actions had actually contributed to the likelihood of injury.[691] This may matter in certain medical negligence situations. Suppose a claimant undergoes two operations at

and Arran Health Board [1987] 2 All E.R. 417 (where two or more competing causes of injury, no inference to be drawn that the tortious cause was responsible); and note *Collyer v Mid Essex Hospital Services NHS Trust* [2019] EWHC 3577 (QB) at [138]–[140] (claimant must prove that negligence more likely than not caused his injury: not enough to show negligence least unlikely cause).

683 [1973] 1 W.L.R. 1. See also para.2-45.

684 [2002] UKHL 22; [2003] 1 A.C. 32.

685 Notably that in *McGhee* it is arguable that the two possible causes actually combined to injure the pursuer, dermatitis being caused (and worsened) by progressive accumulation of matter on the skin. If so, it follows that the "guilty" dust had positively contributed to the pursuer's injury, which would make the defenders liable on ordinary principles of joint causation. This was not true in *Wilsher*, where it was a question of one cause or another: there was no question of combination between the possible causes.

686 See the opinion of Lord Wilberforce at [1973] 1 W.L.R. 1, 5–6.

687 Notably by Lord Bridge in *Wilsher*: [1988] A.C. 1074, 1088 onwards.

688 [2002] UKHL 22; [2003] 1 A.C. 32: above, para.2-53.

689 The approval of the dicta in *McGhee* seems to have been limited to such cases: see [2002] UKHL 22; [2003] 1 A.C. 32 at 57 (Lord Bingham) and 118 (Lord Rodger). This was of course the situation in *Fairchild* itself, where it was clear that the claimants had been poisoned by asbestos, but unclear which employer's asbestos had been responsible.

690 In *Fairchild* it was accepted that all the potential defendants (previous employers) had been negligent. But this is not essential: see *Barker v Corus (UK) Plc* [2006] UKHL 20; [2006] 2 A.C. 572.

691 Because of *Barker v Corus (UK) Plc* [2006] UKHL 20; [2006] 2 A.C. 572 (which, despite having

the hands of different defendants, in both of which he is not warned about a possible side-effect. If that side-effect eventuates but it is not clear which operation it arose from, then on the basis of *Fairchild* the claimant will be relieved of the necessity of proving that the defendant's operation was responsible.

(ii) Subsequent hypothetical acts

Causation: subsequent hypothetical acts Where medical negligence is shown, the question will frequently arise as to what further actions would have been taken had there been no negligence. For example, if a hospital negligently fails to diagnose a condition affecting a patient, there may be an issue as to what further steps would have been taken had a proper diagnosis been made. In such a case, it is the practice to assume that the claimant would subsequently have been properly treated, and determine causation in that basis. If, on that assumption, the injury would have been suffered anyway, then causation has not been proved, and the possibility that the claimant would have received a higher level of care that that to which he was entitled is disregarded.[692] Thus in *Bolitho v City and Hackney HA*[693] a hospital doctor negligently failed to attend to a sick child, who subsequently suffered brain damage and died. The authority resisted the estate's claim on the basis that even if the doctor had attended, she would have recommended no treatment and the damage would have occurred anyway. The House of Lords held that only if the hypothetical later decision to do nothing would itself have been negligent within the *Bolam* principle would causation be established between the initial negligence and the subsequent injury. In the event the claim failed. On the other hand, where the subsequent actor had to make a genuine choice (for example, as to allocation of scarce intensive care beds in a case of an original negligent failure to request such facilities) there is much to be said for allowing the claimant to recover proportionately on the basis of the loss of a chance.[694] 9-111

The converse of *Bolitho* is, of course, that if it is shown that the person to whom the patient should have been referred would not have given the necessary treatment but would have been negligent in not doing so, the defendant will remain liable.[695] This applies not only where (as in *Bolitho*) the subsequent actor was someone for whose negligence the defendant was itself liable, but also where the subsequent actor was an unconnected third party.[696] The point is illustrated by *Wright v Cambridge Medical Group*.[697] Doctors negligently failed to refer a little girl with a hip infection to a local hospital with sufficient promptness. Immediate 9-112

---

been reversed in the context of mesothelioma claims by the Compensation Act 2006, remains good law in all other cases where the *Fairchild* principle applies: see *International Energy Group Ltd v Zurich Insurance Plc UK* [2015] UKSC 33; [2016] A.C. 509). See paras 4-41 onwards.

692 "In considering how the defendant would have acted in the hypothetical situation, it is assumed that he would have acted in accordance with his obligations to the claimant, but it is also assumed that he will not have gone beyond his duty." See *Smith v NHS Litigation Authority* [2001] Lloyd's Rep. Med. 90 (Andrew Smith J).

693 [1998] A.C. 232. See too *Zarb v Odetoyinbo* [2006] EWHC 2880 (QB); (2006) 93 B.M.L.R. 166.

694 On the basis of the principle in *Allied Maples Ltd v Simmons & Simmons* [1995] 1 W.L.R. 1602; see para.2-78 onwards.

695 See the later *Gouldsmith v Mid Staffordshire General Hospitals NHS Trust* [2007] EWCA Civ 397; [2007] LS Law Med. 363.

696 See Lord Browne-Wilkinson at [1998] A.C. 232, 239–240.

697 [2011] EWCA Civ 669; [2013] Q.B. 312; also *Marshall v Hull & East Yorkshire Hospitals NHS Trust* [2014] EWHC 4326 (QB). See K. Amirthalingam, "Causation and the medical duty to refer" (2012) 128 L.Q.R. 208.

treatment would have cured her: as it was she became disabled. All three members of the Court of Appeal accepted that as a matter of law it was not open to the doctors to escape liability by arguing (as they did) that even if they had referred the claimant on time, the treatment she received would have been incompetent and ineffective and hence they had personally caused her no loss.[698]

(iii) Loss of a chance of recovery

9-113 **Causation: loss of a chance of recovery**[699] A common feature of claims for medical negligence is that an injured claimant can prove no more than that the defendant's fault deprived him of a chance of full recovery, or alternatively that it increased the chance of his succumbing to his present injury. The normal rule here is that this is not enough. In so far as the claimant wishes to recover for a given illness or susceptibility, he must prove on a balance of probability that the defendant's negligence caused it. If he can, he recovers in full. If not he recovers nothing. But what he cannot do in England[700] is allege simply that he has been deprived of a chance of a cure, or of a disease-free future, and then base his claim on the value of that lost chance. Thus in *Hotson v East Berkshire Area Health Authority*[701] the claimant injured his hip and suffered a stoppage of blood-flow; but when he was taken to hospital the defendants negligently failed to diagnose the fact or treat him on time. The lack of blood in due course caused avascular necrosis. The trial judge found that, had the claimant been promptly treated, necrosis might still have followed, but there was a 25 per cent chance that it would not. He duly awarded 25 per cent of full compensation for the claimant's condition[702]; but his decision was reversed in the House of Lords. The claimant had failed to prove, on a balance of probabilities, that the necrosis resulted from the defendants' negligence rather than the natural progression of his original injury.[703] The principle in *Hotson's* case proved controversial[704]; but a majority of the House of Lords upheld it in *Gregg v Scott*.[705] A physician negligently failed to diagnose a cancerous growth. Had he acted properly the patient would have had a 45 per cent chance of a cure, but as it was his chances of recovery were now 20 per cent or less. The judge awarded noth-

---

698 There is some logic to this. If subsequent actual medical negligence does not break the chain of causation between the original injury and the damage (e.g. *Webb v Barclays Bank Plc* [2001] EWCA Civ 1141; [2002] P.I.Q.R. P8), the same should go a fortiori for subsequent hypothetical negligence.

699 M.A. Jones, *Medical Negligence*, 5th edn (2018), paras 5-100 to 5-130.

700 Some American jurisdictions hold the contrary. See, e.g. *Matsuyama v Birnbaum*, 890 NE 2d 819 (2008), where the Supreme Judicial Court of Massachusetts, after exhaustive discussion, allowed recovery.

701 [1987] A.C. 750. See too *Richardson v Kitching* [1995] 6 Med. L.R. 257. The same principle was applied to a failure to warn case in Australia in *Green v Chernoweth* [1998] 2 Qd. R. 572.

702 [1985] 1 W.L.R. 1036.

703 [1987] A.C. 750.

704 For perceptive coverage, see, e.g. H. Reece, "Losses of Chances in the Law" (1996) 59 M.L.R. 188; J. Stapleton "Cause-in-Fact and the Scope of Liability for Consequences" (2003) 119 L.Q.R. 388; J. Edelman, "Loss of a chance" (2013) 21 Torts Law J. 1.

705 [2005] UKHL 2; [2005] 2 A.C. 176. See J. Spencer, "Damages for lost chances: lost for good?" [2005] C.L.J. 282; E. Peel, "Loss of a chance in medical negligence" (2005) 121 L.Q.R. 364. *Gregg v Scott* was ultimately followed by the High Court of Australia in the carefully reasoned *Tabet v Gett* [2010] HCA 12; (2010) 240 C.L.R. 537.

ing, and his decision was upheld. The House agreed with the Court of Appeal[706] that it would be unacceptably radical to regard a lost chance of health as a kind of damage compensable in tort[707] in its own right,[708] and went on to say that the "all-or-nothing" approach operated as much in claimants' as in defendants' favour,[709] and that there was no reason to make an exception to it in medical malpractice suits.[710]

Despite *Hotson* and *Gregg*, however, it is suggested that damages based on the loss of a chance of avoiding a given complaint remain available in two situations. The first is where the question of the outcome of medical negligence depends on the hypothetical later action of a third party. Here, there may be room to apply the principle in *Allied Maples Group Ltd v Simmons & Simmons*.[711] Suppose a doctor negligently fails to refer a patient's suggestive symptoms to an outside specialist. Suppose also that if he had done so there is a 40 per cent chance that the specialist would have decided that the symptoms required treatment. In such a case it is suggested that the patient can recover for loss of that 40 per cent chance.[712] Secondly, when the negligence of the defendants is proved to have resulted in some condition or injury and that condition itself increases the risk of some further illness or disability, the chance of succumbing to that further illness or disability is recoverable on the normal principles relating to the measure of damages, since this is regarded as a matter of quantification and not of liability.[713] Thus where medical negligence results in brain damage carrying, say, a 20 per cent risk of epilepsy later in life, compensation for the original damage will include compensation for the chance of succumbing to epilepsy.[714] 9-114

(iv) Causation and failure to warn

Causation: "failure to warn" cases A patient alleging injury by way of the materialisation of a risk of which he was not and should have been warned must prove that his injury results from that breach of duty. He must thus prove that, had he been warned of the risk, he would not have consented to the treatment.[715] Although there is room for some argument as to whether the criterion here is objective or subjective, it is suggested that the better view is that the sole question is 9-115

706 See [2002] EWCA Civ 1471; (2003) 71 B.M.L.R. 16; also E. Peel "'Loss of a Chance' Revisited: Gregg v Scott" (2004) 66 M.L.R. 623.

707 In *de la Giroday v Brough* (1997) 33 B.C.L.R. (3d) 171 a Canadian court held that if a doctor was sued in contract rather than tort, there was no requirement for proof of loss to complete the cause of action, and there could therefore be recovery for loss of a chance. Despite the apparent logic of this solution, it seems inconceivable that it would be followed in England.

708 [2005] UKHL 2; [2005] 2 A.C. 176 at [85]–[90] (Lord Hoffmann). See too Lord Phillips at [190]: "Awarding damages for the reduction of the prospect of a cure, when the long term result of treatment is still uncertain, is not a satisfactory exercise."

709 [2005] UKHL 2; [2005] 2 A.C. 176 at [195] and [225] (Lady Hale).

710 [2005] UKHL 2; [2005] 2 A.C. 176 at [84] (Lord Hoffmann)

711 [1995] 1 W.L.R. 1602 (a non-medical case but still in point).

712 Accepted, it seems, in *Smith v NHS Litigation Authority* [2001] Lloyd's Rep. Med. 90 (where, however, the claimant failed for other reasons); and apparently also by Lord Hoffmann in *Gregg v Scott* [2005] UKHL 2; [2005] 2 A.C. 176 at [83].

713 See *Gregg v Scott* [2005] UKHL 2; [2005] 2 A.C. 176 at [176] (Lord Phillips).

714 However, even if the claimant has suffered some element of illness this principle does not allow a claim for the loss of the chance of a cure to be dressed up as a claim for consequential loss: *Gregg v Scott* [2005] UKHL 2; [2005] 2 A.C. 176 at [67]–[71] (Lord Hoffmann), [199]–[208] (Lady Hale).

715 *Ferguson v Hamilton Civic Hospitals* (1983) 144 D.L.R. (3d) 219; *White v Turner* (1981) 120 D.L.R. (3d) 269. But note that a court may be fairly ready to infer this in a suitable case: *McAllister v Lewisham HA* [1994] 5 Med. L.R. 343, noted [1995] C.L.J. 30.

whether *this* patient would have consented, the reaction of the hypothetical "reasonable patient" being out of account.[716] A problem may arise where no adequate warning was given of the risks of a given treatment and it is clear that had one been forthcoming the patient would have refused it, but on the evidence he would later have changed his mind and undergone the same treatment, carrying the identical risk. If the risk eventuates, is the injury caused by the failure to warn? In *Chester v Afshar*[717] the House of Lords held that it was. Even if this involved some departure from the normal rules of causation (since the claimant could not argue that, but for the defendant's negligent failure to warn, she would not have incurred the risk[718]), the importance attached to the claimant's right to make an informed decision justified applying a special rule.[719] In addition, it is suggested that a doctor guilty of failure to warn will be liable only for the eventuation of the risk he ought to have warned about. If a doctor causes a patient to undergo treatment by negligently failing to warn him of the risk of laryngeal damage, he should hardly be liable if the patient in fact succumbs to an adverse reaction to the anaesthetic.[720]

(h) Medical negligence: damages

9-116 **Damages in medical negligence cases**[721] Generally speaking,[722] no special principles govern awards of damages in claims for medical negligence. The general

[716] This is consistently assumed in the cases. See, e.g. *Smith v Barking, Havering & Brentwood HA* [1994] 5 Med. L.R. 285; *Smith v Salford HA* [1994] 5 Med. L.R. 321. The point has been specifically decided in this way, after careful canvassing of the arguments, in Australia: *Ellis v Wallsend District Hospital* (1989) 17 N.S.W.L.R. 553. *Contra*, however, in Canada: *Reibl v Hughes* (1980) 114 D.L.R. (3d) 1; and cf. *Smith v Arndt* (1997) 148 D.L.R. (4th) 448.

[717] [2004] UKHL 41; [2005] 1 A.C. 134; R. Heywood, "Informed Consent through the Back Door" [2005] N.I.L.Q. 266. See para.2-15. Note the limits of *Chester*'s case, however. Where a doctor explains treatment in detail but then negligently fails to carry out part of it, causation must be proved in the ordinary way. It is not open to the claimant to dress this up as a case of failure to warn and thus avoid the burden of proving causation: see *Correia v University Hospital of North Staffordshire NHS Trust* [2017] EWCA Civ 356; [2017] E.C.C. 37.

[718] Which may be doubtful. It is hard to see why the claimant should not have succeeded on orthodox causation grounds. She was claiming for injury, not for loss of the chance of avoiding it: cf. *Gregg v Scott* [2005] UKHL 2; [2005] 2 A.C. 176. But for the defendant's failure to warn her she would not have been injured when she was. If she had had the same operation later, there was a 99 per cent chance that she would not have suffered the same injury then. She had therefore proved "but-for" causation on an overwhelming balance of probabilities. See *Marshall v Hull & East Yorkshire Hospitals NHS Trust* [2014] EWHC 4326 (QB) at [79]; also *Crossman v St George's Healthcare NHS Trust* [2016] EWHC 2878 (QB); (2017) 154 B.M.L.R. 204; and *Meadows v Khan* [2017] EWHC 2990 (QB); [2018] 4 W.L.R. 8 at [52]–[55] (Yip J) (appealed on other grounds, [2019] EWCA Civ 152; [2019] 4 W.L.R. 26). In an identical Australian case, *Chappell v Hart* (1998) 72 A.L.J.R. 1344, a majority of the High Court seemingly accepted this point: see at pp.1347–1348 (Gaudron J), 1359 (Gummow J) and 1370 (Kirby J). On this point see P. Cane, "A Warning About Causation" (1999) 115 L.Q.R. 21; M. Stauch, "Taking the Consequences for Failure to Warn of Medical Risks: Chappel v Hart" (2000) 63 M.L.R. 261; and C. Purshouse, "Causation, coincidences and Chester v Afshar" (2017) 33 P.N. 220.

[719] [2004] UKHL 41; [2005] 1 A.C. 134 at [24] (Lord Steyn), [86]–[87] (Lord Hope), [101] (Lord Walker). But the patient bears the burden of proving that he would indeed have put off the treatment: *Duce v Worcestershire Acute Hospitals NHS Trust* [2018] EWCA Civ 1307; [2018] P.I.Q.R. P18. There has been notable reluctance since to extend the case outside medical malpractice: e.g. *White v Paul Davidson & Taylor* [2004] EWCA Civ 1511; [2005] P.N.L.R. 15 at [30]–[35] (Arden LJ).

[720] So held in Australia: *Wallace v Kam* [2013] HCA 19; (2013) 297 A.L.R. 383 (see too Gummow J in *Chappell v Hart* (1998) 72 A.L.J.R. 1344, 1357). cf. the non-medical decision in *Darby v National Trust* [2001] EWCA Civ 189; [2001] P.I.Q.R. P27.

[721] M.A. Jones, *Medical Negligence*, 5th edn (2018), Ch.12.

principles relating to the measure of damages in claims for personal injuries apply.[723] Psychiatric injury can be compensated in a suitable case.[724] Where that very kind of harm is the type of harm against which the professional undertook to safeguard the patient, damages for mental distress will be recoverable. Thus it was held in *Kralj v McGrath*[725] that damages for a grossly mismanaged childbirth could include compensation for the mother's shock and distress at losing her child.[726] Where medical negligence causes no actual injury, there is of course no cause of action in negligence.[727] However, it should be noted that where the negligence amounts to a breach of a claimant's entitlements under the Human Rights Act, then there may be scope for an award of damages on a more generous basis than otherwise available under the ordinary rules of English law.[728]

3. Law[729]

(a) General

A technical distinction must be drawn here between solicitors and barristers. It is clear that solicitors owe duties to their clients in both contract and tort.[730] Barristers are in a slightly different position, since there is presumptively[731] no contract between a barrister and his lay client: nevertheless, it is now abundantly clear that this does not bar an action in the tort of negligence.[732] Prima facie, therefore, a bar- **9-117**

---

722 There are of course exceptions: see, e.g. the failed sterilisation cases, para.9-96 onwards.

723 Ch.27.

724 *Farrell v Avon HA* [2001] Lloyd's Rep. Med. 458 (father has claim for psychiatric injury as primary victim on being falsely told baby dead and given wrong deceased infant to cuddle); *Froggatt v Chesterfield and North Derbyshire Royal Hospital NHS Trust* [2002] All E.R. (D) 218 (Dec) (unnecessary mastectomy: husband and son recover for psychiatric injury caused as a result). See too *B v South Tyneside Healthcare Trust* [2004] EWHC 1169 (QB); [2004] Lloyd's Rep. Med. 505 (psychiatric injury after birth of malformed foetus, though no negligence on the facts).

725 [1986] 1 All E.R. 54.

726 See too *Williamson v East London & City HA* [1998] Lloyd's Rep. Med. 6 (distress at loss of breast). See too *Landau v Werner* (1961) 105 S.J. 1008 CA (psychiatrist improperly having sexual relations with patient).

727 A point neatly illustrated by the Northern Irish decision in *A v A Health and Social Services Trust* [2011] NICA 28; [2012] N.I. 77 (child born coloured rather than white owing to allegedly negligent mix-up of donors' sperm: no compensable damage). See O. Buttler, "Remedying wrongs in IVF negligence: grasping the nettle?" (2011) 127 L.Q.R. 203 (on the first instance decision, to the same effect); and S. Sheldon, "Only skin deep? The harm of being born a different colour to one's parents" (2011) 19 Med. L. Rev. 657.

728 This may arise in particular in two cases. In *McGlinchey v United Kingdom* [2003] Lloyd's Rep. Med. 264 inadequate medication was provided to a prisoner, which broke his rights under art.3 of the ECHR (inhuman or degrading treatment) but was not actionable in England because he suffered no injury as a result. The ECtHR upheld the complaint and awarded a fairly modest sum by way of compensation. No doubt were this to happen again there would be an award under s.8 of the 1998 Act. And in *Rabone v Pennine Care NHS Foundation Trust* [2012] UKSC 2; [2012] 2 A.C. 72 it was held that in the event of a death that also amounted to infringement by the state of the right to life under art.2 ECHR, compensation had to be made available to a more generous class of claimants than provided for in the Fatal Accidents Act 1976. See generally A. Tettenborn, "Wrongful Death, Human Rights and the Fatal Accidents Act" (2012) 128 L.Q.R. 327.

729 See *Jackson & Powell on Professional Liability*, 8th edn (2017) Chs 11 and 12.

730 See para.9-119.

731 But note the Courts and Legal Services Act 1990 s.61, allowing barristers to enter into contractual relations if they wish. In practice this dispensation is hardly if ever invoked.

732 *Rondel v Worsley* [1969] 1 A.C. 191, 232 (Lord Reid), 246–247 (Lord Morris), 281 (Lord Upjohn).

rister, like any other professional person, is under a tortious duty to exercise a reasonable degree of skill and care in his professional undertakings.[733]

(b) Duties owed by lawyers

(i) Duties to clients

9-118 **Duties owed to clients** When a solicitor is engaged for reward[734] there is no doubt as to the existence of a contractual duty to exercise skill and care on behalf of his client.[735] Nor is there now any doubt that, even in the absence of a contract, a solicitor who gratuitously offers his services to a client on a professional basis owes a similar duty in tort to that client.[736] A solicitor may be liable for the negligence of an agent employed by him in the discharge of his central functions (for example, where under the old practice country solicitors appoint London agents to conduct litigation on their behalf[737]). He is not, however, answerable for the acts of other professional advisers whom he consults on behalf of his client,[738] unless he is guilty of personal fault in failing to supervise them.[739]

9-119 **Duties to client in tort and contract**[740] It was once thought that a solicitor in a contractual relationship with his client owed no parallel duty in tort.[741] But this view was decisively rejected by Oliver J in *Midland Bank v Hett, Stubbs & Kemp*[742] on

---

See too *Saif Ali v Sydney Mitchell & Co* [1980] A.C. 198.

733 *Saif Ali v Sydney Mitchell & Co* [1980] A.C. 198, 215 (Lord Wilberforce), 210–219 (Lord Diplock), 231 (Lord Salmon).

734 Including, it is submitted, a solicitor acting for a legally-aided client, even if his contribution be nil, and a solicitor paid for by a third party, such as an insurance company or trade union.

735 See *Nocton v Lord Ashburton* [1914] A.C. 932, 956 (Lord Haldane).

736 A point made abundantly clear by Lord Neuberger MR in *Padden v Bevan Ashford Solicitors* [2011] EWCA Civ 1616; [2012] 1 W.L.R. 1759 at [41] (inadequate advice to wife called upon to charge her property for husband's liability; fact that solicitors advised free of charge did not lighten onerous duty placed on them). Note, however, that the distinction between tort and contract may continue to be significant to liability, especially where the complaint is failure to advise, since there can be no duty to do so unless and until a retainer, or some similar arrangement, exists. See *Aroca Seiquer y Asociados v Adams* [2018] EWCA Civ 1589; [2018] P.N.L.R. 32, where the point was accepted (though a contract of retainer was in the event found).

737 *Simmons v Rose* (1862) 31 Beav. 1. The practice is obsolescent but not entirely extinct. This head of liability may now be best explained as based on the liability of a service provider undertaking to look after a client's interests for any negligence taking place in the service provided by him, whether the party at fault be himself, a servant or an independent contractor: cf. *Woodland v Swimming Teachers Association* [2013] UKSC 66; [2014] A.C. 537, and para.6-67.

738 *Gregory v Shepherds* [2000] P.N.L.R. 769 (no liability as such for negligence of Spanish lawyer in handling Spanish conveyancing transaction on instructions of English solicitor). Compare *Phelps v Stewarts (A Firm)* [2007] EWHC 1561 (Ch); [2007] P.N.L.R. 32 (same result in relation to negligent tax consultant engaged by solicitors). It is suggested that the results in these cases are unaffected by the decision in *Woodland v Swimming Teachers Association* [2013] UKSC 66; [2014] A.C. 537 (see the previous note), since tax consultancy and foreign legal services are not part of the core services undertaken by solicitors.

739 As in *Gregory v Shepherds* [2000] P.N.L.R. 769 (English solicitors liable for own negligence in failing to check whether Spanish lawyer had completed necessary paperwork).

740 See para.9-06.

741 e.g. *Groom v Crocker* [1939] 1 K.B. 194; *Clark v Kirby-Smith* [1964] 1 Ch. 506.

742 [1979] Ch. 384. For vigorous, but ultimately unsuccessful, criticism, see J. Kaye, "The Liability of Solicitors in Tort" (1984) 100 L.Q.R. 680.

the basis that it was inconsistent with *Hedley Byrne v Heller*[743] and *Esso Petroleum Co Ltd v Mardon*[744]; and Oliver J's opinion has since been accepted by the House of Lords.[745] It follows that any solicitor acting for reward now owes concurrent duties in contract and tort—a matter that may be of some importance in, for example, limitation cases. Barristers presumptively have no contract with their clients,[746] but there is now no doubt that they do owe them a duty in tort.[747]

Duties to clients: trustees and personal representatives Solicitors or barristers instructed by trustees or personal representatives are prima facie regarded as acting for them alone; it is they who are the client, and no-one else. It follows from this that in general a lawyer owes no duty, whether in contract or in tort, to the beneficiaries of the trust or the heirs, and hence that any proceedings for negligence must be brought by the trustees or representatives.[748] Conversely, the benefit of a duty owed by a solicitor to a living person will not generally pass or be available to that person's personal representatives.[749] 9-120

(ii) Duties to third parties[750]

Duties to non-clients Prima facie a lawyer's professional duty is owed to his client alone.[751] Nevertheless, this is by no means an absolute rule, and there is no reason why, in a suitable case where there is adequate proximity between the parties, he should not also owe a duty in tort to a third party. Despite some discourag- 9-121

743 [1964] A.C. 465. See also *Chittick v Maxwell* (1993) 118 A.L.R. 728.

744 [1976] Q.B. 801.

745 *Henderson v Merrett Syndicates Ltd* [1995] 2 A.C. 145 (strictly speaking, this case concerned Lloyds agents and not solicitors: but Oliver J's judgment in *Hett, Stubbs & Kemp* was specifically approved). The Court of Appeal had earlier reached the same view: *Forster v Outred & Co* [1982] 1 W.L.R. 86

746 Though they may, if they wish, enter into such contracts: Courts and Legal Services Act 1990 s.61(1). Few, if any, do.

747 Since *Saif Ali v Sydney Mitchell & Co* [1980] A.C. 198; see now *Hall (Arthur JS) & Co v Simons* [2002] 1 A.C. 615, para.9-137 below.

748 See *Roberts v Gill & Co.* [2010] UKSC 22; [2011] 1 A.C. 240; and the earlier decisions in *Yeatman v Yeatman* (1887) 7 Ch. D. 210; and *Re Field* [1971] 1 W.L.R. 555. As for the measure of damages see below, para.9-157. Presumably, however, there is nothing to stop a lawyer expressly or impliedly accepting a duty of care directly to the beneficiary. cf. the Scots decision in *Marquess of Aberdeen and Temair v Turcan Connell* [2008] CSOH 183; [2009] P.N.L.R. 18 (both trustee and landowner beneficiary clients of solicitors).

749 *Reader v Molesworths Bright Clegg* [2007] EWCA Civ 169; [2007] 1 W.L.R. 1082 (duty of solicitors to litigant to watch for end of limitation period did not comport duty similarly to advise his estate after his death). See too the Scots decision in *McLeod v Crawford* [2010] CSOH 101; 2011 S.C.L.R. 133 (solicitors acting for moribund personal injury client not liable for settling claim outright, rather than provisionally, so as to protect dependants' interests were he to die shortly afterwards (as happened)).

750 See Jackson & Powell on *Professional Liability*, 8th edn (2017), para.11-043 onwards; also S. Whittaker, "Privity of contract and the tort of negligence" (1996) 16 O.J.L.S. 191; J. Dwyer, "Solicitors' Duty in Tort to Persons Other Than Their Clients" (1994) 2 Tort L. Rev. 29.

751 *Yeatman v Yeatman* (1887) 7 Ch. D. 210; *White v Jones* [1995] 2 A.C. 207, 256 (Lord Goff). See also *Roberts v Gill & Co.* [2010] UKSC 22; [2011] 1 A.C. 240; and *Whitehead v Hibbert Pownall & Newton (a firm)* [2008] EWCA Civ 285; [2009] 1 W.L.R. 549 (solicitor instructed specifically by mother to bring proceedings in respect of birth of handicapped child: mother unexpectedly dies: solicitor owes no duty to child's father to advise as to the possibility of continuing the claim); also *Connaught Income Fund, Series 1 (In liquidation) v Hewetts* [2016] EWHC 2286 (Ch) (solicitors instructed by buyer of commercial property owed no general duty to investment scheme providing funds to buyer); and *Joseph v Farrer & Co LLP* [2017] EWHC 2072 (Ch); [2018] P.N.L.R. 1 at [36].

ing older authorities,[752] in 1979 Megarry J in *Ross v Caunters*[753] had no difficulty in accepting this point. Hence he held solicitors liable to a claimant when they drew up a will naming her as a beneficiary but failed to warn the testator that the claimant would lose the legacy if her spouse witnessed the will. "A solicitor," he said, "who is instructed by his client to carry out a transaction that will confer a benefit on an identifiable third party owes a duty of care towards that third party in carrying out that transaction".[754] In Ross Megarry J founded the duty alternatively on an extension of the *Hedley Byrne* principle or, more probably, a direct application of the principle in *Donoghue v Stevenson*.[755] Of these two the former seems more convincing, but in most cases it is probably better today to apply the general principles of negligence law under such cases as *Caparo Plc v Dickman*.[756]

9-122 **Duties to third parties: will cases** The majority of the third party cases concern negligence in and about the execution of wills and gifts. Although the principle of liability was laid down in *Ross v Caunters*,[757] the leading case is now *White v Jones*.[758] A dilatory solicitor, instructed by a testator to draw up a will in favour of the claimants, failed to do so, whereupon the client died and the claimants received nothing.[759] The House of Lords, by a majority, held the claimants entitled to recover the would-be legacy from the solicitor.[760] Lord Goff, while accepting the general principle that a solicitor owed no duty to those other than his client,[761] pointed out that the solicitor had obviously failed to effectuate the testator's intentions[762]; that even if the client himself had suffered no loss justice seemed to demand a remedy[763]; that it was not an insuperable objection that the loss was merely economic[764]; and that there was little danger of over-extended liability.[765]

9-123 The principle in *White v Jones* has been refined in a number of decisions. There is no doubt that it covers simple misdrafting,[766] and in addition failure to check a

---

[752] Notably the House of Lords' decision in the Scots appeal of *Robertson v Fleming* (1861) 4 Macq. 167.

[753] [1980] 1 Ch. 297. See now *White v Jones* [1995] 2 A.C. 207, below.

[754] See [1980] 1 Ch. 297, 322; also *Al-Kandari v JR Brown & Co* [1988] Q.B. 665, 671–672 (Lord Donaldson MR).

[755] See [1980] 1 Ch. 297, 322; also pp.314–315.

[756] [1990] 2 A.C. 605. As Lord Goff observed in *White v Jones* [1995] 2 A.C. 207, 267–268, it is difficult to construct any meaningful assumption of responsibility by a solicitor to a potential beneficiary under a will he is drafting.

[757] [1980] 1 Ch. 297.

[758] [1995] 2 A.C. 207 (upheld in Australia in *Hill v Van Erp* (1997) 188 C.L.R. 159). See too *Feltham v Freer Bouskell* [2013] EWHC 1952 (Ch); [2014] P.N.L.R. 2 (delay in preparing will caused beneficiary to draw up home-made will, which had to be expensively defended in court); T. Rosen Peacocke, "The remedy in White v Jones cases: smoothing the analytical wrinkles' (2008) 24(3) P.N. 138.

[759] And cf. *Hawkins v Clayton* (1988) 79 A.L.R. 69 (solicitor with custody of will bound to bring death of testator to notice of executor, and liable in negligence to the latter when he did not).

[760] In this connection note also *Feltham v Freer Bouskell* [2013] EWHC 1952 (Ch); [2014] P.N.L.R. 2, where it was suggested at [99] onwards that where the loss to the claimant depended in any way on the hypothetical action of the testator, an award should be made on a "loss of a chance" basis.

[761] [1995] 2 A.C. 207, 256.

[762] [1995] 2 A.C. 207, 260.

[763] [1995] 2 A.C. 207, 259–260.

[764] [1995] 2 A.C. 207, 268.

[765] [1995] 2 A.C. 207, 269.

[766] *Horsfall v Haywards* [1999] P.N.L.R. 583 (instructions to leave to X for life, remainder to Y; will in fact left to X absolutely). Note that there is no need to show that the would-be testator's desire to

will for due execution when returned.[767] In *Carr-Glyn v Frearsons*[768] it was extended to cover failure to warn a testatrix that where she left her interest in a house held on joint tenancy to a legatee, it would be necessary to sever the joint tenancy to make the gift effective. On the other hand, it is also clear that the duty is subject to a number of important qualifications. First, it is limited to a duty to ensure execution of the testator's instructions. It has thus been held not to extend to a failure to advise further about how to minimise adverse tax consequences,[769] or as to whether the instructions reflected what the testator actually might have wanted.[770] Nor, it seems, will a solicitor be liable to a would-be beneficiary if he wrongly advises the testator that a bequest to him is impossible in law.[771] It has also been said that in so far as a disappointed legatee has a right to rectify the testator's will, he must take reasonable steps to do so and if he does not his claim may fail for lack of mitigation[772]; but this, with respect, is highly doubtful.[773] Secondly, in *Worby v Rosser*[774] it was held to be owed only to the would-be legatee or beneficiary. Hence a solicitor drafting a will for a client who he allegedly should have known was in fact incompetent was held not liable to legatees under a previous, valid, will for their expenses of establishing their entitlement. Thirdly, no duty will be owed where the solicitor would have been liable to the estate, so as to avoid the problem of double liability.[775]

Duties to third parties: gift cases The *White v Jones* principle has been held not to extend to the misdrafting of an inter vivos gift or promise[776] or other negligent 9-124

benefit the legatee continued until his death: *Humblestone v Martin Tolhurst Partnership* [2004] EWHC 151 (Ch); [2004] P.N.L.R. 26.

767 *Humblestone v Martin Tolhurst Partnership* [2004] EWHC 151 (Ch); [2004] P.N.L.R. 26. See too *Martin v Triggs Turner Bartons* [2009] EWHC 1920 (Ch); [2010] P.N.L.R. 3 (costs of a failed attempt at rectification of the will may be recoverable).

768 [1999] Ch. 326; followed in *Vagg v McPhee* [2013] NSWCA 29; (2013) 85 N.S.W.L.R. 154. See A. Brierly and R. Kerridge, "Will making and the avoidance of negligence claims" [1999] Conv. 399.

769 *Cancer Research Campaign v Ernest Brown* [1998] P.N.L.R. 592. Nor yet how to frustrate a claim by a third party under the family provision legislation: *Badenach v Calvert* [2016] HCA 18; (2016) A.L.J.R. 610.

770 *Littlewood v Wilkinson Woodward (A Firm)* [2009] P.N.L.R. 29.

771 So held in Scotland: *Fraser v McArthur Stewart* [2008] CSOH 159; 2009 S.L.T. 31; [2009] P.N.L.R. 13.

772 *Walker v Medlicott* [1999] 1 W.L.R. 727.

773 Since in general it is not open to a defendant sued for damages to argue that the claimant should, however reasonably, have recouped his loss from someone else liable to palliate it or make it good: see in particular *Peters v East Midlands Health Authority* [2009] EWCA Civ 145; [2010] Q.B. 48; and *Haugesund Kommune v Depfa ACS Bank* [2010] EWHC 227 (Comm); [2010] P.N.L.R. 21 (reversed on other grounds, [2011] EWCA Civ 33; [2011] 3 All E.R. 655).

774 [2000] P.N.L.R. 140. See too *Gibbons v Nelsons* [2000] P.N.L.R. 734 (failure to warn that will had effect of exercising power of appointment: no duty to those entitled in default of exercise); also *Sutherland v Public Trustee* [1980] 2 N.Z.L.R. 536.

775 *Carr-Glyn v Frearsons* [1999] Ch. 326 (where, however, it was held that there was no possibility of double liability); and cf. *Corbett v Bond Pearce* [2001] EWCA Civ 531; [2001] 3 All E.R. 769. See generally J. O'Sullivan, "Solicitors, Executors and Beneficiaries: Who can sue and be sued?" (2003) 19 P.N. 494.

776 *Hemmens v Wilson Browne & Co* [1995] Ch. 223, following suggestions by Lord Goff in *White v Jones* [1995] 2 A.C. 207, 262; J. O'Sullivan, "Professional liability to third parties for inter vivos transactions" (2005) 21 P.N. 142. The ostensible reason is that the would-be donor could always have changed his mind, and hence causation was not established. Sed quaere. If the evidence was that the donor would not have changed his mind, why logically should this make any difference? Compare the Scots decision in *Steven v Hewats* [2013] CSOH 61; [2013] P.N.L.R. 22 refusing despite *Hem-*

failure to make it effective.[777] So where a rich man instructed solicitors to make arrangements for regular munificent gifts by his trustees to a lover, no duty was imposed vis-à-vis ther latter to take steps to make the arrangement irrevocable.[778]

9-125 **Duties to third parties: conveyancing transactions** There is no doubt that a solicitor undertaking conveyancing may owe a duty to some third parties, especially those whose interests are not opposed to his client's.[779] However, owing to the opposed interests of the parties to a conveyancing transaction, it is rare for duties to be owed by one party's solicitor to the other party.[780] The only case where a duty is owed is, it seems, where specific information is given in circumstances indicating an acceptance of responsibility for its correctness.[781] Whether answers to enquiries before contract come in this category is unclear. In *Gran Gelato Ltd v Richcliff (Group) Ltd*[782] it was held that they did not; however, later decisions, with some justification, have thrown some doubt on this,[783] and it should be noted that in *First National Commercial Bank Plc v Loxleys*[784] the Court of Appeal refused to strike out a claim on very similar facts. Outside such situations, the position seems clear: no duty will be owed. In the Scots case of *Steel v NRAM Ltd*[785] solicitors for a borrower who had paid off part of a loan on the basis that an appropriate part of the security would be released inadvertently drafted and sent to the lenders a release of the entire security. The lenders equally inadvertently executed it; the borrower later collapsed, leaving the lenders unsecured. The lenders sued the solicitors for negligence: but the Supreme Court, reversing the Inner House, held that no duty had existed. It was, it was said, inappropriate in the circumstances to expect solicitors for one side in a conveyancing transactiuon to take care to protect the interests of the other.[786]

9-126 **Duties to third parties: other cases** In general, whether a lawyer is liable to a third party for negligence depends on whether his obligation vis-à-vis his client can be said to be undertaken or imposed for the benefit of that third party. Normally it will not.[787] For instance, in the ordinary course of adversarial litigation[788] or negotia-

---

mens to dismiss a claim by a donee inter vivos in respect of misdrafting by a solicitor which caused the gift to be chargeable to IHT on the donor's subsequent death.

777 *Joseph v Farrer & Co LLP* [2017] EWHC 2072 (Ch); [2018] P.N.L.R. 1.

778 *Joseph v Farrer & Co LLP* [2017] EWHC 2072 (Ch); [2018] P.N.L.R. 1.

779 See, e.g. *Dean v Allin & Watts* [2001] EWCA Civ 758; [2001] P.N.L.R. 39 (duty to client's lender to ensure lender's security not affected by invalidity).

780 *Gran Gelato Ltd v Richcliff (Group) Ltd* [1992] Ch. 560, 570 (Nicholls V-C; see too *P&P Property Ltd v Owen White & Catlin LLP* [2018] EWCA Civ 1082; [2019] Ch. 273 (solicitor for fraudulent seller owed no duty to defrauded buyer).

781 cf. *Edwards v Lee*, *The Times*, 5 November 1991 (solicitor gave clean reference to other party on client he knew to have 13 fraud charges outstanding).

782 [1992] Ch. 560; cf. *Wilson v Bloomfield* (1979) 123 S.J. 860. It should be noted that *Gran Gelato* was cited without adverse comment by by Lord Wilson JSC in *Steel v NRAM Ltd* [2018] UKSC 13; [2018] 1 W.L.R. 1190 at [29].

783 See *McCullagh v Lane Fox & Partners Ltd* [1996] P.N.L.R. 205, 227 onwards (Hobhouse LJ). Note also that Gran Gelato has been disowned in Ireland (*Doran v Delaney* [1998] 2 I.L.R.M. 1) and strongly doubted in Australia (*Bebonis v Angelos* [2003] NSWCA 13; (2003) 56 N.S.W.L.R. 12).

784 [1997] P.N.L.R. 211.

785 [2018] UKSC 13; [2018] 1 W.L.R. 1190. See E. Gordon, "Out with the old, in with the older? Hedley Byrne reliance takes centre stage" [2018] C.L.J. 251.

786 See [2018] UKSC 13; [2018] 1 W.L.R. 1190 at [25]–[32].

787 *White v Jones* [1995] 2 A.C. 207, 256 (Lord Goff).

tion,[789] or where parties' interests are otherwise opposed,[790] no duty is owed to the client's adversary. Hence in *Connolly-Martin v Davis*[791] a barrister who advised his clients, wrongly, that they were not bound by an undertaking to preserve the funds in dispute was held to owe no duty to the other side. Nor is the unwillingness to acknowledge a duty limited to contentious business. A solicitor, for instance, who is duped into registering a forged mortgage release at the behest of a dishonest mortgagor owes no duty to the creditor.[792] So too in *Clarke v Bruce Lance & Co*[793] the Court of Appeal held that a solicitor who had acted for the testator in drawing up a will in which the claimant was a beneficiary owed no duty to the claimant when acting for the testator in another transaction which had the effect of diminishing the value of the claimant's benefit under the will.[794]

However, even in the case of parties whose interests may be opposed, if a solicitor assumes a duty independent of his role as one party's adviser, which is intended to protect, or to confer a benefit on, the other party, he may still owe a duty to that other party. In general, it is submitted that a solicitor will owe a duty of care to a third party where either (1) there is identity of interest between the client and the third party, and the performance of the duty to the client is intended to benefit the third party; or (2) he gives advice or information, intending that a person other than the client act on that advice or information, without other independent professional advice; or (3) he has specifically undertaken a responsibility to the third party independent from his status as the client's adviser. **9-127**

Thus lawyers drafting a tax avoidance scheme for a husband may owe a duty to the chief beneficiary, his wife[795]; and the same may possibly apply to those advising on inheritance tax vis-à-vis the beneficiaries who stand to gain (or lose).[796] Again, solicitors instructed by a borrower to arrange secured lending have been held to owe a duty to the lender to ensure the security is effective.[797] Similarly, a lawyer apparently instructed on behalf of a given person owes a duty to that person to take **9-128**

---

788 *Business Computers International Ltd v Registrar of Companies* [1988] Ch. 229; *New Zealand Social Credit Political League Inc v O'Brien* [1984] 1 N.Z.L.R. 84; *German v Major* (1985) 20 D.L.R. (4th) 703.

789 e.g. *Clarke v Bruce Lance & Co* [1988] 1 W.L.R. 881 (will); *Gran Gelato Ltd v Richcliff Group Ltd* [1992] Ch. 560, *Allied Finance v Haddow* [1983] N.Z.L.R. 22 (conveyancing); also the New Zealand decision in *Burmeister v O'Brien* [2010] 2 N.Z.L.R. 395 and the Scottish *Frank Houlgate Investment Co Ltd v Biggart Baillie LLP* [2011] CSOH 160; [2012] P.N.L.R. 2 (solicitors duped into acting for fraudster: no duty of care to counterparty, the victim of the fraud). See also *Kamahap Enterprises v Chu's Central Market Ltd* (1989) 64 D.L.R. (4th) 167; *Collins Borrow v Bank of Montreal* [1987] 1 W.W.R. 755.

790 *Edenwest Ltd v CMS Cameron McKenna (A Firm)* [2012] EWHC 1258 (Ch); [2013] B.C.C. 152 (solicitors to receiver owe no duty to company); see too the Australian case of *Lee v Abedian* [2016] QSC 92; [2017] 1 Qd.R. 549 (solicitor for one side in property deal preparing report suggesting fraud by other party: no duty of care).

791 [1999] P.N.L.R. 826.

792 *Chief Land Registrar v Caffrey & Co* [2016] EWHC 161 (Ch); [2016] P.N.L.R. 23.

793 [1988] 1 W.L.R. 881.

794 A further consideration was that this was not a case where if there was negligence there was no other effective remedy; [1988] 1 W.L.R. 881 at 889.

795 *Matthew v Maughold Life Assurance Co Ltd* [1955–95] P.N.L.R. 309; cf. *Re Foster* (1985) 129 S.J. 333 (solicitors instructed to register company charge owe duty to guarantors of company's liability thereby accelerated). See also *Daniels v Thompson* [2004] EWCA Civ 307; [2004] P.N.L.R. 33 (negligent IHT advice: CA left open the possibility of action by beneficiaries of estate). There seems no reason why liability analogous to *White v Jones* [1995] 2 A.C. 207 should not apply here.

796 *Rind v Theodore Goddard (A Firm)* [2008] EWHC 459 (Ch); [2008] P.N.L.R. 24; cf. *Steven v Hewats* [2013] CSOH 61; [2013] P.N.L.R. 22 (mishandling of lifetime gift with dire IHT consequences).

797 *Dean v Allin & Watts* [2001] EWCA Civ 758; [2001] P.N.L.R. 39 (security failed under Law of

reasonable precautions to check the authenticity of those instructions[798]; and a solicitor giving a formal reference on his client's trustworthiness to the other side in, say, a conveyancing transaction remains under a duty to take care in what he says.[799] Yet another example is *Al-Kandari v JR Brown & Co.*[800] The defendants, who acted for the husband in contested custody proceedings, gave an undertaking to the court to retain their client's passport and not to release it to him without the court's consent. They broke the undertaking; the husband, armed with the passport, kidnapped the claimant wife and their children, and removed the latter to Kuwait. The defendants were held to owe a duty to the claimant which they breached by not warning her of the risk that arose once the passport was no longer in their hands.

(iii) Duties as trustee or under the law of trusts

9-129 **Liability under the law of trusts** In addition to any duties in contract or tort, a lawyer may owe a duty to a client as trustee of the latter's funds. This arises particularly[801] where the solicitor for a purchaser or mortgage lender is entrusted with the price or mortgage monies for transmission to the vendor.[802] In such a case the solicitor's duty is to disburse the monies according to his instructions or account for them to the client: if he fails to do this, he is presumptively liable for breach of trust,[803] whether he disburses the funds at the wrong time,[804] omits to ap-

Property (Miscellaneous Provisions) Act 1989 s.2).

798 *Al-Sabah v Ali* [1999] E.G.C.S. 11 (impostor forged claimant's signature and instructed solicitors to dispose of her property: solicitors liable to claimant for expenses of re-establishing title). See too *Penn v Bristol & West Building Society* [1997] 1 W.L.R. 1356 (similar); *Johnson v Bingley Dyson & Finney* [1997] P.N.L.R. 392 (duty of solicitor to verify authenticity of enduring power of attorney under which instructions given); *Esser v Brown* (2003) 223 D.L.R. (4th) 560 (notary instructed to sell property by one co-owner acting in fraud of the other: held to owe duty to latter).

799 cf. *Edwards v Lee*, *The Times*, 5 November 1991 (solicitor gave clean reference on client he knew to have 13 fraud charges outstanding; no defence that this was information received in confidence from the client). *Aliter* with a less formal enquiry, which would perhaps not give rise to a "special relationship" at all: cf. *Ouwens v Ace Builders P/L* (1989) 59 S.A.S.R. 54 (no liability in solicitors answering unconnected claimant's "arm's length" questions about client's inheritance).

800 [1988] Q.B. 665; cf. *Klingspon v Ramsey* [1985] 5 W.W.R. 411 and the Singapore decision in *Anwar v Ng Chong* [2014] SGCA 34; [2014] 3 S.L.R. 761 (solicitors instructed to draft loan without client's son's guarantee disobeyed instruction: liable to son) (criticised, A. Kum et al, "The conceptual basis of the solicitor's liability to a third party" (2016) 32 P.N. 32).

801 But not exclusively. The same position can equally arise with a straightforward express trust (as in *Daniel v Tee* [2016] EWHC 1538 (Ch); [2016] 4 W.L.R. 115; and *Levack v Philip Ross & Co (a firm)* [2019] EWHC 762 (Comm); [2019] P.N.L.R. 20), or with monies held pending a loan to any other borrower against security over its assets. See, e.g. *Gabriel v Little* [2013] EWCA Civ 1513; (2013) 16 I.T.E.L.R. 567 (though no such trust was found on the facts) (the point did not feature on appeal in *BPE Solicitors v Hughes-Holland* [2017] UKSC 21; [2018] A.C. 599).

802 This is not the only case. The same position can equally arise with, for instance, monies held for loan to a company against security over the company's assets (e.g. *Bellis v Challinor* [2015] EWCA Civ 59; [2016] W.T.L.R. 43; or held against payment for services (*Chang v Mishcon de Reya* [2015] EWHC 164 (Ch)) (though in neither case was a trust found to exist on the facts).

803 See para.9-21; *Target Holdings Ltd v Redferns* [1996] A.C. 421; *Lloyds TSB Bank Plc v Markandan & Uddin* [2012] EWCA Civ 65; [2012] 2 All E.R. 884); *Nationwide Building Society v Davisons Solicitors* [2012] EWCA Civ 1626; [2013] P.N.L.R. 12). It should be noted, however, that mere negligence in protecting the client's interest, for instance by failing to notice matters that might raise suspicions and warn the client of them, is not covered: here liability is simply for negligence. See *Bristol & West Building Society v Mothew* [1998] Ch. 1; and *Birmingham Midshires Building Society v Infields* (1999) 66 Con. L.R. 20.

804 *Target Holdings Ltd v Redferns* [1996] A.C. 421.

ply them to pay off prior charges,[805] transfers them to impostors not entitled to receive them,[806] or pays them over against a forged transfer.[807] Where such a breach is committed his duty is not strictly to compensate the beneficiary for his net loss, as in tort,[808] as to restore the trust monies so as to put the trust fund in the position it would have occupied had the terms of the trust been observed.[809] However, in practice the measure of compensation is in most cases much the same,[810] and indeed the House of Lords and the Supreme Court have both criticised the idea that a technical change in the cause of action should make a large difference in the measure of recovery.[811]

Liability for breach of trust is not dependent on fault. However, it may be possible for the solicitor to invoke s.61 of the Trustee Act 1925, which gives the court a discretion to exonerate a trustee from liability if he proves that he has acted honestly and reasonably, and ought fairly to be excused for his breach of trust.[812] But the standard under s.61 is an exacting one, and in practice it can be difficult for a solicitor to invoke it in order to extricate himself from liability.[813] It should also be noted that where funds are held on trust, the duties arising under the trust are **9-130**

---

805 *AIB Group (UK) Plc v Mark Redler & Co* [2014] UKSC 58; [2015] A.C. 1503.

806 *Mortgage Express Ltd v Iqbal Hafeez Solicitors* [2011] EWHC 3037 (Ch); *Lloyds TSB Bank Plc v Markandan & Uddin* [2012] EWCA Civ 65; [2012] 2 All E.R. 884; *Purrunsing v A'Court & Co* [2016] EWHC 789 (Ch); [2016] 4 W.L.R. 81.

807 *Nationwide Building Society v Davisons Solicitors* [2012] EWCA Civ 1626; [2013] P.N.L.R. 12.

808 "[T]he common law rules of remoteness of damage and causation do not apply" (Lord Browne-Wilkinson in *Target Holdings Ltd v Redferns* [1996] A.C. 421, 434); *AIB Group (UK) Plc v Mark Redler & Co Solicitors* [2014] UKSC 58; [2015] A.C. 1503 at [98] (Lord Reed). Equally there is no scope for reduction of any award for contributory negligence, whether under the Law Reform (Contributory Negligence) Act 1945 or otherwise: *Lloyds TSB Bank Plc v Markandan & Uddin* [2012] EWCA Civ 65; [2012] 2 All E.R. 884.

809 See, e.g. *Target Holdings Ltd v Redferns* [1996] A.C. 421, 434–435 (Lord Browne-Wilkinson); *AIB Group (UK) Plc v Mark Redler & Co* [2014] UKSC 58; [2015] A.C. 1503 at [92]–[93] (Lord Reed).

810 But not in all. One case where this made a difference was *Various Claimants v Giambrone & Law (A Firm)* [2017] EWCA Civ 1193; [2018] P.N.L.R. 2 (lawyers liable for releasing buyers' deposits on Calabrian real estate without obtaining stipulated guarantees, without reference to whether guarantees would have been worth anything). For a critical comment see P. Davies, "Equitable compensation and the SAAMCO principle" (2018) 134 L.Q.R. 165.

811 See Lord Browne-Wilkinson in *Target Holdings Ltd v Redferns* [1996] A.C. 421, 436–439; *AIB Group (UK) Plc v Mark Redler & Co* [2014] UKSC 58; [2015] A.C. 1503 at [64]–[66] (Lord Toulson). On this see A. Shaw-Mellors, "Equitable compensation for breach of trust: still missing the target?" [2015] J.B.L. 165.

812 See Rimer LJ in *Lloyds TSB Bank Plc v Markandan & Uddin (A Firm)* [2012] EWCA Civ 65; [2012] 2 All E.R. 884 at [61]. For cases where solicitors in breach of trust benefited from the section, see *Nationwide Building Society v Davisons Solicitors* [2012] EWCA Civ 1626; [2013] P.N.L.R. 12 (solicitors entirely innocently duped into releasing loan monies to bogus solicitors in league with fraudsters); *Ikbal v Sterling Law* [2013] EWHC 3291 (Ch); [2014] P.N.L.R. 9 (release against forged transfer). The cases are discussed in J. Lowry & R. Edmunds, "Relieving the trustee-solicitor: a modern perspective on section 61 of the Trustee Act 1925?" (2017) 133 L.Q.R. 223.

813 See e.g. *Purrunsing v A'Court & Co* [2016] EWHC 789 (Ch); [2016] 4 W.L.R. 81 at [38]; also *P&P Property Ltd v Owen White & Catlin LLP* [2018] EWCA Civ 1082; [2019] Ch. 273, especially at [111]. Note that if the solicitor cannot disprove negligence of a kind related to the loss suffered, the jurisdiction to relieve falls away, even if the fault was in fact non-causative: *Santander UK v RA Legal Solicitors* [2014] EWCA Civ 183; [2014] P.N.L.R. 20. Furthermore, s.61 cannot be invoked so as to reduce any award on account of contributory negligence: *Lloyds TSB Bank Plc v Markandan & Uddin (A Firm)* [2012] EWCA Civ 65; [2012] 2 All E.R. 884. See generally, on the application of s.61 to solicitors, M. Haley, "Section 61 of the Trustee Act 1925: a judicious breach of trust?" [2017] C.L.J. 537, 557 onwards.

generally narrower than those under the solicitor's retainer[814]: thus even in respect of the disbursement of funds the solicitor may well be guilty of negligence without in addition being in breach of trust.[815]

(iv) Fiduciary duties

9-131 **Fiduciary liabilities** In addition to possible liability for breach of contract or tort, or breach of trust, a lawyer owes certain fiduciary duties to his client, for breach of which he may be liable to pay compensation.[816] Thus solicitors are guilty of breach of fiduciary duty if they disclose information received from a client which is confidential, or which (even if it is technically public) would harm the client's interests[817]; if they enter into a business in partnership with a client without disclosing the full facts so as to enable the clients to make a properly informed decision[818]; if they pay away client's monies to a borrower in the knowledge that certain conditions of the loan have not been satisfied[819]; and if, when acting for both lender and borrower, they deliberately fail to pass on to the lender relevant information obtained from the borrower while acting for him.[820] Similarly, too, with a solicitor who acts for two parties in circumstances where his ability to provide full loyalty to either is compromised.[821] In practice, it should be noted, many of these duties can equally be expressed as implied terms of any contract between lawyer and client.[822] Besides duties owed as fiduciaries, lawyers may also of course be liable to other remedies in the law of trusts, such as claims for dishonest assistance in a breach of trust where they know facts indicating that a transaction is dishonest by the standards of ordinary people,[823] or for knowing receipt of trust property.[824]

---

814 See *Bristol & West Building Society v Mothew* [1998] Ch. 1, 24 (Millett LJ); *Target Holdings Ltd v Redferns* [1996] A.C. 421, 436 (Lord Browne-Wilkinson).

815 e.g. *Bristol & West Building Society v Mothew* [1998] Ch. 1 (failing to pass on relevant information to lender); also *Lloyds TSB Bank Plc v Markandan & Uddin (A Firm)* [2012] EWCA Civ 65; [2012] 2 All E.R. 884 at [42]–[46]; and *DB UK Bank Ltd v Edmunds & Co* [2014] P.N.L.R. 12 (Ch) (failure to register lender's interest after completion). For a non-conveyancing case of the same type see *BPE Solicitors v Hughes-Holland* [2017] UKSC 21; [2018] A.C. 599 (solicitors for lender at fault, but not in breach of trust, in failing to mention suspicious features).

816 See generally para.9-22.

817 e.g. information that a client for whom they are acting in a commercial conveyancing transaction is a convicted fraudster: see *Hilton v Barker Booth & Eastwood* [2005] UKHL 8; [2005] 1 W.L.R. 567 at [34] (Lord Walker). Like all duties of confidentiality this is subject to a public interest defence, at least outside the confines of legal professional privilege: see *Saab v Dangate Consulting Ltd* [2019] EWHC 1558 (Comm); [2019] P.N.L.R. 29 at [216]–[218] (Cockerill J, giving the example of a client's disclosure to his lawyer of an imminent bomb attack).

818 *Longstaff v Birtles* [2001] EWCA Civ 1219; [2002] 1 W.L.R. 470. See too *Swindle v Harrison* [1997] 4 All E.R. 705 (undisclosed profits from loan to client).

819 e.g. *Bristol & West Building Society v May, May & Merrimans* [1996] 2 All E.R. 801. Inadvertent wrongdoing will, however, generally not suffice: see *Bristol & West Building Society v Mothew* [1998] Ch. 1; and *Birmingham Midshires Building Society v Infields* (1999) 66 Con. L.R. 20.

820 *Nationwide Building Society v Balmer Radmore (A Firm)* [1999] P.N.L.R. 606.

821 See e.g. *Hilton v Barker Booth & Eastwood* [2005] UKHL 8; [2005] 1 W.L.R. 567; *Ball v Druces & Attlee (No 2)* [2004] EWHC 1402 (QB); [2004] P.N.L.R. 39. And cf. *Clark Boyce v Mouat* [1994] 1 A.C. 428 (same principle accepted, though claim failed on the facts). The question of conflict of interest is dealt with in more detail below: see para.9-153.

822 Thus in *Hilton v Barker Booth & Eastwood* [2005] UKHL 8; [2005] 1 W.L.R. 567, where solicitors improperly compromised their loyalty to a conveyancing client, all parties were content to treat the duty as a contractual one.

823 See, e.g. *Underhill & Hayton's Law of Trusts and Trustees*, 19th edn (2016), Ch.24; and *Lewin on*

(c) Wasted costs orders

9-132 **Liability under the Senior Courts Act 1981 s.51: "wasted costs orders"** Under s.51 of the Senior Courts Act 1981,[825] where a legal representative has been guilty of any "improper, unreasonable, or negligent act or omission", the court may order him to pay any costs wasted as a result. This jurisdiction, which extends somewhat vague powers previously available at common law,[826] covers solicitors and barristers (though not in-house lawyers, except when they are exercising rights of audience[827]) in any case where they are exercising a "right to conduct litigation",[828] a phrase apt to cover not only actual proceedings in court but any act in connection with litigation.[829] Orders may be obtained by a party against either his own or his opponent's lawyers.[830] It is a summary jurisdiction applying at any stage in the proceedings up to and including the proceedings relating to the detailed assessment of costs,[831] normally exercised by the trial judge, though only after giving the representative a chance to be heard.[832]

9-133 "Improper" for these purposes includes, but is not limited to, actual breaches of the rules of professional etiquette: it embraces any conduct that would be regarded

---

Trusts, 19th edn (2016), Ch.40. For examples, see *Pulvers (A Firm) v Chan* [2007] EWHC 2406 (Ch); [2008] P.N.L.R. 9 (solicitors handling mortgage money knowingly paid it away to mortgage fraudsters); *Clydesdale Bank Plc v Workman* [2013] EWHC B38 (Ch); [2014] P.N.L.R. 18 (appeal allowed on the facts, [2016] EWCA Civ 73; [2016] P.N.L.R. 18) (knowingly helping property owner pay away purchase monies in defiance of unregistered charge); also *Nolan v Minerva Trust Co Ltd* [2014] JRC 78A (Jersey Royal Court); and *Group Seven Ltd v Nasir* [2019] EWCA Civ 614; [2019] 3 W.L.R. 1011. In the latter case at [702] the CA left it open whether knowing failure to observe regulatory requirements automatically amounted to dishonesty. Morgan J had held at first instance that it did not (see [2017] EWHC 2466 (Ch); [2018] P.N.L.R. 6 at [454]–[472]). It is tentatively suggested that this is correct; there is no reason to assimilate technical infractions to moral obliquity, which is the essence of dishonest assistance.

824 For details of this liability, see, e.g. *Underhill & Hayton's Law of Trusts and Trustees*, 19th edn (2016), Ch.24; and *Lewin on Trusts*, 19th edn (2016), Ch.42. For examples, see *Pulvers (A Firm) v Chan* [2007] EWHC 2406 (Ch); [2008] P.N.L.R. 9, above (solicitors also liable for knowing receipt).

825 As rewritten by s.4 of the Courts and Legal Services Act 1990. Note that this provision also covers the unified Family Court, and in addition the County Court. In addition, ss.111 and 112 of the 1990 Act inserted a new s.19A into the Prosecution of Offences Act 1985 to provide an analogous jurisdiction in the case of criminal courts. See generally CPR, 48.7 (civil cases) and in criminal cases the Costs in Criminal Cases (General) Regulations 1986 (SI 1986/1335), regs.3A–3D (as amended) and the *Practice Direction (Costs in Criminal Proceedings)* [2015] EWCA 1568 (as amended by the *Practice Direction (Costs in Criminal Proceedings) 2015 Amendment No.1* [2016] EWCA Crim 98), para.4.2.

826 On which see *Myers v Elman* [1940] A.C. 282; and *Orchard v S.E. Electricity Board* [1987] Q.B. 565.

827 See *R v Lambeth BC, ex p. Wilson* (1998) 30 H.L.R. 64; and Senior Courts Act 1981 s.51(13). So too in immigration cases with Home Office presenting officers: *Re Awuah (Wasted Costs Orders)* [2017] UKFTT 555 (IAC); [2018] P.N.L.R. 7 at [22]–[23]. See generally *Lloyd & Son Ltd (In Administration) v PPC International Ltd* [2016] EWHC 2162 (QB); [2017] P.N.L.R. 1.

828 1981 Act s.51(13). Thus dilatory solicitors who had come off the record well before proceedings were started were not amenable (*Byrne v Sefton Health Authority* [2001] EWCA Civ 1904; [2002] 1 W.L.R. 775); nor is a solicitor liable for merely failing to bring a timeous appeal (*Radford & Co v Charles* [2003] EWHC 3180 (Ch); [2004] P.N.L.R. 25).

829 *Medcalf v Mardell* [2002] UKHL 27; [2003] 1 A.C. 120 at [18]–[20] (Lord Bingham).

830 *Medcalf v Mardell* [2002] UKHL 27; [2003] 1 A.C. 120 at [18]–[19] (Lord Bingham).

831 CPR, 53.1PD. There is no jurisdiction to make such an order at a later stage: *Sharma v Hunters (Wasted Costs)* [2011] EWHC 2546 (CoP); [2012] P.N.L.R. 6.

832 1981 Act s.51(6); CPR r.48.7(2); *S v M* [1998] 3 F.C.R. 665.

as improper by the consensus of professional opinion.[833] Examples include swearing false affidavits,[834] failing to disclose material[835] or give a notice[836] required by rules of court,[837] engineering hopeless applications in order to delay inevitable orders for eviction or payment of tax,[838] seriously slapdash drafting,[839] and making groundless applications on behalf of a penniless litigant in order to harass the other side.[840] And similarly with lawyers who take no steps in proceedings and then abandon them at the last moment,[841] or simply fail to appear for a hearing at all.[842] It is also "improper" in this connection to allege fraud or crime without admissible and credible evidence.[843] "Unreasonable" means any activity designed to harass the other side or achieve some end other than to help to resolve the dispute.[844] "Negligent" means any conduct which no reasonably competent practitioner would engage in[845]; for example, risking non-appearance by over-ambitious scheduling,[846] dispatching an inadequately-instructed clerk to appear on an application,[847] causing a criminal trial to be aborted by making incautious remarks in the jury's hearing,[848] acting with reason to know one is without authority to do so,[849] or misdesignating parties and hence causing a need for expensive interlocutory proceedings to put matters right.[850] Even here, however, mere negligence is not

---

833 *Ridehalgh v Horsfield* [1994] Ch. 205, 232.

834 *Re a Company (No.00679 of 1995)* [1996] 1 W.L.R. 491.

835 *CMCS Common Market Commercial Services AVV v Taylor (Wasted Costs)* [2011] EWHC 324 (Ch); [2011] P.N.L.R. 17 (allowing client to redact disclosed documents without explanation); *HU v SU* [2015] EWFC 18; [2015] P.N.L.R. 20.

836 *R. v SVS Solicitors (Wasted Costs)* [2012] EWCA Crim 319; [2012] P.N.L.R. 21 (notice of hearsay evidence under Criminal Procedure Rules).

837 *CMCS Common Market Commercial Services AVV v Taylor (Wasted Costs)* [2011] EWHC 324 (Ch); [2011] P.N.L.R. 17 (allowing client to redact disclosed documents without explanation); *R v SVS Solicitors (Wasted Costs)* [2012] EWCA Crim 319; [2012] P.N.L.R. 21 (notice of hearsay evidence under Criminal Procedure Rules).

838 *Woolwich Building Society v Fineberg* [1998] P.N.L.R. 216; *Morris v Roberts (Inspector of Taxes)* [2005] EWHC 1040 (Ch); [2005] P.N.L.R. 41.

839 *R. (Okondu) v Home Secretary (Wasted Costs)* [2014] UKUT 377 (IAC); [2015] I.N.L.R. 99; cf. *Secretary of State for the Home Department v Zinovgev* [2003] EWHC 100; [2004] P.N.L.R. 6 (production-line appeals on behalf of numerous asylum-seekers with no consideration of individual merits: wasted costs order made, and solicitor reported by judge to Law Society).

840 *Tolstoy (Count) v Aldington (Lord)* [1996] 1 W.L.R. 736.

841 *R (Gassama) v Home Secretary* [2012] EWHC 3049 (Admin); [2013] P.N.L.R. 10.

842 *R v Rodney* [1997] P.N.L.R. 489; *Snowden v Ministry of Defence* [2001] EWCA Civ 1524.

843 *Medcalf v Mardell* [2002] UKHL 27; [2003] 1 A.C. 120; *R. (Hubert) v Manchester Crown Court* [2015] EWHC 3734 (Admin). However, that evidence may in a suitable case comprise privileged material unavailable to the other side: see *Medcalf's* case.

844 *Ridehalgh v Horsfield* [1994] Ch. 205, 232. See also *Re A Barrister (Wasted Costs Order) (No.1 of 1991)* [1993] Q.B. 293 (decided under the analogous s.19A of the Prosecution of Offences Act 1985).

845 *Ridehalgh v Horsfield* [1994] Ch. 205, 232–233. See too *Filmlab Systems Int'l Ltd v Pennington* [1995] 1 W.L.R. 673 and *R. v Horsham DC, ex p. Wenman* [1995] 1 W.L.R. 680. Effectively this incorporates the "*Bolam* test". Note that, for these purposes, a barrister is liable for the fault of his clerk even if himself entirely blameless: *R v Rodney* [1997] P.N.L.R. 489.

846 *R v Henrys Solicitors* [2012] EWCA Crim 1480; [2012] P.N.L.R. 32 (morning and afternoon appointments 50 miles apart).

847 *Shah v Singh* [1996] P.N.L.R. 83.

848 *R v Qadi* [2000] P.N.L.R. 137.

849 *Thames Chambers Solicitors v Miah* [2013] EWHC 1245 (QB); [2013] P.N.L.R. 30 (acting for known bankrupt without authority from trustee).

850 *Veasey v Millfeed Co* [1997] P.N.L.R. 100.

enough: there must be a sufficiently serious degree of fault to justify some professional penalty.[851]

To be amenable to a wasted costs order, a lawyer must in some way be in breach of his duty to the court.[852] A mere breach of duty to his client[853] or the legal aid authorities[854] is not enough: nor, as such, is acting for an impecunious client in the knowledge that the latter may not be good for any costs.[855] Similarly, presentation of a hopeless case is not of itself sufficient. There must be in addition an element of abuse of the court's process,[856] such that no reasonable lawyer would have proceeded in the circumstances.[857] Furthermore, the jurisdiction should be exercised with one eye on the constitutional position of the advocate,[858] to the fact that to some extent lawyers have to be able to trust even dubious clients,[859] and to the consideration that decisions in litigation often have to be taken at some speed; it should therefore only be exercised in respect of conduct that is quite plainly unjustifiable.[860] A solicitor will normally not have an order made against him in so far as he has acted on the basis of a commonly held professional opinion,[861] or the advice of apparently competent counsel,[862] but this is not an absolute rule.[863] The wasted costs jurisdiction, despite its emphasis on wrongdoing, is essentially compensatory. It follows that even if a representative is subject to a wasted costs order, he should only 9-134

---

851 "[T]here must be something akin to an abuse of process if the conduct of the legal representative is to make him liable to a wasted costs order"—Peter Gibson LJ in *Persaud v Persaud* [2003] EWCA Civ 394; [2003] P.N.L.R. 26 at [27].

852 *Radford & Co v Charles* [2003] EWHC 3180 (Ch); [2004] P.N.L.R. 25.

853 *Radford & Co v Charles* [2003] EWHC 3180 (Ch); [2004] P.N.L.R. 25 (failing to bring an appeal in time, followed by an unsuccessful attempt to extend).

854 *Persaud v Persaud* [2003] EWCA Civ 394; [2003] P.N.L.R. 26.

855 See, e.g. *Tinseltime Ltd v Roberts (Costs)* [2012] EWHC 2628 (TCC); [2013] P.N.L.R. 4; *Heron v TNT (UK) Ltd* [2013] EWCA Civ 469; [2014] 1 W.L.R. 1277 (complaints of knowingly acting for impecunious client not having obtained ATE insurance).

856 *Ridehalgh v Horsfield* [1994] Ch. 205, 233–234; *Tolstoy (Count) v Aldington (Lord)* [1996] 1 W.L.R. 736; cf. *Orchard v S.E. Electricity Board* [1987] Q.B. 565 (decided under the old law).

857 See *Dempsey v Johnstone (Wasted Costs)* [2003] EWCA Civ 1134; [2004] P.N.L.R. 2.

858 *Medcalf v Mardell* [2002] UKHL 27; [2003] 1 A.C. 120 at [51] onwards (Lord Hobhouse).

859 *Hedrich v Standard Bank London Ltd* [2008] EWCA Civ 905; [2009] P.N.L.R. 3 (no order against lawyers who accepted dishonest client's word that awkward documents not available for discovery). See too *Re Boodhoo* [2007] EWCA Crim 14; [2007] 4 All E.R. 762 (no order against solicitor who immediately withdrew from representing criminal client after latter absconded, since client's wishes and desires no longer clear).

860 *Ridehalgh v Horsfield* [1994] Ch. 205. Of course a solicitor acting entirely blamelessly will always escape liability: *Nelson v Nelson* [1997] 1 W.L.R. 233.

861 *R v X (Wasted Costs)* [2013] EWCA Crim 775; [2014] 1 W.L.R. 786 (common, but erroneous, view about prior disclosure of alibi evidence in criminal proceedings).

862 *Reaveley v Safeway Stores Plc* [1998] P.N.L.R. 526; *Afzal v Chubb Guarding Services Ltd (Wasted Costs)* [2002] EWHC 822 (TCC); [2003] P.N.L.R. 33 (failure under counsel's advice to disclose to other side adverse report suggesting client's claim fraudulent: not improper conduct in the circumstances).

863 See *Tolstoy (Count) v Aldington (Lord)* [1996] 1 W.L.R. 736 (solicitor liable for harassing opponent despite advice from leading and junior counsel that his action was permissible); *Isaacs Partnership v Umm-Al-Jawaby Oil Service Co Ltd (Wasted Costs)* [2003] EWHC 2539 (QB); [2004] P.N.L.R. 9 (solicitors in wrongful dismissal claim insist on suing the wrong defendant, despite clear indications of their error: liable to wasted costs order despite having relied on counsel's advice, since this was an elementary point easily comprehensible to the ordinary lawyer, and in any case counsel had not been adequately informed before advising).

be held liable for those costs whose waste is shown to have resulted from any misconduct.[864]

9-135 Three further limitations to the wasted costs jurisdiction must be noted. First, it must take account of the fact that the lawyer may not be able to defend himself without using privileged material which he is unable to disclose without his client's leave. Unless the court is convinced that such material has been presented or, even if presented, could not have exonerated the lawyer, it was held by the House of Lords in *Medcalf v Mardell*[865] that no order should be made. Secondly, the wasted costs procedure is essentially a summary one, unsuited to extended argument over disputed facts: as Lord Bingham MR has observed, hearings should take hours rather than days, and any tendency to expensive satellite litigation should be firmly repressed.[866] It follows that if serious or difficult issues of fact are likely to arise, then the procedure is inappropriate,[867] despite any possible unfairness to potential applicants and the fact that any disciplinary effect on errant lawyers may be emasculated.[868] Thirdly, the jurisdiction is a discretionary one. Thus if the person seeking an order could equally well get his costs from a losing and solvent opponent, this is a factor against making it at all,[869] as is the fact that any order, if made, would have effects disproportionate to any wrongdoing.[870]

(d) Immunities

9-136 **Collateral challenge and abuse of process** An action for negligence against a lawyer may, like any other action,[871] be struck out if it amounts to an impermissible collateral challenge to the previous decision of a court of competent

---

[864] *Ridehalgh v Horsfield* [1994] Ch. 205, 232, 237; *Brown v Bennett (No.2)* [2002] 1 W.L.R. 713 at [52]–[54], [187]; *Le Brocq v Liverpool Crown Court* [2019] EWCA Crim 1398; [2019] 4 W.L.R. 108. Proof must be on a balance of probabilities, and there is no room for a partial award based on loss of a chance: *Brown v Bennett (No.2)* [2002] 1 W.L.R. 713 at [53]–[54] (Neuberger J).

[865] [2002] UKHL 27; [2003] 1 A.C. 120 at [20]–[24] (Lord Bingham); approving dicta in *Ridehalgh v Horsfield* [1994] Ch. 205, 237. See too *Dempsey v Johnstone (Wasted Costs Order)* [2003] EWCA Civ 1134; [2004] P.N.L.R. 2.

[866] *Ridehalgh v Horsefield* [1994] Ch. 205, 210–239.

[867] *B v Pendlebury* [2002] EWHC 1797 (QB); [2003] P.N.L.R. 1 ("formidable" challenge to accuracy of documentary evidence relevant to lawyer's conduct: s.51 inappropriate); *Kagalovsky v Balmore Invest Ltd* [2015] EWHC 1337 (QB); [2015] P.N.L.R. 26. Nevertheless, a judge should always consider whether strict case management could bring any hearing within reasonable bounds: see *Wagstaff v Colls (Wasted Costs Order)* [2003] EWCA Civ 469; [2003] P.N.L.R. 29.

[868] A point noted by Turner J in *B v Pendelbury*: see [2002] EWHC 1797 (QB); [2003] P.N.L.R. 1 at [24]–[25].

[869] *Koo Golden East Mongolia v Bank of Nova Scotia* [2008] EWHC 1120 (Admin); [2008] P.N.L.R. 32; *Harrison v Harrison* [2009] EWHC 428 (QB); [2009] 1 F.L.R. 1434. On the other hand, the claimant faces something like Morton's fork here, since if the losing party cannot pay the costs, Lord Hobhouse has equally cautioned against using the jurisdiction "to obtain from a party's lawyers what cannot be obtained from the party himself" (see *Medcalf v Mardell* [2002] UKHL 27; [2003] 1 A.C. 120 at [58]).

[870] *R. (Hide) v Staffordshire County Council* [2007] EWHC 2441 (Admin); [2008] P.N.L.R. 13 (inappropriate to bankrupt improperly over-zealous solicitor). See too *F v M (Wasted Costs)* [2015] EWHC 3259 (Fam); [2016] P.N.L.R. 13 (amount may be reduced if applicant himself at fault).

[871] e.g. actions against the police for assault aimed at impugning confessions on the basis of which the claimant has been convicted of a criminal offence: *Hunter v Chief Constable of West Midlands* [1982] A.C. 529. For its application to professional negligence proceedings, albeit against non-lawyers, see *Arts & Antiques Ltd v Richards* [2013] EWHC 3361 (Comm); [2014] P.N.L.R. 10 (insurance brokers).

jurisdiction. Thus in *Smith v Linskills*[872] a convicted burglar attempted to sue his solicitor for negligence, alleging that had his defence been properly conducted he would have been acquitted. The Court of Appeal struck out the action as an abuse of process: unless compelling new evidence was produced which "entirely change[d] the aspect of the case",[873] it was contrary to public policy to allow the conviction to be effectively re-litigated in the civil courts. A similar principle may apply to attempts to impugn a final judgment in contested civil proceedings,[874] though here the jurisdiction is much more sparingly exercised.[875] But the limits of this rule must be noted. It applies only to proceedings where the claimant has had a reasonable opportunity to present his case, and not (for example) to cases where the defendants' negligence deprives the claimant of the chance of a successful appeal,[876] or of the services of a suitable expert to support his story.[877] Furthermore, the bar on collateral attack is much less stringently applied in the case of consent orders,[878] even where those orders embody a settlement which has by law to be approved by the court.[879] Although in such a case subsequent proceedings in negligence are prima facie abusive, they will normally be allowed to proceed if (a) good reason is shown why steps were not taken to challenge the original decision by appeal or otherwise[880]; and (b) the claimant has been deprived of either a reasonable opportunity to appreciate that substantially better terms could have been obtained, or has been placed in the position of having to accept a settlement significantly less advantageous than he should have had.

---

[872] [1996] 1 W.L.R. 763. See too *Somasundaram v M. Julius Melchior* [1988] 1 W.L.R. 1394; *Workman v Deansgate 123 LLP* [2019] EWHC 360 (QB); [2019] P.N.L.R. 18; and *Day v Womble Bond Dickinson (UK) LLP* [2020] EWCA Civ 447; [2020] P.N.L.R. 19. If the proceedings were ultimately favourable to the claimant, his action for damages will of course be allowed to proceed, since then it does not impugn anything: *Acton v Graham Pearce* [1997] 3 All E.R. 909.

[873] [1996] 1 W.L.R. 763, 771; see too *Hunter v Chief Constable of West Midlands* [1982] A.C. 529, 545 (Lord Diplock).

[874] See, e.g. *Laing v Taylor Walton (A Firm)* [2007] EWCA Civ 1146; [2008] P.N.L.R. 11 (simple attack on otherwise impeccable finding of fact in previous proceedings); *Ahmad v Wood* [2018] EWHC 996 (QB); [2018] P.N.L.R. 28 (previous matrimonial proceedings: attack on amount awarded); also L. Haller, "Abuse of process, collateral attack and claims against lawyers" (2015) 34 C.J.Q. 377.

[875] See *Nesbitt v Holt* [2007] EWCA Civ 249; [2007] P.N.L.R. 24 (client's allegation that claim had been settled without authority not abusive, despite previous decision by employment tribunal that settlement had been with authority: allegation only abuse of process if advancement manifestly unfair to other side). See too Lord Bingham CJ's judgment in the Court of Appeal in *Hall (Arthur JS) & Co v Simons* [2002] 1 A.C. 615. In the House of Lords, however, Lord Hoffmann doubted whether the principle could apply where a lawyer was sued for negligence in conducting civil proceedings (see [2002] 1 A.C. 615, 701). Lord Steyn said: "It would not ordinarily be necessary to rely on the *Hunter* principle in the civil context but I would accept that the policy underlying it should still stand guard against unforeseen gaps." ([2002] 1 A.C. 615, 680).

[876] *Walpole v Partridge & Wilson* [1994] Q.B. 106.

[877] A contrary decision in *Palmer v Durnford Ford* [1992] Q.B. 483 was discountenanced in *Walpole v Partridge & Wilson* [1994] Q.B. 106.

[878] See *Hall (Arthur JS) & Co v Simons* [2002] 1 A.C. 615, 647 (Lord Bingham CJ in the Court of Appeal).

[879] For example, settlements of claims by minors, or for ancillary relief in matrimonial cases. Where the consent order embodies a settlement that does not have to be approved, it is indeed doubtful whether the "collateral attack" principle applies at all: see *Saif Ali v Sydney Mitchell* [1980] A.C. 198, 223 (Lord Diplock).

[880] For a neat example see *LR v Witherspoon* [1999] P.N.L.R. 776 CA (Civ Div) (action against solicitors for delay in prosecuting contact proceedings; because of delay, decision against claimant since not in best interests of child to upset established arrangements: no strike-out on basis of "collateral attack" rule).

9-137 **Erstwhile advocates' immunity** Until 2001 it was accepted that advocates[881] were immune from suit, whether by their clients or anyone else,[882] in respect of their conduct and management of a case in court[883] and preparations for it.[884] This was variously justified by arguing that such claims were apt to amount to a collateral attack on the proceedings concerned,[885] that all statements in court should remain immune to action, or that the advocate owed a duty to the court from which he should not be distracted.[886] However, in *Hall (Arthur J.S.) & Co v Simons*[887] the House of Lords, by a majority of four to three,[888] decided that these arguments were no longer persuasive, and that advocates (there, legal advisers who had settled civil proceedings at or near the door of the court on allegedly improvident terms) were on principle liable for negligence in the same way as other professionals. Any problems of collateral attack could, said Lords Steyn, Browne-Wilkinson and Hoffmann, be adequately dealt with by the doctrine of abuse of process[889]; the immunity from suit accorded statements in the course of legal proceedings was no justification for immunising those guilty of forensic misjudgment or bungling[890]; and the regular use of the wasted costs jurisdiction against incompetent advocates had showed that the prospect of liability had not noticeably compromised the bar's ethical standards.[891]

---

881 Including latterly solicitors acting as advocates: see *Saif Ali v Sydney Mitchell & Co* [1980] A.C. 198, 215, 224 and 227.

882 e.g. *Welsh v Chief Constable of Merseyside* [1993] 1 All E.R. 692.

883 See in particular *Rondel v Worsley* [1969] 1 A.C. 191; and *Saif Ali v Sydney Mitchell & Co* [1980] A.C. 198.

884 *Rees v Sinclair* [1974] 1 N.Z.L.R. 180, 187; adopted in *Saif Ali v Sydney Mitchell & Co*, above.

885 Indeed, quite apart from any question of forensic immunities, no action would lie which constituted a collateral attack on an earlier judgment: e.g. *McIlkenny v Chief Constable of the West Midlands* [1980] Q.B. 283; *Somasundaram v M. Julius Melchior* [1989] 1 W.L.R. 940; and *Hunter v Chief Constable of the West Midlands* [1982] A.C. 529. See further para.9-136.

886 See Lord Bingham CJ in the CA in *Hall (Arthur JS) & Co v Simons* [2002] 1 A.C. 615, 624; also *Saif Ali v Sydney Mitchell & Co* [1980] A.C. 198, 212, 222, 227, 230.

887 [2002] 1 A.C. 615; on which see generally D. Capper, "The demise of the advocate's immunity" (2006) 57 N.I.L.Q. 391. New Zealand has followed suit (*Chamberlains v Lai* [2007] 2 N.Z.L.R. 7), but not Australia (*D'Orta-Ekenaike v Victoria Legal Aid* (2005) 223 C.L.R. 1; and *Attwells v Jackson Lalic Lawyers Pty Ltd* [2016] HCA 16; (2016) 331 A.L.R. 1), nor Scotland, at least with regard to civil cases (*Wright v Paton Farrell* [2006] CSIH 7; 2006 S.C. 404). In *Janin Caribbean Construction Ltd v Wilkinson* [2016] UKPC 26; [2017] P.N.L.R. 5 the Privy Council accepted that the appropriateness of retaining the immunity might well depend on local conditions (and upheld it in Grenada).

888 Lords Steyn, Browne-Wilkinson, Hoffmann and Millett. The dissentients were Lords Hope, Hutton and Hobhouse. The dissenting Law Lords agreed that advocates' immunity should no longer apply to civil proceedings, and hence concurred in the result: but they thought that it still should have a part to play in criminal proceedings. The decision remains controversial: Australia retains immunity, albeit in a curtailed form (*Attwells v Jackson Lalic Lawyers Pty Ltd* [2016] HCA 16; (2016) 331 A.L.R. 1).

889 See [2002] 1 A.C. 615, 679–680, 684, 691–704. cf. cases such as *Hunter v Chief Constable of West Midlands* [1982] A.C. 529; *Somasundaram v M. Julius Melchior* [1989] 1 W.L.R. 940; and *Smith v Linskills* [1996] 1 W.L.R. 763; also para.9-136.

890 See [2002] 1 A.C. 615, 697–698 (Lord Hoffman), 679 (Lord Steyn).

891 See [2002] 1 A.C. 615, 689–695 (Lord Hoffmann). His Lordship also made the point that in any case fault was often difficult to prove, and ample means existed to dismiss unpropitious claims at an early stage. For good measure, Lord Millett also added (at 751) that the continuation of any blanket immunity afforded to advocates might face problems under the European Convention on Human Rights. No doubt his Lordship was contemplating art.6.1 of the Convention and *Osman v United Kingdom* (1998) 29 E.H.R.R. 245.

(e) What amounts to breach of duty

Breach of duty A lawyer is not "bound to know all the law".[892] His duty is, like that of every other professional person, to exercise that reasonable degree of skill and care to be expected of a competent and reasonably experienced solicitor.[893] Thus it has been said that a solicitor will be liable in general: 9-138

> "for the consequences of ignorance or non-observance of the rules of practice of this Court; for the want of care in the preparation of the cause for trial; or the attendance thereon with his witnesses, and for the management of so much of the conduct of a cause as is usually and ordinarily allocated to his department of the profession. Whilst on the other hand, he is not answerable for an error in judgment upon points of new occurrence, or of nice and doubtful construction."[894]

Thus in determining when an error made by a lawyer is negligent, he should not be judged by the standard of what "a particularly meticulous and conscientious practitioner"[895] would elect to do but by what "the reasonably competent practitioner would do having regard to the standards normally adopted in his profession".[896] Nor need he exhibit a high degree of suspicion, even in areas where fraud is clearly possible.[897] Conversely, however, an error by a lawyer may constitute negligence, without that error being morally blameworthy or indicative of general incompetence.[898]

Proving negligence The onus of proving negligence in an action against a lawyer lies on the claimant,[899] as it does in relation to professional liability generally. In practice a good deal of latitude may be shown. As Lord Salmon observed (in connection with barristers): 9-139

> "Diametrically opposite views may and not infrequently are taken by barristers, and indeed by judges, each of whom has exercised reasonable, and sometimes far more than reasonable, care and competence. The fact that one of them turns out to be wrong certainly does not mean that he has been negligent."[900]

---

892 These comfortable words appear in *Montriou v Jeffreys* (1825) 2 C. & P. 113, 116. Note also, however, *Central Trust Co v Rafuse* (1987) 31 D.L.R. (4th) 62: "where a solicitor does not have the knowledge of the statutes pertaining to a transaction, then he has an obligation to inform himself of those provisions".

893 See *Hall (Arthur JS) v Simons* [2002] 1 A.C. 615, 726 (Lord Hope), 737 (Lord Hobhouse); and cf. *Bolam v Friern HMC* [1957] 1 W.L.R. 582. He can, of course, agree to a higher standard, or even guarantee results: but such an undertaking is not to be lightly inferred. See, e.g. *Barclays Bank Plc v Weeks Legg & Dean* [1999] Q.B. 309; *Midland Bank plc v Cox McQueen* [1999] P.N.L.R. 593; and *UCB Corporate Services Ltd v Clyde & Co* [2000] P.N.L.R. 841.

894 *Godefroy v Dalton* (1830) 6 Bing. 460, 467–468 (Tindal C.J.); approved by Scrutton LJ in *Fletcher & Son v Jubb Booth & Helliwell* [1920] 1 K.B. 275 at 280.

895 *Midland Bank Trust Co Ltd v Hett, Stubbs & Kemp* [1979] Ch. 384, 403 (Oliver J).

896 *Midland Bank Trust Co Ltd v Hett, Stubbs & Kemp* [1979] Ch. 384, 403. The standards of the profession include, where appropriate, guidance issued by the Law Society or other supervisory bodies from time to time: *Robins v Meadows & Moran* [1991] 2 E.G.L.R. 137.

897 *Young v Hamilton* [2014] NICA 48; [2014] P.N.L.R. 30; also *Redstone Mortgages Ltd v B Legal Ltd* [2014] EWHC 3398 (Ch).

898 *Sykes v Midland Bank Executor & Trustee Co Ltd* [1971] 1 Q.B. 113; *Creech v Mayorcas* (1966) 198 E.G. 1091.

899 *Stewart Wrightson Group Ltd v Crocker* (1979) 124 S.J. 83.

900 *Saif Ali v Sydney Mitchell & Co* [1980] A.C. 198, 231. Similarly a claimant is normally expected to lead positive evidence as to why the lawyer was negligent: *Moy v Pettman Smith* [2005] UKHL 7; [2005] 1 W.L.R. 581 at [19].

Thus where a senior tax barrister advised that a tax avoidance scheme would be effective, but after a protracted appeal to the House of Lords it was held not to be, Lloyd J had no difficulty in deciding that he had not been proved negligent in the circumstances.[901] It should be noted that, in deciding whether a lawyer has been negligent, all the circumstances, including the exigencies of the situation, are in account. A lawyer with time for reflection may be expected to take account not only of the existing understanding of the law but of the possibility it may be upset.[902] Conversely, conduct normally blameworthy may be justifiable in a case of urgency where the time for reflection is limited.[903]

9-140 As with medical negligence, conformity to the general practice of the profession is normally but not invariably an answer to a claim in negligence.[904] In *Simmons v Pennington*[905] the defendants, acting on behalf of vendors of land, in answering a requisition acted in accordance with the general practice of conveyancers. They escaped liability, even though a court later held that the answer entitled the purchaser to rescind. On the other hand, compliance with accepted practice is not conclusive against negligence: if the risks are obvious, the defendant remains liable.[906] Thus in *Edward Wong Finance Co Ltd v Johnson Stokes & Master*[907] solicitors acting for mortgagees followed the then usual practice[908] of paying the purchase price to the vendors' solicitors against the latter's undertaking to pay off existing encumbrances. The vendors' solicitors decamped with the money, and the mortgagees failed to get an unencumbered title. Their solicitors were held liable to them in negligence by the Privy Council, despite admitted compliance with the then general practice. The defendants ought to have foreseen the risk of loss should the vendors' solicitor be dishonest, and should have taken precautions to avoid that

---

901 *Matrix Securities Ltd v Theodore Goddard* [1998] P.N.L.R. 290.

902 See, e.g. *Dean v Allin & Watts* [2001] EWCA Civ 758; [2001] P.N.L.R. 39 (solicitors should have known interpretation of s.2 of the Law of Property (Miscellaneous Provisions) Act 1989 was opaque, and acted accordingly); and *Williams v Thompson Leatherdale* [2008] EWHC 2574 (QB); [2009] P.N.L.R. 15 (foreseeability of revolution in financial provision resulting from *White v White* [2001] 1 A.C. 596).

903 *Patel v Daybells (A Firm)* [2001] EWCA Civ 1229; [2002] P.N.L.R. 6 (urgency of conveyancing transaction relevant to whether negligent for purchaser's solicitors to rely simply on vendors' solicitors' undertaking to discharge mortgage). And cf. *Moy v Pettman Smith* [2005] UKHL 7; [2005] 1 W.L.R. 581 (swift advice with regard to whether claimant should accept payment in).

904 *Simmons v Pennington* [1955] 1 W.L.R. 183; *Midland Bank Trust Co Ltd v Hett Stubbs & Kemp* [1979] Ch. 384, 403 (Oliver J); *Thorpe v Fellowes (a firm)* [2011] EWHC 61 (QB); [2011] P.N.L.R. 13 at [76] (Sharp J).

905 [1955] 1 W.L.R. 183. But note the important case of *Brown v Gould & Swayne* [1996] P.N.L.R. 130, where Millett LJ suggested that questions of acceptable conveyancing practice should now be regarded as largely questions of law.

906 "[T]he mere fact that a practice is universal does not, of itself, immunise the professional concerned from potential liability, if it is a practice which, on reasonable consideration, the professional concerned ought to have identified as giving rise to a significant risk" (Clarke J in *ACC Bank Plc v Johnston & Co* [2010] IEHC 236; [2010] 4 I.R. 605; [2011] P.N.L.R. 19 at [6.23]). The practice there, which Clarke J condemned, consisted in completing a very large land transaction not by paying the vendor, but paying the latter's solicitor against its mere undertaking to pay over the completion monies to the vendor. See too *Edward Wong Finance Co Ltd v Johnson Stokes & Master* [1984] A.C. 296, 305–306.

907 [1984] A.C. 296. See too the Irish decision in *ACC Bank Plc v Johnston & Co* [2010] IEHC 236; [2010] 4 I.R. 605; [2011] P.N.L.R. 19 (similar practice: similar result); also *Martin Boston & Co v Roberts* [1996] P.N.L.R. 45 (failure to obtain real rather than personal security for costs negligent even though established practice).

908 Usual in Hong Kong at the time; less so, no doubt, today.

risk.[909] Conversely, the fact that a lawyer has failed to follow professional guidance is evidence that he was at fault, though not conclusive.[910]

Where there is a difference of opinion in the profession on what constitutes proper practice, it is clear that the *Bolam* test[911] applies to lawyers as much as to medical practitioners. This means that a defendant conforming to a practice accepted as proper by a responsible body of professional opinion should not be held liable merely because others disagree.[912] Nevertheless, as with medical negligence[913] the courts have the last word in deciding on the propriety of the practice adopted by the defendant. So, for example, in *G & K Ladenbau Ltd v Crawley & de Reya*,[914] Mocatta J held solicitors for a purchaser of a block of vacant land liable for professional negligence when they failed to make a search of the commons register. Despite accepting that it was not their practice, nor indeed the practice of a considerable body of the profession, to search such registers, he preferred the evidence of the claimants' experts that proper careful practice demanded such a search. It is relevant that, as in *Edward Wong* above, this was a case in which the court found that the transaction should have rung "warning bells" that whatever usual practices might be, special precautions were required. 9-141

Standards to be applied The standard demanded of a lawyer will, as noted earlier, be that of the reasonably competent practitioner. In addition it goes without saying that observance or disregard of the requirements of the SRA's or BSB's Code of Conduct will be highly relevant to a determination whether a lawyer has fallen below those standards.[915] Moreover, a lawyer is to be judged according to the standards of practitioners of his own specialism and apparent level of practice, with no allowance made for personal inexperience.[916] Where the client engages a solicitor professing particular expertise in a particular branch of the law it has been said that he is: 9-142

> "entitled to expect from that solicitor or firm a standard of care and skill commensurate with the skill and experience which that solicitor or firm has. The uniform standards of care postulated for the world at large in tort hardly seem appropriate when the duty is not only imposed by the law of tort but arises from a contractual obligation existing between the client and the particular solicitor in question."[917]

Thus when a firm, such as a firm of City solicitors, holds itself out as having

---

909 Their Lordships were doubtless influenced by evidence that the Hong Kong Law Society was aware of, and had warned practitioners of, the risk inherent in the customary conveyancing practice.

910 *Johnson v Bingley, Dyson & Finney* [1997] P.N.L.R. 392.

911 See *Bolam v Friern HMC* [1957] 1 W.L.R. 582 at 587; above, para.9-76.

912 See *McFarlane v Wilkinson* [1997] P.N.L.R. 578 (solicitors); *Matrix Securities Ltd v Theodore Goddard* [1998] P.N.L.R. 290; and *Bark v Hawley* [2004] EWHC 144 (QB); [2005] P.N.L.R. 3 (barristers); and the Northern Ireland decision in *McIlgorm v Bell Lamb & Joynson* [2001] P.N.L.R. 28 (both). Other instances are *Football League Ltd v Edge Ellison* [2006] EWHC 1462 (Ch); [2007] P.N.L.R. 2; and *Barker v Baxendale Walker Solicitors* [2016] EWHC 664 (Ch); [2016] S.T.I. 1266 (appealed on other grounds at [2017] EWCA Civ 2056; [2018] 1 W.L.R. 1905).

913 See para.9-77.

914 [1978] 1 W.L.R. 266.

915 *Lloyd Cheyham & Co Ltd v Eversheds* [1985] 2 Lloyd's Rep. P.N. 154.

916 *Argyll (Duchess) v Beuselinck* [1972] 2 Lloyd's Rep. 172, 183 (Megarry J). This is in line with decisions elsewhere; cf. the road traffic case of *Nettleship v Weston* [1971] 2 Q.B. 691, 709 (Lord Denning MR).

917 *Matrix Securities Ltd v Theodore Goddard* [1998] P.N.L.R. 290 (high level of duty expected from senior tax silk); *Swain Mason v Mills & Reeve* [2011] EWHC 410 (Ch); [2011] S.T.C. 1177, especially at [149] (upheld, save as to costs, at [2012] EWCA Civ 498; [2012] S.T.C. 1760) (tax

expertise in a particular field, it seems right that the standard of the competent practitioner be judged in the light of its particular speciality and in accordance with the general principles of professional liability.[918] Whether the standard of care required differs according to the standing or seniority of the actual lawyer is more doubtful, but the better view appears to be that it cannot.[919] If the inexperienced are not held to a lower duty, the experienced should not be bound to a more exacting one.

9-143 **Solicitor acting on counsel's advice** Older authorities[920] stated baldly that a solicitor could not be liable for negligence if he had relied on counsel's advice. Today, however, it is clear that there is no such absolute rule. It is more accurate to say that a solicitor is presumptively entitled to assume that properly instructed[921] counsel is competent and take him at his word.[922] But he must consider at least the prima facie validity of counsel's advice, at least in common areas of practice[923]; and he may not be able to shelter behind it if it shows some elementary error[924] or is "glaringly wrong".[925] The law, it has been said:

> "does not operate so as to give a solicitor an immunity in every such case. A solicitor is highly trained and rightly expected to be experienced in his particular legal fields. He is under a duty at all times to exercise that degree of care, to both client and the court, that can be expected of a reasonably prudent solicitor. He is not entitled to rely blindly and with no mind of his own on counsel's views."[926]

In certain exceptional cases, moreover, it may be incumbent on a solicitor to warn the client that counsel's advice cannot be guaranteed to be correct.[927]

---

advice by firm with specialist tax department: client entitled to advice of standard typical of such firms). See too the earlier *Argyll (Duchess) v Beuselinck* [1972] 2 Lloyd's Rep. 172, 183.

918 See above, and also *Wright v Lewis Silkin LLP* [2015] EWHC 1897 (QB); [2015] P.N.L.R. 32 at [106]–[116] (Hamblen J). An appeal was dismissed at [2016] EWCA Civ 1308; [2017] P.N.L.R. 16, but not on this point.

919 *McFaddens v Platford* [2009] EWHC 126 (TCC); [2009] P.N.L.R. 26 at [50] (HH Judge Toulmin QC). Contrary dicta, however, appear in *Argyll (Duchess) v Beuselinck* [1972] 2 Lloyd's Rep. 172, 183 (Megarry J); and *Williams v Leatherdale & Francis* [2008] EWHC 2574 (QB); [2009] P.N.L.R. 15 at [67] (Field J).

920 e.g. *Kemp v Burt* (1833) 4 B. & Ad. 424; *Manning v Wilkin* (1848) 12 L.T. (O.S.) 249.

921 For a case of improperly instructed counsel, see *Estill v Cowling, Swift & Kitchen* [2000] Lloyd's Rep. P.N. 378.

922 *Francis v Francis & Dickerson* [1956] P. 87; *Hellard v Irwin Mitchell* [2013] EWHC 3008 (Ch) at [76].

923 See *Locke v Camberwell HA* [1991] 2 Med. L.R. 249 at 254, per Taylor LJ (solicitor must "exercise his own independent judgment."); also *Hickman v Blake Lapthorn* [2005] EWHC 2714 (QB); [2006] P.N.L.R. 20. The more esoteric the area, the more implicit the reliance may be: see e.g. *Manor Electronics Ltd v Dickson* (1990) 140 N.L.J. 590 (search orders).

924 e.g. *Green v Collyer-Bristow* [1999] Lloyd's Rep. P.N. 798 (conveyancer overlooking Law of Property (Miscellaneous Provisions) Act 1989); *Green v Hancocks* [2001] P.N.L.R. 286; affirmed [2001] Lloyd's Rep. P.N. 212 (elementary point on title to sue); and *Pritchard Joyce & Hinds v Batcup* [2009] EWCA Civ 369; [2009] P.N.L.R. 28 (simple limitation issue).

925 The phrase is Taylor LJ's: *Locke v Camberwell HA* [1991] 2 Med. L.R. 249, 254 (if solicitor "reasonably thinks counsel's advice is obviously or glaringly wrong, it is his duty to reject it."). See too *Firstcity Insurance Ltd v Orchard* [2003] P.N.L.R. 9 at [82] (Forbes J); and *Dunhill v Brook & Co* [2018] EWCA Civ 505 at [49] (Leveson P).

926 *Davy-Chiesman v Davy-Chiesman* [1984] Fam. 48 at 63. See too *Matrix Securities Ltd v Theodore Goddard* [1998] P.N.L.R. 290, 317.

927 For instance, where the matter is one of clear uncertainty, as with obscure covenants attaching to

(f) Specific duties

(i) *The duty to advise*

The duty to advise A lawyer owes a duty to give his client reasonably careful, competent and comprehensive[928] advice concerning any transaction in respect of which he is instructed. Thus he must keep the client informed of the progress of the transaction,[929] and warn of any specific risks inherent in it,[930] such as a possible ultra vires problem with municipal lending,[931] the possibility that a borrower offering shares as security does not in fact own them,[932] the risk of liability for breach of fiduciary duty in a property deal,[933] or the dangers inherent where a wife contemplates burdening her share in the matrimonial home to support her husband's business indebtedness.[934] In a conveyancing transaction he must bring to his notice matters such as the risk of exchanging contracts before a purchaser has paid a deposit,[935] a defect in the title to, or adverse right of way over, a property to be bought,[936] the lack of a NHBC guarantee on a new house,[937] a recent sale at a much lower price[938] or an absence of relevant planning permission for prior works[939] or a known future proposed use.[940] With foreign real estate it may be incumbent on him to warn of endemic local criminality and fraud.[941] When acting for a lender he must advise the lender of any matters specifically mentioned in the latter's instructions, 9-144

properties in smart London squares, there may be a duty to warn that counsel's advice is not necessarily the last word: *Herrmann v Withers LLP* [2012] EWHC 1492 (Ch); [2012] P.N.L.R. 28.

928 e.g. where a wife contemplates charging her share in the matrimonial home for her husband there must be more than formulaic advice not to enter into the transaction at all: *Padden v Bevan Ashford Solicitors* [2011] EWCA Civ 1616; [2012] 1 W.L.R. 1759; and cf. another formulaic advice case, *Procter v Raleys Solicitors* [2015] EWCA Civ 400; [2015] P.N.L.R. 24. See too *Padden v Bevan Ashford Solicitors (No 2)* [2013] EWCA Civ 824; [2013] P.N.L.R. 34 (wife thought burdening her property would prevent husband's prosecution for fraud: solicitors ought to have advised that this was unlikely). So too with commercial clients: see *Redstone Mortgages Ltd v B Legal Ltd* [2014] EWHC 3398 (Ch) (need for advice as to effect of shared ownership lease on value of security).

929 *Groom v Crocker* [1939] 1 K.B. 194 at 222. cf. *Jenmain Builders Ltd v Steed & Steed* [2000] P.N.L.R. 616 (duty to warn purchaser client that he was in "contract race").

930 *Boyce v Rendells* (1983) 268 E.G. 268 at 272; *Ohna v Goldberg* [2014] EWHC 4693 (Ch).

931 *Haugesund Kommune v Depfa ACS Bank (No 2)* [2010] EWHC 227 (Comm); [2010] P.N.L.R. 21 (reversed, but not on this point, in *Haugesund Kommune v Depfa ACS Bank* [2011] EWCA Civ 33; [2011] 3 All E.R. 655).

932 *Clack v Wrigleys Solicitors LLP* [2013] EWHC 413 (Ch) (in fact no damage suffered, since shares worthless anyway).

933 See the Scots decision in *Keith v Davidson Chalmers*, 2004 S.C. 287.

934 *Etridge v Pritchard Englefield* [1999] P.N.L.R. 839; *McGregor v Michael Taylor & Co* [2002] 2 Lloyd's Rep. 468; *Padden v Bevan Ashford Solicitors* [2011] EWCA Civ 1616; [2012] 1 W.L.R. 1759. See too the Irish Supreme Court's decision in *O'Carroll v Diamond* [2005] IESC 21; [2005] P.N.L.R. 34.

935 *Morris v Duke-Cohan & Co* (1975) 119 S.J. 821.

936 See e.g. *Pilkington v Wood* [1953] Ch. 770; *Piper v Daybell Court & Cooper & Co* (1969) 210 E.G. 1047. So too with major development plans affecting it: *Orientfield Holdings Ltd v Bird & Bird LLP* [2015] EWHC 1963 (Ch); [2015] P.N.L.R. 33.

937 *Rickards v Jones (No 2)* [2002] EWCA Civ 1344; [2003] P.N.L.R. 13.

938 *Eden (NI) Ltd v Mills Selig (A Firm)* [2016] NIQB 71; [2017] P.N.L.R. 2 (though there the claim failed on causation grounds).

939 *Oates v Pitman* [1998] P.N.L.R. 683 (liability admitted); *G. P. & B. v Bulcraig & Davies* (1988) 12 E.G. 103; also *Various Claimants v Giambrone & Law (A Firm)* [2017] EWCA Civ 1193; [2018] P.N.L.R. 2 (a case about newbuild villas in Calabria).

940 *AW Group Ltd v Taylor Walton (A Firm)* [2014] EWCA Civ 592.

941 *Various Claimants v Giambrone & Law (A Firm)* [2017] EWCA Civ 1193; [2018] P.N.L.R. 2 (properties in Calabria).

together with other matters raising serious suspicions as to the behaviour of the borrower,[942] such as unusual features in the transaction[943] or a recent sale at a price much less than the valuation.[944] In advising employers on the drafting of employment contracts he must warn of matters that might be unexpectedly favourable to the employee[945]; conversely, in advising employers on dismissing a senior employee he must apprise them of contractual terms favourable to their position.[946] In litigation, he must advise properly on the prospects of success.[947] Depending on the circumstances, the duty to advise may include a duty to take account of the fact that the law is uncertain,[948] or indeed that it may be changed by judicial decision.[949]

9-145 Once a lawyer has given the client competent advice and ensured that it reaches the client[950] and is understood,[951] the final decision is the client's: the solicitor owes him no duty to save him from his own folly if he decides to take the risk.[952] A lawyer is not generally required to remind his client of advice once given.[953] On the other hand, if later events reveal that advice to have been mistaken, it must be corrected.[954]

---

[942] e.g. *Bristol & West Building Society v Mothew* [1998] Ch. 1 (second charge throwing doubt on mortgagors' ability to repay); *Swindle v Harrison* [1997] 4 All E.R. 705; [1997] P.N.L.R. 641 (hidden arrangements for borrower to profit from loan); *Mortgage Express Ltd v Abensons Solicitors* [2012] EWHC 1000 (Ch); [2012] 2 E.G.L.R. 83 (mortgagor buying from company he himself owned); *Godiva Mortgages Ltd v Keepers Legal LLP* [2012] EWHC 1757 (Ch) (no control over deposit and seller paying buyer's costs).

[943] *Capital Home Loans Ltd v Hewit & Gilpin Solicitors Ltd* [2016] NIQB 13; [2016] P.N.L.R. 24 (price paid partly in shares in vendor, and advance used to pay solicitors' fees).

[944] *E. Surv Ltd v Goldsmith Williams Solicitors* [2015] EWCA Civ 1147; [2016] 4 W.L.R. 44 (remarkable discrepancy between valuation and recent purchase price).

[945] *Newcastle International Airport Ltd v Eversheds LLP* [2013] EWCA Civ 1514; [2014] 1 W.L.R. 3073 (drafting glitch gave employee disproportionately bloated bonus: in fact action failed on causation grounds).

[946] *Commodities Research Unit International (Holdings) Ltd v King & Wood Mallesons LLP* [2016] EWHC 727 (QB); [2016] P.N.L.R. 29 (appeal dismissed, [2017] EWCA Civ 1197; [2018] P.N.L.R. 3).

[947] e.g. the Scottish decision in *Campbell (or Pearson) v Imray* [2004] P.N.L.R. 1 (solicitors negligent in advising that action statute-barred without adverting to the possibility of an application to lift the bar).

[948] *Herrmann v Withers LLP* [2012] EWHC 1492 (Ch); [2012] P.N.L.R. 28 (negligent to fail to warn of uncertainty of purchaser's right to use communal garden, despite eminent conveyancing counsel's advice that all was well). See too *Barker v Baxendale Walker Solicitors (a Firm)* [2017] EWCA Civ 2056; [2018] 1 W.L.R. 1905 (aggressive tax scheme likely to be challenged by Revenue; duty to advise of uncertainties giving rise to successful claim following attack and settlement with Revenue).

[949] *Williams v Thompson Leatherdale* [2008] EWHC 2574 (QB); [2009] P.N.L.R. 15 (barrister—but not solicitor—advising on ancillary relief negligent in not advising delay pending decision in *White v White* [2001] 1 A.C. 596). But obviously not with unforeseeable changes: *Schumann v Veale Wasbrough* [2015] EWCA Civ 441; [2015] P.N.L.R. 25.

[950] Where lawyers are instructed by employees of a client whose interests might conflict with the client's own, they may be in breach unless they send a copy of the advice directly to the client. See *Newcastle International Airport Ltd v Eversheds LLP* [2013] EWCA Civ 1514; [2014] 1 W.L.R. 3073.

[951] See *Booth v Davey* (1988) 138 N.L.J. 104. An action for alleged failure to inform the client of a restrictive covenant failed on a finding that the draft contract had been read through to, and assented to by, the client. But Fox LJ commented that the result might have been different had there been evidence that the client, to the solicitor's knowledge, did not understand the import of the covenant.

[952] *Dutfield v Gilbert H. Stephens & Sons* (1988) 18 Fam. Law 473.

[953] *Yager v Fishman & Co* [1944] 1 All E.R. 552; but see *Mathew v Maughold Life Assurance Co* [1955–95] P.N.L.R. 309.

[954] So decided in Australia: *Hall v Foong* (1996) 65 S.A.S.R. 281.

Extent of duty to advise Where a lawyer is asked to advise on one matter, the general rule is that he is not required to advise on different points, even though they may be related.[955] Thus solicitors instructed to handle a sale and leaseback arrangement for a large and sophisticated client escaped liability for failing to draw their clients' attention to a potential VAT trap.[956] Similarly, solicitors instructed to advise a client on liability for damage to adjoining property inflicted by the client's contractors was held not liable for failing to advise the client to notify his own insurers timeously.[957] On the other hand, a solicitor may be required to deal with very closely connected, though technically extraneous, issues[958]; furthermore, in so far as the solicitor has reason to suspect that the client is not aware of them, he may have at least to draw possible difficulties to the client's attention even if technically outside his retainer.[959] Thus it may be necessary for a solicitor advising on the possibility of escaping a lease to point out a clear trap in the break clause[960]; to warn a client of little business experience about the possible tax consequences of a particular transaction[961]; and to advise a couple who consult him about mutual bequests to each other, of the effect of marriage on such a transaction.[962] In practice, it is submitted that the precise scope of the duty to advise a client depends on the circumstances of the professional relationship between the particular solicitor and his client. Donaldson LJ has warned that an inexperienced client "will need and will be entitled to expect the solicitor to take a much broader view of the scope of his retainer and of his duties, than will be the case with an experienced client".[963] It should also be noted that even though a lawyer does not have to advise on a certain 9-146

[955] e.g. *Griffiths v Evans* [1953] 1 W.L.R. 1424 (if instructed to advise with regard to statutory industrial injury payments, no duty to advise about potential claim in negligence at common law). See too *Lyons v Fox Williams LLP* [2018] EWCA Civ 2347; [2019] P.N.L.R. 9 (solicitors engaged to advise on insurance claim owe no duty to advise of other policies that might have responded).

[956] *Virgin Management v De Morgan Group* [1996] E.G.C.S. 16; see too *Swain Mason v Mills & Reeve* [2012] EWCA Civ 498; [2012] S.T.C. 1760 (solicitors retained to advise on management buy-out not liable for failure to draw attention to potential IHT liability if seller died shortly afterwards, even if they knew seller was in poor health).

[957] *Carradine Properties Ltd v DJ Freeman & Co* [1955–95] P.N.L.R. 219; (1982) 126 S.J. 157 (the claimant's managing director was himself very experienced in insurance matters). See too *John Mowlem Construction Ltd v Neil F. Jones & Co* [2004] EWCA Civ 768; [2004] P.N.L.R. 45 (no duty in solicitors acting for defendant to professional negligence claim to remind defendants to renew indemnity insurance cover).

[958] See, e.g. *Inventors Friend Ltd v Leathes Prior (a firm)* [2011] EWHC 711 (QB); [2011] P.N.L.R. 20 (drafting of distribution agreement: solicitors in breach by protecting distributor as instructed in event that it sold IP rights, but not if it merely licensed them).

[959] "A client cannot expect a solicitor to undertake work he has not asked him to do, and will not wish to pay him for such work. But if in the course of doing the work he is instructed to do the solicitor comes into possession of information which is not confidential and which is clearly of potential significance to the client, I think that the client would reasonably expect the solicitor to pass it on and feel understandably aggrieved if he did not." (Bingham LJ in *Mortgage Express Ltd v Bowerman & Partners* [1996] 2 All E.R. 836, 842. See also *Crédit Lyonnais SA v Russell Jones & Walker (A Firm)* [2002] EWHC 1310; [2003] P.N.L.R. 2 at [21]–[25].)

[960] *Crédit Lyonnais SA v Russell Jones & Walker (A Firm)* [2002] EWHC 1310; [2003] P.N.L.R. 2.

[961] *Hurlingham Estate Ltd v Wilde & Partners* [1997] 1 Lloyd's Rep. 525.

[962] *Hall v Meyrick* [1957] 2 Q.B. 455 at first instance. The Court of Appeal were divided on the point, which did not in the event arise because the claim was held to be statute-barred.

[963] *Carradine Properties Ltd v DJ Freeman & Co* [1955–95] P.N.L.R. 219, 226. Hence a Northern Ireland solicitor dealing with a retiree's project of downsizing and providing a child with a house was held negligent in not warning of the danger of agreeing to buy a new property without a binding contract to sell the old one: *Baird v Hastings & Co* [2013] NIQB 143; [2014] P.N.L.R. 17 (appealed on the facts, [2015] NICA 22).

matter, if he chooses to do so he is likely to owe the client a duty of care in respect of the advice he does give.[964]

9-147 A solicitor is not generally obliged to advise his client on non-legal matters, i.e. on matters of business or the prudence of a particular transaction other than its legal aspects.[965] As Lord Jauncey put it in the Privy Council:

> "When a client in full command of his faculties and apparently aware of what he is doing seeks the assistance of a solicitor in the carrying out of a particular transaction, that solicitor is under no duty whether before or after accepting instructions to go beyond those instructions by proffering unsought advice on the wisdom of the transaction."[966]

The point was trenchantly confirmed in a later Privy Council case, *Riley v Pickersgill*.[967] A businessman arranged for X Ltd, a company he owned, to lease premises, he guaranteeing the rent and taking an indemnity from Y Ltd, to which he then sold his shares in X. His guarantee was called in, but when called on for an indemnity Y turned out to be judgment-proof. He failed in a claim for negligence against his solicitors, who had handled the transaction, for failing to advise him to check Y's financial standing. This was an obvious business risk against which he could have been expected to guard himself. So too a solicitor is under no duty to advise a client, at least where the latter is of relative sophistication, about the dangers of agreeing to buy a property from the proceeds of other property before being assured of receipt of the latter.[968] On the other hand, where the solicitor takes it upon himself to offer general advice he must do so carefully. A solicitor who undertook to obtain a structural report on property for his client was liable when he negligently instructed an unqualified person.[969] Similarly, where a solicitor is aware that his client is inexperienced and relies on him for more than strictly legal advice, he may owe a duty to give that advice or to advise on other sources from which proper advice may be obtained.[970]

(ii) The duty to explain documents

9-148 **Duty to explain documents** In acting for a client, a solicitor is bound to explain any legal document as fully and adequately as the needs of the client indicate.[971] For example, a solicitor who failed to explain to clients taking an underlease that the

---

964 *Holt v Payne Skillington* [1996] P.N.L.R. 179.

965 *Yager v Fishman & Co* [1944] 1 All E.R. 552, 557–558.

966 *Clark Boyce v Mouat* [1994] 1 A.C. 428, 437.

967 [2004] UKPC 14; [2004] P.N.L.R. 31. See too *John Mowlem Construction Ltd v Neil F. Jones & Co* [2004] EWCA Civ 768; [2004] P.N.L.R. 45 (no duty in solicitors acting for defendant to professional negligence claim to remind defendants to renew indemnity insurance cover); *Football League Ltd v Edge Ellison (a firm)* [2006] EWHC 1462 (Ch); [2007] P.N.L.R. 2 (no duty to warn highly professional League that counterparty to contract might become insolvent owing them money; *Kandola v Mirza Solicitors LLP* [2015] EWHC 460 (Ch); [2015] P.N.L.R. 19 (uncreditworthiness of real estate seller).

968 See the Irish decision in *Flynn v King* [2017] IEHC 735; [2018] P.N.L.R. 15.

969 *Collard v Saunders* [1971] C.L.Y. 1116.

970 *Neushul v Mellish & Harkavy* (1967) 111 S.J. 399; *Carradine Properties Ltd v DJ Freeman & Co* [1955–95] P.N.L.R. 219; and see M. Brazier [1976] Conv. 179 at 191–194. cf. *Agouman v Leigh Day (A Firm)* [2016] EWHC 1324 (QB); [2016] P.N.L.R. 32 (safe investment of funds recovered for unsophisticated African clients in the Ivory Coast).

971 Including advising on the possibility of a dispute arising from those documents: *Balogun v Boyes Sutton & Perry* [2017] EWCA Civ 75; [2017] P.N.L.R. 20 (discrepancy between headlease and sublease).

head lessor had an absolute right to withhold his consent to change of user was found liable to the clients in negligence.[972] Where a solicitor takes counsel's advice it is his duty rather than counsel's to ensure that the client fully comprehends the implications of it.[973] In a case where instructions from a client to draft documents come through those whose interests may be not the same as the client's, there may be a duty to give advice on their implications directly to the client as well as to the person providing the instructions.[974]

(iii) The duty to keep the client informed

Duty to provide information Where a solicitor is in possession of, or comes across, information while acting for his client, he must normally pass this information on to the latter in so far as it is relevant to the client's interests and the transaction in which he is instructed.[975] Moreover, this duty applies even if the solicitor is acting for another party as well and disclosing the information would be a breach of duty vis-à-vis that other. Thus a solicitor acting for both mortgagor and mortgagee must pass on to the latter information that there has been a recent or contemporaneous sale at a substantially lower price,[976] that the price actually being paid is substantially less than the stated amount,[977] or that part of the alleged price has never actually passed through his hands,[978] since all these factors may indicate fraud or an over-valued security. And the House of Lords has held a solicitor acting for vendor and purchaser liable to the vendor for failing to tell him that the purchaser had a number of convictions suggesting that he was dishonest and might fail to carry the transaction through (which, in the event, happened).[979] 9-149

972 *Sykes v Midland Bank Executor & Trustee Co Ltd* [1971] Q.B. 113; *County Personnel v Alan R. Pulver & Co* [1987] 1 W.L.R. 916. But a general explanation will normally suffice, even though particular details be missed out: see *Reeves v Thrings & Long* [1996] P.N.L.R. 265; and *Rentokil Initial 1927 plc v Goodman Derrick LLP* [2014] EWHC 2994 (Ch) at [134].

973 *Mathew v Maughold Life Assurance Co* [1955–95] P.N.L.R. 309; *The Times,* 19 February 1987. But sophisticated commercial clients are entitled to less protection in this respect: *Accident Assurance Ltd v Hammonds Suddards Edge* [2005] EWHC 202 (Ch); [2005] P.N.L.R. 29.

974 See *Newcastle International Airport Ltd v Eversheds LLP* [2013] EWCA Civ 1514; [2014] 1 W.L.R. 3073 (employers, remarkably, left it to senior employees to instruct solicitors on their behalf to draft their own employment contracts: contracts contained wildly over-munificent bonuses: held, breach of duty for solicitors not to send copy of draft, with clear advice on its implications, directly to employers' human resources department as well as to employees themselves).

975 "A solicitor must put at his client's disposal not only his skill but also his knowledge, so far as is relevant; and if he is unwilling to reveal his knowledge to his client, he should not act for him. What he cannot do is to act for the client and at the same time withhold from him any relevant knowledge that he has …" (Megarry J in *Spector v Ageda* [1973] Ch. 30, 48). Note the mortgagee case of *E.Surv Ltd v Goldsmith Williams Solicitors* [2015] EWCA Civ 1147; [2016] 4 W.L.R. 44, making it clear that the requirements of publications such as the Council of Mortgage Lenders Handbook are not necessarily exhaustive in this respect.

976 *Mortgage Express Ltd v Bowerman* [1996] 2 All E.R. 836; *Bristol & West Building Society v Fancy & Jackson* [1997] 4 All E.R. 582, 605–606; *Nationwide Building Society v Balmer Radmore* [1999] P.N.L.R. 606, 652–653.

977 *Nationwide Building Society v Balmer Radmore* [1999] P.N.L.R. 606, 646.

978 *Bristol & West Building Society v Fancy & Jackson* [1997] 4 All E.R. 582; *Nationwide Building Society v Balmer Radmore* [1999] P.N.L.R. 606, 648. And similarly with other indications of possible fraud: see *Darlington Building Society v O'Rourke* [1999] P.N.L.R. 365, 371–372; and *Anglia, Hastings & Thanet Building Society v House & Son* [1955–95] P.N.L.R. 209; (1981) 260 E.G. 1128.

979 *Hilton v Barker Booth & Eastwood* [2005] UKHL 8; [2005] 1 W.L.R. 567. Earlier decisions suggesting a more limited duty, such as *National Home Loans Corp plc v Giffen Couch & Archer* [1998]

(iv) The duty to take care in carrying through a transaction

9-150 Solicitors instructed to carry out a particular transaction owe a duty to ensure that, as far as possible, the affair proceeds according to plan. Thus care must be taken to read documents thoroughly,[980] to draft documentation effectively,[981] properly[982] and as unambiguously as possible,[983] with where necessary suitable co-ordination between the members of the firm involved[984]; and to obtain, and where necessary check, relevant information from the counterparty.[985] Similarly, solicitors acting for purchasers must take steps to register any title obtained[986]; and those acting for mortgagees must take proper steps to ensure that the mortgage documents are valid, and that the signatures on them are genuine.[987]

(v) The duty to take care in conduct of litigation

9-151 A lawyer is under a duty to take care at all stages during litigation, whether in court or out of it.[988] A solicitor who delays issuing proceedings so that his client's action becomes statute-barred will almost certainly[989] be held to be negligent.[990] Similarly he will be liable if he issues proceedings against the wrong parties,[991] save in exceptional circumstances.[992] Delay in prosecuting litigation once started so that the action is struck out for want of prosecution,[993] or even if not struck out, is to the detriment of the client in other respects,[994] are other common examples of negligence in the conduct of litigation. The duty to conduct litigation with care also

1 W.L.R. 207, must it is submitted now be regarded as doubtful.

980 See the Hong Kong decision in *Hondon Development Ltd v Powerise Investments Ltd* [2005] 3 HKLRD 605; [2006] P.N.L.R. 1 (solicitors negligent in not spotting discrepancy in size of shop unit apparent from conveyancing documents).

981 *UCB Corporate Services Ltd v Clyde & Co* [2000] P.N.L.R. 841 (lenders' security as drafted ineffective under Statute of Frauds 1677: City solicitors who advised them on it understandably held negligent).

982 *Wellesley Partners LLP v Withers LLP* [2015] EWCA Civ 1146; [2016] Ch. 529

983 See *Queen Elizabeth's School Blackburn Ltd v Banks Wilson* [2001] EWCA Civ 1360; [2002] P.N.L.R. 14 (imprecise drafting caused legal expenses of establishing true position); also *Balogun v Boyes Sutton & Perry* [2017] EWCA Civ 75; [2017] P.N.L.R. 20 (solicitors in breach in failing to ensure underlease of restaurant gave unambiguous access to communal ventilation, though case failed on causation grounds). The *Queen Elizabeth* case is criticised in S. Gee, "The solicitor's duty to warn that a court might take a different view" (2003) 19 P.N. 362, but (it is suggested) not particularly convincingly.

984 *Swain Mason v Mills & Reeve* [2011] EWHC 410 (Ch); [2011] S.T.C. 1177 at [150] (Arnold J) (appeal dismissed, save as to costs, [2012] EWCA Civ 498; [2012] S.T.C. 1760).

985 See *Cottingham v Attey Bower* [2000] P.N.L.R. 557 (vendor provides no evidence of planning consent for extension: in fact none granted: purchaser's solicitor negligent not to enquire further).

986 See the Irish case of *Rosbeg Partners Ltd v L.K. Shields (A Firm)* [2018] IESC 23; [2018] P.N.L.R. 26.

987 *Zwebner v Mortgage Corp'n Ltd* [1998] P.N.L.R. 769.

988 Since *Hall (Arthur JS) & Co v Simons* [2002] 1 A.C. 615; above, para.9-137.

989 Though not absolutely invariably, e.g. where limitation law is unexpectedly changed by judicial decision.

990 *Fletcher & Jon v Jubb Booth & Helliwell* [1920] 1 K.B. 275.

991 *Losner v Michael Cohen & Co* (1975) 119 S.J. 340. See too *Gill v Lougher* (1830) 1 In. & J. 170 (wrong court).

992 *Martin Boston v Roberts* [1996] P.N.L.R. 45.

993 *Fitzpatrick v Batger & Co Ltd* [1967] 1 W.L.R. 706. This may require very forceful advice to the client: see the Irish decision in *Emerald Isle Assurances & Investments Ltd v Dorgan* [2016] IECA 12.

994 e.g. *Stewart v Patterson Donnelly Solicitors* [2014] NIQB 103; [2015] P.N.L.R. 7 (intervening

includes a duty to collate evidence and ensure it is available to the court,[995] and not to withdraw without adequate notice.[996] Similarly a solicitor or barrister is under a duty to exercise care in settlement negotiations and may be liable if he advises his client to settle for a sum that is too high or low, as the case may be.[997] The client's financial interests must be properly protected, for example by obtaining proper security for costs,[998] or taking proper steps to safeguard any sums recovered.[999] But advice, while it must be sufficient to inform the client's decision as to how to proceed, need not be exhaustive: as Baroness Hale has put it, "there is still a respectable body of professional opinion that the client pays for the advocate's opinion, not her doubts".[1000]

However, the impact of the *Bolam*[1001] rule, to which lawyers are subject, needs to be taken into account: a lawyer who elects to run litigation in a particular way will not be negligent if a responsible body of professional opinion supports the approach taken.[1002] As Lord Bingham has said, "advocacy is more an art than a science. It cannot be conducted according to formulae. Individuals differ in their style and approach."[1003] Furthermore, with respect to decisions taken in the fast-moving scenario of court proceedings, account will be taken of the need to make quick decisions without the possibility of leisured research.[1004] **9-152**

(vi) The duty to avoid a conflict of interest

A lawyer owes a duty to his client, both as a matter of fiduciary duty and as an implied regulatory[1005] and contractual[1006] obligation, not to act for another in a situ- **9-153**

insolvency of other party); *Emerald Isle Assurances & Investments Ltd v Dorgan* [2016] IECA 12 (indolent lawyers: strike out more likely, thus affecting settlement value).

995 *Browning v Brachers* [2004] EWHC 16 (QB); [2004] P.N.L.R. 28 (liability in solicitors for failing to assemble evidence on time, with result that client prevented from relying on it at trial) (appealed on other grounds, [2005] EWCA Civ 753; [2005] P.N.L.R. 44).

996 *Kim v Oh* [2013] NZHC 925; [2013] 2 N.Z.L.R. 825.

997 e.g. *Hall (Arthur JS) & Co v Simons* [2002] 1 A.C. 615; and more recently *Perry v Raleys Solicitors* [2019] UKSC 5; [2019] 2 W.L.R. 636 (negligent advice not to pursue one head of claim). See too *Dunhill v Brook & Co* [2018] EWCA Civ 505 at [45]–[46] (Leveson P).

998 *Martin Boston v Roberts* [1996] P.N.L.R. 45.

999 *Agouman v Leigh Day (A Firm)* [2016] EWHC 1324 (QB); [2016] P.N.L.R. 32 (recoveries obtained for Ivorian claimants left in Ivorian bank, where swiftly annexed by local strongmen manipulating judicial system).

1000 *Moy v Pettman Smith* [2005] UKHL 7; [2005] 1 W.L.R. 581 at [28].

1001 *Bolam v Friern HMC* [1957] 1 W.L.R. 582.

1002 See, e.g. *Firstcity Insurance Ltd v Orchard* [2003] P.N.L.R. 9 (counsel declined to run a tendentious point at first instance which in fact was good, with the result that although the claimant won in the CA he was mulcted in costs: no liability); *Boyle v Thompsons Solicitors* [2012] EWHC 36 (QB); [2012] P.N.L.R. 17 (not negligent for personal injury claimant's solicitors to fail to seek further expert report, with the risks entailed if it should prove unfavourable).

1003 *Ridehalgh v Horsefield* [1994] Ch. 205, 236. These words, though used in connection with wasted costs orders, were approved in the general negligence context by Lord Steyn in *Hall (Arthur JS) & Co v Simons* [2002] 1 A.C. 615, 681–682.

1004 *Hall (Arthur JS) & Co v Simons* [2002] 1 A.C. 615, 681–682 (Lord Steyn); *Moy v Pettman Smith* [2005] UKHL 7; [2005] 1 W.L.R. 581 at [59]–[60] (Lord Carswell). See too, for similar comments, *Dunhill v Brook & Co* [2018] EWCA Civ 505 at [45]–[48] (Leveson P).

1005 See the 2018 *SRA Code of Conduct*, para.6 and the 2020 *BSB Code of Conduct* rr.C21 and C25.

1006 "A solicitor's duty of single-minded loyalty to his client's interest, and his duty to respect his client's confidences, do have their roots in the fiduciary nature of the solicitor-client relationship. But they may have to be moulded and informed by the terms of the contractual relationship."—Lord Walker ation where there would be a potential conflict of interest.[1007] If such a situation arises, he must decline to act for one or the other: if he continues so to do, he will be amenable to an injunction and liable in damages for any loss caused.[1008] Such a conflict will normally arise where one firm of solicitors represents the two parties on opposite sides in litigation,[1009] or any other potentially contentious matter,[1010] though perhaps not invariably so.[1011]

9-154 **Confidential information protected independently of conflict of interest** The fiduciary relationship precluding a solicitor from acting from an opponent is coterminous with the retainer itself, and does not survive the end of it.[1012] Nevertheless, even after the retainer is at an end the client is entitled to protection against any risk that confidential information revealed to his lawyer will pass to someone with whom he comes into conflict.[1013] Whether a remedy will be given depends on the circumstances,[1014] and particularly on whether confidential information was held likely to affect the interests of the former client which was at a real or appreciable risk of disclosure.[1015] The presumption is against the lawyer: unless it is clear that there can be no leakage or misuse, deliberate or otherwise, of confidential information, there will be a breach of duty.[1016] On the other hand, if the court is satisfied that there is no possibility of such misuse, then a firm of solicitors may act for one

---

in *Hilton v Barker Booth & Eastwood* [2005] UKHL 8; [2005] 1 W.L.R. 567 at [30]. See too *Hospital Products Ltd v United States Surgical Corp'n* (1984) 156 C.L.R. 41 at 97 (Mason J).

[1007] *Rakusen v Ellis, Munday & Clarke* [1912] 1 Ch.831; *Clark Boyce v Mouat* [1994] 1 A.C. 428; *Hilton v Barker Booth & Eastwood* [2005] UKHL 8; [2005] 1 W.L.R. 567 at [30]–[31]; *Markey v McMahon* [2012] NIQB 35 at [25]–[26]; *Western Avenue Properties Ltd v Soni* [2017] EWHC 2650 (QB); [2018] P.N.L.R. 10. Where a solicitor has possibly obtained information through having acted adversely to the claimant (e.g. by disclosure or in the course of mediation), an injunction may be granted to prevent him acting adversely to the claimant for another client in a similar matter, but there is a fairly heavy burden of proof on the claimant to show a likelihood of misuse of the information involved: see, e.g. *Glencairn IP Holdings Ltd v Product Specialities Inc* [2019] EWHC 1733 (IPEC); [2019] P.N.L.R. 31.

[1008] *Morkot v Watson & Brown Solicitors* [2014] EWHC 3439 (QB); [2015] P.N.L.R. 9 (purchasers' solicitor hand-in-glove with vendors: liable in damages to purchasers who lost money); see too *Ball v Druces & Attlee (No. 2)* [2004] EWHC 1402 (QB); [2004] P.N.L.R. 39. cf. *Longstaff v Birtles* [2001] EWCA Civ 1219; [2002] 1 W.L.R. 470; and *Day v Mead* [1987] 2 N.Z.L.R. 443 (both cases of advice by solicitors to invest in businesses in which firm interested).

[1009] *Marks & Spencer Plc v Freshfields Bruckhaus Deringer* [2004] EWHC 1337 (Ch); [2004] 1 W.L.R. 2331; *Western Avenue Properties Ltd v Soni* [2017] EWHC 2650 (QB); [2018] P.N.L.R. 10.

[1010] Such as landlord and tenant negotiating over a lease (*Markey v McMahon* [2012] NIQB 35) or buyer and seller of a business (*Taylor v Schofield Peterson* [1999] 3 N.Z.L.R. 434).

[1011] It may be that a lawyer may act both for and against a client in two entirely unrelated contentious matters: see *Marks & Spencer Plc v Freshfields Bruckhaus Deringer* [2004] EWHC 1337 (Ch); [2004] 1 W.L.R. 2331 at [16] (Lawrence Collins J: need for "some reasonable relationship between the two matters"); and the Australian decision in *Australian Liquor Marketers Pty Ltd v Tasman Liquor Traders Pty Ltd* [2002] VSC 324. Paragraph 6.2 of the 2018 *SRA Code of Conduct* does not in so many words allow this, but the definition of "conflict of interest" may well mean that such a case does not involve a conflict in the first place, so that the omission is irrelevant.

[1012] *Bolkiah (Prince Jefri) v KPMG* [1999] 2 A.C. 222, 235 (Lord Millett).

[1013] e.g. *Georgian American Alloys Inc v White & Case LLP* [2014] EWHC 94 (Comm); [2014] 1 C.L.C. 86; see too *Bolkiah (Prince Jefri) v KPMG* [1999] 2 A.C. 222, 236 (Lord Millett). The reason is that the solicitor is bound to put any relevant knowledge he has at the disposal of those instructing him, and thus would be subject to irreconcilable obligations to the old and new clients. The 2018 *SRA Code of Conduct*, para.6.3 and the 2020 *BSB Code of Conduct* r.C15, spell this out in the regulatory field.

[1014] See generally K. Stafford, "Chinese Walls and Confidential Information" (2003) 19 P.N. 306.

[1015] *Russell McVeagh McKenzie Bartleet & Co v Tower Corporation* [1998] 3 N.Z.L.R. 641, 648–651.

[1016] e.g. *Ball v Druces & Attlee* [2002] P.N.L.R. 23 (litigation between ex-partners in joint venture:

side in litigation despite having been previously retained by the other.[1017] In practice a "Chinese wall" arrangement, with perhaps additional undertakings as to contact between particular lawyers, or some similar arrangement,[1018] is likely to suffice.[1019]

Solicitor may act for two parties to transaction There is no legal objection as such to the same solicitor acting for two parties to a transaction whose interests may not be the same, provided both parties have given their informed consent to his doing so.[1020] The practice has frequently been criticised.[1021] Nevertheless, dual capacity is both practically convenient and widespread. A common example is where, in the case of residential conveyancing, the same firm acts for both mortgagor and mortgagee; less common, though still significant, is the case where it acts for both vendor and purchaser. Yet another example is where in a professional negligence action the same solicitors represent the defendant and his professional indemnity insurers. However, where in such a case the solicitor makes a mistake to the detriment of one party, the courts will be very ready to find such a mistake to be negligent on the basis that the solicitor should never have put himself in a position where such a risk of conflict could arise.[1022] In all such situations, a solicitor continues to owe the same duty to each client as he would were he acting for him **9-155**

erstwhile solicitors for joint venture restrained from representing defendants in absence of evidence that no conflict); also *Re Z* [2009] EWHC 3621 (Fam); [2010] 2 F.L.R. 132. See too the Canadian decision in *MacDonald Estate v Martin* [1990] 3 S.C.R. 1235 (solicitor who had previously worked for opponent disqualified: affidavit of no conflict not enough in absence of verifiable methods to protect confidences). For the case where a solicitor has acted for A and B jointly and now wishes to act for A against B, see *Singla v Stockler* [2012] EWHC 1176 (Ch); [2012] B.P.I.R. 1061.

1017 *Christie v Wilson* [1998] P.N.L.R. 748; and cf. *CPR v Aikens* [1998] 6 W.W.R. 351. Compare *Hornan v Latif Group SL* [2003] EWHC 536 (Ch); [2003] B.C.C. 976 (not enough to allege vague possibility of conflict).

1018 e.g. *Halewood International Ltd v Addleshaw Booth & Co* [2000] P.N.L.R. 788 (risk of leakage may be adequately prevented where solicitors in one firm work in separate premises).

1019 e.g. *Koch Shipping Inc v Richards Butler* [2002] EWCA Civ 1280; [2003] P.N.L.R. 11 (solicitor joined firm involved in hostile arbitration against erstwhile client of hers: Chinese wall arrangement, plus undertaking that she would not enter the offices of or talk to those involved in arbitration, held sufficient to preclude any real risk of leakage); *Gus Consulting GmbH v Leboeuf Lamb Green & Macrae* [2006] EWCA Civ 683; [2006] P.N.L.R. 32 (similar); *Bank of Montreal v Dresler* (2003) 224 D.L.R. (4th) 337 (no conflict where reasonably informed person would conclude no likelihood of inadvertent disclosure).

1020 See *Clark Boyce v Mouat* [1994] 1 A.C. 428; *Farrington v Rowe McBride & Partners* [1985] 1 N.Z.L.R. 83, 90. There may nevertheless be some situations where the conflict is so glaring that even with disclosure it is impermissible for the same solicitor to act: ibid. cf. *Taylor v Schofield Peterson* [1999] 3 N.Z.L.R. 434 (acting for seller and buyer of business who were in dispute). Today the matter is dealt with by the 2018 *SRA Code of Conduct*, para.6.2, allowing the solicitor so to act, but only if the clients have a substantially common objective or are competing for the same objective, and in addition (i) effective safeguards against leakage of confidential information are in place; and (ii) the solicitor is satisfied that it is reasonable to act.

1021 e.g. *Goody v Baring* [1956] 1 W.L.R. 448; *Smith v Mansi* [1963] 1 W.L.R. 26.

1022 *Nash v Phillips* (1974) 232 E.G. 1219; *Dogma Properties v Gale* (1984) New L.J. 453; *Blackwell v Barroile Pty Ltd* (1994) 123 A.L.R. 81.

alone,[1023] despite the fact that he may owe duties of confidence to one or the other.[1024]

9-156 **Solicitors acting for two parties: duty to disclose information** A solicitor is bound at all times to take all reasonable steps to protect the interests of his client, whether by passing on relevant information which comes into his hands or otherwise. This duty is entirely unaffected by the fact that he may be acting for two parties at the same time.[1025] Thus, for example, a solicitor acting for both mortgagor and mortgagee must pass on to the latter information indicative of fraud or over-valuation, such as recent or contemporaneous sales at a substantially lower price,[1026] or the fact that part of the alleged price has never actually passed through his hands.[1027] If he does not, he may be liable to the mortgagee for any loss suffered. Similarly, in *Hilton v Barker Booth & Eastwood*[1028] solicitors acting for vendor and purchaser were held liable by the House of Lords for failing to protect the former's interests by informing them that their purchaser was a convicted fraudster who might well prove (as he did) to be insubstantial. In the event that observing the duty incumbent on a solicitor acting for both parties puts him into a serious conflict, there is no doubt as to his duty: he must decline to act for one or other.[1029]

(g) Damages

(i) *Need to prove loss and causation*

9-157 **Need to prove loss** Whether the claimant sues in contract or tort, he must of course establish that he[1030] has suffered a loss. If he cannot, he will fail in tort and recover only nominal damages in contract. For example, in *Kennedy v Van*

[1023] *Hilton v Barker Booth & Eastwood* [2005] UKHL 8; [2005] 1 W.L.R. 567 (solicitors acting for vendor and purchaser liable for failing to tell vendor that purchaser a convicted fraudster). See too *Moody v Cox & Hatt* [1917] 2 Ch. 71 at 81; *Mortgage Express v Bowerman & Partners* [1996] 2 All E.R. 836, 844; *Bristol & West B.S. v Mothew* [1998] Ch. 1, 110–20; *Nationwide Building Society v Balmer Radmore* [1999] P.N.L.R. 606, 641.

[1024] *Hilton v Barker Booth & Eastwood* [2005] UKHL 8; [2005] 1 W.L.R. 567. See generally C. Hollander, "Conflicts of Interest and the Duty to Disclose Information" (2004) 23 C.J.Q. 257. Any contrary suggestions in *Nationwide Building Society v Balmer Radmore* [1999] P.N.L.R. 606 at 638 must now be seen as discredited.

[1025] *Mortgage Express Ltd v Bowerman & Partners* [1996] 2 All E.R. 836, 844–845 (Millett LJ); *Hilton v Barker Booth & Eastwood* [2005] UKHL 8; [2005] 1 W.L.R. 567 at [35]–[46] (Lord Walker).

[1026] *Mortgage Express Ltd v Bowerman* [1996] 2 All E.R. 836; *Bristol & West Building Society v Fancy & Jackson* [1997] 4 All E.R. 582, 605–606; *Nationwide Building Society v Balmer Radmore* [1999] P.N.L.R. 606, 652–653.

[1027] *Bristol & West Building Society v Fancy & Jackson* [1997] 4 All E.R. 582; *Nationwide Building Society v Balmer Radmore* [1999] P.N.L.R. 606, 648.

[1028] [2005] UKHL 8; [2005] 1 W.L.R. 567 (reversing [2002] EWCA Civ 723; [2003] P.N.L.R. 32). Cases favouring a more limited duty of disclosure, such as *Bristol & West Building Society v Baden, Barnes & Groves* [2000] Lloyd's Rep. P.N. 788, must now be regarded as wrongly decided.

[1029] See *Halifax Mortgage Services v Stepsky* [1996] Ch. 1; *Nationwide Building Society v Balmer Radmore* [1999] P.N.L.R. 606, 638 et seq.; *Hilton v Barker Booth & Eastwood* [2005] UKHL 8; [2005] 1 W.L.R. 567.

[1030] The loss must in general have been suffered by the claimant himself. A loss suffered by a third party, such as a company intimately connected with him, will not do: see, e.g. *Xenakis v Birkett Long LLP* [2014] EWHC 171 (QB); [2014] P.N.L.R. 16 (solicitors' negligence in arranging for guarantee forced claimants to support ailing business: no claim in so far as support came from claimants' private company).

Emden[1031] solicitors negligently allowed clients to pay a premium of £50,000 for assignment of a residential lease at a time when charging such premiums was illegal. But the law was subsequently changed so that the clients could themselves charge a premium when they sold the lease on. The clients, having suffered no loss, recovered nothing in respect of the premium they had paid. Similarly, where purchasers' solicitors negligently failed to spot certain building restrictions on land but the land was in any case worth more than was paid for it, the purchasers recovered nothing.[1032] Again, where an insolvent client subject to an individual voluntary arrangement sued solicitors for mismanaging arbitration proceedings, he failed to recover substantial damages on the basis that the assets thereby diminished belonged not to him, but to his administrator.[1033] However, the limitations on this principle must be noted. A client may still suffer a loss even though the deficiency is made good by a third party[1034]; and it seems that where a trustee or personal representative sues for loss to the estate, the lack of personal loss to him is out of account.[1035] It should also be remembered that a claimant has an unfettered choice as to whom he turns to in order to make good his loss[1036]: from which it follows that a lawyer may be liable for a loss however reasonable it might be to expect the client to look to some third party instead for reparation.[1037]

Need to prove causation As elsewhere in the law of tort, the claimant bears the burden of proving not only a loss suffered, but that his loss was caused by the defendant's negligence.[1038] Thus in *Sykes v Midland Bank Executor & Trustee Co Ltd*[1039] the claimants, who were taking an under-lease of premises, established that the defendants had been negligent in not drawing their attention to the fact that the 9-158

1031 [1996] P.N.L.R. 409. cf. *Aylwen v Taylor Joynson Garrett* [2001] EWCA Civ 1171; [2002] P.N.L.R. 1 (loss of house due to solicitors' negligence, but house subject to negative equity anyway: no recovery); and *Parker v SJ Berwin & Co* [2008] EWHC 3017 (QB); [2009] P.N.L.R. 17.

1032 *Ford v White* [1964] 1 W.L.R. 885. See too a converse case, *Hay v Gourley McBain*, 2008 S.L.T. (Sh Ct) 101; [2009] P.N.L.R. 7 (sellers' solicitors negligently expose sellers to an unanswerable claim for £30,000 for breach of title covenants: but no recovery, since land sold for £50,000 more than market value).

1033 *Welburn v Dibb Lupton Broomhead* [2002] EWCA Civ 1601; [2003] P.N.L.R. 28.

1034 cf. the surveyors' case of *Gardner v Marsh & Parsons* [1997] 1 W.L.R. 489.

1035 *Chappell v Somers & Blake* [2003] EWHC 1644 (Ch); [2004] Ch. 19 (solicitors negligently delay in distributing estate including rental property: liable to administratrix for rentals lost by beneficiaries even though administratrix suffered no loss personally). Neuberger J thought, surely rightly, that a trustee would be similarly treated: [2003] EWHC 1644 (Ch); [2004] Ch. 19 at [27]–[38]. Compare the Scots decision in *Marquess of Aberdeen and Temair v Turcan Connell* [2008] CSOH 183; [2009] P.N.L.R. 18.

1036 *Peters v East Midlands Strategic HA* [2009] EWCA Civ 145; [2010] Q.B. 48.

1037 See *Haugesund Kommune v Depfa ACS Bank (No 2)* [2010] EWHC 227 (Comm); [2010] P.N.L.R. 21 (reversed on other grounds, [2011] EWCA Civ 33; [2011] 3 All E.R. 655) (lawyers fail to notice ultra vires problem in municipal financing: lenders recover full amount lent, and fact that some monies recoverable from municipalities on unjust enrichment basis irrelevant).

1038 Nevertheless, courts may be prepared to draw some favourable inferences. As Jacob LJ put it in *Levicom International Holdings BV v Linklaters* [2010] EWCA Civ 494; [2010] P.N.L.R. 29 at [284]: "When a solicitor gives advice that his client has a strong case to start litigation rather than settle and the client then does just that, the normal inference is that the advice is causative. Of course the inference is rebuttable—it may be possible to show that the client would have gone ahead willy-nilly. But that was certainly not shown on the evidence here."

1039 [1971] 1 Q.B. 113 For other cases where proper advice would not have been appreciated or followed, see *Nash v Phillips* (1974) 232 E.G. 1219; *Lynne v Gordon Doctors & Walton* (1991) 135 S.J. 29; *White v Paul Davidson & Taylor* [2004] EWCA Civ 1511; [2005] P.N.L.R. 15; and *Newcastle International Airport Ltd v Eversheds LLP* [2013] EWCA Civ 1514; [2014] 1 W.L.R. 3073.

head lessor had an absolute right to refuse consent to a change of user, but were awarded only nominal damages because the Court of Appeal found that they would have taken the underlease even if properly advised[1040]: so too where a claimant is so enthusiastic that a warning would have made no difference.[1041] Furthermore, where the real cause of the claimant's loss is some failure on his part to secure his own interests,[1042] or the intervening act of a third party,[1043] he will recover nothing in respect of it.

(ii) Measure of recovery

9-159 **Measure of recovery in general** The claimant complaining of legal malpractice is entitled to be put in the position he would have been in had the defendant performed his duty. In many cases this means that he recovers the amount by which he is out of pocket as a result of relying on the defendant's advice.[1044] Conveyancing transactions provide a straightforward example. Thus in *Oates v Pitman*[1045] purchasers' solicitors negligently failed to notice that the planning laws precluded the intended use of premises as a nursing home. The purchasers recovered the difference between the price paid and the actual value of the premises, but not the profits they would have made if the restriction had not existed: this was because, had the solicitors acted properly, they would not have purchased those premises at all.[1046] Loan transactions are similarly treated. Where solicitors' negligence causes lenders to lend on overvalued property, the lenders can recover the amount lent less any recovery from the debtor and the property itself, plus any interest they would otherwise have earned on their money had they not committed it, but nothing in respect of the interest that ought to have been paid by the borrower.[1047] It should be noted, however, that the price-value differential is not always the appropriate measure of recovery. It may be more fitting to award the claimant his costs of

[1040] See too *Etridge v Pritchard Englefield* [1999] P.N.L.R. 839 (failure to advise wife properly about effect of guarantee of husband's debts, but wife would have concluded transaction anyway); and *White v Paul Davidson & Taylor* [2004] EWCA Civ 1511; [2005] P.N.L.R. 15. The latter case made it clear that, if and in so far as *Chester v Afshar* [2004] UKHL 41; [2005] 1 A.C. 134, modified the law of causation (on which see para.9-115), it was not to be extended outside the field of medical malpractice.

[1041] *Capital Home Loans Ltd v Hewit & Gilpin Solicitors Ltd* [2016] NIQB 13; [2016] P.N.L.R. 24.

[1042] *Simmons v Pennington* [1955] 1 W.L.R. 183 CA (failure to insure); *Frank v Seifert, Sedley & Co* (1964) 108 S.J. 523 (failure to complete).

[1043] Assuming that the third party's act was sufficient to break the chain of causation. It was not in *Cook v Swinfen* [1968] 1 W.L.R. 635.

[1044] Subject to the general limitations on recovery, such as the duty to mitigate loss. See, e.g. *British Racing Drivers' Club v Hextall Erskine* [1996] 3 All E.R. 667 (where damages include costs payable to third party, duty to demand taxation of those costs).

[1045] (1998) 76 P. & C.R. 490. See too *Ford v White* [1964] 1 W.L.R. 885 (solicitors fail to notice building restrictions on land being purchased: land free of restrictions would have been worth £1,000 more: no recovery of £1,000, but only diminution in value (which in the event was nil). It has been held that the same applies to the purchase of a business: see the Irish decision in *Kelleher v O'Connor* [2010] IEHC 313; [2011] P.N.L.R. 3 (solicitors fail to warn of food hygiene problem in restaurant being bought by client: measure of damages is price, less actual value).

[1046] Though presumably if the claimants could have shown that they would otherwise have invested their money in a profitable manner, or laid it out at interest, they could recover those gains, since but for the defendants' negligence they would not have been foregone: cf. the deceit case of *East v Maurer* [1991] 1 W.L.R. 461.

[1047] By analogy from the valuers' decision in *Swingcastle v Alastair Gibson* [1991] 2 A.C. 223. The reason is that, had the solicitors given proper advice, the claimants would not have lent at all on the terms they did.

unwinding a transaction entered into as a result of his lawyers' incompetence,[1048] for example the cost of paying to escape from a disadvantageous lease,[1049] or loss incurred in selling on an unviable business.[1050]

Nevertheless, the "out-of-pocket loss" measure of recovery is not invariable. If the claimant can show that, had the lawyer acted with due care, he would have made a particular gain, or obtained the benefit of a valuable asset, then damages are recoverable in respect of the failure to realise the gain concerned. So where solicitors failed to ensure purchasers obtained the protected leasehold they sought, damages were the capital cost of obtaining such an interest[1051]; and where vendors' solicitors negligently delayed sending documentation to a purchaser who as a result withdrew, the vendors were held entitled to recover in respect of the profit they would have made on the sale.[1052] Again, if lawyers negligently fail to structure a joint venture transaction so as to allow their client to make a profit, they will be liable for the profit foregone.[1053] The decision in *White v Jones*,[1054] allowing a disappointed beneficiary of a will to recover from negligent solicitors, is another example of the same principle. **9-160**

Consequential losses The claimant can, in addition, recover consequential losses, provided they result from the defendant's negligence and are not too remote. These may include, for example, loss of profits resulting from a failure to advise properly on a transaction,[1055] or from a failure due to lawyers' negligence to obtain land[1056] or an option over it[1057]; a mother's expense in trying to recover children spirited **9-161**

1048 See *South Australia Asset Management Corporation and York Montague Ltd* [1997] A.C. 191, 218-219 (Lord Hoffmann).

1049 *County Personnel Ltd v Alan R. Pulver* [1987] 1 W.L.R. 916. See too *Hayes v James & Charles Dodd* [1990] 2 All E.R. 815. This may include expenditure on improvements wasted as a result: see, e.g. *Geoffrey Funnel v Adams* [2007] EWHC 2166.

1050 *Scott v Kennedys Law LLP* [2011] EWHC 3808 (Ch); see too, e.g. *Doran v Delaney (No. 2)* [1999] 1 I.L.R.M. 225.

1051 *Murray v Lloyd* [1989] 1 W.L.R. 1060. Similarly with solicitors who bungle the renewal of a lease: *Nahome v Last Cawthra Feather* [2010] EWHC 76 (Ch); [2010] P.N.L.R. 19.

1052 *Stovold v Barlows* [1996] P.N.L.R. 19. (In fact the damages were reckoned on a loss of chance basis, but this does not affect the point in the text.) cf. *Jenmain Builders Ltd v Steed & Steed* [2000] P.N.L.R. 616 (solicitors' negligence caused clients to lose purchase: no liability for lost putative profits on deal, but only because no such profits proved). See too *Leggett v Giambrone Law LLP* [2020] EWHC 724 (QB); [2020] P.N.L.R. 18.

1053 *Ball v Druces & Attlee (No.2)* [2004] EWHC 1402; [2004] P.N.L.R. 39 (solicitors negligently arrange transaction as charitable venture with no profits withdrawable: recovery for profits that might have been earned had deal been structured properly). See too the similar result in *Fulham Leisure Holdings Ltd v Nicholson Graham & Jones* [2006] EWHC 2017 (Ch); [2007] P.N.L.R. 5 (reversed on purely factual issues, [2008] EWCA Civ 84; [2008] P.N.L.R. 22).

1054 [1995] 2 A.C. 207.

1055 As in, e.g. *Vasiliou v Hajigeorgiou* [2010] EWCA Civ 1475; or *Wellesley Partners LLP v Withers LLP* [2015] EWCA Civ 1146; [2016] Ch. 529.

1056 *Watts v Bell & Scott* [2007] CSOH 108; 2007 S.L.T. 665; [2007] P.N.L.R. 30 (solicitors fail to put in client's tender for development property: liable for lost development profits). Similarly, where a lawyer's conveyancing bungle led to a property developer receiving payment late and deprived him of the opportunity to invest the money profitably in another project, a Scottish court refused to regard the claim as unarguable: *Henderson v Wotherspoon* [2013] CSOH 113; [2013] P.N.L.R. 28. Sed quaere.

1057 *Joyce v Bowman Law Ltd* [2010] EWHC 251 (Ch); [2010] P.N.L.R. 22.

abroad by an estranged father owing to her solicitors' negligence[1058]; and in certain cases, injury to health.[1059]

9-162 **Net loss only recoverable** The claimant is, of course, entitled to net loss only: credit must be given for any gains made.[1060] But the general exceptions to the deductibility rule, for example the principle that insurance recoveries are out of account, apply equally to actions against legal practitioners.[1061]

9-163 **Non-pecuniary loss** When some physical inconvenience is a foreseeable result of the lawyer's breach of duty,[1062] that loss is it seems recoverable.[1063] As for damages for distress or vexation, on principle these are available only if an object of the contract between solicitor and client is the provision of peace of mind or freedom from distress.[1064] Effectively this means that where the interest which the solicitor is retained to protect is a financial or business one, no such damages are recoverable (even if distress is otherwise foreseeable). Thus they were denied in *Hayes v James & Charles Dodd*[1065] where a solicitors' bungle over rights of way caused a garage owner to lease a useless workshop; and similarly in *Johnson v Gore Wood*[1066] the House of Lords upheld a Court of Appeal decision denying them in the case of mishandled litigation concerning a failed land deal.[1067] But with litigation over matters of a more personal nature, for example when a solicitor negligently fails to obtain a non-molestation order against an ex-boyfriend, then it seems damages for distress may be recovered.[1068] So solicitors whose negligence allowed the claimant's "tug-of-love" child to be spirited out of the country by her estranged husband were held liable for £20,000 general damages in respect of the

---

1058 *Hamilton-Jones v David & Snape (a firm)* [2003] EWHC 3147 (Ch); [2004] 1 W.L.R. 924.

1059 e.g. *Malyon v Lawrence Messer & Co* [1968] 2 Lloyd's Rep. 539 (compensation neurosis resulting from solicitors' incompetence). See too *McLoughlin v Grovers* [2001] EWCA Civ 1743; [2002] Q.B. 1312 (psychiatric damage allegedly caused as a result of imprisonment following wrongful conviction doe to solicitors' negligence: strike-out refused).

1060 e.g. *Sheerness Port Ltd v Brachers* [1997] I.R.L.R. 214 (negligent arrangement of downsizing operation led to massive redundancy costs: solicitors liable, but claimant must give credit for increased profitability of slimline business). See too *Hay v Gourley McBain*, 2008 S.L.T. (Sh Ct) 101; [2009] P.N.L.R. 7 (solicitors' negligence causes seller of land to face unanswerable £30,000 damages claim from buyer for breach of covenants as to title; but since land sold for £50,000 more than its value in any case, gain outweighs loss; no recovery).

1061 *Portman Building Society v Bevan Ashford* [2000] P.N.L.R. 336 CA (mortgage lender retains right to sue negligent solicitors, despite having already claimed under mortgage indemnity policy). Less defensibly, this remains the case even if the underwriters have waived any right to subrogation: *Bristol & West Building Society v May, May & Merrimans (No.2)* [1998] 1 W.L.R. 336. The *Portman* case was overruled on another point in *BPE Solicitors v Hughes-Holland* [2017] UKSC 21; [2018] A.C. 599, but not so as to affect the issue here.

1062 But not otherwise: *Cook v Swinfen* [1967] 1 W.L.R. 457 at 462 (nervous breakdown due to mishandled litigation too remote).

1063 *Bailey v Bullock* [1950] 2 All E.R. 1167 (inconvenience of living with in-laws when a solicitor negligently delayed in recovering possession of the claimant's home); *Wapshott v Davis Donovan & Co* [1996] P.N.L.R. 361 (burgeoning family living in cramped flat after solicitors missed dubiety of title).

1064 *Hayes v James & Charles Dodd* [1990] 2 All E.R. 815, 824 (Staughton LJ); cf. the surveyors' case of *Farley v Skinner* [2001] UKHL 49; [2002] 2 A.C. 732, below, para.9-204 onwards.

1065 [1990] 2 All E.R. 815.

1066 [2002] 2 A.C. 1.

1067 See too *Channon v Lindley Johnstone (A Firm)* [2002] EWCA Civ 353; [2002] P.N.L.R. 41 (financial provision litigation: same result, even though arose from non-commercial divorce litigation).

1068 See *Heywood v Wellers* [1976] Q.B. 446; also *Dickinson v Jones Alexander & Co* [1993] 2 F.L.R. 521.

claimant's distress.[1069] Similarly, where solicitors' incompetence causes a claimant to be made bankrupt he can recover something in respect of the stigma resulting,[1070] and it may be that the same applies where solicitors fail to represent relatives properly at an inquest,[1071] or a person is wrongly convicted and imprisoned owing to his lawyer's negligence.[1072]

Timing Many cases of lawyers' negligence concern claimants concluding a transaction of some sort as a result of their lawyers' negligence. In this situation, damages are presumptively measured by reference to events and values as at the time of the transaction concerned. For example, in the case of a property purchase the claimant generally recovers the price-value differential as it existed at the time of the purchase, and no later[1073]; and in the case of a loan on security, any discrepancy in value as at the time the advance was made.[1074] But this is not an absolute rule: where justice would only be done by taking account of subsequent events, a later date may be taken. So where solicitors for property developers buying a site negligently failed to obtain necessary rights over neighbouring land, the developers recovered the cost actually incurred at a later stage to obtain those rights and not the smaller sum they would have cost at the time the site was purchased.[1075] Again, where the claimant obtains the costs of escaping from a transaction occasioned by his solicitors' negligence,[1076] these will clearly reflect values at a later time. Moreover, this principle cuts both ways: subsequent events may not only increase recovery, but reduce it. Hence where solicitors negligently caused purchasers to buy a Spanish property with an unknown mortgage still outstanding, but the mortgage was subsequently released at no charge to the buyers, the award of damages took account of this fact.[1077] 9-164

The "SAAMCO limitation" The important surveyors' case of *South Australia Asset Management Co v York Montague Ltd*[1078] (often abbreviated to *SAAMCO*) establishes that a claimant relying on a failure to advise him properly will recover only the damage he has suffered as a specific result of the advice having been wrong. Even though his total loss stemming from reliance on the advice may be greater, and entirely foreseeable, the excess is irrecoverable unless the solicitor has (unusually) undertaken to guide his entire decision process and take responsibility 9-165

1069 *Hamilton-Jones v David & Snape* [2003] EWHC 3147 (Ch); [2004] 1 W.L.R. 924.

1070 *Rey v Graham & Oldham* [2000] B.P.I.R. 354.

1071 See *Shaw v Leigh Day* [2017] EWHC 825 (QB); [2017] P.N.L.R. 26 (refusal to strike claim).

1072 See *McLoughlin v Grovers* [2001] EWCA Civ 1743; [2002] Q.B. 1312 (strike-out refused); cf. *Shilcock v Passman* (1836) 7 C. & P. 289; *Beckett v Walker* [1985] C.L.Y. 129.

1073 e.g. *Wapshott v Davis Donovan & Co* [1996] P.N.L.R. 361; *Griffiths v Last Cawthra Feather* [2002] P.N.L.R. 27. And cf. the surveyors' case of *Philips v Ward* [1956] 1 W.L.R. 471. Theoretically at least, inflation is taken care of by an award of interest on the damages.

1074 e.g. *South Australia Asset Management Corporation v York Montague Ltd* [1997] A.C. 191; *Lloyds Bank Plc v Crosse & Crosse* [2001] P.N.L.R. 34.

1075 See the Scots decision in *Kirkton Investments Ltd v VMH LLP* [2011] CSOH 200; [2012] P.N.L.R. 11.

1076 As in *County Personnel Ltd v Alan R Pulver & Co* [1987] 1 W.L.R. 916; above, para.9-159. See too *Snipper v Enever Freeman & Co* [1991] E.G.L.R. 270.

1077 *Gregory v Shepherds* [2000] P.N.L.R. 769. See too *Kennedy v Van Emden* [1996] P.N.L.R. 409 (subsequent change in the law); *Bacciottini v Gotelee & Goldsmith* [2016] EWCA Civ 170; [2016] 4 W.L.R. 98 (condition attached to planning permission released); *LSREF III Wight Ltd v Gateley LLP* [2016] EWCA Civ 359; [2016] P.N.L.R. 21 (destructive clause in lease the subject of security for a debt: landlord's rights later bought out).

1078 [1997] A.C. 191. See also para.9-201.

for any consequences of his advice being wrong.[1079] There is no doubt that this principle applies equally to lawyers.[1080] Hence where, through a solicitor's negligent advice, the claimant purchases a property he would not otherwise have bought, his damages will not normally include any sum in respect of either a subsequent decline in property values generally, or any other unconnected factor depreciating the particular property.[1081] Again, a lender misadvised as to the legal enforceability of a loan agreement cannot recover where the loan is lost through the borrower's inability to repay it[1082]; and a lender misled as to the purpose of a loan cannot recover in so far as he would still have lost his money even if he had known the facts.[1083] Yet again, solicitors who negligently fail to warn lenders that the necessary security is not in place before releasing loan monies,[1084] or that there are suspicious features indicating a possible overvaluation which suggest that any lender should steer clear,[1085] are liable only for the loss flowing from the deficiency in the security.

9-166 Although the *SAAMCO* limitation began as a limitation of liability for negligent advice, it reflects a more general rule: namely, that a wrongdoer is not liable except for the kind of loss which the duty breached was designed to prevent.[1086] So failing to warn a joint tenant that a devise of his share is ineffective in the absence of prior severance engenders liability to the disappointed beneficiary but not to the estate thus diminished[1087]; and it has been held that if a solicitor fails to prosecute

---

[1079] *South Australia Asset Management Corporation v York Montague Ltd* [1997] A.C. 191, 241 (Lord Hoffmann); *BPE Solicitors v Hughes-Holland* [2017] UKSC 21; [2018] A.C. 599 at [25]–[45] (Lord Sumption). See also J. Thomson, "SAAMCO revisited" [2017] C.L.J. 476; H. Evans, "Solicitors and the scope of duty in the Supreme Court" (2017) 33 P.N. 193.

[1080] See, e.g. *Lloyds Bank Plc v Crosse & Crosse* [2001] EWCA Civ 366; [2001] P.N.L.R. 34; *BPE Solicitors v Hughes-Holland* [2017] UKSC 21; [2018] A.C. 599.

[1081] e.g. *Lloyds Bank Plc v Crosse & Crosse* [2001] EWCA Civ 366; [2001] P.N.L.R. 34 (failure to spot troublesome restrictive covenant: solicitors liable only for depreciation due to the covenant, not whole loss); *Cottingham v Attey Bower* [2000] P.N.L.R. 557 (failure to advise that extension illegally built: damages limited to the loss due specifically to lack of planning consent); *Credit & Mercantile Plc v Nabarro* [2014] EWHC 2819 (Ch); [2015] P.N.L.R. 14 (undevelopable land). See too *Trust Co of Australia v Perpetual Trustee Co* (1997) 42 N.S.W.L.R. 237; and the Irish decision in *Rosbeg Partners v L.K. Shields (A Firm)* [2018] IESC 23; [2018] P.N.L.R. 26 (solicitors who negligently failed to register title, thus rendering land unsaleable, liable only for costs of doing so, plus any diminution in value before matter could be put right).

[1082] *Haugesund Kommune v Depfa ACS Bank* [2011] EWCA Civ 33; [2011] 3 All E.R. 655. cf. *Broker House Insurance Services Ltd v OJS Law* [2010] EWHC 3816 (Ch); [2011] P.N.L.R. 23. Compare *BPE Solicitors v Hughes-Holland* [2017] UKSC 21; [2018] A.C. 599 (failure to advise of possible misuse of loan funds: no liability where non-repayment due simply to uncreditworthiness of borrower).

[1083] *BPE Solicitors v Hughes-Holland* [2017] UKSC 21; [2018] A.C. 599.

[1084] *AIB Group (UK) Plc v Mark Redler & Co* [2013] EWCA Civ 45; [2013] P.N.L.R. 19 at [10] (Patten LJ); also the Irish decision in *KBC Bank Ireland Plc v BCM Hanby Wallace (A Firm)* [2012] IEHC 120; [2013] P.N.L.R. 7 (reversed on other grounds, [2013] IESC 32; [2013] P.N.L.R. 33).

[1085] As in *Portman Building Society v Bevan Ashford* [2000] P.N.L.R. 344. In that case there was held to be full liability, but this result was stated to be wrong by Lord Sumption in *BPE Solicitors v Hughes-Holland* [2017] UKSC 21; [2018] A.C. 599 at [52]. The same, it is suggested, goes for a series of other cases on similar facts, such as of *Leeds & Holbeck Building Society v Alex Morison & Co*, 2001 S.C.L.R. 41; [2001] P.N.L.R. 346; *Newcastle Building Society v Paterson Robertson & Graham*, 2001 S.C. 734; [2001] P.N.L.R. 870; and *Michael Gerson Investments Ltd v Haines Watts* [2002] P.N.L.R. 34.

[1086] *South Australia Asset Management Corporation v York Montague Ltd* [1997] A.C. 191, 210 (Lord Hoffmann).

[1087] *Carr-Glyn v Frearsons* [1999] Ch. 326, 337 (Chadwick LJ).

proceedings with due expedition, he may be liable if the action is struck out for delay, but not generally if the defendant becomes bankrupt in the meantime.[1088]

Qualification to the "SAAMCO limitation" However, the *SAAMCO* principle is subject to an important limit. Where a lawyer gives advice generally on the advisability of a transaction, rather than on some limited aspect of it, so that he can be regarded as "guiding the whole of the decision-making process",[1089] he is normally regarded as accepting liability for any foreseeable loss suffered.[1090] An example might be where a non-commercial client seeking to invest a legacy in property development asked a solicitor in general terms to choose between a number of schemes on offer and the solicitor advised one of them having failed to notice signs that the property was subject to inappropriate planning restrictions: in such a case, it is suggested that he would be potentially liable for the investor's whole loss, even if partly resulting from a downturn in the market. **9-167**

Loss of a chance[1091] Prima facie the burden is on the claimant to prove, on a balance of probabilities, that the defendant lawyer's negligence was a cause of his loss: if he can do so, he recovers in full, while otherwise he receives nothing.[1092] In certain cases, however, the claimant, whether he sues in contract or tort,[1093] may recover damages based on the loss of the chance of making a gain or avoiding a loss. One such instance concerns bungled litigation, referred to below.[1094] But in *Allied Maples Ltd v Simmons & Simmons*[1095] the Court of Appeal made it clear that the principle was wider than this, and that wherever the chance of making a gain or avoiding a loss depended substantially on the hypothetical actions of a third party, *prima facie* a "loss of chance" award was appropriate. Solicitors advising the purchasers of a company negligently failed to warn them that the sellers' warranties against contingent liabilities were inadequate. Although the purchasers could not prove on a balance of probabilities that the sellers would have agreed to an extended warranty if asked, it was held that they were entitled to an award based on the chance **9-168**

1088 *Pearson v Sanders Witherspoon* [2000] P.N.L.R. 110.

1089 The phrase is Lord Sumption's: *BPE Solicitors v Hughes-Holland* [2017] UKSC 21; [2018] A.C. 599 at [40]. In such a case he regarded it as "pragmatic justice" that the solicitor should be liable for the whole loss.

1090 See *South Australia Asset Management Corporation v York Montague Ltd* [1997] 1 A.C. 191, 214 (Lord Hoffmann).

1091 N. Jansen, "The Idea of a Lost Chance" (1999) 19 O.J.L.S. 271. For extensive discussion of the rules relating to loss of a chance, including how multiple contingencies are to be treated, see *Assetco Plc v Grant Thornton UK LLP* [2019] EWHC 150 (Comm); [2019] Bus. L.R. 2291 at [428]–[455].

1092 e.g. *Sykes v Midland Bank Executor and Trustee Co Ltd* [1971] 1 Q.B. 113.

1093 Most cases allowing such recovery have been in contract, but not all: for a case where it was accepted that the same rule applied in tort, see *Khan v R.M. Falvey* [2002] EWCA Civ 400; [2002] P.N.L.R. 28.

1094 See para.9-170.

1095 [1995] 1 W.L.R. 1602; see too *Lord Briggs in Perry v Raleys Solicitors* [2019] UKSC 5; [2019] 2 W.L.R. 636 at [17]–[22]. For a virtual carbon copy of *Allied Maples*, see the later *Perkin v Lupton Fawcett* [2008] EWCA Civ 418; [2008] P.N.L.R. 30. See too *McGregor v Michael Taylor & Co* [2002] 2 Lloyd's Rep. 468 (solicitors at fault in failing to advise wife of possibility of setting aside charge over her share of shared home: 75 per cent loss of chance award); *Magical Marking Ltd v Ware & Kay LLP* [2013] EWHC 59 (Ch) (misadvice to company about right to remove director: loss of chance of amicable arrangement for departure); *Wellesley Partners LLP v Withers LLP* [2015] EWCA Civ 1146; [2016] Ch. 529 (loss of chance of opening profitable business in New York); *Moda International Brands Ltd v Gateley LLP* [2019] EWHC 1326 (QB); [2019] P.N.L.R. 27 (loss of chance to stipulate for profit share due to drafting error). cf. the earlier cases of *Hall v Meyrick* [1957] 2 Q.B. 455; and *Dunbar v A & B Painters Ltd* [1986] 2 Lloyd's Rep. 38.

that such an agreement would have been forthcoming. For these purposes there must be a real and substantial chance: a fanciful or speculative one will generally be ignored.[1096]

9-169 The "loss of chance" principle applies as much in favour of the defendant as the claimant.[1097] Thus in *Stovold v Barlows*,[1098] vendors' solicitors negligently failed to transmit the documentation to prospective purchasers on time; the purchasers withdrew, and the property was sold later for a great deal less. Even though the vendors proved on the balance of probabilities that had the documents arrived on time the purchasers would not have withdrawn, it was held that the vendors' damages fell to be discounted by the probability that they might have declined to proceed in any case. This can be significant where a claim against lawyers includes a claim for consequential loss of a profitable business opportunity: even if the opportunity would more likely than not have materialised, there should it seems be a discount for the chance that it would not have done so.[1099] Where several contingencies would have affected the likelihood of the claimant gaining a particular benefit, the presumptive practice is to multiply them together.[1100] But this is only justified if they are truly independent of each other: if they are in some way interdependent, then a more nuanced approach than the purely mathematical one is called for.[1101]

9-170 **Bungled litigation: measure of damages**[1102] The best-established instance of a "loss of chance" award arises where a lawyer negligently causes a client to lose in litigation: in such a case the measure of recovery is the client's loss of the chance of winning. Hence if the client had a 40 per cent chance of recovering £10,000, the measure of loss will be £4,000. The leading case is *Kitchen v RAFA*.[1103] The claimant's husband was electrocuted at home; his widow's solicitors then negligently allowed her claim against the electricity suppliers to become statute-barred. She was awarded £2,000 in her professional negligence action, on the basis that, had she succeeded in a Fatal Accidents Act action, she would have recovered £3,000, and that her chances of success would have been two-thirds. Lord Evershed MR said:

1096 As a rule of thumb Proudman J has expressed the view that any chance less than 10 per cent should be disregarded: *Harding Homes (East Street) Ltd v Bircham Dyson Bell* [2015] EWHC 3329 (Ch) at [167]. (Note that the actual result in that case was doubted by Bryan J in *Assetco Plc v Grant Thornton UK LLP* [2019] EWHC 150 (Comm); [2019] Bus. L.R. 2291 at [447]; but this does not affect this point).

1097 See *Stovold v Barlows* [1996] P.N.L.R. 19; and *Assetco Plc v Grant Thornton UK LLP* [2019] EWHC 150 (Comm); [2019] Bus. L.R. 2291 at [411]–[417] (Bryan J).

1098 [1996] P.N.L.R. 19. In the earlier *Martin Boston & Co v Roberts* [1996] P.N.L.R. 45 solicitors who failed to advise clients to insist on a guarantee from X were held liable in full, with no discount to reflect the possibility that X would not have given it. But *Allied Maples* was not referred to, and it is submitted that this case is of doubtful authority on the point.

1099 *Wellesley Partners LLP v Withers LLP* [2015] EWCA Civ 1146; [2016] Ch. 529, esp. at [44] (Floyd LJ). By contrast general claims for loss of profits over a period of time seem to be decided on a balance of probabilities basis (e.g. *Vasiliou v Hajigeorgiou* [2010] EWCA Civ 1475). This is a difficult distinction to draw or understand: see A. Tettenborn, "Professional Liability and Remoteness" (2016) 32 P.N. 66, 67–68.

1100 *Assetco Plc v Grant Thornton UK LLP* [2019] EWHC 150 (Comm); [2019] Bus. L.R. 2291 at [447]–[448].

1101 See Bryan J in *Assetco Plc v Grant Thornton UK LLP* [2019] EWHC 150 (Comm); [2019] Bus. L.R. 2291at [422], following cases such as *Tom Hoskins Plc v EMW Law (A Firm)* [2010] EWHC 479 (Ch); [2010] E.C.C. 20.

1102 See the useful summary of the law in *Harrison v Bloom Camillin* [2001] P.N.L.R. 7 at [87] onwards.

1103 [1958] 1 W.L.R. 563.

> "[A]ssuming that the plaintiff has established negligence, what the court has to do in such a case as the present is to determine what the plaintiff has lost by that negligence. The question is: Has the plaintiff lost some rights of value, some chose in action of reality and substance? In such a case it may be that its value is not easy to determine, but it is the duty of the courts to determine that value as best as it can."[1104]

For these purposes, the claimant must demonstrate an appreciable chance that he would have won on the merits. The mere "nuisance-value" of a demonstrably bad claim will not suffice.[1105] But once the claimant has leapt this hurdle the court must do its best to assess the value of the claim[1106] and the chance of success.[1107] In addition to the value of the claim, the client may of course recover any costs he has had to pay, or has been prevented from recovering from the other side, as a result of his lawyers' incompetence,[1108] plus any other foreseeable consequential loss.[1109] It should be noted that, before a claimant can invoke the rule in *Kitchen's* case, he must demonstrate on a balance of probabilities that he would in fact have prosecuted the action.[1110] In addition, it has not surprisingly been held that the claim must on the facts have been an honest one. Whatever the prospects of success of a known bad claim, as Lord Briggs pithily put it in *Perry v Raleys Solicitors Ltd*,[1111] the court "simply has no business rewarding dishonest claimants".

The "loss of a chance" principle referred to above applies as much to a defendant who loses when he should have won as it does to a claimant. In *Newline Corporate Name Ltd v Morgan Cole (A Firm)*[1112] solicitors failed to advise professional indemnity insurers faced with a claim that they probably had a watertight defence. The insurers recovered the amount that they had paid out in damages and costs, discounted by 15 per cent to take account of the chance that the defence would not have succeeded. Nearly all the cases turn on lost civil litigation. It is questionable whether their reasoning can be extended to criminal proceedings so as to allow proportionate recovery of the damages associated with wrongful convic- **9-171**

[1104] at 274–275; and see *Gregory v Tarlo* (1964) 108 S.J. 219; *Maylon v Lawrence Messer and Co* [1968] 2 Lloyd's Rep. 539.

[1105] See *McFarlane v Wilkinson* [1997] P.N.L.R. 578, 606; *Harrison v Bloom Camillin* [2001] P.N.L.R. 7 at [87].

[1106] Which means a sober assessment of the chances of recovery and emphatically not a re-trial of the putative proceedings: *Haithwaite v Thomson Snell & Passmore (A Firm)* [2009] EWHC 647 (QB); [2009] P.N.L.R. 27; and *Perry v Raleys Solicitors* [2017] EWCA Civ 314; [2017] P.N.L.R. 27 at [38] (Gloster LJ) (an appeal was allowed by the Supreme Court—see [2019] UKSC 5; [2019] 2 W.L.R. 636—but the point made by her Ladyship remains sound).

[1107] Including the chances of success where causation was in issue in the original proceedings: *Dixon v Clement Jones* [2004] EWCA Civ 1005; [2005] P.N.L.R. 6.

[1108] A straightforward example is *Brinn v Russell Jones & Walker* [2002] EWHC 2727 (QB); [2003] P.N.L.R. 16 (solicitors bungle libel proceedings against X; claimant thereby forced to sue Y, another publisher, to clear his name: award of unrecovered costs in proceedings against Y). See too *Adrian Alan Ltd v Fuglers* [2002] EWCA Civ 1655; [2003] P.N.L.R. 14; *Browning v Brachers* [2004] EWHC 16 (QB); [2004] P.N.L.R. 28 (reversed on factual grounds, [2005] EWCA Civ 753; [2005] P.N.L.R. 44).

[1109] So decided in Northern Ireland: *Macmahon v Doran & Co* [2001] P.N.L.R. 35 (upheld on other grounds in the NI Court of Appeal: [2002] P.N.L.R. 33) (cash flow losses stemming from failure to collect on putative judgment).

[1110] *Harrison v Bloom Camillin* [2001] P.N.L.R. 7 at [83] (Neuberger J); *Perry v Raleys Solicitors* [2019] UKSC 5; [2019] 2 W.L.R. 636 at [20], [27] (Lord Briggs).

[1111] [2019] UKSC 5; [2019] 2 W.L.R. 636 at [27].

[1112] [2007] EWHC 1628 (Comm); [2008] P.N.L.R. 2; see too *Commodities Research Unit International (Holdings) Ltd v King & Wood Mallesons LLP* [2016] EWHC 727 (QB); [2016] P.N.L.R. 29 (appeal dismissed, [2017] EWCA Civ 1197; [2018] P.N.L.R. 3).

tion and imprisonment. There is some authority that they can.[1113] On the other hand, the idea that a chance of acquittal is something of value akin to a chance of recovering £10,000 is somewhat curious, and there is much to be said for requiring proof on a balance of probabilities in such cases.[1114]

9-172 In assessing the amount of any putative recovery, the amount of any likely settlement is taken into account,[1115] taking due notice of the circumstances, including those of the parties themselves.[1116] Where the claim is inflated, the court should decide what, on the whole, was likely to have been awarded.[1117] If there are claims and counterclaims, each should be evaluated and a percentage deduction determined, and then the sums set-off against each other.[1118] Where any recovery would have been reduced by the amount of any social security benefits received by the claimant, it seems the net recoverable amount should be taken, with any percentage discount being applied to that sum.[1119] The value of the claim should generally be taken as at the time of the putative decision, since it is that value of which the claimant has been deprived.[1120] It seems, therefore, that where some new event occurs subsequent to that date which goes to augment or reduce the claimant's original loss, that event is out of account in the action against the solicitor.[1121] However, there is an important qualification to this principle. Where, at the time of the notional trial, a question of prognosis would have arisen (for example, as to whether a personal injury claimant's condition was likely to deteriorate), then it seems that any subsequent events which make that prognosis unnecessary are in account.[1122] The assessment of the chances of success is in its nature a matter of informed

---

1113 *Acton v Graham Pearce & Co* [1997] 3 All E.R. 909.

1114 So decided in Canada: *Folland v Reardon* (2005) 249 D.L.R. (4th) 167.

1115 *Harrison v Bloom Camillin* [2001] P.N.L.R. 7 at [82] onwards (Neuberger J). But where there is no indication that a settlement would have yielded a substantially different sum from that which would have been awarded by the court, then little if any account should be taken of it: *Charles v Hugh James Jones & Jenkins* [2000] 1 W.L.R. 1278 at 1294 (Swinton Thomas LJ).

1116 *Brinn v Russell Jones & Walker* [2002] EWHC 2727 (QB); [2003] P.N.L.R. 16 (loss of chance of libel settlement from the *Oldie*, a small and cash-strapped monthly magazine: small likelihood of substantial offer highly relevant).

1117 See *Browning v Brachers* [2004] EWHC 16 (QB); [2004] P.N.L.R. 28.

1118 *Browning v Brachers* [2004] EWHC 16 (QB); [2004] P.N.L.R. 28. But it is not normally appropriate to perform a separate calculation for each part of a claimant's claim: *Dudarec v Andrews* [2006] EWCA Civ 256; [2006] 1 W.L.R. 3002 at [54] (Sedley LJ).

1119 So decided in Australia: *Green v Berry* [2001] Qd. R. 605.

1120 *Charles v Hugh James Jones & Jenkins* [2000] 1 W.L.R. 1278 at 1290 (Swinton Thomas LJ); *Hunter v Earnshaw* [2001] P.N.L.R. 42; *Edwards v Hugh James Ford Simey (A Firm)* [2019] UKSC 54; [2019] 1 W.L.R. 6549.

1121 A conclusion provisionally accepted by Swinton Thomas LJ in *Charles v Hugh James Jones & Jenkins* [2000] 1 W.L.R. 1278, 1290, and applied in the Scots decision in *Campbell (or Pearson) v Imray* [2004] P.N.L.R. 1 (claimant's condition deteriorated between putative hearing and trial of professional negligence action, vastly increasing her loss: nevertheless, subsequent increase out of account). See too *Hunter v Earnshaw* [2001] P.N.L.R. 42; *Nikolaou v Papasavas, Phillips & Co* (1988) 82 A.L.R. 617. The point was left open by the Supreme Court in *Edwards v Hugh James Ford Simey (A Firm)* [2019] UKSC 54; [2019] 1 W.L.R. 6549 at [24].

1122 See *Charles v Hugh James Jones & Jenkins* [2000] 1 W.L.R. 1278; *Dudarec v Andrews* [2006] EWCA Civ 256; [2006] 1 W.L.R. 3002; *Whitehead v Hibbert Pownall & Newton (a firm)* [2008] EWCA Civ 285; [2009] 1 W.L.R. 549. Sed quaere: as was pointed out in *Campbell (or Pearson) v Imray* [2004] P.N.L.R. 1 at [21], the result may be that the claimant recovers more (or less) from his solicitor than he could have recovered from the original defendant. Hence in *Edwards v Hugh James Ford Simey* [2018] EWCA Civ 1299; [2018] P.N.L.R. 30 at [69] Irwin LJ accepted that subsequent events which could have been foreseen at the notional trial date should be in account, despite the general rule that the relevant time was that of the notional trial date. The issue was not dealt with on appeal at [2019] UKSC 54; [2019] 1 W.L.R. 6549.

impression.[1123] In a suitable case where the claimant would almost certainly have won, a figure of 100 per cent may be appropriate.[1124] Where the chances of success under different heads of loss are appreciably different, a separate computation should be made for each.[1125] Furthermore, there is an evidential burden on a defendant to show that the action would have failed; in the event of doubt, the issue should be decided in favour of the claimant.[1126] In so far as a point of law would have arisen, there is no necessary objection to assessing the chances of success. However, it will generally be assumed that the putative court deciding the case would have got the law right.[1127]

(iii) Limitations on damages

Remoteness of damage Although the claimant can in principle claim for all losses consequential on the defendant's negligence,[1128] and such claims are not infrequently allowed,[1129] those losses must be reasonably foreseeable or otherwise in the contemplation of the parties. Thus, in *Pilkington v Wood*,[1130] a solicitor was negligent in not advising his client of a defect in title in a house he bought in Hampshire, which came to light when he tried to sell it. The claimant recovered the diminution in value but not his expenses in travelling to and fro from Lancashire, where he had obtained employment, to visit his wife who was still living in the unsaleable house. The latter expenses were not foreseeable and hence too remote. Similarly, where solicitors' negligence caused a farmer to lose a right of preemption over certain land, he recovered the value of the right but not that of the milk quota associated with the land: the latter was too remote.[1131] It should be noted that where (as is normally the case) a solicitor is liable to his client in both contract and tort, the relevant remoteness rule is that applicable in contract.[1132] **9-173**

Failure to mitigate loss A claimant suing his lawyer for negligence must, like any other claimant, mitigate his loss. Thus a person having to pay litigation costs as a result of a lawyer's fault is expected to minimise the loss by demanding detailed assessment where appropriate[1133]; and a lender against leasehold property who is not warned of a clause depreciating the lease as a security must take an opportunity offered to buy out the landlord's rights, and cannot claim any losses resulting from **9-174**

1123 For the proper approach where there are a number of contingencies, see *Hanbury v Hugh James Solicitors* [2019] EWHC 1074 (QB); [2019] P.N.L.R. 25 (unless contingencies genuinely independent, mechanistic multiplication of chances inappropriate).

1124 *Harrison v Bloom Camillin* [2001] P.N.L.R. 7 at [87] (Neuberger J). See too *Somatra v Sinclair Roche & Temperley (No 2)* [2003] EWCA Civ 1474; [2003] 2 Lloyd's Rep. 855 (solicitors' bad advice to insurance claimant led to settlement of claim at two-thirds, whereas it otherwise would have settled at 75 per cent: award of total difference upheld).

1125 *Harrison v Bloom Camillin* [2001] P.N.L.R. 7 at [88] (Neuberger J).

1126 *Mount v Barker Austin* [1998] P.N.L.R. 493, 511 (Simon Brown LJ).

1127 *Harrison v Bloom Camillin* [2001] P.N.L.R. 7 at [101] (Neuberger J).

1128 See para.9-161.

1129 See para.9-161.

1130 [1953] Ch. 770. See too *Scott v Kennedys Law LLP* [2011] EWHC 3808 (Ch) (purchase of guest-house useless to claimant because of hidden planning condition; claim for capital loss but not cancellation of holiday, this being unforeseeable); *Cook v Swinfen* [1967] 1 W.L.R. 457 (failure to prevent harassment: further neurosis unforeseeable).

1131 *Parry v Edwards Geldard* [2001] P.N.L.R. 44.

1132 i.e. the rule in *Hadley v Baxendale* (1854) 9 Ex 354. See *Wellesley Partners LLP v Withers LLP* [2015] EWCA Civ 1146; [2016] Ch. 529, finally settling a long-running controversy over the matter.

1133 *British Racing Drivers' Club v Hextall Erskine* [1996] 3 All E.R. 667.

his failure to do this.[1134] One important limitation needs to be noted, however. Despite some suggestions to the contrary,[1135] the duty to mitigate does not generally include a duty to exercise a right of recovery, even an eminently reasonable one, against a third party, since to decide otherwise would be to disregard the rule that a claimant is entitled to choose untrammelled between two or more possible causes of compensation.[1136]

9-175 **Contributory negligence** Generally speaking the courts recognise that a client should not have himself to take steps to check on a lawyer's professionalism[1137]; nevertheless, in a suitable case damages may be reduced to take account of the claimant's contributory negligence.[1138] In this respect, while businessmen may be held to a fairly robust standard of care,[1139] as against non-business clients courts do not seem particularly willing in practice to find contributory negligence.[1140]

4. Surveyors and Valuers[1141]

(a) Duties owed

(i) Duties to clients

9-176 **Duties to clients** As with doctors and lawyers, there is no doubt that a surveyor or valuer owes a duty of care to his paying client in both contract[1142] and tort[1143]; this is a matter of some little importance, particularly where limitation of actions

1134 *LSREF III Wight Ltd v Gateley LLP* [2016] EWCA Civ 359; [2016] P.N.L.R. 21.

1135 See, e.g. *Capital Home Loans Ltd v Hewit & Gilpin Solicitors Ltd (Sued as a Firm)* [2016] NIQB 13; [2016] P.N.L.R. 24.

1136 *Haugesund Kommune v Depfa ACS Bank* [2010] EWHC 227 (Comm); [2010] P.N.L.R. 21 (appeal allowed on other grounds at [2011] EWCA Civ 33; [2011] P.N.L.R. 14).

1137 For a statement that a client should not too readily be penalised for failing to duplicate precautions that should be his lawyer's concern, see the Irish decision in *KBC Bank Ireland Plc v BCM Hanby Wallace (A Firm)* [2013] IESC 32; [2013] P.N.L.R. 33 at [89]–[90] (Fennelly J).Also note that where a company suffers loss owing to negligent failure to advise it to observe shareholder protection mechanisms, a contributory negligence reduction is unlikely to be made on account of its directors' own fault, in so far as to do so would unfairly penalise the shareholders: see British Racing Drivers Club Ltd v Hextall Erskine & Co [1996] 3 All E.R. 667 (advice on what is now s.190 of the Companies Act 2006).

1138 e.g. *Omega Trust Co Ltd v Wright, Son & Pepper (No 2)* [1998] P.N.L.R. 337; *Bristol & West Building Society v Fancy & Jackson* [1997] 4 All E.R. 582; *Football League Ltd v Edge Ellison* [2006] EWHC 1462 (Ch); [2007] P.N.L.R. 2. See too *KBC Bank Ireland Plc v BCM Hanby Wallace (A Firm)* [2013] IESC 32; [2013] P.N.L.R. 33 (borrower fairly obviously untrustworthy: possible for lender to be contributorily negligent, despite having employed solicitors, by failing to follow up suspicions).

1139 *Omega Trust Co Ltd v Wright, Son & Pepper (No 2)* [1998] P.N.L.R. 337 (lender's solicitors negligently fail to carry out bankruptcy search against borrower: lender recovers, but held 70 per cent to blame for losses); *Bristol & West Building Society v Fancy & Jackson* [1997] 4 All E.R. 582 (action against solicitors by mortgage lender when borrower defaulted: damages reduced to reflect imprudence of lending practice). See too *Capital Home Loans Ltd v Hewit & Gilpin Solicitors Ltd* [2016] NIQB 13; [2016] P.N.L.R. 24 (bank lending against obviously less-than-candid mortgage application).

1140 For a spectacular example, see the Scots decision in *Campbell (or Pearson) v Imray* [2004] P.N.L.R. 1 (claim about to become time-barred; potential pursuer repeatedly failed to answer urgent letters from her solicitors asking her to see them; no contributory negligence. Sed quaere: this seems remarkably generous in the circumstances).

1141 See Jackson & Powell on *Professional Liability*, 8th edn (2017), Ch.10.

1142 Under the Supply of Goods and Services Act 1982 s.13 and the Consumer Rights Act 2015 s.49 as or the right to pre-judgment interest is in issue.[1144] There would equally seem to be no reason in principle why a surveyor should not be liable in tort to a client for whom he provides services gratuitously.[1145] In suitable cases, in particular where commercially sensitive information is involved, a surveyor will also owe a fiduciary duty to his client.[1146]

(ii) Duties to non-clients

Duties to third parties Whether a surveyor or valuer owes a duty to someone other than his client depends on whether a sufficient relation of proximity can be established between the parties.[1147] When a surveyor prepares a report commissioned by a client which he knows is intended to be shown by the client to a third party who will rely on it, this is likely to be the case. Thus in *Cann v Wilson*,[1148] approved by the House of Lords in *Hedley Byrne & Co Ltd v Heller & Partners Ltd*,[1149] valuers instructed by a mortgagor sent their valuation to the mortgagee's solicitors and confirmed it to them on a subsequent inquiry. They were held to owe a duty in negligence to the mortgagee. But mere foreseeability of reliance or loss is not enough: some intent to report for the benefit of the third party, implying an undertaking of responsibility to him, must be shown. Thus valuers have been held to owe no duty to assignees of their clients' contractual rights[1150]; and where a valuation is prepared for a lender, it has been doubted whether any duty is owed to an undisclosed principal of that lender who is providing some of the money.[1151] Similarly, a valuer employed by a receiver to value property to be sold owes no direct duty to the owner of the property concerned[1152]; and a surveyor inspecting dilapidated premises on behalf of the landlord in connection with a dispute with the tenant owes no duty to a passer-by injured as a result of the disrepair.[1153] **9-177**

Liability to mortgagees and purchasers When a surveyor acts for the owner or **9-178**

regards business and consumer clients respectively.

1143 Since the decision in *Henderson v Merrett Syndicates Ltd* [1995] 2 A.C. 145 cleared the way for general concurrent liability in contract and tort.

1144 In particular, because (i) time runs in contract from the time of breach, but in the tort of negligence from the time when damage is suffered, which may be a good deal later; and (ii) a contract claimant cannot claim the benefit of s.14A of the Limitation Act 1980, which deals with latent damage (see *Iron Trades Mutual Insurance Ltd v Buckenham* [1990] 1 All E.R. 808; approved in *Société Commerciale de Réassurance v ERAS Ltd* [1992] 2 All E.R. 82). On interest see generally *Nykredit Mortgage Bank plc v Edward Erdman Group Ltd (Interest on Damages)* [1997] 1 W.L.R. 1627.

1145 On the other hand, where gratuitous advice is given informally and relates to commercial matters such as the viability of a proposed development, it may be difficult to show reasonable reliance: see, e.g. *Civic Structures v Clark Quinney & Co* [1991] 2 E.G.L.R. 165.

1146 See, e.g. *Satnam Ltd v Dunlop Haywood* [1999] 3 All E.R. 652 (information about potential development site obtained from one client passed by surveyor to another).

1147 See, e.g. *Raja v Austin Gray* [2002] EWCA Civ 1965; [2003] Lloyd's Rep. P.N. 126; and generally above, para.9-09 onwards.

1148 (1888) 39 Ch.D. 39

1149 [1964] A.C. 465 at 489, 502, 535.

1150 *Barex Brokers Ltd v Morris Dean* [1999] P.N.L.R. 344.

1151 *Omega Trust Ltd v Wright, Son & Pepper* [1997] P.N.L.R. 424; *First National Commercial Bank Plc v Loxleys* [1997] P.N.L.R. 211.

1152 *Raja v Austin Gray* [2002] EWCA Civ 1965; [2003] Lloyd's Rep. P.N. 126. But note that the receiver would have been liable here: see below, para.9-241 onwards. The fact that the claimant had a remedy against someone doubtless influenced the decision.

1153 *Harrison v Technical Sign Co Ltd* [2013] EWCA Civ 1569; [2014] P.N.L.R. 15 (tenant liable: no contribution available from surveyor). Nor, indeed, does he owe a duty to the tenant: ibid.

purchaser of property and it is made clear to him that the valuation is for mortgage purposes and will be passed on to and relied on by the mortgagee, he owes a duty to the mortgagee.[1154] The duty so owed is to make a careful appraisal and valuation of the property to assess whether it is suitable security for the proposed loan. No conflict of interest is present between the client and the third party, since it is the client who seeks the surveyor's assistance in obtaining the valuation which will enable him to be granted a mortgage. Similarly, when a report is commissioned by vendors of property which the surveyors are aware is intended for the benefit of the purchasers,[1155] who will be shown the report and rely on its contents, a duty is owed to those purchasers.[1156] It would seem that a duty may also be owed where in the circumstances the surveyor ought to have known that his report, commissioned by the vendors, would be relied on by the purchaser.[1157] But in the absence of such knowledge or notice, the purchaser cannot recover simply because there has been a breach of duty to the client.[1158]

9-179 **Liability to mortgagors** After some doubt, it is now clear that on principle a surveyor engaged by a potential mortgagee of residential property[1159] owes a duty not only to that person but also to the proposed residential purchaser. This is significant, since unless the surveyor is the employee of the mortgagee[1160] it is highly unlikely that the latter will be liable.[1161] The matter was put beyond doubt by the House of Lords in *Smith v Eric S. Bush*,[1162] where their Lordships made it clear that in such a case there was no difficulty in constructing an assumption of responsibility by the surveyors to the eventual purchasers. Despite earlier scepticism,[1163] moreover, it now seems accepted that this rule applies equally to relatively expensive, as well as modest, house purchases.[1164] However, there is an unstated element of consumer protection involved here, and accordingly it has been held that

---

[1154] *Cann v Wilson* (1888) 39 Ch.D. 39, above; *Singer and Friedlander Ltd v John D Wood & Co* [1955–95] P.N.L.R. 70; (1977) 243 E.G. 212; *Bank of Scotland v Fuller Peiser*, 2002 S.C.L.R. 255; [2002] P.N.L.R. 13 (where, however, there was an effective exemption clause). But there must be foreseeable reliance: *Ta Ho Ma Pty Ltd v Allen* (1999) 47 N.S.W.L.R. 1.

[1155] But not otherwise: see the Scotch case of *Howes v Crombie*, 2001 S.C.L.R. 921; [2002] P.N.L.R. 3 (letter from chartered engineer to vendor: engineer not liable, since he did not know of imminence of sale).

[1156] *Bourne v McEvoy Timber Preservations Ltd* (1976) 237 E.G. 496. But presumably the survey must be prepared with a sale in mind: a survey obtained, e.g. for insurance purposes, would almost certainly not give rise to liability vis-à-vis a purchaser who was subsequently shown it. cf. in another context, *The Morning Watch* [1990] 1 Lloyd's Rep. 547 (classification survey of ship cannot be relied on by buyer).

[1157] See the previous note: also *Wooldridge v Stanley Hicks & Son* (1953) 163 E.G. 513; *Hingorani v Blower* (1976) 238 E.G. 883.

[1158] *Le Lievre v Gould* [1893] 1 Q.B. 441.

[1159] Most cases so far have concerned residential property. It remains open—and, indeed, perhaps rather doubtful—whether the purchaser of a factory would be allowed to sue his financier's surveyor if it turned out that the factory contained unnoticed defects. In the Scots decision in *Wilson v D.M. Hall & Sons* [2005] P.N.L.R. 22 the Court of Session declined to hold that a lender's surveyor owed any duty to a property developer whom the lender was financing.

[1160] As in *Beaton v Nationwide Building Society* [1991] 2 E.G.L.R. 145.

[1161] Lord Templeman in *Smith v Eric S. Bush* [1990] 1 A.C. 831 said that the mortgagee could not be liable merely for passing on a negligent report. Despite the contrary being held not totally unarguable in *Beresforde v Chesterfield BC* [1989] 2 E.G.L.R. 149, it is submitted that he was right.

[1162] [1990] 1 A.C. 831, approving *Yianni v Edwin Evans & Sons* [1982] Q.B. 438.

[1163] See *Yianni v Edwin Evans & Sons* [1982] Q.B. 438, 455 (Park J).

[1164] *Beaumont v Humberts* [1990] 2 E.G.L.R. 166 (in fact the claim failed for lack of proof of fault). But it seems that the expense of the house, and the buyer's correspondingly likely sophistication, may where the purchaser is not a residential buyer but a "buy-to-let" investor, presumptively no duty is owed.[1165] No doubt the same is likely to apply to a purchaser of business premises.

Other duties In addition to duties in contract and tort, a surveyor may in addition owe certain fiduciary duties to his client for breach of which he will potentially be liable in damages[1166] and also amenable to other remedies.[1167] 9-180

(iii) Exclusion of duty[1168]

At common law a surveyor may freely limit or exclude his liability to his client or anyone else.[1169] Any attempt to do this is, however, now controlled by statute. As regards commercial claimants the Unfair Contract Terms Act 1977 by s.2(2) imposes a condition of reasonableness in respect of any purported exclusion or limitation of liability, whether to clients or to third parties.[1170] As regards non-commercial claimants, a distinction is drawn: the duty to the client himself cannot be excluded or limited at all,[1171] while the duty to third parties may be excluded by notice, subject to s.62 of the Consumer Rights Act 2015, invalidating any exclusion of liability which contrary to the requirement of good faith causes a significant imbalance in the parties' rights and obligations. 9-181

Exclusion of liability: non-business claimants As we have seen, under the 2015 Act the contractual duty to the client himself cannot be excluded.[1172] As regards those other than clients (in practice house-buyers relying on surveys provided for lenders, or possibly vendors), when the Unfair Contract Terms Act 1977 applied to 9-182

---

affect the validity of any purported exclusion of liability under the Unfair Contract Terms Act 1977 or similar legislation. See *Smith v Eric S. Bush* [1990] 1 A.C. 831, 858 (Lord Griffiths); also *Stevenson v Nationwide Building Society* (1974) 272 E.G. 663; and *McCullagh v Lane Fox & Partners Ltd* [1996] P.N.L.R. 205.

1165 *Scullion v Bank of Scotland Plc (t/a Colleys)* [2011] EWCA Civ 693; [2011] 1 W.L.R. 3212. See in particular Lord Neuberger MR at [49]–[52], pointing out that (a) commercial investors were less deserving of protection than those merely seeking somewhere to live; and (b) their reliance on the lender's report, rather than on advice obtained independently, was a good deal less likely in practice.

1166 See, e.g. *Satnam Investments Ltd v Dunlop Heywood & Co Ltd* [1999] 3 All E.R. 652 (developer's surveyor passing on details of business opportunity to rival developer).

1167 For instance, were a surveyor to use confidential information derived from a client to carry out a successful property deal on his own account he would potentially be liable to account for any profits received.

1168 See generally above, para.9-36 onwards.

1169 Note in this context the Contracts (Rights of Third Parties) Act 1999 s.1(6), which now specifically allows third parties to take advantage of exemption clauses.

1170 Note that exclusion of liability for these purposes includes stipulating that no promise to take care is made, nor any obligation of care accepted, to a given person relying on the information provided. Despite a speciously attractive argument that liability for negligent misstatement depends on an acceptance of responsibility and hence that in such a case there is no liability to be excluded, in *Harris v Wyre Forest District Council* [1990] 1 A.C. 831 the House of Lords unhesitatingly held the 1977 Act applicable to stipulations on this sort.

1171 This is by a combination of s.49 of the Consumer Rights Act 2015, imposing a contractual duty of care, and s.57, preventing its exclusion. Theoretically the duty in tort could be excluded, subject to s.62, referred to below: but except in rare cases (for example where an action in contract is statute-barred but one in tort is not) this will make no difference.

1172 Moreover, this prohibition also includes terms preventing a duty arising in the first place, thus cementing the result in *Harris v Wyre Forest DC* [1990] 1 A.C. 831 under the 1977 Act: see s.57(5) of the 2015 Act.

such claimants, it was held in *Smith v Eric S. Bush*[1173] that where mortgagees' surveyors attempted to exclude liability to the borrower who they knew was likely to rely on their report, this exclusion was unreasonable in the circumstances.[1174] It seems likely that the same would apply today under s.62.[1175] In another case under the old law, however, it was also held that it was reasonable to exclude liability in respect of a substantial property likely to appeal only to the sophisticated and well-heeled.[1176] Whether this indulgence will be carried over into s.62 may be more doubtful.

9-183 **Exclusion of liability: business claimants** It is suggested that the approach is likely to be less strict on purported exclusions of liability covered by the Unfair Contract Terms Act 1977 where the property concerned is commercial, or the potential claimant is acting in the course of a business.[1177] Thus in *Omega Trust Ltd v Wright, Son & Pepper*[1178] financiers commissioned a valuation of properties offered as security by a commercial borrower. The valuation specifically excluded liability to anyone except the financiers commissioning it, but was nevertheless relied on by other lenders who had agreed to advance part of the money. The Court of Appeal unhesitatingly upheld the exclusion clause as being reasonable in the circumstances. Similarly, in the Scots decision in *Bank of Scotland v Fuller Peiser*,[1179] involving a mirror image of the situation in *Smith v Eric S. Bush*, a valuation was provided to a purchaser containing a clause to the effect that it was for her benefit alone and that no liability would be accepted to anyone else. It was passed on to a mortgage lender, who relied on it. It was held that the clause was effective in its terms to prevent any duty of care arising to the lender, and that in the light of the lender's status as an experienced mortgage lender, the exclusion did not run foul of the Unfair Contract Terms Act 1977.

9-184 **Exclusions and limitations on a professional's instructions** One other point calls for particular notice in connection with exclusion clauses: namely, the effect of a statement limiting the degree of inspection that has been, or will be, carried out.[1180] Where the first time the client is aware of this is when he is presented with the report, it cannot strictly speaking qualify the surveyor's obligation to inspect;

[1173] [1990] 1 A.C. 831.

[1174] It is suggested that a similar result might well be reached were the clause to be tested against the criterion of whether, contrary to the requirement of good faith, it causes a significant imbalance in the parties' rights and obligations (the test in the Consumer Rights Act 2015 s.62(4)).

[1175] Note also that s.62 is, like s.2 of the 1977 Act as interpreted in *Harris v Wyre Forest DC* [1990] 1 A.C. 831, wide enough to cover a notice purporting to prevent any duty arising as well as one disclaiming liability for breach of an existing duty: the notices affected include any notice which "relates to rights or obligations as between a trader and a consumer" (s.61(4)(a)), a phrase which could not be wider.

[1176] See *McCullagh v Lane Fox & Partners Ltd* [1996] P.N.L.R. 205.

[1177] See *Stevenson v Nationwide Building Society* (1984) 272 E.G. 663. Indeed, liability to such people who have not contracted for protection is narrow anyway: see *Scullion v Bank of Scotland Plc (t/a Colleys)* [2011] EWCA Civ 693; [2011] 1 W.L.R. 3212 (valuer to mortgagee owes no duty to buy-to-let mortgagor).

[1178] [1997] P.N.L.R. 424. It should be noted, however, that a differently-constituted Court of Appeal had a month earlier regarded the matter as less clear-cut: see *First National Commercial Bank Plc v Loxleys* [1997] P.N.L.R. 211.

[1179] 2002 S.C.L.R. 255; [2002] P.N.L.R. 13.

[1180] For example, a clause in a domestic survey report that surveyors have not inspected woodwork or other parts of the structure which are covered unexposed or inaccessible. See M. Brazier, "The Innocent Purchaser and his Professional Adviser" [1976] Conv. 179; also M. Brazier, "Surveyors' nevertheless it would clearly prevent the client suing in respects of defects that would only be apparent from scrutiny of the parts not inspected.[1181] Where notice of the limitation of the surveyor's undertaking is given to the client in advance, however, it seems likely that it will be effective despite the 1977 Act. It will be regarded as limiting what the surveyor was employed to do in the first place, rather than as excluding any would-be liability.[1182] It can hardly be negligent not to look at inaccessible parts when one has promised only to inspect the accessible ones.[1183]

(b) Negligence

(i) General

Breach of duty: general In deciding what is negligence on the part of a surveyor,[1184] care must be taken to identify the exact scope of his terms of engagement. This is because, while it is true that whenever a surveyor is retained for reward by a client, a term is implied into the contract that he will exercise reasonable care and skill in carrying out his instructions,[1185] this leaves unanswered the question what he was instructed to do. For example, the distinction between a full structural survey, valuation with limited survey, and a valuation report is too often not clearly understood by clients.[1186] Nevertheless, they all give rise to very different obligations on the part of the surveyor concerned.[1187] It should be added, however, that however limited a surveyor's terms of engagement, a court is unlikely to construe them as ousting the surveyor's fundamental duty to inspect properly and warn of untoward matters.[1188] **9-185**

Standard of care A surveyor, like any other professional person, is liable for negligence if and only if "he acted in a way which no surveyor of ordinary skill **9-186**

Negligence: A Survey" [1981] Conv. 96.

1181 Since he would not then be able to demonstrate reasonable reliance.

1182 Similarly, it would seem, with s.64(1)(a) of the Consumer Rights Act 2015 (no attack permitted on term relating to "the main subject matter of the contract").

1183 Subject to one caveat: s.3(2)(b)(i) of the 1977 Act specifically catches attempts by a contractor to allow himself "to render a contractual performance substantially different from that which was reasonably expected of him". But if a surveyor's terms of engagement prominently and specifically state he will not inspect certain parts of the house, how can it be reasonable of his client to expect him to do so? For a general discussion, see M. Brazier [1981] Conv. 96 at 105–107.

1184 On which expert evidence will normally be necessary: see *Wattret v Thomas Sands Consulting Ltd* [2015] EWHC 3455 (TCC); [2016] P.N.L.R. 15.

1185 In tort, and also in contract under the Supply of Goods and Services Act 1982 s.13 (business clients) and s.49 of the Consumer Rights Act 2015 (other clients).

1186 *Sutcliffe v Sayer* [1987] 1 E.G.L.R. 155 (but details of the various types of survey, and the differences between them, can now be readily found via the RICS website: *http://www.rics.org*). Of course the standard of care to be applied by the surveyor, once it is clear precisely what he has to do, remains uniform: see *Cross v David Martin & Mortimer* [1989] 1 E.G.L.R. 154.

1187 See, e.g. *Whalley v Roberts & Roberts* [1990] 1 E.G.L.R. 164 (limited scope of mortgage valuation, as against, e.g. full structural survey). For a neat illustration see the Scots decision in *Phimister v DM Hall LLP* [2012] CSOH 169; 2013 S.L.T. 261; [2013] P.N.L.R. 6 (valuer for mortgage purposes not in breach by passing on vendor's (over-generous) statement as to area of plot rather than measuring it himself).

1188 *Webb Resolutions Ltd v E.Surv Ltd* [2012] EWHC 3653 (TCC); [2013] P.N.L.R. 15 (instructions from mortgage lender mandating professional standards but then requiring tick-box valuation and stating that all further comment would be ignored: nevertheless, obligation to mention matters of concern where relevant).

would be guilty of, if acting with ordinary care".[1189] As might be expected, a surveyor is not to be judged on hindsight.[1190] Failure to follow accepted professional practice is obviously evidence,[1191] though not conclusive evidence,[1192] of negligence. Equally obviously, it is no answer to a claim in negligence that the surveyor carrying out the inspection and valuation lacks experience[1193]; the standard is that of the "average skilled professional". For these purposes, the *Bolam* test[1194] applies to surveyors as it does to other professionals.[1195] Though as yet there has not been judicial intervention to condemn accepted practice as improper, no doubt it will come in a suitable case.

(ii) Valuation

9-187 **Breach of duty: valuation**

> "The valuation of land ... is a task which rarely, if ever, admits of precise conclusion. Often beyond certain well-founded facts so many imponderables confront the valuer that he is obliged to proceed on assumptions. Therefore, he cannot be faulted for achieving a result which does not admit of some degree of error. Thus, two able and experienced men, each confronted with the same task might come to different conclusions without anyone being justified in saying that either of them lacked competence and reasonable care ..."[1196]

In practice, however, standards are today carefully laid down, notably in publications issued by the Royal Institution of Chartered Surveyors and the like.[1197]

9-188 A surveyor must of course act in accordance with his instructions.[1198] Assuming he does this, he is expected to be acquainted with local conditions,[1199] comparable sales[1200] and market values, to be aware of current market trends,[1201] and to take all

[1189] *Strover v Harrington* [1988] Ch. 390 (not contrary to good practice to fail to check vendor's statements about connection to sewers, hence no liability); see too *Corisand Investments Ltd v Druce & Co* (1978) 248 E.G. 315, 318.

[1190] See *Hacker v Thomas Deal & Co* [1991] 2 E.G.L.R. 161 (a dry rot case).

[1191] e.g. *Watts v Morrow* (1991) 7 P.N. 54 (varied on appeal, [1991] 1 W.L.R. 1421), where the unrecommended and indolent practice of dictating a report from site rather than working from detailed site notes was held negligent.

[1192] *P. K. Finans International (UK) Ltd v Andrew Downs & Co* [1992] 1 E.G.L.R. 172.

[1193] *Kenney v Hall, Pain and Foster* (1976) 239 E.G. 355.

[1194] See para.9-76. The reference is to *Bolam v Friern HMC* [1957] 1 W.L.R. 582. On the importance of common practice and expert evidence in surveyors' cases, see *Pfeiffer v E. & E. Installations* [1991] 1 E.G.L.R. 162.

[1195] See *Theodore Goddard v Fletcher-King* [1997] 2 E.G.L.R. 131.

[1196] *Singer & Friedlander Ltd v John D Wood & Co* [1955–95] P.N.L.R. 70, 74 (Watkins J); (1977) 243 E.G. 212 at 213. On the other hand, courts on occasion have been known to decry certain valuation techniques: see, e.g. *Preferred Mortgages Ltd v Countrywide Surveyors Ltd* [2005] EWHC 2820 (Ch); [2006] P.N.L.R. 9.

[1197] In particular, the so-called "Red Book", periodically re-issued (and available for free download at *http://www.rics.org*. The latest edition dates from late 2018 and takes effect from January 2019.

[1198] *Helm Housing Ltd v Myles Danker Associates Ltd* [2015] NIQB 73; [2016] P.N.L.R. 4 (valuation on wrong basis: liability).

[1199] See the Red Book, referred to above; also *Baxter v F. W. Gapp & Co Ltd* [1938] 4 All E.R. 457; *Wallshire Ltd v Aarons* [1989] 1 E.G.L.R. 147. It goes without saying that he must factor in very local annoyances, such as a railway line or rough estate, in close proximity: see *Webb Resolutions Ltd v E.Surv Ltd* [2012] EWHC 3653 (TCC); [2013] P.N.L.R. 15.

[1200] e.g. *John D Wood (Residential) Ltd v Knatchbull* [2002] EWHC 2822 (QB); [2003] P.N.L.R. 17 (negligence in estate agent and valuer acting for seller not to draw seller's attention to comparable house that sold for £60,000 more than seller's price); also see *Helm Housing Ltd v Myles Danker* these matters where relevant into account.[1202] Where the task undertaken by the defendant necessarily demands some knowledge of the law, a surveyor failing to take account of rules of planning law or land compensation may be found to be negligent. Thus in *Weedon v Hindwood Clarke & Esplin*[1203] a valuer instructed to negotiate compensation with the district valuer for land compulsorily acquired was found negligent in not being aware of a recent judgment changing the basis of valuation for such land. Similarly, in valuing commercial premises an understanding of general market conditions affecting their value may be important.[1204]

9-189 Over-valuation is not per se conclusive evidence of professional negligence: nevertheless, gross over-valuation, unless explained, "may be strong evidence of negligence".[1205] In 1977 Watkins J usefully elaborated[1206] what is generally required to complete a proper and careful valuation.[1207] There must be (1) a careful investigation of the property in which all relevant inquiries are pursued; (2) a skilful interpretation of facts disclosed; and (3) the employment of a well-practised method of conclusion.[1208] Where a valuation is for mortgage purposes only, but is relied on by the mortgagor so as to create a duty to him, he can reasonably assume only that the report indicates that the property is sufficient security for the proposed loan.[1209] He cannot rely on the valuation as indicating that the property is worth the proposed purchase price.[1210] In the case of leasehold property, the terms of the lease may be

---

Associates Ltd [2015] NIQB 73; [2016] P.N.L.R. 4. But the surveyor must take account of the limitations of such comparable figures, for example where owing to deep discounting in a new development they do not reflect actual prices paid: see *Platform Funding Ltd v Anderson & Associates Ltd* [2012] EWHC 1853 (QB) and *Webb Resolutions Ltd v E.Surv Ltd* [2012] EWHC 3653 (TCC); [2013] P.N.L.R. 15. For how far comparables should take account of market movements, see *Dunfermline Building Society v CBRE Ltd* [2017] EWHC 2745 (Ch); [2018] P.N.L.R. 13.

1201 *Singer & Friedlander Ltd v John D Wood & Co* [1955–95] P.N.L.R. 70; (1977) 243 E.G. 212; *Corisand Investments Ltd v Druce & Co* (1978) 248 E.G. 315.

1202 See, e.g. *Blemain Finance Ltd v E.Surv Ltd* [2012] EWHC 3654 (TCC) (no evidence of proper grounds for valuation: negligence established). See also *Bank of Ireland (UK) Plc v Patterson (t/a Patterson Miller)* [2014] NIQB 140. If a valuer deliberately ignores obvious matters, for example by indolently producing "production-line" valuations, there is scope for liability in deceit: *Mortgage Express v Countrywide Surveyors Ltd* [2016] EWHC 224 (Ch).

1203 (1974) 234 E.G. 121; *Jenkins v Betham* (1855) 15 C. & B. 167. And see *McIntyre v Herring Son & Daw* [1988] 1 E.G.L.R. 231 (failure to advise of the significance for leasehold enfranchisement purposes of the terms of the relevant statute).

1204 *Capita Alternative Fund Services (Guernsey) Ltd v Drivers Jonas (A Firm)* [2012] EWCA Civ 1417; [2013] 1 E.G.L.R. 119.

1205 *Baxter v F. W. Gapp & Co* [1939] 2 All E.R. 752, 758 (Du Parcq LJ).

1206 In *Singer & Friedlander Ltd v John D Wood & Co* [1955–95] P.N.L.R. 70 at 74; (1977) 243 E.G. 212, 213.

1207 Compare the overall rule appearing at various points in the RICS Red Book: it is the estimated amount for which an asset or liability should exchange on the valuation date between a willing buyer and a willing seller in an arm's length transaction after proper marketing and where the parties had each acted knowledgeably, prudently and without compulsion. On the details of valuation of more complex commercial property, see *Barclays Bank Plc v Christie Owen & Davies Ltd* [2016] EWHC 2351 (Ch); [2017] P.N.L.R. 8.

1208 For a case where a valuer was held negligent for producing an essentially unreasoned valuation, see *Blemain Finance Ltd v E.Surv Ltd* [2012] EWHC 3654 (TCC).

1209 *Nash v Evens & Matta* [1988] 1 E.G.L.R. 130. See too the Scots decision in *Phimister v DM Hall LLP* [2012] CSOH 169; 2013 S.L.T. 261; [2013] P.N.L.R. 6 (valuer for mortgage purposes accepted area of land as stated without measuring it, but valued it correctly: no liability where area less and fewer houses buildable as a result).

1210 For an example of a case of valuers held negligent on this basis, see *Webb Resolutions Ltd v E.Surv Ltd* [2012] EWHC 3653 (TCC); [2013] P.N.L.R. 15.

highly relevant to the interest being valued: failure to investigate them may accordingly be negligence.[1211]

9-190 **Valuation: the "bracket"** In *Singer & Friedlander Ltd v John D Wood & Co*[1212] Watkins J suggested that in normal conditions[1213] an error of 10 per cent, or in exceptionally difficult cases 15 per cent, might be regarded as a permissible "bracket" in valuation cases.[1214] This figure has in practice hardened almost into a rule of law, at least in respect of fairly ordinary properties where comparable valuations are available. In such a situation it has been pretty consistently held that where a good faith valuation[1215] is within that margin of error, this automatically forecloses the negligence issue and exonerates the valuer even if there is clear evidence that he has been at fault in reaching it.[1216] Conversely, there are dicta that where the valuation is outside the margin, the claimant may succeed without proving any particular instances of fault.[1217] The 10 per cent "bracket" is, however, relevant only to the question of whether the defendant was at fault. It plays no part in the assessment of damages. Thus where a valuer overvalues a £1 million house at £1.15 million, he will be liable for £150,000 and not £50,000: the fact that he would have escaped liability altogether had he valued it at £1.1 million is irrelevant.[1218]

(iii) Surveys: failure to observe defects in property

9-191 **Breach of duty: failure to observe defect** A surveyor who fails to conduct an adequate inspection of the property and/or to observe a material defect in the property is negligent if (a) the reasonably competent and experienced surveyor[1219] would have identified and reported the defect; (b) the defect is of a kind, which in

---

[1211] e.g. *K/S Lincoln v CB Richard Ellis Hotels Ltd* [2010] EWHC 1156 (TCC); [2010] P.N.L.R. 31 (freehold hotels subject to leases: valuers negligent in not factoring in term which might cause the expected rent to be sharply reduced).

[1212] [1955–95] P.N.L.R. 70, 74. See too *Webb Resolutions Ltd v E.Surv Ltd* [2012] EWHC 3653 (TCC); [2013] P.N.L.R. 15 at [22]–[29] (Coulson J).

[1213] But see *Corisand Investments Ltd v Druce & Co* (1978) 248 E.G. 315 (valuation of hotel in booming and mobile market; 37 per cent error not of itself evidence of negligence).

[1214] The court must "stand back and ask whether there is by the standards of the profession, a margin of error which can be tolerated or which can only sensibly be stigmatised as negligence"—Judge Stewart QC in *Mount Banking Corp. v Brian Cooper & Co* [1992] 2 E.G.L.R. 142. For a useful discussion of the "bracket", see Wilkinson (1995) 145 New L.J. 1267.

[1215] It has been said, sensibly, that a valuer will be negligent if he reaches a valuation and then arbitrarily adds the margin of error to gratify the would-be mortgagor: *Webb Resolutions Ltd v E.Surv Ltd* [2012] EWHC 3653 (TCC); [2013] P.N.L.R. 15 at [112]–[113].

[1216] See *Titan Europe 2006–3 Plc v Colliers International UK Plc (In Liquidation)* [2015] EWCA Civ 1083; [2016] P.N.L.R. 7; approving earlier authority such as *K/S Lincoln v CB Richard Ellis Hotels Ltd* [2010] EWHC 1156 (TCC); [2010] P.N.L.R. 31; and more recently *Dunfermline Building Society v CBRE Ltd* [2017] EWHC 2745 (Ch); [2018] P.N.L.R. 13 at [33]. Whether the rule is sensible is another matter. If a valuer negligently misses the fact that a £1 million house suffers from deathwatch beetle and as a result overvalues it at £1.09 million, why should he escape scot-free?

[1217] *Legal & General Mortgage Services Ltd v HPC Professional Services* [1997] P.N.L.R. 567, 574.

[1218] See *Scotlife Homeloans v Kenneth James & Co* [1995] E.G.C.S. 70; *South Australia Asset Management Corp'n v York Montague Ltd* [1997] A.C. 191, 221 (Lord Hoffmann). And cf. the business sale case of *Lion Nathan Ltd v CC Bottlers Ltd* [1996] 1 W.L.R. 1438.

[1219] "[D]efects which were of such a nature as a prudent person would have put right and which would have been apparent to the defendant exercising the ordinary skill of an ordinary competent chartered surveyor, and taking into account the type and age of the property": *Fisher v Knowles* (1982) 262 E.G. 1083.

the type of survey which the surveyor was instructed to carry out, he should have discovered[1220]; and (c) the defect would have a material effect on the value or amenity of the property.[1221] Failure to warn the claimant of a relevant defect in the property may result from a failure to inspect that part of the property, or a failure to observe the defect in the course of inspection, or a failure to warn the claimant of the defect in the report: whatever it is, it makes no difference to liability. In particular, failure to identify and report on visible signs of rot[1222] or woodworm[1223] or other infestation[1224] or of subsidence[1225] is very good evidence of negligence.[1226] Where a proper warning of a possible defect has been given, together with advice as to what to do about it (for example, where the client is warned of the risk of subsidence and counselled to insure against it) this will normally discharge the surveyor's duty of care.[1227]

Where the alleged negligence is a failure to inspect a particular matter which would have revealed a defect, it becomes crucial to define the proper scope of the survey, since surveys vary enormously.[1228] Thus in a number of judgments, failure to gain access to and inspect roof spaces has been held to be negligent in the case of a structural survey[1229] but not in relation to more limited surveys and valuations.[1230] In the latter, very common, case, there will normally be no duty "in the absence of any suspicious circumstances" to "cause carpets and linoleums to be lifted to go underneath floors and make a detailed examination of every hidden corner of the building"[1231] (though where visible parts of the premises give rise to suspicious circumstances,[1232] indicative of hidden dry rot or some other relevant defect, there is authority that he may well be required to extend the scope of his **9-192**

1220 *Stewart v H.A. Brechin & Co*, 1959 S.C. 306; discussed in Jackson & Powell on *Professional Liability*, 8th edn (2017), para.10-090 onwards.

1221 *Nash v Evens & Matta* [1988] 104 E.G. 131. In *Lloyd v Butler* [1990] 2 E.G.L.R. 155 Henry J observed that even on a mere valuation, anything very obviously likely to need repair within a relatively short time in relation to the duration of the loan ought to be reported.

1222 *Wooldridge v Stanley Hicks & Son*, above; *Horbury v Craig Hall & Rutley* (1991) 7 P.N. 206.

1223 *Denny v Budgen* (1955) 166 E.G. 433 (woodworm in floors).

1224 *Philips v Ward* [1956] 1 W.L.R. 471 (death-watch beetle).

1225 *Lawrence v Hampton & Sons* (1964) 190 E.G. 197.

1226 On the other hand, such defects can spread very quickly, and the mere fact that they are found some little time after the survey is weak evidence, if any, that there were visible signs at that time: *Hacker v Thomas Deal & Co* [1991] 2 E.G.L.R. 161.

1227 *Eley v King & Chasemore* [1989] 1 E.G.L.R. 181 CA.

1228 See, e.g. the principles set out in the RICS "Red Book" (latest edition 2014 with updates), laying down with some precision what the Institution expects of surveyors and valuers carrying out different types of survey. Under the RICS scheme there are essentially three levels of survey: Level One, showing general condition of the property and highlighting any urgent defects; Level Two, including in addition a market valuation, insurance rebuild costs, advice on defects relevant to value, and ongoing maintenance advice; and Level Three, the most comprehensive type. Nevertheless, there is authority that if a surveyor chooses to advise on matters outside his retainer, he must normally take care in doing so: cf. *Holt v Payne Skillington* [1996] P.N.L.R. 179.

1229 *Hill v Debenham Tewson & Chinnocks* [1955–95] P.N.L.R. 44; (1958) 171 E.G. 835; *Stewart v H. A. Brechin & Co*, above; *Conn v Munday* (1955) 166 E.G. 465.

1230 *Ker v John H. Allan & Son*, 1949 S.L.T. 20; *Thorne v Harris* (1953) 163 E.G. 324. The extent to which a surveyor must attempt to gain access to difficult areas of the building will vary with the nature of the survey; see *Hill v Debenham Tewson & Chinnocks* [1955–95] P.N.L.R. 44; (1958) 171 E.G. 835 and contrast with *Bishop v Watson, Watson & Scholes* (1972) 224 E.G. 1881.

1231 *Ker v John H. Allan & Son*, above.

1232 On which see, e.g. *Hipkins v Jack Cotton Partnership* [1989] 2 E.G.L.R. 157; and *Bere v Slades* [1989] 2 E.G.L.R. 160. And cf. *Henley v Cloke & Sons* [1991] 2 E.G.L.R. 141.

inspection,[1233] or at least warn the client).[1234] The limited nature of a survey to ascertain the value of a property as security for a mortgage advance is such that the duty owed in tort to mortgagor or mortgagee is similarly limited in scope.[1235]

9-193 Parts of premises particularly susceptible to rot must be carefully observed,[1236] and the surroundings of the building noted for any evidence of such matters as subsidence.[1237] Surveyors must be cautious about evidence of recent redecoration in case defects are being covered up[1238] and should not rely blindly on information given by vendors.[1239] Where the defendant observed but misread a possible indication of a defect it must be established that his error of judgment was negligent.[1240] The more defects which later manifest themselves which were not observed and identified, the easier it is to prove negligence.[1241] Finally, once a surveyor identifies a relevant defect in the property, he should normally warn his client in the report of that defect even if he considers it of minor importance.[1242]

(iv) Advice, representation etc

9-194 **Breach of duty: advice and representation** Surveyors increasingly take on the role of advising clients on property dealings, and in doing so owe a duty of care. In *Kenney v Hall, Pain & Foster*[1243] the defendants were held liable for negligent advice given to the claimant about the value of his property before he engaged them to sell it; their over-valuation had induced the claimant to commit himself to buy further properties beyond his means. Similarly where a surveyor represents a client at, for example, a rent review arbitration, he must show the skill and competence of a reasonable surveyor, and will be negligent if they fail to take into account relevant factors,[1244] submit relevant material to the arbitrator[1245] or present all the evidence adequately.[1246]

1233 *Wooldridge v Stanley Hicks & Son* (1953) 162 E.G. 513; *Roberts v Hampson* [1990] 1 W.L.R. 94.

1234 It is suggested that this must satisfy the duty. A surveyor's agreement to carry out a simple mortgage valuation can hardly be expanded into a commission for a structural survey because of the appearance of suspicious signs whose significance might be confirmed by the latter.

1235 See, e.g. *Whalley v Roberts & Roberts* [1990] 1 E.G.L.R. 164.

1236 *Lowy v Woodruffe Buchanan & Coulter* (1950) 156 E.G. 375.

1237 *Daisley v B. S. Hall & Co* (1973) 225 E.G. 1533.

1238 *Hingorani v Blower* (1976) 238 E.G. 883; *Morgan v Perry* (1974) 229 E.G. 1737.

1239 *Strover v Harrington* [1988] Ch.390. See too the valuation case of *Webb Resolutions Ltd v E.Surv Ltd* [2012] EWHC 3653 (TCC); [2013] P.N.L.R. 15 (failure to check vendors' figures).

1240 See *Leigh v Unsworth* (1974) 230 E.G. 501; *Kerridge v James Abbott & Partners* [1992] 2 E.G.L.R. 162.

1241 *Hill v Debenham Tewson & Chinnocks* [1955–95] P.N.L.R. 44; (1958) 171 E.G. 835.

1242 *Lees v English & Partners* (1977) 242 E.G. 293.

1243 (1976) 239 E.G. 355; [1977] Conv. 233. See too *Freemont (Denbigh) Ltd v Knight Frank LLP* [2014] EWHC 3347 (Ch); [2015] P.N.L.R. 4.

1244 *C.I.L. Securities v Briant Champion Long* [1993] 2 E.G.L.R. 164; also *John D. Wood & Co v Knatchbull* [2002] EWHC 2822 (QB); [2003] P.N.L.R. 17 (failure to take account of comparable property when advising vendor about sale price).

1245 *Rajdev v Becketts* [1989] 2 E.G.L.R. 144.

1246 *Thomas Miller & Co v Richard Saunders & Partners* [1989] 1 E.G.L.R. 267.

(c) Damages

(i) Need to prove loss and causation

Need to prove loss A claimant faced with negligence on the part of his surveyor must prove loss in order to claim damages. So, for example, if he relies on a negligent report on the state of a property but pays no more than the property is worth, presumptively no substantial damages are recoverable.[1247] 9-195

Causation The essence of a claim in negligence against a surveyor is generally that in reliance on his report the claimant either purchased property or lent money on the security of it in circumstances in which, but for the surveyor's negligence, he would not have done so. The claimant must therefore establish that he did so rely on the relevant report, and that had he been properly informed he would not have acted as he did.[1248] This is not generally a matter of difficulty where the claimant is the client who engaged the surveyor, or a mortgagee on whose behalf a report is obtained by the prospective purchaser. But in *Shankie-Williams v Hervey*,[1249] while it was accepted that a duty might arise to the purchaser of property in respect of a report obtained by the vendors from a dry rot specialist to help them sell the property, the claimant purchaser's claim failed in the absence of evidence that they had actually seen the report. Again, in *HIT Finance v Lewis & Tucker*[1250] the claimant lender complained that the defendant had over-estimated not only the value of the property but also the borrower's personal capacity to repay the advance. His claim in respect of the latter failed, among other reasons because the real cause of the claimant's loss was the inadequacy of the security on which he had lent. 9-196

Unreasonable action by the claimant may break the chain of causation between his loss and the defendant's fault, but this is in practice a difficult plea to make out. In *Kenney v Hall, Pain & Foster*[1251] the claimant was given a gross over-valuation of his own property by the defendants. He committed himself to buy a property beyond his means and to extensive repairs and improvements on that property. This was despite a warning from another estate agent that the asking price for his own property was too high. Goff J rejected submissions by the defendant that the claimant had acted unreasonably in committing himself to a new property before arranging to sell his own, and that after being warned of the over-valuation he was no longer acting on the defendants' advice. He held that the claimant had continued to rely substantially on the inaccurate and negligent advice given to him by the defendants.[1252] 9-197

1247 Implicit in *Philips v Ward* [1956] 1 W.L.R. 471; see too, e.g. *Farley v Skinner (No.2)* [2000] P.N.L.R. 441 (reversed on other grounds, [2001] UKHL 49; [2002] 2 A.C. 732).

1248 See *Dancorp Developers Ltd v Auckland CC* [1991] 3 N.Z.L.R. 337 (complaint of failure to warn about site contamination failed, since on the evidence claimants would have gone ahead with development in any case).

1249 (1986) 279 E.G. 316 CA.

1250 [1993] 2 E.G.L.R. 231; (1993) 9 P.N. 33.

1251 (1976) 239 E.G. 355.

1252 Quaere, however, whether it might be more appropriate to reduce the claimant's damages under the contributory negligence legislation in such a case.

(ii) *Measure of recovery*

9-198 On principle, the measure of damages available against a negligent surveyor or valuer is the loss foreseeably resulting from the negligence or misvaluation,[1253] subject to the usual qualifications affecting all damage awards.[1254] The measure of recovery in the commonest case, where the claimant has purchased property in reliance on a negligent survey or valuation, will normally be the difference in value between the price actually paid for that property and its true market value.[1255] For these purposes, the "true market value" generally means the amount the property would have fetched on the market at the time the advice was received.[1256] It follows from the above that if the value put on the property by the valuer is higher than the price paid, the overplus is out of account.[1257] But if it is lower, it is suggested that the claimant is limited to the difference between the valuation and the true value: in so far as he chose to pay more than the valuer said the property was worth, this element of his loss is hardly a loss attributable to the valuer's negligence.[1258]

9-199 Just as the value of the property in the condition wrongly attributed to it by the defendant is out of account, so is the cost of putting it into such condition, even if the claimant, having bought the house, proceeds reasonably to incur it,[1259] and apparently even if the surveyor was specifically instructed to advise on the costs of

---

[1253] "[T]he proper measure of damage is the amount of money which will put [the claimant] into as good a position as if the surveying contract had been properly fulfilled"—Denning LJ in *Philips v Ward* [1956] 1 W.L.R. 471, 473.

[1254] e.g. the principle that net loss only is recoverable. See *John D. Wood (Residential) Ltd v Knatchbull* [2002] EWHC 2822 (QB); [2003] P.N.L.R. 17 (estate agent negligently allowed seller to sell too cheaply: recovery of difference reduced by (a) the extra commission saved; and (b) the use of the sale monies due to the fact that the actual sale had taken place earlier than it would have had vendor been properly advised). The same case allowed recovery on the basis of a loss of chance: the vendor recovered the difference between the actual and the "proper" sale price discounted by the chance that he would not in fact have obtained the latter.

[1255] Referred to by Nourse LJ as the "prima facie rule": *Patel v Hooper & Jackson* [1999] 1 W.L.R. 1792, 1801. See too *Oswald v Countrywide Surveyors Ltd* (1996) 50 Const. L.R. 1; and cf. *Ford v White* [1964] 1 W.L.R. 885. In *HTW Valuers (Cen Qd) Ltd v Astonland Ltd* [2004] HCA 54; (2004) 79 A.L.J.R. 190 the High Court of Australia seemingly held that, where a valuer's negligent advice leads a claimant to buy an overvalued property, the claimant could recover the difference between the purchase price and the amount he reasonably resells for, even if less than the value at the time of purchase.

[1256] *Shaw v Halifax (South West) Ltd* [1996] P.N.L.R. 451 (no account of rise in values between valuation and exchange of contracts); see too *Wapshot v Davies Donovan* [1996] P.N.L.R. 361. Where this might yield different figures according to how the property was hypothetically marketed, the claimant's own intentions may well be decisive: see *Duncan Investments Ltd v Underwoods* [1998] P.N.L.R. 754 (negligent valuation of portfolio of properties: since claimant had intended to sell properties individually, this value and not their value *en bloc* was taken).

[1257] See the solicitors' negligence case of *Ford v White* [1964] 1 W.L.R. 885. The reason is that, had the valuer not been negligent, the buyer would not have bought the house at the price he did: he would thus not have benefited from the increase in value. Note, however, that, faute de mieux, the surveyor's valuation may be some evidence of the diminution in value: *Steward v Rapley* [1989] 1 E.G.L.R. 159.

[1258] cf. *Hardy v Wamsley-Lewis* (1967) 203 E.G. 1039. This can alternatively be regarded as a variant on the rule in *South Australia Asset Management Co v York Montague Ltd* [1997] A.C. 191 referred to below at para.9-201. But where the overpayment can be attributed to inflation in prices between the time of the advice and that of the commitment to purchase, the result may well be different: cf. *Shaw v Halifax (South West) Ltd* [1996] P.N.L.R. 451.

[1259] *Watts v Morrow* [1991] 1 W.L.R. 1421; *Holder v Countrywide Surveyors Ltd* [2002] EWHC 856 (TCC); [2003] P.N.L.R. 3. See too the contract case of *Moore v National Westminster Bank Plc* [2018] EWHC 1805 (TCC); [2018] P.N.L.R. 33 (same measure where no report provided at all). But if the cost of repair was substantially lower than the difference in value, *quaere* if the claimant would repair.[1260] Such cost may, however, be some guide *faute de mieux* as to the difference in value.[1261] It should be noted that, as in the law of damages generally, the fact that the purchaser has recouped his loss from another source is generally left out of account: thus in *Gardner v Marsh & Parsons (A Firm)*[1262] the purchaser of a leasehold flat recovered in full for defects overlooked by his surveyor, even though they were later remedied by the landlord at his own expense.

In the converse case where surveyors misadvise a vendor as to the price at which he should sell, it is suggested that, by parity of reasoning the measure of damages is the difference between the actual value and the price at which the claimant in fact sold.[1263] Where the misadvice is as to the rental at which land should be leased, then (at least if the lease is a long-term one) the best way to measure damages is, it seems, the difference between the capital value of the reversion that the claimants would have obtained if A had fulfilled his obligations and the capital value of the reversion in fact obtained.[1264] 9-200

Measure of damages available to mortgagees Where money is advanced by a mortgagee on the basis of a negligent valuation, the House of Lords in *South Australia Asset Management Co (SAAMCO) v York Montague Ltd*[1265] made it clear that in principle the lender can recover the losses suffered by him as a result of the valuation being inaccurate, but no more. This sum[1266] is computed by first taking the capital sum advanced,[1267] less what was (or, if greater, what should have been) recovered by realising the security and/or suing the debtor. There is then added to 9-201

be expected to incur it to mitigate his loss. cf. *Daisley v B. S. Hall & Co* (1972) 225 E.G. 1553.

1260 *Smith v Peter North & Partners* [2001] EWCA Civ 1553; [2002] P.N.L.R. 12 (surveyors asked to value equestrian property, and estimate cost of repairs necessary to bring it up to scratch: expenses underestimated, but no recovery because property worth more than price paid). Sed quaere: if the surveyors had not been negligent the purchasers would doubtless have bought another property not needing exorbitant expenditure.

1261 *Steward v Rapley* [1989] 1 E.G.L.R. 159; *Oswald v Countrywide Surveyors Ltd* (1996) 50 Const. L.R. 1; *Moore v National Westminster Bank Plc* [2018] EWHC 1805 (TCC); [2018] P.N.L.R. 33 at [23].

1262 [1997] 1 W.L.R. 489.

1263 As suggested by Jack J in *Malmesbury (Earl) v Strutt & Parker* [2007] EWHC 999 (QB); [2007] P.N.L.R. 29 at [185].

1264 *Malmesbury (Earl) v Strutt & Parker* [2007] EWHC 999 (QB); [2007] P.N.L.R. 29; see too the earlier *Inter-Leisure Ltd v Lamberts* [1997] N.P.C. 49.

1265 [1997] A.C. 191; also *Bank of Ireland v Faithful & Gould Ltd* [2014] EWHC 2217 (TCC); [2014] P.N.L.R. 28; and generally *BPE Solicitors v Hughes-Holland* [2017] UKSC 21; [2018] A.C. 599. For the scope of application of the "SAAMCO cap" to mortgagees' advisers acting as project managers, see *Lloyds Bank Plc v McBains Cooper Consulting Ltd* [2018] EWCA Civ 452; [2018] P.N.L.R. 23. See in general J. Stapleton, "Negligent valuers and falls in the property market" (1997) 113 L.Q.R. 1; J. O'Sullivan, "Negligent Professional Advice and Market Movements" [1997] C.L.J. 19; J. Thomson, "SAAMCO revisited" [2017] C.L.J. 476.

1266 Which is available to the lender even though it has personally suffered less, or no, loss, because (for example) it has syndicated the loan (see *Paratus AMC Ltd v Countrywide Surveyors Ltd* [2011] EWHC 3307 (Ch); [2012] P.N.L.R. 12 at [54] ff; and *Titan Europe 2006-3 Plc v Colliers International UK Plc* [2015] EWCA Civ 1083; [2016] P.N.L.R. 7), or it is a mere subsidiary put in funds by a parent corporation (*Legal & General Mortgage Services Ltd v Underwoods* [1997] P.N.L.R. 567). These developments are criticised, though ultimately unconvincingly, in N. Goh, "Syndicated Loans, Recovery of Third-Party Loss and the Res Inter Alios Acta Principle" [2016] L.M.C.L.Q. 368.

1267 Where the lender was already exposed to the borrower, and the valuation in question was taken to support an increase in borrowing, only the amount of the extra monies made available in reliance on the valuation advanced can be recovered: see *Tiuta International Ltd (In Liquidation) v De Villiers Chartered Surveyors Ltd* [2017] UKSC 77; [2017] 1 W.L.R. 4627. In the same case it was held it (i) any expenses incurred in enforcing the security; and (ii) the interest (if any) that would otherwise have been earned by the claimant on the capital sum advanced against the inadequate security[1268] (but not the interest that should have been paid by the mortgagor himself[1269]). However, the amount by which the security has been over-valued generally forms a cap for any such award. This is largely on the basis that any loss over and above this figure cannot result from the over-valuation. However, Lord Hoffmann also gave a further reason: namely, that since a valuer did not make any statement about the possible future value of the security, it would be unfair to impose on him an open-ended liability for all loss suffered owing, for example, to a general decline in property values, even if such a loss might have been foreseeable.[1270] The result is that, while there is no bar on the lender being compensated for losses due to a collapse in property values,[1271] such loss can only be claimed up to the amount of the over-valuation.[1272] The principles in the *SAAMCO* case are not limited to over-valuation cases. In any case where the defendant's negligent misrepresentation leads the claimant to lend on the security of property, the claimant is generally limited to the amount, if any, by which the lender has been misled as to the value of the security he is getting.[1273]

9-202 In any case of over-valuation of mortgaged property, the mortgagee is expected to mitigate his loss by realising his security providently and in good time once the borrower has defaulted. In so far as he fails to do so, and property values subsequently decline, this further loss is borne by him alone.[1274] However, the limits to the duty to mitigate are important. In particular, it now seems that despite some contrary authority[1275] the mortgagee is under no duty to mitigate by proceeding against the mortgagor personally, or against any other security available to him, and that the availability of such a remedy does not affect the sum payable by the defendant. This is because of the principle that it does not lie in the mouth of a

to be immaterial that the further advance technically took the form of an entirely new advance, part of which was to be used to pay off the existing indebtedness.

1268 But the amount of such sums must be proved: *Mortgage Express v Countrywide Surveyors Ltd* [2016] EWHC 1830 (Ch); [2016] P.N.L.R. 35. In a suitable case, the lender may alternatively recover extra interest charges incurred from having had to borrow the money: *Birmingham Midshires Building Society v Phillips* [1998] P.N.L.R. 468. It seems that the right to claim the cost to the lender of the funds is a general one not limited to interest costs as such: thus a lender who has hedged by entering into an interest rate swap is not barred from claiming the costs associated with the swap. See *Mortgage Agency Services Number One Ltd v Edward Symmons LLP* [2013] EWCA Civ 1590.

1269 Since had the surveyor acted properly there would have been no loan in the first place, and hence no interest paid: see *Swingcastle Ltd v Alastair Gibson* [1991] 2 A.C. 223.

1270 Thus in Australia the *South Australia* case has not been followed where the valuers expressed the view that their valuation was good for three to five years: *Kenny & Good Pty Ltd v MGICA* (1999) 73 A.L.J.R. 901. Two judges (McHugh and Gummow JJ) thought *South Australia* correct but distinguishable: the other three (Gaudron, Kirby and Callinan JJ) inclined to the view that it was wrong. By contrast, South Australia has been accepted as correct in New Zealand: *Bank of New Zealand v N.Z. Guardian Trust Co* [1999] 1 N.Z.L.R. 664, 682–683.

1271 As the Court of Appeal had held: [1995] Q.B. 375.

1272 Where the claimant has already recovered a sum from a third party, he may set that sum against that portion of his loss that is irrecoverable under the *South Australia* case, thus preserving full recovery from the surveyor: see *Law Debenture Trust Corp'n plc v Hereward Phillips* [1999] P.N.L.R. 725.

1273 *Bristol & West Building Society v Mothew* [1998] Ch. 1 (statement to prospective first mortgagee that no second charges contemplated). See too *Scullion v Bank of Scotland Plc (t/a Colleys)* [2011] EWCA Civ 693; [2011] 1 W.L.R. 3212 at [62]–[68] (Lord Neuberger MR).

1274 *Western Trust & Savings Ltd v Clive Travers & Co* [1997] P.N.L.R. 295 (a solicitors' case, but the same principles apply).

1275 Notably *London & South of England Building Society v Stone* [1983] 1 W.L.R. 1242, where the existence of such a duty (though not the breach of it) was accepted.

defendant liable for a loss to argue that the claimant ought to have looked elsewhere in order to recoup it.[1276]

Consequential and other losses As well as damages of the kinds mentioned above, there may be further consequential losses recoverable against a negligent surveyor. Thus in the case of negligent inspection on behalf of a purchaser of residential property there can potentially be claims for such matters as alternative accommodation while problems are sorted out,[1277] stamp duty on the amount overpaid by the claimant,[1278] and if the house is entirely uninhabitable the cost of buying and moving into another.[1279] In the case of failure to spot defects in commercial property there may be liability for lost trading or development profits.[1280] In either case there may also be a claim for expenditure wasted.[1281] Where the purchaser has, to the clear knowledge of the buyer, bought the property for immediate resale, there may it seems be liability for resale profits lost through failure to notice defects.[1282] But all consequential losses must be reasonably foreseeable: thus where surveyors failed to notice defects that made a house difficult to re-sell, the purchaser failed to recover extra commuting costs caused by his relocation to another job.[1283] 9-203

Personal injury, inconvenience and distress In a suitable case there is no reason why damages for personal injury should not be available from a surveyor: for example, where he fails to notice dangerous loose bricks one of which later falls on a purchaser's head.[1284] In addition to this, there is clear authority that compensation is available for the physical inconvenience and discomfort resulting from a breach of duty: for example where a claimant has to live with building works aimed at rectifying defects that ought to have been spotted.[1285] Less straightforward is recovery for mere distress,[1286] notably where a surveyor fails to notice some disamenity in a property and a purchaser claims to have suffers disappointment or 9-204

1276 See in particular *Peters v East Midlands Strategic HA* [2009] EWCA Civ 145; [2010] Q.B. 48 at [39]–[41] (Dyson LJ); also cases such as *Haugesund Kommune v Depfa ACS Bank* [2010] EWHC 227 (Comm); [2010] P.N.L.R. 21 (reversed on other grounds, [2011] EWCA Civ 33; [2011] 3 All E.R. 655).

1277 e.g. *Patel v Hooper & Jackson* [1999] 1 W.L.R. 1792.

1278 *Patel v Hooper & Jackson* [1999] 1 W.L.R. 1792, above.

1279 See the suggestion of Romer LJ in *Philips v Ward* [1956] 1 W.L.R. 471, 478.

1280 See the Scots decision in *Manorgate Ltd v First Scottish Property Services Ltd* [2013] CSOH 108; [2014] P.N.L.R. 1 (failure by record search agent to spot archaeological impediments to development: trading profits recoverable, though claim for development profits failed on the facts).

1281 Thus in *Manorgate Ltd v First Scottish Property Services Ltd* [2013] CSOH 108; [2014] P.N.L.R. 1 there was also a claim for costs incurred before impediments to development, which the defendants had failed to spot, were fully apparent.

1282 See *MPG Investments LLP v Connells Survey & Valuation Ltd* [2012] EWHC 4071 (Ch), apparently refusing to strike out such a claim; also the solicitors' case of *Watts v Bell & Scott* [2007] CSOH 108; 2007 S.L.T. 665; [2007] P.N.L.R. 30.

1283 See the Scots decision in *Douglas v Stuart Wyse Ogilvie Estates Ltd*, 2001 S.L.T. 689; and cf. the solicitors' negligence case of *Pilkington v Wood* [1953] Ch. 770.

1284 *Allen v Ellis* [1990] 1 E.G.L.R. 170.

1285 See *Watts v Morrow* [1991] 1 W.L.R. 1421, esp. at 1445 (Bingham LJ). See too, e.g. *Patel v Hooper & Jackson* [1999] 1 W.L.R. 1792 (£2,000 each for couple in uninhabitable house); *Hoadley v Edwards* [2001] P.N.L.R. 41 (£5,000 for being forced to live on a virtual building site); *Holder v Countrywide Surveyors Ltd* [2002] EWHC 856 (TCC); [2003] P.N.L.R. 3; and, generally, *Farley v Skinner* [2001] UKHL 49; [2002] 2 A.C. 732, esp. at [35] (Lord Browne-Wilkinson).

1286 See A. Tettenborn, "Non-Pecuniary Loss: The Right Answer, but Bad Reasoning" (2003) 2 J.O.R. 94.

vexation as a result.[1287] In such a case, it seems, distress damages are available provided the avoidance of distress or annoyance forms at least one of the objects of the contract[1288] between surveyor and client, but not otherwise.[1289] In the leading case, *Farley v Skinner*,[1290] surveyors acting for the purchaser of a house near Gatwick Airport were specifically instructed to report on aircraft noise, but negligently reported that no problem arose. An award of £10,000 for distress and vexation was upheld, it being clear from the circumstances that the avoidance of such distress was at least one of the objects of the contract between them and the purchaser. However, the limitations of *Farley* must be noted. In the earlier decision in *Watts v Morrow*,[1291] the Court of Appeal had said that ordinarily damages for distress were *not* recoverable against a surveyor who failed to notice defects, and this decision was seemingly accepted as correct by the House of Lords. The distinction seems to be that, while *Watts* was an "ordinary" negligence case, in *Farley* the defendants had specifically been instructed to deal with the particular cause of distress in issue. It seems to follow that, despite *Farley*, damages for distress remain irrecoverable in the absence of some such explicit instruction as was present in that case.[1292]

9-205 **Timing** For the purpose of reckoning damages against a valuer, the relevant time is presumptively the date of purchase.[1293] But where justice so demands, subsequent events may be in account. So in *McKinnon v e.surv Ltd*[1294] purchasers' surveyors negligently failed to detect signs of possible movement: at that time there was no means of telling whether movement might not be actually taking place, and the disparity between the price paid and the market value was hence very large. Later it emerged that the premises had in fact stabilised, and the difference in value was accordingly much less. It was held that the later events were in account in assess-

---

[1287] The distinction between inconvenience (always compensable) and distress (compensable only *sub modo*) can at times be narrow. In *Farley v Skinner* [2001] UKHL 49; [2002] 2 A.C. 732, the House of Lords apparently accepted that misery caused by uncovenanted aircraft noise fell under both heads. See [2001] UKHL 49; [2002] 2 A.C. 732 at [30] (Lord Steyn), [57]–[60] (Lord Hutton), [108] (Lord Scott (apparently)). See generally A. Tettenborn, "Non-Pecuniary Loss: The Right Answer, but Bad Reasoning" (2003) 2 J.O.R. 94, above.

[1288] *Farley v Skinner* was argued as a contract case, but as a surveyor is concurrently liable in contract and tort, it would be nonsensical if tortious liability were treated differently. In the case of tort, no doubt the object of the surveyor's engagement must have been to preserve peace of mind etc. Thus it is suggested that if the survey in *Farley v Skinner*, below, had been made for a mortgage lender and shown to the purchaser (who would thus have an action in tort but not in contract) the result would have been the same.

[1289] See *Watts v Morrow* [1991] 1 W.L.R. 1421 at 1445 (Bingham LJ); *Farley v Skinner* [2001] UKHL 49; [2002] 2 A.C. 732 at [16] (Lord Steyn), [34] (Lord Clyde), [47] (Lord Hutton).

[1290] [2001] UKHL 49; [2002] 2 A.C. 732.

[1291] [1991] 1 W.L.R. 1421.

[1292] Though it is, with respect, difficult to see why this should be so. Surely one of the objects of any contract to survey a house for a purchaser is avoidance of distress caused by buying a seriously substandard property. See A. Tettenborn, "Non-Pecuniary Loss: The Right Answer, but Bad Reasoning" (2003) 2 J.O.R. 94, 107.

[1293] See *Philips v Ward* [1956] 1 W.L.R. 471, 475 (Denning LJ); *Holder v Countrywide Surveyors Ltd* [2002] EWHC 856 (TCC) [2003] P.N.L.R. 3, 49 (difference at date of purchase, not of discovery of defects); *Scullion v Bank of Scotland Plc (t/a Colleys)* [2010] EWHC 2253 (Ch); [2011] P.N.L.R. 5 (reversed on other grounds, [2011] EWCA Civ 693; [2011] 1 W.L.R. 3212). In the latter case, indeed, the "time of purchase" rule was regarded as an aspect of *South Australia Asset Management v York Montague Ltd* [1997] A.C. 191, under which subsequent drops in value were regarded as outside the scope of the valuer's duty to appraise premises at a fixed point in time.

[1294] [2003] EWHC 475 (Ch); [2003] 2 E.G.L.R. 57.

ing, and hence reducing, the claimant's damages. Again, in *Devine v Jefferys*[1295] the claimant paid too much for a house as a result of a negligent overvaluation. But later, when he encountered negative equity and defaulted on payments, the lender accepted a surrender of the house in full settlement of the mortgage debt. The claimant was held to have lost, and hence to be entitled to, nothing.

Contributory negligence Damages against a negligent surveyor may, in a suitable case, be reduced on account of contributory negligence. Thus lenders providing funds are generally expected to take care to protect their interests, for instance by confirming the true purchase price[1296]; querying wildly discrepant valuations from different valuers[1297]; and carrying out at least rudimentary checks on a borrower's credit status.[1298] No doubt a person purchasing a property on the basis of a valuation would equally be expected to take at least some steps to protect his own interests.[1299] In extreme cases an over-risky business model may itself count as contributory negligence, as where lenders combine a very high loan-to-value proportion with failure to make any other substantial checks on the borrower's status.[1300] But a high loan-to-value ratio on its own is unlikely to be so categorised[1301]; and indeed, courts are unwilling to attribute contributory fault to a claimant who acted in accordance with common practice.[1302] **9-206**

Although a surveyor's liability for misvaluation is generally limited to the loss resulting from that misvaluation, it seems, slightly oddly, that a reduction will be made for contributory negligence on the claimant's part even where this relates to some unconnected matter. Thus in *Platform Home Loans Ltd v Oyston Shipways*[1303] lenders guilty of negligence in failing to make sufficient checks on a borrower's status suffered a 20 per cent reduction when they sued their surveyors for overvaluing the security. Their argument that their own negligence had nothing to do with the loss for which the defendants were liable, and hence no deduction to be made, had a good deal of logic: nevertheless, it was decisively was rejected by both the Court of Appeal and the House of Lords. However, where such a deduction does fall to be made, it is by parity of reasoning made from the whole of the claimant's **9-207**

1295 [2001] P.N.L.R. 16.

1296 *Platform Home Loans Ltd v Oyston Shipways Ltd* [1998] Ch. 466 (the case went to the HL on another point: see [2000] 2 A.C. 190).

1297 *Cavendish Funding Ltd v Henry Spencer* [1998] P.N.L.R. 123.

1298 *First National Commercial Bank Plc v Andrew S. Taylor Ltd* [1997] P.N.L.R. 37; see too *Omega Trust Ltd v Wright, Son & Pepper (No 2)* [1998] P.N.L.R. 337; and *Paratus AMC Ltd v Countrywide Surveyors Ltd* [2011] EWHC 3307 (Ch); [2012] P.N.L.R. 12.

1299 For example, if a purchaser were alerted before exchange of contracts to possible subsidence that had gone unnoticed by his surveyor, but nevertheless proceeded without making further checks.

1300 See *Paratus AMC Ltd v Countrywide Surveyors Ltd* [2011] EWHC 3307 (Ch); [2012] P.N.L.R. 12 (90 per cent LTV with hardly any checks would have been 60 per cent contributorily negligent had defendants been liable); *Webb Resolutions Ltd v E.Surv Ltd* [2012] EWHC 3653 (TCC); [2013] P.N.L.R. 15 (same for 95 per cent LTV and no checks).

1301 *Banque Bruxelles Lambert SA v Eagle Star Insurance Co Ltd* [1994] 2 E.G.L.R. 108, 137 (Phillips J); *Paratus AMC Ltd v Countrywide Surveyors Ltd* [2011] EWHC 3307 (Ch); [2012] P.N.L.R. 12 at [80] ff. Note also *Webb Resolutions Ltd v E.Surv Ltd* [2012] EWHC 3653 (TCC); [2013] P.N.L.R. 15 (85 per cent LTV not as such negligent, even though 95 per cent was when combined with lack of other checks).

1302 *Blemain Finance Ltd v E.Surv Ltd* [2012] EWHC 3654 (TCC). See too *Banque Bruxelles Lambert SA v Eagle Star Insurance Co Ltd* (1994) 68 B.L.R. 39.

1303 [1998] Ch. 466 (the case went to the H.L. on another point: [2000] 2 A.C. 190); see too *Bank of Ireland v Faithful & Gould Ltd* [2014] EWHC 2217 (TCC); [2014] P.N.L.R. 28. See A. Dugdale, "Contributory Negligence applied to Economic Loss" (1999) 62 M.L.R. 281.

loss, and not just from that part of it recoverable from the defendant. Thus in the *Platform* case, the claimants had suffered a total loss of £600,000, of which under the principles in *South Australia Asset Management Co v York Montague Ltd*[1304] the sum of £500,000 was actually recoverable. It was held that the claimants recovered £480,000 (i.e. £600,000 less 20 per cent) and not £400,000 (i.e. £500,000 less 20 per cent).[1305]

5. Architects and Consulting Engineers[1306]

(a) Duties

(i) Duties to clients

9-208 **Duties to clients** An architect or consulting engineer[1307] of course owes a contractual duty to his client to exercise reasonable skill.[1308] Nor is the architect's duty of care limited to issues of simple design and construction. Architects commonly are concerned with the issue of certificates in the course of construction contracts for the purpose of allowing the builders to claim payment for it; they owe a duty to the clients to take care in inspecting the work, and will be held liable if they negligently certify work which has been badly done so that the client has to pay for it.[1309] With regard to tort, it also seems clear that an architect or engineer who designs a house so dangerous that it actually injures the client or damages an item of his property (other than something forming part of the premises themselves) would be liable in tort.[1310] There was once some doubt over whether he could concurrently be liable to his client in tort for defective design or advice causing merely economic loss; where, for instance, work was necessary to put right defects, or where an office building was unusable and as a result the client lost profits.[1311]

1304 [1997] A.C. 191.

1305 Thus yielding the peculiar result that a claimant guilty of 20 per cent contributory negligence recovered only 4 per cent less than he would have recovered if blameless.

1306 See Jackson & Powell on *Professional Liability*, 8th edn (2017), Ch.9.

1307 The term "architect" will be taken here, except where the context requires otherwise, to include a consulting engineer or similar professional.

1308 Today by statute: Supply of Goods and Services Act 1982 s.13 (commercial clients) and s.49 of the Consumer Rights Act 2015 (others). In practice the level of skill is often set by express contract: thus the 2010 *RIBA standard conditions of appointment* (revised 2012) by cl.2.1 require the architect to exercise reasonable skill, care and diligence in accordance with the normal standards of the architectural profession in performing his services and discharging his obligations. Clauses of this type add little, if anything, to the common law duty: see *199 Knightsbridge Development Ltd v WSP UK Ltd* [2014] EWHC 43 (TCC) at [101]–[102] (Edwards-Stuart J).

1309 *Sutcliffe v Thackrah* [1974] A.C. 727 (deciding that no quasi-arbitral immunity applied); see too *Lloyds Bank Plc v McBains Cooper Consulting Ltd (No.2)* [2016] EWHC 2045 (TCC); [2017] P.N.L.R. 11 (varied on appeal, but not on this ground, at [2018] EWCA Civ 452; [2018] P.N.L.R. 23). That liability here is based on negligence and not on any stricter duty was confirmed without hesitation by Coulson J in *Dhamija v Sunningdale Joineries Ltd* [2010] EWHC 2396 (TCC); [2011] P.N.L.R. 9.

1310 cf. *Baxall Securities Ltd v Sheard Walshaw Partnership* [2001] P.N.L.R. 9 (reversed on appeal on other grounds, [2002] EWCA Civ 9; [2002] P.N.L.R. 24) (damage to stock from ingress of rainwater); also *Targett v Torfaen BC* [1992] 3 All E.R. 27 (a case of liability to a local authority tenant).

1311 See *Bagot v Stevens Scanlan* [1966] 1 Q.B. 197.

It now seems probable, however, that he can be so liable.[1312] The point matters largely in connection with limitation. If a claimant relies on a breach of contract by the architect, time runs from when the building was badly designed, whereas if he founds his action on a breach of duty in tort, time does not run until some damage is suffered, which may be a good deal later.[1313]

(ii) *Duties to others*[1314]

Personal injury and property damage With regard to personal injury or damage to property other than the premises themselves, there is no doubt that an architect or consulting engineer is under a duty of care[1315]: if negligent, he may be liable in tort to any third party suffering damage as a result.[1316] So in *Rimmer v Liverpool City Council*[1317] defendants were held liable for the act of their architect in designing a council flat with an over-thin glass partition which cut the claimant when he fell against it. An architect is equally liable under this principle for damage to property other than the building itself, for instance where badly designed guttering causes ingress of water which damages stock in an industrial unit.[1318] Another case is where misdesign of one property causes physical damage to neighbouring property.[1319] But the limitations to this need to be noted. In particular, where a number of properties are constructed as a single entity, as with an apartment block 9-209

[1312] See *Congregational Union v Harriss & Harriss* [1988] 1 All E.R. 15; *Ketteman v Hansel Properties Ltd* [1987] A.C. 189; and *Wessex RHA v HLM Design* (1994) 40 Con. L.R. 1. True, in *Robinson v PE Jones (Contractors) Ltd* [2011] EWCA Civ 9; [2012] Q.B. 44 the Court of Appeal held, after exhaustive analysis, that *builders* did not owe concurrent duties; but both Jackson LJ (at [51] and [74]) and Stanley Burnton LJ (at [93]) seemingly accepted that architects continued to do so. Presumably this means that in a design and build contract the court will now have as best it can to separate out the "design" and "build" elements, with concurrent liability applying to the former only.

[1313] Nor can the client invoke the latent damage provisions of s.14A of the Limitation Act 1980 if his action lies solely in contract. See para.31-74.

[1314] J. Keeler, "Paying for Mistakes–Professional Negligence and Economic Loss" (1979) 53 A.L.J. 412.

[1315] The fact that the architect, or his employer, is vendor or lessor of the premises in question will not insulate him from liability. See *Rimmer v Liverpool City Council* [1985] Q.B. 1 (distinguishing *Cavalier v Pope* [1906] A.C. 428); *Targett v Torfaen DC* [1992] 3 All E.R. 27. He would probably also be liable under s.3 of the Defective Premises Act 1972.

[1316] *Clay v AJ Crump & Sons Ltd* [1964] 1 Q.B. 533; cf. *Clayton v Woodman* [1962] 2 Q.B. 533; and see also *Voli v Inglewood Shire Council* (1963) 110 C.L.R. 74, 85 (Windeyer J). Note also that specific limitations on an architect's brief will not necessarily protect him from liability for obvious dangers to third parties: *Pantaleone v Alaouie* (1989) 18 N.S.W.L.R. 121.

[1317] [1985] Q.B. 1. See also *Clay v AJ Crump & Sons Ltd* [1964] 1 Q.B. 533 (architect supervising demolition liable to passer-by injured by collapsing wall); *Targett v Torfaen BC* [1992] 3 All E.R. 27 (council liable for designing council house without adequate stair rails, causing tenant to fall badly); *McManus v City Link Development Co Ltd* [2015] CSOH 178 (illness to residents allegedly from causing construction on contaminated land: appealed on other grounds at [2017] CSIH 12; 2017 Hous. L.R. 84).

[1318] *Baxall Securities Ltd v Sheard Walshaw Partnership* [2001] P.N.L.R. 9 (reversed on appeal on other grounds, [2002] EWCA Civ 9; [2002] P.N.L.R. 24); see too *Bellefield Computer Systems Ltd v Turner & Sons Ltd* [2000] B.L.R. 97; and *Pearson Education Ltd v Charter Partnership Ltd* [2005] EWHC 2021 (TCC); [2006] P.N.L.R. 14 (designer owes duty to later lessee for loss of stock due to water ingress. The point did not arise on appeal: [2007] EWCA Civ 130; [2007] B.L.R. 324). Cf. *Biffa Waste Services Ltd v Maschinenfabrik Ernst Hese GmbH* [2008] EWHC 6 (TCC); [2008] P.N.L.R. 17 (appealed on other matters, [2008] EWCA Civ 1257; [2009] Q.B. 725).

[1319] For, instance where consulting engineers overestimate the stability of a construction site, causing damage to neighbouring buildings: *Offer-Hoar v Larkstore Ltd* [2006] EWCA Civ 1079; [2006] 1 W.L.R. 2926.

or row of townhouses, and later sold into separate ownership, later damage caused by bad design of one unit to another unit is not damage to "other property."[1320]

9-210 It seems that an architect's liability in tort for injury or damage caused by misdesign is limited to cases where there is no reasonable likelihood of intermediate inspection, thus approximating his position to that of a manufacturer of goods.[1321] Thus, where the defect is one that is likely to be spotted by a surveyor acting for a would-be purchaser, the architect will not normally be liable.[1322] Furthermore, it seems likely that architects and consulting engineers will only be liable if engaged wholly or partly to avert the danger which the claimant now complains of.[1323]

9-211 **Economic loss—liability to purchasers etc** The above liability, however, is limited to personal injury or damage to other property not forming part of the premises in question. The question of the architect's liability to third parties for economic loss, including damage to the misdesigned property itself, must be looked at in the light of the House of Lords' decision in *Department of the Environment v Thomas Bates & Son Ltd*.[1324] That finally established that at common law[1325] a builder putting up premises owed no duty in negligence to a subsequent owner of them.[1326] By parity of reasoning, the same must be true of an architect. Thus in *Bellefield Computer Systems Ltd v Turner & Sons Ltd*[1327] a building caught fire allegedly as a result of the defective design of an internal firewall by architects on behalf of a previous owner. The architects were held to have owed no duty of care to the present owners of the premises for the loss suffered by them.[1328] Similarly, a Scottish court has held that architects engaged by A Ltd to design garage premises

---

[1320] See *Payne v Setchell Ltd* [2002] P.N.L.R. 7 (adjoining cottages built on a bad concrete slab are a single unit for tort purposes); *Broster v Galliard Docklands Ltd* [2011] EWHC 1722 (TCC); [2011] P.N.L.R. 34 (apartment block misdesigned as a whole; debris from one apartment damages another; no tort action).

[1321] See para.10-37 onwards.

[1322] See *Baxall Securities Ltd v Sheard Walshaw Partnership* [2002] EWCA Civ 9; [2002] P.N.L.R. 24 (criticised, I. Duncan Wallace, "Lucky architects: snail in an opaque bottle?" (2003) 119 L.Q.R. 18; and see too Lord Phillips CJ's slightly sceptical comments in *Pearson Education Ltd v Charter Partnership Ltd* [2007] EWCA Civ 130; [2007] B.L.R. 324 at [32]).

[1323] This is the case with surveyors (see *Harrison v Technical Sign Co Ltd* [2013] EWCA Civ 1569; [2014] P.N.L.R. 15), and was accepted to be true of environmental consulting engineers in the Scots decision in *McManus v City Link Development Co Ltd* [2015] CSOH 178 at [132]–[144] (appealed on other grounds at [2017] CSIH 12; 2017 Hous. L.R. 84).

[1324] [1991] 1 A.C. 499. See too *Murphy v Brentwood DC* [1991] 1 A.C. 398; I. Duncan Wallace, "Anns beyond repair" (1991) 107 L.Q.R. 228. Irish courts, by contrast, seem to be more generous here: e.g. *McGhee v Alcorn* [2016] IEHC 59; [2016] P.N.L.R. 25.

[1325] For the position under the Defective Premises Act 1972, see para.9-215.

[1326] Tentative suggestions by Lord Bridge in *Murphy*'s case, above, at 475, that there might be an exception where negligent construction or design caused danger to third parties and expense was incurred averting it, were comprehensively discountenanced in *Thomas v Taylor Wimpey Developments Ltd* [2019] EWHC 1134 (TCC); [2019] P.N.L.R. 26 and must now be taken as heterodox.

[1327] [2000] B.L.R. 97. See too *Preston v Torfaen BC* [1955–95] P.N.L.R. 625; *The Times,* 21 July 1993 (consulting engineer who prepared site report for builder/vendor owed no duty in respect of economic loss suffered by subsequent purchaser of defective house); *Machin v Adams* (1997) 84 B.L.R. 79 (architect reporting to building owner on state of premises owes no duty to purchaser); *Howes v Crombie*, 2001 S.C.L.R. 921; [2002] P.N.L.R. 3 (ditto). Decisions upholding a wider liability elsewhere in the Commonwealth (e.g. *Animal Concerns Research & Education Society v Tan Boon Kwee* [2011] SGCA 2; [2011] 2 S.L.R. 146) would be unlikely to be followed in England.

[1328] It is also worth noting that the CA roundly rejected an argument that the building was a "complex structure" and that the claimants should be able to recover on the basis that a defect in one part of it had damaged separate property of theirs. The contrary decision in *Jacobs v Moreton* (1994) 72 B.L.R.

owed no duty to B Ltd, a subsidiary of A Ltd, who suffered loss because the premises had allegedly been badly planned.[1329]

Economic loss—other cases In general, architects owe no duty to third parties generally in tort in respect of economic loss. So consulting engineers on a major construction project will presumptively owe no duty to participants other than those employing them or with whom they have contractual relations.[1330] Again, in the important decision in *Pacific Associates Inc v Baxter*[1331] the Court of Appeal held that where architects were retained to certify work for the purposes of deciding whether builders were entitled to be paid for it, they owed no duty to the builders, and so were not liable for negligently failing to certify work that had in fact been properly done.[1332] **9-212**

Nevertheless, in a few cases the architect remains liable. Where he is engaged by one of a group of associated companies collaborating on a project, he may be liable in tort to an associated company of the employer.[1333] Similarly, where there is direct communication between the architect and the third party there may be room for the inference of a duty to take care. Hence an architect engaged to certify to potential purchasers that work on a newbuild project has been properly done for the benefit of giving them reassurance will be liable if such certificates are negligently issued.[1334] Furthermore, there must be remembered the situation exemplified by the controversial decision in *Junior Books Ltd v Veitchi Co Ltd*,[1335] where it was held that nominated sub-contractors engaged under a building contract to lay a floor owed a duty to the building owner to lay it properly. If this decision is right,[1336] presumably an architect nominated as a sub-contractor in similar circumstances would equally be liable. **9-213**

105 was subjected to sustained criticism, and must now be regarded as discredited. See too *Preston v Torfaen BC* [1955–95] P.N.L.R. 625; *The Times,* 21 July 1993 (consulting engineer who prepared site report for builder/vendor owed no duty in respect of economic loss suffered by subsequent purchaser of defective house); *Machin v Adams* (1997) 84 B.L.R. 79 (architect reporting to building owner on state of premises owes no duty to purchaser).

[1329] *Strathford East Kilbride Ltd v HLM Design Ltd*, 1999 S.L.T. 121.

[1330] *Galliford Try Infrastructure Ltd v Mott MacDonald Ltd* [2008] EWHC 1570 (TCC); [2009] P.N.L.R. 9; *Riva Properties Ltd v Foster + Partners Ltd* [2017] EWHC 2574 (TCC); (2017) 175 Con. L.R. 45 at [135]–[151] (Fraser J). See also *Turton & Co Ltd v Kerslake & Partners* [2000] 3 N.Z.L.R. 406.

[1331] [1989] 2 All E.R. 159; see also to the same effect, *Leon Engineering Co v Ka Duk Investments Co* (1989) 47 Build. L.R. 139; and *Spandeck Engineering Pte Ltd v Defence Science & Technology Agency* [2007] SGCA 37; [2007] 4 S.L.R. (R.) 100. cf. *Auto Concrete Ltd v South Nation* (1992) 89 D.L.R. (4th) 393.

[1332] The converse, however, does not apply: the architect does owe a duty to the building owner employing him for certifying as good work in fact bad. See *Sutcliffe v Thackrah* [1974] A.C. 727.

[1333] e.g. *Mirant Asia-Pacific Ltd v OAPIL* [2005] EWCA Civ 1585; [2006] B.L.R. 187 (failure to evaluate construction site: liability not only to client but also to associated company of client involved in construction project).

[1334] *Hunt v Optima (Cambridge) Ltd* [2013] EWHC 681 (TCC); 148 Con. L.R. 27 (successfully appealed on causation grounds at [2014] EWCA Civ 714; [2015] 1 W.L.R. 1346); *McGhee v Alcorn & Friel* [2016] IEHC 59; [2016] P.N.L.R. 25. It is suggested that the same would apply to financiers who agreed to advance funds only against suitable certification from architects.

[1335] [1983] 1 A.C. 520. See paras 7-128 and 7-145.

[1336] Which is open to some doubt, as reconciling it with *Murphy*'s case is not easy—so much so that in *Architype Projects Ltd v Dewhurst Macfarlane & Partners (A Firm)* [2003] EWHC 3341 (TCC); [2004] P.N.L.R. 38 at [64] a judge would have declined to follow it, except on identical facts. Nevertheless, *Junior Books* was cited, with neither enthusiasm nor outright disapproval, by Lords Keith and Bridge in *Murphy* ([1991] 1 A.C. 398 at 466, 481), and by the House in *Henderson v Merrett Syndicates Ltd* [1995] 2 A.C. 145 at 196 (Lord Goff).

9-214 **Liability for independent contractors** In performing his central functions of design and supervision an architect is, it seems, liable both for his own negligence and for that of anyone to whom he delegates those tasks.[1337] But where independent contractors are instructed in respect of specialist tasks outside an architect's normal expertise, then provided they were properly so employed,[1338] are reasonably employed and supervised,[1339] and their work (where possible) properly appraised and checked,[1340] the architect is not without more liable for their negligence.[1341]

9-215 **Liability under the Defective Premises Act 1972** An architect may be liable in the same way as a builder to a house-owner under s.1 of the Defective Premises Act 1972 as a "person taking on work for or in connection with the provision of a dwelling" if he fails to exercise a suitable degree of professional skill.[1342]

(b) Breach of duty

(i) *Design and supervision*

9-216 **Design and supervision** The duty of an architect or consulting engineer is normally to exercise reasonable skill in design and supervision, though he may expressly or impliedly undertake a higher duty by contract.[1343] The level of skill he

[1337] *Moresk Cleaners Ltd v Hicks* [1966] 2 LIoyd's Rep. 338; see too *Cooperative Group Ltd v John Allen Associates Ltd* [2010] EWHC 2300 (TCC); (2010) 28 Const. L.J. 27 at [180] (Ramsay J). This seems consistent with the obligation to exercise reasonable skill, care and diligence contained in the RIBA Standard Conditions of Appointment 2010 (2012 revision) and with Lord Sumption JSC's analysis of non-delegable duties in *Woodland v Swimming Teachers Association* [2013] UKSC 66; [2014] A.C. 537 at [7], even though it lacks the element of vulnerability mentioned there by his Lordship.

[1338] A point made clear by Ramsey J in *Cooperative Group Ltd v John Allen Associates Ltd* [2010] EWHC 2300 (TCC); (2010) 28 Const. L.J. 27 at [180]. So too, where an architect improperly delegated jobs he ought to have done himself: *Moresk Cleaners Ltd v Hicks* [1966] 2 Lloyd's Rep. 338 (semble).

[1339] On what amounts to reasonable employment, see *Cooperative Group Ltd v John Allen Associates Ltd* [2010] EWHC 2300 (TCC); (2010) 28 Const. L.J. 27 at [180] (Ramsey J). Obviously an architect may be liable if there are clear indications that the person appointed is not in fact an appropriate expert: e.g. *District of Surrey v Carroll-Hatch and Associates Ltd* (1979) 101 D.L.R. (3d) 218.

[1340] For cases where this requirement was unsatisfied, see, e.g. *Richard Roberts Holdings Ltd v Douglas Smith Stimson Partnership (No.2)* (1990) 46 B.L.R. 50; and *Sealand of the Pacific v Robert C McHaffie Ltd* (1974) 51 D.L.R. (3d) 702.

[1341] *Merton LBC v Lowe* (1982) 18 B.L.R. 130 (specialised ceiling installation advice); *Cooperative Group Ltd v John Allen Associates Ltd* [2010] EWHC 2300 (TCC); (2010) 28 Const. L.J. 27 (piling advice). See too *IBA v EMI Electronics Ltd* (1980) 14 Build. L.R. 1; *Investors in Industry Ltd v South Bedfordshire DC* [1986] Q.B. 1034.

[1342] For examples of architects' liability under the Defective Premises Act 1972, see *Payne v Setchell Ltd* [2002] P.N.L.R. 7 (though the claim there was statute-barred); and *Bole v Huntsbuild Ltd* [2009] EWCA Civ 1146; (2009) 127 Con. L.R. 154. This liability, it seems, includes liability for the fault of independent contractors employed by the defendant: see para.6-65.

[1343] *George Hawkins v Chrysler U.K. Ltd* (1986) 38 Build. L.R. 36. For an example of a higher duty being accepted by a consulting engineer, see *Greaves v Baynham Meikle* [1975] 1 W.L.R. 1095. In practice the engagement of an architect or consulting engineer is likely to be on the basis of a standard agreement such as some form of RIBA's Professional Services Contract 2018; and the details of the obligations undertaken will be found in that agreement. An architect will normally be expected to be familiar with the RIBA Job Book and other similar industry publications: see *Riva Properties Ltd v Foster + Partners Ltd* [2017] EWHC 2574 (TCC); (2017) 175 Con. L.R. 45 at [154] (Fraser J).

must show is that of an ordinarily competent architect of his type[1344]; he is not to be judged on hindsight,[1345] and, as in other cases of professional negligence, the fact that he is unusually skilled or experienced will not alter the standard of care to be expected.[1346] The fact that he has observed standards generally accepted in the profession is a strong indication that he was not negligent, but it is not conclusive.[1347] He is generally entitled to assume that the premises he has designed will not be misused,[1348] and that other professionals involved with the project will perform reasonably satisfactorily.[1349] The content of an architect's duty depends very largely on the terms of his engagement; if not employed to carry out a particular function, it can hardly be negligent for him not to do it. So, for instance, an engineer employed simply to supervise the laying of foundations would not be liable for failing to inspect other parts of the building for defects,[1350] and an architect employed to design an ordinary billiard room will not be liable merely because it is not big enough for full-scale competition snooker.[1351] On the other hand, an architect employed to supervise construction generally may be negligent if he limits himself merely to perfunctory inspections at regular intervals,[1352] and there may be a duty to warn against obvious and immediate dangers even in the absence of specific instructions to do so.[1353]

Thus architects and engineers have been held liable for failing to check the size of a site[1354]; for designing premises with partitions that were dangerous to the oc- **9-217**

1344 *Greaves v Baynham, Meikle* [1975] 1 W.L.R. 1095, 1101 (Lord Denning MR). For a similar statement specifically dealing with consulting engineers, see *Brickhill v Cooke* [1984] 3 N.S.W.L.R. 396.

1345 *IBA v EMI Electronics Ltd* [1955–95] P.N.L.R. 179; (1980) 14 Build. L.R. 1, 31 (Lord Edmund-Davies).

1346 *Wimpey Construction Ltd v Poole* [1984] 2 Lloyd's Rep. 499, 506 (Webster J). cf. the comments of Megarry VC in *Argyll (Duchess) v Beuselinck* [1972] 2 Lloyd's Rep. 172, 183–184. If, however, an architect holds himself out as having a particular expertise, then the level of skill to be expected would no doubt be adjusted accordingly: cf. the lawyers' negligence case of *Matrix-Securities Ltd v Theodore Goddard* [1998] S.T.C. 1 (tax lawyers expected to show expertise of specialist tax lawyers).

1347 See *Worboys v Acme Investments Ltd* (1969) 210 E.G. 335. The same goes for the various codes of practice applicable to the profession, though obviously these must be correctly applied; see *IBA v EMI Electronics Ltd* (1980) 14 Build. L.R. 1, especially at 36–37 (application to building for which unsuitable).

1348 cf. *Introvigne v Commonwealth* (1980) 32 A.L.R. 251. But he may be under a duty to anticipate ordinary negligence by employees of the occupier: *Sahib Foods Ltd v Paskin Kyriakides Sands* [2003] EWCA Civ 1832; [2004] P.N.L.R. 22 (architects fail to fireproof industrial kitchen adequately: liable for effect of fire caused by negligent frying operations, though subject to deduction for contributory negligence).

1349 *Department of National Heritage v Steenson Varming Mulcahy* (1998) 60 Con. L.R. 33 (a consulting engineer case: engineers on British Library project entitled to assume cabling would be installed properly); see too *Bellefield Computer Services Ltd v E Turner & Sons Ltd (No.2)* [2002] EWCA Civ 1823; [2003] Lloyd's Rep. P.N. 53; and *Goldswain v Beltec Ltd* [2015] EWHC 556 (TCC); [2015] C.I.L.L. 3645. It follows that if a more proactive level of supervision is required, it is advisable to stipulate for it by contract.

1350 But a court may be prepared to imply a duty to point out obvious defects even in parts of the building the architect is not responsible for; cf. *Kensington, Chelsea & Westminster AHA v Wetten Ltd* [1984] 1 Const. L.R. 114. And an architect who does exactly as told by his client may nevertheless be liable for obvious dangers to third parties: cf. *Pantaleone v Alaouie* (1989) 18 N.S.W.L.R. 121.

1351 *Stormont Main W.M.C. v J. Roscoe Milne* (1989) 13 Con. L.R. 127.

1352 *McGlinn v Waltham Contractors Ltd* [2007] EWHC 149 (TCC); (2007) 111 Con. L.R. 1.

1353 *Hart Investments Ltd v Fidler* [2007] EWHC 1058 (TCC); [2007] P.N.L.R. 26.

1354 *Columbus v Clowes* [1903] 1 K.B. 244

cupants,[1355] unfit for their purpose,[1356] not in accordance with their instructions,[1357] inadequately fireproofed[1358] or waterproofed[1359] or which contravened the Building Regulations[1360]; for not taking into account technical information that showed a television mast was likely to fall down in a high wind[1361]; for failing to take reasonable steps to check the suitability of materials,[1362] or the quality of work done,[1363] at least for obvious defects[1364]; and for failing adequately to supervise building or demolition operations to prevent them becoming dangerous.[1365] Standard terms often require him to keep the client informed of progress and of any issue that may materially affect the project.[1366] But his duty does not extend beyond the end of his employment,[1367] unless he undertakes to give post-completion advice, in which case he comes under a new duty to take care in providing that advice.[1368]

(ii) Advice

9-218 **Breach of duty: advice** An architect may be liable in negligence if he offers misleading advice on matters pertinent to his engagement. Thus an architect who provides misleading estimates of likely cost,[1369] or fails to take account of the probable impact of inflation,[1370] may be liable in negligence to the client. An architect who negligently recommended a firm of builders as "very reliable" was found liable on evidence that the builders were in no sense either financially or professionally responsible.[1371] There can equally be liability for failure to advise on important

[1355] *Rimmer v Liverpool City Council* [1985] Q.B. 1.

[1356] *National Museums and Galleries on Merseyside Board of Trustees v AEW Architects and Designers Ltd* [2013] EWHC 2403 (TCC).

[1357] *National Museums and Galleries on Merseyside Board of Trustees v AEW Architects and Designers Ltd* [2013] EWHC 2403 (TCC).

[1358] e.g. *Bellefield Computer Services Ltd v E Turner & Sons Ltd (No.2)* [2002] EWCA Civ 1823; [2003] Lloyd's Rep. P.N. 53; *Sahib Foods Ltd v Paskin Kyriakides Sands* [2003] EWCA Civ 1832; [2004] P.N.L.R. 403.

[1359] *Pearson Education Ltd v Charter Partnership Ltd* [2007] EWCA Civ 130; [2007] B.L.R. 324.

[1360] *Wharf Properties v Cummine Ass'tes* [1991] 2 H.K.L.R. 6. See Dugdale & Stanton, *Professional Negligence* (3rd edn, 1998), para.17–17 onwards.

[1361] *IBA v EMI Electronics Ltd* (1980) 14 Build. L.R. 1; cf. *Pullen v Gutteridge Haskins* [1993] 1 V.R. 27.

[1362] *Merton LBC v Lowe* (1981) 18 Build. L.R. 130; *Sealand of the Pacific v McHaffie* (1974) 51 D.L.R. (3d) 702. And cf. the engineer's case of *Edgeworth Construction v Lea* (1994) 107 D.L.R. (4th) 169.

[1363] *Rogers v James* (1891) 8 T.L.R. 67; *Corfield v Grant* (1993) 59 Build. L.R. 102; *Brown v Gilbert-Scott*, unreported, 30 March 1993, QBD. See also *Florida Hotels v Mayo* (1965) 113 C.L.R. 588; and the Scottish decision in *Jameson v Simon* (1899) 1 F. 1211.

[1364] An architect is not in breach of duty merely for failing to spot bad workmanship that has been deliberately and effectively concealed by those who did it: *Gray v TP Bennett & Son* (1987) 43 Build. L.R. 63; (1987) 13 Con. L.R. 22.

[1365] *Clay v AJ Crump & Sons Ltd* [1964] 1 Q.B. 533; *Re-Source America International Ltd v Platt Site Services Ltd* [2004] EWCA Civ 665; (2004) 95 Con. L.R. 1. But a duty to supervise is not a duty to inspect everything exhaustively; an architect may legitimately take some risks.

[1366] See *RIBA Standard Conditions of Appointment 2010* (2012 revision) cl.2.2.

[1367] *New Islington & Hackney HA v Pollard Thomas & Edwards* [2001] B.L.R. 74.

[1368] Which may include warning of his own previous incompetence: *Davies v Baart*, unreported 6 January 1993, QBD.

[1369] *Moneypenny v Hartland* (1826) 2 C. & P. 278; cf. *Gable House Estates v Halpern Partnership* (1995) 48 Con. L.R. 1 (negligent estimate of profitability of project).

[1370] *Nye Saunders & Partners v AE Bristow* (1987) 37 Build. L.R. 92 CA.

[1371] *Pratt v George J. Hill Associates (a firm)* (1987) 38 Build. L.R. 25.

matters.[1372] Architects may be expected, like surveyors, to have at least a limited knowledge of the law.[1373] An architect will not be expected to advise a sophisticated client on matters the client is likely to be already familiar with, unless specifically instructed.[1374] It has been held that a construction professionsal cannot be liable for giving negligent advice on a subject which the recipient of the advice knows as much about as he does,[1375] but this may be regarded as doubtful.

(c) Damages

Damages The measure of damages for personal injury and property damage need not concern us here. In the case of bad design of a building, the measure of recovery is prima facie the reasonable cost of correcting the defects.[1376] However, the claimant will be limited to any diminution in value if either he does not intend to do the work,[1377] or the coat of doing so is wholly unreasonable.[1378] Provided the claimant acts reasonably, he is not prevented from claiming the costs of correction at a later stage, even if substantially greater than at the time the works were carried out.[1379] For other breaches of duty, such as bad advice, it is suggested that the claimant is entitled to be put in the position he would have occupied if the duty to advise had been properly performed.[1380] Consequential damages, for instance, wasted expenditure or loss of profits, are also available.[1381] Similarly, where as a result of an architect's negligence the claimant finds himself liable to a third party, he can **9-219**

1372 e.g. the likelihood of cost overruns: see *Plymouth & South West Co-operative Society v Architecture Structure & Management Ltd* [2006] EWHC 5 (TCC); 108 Con. L.R. 77; [2006] C.I.L.L. 2366.

1373 *B. L. Holdings Ltd v Wood* (1978) 10 Build. L.R. 48; (1979) 12 Build. L.R. 1 (no negligence on the facts): see Dugdale & Stanton, *Professional Negligence* (3rd edn, 1998), para.17–15.

1374 See *Riva Properties Ltd v Foster + Partners Ltd* [2017] EWHC 2574 (TCC); (2017) 175 Con. L.R. 45 at [130]-132] (Fraser J).

1375 See the engineers' case of *G. Percy Trentham v Beattie Wilkinson*, 1987 S.L.T. 449. But note that in a suitable case damages may be reduced on account of contributory negligence: *Crédit Agricole SA v Murray* [1995] N.P.C. 33 (semble).

1376 *McGlinn v Waltham Contractors Ltd (No 3)* (2007) 111 Con. L.R. 1 at [787]; also *West v Ian Finlay & Associates (A Firm)* [2013] EWHC 868 (TCC) at [250] (Edwards-Stuart J) (decision reversed on unconnected grounds, [2014] EWCA Civ 316; [2014] B.L.R. 324); compare the construction decision in *East Ham BC v Bernard Sunley & Sons Ltd* [1966] A.C. 406. The claimant must of course mitigate his loss (*George Fischer Holding Ltd v Multi Design Consultants Ltd* (1998) 61 Con. L.R. 85): but where works have already been carried out on professional advice, the defendant will have some difficulty in repelling an inference that the expenditure was reasonable: cf. the property damage case of *Skandia Property UK Ltd v Thames Water Plc* [1999] B.L.R. 338.

1377 See *Nordic Holdings Ltd v Mott McDonald Ltd* (2001) 77 Con. L.R. 88; and *London Fire & Emergency Planning Authority v Halcrow Gilbert Associates Ltd* [2007] EWHC 2546 (TCC); and cf. generally the builders' case of *Ruxley Electronics & Construction Ltd v Forsyth* [1996] A.C. 344.

1378 So held in the construction case of *Ruxley Electronics & Construction Ltd v Forsyth* [1996] A.C. 344. That there is no reason to treat architects any differently is suggested by Ramsey J in *Cooperative Group Ltd v John Allen Associates Ltd* [2010] EWHC 2300 (TCC); (2010) 28 Const. L.J. 27 at [369]–[370].

1379 *London Congregational Union v Harriss & Harriss* [1985] 1 All E.R. 335; see too *Catlin Estates Ltd v Carter Jonas (a firm)* [2005] EWHC 2315 (TCC); [2006] P.N.L.R. 15; and cf. *Dodd Properties Ltd v Canterbury CC* [1980] 1 W.L.R. 433.

1380 e.g. *Ampleforth Abbey Trust v Turner & Townsend Management Ltd* [2012] EWHC 2137 (TCC); (2012) 144 Con. L.R. 115. See too *Riva Properties Ltd v Foster + Partners Ltd* [2017] EWHC 2574 (TCC); (2017) 175 Con. L.R. 45 at [207]–[214] (Fraser J) (losses caused by economic downturn not within scope of architects' duty to advise).

1381 See, e.g. *Earl's Terrace Properties Ltd v Nilsson Design Ltd* [2004] EWHC 136 (TCC) (negligent architect: loss of use of funds while defects sorted out); *John Grimes Partnership Ltd v Gubbins* [2013] EWCA Civ 37; [2013] P.N.L.R. 17 (property development designs provided late: consulting engineer liable for foreseeable loss in development value of land due to delay).

claim the amount of that liability, or where appropriate a sum paid in reasonable settlement of a third party's claim.[1382] Where an architect is guilty of negligence in design, advice or similar work, he will generally remain liable to the client even though the latter has since disposed of the property for full value.[1383]

9-220 It should be noted, however, that where an architect provides specific advice, the principle in *South Australia Asset Management Corp'n v York Montague Ltd*[1384] may apply so as to limit his liability to the specific consequences of that advice being wrong. So in *HOK Sport Ltd v Aintree Racecourse Ltd*[1385] architects gave wrong advice on the possible capacity of a new racecourse stand. Their liability was limited to the prospective shortfall in ticket monies, and did not extend to other losses caused by the lessened profitability of the scheme.

9-221 **Non-economic loss** In the case of commercial premises, there seems little doubt that the liability of an architect or structural engineer for negligence is limited to physical and financial loss.[1386] With residential premises, however, there seems no reason why there should not be an award for discomfort or physical inconvenience caused by having to live in a defective house[1387]; and where an architect is instructed specifically to deal with a particular matter going to the comfort or amenity of the occupants, it is equally suggested that a modest award for distress and vexation may be in order.[1388]

9-222 **Contributory negligence** In a suitable case liability may be reduced for contributory negligence by the employer,[1389] for example in giving misleading indications of the premises' proposed use.[1390]

[1382] cf. *Biggin v Permanite Ltd* [1951] 2 K.B. 314; and McGregor, *Damages*, 20th edn (2017), para.21–038; also *P & O Developments Ltd v Guys & St Thomas's Hospital* [1999] B.L.R. 1.

[1383] On the principle in *Alfred McAlpine Construction Ltd v Panatown Ltd* [2001] 1 A.C. 518: see *Catlin Estates Ltd v Carter Jonas (a firm)* [2005] EWHC 2315 (TCC); [2006] P.N.L.R. 15.

[1384] [1997] A.C. 191.

[1385] [2002] EWHC 3094 (TCC); [2003] B.L.R. 155.

[1386] cf. the solicitors' case of *Hayes v James & Charles Dodd* [1990] 2 All E.R. 815.

[1387] Such damages were awarded against architects in the Irish case of *Mitchell v Mulvey Developments Ltd* [2014] IEHC 37. Although that case would not be followed on liability in England because of *Murphy v Brentwood DC* [1991] 1 A.C. 398, the award of damages on this basis is unexceptionable. cf. in England the surveyors' cases of *Watts v Morrow* [1991] 1 W.L.R. 1421; and *Farley v Skinner* [2001] UKHL 49; [2002] 2 A.C. 732.

[1388] A decision to the contrary, in *Knott v Bolton* (1995) 45 Con. L.R. 127, was specifically discountenanced in *Farley v Skinner* [2001] UKHL 49; [2002] 2 A.C. 732. Such awards have been made in the Antipodes: see *Campbelltown CC v Mackay* (1989) 15 N.S.W.L.R. 501; and *Rowlands v Collow* [1992] 1 N.Z.L.R. 178.

[1389] Including those employed by him, but not independent contractors—even those for whose negligence he might otherwise have been liable in damages. See *Willmott Dixon Construction Ltd v Robert West Consulting Ltd* [2016] EWHC 3291 (TCC); [2017] P.N.L.R. 17.

[1390] See *Sahib Foods Ltd v Paskin Kyriakides Sands* [2003] EWCA Civ 1832; [2004] P.N.L.R. 22. In *Plymouth & South West Co-operative Society v Architecture Structure & Management Ltd* [2006] EWHC 5 (TCC); 108 Con. L.R. 77; [2006] C.I.L.L. 2366 the possibility was accepted of contributory negligence by continuing with a scheme likely to be ruinously expensive following poor advice by architects, but no such negligence was found on the facts.

6. FINANCE PROFESSIONALS[1391]

(a) Accountants and auditors

General Accountants and auditors perform a number of very different functions: preparing and auditing company accounts, providing tax or general financial advice, advising on particular projects or litigation, and so on. What amounts to negligence in each of these contexts will of course vary: nevertheless, some general principles can be stated as to the liability of accountants. 9-223

(i) *Duties to clients*

Duties to clients A negligent accountant can clearly be held liable to his client in contract.[1392] It has not been definitively held that he can also be sued in tort,[1393] but since *Henderson v Merrett Syndicates Ltd*[1394] it seems abundantly clear that he can.[1395] As with other professionals, the importance of this lies largely in procedural matters such as when time begins to run for the purposes of the Limitation Act 1980, or the time from which interest on damages runs. Subject to the statutory controls over exception clauses generally,[1396] however, these duties can on principle be limited or excluded. 9-224

(ii) *Duties to others*

Accountants and auditors: duties to third parties On principle, an accountant may owe a duty of care not only to the person who employs him but also to others relying on any report he makes,[1397] or otherwise foreseeable as likely to be affected by his negligence.[1398] The question is when he will do so. In the absence of evidence of some undertaking to, or direct communication with, third parties other than his direct client,[1399] it is submitted that the general rule is that no duty is owed to anyone other than the person for whom the accountant acts.[1400] In addition it is clear that on principle such liability may be prevented from arising by a suitable 9-225

1391 See *Jackson & Powell on Professional Liability*, 8th edn (2017), Ch.15.

1392 See Supply of Goods and Services Act 1982 s.13 and Consumer Rights Act 2015 s.49, dealing respectively with business and non-business clients.

1393 The matter was expressly left open by the New South Wales Court of Appeal in *Simonius Vischer v Hold & Thompson* [1979] 2 N.S.W.L.R. 322.

1394 [1995] 2 A.C. 145. Strictly speaking the decision concerned the liability of a Lloyd's agent: but the reasoning of the House of Lords was perfectly general.

1395 In *West Wiltshire DC v Garland* [1995] Ch. 297; and *Sasea v KPMG* [1999] B.C.C. 857 (reversed on other grounds, [2000] 1 All E.R. 676), courts refused to strike out tortious claims.

1396 See para.9-36 onwards. Note that there is one statutory control peculiar to accountants. Sections 532–534 of the Companies Act 2006 put careful limits on statutory auditors' rights to exclude liability to the company employing them: essentially such limits must be agreed from year to year, and may only limit any liability to an amount which is fair and reasonable. This provision, where applicable, pre-empts the Unfair Contract Terms Act 1977: see s.534(3)(b)(i).

1397 e.g. *JEB Fasteners Ltd v Marks Bloom & Co* [1981] 3 All E.R. 289 (though the claim failed on causation, upheld on appeal: [1983] 1 All E.R. 583).

1398 e.g. *Law Society v KPMG Peat Marwick* [2000] P.N.L.R. 831, below (solicitors' auditors owe duty to Law Society, who had to compensate fraud victims).

1399 As in cases such as *JEB Fasteners Ltd v Marks Bloom & Co* [1981] 3 All E.R. 289, para.9-228.

1400 See *Anthony v Wright* [1995] 1 B.C.L.C. 236 (auditor engaged by trustee company owes no duty to beneficiaries of trust); *Abbott v Strong* [1998] 2 B.C.L.C. 420; and *Arrowhead Capital Finance Ltd (In Liquidation) v KPMG LLP* [2012] EWHC 1801 (Comm); [2012] P.N.L.R. 30 (accountants disclaimer of third party liabilities,[1401] though such disclaimers are subject, in the same way as all disclaimers, to control under the general law relating to exception clauses.[1402]

9-226 Nevertheless, the above rule is only presumptive, and there are a number of situations where a duty to third parties, particularly those closely connected to the client, may be owed. Thus there may well be a duty where a firm of auditors' corporate client is a member of a group of companies effectively run as one.[1403] Again, accountants who negligently advised a company that a proposed arrangement between it and its directors was lawful were held liable to the directors when it was not and they were disqualified as a result[1404]; and similarly, it is suggested that where accountants are instructed by a husband to arrange a tax-saving scheme for himself, his wife and children, they will on principle be liable to the latter if they botch it.[1405] Moreover, it has also been held that where shares in a closely-held company fall to be sold at a price to be fixed by valuation, the accountants performing the valuation may owe duties to either party.[1406]

9-227 Furthermore, there may also be liability where accountants' advice is clearly meant to protect the interests of a third party and it is possible to infer some kind of acceptance of responsibility for it by the accountant. Thus, while auditors generally do not owe duties to persons buying into a company or business,[1407] it may be different with accounts prepared specifically for a named would-be buyer.[1408] Similarly, accountants or auditors may be liable to third parties on some basis other

---

engaged by company owe no duty to shareholders); *Devine v McAteer* [2014] NICA 50 (tax advice to husband cannot be relied on by wife). And see the actuary case of *Precis (521) Ltd v William H Mercer Ltd* [2005] EWCA Civ 114; [2005] P.N.L.R. 28. The question of the liability of company accountants or auditors to investors and buyers is dealt with in the following paragraphs.

[1401] *Barclays Bank Plc v Grant Thornton UK LLP* [2015] EWHC 320 (Comm); [2015] 1 C.L.C. 180.

[1402] Accepted in *Barclays Bank Plc v Grant Thornton UK LLP* [2015] EWHC 320 (Comm); [2015] 1 C.L.C. 180; where it was also accepted that the reasoning in *Harris v Wyre Forest DC* [1990] 1 A.C. 831 applied to such clauses, so as to subject them to control even though expressed as devices to prevent any duty arising in the first place. In the event that the claimant is a consumer, the relevant legislation is s.62 of the Consumer Rights Act 2015, subjecting such clauses to a test of whether, in breach of a duty of good faith, they unduly imbalance the relation between accountant and claimant.

[1403] *BCCI SA v Price Waterhouse* [1998] P.N.L.R. 564 (failure to spot irregularity in BCCI group: auditors arguably liable to all members of group, even though employed by only one): see too *Riyad Bank v Ahli United Bank Plc* [2006] EWCA Civ 780; [2006] 2 Lloyd's Rep. 292 (advisers to bank setting up Shari'a investment arm owe direct tortious duty to the latter). But the purpose for which the claimant relied on the advice may be all-important: cf. *Barings Plc (In Liquidation) v Coopers & Lybrand* [2002] P.N.L.R. 16, where a "group claim" of this kind failed on that basis.

[1404] *Coulthard v Neville Russell* [1998] P.N.L.R. 276. Compare *Christensen v Scott* [1996] 1 N.Z.L.R. 273 (accountants advising family company owe duty of care to family members in capacity of guarantors of liabilities). However, in a case of this sort the claimant may find difficulty in claiming any loss that simply reflects the diminution in the value of his shareholding due to a wrong done to the company: see *Johnson v Gore Wood* [2002] 2 A.C. 1.

[1405] Solicitors have been held so liable: *Matthew v Maughold Life Assurance Co Ltd* [1955–95] P.N.L.R. 309. In *Richards v Hughes* [2004] EWCA Civ 266; [2004] P.N.L.R. 35 the Court of Appeal doubted, *obiter*, whether accountants who bungled a tax-saving school fees scheme were liable to the children whose own trust monies had to be spent as a result. Sed quaere.

[1406] *Killick v PriceWaterhouseCoopers* [2001] P.N.L.R. 1; see too the similar *Pearce v European Reinsurance Consultants Run-off Ltd* [2005] EWHC 1493 (Ch); [2006] P.N.L.R. 8.

[1407] *Caparo Plc v Dickman* [1990] 2 A.C. 605; below, para.9-228.

[1408] *JEB Fasteners Ltd v Marks Bloom & Co* [1981] 3 All E.R. 289; affirmed on causation, [1983] 1 All E.R. 583 (though the circumstances may indicate otherwise: *Peach Publishing Ltd v Slater & Co* [1998] P.N.L.R. 364). See too *Royal Bank of Scotland plc v Bannerman Johnstone Maclay* [2005] CSIH 39; 2005 S.C. 437; [2005] P.N.L.R. 43 (accountants knew bank support of company conditional on view of accounts: Scots court holds duty owed to bank); *Trustees Executors & Agency* than reliance. So in *Law Society v KPMG Peat Marwick*,[1409] where auditors to a firm of solicitors failed to spot signs of ongoing fraud, they were held liable to the Law Society, which had to compensate the victims of the fraud.

The problem of third-party liability has arisen in particular in connection with company accounts and auditors' reports that have been relied on by third parties in buying shares or lending to the company, or by predators in taking over the company concerned. In *JEB Fasteners Ltd v Marks, Bloom*[1410] Woolf J held that accountants who prepared annual accounts for a company in the knowledge that they were intended for the benefit of the claimants, who were at the time negotiating to take it over, owed the claimants a duty of care. A number of Commonwealth authorities reached the same result.[1411] However, the decision of the House of Lords in *Caparo Industries Plc v Dickman*[1412] shows that this is a very limited liability indeed. The claimants bought some shares in F Ltd with a view to a possible takeover. Later, having received copies of the accounts, audited and approved by the defendants, they launched a bid that was ultimately successful. When they discovered alleged inaccuracies in the accounts concealing large unexpected losses in F Ltd, they sued, *inter alios*, the auditors. The latter took the preliminary point that they owed no duty of care. The House of Lords[1413] held they were right: the duty of care in respect of negligent misstatement was, they said, limited to statements made with a view to reliance by the claimant for a particular purpose. It did not apply where a statement was put into more or less general circulation[1414] (as in the case of standard company accounts), however foreseeably claimants might rely on them.[1415] Although *JEB Fasteners Ltd v Marks, Bloom*[1416] was cited without disapproval by Lord Bridge in *Caparo*, it now seems clear that it can be justified, if at all, only on the basis that the accounts there were prepared in some sense for the 9-228

Co of NZ v Price Waterhouse [2000] P.N.L.R. 673 (auditors' liability to bondholders for failing to note matters giving rise to right to accelerate liability).

1409 [2000] 1 W.L.R. 1921; [2000] 4 All E.R. 540 CA. In New Zealand auditors in a similar position were held directly liable to the fraud victims themselves (*Price Waterhouse v Kwan* [2000] 3 N.Z.L.R. 39): sed quaere. See too *Andrew v Kounnis Freeman* [1999] 2 B.C.L.C. 641 (accountants arguably liable to CAA for negligently certifying bankrupt tour operator solvent, with result that CAA put to expense repatriating passengers when operator failed).

1410 [1981] 3 All E.R. 289. The claim failed on causation (upheld on appeal, where the duty of care was not in issue: [1983] 1 All E.R. 583). cf. Denning LJ's dissenting judgment in *Candler v Crane Christmas* [1951] 2 Q.B. 164, later vindicated in *Hedley Byrne & Co Ltd v Heller & Partners Ltd* [1964] A.C. 465, and also the Scots decision in *Twomax Ltd v Dickson M'Farlane & Robinson*, 1982 S.C. 113.

1411 e.g. *Haig v Bamford* (1975) 53 D.L.R. (3d) 81; *Scott Group Ltd v McFarlane* [1978] 1 N.Z.L.R. 553. But see *Caparo v Dickman*, below.

1412 [1990] 2 A.C. 605. See J. Weir, "Statutory auditor not liable to purchaser of shares" [1990] C.L.J. 212; J. Fleming, "The Negligent Auditor and Stakeholders" (1990) 106 L.Q.R. 349. The Canadian courts have since followed it (*Hercules Management v Ernst & Young* [1997] 2 S.C.R. 115), as have the Australian (*Lowe v A.G.C.* [1992] 2 V.R. 671; *Esanda Ltd v Peat Marwick* (1997) 15 A.C.L.C. 483).

1413 Reversing the Court of Appeal, which had held ([1989] Q.B. 653) that Caparo were owed a duty qua existing shareholders, though not otherwise. This distinction was rejected by the House of Lords as anomalous and unreasonable.

1414 See [1990] 2 A.C. 605, 621 (Lord Bridge).

1415 This is understandable: liability to any foreseeable relier would seriously raise the spectre of liability "in an indeterminate amount of an indeterminate time to an indeterminate class" decried by Cardozo J in the New York decision of *Ultramares Corp v Touche*, 255 N.Y. 170, 179, 174 N.E. 441, 450 (1931).

1416 [1981] 3 All E.R. 289.

claimants specifically, so as to show an undertaking of responsibility to them[1417]; it is clear that the auditor will not be liable merely because he knows a potential predator has an interest in the company concerned.[1418] Nor will he be liable to others concerned with the company's profitability, such as guarantors[1419] or (it is submitted) creditors. What amounts to a sufficient undertaking of responsibility for these purposes remains rather uncertain.[1420] But direct advice to the predator at a meeting set up for the purpose[1421] may well suffice, unless there is evidence that either the advice was qualified,[1422] or the recipients really relied on some extraneous factor, such as the word of a third party.[1423]

9-229 Although *Caparo*'s case concerned statutory auditors appointed under the provisions of the companies legislation, its reasoning is equally applicable to others involved in preparing the accounts. It is therefore submitted that in so far as auditors are free from liability, so are, for example, the accountants who actually draw up the accounts. Furthermore, it is suggested that the same result will follow even where the accounts are not required by law but are prepared as a matter of good business practice.[1424] Similarly, there is no reason to limit the principle in that case to those taking over a company. Ordinary investors must be subject to the same rule, as (it has now been decided) are those who give credit to the company.[1425] It may be that, despite *Caparo*, accountants remain potentially liable to predators for statements other than those contained in the company accounts themselves. In *Morgan Crucible Ltd v Hill Samuel Ltd*[1426] the Court of Appeal refused to strike out a claim in negligence arising from defensive statements made by the accountants to a company that was the target of a hostile bid. Whether direct statements of this type will give rise to liability must depend very much on the facts of the case and the degree of proximity between the parties.

1417 cf. the Australian decision in *Columbia Coffee & Tea v Churchill* (1992) 29 N.S.W.L.R. 141, where *Caparo* was distinguished and such an undertaking was found; also *Dimond Manufacturing Co Ltd v Hamilton* [1969] N.Z.L.R. 609.

1418 *James McNaughton Paper Group Ltd v Hicks Anderson* [1991] 2 Q.B. 113. *Scott Group Ltd v McFarlane* [1978] 1 N.Z.L.R. 553, in so far as inconsistent with this reasoning, cannot be good law in England (see also the scepticism expressed on this case in *Caparo plc v Dickman* [1990] 2 A.C. 605, 624 (Lord Bridge), 644–646 (Lord Oliver)).

1419 *Rushmer v Mervyn Smith (t/a Mervyn E Smith & Co)* [2009] EWHC 94 (QB); [2009] Lloyd's Rep. P.N. 41.

1420 cf. *Columbia Coffee & Tea v Churchill* (1992) 29 N.S.W.L.R. 141; and *Surrey Credit Union v Willson* (1991) 73 D.L.R. (4th) 207, both distinguishing *Caparo* (sed quaere as to the latter). An example of a report required and produced for a specific purpose and thus potentially engendering liability appears in *Deloitte Haskins & Sells v Mutual Life Nominees* [1993] A.C. 774, where a company auditor would, but for certain statutory provisions, have owed a duty to the trustee of a deposit protection fund for not making a proper report that would have revealed an impending insolvent liquidation.

1421 *ADT v BDO Binder Hamlyn* [1996] B.C.C. 808.

1422 As in *Peach Publishing Ltd v Slater & Co* [1998] P.N.L.R. 364.

1423 *Electra Private Equity Partners v KPMG Peat Marwick* [1998] P.N.L.R. 135.

1424 Which may matter, e.g. if a claimant is induced to buy into a partnership by negligently-prepared partnership accounts.

1425 *Al Saudi Banque v Clarke Pixley* [1989] 2 All E.R. 361; *CCB v Crawford Smith* [1994] 3 Build. L.R. 147.

1426 [1991] Ch. 259. But cf. *Al-Nakib Investments (Jersey) Ltd v Longcroft* [1990] 1 W.L.R. 1390, holding directors of the target company not liable for such statements. See also *Lowe Lipman v A.G.C.* [1992] 2 V.R. 671; *Galoo v Bright Grahame Murray* [1994] 1 W.L.R. 1360; *West Wilts DC v Garland* [1995] Ch. 297; and *Electra Private Equity Partners v KPMG Peat Marwick* [1998] P.N.L.R. 135. cf. *Berg Sons & Co v Adams* (1992) 8 P.N. 167.

(iii) Breach of duty

Accountants and auditors: breach of duty An accountant, like any other professional, is required to show the level of skill to be expected of a reasonable practitioner in his field. As elsewhere in professional negligence, the following of common professional practice is strong, though not conclusive, evidence of lack of fault.[1427] The work accountants do is very varied and not surprisingly the precise details of an accountant's duty, in tort as in contract,[1428] depend on precisely what he was employed to do. An accountant employed to fill in tax returns, for example, is not liable for failing to draw his employer's attention to fraud,[1429] and accountants advising on disposing of a shareholding are not bound to give unsolicited advice on corporation tax.[1430] This principle is particularly important in the case of the statutory accounts required by Pt 15 of the Companies Act 2006, since the legislation and regulations lay down the scope of what is required, and hence govern very largely the liability of the accountant preparing them.[1431] 9-230

(iv) Breach of duty: audit

Auditing duties In practice, the most significant function of accountants, and the one that most often reaches the courts, is that of auditor. Here the standard of care is the skill to be expected of a reasonably competent professional; in general, an auditor must "make a reasonable and proper investigation of accounts and stock sheets, and if a reasonably prudent man would have concluded on that investigation that there was something wrong call his employer's attention to the fact."[1432] He is not obliged, however, to "turn every stone and open every cupboard".[1433] He is of course not liable for failing to find irregularities that would not have been found by a reasonably competent auditor.[1434] Having discovered irregularities he must take adequate steps to see them remedied.[1435] Thus if he finds evidence of peculation[1436] or improper transfers of funds from the client's accounts,[1437] it is his duty to draw the client's attention to the fact.[1438] 9-231

It used to be thought that an auditor's duty varied fairly radically according to whether there was, or was not, any obvious sign of irregularity in the accounts presented; only if such signs were present was any very thorough investigation 9-232

1427 See, e.g. *Pacific Acceptance Corporation Ltd v Forsyth* (1970) 92 W.N. (N.S.W.) 29, 75 (Moffitt J).; *Lloyd Cheyham & Co Ltd v Littlejohn* [1986] PCC 389.

1428 No case explicitly decides that the scope of an accountant's retainer delimits his duty in tort as in contract; but common sense dictates that this must be so. It cannot be negligent for him to fail to do something he was not employed to do in the first place.

1429 *Leech v Stokes* [1937] I.R. 787.

1430 *Pegasus Management Holdings SCA v Ernst & Young (A Firm)* [2010] EWCA Civ 181; [2010] 3 All E.R. 297.

1431 See, e.g. *Re London & General Bank (No.2)* [1895] 2 Ch. 673.

1432 *Henry Squire Cash Chemist Ltd v Ball, Baker* (1911) 27 T.L.R. 269 at 271, per Alverstone CJ.

1433 See Bingham LJ's judgment in *Caparo Plc v Dickman* [1989] Q.B. 653 (unaffected by the reversal of the decision at [1991] 2 A.C. 249).

1434 e.g. *Calne Gas Co v Curtis* (1918) 59 Acct. L.R. 17.

1435 *Re London & General Bank (No.2)* [1895] 2 Ch. 673.

1436 *Sasea Finance Ltd v KPMG* [2000] 1 All E.R. 676 (auditors failed to spot company insolvent owing to frauds practised on it: liable for dividend improperly paid out as a result).

1437 See *West Wiltshire DC v Garland* [1995] Ch. 297 (district auditor failing to take steps concerning improper uses of public monies).

1438 See too the multifarious *Statements of Accounting Standards* issued by the Financial Reporting Council.

called for.[1439] But this somewhat lax view is now outdated[1440]; it now seems clear that the auditor's duty is not subject to rigid categories. The question is simply whether, on the facts, the auditor has failed to come up to a reasonable professional standard: hence it has been said that his duty is very generally to investigate any "irregular or unusual matters" that might indicate a "real possibility that something is wrong".[1441] So, in the instructive Australian case of *Pacific Acceptance Corporation Ltd v Forsyth*,[1442] auditors were held liable for having failed to query loans made by a branch manager which were apparently in order but which were clear on closer inspection to have been made to insolvent companies controlled by the manager.

9-233 **Auditors and criminality** There is no doubt that auditors may be liable for negligently failing to prevent a company from being defrauded by its employees,[1443] or from inadvertently falling foul of the criminal law.[1444] Difficulties used to arise, however, where the fraudsters were themselves the company's controllers and formed part of its directing mind and will, since then the company in suing its auditors was in a technical sense seeking to rely on its own criminality. In *Stone & Rolls Ltd (in liquidation) v Moore Stephens (A Firm)*[1445] a company controlled by S, a fraudster and effective sole shareholder, had defrauded a bank of some $100 million in a sophisticated letter-of-credit fraud. Having been held liable to the bank, the company then sought to recover the amount of that liability from its auditors, who had (allegedly) been negligent in failing to spot the fraud and stop it. The House of Lords, by a majority, struck out the claim on the basis of the maxim ex turpi causa non oritur actio. But *Stone & Rolls* was subjected to severe attack[1446] its ambit was increasingly limited, and the decision itself was in effect deprived of any authority by the Supreme Court in *Singularis Holdings Ltd v Daiwa Capital Markets Europe Ltd*.[1447] There, a company was permitted to sue its brokers (who were effectively its bankers) for negligently allowing a shareholder to make away with its assets, despite the fact that the despoiler was also the person who had acted

1439 The clearest exposition of this view was in *Re London & General Bank (No. 2)* [1896] 2 Ch. 673 at 683 (Lindley LJ); and see too Lopes LJ's *bon mot* in *Re Kingston Cotton Mill (No.2)* [1896] 2 Ch. 279, 281–289, that an auditor was a watch-dog and not a bloodhound.

1440 *Re Thomas Gerrard & Son Ltd* [1968] 1 Ch. 455 at 473, per Pennycuick J.

1441 *Pacific Acceptance Corporation Ltd v Forsyth* (1970) 92 W.N. (N.S.W.) 29 at 62, per Moffitt J. See generally the Statement of Accounting Standards issued by the accounting profession, SAS 110.

1442 (1970) 92 W.N. (N.S.W.) 29.

1443 See, e.g. *Sasea Finance Ltd v KPMG* [2000] 1 All E.R. 676; *Barings Plc v Coopers & Lybrand (No 7)* [2003] EWHC 1319 (Ch); [2003] P.N.L.R. 34.

1444 As in, e.g. *Coulthard v Neville Russell* [1998] P.N.L.R. 276 (technical company assistance in purchasing own shares); and *Griffin v UHY Hacker Young & Partners* [2010] EWHC 146 (Ch); [2010] P.N.L.R. 20 (breach of "phoenix" provisions of Companies Acts). cf. the Singapore decision in *United Project Consultants Pte Ltd v Leong Kwok Onn* [2005] 4 S.L.R. 214.

1445 [2009] UKHL 39; [2009] 1 A.C. 1391. The effective claimant, of course, was the bank victim of the fraud, who had put the company into liquidation and then persuaded the liquidator to sue for its benefit. For an approving note, see P. Watts, "Audit Contracts and Turpitude" (2010) 126 L.Q.R. 14; for a less approving one, E. Ferran, "Corporate Attribution and the Directing Mind and Will" (2011) 127 L.Q.R. 239.

1446 It was referred to by Lord Neuberger in *Jetivia SA v Bilta (UK) Ltd* [2015] UKSC 23; [2016] A.C. 1 at [30] as a case to be put "on one side in a pile and marked 'not to be looked at again'". It is also worth noting, more generally, that in *Patel v Mirza* [2016] UKSC 42; [2017] A.C. 467 the Supreme Court, while not commenting directly on *Stone & Rolls*, emphasised the need to tailor the application of the ex turpi causa maxim to those cases where public policy genuinely demands the dismissal of a suit.

1447 [2019] UKSC 50; [2019] 3 W.L.R. 997.

as the company's collective mind and will. As Lady Hale said, to attribute that person's acts to the company would denude the duty owed by professional advisers of much of its significance.[1448]

Auditors: statutory protection In any proceedings for negligence against an auditor of a company, the court has a power to grant relief from liability on such terms as it thinks fit if it appears that he has "acted honestly and reasonably", and that having regard to all the circumstances of the case he "ought fairly to be excused".[1449] Similar provisions apply to auditors to charities and some other organisations.[1450] This provision may apply (despite its wording) even to an auditor guilty of a degree of negligence,[1451] either to excuse him entirely, or to adjust the level of liability to that which is fair in the circumstances.[1452] 9-234

(v) *Breach of duty: advice*

Advice Accountants provide advice on all kinds of matters, from share valuations[1453] to tax[1454] to advice on tendering for work[1455] to company administration to advice on how to administer the financial side of a business, not to mention technical advice as to how particular transactions should be treated for accounting and regulatory purposes.[1456] In giving such advice, an accountant must show a reasonable level of care, including where necessary a knowledge of the law.[1457] Although it seems that in general the duty owed by an accountant advising on a course of action ceases to apply after the time of reliance but no further, circumstances may indicate a continuing duty.[1458] It is suggested that a rule analogous to the *Bolam* 9-235

1448 See [2019] UKSC 50; [2019] 3 W.L.R. 997 at [35]. On the issue, see R. Leow, "Attribution and Illegality Again" (2020) 136 L.Q.R. 181.

1449 Companies Act 2006 s.1157. This is based on a parallel provision for trustees in s.61 of the Trustee Act 1925.

1450 See Charities Act 2011 s.191; Open-Ended Investment Companies Regulations 2001 (SI 2001/1228) reg.63.

1451 *Maelor-Jones v Heywood-Smith* (1989) 54 S.A.S.R. 285, 294 (Olssen J, applying equivalent South Australian provisions). But it effect is, it would seem, limited to claims brought by the company: *Dimond Manufacturing Co Ltd v Hamilton* [1969] N.Z.L.R. 609, 629, 630, 640, 645.

1452 As in *Barings Plc v Coopers & Lybrand (No 7)* [2003] EWHC 1319 (Ch); [2003] P.N.L.R. 34 (auditor's negligence: account taken of gains to associated companies in same group as claimant, even though not strictly deductible from losses).

1453 On share valuations by accountants see, e.g. *Goldstein v Levy Gee* [2003] EWHC 1574 (Ch); [2003] P.N.L.R. 35. Analogous principles often apply here to those obtaining in relation to valuations of land, for example as to the permissible "bracket" of error: see *Goldstein v Levy Gee* [2003] EWHC 1574 (Ch); [2003] P.N.L.R. 35; *Dennard v PricewaterhouseCoopers LLP* [2010] EWHC 812 (Ch); and above, para.9-190.

1454 See Reed, "Professional Negligence and the Tax Adviser" [2004] *Private Client Business* 318. Also cases such as *Mehjoo v Harben Barker (A Firm)* [2014] EWCA Civ 358; [2014] 4 All E.R. 806 (extent of tax adviser's duty to engage in general tax planning activities for client: no breach in the circumstances).

1455 *Whiteleys (a firm) v Trafalgar Consultancy Ltd* [2006] EWCA Civ 503; [2006] All E.R. (D) 75 (May).

1456 For an example, see *Manchester Building Society v Grant Thornton UK LLP* [2019] EWCA Civ 40; [2019] 1 W.L.R. 4610.

1457 e.g. *Coulthard v Neville Russell* [1998] P.N.L.R. 276 (misadvice about impact of company law).

1458 So held in Australia: *Swan & Baker Pty Ltd v Marando* [2013] NSWCA 233 (duty to warn of impending collapse of investment fund while investor had benefit of cooling-off period).

rule[1459] applies here: even if the advice is wrong,[1460] the accountant will not be liable if a respectable body of opinion would have supported it.[1461]

(vi) Conflict of interest

9-236 **Conflict of interest** In addition to a duty of care, an accountant owes his client a duty, similar to that owed by a solicitor, not to put himself in a position where he may face a conflict of interest. This problem arises particularly in the field of forensic accountancy, where the risk of confidential information is acute. Thus in *Young v Robson Rhodes*[1462] accountants who were acting for the claimants in proceedings against another accountancy firm were prevented from merging with the latter firm except on terms that during the pendency of the litigation there should be in place foolproof arrangements to prevent leakage of information. Furthermore, while the above duty persists only as long as the accountant-client relation, even after the relationship has finished there remains a duty not to misuse confidential information or to do anything that may facilitate its misuse. Thus in *Prince Jefri Bolkiah v KPMG*[1463] forensic accountants who had previously acted for the claimant were subsequently instructed by the Government of Brunei, which wished to sue him for the return of monies they said he had unlawfully spirited away. The claimant obtained an injunction preventing the defendants accepting the instructions, which was upheld in the House of Lords, despite the latter's plea that they had instituted what they regarded as an effective information barrier within the firm. Only if it was absolutely clear that there could be no leakage or misuse, deliberate or otherwise, of confidential information, would the defendants' actions have been permissible; and of this their Lordships were unconvinced.

(vii) Damages: loss and causation

9-237 **Necessity for proof of loss and causation** In an accountants' negligence suit the claimant must, of course, show not only that the defendant was at fault, but that he has suffered a loss as a consequence. Thus the victim of negligent advice who would not have relied on it cannot recover.[1464] Again, where a claimant took over a company, allegedly in reliance on a negligent accountant's report which failed to reveal previous defalcations, he was held to have suffered no loss because the despite the thefts the underlying asset value of the company remained substantially the same.[1465] Any negligence by an accountant must have caused the loss complained of by the claimant. An instance of a claimant failing on causation

---

1459 *Bolam v Friern HMC* [1957] 1 W.L.R. 582, above, para.9-76.

1460 If it is correct there will be no liability, even if the client is put to expense because the Revenue disagree: *Grimm v Newman* [2002] EWCA Civ 1621; [2003] 1 All E.R. 67.

1461 In *Halsall v Champion Consulting Ltd* [2017] EWHC 1079 (QB); [2017] P.N.L.R. 32 it was seemingly assumed that Bolam applied in the accounting context. cf. the lawyer's tax advice case of *Matrix Securities Ltd v Theodore Goddard* [1998] P.N.L.R. 290.

1462 [1999] 3 All E.R. 524.

1463 [1999] 2 A.C. 222.

1464 e.g. *Davenhall v Franks & Co* [2002] EWCA Civ 1961; *Beary v Pall Mall Investments (A Firm)* [2005] EWCA Civ 415; [2005] P.N.L.R. 35.

1465 *Dixon v Deacon* (1990) 70 D.L.R. (4th) 609. See also *Galoo v Bright Grahame Murray* [1995] 1 All E.R. 16 (no loss from making of loan, since moneys advanced balanced by right to repayment); and *Demarco v Bulley Davey* [2006] EWCA Civ 188; [2006] P.N.L.R. 27 (no financial loss from being bankrupted rather than entering IVA); *Murfin v Ford Campbell* [2011] EWHC 1475 (Ch); [2011] P.N.L.R. 28 (loss of potential set-off against liability that in the event never accrued). cf. *David* grounds came in *JEB Fasteners Ltd v Marks, Bloom*,[1466] above, where the claimants failed because at the time they acted they already knew of the inaccuracy of the accounts prepared by the defendants. Similarly, where an accountant acting for the seller of a business negligently failed to tell his client of the possibility of rollover relief under the capital gains tax legislation, the client failed when it became clear he would not have reinvested the proceeds in qualifying assets in any event.[1467] The fact that some employee of the client misled the accountant will not as such negative causation, if the accountant was employed in whole or in part to detect such misleading statements.[1468] It is enough, however, if the accountant's negligence played a "real and substantial" part in causing the claimant to suffer loss, even if it was not the sole cause.[1469]

As with other professionals, accountants are subject to the rule in *South Australia Asset Management Corporation v York Montague Ltd*[1470] and *BPE Solicitors v Hughes-Holland*,[1471] that a professional providing advice is liable only for the consequences of the specific advice being incorrect, and not (unless he undertook responsibility to guide the whole of the client's decision process and take responsibility for any defects in it) for other losses, however foreseeable. So in *Manchester Building Society v Grant Thornton UK LLP*[1472] accountants negligently misadvised a lender on what were acceptable accounting techniques for the purposes of reckoning capital adequacy, a matter which incidentally affected the amount the lender was permitted to lend. The accountants were held not liable for losses suffered when the lender in reliance on their advice lent more than was in fact permissible, lost heavily on those loans owing to a market downturn, and had to close out certain swaps at large expense to rectify the situation. These losses, it was held, did not result from the incorrect advice given, but were a matter of simple market forces; and there was no indication that the accountants had done anything more than provide discrete advice, or had undertaken to guide the lender's decision process as a whole. 9-238

(viii) Damages: measure of recovery

Assuming the claimant can show reliance and loss, the measure of damages is the sum that will put the claimant in the position he would have been in had the accountant performed his duty. In the common case of negligent advice, the measure of damages is generally the amount by which he is out of pocket[1473] as a result of 9-239

Securities P/L v Commonwealth Bank (1990) 93 A.L.R. 271.

1466 [1981] 3 All E.R. 289; on appeal [1983] 1 All E.R. 583. See also *Deloitte Haskins & Sells v Mutual Life Nominees Ltd* [1993] A.C. 774 PC.

1467 *Davenhall v Franks & Co* [2002] EWCA Civ 1961. See too *Beary v Pall Mall Investments (A Firm)* [2005] EWCA Civ 415; [2005] P.N.L.R. 35 (another case of advice that would not have been taken).

1468 *Barings Plc (In Liquidation) v Coopers & Lybrand (Issues re liability)* [2003] EWHC 1319 (Ch); [2003] P.N.L.R. 34 (accountants liable for failing to spot unauthorised activity by trader, despite information received from trader and others stating that nothing had been concealed).

1469 *JEB Fasteners Ltd v Marks Bloom & Co* [1983] 1 All E.R. 583, 589 (Stephenson LJ); see also at 588 (Donaldson LJ).

1470 [1997] A.C. 191.

1471 [2017] UKSC 21; [2018] A.C. 599.

1472 [2019] EWCA Civ 40; [2019] 1 W.L.R. 4610.

1473 The mere fact that the claimant is a corporate vehicle wholly financed by a third party and thus personally may have lost nothing is, it is suggested, generally to be disregarded: compare the surveyor cases of *Titan Europe 2006-3 Plc v Colliers International UK Plc* [2015] EWCA Civ 1083;

relying on the advice in question, plus any consequential loss.[1474] So where assets to be sold by a client are undervalued, the client recovers that part of the price foregone.[1475] Where a client takes over a company on the basis of audited figures that are wrong, he prima facie recovers the difference, if any, between what he paid for the company and what it was in fact worth at that time.[1476] Again, where tax accountants misadvise clients over their tax affairs, the measure of damages is the extra tax unnecessarily payable.[1477] In a suitable case there may be an award for loss of a chance.[1478] But as with valuers' negligence,[1479] the scope of the duty broken is vital to the computation of damages. An accountant providing negligent advice (or negligently failing to provide advice at all) is liable only for the consequences of the advice being negligent (or lacking). Thus auditors failing to spot that a company is insolvent may be liable for the amount of a dividend unlawfully declared,[1480] but will not be liable for the consequences of further loans being made to that company by others in the same group: this is a question of an ordinary business risk, on which it is not their function to advise.[1481] Similarly, even if accountants fail to spot that a company is in fact insolvent such that it ought to be put into liquidation, they are not liable for ordinary trading losses incurred merely as a result of the company continuing in existence,[1482] though they may be liable in so far as the company's

---

[2016] P.N.L.R. 7; and *Legal & General Mortgage Services Ltd v Underwoods* [1997] P.N.L.R. 567. But where the claimant sues on the basis that the negligence of the defendant has caused it to make an irrecoverable loan to a borrower, account must be taken of any refinancing by the third party which involves repayment of that loan, since this causes the alleged loss to disappear: see *Swynson Ltd v Lowick Rose LLP (in liquidation)* [2017] UKSC 32; [2018] A.C. 313.

1474 For example, any loss resulting from bankruptcy caused by accountants' negligence: see *Demarco v Bulley Davey* [2006] EWCA Civ 188; [2006] P.N.L.R. 27. Subsequent events may, of course, equally go to reduce damages. See, e.g. *Murfin v Ford Campbell* [2011] EWHC 1475 (Ch); [2011] P.N.L.R. 28 (accountants' negligence allegedly causes claimant to incur liability: liability later eliminated for other reasons); and *Swynson Ltd v Lowick Rose LLP* [2017] UKSC 32; [2018] A.C. 313 (irrecoverable loan later paid off by third party in refinancing transaction).

1475 *Dennard v PricewaterhouseCoopers LLP* [2010] EWHC 812 (Ch) (reduced there to represent the element of chance).

1476 *West Coast Finance v Gunderson, Stokes, Walton* (1975) 56 D.L.R. (3d) 460; *Scott Group v Macfarlane* [1978] 1 N.Z.L.R. 553, 585 et seq. (Cooke J). (*Contra*, however, at 576 onwards, per Woodhouse J). But in a suitable case, where a claimant cannot be expected to liquidate his investment immediately, a later time may be taken: see *Twomax Ltd v Dickson M'Farlane & Robinson*, 1982 S.C. 113. In any event it seems that the claimant can recover the costs of a re-audit; *Tormont Holdings v Thorne Gunn & Helliwell* (1975) 62 D.L.R. (3d) 465.

1477 e.g. *Midland Packaging Ltd v HW Accountants Ltd* [2010] EWHC 1975 (QB); [2011] P.N.L.R. 1.

1478 *Dennard v PricewaterhouseCoopers LLP* [2010] EWHC 812 (Ch); also *Altus Group (UK) Ltd v Baker Tilly Tax & Advisory Services LLP* [2015] EWHC 12 (Ch); [2015] S.T.I. 158.

1479 See *South Australia Asset Management Co v York Montague Ltd* [1997] A.C. 191, above, para.9-201.

1480 *Sasea Finance Ltd v KPMG* [2000] 1 All E.R. 676. See too *Assetco Plc v Grant Thornton UK LLP* [2019] EWHC 150 (Comm); [2019] Bus. L.R. 2291 at [967]–[969] (Bryan J).

1481 See *Bank of Credit & Commerce International (in liq) v Price Waterhouse (No.4)* [1999] B.C.C. 351; and compare *Manchester Building Society v Grant Thornton UK LLP* [2019] EWCA Civ 40; [2019] 1 W.L.R. 4610 (misadvice by accountants causing underestimation of regulatory capital requirements: no liability for market losses resulting from extra loans made in reliance on that advice). For another instance, cf. the actuaries' case of *Andrews v Barnett Waddingham (a firm)* [2006] EWCA Civ 93; [2006] P.N.L.R. 24 (misadvice as to whether annuity protected under Policyholders Protection Act 1975 irrelevant where underwriter of annuity not insolvent anyway).

1482 *Assetco Plc v Grant Thornton UK LLP* [2019] EWHC 150 (Comm); [2019] Bus. L.R. 2291 at [932]–[934], following dicta of Langley J in *Equitable Life Assurance Society v Ernst & Young* [2003] EWHC 112 (Comm); [2003] P.N.L.R. 23 at [85].

method of trading is affected by failure to spot (for example) widespread fraud.[1483] In a suitable case damages may, of course, fall to be reduced where the claimant has been contributorily negligent.[1484]

Although normally damages against a negligent accountant will be limited to financial losses, this is not an absolute rule. In *Demarco v Bulley Davey*[1485] accountants negligently caused a client to be made bankrupt rather than arranging an IVA. Although no financial loss was shown (since the monetary effect of either procedure was much the same), the claimant recovered £6,000 general damages in respect of the stigma attaching to his bankruptcy. 9-240

(b) Accountants as receivers

Accountants and receivers The appointment of a receiver[1486] is a very general remedy available in equity.[1487] Strictly speaking the liability of a receiver to the owner of the property concerned is of no interest to a tort lawyer, since it is now clear that it is a liability in equity and not in tort.[1488] Nevertheless, receivers are in practice nearly always accountants or similar financial professionals, and their liability as suchis an important aspect of their liability which deserves brief coverage here. It matters in particular in one case, namely, where a mortgagee or chargee,[1489] acting under a power contained in the relevant instrument, appoints a receiver to realise his security. 9-241

A receiver appointed in these circumstances, while theoretically an agent of the debtor, acts under the general direction of the chargee. It is to the chargee that his first duty is owed. Thus, where he takes over a business he may close it down forthwith and sell the assets for what they will fetch, even if this is disastrous to the chargor.[1490] Similarly, if he decides to sell assets, he owes the chargor no duty of care with regard to the actual timing of the realisation of those assets (since this would unduly hamper the chargee's right to realise his security[1491]). The receiver's only duty in this respect is one of good faith: that is, not to act fraudulently or for 9-242

[1483] See *Assetco Plc v Grant Thornton UK LLP* [2019] EWHC 150 (Comm); [2019] Bus. L.R. 2291, especially at [919]–[966].

[1484] e.g. *Barings Plc (In Liq) v Coopers & Lybrand* [2003] EWHC 1319 (Ch); [2003] P.N.L.R. 34 (accountants negligently failed to draw attention to suspicious signs of unauthorised trading: damages reduced to take account of failings in claimants' own internal procedures). See too *Slattery v Moore Stephens* [2003] EWHC 1869 (Ch); [2004] P.N.L.R. 14 (tax adviser negligently failed to shelter earnings from UK tax: taxpayer's claim reduced by 50 per cent for his failure to act on the Revenue's pointed suggestion that earnings in fact taxable).

[1485] [2006] EWCA Civ 188; [2006] P.N.L.R. 27.

[1486] Who is almost invariably an accountant. Note that this is a specific reference to a receiver. The duties of a person acting as a statutory officer in insolvency, such as an administrator, are different and derived from a separate legislative framework, beyond the scope of this work. See *Davey v Money* [2018] EWHC 766 (Ch); [2018] Bus. L.R. 1903 at [252]–[254].

[1487] See generally *Kerr & Hunter on Receivers and Administrators*, 20th edn (2017).

[1488] *Downsview Nominees Ltd v First City Corp* [1993] A.C. 295; *Medforth v Blake* [2000] Ch. 86, 97 (Scott V-C).

[1489] Including a company debenture-holder-cum-floating chargee, the commonest situation where the problem arises.

[1490] *Re B. Johnson & Co* [1955] Ch. 634, 661 (Jenkins LJ).

[1491] *Tse Kwong Lam v Won Chit Sen* [1983] 1 W.L.R. 1394, 1434. See also the *Standard Chartered* case at 1417; also *Centenary Homes Ltd v Liddell* [2020] EWHC 1080 (QB). The creditor, not surprisingly, has the same immunity: *China & South Sea Bank v Tan* [1990] A.C. 536. *A fortiori*, the creditor owes no duty to the debtor or any guarantor in deciding when to appoint a receiver: *Shamji v Johnson Matthey Bankers Ltd* [1991] B.C.L.C. 36. Whether this is entirely fair to the debtor is open an improper motive.[1492] Put another way, breach of this duty necessarily involves intentional conduct amounting to more than mere negligence, and encompassing either an improper motive or an element of bad faith, but it need not amount to dishonesty.[1493] It is not enough for these purposes to show that the sale was to an associate of the mortgagee appointing the receiver.[1494]

9-243 However, once a receiver has determined on a course of action, such as sale of the assets or the continuing of the business, he must normally carry this out with due care. This duty of care operates on analogous principles to the duty owed by a mortgagee to his mortgagor.[1495] Thus if he chooses to realise the security forthwith, he owes a duty,[1496] certainly to the chargor himself[1497] and possibly to any surety of his,[1498] to get a reasonable amount for it.[1499] Similarly, a receiver must show proper diligence in carrying on a business. Thus in *Medforth v Blake*[1500] it was held that receivers managing a pig-farming business owed the chargor at least some duty to do so in a commercial manner and keep costs under control. In so far as the receiver acts as the chargee's agent or on his orders, the chargee will be liable equally with him,[1501] but not otherwise.[1502] The receiver's duty of care, however, is not owed to anyone other than the debtor, a co-mortgagor or incumbrancer

---

to some doubt: compare the New Zealand Receiverships Act 1993 s.18, requiring the receiver to have reasonable regard to the interests of the debtor and his unsecured creditors, subject to his overriding duty to the creditor.

1492 For example, where (as in *Downsview Nominees Ltd v First City Corp'n* [1993] A.C. 295) the receiver refuses an offer by a subsequent incumbrancer to purchase his interest for the full amount owing, thus showing an intention to do something other than simply realise his security as advantageously as possible.

1493 *Devon Commercial Property Ltd v Barnett* [2019] EWHC 700 (Ch) at [188].

1494 *Devon Commercial Property Ltd v Barnett* [2019] EWHC 700 (Ch) at [194].

1495 Lord Denning MR implied as much in *Standard Chartered Bank Ltd v Walker* [1982] 1 W.L.R. 1410, 1414. For the principle as between mortgagor and mortgagee, see *Cuckmere Brick Ltd v Mutual Finance Ltd* [1971] Ch. 949.

1496 Which seems to include liability for independent contractors, such as valuers, employed by him: see *Cuckmere Brick Co Ltd v Mutual Finance Ltd* [1971] Ch. 949 at 973 (Cross LJ); *Raja v Austin Gray* [2002] EWCA Civ 1965; [2003] Lloyd's Rep. P.N. 126; and G. Lightman & G. Moss, *The Law of Receivers and Administrators of Companies* (6th edn, 2017), para.13-044 onwards. But the independent contractor is not himself liable directly to the claimant: see *Raja*, above.

1497 Including someone whose property stands charged with the debt, even if not personally liable to pay it: *Knight v Lawrence* [1993] B.C.L.C. 215.

1498 In *Standard Chartered Bank Ltd v Walker* [1982] 1 W.L.R. 1410; and *American Express International Banking Corp'n v Hurley* [1985] 3 All E.R. 564, the duty was held to be owed to guarantors; and in *Raja v Austin Gray EWCA* [2002] EWCA Civ 1965; [2003] Lloyd's Rep. P.N. 126 the CA thought it was also person whose property was mortgaged to support the debt. But the correctness of this was doubted by Lightman J in *Burgess v Auger* [1998] B.C.L.C. 478.

1499 *Standard Chartered Bank Ltd v Walker* [1982] 1 W.L.R. 1410; also *American Express International Banking Corp'n v Hurley* [1985] 3 All E.R. 564. See too the administrators' case of *Brewer v Iqbal* [2019] EWHC 182 (Ch); [2019] P.N.L.R. 15 at [79]–[89].

1500 [2000] Ch. 86; see too A. Kenny, "Equity, commercial sense and the borrower" [1999] Conv. 434.

1501 As in *Standard Chartered Bank v Walker* [1982] 1 W.L.R. 1410, where the bank was liable for the acts of the receiver, since it had largely directed its operations.

1502 Thus in *American Express v Hurley* [1985] 3 All E.R. 564 it was held that the receiver had acted purely as agent for the debtor until it went into liquidation, and thereafter for the bank. But it was stressed in that case that the question whether the receiver is an agent for the creditor is a question of fact in all cases. See generally the CA decision in *National Bank of Greece v Pinios Shipping Co (The Maira)* [1990] 1 A.C. 637 (reversed on other grounds in the HL: ibid.). Just conceivably a chargee who appoints a receiver it ought to know to be incompetent may be liable to the debtor: *Shamji v Johnson Matthey Bankers Ltd* [1991] B.C.L.C. 36, 42.

interested in the mortgaged property,[1503] or possibly the debtor's guarantor. Thus it cannot be invoked by a shareholder,[1504] creditor,[1505] subsequent incumbrancer[1506] or (it would seem) the beneficiary of property held on trust by the debtor.[1507]

(c) Stockbrokers

Stockbrokers Although there is little authority, there is no doubt that a stockbroker owes a duty to his clients to exercise reasonable professional care in executing his commissions, conducting their affairs[1508] and also (it is submitted) when advising them, if he does so.[1509] It seems that this duty is owed concurrently in tort and in contract.[1510] However, investment is a risky business, and although glaringly misguided advice will attract liability,[1511] a court will not lightly hold an adviser liable where an investment decision turns out in retrospect to have been unfortunate.[1512] In practice, many of the standards to be met by stockbrokers are laid down in rules made by the Financial Conduct Authority[1513] under s.64A of the Financial Services and Markets Act 2000.[1514] Standards laid down by these instruments are likely strongly to inform what counts as negligence in a broker[1515]; furthermore, breach of the latter gives rise, in favour of non-institutional clients, to a separate action for breach of statutory duty.[1516] 9-244

1503 *Downsview Nominees Ltd v First City Corp Ltd* [1993] A.C. 295; *Alpstream AG v PK Airfinance SàRL* [2015] EWCA Civ 1318; [2016] 2 P. & C.R. 2.

1504 *Burgess v Auger* [1998] B.C.L.C. 478.

1505 *Latchford v Beirne* [1981] 3 All E.R. 705, per Milmo J (semble); *Hague v Nam Tai Electronics Inc* [2008] UKPC 13; [2008] P.N.L.R. 27; [2008] B.C.C. 295.

1506 *Downsview Nominees Ltd v First City Corp* [1993] A.C. 295.

1507 This seems to follow from the analogy of *Parker-Tweedale v Dunbar Bank Plc* [1991] Ch. 26.

1508 An example of a case not concerning execution of commissions was *Singularis Holdings Ltd v Daiwa Capital Markets Europe Ltd* [2019] UKSC 50; [2019] 3 W.L.R. 997 (negligently allowing cash on deposit for client to be fraudulently spirited away).

1509 In *Briggs v Gunner* (1979) 129 N.L.J. 116, Foster J seems to have thought, despite *Hedley Byrne v Heller* [1964] A.C. 465, that a broker's only duty when giving advice was to be honest. It is submitted, with respect, that this is contrary to principle; it is also difficult to reconcile with *Stafford v Conti Commodity Services* [1981] 1 All E.R. 691, where Mocatta J clearly thought all investment advisers owed a duty to be careful. See also *Central BC Planners Ltd v Hocker* (1970) 70 W.W.R. 561.

1510 So held in Ireland: *Haughey v J&E Davy* [2014] IEHC 206, [31], [36] (Charleton J). See too *Stafford v Conti Commodity Services* [1981] 1 All E.R. 691, where the point was conceded.

1511 *Haughey v J&E Davy* [2014] IEHC 206 (lay client of limited sophistication pushed into heavy margin trading).

1512 See, e.g. *Stafford v Conti Commodity Services*, above.

1513 Previously the Financial Services Authority.

1514 Notably those contained in the Conduct of Business Sourcebook (COBS), available in the FCA Handbook, published from time to time.

1515 See the financial adviser cases of *Seymour v Ockwell* [2005] EWHC 1137 (QB); [2005] P.N.L.R. 758 at [77]; and *Shore v Sedgwick Financial Services Ltd* [2007] EWHC 2059 (QB); [2008] P.N.L.R. 10 at [161] (appealed on other grounds, [2008] EWCA Civ 863; [2008] P.N.L.R. 37) (Beatson J); also the banking case of *Rubenstein v HSBC Plc* [2012] EWCA Civ 1184; [2013] P.N.L.R. 9.

1516 See s.138D. This may be important, since among other things the Conduct of Business Sourcebook requires brokers to ensure investments advice is suitable overall for their clients (COBS 9.2), which may go beyond the requirements of the common law. Compare on this point the banking case of *Green v Royal Bank of Scotland Plc* [2013] EWCA Civ 1197; [2014] P.N.L.R. 6.

(d) Financial professionals and advisers[1517]

9-245 **General** This section deals briefly with the liabilities of financial, pension and similar advisers. It summarises their liabilities to clients and others.

9-246 **Liability to clients** A financial adviser is, like any professional, liable to his client for negligence at common law in contract or tort.[1518] In addition, where the claimant is a private person[1519] s.138D of the Financial Services and Markets Act 2000 makes him liable for breach of statutory duty if he disobeys rules made by the Financial Conduct Authority[1520] or (if the rules so state) by the Prudential Regulation Authority[1521]; a liability quite separate from that at common law.[1522] This aside, financial advisers may well also owe fiduciary duties to clients, thus (for example) creating a liability to account for any commissions received from third parties and not sufficiently disclosed.[1523]

9-247 **Liability to third parties** A financial adviser may also in a suitable case owe a duty to third parties, in so far as any advice given is clearly intended to protect their interests. Thus in *Gorham v British Telecommunications Plc*[1524] pension advisers incorrectly advised a breadwinner as to the kind of pension he should obtain: the result was that when he unexpectedly died his dependents received less than they ought to have. The Court of Appeal held that a duty had been owed to them: it was, said Pill LJ, "fundamental to the giving and receiving of advice upon a scheme for pension provision and life insurance" that the interests of the customer's dependants must arise for consideration.[1525] Where an adviser knows that information provided will be passed to a third party and relied on by the latter, this may indicate an acceptance of responsibility to him.[1526] But it is by no means conclusive, and

[1517] *Jackson & Powell on Professional Liability*, 8th edn (2017), Ch.15.

[1518] *Henderson v Merrett Syndicates Ltd* [1995] 2 A.C. 145. But the tortious duty is likely to be co-extensive with any contractual duty, even a limited one: *Titan Steel Wheels Ltd v Royal Bank of Scotland Plc* [2010] EWHC 211 (Comm); [2010] 2 Lloyd's Rep. 92.

[1519] Defined as a company not carrying on a business, or an individual not himself engaged in financial services: Financial Services and Markets Act (Rights of Action) Regulations 2001 (SI 2001/2256) reg.3. See generally *Titan Steel Wheels Ltd v Royal Bank of Scotland Plc* [2010] EWHC 211 (Comm); [2010] 2 Lloyd's Rep. 92.

[1520] Unless the rule provides to the contrary: s.138D(3). Notably this means that the adviser must comply with any relevant obligations contained in the Conduct of Business Sourcebook compiled by the FCA.

[1521] Note, however, that this provision has been construed as only creating liability to a client or customer: *Sivagnanam v Barclays Bank Plc* [2015] EWHC 3985 (Comm). Furthermore, except where advice is actually provided, this creates no further duty at common law: *Green v Royal Bank of Scotland Plc* [2013] EWCA Civ 1197; [2014] P.N.L.R. 6.

[1522] So that, for instance, a court should avoid the temptation of applying common law reasoning to the scope of the statutory duty: *Rubenstein v HSBC Bank Plc* [2012] EWCA Civ 1184; [2012] 2 C.L.C. 747; and A. Milner, "Liability for negligent investment advice following extraordinary market turmoil" (2013) 29 P.N. 59. On the statutory remedy in particular see K. Stanton, "Investment Advice: the statutory remedy" (2017) 33 P.N. 153.

[1523] See, e.g. *Seymour v Ockwell* [2005] EWHC 1137; [2005] P.N.L.R. 39; also *Medsted Associates Ltd v Canaccord Genuity Wealth (International) Ltd* [2019] EWCA Civ 83; [2019] 1 W.L.R. 4481 (though there the court doubted whether on the facts the relationship was fiduciary).

[1524] [2000] 1 W.L.R. 2129.

[1525] [2000] 1 W.L.R. 2129, 2141. See too *Richards v Hughes* [2004] EWCA Civ 266; [2004] P.N.L.R. 35.

[1526] *Morgan Crucible Co Plc v Hill Samuel & Co Ltd* [1991] Ch. 295 (merchant bank's financial state-every case must depend on its own facts. Thus in *Seymour v Ockwell*,[1527] where a defendant recommended an unsuitable investment to another financial adviser who herself passed it on to her client, it was held that this evidenced neither an acceptance of responsibility nor a relation of proximity so as to allow the latter to sue the defendant direct.

Scope of duty Where positive financial advice is provided which it is clear is likely to be relied on by a client or customer, there is presumptively a duty of care to make sure it is considered and correct.[1528] Thus in a series of cases banks have been held liable where they have misadvised customers on particular investments.[1529] On the other hand, a positive duty to give advice will not be inferred from the mere fact that a financial organisation enters into a transaction with a customer.[1530] But the extent of any duty owed depends ultimately on the terms of a financial adviser's retainer.[1531] Thus while an adviser will readily be held to owe a duty to advise on matters directly pertinent to the transaction in question,[1532] he will not generally come under any duty to advise about collateral matters.[1533] 9-248

Breach of duty A financial adviser is bound to reach the standards of "the ordinary skilled man exercising and professing to have the special skill of financial adviser",[1534] taking into account all the factors relevant to the client's position[1535] and warning of any pertinent risks[1536] or relevant matters the client might have missed.[1537] The principle in *Bolam v Friern HMC*,[1538] protecting those who act in 9-249

---

ments and profit forecasts provided to client in knowledge that predator would rely on them: arguable duty of care).

1527 [2005] EWHC 1137; [2005] P.N.L.R. 39.

1528 *Cornish v Midland Bank Plc* [1985] 3 All E.R. 513, esp. at 516–517 (Croom-Johnson LJ), 520 (Glidewell LJ).

1529 e.g. *Woods v Martins Bank Ltd* [1959] 1 Q.B. 55; *Cornish v Midland Bank Plc* [1985] 3 All E.R. 513; *Verity v Lloyds Bank Plc* [1995] CLC 1557; *Rubenstein v HSBC Bank Plc* [2012] EWCA Civ 1184; [2012] 2 C.L.C. 747.

1530 e.g. *Barclays Bank Plc v Khaira* [1992] 1 W.L.R. 623; and *Bankers Trust International Plc v PT Dharmala Sakti Sejahtera* [1996] C.L.C. 518; see too *JP Morgan Bank v Springwell Navigation Corp* [2008] EWHC 1186 (Comm) (appealed on other grounds at [2010] EWCA Civ 1221; [2010] 2 C.L.C. 705).

1531 *Denning v Greenhalgh Financial Services Ltd* [2017] EWHC 143 (QB); [2017] P.N.L.R. 19 at [47] (Green J). This will very often be co-extensive with the adviser's regulatory duties: see *Seymour v Ockwell* [2005] EWHC 1137; [2005] P.N.L.R. 39; and cf. *Lloyd Cheyham & Co Ltd v Eversheds* (1985) 2 Lloyds P.N. 154.

1532 e.g. *Bateson v Savills Private Finance Ltd* [2013] EWHC 719 (QB); [2013] P.N.L.R. 20 (mortgage adviser: duty to warn of redemption penalties and fact that where several properties mortgaged, all were cross-charged).

1533 e.g. *Denning v Greenhalgh Financial Services Ltd* [2017] EWHC 143 (QB); [2017] P.N.L.R. 19 (pension adviser: no duty to advise client that might have claim against previous adviser).

1534 *Lenderink-Woods v Zurich Assurance Ltd* [2016] EWHC 3287 (Ch); [2017] P.N.L.R. 15 at [74] (Norris J).

1535 Such as the level of riskiness demanded (*Seymour v Ockwell* [2005] EWHC 1137; [2005] P.N.L.R. 39 and *Rubenstein v HSBC Bank Plc* [2012] EWCA Civ 1184; [2012] 2 C.L.C. 747), or the domicile of the client in tax advice (*Lenderink-Woods v Zurich Assurance Ltd* [2016] EWHC 3287 (Ch); [2017] P.N.L.R. 15). For a discussion of what is relevant, see *Gestmin SGPS SA v Credit Suisse (UK) Ltd* [2013] EWHC 3560 (Comm).

1536 *Shore v Sedgwick Financial Services Ltd* [2007] EWHC 2509 (Admin); [2008] P.N.L.R. 10 at [143]–[144] (risks of withdrawing too much from pension pot).

1537 *Bateson v Savills Private Finance Ltd* [2013] EWHC 719 (QB); [2013] P.N.L.R. 20 (mortgage adviser: duty to warn of redemption penalties and fact that where several properties mortgaged, all were cross-charged).

accordance with a rational and recognised practice in the profession, applies.[1539] As with professional liability generally, the level of care demanded depends on the nature of the adviser's business and the field of his practice (though not the length of his experience).[1540] In a suitable case a duty may be satisfied by taking advice from an apparently competent third party; but the adviser may still be negligent if there are indications that that advice may be misguided.[1541] The fact that a person has satisfied all regulatory requirements will not necessarily exonerate him.[1542] Nevertheless, the standards imposed on an adviser by a relevant regulatory body are a highly relevant indicator of the level of duty required of him at common law,[1543] which may incorporate any applicable requirements,[1544] but only if this is consistent with the scheme of liability contemplated by the relevant regulatory scheme.[1545]

9-250 **Damages** Damages for misguided investment advice will normally comprise the difference between the claimant's present position and the position he would have been in had he received proper advice. In practice this normally means the amount of any capital losses,[1546] plus or minus any gains or losses that would have been realised with such advice.[1547] To this must be added any consequential losses.[1548] But it seems that damages for distress and disappointment are not available.[1549]

7. INSURANCE BROKERS[1550]

(a) Duties of care

9-251 **General duty** An insurance broker, as a professional person and also as agent of the assured, is under a duty to show a reasonable level of skill and care in advising on, arranging and administering insurance on his behalf. Most often the law is concerned with the duties he owes his client, who may be either the assured or

1538 [1957] 1 W.L.R. 582.

1539 *Lenderink-Woods v Zurich Assurance Ltd* [2016] EWHC 3287 (Ch); [2017] P.N.L.R. 15 at [74] (Norris J). But this may not be so as regards advice as to the risks inherent in a transaction: *O'Hare v Coutts & Co* [2016] EWHC 2224 (QB).

1540 *Seymour v Ockwell* [2005] EWHC 1137; [2005] P.N.L.R. 39 at [92].

1541 *Seymour v Ockwell* [2005] EWHC 1137; [2005] P.N.L.R. 39 (investment advised by third party based in notoriously under-regulated jurisdiction, and obviously inadequately secured).

1542 *Gorham v British Telecommunications Plc* [2000] 1 W.L.R. 2129, 2141, 2144 (Pill and Schiemann LJJ) (see M.A. Jones (2001) 17 P.N. 190); *Lenderink-Woods v Zurich Assurance Ltd* [2016] EWHC 3287 (Ch); [2017] P.N.L.R. 15 at [94]–[96] (Norris J).

1543 *Seymour v Ockwell* [2005] EWHC 1137; [2005] P.N.L.R. 39 at [77]; *Shore v Sedgwick Financial Services Ltd* [2007] EWHC 2509 (Admin); [2008] P.N.L.R. 10 at [161] (Beatson J).

1544 *Loosemore v Financial Concepts* [2001] 1 Lloyd's Rep. P.N. 235, 241.

1545 *Flex-E-Vouchers Ltd v Royal Bank of Scotland Plc* [2016] EWHC 2604 (QB) (action for breach of statutory duty under s.138D limited to private clients: inappropriate to incorporate requirements into contract with non-private client).

1546 This may be equally appropriate with a retirement plan, where a capital value may quite easily be assigned: *Primavera Ltd v Allied Dunbar Assurance Plc* [2002] EWCA Civ 1327; [2003] P.N.L.R. 12.

1547 *Seymour v Ockwell* [2005] EWHC 1137; [2005] P.N.L.R. 39 at [168]–[169].

1548 For example, professional advice: *Primavera Ltd v Allied Dunbar Assurance Plc* [2002] EWCA Civ 1327; [2003] P.N.L.R. 12.

1549 *Seymour v Ockwell* [2005] EWHC 1137; [2005] P.N.L.R. 39.

1550 *Jackson & Powell on Professional Liability* 8th edn (2017), Ch.16.

another insurer (in the case of reinsurance), or even another broker.[1551] But on occasion there may also be duties to third parties.

(i) Duties to clients

Liability in contract and tort Although the broker is traditionally paid by the insurer, it seems clear that there is a contract between him and his client, carrying with it an implied obligation of reasonable care.[1552] In addition, it has been accepted for some little time that the broker owes his client a concurrent duty in tort,[1553] though no doubt the scope of any tortious duty will depend on the terms of any contract between him and his client, and is unlikely to go further than the contractual obligation. Not infrequently a broker will employ a sub-broker to place the risk. In such a case it is clear that as a general rule there will be no direct contractual relations between client and sub-broker.[1554] Nevertheless there is no reason why on principle the sub-broker, if negligent, should not owe the client a duty in tort[1555]; though it must be added that unless there is a fairly close relation between client and sub-broker a court is unlikely to find an adequate undertaking of responsibility to establish proximity between the parties.[1556] Even if there is no duty between client and sub-broker, however, the broker will prima facie be liable for the negligence of the sub-broker,[1557] with the right to sue the latter for an indemnity.[1558] In addition to duties in contract and tort, insurance brokers may also owe certain fiduciary duties to their clients.[1559] 9-252

[1551] Notably where he is a placing, and the other broker a producing, broker. The duty in such a case is similar, save that the placing broker is generally entitled to assume that the producing broker understands the ultimate client's needs: see *Dunlop Haywards (DHL) Ltd v Barbon Insurance Group Ltd* [2009] EWHC 2900 (Comm); [2010] Lloyd's Rep. I.R. 149 at [241]–[243] (Hamblen J).

[1552] See s.13 of the Supply of Goods and Services Act 1982 (commercial clients) and s.49 of the Consumer Rights Act 2015 (others). Consideration is provided, it would seem, by the assured giving the broker his business and hence the chance to earn commission.

[1553] e.g. *Cherry Ltd v Allied Insurance Brokers Ltd* [1978] 1 Lloyd's Rep. 274; *Forsikringsaktieselskapet Vesta v Butcher* [1988] 1 Lloyd's Rep. 19 (affirmed [1989] A.C. 852). In the latter case the point mattered: the issue was the applicability of the Law Reform (Contributory Negligence) Act 1945, which only affects a claim which could have been brought in the tort of negligence. See too *Youell v Bland Welch & Co Ltd (No.2)* [1990] 2 Lloyd's Rep. 431, 455–460 (the *Superhulls Cover* case) on the same point.

[1554] This being the normal rule with sub-agents: *Calico Printers Ass'n v Barclays Bank Ltd* (1931) 145 L.T. 151. For an application of it to brokers see *Prentis Donegan Ltd v Leeds & Leeds Co, Inc* [1998] 2 Lloyd's Rep. 326.

[1555] See *Tudor Jones & Marsh McLennan v Crowley Colosso* [1996] 2 Lloyds Rep. 619; *Involnert Management Inc v Aprilgrange Ltd* [2015] EWHC 2225 (Comm); [2015] 2 Lloyd's Rep. 289 at [278] (Leggatt J).

[1556] See *Pangood Ltd v Barclay Brown & Co Ltd* [1999] P.N.L.R. 678; *Involnert Management Inc v Aprilgrange Ltd* [2015] EWHC 2225 (Comm); [2015] 2 Lloyd's Rep. 289.

[1557] cf. *Coolee Ltd v Wing Heath & Co* (1930) 38 Ll.L. Rep. 188. This is the general rule in agency law (cf. *Henderson v Merrett Syndicates Ltd* [1995] 2 A.C. 145); and reflects the principle stated in *Woodland v Swimming Teachers Association* [2013] UKSC 66; [2014] A.C. 537.

[1558] As in, e.g. *Tudor-Jones v Crowley Colosso Ltd* [1996] 2 Lloyd's Rep. 619; or *European International Reinsurance Co Ltd v Curzon Insurance Ltd* [2003] EWCA Civ 1074; [2003] Lloyd's Rep. I.R. 793. Contributory negligence may of course apply: see e.g. *Ocean Finance & Mortgages Ltd v Senior Wright Ltd* [2016] EWHC 160 (Comm); [2016] Lloyd's Rep. I.R. 319.

[1559] See, e.g. *North & South Trust Co v Berkeley* [1971] 1 W.L.R. 470 (brokers acting for insured and also for loss-adjusters).

(ii) Duties to others

9-253 **Duties to third parties** Prima facie a broker is liable only to his client,[1560] and is under no duty to protect the interests of others, such as the insurer, even if loss to them is foreseeable.[1561] However, there is no reason why he should not in addition owe duties in tort to third parties, provided a sufficient degree of proximity is shown.[1562] Thus there may be such a duty where the broker makes a positive (and negligent) representation to the insurer. So in *Youell v Bland Welch & Co Ltd (No.2)* (the *Superhulls Cover* case)[1563] brokers were held liable to underwriters whom they misinformed as to the level of reinsurance cover available for the risk they sought to place. Again, where the broker is also a coverholder (that is, a broker who is given power to bind the insurer, at least to a limited extent), it has not surprisingly been held that he owes a duty of care to the underwriter whose credit he pledges.[1564]

9-254 Apart from a possible duty to insurers, brokers may in a suitable case be held to owe duties to other third parties interested in the insured risk. Thus it seems clear that where a broker instructed by A to arrange cover for the benefit of A and B negligently fails to do so, it will be liable not only to A but to B as well.[1565] Again, in *Punjab National Bank v De Boinville*[1566] sellers of goods who were unsure whether their buyer was solvent instructed brokers to take out insurance against non-payment, and then assigned the policies to the bank financing the transaction. The buyers failed to pay, and as matters turned out the insurance was ineffective owing to the brokers' negligence. The Court of Appeal, in view of the fact that the bank had been involved from the start in the negotiations, held that it was entitled

---

1560 The mere fact that a third party stands to lose as a result of the broker's negligence is not enough of itself: see, e.g. *Macmillan v Knott Becker Scott Ltd* [1990] 1 Lloyd's Rep. 98 (brokers negligently failing to arrange effective liability insurance not liable to claimant left with worthless claim against insolvent defendant). A similar case is *Verderame v Commercial Union Assurance Co Plc* [2000] Lloyd's Rep. P.N. 557 (brokers to company owe no duty to shareholders: though note that the same result could also be reached under the principle in *Johnson v Gore Wood & Co* [2002] 2 A.C. 1).

1561 See, e.g. *Pryke v Gibbs Hartley Ltd* [1991] 1 Lloyd's Rep. 602, 615.

1562 A straightforward instance being *BP Plc v Aon Ltd (No.2)* [2006] EWHC 424 (Comm); [2006] 1 All E.R. (Comm) 789; [2006] Lloyd's Rep. I.R. 577 (London subsidiary of American broker, which in practice handled affairs of client, owed duty to client with regard to nomination of risks under open cover). But this will not always be so: e.g. *Pangood Ltd v Barclay Brown & Co Ltd* [1999] 1 All E.R. (Comm.) 460; [1999] P.N.L.R. 678.

1563 [1990] 2 Lloyd's Rep. 431 (misstatement to proposed underwriters about reinsurance cover available): see also *Avon Insurance plc v Swire Fraser Ltd* [2000] Lloyd's Rep. IR 535 (representations to underwriters to persuade them to give binding authority to coverholder: broker owed duty, though in the event no negligence shown).

1564 e.g. *Woolcott v Excess Insurance Co Ltd* [1978] 1 Lloyd's Rep. 633 (brokers writing risks when they had knowledge of matters that should have led them to decline it). A new trial was ordered on certain matters (see *Woolcott v Excess Insurance Co Ltd* [1979] 1 Lloyd's Rep. 231): but this does not affect the point. See too *Avon Insurance Plc v Swire Fraser Ltd* [2000] Lloyd's Rep. IR 535.

1565 See *Crowson v HSBC Insurance Brokers Ltd* [2010] Lloyd's Rep. I.R. 441 (broker potentially liable if instructed to arrange insurance both for person instructing him and someone else, or where the policy intended to benefit a third party). For an example see *BP Plc v Aon Ltd (No.2)* [2006] EWHC 424 (Comm); [2006] 1 All E.R. (Comm) 789 (broker arranges insurance for an associated company of the insured). Other instances might be where a site owner in a construction contract arranges to insure the works for the benefit of contractors working on the site, or where brokers acting for a husband fail to arrange effective cover for his wife's jewellery. Another instance is where a broker arranges insurance for an associated company of the insured.

1566 [1992] 1 W.L.R. 1138.

to sue the brokers in tort. Yet again, in *Bromley LBC v Ellis*[1567] a car was sold: the seller's insurance brokers assured the buyer that the benefit of the seller's insurance would be transferred to him but then negligently failed to tell him that the underwriters had refused to effect the transfer. The brokers were held liable to the buyer when the latter, uninsured, carelessly ran into a Rolls-Royce and was held personally liable for somewhat expensive repairs to it.

(b) Breach of duty

(i) Proof of negligence

Proof of negligence A broker's duty, whether in contract or tort, is to show that degree of skill and care to be expected of a reasonable broker[1568] to take reasonable steps to obtain, and where necessary maintain, cover which clearly meets the client's needs and is suitable for the client.[1569] The degree of specialisation is in account. Thus a marine broker will be expected to reach the standard of a reasonable marine broker, but if marine insurance is arranged by a general purpose broker the latter need merely show the expertise to be expected of a reasonable general insurance broker[1570] (though no doubt if the matter was particularly complex or specialised he would be expected to take expert advice[1571]). The rule in *Bolam v Friern HMC*[1572] applies to insurance brokers as to any other professional, so that a broker who acts in accordance with a responsible broking practice will escape liability.[1573] For obvious reasons, evidence of good professional practice is highly relevant here.[1574] 9-255

(ii) Failure to arrange insurance as instructed

Duty to arrange insurance as instructed A broker owes a duty to arrange (or, as the case may be, renew) insurance according to the client's instructions. If he fails to do this at all, he is clearly liable[1575]; and similarly where he fails to do it on time,[1576] where he does take out a policy but it is ineffective to cover the risk he is 9-256

1567 [1971] 1 Lloyd's Rep. 97.

1568 See, e.g. *Chapman v Walton* (1833) 10 Bing. 57, 63–64 (Tindal CJ); *Alexander Forbes Europe Ltd v SBJ Ltd* [2002] EWHC 3121 (Comm); [2003] P.N.L.R. 15 at [36].

1569 *Ground Gilbey Ltd v Jardine Lloyd Thompson UK Ltd* [2011] EWHC 124 (Comm); [2011] P.N.L.R. 15 at [73] (Blair J).

1570 See, e.g. *Sharp & Roarer Investments Ltd v Sphere Drake Insurance Plc* [1992] 2 Lloyd's Rep. 501, 523.

1571 cf. *Sarginson v Keith Moulton & Co* (1942) 73 Lloyd's L.L. Rep. 104 at 107.

1572 [1957] 1 W.L.R. 582.

1573 See *FNCB Ltd v Barnet Devanney (Harrow) Ltd* [1999] Lloyd's Rep. IR 43 at 46 (reversed on other grounds, [2000] P.N.L.R. 248).

1574 *Harvest Trucking Co Ltd v Davis* [1991] 2 Lloyd's Rep. 638 at 643.

1575 As in, e.g. *United Marketing Co v Hasham Kara* [1963] 1 Lloyd's Rep. 331 (failure to renew insurance as promised: liability for subsequent uninsured loss). And cf. the antique decision in *Wilkinson v Coverdale* (1793) 1 Esp. 75 (defendant broke gratuitous promise to insure claimant's property without telling claimant: liable in negligence for uninsured loss).

1576 *Avondale Blouse Co Ltd v Williamson* (1947–48) 81 Lloyd's L. Rep. 492 (failure immediately to transfer risk: goods lost uninsured in the interim. In fact the action failed, but for other reasons). cf. *Cock Russell & Co v Bray Gibb & Co Ltd* (1920) 3 Lloyd's L.L. Rep. 71.

instructed to insure,[1577] or where the policy he arranges fails to reflect properly what he was instructed to do.[1578] Instructions may in a suitable case be implied.[1579] But if instructions are ambiguous, then the broker is not liable provided he takes an interpretation of them which is reasonable in the circumstances.[1580] Strictly speaking, the broker's duty is only to take reasonable care to arrange cover as instructed: he does not guarantee to obtain coverage come what may. Thus if he cannot reasonably get it, he is not liable.[1581] However, even then he must tell his client that he has been unable to place the risk, so as to give the latter a chance to try to obtain cover elsewhere.[1582]

(iii) Failure to obtain insurance suitable for client

9-257 **Duty to obtain insurance suitable for the client's needs** A broker must take reasonable steps to ensure that any insurance satisfies the client's needs[1583] in the light of the information given to him.[1584] Cover may be insufficient as regards risk: thus reinsurance on ships in course of construction may be inadequate if it automatically expires after 48 months[1585]; insurance on a yacht may similarly be inappropriate if it does not cover the vessel while the owners are staying on board[1586] or it is being used to provide crew accommodation in port[1587]; and brokers have been held negligent in failing to cover a warehouseman for goods held as a bailee[1588] and for insuring a car on the basis that the insured is not a part-time musician without checking the facts first.[1589] Cover must also, fairly obviously, be adequate in

---

1577 See, e.g. *The Tiburon* [1990] 2 Lloyd's Rep. 418; and *Mander v Commercial Union Assurance Co plc* [1998] Lloyd's Rep. I.R. 93 (both cases of ineffective declarations under open cover); also *Standard Life Assurance Ltd v OAK Dedicated Ltd* [2008] EWHC 222 (Comm); [2008] P.N.L.R. 26; [2008] 1 C.L.C. 59 (cover useless because of effect of excess).

1578 *Fine's Flowers v General Accident of Canada* (1977) 81 D.L.R. (3d) 139 (instructions to obtain "full coverage" but broker only insured selected risks); see too *Dixon & Co v Devitt* (1916) 86 L.J.K.B. 315.

1579 So, for example, a broker instructed to obtain reinsurance is impliedly instructed to ensure its terms and warranties are as far as possible back-to-back with the main policy: see, e.g. *British Citizens Assurance Co v Woolland & Co* (1921) 8 Lloyd's L.L. Rep. 89; and cf. *Youell v Bland Welch & Co Ltd (No.2)* [1990] 2 Lloyd's Rep. 431 (the *Superhulls Cover* case).

1580 e.g. *Vale v Van Oppen & Co Ltd* (1921) 37 T.L.R. 367.

1581 See the old case of *Smith v Cadogan* (1788) 2 T.R. 188n (broker "is not obliged to get insurance at all events"); also *Avonale Blouse Co Ltd v Williamson* (1947–48) 81 Lloyd's. L. Rep. 492 (instructions to transfer burglary risk to new premises immediately: no negligence in delay, since underwriters declined to act without survey).

1582 *Smith v Lascelles* (1788) 2 T.R. 187; cf. *Aneco Reinsurance Underwriting Ltd v Johnson & Higgs Ltd* [2001] UKHL 51; [2002] 1 Lloyd's Rep. 157 (reinsurance broker liable for failing to tell insurer before latter accepted risk that risk effectively unreinsurable on any terms).

1583 And which does so clearly: a client wishes straightforward cover, not litigation, even if the cover is in fact effective. See *Standard Life Assurance Ltd v OAK Dedicated Ltd* [2008] EWHC 222 (Comm); [2008] P.N.L.R. 26; also *Ground Gilbey Ltd v Jardine Lloyd Thompson UK Ltd* [2011] EWHC 124 (Comm); [2011] P.N.L.R. 15 (warranty of uncertain extent).

1584 Note, however, that where the defendant is a placing, and the claimant a producing, broker, this duty applies only to a limited extent if at all: see *Dunlop Haywards (DHL) Ltd v Barbon Insurance Group Ltd* [2009] EWHC 2900 (Comm); [2010] Lloyd's Rep. I.R. 149 at [241]–[243] (Hamblen J).

1585 *Youell v Bland Welch & Co Ltd (No.2)* [1990] 2 Lloyd's Rep. 431 (the *Superhulls Cover* case).

1586 *Strong & Pearl v Allison & Co Ltd* (1926) 25 Lloyd's L. L. Rep. 504.

1587 *The Moonacre* [1992] 2 Lloyd's Rep. 501.

1588 *Ramco Ltd v Weller Russell & Laws IB Ltd* [2008] EWHC 2202 (QB); [2009] P.N.L.R. 14.

1589 *McNealy v Pennine Insurance Co Ltd* [1978] 2 Lloyd's Rep. 18. Musicians and performers are notoriously regarded as bad risks by underwriters.

amount.[1590] Further, a broker is bound to take care in selecting an insurer, and may thus be liable if the insurer is unauthorised and the policy unenforceable,[1591] or if the underwriter is of doubtful financial standing.[1592] In a suitable case the broker may also be bound to take steps to protect the insured's interests even after cover has been arranged[1593]; in addition if after placement he discovers information with potentially deleterious effect on the cover he must protect the client's interests by adverting to it and seeking further instructions.[1594]

(iv) Negligent advice

Duty to advise A broker clearly instructed to obtain cover of a given class is not normally bound to advise the client if it would be in his interests to obtain more extensive cover. But there may be a duty to advise of the types of cover available and enquire which one the client wants: thus brokers have been held negligent in insuring premises without advising the clients of the desirability of obtaining cover for the full cost of reinstatement.[1595] Furthermore, there is a duty to advise on matters that, perhaps unknown to the client, may affect the validity of cover.[1596] Similarly, even after the risk has been placed brokers may be under a duty to advise of particularly onerous clauses in the policy[1597] or other matters which may adversely affect the interests of the client.[1598] There may in some cases be a duty to remind the assured to take steps to protect his interests, for example by making 9-258

[1590] *Eurokey Recycling Ltd v Giles Insurance Brokers Ltd* [2014] EWHC 2989 (Comm); [2015] P.N.L.R. 5 (wholly inadequate business interruption cover).

[1591] cf. *Bates v Barrow* [1995] 1 Lloyd's Rep. 680.

[1592] e.g. *Lewis v Tressider Andrews Pty Ltd* [1987] 2 Qd. R. 533.

[1593] *BP Plc v Aon Ltd* [2006] EWHC 424 (Comm); [2006] 1 All E.R. (Comm) 789; [2006] Lloyd's Rep. I.R. 577 (failure to make declarations required under open cover). See too *Osman v J Ralph Moss* [1970] 1 Lloyd's Rep. 313 (failure to tell policyholder of collapse of insurer).

[1594] *HIH Casualty & General Insurance Ltd v JLT Risk Solutions Ltd* [2007] EWCA Civ. 710; [2007] 2 All E.R. (Comm) 1106 at [116] (Longmore LJ). For an instance see *Ground Gilbey Ltd v Jardine Lloyd Thompson UK Ltd* [2011] EWHC 124 (Comm); [2011] P.N.L.R. 15 (failure to deal adequately with post-issue requirement from underwriters to deal with risk).

[1595] *Bollom (JW) & Co Ltd v Byas Mosley & Co Ltd* [1999] Lloyd's Rep. P.N. 598.

[1596] See, e.g. *O & R Jewellers Ltd v Terry* [1999] Lloyd's Rep. IR 436 (duty to advise jewellers of need to disclose fact that managing director a convicted burglar); *Fisk v Brian Thornhill & Son* [2007] EWCA Civ 152; [2007] P.N.L.R. 21 (failure to warn of new onerous warranty when renewing cover); *Jones v Environcom Ltd* [2010] EWHC 759 (Comm); [2010] P.N.L.R. 27 (appealed on other grounds, [2011] EWCA Civ 1152; [2012] P.N.L.R. 5) (failure to draw attention of insured to duty of disclosure on renewal).

[1597] *Youell v Bland Welch & Co Ltd (No.2)* [1990] 2 Lloyd's Rep. 431 (the *Superhulls Cover* case) (duty of reinsurance broker to warn insurers of time-limit in reinsurance treaty); *George Barkes (London) Ltd v LFC (1988) Ltd* [2000] P.N.L.R. 21 (unexpected clause in burglary insurance).

[1598] e.g. *Youell v Bland Welch & Co Ltd (No.2)* [1990] 2 Lloyd's Rep. 431 (the *Superhulls Cover* case) (duty to warn insurers that reinsurance cover about to expire); *Alexander Forbes Europe Ltd v SBJ Ltd* [2002] EWHC 3121 (Comm); [2003] P.N.L.R. 15 (duty to remind assured to notify claims arising under "claims made" policy); *Osman v J Ralph Moss* [1970] 1 Lloyd's Rep. 313 (failure to tell policyholder of collapse of insurer); *HIH Casualty & General Insurance Ltd v JLT Risk Solutions Ltd* [2007] EWCA Civ 710; [2007] 2 Lloyd's Rep. 278 (duty in reinsurance brokers to advise of post-placement breaches of warranty by ultimate assured so as to prevent insurers paying out without liability and thus not having recourse against reinsurers).

a notification.[1599] Where a broker undertakes to give advice on specific matters, that advice must, of course, be given with reasonable care.[1600]

(v) *Failure to provide full and correct information to insurer*

9-259 **Providing information to the insurer** In commercial insurance law, the broker being the agent of the assured, any misrepresentation or non-disclosure of a material fact[1601] on his part may be invoked by the insurer to avoid or qualify its liability even if the assured is entirely innocent.[1602] Nevertheless, in such a case the broker himself may be liable to the assured,[1603] though to establish such liability negligence must obviously be proved.[1604] Similarly, when a broker completes a proposal form for the assured which contains misrepresentations he will normally be liable if he had reason to suspect that the information was false,[1605] though if the assured approves the form once it has been filled in, then any subsequent loss may well be regarded as not having been caused by that negligence.[1606]

9-260 This principle is, however, now limited to commercial insurance. As regards consumer insurance, under the provisions of the Consumer Insurance (Disclosure and Representations) Act 2012[1607] the broker is regarded not as the assured's agent to give information but the underwriter's to receive it. It follows that the underwriter will no longer have the right to disclaim liability where brokers are guilty of misrepresentation or non-disclosure, and therefore this head of liability to the client is likely to disappear. On the other hand, the broker will remain potentially liable for misadvising the client on what has to be disclosed.[1608]

(c) Damages

9-261 **General measure of damages: failure to obtain proper insurance** Where a broker negligently fails to insure according to instructions, or to advise of relevant limitations of cover, the measure of damages in such a case is prima facie the

---

1599 *Ocean Finance & Mortgages Ltd v Senior Wright Ltd* [2016] EWHC 160 (Comm); [2016] Lloyd's Rep. I.R. 319.

1600 e.g. *Sarginson v Keith Moulton & Co* (1942) 73 Lloyd's L. Rep. 104 (advice about possibility of valid insurance).

1601 For what is material, see *Macgillivray on Insurance Law* (14th edn, 2019), Chs 16–17; and generally *Pan Atlantic Insurance Co v Pine Top Insurance Co Ltd* [1995] 1 A.C. 501.

1602 The duty is now statutory: Insurance Act 2015 Pt 2 (commercial insurance); Consumer Insurance (Disclosure and Representations) Act 2012 s.2 (consumer insurance). See *MacGillivray on Insurance Law* (14th edn, 2019), Chs 16 to 20.

1603 See, e.g. *Maydew v Forrester* (1814) 5 Taunt 615; *Cooley v Wing Heath & Co* (1930) 47 T.L.R. 78 (non-disclosure); *Everett v Hogg Robinson (Insurance) Ltd* [1973] 2 Lloyd's Rep. 217; *Aneco Reinsurance Underwriters Ltd v Johnson & Higgins Ltd* [1998] 1 Lloyd's Rep. 565 (appealed on other grounds: [2001] UKHL 51; [2002] 1 Lloyd's Rep. 157) (misrepresentation).

1604 For a rare case in which it was not, see *Bell v Tinmouth* (1988) 53 D.L.R. (4th) 731 (broker misrepresented facts having reasonably relied on facts supplied by third party nominated by assured).

1605 *Involnert Management Inc v Aprilgrange Ltd* [2015] EWHC 2225 (Comm); [2015] 2 Lloyd's Rep. 289.

1606 *Kapur v Francis & Co* [2000] Lloyd's Rep. I.R. 361; see too *O'Connor v Kirby & Co* [1972] 1 Q.B. 90.

1607 Sch.2 para.2(b) (in force from 6 April 2013 and applicable to consumer insurance contracts entered into from that date).

1608 For details of what needs to be disclosed in a consumer insurance contract and the effects of misrepresentation by the assured, see the Consumer Insurance (Disclosure and Representations) Act 2012 Sch.1.

uninsured loss suffered by the assured in respect of which he would have had a right to indemnity had the broker acted properly.[1609] Normally this loss takes the form of direct loss such as damage to property, but it may equally well be a liability in damages which the claimant has to meet personally but would otherwise have been paid by the insurer.[1610] If the complaint is that the insurance obtained is inadequate, rather than non-existent, the prima facie measure is the difference between the amount actually payable and the amount that should have been payable.[1611] However, this is only a prima facie rule. If suitable cover would have been unavailable, there will be no damages[1612]; conversely, the damages may be increased if there is consequential loss,[1613] such as the expense of a fruitless suit against the insurer.[1614]

Other claims against brokers Claims against brokers for failure to get effective or adequate cover are not the only possibility. There may, for example, be a liability in damages where the broker is instructed to advise about the availability of cover generally and fails to do so or does so negligently. Here, on principle, liability extends to all the consequences of that negligence. Thus in *Aneco Insurance Underwriting Ltd v Johnson & Higgs Ltd*[1615] reinsurance brokers instructed to take out $10 million cover for a proposed $30 million risk negligently omitted to inform their clients that this risk was effectively unreinsurable. Had they known these facts, the clients would have declined to write the risk at all; as it was they did so and lost the full $30 million. The brokers were held liable for this sum. **9-262**

However, any extended liability of this sort is potentially subject to the limitations in *South Australia Asset Management Co (SAAMCO) v York Montague Ltd*.[1616] In the *Aneco* case this limitation did not apply, since the brokers' duty was construed as one to advise generally on the feasibility of the original risk rather than simply to provide information.[1617] But it may well apply elsewhere. For instance, if brokers negligently advise that cover arranged by them is unlimited whereas in fact it is limited to a relatively low sum, with the result that the assured suffers a partly **9-263**

1609 See, e.g. *Park v Hammond* (1816) 6 Taunt 495; *Smith v Price* (1862) 2 F & F 748; *General Accident Assurance Ltd v Minet & Co Ltd* (1942) 74 Lloyd's LL Rep. 1; *Ramwade Ltd v Emson & Co* [1987] RTR 72; *BP Plc v Aon Ltd* [2006] EWHC 424 (Comm); [2006] 1 All E.R. (Comm) 789; [2006] Lloyd's Rep. I.R. 577 at [317]–[318].

1610 e.g. *Fraser v Furman Productions Ltd* [1967] 3 All E.R. 57 (employers' liability). See too the motor insurance cases of *Osman v J Ralph Moss Ltd* [1970] 1 Lloyd's Rep. 313; and *Bromley LBC v Ellis* [1971] 1 Lloyd's Rep. 97.

1611 See the Canadian decision in *Coyle v Ray Fredericks Insurance Ltd* ((1984) 64 N.S.R. 93 (insurance obtained for value rather than replacement cost).

1612 See, e.g. *Jones v Environcom Ltd* [2010] EWHC 759; [2010] P.N.L.R. 27 (appealed at [2011] EWCA Civ 1152; [2012] P.N.L.R. 5) (brokers negligent in not ensuring clients understood duty of disclosure, but in event risk uninsurable anyway). See too *BP Plc v Aon Ltd* [2006] EWHC 424 (Comm); [2006] 1 All E.R. (Comm) 789; [2006] Lloyd's Rep. I.R. 577 at [317] onwards.

1613 *Arbory Group Ltd v West Craven Insurance Services* [2007] P.N.L.R. 23 QBD (business interruption insurance wholly inadequate owing to brokers' negligence: insured recovers extra loss due to further disruption caused by underpayment). See too *Osman v J Ralph Moss Ltd* [1970] 1 Lloyd's Rep. 313 (negligence of broker left motorist inadvertently uninsured: brokers liable for amount of criminal fine). The result in *Osman* was approved in *Patel v Mirza* [2016] UKSC 42; [2017] A.C. 467 at [242].

1614 As in *Ramco Ltd v Weller Russell & Laws Insurance Brokers Ltd* [2008] EWHC 2202 (QB); [2009] P.N.L.R. 14.

1615 [2001] UKHL 51; [2002] 1 Lloyd's Rep. 157. See too *Youell v Bland Welch & Co Ltd (No.2)* [1990] 2 Lloyd's Rep. 431 (the *Superhulls Cover* case), where a similar result was reached by concession.

1616 [1997] A.C. 191.

1617 See [2001] UKHL 51; [2002] 1 Lloyd's Rep. 157 at 180, 181, 186-187; also *BPE Solicitors v Hughes-Holland* [2017] UKSC 21; [2018] A.C. 599 at [43] (Lord Sumption).

uninsured loss, then it is suggested that damages are likely to be limited to the difference between the actual loss and the limit of the cover.

9-264 **Additional and consequential damages** Damages against an insurance broker are not restricted to the sum for which, but for the broker's breach of duty, the underwriters would have been liable. Thus where the assured reasonably litigates his claim against the underwriters and loses, he can claim his costs from the brokers the costs of those proceedings.[1618] Similarly, a motorist left driving uninsured as a result of his brokers' bungle can recover if as a result he is fined for doing so.[1619] So too, if inadequate business interruption insurance is arranged the assured can recover for any profits lost.[1620] However, the scope for such extra damages is limited. First, they must be within the scope of the duty owed by the broker.[1621] Thus while a broker who fails to warn the client to take warranted fire precautions may be liable for cover lost, it is not open to the client to argue (for instance) that the failure to warn itself caused his premises to be burnt down, and claim a complete indemnity for the loss of them.[1622] Secondly, it seems clear that a claim against insurance brokers is not one where damages for distress or anxiety can be claimed.[1623] It has been said in addition that where brokers fail to arrange proper cover there can be no damages for extra losses caused by the fact that the claimant received payment late from the brokers rather than promptly from the underwriters[1624]: but this may well be open to question.[1625]

9-265 **Claimant limited to net loss, if any** The claimant is, of course, only entitled to recover to the extent that he has actually suffered a net loss. It follows that the broker is entitled to credit for any gains or savings made by him. In particular, despite one curious decision of the Privy Council to the contrary,[1626] it is suggested that this means that where cover arranged is ineffective and as a result the assured recovers (or never pays) the premium, his recovery should be reduced accordingly.[1627] Similarly, where the cover is effective but inadequate or inappropriate, any damages should be docked by the amount of any extra premium that the assured would have had to pay for proper cover.[1628] On the same basis, if a broker fails to arrange valid reinsurance but the insurers nevertheless pay out knowing they

---

1618 *Strong v Allison & Co Ltd* (1926) 25 Lloyd's LL Rep. 504, esp. at 508. For the measure of costs recoverable, see *The Tiburon* [1992] 2 Lloyd's Rep. 26.

1619 *Osman v J Ralph Moss Ltd* [1970] 1 Lloyd's Rep. 313.

1620 *Arbory Group Ltd v West Craven Insurance Services* [2007] Lloyd's Rep. I.R. 491; [2007] P.N.L.R. 23; *Eurokey Recycling Ltd v Giles Insurance Brokers Ltd* [2014] EWHC 2989 (Comm); [2015] P.N.L.R. 5.

1621 Under the principle in *South Australia Asset Management v York Montague Ltd* [1997] A.C. 191.

1622 *Jones v Environcom Ltd* [2011] EWCA Civ 1152; [2012] P.N.L.R. 5.

1623 cf. *Verderame v Commercial Union Assurance Co Plc* [2000] Lloyd's Rep. P.N. 557.

1624 *Ramwade Ltd v Emson & Co* [1987] R.T.R. 72. See too *Verderame v Commercial Union Assurance Co Plc* [2000] Lloyd's Rep. P.N. 557.

1625 The reason given is the rule that insurance payouts are regarded as damages, and there can be no damages for late payment of damages: see *Sprung v Royal Insurance (UK) Ltd* [1997] C.L.C. 70. But this does not follow. There is every difference between making good late payment of one's own obligation and compensating for non-receipt of money from a third party. It is also worth noting that, as from May 2017, the rule barring compensation for late payment of claims is itself suppressed by statute: Insurance Act 2015 s.13A. See too A. Tettenborn, "The Negligent Broker", in R. Thomas (ed), *The Modern Law of Marine Insurance*, Vol. 4, 67.

1626 *Eagle Star Insurance Co Ltd v National Westminster Finance (Australia) Ltd* (1985) 58 A.L.R. 165.

1627 See *Charles v Altin* (1854) 15 C. & B. 46, 63; *The Moonacre* [1992] 2 Lloyd's Rep. 501.

1628 See *Bollom v Byas Mosley* [2000] Lloyd's Rep. I.R. 136; *George Barkes (London) Ltd v LFC (1988)*

have a defence, it is not surprising that nothing is recoverable.[1629] Again, on occasion, a payment from a third party may go to reduce the damages, at least if the third party intended to make good the loss.[1630]

On the other hand, although the defendant is generally entitled to credit for amounts received from the actual insurer, and may be so entitled in respect of other third party receipts, this rule does not extend to payments received from other insurers,[1631] whether or not the insurer concerned is entitled to subrogation to the claimant's rights.[1632] So in *FNCB Ltd v Barnet Devanney (Harrow) Ltd*[1633] brokers negligently omitted to ensure that cover on a country house extended to the mortgagees. In fact the mortgagees were paid because they had arranged secondary contingency cover with other underwriters; nevertheless, they successfully sued the brokers in addition for the amount of the insurance monies they had not received under the primary policy. 9-266

(d) Causation of loss

Causation It is not enough for the claimant to show that the broker was negligent: he must in addition show that the broker's negligence caused the loss he is complaining of. So a client cannot complain if the insurance that should have been obtained would not in fact have covered him in the events that happened,[1634] and a fortiori if he would have been uninsurable even if the broker had acted properly.[1635] Again, if it is plain that, even assuming the broker had placed the risk properly, the underwriters would have rightly refused to pay anything for some unconnected reason, then there will be no substantial damages.[1636] But this is a difficult plea to sustain: in the absence of convincing evidence that the claim would not in fact have been paid, the claimant is likely to succeed.[1637] 9-267

In many cases of the above type, it will be found that there was some likelihood 9-268

Ltd [2000] P.N.L.R. 21. In the latter case, a County Court decision, the judge pointedly declined to follow the Privy Council in *Eagle Star Insurance Co Ltd v National Westminster Finance (Australia) Ltd* (1985) 58 A.L.R. 165, above (!).

1629 *HIH Casualty & General Insurance Ltd v JLT Risk Solutions Ltd* [2007] EWCA Civ 710; [2007] 2 Lloyd's Rep. 278 (failure by brokers to advise of breaches of warranty invalidating insurance and reinsurance, but insurers subsequently pay out knowing of breach). See too *Harvest Trucking Co Ltd v Davis* [1991] 2 Lloyd's Rep. 638. But the assured's right to recovery, it seems, revives if he has returned the payout: *Maydew v Forester* (1814) 5 Taunt 615.

1630 *Talbot Underwriting Ltd v Nausch, Hogan & Murray Inc* [2006] EWCA Civ 889; [2006] 2 All E.R. (Comm) 751.

1631 On the basis (however illogically) of the rule in *Bradburn v Gt Western Ry Co* (1875) L.R. 10 Ex. 1.

1632 Because of the rule in *Bradburn v Great Western Ry Co* (1874) L.R. 10 Ex 1.

1633 [2000] P.N.L.R. 248.

1634 *Channon v Ward* [2017] EWCA Civ 13; [2018] Lloyd's Rep. I.R. 239.

1635 *Jones v Environcom Ltd* [2011] EWCA Civ 1152; [2012] P.N.L.R. 5 (failure to warn about warranty which client would never have satisfied).

1636 e.g. *Newbury International Ltd v Reliance National Insurance Co (UK) Ltd* [1994] 1 Lloyd's Rep. 83 (non-disclosure by brokers, but insurers could, and would, have declined to pay for the separate reason of lack of any insurable interest). See too *Gunns v Par Insurance Brokers* [1997] 1 Lloyd's Rep. 173; also *Fraser v Furman Productions Ltd* [1967] 3 All E.R. 57 (though there it was found that the underwriters could not have repudiated liability, and even if they could they would have paid ex gratia); and *Daland Ltd v Butterworth Spengler Commercial Ltd* [2018] EWHC 2558 (Comm); [2019] P.N.L.R. 6. See generally *Macgillivray on Insurance Law*, 14th edn (2019), paras 38-37 to 38-44.

1637 *Quaere* where the burden of proof lies here. Diplock LJ in *Fraser v Furman Productions Ltd* [1967] 3 All E.R. 57 at 63–64, thought it was on the defendant, but this may be going too far. The better that the insurer would in fact have paid even if not liable to do so, whether ex gratia or for other good commercial reasons. Since the claimant can recover only his actual loss, it follows that in such a case damages may have to be reckoned on the basis of the loss of a chance of receiving payment, on the principle of the decision in *Allied Maples Group Ltd v Simmons & Simmons*.[1638] So in *Everett v Hogg Robinson Ltd*[1639] brokers negligently made a misrepresentation to the underwriters which the latter correctly invoked to avoid liability. The brokers argued that the underwriters would, even absent the misrepresentation, have repudiated on the basis of the assured's undisclosed claims record, but Kerr J found that the underwriters would probably have compromised the claim for commercial reasons, and merely reduced the award by one-third to take account of the possibility that they would not have.[1640] Where the claimant's putative right against the underwriters is uncertain—for instance where it is arguable whether non-disclosure would have allowed repudiation at all—and the assured reasonably accepts a settlement of his claim, he is it seems entitled to recover the difference between the amount received under the settlement and the full amount.[1641]

9-269 **Assured's own act may negative causal link** If a broker makes a misrepresentation when filling in a proposal form, whereupon the client then checks it, notices the statement in it but nevertheless signs it, it may be held when the underwriters refuse cover that the cause of the loss is the assured's own act rather than the broker's negligence.[1642] One older case goes further than this, and holds that the same result applies where the assured signs the form but only after a cursory glance.[1643] But it is suggested that today such cases are likely to be treated as involving mere contributory negligence on the part of the client, if that.[1644]

(e) Damages: mitigation of loss and contributory negligence

9-270 **Mitigation of loss** On principle there is no reason why the principle of mitigation of loss should not apply to claims against brokers as to any other negligence claim.[1645] However, it is likely to be of limited importance in practice. It has admittedly been suggested that it is open to the broker in breach of duty to prove that the assured might reasonably have got something from the underwriter by way of set-

view, it is suggested, is that it is always up to the claimant to prove his loss, though no doubt with an evidential burden on the defendant to in regard to certain defences. cf. *Toikan Insurance Broking Pty Ltd v Plasteel Windows (Australia) Pty Ltd* (1988) 15 N.S.W.L.R. 641.

[1638] [1995] 1 W.L.R. 1602.

[1639] [1973] 2 Lloyd's Rep. 217. cf. *O & R Jewellers Ltd v Terry* [1999] Lloyd's Rep. I.R. 436; and *Ramco Ltd v Weller Russell & Laws Insurance Brokers Ltd* [2008] EWHC 2202 (QB); [2009] P.N.L.R. 14.

[1640] cf. too *Cee Bee Marine Ltd v Lombard Insurance Co Ltd* [1990] 2 N.Z.L.R. 1.

[1641] *Unity Insurance Brokers Pty Ltd v Rocco Pezzano Pty Ltd* (1998) 72 A.L.J.R. 937; see too *Mander v Commercial Union Assurance Co Ltd* [1998] Lloyd's Rep. I.R. 93, especially at 141–149; and *Dalamd Ltd v Butterworth Spengler Commercial Ltd* [2018] EWHC 2558 (Comm); [2019] P.N.L.R. 6 at [133], plus the authorities cited there. But according to the latter case at [130]–[132] the assured must actually pursue the underwriter: if the cover is in fact good, he cannot proceed directly against the broker without even attempting to recover from the insurer.

[1642] See *Kapur v Francis & Co* [2000] Lloyd's Rep. I.R. 361.

[1643] *O'Connor v Kirby & Co* [1972] 1 Q.B. 90.

[1644] See para.9-271 onwards.

[1645] e.g. in respect of consequential losses: cf. *Ramco Ltd v Weller Russell & Laws Insurance Brokers Ltd* [2008] EWHC 2202 (QB); [2009] P.N.L.R. 14 at [70] (claim for abortive legal expenses against underwriters: failure to apply for leave to appeal possible failure to mitigate).

tlement, and hence to the extent of the excess[1646] he has failed to mitigate his loss.[1647] However, the better position, it is submitted, is that no credit need be granted here. A claimant is generally under no duty to claim his loss from a third party other than the defendant, however straightforward the claim against the former may be[1648]: and in a case where the broker has failed to get for the assured what he promised, namely an enforceable claim, there seems no reason to make any exception to the rule in this case.[1649]

Contributory negligence Even where a broker has been negligent, damages may be reduced on account of contributory negligence if (for example) the client should have realised that his cover was defective or inadequate.[1650] Such reductions are not uncommon in reinsurance cases. So in *Forsikrings A/S Vesta v Butcher*[1651] reinsurance brokers negligently omitted to follow instructions to check certain provisions in a proposed reinsurance treaty. The original insurers for their part failed to goad them into action. Damages were cut by 75 per cent. Another example is *Youell v Bland Welch & Co Ltd (No.2)* (the *Superhulls Cover* case).[1652] Brokers negligently arranged reinsurance cover which differed significantly from the original risk. Although they had copies of the reinsurance treaty, the client insurers failed to notice the difficulty: as a result recovery was reduced by 20 per cent. While a reduction for contributory negligence is possible, in practice the courts show a good deal of indulgence towards assureds who assume that their brokers have acted properly and do not take steps to double check.[1653] So the owner of a boat is not expected to comprehend the precise significance of a technical term in the policy[1654]; nor is an 9-271

1646 Or possibly the amount of the excess multiplied by the chance of extracting it from the insurer: *Mander v Commercial Union Assurance Co Ltd* [1998] Lloyd's Rep. I.R. 93, 148. cf. *Ground Gilbey Ltd v Jardine Lloyd Thompson UK Ltd* [2011] EWHC 124 (Comm); [2011] P.N.L.R. 15, especially at [109].

1647 *Mander v Commercial Union Assurance Co Ltd* [1998] Lloyd's Rep. I.R. 93, 148. But this right in the broker, if it existed at all, was always a difficult one to make out: see e.g. *Alexander Forbes Europe Ltd v SBJ Ltd* [2002] EWHC 3121 (Comm); [2003] P.N.L.R. 15 (no need to mitigate by starting speculative proceedings against underwriters).

1648 See *Peters v East Midlands Health Authority* [2009] EWCA Civ 145; [2010] Q.B. 48; and the lawyers' negligence decision in *Haugesund Kommune v Depfa ACS Bank* [2010] EWHC 227 (Comm); [2010] P.N.L.R. 21 (reversed on other grounds, [2011] EWCA Civ 33; [2011] 3 All E.R. 655).

1649 Indeed, the holding in *Haugesund Kommune v Depfa ACS Bank* [2010] EWHC 227 (Comm); [2010] P.N.L.R. 21 (reversed on other grounds, [2011] EWCA Civ 33; [2011] 3 All E.R. 655) is against application of the doctrine. There lawyers who failed to ensure that a loan to a public authority was enforceable against it were held liable for the value of that loan, despite evidence that the lenders had an enforceable claim to return of their monies under the law of unjust enrichment. An unenforceable claim is a fortiori.

1650 A proposition cemented by *Forsikrings A/S Vesta v Butcher* [1988] 2 All E.R. 43 (affirmed on other grounds, [1989] A.C. 852).

1651 [1988] 1 Lloyd's Rep. 19 (affirmed on other grounds, [1989] A.C. 852).

1652 [1990] 2 Lloyd's Rep. 431. See too *Jones v Crowley Colosso Ltd* [1996] 2 Lloyd's Rep. 619; *National Insurance & Guarantee Corp'n v Imperio Reinsurance (UK) Ltd* [1999] Lloyd's Rep. I.R. 249.

1653 See *Youell v Bland Welch & Co Ltd (No.2)* [1990] 2 Lloyd's Rep. 431 at 453–454 (the *Superhulls Cover* case) (Phillips J); also *Arbory Group Ltd v West Craven Insurance Services* [2007] P.N.L.R. 23 (where brokers undertake to get documentation right, not contributorily negligent for insured not to check them exhaustively).

1654 *The Moonacre* [1992] 2 Lloyd's Rep. 501 (extent of a rather obscure warranty against use of a vessel "as a houseboat").

insured expected automatically to appreciate the existence and effect of a warranty nestling deep inside the small print of the proposed policy.[1655]

[1655] *Bollom & Co Ltd v Byas Mosley Ltd* [1999] Lloyd's Rep. I.R. 598.

Chapter 10

PRODUCT LIABILITY AND CONSUMER PROTECTION

Table of Contents

1. Product Liability in General[1]

This chapter is concerned with liability for defective and unsafe products. This is a subject spanning tort, contract and for that matter criminal law: but for obvi- 10-01

[1] J. Stapleton, *Product Liability* (Oxford: OUP, 1994); C. Miller & R. Goldberg, *Products Liability*, 2nd edn (Oxford: OUP, 2004); C. Miller, *Products Liability and Safety Encyclopaedia*. For a medical perspective, see M. Jones, *Medical Negligence*, 5th edn (London: Sweet & Maxwell, 2018), Ch.10; and R. Goldberg, *Medicinal Product Liability and Regulation* (Hart). And, for the American position, see M.S. Shapo, *Shapo on the Law of Products Liability*, 7th edn (Elgar, 2017).

ous reasons, the chapter will concentrate on the first of these. For the sake of completeness, however, some reference will be made to the other two. Logically, it may seem a little odd to partition off a particular class of injury merely because it happens to have been caused by a defect in a thing rather than (say) inaccurate information, or a service that goes wrong.[2] On the other hand, there are pragmatic reasons justifying this separate chapter. First, the idea of product liability as a discrete topic has long shaped legal thought, both in the US and England, and more recently in the EU. The Law Commission[3] and the Pearson Commission[4] both regarded it as raising particular issues and worth treating on its own; and the European Commission accepted that, in the event of harmonisation of liability for products and services, different rules would have to apply.[5] Secondly, products are increasingly subject to special legal regimes, the most important being the statutory scheme of liability under Pt 1 of the Consumer Protection Act 1987, introduced as a result of the EC Directive of July 1985 concerning liability for defective products.[6] Thirdly, even where liability is based on general principles such as negligence, a number of specific topics are in practice peculiar to product liability cases.[7]

10-02 **Defective and dangerous products** There are two kinds of complaint that can be made against a product. One is that it is dangerous and has actually injured the claimant or damaged other property[8] of his. The other is that it cannot be used to full advantage, either because if used it is likely to cause damage, or because it simply does not work, and that the claimant has suffered loss as a result. There is no reason on principle why the law of tort should not cover both.[9] As a broad rule, however, the approach of English law has been to limit it to claims of the former sort, and to leave victims of the latter to their rights (if any) in contract. This ap-

2 See J. Stapleton, *Product Liability*, pp.323 onwards for a resolute attack on the products/services dichotomy.

3 *Liability for Defective Products* (1977) Cmnd.6831.

4 *Royal Commission on Civil Liability and Compensation for Personal Injury* (1978) Cmnd.7054, Ch.22.

5 For the proposal for a draft Directive on liability for services, see Draft Directive 91/C 12/11 (18 January 1991). Unlike the Directive on product liability, the basis of liability here is negligence, albeit with a reversed burden of proof. For a brief account of it, see N. Palmer and E. McKendrick, *Product Liability in the Construction Industry* (1993), pp.192 onwards.

6 Directive 85/374. For coverage of the 1987 Act, which will almost certainly remain in force despite Brexit, see para.10-45 onwards. Another example is the Employer's Liability (Defective Equipment) Act 1969, making employers strictly liable in certain cases for faulty work equipment (see Ch.12). Others include the Vaccine Damage Payments Act 1979, providing for fixed-sum payments to those suffering severe disablement as a result of certain vaccinations; and s.2 of the Automated and Electric Vehicles Act 2018 (not yet in force), imposing an element of strict liability on the insurers of automated vehicles that cause accidents when driving themselves.

7 Straightforward examples are the jurisprudence concerning "probability of intermediate examination" (para.10-37), the flourishing case law on the "duty to warn" (para.10-30), and the requirement for tort purposes of damage to "other property" (para.10-22).

8 And not simply itself. If a television set burns out and wrecks itself but nothing else, this is technically damage to property; nevertheless the gravamen of the owner's complaint is that it did not work, not that it was dangerous. For discussion of what counts as "other property", see para.10-22.

9 As indeed may be the case in more generous jurisdictions such as Canada: e.g. *Rivtow Marine v Washington Iron Works* [1974] S.C.R. 1189, where the owner of a badly-manufactured and unsafe crane recovered in tort for the loss of profits incurred in making it safe to use. A minority of US jurisdictions follow a similar rule: see e.g. *Santor v A & M Karagheusian, Inc*, 44 N.J. 52; 207 A.2d 305 (1965). See generally D. Nolan, "Preventive Damages" (2016) 132 L.Q.R. 68.

proach is also that of the Consumer Protection Act 1987,[10] which specifically limits the types of loss claimable thereunder to personal injury and discrete property damage.[11]

2. Liability in Contract

Contractual liability of sellers etc[12] The contractual liability of sellers and suppliers of goods is technically outside the province of this work. Nevertheless, in practice it is at least as important as tort liability, and some understanding of the liability of a seller under ss.13 and 14 of the Sale of Goods Act 1979 and ss.9–14 of the Consumer Rights Act 2015 (and their equivalent in the case of analogous transactions, such as lease or hire purchase[13]) is necessary for a proper appreciation of the position in tort.[14] It must also be remembered that it is now possible, if the parties so intend, for a seller's liability under a contract of sale to extend not only to his immediate buyer, but also to any third party whom the parties wish to benefit.[15] **10-03**

Contract: compliance with description In any sale of goods by description,[16] there is by s.13 of the Sale of Goods Act 1979 and s.11 of the Consumer Rights Act 2015 an implied term that the goods will comply with any description applied to them. This can clearly have product liability consequences. If, for instance, petrol were sold as diesel fuel, the buyer would no doubt be able to sue in respect of his wrecked car engine.[17] Nevertheless, the significance of these provisions should not be overstated. Only statements about goods that go to identify their essential quality are regarded as part of their "description" in this connection; the mere fact that goods are defective does not prevent them complying with their description. For instance, it has been held that herring meal may be properly described as such, and hence that there is no failure to supply goods answering the contract description, even though the meal contains small amounts admixed of a different substance that poisons animals eating it.[18] **10-04**

---

10 See para.10-47 onwards.

11 And indeed, in the latter case, damage to private (rather than commercial) property: s.5(3). There is also a financial limit; only damage of over £275 is covered: s.5(4).

12 For general coverage of this subject, see *Benjamin on Sale*, 10th edn (London: Sweet & Maxwell, 2017), Ch.11.

13 Hire purchase: Supply of Goods (Implied Terms) Act 1973 ss.10-11; and Consumer Rights Act 2015 s.7. Other contracts: Supply of Goods and Services Act 1982 ss.3-4; and Consumer Rights Act 2015 s.8. These provisions are almost exactly equivalent to those applying to sales, and will not be mentioned further.

14 For an example of where the boundary mattered, see *Wood v Days Health UK Ltd* [2016] EWHC 1079 (QB) (where NHS supplied equipment at a charge, it sold it and was liable for defects accordingly. If it had merely bought it on the patient's behalf, it would not have been liable).

15 Under the Contracts (Rights of Third Parties) Act 1999 s.1.

16 A term which may include sales of specific goods: e.g. *Beale v Taylor* [1967] 1 W.L.R. 1193.

17 A claim of precisely this nature was settled for £400 by Asda Supermarkets in 1995: see *Daily Mail*, 27 November 1995.

18 *Ashington Piggeries Ltd v Christopher Hill Ltd* [1972] A.C. 441. The claimants succeeded under what is now s.14(2) of the 1979 Act, however (see below). See too *Proton Energy Group SA v Orlen Lietuva* [2013] EWHC 2872 (Comm); [2014] 1 Lloyd's Rep. 100.

10-05 **Contract: satisfactory quality** Whenever the seller sells in the course of a business,[19] there is an implied term under s.14 of the Sale of Goods Act 1979 and (in the case of consumers) s.9 of the Consumer Rights Act 2015 that the goods are of "satisfactory quality": that is, that they meet the standard that a reasonable person would regard as satisfactory, taking account of any description of the goods, the price (if relevant) and all the other relevant circumstances.[20] Goods that are defective in normal use[21] will normally therefore give a remedy to the buyer under this section. Not surprisingly, the satisfactory quality duty does not apply in respect of defects specifically notified to the buyer; nor to those which any inspection actually made by the buyer ought to have revealed.[22]

10-06 **Contract: fitness for purpose** In the case of sales in the course of a business, s.14(3) of the Sale of Goods Act 1979 and s.10 of the Consumer Rights Act 2015 imply a term that goods are fit for any particular purpose that the buyer may have made known to the seller (unless the seller proves that the buyer did not rely, or it was unreasonable for him to rely, on his skill or judgment).[23] Like the duty to supply goods of satisfactory quality, this obligation is also apt to catch most cases of goods (especially consumer goods) defective in normal use, since where no specific purpose is notified to the seller he is deemed to promise that the goods are fit for any of the purposes for which those goods are ordinarily used.[24]

10-07 **General features of contractual liability** Actions under the Sale of Goods Act and the equivalent consumer legislation have a number of advantages over proceedings in tort. There is no need to prove fault, only defectiveness, thus making the remedy potentially wider than in the tort of negligence.[25] Furthermore, in contrast to the position in tort, no distinction is drawn between dangerous and ineffective goods, or between physical and economic loss; all losses are recoverable, provided they are not too remote. So if a television set goes wrong the buyer can sue for the cost of repairing it as much as for any injury to himself or damage done to his living room. On the other hand, such liability only applies between parties to a contract of sale. Thus the buyer has no action against the manufacturer or wholesaler with whom he had no contract[26]; equally unprotected are workers, bystanders or donees.[27]

---

19 For what this means, see *Stevenson v Rogers* [1999] Q.B. 1028; and *McDonald v Pollock* [2012] CSIH 12; 2013 S.C. 22. Effectively, any sale of a business asset is covered even if the seller is not generally in the business of selling that kind of asset.

20 1979 Act s.14(2A); the 2015 Act s.9(2). In the case of consumer goods, statements made about the goods by those in the distribution chain are also relevant: the 2015 Act ss.9(6), 9(7).

21 Note that where goods have more than one normal use they must generally be fit for all of them: see the 1979 Act s.14(2B)(a) and the 2015 Act s.9(3)(a).

22 See s.14(2C)(a) and (b) of the 1979 Act; s.9(4) of the 2015 Act.

23 Proviso to s.14(3) of the 1979 Act; see too s.10(4) of the 2015 Act.

24 Sellers were thus liable in *Preist v Last* [1903] 2 K.B. 148 (exploding hot-water bottle unfit for usual purpose); and *Kendall (Henry) Ltd v William Lillico Ltd* [1969] 2 A.C. 31 (general animal food toxic to turkeys). But there are limits: e.g. *Jewson Ltd v Kelly* [2003] EWCA Civ 1030; [2004] 1 Lloyd's Rep. 505 (heating boiler entirely fit for purpose despite being highly extravagant on fuel).

25 See, e.g. *Frost v Aylesbury Dairy Co Ltd* [1905] 1 K.B. 608.

26 Compare developments in the USA, where many States allowed the manufacturer's contractual liability to enure to the benefit of the ultimate consumer: e.g. *Henningsen v Bloomfield Motors, Inc*, 161 A.2d 69 (1960) (New Jersey). But this oddly hybrid form of liability was later overtaken by a genuine common law strict liability: see para.402A of the *Restatement (2d) of Torts*. See generally W. Prosser, "The Assault on the Citadel" (1960) 69 Yale L.J. 1099; J. Stapleton, *Product Liability* (Oxford: OUP, 1994), Ch.2; M.S. Shapo, *Shapo on the Law of Product Liability*, 7th edn (Elgar,

Furthermore, even inter partes liability to commercial buyers can, subject to the provisions of the Unfair Contract Terms Act 1977,[28] be excluded.

3. Negligence

(a) Generally

The rule in Donoghue v Stevenson Tort liability to the world at large for injury due to negligence in the production of goods is almost entirely a twentieth-century phenomenon,[29] though admittedly foreshadowed by earlier dicta.[30] It is based on the foreseeability of damage to members of the public through defectively manufactured articles, and stems from the leading authority of *Donoghue v Stevenson*.[31] A bottle of ginger beer was bought in a café by a purchaser. She gave it to the pursuer, who drank it. Allegedly poisoned as the result of the presence of a decomposed snail in the bottle, the pursuer—who of course had no contractual claim against anyone—sued the manufacturers in tort. On a preliminary point of law as to whether the manufacturers owed her a duty of care, the House ruled by a bare majority that they did, overturning previous authority that the lack of privity of contract barred the action.[32] The general principle was stated by Lord Atkin: 10-08

> "A manufacturer of products which he sells in such a form as to show that he intends them to reach the ultimate consumer in the form in which they left him with no reasonable possibility of intermediate examination, and with the knowledge that the absence of reasonable care in the preparation or putting up of the products will result in an injury to the consumer's life or property, owes a duty to the consumer to take reasonable care."[33]

Extent of the principle Despite early suggestions that it might be limited to food and drink,[34] it is now clear that *Donoghue v Stevenson* applies to products gener- 10-09

2017), Ch.7. It would be theoretically possible for English courts to allow a consumer to sue as third party beneficiary under a contract between, say, manufacturer and wholesaler pursuant to the Contracts (Rights of Third Parties) Act 1999. But it is submitted that this is unlikely unless the contract in question contains clear provisions to that effect.

27 Such as the pursuer in *Donoghue v Stevenson* [1932] A.C. 562. Note, however, the concept of agency may help the buyer's family: e.g. *Lockett v A & M Charles* [1938] 4 All E.R. 170 (family party poisoned by restaurant meal can all sue in contract under what is now s.9 of the Consumer Rights Act 2015).

28 See s.6, allowing exclusion provided the term satisfies the "requirement of reasonableness"; this requirement is defined in s.11. The equivalent provisions on consumer liability under the Consumer Rights Act 2015 cannot, however, be excluded: see s.31 of that Act.

29 Nineteenth-century and indeed early twentieth-century authority was pretty unanimous against such recovery: See *Winterbottom v Wright* (1842) 10 M. & W. 109; *Longmeid v Holliday* (1851) 6 Exch. 761; *George v Skivington* (1869) L.R. 5 Ex. 1; *Bates v Batey* [1913] 3 K.B. 351.

30 e.g. *Heaven v Pender* (1883) 11 Q.B.D. 503 at 510, per Lord Esher. Note, however, that the facts of this case were closer to occupiers' than to manufacturers' liability.

31 [1932] A.C. 562. Strictly speaking this was a Scots case (the events took place in Paisley, near Glasgow), but it was accepted that there was no relevant difference between Scots and English law. The development in it had been anticipated by some 15 years in the USA: *McPherson v Buick Motor Co*, 217 N.Y. 382 (1916).

32 See cases referred to in fn.29. This was not quite as perverse as it sounds. Whoever bought from the manufacturer might have been satisfied with defective goods; if so, why should the manufacturer who had performed his obligations to his immediate buyer be under a greater liability to anyone else?

33 [1932] A.C. 562 at 599.

34 Unsuccessfully argued in *Grant v Australian Knitting Mills Ltd* [1936] A.C. 85.

ally without discrimination as to type. For example, vehicles,[35] tyres,[36] clothing,[37] bottles,[38] and chemicals[39] have all been included within it, as have structures such as a kiosk,[40] tombstone[41] or staircase.[42] It may even be that it extends to products containing information likely to cause actual harm; for example, a misleading do-it-yourself manual or hiker's map.[43] This list is neither exhaustive nor closed. The rule, moreover, covers not only products themselves, but also their containers[44]; it also takes into account warnings and labels.[45] It is normally applied to items sold or constructed for payment, but there is no reason not to extend it to, for example, free samples[46] or for that matter goods supplied other than in the course of a business.[47]

10-10 **Buildings** At first it was held that builders and architects were an exception to *Donoghue v Stevenson*, so that purchasers and others injured by defects had no remedy against them even if they were negligent.[48] It is now established, however, that realty is in no special position in this respect.[49]

10-11 **Who can be sued?** Liability under *Donoghue v Stevenson*[50] began with manufacturers; it is not of course limited to them. It has been extended to negligent designers,[51] installers,[52] erectors[53] and assemblers.[54] And similarly with repairers:

---

35 *Herschtal v Stewart & Ardern Ltd* [1940] 1 K.B. 155.

36 *Carroll v Fearon* [1998] P.I.Q.R. P416.

37 *Grant v Australian Knitting Mills Ltd* [1936] A.C. 85.

38 *Hart v Dominion Stores Ltd* (1968) 67 D.L.R. (2d) 675.

39 *Vacwell Engineering Co Ltd v BDH Chemicals Ltd* [1971] 1 Q.B. 88 (on appeal [1971] 1 Q.B. 111); *Wright v Dunlop Rubber Co Ltd* (1973) 13 K.I.R. 255.

40 *Paine v Colne Valley Electricity Supply Co Ltd* [1938] 4 All E.R. 803.

41 *Brown v Cotterill* (1934) 51 T.L.R. 21.

42 *McGee v RJK Building Services Ltd* [2013] CSOH 10; 2013 S.L.T. 428.

43 Accepted in Scotland: *Munro v Sturrock (t/a Scotmaps)* [2012] CSIH 35 (though the claim failed on the facts).

44 *Watson v Buckley, Osborne, Garrett & Co Ltd* [1940] 1 All E.R. 174. For inadequate warning, see *Labrecque v Saskatchewan Wheat Pool* [1977] 6 W.W.R. 122.

45 *Kubach v Hollands* [1937] 3 All E.R. 907 (chemicals mislabelled, with disastrous results; manufacturer only escapes liability on grounds of intermediate examination). Inadequate warning on label: *Vacwell Engineering Co Ltd v BDH Chemicals Ltd* [1971] 1 Q.B. 88 (settled on appeal without affecting the point: [1971] 1 Q.B. 111).

46 As suggested by Denning LJ in *Hawkins v Coulsdon & Purley Urban DC* [1954] 1 Q.B. 319 at 333.

47 e.g. the baker of a poisonous cake donated to a W.I. stall. cf. *Swanson v Hanneson* (1972) 26 D.L.R. (3d) 201 (owner of car who botched repairs liable to person killed). Note that this may be important, since Pt I of the Consumer Protection Act 1987 is inapplicable here: s.4(1)(c).

48 e.g. *Otto v Bolton & Norris* [1936] 2 K.B. 46.

49 Established beyond doubt in *Murphy v Brentwood DC* [1991] 1 A.C. 398; see at 462, per Lord Keith; at 475, per Lord Bridge; at 487–488, per Lord Oliver. cf. *Clapham v Peacock (t/a Allflames)* [2018] EWHC 518 (TCC). Note, however, that a vendor of dangerous property may still escape liability unless he can be brought within the Defective Premises Act 1972: see para.7-151.

50 [1932] A.C. 562.

51 *Hindustan S.S. Co v Siemens Bros & Co Ltd* [1955] 1 Lloyd's Rep.167; *IBA v EMI (Electronics) Ltd* (1981) 14 B.L.R. 1.

52 *Hartley v Mayoh & Co* [1953] 2 All E.R. 525 (electricity meter wrongly wired; installer liable to fireman electrocuted as a result. Note that the Court of Appeal decision, reported in [1954] 1 Q.B. 383, was concerned only with the liability of the occupiers of the factory and not with that of the installers).

53 *Brown v Cotterill* (1934) 51 T.L.R. 21 (tombstone fell on the claimant in churchyard; monumental mason who negligently put it up held liable).

54 *Malfroot v Noxal Ltd* (1935) 51 T.L.R. 551 (assembler, who fitted a side-car to a motorcycle so

"Where the facts show that no intermediate inspection is practicable", said Goddard LJ, "a repairer of a chattel stands in no different position from that of a manufacturer, and does owe a duty to a person who, in the ordinary course, may be expected to make use of the thing repaired".[55] So repairers were liable when a negligently replaced wheel came off a lorry and knocked over a pedestrian[56]; and when bungled work on a lift caused it to fall to the bottom of the shaft and injure a passenger.[57] Indeed, a repairer may owe a duty not only to carry out the stipulated repairs with due skill, but also to point out to the owner any other dangerous defects that have become apparent.[58]

Distributors etc Not only those involved in production are covered; so also are those further down the distribution chain.[59] Thus a wholesaler must take reasonable steps to check the safety of what he distributes. In the case of products which cannot practically be examined while in his hands, his duty is no doubt limited to taking reasonable steps to deal with reputable suppliers[60]; but in other cases he may have to do more. So in *Watson v Buckley, Osborne, Garrett & Co Ltd*,[61] hair-dye was distributed without any preliminary test being made. The distributors were held liable to a customer who was injured as a result of having his hair treated with it. Retailers, who are of course liable in contract, may also be liable in tort, for example, if they sell goods they have reason to know may be defective, or if they disregard instructions issued by manufacturers or distributors,[62] or if they sell goods with reason to know they are likely to be used to harm others,[63] at least where they 10-12

negligently that it came off and injured the passenger, held liable). See too *Howard v Furness Houlder Argentine Lines Ltd* [1936] 2 All E.R. 781 (assembly of a valve).

55 *Haseldine v Daw & Son Ltd* [1941] 2 K.B. 343, 379 (Goddard LJ).

56 *Stennett v Hancock & Peters* [1939] 2 All E.R. 578; *Power v Bedford Motor Co & Harris* [1959] I.R. 391; *McPherson's Ltd v Eaton* [2005] NSWCA 435; (2005) 65 N.S.W.L.R. 187.

57 *Haseldine v Daw & Son Ltd* [1941] 2 K.B. 343. See too *Swanson v Hanneson* (1972) 26 D.L.R. (3d) 201 (motorist liable for lethally botched do-it-yourself repairs).

58 *Nicholson v John Deere Ltd* (1987) 34 D.L.R. (4th) 542; affirmed (1988) 57 D.L.R. (4th) 639. But a third party injured by such a defect would presumably only recover if he proved that the owner would have repaired the defect in question had he been told about it.

59 For the position of such people under the Consumer Protection Act 1987 Pt I, see para.10-80. It has been suggested, with some reason, that suppliers are unlikely to be liable as such unless there is some matter to put them on notice of the presence of a possible defect: see *Gill v Ethicon SaRL (No 5)* [2019] FCA 1905 at [3628]–[3634] (Katzmann J).

60 cf. *Watson v Buckley* [1940] 1 All E.R. 174 at 181, where distributors were held liable for selling poisonous hair-dye. Stable J stressed their incautiousness in deciding whom to buy from; they had been "dealing with a gentleman who had emerged quite unexpectedly from Spain". Compare *McPherson's Ltd v Eaton* [2005] NSWCA 435; (2005) 65 N.S.W.L.R. 187, where judgment against a retailer of asbestos-contaminated hardboard was set aside, it being wrong to impose on the latter a duty positively to investigate everything it sold for hidden hazards.

61 [1940] 1 All E.R. 174; and see *Goodchild v Vaclight*, *The Times*, 22 May 1965 (importer). The Thalidomide cases involved a similar principle; the drug was imported from Germany and Distillers Ltd, the defendants, were distributors, not manufacturers. See M. Brazier and E. Cave, *Medicine, Patients and the Law*, 6th edn (Penguin, 2016), Ch.10.

62 *Kubach v Hollands* [1937] 3 All E.R. 907 (seller of chemicals failed to test them before sale as instructed; liable for injuries suffered by third party user); and, more recently, *Faisal v Younis* [2018] EWHC 1111 (QB) (negligence of shopkeeper in displaying caustic soda with non-childproof cap within easy reach of small boy who ate some: liability apportioned two-thirds to manufacturer and one-third to retailer). See also *Holmes v Ashford* [1950] 2 All E.R. 76. cf. *Prendergast v Sam & Dee* [1989] 1 Med. L.R. 36 (doctor writes illegible prescription; chemist misreads it and supplies wrong medicine; chemist and doctor both liable to poisoned patient).

63 e.g. *Andrews v Hopkinson* [1957] 1 Q.B. 229 (dealer in second-hand cars). See too the Canadian deci-

do not make it clear to the buyer that the goods are sold with all faults and hence that they should not be used without prior checking.[64] Similar principles apply to second-hand dealers,[65] and to others, such as universities, making products available to those who work with them.[66]

10-13 **Utility supplies** Suppliers of electricity, water, gas etc are equally liable to take due care in so doing. Thus when water supplied by a local authority was plumbosolvent so that it became poisonous when passed through lead piping, and no warnings of the necessary precautions to be taken were given, the authority was held liable.[67]

10-14 **Liability of those undertaking quality control and certification** A number of products may not be marketed at all without extensive prior testing and approval by outside bodies, for instance, medicines.[68] And even where this is not the case products are often voluntarily submitted for checks[69] by experts or certification bodies of one sort or another. The possibility must therefore arise of suing such organisations as an alternative to the actual manufacturers or distributors. Hence the importance of the question: how far do they owe a duty of care to ultimate consumers and others who may suffer if they fail to do it properly?[70] It is suggested that the answer depends on the purpose of the inspection (or the requirement for inspection): if, but only if, it is to protect the claimant against the damage suffered, then there may be liability.

10-15 In practice, it is suggested that those whose function it is to inspect particular items for safety are likely to owe a duty, especially where danger to human life or health is involved: but otherwise claimants face an uphill battle. Thus in a 1969 case[71] private consulting engineers engaged with the specific aim of ensuring the safety of a building hoist were held liable to a workman injured when it collapsed;

---

sion in *Good-wear Treaders v D & B Holdings* (1979) 98 D.L.R. (3d) 59.

64 See *Hurley v Dyke* [1979] R.T.R. 265 (auction seller of dangerous car "with all faults" not liable for subsequent injury to third party).

65 See, e.g. *Herschtal v Stewart and Ardern Ltd* [1940] 1 K.B. 155 (seller of reconditioned car); *Andrews v Hopkinson* [1957] 1 Q.B. 229. Note that it is an offence to sell a car for use on the road which one knows to be defective (Road Traffic Act 1988 s.75); however, breach of this section does not give rise to an action for breach of statutory duty (*Badham v Lambs* [1946] K.B. 45).

66 See *Lewis v Ultra Violet Products Ltd* unreported 14 June 1999 (research student suffering ultraviolet burns from university scientific apparatus: university liable for failure to warn).

67 *Barnes v Irwell Valley Water Board* [1939] 1 K.B. 21. See also *Read v Croydon Corp* [1938] 4 All E.R. 631 (water infected with typhoid). In the later *AB v South West Water Services Ltd* [1993] Q.B. 507 a water authority admitted liability for supplying water admixed with aluminium sulphate; the case was argued purely on the measure of damages.

68 Under the Human Medicines Regulations 2012 (SI 2012/1916). Motor vehicles are another example: see Road Traffic Act 1988 ss.65, 65A and regulations made under these provisions.

69 e.g. a new ship will invariably be submitted to a classification society before first use; mineral water will normally be tested by an independent laboratory; and so on.

70 We are talking here of direct liability to the claimant suffering loss or damage. Such organisations may of course also be liable in contract or (if sufficient proximity is shown) tort to producers whom they have advised and who have found themselves liable to third parties: see, e.g. *Argos Ltd v Leather Trade House Ltd* [2012] EWHC 1348 (QB); [2012] E.C.C. 34.

71 *Driver v William Willetts Ltd* [1969] 1 All E.R. 665. See too dicta of Denning LJ in *Candler v Crane Christmas & Co* [1951] 2 K.B. 164 at 178–179 (hypothetical liability of food analyst); and cf. *Ostash v Sonnenberg* (1967) 68 D.L.R. (2d) 311. For classification societies, see D.R. Thomas (ed.), *Liability Regimes in Contemporary Maritime Law* (Routledge, 2007), Ch.7.

and in *Perrett v Collins*[72] a defendant who wrongly certified an aircraft fit to fly was held to have owed a duty of care to a passenger injured when it crashed. And in the *CJD Litigation*[73] in 1996 Morland J was prepared to hold that the Medical Research Council could be liable in negligence for having continued to promote research into, and consequent production of, hormone products after their ingestion had been shown to carry risks of serious disease. From this it would seem to follow that if a manufacturer entrusted the testing of its products for safety to an independent contractor, it is likely that the latter would owe a duty to anyone injured as a result of failure to spot a defect. There is no case unequivocally holding liable a public body charged with the duty of inspecting particular items, but the possibility remains open.[74]

On the other hand, attempts to fix liability on quality control inspectors and the like for matters other than personal injury have normally failed. Thus those, such as classification societies, charged with inspecting ships and aircraft have escaped liability for economic loss[75] and even property damage[76]; and in Canada a similar result followed where a disappointed purchaser sued an independent tester.[77] As for actions against licensing bodies and the like for failure to warn of defects, or cause products to be taken off the market, these have failed even where personal injury was in issue.[78] It therefore seems that the chances of establishing a duty of care in a body such as the Committee on the Safety of Medicines deciding whether to license a new drug under the Medicines Act 1968[79] are relatively small.[80] 10-16

Independent contractors There is no liability under *Donoghue v Stevenson* for the negligence of independent contractors, provided they were chosen with due 10-17

---

72 [1999] P.N.L.R. 77.

73 Reported under that name at [1996] 7 Med. L.R. 309.

74 The judgment in *Murphy v Brentwood DC* [1991] 1 A.C. 398 exonerating local authorities in respect of building inspections concerned only liability for economic loss. The question of physical damage was pointedly left open by Lord Keith:see at 463. In *Tesco Stores Ltd v Wards Construction Co* (1995) 76 B.L.R. 99 it was stated that such liability, if it existed at all, would be limited to personal injury: hence the lessee of a store which caught fire had no action for the value of lost stock against the local authority which allowed the building to be erected. See too *Attis v Canada* (2008) 300 D.L.R. (4th) 415 (no remedy in Canada against public body charged with overseeing safety of medicines).

75 Thus purchasers of such things have failed, whether of ships (*The Morning Watch* [1990] 1 Lloyd's Rep. 547; *Reeman v Department of Transport* [1997] 2 Lloyd's Rep. 648) or aircraft (*Philcox v Civil Aviation Authority* unreported 25 May 1995).

76 *The Nicholas H* [1996] 1 A.C. 211 (no liability for loss of cargo that went down with unseaworthy ship, though admittedly decision was partly on basis that Hague Rules regime would otherwise be subverted). See M. Clarke, "Negligence-under Control and under Contract" [1994] C.L.J. 220.

77 *Hughes v Sunbeam Corp (Canada) Ltd* (2003) 219 D.L.R. (4th) 467 (defective smoke-alarm: but claim was merely for replacement cost).

78 *Smith v Secretary of State for Health* [2002] EWHC 200 (QB); [2002] Lloyd's Rep. Med. 333 (no common law duty in Secretary of State, through Committee on Safety of Medicines, to pass on warnings about dangers attaching to aspirin in certain circumstances). See too *Graham Barclay Oysters Pty Ltd v Ryan* (2003) 77 A.L.J.R. 183 (supervisory authorities owed no duty to public to close oyster beds on account of risk of hepatitis virus contamination).

79 For discussion of attempts to fix liability on drugs licensing bodies, see M. Brazier and E. Cave, *Medicine, Patients and the Law*, 6th edn (Penguin, 2016), Ch 10; and cf. *Griffin v US*, 500 F.2d 1059 (1974).

80 Note that where quality control is under the aegis of EU legislation, there is no general principle of EU law requiring certifiers to be civilly liable for negligence: *Schmitt v TÜV Rheinland LGA Products GmbH* (Case C-219/15) EU:C:2017:128; [2017] 3 C.M.L.R. 8.

care.[81] However, the independent contractor may himself in certain cases be liable to the claimant.[82]

10-18 **Who can sue?** Anybody who suffers personal injury or damage to property can on principle sue under *Donoghue v Stevenson*, whether buyer,[83] hirer,[84] user,[85] bystander[86] or anyone else.[87] Conceivably, however, there may be exceptions based on public policy. While a bailee of a car is no doubt able to recover from the manufacturer if injured by a defect in it, it is by no means clear that a thief or joy-rider could do the same.[88]

(b) Damage

10-19 **For what damage?** The action under *Donoghue v Stevenson* lies for physical damage only; that is: (1) personal injury[89]; and (2) damage to property other than that alleged to be defective. A person suffering financial loss because he was supplied with defective goods cannot claim.[90] For example, in *Simaan General Contracting Co v Pilkington Glass Ltd (No.2)*[91] contractors building a bank incurred extra costs because glass manufactured by the defendants turned out to be the wrong colour and unacceptable to their clients; they were nevertheless held not to be owed a duty of care by the defendants. Furthermore, where a product causes damage to

---

81 *Taylor v Rover Co Ltd* [1966] 1 W.L.R. 1491 (chisel manufacturer entrusted hardening to third party: not liable for injury caused by third party's negligence). For a case where there was held to be personal negligence despite the employment of an independent contractor, see *Winward v TVR Engineering Ltd* [1986] B.C.L.C. 366 (carburettor fitted to specialist car caught fire; even though bought in from Ford Motor Co, should have been tested before use).

82 cf. *Stennett v Hancock & Peters* [1939] 2 All E.R. 578; and para.10-11.

83 *Grant v Australian Knitting Mills Ltd* [1936] A.C. 85.

84 See *Andrews v Hopkinson* [1957] 1 Q.B. 229.

85 e.g. in *Donoghue v Stevenson* itself; or *Wright v Dunlop* (1973) 13 K.I.R. 255 (worker).

86 e.g. *Stennett v Hancock* [1939] 2 All E.R. 578 (pedestrian injured when lorry lost wheel).

87 Such as a schoolgirl injured by a mislabelled chemical (*Kubach v Hollands* [1937] 3 All E.R. 907), or a visitor to a cemetery hit by a falling tombstone (*Brown v Cotterill* (1934) 51 T.L.R. 21); see too *Power v Bedford Motor Co Ltd* [1959] I.R. 391.

88 Compare *Ashton v Turner* [1981] Q.B. 137; and *Joyce v O'Brien* [2013] EWCA Civ 546; [2014] 1 W.L.R. 70.

89 Including, almost certainly, psychiatric injury: see *Mustapha v Culligan of Canada Ltd* [2008] SCC 27; (2008) 293 D.L.R. (4th) 29 (flies found in bottled water: possibility of recovery accepted, though case failed on facts). It has been held in Australia that, where there would be liability for personal injury, there can be recovery for worry caused, and medical treatment necessitated, by fact that the claimant might have been injured: see the defective serum case of *APQ v Commonwealth Serum Laboratories Ltd* [1999] 3 V.R. 633. One English case lends some support to this: see *CJD Litigation: Group B Plaintiffs v Medical Research Council* (1997) [2000] Lloyd's Rep. Med. 161; (1997) 41 B.M.L.R. 157. But it is unlikely today that an English court would follow this expansive rationale: compare *Rothwell v Chemical & Insulating Co Ltd* [2007] UKHL 39; [2008] 1 A.C. 281.

90 But note *The Orjula* [1995] 2 Lloyd's Rep. 395, where Mance J queried whether an owner who had no realistic option to dispose of the damaged property (in that case, leaking drums of hazardous chemicals on a ship) might be in a different position. Sed quaere.

91 [1988] Q.B. 758. See too *Hamble Fisheries v Gardner* [1999] 2 Lloyd's Rep.1 (boat supplied with defective engine: no action against engine manufacturer for towage expenses due to breakdown); *Finesse Group Ltd v Bryson Products (A Firm)* [2013] EWHC 3273 (TCC); [2013] 6 Costs L.R. 991 (ineffective adhesive); *Barking & Dagenham LBC v GLS Educational Supplies Ltd* [2015] EWHC 2050 (TCC). Also, in the Commonwealth, see *Minchillo v Ford* [1995] 2 V.R. 594; *Bow Valley Husky v St John Shipbuilding Co* [1997] 3 S.C.R. 1210. In *Swick Nominees Ltd v Leroi International Inc* [2015] WASCA 35; (2015) 28 W.A.R. 376 a contrary concession was regarded as thoroughly misguided by Murphy JA and Edelman J at [361]–[411].

itself owing to its own defectiveness (as where a car with defective brakes runs into a wall and is destroyed), the owner is similarly unable to sue the manufacturer in tort.[92] It should be noted, moreover, that this tort bar applies even though the action is framed as one for failure to warn rather than negligent manufacture. Thus in *Hamble Fisheries Ltd v Gardner*[93] a marine engine failed when a piston shattered. Even though the engine manufacturer had known of the pistons' weakness for some time and had been negligent in failing to warn users of them, the claimants' action against him for towage and repair expenses failed.

Punitive damages[94] It was once thought, on the basis of the limitations put on the award of exemplary damages by the decisions in *Rookes v Barnard*[95] and *Cassell & Co Ltd v Broome*,[96] that there was no room for an award of exemplary damages in a negligence case, which of course included products liability.[97] This was because such damages had never been given for negligence prior to *Rookes*; furthermore, even where they were available, they could be had only for a tort committed either by a public authority or by a private party deliberately with a view to the gain exceeding any compensatory damages payable, which itself would exclude all but a small minority of product liability litigation. It is now clear, however, that such damages are available on principle for any tort,[98] and it may well be that the second limitation has also disappeared.[99] If so, it follows that there is jurisdiction to award such damages in a products liability action,[100] at least where there has been a deliberate and outrageous disregard of the claimant's rights,[101] and possibly even 10-20

[92] See *Hamble Fisheries v Gardner* [1999] 2 Lloyd's Rep.1 (boat supplied with defective pistons: no action against engine manufacturer for costs of repair when piston failed); and cf. *Nitrigin Eireann Teoranta v Inco Alloys* [1992] 1 W.L.R. 498 (defective tubing fitted to industrial plant cracks, then later ruptures and devastates plant: for purposes of limitation, no cause of action when tube itself cracked). A similar rule applies to building works on land: see *Murphy v Brentwood DC* [1991] 1 A.C. 398 at 469, per Lord Keith, at 476–478, per Lord Bridge, at 497, per Lord Jauncey; *Bellefield Computer Services Ltd v E Turner & Sons Ltd* [2002] EWCA Civ 1823; [2003] Lloyd's Rep. P.N. 53, and paras 7-144 onwards. But note that it may be possible in a few cases for a court to construct a special relationship giving rise to a duty of care not to cause economic loss: cf. the Scots decision in *Tartan American Machinery Corp v Swan & Co*, 2004 S.C. 276 (packing supervisors may owe duty in respect of damage caused by insufficient packing of machinery).

[93] [1999] 2 Lloyd's Rep. 1. See too *Bow Valley Husky v St John Shipbuilding Co* [1997] 3 S.C.R. 1210; *Man B&W Diesel SE Asia Pte Ltd v PT Bumi International Tankers* [2004] 2 S.L.R. 300. American jurisprudence is to the same effect: *Sea-Land Service, Inc v General Electric Co*, 134 F.3d 149 (1998).

[94] See para.27-134.

[95] [1964] A.C. 1129.

[96] [1972] A.C. 1027.

[97] See *AB v South West Water Services Ltd* [1993] Q.B. 507 (contaminated drinking water).

[98] *Kuddus v Chief Constable of Leicestershire* [2001] UKHL 29; [2002] A.C. 122.

[99] Lord Nicholls was decidedly sceptical about it in *Kuddus*: see [2001] UKHL 29; [2002] A.C. 122 at [66]–[67].

[100] As in the US, where there is a well-developed jurisprudence on the matter: see, e.g. M.S. Shapo, *Shapo on the Law of Products Liability*, 7th edn (Elgar, 2017), Ch.29. A notorious instance is *Grimshaw v Ford Motor Co*, 174 Cal. Rptr. 348 (1981) (the "*Ford Pinto*" case).

[101] e.g. where a defendant continues to market a product in full knowledge of its injurious propensities.

where all that is shown is a very high degree of negligence.[102] Whether such awards will now be made in practice remains to be seen.[103]

10-21 **"Damage"** The proposition that a manufacturer is liable if his product causes "damage" to other property raises a number of issues. First, does *Donoghue v Stevenson* cover products which do not positively cause harm but merely fail to prevent it (for example, where the claimant's house burns down because a defective smoke alarm in it fails to give timely warning of a fire)? The answer is that it does.[104] Secondly, does "damage" under *Donoghue v Stevenson* include loss by theft: for example, where a negligently manufactured burglar alarm fails to work and the claimant's silver vanishes? There is some indirect authority that it does.[105] But this, it is suggested, is a little doubtful. The better position is that, while there may be liability here, the loss is more accurately categorised as economic loss and therefore the claimant must show a sufficient degree of proximity in order to establish a duty of care.[106] Thirdly, it should be remembered that "damage" for these purposes seems to include not only direct physical lesion, but also less direct affectation such as serious contamination.[107]

10-22 **Damage to "other property"** At this point a difficulty arises; for the purposes of the rule in *Donoghue v Stevenson*, what is to count as damage to "other property"? This is particularly troublesome where what fails is a component part of some larger item. Suppose, for instance, a defective tyre explodes and damages the car it is fitted to; or a haulage contractor buys an articulated lorry and a defect in the brakes on the towing unit causes the trailer to be wrecked as well. Is this damage to the defective product itself, or can the car or trailer be regarded as "other

---

[102] The Privy Council awarded such damages for mere gross negligence in the (non-product liability) case of *A v Bottrill* [2002] UKPC 44; [2003] 1 A.C. 449. Although this concerned New Zealand law, it is at least suggestive as regards English law since *Kuddus*.

[103] For exemplary damages generally, see para.27-134 onwards.

[104] *Howmet Ltd v Economy Devices Ltd* [2014] EWHC 3933 (TCC); (2014) 157 Con. L.R. 1, especially at [209] (defective fire protection device can make manufacturer liable for resulting fire, though in the event causation not proved; appealed on other grounds, [2016] EWCA Civ 847; [2016] B.L.R. 555; 168 Con. L.R. 27). See too *Bellefield Computer Services Ltd v E Turner & Sons Ltd* [2000] B.L.R. 97 (assumed, architects potentially liable for defective fire-wall in building which failed to prevent spread of fire: case turned on whether damage to "other property"). Quaere, however, where the claimant cannot show that he relied on the product. It would be odd, for example, if the manufacturer of a defective smoke alarm had to compensate not only the owner who relied on it, but also his neighbour, to whose house the fire spread because of its ineffectiveness. The House of Lords' decision in *Stovin v Wise* [1996] A.C. 923 seems to suggest that positive duties are unlikely to be extended in this way.

[105] See *Stansbie v Troman* [1948] 2 K.B. 48 (workman negligently leaves door unlocked: liable for resulting theft, it being apparently assumed that *Donoghue v Stevenson* applied).

[106] cf. *Bailey v HSS Alarms Ltd*, *The Times*, 20 June 2000 (burglar alarm monitoring company sued for negligence over goods stolen: claimants succeed, but only on a showing that it was fair, just and reasonable to impose liability in the circumstances).

[107] See *The Orjula* [1995] 2 Lloyd's Rep. 395 (container affected by acid: successful tort claim for cost of decontamination); also the insurance case of *Omega Proteins Ltd v Aspen Insurance UK Ltd* [2010] EWHC 2280 (Comm); [2011] 1 All E.R. (Comm) 313 (meat "damaged" when mixed with other meat unsaleable under food laws, even though no physical lesion). And cf. *Blue Circle Industries Ltd v Ministry of Defence* [1999] Ch. 289; and *Magnohard Ltd v United Kingdom Atomic Energy Authority*, 2004 S.C. 247; 2003 S.L.T. 1083 (radioactive contamination, whether or not hazardous, is "damage" within Nuclear Installations Act 1965).

property" so as to attract tort liability?[108] This is a question which it is hard to answer logically, since any product can theoretically be viewed either as an indivisible entity or as a congeries of its individual parts.[109] It is submitted, however, that it ought to be dealt with as follows.

"Other property": components fitted by owner Where the owner himself fitted (or arranged to have fitted) the offending component, it is submitted that he will always be able to sue. Thus if A fits to his car new brake pads negligently manufactured by B which fail and cause the car to crash, A will have an action in negligence against B for the loss of his car.[110] It ought to be sufficient, in other words, if at the time of its acquisition by the claimant, the defective product was not incorporated in the item suffering the damage.[111] On the other hand, this case must it seems be distinguished from that where a claimant assembles a number of ingredients to make something completely new. If a defect in one of those ingredients renders useless the new product as a whole, then this counts as damage to the product itself and hence falls outside the ambit of tortious liability. The point was neatly demonstrated in *Bacardi-Martini Beverages Ltd v Thomas Hardy Packaging Ltd*.[112] Carbon dioxide contaminated with benzene was incorporated into fizzy drinks, which as a result were unsaleable and had to be destroyed. The Court of Appeal was clear that the drinks manufacturer had no claim in tort against the producer of the carbon dioxide.[113] 10-23

"Other property": components fitted by manufacturer etc Where the incorporation or fitment was made by the manufacturer or someone else involved in the distribution chain (e.g. an assembler or dealer), it is suggested that the owner's right to sue will depend on whether the offending product can, looking at the matter from a commercial or common sense point of view, be regarded as an integral part of what he acquired.[114] Only if the answer is no, it is suggested, will there be 10-24

108 Assuming, of course, the manufacturer concerned can be proved to have been negligent.

109 As an American judge put it (in the context of strict products liability): "Since all but the very simplest of machines have component parts, [a contrary] holding would require a finding of 'property damage' in virtually every case where a product damages itself. Such a holding would eliminate the distinction between warranty and strict products liability." (*Northern Power & Engineering Corp v Caterpillar Tractor Co*, 623 P.2d 324 at 330 (1981)).

110 As in *Nitrigin Eireann Teoranta v Inco Alloys* [1992] 1 W.L.R. 498 (defective tubing fitted to industrial plant ruptures and devastates plant: duty of care admitted in relation to everything other than tubing). cf. *M/S Aswan Engineering v Lupdine Ltd* [1987] 1 W.L.R. 1 at 21, per Lloyd LJ.

111 Some American courts draw a distinction between accessories fitted by the owner and replacements for essential parts, and bar a tort action in respect of the latter (e.g. *Sea-Land Service, Inc v General Electric Co*, 134 F.3d 149 (1998)). It is suggested, however, that this solution is unlikely to commend itself in England.

112 [2002] EWCA Civ 549; [2002] 2 Lloyd's Rep. 379.

113 In fact the case turned not on tortious liability as such, but on a clause in the CO2 sale contract limiting the seller's liability to "direct physical damage to property." This clause was held to incorporate the "other property" limitation in tort law: the damage was accordingly held to be outside the seller's responsibility.

114 See, e.g. *Linklaters Business Services v Sir Robert McAlpine Ltd* [2010] EWHC 2931 (TCC); (2010) 133 Con. L.R. 211, especially at [115]–[119] (doubted whether subcontracted assemblers of insulated piping liable in tort to building owners when defectiveness of insulation caused pipe to corrode: insulation and pipe were essentially one and the same thing); also the building cases of *Bellefield Computer Services Ltd v E Turner & Sons Ltd* [2000] B.L.R. 97; and *Payne v John Setchell Ltd* [2002] P.N.L.R. 7 at [183]. Compare also the American approach of asking "What was the object of the bargain?" If it was the composite property, tort is barred (see, e.g. *Shipco v Avondale*, 825 F. 2d 925, 928 (1987)).

potential liability in tort.[115] What counts as an "integral part" will obviously be a matter of degree. It is submitted that where the defective item cannot be readily separated from the damaged property, or is unlikely to be used separately from it, it should normally be regarded as integral. Thus, there should be no liability where a tyre bought already fitted to a car explodes[116]; but in the case of the articulated lorry, where both units can be readily used without the other, the result may well be different. Two cases can illustrate these points. In *M/S Aswan Engineering v Lupdine Ltd*.[117] A bought from B mastic manufactured by B and packed in plastic pails made by C. Because of alleged defects, the pails melted in the Middle Eastern sun and the mastic was lost. A sued C in negligence. The Court of Appeal strongly doubted whether C owed a duty to A.[118] It was artificial to separate the pails from their contents; as Lloyd LJ pithily put it, the claimants were buying mastic *in* pails, not mastic *and* pails.[119] Similarly, in *The Orjula*,[120] shippers of drums of acid negligently packed the drums in defective staging. The staging collapsed; the drums were holed and leaked, damaging a container in which they had been placed. Mance J held that a duty of care was owed in respect of the damage to the container, but not the damage to the drums themselves: the staging and the drum counted as a single item for product liability purposes.

10-25 **"Other property": components fitted by third parties** There is no English authority on the position where the offending component was fitted by someone other than the owner or a party in the distribution chain. Suppose, for example, that A buys a second-hand car from B which is then wrecked owing to defective brakes fitted by B; or again, imagine a ship suffers damage because of a defective valve fitted by a previous bareboat charterer while the vessel was in his hands. It is tentatively suggested that such components fall to be treated in the same way as those fitted by the claimant himself for the purpose of determining the component manufacturer's liability.[121] In the case of the car destroyed by defective brakes, it would be anomalous if the brake manufacturer's liability were to depend on the

---

115 Canadian courts, by contrast, on occasion allow recovery in such cases: see *Plas-Tex Canada Ltd v Dow Chemicals of Canada Ltd* (2005) D.L.R. (4th) 650 (pipes shatter because of defective resin used in manufacture; owners of pipes can sue).

116 It is suggested that the contrary suggestion of Lloyd LJ in *M/S Aswan Engineering v Lupdine Ltd* [1987] 1 W.L.R. 1, 21 should not be followed.

117 [1987] 1 W.L.R. 1. See too *Muirhead v Industrial Tank Specialities Ltd* [1986] Q.B. 507 (manufacturers of motors not liable for repairs to pumps to which they were fitted, and which were damaged when motors cut out); and the Singapore decision in *Man B&W Diesel SE Asia Pte Ltd v PT Bumi International Tankers* [2004] 2 S.L.R. 300 (ship grounded owing to failure of engines: engines negligently manufactured by subcontractors engaged by builders: no tort action by shipowners against subcontractors). In *Bahamasair Holdings Ltd v Messier Dowty Inc* [2018] UKPC 25; [2019] 1 All E.R. 285 this principle may have been lost sight of. Where a part of the landing gear of an aircraft failed, making the machine a total loss, the manufacturer of the relevant part was held liable to the aircraft owner for failure to warn. There is no indication, however, that the part that failed was a replacement, rather than an original, part.

118 A in fact failed on foreseeability grounds, so the question of duty did not fall to be decided.

119 See [1987] 1 W.L.R. 1 at 21.

120 [1995] 2 Lloyd's Rep. 395; A. Tettenborn, "Maritime Consumers? The Consumer Protection Act and Shipping Law" [1986] L.M.C.L.Q. 6.

121 So held by the US Supreme Court, after extensive discussion, in *Saratoga Fishing Co v Martinac* 520 U.S. 875 (1997); [1997] A.M.C. 2113. The position under the Products Liability Directive is different: see para.10-84.

fortuitous circumstance of whether the brakes were last replaced before or after he himself bought the vehicle.

(c) Liability

(i) General

Donoghue v Stevenson: proof of negligence In many cases this gives rise to little difficulty. The duty of the defendant is to take such care as is reasonable in the circumstances[122]; and often the claimant will have clear evidence of defectiveness and of negligence in the defendant. Provided the damage is foreseeable, the claimant will thus recover.[123] Some early cases suggested that the principle res ipsa loquitur could not apply to such cases of product liability,[124] but this heresy now seems to be exploded. In *Carroll v Fearon*[125] the Court of Appeal explicitly discountenanced the idea that product liability cases formed any exception to the general rule. It accordingly held the manufacturers of a defective tyre liable for injuries suffered in an accident when it exploded, despite the lack of specific evidence as to how the defect had arisen. Today it seems accepted that in a suitable case the maxim may be used to aid a claimant otherwise lacking specific evidence of negligence.[126] **10-26**

The duty of the defendant is, of course, only to do what is reasonable, rather than to guard against every risk, however small. It follows that a very slight risk of injury may be run without the defendant necessarily being negligent.[127] Furthermore, in calculating what is reasonable, all the circumstances are in account. For example, in the leading Scottish case on tobacco liability one reason why the defendant cigarette manufacturers escaped liability was that it was not reasonable to expect cigarette manufacturers to cease production even in the face of strong indications of a link with cancer: they were entitled to take account of public demand, the fact that the danger was not latent, and the right of consumers to enjoy hazardous **10-27**

---

122 On the level of duty, see, e.g. *Stokes v GKN (Bolts and Nuts) Ltd* [1968] 1 W.L.R. 1778 at 1783.

123 If it is not foreseeable, then the claim fails on orthodox negligence grounds: e.g. *Hamilton v Papakura DC* [2002] UKPC 9; [2002] 2 N.Z.L.R. 308 (fact that water complied with statutory standards strong indication of lack of fault).

124 e.g. *Donoghue v Stevenson* [1932] A.C. 562 at 622 (Lord Macmillan). See too *Mason v Williams & Williams* [1955] 1 W.L.R. 549.

125 [1998] P.I.Q.R. P416. See too *Howmet Ltd v Economy Devices Ltd* [2014] EWHC 3933 (TCC); (2014) 157 Con. L.R. 1, where at [199]–[201], Edwards-Stuart J thought that even where defects in a fire safety device were unexplained and might have been due to components bought in elsewhere, the failure to have a rigorous system of testing might itself be evidence of negligence. The case was appealed on other grounds at [2016] EWCA Civ 847; [2016] B.L.R. 555; 168 Con. L.R. 27

126 See *Divya v Toyo Tire & Rubber Co Ltd* [2011] EWHC 1993 (QB); also the earlier decisions in *Hill v James Crowe (Cases) Ltd* [1978] 1 All E.R. 812; and *Evans v Triplex Safety Glass Co* [1936] 1 All E.R. 283, and the Canadian decisions in *Farro v Nutone Electrical Ltd* (1990) 72 O.R. (2d) 637 (electric fan which caught fire later mislaid by investigators: inference of negligent defect); and *Johansson v General Motors of Canada Ltd*, 2012 NSCA 120; (2012) 324 N.S.R. (2d) 252 (car mysteriously swerving).

127 See *Graham Barclay Oysters Pty Ltd v Ryan* (2003) 77 A.L.J.R. 183 (High Court of Australia refused to find oyster farmers negligent for failing to cease production when there was a small, but quantifiable, risk of hepatitis contamination following floods in their spawning grounds). cf. *Hamilton v Papakura DC* [2002] UKPC 9; [2002] 2 N.Z.L.R. 308, where the Privy Council clearly thought very slight traces of contaminants in water supply acceptable.

pleasures if they wanted.[128] The fact that the product complies with minimum standards set by governmental or other organisations is evidence against negligence in the producer,[129] though no doubt it is not conclusive. Conversely, if the product does not comply with such standards it is suggested that this is evidence, though not conclusive evidence, of negligence.

(ii) Manufacturing and design defects

10-28 **Manufacturing and design defects**[130] Most cases under *Donoghue v Stevenson* have concerned manufacturing defects; that is, products which left the manufacturer[131] with something unintentionally wrong with them. Here, absent fairly clear evidence that the defect was unforeseeable or not reasonably avoidable, the defendant will rarely escape liability in practice. In "design defect" cases, by contrast, the product is manufactured as intended, but the design itself provides some foreseen or unforeseen danger which it is alleged evidences negligence.[132] Most drug cases, as in the Thalidomide or Opren litigation, fall in this category. But it extends much further, to include (for example) inherently unstable cranes,[133] cars which are overprone to catch fire in the event of an accident,[134] or products which continue to make use of noxious chemicals after the danger of such substances has become apparent.[135] Here the claimant, while clearly owed a duty of care, faces extra difficulty.

10-29 First he bears the burden of proving that the risk ought to have been foreseen at the time the product left the defendant's control; in the drug cases, for example, by showing inadequate testing.[136] And secondly, there is the problem of risk and benefit. A manufacturer may be justified in taking even a known or foreseeable risk if the benefits of the product to society[137] or the individual[138] warrant it, particularly if an adequate warning is incorporated.[139] For example, cheap cars have fewer safety features than luxury models; nevertheless, despite the increased risk of injury, this does not as such make the manufacturer of such cars negligent. Or it may be impossible to avoid danger without withdrawing the product entirely; matches must burn, whisky can intoxicate and medicine on occasion will create side-effects, and it can hardly be negligent as such to produce such things. In general, it is suggested that,

128 *McTear v Imperial Tobacco Ltd*, 2005 2 S.C. 1 at [7.172]. A similar claim fared the same way in New Zealand: *Pou v British-American Tobacco Ltd* [2006] 1 N.Z.L.R. 661.

129 *Hamilton v Papakura DC* [2002] UKPC 9; [2002] 2 N.Z.L.R. 308 (fact that water complied with statutory standards strong indication of lack of fault).

130 See para.10-57 onwards, for discussion of this problem under the 1987 Act.

131 Or repairer, distributor etc as the case may be.

132 cf. *Davie v New Merton Board Mills* [1959] A.C. 604 at 626, per Viscount Simonds; *Hindustan Shipping Co Ltd v Siemens Bros Ltd* [1955] 1 Lloyd's Rep. 167 at 177, per Willmer LJ.

133 *Rivtow Marine v Washington Iron Works* (1973) 40 D.L.R. (3d) 530.

134 For a well-known American example, see the "Ford Pinto case": *Grimshaw v Ford Motor Co*, 174 Cal.Rptr. 348 (1981).

135 e.g. *Wright v Dunlop Rubber Co* (1973) 13 K.I.R. 255.

136 On which, cf. *Best v Wellcome Foundation* [1993] 3 I.R. 421.

137 Quaere: can account be taken of the fact that production creates employment which would otherwise be lost? An American federal court has said not, in the case of tobacco: *Cipollone v Liggett Group, Inc*, 644 F. Supp. 283 (1986).

138 Compare the American decision in *Cipollone v Liggett Group, Inc*, 644 F. Supp. 283 (1986) (fact that smokers enjoy cigarettes relevant to determination of whether manufacturers negligent).

139 For the duty to warn, see para.10-30.

provided a product satisfies a genuine demand, is as safe as it can be made at reasonable cost, and its danger is not out of all proportion to its social benefits,[140] an action in negligence will fail. Hence it seems that, at least with regard to negligence, the chances of success against such persons as the makers of fast cars,[141] chain saws and (more controversially) tobacco are low.

(iii) Failure to warn

The duty to warn Whether or not producing a dangerous product is negligent, failing to label it adequately or to provide sufficient warnings about it may well be. So a manufacturer of chemicals was held liable for failing to warn of the hazard of serious explosion when it came into contact with water[142]; a similar conclusion was reached in the case of a flammable wall-coating which contained no indication of its combustibility[143]; and there are numerous other illustrations.[144] A fortiori, if safety instructions are actually misleading there can equally be liability.[145] It is not inconceivable that a duty to warn might extend to products other than the product itself. Physicians, for example, in prescribing generic drugs based on a proprietary pharmaceutical may well rely on information provided by the producer of the latter; again, a product innocuous in itself might well be regularly used in conjunction with a dangerous one. No English authority has yet gone this far, however; and it is suggested that in view of the necessity of keeping liability within reasonable bounds such liability should rarely, if ever, be held to exist.[146] **10-30**

Whether a duty to warn arises will depend on the circumstances, including not only the level of danger but also the practicality of issuing a warning[147] and the obviousness of the danger to the reasonable user. Thus in the Scots tobacco decision in *McTear v Imperial Tobacco Ltd*[148] the claim failed partly because at the time the pursuer's husband had started to smoke the possible dangers of smoking were well-known to anyone who cared to heed them.[149] Where the duty applies, the warn- **10-31**

---

140 cf. the Canadian case of *O'Fallon v Inecto Rapid* [1940] 4 D.L.R. 276. See too P. Ferguson, "Pharmaceutical Products Liability" [1993] J.R. 226.

141 cf. the American decision in *Schemel v General Motors*, 384 F.2d 802 (1967) (not negligent per se to produce car capable of 115mph).

142 *Vacwell Ltd v BDH Chemicals Ltd* [1971] 1 Q.B. 88.

143 *E Hobbs (Farms) Ltd v Baxenden (Chemical Co) Ltd* [1992] 1 Lloyd's Rep. 54.

144 See *Watson v Buckley etc* [1940] 1 All E.R. 174 (hair-dye likely to cause serious reaction); *Carroll v Fearon* [1998] P.I.Q.R. P146 (tyre likely to explode); *Bow Valley Husky v St John Shipbuilding Co* [1997] S.C.R. 1210 (flammable pipe cladding sold for use on oil-rigs); *Hollis v Dow Corning Corp* (1996) 129 D.L.R. (4th) 609 (breast implant likely to rupture after installation). For the American position, which is much more developed, see J. Henderson & A. Twerski, "Doctrinal Collapse in Products Liability: The Empty Shell of Failure to Warn" 65 N.Y.U.L.R. 265 (1990); M.S. Shapo, *Shapo on the Law of Products Liability*, 7th edn (2017), Ch.19.

145 See the Canadian decision in *A & L Plumbing & Heating Ltd v Ridge Tool Co* (2010) 350 Sask. R. 148 (user encouraged to keep hand on rope that went round drum, with result that hand snagged).

146 Compare the US Supreme Court decision in *Air & Liquid Systems Corp v DeVries*, 139 S.Ct. 986 (2019) (equipment that required asbestos add-ons to work: duty to warn of danger emanating from the latter). One California court has, perhaps worryingly, held a proprietary drug producer potentially liable for failing to warn a user of generics based on it. See *Conte v Wyeth, Inc*, 85 Cal.Rptr. 3d 299 (2008); (2009) 105 B.M.L.R. 122.

147 *Coal Pension Properties Ltd v Nu-Way Ltd* [2009] EWHC 824 (TCC); [2009] N.P.C. 65

148 2005 2 S.C. 1.

149 See 2005 2 S.C. 1 at [7.167] onwards. A similar conclusion was reached in New Zealand in *Pou v British-American Tobacco Ltd* [2006] 1 N.Z.L.R. 661. See too *B (A Child) v McDonald's Ltd* [2002]

ing must for obvious reasons be such as to make the user as safe as reasonably possible.[150] In an appropriate case, a warning to retailers or other professional users, rather than to the ultimate consumer, may suffice.[151] This is likely to be particularly important[152] in the case of drugs and other complex products where the end user may not be sufficiently qualified to take proper account of any warning given, and in other cases where warning each individual user would be impracticable.[153] On occasion, it is suggested that those other than manufacturers, such as retailers, distributors or local affiliates of the manufacturer, may themselves come under a duty to warn.[154]

10-32 **Failure to warn: dangers subsequently appearing** The above duty to warn is limited to dangers that should have been apparent when the product left the defendant's hands, hindsight being out of account.[155] However, even after this time, if a clear indication of a serious danger is received, the manufacturer may be under a duty to take reasonable steps to bring it to the attention of those likely to be affected.[156] Thus in *E Hobbs (Farms) Ltd v Baxenden (Chemical Co) Ltd*[157] manufacturers selling supposedly flameproof wall-coverings discovered subsequently that they were more flammable than they seemed. They were held to owe a duty to bring this to the attention of previous customers. Moreover, it is possible that this duty may also attach to someone who was not himself the manufacturer, but has taken over the manufacturer's business and continued to market the

EWHC 490 (QB) (no duty to warn of danger of scalding by hot drinks served in fast food outlet); *Deshane v Deere & Co* (1994) 106 D.L.R. (4th) 385 (patent danger in forage harvester). In *Bow Valley Husky v St John Shipbuilding Co* [1997] 3 S.C.R. 1210 it was suggested by the Canadian Supreme Court that obviousness was not enough per se to negative a duty to warn, and that the claimant must be shown to have agreed to accept the risk so as to be volens. Sed quaere.

150 *Vacwell v BDH* [1971] 1 Q.B. 88 (chemical; warning of "harmful vapour" does not absolve manufacturers in case of violent explosion on contact with water). See too *Can-Arc Helicopters Ltd v Textron Ltd* (1992) 86 D.L.R. (4th) 404. By contrast, see *Cassels v Marks & Spencer Plc* [2002] 1 I.R. 179 (warning to "keep away from fire" sufficient to absolve defendants who sold inflammable cotton dress that burst into flames when child left alone next to open fire).

151 See *Holmes v Ashford* [1950] 2 All E.R. 76. For some scepticism on the applicability of the so-called "learned intermediary" defence, see *Peterson v Merck Sharpe & Dohme (Aust) Pty Ltd* [2010] FCA 180; (2010) 266 A.L.R. 1 at [796]–[798].

152 Though not exclusively so: cf. *Lewis v University of Bristol* unreported June 14, 1999 CA below; and the Massachusetts decision in *Carrel v National Cord & Braid Corp*, 852 N.E.2d 100 (2006) (bungee-jumping equipment: sufficient to warn organisers of events).

153 See *Lewis v University of Bristol* unreported 14 June 1999 CA (ultra-violet apparatus burned researcher who failed to appreciate danger: sufficient to provide adequate instruction and warning to university rather than actual user). See too *Bow Valley Husky Ltd v St John Shipbuilding Co* [1997] 3 S.C.R. 1210, where it was suggested that this "learned intermediary" defence was likely to be limited in practice to the situations mentioned in the text. Hence where pipe-cladding for oil-rigs was unusually flammable, it was not sufficient for the manufacturers to warn the suppliers.

154 So held in Canada: see the Alberta decision in *Hutton v General Motors of Canada Ltd* [2010] ABQB 606; [2011] 4 W.W.R. 284 (Canadian distribution branch of General Motors under duty to warn Canadian user of defect in car, despite car itself having been manufactured by the American parent company (in Mexico)).

155 Under the "no hindsight" principle exemplified by the medical negligence case of *Roe v Ministry of Health* [1954] 2 Q.B. 66.

156 Presumably on the basis that he who without fault creates a situation of danger is bound to act reasonably to alleviate it: e.g. *Wright v Lodge* [1993] 4 All E.R. 299.

157 [1992] 1 Lloyd's Rep. 54. See too *Nicholson v John Deere Ltd* (1987) 57 D.L.R. (4th) 639; and *United Central Bakeries Ltd v Spooner Industries Ltd* [2013] CSOH 150.

product.[158] On the other hand, in deciding whether to give a warning the necessity of desirability of avoiding undue alarm will also be taken into account.[159] It should be noted that there exist statutory powers to compel manufacturers and others to issue warnings about suspect products.[160] No doubt the fact that such an order had been made would furnish some evidence of negligence in a manufacturer who had not included such a warning, and be a strong indication of negligence in a manufacturer who failed to obey it once made.

Effect of warning In either case of failure to warn, the claimant still has to prove causation: i.e. that had there been a warning it would have been heeded and hence his loss would not have been suffered.[161] Since warnings are often disregarded in practice, this is likely to be a heavy burden which will make it difficult for many claimants to succeed on a "failure to warn" basis.[162] **10-33**

(iv) Failure to recall defective products

Duty to recall In extreme cases where a product proves dangerous after it has left the defendant's control, it is suggested that there may be a duty to recall it.[163] If the claimant can prove that he would have heeded such a call and thus avoided injury, it follows that he will have a potential cause of action against the manufacturer.[164] If a recall is made, not surprisingly the manufacturer may be liable for failing to carry out the relevant modifications properly.[165] **10-34**

---

158 Suggested by Tuckey and Nourse LJJ in *Hamble Fisheries Ltd v Gardner* [1999] 2 Lloyd's Rep. 1 at 7, 10. See too *Hutton v General Motors of Canada Ltd* [2010] ABQB 606; [2011] 4 W.W.R. 284 (Canadian distribution branch of General Motors).

159 See *Thompson v Johnson & Johnson* [1991] 2 V.R. 449 (possibility of toxic shock syndrome resulting from use of tampons).

160 Consumer Protection Act 1987 s.13(1)(b). Such orders can be issued if the Secretary of state believes goods to be unsafe within the General Product Safety Regulations 2005 (SI 2005/1803): see General Product Safety Regulations 2005 (SI 2005/1803) regs 12, 13.

161 See *Carroll v Fearon* [1998] P.I.Q.R. P146; *Best v Wellcome Foundation* [1993] 3 I.R. 421.

162 Thus in *Carroll v Fearon* [1998] P.I.Q.R. P146 the claimant failed to show that a warning of the defectiveness of the tyre would have made any difference (though she succeeded on the basis of negligent manufacture). Lack of proof that a warning would have been heeded also defeated the tobacco claimant in *Pou v British-American Tobacco Ltd* [2006] 1 N.Z.L.R. 661. In *Hollis v Dow Corning Ltd* (1996) 129 D.L.R. (4th) 609, La Forest J suggested in the Supreme Court of Canada that in "learned intermediary" cases of this sort the claimant did not have to prove that the intermediary would have acted on the warning. In his view either the burden of proof was on the defendant, or (more radically) there should be a conclusive presumption that he would have done so. With respect, it is submitted that neither proposition is good law in England.

163 Under the General Product Safety Regulations 2005 (SI 2005/1803) reg.15, the Secretary of State or a local authority may require recall of any product reasonably believed to be dangerous.

164 See, e.g. *Walton v British Leyland UK Ltd* unreported 1978 (see [1980] Product Liability International, August, p.156). On the American jurisprudence in this area, which is much better developed than the English, see Matula (1996) 32 Tort & Ins. L.J. 87.

165 *Hutton v General Motors of Canada Ltd* [2010] ABQB 606; [2011] 4 W.W.R. 284 (air-bags on cars deployed when they should not; modification inadequate to prevent reprise of problem; liability imposed).

(d) Causation

10-35 **Causation**[166] As in the rest of the law of negligence, the burden of proof of this falls on the claimant in a product liability action. Unless he can prove not only that the defendant manufacturer was negligent but also that this amounted to at least a substantial cause[167] of his injury, he will fail. This may be significant in product liability situations. The claimant who becomes ill having taken a defective drug may only be able to show that the drug was one of a number of possible causes of his illness.[168]

10-36 More difficult issues arise where it is clear what the cause of the claimant's damage is, but not who was responsible. One problem is where a claimant has been exposed repeatedly to a dangerous substance (of whose hazards, say, no proper warning was given) manufactured by a series of different manufacturers, but it is not clear which bout of exposure made him ill. Although theoretically he should fail in such a case for lack of proof as to whose negligence caused his damage, the inference seems irresistible that here he would be able to invoke the exceptional rule in *Fairchild v Glenhaven Funeral Services Ltd*[169] and recover in full from any defendant who cannot positively exculpate himself. A yet more awkward case, where again the claimant ought logically to fail on causation grounds, is where he has been injured by a single exposure to a substance, but that substance is produced by a number of manufacturers and it is not clear whose product injured him.[170] American courts have on occasion been prepared to modify the law of causation here, at least to make the defendant liable for a part of the loss proportional to his market share.[171] But the House of Lords was decidedly non-committal as to whether the English courts would adopt any such rule.[172] For the moment, it seems that an English claimant will continue to fail in such a situation.

---

166 See generally Ch.2; *Best v Wellcome Foundation* [1993] 3 I.R. 421; Goldberg [1996] A-A. L. Rev. 286; Goldberg (1996) 4 Med. L. Rev. 32.

167 And not, it seems, any lower test. In *Hanke v Resurfice Corp* [2007] 1 S.C.R. 333; [2007] 4 W.W.R. 1, the Supreme Court of Canada confirmed that in ordinary product liability cases the standard rules of causation applied, and would not be relaxed in favour of a "material contribution" criterion. Similarly in the tobacco case of *Pou v British-American Tobacco Ltd* [2006] 1 N.Z.L.R. 661 Lang J refused to make any exception to the normal rules. On the other hand, courts can sometimes be highly creative within those rules: cf. *Samaan v Kentucky Fried Chicken Pty Ltd* [2012] NSWSC 381 (salmonella poisoning; claim against restaurant; court inferred causation simply from evidence that restaurant in question had regularly infringed hygiene standards).

168 cf. *Hotson v East Berkshire AHA* [1989] A.C. 750. Moreover, in *McTear v Imperial Tobacco Ltd*, 2005 2 S.C. 1 Lord Nimmo Smith in the Court of Session significantly declined to accept statistical evidence of a correlation between smoking and cancer as probative of the issue before him.

169 [2002] UKHL 22; [2003] 1 A.C. 32, on which see para.2-53. In this case, which concerned asbestos, the serial defendants were employers rather than manufacturers; but that can hardly make any difference.

170 For example, where it is not clear whose defective batch of some generic drug poisoned the claimant.

171 See the well-known decision in *Sindell v Abbott Laboratories* 607 P. 2d 924 (1980); and generally E. Handsley, "Market Share Liability and the Nature of Causation in Tort" (1993) 1 Torts L.J. 24. A Dutch court went further and held the defendant in a similar case liable in full (*Hoge Raad*, 9 October 1992, N.J. 1994, 535); see J. Teulings, "DES and the Market Share Liability in the Netherlands" (1994) 110 L.Q.R. 228. cf. too the (Irish) Civil Liability Act 1961 s.11(3).

172 *Fairchild v Glenhaven Funeral Services Ltd* [2002] UKHL 22; [2003] 1 A.C. 32 at [78], per Lord Hoffmann.

(e) Qualification of negligence liability

(i) Probability of intermediate examination

Prospect of intermediate examination may affect liability In *Donoghue v Stevenson*[173] Lord Atkin qualified the principle of manufacturers' liability by referring specifically to products intended "to reach the consumer in the form in which they left him, with no reasonable possibility of intermediate examination." The reason for this limitation was twofold: first, an intermediate examination may affect causation, and secondly, a manufacturer should be able to satisfy his duty of care by supplying goods which are safe when used by a reasonable intermediary.[174] As Lord Macmillan put it: 10-37

> "I can readily conceive that where a manufacturer has parted with his product and it has passed into other hands, it may well be exposed to vicissitudes which may render it defective or noxious. It may be a good general rule to regard responsibility as ceasing when control ceases. So also, where between the manufacturer and the user there is interposed a party who has the means and opportunity of examining the manufacturer's product before he reissues it to the actual user. … the intervention of any exterior agency is intended to be excluded."[175]

Intermediate examination: "probability" or "possibility"? The limitation originally placed on *Donoghue v Stevenson* liability was a severe one; but it was perhaps understandable, if only because in 1932 there was no provision for contribution between tortfeasors,[176] and therefore it might well be unduly drastic to make a manufacturer liable for an accident that was predominantly someone else's fault. This is no longer so, however; and in the light of subsequent authority, the phrase "probability of intermediate examination" is now more accurate.[177] This represents a noticeable extension of the manufacturer's liability. The point is nicely illustrated by *Griffiths v Arch Engineering Co Ltd*.[178] The defendants hired out a dangerous grinding-wheel to a firm of contractors, one of whose workmen was injured using it. They were held liable to the workman, even though an intermediate examination was clearly a possibility. The prospect of such an examination, said Chapman J,[179] would exonerate the defendant if, and only if, he had reason to 10-38

173 [1932] A.C. 562 at 599 (see too at 578).

174 cf. *Kubach v Hollands* [1937] 3 All E.R. 907.

175 [1932] A.C. 562 at 622.

176 A point made in J.A. Weir, "Negligence-Duty of Care-Foreseeability" [1964] C.L.J. 23, 24–25. Contribution was first introduced by the Law Reform (Married Women and Tortfeasors) Act 1935 s.6. See now Civil Liability (Contribution) Act 1978 s.1.

177 "Perhaps, therefore, without disrespect, the word 'probability' may be substituted for 'possibility'. If there be such a probability the relationships between manufacturer and ultimate user or consumer will not be proximate."—Goddard LJ in *Paine v Colne Valley Electricity Supply Co Ltd* [1938] 4 All E.R. 803 at 808-809. See too *Haseldine v Daw & Son Ltd* [1941] 2 K.B. 343 at 376; *Holmes v Ashford* [1950] 2 All E.R. 76; *Mason v Williams & Williams Ltd* [1955] 1 W.L.R. 549; *Hindustan SS Co Ltd v Siemens Bros* [1955] 1 Lloyd's Rep. 167. For a case where such a probability seems to have been found as a reason to deny liability, see the Scots decision in *Renfrew Golf Club v Motocaddy Ltd* [2016] CSIH 57; 2016 S.C. 860 (electric golf caddy mysteriously self-ignited and damaged clubhouse where stored; recovery in negligence denied, apparently on the basis that there had been any number of prospects of intermediate interference).

178 [1968] 3 All E.R. 217.

179 [1968] 3 All E.R. 217 at 222. For similar dicta, see too *Gallagher v McDowell Ltd* [1961] N.I. 26 at 42, per Lord McDermott LCJ.

believe that whoever carried out any subsequent examination would use the opportunity to indicate the risk and warn subsequent users.

10-39 If there is no relevant probability of intermediate examination, then an actual examination by a third party will normally make no difference. For example, in *Lambert v Lewis*[180] manufacturers supplied a defective towing coupling to retailers, who sold it to a customer for use on a Land Rover. The latter, though apparently aware of the defect, continued to use it for some months. The coupling broke and a collision occurred with another car. The trial judge nevertheless held the manufacturers liable to the persons in the other car.[181] But it should be noted that egregious folly on some third party's part may have the effect of breaking the chain of causation. Thus in *Taylor v Rover Co Ltd*[182] employers bought in chisels from specialist manufacturers, who in turn engaged independent contractors to harden them. Owing to negligence in the hardening process a chisel splintered and injured an employee of the first defendants. They did not withdraw the chisel from use, and about four weeks later another piece flew off and it injured the claimant. The employers were held liable to the claimant, but the manufacturers were not: apart from the fact that they had entrusted the hardening to an apparently competent third party, the employers' continued use of the chisel broke the chain of causation between the negligent manufacture and the injury.

(ii) Default of the claimant

10-40 **No liability for consequence of knowing use** If the claimant himself discovers a product is defective, but proceeds to use it, this may be sufficient to break the chain of causation between the defendant's negligence and his loss. As Lord Wright put it in *Grant v Australian Knitting Mills Ltd*[183]:

> "The principle of *Donoghue's* case can only be applied where the defect is hidden and unknown to the consumer, otherwise the directness of cause and effect is absent: the man who consumes or uses a thing which he knows to be noxious cannot complain in respect of whatever mischief follows, because it follows from his own conscious volition in choosing to incur the risk or certainty of mischance."

Thus in *Gledhill v Liverpool Abattoir Ltd*[184] a slaughterman injured through using unsuitable equipment provided by the defendants failed in his action against them on proof that he had known all along of the unsuitability. Similarly, in the New Zealand decision in *Pou v British-American Tobacco Ltd*,[185] the claimant in a

---

180 [1978] 1 Lloyd's Rep. 610. This was not appealed when the case went to the House of Lords: see *Lexmead (Basingstoke) Ltd v Lewis* [1982] A.C. 225. A similar conclusion was reached in the real property case of *Pearson Education Ltd v Charter Partnership Ltd* [2005] EWHC 2021 (TCC); [2006] P.N.L.R. 14; affirmed [2007] EWCA Civ 130; [2007] B.L.R. 324 (intermediate examination of building made no difference to claim against designers).

181 The manufacturers' liability to the claimants was not contested on appeal: see [1982] A.C. 225.

182 [1966] 1 W.L.R. 1491.

183 [1936] A.C. 85 at 105. Compare *Lexmead (Basingstoke) Ltd v Lewis* [1982] A.C. 225 (claimant who knowingly uses defective goods cannot complain of resulting damage under Sale of Goods Act 1979).

184 [1957] 1 W.L.R. 1028. See too *Nitrigin Eireann Teoranta v Inco Alloys Ltd* [1992] 1 W.L.R. 498 (where, however, the defence failed on the facts); and *Howmet Ltd v Economy Devices Ltd* [2016] EWCA Civ 847; [2016] B.L.R. 555; 168 Con. L.R. 27.

185 [2006] 1 N.Z.L.R. 661.

tobacco suit failed because, among other things, she had voluntarily continued to smoke knowing of the hazards that might attach to that activity.[186] On the other hand, a claimant who acts reasonably in the circumstances, for instance by unloading a dangerous barge in a situation of some urgency, will not be barred merely because he knew the risk he was running.[187] Furthermore, barring the risk-taking claimant entirely is an extreme solution; and while it may be appropriate to a claimant knowingly and recklessly endangering himself,[188] it is suggested that in most cases today the claimant will merely have his damages reduced on account of contributory negligence.[189]

(iii) Defect arose after product left defendant's hands

Subsequently-appearing defects out of account There will be no liability if the chattel was not dangerous at the time when the defendant parted with it, and he had no reason to anticipate that it would become dangerous.[190] It is for the claimant to prove that the article was defective at the time it left the manufacturer, which he might succeed in doing if he can show on a balance of probability that nothing had occurred since then to add to the defect.[191] 10-41

(iv) Unexpected or misguided use

No liability for consequences of unforeseeable use There is generally no liability under *Donoghue v Stevenson* if the use to which the chattel is put is illegitimate or substantially different from that for which it was intended by the manufacturer.[192] So in the Scottish decision of *Eccles v Cross*[193] the manufacturers 10-42

---

186 On the other hand, Lang J accepted that had she proved that she only continued to smoke because addicted, and that she had taken all reasonable steps to stop, this defence would not have been open.

187 *Denny v Supplies & Transport Co Ltd* [1950] 2 K.B. 374. cf. *Targett v Torfaen BC* [1992] 3 All E.R. 27 (occupier did not lose right to sue for injury resulting from dangerous defect in house merely because he continued to occupy it having discovered its state, as he had to live somewhere).

188 cf. *Morris v Murray* [1991] 2 Q.B. 6 (not a products liability case, but on the same principle).

189 cf. *Farr v Butters Bros Ltd* [1932] 2 K.B. 606 (claimant killed while erecting obviously dangerous crane held contributorily negligent). There he failed entirely, because at that date contributory negligence was a complete defence. Today there would be apportionment under the Law Reform (Contributory Negligence) Act 1945. So too with a claimant disregarding a clear warning: cf. the Washington decision in *Matthias v Lehn & Fink Products Corp*, 424 P.2d 284 (1967). However, the decision in *Howmet Ltd v Economy Devices Ltd* [2016] EWCA Civ 847; [2016] B.L.R. 555; 168 Con. L.R. 27 may presage a stricter view in future.

190 Inference from *Pattendon v Beney* (1934) 50 T.L.R. 204, per Horridge J and especially Scrutton LJ at 204. See too *Smith v Inglis* (1978) 83 D.L.R. (3d) 215; and *Dollaire v PE Mantel* (1990) 62 D.L.R. (4th) 182 (safety features dispensed with by user).

191 See, for an example, *Divya v Toyo Tire & Rubber Co Ltd (t/a Toyo Tires of Japan)* [2011] EWHC 1993 (QB) (high-speed tyre blow-out otherwise unexplained: judge prepared to infer that there must have been a defect in the tyre at the time of manufacture); also *Smith v Inglis* (1978) 83 D.L.R. (3d) 215. And cf. *Evans v Triplex Safety Glass Co* [1936] 1 All E.R. 283. But Scottish courts may be more cautious here. In the broadly similar *McGlinchey v General Motors UK Ltd* [2012] CSIH 91, the Inner House of the Court of Session, faced with an inexplicable handbrake failure which injured a motorist, held that the judge had rightly declined to draw from this the inference of a manufacturing defect, and dismissed the claim.

192 See *M/S Aswan v Lupdine Ltd* [1987] 1 W.L.R. 1, 23 (Lloyd LJ).

193 1938 S.C. 697.

of temporary lighting were held not liable when it was used as a permanent fixture and a workman was electrocuted as a result. On the other hand, presumably the manufacturer cannot take advantage of this defence if the accident would have occurred even in normal use,[194] nor if the misuse is itself foreseeable.[195] So failure to encase dangerous medicine in a child-proof bottle may well be negligent, even though *ex hypothesi* it can only cause harm in the case of misuse by a child.

(v) Abnormally sensitive claimants

10-43 **No liability for damage caused by unusual sensibility** At least where ordinary articles of commerce are concerned, it is suggested that a manufacturer need not take account of risks to abnormally sensitive claimants. Thus even though it may be known that a small minority of people are allergic, for example, to tweed, it does not follow that the manufacture of tweed garments is itself negligent, or even that all manufacturers of tweed garments should have to warn of the risks of allergy.[196] However, it is submitted that this merely reflects the fact that a manufacturer may normally assume consumers will know their own weaknesses and act accordingly. Where this is not the case, the duty to warn is likely to be stricter. A pharmaceutical manufacturer who failed to warn of some known rare but fatal side-effect would hardly escape liability on the basis that only those of abnormal sensitivity were likely to be at risk.

(vi) Exclusion of duty

10-44 **Exclusion of liability** On principle, there is no reason why *Donoghue v Stevenson* liability cannot be excluded by contract: for example, where the potential claimant has bought goods direct from a manufacturer subject to a limited warranty, or where in consideration of a specific guarantee provided by the manufacturer he agrees to give up his rights at common law.[197] Indeed, such exclusion is possible even though the claimant is not in contractual relation with the manufacturer at all: for example, a contract between the claimant and his seller which purports in terms to exempt the manufacturer from liability will be effective to do so.[198] It should be noted, however, that even where liability might otherwise be excluded, such exclusions may be subject to statutory control.[199] Where A sells goods to B who sells to

---

194 cf. *McCain Foods Ltd v Grand Fall Industries Ltd* (1990) 67 D.L.R. (4th) 639.

195 cf. *Devilez v Boots Ltd* (1962) 106 S.J. 552 (manufacturer of corrosive medicament must guard against possibility of mishandling of container).

196 See *Griffiths v Peter Conway* [1939] 1 All E.R. 685 (a case actually decided under s.14 of the Sale of Goods Act; however, it is suggested that the same principles apply in tort).

197 On the other hand, where the manufacturer sells goods to X who sells to the claimant, an exemption clause between the manufacturer and X cannot affect the claimant's rights (see *Western Processing and Cold Storage v Hamilton Construction Co and Dow Chemical of Canada* (1965) 51 D.L.R. (2d) 245). See also *The Diamantis Pateras* [1966] 1 Lloyd's Rep. 179. cf. on the other hand, where a person puts goods into circulation "with all faults" this may break the chain of causation as regards subsequent injury; cf. *Hurley v Dyke* [1979] R.T.R. 265.

198 Contracts (Rights of Third Parties) Act 1999 s.1(6).

199 Thus liability for negligence resulting in death or personal injury cannot be excluded in any contract: Unfair Contract Terms Act 1977 s.2(1) and Consumer Rights Act 2015 s.65(1). Liability in negligence resulting in other damage can be excluded, but not if (in the case of a consumer contract) the term, contrary to the requirement of good faith, causes a significant imbalance in the parties' rights and obligations, or (in the case of any other contract) it fails to satisfy the requirement of

C, an exemption clause between A and B cannot generally affect the rights of C or anyone else suffering injury or damage.[200] Nevertheless, where goods are sold "with all faults" and it is clear that they may well be defective, this may amount to a sufficient warning to the immediate buyer and allow the seller to argue that he has satisfied any duty of care as against third parties who may be injured by them. Thus in *Hurley v Dyke*[201] defendants sold a seriously defective old car at auction to a buyer who immediately resold it: shortly after, the claimant was injured as a result of the defects. The House of Lords upheld a decision by the Court of Appeal that even if the seller had known of the possible defects, they had satisfied any duty they owed to the claimant.

4. The Consumer Protection Act 1987 Part I

(a) Generally

Shortcomings of negligence liability The principal and obvious shortcoming of the traditional *Donoghue v Stevenson* cause of action is the need to prove fault.[202] A less apparent problem, but still highly important, concerns imports. The importer of a defective product and others in the distribution chain as often as not have no chance to check the quality of what they distribute and hence cannot be held negligent: if so, the consumer or other victim is left, apart from a possible claim in contract against the retailer,[203] with at best a cause of action in tort against an inaccessible defendant. Further, guarantees offered by manufacturers are often also of limited use. There may be difficulty in proving that they are contractually binding; the manufacturer may be abroad; and in any case manufacturers are under no obligation to offer them. 10-45

The Consumer Protection Act 1987 A number of English initiatives for the reform, inter alia, of product liability eventually came to nothing.[204] The 1987 Act now in force is the product of EU pressure, based partly on harmonising zeal and partly on the experience of the US,[205] to introduce a measure of liability without 10-46

reasonableness. See s.62(1) of the 2015 Act and s.2(2) of the 1977 Act.

200 *Simaan General Contracting Co v Pilkington Glass Ltd (No.2)* [1988] Q.B. 758 at 772 et seq. (discountenancing suggestions by Lord Roskill in *Junior Books Ltd v Veitchi Co Ltd* [1983] 1 A.C. 520 at 546 that in certain cases a manufacturers' exempting conditions might qualify his liability towards third parties); *Western Processing and Cold Storage Ltd v Hamilton Construction Co Ltd* (1965) 51 D.L.R. (2d) 245.

201 [1979] R.T.R. 265. See too the old case of *Ward v Hobbs* (1878) L.R. 4 App. Cas. 13.

202 Though perhaps this should not be overplayed. In a large number of product liability cases the difficulty is not so much proof of fault as proof of causation, which is necessary even under a strict liability regime.

203 And not even that if the claimant is a donee, or a passer-by, for example.

204 See in particular Law Commission, *Liability for Defective Products* (1977) Cmnd.6831; and the *Pearson Commission on Civil Liability and Compensation for Personal Injury* (1978) Cmnd.7054, Ch.22. The latter stopped short of recommending the abolition of the law of torts and the substitution of automatic insurance, but recommended instead that in the main the basis of liability should be changed from negligence to strict liability.

205 Where a greater or lesser degree of strict liability has long been accepted, originally on the lines of s.402A of the *Restatement (2d) of Torts* and more recently in many jurisdictions on the more streamlined basis of Ch.1 of the *Restatement (3d) of Torts*. The literature is immense. An excellent English summary of the main features is J. Stapleton, *Products Liability* (1994), Chs 2 and 4; for a fuller coverage, see M.S. Shapo, *Shapo on the Law of Products Liability*, 7th edn (2017), Ch.7.

fault into the product liability arena. This culminated in a Directive of July 1985,[206] drafted with these aims and also partly in order to replace existing similar schemes,[207] which in turn was given effect to by Pt I of the Consumer Protection Act 1987.[208] It applies to any products supplied after March 1988. Although based on an EU directive, as a UK statute it continues to apply despite Brexit, though subject to a few changes taking effect at the end of the transition period, which will be referred to below.[209]

10-47 **Interpretation** Section 1(1) provides as follows:

> "This Part shall have effect for the purpose of making such provision as is necessary in order to comply with the product liability Directive and shall be construed accordingly."

The subsection enables judges to pay heed to the Directive and decisions of the European Court when interpreting the Act.[210] In any case it is clear that where English legislation aims to give effect to EU law, the courts will strain to resolve any ambiguities in favour of the latter. Occasionally there seems to be a conflict between the Directive and the 1987 Act.[211] Here it is arguable that as a matter of strict law the wording of the Act ought to prevail.[212] Nevertheless, in *A v National Blood Authority*[213] it was accepted without argument on the point that, if there was

---

206 Council Directive on the approximation of the laws, regulations and administrative provisions of the Member States concerning liability for defective products, Dir. 85/374; [1985] O.J. L210/29. For a useful and constructive criticism, see D. Fairgrieve & G. Howells, "Rethinking Product Liability: A Missing Element in the European Commission's Third Review of the European Product Liability Directive" (2007) 70 M.L.R. 962.

207 The Directive is presumptively pre-emptive, but under art.13 it specifically preserves "any rights which an injured person may have according to the rules of the law of contractual or non-contractual liability" or a "special liability system" already existing. This has been held to mean that it pre-empts any other strict (as against fault-based) tort liability in a manufacturer or anyone else in the supply chain for personal injury or damage to domestic property, even if pre-existing: see *Skov AEG v Bilka Lavprisvarehus A/S* (C402/03) [2006] E.C.R. I-199; [2006] 2 C.M.L.R. 16, *Cass Comm* 26.5.2010, 08-18545 (also reported as *Acte IARD (Société) v Ettax (Société)* [2010] E.C.C. 24); and *Novo Nordisk Pharma GmbH v S* [2014] EUECJ C-310/13. But it permits parallel liability in respect of damage which it does not cover, such as harm to commercial property (*Moteurs Leroy Somer v Société Dalkia France* (C-285/08) [2009] E.C.R. I-4733; applied in *Cass Comm* 26.5.2010, 07-11744 (also reported as *Dalkia France v Moteurs Leroy Somer* [2010] E.C.C. 32)) or strict liability on service providers, even if premised on a defect in the equipment used (*Centre hospitalier universitaire de Besançon v Dutrueux* (Case C-495/10) [2012] 2 C.M.L.R. 1 (claim by hospital patient in respect of overheating bed, based on French provisions making hospitals strictly liable for injuries caused by defects in equipment)). For what amounts to a "special liability system" see *Novo Nordisk Pharma GmbH v S* [2014] EUECJ C-310/13.

208 The Directive was not incorporated verbatim, and there are some inconsistencies between the two documents. For an account of the difficulties of incorporation, see G. Howells, "Implications of the Implementation and Non-Implementation of the EC Products Liability Directive" (1990) 41 N.I.L.Q. 22, 33. For a jaundiced account of some of the Act's pitfalls, see D. Body, "Product liability claims under the Consumer Protection Act 1987: some practical problems" [2012] J.P.I.L. 79.

209 For example, as to the liability of importers: see below, para.10-78.

210 And also, at least in practice, to decisions of the courts of other EU members. A number of such decisions were referred to in the leading decision in *A v National Blood Authority* [2001] 3 All E.R. 289.

211 Notably in relation to s.4(1)(e) (the "development risks defence") (though the ECJ was not convinced on this point: *Commission v UK* (Case C-300/95) [1997] 3 C.M.L.R. 923). See para.10-72.

212 Despite s.2(1) of the European Communities Act 1972. This is because Directives do not generally have horizontal direct effect except as against governmental and analogous bodies.

213 [2001] 3 All E.R. 289 at 308. See too *Gee v DePuy International Ltd* [2018] EWHC 1208 (QB); [2018] Med. L.R. 347 at [67] (Andrews J).

a conflict, the wording of the Directive ought to be applied.[214] The aim of the Directive is, among other things, to provide a high degree of protection to consumers, and it should be interpreted accordingly.[215]

The law as stated in the previous paragraph continues to apply despite the UK's exit from the EU in January 2020, up to the end of the transition period.[216] Thereafter, courts in England, as in the rest of the UK, cease to be bound by later EU jurisprudence in interpreting the Act, though they may take account of it.[217] The practical effect of this change is likely to be minimal, however. **10-48**

The strict liability rule The vital provision is in s.2(1) of the 1987 Act: **10-49**

> "Subject to the following provisions of this Part, where any damage is caused wholly or partly by a defect in a product, every person to whom subsection (2) below applies [i.e. the manufacturer and various others] shall be liable for the damage."

The omission of any reference to negligence is deliberate: defectiveness, not fault, is the criterion of recovery.[218] This does not, of course, mean that liability is absolute: a number of defences are provided, and their cumulative effect may well be that in practice few claimants will succeed under the 1987 Act who would not have succeeded under negligence. Nevertheless, formally at least, the claimant relying on the 1987 Act need not trouble with proving negligence in the defendant. Having briefly described the principle of liability under s.2(1), six particular matters call for extended discussion in connection with the statutory scheme.

(b) What is a "product"?

Statutory definitions Section 1(2) says that a product: **10-50**

> "… means any goods or electricity and … includes a product which is comprised in another product, whether by virtue of being a component part or raw material or otherwise."

"Goods", by s.45, include ships[219] and aircraft, and any substance, including food

[214] If the national law were to be applied and later found to be in manifest conflict with the Directive, then it seems the relevant government would be liable to the party prejudiced for any loss suffered: see the principle adumbrated by the ECJ in *R. v Secretary of State for Transport Ex p. Factortame Ltd (No.3)* (C221/89) [1991] 3 C.M.L.R. 589; and *Köbler v Austria* (C224/01) [2003] 3 C.M.L.R. 28.

[215] The recitals to the Directive refer, among other things, to the need for a "fair apportionment of the risks inherent in modern technological production" and repeatedly to the "protection of the consumer"; and in *Boston Scientific Medizintechnik GmbH v AOK Sachsen-Anhalt-Die Gesundheitskasse* (C-503/13) [2015] 3 C.M.L.R. 6; (2015) 144 B.M.L.R. 225 at AG40 it was suggested that in interpreting it account "must be taken of art.168(1) TFEU and the second sentence of art.35 of the Charter of Fundamental Rights of the European Union, which require a high level of human health protection in the definition and implementation of all Union policies and activities".

[216] As at the time of writing, 31 December 2020: European Union (Withdrawal Agreement) Act 2020 s.33.

[217] European Union (Withdrawal) Act 2018 ss.6(1), 6(2) (as amended). As from 31 December 2020 the Supreme Court gains the ability to depart from prior EU jurisprudence as well: s.6(5) (as amended).

[218] A point stressed in the leading English authority on the 1987 Act, *A v National Blood Authority* [2001] 3 All E.R. 289.

[219] On ships, see A. Tettenborn, "Maritime Consumers? The Consumer Protection Act 1987 and Shipping Law" [1988] L.M.C.L.Q. 211.

and drugs. It is thus wide, including (for instance) transfused blood.[220] It seems to follow that it also covers other biological products, such as semen,[221] and presumably organs for transplant.[222] However, the specific reference to "goods" indicates that the Act is limited to damage caused by physical assets: services, information and advice are not included. On the other hand, in so far as (say) software embedded in other goods causes them to fail in a dangerous way, there can be liability.[223] Moreover, information contained on a label or in a book of instructions may be relevant, since (as we shall see) the matters relevant to the decision whether a product is defective include its get-up and any instructions or warnings provided.[224]

10-51 **Information**[225] Although instructions and labels referable to a physical product fall to be aggregated with it for the purpose of deciding whether the product as a whole is or is not defective,[226] it is suggested that the Directive and the 1987 Act are essentially concerned with dangers arising from the physical propensities of a thing. Purely informational defects are, it is submitted, outside it.[227] So, despite one indirect suggestion to the contrary,[228] it is suggested that a book or pamphlet should not be regarded as defective merely because its content is misleading, even if dangerously so,[229] so as to make the publisher[230] liable.[231]

10-52 **Computer software** Where it is supplied on a tangible medium such as a compact disk, it is suggested that computer software will generally count as goods rather than as simple information.[232] It follows that if a malfunction or glitch in the software

---

220 *A v National Blood Authority* [2001] 3 All E.R. 289.

221 Held a "product" under New York product liability law: *Donovan v Idant Laboratories*, 625 F. Supp. 256 (E.D. Pa, 2009).

222 If transfused blood is covered (see *A v National Blood Authority* [2001] 3 All E.R. 289 above), it would be odd if a transplanted kidney were not.

223 See the German decision in *BGH* 16.6.2009, VI ZR 107/08 (software controlling airbag). This may become more significant with the growth of the internet of things.

224 s.3(2)(a).

225 S. Whitaker, "European Product Liability and Intellectual Products" (1989) 105 L.Q.R. 125.

226 See para.10-63.

227 As a court in California put it, declining to hold book publishers liable for misinformation, "the purposes served by products liability law also are focused on the tangible world and do not take into consideration the unique characteristics of ideas and expression.": *Winter v G Putnam's Sons, Inc*, 938 F.2d 1033 at 1034 (1991).

228 In *St Albans City Council v ICL Ltd* [1996] 4 All E.R. 481 at 493 Glidewell LJ thought a book containing dangerous misinformation would count as defective goods within s.14 of the Sale of Goods Act 1979.

229 As with, e.g., a "do-it-yourself" manual which contained dangerous misinformation.

230 Or possibly even the printer? Or the binder? They both in a sense "produce" it.

231 The trend in the US is so to hold: e.g. *Winter v G Putnam's Sons*, 938 F. 2d 1033 (1991) (Californian mycophagists poisoned after relying on the *Encyclopedia of Mushrooms*: no action against publishers under strict products liability law), and also the Florida decision in *Cardozo v True*, 342 So. 2d 1053 (1977) (cookbook containing potentially lethal recipe). There are decisions to the contrary, for example *Aetna Casualty Co v Jeppesen & Co*, 642 F. 2d 339 (1981) (misleading aerial chart): but they have been roundly criticised (e.g. Noah, "Office, Publishers and Product Liability", 77 Ore. L. Rev. 1195 (1998)). cf. A. Tettenborn, "Wild oats and the sale of Goods" [1986] C.L.J. 389 (a note on the Sale of Goods Act case of *Wormell v RHM* [1986] 1 W.L.R. 336).

232 Software was held to be goods in connection with liability under the Sale of Goods Act 1979: *St Albans City Council v ICL Ltd* [1995] F.S.R. 686 (appeal dismissed on other grounds: [1996] 4 All E.R. 481). It has been suggested (C. Miller & R. Goldberg, *Product Liability*, 2nd edn (Oxford: OUP, 2004) para.9.102; and Chissick & Kelman, *Electronic Commerce Law & Practice*, (London: Sweet & Maxwell, 2000), p.70) that a distinction should be drawn here between bespoke and standard

as written causes a machine to malfunction and injure the claimant there will be liability under the 1987 Act.[233] However, where software is supplied non-physically—for example, over the internet—it seems hard to escape the conclusion that no "product" is involved and hence there can be no liability.[234]

Land and premises The mere fact that something has been incorporated into land does not prevent it being a "product"; s.45 indeed defines "goods" as including "things comprised in land by virtue of being attached to it". So, for instance, a manufacturer of building materials which contained large quantities of asbestos could be liable to an injured occupier under s.2(1). However, by ss.46(3) and 46(4) there can only be liability in respect of things forming part of land where those things have been incorporated in land pursuant to a contract (for example a building contract). A mere sale of land together with chattels affixed to it is outside the Act. So if a builder-developer sold a house with a defective chimney, he would not be liable under the Act to a buyer who was asphyxiated as a result: but if he constructed a defective metal flue which he then inserted into the chimney, he would be responsible. 10-53

Primary agricultural and fishery produce This is a product under the Act: a harvester of poisoned oysters, a farmer producing corn with pesticide residues, and presumably a landowner shooting and selling diseased rabbits, will therefore be liable.[235] 10-54

(c) When is a product "defective"?

"Defect"[236] Section 3(1) states that there is a defect in a product for the purposes of the Act: 10-55

> "if the safety of the product is not such as persons generally are entitled to expect[237]; and for those purposes "safety", in relation to a product, shall include safety with respect to products comprised in that product and safety in the context of risks of damage to property, as well as in the context of risks of death or personal injury."

For the purpose of determining this, s.3(2) lays down guidelines and provides that

software, with only the latter treated as a product. But no such distinction is drawn with other goods, and it seems unlikely that it will be adopted here.

233 A point that may become highly significant with, for example, driverless vehicles. See the Department of Transport's 2015 publication *The Pathway to Driverless Cars: A detailed review of regulations for automated vehicle technologies*, Ch.7. The matter here is partly pre-empted by legislation: see s.2 of the Automated and Electric Vehicles Act 2018, which (when in force, which as yet it is not) will impose a measure of strict liability in respect of such vehicles when driving themselves.

234 Unless it can be said that the physical manifestation of the program on the host mainframe is a product which is "supplied" when a copy is transmitted.

235 Until 2000 liability under the Act was excluded in respect of any damage caused by primary produce before it had undergone an "industrial process". So, for example, a farmer who sold contaminated peas could not be sued, though the canner who tinned them could. Following amendment of the Directive this exemption was removed as from 4 December 2000, when s.2(4) of the 1987 Act was repealed.

236 R. Freeman, "Strict product liability laws" [2001] J.P.I.L. 26; G. Howells & M. Mildred, "Infected Blood: Defect and Discoverability" (2002) 65 M.L.R. 95. For the position under analogous American strict liability law, see M. Shapo, *Shapo on the Law of Products Liability*, 7th edn (2017), Ch.9.

237 The wording of the Directive is: "which a person is entitled to expect."

"all the circumstances" are in account, including the manner and purposes of marketing, get-up, the use of any mark in relation to the product, instructions and warnings, and what might reasonably be expected to be done with or in relation to the product. It should be noted, however, that a defect must affect safety: a defect regarding mere usability is not within the Act.[238]

10-56 **Proof of defectiveness** Although the Act pointedly dispenses with the need to prove fault, the claimant must still prove defectiveness.[239] It is not enough merely to show that the product failed and caused damage[240]; nor that a product is defective and that damage occurred, if that damage might equally have had some other cause.[241] On the other hand, the court may on occasion accept proof by inference. Thus in a suitable case it has been said to be open to a judge to find a product defective if it failed in use and no other plausible explanation is available: for instance, if a deep-fat fryer unaccountably catches fire,[242] or the handlebars on a child's bicycle inexplicably sheer while it is being ridden.[243]

---

238 *Busby v Berkshire Bed Co Ltd* [2018] EWHC 2976 (QB) at [142] (fall from double bed during energetic activity on it: although bed missing casters, not defective within s.3 and no claim under 1987 Act).

239 What is the position where the claimant cannot prove an actual inadequacy, but can show that identical products have failed and thus that there is an appreciable chance that this item was not properly functional? In *Boston Scientific Medizintechnik GmbH v AOK Sachsen-Anhalt-Die Gesundheitskasse* (C-503/13) [2015] 3 C.M.L.R. 6; (2015) 144 B.M.L.R. 225, a case concerning pacemakers, the ECJ decided that, at least in the medical context where safety was a primary consideration, "where it is found that such products belonging to the same group or forming part of the same production series have a potential defect, it is possible to classify as defective all the products in that group or series, without there being any need to show that the product in question is defective" (see [41]). In addition it decided that the proper protection of consumers against damage caused by defective products required that the costs of surgery to replace the pacemaker should also be recoverable: see [47]–[50]. For proceedings following this holding see the German decision in *BGH* 09.06.2015, Az. VI ZR 284/12 & VI ZR 327/12 (four failures in pacemakers out of 46,000, some 17–20 times the normal risk, suffices to create liability). See generally B. van Leeuwen & P. Verbruggen, "Resuscitating EU Product Liability Law?" (2015) 23 Eur. Rev. Priv. L. 899.

240 *Foster v Biosil Ltd* (2000) 59 B.M.L.R. 178 (unexplained rupture of breast implant: no liability in absence of proof of what went wrong); *Richardson v London Rubber Co Ltd* [2000] Lloyd's Rep. Med. 280 (unexplained failure of condom); *Love v Halfords Ltd* [2014] EWHC 1057 (QB); [2014] P.I.Q.R. P20 (defect in cycle could have been due to mishandling). Indeed, it has been said that such presumptions would be contrary to EU law: see *W v Sanofi Pasteur MSD SNC* [2017] EUECJ C-621/15; [2017] 4 W.L.R. 171; [2018] 1 C.M.L.R. 16 at [36]–[37]; and *Gee v DePuy International Ltd* [2018] EWHC 1208 (QB); [2018] Med. L.R. 347 at [79]–[80] (Andrews J). But courts elsewhere in Europe do not necessarily accept this: see the French decision in *Aix-en-Provence*, 2.10.2001, 2001 D. (IR) 3092.

241 *Hufford v Samsung Electronics (UK) Ltd* [2014] EWHC 2956 (TCC); [2014] B.L.R. 633 (house fire might have originated either in a refrigerator or in material strewn around it: claimant lost)); see also *Gee v DePuy International Ltd* [2018] EWHC 1208 (QB); [2018] Med. L.R. 347 at [98].

242 See the the German decision in *OLG Koblenz* 12.02.2014, 5 U 762/14.

243 As in *Ide v ATB Sales Ltd* [2008] EWCA Civ 424; [2008] P.I.Q.R. P13. For other similar cases, see *Baker v KTM Sportmotorcycle UK Ltd* [2017] EWCA Civ 378; [2018] E.C.C. 35 (brakes on two-year-old fully-maintained motorcycle inexplicably seized, throwing and injuring its rider); and *Al-Iqra v DSG Retail Ltd* [2019] EWHC 429 (QB); [2019] P.I.Q.R. P11 (electric heater ignited, causing house fire). American authority on strict product liability shows a similar tendency: see, e.g. *Moores v Sunbeam Products, Inc*, 425 F.Supp.2d 151 (Me 2003). In *W v Sanofi Pasteur MSD SNC* [2017] EUECJ C-621/15; [2017] 4 W.L.R. 171; [2018] 1 C.M.L.R. 16 the ECJ held that there was no inconsistency between such practices and art.4 of the Directive, since this was a matter of national (procedural) law, and besides it was right to construe the Directive generously in favour of victims.

Manufacturing and design defects We mentioned above, in connection with negligence liability, a difference between manufacturing defects (i.e. unintended imperfections in a product such as the presence of mechanical flaws, foreign bodies or contaminants) and design defects (where something is produced exactly as intended but is alleged to be unsafe because of the way it was designed).[244] An analogous distinction has occasionally been mentioned under the 1987 Act between so-called "standard" and "non-standard" (or "rogue") products,[245] and clearly has some relevance: for example, in deciding whether a given item is defective, it falls to be compared with a product in its normal state as regards non-standard products but with other products on the market as regards standard ones.[246] But in *A v National Blood Authority*[247] Burton J declined to accept the prevailing American view[248] that a different standard of defectiveness applied to each category. No such distinction appeared in the Act or the Directive: in all cases the issue was the public's legitimate expectation of safety.[249] 10-57

Defective electricity Although electricity is a "product", it is not entirely easy to see how it can be "defective". It might, however, be so if a sudden "spike" or fall in the supply due to a fault in the generating plant caused injury by flashover or damage to (say) a home computer.[250] It is suggested, however, that a power cut would not amount to a "defect", even if it caused spoilage of (say) frozen meat: this surely a case of non-supply, rather than defective supply. 10-58

Defects: safety "such as persons generally are entitled to expect" The phrase "such as persons generally are entitled to expect" involves an objectively reasonable expectation. The relevant time for such expectation to be measured has been said to be when the product is first marketed, though hindsight may be employed to determine whether that standard was in fact met.[251] The phrase refers to objec- 10-59

---

244 See para.10-28, discussing the same point in connection with negligence liability.

245 e.g. A. Stoppa, "The Concept of Defectiveness in the Consumer Protection Act 1987: a critical analysis" (1992) 12 L.S. 210, 214 onwards. In *A v National Blood Authority* [2001] 3 All E.R. 289, 317 onwards, Burton J preferred these terms, regarding the terms "design defects" and "manufacturing defects" as US imports foreign to European jurisprudence. But whether this makes much difference is open to doubt.

246 Compare the Scottish decision in *Hastings v Finsbury Orthopaedics Ltd* [2019] CSOH 96; 2019 S.L.T. 1411 (novel form of hip replacement to be compared to others on the market at the time). In particular, in the US the *Restatement 3d of Torts*, §2(b) requires evidence of a possible alternative design in any claim relying on a "design defect." But it is extremely unlikely that such a requirement would be held to apply in the European context (though doubtless the presence or absence of such an alternative would be relevant as a matter of evidence).

247 [2001] 3 All E.R. 289 at 319. See R. Goldberg, "Paying for Bad Blood: Strict Product Liability after the Hepatitis C Litigation" (2002) 10 Med. L. Rev. 165.

248 e.g. J. Wade, "On the Nature of Strict Tort Liability for Products", 44 Miss. L.J. 825, 837-38 (1973); see also *Troja v Black & Decker Mfg Co*, 488 A. 2d 516, 519 (1985); *Restatement (3d) of Torts*, para.2(a)(b)(c).

249 [2001] 3 All E.R. 289, 317–318. See too *Gee v DePuy International Ltd* [2018] EWHC 1208 (QB); [2018] Med. L.R. 347 at [93] (Andrews J); and V. Westphalen, ***Produkthaftungshandbuch*** (1990), at paras 23-24 (discussing the Directive in the German context).

250 So held by the German supreme court: *BGH* 25.2.2014, Az. VI ZR 144/13 (voltage spike damages household equipment). See too P. Kolba [1998] Cons. L.J. 81).

251 *Gee v DePuy International Ltd* [2018] EWHC 1208 (QB); [2018] Med. L.R. 347 at [84] (Andrews J). With respect, this may be open to question. If legitimate expectations change over the time a product is on the market (for example on poisonous pollution from cars), a producer should clearly escape in respect of an early product; but should he be exonerated if he continues to produce it after

tive qualities, rather than to any actual belief[252]: as such it is clearly meant to introduce some flexibility.[253] A person cannot legitimately expect a car to have armour-plating even if this would reduce the chances of injury in an accident: again, merely because some cars have special safety features such as anti-lock brakes, this does not necessarily mean that cheaper models without such features are therefore defective.[254] Similarly, if a product is reasonably safe it may be non-defective even if as a result of a manufacturing error it is not up to normal standards.[255] However, it should be noted that the criterion of what is defective remains a stringent one. Thus in *A v National Blood Authority*,[256] concerning transfused blood containing the hepatitis C virus, it was held that concept referred to the public's legitimate expectation, not its actual expectation. Hence the fact that the public knew that there was an inevitable risk that some blood would be contaminated despite all possible precautions did not prevent liability arising in respect of that which was contaminated: a recipient had a right to expect that the blood he got would be safe.[257]

10-60 **"All the circumstances"** The specific matters referred to in s.3(2) are fairly straightforward. The reference to marketing and get-up emphasises the point that (for instance) the same tin of meat may be safe sold as cat food but defective if distributed for human consumption; and that model cars with sharp projections may

---

the change in expectations? A better criterion might be the time the particular product of which complaint is made left the producer's control.

252 *A v National Blood Authority* [2001] 3 All E.R. 289, 311 (Burton J); *Wilkes v Depuy International Ltd* [2016] EWHC 3096 (QB); [2018] Q.B. 627 at [69] (Hickinbottom J).

253 It has thus been said in Germany (rightly, it is suggested) that "a manufacturer can be expected to take more far-reaching measures where there is serious danger to human life or health than in the case where what is to be feared is only damage to property or possessions or slight injury": see *BGH* 5.2.2013, VI ZR 1/12 at [13].

254 In *Gee v DePuy International Ltd* [2018] EWHC 1208 (QB); [2018] Med. L.R. 347 at [96] Andrews J denied, in a case concerning artificial hips, that the Directive or the 1987 Act imposed a warranty of performance on a producer. Compare the German decisions in *OLG Düsseldorf* 20.12.2002, 14 U 99/02 at [58] (under the Directive, food manufacturers are "not bound to formulate edible products from the beginning so as to promote the highest degree of health", and hence no liability merely for producing confectionery very unhealthily high in sugar); and *BGH* 5.2.2013, VI ZR 1/12 at [15] ("absolute safety cannot be expected of every product in every situation"). There is a similar move in the US: see the New York decision in *Pigliavento v Tyler*, 669 N.Y.S.2d (1998) (safety rail available as optional extra for cement mixer: mixer not defective within American strict liability law merely because purchaser chose to forgo safety feature). See too Hickinbottom J in *Wilkes v Depuy International Ltd* [2016] EWHC 3096 (QB); [2018] Q.B. 627, especially at [65] (hip replacement cannot be expected to be foolproof, especially where implanted in overweight and very active patient).

255 So held in *Tesco Stores Ltd v Pollard* [2006] EWCA Civ 393 (manufacturing glitch made container of dishwasher powder less childproof than it should have been, with result that child ate contents: nevertheless, held reasonably safe and not defective).

256 [2001] 3 All E.R. 289, 334 onwards.

257 See too the German Supreme Court decision in *BGHZ 181, 253; BGH VI ZR 107/08*, 16.6.2009, especially at [16] (liability for airbag which unexpectedly deployed on rough road: question is not subjective but objective, whether product "offers degree of safety regarded as obligatory by prevailing public opinion in the area concerned"). *A v National Blood Authority* was also accepted in this respect by the Federal Court of Australia, applying similar legislation, in *Gill v Ethicon SaRL (No 5)* [2019] FCA 1905 at [3170]. Note, however, that this interpretation is not entirely uncontroversial. The Austrian Supreme Court, interpreting "defect," held in 1997 that an electrical voltage surge did not amount to a "defect" since this was an unavoidable risk that everyone knew about. See *OGH* 16.04.1997, 7 OB 2414/96t, (noted P. Kolba [1998] Cons. L.J. 81).

be defective if sold as toys but not if marketed as adult collectors' items. Advertising may no doubt also play a part: wall-coverings may not be defective merely because they are combustible, but if advertised as flame-proof, or for use in industrial kitchens, they doubtless would be.[258] And similarly with foreseeable uses: an axe is not defective merely because it would be highly dangerous to use it as a meat cleaver. The fact that a product satisfied, or did not satisfy, an official or industry standard is relevant to whether it was defective, but not conclusive either way.[259]

Apart from specific instances, s.3(2) of the 1987 Act says that "all the circumstances" are in account in deciding whether a product is defective. Nevertheless, it seems that this phrase cannot be taken quite *au pied de la lettre*. In *A v National Blood Authority*[260] Burton J expressed the view that it was improper to take into account at least two matters, namely (a) the practicality and cost of possible measures to avoid the defect; and (b) the social benefits of the product as compared to its risks. To do otherwise, he said, would subvert the intention of the Act and the Directive and frustrate the ex post facto strict liability it was meant to impose.[261] However, it may well be that these remarks may have to be modified, at least with regard to (a), in cases involving standard products. Even if there is no difference in principle between standard and non-standard products, it seems unlikely that, say, a car or chain-saw produced as designed would be regarded as defective merely because some fantastically expensive or awkward addition might have increased its safety: the legitimate expectation of the public cannot extend that far.[262] **10-61**

Inherently dangerous products The mere fact that a product may cause injury clearly cannot be enough to render it "defective". Knives must cut and guns shoot; by their nature whisky will intoxicate and cigarettes kill,[263] and coffee occasionally scald: yet they cannot be defective for that reason alone.[264] The problem is how **10-62**

---

258 cf. *Hobbs Farms v Baxenden Chemicals Ltd* [1992] 1 Lloyd's Rep. 54 (a negligence case: combustible wall-coverings defective because marketed as flame-proof).

259 *Gee v DePuy International Ltd* [2018] EWHC 1208 (QB); [2018] Med. L.R. 347 at [170]–[178], following Pollard v Tesco Stores Ltd [2006] EWCA Civ 393, in which a product had been held non-defective despite non-compliance.

260 [2001] 3 All E.R. 289, 334 onwards.

261 [2001] 3 All E.R. 289, 335–336. Compare *Wilkes v Depuy International Ltd* [2016] EWHC 3096 (QB); [2018] Q.B. 627 at [66]–[67], where Hickinbottom J expressed some doubts as to whether this was so. In *AH v Greater Glasgow Health Board* [2018] CSOH 57; 2018 S.L.T. 535 at [114], a Scottish court discussing the defectiveness of vaginal mesh inserts was inclined to accept the view expressed in *Wilkes*, as was Andrews J in *Gee v DePuy International Ltd* [2018] EWHC 1208 (QB); [2018] Med. L.R. 347 at [143].

262 Compare *Wilkes v Depuy International Ltd* [2016] EWHC 3096 (QB); [2018] Q.B. 627 at [66]–[67], where Hickinbottom J expressed some scepticism as to the irrelevance of risk-benefit generally. So too did Andrews J in *Gee v DePuy International Ltd* [2018] EWHC 1208 (QB); [2018] Med. L.R. 347 at [144]–[167]. On the Wilkes decision, see J. Eisler, ""One step forward and two steps back in product liability: the search for clarity in the identification of defects" [2017] C.L.J. 230; and D. Nolan, "Strict product liability for design defects" (2018) 134 L.Q.R. 176.

263 Compare the New Jersey asbestos decisions in *Beshada v Johns-Manville Corp*, 447 A. 2d 539 (1982); and *Feldman v Lederle Laboratories*, 479 A. 2d 374 (1984), both based on the strict liability rule in para.402A of the *Restatement 2d of Torts*. But there may of course be liability for failure to warn of dangers.

264 See *B (A Child) v McDonald's Restaurants Ltd* [2002] EWHC 490 (QB) (piping hot tea and coffee in substantial polystyrene cups not defective products: customers liked their beverages thus, and knew the risks); and see the careful German judgment in *OLG Düsseldorf* 20.12.2002, 14 U 99/02 denying recovery under the Directive to a chocoholic now suffering from chronic diabetes. The same

this can be reconciled with s.6. One possible argument is that the advantages of utility and consumer choice on balance outweigh the risk of injury.[265] Unless a very similar product could have been produced without the inherent danger, then there is no defect.[266] But this is precluded because risk/utility analysis of this sort has been rejected as a criterion of defectiveness under s.6.[267] In *A v National Blood Authority*[268] Burton J suggested an alternative explanation: namely, that that such products were not only inherently dangerous but known to everyone to be so, and hence their danger had to be factored into the public's reasonable expectation.[269] This approach has the advantage of putting clearly within s.6 products that, although produced impeccably according to plan, are in fact unexpectedly dangerous, such as drugs with disastrous uncovenanted side-effects.[270] But with respect, it may go too far in demanding general knowledge of the risk.[271] Some drugs, while clearly therapeutic, are well-known to have horrific side-effects: it would be curious if they were now to be regarded as defective because this was known merely to the medical profession rather than the public as a whole.[272] Again, suppose an industrial chemical is known to be apt to explode without warning even if entirely pure and made and handled impeccably: it is suggested that it would not for that reason be regarded as defective, even if the public had never heard of it or the danger it embodied.[273]

10-63 **Warnings and instructions** Among the relevant criteria for defectiveness in s.3 of the Act are "any instructions for, or warnings with respect to, doing or refraining from doing, anything with or in relation to the product".[274] In many cases,

has been said in Australia in a case applying fairly similar legislation: *Gill v Ethicon SaRL (No 5)* [2019] FCA 1905 at [3192]. Compare the comment of an American judge in a tobacco case: "[S]trict liability should not be used as a tool of social engineering to mandate that manufacturers bear the entire risk and costs of injuries caused by their products" (*Buckingham v RJ Reynolds*, 731 A. 2d 381 (1998)).

265 cf. *Barker v Lull Engineering Co, Inc*, 20 Cal. 3d 413, 143 Cal.Rptr. 225, 573 P. 2d 443 (1978).

266 See, e.g. the American decisions in *Kelley v RG Industries, Inc*, 304 Md. 124; 497 A. 2d 1143 (1985) (handgun not unreasonably dangerous, and hence not defective, as such); and *Vautour v Body Masters Sports Indus., Inc*, 784 A. 2d 1178 (2001).

267 *A v National Blood Authority* [2001] 3 All E.R. 289, 335–336.

268 [2001] 3 All E.R. 289, 312. This reasoning was followed in *B (A Child) v McDonald's Restaurants Ltd* [2002] EWHC 490 (QB) (hot tea and coffee in substantial polystyrene cups not defective as such: risk was notorious).

269 cf. G. Howells, *Law of Product Liability*, para.1.19. A German court interpreting the Directive has articulated a further reason, often present to mind but rarely expressed: people's freedom to have what is not good for them. See *OLG Düsseldorf* 20.12.2002, 14 U 99/02 at [58] (demanding that manufacturers—there of confectionery—make it impossible to take deliberate risks "puts unacceptable limits on freedom and autonomy").

270 Thus at least making sure that there would be liability were the Thalidomide tragedy to recur today. For drugs and defectiveness generally, see M-E. Arbour, "Compensation for Damage Caused by Defective Drugs: European Private Law between Safety Requirements and Free-Market Values" (2004) 10 Eur. L.J. 87; M. Brazier and E. Cave, *Medicine, Patients and the Law*, 6th edn (Penguin, 2016), Ch.10.

271 G. Howells, *Law of Product Liability*, above, justifies the need for public knowledge on the basis that users' choice to run a risk needs to be informed. But it has to be remembered that non-users, to whom this argument does not apply at all, can also sue under the Act.

272 cf. *Restatement 2d, Torts*, para.402A comment k (giving the example of rabies treatments).

273 Hence Andrews J's interesting suggestion in *Gee v Depuy International Ltd* [2018] EWHC 1208 (QB); [2018] Med. L.R. 347 at [112] that in such cases one should ask whether such products were abnormally hazardous.

274 See s.3(2)(a). For a case of a sufficient warning, see *Worsley v Tambrands Ltd* [2000] P.I.Q.R. 95

especially of "standard products",[275] the adequacy of warnings and instructions may make all the difference.[276] A chain-saw is not defective as such: without adequate safety instructions, it probably is.[277] With regard to warnings, where the danger is a known one, presumably the standard will bear some similarity to that in negligence, despite the strict liability thrust of the Act[278]; was it reasonable to require the manufacturer to provide a warning in the circumstances? Dangers obvious to the user do not need to be warned against[279]; presumably the same would apply to very remote possibilities. But if the danger is entirely unknown, then the position may be different. Suppose a new drug is highly effective but, unknown to anyone, has the propensity to produce horrendous side-effects when given to a small class of patients. It is submitted that, in line with the strict liability approach in the Act, it would be regarded as defective in the absence of some clear warning as to the side-effects.[280] In some cases a warning to an intermediary might suffice,[281] for example with pharmaceuticals, where a warning to the prescribing physician might well be enough. In others, it is suggested that a manufacturer may be entitled to expect the intermediary to provide it.[282] A warning may be required of the nature of a product where this is necessary to avoid danger.[283] There seems, however, to be no duty under the Act (unlike the common law[284]) to warn of dangers that subsequently become apparent.

Foreseeability of damage: relevance In the case of "non-standard" products,[285] there is no doubt that foreseeability of damage is irrelevant. If a drug contains an impurity which in fact causes a user to suffer injury, it should not matter whether 10-64

(explicit warning on tampons with regard to toxic shock syndrome).

275 See para.10-57.

276 Compare *OGH* 22.2.2011, 8 Ob 14/11h (Austrian Supreme Court), reported as *Re Defective Instructions on Oven Cleaner* [2012] E.C.C. 10 (instructions on corrosive product must include instructions on emergency procedures when skin affected).

277 cf. the Sale of Goods Act case of *Wormell v RHM* [1986] 1 W.L.R. 336 (reversed on the facts, [1987] 1 W.L.R. 1091).

278 "When the factual issue is not whether the product itself is defective but whether the manufacturer has provided adequate warnings, the existence of a product defect and a breach of duty are defined by the same standard-reasonable care under the circumstances": *Smith v ER Squibb*, 273 N.W. 2d 476 at 480 (1979), decided under American strict liability law.

279 cf. *B (A Child) v McDonald's Restaurants Ltd* [2002] EWHC 490 (QB) (no duty to warn in relation to hot coffee).

280 The producer might, of course, have a defence under the "development risks" provision in s.4(1)(e). But this is irrelevant to the question of defectiveness. Note, however, in this context the French decision in Cass.Civ. 26.09.2018, No. 17-21271, also reported as *Consorts X v Office National d'Indemnisation des Accidents Médicaux, des Affections Iatrogènes et des Infections Nosocomiales* [2018] E.C.C. 36, suggesting that some products are so dangerous within the Directive that they remain defective even with a warning.

281 See *AH v Greater Glasgow Health Board* [2018] CSOH 57; 2018 S.L.T. 535 at [125]; and *Gee v DePuy International Ltd* [2018] EWHC 1208 (QB); [2018] Med. L.R. 347 at [169]; and also cf. the negligence case of *Holmes v Ashford* [1950] 2 All E.R. 76. See generally P. Ferguson, "Liability for pharmaceutical products: a critique of the 'learned intermediary' rule" (1992) 12 O.J.L.S. 60.

282 e.g. where A supplies B with chemicals for B to make up into children's chemistry sets. The chemicals no doubt require precise instructions and warnings as to use: but this is clearly something for B to provide, and the chemicals could hardly be said to be "defective" when they left A's factory because at that stage no warning was included.

283 For example, a statement on bottled gas canisters as to whether they contain butane or more volatile propane: see the French decision in *Cass Civ 1ère*, 04.02.2015, 13-19781.

284 See para.10-32.

285 See para.10-57.

at the time of production it was foreseeable that the impurity would be harmful, or even present. Indeed, it could be said that this is the essence of imposing liability without fault. Where standard products are involved, the matter used to be less certain: but it now seems that a similar rule applies: foreseeability of damage is out of account, and the only question is whether the public's legitimate expectation of safety has been satisfied.[286]

10-65 **Misuse** Prima facie it is suggested that a product is not defective merely because it is dangerous when misused. A foolish consumer who used bleach to wash up could hardly complain if it burnt his hands.[287] However, foreseeable misuse may well be in a different category, such that a manufacturer is not entitled to disregard it: indeed, s.3(2)(b) of the 1987 Act specifically requires the court to take account of what may reasonably be expected to be done with the product. So if foreseeable misuse is likely to have harmful consequences there may arise a duty to warn, at least where the risks are not obvious. In particular this may be relevant where the product may foreseeably come into the hands of children, whose propensity to misuse products is notorious. Thus dangerous medicine might well be defective if not provided in child-proof containers. If sued by a poisoned child who had swallowed the contents of a non-protected container, it is submitted that it would be idle for the manufacturer to argue that medicine was not meant to be used that way.

10-66 **Sensitive claimants** It is clear that under negligence liability and sale of goods law, a product which is safe for persons generally does not make the producer liable merely because it is harmful to a small minority of extra-sensitive claimants (e.g. sufferers from a rare allergy).[288] It is suggested that a similar rule ought to apply under the 1987 Act, on the basis that the public's legitimate expectation of safety extends to those of ordinary sensitivity, but not to those beyond it.

(d) What defences are available?

10-67 **Compliance with a legal requirement** Section 4(1)(a) provides a defence if "the defect is attributable to compliance with any requirement imposed by or under any enactment or with any Community obligation",[289] the burden of proof being on the defendant. Clearly this precludes complaint if the only possible defectiveness arises from something the manufacturer was bound to include in the product. But this is likely to be rare; most safety requirements merely set minimum standards which manufacturers can surpass if they want. A more important question is: does s.4(1)(a) pre-empt the action under s.2(1) provided these minimum standards set by law have been met? For example, children's nightdresses must satisfy certain standards of fire

286 *A v National Blood Authority* [2001] 3 All E.R. 289, 317-318. See too F. v. Westphalen, *Produkthaftungshandbuch* (1990), at para.23-24 (discussing the Directive in the German context).

287 cf. the Sale of Goods Act case of *Wormell v RHM* [1987] 1 W.L.R. 1091 (weedkiller used in plain disregard of instructions; no liability for failure to warn of result).

288 This is undoubtedly the position under the strict liability provision in s.14 of the Sale of Goods Act 1979: *Griffiths v Peter Conway Ltd* [1939] 1 All E.R. 685 (buyer allergic to Harris tweed: no liability under s.14).

289 After the end of the EU exit transition period, only retained EU law obligations will trigger this defence. See Product Safety and Metrology etc. (Amendment etc.) (EU Exit) Regulations 2019 (SI 2019/696) Sch.3 para.4, given effect by Sch.5 of the European Union (Withdrawal Agreement) Act 2020.

resistance: does this prevent a claimant arguing that these standards are too low, and that even though a nightdress satisfies them it is nevertheless so inflammable as to be defective? It is suggested that the answer is no.[290] It would be odd, to say the least, if the effect of safety regulations was actually to reduce the exposure of the manufacturer to civil liability.

Uncirculated products It is a defence that the defendant "did not at any time supply the product to another": see s.4(1)(b). The effect of this is that there can be no liability in respect of goods which have not been put into circulation at all by the defendant. Suppose, for example, a car is manufactured with faulty brakes. An employee of the manufacturer injured while attempting to park it in the factory compound will not be able to sue; nor, if the car is stolen by a joy-rider, will a bystander who is run down. On the other hand, if the accident happened to an employee at a retail outlet, or to a journalist test-driving the vehicle, it would be covered.[291] Although s.4(1) uses the word "supply", the equivalent wording of the Directive, which is likely to inform any interpretation, is "put into circulation".[292] For these purposes a product is, it seems, put into circulation when it leaves the control of the producer or a distribution network controlled by him.[293] However, it seems that there may also be a "putting into circulation" where goods are used within an institution such as a hospital,[294] or made available to those hiring premises such as exhibition halls.[295] The burden of proof of the "no supply" defence is on the defendant. However, presumably this only applies where the defendant is alleged to come within s.2(2)[296]; where the essence of the claimant's allegation is that the defendant was a supplier within s.2(3), it presumably remains up to him to prove it. **10-68**

Subsequent defects Section 4(1)(d) provides a defence if "the defect did not exist in the product at the relevant time". In the case of producers, importers and others covered by s.2(2), this means that the defendant escapes if the defect came into **10-69**

---

290 A point confirmed by Andrews J in *Gee v DePuy International Ltd* [2018] EWHC 1208 (QB); [2018] Med. L.R. 347 at [170]–[178]. The same is true with negligence and compliance with statutory duties as to health and safety; see *Bux v Slough Metals Ltd* [1973] 1 W.L.R. 1358; and *Best v Wellcome Foundation* [1983] 3 I.R. 421.

291 Since there would then be a supply to the retailer or the journalist (note that "supply" may include a loan: s.46(1)). The distinction is bizarre and difficult to defend: see J. Stapleton, *Product Liability* (Oxford: OUP, 1994), pp.336 onwards.

292 art.7(a).

293 See the ECJ decision in *O'Byrne v Sanofi Pasteur MSD Ltd*, Case 127/04, [2006] 1 W.L.R. 1606; [2006] 2 C.M.L.R. 24 (a case on art.10 of the Directive, but the wording is the same). For subsequent proceedings, see *O'Byrne v Aventis Pasteur MSD Ltd* [2008] UKHL 34; [2008] 4 All E.R. 881 and the acid comments in G. Howells, "O'Byrne v Aventis Pasteur SA - how many trips to Luxembourg are necessary?" [2009] J.B.L. 97; also the equally opaque result of yet a further reference to the ECJ in *Aventis Pasteur SA v OB*, C-358/08, [2010] 1 W.L.R. 1375; explained by the Supreme Court in *O'Byrne v Aventis Pasteur MSD Ltd* [2010] UKSC 23; [2010] 1 W.L.R. 1412.

294 Under the ECJ's decision in *Veedfald v Arhus Amtskommune* [2003] 1 C.M.L.R. 41 (injury to hospital patient from contaminated cleansing fluid made in-house: held, the fluid had nevertheless been "put into circulation" within intent of the Directive). On the meaning of "put into circulation" under the Directive and its potentially wide application, see the German decision in *OLG Hamm*, 02.11.2016 – 21 U 14/16 (farmer agisting horse on own farm fed it with his own silage, which turned out defective: liable under Directive when horse fell ill as a result).

295 So held in Austria: *OGH* 30.09.2002, 1 Ob 169/02p (reported as *Re Defective Room Dividers* [2004] E.C.C. 20).

296 i.e. a "producer" etc.

existence after he parted with it.[297] In the case of those sued as suppliers within s.2(3), the defect must have arisen after the last disposal by a person who was covered by s.2(2).[298] So if a person poisoned by tainted meat proceeds against the butcher who sold it, and the latter cannot name his source of supply, he may nevertheless escape liability by showing that at the time the meat left the abattoir it was wholesome, and became noxious, for example, en route to his shop. Again, if a surgical implant is shown to have been perfect when fitted and only to have failed subsequently the defence will be made out.[299] The burden of proof lies on the defendant in respect of this defence,[300] though presumably the claimant must initially show that the product was defective at some time.

10-70 **Non-profit activities** Section 4(1)(c) provides two defences: a wide one in the case of suppliers, and a narrower one in the case of producers, importers and others covered by s.2(2). Suppliers escape liability entirely if they prove that they did not supply in the course of a business, thus protecting holders of church fêtes and the like.[301] Producers must prove this, but must also show in addition that they never supplied the goods in question with a view to profit.[302] This is a very ungenerous exception that seems inapt to cover much more than the baker of home-made cakes for a charity shop.[303]

10-71 **Components** A component manufacturer has a defence if he can show that the defect is a defect in the subsequent product in which the component was included, and such defect is wholly due to the design of the finished product, or to compliance with instructions from the manufacturer of the finished product: see s.4(1)(f).[304] So, for example, if a car manufacturer orders brake parts to a clear, but wholly inadequate, standard, the manufacturer of the parts escapes liability if the brakes fail (though the manufacturer of the car, of course, does not).

---

297 Thus arguably exonerating an electricity generating company if a voltage "spike" occurs as a result, not of events at the power station, but of problems in a part of the distribution network not under the generator's control. This may be important in practice, given the propensity of such "spikes" to wreak havoc in home computers.

298 See s.4(2).

299 As happened in *Piper v JRI (Manufacturing) Ltd* [2006] EWCA Civ 1344; (2006) 92 B.M.L.R. 141 (failure of prosthesis after fitment).

300 See *Love v Halfords Ltd* [2014] EWHC 1057 (QB); [2014] P.I.Q.R. P20 at [29]. To this extent it is difficult to support the reasoning in the Scottish decision in *McGlinchey v General Motors UK Ltd* [2011] CSOH 206; 2012 Rep. L.R. 20 (defect in handbrake on car; unclear when arose; defenders assoilzied). The point did not arise on appeal at [2012] CSIH 91.

301 Though presumably not charity shops. A business remains a business even if its profits go to good causes. And a hospital, even one practising free state socialised medicine (as with the NHS) is not within the exception in respect of what it produces in the course of providing therapy: see the decision of the European Court in *Veedfald v Århus Amtskommune* [2003] 1 C.M.L.R. 41.

302 s.4(1)(c)(ii). The Directive, art.7, requires that the product "was neither manufactured by [the producer] for sale or any form of distribution for economic purpose nor manufactured or distributed by him in the course of his business".

303 Or, possibly, gifts such as food parcels for refugees supplied by trading corporations.

304 The burden of proof is troublesome here. In cases such as this the claimant will surely not be able to show that the component was defective at all; but if so, it is a little difficult to see why the defendant will ever have to prove anything.

Development risks[305] This is a controversial defence, whose inclusion is optional under the Directive.[306] The 1987 Act adopted it for a variety of reasons, such as encouragement of technological innovation, keeping down insurance costs, preserving a competitive advantage and (no doubt) to protect the pharmaceutical industry. By s.4(1)(e) it is a defence to prove: 10-72

> "that the state of scientific and technical knowledge at the relevant time[307] was not such that a producer of products of the same description as the product in question might be expected to have discovered the defect if it had existed in his products while they were under his control."

It should be noted that the underlying Directive is slightly stricter, referring simply to whether the defect could have been discovered (i.e. by anyone) given the state of scientific and technical knowledge at the time when the producer put the product into circulation.[308] This matters: information available to scientific researchers but not producers will defeat the defence under the Directive but not under the strict wording of the Act. In *A v National Blood Authority*,[309] however, it was accepted that the wording of the Directive should prevail in this respect, though this is not necessarily the last word.[310]

It should be noted that s.4(1)(e) substantially qualifies the "hindsight" rule which 10-73
it has been suggested is inherent in the concept of "defect",[311] and introduces an element of foreseeability that would not have otherwise been there. It therefore has the effect of considerably watering down the idea of liability without fault, and providing producers with ample opportunities to discourage potential claimants by making allegations about the state of technology at the time of production. To this extent, s.4(1)(e) may have the effect of subverting the strict liability regime of the 1987 Act. However, the section is narrowly construed.[312] In particular, it is now clear that it only protects the producer if the possibility of the defect could not have been discovered.[313] If the hypothetical producer could have known that the defect might

---

305 C. Newdick, "The Development Risk Defence of the Consumer Protection Act 1987" [1988] C.L.J. 455; C. Newdick, "Risk, Uncertainty and Knowledge in the Development Risk Defence" (1992) 20 Anglo-Am. L.R. 309.

306 See arts 7(e) and 15(1)(b). France, Belgium and Luxembourg omit it; Germany does not apply it to the development of drugs.

307 i.e. that of supply by the producer: s.4(2).

308 See 85/374/EC art.7(e): defence for producer if "the state of scientific and technical knowledge at the time when he put the product into circulation was not such as to enable the existence of the defect to be discovered".

309 [2001] 3 All E.R. 289, 326–327. cf. *Commission v UK* [1997] 3 C.M.L.R. 923, where the ECJ thought, perhaps optimistically, that s.4(1)(e) had not failed properly to transpose the terms of 85/374/EC art.7(e).

310 See para.10-47.

311 See para.10-64.

312 Though how narrowly is a matter of some controversy. It has been said in Germany (see *BGH* 9.5.1995, NJW 1995, 2162) that the defence only applies to "standard products". But the Directive contains no such limitation, and in *A v National Blood Authority* [2001] 3 All E.R. 289, 317–319 Burton J thought it could apply even to non-standard products.

313 Note an obvious point: scientific knowledge is not the same as accident experience. In *Abouzaid v Mothercare (UK) Ltd, The Times,* 20 February 2001, it was understandably held that s.4(1)(e) could not protect the producer of a dangerous pushchair attachment which half-blinded a child merely because no such accident had ever happened before. On the other hand, it has been held in Australia, interpreting provisions essentially identical to art.7(e), that it is not enough that contemporary technical knowledge might raise a mere suspicion: it must be sufficient to establish the defect. See *Peterson*

be present, it is irrelevant that he has no means of knowing if it exists in a specific item, or that there is no foolproof way of screening products for it or otherwise eliminating it.[314] Furthermore, assuming the wording of the Directive is taken, the requirement that the state of knowledge "was not such as to enable the existence of the defect to be discovered" is also strictly construed. If any hypothetical researcher could have discovered the possibility of the defect, however obscure the source of the information,[315] the defence will not apply. Indeed, in *A v National Blood Authority*[316] Burton J seemingly thought that existing knowledge could be discounted only where in the form of "an unpublished document or unpublished research not available to the general public, retained within the laboratory or research department of a particular company".[317]

(e) Defendants

10-74 **Persons liable under the Act** Sections 2(2) and 2(3) of the 1987 Act make four categories of person liable. These are (a) producers; (b) those who hold themselves out as producers; (c) importers; and (d) suppliers. The first three are liable automatically: the fourth, only if they fail to state whom they bought the product from. It should also be noted that activities carried out otherwise than with a view to profit do not count for these purposes.[318]

10-75 **"Producers"** Section 1(2) defines "producer" so as to include the following three categories:

(a) "The person who manufactured[319] [the product]." This covers the manufacturer of a component as well as the manufacturer of the finished product. So if brakes manufactured by X are installed in a car manufactured by Y and they fail, both X and Y will be liable: X because the brakes were defective, Y because the car as a whole was sub-standard.

(b) "In the case of a substance which has not been manufactured but has been won or abstracted, the person who won or abstracted it." This applies to such persons as the resources company that mines some mineral which turns out

v Merck Sharpe & Dohme (Australia) Pty Ltd [2010] FCA 180; (2010) 266 A.L.R. 1 at [928]–[929] (Jessup J) (appeal dismissed, [2011] FCAFC 128; (2011) 284 A.L.R. 1).

314 *A v National Blood Authority* [2001] 3 All E.R. 289, 361-365. See too the "defective condom" case, *Richardson v London Rubber Co Ltd* [2000] Lloyd's Rep. Med. 280 (once shown manufacturers could have known of possibility that condom might disintegrate in use, would have defeated s.4(1)(e) defence *in limine*: practicality of eliminating defect irrelevant. As it happened, the action failed for other reasons). But this approach is controversial in the European context. A Dutch court has rejected it: *Scholten v Sanguin Foundation*, 03.02.1999, NJ 1999, 621 (blood products).

315 e.g. in a recondite journal in a recondite country such as French Polynesia.

316 [2001] 3 All E.R. 289.

317 [2001] 3 All E.R. 289 at 327. cf. the slightly more generous view expressed by the Advocate-General in *Commission v UK* [1997] 3 C.M.L.R. 923, 934.

318 See s.4(1)(c).

319 Note that a mere repairer or reconditioner is not a manufacturer, even though goods leave his premises (one hopes) in a different and better state than they entered them. But delineation may be difficult. It must be arguable that where, say, a car or computer is so completely reconstructed as to amount to an essentially different thing, then the rebuilder will be a manufacturer. A case close to the line is a German decision (*KG (Berlin)* 03.04.2014, Az. 20 U 253/12) that a doctor who modifies an artificial hip is not a producer so as to incur liability under the Directive. See C. Miller & R. Goldberg, *Product Liability* 2nd edn, (Oxford: OUP, 2004), para.8.10.

to be dangerous (for example, blue asbestos), or the distiller of sea-salt from contaminated sea water.

(c) "In the case of a product which has not been manufactured, won or abstracted but essential characteristics of which are attributable to an industrial or other process having been carried out (for example, in relation to agricultural produce), the person who carried out that process." This covers agricultural produce and game which has been subjected to some process. For example, it makes liable the farmer who harvests poisonous peas or grows cattle with toxic hormones, the drier of defective fruit, and (it would seem) the abattoir owner in the case of tainted meat.

It should be noted that, while there is a limited exception for non-business supply,[320] there is no free-standing requirement that a product be supplied for money: free samples and promotional gifts are as much within the Act as ordinary merchandise.

Producers abroad The provisions of the Act would seem to apply to producers not only in England, but anywhere within the European Economic Area (EEA)[321] (all the countries of which have agreed to enact legislation similar to the 1987 Act). It is an open question whether the provisions of the Act apply extra-territorially outside the EEA, so as to make (say) an American or Korean producer liable. It is tentatively submitted, however, that they do.[322] In any case, as will appear below, where goods are produced outside the EEA, the importer of them into the EEA will be liable. **10-76**

Those who hold themselves out as producers Section 2(2)(b) applies liability to: **10-77**

> "any person who, by putting his name on the product or using a trade mark or other distinguishing mark in relation to the product, has held himself out to be the producer of the product."

This clearly applies to manufacturers who "out-source" actual production. So, for instance, if a European television maker sub-contracts production to another firm but puts its own name on the finished product, it will be liable in the same way as if it had produced it itself.[323] Similarly with a food company which buys in canned fish that it then labels and markets under its own name.[324] (The actual producer will,

---

320 See s.4(1)(c).

321 i.e. the EU and the ex-EFTA Member States collectively (except for Switzerland and Liechtenstein); see the European Economic Area Act 1993. This means effectively the current members of the EU, plus Norway and Iceland. See generally T. Blanchet, R. Piipponen & M. Westman-Clément, *The Agreement on the European Economic Area* (1994), Ch.VI.

322 It is true that in *Allen v Depuy International Ltd* [2014] EWHC 753 (QB); [2015] 2 W.L.R. 442 it was held that the 1987 Act did not have extraterritorial application so as to apply to damage done outside the EEA by products manufactured in it. But the converse does not follow: the aim of the Act and the underlying Directive is clearly to protect those suffering product damage within the EEA, and there seems no reason to disapply the Act merely because the defendant's act leading to the damage (i.e. the manufacture) took place somewhere else.

323 For an example of potential liability arising from such outsourcing see *Busby v Berkshire Bed Co Ltd* [2018] EWHC 2976 (QB) esp. at [21]. If the other firm is abroad, e.g. in South Korea, the European firm will in addition be liable as an importer; see para.10-78.

324 Quaere whether including the words "produced for X" in the small print on the label would mean

of course, also be liable under s.2(2)(a).) It is often assumed[325] that a similar liability attaches under this provision to an "own-brander" such as a supermarket chain which buys in produce, but puts its own name on it before marketing it. But this is open to some doubt. A supermarket which puts its name on a product does not (it is submitted) come within the description of one who has "held himself out to be the producer;" at most it says that the product has its imprimatur. Few, after all, can believe that (say) Tesco plc actually produces all its own-branded goods itself. If this is right, the "own-brander" is subject only to the more limited liability of a supplier to name his source of supply (on which see below).[326]

10-78 **Importers** Section 2(2)(c) applies liability to:

> "any person who has imported the product into a Member State from a place outside the Member States[327] in order, in the course of any business of his, to supply it to another."

Hence, even if the extra-EEA producer cannot be sued, the importer into the EEA can.[328] It should be noted that under the provisions of the Brussels I Recast Regulation,[329] the English courts will have jurisdiction over the importer, even if not normally resident in England, provided the damage was incurred in England.

10-79 It should be noted that in respect of events after the end of the UK–EU transition period,[330] s.2(2)(c) referred to above applies instead only to importers into the UK.[331] Two effects follow. First, where goods manufactured in the EEA are imported into the UK, the claimant obtains a further potential defendant in the shape of the UK importer. Secondly, where goods are imported from a non-European state via the EEA, the liable defendant changes from the importer into the EEA to the UK importer (if different).

10-80 **Suppliers**[332] Section 2(3) runs as follows:

> "Subject as aforesaid, where any damage is caused wholly or partly by a defect in a product, any person who supplied[333] the product (whether to the person who suffered the damage, to the producer of any product in which the product in question is comprised or

the defendant did not hold itself out as producer. It is submitted that this is unlikely.

325 e.g. *Tesco Stores Ltd v Pollard* [2006] EWCA Civ 393.

326 A similar uncertainty appears in the case of franchisors. Do (say) McDonalds, Pizza Hut or Starbucks hold themselves out as producing food or drink actually prepared by their franchisees? It has apparently been assumed they do (e.g. *B (A Child) v McDonald's Restaurants Ltd* [2002] EWHC 490 (QB)); and it is tentatively suggested that this is right. The nature of the franchise relationship, and the separation between franchisor and franchisee, is much less clear to the average customer than in the case of a multiple store such as Tesco Plc.

327 See para.10-76 for what this means.

328 Where goods are imported into the EU from a state which is a member of the EEA but not of the EU, the EU importer is also liable unless the non-EU state in question has ratified the Lugano Convention on jurisdiction so as to guarantee that its residents are subject to jurisdiction elsewhere in the EEA. If it has, the EFTA importer is exclusively liable. See the 1993 Agreement establishing the EEA (1993 Cm.2073), Annex III.

329 Regulation (EU) No 1215/2012 art.7(2) (assuming the defendant to be domiciled in an EEA state).

330 At the time of writing, 31 December 2020: see s.33 of the European Union (Withdrawal Agreement) Act 2020.

331 See Sch.3 to the Product Safety and Metrology etc. (Amendment etc.) (EU Exit) Regulations 2019 (SI 2019/696), activated at the end of the transition period by Sch.5 Pt 1 to the European Union (Withdrawal Agreement) Act 2020.

332 See C. Hodges, "Product liability of suppliers: the notification trap" (2002) 27 E.L. Rev. 758.

333 For the definition of "supply", see s.46(1). It covers not only sale, but hiring, letting on hire-

to any other person) shall be liable for the damage if

(a) the person who suffered the damage[334] requests the supplier to identify one or more of the persons (whether still in existence or not) to whom subsection (2) above applies in relation to the product [i.e. producers, those holding themselves out as producers, and importers];
(b) that request is made within a reasonable period after the damage occurs and at a time when it is not reasonably practicable for the person making the request to identify all those persons; and
(c) the supplier fails, within a reasonable period after receiving the request, either to comply with the request or to identify the person who supplied the product to him."

In order to come within this section, the supplier does not have to have supplied the goods to the actual claimant: any supply will suffice. Thus where a consumer is injured by a defective product, the wholesaler, as much as the retailer, is bound to provide the requisite information. Where goods are supplied by way of hire-purchase or conditional sale, the "supplier" is deemed to be the dealer and not the finance company with whom the contract is actually made.[335] In the case of a ship or aircraft, a charter for the purpose of carrying goods or passengers is not however considered a "supply".[336] It should be noted that this is merely a "fall-back" liability. All a supplier needs to do in order to escape liability under this provision is to identify such a person[337] as is referred to in s.2(3); he is not a guarantor of that person's liability, and it does not matter that he is inaccessible, or judgment-proof, or immune from liability under the Act.[338] Nevertheless, the supplier may on occasion find it difficult to escape liability in practice, since very often it will be difficult to identify the persons specified[339]: the supply may have happened some time ago, he may have obtained supplies from two different sources and be unable to identify which, and the relevant records may not still be extant.

Two qualifications should be noted to s.2(3). First, it does not apply to those who supply otherwise than in the course of a business.[340] And secondly, the provision in s.1(3) should be noted. This provides that: **10-81**

---

purchase and virtually any other transfer, including gift. It may not, however, apply to a mere licence to use. Thus where a child is injured using a defective swing provided outside a shop, it seems doubtful if the shop is a "supplier".

334 Or, in the case of wrongful death actions, his personal representatives: s.6(2). No doubt a request from an agent, such as a solicitor, would suffice.

335 s.46(2).

336 s.46(9). This is introduced, one suspects, to prevent lease financiers of ships and aircraft from being drawn into the product liability net. Effectively this means that an injured passenger is limited to a claim under the Act against the builder, rather than the airline or shipping company, or the bank (if any) that own the aircraft. Compare generally *Stott v Thomas Cook Tour Operators Ltd* [2014] UKSC 15; [2014] A.C. 1347.

337 And presumably, if there is more than one person qualifying as "producer", it is enough if the supplier identifies one of them.

338 e.g. because the first supplier of the product is a charity which supplied it otherwise than with a view to profit (see s.4(1)(c)), or even (semble) because the goods became defective while in the supplier's own hands!

339 The Austrian Supreme Court has held, interpreting the Directive, that identification must include the proper legal designation of the supplying or importing business and all other information necessary to allow the claimant to sue it: see *OGH* 21.12.2004, 5 OB 217/04D, reported as *Re A Faulty Baguette* [2006] E.C.C. 17. Sed quaere.

340 See s.4(1)(c).

"a person who supplies any product in which products are comprised, whether by virtue of being component parts or raw materials or otherwise, shall not be treated by reason only of his supply of that product as supplying any of the products so comprised."

The significance of this somewhat opaque provision is as follows. Suppose X buys a car with defective brakes from Y, a dealer, and a passenger is injured as a result. If the passenger proceeds against Y, Y can escape liability by identifying the producer[341] of the car. He need not go further and identify the producer of the actual brakes, since the latter is deemed not to have supplied them.

(f) Claimants

10-82 The persons entitled to be claimants are not specified in detail in the Act, although with regard to loss or damage to property s.5(5) speaks of "a person with an interest in the property". Leaving this aside, the answer must be anyone suffering damage of the kind covered by the Act[342] as a result of a defect in a product.

(g) Damage recoverable[343]

10-83 Damage is essential to liability under the 1987 Act. Section 5(1) defines it as "death or personal injury[344] or any loss of[345] or damage to any property (including land)." Pure economic loss is therefore excluded (as under *Donoghue v Stevenson*[346]), though no doubt consequential loss is available in the normal way.[347] Liability for damage to property is, however, restricted in two ways. First, s.5(3) states that there is no liability if the property lost or damaged is not:

---

341 Or *soi-disant* producer, or importer, as the case may be.

342 On which see para.10-83.

343 See generally A. Bell, "Product Liability Damages in England and Wales" (1992) 20 An. Am. L.R. 371.

344 In *Richardson v London Rubber Co Ltd* [2000] Lloyd's Rep. Med. 280, it was apparently accepted that an unwanted pregnancy resulting from use of a defective condom counted as "damage" within the Act. (The action in fact failed, but for other reasons.) Sed quaere whether this ought to count per se as personal injury; also whether, if the action succeeded, any damages would face the same limits as in actions for failed sterilisation (see *Rees v Darlington Memorial Hospital NHS Trust* [2003] UKHL 52; [2004] 1 A.C. 309; see para.7-99).

345 The reference to "loss of or damage to any property" might be thought to cover mere theft (e.g. where a householder's silver is stolen because of a defect in a burglar alarm). It is suggested, however, that it does not, since (a) the definition of "defect" in the Act refers to a product's safety, and the definition of "safety" refers only to a propensity to cause damage to (rather than loss of) other property (see s.3(1)); (b) the Directive, in defining "damage" (para.9), makes no reference to loss; and (c) there seems no strong social imperative to protect consumers against mere theft.

346 [1932] A.C. 562; see para.10-22.

347 However, there is a possible clash with the Directive here, which in art.9(a) refers more widely to "damage caused by death or by personal injuries" (French: "*le dommage causé par la mort ou par des lésions corporelles*"; German: "*den durch Tod und Körperverletzungen verursachten Schaden*"). This might allow a user of goods to sue for his loss where a malfunction of those goods causes him to be liable for injury to third parties. The Austrian Supreme Court has certainly assumed so: *OGH* 16.07.1998, 6 Ob 157/98a, reported as *Re Damage Caused By Kitchen Stove* [2000] E.C.C. 137 (failure of oven to heat food properly caused salmonella in third parties who ate it, for which oven owner liable: accepted, owner has potential claim under Directive, though the claim failed for other reasons). In *Boston Scientific Medizintechnik GmbH v AOK Sachsen-Anhalt-Die Gesundheitskasse* (C-503/13) [2015] 3 C.M.L.R. 6; (2015) 144 B.M.L.R. 225 the ECJ held that a claim lay under the Directive for the cost of an operation to replace a defective pacemaker, on the basis that this counted as compensation for personal injury.

"(a) of a description of property ordinarily intended for private use, occupation or consumption[348]; and

(b) intended by the person suffering the loss or damage mainly for his own private use, occupation or consumption."

This excludes damage to business property such as a factory; it should be noted that property may also count as business property even if held by a non-profit organisation.[349] Furthermore, since (a) and (b) are cumulative requirements, it also excludes liability for damage to a shopkeeper's stock-in-trade of consumer goods. Presumably the interest in property that suffices for a claim under the Act is the same as at common law; if so, where damage is done to a house owned by X but let to Y, Y will be able to sue but X will not (unless he can prove damage to the reversion). Secondly, s.5(4) states that no damages are claimable under the Act in respect of damage to property[350] if the claimant's total damage (excluding interest)[351] does not exceed £275.[352] His remedy for any lesser amount will be in negligence.

Damage to the product itself Section 5(2) makes clear that the Act is concerned with damage to other property; there is no liability for "loss of or any damage to the product itself or for the loss of or any damage to the whole or any part of any product which has been supplied with the product in question comprised in it". Thus where a newly-purchased car crashes because a defective tyre bursts at speed, the car manufacturer will not be liable for its replacement cost because this is damage to the "product itself" (i.e. the car he produced). Nor will the tyre manufacturer, because this is damage to a "product which has been supplied with the product in question [i.e. the tyre he produced] comprised in it". Note that, in order to escape liability, it is not enough for the component maker to show his component has been "comprised" in another product: the composite product must actually have been *supplied* with the defective component incorporated in it. So a motorist whose car is wrecked by the failure of a defective tyre which he himself has had fitted can proceed against the tyre maker under s.2(1); this right will be lost only if and when there is a subsequent "supply" of the car to somebody else. On the other hand, it seems any supply will have this effect, whether new or second-hand, and whether or not in the course of a business.[353] So were the motorist in the above example to sell his car privately to a friend before failure of the tyre, the friend would have no cause of action against the tyre manufacturer.[354] 10-84

Punitive damages Despite the liberalisation of the law on exemplary damages 10-85

[348] What of property with two ordinary uses, both business and pleasure, e.g. a personal computer? If intended for pleasure, it is submitted that a claim will lie under the Act.

[349] *Renfrew Golf Club v Motocaddy Ltd* [2016] CSIH 57; 2016 S.C. 860 (golf clubhouse).

[350] No such limitation applies in the case of personal injury.

[351] The subsection refers to "the amount which would fall to be so awarded to that person". It seems to follow that if the claimant's property loss is more than £275 but his award falls to be reduced below that sum by virtue of his contributory negligence, he recovers nothing.

[352] So if the claimant's damage is £300 he recovers in full: if £200, nothing.

[353] Although by s.4(1)(c) there can be no liability in a non-business seller, such a sale is clearly a "supply" within the meaning of the Act: see s.46(1). Note that even a gratuitous transfer will do: ibid.

[354] Contrary to what has been suggested to be the position in respect of negligence at common law: see para.10-25. Note, however, a slight difference between the wording of s.5(2) of the Act and that of the Directive para.9, which defines damage more laconically as: "damage to, or destruction of, any item of property other than the defective product itself." It is just arguable (though unlikely) that this would be regarded as inconsistent with the statutory exclusion of liability in respect of goods sup-

in *Kuddus v Chief Constable of Leicestershire*,[355] it is suggested that they are not available in an action under the 1987 Act. The Directive refers to "damage caused by death or personal injuries" and "damage to, or destruction of, any item of property",[356] which seems to be limited to compensatory damages. Since it seems that member states are not permitted to grant recovery in the area covered by the Directive to a greater extent than the Directive provides,[357] it should follow that exemplary damages are not permitted. In any case, most situations where personal injuries are involved are likely to involve negligence, so the issue is likely to be moot anyway.

(h) Limitation[358]

10-86 **Timing and limitation** The Act applies only to goods supplied by a producer after 1 March 1988.[359] Limitation periods are as for the general law, subject to two exceptions.[360] First, actions in respect of damage to property are subjected to the same period of limitation as injuries to the person, namely three years, rather than the normal six.[361] Secondly, the "long-stop" period is reduced from 15 to 10 years from the time when a producer or other person subject to s.2(2) supplied the product to another[362]; or in the case of a supplier, from the time of last supply by such a person.[363] So "long-tail" claims brought after the 10-year cut-off may still have to be argued in negligence. Similar provisions apply to fatal accidents actions in respect of defective products.[364]

10-87 **Limitation: when time begins to run** In actions for damages under the 1987 Act, time begins to run[365] (i) from the time the cause of action accrued; or (ii) if later, from when the claimant had knowledge[366] of the injury or damage within s.14(1A) of the Limitation Act 1980.[367] In personal injury cases the date of accrual is presum-

plied with defective products comprised in them. On "other property" in connection with negligence, see para.10-23.

355 [2001] UKHL 29; [2002] A.C. 122.

356 art.9(a), (b).

357 *Commission v France* (C52/00) [2002] E.C.R. I-3827 (500 ECU lower limit for property damage cannot be ousted).

358 For limitation generally in tort, see Ch.31.

359 The date when Pt I came into force: see s.50(7), and SI 1987/1680.

360 The periods concerned are laid down in s.11A of the Limitation Act 1980, added thereto by s.6(6) of and Sch.1 to the 1987 Act.

361 Limitation Act 1980 s.11A(4).

362 Although the reference in the 1987 Act is to "supply," the criterion in art.10 of the Directive, which in practice is likely to control, is "put into circulation". For these purposes, it seems, goods are "put into circulation" when they leave the hands of the manufacturer and any distributor wholly under his control. See the decision of the ECJ in *O'Byrne v Sanofi Pasteur MSD Ltd*, Case 127/04, [2006] 1 W.L.R. 1606; [2006] 2 C.M.L.R. 24.

363 Limitation Act 1980 s.11A(3), referring to s.4 of the 1987 Act. For whether the jurisdiction to substitute another defendant after the expiry of the limitation period can be used to sidestep this provision, see *O'Byrne v Aventis Pasteur MSD Ltd*, Case 127/04, [2006] 1 W.L.R. 1606; [2006] 2 C.M.L.R. 24 (a case on art.10 of the Directive, but the wording is the same); and the subsequent proceedings, in *Aventis Pasteur SA v OB*, C-358/08, [2010] 1 W.L.R. 1375; *O'Byrne v Aventis Pasteur MSD Ltd* [2010] UKSC 23; [2010] 1 W.L.R. 1412.

364 See ss.12 and 14(1A) of the 1980 Act.

365 Other than for the purpose of the 10-year "long-stop" provision.

366 Including constructive knowledge: see s.14(3) of the 1980 Act.

367 See Limitation Act 1980 s.11A(4). Note that the "latent damage" provisions in ss.14A and 14B of

ably when the injury was suffered (whether or not the claimant knew about it)[368]; in property damage cases, by contrast, it is when the owner is aware of the material facts about the damage.[369] The definition of "knowledge" in personal injury and property damage cases alike is virtually the same as that applicable in the general law by virtue of s.14(1) and (3) of the 1980 Act,[370] save that in property damage actions no account is taken of knowledge gained before the claimant had a right of action.[371]

Limitation: extension of period The discretion in s.33 of the Limitation Act 1980 to disapply a primary limitation period applies equally to actions under the Consumer Protection Act 1987. But no extension is possible in respect of damage to property,[372] or where it would override the 10-year "long-stop" provision.[373] **10-88**

(i) Miscellaneous matters

Contributory negligence The Law Reform (Contributory Negligence) Act 1945 applies to actions under the 1987 Act.[374] **10-89**

Exclusion of liability Section 7 prevents the statutory liability being excluded or limited by any contract term, notice, or by any other provision.[375] This is wider than the equivalent provision in the Unfair Contract Terms Act 1977, in that it completely prevents exclusion of liability for property damage, rather than subjecting it to a "reasonableness" test.[376] Section 7 does not, however, affect claims for contribution and indemnity.[377] **10-90**

Nuclear installations The special regime applicable to nuclear accidents under the Nuclear Installations Act 1965 is preserved and the Act does not apply to them.[378] **10-91**

---

the 1980 Act do not apply to actions under the 1987 Act, being limited to liability in negligence.

368 cf. *Cartledge v Jopling* [1963] A.C. 758.

369 See Consumer Protection Act 1987 s.5(5). But subss.5(6) and 5(7) then go on to define knowledge of the relevant facts in very similar terms to the definition of "knowledge" within s.14 of the Limitation Act 1980.

370 See s.14(1A).

371 e.g. where I buy a house which I know has already suffered damage from a defective boiler in the house next door, and the house later suffers further damage, my knowledge runs from the date of purchase.

372 Limitation Act 1980 s.33(1A)(b).

373 Limitation Act 1980 s.33(1A)(a). But in *Smithkline Beecham Plc v Horne-Roberts* [2001] EWCA Civ 2006; [2002] 1 W.L.R. 1662, the Court of Appeal held that this did not preclude the substitution of a defendant in the case of misnomer. There has since been a reference to the ECJ on the point: *O'Byrne v Aventis Pasteur MSD Ltd*, Case C-127/04 (2004). See para.10-68 fn.293.

374 s.6(4).

375 Contrast the Directive para.12, which merely prevents exclusion of the *producer's* liability for personal injury.

376 See s.2(2) of the Unfair Contract Terms Act 1977.

377 Since it only applies in favour of a person who has suffered damage, or his relatives. cf. *Thompson v T Lohan (Plant Hire) Ltd* [1987] 1 W.L.R. 649.

378 s.6(8).

5. BREACH OF STATUTORY DUTY: THE CONSUMER PROTECTION ACT 1987 PART II

10-92 **Unsafe products** Prevention is often better than cure. In this connection it is worth noting the provisions of Pt II of the Consumer Protection Act 1987. Under s.11, and also under the General Product Safety Regulations 2005,[379] the Secretary of State is enabled to lay down safety regulations in relation to goods, their construction and composition and, where appropriate, to require warnings to be furnished.[380] It is a criminal offence under s.12 to supply (or to expose or possess for supply[381]) goods in the course of a business that do not comply with such regulations. By s.41(1) infringement of this provision expressly gives rise to an action for breach of statutory duty;[382] however, where the claimant is a consumer this is of limited significance.[383] Liability (which cannot be excluded[384]) is not dependent on negligence, since although there is a "due diligence" defence provided, it applies only to criminal proceedings.[385] It is also a criminal offence to supply dangerous goods as such in the course of a business[386]; but breach of this prohibition does not give rise to civil liability,[387] and it is therefore of little relevance here.

---

379 SI 2005/1803.

380 Such regulations are legion. A straightforward, but entirely unremarkable, example is the Electrical Equipment (Safety) Regulations 2016 (SI 2016/1101).

381 This provision is worth noting; contrast Pt I of the 1987 Act, which imposes no liability in respect of goods never supplied by the defendant.

382 For an example of such a claim (though unsuccessful on the facts), see *Howmet Ltd v Economy Devices Ltd* [2016] EWCA Civ 847; [2016] B.L.R. 555; 168 Con. L.R. 27 (dangerous electric fire-safety probe). An example of a successful statutory duty claim under the predecessor of the Electrical Equipment (Safety) Regulations 2016 was *Stoke-on-Trent College v Pelican Rouge Coffee Solutions Group Ltd* [2017] EWHC 2829 (TCC) (defective drinks vending machine set fire to building).

383 This is because the maximal nature of the Product Liability Directive precludes the imposition of strict liability under the Regulations where it would not arise under the Directive: see *Wilson v Beko Plc* [2019] EWHC 3362 (QB); [2020] P.I.Q.R. P8. This will remain the position after the end of the transition period (since, save for the Supreme Court, English courts remain bound by pre-existing EU jurisprudence: see s.6 of the European Union (Withdrawal) Act 2018, which only releases them from following subsequent EU developments).

384 s.41(4).

385 s.39(1).

386 General Product Safety Regulations 2005 (SI 2005/1803) regs 5, 8.

387 General Product Safety Regulations 2005 (SI 2005/1803) reg.42.

CHAPTER 11

OCCUPIERS' LIABILITY AND DEFECTIVE PREMISES

TABLE OF CONTENTS

1. LIABILITY OF OCCUPIERS TO VISITORS FOR CONDITION OF PREMISES

Common law At common law, occupiers' liability was one of several cases of liability based on negligence which evolved before a general principle of liability was propounded in *Donoghue v Stevenson*.[1] As the rules had been worked out in some detail before that case, they differed from those which might have been expected to be derived from that decision.[2] Two features stood out. First, what an occupier could and could not do without attracting liability was treated to a large extent as a matter of law, rather than a matter of fact which turned on what was reasonable in a given case. Secondly, the scope of an occupier's duties towards 11-01

[1] [1932] A.C. 562. See F. Parker & N. Parry, "Private Property, Public Access and Occupier's Liability" (1995) 15 L.S. 335.

[2] Though, but for the Occupiers' Liability Act 1957, the occupiers' rules might well have gradually been assimilated into the general law. Some American authority tended this way (e.g. *Rowland v Christian*, 443 P.2d 561 (1968)). And in *Australian Safeway Stores P/L v Zaluzna* (1987) 61 A.L.J.R. 180 at 182–183, on an appeal from Victoria (which then still applied the common law rules), a majority of the High Court of Australia thought occupiers' liability should no longer be treated as separate from general negligence. On the relation between occupiers' liability and the common law, see P. Handford and B. McGivern, "Two Problems of Occupiers' Liability Part One—The Occupiers' Liability Acts and the Common Law" (2015) 39 Melb. U. L. Rev. 128.

those on his land depended crucially on their status. Trespassers and other unlawful visitors were owed no duty at all except in respect of intentional or reckless injury. As regards lawful visitors, a distinction was drawn between persons entering under a contract and those entering merely by invitation or permission, express or implied, on the part of the occupier. In the class of contractual visitors a further distinction was drawn between persons entering under a contract for the use of the premises and those entering under a contract in which the use of the premises was only ancillary to some other purpose. In the heterogeneous class of persons who entered without contract, there was the all-important distinction between "invitees", in the purpose of whose visit the occupier had a material interest, and "licensees", for example those visiting for purely social purposes. The latter were owed a much more exiguous duty.[3]

2. The Occupiers' Liability Act 1957

11-02 **Generally** This Act gave effect to recommendations in the Law Reform Committee's Third Report.[4] Its main purpose was to provide new rules, and a "common duty of care," to replace the rules of the common law under which the duty owed by an occupier of premises differed according as the visitor was an invitee or a licensee. Under the Act, the substance of occupiers' liability became much more like the ordinary law of negligence. Nevertheless, the law of occupiers still contains a number of features not found in the rest of the law, and for that reason it is still helpful to treat it separately.

(a) Scope of the 1957 Act

11-03 **Scope of occupier's liability: "occupancy duty" and "activity duty"** The common law of occupier's liability, with its distinctions between licensees, invitees, trespassers and the like, was limited in application to dangers due to the state of the premises, sometimes known as "occupancy duties". By contrast, where a danger arose from activities on land, such as shooting or driving vehicles, rather than from the state of the land itself, any duty arising ("activity duty") was governed by the general rules of negligence, in which issues such as the status of the claimant were largely irrelevant.[5]

11-04 The Act is not entirely clear on this point, s.1(1) providing that the rules in it:

> "shall have effect in place of the rules of the common law, to regulate the duty which an occupier of premises owes to his visitors in respect of dangers due to the state of the premises or to things done or omitted to be done on them."

It could be argued that these words are wide enough for the Act to apply to all

[3] See the 11th edn of the present work, pp.667 onwards.; P. North, *Occupiers' Liability* (1971), pp.1–15. Illustrative authorities include *Francis v Cockrell* (1870) L.R. 5 Q.B. 184 and 501; *Maclenan v Segar* [1917] 2 K.B. 325; *Indermaur v Dames* (1866) L.R. 1 C. & P. 274; *Fairman v Perpetual Investment Building Society* [1923] A.C. 74; *Jacobs v LCC* [1950] A.C. 361. For a comparative survey, see B. McMahon, "Conclusions on judicial behaviour from a comparative study of Occupiers' Liability" (1975) 38 M.L.R. 39.

[4] See Law Reform Committee, *Third Report: Occupiers' Liability to Invitees, Licensees and Trespassers* (1954) Cmd.9305.

[5] *Gallagher v Humphrey* (1862) 6 L.T. 684; *Slater v Clay Cross Co Ltd* [1956] 2 Q.B. 264; *Riden v AC Billings & Sons Ltd* [1957] 1 Q.B. 46, 56 (affirmed [1958] A.C. 240).

injuries on land due to the negligence of the occupier, thus erasing the common law distinction. But while there may of course be liability for dangers in the state of land due to activities on it,[6] or failure to supervise those carried on by others,[7] and the boundary may be a narrow one,[8] it now seems clear that the specific reference to the "state of the premises" limits the effect of the Act to occupancy duties.[9] As Lord Hoffmann has observed, the mere fact that a person may get into danger on a given piece of land is not itself a peril due to the state of the premises, and even if the occupier's acts or omissions may concurrently affect his safety this does not widen the ambit of the subsection.[10] Furthermore, this seems right in principle; if A's activity hurts B, the regime governing it should be the same whether or not B happens to have been on A's land at the time. Thus injuries due to the occupier failing properly to supervise a firework display,[11] shooting a person on his land,[12] inadequately controlling thugs in a nightclub,[13] failing to teach a visitor to use sports equipment,[14] or failing to ensure safe working conditions for a contractor,[15] have

---

[6] e.g. *Lear v Hickstead Ltd* [2016] EWHC 528 (QB); [2016] 4 W.L.R. 73 (parking arrangements alleged (unsuccessfully) to create danger for which defendants liable); *Bosworth Water Trust v SSR* [2018] EWHC 444 (QB) (failure to give proper warnings about dangers of crazy golf).

[7] e.g. *Bottomley v Todmorden Cricket Club* [2003] EWCA Civ 1575; [2004] P.I.Q.R. P18 (firework display organised by third party).

[8] See, e.g. the Scottish case of *Anderson v Imrie* [2018] CSIH 14; 2018 S.C. 328, where Lords Brodie and Drummond Young, at [28] and [53], thought a case of injury to a child on a dangerous farm gate was better viewed as involving child supervision rather than occupiers' liability. Sed quaere. In this particular case, why not both?

[9] See *Fowles v Bedfordshire CC* [1995] P.I.Q.R. P380; *Revill v Newberry* [1996] Q.B. 567 at 574 onwards; *Bottomley v Todmorden Cricket Club* [2003] EWCA Civ 1575; [2004] P.I.Q.R. P18 at [31], per Brooke LJ; *Kolasa v Ealing Hospital NHS Trust* [2015] EWHC 289 (QB) at [44]–[47]. The text here was approved by Martin Spencer J in *Spearman v Royal United Bath Hospitals NHS Foundation Trust* [2017] EWHC 3027 (QB); [2018] Med. L.R. 244 at [58]–[59]. For earlier expressions of the same view see F. Odgers, "Occupiers' Liability: A Further Comment" [1957] C.L.J. 39; P. North, *Occupiers' Liability* (1971), pp.80–82.

[10] *Tomlinson v Congleton BC* [2003] UKHL 47; [2004] 1 A.C. 46 at [26]–[27]. Strictly speaking this case concerned the interpretation of the Occupiers' Liability Act 1984: but the wording interpreted is the same, and hence its reasoning clearly applies to the 1957 Act. Similar cases are *Keown v Coventry NHS Trust* [2006] EWCA Civ 39; [2006] 1 W.L.R. 953 (when a child climbed on, and fell off, a fire escape, not within 1984 Act since no complaint as to the dangerous state of the premises); *Baldacchino v West Wittering Estate Plc* [2008] EWHC 3386 (QB) (similarly with regard to injuries suffered from diving off impeccably maintained navigation beacon); and *Hatcher v ASW Ltd* [2010] EWCA Civ 1325, a case under the Occupiers' Liability Act 1984 (child injured while climbing on buildings in abandoned Cardiff steelworks equipped with formidable anti-trespasser defences: held, no danger *due to state of premises*). A case on the other side of the line was *Liddle v Bristol City Council* [2018] EWHC 3673 (QB) (embedded rail tracks snaring cyclist). See too *Donoghue v Folkestone Properties Ltd* [2003] EWCA Civ 231; [2003] Q.B. 1008 at [53], per Lord Phillips; *Siddorn v Patel* [2007] EWHC 1248 (QB).

[11] *Bottomley v Todmorden Cricket Club* [2003] EWCA Civ 1575; [2004] P.I.Q.R. P18.

[12] *Revill v Newberry* [1996] Q.B. 567 (see Neill LJ at 574 onwards).

[13] *Everett v Comojo (UK) Ltd* [2011] EWCA Civ 13; [2012] 1 W.L.R. 150.

[14] *Fowles v Bedfordshire CC* [1995] P.I.Q.R. P380; *Poppleton v Trustees of the Portsmouth Youth Activities Committee* [2007] EWHC 1567 (QB) (the question was not discussed on appeal: [2008] EWCA Civ 646; [2009] P.I.Q.R. P1); *Pinchbeck v Craggy Island Ltd* [2012] EWHC 2745 (QB), especially at [42] (bad supervision of adult adventure playground); *Pook v Rossall School* [2018] EWHC 522 (QB); [2018] E.L.R. 402 (alleged failure to supervise school athletes). So also with an occupier whose negligence consists in knowingly allowing contractors to work on his land without proper regard for the safety of their own employees: *Tafa v Matsim Properties Ltd* [2011] EWHC 1302 (QB).

[15] *Yates v National Trust* [2014] EWHC 222 (QB); [2014] P.I.Q.R. P16, esp. at [37] (tree surgeon); also *McCarthy v Marks & Spencer Plc* [2014] EWHC 3183 (QB), especially at [61] and [81] (building

been held to fall outside the occupier's liability regime and within that of general negligence.[16] In any case, where the claimant's status is not in issue there is often little practical difference between his remedy under the Act and that at common law. The issue in many cases will be one of fact: was the claimant foreseeable,[17] and has the duty to take reasonable care been broken?[18] Indeed, even in clear "occupancy duty" cases the courts have on occasion simply ignored the Act.[19]

11-05 **Concurrent duties** There is no doubt that liability under the Act (like occupier's liability at common law) may coexist with duties owed in some other capacity, for example as a school, hospital authority, employer,[20] or event organiser[21]; in such a case the claimant can rely on whichever cause of action is more advantageous to him. "Occupation of premises is a ground of liability and is not a ground of exemption from liability."[22] Hence the fact that the claimant would fail were he to bring an action under the Act is no reason to deny liability if he sues in some other capacity,[23] or indeed for ordinary negligence at common law.[24]

11-06 **"Premises"** The Act regulates the liability of occupiers of "premises".[25] It is submitted that "premises" is here used in its legal and not its popular connotation to mean "land", whether or not there are buildings on it. Thus the term has been held to cover such things as railway lines,[26] open land next to a path,[27] an airport

---

contractors dealing with asbestos).

16 Or as often as not, in the case of a business occupier, health and safety legislation such as the Provision and Use of Work Equipment Regulations 1998 (SI 1998/2306). In practice the majority of claims for accidents at work tend to be brought under such provisions with the 1957 Act used as a mere fall-back. Normally these duties do not affect private residential occupiers, though this is not entirely true: see generally *Kmiecic v Isaacs* [2011] EWCA Civ 451; [2011] I.C.R. 1269.

17 On which the claimant's status may well be relevant de facto. Trespassers are, one hopes, generally less foreseeable than lawful visitors.

18 But the question might conceivably be relevant in other ways. For example, it may be important with regard to the construction of an occupier's liability insurance policy, which will often cover him for liability as occupier but not otherwise. Thus in *New Zealand Ins Co v Prudential Ins Co* [1976] 1 N.Z.L.R. 84, a court was asked (and declined) to decide the source of the liability of a deceased occupier who committed suicide leaving poison in the kitchen which a visitor later accidentally drank. See P. North, *Occupiers' Liability* (1971), pp.79–87.

19 See, e.g. *Davies v Borough of Tenby* [1974] 2 Lloyd's Rep. 469; *Ward v Tesco Stores Ltd* [1976] 1 W.L.R. 810.

20 See, e.g. *Reffell v Surrey CC* [1964] 1 W.L.R. 358; *Ward v Hertfordshire CC* [1970] 1 W.L.R. 356; *Munnings v Hydro-Electric Commission* (1971) 45 A.L.J.R. 378; *Murphy v Brentwood DC* [1991] 1 A.C. 398 at 433, per Nicholls LJ. See P. North, *Occupiers' Liability* (1971), pp.66–87.

21 See *Geary v Wetherspoon Plc* [2011] EWHC 1506 (QB); [2011] N.P.C. 60 (no liability in bar owner when patron injured sliding down banisters, since no danger due to state of premises: but might be different if defendant organised competitions involving such activities (at [60])).

22 *Commissioner for Railways v McDermott* [1967] 1 A.C. 169 at 186.

23 e.g. *Westwood v Post Office* [1974] A.C. 1 (workman injured in lift room where he should not have been: employers liable qua employers for breach of statutory duty, but not qua occupiers, since claimant trespassing).

24 e.g. *AC Billings & Son v Riden* [1958] A.C. 240; *Sharpe v ET Sweeting & Son Ltd* [1963] 1 W.L.R. 665 (builders and contractors leave site in dangerous condition: liable at common law even if not "occupiers" within 1957 Act). In *Bailey v Armes* [1999] E.G.C.S. 21, the CA seemingly accepted that an occupier might be liable at common law (though not in the case before them) for injury due to dangers on land he did not occupy, but to which his land gave access: but this seems questionable (cf. *Armstrong v Keepmoat Homes Ltd*, unreported 3 February 2012).

25 s.1(1).

26 *Videan v British Transport Commission* [1963] 2 Q.B. 650. Similarly with a track across an open

runway,[28] and (it seems) the waters of a harbour.[29] So it seems likely that the Act would govern the liability of, say, the owner of a field with toxic berries growing on it which poisoned a child visitor who ate them.

Fixed or movable structures Following the recommendations of the Law Reform Committee,[30] s.1(3) of the Act provides that the rules it lays down apply to regulate "the obligations of a person occupying or having control over any fixed or movable structure, including any vessel, vehicle or aircraft".[31] Fixed or movable structures are undefined, and there may be difficulties in the application of the subsection to particular instances. But the general rule now is that wherever at common law there was a distinction between the duty owed to an invitee and that owed to a licensee in respect of the defective or dangerous condition of an object or appliance, the Act will apply. There is little difficulty with substantial things such as ships, aircraft or vehicles.[32] Less substantial things, such as fairground attractions[33] or even ladders,[34] may give rise to occupier's liability. But the owner by letting someone else use them may well have relinquished possession and thus not be an occupier at all. Hence in *Wheeler v Copas*[35] a bricklayer injured when a farmer lent him a defective ladder was held to have no claim under the 1957 Act; he succeeded instead under the general law of negligence. 11-07

(b) Who is an occupier?

Who is an occupier?[36] The Act does not define an "occupier". The rules of the common law, therefore, continue to determine this question.[37] Furthermore, little guidance as to who is an occupier for the purpose of occupiers' liability is to be obtained from the use of the word "occupier" in other branches of the law. There 11-08

---

field: *Vodden v Gayton* [2001] P.I.Q.R. P4 (a case under the Occupiers' Liability Act 1984).

27 *Singh v Cardiff City Council* [2017] EWHC 1499 (QB).

28 *Monarch Airlines Ltd v Luton Airport Ltd* [1998] 1 Lloyds Rep. 403.

29 See *Anchor Lines Ltd v Dundee Harbour Trustees* (1922) 10 Ll. L. Rep. 47; *St Just S.S. Co v Hartlepool Port Commissioners* (1929) 34 Ll. L. Rep. 34 (harbour owners occupiers at common law); *Carisbrooke Shipping Ltd v Bird Port Ltd* [2005] EWHC 1974 (Comm); [2005] 2 Lloyd's Rep. 626 (under the 1957 Act); also *George v Coastal Marine 2004 Ltd* [2009] EWHC 816 (Admty); [2009] 2 Lloyd's Rep. 356 (though not on the facts). See too Marsden and Gault, *Collisions at Sea*, 14th edn (London: Sweet & Maxwell, 2015), para.13-023.

30 (1955) Cmd.9305, paras 42 and 83.

31 See s.1(3)(a). The common law was similar: see e.g. *Pratt v Richards* [1951] 2 K.B. 208 (scaffolding platform); *London Graving Dock Co v Horton* [1951] A.C. 737 (staging); *Fosbroke-Hobbes v Airwork Ltd* [1937] 1 All E.R. 108 (aircraft).

32 But note that in the case of passengers on commercial ships or aircraft the liability provisions of the relevant international carriage conventions will nearly always pre-empt any occupiers' liability claim. See *Adams v Thomson Holidays Ltd* [2009] EWHC 2559 (QB); and the Irish decision in *Hennessey v Aer Lingus Ltd* [2012] IEHC 124; and generally *Stott v Thomas Cook Tour Operators Ltd* [2014] UKSC 15; [2014] A.C. 1347.

33 cf. *Furmedge v Chester-Le-Street DC* [2011] EWHC 1226 (QB) (inflatable interactive sculpture some 150 feet square, through which the public were invited to walk: operator, not underlying landowner, held occupier).

34 See *Maddocks v Clifton* [2001] EWCA Civ 1837 (ladder a more or less permanent feature of barn) and the Northern Irish case of *Leitch v Reid* [2003] N.I.Q.B. 45.

35 [1981] 3 All E.R. 405.

36 P. North, *Occupiers' Liability* (1971), Ch.2.

37 See, e.g. *Greenhalgh v British Railways Board* [1969] 2 Q.B. 286; *Shtern v Cummings* [2014] UKPC 18 at [17].

may be more than one occupier of the same premises, each under a duty to use care dependent on his degree of control, and each liable to a visitor (with a claim to contribution over).[38] So where a householder hands over his premises to builders, each may well be an occupier as against a visitor who is injured, with liability in one, or other, or both.[39]

11-09 **Owners, lessees and licensees** An owner-occupier is obviously an occupier within the Act.[40] However, the status of occupier is normally dependent on some degree of actual physical control.[41] Thus a landlord who lets premises to a tenant is treated as parting with all control and is not an occupier under the Act, even where he has undertaken to repair.[42] On the other hand, a landlord remains the occupier of parts of premises retained by him and excluded from the demise, such as a path in a housing estate, a common staircase, an entrance hall, a roof, or a forecourt.[43] A licensor, as against a lessor, may remain occupier of any part of the property he "lets", if he retains a sufficient degree of practical control over it.[44] Thus requisitioning authorities and those in possession by way of compulsory purchase have been treated as occupiers of the requisitioned premises, even where the premises have been in use, in part or whole, by persons licensed by the authority[45]; and again, where a farmer turned over a barn to her mother for use as an equestrian centre she was held to remain the occupier.[46] However, if the licence involves a parting with exclusive possession to the tenant, it is suggested that the technical difference between lease and licence should be disregarded and that the licensor should not count as an occupier. Where no-one is in physical control of premises, for example where they have been abandoned, it is submitted that whoever has legal title should be deemed to be the occupier. Thus it has been held that the buyer of empty house becomes the occupier of it on conveyance, even if he has not taken possession of

---

38 *Wheat v E Lacon & Co Ltd* [1966] A.C. 552 at 577–579, 581, 585–586, 587, 589; *Fisher v CHT Ltd (No.2)* [1966] 2 Q.B. 475; *AMF International Ltd v Magnet Bowling Ltd* [1968] 1 W.L.R. 1028 at 1052; *Couch v McCann* (1977) 77 D.L.R. (3d) 387; *Ferguson v Welsh* [1987] 1 W.L.R. 1553.

39 That one of two occupiers could be liable to the exclusion of the other was confirmed by the Scots decision in *Anderson v Imrie* [2016] CSOH 171; 2017 Rep. L.R. 21 (appealed on other grounds, [2018] CSIH 14; 2018 S.C. 328) (a case concerned with the Occupiers' Liability (Scotland) Act 1960, but there is no reason to think it inapplicable to the 1957 Act).

40 Even, it seems, if the land is otherwise publicly accessible: compare *Schiller v Mulgrave Shire Council* (1973) 129 C.L.R. 116 (wilderness nature reserve). See too *Clancy v Commissioners of Public Works in Ireland* [1992] 2 I.R. 460 (ruined castle open to the public). But the requirements laid on such an occupier will doubtless be somewhat limited.

41 cf. *Ellis v Scruttons Maltby Ltd* [1975] 1 Lloyd's Rep. 564 (time-charterer of a ship not occupier of the hold; he can tell the ship where to go, but does not have physical control if it). See too *Page v Read* (1984) 134 N.L.J. 723 (painter working on private house not liable as "occupier" of roof when sub-contractor fell off).

42 *Wheat v E Lacon & Co Ltd* [1966] A.C. 552, 579 (Lord Denning); see too *Drysdale v Hedges* [2012] EWHC B20 (QB); [2012] 3 E.G.L.R. 105; *Dodd v Raebarn Estates Ltd* [2017] EWCA Civ 439; [2017] 2 P.&C.R. 14; and *Essex CC v Davies* [2019] EWHC 3443 (QB); [2020] P.I.Q.R. P7. He does, however, owe certain duties qua landlord, both at common law and under ss.3 and 4 of the Defective Premises Act 1972: see para.11-83 onwards.

43 *Wheat v E Lacon & Co Ltd* [1966] A.C. 552 at 579; *Fairman v Perpetual Investment Building Society* [1923] A.C. 74; *Jacobs v LCC* [1950] A.C. 361; *Esdale v Dover DC* [2010] EWCA Civ 409.

44 *Wheat v E Lacon* [1966] 1 Q.B. 335; *Greene v Chelsea BC* [1954] 2 Q.B. 127.

45 *Hawkins v Coulsdon & Purley Urban DC* [1954] 1 Q.B. 319; *Greene v Chelsea BC* [1954] 2 Q.B. 127; *Harris v Birkenhead Corp* [1976] 1 W.L.R. 279

46 *Maddocks v Clifton* [2001] EWCA Civ 1837.

it.[47] In Ireland the owner of an uninhabitable but picturesque castle who held it on trust to allow public access was regarded as an occupier[48]; and in Australia a local authority was similarly treated in respect of a wilderness area held on trust for the public.[49]

Other occupiers Apart from owners and lessees, a person is likely to be regarded as an "occupier" if he has a sufficient degree of control over premises to be able to ensure their safety, and to appreciate that a failure on his part to use care may result in injury to a person coming on to them.[50] The control need be neither entire nor exclusive. So someone with the immediate supervision and control of premises, such as a builder in de facto control of part of a house, may be an occupier, whether or not he has the power of permitting or prohibiting the entry of other persons to it. Furthermore, it is submitted that someone who does have the legal right to invite or permit others to come on them, such as the concessionaire of space at a fairground,[51] will almost certainly be an occupier. It is submitted that for these purposes the occupier's control need not necessarily be lawful: thus, it is suggested, there is no reason why a squatter should not be liable under the Act. In a suitable case one may of course occupy premises through a servant or agent.[52] **11-10**

On the basis of the above principles, therefore, a builder or contractor may be liable as an occupier, for example if he has practical control of part of the premises[53]: **11-11**

> "The answer in each case depends on the particular facts of the case and especially on the nature and extent of the occupation or control in fact enjoyed or exercised by the defendants over the premises."[54]

Thus in *Bunker v Charles Brand & Son Ltd*[55] contractors building a tunnel were held to owe a duty under the 1957 Act in respect of the state of the tunnelling machine they were using. So also, someone who regularly maintains premises may

47 *Harris v Birkenhead Corp* [1976] 1 W.L.R. 279 (actually about compulsory purchase, but presumably the same applies to a consensual buyer). See too *Dawson v Page* [2012] CSOH 33; 2012 Rep. L.R. 56 (affirmed for other reasons, [2013] CSIH 24; 2013 S.C. 432) (person who moves out during building works).

48 *Clancy v Commissioners of Public Works in Ireland* [1992] 2 I.R. 460.

49 *Schiller v Mulgrave Shire Council* (1973) 129 C.L.R. 116.

50 See *Wheat v E Lacon & Co Ltd* [1966] A.C. 552, 577–579 (Lord Denning); cf. *Duncan v Cammell, Laird & Co Ltd* [1943] 2 All E.R. 621, 627 (Wrottesley J); F. Odgers (1966) 82 L.Q.R. 465. Where a business is carried on by a company on premises, it is generally the company that is the occupier: *Shtern v Cummings* [2014] UKPC 18, below, para.11-12.

51 *Humphreys v Dreamland (Margate) Ltd* (1930) 144 L.T. 529, 531; *Furmedge v Chester-Le-Street DC* [2011] EWHC 1226 (QB) (inflatable interactive sculpture some 150 feet square in public park, through which the public were invited to walk: concessionaire, not local authority, held occupier).

52 *Wheat v E Lacon & Co* [1966] A.C. 552, 571; *Stone v Taffe* [1974] 1 W.L.R. 1575, 1580. Indeed, a corporation can occupy them in no other way.

53 *Ferguson v Welsh* [1987] 1 W.L.R. 1553 is a classic example. See too *Prenton v General Steam Navigation Co Ltd* (1944) 77 Ll. L. Rep. 174; *Hartwell v Grayson Rollo & Clover Docks Ltd* [1947] K.B. 901; *Kearney v Eric Waller Ltd* [1967] 1 Q.B. 29; *AMF International Ltd v Magnet Bowling Ltd* [1968] 1 W.L.R. 1028 at 1052. In the latter case building owners and building contractors were both held to be occupiers and to have been negligent, with responsibility assessed at 40 per cent and 60 per cent respectively.

54 *Creed v McGeoch & Sons Ltd* [1955] 1 W.L.R. 1005 at 1009. See too *Lyne v Grayston Scaffolding* (1983) 133 N.L.J. 829.

55 [1969] 2 Q.B. 480. See also *Pannett v P McGuinness & Co Ltd* [1972] 2 Q.B. 599.

be an occupier; thus in *Collier v Anglian Water Authority*,[56] a water authority which kept a sea-wall in repair for the local authority was held liable as occupier to a holidaymaker who tripped over a loose paving-stone. But the element of maintenance must be substantial: merely cutting the grass in summer will not suffice.[57] Some difficulty arises over those who occupy land which gives access to other premises over which they have no interest: for example, where a first-floor window abuts on the unfenced roof of a factory next door. They have, in a sense, de facto control of the neighbouring premises: but in *Bailey v Armes*,[58] the Court of Appeal held that this did not make them occupiers of the neighbouring premises.

11-12 **Corporations** A corporation can of course be an occupier, acting through its employees. Indeed, where commercial premises are vested in a private one-person company, it is likely that the latter will be regarded as occupier to the exclusion of the owner of the shares, even if the latter is in practice in physical control of the building concerned.[59]

11-13 **Trustees, clubs and unincorporated associations** Premises vested in trustees on behalf of an unincorporated association or members' club raise difficulties, for instance where a visitor is injured because of the disrepair of the premises.[60] Who is the occupier for the purposes of the 1957 Act? The association itself, having no legal personality, cannot be; and even if it could, it would not be able to be sued.[61] Nor do the members of its committee or governing body as such owe any duty.[62] On principle, however, it is submitted that there is no reason why the trustees, as legal owners, should not be regarded as occupiers: in the absence of any right of exclusive possession in anyone else, they would seem to have the requisite degree of control.[63] Furthermore, it would seem that where a given official or committee

---

56 *The Times*, 26 March 1983. Of course, if repairs are so botched as to make the premises more dangerous than they were originally, the repairer will be liable under *Donoghue v Stevenson*, independently of whether he is an occupier.

57 *Prentice v Hereward HA* unreported 29 April 1999, per Douglas Brown J.

58 [1999] E.G. 21 (C.S.). Some duty may, however, be owed even in respect of adjacent property. In *George v Coastal Marine 2004 Ltd* [2009] EWHC 816 (Admlty); [2009] 2 Lloyd's Rep. 356, a ship was damaged when she grounded awkwardly at a wharf occupied by the defendants. Even though the foreshore on which the vessel settled was probably vested in the Crown, Gloster J took the view that there could be liability under the 1957 Act for failure to warn of the danger (though in fact the defendant succeeded on other grounds).

59 See the Privy Council decision in *Shtern v Cummings* [2014] UKPC 18 (person injured in hotel by electrically defective refrigerator has no action against controlling shareholder of operating company, despite physical presence of latter).

60 Though in practice it is thought that most reputable liability insurers would decline to take technical points here.

61 It is true that an unincorporated association can be vicariously liable (see *Heatons Transport (St Helens) Ltd v Transport and General Workers' Union* [1973] A.C. 15; *Various Claimants v Catholic Child Welfare Society* [2012] UKSC 56; [2013] 2 A.C. 1 at [20] (Lord Phillips). But this assumes that proceedings can be brought against it in the first place. If it cannot be sued at all, the claimant still faces an insurmountable obstacle. In both the above cases the difficulties of suit, for various reasons, did not apply.

62 *Robertson v Ridley* [1989] 1 W.L.R. 872 (a case of injury on club premises, though oddly the 1957 Act was never mentioned).

63 Particularly since otherwise there would be no occupier at all. Compare *Schiller v Council of the Shire of Mulgrave* (1973) 129 C.L.R. 116; and *Clancy v Commissioners of Public Works in Ireland* [1992] 2 I.R. 460, where trustees of heritage sites were held to owe occupiers' duties. In *Prole v Allen* [1950] 1 All E.R. 476 a trustee of a club was held to owe a duty of care at common law; but he

member has responsibility for keeping the premises in repair, he may himself owe a duty of care to visitors.[64] The basis of this is not clear, but arguably he could be regarded as an occupier,[65] in the same way as a person undertaking extensive responsibility for repairs to someone else's property.[66] In addition, it appears that he may be vicariously liable for the negligence of those whom he appoints or supervises (despite not being technically their employer[67]). In *Grice v Stourport Tennis Club*,[68] a case of injury due to the defective state of club premises, the Court of Appeal declined to strike out a claim against two members of the club as representing the membership as a whole. But this, it is submitted, must be doubtful, since the only basis for such an action would be that each individual member was personally responsible for the state of the premises. It is suggested that this is very dubious. Even if members use club premises, but they cannot sensibly be regarded as occupiers of them; and if so, it is difficult to think of any other basis for making them liable.

Highways A highway authority is not regarded as the occupier of a public road or footpath.[69] Nor is the owner of the underlying subsoil.[70] However, the highway authority does owe a statutory duty under the Highways Act 1980 to keep the surface of the highway in repair.[71] **11-14**

(c) Who is a visitor?

Who is a visitor? The rules of the common law as to the persons to whom a duty is owed by the occupier are not altered by the Act. Accordingly the persons who are to be treated as visitors are the same as those who would at common law have been treated as invitees or licensees: that is, those who enter (or otherwise use[72]) premises by express or implied permission of the occupier.[73] **11-15**

---

also had specific responsibilities concerning the repair of the premises (but note *Taylor v Quigley* [2016] CSOH 178; 2017 Rep. L.R. 37, where such an action against an owner failed). In practice one suspects that where there is current insurance in the trustees' names, liability insurers will rarely if ever take the point that the wrong defendant has been sued, or that the trustees arguably lack any insurable interest.

64 See *Prole v Allen* [1950] 1 All E.R. 476 at 477; *Grice v Stourport Tennis Club* unreported 28 February 1997 CA. And cf. *Vowles v Evans* [2003] EWCA Civ 318; [2003] 1 W.L.R. 1607 (referee appointed by amateur rugby organisation owes direct duty to players).

65 Though, peculiarly, the 1957 Act was never mentioned in *Grice*'s case, above.

66 See *Collier v Anglian Water Authority*, *The Times*, 26 March 1983.

67 *Grice v Stourport Tennis Club* unreported 28 February 1997. Sed quaere: is this reconcilable with *Bainbridge v Postmaster-General* [1906] 1 K.B. 178, holding that a senior employee is not vicariously liable for the torts of those under his supervision?

68 Unreported 28 February 1997 CA. See too *Melhuish v Clifford* unreported 18 August 1998; and the Irish decision in *Murphy v Roche* [1987] 1 I.R. 656.

69 *Whiting v Hillingdon LBC* (1970) 68 L.G.R. 437. Aliter where a road has not been dedicated: see *Coleshill v Manchester Corp* [1929] 1 K.B. 776.

70 *McGeown v NI Housing Executive* [1995] 1 A.C. 233 (housing authority not liable for defect in path approaching council house since path was dedicated as a highway). In *Vodden v Gayton* [2001] P.I.Q.R. P4 the owner of a field across which a bridleway ran was held to be the occupier of the bridleway: but with respect this seems highly doubtful. See now *Barlow v Wigan MBC* [2020] EWCA Civ 696 esp. at [9]–[13].

71 ss.41, 58. See paras 7-217 to 7-219.

72 See *George v Coastal Marine 2004 Ltd* [2009] EWHC 816 (Admty); [2009] 2 Lloyd's Rep. 356 at [20] (boat owner visitor to wharf where boat moored, even though adjacent sea-bed vested in the Crown). So (it is suggested) a user of a street ATM machine set into a bank wall would be a visitor

11-16 **Permission to enter** Express permission causes little difficulty. Permission may, however, equally be implicit; for example, as regards the public part of a shop or pub, or roads on a new housing estate not yet dedicated to the public,[74] or places of public resort such as courts or public libraries. It may sometimes be inferred when the public habitually use the premises to the knowledge of the occupier and no steps are taken to prevent this; for example, in the case of a field known by the occupier to be regularly used as a short cut.[75] But there will be no implied licence where the occupier takes what steps he can to assert his rights, such as by warning off interlopers,[76] or by fencing his land and keeping it properly fenced.[77] As Lord Goddard said in *Edwards v Railway Executive*[78]: "Repeated trespass itself confers no licence … how is it to be said that [the occupier] has licensed what he cannot prevent?" Persons entering premises to communicate with people in them, or for other lawful purposes, are lawful visitors as long as they confine themselves to that part of the premises which provides the usual access to them, unless they have been forbidden to enter either by an express prohibition or a general notice.[79] If they stray from the usual access, they become trespassers.[80]

11-17 **Permission given by employees and others** Difficulties may arise when the claimant is permitted to enter, not by the occupier himself, but by his employees. If the employee is acting within the scope of the actual authority which his employer has given him, then clearly the entrant is a visitor and not a trespasser. But what if the employee is disobeying instructions? In *Stone v Taffe*,[81] the Court of Appeal held that in such a case the entrant, if bona fide, was a visitor rather than a trespasser where the employee, though breaking his instructions, was still "in the course of his employment" according to the usual rules of vicarious liability.[82] The situation is similar where the invitation comes from an independent contractor who is himself an occupier, though here there is a further twist. Suppose A invites B (for example, a building contractor) on to his land, and B, having apparent control of the land, then invites C on to it without A's permission. If B has A's ostensible authority to do this,

---

as against the bank if he suffered injury because of, say, falling debris.

73 s.1(2); and see *Greenhalgh v British Railways Board* [1969] 2 Q.B. 286.

74 *Coleshill v Manchester Corp* [1929] 1 K.B. 776. Aliter when the roads have been dedicated: see para.11-13.

75 *Lowery v Walker* [1911] A.C. 10. cf. *Cooke v Midland GW Ry of Ireland* [1909] A.C. 229.

76 *Hardy v Central London Ry* [1920] 3 K.B. 459; *Robert Addie & Sons (Collieries) Ltd v Dumbreck* [1929] A.C. 358.

77 *Edwards v Railway Executive* [1952] A.C. 737.

78 [1952] A.C. 737, 746. Note also that the cases where implied licences were found to exist on slender evidence were decided at a time when a trespasser was unable to sue for negligent injury, but the courts nevertheless wanted to give a remedy. Since today a trespasser has a claim in negligence under the Occupiers' Liability Act 1984, it is submitted that the facts would no longer be stretched to make such a claimant into a licensee. cf. *Herrington v British Railways Board* [1972] A.C. 877, 895 (Lord Reid), 914 (Lord Wilberforce), 928 (Lord Pearson), 933 (Lord Diplock); *Pannett v P McGuinness & Co Ltd* [1972] 2 Q.B. 599, 605–606 (Lord Denning MR).

79 *Dunster v Abbott* [1954] 1 W.L.R. 58; *Robson v Hallett* [1967] 2 Q.B. 939, 953–954 (Diplock LJ). Note, however, that a policeman has no implied licence to wander over private premises merely to see if anything is amiss: *Great Central Ry v Bates* [1921] 3 K.B. 578.

80 *Mersey Docks and Harbour Board v Proctor* [1923] A.C. 253; *Hillen v ICI (Alkali) Ltd* [1936] A.C. 65. But see *Braithwaite v South Durham Steel Co* [1958] 1 W.L.R. 986.

81 [1974] 1 W.L.R. 1575.

82 With respect, perhaps a more appropriate test would have been whether or not the servant was acting within his apparent authority, as it seems more a question of agency than employment.

C will be a lawful visitor vis-à-vis both A and B. If he has not, C will be a lawful visitor vis-à-vis B, but a trespasser vis-à-vis A.[83]

Limited permission A licence to enter is limited to those places into which the visitor may reasonably be supposed to be likely to go, in the reasonable belief that he is entitled or invited to be there.[84] A hotel guest, therefore, who wanders about in the dark and is injured in a service room enters a part of the hotel to which he is not invited.[85] The same goes for a person forsaking a path to take a short cut over a grassed area,[86] a visitor to a public beach who tries to dive off a navigation beacon;[87] and a cheat who runs across council land to escape from an unpaid taxi-driver.[88] But a customer at a pub is invited to use the lavatory and remains a lawful visitor while making a reasonable search for it.[89] And an involuntary or accidental encroachment outside the licensed area does not convert a lawful visitor into a trespasser.[90] Similarly, permission to enter may be limited as to time. Thus a customer who, without the publican's consent, stays in the bar after closing time thereby becomes a trespasser.[91] Furthermore, an indefinite licence may always be revoked; in such a case the licensee has a reasonable time in which to leave, after which he becomes a trespasser.[92] Furthermore, a licence will frequently be limited as to purpose.[93] A licence to enter for lawful purposes, for instance, does not imply a licence to enter in order to steal.[94] Again, in the important decision in *Tomlinson v Congleton BC*[95] it was accepted that where occupiers of a country park allowed 11-18

---

83 *Ferguson v Welsh* [1987] 1 W.L.R. 1553.

84 e.g. *Kolasa v Ealing Hospital NHS Trust* [2015] EWHC 289 (QB) (hospital: three-foot wall on ambulance ramp backing 30-foot drop; drunk patient climbed on wall and fell off); *Driver v The Painted House Trust* [2014] EWHC 1929 (QB) (tipsy visitor used a wall to relieve herself and fell over it).

85 *Lee v Luper* [1936] 3 All E.R. 817. See too *Mason v Langford* (1888) 4 T.L.R. 407; *Prole v Allen* [1950] 1 All E.R. 476.

86 *Maloney v Torfaen County BC* [2005] EWCA Civ 1762; [2006] P.I.Q.R. P21.

87 *Baldacchino v West Wittering Estate Plc* [2008] EWHC 3386 (QB).

88 *Harvey v Plymouth City Council* [2010] EWCA Civ 860; [2010] P.I.Q.R. P18.

89 *Gould v McAuliffe* [1941] 2 All E.R. 527.

90 See *Braithwaite v South Durham Steel Co* [1958] 1 W.L.R. 986; *Public Transport Commission (NSW) v Perry* (1974) 14 A.L.R. 273 (rail passenger having fit and falling onto track). This seems the best explanation for *Spearman v Royal United Bath Hospitals NHS Foundation Trust* [2017] EWHC 3027 (QB); [2018] Med. L.R. 244 (confused visitor to hospital climbed five staircases, went into non-public part and fell off a flat roof: held, a lawful visitor). Martin Spencer J seemingly suggested at [56] that an honest mistake sufficed, but this arguably goes too far: it seems unacceptable to a landowner to burden him with the consequences of unreasonable errors.

91 *Stone v Taffe* [1974] 1 W.L.R. 1575; this was accepted by the Court of Appeal, although the claimant's husband was held to be lawfully on the premises because on the facts he had reason to believe that the occupier had consented to his presence after closing-time.

92 *Robson v Hallett* [1967] 2 Q.B. 939. The occupier must, however, make it quite clear that the licence is revoked: e.g. *Snook v Mannion* [1982] Crim. L.R. 601 (telling policeman to "fuck off" not unequivocal enough: sed quaere).

93 "When you invite a person into your house to use the stairs, you do not invite him to slide down the banisters ... " (Scrutton LJ in *The Carlgarth* [1927] P. 93, 110). See too *Mersey Docks & Harbour Board v Proctor* [1923] A.C. 253, 260 (Lord Cave). For a literal application of Scrutton LJ's dictum, see *Geary v Wetherspoon Plc* [2011] EWHC 1506 (QB); [2011] N.P.C. 60 where a bar patron did slide down the banisters, suffered injury, and duly failed in her claim.

94 See the burglary case of *R. v Jones & Smith* [1976] 1 W.L.R. 672. Similar is *Auffrey v Province of New Brunswick* (1975) 48 D.L.R. (3d) 304, reversed on the facts (1977) 70 D.L.R. (3d) 751 (visitor to rubbish dump trespasser when came not to deposit rubbish but to steal it).

95 [2003] UKHL 47; [2004] 1 A.C. 46. For a similar holding, see yet another unauthorised swimming

activities such as kayaking on an ornamental lake but expressly prohibited swimming, a person who chose to dive into it was a trespasser.

11-19 **Children as visitors** Whether a child prima facie trespassing can claim to be a licensee depends on the same considerations as apply in the case of an adult.[96]

> "The mere fact that the occupier has upon his premises a dangerous object alluring to children does not make him liable to a trespassing child who meddles with and is injured by it; but the presence of such an object in a place accessible to children may aid the inference of an implied licence."[97]

It is possible, however, for an occupier to contend that the only licence he has granted in respect of children too young to appreciate danger is a licence to enter in the company and care of some competent guardian.[98] The notion of the conditional licence, however, involves difficulties and disadvantages which led Devlin J to doubt whether it was entirely satisfactory.[99]

11-20 **Visitors entering by right** Persons who enter premises for any purpose in the exercise of a right conferred by law are visitors, whether or not the occupier in fact consents to their presence.[100] These include, for example police with search warrants or in the act of pursuing fugitive criminals,[101] in certain cases the emergency services,[102] and a numerous class of enforcement officers and other officials with statutory rights of entry. However, persons entering land pursuant to the "right to roam" granted by the Countryside and Rights of Way Act 2000 are not regarded as visitors under the 1957 Act.[103] Instead they are owed a modified duty under the Occupiers' Liability Act 1984.[104] It is also expressly provided by statute that a person entering any premises in exercise of rights conferred by virtue of an access agreement or order under the National Parks and Access to the Countryside Act 1949, is

---

case, *Rhind v Astbury Water Park Ltd* [2004] EWCA Civ 756; [2004] N.P.C. 95. In *Darby v National Trust* [2001] EWCA Civ 189; [2001] P.I.Q.R. P27 it was seemingly held that where visitors to a stately home regularly swam in an ornamental pond without authorisation this might amount to an implied licence to do so: sed quaere whether this is reconcilable with the authorities just mentioned.

96 *Addie & Sons (Collieries) Ltd v Dumbreck* [1929] A.C. 358. cf. however, *Bye v Bates* (1989) 51 S.A.S.R. 67 (child despatched home by occupier unaccompanied who returned and was burned by unguarded electrical equipment apparently a visitor; quaere if an adult would have been so indulgently treated).

97 See Cmd.9305 (1955), para.30. It used to be commonplace for the courts to hold that an "allurement" amounted to an implied invitation to children so as to sidestep the rule that no duty was owed to a trespassing child; e.g. *Cooke v Midland GW Ry of Ireland* [1909] A.C. 229; *Latham v Johnson* [1913] 1 K.B. 398 at 416. But in view of the fact that a trespasser is now owed a duty, this device is clearly outdated, and is unlikely to be readily adopted in the future.

98 e.g. *Phipps v Rochester Corp* [1955] 1 Q.B. 450; *D v Dept of the Environment (NI)* [1993] B.N.I.L. 106.

99 *Phipps v Rochester Corp* [1955] 1 Q.B. 450 at 470. Of course, In a suitable case an innocent but foolish child may have his damages substantially reduced on the basis of contributory negligence: *Adams v SEB*, *The Times*, 21 October 1993.

100 Occupiers' Liability Act 1957 s.2(6).

101 e.g. Police and Criminal Evidence Act 1984 s.17.

102 e.g. firemen: see *Hartley v Mayoh & Co* [1954] 1 Q.B. 383; and Fire and Rescue Services Act 2004 s.44(2).

103 Occupiers' Liability Act 1957 s.1(4), as substituted by Countryside and Rights of Way Act 2000 s.13.

104 See paras 11-79 to 11-82.

not, for the purposes of this Act, a visitor of the occupier of those premises.[105] However, here too there may be a duty under s.1 of the Occupiers' Liability Act 1984.

Highway users As at common law,[106] persons using a public right of way do not count as visitors under the Act vis-à-vis the owner of the subsoil.[107] Furthermore, this rule seems to apply even though the claimant is acting at the express invitation of the occupier, for example where he is using the footpath as a means of access to those very premises.[108] This does not mean, however, that he is necessarily without redress. In *Thomas v British Railways Board*[109] the absence of any remedy under the 1957 Act was circumvented in favour of such a claimant by invoking the occupier's duty at common law. A little girl got through a broken stile next to a railway and was hit by a train. By a majority, the defendants were held liable for breach of statutory duty. Unanimously, they were also held liable in negligence at common law in failing to repair the stile, apparently on the basis that in running the railway without taking care to keep the stile in repair they had broken their "activity duty".[110] Again, an employer's duty as employer to safeguard his employees may include a duty in respect of highway dangers.[111] 11-21

Private rights of way A person using a private right of way, such as an easement, over another's land, was not a visitor at common law[112] and equally is not in 11-22

105 See s.1(4). Section 60(1) of the National Parks and Access to the Countryside Act 1949, provides that where an access agreement or order is in force as respects any land, a person who enters upon such land for the purpose of open-air recreation, without doing damage, shall not be treated as a trespasser or incur any other liability by reason only of so entering or being on the land. But s.66(2) of the Act provides that the operation of s.60(1) shall not increase the liability, under any enactment not contained in the Act or under any rule of law, of a person interested in that land or adjoining land.

106 *Gautret v Egerton* (1867) L.R. 2 C. & P. 371. Note, however, that if the occupier of land next to the highway allows something projecting from his land to endanger highway users, there may be a liability in public nuisance: see the Irish decision in *O'Shaughnessy v Dublin City Council* [2017] IEHC 774 (projection onto pavement under railway bridge).

107 See *Greenhalgh v BRB* [1969] 2 Q.B. 286 (where a counter-argument based on s.2(6) of the Act was rejected); *McGeown v NI Housing Executive* [1995] 1 A.C. 233. Cf. *Whiting v Hillingdon LBC* (1970) 68 L.G.R. 437; *Smith v National Farmers Union Mutual Insurance Society Ltd* [2019] NICA 63 at [43]. The suggestion to the contrary in *O'Shaughnessy v Dublin City Council* [2017] IEHC 774 at [41] is heterodox. Ironically, although a landowner escapes liability to people *on* a path over his land, he faces more hazard as soon as they stray *off* it, since then he owes a duty under the 1984 Act, or if the straying is tolerated, under the 1957 Act. See e.g. *McKaskie v Cameron* (HH Judge Howarth, Blackpool County Court, 1 July 2009) (farmer liable under 1957 Act where cattle mauled walker who strayed off path to use a tolerated shortcut); also *Barlow v Wigan MBC* [2020] EWCA Civ 696 esp. at [9]–[13].

108 *Campbell v Northern Ireland Housing Executive* [1996] 1 B.N.I.L. 99, dismissing doubts expressed by Lord Browne-Wilkinson in *McGeown v NI Housing Executive* [1995] 1 A.C. 233, 247–248 as to whether an invitee was necessarily within the rule.

109 [1976] Q.B. 912.

110 This, at least, seems to have been the view of Lord Denning MR and Goff LJ. Scarman LJ thought that at common law the Board owed an "occupancy duty" to the claimant as a non-visitor under *British Railways Board v Herrington* [1972] A.C. 877. But this avenue of escape has now been closed: see Occupiers' Liability Act 1984 s.1(7), specifically precluding a duty to highway users.

111 *Smith v National Farmers Union Mutual Insurance Society Ltd* [2019] NICA 63 (worker slipping on compacted snow on pavement outside employer's premises; employer liable, though not under 1957 Act).

112 *Greenhalgh v BRB* [1969] 2 Q.B. 286 at 293, per Lord Denning MR.

general a visitor for the purpose of the 1957 Act. The point was put beyond doubt in *Holden v White*[113] in 1982, where a milkman using a private right of way across the defendant's land was held to have no cause of action under the 1957 Act when a manhole cover disintegrated underneath him. Three factors, however, complicate the situation. First, the rule that an occupier is not liable to those exercising private rights of way does not seem to apply where the lessor of a building such as a block of flats or offices retains control of the common means of access (such as entrance halls, lifts and stairs). People using such facilities were at common law regarded as his visitors,[114] and since the Act utilises the common law definition of lawful visitor, it follows they must be protected under it. Secondly, it now seems that those exercising private rights of way are owed a duty of care under the Occupiers' Liability Act 1984.[115] Thirdly, users of private rights of way may have other remedies open to them, such as the implied contractual obligation of the lessor of a dwelling-house to maintain not only the house itself but the means of access thereto.[116]

11-23 **Trespassers** Trespassers are not visitors and are wholly outside the 1957 Act.[117] The duty which an occupier owes to them is governed largely by the Occupiers' Liability Act 1984 and is discussed at length elsewhere.[118]

(d) The common duty of care

11-24 **The common duty of care** Section 2 of the Act provides:

> "(1) An occupier of premises owes the same duty, the 'common duty of care', to all his visitors, except in so far as he is free to and does extend, restrict, modify or exclude his duty to any visitor or visitors by agreement or otherwise.
>
> (2) The common duty of care is a duty to take such care as in all the circumstances of the case is reasonable to see that the visitor will be reasonably safe in using the premises for the purposes for which he is invited or permitted by the occupier to be there."

11-25 This reflects the recommendation of the Law Reform Committee that (contrary to the situation at common law) all lawful visitors should be owed the same duty of care.[119] The issue is now simply one of fact to be determined with regard to all the circumstances of the case. As s.2(3) provides:

> "The circumstances relevant for the present purpose include the degree of care, and of want of care, which would ordinarily be looked for in such a visitor, so that (for example) in proper cases—
>
> (a) an occupier must be prepared for children to be less careful than adults; and
>
> (b) an occupier may expect that a person, in the exercise of his calling, will appreci-

---

[113] [1982] Q.B. 679. See too *Vodden v Gayton* [2001] P.I.Q.R. P4 (sed quaere on the facts of that case, since the track there was also a highway).

[114] *Fairman v Perpetual Investment Society* [1923] A.C. 74; *Jacobs v LCC* [1950] A.C. 361.

[115] See para.11-80; also M.A. Jones, "The Occupiers' Liability Act 1984" (1984) 47 M.L.R. 713, 716.

[116] See *King v South Northants DC* (1992) 90 L.G.R. 121.

[117] Occupiers' Liability Act 1957 s.1(2). But note that a person may be a trespasser vis-à-vis A but not vis-à-vis B: *Ferguson v Welsh* [1987] 1 W.L.R. 1553.

[118] See para.11-62 onwards.

[119] Cmd.9305 (1954), para.78.

ate and guard against any special risk ordinarily incident to it, so far as the occupier leaves him free to do so."

The common duty of care is more than a duty to avoid negligent acts, but extends to negligent omissions as well. Not only must the occupier avoid creating dangers himself: he must also take reasonable steps to protect his visitors from dangers which he did not himself create,[120] as where he fails to warn of a hazard not otherwise apparent,[121] or to take steps to remove a danger that materialises without his negligence.[122] On the other hand, it is submitted that there must be some danger arising from the state of the premises. The mere fact that they lack some given amenity will not do, even if injury may be foreseeable as a result.[123] It should also be noted that even if the defendant is at fault in providing unsafe premises, he will be liable only for injuries likely to result from the particular unsafe feature.[124] There is some doubt whether an occupier's duty extends to protecting visitors from succumbing to dangers on neighbouring land not in his occupation, for instance by suitable fencing; but the better view is that it does not.[125] Similarly, it seems there is no duty in respect of dangers emanating from other land but affecting the defendant's own visitors.[126] On the other hand, if a danger is present on the oc- 11-26

[120] Thus, sometimes occupiers have even been held liable for negligently failing to control dangerous visitors liable to cause injury to others, as where football hooligans hurled all too detachable paving slabs at a policeman: *Cunningham v Reading Football Club* [1992] P.I.Q.R. P141. See too *Hosie v Arbroath Football Club*, 1978 S.L.T. 122; *Allison v Rank City Wall Canada Ltd* (1984) 6 D.L.R. (4th) 144. cf. *Skuse v Commonwealth* (1985) 62 A.L.R. 108, where on the facts the defendants were held not liable as occupiers of a court-house when they failed to stop a disgruntled litigant shooting a lawyer.

[121] e.g. *Moon v Garrett* [2006] EWCA Civ 1121; [2007] P.I.Q.R. P3 (failure to warn deliveryman of trench in his path); *English Heritage v Taylor* [2016] EWCA Civ 448; [2016] P.I.Q.R. P14 (no warning of sheer drop next to path: sed quaere whether this may be over-generous). But there must nevertheless be evidence that such a warning would, if given, have made a difference: see *Victoria v Subramanian* (2007) 19 V.R. 312.

[122] As with slippery supermarket spillages (e.g. *Ward v Tesco Stores Ltd* [1976] 1 W.L.R. 810; and see too the Irish case of *Duffy v Carabane Holdings Ltd* [1996] 2 I.L.R.M. 86 (nightclub floor strewn with liquor and shards of glass)). For another example, see *G4S Care and Justice Services (UK) Ltd v Manley* [2016] EWHC 2355 (QB) (failure quickly to restore lighting in prison after power-cut: disabled prisoner injured).

[123] See *Berryman v Hounslow LBC* (1998) 30 H.L.R. 567 CA (non-functioning of lift in block of flats not within s.2 even though claimant foreseeably injured through having to carry heavy shopping up the stairs). This may also explain the Irish decision in *Byrne v Ardenheath Co Ltd* [2017] IECA 293 (not negligent to fail to provide pedestrian-only exits from car park).

[124] *Darby v National Trust* [2001] EWCA Civ 189; [2001] P.I.Q.R. P27 (owner of stately home negligent in not warning against swimming in pond because of danger of Weil's disease, but not liable to swimmer who drowned rather than succumbing to contagion). But this principle is applied fairly generously as regards claimants: cf. *Jolley v Sutton LBC* [2000] 1 W.L.R. 1082 (council liable for derelict boat left ready to fall onto children playing with it: fact that precise means of injury unforeseeable irrelevant).

[125] *Armstrong v Keepmoat Homes Ltd*, QBD (Newcastle District Registry), unreported 3 February 2012 (occupiers of a grassed area separated by a hedge from a busy dual carriageway not liable when a child went through an obvious gap in the hedge into the path of a car). The reason is simple and logical: if a claimant is injured by a danger on neighbouring land, how can he complain of the defendant occupier's failure to ensure his reasonable safety *in using his premises*? But there are cases suggesting the opposite: e.g. *McLuskey v Lord Advocate*, *The Times*, 17 August 1993 (decided under the Occupiers' Liability (Scotland) Act 1960); and cf. *Perkowski v Wellington Corp* [1959] A.C. 53.

[126] See *Kelly v Riverside Inverclyde (Property Holdings) Ltd* [2014] CSOH 86 (vicious seagull attack on defender's premises: pursuer failed for lack of proof that seagull had nested on that land rather than neighbouring property).

cupier's land, he does not escape liability merely because the actual injury takes place elsewhere.[127]

11-27 **Entry under contract between occupier and visitor** Under s.5 of the Act, where a person enters premises pursuant to a right arising under a contract between himself and the occupier,[128] an obligation to satisfy the common duty of care will be implied in the contract. In other words, the contractual duty owed by an occupier vis-à-vis his visitors is presumptively the same as the tortious one. It is, however, open to the occupier by specific provision in the contract to increase or (subject to what is said below[129]) reduce those duties.

11-28 **Examples of liability** An occupier has, on the facts, been held liable: for creating dangers, for example by polishing a floor so highly as to be dangerous,[130] providing an unstable deck-chair[131] or a lift apt to ensnare the fingers of unwary users,[132] or switching on electricity when a decorator is working near exposed live cables[133]; for failure to alleviate hazards by leaving asbestos unremoved,[134] an icy driveway unsalted,[135] a hole in a garden unfilled[136], a builder's trench unguarded[137] or a known rickety balcony accessible to partygoers[138]; for leaving a trolley in a supermarket aisle so as to trip a shopper engrossed in eye-level merchandise[139]; for omitting to light stairs adequately,[140] stack cargo properly,[141] or remove potential hazards likely to injure playing children[142]; and for failure to warn of hazards such as shallow water under a diving-board.[143] Occupiers have equally been held liable

---

127 *Shepherd v Travelodge Hotels Ltd* [2014] CSOH 162; [2015] Rep. L.R. 2 (spilt oil seeped into the shoes of a motorcyclist visiting a hotel car park; motorcyclist later slipped elsewhere, having ridden many miles). See too *Amaca Pty Ltd v King* (2011) 35 V.R. 280 (asbestos in premises causing later illness).

128 For the effect of contracts between the occupier and persons other than the visitor, see para.11-56.

129 See para.11-45.

130 *Adams v SJ Watson & Co* (1967) 117 N.L.J. 130. See too *Appleton v Cunard S.S. Co* [1969] 1 Lloyd's Rep. 150. So too with leaving a floor wet; see *Jedruch v Tesco Ireland Ltd* [2018] IEHC 205 (slippage on lavatory floor left swimming in water).

131 *Hollingworth v Southern Ferries Ltd* [1977] 2 Lloyd's Rep. 70.

132 *Sandford v Eugene* (1970) 115 S.J. 33, per Hinchliffe J.

133 *Fisher v CHT Ltd (No.2)* [1966] 2 Q.B. 475. See too *Lough v Intruder Detention & Surveillance Fire & Security Ltd* [2008] EWCA Civ 1009 (householder 25 per cent responsible for letting repairman doing non-urgent work use temporarily unbanistered staircase rather than telling him to come back later). The latter decision, with respect, seems somewhat generous to the claimant.

134 *Amaca Pty Ltd v King* (2011) 35 V.R. 280.

135 *Waldick v Malcolm* [1991] 2 S.C.R. 456. For other slipping cases see *Jennings v British Railways Board* (1984) 134 N.L.J. 584 (not clearing litter); *Garner v Walsall Hospitals NHS Trust* [2004] EWCA Civ 702 (not cleaning slimy manhole cover).

136 *Butcher v Southend-on-Sea BC* [2014] EWCA Civ 1556.

137 *Moon v Garrett* [2006] EWCA Civ 1121; [2007] P.I.Q.R. P3. See too *Hall v Holker Estate Co Ltd* [2008] EWCA Civ 1422; [2008] N.P.C. 143 (goalpost that fell on footballer).

138 *Libra Collaroy Pty Ltd v Bhide* [2017] NSWCA 196.

139 *Palfrey v Morrisons Supermarkets Plc* [2012] EWCA Civ 1917.

140 *Stone v Taffe* [1974] 1 W.L.R. 1575.

141 *The Vladimir Timofeyev* [1983] 1 Lloyd's Rep. 378 (stevedore fell into unexpected chasm in badly-loaded cargo of timber).

142 *Jolley v Sutton LBC* [2000] 1 W.L.R. 1082 (derelict boat left ready to fall onto children playing with it).

143 *Davies v Borough of Tenby* [1974] 2 Lloyd's Rep. 469. See too *McCarrick v Park Resorts Ltd* [2012] EWHC B27 (QB) (unguarded and deceptively shallow pool). But not so where the danger is obvious: *Risk v Rose Bruford College* [2013] EWHC 3869 (QB); [2014] E.L.R. 157 (dive into paddling-

for failure to anticipate problems caused by human agency, as where a supermarket allowed uncontrolled children to career into customers,[144] or no notices were posted to forewarn golfers on a fairway of flying balls.[145] This may even cover deliberate wrongdoing, as where a spectator was trampled at a football match when hooligans forced their way into the ground through an inadequately-maintained exit barrier.[146]

Examples of non-liability An occupier has, on the facts, been held not liable: to a motel customer who climbed onto a log and fell off it,[147] a walker in a park who fell off a rustic bridge with a low parapet,[148] or a hotel guest who leaned out of a second-floor window and fell out[149]; to a walker in a cathedral close who tripped over a small concrete protuberance[150]; to a supermarket customer who fell over a pile of cartons in a gangway[151]; to a shopper who fell down a few stone stairs unequipped with a hand-rail outside a Georgian shop[152]; to an unsteady reveller who toppled over a low balustrade at the Ritz Hotel[153]; to a child of eight falling against a brick and flint wall in a school playground[154]; and to a footballer breaking his leg against a concrete wall near the touch-line.[155] Domestic occupiers have escaped liability where a domestic visitor tripped over a lowered washing-line,[156] and where a party-goer dived into a shallow paddling-pool[157] or suffered injury in horse-play on a bouncy castle.[158] Employers were held not liable where a lightly-used approach road in their occupation included no segregated footpath, with the result that an employee walking to work was knocked down by a car.[159] **11-29**

pool by foolish youth).

144 *Beardmore v Franklins Management Services Pty Ltd* [2003] 1 Qd R. 1.

145 *Phee v Gordon* [2013] CSIH 18; 2013 S.C. 379.

146 *Hosie v Arbroath Football Club*, 1978 S.L.T. 122. See too *Bluett v Suffolk County Council* [2004] EWHC 378 (QB) (inadequate security leading to drug-fuelled attack on claimant in authority home). But the disinclination of courts to make A liable for the criminal acts of B make successful claims rare (cf. *Modbury Triangle Shopping Centre Pty Ltd v Anzil* (2000) 205 C.L.R. 254, denying recovery on this basis for a brutal attack in an unlit car-park). Furthermore, in England occupiers' liability claims for the direct result of a deliberate attack are unlikely, save in recourse proceedings, because the criminal injuries compensation scheme gives the claimant access to no-fault compensation from the taxpayer in any case.

147 *Phillis v Daly* (1988) 15 N.S.W.L.R. 65.

148 *Sutton LBC v Edwards* [2016] EWCA Civ 1005; [2017] P.I.Q.R. P2. See too *Singh v Cardiff City Council* [2017] EWHC 1499 (QB) (no liability when tipsy pedestrian strayed from footpath and fell from unfenced open land into stream).

149 *Lewis v Six Continents Plc (formerly Bass Plc)* [2005] EWCA Civ 1805.

150 *Rochester Cathedral v Debell* [2016] EWCA Civ 1094.

151 *Doherty v London Co-operative Society* (1966) 110 S.J. 74; 116 N.L.J. 388; cf. *Ward v Tesco Stores Ltd* [1976] 1 W.L.R. 810.

152 *Brown v Lakeland Ltd* [2012] CSOH 105; 2012 Rep. L.R. 140. See too *Wheat v E Lacon & Co Ltd* [1966] A.C. 552 (visitor killed owing to the inadequacy of a handrail and the absence of a bulb in a light at the top of stairs). cf. *Martin v Greater Glasgow Health Board*, 1977 S.L.T. 66; and *Green v Building Scene Ltd* [1994] P.I.Q.R. P259 CA.

153 *Ward v Ritz Hotel (London) Ltd* [1992] P.I.Q.R. P315.

154 *Ward v Hertfordshire CC* [1970] 1 W.L.R. 356. cf. *Comer v St Patrick's School*, ureported November 13, 1997 (participant in sports day fathers' race in similar predicament).

155 *Simms v Leigh Rugby Football Club* [1969] 2 All E.R. 923. See too *Wheeler v Trustees of St Mary's Hall, Chislehurst, The Times,* 10 October 1989.

156 *Breen v Newbury* [2003] EWHC 2959 (QB).

157 *Cockbill v Riley* [2013] EWHC 656 (QB).

158 *Perry v Harris (a Minor)* [2008] EWCA Civ 907; [2009] 1 W.L.R. 19.

159 *Mullen v Kerr* [2017] NIQB 69.

11-30 **Factors in account** In determining whether what was done or not done by the occupier was in fact reasonable, and whether in the particular circumstances of the case the visitor was reasonably safe, the court is free to consider all the circumstances,[160] such as the foreseeability of injury,[161] how obvious the danger is,[162] the age or infirmity of the visitor,[163] the purpose of his visit, the conduct to be expected of him, and the state of knowledge of the occupier.[164] The difficulty and expense of removing the danger is a relevant factor,[165] as is the time in which a reasonable occupier may be expected to spot and deal with a hazard,[166] the practice of occupiers generally,[167] and any relevant official or semi-official safety rules.[168] The presence of a reasonable system for dealing with possible dangers, such as regular patrols, is a powerful indicator that any duty of care has been satisfied.[169] Thus it has been held unreasonable to expect a local authority to supervise a municipal

---

[160] In *Butcher v Southend-on-Sea BC* [2014] EWCA Civ 1556 at [11] Bean LJ unsurprisingly held that the list of factors appearing in this paragraph should in no way be regarded as a simple check-list.

[161] *West Sussex CC v Pierce* [2013] EWCA Civ 1230; [2014] P.I.Q.R. P5 (freak accident from sharp projection underneath school water-fountain: no liability); see too *Sutton LBC v Edwards* [2016] EWCA Civ 1005; [2017] P.I.Q.R. P2. Hindsight clearly needs to be avoided in this connection: *McCarthy v Marks & Spencer* [2014] EWHC 3183 (QB) at [94] (asbestos in roof void).

[162] Examples of obvious dangers carrying no liability were *Sutton LBC v Edwards* [2016] EWCA Civ 1005; [2017] P.I.Q.R. P2, esp at [42]–[43] (bridge in park with low parapet); and *Singh v Cardiff City Council* [2017] EWHC 1499 (QB) (unfenced open land leading down to stream). A case on the other side of the line was *Ireland v David Lloyd Leisure Ltd* [2013] EWCA Civ 665 (barbell in rack in gym severed weightlifter's finger: liability for lack of warning of this). See too *Cook v Swansea City Council* [2017] EWCA Civ 2142, especially at [34].

[163] For a neat example, see *Pollock v Cahill* [2015] EWHC 2260 (QB) (open casement window in bedroom occupied by blind man).

[164] In a suitable case, as in the rest of the law of negligence, res ipsa loquitur may apply. See, e.g. *Ward v Tesco Stores Ltd* [1976] 1 W.L.R. 810; *Kealey v Heard* [1983] 1 W.L.R. 573; *Hassan v Gill* [2012] EWCA Civ 1291; [2013] P.I.Q.R. P1 (slipping on grape at fruit stall: evidentiary burden not discharged by two-hourly sweep of area); *Dawkins v Carnival Plc (t/a P & O Cruises)* [2011] EWCA Civ 1237; [2012] 1 Lloyd's Rep. 1 (slippage on pool of liquid in popular walk-through location on cruise ship; inference drawn, in absence of clear evidence, that puddle had probably been there long enough to attract a duty to mop it up).

[165] e.g. *Tedstone v Bourne Leisure Ltd (t/a Thoresby Hall Hotel & Spa)* [2008] EWCA Civ 654 (occupier of jacuzzi not bound to mop up all spills immediately); *Sutton v Syston Rugby Football Club Ltd* [2011] EWCA Civ 1182 (no need for minute inspection of rugby pitch for debris). See too *Cook v Swansea City Council* [2017] EWCA Civ 2142, especially at [35] (cost of regular gritting of car parks); also the Scots decision in *Cairns v Dundee City Council* [2017] CSOH 86; [2017] Rep. L.R. 96. A fortiori where removal of the danger would itself be unsafe: see *Hughes (A Minor) v Newry & Mourne District Council* [2012] NIQB 54 (child injured by firework abandoned in park: no liability in council for failure to remove, since operatives sent to tidy up likely to be set upon by thugs who frequented park). In Australia it has been held that the threat to employment caused by demanding extensive precautions is a relevant factor: *Hennessy v Patrick Stevedores Operations* [2014] NSWSC 1716 (reversed on other grounds: [2015] NSWCA 253).

[166] *Shepherd v Travelodge Hotels Ltd* [2014] CSOH 162; 2015 Rep. L.R. 2 (not negligent to fail to clear up spilt oil for 30 minutes); see too *Knight v Rentokil Initial Facilities Services Ltd* [2008] EWCA Civ 1219 (very transient hazard at airport). cf. however *Ward v Tesco Stores Ltd* [1976] 1 W.L.R. 810 (fault in failure to mop up spill in supermarket for 15 minutes).

[167] *Waldick v Malcolm* [1991] 2 S.C.R. 456 (custom of not salting driveways even in extreme weather, though there this was overridden by other factors in favour of liability).

[168] See *AB (a protected party by his litigation friend, CD) v Pro-Nation Ltd* [2016] EWHC 1022 (QB) (building regulations); *McCarrick v Park Resorts Ltd* [2012] EWHC B27 (QB) (HSE guidance); *Wilson v Haden (t/a Clyne Farm Centre)* [2013] EWHC 229 (QB) (British Standards).

[169] *Beaton v Ocean Terminal Ltd* [2018] CSOH 74; 2018 Rep. L.R. 110 (system to deal with wet floor due to roof leak); *Walker v Lyons* [2018] IEHC 21 (system for cleaning hospital pantry: no breach of duty under equivalent Irish legislation).

swing at all times, or otherwise disable it, in case a child falls off it.[170] Similarly the court is entitled to take into account the likelihood of the danger materialising[171]: if one allows a reputable organisation to use land, one may well justifiably assume that it will act responsibly.[172] Again, the precautions expected of a householder are likely to be less than those of a professional.[173] With amenity or wilderness land, the desirability of keeping it in an unaltered state is relevant.[174] Furthermore it seems the occupier is entitled to take at least some account of aesthetic matters,[175] and to leave his premises in their original condition even though particular safety features may later become available.[176] It should also be noted that s.1 of the Compensation Act 2006[177] may be relevant here. This requires a court in any negligence action to have regard to whether requiring steps to avoid an accident might prevent, limit or discourage desirable activity. This may well incline a court to be indulgent to the occupiers of amenity land, cycle paths and the like faced with a claim that demanding precautions ought to have been taken[178] (though in practice this seems to have been the approach anyway[179]).

An occupier who reasonably acts on professional or semi-professional advice is also likely to escape liability.[180] Conversely, failure to obtain or follow such advice, **11-31**

---

170 *Simonds v Isle of Wight CC* [2003] EWHC 2303 (QB); [2004] E.L.R. 59.

171 *Perry v Harris (a Minor)* [2008] EWCA Civ 907; [2009] 1 W.L.R. 19 (see para.7-226) (insufficient likelihood of injury on bouncy castle to justify extensive safety measures); *Tacagni v Penwith District Council* [2013] EWCA Civ 702 (no sufficient likelihood of falls to justify making occupier fence off six-foot drop onto road).

172 See *Cole v Davis-Gilbert* [2007] EWCA Civ 396; [2007] All E.R. (D) 20 (March) (occupier of village green entitled to assume British Legion, having set up temporary maypole, will plug hole so passer-by does not step into it).

173 *Perry v Harris (A Minor)* [2008] EWCA Civ 907; [2009] 1 W.L.R. 19 (householder not liable for failure to observe detailed health and safety instructions accompanying bouncy castle hired by him for party).

174 *Cowan v The Hopetoun House Preservation Trust* [2013] CSOH 9; 2013 Rep. L.R. 62 (no need to fence ha-ha at stately home, though duty to warn visitors at night). See too the Australian decision in *Department of Natural Resources v Harper* [2000] 1 V.R. 1 (no duty to warn about danger of falling trees in national park).

175 cf. *Phillis v Daly* (1988) 15 N.S.W.L.R. 65 (no liability to motel customer who fell off a log acting as a rustic boundary to a car-park; it could have been replaced with a foolproof but unsightly fence, but the occupier acted reasonably in not doing so).

176 See *McGivney v Golderslea* (2001) 17 Const. L.J. 454 (ordinary glass in door shattered on impact and cut visitor: CA deny liability, since such glass acceptable when building put up even though building regulations today require toughened glass). Presumably, however, this would not apply in extreme cases. Could an industrialist escape liability under the 1957 Act to his employees if he continued to operate a factory replete with blue asbestos, merely because the premises were built in 1850 when such materials were acceptable? It seems unlikely.

177 See para.7-188. See also the Social Action, Responsibility and Heroism Act 2015, under s.2 of which the court in an action for negligence or breach of statutory duty "must have regard to whether the alleged negligence or breach of statutory duty occurred when the person was acting for the benefit of society or any of its members." See para.7-190. This Act (applicable to events after 13 April 2015) might well be relevant in the case of amenity land, playgrounds etc.

178 Thus the 2006 Act was invoked in *Sutton v Syston Rugby Football Club Ltd* [2011] EWCA Civ 1182 as one reason for not holding a rugby club liable for failing to inspect its pitch minutely before every match in case it might contain debris.

179 See cases such as *Simonds v Isle of Wight CC* [2003] EWHC 2303 (QB); [2004] E.L.R. 59. In *Wilkin-Shaw v Fuller* [2012] EWHC 1777 (QB); [2012] E.L.R. 575 at [42] (not an occupier's case), Owen J suggested that the 2006 Act added nothing to the common law.

180 *Wattleworth v Goodwood Road Racing Co Ltd* [2004] EWHC 140 (QB); [2004] P.I.Q.R. P25 (motor racetrack proprietors not liable for hazard when took advice of sport's governing body); also *Browning v Odyssey Trust Co Ltd* [2014] NIQB 39 (precautions in ice-hockey stadium in accord-

or to perform an adequate risk assessment, may well tip the balance in favour of liability.[181] The fact that an occupier has been convicted of an offence the gist of which is failing to take due care (for example under health and safety legislation) is a powerful, and indeed sometimes compelling, indication that he failed to come up to the acceptable civil standard.[182]

11-32 **Obvious dangers and ordinary risks** No duty is owed as occupier[183] in respect of dangers which are entirely usual or obvious to a reasonable visitor[184] such as the fact that a sea wall covered with seaweed may be slippery,[185] that a rustic path may trip,[186] that a concrete drive in front of a house may be uneven,[187] that one can fall off an escalator,[188] that car parks may be icy in winter,[189] or that piping hot coffee may scald if spilt.[190] Nor is there any duty to protect visitors in respect of the ordinary risks of activities which they elect to engage in on land: to say otherwise would elevate paternalism over ordinary freedom. In *Tomlinson v Congleton BC*[191] the House of Lords trenchantly affirmed this principle. It accordingly denied

---

ance with governing body rules, so no liability when spectator hit by puck). Similar cases are *Hufton v Somerset County Council* [2011] EWCA Civ 789; [2011] E.L.R. 482 (school pupil slipped on a puddle of water in a school hall: school exonerated, on basis that it had an adequate system in place for preventing such hazards). Similarly, the National Trust was exonerated in *Bowen v National Trust* [2011] EWHC 1992 (QB) when despite impeccable risk-assessment a tree branch on an amenity property fell, killing a child.

[181] See *Bailey v Command Security Ltd*, ureported 25 October 2001 QBD (security guard fell off unfenced lift aperture; occupiers liable together with employers, subject to 25 per cent contributory negligence); *Phee v Gordon* [2013] CSIH 18; 2013 S.C. 379 (golfer struck by ball negligently mishit from another tee; course owners 80 per cent liable, partly on basis of lack of proper formal assessment of danger); also *Corbett v Cumbria Kart Racing Club* [2013] EWHC 1362 (QB); and *C v City of Edinburgh Council*, 2018 S.L.T. (Sh Ct) 34 (large sign at school fell on parent's head in high wind after screws rusted: liability for not conducting risk assessment and regular checks). But note Sharp J's comment in *West Sussex CC v Pierce* [2013] EWCA Civ 1230; [2014] P.I.Q.R. P5 at [12]: in all cases the question is whether reasonable care was taken, and simply asking whether a proper risk assessment was undertaken is an unacceptable judicial shortcut.

[182] See *James v White Lion Hotel* [2020] P.I.Q.R. P10 (QBD) (guest fell out of low sash window without limiters; hotel owner convicted; held liable).

[183] But a duty may be owed in some other respect: for instance, if an occupier lends his aid to someone carrying out an obviously dangerous activity and then in doing so fails to take proper care. See *Biddick v Morcom* [2014] EWCA Civ 182 (undertaking by householder to support trap door under workman).

[184] In *White v Doherty* [2019] IECA 295 at [29] the Irish Court of Appeal, construing similar but not identical Irish legislation, drew the distinction in terms of usual and unusual dangers. This may be more informative than asking whether the danger is obvious. A hidden rabbit-hole on a woodland walk is not an obvious danger, but it is a usual one, and there should be no liability in respect of it.

[185] *Staples v West Dorset DC* [1995] P.I.Q.R. P439 (holidaymaker slipping on the Cobb at Lyme Regis). See too *Darby v National Trust* [2001] EWCA Civ 189; [2001] P.I.Q.R. P27 (ill-advised visitor drowned while swimming in pond outside stately home); *Department of Natural Resources v Harper* [2000] 1 V.R. 1 (no duty to warn about danger of falling trees in national park). However, in *English Heritage v Taylor* [2016] EWCA Civ 448; [2016] P.I.Q.R. P14 the Court of Appeal refused to interfere with a finding that a sheer drop on the ramparts of a castle was not obvious. With respect this seems over-generous to the claimant (though he was held 50 per cent to blame).

[186] See the Scots decision in *Leonard v Loch Lomond & Trossachs National Park Authority* [2015] CSIH 44; 2016 S.C.L.R. 102.

[187] See the Australian decision in *Neindorf v Junkovic* [2005] HCA 75; (2006) 222 A.L.R. 631.

[188] *Lavin v Dublin Airport Authority Plc* [2016] IECA 268 (decided under the Irish occupiers' liability legislation).

[189] *Cook v Swansea City Council* [2017] EWCA Civ 2142 especially at [34].

[190] *B (A Child) v McDonald's Restaurants Ltd* [2002] EWHC 490 (QB).

[191] [2003] UKHL 47; [2004] 1 A.C. 46.

recovery to a swimmer injured by swimming in a lake who argued that his injury had been foreseeable and that he would not have suffered it had he been prevented from swimming at all. Lord Hoffmann put the point thus:

> "I think it will be extremely rare for an occupier of land to be under a duty to prevent people from taking risks which are inherent in the activities they freely choose to undertake upon the land. If people want to climb mountains, go hang gliding or swim or dive in ponds or lakes, that is their affair. Of course the landowner may for his own reasons wish to prohibit such activities. He may think that they are a danger or inconvenience to himself or others. Or he may take a paternalist view and prefer people not to undertake risky activities on his land. He is entitled to impose such conditions ... But the law does not require him to do so."[192]

Thus children who choose to mountaineer on fire-escapes,[193] holidaymakers and revellers who dive into obviously shallow pools,[194] skiers who elect to ski near a precipice,[195] and others acting in clearly dangerous ways,[196] are likely to obtain little sympathy. Furthermore, where the claimant's injuries are caused by his own perverse or unpredictable conduct, this may well in a suitable case be regarded as breaking the chain of causation.[197] On the other hand, this exoneration of the occupier is, it seems, premised on the avoidability of the danger: thus in *Liddle v Bristol City Council*[198] it was said that while obvious hazards on an unfenced quayside would not give rise to liability to a lone cyclist suffering injury, it might be different were large crowds to be present at the same spot.

Activities of third parties Elsewhere in the law of tort the courts are somewhat disinclined to hold defendants liable for failure to guard against the deliberate activities of third parties,[199] demanding a high degree of foreseeability or a close relationship between the parties. It is suggested that a similar tendency is likely to apply in occupier's liability cases, for example where a claimant alleges that the ill-lit nature of a car park or vestibule acts as an attractant for potential robbers.[200] **11-33**

---

192 [2003] UKHL 47; [2004] 1 A.C. 46 at [45]. See too [59], per Lord Hutton and [81], per Lord Hobhouse. Strictly speaking this was a case under the Occupiers' Liability Act 1984: but the reasoning applies equally to liability under the 1957 Act.

193 *Keown v Coventry NHS Trust* [2006] EWCA Civ 39; [2006] 1 W.L.R. 953 (a case under the 1984 Act, but still in point).

194 See *Grimes v Hawkins* [2011] EWHC 2004 (QB) (teenage visitor disabled after misjudging dive into entirely ordinary domestic swimming pool; householder understandably held not liable); also *Risk v Rose Bruford College* [2013] EWHC 3869 (QB); [2014] E.L.R. 157 (dive into paddling-pool at student union event); also *Evans v Kosmar Villa Holiday Plc* [2007] EWCA Civ 1003; [2008] 1 W.L.R. 297 (action against tour operator under Package Travel, Package Holidays and Package Tours Regulations 1992, but raising the same issues). See too *Unger v City of Ottawa* (1989) 58 D.L.R. (4th) 98 (no liability when drunken swimmer dived off a life-guard's chair into three feet of water).

195 See the Scots decision in *Struthers-Wright v Nevis Range Development Co Plc* [2006] CSOH 68.

196 See, e.g. *Clark v Bourne Leisure Ltd* [2011] EWCA Civ 753 (no negligence where disabled bar patron tried to steer wheelchair down a flight of stairs obvious as such to a casual glance, in the belief that they constituted a wheelchair ramp).

197 *Jolley v Sutton LBC* [1998] 1 W.L.R. 1546, 1555 (Woolf and Roch LJJ) (reversed for other reasons at [2000] 1 W.L.R. 1082). cf. *Unger v City of Ottawa* (1989) 58 D.L.R. (4th) 98 (no liability when drunken swimmer dived off a life-guard's chair into three feet of water).

198 [2018] EWHC 3673 (QB) at [109]–[110].

199 e.g. *Smith v Littlewoods Organisation Ltd* [1987] A.C. 241; *Topp v London Country Bus (South West) Ltd* [1993] 1 W.L.R. 1076.

200 See the Australian decisions in *Modbury Triangle Shopping Centre Ltd v Anzil* (2000) 175 A.L.R.

(e) Specific issues

11-34 **Lighting** If a visitor is injured in the dark by a danger which would have been obvious enough in the light, his right to recover depends to a large extent on whether he was invited to use the premises in the dark or not.[201] If he was, the occupier owes a duty to protect him by lighting, guarding or otherwise.[202] Even then, however, it may well amount to contributory negligence to walk about in the dark without a light.[203]

11-35 **"Do-it-yourself" repairs** In general, it is not a breach of duty for the occupier himself to undertake minor repairs such as fixing a handle to a door.[204] Moreover, if he does so, he will only be held to the standard of the reasonably competent amateur.[205] However, he may be in breach of duty if he undertakes to do himself work involving such highly specialised skill and knowledge that an ordinary occupier would employ experts to do it for him, such as electrical wiring, the maintenance of lifts, the installation of boilers and the like.[206]

11-36 **Liability to children**[207] The Act specifically states that an occupier must be prepared for children to be less careful than adults,[208] for the obvious reason that something which would not be a danger to an adult may very well be one to a child, and a warning sufficient for the former may be inadequate for the latter. So in *Moloney v Lambeth LBC*[209] an occupier was held liable to a four-year-old boy who fell through the bars of a balustrade. If a person the size of the claimant lost his balance he was liable to go through the gap. The following have at one time or another been held dangerous specifically to children: attractive but poisonous berries in a park,[210] an insecure wall on which children were known to be in the habit of bird's-nesting,[211] a tree, not far from a footpath, which could be climbed by children and close over which there was a live electric cable,[212] and a house in course of

---

164 (no liability for assault in unlit car-park); and *Strata Plan 17226 (Proprietors) v Drakulic* (2002) 55 N.S.W.L.R. 659 (owner of common parts of apartment building not liable for mugging of returning resident allegedly due to ill-lit state).

201 *Hogan v P & O Steam Navigation Co* [1959] 2 Lloyd's Rep. 305.

202 *Campbell v Shellbourne Hotel* [1939] 2 K.B. 534 (unlit passage in hotel). And see *Stone v Taffe* [1974] 1 W.L.R. 1575. cf. *Schlarb v L & NE Ry* [1936] 1 All E.R. 71, where the railway was held liable to passengers who fell off the platform in fog.

203 *Ghannan v Glasgow Corp*, 1950 S.C. 23 (pursuer held two-fifths to blame); and see *Devine v London Housing Society Ltd* [1950] 2 All E.R. 1173; *Rochman v Hall Ltd* [1947] 1 All E.R. 895.

204 *Wells v Cooper* [1958] 2 Q.B. 265.

205 *Wells v Cooper* [1958] 2 Q.B. 265.

206 *Wells v Cooper* [1958] 2 Q.B. 265, 274. Note that many electrical works must now be carried out by qualified persons or inspected by the local authority, in so far as they come under Pt P of Schedule 1 to the Building Regulations 2010 (SI 2010/2214, as amended). This may affect the question of negligence in particular situations.

207 See R. Kidner, "The duty of occupiers towards children" (1988) 39 N.I.L.Q. 150.

208 Occupiers' Liability Act 1957 s.2(3)(a).

209 (1966) 198 E.G. 895; (1966) 64 L.G.R. 440; and see *French v Sunshine Holiday Camp (Hayling Island)* (1963) 107 S.J. 595. The Building Regulations 2010 (SI 2010/2214) now require all new staircases to carry close-fenced balustrades and to have various other safety features.

210 *Glasgow Corp v Taylor* [1922] 1 A.C. 44.

211 *Boyd v Glasgow Iron & Steel Co*, 1923 S.C. 758.

212 *Buckland v Guildford Gas Light & Coke Co* [1949] 1 K.B. 410.

demolition.[213] However, while foolhardiness can be expected in children, so also may a reasonable degree of parental supervision and control. As Devlin J. put it in *Phipps v Rochester Corp*[214]:

> "But the responsibility for the safety of little children must rest primarily on the parents; it is their duty to see that such children are not allowed to wander about by themselves, or at the least to satisfy themselves that the places to which they do allow their children to go unaccompanied are safe for them to go to. It would not be socially desirable if parents were, as a matter of course, able to shift the burden of looking after their children from their own shoulders to those of persons who happen to have accessible bits of land. Different considerations may well apply to public parks or to recognised playing grounds where parents allow their children to go unaccompanied in the reasonable belief that they are safe."[215]

Visitors entering premises to carry out works of construction, maintenance, repair etc By s.2(3)(b) of the 1957 Act, an occupier "may expect that a person, in the exercise of his calling, will appreciate and guard against any special risks ordinarily incident to it". The reason for this is self-explanatory.[216] A window-cleaner's job, for instance, is inherently dangerous, and questions as to the adequacy of hand-holds and the like are for him and not the occupier to determine. Furthermore, an occupier may normally expect a workman's employers to take steps to guard him against such risks.[217] Thus, where two chimney-sweeps were killed by carbon monoxide fumes while sealing up a sweep-hole, it was the view of Lord Denning that: 11-37

> "the occupier here was under no duty of care to these sweeps, at any rate in regard to the dangers which caused their deaths. If it had been a different danger, as for instance if the stairs leading to the cellar gave way, the occupier might no doubt be responsible, but not for these dangers which were special risks ordinarily incidental to their calling."[218]

Again, the occupier was exonerated where an experienced window cleaner lost his balance when ornamental trelliswork broke away[219]; and on similar reasoning, the

213 *Davis v St Mary's Demolition & Excavation Co* [1954] 1 W.L.R. 592; *Harris v Birkenhead Corp* [1976] 1 W.L.R. 279.

214 [1955] 1 Q.B. 450. See too *B (A Child) v London Borough of Camden* [2001] P.I.Q.R. P9 (four-year-old burnt by very hot pipes in flat: landlords exonerated in action under s.4 of the Defective Premises Act. Parents in such situations could be expected to take proper precautions to protect their children); and *Bourne Leisure Ltd v Marsden* [2009] EWCA Civ 671; [2009] N.P.C. 93 (pond at caravan site a danger obvious to parents if not toddlers: no liability when unsupervised child fell in and drowned).

215 [1955] 1 Q.B. 450 at 472. And see *O'Connor v British Transport Commission* [1958] 1 W.L.R. 346. *Phipps* was followed in *Simkiss v Rhondda BC* (1983) 81 L.G.R. 460.

216 And indeed applies generally, even where the 1957 Act is not applicable: see *Yates v National Trust* [2014] EWHC 222 (QB); [2014] P.I.Q.R. P16 at [40] (Nicol J).

217 See *Fairchild v Glenhaven Funeral Services Ltd* [2001] EWCA 1881; [2002] 1 W.L.R. 1052 (appealed to HL on other grounds, [2002] UKHL 22; [2003] 1 A.C. 32) (workman injured clearing asbestos from building: occupier not liable, since entitled to assume workman's employer would take reasonable care to safeguard him from danger). But if the occupier himself undertakes to provide equipment he may be liable for failure to supervise those who erect it: see *Kealey v Heard* [1983] 1 W.L.R. 573 (defective scaffolding).

218 *Roles v Nathan* [1963] 1 W.L.R. 1117 at 1123-1125. See too *Richards v Brooks Wharf & Bull Wharf Ltd* [1965] 2 Lloyd's Rep. 304 at 311, per Thompson J (upheld at [1966] 1 Lloyd's Rep.145) (dock worker); *Phillips v Perry* unreported 6 March 1997 (deliveryman); *Sydney CC v Dell'Oro* (1974) 132 C.L.R. 97 (electrician); *Epp v Ridgetop Builders* (1979) 94 D.L.R. (3d) 505 (surveyor).

219 *Caddis v Gettrup* (1967) 202 E.G. 517.

occupier of a building site was not liable to experienced roofers for failing to urge them to use crawling boards.[220]

11-38 On the other hand, the risk must be one specifically associated with the visitor's calling. Were a window-cleaner to trip on a defective staircase, there is no reason why the occupier should not be liable.[221] Similarly a joiner fitting a door is not saddled with the risk of a collapsing lintel,[222] nor a telephone engineer with that of weak hardboard roofing: these risks relate not to the job being done but to the premises themselves.[223]

11-39 **Firemen and rescue services** These deserve special mention at this point. Because of s.2(3)(b) an occupier is not liable to a fireman merely because the state of his premises makes fire-fighting more hazardous.[224] However, it was made clear in *Ogwo v Taylor*[225] that an occupier who negligently starts a fire in his own premises may be liable under the general law of negligence to a fireman who is foreseeably injured while trying to put it out, even though fire-fighting is part of his job.

11-40 **Warning of danger** Section 2(4) provides:

> "In determining whether the occupier of premises has discharged the common duty of care to a visitor, regard is to be had to all the circumstances, so that (for example)—(a) where damage is caused to a visitor by a danger of which he had been warned by the occupier, the warning is not to be treated without more as absolving the occupier from liability, unless in all the circumstances it was enough to enable the visitor to be reasonably safe."

11-41 This provision seems at first sight self-evident. It was, however, introduced to reverse the common law decision in *London Graving Dock Co v Horton*,[226] where the House of Lords had in effect held that any notice to or knowledge by the visitor of the risk, provided he recognised the full significance of that risk, was ipso facto sufficient to exculpate the occupier. Under s.2(4)(a), by contrast, a warning by the occupier is one of the circumstances to be considered, but is not an absolute

---

220 *Clare v Whittaker & Son Ltd* [1976] I.C.R. 1. See too *Hood v Mitie Property Services (Midlands) Ltd* [2005] All E.R. (D) 11 (Jul).

221 See the Law Reform Committee's Report, Cmd.9305, para.77(iii). See too *Lough v Intruder Detention & Surveillance Fire & Security Ltd* [2008] EWCA Civ 1009 (householder 25 per cent responsible for letting repairman doing non-urgent work use temporarily unbanistered staircase rather than telling him to come back later). The latter decision, with respect, seems uncommonly generous to the claimant.

222 *Eden v West & Co* [2002] EWCA Civ 991; [2003] P.I.Q.R. Q2; and cf. *Simpson v Al Dairies Ltd* [2001] EWCA Civ 13 (liability to fireman who fell into unguarded trench in farmyard hidden by surface water).

223 *Woollins v British Celanese Ltd* (1966) 1 K.I.R. 438; 110 S.J. 686 CA. See too *Bird v King Line* [1970] 2 Lloyd's Rep. 349 (boiler scaler slipping on bottles); and *Flagg v Kent CC* unreported 23 April 1993 (fireman negotiating practice obstacle course recovered in respect of damage caused by protruding bar not part of exercise).

224 *Sibbald (or Bermingham) v Sher Bros*, 1980 S.L.T. 122. But cf. *Merrington v Ironbridge Metal Works Ltd* [1952] 2 All E.R. 1101 and *Hartley v British Railways Board*, *The Times*, 2 February 1981, for the situation where there is some special or unusual danger.

225 [1988] 1 A.C. 431: see too *Salmon v Seafarer Restaurants Ltd* [1983] 1 W.L.R. 1264. Quaere whether a defence analogous to s.2(3)(b) ought to be available here: cf. the American "firemen's rule," exemplified in cases such as *Krauth v Geller*, 157 A.2d 129 (1960). See further para.7-35.

226 [1951] A.C. 737.

bar to recovery.[227] The question is whether, on the facts of the particular case, the warning is enough to enable the visitor to be reasonably safe, and hence to show that the occupier has discharged his duty of care.[228] Thus a verbal warning given insufficiently seriously,[229] or a notice placed in an unsuitable place[230] will not do. As one might expect, the more drastic the danger, the more specific the warning of it must be.[231] However, an occupier who fails to warn of a particular danger will not be liable if the visitor succumbs to an entirely different peril, even if the warning would in fact have prevented this.[232]

Visitor's knowledge of the risk The provisions as to warnings referred to above are a statutory example of the general proposition that, in determining whether the occupier has discharged the common duty of care, regard is to be had to all the circumstances. In the light of this, it is clear that mere knowledge of a risk is no longer a complete bar to a visitor's right to recover[233]; the defendant must go further and show that the visitor was *volens* in that he must be taken to have agreed to bear that risk. Thus in *Bunker v Brand (Charles) & Son Ltd*[234] the claimant walked over hazardous tunnelling equipment with knowledge of the dangers involved; nevertheless, on the evidence, he was held not to have agreed to bear the risk of the injuries he suffered as a result.[235] 11-42

(f) Defences

Volenti non fit injuria This was always a defence available to the occupier, and s.2(5) of the 1957 Act expressly preserves it[236]: 11-43

> "The common duty of care does not impose on an occupier any obligation to a visitor in respect of risks willingly accepted as his by the visitor (the question whether a risk was so accepted to be decided on the same principles as in other cases in which one person owes a duty of care to another)."

So, where a visitor knowingly exposes himself, while on the premises, to a particular physical risk, the occupier may raise against him the defence of volenti

227 *Bunker v Charles Brand & Sons Ltd* [1969] 2 Q.B. 480.

228 Contrast the situation where the occupier exhibits a notice excluding his liability; the effect here is not to satisfy the duty of care, but to prevent it arising in the first place.

229 *Bishop v JS Starnes & Sons* [1971] 1 Lloyd's Rep. 162. Compare *Roles v Nathan* [1963] 1 W.L.R. 1117, where the warning was held sufficient (especially per Lord Denning MR at 1124-1125 and Harman LJ at 1127-1128). cf. *Nasser v Rumford* (1977) 77 D.L.R. (3d) 287; (1978) 83 D.L.R. (3d) 208.

230 *Coupland v Eagle Bros* (1969) 210 E.G. 581; *Woollins v British Celanese Ltd* (1966) 1 K.I.R. 438.

231 *Rae v Mars (UK) Ltd* [1990] 3 E.G. 80.

232 *Darby v National Trust* [2001] EWCA Civ 189; [2001] P.I.Q.R. P27 (National Trust not liable for death of visitor who swam and drowned in pond merely because it had been negligent in failing to warn of entirely unrelated danger of catching Weil's disease).

233 But it may apparently qualify the level of care required, where the visitor knows that the occupier is old and frail, and unlikely to be able to appreciate the risk and put repairs in hand: see *Seymour v Flynn* unreported 4 February 1992 CA.

234 [1969] 2 Q.B. 480.

235 See too *Slater v Clay Cross Co* [1956] 2 Q.B. 264, 271 (Denning LJ). cf. in the context of general negligence, *Targett v Torfaen BC* [1982] 3 All E.R. 27; and *Smith v Baker & Sons* [1891] A.C. 325.

236 The statutory defence has been confirmed to be "indistinguishable from the common law defence of *volenti*"—see *Geary v Wetherspoon Plc* [2011] EWHC 1506 (QB); [2011] N.P.C. 60 at [36] (Coulson J).

non fit injuria. Thus in *Simms v Leigh Rugby Football Club*[237] Wrangham J held that a visiting rugby league football player willingly accepted the risks necessarily involved in playing on a field with a concrete wall some seven feet from the touchline, such walls being permitted under the rules of the game.

11-44 But a claimant will be volens only if the danger which causes his injury is the one which he willingly accepted—and this usually means that he must have known the precise risk in advance.[238] Thus in *White v Blackmore*[239] the defence failed against a spectator watching stock-car racing who was catapulted into the air by the safety ropes. The relevant risk did not arise from participation in a dangerous sport, to which the claimant had consented, but from the organisers' failure properly to lay out the safety arrangements, a failure of which the claimant clearly did not knowingly take the risk. On the other hand, if the claimant's knowledge is not sufficient to trigger a defence of volenti non fit injuria, it may still allow the defendant to reduce any damages on account of contributory negligence. Even if a claimant does have full knowledge of the risk, he will not be *volens* if his action is reasonable in the circumstances.[240] So the defence could hardly be raised against a fireman rescuing a victim from a fume-filled factory merely because he knew of the precise danger before he went in. The Unfair Contract Terms Act 1977, referred to below, specifically preserves the defence of volenti,[241] although it does also provide—not surprisingly—that a notice purporting to exclude liability will not, without more, entitle the defendant to invoke it.[242]

11-45 **Contributory negligence** The Law Reform (Contributory Negligence) Act 1945 applies to an action for breach of the common duty of care.[243] However, a visitor who is extremely careless for his own safety may fail completely on grounds of causation. Thus in *Munro v Porthkerry Park Holiday Estates Ltd*[244] a drunken patron at a cliff-top bar tried to climb a low chain-link fence, and fell to his death over a cliff beyond it. His estate failed completely in an action for negligence against the owners of the bar.

11-46 **Exclusion of liability by the occupier** A suitably worded notice giving precise warning of a danger may have the effect of discharging the occupier's duty on the basis that he has taken all reasonable care in the circumstances. But even where this was not the case, at common law an occupier could in addition limit or entirely exclude his liability vis-à-vis his visitors by a suitably worded contract term or notice.[245] The position is the same under the 1957 Act: by s.2(1) the occupier owes his visitors the common duty of care, "except in so far as he is free to and does

---

237 [1969] 2 All E.R. 923.

238 cf. *Murray v Bitango* [1996] 7 W.W.R. 163 (claimant not *volens* unless risk "virtually certain").

239 [1972] 2 Q.B. 651; see too *Latchford v Spedeworth International Ltd* (1984) 134 N.L.J. 36; and *Browning v Odyssey Trust Co Ltd* [2014] NIQB 39 at [17]. Also cf. *Hanson v City of Saint John* (1974) 39 D.L.R. (3d) 417 (Sup. Ct of Can.).

240 [1958] A.C. 240 at 266.

241 By s.2(3).

242 So too the Consumer Rights Act 2015: see s.65(2).

243 *Wheat v E Lacon & Co Ltd* [1966] A.C. 552 at 557, 560, 563, 564, 570. See too *McDowell v FMC (Meat)* (1968) 5 K.I.R. 456; *Bunker v Brand (Charles) & Sons Ltd* [1969] 2 Q.B. 480; *Stone v Taffe* [1974] 1 W.L.R. 1575 by one-half. See para.3-58 onwards.

244 (1984) 81 L.S. Gaz. 1368. See too *Brayshaw v Leeds City Council* [1984] 2 C.L. 234.

245 See *Ashdown v Samuel Williams & Son Ltd* [1957] 1 Q.B. 409 (arising out of events taking place before the Act came into force).

extend, restrict, modify or exclude his duty to any visitor or visitors by agreement or otherwise".[246] The introduction of the words "in so far as he is free to do so" indicates that the occupier is to have no greater power to exclude or restrict his duty than he has under the general law. It must be remembered, however, that the Unfair Contract Terms Act 1977 and the Consumer Rights Act 2015 now limit the occupier's power of exclusion.[247]

Exclusion by contract or notice Exclusion by contract between occupier and visitor gives rise to little difficulty. Subject to the provisions of the Unfair Contract Terms Act 1977, the Consumer Rights Act 2015, and other similar legislation,[248] the common duty of care can, like any other duty in tort, be excluded. Furthermore, it is now clear that a suitably-worded contract may be effective to exclude the liability of someone who is not a party to it.[249] Liability can also (again subject to contrary legislation) be excluded by agreement or notice falling short of a contract,[250] such as printed conditions accepted by a gratuitous entrant,[251] or a suitably worded notice exhibited on the premises themselves. Thus in *White v Blackmore*[252] the Court of Appeal held that notices at a motor racing circuit absolving the organisers from all liability for accidents "howsoever caused" was effective to exclude a claim by the widow of a spectator killed as a result of the negligent arrangement of the ropes fencing off the track. Roskill LJ said: 11-47

> "Parliament must be taken to have known the law [as laid down in *Ashdown's* case] and to have decided as a matter of policy not to alter it, but on the contrary to preserve and continue any pre-existing rights possessed by an occupier to extend, restrict, modify or exclude his duty by agreement or otherwise. ..."[253]

The theory behind such exclusion of liability by agreement falling short of contract is said to be one of conditional licence: the occupier is allowing the visitor onto his land on condition that the occupier is not to be liable for loss or damage, and the visitor cannot make use of the licence so granted without being bound by the condition attached to it.[254]

The power of the occupier to exclude his duty is thus wide. Indeed, it seems clear 11-48

---

[246] For the distinction between excluding a duty and satisfying it by use of a suitable warning, see *White v Blackmore* [1972] 2 Q.B. 651, 669 (Buckley LJ), 674 (Roskill LJ).

[247] See para.11-51.

[248] e.g. Road Traffic Act 1988 s.149, preventing exclusion of liability by a driver vis-à-vis his passengers. Presumably this would apply to liability arising out of the state of the vehicle and thus be covered by the 1957 Act.

[249] Contracts (Rights of Third Parties) Act 1999 s.1(6). For example, a building contractor working on an occupier's premises may now in his contract with a subcontractor exclude the occupier's liability for loss or damage to the subcontractor's plant and equipment on site.

[250] Whether a given arrangement purporting to exclude liability does or does not amount to a contract is a vexed question. Compare *Wilkie v LPTB* [1947] 1 All E.R. 258 at 260, per Lord Greene MR, with *Gore v Van Der Lann* [1967] 2 Q.B. 31. But for present purposes the distinction does not matter.

[251] cf. in the context of the general law, *Wilkie v LPTB* [1947] 1 All E.R. 258 (exclusion of liability to bus passenger on a free pass). Presumably an oral disclaimer would also be effective.

[252] [1972] 2 Q.B. 651. See A.L. Goodhart (1972) 88 L.Q.R. 453; D. Bowett, "Tort Liability and Exemption Notices" [1972A] C.L.J. 207. See too *Ashdown v Samuel Williams & Son Ltd* [1957] 1 Q.B. 409, decided at common law. That case would be decided differently today because of the Unfair Contract Terms Act 1977.

[253] [1972] 2 Q.B. 651 per Roskill LJ at 674.

[254] *Wilkie v LPTB* [1947] 1 All E.R. 258, 260. See too *Ashdown v Samuel Williams & Son Ltd* [1957] 1 Q.B. 409, 428 (Parker LJ).

that it extends both to "occupancy duty" covered by the Act and "activity duty" covered by the common law.[255] Thus in the common law case of *Ashdown v Samuel Williams & Son Ltd*[256] a notice was held effective to exclude liability where employees of the defendant occupier negligently shunted railway wagons so as to injure the claimant visitor—a classic case of an "activity duty". On the other hand, the notice must be sufficiently explicit in its terms, and would no doubt in cases of ambiguity be construed *contra proferentem*. As Parker LJ said in *Ashdown's* case:

> "Each case must, of course, depend upon its own facts, and in particular on what the licensee knows as to the use of the land. Where, for instance, an occupier of land used as a shooting school desires to exclude liability for negligent shooting, he may well have to bring to the knowledge of the proposed licensee that the land is so used. A mere reference to negligence without a warning as to the user of the land might well be insufficient."[257]

11-49 Where an occupier seeks to rely on a notice, he need not show actual knowledge on the part of the visitor; it is clear from *Ashdown v Samuel Williams & Son Ltd*[258] and from *White v Blackmore*[259] that all that is required is that reasonable efforts were made to bring it to his attention. As Jenkins LJ said in *Ashdown*:

> "I see no reason in principle for holding that something more is needed to give a mere non-contractual licensee constructive knowledge of a condition restricting or excluding his ordinary right to be treated with reasonable care while on the land to which the licence relates, than is required to give a party to a contract constructive knowledge of a term restricting or excluding some right of action he would or might otherwise have under the general law."[260]

Thus, although the ultimate origin of the occupier's right to exclude his liability by notice may be the same notion as underlies volenti non fit injuria, the rules governing the validity of such notices have evolved into something separate and wider. So in *White v Blackmore*[261] itself the Court of Appeal held that the defendant failed in his defence of volenti, because the deceased was not aware of the particular danger—badly laid-out ropes—which killed him; nevertheless, the defence based on the excluding notice succeeded.

11-50 **Common law limitations on the effect of excluding notice** Normally the court will infer the visitor's agreement to the condition from the mere fact that he enters the property with actual or constructive notice of it. Arguably, however, this only applies where the visitor has, in practical rather than in strictly legal terms, a free choice as to whether or not to enter in the first place. Thus in *Burnett v British Waterways Board*[262] the Court of Appeal held that a lighterman, injured by a defective rope from a dock while he was working on a barge, was not bound by a notice,

---

[255] On the distinction, see para.11-03.
[256] [1957] 1 Q.B. 409.
[257] [1957] 1 Q.B. 409 at 429–430.
[258] [1957] 1 Q.B. 409.
[259] [1972] 2 Q.B. 651.
[260] [1957] 1 Q.B. 409 at 425. For a case in which the notice was held to be inadequate, see *Lynch v Brewer's Warehousing Co Ltd* (1974) 44 D.L.R. (3d) 677.
[261] [1972] 2 Q.B. 651.
[262] [1973] 1 W.L.R. 700. See J. Lowe, "The Exclusion of Liability for negligence" (1974) 37 M.L.R. 218.

although its wording was apt to cover the accident and the lighterman knew what it said. "He was an employee on a barge, part of a train of barges, and by the time he had got to the dock it was certainly beyond his ability to make a choice and not go in."[263] Similarly, it was suggested in *White v Blackmore* that police officers and ambulance crew would not have been affected by the notice.[264] If these cases are correct, they impose a severe limit on a landowner's ability to exclude liability, since they seem to mean that liability can never be excluded vis-à-vis visitors entering in the course of their employment. This is a drastic result, and suggests that in this respect the principle in *Burnett v British Waterways Board*[265] might perhaps be open to reconsideration.

Exclusion of liability: visitors entering by right It will be remembered that those with a right of entry to premises, such as police executing search warrants, are regarded by the 1957 Act as visitors even if the occupier does not consent to their presence.[266] If the basis of the occupier's right to limit his liability is his right to exclude potential visitors who do not accept his conditions,[267] it no doubt follows that he cannot qualify his liability as against entrants as of right; he has to admit such persons willy-nilly.[268] Similarly, it is suggested that where the claimant has a right of entry under the provisions of the Countryside and Rights of Way Act 2000, there can be no exclusion of the provisions of the Occupiers' Liability Act 1984[269] (which make the occupier liable for intentional or reckless harm). **11-51**

Exclusion of liability: statutory controls While residential occupiers not acting in the course of a business retain complete freedom to exclude liability as they wish, statute places considerable restrictions on other attempts to exclude or restrict their liability for negligence with regard to lawful visitors. As regards non-business visitors the relevant provision is the Consumer Rights Act 2015; for others it is the Unfair Contract Terms Act 1977. **11-52**

Exclusion of liability: non-business visitors Under s.65 of the Consumer Rights Act 2015 an occupier who occupies premises as a trader (by which is meant anyone acting in the course of a business, craft or profession,[270] together with any government department or local or public authority[271]) cannot by contract or notice exclude **11-53**

---

263 Waller J in the same case at first instance, [1972] 1 W.L.R. 1329 at 1334; approved by Lord Denning MR at [1973] 1 W.L.R. 700 at 705.

264 [1972] 2 Q.B. 651 at 677, per Roskill LJ. In many cases the emergency services have rights of entry anyway (on which see para.11-19). But Roskill LJ's reasoning may apply even where they do not: for example, where a policeman is ordered by his superiors to make routine enquiries of a householder.

265 [1973] 1 W.L.R. 700.

266 1957 Act s.2(6).

267 See para.11-46.

268 cf. P. North, *Occupiers' Liability* (1971), p.131.

269 Occupiers' Liability Act s.1(6C), inserted by the 2000 Act.

270 Consumer Rights Act 2015 s.2(2). Quaere whether this definition includes land occupied for communal, charitable or eleemosynary purposes. It is suggested that it does if they provide paid-for services or charge for entry (as in the case of private schools or hospitals, charity shops, Salvation Army hostels, village halls, or gentlemen's clubs), but not otherwise (for example, churches, Christian Science reading-rooms, or citizens' advice bureaux).

271 Consumer Rights Act 2015 s.2(7). The reference to local authorities means that most schools are covered, but there must be some doubt over foundation schools independent of local authority control (though it is likely that they will be covered). But entirely private institutions, such as free evening

liability for death or personal injury arising under the 1957 Act, or for that matter any other liability in negligence at common law arising out of the state of those premises,[272] as regards a person visiting for non-business purposes.[273] This is, however, subject to one exception. Where the visitor is on the premises for recreational purposes, it remains possible for the occupier by notice or contract to exclude liability for negligence arising out of the state of the premises,[274] unless his business includes the provision of recreation.[275] This will thus cover the case of a factory owner admitting sightseers, a farmer allowing the public to walk over his land, or a local authority entertaining pensioners to a meal; depending on the width of the concept of recreation, it might also cover a church admitting worshippers or a business admitting a school party. But it would not include visitors admitted to an amusement park or caravan site.

11-54 Other liability, for example liability for damage to visitors' property (for example, clothing, equipment or parked cars), can be excluded, but only in so far as the exclusion is not "unfair".[276] For these purposes an exclusion is unfair if, taking account of all the circumstances, it is one that, contrary to the requirement of good faith, causes a significant imbalance in the parties' rights and obligations to the detriment of the visitor.[277] In practice one suspects that such exclusions are unlikely to be upheld in the absence of some very clear justification.

11-55 **Exclusion of liability: business visitors** Exclusion of liability to those visiting premises for business purposes, such as repairers, salesmen, business customers, government functionaries or for that matter legal advisers, is dealt with by the Unfair Contract Terms Act 1977. Similar but not identical to the Consumer Rights Act 2015, this covers liability arising from things done or to be done by a person in the course of a business, or from the occupation of premises used for business purposes;[278] business purposes being defined as including professions and the activities of government and local authorities.[279] Under s.2(1) of the Act, liability for death or personal injury resulting from negligence, including breach of the common duty of care under the 1957 Act,[280] cannot be excluded at all.[281] Under s.2(2), other liability, for example for damage to a visitor's property, can only be excluded

classes, would not seem to be. Presumably NHS hospitals all count as public authorities, though this cannot be regarded as certain.

272 See s.65(4).

273 The term used is the slightly misleading one of "consumer", but this is defined as "an individual acting for purposes that are wholly or mainly outside that individual's trade, business, craft or profession": s.2(3).

274 But not, it would seem, for things done on them. Thus a farmer can exclude liability to walkers if they fall over a badly-maintained stile, but not if he negligently allows them to be peppered while he is out shooting rabbits.

275 See s.66(4).

276 See ss.62(1), 62(2).

277 See ss.62(4), 62(6).

278 Where the parts of premises used for business are clearly marked off, there is no reason why the rest of them should not be regarded as private. Thus while a shopkeeper clearly ought not to be able to exclude liability in respect of the shop itself, it would be odd if he could not do so in respect of the living accommodation above.

279 See ss.1(3), 14; also para.11-53.

280 See s.1(1) of the 1977 Act.

281 Subject to one curious exception for recreational or educational visitors: s.1(3). One can only imagine that this might protect, for example, a teacher accompanying a school party, who might arguably not be a non-business visitor within the Consumer Rights Act 2015.

if the exclusion satisfies a "requirement of reasonableness". This is defined in s.11(3)[282]: the term excluding or limiting liability must be such that it should be fair and reasonable to allow reliance on it, having regard to all the circumstances obtaining when the liability arose or (but for the notice) would have arisen. It is further provided[283] that where, by reference to a contract term or notice, a person seeks not to exclude liability entirely but to restrict it to a specified sum of money, regard shall be had to the resources which he could expect to be available to him for the purpose of meeting the liability should it arise, and the possibility of insuring against the risk. Where a term is challenged under the Act, the burden of proof is on the person seeking to rely on it to show that it satisfies the requirement of reasonableness.[284] In practice, it is suggested that the courts may well tend to uphold exclusions as against business visitors, particularly if the occupier accepts liability but only up to a particular limit,[285] or limits liability to cases of deliberate or reckless conduct.[286]

Effect of contract on occupier's liability to third party A contract between the occupier and the visitor may always increase or (subject to the restrictions in the Unfair Contract Terms Act 1977 and the Consumer Rights Act 2015) reduce the occupier's duty. Special statutory provisions apply, however, where an occupier is bound by contract with A to let B onto his premises; for example, where a householder contracts with a firm of builders to admit their employees to carry out works on his house, or where the landlord of a block of flats agrees to let his tenants' visitors use the common parts.[287] At common law B, not being a party to the contract, could not take any benefit from it: but this is reversed in the context of occupiers' liability by s.3(1). Effectively, the contract between the occupier and A may increase the former's liability to B, but may not reduce it below the common duty of care.[288] In fact, s.3(1) is now largely redundant. Under s.1 of the Contracts (Rights of Third Parties) Act 1999 a contract entered into between an occupier and A to increase the occupier's duty to B will be enforceable by B in any case. Moreover, in one respect the 1999 Act is wider than s.3(1) of the 1957 Act. This is because it applies to any third party, whereas s.3(1) only benefits a third party whom the occupier is actually bound by contract to admit to the premises. 11-56

282 Technically this applies in relation to a notice that does have contractual effect. As regards a contract term, the requirement is identical, save that the relevant time is when the contract was entered into, not when the would-be liability arose. See s.11(1).

283 s.11(4).

284 s.11(5). It is not open to the court to uphold the term in part only: *Mitchell (George) (Chesterhall) Ltd v Finney Lock Seeds Ltd* [1983] 2 A.C. 803, at 815–816 (Lord Bridge). This case was decided under other statutory provisions, but the reasoning must be applicable to the point here.

285 cf. *Ailsa Craig Co Ltd v Malvern Shipping Co Ltd* [1983] 1 W.L.R. 964 at 966 (Lord Wilberforce).

286 See *Monarch Airlines Ltd v Luton Airport Ltd* [1998] 1 Lloyd's Rep. 403 (limitation to deliberate or reckless conduct upheld where runway disintegrated under aircraft).

287 And conversely, when a tenant agrees with the landlord (as he almost invariably does) to admit the landlord's agents to carry out repairs, other prospective tenants to view the premises etc. Agreements between landlord and tenant are specifically brought within s.3(1) by s.3(4), which also makes it clear that it applies to statutory tenancies even though they may not technically amount to contracts.

288 Setting at rest doubts raised at common law by *Fosbroke-Hobbes v Airwork Ltd* [1937] 1 All E.R. 108, 112. Quaere whether the occupier could, in such a case, take away with one hand what he had given with the other, by putting up a prominent notice on the premises disclaiming liability to B. There seems no reason on principle why he should not: his liability to B would be excluded, not by the terms of his contract with A (which the Act prohibits) but by the separate notice (which it does not).

(g) Independent contractors

11-57 **Liability of occupier for his independent contractors** At common law it was arguable that an occupier's duty, at least vis-à-vis his invitees, was non-delegable and hence that he was liable for the negligence not only of his servants but also of any independent contractors he employed.[289] But if this ever was the case, s.2(4)(b) of the 1957 Act makes it clear that it no longer is:

> "Where damage is caused to a visitor by a danger due to the faulty execution of any work of construction, maintenance or repair by an independent contractor employed by the occupier, the occupier is not to be treated without more[290] as answerable for the danger if in all the circumstances he had acted reasonably in entrusting the work to an independent contractor and had taken such steps (if any) as he reasonably ought in order to satisfy himself that the contractor was competent and that the work had been properly done."

"Faulty execution" for these purposes comprises culpable omissions to maintain or repair as well as negligent acts,[291] and "construction, maintenance or repair" covers almost all conceivable works on land or structures, including demolition.[292] Even if it were possible to conceive of some negligence by an independent contractor that was not directly covered by these words,[293] it is suggested that the courts would read the section expansively, as clearly intended to oust any occupier's liability for independent contractors, and deny a remedy accordingly.[294]

11-58 It follows from this that, where the occupier has: (1) acted reasonably in selecting and entrusting work to the independent contractor concerned[295]; (2) taken reasonable steps (if possible) to supervise the carrying out of the work; and (3) used reasonable care to check that the work has been properly done,[296] he will be held to have discharged his common duty of care.[297] Of course, an occupier may find

---

289 This resulted from the rather Delphic decision in *Thomson v Cremin* [1956] 1 W.L.R. 103n; [1953] 2 All E.R. 1185.

290 For doubts as to the effect of the words "without more", see P. North, *Occupiers' Liability* (1971), p.144; F. Newark, "The Occupiers' Liability Act (Northern Ireland) 1957" (1956–1958) 12 N.I.L.Q. 203, 213. On s.2(4)(b) see too *Ferguson v Welsh* [1987] 1 W.L.R. 1553.

291 Since the dilatory should be in no different position from the plain incompetent. See *AMF International Ltd v Magnet Bowling Ltd* [1968] 1 W.L.R. 1028, especially at 1043; and *Prentice v Hereward Housing Association* unreported 29 April 1999.

292 See *Ferguson v Welsh* [1987] 1 W.L.R. 1553, 1560, where Lord Keith gave a purposive interpretation to the section and held that demolition operations were covered by "construction".

293 Suppose a cook engaged for the evening leaves a slippery floor on which a visitor slips and is injured: on most readings this would not be a work of "construction, maintenance or repair".

294 cf. *Ellis v Scruttons Maltby Ltd and Cunard SS Co Ltd* [1975] 1 Lloyd's Rep. 564 (shipowner not liable for activities of independent stevedores in the hold). But note a suggestion to the contrary in *Stone v Taffe* [1974] 1 W.L.R. 1575, 1580. The words in this paragraph were approved by Picken J in *Lear v Hickstead Ltd* [2016] EWHC 528 (QB); [2016] 4 W.L.R. 73 at [27]–[29].

295 It is for the occupier to prove that an independent contractor has been employed to do the work in question: *Christmas v Blue Star Line Ltd* [1961] 1 Lloyd's Rep. 94.

296 For a case where an occupier knew that independent work had created a danger but did nothing about it, see *Alexander v Freshwater Properties Ltd* [2012] EWCA Civ 1048 (landlord of apartment block allowing builder to remove door handle from heavy entrance door, leaving door likely to trap unwary fingers).

297 For illustrations, see *O'Connor v Swan & Edgar Ltd* (1963) 107 S.J. 215 (occupiers not liable but contractors held liable for injuries caused by fall of ceiling plastered by contractors); *Gaffney v Aviation & Shipping Co Ltd* [1966] 1 Lloyd's Rep. 249, 251-252 (shipowners' liability for stevedores' negligence in stowing); *Cook v Broderip* [1968] C.L.Y. 2690 (occupier not liable for contractor's negligence in putting in new switch fuse in flat). Cases at common law include *Haseldine v Daw &*

himself liable for the negligence of an independent contractor on some independent ground, such as the non-delegable duty of an employer to provide his employee with a safe place of work,[298] or the duty of a school, hospital or entertainment business to keep patrons safe in providing its services.[299] But this is not strictly a matter of occupiers' liability.

On the other hand, an occupier may be liable for personal fault if he fails to take care to ensure the competence of the contractor, to supervise him properly or to check for obvious defects in the work.[300] Normally, it seems, an occupier will be entitled to assume that where he invites an independent contractor, such as a builder, onto his premises, that contractor will not himself endanger his own employees, thus relieving the occupier of the necessity to do more by way of supervision.[301] But it seems that this is not invariably so. Thus, in *Bottomley v Todmorden Cricket Club*[302] an occupier who engaged a showman to provide a firework display was held liable for failing to prevent an obvious piece of negligence which resulted in injury to an employee of the showman. Nevertheless, it is suggested that this decision puts a very heavy and possibly unwarrantable burden on the occupier, and that decisions of this kind are likely to be rare in practice. It has been suggested that, in engaging an independent contractor, the occupier owes a duty to satisfy himself not only that the latter is competent, but that he carries adequate liability insurance; hence the occupier will be liable if, owing to the lack of insurance, a visitor injured by the contractor's negligence goes uncompensated.[303] But this seems heterodox. The common duty of care is to see that visitors will be reasonably safe,[304] words that do not readily translate into an additional duty to safeguard the visitor's right to compensation if he is injured without any other fault on the occupier's part. In *Naylor v Payling*[305] the Court of Appeal took this point, discountenanced the earlier suggestions and exonerated nightclub owners whose only fault was failure to enquire into the insurance coverage of an independent doorman engaged by them, **11-59**

Son Ltd [1941] 2 K.B. 343; and *Wilkinson v Rea Ltd* [1941] 1 K.B. 688.

298 A classic example is where an employee is injured at his place of work owing to the negligence of independent maintenance contractors engaged by the employer. The employer will be liable qua employer, but not qua occupier.

299 As established by *Woodland v Swimming Teachers Association* [2013] UKSC 66; [2014] A.C. 537.

300 "In the case of the construction of a substantial building, or of a ship, … the building owner, if he is to escape subsequent tortious liability for faulty construction, should not only take care to contract with a competent contractor or shipbuilder, but also to cause that work to be supervised by a properly qualified professional man such as an architect or surveyor, or a naval architect or Lloyd's surveyor. Such cases are different in fact and in everyday practice from having a flat re-wired." See *AMF International Ltd v Magnet Bowling Ltd* [1968] 1 W.L.R. 1028, 1044 (Mocatta J).

301 Indeed, in *Fairchild v Glenhaven Funeral Services Ltd* [2001] EWCA Civ 1881; [2002] 1 W.L.R. 1052 at [150], Brooke LJ had suggested that occupiers should not have to be concerned at all with the question whether employers they admitted to their land would take proper care vis-à-vis their own employees. (The decision was reversed on other grounds at [2002] UKHL 22; [2003] 1 A.C. 32).

302 [2003] EWCA Civ 1575; [2004] P.I.Q.R. P18. See too *Ferguson v Welsh* [1987] 1 W.L.R. 1553, 1560 (Lord Keith) for an earlier suggestion that such liability might be possible. On the other hand there may be some doubt as to whether this is liability coming under the 1957 Act: *Tafa v Matsim Properties Ltd* [2011] EWHC 1302 (QB).

303 *Gwilliam v West Hertfordshire Hospitals NHS Trust* [2002] EWCA Civ 1041; [2003] Q.B. 443 at [38], per Waller LJ. The issue did not arise because the defendant there, a hospital organising a fund-raising stunt, was held not to have been negligent in any case.

304 Occupiers' Liability Act 1957 s.2(2).

305 [2004] EWCA Civ 560; [2004] P.I.Q.R. P36. See too *Bottomley v Todmorden Cricket Club* [2003] EWCA Civ 1575; [2004] P.I.Q.R. P18 at [25]–[29], per Brooke LJ.

with the result that a patron injured through the bouncer's over-enthusiastic performance of his duties was left with a worthless claim against a judgment-proof defendant.[306]

11-60 **Independent contractors: contractual liability of the occupier** We saw above[307] that where an occupier contracts with A to let B onto his premises, he owes a contractual duty to B to show the common duty of care, unless he has by the terms of the contract undertaken a higher duty. For the avoidance of uncertainty, and again to remove doubts that had arisen at common law,[308] s.3(2) of the 1957 Act provides specifically that in the absence of express provision, such a contract will not make the occupier liable to B for the negligence of independent contractors, provided that he acted reasonably in employing them:

> "A contract shall not by virtue of this section have the effect, unless it expressly so provides, of making an occupier who has taken all reasonable care answerable to strangers to the contract for dangers due to the faulty execution of any work of construction, maintenance or repair or other like operation by persons other than himself, his servants and persons acting under his direction and control."

Although the wording of this subsection differs in detail from that of s.2(4)(b) above it is not thought that any difference in the application of the general principle is intended.[309]

(h) Damage covered by the 1957 Act

11-61 **Damage covered by the 1957 Act** Most occupiers' liability actions are for personal injury,[310] but there is no doubt that the 1957 Act covers damage to property as well. Thus s.1(3)(b) applies the provisions of the Act to "the obligations of a person occupying or having control over any premises or structure in respect of damage to property, including the property of persons who are not themselves his visitors". Here again the Act merely substitutes the common duty of care for the special duties, if any, owed to invitees and licensees at common law for damage to goods caused by the condition of the premises. It does not create a liability if there was none at common law, for example for theft of goods.[311] The extension to

---

306 It should be noted, however, that lack of insurance cover may be an indication that the independent contractor is incompetent or likely to endanger others' safety: to that extent, there may still be a limited duty to enquire whether there is any. This was the view taken by Lord Woolf in *Gwilliam v Hertfordshire Hospitals NHS Trust* [2002] EWCA Civ 1041; [2003] Q.B. 443 at [15]; and by Latham and Neuberger LJJ in *Naylor v Payling* [2004] EWCA Civ 560; [2004] P.I.Q.R. P36 at [19]–[25] and [34].

307 See para.11-26.

308 Where arguably the occupier's contractual duty was non-delegable: e.g. *Francis v Cockrell* (1870) L.R. 5 Q.B. 184 at 501.

309 Compare *Maguire v Sefton Metropolitan BC* [2006] EWCA Civ 316; [2006] 1 W.L.R. 2550.

310 Including psychiatric injury, for example from being stuck in a lift, as in the Irish case of *Dicker v The Square Management Ltd* [2016] IEHC 570.

311 "There is no warrant at all on the authorities, so far as I know, for holding that an invitor, where the invitation extends to the goods as well as the person of the invitee, thereby by implication of law assumes a liability to protect the invitee and his goods, not merely from physical dangers arising from defects in the premises, but from the risk of the goods being stolen by some third party. That implied liability, so far as I know, is one unknown to the law": *Tinsley v Dudley* [1951] 2 K.B. 18 at 31, per Jenkins LJ. See too *Edwards v West Herts Group Hospital Management Committee* [1957] 1 W.L.R.

property of those who are not visitors is to cover the situation where (for example) A's car is driven by B on to C's land and is damaged there owing to the state of the land; in such a situation A would not be C's visitor, but could nevertheless sue.[312] Where A hires B's vehicle or engages B to carry his property in it, s.5(3) of the Act makes it clear that B's liability as carrier or bailee is unaffected by the provisions of the Act.[313]

3. LIABILITY TO TRESPASSERS

(a) Introduction

Trespassers A trespasser is a person who has neither right nor permission to enter on premises, who "goes on the land without invitation of any sort and whose presence is either unknown to the proprietor or, if known, is practically objected to".[314] It must, of course, be remembered that not every trespasser is a miscreant. 11-62

> "The term trespasser is a comprehensive word; it covers the wicked and the innocent; the burglar, the arrogant invader of another's land, the walker blithely unaware that he is stepping where he has no right to walk, or the wandering child—all may be dubbed as trespassers."[315]

A trespasser is not a "visitor" as defined in the Occupiers' Liability Act 1957.[316] Hence that Act does not govern an occupier's liability to trespassers; instead, this subject is largely dealt with by the Occupiers' Liability Act 1984, together with a modest admixture of the common law.

Brief history of the law before the Occupiers' Liability Act 1984[317] At one time, an occupier was liable to a trespasser if he injured him intentionally or recklessly,[318] but not for mere negligence. The reason was a combination of the idea that wrongdoers should act at their own risk—ex turpi causa non oritur actio—and a 11-63

415; *AMF International Ltd v Magnet Bowling Ltd* [1968] 1 W.L.R. 1028, 1050; and A.L. Goodhart (1957) 73 L.Q.R. 313.

312 Presumably, however, there must be some relation between the damaged property and a person who counts as a visitor. The wording can hardly have been intended to make an occupier liable for damage to the car of a trespasser, or of someone using the highway above his land, even though on a literal reading of the section the car is "the property of persons who are not themselves his visitors".

313 A point made clearly in Cmd.9305 (1954), para.56.

314 *Addie & Sons (Collieries) Ltd v Dumbreck* [1929] A.C. 358, 371 (Lord Dunedin).

315 *British Railways Board v Herrington* [1972] A.C. 877 at 904, per Lord Morris: see e.g. *Phillips (A Minor) v South Eastern Education & Library Board* [2015] NIQB 91 (small boy climbing into school grounds to retrieve ball).

316 cf. Scotland, where s.2(1) of the Occupiers' Liability (Scotland) Act 1960 protects visitors and trespasser alike, the claimant's status merely going to affect what a reasonable occupier is expected to do to keep him safe. See *Titchener v British Railways Board* [1983] 1 W.L.R. 1427. A similar approach is taken by some Australian jurisdictions: e.g. ss.14A–14D of the Victorian Wrongs Act 1958, as amended in 1983.

317 For statements of the earlier law in fuller detail, see the fourteenth edition of this work, paras 1048-1059; P. North, *Occupier's Liability*, (Butterworths, 1971), Ch.11; see also A.L. Goodhart, "An Infant Trespasser on Railway Lines" (1963) 79 L.Q.R. 586 and (1964) 80 L.Q.R. 559; P. Atiyah (1965) 81 L.Q.R. 186; J. Fleming (1966) 82 L.Q.R. 25.

318 Such as by setting man-traps: *Townsend v Wathen* (1808) 9 East. 277. Ireland has a neat solution here: see the Occupiers' Liability Act 1995 s.4(1) (Eire), limiting liability to trespassers to cases of deliberate harm or reckless disregard.

disinclination to subject a landowner to duties that might "seriously impede the conduct of his lawful activities."[319] Thus in *Addie & Sons (Collieries) Ltd v Dumbreck*[320] defenders were held not liable when a trespassing child was killed by machinery carelessly started without checking to see whether anyone was playing on it.[321] Though it had its supporters,[322] the non-liability rule could be harsh,[323] especially to children,[324] and was increasingly sidestepped by a number of more or less artificial devices.[325] As a result, in 1972 the House of Lords in *British Railways Board v Herrington*[326] discarded the old rule and the fictions that had circumvented it,[327] and held that a trespasser (here a trespassing child injured on a live rail) was, after all, owed a limited duty of care. Unfortunately, however, the precise level of the duty of care owed under *Herrington*, and how it differed from the common duty of care, remained obscure. There were attempts to mark it off by suggesting that a defendant could not be liable without actual knowledge that trespassers were likely to be on his land, or that, exceptionally, his assets (or lack of them) should be in account in assessing what was expected of him.[328] But these were later discountenanced,[329] and in their absence, one was left with little more than a Delphic description of the duty as being one of "ordinary humanity".[330]

11-64 **The Occupiers' Liability Act 1984** The Act was passed following a recommendation of the Law Commission[331] that the duty adumbrated in the decision in

---

319 *Commissioner for Railways v Quinlan* [1964] A.C. 1054, 1086 (Lord Radcliffe).

320 [1929] A.C. 358; *Adams v Naylor* [1944] 1 K.B. 750; [1946] A.C. 543; *Grand Trunk Ry of Canada v Barnett* [1911] A.C. 361.

321 See particularly Lord Hailsham at [1929] A.C. 358, 365.

322 See J.A. Weir, *Casebook on Tort*, 2nd edn (London: Sweet & Maxwell, 1970), pp.68 and 99.

323 M. Millner, *Negligence in Modern Law* (Butterworths, 1967) pp.53 and 54; *Fleming's Law of Torts*, 10th edn (Thomson Reuters Australia, 2012), para.22.160; F. Odgers, "Tort—Invitees, Licensees and Trespassers" [1955] C.L.J. 1; *Videan v British Transport Commission* [1963] 2 Q.B. 650, 663 (per Lord Denning MR).

324 cf. the occupiers' liability legislation of Alberta, which provides for a duty of care to child, but not adult, trespassers: R.S.A. 0-3, ss.12–13.

325 For example, "allurement", whereby a child attracted by some alluring feature was treated as impliedly invited (e.g. *Cooke v Midland Gt Western Ry* [1909] A.C. 229); the doctrine that acquiescence in repeated trespass could be equiparated with an implied licence (e.g. *Lowery v Walker* [1911] A.C. 10): and later the confining of the trespasser exception to pure "occupancy duties" (e.g. *Videan v BTC* [1963] 2 Q.B. 650, 664–668 (Lord Denning MR)). In *Phillips (A Minor) v South Eastern Education & Library Board* [2015] NIQB 91 Deeny J at [18] expressed the strong view that these common law devices had essentially disappeared since the enactment of the 1984 Act (or in that case its Northern Ireland equivalent).

326 [1972] A.C. 877. The case was followed enthusiastically in the Commonwealth: e.g. *Veinot v Kerr-Addison Mines Ltd* (1975) 51 D.L.R. (3d) 533 (Canada); *Southern Portland Cement v Cooper* [1974] A.C. 623 (Australia). There were similar developments in a number of US states: e.g. *Soule v Massachusetts Electric Co*, 378 Mass. 177; 390 N.E.2d 716 (1979).

327 The "implied licence" cases were excoriated as legal fiction by Lords Reid ([1972] A.C. 877 at 894, 899), Wilberforce (at 914), Pearson (at 928), and Diplock (at 932-933). "Allurements" were similarly treated by Lord Wilberforce (at 914). The distinction between "activity duties" and "occupancy duties" was rejected by Lords Reid (at 895), Morris (at 910), Pearson (at 929) and Diplock (at 942).

328 For the former suggestion, see [1972] A.C. 877 at 941, per Lord Diplock: for the latter, see [1972] A.C. 877 at 942, per Lord Diplock; at 899, per Lord Reid; and at 920, per Lord Wilberforce.

329 See *Southern Portland Cement Ltd v Cooper* [1974] A.C. 623, esp. at 644, per Lord Reid.

330 The words were Lord Pearson's: [1972] A.C. 877, 922-923. cf. Lord Morris, who (at 909) referred to "common humanity".

331 Law Com. No.75, *Liability for Damage or Injury to Trespassers and Related Questions of Occupiers' Liability* (1976).

Herrington[332] be largely put in statutory form. Hence s.1(1) of the Act provides that it replaces the common law rules concerning liability for personal injury to trespassers and other entrants outside the protection of the 1957 Act. Because it uses the same terms of application as the 1957 Act (referring in s.1(1)(a) to dangers due to "the state of the premises or to things done or omitted to be done on them") it follows that its ambit is the same: hence, like the 1957 Act it appears that it applies only to cases where injury can truly be said to be due to the "state of the premises",[333] and only to "occupancy duties".[334] Thus in *Revill v Newberry*[335] it was held irrelevant to a case where an occupier shot a trespasser who was trying to burgle him. It should be noted, however, that unlike the 1957 Act its effect is specifically limited to personal injury claims.[336] Claims for property damage are outside its ambit and are dealt with below.[337]

(b) The duty of care under the 1984 Act

Trespassers owed "such care as is reasonable" The main provision of the Occupiers' Liability Act 1984 is s.1(4), by which an occupier owes the trespasser[338] a duty to take "such care as is reasonable in all the circumstances of the case to see that the trespasser does not suffer injury on the premises" by reason of any danger on them, provided three conditions are met. These are: (a) that the occupier knows of, or has reasonable grounds to believe, the existence of the danger on his land[339]; (b) that he knows, or has reasonable grounds to believe, that the trespasser is in the vicinity of the danger, or is likely to come into it[340]; and (c) that "the risk is one against which, in all the circumstances of the case, he may reasonably be expected to offer some protection".[341] In respect of (a) and (b) above, it should be noted that the threshold which must be crossed by the claimant is high. It is not enough to show that, had the defendant been reasonably vigilant, he would have known of the possible presence of the trespasser and his proximity to the danger: instead, it must **11-65**

---

332 [1972] A.C. 877.

333 See *Hatcher v ASW Ltd* [2010] EWCA Civ 1325 (child injured climbing on abandoned Cardiff steelworks: held, no liability, since no danger due to state of premises); similarly *Buckett v Staffordshire CC*, unreported 13 April 2015 QBD (ordinary school skylight); see too *Phillips (A Minor) v South Eastern Education & Library Board* [2015] NIQB 91 (well-maintained fence round school grounds); and *Wray v Derry City and Strabane DC* [2020] NIQB 39 at [60]–[62].

334 *Tomlinson v Congleton BC* [2003] UKHL 47; [2004] 1 A.C. 46 at [26]–[27], per Lord Hoffmann; followed by the Court of Appeal in *Keown v Coventry NHS Trust* [2006] EWCA Civ 39; [2006] 1 W.L.R. 953.

335 [1996] Q.B. 567 at 574 onwards, per Neill LJ. cf. *Hackshaw v Shaw* (1984) 59 A.L.J.R. 156.

336 See s.1(1) (persons "suffering injury").

337 See para.11-78.

338 The Act in addition protects others apart from trespassers, notably those using private rights of way: see para.11-80. But we concentrate on trespassers here.

339 s.1(3)(a).

340 s.1(3)(b). Note that an occupier may have grounds to believe that a trespasser will be on his land at some times but not others. See *Donoghue v Folkestone Properties Ltd* [2003] EWCA Civ 231; [2003] Q.B. 1008 (no liability to drinker who chose to cool off by taking an illicit midnight swim from a pier and was injured thereby. Even if defendants might have expected trespassers during ordinary hours, there was no reason for them to envisage their presence in the middle of the night). Similarly trespass may be foreseeable in some, but not other, parts of the defendant's property: *Higgs v Foster (t/a Avalon Coaches)* [2004] EWCA Civ 843 (trespassing policeman injured fossicking in recondite part of coach-yard: no liability).

341 s.1(3)(c).

be shown that he had actual knowledge of facts that would have led a reasonable person to the requisite conclusions.[342]

11-66 **The limits of the duty of care under the 1984 Act** Assuming the necessary degree of knowledge in the occupier, the Act seems to envisage a two-stage inquiry: (i) was the risk one against which the occupier "may reasonably be expected to offer some protection"? (s.1(3)(c)); and (ii) if so, did he take "such care as is reasonable in all the circumstances"? (s.1(4)). Since s.1(4) presumably takes account of the fact that any reasonable occupier is more solicitous for lawful visitors than for trespassers, s.1(3)(c) must have some different function: namely, to make it clear that some classes of trespasser can never complain of the state of the premises, however negligent the occupier. But who are these excepted classes?

11-67 It is submitted that this matter is best approached from the point of view of the injured trespasser. The essential question should be: "would this claimant be unreasonable if he were to complain of the state of the premises?" In some outrageous cases, the answer is clearly yes. An obvious example is the burglar tripping on a missing stair and then suing the householder for his injuries.[343] Similarly, it is submitted, with any adult who knowingly, and without reasonable excuse of any kind, goes where he is not meant to be (for example the tramp who, on his way to the garden shed where he intends to sleep, breaks his leg on an uneven path). Such a person can have no reasonable expectation that the premises will be kept safe for him.[344] By contrast, a child who goes on another's land for an innocent purpose[345] would seem to be reasonable in expecting some care to be taken for his safety; and the same, it is suggested, goes for an adult who trespasses where he neither knows nor ought to know he is doing so,[346] and possibly for an adult who trespasses knowingly, but does so as a result of some emergency.[347] Of course whether in such circumstances the occupier will be in breach of such a duty is another question, and to this we now turn.

---

[342] So held in *Swain v Puri* [1996] P.I.Q.R. P442 (requisite knowledge not shown in the case of a mischievous but agile small boy climbing onto roof and falling through skylight). See too *White v St Albans CC, The Times*, 12 March 1990; *Hatcher v ASW Ltd* [2010] EWCA Civ 1325 (child injured climbing on abandoned Cardiff steelworks notwithstanding presence of formidable anti-trespasser defences: held, no liability, since presence not reasonably foreseeable).

[343] As the Law Commission intended: Law Com. No.75, s.28. Quaere whether *ex turpi causa* would also bar the claimant? *Revill v Newberry* [1996] Q.B. 567 at 576 suggests—perhaps surprisingly—that the answer is No. But cf. J. Spencer, "Ask for it, get it and sue for it" [1977] C.L.J. 242, 243.

[344] This seems consistent with cases such as *Keown v Coventry NHS Trust* [2006] EWCA Civ 39; [2006] 1 W.L.R. 953 (not reasonable to expect protection for child who climbed on fire escape and fell off), and the similar *Baldacchino v West Wittering Estate Plc* [2008] EWHC 3386 (QB) (not reasonable to expect precautions against swimmer diving off navigation beacon).

[345] What about a child who goes to steal? The Law Commission (Law Com. No.75, para.32) suggest that at least sometimes he ought to be protected: sed quaere.

[346] Trespass being a tort of strict liability. cf. *Veinot v Kerr-Addison Mines Ltd* (1975) 51 D.L.R. (3d) 533, where under the rule in *Herrington* the Supreme Court of Canada allowed an unwitting adult trespasser to recover.

[347] e.g. the victim of an attempted robbery who runs into nearby office premises in order to escape his assailant: cf. *Public Transport Commission v Perry* (1975-6) 137 C.L.R 107 (rail passenger who falls onto line as a result of a fit not a trespasser: but even if she was, still owed a duty of care).

(c) Standard of care owed to trespassers

11-68 **The standard of care** Assuming the trespasser is owed a duty of care, the Act is vague on the standard of care that he is owed ("reasonable in all the circumstances"[348]). Perhaps all one can say with confidence is that, since there is no indication in the Act that the standard is other than objective, the suggestions in *Herrington v BRB*[349] that the resources of the individual defendant ought to be in account, have been clearly rejected.[350] In deciding whether the precautions taken by the defendant were reasonable in all the circumstances,[351] it is suggested that two circumstances are particularly relevant. The first is the seriousness of the danger. An occupier must presumably take more steps to keep a trespasser out of or away from high-tension cable[352] than from something not obviously harmful such as a pile of stones.[353] The second circumstance is the type of trespasser who is likely to come. The cases make it abundantly clear that an occupier must take greater care for the safety of child trespassers than adults. There is no theoretical objection to a claim by an adult trespasser, but in practice it is much less likely to succeed, principally because an occupier will usually show sufficient diligence in keeping an adult away from the danger if he puts up notices saying "Danger, keep out".[354] Thus in *Ratcliff v McConnell*[355] the Court of Appeal denied recovery to a 16-year-old youth who, while trespassing in a college swimming-pool, dived in, hit the bottom and suffered brain damage. Stuart-Smith LJ stated that it would normally suffice for occupiers in such a case to make it clear that the claimant was not meant to be there,[356] and denied that there should be any duty to warn adults of dangers that would be obvious to a reasonable person.[357] Similarly in *Tomlinson v Congleton BC*[358] the House of Lords denied that a local authority had acted unreasonably in failing to fence off a potentially dangerous lake in case adults swam in it and suffered injury. On the other hand, if the occupier can reasonably anticipate the presence of children, he is likely to be expected to take more active steps, such as keeping up his fences[359]; if the danger is great and he is unable or unwilling to erect a fence, then he may well have to set a watchman to warn children off.[360]

11-69 The cases discussed so far raise a fairly simple issue: "did the occupier take reasonable steps to warn the trespasser off or keep him out?" Unfortunately, cases can arise where the issue is nothing like as simple. For instance, what happens where, despite reasonable efforts to keep trespassers out, trespassers enter and the occupier knows or ought to know of this? He could safeguard them from danger if

---

348 See s.1(4).

349 [1972] A.C. 877 at 899, 920 and 942.

350 As the Law Commission wished: above, s.29.

351 See Occupiers' Liability Act 1984 s.1(5), making it clear that at least in some cases reasonable warning of the danger may do.

352 cf. *Southern Portland Cement Ltd v Cooper* [1974] A.C. 623.

353 cf. *Latham v R Johnson & Nephew Ltd* [1913] 1 K.B. 398.

354 See *Ratcliff v McConnell* [1999] 1 W.L.R. 670, below.

355 [1999] 1 W.L.R. 670.

356 [1999] 1 W.L.R. 670 at 681.

357 [1999] 1 W.L.R. 670 at 680-681.

358 [2003] UKHL 47; [2004] 1 A.C. 46.

359 e.g. *Scott v Associated British Ports Ltd* unreported 22 November 2000 (glue-sniffing youth injured while riding perched on railway truck: CA suggest a duty to fence under 1984 Act, although they dismiss claim on basis of volenti non fit injuria under s.1(6)).

360 As in *Pannett v PM McGuinness & Co Ltd* [1972] 2 Q.B. 599 (decided at common law).

he curtailed his activities to abate the risk, but he does not do so, and a trespasser is injured. Is the occupier liable to the trespasser for failing to abate the danger from which he made reasonable efforts to fence him out?[361] It is suggested that an occupier could be liable in such a case, and that whether or not he is so liable must depend on how severe the danger is, and how inconvenient it would be for the occupier to abate it. It is a question of degree. A demolition contractor should be liable if, without checking first, he knocks a house down on the head of a squatter whose presence he should have foreseen, despite his efforts to keep squatters out; but railway operators should not be expected to run all their trains at walking-pace just because they know, in general terms, that trespassers sometimes get on to the tracks even when fences are well maintained.[362]

11-70 **Obvious dangers** As under the 1957 Act,[363] an occupier is highly unlikely to be considered negligent for failing to prevent, or warn of the dangers of, obviously dangerous activities which adult trespassers choose to engage in on his land. Thus in the important case of *Tomlinson v Congleton BC*[364] occupiers were exonerated when a claimant chose, in disregard of "no swimming" notices, to dive into an ornamental lake and broke his neck as a result. Although children may well be more generously treated in this regard, it is submitted that to some extent the occupier may be able to expect accompanied children to be protected by a certain degree of supervision from parents and others.[365]

11-71 **Measures to keep out trespassers** Problems have arisen in the past where the trespasser is injured, not by the land, but by the steps taken by the occupier to keep him off it. In a series of old cases the law drew a distinction between "deterrent dangers" and "retributive dangers". The occupier could, with impunity, set around his property dangers such as broken glass on the top of walls,[366] spikes,[367] dogs,[368] etc. provided these were obvious from the outside and set there solely to deter trespassers from entry. However, he was not allowed to set within his property hidden dangers such as spring-guns[369] to punish the trespasser having entered. This counted as deliberate injury and was always outside the common-law immunity. In

---

361 cf. *Umek v LTE* (1984) 134 N.L.J. 522. cf. *Auffrey v Province of New Brunswick* (1977) 70 D.L.R. (3d) 751; *Phillips v Canadian National Ry* (1976) 61 D.L.R. (3d) 253; *Public Transport Commission (NSW) v Perry* (1977) 14 A.L.R. 273.

362 cf., though, *Umek v LTE* (1984) 134 N.L.J. 522 (London Transport ought to have warned train drivers about employees crossing track contrary to repeated orders).

363 See para.11-32.

364 [2003] UKHL 47; [2004] 1 A.C. 46. See too *Geary v Wetherspoon Plc* [2011] EWHC 1506 (QB); [2011] N.P.C. 60 (patron of bar, after a few drinks, choosing to slide down banisters and falling off, with disastrous results); *Buckett v Staffordshire CC*, unreported 13 April 2015 QBD (no expectation of protection against dangers of falling through school skylight while trespassing on school roof).

365 cf. *Phipps v Rochester Corp* [1955] 1 Q.B. 450, decided under the 1957 Act; see para.11–36.

366 *Deane v Clayton* (1817) 7 Taunt. 489 at 521.

367 *Jordin v Crump* (1841) 8 M. & W. 782.

368 *Brock v Copeland* (1794) 1 Esp. 203; *Sarch v Blackburn* (1830) 4 C. & P. 297; though he may find himself liable in some cases under s.2 of the Animals Act 1971. The Guard Dogs Act 1975 may also affect the position now: see *Cummings v Grainger* [1977] Q.B. 397.

369 *Bird v Holbrook* (1828) 4 Bing. 628. The Offences against the Person Act 1861 s.31, makes it illegal to set man-traps or spring-guns except in, and for the protection of, a dwelling-house. In *Illott v Wilkes* (1820) 3 B. & A. 304, a person injured when trespassing on land where he knew there were spring-guns set was held not entitled to recover as he had voluntarily run the risk. Sed quaere.

Cummings v Grainger[370] the Court of Appeal approved the old cases on deterrent dangers, with particular reference to fierce dogs—although they did suggest that it would be an unreasonable deterrent to keep a guard dog in circumstances prohibited by the Guard Dogs Act 1975.[371] With respect, the Court of Appeal was right to approve the cases on deterrent dangers. An occupier can hardly be the more liable for injury caused by his efforts to keep trespassers out now that he sometimes owes a positive duty to try to keep them out—whereas it used to be entirely in his discretion whether he bothered to do so or not.

Examples of liability Occupiers have surprisingly rarely been held in breach of duty under the 1984 Act. But they were held to have been negligent where a youth got onto railway land and was injured riding a freight train.[372] At common law, as well as *Herrington v British Railways Board*[373] itself (which it seems would be decided the same way today), they had been held liable where occupiers dumped quarry spoil around the base of a pole carrying a high-tension electric cable, until the cable came within easy reach of the top of the heap, so that a boy of 13 touched it and was severely injured[374]; where demolition contractors removed the hoardings surrounding the site, lit a fire, and—although they knew children tended to wander on to the site—left it unattended, whereupon a boy of five entered the site and fell into it[375]; where a local authority failed to mend a defective fence surrounding a decrepit wall, although it knew that children regularly played on the site[376]; and where a local authority failed to block up the doors and windows of an empty house which it had acquired for demolition, so that a child of four wandered in and fell out of an upstairs window.[377] In Canada, an occupier who put a pole across his private road, which led on from a public road, was held liable to a trespasser who drove down the private road by mistake and collided with the pole: the occupier knew the public used to stray down his road, and could have averted the danger by painting the pole to make it visible.[378] In Ireland, the occupier of an electricity substation was held liable to a boy of 11 who was electrocuted when he climbed over a perimeter fence made temporarily climbable during rebuilding.[379] **11-72**

Examples of non-liability On the other hand, occupiers have been held not negligent under the 1984 Act where a 15-year-old climbed an eight-foot fence into an electricity substation to steal metal and was badly burnt[380]; where a nine-year-old scaled a seven-foot fence, climbed onto the roof of a disused factory and fell **11-73**

---

370 [1977] Q.B. 397.

371 This Act prohibits on pain of a fine the use of a guard dog unless it is either chained up, or under the supervision of a handler. It does not extend to farms or dwellings: s.7.

372 *Scott v Associated British Ports Ltd* unreported 22 November 2000 CA. However the claim failed on the basis of volenti non fit injuria.

373 [1972] A.C. 877. Contrast, though, *Davies v British Railways Board* (1984) 134 N.L.J. 888, where a claim similar to *Herrington* failed where the claimant was 12.

374 *Southern Portland Cement Ltd v Cooper* [1974] A.C. 623.

375 *Pannett v PM McGuinness & Co Ltd* [1972] 2 Q.B. 599.

376 *Melvin v Franklins (Builders) Ltd* (1973) 71 L.G.R. 142 CA.

377 *Harris v Birkenhead Corp* [1976] 1 W.L.R. 279 CA.

378 *Veinot v Kerr-Addison Mines Ltd* (1975) 51 D.L.R. (3d) 533 (Sup. Ct.).

379 *McNamara v Electricity Supply Board* [1975] I.R. 1.

380 *Ward v Norweb Plc* unreported 30 October 1991 CA. See too *Platt v Liverpool City Council* unreported 1 May 1997 CA (no liability where fenced-off derelict house collapsed onto youth who wriggled under or over fence).

through a skylight[381]; where a ten-year-old chose to walk along a wall barring a 30-foot drop and fell off[382]; where a student dived into an unsupervised college swimming-pool out of hours and became tetraplegic[383]; where trespassers insisted on swimming in obviously dangerous waters despite "no-swimming" notices[384]; and where a resident of a housing estate left a defined path to take a short-cut and fell into an underpass.[385] At common law a court refused to hold a local authority liable to a child who was injured when, playing on a rubbish-tip, he set fire to an empty aerosol: superhuman efforts were not to be expected to child-proof the tip.[386] In an Irish case, a claim failed where the claimant, turned out of a hotel bar at 2am, knowingly wandered round the unlit back of the hotel, fell and injured himself[387]; and in Canada a cemetery owner was held not liable to a person who, wanting to visit a grave and finding the gates locked against him, tried to climb over the fence, which gave way beneath him.[388]

(d) Defences

11-74 **Exclusion of the duty owed under the Occupiers' Liability Act 1984** Unlike the Occupiers' Liability Act 1957,[389] the Occupiers' Liability Act 1984 is silent on whether the duty it creates can be excluded by notice or otherwise. Logically, there is some ground for arguing that it cannot. This is because the basis of the occupier's right to exclude his duty to lawful entrants is said to be implied licence[390]; the visitor knows that he is permitted on the land only on condition that he holds the occupier harmless from liability, and once he has taken advantage of the permission he is bound by the condition on which it was given. Such reasoning is inapplicable to the trespasser, who has no permission from the occupier, conditional or otherwise, to be there at all. There are, moreover, additional arguments from legal policy that at least some duties created by statute should not be subject to contrary agreement,[391] and also that the duty owed to a trespasser should be regarded as a bare minimum from which no derogation ought to be permitted.[392]

11-75 On the other hand, if the duty under the 1984 Act cannot be excluded, the anomalous position arises that a trespasser is better protected than a lawful visitor, since it is clear that the "common duty of care" owed to the latter can (subject always to the restrictions in the Unfair Contract Terms Act 1977 and the Consumer

---

381 *Swain v Puri* [1996] P.I.Q.R. P442.

382 *Price v City of Nottingham* unreported 1 July 1998 CA.

383 *Ratcliff v McConnell* [1999] 1 W.L.R. 670.

384 *Tomlinson v Congleton BC* [2003] UKHL 47; [2004] 1 A.C. 46; *Rhind v Astbury Water Park Ltd* [2004] EWCA Civ 756; [2004] N.P.C. 95.

385 *Maloney v Torfaen CBC* [2005] EWCA Civ 1762; [2006] P.I.Q.R. P21.

386 *Penny v Northampton BC* (1974) 72 L.G.R. 733.

387 *O'Keefe v Irish Motor Inns Ltd* [1978] 1 I.R. 85.

388 *Yelic v Town of Gimli* [1987] 1 W.W.R. 537.

389 s.2(1); see para.11-46.

390 See para.11-47.

391 e.g. employers' statutory health and safety duties: *Baddeley v Granville (Earl)* (1887) 19 Q.B.D. 423.

392 cf. *Salmond & Heuston on Torts*, 21st edn (London: Sweet & Maxwell, 1996), p.282; M.A. Jones, "The Occupiers' Liability Act 1984" (1984) 47 M.L.R. 713, 723–725. A further argument is that the Law Commission inserted a clause (cl.2(4)) into its draft Bill allowing exclusion of the duty, but that Parliament—doubtless designedly—omitted that clause when passing the Act. cf. the position in Ireland, where the Occupiers' Liability Act 1995 s.5(3), invalidates any clause which would reduce the occupier's duty to anyone, whether trespasser or otherwise, below the bare minimum owed to trespassers.

Rights Act 2015) be excluded.[393] Moreover, despite the superficial attractiveness of the "implied licence" argument, it is submitted that there is no clear legal reason why an occupier should not be able to say, "Do not come on my land: but if you do come on it, while I in no way condone what you have done, I insist that you do so at your own risk".[394] On balance, it is submitted that the marginally better view is that the duty under the 1984 Act can be excluded by notice. In any case the same result can be reached another way. A duty of care under the 1984 Act is owed only if the occupier can "reasonably be expected" to offer protection against the risk concerned to that claimant. And it is submitted that, where an occupier displays adequate[395] notices warning that he accepts no liability, it will be very hard for a trespasser who enters having read such a notice (or in circumstances where he ought to have read it) to argue that the occupier can "reasonably be expected" to owe him any duty at all.

Assuming that the duty to a trespasser can be excluded, is such exclusion subject to the rules in the Unfair Contract Terms Act 1977 and the Consumer Rights Act 2015 that a business cannot exclude its liability for negligence causing personal injury? Oddly enough, the answer seems to be no. This is because "negligence" in both these Acts is specifically limited to negligence at common law and under the Occupiers' Liability Act 1957[396]; and, of course, liability under the 1984 Act arises neither at common law nor under the 1957 Act.[397] On the other hand, it seems that where the trespasser is a non-business visitor, any exclusion must be fair (i.e. not such as, in breach of the duty of good faith, to cause an untoward imbalance in the parties' rights).[398] **11-76**

Volenti non fit injuria and the 1984 Act By s.1(6) of the Occupiers' Liability Act 1984, the defence of volenti non fit injuria is preserved, in respect of risks "willingly accepted" by the entrant.[399] This defence has been applied to both children and adult trespassers who have deliberately run clear and obvious risks, for example, by diving into a shallow swimming-pool after hours,[400] or hitching illicit rides on slow-moving railway wagons.[401] **11-77**

---

393 cf. the Law Commission's point (Law Com. No.75, s.66): "It would in our view be extraordinary if, to avoid a notice being brought into operation against her, a person in the position of [the plaintiff in *Ashdown v Williams* [1957] 1 Q.B. 409] were able to argue that she was a trespasser rather than a lawful entrant."

394 By way of analogy, assume P lends D his bicycle on condition that if D makes off with it he has to pay £200. If D did make off with the machine, surely P could recover the £200 without being forced to argue that he had condoned the theft? And cf. *Arthur v Anker* [1997] Q.B. 564 (right to wheelclamp trespassing car may be given by suitably-worded notice, though this is now possibly overtaken by s.54 of the Protection of Freedoms Act 2012).

395 Quaere whether a notice would be adequate with regard to a child who could not read? Presumably not: but in the case of a very young child, perhaps the occupier would have a defence analogous to the rule in *Phipps v Rochester Corp* [1955] 1 Q.B. 450; see para.11-36.

396 See s.1(1) of the 1977 Act and s.65(4) of the 2015 Act.

397 It is also ironic that liability under *Herrington v British Railways Board* [1972] A.C. 877, being liability at common law, *was* covered by s.2(1) of the Unfair Contract Terms Act. Such are the pitfalls of statutory drafting!

398 This is because s.62 of the 2015 Act applies generally to any clause or notice affecting any liability of a trader to a consumer, as defined in s.2 of that Act.

399 A parallel provision to s.2(5) of the 1957 Act: see para.11-43.

400 See *Ratcliff v McConnell* [1999] 1 W.L.R. 670, especially at 683.

401 *Scott v Associated British Ports Ltd* unreported 22 November 2000 CA.

11-78 **Damage to property of trespasser** Presumably under the common law rule in *Herrington v British Railways Board*[402] occupiers owed trespassers at least a vestigial duty to safeguard their property. The Law Commission, and doubtless the Occupiers' Liability Act 1984, intended to abolish this liability, leaving trespassers protected only in respect of personal injury.[403] Unfortunately this does not seem to have been done. Section 1(1) of the 1984 Act makes it clear that the Act replaces the common law only "in respect of [trespassers] suffering injury"; "injury" being later defined as personal injury.[404] It seems to follow that the common law remains with respect to damage to trespassers' property, and the occupier remains potentially liable for damage to a trespasser's clothes, car etc. Normally this is unlikely to be very important. The notion of a duty of "ordinary humanity"[405] to property is a bizarre one, and there were few if any cases of owners recovering for damage to property under *Herrington*.[406] But cases where there might be liability are imaginable. Might a farmer not owe a duty—albeit a low one—in respect of cattle straying on his land? Or might a dock company not owe a duty of care to a vessel in respect of hidden hazards of a given wharf, despite the fact that the ship had, through oversight, technically trespassed by docking at the wrong wharf?[407] The prospect of common law claims in respect of trespassers' property cannot be written off entirely.

4. LIABILITY TO OTHER NON-VISITORS ON THE DEFENDANT'S PREMISES

11-79 Section 1 of the Occupiers' Liability Act 1984 applies not simply to trespassers, but to anyone who is on the occupier's land but is not his visitor. As well as unlawful interlopers, a number of persons lawfully on land may fall into this category: for example, those using private (but not public[408]) rights of way, and those availing themselves of the provisions of the National Parks and Access to the Countryside Act 1949 and the Countryside and Rights of Way Act 2000.

11-80 **Private rights of way** In *Holden v White*[409] it was held that a milkman exercising a private right of way while delivering milk to a house some distance away was not a visitor under the 1957 Act as regards the owner of the land he was traversing. In 1982 this was fatal to his claim: but today it seems clear that he would be held

402 [1972] A.C. 877.

403 Law Com. No.75, para.30.

404 See s.1(9). Section 1(8) might seem to preclude actions by trespassers for property damage: "when a person owes a duty by virtue of this section, he does not by reason of any breach of the duty, incur any liability in respect of any loss of or damage to property." But it does not, since the duty under *Herrington* in respect of property damage arises at common law, and not by reason of any breach of the 1984 Act.

405 Lord Pearson's formulation of the duty under *Herrington*: see [1972] A.C. 877, 922–923.

406 In *Tutton v AD Walter Ltd* [1986] Q.B. 61 the judge thought, but did not decide, that there might be *Herrington* liability to a trespassing swarm of bees. See J. Spencer, "A Duty of Common Humanity to Bees" [1986] C.L.J. 15.

407 An analogous case was *HMS Glatton* [1923] P. 215, where a vessel failed to recover against a harbour authority when she struck an unmarked wreck, on the grounds that she was using that part of the harbour at a prohibited time. But that case was decided before *Herrington* and the 1984 Act and—it is submitted—might well be differently decided today.

408 Because of s.1(7).

409 [1982] Q.B. 679.

to have been owed a duty of care under the 1984 Act,[410] as confirmed by the decision in *Vodden v Gayton*,[411] holding that a visitor injured while using a right of way over a badly-rutted track could sue the owner of the underlying subsoil.[412] What level of duty a non-visitor of this kind will be owed, of course, is another matter; for while he is not a wrongdoer like a trespasser, the occupier has not necessarily consented to his presence on his land, and presumably any duty owed by him should reflect this fact.

National parks and access to the countryside[413] Visitors availing themselves of rights of access to open land under the provisions of the National Parks and Access to the Countryside Act 1949 and the Countryside and Rights of Way Act 2000[414] are not visitors of the occupier.[415] They are therefore subject to the provisions of the Occupiers' Liability Act 1984. In the case of the 2000 Act,[416] however, the duty owed to them is modified in a number of respects. First, no duty at all is owed in respect of natural features of the landscape, of anything growing on it,[417] or of any river, stream, ditch or pond[418] forming part of it.[419] Hence there is no duty to warn foolish visitors not to swim or pick poisonous berries. However, the exemption is relatively narrow. The duty remains in respect of (say) derelict agricultural equipment left on land which may trip up and injure the unwary walker. It should be noted, moreover, that this exemption is entirely lost in respect of acts done with intent to cause injury or recklessly as to whether injury is caused.[420] Secondly, there is no duty in respect of walls, fences or gates, except when gates or stiles are being properly used.[421] Thus a child injured when climbing on a decrepit dry stone wall would have no claim.[422] On the other hand, there is a (potentially onerous) duty to maintain, say, stiles so that they do not collapse under the pressure of hordes of ramblers. Thirdly, regard is to be had in fixing any duty to (a) the fact that the existence of that right ought not to place an undue burden (whether financial or otherwise) on the occupier; and (b) the importance of maintaining the character of the countryside, including features of historic, traditional or archaeological interest; and (c) any code of conduct issued by the Countryside Agency. **11-81**

Three further minor points are worth making. First, although the new ss.1(6A)-(6C) of the 1984 Act refer to duties owed "by virtue of this section", it is to be hoped **11-82**

[410] Note, however, a possible lacuna. The 1984 Act does not give a cause of action for damage to property. Hence it seems that if a deliveryman's van was eviscerated by a pothole in a private right of way, he would have no cause of action at all, unless a court was prepared to say he was owed a duty at common law as a non-visitor analogous to that in *Herrington v British Railways Board* [1972] A.C. 877.

[411] [2001] P.I.Q.R. P4.

[412] Note, however, that the result in *Vodden v Gayton* is problematic, since there the track was also a highway, in respect of which there is no liability because of s.1(7) of the 1984 Act. Curiously, counsel for the defendant disclaimed reliance on the section.

[413] See generally P. Kenny, "Is new right to roam final straw?" [2001] Conv. 296.

[414] The latter provisions apply to events after 19 September 2004.

[415] Occupiers' Liability Act 1957 s.1(4), as amended by the Countryside and Rights of Way Act 2000.

[416] Though not, apparently, in the case of the 1949 Act.

[417] Including plants or trees deliberately cultivated: Occupiers' Liability Act 1984 s.1(6B).

[418] Including a pond or cut deliberately created: Occupiers' Liability Act 1984 s.1(6A)(a).

[419] See the 1984 Act ss.1(6A)(a), inserted by s.13 of the 2000 Act.

[420] Occupiers' Liability Act 1984 s.1(6C).

[421] See the 1984 Act s.1(6A)(b), inserted by s.13 of the 2000 Act.

[422] Though presumably a child injured playing in a tumbledown barn would be owed a duty: a building can hardly be categorised as a mere "wall".

that they will be construed as exonerating the landowner from any liability at common law as well. Secondly, the 2000 Act says nothing about those using existing public rights of way, who under the previous law were owed no duty whatever. Presumably this rule remains, particularly since s.12(1) of the 2000 Act states that it does not increase the occupier's liability under any other enactment or rule of law in respect of the state of the land or of things done or omitted to be done on it. And lastly, presumably the occupier's duty to those exercising the "right to roam" cannot be excluded by any contract or notice.

5. Liability of Landlord

11-83 As we have seen, a landlord by demise is not the "occupier" of those parts of the property which he parts with, even if he does in fact retain some measure of control over their maintenance or repair[423]; it follows that he owes no duty in respect of them under the 1957 Act.

11-84 **Landlord's liability at common law** It was originally thought that a landlord was not liable at all in tort[424] for damage caused by defects in the property let,[425] whether or not he knew of them[426] or even had been responsible for introducing them in the first place.[427] It was regarded as equally irrelevant that the defect arose during the currency of the lease, or that it was one that the landlord was under the terms of the lease obliged to repair.[428] This common law immunity, exemplified by the 1906 decision in *Cavalier v Pope*,[429] was subsequently removed by judicial decision in respect of defects created by the landlord's negligence, whether before[430] or after[431] the lease was entered into. It still exists, however, where the landlord is guilty of mere nonfeasance, as where he lets premises knowing of some dangerous defect in them which was not of his own making, or even in the case of positive acts which cannot be regarded as something relating to "construction, repair, maintenance or demolition".[432] Thus in *Boldack v East Lindsey DC*,[433] the defendants escaped liability where a large flagstone, left upright next to a council house and never removed, fell on and injured a small boy. Again, it has been held that letting a

423 See para.11-09.

424 He might, of course, be liable to his tenant in contract. This can be important, given the implied obligations of repair in many tenancies of dwelling-houses; e.g. *King v South Northants DC* (1992) 90 L.G.R. 121. But liability of that kind obviously cannot affect the landlord's position as against third parties.

425 The landlord's immunity covered dangers created on all kinds of property, e.g. fields etc. and was not limited to buildings: *Shirvell v Hackwood Estates Co* [1938] 2 K.B. 577; *Cheater v Cater* [1918] 1 K.B. 247.

426 *Cavalier v Pope* [1906] A.C. 428; *Lane v Cox* [1897] 1 Q.B. 415.

427 See *Travers v Gloucester Corp* [1947] K.B. 71 (negligently installed geyser which gassed user of bathroom).

428 *Cavalier v Pope* [1906] A.C. 428; *Malone v Laskey* [1907] 2 K.B. 141; *Ball v London CC* [1949] 2 K.B. 159.

429 [1906] A.C. 428 (landlord negligently failed to observe duty to keep property in repair; not liable to tenant's wife who fell through rotten floor).

430 *Rimmer v Liverpool CC* [1985] Q.B. 1; *Targett v Torfaen BC* [1992] 3 All E.R. 27.

431 *AC Billings & Son v Riden* [1958] A.C. 240.

432 Where s.3 of the Defective Premises Act 1972 now applies: below, para.11-85.

433 (1999) 31 H.L.R. 41. Note, however, the Irish decision in *Ward v McMaster* [1985] I.R. 29, where Costello J denied that *Cavalier v Pope* remained good law at all. cf. *Siney v Dublin Corp* [1980] I.R. 400.

property with a slippery step next to a long drop is still within the immunity.[434] Whatever the position with regard to leases, the Northern Ireland High Court has held that no immunity applies where the defendant is a licensor, as opposed to a lessor[435]; such persons were, it was said, liable in negligence in the ordinary way.

Liability under the Defective Premises Act 1972 Paralleling the developments at common law, ss.3 and 4 of the Defective Premises Act 1972[436] provide a statutory remedy against the landlord in certain cases. Section 3[437] deals with defects existing at the time the lease is entered into, and provides: 11-85

> "Where work of construction, repair, maintenance or demolition or any other work is done on or in relation to premises, any duty of care owed, because of the doing of the work, to persons who might reasonably be expected to be affected by defects in the state of the premises created by the doing of the work shall not be abated[438] by the subsequent disposal of the premises by the person who owed the duty."

Three points arise in connection with this section. First, it is submitted that "premises" means simply the land subject to the demise in question,[439] and is not limited to buildings or structures. The common law immunity, which the section aimed to abolish, certainly applied to all land without discrimination,[440] and it would be odd if Parliament had intended to leave a landlord immune where (for example) he let out an undeveloped field which to his knowledge had been sprayed with some poisonous chemical. Secondly, it is suggested that the phrase "work of construction, repair, maintenance or demolition or any other work" covers not only active operations such as structural repairs or extensions, but also culpable failure to carry out maintenance or repairs which any reasonable property owner would take steps to perform.[441] It would be, to say the least, perverse if a landlord could escape liability for letting a house known to have a garden full of broken glass or an unexploded bomb in the cellar, merely on the ground that he himself had not put

---

434 *Drysdale v Hedges* [2012] EWHC B20 (QB); [2012] 3 E.G.L.R. 105. See too *Essex CC v Davies* [2019] EWHC 3443 (QB); [2020] P.I.Q.R. P7 (lessor of college not liable for carbon monoxide injuries to employees of college).

435 *Graham v NI Housing Executive* (1986) 8 N.I.J.B. 93 (housing authority liable to squatter-licensee).

436 For consideration of the Act in detail, see P. North, "The Defective Premises Act 1972" (1973) 36 M.L.R. 628; and Spencer, "The Defective Premises Act 1972—Defective Law and Defective Law Reform" [1974] C.L.J. 307; [1975] C.L.J. 48. See also Law Com. No.40, *Civil Liability of Vendors and Lessors of Defective Premises* (1970), on which the Act was based.

437 For cases under this section, see, e.g. *Ryan v Camden LBC* (1983) 13 Fam. Law 81; *McDonagh v Kent AHA* (1984) 134 N.L.J. 567. Note that it only applies to leases entered into after the Act came into effect.

438 A very technical argument could be raised that these words leave the law unchanged since they do not actually create a cause of action; they merely provide that a cause of action that did not exist in the first place "shall not be abated". But it is almost inconceivable that any court would accept this.

439 See J. Spencer, "The Defective Premises Act 1972—Defective Law and Defective Law Reform" [1975] C.L.J. 48, 58-59.

440 Since the immunity at common law covered dangers created on all kinds of property, and was not limited to buildings: see *Shirvell v Hackwood Estates Co* [1938] 2 K.B. 577 and *Cheater v Cater* [1918] 1 K.B. 247.

441 See, e.g. *Hannon v Hillingdon Homes Ltd* [2012] EWHC 1437 (QB); [2012] P.T.S.R. D37 (staircase with no banister). Compare *AMF International Ltd v Magnet Bowling Ltd* [1968] 1 W.L.R. 1028, especially at 1043, where the reference in s.2(4)(b) of the Occupiers' Liability Act 1957 to the "faulty execution" of works of maintenance etc was held to cover nonfeasance as well as misfeasance. See para.11-57.

them there.[442] Thirdly, it should be noted that the works need not have been carried out by the landlord or anyone connected with him.[443] Thus the section would catch a landlord who let a house knowing that contractors acting for a previous owner had carried out repairs badly, so as to leave the building dangerously defective.

11-86 **Defective Premises Act 1972 s.4** Unlike s.3, s.4 of the Act[444] deals with defects arising during the currency of the lease.[445] Its effect is to impose on the landlord a statutory duty of care (which is not the same as the occupier's common duty of care) in respect of defects arising in leased premises where either he has the duty to repair under the lease,[446] or (even where he is under no duty to repair) the premises are let under a tenancy giving him "the right to enter the premises to carry out any description of maintenance or repair of the premises".[447] In the latter case, however, the landlord is under no duty to the tenant in respect of defects which the lease expressly requires the latter to repair.[448] The landlord's duty under s.4 is simply to take such care as is reasonable in the circumstances to see that those likely to be affected by the defect are reasonably safe.[449] It should be noted that liability is not dependent on actual knowledge,[450] but merely the means of knowledge.[451] Thus the landlord can be liable for general failure to repair or maintain even if not given

---

442 The examples are Spencer's: see J. Spencer, "The Defective Premises Act 1972—Defective Law and Defective Law Reform: Part II" [1975] C.L.J. 48, 57–58. Or compare the facts of *Collins v Hopkins* [1923] 2 K.B. 617 (failure to warn that the outgoing tenant of a house had died there of a highly infectious disease). Nevertheless, there are limits to the concept of "construction, repair, maintenance or demolition". They are not apt to cover the case where the design of the premises is itself dangerous: see *Drysdale v Hedges* [2012] EWHC B20 (QB); [2012] 3 E.G.L.R. 105 (leaving slippery paint on front steps of let house, with long drop next to them, might be misguided, but not a matter relating to repair etc).

443 Thus s.3 is clearly wider than the principle in *Rimmer v Liverpool CC* [1985] Q.B. 1, which was limited to defects created by the landlord.

444 Which replaces a narrower provision in the Occupiers' Liability Act 1957 s.4. Note that in Wales a more generous regime will apply as from the activation of the Renting Homes (Wales) Act 2016 ss.91–99. This applies to both leases and licences, and puts the landlord under a general duty to maintain the premises in repair and fit for habitation throughout the relevant period, with repairs to be done as soon as the landlord has notice of their necessity.

445 See s.4(3). It applies mutatis mutandis to licences: s.4(6).

446 s.4(1).

447 s.4(4). The duty would seem to apply where the landlord has any duty to repair and/or right of entry, whether or not the duty or right concerned the particular defect complained of. On the definition of a right of entry for repairs under s.4, see *McAuley v Bristol CC* [1992] Q.B. 134 (includes obligation to afford "reasonable facilities" to landlord's workmen).

448 s.4(4). Note, however, that this immunity applies only to actions by the tenant himself. The landlord's duty to third parties other than the tenant is unaffected: *Boldack v East Lindsey DC* (1999) 31 H.L.R. 41.

449 For an example of liability under the section, see *Stockley v Knowsley MBC* (1986) 279 E.G. 677 CA (landlord liable for not doing anything about frozen pipes and subsequent flood, despite having been asked to): *Smith v Bradford Corp* (1982) 44 P. & C.R. 171 (landlord liable for state of patio). An argument that the section created any stricter liability was decisively rejected by Jay J in *Lafferty v Newark & Sherwood District Council* [2016] EWHC 320 (QB); [2016] H.L.R. 13, and also by the Northern Ireland Court of Appeal in *Argue v Northern Ireland Housing Executive* [2016] NICA 18; [2018] N.I. 43.

450 Defective Premises Act 1972 s.4(2). This reversed the position under the erstwhile s.4 of the Occupiers' Liability Act 1957, on which see *O'Brien v Robinson* [1973] A.C. 912.

451 In *Pritchard v Caerphilly CBC* (Cardiff County Court, 26.11.2013), 2013 WL 6980728, it was confirmed that the means of knowledge necessary to impose liability was the same whether based on a duty to repair under s.4(1) or a right to carry out repairs under s.4(4).

actual notice of the defect.[452] On the other hand, s.4 is based on the duty of the landlord to keep premises in repair, which means that it does not cover defects, even dangerous ones, that are inherent in the building and cannot be categorised as "disrepair".[453] By s.6(3), the duty under s.4 cannot be excluded or restricted, and is in addition to any other duty owed by the landlord.[454] It is in practice a highly important duty in the context of council and housing association lettings, since the duty to repair in such cases will very often be on the landlord.[455]

The duty under s.4 is owed to "all who might reasonably be expected to be affected by defects in the state of the premises", words which have been held to cover not only the tenant himself,[456] but also guests,[457] and indeed are apt to embrace not only those on the premises but also those who are outside it—neighbours, users of the highway etc—in so far as they might reasonably be expected to be affected. In principle, it is also owed to those who are foreseeably affected whilst on the property, even if they are not "visitors" and the occupier does not owe them the common duty of care—for example trespassers, users of public and private rights of way, and entrants under the National Parks and Access to the Countryside Act 1949. Surprisingly, therefore, towards them the landlord now appears to be under a more onerous duty than the occupier himself. **11-87**

6. Liability to Persons not on the Premises

There is a duty on the occupier of premises to maintain them in such a condition as not to be a nuisance. Moreover, apart from nuisance, there is a duty on the part of the occupier to take care to maintain the premises in a reasonably safe condition. This duty is owed to anyone who is likely to suffer injury or damage if the duty is neglected, whether on the highway or a private road or on adjoining premises.[458] Furthermore, under s.4 of the Defective Premises Act 1972 a landlord **11-88**

---

452 *Sykes v Harry* [2001] EWCA Civ 167; [2001] Q.B. 1014 (landlord liable to tenant poisoned by improperly maintained gas fire despite lack of formal notice, though tenant contributorily negligent for not letting him know); *Rogerson v Bolsover District Council* [2019] EWCA Civ 226; [2019] Ch. 450 (unsafe manhole cover in garden).

453 *Dodd v Raebarn Estates Ltd* [2017] EWCA Civ 439; [2017] 2 P.&C.R. 14 (staircase built without rail). See too *Alker v Collingwood Housing Association* [2007] EWCA Civ 343; [2007] 1 W.L.R. 2230; and *Sternbaum v Dhesi* [2016] EWCA Civ 155; [2016] H.L.R. 16.

454 s.6(2). Outside this section a landlord could be liable for an omission (a) in contract, for breach of a covenant to repair or (in some cases) a condition that the premises be fit for habitation; or (b) for breach of the duty imposed on builders by s.1 of the Defective Premises Act. For s.1, see North, 36 M.L.R. 628; J. Spencer, "The Defective Premises Act 1972—Defective Law and Defective Law Reform: Part I" [1974] C.L.J. 307.

455 See, e.g. ss.8–9C Landlord and Tenant Act 1985 (implied undertaking by landlord to keep certain small houses fit for human habitation) and ss.11 and 12 (implied covenant by lessor to repair structure and exterior of dwelling-house and certain installations in it, where the lease is for less than seven years: no exclusion or limitation of this obligation except on authority of county court). On the scope of s.11, see the Court of Appeal decisions in *Wainwright v Leeds City Council* (1984) 82 L.G.R. 657; and *Quick v Taff-Ely BC* [1986] Q.B. 809; and that of the Supreme Court in *Edwards v Kumarasamy* [2016] UKSC 40; [2016] A.C. 1334. In Wales these provisions will be replaced by ss.91–92 of the Renting Homes (Wales) Act 2016, when in force.

456 See *Smith v Bradford MBC* (1982) 44 P. & C.R. 171; *Barrett v Lounova (1982) Ltd* [1990] 1 Q.B. 348.

457 e.g. *Dodd v Raebarn Estates Ltd* [2017] EWCA Civ 439; [2017] 2 P.&C.R. 14.

458 In Canada, it has been held that an occupier owes a duty to others in connected premises not to allow his own part to become so dilapidated as to cause the local authority to demolish the whole as a danger: *Foley v Shamess* (2008) 297 D.L.R. (4th) 287.

now owes a statutory duty of care to persons off as well as on the premises which he lets.[459] This is in addition to any such duty which he may owe at common law.

[459] See para.11-86.

CHAPTER 12

EMPLOYERS' LIABILITY[1]

TABLE OF CONTENTS

1. INTRODUCTION

This chapter is concerned with an employer's liability to its employees. Liability arises under the torts of negligence and breach of statutory duty but separate treatment of employers is justified by the distinctive nature of the applicable negligence principles and the particular importance of liability for breach of statutory duty. Both can be seen as a response to the doctrine of "common employment" which emerged in the mid-nineteenth century. According to this an employer could not be held vicariously liable to an employee for injury caused by the negligence of another employee as employees were regarded as having agreed to run the risk of negligence on the part of fellow employees.[2] Although an employer would still be liable if the injury stemmed from a breach of the employer's personal duty of care to the employee, the fact that many work injuries were the direct result of another employee's negligence, meant that this doctrine greatly limited an employer's potential liability. The recognition[3] in the late nineteenth century that an employer's breach of a statutory safety duty would give rise to liability for breach of statutory duty went some way to redressing the balance and the introduction of the notion in the late 1930s that the employer's personal duty of care could not be delegated to others negated to some extent the impact of the common employment doctrine.[4] The doctrine of "common employment" was abolished by legisla- **12-01**

---

[1] For detailed consideration see D. Bennett, *Munkman on Employer's Liability*, 17th edn (2019); in respect of health and safety provisions see M. Ford and J. Clarke, *Redgrave's Health and Safety*, 9th edn (2016).

[2] *Priestley v Fowler* (1837) 3 M. & W. 1; 150 E.R. 1030.

[3] *Groves v Lord Wimborne* [1898] 2 Q.B. 402.

[4] *Wilsons and Clyde Coal Co Ltd v English* [1938] A.C. 57. As a consequence of the non-delegable nature of the duty, an employee injured due to the negligence of a fellow employee to whom a safety responsibility had been delegated, would be able to claim against his employer for breach of personal

tion in 1948[5] and an employee injured by the negligence of a fellow employee can now claim against the employer on the basis of vicarious liability. Where the employee's negligence is unrelated to safety systems or statutory duties, the vicarious liability claim may stand alone but otherwise has often overlapped with claims for breach of personal duty or breach of statutory duty. No special rules apply to vicarious liability claims against the employer and they are not considered in this chapter, which focuses on the distinctive nature of employers' liability for breach of the personal duty of care and breach of statutory duty. The distinction between the employer's vicarious liability for the negligence of a claimant's fellow employee and primary liability for breach of the employer's personal duty of care is essentially a distinction between casual acts of negligence by an individual employee and some failure in the managerial system to provide for employees' safety. For accidents occurring after 1 October 2013, the scope of the action for breach of statutory duty is much reduced,[6] and increasing emphasis will inevitably be placed on the employer's personal duties at common law.

12-02 **Breach of statutory duty—post 1 October 2013** A major change to civil liability for breach of statutory duty, including liability under the many health and safety regulations, was made by s.69 of the Enterprise and Regulatory Reform Act 2013, which came into force on 1 October 2013. Section 69 amended s.47 of the Health and Safety at Work etc. Act 1974 so far as it relates to civil liability. Section 47 now provides that breach of a duty imposed by a statutory instrument "containing health and safety regulations" made under s.15, or breach of a duty imposed by an existing statutory provision,[7] shall not be actionable except so far as regulations under s.47 so provide.[8] The government's rationale for this change was to ensure that a claim for damages for breach of health and safety duties could only succeed where an injured employee can prove that the employer has been negligent. This was part of its drive to reduce the "burden of health and safety", and the perception that there is unfairness when regulations impose a strict duty on employers rendering them liable to pay compensation despite reasonable care having been taken to protect employees from harm. Whether the imposition of a stricter form of liability than negligence on employers truly does give rise to unfairness is highly debateable, given that: (1) employers are already under a duty to comply with health and safety legislation, since breach will normally constitute a criminal offence; (2) liability to employees is (or should be) covered by insurance, which has been compulsory since 1972[9]; and (3) there is a strong economic argument in favour of strict liability combined with compulsory insurance for harm to employees, in that it "internalises" the real cost of production of goods and services into the price

---

duty although under the common employment rule, not for vicarious liability.

5 Law Reform (Personal Injuries) Act 1948 s.1.

6 See para.12-02.

7 The list of relevant existing statutory provisions (as defined in s.53 of the Act) is set out in Sch.1 to the Health and Safety at Work etc. Act 1974. The actionability of legislation which is not made under HSWA 1974 s.15 nor by the primary legislation specified in Sch.1 to the Enterprise and Regulatory Reform Act 2013 is not affected by s.69. This includes regulations made under the European Communities Act 1972 s.2(2) and/or under the Merchant Shipping Acts 1979 and 1995.

8 Limited exceptions have been made in relation to risk assessments in respect of new or expectant mothers and working during compulsory maternity leave: Health and Safety at Work etc. Act 1974 (Civil Liability) (Exceptions) Regulations 2013 (SI 2013/1667).

9 The Employers' Liability (Compulsory Insurance) Act 1969 came into force on 1 January 1972.

charged to the employer's customers.[10] The change applies to breaches of duty occurring on or after 1 October 2013,[11] and so the previous law continues to apply to claims arising from breaches of duty which occurred before that date. Moreover, it is arguable that even for claims arising on or after that date the measure of what constitutes reasonable care for the safety of employees in the tort of negligence should be mediated by reference to the health and safety legislation. After all, if it is a criminal offence to fail to comply with the relevant statutory duty it is difficult to see how the employer can argue that it was *reasonable* to breach the duty.[12] A pursuer's argument to this effect was accepted in *Gilchrist v Asda Stores Ltd*,[13] although here, the defender offered no substantial argument to the contrary. In *Kennedy v Cordia (Services) LLP*,[14] Lord Reed and Lord Hodge (with whom Lady Hale, Lord Wilson and Lord Toulson agreed) said: "the expansion of the statutory duties imposed on employers in the field of health and safety has given rise to a body of knowledge and experience in this field, which ... creates the context in which the court has to assess an employer's performance of its common law duty of care". In the same case, the Supreme Court determined that employers' duties at common law have themselves evolved to encompass duties to conduct risk assessments and therefore, to some extent, to anticipate risks. It is to be expected that cases interpreting the Regulations will continue to be referred to, but their precise future influence in actions brought in negligence and under unaffected legislation is difficult to predict. In *Cockerill v CXK*,[15] a case stemming from an accident which occurred on 1 October 2013, it was common ground that in assessing the nature of the common law employer's duty it is permissible to have regard to the statutory duties "in order to understand in more detail what steps reasonable and conscientious employers can be expected to take to provide a reasonably safe workplace and system of work".[16] However, it should also be remembered that Parliament had intended to make a "perceptible change" to the legal relationship between employer and employee: it would not be the case that all breaches of the regulations would be regarded as negligent.[17]

---

10 See *Cairns v Northern Lighthouse Board* [2013] CSOH 22; 2013 S.L.T. 645 at [37], [38] and [43], per Lord Drummond Young (see para.1-74).

11 Enterprise and Regulatory Reform Act 2013 s.69(10); SI 2013/2227 art.2(f).

12 See N. Tomkins, "Civil health and safety law after the Enterprise and Regulatory Reform Act 2013" [2013] J.P.I.L. 203; and P. Limb and J. Cox, "Section 69 of the Enterprise and Regulatory Reform Act 2013—plus ca change?" [2014] J.P.I.L. 1. The difference between strict liability and negligence will tend to come into clearer focus where the damage was unforeseeable (for which there can be no liability in negligence), rather than where the issue is whether the precautions taken by the employer in the face of foreseeable harm were reasonable. In the latter case it is arguable that the statutory duty will set the standard of what was reasonable. See also A. Roy, "Without a safety net: litigating employers' liability claims after the Enterprise Act" [2015] J.P.I.L. 15.

13 [2015] CSOH 77; 2015 Rep. L.R. 95. Equally, in another case in which the alleged breach occurred after 1 October 2013; *Jones v Scottish Opera* [2015] CSOH 64; 2015 S.L.T. 401 at [19], counsel proposed that the content of the negligence duty was "informed by" the applicable Regulations. Without commenting on this proposal, the court found that a common law duty of care was owed on *Caparo* principles, and that it had been breached.

14 *Kennedy v Cordia (Services) LLP* [2016] UKSC 6; [2016] 1 W.L.R. 597 at [64]; see para.12-35.

15 [2018] EWHC 1155 (QB).

16 [2018] EWHC 1155 (QB) at [17], per Judge Collins Rice.

17 [2018] EWHC 1155 (QB) at [18]. See also, e.g. *Dehenes v T. Bourne and Son* 2019 S.L.T. (Sh Ct) 219, 2 May 2019, Sheriff Personal Injury Court at [10]: though the regulations are no longer directly enforceable in a damages claim, and such a claim lies in negligence, "... in considering the scope and standard of duty of care owed, and whether that duty is breached, it is relevant to consider, in

12-03 **Insurance position** Apart from the existence of a range of non-delegable duties at common law, and of special duties under statute and regulation, it is also important to note that employers have (with exceptions) been obliged to insure against liability in respect of bodily injury or disease to their employees since 1972, when the Employers' Liability (Compulsory Insurance) Act 1969 came into force.[18] Breach of the obligation under the Employers' Liability (Compulsory Insurance) Act 1969 has been held not to be actionable in damages by an employee who may thereby be unable to obtain damages.[19] The Third Parties (Rights against Insurers) Act 1930 has also been particularly important in this context. This statute was originally introduced to support the newly introduced compulsory liability insurance applicable to road traffic accidents, but is of general application. It allows a party with a claim against an insolvent insured party to establish the existence and amount of the insured's liability—if necessary by first bringing proceedings to restore the insured to the register of companies—and then to take over the rights of the insured, seeking indemnity from the liability insurer. The Third Parties (Rights against Insurers) Act 2010 replaced the 1930 Act. Among other improvements, the Act allows claimants to proceed against the insurer without first proceeding against the insolvent party.[20]

the exercise of assessing the defender's duty to take reasonable care towards the pursuer as their employee, the defender's obligations under the regulations which they still require to comply with as a matter of law." The Manual Handling Operations Regulations 1992 (paras 12-82 to 12-84) indicated what would be a suitable or sufficient risk assessment and in the present case, the absence of such a sufficient assessment constituted a breach of the common law duty of care. See by way of contrast the comments of Judge Gore QC in *Tonkins v Tapp* [2018] Lexis Citation 130 at [103]–[106], disagreeing with Judge Collins Rice and suggesting that he would not follow the decision in *Cockerill* if that had been applicable. Judge Gore suggested at [104] that it could not consistently be said that employers remained bound by the provisions and at the same time that Parliament intended to make a perceptible change through s.69. However, he did not note the point made by Judge Collins Rice, that the statutory duties continue to bind employers despite the absence of civil liability.

18 s.1(1) sets out the duty to insure and maintain insurance under approved policies with authorised insurers. The exceptions to the duty to insure are set out in s.3 (as extensively amended by a series of later statutes).

19 *Campbell v Peter Gordon Joiners Ltd* [2016] UKSC 38; [2016] A.C. 1513.

20 Necessary changes to the Act were made by s.19 of the Insurance Act 2015; see also the Third Parties (Rights against Insurers) Regulations 2016 (SI 2016/570). So far as not already in force, the Third Parties (Rights against Insurers) Act 2010 came into force on 1 August 2016. The Act is based on proposals of the Law Commission and Scottish Law Commission, *Third Parties—Rights Against Insurers* (2001) (Law Com. No.272; Scot Law Com. No.184, Cm.5217). However, this legislation cannot provide a practical remedy where the employer is insolvent and the employer's liability insurer cannot be traced. This is more likely to occur with medical conditions which have a long latency period from exposure to a toxic agent and the manifestation of symptoms, such as mesothelioma following exposure to asbestos (which can have a latency of 30 to 40 years). Parliament has introduced a statutory compensation scheme specifically for employees who contract mesothelioma who would have had a good claim against their employer but are unable to recover compensation because the employer is insolvent and the insurer cannot be traced. See the Mesothelioma Act 2014 and the Diffuse Mesothelioma Payment Scheme Regulations 2014 (SI 2014/916) (as amended by the Diffuse Mesothelioma Payment Scheme (Amendment) Regulations 2014 (SI 2014/917) and the Diffuse Mesothelioma Payment Scheme (Amendment) Regulations 2015 (SI 2015/367)), establishing the Diffuse Mesothelioma Payment Scheme which applies where the person was first diagnosed with the disease on or after 25 July 2012.

2. LIABILITY FOR BREACH OF PERSONAL DUTY OF CARE

(a) Nature of the employer's duty

Governed by the general principles As Lord Hoffmann stated in *White v Chief Constable of South Yorkshire Police*[21]: "The liability of an employer to his own employees for negligence ... is not a separate tort with its own rules. It is an aspect of the general law of negligence." Hence, it was held that an employer is only under a duty of care to an employee in relation to psychiatric illness caused by shock, if the generally applicable tests for recognising such a duty have been satisfied.[22] Nevertheless, the close relationship between employer and employee does shape the nature of the duty. The employer's control and the employee's reliance is sufficient to justify an exception to the mere omission rule and justify a duty to take care to protect the employee from harm. Most obviously, the duty extends to persuading employees to use safety equipment but it will also, for example, require the provision of proper medical care for an employee who has collapsed at work.[23] Similarly, it may extend to providing employees with protection from the acts of third parties.[24] The primary purpose of the duty is to protect the health and safety of the employee. It extends to activities incidental to work such as using washroom facilities[25] or leaving the workplace at the end of the work period.[26] The employee's mental health comes within its scope and there is developing case law as to the liability of an employer for psychiatric illness caused by the stress of the job.[27] Anxiety resulting from a physiological condition caused by the employer's negligence is not a recoverable head of claim, unless the condition is sufficiently serious to amount to actionable damage.[28] **12-04**

---

21 [1999] 2 A.C. 455 at 506.

22 For these tests, see para.7-69 onwards.

23 Note *Barrett v Ministry of Defence* [1995] 1 W.L.R. 1217, where the employer's duty was held not to extend to controlling drinking of alcohol at a workplace facility out of work hours but did apply once the employer had assumed a responsibility for the care of a drinker who had collapsed.

24 *Rahman v Arearose Ltd* [2001] Q.B. 351: restaurant owner liable for failing to take care to reduce the known risk of gang attacks on staff; *Charlton v Forrest Printing Ink Co Ltd* [1980] I.R.L.R. 331: duty to take precautions against attacks on employees taking cash to a bank; *Cook v Bradford Community Health NHS Trust* [2002] EWCA Civ 1616; [2003] M.H.L.R. 111: duty of hospital to avoid risks to staff from psychiatric patients known to be dangerous. The duty can extend to evacuating employees working in areas which become dangerous, e.g. through the outbreak of war: *Longworth v Coppas International (UK) Ltd*, 1985 S.L.T. 111.

25 *Davidson v Handley Page Ltd* [1945] 1 All E.R. 235.

26 *Bell v Blackwood Morton & Sons Ltd*, 1960 S.C. 11. The employer's duty covers the performance of work done by the employee and anything reasonably incidental to it, and is not owed outside the course of employment. In *Vaughan v Ministry of Defence* [2015] EWHC 1404 (QB) a marine who dived into shallow water at a beach while off duty during a training week was held not to have been acting in the course of employment and was not on duty: thus, the employer's non-delegable duty was not owed to him.

27 The leading decision is *Barber v Somerset CC* [2004] UKHL 13; [2004] 1 W.L.R. 1089. See further para.12-37.

28 *Rothwell v Chemical and Insulating Co Ltd* [2007] UKHL 39; [2008] 1 A.C. 281: no recovery in respect of anxiety caused by the knowledge that exposure to asbestos had led to pleural plaques—an irreversible structural change to the lungs which whilst not harmful in itself, indicates (but does not cause) a risk of the future development of malignant conditions. Even when taken together with the anxiety, this condition was considered to fall within the de minimis principle, so that it did not amount to actionable damage (even though in previous cases, damages had been calculated at a substantial level: see *Hindson v Pipe House Wharf (Swansea) Ltd* [2007] EWHC 273 (QB), where

12-05 **Financial losses** Without a specific assumption of responsibility, the duty will not extend to protecting the property of the employee[29] or his financial interests. Thus, in *Reid v Rush & Tompkins Group Plc*[30] the Court of Appeal held that an employer posting an employee overseas owes no duty either to provide him with insurance or advise him to take out such insurance himself. But in *Spring v Guardian Assurance*[31] the House of Lords held that an employer providing a reference for an employee may be subject to a duty of care and liable for economic loss suffered by the employee as a result of a negative reference compiled on the basis of careless research,[32] and in *Lennon v Commissioner of Police of the Metropolis*[33] the Court of Appeal held that a specific assumption of responsibility stemming from an undertaking about housing allowances, did give rise to a duty of care and liability in respect of financial losses suffered by the employee. The court in *Lennon* noted that this was an example of a tortious duty of care going beyond the concurrent contractual duty owed by the employer.[34] Where the duty arises from the relation-

---

general damages were assessed at £15,500, with additional sums for the risk of future financial loss and potential care costs). See further para.7-97. In Scotland, pleural plaques are defined by statute as amounting to "personal injury which is not negligible" which "constitute actionable harm for the purposes of an action in damages for personal injury": Damages (Asbestos-Related Conditions) (Scotland) Act 2009 s.1(1) and (2). A challenge to this legislation by way of judicial review was launched by some insurers on grounds of conflict with the European Convention and on common law grounds (the legislation was an unreasonable, irrational, and arbitrary exercise of legislative authority), but this was rejected by the Supreme Court: *Axa General Insurance Ltd v HM Advocate* [2011] UKSC 46; [2012] 1 A.C. 868; 2011 S.L.T. 1061. Similar provisions, providing that pleural plaques constitute more than de minimis harm and are to be compensatable, were enacted in Northern Ireland in the Damages (Asbestos-related Conditions) Act 2011. In *McCauley v Harland and Wolff Plc* [2015] NICA 28; [2016] N.I. 254, the Court of Appeal (Northern Ireland) held that case law developed before the decision of the House of Lords in *Rothwell* was nevertheless flawed, to the extent that it approached asymptomatic plaques as "significant bodily harm" with "grave consequences". The injury was not in fact significant on its own, even if it was to be treated as compensatable. Asymptomatic plaques taken on their own would justify an award of around £3,000, but to this should be added an award for the anxiety and distress which was understandable as the plaques indicated exposure to asbestos. In the absence of grave psychiatric consequences, most awards would be between £5,000 and £15,000. Discussing this in relation to the Scottish legislation, see *W v Advocate General for Scotland* [2015] CSOH 111; [2015] S.L.T. 537.

29 *Deyong v Shenburn* [1946] K.B. 227.

30 [1990] 1 W.L.R. 212. See also *Outram v Academy Plastics Ltd* [2001] I.C.R. 367, where it was held that the duty of care did not extend to advising the employee to join a pension scheme.

31 [1995] 2 A.C. 296.

32 Unfavourable comments about an employee should be confined to matters into which reasonable investigation has been made and there must be reasonable grounds for believing the statements to be true. Thus, a suspicion of dishonesty by the employee should not be raised in the reference if the charges of dishonesty have never been put to him, and have never been the subject of proper investigation or formal disciplinary proceedings: *Cox v Sun Alliance Life Ltd* [2001] EWCA Civ 649; [2001] I.R.L.R. 448. *Spring* does not apply where no reference has ever been provided by the employer: *Legal & General Assurance Ltd v Kirk* [2001] EWCA Civ 1803; [2002] I.R.L.R. 124 (no liability where, due to a dispute about a claim for the return of £7,500 in commission, the employee did not apply for another job in the financial services industry because the dispute would have been referred to in any reference and would have prevented another employer offering him a job). See also *Aspin v Metric Group Ltd* [2004] EWHC 1265 (QB): no duty owed by an employer to an employee in giving reasons for dismissing the employee or in disseminating those reasons. The duty of care owed in respect of the giving of references was specific to the giving of references, and does not apply more generally to the reasons surrounding the dismissal.

33 [2004] EWCA Civ 130; [2004] 1 W.L.R. 2594; [2004] 2 All E.R. 266. *Outram* was distinguished on the ground that the duty arose from a specific assumption of responsibility rather than the general relationship.

34 In *Crossley v Faithful & Gould Holdings Ltd* [2004] EWCA Civ 293; [2004] I.C.R. 1615; [2004] 4

ship rather than a specific undertaking, it will mirror the implied duty arising under the contract of employment and the employee may claim under both contract and tort concurrently.[35] In *Greenway v Johnson Matthey Plc*[36] the Court of Appeal held that the purpose of the employer's duty to employees is to safeguard the health, safety and welfare of employees, and this is true both of tort law and of implied contractual duties between employer and employee. The Court of Appeal considered that sensitisation to chlorinated or halogenated platinum salts, caused by exposure, was not a personal injury. Thus, the consequences of these physiological changes were categorised as unrecoverable economic losses. On appeal, the Supreme Court reversed this decision.[37] Actionable personal injury for the purposes of a claim in negligence or breach of statutory duty included a physical change which made a person appreciably worse off in respect of health, capability, or physical capacity to enjoy life. Since the sensitisation affected their capacity to work, the claimants were appreciably worse off as a result of the physical changes. This, it was suggested, made the case clearly distinguishable from *Rothwell v Chemical and Insulating Co Ltd*,[38] where the claimants suffered from asymptomatic pleural plaques. Since the physical changes were classified as personal injury in their own right, the company's argument that the claimants were in reality claiming for loss of earnings, and therefore for pure economic loss, fell away.

Duty to employees The duty is peculiar to the employer-employee relationship.[39] 12-06
It is not owed to one who is not an employee, though on ordinary principles there

All E.R. 447, the Court of Appeal held that a general duty on the employer to take reasonable care for the economic well-being of an employee could not be implied as a term of the employment contract as it would impose an unfair burden on employers. It was not the function of an employer to act as an employee's financial adviser and it was not fair to require the employer to consider the employee's financial circumstances when it took lawful business decisions which might affect the employee's economic welfare. cf. *Scally v Southern Health and Social Services Board* [1992] 1 A.C. 294 where the House of Lords was prepared to imply a term into a contract of employment requiring an employer to take reasonable steps to bring the existence of a contingent right to the notice of an employee, even though the effect was to sustain a claim for purely economic loss. See also *Hagen v ICI Chemicals and Polymers Ltd* [2002] I.R.L.R. 31 QBD, where it was held that employers can owe a duty of care that statements made to employees about the terms of a transfer of an undertaking in which they were employed to another employer were made with reasonable care. Elias J found that there was an implied contractual duty to take reasonable care in making such statements (which related to the terms of the employees' pension rights with the new employer) where the transfer would have an impact on the future economic interests of the employees, the transfer was unlikely to take place if a significant body of the employees objected, the employer had access to information that was unavailable to the employees, and the employer knew that its information or advice would carry significant weight with the employees. There was also a corresponding duty in the tort of negligence.

35 *Matthews v Kuwait Bechtel Corp* [1959] 2 Q.B. 57.

36 [2016] EWCA Civ 408; [2016] 1 W.L.R. 4487.

37 *Dryden v Johnson Matthey Plc* [2018] UKSC 18; [2019] A.C. 4034.

38 [2007] UKHL 39; [2008] A.C. 281.

39 But note that the Crown owes it to Crown servants: Crown Proceedings Act 1947 s.2(1)(b). However, no duty is owed to soldiers in battle conditions since it is not fair, just or reasonable to impose a duty of care when engaging the enemy during hostilities: *Mulcahy v Ministry of Defence* [1996] Q.B. 732. The position will be different if the injury was not incurred during "battle conditions": see paras 5-13 and 13-52. The employer's duties to provide safe equipment and a safe system of work have been of particular importance in relation to the armed forces, where the extra-territorial application of the Human Rights Act was interpreted restrictively until the decision of the Supreme Court in *Smith v Ministry of Defence* [2013] UKSC 41; [2014] A.C. 52; see further para.13-53.

would still be the normal duty to show reasonable care.[40] Thus, the employer of an independent contractor does not owe it to the contractor,[41] nor does an independent contractor owe it to the employee of the person who engages him.[42] Generally, the employer of an independent contractor does not owe the duty to an employee of the contractor. However, there appear to be exceptional cases where the duty may be owed to employees of sub-contractors. An example is *EH Humphries (Norton) Ltd, Thistle Hotels Plc v Fire Alarm Fabrication Services Ltd*,[43] where the subcontractor was bound to carry out work in "close liaison" with the contractor's manager. Equally, the public interest in safety standards (and perhaps the compulsory nature of employers' liability insurance) may incline courts to recognise a worker as an employee rather than an independent contractor for these purposes.[44] Where the injured worker is on loan from another employer, the borrowing employer will be treated as owing a duty in relation to aspects of the work under its control despite the worker not satisfying the tests for an employee used for vicarious liability.[45] In *Spalding v Tarmac Civil Engineering Ltd*,[46] where A hired from B a mechanical excavator and a driver, it was held that A was the employer as far as the working of the excavator was concerned, but that B remained the employer as far as its maintenance was concerned. If, in a situation like this, the driver had been injured through a defect in the machine, it would be B and not A, who would be liable to him. With regard to the provision of a safe place of work, it may well be that the hirer or borrower is liable independently under the Occupiers' Liability Act 1957.[47] With regard to the provision of a safe system of work, the employer who can tell the worker how to perform the job will nearly always be the one liable to the worker for injury caused by an unsafe system. If in *Spalding*'s case the driver was injured as a result of the way he was told to work the excavator or the incompetence of fellow workers, the duty should lie on A, the temporary

---

40 *Inglefield v Macey* (1967) 2 K.I.R. 146.

41 *Jones v Minton Construction* (1973) 15 K.I.R. 309.

42 *Taylor v Rover Co Ltd* [1966] 1 W.L.R. 1491.

43 [2006] EWCA Civ 1496; [2007] I.C.R. 247. Note also *Rice v Secretary of State for Trade and Industry* [2007] EWCA Civ 289; [2007] I.C.R. 1469, where a common law duty was said to arise within a statutory hybrid relationship between the National Dock Labour Board and dock workers: see para.8-10 and para.13-67.

44 *Lane v Shire Roofing Co (Oxford) Ltd* [1995] I.R.L.R. 493. Applying this policy, the Court of Appeal held that those hired "on the lump" to undertake roofing work were employees and were owed a duty of care by the employer.

45 See para.6-09 onwards. For the purposes of vicarious liability, loaned employees will normally be regarded as employees of the general rather than the borrowing employer: *Mersey Docks & Harbour Board v Coggins & Griffiths (Liverpool) Ltd* [1947] A.C. 1; para.6-23. In *Morris v Breaveglen Ltd* [1993] I.C.R. 766, where there was held to be no transfer of employment in relation to a borrowed general labourer, the Court of Appeal indicated that a different test might be required where breach of the personal duty rather than vicarious liability was in issue. An influential case where the Court of Appeal appears to have accepted that there is a difference in the applicable tests is *Denham v Midland Employers Mutual Assurance Ltd* [1955] 2 Q.B. 437. A "borrowed" employee who had been killed through negligence of the employees of the "borrowing" company was treated as not employed by the borrowing company for these purposes, so that the liabilities would be covered by the employer's public liability insurance, not its employers' liability insurance. Both Slesser LJ and Denning LJ expressed the view that for the purposes of vicarious liability, the deceased would have been treated as an employee of the borrowing company because he was working under its control.

46 [1966] 1 W.L.R. 156. The Court of Appeal apportioned between A and B. This result was reversed by the House of Lords, because of a contractual term intended to ensure (as between the parties) that B alone would be liable for the driver's negligence: [1967] 1 W.L.R. 1508.

47 *Savory v Holland and Hannen and Cubitts (Southern) Ltd* [1964] 1 W.L.R. 1158.

employer rather than the permanent employer, B. But where the permanent employer allows the employee to operate plant or equipment without proper instruction, and the injury was caused by lack of instruction when the employee was using the borrowing employer's plant, the permanent employer will be in breach of his duty to provide a safe system of work.[48] If the borrowing employer has also been negligent, then he is liable to the employee and there may be apportionment of the loss between the two employers.[49]

Duty owed to rescue services employees Employers of those with occupations carrying inherent dangers are not thereby exempt from the duty. In *King v Sussex Ambulance NHS Trust*,[50] Hale LJ said: **12-07**

> "There is no special rule in English law qualifying the obligations of others towards fire-fighters, or presumably police officers, ambulance technicians and others whose occupations in the public service are inherently dangerous ... Such public servants accept the risks which are inherent in their work, but not the risks which the exercise of reasonable care on the part of those who owe them a duty of care could avoid. An employer owes his employees a duty to take reasonable care to provide safe equipment and a safe system of work, which includes assessing the tasks to be undertaken, training in how to perform those tasks as safely as possible, and supervision in performing them."

King concerned the ambulance service. In *Buck v Nottinghamshire Healthcare NHS Trust*,[51] Waller LJ cited Hale LJ's dictum when holding the Trust liable for failing to have a safe system for protecting nurses from attack by a disturbed patient, and in *Wembridge Claimants v Winter*[52] Irwin J applied Hale LJ's dictum in rejecting an argument that the fire service owed no duty to fire officers fighting a fire.[53] Irwin J also rejected the contention that the fire service should enjoy an immunity from suit in respect of decisions taken in the heat of the moment by those in charge in the emergency services. There is no "fireground immunity" analogous to "combat immunity".[54] The decision of the Court of Appeal in *Capital and Counties Plc v Hampshire CC*[55] did not support such an immunity, though in considering whether there has been a breach of duty the court should "make every allowance for the difficulty of exercising command and making swift decisions on a fireground".[56]

---

48 *Morris v Breaveglen Ltd* [1993] I.C.R. 766 CA.

49 *Nelhams v Sandells Maintenance Ltd* [1996] P.I.Q.R. P52 CA; *McGarvey v Eve NCI Ltd* [2002] EWCA Civ 374 (claimant employed by subcontractors, E, but told to perform such work as D's foreman instructed. D negligent in telling claimant to use a piece of equipment that was unsuitable for the job, i.e. ladders that were too short); *Humpheryes v Nedcon UK Ltd* [2004] EWHC 1260 (QB).

50 [2002] EWCA Civ 953; [2002] I.C.R. 1413 at [21]; cited with apparent approval by Lord Carnwath JSC in *Smith v Ministry of Defence* [2013] UKSC 41; [2014] A.C. 52 at [171].

51 [2006] EWCA Civ 1576; (2006) 93 B.M.L.R. 28.

52 [2013] EWHC 2331 (QB) at [206], [217].

53 In view of the decision of the House of Lords in *Ogwo v Taylor* [1988] A.C. 431, para.7-36, the defendants' argument would have had led to the extraordinary conclusion that fire officers could sue a negligent occupier of premises but not their negligent employer. Irwin J also rejected the fire service's argument that they owed no duty of care to police officers injured in the same incident (at [219]).

54 [2013] EWHC 2331 (QB) at [225], [228]. See para.13-53, discussing *Smith v Ministry of Defence* [2013] UKSC 41; [2014] A.C. 52 and "combat immunity".

55 [1997] Q.B. 1004; see paras 7-54 and 13-46.

56 [2013] EWHC 2331 (QB) at [225]. Irwin J considered that the *Bolam* test (see para.7-196) did not apply to the assessment of breach of duty (at [223]).

12-08 **Duty owed by parent company** The existence of a duty between employer and employee does not negate the potential for duties to be owed by other parties in respect of the worker's safety, on ordinary negligence principles. In *Chandler v Cape Plc*[57] the Court of Appeal found that the parent company of a subsidiary which had employed the claimant owed a duty of care to the claimant in respect of his exposure to asbestos. The court made clear that it was not concerned with "piercing the corporate veil", and that the duty was one owed by the defendant on the application of ordinary negligence principles: "in appropriate circumstances the law may impose on a parent company responsibility for the health and safety of its subsidiary's employees". Those circumstances were not exhausted by the situation in *Chandler*.[58] It was conceded that the system of work in operation in *Chandler* was defective. The subsidiary was no longer in existence, and its employers' liability insurance policy had in any event excluded liability for asbestosis, the condition suffered by the claimant, so that there was no possibility of direct recourse against an insurer.[59] The Court of Appeal recognised that this was the first reported case in which a parent company was found to owe a duty to employees of another company within the group. An analogous line of authority was said to be that on the duty of a person to intervene to prevent damage to another.[60] Although it could be said that the parent company had assumed a responsibility to the claimant, "assumption" in this context was said to be a misnomer, and "attachment" of responsibility "might be more accurate".[61] The court emphasised that there does not have to be an unusual relationship between the parent and its subsidiary for the duty to apply. Relevant circumstances justifying the existence of a duty and exemplified in *Chandler* were identified as: (1) that the businesses of the parent and subsidiary are in a relevant respect the same; (2) the parent has, or ought to have, superior knowledge on some relevant aspect of health and safety in the particular industry; (3) the subsidiary's system of work is unsafe as the parent company knew, or ought to have known; and (4) the parent knew or ought to have foreseen that the subsidiary or its employees would rely on its using that superior knowledge for the employees' protection.[62] Here, the subsidiary's unsafe working practice was inherited from the parent company. The factors set out in (1)–(4), however, did not exhaust the possibilities, and the case merely illustrated the way in which the requirements of *Caparo Industries Plc v Dickman*[63] may be satisfied between a parent company, and the employee of a subsidiary.[64]

12-09 While some, subsequent cases have distinguished *Chandler v Cape*, finding some or all of the factors set out by the Court of Appeal to be lacking, other decisions

---

57 [2012] EWCA Civ 525; [2012] 1 W.L.R. 3111; discussed by Petrin "Assumption of responsibility in corporate groups: Chandler v Cape plc" (2013) 76 M.L.R. 603.

58 [2012] EWCA Civ 525; [2012] 1 W.L.R. 3111 at [80].

59 Subsequently the subsidiary's liability insurer, exercising rights of subrogation in Cape's name, sought an indemnity from the parent company under the Civil Liability (Contribution) Act 1978 or under the indemnities in the sale agreement. In May 2016 (*Cape Distribution Ltd v Cape Intermediate Holdings Plc* [2016] EWHC 1119 (QB); [2016] Lloyd's Rep. I.R. 499) the court determined a number of preliminary issues; further issues in the litigation were resolved in *Cape Distribution Ltd v Cape Intermediate Holdings Plc* [2016] EWHC 1786 (QB); [2017] Lloyd's Rep. I.R. 1.

60 *Smith v Littlewoods Ltd* [1987] A.C. 241, para.7-60.

61 [2012] EWCA Civ 525; [2012] 1 W.L.R. 3111 at [64].

62 [2012] EWCA Civ 525; [2012] 1 W.L.R. 3111 at [80].

63 [1990] 2 A.C. 605.

64 This sentence was adopted by Tomlinson LJ in *Thompson v Renwick Group Plc* [2014] EWCA Civ 635; [2014] P.I.Q.R. P18 at [33].

have continued to build on *Chandler* to find duties owed directly by parent companies in a range of circumstances. *Thompson v Renwick Group Plc*[65] falls into the former category. Here, the Court of Appeal concluded that a holding company had not assumed a duty of care to employees of its subsidiary in health and safety matters simply because the parent company had appointed an individual as a director of the subsidiary company with responsibility for health and safety matters. That individual was not acting on behalf of the parent company, but acting pursuant to his fiduciary duty to the subsidiary as a director. Moreover, on the facts of *Thompson*, there was no evidence that the parent holding company carried on any business at all, other than holding shares in other companies. It was not a situation where the parent company was better placed, because of its superior knowledge or expertise, to protect the employees of subsidiary companies against the risk of injury and where, because of that, it was fair to infer that the subsidiary would rely on the parent deploying its superior knowledge in order to protect its employees from the risk of injury.[66]

The approach in *Chandler v Cape* has been further considered in claims brought, not by employees, but by those living in the vicinity of mining and other operations, and affected by pollution, with evident implications for future cases relating to employees. In *Vedanta Resources Plc v Lungowe*,[67] a claim alleging personal injury, damage to property, and loss of income, amenity and enjoyment of land, was brought in the English courts in relation to the activities in Zambia of a mining company, "KCM". The claimants were not employees, but the duty to employees by a parent company in *Chandler v Cape*[68] was influential in the decision. The actions were brought not only against KCM, but also against its UK parent company, "Vedanta". Hearing preliminary issues, the Supreme Court upheld the Court of Appeal's decision both that the claims were within the jurisdiction of the English courts, and that there was a real issue to be tried between the claimants and Vedanta, the parent company. Lord Briggs, with whom all the other Justices agreed, concluded that there was no special category of negligence case involving the liability of parent companies for the activities of their subsidiaries. Applying the approach of Sales LJ in *AAA v Unilever Plc*,[69] a duty will be owed by the parent if ordinary principles of the law of tort regarding the imposition of a duty toward the claimant are satisfied in the particular case: the indicia in *Chandler* are merely helpful guidelines. In *AAA v Unilever Plc*, Sales LJ proposed two basic types of case in which a parent may owe duties in respect of the activities of their subsidiaries. These are: (i) where the parent has effectively taken over the management of the relevant activity of the subsidiary either in place of or jointly with the subsidiary; and (ii) where the parent has advised the subsidiary on how it should manage the particular risk concerned.[70] The Supreme Court in *Lungowe* was reluctant, however, **12-10**

---

65 [2014] EWCA Civ 635; [2014] P.I.Q.R. P18.

66 [2014] EWCA Civ 635; [2014] P.I.Q.R. P18 at [37].

67 [2019] UKSC 20; [2019] 2 W.L.R. 1051.

68 [2012] EWCA Civ 525; [2012] 1 W.L.R. 3111; see para.12-08.

69 [2018] EWCA Civ 1532; [2018] B.C.C. 959 at [36].

70 In *AAA* itself, [2018] EWCA Civ 1532; [2018] B.C.C. 959, it was concluded that no duty of care was owed by the parent company to the claimant employees of a Kenyan subsidiary. There had been violent unrest following an election, and this led to murders, rapes and assaults of employees. In this case, a duty was not arguable so that there was no "anchor" defendant justifying service of proceedings in the UK. The evidence showed that the subsidiary did not receive relevant advice from Unilever in relation to violent unrest and crisis management; and that the subsidiary understood that

to restrict the potential duty to these categories, and appeared to set out a much broader set of factors which would point towards a duty. Lord Briggs pointed to three routes to the imposition of a duty.[71] First, there may be a general group-wide policy in place, which has inherent flaws. Secondly, the parent may go beyond proclaiming policies for the group and may take active steps (by training, supervision, or enforcement) to see that they are implemented. Thirdly, and perhaps most controversially, the parent may incur the relevant duty to third parties if "it holds itself out as exercising that degree of supervision and control of its subsidiaries",[72] even if it does not do so in fact. This is not necessarily an issue of reliance: rather, the parent's omission appears to be an abdication of a "responsibility which has been publicly undertaken". There was no reason to doubt the judge's view that there was sufficient material available to the court to demonstrate that the claimants had an arguable case. It should be noted that both the judge, and the Supreme Court, recognised that the final resolution of the question whether a duty was owed would depend on evidence that would be available only should the trial proceed.

12-11 In *His Royal Highness Okpabi v Royal Dutch Shell Plc*,[73] predating the Supreme Court's decision in *Vedanta Resources Plc v Lungowe*,[74] the Court of Appeal decided a case in which the claimants had been affected by the consequences of polluting activities in Nigeria. The first defendant ("RDS") was the parent company of the Shell group; the second defendant was a subsidiary of the first defendant, incorporated in Nigeria, and an exploration and production company. The question of whether RDS could owe a duty of care to the claimants was essential to the question of the court's jurisdiction. By a majority, the Court of Appeal held that the claimants could not demonstrate a properly arguable case that RDS owed them a duty of care on the basis of an assumed responsibility for devising a material policy which was the subject of the claim, or on the basis that it controlled or shared control of the operations which were the subject of the claim. The issuing of mandatory policies for a group could not, it was suggested, mean that a parent has taken control of the operation of a subsidiary such as to give rise to a duty of care in favour of all of those affected by the policies.[75] Dissenting, Sales LJ suggested that the claimants' argument was that RDS had taken control of management of the operation and security of the pipeline and facilities to a material degree; and that if this factual allegation were to be established, this would be "a true *Chandler v Cape* type case". Taking a different view of the likelihood that sufficient new evidence would be produced by the claimants, Sir Geoffrey Vos in a concurring judgment warned of "the unlikelihood ... of an international parent like RDS undertaking a duty of care to all those affected by the operations of all its subsidiaries".[76] In *Vedanta Resources Plc v Lungowe*, the Supreme Court referred to *Okpabi* and made clear that the issuing of mandatory policies may, in some circumstances, be the basis for a duty on the part of the parent company, if that policy contained inherent flaws. This was essentially similar to the position in

---

it was responsible for devising its own risk management policy and for handling the severe crisis that unfolded.

[71] [2019] UKSC 20; [2019] 2 W.L.R. 1051 at [52]–[53].

[72] [2019] UKSC 20; [2019] 2 W.L.R. 1051 at [53].

[73] [2018] EWCA Civ 191; [2018] Bus. L.R. 1022.

[74] [2019] UKSC 20; [2019] 2 W.L.R. 1051; see para.12-10

[75] [2018] EWCA Civ 191; [2018] Bus. L.R. 1022 at [89].

[76] [2018] EWCA Civ 191; [2018] Bus. L.R. 1022 at [206].

Chandler v Cape itself, where the subsidiary had inherited an unsafe system of work from its parent company; and the same result might be expected whether it was an employee of the subsidiary, or a third party, whose safety was affected.[77] The approach of the majority would therefore appear now to have been disapproved by the Supreme Court.

Secondary exposure to risk An employer's failure to take reasonable steps to protect employees from exposure to risk, for example from toxic substances such as asbestos dust, may also result in the exposure of family members or, indeed, members of the public to such a risk. However, the fact that there would have been liability to an employee does not mean there must also be liability to those suffering as a result of secondary exposure. Whether there is liability will depend upon the foreseeability of damage to the particular claimant. In *Maguire v Harland & Wolff Plc*[78] the majority of the Court of Appeal rejected a claim by the wife of an employee who had developed mesothelioma as a result of exposure to asbestos dust when washing her husband's dusty work clothes. The majority of the Court held that at the time when the exposure occurred, in the early 1960s, the risks of familial exposure were not recognised by the industry or the medical profession.[79] Judge LJ said: **12-12**

> "It does not necessarily follow that an employer who should have appreciated the risk of harm to his employees, and taken precautions for their safety, should simultaneously have appreciated, and addressed, a familial risk arising from secondary exposure."[80]

Courts have subsequently been required to consider the relevant date at which it can be said that at least some employers should have become aware that there was no safe level of exposure to asbestos, and that a risk was therefore posed to family members by "secondary" exposure to asbestos dust, whether on overalls or other clothing, or on the employee's hair, for example. In *Maguire*, the majority had determined that this knowledge could not reasonably be expected before the publication, in 1965, of a major study into the effects of low-level exposure to asbestos, by Newhouse and Thomson.[81] In *Gibson v Babcock International Ltd*,[82] the deceased's husband (who had himself died from mesothelioma) had been employed by the defenders from 1962–1974. Adopting the majority's approach in *Maguire*, Lady Carmichael reached the conclusion that from at latest October 1965, when the Newhouse and Thomson article was given wide currency through an article in the *Sunday Times*, a large employer such as the defenders ought reasonably to have been aware that even lower levels of exposure would pose a risk not only to employees, but also to their families. There was a duty to reduce exposure **12-13**

---

77 *Vedanta Resources Plc v Lungowe* [2019] UKSC 20; [2019] 2 W.L.R. 1051 at [52].

78 [2005] EWCA Civ 1; [2005] P.I.Q.R. P21.

79 Contrast the settlement of a claim by the Ministry of Defence in 2007, in favour of a daughter (Deborah Brewer) who used to hug her father when he returned from work in his dusty overalls. The date of exposure—including the period from 1966—was vital: see further para.12-13.

80 [2005] EWCA Civ 1; [2005] P.I.Q.R. P21 at [51]. Mance LJ noting that it would be a "particularly hard case" if the claimant's case failed when the defendant was "admittedly in substantial breach of its duty to [the employee]", took a different view of the facts and held that there was sufficient foreseeability of familial risk to ground liability.

81 M.L. Newhouse and H. Thompson, "Mesothelioma of pleura and peritoneum following exposure to asbestos in the London area", *British Journal of Industrial Medicine* (1965) 22, 261–296 (6/50).

82 [2018] CSOH 78; 2018 S.L.T. 886.

to the lowest level practicable; and there were simple, effective ways of doing so. Before 1965, it was not appreciated that such risks were posed to family members; from 1965, the position was different. A compatible conclusion was reached in the English High Court in *Carey v Vauxhall Motors Ltd*,[83] where the deceased's husband had been employed by the defendants from 1976–1979. It was concluded that by 1965, it had become common knowledge that there could be no safe or permissible level of exposure, direct or indirect, to asbestos dust. The defendant's liability was not affected by the existence of exposure during an earlier period, from 1961–1962. Even before these recent decisions, it had already been recognised that where the exposure of family members or the public to dangerous pollutants from a workplace can be foreseen, the employer's liability will not be limited to its own workforce. In *Margereson and Hancock v JW Roberts Ltd*,[84] the Court of Appeal held the employer liable for the mesothelioma suffered by members of the public who, as children, had been exposed to asbestos dust which had escaped from the workplace in vast quantities. Russell LJ approved the observation of Holland J at first instance that:

> "There is nothing in the law that circumscribes the duty of care by reference to the factory wall … If the evidence shows with respect to a person outside the factory that he or she was exposed to the knowledge of the defendants, actual or constructive, to conditions of dust emissions not materially different to those giving rise within the factory to a duty of care, then I can see no reason not to extend to that extra-mural neighbour a comparable duty of care."[85]

12-14 **Non-delegable duty** The most distinctive feature of the employer's duty of care to his employee is its non-delegable nature.[86] The employer can delegate the performance of the duty to others, whether employees or independent contractors, but cannot delegate responsibility for its negligent performance. This was established by *Wilsons and Clyde Coal Co Ltd v English*.[87] There, the employer had entrusted the task of organising a safe system of work to an employee and through his negligence another employee was injured. The employer could not have been held liable for its own negligence since it had taken all reasonable care in entrusting the job to a competent employee, nor could it have been held liable vicariously since common employment would have been a defence. Thus, the basis of the decision is that the employer was liable for a breach of a personal duty to see that care was taken by the person whom they appointed. It is true that this person happened to be an employee, but their liability was personal, not vicarious. In the words of Lord Wright: "It is the obligation which is personal to him, and not the performance."[88] However, the liability is negligence-based rather than strict. It is to take reasonable care to see that employees are safe. What that requires will vary with the nature of the risk. In *Kondis v State Transport Authority*[89] the High Court

---

83 [2019] EWHC 238 (QB).
84 [1996] P.I.Q.R. P358.
85 [1996] P.I.Q.R. P154 at P182.
86 In *Farraj v King's Healthcare NHS Trust* [2009] EWCA Civ 1203; [2010] 1 W.L.R. 2139 at [103] Sedley LJ suggested that: "Bearing in mind … the peculiar considerations of policy and law which for over a century drove the law of master and servant to and fro, caution is needed in importing the palliative concept of the non-delegable duty into other legal relationships."
87 [1938] A.C. 57.
88 *Wilsons and Clyde Coal Co Ltd v English* [1938] A.C. 57 at 81.
89 (1984) 154 C.L.R. 672.

of Australia held an employer in breach of its duty to provide a safe system of work when an independent contractor dropped part of a crane which hit an employee. The contractor's failure to adopt a safe system of work was held to constitute a failure by the employer to satisfy the non-delegable duty to provide a safe system. In *McDermid v Nash Dredging & Reclamation Co Ltd*[90] the House of Lords held the employer liable for injury to an employee which occurred at the work site of a Dutch company where he had been instructed to work. The injury was caused by the failure of the Dutch company to have a safe system of work. The English employer was held to have delegated performance of its duty to the Dutch company and was responsible for its failure.[91]

The non-delegable nature of the duty in situations where its performance is to some extent delegated to an independent contractor or (as in this case) another separate organisation was explored by Christopher Clarke J in *Hopps v Mott MacDonald and Ministry of Defence*.[92] The claimant, a civilian employee of the first defendant, was engaged in reconstruction work in Iraq in April 2003, after the "war phase" of the invasion. He was being carried in a soft-skinned vehicle when a bomb exploded, causing him physical injury. The judge reasoned that although some elements of employees' safety had been delegated to the Ministry of Defence, which also conceded that it had assumed a responsibility for the civilians' safety, the first defendant was not absolved of responsibility in circumstances where "the duty to take reasonable care was not fulfilled by it and the Ministry of Defence between them".[93] It appears therefore that although the performance of the duty may be delegated, the duty to take reasonable care remains the duty of the employer. Clearly, in such cases (where the party to whom performance is delegated is not an employee), non-delegable duties retain their importance despite the demise of the doctrine of common employment. By contrast, in *Cook v Square D Ltd*[94] the Court of Appeal held the employer not liable to an employee injured by a fall caused by defective flooring at the Saudi Arabian work site to which he had been sent. It was held that the employer had not delegated its responsibility and had acted with reasonable care in being satisfied that the occupier of the work site was a reliable company aware of its safety responsibility to workers. **12-15**

---

90 [1987] A.C. 906.

91 In *A (A Child) v Ministry of Defence* [2003] EWHC 849 (QB); [2003] P.I.Q.R. P33. Bell J usefully reviewed *Kondis*, *McDermid* and other authorities and concluded that the defendant's duty to its service personnel in relation to medical care was satisfied by providing access to an appropriate health care provider. It was not responsible for the negligence of that provider. He described the employer's duty as "at the most to provide a safe *system* of working or to take reasonable care to see that one is provided (a negligence duty)". The Court of Appeal affirmed his analysis and decision: [2004] EWCA Civ 641; [2005] Q.B. 183.

92 [2009] EWHC 1881 (QB).

93 [2009] EWHC 1881 (QB) at [50]. In *Uren v Corporate Leisure (UK) Ltd* [2011] EWCA Civ 66; [2011] I.C.R. D11 the Court of Appeal concluded that the duty to conduct a risk assessment under reg.3(1) of the Management of Health and Safety at Work Regulations 1999 was so closely linked to the common law duty to take care for the safety of employees that it too must be non-delegable ("it would be remarkable if the duty to undertake a risk assessment were delegable and yet the general responsibility for safety were not", per Smith LJ at [71]). Although breach of the duty to conduct an appropriate risk assessment could not be directly causative of injury, it will be indirectly causative where a proper assessment would have led to a precaution being taken to remove a particular risk. See further para.12-55 on the relationship between duties to conduct risk assessments and substantive duties to minimise or remove risks.

94 [1992] I.C.R. 262.

(b) Aspects of the employer's personal duty

12-16 **Heads of duty** The duty is often explained under four heads: the provision of safe staff; safe equipment; safe place of work; and a safe system of work.[95] These heads provide a useful framework for analysing the duty but it should be remembered that they are part and parcel of one duty within the law of negligence. To use the words of Lord MacDermott, they "are not absolute in nature. They lie within, and exemplify, the broader duty of taking reasonable care for the safety of his workmen which rests on every employer."[96] So an employer cannot escape liability simply because it may be difficult to assign his conduct to one of the four heads. The key question is whether it was in breach of the duty of care.

12-17 **Safe staff** The employer's duty to his employee to employ competent fellow-workers has long been recognised.[97] While the defence of common employment prevailed, an employer escaped vicarious liability for an injury to an employee at the hands of another employee, but remained answerable for its own default in failing to employ a competent employee. This aspect of the duty has diminished in importance since the abolition of common employment, but should not be disregarded. Thus, in *Hudson v Ridge Manufacturing Co Ltd*[98] the company was held liable on this ground for continuing to employ a man who was known to be addicted to acts of horseplay and who by such an act injured the claimant. Counsel for the claimant put the case expressly on the ground of the employer's duty to provide competent employees, thereby avoiding any difficulties that might have arisen with regard to course of employment had he put it on the ground of vicarious liability.[99] The duty extends to the appointment of staff who are independent contractors so that if the employer negligently selects an independent contractor or employed an insufficient number of such contractors with resulting injury to an employee, it will be in breach of its personal duty.[100] An obvious development from the duty to provide competent staff is that the employer must instruct staff properly. It is not enough to supply adequate equipment unless staff are instructed in their use.[101] This aspect of the duty may extend to failing to control staff who are harassing an employee. In *Waters v Commissioner of Police of the Metropolis*[102] the House

---

95 *Wilsons and Clyde Coal Co Ltd v English* [1938] A.C. 57 at 78 and 86 by Lords Wright and Maugham.

96 *Winter v Cardiff RDC* [1950] 1 All E.R. 819 at 823.

97 *Black v Fife Coal Co Ltd* [1912] A.C. 149.

98 [1957] 2 Q.B. 348, especially at 350; distinguished in *Coddington v International Harvester Co of GB Ltd* (1969) 6 K.I.R. 146. An isolated, unforeseeable, incident of horseplay would not be sufficient: *Smith v Crossley Bros Ltd* (1951) 95 S.J. 655 CA.

99 There would be no vicarious liability if the employee's conduct was such as to be outside the course of his employment. See further para.6-29. See *Harrison v Michelin Tyre Co Ltd* [1985] 1 All E.R. 918; [1985] I.C.R. 696 QBD, where an employer was held vicariously liable for the negligence of an employee who had engaged in a prank, on the basis that the employee was nonetheless still acting within the course of his employment.

100 *Pinn v Rew* (1916) 32 T.L.R. 451. See further para.6-63.

101 *General Cleaning Contractors Ltd v Christmas* [1953] A.C. 180; *Drummond v British Building Cleaners Ltd* [1954] 1 W.L.R. 1434.

102 [2000] 1 W.L.R. 1607. See also *Moore v Welwyn Components Ltd* reported as one of the co-joined appeals in *Hartman v South Essex Mental Health and Community Care NHS Trust* [2005] EWCA Civ 6; [2005] I.C.R. 782, where the employer was liable for the bullying of the claimant by a colleague; and *Banks v Ablex Ltd* [2005] EWCA Civ 173; [2005] I.C.R. 819, where the employer did not incur primary liability for the harassment of the claimant by a fellow employee as it could not

of Lords, treating a police officer's status as analogous to an employee, considered it arguable that there was a breach of duty where an employer knew that acts done by employees during their employment might cause physical or mental harm to a particular fellow employee and did nothing to supervise or prevent such acts when he had the power to do so. In *Clark v Chief Constable of Essex*,[103] the defendant Chief Constable was held liable in negligence to a police officer who had been caused foreseeable mental and physical harm through bullying, intimidation and unlawful use of disciplinary proceedings. One route to this conclusion was through "vicarious" liability for the acts of police officers; another was through the defendant's own duty to provide a safe place of work.

Safe equipment Responsibility for the safety of equipment provided to the employee is now governed by s.1(1) of the Employer's Liability (Defective Equipment) Act 1969 which was passed to reverse the ruling in *Davie v New Merton Board Mills Ltd*.[104] The statutory duty is expressly non-delegable. An employer is made personally answerable in negligence if: 12-18

"(a) an employee suffers personal injury in the course of his employment in consequence of a defect in equipment provided by his employer for the purposes of the employer's business; and

(b) the defect is attributable wholly or partly to the fault of a third party (whether identifiable or not)."

Contributory negligence of the employee is a defence,[105] and the employer is left free to recover indemnity from the third party. The Crown is made liable to persons in Crown service even though they may not strictly be employees.[106] "Course of employment", in which an employee has to sustain injury in order to recover, is not defined, which means that it has to be determined according to the ordinary tests.[107] Nor is "equipment" exhaustively defined: it is said to "include any plant and machinery, vehicle, aircraft and clothing".[108] It has been held to include not only the tools with which the employees work but also the material on which they

---

have foreseen the significant injury to the mental health of the claimant and had no reason to believe that the offending employee would not heed the warning given to him. Note also that in *Majrowski v Guy's and St Thomas's NHS Trust* [2006] UKHL 34; [2007] 1 A.C. 224, the House of Lords held that an employer could be vicariously liable for conduct of an employee which constituted the statutory tort of harassment under the Protection from Harassment Act 1997. This development, and subsequent case law, are discussed in Chs 6 and 14. In *Green v DB Group Services (UK) Ltd* [2006] EWHC 1898 (QB); [2006] I.R.L.R. 764, Owen J found the employer to be vicariously liable because the harassing employee's conduct was sufficiently close to his work (at [154]), but found that it was not directly liable for breach of personal duty because its HR Department had taken reasonable steps to avoid the victim coming into contact with the harasser (at [168]).

103 [2006] EWHC 2290 (QB).

104 [1959] A.C. 604. In *Davie* the House of Lords held that an employer was not liable where it had purchased from a reputable manufacturer a defective chisel which shattered in use causing injury to an employee. The chisel had been negligently manufactured but the resulting defect could not be discovered by reasonable inspection. The Lords refused to treat the purchase of equipment from a supplier as a delegation of the employer's personal safety duty.

105 *James v Durkin (Civil Engineering Contractors)*, *The Times*, 25 May 1983.

106 Employer's Liability (Defective Equipment) Act 1969 s.1(4).

107 See further para.6-29 onwards.

108 Employer's Liability (Defective Equipment) Act 1969 s.1(3). A ship is "equipment": *Coltman v Bibby Tankers Ltd (The Derbyshire)* [1988] A.C. 276.

work.[109] "Defect" too, is undefined. Lindley LJ said long ago: "I take defect to include everything which renders the plant etc unfit for the use for which it is intended when used in a reasonable way and with reasonable care."[110] The policy of the Act suggests that "fault of a third party" should cover a situation where the third party responsible for maintaining equipment has negligently failed to correct a defect which was itself not attributable to anyone's fault.[111] Where a piece of defective equipment is used by a workman on a job for which it is not intended and he is injured because of the extra strain which this use places on it and which causes the defect to operate, the answer is likely to rest on causation, i.e. whether the injury is attributable to the defect or to the wrong use; and, if to the defect, how far wrong use contributed to it, which might let in a plea of contributory negligence. The Provision and Use of Work Equipment Regulations 1992 have been held[112] to impose a strict duty to ensure that work equipment is suitable for the purpose for which it is used and maintained in an efficient state and in good repair. This goes further than the 1969 Act as there can be liability under the Regulations even if there is no fault of a third party.[113] However, with the prospective removal of civil liability for breach of these Regulations by s.69 of the Enterprise and Regulatory Reform Act 2013, the importance of the 1969 Act can be expected to grow.[114]

12-19 **Maintenance of equipment** "The obligation to provide and maintain proper plant and appliances is a continuing obligation."[115] The duty is not absolute; there has to be fault in someone. So an employer is not liable for a latent defect due to no one's fault and which cannot be detected on reasonable examination.[116] If it knows the equipment is dangerous and does nothing about it, it will be liable.[117] There will also be liability if it retains in use a piece of equipment known to be defective.[118] Reasonable care is taken if the appliances used are of the type usual for the work in question.[119] The duty is "limited to reasonable exercise of care and skill to guard against danger which as reasonable people the employers ought to have anticipated",[120] so that the employer was not liable when a piece of wood was thrown off from a circular saw, properly guarded according to the regulations, and injured the operator.[121] The employer will not be liable where it would be reasonable to leave

---

109 *Knowles v Liverpool City Council* [1993] 1 W.L.R. 1428: employees working on a flagstone.

110 *Yarmouth v France* (1887) 19 Q.B.D. 647 at 658.

111 Alternatively, there might be a common law action under *Wilsons & Clyde Coal Co Ltd v English* [1938] A.C. 57. As the object of the Act was to restore the principle in *Wilsons'* case, it can hardly have abrogated it.

112 *Stark v Post Office* [2000] I.C.R. 1013; [2000] P.I.Q.R. P105. See now the Provision and Use of Work Equipment Regulations 1998 (SI 1998/2306), para.12-60.

113 See further para.12-69.

114 The 1969 Act was not listed in Sch.1 to the Health and Safety at Work etc. Act 1974 and is unaffected by s.69.

115 per Lord Wright in *Wilsons & Clyde Coal Co v English* [1938] A.C. 57 at 84.

116 *Toronto Power Co v Paskwan* [1915] A.C. 734 at 738. For the importance of reasonable examination, see *Pearce v Round Oak Steel Works* [1969] 1 W.L.R. 595.

117 As where a film actress was required to cover her feet with inflammable material during the filming of a scene and this caught fire and injured her: *Naismith v London Film Productions Ltd* [1939] 1 All E.R. 794.

118 *Taylor v Rover Co Ltd* [1966] 1 W.L.R. 1491.

119 *Davie v New Merton Board Mills Ltd* [1959] A.C. 604.

120 per Lord Wright in *Nicholls v F Austin (Leyton) Ltd* [1946] A.C. 493 at 503.

121 *Nicholls v F Austin (Leyton) Ltd* [1946] A.C. 493.

to the employee the task of selecting the equipment,[122] nor where the employee fails to make proper use of the equipment,[123] provided in both cases the employee has been given adequate instruction as to the selection and use of the equipment. Effective maintenance may require both a system of inspection[124] and/or defect reporting[125] and a system for withdrawing defective equipment from use for repair or replacement.[126]

Protective equipment The provision of appropriate safety equipment such as goggles, safety gloves and shoes, safety belts and so on, is a key part of the duty. Neill LJ in *Crouch v British Rail Engineering Ltd*[127] said that the extent of the duty would depend on: **12-20**

> "the risk of injury, the gravity of any injury which may result, the difficulty of providing equipment ... the availability of that protective equipment ... and the distance which any individual workman might have to go to fetch it, the frequency on which the [claimant] was likely to need that protective clothing or equipment and, last but not least, the experience and degree of skill to be expected of the [claimant]."

Thus, as in *Crouch*, there may be liability if the equipment is not readily accessible with the result that employees are encouraged to take the chance of not using it. In some situations the danger may be such that the employer's duty will extend to taking reasonable steps to enforce the use of such equipment.[128] On the other hand, there may be cases where the employer can rely on the experience of the employee to use the equipment and no further persuasion is necessary.[129]

Safe place of work and access to it There is a duty to see that a reasonably safe place of work is provided and maintained. The place of employment should be as safe as the exercise of reasonable care and skill permits[130]; it is not enough for the employer to show that the danger on the premises was known and fully understood by the employee.[131] On the other hand, there will be no liability if there is no real **12-21**

---

[122] *Richardson v Stephenson Clarke Ltd* [1969] 1 W.L.R. 1695.

[123] *Parkinson v Lyle Shipping Co* [1964] 2 Lloyd's Rep. 79. This includes an act of folly on the workman's part in selecting the wrong tool for the job in hand: *Leach v British Oxygen Co* (1965) 109 S.J. 157.

[124] *Henderson v Henry E Jenkins & Sons* [1970] A.C. 282: reasonableness of requiring inspection of lorry hydraulic brake fluid pipes depended on whether use of lorry created a particular risk of corrosion.

[125] *Barkway v South Wales Transport Co Ltd* [1950] 1 All E.R. 392, which unlike the [1950] A.C. 185, reports the case on this point.

[126] *Johnstone v Clyde Navigation Trustees* (1948–49) 82 Lloyd's Law Rep. 187.

[127] [1988] I.R.L.R. 404 at 408.

[128] *Bux v Slough Metals Ltd* [1973] 1 W.L.R. 1358.

[129] *Qualcast (Wolverhampton) Ltd v Haynes* [1959] A.C. 743: experienced employee could be relied upon to wear foot protection when ladling molten metal, so no warning was necessary.

[130] *Naismith v London Films Productions Ltd* [1939] 1 All E.R. 794; *Stafford v Antwerp S.S. Co* [1965] 2 Lloyd's Rep. 104; *Newland v Rye-Arc* [1971] 2 Lloyd's Rep. 64. Under the Construction (Working Places) Regulations 1966 (SI 1966/94, as amended), reg.6(1) a defendant was required specifically to plead that it was not "reasonably practicable" if he wished to rely on that defence: *Bowes v Sedgefield DC* [1981] I.C.R. 234. See now the Construction (Design and Management) Regulations 2015 (SI 2015/51). Civil liability for breach of the duties in Pt 4 of the 2015 Regulations (relating to health and safety on construction sites), in those cases to which such civil liability still applies, is not confined to employees.

[131] *Umek v LTE* (1984) 134 N.L.J. 522. The employee's degree of knowledge would be relevant to

risk to employees acting with sufficient care.[132] In considering whether the place of work is safe or not, regard must be paid to its nature. If it is a roof, scaffold or tunnel, the standard of safety to be applied is that of a reasonably prudent employer who provides a roof, scaffold or tunnel at which his men are to work. The failure to provide crawling boards for a risky operation on a roof and reliance solely on the experience of the workman was held to constitute negligence.[133] A place which is safe in construction may become unsafe through some obstruction being placed on it or through the presence of something on the floor which makes it slippery. In such cases the test to be applied is whether a reasonable employer, in the circumstances of the case, would have caused or permitted the existence of the state of affairs complained of. In *Latimer v AEC Ltd*[134] the floor of a factory became flooded by an exceptionally heavy rainfall, and when the flood subsided the floor became slippery from oil which was usually contained in a channel in the floor. Sawdust was put down, but the supply was insufficient to cover the whole of the floor, and a workman slipped and was injured. It was held that there was no breach of duty. The test was:

> "Has it been proved that the floor was so slippery that, remedial steps not being possible, a reasonably prudent employer would have closed down the factory rather than allow his employees to run the risk involved in continuing work?"[135]

Again, in *O'Reilly v National Rail and Tramway Appliances*[136] it was held that the defendants were not in breach of their duty to provide a safe place of work where (a) the place had become unsafe owing to a transient and exceptional danger; and (b) the only knowledge of that danger was that of employees, who were neither foremen nor charge-hands and whose knowledge could not, therefore, be imputed to the defendants. The non-delegable nature of the duty means that the employer will be held liable for injuries caused to employees by defects in the structure resulting from the work of independent contractors.[137] Whether the same applies where the defect is caused by the negligence of a supplier of parts for the structure is more doubtful.[138] In *Mason v Satelcom Ltd*,[139] at first instance, an employer was held liable for negligence in failing to provide its field service engineer with a ladder suitable for reaching equipment to be serviced. The employee found a ladder at the premises, but it was unsuitable, and he fell off. Damages were reduced by a third to reflect the employee's contributory negligence. The judge also allowed a contribution claim against the owner of the premises but this was reversed by the

---

contributory negligence.

132 *Jaguar Cars Ltd v Coates* [2004] EWCA Civ 337: no liability for failing to provide a handrail for a four step flight of steps of a kind commonly used.

133 *Jenner v Allen West & Co Ltd* [1959] 1 W.L.R. 554.

134 [1953] A.C. 643. In this case, as in others cited here, a claim for breach of the common law duty is often joined with a claim for breach of statutory duty.

135 per Lord Tucker at 659.

136 [1966] 1 All E.R. 499.

137 *Paine v Colne Valley Electricity Supply Co Ltd* [1938] 4 All E.R. 803.

138 See the High Court decision in *Sumner v William Henderson & Sons Ltd* [1964] 1 Q.B. 450, where Phillimore J held that a purchase of a part for a building (electrical cable) was to be treated in a similar way to the purchase of equipment from a supplier and that following *Davie v New Merton Board Mills*, the employer did not owe a non-delegable duty in such a case. In light of the legislative reversal of *Davie* in relation to equipment purchase, courts might be prepared to impose a non-delegable duty in respect of the purchase parts for the structure.

139 [2007] EWHC 2540 (QB); [2008] P.I.Q.R. P4.

Court of Appeal.[140]

Distant places of work The fact that the place of work is not under the control of the employer is only one factor in deciding whether the obligation to provide a safe place of work has been discharged.[141] Although generally an employer owes no duty to employees as to the safety of the premises occupied by another, it will have to provide a system of work suitable for those premises.[142] For example, window cleaning firms are not bound to inspect the premises of those whose windows they clean before sending men to clean them, but they must be taken to know that window sashes may move unexpectedly and should give instructions and provide any necessary implements accordingly.[143] If an employer is found to have delegated responsibility for providing a safe place of work to the occupier of the premises to which employees are sent, it may be personally liable if the occupier failed to use reasonable care. In determining an employer's responsibility: 12-22

> "one has to look at all the circumstances of the case, including the place where the work is to be done, the nature of the building on the site concerned (if there is a building), the experience of the employee who is so despatched to work at such a site, the nature of the work he is required to carry out, the degree of control that the employer can reasonably exercise in the circumstances, and the employer's own knowledge of the defective state of the premises."[144]

In *Johnson v Coventry Churchill International Ltd*,[145] the employer, an agency, was held liable when an employee it sent to Germany to work on a construction site was injured due to a lack of site safety. The operators of the site were negligent in having no adequate system of site inspection and hence, the employment agency was in breach of its non-delegable duty to see that care was taken. In contrast, in *Cook v Square D Ltd*[146] the employer was not liable when an employee sent to work in Saudi Arabia was injured when he fell through a hole in the floor at the work site. It was held that the employer had not delegated its responsibility; rather it had satisfied itself that the occupier of the site was reliable and aware of its responsibility for the safety of workers on the site.[147] This does not preclude a claim for contribu-

---

140 [2008] EWCA Civ 494; [2008] I.C.R. 971. There was no appeal on the question of the employer's liability.

141 *Wilson v Tyneside Window Cleaning Co* [1958] 2 Q.B. 110. See the comment of Pearce LJ at 121:

> "Whether the employee is working on the premises of the employer or those of a stranger, that duty is still, as it seems to me, the same; but as a matter of common sense its performance and discharge will probably be vastly different in the two cases."

142 See *Garcia v Harland and Wolff Ltd* [1943] 2 All E.R. 477 at 483, 485; *Smith v Austin Lifts Ltd* [1959] 1 W.L.R. 100 at 118, per Lord Denning: "employers who send their workmen to work on the premises of others cannot renounce all responsibility for their safety. The employers still have an overriding duty to take reasonable care not to expose their men to unnecessary risk. They must, for instance, take reasonable care to devise a safe system of work … and if they know or ought to know of a danger on the premises to which they send their men, they ought to take reasonable care to safeguard them from it. What is reasonable care depends, of course, on the circumstances …"

143 *General Cleaning Contractors Ltd v Christmas* [1953] A.C. 180; see also *Wilson v Tyneside Window Cleaning Co* [1958] 2 Q.B. 110.

144 *Cook v Square D Ltd* [1992] I.C.R. 262 at 269, per Farquharson LJ. Such an inquiry is highly fact-sensitive: *Berry v Ashtead Plant Hire Co Ltd* [2011] EWCA Civ 1304; [2012] P.I.Q.R. P6.

145 [1992] 3 All E.R. 14.

146 [1992] I.C.R. 262.

147 The position might have been different if a number of employees were going to work at a foreign

tion against the occupier.[148]

12-23 Employers' duties in relation to fatal accidents of employees in remote places of work were considered in *Dusek v Stormharbour Securities LLP*,[149] and *Cassley v GMP Securities Europe LLP*.[150] In *Dusek* the employee had been required to take a helicopter trip across the Andes. The weather was stormy and the helicopter crashed, killing all on board. The helicopter was chartered by a Peruvian company with whom the defendant employers were working on an investment project. One carrier advised against using the proposed route because of the dangers involved; however, the Peruvian company went ahead with a carrier that would offer the route. The accident was caused when the crew made a flawed decision to fly the return route in bad weather. The employer owed a duty to take reasonable care to ensure that the employee was safe while travelling to and from work overseas. Given the obvious potential dangers in the trip, the employer owed a duty to inquire into its safety and to conduct a risk assessment. Doing nothing was a breach of the duty of care. Had it conducted a proper risk assessment, the company would have advised its employee not to take the flight. Therefore, causation was established. In *Cassley* the employee was killed when a private charter flight crashed. The carrier had an inadequate culture of safety. A duty was again owed, applying *Dusek*, since travel on private charter flights was an integral part of the employee's work. Again, the employer had taken no steps to discharge that duty. However, in this instance the claim failed on causation. The carrier secured by a charterer had been changed at the last minute. Even if proper enquiries had been made, they would not have related to the carrier which was finally selected. The charterer of the flight also owed a duty of care under *Caparo* principles, although this duty is not non-delegable and the charterer had made reasonable enquiries and thus was not in breach of duty.

12-24 **Safe system of work** This is an over-arching obligation, supporting and supplementing the other aspects of the personal duty. At its lowest, it requires appropriate instruction of the workforce as to the safe performance of the task.[151] But with a task of any complexity, it requires the use of a safe system of work. This may involve the organisation of the work, the procedure to be followed in carrying it out, the sequence of the work, the taking of safety precautions and the stage at which they are to be taken, the number of workers to be employed and the parts to be taken by them, and the provision of any necessary supervision.[152] It can, however, be ap-

site, or one or two were going for a considerable period of time. In that case it would be reasonable for the employer to inspect the site and satisfy himself that the occupiers were conscious of their safety obligations: [1992] I.C.R. 262 at 272.

[148] See *Intruder Detection and Surveillance Fire and Security Ltd v Fulton* [2008] EWCA Civ 1009. An occupier of premises was held liable to make contribution to an employer in respect of injuries sustained by its employee at the occupier's premises (a domestic property). The occupier had been persuaded to allow entry to the injured employee and a supervising employee of the claimant, in order to upgrade the security system. The property was in the process of refurbishment, and the banisters to the upper landing had been removed. No amount of warning could make the premises reasonably safe for this purpose. On the facts, the occupier's share of responsibility was placed at 25 per cent.

[149] [2015] EWHC 37 (QB).

[150] [2015] EWHC 722 (QB).

[151] *General Cleaning Contractors Ltd v Christmas* [1953] A.C. 180 at 189, per Lord Oaksey.

[152] See *Speed v Thomas Swift & Co Ltd* [1943] K.B. 557, especially, per Lord Greene at 563.

plied to a single operation. In *Winter v Cardiff RDC*[153] Lord Oaksey said that where "the mode of operation is complicated or highly dangerous or prolonged or involves a number of men performing different functions", or where it is "of a complicated or unusual character", a system should be prescribed, but "where the operation is simple and the decision how it shall be done has to be taken frequently, it is natural and reasonable that it should be left to the … workman on the spot". When there is an obligation to prescribe a system, the obligation is "to take reasonable steps to provide a system which will be reasonably safe, having regard to the dangers necessarily inherent in the operation".[154] Thus, it is a question of fact whether a system should be prescribed, and in deciding this question regard must be had to the nature of the operation, and whether it is one which requires proper organisation and supervision in the interests of safety. When the operation is one regulated by statute or statutory regulations, compliance with those provisions is evidence, but not conclusive evidence, that the common law duty has been fulfilled[155] because "the reasonable employer is entitled to assume prima facie, that the dangers which occur to a reasonable man have occurred to Parliament or the framers of the regulations",[156] but in exceptional cases or where some special peril is anticipated the common law duty is not restricted by the statutory requirements.[157] A safe system of work will often require that the employer has undertaken an adequate risk assessment.[158] The significance of the duty to undertake an adequate risk assessment, and to act on it accordingly, has become increasingly plain since the decision of the Supreme Court in *Kennedy v Cordia (Services) LLP*.[159] *Kennedy* has been discussed and followed in a range of negligence cases since liability was removed from all but negligent breaches of industrial safety legislation by the Enterprise and Regulatory Reform Act 2013 s.69, for example: *Chisholm v D & R Hankins (Menea) Ltd*[160]; *Cassells v Allan*[161]; *Cockerill v CXK Ltd*[162]; and *Dehenes v T Bourne and Son*.[163]

With the shift in the main work activity from manufacturing to services, the requirement for a safe system of work has been extended to protect employees from **12-25**

---

[153] [1950] 1 All E.R. 819 at 823.

[154] per Lord Tucker in *General Cleaning Contractors Ltd v Christmas* [1953] A.C. 180 at 195.

[155] *Franklin v Gramophone Co Ltd* [1948] 1 K.B. 542, per Somervell LJ at 558; *Chipchase v British Titan Products Co Ltd* [1956] 1 Q.B. 545.

[156] *England v NCB* [1953] 1 Q.B. 724 at 732, per Somervell LJ (the decision of the Court of Appeal was varied by the House of Lords: [1954] A.C. 403).

[157] *NCB v England* [1954] A.C. 403; *Bux v Slough Metals Ltd* [1973] 1 W.L.R. 1358 (breach of common law duty but not of statutory duty). But note that even where failure to give instructions does not amount to negligence at common law, there may still be a breach of statutory duty: *Boyle v Kodak Ltd* [1969] 1 W.L.R. 661.

[158] See *Vaile v London Borough of Havering* [2011] EWCA Civ 246; [2011] E.L.R. 274 where an education authority was held liable to a teacher injured in an attack by a 14-year-old autistic pupil. Although the claimant could not identify what precise steps should have been taken in order to prevent the attack, this was the result of a failure to assess the risks posed by the pupil in light of his behaviour, and a proper risk assessment would have led to the identification of steps which would have avoided the injuries. See further para.12-55 in relation to an employer's statutory duty to undertake risk assessments under the Management of Health and Safety at Work Regulations.

[159] [2016] UKSC 6; [2016] 1 W.L.R. 597; discussed in para.12-35.

[160] [2018] EWHC 3407 (QB).

[161] [2019] CSOH 14.

[162] [2018] EWHC 1155 (QB).

[163] 2019 S.L.T. (Sh Ct) 219, 2 May 2019, Sheriff Personal Injury Court.

mental stress and its consequences. In *Walker v Northumberland CC*[164] the employer was held liable for the psychiatric illness suffered by a social work employee as a result of work stress. The employer had failed to respond to a request for assistance from the employee when it knew that he had already suffered an earlier breakdown because of the burden of work placed upon him and the lack of a system to provide relief. The first breakdown made the second breakdown more readily foreseeable, but in many cases of this nature the employer will simply be unaware of the particular circumstances which give rise to a risk of psychiatric injury to the particular employee, given that many white collar managerial jobs are stressful, and it may be argued that, unknown to the employer, the claimant was unduly susceptible to the risk of psychiatric illness.[165] Moreover, the damage must take the form of a recognised psychiatric illness or disorder. There is no duty to protect an employee from unpleasant emotions such as grief, anger and resentment or normal human conditions such as anxiety or stress, since "these do not involve any form of 'injury' at all".[166]

12-26 **Supervision** When there is a duty to provide a safe system of work, the employer does not discharge the whole duty merely by providing it, but must take reasonable steps to see that it is carried out.[167] This involves instruction of the employee in the system[168] as well as some measure of supervision. It does not mean "that an employer is bound, through his foreman, to stand over workmen of age and experience every moment they are working and every time that they cease work, in order to see that they do what they are supposed to do".[169] The employer must take reasonable care to see that the system is followed, and it is a question of degree and of fact whether this has been done in every individual case. In *Nolan v Dental Manufacturing Co Ltd*[170] a workman was blinded while sharpening a tool on a grinder when a chip flew off and entered his eye. It was held that the common law duty of the defendants was not only to provide him with goggles but also to issue "strict orders that they were to be used, and to supervise their workmen, at any rate to a reasonable extent, in order to ensure that their orders were obeyed". In some circumstances the risk may be so great that the employer has a duty to issue an absolute prohibition against using a dangerous method of working.[171] On the other

---

164 [1995] 1 All E.R. 737.

165 See further para.12-39.

166 *Fraser v State Hospitals Board for Scotland*, 2001 S.L.T. 1051 at [129], per Lord Carloway.

167 *Barcock v Brighton Corp* [1949] 1 K.B. 339 at 343; *Crookall v Vickers-Armstrong Ltd* [1955] 1 W.L.R. 659.

168 *General Cleaning Contractors Ltd v Christmas* [1953] A.C. 180. In *Kerry v Carter* [1969] 1 W.L.R. 1372, the Court of Appeal held that the defendant should have inquired into the experience of the claimant, an apprentice, in working circular saws and should have supervised him more closely.

169 per Singleton LJ in *Woods v Durable Suites Ltd* [1953] 1 W.L.R. 857 at 862.

170 [1958] 1 W.L.R. 936 at 942, per Paull J. See also *Pape v Cumbria CC* [1992] I.C.R. 132; [1992] 3 All E.R. 211 QBD, where the employers were held liable for the claimant's dermatitis caused by contact with cleaning products, notwithstanding the provision of protective gloves, on the basis of a failure to warn cleaning staff of the danger of sustained exposure of the skin to the chemicals and a failure to instruct staff to wear protective gloves at all times; cf. *Qualcast (Wolverhampton) Ltd v Haynes* [1959] A.C. 743 where the employer provided protective boots against the obvious danger of splashes of molten metal, but did not urge employees to wear them; the claimant wore his own boots and the employer was held not liable.

171 *King v Smith* [1995] I.C.R. 339, CA: window cleaner standing on the exterior sill of a second floor window, with no means of attaching a safety harness.

hand, it may be reasonable to expect experienced workers to guard against obvious dangers[172]; and it has been said that it is not necessary:

> "for an employer to tell a skilled and experienced man at regular intervals things of which he is well aware unless there is reason to believe that that man is failing to adopt the proper precautions or, through familiarity, becoming contemptuous of them."[173]

Duty to warn of obvious dangers Despite this, in *Ammah v Kuehne+Nagel Logistics Ltd*,[174] the Court of Appeal emphasised that in many circumstances, there is a duty on employers to warn employees of even obvious risks. Richards LJ quoted a passage from *General Cleaning Contractors Ltd v Christmas*,[175] where leaving it to individual employees to take precautions against an obvious danger amounted to a failure to discharge the employer's duty to provide a reasonably safe system of work. Indeed the likelihood that individuals will often overlook obvious dangers is part of the rationale for the existence of the duty: 12-27

> "… It is, I think, well known to employers … that their workpeople are very frequently, if not habitually, careless about the risks which their work may involve. It is, in my opinion, for that very reason that the common law demands that employers should take reasonable care to lay down a reasonably safe system of work."

In *Ammah* itself, the Court of Appeal dismissed the claim because there was evidence that the claimant had indeed been warned not to stand on boxes to reach things from high shelves, and that he had been advised of available safe means of doing so.

If it is probable that the worker would not have used the safety equipment provided, or obeyed instructions to use them, the employer will not be liable.[176] Where the employer does not instruct the employee as to what equipment to use and the latter does not trouble to find out, responsibility will be apportioned.[177] The employer will be liable, however, if it can be shown that the employee would have made use of the proper equipment had it been provided. 12-28

(c) Standard of care expected of an employer

General Taking reasonable care is always a question of fact.[178] In *Qualcast (Wolverhampton) Ltd v Haynes*[179] the House of Lords emphasised this point and deprecated the tendency to present decisions on questions of fact, such as these, as propositions of law. However, some general guidance can be drawn from the case 12-29

---

172 *Wilson v Tyneside Window Cleaning Co* [1958] 2 Q.B. 110.

173 *Baker v T Clarke (Leeds) Ltd* [1992] P.I.Q.R. P262 at 267, per Stuart-Smith LJ. See also *Rozario v The Post Office* [1997] P.I.Q.R. P15 CA.

174 [2009] EWCA Civ 11.

175 *General Cleaning Contractors Ltd v Christmas* [1953] A.C. 180 at 189–190, per Lord Oaksey.

176 *McWilliams v Sir William Arrol & Co Ltd* [1962] 1 W.L.R. 295; see para.2-13.

177 *Ross v Associated Portland Cement Manufacturers Ltd* [1964] 1 W.L.R. 768.

178 It must therefore be established on the balance of probabilities. The need to establish breach of duty was reiterated by the Court of Appeal in *Brett v University of Reading* [2007] EWCA Civ 88. In this case, the evidence was taken to establish that there had been exposure to asbestos at work. Applying the principles in *Fairchild v Glenhaven Funeral Services Ltd* [2002] UKHL 22; [2003] 1 A.C. 32, this would be sufficient indication of a causal link between his employment and his mesothelioma, since the exposure would increase the risk of the disease. However, the evidence "did not begin to establish a breach of duty on the part of the [defendant]" (Maurice Kay LJ at [26]).

179 [1959] A.C. 743.

law. The standard of care required has been described as "high",[180] but this means no more than that the precautions required vary with the circumstances, and the dangers involved in a work situation may require considerable care.[181] The common practice of other employers in the same work area may provide guidance. Thus, in *Thompson v Smiths Shiprepairers (North Shields) Ltd*[182] it was held that where there had long been a general practice of inaction with regard to the possibility of deafness through industrial noise, the defendants were only liable for failure to take steps once there was awareness of the danger and protective equipment had become available.[183] But the employer must allow for the fact that employees may be inadvertent or become heedless of the risks, particularly where they are encountered on a regular basis. This will involve taking reasonable steps, not only to instruct employees on safety procedures, but also to ensure that the procedures are followed.[184] Failure to follow common practice is not necessarily negligent, as for example, where there is conflicting evidence as to its utility.[185] In the context of a hospital, for example, where the employer also owes duties to other parties (in this instance, the patients), complex questions may arise concerning the nature of the duty to employees and others. The content of the duty owed to the employee may in principle be quite different from the content of the duty owed to others.[186]

12-30 The duty is owed to each employee individually, so that all the circumstances relevant to each employee must be taken into account. This is of special relevance in respect of stress-related injury.[187] If the employee is known to have only one eye a greater degree of care must be shown towards him than towards a man with two eyes, so that if he is employed at work involving the risk of a chip of metal entering his eye, goggles should be provided for him, although this may not be necessary for a man with two eyes.[188] An employer's lack of knowledge of the risk to employees may itself be evidence of a negligent failure to assess risk[189] but if the

---

180 *Winter v Cardiff Rural DC* [1950] 1 All E.R. 819 at 822, per Lord Porter.

181 *Davie v New Merton Board Mills Ltd* [1959] A.C. 604 at 620, per Viscount Simonds: "the subject-matter may be such that the taking of reasonable care may fall little short of absolute obligation."

182 [1984] Q.B. 405. See also *Gray v Stead* [1999] 2 Lloyd's Rep. 559 CA; and *Heyes v Pilkington Glass Ltd* [1998] P.I.Q.R. P303 CA, on following common practice in the relevant industry.

183 Mustill J suggested, [1984] Q.B. 405 at 423, that the question was: "From what date would a reasonable employer, with proper but not extraordinary solicitude for the welfare of his workers, have identified the problem of excessive noise in his yard, recognised that it was capable of solution, found a possible solution, weighed up the potential advantages and disadvantages of that solution, decided to adopt it, acquired a supply of the protectors, set in train the programme of education necessary to persuade the men and their representatives that the system was useful and not potentially deleterious, experimented with the system, and finally put it into full effect?" On the practicability of precautions against noise induced deafness see *Harris v BRB (Residuary) Ltd* [2005] EWCA Civ 900; [2005] I.C.R. 1680; [2006] P.I.Q.R. P10; and the Control of Noise at Work Regulations 2005 (SI 2005/1643), applying not only to employees but also to others at work. For discussion of *Harris* see T.D. Huckle, "Not Listening or Just Not Hearing …? The Noise Exposure Threshold in Deafness Claims" [2007] J.P.I.L. 23.

184 *Clifford v Charles H Challen & Son Ltd* [1951] 1 K.B. 495.

185 *Brown v Rolls Royce Ltd* [1960] 1 W.L.R. 210: differing evidence as to utility of barrier creams.

186 *Buck v Nottinghamshire Healthcare NHS Trust* [2006] EWCA Civ 1576; (2006) 93 B.M.L.R. 28.

187 See para.12-37.

188 *Paris v Stepney BC* [1951] A.C. 367.

189 *Baker v James Bros & Sons Ltd* [1921] 2 K.B. 674 at 680, McCardie J: "the absence of knowledge may itself be the basis of the charge of negligence." Note that there is a statutory duty on employers actively to assess risks to employees: Management of Health and Safety at Work Regulations 1999 (SI 1999/3242).

harm was truly unforeseeable there will be no breach of duty.[190] In the case of occupational disease foreseeability of the risk of injury of the same type is sufficient; the defendant does not have to foresee the precise disease that the employee is likely to contract.[191] The knowledge of employees in a management position may be imputed to the employer[192] but this may not be the case with knowledge of a mere employee.[193] Where there is knowledge of the risk, the response of the employer must be reasonable. And if the employer had particular knowledge of some fact which makes harm to the claimant more likely than would otherwise be the case, then as a reasonable man he must take account of that. A greater than average knowledge of the risks will entail more than the average or standard precautions.[194]

Sufficient knowledge Where knowledge of the risks to employees within an industry is developing over time issues will arise as to when an employer's knowledge has reached the point at which it would be unreasonable to fail to take precautions against that risk and whether different employers are subject to different criteria. In *Baker v Quantum Clothing Group Ltd*[195] the question was when it would have been reasonable to expect an employer to be aware of the risks of deafness from exposing an employee to noise rated between 85 and 90dB(A)lepd. A Code of Practice issued by the Department of Employment in 1972 recommended that a noise level of 90dB(A)lepd should not be exceeded. The judge held that it would have been unreasonable to expect most employers to have been aware of the problem of noise levels between 85 and 90dB(A)lepd until publication of a consultative document in 1987, but that two of the employers had greater awareness of the problem from 1983 and so were in breach of their duty in not providing protection from the beginning of 1985. In the Supreme Court a majority[196] considered that the correct approach to the common law duty was to take as a starting point the relevant Code of Practice, which required protection where there was exposure to decibel levels in excess of 90dB(A)lepd, but did not require protection against the slightly lower levels to which the claim related. Applying "classic statements" on the content of the employer's duty,[197] it was held that a reasonable employer could legitimately rely upon the standards set by the Code of Practice, unless certain exceptions applied, namely that the established practice was "clearly bad", or, if the situation was one where there was developing knowledge about the risks involved, and the employer had "greater than average knowledge of the risks".[198] In such circumstances the employer would be treated differently from the "average employer" in that they were required to act on the knowledge that they 12-31

---

[190] *Pearce v Stanley Bridges Ltd* [1965] 1 W.L.R. 931.

[191] *Jeromson v Shell Tankers (UK) Ltd* [2001] EWCA Civ 101; [2001] I.C.R. 1223: where it was known that exposure to asbestos dust could produce lung disease it was irrelevant that the specific link between asbestos and mesothelioma was not established until a later date.

[192] *Taylor v Rover Co Ltd* [1966] 1 W.L.R. 1491.

[193] *Cole v De Trafford (No.2)* [1918] 2 K.B. 523 at 537: Scrutton LJ: "knowledge is not imputed to [the employer] because a fellow workman knew and negligently did not remedy or ought to have found out danger and negligently did not discover it."

[194] *Stokes v Guest, Keen & Nettlefold (Bolts & Nuts) Ltd* [1968] 1 W.L.R. 1776 at 1783, per Swanwick J.

[195] [2011] UKSC 17; [2011] 1 W.L.R. 1003.

[196] Lords Mance, Dyson and Saville.

[197] In *Stokes v Guest Keen and Nettlefold (Bolt & Nuts) Ltd* [1968] 1 W.L.R. 1776; and *Thompson v Smiths Shiprepairers (North Shields) Ltd* [1984] Q.B. 405.

[198] [2011] UKSC 17; [2011] 1 W.L.R. 1003 at [23], per Lord Mance JSC. Contrast the dissenting

actually had, even though this appears to penalise employers "who have a safety department and medical officers and take noise more seriously than the ordinary reasonable employer".[199]

12-32 **Application to cases of mesothelioma** With cases of low level exposure to asbestos, liability has been defeated on the basis that there has been no breach of duty either at common law or in the case of those statutory duties interpreted as akin to negligence. The general approach to breach of duty, as elaborated in *Baker v Quantum Clothing*, remains applicable to mesothelioma cases, notwithstanding the modification of the test for causation in such cases.[200] In *Williams v University of Birmingham*[201] the Court of Appeal held that the correct test in relation to breach of duty in mesothelioma cases was not whether the defendant exercised reasonable care to avoid exposing the claimant to a *material increase of the risk* of developing mesothelioma, but whether the defendant exercised reasonable care to ensure that the claimant was not exposed to a foreseeable risk of asbestos-related injury (with the question of foreseeability to be judged by reference to the state of knowledge and practice at the time). The test for establishing causation may have been modified by the House of Lords in *Fairchild*, but there was nothing to suggest that the test for breach of duty in mesothelioma cases had been altered so that a claimant only had to demonstrate that the defendant failed to take reasonable steps to ensure that the claimant or victim was not exposed to a "material increase in the risk of mesothelioma".[202] In *Bussey v 00654701 Ltd (formerly Anglia Heating)*[203] the Court of Appeal provided important clarification of an issue raised by the decision in *Williams*, without questioning the result of the decision itself nor other aspects of its reasoning. In *Bussey*, the first instance judge had felt bound by *Williams* to decide that the claimant could not succeed if his exposure by the defendant, which took place between 1965 and 1968, was at a level below that provided

opinions of Lord Kerr and Lord Clarke which emphasised the duty of all employers to give positive thought to the risks posed to employees by their undertaking, irrespective of established practice. A Code of Practice could not absolve employers from a common law duty to protect their employees from a discoverable risk of harm at lower noise levels.

199 [2011] UKSC 17; [2011] 1 W.L.R. 1003 at [25] per Lord Mance; see also para.7-163.

200 See *Fairchild v Glenhaven Funeral Services Ltd* [2002] UKHL 22; [2003] 1 A.C. 32, para.2-53 onwards.

201 [2011] EWCA Civ 1242; [2012] P.I.Q.R P4.

202 [2011] EWCA Civ 1242; [2012] P.I.Q.R P4 at [40]. See also *Asmussen v Filtrona United Kingdom Ltd* [2011] EWHC 1734 (QB) at [55] (approved by Aikens LJ in *Williams v University of Birmingham* [2011] EWCA Civ 1242; [2012] P.I.Q.R P4 at [37]); *McDonald v Department for Communities and Local Government* [2014] UKSC 53; [2015] A.C. 1128 (on the state of knowledge at the time injury was not foreseeable from the level of exposure to asbestos experienced by the claimant); *McGregor v Genco (FC) Ltd* [2014] EWHC 1376 (QB) (to similar effect); *Hill v John Barnsley & Sons Ltd* [2013] EWHC 520 (QB) (claimant succeeded on the basis of the levels of exposure to asbestos established, and the employers' failure to take adequate precautions); *McCarthy v Marks and Spencer Plc* [2014] EWHC 3183 (QB) (where mesothelioma had not been foreseeable by the standards of the time); *Woodward v Secretary of State for Energy and Climate Change* [2015] EWHC 3604 (QB) (where the employer had acted reasonably in following guidance set out at the time by the Health and Safety Executive); *Smith v Portswood House Ltd* [2016] EWHC 939 (QB) (where foreseeability at the time of the alleged exposure was to be judged according to the requirements of a *Factories Inspectorate Technical Note* issued in 1970). These decisions must now be read subject to the decision in *Bussey v 00654701 Ltd (formerly Anglia Heating)* [2018] EWCA Civ 243; [2018] 3 All E.R. 354, which calls into question some of their reasoning. In particular, it clarifies that the Technical Note referred to in Smith v Portswood House does not set a definitive "acceptable level" for exposure. See the main text of this paragraph.

203 [2018] EWCA Civ 243; [2018] 3 All E.R. 354.

in Technical Data Note 13 ("TDN13"), which was published by HM Factory Inspectorate in 1970. It appeared that the Court in *Williams* had referred to this as establishing what was considered to be an "acceptable level" of exposure at the relevant time. In *Bussey* the Court of Appeal considered that TDN13 did not set such a definitive level for exposure either in 1970, or before that time. Rather, the test for the content of the employer's duty where knowledge was developing continued to be that set out by Swanwick J in *Stokes v Guest Keen and Nettlefold*.[204] Applying the general foreseeability test to the circumstances of Bussey itself, the question was whether the employer ought to have foreseen, during the period 1965–1968, that if Mr *Bussey* cut and caulked pipes in the manner he did, he would be exposed to an unacceptable risk of asbestos-related injury? TDN13 did not set out a bright line and when he treated it as significant, Aikens LJ in *Williams* had not been setting out a principle of law. A more nuanced approach was required, asking what knowledge an employer ought to have acquired at the relevant time and determining what risks the employer should have foreseen. TDN13 should not be seen as a universal test of foreseeability in mesothelioma cases. By 1965, it had begun to be realised that there was no safe level of exposure, and that exposure to "relatively small quantities" of asbestos dust was associated with the risk of mesothelioma. Rather, TDN13 set out the levels that would trigger a prosecution by the Factory Inspectorate. The issue of foreseeability needs to be considered in light of what the employer knew or ought to have known at the relevant time. In *Bussey* itself, this question had not been considered at trial, and the case was returned to the trial judge for redetermination.[205]

Risk The mere foreseeability of a risk does not give rise to breach of duty if it is one which could be met by employees taking obvious precautions. Thus, in *Jaguar Cars Ltd v Coates*[206] the Court of Appeal held that steps without a handrail posed no real risk to those using them with reasonable care and that the judge who had held there to be a breach, had "erred by equating foreseeability of risk with a finding of a duty to install a rail". Where the employer ought to realise that a work practice poses serious risk to employees, the onus is on the employer to show that it was impractical to control or eliminate the risk. In *Brown v Corus (UK) Ltd*[207] the claimants developed hand/arm vibration syndrome as a result of using vibrating tools and being exposed to vibration greatly exceeding the recommended maximum. The employer was aware of the risk of such injury. The trial judge found the employer to be in breach of duty in failing to provide proper training in the use of the tool or proper medical surveillance but he also held that these breaches were not causative because even if training and surveillance had been provided, the injuries would still have occurred. He also held that the employer was not in breach in failing to secure a reduction in the exposure to vibration because he considered (on the basis of no evidence) that the costs of reduction through either restricted working time or using mechanical alternatives to handheld tools, would have been **12-33**

204 [1968] 1 W.L.R. 1776; see para.12-30.

205 See also *Hawkes v Warmex Ltd* [2018] EWHC 205 (QB): an employer would be liable if any form of asbestos-related disease was foreseeable, and it had failed to reduce exposure to the greatest extent practicable; if read correctly, there was no conflict between the approach in *Jeromson v Shell Tankers Ltd* [2001] EWCA Civ 101; [2001] I.C.R. 1223 (see para.12-30); and *Williams v University of Birmingham*.

206 [2004] EWCA Civ 337.

207 [2004] EWCA Civ 374; [2004] P.I.Q.R. P30.

unreasonably high. The Court of Appeal reversed this latter finding. Scott Baker LJ said:

> "Once [the judge] had concluded that the appellants had been subjected to excessive levels of vibration the burden shifted to the respondents to justify why that situation was allowed to continue. It was not open to the judge to speculate on matters such as cost and resistance to change in working practices. These were matters which required evidence if the [employer] wished to use them to justify maintaining unchanged the excessive level of vibration.... It is not open to [the employer] to provide a system that is unsafe and fail to improve it expecting the employee to justify what should have been done."[208]

The court concluded that the failure to reduce vibration exposure was "in plain breach of duty" and was causative of the damage.

12-34 If a significant risk cannot be reduced to safe levels, then the employer must warn employees and prospective employees[209] of the danger so that they can take an informed decision about undertaking the work and the risk. Over 50 years ago, Devlin LJ said that "there is no legal duty upon an employer to prevent an adult employee from doing work which he or she is willing to do"[210] but it is suggested that some risks may be so significant that to allow even a fully informed employee to continue with the risky work will constitute a breach of duty.[211] Thus, in *Doherty v Rugby Joinery (UK) Ltd*[212] the Court of Appeal held that once the employer should have been aware of the symptoms of vibration syndrome affecting some employees,

---

208 [2004] EWCA Civ 374; [2004] P.I.Q.R. P30 at [34]. See also *Brookes v South Yorkshire Passenger Transport Executive* [2005] EWCA Civ 452; and *Doherty v Rugby Joinery (UK) Ltd* [2004] EWCA Civ 147; [2004] I.C.R. 1272 on the dates from which employers should have been aware of the risk to employees of developing vibration white finger. The Control of Vibration at Work Regulations 2005 (SI 2005/1093) (implementing the European Physical Agents (Vibration) Directive 2002/44/EC) impose duties on employers to protect employees who may be exposed to vibration at work, and other persons who might be affected by the work, whether they are at work or not. The Regulations, inter alia, require the elimination of vibration at source or, where this is not reasonably practicable, a reduction to as low a level as is reasonably practicable, and set daily exposure limits. They came into force on 6 July 2005. See also *Harris v BRB (Residuary) Ltd* [2005] EWCA Civ 900; [2005] I.C.R. 1680; [2006] P.I.Q.R. P10, where the Court of Appeal held the employer liable for failing to provide ear protection against known noise exposure. Neuberger LJ commented at [66]: "the defendant, having been aware of the problem and of the possible solution, either failed to translate words and thoughts into action, or took the view that to do so would be more trouble than it was worth, and that it would be better to run the risk of facing the possibility of future claims."

209 In *White v Holbrook Precision Castings Ltd* [1985] I.R.L.R. 215 at 218, Lawton LJ said: "If a job has risks to health and safety which are not common knowledge but of which an employer knows or ought to know and against which he cannot guard by taking precautions, then he should tell anyone to whom he is offering the job what those risks are if, on the information available to him, knowledge of those risks would be likely to affect the decision of a sensible, level-headed prospective employee about accepting the offer."

210 *Withers v Perry Chain Co Ltd* [1961] 1 W.L.R. 1314 at 1320. In *Henderson v Wakefield Shirt Co Ltd* [1997] P.I.Q.R. P413 the Court of Appeal held that if an employee developed work-related symptoms a reasonable employer would reconsider whether the equipment provided or the particular system of work created any particular risk to the employee. But if there were no reasonable changes that could be made, the employer does not have to offer a wholly different job to, or to dismiss or remove, the employee. See now, however, *Coxall v Goodyear Great Britain Ltd* [2002] EWCA Civ 1010; [2003] 1 W.L.R. 536 and *Lane Group Plc v Farmiloe* [2004] P.I.Q.R. P22 (EAT), below.

211 Devlin LJ's dictum is echoed in the guidance of Hale LJ in *Hatton v Sutherland* [2002] EWCA Civ 76; [2002] I.C.R. 613; [2002] 2 All E.R. 1, in relation to stress and was cited with approval by Lord Rodger in the House of Lords in that case, although he did reserve the question of how the reasoning was affected by requirements to carry out risk assessment: *Barber v Somerset CC* [2004] UKHL 13; [2004] 1 W.L.R 1089 at [30]. See further para.12-37.

212 [2004] EWCA Civ 147; [2004] I.C.R. 1272.

its duty was not simply to restrict them to use of the tools for no longer than the maximum recommended period, but to ensure that they did not use vibrating tools at all. In *Coxall v Goodyear Great Britain Ltd*[213] the Court of Appeal held that the question of whether an employer was under a duty to remove an employee from work which exposed him to a risk of physical danger depended on the magnitude of the risk. The defendants had been negligent in failing to follow the advice of their works doctor and either move the claimant (who developed occupational asthma) to alternative work or dismiss him. In *Lane Group Plc v Farmiloe*[214] the Employment Appeal Tribunal applied *Coxall*, holding that if an employer had continued to employ a worker in breach of the Personal Protective Equipment Regulations 1992 it would have been in breach of its common law duty of care to the employee. Thus "there may be cases where an employer is under a duty at law to dismiss the employee so as to protect him from danger".[215] At the least, the employer must supply the necessary protective clothing or appliances and take reasonable steps to see that they are used.[216] This may be done by giving the workmen instruction in the protective steps to be taken[217]; but if management knows that these steps are not being taken and does nothing to enforce them, the employer will be liable.[218]

Duty to conduct risk assessments In *Kennedy v Cordia (Services) LLP*,[219] the Supreme Court emphasised that it has become generally accepted that a prudent employer will conduct a risk assessment in connection with its operations, so that it can take suitable precautions to avoid injury to its employees. Importantly, this is the case whether (as in the instant case) there is a statutory duty to do so, or not. Further, the requirement to carry out such an assessment, whether statutory or not, "forms the context in which the employer has to take precautions in the exercise of reasonable care for the safety of its employees". Citing *Threlfall v Kingston-upon-Hull City Council*[220] and *Fytche v Wincanton Logistics Plc*,[221] both of which concerned breach of regulations rather than common law duties, the Supreme Court emphasised that the duty to conduct a risk assessment "is logically anterior to determining what precautions a reasonable employer would have taken in order to fulfil his common law duty of care". The significance of this is that an employer's duty at common law in relation to omissions—here, the omission to provide protective footwear to reduce the risk of slipping on ice and snow—is not confined to taking such precautions as are commonly taken, or which would be taken by "anyone". The employee working away from the employer's premises is not in the same position as anyone else, as they have less choice about whether to encounter risks. At common law, the employer has a duty to seek out risks and to "inquire into possible means of reducing that risk". If these inquiries had been made in the instant case, Cordia would have discovered that attachments to footwear were available at 12-35

---

213 [2002] EWCA Civ 1010; [2003] 1 W.L.R. 536.

214 [2004] P.I.Q.R. P22 (EAT).

215 [2004] P.I.Q.R. P22 (EAT) at [43].

216 *Finch v Telegraph Construction and Maintenance Co* [1949] 1 All E.R. 452; *Nolan v Dental Manufacturing Co Ltd* [1958] 1 W.L.R. 936 at 941–942; *McWilliams v Sir William Arrol & Co Ltd* [1962] 1 W.L.R. 295.

217 *Woods v Durable Suites Ltd* [1953] 1 W.L.R. 857; *Quinn v Horsfall and Bickham Ltd* [1956] 1 W.L.R. 652.

218 *Clifford v Charles H Challen & Son Ltd* [1951] 1 K.B. 495.

219 [2016] UKSC 6; [2016] 1 W.L.R. 597.

220 [2010] EWCA Civ 1147; [2011] I.C.R. 209 (see para. 12-56).

221 [2004] UKHL 31; [2004] 4 All E.R. 221; [2004] I.C.R. 975 (see paras 12-59 and 12-60).

modest cost which would have reduced the risk of slipping; and that other employers had provided them. Therefore, the Lord Ordinary had been entitled to conclude that Cordia were negligent.

12-36 In *Cockerill v CXK Ltd*,[222] it was again emphasised, relying on *Kennedy v Cordia Services LLP*,[223] that risk assessments play a significant role in the content and discharge of an employer's duty of care. It remained relevant to consider reg.3(1) of the Management of Health and Safety at Work Regulations 1999, requiring a suitable and sufficient risk assessment. While this no longer creates an actionable duty to carry out a risk assessment, making such a risk assessment "is an obvious measure for an employer to take in discharge of its duty of care".[224] The decision in *Cockerill* illustrates both the continued relevance of some of the Regulations and the change in the law brought about by Enterprise and Regulatory Reform Act 2013 s.69.[225] The employer had not conducted its own risk assessment, but on the evidence had considered an existing risk assessment in relation to premises which it had hired on a short-term basis. Whether or not this omission was capable of being a technical breach of the Regulations (a point which was not decided), it would not be considered negligent. Reliance on the existing risk assessment was reasonable and a new assessment was unlikely to have made any difference to the precautions taken. The risk (posed by an uneven step) was not one which would be appreciated only by application of expertise or special knowledge, and the employee was not in a particularly vulnerable position in relation to the risk.[226] The existing precautions—marking the step with hazard tape—amounted to a reasonable response. The significance of risk assessment for the analysis of breach of the duty of care at common law is also illustrated by the decision in *Cassells v Allan*.[227] Here, the deceased had been run down by a coach while "greeting" the vehicle in the car park in the course of her employment. The second defendant's risk assessment did not consider the risk involved in this practice, and this was a negligent omission. Consideration of the risk would have led to the practice being discontinued so that the omission was a cause of the injury. The fact that, after an incident, a risk assessment is broadened to include the risk that has now eventuated, does not imply that the original omission of the risk assessment was negligent: this would be to judge the issue with hindsight. In *Shelbourne v Cancer Research UK*,[228] an employer had not been negligent in failing to include in their risk assessment the possibility that an inebriated employee would act dangerously on the dance floor at an office party. Context was all-important, and previous parties had not given rise to any similar behaviour.

---

[222] [2018] EWHC 1155 (QB).

[223] [2016] UKSC 6; [2016] 1 W.L.R. 597; see para.13-35.

[224] See also *Dehenes v T Bourne and Son*, 2019 S.L.T. (Sh Ct) 219, 2 May 2019, Sheriff Personal Injury Court. The Manual Handling Operations Regulations 1992 were relevant in defining the common law duty of care, and in particular in defining what was a suitable and sufficient risk assessment: "The state of knowledge which has built up amongst employers over the last few decades as regards health and safety is also important to consider. This includes the concept of carrying out a suitable and sufficient risk assessment" (ibid. at [10]).

[225] See paras 12-02 and 12-46.

[226] [2018] EWHC 1155 (QB) at [82].

[227] [2019] CSOH 14.

[228] [2019] EWHC 842 (QB); [2019] P.I.Q.R. P16.

Occupational stress In *Barber v Somerset CC*[229] the House of Lords considered the standard of care expected of an employer in respect of the prevention of stress causing psychiatric illness to employees. The claimant was a teacher who had been off work with stress and depression caused by his workload. On his return to work, he complained to the management about his work pressures but did not refer to his stress. Management was unsympathetic and after no measures were taken to help him, the stress-related illness returned and he had to leave work. The trial judge found the employer to be in breach of its duty; the Court of Appeal[230] reversed the finding but the House of Lords restored it with a damages award of £72,500. Delivering judgment of the Court of Appeal, Hale LJ gave guidance on the handling of occupational stress claims: there are no occupations which are inherently dangerous to mental health since it is not the job, but the interaction between the individual and the job which causes the harm: 12-37

> "Stress is a subjective concept: the individual's perception that the pressures placed upon him are greater than he may be able to meet. Adverse reactions to stress are equally individual, ranging from minor physical symptoms to major mental illness."[231]

However, the nature of psychiatric illness is such that it is inevitably more difficult to foresee than physical injury. Issues which go to the foreseeability of the psychiatric harm include:

(1) The nature and extent of the work being done by the employee (is the employer putting pressure on the individual employee; are there signs that other employees are also suffering from the effects of stress?)
(2) The signs from the employee himself, and in this context there is a distinction between "signs of stress and signs of impending harm to health. Stress is merely the mechanism which may but usually does not lead to damage to health".
(3) "Unless he knows of some particular problem or vulnerability, an employer is usually entitled to assume that his employee is up to the normal pressures of the job. It is only if there is something specific about the job or the employee or the combination of the two that he has to think harder. But thinking harder does not necessarily mean that he has to make searching or intrusive enquiries. Generally he is entitled to take what he is told by the employee at face value."

So if the employee has been off work sick and then returns to work without giving any indication to the employer that there is a continuing problem this can usually be taken to imply that the employee believes himself fit to return to the work which he was doing before.[232] In the House of Lords, Lord Scott endorsed[233] the guidance in the Court of Appeal's judgment, although Lord Walker specifically endorsed

[229] [2004] UKHL 13; [2004] 1 W.L.R. 1089; [2004] I.C.R. 457.

[230] The case was joined with others and is reported as *Hatton v Sutherland* [2002] EWCA Civ 76; [2002] I.C.R. 613; [2002] 2 All E.R. 1.

[231] [2002] EWCA Civ 76; [2002] 2 All E.R. 1 at [24].

[232] [2002] EWCA Civ 76; [2002] 2 All E.R. 1 at [26]–[29]. See also at [43] of Hale LJ's judgment where the guidance is summarised. See *Pakenham-Walsh v Connell Residential* [2006] EWCA Civ 90; [2006] All E.R. (D) 275, where it was held that the stress suffered by an estate agent was unforeseeable given the lack of absence from work, complaint or other warning signs; *Rothwell v Chemical & Insulating Co* [2007] UKHL 39; [2008] 1 A.C. 281, where the House of Lords held that psychiatric injury resulting from anxiety due to exposure to noxious substances at work was not foreseeable and hence no duty was owed under the *Barber* principle (see further para.7-97); *French v Sussex CC*

only the Court's observation that an employer is entitled to take what he is told by the employee at face value.[234] However, whilst the Court of Appeal and Lord Scott, dissenting, in the Lords considered that, on the facts of *Barber*, the management did not have a sufficiently clear warning of the danger of stress-related illness, Lord Walker and the majority concluded that although close to the borderline, the employer was in breach of duty: when the complaint was made to management it should have investigated further instead of "brushing him off unsympathetically" or "simply telling him to prioritise his work".

12-38 In *Yapp v Foreign and Commonwealth Office*[235] the Court of Appeal reviewed *Barber* and subsequent cases in relation to occupational stress and arrived at a summary of how questions of foreseeability and remoteness should be applied:

(1) In considering, in the context of the common law duty of care, whether it is reasonably foreseeable that the acts or omissions of the employer may cause an employee to suffer a psychiatric injury, such an injury will not usually be foreseeable unless there were indications, of which the employer was or should have been aware, of some problem or psychological vulnerability on the part of the employee (derived from *Barber v Somerset*).

(2) That approach extends to cases where the employer has committed a one-off act of unfairness such as the imposition of a disciplinary sanction.

(3) In neither kind of case should that be regarded as an absolute rule: *Barber* contains no more than guidance and each case must turn on its own facts.

(4) In claims for breach of the common law duty of care it is immaterial that the duty arises in contract as well as tort: they are in substance treated as covered by tortious rules. In order to establish whether the duty is broken, it will be necessary to establish whether psychiatric injury was reasonably foreseeable; and if that is established, no issue as to remoteness can arise when such injury eventuates.

(5) In claims for breach of express contractual term, the contractual test of remoteness will be applicable.

In *Yapp* itself, the claimant had been suddenly withdrawn from his post in response to allegations of misconduct which proved to be untrue. He later developed a depressive illness. There were no prior signs of vulnerability to stress. The Court pointed out that, in principle, an employer's conduct in a particular case may be so devastating that it is foreseeable that even a person of ordinary robustness might develop a depressive illness as a result. In this particular case, however, it was concluded that it was not reasonably foreseeable that the defendant's action in withdrawing the claimant from his post without giving him the opportunity to state

---

[2006] EWCA Civ 312; *The Times,* 5 April 2006, where the Court of Appeal struck out an occupational stress claim on the grounds that the stress was not foreseeable (see para.7-79); *Deadman v Bristol City Council* [2007] EWCA Civ 822; [2008] P.I.Q.R. P2, where it was held that the employer's breach of procedure in investigating a complaint against the claimant employee, was not a foreseeable cause of the claimant's psychiatric illness given that "to all appearances he was a person of robust good health" (at [32]); *Easton v B&Q* [2015] EWHC 880 (QB), where the claimant on his return to work had given no indication that his work was unmanageable or that it was likely to make his illness recur.

[233] [2004] UKHL 13; [2004] 1 W.L.R. 1089 at [5].

[234] [2004] UKHL 13; [2004] 1 W.L.R. 1089 at [6]: "This is, I think, useful practical guidance, but it must be read as that, and not as having anything like statutory force."

[235] [2014] EWCA Civ 1512; [2015] I.R.L.R. 112 at [119].

his case might lead him to develop psychiatric illness.[236] *K v Chief Constable of the Police Service of Scotland*[237] also concerned the conduct of an investigation into the pursuer's conduct. At first instance the employer was found to be in breach of duty in moving the pursuer from her existing role without objective evaluation or scrutiny and without presenting them to the pursuer, and in wrongfully stating that the move was temporary, but on appeal the Inner House concluded that the harm was not foreseeable. A case where the psychological harm to the claimant was found to be unforeseeable is *Piepenbrock v London School of Economics and Political Science*.[238] It was held that the defendant employer had no relevant prior information as to the claimant's personality or medical issues which should have put it on notice of his vulnerability to mental ill-health. Although it should have resolved the complaints against him expeditiously, its breaches did not create a foreseeable risk of psychiatric injury.

The fact that psychiatric illness can be foreseen by the employer will not result in liability if the illness results from unforeseeable circumstances. In *Pratley v Surrey CC*[239] it was held that it was reasonable for the claimant's supervisor to wait for her return from holiday before dealing with her workload issues and that the employer was not liable for the claimant's immediate breakdown on her return, since that was not foreseeable, notwithstanding that there was a foreseeable risk of a breakdown in the future if the claimant's workload was not reduced. Knowledge that the employee is undergoing counselling is not necessarily sufficient warning of psychiatric vulnerability.[240] In *Hartman v South Essex Mental Health and Community Care NHS Trust*[241] the claimant in the lead case had disclosed her history of depression to her employer's occupational health department but the court held that it was not appropriate to attribute this knowledge to the employer. In another of the co-joined appeals in *Hartman*, the case of *Best v Staffordshire University*, where the claimant had been aware of his employer's counselling service but had never used it, it could not be said the employer should have been aware of his vulnerability. It should be noted that knowledge of vulnerability is not necessary if the employee can recover under the normal rules relating to recovery for psychiatric injury.[242] Thus, if stress is foreseeable because of the traumatic nature of the employee's work experience and the employer carelessly fails to provide **12-39**

---

236 [2014] EWCA Civ 1512; [2015] I.R.L.R. 112 at [124].

237 [2019] CSOH 9; reversed at [2020] CSIH 18.

238 [2018] EWHC 2572 (QB); [2018] E.L.R. 596.

239 [2003] EWCA Civ 1067; [2004] I.C.R. 159; [2004] P.I.Q.R. P17.

240 *Croft v Broadstairs & St Peter's Town Council* [2003] EWCA Civ 676: receipt of written disciplinary warning caused claimant to suffer nervous breakdown. Two council members knew she was having counselling but neither they nor the council was aware of her psychiatric vulnerability. Warning would not have been sent if this had been known. Court of Appeal held there to be insufficient knowledge to found liability. See also *Bonser v UK Coal Mining Ltd (formerly RJB Mining (UK) Ltd)* [2003] EWCA Civ 1296; [2004] I.R.L.R. 164—not foreseeable that an employee subjected to an increasing workload would have a breakdown when given a 40-hour project a week before her holiday leave; and *Cross v Highlands and Islands Enterprise* [2001] I.R.L.R. 336; *Fraser v State Hospitals Board for Scotland*, 2001 S.L.T. 1051, where the claims failed on the basis of a lack of foreseeability.

241 [2005] EWCA Civ 6; [2005] I.C.R. 782; [2005] P.I.Q.R. P19. The judgment determined six co-joined appeals. Scott Baker LJ, giving the judgment on behalf of Lord Phillips MR and Tuckey LJ, gave a helpful summary of *Hatton* and subsequent case law.

242 See para.7-91 onwards. And see *Holladay v East Kent Hospitals NHS Trust* [2003] EWCA Civ 1696; (2004) 76 B.M.L.R. 201 where the Court of Appeal held that the defendant employers were vicariously liable for foreseeable psychiatric injury, where the claimant had been wrongly arrested for theft and possession of controlled drugs, as a result of the negligence of fellow employees.

adequate support, there may be liability.[243] Again, if stress is unforeseeable but is the result of a foreseeable risk of physical injury, there may be liability under the principle in *Page v Smith*,[244] notwithstanding the employer's lack of awareness of any vulnerability.[245]

12-40 **Care in respect of known stress vulnerability** In *Barber v Somerset CC*,[246] Lord Walker commented that lack of resources for more staff was not an excuse as "even a small reduction in [the claimant's] duties, coupled with the feeling that the management was on his side, might by itself have made a real difference. ... Supply teachers cost money, but not as much as the cost of the permanent loss through psychiatric illness of a valued member of the school staff."[247] He did not comment on other guidance given by Hale LJ, in particular, that "if the only reasonable and effective step would have been to dismiss or demote the employee, the employer will not be in breach of duty in allowing a willing employee to continue the job".[248] Lord Rodger in Barber did approve similar guidance in relation to physical injury given by Devlin LJ: "It cannot be said that an employer is bound to dismiss an employee rather than allow her to run a small risk."[249] Whether it is appropriate to regard potentially long-term psychiatric illness as a "small risk" must depend upon the facts. However, the lengthy process involved in dismissal for stress-based incapacity may suggest that an employer acts reasonably in seeking to assist the employee to adapt to the perceived stressful conditions.[250] Again, it may not be reasonable to require the employer to make key management changes simply to

243 See, for example, *Melville v The Home Office* [2005] EWCA Civ 6; [2005] I.C.R. 782, decided as part of the group of cases under the name of *Hartman v South Essex Mental Health and Community Care NHS Trust*. As part of his employment, the claimant had to cut down the body of a suicide victim. His employer failed to implement its own system of care support for employees experiencing such trauma and was held liable for his resulting stress-related illness. Contrast *French v Sussex CC* [2006] EWCA Civ 312; *The Times*, 5 April 2006: no duty of care was owed by a chief constable to police officers who allegedly sustained psychiatric injury as a result of the stress of being exposed to criminal and/or disciplinary proceedings through no fault of their own. It was not reasonably foreseeable that corporate failings on the part of the police service would cause psychiatric harm in this way. Moreover, as a matter of principle, there was no duty of care owed by an employer to an employee not to cause an untoward event that could foreseeably lead to proceedings (such as a public inquiry or a criminal prosecution) in which the employee's conduct would be in issue.

244 [1996] 2 A.C. 155. See further para.7-70.

245 *Donachie v Chief Constable of the Greater Manchester Police* [2004] EWCA Civ 405; *The Times*, 6 May 2004: police officer physically endangered because of negligently run surveillance operation; extreme stress of operation led to a clinical psychiatric state that resulted in an acute rise in blood pressure and caused a stroke; psychiatric injury not foreseeable but Chief Constable found liable for the stroke because physical injury was foreseeable, even though that (assault by suspects under surveillance) was not of the kind the claimant actually suffered, and it was caused by an unforeseeable mechanism.

246 [2004] UKHL 13; [2004] 1 W.L.R. 1089; [2004] I.C.R. 457.

247 [2004] UKHL 13; [2004] 1 W.L.R. 1089; [2004] I.C.R. 457 at [67]–[68].

248 [2002] EWCA Civ 76; [2002] I.C.R. 613; [2002] 2 All E.R. 1 at [43]. Less controversially, Hale LJ said that "the size and scope of the employer's operation, its resources and the demands it faces are relevant in deciding what is reasonable; these include the interests of other employees and the need to treat them fairly, for example, in any redistribution of duties".

249 [2004] UKHL 13; [2004] 1 W.L.R. 1089; [2004] I.C.R. 457 at [30], endorsing the passage of Devlin LJ in *Withers v Perry Chain Co Ltd* [1961] 1 W.L.R. 1314 at 1320.

250 See *Vahidi v Fairstead House School Trust Ltd* [2005] EWCA Civ 765; [2005] E.L.R. 607: no liability to teacher who collapsed under the strain of making fundamental changes to her methods of teaching.

avoid the employee's known vulnerability to stress.[251] Having said that, it has been made clear that the provision of counselling services is not a panacea and will not necessarily suffice to discharge the duty.[252] On the other hand, where the employer's counselling service could only have provided low-level emotional support and would not have prevented the onset of the claimant's psychiatric condition the claim will fail.[253]

Dismissal and psychiatric harm No claim for psychiatric harm or distress can arise out of the *manner* in which an employee is dismissed.[254] However, if an employee has acquired a cause of action (whether in contract or in tort) before the dismissal he is still entitled to pursue that cause of action notwithstanding a subsequent unfair dismissal and the statutory right to a remedy for that unfair dismissal that arises.[255] So, although damages for psychiatric harm are not recoverable in an action for wrongful dismissal, there may be a common law claim in relation to events that preceded the dismissal (including events leading up to the dismissal).[256] The analogous case of the initiation of disciplinary proceedings was raised in the case of *Coventry University v Mian*.[257] The question was whether the decision to initiate such proceedings was unreasonable in the sense of being outside the range of reasonable decisions open to an employer in the circumstances. This should not be approached with hindsight nor confused with the merits of the case. **12-41**

---

251 See *Foumeny v University of Leeds* [2003] EWCA Civ 557; [2003] E.L.R. 443: only reversal of the management decision to merge academic departments and restoration of the claimant to the position of head of department would have suited him and averted stress. These were not reasonable steps for the employer to take. In *Flood v University Court of the University of Glasgow* [2008] CSOH 98; 2008 S.C.L.R. 719, a claim failed before the Outer House of the Court of Session, because the pursuer had not identified the steps that would have been taken by a reasonable employer to protect her from harm. On appeal, this approach was reversed by the Inner House. The pursuer alleged that she had been required to perform duties additional to those contracted for; that urgent steps ought to have been taken to reduce her workload; and that this had not been done despite a series of assurances. This amounted to sufficient notice of her case, which should therefore proceed: *Flood v University Court of the University of Glasgow* [2010] CSIH 3; 2010 S.L.T. 167.

252 See in particular *Daw v Intel Corp (UK) Ltd* [2007] EWCA Civ 70; [2007] 2 All E.R. 126, see in particular [43]–[45]. On the facts of the case, only a reduction in workload could have removed the problems caused to the "capable and loyal employee". The point was reiterated in *Dickins v O2 Plc* [2008] EWCA Civ 1144; [2009] I.R.L.R. 58.

253 *Pratt v Scottish Ministers* [2013] CSIH 17; 2013 S.L.T. 590, where the claim failed on both causation and breach of duty. The claimant had received professional counselling following an incident when he had ingested blood from a prisoner known to be a drug addict and his psychiatric reaction was caused by a morbid fear of blood borne disease fuelled by abnormal and irrational beliefs. The medical evidence indicated that the sort of counselling he could have received from his employer (characterised as "a cup of tea and a chat") would have made no difference. There was no breach of duty because an "employer can only reasonably be expected to take steps which are likely to do some good": *Hatton v Sutherland* [2002] EWCA Civ 76; [2002] I.C.R. 613 at [34], per Hale LJ.

254 *Johnson v Unisys Ltd* [2001] UKHL 13; [2003] 1 A.C. 518 (breach of the implied term of trust and confidence cannot be relied on to found a claim at common law for unfair dismissal because the statutory code for unfair dismissal provides statutory remedies for breach of the right not to be unfairly dismissed).

255 *Eastwood v Magnox Electric Plc* [2004] UKHL 35; [2005] 1 A.C. 503.

256 *Eastwood v Magnox Electric Plc* [2004] UKHL 35; [2005] 1 A.C. 503; *Monk v Cann Hall Primary School* [2013] EWCA Civ 826; [2014] P.I.Q.R. P3. In such a case care will have to be taken to identify the date of dismissal (particularly in the case of constructive dismissal); and for the claim to succeed the evidence will have to point to the employer's pre-dismissal breach of duty as the cause of the claimant's psychiatric illness, as opposed to the dismissal itself.

257 [2014] EWCA Civ 1275; [2014] E.L.R. 455.

On the facts of the particular case, the decision to commence disciplinary proceedings was not unreasonable in this sense and there was no breach of the duty of care.

12-42 **Causation** In addition to the problem of proving breach of duty, proving causation is also problematic for many employees in claims for occupational stress. They have to demonstrate that the psychiatric illness is due not simply to stress at work but that it was the employer's specific breach of duty that caused the damage. This is complicated by the fact that there are many other stressful factors in ordinary life that can contribute to mental breakdown. In *Hatton* the Court of Appeal commented that: "Where there are several different possible causes, as will often be the case with stress related illness of any kind, the claimant may have difficulty proving that the employer's fault was one of them."[258]

12-43 **Material contribution** On the other hand, the employee does not have to prove that the breach of duty was the sole cause, merely that it made a material contribution to his mental illness.[259] The difficulty has been in determining whether and when damages fall to be apportioned where there are other potential causes. Equally, the existence of one or more other potential causes has also been distinguished from the situation where damages fall to be reduced because of the likelihood of future harm irrespective of the tort, where there is a susceptible claimant. In *Garrod v North Devon NHS Primary Care Trust*,[260] Henriques J reduced damages to reflect the vulnerability of a particular claimant to stress, relying on Hale LJ's suggestion in *Hatton* that where:

> "it is established that the constellation of symptoms suffered by the claimant stems from a number of different extrinsic causes then a sensible attempt should be made to apportion liability accordingly."[261]

In *Dickins v O2 Plc*,[262] the Court of Appeal unanimously declared (albeit obiter) that this was not the right approach; but the route taken in *Dickins* has itself not been followed in more recent cases as explained in the following paragraph. In *Dickins*, the trial judge had reduced the claimant's damages to reflect the fact that other non-tortious factors, including her vulnerable personality and relationship with her partner, had interacted with her employer's negligence in bringing about the harm. The claimant did not appeal against this reduction in damages. But Smith LJ (with the agreement of Wall LJ and Sedley LJ) was of the view that the approach, based as it was on dicta of Hale LJ which were incompatible with the decision of the Court

---

[258] [2002] EWCA Civ 76; [2002] 2 All E.R. 1 at [35]. See also *MacLennan v Hartford Europe Ltd* [2012] EWHC 346 (QB) (no proven causal link between stress and chronic fatigue syndrome, either generally or in the claimant's particular case; the case would also have failed for lack of foreseeability on the part of her employer); *Saunders v Chief Constable of Sussex* [2012] EWCA Civ 1197 (even if relevant support had been available to the claimant on his return to work, he would probably not have sought help, nor acted differently); *Bailey v Devon Partnership NHS Trust* (unreported 11 July 2014 QBD District Registry (Exeter)) (claimant would not have informed the employer of her difficulties even if the employer had been more proactive; and many factors were involved in her illness).

[259] [2002] EWCA Civ 76; [2002] 2 All E.R. 1; applying *Bonnington Castings Ltd v Wardlaw* [1956] A.C. 613.

[260] [2006] EWHC 850 (QB); [2007] P.I.Q.R. Q1.

[261] [2006] EWHC 850 (QB); [2007] P.I.Q.R. Q1 at [71].

[262] [2008] EWCA Civ 1144; [2009] I.R.L.R. 58.

of Appeal in *Bailey v Ministry of Defence*,[263] was not appropriate to a stress case of this type. In *Bailey*, the Court of Appeal allowed recovery in full where the claimant could establish that the defendant's breach made a "material contribution to" an indivisible injury, which is to say that its causal potency was more than negligible. Smith LJ stated the position as follows:

> "... apportionment of the whole of the damages is usually carried out only in cases where the injury is divisible. In such cases the seriousness of the medical condition in question is often related to the degree of exposure to the agent causing it; in other words the condition is 'dose-related'. The true nature of such cases is that the tort has caused only part of the overall injury."[264]

It followed that although Hale LJ in *Hatton* treated *Rahman v Arearose*[265] as a case where damage for mental injury was apportioned even though the injury was not divisible, *Rahman* should be seen as a case where the court (rightly or wrongly) accepted expert evidence that the claimant was suffering from more than one distinct psychiatric condition, and that each of these was attributable to a different cause. As such, it fell within the definition of cases where "the tort has caused only part of the overall injury", and therefore of divisible injury. In a case in which the claimant has been "tipped over the edge" into a breakdown by a series of factors, the Court in *Dickins* felt that the analysis in *Rahman* is not appropriate. There is only one indivisible injury, albeit with multiple contributing causes. Essentially, the Court of Appeal in *Dickins* took the view that such damage generally is indivisible. Although Hale LJ's observations were qualified by the caveat that damage should not be apportioned where the injury was to be regarded as genuinely indivisible, there was a tension between the interpretation of the relevant damage in such cases in *Hatton*, and in *Dickins v O2*. As Sedley LJ observed, the decision in *Bailey v Ministry of Defence*[266] would now be binding on lower courts in these circumstances, rather than the obiter observations of Hale LJ in *Hatton*.

In *BAE Systems (Operations) v Konczak*[267] a later Court of Appeal has resolved this tension in favour of the remarks of Hale LJ: to the extent that there is a difference, *Hatton* should be followed. They did so without reference to the decision in *Bailey v Ministry of Defence*, which has remained controversial and open to interpretation.[268] In *Konczak*, the Court of Appeal distinguished between two remarks of Hale LJ in *Hatton*. Among Hale LJ's "practical propositions" were proposition 15: **12-44**

> "Where the harm suffered has more than one cause, the employer should only pay for the proportion of the harm suffered which is attributable to his wrongdoing, unless the harm is truly indivisible ...";

and proposition 16:

> "The assessment of damages will take account of any pre-existing disorder or vulnerability and of the chance that the claimant would have succumbed to a stress-related disorder in any event".

263 [2008] EWCA Civ 883; [2009] 1 W.L.R. 1052.
264 [2008] EWCA Civ 883; [2009] 1 W.L.R. 1052 at [44].
265 [2001] Q.B. 351.
266 [2008] EWCA Civ 883; [2009] 1 W.L.R. 1052.
267 [2017] EWCA Civ 1188; [2018] I.C.R. 1 at [70].
268 See para.2-33.

Proposition 16 looks to the future, in light of the claimant's vulnerability, and may lead to a reduction in damages to reflect the likelihood that harm would have occurred in any event. Proposition 15, however, relates to competing causes of harm already suffered. Underhill LJ declared that "both propositions are tools which enable a tribunal to avoid over-compensation in these difficult cases".[269] Underhill LJ suggested that the court in *Dickins* had overstated the difference between its own approach, and that of Hale LJ in *Hatton*: Hale LJ recognised the existence of "truly indivisible" injuries and agreed that in such cases, there was no basis for apportionment under proposition 15. The difference lay in an assumption on the part of the Court in *Dickins v O2* that such injuries generally were indivisible. However, the Court of Appeal in *BAE Systems* appears to have added an important gloss to Hale LJ's proposition 15. According to Underhill LJ,[270] in any case of this type "the tribunal should try to identify a rational basis on which the harm suffered can be apportioned between a part caused by the employer's wrong and a part which is not so caused". This exercise, it was emphasised, was concerned with the divisibility of the harm, and not the divisibility of the cause. This approach takes as its starting point that there should be an attempt to divide the injury, pointing to a preference for apportionment where this can be consistent with the injury suffered. Underhill LJ added that on his reading of *Rahman* and *Hatton*, in the "difficult" case where an employee is "tipped over the edge" by a particular incident, the tribunal "should seek to find a rational basis for distinguishing between a part of the illness which is due to the employer's wrong and a part which is due to other causes".[271] This did not assist the defendant in *BAE* itself, since no such rational basis had been identified. Plainly, however, future defendants will seek to establish through expert evidence that there is a rational basis that tribunals may use in following the emphasis placed on apportionment in *BAE Systems*. As Irwin LJ added, in a concurring judgment, the difficulty may be seen as one of medicine or science, rather than legal principle.[272] Nonetheless, the instruction to future courts to try to find a rational basis for apportionment is a matter of legal emphasis, and no doubt reflects Irwin LJ's further observation that "compensation should never become windfall".[273]

12-45 **Compliance with statutory obligations** The fact that the employer has complied with statutory safety regulations does not preclude liability for breach of the personal duty of care, though breach of those regulations may well suggest breach of the duty of care, even (potentially) where the key goal of those regulations is not the protection of employees.[274] In *Bux v Slough Metals*,[275] for example, the employer complied with the statutory duty to provide protective goggles but was held in breach of the common law duty in failing to persuade employees to use the goggles. The statutory duties may offer guidance as to what might be regarded as reasonable care but no more than that. Where the employer cannot comply with statutory safety regulations if the employee continues in the job, it will be a breach of the employer's common law duty of care to the employee to fail to move the employee

269 [2017] EWCA Civ 1188; [2018] I.C.R. 1 at [62].
270 [2017] EWCA Civ 1188; [2018] I.C.R. 1 at [71].
271 [2017] EWCA Civ 1188; [2018] I.C.R. 1 at [72].
272 [2017] EWCA Civ 1188; [2018] I.C.R. 1 at [93].
273 [2017] EWCA Civ 1188; [2018] I.C.R. 1 at [92].
274 See *Buck v Nottinghamshire Healthcare NHS Trust* [2006] EWCA Civ 1576; (2006) 93 B.M.L.R. 28 (breach of regulations applicable to high security hospitals, where compliance with the regulations would provide protection to hospital staff).
275 [1973] 1 W.L.R. 1358.

to an alternative job or, if there is no alternative, to continue to employ the employee.[276]

3. BREACH OF STATUTORY DUTY

Enterprise and Regulatory Reform Act 2013 s.69 The Enterprise and Regulatory Reform Act 2013 s.69 has had a radical effect on the liability of employers to their employees in respect of breach of industrial safety legislation.[277] Section 69 amended s.47 of the Health and Safety at Work etc. Act 1974 to provide that, as from 1 October 2013,[278] breach of a duty imposed by a statutory instrument containing health and safety regulations made under s.15 of the 1974 Act, or breach of a duty imposed by an existing statutory provision,[279] shall not be actionable except so far as regulations under s.47 so provide. This reverses the previous position under the Act, which by s.47(2) provided that breach of a duty imposed by health and safety regulations shall, so far as it causes damage, be actionable except in so far as the regulations provide otherwise.[280] The effect is that from 1 October 2013, with very limited exceptions,[281] employees harmed by their employers' breach of statutory duty can only bring an action in the tort of negligence. Thus, the following paragraphs of this section of the chapter apply directly only to claims where the cause of action accrued *before* 1 October 2013. Despite this, it is arguable that the detail of the health and safety regulations will often remain relevant to employees' actions in negligence. Breach of the regulations will normally constitute a criminal offence. Negligence sets a standard of reasonable care in the face of a foreseeable risk of harm to employees. Many of the health and safety regulations require employers to take such precautions as are "practicable" or "reasonably practicable". If an employer is in breach of the regulations it may be difficult to argue that he has nonetheless acted reasonably whilst at the same time committing a criminal offence, an offence that has been created by Parliament specifically for the protection of the health and safety of employees and which can be seen as setting the appropriate standard of behaviour.[282] Two differences will be apparent. First, the burden of proof (that it was "practicable" to take precautions) will effectively shift 12-46

[276] *Lane Group Plc v Farmiloe* [2004] P.I.Q.R. P22 (EAT) at [13]–[19].

[277] See para.12-02.

[278] In *Johnson v University of Bristol* [2017] EWCA Civ 2115, a claim framed in terms of the Provision and Use of Work Equipment Regulations 1998 and the Workplace (Health, Safety and Welfare) Regulations 1992, was said to give rise to no significant matters of law, because whatever was said in the judgment about the civil consequences of the regulations no longer had any applicability to the circumstances of contemporaneous or future events. Therefore, the Court would not embark upon a full judgment, and offered a short form judgment in its place.

[279] The list of relevant existing statutory provisions (as defined in s.53 of the Act) is set out in Sch.1 to the Health and Safety at Work etc. Act 1974.

[280] See para.12-52.

[281] See the Health and Safety at Work etc. Act 1974 (Civil Liability) (Exceptions) Regulations 2013 (SI 2013/1667); though regulations made under other statutes (see para.12-02 fn.7), and statutes such as the Employer's Liability (Defective Equipment) Act 1969 which are not listed in Sch.1, are unaffected.

[282] In a Ministerial Statement in the House of Lords Viscount Younger made the point that s.69 of the Enterprise and Regulatory Reform Act 2013 did not undermine core health and safety standards and that employers' statutory duties "will remain relevant as evidence of the standards expected of employers in future civil claims for negligence": see N. Tomkins, "Civil health and safety law after the Enterprise and Regulatory Reform Act 2013" [2013] J.P.I.L. 203 at 207; and P. Limb and J. Cox, "Section 69 of the Enterprise and Regulatory Reform Act 2013—plus ca change?" [2014] J.P.I.L. 1 at 7.

to the claimant. Under the regulations, the burden of proving that it was not practicable or not reasonably practicable to take precautions generally rests with the employer. In a negligence action the employee will have to establish this as part of proving that the employer took an unreasonable risk.[283] Secondly, there are arguably some regulations where the employer may be found to be in breach for harm that was unforeseeable. If the harm truly was unforeseeable there will be no liability in negligence. This is likely to be rare, since the existence of a statutory duty to take precautions will make it difficult for the employer to argue that the damage was unforeseeable.[284] The argument is more likely to revolve around whether the harm suffered by the employee falls within the scope of the particular regulation.[285] If it does not, then the regulation would not have assisted the employee in any event, and the issue will simply be whether there has been a breach of duty applying ordinary negligence principles.

12-47 **Industrial safety legislation** It has been established since *Groves v Lord Wimborne*[286] that breach of penal legislation designed to promote industrial safety can give rise to an action for breach of statutory duty by an injured worker. The action for breach of statutory duty provided a means of avoiding the doctrine of common employment, and the legislation was often stricter in the standards applied than the tort of negligence. For many years the two actions have been routinely combined in claims by injured employees against their employers. The degree of protection conferred by an action for breach of statutory duty varies considerably with the wording of the particular provision. Sometimes legislation has been treated as imposing an absolute obligation on the employer. For example, in *John Summers & Sons Ltd v Frost*[287] it was held that s.14(1) of the Factories Act 1937, which provided that every dangerous part of any machinery must be securely fenced, created an absolute obligation, in the sense that it was not a defence to show that it was

---

283 There is also some authority for the view once breach of the statutory duty is established it is for the employer to prove the breach did not cause the claimant's injury, thus placing the burden of proof with respect to causation on the defendant: *Chief Constable of Hampshire v Taylor* [2013] EWCA Civ 496; [2013] I.C.R. 1150 at [19]. Sed quaere: see further para.2-13 fn.39.

284 Though see *Blair v Chief Constable of Sussex Police* [2012] EWCA Civ 633; [2012] I.C.R. D33 at [14] where the Court of Appeal held the defendants to be in breach of the Personal Protective Equipment at Work Regulations 1992 because it would have been possible (and not impractical) to prevent significant injury to the claimant by providing stronger boots. Longmore LJ commented: "I emphasize that this is not to say that the Chief Constable was in any way negligent at common law. Likelihood or foresight of injury does not come into the matter. Nor is it of any relevance to consider whether it would be sensible (as opposed to impractical) to provide [stronger] boots to trainees who would be unlikely to be wearing them in the course of their operational duties as police constables."

285 See, e.g. *Fytche v Wincanton Logistics Plc* [2004] UKHL 31; [2004] I.C.R. 975, para.12-59.

286 [1898] 2 Q.B. 402.

287 [1955] A.C. 740. For discussion of *Groves v Lord Wimborne* and points of distinction between claims based on breach of the Factory Acts and a claim based on breach of safety regulations under the Merchant Shipping Act 1995 s.121; and the Fishing Vessel (Safety Provisions) Rules 1975 (SI 1975/330) (revoked by the Fishing Vessels (Codes of Practice) Regulations 2017, SI 2017/943); see *Todd v Adams and Chope (t/a Trelawney Fishing Co) (The "Margaretha Maria")* [2002] EWCA Civ 509; [2002] 2 Lloyd's Rep. 293 at [33]–[35]. The Court of Appeal concluded that Parliament had not intended that breach of these provisions should give rise to a civil action for breach of statutory duty. cf. *Cairns v Northern Lighthouse Board* [2013] CSOH 22; 2013 S.L.T. 645, where Lord Drummond Young distinguished *Todd*, holding that breach of reg.5 of the Merchant Shipping and Fishing Vessels (Health and Safety at Work) Regulations 1997 (SI 1997/2962), made under s.85 of the Merchant Shipping Act 1995, did confer a right to a civil remedy. Regulations made under the Merchant Shipping Act 1995 retain civil liability as they are not within the terms of s.69 Enterprise and Regulatory Reform Act 2013.

impracticable to fence, even though fencing would make the machine unusable. Some statutory duties are qualified by the phrase "so far as is reasonably practicable", and the assessment of what is reasonably practicable can involve a calculation somewhat similar to that in deciding what constitutes reasonable care for the tort of negligence. However, it is important not to be drawn into treating statutory provisions as creating something equivalent to negligence standards, just because they include a reference to reasonableness. In *Edwards v National Coal Board*[288] Asquith LJ suggested that where there is "gross disproportion" between the risk and the measures necessary to avoid the risk, the risk being "insignificant" in relation to the cost, then the measures were not reasonably practicable. In *Baker v Quantum Clothing*,[289] a case requiring interpretation of s.29 of the Factories Act 1961,[290] the Court of Appeal underlined that there is a difference between a "gross disproportion" test as set out by Asquith LJ in *Edwards v National Coal Board*, and the test for negligence at common law. Smith LJ emphasised that for an employer to avoid liability:

> "... he has to show that the burden of eliminating the risk substantially outweighed the 'quantum of risk'. When that forensic process is compared and contrasted with the process by which liability at common law is established, it is hard to understand how lawyers and judges have so often fallen into the error of thinking that there is no significant difference between the two."[291]

The Supreme Court[292] reversed the judgment of the Court of Appeal. Lord Mance, in the majority, said that the point did not need to be resolved given his approach to "safety",[293] but nonetheless he considered that the "gross disproportion" test was an "unjustified gloss" on the statutory wording.[294] His Lordship did not refer expressly to *Edwards v National Coal Board*, but took the view that: "The criteria relevant to reasonable practicability must on any view very largely reflect the criteria relevant to satisfaction of the common law duty of care. Both require consideration of the nature, gravity and imminence of the risk and its consequences, as well as of the nature and proportionality of the steps by which it might be addressed, and a balancing of the one against the other."[295] Lord Mance rejected any assumption that the statutory duties must necessarily be intended to be stricter than the common law, arguing that the imposition of criminal liabilities implied that the duties should not be interpreted too broadly. Lord Dyson, also in the majority, did not comment on the "gross disproportion" test, but referred to *Edwards v National Coal Board* as the leading authority on the meaning of "reasonably practicable" in industrial safety legislation. Since Lord Mance's comments on "gross disproportion" were not necessary to his decision, and he did not mention *Edwards* expressly, it is suggested that the authority of that decision is unaffected. There is some difficulty describing the gross disproportion test as a "gloss" on the statutory language given that the interpretation was well established long before the Factories Act 1961

288 [1949] 1 All E.R. 743 at 747.
289 [2009] EWCA Civ 499; [2009] P.I.Q.R. P19.
290 The majority of the Factories Act 1961 was repealed by the Workplace (Health, Safety and Welfare) Regulations 1992 (SI 1992/3004), including s.29, which therefore applies only to pre-1993 events and is to this extent unaffected by s.69 Enterprise and Regulatory Reform Act 2013, para.12-46.
291 [2009] EWCA Civ 499; [2009] P.I.Q.R. P19 at [87].
292 *Baker v Quantum Clothing Ltd* [2011] UKSC 17; [2011] 1 W.L.R. 1003.
293 See paras 12-49 and 12-50.
294 [2011] UKSC 17; [2011] 1 W.L.R. 1003 at [84].
295 [2011] UKSC 17; [2011] 1 W.L.R. 1003 at [82].

was drafted. In *Walsh v CP Hart & Sons Ltd*,[296] decided by reference to the Work at Height Regulations 2005,[297] a court applied both *Edwards*, and *Quantum*, when interpreting "reasonable practicability". Reasonable practicability under the Regulations did not call for a mere balancing act. Rather, the employer needed to show that the cost and difficulty of the steps to be taken substantially outweighed the quantum of risk involved. A mere balancing act "is not what was intended by the legislation, the policy of which is to put safety first and not provide the employer with an easy escape avenue but rather a 'long stop' defence in very limited circumstances."[298] In *Goldscheider v Royal Opera House Covent Garden Foundation*,[299] a case of serious hearing impairment caused by exposure to noise during orchestral rehearsals, the Court of Appeal made the point that it will be very difficult for a defendant to establish that all "reasonably practicable" steps have been taken, if it has subsequently made adaptations that avoid the risk.[300] Reasonable practicability is in this sense different from foreseeability, which is not to be judged with hindsight.

12-48 Other regulations may require an employer to do what is "practicable" to achieve a particular result. For example, the Mines and Quarries Act 1954 s.157, provided a defence to all the duties laid down in that Act if it was impracticable to avoid or prevent the contravention.[301] On the face of it, "practicability" leaves the defendant subject to a stricter standard than "reasonable practicability", and it has been taken to mean that if there were additional precautions which could have been taken (reasonably or not), there will have been a breach. The applicable case law is not uniform.[302] One important advantage for an employee of an action for breach of statutory duty over a claim based on negligence is that the onus of proving that it was impracticable or not reasonably practicable to comply with the statutory requirement is the defendant's.[303]

12-49 **Safety and dangerousness** In addition to any specific qualifications of statutory duties ("so far as practicable" or "reasonably practicable"), other terms are also used which lead to comparison (and sometimes contrast) with the tort of negligence. The concept of what is "safe" or what is "dangerous" sometimes involves notions of foreseeability. So it has been said that a machine is "dangerous" only if it is foreseeably likely to injure someone, taking account of carelessness by the worker.[304] Here,

---

296 [2020] EWHC 37 (QB).

297 The accident occurred on 8 April 2013.

298 *Walsh v CP Hart & Sons Ltd* [2020] EWHC 37 (QB) at [45].

299 [2019] EWCA Civ 711; [2020] I.C.R. 1 at [42].

300 Here, the orchestra pit had subsequently been reconfigured to reduce exposure to noise on the part of musicians. The claim was for breaches of duty under the Control of Noise Regulations 2005. In relation to "safety" of the workplace in this claim, and particularly foreseeability, see para.12-50.

301 A duty to take such steps as may be necessary for keeping a road or working place secure, under the Mines and Quarries Act 1954 s.48, was not an absolute duty but a duty to exercise care in the light of knowledge at the time: *Brown v National Coal Board* [1962] A.C. 574.

302 For interpretations of the terms "practicable" and "reasonably practicable" see, e.g. *Jayne v National Coal Board* [1963] 2 All E.R. 220; and *Sanderson v National Coal Board* [1961] 2 Q.B. 244; distinguishing *Brown v National Coal Board* [1962] A.C. 574. For interpretation of "reasonably practicable" see also *R. v HTM Ltd* [2006] EWCA Crim 1156; [2007] 2 All E.R. 665.

303 *Nimmo v Alexander Cowan & Sons Ltd* [1968] A.C. 107; applied in *McDonald v Department for Communities and Local Government* [2013] EWCA Civ 1346; [2014] P.I.Q.R. P7 at [86]–[91], [115].

304 "It seems to me that machinery or parts of machinery is and are dangerous if in the ordinary course of human affairs danger may be reasonably anticipated from the use of them without protection",

the idea of "dangerousness" helps define the applicability of the duty,[305] whereas the authorities dealing with "safety" as an objective state of affairs are concerned with the content of the duty, for example to ensure that a workplace is "safe".[306] It is not entirely surprising that the role of foreseeability has varied depending on the concept being applied. However, in *Baker v Quantum Clothing Group Ltd*[307] the Supreme Court held by a majority that "safety" is always dependent on ideas of foreseeability judged according to the standards of the time at which the risk was encountered; and that the authorities interpreting s.14 of the Factories Act 1961 (relating to "dangerous" equipment) are also of relevance to the interpretation of s.29 of that Act, which set out a duty to keep the workplace "safe" so far as reasonably practicable. Section 14, however, was not qualified by a provision that the dangers should be removed so far as reasonably practicable, and the minority thought this a pertinent reason why "safe" in s.29 should not necessarily be interpreted as the antonym of "dangerous" in s.14. It is suggested that reading "safe" and "dangerous" as simple "antonyms" in this way is to take them out of their statutory context and, in a sense, to give them invariable meanings of the sort which the majority said it was rejecting when it denied that s.29 referred to an absolute notion of safety.

Safety "Safety" was considered in *Larner v British Steel Plc*.[308] Here, the Court of Appeal held that in determining whether a place of work had been kept "safe" (for the purposes of the Factories Act 1961 s.29(1)) for any person working there, it would be wrong to import a test of "reasonable foreseeability" of danger. The obligation imposed by the section was strict, with no reference to foreseeability, reasonable or otherwise, and such a requirement would have the effect of limiting successful claims for breach of statutory duty to circumstances where the worker would also succeed in a parallel claim for negligence. *Larner v British Steel* was accepted by the Court of Appeal as not only binding, but also correct in principle, in *Baker v Quantum Clothing*.[309] The "safety" of a place of work was to be judged objectively without reference to reasonable foresight of injury, though if the risk in question was one which the employer cannot reasonably have been expected to have known about, then the employer should be able to show that no steps to avoid **12-50**

---

per Wills J in *Hindle v Birtwistle* [1897] 1 Q.B. 192 at 195; cited by Lord Reid with approval in *John Summers & Sons Ltd v Frost* [1955] A.C. 740 at 765. See also the comment of Lord Keith in *John Summers* at 774: "it was a dangerous machine, or dangerous part of a machine, according to the test of reasonable foreseeability of accident, repeatedly and, in my opinion, correctly laid down in various cases in which this question has been considered". See also *Close v Steel Co of Wales Ltd* [1962] A.C. 367 HL: worker's injury was not reasonably foreseeable and therefore the drill bit which shattered and injured his eye was not a "dangerous part of … machinery".

305 *John Summers & Sons Ltd v Frost* [1955] A.C. 740 required interpretation of s.14 of the Factories Act 1937, which stated that "Every dangerous part of any machinery … shall be securely fenced …". This was an absolute duty, but it applied only where the danger was foreseeable.

306 *Latimer v AEC Ltd* [1953] A.C. 643 dealt with neither "safety" nor "dangerousness". Here, the question was whether a floor was maintained in an "efficient state", and this was treated as a matter of degree depending on the foreseeability of injury. On the other hand, it was significant that the condition in question was transient (the floor was slippery with an accumulation of oil and water, rather than poorly constructed or in disrepair).

307 [2011] UKSC 17; [2011] 1 W.L.R. 1003.

308 [1993] I.C.R. 551; [1993] 4 All E.R. 102.

309 [2009] EWCA Civ 499; [2009] P.I.Q.R. P19.

the risk were "reasonably practicable",[310] thus avoiding liability. On appeal to the Supreme Court, the approach of the Court of Appeal to "safety" was disapproved and *Larner v British Steel* was overruled.[311] The majority concluded that the interpretation of "safety" should reflect reasonable foreseeability judged in accordance with the standards of the time, in line with cases interpreting s.14 of the same Act.[312] There was no such thing as an unchanging notion of "safety". Although it was not disputed that the burden of showing that it was not reasonably practicable to make the workplace "safe" lay with the employer, the employee must do more than show that an injury occurred and was likely with hindsight. The employee must also show that there was a reasonable foreseeability of harm and that the risk of harm was not acceptable, before the workplace could be shown not to have been "safe". Safety, according to the majority, was a matter of opinion. The minority rejected this view, emphasising that the section did not refer to reasonable safety, and arguing that a workplace which was believed (even reasonably) to be safe at the time of exposure was not necessarily safe for the purposes of the statute. The question, rather, should be whether there were reasonably practicable steps that could have been taken in view of the knowledge existing at the time of exposure. In line with the approach of the Court of Appeal, the minority would therefore have dealt with issues of reasonableness largely in connection with "reasonable practicability", where the burden is on the employer. Lord Clarke, in the minority, emphasised that the purpose of the statutory duty was first and foremost to protect employees, not employers, and that a balance between these interests was established through the qualification that employers may show they have taken all steps that are "reasonably practicable". His Lordship suggested that s.29 was different from common law duties in that it was "results-oriented": there was a duty to achieve a particular result (that the workplace should be safe, not reasonably safe or believed to be safe), but the content of the duty was only to do what was reasonably practicable to this end.[313] In *Goldscheider v Royal Opera House Covent Garden Foundation*,[314] it was emphasised that the precise injury suffered does not need to be foreseen, and perhaps does not need to be reasonably foreseeable, for the claimant to show that it was "unsafe". Here, the Regulations were enacted to protect employees from exposure to excessive noise at work. It was not foreseen that exposure at the levels shown would cause "sudden" injury; but exposure at these levels was considered likely to cause long-term injury. Once the defendant had failed to show reduction of exposure to the lowest level that was reasonably practicable, the fact that the foreseeable risk was of long-term injury was irrelevant. Notably, the court cited common law authority on remoteness of damage to sup-

---

310 See para.12-47.

311 *Baker v Quantum Clothing Group Ltd* [2011] UKSC 17; [2011] 1 W.L.R. 1003.

312 See para.12-49.

313 Lord Kerr agreed, at [177], that "a place is safe or it is not. A place which is not safe cannot be said to be safe merely because it is believed to be, however justified the belief." The effect of applying the s.14 authorities on "dangerousness" to the s.29 duty is that claimants encounter more obstacles to a claim under s.29 than under s.14. First they must show that the workplace was not "safe" according to the standards of the time (effectively importing a foreseeability requirement), and the employer then has the opportunity to show that steps to make the workplace safe would not be reasonably practicable. The majority's approach therefore significantly increases the protection of employers where s.29 is concerned.

314 [2019] EWCA Civ 711; [2020] I.C.R. 1 at [46].

port this contention.[315] In *D v Amec Group Ltd*,[316] it was accepted by the Inner House of the Court of Session that "safety" for the purposes of the Fire (Scotland) Act 2005 s.53 extended to protection of mental as well as physical integrity. The content of the applicable duty was to ensure safety as far as "reasonably practicable". Although "safety" encompassed mental integrity, the employee had failed to identify any fire safety measure which would have prevented him from suffering harm, and therefore had not established any breach on the part of the employer when he suffered post-traumatic stress disorder following a fire in a factory.

Inconsistent regulation It is apparent, then, that over the years there has been much variation in the standards applied to breaches of industrial safety legislation. Moreover, unless the facts of the case fall within the precise statutory wording the claimant will be unable to maintain an action for breach of statutory duty,[317] even though the facts may be analogous to the circumstances which the legislation was intended to cover and objectively might warrant such protection. The claimant would then have to rely on an action in negligence. This inconsistency is probably partly due to the process of adapting legislation with one purpose (the promotion of industrial safety through penal sanctions) to an entirely different purpose, namely providing compensation for injured workers, but it is also due to the accident of language and the historically somewhat piecemeal process of parliamentary regulation of industrial safety.[318] 12-51

Health and Safety at Work etc. Act 1974 Regulations made under the Health and Safety at Work etc. Act 1974[319] gradually replaced the previous piecemeal system of industrial safety legislation to be found in various statutes which governed specific types of premises, such as the Factories Act 1961, the Mines and Quarries Act 1954 and the Offices, Shops and Railway Premises Act 1963. The scheme of the 1974 Act was simple. A series of duties phrased in very general terms were imposed on employers and others by ss.2–7 of the Act. For breach of such general health and safety duties no civil action lay.[320] However, s.15 empowered the Secretary of State to make regulations to replace the existing statutory provisions. Section 47(2) provided that a civil action would lie for breach of these new regulations, except where the regulations provide otherwise.[321] That presumption was reversed by s.69 of the Enterprise and Regulatory Reform Act 2013, amending s.47 so that, as from 1 October 2013, breach of health and safety regulations is not actionable (for claims arising after that date) except so far as regulations made under 12-52

---

[315] *Hughes v Lord Advocate* [1963] A.C. 837; *Page v Smith* [1996] 1 A.C. 155.

[316] [2017] CSIH 75; 2018 S.C. 247.

[317] See para.12-59.

[318] G. Williams, "The Effect of Penal Legislation in the Law of Tort" (1960) 23 M.L.R. 233 at 243 commented that the language used in legislation seemed to be largely haphazard.

[319] The Act was based on the report of the Robens Committee; Cmnd.5034; and see Simpson (1973) 36 M.L.R. 192.

[320] s.47(1)(a). The 1974 Act did not affect "the extent (if any) to which breach of a duty imposed by any of the existing statutory provisions was actionable".

[321] So the fact that the fire and rescue services were not explicitly excluded from the operation of the 1974 Act meant that their employees are owed the relevant duties created by regulations under the Act: *Wembridge Claimants v Winter* [2013] EWHC 2331 (QB).

the 1974 Act so provide.[322] The following discussion of the law is therefore largely relevant to causes of action accruing before 1 October 2013 (except in so far as health and safety regulations provide evidence of the standard of care required of an employer for the purpose of the tort of negligence), although regulations which were not made under the 1974 Act are outside the terms of s.69. A series of EC health and safety directives from the late 1980s and early 1990s[323] required the implementation of a new, coherent scheme for industrial safety. The "framework" Directive was implemented by the Management of Health and Safety at Work Regulations 1992,[324] which were revoked and re-enacted by the Management of Health and Safety at Work Regulations 1999.[325] These Regulations, which provide for risk assessments by employers, health and safety arrangements, and health surveillance of employees, impose general duties somewhat akin to those provided for in the 1974 Act.[326] Originally, breach of these general duties did not give rise to any civil action, except for breaches of reg.16 or 19,[327] though breach of other, more specific, regulations did give rise to a civil action, unless specifically excluded. The prohibition on civil actions arising out of breach of the Management of Health and Safety at Work Regulations 1999 was removed, from 27 October 2003, but only in relation to actions by employees,[328] and has effectively been restored as of 1 October 2013 by the amendment of s.47 of the 1974 Act by s.69 of the Enterprise and Regulatory Reform Act 2013. The status of the Regulations on the date of the

---

[322] See paras 12-02 and 12-46. The only regulations providing for civil actions are the Health and Safety at Work etc. Act 1974 (Civil Liability) (Exceptions) Regulations 2013 (SI 2013/1667) which amend the Management of Health and Safety at Work Regulations 1999 (SI 1999/3242) reg.22, to provide that breach of a duty imposed by reg.16, 16A, 17 or 17A of the 1999 Regulations shall, so far as it causes damage, be actionable by a new or expectant mother.

[323] Directives 89/391 (the "framework" Directive), 89/655, 89/656, 90/269, 90/270 and 91/283. See further Directive 2000/54, 18 September 2000 on the protection of workers from risks related to exposure to biological agents at work: [2000] OJ L262/21; and Directive 2000/39, 8 June 2000 on the protection of the health and safety of workers from risks related to chemical agents at work: [2000] OJ L142/47. Directive 2001/45 of 27 June 2001 amends Directive 89/655 concerning minimum health and safety requirements for the use of work equipment at work: [2001] OJ L195/46.

[324] SI 1992/2051. In *Robb v Salamis Ltd* [2006] UKHL 56; [2007] I.C.R. 175 Lord Hope said that he preferred to reserve his opinion as to whether these Regulations gave rise to civil liability.

[325] SI 1999/3242. The framework Directive does not cover the impact of stress at work on the mental health of employees: *Cross v Highlands and Islands Enterprise*, 2001 S.C.L.R. 547; [2001] I.R.L.R. 336, Court of Session, OH.

[326] In *Commission of the European Communities v United Kingdom* (C-127/05) [2007] I.C.R. 1393; [2007] All E.R. (EC) 986; [2007] 3 C.M.L.R. 20, the European Court of Justice held that the UK was not in contravention of the framework directive (Directive 89/391) by limiting the duty imposed upon employers in the Health and Safety at Work etc. Act 1974 s.2(1) to a duty to ensure the safety and health of workers in all aspects related to work only "so far as was reasonably practicable". The directive had not imposed on Member States a duty to prescribe a no-fault liability regime for employers. Variations and inconsistencies in interpretation of the many Regulations, in light of this decision and many decisions of the House of Lords and Court of Appeal, are analysed by S. Allen, "The complexity of employers' liability law" [2009] J.P.I.L. 243.

[327] Regulation 16 requires employers to undertake a risk assessment in respect of new or expectant mothers and reg.19 requires employers to protect young persons employed from any risks to their health or safety which are a consequence of their lack of experience, or absence of awareness of existing or potential risks or the fact that young persons have not yet fully matured.

[328] Regulation 22 of the Management of Health and Safety at Work Regulations 1999 extended to employees the protection enjoyed by their employers against claims brought by third parties, in circumstances where the employee may have owed a duty to third parties under reg.14. That protection ceased to be relevant from 1 October 2013. Regulation 22 is now limited to actions by a new or expectant mother for breach of a duty imposed by reg.16, 16A, 17 or 17A.

UK's withdrawal from the EU (31 January 2020) was maintained as a result of the European Union (Withdrawal) Act 2018 s.2(1), which states that: "EU-derived domestic legislation, as it has effect in domestic law immediately before exit day, continues to have effect in domestic law on and after exit day". "EU-derived legislation" includes regulations passed in order to give effect to EU Directives. Section 25 of the European Union (Withdrawal Agreement) Act 2020 amends s.2(1) to extend its effect beyond the end of the transition period (with a commencement date to be determined).

Duty owed to persons at work under defendant's control Some of the Regulations impose duties not only in respect of employees, but also in respect of persons at work and under a defendant's control. In *Kmiecic v Isaacs*[329] the Court of Appeal emphasised that this did not mean that the Regulations impose duties on ordinary householders toward workers on their premises. Even if the householder controlled access to the premises (in this instance, by barring access to a roof through a bedroom window), this did not mean that the householder controlled the work, which determined whether a duty was owed under the Construction (Health, Safety and Welfare) Regulations 1996,[330] and the Work at Height Regulations 2005. "Control" over construction work includes control over access and duties arise in respect of access; but this does not mean that controlling access is sufficient to show that an occupier exercises control over construction work. In any given case, whether or not an occupier exercises "control" over the work is a question of fact, as explained in *McCook v Lobo*.[331] It would be absurd to think that requiring anyone who asks for repair work to be done on their house to assume responsibility under the Regulations would improve the safety of workers, which was the rationale of the Framework Directive and Implementing Directive 92/57 of 24 June 1992.[332] The reason for the claim against the householder in *Kmiecic* was that the employer had not insured his employee. Nor had the immediate employer in *Tafa v Matsim Properties Ltd*,[333] but here it was held that the second and third defendants did have sufficient control to come under the duties in the 1996 and 2005 Regulations. It was suggested that the nature of "control" in these two sets of Regulations was different, in that in order to owe a duty under the 1996 Regulations, the defendant must control the manner in which the work is carried out, whereas the 2005 Regulations impose a duty on anyone who controls the person conducting the work. The meaning of risks arising "at work" has needed examination in connection with some of the Regulations. In both *Kennedy v Cordia (Services) LLP*[334] and *Parr v Wirral University Teaching Hospital NHS Foundation Trust*,[335] the risk of slipping on snow and ice while outside as an ancillary, not central, part of employment was held not to be a risk "while at work" for the purposes of the Personal Protective Equipment at Work Regulations 1992 reg.4, or (in *Kennedy*) the Management of Health and Safety at Work Regulations 1999. However, the former decision was reversed by 12-53

[329] [2011] EWCA Civ 451; [2011] I.C.R. 1269; [2011] P.I.Q.R. P13.

[330] Revoked by the Construction (Design and Management) Regulations 2007 (SI 2007/320), which were in turn revoked by the Construction (Design and Management) Regulations 2015 (SI 2015/51).

[331] [2002] EWCA Civ 1760; [2003] I.C.R. 89.

[332] For a similar result in a case argued in negligence, where an elderly couple owed no duty of care to a volunteer working on their house, see *McElhatton v McFarland* [2012] NIQB 114.

[333] [2011] EWHC 1302 (QB).

[334] [2014] CSIH 76; 2014 S.L.T. 984.

[335] County Court, Liverpool, 5 November 2014.

the Supreme Court in *Kennedy v Cordia (Services) LLP*.[336] The pursuer, as a home carer, was "at work" when travelling to a client's home. Since the risk could not be avoided, it had to be evaluated, with merely "giving instructions" to employees a last resort. The defenders had given no consideration to the possibility of individual protective measures before merely giving instructions, and could therefore be said to be in breach of the 1999 and 1992 Regulations.[337]

12-54 In *Ceva Logistics Ltd v Lynch*[338] the owner and operator of a warehouse was held to be in breach of duty under the Workplace (Health, Safety and Welfare) Regulations 1992 to a visiting electrician who was not an employee, and who suffered injury on the premises. The defendant was not in control of the way in which the electrician carried out his electrical work, but was in control of operations within the warehouse and could make and enforce rules of conduct to assure the safety of those on site. Since the electrician was injured when he was struck by a vehicle in the warehouse, the injury fell within the matters over which the defendant had control, and the defendant owed the relevant duties under the Regulations. The defendant ought to have ensured separation of pedestrians and vehicles within the warehouse. The need for control in relation to the risk was, by contrast, fatal to the pursuer's claim against surveyors in *Winn-Pope v ES Access Platforms Ltd*,[339] involving alleged breaches of the Work at Height Regulations 2005. The pursuer was the driver and operator of equipment hired to surveyors in order to enable them to inspect the roof of a building. He had unexpectedly chosen to follow one of the surveyors onto the roof, apparently in order to continue a conversation, when he suffered a fall. The surveyors were in control of the work, but this work was not intended to include the pursuer, who ought to have worn a harness which would have made it impossible for him to leave the raised basket. He had come onto the roof for his own purposes. The defendants therefore did not control the pursuer, and did not owe him the relevant duty.

12-55 **Duty to conduct risk assessment** Whatever the position in relation to civil actions for breach of the Management of Health and Safety at Work Regulations 1992,[340] in *Robb v Salamis*[341] Lord Hope considered that it was proper to take into account an employer's obligations under reg.3(1) of the Regulations—which requires an employer to make a suitable assessment of the risks to health and safety to which employees are exposed whilst at work, and the risks to health and safety to which persons not in his employment are exposed arising out of the conduct of his undertaking—when construing other regulations which did impose civil liability (in particular regs 4 and 20 of the Provision and Use of Work Equipment Regulations 1998). Thus, a failure to undertake the risk assessments required under the Management of Health and Safety at Work Regulations may be a factor in considering whether an employer is in breach of other regulations. This point is reinforced by the decision of the Court of Appeal in *Allison v London Underground Ltd*,[342] where it was held that in considering the adequacy of training in the use of work equipment under reg.9 of the Provision and Use of Work Equipment Regula-

336 [2016] UKSC 6; [2016] 1 W.L.R. 597.
337 See also para.12-02 and para.12-35.
338 [2011] EWCA Civ 188; [2011] I.C.R. 746.
339 [2012] CSOH 87; 2012 S.L.T. 929.
340 Discussed in para.12-52.
341 [2006] UKHL 56; [2007] I.C.R. 175; [2007] 2 All E.R. 97.
342 [2008] EWCA Civ 71; [2008] I.C.R. 719; [2008] P.I.Q.R. P10.

tions 1998 the court had to take into account the employer's obligation to carry out a risk assessment under reg.3 of the Management of Health and Safety at Work Regulations 1999. Smith LJ commented that reg.3:

> "requires the employer to carry out a suitable and sufficient risk assessment for the purposes of identifying the measures he needs to take to comply with the requirements and prohibitions imposed upon him by or under the relevant statutory provisions. What the employer *ought* to have known will be what he *would* have known if he had carried out a suitable and sufficient risk assessment. Plainly, a suitable and sufficient risk assessment will identify those risks in respect of which the employee needs training. Such a risk assessment will provide the basis not only for the training which the employer must give but also for other aspects of his duty, such as, for example, whether the place of work is safe or whether work equipment is suitable."[343]

In *Threlfall v Kingston-upon-Hull City Council*,[344] Smith LJ again emphasised the connection between a duty to conduct a risk assessment (on this occasion, in reg.6 of the Personal Protective Equipment at Work Regulations 1992[345]), and a duty to provide "suitable" equipment (under reg.4 of the same Regulations). For equipment to be suitable in accordance with reg.4, it had to be at least appropriate for the risk and, as far as practicable, effective to prevent or adequately control the risk. The identification of risk is therefore essential to the judgment of suitability, and it was not open to the judge to base his assessment of the suitability of equipment on an inadequate risk assessment by the employer. Here, the claimant had suffered lacerations to his hand from a concealed sharp object when clearing garden refuse. He had been supplied with ordinary gardening gloves which would not protect from such lacerations. Although the risk of such lacerations was not high, this did not mean that the gloves could be said to be suitable. Gloves which would protect against such lacerations were available, albeit at greater cost. Smith LJ said that an adequate risk assessment would have considered the risk of laceration from sharp objects, and the suitability of the equipment should be judged accordingly. In general terms, Smith LJ described the difference made by the statutory health and safety duties in terms of a duty to anticipate and guard against risks: **12-56**

> "In many instances, a statutory duty to conduct … a risk assessment has been imposed. Such a requirement (whether statutory or not) has to a large extent taken the place of the old common law requirement that an employer had to consider (and take action against) those risks which could reasonably be foreseen. The modern requirement is that he should take positive thought for the risks arising from his operations."[346]

The decision of the Supreme Court in *Kennedy v Cordia* illustrates that the "modern requirement" applies also in the context of a negligence action at common law.[347] In *Threlfall*, a failure to undertake a risk assessment was not itself sufficient basis for liability. It still needed to be shown that the equipment was not suitable. But effectiveness was at the heart of suitability,[348] and effectiveness was judged in relation to the avoidance of the risks that ought to have been identified. Given that an

---

343 [2008] EWCA Civ 71; [2008] I.C.R. 719; [2008] P.I.Q.R. P10 at [57].
344 [2010] EWCA Civ 1147; [2011] I.C.R. 209.
345 SI 1992/2966.
346 [2010] EWCA Civ 1147; [2011] I.C.R. 209 at [35].
347 See para.12-35.
348 [2010] EWCA Civ 1147; [2011] I.C.R. 209 at [41]. See *Blair v Chief Constable of Sussex Police* [2012] EWCA Civ 633; [2012] I.C.R. D33 at [6] per Longmore LJ, applying the approach set out

adequate risk assessment would have considered the risk of laceration, the equipment was not, in the circumstances, "suitable". The judge below had come close to adopting the common law standard, which was thought not to be the standard of the Regulations.[349]

12-57 The content of the Regulations made under the Health and Safety at Work etc. Act 1974 in some respects resembles the older statutory provisions. A mixture of duties is imposed on employers. Some are absolute[350] and safety must be guaranteed. Others require that employers do what is reasonably practicable.[351] The number of Regulations is large and it is not possible here to do more than provide an outline of what have been the most significant Regulations in terms of civil litigation by employees.[352] It has been suggested that the Regulations should not be construed so as to overlap.[353]

---

in *Threlfall*: "Thus a structured approach to the 1992 Regulations is required. It is first necessary to identify the risk of injury, and then to ask if the equipment in fact provided was, so far as practicable, effective to prevent or adequately control that risk. It is only if the equipment was effective or it was not practicable to make it effective that there is any need to consider whether the equipment is appropriate …".

349 See also *Chief Constable of Hampshire v Taylor* [2013] EWCA Civ 496; [2013] I.C.R. 1150, emphasising that the task on which an employee is engaged at the time of injury should not be subjected to such fine analysis that the risks against which protection is to be afforded are artificially limited in scope, since this would undermine the protection of the Regulations (at [17]). The claimant was engaged in dismantling a cannabis factory and gashed her hand attempting to open a window to alleviate the fumes; it was held that she should have been supplied with thick gloves. Dismantling the factory involved a range of tasks, and it was no answer that her injury was not caused by removal of the plants themselves. See further *McPake v SRCL Ltd* [2013] CSOH 157; 2014 Rep. L.R. 41 (clinical waste management company in breach of reg.4 of the Personal Protective Equipment at Work Regulations 1992 for a needle-stick injury sustained by a driver collecting clinical waste from a hospital; reg.4 had to be considered in light of the requirement to undertake a risk assessment imposed by reg.6).

350 Regulation 6(1) of the Provision and Use of Work Equipment Regulations 1992 (SI 1992/2932), requiring every employer to ensure that work equipment is maintained in an efficient state, an efficient working order and in good repair, imposed an absolute duty: *Stark v Post Office* [2000] P.I.Q.R. P105. See now the Provision and Use of Work Equipment Regulations 1998 (SI 1998/2306).

351 See the Manual Handling Operations Regulations 1992 (SI 1992/2793); on which see *Koonjul v ThamesLink Healthcare Services* [2000] P.I.Q.R. P123, CA; *Swain v Denso Marston Ltd* [2000] I.C.R. 1079; [2000] P.I.Q.R. P129, CA. See also J. Hendy, "Industrial Accident Claims: Reasonable Practicability" [2001] J.P.I.L. 209. Even where avoidance is not reasonably practicable, the employer is under a duty to conduct a risk assessment and take steps to reduce risks. The dangers for employers of treating risk assessment as a "tick box" exercise are well illustrated by *Denton Hall Legal Services v Fifield* [2006] EWCA Civ 169; [2006] Lloyd's Rep. Med. 251 (a case involving the Management of Health and Safety at Work Regulations 1992 and the Health and Safety (Display Screen Equipment) Regulations 1992).

352 Regulations include the Management of Health and Safety at Work Regulations 1999 (SI 1999/3242); Provision and Use of Work Equipment Regulations 1998 (SI 1998/2306); Personal Protective Equipment at Work Regulations 1992 (SI 1992/2966); Workplace (Health, Safety and Welfare) Regulations 1992 (SI 1992/3004); Manual Handling Operations Regulations 1992 (SI 1992/2793); Control of Noise at Work Regulations 2005 (SI 2005/1643); Control of Substances Hazardous to Health Regulations 2002 (SI 2002/2677; as amended by SI 2003/978 and SI 2004/3386); Control of Lead at Work Regulations 2002 (SI 2002/2676); Control of Asbestos Regulations 2012 (SI 2012/632, which consolidate the Asbestos Regulations); Ionising Radiations Regulations 2017 (SI 2017/1075); Ionising Radiation (Medical Exposure) Regulations 2017 (SI 2017/1322); Justification of Practices Involving Ionising Radiation Regulations 2004 (SI 2004/1769); Control of Artificial Optical Radiation at Work Regulations 2010 (SI 2010/1140); Health and Safety (Display Screen Equipment) Regulations 1992 (SI 1992/2792); Work at Height Regulations 2005 (SI 2005/735; as amended by SI 2007/114); Supply of Machinery (Safety) Regulations 2008 (SI 2008/1597); Merchant Ship-

The ambit of the regulations Apart from the question of the standard of liability to be applied by any particular statute or set of regulations, the central issue in most of these cases is whether the circumstances in which the employee sustained injury are covered by the statutory rules. The territorial extent of the Regulations was considered in *Bass v Ministry of Defence*.[354] Referring to remarks of Lord Carnwath in *Smith v Ministry of Defence*,[355] it was concluded that the Management of Health and Safety at Work Regulations did not apply to activities overseas (in this instance, protection of armed forces personnel from risk of specified diseases), whether or not the relevant decisions as to risk prevention were taken within the UK. Such a distinction would lead to great difficulty.[356] As in all other cases involving the tort of breach of statutory duty, the claimant must prove that the damage fell within the ambit of the statutory provision.[357] This is a matter of statutory construction. For example, in *Close v Steel Co of Wales Ltd*[358] the House of Lords held that the duty to fence "every dangerous part of any machinery" in the Factories Act 1937[359] was confined to preventing the operator himself from coming into contact with moving parts of the machinery, and thus did not give rise to liability if a fragment of the machine or of the material on which it was working 12-58

ping and Fishing Vessels (Health and Safety at Work) Regulations 1997 (SI 1997/2962); Merchant Shipping and Fishing Vessels (Manual Handling Operations) Regulations 1998 (SI 1998/2857); Merchant Shipping and Fishing Vessels (Provision and Use of Work Equipment) Regulations 2006 (SI 2006/2183; as amended by SI 2008/2165); Merchant Shipping and Fishing Vessels (Lifting Operations and Lifting Equipment) Regulations 2006 (SI 2006/2184; as amended by 2008/2166); Merchant Shipping and Fishing Vessels (Control of Noise at Work) Regulations 2007 (SI 2007/3075); Merchant Shipping and Fishing Vessels (Control of Vibration at Work) Regulations 2007 (SI 2007/3077 as amended by SI 2010/1110); Construction (Design and Management) Regulations 2015 (SI 2015/51); Control of Electromagnetic Fields at Work Regulations 2016 (SI 2016/588). See also the Health and Safety (Miscellaneous Amendments and Revocation) Regulations 2017 (SI 2017/304); Merchant Shipping and Fishing Vessels (Health and Safety) (Miscellaneous Amendments) (EU Exit) Regulations 2018 (SI 2018/1202); and the Health and Safety (Amendment) (EU Exit) Regulations 2018 (SI 2018/1370).

353 *Mason v Satelcom Ltd, East Potential Ltd* [2008] EWCA Civ 494; [2008] I.C.R. 971 at [21], per Longmore LJ, and at [54], per Ward LJ. This was applied in *Heeds v Chief Constable of Cleveland* [2018] EWHC 810 (QB); [2019] I.C.R. 513 to exclude the operation of the Provision and Use of Work Equipment Regulations 1998, where there would have been liability, and to apply instead the Workplace (Health, Safety and Welfare) Regulations 1992, where there was no liability.

354 [2020] EWHC 36 (QB).

355 [2013] UKSC 41; [2014] A.C. 52 at [38].

356 In this case, however, it was also held that the Regulations would add nothing to the common law duty to conduct a risk assessment.

357 See para.8-50 onwards.

358 [1962] A.C. 367. See also *Nicholls v F Austin (Leyton) Ltd* [1946] A.C. 493; *Kilgollan v William Cooke & Co Ltd* [1956] 1 W.L.R. 527 CA; *Rutherford v RE Glanville & Sons etc Ltd* [1958] 1 W.L.R. 415 CA; cf. *Johnson v J Stone & Co Ltd* [1961] 1 W.L.R. 849. In *Littler v GL Moore (Contractors) Ltd* [1967] 1 W.L.R. 1241, *Close v Steel Company of Wales Ltd* was distinguished and an employer who had failed to supply goggles in accordance with the Construction (General Provisions) Regulations 1961 reg.52 was held liable to an employee whose eye was injured by a particle which flew off a tool. See also *Millard v Serck Tubes Ltd* [1969] 1 W.L.R. 211 CA; *Cross v Midland etc Iron and Steel Co* [1965] A.C. 343. In *Young v Charles Church (Southern) Ltd* (1998) 39 B.M.L.R. 146, the Court of Appeal held that breach of the Construction (General Provisions) Regulations 1961 reg.44(2) applied to an employee who suffered psychiatric damage as a result of witnessing the electrocution of a fellow worker, at least where he was working very close to the danger—the regulation was not limited to physical electrocution. See now the Construction (Design and Management) Regulations 2015 (SI 2015/51).

359 See now the Supply of Machinery (Safety) Regulations 2008 (SI 2008/1597), implementing Directive 2006/42/EC, itself revoking the "Machinery Directive", Directive 98/37/EC. The 2006 Directive and the 2008 Regulations came into force on 29 December 2009.

flew out and struck the operator.[360] Nor did the duty to fence extend to dangers from materials which were in motion in the machine, nor to dangers due to the machinery breaking down or behaving in an unexpected way,[361] nor to preventing a tool which the operator was using from coming into contact with the dangerous machinery.[362] In *Tate v Swan Hunter & Wigham Richardson Ltd*[363] an electrician employed by the defendants was engaged in work on a gantry some 80 feet above the ground. Planks were placed on the gantries for men to move from one part of the structure to another. The electrician stepped backwards and fell through a gap in the planks to his death. The Factories Act 1937 s.25(3) provided that all openings in floors should be securely fenced, except in so far as the nature of the work renders such fencing impracticable. The Court of Appeal held that the plank way was not a "floor" within the meaning of this section and so defendants were not in breach of a statutory duty to fence the opening. On the other hand, an employee who injured his back attempting to remove a plank obstructing a walkway was held to be within the scope of reg.30(2) of the Construction (Working Places) Regulations 1966 prohibiting obstructions on walkways.[364] A man who was struck by masonry falling from the side of a shaft in a block of flats under construction had no remedy under a regulation for the protection of a workman "from being struck by any falling material or article",[365] and a man who injured himself when a defective toilet-seat came adrift from the pan had no remedy under s.7 of the Factories Act 1961, providing for "sufficient and suitable sanitary conveniences", this being designed to prevent infection rather than injury to the user.[366]

12-59 This type of problem is not confined to the statutory duties created under the older industrial safety legislation. In *Fytche v Wincanton Logistics Plc*[367] the claimant developed frostbite in one of his toes as a result of water entering a steel capped safety boot, provided by his employers, through a small hole in the sole which was not discoverable by either the employer or the employee. Regulation 7 of the Personal Protective Equipment at Work Regulations 1992[368] provides that "every employer shall ensure that any personal protective equipment provided to his employees is maintained … in an efficient state, in efficient working order and in good repair". By a majority, the House of Lords held that this obligation applies only to the risk in respect of which the protective equipment is supplied, not *any* risk that may arise if the equipment is not in an efficient state or good repair. The provision of steel capped safety boots was intended to protect the employee against the risk of injury from falling weights or contact with hard or sharp objects. It was

---

[360] See also *Nicholls v F Austin (Leyton) Ltd* [1946] A.C. 493 at 505, per Lord Simonds: "The fence is intended to keep the worker out, not to keep the machine or its product in."

[361] *Eaves v Morris Motors Ltd* [1961] 2 Q.B. 385 CA.

[362] *Sparrow v Fairey Aviation Co Ltd* [1964] A.C. 1019 HL. Although the statute did require the fencing of a "nip" between the machine and the materials it was processing: *Cross v Midland and Low Moor Iron and Steel Co Ltd* [1965] A.C. 343; *Johnson v FE Callow Ltd* [1971] A.C. 335; and gave rise to liability where the unfenced dangerous part threw the workman's hand against the materials being worked upon: *Wearing v Pirelli Ltd* [1977] 1 W.L.R. 48.

[363] [1958] 1 W.L.R. 39 CA.

[364] *McGovern v British Steel Corp* [1986] I.C.R. 608. See now Construction (Design and Management) Regulations 2015 (SI 2015/51).

[365] *Bailey v Ayr Engineering and Constructional Co Ltd* [1959] 1 Q.B. 183 CA.

[366] *Hands v Rolls-Royce Ltd*, unreported, noted at (1972) 69 L.S. Gaz. 504. Sed quaere: the section also says that lavatories shall be properly lighted, a requirement surely directed towards safety rather than health.

[367] [2004] UKHL 31; [2004] I.C.R. 975; [2004] 4 All E.R. 221.

[368] SI 1992/2966.

not to protect the employee from the risk of frostbite when working in extreme weather conditions.

(a) Provision and Use of Work Equipment Regulations

Work equipment and the coverage of the Regulations The Provision and Use of Work Equipment Regulations 1998[369] reg.4(1) provides that every employer[370] shall ensure that work equipment[371] is so constructed or adapted as to be suitable for the purpose for which it is used or provided. The duty in reg.4 is strict, and the definition of "work equipment" (reg.2(1)) which is "provided for use or used by an employee at his work" (reg.3(2)) will therefore be vital in defining the ambit and limits of the strict liability thereby created. The meaning of these provisions has been subject to close analysis by the House of Lords in *Spencer-Franks v Kellogg Brown & Root*,[372] and *Smith v Northamptonshire CC*,[373] and the Court of Appeal in (amongst others) *Mason v Satelcom*.[374] Earlier, in *Hammond v Commissioner of* 12-60

369 SI 1998/2306. The Regulations revoked and replaced the Provision and Use of Work Equipment Regulations 1992 (SI 1992/2932). See also the Personal Protective Equipment at Work Regulations 1992 (SI 1992/2966), on which see *Fytche v Wincanton Logistics Plc* [2004] UKHL 31; [2004] I.C.R. 975; [2004] 4 All E.R. 221, see para.12-59; and *Threlfall v Kingston-upon-Hull City Council* [2010] EWCA Civ 1147; [2011] I.C.R. 209, para.12-56.

370 Note that by reg.3(3) the Provision and Use of Work Equipment Regulations 1998 also apply to any person who has control to any extent (and to the extent of his control) over (i) work equipment; (ii) a person at work who uses or supervises or manages the use of work equipment; or (iii) the way in which work equipment is used at work. In *Casson v Hudson* [2017] EWCA Civ 125; [2017] P.I.Q.R. P12, a prisoner on day release was injured falling from a ladder while carrying out decorating work at a church, and claimed against the church for his injuries. His claim failed. The ladder was in good condition; he had been required not to use ladders when taking his placement; and the church did not supervise his work or offer him instruction. Within the terms of reg.3(3), even if the ladder was "work equipment" (which the court below had held it was not, given the prohibition on use of ladders), the church would only have control of "(i) work equipment", and not of "(ii) a person at work who uses or supervises ... work equipment; or (iii) the way in which work equipment is used at work". Thus, the only duty that would be brought into play would be the duty of maintenance under reg.5. Duties to provide training and to ensure the suitability of the equipment would not be triggered. In *Mason v Satelcom* [2008] EWCA Civ 494; [2008] I.C.R. 971, a service engineer fell from a ladder that was too short for the job he was undertaking, having found the ladder in the room where the equipment was to be serviced. His employers were found to have been negligent and in breach of the Work Equipment Regulations in failing to provide a suitable ladder. Relying on reg.3(3), the employers brought proceedings against the occupier of the room in question on the basis that although the occupier did not supply the ladder, they could have removed it or placed a notice on it. The Court of Appeal reversed the judge's decision that the occupier should contribute 25 per cent of the claimant's damages. The occupier did not have control of the ladder to a relevant extent; or, if they did have control of the ladder, the extent of their control did not justify liability on their part. See also *Hyndman v Brown and Bradley* [2012] NICA 3, where the Court of Appeal in Northern Ireland held that the second defendant, who had loaned a harvester to the claimant's employer, did not have control of the harvester at the time of the accident. It was appropriate for the work and well-maintained, and the claimant's employer was an experienced contractor. The second defendant had no control over the staff selected to operate the machinery and no control over how they operated it.

371 Regulation 2(1) provides that work equipment is "any machinery, appliance, apparatus, tool or installation for use at work (whether exclusively or not)".

372 [2008] UKHL 46; [2008] I.C.R. 863; [2009] 1 All E.R. 269.

373 [2009] UKHL 27; [2009] 4 All E.R. 557; [2009] I.C.R. 734. This case concerned reg.5 of the Provision and Use of Work Equipment Regulations 1998 (see para.12-69), but the case turned upon the definition of "work equipment". It is explored in para.12-65.

374 [2008] EWCA Civ 494; [2008] I.C.R. 971.

Police for the Metropolis,[375] the Court of Appeal had taken a more restrictive approach, now disapproved by the House of Lords, in which "work equipment" applied only to the "tools of the trade" provided by an employer for use by his employees when they are at work, but not other objects provided by others or on which the employee was working. So a mechanic employed by the Commissioner of Police who was working on a van owned by the Metropolitan Police Authority was not covered by the Regulations when a bolt on the van sheared off. The van could have been the work equipment of a police officer driving it, but not of the police mechanic repairing it, at least when the van was not the property of the employer of the mechanic. Regulation 3(2) provides that: "The requirements imposed by these Regulations on an employer in respect of work equipment shall apply to such equipment provided for use or used by an employee of his at work." In *PRP Architects v Reid*,[376] the Court of Appeal distinguished *Hammond* and held that an employee leaving at the end of a day's work who used a lift located in the lobby of the building where the employee worked (the lift being situated in the common parts of the building and not leased to the employer) was using it at work within the meaning of reg.3(2). Although as with the wheel bolt in *Hammond* the lift was the property of a third party, it was "a facility used in the course of work, which is different from an object worked on".[377] In *Rooney v Western Education and Library Board*,[378] a canteen assistant suffered personal injury from a broken cup or mug while drying staff crockery. It was held that a staff mug or cup was "work equipment" for the purposes of the Provision and Use of Work Equipment Regulations (Northern Ireland) 1999. Though not supplied by her employers, it had become part of the generally used crockery in the canteen, and in drying it, she was using it at work: "use" in reg.2(1) expressly included cleaning, and drying is part of cleaning.

12-61 In *Spencer-Franks v Kellogg Brown & Root*,[379] *Hammond* was disapproved. A door closer which was being repaired by the claimant when it caused injury to him was within the definition of "work equipment" to which the Regulations applied. The claimant was employed by K to work on a North Sea oil platform operated by another company, T. He was asked to inspect and repair the "door closer", and was struck in the face by a linkage arm when a screw came out. He brought an action for damages against K and T, based upon breach of obligations under the 1998 Regulations. The issues considered by the House of Lords were whether the door closer was "work equipment" and if so whether the claimant had been "using" that equipment within the meaning of the 1998 Regulations. The case against the pursuer's employer K was not given any separate consideration from that of the

---

[375] [2004] EWCA Civ 830; [2004] I.C.R. 1467; [2005] P.I.Q.R. P1. This was a decision on the Provision and Use of Work Equipment Regulations 1992. The Court of Appeal held in *Hammond* that a mechanic employed by the Metropolitan Police Authority was not covered by the Regulations when a bolt on the van sheared off. The van was not the work equipment of the employee repairing it. *Hammond* was disapproved by the House of Lords in *Spencer-Franks v Kellogg Brown & Root* [2008] UKHL 46; [2008] I.C.R. 863; [2009] 1 All E.R. 269.

[376] [2006] EWCA Civ 1119; [2007] I.C.R. 78; [2007] P.I.Q.R. P4. Contrast *Heeds v Chief Constable of Cleveland* [2018] EWHC 810 (QB); [2019] I.C.R. 513, where a door was held not to be work equipment. Though a specialist door, it was "nevertheless a door". The case was approached instead under the Workplace (Health, Safety and Welfare) Regulations 1992, reg.18, where liability was less strict, and for this reason the claim failed.

[377] [2006] EWCA Civ 1119; [2007] I.C.R. 78; [2007] P.I.Q.R. P4 at [19], per Pill LJ.

[378] [2015] NIQB 87.

[379] [2008] UKHL 46; [2008] I.C.R. 863; [2009] 1 All E.R. 269.

second defender, T. This was because there was a contractual indemnity in favour of T, so that it was not worthwhile for K to seek to establish that only T was liable. The 1998 Regulations impose duties and liabilities not only upon employers, but also (and going beyond the requirements of Directive 89/655 which it implements) upon others if and to the extent that they have "control" over "work equipment". If the door closer was "work equipment" and if repairing it fell within the Regulations, then it seemed obvious that T as the operator of the platform had control over it. As such, it was unlikely that K alone would be liable. But in principle, should T be the only liable party? Lord Hoffmann thought that if it had been in issue, the liability of the employer (K) might depend upon whether the equipment had been "provided for use" by K, which in turn might depend whether the platform could be said to be "the site of an undertaking by KBR as well as Talisman". Lord Rodger differed in his analysis of the wording of the Regulation. He pointed out that the Regulation used the expression "provided for use" without mentioning *who* had to provide the equipment for use: it did not have to be provided by the employer. In distinguishing *Hammond v Commissioner of Police for the Metropolis*,[380] Lord Rodger and Lord Hoffmann emphasised that equipment cannot be "work equipment" with regard to one employee, but not with regard to others. An item cannot "slip in and out of being work equipment".[381] This would not assist employers in improving the safety of their workers. As Lord Hoffmann put it, the relevant question should have been whether Mr Hammond was a worker "in the undertaking to which it had been supplied". The claimant in *Hammond* would also fit this description, even if his only "use" of the equipment was to repair it. The Court of Appeal had been wrong to suggest that "repairing" an object did not amount to "using" that equipment. "Repair" is listed as an example of "using" in the Regulations themselves. Nor, as an alternative, did the House accept that minor repairs could amount to "use" while major repairs were something separate and different.

Departure from wording of Regulation Members of the House of Lords in *Spencer-Franks* drew attention to the fact that the wording used in reg.3(2) could conceivably impose very broad liability on an employer in respect of equipment which satisfied the definition of "work equipment" in reg.2(1), but in respect of which they had little or no connection. On the face of it, they would owe a duty if the equipment is simply "used" by an employee. Lord Hoffmann thought this could not have been the intention of Parliament, and described it as a case "in which the draftsman thought he could clarify the meaning of a directive but would have done better to leave its language alone".[382] The Directive did not include the alternative "or used" as amounting to a sufficient connection. Lord Hoffmann took a very simple approach to the definition of "work equipment" in reg.2(1). The regulation includes within the definition any equipment "for use at work", which clearly focuses on the purpose of the equipment. In this instance, everyone using the control room used the door, and therefore used the closer. It was, clearly, work equipment. Lord Rodger appears to have been less troubled by the possibility that the wording of reg.3(2) might, taken literally, lead to quite extensive strict liability. One reason for this is that he took a broader approach to the purpose of the Regulations. These, he said, were primarily designed to improve safety: 12-62

380 [2004] EWCA Civ 830; [2004] I.C.R. 1467.
381 [2008] UKHL 46; [2008] I.C.R. 863 at [35], per Lord Rodger.
382 [2008] UKHL 46; [2008] I.C.R. 863 at [26].

"Their main purpose is not to give those who have been injured a straightforward route to damages, but to prevent them being injured in the first place. If this results in a broad swathe of strict liability in damages, that is simply one consequence of the correspondingly broad scope of the measures adopted to achieve that purpose."[383]

The immediate purpose of the Regulations was "to give full effect to the proposals of the Health and Safety Commission which went further than the minimum requirements of the directive".[384] Lord Rodger also took a more nuanced approach to the meaning of "work equipment" in reg.2(1). The meaning of "work equipment" was restricted slightly by its context: "The machinery and apparatus etc of an undertaking are there to perform a useful, practical function in relation to the purposes of the undertaking."[385] This, he argued, is an essential aspect of the idea of being "for use at work"–the wording used in reg.2(1). On Lord Rodger's view, a piece of work equipment which requires repair—like the closer in this case, or like the police vehicle in *Hammond*—remains a piece of work equipment even if it was being worked upon, cleaned, repaired, and so on. But if something was present *only* for repair, cleaning etc it would not be serving a useful, practical purpose in the undertaking. As such, while Lord Hoffmann proposed that the ambit of strict liability must be restricted by reference to reg.3(2), itself interpreted in the light of the Directive which it implemented, Lord Rodger introduced at least some substantive restriction to what counts as "work equipment" within reg.2(1). On Lord Rodger's account, the broad wording of reg.3(2) would be less troublesome—the equipment would have to serve a useful, practical purpose to the undertaking in question before "using" it could trigger the obligation under the following Regulations.

12-63 The Court of Appeal in *Hammond* had been troubled by the example of the employee of a garage, injured through defectiveness of a car brought to the garage for repair by a third party, seeking damages from his employer under the 1998 Regulations. Lord Rodger's approach would not treat the car, which is there solely for repair, as "work equipment" at all; whereas the police vehicle in *Hammond* itself clearly was. A door or any other piece of useful equipment which requires repair does not thereby *cease* to be work equipment; but bringing it for repair does not make it work equipment. Lord Rodger's approach provides a potential solution to a variety of problems posed by the wording of the regulation, by giving a more substantial role to reg.2(1). But it has not been taken up in subsequent cases, which have tended to prefer the route taken by Lord Hoffmann and have therefore placed more emphasis on reg.3(2), tending in addition to read it as though its wording conformed more closely to the wording of the Directive which it transposed. The wording of the Directive makes reference to equipment which is "made available to workers" and this has been taken to imply selection by the employer. The wording of reg.3(2) is clearly broader than this and the courts have assumed that this leads to the potential for broader strict liability than Parliament intended: the wording has been taken, as Lord Hoffmann took it, to be a drafter's oversight. This is, of course, contestable. But the courts have been in the position of departing from the literal words of the regulation, guided by their own view as to what parliamen-

---

383 [2008] UKHL 46; [2008] I.C.R. 863 at [34].
384 [2008] UKHL 46; [2008] I.C.R. 863 at [32].
385 [2008] UKHL 46; [2008] I.C.R. 863 at [51].

tary intent required. This is clearly the case with the majority opinions in *Smith v Northamptonshire CC*.[386]

Equipment not provided by the employer In *Couzens v T McGee & Co Ltd*,[387] the Court of Appeal encountered a variation on this problem, and decided that if equipment which had not been provided by the employer was used at work, even if for a useful purpose, it would not be "work equipment" unless the employer expressly or impliedly permitted its use. Clearly, some equipment supplied by the employee can be work equipment, as determined by the Court of Appeal in *Mason v Satelcom*.[388] The Court of Appeal also suggested that permission may be "deemed" where an employer knows of the use of equipment and does nothing to stop it. In this instance, a lorry driver was injured when his vehicle turned over. He argued that the accident was caused by an angled piece of scrap metal which he carried in the door of his cab and used as a kind of scraper, and that the employer should have provided a safe place for the tool. The employer did not know and had no reason to know that he had an implement of this kind, and the Court of Appeal held that they could not be liable for it. It seems clear that the Court supplied what it considered to be a justifiable interpretation of parliamentary intent in respect of the Regulations, thus continuing the courts' search for principles which limit the ambit of the strict liability in the Regulations but which are not present in their wording. Smith LJ said that: 12-64

> "… by applying the regulations to 'equipment provided for use or used by an employee … at work' …, Parliament extended the scope of the regulations to items of equipment which the worker himself had provided and used. I do not think it conceivable that Parliament could have intended to impose strict liability on an employer in respect of an item of equipment about which he did not know and could not reasonably have been expected to know."[389]

In *Smith v Northamptonshire CC*,[390] the House of Lords considered the applicability of the Regulations to equipment which was not provided by an employer, nor used on their premises, but which they knew to be used at another location in the course of the injured employee's work. The case concerned the reg.5 duty to keep work equipment in an efficient state, efficient working order, and good repair, but the key issue was whether the equipment in question was to be regarded as "work equipment" within the meaning of the Regulations. The claimant was employed by the respondent Council as a driver and carer. As part of her job she was required to collect people in need of care from their homes, and take them by minibus to a day centre. One of the people she regularly collected was confined to a wheelchair and in order to get her to the minibus the claimant had to use a fixed wooden ramp leading out from the living room. The claim arose because on one occasion the edge of the ramp crumbled below her foot, causing her to fall and sustain injury. The Council was well aware of the presence of the ramp and of the claimant's use of it for the purposes of performing her job, and had reviewed its safety for the purpose. On the other hand, it was accepted that the defect which caused the injury was a latent one which they could not have observed even on 12-65

---

386 [2009] UKHL 27; [2009] 4 All E.R. 557; [2009] I.C.R. 734. See para.12-65.
387 [2009] EWCA Civ 95; [2009] P.I.Q.R. P14.
388 [2008] EWCA Civ 494; [2008] I.C.R. 971.
389 [2009] EWCA Civ 95; [2009] P.I.Q.R. P14 at [33].
390 [2009] UKHL 27; [2009] 4 All E.R. 557; [2009] I.C.R. 734.

reasonable inspection. Given the strictness of the reg.5 duty,[391] if the ramp was "work equipment" for the use of or used by the employee (within regs 2(1) and 3(2)), then the Council would be liable. By a bare majority (Lord Hope and Baroness Hale dissenting), the House of Lords held that the ramp did not fall within the definition of work equipment to which the Regulations applied, and therefore its collapse gave rise to no liability. The majority judges were not alone in feeling compelled to read additional words into the Regulations in order to restrict their effect. Lord Hope referred to the concept of "control" which applied to the liability of non-employers under reg.3(3), and argued that the absence of this word from the provisions applying to employers under reg.3(2) did not mean that the concept of control had no place in respect of employer liability. He agreed with Lord Mance, for the majority, that there needs to be some sufficient "nexus" between the work equipment and the undertaking, but unlike Lord Mance he thought there was such a nexus in this case. Lord Hope's preferred tests were authorisation, and control, of the employee's *use of the equipment* (rather than of the equipment itself). He emphasised that the Council would have "had to have made other arrangements" if they had not considered the ramp suitable. He also thought that if the relevant test was incorporation and adoption of the ramp as part of the undertaking, this too would be satisfied; as indeed would a test (derived from Lord Mance's majority opinion), that there was "consent and endorsement" for its use. On all these grounds, he thought there was a sufficient nexus with the undertaking to justify absolute liability in respect of maintenance and repair. But it should be remembered that the language of the regulation does not require any of these connections explicitly. Also in dissent, Baroness Hale took a different route to the same conclusion. The employer must be subject to *at least* the same liabilities as a non-employer under reg.3(3); the test for the liability of a non-employer was "control"; in this instance, the Council had sufficient control over the use of the ramp (rather than over its condition), because it had a choice whether to allow its employee to use it, or to provide an alternative (for example, a portable ramp). This approach treats the particular case as within the ambit of the Regulations without seeking to establish where their outer limits are: they must cover this case because they cover cases of control of this sort where non-employers are concerned. Baroness Hale pointed out that the real objection to liability in this instance was not lack of choice on the part of the employer (they did have this choice), but lack of negligence. Like Lord Rodger in *Spencer-Franks v Kellogg Brown & Root*, she emphasised that the source of the Regulations was not solely the Directive, but (more directly) the Health and Safety at Work etc. Act 1974. There was no indication that Parliament aimed to include any element of lack of care in the conditions for their application.

12-66 The majority judges emphasised the need to limit the strict liability in the Regulations. Lord Mance in particular, with whom Lord Carswell agreed, was concerned about the application of the Regulations "at places with which an employer has no connection except that his or her employee has while working to visit them". In such cases, in Lord Mance's view, the appropriate test was "control". Unlike both the first instance judge and the dissenting judges, Lord Mance thought that this concerned control *of the equipment*, not simply of the employee's use of the equipment. This contrasts with Baroness Hale's emphasis on the Council's *choice* of whether to use the equipment. In essence, Baroness Hale's approach may be described in terms of the Council's choice of whether to take the risk of their

391 See para.12-69.

employee using a particular piece of equipment when they could have provided a different one. Lord Mance focused much more narrowly on the question of whether the Council could have been expected to have known about the defect—a negligence type question. Lord Neuberger said that the policy arguments were balanced, but equated "control" with control *over the equipment* by analogy with reg.3(3), in direct contrast to the approach of both dissenting judges. Yet it would appear plain that in requiring "control" on the part of the non-employer, Parliament was imposing an additional qualification on their liability. It could be argued that Baroness Hale's approach—although she too preferred to avoid the policy discussion—corresponds with Lord Rodger's analysis in *Spencer-Franks v Kellogg Brown & Root* that the purpose of the Regulations is primarily to increase standards of health and safety. The Council had a choice of whether to provide an alternative means of achieving the same goal, whose maintenance would be under their control. This would increase safety standards. Their choice to use the equipment already available should not be free of risk to them, nor should it be at the employee's risk. This approach, however, did not win the day.

Suitability of work equipment The question of what is "suitable" for the purpose for which the equipment is provided has to be assessed without reference to the cost of the equipment. In *Skinner v Scottish Ambulance Service*[392] the claimant suffered a needle-stick injury, and claimed that his employers should have provided a different, safer, model which was available. The employers argued that the question of what was suitable had to take account of the cost of the alternative model (which was more than five times more expensive than the type of needle used by the defendants), but it was held that "suitable" meant "suitable in any respect which it is reasonably foreseeable will affect the health or safety of any person" without reference to its cost. In *Robb v Salamis (M&I) Ltd*,[393] the claimant was an offshore scaffolder working on a semi-submersible production platform who was injured when he was descending from an upper bunk in his cabin and the ladder gave way causing him to fall. In the House of Lords it was accepted that the claimant was "at work" and that the ladder was "work equipment" within the meaning of the Provision and Use of Work Equipment Regulations 1998. Lord Hope considered that in determining whether there had been a breach of the Provision and Use of Work Equipment Regulations 1998 regs 4 (providing that work equipment must be suitable for the purpose for which it is used or provided) or 20 (providing that work equipment must be stabilised by clamping or otherwise where necessary for purposes of health and safety) the court should have regard both to the employer's obligations under reg.3 of the Management of Health and Safety at Work Regulations (to conduct a risk assessment) and the Framework Directive (Directive 89/391 of 12 June 1989) and the Work Equipment Directive (Directive 89/655 of 30 November 1989) which the Provision and Use of Work Equipment Regulations 1998 were designed to implement. His Lordship commented that: "The dominant 12-67

[392] 2004 S.C. 790; 2004 S.L.T. 834 (Inner House, Ex Div). See also *Crane v Premier Prison Services Ltd* [2001] C.L.Y. 3298 (QBD) where a van used for the transport of prisoners in which the employee was expected to move about while the vehicle was in motion was in breach of reg.5 of the 1992 Regulations because there were no adequate handholds; *Beck v United Closures & Plastics Plc*, 2001 S.L.T. 1299: claimant trapped his hand in two heavy doors at his place of work; the doors fell within the definition of "work equipment" in the Provision and Use of Work Equipment Regulations 1992 reg.2, and were not "suitable" for their purpose by virtue of their faulty locking mechanism, the positioning of the handles and the faulty bracket.

[393] [2006] UKHL 56; [2007] I.C.R. 175; [2007] 2 All E.R. 97.

purpose of all these provisions is to encourage improvements in the safety and health of workers at work."[394] Although the question of what is "necessary" (in reg.20) imported the notion of guarding against only a reasonably foreseeable mischief, the determination of what is "foreseeable" had to be considered in the context of the Directives, which impose an absolute and continuing duty extending to every aspect related to employees' work. Thus, said Lord Hope: "The obligation is to anticipate situations which may give rise to accidents. The employer is not permitted to wait for them to happen."[395] So the fact that there had been no previous accidents of a similar nature was irrelevant. The Work Equipment Directive requires an assessment of risk before the work equipment is used or provided, to identify the risks to health and safety if things go wrong. It was:

> "a short and simple step, for example, to appreciate that if a ladder becomes unstable or slips while it is being used the worker is likely to be injured. That is the risk that must be faced wherever and whenever a ladder is provided. The risk of injury if such events occur is reasonably foreseeable. Work equipment that is not so constructed or adapted as to eliminate that risk is not suitable within the meaning of regulation 4(1)."[396]

As Lord Clyde observed:

> "the precise mechanics of the accident do not require to be foreseeable for the risk of injury to be foreseeable. It is enough to find that the ladder could be removed and replaced in a way which would not be secure and that if it was thereby insecure an accident was likely to occur."[397]

Moreover, in assessing the risk, an employer must take account of the possibility of carelessness by others. The employer:

> "must consider not only the skilled and careful man who never relaxes his vigilance. He must take into consideration 'the contingency of carelessness on the part of the workman in charge of it and the frequency with which that contingency is likely to arise': *Hindle v Birtwistle* [1897] 1 Q.B. 192, 195 *per* Wills J; *John Summers & Sons Ltd v Frost* [1955] A.C. 740, 765 *per* Lord Reid. The ladder was not suitable for the purpose for which it was used and provided because a person replacing it might not replace it properly due to carelessness, and because a fall from a ladder which had not been replaced properly was likely to cause injury. That risk could have been avoided by screwing the ladder to the side of the bunks, as was done after the accident."[398]

Note also Lord Clyde's observation that while the Directives lay down minimum

---

394 [2006] UKHL 56; [2007] I.C.R. 175; [2007] 2 All E.R. 97 at [15].

395 [2006] UKHL 56; [2007] I.C.R. 175; [2007] 2 All E.R. 97 at [24].

396 [2006] UKHL 56; [2007] I.C.R. 175; [2007] 2 All E.R. 97 at [25], per Lord Hope.

397 [2006] UKHL 56; [2007] I.C.R. 175; [2007] 2 All E.R. 97 at [39]. Note however Lord Clyde's reservations, at [46], as to whether the word "necessary" involved a requirement of "reasonable foreseeability". See also the decision of the Court of Appeal in *Hide v Steeplechase Co (Cheltenham) Ltd* [2013] EWCA Civ 545; [2014] I.C.R. 326; [2014] 1 All E.R. 405, where a jockey was injured as his horse fell and he hit a post on the rail running around the track. The judge had been wrong to import the common law idea of "reasonable foreseeability" into the Regulations. Rather, a defendant could escape liability under reg.4 by showing the injury was caused by the particular types of event set out in art.5(4) of Directive 89/391: occurrences due to unforeseeable circumstances beyond his control; and occurrences due to exceptional events whose consequences were unavoidable. The claim should not have been dismissed on the basis that the way the claimant was injured was unusual. In *Kennedy v Chivas Brothers Ltd* [2013] CSIH 57; 2013 S.L.T. 981 at [18]–[19], the Inner House of the Court of Session agreed with the analysis in *Hide*.

398 [2006] UKHL 56; [2007] I.C.R. 175; [2007] 2 All E.R. 97 at [8], per Lord Hope; see also [26]–[30].

standards of protection for the health and safety of workers, it may be that they are not necessarily intended simply to preserve common law standards, which may now be too low by reference to modern requirements:

> "The degree of foresight and the definition of the level of risk may remain matters for future consideration in the general development of the law in this area towards the greater safety of the workplace and the consequently higher levels of obligation on the employer."[399]

This observation is all the more pertinent given the impact of s.69 of the Enterprise and Regulatory Reform Act 2013, and the inevitable emphasis on common law negligence.[400]

Need for evidence In *Arriva Trains Northern Ltd v Eaglen*,[401] the Court of Appeal emphasised the need for evidence to show that there was a foreseeable risk of injury (here, aggravation of a painful back condition). Since there was no such evidence, no breach of reg.4 had been established. **12-68**

Absolute duty in reg.5 Regulation 5(1) of the 1998 Regulations provides that every employer shall ensure that work equipment is maintained in an efficient state, in efficient working order and in good repair.[402] In *Ball v Street*[403] the Court of Appeal held that this imposed an absolute duty, and that it was irrelevant that the type of accident which occurred was unforeseeable. The regulation was designed to make it easier for an injured workman to bring a claim by simply requiring him to prove that the mechanism of the machine failed to work efficiently or was not in good repair and that this failure caused the accident. However, the claimant is required to show on the balance of probabilities that it was a defect in the equipment that caused the accident. In *Bond v Tom Croft (Bolton) Ltd*,[404] the employer suggested that operator misuse was an alternative cause of the accident. The claimant failed to show that there was a defect in the ladder from which he fell, the judge preferring, on the basis of expert evidence, the suggestion that the claimant had fallen because he was "overreaching" (stretching beyond the safe limit while working on the ladder). The burden did not pass to the employer to show that the injury was not caused by a defect. The fact that work equipment was required to be "suitable" for the purposes of reg.4 did not affect the nature and level of the absolute obligation of maintenance in reg.5.[405] In *Johnstone v AMEC Construction Ltd*[406] the Inner House of the Court of Session accepted that the very fact that a barrier fence **12-69**

---

399 [2006] UKHL 56; [2007] I.C.R. 175; [2007] 2 All E.R. 97 at [48].

400 See para.12-02.

401 [2008] EWCA Civ 352.

402 In *Yorkshire Traction Co Ltd v Searby* [2003] EWCA Civ 1856; (2004) 148 S.J.L.B. 61 the Court of Appeal concluded that a failure to provide a screen to protect the driver of a bus from attack by passengers did not constitute a breach of the Provision and Use of Work Equipment Regulations 1992 reg.5.

403 [2005] EWCA Civ 76; [2005] P.I.Q.R. P22.

404 [2018] EWHC 1290 (QB).

405 The strictness of the reg.5 duty was also emphasised by the House of Lords in *Smith v Northamptonshire CC* [2009] UKHL 27; [2009] 4 All E.R. 557; [2009] I.C.R. 734. The reg.5 duty was described by Lord Hope as "absolute" although in this instance, for the reasons explored in para.12-65, the defective ramp did not fall within the definition of "work equipment". cf. *Horton v Taplin Contracts Ltd* [2002] EWCA Civ 1604; [2003] I.C.R. 179; [2003] P.I.Q.R. P12 at [10] where the Court of Appeal indicated that reg.20 of the Provision and Use of Work Equipment Regulations 1992 (which provided that "every employer shall ensure that work equipment or any part of work

failed to remain in position and was blown over by the wind meant that it was not maintained in an efficient state, in efficient working order and in good repair, as required by reg.5.[407]

12-70 In *Sherlock v Chester City Council*[408] the Court of Appeal held that, notwithstanding the fact that the claimant was experienced and trained in the use of a portable bench saw, his employers, having failed to assess the risk adequately and ask what was required so as to ensure that the claimant was alerted to or reminded of the need for appropriate precautions, were in breach of reg.8 of the Provision and Use of Work Equipment Regulations 1998, which provides that:

> "Every employer shall ensure that all persons who use work equipment have available to them adequate health and safety information and, where appropriate, written instructions pertaining to the use of the work equipment."

12-71 **Training in use of equipment** More generally, an employer may be liable for failure to train the employee in the use of equipment, even if that equipment is suitable within the meaning of reg.4. In *Pennington v Surrey CC*,[409] a fire officer was injured while using a particular type of power ram which he had not used before. Regulation 11(1) provides that every employer shall ensure that measures are taken which are effective to prevent access to any dangerous part of machinery or to any rotating stock-bar; or to stop the movement of any dangerous part of machinery or rotating stock-bar before any part of a person enters a danger zone. Effective measures include the provision of fixed guards or other guards or protection devices to the extent that it is practicable to do so, but where this is not practicable the employer must provide information, instruction, training and supervision. A majority of the Court of Appeal held that though there was no breach of reg.4, since the ram was suitable equipment when used by a trained fire officer, and there were no reasonably practicable methods of providing a guard, the employers were in breach of reg.11(2)(d) of the 1998 Regulations for failing to provide the claimant with instruction and training in the use of the power ram. This also amounted to an unsafe system of work at common law.

12-72 Evidently, training must be adequate if it is to satisfy the duty in reg.9. In *Milroy*

---

equipment is stabilised by clamping or otherwise where necessary for the purposes of health or safety"), though suggestive of absolute liability actually required foreseeability because "a step is realistically only 'necessary' when the mischief to be guarded against can be reasonably foreseen." For discussion of *Horton* see Fetto and Karseras (2003) 153 N.L.J. 53. On the general relationship between assessment of risks and duties under Health and Safety Regulations to provide suitable equipment, training etc, see para.12-55.

406 [2010] CSIH 57; 2011 S.C.L.R. 178; 2010 Rep. L.R. 96.

407 Applying the dictum of Lord Reid in *Millar v Galashiels Gas Company* [1949] A.C. 275, 290: "If the duty is proper maintenance and maintenance is defined as maintenance in efficient working order, then, once it is established that the duty goes beyond a duty to exercise care the fact that on a particular occasion the mechanism was not in working order shows that there had not been proper maintenance." There was also a breach of reg.4 on the facts of *Johnstone*. The fence was treated as work equipment which was used by the appellant, a security guard who was patrolling the perimeter and was injured when he first tried to replace the fence, and then to step over it. See also *Swilas v Clyde Pumps Ltd*, 2012 S.L.T. (Sh Ct) 146 where perimeter gates were held to be "work equipment" so far as a security guard was concerned. The fact that they were also part of the fabric of the premises was irrelevant; *Hodgkinson v Renfrewshire Council* [2011] CSOH 142.

408 [2004] EWCA Civ 201.

409 [2006] EWCA Civ 1493; [2007] P.I.Q.R. P11.

v British Telecommunications Plc[410] there were breaches both of reg.9 of the 1998 Regulations and reg.4 of the Electricity at Work Regulations 1989. A new system for working with elevated work platforms was introduced, although training was largely by amendment to on-line manuals, with brief follow-up training at the same time as training in other unconnected issues. This was inadequate and prevented the changes from being properly understood. In *Allison v London Underground Ltd*,[411] employers were in breach of reg.9 of the Provision and Use of Work Equipment Regulations 1998 (providing that the employer shall ensure that all persons who use work equipment have received "adequate training" for purposes of health and safety) because they had not carried out a "suitable and sufficient" risk assessment (as required by reg.3 of the Management of Health and Safety at Work Regulations 1999), which would have revealed the need for training in the use of a traction brake controller on a train. Smith LJ commented that:

> "To say that the training is adequate if it deals with the risks which the employer knows about is to impose no greater a duty than exists at common law. In my view the statutory duty is higher and imposes on the employer a duty to investigate the risks inherent in his operations, taking professional advice where necessary."[412]

In light of the Supreme Court's judgment in *Kennedy v Cordia (Services) LLP*,[413] it is possible that the duty to conduct risk assessments in order to identify training needs will also be recognised at common law, as an aspect of the duty to provide a safe system of work.

Protection against specified hazards Regulation 12(1) imposes a duty on employers to take measures to ensure that exposure of a person using work equipment to risk arising from a list of specified hazards is either prevented or, where that is not reasonably practicable, adequately controlled. The required measures are defined in reg.12(2)(a) as measures "other than" the provision of personal protective equipment, or of instruction, training and supervision "so far as is reasonably practicable". Regulation 12(2)(b) requires that this will, where appropriate, include measures to minimise the effects of the hazard as well as to reduce the likelihood of its occurring. This distinctive wording was considered by the Court of Appeal in *Whitehead v Trustees of the Chatsworth Settlement*.[414] A gamekeeper, disregarding what he knew to be safe practice, attempted to cross a stile without removing live ammunition from his rifle. The stile crumbled and the rifle discharged two bullets into his leg. The danger from the gun was accepted to fall into the listed hazards. The Court decided that the wording of reg.12(1) ("to take measures" to prevent or adequately control) meant that in the case both of prevention, and of control, reasonable practicability was relevant. The meaning of reg.12(2) was that measures intended to safeguard the user from risk may include, but must not be limited to, provision of protective equipment, training, instruction, supervision and so on, so far as it was reasonably practicable to take additional measures. Although the duty can extend to injury caused by the claimant's own misuse of equipment, in this instance the claimant was working alone and appropriate training and instruction had been given. There were no further protective measures that were reasonably 12-73

410 [2015] EWHC 532 (QB).
411 [2008] EWCA Civ 71; [2008] I.C.R. 719; [2008] P.I.Q.R. P10.
412 [2008] EWCA Civ 71; [2008] I.C.R. 719; [2008] P.I.Q.R. P10 at [55].
413 [2016] UKSC 6; [2016] 1 W.L.R. 597; see para.12-35.
414 [2012] EWCA Civ 263; [2013] 1 W.L.R. 251.

practicable either to prevent or control the hazard. The employer was, therefore, not in breach of the duty.

(b) Workplace (Health, Safety and Welfare) Regulations

12-74 The Workplace (Health, Safety and Welfare) Regulations 1992[415] address issues of ventilation, cleanliness, lighting, condition of floors, and working facilities in most (though not all[416]) types of workplaces. They apply only to workers, not visitors to the premises,[417] though they will apply to independent contractors working on premises provided the duty in question relates to matters within the control of the defendant.[418] The two most important provisions, in terms of litigation by injured employees, are regs 5 and 12.[419] Regulation 5(1) provides that:

> "The workplace and the equipment, devices and systems to which this regulation applies shall be maintained (including cleaned as appropriate) in an efficient state, in efficient working order and in good repair."

Unlike reg.12(3),[420] this states a strict or absolute duty. Nevertheless, it was agreed in *Cruz v Chief Constable of Lancashire Police*[421] that it can only be said that a workplace has not been maintained in an efficient state if there was a foreseeable risk of injury. Further, the foreseeable risk must be a risk to employees, and not to others. In this case, a cell door in a police station had been left partly open, rather than fully open and flush with the wall of a corridor. Usually, the doors of empty cells were left fully open. This, however, was for operational rather than safety reasons, as it allowed quicker access to the cells with detained persons. This reduced the risk of injury to those individuals, but was not done in order to preserve the safety of employees. In this instance, a comprehensive risk assessment had not identified risks associated with partially open cell doors, and it was concluded that the partially open door had posed no material risk of injury to those who worked in the corridors.

12-75 In *Irvine v Commissioner of Police of the Metropolis*[422] there was a breach of reg.5 when an employee tripped on a raised piece of carpet and fell. The carpet constituted part of the workplace which was not "in an efficient state" of repair. The

---

415 SI 1992/3004.

416 See reg.3(1) excluding ships, construction sites and mines, which are covered by other Regulations.

417 *Donaldson v Hays Distribution Services Ltd* 2005 1 S.C. 523; 2005 S.L.T. 733; *Brown v East Lothian Council* [2013] CSOH 62; 2013 S.L.T. 721 (premises hired for a fitness class were not made available to a fitness instructor "as a place of work", as opposed to a place where she, as a self-employed person, was working).

418 *Ceva Logistics Ltd v Lynch* [2011] EWCA Civ 188; [2011] I.C.R. 746, see para.12-54.

419 reg.13 created a duty, so far as was reasonably practicable, to take suitable and effective measures to prevent falls from a distance likely to cause personal injury. See *Parker v PFC Flooring Supplies Ltd* [2001] P.I.Q.R. P7: defendants in breach of reg.13 when the claimant fell from a roof (*Parker* was affirmed at [2001] EWCA Civ 1533 on the defendant's liability in negligence, but the issue of breach of statutory duty was not addressed); *Wright v Romford Blinds and Shutters Ltd* [2003] EWHC 1165 (QB): defendants in breach of reg.13 when claimant fell from the roof of a van. Regulation 13 has now been replaced by the Work at Height Regulations 2005 (SI 2005/735), which are directed at eliminating the risks involved in working at height if reasonably practicable to carry out the work otherwise than at height, and minimising those risks which cannot be avoided in this way. For consideration of the 2005 Regulations see *Bhatt v Fountain Motors Ltd* [2010] EWCA Civ 863; [2010] P.I.Q.R. P17.

420 See para.12-78.

421 [2016] EWCA Civ 402.

422 [2004] EWHC 1536 (QB); [2005] P.I.Q.R. P11.

defendant was held strictly liable for the breach. By contrast in *Caerphilly CBC v Button*[423] the Court of Appeal considered that reg.5 was not easily applicable to a case where an employee was injured tripping over a kerb placed on a loose slope in a car park at work. The case did not involve "equipment, devices and systems", which were the main concern of reg.5, and it would be artificial to say that the kerb was not in an "efficient state". The case was dealt with under reg.12, and as a claim in negligence at common law. In *Munro v Aberdeen City Council*,[424] the Outer House of the Court of Session distinguished between transient states of premises, to which the "absolute" duty in reg.5 would not apply, and continuing states. Here, the employee was injured when she slipped and fell in an icy car park. The Court of Session held that this did not fall within reg.5. Nor did it fall within reg.12(1), which applies to structural issues. Since reg.12(3) requires only "reasonably practicable" steps to be taken, the claim was bound to fail. A contrasting case is *Wilkinson v Hjaltland Housing Association Ltd*.[425] Here, a care worker tripped and fell when she stepped in a hole left by the removal of a fountain, where the presence of the hole was disguised by a snowstorm. The hole was positioned on a well-used shortcut which qualified as a traffic route; the hole was not a "transient" condition (like the ice in *Munro*); and in any event, reg.12(2) expressly provides that a traffic route should have no hole. Unlike reg.12(3), the duty in reg.12(2) is strict.

Equipment does not fail to be in an efficient state, or in efficient working order, 12-76
if it is used for a purpose for which it is not designed or provided. In *Wallace v Glasgow City Council*[426] there was no breach of reg.5 when a toilet bowl toppled while the pursuer was standing on it in order to open a window to ventilate the room. There was, however, a breach of reg.15, which provides that windows, skylights and ventilators which are capable of being opened shall not be likely to be opened in a way which exposes the person opening it to a risk to their health and safety, taken together with the duty to conduct risk assessments set out in reg.3 of the Management of Health and Safety at Work Regulations 1999.[427] A pole should have been readily available for use by those seeking to open the window.[428]

The Workplace (Health, Safety and Welfare Regulations) 1992 have no applica- 12-77
tion to falls from ladders, which should be dealt with under the Provision and Use of Work Equipment Regulations 1998,[429] or the Work at Height Regulations 2005.[430] Regulation 13 of the 1992 Regulations deals with "the risk of falling as a result of a danger inherent in the workplace not a danger inherent in some piece of equipment which happens to be brought into the workplace".[431]

Regulation 12(1) provides that: 12-78

"Every floor in a workplace and the surface of every traffic route in a workplace shall be

423 [2010] EWCA Civ 1311; [2011] I.C.R. D3.

424 [2009] CSOH 129; 2009 S.L.T. 964. See also *McKeown v Inverclyde Council* [2013] CSOH 141; 2013 S.L.T. 937 at [40]: reg.5 does not apply to transient conditions, such as ice (though reg.12(3) did cover a slip on ice by the claimant).

425 2015 Rep. L.R. 62 (Sheriff Court).

426 [2011] CSIH 57; 2011 Rep. L.R. 96.

427 SI 1999/3242. See para.12-55.

428 Damages, however, were reduced by 50 per cent for contributory negligence because this was not a case of momentary inattention but a deliberate act which was acknowledged to be dangerous.

429 *Mason v Satelcom Ltd, East Potential Ltd* [2008] EWCA Civ 494; [2008] I.C.R. 971 at [23], per Longmore LJ.

430 Work at Height Regulations 2005 (SI 2005/735).

431 *Mason v Satelcom Ltd, East Potential Ltd* [2008] EWCA Civ 494; [2008] I.C.R. 971 at [23], per Longmore LJ.

of a construction such that the floor or surface of the traffic route is suitable for the purpose for which it is used";

and reg.12(3) that:

"So far as is reasonably practicable, every floor in a workplace and the surface of every traffic route in a workplace shall be kept free from obstructions and from any article or substance which may cause a person to slip, trip or fall."

In *Lowles v The Home Office*[432] the Court of Appeal held that an unexpected threshold, constituting a step of unusual intermediate height at the top of a ramp, for which there was no apparent reason, constituted an obstruction in the floor or the surface of the traffic route, in breach of reg.12(1). In *McGhee v Strathclyde Fire Brigade*[433] the employers were held liable where a fire officer slipped on a worn, tiled floor which had been polished. They were found to be in breach of both reg.12(1) and (3). Regulation 12(1) was said to create a continuing duty, unqualified by reasonable practicality. Although the fact that the claimant slipped was not proof of breach of duty, because both reg.12(1) and (3) required some degree of foreseeability of risk, the employers met the requirements of reg.12(1) only if there was no real risk of a person using it as a means of passage and thereby sustaining injury. Regulation 12(3) was limited by the qualification of reasonable practicality, but this involved considering the practical measures which could reasonably have been taken to keep the floor free from substances which might cause a person to slip. Since the freshly polished floor created a risk, even though a relatively low risk, that someone might slip on it there was also a breach of reg.12(3).[434]

12-79 The content of the reg.12(3) duty, and the applicability of the various duties in reg.12, were considered by the Court of Appeal in *Craner v Dorset CC*.[435] The evidence in the case was thin,[436] but the Court of Appeal held that a judge had been entitled to hold the defendant liable where a school caretaker alleged that a protruding paving stone had caused an injury to his knee while he was pushing a trolley along a path at the school. Longmore and Arden LJJ advised that in future such cases should be argued in terms of reg.12(1) and (2), which refer to unevenness, and not in terms of reg.12(3), which refers to obstructions. Although reg.12(3) creates a less strict liability, since it refers to steps that are "reasonably practicable", the Court nevertheless held that whatever the wording of the regulation, it imposed a stricter liability than at common law. Longmore LJ observed that the accident was not a "freak accident" as the defendants alleged, since this sort of accident was frequently observed: "However much the courts may not wish to encourage a

---

[432] [2004] EWCA Civ 985.

[433] 2002 S.L.T. 680 (Outer House).

[434] See also *Anderson v Newham College of Further Education* [2002] EWCA Civ 505; [2003] I.C.R. 212 where the Court of Appeal held the defendants to be in breach of reg.12(3) when a caretaker tripped over a frame supporting a white board stored with its wheeled feet, some two feet in length, protruding into a classroom and creating an obvious hazard. The danger would have been avoided if it had been stored properly facing the wall. The claimant was held 50 per cent contributorily negligent. cf. *Gillie v Scottish Borders Council* [2013] CSOH 76; 2013 Rep. L.R. 86, where a school janitor slipped and fell on stairs, probably because of petroleum jelly left by students as a practical joke on their final day. The probability of this was low and it was not reasonably practicable for the school to ensure that the stair was kept free of the substance.

[435] [2008] EWCA Civ 1323; [2009] I.C.R. 563.

[436] Note also *Burgess v Napier* [2009] CSOH 6; 2009 Rep. L.R. 55: exam invigilator at a university claimed she had been injured falling over a wastepaper basket when carrying a stack of exam papers out of the examination room; but the evidence was not found sufficiently compelling.

compensation culture, the fact remains that the Regulations exist."[437] It was not a defence that other maintenance issues had a higher priority, even if this was entirely reasonable. The Court distinguished *Marks and Spencer Plc v Palmer*,[438] where the claimant had tripped over a weather strip 9mm high which had been inserted in the floor of the staff exit at the defendants' Boston branch. A weather strip was a "convenient, desirable and regularly used fitting": an uneven paving stone is not.

In *Bassie v Merseyside Fire and Civil Defence Authority*,[439] the employers were held to be in breach of reg.12(3) of the Workplace (Health, Safety and Welfare) Regulations 1992 when a fireman slipped on an invisible layer of fine dust in the fire station while on a training exercise. It would have been reasonably practicable to keep the floor free of dust by damp mopping. In *Burgess v Plymouth City Council*,[440] the Court of Appeal held that the employers were liable for breach of reg.12(3) when a school cleaner tripped over a plastic lunchbox container in plain view on the floor. The container was an obstruction or an article which "may cause a person to … fall", and it was reasonably practicable to have stowed the container away. The failure to do so constituted a breach of the regulation. The claimant was found 50 per cent contributorily negligent. Under reg.5(2) of the Construction (Health, Safety and Welfare) Regulations 1996 the duty was to keep the place of work safe within the limits of reasonable practicability.[441] **12-80**

In *Lewis v Avidan Ltd*[442] the claimant slipped on a patch of water which had leaked from a concealed pipe just before the accident. The Court of Appeal found that there was no breach of reg.5 since, given that the defendants had not been negligent, the floor was maintained in an efficient state. Even if the pipe itself constituted equipment for the purposes of reg.5, it was not equipment a fault in which was liable to result in a failure to comply with the regulations. A fault in the pipe would be liable to produce a flood which would render the floor slippery, but that in itself would not result in a breach of reg.12(3) which is qualified by reasonable practicality. The mere fact of an unexpected flood did not mean that a floor was **12-81**

---

437 [2008] EWCA Civ 1323; [2009] I.C.R. 563 at [8].

438 [2001] EWCA Civ 1528, where Waller LJ emphasised that the correct approach to the question of whether a traffic route was "suitable" was to ask whether, by reference to the factors arising before the accident took place and not with the benefit of hindsight, the route was suitable; "suitability" required a qualitative assessment. In *Taylor v Wincanton Group Ltd* [2009] EWCA Civ 1581, Waller LJ accepted that this may be much the same as making a risk assessment, the approach taken by Smith LJ in *Allison v London Underground* [2008] EWCA Civ 71; [2008] I.C.R. 719, para.12-55. See also *Caerphilly CBC v Button* [2010] EWCA Civ 1311; [2011] I.C.R. D3 (claimant tripped over three inch high kerbstone; traffic route found not "suitable").

439 [2005] EWCA Civ 1474; (2005) 149 S.J.L.B. 1352. See also *McKeown v Inverclyde Council* [2013] CSOH 141; 2013 S.L.T. 937 where the local authority was held in breach of reg.12(3) when a school janitor slipped on an icy step of a fire escape. The council had a reasonable system for gritting the school premises in icy weather but "it existed only on paper and was never actually put into action."

440 [2005] EWCA Civ 1659; [2006] I.C.R. 579.

441 The regulation required the employer to achieve a certain result, but only within the bounds of reasonable practicability. The employer will be liable unless he shows, the burden being on him, that it was not reasonably practicable for him to avoid the danger which arose: *Brown v Grosvenor Building Contractors Ltd* [2006] EWCA Civ 590. However, if there was in fact no foreseeable risk of harm which the employer should have recognised there will be no breach of the regulation. In *McFarlane v Scottish Borders Council*, 2005 S.L.T. 359, a claim for breach of reg.5(2) of the Construction (Health, Safety and Welfare) Regulations 1996, the defendant was unable to establish that it was not practicable to take precautions in the absence of evidence as to cost or other disadvantages. The Construction (Health, Safety and Welfare) Regulations 1996 were revoked and replaced by the Construction (Design and Management) Regulations 2007 (SI 2007/320) which were in turn revoked by the Construction (Design and Management) Regulations 2015 (SI 2015/51).

442 [2005] EWCA Civ 670; [2006] P.I.Q.R. P6.

not in an efficient state for the purposes of reg.5(1). *Lewis v Avidan Ltd* should be contrasted with *Ellis v Bristol City Council*,[443] where the Court of Appeal concluded that the employers were in breach of reg.12 when a care assistant at a home for the elderly slipped in a pool of urine left by one of the residents on a floor of the home. The surface was smooth vinyl and was slippery when wet. The evidence indicated that the majority of the residents were incontinent and they urinated on the floor several times a week. Regulation 12(1) and (2) required the court to consider the suitability of the floor in the context of the circumstances of its use. This included not only the temporary nature of the hazard but also the frequency and regularity of the occurrence. In *Aldenham v Deacon*,[444] a school nurse sustained injuries when she slipped on a wet floor on her return from lunch. Eady J held that liability under reg.12(3) was established because the corridor could have been cleaned in the evenings when it was less frequented. This would have reduced the risk of injury, and the essence of reg.12(3) was reduction of risk. The known risk should be balanced against the effort and expense of eliminating it. Similarly, in *McLeish v Lothian NHS Board*,[445] a nurse who fell on the wet floor of a ward succeeded in a claim. The positioning of a cleaning trolley in the doorway did not amount to a warning. On this basis, she had received no warning, either verbal or visible, that the floor was wet; the wet floor sign was not deployed and no alternative wet floor warning was given; and the wet floor sign was a reasonably practicable measure.

(c) Manual Handling Operations Regulations

12-82 The Manual Handling Operations Regulations 1992[446] reg.4(1)(a) provides that each employer shall, so far as is reasonably practicable, avoid the need for employees to undertake any manual handling operations at work which involve a risk of their being injured. Where it is not reasonably practicable to avoid the need for employees to undertake any manual handling operations which involve a risk of their being injured then the employer must:

(i) make a suitable and sufficient assessment of all such manual handling operations to be undertaken by them;
(ii) take appropriate steps to reduce the risk of injury to the lowest level reasonably practicable; and
(iii) take appropriate steps to provide employees with general indications and, where reasonably practicable to do so, precise information on the weight of each load and the heaviest side of any load whose centre of gravity is not positioned centrally.[447]

A manual handling operation means "any transporting or supporting of a load

---

443 [2007] EWCA Civ 685; [2007] I.C.R. 1614; [2007] P.I.Q.R. P26; applied in *Cheung v Zhu* [2011] EWHC 2913 (QB).

444 [2008] EWHC 2343 (QB).

445 [2017] CSOH 71; 2017 Rep. L.R. 90.

446 SI 1992/2793. See J. Levy, "Manual Handling cases—Music to the Ears" [2001] J.P.I.L. 130.

447 SI 1992/2793 reg.4(1)(b). The three elements of reg.4(1)(b) should be read conjunctively. An employer cannot argue that it was unable to provide information or guidance about the weight of a load because it did not know the weight if it has failed to carry out an appropriate assessment: *Swain v Denso Marston Ltd* [2000] I.C.R. 1079; [2000] P.I.Q.R. P129 CA. The provisions of reg.4(1) were found to be relevant to definition of the employer's common law duty to its employees, and particularly the definition of a suitable and sufficient risk assessment, in *Dehenes v Bourne* 2019 S.L.T. (Sh Ct) 219.

(including the lifting, putting down, pushing, pulling, carrying or moving thereof) by hand or by bodily force".[448] Clearly these regulations have a potentially very wide application,[449] though the most common situation to result in litigation would seem to be back injuries.[450]

Distinct duties In *Egan v Central Manchester and Manchester Children's University Hospitals NHS Trust*,[451] the Court of Appeal has clarified that the various duties listed in reg.4(1)(a) are distinct and should be considered separately. Where an employer had not carried out a risk assessment in respect of use of a particular piece of equipment (a hoist for transporting a patient into a bath), it was not enough to dispose of the claim for the judge to consider whether that risk assessment would, in the circumstances, have made any difference. There was also a positive duty in reg.4(1)(a)(ii) to reduce risks to the lowest level reasonably practicable, and this was an additional duty. If a risk of injury was established, the burden of proof was on the employer to prove that it had taken all reasonable steps to reduce that risk.[452] Here, the employer was liable since there were steps that could reasonably have been taken to reduce the risk of injury. The claimant however was an experienced nurse and took an equal share in responsibility. Hence, her damages were reduced by 50 per cent. **12-83**

The test for whether manual handling operations involve a risk of being injured is that "there must be a real risk, a foreseeable possibility of injury; certainly nothing approaching a probability".[453] Moreover, the employer is not entitled to assume that all his employees will on all occasions behave with full and proper **12-84**

---

448 SI 1992/2793 reg.2. This does not cover work on a "chicken trussing line" because a manual handling operation under reg.4 involves the transporting or supporting of a load: *Hughes v Grampian Country Food Group Ltd* [2007] C.S.I.H. 32; 2007 S.L.T. 635 (employee's injury caused by repetitive movements of the actual trussing process rather than the transporting or supporting of a load). It has been held that the Regulations do not apply where it is not the claimant but a third party who is supporting the load: *Smith v Scottish Ministers* 2015 G.W.D. 17–292 (Sheriff Court).

449 In *King v RCO Support Services Ltd and Yorkshire Traction Co Ltd* [2001] I.C.R. 608; [2001] P.I.Q.R. P15 the claimant was injured when he slipped on the ungritted part of an ice-covered bus yard while engaged in the process of spreading grit with a barrow and shovel. In *Wright v Romford Blinds and Shutters Ltd* [2003] EWHC 1165 (QB) the employer was held to be in breach of reg.4(1)(b)(ii) in allowing the claimant to work from a flat roof rack on top of a van.

450 See, e.g. *Koonjul v ThamesLink Healthcare Services NHS Trust* [2000] P.I.Q.R. P123, CA; *O'Neill v DSG Retail Ltd* [2002] EWCA Civ 1139; [2003] I.C.R. 222; *King v Sussex Ambulance NHS Trust* [2002] EWCA Civ 953; [2002] I.C.R. 1413; *Taylor v Glasgow City Council*, 2002 S.C. 364; 2002 S.L.T. 689; *Davidson v Lothian and Borders Fire Board*, 2003 S.C.L.R. 750; 2003 S.L.T. 939; *Fleming v Stirling Council*, 2000 S.C.L.R. 779; 2001 S.L.T. 123; *Goodchild v Organon Laboratories Ltd* [2004] EWHC 2341 (QB); *Bennetts v Ministry of Defence* [2004] EWCA Civ 486; *Gravatom Engineering Systems Ltd v Parr* [2007] EWCA Civ 967; *Cooper v Bright Horizons Family Solutions Ltd* [2013] EWHC 2349 (QB).

451 [2008] EWCA Civ 1424; [2009] I.C.R. 585; applied in *Ghaith v Indesit Co UK Ltd* [2012] EWCA Civ 642; [2012] I.C.R. D34.

452 *Egan* was followed on this point by the Court of Appeal in *Sloan v Rastrick High School Governors* [2014] EWCA Civ 1063; [2015] P.I.Q.R. P1. The trial judge had erred in placing the burden on the employee. However, the employer had discharged the burden. See also *Kennedy v Chivas Brothers Ltd* [2013] CSIH 57; 2013 S.L.T. 981 at [29]: Regulation 4 "only requires an employer to do what is reasonably practicable. It is clear, however, that the onus of proving that a particular step is not reasonably practicable rests on the employer." Moreover, the employer must plead the point: also at [29].

453 *Koonjul v ThamesLink Healthcare Services* [2000] P.I.Q.R. P123 at 126, per Hale LJ. See also *Bennetts v Ministry of Defence* [2004] EWCA Civ 486 at [39], per Carnwath LJ: "even a 'slight' risk may be a relevant risk in the sense that it brings Regulation 4 into play", citing *Hawkes v London Borough of Southwark*, unreported, 1998, CA. The requirement in *Koonjul* for a "real risk" was ap-

concern for their own safety.[454] There may be a duty to provide training for manual handling even where the attendant risks might appear obvious. In *Smith v S Notaro Ltd*,[455] the defendants were in breach of reg.4 in failing to provide training for manual handling over uneven ground.[456] On the other hand, the court must also consider the background against which the incident took place and assess the alleged obligation in its real context. So there was no breach of the Regulations where a care assistant had injured her back when pulling a low wooden bed from against a wall.[457] The court was entitled to take account of the size of the employer (a small residential home with a small number of staff), that the claimant was an experienced member of staff and had received prior training in bending and lifting techniques. It would be impracticable to require the employer to assess each task and provide guidance as to how those tasks were to be carried out where innumerable everyday domestic tasks were involved. But where an employer had failed to take appropriate steps to reduce the risk by failing to give the training necessary to increase awareness of the risk of back injury from twisting while carrying a load there was a breach of reg.4.[458] Where the accident arose from a wholly unforeseen risk, where, for example, the employee had created that risk by acting contrary to normal procedures for the task, the claim may fail on the basis that any breach of the regulations was not the cause of the injury.[459] The need for proof of a causal link between a failure to conduct a proper risk assessment and injury sustained by the employee is emphasised by the Court of Appeal's decision in *West Sussex CC v Fuller*.[460] The burden of proving this causal link is on the claimant. It was remarked that in many workplace situations, a failure by the employer to assess the risks of injury involved in a manual handling operation and to take appropriate steps to reduce the risk of injury to the lowest level practicable, would effectively cast on to the employer the evidential burden of showing that its failure was not at least a cause of the accident. However, that was because there would be an obvious connection between the

plied in *Stuart v Lewisham and Greenwich NHS Trust* [2017] EWCA Civ 2091; (2018) 160 B.M.L.R. 180. The Recorder had effectively found that there was no "real risk" where a midwife lifted an oxygen box weighing no more than 8kg. This would not pose a risk to most people, and as such the duty to conduct a risk assessment did not apply.

454 *Koonjul v ThamesLink Healthcare Services* [2000] P.I.Q.R. P123.

455 [2006] EWCA Civ 775.

456 See also *Walsh v TNT UK Ltd* [2006] CSOH 149; 2006 S.L.T. 1100 (employer in breach of reg.4(1)(b)(ii) of the 1992 Regulations in failing to send the employee on refresher courses on manual handling).

457 *Koonjul v ThamesLink Healthcare Services* [2000] P.I.Q.R. P123 CA; referred to for guidance in relation to breach of the employer's common law duty of care in *Cockerill v CXK Ltd* [2018] EWHC 1155 (QB): see further, para.12-35.

458 *O'Neill v DSG Retail Ltd* [2002] EWCA Civ 1139; [2003] I.C.R. 222. See also *Skinner v Aberdeen City Council*, 2001 Rep. L.R. 118 (Court of Session, OH): employer's failure to train or instruct the claimant on how to approach the task of lifting some broken slabs, in order to reduce the risk of injury to the lowest possible level, amounted to a breach of reg.4(1)(b)(i) and reg.4(1)(b)(ii). In *Costa v Imperial London Hotels Ltd* [2012] EWCA Civ 672 it was held that an absence of refresher training is capable of constituting a breach of reg.4, on the basis of a failure to take appropriate steps to reduce the risks to the lowest level reasonably practicable, but it must still be shown that the absence of refresher training caused the injury (i.e. that the training would have led the claimant to alter their practice, and that it would have avoided the particular injury).

459 *Bennetts v Ministry of Defence* [2004] EWCA Civ 486, where the claimant's back injury was caused not by the weight of the postal bag she was attempting to move, nor the height to which the bag was lifted, but as a result of her pulling at a bag that had snagged on a trolley. This (the claimant's decision to proceed in this way) was an event that was unforeseen, and therefore would not have been identified by a risk assessment by the employers.

460 [2015] EWCA Civ 189.

injury and the risks associated with the activity being undertaken. Here, the cause of the accident was unconnected with the risk generated by the operation in question and the incident leading to injury did not fall within the ambit of the risk that the local authority had been required to assess.

(d) Control of Substances Hazardous to Health Regulations

Regulation 7(1) of the Control of Substances Hazardous to Health Regulations 2002[461] requires every employer to ensure that the exposure of his employees to substances hazardous to health is either prevented or, where this is not reasonably practicable, adequately controlled. It is in the nature of these Regulations that they may be invoked in relation to exposure over a number of years, and with delayed effects, so that their applicability may be less immediately truncated by the commencement of the Enterprise and Regulatory Reform Act 2013 s.69 than some of the other regulations.[462] The regulations apply between an employer and employee. Although by reg.3 they are owed to third parties who are affected by substances used at work, it has been concluded that they are not imposed on a hospital trust for the benefit of a patient in a case of infection, where there is no relevant substance being used at work: MRSA is not a "substance arising out of or in connection with work at the work place".[463] Contrast, however, *Miller v Greater Glasgow Health Board*,[464] where it was found at least arguable that a patient who contracts MRSA may be able to rely on the Regulations. Regulation 7(3) provides that where it is not reasonably practicable to prevent exposure to a substance hazardous to health, the employer must apply protection measures appropriate to the activity and consistent with the risk assessment. In *Dugmore v Swansea NHS Trust*[465] the Court of Appeal considered the meaning of the words "reasonably practicable" in a previous version of the Regulations.[466] The claimant was a nurse who developed a latex allergy as a result of using powdered latex gloves. The Court of Appeal held that the duty to ensure that exposure was prevented or adequately controlled under reg.7(1) was absolute. The defence of reasonable practicability qualified only the duty of total prevention, not the requirement to see that exposure is adequately controlled. It was for the employers to prove that it was not reasonably practicable to replace latex gloves with vinyl gloves (it "was not rocket science waiting to be invented"). With a simple step of this nature questions of the degree and magnitude of the risk did not arise, but even if they did the onus was on the employers to go out and find out about them. The regulation does not refer to the foreseeability of the risk: 12-85

> "To import into the defence of reasonable practicability the same approach to foreseeability of risk as is contained in the common law of negligence would be to reduce the

---

461 SI 2002/2677 (as frequently amended).

462 See, for example, *Cotton v Helphire Ltd* [2019] EWHC 508 (QB), a claim for breach of reg.11, requiring health surveillance under certain circumstances. In this instance, however, it had not been established that the claimant's condition was work-related, nor that the employer should have understood his symptoms to be those of a work-related disease triggering the health surveillance duty.

463 *Billington v South Tees Hospitals NHS Foundation Trust*, County Court (Bristol), 6 January 2015.

464 [2010] CSIH 40; 2011 S.L.T. 131, [52]–[56].

465 [2002] EWCA Civ 1689; [2003] I.C.R. 574; [2003] 1 All E.R. 333; discussed by Fetto and Karseras (2003) 153 N.L.J. 53.

466 The Control of Substances Hazardous to Health Regulations 1988 (SI 1988/1657). The employer's duty was expressed in similar terms to that required by the 2002 Regulations.

> absolute duty to something much closer to the common law, albeit with a different burden of proof."[467]

Moreover, it could not be adequate control to require the employee to wear powdered latex gloves when other barriers were available. The purpose of the Regulations is protective and preventive, and they involve positive obligations to seek out the risks and take precautions against them. Thus:

> "It is by no means incompatible with their purpose that an employer who fails to discover a risk or rates it so low that he takes no precautions against it should nevertheless be liable to the employee who suffers as a result."[468]

This approach was affirmed and applied by the Court of Appeal in *Allison v London Underground Ltd*,[469] a case applying reg.9 of the Provision and Use of Work Equipment Regulations 1998.[470]

12-86 In *Wembridge Claimants v Winter*[471] Irwin J held that the defendant fire and rescue service was in breach of reg.6 (assessment of the risk to health created by work involving substances hazardous to health), reg.7 (prevention or control of exposure to substances hazardous to health) and reg.12 (information, instruction and training for persons who may be exposed to substances hazardous to health) of the Control of Substances Hazardous to Health Regulations 2002,[472] following a large explosion of fireworks stored in a steel shipping container in which two fire officers died and a number of others were injured. There had been a failure to pass on information about the nature of the incident which would have improved the dynamic risk assessments at the fireground. The decision to fight the fire at the site was not a breach of the Regulations, but a negligent failure to evacuate the fireground earlier meant that the risks of injury were not reduced or avoided, and the negligent implementation of the decision to evacuate also constituted a breach of reg.7.

---

467 [2002] EWCA Civ 1689; [2003] 1 All E.R. 333 at [23], per Hale LJ (relied on in the context of the Workplace (Health, Safety and Welfare) Regulations 1992 in *Cruz v Chief Constable of Lancashire Police* [2016] EWCA Civ 402, para.12-74). See also the discussion of the advantages offered to claimants by the Control of Substances Hazardous to Health Regulations in comparison to common law in respect of MRSA in D. Bennett, "Litigating hospital acquired MRSA as a disease" [2004] J.P.I.L. 197.

468 [2002] EWCA Civ 1689; [2003] 1 All E.R. 333 at [27].

469 [2008] EWCA Civ 71; [2008] I.C.R. 719; see para.12-55.

470 Contrast the approach taken to the words "reasonably practicable" in *R. v HTM Ltd* [2006] EWCA Crim 1156; [2006] I.C.R. 1383; [2007] 2 All E.R. 665, where the issue was whether they modified an employer's duties under s.2 of the Health and Safety at Work etc. Act 1974 for the purposes of criminal liability. The Court of Appeal (at [23]) did not disagree with the approach taken to reg.7 in *Dugmore v NHS Trust*.

471 [2013] EWHC 2331 (QB).

472 As well as reg.5 (risk assessment) and reg.9 (information, instruction and training) of the Dangerous Substances and Explosive Atmospheres Regulations 2002 (SI 2002/2776).

4. DEFENCES

12-87 The general defences of ex turpi causa non oritur actio,[473] volenti non fit injuria[474] and contributory negligence[475] all apply to actions by employees against their employers in relation to the employers' non-delegable duty of care in respect of health and safety. The volenti defence is rarely likely to succeed in an action for negligence against an employer.[476] This does not mean that employers must remove all risks. Many jobs are inherently dangerous and the employer will have done enough, at least for the purposes of the tort of negligence, if he acts reasonably to minimise the risks. Care also has to be taken when applying the defence of contributory negligence to claims by employees to make due allowance for human error when faced with a repetitive routine and familiarity with the inherent dangers of the job. This is particularly the case where the defendant is held liable for breach of a statutory duty.[477] Here the standard by which the claimant's contributory negligence is judged is sometimes less exacting than that used for ordinary negligence, because the courts are conscious that, in many instances, statutory duties are imposed on employers in order to protect employees from their own carelessness, and allowing the defence to apply too readily may effectively undermine the policy of the statute.

12-88 **Volenti non fit injuria** As a matter of public policy, if Parliament has required certain precautions to be taken by an employer to protect his employees, the employer should not be entitled to neglect those precautions and then to rely on an express or implied agreement between himself and an employee that the latter, if injured, will bear the loss alone.[478] Thus, in *Wheeler v New Merton Board Mills Ltd*,[479] it was held that the defence of volenti was no answer to a claim made against an employer in respect of injury caused through a breach of a duty imposed on him by statute. In *Imperial Chemical Industries Ltd v Shatwell*,[480] the House of Lords approved that decision, but held that although the defence of volenti is not available where the employer is in breach of his own statutory duty, there is nothing to prevent him relying on it when he himself was not in breach of a statutory duty and was not vicariously liable for breach of a statutory duty through the neglect of some person whose commands the claimant felt bound to obey. In *Shatwell*, two experienced shotfirers of equal rank were injured having collaborated in a method of work which they both knew to be dangerous and contrary to statutory regulations, which placed the statutory duty on the shotfirers personally and not their employers. The House of Lords held that an action by one of the shotfirers against the employers as being vicariously liable for the breach of statutory duty by the

---

473 See para.3-48.

474 See para.3-126.

475 See para.3-58 onwards.

476 See para.3-126.

477 See para.3-80.

478 *Imperial Chemical Industries Ltd v Shatwell* [1965] A.C. 656 at 687, per Lord Pearce; *Burnett v British Waterways Board* [1973] 1 W.L.R. 700, per Phillimore LJ.

479 [1933] 2 K.B. 669 CA; reluctantly following *Baddeley v Earl Granville* (1887) 19 Q.B.D. 423. But there are other reasons why a defence of volenti will rarely succeed against an employee: see paras 3-126 to 3-130.

480 [1965] A.C. 656 HL; Brodetsky (1964) 27 M.L.R. 733. See also paras 3-129 and 3-130.

other failed, because the employers were entitled to rely on the defence of volenti.[481] Their Lordships considered that it would be unfair not to allow the employers to rely on volenti. Lord Pearce said that the defence should be available where the employer was not himself in breach of statutory duty and was not vicariously in breach of statutory duty through the fault of an employee whose commands the claimant was bound to obey, and where the claimant assented to and took part in the breaking of the statutory duty.

12-89 **Defendant's breach of duty coextensive with that of the claimant** This situation (in *ICI v Shatwell*) is closely analogous to the position where it is the claimant's own wrongful act which puts the employer in breach of statutory duty. A statute may impose the same duty on both claimant and defendant. In such a case, the claimant's physical act is usually a breach of duty both by himself and by the defendant. Thus, in *Ginty v Belmont Building Supplies Ltd*,[482] a regulation required crawling-boards to be provided and used for work on fragile roofs. The defendant employer provided them, but the claimant, in breach of orders failed to use them, and so fell and suffered injury. The only wrongful act was the claimant's but through that act of the employee, the defendant was vicariously in breach of the regulation and liable to prosecution. Pearson J held that he had a good defence to the employee's civil action on the basis that where it was the claimant's own wrongful act which put the defendant in breach of statutory duty, the defendant will not be liable, provided the claimant was the sole cause of his own loss. It would be absurd if a workman who deliberately disobeyed his employer's orders, and thereby put the employer in breach of a regulation, could claim damages for injury caused to him solely by his own wrongdoing. As Lord Diplock put it in *Boyle v Kodak Ltd*: "To say 'you are liable to me for my own wrongdoing' is neither good morals nor good law."[483] In that case, the House of Lords approved the rule laid down in *Ginty*, but like Pearson J, was careful to hedge it with restrictions. The question must be asked "Whose fault was it?" This defence will apply only where the claimant is the sole author of his own misfortune.[484] The employer will be liable if he was himself at fault. Thus if, as in *Boyle v Kodak Ltd*, the employer should have warned the claimant and instructed him in what was needed to comply with the regulations, or if he is vicariously responsible for the conduct of another employee,[485] the defence does not apply.[486] However, in such a case the claimant's damages may be reduced for his

---

481 See also *Bolt v William Moss & Sons* (1966) 110 S.J. 385.

482 [1959] 1 All E.R. 414.

483 [1969] 1 W.L.R. 661 at 673.

484 See *McCreesh v Courtaulds Plc* [1997] P.I.Q.R. P421, in which both the employer and employee were in breach of statutory duty to have a guard on a circular saw. The Court of Appeal held that if the court finds that the employer's breach of statutory duty is causally relevant to the accident, then even though the employee has adopted a manifestly dangerous practice, it is not open to the judge to exonerate the defendants entirely. A practice of allowing a circular saw to be used unguarded and the failure to provide instructions as to the saw's use contributed to the accident, notwithstanding that the claimant had experience of working with such saws. The defendants were held 25 per cent responsible.

485 *Ross v Associated Portland Cement Manufacturers Ltd* [1964] 1 W.L.R. 768 at 777.

486 cf. *Jenner v Allen West & Co Ltd* [1959] 1 W.L.R. 554 CA; *Byers v Head Wrightson & Co Ltd* [1961] 1 W.L.R. 961; *Leach v Standard Telephones and Cables Ltd* [1966] 1 W.L.R. 1392; *Quinn v JW Green (Painters) Ltd* [1966] 1 Q.B. 509 CA; *Stocker v Norprint* (1971) 10 K.I.R. 10. See also *Donaghey v Boulton and Paul Ltd* [1968] A.C. 1; *Parker v PFC Flooring Supplies Ltd* [2001] P.I.Q.R. P7; affirmed at [2001] EWCA Civ 1533 on the question of negligence (though breach of

contributory negligence.[487] The difference between *Ginty v Belmont Building Supplies Ltd* and *Imperial Chemical Industries Ltd v Shatwell* is that in the latter case the court could not say that the injury was caused solely by the claimant's conduct, and therefore volenti was invoked in order to prevent the concept of vicarious liability producing the result that was avoided in *Ginty v Belmont Building Supplies Ltd* on the basis that the defendant did not cause the loss.

In *Brumder v Motornet Service and Repairs Ltd*[488] the defence in *Ginty* and *Boyle v Kodak* was extended by the Court of Appeal to a case where the claimant was the sole director and shareholder of the defendant, and had breached a different duty (namely, a duty of care owed to the company) from the duty whose breach was the basis of his action for personal injuries. The defendant company was in breach of its absolute duty under the Provision and Use of Work Equipment Regulations 1998 reg.5, when the compressor in a raised hydraulic ramp failed. The claimant lost a finger attempting to descend from the ramp. It was found that the claimant, as sole director, had not given any consideration to health and safety and had not conducted a risk assessment nor sought to ensure that statutory obligations were met. The Court of Appeal rejected the judge's finding of 100 per cent contributory negligence as contrary to principle. However, it extended the defence in *Boyle* and *Ginty* to this situation. This extension of a defence which was previously understood to be tightly confined could pose some difficulties, since the claimant's breaches of duty in this instance were different in kind from the defendant's breach of the absolute duty under reg.5. So, for example, it was suggested that the company would be able to recover its losses from the claimant if he should succeed in his action, so that the result would be circuitous actions.[489] This argument was also used in *Ginty*. But where the duties breached by the parties are different in kind it is difficult to be sure that this would be the case. For example, was the claimant's failure causative of the defendant's breach of duty, or would the ramp have failed even if a risk assessment had been carried out? In a short concurring judgment, Longmore LJ based his agreement more directly on the policies which he identified as underlying absolute duties, most particularly the aim of encouraging high standards of compliance.[490] It is open to question whether leaving an individual director without compensation for personal injury is an ideal means of encouraging compliance, but the decision clearly extends the defence beyond cases where the breaches of duty are "coextensive". 12-90

Contributory negligence Contributory negligence is a defence both to an action in negligence and breach of statutory duty. In general, however, the carelessness of employees as claimants is treated more leniently than the negligence of employers, even where liability rests upon the vicarious responsibility of the employer for the negligence of another employee. So, "[i]t is not for every risky thing which a workman in a factory may do in his familiarity with the machinery 12-91

statutory duty was not dealt with on appeal).

487 For discussion of the effect of *Boyle v Kodak Ltd* on the correct approach to causation and contributory negligence see *O'Neill v DSG Retail Ltd* [2002] EWCA Civ 1139; [2003] I.C.R. 222 at [79]–[85]; and *Anderson v Newham College of Further Education* [2002] EWCA Civ 505; [2003] I.C.R. 212 (see para.3-58 fn.199) respectively.

488 [2013] EWCA Civ 195; [2013] 1 W.L.R. 2783.

489 [2013] EWCA Civ 195; [2013] 1 W.L.R 2783 at [49], [51].

490 [2013] EWCA Civ 195; [2013] 1 W.L.R. 2783 at [62].

that a [claimant] ought to be held guilty of contributory negligence".[491] The House of Lords has accepted that precisely the same conduct by an employee might lead to a different conclusion on negligence, depending upon whether the employee is suing as a claimant or whether a third party (possibly another employee) is suing the employer as vicariously liable for the employee's conduct.[492] The fact that the deceased was carrying out her duties as an employee with attendant risks, albeit carelessly, was also considered a relevant factor in *Cassells v Allan*,[493] where Mrs Cassells had died as a result of a collision with a coach: "Mrs Cassells did not create a sudden hazard, by running in front of the bus. She was a person on foot, vulnerable to injury by a large vehicle, and acting in the course of her employment." Although she had approached a moving vehicle, the driver and the employer should bear the greater part of the responsibility. Where the employee's claim is based on the employer's breach of statutory duty, the underlying policy of the legislation is also a factor in setting the standard of care for contributory negligence. Thus, in *Staveley Iron and Chemical Company Ltd v Jones*[494] Lord Tucker commented that:

> "In Factory Act cases the purpose of imposing the absolute obligation is to protect the workmen against those very acts of inattention which are sometimes relied upon as constituting contributory negligence so that too strict a standard would defeat the object of the statute."

In some instances an allegation of contributory negligence simply points to a breach of the employer's duty to take reasonable care to protect employees from their own carelessness or inadvertence.[495]

12-92 Where an accident has occurred as a result of "human fallibility, aberration or lapse in attention, or inadvertence" by an employee, this does not form the basis for a finding of contributory negligence where the employer is in breach of the absolute statutory duty imposed by reg.11(1) of the Provision and Use of Work Equipment Regulations 1998 (requiring measures which are effective to prevent access to any dangerous part of machinery or to any rotating stock-bar; or to stop the movement of any dangerous part of machinery or rotating stock-bar before any part of a person enters a danger zone). The statutory provisions are intended to protect employees

---

[491] *Flower v Ebbw Vale Steel Iron & Coal Ltd* [1934] 2 K.B. 132 at 140, per Lawrence J, approved by Lord Wright at [1936] A.C. 206 at 214. See also *Caswell v Powell Duffryn Associated Collieries Ltd* [1940] A.C. 152, para.8-64. See further *Casson v Spotmix Ltd (in Liquidation)* [2017] EWCA Civ 1994, where the claimant's hand was trapped in machinery he had been cleaning while it was in operation. Too much emphasis had been placed by the trial judge on the fact that the claimant, with hindsight, acknowledged that this was a dangerous procedure; and more attention should have been paid to the fact that other employees cleaned the machine in the same way. There should have been no finding of contributory negligence. The basis of liability was failure to provide adequate training in how to clean the machine.

[492] *Staveley Iron & Chemical Co Ltd v Jones* [1956] A.C. 627 at 642, 648.

[493] [2019] CSOH 14; see also para.12-36.

[494] [1956] A.C. 627 at 648; *Sherlock v Chester City Council* [2004] EWCA Civ 201 at [30] and [32], per Latham LJ. See also para.8-64.

[495] *General Cleaning Contractors Ltd v Christmas* [1953] A.C. 180. In *Bhatt v Fountain Motors Ltd* [2010] EWCA Civ 863; [2010] P.I.Q.R. P17 where breaches of the Work at Height Regulations 2005 exposed an employee to unnecessary risk of injury Richards LJ observed, at [34], that an employee's "failure to follow the prescribed procedure when doing work he should not have been required to do at all, and when using equipment that he should not have been required to use if the work was to be done, does not mean that the accident was caused by him alone. It goes only to contributory negligence"; applied in *Sharp v Top Flight Scaffolding* [2013] EWHC 479 (QB) (where breach of the same Regulations arose from a failure to ensure that the claimant was properly trained or supervised).

against accidents caused by inattention or inadvertence: "The protection does not extend only to employees who are fully alert. A momentary lapse, such as occurred in the present case, falls short of being described as a lack of reasonable care on the part of the pursuer."[496] This approach was cited in *Sowmez v Kebaberry Wholesale Ltd*,[497] but distinguished where the claimant had deliberately overridden a safety device in order to clean a meat mincer while it was rotating. There was a reduction of damages of 20 per cent to reflect deliberate and considered choice to override a safety feature.

Issues may arise where injured employees make choices after the event of the accident thereby deliberately (in the case of suicide) or carelessly exposing themselves to further harm. In *Corr v IBC*,[498] the House of Lords held that an employee who committed suicide as a consequence of depression following a serious accident at work had not thereby broken the chain of causation. His employers were liable for the death as well as the initial injury. Since the trial judge had ruled that there was no liability, he had not made sufficient findings of fact on which to base a conclusion as to contributory negligence, but the House appeared divided on the question of whether, in principle, damages ought to be awarded to reflect contributory negligence by the employee in such a case.[499] In *Spencer v Wincanton Holdings Ltd*,[500] the claimant had had a leg amputated after an accident at work. He suffered a second accident, causing him to be confined to a wheelchair, when he attempted to fill his car with fuel without attaching his prosthetic leg. The Court of Appeal held that the claimant's actions were not sufficiently unreasonable to justify treating the effects of the second accident as too remote from the original injury or as breaking the chain of causation, as in the case of *McKew v Holland & Hannen & Cubitts (Scotland) Ltd*[501]: such questions were questions of fairness so that a judgment as to remoteness depended on value judgments. Rather, there was a reduction in damages by one third to reflect contributory negligence. There may also be reductions for contributory negligence where employees make their own decisions to face unnecessary risks, but under the influence of other employees in positions of authority. This was the case in *Ministry of Defence v Radclyffe*[502] where the injured claimant took an "ill-judged decision to face an obvious risk" (jumping 65 feet from a road bridge into a reservoir), but "under great pressure" from his senior officer, who was responsible for safety and who also jumped from the bridge, to do so. Damages were reduced by 40 per cent. **12-93**

---

[496] *McGowan v W & JR Watson Ltd* [2006] CSIH 62; 2007 S.C. 272; 2007 S.L.T. 169 at [14]. See also *Kennedy v Chivas Brothers Ltd* [2013] CSIH 57; 2013 S.L.T. 981 at [38], refusing to make a finding of contributory negligence in relation breaches of reg.4 of the Provision and Use of Work Equipment Regulations 1998 and reg.4 of the Manual Handling Operations Regulations 1992: "The point of the legislation is to ensure a safe working environment and work practices, and to impose strict liability on the employer if those standards are not met. Momentary acts of inattention are to be expected, especially when employees are under pressure or are performing repetitive tasks. For that reason a finding of contributory negligence should only be made in a clear case; generally speaking this will be one where the employee has made a conscious decision to embark upon a risky course of action." See further para.3-80.

[497] [2008] EWHC 3366 (QB).

[498] [2008] UKHL 13; [2008] 1 A.C. 884; see further paras 2-140, 3-70, 3-116 and 7-40.

[499] Although there is some apparent contradiction in holding that suicide through depression is a foreseeable consequence of industrial injury, and then holding the deceased partly responsible, there was a deduction made in the suicide in prison case, *Reeves v Commissioner of Police of the Metropolis* [2000] 1 A.C. 360.

[500] [2009] EWCA Civ 1404; [2010] P.I.Q.R. P8; para.2-130.

[501] [1969] 3 All E.R. 1621 HL.

[502] [2009] EWCA Civ 635 at [26].

gains or deficits caused by inattention or inadvertence.[85] The protection does not extend only to employees who are skilfully alert. A momentary lapse, such as occurred in the present case, falls short of being described as a lack of reasonable care on the part of the pursuer."[86] This approach was taken in *Smith v Kilbowie Hotels Ltd*,[87] but distinguished where the claimant had deliberately overridden a safety device in order to clean a machine while it was running. There was a reduction of damages of 20 per cent to reflect deliberate and considered choice to [illegible] safety feature.

---

[86] [illegible]

[87] [2018] EWHC [illegible] (QB).

[91] [1969] 3 All E.R. 1621 HL.

[92] [2011] EWCA Civ 66 at [20].

CHAPTER 13

PUBLIC SERVICE LIABILITY

TABLE OF CONTENTS

1. INTRODUCTION

Areas of liability This chapter considers three areas of public service liability: liability for common law negligence; liability under ss.6–8 of the Human Rights Act 1998 which make it unlawful for a public body to act in contravention of a right contained in the European Convention for the Protection of Human Rights, and provide a right of action before domestic courts; and thirdly, liability for misfeasance in public office. Public service liability for the tort of breach of statutory duty is discussed in Ch.9 and has a close bearing upon negligence liability. **13-01**

Public services through their employees' conduct may be liable under other torts, for example, the police service may be liable for the trespass torts of battery and false imprisonment; services responsible for activities affecting land use may be liable for nuisance; statements to the media may give rise to defamation liability, and so on. These areas of liability are not separately considered here as in principle, no special rules apply by virtue of a public service being the defendant.[1] However, the Human Rights Act action runs parallel with (and sometimes overlaps) a number of these torts. Equally, there are areas of negligence liability such as road accidents caused by a public service vehicle, where there is no special "public service element" affecting the operation of the rules and these situations are not considered either. The chapter focuses on the principles which are special to the public service sector.

2. NEGLIGENCE LIABILITY

13-02 **Special considerations** Five issues are discussed in this section. The first is whether the public or discretionary nature of a decision taken by a public service makes its conduct non-justiciable, that is, incapable of being assessed by a court. This is a threshold question. If the matter is not justiciable then the court cannot examine any further issues related to duty or breach. The second issue is whether there are policy reasons having particular relevance for public authorities. In many of the leading cases, this question is expressed in terms of the way the "*Caparo*[2] test" of fairness, justice and reasonableness applies to public services; but the most recent decisions of the Supreme Court, and especially *Poole BC v GN*,[3] cast doubt on this way of approaching the issue and recast the nature of the enquiry as summarised in the following paragraph. For example, it may be relevant that services have competing interests to balance. Since the decision in *Poole*, this issue is cast in terms of inconsistency with exercise of their statutory powers and duties. While this could be said to be a policy issue, it is expressed narrowly. The third issue has been framed in terms of proximity, and has arisen, in particular, in relation to regulatory services where the question is whether the purpose of the service can be regarded as being to benefit individuals as opposed to the public as a whole. This, however, must now be read subject to the increased emphasis on "assumption of responsibility" in such cases, since they are treated as part of the category of claims based on failures to confer a benefit, and subject to the general rules on such claims.[4] The fourth question concerns the application to the public service sector of the general position in respect of omissions, that is, the absence of a duty to act positively to protect others. The rule is of particular significance as the role of a public service often involves intervening positively to protect the public from harm, and in a series of recent cases has been identified by the Supreme Court as the key consideration in negligence actions against public authorities. Certainly this encompasses many situations which would in the past have been approached in

---

[1] On the other hand, the applicable liability principles in these torts may be influenced by many factors, such as the potential engagement of Convention rights; or the presence of a "statutory scheme" (see for example *Marcic v Thames Water Utilities* [2003] UKHL 66; [2004] 2 A.C. 42, and para.13-07 and 13-118).

[2] *Caparo Industries Plc v Dickman* [1990] 2 A.C. 605. See further para.7-17.

[3] [2019] UKSC 25; [2019] 2 W.L.R. 1478.

[4] See further para.13-03.

terms of "proximity", and leads to much less direct emphasis on free-ranging policy considerations. Rather, policy concerns are treated as identified with "categories" of case. The final issue concerns the standard of care to be expected of the public sector. For a time, it appeared that there would be a greater willingness to accept that public services owe a duty of care, so that the focus of litigation would shift to whether there had been a breach of the required standard of care. Applicable standards of care are indeed very important in areas where duties have been recognised. But the tendency has been for duty, rather than breach, to remain the key concept in controlling liability.[5]

Reinterpretation In its decision in *Poole BC v GN*,[6] the Supreme Court reinterpreted many of the key negligence decisions relating to public service liability, identifying the key concept for analysis of the field as the distinction between "harming the claimant" and "failing to confer a benefit". Lord Reed suggested that decisions in this area had for many years remained unduly influenced by the decision in *Anns v Merton*,[7] even after the House of Lords had departed from it, and that the significance of the distinction between causing harm and failing to confer a benefit set out in *Stovin v Wise*[8] and *Gorringe v Calderdale*[9] had not been fully realised until the decisions in *Michael v Chief Constable of South Wales*[10] and *Robinson v Chief Constable of West Yorkshire Police*.[11] In light of this new emphasis, the decision in *Poole* proposes a reorientation in the law relating to negligence liability of public bodies, in which the distinction between harming and failing to benefit is key, and in which the central notion in failure to benefit cases is whether there has been an assumption of responsibility. There is much less direct appeal to policy considerations, some of which have been redescribed in other terms. Generally, the Supreme Court in *Poole* proposed that public authorities will owe a duty on the same basis as private individuals, unless such duties would be inconsistent with their statutory powers and duties.[12] It was recognised by Lord Reed that many of the decisions reached between *X (Minors) v Bedfordshire CC*,[13] and *Poole* itself, would have to be reinterpreted, if they were to fit the framework set out in *Poole*. He suggested however that such a reinterpretation was generally possible: 13-03

> "Although the decisions themselves are generally consistent with the principles explained in *Gorringe* and later cases and can be rationalised on that basis, their reasoning has in some cases, and to varying degrees, been superseded by those later developments."[14]

Naturally, this requires the present chapter to include more than one explanation of some of the key decisions.

---

5 See the discussion by S. Bailey, "Public authority liability in negligence: the continued search for coherence" (2006) 26 L.S. 154, and more recent decisions reaffirming "no duty" situations charted in paras 13-23, 13-24 and 13-34, for example.
6 [2019] UKSC 25; [2019] 2 W.L.R. 1478.
7 [1978] A.C. 728; [1977] 2 W.L.R. 1024.
8 [1996] A.C. 923; [1996] 3 W.L.R, 388.
9 [2004] UKHL 15; [2004] 1 W.L.R. 1057.
10 [2015] UKSC 2; [2015] A.C. 1732; see para.13-37.
11 [2018] UKSC 4; [2018] A.C. 736; see paras 13-42 onwards.
12 [2018] UKSC 4; [2018] A.C. 736 at [65].
13 [1995] 2 A.C. 633.
14 [2018] UKSC 4; [2018] A.C. 736 at [34].

(a) Justiciability

13-04 **Non-justiciability** Notwithstanding more recent developments, the House of Lords decision in *X (Minors) v Bedfordshire CC*[15] remains the leading authority explaining the basis on which the discretionary nature of a public service decision may preclude the existence of a duty of care on the basis of "non-justiciability". It simplified the approach to such questions by comparison with the previous leading authority, *Anns v Merton LBC*.[16] Aspects of the approach in *X v Bedfordshire*, particularly the apparent reliance on a public law concept of reasonableness, have been subject to further simplification.[17] Here we deal with the core of its approach to justiciability, discretion, and policy decisions reached by public bodies.

13-05 In *X (Minors) v Bedfordshire*, Lord Browne-Wilkinson said that the first question in a case involving a discretionary decision was "is the negligence relied upon negligence in the exercise of a statutory discretion involving policy considerations: if so the claim will pro tanto fail as being non-justiciable". The claim will fail because the court will be unable to evaluate the exercise of discretion to determine whether there was negligence or not. On the facts he held that social work decisions as to the removal of children, the allocation of suitable social workers and the need for investigation of abuse allegations, did not raise non-justiciable policy issues whereas an allegation that the social services department had failed to provide a level of service appropriate to the claimants' needs might do so. As Lord Browne-Wilkinson acknowledged, the first attempt to lay down the principles applicable in deciding whether or not a decision was one of policy was made by Lord Wilberforce in *Anns*, in which he contrasted policy decisions with operational decisions. The issue was whether a local authority with a statutory discretion to inspect the foundations of buildings to ensure they were adequate, could owe a duty of care to a subsequent purchaser of a building who suffered loss because the foundations had not been adequately inspected. Lord Wilberforce considered that if the inspection failure had resulted from a policy decision, for example, a limit on the availability of inspectors because of resource constraints, no duty would be owed. But if the failure was operational in nature, such as a failure to examine foundations sufficiently closely during an inspection, then a duty could be owed.[18] In *Rowling v Takaro Properties Ltd*[19] Lord Keith related the issue of policy to that of justiciability, explaining that a policy decision was one which was "unsuitable for judicial resolution, of which notable examples are discretionary decisions on the allocation of scarce resources or the distribution of risks". This explanation had been adopted by Browne-Wilkinson VC himself in *Lonrho Plc v Tebbit*[20] where he refused to strike out Lonhro's claim that the Secretary of State had negligently delayed releasing Lonhro from its undertaking not to acquire shares in House of Fraser until it was too late for them to make a bid. It was argued that the delay was the result of a policy decision to hear representations from the House of Fraser

---

[15] [1995] 2 A.C. 633.

[16] [1978] A.C. 728.

[17] See para.13-10.

[18] Lord Wilberforce conceded that such operational powers could involve an element of discretion but concluded that "it can safely be said that the more 'operational' a power or duty may be, the easier it is to superimpose upon it a common law duty of care".

[19] [1988] A.C. 473.

[20] [1991] 4 All E.R. 973 at 981. His refusal to strike out the action was upheld by the Court of Appeal without further comment on the policy issue.

before any release was given to Lonhro. This argument was dismissed on the ground that it was "manifestly" not a policy reason in the sense used in *Rowling* as the "timing of the release did not involve the allocation of resources or the distribution of risks … nor any other policy considerations".

Policy decisions In a roughly contemporaneous decision to that in *Bedfordshire*, the Canadian Supreme Court decision in *Brown v British Columbia*[21] also considered the nature of policy decisions. The issue was whether the decision of a highway authority to continue a light summer schedule of road maintenance into the winter, was a policy rather than an operational decision. Cory J, giving the judgment of the majority, described the policy/operational distinction as follows: 13-06

> "True policy decisions involve social, political and economic factors. In such decisions, the authority attempts to strike a balance between efficiency and thrift, in the context of planning and predetermining the boundaries of its undertakings and their actual performance. True policy decisions will usually be dictated by financial, economic, social and political factors or constraints. The operational area is concerned with the practical implementation of the formulated policies; it mainly covers the performance or carrying out of a policy. Operational decisions will usually be made on the basis of administrative direction, expert or professional opinion, technical standards or general standards of reasonableness."

He rejected the argument that "policy decisions must be limited to threshold decisions, i.e. broad initial decisions as to whether something will or will not be done", holding instead that they can be "made by persons at all levels of authority" and that it was the "nature of the decision itself that must be scrutinised rather than the position of the person who makes it".[22] Applying these principles, he concluded that the decision "was clearly one of policy" and could "not be reviewed on a private standard of reasonableness". In a similar vein, Lord Woolf MR in *Kent v Griffiths*[23] commented that an important feature of the case was that:

> "there is no question of an ambulance not being available or of a conflict in priorities. I recognise that where what is being attacked is the allocation of resources, whether in the provision of sufficient ambulances or sufficient drivers different considerations could apply. There then could be issues which are not suited for resolution by the courts."

In *Dobson v Thames Water Utilities Ltd*,[24] Ramsay J considered the policy/ 13-07

---

[21] (1994) D.L.R. (4th) 1. *Brown* was not cited in *Bedfordshire* which was argued before the Lords in 1994.

[22] A narrower approach was taken by Linden JA in *Swanson Estate v Canada* (1991) 80 D.L.R. 4th 741. He argued that the special protection "must be limited only to those functions of government that are considered to be 'governing' and not available to those tasks of government that might be styled 'servicing' ". Applying this criterion, he held that the decision of the regional director of a licensing body to allow an airline to continue unsafe flying practices, was not part of a "governmental" function. The factors on which he based this conclusion were that the decision maker was not an elected official, the decision involved no polycentric or multi-faceted questions such as the choice between efficiency and thrift, it was not a macro-decision affecting the welfare of the nation and neither was it a budgetary decision based on the availability of resources.

[23] [2001] Q.B. 36. This case did not concern a striking out action, but proceeded on the basis of facts established on the balance of probabilities. This helps to explain the confidence with which Lord Woolf decided that no policy issues were involved. In many other cases considered in this chapter, the duty issue has arisen in the context of a striking out action.

[24] [2007] EWHC 2021 (TCC); [2008] 2 All E.R. 362.

operational distinction in relation to a claim in negligence and nuisance against a sewerage undertaker for failing to take steps to prevent the contents of sewers giving rise to odour and attracting mosquitoes. The defendant argued that the claim should be struck out as it had a statutory duty to deal with the contents of sewers under the Water Industry Act 1991 and that any common law claim would be inconsistent with the statutory scheme. Ramsay J refused to strike out the claim, commenting that "if there is a different cause of action which is not inconsistent ... there is nothing to preclude a claim being made on that basis. Policy matters are likely to lead to such inconsistency ... whilst operational matters are less likely to do so. It must be a question of fact and degree".[25] He noted that the "boundary may be difficult to draw and may depend on such uncertain phrases as matters or decisions relating to 'policy' or 'capital expenditure' matters or decisions as contrasted with 'operational' or 'current expenditure' matters or decisions".[26] Thus "where an allegation is tantamount to requiring major plant renewal that will fall on one side of the line whilst an allegation that a filter should be cleaned will lie on the other side".[27] The difficulty in boundary drawing was well illustrated by the claim itself. The statutory regulator, Ofwat, intervened in the litigation to argue that the claim would "raise the intractable issues of proving that the 'failure' of Thames Water was caused by inadequate funding; ... that [its] decision as to how to frame its submissions to Ofwat ... was so unreasonable as to be negligent; and of showing what Ofwat would have done if during the relevant price review the defendant had made further submissions ... regarding the need for capital funding for odour abatement".[28] The defendants appealed on a number of points relating to the available damages, but there was no appeal on the threshold issue of whether the claimants were precluded from bringing an action at common law on the grounds that the action was potentially inconsistent with a statutory claim under the Water Industry Act 1991. The Court of Appeal made clear in *Dobson v Thames Water Utilities Ltd*,[29] that if the claim had been one where no negligence was alleged, the position would have been covered by the House of Lords decision in *Marcic v Thames Water Utilities*.[30]

13-08 **Policy and justiciability** In *Stovin v Wise*,[31] Lord Hoffmann commented that "[p]ractically every decision about the provision of [public] benefits, no matter how trivial it may seem, affects the budget of the public authority in either timing or amount" and criticised the policy/operational distinction in general and the Canadian case law in particular. However, he was criticising the use of the policy/operational distinction to determine the question of duty whereas the approach of Lord Browne-Wilkinson requires the claimant to establish the absence of a non-justiciable policy issue as one of the conditions for establishing a duty: it is, rather, a threshold issue. It is suggested that Lord Hoffmann's comments may give too

25 [2007] EWHC 2021 (TCC); [2008] 2 All E.R. 362 at [143].
26 [2007] EWHC 2021 (TCC); [2008] 2 All E.R. 362 at [140].
27 [2007] EWHC 2021 (TCC); [2008] 2 All E.R. 362 at [143].
28 [2007] EWHC 2021 (TCC); [2008] 2 All E.R. 362 at [167].
29 [2009] EWCA Civ 28; [2009] 3 All E.R. 319. In respect of damages, see para.13-131.
30 [2003] UKHL 66; [2004] 2 A.C. 42; see paras 19-77 and 19-134.
31 [1996] A.C. 923 at 951.

wide an interpretation of what is a policy question in this context. A better explanation is that provided by Lord Slynn in *Phelps v Hillingdon BC*[32] where he said:

> "It is only where what is done has involved the weighing of competing public interests or has been dictated by considerations on which Parliament could not have intended that the courts would substitute their views for the views of ministers or officials that the courts will hold that the issue is not justiciable on the ground that the decision was made in the exercise of a statutory discretion."

Thus, in *A v Essex CC*[33] Hale LJ considered the policy of an adoption agency about disclosure of information to be the kind of policy which could not be challenged by the courts as Parliament had entrusted the task to the agencies under the general guidance of the Secretary of State.[34]

Parallel issues of justiciability arise in relation to positive duties under art.2 ECHR.[35] One difficulty posed by the decision in *Smith v Ministry of Defence* is that issues of justiciability were considered to attach both to military decisions made on the ground in the course of active engagement (potentially giving rise to "combat immunity"); and also in relation to decisions of policy at a high level. Thus, Lord Hope thought it would be easy to find that allegations are beyond the reach of art.2 if they are about issues of "training, procurement or the conduct of operations" which were taken "at a high level of command and closely linked to the exercise of political judgment and issues of policy." Indeed the more political a decision, the slower a court should be to impose liability either at common law or under art.2.[36] But Lord Hope added the same would be true of decisions that "relate to things done or not done when those who might be thought to be responsible for avoiding the risk of death or injury to others were actively engaged in direct contact with the enemy". Both of these are based on considerations of justiciability. Claims could only be brought in the "middle ground" between these two.[37] The interconnected nature of the complaints was treated by Lord Mance, in dissent, as posing serious difficulties, and he argued that the availability of claims limited to the "middle ground" was unattractive.[38] Notably, he preferred to consider common law first, so that established thinking of the domestic courts could guide any novel conclusions in relation to art.2. A case which was agreed to fall into the "middle ground" described in *Smith* was *R. (on the application of Long) v Secretary of State for Defence*.[39] 13-09

Ambit of discretion In *X (Minors) v Bedfordshire CC*[40] Lord Browne-Wilkinson said that a further question to be asked in discretion cases was: "were the acts alleged to give rise to the cause of action within the ambit of the discretion conferred on the local authority?" This test invited the courts to apply the public law test for determining whether conduct was outside the ambit of discretion, namely, was the 13-10

---

32 [2001] 2 A.C. 619.
33 [2003] EWCA Civ 1848; [2004] 1 W.L.R. 1881 at [48].
34 See also *Paton v Scottish Ministers* [2019] SAC (Civ) 31: a decision in relation to the recall of an offender to prison was considered to be non-justiciable, as within the decision-maker's discretion.
35 *Smith v Ministry of Defence* [2013] UKSC 41; [2014] A.C. 52.
36 *Smith v Ministry of Defence* [2013] UKSC 41; [2014] A.C. 52 at [65].
37 *Smith v Ministry of Defence* [2013] UKSC 41; [2014] A.C. 52 at [76].
38 *Smith v Ministry of Defence* [2013] UKSC 41; [2014] A.C. 52 at [149].
39 [2015] EWCA Civ 770; [2015] 1 W.L.R. 5006; paras 13-93 and 13-97.
40 [1995] 2 A.C. 633.

decision "so unreasonable that no reasonable authority could have made it".[41] In effect, the unreasonableness of the authority's conduct was treated as a threshold issue going to whether a duty was owed rather than a standard of care issue going to whether there had been a breach of duty. Arguably the test did not form part of the ratio of *Bedfordshire*[42] and in *Barrett v Enfield LBC*[43] Lord Hutton said it was:

> "preferable for the courts to decide the validity of the claim by applying directly the common law concept of negligence than by applying as a preliminary test the public law concept of unreasonableness to determine if the decision fell outside the ambit of the statutory discretion."

Again, in *Phelps v Hillingdon LBC*[44] Lord Slynn said that the fact that acts were "carried out within the ambit of a statutory discretion is not in itself a reason why it should be held that no claim in negligence can be brought". In *Carty v London Borough of Croydon*[45] after an exhaustive review of the authorities, Dyson LJ concluded that there were just two areas of potential enquiry: "the first is whether the decision is justiciable at all. And the second is to apply the classic three stage test enunciated in *Caparo*."[46] He suggested that "the *Caparo* test is sufficiently flexible to allow [the ambit of discretion] to be taken into account in deciding whether there has been a breach of the duty of care"[47] and earlier in the judgment explained:

> "there is a spectrum at one end of which lie decisions which are heavily influenced by policy and which come close to being non-justiciable … in relation to which the court is unlikely to find negligence proved unless they are ones which no reasonable … authority could have made. At the other end of the spectrum are decisions involving pure professional judgment … in relation to these, the court will only find negligence on the part of the person who made the decision … if he failed to act in accordance with a practice accepted as proper by a responsible body of persons of the same profession."[48]

This approach suggests that the "unreasonableness" of a decision should normally be regarded as relevant to whether there has been a breach and not whether there is a duty. Where the decision is at the policy end of the spectrum, then its unreasonableness may be a reason for courts considering that it remains justiciable. In *A v Essex CC*[49] Hale LJ said that the policy decision as to the level of information to be given to potential adopting parents was "classically an area of discretion

---

41 [1995] 2 A.C. 633 at 740. Lord Browne-Wilkinson cautioned that the test was confined to the unreasonableness of the decision and did not introduce the broader public law concept of ultra vires under which decisions could be invalid "for reasons other than *Wednesbury* unreasonableness".

42 In *Barrett v Enfield LBC* [2001] 2 A.C. 550 at 585, Lord Hutton said that as the claims in *Bedfordshire* were struck out on grounds of justice and reasonableness and not ambit of discretion, Lord Browne-Wilkinson's speech did not preclude a ruling that a duty could be owed even if the decisions were within the ambit of discretion.

43 [2001] 2 A.C. 550 at 586.

44 [2001] 2 A.C. 619 at 653. See also *S v Gloucestershire CC* [2001] Fam. 313; [2000] 3 All E.R. 346 at 369, another claim against a welfare authority by a child allegedly abused by foster parents, where May LJ giving the judgment of the Court of Appeal held that a duty was owed but said: "In considering whether a discretionary decision was negligent, the court will not substitute its view for that of the local authority unless the discretionary decision was plainly wrong."

45 [2005] EWCA Civ 19; [2005] 1 W.L.R. 2312.

46 [2005] EWCA Civ 19; [2005] 1 W.L.R. 2312 at [28]. Mummery LJ at [82] expressed the same view.

47 [2005] EWCA Civ 19; [2005] 1 W.L.R. 2312 at [32].

48 [2005] EWCA Civ 19; [2005] 1 W.L.R. 2312 at [26].

49 [2003] EWCA Civ 1848; [2005] 1 W.L.R. 1881 at [48].

which can only be challenged if it falls outside the realms of reasonableness". In *Connor v Surrey County Council*,[50] Laws LJ reviewing the authorities said that "(1) Where it is sought to impugn, as the cause of the injury, a pure choice of policy under a statute which provides for such a choice to be made, the court will not ascribe a duty of care to the policy-maker". However, "(2) If a decision, albeit a choice of policy, is so unreasonable that it cannot be said to have been taken under the statute, it will (for the purpose of the law of negligence) lose the protection of the statute". Laws LJ expressly had in mind the *Wednesbury* form of unreasonableness.

Crown act of state and non-justiciability Non-justiciability is recognised as underpinning some, and perhaps all, aspects of the doctrine of "Crown act of state". The doctrine precludes tort actions in relation to "acts which are by their nature sovereign acts, acts which are inherently governmental, committed in the conduct of the foreign relations of the Crown",[51] and is therefore a separate application of "non-justiciability", and is not confined to the tort of negligence. It does not however apply to actions under the Human Rights Act 1998. In *Rahmatullah*, there was divergence between Justices of the Supreme Court as to whether "Crown act of State" could be entirely explained in terms of "non-justiciability or abstention",[52] or whether there are in fact two aspects to the doctrine: a relatively narrow principle of non-justiciability, and a "tort defence".[53] Baroness Hale DPSC offered the solution of a non-justiciability principle, which was nevertheless wider than the one espoused in the courts below. On this basis, the non-justiciability principle extended to "aspects of the conduct of military operations abroad as well as the high policy decision to engage in them",[54] and the questions raised could be seen as non-justiciable "even though their subject matter was entirely suitable for determination by a court".[55] Crown act of state relates to sovereign acts; committed abroad; in the conduct of the foreign policy of the state; so closely connected to that policy to be necessary in pursuing it; and at least extending to the conduct of military operations which are themselves lawful in international law.[56] The interpretation of Crown act of state fell to be further considered in *Alseran v Ministry of Defence*,[57] which continued the claims by Iraqi civilians under both the law of tort, and the HRA.[58] Leggatt J understood the Supreme Court to have declared in *Rahmatulla* that the application of the Crown act of state doctrine does not depend on establishing that either the allegedly wrongful act or the wider military operation of which the act formed part, or the policy decision to engage in that operation, was lawful in international law. 13-11

50 [2010] EWCA Civ 286; [2011] Q.B. 469, at [103].

51 *Rahmatullah v Ministry of Defence and another* [2017] UKSC 1; [2017] A.C. 649 at [33], per Baroness Hale.

52 This was the view of Lord Mance JSC, with whom Lord Hughes JSC agreed. Non-justiciability was also identified as the basis of the related doctrine of foreign act of state in the judgments of Lord Mance JSC, and of Lord Neuberger JSC, in *Belhaj v Straw* [2017] UKSC 3; [2017] A.C. 964. In that case however, the doctrine was not effective and the claims proceeded to trial.

53 This was the view of Lord Sumption JSC.

54 [2017] UKSC 1; [2017] A.C. 649 at [33].

55 [2017] UKSC 1; [2017] A.C. 649 at [33].

56 [2017] UKSC 1; [2017] A.C. 649 at [37]. It was accepted that the doctrine would not extend to acts of torture, for example.

57 [2017] EWHC 3289 (QB); [2019] Q.B. 1251.

58 See further para.13-130.

(b) Fair just and reasonable[59]

13-12 **The restrictive Bedfordshire approach** In *X (Minors) v Bedfordshire CC*[60] Lord Browne-Wilkinson held that it would not be fair, just and reasonable to impose a duty of care on the public services in relation to most of the claims in question. The case grouped together claims concerning the decisions of welfare authorities in relation to child abuse, of education authorities in relation to special needs provision and the advice given to children by education staff. In the child abuse cases it was alleged that welfare authorities had negligently investigated two situations with the result that in one case a child had been wrongly taken away from its mother and in the other case, the children had been wrongly left with their mother. The child and mother in the first case and the children in the second case, claimed compensation. The authority argued that the claims should be struck out without trial as whatever the facts, it would not be fair and just to impose a duty. Lord Browne-Wilkinson, giving the leading speech in the House of Lords, upheld this argument. Two of the reasons for finding the imposition of a duty to be unfair were linked to the nature of the discretion: first, the difficult nature of the decisions which had to balance the risk of taking action too soon against the risk of not taking it soon enough and had to balance the views of an interdisciplinary team which included police and doctors; and secondly, the fear that the possibility of liability would lead to a defensive approach with decisions being postponed until litigation-proof evidence had been found. Other reasons for holding a duty to be unfair were the concern that a duty would lead to a diversion of resources from the provision of care to the defence of claims, and that parents had an adequate existing remedy against the authority through the statutory complaints process. He also held that social workers individually owed no duty to the families as any such duty would put them in conflict with their primary duty to advise the authority in relation to the action to be taken. Likewise, he rejected the education claims which were based simply on the alleged negligent assessment of the children's needs and the subsequent decisions as to educational provision. Here too, he considered that it would not have been fair, just and reasonable to impose a duty as the statutory framework required co-operation between disparate agencies and also provided alternative remedies through a grievance procedure. In *Poole BC v GN*,[61] Lord Reed drew attention to the way in which Lord Browne-Wilkinson approached *Caparo*'s proposal that the law of negligence should proceed incrementally and by analogy, noting that the

---

[59] In *Tortious Liability of Statutory Bodies: A Comparative and Economic Analysis of Five English Cases* (1999) Markesinis, Auby, Coester-Waltjen and Deakin; the authors identified four groups of arguments used to justify restricting the duty imposed on public bodies on grounds of fairness: liability makes bad economic sense in that it may lead to diversion of resources or defensive practice; liability would inhibit freedom of action; it is inappropriate for courts to tell elected bodies how to exercise their powers; and victims often have alternative remedies. The authors question the economic and inhibitory arguments as unsupported by empirical evidence, argue that legal as well as political controls may be necessary, and question whether alternative remedies are as effective. Whilst for a time the case law seemed to suggest that the courts were recognising the strength of these counter-arguments (para.13-16 onwards), the first in particular subsequently gained ground. The Human Rights Act itself provides a relevant "alternative remedy" in some negligence cases, and the House of Lords and Supreme Court have taken a stance against "gap-filling" in cases where the Human Rights Act did not apply.

[60] [1995] 2 A.C. 633.

[61] [2019] UKSC 25; [2019] 2 W.L.R. 1478. See para.13-03.

restrictive police cases, such as *Hill v Chief Constable of West Yorkshire*,[62] and other cases dealing with regulators,[63] provided the closest analogy.

By contrast, Lord Browne-Wilkinson held that a duty could be fair, just and reasonable in the case of the education claims stemming from offering a specialist advisory service to children and parents. Hence, advice given by education staff and the failure of staff to refer children to the specialist advice service could give rise to a duty. The conduct involved was sufficiently distinct from the underlying statutory scheme that a duty would not upset the working of the scheme and the provision of advice direct to the claimants by education staff gave rise to an assumption of responsibility to them by the authority. Lord Browne-Wilkinson concluded: 13-13

> "Once the decision is taken to offer such an [advisory] service, a statutory body is in general in the same position as any private individual holding itself out as offering such a service ... The position is directly analogous with a hospital ... in such a case the authority running the hospital is under a duty to those whom it admits to exercise reasonable care in the way in which it runs it."[64]

Lord Browne-Wilkinson also considered that the education staff themselves might owe duties in so far as they held themselves out as having special skills to advise the claimants. To that extent the authority could be vicariously liable as well as directly liable to the claimants.

Barrett and children in care In *Barrett v Enfield LBC*[65] the House of Lords refused to strike out a claim by a child, who had been in care, alleging that the authority had been negligent in the choice of inappropriate and abusing foster parents and had thereby caused him to suffer injury. The Lords distinguished *Bedfordshire* on the ground that it was concerned with the decision to take a child into care whereas *Barrett* was concerned with decisions about the child after it had been taken into care. Lord Slynn said that the factors which had led the court in *Bedfordshire* to conclude that it would not be reasonable to impose a duty did not "necessarily have the same force separately or cumulatively in the present case". He distinguished the policy reason based on the difficulty of the task on the ground that decisions about children in care did not involve the same difficult discretion as those about taking children into care. However, he rejected the substance of the other policy reasons. He considered that fear of defensive conduct should be given "little if any weight" as "if the conduct in question is of a kind which can be measured against the standards of the reasonable man, then I do not see why the law in the public interest should not require those standards to be observed".[66] He also countered the *Bedfordshire* argument based on the availability of complaints procedures, with the observation that these remedies were "not likely to be as efficacious as the recognition by the court that a duty of care may be owed at common law" and endorsed the view that the imposition of a duty of care could contribute to the maintenance of high standards of public service. In *Poole BC v* 13-14

62 [1989] A.C. 53.
63 *Yuen Kun Yeo v Attorney General of Hong Kong* [1988] A.C. 175.
64 [1995] 2 A.C. 633 at 763.
65 [2001] 2 A.C. 550. See also *S v Gloucestershire CC* [2001] Fam. 313; [2001] 2 W.L.R. 909, where the Court of Appeal followed the approach in *Barrett* and refused to strike out claims that a social work authority was liable to children for negligently failing to prevent their abuse by foster parents.
66 [2001] 2 A.C. 550 at 568.

GN,[67] Lord Reed proposed that the key feature of *Barrett* that distinguished it from *Bedfordshire* as a matter of principle was that the local authority had, by taking the child into care, "assumed responsibility for his care", as proposed by Lord Hutton in *Barrett* in a concurring speech. This amounts to a reinterpretation, and would suggest not so much a less restrictive approach to the policy questions, as a distinction based upon the presence of an "assumption of responsibility". Notably, the House of Lords in *Barrett* clearly regarded themselves as stepping away from *X v Bedfordshire*, suggesting that policy arguments should be given close attention rather than being applied in a new context uncritically. The newly categorised approach in *Poole* and other recent Supreme Court decisions[68] may seem to propose that policy concerns once dealt with are not generally to be reopened.

13-15 **Phelps and the improvement of standards** A year after the decision in *Barrett*, a seven member House of Lords in *Phelps v Hillingdon LBC*[69] confirmed the suggestion in *Bedfordshire* that a duty of care could be owed by education authority staff giving advice about special needs, and appeared to confirm a change in emphasis in relation to policy arguments, which had been apparent in *Barrett*. In *Phelps* the claimant sought damages for the negligence of the authority's educational psychologist in failing to diagnose her dyslexia when she was tested at the age of 11. As a result she received inappropriate schooling and her development suffered. She was diagnosed with dyslexia after leaving school and sought damages for the loss of earnings she would have made if she had received the appropriate education and for the cost of tuition to overcome the disability. At trial it was held that the psychologist was liable to her for breach of a duty of care and the authority was vicariously liable. The Court of Appeal reversed this decision on the ground that no duty was owed. The court considered that the psychologist owed a duty to the authority and that any additional duty to the child would result in a conflict of interest.[70] The court also felt that imposition of a duty would lead to a proliferation of education malpractice claims with a consequent diversion of resources to fighting vexatious claims. The House of Lords restored the decision of the trial judge and confirmed the award of damages. Lord Slynn saw no difficulty in holding that the psychologist owed a duty both to the authority and to the child. Lord Nicholls said that the duty would extend to teachers of all pupils and not just those with special educational needs. He also said that he was "not persuaded by fears" that resources would be diverted from teaching to litigation or that schools would focus on defensive record keeping. Rather, the courts would weed out hopeless claims and ensure the door was not open to claims based on poor quality teaching.[71] Lord Clyde similarly argued that "[a]ny fear of a flood of claims may be countered by the consideration that in order to get off the ground the claimant must be able to demonstrate that the standard of care fell short of that set by the *Bolam* test" which would allow for different approaches to teaching method and practice. He also considered that a duty might "have the healthy effect of securing

---

67 [2019] UKSC 25; [2019] 2 W.L.R. 1478 at [47].

68 See the discussion in para.13-03.

69 [2001] 2 A.C. 619.

70 In *Barrett v Enfield LBC* [2001] 2 A.C. 550 at 557, Lord Browne-Wilkinson said that he had come to the conclusion that an educational psychologist's duty was owed only to the authority and that he had been wrong in *Bedfordshire* to suggest that a duty could be owed to the child.

71 [2001] 2 A.C. 619 at 667.

that high standards are sought and secured".[72] In *Poole BC v GN*,[73] the Supreme Court commented that the House of Lords in *Phelps* had called into question the policy-based reasoning applied to education cases in *X v Bedfordshire*, which would have led to a denial of the duty of care. However, it proposed that the key feature of the case was the question of whether there was an "assumption of responsibility" towards the child. This is a reinterpretation of the approach in *Phelps* itself, which was couched in terms of whether the duty was owed to the child or its parents, or simply to the employing local authority. *Phelps*, therefore, is now interpreted as a case where there was an assumption of responsibility.

Greater emphasis on duty An approach which places confidence in questions of breach of duty as a sufficient means of rejecting bad claims has not generally been in evidence in the most recent cases relating to public service liability.[74] However, in cases which are held to be actionable following the approach in decisions such as *Robinson v Chief Constable of West Yorkshire*[75] and *Poole BC v GN*,[76] applying an appropriate standard of care will be an important control over liability.[77] In general, there has been increased emphasis on the need to protect public authorities from excessive litigation, which is best achieved through the rejection of the duty of care rather than through assessment of breach in individual cases.[78] There may also be more general reasons. First, *Barrett* and *Phelps* were influenced by the decision of the European Court of Human Rights in *Osman v UK*,[79] which appeared to hold that striking out negligence claims on the basis of policy concerns was itself a violation of art.6 of the ECHR. Once that misunderstanding had been laid to rest,[80] UK courts became more confident about finding there is no duty of care. Secondly, an action is now available against public authorities pursuant to the Human Rights Act 1998 where Convention rights are engaged. The relatively limited scope of monetary remedies under the Act may lead to the sense that *compensation for losses* (as opposed to vindication of rights) is a disproportionate response to some of the breaches of duty concerned. The duties established in *Barrett* and *Phelps* may to some extent be a product of a stage in the House of Lords' understanding of the relationship between tort liability and Convention rights. However, the status of their authority within the areas of child welfare and educational negligence remains undiminished, and they have now been reinterpreted by the Supreme Court as cases where there is an "assumption of responsibility". Equally, the majority of the Supreme Court in *Smith v Ministry of Defence*[81] decided, perhaps surprisingly, that the role played by policy in decisions alleged to have led to the deaths of the claimants' relatives was best identi- 13-16

72 [2001] 2 A.C. 619 at 672.
73 [2019] UKSC 25; [2019] 2 W.L.R. 1478 at [50]–[51].
74 See paras 13-24 to 13-26.
75 [2018] UKSC 4; [2018] A.C. 736.
76 [2019] UKSC 25; [2019] 2 W.L.R. 1478. See para.13-03.
77 The Supreme Court underlined the need for an appropriate standard of care in *Robinson v Chief Constable of West Yorkshire Police* [2018] UKSC 4; [2018] A.C. 736, para.13-42.
78 See the discussion of *Smith v Chief Constable of Sussex Police* [2008] UKHL 50; [2009] 1 A.C. 225; and *Michael v Chief Constable of South Wales* [2015] UKSC 2; [2015] A.C. 1732; para.13-35 to 13-39.
79 (1998) 29 E.H.R.R. 245; para.13-33.
80 See para.13-84.
81 [2013] UKSC 41; [2014] A.C. 52.

fied at trial, in light of the evidence, so that the claims should not be struck out. In remarks which related to claims under art.2 ECHR, Lord Hope said that the trial judge would nevertheless be expected to recognise the "very wide measure of discretion" to be accorded to those responsible on the ground for the planning and conduct of operations during which the soldiers lost their lives.

13-17 **Direct and vicarious liability** Even on the analysis adopted in *Barrett* and *Phelps*, there may be limited scope for direct liability claims against an authority. In *Bedfordshire*, Lord Browne-Wilkinson struck out the direct liability claim against the social work authority but not that against the education authority. It was in a different position because the claim was not based on a policy decision it had taken but on the fact that it was offering an advisory service and could be said to owe a duty of care in respect of the way in which it ran the service. In *Phelps* the authority was found to be liable vicariously for the negligence of its employees rather than directly liable. Lord Slynn pointed to the limited scope for direct claims against an authority for where such claims were based on decisions pursuant to a policy adopted by the authority they were likely to be non-justiciable. As an example of possible direct liability, he suggested a case where the authority had appointed professionals "who at the outset transparently were neither qualified nor competent to carry out the duties".[82] Where the authority has carelessly managed or trained its staff, there could similarly be a direct claim based on failure to run its services with reasonable care. But claims which are not based on organisational failure, are likely to be brought against the authority by the route of vicarious liability. This rests on establishing that the authority's employee owes a personal duty of care to the claimant. However, in determining whether a personal duty is owed, the impact on the authority's policy making role cannot be ignored. Thus, in *Bedfordshire* Lord Browne-Wilkinson suggested that it would undermine the policy of denying a direct duty on the part of the employer if liability could be imposed by the route of an employee's duty and the employer's vicarious liability.[83] Hence, in the child care cases it was held that the employer did not owe a direct duty and was not vicariously liable because its employees did not owe a personal duty. Conversely, in the education cases, he considered it possible that the authority both owed a direct duty and was vicariously liable for a personal duty owed by its employees. In *Phelps* the authority was found to be vicariously rather than directly liable but Lord Slynn again recognised that "there might be cases where to recognise a vicarious liability might so interfere with the performance of the authority's duties that it would be wrong to do so".[84] He noted that it would be for the authority to establish that this was the case. Neither *Bedfordshire* nor *Phelps* discussed the fairness of imposing a liability on the individual employee. That issue was raised in the much earlier case of *Ministry of Housing v Sharp*[85] where the Court of Appeal agreed that the

---

82 [2001] 2 A.C. 619 at 658.

83 [1995] 2 A.C. 633 at 754.

84 [2001] 2 A.C. 619 at 653. Again, in *Carty v London Borough of Croydon* [2005] EWCA Civ 19; [2005] 1 W.L.R. 2312 at [83], Mummery LJ expressed his concern about allowing a "circular" and "backdoor" route to imposing liability on an authority: "circular" in that the duty on the employee stemmed from the statutory duty placed on the employer; and "backdoor" in that the personal duty would then give rise to vicarious liability on the part of the authority in circumstances where the statutory duty imposed no direct liability.

85 [1970] 2 Q.B. 223.

authority was directly liable to the claimant but divided on the question of individual liability with Lord Denning being in favour and Cross LJ against.

Rejection of policy reasons Within their areas of application, the House of Lords decisions in *Barrett* and *Phelps* undermined the *Bedfordshire* policy reasons for denying a duty of care on grounds of fairness. These policy reasons were subject to further detailed critical analysis in the speech of Lord Bingham in *JD v East Berkshire Community Health NHS Trust*.[86] On the *Barrett* and *Phelps* approach, it seemed that generalised policy reasons would no longer be regarded as sufficient to deny a duty of care; rather attention had to be paid to the particular circumstances of an individual case. This no doubt reflected the understanding of negligence law, in the light of ECHR art.6, adopted by the European Court of Human Rights in *Osman v UK*.[87] The more sceptical approach to policy arguments evident in these cases led to a revised view of the scope of duties owed in relation to the physical and educational welfare of children. It was also recognised in a leading House of Lords decision concerning police duties[88] and was evident in *Arthur JS Hall & Co v Simons*,[89] a House of Lords decision contemporaneous with *Phelps*, in which the policy reasons supporting advocates' immunity were rejected. Scepticism about immunities in particular can be observed in the Supreme Court decisions of *Jones v Kaney*,[90] in which the immunity of expert witnesses was abolished, and *Smith v Ministry of Defence*,[91] where the majority confined the ambit of combat immunity. Only the policy protection of judges, witnesses of fact and the armed forces remain in place, though the latter has been restrictively interpreted. More recently, the Supreme Court has moved away from seeing *Caparo* as laying down a three part "test", with implications for the direct appeal to policy arguments. Subsequent paragraphs will detail the present balance reached in relation to various public services. 13-18

(i) Child welfare

Duty to the child Following *Barrett v Enfield LBC*[92] it is clear that a duty of care is owed to a child who has been taken into care by an authority. *Barrett* limited the authority of *Bedfordshire* to the proposition that decisions about taking a child into care did not give rise to a duty. However, in *D v East Berkshire Community NHS Trust*[93] the Court of Appeal held that this proposition was no longer applicable. In 13-19

86 [2005] UKHL 23; [2005] 2 A.C. 373 at [31]–[36]. Lord Bingham was dissenting but his critical analysis of the *Bedfordshire* policy reasons provides the background to his dissent rather than the reason for it. For the majority view, see para.13-24. For analogous reasons, Lord Bingham was also in the minority in *Smith v Chief Constable of Sussex Police* [2008] UKHL 50; [2009] 1 A.C. 225; para.13-35, where he argued in favour of a narrow "liability principle" in exceptional cases.

87 (1998) 29 E.H.R.R. 245.

88 *Brooks v Commissioner of Police for the Metropolis* [2005] UKHL 24; [2005] 1 W.L.R. 1495, where at [28] Lord Steyn observed: "Nowadays, a more sceptical approach to the carrying out of all public functions is necessary."

89 [2002] 1 A.C. 615.

90 [2011] UKSC 13; [2011] 2 A.C. 398.

91 [2013] UKSC 41; [2014] A.C. 52.

92 [2001] 2 A.C. 550. See also *S v Gloucestershire CC* [2001] Fam. 313, where the Court of Appeal followed the approach in *Barrett* and refused to strike out claims that a social work authority was liable to children for negligently failing to prevent their abuse by foster parents.

93 [2003] EWCA Civ 1151; [2004] Q.B. 558.

East Berkshire the claims stemmed from the accusations of medical authorities that parents had been abusing their children. These accusations proved unfounded but resulted in the temporary removal of the children from their parents. Both parents and children claimed to be owed a duty of care by the medical authorities. Although not involving a claim against social services as in *Bedfordshire*, the claim did arise from the investigation of child abuse. Lord Phillips MR giving the judgment of the Court of Appeal held that the policy reasons justifying denial of a duty in *Bedfordshire* could no longer apply because of the Human Rights Act 1998. This enabled parents and children to claim that an authority which negligently removed children into care, was in breach of s.6 of the Act. Section 6 required a public body to comply with the articles of the European Convention for the Protection of Human Rights including art.8 which required respect for family life.[94] As, subsequent to the Act coming into force in October 2000, parents and children could make a claim based on breach of the duty in s.6 against a public service, there was no point in protecting the service from a common law negligence claim. To the extent that such a claim might upset the process of taking a discretionary decision or might lead to defensive conduct and diversion of resources, this would happen anyway as a result of the s.6 claim. Thus, Lord Phillips concluded: "the decision in *Bedfordshire* cannot survive the 1998 Act."[95] The events in *Berkshire* occurred before 2000 and hence a Human Rights Act claim was not available to the claimants but Lord Phillips reasoned:

> "This cannot constitute a valid reason of policy for preserving a limitation of the common law duty of care which is not otherwise justified. On the contrary, the absence of an alternative remedy for children who were the victims of abuse before October 2000 militates in favour of the recognition of a common law duty of care once the public policy reasons against this have lost their force."

Consequently, he said:

> "it will no longer be legitimate to rule that, as a matter of law, no common law duty of care is owed to a child in relation to the investigation of suspected child abuse and the initiation and pursuit of care proceedings. It is possible that there will be factual situations where it is not fair, just or reasonable to impose a duty of care but each case will fall to be determined on its own individual facts."[96]

However, he held that no duty would be owed to the parents as: "It will always be in the parents' interest that the child should not be removed" and hence "the child's interests are in potential conflict with the interests of the parents" with the result that

---

94 For the application of art.8 to this situation, see para.13-119.

95 [2003] EWCA Civ 1151; [2004] Q.B. 558 at [83]. Wright, "Immunity no more" (2004) 20 P.N. 58 at 63, criticised *D v East Berkshire* as an "illegitimate attempt to overrule a House of Lords' decision [*Bedfordshire*]" and argued that the same result could have been achieved legitimately on the basis of the undermining of *Bedfordshire* in *Barrett* and *Phelps*. In the House of Lords in *D v East Berkshire* [2005] UKHL 23; [2005] 2 A.C. 373, the Court of Appeal's decision in relation to the duty to the child was not in question but Lord Bingham, at [21], noted Wright's criticism. In *Leeds City Council v Price* [2005] EWCA Civ 289; [2005] 1 W.L.R. 1825, shortly after *D v East Berkshire* in the Court of Appeal and before the judgment of the House of Lords, a Court of Appeal including Lord Phillips declined to depart from a House of Lords authority and to follow a subsequent judgment of the European Court of Human Rights instead, suggesting that this would be "iconoclasm of a different dimension" from their decision in *D v East Berkshire* (at [33]).

96 [2003] EWCA Civ 1151; [2004] Q.B. 558 at [84].

there were "cogent reasons of public policy for concluding that, where child care decisions are being taken, no common law duty of care should be owed to the parents".[97] The decision in respect of the duty to the children was not appealed but that in respect of the denial of a duty to the parents was taken to the House of Lords.[98]

D v East Berkshire was affirmed, but in certain respects reinterpreted, in *Poole BC v GN*.[99] The Supreme Court firmly rejected the Court of Appeal's suggestion in *Poole* that *D v East Berkshire* had been impliedly overruled by later, more restrictive decisions such as *Mitchell v Glasgow City Council*[100] and *Michael v Chief Constable of South Wales*,[101] where the House of Lords and Supreme Court had declined to alter the common law in order to bring it closer to the protection offered by the Human Rights Act 1998. Rather, the argument put by the Court of Appeal in *D v East Berkshire* had simply knocked away the policy arguments against the existence of a duty to the children, which had been based on the adverse effects of litigation or the threat of litigation.[102] Once these policy reasons had been dismissed, the decision was consistent with the principles to be gleaned from the later, restrictive cases. Most particularly, the doctors and social workers were claimed to have harmed the child by removing her, rather than failing to benefit by deciding not to remove her.[103] The parents' claims were reconceived as having failed because the imposition of a duty as claimed would be "inconsistent with the statutory framework", because the duty would be inclined to interfere with the exercise of the powers and duties in the manner intended by Parliament. This is a way of expressing the same point more narrowly, without the label of "policy". It is an awkward aspect of the approach set out in *Poole* that it dictates a sharp distinction in applicable principle between claims by children who argue that they have been wrongly taken into care, and children who claim that they have been wrongly not removed from their parents, through decisions made following the same processes. In case of a failure to remove, a successful claim will depend on showing an assumption of responsibility, and this is not the case where the claim is that the removal of a child from a parent has caused harm. **13-20**

The claim in *Poole BC v GN*[104] was that the local authority had failed to protect children from the abuse of third parties, their neighbours, and that they owed a common law duty to do so which was based upon their statutory duty under s.17 of the Children Act 1989. The Supreme Court dismissed this claim. A duty at common law could not be based upon a statutory duty; rather, public authorities "are prima facie subject to the same general principles of the law of negligence as private individuals and organisations". This was plainly a "failure to benefit" claim, and there is generally no liability for failures to benefit in the absence of "some particular reason **13-21**

97 [2003] EWCA Civ 1151; [2004] Q.B. 558 at [86].
98 See para.13-24.
99 [2019] UKSC 25; [2019] 2 W.L.R. 1478.
100 [2009] UKHL 11; [2009] 1 A.C. 874.
101 [2015] UKSC 2; [2015] A.C. 1732.
102 *Poole v GN* [2019] UKSC 25; [2019] 2 W.L.R. 1478, [53]. This is consistent with Lord Phillips' remarks in *Watkins v Secretary of State for the Home Office* [2006] UKHL 17; [2006] 2 A.C. 395 (see para.13-119), emphasising that the Court of Appeal decision in *D v East Berkshire* had involved a change of perspective on policy reasoning specifically, and did not amount to a fundamental change in legal principle.
103 *Poole v GN* [2019] UKSC 25; [2019] 2 W.L.R. 1478, [56].
104 [2019] UKSC 25; [2019] 2 W.L.R. 1478.

justifying such liability". None of the recognised reasons for such liability was present in this case. Landlords do not owe a duty of care to those affected by their tenants' anti-social behavior,[105] so this was not a case where there could be a duty based on having "created a source of danger". Rather, the claim was based on an "assumption of responsibility", but no such assumption could be established in this case, either from the nature of the function carried out by the local authority, or from the actions of the council in this particular case. On the latter point, there was no indication of what specific actions might be the basis for such a claim at trial, and therefore it was appropriate that the action should be struck out. While *X v Bedfordshire*[106] is no longer to be understood as laying down that local authorities do not owe a duty of care to children in relation to social services functions in any circumstances, the present claim did not indicate that any special circumstances justifying such a duty existed. Notably, the Supreme Court added that there were no clear particulars of an appropriate breach of duty in the claim. The argument was that the children should have been removed from their home and taken into care; but the statutory framework allows for care orders to be obtained only where there is a lack of reasonable parental care. That did not match the circumstances in this case, where the threat to the children's welfare was from a different source, and there were therefore no grounds for removing the children.

13-22 **Abuse by foster parents** In *NA v Nottinghamshire County Council*[107] the Court of Appeal held that a local authority was not vicariously liable for abuse perpetrated by foster carers on children placed in their care by the authority, nor did the authority owe a non-delegable duty of care to children in these circumstances.[108] On appeal, the Supreme Court agreed[109] that a local authority does not come under a non-delegable duty, since such a duty could create a conflict with the authority's statutory duty to the child under the Child Care Act 1980 and the local authority's interests in avoiding potential liability. A non-delegable duty would also amount to a form of state insurance for the actions of the child's family members. However, the Supreme Court reversed the Court of Appeal on the issue of vicarious liability, concluding that the local authority could be vicariously liable for the actions of foster carers. Applying *Cox v Ministry of Justice*,[110] several factors were considered to be relevant to this conclusion; the torts were committed in the course of an activity carried out for the benefit of the local authority; the placement of children with foster parents rendered the children particularly vulnerable to abuse; the local authority exercised a significant degree of control over both what the foster parents did and how they did it; and local authorities could more easily compensate the victims of abuse.[111]

---

105 A position confirmed in *Mitchell v Glasgow* [2009] UKHL 11; [2009] A.C. 874.

106 [1995] 2 A.C. 633; [1995] 3 W.L.R. 152.

107 [2015] EWCA Civ 1139; [2016] Q.B. 739.

108 On which see *Woodland v Swimming Teachers Association* [2013] UKSC 66; [2014] A.C. 537, para.6-70.

109 *Armes v Nottinghamshire County Council* [2017] UKSC 60; [2018] A.C. 355.

110 [2016] UKSC 10; [2016] A.C. 660; see para.6-35.

111 *Armes v Nottinghamshire Courty Council* [2017] UKSC 60; [2018] A.C. 355 at [59]–[64]. Though as Lord Hughes pointed out (at [77]) in his dissenting judgment "(deep pockets or insurance) ... cannot by itself be a principled ground for vicariousl liability and tends to be circular".

Child welfare and child support In *Rowley v Secretary of State for Work and Pensions*,[112] claims were brought by three children and their mother alleging that negligent enforcement of maintenance payments by the Child Support Agency (CSA) had resulted in economic losses, as well as psychological injury to the first child claimant, who suffered from cerebral palsy. All of the claims were struck out for a variety of reasons. There was no voluntary assumption of responsibility since the Secretary of State was statutorily obliged under the Child Support Act 1991 to make a maintenance assessment; and the relationship between the CSA and the claimants was not sufficiently similar to a solicitor-client relationship to be treated as analogous to that established duty category. These are essentially issues of proximity. Dyson LJ giving the judgment of the Court further held however that such a duty would not be "fair, just and reasonable". The Child Support Act 1991 "provided a sufficiently comprehensive remedy" to conclude "that a duty of care would be inconsistent with the statutory scheme".[113] Claims could also be referred to the ombudsman, and the cost of litigation "might well be out of proportion to the sums likely to be realistically at stake". *Rowley* is part of a series of decisions rejecting claims for civil remedies framed in tort or in terms of Convention rights, and brought against the Child Support Agency and the Secretary of State in respect of the Child Support Act 1991.[114] However the reasoning deployed is plainly of much broader application. For example in *Murdoch v Department for Work and Pensions*,[115] Walker J applied *Rowley* and ruled that an action in negligence would be inconsistent with the statutory scheme relating to the payment of incapacity benefit and income support. The relevant statute made plain the intended finality of the determination of entitlement under the Act. There would also have been no duty in any event following the approach in *Customs and Excise Commissioners v Barclays Bank Plc*.[116] It appeared from these authorities that action in discharge of a statutory duty does not in itself amount to an "assumption of responsibility", for it is not voluntary; there was no special degree of proximity; any such development would be more than incremental; and it would not be "fair, just and reasonable" to offer a common law remedy where other remedies existed.[117] Without doubting the outcome in *Rowley*, the Supreme Court in *Poole BC v GN*[118] nevertheless suggested that there are some circumstances in which conduct undertaken in the performance of an obligation—including a statutory obligation—may nevertheless give rise to an assumption of responsibility, naming both *Barrett v Enfield*, and *Phelps v Hillingdon*, as examples of this. Neither case had previously been rationalised as depending on an assumption of responsibility. 13-23

---

112 [2007] EWCA Civ 598; [2007] 1 W.L.R. 2861.

113 [2007] EWCA Civ 598; [2007] 1 W.L.R. 2861 at [74]. Remedies to the parent included a right of appeal, right to receive interest on payments on arrears, and the right to seek judicial review.

114 See also *R. (Kehoe) v Secretary of State for Work and Pensions* [2005] UKHL 48; [2006] 1 A.C. 42; para.13-110: the absence of a direct enforcement mechanism for parents did not engage art.6(1); and *Kehoe v UK* (2010/06) [2008] 2 F.L.R. 1014; (2009) 48 E.H.R.R. 2, where an application in respect of this claim was dismissed by the European Court of Human Rights: para.13-110. See also *Treharne v Secretary of State for Work and Pensions* [2008] EWHC 3222 (QB); [2009] 1 F.L.R. 853 (a Human Rights Act claim based on art.8 of the ECHR); para.13-116

115 [2010] EWHC 1988 (QB); [2011] P.T.S.R. D3.

116 [2006] UKHL 28; [2007] 1 A.C. 181.

117 On this last point see also for example *Home Office v Mohammed* [2011] EWCA Civ 351; [2011] 1 W.L.R. 2862, discussed in para.13-69.

118 [2019] UKSC 25; [2019] 2 W.L.R. 1478.

13-24 **No duty to suspect parent** In the appeal in *D v East Berkshire Community Health NHS Trust*[119] the majority of the House of Lords confirmed the decision of the Court of Appeal that no duty of care was owed to parents who were being investigated in cases of suspected child abuse. Three strands of reasoning appear in the majority speeches of Lords Nicholls, Rodger and Brown. The main concern was with the conflict of interest which would result from the imposition of such a duty. As Lord Nicholls put it:

> "The doctor is charged with the protection of the child, not with the protection of the parent. The best interests of a child and his parent normally march hand-in-hand. But when considering whether something does not feel 'quite right', a doctor must be able to act single-mindedly in the interests of the child. He ought not to have at the back of his mind an awareness that if his doubts about intentional injury or sexual abuse prove unfounded he may be exposed to claims by a distressed parent."[120]

A second strand of reasoning focused on the investigatory nature of the conduct in question. Lord Nicholls said:

> "In this area of the law, concerned with the reporting and investigation of suspected crime, the balancing point between the public interest and the interest of a suspected individual has long been the presence or absence of good faith. A report, made to the appropriate authorities, that a person has or may have committed a crime attracts qualified privilege. A false statement ('malicious falsehood') attracts a remedy if made maliciously. Misfeasance in public office calls for an element of bad faith or recklessness. Malice is an essential ingredient of causes of action for the misuse of criminal or civil proceedings."[121]

It should not be open to the claimant to circumvent the malice requirement by alleging a negligence duty. The third strand of the reasoning focused on the derivative nature of the claim. Lord Rodger, in particular, highlighted that the claimants were seeking to introduce an exception to the "settled policy of the law [which] is opposed to granting remedies to third parties for the effects of injuries to other people".[122] The parents were arguing that they should recover for distress suffered as a result of the careless performance of a duty primarily owed to the child. Both Lords Rodger and Brown concluded that recovery in such a case would be incompatible with the restricted duty owed to parents who suffered psychiatric injury as a consequence of negligent injury to a child.[123] Lord Bingham's dissent was based on a combination of the close proximity between the doctor and the parent, the belief that the duties to parent and child could be regarded as consonant rather than conflicting and the concern that if the common law failed to evolve to

---

119 [2005] UKHL 23; [2005] 2 A.C. 373.

120 [2005] UKHL 23; [2005] 2 A.C. 373 at [85]. See also Lord Rodger at [110]: "Of its very nature this kind of duty of care to the parents would cut across the duty of care to the children." and Lord Brown at [129]: "I find it impossible to see how such a duty could fail to impact upon the doctor's approach to his task and create a conflict of interest." Their Lordships cited the denial of a similar duty by the Australian High Court decision in *Sullivan v Moody* (2001) 207 C.L.R. 562; and the Privy Council endorsing the decision of the New Zealand Court of Appeal in *B v Att Gen of New Zealand* [2003] UKPC 61; [2003] 4 All E.R. 833.

121 [2005] UKHL 23; [2005] 2 A.C. 373 at [77]. Lord Brown at [134] made the analogous point that liability for blackening the parent's reputation would only arise if the defendant's malice defeated the defence of qualified privilege.

122 [2005] UKHL 23; [2005] 2 A.C. 373 at [105].

123 [2005] UKHL 23; [2005] 2 A.C. 373, Lord Rodger at [108] and Lord Brown at [133].

fashion an appropriate remedy, it would be leaving the problem to be "swept up by the [European] Convention".[124] He would, he said, choose evolution. This however has not been the theme of recent case law in this and analogous areas. "Sweeping up" by the Human Rights Act action rather than tort may be considered appropriate, and there appears to have been an expectation that tort will therefore not evolve even in cases where the Human Rights Act does not apply, for example because it was not in force at the time of the events: see in particular *Jain v Trent Strategic HA*,[125] and *Van Colle v Chief Constable of Hertfordshire*.[126]

The events in *D v East Berkshire* pre-dated the commencement of the Human Rights Act, but there has been no subsequent departure from its finding that a suspect parent is owed no duty of care, primarily on the basis of a potential "conflict of interest"; nor have exceptional cases been found where such a duty is justified. This may be a hallmark of the "conflict of interest" reasoning and of analogous arguments, since it is supposed that protection of decision-making from the relevant conflict requires a general rule, without exceptions.[127] In *D v Bury MDC*,[128] the approach in *East Berkshire* was applied where a five-month-old baby found to be suffering from fractures was removed from his parents. The Council failed to carry out a risk assessment, which was eventually done by a national children's charity, indicating that the child suffered from brittle bone syndrome and the injuries were not non-accidental. The difficulty in this case was that the Court found that it could not assess what injury (if any) had been caused to the child by the separation, and the parents' claim was barred by the reasoning in *D v East Berkshire*. It may be asked whether the decision whether or not to carry out a risk assessment is really affected by the conflict of interest difficulty, since it is also in the child's best interests to have this sort of assessment. This is not a case where the conflict of interest point seems particularly strong. Even so, no duty was owed to the suspected parents to carry out proper procedures.[129] *B v Reading BC*[130] was an appeal arising from a judge's decision to strike out a claim in negligence brought by a father against a local authority which had incorrectly suspected him of sexually abusing his daughter, and had begun care proceedings. The judge followed the reasoning in *D v East Berkshire*. The claim was originally framed so as to allege that the **13-25**

124 See [2005] UKHL 23; [2005] 2 A.C. 373 at [47], [44] and [50]. Damages under the Human Rights Act were awarded at first instance to parents whose children had been placed in foster care without their consent in *Williams v Hackney LBC* [2015] EWHC 2629 (QB); on appeal however, it was concluded that the placement had not been in breach of art.8: *Williams v Hackney LBC* [2017] EWCA Civ 26; [2017] 3 W.L.R. 59. Damages were awarded under the Human Rights Act against both police and social services in *D (Children) v Wakefield MDC* [2016] EWHC 3312 (Fam); [2017] 2 F.L.R. 1353. The injury was directly that of the parent, who was wrongly accused and had her children removed despite the availability of exonerating evidence: see para.13-115.

125 [2009] UKHL 4; [2009] 1 A.C. 853.

126 [2008] UKHL 50; [2009] 1 A.C. 225; para.13-91.

127 The alternative argument, put by Lord Bingham in *D v East Berkshire* itself, is that gross departures from basic professional standards of care do not need to be protected in this way, and indeed that such departures are to be deterred.

128 [2006] EWCA Civ 1; [2006] 1 W.L.R. 917.

129 In *AD v United Kingdom* (28680/06) [2010] 2 F.L.R. 1, the European Court of Human Rights upheld complaints arising from the facts of *D v Bury*. The focus was upon the proportionality of interference with the applicants' rights under art.8 ECHR, in marked contrast with the "conflict of interest" approach applied in domestic tort law. Presumably, in any future case argued under the Human Rights Act 1998 rather than in tort, this will be the approach taken, thus suggesting the possibility of a remedy under the HRA to suspected parents in situations of this type. See also para.13-119.

130 [2007] EWCA Civ 1313; [2008] 1 F.L.R. 797.

authority was vicariously liable for the negligence of an individual social worker. The father sought leave to amend his claim to allege a breach by the authority of a direct duty owed to B to have in place appropriate policies and processes. The Court of Appeal refused leave to amend the claim, on the basis that it was out of time. The Court also observed however that there was nothing in the reasoning of the House of Lords in *D v East Berkshire* which suggested that the "conflict of interest" reasoning applied only to vicarious, as opposed to direct duty, claims. Indeed, in either case the duty could be breached only if an individual social worker acted as a reasonably competent social worker would not have acted, or failed to act as a reasonably competent social worker would have acted. In either case, the same issue (a potential conflict of interest between the child, and the suspected parent), applied because in both cases it would need to be shown that the social worker acted in breach of duty. Therefore, in neither case was it "fair, just and reasonable" to impose a duty, because in each case a potential conflict of interest arose.[131] In *L v Pembrokeshire*,[132] it was explicitly held by the Court of Appeal that the commencement of the Human Rights Act 1998 and the new status of art.8 ECHR in particular had not swept away the policy reasoning in *D v East Berkshire* as it applies to parents. Therefore, a claim by a parent for alleged negligence in placing her child on the Child Protection Register was struck out, though the events occurred after October 2000. The need to protect those who had a duty to enforce the law in good faith, so that they are not inhibited in that duty, was predominant.

13-26 **Conflict of interest** Arguments based on conflict of interest have become well established, and have been invoked outside the child protection area. Such an argument has been considered strong enough to prevail even in a case where it was felt by the House of Lords that there was a likelihood—or in the case of Lord Scott a probability—that the actions of the defendant public authority were incompatible with the Convention rights of the claimant.[133] This contributes to an unfolding pattern where HRA liability is capable of running ahead of tort liability (though the reverse may also be true).[134] The problem of conflicting duties was recognised by the Supreme Court in *Poole BC v GN*.[135]

13-27 **Duty to protect adopting or fostering parent** The question whether a duty of care is owed to parents to whom a child is allocated for fostering or adoption was considered as a side issue in *W v Essex CC*.[136] Foster parents and their natural children claimed that the welfare authority had negligently allocated to the family a foster child with a record of abusing fellow children. The foster child had physically abused the natural children and that caused the parents psychiatric injury. Following the approach taken in *Barrett*, the House of Lords held that the parents'

---

[131] See also the proceedings brought by B alleging negligence against an investigating police officer; and conspiracy and misfeasance in a public office against the police officer and a social worker: *B v Reading BC* [2009] EWHC 998 (QB); [2009] 2 F.L.R. 1273; paras 13-36 and -13-135.

[132] [2007] EWCA Civ 446; [2007] 1 W.L.R. 2991.

[133] *Jain v Trent Strategic HA* [2009] UKHL 4; [2009] 1 A.C. 853; see para.13-51. Lord Scott said at [17] that it was "very difficult to see how the [statutory] procedures can be regarded as compliant with Art.6".

[134] In relation to false imprisonment, see the decision of the Supreme Court in *R. (Jalloh) v Secretary of State for the Home Department* [2020] UKSC 4; [2020] 2 W.L.R. 418.

[135] [2019] UKSC 25; [2019] 2 W.L.R. 1478.

[136] [2001] 2 A.C. 592.

claim should not be struck out but most of the focus was on the psychiatric nature of the injury. The duty issue was fully considered by the Court of Appeal in *A v Essex CC*.[137] The defendant authority had failed to send the claimants a medical report on the child they were considering for adoption. Had they received the report with its reference to the child's severe behavioural problems, they would not have gone ahead with the adoption. They adopted the child. He was violent towards them and as a result, they suffered psychiatric illness. Hale LJ held that the authority did owe a duty of care to implement its decision to send the claimants the medical report; that its administrative failure to do so was negligent; and that as it was foreseeable that the child would physically injure them, psychiatric injury was recoverable under the principle in *Page v Smith*.[138] However, she held that the authority's employees owed no duty to the parents in respect of the content of the reports or any decision as to how much information to reveal to them. As in the *East Berkshire* decision, the denial of duty stemmed from the conflicts of interests involved in the process. Hale LJ pointed to the closely regulated statutory framework which was designed to ensure the best practice in a "sensitive exercise in social engineering" which had to balance "the interests of all three parties in the adoption triangle" and also to the difficult balance between pessimism and optimism in the report: too much pessimism could render the child unadoptable and too much optimism could risk the breakdown of the adoption.[139] Finally, she confirmed that "unless they fell outside the realms of reasonableness"[140] no duty could be owed in relation to policy decisions concerning the adoption process as such decisions had been entrusted by Parliament to the adoption agencies. The distinction in this decision is between matters of legitimate judgment where no duty is owed and matters of administrative competence where a duty is owed. In *W v Essex CC* the claimants had been given an assurance that no sexual abuser would be placed in their home.[141] The failure to honour that assurance might have been negligent or deliberate but it was not a matter of legitimate judgment. Hence, it is suggested that a duty would be owed in such circumstances. All the more so, as the claimants relied on the assurance in not taking any precautions to protect their natural children.

In *B v A CC*,[142] the Court of Appeal followed *A v Essex CC* in holding that the authority which arranged an adoption by the claimants, owed them a duty of care to ensure that their identities remained secret as that was what it had undertaken to do. Buxton LJ rejected the authority's suggestion that imposition of a duty of care would inhibit the general adoption process, arguing that it should not give such an undertaking unless it has considered the consequences and if it feared it would not be able to maintain confidentiality, then it should discuss the implications with the potential adopters before they committed themselves.[143] There was no liability on the facts, as the claimants could not establish that the negligent breach of confidentiality had been a cause of the alleged harassment and suffering in respect of which they claimed. **13-28**

---

137 [2003] EWCA Civ 1848; [2004] 1 W.L.R. 1881.

138 [1996] A.C. 155. See further para.7-70.

139 [2003] EWCA Civ 1848; [2004] 1 W.L.R. 1881 at [53] and [54]. She also noted at [55] that prospective adopters have to keep a cool head and like all parents "be prepared for the downs as well as the ups".

140 [2003] EWCA Civ 1848; [2004] 1 W.L.R. 1881 at [48].

141 The facts are more fully related in the Court of Appeal decision: [1999] Fam. 90.

142 [2006] EWCA Civ 1388; [2007] P.I.Q.R. P17.

143 [2006] EWCA Civ 1388; [2007] P.I.Q.R. P17 at [25]–[26].

13-29 **Need to show causation** The case of *Lambert v Cardiff CC*,[144] illustrates that even where there have been acknowledged breaches of duty in failing to pass on information to foster carers, it must still be established that these breaches have caused the foster carer to behave differently if causation of harm is to be established. In this case, the judge held that on the evidence, the claimants would still have gone ahead with the fostering agreement if they had known relevant aspects of the child's history. There was no liability therefore in respect of these breaches of duty. Neither did the defendant council owe a duty to control the child after the end of the fostering agreement, or to prevent her from harassing the claimants.

(ii) Educational welfare

13-30 The leading decision in *Phelps*[145] was followed by the Court of Appeal in *Carty v London Borough of Croydon*.[146] There it was alleged that the defendant was vicariously liable for the negligence of an education officer in failing to reassess the claimant's special needs after the breakdown of his special school placement and in failing to amend the statement of special educational needs to name an appropriate school.[147] The defendant argued first that the principle in *Phelps* had no application to an education officer who was not a "professional" and was performing an administrative function. Giving the leading judgment of a unanimous court, Dyson LJ rejected this argument, holding that such officers were professionals and in any case:

> "there was no rational ground for holding that social workers can owe a duty of care to children for whom they assume a responsibility, but that, simply on the grounds they are not professional persons, education officers cannot owe such a duty to the children for whom they assume responsibility."[148]

Secondly, the defendant argued that imposition of a duty would not be fair as it would expose education officers to claims by children once they attained majority in respect of events many years earlier and in respect of paperwork which might no longer exist.[149] Dyson LJ rejected this argument on the ground that it was equally applicable to other types of activity whether by private persons or public authorities which affected children. If this "delayed litigation" argument was good, it would have been a complete answer to the claims in *Barrett* and *Phelps*.[150] Having found the education officer to owe a duty, the court held that there was no breach as the decision concerning the claimant had been taken after careful assessment of his needs with the benefit of expert advice. *Phelps* and *Carty* suggest that educational workers taking decisions about children are unlikely to be able to escape

144 [2007] EWHC 869 (QB); [2007] 3 F.C.R. 148.

145 [2001] 2 A.C. 619. See para.13-15.

146 [2005] EWCA Civ 19; [2005] 1 W.L.R. 2312.

147 It was also alleged that the officer was negligent in allowing the claimant to remain in another school for a period of years without annual reviews or reassessments.

148 [2005] EWCA Civ 19; [2005] 1 W.L.R. 2312 at [48]. Earlier at [45], Dyson LJ had remarked: "The phrase 'professional person' is not a term of art." Mummery LJ at [85], expressly agreed that classification as a professional was irrelevant to whether a duty of care was owed.

149 Note that the damage is classed as a personal injury: *Bracknell Forest BC v Adams* [2004] UKHL 29; [2005] 1 A.C. 76. See para.1-34.

150 [2005] EWCA Civ 19; [2005] 1 W.L.R. 2312 at [51]. Citing *Barrett* and *Phelps*, he also rejected that argument that the statutory appeal procedure provided an adequate remedy.

a duty of care given the presence of an assumption of responsibility in these cases. However, *Carty* also shows that potential liability will be limited by the need to establish that there has been a breach of duty. The subsequent decision of the similarly constituted Court of Appeal in *Devon CC v Clarke*[151] also illustrates the difficulty of establishing causation and quantum in such cases.[152] Further illustration of the difficulties of establishing breach of duty and causation is provided by the decisions in *Crowley v Surrey CC*[153] (on the balance of probabilities, the claimant as a child did not have a readily diagnosable language disorder that the defendants or their employers ought to have discovered), and *Nuttall v Mayor and Burgesses of Sutton LBC*[154] (no evidence that the relevant educational authority had been negligent in failing to place the claimant in a special school any sooner; also no evidence that had they done so, the claimant would have derived long-term benefit from this). The interpretation of applicable limitation periods may also play an important role in these cases.[155]

(iii) Police services

Police services In *Hill v Chief Constable of West Yorkshire*[156] where the claimant had alleged that the police had been negligent in failing to apprehend a mass murderer and were liable for the death of her daughter who was the murderer's last victim, it was held that there was insufficient proximity between the police and a member of the general public to give rise to a duty of care in relation to the apprehension of the criminal. But in addition the House of Lords held that on public interest grounds, no duty would be owed in relation to the investigation of crime.[157] The reasons bore some similarity to those justifying denial of a duty in *Bedfordshire*. First, the fear of liability might lead to the police function "being carried on in a detrimentally defensive frame of mind". Secondly, defending litigation would lead to "a significant diversion of police manpower and attention from their most important function, the suppression of crime" and thirdly, the court was not an appropriate body to determine the reasonableness of a discretionary policing decision. In *Hughes v National Union of Mineworkers*[158] it was held that the **13-31**

151 [2005] EWCA Civ 266; [2005] 2 F.L.R. 747. Dyson and Mummery LJJ were again members of the court with the judgment of the court this time, being given by the latter.

152 Mummery LJ at [9] cited from Markesinis and Stewart Negligent Misdiagnosis of Learning Disabilities published in *Tort Liability of Public Authorities*, Fairgrieve, Andenas and Bell (eds) (BIICL, 2002):

> "the hurdles of causation are formidable … [the claimants] would have to satisfy the court, that if their difficulties had been discovered in time, the school ought to have taught them in a different was and then, if that had happened, their ultimate educational attainment would have improved. These are not insubstantial problems; and overcoming them still leaves open the question of the extent, in financial terms, of the future loss. The quantum problems are thus also likely to be formidable."

On the facts, the Court of Appeal concluded that though the issues were difficult, there was sufficient evidence to support the trial judge's finding of causation and £25,000 for loss of earnings as compared with the £73,000 claimed.

153 [2008] EWHC 1102 (QB); [2008] E.L.R. 349.

154 [2009] EWHC 294 (QB).

155 *Adams v Bracknell Forest BC* [2004] UKHL 29; [2005] 1 A.C. 76.

156 [1989] A.C. 53.

157 [1989] A.C. 53 at 63.

158 [1991] 4 All E.R. 278.

same policy denying a duty also applied to "on the spot operational decisions" in the course of policing serious public disorder. *Hill* was followed by the Court of Appeal in *Osman v Ferguson*[159] which concerned the alleged negligent failure of the police to arrest a known suspect in time to prevent harm to the claimant and where, in distinction to *Hill's* case, the relationship of the police and the claimant might have been close enough to support a finding of proximity. McCowan LJ held that the policy reasons for denying a duty applied even where there was a relationship of proximity and where the police function concerned prevention of crime rather than an investigation.[160] In *Ancell v McDermott*[161] the Court of Appeal held that a duty should be denied in respect of the police function of maintaining the safety of highways. In *Ancell* it was alleged that the police had acted negligently in failing to warn road users of a dangerous oil spillage on the road. Beldam LJ stressed the "formidable diversion of police manpower" that would result from having to defend such cases were a duty to be owed.[162] In *Elguzouli-Daf v Commissioner of Police*[163] the Court of Appeal applied the reasoning in *Hill* to hold that the Crown Prosecution Service owed no duty of care to those it was prosecuting. The broader "conflict of interest" argument[164] would also presumably lead to the same conclusion.

13-32 A further application of the reasoning in *Hill*, before *Osman v UK*, was the decision of the House of Lords in *Calveley v Chief Constable of Merseyside Police*.[165] Here police officers claimed against a Chief Constable on the ground that disciplinary proceedings had been negligently conducted. Giving the opinion of a unanimous House of Lords, Lord Bridge rejected the negligence claim on the ground that it would be contrary to public policy to impose a duty of care on investigating police officers to those suspected of crime and "[i]f no duty of care is owed by a police officer investigating a suspected crime to a civilian suspect, it is difficult to see why a police officer who is subject to [a disciplinary] investigation should be in any better position".[166] The decision in *Calveley* was in turn influential in the Supreme Court's decision in *James-Bowen v Commissioner of Police of the Metropolis*.[167] No duty of care was owed to police officers when a decision was made to settle a claim for the Chief Constable's vicarious liability for the alleged torts of the officers. If there was no duty of care when disciplinary investigations had been initiated by the police in *Calveley*, then no such duty could be owed where an action was initiated by a third party, since the Chief Constable's role was less proactive. In addition, the defendant Chief Constable should be enabled to make decisions freely in light of her public duty. For these and other reasons (for example, the likelihood that the interests of the employer and employee would be

---

159 [1993] 4 All E.R. 344.

160 Notice that the manner in which the *Hill* policy reasons were applied to this case—as though they created a "blanket immunity"—led to a finding that the UK had been in breach of EHCR art.6, in *Osman v UK* [1999] 1 F.L.R. 193 (European Court of Human Rights). The courts' response to this has helped to shape many areas of public authority liability, as noted in para.13-16.

161 [1993] 4 All E.R. 355.

162 [1993] 4 All E.R. 355 at 366.

163 [1995] Q.B. 335. See also *Kumar v Commissioner of Police* unreported 31 January 1995 where the Court of Appeal upheld the striking out of an allegation that the police were negligent in pursuing a hopeless prosecution against the claimant.

164 Explored in connection with child welfare decisions in para.13-24.

165 [1989] A.C. 1228. Claims brought for breach of statutory duty and misfeasance in public office were also rejected: see paras 8-30 and 13-133.

166 [1989] A.C. 1228 at 1238.

167 [2018] UKSC 40; [2018] 1 W.L.R. 4021.

at odds where settlement of vicarious liability claims was in issue), it would not be "fair, just and reasonable" to impose a duty.

Osman v UK and ECHR art.6 The application of the *Hill* policy reasoning in *Osman v Ferguson* led to a controversial decision of the European Court of Human Rights, holding the UK in breach of art.6 of the ECHR.[168] The chief controversy of this decision was that it appeared to suggest that for negligence law to be compatible with art.6, policy arguments in respect of the duty of care should be considered "on their merits" in each individual case. This was widely understood to amount to a finding that negligence actions should not be struck out on policy grounds; all the facts of the case should be considered.[169] This interpretation influenced the approach of the House of Lords in *Barrett v Enfield*[170] and *Phelps v Hillingdon*.[171] Later, in *Z v UK*,[172] the European Court of Human Rights altered its stance on this point and admitted that it had proceeded on the basis of a misunderstanding of English negligence law, and particularly the role of policy factors under *Caparo v Dickman*.[173] The Court now realised that policy factors formed an important substantive element in determining whether a duty arose at common law, and were not used as a procedural device preventing a claimant from asserting his or her rights. Policy factors are essential to the determination of whether the claimant has a right to assert at all; and art.6 will not be breached simply because an action is struck out on policy grounds. However, it still appeared that "blanket" immunities would be considered incompatible with art.6. In some of its most recent decisions, the Supreme Court has taken a further step away from applying *Caparo* as though it had laid out a "three part test", preferring to highlight the aspect of the reasoning in *Caparo* which focused on incremental development and the significance of decided duty cases.[174] As a result, there is less direct appeal to policy considerations. However, in proceeding incrementally, the considerations which have affected the development of existing categories of case should be recognised. 13-33

Developments since Osman v UK In *Brooks v Commissioner of Police for the Metropolis*[175] the House of Lords had an opportunity to review the status of the *Hill* decision in the light of *Osman* and *Z v UK*. The claimant was present when his friend, Stephen Lawrence, was abused and murdered in a racist attack. He claimed that the defendant owed him a duty of care to support him as a victim of crime, to give reasonable support to him as a witness, and to give reasonable weight to his evidence. His allegation was that the defendant's failure to use reasonable care in 13-34

---

168 *Osman v UK* (1998) 29 E.H.R.R. 245.

169 An alternative reading of the Court's comments in *Osman v UK* is that policy factors should not be applied in a *blanket* fashion from one case to another. Arguably, the Court of Appeal in *Osman v Ferguson* did not deal adequately with the differences between that case and *Hill* itself, simply applying generic policy reasoning to rule out the claim.

170 [2001] 2 A.C. 550.

171 [2001] 2 A.C. 619.

172 [2001] 2 F.C.R. 246; [2001] 2 F.L.R. 612; (2002) 34 E.H.R.R. 3. This claim arose from some of the failed actions in *X v Bedfordshire*. Notably, although there was no breach of ECHR art.6, the European Court of Human Rights found violations of other substantive articles and of art.13 (absence of an appropriate domestic remedy).

173 Nevertheless, *Osman v UK* remains the authoritative source in respect of the positive operational duty of States to protect the right to life of its citizens under ECHR art.2: see para.13-90 onwards.

174 paras 13-42 to 13-45 in relation to police negligence.

175 [2005] UKHL 24; [2005] 1 W.L.R. 1495.

these respects exacerbated the post-traumatic stress disorder he suffered as a result of the attack. The House of Lords unanimously held that the claim should be struck out on the ground that no duty was owed. Lord Steyn said that the "three alleged duties are undoubtedly inextricably bound up with the police function of investigating crime which is covered by the principle in *Hill*".[176] He also said that *Hill* "had remained unchallenged in our domestic jurisprudence and in European jurisprudence for many years"[177] and would be decided in the same way today. But Lords Steyn, Bingham and Nicholls all said that "they were not endorsing the full width of all the observations in *Hill*"[178] and indicated that "exceptional cases on the margins of the *Hill* principle will have to be considered if and when they occur."[179]

13-35 Leaving aside cases where there is an assumption of responsibility,[180] such "exceptional cases" have not so far been recognised, and their existence now appears unlikely given not only the outcomes but also the reasoning by the majority justices in *Smith v Chief Constable of Sussex Police*,[181] and *Michael v Chief Constable of South Wales Police*,[182] albeit that the applicable reasoning appears to have undergone a change, and will not extend to cases where a positive act causes physical injury to a claimant.[183] In *Smith*, the House of Lords struck out a claim by the victim of a savage assault by his former partner, the claimant arguing that the police had failed to protect him from the assailant despite repeated warnings of the danger. Lord Bingham, dissenting, would have recognised that this case fell within a narrow "liability principle", which would arise in circumstances falling short of an assumption of responsibility (although he also would have found such an assumption on the facts). According to Lord Bingham, "if a member of the public (A) furnishes a police officer (B) with apparently credible evidence that a third party whose identity and whereabouts are known presents a specific and imminent threat to his life or physical safety, B owes A a duty to take reasonable steps to assess such threat and, if appropriate, take reasonable steps to prevent it being executed".[184] The other members of the House of Lords differed from Lord Bingham in their approach as well as in the outcome, Lord Hope concluding clearly that within the core of the *Hill* "principle", the policy goals served by that case could not be secured if the duty of care depended on a case by case analysis. Rather, a "robust approach" was needed to avoid wasteful diversion of police time. Lord Brown argued that there was no need for common law to develop in order to cover such cases, which he thought were much better ruled out "on a class basis". This looks very much like the *Hill* immunity, though it is subject to an exception for assumption of responsibility, and in theory at least there may be a duty of care outside the "core" application of *Hill*, justifying the assertion that the principle does not amount to an "im-

---

[176] [2005] UKHL 24; [2005] 1 W.L.R. 1495 at [33].
[177] [2005] UKHL 24; [2005] 1 W.L.R. 1495 at [33] at [30].
[178] [2005] UKHL 24; [2005] 1 W.L.R. 1495 at [33] at [3], [6] and [28].
[179] Lord Steyn at [34], referring to cases of outrageous negligence and Lord Nicholls at [6] referring to cases where the absence of a remedy would be an affront to the principles underlying the common law.
[180] See para.13-40.
[181] Reported together with *Van Colle v Chief Constable of Hertfordshire* [2008] UKHL 50; [2009] 1 A.C. 225 (for discussion of *Van Colle*, which was a claim under the Human Rights Act, see para.13-91).
[182] [2015] UKSC 2; [2015] A.C. 1732.
[183] *Robinson v Chief Constable* [2018] UKSC 4; [2018] A.C. 736; see paras 13-42 to 13-45.
[184] Reported together with *Van Colle v Chief Constable of Hertfordshire* [2008] UKHL 50; [2009] 1 A.C. 225 at [44]: this defines the content of Lord Bingham's proposed "liability principle".

munity" by a different name. The existence of a remedy under the Human Rights Act 1998 was an important link in Lord Brown's reasoning, since he considered extension of the common law to be "simply unnecessary" given the existence of an alternative remedy in domestic law. Lord Phillips' approach was more balanced. He agreed in the result with the majority, but thought it "hard to judge" whether the policy concerns in *Brooks* really justified the rule against a duty in such cases.

The broad reach of the *Hill* principle is illustrated by *B v Reading BC*.[185] A father who had been wrongly accused of sexually assaulting his three-year-old daughter brought actions in negligence against an investigating police officer, and in misfeasance in a public office against the police officer and a social worker. Mackay J noted the comments of Lord Nicholls in *Brooks* concerning the possibility of exceptional cases falling outside the core principle in *Hill* but added that "No decided case has been put before me in which such an exceptional circumstance has been found to fall outside the *Hill* principle".[186] Nor could there be said to be an "assumption of responsibility" to a suspected parent. Claims in misfeasance and conspiracy also failed because there was no evidence of bad faith. Despite a series of grossly leading questions being put to the child in interview, and despite the fact that the most damning remarks alleged to have been made by the child proved, on examination of interview recordings, never to have been said at all, neither the claim in negligence nor misfeasance succeeded. The reasoning against police liability in the UK case law has not been accepted in Canada, where the Supreme Court has recognised that the police may owe a duty in the manner of their investigation not just to potential victims of crime in circumstances of close proximity,[187] but also to *suspects*.[188] This directly contrasts with the core application of the *Hill* policy reasoning. **13-36**

Both the courts' continued commitment to the *Hill* principle, and the potential significance of the alternative remedy under HRA, referred to in the previous paragraph, are illustrated by the decision of the Supreme Court in *Michael v Chief Constable of South Wales Police*.[189] The claim concerned the murder of a woman after she had placed two 999 calls to police. Due to an alleged failure to transcribe her words accurately, her initial call was downgraded to a lower priority level requiring a response within 60 minutes, rather than the highest priority requiring a response within five minutes. During this time, her former partner returned and fatally attacked her. It was argued by the claimants that the call handler had failed to appreciate the urgency of the call, and it appears that she did not hear the deceased say that her former partner had threatened to return and "kill" (rather than "hit") her. A negligence claim was struck out by the Supreme Court but a claim based on art.2 ECHR and the Human Rights Act was allowed to proceed to trial. Evidently the case bears comparison with *Smith*. For the majority, Lord Toulson urged that in this instance, the question was not whether the police should benefit from a special "immunity" from actions in negligence but whether they should be **13-37**

---

185 [2009] EWHC 998 (QB); [2009] 2 F.L.R. 1273.

186 [2009] EWHC 998 (QB); [2009] 2 F.L.R. 1273 at [30].

187 Such a duty had already been recognised by Canadian courts in cases of close proximity: *Jane Doe v Metropolitan Toronto (Municipality) Commissioners of Police* (1998) 160 D.L.R. (4th) 697.

188 *Hill v Hamilton-Wentworth Regional Police Services Board* [2007] 3 S.C.R. 129; (2007) 285 D.L.R. (4th) 620 (SCC). For comment see N. Rafferty (2008) 24 P.N. 78; E. Chamberlain (2008) 124 L.Q.R. 205.

189 [2015] UKSC 2; [2015] A.C. 1732.

liable in circumstances where ordinarily no duty of care would be owed[190]: this reasoning is compatible with the general approach to public authority liability set out in *Poole BC v GN*.[191] The refusal of the courts to impose a private law duty on the police to exercise reasonable care to safeguard potential victims of crime, except where there is a "representation and reliance", did not involve giving special treatment to the police.[192] Rather, they reflected the law's general approach to omissions.[193] These features of the majority judgment were doubted by Baroness Hale, pointing out that there would have been little need to create and maintain the *Hill* principle through cases such as *Smith* and *Brooks* if the cases merely turned on the ordinary principles of negligence: the absence of omissions liability, in particular, is not generally complete but subject to exceptions.[194] The majority agreed with counsel for the claimants that the likely effects of liability on the actions of the police, which had been part of the justification for the decision in *Hill*, were hard to predict, but argued that any alleged positive impact on policing was also to be discounted for the same reason (namely, lack of evidence). On the other hand the court could be sure that the existence of such a duty would have "potentially significant financial implications" for the police.[195] In relation to the argument that common law should develop in harmony with the positive duties of the state under arts 2 and 3, Lord Toulson argued that tort should not be used to remedy interferences with Convention rights, partly because of its higher damages awards: he saw no reason "for gold plating the claimant's Convention rights by providing compensation on a different basis from the claim under the Human Rights Act 1998".[196] He was also concerned that the common law duty urged by the claimants would be wider than the positive duty recognised by the Convention.[197]

13-38 Lord Kerr and Baroness Hale, in dissent, proposed creation of a test based upon proximity for application to such claims. This was however rejected by the majority. Their approach, as Baroness Hale expressed it, would recognise proximity in circumstances where the police "know or ought to know of an imminent threat of death or personal injury to a particular individual which they have the means to prevent".[198] This would marry the test for a duty of care in such cases with the test for violation of the positive operational duty to protect life under art.2[199] and would bring negligence in this area into harmony with duties under the HRA. By contrast, Lord Toulson dealt with the HRA claim in a single paragraph and said merely that it would be wrong to disturb the findings of both lower courts on what were to be seen as factual matters that enabled the art.2 claim to proceed to trial. By implication, the Human Rights Act claim suffered none of the barriers explored above and was simply dependent on interpretation of the facts of the case: should the call handler have heard the deceased clearly or asked the deceased to repeat what she said; and should she have appreciated that there was a clear and imminent threat

---

190 [2015] UKSC 2; [2015] A.C. 1732 at [116].
191 Para.13-03.
192 [2015] UKSC 2; [2015] A.C. 1732 at [115].
193 On liability for omissions, see paras 7-51 onwards.
194 [2015] UKSC 2; [2015] A.C. 1732 at [190].
195 [2015] UKSC 2; [2015] A.C. 1732 at [122].
196 [2015] UKSC 2; [2015] A.C. 1732 at [125].
197 [2015] UKSC 2; [2015] A.C. 1732 On the breadth of the positive Convention duty, see para.13-90 onwards.
198 [2015] UKSC 2; [2015] A.C. 1732 at [144].
199 See further para.13-90.

to her life? Thus the HRA claim turns on questions which are very similar to those asked in the tort of negligence, in relation to breach, with none of the obstacles posed by the need to establish a duty. For the majority, it is the difference in available remedies which appears to justify the continued additional hurdles to a negligence claim.

Before the decision of the Supreme Court in *Michael*, in *DSD v Commissioner of Police for the Metropolis*,[200] Green J found the defendant liable under the HRA for violations of positive duties arising under art.3 ECHR. He identified a series of systemic failings which caused the police to fail to apprehend a serial rapist and to cut short the series of attacks that he perpetrated on women, including the claimants. The circumstances are very similar to those in *Hill* itself. Although Lord Toulson in *Michael* referred to *DSD*, he said that he would not wish to influence the Court of Appeal's consideration of the case.[201] Subsequently, the Court of Appeal affirmed Green J's decision,[202] and this in turn was upheld by the Supreme Court.[203] In relation to the law of negligence, both *Michael* and *DSD* raise the question of how far the policy reasons underlying the *Hill* decision can ultimately be retained if the same issues are capable of founding an HRA claim. While the absence of a duty in respect of investigation of crime is no longer referred to as an "immunity", it is still worth noting that immunities are now regarded by the courts as to be retained only to the extent that they serve a clear purpose. If the same issues are to be litigated in any event, this plainly weakens the argument for an immunity.[204] In the same way, the possibility of litigation in an HRA action might be thought to undermine the objectives of the *Hill* "principle", albeit that the purposes of the two actions may be different. Since *Michael*, the Supreme Court has taken up Lord Toulson's approach, and reinterpreted the cases falling within the *Hill* principle as turning on the general absence of a duty of care for failures to benefit, rather than on special policy considerations.[205] 13-39

Assumption of responsibility by the police Situations where responsibility is assumed by the police are recognised as constituting an exception to the *Hill* principle at common law, and as an established category of liability where there is a failure to confer a benefit. This is consistent with the approach to local authority liability in relation to failures to benefit in the child welfare and education cases, where the difference between causing harm and failure to benefit is now also regarded as central.[206] The defendant in *Brooks*[207] accepted that cases of assumption of responsibility by the police fell outside the *Hill* principle. The leading example of this is *Swinney v Chief Constable of Northumbria Police*[208] where the Court of Ap- 13-40

200 [2014] EWHC 436 (QB).
201 [2015] UKSC 2; [2015] A.C. 1732 at [128].
202 *DSD v Commissioner of Police for the Metropolis* [2015] EWCA Civ 646; [2016] Q.B. 161; see para.13-102 for discussion.
203 [2018] UKSC 11; [2019] A.C. 196. See para.13-102.
204 As recognised in *Smart v Forensic Science Service Ltd* [2013] EWCA Civ 783; [2013] P.N.L.R. 32, para.13-57.
205 *Robinson v Commissioner of West Yorkshire Police* [2018] UKSC 4; [2018] A.C. 736.
206 See para.13-03.
207 [2005] UKHL 24; [2005] 1 W.L.R. 1495; para.13-34.
208 [1997] Q.B. 464. The claimant lost at the subsequent trial on the ground that the police were not in breach of the duty: *Swinney v Chief Constable of Northumbria Police (No.2)* (1999) 11 Admin L.R. 811.

peal held it arguable that the police owed a duty of care to an informant to whom they had assumed a responsibility by giving him an undertaking of confidentiality. The court also considered that the public interest in the encouragement of the free flow of information to the police could outweigh the interest in the police carrying out the function of investigating and suppressing crime uninhibited by the spectre of negligence litigation.[209] In *An Informer v A Chief Constable*,[210] the Court of Appeal declined to extend this reasoning to recognise a duty to protect the economic interests of a police informer, deciding that the case fell within the *Hill* principle. Two members of the Court, Arden LJ and Pill LJ, focused on the particular circumstances of the alleged duty, acknowledging that stronger cases may arise in future.[211] In *CLG v Chief Constable of Merseyside*,[212] the Court of Appeal also declined to extend the reasoning in *Swinney* to protect witnesses, rather than informants. The claimant witnesses were forced to move house when their address was inadvertently revealed to those who might reasonably be expected to do them harm, partly through the actions of both the police and the CPS. Applying the reasoning in *Brooks*, whilst there might be an ethical case for arguing that the claimant witnesses were entitled to expect the same support from the police as an informant, this did not convert into a duty of care, and there was no assumption of responsibility comparable to that in *Swinney*.[213] An assumption of responsibility was however found to be arguably present in *Sherratt v Chief Constable of Greater Manchester*,[214] a case whose facts are relatively close to those in *Michael v Chief Constable of South Wales*.[215] Here, a woman had committed suicide. Her mother had placed an emergency call requesting assistance because she feared the deceased would take an overdose. A duty of care was arguable because there was sufficient evidence that the call handler had assured the mother that police would attend and take steps to ensure her daughter's safety, taking her to hospital should this be necessary. Therefore, the mother took no further steps of her own, for example by calling for an ambulance. The call handler appears to have downgraded the call from "emergency" to "priority", and the officers did not attend until over three hours later. It did not matter that the assurance was made to the mother, while it was her daughter who was owed the claimed duty; nor was it relevant that the duty was to prevent the daughter from harming herself.[216]

---

209 Note also the case of *Costello v Chief Constable of Northumbria Police* [1999] 1 All E.R. 550; [1999] I.C.R. 752, in which a police officer was assaulted by a prisoner while another officer who was present specifically for the claimant's protection did nothing to help. The second officer admitted that he was under a "police duty" to assist his colleague, and the Court of Appeal held that he had assumed a responsibility which could also give rise to a duty of care in negligence. The policy issues which would preclude a duty either to a member of the public or to a fellow officer outside such extraordinary facts were noted by the Court of Appeal.

210 [2012] EWCA Civ 197; [2013] Q.B. 579.

211 See also *PBD v Chief Constable of Greater Manchester* [2013] EWHC 3559 (QB), Silber J concluding that neither duty, nor breach had been established. The claimants alleged negligence causing psychiatric damage and economic loss where they had been forced to enter the witness protection programme, the first claimant's name having been revealed to his former criminal associates during the course of a new prosecution. The relationship here was considered less proximate than the relationship in *An Informer*.

212 [2015] EWCA Civ 836.

213 [2015] EWCA Civ 836 at [24].

214 [2018] EWHC 1746 (QB); [2019] P.I.Q.R. P1.

215 [2015] UKSC 2; [2015] A.C. 1732; see para.13-37.

216 A case which proved hard to categorise is *Chief Constable of Essex v Transport Arendonk BvBa*

Even in a case which falls outside the *Hill* principle, it still must be established that a duty of care is owed, and here too a voluntary assumption of responsibility may be required. In *Desmond v Chief Constable of Nottinghamshire Police*,[217] the claimant had been questioned after an allegation of sexual assault but it proved that he had not been involved in the incident and no prosecution was pursued. When the claimant later sought employment as a teacher, he applied for an enhanced criminal record certificate. The Chief Constable authorised release of information about the suspicion of sexual assault, but no information was supplied concerning its resolution. No attempt was made by the police disclosure unit to contact the investigating officer nor to locate his pocket book. The Court of Appeal struck out the action as disclosing no arguable duty of care. The officers were performing statutory duties and if the policy of the statute was not to create a liability, the same policy should "ordinarily exclude" a common law duty of care.[218] There would need to be particular circumstances, such as the assumption of responsibilities or carrying out of acts, to justify such a duty. In this instance, there could not be said to be a voluntary assumption of responsibility, because the defendant acted under a statutory duty. It was argued that to be voluntarily assumed, a duty must not be identical to a duty imposed by statute.[219] It was also considered relevant that the claimant might have other remedies, albeit of a different type. This included the potential for a remedy under HRA for interference with art.8 rights, a claim for which was still continuing in *Desmond* itself. Reasoning said to be similar to that in *Desmond* was used in *C v T BC*,[220] to deny a duty of care on the part of a local authority providing information to the police for use in the creation of an Enhanced Criminal Record Certificate; there were other remedies available and a duty would deter those who would otherwise provide information to the police which would assist in safeguarding. In *Desmond v Foreman*,[221] Tugendhat J held that the claimant had a real prospect of succeeding in an argument based on art.8 ECHR and the Data Protection Act 1998, and also had a real prospect of defeating a defence of qualified privilege in defamation. In *Robinson v Chief Constable of South Yorkshire Police*,[222] Lord Reed stopped short of questioning the correctness of *Desmond*, but did suggest that some of its broader statements were incorrect. 13-41

Scope of the Hill principle In *Robinson v Chief Constable of West Yorkshire Police*,[223] three members of the Supreme Court determined that the *Hill* principle was confined to cases of omission (or failure to benefit), and did not apply to positive acts causing personal injury on the part of the police. There were no dissents as to the outcome of the case, but two members of the Court, Lord Mance and Lord 13-42

[2020] EWHC 212 (QB); [2020] R.T.R. 22: it was argued that the police had either created a danger, or assumed responsibility, when they arrested the driver of a heavy goods vehicle which was parked in a layby and prevented him from calling his employers, and where there was a break in and thefts from the vehicle. His instructions were to remain with the vehicle overnight. The claim was not struck out as it was not clearly resolved by previous authorities.

217 [2011] EWCA Civ 3; [2011] 1 F.L.R. 1361; [2011] Fam. Law 358.

218 [2011] EWCA Civ 3; [2011] 1 F.L.R. 1361; [2011] Fam. Law 358 at [39].

219 Note however the discussion in para.13-72: *conduct* pursuant to a statutory duty may be capable of amounting to an assumption of responsibility.

220 [2014] EWHC 2482 (QB); [2015] E.L.R. 1.

221 [2012] EWHC 1900 (QB).

222 [2018] UKSC 4; [2018] A.C. 736.

223 [2018] UKSC 4; [2018] A.C. 736.

Hughes, adopted a very different analysis of the nature of the *Hill* principle and its applicability. In *Robinson*, officers had attempted to arrest a suspect on a busy shopping street, and three men had collided with the claimant, who suffered injuries as a result. The Court of Appeal had applied *Hill* and its policy reasoning to deny liability. Lord Reed (with whom Baroness Hale and Lord Hodge agreed) concluded, however, that where positive actions by the police caused physical injury, the police would be liable in the same way as any other person. There was no need to apply the *Caparo* test, which was described as applying only to "novel claims". Moreover, the central point of *Caparo* was said to be not that it set out a "tripartite" test, since the decision had denied the possibility of a general test for negligence. Rather, its central point was that development of the law should be "incremental" and based upon the starting point of established categories. The policy reasons expressed in *Hill* would have no application to such a claim, which fell within an established duty category, namely positive acts causing physical injury. Lord Reed went further, suggesting that the *Hill* case was concerned with policy considerations chiefly because it was decided in the era of *Anns v Merton*, and seeking to explain more recent decisions applying *Hill* not in terms of policy, but in terms of their concern with omissions rather than positive acts, and in terms of other established, general reasons for denying a duty. For example, *Brooks v Commissioner of Police of the Metropolis*[224] was explained as involving actions which were "merely insensitive": such actions "are not normally actionable", even if they result in psychiatric illness.[225] Policy discussion in the leading cases should not be "consigned to history"; but the fact that the police did not owe positive duties was not merely a result of policy reasoning by a "recent generation of judges". Rather it built on long-established principles.

13-43 Lord Reed's opinion further develops the logic of *Michael v Chief Constable of South Wales*,[226] which had held that the police were not liable because their actions fell within the category of omissions, and not because the police are specially protected through the application of policy reasoning. It also prefigures the compatible reasoning in relation to public authority liability in *Poole BC v GN*.[227] It applies that logic to a case of commission, arguing that the case should not be seen as a novel one simply because the tortfeasors were police officers acting in the restraint of crime. It is suggested that there are some difficulties raised by the reasoning in *Michael*, considered in this and the following paragraph. First, Lord Reed's approach depends upon the definition of a particular case as falling within an "established duty category". In particular, it would appear to include in a single, unproblematic category any case where a positive act causes physical injury. But why is this the appropriate definition of the relevant "established duty category"? Why is it not possible for the nature of the defendant's activities to take a case into the realms of the "novel", or indeed, into the realms of a category which has previously been considered, and treated as problematic? Less than two weeks after the decision in *Robinson*, in *D v Commissioner of Police for the Metropolis*,[228] all five members of a differently constituted Supreme Court seemed to treat duties in the investigation and suppression of crime in precisely these terms. They described the

---

224 [2005] UKHL 24; [2005] 1 W.L.R. 1495; see para.13-34.
225 [2018] UKSC 4; [2018] A.C. 736 at [60].
226 [2015] UKSC 2; [2015] A.C. 1732; see para.13-37.
227 [2019] UKSC 25; [2019] 2 W.L.R. 1478.
228 [2018] UKSC 11; [2019] A.C. 196.

police as being exempt from a duty of care in cases where they are engaged in the investigation of crime, without reference to any distinction between acts and omissions, and explained that exemption in policy terms. While D is centrally concerned with duties under art.3 ECHR and was a claim under the HRA,[229] the distinction with common law was essential to the decision. Lord Kerr, with whom Baroness Hale and Lord Neuberger both agreed, said that "no assumption should be made that the policy reasons which underlay the conclusion that an exemption of police from liability at common law apply mutatis mutandis to liability for breach of Convention rights".[230] Lord Neuberger, with whom Baroness Hale also agreed, referred to the line of cases from *Hill* to *Michael*, and said that:

> "Those cases establish that, absent special factors, our domestic law adopts the view that, when investigating crime, the police owe no duty of care in tort to individual citizens. That is because courts in this country consider that the imposition of such a duty would, as Lord Hughes puts it, 'inhibit the robust operation of police work, and divert resources from current inquiries; it would be detrimental, not a spur, to law enforcement'."[231]

This appears to present the investigation of crime as belonging to a separate and problematic category, irrespective of whether the negligence consists of acts, omissions, or both. Lord Reed's approach in *Robinson* treats the distinction between positive acts and omissions, and between physical harm and other types as loss, as not only central, but uniquely significant. Notably, he dismissed the House of Lords decision in *Marc Rich v Bishop Rock Marine*[232] as a case "in which the reasoning was essentially directed to considerations relevant to economic loss", despite the fact that it was a case of physical damage and loss in which the relevance of *Caparo* was precisely in issue. In *Robinson*, Lord Mance argued, it is suggested correctly, that it is unrealistic to suppose that courts will not take account of policy considerations when developing an "established category" of case. Such considerations are likely to be especially pertinent in deciding which category a case should be said to fall within.

Secondly, as demonstrated by Lord Mance and Lord Hughes in their separate judgments, to treat more recent decisions as though they do not proceed on the basis of policy considerations would be inconsistent with the reasoning of those cases, including many decided long after *Caparo* and the demise of *Anns*, and requires a considerable degree of rewriting. This point was also made by Baroness Hale in her dissenting opinion in *Michael*. Such a reinterpretation of earlier decisions may have considerable repercussions. This point, about reinterpretation, was subsequently directly considered by Lord Reed in the local authority case of *Poole BC v GN*.[233] Thirdly, Lord Reed's attempt to describe some cases in terms of established principle, rather than policy concerns, is at times unconvincing for other reasons. For example, *Brooks* was treated by the House of Lords which decided the case as involving positive and direct negligence by the police, not as a case where their actions were merely "inconsiderate", and the applicability of the *Hill* policy reasoning was expressly debated (and accepted) by the House. In summary, an attempt to marginalise policy reasoning in an area previously dominated by policy considera- 13-44

[229] See para.13-102.
[230] [2018] UKSC 11; [2019] A.C. 196 at [69].
[231] [2018] UKSC 11; [2019] A.C. 196 at [97].
[232] [1996] A.C. 211.
[233] [2019] UKSC 25; [2019] 2 W.L.R. 1478.

tions both where there is a positive act resulting in injury (where it now appears there will be a duty), and where there is a mere omission (leading to no liability, except where relevant exceptions, principally an assumption of responsibility, apply), is potentially problematic. While accepting that the breadth of application of the policy reasoning from *Hill* has been open to valid criticism, to divide the cases too starkly into those concerning positive acts, which will succeed, and those concerning omissions, which will fail, even with recognised exceptions such as "assumption of responsibility", is inclined to resort to a formulaic solution in an area currently filled with policy concerns. When applied to cases beyond the realm of personal injury, it will at least need more refinement. The subsequent decision in *Poole BC v GN* indicates that it may need to allow for issues such as the notion of conflicting public and private duties, exemplified in the present context by *Elguzouli-Daf v Commissioner of Police of the Metropolis*,[234] as recently discussed by the Supreme Court in *SXH v Crown Prosecution Service*,[235] but also arising in many other cases involving public authorities.

13-45 The decision in *Robinson* also casts some further doubt on the decision, and at least the approach, in *Rathband v Chief Constable of Northumbria Police*.[236] Here, the *Hill* principle operated to defeat a claim by a police officer against his Chief Constable as quasi-employer. Males J recognised that the "starting point" was different in a claim brought by a police officer, since a Chief Constable owes to officers within his force a non-delegable duty to provide a safe system of work (as recognised in *Mullaney v Chief Constable of West Midlands*[237]). He reasoned however that this duty may be excluded by reason of the public policy arguments encapsulated in the *Hill* principle, and that at least in some such cases, these policy arguments would outweigh those underpinning the non-delegable duty. Males J also suggested that there was no "assumption of responsibility" in the particular case, so that the *Hill* principle could be decisive in relation to what was "fair, just and reasonable". No HRA claim based on art.2 ECHR was made in this case. It is suggested that the relationship between the non-delegable duty owed to quasi employees, and the presence of an "assumption of responsibility", merits further reflection. The decision in *Robinson* suggests that the *Hill* policy arguments may not take priority.

(iv) Rescue services

13-46 **Rescue services** As noted below[238] the omission rule is the main limit to the duty owed by rescue services such as the fire authority or the coastguard. The service will owe no duty of care, at least to strangers, in respect of its failure to act. But where the service has created additional danger or assumed responsibility to the claimant, in principle a duty may arise. In *Capital & Counties Plc v Hampshire CC*[239] Stuart-Smith LJ considered seven arguments suggesting that a duty would be unfair even where the fire service had added to the danger. These were that a duty would result in: defensive fire fighting rather than an improvement in standard;

---

234 [1995] QB 335; [1995] 2 W.L.R. 173.
235 [2017] UKSC 30; [2017] 1 W.L.R. 1401; see para.13-117.
236 [2016] EWHC 181 (QB).
237 [2001] EWCA Civ 700; [2001] Po. L.R. 150.
238 See para.13-78.
239 [1997] Q.B. 1004 at 1043.

private litigation being inappropriately used to investigate failures; undesirable actions against services operating for the collective welfare; floodgates opening to many claims; distraction of officers from their ordinary duties; massive claims against the taxpayer; and disruption of the insurance regime. The arguments were dismissed as too general or unsubstantiated. In particular, it was noted that similar arguments would apply to the NHS for which liability was accepted, and that the analogy with the police investigation and suppression of crime was not close. Following both *Capital & Counties Plc*, and *Smith v Ministry of Defence*,[240] the possible existence of positive duties to assure the safety of employees of the fire service was recognised by Irwin J in *Wembridge Claimants v Winter*.[241] Proximity issues such as those which were determinative in *Capital & Counties* would have no effect in an action brought by employees. Following the approach in *Smith*, it would be better for the question whether a duty was owed to be determined in light of all the facts of the case. No "fireground immunity" existed analogous to "combat immunity".[242] However, as Lord Woolf MR noted in *Kent v Griffiths*,[243] if the claim attacked the prioritisation of the rescue or the resources allocated to it, a court might reject a duty on the ground that the issues were not justiciable.[244]

(v) Participants in legal proceedings

13-47 **Advocates** The position of court advocates is considered here as there are elements of public service in their work and because the policy arguments which originally led to a denial of a duty were influential in denial of a duty on the part of the police in *Hill v Chief Constable of West Yorkshire*.[245] However, the abolition of advocates' immunity has not been followed by wholesale retreat from the "no duty" position of the police in respect of the investigation and suppression of crime. Rather, the term "immunity" has been avoided in that context. However, some immunities do continue to be recognised—albeit subject to more careful delineation—in relation to legal proceedings. These are not confined to the tort of negligence.

13-48 The 1967 decision of the House of Lords in *Rondel v Worsley*[246] established that an advocate, whether barrister or solicitor, did not owe a duty to the client in respect of the conduct of a criminal case in court and in *Saif Ali v Sydney Mitchell & Co*[247] this immunity was applied to the context of a civil trial and to pre-trial work which was so intimately connected with the conduct of the case in court that it could fairly be said to be a preliminary decision affecting the way in which it would be conducted. The immunity was justified on a number of public policy grounds: the "cab rank" rule under which an advocate has to accept any client who can pay, the policy against re-litigating court decisions, and concern that any duty to the client might conflict with the advocate's duty to the court. In *Arthur JS Hall & Co v Simons*[248] which was concerned with allegations of advocates' negligence in the

---

240 [2013] UKSC 41; [2014] A.C. 52.
241 [2013] EWHC 2331 (QB).
242 See further para.13-52.
243 [2001] Q.B. 36.
244 See para.13-06.
245 [1989] A.C. 53.
246 [1969] 1 A.C. 191.
247 [1980] A.C. 198.
248 [2002] 1 A.C. 615. See para.9-137.

handling of civil claims, the House of Lords unanimously held that public policy no longer justified an immunity in the context of civil proceedings.[249] The cab rank rule was said to have no great impact; there was no evidence that conflicts of interest presented a real problem and, in any case, other professionals like doctors owed a duty despite similar problems; the fear of re-litigation was met by the development of a rule allowing such claims to be struck out for abuse of process. Furthermore, there were policy reasons for a duty: it would provide a remedy for the client and it would encourage public confidence in advocacy by requiring it to meet a standard of care. Whilst a majority of four Law Lords further held that the immunity was no longer justified in the context of criminal proceedings, a minority of three considered such an immunity was justified because criminal proceedings had a public rather than a private function, criminal advocates were performing a public duty and should not suffer harassment as a result.[250] In practice, the difficulties of proving breach may continue to keep advocates' liability within limits.[251]

13-49 **Judges, witnesses and parties**[252] On public policy grounds neither a judge nor a witness of fact in legal proceedings owes a duty of care to anyone harmed by their negligence. This point is considered briefly here as the courts are a public service and the policy grounds concern the need to ensure the proper functioning of that service. Judges have a long established public policy immunity from an action in negligence and this immunity extends to a magistrate who has an honest belief that he was acting within his jurisdiction.[253] Judicial immunity extends to those exercising a quasi-judicial function, e.g. an arbitrator, where their judgment is based on the

---

[249] In *Awoyomi v Radford* [2007] EWHC 1671 (QB); [2008] Q.B. 793, Lloyd-Jones J held that the decision in *Hall* had retrospective effect back as far as the events in 1991 which gave rise to the *Hall* litigation. Note that The Court of Session has held that the policy reasons which impressed the Lords in *Hall* do not apply in Scotland and hence, the immunity remains effective in Scots law: *Wright v Paton Farrell* [2003] P.N.L.R. 20. On appeal, the Inner House of the Court of Session found against the pursuer but on the different ground that no damage had been pled, and that this was essential: *Wright v Paton Farrell* [2006] CSIH 7; 2006 S.C. 404; [2007] P.N.L.R. 7. For discussion of the Scottish position see Gordon, "Not Yet Dead" (2007) 70 M.L.R. 471.

[250] Lord Hobhouse stressed the distinction between the commercial character of civil proceedings and the public interest nature of criminal proceedings: [2002] 1 A.C. 615 at 745. Lord Hutton stressed harassment, arguing that clients in criminal proceedings were more likely to be "unpleasant, unreasonable and disreputable" than those in civil proceedings: [2002] 1 A.C. 615 at 733. Lord Hope considered that there was a real risk that but for the immunity, advocates might be tempted to pursue every conceivable point on behalf of clients to the detriment of the efficiency of the criminal justice system: [2002] 1 A.C. 615 at 717.

[251] In *Moy v Pettman Smith* [2005] UKHL 7; [2005] 1 W.L.R. 581, the House of Lords emphasised that courts should not be over-critical of barristers' decision-making for the purposes of assessing the breach of duty. Note also *McFaddens (A Firm) v Platford* [2009] EWHC 126 (TCC); [2009] P.N.L.R. 26, where the applicable standard reflected the fact that the advice was given in circumstances of urgency. Causation may also be an issue, but at least in claims for economic loss it seems clear that "loss of chance" may be an available basis for a claim, as it is against solicitors. Advocates' liability is more fully considered in paras 9-136 to 9-137.

[252] For detailed consideration of judicial immunity see paras 5-101 onwards. See also para.9-40.

[253] *Sirros v Moore* [1975] Q.B. 118. See also ss.31–35 of the Courts Act 2003 providing that a magistrate cannot be liable for an act beyond his jurisdiction unless he acts in bad faith (see paras 5-121 to 5-124). In *Re McC* [1985] A.C. 528 at 550, Lord Bridge suggested that judges of inferior courts remained "liable for acts beyond their jurisdiction". The case upheld the liability of magistrates and although their immunity was reinstated by the Courts and Legal Service Act 1990 s.108 (now ss.31–35 of the Courts Act 2003), the principle of liability is likely to apply to judges of other inferior courts. See further para.5-106.

submissions of the parties rather than a direct investigation of the facts.[254] Prior to *Jones v Kaney*,[255] all witnesses in legal proceedings had immunity both in relation to evidence given in court and in relation to work on the evidence which can be said to form part of its presentation in court.[256] The basis of this immunity was the need to enable witnesses to give evidence fearlessly. The immunity of expert witnesses in relation to negligence has been removed by the Supreme Court.[257] While expert witnesses presumably continue to enjoy other immunities in common with other participants in legal proceedings,[258] expressly so in relation to defamation,[259] the restrictive requirements associated with establishing a duty of care in negligence appear to have persuaded the majority of the Supreme Court that no difficulty would be created by withdrawal of the negligence immunity. The role of expert witness was considered much more akin to the role of an advocate rather than the role of a witness of fact in most circumstances. Presumably, in instances where this is not the case, no duty of care will be owed in any event, on ordinary principles. Lord Collins, who joined the majority in the decision, would have preferred to expressly maintain an immunity properly so-called for hostile witnesses,[260] but it is likely that such witnesses would owe no duty. The dissenting judges, Lord Hope and Baroness Hale, thought the issues raised, and particularly the precise boundaries of the area of potential liability of expert witnesses, were not easily resolved by a court and would have preferred to see exploration by the Law Commission.[261] The present position is uncertain to the extent that the ambit of the duty of care is itself uncertain; but also to the extent that areas of immunity for those involved in legal proceedings undoubtedly remain, and the boundaries are somewhat unclear. The "core immunity" has been said to continue outside the circumstances of a case like *Jones v Kaney*, where negligence on the part of a "friendly" expert is alleged, so that alleged negligence by the police in revealing a party's identity in the course of a prosecution was covered by immunity.[262] Outside the ambit of negligence, witness statements given to the police where no prosecution follows have also been held to attract immunity in the form of absolute privilege for the purposes of a

---

254 *Sutcliffe v Thackrah* [1974] A.C. 727. The immunity does not apply where there is no defined dispute between the parties, e.g. to an accountant appointed to value a company, *Arenson v Casson Beckman Rutley & Co* [1977] A.C. 405. See further paras 9-40 and 9-41.

255 [2011] UKSC 13; [2011] 2 A.C. 398.

256 *Evans v London Hospital Medical College* [1981] 1 W.L.R. 184. The extent of expert witness immunity was reviewed by the Court of Appeal in *Stanton v Callaghan* [2000] Q.B. 75. Chadwick LJ held that the immunity extended to an expert agreeing a joint report with the other side's expert prior to a civil trial as it was necessary "in order to avoid the tension between the desire to assist the court and fear of the consequences of a departure from previous advice". Otton LJ seemed to take a more pragmatic approach, holding that in each case it was a question whether "it would serve the interests of justice to grant immunity". Thus, a large firm of accountants providing expert advice on the basis of letters of engagement which provide an opportunity for excluding liability are in an entirely different position from a doctor providing an expert opinion with the minimum of legal formality or protection. In *Walsh v Staines* [2008] EWCA Civ 1324; [2009] C.P. Rep. 16, the Court of Appeal held that the immunity applies to all statements made in or about legal proceedings, including statements made by a solicitor in support of a cross-undertaking in damages.

257 *Jones v Kaney* [2011] UKSC 13; [2011] 2 A.C. 398.

258 See further para.15-78.

259 See for example Lord Phillips in *Jones v Kaney* [2011] UKSC 13; [2011] 2 A.C. 398 at [62].

260 Lord Phillips in *Jones v Kaney* [2011] UKSC 13; [2011] 2 A.C. 398 at [73].

261 Lord Phillips in *Jones v Kaney* [2011] UKSC 13; [2011] 2 A.C. 398 at [173] and [190] respectively.

262 *A and B v Chief Constable of Hampshire Constabulary* [2012] EWHC 1517 (QB). See further para.9-42.

defamation action.[263] In the rare case where such a statement is part of conduct which amounts to a prosecution by the sole witness (or group of witnesses in collusion),[264] then the giver of the statement may in principle be liable for the tort of malicious prosecution, which is an action based on malicious abuse of the process of law.

13-50 In *X (Minors) v Bedfordshire CC*[265] Lord Browne-Wilkinson held that the psychiatrist instructed to examine a child to discover whether they had been abused and the identity of the abuser, could not owe a duty as the investigations had an immediate link with possible legal proceedings for the protection of the child. Subsequently, however, in *Darker v Chief Constable of West Midlands Police*[266] Lord Hope said that "there is no good reason on grounds of public policy to extend the immunity ... to things done [by witnesses] which cannot fairly be said to form part of their participation in the judicial process as witnesses". In relation to the police, he concluded that the immunity should "not be used to shield the police from action for things done while they were acting as law enforcers or investigators". In *D v East Berkshire NHS Trust*[267] Lord Phillips MR citing *Darker*, suggested that the psychiatrist's work in *Bedfordshire* "probably fell into the category of investigations" and outside the protection, and held that the medical staff in the *Berkshire* case were not protected by witness immunity and could owe a duty. In *Singh v Reading BC*,[268] a case of defamation, the Court of Appeal described the "core immunity" as relating to the giving of evidence, and its rationale as "to ensure that persons who may be witnesses in other cases in the future will not be deterred from giving evidence by fear of being sued for what they say in court". The immunity would only be extended beyond this as far as was required "in order to prevent the core immunity from being outflanked"; and otherwise "the principle that a wrong should not be without a remedy prevails".[269] In *Daniels v Chief Constable of South Wales*[270] Lloyd Jones LJ explained that the immunity was "essentially a witness immunity concerned with the giving of evidence and the making of statements in judicial proceedings", which has been extended in certain necessary ways.[271] There is no general immunity from suit for a prosecutor in respect of the initiation, continuation, and conduct of criminal proceedings. As such, acts and omissions of a police force in the course of informing the CPS for the purposes of a prosecution might fall outside the core immunity, and the alleged withholding or concealment of evidence was analogous to the fabrication of evidence in *Darker*. Thus, a claim for misfeasance in public office in relation to the preparation of the case was not necessarily barred and could be tried.[272] Thus even in relation to torts other than

[263] *Westcott v Westcott* [2008] EWCA Civ 818; [2009] Q.B. 407.

[264] *Martin v Watson* [1996] A.C. 74. The range of cases in which this will be concluded will be narrow: *H v AB* [2009] EWCA Civ 1092; *The Times,* 28 October 2009. A case which arguably fell within the range was *Ministry of Justice v Scott* [2009] EWCA Civ 1215 (five prison guards gave witness statements to the CPS, alleging that a prisoner had assaulted one of the guards).

[265] [1995] 2 A.C. 633 at 755.

[266] [2001] 1 A.C. 435 at 448. The decision was concerned with police evidence which had been fabricated and it was held that the protection did cover such evidence.

[267] [2003] EWCA Civ 1151; [2004] Q.B. 558 at [116].

[268] [2013] EWCA Civ 909; [2013] 1 W.L.R. 3052.

[269] [2013] EWCA Civ 909; [2013] 1 W.L.R. 3052 at [66].

[270] [2015] EWCA Civ 680.

[271] [2015] EWCA Civ 680 at [40].

[272] Referring to *Daniels*, the Court of Appeal in *CLG v Chief Constable of Merseyside Police* [2015] EWCA Civ 836 nevertheless concluded that transmission of a witness statement by the police to the

negligence, the usual caution as to the necessity of retaining or recognising an immunity also extends to the immunities of those involved in legal proceedings. Illustrating that the issues are not sharply different in relation to other torts, the decisions discussed here in relation to duty of care were cited by the court in *Singh* notwithstanding that the basis of the claim was defamation.

A litigant does not owe a duty to his adversary in relation to the conduct of the proceedings. Here the policy reason for the immunity is that the safeguards against impropriety should be found in the rules and procedures of the court rather than in the law of tort.[273] This has important implications for some public authorities. In *Jain v Trent Strategic HA*[274] (no duty of care owed by the applicant for ex parte order to the party against whom the order is sought), Lord Scott reviewed and reaffirmed these principles, citing the earlier decision of the House of Lords in *Customs and Excise Commissioners v Barclays Bank Plc*[275] (no duty of care owed by a bank which is the subject of a freezing order, to the party seeking the order). Lord Rodger, in the *Barclays Bank* case, had said: **13-51**

> "When parties embark on contested court proceedings, even under the rules of procedure in force today, they are entitled to treat the other side as opponents to vanquish. So they do not owe them a duty of care."[276]

Lord Scott's conclusion in *Jain* on this "stream of cases" was that:

> "where the preparation for, or commencement or conduct of, judicial proceedings before a court, or of quasi-judicial proceedings before a tribunal such as a registered homes tribunal, has the potential to cause damage to a party to the proceedings, whether personal damage such as psychiatric injury or economic damage as in the present case, a remedy for the damage cannot be obtained via the imposition on the opposing party of a common law duty of care. The protection of parties to litigation from damage caused to them by the litigation or by orders made in the course of the litigation must depend upon the control of the litigation by the court or tribunal in charge of it and the rules and procedures under which the litigation is conducted."[277]

It was possible that the relevant procedures themselves were incompatible with the Convention rights of those against whom the ex parte proceedings were brought, but the common law was unable to provide a remedy. Lord Carswell commented that the earlier Court of Appeal decision in *Martine v South East Kent HA*[278] had been predicated on the magistrates hearing the application carrying out their safeguarding functions "in a satisfactory manner",[279] but agreed with Lord Scott's reasons for deciding that no duty of care was owed at common law. He thought that the case should sound as a strong warning to magistrates not to make orders on ex

CPS was covered by the immunity, even though it was done negligently, and despite the fact that it was not the nature of the statement itself that was in issue, but what was subsequently done with it (revealing the address of the claimant witnesses to third parties). Holding the police liable for communicating the contents of the statement to the CPS would "outflank the immunity to which they were entitled in relation to the evidence once given in court" (at [32]).

273 *Business Computers International Ltd v Registrar of Companies* [1988] Ch. 229.

274 [2009] UKHL 4; [2009] 1 A.C. 853.

275 [2006] UKHL 28; [2007] 1 A.C. 181.

276 [2006] UKHL 28; [2007] 1 A.C. 181 at [47].

277 [2009] UKHL 4; [2009] 1 A.C. 853 at [35].

278 (1993) 20 B.M.L.R. 51.

279 [2009] UKHL 4; [2009] 1 A.C. 853 at [50].

parte applications for cancellation without enabling the owners to state their case, unless there were strong reasons to do so, and particularly that they are satisfied that there is "a serious risk of immediate harm".[280]

(vi) Armed forces

13-52 **Armed forces** Until its prospective repeal by the Crown Proceedings (Armed Forces) Act 1987, the Crown had a statutory immunity from tort proceedings in respect of death of or injuries to a member of the armed forces caused by another member of the forces in the execution of his or her duties. The immunity was set out in s.10(1) of the Crown Proceedings Act 1947, and continues to apply to events before the commencement of the 1987 Act.[281] Section 10(1)(b) of the Crown Proceedings Act 1947 confirmed that such injuries would be treated as "attributable to service" for the purposes of a service pension. As such, s.10 provided the gateway to no-fault compensation at the level of a state pension. In *Mulcahy v Ministry of Defence*[282] the question was whether after the abolition of the immunity, a duty of care was owed by one member of the forces to another in the context of active service. The claimant's hearing was adversely affected by an officer's careless and accidental firing of a heavy gun during the first Iraq war. The Court of Appeal, influenced by the Australian decision in *Shaw Savill v Commonwealth*,[283] held that it would not be fair, just and reasonable to impose a duty of care on one soldier to another whilst in the course of hostilities. Sir Iain Glidewell said: "it could be highly detrimental to the conduct of military operations if each soldier had to be conscious that even in the heat of battle, he owed [a duty of care] to his comrade."[284] As such, an area of "combat immunity" is recognised. In *Shaw Savill*, Dixon J had suggested that a duty of care might arise where the injury did not arise out of "active operations against the enemy" but other wartime activities such as maintenance of a warship. Similar reasoning would justify a duty of care in relation to peacetime activities such as battlefield training exercises.[285] Events unconnected with combat (such as personal injury from exposure to asbestos dust) are outside the ambit of the immunity, as are injuries to civilians.[286] In *Matthews v Ministry of Defence*,[287] a claim for injury through exposure to asbestos to which s.10 of the Crown Proceedings Act applied, the House of Lords considered that there was no conflict between a statutory immunity of this sort, particularly since it provided access to alternative compensation in the form of a pension, and art.6 of the ECHR. In *Roche v UK*, the European Court of Human Rights (by a majority) agreed.[288]

13-53 The extent of "combat immunity" was interpreted restrictively by the Supreme

---

280 [2009] UKHL 4; [2009] 1 A.C. 853 at [51].

281 s.2 of the Crown Proceedings (Armed Forces) Act 1987 enables the Secretary of State to revive s.10 if it is necessary or expedient to do so, either because of national danger or great emergency, or "for the purposes of any warlike operations" in any part of the world.

282 [1996] Q.B. 732.

283 (1940) 66 C.L.R. 344.

284 [1996] Q.B. 732 at 750.

285 See also the nuclear testing litigation, *AB v Ministry of Defence* [2012] UKSC 9; [2013] 1 A.C. 78. The claims failed but not for lack of duty.

286 See the action brought by a civilian in *Hopps v Mott Macdonald Ltd* [2009] EWHC 1881 (QB). The action failed on the basis that no breach was shown.

287 [2003] UKHL 4; [2003] 1 A.C. 1163.

288 [2005] ECHR 32555/96; (2005) 42 E.H.R.R. 599.

Court in *Smith v Ministry of Defence*.[289] *Smith* concerned claims both at common law, and under the HRA. In respect of the claims at common law, counsel for the Ministry of Defence had advanced arguments based both on combat immunity, and on application of the general "fair, just and reasonable" test. Lord Hope, with whom Lord Walker, Lady Hale and Lord Kerr agreed, accepted that combat immunity is "best thought of as a rule"[290]; but he interpreted this rule narrowly, taking as the paradigm of combat immunity those decisions made in the heat of battle: such decisions could not fairly be questioned in litigation. At first instance, Owen J had interpreted combat immunity as not confined to cases involving the presence of the enemy, and ruled that the immunity applied to all active operations in which service personnel are exposed to attack, or a threat of attack. This extended to decisions taken in the planning of the operations in which injury was sustained, though not to the planning and preparation for possible future operations, and it was on this basis that not all of the common law claims had been struck out.[291] Lord Hope, however, considered the judgment of Owen J to amount to an unjustified extension of the immunity, as it could apply to decisions taken far away in place and time from the active operations themselves.[292] Lord Hope described the rule as "a particular application of what is fair, just and reasonable". Nevertheless, it operated like a rule, and should be approached in a restricted way. Combat immunity was an exceptional defence available to governments and individuals who cause damage, injury or death "in the course of actual or imminent armed conflict", amounting to an exception to the principle in *Entick v Carrington* that the executive cannot simply rely on the interests of the state as a justification for the commission of wrongs. The doctrine should be narrowly construed, and any extension of an existing immunity needs to be carefully justified.[293] Although counsel had argued that, beyond the extent of the immunity, public policy reasons existed which would justify the non-existence of a duty of care, it is suggested that surprisingly little argument was devoted to this possibility by the majority. Rather, Lord Hope took the view that any further questions about the existence of a duty could not be determined without hearing evidence. He also appeared to argue that questions of breach of duty would be particularly significant in controlling the operation of negligence outside the area of combat immunity, suggesting that courts must pay attention to the context in which decisions were reached in deciding whether or not the duty has been breached, and that duties must not be "unrealistic or excessively burdensome".[294] At the same time, he described what amounts to a fair, just and reasonable outcome in terms of a "balance", which could not be struck in a general way and must reflect a factual enquiry. This approach appears to run counter to the general preference for resolving questions of policy at the duty stage.[295]

The significance of the majority approach can be illustrated by way of contrast **13-54**
with the dissenting judgments of Lords Mance and Carnwath. Lord Mance in

289 [2013] UKSC 41; [2014] A.C. 52. The Human Rights Act aspects of the decision are considered in paras 13-88 (jurisdictional extent, and art.1), and 13-93 (right to life, art.2).

290 [2013] UKSC 41; [2014] A.C. 52 at [83].

291 See also the earlier decision of Owen J in *Multiple Claimants v Ministry of Defence* [2003] EWHC 1134 (QB); and the successful claim for damages for psychiatric injury on the basis of failure to diagnose and treat, in *New v Ministry of Defence* [2005] EWHC 1647 (QB).

292 [2013] UKSC 41; [2014] A.C. 52 at [89].

293 [2013] UKSC 41; [2014] A.C. 52 at [90], [92], [94].

294 [2013] UKSC 41; [2014] A.C. 52 at [99].

295 Outlined in para.13-16.

particular stressed the importance of asking *what duty was owed* in relation to a death in active operations. Lord Hope, by contrast, emphasised the unassailable nature of *decisions* made in the course of active operations as the core of combat immunity, which was itself a limited exception to the rule that the interests of the state do not take priority over individual rights. Lord Hope was reluctant to extend the area of "no duty" beyond this zone. Lord Mance proposed a larger area of "non-justiciability"[296]; and the need (for this reason) to avoid litigation both after, and during active engagement with an enemy. Both dissenting judges referred to decisions such as *Van Colle* and *Brooks* in which duties of care were denied not because decisions were made "in the heat of the moment", but for policy reasons.[297] Their point was that Lord Hope's majority judgment gave little weight to the presence of policy factors in relation to decisions taken in advance of active engagement, and is unusual among recent decisions of the highest courts in preferring to leave balancing questions to the tribunal of fact.[298] It is suggested that this is because of the way that combat immunity was identified by the majority with decisions unassailable because of battle or combat conditions, rather than as part of a continuum of policy questions underpinned by the subordination of interests ordinarily protected by private law to other objectives in the context of war. This subordination is not unlimited, but the majority judgments supply little information about how to approach duties outside the range of decisions taken in the course of active operations, to which combat immunity must now be said most centrally to apply.

(vii) Immunities

13-55 **Immunities** The difference between "no duty" and "immunity" is hard to define with certainty. The protection formerly given to advocates was referred to as an immunity and the protection given to the police in *Hill* and *Osman* and to social workers in *Bedfordshire* was also initially termed an immunity, although later cases refer to the "*Hill* principle" rather than the *Hill* immunity, and the interpretation in the most recent cases suggests an application of general principles rather than special treatment for the police. The term may be misleading in many cases in that it suggests a status independent of the fairness, justice and reasonableness criteria, but the *generality* of the exclusion of a duty is an important factor, often aimed at deterring litigation. The overturning of advocates' and expert witnesses' immunity and restriction of immunity in child welfare cases tends to suggest that their basis was simply the public interest and perceptions of what that requires have been changing. On the other hand, the surviving immunity from civil actions applicable to witnesses of fact and others involved in litigation may be different in kind from these "no duty" situations; as also was the statutory immunity in s.10 of the Crown Proceedings Act 1947 (above), and perhaps the combat immunity recognised in *Smith*.

13-56 Where the "immunity" in question simply reflects the outcome of ordinary duty of care principles, the term is also misleading in that it seems to suggest protection from a liability which would otherwise exist, that is, a special rule applied to a situation where the ordinary rules would have resulted in a duty being owed. As we have seen, it was this appearance of a two stage process which led the European

---

[296] [2013] UKSC 41; [2014] A.C. 52 at [125].
[297] See paras 13-34 and 13-35.
[298] See further para.13-16.

Court of Human Rights to consider that the "immunity" applied in *Osman* deprived the claimant of a fair trial of what would otherwise have been a right to claim.[299] The term "immunity" should be avoided to the extent that it is simply a misleading label applied to the conclusion that imposition of a duty would be unreasonable, particularly where the possibility remains of exceptional cases based (for example) on an assumption of responsibility (as is conceded in the case of police negligence). As Lord Browne-Wilkinson put it in *Barrett v Enfield LBC*[300]:

> "A holding that it is not fair, just and reasonable to hold liable a particular class of defendants whether generally or in relation to a particular type of activity is not to give immunity from a liability to which the rest of the world is subject. It is a prerequisite to there being any liability in negligence at all that as a matter of policy it is fair, just and reasonable in those circumstances to impose liability in negligence."

Similarly in *Brooks v Commissioner of Police for the Metropolis*[301] Lord Steyn, giving the opinion of the majority of the House of Lords, whilst affirming the core of the *Hill* decision, said: "It would be best for the principle in *Hill* to be reformulated in terms of the absence of a duty of care rather than a blanket immunity."[302]

Restriction of immunities In a number of recent cases, including *Jones v Kaney*,[303] courts have emphasised that immunities are exceptional and must be clearly justified. Equally, existing immunities are not to be extended to new circumstances in the absence of clear reasons. In *Smith v Ministry of Defence*,[304] combat immunity was more narrowly interpreted than had been the case in previous first instance decisions; while in *Smart v Forensic Science Service*,[305] the Court of Appeal held there was no justification for maintaining an immunity against proceedings in negligence where a claim based on deceit was allowed to proceed, so that the evidence was in any event subject to litigation. Similarly in *Singh v Reading BC* the Court of Appeal said that immunity for those involved in judicial proceedings should not be extended further than was necessary to protect the "core immunity".[306] In each instance, the key principle that "wrongs should be righted" takes priority in the absence of clear reasons. Thus it may be said that immunities are rare and subject to careful assessment by the courts. On the other hand, ordinary principles governing the duty of care are themselves capable of offering significant protection. 13-57

(c) Proximity

Proximity Proximity questions concern the relationship between the parties. We have seen that in the case of the welfare and education services, reasonableness rather than proximity has more often been the key question. In the case of the police service, policy considerations have often been identified in the denial of duties, and 13-58

[299] See *Osman v UK* (1998) 5 B.H.R.C. 293.
[300] [2001] 2 A.C. 550 at 559.
[301] [2005] UKHL 24; [2005] 1 W.L.R. 1495. See para.13-34.
[302] [2005] UKHL 24; [2005] 1 W.L.R. 1495 at [27]. He also said that "[n]owadays, a more sceptical approach to the carrying out of all public functions is necessary".
[303] [2011] UKSC 13; [2011] 2 A.C. 398.
[304] [2013] UKSC 41; [2014] A.C. 52.
[305] [2013] EWCA Civ 783; [2013] P.N.L.R. 32.
[306] [2013] EWCA Civ 909; [2013] 1 W.L.R. 3052.

close proximity has not generally been sufficient to dispel these. The exception is where a voluntary assumption of responsibility takes the case outside the principles generally applicable to a "failure to benefit" case. In the case of rescue services and those responsible for maintenance of the highway, the application of general principles in relation to omissions or failure to benefit has been at the forefront. Proximity per se has played a greater role in relation to the regulatory services. Their negligent conduct may be the indirect cause of harm to a claimant, the direct cause being the activity which was negligently regulated, and the regulatory service will normally have no direct contact with the claimant. Proximity has also been used as a guiding principle in respect of the liability of custodial agencies and in a subsidiary role in respect of the police. These categories are explored below. However, not all cases of public service negligence raising issues of proximity fall within the categories. For example, in *Sebry v Companies House*[307] the defendant was a governmental executive agency, rather than a regulator. An incorrect and careless entry in the Register of Companies caused terminal damage to a company. Although the information was published to the whole world, which would ordinarily imply a lack of proximity, in this instance the claim was not one of reliance on the statement by a claimant but a claim that reliance on the statement by third parties had caused loss to the company. It was the closeness of the relationship between company and defendant which was in issue. It was concluded that the registrar owes a duty of care when entering a winding up order on the register to take reasonable care to ensure that the order is not registered against the wrong company. That duty is owed to any company which is not in liquidation but which is wrongly recorded on the register as having been wound up by order of the court. The duty extends to taking reasonable care to enter the order on the record of the company named in the order, and not any other company. It does not extend to checking information supplied by third parties. A special relationship could be said to arise between the registrar of companies and the company concerned; and there was an assumption of responsibility in altering the register to reflect new information.

(i) *Regulatory agencies*

13-59 **Regulatory agencies** Where a regulatory agency has sufficient control over an activity and the purpose of the scheme is to protect the class to which the claimant belongs, then there may be sufficient proximity to justify a duty. On the no duty side of the line is *Yuen Kun-yeu v Att Gen of Hong Kong*[308] where depositors who lost money on the collapse of a regulated financial institution, claimed against the regulatory authority alleging that it had negligently failed to deregister the institution. Giving judgment of the Privy Council, Lord Keith concluded that the applicable legislation "placed a duty on the (regulator) to supervise companies in the general public interest, but no special responsibility towards individual members of the public". Two factors led to that conclusion. First, that rather than acting in the interests of just one particular group, the regulator had to balance the interests of different groups, potential depositors whose loss might be averted by de-registration and existing depositors for whom de-registration would have a disastrous effect. Secondly, the regulator had no power to control the day-to-day

---

[307] [2015] EWHC 115 (QB); [2016] 1 W.L.R. 2499.
[308] [1988] A.C. 175.

activities of the regulated financial institutions, so that depositors were not entitled to rely on the fact of registration as a guarantee of the soundness of a particular company.[309] On the other side of the line is *Perrett v Collins*[310] where the Court of Appeal held that an agency responsible for inspecting the construction of light aircraft did owe a duty of care to those injured in a crash resulting from faulty construction by the builder. Hobhouse LJ found proximity on the ground that the defendant had a "measure of control over and responsibility for a situation, which if dangerous, will be liable to injure the [claimant]". He distinguished two other inspection cases, *Philcox v Civil Aviation Authority*[311] and *Reeman v Department of Transport*,[312] on the ground that the claims had been brought by the owner of the plane and boat respectively whereas the purpose of the inspection scheme was to protect those being carried against personal injury and not the owners against damage to their property. Although the *Perrett* decision was based on proximity, the control and purpose factors could also be viewed as relevant to the reasonableness of any duty and hence, in the regulatory agency cases as in others, the criteria of proximity and reasonableness have a tendency to overlap. Another successful action against a regulatory authority was *Watson v British Boxing Board of Control*.[313] The claimant, a boxer, succeeded in his argument that the regulatory body with responsibility for the sport owed him a duty to provide immediate ringside medical attention. There was sufficient proximity between the parties, since a limited number of individuals made up the membership of the defendants, and injuries of the sort incurred were almost inevitable. In *Wattleworth v Goodwood Road Racing Co Ltd*,[314] the claimant's husband had died during an amateur track day at Goodwood, when his car collided three times with a tyre wall. The action was brought against the occupiers on the basis of their occupancy duty, and also against the RAC (the national body with power to licence motor racing vehicles) and the

---

309 [1988] A.C. 175 at 196–197. See also *Davis v Radcliffe* [1990] 1 W.L.R. 821 PC; and *Curran v Northern Ireland Co-Ownership Housing Association Ltd* [1987] A.C. 718, where the agency, which was responsible for administering grants for home improvement work, was held not liable to a claimant who discovered that such work on the house he had purchased had been carried out defectively. The House of Lords noted that the agency had no powers of control: "Once approval has been given for a grant, the executive has no powers to control the building owner, still less the builder whom he chooses to employ, in the execution of the work." It had a power to withhold the grant if it discovered that the work was defective but Lord Bridge considered that the purpose of this power was the protection of the "public revenue" and not the subsequent purchasers of the property.

310 [1999] P.N.L.R. 77. In *Thames Trains Ltd v Health & Safety Executive* [2003] EWCA Civ 720, the Court of Appeal cited *Perrett*, dismissing the Executive's application to strike out the claims of victims of the Ladbroke Grove rail crash. It could be reasonably argued that the Executive should be made liable, not for failing to use statutory powers involving expenditure of money, but for the negligent exercise, or failure to exercise, its statutory powers through the Railway Inspectorate, if its action or inaction was plainly wrong.

311 (1995) L.S. Gaz. 33; *The Times*, 8 June 1995.

312 [1997] P.N.L.R. 618. Hobhouse LJ followed *Swanson Estate v Canada* (1991) 80 D.L.R. (4th) 741, where Transport Canada which had responsibility for regulating the safety of commercial airlines was held liable to the victims of a plane crash caused after it had negligently allowed the airline to continue unsafe flying practices which led to the crash. Transport Canada had extensive control including powers to interview pilots, revoke the appointment of airline management and suspend the operating licence. See also *Seddon v Driver and Vehicle Licensing Agency* [2019] EWCA Civ 14; [2019] 1 W.L.R. 4593: no duty of care was owed by the DVLA to the purchaser of a classic car who had relied upon a vehicle registration certificate. The purchaser's reliance was outside the statutory purpose of the certificate.

313 [2001] Q.B. 1134.

314 [2004] EWHC 140 (QB); [2004] P.I.Q.R. P25.

FIA (the body governing international competitive motor racing), both of which had previously inspected the track. The RAC was held to owe a duty to the deceased, which it had however discharged (there was no breach); the FIA did not have sufficient involvement with the safety of individuals in the position of the deceased to owe a duty at all.[315]

(ii) Custodial agencies

13-60 **Custodial agencies** The leading House of Lords decision in *Home Office v Dorset Yacht Co Ltd*[316] illustrates the significance of the proximity requirement. In *Dorset Yacht* the alleged negligence of the prison officers had allowed young offenders training on an island to make their escape by seizing the claimant's yacht which was moored nearby. The House of Lords held there was sufficient proximity between the officers and the claimant to justify a duty of care. Lord Morris based the duty on the officers' control of the detainees and would have been prepared to extend the duty to residents in the area of the escape. Lord Diplock took a narrower view, holding that the duty was to prevent the detainee from escaping and was owed only to those whose property was likely to be damaged in the course of the escape[317] and hence, reserved his opinion on *Holgate v Lancashire Mental Hospitals Board*[318] where the negligent release of a mental patient had resulted in liability. In *Palmer v Tees HA*[319] the Court of Appeal held that a custody authority responsible for a negligent release of a patient did not owe a duty to a victim unless that victim had been identifiable. If the identity of the victim was unknown, there was insufficient proximity. A similar result would probably be achieved through application of art.2 ECHR, which requires positive steps where there is an imminent risk to the life of the claimant. The court in *Palmer* disapproved the decision in *Holgate*.

---

315 An analogous case brought not against a regulatory agency but a surveyor, who had inspected a shopfront shortly before pedestrians were severely injured by detached fascia falling from the building, is *Harrison v Technical Sign Co Ltd* [2013] EWCA Civ 1569; [2014] P.N.L.R. 15. *Perrett v Collins* was distinguished since there, the purpose of the inspection was to assess the aircraft's fitness to fly and the risk to the public in case of negligence was obvious; while in *Harrison* itself, proximity was lacking because the purpose of the inspection was in no sense to secure the safety of members of the public.

316 [1970] A.C. 1004.

317 [1970] A.C. 1004 at 1186. This difference of view would be crucial in a case such as *Greenwell v Prison Officers* (1951) 101 L.J. 486 where damage was done not during the course of the escape but after the escape, albeit in the locality of the prison. The county court judge held the authority liable in *Greenwell* for negligently deciding to keep a detainee with a bad record in an open prison from which he had escaped to cause the damage in question. Lord Morris agreed with the statement of the judge in *Greenwell* that a duty was owed to near-by residents to prevent injury being done to their property by detainees but doubted whether the finding of negligence was justified. Lord Diplock disapproved *Greenwell* on similar grounds but went on to comment that no duty should be owed to "a person whose property was damaged merely because the damage to him happened to be caused by a criminal who had escaped from custody before completion of his sentence".

318 [1937] 4 All E.R. 19. The medical officer of the hospital order the release on "holiday licence" of a compulsorily detained patient with convictions for violence, without checking the supervision arrangements for release period. The patient visited the claimant's house and assaulted her.

319 [1999] Lloyd's Rep. Med. 351.

(iii) *Police*

In *Hill v Chief Constable of West Yorkshire*[320] a duty was denied on policy grounds but it was also rejected for lack of proximity. The claim had been brought on behalf of the last victim of a murderer who, it was alleged, the defendant had negligently failed to catch. The likely victim was not identifiable but merely one of a very large number of women at risk and for that reason the House of Lords held that there was insufficient proximity to found a duty. Similarly, in *Alexandrou v Oxford*[321] the Court of Appeal held that there was no special relationship sufficient to found a duty between the police and a member of the public making an emergency call to the police. Glidewell LJ considered that if a duty arose in response to such a call, it would also be "owed to all members of the public who gave information of a suspected crime against themselves or their property".[322] There could not be a special relationship, that is, proximity, with such a wide class. As in *Hill*, the alternative ground of the decision was that of general policy. With the suggestion in *Brooks*[323] that the application of the policy principle in *Hill* might have to be reconsidered in cases on the margins, it seemed possible that the issue of proximity would take on more significance. However, *Smith v Chief Constable of Sussex Police* appears to be one where proximity was established, yet did not suffice to dispel the general policy factors. Within the "core" of the *Hill* principle, where there is a failure in the suppression of crime, it is necessary to show something stronger than proximity per se, namely an assumption of responsibility. This is now rationalised in terms of an exception to the general omissions rule, rather than as a special rule in relation to the police. In *Michael v Chief Constable of South Wales*[324] direct discussion with the victim of crime through a "999" call was insufficient, on the facts, to give rise to an assumption of responsibility, and it therefore appears that such an assumption will not easily be established. In *Smith* Lord Brown said that the question was whether a duty of care "should be found to exist when the police, without having assumed any particular responsibility towards the eventual victim, are engaged rather in discharging their more general duty of combating and investigating crime".[325] However, in *Robinson v Chief Constable of West Yorkshire Police*, the Supreme Court determined that where the alleged negligent act was a positive act causing personal injury, the case will fall into a recognised duty situation so that questions of proximity and fairness do not fall to be considered.[326] 13-61

(d) Omissions

Statutory duties and powers Public services such as those responsible for roads or rescues, may cause harm to a member of the public by negligently failing to perform the service adequately. The question in such cases is whether the service can shelter behind the special status of omissions, according to which a person who 13-62

---

320 [1989] A.C. 53.

321 [1993] 4 All E.R. 328.

322 [1993] 4 All E.R. 328 at 338.

323 *Brooks v Commissioner of Police for the Metropolis* [2005] UKHL 24; [2005] 1 W.L.R. 1495. See para.13-34.

324 [2015] UKSC 2; [2015] A.C. 1732.

325 [2008] UKHL 50; [2009] 1 A.C. 225 at [122].

326 [2018] UKSC 4; [2018] A.C. 736; see para.13-42.

negligently fails to act in order to prevent harm, as opposed to acting negligently and thereby causing harm, owes no duty to the victim of the failure.[327] In both *Poole BC v GN*,[328] and *Robinson v Chief Constable of South Yorkshire Police*,[329] the distinction between acts and omissions was accorded the key role in explaining the decisions in relation to public service liability. It is clear that the fact that the service has a statutory duty or power to take action is not sufficient to give rise to a common law duty. The statute itself may provide for liability for failure to act as is the case with s.41 of the Highways Act 1980[330] which provides for liability for failure to maintain the highway. In the absence of an express liability provision, the courts may conclude that Parliament intended that breach of the statutory duty should give rise to a private law action for the tort of breach of statutory duty.[331] But in the absence of either an express or an implied right to a private law action, the statutory duties and powers of a public service do not themselves justify an exception to the omission rule. In *Stovin v Wise*[332] the House of Lords held that a statutory power could not justify a common law duty of care, and in *Gorringe v Calderdale MBC*[333] it held that a statutory duty which did not expressly or impliedly give rise to a private law right, could not generate a common law duty of care. Any such duty must arise through ordinary common law principles. The result, as May LJ has put it,[334] is that:

> "Although statutory duties or powers which do not give rise to a private law right of action may constitute part of the relevant factual background, the existence of those duties or powers cannot reinforce parasitically the existence of a common law duty of care in the public authority. In short ... the existence of a common law duty depends on unvarnished common law principles."

In the case of omissions where the defendant does not directly inflict the personal or physical injury, May LJ said that the unvarnished common law principles required reliance by the claimant as a "necessary ingredient" of the duty and assumption of responsibility by the defendant as a "helpful guide". In *Poole*, however, assumption of responsibility was treated as the key consideration, and reliance is a key component of establishing such an assumption. These factors will be explored in the subsequent paragraphs

(i) Statutory powers and duties

13-63 **Statutory powers** The leading authority on the relevance of statutory powers to the application of the omission rule is *Stovin v Wise*.[335] In *Stovin* the defendant car driver emerged from a side road and collided with the claimant. When sued, the defendant joined a local highway authority as a third party arguing that it owed the motorists a duty of care to improve the poor visibility at the intersection. The author-

[327] See paras 7-51 and following for an explanation of the rule.

[328] [2019] UKSC 25; [2019] 2 W.L.R. 1478.

[329] [2018] UKSC 4; [2018] A.C. 736.

[330] See paras 7-217 to 7-219.

[331] See Ch.8.

[332] [1996] A.C. 923.

[333] [2004] UKHL 15; [2004] 1 W.L.R. 1057.

[334] *Sandhar v Department of Transport, Environment and the Regions* [2004] EWCA Civ 1440; [2005] 1 W.L.R. 1632 at [37] and [38].

[335] [1996] A.C. 923.

ity had statutory powers to enable it to do this work and, it seemed, had decided to do it but had not implemented that decision. The question was whether the authority owed a duty of care to the claimant to do that work. A normal application of the omission rule would lead to the conclusion that it owed no duty. The only basis for making an exception to the rule was the fact that the authority had a statutory power to take measures for the safety of road users. Lord Hoffmann, giving the leading majority speech, said:

> "[T]he minimum pre-conditions for basing a duty of care upon the existence of a statutory power, if it can be done at all, are, first, that it would in the circumstances have been irrational not to have exercised the power, so that there was in effect a public law duty to act, and secondly, that there are exceptional grounds for holding that the policy of the statute requires compensation to be paid to persons who suffer loss because the power was not exercised."

Applying this test to the facts, he found that the authority's conduct was not irrational as the timing of the work was "as much a matter of discretion as the decision in principle to do it". Further, even if the failure to do the work was irrational in the sense that the authority ought as a matter of public law to have done the work, the second condition was not satisfied. Lord Hoffmann said:

> "It seems impossible to discern a legislative intent that there should be a duty of care in respect of the use of that power, giving rise to a right to compensate persons injured by a failure to use it, when there was at the time [when statute first granted the power in 1925] no such liability even for breach of the statutory duty to maintain the highway ... the creation of a duty of care ... would inevitably expose the authority's budgetary decisions to judicial inquiry. This would distort the priorities of local authorities, which would be bound to try to play it safe by increasing their spending on road improvements rather than risk enormous liabilities for personal injury accidents. They will spend less on education or social services."[336]

In *Mitchell v Glasgow City Council*,[337] the House of Lords considered a case where the deceased was attacked and killed by his neighbour, Drummond, shortly after a meeting with the defendant housing authority, of whom both Drummond and the deceased were tenants. As originally framed, the claim proposed that the defendant was in breach of a duty to act on repeated complaints that Drummond had attacked and threatened to kill the deceased, by exercising its powers to recover possession of the property of which he was a tenant. The pursuers did not continue with this claim, since it was inconsistent with clear authority that (in the words of Lord Hope) "a local authority is not normally liable for errors of judgment in the exercise of its discretionary powers under a statute".[338] The only potential route to delictual **13-64**

336 [1996] A.C. 923 at 953. He had previously commented at 953, that Parliament might have chosen to confer a power rather than impose a duty because the "subject matter did not permit a duty to be stated with sufficient precision". After noting that authorities might defensively over-invest in roads to avoid liability and arguing that road standards were a matter of discretion for the authority, he concluded saying:

> "On the other hand denial of liability does not leave the road user unprotected ... there is compulsory insurance to provide compensation for the victims. There is no reason of policy or justice which requires the highway authority to be an additional defendant."

337 [2009] UKHL 11; [2009] 1 A.C. 874.

338 [2009] UKHL 11; [2009] 1 A.C. 874 at [7].

liability was to argue that the defenders should have warned the deceased about a meeting which had been called with Drummond, and the likelihood that he would react violently. This claim failed.[339]

13-65 **Irrationality** It is now doubtful whether an irrational failure to exercise a power can ever give rise to a common law duty of care. In *Stovin*, Lord Hoffmann had suggested that failure to exercise a power would be irrational where it was exercised to provide a service as a matter of routine but arbitrarily withheld on the occasion in question. The routine exercise might create a general expectation in the community that the power would continue to be exercised and a realisation by the authority that there was a general reliance on its exercise.[340] Lord Hoffmann left open the question whether the previous House of Lords decision in *Anns v Merton LBC*[341] holding a local authority under a duty to the flat owner in respect of its negligent failure to exercise a statutory power to inspect its foundations, could be justified under the general reliance principle. Subsequently, Stuart-Smith LJ giving the judgment of the Court of Appeal in *Capital and Counties Plc v Hampshire CC*,[342] rejected the argument that a fire brigade could owe a positive duty of care in rescuing on the basis of the general reliance principle and said that there appeared to be "no case, except *Anns* itself, which could be said to be an example of [the] application [of the principle]" and that there was clear authority against such a principle in decisions such as *Alexandrou v Oxford*[343] where it was held that there was no duty on the police to take care in responding to an emergency call.[344] However, the Court of Appeal invoked irrationality to justify a duty in *Larner v Solihull MBC*[345] where the claimant argued that she would not have crashed had the defendant acted with care and placed warning signs pursuant to its statutory duty to take measures to prevent accidents. Her claim failed on the facts but Lord Woolf MR said that the authority could be liable in negligence at common law if it had acted wholly unreasonably in failing to provide a sign and its default thus fell outside the ambit of discretion under the statutory duty. Subsequently, this suggestion has been firmly disapproved by the House of Lords in *Gorringe v Calderdale MBC*[346] with Lord Hoffmann saying:

---

339 See the discussion at para.13-72.

340 Lord Hoffmann cited the examples of general reliance given by Mason J in *Sutherland Shire Council v Heyman* (1985) 157 C.L.R. 424 HC at 464: the control of air traffic, the safety inspection of aircraft and the fighting of a fire. In the case of the highway authority, there was no general reliance on the routine removal of road hazards and no arbitrary deprivation of a benefit.

341 [1978] A.C. 728.

342 [1997] Q.B. 1004.

343 [1993] 4 All E.R. 328.

344 In *OLL Ltd v Secretary of State for Transport* [1997] 3 All E.R. 897, when rejecting the application of the general reliance principle to the coastguard, May J commented that he read the analysis of Stuart-Smith LJ as "in effect saying that in English Law no duty of care arises in cases such as this [response to an emergency] from a general expectation".

345 [2001] R.T.R. 32; [2001] P.I.Q.R. P17. Keith J applied the general reliance approach in *R. (on the application of A) v Secretary of State for the Home Department* [2004] EWHC 1585 (Admin); (2004) 154 N.L.J. 1411, but the decision is doubtful in the light of *Gorringe* and in *R. (Atapattu) v Secretary of State for the Home Department* [2011] EWHC 1388 (Admin), it was said that it could no longer be safely relied upon.

346 [2004] UKHL 15; [2004] 1 W.L.R. 1057. Lord Hoffmann at [37]; Lord Scott at [72]; and Lord Rodger at [92].

> "I find it difficult to imagine a case in which a common law duty can be founded simply upon the failure (however irrational) to provide some benefit which a public authority has power (or a public law duty) to provide."[347]

However, in a case where a duty of care would arise on ordinary negligence principles—for example, where the defendant is an employer owing duties to a claimant employee in respect of personal injury—it is possible that the duty may be *breached* by a failure to exercise a statutory power.[348] In any such case, there must be no conflict between the common law duty, and the statutory scheme; but that is a different question from the one addressed by *Stovin* and *Gorringe*.

Statutory duty In *Stovin v Wise*[349] Lord Hoffmann said: 13-66

> "If a [statutory] duty does not give rise to a private law right to sue for breach [i.e. for the tort of breach of statutory duty], it would be unusual if it nevertheless gave rise to a duty of care at common law which made the public authority liable to compensation for foreseeable loss caused by the duty not being performed … If the policy of the act is not to create a statutory liability to pay compensation, the same policy should ordinarily exclude the existence of a common law duty of care."

In *Gorringe v Calderdale MBC*[350] the House of Lords considered whether a statutory duty could give rise to a common law duty of care. The claimant was injured in a road accident which she claimed could have been avoided if the defendant had acted with reasonable care and placed warning signs on the highway. The Road Traffic Act 1988 imposed on the authority a duty to "take measures appropriate to prevent accidents". The claimant argued that this broad statutory duty gave rise to a common law duty of care. This was unanimously rejected by the House of Lords. Lord Scott said:

> "If a statutory duty does not give rise to a private right to sue for breach [i.e. for the tort of breach of statutory duty], the duty cannot create a duty of care that would not have been owed at common law if the statute were not there. If the policy of the statute is not consistent with the creation of a statutory liability to pay compensation for damage caused by a breach of the statutory duty, the same policy would exclude the use of the statutory duty in order to create a common law duty of care that would be broken by a failure to perform the statutory duty … I do not accept that a common law duty of care can grow parasitically out of a statutory duty not intended to be owed to individuals."[351]

He concluded that the statutory duty could not have intended "to create specific duties owed to individuals"; as it was "entirely general" in phrasing and "imposed a 'target duty' and no more than that". Hence, no common law duty of care could be based on the statutory duty. A similar conclusion was reached in relation to the Highways Act 1980 s.130, in *Ali v City of Bradford Metropolitan DC*.[352] The section was concerned with the rights of the public at large, and gave rise to no civil action for damages on the part of a pedestrian who fell and was injured descend-

---

347 [2004] UKHL 15; [2004] 1 W.L.R. 1057 at [32]. He previously commented that the speculation as to the possibility of a duty in *Stovin*, might have been ill-advised.

348 *Connor v Surrey County Council* [2010] EWCA Civ 286; [2011] Q.B. 429; para.13-10.

349 [1996] A.C. 923 at 952.

350 [2004] UKHL 15; [2004] 1 W.L.R. 1057.

351 [2004] UKHL 15; [2004] 1 W.L.R. 1057 at [71].

352 [2010] EWCA Civ 1282; [2012] 1 W.L.R. 161.

ing steps made unsafe by debris. A claim in nuisance alleging a positive duty to remove a hazard was rejected on the basis that—following the decision in *Marcic v Thames Water Utilities*[353]—"for the courts to impose such a liability through the law of nuisance would be to use a blunt instrument to interfere with a carefully regulated statutory scheme". Thus the Court of Appeal rejected an attempt to outflank restrictions on duty of care in negligence by arguing that there was a positive duty in nuisance instead.

13-67 Some scope remains for statutory duties to influence the nature of relationships in such a way that recognition of a duty of care is appropriate. In *Rice v Secretary of State for Trade and Industry*,[354] the Court of Appeal held that a statutory body, the National Dock Labour Board (NDLB), owed a common law duty of care to protect dock workers from asbestos risks when they were employed to unload cargo by a registered employer. The NDLB was under a statutory duty to make provision for the welfare of dock workers and, when not unloading cargo for a registered employer, the statute provided that they were employed by the NDLB. Hence, their relationship was a "hybrid" employment relationship.[355] May LJ considered *Stovin*, *Bedfordshire* and *Phelps*, and summarised the law as follows:

> "a statute containing broad target duties owed to the public at large and which does not confer on individuals a right of action for breach of statutory duty, is unlikely to give rise to a common law duty of care … . There may, however, be relationships, arising out of the existence and exercise of statutory powers or duties, between a public authority and one or more individuals from which the public authority is taken to have assumed responsibility to guard against foreseeable injury or loss to the individuals caused by breach of the duty. There is then a sufficient relationship of proximity and it is fair, just and reasonable that a duty of care should be imposed."[356]

May LJ found that the relevant statute "properly construed did not create a private remedy. But the policy of the statute was clearly aimed at protecting the health of the dock workers." He concluded that:

> "the policy of the statute can only be seen as enabling a relationship such that the law should impose a common law duty of care. This was not a broad target power or duty directed at the public at large…. Although the NDLB were a body created by statute to whom the principles discussed in *Stovin v Wise* and *Gorringe* apply, they would in my view have undertaken an equivalent common law duty if they had been a private organisation in an equivalent relationship with the dock workers and performing and undertaking equivalent functions."[357]

At trial, it was held that the defendants had breached their duty and that this had caused the diseases suffered by the dock workers. Damages were awarded accordingly.[358]

---

353 [2003] UKHL 66; [2004] 2 A.C. 42, para.13-118.
354 [2007] EWCA Civ 289; [2007] I.C.R. 1469.
355 [2007] EWCA Civ 289; [2007] I.C.R. 1469 at [44].
356 [2007] EWCA Civ 289; [2007] I.C.R. 1469 at [42].
357 [2007] EWCA Civ 289; [2007] I.C.R. 1469 at [44]. See further para.8-10.
358 *Rice v Secretary of State for Business Enterprise & Regulatory Reform* [2008] EWHC 3216 (QB).

(ii) *Common law basis for duty*

Common law basis for a duty Just as the existence of a statutory power or duty does not generate a common law duty neither does it preclude such a duty.[359] In *Sandhar v Department of Transport*[360] May LJ, giving the leading judgment of the Court of Appeal, considered whether the "unvarnished" common law principles would justify a duty. The claimant's husband had been killed when his car skidded on an icy road which it was said the defendant should have gritted.[361] He said that in the case of omissions where the defendant does not directly inflict the personal or physical injury, common law principles required reliance by the claimant as a "necessary ingredient" of the duty and assumption of responsibility by the defendant was a "helpful guide". He rejected the claim as there was no evidence that the deceased had relied on the gritting process[362] or that the defendant had "assumed a general responsibility to all road users to ensure that all roads would be salted in freezing conditions". He commented: 13-68

> "an assumption of responsibility sufficient to create a duty of care normally requires a particular relationship with an individual or individuals ... a general expectation cannot alone support an assumption of responsibility."[363]

Compatibility with statutory scheme Though the existence of a statutory duty or power does not mean that no private law duty can arise, a growing body of case law suggests that in the context of a "statutory scheme" designed to benefit groups of people including potential claimants, no private law duty will arise unless it is compatible with that scheme. Thus the existence of the statutory duty will not in itself create an assumption of responsibility,[364] nor proximity with an individual claimant, but more generally, remedies at private law may not be considered compatible with the statutory scheme. What amounts to incompatibility is a difficult question but the availability of other means of redress (even if not as generous as private law remedies), or statutory provisions intended to achieve finality in decision-making, are indications that the private law duty is inappropriate. Key cases in these respects are *Rowley v Secretary of State for Work and Pensions*,[365] and *R. (on the application of Kehoe) v Secretary of State for Work and Pen-* 13-69

---

359 In *Gorringe v Calderdale MBC* [2004] UKHL 15; [2004] 1 W.L.R. 1057 at [38], Lord Hoffmann said "the fact that the public authority acted pursuant to a statutory power or public duty does not necessarily negative the existence of a duty". See also *Connor v Surrey County Council* [2010] EWCA Civ 286; [2011] Q.B. 429, where the breach of a recognised duty took the form of a negligent failure to act pursuant to statutory powers (para.13-10); *Rice v Secretary of State for Trade and Industry* [2007] EWCA Civ 1282; [2007] I.C.R. 1469 (para.13-67).

360 [2004] EWCA Civ 1440; [2005] 1 W.L.R. 1632.

361 The facts occurred in 1996. They were governed by the retrospective application of the decision in *Goodes v East Sussex CC* [2000] 1 W.L.R. 1356, to the effect that the duty to maintain roads under s.41 of the Highways Act 1980, did not extend to de-icing roads. Had the facts occurred after October 2003, they would have been governed by the prospective reversal of *Goodes* by s.111 of the Railways and Transport Safety Act 2003.

362 May LJ found that the terms of the defendant's widely distributed leaflet made a case of reliance unsustainable as the leaflet said: "You should never assume that a road has been salted." See [2004] EWCA Civ 1440; [2005] 1 W.L.R. 1632 at [44].

363 [2004] EWCA Civ 1440; [2005] 1 W.L.R. 1632 at [43].

364 See para.13-71.

365 [2007] EWCA Civ 598; [2007] 1 W.L.R. 2861.

sions,[366] but the influence of this reasoning is much broader. For example in *Murdoch v Department for Work and Pensions*,[367] some aspects of the claim were considered to be inappropriate subject matter for a private law duty because they amounted to questioning "protected decisions" (that is, decisions where the statute concerned showed an intention that the decisions made pursuant to it were to be final); other elements did not give rise to a duty of care because there was an available action for recovery of debts in the County Court, and the addition of a negligence action would add undesirable complexity. Further illustrating the approach and applying *Rowley* to a local authority performing its duty to allocate social housing is *Darby v Richmond Upon Thames LBC*.[368] The claimant's son, who had leukaemia, was housed with his sister and her baby. The deceased informed the local authority that he would be rendered vulnerable to infection by being housed with a young child but was not allocated new housing. When his sister and her baby contracted an infection, he developed influenza and died. No duty of care was owed to him by the local authority in allocating housing. Where a public authority is required to apply a statutory scheme there is no assumption of responsibility. In addition, the existence of remedies under the scheme indicated that a remedy in negligence would be inconsistent with the scheme; and provision of information (here, as to vulnerability to infection) did not of itself create a duty of care. The action was struck out. In *Home Office v Mohammed*,[369] the complaints (that permanent leave to remain had not been granted when, as a matter of formal policy, it should have been) fell within the Parliamentary Ombudsman's remit which may lead to a recommendation of compensation. This was one factor which persuaded the Court of Appeal that it was not a suitable case in which to allow incremental development at the margins of the law. A claim based on inconsistency with art.8 rights was held to be arguable in this instance and that claim too offered the possibility of an appropriate remedy.

13-70 **Failure to protect from third parties** In *Mitchell v Glasgow City Council*[370] Lords Hope and Brown identified a range of circumstances in which a defendant may be liable for harm done by a third party. Although the defendant was a public authority, these circumstances were of general application, since they describe the situations where common law principles may give rise to a positive duty to protect. Each identified broadly the same three categories of case where failure to protect from the acts of a third party may amount to breach of a duty of care and where, as Lord Hope put it, the imposition of such a duty will be "readily understandable":

(i) the defendant created the risk or danger that the third party may cause harm to the claimant;
(ii) the third party is under the control or supervision of the defendant, as in *Dorset Yacht v Home Office*[371];
(iii) The defendant assumed a relevant responsibility towards the claimant.

Foreseeability or likelihood of harm was insufficient to justify a duty to intervene

366 [2005] UKHL 48; [2006] 1 A.C. 42.
367 [2010] EWHC 1988 (QB); [2011] P.T.S.R. D3.
368 [2015] EWHC 909 (QB).
369 [2011] EWCA Civ 351; [2011] 1 W.L.R. 2862.
370 [2009] UKHL 11; [2009] 1 A.C. 874.
371 [1970] A.C. 1004.

to protect from third party acts: Lord Goff's opinion in *Smith v Littlewoods*[372] was correct on this point and is now authoritative in respect of omissions liability in negligence. The principles set out in Mitchell were regarded as of general application, and as guiding liability across the law of public service liability, in the Supreme Court's decision in *Poole BC v GN*.[373]

Assumption of responsibility An assumption of responsibility, if it is to dispel the usual principle against liability for omissions, must be specifically addressed to the risk or damage in question; and it must in some sense be genuinely voluntary. It has been held in a number of authorities that simply doing what a statute obliges the defendant to do will not form the basis of a voluntary assumption. Nevertheless, it was proposed in *Poole v GN*[374] that *conduct* in pursuit of a statutory duty may indeed give rise to an assumption of responsibility. It appears from the discussion of assumption of responsibility in *Poole* that there has been some broadening in what is encompassed in this notion in relation to public service liability. This is most likely a consequence of reinterpreting so much of the existing case law in terms of omissions qualified by assumption of responsibility: the notion must now fit a broader range of the decided cases. Prior to *Poole*, it was thought clear that something more than a general relationship between claimant and defendant must be shown if a voluntary assumption of responsibility towards the claimant is to reverse the general principle against omissions liability. The assumption would have to be specific, voluntary, and within the scope of the risk alleged. It must not merely replicate a statutory duty.[375] 13-71

Specific assumption Illustrating the first of the points in the preceding paragraph (the assumption must be specific), Lord Hope explained in *Mitchell v Glasgow City Council*[376] that a duty to warn would arise "only where the person who is said to be under a duty has by his words or conduct assumed responsibility for the safety of the person at risk". A specific assumption of responsibility may then be found to take the case outside the usual rule, which would otherwise dictate that there was no such positive duty. Hence, such an assumption is one of the three circumstances in which a duty to control the acts of third parties will arise. The general relationship of landlord and tenant will not suffice. Lord Brown emphasised that "A may be liable if he assumes specific responsibility for B's safety then carelessly fails to protect B".[377] Lord Rodger also envisaged that any effective "assumption of responsibility" would have to be specific and that the contractual and statutory powers and duties associated with the tenancy would not suffice: "The pursuers point to no undertaking or other circumstance which would show that, exceptionally, the Council had made themselves responsible for protecting Mr Mitchell."[378] Evidence of a specific assumption of responsibility was required. The principles in *Mitchell* were applied by the Court of Appeal in *X & Y v London Borough of Hounslow*.[379] The claimants were vulnerable adults who were subjected to appalling abuse in their 13-72

372 [1987] A.C. 241.

373 [2019] UKSC 25; [2019] 2 W.L.R. 1478

374 [2019] UKSC 25; [2019] 2 W.L.R. 1478.

375 See para.13-74.

376 [2009] UKHL 11; [2009] 1 A.C. 874 at [29].

377 [2009] UKHL 11; [2009] 1 A.C. 874 at [82]. Lord Brown identified *Costello v Chief Constable of Northumbria Police* [1999] 1 All E.R. 550 as an example of this.

378 [2009] UKHL 11; [2009] 1 A.C. 874 at [63].

379 [2009] EWCA Civ 286; [2009] 2 F.L.R. 262; [2009] N.P.C. 63.

own flat, of which the defendants were landlords, by young people who were known to be entering their home and one of whom had previously assaulted one of the claimants in a supermarket. The Court of Appeal emphasised that a high degree of foreseeability would not suffice, and that the case did not fall within the three categories set out in *Mitchell* where a duty to prevent harm being done by others might be owed. The judge (who had accepted that a duty was owed by the defendants) had erred in not asking himself a sufficiently structured set of questions along these lines; and in not seeking to identify a specific assumption of responsibility. Since the emphasis in cases of omission was on *specific* assumptions of responsibility, it would be essential to show that if an individual employee of the defendant had assumed a duty, that individual had also breached the duty. In this case, the only employee who might possibly be said to have assumed responsibility had clearly acted appropriately. However, in *Poole BC v GN*,[380] Mitchell was treated as having turned on the general principle that there was no assumption of responsibility on the part of a landlord for the actions of his tenants. Beyond this, it was significant that there are some cases in which performance of statutory duties or action in pursuit of statutory powers might give rise to an assumption of responsibility, and it was suggested that this was illustrated by cases such as *Phelps v Hillingdon*[381] and *Barrett v Enfield*.[382] It appears therefore that not all assumptions of responsibility will require to be specific in the sense discussed in *Mitchell*. This reflects the fact that assumption of responsibility was accorded a much broader explanatory role in *Poole* than has hitherto been recognised. There has been some expansion in the meaning of the expression at least in relation to the understanding to be found in *Mitchell*. In *Poole*, the Supreme Court considered first whether the general conduct of the local authority (in housing the claimant family) gave rise to an assumption of responsibility, finding that it did not. It was then considered whether there were specific actions of the authority which might give rise to an assumption of responsibility (the specific assumption): here, no sufficient facts had been indicated to suggest such an assumption. Therefore, there were two available routes to showing an assumption of responsibility, even where conduct is pursuant to a statutory duty.

13-73 Before *Poole*, it had been accepted that there is scope for duties to arise where a specific assumption of responsibility is found to exist in light of the defendant's conduct. The Court of Appeal thought that *Selwood v Durham County Council*[383] was arguably one such case, even though the assumption, if present, was to be inferred from the circumstances. Here, the claimant was a social worker who was attacked by a patient. She was involved in proceedings concerning the patient's two children, and the patient had made threats against her which, as in *Mitchell*, were not communicated to her. Smith LJ proposed that an assumption of responsibility might arguably be inferred from the working arrangements and protocols operating in the conduct of the case. Departing from the general inclination of the courts, the Court of Appeal also suggested that even in the absence of an assumption of responsibility, policy factors in this case might militate in favour of, rather than against, a duty of care. The circumstances were considered to be close to a relationship of employment, and this influenced the result. More typical is the decision in

380 [2019] UKSC 25; [2019] 2 W.L.R. 1478.
381 [2001] 2 A.C. 398; [2000] 3 W.L.R. 776.
382 [2001] 2 A.C. 550; [1999] 3 W.L.R. 79.
383 [2012] EWCA Civ 979; [2012] P.I.Q.R. P20. An art.2 claim was also not struck out.

Furnell v Flaherty.[384] Members of the Health Protection Agency had not assumed responsibility to members of the public and had no "proximate engagement" with those likely to be affected by an E-coli outbreak at a petting farm. The Agency was acting primarily for the public good and not in the private interests of affected individuals.

Voluntary assumption The second requirement identified in para.13-71 (responsibility must be voluntarily assumed and not simply imposed by statute) was clearly stated by the Court of Appeal in *Rowley v Secretary of State for Work and Pensions*,[385] giving effect to statements in *Gorringe v Calderdale*[386]: if a statutory duty which is not itself actionable gives rise to a duty at common law, that would be surprising. The need for a voluntary assumption independent of statutory duties formed the basis of the decision in *Sandford v London Borough of Waltham Forest*,[387] that the defendant council did not owe a duty at common law to provide aids and equipment which it had assessed should be provided. The provision of these items fell, in effect, within the statutory duty owed under the National Health Service and Community Care Act 1990, to undertake the assessment in question. Similarly in *St John Poulton's Trustee in Bankruptcy v Ministry of Justice*,[388] the duty of the court under the Insolvency Rules 1986, to send notice of a bankruptcy petition to the Chief Land Registrar, did not give rise to a private right of action. The duty arose through the operation of the Rules and not through anything said or done by the court or its officers. This was no more voluntary than the position of the bank served with a freezing order in *Customs and Excise Commissioners v Barclays Bank*,[389] and could not be interpreted as a voluntary assumption of responsibility. Similarly in *Seddon v Driver and Vehicle Licensing Agency*,[390] no duty was found to be owed by the DVLA to the purchaser of a classic car, who had relied on the vehicle registration certificate which stated that the car was a classic. The defendant was under a statutory obligation to issue registration certificates to collect the correct taxes and ensure all vehicles were registered. This obligation did not extend to a duty of care to prospective purchasers. Amongst other reasons, as the issue of certificates was not voluntary there was no voluntary assumption of responsibility, and the purchaser was seeking to rely on the document for purposes other than its statutory purpose (namely the collection of tax, the raising of revenue for the government and ensuring vehicles operating on the roads in the UK are registered).[391] The status of the requirement that the assumption must be truly voluntary is however doubtful following remarks of Lord Reed in *Poole BC v GN*,[392] drawing attention to Lord Hoffmann's stated opinion in *Barclays Bank* that conduct pursuant to a statutory duty might generate a duty of care in the same way as the same conduct undertaken voluntarily. Lord Hoffmann proposed that assumptions of responsibility may arise from conduct pursuant to an obligation in many contexts, including statutory obligations. 13-74

---

384 [2013] EWHC 377 (QB); [2013] P.T.S.R. D20.

385 [2007] EWCA Civ 598; [2007] 1 W.L.R. 2861. See also *Darby v Richmond Upon Thames LBC* [2015] EWHC 909 (QB).

386 [2004] UKHL 15; [2004] 1 W.L.R. 1057.

387 [2008] EWHC 1106 (QB); [2008] B.L.G.R. 816.

388 [2010] EWCA Civ 392; [2011] Ch. 1.

389 [2006] UKHL 28; [2007] 1 A.C. 181.

390 [2019] EWCA Civ 14; [2019] 1 W.L.R. 4593.

391 [2019] EWCA Civ 14; [2019] 1 W.L.R. 4593 at [58].

392 [2019] UKSC 25; [2019] 2 W.L.R. 1478, [72].

13-75 **Responsibility following creation of danger** *Kane v New Forest DC*[393] illustrates how a positive duty may flow from the creation of a danger by the defendant. The defendant authority gave planning permission for a footpath which ended on the inside bend of a main road where vegetation reduced a driver's visibility of anyone emerging from the path to 10m. The defendant was aware of the danger created by the path but had not taken steps to improve the sightlines before the claimant was hit by a car when emerging from the path. The lack of visibility meant the driver had no chance of avoiding the claimant. The Court of Appeal refused to strike out the claimant's action against the defendant. May LJ said that by constructing the path, the defendant (at [33]):

> "assumed a responsibility to those including the claimant who might use the footpath to see that it was not open until the danger was removed. That is an entirely orthodox application of common law principles of negligence."

He continued:

> "There is nothing in *Stovin v Wise* which suggests a different conclusion. In *Stovin* the county council had not created the hazard. In the present case the [defendants] had created the hazard. Nor on the facts of this case are the [defendants] immune from a claim in negligence because they were exercising a statutory function."[394]

A similar case is *Yetkin v Mahmoud*,[395] where a highway authority had created a danger through its positive action in planting shrubs in a central reservation, obscuring the claimant pedestrian's view of the road. In *Mitchell v Glasgow City Council*,[396] creation of a danger was recognised by the House of Lords as one of the categories where duties to act to prevent harm may be recognised. The case of *Att Gen of the British Virgin Islands v Hartwell*[397] was treated as falling within this category, since the police authorities had entrusted a gun to an inexperienced police officer who had shown signs of "instability and unreliability". The remarks in *Mitchell* therefore confirm that "creation of a danger" is a separate category of cases where imposition of a positive duty may be (to use Lord Hope's expression) "readily understandable".

13-76 **Borderline cases** In *Gorringe*[398] Lord Hoffmann cited two cases which illustrate the potential difficulty of determining whether there should be liability for a failure to act. The first case was *East Suffolk Rivers Catchment Board v Kent*.[399] The Board, which had a statutory power to repair a sea wall, undertook repairs so negligently that the claimant's land remained flooded for much longer than would

---

393 [2001] EWCA Civ 878; [2002] 1 W.L.R. 312.

394 [2001] EWCA Civ 878; [2002] 1 W.L.R. 312 at [33]. Dealing with the immunity point, May LJ went on to say:

> "It may be, depending on the facts, that the ordinary exercise of a statutory power to grant or refuse planning permission, would not create a duty of care at common law … But I reject the submission that a planning authority has blanket immunity from claims in negligence whatever the facts. That is simply not consonant with recent developments of the law both in this jurisdiction and in Strasbourg."

395 [2010] EWCA Civ 776; [2011] 2 Q.B. 827.

396 [2009] UKHL 11; [2009] 1 A.C. 874.

397 [2004] UKPC 12; [2004] 1 W.L.R. 1273.

398 [2004] UKHL 15; [2004] 1 W.L.R. 1057 at [41] and [42].

399 [1941] A.C. 74.

have been the case had the work been done with care. The majority of the House of Lords held that the Board owed no duty of care to act positively and hence, could not be liable for the inefficient action it did take. Lord Atkin famously dissented and Lord Hoffmann explained that the basis of this dissent was his view that "by going on to the land and commencing work, the Board had done an act which created a common law duty to complete the work with reasonable dispatch".[400] The difference between Lord Atkin and the majority was not over the principles, it was simply about whether the commencement of work was sufficient to give rise to the duty. The second case was the Court of Appeal decision in *Bird v Pearce*[401] where a highway authority was held liable for negligently removing warning lines at a road junction. The absence of warning lines contributed to the accident in which the claimant was injured. Lord Hoffmann said that the reasoning of the court "appears to have been that by painting the lines in the first place, the [authority] had created an expectation on the part of users that there would be lines to warn". He continued:

> "This may be a rather artificial assumption and I express no view about whether the case was rightly decided. But I would certainly accept the principle that if a highway authority conducts itself so as to create a reasonable expectation about the state of the highway, it will be under a duty to ensure that it does not thereby create a trap for the careful motorist who drives in reliance upon such an expectation."[402]

Rescue services Cases concerning the rescue services also illustrate the difficulty of determining what amounts to an undertaking of responsibility. In both *Capital and Counties Plc v Hampshire CC*[403] and *Alexandrou v Oxford*[404] it was held that the mere response by the fire or police service to an emergency call did not give rise to an assumption of responsibility sufficient to found a duty. However, in *Kent v Griffiths*[405] the Court of Appeal held the ambulance service did owe a duty of care when responding to an emergency.[406] Lord Woolf justified this on the ground that "it was not a case of general reliance but of specific reliance". By responding, the service had assumed a responsibility for the care of the patient. He distinguished the police and fire service cases saying: 13-77

> "The ambulance service is part of the health service. Its care functions include transporting patients to hospital … It is therefore appropriate to regard the [service] as providing services of the category provided by hospitals and not as providing services equivalent to those rendered by the police or the fire service."[407]

In *Capital & Counties*, Stuart-Smith LJ endorsed the view that a casualty depart-

400 [2004] UKHL 15; [2004] 1 W.L.R. 1057 at [41].

401 [1979] R.T.R. 369.

402 [2004] UKHL 15; [2004] 1 W.L.R. 1057 at [43]. Lord Scott explained the decision on the basis that by destroying the white lines the defendant had "created a potential source of danger that had not existed before" at [65]. May LJ in *Sandhar v Department of Transport* [2004] EWCA Civ 1440; [2005] 1 W.L.R. 1632 at [41], commented that the Lords in *Gorringe* were doubtful whether *Bird* was correctly decided on its facts.

403 [1997] Q.B. 1004.

404 [1993] 4 All E.R. 328.

405 [2001] Q.B. 36.

406 A doctor had called the ambulance service to take the claimant who suffered an asthma attack to hospital. The service responded negligently by taking 40 minutes to travel the short distance from the hospital to the claimant's home. The claimant suffered a respiratory arrest which would not have occurred had the ambulance not been so late in responding. Turner J held the service liable and the Court of Appeal affirmed his decision.

407 [2001] Q.B. 36 at 53. A further distinction, not mentioned by Lord Woolf, between the fire and health

ment "which closes its doors and says that no patients can be received" owed no duty of care[408] and added that:

> "likewise a doctor who happened to witness a road accident ... is not under any legal obligation [to assist the victim] and the relationship of doctor and patient does not arise. If he volunteers assistance, his only duty as a matter of law is not to make the victim's condition worse."

In the light of the distinction drawn between health services and the fire service in *Kent*, this view may need to be reconsidered.[409]

13-78 **Direct infliction of damage** Where the negligence of the public service has directly inflicted damage then a duty may arise under normal common law principles. The distinction between omissions and direct infliction is well illustrated by *Capital and Counties Plc v Hampshire CC*.[410] The fire service was held under no duty in respect of its mere failure to extinguish a fire because such conduct had not added to the damage which would have occurred if it had simply failed to attend the fire, but it was held under a duty in respect of its decision to switch off the sprinkler unit at the site of one fire because that directly added to the damage. If the fire service had never attended that fire, the sprinkler system would have limited its spread. By attending and switching off the system, the service had contributed to the spread of the fire. In *AJ Allan (Blairnyle) Ltd v Strathclyde Fire Board*[411] the Inner House of the Court of Session concluded that the policy-based, restrictive approach to public authority liability developed by the Supreme Court must also be applied in Scotland, so that earlier Scottish authorities had to be disapproved. In the instant case, the defendant fire board had attended to extinguish a fire in the roofspace of an outbuilding adjacent to a farmhouse and after a visual inspection, left the scene; the fire reignited and destroyed the farmhouse. The board was considered to have breached no duty of care as it had not assumed responsibility for containing and extinguishing the fire merely by attending; nor had it negligently inflicted fresh damage. Again, in *Knightley v Johns*[412] the police were held to be under a duty in respect of personal injury suffered due to their mishandling of a road accident whereas if the injury had resulted from their failure to attend the accident or take steps to prevent it, there would have been no duty.[413]

---

situations is that whilst fire damage is usually covered by insurance, health "damage" is not. A case of personal injury suffered as a result of a failure by the fire service to respond to an emergency call would test whether it was the health service or personal injury context in *Kent* which gave rise to the undertaking. Lord Woolf qualified the duty in one respect:

> "An important feature of this case is that there is no question of an ambulance not being available or of a conflict in priorities. I recognise that where what is being attacked is the allocation of resources, whether in the provision of sufficient ambulances or sufficient drivers different considerations could apply. There then could be issues which are not suited for resolution by the courts."

See further para.13-06.

408 Endorsing the view of Nield J in *Barnett v Chelsea and Kensington Hospital* [1969] 1 Q.B. 428.

409 In *Lowns v Woods* [1995] 36 N.S.W.L.R. 344; (1996) Aus. Torts Rep. 81–376, the New South Wales Court of Appeal did impose a duty on a doctor to assist a non-patient.

410 [1997] Q.B. 1004.

411 [2016] CSIH 3; 2016 S.C. 304.

412 [1982] 1 W.L.R. 349.

413 As is illustrated by *Ancell v McDermott* [1993] 4 All E.R. 355, where the police were held under

A contrasting decision is that of *OLL v Secretary of State for Transport*[414] where the coastguard undertaking a rescue not only misdirected their own lifeboat but also the Royal Navy helicopter. As a result there was a delay in reaching children whose canoeing trip had got into difficulties. It was argued that the misdirection to the Royal Navy was analogous to the turning off of the sprinkler in *Capital and Counties*, it made the situation worse than it would have been. May J rejected the argument on the ground that "[m]isdirecting other rescuers does not of itself inflict direct physical injury" and liability could not be imposed "by assessing a level of intervention which falls short of intervention which results in positive injury directly inflicted".[415]

(e) Standard of care

General To the extent that public services owe a duty of care, an important additional question concerns the required standard of care. The starting point as in other areas of professional work, will be the standard of the competent professional in the area of public service concerned. In *Phelps v Hillingdon LBC*[416] Lord Clyde suggested that "[a]ny fear of a flood of claims may be countered by the consideration that in order to get off the ground the claimant must be able to demonstrate that the standard of care fell short of that set by the *Bolam* test".[417] In *X & Y v London Borough of Hounslow*,[418] while emphasising that the relevant test for breach was the *Bolam* test, the Court of Appeal also underlined that even if the claim is that a *direct* duty of care owed by the public authority has been breached, a specific breach of duty (and therefore generally a specific individual in breach) had to be identified. Two issues which are likely to be of particular relevance are the ambit of the discretion given to the service and the resources available to it. In *Wembridge Claimants v Winter*,[419] Irwin J took the view that the *Bolam* test had no application to a claim arising out of decisions made while fighting a fire: "the problem is the speed and complexity of events, rather than making allowance for different intellectual or technical approaches".[420] 13-79

(i) Ambit of discretion

Discretion and reasonableness Given the discretionary nature of many public service decisions, the scope for differing judgments allowed by the *Bolam* test will be of considerable significance. The difficult balance between the freedom to exercise discretion and the importance of professional standards is reflected in the following comment of May LJ in *S v Gloucestershire CC*[421]: 13-80

> "In considering whether a discretionary decision was negligent, the court will not substitute its own view of that of the local authority … unless the decision was plainly

no duty to warn motorists of an oil slick of which they were aware.

414 [1997] 3 All E.R. 897.

415 [1997] 3 All E.R. 897 at 908. See further para.7-54.

416 [2001] 2 A.C. 619.

417 A case where the claimant had shown lack of care within the *Bolam* test in a child welfare case was *Pierce v Doncaster MBC* [2008] EWCA Civ 1416; [2009] 1 F.L.R. 1189.

418 [2009] EWCA Civ 286; [2009] 2 F.L.R. 262; [2009] N.P.C. 63; see para.13-72.

419 [2013] EWHC 2331 (QB).

420 [2013] EWHC 2331 at [223]. The case is currently under appeal.

421 [2001] Fam. 313.

wrong. But decisions, for example, of social workers are capable of being held to have been negligent by analogy with decisions of other professional people."

The complex nature of such decisions and the social importance of the service and its objective may also weigh heavily against the level of risk involved. In *Carty v London Borough of Croydon*[422] Dyson LJ said that where decisions were at the policy end of the spectrum a court is "unlikely to find negligence proved unless they are ones which no reasonable … authority could have made".[423] In *Carty* the decisions in question were matters of judgment and the Court of Appeal found there to be no negligence.

(ii) Resources

13-81 **Resources** One particularly difficult issue is the extent to which courts should take account of the resource constraints faced by public services when considering whether there has been a breach of duty. In *East Suffolk Rivers Catchment Board v Kent*[424] it was suggested that in the light of the resources available and the urgency of the situation, "much may be condoned as well-meant error of judgment, which under other circumstances might be considered unjustifiably risky" and in *Watt v Hertfordshire CC*[425] Morris LJ considered the fire station's lack of resources in terms of space and vehicles to be relevant. In *Knight v Home Office*,[426] dealing with the adequacy of facilities at a prison hospital, Pill J said that whilst the limited resources available for the public service had to be borne in mind as one factor:

> "It is not a complete defence to a government department … to say that no funds are available for additional safety measures … To take an extreme example if the evidence was that no funds were available to provide any medical facilities in a large prison there would be a failure to achieve the standard of care appropriate for prisoners."[427]

In *Walker v Northumberland CC*[428] in the context of the duty of a public authority employer to provide a safe system of work, Colman J said of the resources issue: "there can be no basis for treating the public body differently *in principle* from any other commercial employer, although there would have to be taken into account considerations such as budgetary constraints and perhaps lack of flexibility of decision-taking which might not arise with a commercial employer" but went on to comment that "the practicability of remedial measures must clearly take into account the resources and facilities at the disposal of the person or body owing the duty of care and the purpose of the activity giving rise to the risk of injury". Again, in *Hardaker v Newcastle HA*[429] Burnton J considered that a health authority's duty of care was qualified by the resources available to it. But this must be balanced by

---

422 [2005] EWCA Civ 19; [2005] 1 W.L.R. 2312.

423 [2005] EWCA Civ 19; [2005] 1 W.L.R. 2312 at [26]. See above para.13-10.

424 [1941] A.C. 74 at 97.

425 [1954] 1 W.L.R. 835 at 839.

426 [1990] 3 All E.R. 237.

427 Pill J concluded that the facilities in a prison hospital had to be measured against those to be expected in prison hospitals rather than those to be expected in psychiatric hospitals. However, his reason for applying this standard seemed to be based on not on the resources point but the difference in function of the two types of hospital, the central function of the prison being detention and that of the psychiatric hospital being specialist care.

428 [1995] I.C.R. 702; [1995] 1 All E.R. 737.

429 [2001] Lloyd's Rep. Med. 512 at [54]. See also *Ball v Wirral HA* [2003] Lloyd's Rep. Med. 165 at

the warning of Mustill LJ in *Bull v Devon AHA*[430] that:

> "it is not necessarily an answer to unsafety that there were insufficient resources to enable administrators to do everything which they would like to do … there is perhaps a danger in assuming … that it is necessarily a complete answer to say that even if the system in any hospital was unsatisfactory, it was no more unsatisfactory than those in force elsewhere."

3. LIABILITY UNDER THE HUMAN RIGHTS ACT 1998[431]

Impact of the Act in the area of tort liability Section 6(1) of the Human Rights Act 1998, which came into force in October 2000, makes it unlawful for a public authority to act in a way which is incompatible with a right set out in arts 2–12 and 14 of the European Convention for the Protection of Human Rights, and certain articles of the First and Sixth Protocols.[432] If a public authority has acted in a way which is incompatible with a Convention right, a victim is entitled to bring proceedings against the authority and the court may grant such relief including damages, as it considers just and appropriate, under ss.7 and 8 of the Act. The Law Commission[433] regarded this as creating a new form of tort action for breach of statutory duty. Constitutional tort might be another way of describing the area of liability. The House of Lords and Supreme Court, however, have emphasised the distinct character of the action under the Human Rights Act and have, in particular, separated Human Rights Act remedies from remedies in tort. As such, to call the action "tort" may be inappropriate or at least imprecise. Nevertheless, the statute clearly provides for new civil actions against public authorities in particular, which coexist with the common law of tort and often overlap with it. The growing familiarity of actions for damages under the Human Rights Act may come to place pressure on the law of tort to adapt, particularly where tort actions in the same circumstances are impeded by policy-based restrictions. 13-82

Public authorities Under s.6(3) a public authority includes "any person certain of whose functions are functions of a public nature". Thus, it includes not just the obvious public bodies such as central and local government authorities and the police but also bodies such as utility companies which have both a private commercial function and a public safety role. Those bodies which are "public" when performing some functions, but not otherwise, have been referred to as "hybrid" 13-83

---

[34]; and Jones, *Medical Negligence*, 5th edn (2018) paras 4–151 to 4–155.

430 (1993) 4 Med. L.R. 117.

431 See para.1-75 onwards, and note that the Act does not incorporate the Convention into domestic law, rather it creates domestic rights in the same terms of those in the Convention. Lord Hoffmann in *Re McKerr*[2004] UKHL 12; [2004] 1 W.L.R. 807 at [64], stressed the importance of understanding that the Convention and parallel domestic rights "belong to different legal systems, are owed by different parties, have different contents and different mechanisms for enforcement". See generally, Stanton, Skidmore, Harris and Wright, *Statutory Torts* (2003), Ch.5.

432 arts 1 to 3 of the First Protocol to the Convention and arts 1 and 2 of the Sixth Protocol.

433 *Damages under the Human Rights Act 1998*, Law Com No. 266, para.4.20. An alternative view is that the discretionary nature of the damages remedy suggests the Act creates a remedy for violation of the victim's public law rights rather than a remedy for a private tortious wrong. The Law Commissions' prediction that quantum of damages would for most purposes be modelled on the law of tort has not been taken up by the courts, which have modelled HRA awards on the quantum of Strasbourg awards.

public authorities. In *YL v Birmingham City Council*[434] it was held by the House of Lords that a private registered care home was not to be regarded as exercising functions of a public nature when providing accommodation for persons funded by a local authority. This decision was reversed by statute in the narrow context of its facts, and care homes providing accommodation together with nursing or personal care, in arrangements falling within the relevant statutory provisions, will now be treated as providing a function of a public nature.[435] In *R. (Weaver) v London Quadrant Housing Trust*,[436] a registered Housing Association was considered to be a public authority when terminating a tenancy. It has also been held that an independent inquiry is to be regarded as a public authority for the purposes of the HRA.[437] A court is itself a public body and this is significant to the extent that courts must act compatibly with the Convention rights. It has been suggested that the state itself is not the proper subject of an action under the Human Rights Act, so that the Crown cannot be held liable under the Act on the basis that there has been a breach, where no other liable public authority can be identified. There is a distinction between international law, and domestic law, and the provisions of the HRA create a liability on the part of public authorities rather than the state.[438] Supperstone J took the view that this interpretation survived statements of principle on the part of the House of Lords in *Al-Skeini*,[439] to the effect that the purpose of ss.6 and 7 was to enable remedies to be sought in domestic courts that would otherwise be available in Strasbourg; and that the Act should not be interpreted so as to defeat this purpose. However, successful actions have been brought against relevant Secretaries of State and against the Ministries of Justice and of Defence, for example. Beyond art.6, a number of other substantive articles have had an impact on the potential liability of public services with, for example, the right to respect for family life under art.8 having a particular impact on welfare and child care authorities, and the right to life (art.2) and liberty (art.5) having particular application in actions against police authorities. This section will first consider the relevance of art.6 to common law decisions, and then outline the relevance of a range of Convention rights to public service liability under the Human Rights Act. The broader relationship of the rights based jurisprudence of the Convention and the wrongs based pattern of the common law of tort, is considered in Ch.1.[440]

---

434 [2007] UKHL 27; [2008] 1 A.C. 95.

435 Health and Social Care Act 2008 s.145; repealed by Care Act 2014 and Children and Families Act (Consequential Amendments) Order 2015 (2015/914); and replaced by s.73 of the Care Act 2014. This section also applies to provision of personal care in a place where the adult receiving the personal care is living: where the conditions in the section are satisfied, this too will be a function of a public nature. Note also *Cameron v Network Rail Infrastructure Ltd* [2006] EWHC 1133 (QB); [2007] 1 W.L.R. 163, where it was held that the defendant was not a "core public authority" in relation to its maintenance functions.

436 [2009] EWCA Civ 587; [2010] 1 W.L.R. 363.

437 *Foreign and Commonwealth Office v Warsama* [2020] EWCA Civ 142.

438 *Morgan v Ministry of Justice* [2010] EWHC 2248 (QB), Supperstone J; applying remarks of Buxton LJ in *R. (Noorkoiv) v Secretary of State for the Home Department* [2002] EWCA Civ 770; [2002] 1 W.L.R. 3284; Lord Hobhouse in *Wilson v First County Trust Ltd (No.2)* [2003] UKHL 40; [2004] 1 A.C. 816; and of Lord Hoffmann in *Re McKerr* [2004] UKHL 12; [2004] 1 W.L.R. 807. The latter emphasised (at [63]) that the HRA creates domestic law remedies enforceable in domestic courts, distinct from the international law remedies available in Strasbourg.

439 *R. (Al-Skeini) v Secretary of State for Defence* [2007] UKHL 26; [2008] 1 A.C. 153.

440 See para.1-75 onwards.

(a) Article 6 and common law liability

The controversy Article 6 provides that: "In the determination of his civil rights and obligations everyone ... is entitled to a fair and public hearing ... by an independent and impartial tribunal." As with other articles, any departure from this right must be proportionate to the objective in question. Thus, for example, an executive certificate issued on grounds of national security, public safety and public order, which barred a contractor from complaining of religious discrimination under the Fair Employment (Northern Ireland) Act 1976 was found by the European Court of Human Rights (ECtHR) to be a disproportionate denial of access to the court for the determination of a statutory civil right.[441] The certificate was a procedural bar to what would otherwise have been a right to a hearing. As we have seen, in *Osman v UK*[442] the ECtHR applied art.6 to a bar which stemmed from the substantive law. The claimant's action against the police had been struck out by the Court of Appeal on the basis that the police owed no duty of care to citizens in relation to the prevention and detection of crime.[443] The ECtHR held that the application of this blanket exclusionary rule constituted a breach of the right to access to the courts and that it was necessary for the English courts to decide on the facts of each case whether the public interest in efficient policing outweighed the merits of the claim. This decision appeared to undermine the ability of the English courts to strike out actions on the basis of established substantive principles of tort law, so far as they were based in policy. However, in *Z v UK*[444] the ECtHR recognised that it had misunderstood the domestic law in its *Osman* decision. Citing Lord Browne-Wilkinson's explanation in *Barrett*[445] of the nature of tort immunities, the Court concluded that "the inability of the applicants to sue the local authority flowed not from an immunity but from the applicable principles governing the substantive right of action in domestic law".[446] Hence, there was no breach of art.6. **13-84**

The substantive/procedural distinction The decision in *Z v UK* recognised that the so-called immunity was substantive rather than procedural in nature and, hence, fell outside art.6. Similarly in *Rahmatullah v Ministry of Defence*[447] the Supreme Court determined that the doctrine of "Crown act of State" was a substantive, not a procedural bar to actions against the Crown, and that it was therefore not incompatible with the right to a fair trial guaranteed by art.6. The House of Lords reviewed the nature of this distinction in *Matthews v Ministry of Defence*.[448] In this case, the claimant had sought a declaration of incompatibility between art.6 and the immunity from suit granted to the Crown by a certificate issued under s.10 of the Crown Proceedings Act 1947. The House of Lords dismissed this argument, making it clear that art.6 did not arise for consideration in that case, given that the immunity granted by s.10 meant that there was no substantive right of action in the first place. Lord Walker, citing the view of the ECtHR that "it may be no more than a question of legislative technique whether the limitation is expressed in terms of **13-85**

---

441 *Tinnelly & Sons Ltd v UK* (1998) 27 E.H.R.R. 249.
442 (1998) 5 B.H.R.C. 293; see para.13-33.
443 An application of the policy-based reasoning in *Hill*: see above para.13-31.
444 [2001] 2 F.C.R. 246; [2001] 2 F.L.R. 612; (2002) 34 E.H.R.R. 3.
445 See para.13-14.
446 [2001] 2 F.C.R. 246; [2001] 2 F.L.R. 612; (2002) 34 E.H.R.R. 3 at [100].
447 [2017] UKSC 1; [2017] A.C. 649. See the discussion in para.13-11.
448 [2003] UKHL 4; [2003] 1 A.C. 1163.

the right or its remedy", concluded that "the uncertain shadow of *Osman v UK* still lies over this area of law".[449] In contrast, Lord Hoffmann said that the distinction between substance and procedure should not be drawn on the basis of formalistic comparison with the way the distinction is used in other areas of law, but with reference to the fundamental principles and purpose behind art.6. This was to protect the rule of law and the separation of powers. It was to prevent the executive intervening with arbitrary discretion to instruct a court to dismiss an action.[450] The purpose of the certificate system giving immunity from tort action was not to give the government an arbitrary power to stop proceedings, but to protect servicemen by ensuring that they received a pension. He took a similar view of the police immunity:

> "[A] rule that people should not be entitled to compensation out of public funds for loss suffered on account of a failure of the police to take reasonable care in conducting a criminal investigation poses no threat to the rule of law ... It may or may not be fair as between victims of negligent police investigations and victims of road accidents but it is not a question of human rights .... These are questions of policy to be developed by the courts, subject if necessary to correction by democratic decision in Parliament. They raise issues of, amongst other things, fairness, but not of human rights."[451]

13-86 In *D v East Berkshire NHS Trust*[452] Lord Phillips MR commented that the "*Osman* shadow" did not stretch "far enough to obscure the position in the appeal in question". That shadow has in any case now receded. As we have seen,[453] the courts are now less likely to use the law of tort to fill "gaps" in the protection of Convention rights, on the basis that the action and remedies under ss.7–8 of the Human Rights Act (considered in the next section) is designed to provide an appropriate domestic remedy in such cases. This has been the case even in those instances where the claimant cannot benefit from the Human Rights Act remedy, for example where the statute was not in force at the time of the alleged breach. Articles 6 and 13 therefore no longer seem to *compel* development in the law of tort. On the other hand, it remains arguable that the Convention rights might act as a source of inspiration or energy for the further development of the common law; or that the existence of such actions will increasingly come to undermine the emphasis on countervailing policy arguments, as they did in *D v East Berkshire NHS Trust* itself. As the adverse experience associated with *Osman v UK* recedes, there may be scope for further uses of the Convention rights in this way.[454] Article 6, like other Convention rights, may also form the basis of a claim against a public authority under the Human Rights Act itself. It is therefore further considered in the next section.

(b) Public authority liability under the Human Rights Act 1998

13-87 **General position** Breach on the part of a public authority of any of the Convention rights annexed to the Human Rights Act 1998 may give rise to an action in domestic law under s.7 of the Human Rights Act, and remedies prescribed by s.8

---

449 [2003] UKHL 4; [2003] 1 A.C. 1163 at [140].

450 [2003] UKHL 4; [2003] 1 A.C. 1163 at [29].

451 [2003] UKHL 4; [2003] 1 A.C. 1163 at [43].

452 [2003] EWCA Civ 1151; [2004] Q.B. 558 at [22]. See para.13-19.

453 e.g. para.13-25.

454 See the analysis by Arden LJ in the Hailsham Lecture 2009, "Human Rights and Civil Wrongs: Tort Law Under the Spotlight" [2010] P.L. 140.

may include a monetary award. If the claimant has secured a remedy in tort, whether in court or through a settlement, this may mean that they do not qualify for a remedy as a "victim" of a violation of Convention rights, as is required by s.7, modeled on art.34 ECHR. However, caution is needed in determining the effect of any settlement. In *Rabone v Pennine Care NHS Foundation Trust*,[455] the Supreme Court considered the Strasbourg jurisprudence on the influence of domestic remedies, finding that it was not easy to extract a clear statement of principle, and that a "broad approach" to the meaning of a settlement, in particular, needed to be taken. For a claimant to be deprived of the status of victim through acceptance of a settlement, the remedy achieved must be concerned with matters which form the basis of his or her Convention claim, and must afford "effective redress" for any Convention breach, including an acceptance that the right has been violated. In *Rabone* itself, the Trust's admission of negligence was, in effect, a sufficient admission in respect of the violation of the positive duty to protect life under art.2, since this violation itself took the form of negligence.[456] However, the settlement of a claim under the Law Reform (Miscellaneous Provisions) Act 1934 in this case did not provide adequate redress for the violation of art.2. This was in part because the settlement of the claim under the 1934 Act was at a lower level than the Court of Appeal found would be appropriate under the Human Rights Act 1998 (as also accepted by the Supreme Court), had liability under that Act been established, but partly also because compensation under the 1934 Act does not purport to compensate for non-pecuniary loss to relatives in the form of bereavement. The claimants here were the parents of an adult child, and therefore did not qualify for bereavement damages under domestic law. In comparison with other decisions of the English courts in relation to Human Rights Act remedies, this places greater emphasis on monetary awards, perhaps because of the particular "tort-like" context of the positive operational duty as it is continuing to emerge.[457] A considerable volume of case law has grown up around the actions under the HRA and around the interpretation of the Convention rights in domestic law, and this section is necessarily selective, concentrating on Human Rights Act claims which are most closely analogous to tort actions, often arising as alternatives or close alternatives to a tort claim in cases against public authorities.

Jurisdictional extent of the HRA: art.1 Article 1 of the Convention provides that contracting states will secure the rights and freedoms defined in the Convention to everyone within their jurisdiction. Prior to *Al-Skeini v UK*,[458] it was thought that the application of the Convention was essentially territorial, with defined exceptions. In *R. (Smith) v Oxfordshire Assistant Deputy Coroner*,[459] the majority of the Supreme Court also interpreted the Strasbourg jurisprudence existing at that time as stating that the rights and freedoms in the Convention could not be divided and tailored to particular circumstances. In both respects, the decision of the Grand Chamber in *Al-Skeini* has had a significant impact on this understanding, as was carefully explained in the judgment of Lord Hope (with the agreement on this point 13-88

455 [2012] UKSC 2; [2012] 2 A.C. 72.
456 See paras 13-89 to 13-92.
457 See further para.13-90.
458 (2011) 53 E.H.R.R. 18.
459 [2010] UKSC 29; [2011] 1 A.C. 1.

of all members of the Supreme Court) in *Smith v Ministry of Defence*.[460] In particular, three points were made by Lord Hope in relation to the current interpretation of art.1. In *Smith* itself, these points together led the Supreme Court to conclude that the state's armed forces overseas are capable of being within its jurisdiction for the purposes of art.1. First, the Strasbourg Court in *Al-Skeini* formulated a general principle with respect to state authority and control, designed to ensure that domestic courts would apply the general principle. The principle could therefore apply to circumstances which the Strasbourg Court itself had not considered, rather than simply explaining a range of exceptional situations. Secondly, the extent of the Convention is not necessarily "essentially territorial". Rather, the general principle is concerned with circumstances where the state had authority and control over the individuals concerned. Thirdly, the Grand Chamber departed from its earlier statements, to the effect that the package of rights in the Convention is indivisible. As a consequence, the court when considering an alleged breach of a Convention right, need not concern itself with the question whether the state is in a position to guarantee other Convention rights to that individual under the circumstances.[461] The decision in *R. (Smith) v Oxford Assistant Deputy Coroner*[462] was therefore departed from. Whilst unanimous on this point, members of the Supreme Court were divided on the question of how art.2 applied to the claims in hand.[463] In addition to claims brought by military personnel, the expanded jurisdictional extent of the HRA has enabled a series of cases to be brought by foreign citizens in respect of British military operations overseas.[464] There have, however, been limits set. In *R. (on the application of Hoareau) v Secretary of State for Foreign and Commonwealth Affairs*,[465] it was held that the decision in *Al-Skeini v UK* had not affected the position in respect of dependent territories. Here, the European Court of Human Rights had not found that the Convention extended to such territories in the absence of a declaration under art.56 by the contracting state. The court therefore applied the approach in *R. (on the application of Bancoult) v Secretary of State for Foreign and Commonwealth Affairs*,[466] holding that neither the Convention, nor the HRA 1998, extended to the Chagos Islands. In *Tomanovic v Foreign and Commonwealth Office*,[467] there was an alleged failure to investigate deaths occurring during the conflict in Kosovo. It was held that the actions of the head of the Kosovan prosecution service were not attributable to the UK, even though he was seconded from the

[460] [2013] UKSC 41; [2014] A.C. 52.

[461] [2013] UKSC 41; [2014] A.C. 52 at [49].

[462] [2010] UKSC 29; [2011] 1 A.C. 1.

[463] See para.13-93. For application of *Al-Skeini v UK and Smith* on this point, see *Kontic v Ministry of Defence* [2016] EWHC 2034 (QB): actions of UK troops in Kosovo were attributable to the U.N., not the Ministry of Defence, but irrespective of this, jurisdiction did not arise from effective control where troops were not in a position to secure the Convention rights, other than arts 2 and 3; and *Al-Saadoon v Secretary of State for Defence* [2016] EWCA Civ 811; [2017] Q.B. 1015: exception to territorial control founded on physical power and control did not extend to every situation in which a Convention party used physical force, but did cover a range of situations where there was an element of control over an individual prior to use of lethal force. During the post-occupation period in Iraq, the UK was exercising some of the public powers normally exercised by the Iraqi government and during this period, fell into the exception to territorial jurisdiction based on exercise of public powers.

[464] See the decisions of the Court of Appeal in *R. (Al-Saadoon) v Secretary of State for Defence* [2016] EWCA Civ 811; [2017] Q.B. 1015; para.13-101; and of the Supreme Court in *Mohammed v Ministry of Defence (No.2)* [2017] UKSC 2; [2017] A.C. 821; para.13-104.

[465] [2019] EWHC 221 (Admin); [2019] 1 W.L.R. 4105.

[466] [2016] UKSC 35; [2017] A.C. 300.

[467] [2019] EWHC 3350 (QB); [2020] 4 W.L.R. 5.

Foreign and Commonwealth Office, and that the provisions of the HRA did not apply.

Article 2: Right to life Article 2 of the ECHR, the right to life, often overlaps with the law of tort, particularly with actions in negligence and trespass to the person. The right to life may be breached in a case where the claimant survives, but where his or her life was endangered. Where states are concerned, the right to life can be said to give rise to at least three types of obligation. First, the State should not itself take life unlawfully; secondly, it should take appropriate steps to protect life; and thirdly, it should investigate appropriately where there is a death which may be thought to violate art.2. The second of these obligations, the duty to protect life, can itself be broken down into two types of obligation. The first obligation requires states to put in place general mechanisms, processes, and procedures for protecting life. An example of breach of this general obligation can be found in *Opuz v Turkey*,[468] where the framework in place in Turkey was found to fall short of an effective system for the prosecution of perpetrators of domestic violence. The second type of obligation relates to operational steps to protect life in individual circumstances where there is an imminent threat. It is this second version of the art.2 obligation to take positive steps to protect life which has most often arisen in parallel with the law of tort. In *Rabone v Pennine Care NHS Foundation Trust*,[469] it was suggested by Lord Mance that under the operational duty to protect life, the European Court of Human Rights "began to develop its own Convention rules of, in effect, tortious responsibility".[470] This created "the difficult line to be drawn between direct Convention rights and national tort law" such as the case in hand. However, a wider range of individuals may benefit from the action under the Human Rights Act, compared with the action in tort, as *Rabone* itself exemplifies. As with all claims under the Human Rights Act, the claimant must be a "victim" of the violation, and this is determined by reference to Strasbourg jurisprudence. In *Morgan v Ministry of Justice*,[471] a fiancée of the deceased was accepted to be a victim, and it was suggested that if she had not been engaged to the deceased, whether or not she was a victim would depend on the facts of the case. *Savage v South Essex Partnership NHS Foundation Trust* further illustrates that "victim" status is not connected to domestic law categories but considered on the facts of the case.[472] Here, the claimant was held to be a victim. In light of ECHR authorities, relevant factors were that "S was her mother to whom she was close", and that "much of her final illness centred around a deluded but sincere concern for the safety of the claimant".[473] The status of the claimants as victims had been doubted earlier by Lord Scott in *Savage v South Essex Partnership Trust*,[474] on the basis that it was not a function of art.2 to add to the class of persons who can seek compensation under domestic law for a death. However, any such objections were swept aside by the Supreme Court in *Rabone v Pennine Care NHS Foundation Trust*,[475] on the basis that the ECtHR had "repeatedly stated that family members of the deceased 13-89

---

468 (2010) 50 E.H.R.R. 28.
469 [2012] UKSC 2; [2012] 2 A.C. 72.
470 [2012] UKSC 2; [2012] 2 A.C. 72 at [121].
471 [2010] EWHC 2248 (QB).
472 [2010] EWHC 865 (QB); [2010] P.I.Q.R. P14; [2010] Med. L.R. 292.
473 [2010] EWHC 865 (QB); [2010] P.I.Q.R. P14; [2010] Med. L.R. 292 at [94].
474 [2008] UKHL 74; [2009] 1 A.C. 681 at [5].
475 [2012] UKSC 2; [2012] 2 A.C. 72 at [44]–[49].

can bring claims in their own right both in relation to the investigative obligation and the substantive obligation". Lord Scott had not considered the Strasbourg jurisprudence on the point. The very fact that art.2 therefore does indeed allow additions to the damages obtainable in relation to a tort involving the death of a family member underlines the significance of the developments in *Savage* and *Rabone* for the law of tort.[476]

13-90 **Positive operational duty to protect life** The relationship of art.2 and liability in tort was considered by the European Court of Human Rights in *Osman v UK*.[477] As already explained[478] the *Osman* case stemmed from the Court Appeal decision in *Osman v Ferguson*.[479] The applicants claimed that the failure of the police to take appropriate protective measures constituted a violation of art.2. The court held that the right to life implied "in certain well defined circumstances a positive obligation to take protective operational measures to protect an individual whose life is at risk from the criminal acts of another individual". To establish breach of this obligation it had to be shown that:

> "the authorities knew or ought to have known at the time of the existence of a real and immediate risk to the life of an identified individual from the criminal acts of a third party and failed to take measures within the scope of their powers which, judged reasonably, might have been expected to avoid that risk."

On the facts "it could not be said that the police ought to have known that the lives of [the claimants' family] were at real and immediate risk" and that having regard to the presumption of innocence, the police "reasonably held the view that they lacked the required standard of suspicion to use [their] powers". Hence, the conduct of the police did not violate art.2.[480]

13-91 Where the operational duty to protect life under art.2 is concerned, *Osman v UK* remains authoritative.[481] The operational duty of the police under art.2 was the subject of detailed consideration by the House of Lords in *Van Colle v Chief*

---

476 *Rabone* was applied on this point and the European jurisprudence examined in *Daniel v St George's Healthcare Trust* [2016] EWHC 23 (QB); [2016] 4 W.L.R. 32. The first claimant had acted as foster parent to the deceased, and would probably be regarded as an indirect victim, affected by the death even if not suffering material damage, as she had a continuing relationship with him. The second claimant, who was the biological son of the first claimant, would not however be regarded as an indirect victim as he had no formally recognised relationship or status in relation to the deceased. In this case, there was no breach of the art.2 duty and causation in the required sense (para.13-92) was in any event not established.

477 (1998) 5 B.H.R.C. 293.

478 See para.13-33.

479 [1993] 4 All E.R. 344.

480 Note: in *Doe v Toronto Commissioner of Police* (1998) 160 D.L.R. (4th) 697, the police knowing that a limited group of women were at risk of attack, preferred to set a trap rather than warning the women. As a result they failed to stop an attack. The Canadian court developed the common law sufficiently to impose liability as well as finding a violation to the right to security provision in the Canadian Charter of Rights. For commentary on *Osman* and *Doe*, see Hoyano, Policing Flawed Police Investigations (1999) 62 M.L.R. 912. See also *Hill v Hamilton-Wentworth Regional Police Services Board* [2007] 3 S.C.R. 129; (2007) 285 D.L.R. (4th) 620 (SCC), para.13-36; N. Rafferty, "The Canadian Supreme Court's approach to the duty question and the tort of negligent investigation" (2008) 24 P.N. 78–92.

481 The *Osman* approach was also applied to a claim arguing positive duties under art.8 in *Bedford v Bedfordshire CC* [2013] EWHC 1717 (QB); [2013] H.R.L.R. 33; [2014] B.L.G.R. 44.

Constable of the Hertfordshire Police.[482] The allegation in this case was that the defendant police authority was aware that a prosecution witness was being intimidated by the accused but failed to take action to protect him. He was murdered by the accused. The House of Lords accepted that a positive obligation to protect the life of a particular individual arises from art.2 where it is established that the authorities knew or ought to have known at the time of the existence of a real and immediate risk to the life of that person. The duty that would then arise is a duty to take measures which, judged reasonably, might be expected to avoid the risk. The claim was rejected, however, on the ground that it could not reasonably be said that the police officer involved should have apprehended the imminent threat of violence against the witness. No lower threshold of knowledge would be applied in circumstances where the conduct of the authorities had exposed the individual to the risk: the *Osman* test for the existence of the positive operational duty was invariable. In *Van Colle v UK*,[483] the European Court of Human Rights also concluded that there had been no violation of art.2, applying the test in *Osman*. It could not be said that the facts involved higher risk factors than in *Osman* itself. Two members of the Court, though concurring in the result, implied that *Osman* set too demanding a test and should be revisited. Although *Osman* has been said to set a high threshold for the existence of the positive duty,[484] it was stated in both *Van Colle* and *Savage v South Essex Partnership NHS Trust* that this should not be taken to refine the test in any way.[485] A similar conclusion in relation to both an NHS Trust, and a police force, where a woman (G) was murdered by her former partner, was reached in *Griffiths v Chief Constable of Suffolk*.[486] The NHS Trust, when considering whether to admit the former partner to hospital, did not know, nor ought it to have known, of any real or immediate threat to G's life; and there was not a sufficient basis for concluding that there was a risk to the general public. Equally, there was nothing to suggest to the police that there was an imminent risk to G. This was a weaker case than either *Osman* or *Van Colle*. An additional argument for the claimants, G's children, was that there was a protective duty under art.8, to protect G from harassment, and that such harassment was foreseeable. This claim was also dismissed: the Strasbourg jurisprudence did not permit a breach of the positive duties under arts 2 and 3 to be based on a failure to take steps required by art.8; and the police did not breach their duty under art.8.[487] In *Savage v South Essex Partnership NHS Foundation Trust*,[488] the approach of the House of Lords in *Savage* and *Van Colle* was taken to provide helpful guidance to a lower court; but the general method was to apply the approach of the Strasbourg court, described by Mackay J as: "to set out the facts of the case fairly fully, … state the test and then simply state its finding that violation of the article is or is not established". As with other claims based on Convention rights, if a breach of art.2 is shown then there is no need to prove causation in the English law sense: loss of substantial chance of survival is

---

482 [2008] UKHL 50; [2009] 1 A.C. 225.

483 (7678/09) (2013) 56 E.H.R.R. 23.

484 *Officer L, Re* [2007] UKHL 36; [2007] 1 W.L.R. 2135 at [20], per Lord Carswell.

485 *Van Colle v Chief Constable of the Hertfordshire Police* [2008] UKHL 50; [2009] 1 A.C. 225 at [30], per Lord Bingham; *Savage v South Essex Partnership NHS Trust* [2008] UKHL 74; [2009] 1 A.C. 681 at [78], per Baroness Hale.

486 [2018] EWHC 2538 (QB); [2019] Med. L.R. 1.

487 For discussion of liability for breach of art.8, see paras 13-111 to 13-120.

488 [2010] EWHC 865 (QB); [2010] P.I.Q.R. P14; [2010] Med. L.R. 292.

sufficient.[489] Indeed, art.2 may be violated where the person at risk survives. This too distinguishes the Human Rights Act claim, from the claim in tort.

13-92 The existence of two different types of obligation to protect life under art.2 was noted by the House of Lords in *Savage v South Essex Partnership NHS Trust*.[490] In light of the decision of the European Court of Human Rights in *Powell v UK*,[491] it was accepted in *Savage* that the operational duty to protect life in individual circumstances does not generally extend to ordinary negligence alleged to have been committed in the course of treatment in hospital. Such negligence is not sufficient to amount to a violation of art.2. But the situation in *Savage* was different because the deceased was suffering from paranoid schizophrenia and was being treated as a detained patient in an open acute psychiatric ward. She absconded from hospital and committed suicide by throwing herself in front of a train. The House of Lords concluded that the status of the deceased as a *detained* patient made the difference, as she was to be regarded as akin to a prisoner in custody in terms of her vulnerability and dependence. Her circumstances were similar to those in *Keenan v UK*,[492] where a positive operational duty to prevent suicide was recognised to exist. The claim should proceed to trial,[493] and the decisions in *Powell* and *Osman* were not incompatible: they simply dealt with different aspects of the positive duty to protect life. Subsequently, in *Rabone v Pennine Care NHS Foundation Trust*,[494] the Supreme Court found that the operational duty to protect life was owed to a psychiatric patient who was not formally detained. In this instance, the reality of the patient's situation was not markedly different from that of a detained patient. Given the control exercised by the defendant over the deceased, the difference between her situation and that of a detained patient was "one of form, not of substance".[495] In taking this route, the Supreme Court was extending the positive operational duty further than any decision of the Strasbourg Court at that time. Lord Brown, however, was at pains to point out that this was not a reversal of the general approach taken by the House of Lords and later the Supreme Court, most notably in *R. (Ullah) v Special Adjudicator*,[496] namely that the English courts should offer no greater protection of Convention rights through the HRA than was offered by the Strasbourg Court. Rather, this was a case where the Strasbourg Court had yet to rule on the relevant issues in the particular form in which they arose. Lord Dyson concluded, indeed, that the European Court of Human Rights would hold that the operational duty existed in this case. Notably, in *D v Commissioner of Police of the Metropolis*,[497] Lord Kerr regarded *Rabone* as a case signalling retreat from the *Ullah* approach, and as recognising that where there is no directly relevant decision of the ECtHR, domestic courts must reach their own conclusions. With this, he agreed: "Reticence by the courts of the UK to decide whether a Convention right has been violated would be an abnegation of our statutory obligation under sec-

489 [2010] EWHC 865 (QB); [2010] P.I.Q.R. P14; [2010] Med. L.R. 292 at [82].
490 [2008] UKHL 74; [2009] 1 A.C. 681.
491 (2000) 30 E.H.R.R. CD362.
492 (2001) 33 E.H.R.R. 38.
493 See *Savage v South Essex Partnership NHS Foundation Trust* [2010] EWHC 865 (QB); [2010] P.I.Q.R. P14 where Mackay J held that there had been a breach of art.2, on the facts.
494 [2012] UKSC 2; [2012] 2 A.C. 72.
495 [2012] UKSC 2; [2012] 2 A.C. 72 at [34].
496 [2004] UKHL 26; [2004] 2 A.C. 323.
497 [2018] UKSC 11; [2018] 2 A.C. 196; see para.13-102.

tion 6 of the HRA".[498] Several of the judges in *Rabone* referred to the developing nature of the positive operational duty under art.2, and its gradual extension since it was first recognised in *Osman v UK*.[499] Nevertheless, it remains the case that in the "generality of cases" involving medical negligence, there is no operational duty under art.2.[500] It is increasingly difficult to be certain of where the boundary between *Powell* type cases, governed by negligence law principles, and *Osman* or *Rabone* type cases will lie, given rejection by the Supreme Court of a bright line based on formal detention in this case. Subsequently, in *Reynolds v UK*,[501] the European Court of Human Rights found a violation of art.13, in conjunction with art.2, where the applicant's domestic claim in relation to the death of her son while in the care of a NHS Trust had been struck out. He had been a voluntary patient suffering with schizophrenia. There was little discussion of the applicable principles, other than by reference to the Supreme Court's decision in *Rabone*. The UK courts have therefore been at the forefront of developing Convention jurisprudence on this point.

A further development in the positive operational duty to protect life instigated by the UK Supreme Court is the recognition of such duties in the context of planning for and conduct of military operations in situations of armed conflict. In *Smith v Ministry of Defence*,[502] the majority identified the need to ensure that the positive obligations imposed on the state in this context are not disproportionate or unrealistic; and identified decisions that were essentially political in nature, or which were taken in the course of armed conflict, as unsuitable for review through an action under the Human Rights Act. However, the claims under art.2 should not be struck out: as with the claims in negligence, it would not be clear until hearing the evidence whether the positive obligation to take preventative operational measures had been breached. Lord Mance, in dissent, preferred to begin with the common law and particularly with the position (as he saw it) that no duty of care was owed in these circumstances. Strasbourg had not extended its jurisprudence in relation to positive operational duties under art.2 to circumstances analogous to this, and it would be wrong for the domestic courts to advance the jurisprudence in this way: "It should be for the Strasbourg court to decide whether it will review the procurement and training policy of the British army over recent decades in the context of claims under art.2".[503] The facts of *R. (on the application of Long) v Secretary of State for Defence*,[504] were said by the court to fall into the "middle ground" identified by the majority in *Smith v Ministry of Defence*, between high level command on the one hand and things done when engaging directly with the enemy on the other, where positive duties under art.2 might potentially arise. Here, the claimant **13-93**

[498] [2018] UKSC 11; [2019] A.C. 196 at [78].

[499] The "incremental" development of the positive duty was also referred to in *Daniel v St George's Healthcare Trust* [2016] EWHC 23 (QB); [2016] 4 W.L.R. 32. Following the Strasbourg jurisprudence, Lang J concluded that where detainees are concerned, medical practitioners, both inside and outside a prison setting, are subject to the art.2 duty, as well as prison officers and police officers. Equally, since it is the state which is subject to the operational duty, "it can apply not only to the detaining authority but also to other public authorities who from time to time may have responsibility for the detainee, such as a hospital or ambulance service" (at [29]). Here, however, there was no breach of the duty.

[500] [2012] UKSC 2; [2012] 2 A.C. 72 at [33].

[501] (2694/08) (2012) 55 E.H.R.R. 35.

[502] [2013] UKSC 41; [2014] A.C. 52 at [76].

[503] [2013] UKSC 41; [2014] A.C. 52 at [134].

[504] [2015] EWCA Civ 770; [2015] 1 W.L.R. 5006.

was the mother of a soldier who had been killed by civilians in Iraq in 2003. However, the court also pointed out that this did not mean that a breach of art.2 is arguable in every case that falls into the middle ground. Indeed, Lord Hope had explained in *Smith* that whether a case which falls within the middle ground engages or comes within the scope of art.2 is "much more difficult" than deciding whether it falls into the middle ground at all.[505] In *Long*, the duty argued for was to protect the lives of soldiers against negligent failure in the chain of command to ensure compliance with a particular order. The Court of Appeal rejected an argument that since the failure was the result of human error in the chain of command, it must fall outside art.2: this was a system failure by the military authorities to permit soldiers routinely to disregard the order, and this remained the case despite the role of human error. The Court of Appeal also rejected an argument that it was disproportionate to investigate why such a practice developed.

13-94 **By whom is the operational duty owed?** In *Mitchell v Glasgow City Council*,[506] the House of Lords unanimously held that a claim for damages under s.8 of the Human Rights Act 1998, based on a violation of the deceased's art.2 right on the part of the defendant council, should be struck out as irrelevant. Since the deceased was killed by a third party, the claim could only be based on breach of a positive duty to protect the deceased. Lord Hope applied the threshold test from *Osman v UK*, concluding that the Council had not been aware of any "real and immediate" threat to the life of the deceased which would trigger the positive duty. Lord Rodger added however that the positive obligation recognised in *Osman v UK* is not triggered in all circumstances where an authority should be aware of a "real and immediate" threat. Mr Mitchell was not in the custody of the Council, which had also not deprived him of his freedom of movement or in any other way assumed responsibility for his safety. In the absence of any such specific reason, it was not the Council but the Strathclyde Police Authority which had to have in place appropriate systems for preventing criminal violence, and who would be under an operational duty to protect the life of the deceased if they became aware of a real and immediate threat to his safety. This suggests that outside certain categories of case, only those authorities which discharge the state's general duty to protect life will come under the positive operational duty set out in *Osman*.

13-95 **Duties to investigate derived from art.2** In *Re McKerr*[507] the relatives of McKerr who was shot dead by members of the police, claimed that art.2 gave rise to a common law obligation on the minister responsible for the police to arrange for an effective investigation.[508] They argued that under s.6 of the Act, the court as a public authority was obliged to develop the common law in a manner consistent with Convention rights. In rejecting this argument, Lord Nicholls said:

> "I have grave reservations about the appropriateness of the common law now fashioning

---

[505] [2015] EWCA Civ 770; [2015] 1 W.L.R. 5006 at [12], noting also that Lord Hope had provided little assistance as to how this difficult question was to be determined.

[506] [2009] UKHL 11; [2009] 1 A.C. 874. The facts of the case are briefly set out in para.13-64.

[507] [2004] UKHL 12; [2004] 1 W.L.R. 807. See also *Ashley v Chief Constable of Sussex Police* [2005] EWHC 415 (QB), where the claim that there was a duty to investigate a police shooting was withdrawn in the light of *McKerr*. Claims in trespass and misfeasance in a public office, however, proceeded.

[508] The events occurred prior to 2000 and hence, s.6 could not be used as a basis for invoking the art.2 right.

a free standing obligation of this far reaching character. Such a development would be far removed from the normal way in which the common law proceeds. But I need not pursue this wider question. The submission fails for more straightforward, orthodox reasons. The effect of the submission would be that the court would create an overriding common law obligation on the state corresponding to Article 2 of the Convention, in an area of law for which Parliament has long legislated. The courts have always been slow to develop the common law by entering or re-entering a field regulated by legislation. Rightly so, because otherwise there would inevitably be the prospect of the common law shaping powers and duties and provisions inconsistent with those prescribed by Parliament."[509]

Although the common law will therefore not develop to provide a freestanding right to an inquiry, it is clear that the state nonetheless has an obligation arising under the Convention to investigate appropriately in the event of a suspicious death.[510] Where the art.2 rights of the deceased are in issue, any inquiry or inquest must therefore be "art.2 compliant". Following the ground-breaking decision of the Grand Chamber of the European Court of Human Rights in *Silih v Slovenia*,[511] holding that the investigative obligation is not ancillary to a particular death but may arise subsequent to that death, the impact of *Re McKerr* in respect of the investigative obligation has been fundamentally altered. The UK Supreme Court has now accepted that although the Human Rights Act 1998 does not have retrospective effect (a conclusion reached in *Re McKerr*), States are nevertheless under a freestanding and autonomous international law obligation to ensure that any investigation into a death satisfies the procedural requirements of art.2. This obligation applies to investigation of deaths occurring before the commencement of the HRA, just as it applied in *Silih v Slovenia* to investigation of deaths arising before the relevant State had accepted individual rights of petition to the Strasbourg Court.[512] In the latter case, where a decision had been reached after commencement of the HRA to investigate a death which had occurred before commencement of the HRA, it was appropriate for the Court to issue a declaration that the coroner was obliged to conduct the inquest in a way which satisfied the State's procedural obligation under art.2.

There is also a requirement that investigation into a death should begin promptly. **13-96**
In *Re Jordan's Application for Judicial Review*,[513] a claim was based on delay in beginning an inquest into a fatal shooting by the police in Northern Ireland in 1992. In 2001, the European Court of Human Rights had found a failure to carry out a prompt investigation, resulting in a breach of art.2. The victim's father sought a declaration and damages. The Court of Appeal in Northern Ireland appeared to hold as a general rule that a claim for damages should be dealt with once the inquest had fully concluded. The Supreme Court explained that there were countervailing reasons why, in a particular case, there should be no stay of a damages action based on delay. ECHR rights had to be applied in a way which rendered them practical and effective; the right conferred by HRA s.7 was a civil right within art.6, so that a claimant was entitled to have the claim determined within a reasonable time; and any stay of an action had to pursue a legitimate aim, bearing in mind its proportionality, to satisfy the art.6 guarantee of effective access to a court. There needed to be a balancing exercise, rather than a general rule, especially where

509 [2004] UKHL 12; [2004] 1 W.L.R. 807 at [32].
510 *R. (Amin) v Home Secretary* [2003] UKHL 51; [2004] 1 A.C. 653.
511 (71463/01) (2009) 49 E.H.R.R. 37.
512 *Re McCaughey* [2011] UKSC 20; [2012] 1 A.C. 725.
513 [2019] UKSC 9; [2019] H.R.L.R. 8.

claimants were elderly or infirm. It was unclear what decision the Court of Appeal would have reached if it had assessed proportionality and individual circumstances.

13-97 A duty to investigate under art.2 generally arises only if there is a suspected breach of substantive obligations under the article.[514] The operation of this general principle is illustrated by the decision in *R. (on the application of Long) v Secretary of State for Defence*.[515] The claimant argued that there should be an effective investigation into her son's death in active service in Iraq, pursuant to art.2. It was held that only if there was an arguable breach of the state's substantive obligations could an art.2 duty to hold an investigation arise. Where there is such a breach (or suspected breach), then in order to determine whether sufficient investigation has been carried out, the totality of the investigations available (including both criminal and civil proceedings, including proceedings in tort) should be considered. The duty has both investigative and accountability objectives. In *Pearson v United Kingdom*,[516] the content of the duty was clarified by the European Court of Human Rights. On the facts of that particular case, where the deceased had died some time after release from custody and where the allegation was effectively of carelessness on the part of the police and others, the pre-HRA style of inquest was capable of fulfilling the investigative element of the duty. It was also held that the accountability objective could be satisfied by the availability of a civil negligence claim. Notwithstanding the known limits to negligence actions in relation to public authorities, including the police, the Court considered that there remains sufficient scope for such an action to arise in a case where a "special relationship" is found to exist. The existence of exceptions to the *Hill* principle,[517] limited though they may be, is therefore also significant in the context of the investigative duty under art.2. Equally, the Court considered that the availability of disciplinary measures was also relevant to satisfaction of the accountability objective. The claim was therefore inadmissible. In *R. (on the application of Long) v Secretary of State for Defence*, prior investigations by an Army Board of Inquiry, and by a coroner's inquest, were between them sufficient to discharge the positive obligation to investigate a death where art.2 was engaged, since the relevant facts and the lessons to be learned had been sufficiently revealed by these investigations. Further, while the duty to investigate is a continuing one, there was no reasonable prospect that there could be further lessons to be learnt from the events of 2003.

13-98 **Article 3: Prohibition on inhuman or degrading treatment** Although art.3 differs from art.2 in that it does not provide for any exceptions from the negative duty to refrain from inflicting torture or inhuman or degrading treatment,[518] in other respects there are similarities between the two. In particular, art.3 is recognised to give rise to certain positive obligations to protect people from inhuman or degrad-

---

514 See, however, *R. (on the application of Letts) v Lord Chancellor* [2015] EWHC 402 (Admin); [2015] 1 W.L.R. 4497, suggesting that there is an important category of cases where the duty to investigate arises automatically, irrespective of evidence of breach of the substantive obligation on the part of the state; and that suicides by detained mental patients fall into this category.

515 [2015] EWCA Civ 770; [2015] 1 W.L.R. 5006.

516 (40957/07) (2012) 54 E.H.R.R. SE11.

517 See paras 13-40 to 13-42.

518 It does however require that a threshold of seriousness is passed. A case where the threshold was discussed, and found to be passed, is *ZH v Commissioner of Police of the Metropolis* [2013] EWCA Civ 69; [2013] 1 W.L.R. 3021 (police harshly restraining a severely autistic and epileptic teenager at a swimming pool).

ing treatment,[519] and these positive duties are not absolute, but will be discharged through taking appropriate steps. *Z v UK*[520] illustrates the existence of the positive duty. This case concerned a complaint by the children whose claims had been rejected by the House of Lords in *Bedfordshire*. The European Court of Human Rights held that the failure of the child care authorities to intervene to prevent long term neglect of children amounted to degrading treatment of children under art.3. The UK was also found to be in breach of art.13 which provides that everyone whose rights and freedoms are set out shall have "an effective remedy before a national authority". The rejection of their claim by the House of Lords meant there was no effective remedy before the national authority. Subsequent to the commencement of the Human Rights Act in October 2000, someone in their position would have an effective claim for breach of art.3 against the public authority under s.6(1) of the Act. The recognition in *D v East Berkshire NHS Trust*[521] that authorities may owe a duty of care to children also enables courts to provide an effective remedy at common law which will overlap with that under s.8 for breach of art.3.

Breadth of the positive duty The potential breadth of the positive duty to protect against infliction of inhuman or degrading treatment is illustrated by *R. (B) v DPP*.[522] The claimant had been subjected to a serious assault in which part of his ear was bitten off. He had a history of psychotic illness and suffered from hallucinations and paranoid beliefs. On the basis of a medical report, the Crown Prosecution Service formed the view that he would not make a credible witness and there was no reasonable prospect of a conviction. As such, no evidence was offered against the accused at trial and the jury was directed to acquit. Toulson LJ (with the agreement of Forbes J) held that the Crown Prosecution Service had misapplied the Code for Crown Prosecutors, in that it had applied a purely "predictive" approach to whether a jury might convict, rather than asking a more "merits-based" question, which appears to require consideration of what a reasonable fact-finder would conclude (or what the Prosecutor himself might conclude about the sufficiency of the evidence). The decision was in breach of art.3 because it deprived the claimant of the opportunity of the proceedings running their proper course and caused him to feel he was beyond the effective protection of the law. The Court made clear however that it was invoking the positive obligation to protect against inhuman or degrading treatment. **13-99**

Content of the positive duty The content of the positive duty under art.3 is indicated by the decision of the House of Lords in *E v Chief Constable of the Royal Ulster Constabulary*.[523] During several months in 2001, "loyalist" protesters in Belfast tried to stop Roman Catholic children and parents taking their normal route on foot through a loyalist area to a Catholic girls' primary school. The parents and children were confronted by a hostile mob which shouted threats and obscenities and threw missiles (including an explosive device) at them. Several police officers and soldiers were injured, some seriously, though the children escaped physical **13-100**

---

[519] Similar investigative duties to those arising under art.2 have also been held to arise in relation to breaches of arts 3 and 4: *O v Commissioner of Police for the Metropolis* [2011] EWHC 1246 (QB); [2011] H.R.L.R. 29; para.13-101.

[520] [2001] 2 F.C.R. 246; [2001] 2 F.L.R. 612; (2002) 34 E.H.R.R. 3.

[521] [2003] EWCA Civ 1151; [2004] Q.B. 558. See also *McGlinchey v United Kingdom* [2003] Lloyd's Rep. Med. 264, and para.13-19.

[522] [2009] EWHC 106 (Admin); [2009] 1 W.L.R. 2072.

[523] [2008] UKHL 66; [2009] 1 A.C. 536.

injury. The applicant (one of the parents) argued that the action taken to protect them and the children was inadequate, and invoked arts 3 and 14 ECHR. The Constabulary accepted that some of the protestors' activities were sufficiently extreme to engage art.3. The House of Lords dismissed an appeal and rejected the claims. In respect of art.3, the absolute obligation not to cause inhuman or degrading treatment did not extend to preventing others from inflicting such treatment. Rather, art.3 required the state and public authorities to do "all that could reasonably be expected of them" to prevent the infliction of such treatment by others. Proportionality would be applied in judging whether, in all the circumstances, the steps taken were reasonable and the duty thus discharged: the traditional public law test for "unreasonableness" would not be adequate for this purpose. In this case, the police had used information available to them and assessed the likely consequences of taking any other action, and the duty to do all that could reasonably be expected had been discharged.

13-101 **Positive duty to investigate** An important area for claims against public authorities in terms of art.3 concerns conditions of detention. In *R. (K) v Secretary of State for the Home Department*,[524] the Court of Appeal found that art.3 was engaged where the claimant had been caught up in the effects of a riot in an immigration centre; and went on to hold that a duty to investigate analogous to the duty under art.2 arises from the art.3 right. In this case, the Home Department should therefore have investigated the conditions endured by the claimant. However, a declaration to this effect was said to be a sufficient remedy under s.8 of the Human Rights Act. Further consideration was given to the duty to investigate, and particularly to its scope, in *O v The Commissioner of Police for the Metropolis*.[525] This was a claim brought by the victims of trafficking, in respect of art.3, and also art.4 (right not to be placed in slavery or servitude). The claimants were brought illegally to the UK from Nigeria and forced to work without pay. They were also subjected to regular violence. It was accepted that there had been breaches of their rights under arts 3 and 4 on the part of the traffickers. In an action against the police, Wyn Williams J upheld their claim that there had been breaches of the positive duty to investigate, and awarded a declaration and damages under s.8 accordingly. In determining the scope of the duty to investigate, he considered the common law could not assist because, for policy reasons, no positive duties to investigate could be said to exist in the law of England and Wales. It was apparent from the decision of the House of Lords in *Van Colle v Chief Constable of Hertfordshire*[526] that duties to protect Convention rights were to be considered according to Strasbourg principles not by attention to common law, and the policy reasons which lay behind the limitations to common law could not be said to be applicable to actions for violation of Convention rights. Since *Osman v UK* was concerned with the preventive duty under art.2 rather than the duty to investigate events that had already occurred, the leading authority was *Rantsev v Cyprus*.[527] The reasoning in Rantsev was equally applicable to arts 3 and 4. Important principles which emerged from this were that the existence of a duty does not depend on a complaint from the victim or a next of kin, and is triggered when a credible allegation of an infringement of the rights has been made to the police; that the duty may arise even where no victim is identi-

524 [2009] EWCA Civ 219; [2009] U.K.H.R.R. 973.
525 [2011] EWHC 1246 (QB); [2011] H.R.L.R. 29.
526 [2008] UKHL 50; [2009] 1 A.C. 225.
527 (25965/04) (2010) 51 E.H.R.R. 1.

fied by name, though this will be a relevant factor; and that the duty to investigate carries with it a duty to investigate promptly and/or with reasonable expedition.[528] There was no basis for suggesting that a failure to investigate is a breach only where the failure is "egregious". In *R. (Al-Saadoon) v Secretary of State for Defence*[529] the Court of Appeal considered the duty to investigate under art.3 in conditions of armed conflict and occupation. The state did not have a duty to investigate whenever there was a breach of the principle that detainees would not be transferred where was a real risk of torture or other mistreatment; but in principle there would be a duty to investigate where the state transferring the detainee was complicit in torture or other serious mistreatment falling within art.3. What was required of any particular investigation would be highly fact-sensitive. Positive duties to investigate may also arise in some cases of deprivation of liberty under art.5, particularly where an individual within the jurisdiction of a Convention state is the subject of "enforced disappearance" (a concept that is defined in international law).

Article 3 and failure to investigate In *Ruddy v Chief Constable of Strathclyde*,[530] **13-102**
the Supreme Court considered and rejected procedural objections to a damages claim based on violations of art.3, both in relation to an alleged assault by police officers and in relation to an alleged failure to investigate. The Courts below in Scotland had rejected the claims as irrelevant, on the basis that they involved a disguised attempt to challenge decisions through a claim for damages, whereas a judicial review action would be the appropriate course. The Supreme Court drew attention to the fact that the allegations were all of completed acts or failures to act. The applicant was not seeking to have decisions corrected, but was seeking just satisfaction for breach of art.3 rights.[531] Notably, these features also resemble an action in tort. The capacity of the positive duty under art.3, modelled on *Osman v UK*, to allow claimants to by-pass the limitations on claims for police negligence outlined in earlier paragraphs is underlined by the case of *D v Commissioner of Police for the Metropolis*.[532] The police in this instance were held to have breached their duties to investigate a series of violent crimes against women. Rapes and sexual assaults were crimes which fell within the protection of art.3. The Human Rights Act 1998 imposed on the state a duty rigorously to enforce laws which prohibited conduct constituting a violation of art.3, and this required that complaints of ill-treatment amounting to a violation of art.3 be properly investigated. This duty arose even where non-state agents were responsible for the infliction of harm. Further, this would not only be breached by failures which were at a systemic level; serious failures which were merely operational could suffice to breach the positive duty, provided those failures were "egregious" and significant. As Lord Neuberger put it, if there is a duty to investigate, this should be understood to be a duty to investigate effectively.[533] Here, both structural and systemic, and operational failures could be identified, and the judge had correctly identified that an award of damages under the HRA was justified. The considerations which militated against police liability in negligence for failures in investigation did not apply to a claim under the HRA, since the basis of liability was in each case different. Given that it

[528] [2011] EWHC 1246 (QB); [2011] H.R.L.R. 29 at [152], [162]–[164].
[529] [2016] EWCA Civ 811; [2017] Q.B. 1015.
[530] [2012] UKSC 57; 2013 S.C. (U.K.S.C.) 126; [2013] H.R.L.R. 10.
[531] [2012] UKSC 57; 2013 S.C. (U.K.S.C.) 126; [2013] H.R.L.R. 10 at [15].
[532] [2018] UKSC 11; [2019] A.C. 196.
[533] [2018] UKSC 11; [2019] A.C. 196 at [92].

had been decided that the common law duty should not be adapted to harmonise with the ECHR, "so should the latter duty remain free from the influence of the pre-HRA domestic law".[534] Further, there was no room in relation to the HRA for such complexities as the notion of "proximity", which were relevant to negligence actions at common law, nor for the notion of what was "fair, just and reasonable". The issue was simpler: did the state fail to comply with its protective obligation under art.3? Either the police had a protective duty under art.3, or they did not.[535] Thus, the Supreme Court was undeterred by the fact that a duty was here recognised in circumstances very close to the core of the *Hill* principle.[536] The decision maintains the potential of actions under the HRA to provide remedies in circumstances where the common law will not, and which would traditionally be pursued through the common law of tort.

13-103 **Article 5: Right to liberty and security** The right to liberty in art.5 is qualified by the provision for lawful arrest and detention, but only for certain specified purposes. The stated purposes in art.5(1) do not include prevention of a breach of the peace, which is recognised (within bounds) as a relevant defence to false imprisonment at common law.[537] In *Austin v Commissioner of the Metropolitan Police*,[538] the Court of Appeal held that the detention of individuals for a period of seven hours in Oxford Circus, in order to keep them contained and avoid a breach of the peace, was an "imprisonment" at common law, but that it was justified and therefore not a false imprisonment. One of the claimants was a protestor, but was not herself thought to pose a threat of breach of the peace. The other claimant was a passer-by who had been caught up in the police action. Under art.5 however, the Court took the view that the detention did not amount to a deprivation of liberty at all. Article 5 applies only to *arbitrary* deprivations of liberty. On appeal to the House of Lords,[539] the false imprisonment claim did not arise for consideration,[540] and the claimant who had not intended to take part in the demonstration played no further part. Counsel for the remaining claimant conceded that if the art.5 claim failed, so too would the claim at common law.[541] The House of Lords, like the Court of Appeal, found that there was no violation of art.5, because there was no deprivation of liberty within the meaning of that article. Lord Hope considered that the Convention as a whole, and thus art.5 in particular, should be understood as effecting a pragmatic balance between individual rights and the public interest. The reason for this approach is that the detention, if it did amount to a restriction of liberty within the terms of art.5, would not come within the terms of any of the legitimate exceptions which are exhaustively listed in art.5(1).[542] In *Austin v UK*,[543] a majority of the Grand Chamber of the European Court of Human Rights

---

[534] [2018] UKSC 11; [2019] A.C. 196 per Lord Kerr at [68].

[535] [2018] UKSC 11; [2019] A.C. 196 per Lord Kerr at [69] and [70].

[536] See para.13-31 onwards.

[537] The bounds of the common law power to detain in order to prevent a breach of the peace were closely defined by the House of Lords in *R. (Laporte) v Chief Constable of Gloucestershire Constabulary* [2006] UKHL 55; [2007] 2 A.C. 105 (see paras 14-54 onwards).

[538] [2007] EWCA Civ 989; [2008] Q.B. 660.

[539] [2009] UKHL 5; [2009] 1 A.C. 564.

[540] Detailed consideration of false imprisonment including its role in police cases will be found in Ch.15.

[541] This concession seems inconsistent with the reasoning in the Court of Appeal: see further para.14-64.

[542] For critical comment see D. Feldman [2009] C.L.J. 243.

[543] (39692/09) (2012) 55 E.H.R.R. 14.

concluded that there had been no violation of art.5(1). The reasoning of the majority was generally compatible with the analysis of the House of Lords in *Austin v Commissioner of Police of the Metropolis*.[544] The majority emphasised that the Convention must be read as a whole and interpreted so as to promote internal consistency and harmony between its provisions. It referred to the existence of other provisions offering qualified protection to freedom of movement (art.2, Protocol 4, which has not been ratified by the UK), where public order reasons may justify restrictions; and to freedom of assembly (art.11), where the Court has held that restrictions may be justified for the prevention of disorder or crime, or in order to protect the rights and freedoms of others. Equally, it was noted that arts 2 and 3 imply positive obligations on the authorities to take preventive operational measures to protect individuals at risk of serious harm. The underlying principle of art.5, on the other hand, was said to be the protection of the individual from arbitrariness, and the "fundamental" right involved was "protection of the individual against arbitrary interference by the State with his or her liberty".[545] Where restrictions on movement did not follow the "paradigm" of confinement in a cell, the Court could address the specific context and circumstances of the restrictions. Applying these principles to the specific circumstances of this case, there was no reason to depart from the finding of Tugendhat J that the cordon represented the least intrusive and most effective means of averting a real risk of serious injury to people within the crowd. Since the police had consistently attempted to initiate a safe release of individuals beginning five minutes after the initial cordon was completed, in each case being prevented by disorder within the crowd from effecting a safe release, the Court could not identify at what point "restriction on movement" could be said to have become a deprivation of liberty. On the "exceptional" facts of the case, there was no deprivation of liberty within the terms of art.5(1). The three dissenting judges took the view that the majority had allowed a legitimate public interest to justify a restriction of liberty despite the absence of any such potential justification from the terms of art.5 itself. By contrast, the emphasis of the majority was, like that of the domestic courts, on interpreting the reach of art.5 in the context of the Convention as a whole. The majority reached the important conclusion that the fundamental nature of the art.5 right was a reason not to interpret its reach too broadly.

Article 5(1) and military operations The extension of the territorial application of the ECHR in *Al-Skeini v UK*[546] raised the question of whether art.5 of the Convention was well suited to the circumstances of military intervention, including peace-keeping operations. In *Hassan v United Kingdom*,[547] the detention of a civilian in Iraq for a period of nine days did not fall within any of the six exhaustive permitted grounds of detention under art.5(1). Nevertheless, the Grand Chamber of the European Court of Human Rights held that the detention did not violate art.5. Article 5(1) had to be adapted to circumstances in which international humanitarian law provided relevant safeguards against arbitrary detention. In *Mohammed v Ministry of Defence (No.2)*[548] the Supreme Court applied *Hassan* to a case where the military operation was not international in nature, arguing that the 13-104

[544] [2009] UKHL 5; [2009] 1 A.C. 564.
[545] (2012) 55 E.H.R.R. 14 at [60].
[546] (2011) 53 E.H.R.R. 18; see para.13-88.
[547] (2014) 38 B.H.R.C. 358.
[548] [2017] UKSC 2; [2017] A.C. 821. The decision included the leapfrog appeal from *Al-Waheed v*

reasoning in *Hassan* applied in the same way. In this instance, authority for the detention was derived from relevant Security Council Resolutions, and art.5(1) had to adapt to these Resolutions: detention was justified when it was required for imperative reasons of security. Following *Hassan*, the "fundamental purpose" of art.5(1) was to guard against arbitrariness.[549] As detention was subject to the terms of the Security Council Resolutions, it was not arbitrary. The exhaustive list of cases in art.5(1) had to yield to these different circumstances, if Convention states are to play a part in peace-keeping operations. *Hassan* is not to be read as adding a seventh permitted ground for detention, namely military detention in armed conflict. Rather, "[i]ts effect is … to recognise that sub-paragraphs (a) to (f) cannot necessarily be regarded as exhaustive when the Convention is being applied to such a conflict, because their exhaustive character reflects peacetime conditions".[550] There had been no breach of art.5(1) in the case of *Al-Waheed*, and the lawfulness of detention would be ascertained at trial in the case of *Mohammed*.[551] The majority Justices were divided on the question of whether a breach of the procedural requirement in art.5(4) had been established, or whether this could only be determined at trial. Lord Sumption argued that breach had been established, but that this need not necessarily lead to an award of damages.[552]

13-105 **Quashed convictions** In *Webster v Lord Chancellor*,[553] the Court of Appeal emphasised that art.5 is not intended to provide compensation to those whose convictions have been quashed on appeal, having initially been reached by a lawfully constituted court. Applying *Benham v UK*,[554] imprisonment following the claimant's earlier conviction could only be a breach of art.5(1) if the court had: (1) acted without jurisdiction over the cause; (2) exercised its powers in a manner that involved a "gross and obvious irregularity"; or (3) made an order that had no proper foundation in law because of a failure to observe a "statutory condition precedent". Other than in these circumstances, a period of detention will, according to the Court in *Benham v UK*, in principle be lawful if carried out pursuant to a court order. In the present case, the claimant's conviction was quashed, because of misdirections by the trial judge, after the claimant had served two years of his sentence. Section 9(3) HRA specifies that no damages may be awarded under the Act in respect of judicial acts done in good faith. The claimant failed to establish, for the purposes of a claim under art.6, that there had been an absence of good faith on the part of the judge. He also claimed there had been a breach of art.5 in relation to his subsequent imprisonment. Section 9(3) defines an exception in the case of compensation required by art.5(5) of ECHR; but the claimant failed to establish that there had been a "gross and obvious irregularity" sufficient to satisfy the principles set out in *Benham*. Neither claim, therefore, could succeed.[555] An analogous case

Ministry of Defence [2014] EWHC 2714 (QB).

549 [2017] UKSC 2; [2017] A.C. 821 at [63] (Lord Sumption). This has strong echoes of the reasoning of the House of Lords in *Austin v Commissioner of Metropolitan Police* [2009] UKHL 5; [2009] 1 A.C. 564, para.13-103.

550 [2017] UKSC 2; [2017] A.C. 821 at [68].

551 Lords Reed and Kerr JJSC dissented.

552 See further para.13-107.

553 [2015] EWCA Civ 742; [2016] Q.B. 676.

554 (1996) 22 E.H.R.R. 293.

555 To similar effect, see *Wright v Lord Chancellor* [2015] EWHC 1477 (QB): a sentence was unlawful but there had been no irregularity sufficient to amount to a breach of art.5.

is *R. (on the application of Brooks) v Independent Adjudicator*.[556] A young offender had been sentenced to an additional 11 days' custody but this was quashed on judicial review. Since the additional days had been imposed in accordance with a judicial procedure, there had been no breach of art.5(1).

Delay and time limits Article 5(3) provides that everyone arrested or detained "shall be brought promptly before a judge ... and shall be entitled to trial within a reasonable time or to release pending trial". In *Olotu v Home Office*[557] the Court of Appeal held that a person detained on remand beyond the 112 day limit in the relevant statutory regulations was not unlawfully detained and falsely imprisoned. Such a period of detention may nevertheless fall foul of art.5(3). On the other hand in *McCreaner v Ministry of Justice*,[558] a negligence claim brought by an existing prisoner succeeded in circumstances where detention was lawful and claims in false imprisonment and under art.5 therefore both failed. In *Dunn v Parole Board*,[559] the Court of Appeal considered that a delay in reviewing a prisoner's recall to prison by the Parole Board would have to be of considerable magnitude before amounting to a violation of art.5(1). Excessive delay may mean that the factors which justify detention under art.5(1) become disproportionate, or (if statutory powers are exceeded) not "prescribed by law". Since the delay in this case was not of the required magnitude, these questions were not fully considered. In *Zenati v Commissioner of Police of the Metropolis*[560] the claimant's detention was unjustifiably prolonged after the time when his passport, which had been thought to be counterfeit, had been declared to be genuine. The police failed to pass this information to the CPS between 19 January, when it was received, and 9 February. Although the obligation of "special diligence" in reviewing detention was placed on courts, nevertheless where the investigating authority (here, the police) caused the court to fail to act with special diligence, it was those responsible for the delay who would breach art.5(3). It is striking that here too, a claim in tort failed There was no false imprisonment, because the imprisonment was justified by judicial action and also because the claimant was not in any event detained by the police. Thus, the case illustrates again that the scope of art.5 may be broader than the scope of tort liabilities. 13-106

Ancillary rights under art.5 Article 5(4) ECHR specifies a right for those arrested or detained to have the lawfulness of their detention "decided speedily by a court", and release ordered if the detention is unlawful. Article 5(4) may be violated by delayed reviews by the Parole Board, even where release would not have been ordered. Equally, art.5(1) may clearly be breached in circumstances which fall short of a false imprisonment, where an applicant has been deprived of "conditional liberty" through delay in the hearing. Significant questions have surrounded the approach to awarding damages in such cases given the general reluctance to create tort-like remedies in respect of maladministration, and the Supreme Court in *R. (Faulkner) v Secretary of State for Justice*; sub nom. *R. (Sturnham) v Parole* 13-107

[556] [2016] EWCA Civ 1033.
[557] [1997] 1 W.L.R. 328.
[558] [2014] EWHC 569 (QB); [2015] 1 W.L.R. 354.
[559] [2008] EWCA Civ 374; [2009] 1 W.L.R. 728.
[560] [2015] EWCA Civ 80; [2015] Q.B. 758.

Board[561] has provided guidance.[562] The decision of the Supreme Court in *R. (on the application of Kaiyam) v Secretary of State for Justice*[563] identified a clear distinction between unlawful detention in breach of art.5(1), and detention which remains lawful but which nevertheless breaches an ancillary right under art.5. In the latter case, the appropriate remedy is not a declaration of unlawfulness but damages to reflect frustration and anxiety. The Supreme Court therefore declined to follow the judgment of the European Court of Human Rights in *James v UK*.[564] There was a duty to provide rehabilitative courses and opportunities which were required for an offender to show that he was no longer a danger to the public and could be released. However, failure to comply with this duty could not be grounds for the continued detention to be unlawful, since safety of release had not been demonstrated. This was an ancillary duty not specifically set out in art.5 and an award of damages similar to those made for delay in parole hearings was the appropriate remedy. These would not be at a level previously awarded by the European Court of Human Rights, since they would be solely aimed at compensating for frustration and anxiety; the detention itself continued to be lawful. However, in *Brown v Parole Board for Scotland*,[565] the Supreme Court departed from its earlier decision in *Kaiyam*, considering that the decision in *James v UK* could now be perceived to be part of a clear and constant line of decisions, so that it should be followed. It was also now clear that the Supreme Court in *Kaiyam* had misunderstood the implications of locating the obligation to provide an opportunity for rehabilitation in art.5(1), rather than understanding it as an ancillary duty inherent in art.5 as a whole. In particular, the European Court of Human Rights had made clear in *James v UK* itself that the result of finding a breach of art.5(1)(a) in these circumstances would not be that an order would be made for the release of the prisoner, but that this aspect of the decision was not brought to the attention of the Supreme Court. Rather, through a combination of judicial review and subsequent action to ameliorate the prisoner's position, the cause of unlawfulness could itself be removed, while detention continued. UK courts would now follow *James v UK*, recognising that the hurdle for establishing a breach of art.5(1) is a high one. Indeed, the European Court of Human Rights had applied a higher hurdle than the one outlined by the Supreme Court in *Kaiyam*, applying a test of "arbitrariness" rather than unreasonableness; and had made clear that this was to be assessed by reference to the history of custody as a whole, rather than in relation to particular decisions. In *Kaiyam v UK*,[566] the Court had found no violation on this basis and the claims were ruled inadmissible. Inadvertently, the Supreme Court in *Kaiyam* had imposed a more onerous duty on prison authorities than the duties recognised in *James*. *James* would now be followed. In *R. (on the application of Lee-Hirons) v Justice Secretary*[567] a claimant who had been conditionally discharged from a secure hospital was recalled by the Secretary of State. Adequate reasons were given orally at the time of the recall, and there was no breach of duty at common law, nor under art.5(2) of the Convention. The Secretary of State conceded that there had been subsequent breaches of both the common law duty, and art.5(2), when written reasons were not

---

561 [2013] UKSC 23; [2013] 2 A.C. 254.

562 See further para.13-128.

563 [2014] UKSC 66; [2015] A.C. 1344; [2015] 2 All E.R. 822

564 (2012) 56 E.H.R.R.

565 [2017] UKSC 69; [2018] A.C. 1.

566 (2016) 62 E.H.R.R. SE13.

567 [2016] UKSC 46; [2017] A.C. 52.

then supplied until 15 days after the recall. There was no connection between this failure, and the lawfulness of detention, and the failure did not mean the detention was unlawful under art.5(1), nor at common law. The claimant had not shown that the violation of his art.5(2) rights was sufficiently serious to warrant the payment of damages under the HRA. The application of ancillary rights under art.5(4) was also in issue in *Mohammed v Ministry of Defence (No.2)*.[568] The majority Justices were divided on the question whether it had been shown that art.5(4) was breached, given the nature of the review processes in place. Lord Sumption, concluding that there had been a breach, pointed out that such a breach does not necessarily render detention unlawful under art.5(1) (applying *Kaiyam*); and that the question of whether a fair review process would have resulted in earlier release would be answered at trial.[569] Neither *Mohammed*, nor *Lee-Hirons*, was referred to in the decision of the Supreme Court in *Brown v Parole Board for Scotland*.

Apart from the conduct of military operations, individuals may be detained by authorities other than the police and prison authorities, in such a way as to engage art.5.[570] In *HL v UK*,[571] the UK was found in breach of art.5 in respect of a voluntarily detained patient in a mental hospital. Although in principle he was free to leave, in fact his movements were closely tracked, and if he had tried to leave, he would have been compulsorily detained under the Mental Health Act 1983. This had been found not to amount to a false imprisonment at common law in *R. (L) v Bournewood Community & NHS Trust*,[572] because it was justified on the basis of necessity. The European Court of Human Rights held that the test for necessity did not offer sufficient protection, since it did not provide for procedural steps such as review. The fact that the applicant had not resisted detention was also an insufficient basis for a finding that there was no deprivation of liberty. The position has now been dealt with by a series of amendments to the Mental Capacity Act 2005, enacted by the Mental Health Act 2007. In *Surrey County Council v P*,[573] the Supreme Court interpreted the notion of deprivation of liberty in the latter Act, which is expressly to be understood by reference to art.5. Baroness Hale said that the right to physical liberty guaranteed by art.5 "is not a right to do or to go where one pleases. It is a more focused right, not to be deprived of that physical liberty". That right however must be the same for everyone, with or without mental or physical disabilities.[574] The Supreme Court rejected the idea that a deprivation of liberty is to be understood as relative to the liberty of others with similar disabilities. The living arrangements put in place for the claimants therefore did amount to deprivations of liberty, albeit entered into in their best interests. As a result, those arrangements should be subject to periodic review to ensure that they continued to be in the patients' best interests. The case further illustrates the existence of gaps between false imprisonment at common law, and deprivations of liberty under the Convention.[575] 13-108

Article 6: Access to a court Article 6 is a complex provision, but its main ap- 13-109

568 [2017] UKSC 2; [2017] A.C. 821, para.13-104.
569 [2017] UKSC 2; [2017] A.C. 821 at [110].
570 See, e.g. *R. (on the application of Lee-Hirons) v Secretary of State for Justice*, para.13–107.
571 (2005) 40 E.H.R.R. 32.
572 [1999] 1 A.C. 458.
573 [2014] UKSC 19; [2014] A.C. 896.
574 [2014] UKSC 19; [2014] A.C. 896 at [46].
575 For more detailed discussion of the case law, see Ch.14.

plication in this context arises from its conferral of an entitlement to a fair and public hearing by an independent and impartial tribunal, in the determination of civil rights and obligations, as well as criminal charges. The question of what amounts to a civil right (and what amounts to an independent and impartial tribunal) has been raised in connection with consideration of entitlement to welfare services and especially housing. In *R. (Begum) v Tower Hamlets LBC*,[576] the House of Lords was willing to assume that the right to be provided with suitable accommodation was a "civil right" for these purposes, without deciding the point. A similar question arose before the Supreme Court in *R. (A) v Croydon LBC*.[577] This case concerned the determination by local authorities of whether a person was a "child" for the purposes of the duty in the Children Act 1989 s.20(1) to provide accommodation to children. Once again, the art.6 point did not have to be determined. It was observed by Lady Hale however that she would be reluctant, unless driven by Strasbourg authorities, to accept that art.6 requires the "judicialisation" of claims to welfare services. If the right to be accommodated as a child is a civil right, it rests "at the periphery" of such rights. The existing decision-making mechanisms, with the safeguard of judicial review, were adequate for fair determination of such rights, if such they were. Lord Hope considered the Strasbourg case law and expressed confidence that given the present state of those authorities, the duty imposed on a local authority to provide accommodation for a child within their area did not give rise to a civil right within the meaning of art.6(1).

13-110 In *R. (Kehoe) v Secretary of State for Work and Pensions*,[578] the House of Lords held that art.6 was not engaged where no direct enforcement mechanism was provided to a parent seeking child support payments under the Child Support Act 1991. Enforcement was exclusively by the Secretary of State. In *Kehoe v UK*,[579] an art.6 complaint against the UK arising from this state of affairs was dismissed. The European Court of Human Rights accepted that the opportunity to obtain a court order directing the Child Support Agency to take action must be regarded as effectively addressing the applicant's principal concern. That there was another potential mechanism which the applicant would find preferable did not itself establish breach of art.6. In *Jones v Powys Local Health Board*,[580] Plender J concluded that it could not be a violation of art.6 to require a claimant to proceed by way of judicial review, rather than by an action in tort, in order to correct an error that he claims has been made by a panel to which he himself elected to refer his case. However, Plender J also raised, without attempting to resolve, the different question of whether there would be a violation of art.6 if in similar circumstances the claimant had not elected to have his case considered by a panel, or if he was required to proceed by complaint to the Ombudsman.

13-111 **Article 8: Right to respect for private and family life** Article 8 has been invoked by claimants in a very wide range of circumstances. In *Malcolm v Secretary of State for Justice*,[581] Richards LJ referred to the breadth and elusiveness of art.8 and noted "how difficult it can sometimes be to determine whether a particular situ-

[576] [2003] UKHL 5; [2003] 2 A.C. 430.
[577] [2009] UKSC 8; [2009] 1 W.L.R. 2557.
[578] [2005] UKHL 48; [2006] 1 A.C. 42.
[579] (2010/06), [2008] 2 F.L.R. 1014; (2009) 48 E.H.R.R. 2.
[580] [2008] EWHC 2562 (Admin).
[581] [2011] EWCA Civ 1538.

ation falls within it or not".[582] That case concerned exercise in the open air on the part of a prisoner, the Court of Appeal concluding that even if there was a right to such exercise under art.8, no right on the part of a prisoner to a full hour's such exercise each day could be derived from the article. The state is under a positive obligation to protect art.8 rights, and this has led to important changes to domestic private law through transformation of the action for breach of confidence, to allow claims based not on duties of confidence but on a "reasonable expectation of privacy". This action has explicitly been developed in order to give effect to art.8 rights. Although the action to prevent publication of private information (explored in Ch. 27) is not typically employed against state defendants (although it certainly may be), there are other areas where art.8 is clearly likely to be relevant in an action against a public authority. The unsuccessful action in *Wainwright v Home Office* provides an example.[583] Here, the House of Lords declined to extend the law of tort to provide a remedy in respect of intrusion, in a case where the Human Rights Act was not applicable. A strip search of the claimants, visiting their relatives in prison, was carried out in a manner which breached Prison Rules. The subsequent finding by the European Court of Human Rights that the UK had therefore breached the arts 8 and 13 rights of the applicants[584] indicates that in future such a case should give rise to a claim under the Human Rights Act itself, for violation of art.8.

In a range of cases relating to personal information and photographs, public authorities may also be defendants to Human Rights Act actions invoking art.8. In *S v UK*,[585] the European Court of Human Rights held that the UK had violated the art.8 rights of the applicants, who had not been convicted of any crime, by keeping cellular (DNA) samples and fingerprints pursuant to a blanket and indiscriminate policy. Subsequently, the Supreme Court has declared that the applicable guidelines, rather than the governing legislation, were incompatible with the Convention[586]; and new legislative provisions allowing a more limited scheme of retention has been brought into force.[587] In *Wood v Chief of Police for the Metropolis*,[588] the Court of Appeal referred to *S v UK* and held that the defendant had violated the claimant's rights under art.8 in taking and retaining a photograph of the claimant. The claimant was a member of an organisation called "campaign against the arms trade", who attended a general meeting of a corporation which had been involved in organising arms fairs. Police officers (who had been led to expect that trouble might be caused at the meeting) spoke to the claimant afterwards, and took his photograph, which they retained but did not add to a database. The Court of Appeal held that the mere fact that a photograph was taken would not itself engage art.8, and in this respect the outcome would be similar whether the photograph was taken by the state (a "vertical" case or instance of the negative duty not to violate art.8), or by a private media corporation (a "horizontal" case or instance of the state's positive duty to protect art.8, through providing a remedy at law). "Aggravating circumstances" in the form of harassment during the taking of the photograph could make the difference, but these were not present in this case. 13-112

[582] [2011] EWCA Civ 1538 at [26].
[583] [2003] UKHL 53; [2004] 2 A.C. 406.
[584] *Wainwright v UK* (2007) 44 E.H.R.R. 40.
[585] (2009) 48 E.H.R.R. 50.
[586] *R. (on the application of GC) v Commissioner of Police of the Metropolis* [2011] UKSC 21; [2011] 1 W.L.R. 1230.
[587] Protection of Freedoms Act 2012 s.1, inserting a new s.63D on the destruction of fingerprints and DNA profiles into the Police and Criminal Evidence Act 1984: in force 31 October 2013.
[588] [2009] EWCA Civ 414; [2010] 1 W.L.R. 123.

Rather, unnecessary retention of the photographs and the anxiety instilled in the claimant were sufficient to engage art.8 in this case. It should be noted that since the purpose of taking and retaining the photographs was potentially a legitimate one, a question of proportionality therefore arose before there could be a finding of a violation. Here the Court of Appeal was divided (Laws LJ dissenting), but the majority held that the police action was disproportionate in the circumstances of the case. A different conclusion was reached by the Supreme Court in the case of *R. (on the application of Catt) v Association of Chief Police Officers of England, Wales and Northern Ireland*.[589] The claimant had a long history of political protest and attended many public demonstrations. Also, intelligence had been overtly compiled and retained over a long period. The Supreme Court held that the art.8 rights of the claimant were engaged but that the interferences were in each case prescribed by law and proportionate, since they pursued legitimate policing goals. In the case of the retention of information, there was sufficient flexibility in the policy adopted to allow for destruction of the records at an earlier stage if they no longer served a policing purpose. Notably, however, the European Court of Human Rights in *Catt v UK* has ruled that the Supreme Court's conclusion that the interferences were proportionate was incorrect and an art.8 violation was established.[590] While a pressing need to collect the personal data had been demonstrated, there was no such need to *retain* the data. The applicant was dependent on diligent application of highly flexible safeguards, whose effectiveness in permitting deletion of any of the data had not been evidenced. Further, the personal data revealed political viewpoints, which were particularly protected through art.11 ECHR.

13-113 Subsequently, in *R. (on the application of Butt) v Secretary of State for the Home Department*,[591] the Court of Appeal sought to apply the Supreme Court's decisions in *R. (on the application of Catt) v Association of Chief Police Officers of England, Wales and Northern Ireland*,[592] and in *JR38's Application for Judicial Review*,[593] in light of the Strasbourg jurisprudence, to a very different case. The claim concerned the Prevent Duty Guidance for England and Wales and the Higher Education Prevent Duty Guidance, and the gathering of data about a public speaker by the Government's Extremism Analysis Unit. As Etherton LJ framed it, this was a claim for privacy in respect of information publicly available by search of the internet and social media, "being views the claimant has expressed publicly and which he wishes to continue to promote to students and others in order to encourage them to follow his way of thinking and details as to where and how he has promoted those views."[594] In his view, unless precluded by authority, the natural conclusion was that Dr Butt could not have had any legitimate or objectively reasonable expectation of privacy in relation to the information about him recorded and retained by the E.A.U. After consideration of a range of decisions of the Strasbourg court, it was concluded that there was an overarching principle that there could not be a violation unless there was a legitimate expectation of privacy in the subject matter of the complaint, notwithstanding Lord Sumption's remarks about

---

589 [2015] UKSC 9; [2015] A.C. 1065.
590 *Catt v UK* (43514/15), (2019) 69 E.H.R.R. 7.
591 [2019] EWCA Civ 256; [2019] 1 W.L.R. 3873.
592 [2015] UKSC 9; [2015] A.C. 1065; see para.13-112.
593 [2015] UKSC 42; [2016] A.C. 1131. This claim concerned photographs of the claimant taken whilst rioting: art.8 was held not to be engaged as there was no reasonable expectation of privacy in the claimant's public and unlawful activities.
594 [2019] EWCA Civ 256; [2019] 1 W.L.R. 3873 at [67].

the possibility of a violation through "systematic retention and storage" in *R. (Catt)*, and still more demanding statements from the Strasbourg Court in *Catt v UK*.[595] In *Butt*, the Court of Appeal concluded that the claimant had no objectively reasonable expectation of privacy in the information collected, and thus his claim could not succeed. The Court also held that if art.8 had been engaged, the interference would have been justified within art.8(2) and his case was distinguishable from that of *Catt*. His data was collected and had been retained by the E.A.U. for a relatively short period before he commenced proceedings. Furthermore, unlike the situation for Mr Catt, Dr Butt's personal information was not of a particularly sensitive nature (indeed, he was publicising and promoting it). Nor was there any evidence that Dr Butt had ceased to be of any interest in relation to the *Prevent* strategy, whereas Mr Catt's information was kept beyond the point at which he was considered in any sense a potential danger. In *R. (on the application of CL) v Chief Constable of Greater Manchester Police*,[596] the court rejected a suggestion that a separate regime was required for consideration of data retention concerning minors: here, the retention of data in relation to alleged "sexting" incidents involving the claimant was argued to be proportionate and the regime adequately protected the claimant's rights. Though decided before the decision in *Catt v UK*, there are significant differences in the kind of information retained in this case and the rationale for its retention.

The exercise in proportionality and balancing which is familiar in the context of "horizontal" claims is also exercised in claims against public authorities where art.8 rights are engaged but information about individuals is released for legitimate reasons. In *R. (L) v Commissioner of Police of the Metropolis*,[597] the defendant police authority had released information in connection with an "enhanced criminal record certificate", to the effect that the claimant's son had been placed on the Child Protection Register for reasons of neglect. The information was correct, and potentially relevant given that the claimant was seeking employment in a school. The Supreme Court held that art.8 was engaged and that the public interest justification for the disclosure must be weighed in the balance against the claimant's art.8 right. Referring to *Campbell v MGN*,[598] the public interest should not be given presumptive priority over the art.8 rights of the applicant for such a certificate,[599] and the previous approach had been wrong in seeming to invite such priority.[600] Here, however, the decision to release the information would not be quashed, because the risk to children was properly held to outweigh the prejudicial effects of disclosure in this particular case. In *R. (on the application of R) v Chief Constable of Greater Manchester*,[601] the Supreme Court held that disclosure of an acquittal on a charge of rape in an enhanced criminal record certificate was a proportionate interference with art.8 rights. It noted, however, the absence of guidance to employers in how to assess information about an acquittal, and proposed that careful thought should be given to inclusion of details about acquittals. The absence of any 13-114

595 [2019] EWCA Civ 256; [2019] 1 W.L.R. 3873 at [75] and [76].
596 [2018] EWHC 3333 (Admin); [2019] A.C.D. 20.
597 [2009] UKSC 3; [2010] 1 A.C. 410.
598 [2004] UKHL 22; [2004] 2 A.C. 457.
599 It is important to note that the information disclosed did not relate to a criminal conviction, but was included as "other" potentially relevant information.
600 Lord Scott disagreed with this approach, suggesting that the entire point of the ECRC was to protect the vulnerable, and that there was an inherent decision to prioritise this over the art.8 rights of applicants.
601 [2018] UKSC 47; [2018] 1 W.L.R. 4079.

presumptive priority between arts 8 and 10 was emphasised by the Supreme Court in *Re Guardian News and Media Ltd*,[602] a case concerned with reporting restrictions rather than a claim for damages. However, the Supreme Court also noted the decision of the European Court of Human Rights in *Petrina v Romania*,[603] and particularly its assertion that in cases where publication raises a matter "of general interest", art.10(2) "scarcely leaves any room for restrictions on freedom of expression".[604] The anonymity orders were discharged.

13-115 There are numerous other contexts in which a claim under art.8 may form the content of, or be relevant to, an action under the Human Rights Act against public authorities. For example, parents whose children are removed after suspicions of abuse may use art.8 as the core of their claim[605]; while children wrongly removed from the home may add an art.8 claim to a claim based on art.3. Article 8 has also formed the basis of claims challenging the limited scope of the tort of nuisance, particularly in respect of claims by children who claim to have suffered personal injuries and who are unable, on the authority of *Hunter v Canary Wharf*,[606] to bring an action in nuisance. A party who does have relevant rights over their home may also frame their argument about severe amenity nuisance in terms of art.8, as well as Protocol 1 art.1.[607] The special protection offered to the home by art.8 is illustrated by the decision in *Keegan v UK*[608] that where a search warrant was wrongly obtained in respect of the applicants' home, the requirement in respect of a tort action that the warrant should be "maliciously" obtained[609] effectively deprived the applicants of protection of their right under art.8. The test should be proportionality in respect of a legitimate restriction on the right.

13-116 Some limits have, however, been placed on the extension of the art.8 right. In *Anufrijeva v Southwark LBC*[610] the claimant alleged that the authority's failure to provide housing suitable for an elderly family member prevented the family from living together and was in breach of art.8. Family life is not an interest protected by the law of tort[611] and hence this claim went beyond any possible liability in tort. The Court of Appeal rejected the art.8 claim. Lord Woolf said that for there to be a breach of art.8 there had to be an element of culpability at least involving knowledge that family life was at risk. A breach of domestic law would be evidence of culpability. He also considered that art.8 would apply more readily where the family unit and children were involved, and that in the context of welfare support it was hard to conceive of it applying unless the art.3 prohibition on inhuman and degrading treatment was also engaged. Finally, he noted that where the problem was one of the dilatory conduct of the authorities, it would have to be shown that the consequences were serious before there would be an infringement. In *A v Essex*

[602] [2010] UKSC 1; [2010] 2 A.C. 697. See also *Re BBC* [2014] UKSC 25; [2015] A.C. 588, upholding the anonymity of an asylum seeker convicted of an offence against children, where that anonymity was designed to protect him from violence once deported, so that open justice was departed from in the interests of justice and in order to protect X. In the event of any conflict between common law values and Convention values, the Convention values will take priority.

[603] (78060/01), 14 October 2008.

[604] [2010] UKSC 1; [2010] 2 A.C. 697 at [51].

[605] For a successful claim see *D (Children) v Wakefield MDC* [2016] EWHC 3312 (Fam); [2017] 2 F.L.R. 1353.

[606] [1997] A.C. 655.

[607] See para.13-123.

[608] App. No.28867/03, (2006) 44 E.H.R.R. 716.

[609] See para.15-18.

[610] [2003] EWCA Civ 1406; [2004] Q.B. 1124.

[611] See *F v Wirral MBC* [1991] Fam. 69.

CC,[612] the Court of Appeal held that the burdens placed upon a family when a gravely disabled child was excluded from his school (in this case, for valid reasons) could not give rise to a claim for breach of art.8. Sedley LJ said that "[t]he applicability of art.8 has grown since the inception of the Convention, but the contention that the denial by the state of legal rights, engages art.8 by disrupting the individual's or the family's well-being is an argument too far".[613] It was important to emphasise that although the family's predicament was not to be underestimated, the Convention was not "a panacea for every ill". Sedley LJ also referred to Lord Woolf's remarks in *Anufrijeva*, reiterating that in a case of failure to alleviate need, it was hard to envisage that an art.8 claim would succeed unless the family's suffering was sufficiently severe to engage art.3. In *Treharne v Secretary of State for Work and Pensions*,[614] the claim was for damages in relation to failure by the Child Support Agency to enforce a maintenance assessment. A claim framed in negligence inevitably could not succeed after the decision in *Rowley v Secretary of State for Work and Pensions*,[615] so the claim for damages proceeded on the basis that there had been a violation of the claimants' art.8 rights. This claim was comprehensively dismissed by Cranston J. Article 8 did not confer a right to welfare benefits on individuals, and to the extent that it imposed a positive duty on the state to provide such support (particularly in respect of the upbringing of children), this was at a minimal level. More analogously to tort claims and with specific reference to *Marcic v Thames Water Utilities*,[616] the scheme as a whole complied with the requirements of art.8 and its malfunctioning in particular cases was not sufficient to ground a claim under art.8.

A further limit to the extent of art.8 was recognised by the Supreme Court in *SXH v Crown Prosecution Service (United Nations High Commissioner for Refugees Intervening)*.[617] The claimant was a Somali national. She had come to the UK using false travel documents, was arrested, and on arrest immediately claimed asylum. She was remanded in custody, charged with possessing a false identity document. Nearly six months later, she was granted asylum, and sought damages from the CPS on the basis that the decision to prosecute her was an unlawful interference with her art.8 rights, given the high likelihood of success in her claim to asylum. The Supreme Court concluded that if the criminalisation of conduct did not violate art.8, neither did the decision to prosecute. Given that the relevant legislation was Convention-compliant, art.8 was not applicable to the decision to prosecute. It is unclear whether this is dependent on the decision to prosecute being reasonable, in the sense that the evidential test is satisfied. In *SXH* there was a concession that this was the case. By contrast in *Whitehouse v Chief Constable of Scotland*,[618] there was a claim that the prosecution was not based on sufficient evidence. The Inner House held that a decision to prosecute may in some circumstances involve a violation of art.8, so that the case should proceed to trial and, while art.8 may add little to the common law, it may permit an action in circumstances where the common law did not. Here, there would be no need to show malice, which would be essential for the **13-117**

612 [2008] EWCA Civ 364; [2008] H.R.L.R. 31.
613 [2008] EWCA Civ 364; [2008] H.R.L.R. 31 at [23]. A claim under First Protocol, art.2 also failed. On this point, there was an appeal to the Supreme Court, but the appeal was rejected: *A v Essex CC* [2010] UKSC 33; [2011] 1 A.C. 280, para.13-125.
614 [2008] EWHC 3222 (QB); [2009] 1 F.L.R. 853.
615 [2007] EWCA Civ 598; [2007] 1 W.L.R. 2861; see para.13-23.
616 [2003] UKHL 66; [2004] 2 A.C. 42.
617 [2017] UKSC 30; [2017] 1 W.L.R. 1401.
618 [2019] CSIH 52; 2019 S.L.T. 1269; 2020 S.C.L.R. 165. See further para.15-03.

common law claim in malicious prosecution (discussed in Ch.15). However, in *SXH* itself, the Supreme Court added the broad point that the duty of the CPS is to the public, so that recognition of a duty of care towards victims or suspects would put the service in a position of potential conflict. According to Lord Toulson, similar considerations are applicable when considering the applicability of art.8 in the context of a decision to prosecute. That decision places the question of determining guilt before a court; and the court is also responsible for decisions as to bail or remand in custody.[619] This appears to be in contrast with the approach in *D v Commissioner of Police for the Metropolis*,[620] in which the positive duty to investigate was said to be free from considerations of proximity, justice and fairness which arise in relation to negligence actions against the police.[621] Lord Toulson expressed no conclusion on a question which was raised at a late stage in proceedings, namely whether the continuation of a prosecution which had not violated art.8 when initiated could nevertheless become a violation of art.8. No argument had been heard on the question. However, Lord Kerr in a concurring judgment pointed to the decision in *Zenati v Commr of Police of the Metropolis*,[622] where art.5 was considered capable of being breached when a prosecution was unjustifiably prolonged. The same need to keep a prosecution under review could apply to violations of art.8.

13-118 **Nuisance and overlapping liability** There have been particular overlaps between art.8 and the law of tort in claims concerning nuisance. In *Marcic v Thames Water Utilities*,[623] the question was whether the defendant's failure to prevent the claimant's house being affected by flooding was an infringement of his right to respect for his home under art.8. The House of Lords rejected the claim. Lord Hoffmann said:

> "the convention does not accord absolute protection to property ... It requires a fair balance to be struck between the interests of persons whose homes and properties are affected and the interests of other people such as customers and the general public. National institutions ... are accorded a broad discretion in choosing the solution appropriate to their own society or creating their own machinery for doing so."[624]

The court concluded that the statutory system under which the Director General of Water Services struck that balance met the requirements of the article and only where the Director exceeded the broad margin of discretion allowed by the Convention, would the claimant have a remedy under s.8 of the 1998 Act. It was also held that the common law of nuisance did not impose obligations inconsistent with the statutory scheme. In this case the Convention right was construed as compatible with basis of common law liability. Subsequently, in *Dobson v Thames Water Utilities*,[625] Ramsey J held that where the interference was *negligently* created by a sewerage undertaker, so that a nuisance arose through operational negligence rather

---

619 [2017] UKSC 30; [2017] 1 W.L.R. 1401 at [38].

620 [2018] UKSC 11; [2019] A.C. 196.

621 See para.13-102.

622 [2015] EWCA Civ 80; [2015] Q.B. 758; see para.13-106.

623 [2003] UKHL 66; [2004] 2 A.C. 42.

624 [2003] UKHL 66; [2004] 2 A.C. 42 at [71]. The House of Lords followed the European Court of Human Rights ruling in *Hatton v UK* [2002] 1 F.C.R. 732; (2002) 34 E.H.R.R. 1, on this point. There the court in rejecting the claim that Heathrow night flights violated art.8, said that national authorities had a "direct democratic legitimation" and were in principle better placed than an international court to evaluate local needs and conditions.

625 [2007] EWHC 2021 (TCC); [2008] 2 All E.R. 362.

than simple overloading of the sewerage system, a claim was not precluded. In such a case, the common law claim on the part of those with relevant proprietary rights in their home could be supplemented by an action for breach of art.8 by people (in this instance children) who occupied property without enjoying proprietary rights. This, therefore, gives rise to a clear case of overlap between the common law and the HRA action, the latter being available to a wider range of claimants on the same facts. As such, principles relating to the assessment of damages were extremely important and on this point (available remedies), but not on the basic principle of liability in the presence of negligence, there was an appeal to the Court of Appeal.[626] The actions were subsequently tried and damages awarded accordingly, but not to those without proprietary interests, since damages at common law were sufficient.[627] Issues of overlap also arose in *Fearn v Tate Gallery Board of Trustees*.[628] The claimants occupied flats neighbouring the Tate Gallery, and complained of interference with the use and enjoyment of their property from the use of a new viewing platform constructed by the Gallery, directly overlooking their flats and balconies. They were often observed and photographed from the viewing platform. The tort of nuisance had not been extended to cases of overlooking, and the claimants argued that the tort should be extended in order to embody appropriate protection for art.8 rights, thus avoiding a breach of art.6 on the part of the courts. The Court of Appeal rejected this argument for a number of reasons. In particular, nuisance protected property rights, while art.8 offered much broader protection; and it would be difficult to superimpose the art.8(2) justifications for interference with privacy onto the tort of nuisance. Thus, the common law would not be extended to protect the proposed art.8 rights.

Relationship between common law and art.8 Case law in relation to art.8 exemplified that the common law has in some instances responded to Convention rights, but that the more general trend has been towards separation of the actions. The acceptance of a duty to children in *D v East Berkshire NHS Trust*[629] was a direct result of the European court decision in *Z v UK*.[630] Tort law has also changed to lessen the impact of the EHCR decision in *TP and KM v UK*,[631] which stemmed from the *Bedfordshire*[632] decision, but here the link is less direct. In *TP and KM* the ECHR held the UK to be in breach of art.8. The case concerned the child removed from its mother by the welfare authority in order to protect it from suspected abuse by the mother's partner. In fact, the partner was not responsible for the abuse but the authority refused to disclose to the mother a video of the interview with the child which would have revealed this fact. This refusal delayed the return of the child and denied the mother involvement in decisions concerning the care of her child. Hence, there was a breach of art.8. Subsequently, the House of Lords has taken a more restricted approach to the scope of witness immunity.[633] In the light of this development it is suggested that there would now be no common law ground for withholding the video in a *Bedfordshire* situation. As a result the common law on this point 13-119

626 [2009] EWCA Civ 28; [2009] 3 All E.R. 319; see para.13-131.

627 [2011] EWHC 3253 (TCC); (2011) 140 Con. L.R. 135.

628 [2020] EWCA Civ 104; [2020] 2 W.L.R. 1081.

629 [2003] EWCA Civ 1151; [2004] Q.B. 558.

630 [2001] 2 F.C.R. 246; [2001] 2 F.L.R. 612; (2002) 34 E.H.R.R. 3. See para.13-33.

631 [2001] 2 F.C.R. 289; [2001] 2 F.L.R. 549.

632 See para.13-10.

633 See para.13-57; and the view of Lord Phillips MR in *D v East Berkshire NHS Trust* [2003] EWCA Civ 1151; [2004] Q.B. 558 at [116].

should be compatible with the requirements of art.8. In *L v Pembrokeshire CC*,[634] Auld LJ, giving the leading judgment of the Court of Appeal, rejected the argument that art.8, in giving the parent a remedy for interference with his or her family life, had "in one fell blow" removed all the force of the conflict of interest point and required the "consignment to history" of the *East Berkshire* decision. He commented: "that argument overlooks an important difference between the Article 8 right to respect for family life and a putative right of a claimant at common law to a duty of care. Article 8 is not concerned with the establishment of any such duty, but of a threshold of interference by a public authority with family life. It is not based on a breach of duty of care by such authority, which, once surmounted, is for the authority to justify."[635] He concluded:

> "the advent of Article 8 to our domestic law, bringing with it a discrete right to children and parents of respect for their family life, does not undermine or weaken as a matter of public policy the primacy of the need to protect children from abuse, or the risk of abuse, from, among others, their parents. Nor, when those interests are or may be in conflict, does Article 8 so enhance the status of family life as, in the balancing exercise involved, would require the development of the common law by the introduction of a duty of care to parents suspected of abusing their children, a duty precluded by that public policy."[636]

Subsequently, the European Court of Human Rights has held that the facts of *D v Bury MDC*[637] disclosed a breach of the applicant parent's art.8 right.[638] This signals that liability under the Human Rights Act may yet need to develop in such cases, applying a case by case approach to proportionality in contrast with the blanket application of "conflict of interest" reasoning.

13-120 In *Watkins v Secretary of State for the Home Department*[639] Lord Rodger noted that although the tort of misfeasance in public office could not be extended to cover interference with the constitutional right to unimpeded communication with a legal advisor, it might now be possible for the claimant to bring proceedings under s.8 of the Human Rights Act for damages for breach of certain of the guarantees in arts 6 and 8 of the Convention. But this was a reason why the common law does not need to develop to protect the rights; there is a remedy suited to that purpose. *Watkins* is one of a series of decisions in the House of Lords in which the common law and Human Rights Act actions were separated in this way. It is a corollary of the separation of tort duties and remedies, and their counterparts under the Human Rights Act, that there may in principle be liability under the statute where no claim in tort is available. This is illustrated by *Jain v Trent Strategic HA*.[640] Here, the House of Lords thought that a claim for violation of Convention rights on similar facts to this would be at least arguable. Even so, no duty of care would be recognised, as it would not be "fair, just and reasonable" to impose liability. Therefore, it was clear that even tort principles which are overtly premised on policy considerations would be maintained in circumstances where a violation of Convention rights is arguable. This illustrates clearly that the immediate influence of the art.6 elements of the decision in *Osman v UK* had been left behind. It remains to

---

[634] [2007] EWCA Civ 446; [2007] 1 W.L.R. 2991.

[635] [2007] EWCA Civ 446; [2007] 1 W.L.R. 2991 at [32].

[636] [2007] EWCA Civ 446; [2007] 1 W.L.R. 2991 at [41].

[637] [2006] EWCA Civ 1; [2006] 1 W.L.R. 917; see para.13-25.

[638] *AD v United Kingdom* (28680/06) [2010] 2 F.L.R. 1; see para.13-25.

[639] [2006] UKHL 17; [2006] 2 A.C. 395 at [64].

[640] [2009] UKHL 4; [2009] 1 A.C. 853; para.13-51.

be seen whether a new phase has been reached in which a negative reaction to *Osman* no longer influences the law, but there are signs that this is the case. An important indication is the willingness of the Supreme Court to extend "tort-like" duties to protect life under the Human Rights Act, beyond the point already reached by the European Court of Human Rights, in *Rabone v Pennine Care NHS Foundation Trust*,[641] *Smith v Ministry of Defence*,[642] and *D v Commissioner of Police for the Metropolis*,[643] thus outflanking settled policy reasons against liability in tort. Since positive duties also arise under other articles, including art.8, these developments have potentially broader reach.

Article 10: Freedom of expression; art.11: freedom of assembly Articles 10 and 11 have come into contact with the law of tort where public authorities have aimed to use tort remedies against protestors occupying public land and interfering with the rights of the public. In these cases, Convention rights have been raised by protestors in defence against domestic law remedies. They are not, therefore, actions under the Human Rights Act 1998, but illustrate a different dimension to the role played by Convention rights in determining common law rights and duties. The proper approach to such arguments was outlined by the Court of Appeal in *Mayor of London v Samede*,[644] where the Mayor had applied for an order to evict those taking part in a camp at St Paul's Churchyard in London, and earlier in *Mayor of London v Hall*.[645] It was accepted that the arts 10 and 11 rights of the protestors are engaged in these instances; but it was also relevant that the actions of the protestors interfered with the rights of others, including substantial interferences with public rights of way, and with the rights of those wishing to worship. The court noted in *Samede* that it was very difficult to see how the arts 10 and 11 rights of the protestors: **13-121**

> "could ever prevail against the will of the landowner, when they are continuously and exclusively occupying public land, breaching not just the owner's property rights and certain statutory provisions, but significantly interfering with the public and Convention rights of others, and causing other problems (connected with health, nuisance, and the like), particularly … where the occupation has already continued for months, and is likely to continue indefinitely".[646]

While the value of the protestors' cause was irrelevant, the level of disruption caused was significant. The approach in *Samede* clearly involves weighing the protestors' rights against the rights and interests of others, and general public concerns (such as health) are also relevant. The approach was applied in *Islington LBC v Jones*,[647] justifying an order to evict occupiers from a public square on the basis of interferences with the rights of the local authority and of the public; and in *Olympic Delivery Authority v Persons Unknown*[648] to prevent protestors from entering a site intended for use in the 2012 Olympics and disrupting work. In the

641 [2012] UKSC 2; [2012] 2 A.C. 72. See para.13-89.
642 [2013] UKSC 41; [2014] A.C. 52. See para.13-93.
643 [2018] UKSC 11; [2019] A.C. 196. See para.13-102.
644 [2012] EWCA Civ 160; [2012] 2 All E.R. 1039.
645 [2010] EWCA Civ 817; [2011] 1 W.L.R. 504.
646 [2010] EWCA Civ 817; [2011] 1 W.L.R. 504 at [49].
647 [2012] EWHC 1537 (QB).
648 [2012] EWHC 1012 (Ch).

latter case, Arnold J applied the approach in *Re S (A Child)*,[649] suggesting that neither the contractors' rights under Protocol 1 art.1,[650] nor the protestors' rights under arts 10 and 11, took precedence, so that a proportionality approach must be applied to the restriction of each. In *Manchester Ship Canal Developments Ltd v Persons Unknown*,[651] it was considered that the court, as a public authority, had to weigh the rights of the parties even where the landowner was a private party. In this case it was considered that the art.10 and art.11 rights of the trespassers could not possibly outweigh the rights of the landowner; and that any art.8 rights of a trespasser—which would be engaged only if they could establish that the land on which they were trespassing was a "home"—could only outweigh a landowner's right under Protocol 1 art.1 in "exceptional cases". This was not such a case. These decisions illustrate that numerous articles of the Convention may interact with common law rights in a range of ways, and that courts are actively developing approaches to balancing these rights.

13-122 **Article 14: Prohibition of discrimination** States are required by art.14 of the ECHR to protect the Convention rights of everyone without discrimination. In *E v Chief Constable of the Royal Ulster Constabulary*,[652] the claimant argued that the passive approach of the police was in breach of ECHR art.14. The art.14 claim, like the art.3 claim explored above, failed. The House of Lords held that there was no evidence that the police would have handled the situation any differently had the claimant been a Protestant encountering a Catholic protest. As such, there was no evidence that the police had been motivated by sectarian bias. The key test, according to Lord Carswell, is whether there has been a "failure to treat like cases alike".[653] In *A v Essex CC*,[654] Sedley LJ emphasised that *unlawful* discrimination might take the form of treating unalike cases as though they were alike. In other words, it is right to discriminate between cases which are different, and this does not breach art.14. In that case, it was right for the education authority to treat a gravely disabled child differently and therefore to discriminate in his favour. The removal of the child from a school which could not cope with him, pending a more appropriate placement, could not be seen as unlawful discrimination. In *R. (on the application of Johnson) v Secretary of State for the Home Department*[655] the Supreme Court held that there was an arguable claim that art.14 rights, read with art.8, had been violated. The claimant, a Jamaican national born out of wedlock, was subject to deportation but would not have been had his parents been married. This was an accident of birth which was not his fault, and use of this to impose a character test had to be justified. In *Smith v Lancashire Teaching Hospitals NHS Foundation Trust*,[656] the Court of Appeal dealt with a claim that there had been a violation of art.14 in conjunction with art.8, holding that art.14 may be violated even in the absence of violation of art.8, provided the measure complained of had a more than tenuous connection with the values protected by art.8, and was discriminatory and not justified. The claim-

---

649 [2004] UKHL; [2005] 1 A.C. 593

650 See para.13-123.

651 [2014] EWHC 645 (Ch).

652 [2008] UKHL 66; [2009] 1 A.C. 536; para.13-100.

653 [2008] UKHL 66; [2009] 1 A.C. 536 at [64]; quoting from the speech of Lord Hoffmann in *R. (Carson) v Chief Constable of the Royal Ulster Constabulary* [2005] UKHL 37; [2006] 1 A.C. 173 at [14].

654 [2008] EWCA Civ 364; [2009] B.L.G.R. 182; [2008] E.L.R. 321.

655 [2016] UKSC 56; [2017] A.C. 365.

656 [2017] EWCA Civ 1916; [2018] Q.B. 804.

ant had lived with a man in the same household as husband and wife for 11 years until his death resulting from admitted negligence of the defendant. A claim for dependency damages under Fatal Accidents Act 1976 s.1 was settled and the claimant argued that denial of bereavement damages to her as a cohabiting partner was discriminatory. Section 1A(2)(a) of the Fatal Accidents Act 1976 had not extended bereavement damages to cohabitees. The Court found that in all the circumstances of this claim, discrimination between the claimant and a surviving spouse required to be justified in order to avoid infringing art.14 in conjunction with art.8, and there was no evidence of any such justification since dependency damages had been extended to cohabitees of over two years. There was no scope for interpretation of the statutory language as extending to such a cohabitee, and so the appropriate remedy was a declaration of incompatibility with art.14 in conjunction with art.8.

First Protocol art.1: Right to peaceful enjoyment of possessions The right to peaceful enjoyment of possessions was argued to be engaged alongside art.8 in the unsuccessful claim for nuisance and breach of Convention rights in *Marcic v Thames Water Utilities Ltd*.[657] This was a claim brought by a property owner, and it seems that in most such cases the tort of private nuisance will provide a better remedy than an action under the Human Rights Act. Article 1 of the First Protocol may be relevant to public service liability in a range of other circumstances. In *R. (K) v HM Treasury*,[658] K applied for restrictions on her access to funds to be set aside. Her husband's assets had been frozen world-wide on the basis of his involvement in an organisation linked to Al-Qaeda. K was given a licence to withdraw funds for basic family expenses, subject to a monthly reporting requirement. Burton J held that the public interest was wide and that the reporting requirement did not breach art.8 or art.1 of the First Protocol, since it was proportionate under the circumstances.[659] It has been held that deprivation of one's passport does not amount to a violation of Protocol 1 art.1. The fact that a passport is a tangible object is not sufficient to constitute it as a "possession", and its significance or essence is that it represents an intangible privilege or entitlement, which was not "marketable".[660] Nevertheless, in *Atapattu*, a claim at common law for conversion was successful, indicating that some possessions may be protected by conversion though not suitable for protection under Protocol 1 art.1. However, it appears that a legitimate expectation based on a judicial ruling or statutory provision is capable of protection under Protocol 1 art.1. In *The Gas and Electricity Markets Authority v Infinis Plc*[661] the respondents were deprived of a pecuniary benefit when they were refused accreditation for Renewables Obligations Certificates under two Orders in respect of their electricity generating stations. As the damage suffered was pecuniary and could be clearly calculated, "just satisfaction" required that it should be fully compensated, permitting compensation in respect of pecuniary loss where tort would not provide a remedy. 13-123

Changes in government policy may have significant effects on businesses, which 13-124

657 [2003] UKHL 66; [2004] 2 A.C. 42.

658 [2009] EWHC 1643 (Admin); [2009] Lloyd's Rep. F.C. 533.

659 Applying the test for proportionality as required in *Huang v Secretary of State for the Home Department* [2007] UKHL 11; [2007] 2 A.C. 167.

660 *R. (on the application of Atapattu) v Secretary of State for the Home Department* [2011] EWHC 1388 (Admin); followed in *Young v Young* [2012] EWHC 138 (Fam); [2012] Fam. 198 where it was also held that confinement to the UK was not confinement to a sufficiently limited place to engage art.5. A claim under art.8 also failed in each case.

661 [2013] EWCA Civ 70; [2013] J.P.L. 1037.

may turn to Protocol 1 art.1 in pursuit of a remedy. In *Breyer Group Plc v Department of Energy and Climate Change*[662] the Court of Appeal determined that there had been unjustified interference with the possessions of the claimant company, even where loss of goodwill was created by a mere proposal which was therefore not itself unlawful. In this instance, the proposed course of action (reducing a subsidy) would have been unlawful if implemented. Following clear and consistent Strasbourg and domestic jurisprudence, "possessions" in art.1 of the First Protocol ECHR could take the form of goodwill which had already been established by a company but could not be applied to a future income stream.[663] Thus, where existing contracts were abandoned through an unjustified interference, the claimants were entitled to damages. By contrast, in the related, but later claim in *Solaria Energy UK Limited v Department for Business, Energy and Industrial Strategy*,[664] it was held that contractual rights that were not assignable, transmissible, nor realisable could amount to an "asset" protected by Protocol 1 art.1. For goodwill to be treated as an asset, it had to be marketable. The company, which supplied and distributed solar panel products, could not seek damages where the proposal to reduce the crucial subsidy for electricity generated by solar panels caused it to have to renegotiate its contracts. In *Bank Mellat v HM Treasury (No.2)*,[665] the Supreme Court also referred to goodwill as amounting to a "possession" for the purposes of art.1 of the First Protocol ECHR. In *Bank Mellat v HM Treasury*,[666] the Court of Appeal determined that, in accordance with the principles applied in Strasbourg, it was the company and not its shareholders which had the status to recover losses suffered as a consequence of a breach of Convention rights. The bank argued that a wide range of economic interests was protected by Protocol 1 art.1, including tangible and intangible interests; on this point, the Court of Appeal determined that the recoverability of the full range of losses argued for should be considered at trial. The potential breadth of Protocol 1 art.1 in relation to regulatory policy is further illustrated by *R. (Mott) v Environment Agency*.[667] The Supreme Court held that a fisherman's rights under Protocol 1 art.1 had been breached by conditions attached to his licence to catch salmon by the statutory regulator. Although the restrictions imposed were a proper exercise of the defendant's powers to control fishing activity in the interests of protection of the environment, a fair balance nevertheless had to be struck between public and private interests. The conditions amounted to a reduction of 95 per cent of the benefit of the claimant's fishing right and there had been no consideration of the particular impact on the claimant's livelihood, nor of the relative severity of the impact on him, as compared to those whose interest was recreational. Given the severity and disproportion of the impact on him, his Convention rights had been breached, and damages were an appropriate remedy. However, in future cases where the authorities had given appropriate consideration to issues of fair balance, courts should give weight to their assessment.[668]

13-125 **First Protocol art.2: Right to education** Protocol 1 art.2 ECHR provides that

[662] [2015] EWCA Civ 408; [2015] 1 W.L.R. 4559

[663] [2015] EWCA Civ 408; [2015] 1 W.L.R. 4559 at [43], [45].

[664] [2019] EWHC 2188 (TCC); [2019] B.L.R. 610.

[665] [2013] UKSC 39; [2014] A.C. 700

[666] [2016] EWCA Civ 452; [2017] Q.B. 67.

[667] [2018] UKSC 10; [2018] 1 W.L.R. 1022.

[668] In *R. v M* [2017] UKSC 58; [2017] 1 W.L.R. 3006, the claimant's rights under Protocol 1 art.1 had not been violated by the threat of prosecution for trade mark infringement. He was free to sell his goods provided the misleading trade marks were removed, and there was no unjustified interference with his possessions.

"[n]o person shall be denied the right to education". The applicability of this article to school exclusions was considered by the House of Lords in *Ali v Lord Grey School Governors*.[669] The exclusion from school in that case (pending investigation of an allegation of arson) was found to be incapable of amounting to a breach of Protocol 1 art.2. There was a difference of approach within the House of Lords, Lord Bingham asking[670] whether there was a denial of effective access to such educational facilities as the state provides, and Lord Hoffmann asking whether there had been a systemic failure of the education system as a whole. In *A v Essex CC*,[671] Protocol 1 art.2 was considered in connection with facts somewhat closer to educational negligence cases such as *Phelps v Hillingdon LBC*.[672] The case concerned a gravely disabled child, who had been placed in a special school by the local education authority, but whose behaviour was considered too challenging for the school to cope with, posing a danger both to other students and to staff. He was therefore excluded from the school, and it was a period of several months before a more appropriate setting could be found, during which period the child was educated at home. The Court of Appeal found that this interlude amounted to neither a failure of the education system, nor an exclusion from it (the two tests in *Ali v Lord Grey*),[673] and as such it could not amount to a breach of the Convention right to education. Claims under arts 3, 8, and 14 also failed. The Supreme Court dismissed an appeal, but was divided on a number of significant issues. On the appellant's key argument that exclusion from state education at school for a period of 18 months was capable of amounting to a violation of art.2 of the first Protocol, a majority of the court (Baroness Hale and Lord Kerr dissenting) agreed that this was not the case: only "systemic failure" in the education system could amount to a violation of the right. There would not be a violation of the right simply because a state failed to cater "for the special needs of a small, if significant, portion of the population which is unable to profit from mainstream education".[674] Rather, the article "guarantees fair and non-discriminatory access for [a child with special needs] to the limited resources actually available to deal with his special needs". Thus the appellant's primary contention, that there was a positive obligation on the state to make provision for children with special needs, in these circumstances at enormous cost, was rejected. Equally, the appellant could not rely on a breach of domestic law as constituting a violation of the art.2 right: this was established by the *Lord Grey School* case. However, a different majority of the court (Lords Phillips and Kerr, and Baroness Hale) also concluded that there was an arguable case that during the 18 months during which the appellant was excluded from school, he did not in fact have access to the educational resources that were, or might have been made, available. Essentially, he did not receive any education at all. However, both Lord Phillips and Lord Kerr nevertheless concluded that the existence of an arguable case did not justify an extension of time to bring the claim outside the one year limitation period applied to claims under the Human Rights Act 1998. The is-

[669] [2006] UKHL 14; [2006] 2 A.C. 363.
[670] [2006] UKHL 14; [2006] 2 A.C. 363 at [24].
[671] [2008] EWCA Civ 364; [2009] B.L.G.R. 182; [2008] E.L.R. 321; [2010] UKSC 33; [2011] 1 A.C. 280.
[672] [2001] 2 A.C. 619.
[673] Sedley LJ pointed out that in *DH v Czech Republic* (2008) 47 E.H.R.R. 3, the European Court of Human Rights found that Protocol 1 art.2 could be breached where the education system remained intact but failed a specific child. This was a case concerning the diversion of Roma children to "special schools".
[674] [2010] UKSC 33; [2011] 1 A.C. 280 at [75], per Lord Phillips.

sues that arose would turn on the facts of the individual case, and would not be matters of principle; nor was it likely that substantial damages would be awarded. The claim, though arguable, was time barred. A successful claim for violation of this right, applying *A v Essex CC*, was made in *R. (on the application of E) v Islington LBC*.[675] Through repeated changes in where the family was housed, without reference to her need for education, E had missed 50 per cent of her schooling for a particular school year. The impact of the periods of absence was particularly difficult for her, given the problems she faced as a result of her mother's disabilities. This amounted in E's particular case to a denial of the essence of her right to education for that year, and she would be awarded both a declaration, and damages.

(c) Damages under the Human Rights Act 1998

13-126 **Discretionary damages** An award of damages is at the discretion of the court and s.8(3) of the 1998 Act provides that it should only be made if in the light of any other relief it is necessary to "afford just satisfaction". Section 8(2) specifies that damages may be awarded by a court which is able to award damages in civil proceedings.[676] Section 8(4) of the Act provides that in determining whether to award damages or the amount of damages a domestic court must take into account the principles adopted by the ECHR in awarding compensation. This is to ensure consistency between domestic and European awards. In *Anufrijeva v Southwark LBC*,[677] Lord Woolf delivering the judgment of the Court of Appeal, said:

> "In considering whether to award compensation … there is a balance to be drawn between the interests of the victim and those of the public as a whole … The court has a wide discretion in respect of the award of damages for breach of human rights … Damages are not an automatic entitlement but … a remedy of 'last resort'."

He went on to say that an equitable approach should be taken to whether it was "just and appropriate" to award damages and this would involve considering the scale and manner of the violation and whether other remedies were sufficient to vindicate the infringed right. Thus, the onus is on the victim and if, say, he is already entitled to common law damages, an award would not be necessary. The same might be the case if the common law remedy was injunctive relief. The ECHR does not award punitive or exemplary damages and in *R. (KB) v Mental Health Review Tribunal*[678] Burnton J held that: "s.9(3) of the 1998 Act, by prohibiting any award of damages otherwise than by way of compensation, expressly prohibits the award of exemplary damages." In *Watkins v Secretary of State for the Home Department*[679] the House of Lords emphasised that exemplary damages are generally not awarded by the European Court of Human Rights, and since damages under s.8 are modelled on Strasbourg awards, they should not be recoverable under the Human Rights Act. The claimant's argument that the tort of misfeasance in a public office extended to

---

675 [2017] EWHC 1440 (Admin); [2018] P.T.S.R. 349.

676 Thus in *OB (Ukraine) v Entry Clearance Officer* [2019] EWCA Civ 1216, the Court of Appeal refused to award damages in proceedings which had been commenced at the Upper-Tier Tribunal (though damages would also have been refused because the refusal of a visitor visa complained of had in any event been reversed). If damages were sought under s.8, different proceedings would need to be commenced. See also *Mazhar v Lord Chancellor* [2019] EWCA Civ 1558; [2020] 2 W.L.R. 541; para.13-127.

677 [2003] EWCA Civ 1406; [2004] Q.B. 1124 at [56].

678 [2003] EWHC 193 (Admin); [2004] Q.B. 936 at [60].

679 [2006] UKHL 17; [2006] 2 A.C. 395.

cases where there was no "material damage" provided there was a violation of constitutional rights was seen as an attempt to circumvent the non-availability of exemplary damages under the Human Rights Act. The ECHR has also refused to make awards to wrongdoers and it is likely that an award would be reduced to reflect the contribution of the victim to the harm.

Article 5 and damages The relationship between the discretionary nature of damages under s.8, and the requirement of art.5(5) of the Convention that "everyone who has been the victim of arrest or detention in contravention of the provisions of this article shall have an enforceable right to compensation", was considered in the case of *R. (on the application of Downing) v The Parole Board*.[680] It was considered clear that art.5(5) did not give any freestanding right to damages in English law. The provisions of s.8 applied to art.5 cases just as they apply to other claims. In the event, the judge granted a declaration that there had been a violation of art.5 through delay in reviewing the claimant's detention following the end of his tariff period, and exercised his discretion against an award of damages under s.8 given the seriousness of the original crime (murder), and the relatively mild effect of the delay on the claimant.[681] However, art.5(5) damages are unique in that, by s.9(3) of the HRA, the need for a remedy under art.5(5) is the only circumstance in which a claim in relation to judicial acts done in good faith is possible. In *Mazhar v Lord Chancellor*,[682] it was suggested that this should generally be by new proceedings brought against the relevant Minister, in order to protect judicial immunity. 13-127

The approach to damages in cases of delay under art.5(4) has been considered by the Supreme Court in a decision which has broader implications for the approach to damages under the Human Rights Act in general. In *R. (Faulkner) v Secretary of State for Justice; R. (Sturnham) v Parole Board*,[683] the Supreme Court considered joined appeals from contrasting decisions of the Court of Appeal. In the first, the claimant had been denied access to a Parole Board hearing for a period of around 10 months, during which time his release would probably have been ordered, so that the case involved a deprivation of "conditional liberty". In the second, a life prisoner's Parole Board hearing was also delayed, but in this instance his release would probably not have been ordered and thus there was delay in review but no deprivation of conditional liberty. The Supreme Court underlined that neither case involved a deprivation of liberty sufficient to amount to false imprisonment nor to a violation of art.5(1). Both were cases of delay amounting to violations of art.5(4). They were to be distinguished from the case of *James v UK*,[684] where the European Court of Human Rights found a violation of art.5(1). That was because in *James v UK*, the claimants did not have access to relevant courses, without which they had no opportunity to show that they no longer posed a risk to the public: since the justification for detention after the expiry of a tariff period was protection of the public, it followed that the conditions of detention must allow a 13-128

680 [2008] EWHC 3198 (Admin).

681 See also *R. (Biggin) v Secretary of State for Justice* [2009] EWHC 1704 (Admin). Article 5(4) had been breached, but the court did not award damages. Subjective questions concerning the impact on the claimant were relevant. Here the prisoner sought transfer to open from closed conditions, rather than release.

682 [2019] EWCA Civ 1558; [2020] 2 W.L.R. 541. This was a case of transfer of a patient to hospital without consent.

683 [2013] UKSC 23; [2013] 2 A.C. 254.

684 (25119/09) (2012) 56 E.H.R.R. 12.

real opportunity for rehabilitation. That did not apply in the instant cases.[685] In cases involving breaches of art.5(4), where it is established on the balance of probabilities that a violation of art.5(4) has resulted in the detention of a prisoner beyond the date when he would otherwise be released, damages should ordinarily be awarded for the resultant detention. Pecuniary losses shown to have been caused by prolongation of detention should be compensated in full. The fact of recall to prison after release should not ordinarily be taken into account in assessing damages. There should be no award for loss of chance of release nor any adjustment for the degree of probability of release. Where it is not established that an earlier hearing would have resulted in earlier release, there is a strong but not irrebuttable presumption that delay in violation of art.5(4) has caused feelings of frustration and anxiety. Where this is the case, the finding of a violation would not ordinarily constitute sufficient just satisfaction, and an award of damages on a modest scale should also be made. No award should be made where the delay was such that any resultant frustration and anxiety were insufficiently severe to warrant it. Where there is a delay of over three months however, this is unlikely to be the case.[686] Applying these conclusions to the two appeals, an award of damages was plainly justified in the *Faulkner* case, but it had been set at too high a level, and was reduced from £10,000 to £6,500. In the *Sturnham* case, where delay in the hearing had not led to a delay in release, the Court of Appeal had been wrong to refuse to award damages for frustration and anxiety, and the judge's award of £300 was reinstated. Lord Carnwath JSC would have been prepared to accept that refusing to make an award of damages in relation to a delay of six months was consistent with the Strasbourg jurisprudence. However, he did not dissent from Lord Reed's approval of the award, nor from his statement of principles.[687] It should be noted that the quantum of the award in *Sturnham* did not fall to be considered by the Supreme Court, since leave to appeal on the question of quantum had been refused and the Court did not consider it necessary in order to do justice in the appeal. However, the Court made plain that awards for frustration and anxiety in cases of delay are invariably modest[688]; Lord Reed referred to the award of £300 as reasonable in the circumstances of this case[689]; and Lord Carnwath would have considered it compatible with Strasbourg case law not to make an award at all. There are clear indications, therefore, that the quantum of the award was considered acceptable.

13-129 **Assessment of damages** It is rare for the ECtHR to award more than £15,000 for non-pecuniary loss, a lower figure than is the case with domestic courts. In *R. (KB) v Mental Health Review Tribunal*[690] Burnton J reviewed the basis on which damages should be awarded and concluded that: "The English court should take account of the scale of damages awarded by the European Court." He also held that it would be contrary to the principles of the ECHR to award damages for loss of the chance of a favourable tribunal decision and that the likelihood of such a deci-

---

[685] [2013] UKSC 23; [2013] 2 A.C. 254 at [24]. See, the decisions of the Supreme Court in *R. (on the application of Kaiyam) v Secretary of State for Justice* [2014] UKSC 66; [2015] A.C. 1344, not following *James v UK*; and *Brown v Parole Board for Scotland* [2017] UKSC 69; [2018] A.C. 1, determining that *Kaiyam* is not to be followed. See further, para.13-107.

[686] [2013] UKSC 23; [2013] 2 A.C. 254 at [13], where the Court summarised its conclusions in relation to art.5(4) cases arising from delay in review of detention.

[687] [2013] UKSC 23; [2013] 2 A.C. 254 at [127].

[688] [2013] UKSC 23; [2013] 2 A.C. 254 at [67].

[689] [2013] UKSC 23; [2013] 2 A.C. 254 at [97].

[690] [2003] EWHC 193 (Admin); [2004] Q.B. 936 at [47].

sion had to be shown on the balance of probabilities.[691] Subsequently in *Anufrijeva v Southwark LBC*,[692] the Court of Appeal gave the following guidance as to quantum:

> "the levels of damages awarded in respect of torts as reflected in the guidelines issued by the Judicial Studies Board, the levels of awards made by the Criminal Injuries Compensation Board and by the Parliamentary Ombudsman and the Local Government Ombudsman may all provide some rough guidance where the consequences of the infringement of human rights are similar to that being considered in the comparator selected. In cases of maladministration where the consequences are not of a type which gives any right to compensation under our civil law, the awards of the Ombudsman may be the only comparator."

Significantly, the court went on to say:

> "There are good reasons why, where the breach arises from maladministration … the scale of damages should be modest. The cost of supporting those in need falls on society as a whole. Resources are limited and payments of substantial damages will deplete the resources available for other needs of the public including primary care."

The court also advised that Lord Woolf's extra-judicially expressed view that damages should be on the low side in comparison with those for tort, should be ignored and noted that this view had been criticised by the Law Commission in its report *Damages under the Human Rights Act 1998*.[693] However, in *R. (on the application of Greenfield) v Secretary of State for the Home Department*[694] the House of Lords confirmed that awards should not be significantly more or less generous that those of the ECtHR and domestic rules should not be applied. While the statutory language of s.8 refers to the "principles" applicable to awards of damages in Strasbourg, the House of Lords here held that the *quantum* of damages observed in Strasbourg cases should also be followed. Indeed in *R. (Faulkner) v Secretary of State for Justice; R. (Sturnham) v Parole Board*,[695] Lord Reed JSC suggested that the term "principles" in s.8(4) was to be understood in a broad sense, not to be "confined to articulated statements of principle". Not only were statements of general principle on the part of the Strasbourg court uncommon, they should not be taken at face value.[696] At the present stage of development of the damages remedy, courts should be guided primarily by any clear and consistent practice of the European court.[697] In an important statement, Lord Reed, with whom Lords Neuberger, Mance and Kerr agreed, proposed that the remedy under s.8 will in due course become "naturalised", emphasising a number of important differences between the role of an international court, and of a domestic court, when assessing damages. Thus:

> "over time, and as the practice of the European court comes increasingly to be absorbed into our own law through judgments such as this, the remedy should become naturalised. … we should have confidence in our own case law under section 8 once it has developed

691 [2003] EWHC 193 (Admin); [2004] Q.B. 936 at [62]–[64].
692 [2003] EWCA Civ 1406; [2004] Q.B. 1124 at [66], [74] and [75].
693 Law Com No.266, October 2000.
694 [2005] UKHL 14; [2005] 1 W.L.R. 673.
695 [2013] UKSC 23; [2013] 2 A.C. 254.
696 [2013] UKSC 23; [2013] 2 A.C. 254 at [31].
697 [2013] UKSC 23; [2013] 2 A.C. 254 at [39].

sufficiently, and not be perpetually looking to the case law of an international court as our primary source".[698]

For the time being, however, courts will need to assess damages in the light of Strasbourg practice. Lord Reed set out guidance as to the approach to be taken by parties when citing Strasbourg case law in order to direct courts to the underlying principles which the cases are said to express. Notably, that would not, according to Lord Reed, be necessary in cases relating to art.5(4), "which should take the present judgment as its starting point".[699] In other words, principles will over time be identified and extracted from the case law in relation to particular articles of the Convention.[700]

13-130 Reference in the courts to the quantum awarded in Strasbourg has now become routine and domestic courts have had the opportunity to deal with a range of issues arising in respect of quantum. In *Van Colle v Chief Constable of the Hertfordshire Police*,[701] the Court of Appeal left open for future consideration the question whether compensation under the HRA could be awarded for the distress suffered by the parents of a potential police witness who had been murdered following the failure of the police to take proper steps to protect his right to life under art.2. Sir Anthony Clarke MR noted the defendant's argument that "no Strasbourg award includes compensation for the applicant's own suffering except where the applicant was also a direct victim"[702] but as the defendants had not contended that no award should be made to the parents personally, he simply reduced the trial award to each parent from £17,500 to £7,500. The House of Lords reversed the decision of the Court of Appeal on liability without commenting on the assessment of damages.[703] In *R. (B) v DPP*,[704] Toulson LJ simply said that the amount awarded by way of "just satisfaction" in respect of a failure to prosecute, which thereby violated the art.3 rights of the victim, "should be in line with the customary level of Strasbourg awards in this area, which tend to be relatively modest", and awarded £8,000. In *R. (on the application of Waxman) v Crown Prosecution Service*,[705] Moore-Bick LJ awarded £3,500 in relation to a failure to prosecute an individual who was harassing the claimant, thus violating the claimant's art.8 rights. This was a less severe case than some of those considered by the European Court of Human Rights, in which applicants had been left vulnerable to serious physical abuse through failures to prosecute; but the failure did substantially affect the claimant's well-being. In *Savage v South Essex Partnership NHS Foundation Trust*,[706] Mackay J said that it was hard to discern the principles on which Strasbourg awards were determined, but was referred to a table of awards made by the European Court of

---

698 [2013] UKSC 23; [2013] 2 A.C. 254 at [29]; see also [39], referring to the current stage in development of the remedy.

699 [2013] UKSC 23; [2013] 2 A.C. 254 at [100].

700 The general guidance requires parties to prepare a table of authorities including identification of the particular violations which were established; the damages awarded; summaries of the appellants' and respondents' contentions in relation to the case; and a further chronological table of the authorities: [2013] UKSC 23; [2013] 2 A.C. 254 at [101]–[103]. The objective is for counsel to assist courts as much as possible in identifying the principles as to the relevant award of damages which can be extracted from the potential blizzard of authorities generated by Strasbourg cases.

701 [2007] EWCA Civ 325; [2007] 1 W.L.R. 1821.

702 [2007] EWCA Civ 325; [2007] 1 W.L.R. 1821 at [114].

703 [2008] UKHL 50; [2009] 1 A.C. 225.

704 [2009] EWHC 106 (Admin); [2009] 1 W.L.R. 2072; see para.13-99.

705 [2012] EWHC 133 (Admin); [2012] A.C.D. 48.

706 [2010] EWHC 865 (QB); [2010] P.I.Q.R. P14; [2010] Med. L.R. 292.

Human Rights. Taking into account that there had already been a full inquest into the death, he awarded £10,000, stating that this could only be "a symbolic acknowledgement that the defendant ought properly to give her some compensation to reflect her loss".[707] That award was discussed without dispute by the Supreme Court in *Rabone v Pennine Care NHS Foundation Trust*.[708] Here, the Court of Appeal's proposed award of £5,000 to each of the bereaved parents (had it found a violation) was not the subject of an appeal. Lord Dyson thought there was force in the argument that it was too low, but in the absence of an appeal by the claimants on quantum, the award was approved. Relevant factors in determining such an award in the context of breach of the operational duty to protect life included the closeness of family ties, and the serious nature of the breach in this instance. In *O v The Commissioner of Police for the Metropolis*,[709] Wyn Williams J identified substantial distress and frustration to be recognised by the European Court of Human Rights as justifying an award of damages for failure to investigate. In assessing damages, he took into account that the violation was in respect of failure to investigate rather than perpetration of the inhuman treatment, and referred to the restricted period of time during which the failure could be said to have extended the suffering of the claimants. This allowed him to position the case relative to others determined in Strasbourg, and he awarded £5,000 to each claimant. The decision in *Alseran v Ministry of Defence*,[710] dealing with test cases for over 600 similar claims (the "Iraqi civilian litigation") incorporates some important statements of principle for approaching damages awards under the HRA, which may be particularly attuned to test cases. Leggatt J suggested that despite the fact that HRA awards do not require application of the domestic scale of damages, it may sometimes be important to consider domestic awards. In assessing damages, three considerations were described as paramount: (a) transparency: the parties and the public were entitled to a reasoned judgment from which it could be seen how the sum awarded in each case had been arrived at; (b) objectivity: although the assessment of damages inescapably involved an exercise of judgment, justice required the adoption of an approach which was based on external standards and not simply on the intuition of the individual judge; (c) predictability: that was of vital importance in test cases, since there was a very strong public interest in facilitating the settlement of similar claims. In quantifying the claimants' human rights damages claims, the first stage was to identify the injuries which the claimant had suffered as a result of the relevant breach of his Convention rights and assess the amount of compensation that would be awarded for those injuries in accordance with English tort law. The court had then to consider whether to depart from or adjust that sum having regard to wider considerations of what was just and equitable in all the circumstances. The court was entitled to take account of the fact that the country where the claimants resided and suffered harm had a lower cost and standard of living than the UK. Damages would be assessed at around half the amount that would be recoverable on a claim in tort to which English law applied. Each of the claimants were awarded sums of around £10,000 to £15,000 in relation to ill-treatment, in addition to sums of between £2,700 and £3,300 for unlawful detention and additional damages for personal injury and the costs of medical treatment.

[707] [2010] EWHC 865 (QB); [2010] P.I.Q.R. P14; [2010] Med. L.R. 292 at [97].
[708] [2012] UKSC 2; [2012] 2 A.C. 72.
[709] [2011] EWHC 1246 (QB); [2011] H.R.L.R. 29.
[710] [2017] EWHC 3289 (QB); [2019] Q.B. 1251.

13-131 In *Dobson v Thames Water*,[711] the Court of Appeal followed *Hunter v Canary Wharf* and held that the assessment of damages for nuisance should not include an amount representing loss of amenity and interference suffered by members of the household other than the party with the rights required to pursue the action. Rather, damages would reflect the value of the property and diminution in amenity value. A member of the household whose loss was therefore not directly taken into account in the award of damages might have a claim under art.8 provided the nuisance affected their home, the Human Rights Act providing the sort of action which nuisance has not been extended to encompass. Having said that, the award of damages to the household in nuisance would be relevant to the Human Rights Act remedy and (given the modest levels of such awards) the tort award may well be thought to suffice in providing just satisfaction to other occupants in most circumstances. The Court of Appeal also thought it clear that the person with the relevant proprietary right would be unable to expect an additional award to reflect the violation of art.8. Given the modesty of Strasbourg awards, and the relative generosity of tort damages, it was inconceivable that such a "top up" would be found appropriate. Applying these principles, Ramsey J concluded at the trial of the actions that although there had been violations of the art.8 rights of the claimants, no damages under the HRA were "necessary" to afford just satisfaction in addition to the awards made for amenity nuisance.[712] In the case of those without a proprietary interest living in family homes, all the circumstances of the case were to be taken into account. These circumstances included the award of damages in nuisance to those with proprietary interests, which would reflect the actual impact of the nuisance on the amenity of those living in the property. Even where the claimant was not a family member and/or not a minor, so that there was no guarantee that they would receive a share of the damages, it was not established that the award of damages was "necessary". This reflected the fact that "the principal objective of the Convention is to declare any infringement and put a stop to it", and that "the interests of an individual, rather than the wider public, are only part of the matters for consideration".[713] Other relevant circumstances in this case included the fact that the court made declarations in respect of violations of art.8 rights, and that remedies were available under ss.80 and 82 of the Environmental Protection Act 1990 by abatement notices and by way of a complaint to OFWAT under s.94 of the Water Industry Act 1991. The very different case of *D v Commissioner of Police for the Metropolis*[714] provides something of a contrast. Here, awards of damages under the Human Rights Act were made to two claimants who had already been awarded compensation in a civil action against the rapist who had attacked them, and through the Criminal Injuries Compensation Fund. The police were liable for a breach of positive duties under art.3.[715] Green J reasoned that the earlier awards must be taken into account according to s.8(3) of the HRA but that these awards did not remove the justification for an award of damages for violation of the claimants' rights by the defendant police authority. The violation by the defendants was not vindicated by the earlier awards, since these related to the rapes themselves, not to the ad-

711 [2009] EWCA Civ 28; [2009] 3 All E.R. 319.
712 *Dobson v Thames Water Utilities Ltd* [2011] EWHC 3253 (TCC); (2011) 140 Con. L.R. 135.
713 *Dobson v Thames Water Utilities Ltd* [2011] EWHC 3253 (TCC); (2011) 140 Con. L.R. 135 at [1099].
714 [2014] EWHC 2493 (QB); [2015] 1 W.L.R. 1833.
715 The Supreme Court, confirming the outcome ([2018] UKSC 11; [2019] A.C. 196) could see no flaw in the reasoning of Green J in relation to the assessment of damages.

ditional harm and rights violations involved in the failure to investigate. While it was not possible to be entirely clear about which aspects of the harm suffered by the claimants was caused by the police handling of their claims (for example, the failure to believe their accounts and failure to take them seriously), nevertheless there was additional harm flowing from those breaches and therefore an award of damages should be made to each of the two claimants. These awards were set at £22,250 and £19,000, respectively.

4. Misfeasance in Public Office[716]

(a) Nature of the tort

Introduction The tort of misfeasance in public office originated in the electoral corruption cases of the late seventeenth century,[717] was expanded in the nineteenth century to cover the liability of judges of inferior courts for malicious acts within their jurisdiction,[718] and has now been authoritatively defined in the speech of Lord Steyn in *Three Rivers DC v Bank of England (No.3)*.[719] Lord Steyn explained that there were two different forms or limbs of the tort: 13-132

> "First there is the case of targeted malice by a public officer, i.e. conduct specifically intended to injure a person or persons. This type of case involves bad faith in the sense of the exercise of public power for an improper or ulterior motive. The second form is where a public officer acts knowing that he has no power to do the act complained of and that the act will probably injure the plaintiff. It involves bad faith inasmuch as the public officer does not have an honest belief that his act is lawful."[720]

The first form is referred to as "targeted malice" and the second as the "untargeted malice" or "illegality" limb. It can be classed as an "intentional tort" but the key element is an intention to act for an improper motive. Its rationale, according to Lord Steyn, is that "in a legal system based on the rule of law executive or administrative power 'may be exercised only for the public good' and not for ulterior or improper purposes" and hence, it was an exception to "the general rule … that, if conduct is lawful apart from the motive, a bad motive will not make [the defendant] liable."[721]

Targeted malice The difficulty of establishing liability under this limb is illustrated by *Jones v Swansea City Council*.[722] Jones alleged that the Council was liable for misfeasance in public office in maliciously voting for a resolution rescinding consent for a change in the use of commercial premises that he leased from the Council. He claimed that the malice stemmed from the personal antipathy of the leader of the Labour group which had infected all the other members of the group who voted as a block for the resolution. At first instance, the judge said that the evidence of the leader did not establish that he was "not motivated by malice", but concluded that despite the grounds for suspicion, malice had not been established 13-133

716 See Stanton, Skidmore, Harris and Wright, *Statutory Torts* (2003), Ch.4.
717 See *Ashby v White* (1703) 92 E.R. 126; reversed 1 E.R. 417.
718 See *Harman v Tappenden* (1801) 102 E.R. 214.
719 [2003] 2 A.C. 1. See also M. Aronson, "Misfeasance in Public Office: Some Unfinished Business" (2016) 132 L.Q.R. 427.
720 [2003] 2 A.C. 1 at 191.
721 [2003] 2 A.C. 1 at 190. See *Allen v Flood* [1898] A.C. 1. See para.1-59.
722 [1990] 1 W.L.R. 1453.

on the balance of probabilities and that his motive was about "having his own way". In the Court of Appeal, Slade LJ was dissatisfied with this finding and prepared to set it aside, but giving the leading speech in a unanimous House of Lords, Lord Lowry accepted the judge's finding commenting that the events had to be understood in the context of a council "divided by political animosity". The House went on to hold that even if malice were established on the part of the leader, the claimant's claim failed because it alleged that the council was liable for the tort because all the members of the Labour group were infected by the alleged malice and on the evidence this was clearly not the case.[723] Again, in *Calveley v Chief Constable of the Merseyside Police*[724] the House of Lords rejected the claimant's argument that his suspension pending disciplinary investigation was a misfeasance on the ground that there was no evidence that the Chief Constable had acted with malice when suspending him. One rare example of targeted malice is provided by the Canadian case of *Roncarelli v Duplessis*[725] where the Prime Minister of Quebec ordered a licensing commission to revoke the claimant's liquor license as part of a sustained campaign against his church, the Jehovah's Witnesses. The existence of targeted malice does not remove the need to show material damage to the claimant. In *Watkins v Secretary of State for the Home Department*[726] Lord Walker said:

> "Some cases of 'targeted' malice are very clear, such as the early Canadian case of *Roncarelli v Duplessis* [1959] SCR 121 (discussed by the Supreme Court of Canada in *Odhavji Estate v Woodhouse* [2003] SCC 69 at [19]). But the weight of authority is against treating targeted malice as being in a special category, rather than as being at the brightest end of a spectrum (see *Odhavji* at [22] and the decision of this House in *Three Rivers District Council v Governor and Company of the Bank of England* [2003] 2 A.C. 1 at pp.191–192 (Lord Steyn), 219–223 (Lord Hutton), 230–231 (Lord Hobhouse) and 235 (Lord Millett who expressed most strongly the view that there is a single tort of intention). A rule that the targeted malice limb (only) of the tort is actionable without proof of special damage would therefore be unprincipled and difficult to apply."

13-134 **Untargeted malice** The basis of liability for untargeted malice was reviewed in *Three Rivers DC v Bank of England (No.3)*.[727] Here some 6,000 investors who lost deposits when the fraudulently run Bank of Credit and Commerce International (BCCI) collapsed, claimed that the senior officials of the Bank of England acted in bad faith in: (a) licensing BCCI in 1979 when they knew it was unlawful to do so; (b) shutting their eyes to what was happening at BCCI after the license was granted; and (c) failing to close BCCI when the known facts cried out for action in the mid-1980s. The question was whether these allegations were sufficient to ground liability for misfeasance in public office on the part of the Bank of England. The Bank argued that for liability under the second limb it must be shown that the officials knew of the illegality of their acts and of the probability of resulting injury and that recklessness as to the illegality and probable injury was not sufficient. The claimant argued that objective recklessness in the sense of there being an obvious

---

723 The judgments were influenced by the way in which the case was pleaded and leave open the question whether a bare majority of malicious or infected councillors would have been enough to justify liability. A still less restrictive approach would be to impose liability where the malicious councillors were the key to the vote, i.e. the resolution would have been lost but for their malicious and improper votes.

724 [1989] A.C. 1228.

725 (1959) 16 D.L.R. (2d) 689.

726 [2006] UKHL 17; [2006] 2 A.C. 395 at [73].

727 [2001] UKHL 16; [2003] 2 A.C. 1.

risk to which the defendant had failed to give any thought, was sufficient. The House of Lords held that recklessness was sufficient but only in its subjective sense. Lord Steyn commented that to impose liability where the defendant had acted with reckless indifference to the illegality of his act and the probability of its causing injury, was "an organic development, which fits into the structure of our law governing intentional torts" and that "the policy underlying it is sound: reckless indifference to consequences is as blameworthy as deliberately seeking such consequences".[728] But he also said that the difficulty with a test of objective recklessness was that "it could not be squared with a meaningful requirement of bad faith in the exercise of public powers which is the *raison d'etre* of the tort". Hence, the claimant has to prove that the public officer acted with a state of mind of reckless indifference to the illegality of his act and its consequences. The nature of untargeted malice sufficient for the tort was considered by Nicol J in *TBS v Metropolitan Police Commissioner*.[729] Here, the claimant's father had been an undercover police officer who had embarked on a relationship with his mother, an animal rights activist, while assuming a false identity. The claimant was born in 1985, and his father's true identity as a police officer was revealed only in 2012. The claim related to the psychological consequences of these events. Nicol J declined to strike out actions framed in misfeasance, and in negligence. So far as misfeasance was concerned, the claimant asserted that the tortfeasor knew that the claimant "was likely to suffer psychiatric damage or was recklessly indifferent to this consequence". A submission that this was insufficient, and that the claimant needed to show that psychiatric injury was known to be a probable consequence, was rejected. Language used by the House of Lords in *Three Rivers* had varied, but Lord Steyn had used the expression "likely to cause damage" as a test of liability; and Lord Hope had referred to a "serious risk that the plaintiff would suffer loss". The point was too uncertain for striking out to be an appropriate course.

A knowing excess of powers is also essential. Thus in *B v Reading BC*,[730] a social worker and police officer who had made very significant errors in the process of interviewing the claimant's daughter, wrongly concluding that he had sexually abused her, were found neither to have been subjectively reckless in the sense required by *Three Rivers*; nor to have knowingly exceeded their powers. Rather, they had made a "bad misjudgement" in a bona fide exercise of their authority. No duty of care in negligence was owed to the suspected parent,[731] and so the claimant's action failed. In both *Stockwell v Society of Lloyd's*,[732] and *London Borough of Southwark v Dennett*,[733] the Court of Appeal has rejected misfeasance claims on the grounds that the claimant had failed to establish the subjective recklessness required by *Three Rivers*. In *Dennett*, May LJ said: **13-135**

> "The whole thrust of the *Three Rivers* case was that … mere reckless indifference without the addition of subjective recklessness will not do. This element virtually requires the

[728] [2003] 2 A.C. 1 at 192. Note that Lord Millett at 235, took a different view, considering that knowledge was not a substitute for the relevant intention. See also *Douglas v Hello! Ltd* [2005] EWCA Civ 595; [2006] Q.B. 125 at [222], where Lord Phillips said that the element of intention required for the economic torts could not be applied to misfeasance where the gist of the tort is deliberate abuse of power.

[729] [2017] EWHC 3094 (QB).

[730] [2009] EWHC 998 (QB); [2009] 2 F.L.R. 1273.

[731] See para.13-24 onwards.

[732] [2007] EWCA Civ 930; [2008] 1 W.L.R. 2255.

[733] [2007] EWCA Civ 1091; [2008] B.L.G.R. 94.

claimant to identify the persons or people said to have acted with subjective recklessness and to establish their bad faith. An institution can only be reckless subjectively if one or more individuals acting on its behalf are subjectively reckless and their subjective state of mind needs to be established."[734]

In *Carter v Chief Constable of the Cumbria Police*,[735] Tugendhat J emphasised the importance of properly particularising the elements of bad faith. Here, the claims related to disciplinary proceedings, which would be outside the reach of the tort of malicious prosecution (see Ch.16). Claims in negligence had been discontinued. It was held that the claim should be anxiously scrutinised in case the defendant's immunity from a suit in negligence was being circumvented through the device of pleading misfeasance. On this basis, insufficient particulars in support of subjective recklessness had been pleaded, and the claims were struck out. Absence of evidence of malice or knowing excess of powers has been fatal to many recent claims in misfeasance.[736]

13-136 *Muuse v Secretary of State for the Home Department* was a successful claim in misfeasance at first instance, but was reversed on the misfeasance issue on appeal.[737] The claimant held Dutch nationality but was mistakenly detained in custody for 128 days pending consideration of a deportation order, in the mistaken belief that he was a Somali national, despite having an identity card in his possession. The Secretary of State admitted that this had amounted to a false imprisonment for which compensatory damages might be paid, but denied the claim in misfeasance and submitted that neither aggravated nor exemplary damages should be payable. The judge held that the real risk of deportation made the claimant's treatment far worse than a simple false imprisonment. Having listed the number of errors involved and the complete failure to consider the claimant's position in any adequate way, he concluded that there had been a reckless indifference to doing justice and that some of the defendants' officers "did not care" whether the claimant was deported or not. The misfeasance action succeeded, but the judge made clear that he would have awarded exemplary and aggravated damages in any event; as such, the misfeasance action did not add to the damages awarded. The latter point was emphasised by the Court of Appeal. The claim in misfeasance failed because the judge had not made an express finding of reckless indifference to the legality of their actions on the part of the officials, and no such reckless indifference could be inferred from the facts. Even so, the judge's award of exemplary and aggravated damages was not disturbed, since these heads of damage were justified in respect of the claim in false imprisonment.

13-137 **The remoteness test for untargeted malice** A second issue in *Three Rivers* concerned the remoteness test to be applied to untargeted malice. The claimant argued that it was sufficient if the officials could foresee the resulting losses whereas the defendant argued that they had to know that their illegality could cause loss. Lord Steyn rejected the knowledge test on the ground that it did "not readily fit into the standard of proof generally required in the law of tort, and specifically in the case of intentional torts" and "unnecessarily emasculate[d] the effectiveness of the

[734] [2007] EWCA Civ 1091; [2008] B.L.G.R. 94 at [21].

[735] [2008] EWHC 1072 (QB).

[736] Examples not otherwise mentioned in this section are *Abdalla v Transport for London* [2013] EWHC 3916 (QB); *Hargreaves v Chief Constable of Greater Manchester* [2013] EWHC 2478 (QB).

[737] [2009] EWHC 1886 (QB); reversed [2010] EWCA Civ 453.

tort". Instead the choice lay between a test of knowledge that the decision would probably damage the claimant and a test of reasonable foreseeability. Lord Steyn considered that "in both forms of the tort the intent required must be directed at the harm complained of" and that this justified the conclusion that a claimant must establish that the defendant acted "in the knowledge that his act would probably injure the [claimant] or person of a class of which the [claimant] was a member". He commented that the force of the argument "for a rule allowing recovery of all foreseeable losses [a]s necessary in a democracy as a constraint upon abuse of executive power ... is substantially reduced by the recognition that subjective recklessness on the part of a public officer ... about the consequences of his act, in the sense of not caring whether consequences happen or not, is sufficient". In other words, the less restrictive "recklessness" basis of liability was balanced by a more restrictive "knowledge of probability" test of remoteness. In his view this produced "a satisfactory balance between the two competing policy consideration, namely enlisting tort law to combat executive and administrative abuse of power and not allowing public officers, who must always act for the public good, to be assailed by unmeritorious actions". With this guidance the case itself was adjourned for further consideration on the facts.

No proximity required In *Akenzua v Secretary of State for the Home Department*[738] the Court of Appeal had to determine whether in the light of Three Rivers there was any requirement of proximity between defendant and claimant. The allegation in the case was that an immigration officer knowing that the only proper course was to detain and remove from the UK an illegal immigrant with a record of violence, colluded with police officers in setting him at liberty to act as a police informant and that this was reckless as to the risk to potential victims of his violent proclivities. The administrators of the estate of someone he murdered during his period of arranged liberty claimed that this conduct amounted to misfeasance in public office by the immigration officer and that the police officers were also liable for misfeasance. It was accepted that the tort could apply where the consequence of the tort was personal injury rather than property damage.[739] The issue was whether it could only apply where there was proximity between defendant and claimant in the sense of the defendant being able to identify a closely defined class of probable victims which included the claimant. On the facts, there was no such proximity as all persons residing in London were at risk and seven million people could not constitute a class for this purpose. The defendant relied on the reference in Lord Steyn's speech in *Three Rivers* to the requirement that "the defendant acted in the knowledge that his act would probably injure the [claimant] or a person of a class of which the [claimant] was a member".[740] The Court of Appeal rejected this argument. Sedley LJ interpreted the reference to "knowledge of class" as "not a free standing requirement of tort ... [but one] derived from the antecedent proposition that the intent or recklessness must relate ('be directed') to the kind of harm suffered"[741] and said that in the context of *Three Rivers* "the purpose of being required to specify a class is to be able to establish that the harm done lay within the ambit of the material intent or recklessness". Simon Brown LJ 13-138

738 [2002] EWCA Civ 1470; [2003] 1 W.L.R. 741.

739 [2002] EWCA Civ 1470; [2003] 1 W.L.R. 741 at [17], Sedley LJ commented that "any other doctrine would give life to the old reproach that the law was more concerned with property than people".

740 [2003] 2 A.C. 1 at 196.

741 [2002] EWCA Civ 1470; [2003] 1 W.L.R. 741 at [19].

also rejected the defendant's argument that it would be strange if the claim could succeed in misfeasance but fail in negligence for lack of proximity, on the ground that "a claim in misfeasance postulates that the claimant can prove altogether more blameworthy conduct than in a negligence action" and hence, "it is unsurprising that the law should decline to impose a further limiting requirement akin to proximity". The Court upheld the claimants' appeal against the first instance decision that it should be struck out. It also held that whilst the police could not be liable for the misfeasance tort by simply instigating the action of the immigration officer, they could be liable on the basis that it was "a breach of the commission of the peace for a police officer improperly to procure the release by another official of a criminal known to be dangerous". In *Ashley v The Chief Constable of Sussex Police*,[742] Sir Anthony Clarke MR reversed a first instance decision to strike out a claim for misfeasance on the ground that the police owed no duty to the claimant either at common law or under the Convention, stating that the "case in misfeasance does not depend upon a duty of care or a duty under the Convention".[743] Rather, it depended on whether the police "knew that what they were doing was unlawful or … were reckless as to whether it was lawful or not".[744] Without commenting on misfeasance, the House of Lords rejected an appeal against the refusal to strike out the battery element of the claim.[745]

13-139 **Material damage required** The courts have emphasised the importance of the damage requirement for this tort. However, there is still some uncertainty over the precise nature of the damage required. Given that the tort is inherently concerned with excess of powers in bad faith, it is at least arguable that the range of types of damage required for the tort to be actionable should be broader than the equivalent range of damage which will suffice for an action in negligence. It is already established that purely economic losses are more readily recoverable (in the rare case where the other elements of the tort are made out) in an action for misfeasance than in an action for negligence, and that proximity is not required.[746] In *Watkins v Secretary of State for the Home Department*,[747] the House of Lords reversed a decision of the Court of Appeal holding that no damage was required for the tort of misfeasance in public office where a constitutional right such as that of unimpeded communication with legal advisors, had been infringed. Lord Bingham considered that the 1703 decision in *Ashby v White*,[748] on which the Court of Appeal had relied, was concerned with protection of an incorporeal property right and was not a reliable authority for the proposition that the tort was actionable per se.[749] The House of Lords recognised that the tort could be extended to protect constitutional rights without proof of actual damage but for a number of reasons considered that this would not be appropriate. First, there was a concern that it would be difficult to define the scope of protected rights with any precision and this would lead to uncertainty. Secondly, there was a reluctance to extend liability without thorough consultation and consideration by the Law Commission. Thirdly, it was considered

742 [2006] EWCA Civ 1085; [2007] 1 W.L.R. 398.
743 [2006] EWCA Civ 1085; [2007] 1 W.L.R. 398 at [136].
744 [2006] EWCA Civ 1085; [2007] 1 W.L.R. 398 at [137].
745 [2008] UKHL 25; [2008] 1 A.C. 962. See para.1-12.
746 See para.13-138.
747 [2006] UKHL 17; [2006] 2 A.C. 395.
748 (1703) 1 Sm. L.C. 253; 2 Ld. Raym. 938.
749 [2006] UKHL 17; [2006] 2 A.C. 395 at [23].

that the right to unimpeded communication and other constitutional rights would now be adequately safeguarded by the ability to claim under the Human Rights Act 1998. Fourthly, it would be inappropriate to introduce an overlapping tort liability with the possibility of an award of exemplary damages when no such award would be available in proceedings for breach of the Convention rights.

In *Karagozlu v Commissioner of the Police of the Metropolis*,[750] the Court of Appeal held that depriving a prisoner of a residual liberty was sufficient damage to support a cause of action for misfeasance. Sir Anthony Clarke MR said: "we would hold that loss of liberty, if not a form of physical injury, is at least akin to or analogous to physical injury."[751] He cited Holt CJ in *Savill v Roberts*,[752] as treating loss of liberty as a form of material damage and distinguished *Watkins* as not considering the issue of loss of liberty. He further distinguished *R. v Deputy Governor of Parkhurst Prison Ex p. Hague*,[753] where it had been held that a prisoner had no residual liberty vis-à-vis the governor to enable him to sue for false imprisonment, as being a case where action had been taken with the authority of the governor and no allegations of bad faith had been made.[754] He concluded that loss of residual liberty was actionable in misfeasance and suggested that a prisoner put in solitary confinement by a prison officer or a person detained within a lawful police cordon and then handcuffed to a lamppost by a police officer, would have an action if the act of the officer was a misfeasance.[755] In *Iqbal v Prison Officers Association*,[756] a claim in false imprisonment was brought against a trade union whose members had undertaken an unlawful one day strike. The claimant had been confined to his cell as a consequence of the strike. That claim failed on the basis that the trade union was not directly responsible for the additional imprisonment of the claimant which resulted, nor did it intend it. Lord Neuberger MR suggested that claims involving additional periods of confinement due to the inaction of prison officers would be better confined to misfeasance in a public office, and therefore to cases where the inaction was "deliberate or dishonest". In *Malcolm v Ministry of Justice*,[757] this was taken to mean that in cases of loss of residual liberty (in this case, a reduction in time in the open air from 60 to 30 minutes each day), misfeasance provided a safety net to deal with the "most extreme" cases of bad faith and abuse of power. In this case, the inaction was not unlawful, so that there could be no action in misfeasance. But in any event, the claimant had failed to show the required bad faith. An appeal based solely on art.8 ECHR was dismissed by the Court of Appeal.[758] **13-140**

The Court of Appeal considered the nature of the damage required for the tort in the case of *Hussain v Chief Constable of West Mercia*.[759] The claimant taxi driver had been involved in many incidents with members of the public, and was concerned that he had not been treated fairly by the police. He alleged a campaign of racial harassment against him. There was no evidence of a recognised psychiatric illness, but there were stress-related conditions including irritability and physical **13-141**

[750] [2006] EWCA Civ 1691; [2007] 1 W.L.R. 1881.
[751] [2006] EWCA Civ 1691; [2007] 1 W.L.R. 1881 at [39].
[752] (1698) 12 Mod. 208.
[753] [1992] A.C. 58.
[754] [2006] EWCA Civ 1691; [2007] 1 W.L.R. 1881 at [47].
[755] [2006] EWCA Civ 1691; [2007] 1 W.L.R. 1881 at [51].
[756] [2009] EWCA Civ 1312; [2010] Q.B. 732.
[757] [2010] EWHC 3389 (QB).
[758] *Malcolm v Secretary of State for Justice* [2011] EWCA Civ 1538. See para.13-111.
[759] [2008] EWCA Civ 1205.

discomfort. All members of the Court of Appeal agreed that there was insufficient injury to complete the tort. Stanley Burnton LJ referred to the following remarks of Lord Bingham on the subject of "material damage" in *Watkins*:

> "There was no challenge to the judge's findings of bad faith against the three officers, nor to his finding that their conduct had caused the respondent no financial loss or physical or mental injury, which in argument was helpfully described as 'material damage', an expression understood to include recognised psychiatric illness but not distress, injured feelings, indignation or annoyance."[760]

There was significant variation in the way that the Court of Appeal approached this statement. Stanley Burnton LJ thought that it equated "material damage" in misfeasance claims with the requirements for non-physical personal injury in negligence and, by implication, other torts: "where the damage alleged is financial or physical damage to property or injury, the requirements of the tort of misfeasance are not more stringent than those of, for example, negligence."[761] Maurice Kay LJ proposed that there may be variation in the damage requirement between different torts, dependent in part on the nature of the conduct required, and in part on the range of circumstances for which the tort is properly suited:

> "Misfeasance in public office is an intentional tort of considerable gravity. It is a tort of obloquy ... In most of its manifestations, it does not result in physical injury. While it is entirely appropriate to deny actionability where the non-physical consequences are trivial (so avoiding lengthy trials which, at best, result in very modest awards of damages), it is important not to set the bar too high."[762]

On this approach, Lord Bingham meant only that the forms of material damage recoverable in misfeasance *included* recognised psychiatric damage, not that it is limited to that type of non-physical injury; and he would "strive to treat misfeasance in public office exceptionally". The Master of the Rolls saw the force of these points but preferred not to express an opinion on what precisely amounts to actionable damage in the tort, until a suitable case arose. He did, however, note that "there must be injury of some kind, whether psychiatric or physical".

13-142 In *Romantiek BVBA v Simms*,[763] Wyn Williams J considered the novel question of whether the tort could be made out where the only damage caused was that the claimant was prevented from engaging in unlawful trade and therefore earning profits from illegal activities. Apart from doubting that there could be "bad faith" in a relevant sense where the public officer's motive was to prevent unlawful trade, Wyn Williams J also held that loss of prospective profits from illegal trade could not amount to relevant damage for the purposes of the tort. Drawing on the Court of Appeal decision in *Hewison v Meridian Shipping Services PTE Ltd*,[764] this was a variation of the illegality principle encapsulated in the maxim ex turpi causa non oritur actio. In this instance, the relevant maxim could be said to be ex turpi causa non oritur damnum.

---

760 *Watkins v Secretary of State for the Home Department* [2006] UKHL 17; [2006] 2 A.C. 395 at [7].
761 [2008] EWCA Civ 1205 at [15].
762 [2008] EWCA Civ 1205 at [20].
763 [2008] EWHC 3099 (QB).
764 [2002] EWCA Civ 1821; [2003] I.C.R. 766.

(b) Scope of the tort

Public officer The alleged tortfeasor must be a public officer, though it has been said that ordinarily the individual should not be the defendant. Rather, the ordinary approach is to bring an action against an institution or body on the basis that it will be vicariously liable for the misfeasance of its officers, rather than proceeding directly against individuals. This is for the protection of individuals going about their public duty who may be the subject of ill founded claims, and should be the direct subject of a claim only where "absolutely necessary".[765] In *Three Rivers*[766] Lord Steyn said that the office had to be understood in a "relatively wide sense" and thus, citing *Jones*,[767] would extend to "a local authority exercising private law functions as a landlord". In *AA v Southwark LBC*,[768] three of the defendant council's officers were found to have exercised their powers as public officers in relation to a local authority secure tenancy for an improper motive, with the intention of harming the claimant by evicting him when there were no reasonable grounds for doing so and arranging for his possessions to be seized and destroyed unlawfully. Each was liable for misfeasance in a public office and the local authority was also vicariously liable. Other actions in tort and under the HRA (for actions inconsistent with art.8 ECHR) were also established. It is the nature of the office exercising power and not the nature of the power which is crucial. As *Jones* illustrates, a collective public body such as a council can be liable although there is some uncertainty as to the extent to which it must have been infected with malice. In *Rawlinson v Rice*[769] the New Zealand Court of Appeal resolved doubts in the lower court by holding that public office extended to judicial office and that a District Court Judge could be sued for misfeasance in public office. *Three Rivers* and *Bourgoin SA v Ministry of Agriculture Fisheries and Food*[770] illustrates the potential importance of the tort in the regulatory context but its major impact may be in the law enforcement area. In *Brent LBC v Davies*,[771] Zacaroli J held that governors of a grant-maintained school were "public officers" for the purpose of an action in misfeasance in a public office. They were said to fulfil one of the responsibilities of government, while the public had a significant interest in the discharge of their duties. 13-143

Officers with law enforcement responsibility The tort has a significant impact on public officers with law enforcement responsibility: 13-144

(a) *Police officers:* The alleged collusion in the improper release of a violent criminal in *Akenzua*[772] is one example of the kind of situation that can give rise to misfeasance liability. There is obvious scope for the tort in relation to the more extreme instances of police malpractice such as the fabrication of evidence. In *Rees v Commissioner of Police for the Metropolis*, the actions of a police officer who had perverted the course of justice by directly encouraging testimony from an unreliable "witness", also amounted to

---

765 *Adams v Law Society of England and Wales* [2012] EWHC 980 (QB) at [160]–[162].
766 [2003] 2 A.C. 1 at 191.
767 *Jones v Swansea City Council* [1990] 1 W.L.R. 1453.
768 [2014] EWHC 500 (QB).
769 [1998] 1 N.Z.L.R. 454.
770 [1986] Q.B. 716. The case concerned the revocation of an import license for French turkeys by the defendant ministry.
771 [2018] EWHC 2214 (Ch).
772 [2002] EWCA Civ 1470; [2003] 1 W.L.R. 741, see para.13-138.

misfeasance in public office.[773] A different example is provided by *Elliott v Chief Constable of Wiltshire*[774] where the court refused to strike out a misfeasance claim against a police officer alleged to have got a troublesome journalist dismissed from his newspaper by improperly revealing his past criminal convictions to the editor of the paper. In *DIL v Commissioner of Police of the Metropolis*[775] the court considered a claim that officers engaged in covert surveillance operations had developed long-term sexual relationships with the claimants as part of those operations, under the supervision of superior officers. This behaviour amounted to deceit, assault, misfeasance in public office and negligence. The court concluded that it was not open to the police to offer a "neither confirm nor deny" response. Again, it has been suggested that a wilful refusal by a police officer to intervene to stop a violent attack on an individual, could constitute misfeasance.[776] Similarly in *Amin v Imran Khan & Partners*,[777] a claim in negligence, a failure to add a claim for misfeasance where the claimants' son, a young offender of Asian origin, had been killed by a cellmate who was known to be both racist and dangerous, was (amongst other failings) held to be in breach of the defendant solicitor's duty of care: this suggests that the misfeasance claim was thought to have some prospect of success. The police immunity which bars negligence claims in respect of the investigation of crime, has no application to misfeasance claims.[778]

(b) *Crown Prosecutors:* In *Elguzouli-Daf v Commissioner of Police of the Metropolis*[779] Steyn LJ recognised that liability for misfeasance in public office "might attach to the decision of a C.P.S prosecutor" and that "a citizen who is aggrieved by a prosecutor's decision, has in our system potentially extensive private law remedies for a deliberate abuse of power".

(c) *Prison officers:* In *Racz v Home Office*[780] the House of Lords recognised that prison officers who were alleged to have deliberately exceeded their powers under the Prison Rules by maliciously moving the claimant to a strip cell, could be liable for misfeasance in public office. There is a considerable potential for claims in this context and also an overlap with claims under the Human Rights Act 1998.

(d) *Social workers:* In *F v Wirral BC*[781] Stuart-Smith LJ commented that where social workers consciously exceeded their powers in relation to children,

---

773 [2018] EWCA Civ 1587: the claimants succeeded in showing damage sufficient for the actions in misfeasance and malicious prosecution. On the malicious prosecution elements, see paras 15-25; 15-52; 15-57; and 15-60.

774 *The Times,* 5 December 1996.

775 [2014] EWHC 2184 (QB).

776 *R. v Dytham* [1979] Q.B. 722.

777 [2011] EWHC 2958 (QB).

778 See *Bennett v Commissioner of the Police for the Metropolis* (1998) 10 Admin. L.R. 245, where the claimant claimed that the defendant had tricked him into flying to the UK where he was arrested on theft charges. The court dismissed the defendant's application to strike out on the basis of the public policy immunity. The claimant's claim was also struck out on the ground that he had failed to establish malice against the defendant. His earlier claim of misfeasance against the Secretary of State in relation to his certificate of public interest immunity for documents relating to the case, also failed for lack of malice: [1995] 1 W.L.R. 488.

779 [1995] Q.B. 335 at 347.

780 [1994] 2 A.C. 45.

781 [1991] Fam. 69 at 107.

they and the responsible authority might be liable for misfeasance in public office. As in *Elguzouli-Daf*, this suggestion was made in part as justification for denial of a duty of care in negligence.[782]

Vicarious liability In *Racz v Home Office*[783] the Court of Appeal had held that the Home Office could not be vicariously liable for the alleged misfeasance by its prison officers because such officers would have been acting ultra vires. However, the House of Lords refused to strike out the claim on this ground. Lord Jauncey said that vicarious liability would apply where the officers were performing their duties in an unauthorised way as opposed to being on a "frolic of their own". The adoption by the House of a "close connection test" in *Lister v Hesley Hall Ltd*[784] makes it all the more likely that the employing authorities will be held vicariously liable for the misfeasance in public office of their employees; and an action against the employer, not against the individual, appears to be the norm.[785] **13-145**

Improper exercise of power Two issues require consideration where powers are concerned: whether omissions can give rise to liability and whether an improper prosecution can also give rise to liability in misfeasance. In *Three Rivers*[786] Lord Hutton cited Brennan J in *Mengel*'s case[787] for the proposition that "[a]ny act of omission done or made by a public official in purported performance of the functions of the office can found an action for misfeasance in public office" and added that "whether the public official is sued in respect of an act or omission, it must be a deliberate one involving an actual decision and liability will not arise from injury suffered by mere inadvertence or oversight". Lord Millett explained further that: **13-146**

> "a failure to act can amount to misfeasance only where (i) the circumstances are such that the discretion whether to act can only be exercised in one way so that there is effectively a duty to act; (ii) the official appreciates this but nevertheless takes a conscious decision not to act and (iii) he does so with intent to injure the plaintiff or in the knowledge that such injury will be the natural and probable consequence of this failure to act."[788]

He identified *R. v Dytham*[789] as the "one case in the books" exemplifying this.[790] As to the second question, there seems no good policy reason why a malicious decision to prosecute should not be capable of giving rise to a misfeasance action but doubt has been expressed on the matter.[791] A misfeasance action would enable the claimant to avoid the need to prove the lack of reasonable and probable cause

782 See also *B v Reading BC* [2009] EWHC 998 (QB); [2009] 2 F.L.R. 1273; para.13-36, where a misfeasance action based on wrongdoing by a social worker failed on the facts for lack of subjective recklessness and lack of knowing excess of powers.

783 [1994] 2 A.C. 45.

784 [2001] UKHL 22; [2002] 1 A.C. 215. See para.6-29.

785 See para.13-143.

786 [2003] 2 A.C. 1 at 223.

787 *Northern Territory of Australia v Mengel* (1995) 185 C.L.R. 301 (Aust. H.C).

788 [2003] 2 A.C. 1 at 237.

789 [1979] Q.B. 722.

790 But see also *Toumia v Evans*, *The Times*, 1 April 1999, where the Court of Appeal refused to strike out a claim for misfeasance where prison officers refused to unlock the plaintiff's cell as part of unlawful industrial action.

791 *McDonagh v Commissioner of Police for the Metropolis*, *The Times*, 28 December 1989, where at first instance it was suggested that the only cause of action where the prosecution ends in the claimant's favour, is malicious prosecution. In *Clifford v Chief Constable of the Hertfordshire Constabulary* [2011] EWHC 815 (QB) (see also para.15-60), a successful action in malicious

required for the tort of malicious prosecution but the malice requirement of misfeasance should ensure consistency and in each case would protect against attempts to circumvent the lack of a duty of care in negligence.[792] In *Darker v Chief Constable of the West Midlands Police*[793] Lord Clyde said that the same principles of witness immunity applied whatever the cause of action. Consistently with this observation, in *Baxendale-Walker v Middleton*,[794] claims in misfeasance in public office were among those struck out on the basis (inter alia) of immunities on the part of various of the nine defendants. The absolute privilege or immunity held to apply to the disciplinary tribunals involved was therefore treated as extending to the tort of misfeasance in public office; as did the witness immunity enjoyed by the eighth and ninth defendants (the Chairman of the Panel of the Solicitors Disciplinary Tribunal, and the Panel itself).

13-147 **Damages** In *Kuddus v Chief Constable of Leicestershire Constabulary*[795] the House of Lords held that exemplary damages could be awarded for misfeasance in public office where the facts fell within the category of oppressive, arbitrary or unconstitutional actions by servants of the government. In that case, it was accepted that a police officer who had forged the claimant's signature on a document withdrawing an allegation of theft against the police, was liable for misfeasance but the Court of Appeal had struck out the claim for exemplary damages. The House of Lords reinstated the claim. Lord Hutton said that the power to award exemplary damages:

> "serves to uphold and vindicate the rule of law because it makes clear that the courts will not tolerate such conduct. It serves to deter such actions in future as such awards will bring home to officers in command of individual units that discipline must be maintained at all times."[796]

However, Lord Scott doubted whether exemplary damages were ever appropriate in a case against an employer based on vicarious liability and indicated that he would have been receptive to a submission that exemplary damages should no longer be available in any civil proceedings.[797] In *Watkins v Secretary of State for the Home Department*[798] Lord Carswell said:

> "Notwithstanding the fact that the House has ruled in *Kuddus v Chief Constable of*

prosecution, Mackay J said briefly that he also considered that there was a misfeasance, but added no separate damages to reflect this (at [65]). He did not comment on the doubts expressed in McDonagh about the exclusivity of malicious prosecution. In *Daniels v Chief Constable of South Wales* [2015] EWHC 228 (QB) it was suggested that misfeasance in public office may be a suitable cause of action where police officers provide evidence to the CPS with a view to initiating a prosecution. Evidence of misconduct after the prosecution had been initiated could also form the basis for a claim in malicious prosecution. On appeal, in *Daniels v Chief Constable of South Wales Police* [2015] EWCA Civ 680, the claims in misfeasance in public office were allowed to proceed to trial.

792 *Carter v Chief Constable of the Cumbria Police* [2008] EWHC 1072 (QB).

793 [2001] 1 A.C. 435.

794 [2011] EWHC 998 (QB).

795 [2001] UKHL 29; [2002] 2 A.C. 122. See further para.27-143.

796 [2001] UKHL 29; [2002] 2 A.C. 122 at [79].

797 [2001] UKHL 29; [2002] 2 A.C. 122 at [139], [111]. This view was not, however, shared by all members of the House, and Lords Nicholls and Hutton took a more positive approach to exemplary damages.

798 [2006] UKHL 17; [2006] 2 A.C. 395 at [81].

Leicestershire [2001] UKHL 29; [2002] 2 A.C. 122 that exemplary damages may in principle be awarded in cases of misfeasance in public office, I should myself prefer to confine the award of such damages very closely indeed."

Lord Rodger said that it would be wrong to develop the tort of misfeasance "so as to create a situation where exemplary damages could be awarded when they would not be available in equivalent proceedings for breach of the relevant Convention right",[799] and Lord Bingham considered:

> "That exemplary damages may be awarded where a compensatory award is insufficient to mark the court's disapproval of proven misfeasance in public office, and deter repetition, is, as already noted, accepted. But the policy of the law is not in general to encourage the award of exemplary damages, and I would not for my part develop the law of tort to make it an instrument of punishment in cases where there is no material damage for which to compensate."[800]

These remarks reinforced the conclusion that no action should lie in misfeasance where there had been no material damage.

5. CONCLUSION

Coherence In his speech in *Three Rivers*[801] Lord Steyn said that "the coherent *development* of the law required … the place of the tort of misfeasance in public office [to be considered] against the general scheme of the law of tort". Thus, he noted that its availability was a justification for the non-actionability of some negligence claims for maladministration but also that it was not an effective remedy to deal with state liability for breaches of Community law. In *Akenzua*[802] Simon Brown LJ stressed that the fact that proximity was required for the tort of negligence was no reason for it to be applied in the tort of misfeasance. Again, in *D v East Berkshire Community Health NHS Trust*[803] a major reason for rejecting the claim for negligent investigation was that accepting such a claim would undermine the requirement of malice for liability in misfeasance, malicious prosecution or (effectively) defamation.[804] The underlying point is that each of the forms of tort liability applying to public services has a particular role to fulfil. That role can be understood better in comparison and not confusion with the other forms of liability. Misfeasance in a public office concerns abuse of power, while malicious prosecution (considered in Ch.16) concerns abuse of the process of law. 13-148

Maladministration The major gap in the framework of private law liability concerns the lack of a damages remedy for unlawful administrative acts which cause loss to the claimant but do not give rise to liability under one of the existing heads of recovery. An example is that of an individual unlawfully refused a license to pursue a business activity. Such an individual may be able to secure reversal of the decision by judicial review but will not be able claim compensation for loss suf- 13-149

799 [2006] UKHL 17; [2006] 2 A.C. 395 at [64].
800 [2006] UKHL 17; [2006] 2 A.C. 395 at [26].
801 [2003] 2 A.C. 1 at 190.
802 [2002] EWCA Civ 1470; [2003] 1 W.L.R. 741 at [33].
803 [2005] UKHL 23; [2005] 2 A.C. 373.
804 See para.13-24.

fered in the meantime.[805] A similar gap is also illustrated by *Jain v Trent Strategic HA*,[806] although here members of the House of Lords thought it at least possible that there could be liability under the Human Rights Act in future such cases. There is judicial and academic concern[807] about this but, as Sedley LJ has commented, the policy implications of extending liability for damages would be "immense". He suggested that the step should be left to legislation.[808] In its Consultation Paper, *Administrative Redress: Public Bodies and the Citizen*,[809] the Law Commission invited views in respect of the abolition of the tort of misfeasance in public office, as part of a new package of remedies for maladministration which would remove "truly public" activities from the reach of the tort of negligence and create a new action conditional on serious fault. The Commission pointed to the expensive nature of litigation in misfeasance cases and the scarcity of successful claims, despite recent clarification in respect of the ingredients of the tort. Among the key concerns guiding this part of the Consultation is protection of public authorities from frivolous and unfounded litigation, or perhaps simply from excessive claiming where success rates are so low. In effect, "misfeasance" would be subsumed within the new liability for "serious fault". The Consultation received a critical response from tort lawyers, and it was questionable whether the new concepts proposed by the Commission to identify sufficiently serious fault would reduce litigation. The provisional proposals were ultimately withdrawn, the Law Commission noting that it had not succeeded in persuading many consultees that there was a case for reform (though also noting inconsistency in the views of their critics).[810] It is significant that Government was "firmly opposed" to the proposed reforms. As the Law Commission's Summary explains:

> "1.4 Our proposals were contested by many parties, most notably the key stakeholder Government. That opposition and the inability to access appropriate evidence to counter the opposition mean that we feel that it is impractical to attempt to pursue the reform of state liability any further at this time."

Where misfeasance in public office is concerned, the Law Commission said that despite drawing its proposals to a close, it still took the view that the action against individual office-holders was capable of being intrusive and unfair, and that this outweighed its benefits for individual claimants, at least within the context of the

---

805 An individual may only recover damages in an application for judicial review if he would have recovered damages if the claim had been made in an ordinary private law action: Senior Courts Act 1981 s.31(4). For examples of the gap see *R. v Knowsley MBC Ex p. Maguire* (1992) 90 L.G.R. 652; [1992] C.O.D. 478; and *R. (Quark) v Secretary of State for Foreign and Commonwealth Affairs (No.2)* [2003] EWHC 1743 (Admin); [2003] A.C.D. 96, where Collins J dismissed a strong case with regret on the ground that "English law does not provide a remedy in damages for breach of a public law right". An appeal in respect of damages under the Human Rights Act was pursued to the House of Lords, but this claim too was ultimately unsuccessful: [2005] UKHL 57; [2006] 1 A.C. 529.

806 [2009] UKHL 4; [2009] 1 A.C. 853; see para.13-51.

807 In *Sandhar v Department of Transport* [2004] EWCA Civ 1440; [2005] 1 W.L.R. 1632 at [57]. Brooke LJ said he would have welcomed assistance for the claimant from public funds as a remedy for the loss suffered through the defendant's maladministration. See Carnwath LJ writing extra judicially, "Welfare Services—liabilities in tort after the Human Rights Act" [2001] P.L. 475; Fordham, "Reparation for Maladministration" [2003] J.R. 104; Harlow, *Administrative Compensation in State Liability—Tort Law and Beyond* (2004).

808 *R. v Commissioners of Customs and Excise Ex p. F & I Services Ltd* [2001] EWCA Civ 762; [2001] S.T.C. 939.

809 Law Com CP No.187 (2008).

810 Law Commission, *Administrative Redress: Public Bodies and the Citizen* (2010), Law Com. No.322. An analysis of responses is also available via the Law Commission's website.

wider proposals.[811] In respect of state liability generally, the Law Commission recommended the collation and publication of the costs of compensation for central government (including settlements, compensation payments made after judgment, and associated legal costs),[812] in order to provide a firmer foundation for future debate.

[811] Law Commission, *Administrative Redress: Public Bodies and the Citizen* (2010), Law Com. No.322, para.3.70.

[812] Law Commission, *Administrative Redress: Public Bodies and the Citizen* (2010), Law Com. No.322, paras 4.72–4.73.

Chapter 14

TRESPASS TO THE PERSON

Table of Contents

1. Introduction

14-01 **Trespass to the person** It has long been recognised that "[t]he fundamental principle, plain and incontestable, is that every person's body is inviolate".[1] As such, interference, however slight, with a person's elementary civil right to security of the person, and self-determination in relation to his own body, constitutes trespass to the person. Trespass to the person may take three forms, assault, battery and false imprisonment: "An assault is an act which causes another person to apprehend the infliction of immediate, unlawful, force on his person; a battery is the actual infliction of unlawful force on another person", and false imprisonment is "the unlawful imposition of constraint on another's freedom of movement from a particular place".[2] These torts are all descended from the ancient writ of trespass. The two distinctive features of trespass were that it is actionable per se and that the interference with the claimant's interest has to be a "direct" consequence of the defendant's act. Indirect consequences were the subject of a writ of "trespass on the case", later referred to as an "action on the case" or simply "case". This distinction is retained in the modern law, in terms of the rules of remoteness of damage. The claimant can recover in trespass for all the *direct* consequences of the tort, even if they are unforeseeable. However, the distinction is seldom important,[3] as most direct consequences are also foreseeable.

14-02 Trespass to the person is also regarded as a tort of intention, but as will be seen,[4] in this context the term "intention" has a very particular meaning. Although there is a generalised principle of liability for careless conduct (in the form of the tort of negligence) English law has not developed a general principle of liability for the intentional infliction of harm; rather a claimant must demonstrate that his case falls within the specific requirements of one of the particular trespass torts. Furthermore, despite Lord Hoffmann's observation that *Wilkinson v Downton* has nothing to do with the tort of trespass to the person,[5] it is appropriate to consider that case in this chapter, along with the statutory rules on protection from harassment.[6]

14-03 Although the torts of assault, battery and false imprisonment apply to all categories of defendant, in practice most claims are brought against agencies of the state in respect of the manner in which they have carried out their law enforcement functions or their responsibilities in relation to the detention and/or treatment of mentally incapacitated patients. The victims of assault and battery perpetrated by private individuals, while frequently having sound claims, often find that the defendant is not worth suing and have to look to the criminal injuries compensation scheme for financial recompense.[7] On the other hand, claims against the police, prison authorities, or an NHS Trust in respect of medical treatment, tend to focus on the justification for acting in a particular way (such as arresting a suspect or treating a patient without consent). The consequence is that more often than not it is the defences to trespass that feature in the cases rather than the basic elements

---

1 *Collins v Wilcock* [1984] 1 W.L.R. 1172 at 1178, per Robert Goff LJ.

2 *Collins v Wilcock* [1984] 1 W.L.R. 1172 at 1178 at 1178.

3 Though see, e.g. *Allan v New Mount Sinai Hospital* (1980) 109 D.L.R. (3d) 634 (reversed on a pleading point at (1982) 125 D.L.R. (3d) 276) where the distinction was significant.

4 See para.14-04.

5 *Wainwright v Home Office* [2003] UKHL 53; [2004] 2 A.C. 406 at [47].

6 See para.14-19.

7 See para.14-144.

of the relevant torts. This, and the fact that trespass is actionable per se,[8] makes trespass to the person an important tool in the protection of civil liberties.

Trespass: intention and negligence An act does not constitute trespass to the person unless it is done deliberately or negligently.[9] A man pushed by another against a third person commits no battery. The sportsman firing at a clay pigeon commits a battery when his pellet hits a fellow human only if he either intended to hit that person, or if negligence can be proved (assuming that it remains possible to commit trespass negligently[10]). A blow inflicted in a state of automatism is no battery, but if the defendant intended to strike the claimant it is no defence simply that, by reason of mental incapacity, he did not know that what he was doing was wrong.[11] When the defendant is proved to have intended to commit a battery against X, and by mistake strikes Y, that is a battery against Y.[12] Thus, when a soldier fires into the crowd at a rioter intending to strike him, but misses and strikes another person nearby, it is no defence that the defendant did not intend to strike the claimant.[13] The defendant's intention relates to the act constituting trespass; there is no requirement that the defendant intended to harm the claimant.[14] 14-04

In *Letang v Cooper*,[15] Lord Denning attempted to confine trespass to the person to intentional acts and to bar any action for negligent trespass: 14-05

> "If one man intentionally applies force directly to another, the [claimant] has a cause of action for assault and battery, or, if you so please to describe it, in trespass to the person … If he does not inflict injury intentionally but only unintentionally, the [claimant] has no cause of action today in trespass. His only cause of action is in negligence, and then only on proof of want of reasonable care."[16]

However, although Danckwerts LJ concurred with Lord Denning's judgment on negligent trespasses, Lord Denning himself offered as an alternative ratio in *Letang*[17] the idea that any action for trespass to the person, including intentional trespass, was barred after three years as an action for personal injuries arising out of "breach of duty".[18] Hence it is not yet finally established that direct injuries inflicted via negligence are not actionable in trespass.

It was once the view that there was a difference in the onus of proof between 14-06

---

8 Though substantive damages will be awarded where the claimant has sustained personal injury or been deprived of his freedom.

9 *Stanley v Powell* [1891] 1 Q.B. 86; approved *National Coal Board v Evans* [1951] 2 K.B. 861; *Fowler v Lanning* [1959] 1 Q.B. 426; *Letang v Cooper* [1965] 1 Q.B. 232; *Wilson v Pringle* [1987] Q.B. 237.

10 On which see *Fowler v Lanning* [1959] 1 Q.B. 426.

11 *Morriss v Marsden* [1952] 1 T.L.R. 947; cf. *Tindale v Tindale* [1950] 4 D.L.R. 363.

12 *James v Campbell* (1832) 5 C. & P. 372; followed in *Livingstone v Ministry of Defence* [1984] N.I. 356. See also *Haystead v Chief Constable of Derbyshire* [2000] 3 All E.R. 890; [2000] 2 Cr. App. R. 339.

13 *Livingstone v Ministry of Defence* [1984] N.I. 356.

14 "It is the act and not the injury which must be intentional. An intention to injure is not essential to an action for trespass to the person. It is the mere trespass by itself which is the offence": *Wilson v Pringle* [1987] Q.B. 237 at 248.

15 [1965] 1 Q.B. 232.

16 [1965] 1 Q.B. 232 at 239.

17 [1965] 1 Q.B. 232 at 240.

18 For judicial sympathy with this approach see *A v Hoare* [2008] UKHL 6; [2008] 1 A.C. 844 at [17], per Lord Hoffmann (obiter).

bringing an action for personal injuries in negligence and bringing it in trespass, at least in actions which did not arise out of accidents on the highway.[19] In trespass, it was contended, the defendant must disprove negligence. In *Fowler v Lanning*, Diplock J held that there is no such difference in the onus of proof. The onus of proving negligence lies upon the claimant, whether the action is called negligence or trespass.[20]

14-07 One advantage of an action framed in trespass is that the requirement in negligence to establish that the injuries complained of are of a reasonably foreseeable kind does not apply.[21] Trespass is actionable per se, and all the damage flowing directly from that unlawful act is recoverable. Thus, a defendant may be liable for unforeseeable damage—irrecoverable in negligence—arising from trespass to the person.[22] Where, however, the facts are such that a claim could be framed either in negligence or in trespass to the person, the claimant cannot obtain an advantage by suing in trespass rather than negligence. The description given by the claimant to the cause of action is irrelevant.[23] Where the factual situation discloses a substantive cause of action based on negligence, all the rules governing the tort of negligence apply whether in relation to proof of damage, onus of proof, limitation or whatever. The burden of proof in trespass to the person lies with the claimant to establish the interference with his person by the defendant.[24] It is then for the defendant to establish some justification or defence.

14-08 **Defendant's mistake as to a defence** Where the defendant has made a mistake, whether negligently or non-negligently, as to the availability of a defence, he may be liable in trespass depending upon whether the action is false imprisonment on the one hand, or assault and/or battery on the other. In relation to false imprisonment, it has been held by the House of Lords that a prison governor who in good faith, and in reliance on the existing law, calculates the release date of a prisoner which subsequently turns out to have been too late because the law has changed in the interim, is liable in false imprisonment for the additional days that the prisoner is detained.[25] The relevant intention consists of the intention to detain the prisoner combined with the fact of detention. By contrast, in *Ashley v Chief Constable of Sussex*,[26] the House of Lords held in relation to assault and battery that a defendant may invoke the defence of self-defence if he honestly and reasonably (yet mistakenly) believed that he was about to be attacked. The case involved a police officer shooting dead a suspect in the honest, but mistaken, belief that the suspect was about to use lethal force against the police officer. The particular facts of the

---

19 This was because the defence of inevitable accident came to be interpreted to mean that if the defendant could prove that he had not been negligent the claim would fail: *Stanley v Powell* [1891] 1 Q.B. 86.

20 [1959] 1 Q.B. 426. More particularly Diplock J stated that C must plead and give particulars of negligence unless the res ipsa loquitur principle can be invoked.

21 See *Wilson v Pringle* [1987] Q.B. 237.

22 See *Allan v New Mount Sinai Hospital* (1980) 109 D.L.R. (3d) 634.

23 *Letang v Cooper* [1965] 1 Q.B. 232 at 243.

24 Where, however, an alleged battery comprises, in effect, a charge of murder the criminal standard of proof may apply: *Halford v Brookes* [1992] P.I.Q.R. P175.

25 *R. v Governor of Brockhill Prison Ex p. Evans (No.2)* [2001] 2 A.C. 19; see also para.14-26.

26 [2008] UKHL 25; [2008] 1 A.C. 962. In *R. (on the application of Duggan) v Assistant Deputy Coroner for the Northern District of Greater London* [2017] EWCA Civ 142; [2017] 1 W.L.R. 2199, the court held that the criminal law test for self-defence (and not the civil law test stated in *Ashley*) applied at inquests.

case may well be critical to the decision, which reverses prior Court of Appeal authority indicating that an honest and reasonable mistake cannot be a defence to trespass to the person.[27] Notably, a majority of their Lordships (Lord Scott, Lord Rodger and Lord Neuberger) expressly left open the question of whether even a reasonably held, but mistaken, belief would be sufficient if the defendant was not actually in immediate danger of being attacked.[28] And there is certainly good cause to doubt the availability of the defence in such circumstances, for the defendant is not forced into a split-second decision that denies him the opportunity to ascertain with more precision the relevant facts. Thus, for example, if a surgeon were to operate by mistake on the wrong patient, invocation of the defence would be hard to justify given that the surgeon's mistake would lack the reasonableness required by the *Ashley* test.

2. Battery

Battery "The least touching of another in anger is a battery."[29] The direct imposition of any unwanted physical contact on another person may constitute the tort of battery. There is no requirement to prove that the contact caused or threatened any physical injury or harm. "An intention to injure is not essential to an action for trespass to the person. It is the mere trespass by itself which is the offence."[30] The culpable touching may take several forms. Thus, so long as it is direct, anything which amounts to a blow, whether inflicted by hand, weapon or missile, is a battery. It is a battery to throw water over someone or to spit on his face.[31] It is a battery to overturn a chair on which someone is sitting.[32] And in *Dodwell v Burford*,[33] it was held to be a battery when the defendant struck the claimant's horse so that he was thrown and injured.[34] But when the contact is only indirectly consequential on the act of the defendant, as where he lays a trap for the claimant, logically there should be no battery.[35] 14-09

Hostile intent? Not every deliberate touching of another constitutes a battery.[36] A degree of physical contact is an inevitable part of everyday life.[37] In *Wilson v* 14-10

---

27 *Hepburn v Chief Constable of Thames Valley Police* [2002] EWCA Civ 1841 at [24], per Sedley LJ.

28 Even though they all technically left open the question, Lords Scott and Rodger felt the balance of authority was against the defence being available ([2008] UKHL 25; [2008] 1 A.C. 962 at [20] and [55] respectively), while Lord Neuberger was of the opposite view ([2008] UKHL 25; [2008] 1 A.C. 962 at [89]–[90]).

29 *Cole v Turner* (1704) 6 Mod. 149, per Holt CJ.

30 *Wilson v Pringle* [1987] Q.B. 237 at 249.

31 *R. v Cotesworth* (1704) 6 Mod. 172; *Pursell v Horn* (1832) 8 A. & E. 602.

32 *Hopper v Reeve* (1817) 7 Taunt. 698; or the ladder on which he is standing; *Collins v Renison* (1754) Say. 138.

33 (1670) 1 Mod. 29.

34 It has been said that to take a chattel from a man forcibly is in itself an assault: see *Green v Goddard* (1704) 2 Salk. 691, per Powell J Striking A, which act in turn causes injury to B is a battery of B, as where D punched W in the face causing the child in W's arms to fall, striking his head on the floor: *Haystead v Chief Constable of Derbyshire* [2000] 3 All E.R. 890; [2000] 2 Cr. App. R. 339.

35 But note *DPP v K* [1990] 1 W.L.R. 1067 (accused convicted of criminal assault when he dumped acid in a hot air hand/face drier so that acid scalded the next user of the drier).

36 *Cole v Turner* (1704) 6 Mod. 145: "If two or more meet in a narrow passage, and without any violence or design of harm, one touches the other gently, it will be no battery", per Holt CJ.

37 In *F v West Berkshire HA* [1990] 2 A.C. 1 at 73 Lord Goff said that: "That exception is concerned with the ordinary events of everyday life—jostling in public places and such like—and affects all

Pringle,[38] the Court of Appeal said that for a touching to constitute battery it must be shown to be hostile, though hostility was not to be equated with malevolence or ill-will. Lord Goff in *F v West Berkshire HA*[39] doubted the usefulness of the word "hostile" to define the required state of mind in battery. The term was incompatible with the basic principle that "any touching of another's body is, in the absence of lawful excuse, capable of amounting to a battery and a trespass".[40] He preferred to ask whether there was any physical contact imposed on the claimant in excess of that "generally acceptable in everyday life"?[41] If it was, and the claimant did not consent to the contact, the defendant will have committed a battery. A constable who took hold of a woman's arm to require the woman to carry on listening to her committed a battery.[42] Kissing a newly met colleague on the lips may not be motivated by hostility,[43] but clearly falls beyond what is generally acceptable in everyday life. Shaking his hand falls within Lord Goff's exception to the general prohibition on non-consensual touching. No battery is committed even though, unknown to the defendant, the claimant has a fixed aversion to any form of physical contact.

14-11 **Absence of consent** An exception to the general prohibition on non-consensual touching was set out by Lord Goff in *F v West Berkshire HA*. He considered that no action in trespass could lie in respect of "all physical contact generally acceptable in the ordinary conduct of everyday life", such as brushing past another in a crowded corridor.

3. ASSAULT

14-12 **Assault** "An assault is an act which causes another person to apprehend the infliction of immediate, unlawful, force on his person".[44] The defendant's act must also be coupled with the capacity of carrying the intention to commit a battery into effect.[45] Although in popular language an assault includes a battery, a person may be liable for an assault without being liable for a battery.[46] Thus, "[i]f you direct a weapon, or if you raise your fist, within those limits which give you the means of striking, that may be an assault".[47] However, where defendants are in close proximity to the claimant but cannot actually carry out their threats because the claimant

---

persons, whether or not they are capable of giving their consent." But if someone forces his way through the crowd "in a rude and inordinate manner" this could constitute battery: *Cole v Turner* (1704) 6 Mod. 149.

38 [1987] Q.B. 237 at 246–248.

39 [1990] 2 A.C. 1.

40 [1990] 2 A.C. 1 at 73.

41 *Collins v Wilcock* [1984] 1 W.L.R. 1172 at 1178. This includes "touching a person for the purpose of engaging his attention, though of course using no greater degree of physical contact than is reasonably necessary in the circumstances for that purpose"; but "persistent touching to gain attention in the face of obvious disregard may transcend the norms of acceptable behaviour and so be outside the exception": ibid. at 1179. cf. *Donnelly v Jackman* [1970] 1 W.L.R. 562.

42 *Collins v Wilcock* [1984] 1 W.L.R. 1172. Contrast *Pegram v DPP* [2019] EWHC 2673 (Admin): borderline case where police officer took hold of a protestor's arm for a second to get his attention.

43 *R. v Chief Constable of Devon and Cornwall Ex p. CEGB* [1982] Q.B. 458 at 471. Query what is "generally acceptable" touching during the COVID-19 pandemic.

44 *Collins v Wilcock* [1984] 1 W.L.R. 1172 at 1178.

45 *Stephens v Myers* (1830) 4 C. & P. 349; *Read v Coker* (1853) 13 C.B. 850.

46 *Jones v Sherwood* [1942] 1 K.B. 127.

47 *Cobbett v Grey* (1849) 4 Ex. 729 at 744, per Pollock CB.

is under police guard, there is no assault.[48] The defendants lack the means to commit the threatened battery. Threats and vile abuse per se do not constitute a tortious assault even though conduct designed to cause psychiatric harm constitutes a criminal assault.[49] Accordingly, the claim for harassment created by the Protection from Harassment Act 1997 may, in many cases, offer the claimant a more favourable remedy than the tort of assault.[50]

Threatening conduct It is an assault to aim a gun in a hostile manner within shooting distance, although it may be at half cock, because the cocking is a momentary operation.[51] Similarly, if a man makes a rush at the claimant so that a blow would almost immediately have reached him, but is stopped before he is near enough to deal a blow, this is an assault.[52] As the substance of an assault is an act causing reasonable apprehension of a battery, it is submitted that if an unloaded firearm is aimed in such circumstances that, had it been loaded, its discharge would have been likely to cause injury, that is an assault, unless the person at whom it is pointed knows that it is empty.[53] By contrast, a mere gesture, however menacing, is not actionable if it appears at the time that there is no intention to put the menace into immediate effect. In *Tubervell v Savage*,[54] for example, the defendant put his hand to his sword and said: "If it were not assize time I would not take such language from you". It was held to be no assault. Similarly, mere threatening words do not constitute an assault.[55] Nor is it an assault for one person to stand in front of another and refuse to move if there is no threat to touch him.[56] It is, however, assault to take or threaten active measures to block or obstruct another.[57] In *Hepburn v Chief Constable of Thames Valley Police* Sedley LJ commented that: "While it is not an assault simply to get in someone's way, it is a technical assault to obstruct them in circumstances which make it clear that if they go on they will be stopped forcibly".[58] 14-13

48 *Thomas v NUM* [1986] Ch.20 (working miners in a reinforced bus protected by police not assaulted by their striking colleagues).

49 *R. v Ireland* [1998] A.C. 147 (threats made over the telephone); *R. v Constanza* [1997] 2 Cr. App. R. 492.

50 See para.14-19.

51 *Osborn v Veitch* (1858) 1 F. & F. 317 at 318, per Willes J.

52 *Stephens v Myers* (1830) 4 C. & P. 349.

53 *R. v St George* (1840) 9 C. & P. 483 at 490 and 493 (overruled on another point by *R. v Duckworth* [1892] 2 Q.B. 83). There is, however, authority to the contrary: *Blake v Barnard* (1840) 9 C. & P. 626 (but this was a decision based on the pleadings, and in any event would seem to be wrong in principle).

54 (1669) 1 Mod. Rep. 3. But cf. *R. v Light* (1857) 27 L.J.M.C. 1.

55 *Mead's Case* (1823) 1 Lew. C.C. 184; see also *Read v Coker* (1853) 13 C.B. 850; cf. *R. v Ireland* [1998] A.C. 147. Where threatening words cause psychiatric harm they may be actionable under the principle of *Wilkinson v Downton* [1897] 2 Q.B. 57. See the discussion of *Wilkinson v Downton* in *Wainwright v Home Office* [2003] UKHL 53; [2004] 2 A.C. 406; paras 14-14 to 14-17.

56 *Innes v Wylie* (1844) 1 C. & K. 257. See also *Squires v Botwright* [1972] R.T.R. 462.

57 *Innes v Wylie* (1844) 1 C. & K. 257; *Murray v Ministry of Defence* [1985] 12 N.I.J.B. 12.

58 [2002] EWCA Civ 1841 at [17].

4. INTENTIONAL INFLICTION OF INJURY

(a) Liability based on defendant's intention to cause harm

14-14 **Wilkinson v Downton** In *Wilkinson v Downton*[59] the defendant told the claimant that her husband had been seriously injured in an accident. This was untrue, but was intended as a practical joke. The claimant was shocked and suffered a serious reaction. Wright J held the defendant liable because he had "wilfully done an act calculated to cause harm—that is to say, to infringe … [a] right to personal safety, and has in fact thereby caused physical harm".[60] Since the defendant's act was obviously intended to produce some effect of the kind that it did cause, an intention to produce the harm was imputed to the defendant, and it was no answer to say more harm was done than was anticipated. *Wilkinson v Downton* was approved by the Court of Appeal in *Janvier v Sweeney*.[61] The factual circumstances of *Wilkinson v Downton* do not fit the classic definitions of assault or battery because the harm was caused indirectly and there was no application, or threat, of force. For that reason there has been debate as to whether it represents a residuary category of trespass to the person or whether it should be treated as a separate, unclassified tort.[62] The man who poisons someone's drink, who deliberately infects someone with a contagious disease, who startles someone descending a flight of stairs causing a fall, who prevents a doctor from treating a sick patient—in each case he *ought* to be liable even though the specific requirements of assault or battery are not satisfied. For almost a century *Wilkinson v Downton* was regarded as laying down a general principle, but was rarely, if ever, applied. Attempts to adapt the principle to create a common law tort of harassment led to closer attention being paid to the conditions for the principle to apply. More recently, the Supreme Court examined the operation of the principle in *Rhodes v OPO*[63] and held unanimously that the action has three elements: conduct, mental and consequence. In terms of conduct, the Court held that the cause of action under *Wilkinson v Downton* does not extend beyond words or conduct directed at the claimant for which there is no justification or reasonable excuse. The claim would fail therefore where the defendant had written a book about his life which was simply of general interest to the public even if it might be distressing for his son if he read it. The Court found it difficult to envisage any circumstances in which speech which was not deceptive, threatening or possibly abusive, could give rise to liability in tort for wilful infringement of another's right to personal safety. This leaves two related issues: (1) to what consequences (forms of harm) does the principle apply; and (2) what is meant by the mental element?

---

59 [1897] 2 Q.B. 57.

60 [1897] 2 Q.B. 57 at 59. The nature of the physical harm was not, however, clear from the report. Wright J made reference (at 58) to "permanent physical consequences" yet failed to spell out what "permanent physical consequences" he considered normally flow from being informed that one's spouse has broken his legs in an accident.

61 [1919] 2 K.B. 316.

62 In *Wainwright v Home Office* [2003] UKHL 53; [2004] 2 A.C. 406 at [47] Lord Hoffmann considered that *Wilkinson v Downton* "has nothing to do with trespass to the person".

63 [2015] UKSC 32; [2016] A.C. 219.

Consequence: the meaning of injury In *Wong v Parkside Health NHS Trust*[64] the Court of Appeal emphasised that under the principle in *Wilkinson v Downton* the damage that must result is physical harm or a recognised psychiatric illness. A "catalogue of rudeness and unfriendliness" was behaviour which was not to be expected of grown up colleagues in the workplace, but could not be regarded as "behaviour so calculated to infringe [the claimant's] legal right to personal safety that an intention to do so should be imputed to the second defendant".[65] Similarly, in *Wainwright v Home Office*,[66] the House of Lords upheld the decision of the Court of Appeal to the effect that emotional distress alone was not sufficient, but if severe emotional distress caused bodily harm, and the requisite intention existed, then there would be liability. Lord Hoffmann, however, went a long way towards sidelining the rule in *Wilkinson v Downton*, arguing that while at the time of the decision claims in respect of psychiatric harm were not available where the defendant had been negligent, the modern law of negligence ought to be seen as having captured much of the relevant ground now that it more readily permits claims for psychiatric harm. It had, he said, become "unnecessary to fashion a tort of intention or to discuss what the requisite intention, actual or imputed, should be".[67] The Supreme Court in *Rhodes* disagreed. It affirmed that where a recognised psychiatric illness is the product of severe mental or emotional distress, it is sufficient for the rule that the defendant intended to cause severe distress which in fact results in recognisable illness. 14-15

The mental element: intention to cause at least mental or emotional distress In *Wong v Parkside Health NHS Trust*[68] the Court of Appeal held that in order to be categorised as an act "calculated to cause harm" to the claimant the defendant must have intended to violate the claimant's interest in her freedom from such harm, namely physical injury or a recognised psychiatric illness. The defendant's conduct must be such that that degree of harm was so likely to result that the defendant cannot be heard to say that he did not mean it to do so. He will be taken to have meant it to do so by the combination of the likelihood of such harm being suffered as a result of his behaviour and his deliberately engaging in that behaviour.[69] It has been debated whether this will include objective recklessness (Court of Appeal in *Wainwright*)[70] or subjective recklessness (House of Lords in *Wainwright*).[71] The Supreme Court in *Rhodes* stated that where a recognised psychiatric illness is the product of severe mental or emotional distress, it is sufficient for the tort that the defendant intended to cause severe distress which in fact results in recognisable illness.[72] It was not necessary to prove that the defendant intended to cause the illness in question. Recklessness would not, however, be included in the definition of the mental element: "to hold that the necessary mental 14-16

64 [2001] EWCA Civ 1721; [2003] 3 All E.R. 932.
65 [2001] EWCA Civ 1721; [2003] 3 All E.R. 932 at [17].
66 [2003] UKHL 53; [2004] 2 A.C. 406.
67 [2003] UKHL 53; [2004] 2 A.C. 406 at [40].
68 [2001] EWCA Civ 1721; [2003] 3 All E.R. 932.
69 [2001] EWCA Civ 1721; [2003] 3 All E.R. 932 at [12].
70 [2001] EWCA Civ 2081; [2002] Q.B. 1334 at [79], per Buxton LJ.
71 *Wainwright v Home Office* [2003] UKHL 53; [2004] 2 A.C. 406 at [45] per Lord Hoffmann.
72 See also *C v WH* [2015] EWHC 2687 (QB); [2016] P.I.Q.R. Q2 (sexting of vulnerable pupil in special school—perpetrator could not realistically say that the obvious consequences of his actions were unintended).

element is intention to cause physical harm or severe mental or emotional distress strikes a just balance".[73] The line is therefore drawn at intentionality. In *Brayshaw v Partners of Apsley Surgery*[74] the court found it very unlikely that the defendant had the requisite intention to cause harm—the intention of the defendant, misguided as it may have been, was the improvement of the claimant's spiritual (and therefore mental) health and, in the view of the judge, this was a long way from the type of conduct which this tort is intended to catch.

14-17 Given that the rule in *Wilkinson v Downton* is assuredly an intentional tort, then in line with the three more established torts of assault, battery and false imprisonment, "problems as to foreseeability do not arise". For "[i]f the conduct is actionable then compensation should be payable for the intended harm".[75]

(b) Harassment: common law

14-18 **A common law tort of harassment?** In the 1990s a number of cases appeared to suggest that a tort of harassment based on the principle in *Wilkinson v Downton* could be developed.[76] In *Hunter v Canary Wharf Ltd*[77] Lord Hoffmann noted that there was no necessary reason to confine *Wilkinson v Downton* to the intentional infliction of psychiatric injury but noted also that the Protection from Harassment Act 1997 rendered it unnecessary to consider how a common law tort of harassment might have developed. In *Wong v Parkside Health NHS Trust*[78] the Court of Appeal confirmed that the 1997 Act had effectively precluded the development of a common law tort of harassment.

(c) Protection from Harassment Act 1997

14-19 The Protection from Harassment Act 1997 creates both civil remedies[79] and criminal offences[80] in respect of "a course of conduct which amounts to harassment of another" which the defendant "knows or ought to know amounts to harassment".[81] Notwithstanding these references to the actual or constructive knowledge of *the defendant*, the House of Lords has made clear that *an employer* can be held vicariously liable in damages for the conduct of its employees.[82] And it is also clear that the course of conduct may have been pursued either by one

[73] [2015] UKSC 32; [2016] A.C. 219 at [89]. Lord Neuberger (Lord Wilson agreeing) also suggested (obiter) at [119] that there was a powerful case for stating that where an intent to cause distress was an essential ingredient of the tort, it should be enough for the claimant to establish that he suffered sufficient distress as a result of the defendant's statement.

[74] [2018] EWHC 3286 (QB); [2019] 2 All E.R. 997.

[75] *Wainwright v Home Office* [2003] UKHL 53; [2004] 2 A.C. 406 at [50].

[76] See, e.g. *Burnett v George* [1992] 1 F.L.R. 156; *Pidduck v Molloy* [1992] 2 F.L.R. 202; *Burris v Azadini* [1995] 1 W.L.R. 1372; *Khorasandjian v Bush* [1993] Q.B. 727.

[77] [1997] A.C. 655.

[78] [2001] EWCA Civ 1721; [2003] 3 All E.R. 932.

[79] Protection from Harassment Act 1997 s.3(1). The civil standard of proof applies to an application for an injunction made under s.3: *Jones v Hipgrave* [2004] EWHC 2901 (QB); [2005] 2 F.L.R. 174.

[80] s.2(1). See also Public Order Act 1986 s.5; Criminal Justice and Police Act 2001 ss.42 and 42A.

[81] s.1(1). Importantly, the question of what D knows or ought to know is confined only to the matter of what amounts to harassment. By contrast, D need not know, or be able to foresee, the kind of harm which results from the harassment: *Jones v Ruth* [2011] EWCA Civ 804; [2012] 1 W.L.R. 1495 at [32], per Patten LJ.

[82] *Majrowski v Guy's and St Thomas' NHS Trust* [2006] UKHL 34; [2007] 1 A.C. 224.

employee, or "by more than one employee each acting on different occasions in furtherance of some joint design".[83] In addition, s.1(1A) now provides that a person must not pursue a course of conduct:

(a) which involves harassment of two or more persons; and
(b) which he knows or ought to know involves harassment of those persons; and
(c) by which he intends to persuade any person:
  (i) not to do something that he is entitled or required to do; or
  (ii) to do something that he is not under any obligation to do.

This subsection creates a criminal offence, but there is no civil remedy in damages for its breach.[84] On the other hand, a victim is entitled to apply for an injunction in relation to breaches of s.1(1A).[85] The standard applied by the Protection from Harassment Act is objective. The defendant will be taken to have known that his conduct amounts to or involves harassment "if a reasonable person in possession of the same information would think the course of conduct amounted to or involved harassment of the other".[86] The fact that the defendant suffers from a mental illness is irrelevant because otherwise there would be a significant gap in the protection afforded by the Act, particularly since the conduct at which the Act was aimed was likely to be conducted by those of an obsessive or otherwise unusual psychological makeup, or those suffering from an identifiable mental illness.[87] Thus, in a case where the defendant made 95 telephone calls to a small business saying that he would persist in calling until he got to speak to a particular individual, it was held that these repeated calls could amount to harassment even though (i) the initial calls were made by way of legitimate enquiry; and (ii) the defendant thought that it was the recipient of the calls who had behaved unreasonably in failing to connect him to the person sought.[88]

"Harassment" is not defined in the 1997 Act, though s.7(2) states that it "includes alarming the person or causing the person distress" and "conduct" includes speech.[89] It has also been held that the conduct in question "must be grave" since the only difference between the crime and the tort of harassment is the standard of proof; and in any event, "in life one has to put up with a certain amount of annoyance: things have got to be fairly severe before the law, civil or criminal, will intervene".[90] Thus, where a newspaper publishes a series of articles concerning a press officer who has had an affair with a prominent MP, it will not amount to harassment to **14-20**

83 *Daniels v Commissioner of Police of the Metropolis* [2006] EWHC 1622 at [9], per Mackay J.

84 The Protection from Harassment Act 1997 s.3(1) creating the right to a civil remedy for damages was amended to make it clear that it applies only to breach of s.1(1), not s.1(1A).

85 The Protection from Harassment Act 1997 s.3(A). See, e.g. *AMP v Persons Unknown* [2011] EWHC 3454 (TCC); [2011] Info. T.L.R. 25 at [44]–[45], per Ramsey J; *Triad Group Plc v Makar* [2019] EWHC 423 (QB), [44]–[49].

86 s.1(2).

87 *R. v Colohan* (also reported as *R. v C (Sean Peter)*) [2001] EWCA Crim 1251; [2001] 2 F.L.R. 757.

88 *DPP v Hardy* [2008] EWHC 2874 (Admin); (2009) 173 J.P. 10. Contrast, e.g. *Calland v Financial Conduct Authority* [2015] EWCA Civ 192.

89 Protection from Harassment Act 1997 s.7(4). In *Thomas v News Group Newspapers Ltd* [2001] EWCA Civ 1233; [2002] E.M.L.R. 78 at [30] Lord Phillips MR said that: "'Harassment' is, however, a word which has a meaning which is generally understood. It describes conduct targeted at an individual which is calculated to produce the consequences described in s.7 and which is oppressive and unreasonable". This approach was endorsed by the Court of Appeal in *Banks v Ablex Ltd* [2005] EWCA Civ 173; [2005] I.C.R. 819 at [20].

90 *Ferguson v British Gas Trading Ltd* [2009] EWCA Civ 46; [2010] 1 W.L.R. 785 at [18]; *Majrowski v Guy's and St Thomas' NHS Trust* [2006] UKHL 34; [2007] 1 A.C. 224 at [30].

publish those articles since "discussion or criticism of sexual relations which arose within a pre-existing professional relationship, or of sexual relationships which involved the deception of a spouse, or a civil partner, or others with a right not to be deceived, were matters which a reasonable person would not think was conduct amounting to harassment and would think was reasonable, unless there were some other circumstances which made it unreasonable".[91] On the other hand, the relationship between the gravity of the crime and its tortious equivalent is not a precise one since a tort action may lie even though the facts would not persuade a prosecuting authority to pursue the case criminally.[92] Breach of s.1(1) of the Act does not, however, catch a single act of harassment because there must be "a course of conduct".[93] In relation to a breach of s.1(1) the harassment must occur at least twice to be actionable.[94] A series of articles in a newspaper can constitute a course of conduct for this purpose.[95] Sinister and alarming emails which went beyond the "acceptably brusque", and anonymous threatening telephone calls, in the course of a dispute about a commercial debt, have been held to constitute harassment.[96] So too have repeated, groundless demands by a local authority to a council house tenant to pay rent at an alternative (and, for the claimant, inconvenient) location.[97] The court will look at the correspondence as a whole—letters and emails from a housing association to its tenants threatening immediate action to expel them from their houses were deemed to cross the boundary from a heavy handed response to one which was oppressive and unacceptable.[98] But for breach of s.1(1A) (involving harassment of more than one person) a course of conduct can be established if it involves a course of conduct on at least one occasion in relation to each of those persons.[99] The Act does not protect a corporate entity.[100]

14-21 There are defences for conduct pursued for the purpose of preventing or detect-

---

91 *Trimmingham v Associated Newspapers Ltd* [2012] EWHC 1296 (QB); [2012] 4 All E.R. 717 at [262], per Tugendhat J.

92 *Veakins v Kier Islington Ltd* [2009] EWCA Civ 1288; [2010] I.R.L.R. 132 at [12], per Maurice Kay LJ; Rimer and Waller LJJ concurred.

93 *Lau v DPP* [2000] 1 F.L.R. 799—gap of four months between two incidents; insufficient to amount to a "course of conduct"; cf. *Jones v Hipgrave* [2004] EWHC 2901 (QB); [2005] 2 F.L.R. 174—two incidents, eight months apart, could constitute a "course of conduct". For the purposes of the Act, the issue is whether the course of conduct, looked at as a whole, is harassing not whether the incidents individually could be regarded as harassing: *Iqbal v Dean Manson Solicitors* [2011] EWCA Civ 123; [2011] I.R.L.R. 428. A single act of harassment might still fall within the principle of *Wilkinson v Downton*, but following the decision of the House of Lords in *Wainwright v Home Office* [2003] UKHL 53; [2004] 2 A.C. 406 the claimant would have to prove physical or psychiatric damage.

94 Protection from Harassment Act 1997 s.7(3)(a) provides that in the case of conduct in relation to a single person (i.e. involving a breach of s.1(1)), a "course of conduct" must involve conduct on at least two occasions in relation to that person. Furthermore, for conduct to count, it must cross "the boundary between unattractive and even unreasonable conduct and conduct which is oppressive and unacceptable": *Conn v Sunderland City Council* [2007] EWCA Civ 1492; [2008] I.R.L.R. 324 at [12], per Gage LJ.

95 *Thomas v News Group Newspapers Ltd* [2001] EWCA Civ 1233; [2002] E.M.L.R. 78.

96 *Potter v Price* [2004] EWHC 781 (QB).

97 *Allen v Southwark LBC* [2008] EWCA Civ 1478. Similarly, hundreds of automatic calls from a call centre to a bank customer have been held to amount to harassment: *Roberts v Bank of Scotland* [2013] EWCA Civ 882.

98 *Worthington v Metropolitan Housing Trust Ltd* [2018] EWCA Civ 1125; [2018] H.L.R. 32. For its impact on drafting letters threatening legal action, see Shmilovits (2019) 135 L.Q.R. 27.

99 Protection from Harassment Act 1997 s.7(3)(b).

100 Protection from Harassment Act 1997 s.7(5) provides that: "References to a person, in the context of the harassment of a person, are references to a person who is an individual". See also *Daiichi*

ing crime; conduct pursued under any enactment or rule of law or to comply with a condition or requirement imposed by any person under any enactment; or for conduct that was reasonable in the particular circumstances.[101] There is no guidance in the Act as to what constitutes reasonable conduct. However, the Supreme Court has made clear that, "[b]efore an alleged harasser can be said to have had the purpose of preventing or detecting crime… he must have thought rationally about the material suggesting the possibility of criminality and formed the view that the conduct said to constitute harassment was appropriate for the purpose of preventing or detecting it".[102] In addition, it has also been said that the Act was not intended to be used to prevent individuals from exercising a right to protest about issues of public interest and the courts will seek to exercise caution in drawing the line between the legitimate exercise of the right to freedom of expression and unlawful interference with the rights of others.[103] On the other hand, unless there are exceptional circumstances, it will not be reasonable, for the purposes of the defence, to pursue a course of conduct which is clearly in breach of an injunction.[104] Moreover, conduct amounting to harassment for the purposes of the Act is not justified merely because the defendant believes it to be reasonable.[105] Helpfully, in *Dowson v Chief Constable of Northumbria* Simon J offered a summary of what must be proved in order for a claim in harassment to succeed:

"(1) There must be conduct which occurs on at least two occasions,
(2) which is targeted at the claimant,
(3) which is calculated in an objective sense to cause alarm or distress, and
(4) which is objectively judged to be oppressive and unacceptable.
(5) What is oppressive and unacceptable may depend on the social or working context in which the conduct occurs.
(6) A line is to be drawn between conduct which is unattractive and unreasonable, and conduct which has been described in various ways: 'torment' of the victim, 'of an order which would sustain criminal liability'."[106]

Pharmaceuticals UK Ltd v Stop Huntingdon Animal Cruelty [2003] EWHC 2337 (QB); [2004] 1 W.L.R. 1503. cf. *Bayer Plc v Shook* [2004] EWHC 332 (QB). It is clear, however, that whilst only an individual can be a victim of harassment, a perpetrator can be a corporate body (see *Kosar v Bank of Scotland Plc (t/a Halifax)* [2011] EWHC 1050 (Admin); [2011] B.C.C. 500) or an unincorporated body, such as a partnership (see *Iqbal v Dean Manson Solicitors* [2011] EWCA Civ 123; [2011] I.R.L.R. 428—at least for the purposes of civil liability).

101 Protection from Harassment Act 1997 s.1(3). For these purposes a subjective test of reasonableness is applied; and although an actual crime need not have been committed, the crime that D was intending to prevent must have been specific both in the sense that a particular victim and a particular, imminent danger could be identified: *EDO Technology Ltd v Campaign to Smash EDO* [2005] EWHC 2490 (QB). These qualifications mean that the defence cannot be lightly invoked by the police in relation to harassment that is purely incidental to crime prevention: see, e.g. *Dowson v Chief Constable of Northumbria* [2009] EWHC 907 (QB). The "particular circumstances" referred to in s.1(3)(c) must be those prevailing at the time at which reasonableness is to be assessed: *Hourani v Thomson* [2017] EWHC 432 (QB) at [208] (here not reasonable where the defendants had formed their beliefs about the subject too readily and without sufficient critical analysis and research).

102 *Hayes v Willoughby* [2013] UKSC 17; [2013] 1 W.L.R. 935 at [15], per Lord Sumption JSC. *Chief Constable of Surrey v Godfrey* [2017] EWHC 2014 (QB) follows *Hayes* in its treatment of the requirement of rationality test under s.1(3).

103 *EDO Technology Ltd v Campaign to Smash EDO* [2005] EWHC 2490 (QB) at [26], per Walker J.

104 *DPP v Moseley (Joanna), The Times,* 23 June 1999.

105 *DPP v Moseley (Joanna), The Times,* 23 June 1999.

106 [2010] EWHC 2612 (QB) at [142].

In *Levi v Bates*,[107] the Court of Appeal clarified that while in most harassment cases the claimant will be the intended target of the perpetrator's course of conduct (as suggested by Simon J above), it may infrequently happen that a course of conduct which, because it is targeted at him, is clearly harassment as against A, causes just as much alarm and distress to B, even though B is not the intended target of the perpetrator's misconduct, although *foreseeably* likely to be harmed by it. In this case, harassment of the claimant's husband had foreseeably affected his wife. There was no reason why Parliament, in the absence of express words, should by implication be found to have deliberately excluded from the protection of the Act persons who are foreseeably alarmed and distressed by a course of conduct of the targeted type contemplated by the word "harassment".[108] It followed that (2) above should be read as "conduct which is targeted at an individual".

14-22 The civil remedies available to a claimant are damages and/or an injunction. These remedies are available even where the harassment does not cause the claimant to fear that violence will be used. Damages can be awarded for, inter alia, any anxiety caused by the harassment and any resulting financial loss.[109] So far as injunctions are concerned, the court must take into account the prospects of *future* harassment, regardless of any past conduct amounting to harassment, before granting such an order, since an injunction will only be granted where the need for it exists *as of the date of the hearing*.[110] Unusually, the Act provides that breach an injunction granted for the purpose of restraining the defendant from pursuing harassing conduct is a criminal offence.[111]

5. FALSE IMPRISONMENT

(a) What constitutes false imprisonment?

14-23 **Imprisonment** False imprisonment is "the unlawful imposition of constraint on another's freedom of movement from a particular place".[112] The tort is established on proof of: (1) the fact of imprisonment; and (2) the absence of lawful authority to justify that imprisonment. For these purposes, imprisonment is complete deprivation of liberty for any time, however short, without lawful cause.[113] Even confining an individual in a doorway for a few seconds without lawful authority would amount to a false imprisonment.[114] In *R. (on the application of Jalloh (formerly Jollah)) v Secretary of State for the Home Department*,[115] the Supreme Court found imprisonment to have a broad meaning which would include physical barriers, such as locks and bars, physical people, such as guards, and threats, whether of force or

[107] [2015] EWCA Civ 206; [2016] Q.B. 91.
[108] [2015] EWCA Civ 206; [2016] Q.B. 91 at [29].
[109] Protection from Harassment Act 1997 s.3(2).
[110] *APW v WPA* [2012] EWHC 3151 (QB).
[111] Protection from Harassment Act 1997 s.3(6).
[112] *Collins v Wilcock* [1984] 1 W.L.R. 1172 at 1178.
[113] *Bird v Jones* (1845) 7 Q.B. 742; *Meering v Grahame-White Aviation Co* (1919) 112 L.T. 44. But note that bail relieves the prisoner from imprisonment: *Syed Mahamud Yusuf-ud-Din v Secretary of State for India* (1903) 19 T.L.R. 496; L.R. 30 Ind. App. 154.
[114] *Walker v Commissioner of Police of the Metropolis* [2014] EWCA Civ 897; [2015] 1 W.L.R. 312. See Tomlinson LJ at [46]: "a fundamental constitutional principle is at stake. The detention was indeed trivial, but that can and should be reflected in the measure of damages and does not render lawful that which was unlawful."
[115] [2020] UKSC 4; [2020] 2 W.L.R. 418 at [24]; confirming *R. (on the application of Jollah) v Secretary of State for the Home Department* [2018] EWCA Civ 1260; [2019] 1 W.L.R. 394.

legal process. In the case itself, Jalloh had been subject to an unlawful curfew condition. He had been electronically tagged and warned in the clearest possible terms that breaking the curfew could lead to a £5,000 fine or imprisonment for up to six months or both. In such circumstances, the fact he could physically leave his home did not prevent him being "imprisoned". The idea that the claimant was a free agent, able to come and go as he pleased, was deemed "completely unreal".[116] A prisoner, therefore, need not be placed under lock and key for the purposes of this tort. It is enough that his movements are simply constrained at the will of another.[117] The constraint may be actual physical force, amounting to a battery, or merely the apprehension of such force, or it may be submission to a legal process.[118] A mere partial interference with freedom of movement does not amount to an imprisonment. If a road is blocked so that a man is prevented from exercising a right of way and he is compelled to turn back, he has not been imprisoned.[119] Nor is making a charge against a person without actual arrest an imprisonment.[120] But where the claimant was invited to enter a waiting-room by two fellow-employees who waited outside in the immediate neighbourhood while a third man called the police, it was held that there was evidence of an intention to restrict the liberty of the claimant and therefore of an imprisonment.[121] Any restraint within defined bounds which is a restraint in fact may be an imprisonment.[122]

Arrest If a writ or warrant for a man's arrest is exhibited to him and he submits himself to the orders of the officer executing it, he becomes a prisoner even though his person has not been touched.[123] In *Arrowsmith v Le Mesurier*,[124] a constable was entrusted with a warrant for the apprehension of the claimant. He showed the warrant, and the claimant afterwards accompanied him before a magistrate. It was held that there had been no intention to apprehend and no submission to arrest, the warrant had been simply used as a summons to indicate to the claimant that he was required to appear to the charge and that consequently there had been no arrest. In *Berry v Adamson*,[125] the claimant sued for malicious arrest. A writ had been placed in the hands of a sheriff's officer, who gave him notice of it by a messenger who asked him to attend to give a bail bond, which the claimant did. The action failed on the ground that this did not amount to an arrest. An unlawful arrest is a false imprisonment, and if the requirements of the law as to making it clear to the arrested person that he is under lawful restraint, or informing him of the grounds of his arrest, or taking him before the appropriate authorities within a reasonable time 14-24

---

116 [2020] UKSC 4; [2020] 2 W.L.R. 418 at [27]. However, a residence condition that required the claimant to live at a specified address, to seek the permission of the Secretary of State to change that address and not spend more than three consecutive nights away from the address without prior written consent from the Secretary of State did not amount to "imprisonment": *R. (on the application of W) v Secretary of State for the Home Department* [2019] EWHC 254 (Admin).

117 *Bird v Jones* (1845) 7 Q.B. 742 at 744, per Coleridge J.

118 *Warner v Riddiford* (1858) 4 C.B. (N.S.) 180.

119 *Bird v Jones* (1845) 7 Q.B. 742. In similar vein see *Robinson v Balmain New Ferry Co* [1910] A.C. 295.

120 *Simpson v Hill* (1795) 1 Esp. 431.

121 *Meering v Grahame-White Aviation Co* (1919) 122 L.T. 44.

122 *Meering v Grahame-White Aviation Co* (1919) 122 L.T. 44 at 53–54, per Atkin LJ.

123 *Grainger v Hill* (1838) 4 Bing. N.C. 212.

124 (1806) 2 B. & P.N.R. 211; see, however, *Warner v Riddiford* (1858) 4 C.B. (N.S.) 180 at 205, per Willes J.

125 (1827) 6 B. & C. 528.

are not complied with, an arrest which might otherwise be justified will be unlawful, grounding an action in false imprisonment.[126]

14-25 **Claimant's knowledge irrelevant** It is not necessary that the claimant is aware of his imprisonment at the time.[127] Thus a person may be falsely imprisoned while drunk or asleep or while he is of unsound mind. False imprisonment as a form of trespass to the person is actionable per se because, as Lord Griffiths put it in *Murray v Ministry of Defence*[128]: "The law attaches supreme importance to the liberty of the individual and if he suffers a wrongful interference with that liberty it should remain actionable even without proof of special damage."

14-26 **Absence of lawful authority** It is irrelevant whether or not the defendant honestly and reasonably believed that he had the necessary authority to detain the claimant, if, in fact, no such authority existed. Thus, in *R. v Governor of Brockhill Prison Ex p. Evans (No.2)*[129] the House of Lords held that a prison governor who in good faith, and in reliance on the existing law, calculated the release date of a prisoner which subsequently turned out to have been 59 days too late because the law had changed in the interim,[130] was liable in false imprisonment for the additional days that the prisoner was detained. Liability is strict. It was irrelevant that the governor had not been negligent and had acted in good faith in accordance with the law when the release date was calculated. *Ex p. Evans* can be contrasted with *Percy v Hall*,[131] where the Court of Appeal said (obiter) that constables arresting the claimant under byelaws subsequently found to be invalid would not be liable in false imprisonment. There was authority for regarding a byelaw, albeit one later found invalid, as entitled to some recognition at least to the extent of providing a defence to an action in false imprisonment. Arguably, the constables were under a duty to act according to what they believed was the law, thus rendering the arrest necessary (even though the byelaw turned out to be invalid).

14-27 **Defendant's intention** To be liable in false imprisonment, it must be demonstrated that the defendant had the necessary intention, as well as the ability, to detain the claimant. It must be shown that had the claimant attempted to leave premises controlled by the defendant, the defendant would have taken steps to stop him. In *R. v Bournewood Community and Mental Health Services Trust Ex p. L*,[132] a mentally incapacitated patient was admitted to a mental hospital as an informal patient under s.131(1) of the Mental Health Act 1983. The patient, who suffered from autism, lacked any independent capacity to consent to his admission to hospital or to his medical care, and his carers objected to his remaining in hospital. The patient was housed in an unlocked ward, however, and evinced no desire to

---

[126] See para.14-65 onwards.

[127] *Murray v Ministry of Defence* [1988] 1 W.L.R. 692 at 703–704; overruling *Herring v Boyle* (1834) 1 C.M. & R. 377. See also *P v Cheshire West and Chester Council* [2014] UKSC 19; [2014] A.C. 896 at [35].

[128] *Murray v Ministry of Defence* [1988] 1 W.L.R. 692 at 704. By the same token, a claimant's mistaken belief that he has been lawfully arrested does not render lawful an otherwise unlawful arrest: *R. v McKoy* [2002] EWCA Crim 1628; *The Times,* 17 June 2002.

[129] [2001] 2 A.C. 19.

[130] In *R. v Governor of Brockhill Prison Ex p. Evans* [1997] Q.B. 443 the Court of Appeal had held that earlier judgments affirming the mistaken basis for calculating length of sentence should be treated as if they did not exist.

[131] [1997] Q.B. 924.

[132] [1999] 1 A.C. 458.

leave the hospital. The issue arose before the House of Lords of whether L was in fact detained, that is, "imprisoned", in the hospital. While their Lordships unanimously agreed that any detention of the patient was lawful by virtue of the common law principle of necessity, the House divided on whether L was in fact "imprisoned" during his residence in the hospital. Lord Goff (giving the judgment of the majority) found that while L was an informal patient in the hospital, he was not detained there. He was free to leave and not restrained by any physical barriers from choosing to do so. The fact that, had he shown any desire to leave, doctors would have prevented him from doing so, Lord Goff considered to be irrelevant.[133] Lord Steyn (dissenting) considered that the sedation administered to L, the constant monitoring of his movements by staff, and the veto on contact with his carers rendered any suggestion that L was free to leave " … a fairy tale". The European Court of Human Rights subsequently held that the patient's detention constituted a breach of art.5(1) of the European Convention on Human Rights (right to liberty and security), concluding that the fact that he had not resisted his detention was irrelevant, since the right to liberty was too important to be forfeit for that reason alone.[134] The court's reasoning mirrored that of Lord Steyn in the House of Lords.[135] Lady Hale in *Jalloh* commented that it was not easy to grasp the rationale of the narrow majority in *Bournewood* and that it was the only example her Ladyship could find of an art.5 deprivation of liberty which did not amount to imprisonment at common law.[136]

Placing reasonable conditions on the claimant's exit Where the claimant enters the defendant's premises on terms which involve some restriction of his liberty he cannot later complain of false imprisonment. The passenger on an airplane, for example, cannot insist on being allowed to get off the plane in mid-flight. In *Herd v Weardale Steel Co*,[137] the owners of a colliery refused to permit a miner, who had gone down the mine in accordance with the terms of his employment, to be brought to the top by the lift until the end of his shift, which was the proper time for him to return to the surface. It was held that this was not imprisonment, because there was no violation of the terms upon which the claimant had voluntarily descended the mine. Crucially, in *Herd*, it has since been explained, there was a mere omission to lend assistance to the miners; while for the tort of false imprisonment to be com- 14-28

[133] Lord Goff indicated ([1999] 1 A.C. 458 at 486) that in *Meering v Grahame-White Aviation Co Ltd* (1919) 122 L.T. 44 at 54–55 Atkin LJ had drawn a distinction between: "restraint upon the [claimant's] liberty which is conditional upon his seeking to exercise his freedom (which would not amount to false imprisonment), and an actual restraint upon his liberty, as where the defendant decided to restrain the [claimant] within a room and placed a policeman outside the door to stop him leaving (which would amount to false imprisonment)." However, query why the latter case is not also conditional upon the claimant seeking to exercise his freedom—the policeman would have no need to act to restrain the claimant if he did not attempt to leave the room. Contrast, also, the actual decision in *Meering v Grahame-White Aviation Co*.

[134] *HL v United Kingdom (Application No.45508/99)* (2005) 40 E.H.R.R. 32; 17 B.H.R.C. 418; [2005] Lloyd's Rep. Med. 169. See further para.14-122. In response, machinery was introduced for the many thousands of mentally incapacitated people who are regularly deprived of their liberty in hospitals, care homes and elsewhere. The Mental Health Act 2007 s.50 amended the Mental Capacity Act 2005 accordingly: see *P v Cheshire West and Chester Council* [2014] UKSC 19; [2014] A.C. 896. Note also recent changes introduced by the Mental Capacity (Amendment) Act 2019.

[135] *HL v United Kingdom (Application No.45508/99)* (2005) 40 E.H.R.R. 32; 17 B.H.R.C. 418; [2005] Lloyd's Rep. Med. 169 at [91].

[136] *R. (on the application of Jalloh (formerly Jollah)) v Secretary of State for the Home Department* [2020] UKSC 4; [2020] 2 W.L.R. 418 at [23].

[137] [1915] A.C. 67; cf. *Robinson v Balmain New Ferry Co* [1910] A.C. 295; 44 L.Q.R. 464 at 467.

mitted there must *either* be a positive act that causes the confinement of the claimant, *or* a failure to fulfil some special duty to facilitate the claimant's free movement (which will arise out of a particular relationship between the parties).[138]

(b) Continuation of imprisonment

14-29 Anyone who helps to continue a wrongful detention is guilty of false imprisonment, though he is not responsible for the original wrong.[139] In *R. v Governor of Brockhill Prison Ex p. Evans*,[140] the Court of Appeal rejected the formula, approved in earlier judgments, for calculating the allowance for time spent in custody on remand which had been used in determining the claimant's release date. Consequently the claimant had spent an additional period in custody subsequent to the date on which she was lawfully entitled to be released. Her claim for false imprisonment against the prison governor succeeded. Albeit he was not at fault, and honestly believed that on the authority of the earlier judgments he was entitled to continue to detain the claimant, her detention was not lawful. Blameworthiness plays no part in false imprisonment. The sole issue is whether the claimant's detention is justified in law.[141] However, in *Olotu v Home Office*,[142] failure on the part of the Crown Prosecution Service to comply with the Prosecution of Offences (Custody Time Limits) Regulations 1987 resulting in the claimant's detention on remand beyond the 112 day limit imposed by those Regulations did not render her continued detention unlawful and a false imprisonment. The claimant had been lawfully committed into the custody of the prison governor and his duty was to detain her until ordered to deliver her to the Crown Court. He never received such an order and had no independent authority to release her. Unlike the claimant in *Ex p. Evans*, the claimant in *Olotu* had no right to be released, save by order of the court.

14-30 In *Quinland v Governor of Swaleside Prison*,[143] another sentencing error occurred causing the claimant to serve six weeks' imprisonment more than he should have done. The Court of Appeal applied *Olotu v Home Office*,[144] and distinguished *R. v Governor of Brockhill Prison Ex p. Evans (No.2)*,[145] on the basis that the prison governors did not make any arithmetical or other error. The judicial warrant (albeit that it erroneously stated the sentence to be two years and six months instead of two years and three months) could be relied on until set aside. Provided an individual is in custody under an order of the court—as was the case in *Quinland*—the governor is not liable for false imprisonment since he will have had no option but

138 *Prison Officers Association v Iqbal* [2009] EWCA Civ 1312; [2010] Q.B. 732.

139 *Griffin v Coleman* (1859) 4 H. & N. 265.

140 [1997] Q.B. 443.

141 *R. v Governor of Brockhill Prison Ex p. Evans (No.2)* [2001] 2 A.C. 19. See also *Roberts v Chief Constable of the Cheshire Constabulary* [1999] 1 W.L.R. 662; *Clarke v Chief Constable of Northamptonshire* (1999) 149 N.L.J. 899. The statute and rules which provide for remission of part of the sentence of imprisonment for good conduct do not confer any legal right upon the prisoner to be discharged before the end of the original sentence, and an allegation that the claimant has been wrongfully deprived of remission will not support an action for false imprisonment: *Hancock v Prison Commissioners* [1960] 1 Q.B. 117; *Williams v Home Office (No.2)* [1981] 1 All E.R. 1211.

142 [1997] 1 W.L.R. 328. A claim for breach of statutory duty against the Crown Prosecution Service also failed.

143 [2002] EWCA Civ 174; [2003] Q.B. 306.

144 [1997] 1 W.L.R. 328.

145 [2001] 2 A.C. 19.

to obey the warrant.[146] The same is true where a prisoner serving an indeterminate sentence for the protection of the public has his detention prolonged by virtue of a delay by the Parole Board in reviewing his case following the expiry of his tariff. Because such a prisoner remains lawfully incarcerated by statute until the Board gives a direction for his release, he cannot sue for false imprisonment.[147]

(c) Limitations on police detention: Police and Criminal Evidence Act 1984

Duration of police detention Part IV of the Police and Criminal Evidence Act 1984 sets out detailed rules limiting the period for which an arrested person may be detained in police custody, and defining the conditions in which he may be so detained.[148] Section 34(1) provides that a person arrested for an offence shall not be kept in police detention except in accordance with the provisions of that Part of the Act (though s.34 does not apply to a person arrested for breach of the peace[149]). Any significant breach of the provisions of Pt IV would seem to render further detention of that person unlawful and constitute false imprisonment. The Act provides that, normally, a person arrested should be taken only to designated police stations and that at such police stations there be a custody officer,[150] normally of the rank of sergeant or above. The custody officer is initially responsible for the continued detention, unconditional release or release on bail of arrested persons brought there. If at any time a custody officer becomes aware, in relation to any person in police detention, that the grounds for that person's detention have ceased to exist and is not aware of other grounds on which continued detention[151] could be justified, he is bound to order an immediate release.[152] Detention after a time when investigations have revealed that the grounds for the arrest were mistaken **14-31**

---

[146] The prison may, however, find itself liable for negligence if it has assumed responsibility to the prisoner, e.g. to complete the final stage of the process associated with his release in accordance with government policy: *McCreaner v Ministry of Justice* [2014] EWHC 569 (QB); [2015] 1 W.L.R. 354.

[147] *R. (on the application of Sturnham) v Parole Board* [2013] UKSC 23; [2013] 2 A.C. 254 at [13], per Lord Reed JSC. In similar vein see *R. (on the application of James) v Secretary of State for Justice (Parole Board intervening)* [2009] UKHL 22; [2010] 1 A.C. 553. Note also that in *Sturnham's* case three further things were made clear. (1) such detention does not constitute a violation of art.5(1) of the European Convention on Human Rights (despite being in contravention of art.5(4)); (2) in view of the art.5(4) violation, it was said that damages under s.8 of the Human Rights Act 1998 would be payable in respect of the delay where it could be established that an earlier review by the Parole Board would have resulted in an earlier release; (3) even in a case where it could not be shown that an earlier release would have been ordered, a modest sum of s.8 damages should be paid in any case where the prisoner suffered sufficiently severe frustration and anxiety about the prospect of release. See also paras 13-128, 13-129 and 14-145.

[148] The Police and Criminal Evidence Act 1984 s.66 provides that the Secretary of State shall issue codes of practice relating to the exercise by constables of statutory powers of search, detention, entry onto premises, and seizure of property. Breach of a relevant code of practice does not per se give rise to an action in tort (see s.67(10)). However, s.67(11) provides that codes of practice are admissible in evidence and that "if any provision of a code appears to the court or tribunal conducting the proceedings to be relevant to any question arising in the proceedings it shall be taken into account in determining that question".

[149] Arrest and detention for a breach of the peace are not subject to the protections provided for arrested persons in the Act: *Williamson v Chief Constable of West Midlands Police* [2003] EWCA Civ 337; [2004] 1 W.L.R. 14. But the common law provides considerable protection against arbitrary arrest and/or unreasonable detention: see ibid. at [19], per Dyson LJ.

[150] Police and Criminal Evidence Act 1984 s.36.

[151] Police and Criminal Evidence Act 1984 s.37.

[152] Police and Criminal Evidence Act 1984 s.34(2).

becomes unlawful once the custody officer is aware of the relevant facts. A continuance of detention beyond these various junctures constitutes false imprisonment. Equally, after the expiry of the prescribed period of detention, any authority to continue the detention of the arrested person ceases to exist and continued detention is unlawful.[153]

14-32 Sections 37 and 38[154] impose further duties on custody officers: s.40 provides for regular reviews of police detention, and ss.41–45 impose fixed limits on the duration of police detention. Ascertaining the extent to which breach of these provisions renders continued detention unlawful and a false imprisonment is problematic. Section 34(1) on its face suggests that any breach of the conditions for detention provided for in Pt IV results in the detention ceasing to be lawful. But as the various provisions confer a certain amount of discretion on the relevant officers, matters are not entirely straightforward. Where discretionary powers are concerned, the judgment in *Mohammed-Holgate v Duke*[155] must be considered. The court will not substitute its judgment backed by hindsight for that of the officer, but will seek to ensure that the relevant discretionary power was properly and lawfully exercised. Thus, a distinction may be drawn between the custody officer's duty under s.34(2) and that under s.37 of the Act. The former imposes a mandatory duty to order the release of the person detained once the custody officer becomes aware that there are no grounds to justify his further detention. Section 37, by contrast, imposes discretionary duties relating to charging and releasing, with or without bail, persons detained in custody. A person alleging that his continued detention in breach of s.37 constituted false imprisonment must therefore establish that the custody officer misused his discretion, and acted ultra vires in deciding not to release that person.[156]

14-33 **Review of detention** Section 40 of the Act imposes an obligation to review the detention of each person in police detention at regular intervals, normally not later than six hours after the person is first detained and then at nine-hourly intervals. The duty to review is hedged about by a number of exceptions,[157] but a failure to comply with the procedure renders the continued detention in police custody unlawful, and therefore a false imprisonment.[158]

---

153 See *Roberts v Chief Constable of Cheshire* [1999] 1 W.L.R. 662.

154 The Police and Criminal Evidence Act 1984 s.38 provides that the person charged has the right to bail unless certain criteria are fulfilled, and s.38(2) provides that he may be kept in police detention if the criteria for bail are not satisfied. But the section does not confer a power to detain a person who has been unlawfully arrested: *Hutt v Metropolitan Police Commissioner* [2003] EWCA Civ 1911. It cannot turn an initially unlawful arrest into a lawful one.

155 [1984] A.C. 437.

156 Section 37(7)(a) to (d) of the Police and Criminal Evidence Act 1984 provides a comprehensive statutory framework dealing with the alternatives available to a custody officer. Where the custody officer has sufficient evidence to charge the person arrested with the offence for which he was arrested, the person arrested must be released without charge on bail, released without charge and without bail, or charged. In these circumstances there is no power for a custody officer to detain a person pending a decision from the CPS as to whether he should be charged: *G v Chief Constable of West Yorkshire* [2008] EWCA Civ 28; [2008] 1 W.L.R. 550.

157 Police and Criminal Evidence Act 1984 s.40(4).

158 In *Roberts v Chief Constable of Cheshire* [1999] 1 W.L.R. 662, it was irrelevant that detention would have been lawful if the requisite review had been carried out, or that there were in fact grounds for continuing the claimant's detention. See also *Lumba v Secretary of State for the Home Department* [2011] UKSC 12; [2012] 1 A.C. 245 where, in the different context of the detention of foreign nationals pending deportation under the Immigration Act 1971, it was held that the fact that the defendant *could* have acted lawfully to detain the claimant is not a basis on which liability can be avoided

Time-limits on detention Sections 41–45 impose fixed time-limits on detention. The primary rule is that "a person shall not be kept in police detention for more than 24 hours without being charged". Further detention must be authorised under ss.42–45. Where there is no such authorisation, continued detention beyond 24 hours without charge constitutes false imprisonment. Section 42 provides that a police officer of the rank of superintendent or above who is responsible for the police station at which a person is detained may authorise the detention of a person for a further 12 hours (i.e. up to 36 hours) provided that he has reasonable grounds for believing that the following conditions are met. (1) The detention of that person without charge is necessary to secure or preserve evidence relating to an offence for which he is under arrest or to obtain such evidence by questioning him. (2) The relevant offence is an indictable offence. (3) The investigation is being conducted diligently and expeditiously. Continued detention, beyond 24 hours, of a person under arrest for an offence other than an indictable offence or where there are no reasonable grounds to believe that continued detention is necessary will constitute false imprisonment.[159] 14-34

Detention without charge beyond 36 hours must be authorised by a warrant of further detention granted by a magistrates' court under s.43. That warrant will authorise further detention for 36 hours (i.e. up to 72 hours from the time of arrest). Section 44 provides that a second application to extend a warrant of further detention may be made to a magistrates' court, authorising detention for up to a further 36 hours, provided that a total period of 96 hours in police detention is not exceeded. Sections 43 and 44 specify the grounds on which applications for warrants of further detention should be based, including, inter alia, that the offence is an indictable offence and that further detention is necessary. A claimant alleging that the proper grounds for the issue of a warrant, or extension of a warrant, of further detention were not present faces problems in establishing that his continued detention was unlawful. No action for false imprisonment will lie even if the warrant was improperly obtained, because of the intervention of the judicial process. The claimant's remedy must be to sue for the malicious procuration of the warrant by analogy with the action for maliciously obtaining a search warrant.[160] The onus will, however, then lie on the claimant to prove absence of reasonable and probable cause and malice. 14-35

(d) Imprisonment in unauthorised places or conditions

It was held in *Cobbett v Grey*[161] that to hold a prisoner in a part of a prison where inmates in his category should not be confined constituted false imprisonment. Since 1952, s.12(1) of the Prison Act 1952 has authorised the confinement of any prisoner in any prison. In *R. v Deputy Governor of Parkhurst Prison Ex p. Hague*,[162] the House of Lords held that confinement within a prison in conditions, or circumstances, not authorised by the Prison Rules cannot constitute false 14-36

---

if the defendant has in fact acted unlawfully in detaining the claimant. But in such circumstances, the claimant will only receive nominal damages.

159 See *Application for a Warrant for Further Detention* [1988] Crim. L.R. 296. Quaere whether the burden of proof lies on the claimant or the officer. In cases relating to arrest it is the constable who must establish reasonable ground for suspicion; *Holtham v Commissioner of Police for the Metropolis*, *The Times*, 28 November 1987.

160 See para.15-18.

161 (1849) 4 Ex. 729.

162 [1992] 1 A.C. 58.

imprisonment. Their Lordships unanimously held that breach of the 1964 Prison Rules could not give rise to an action for breach of statutory duty because this would allow a back door remedy when the front door was shut.[163] The Prison Act authorises the restraint of a prisoner within boundaries defined by the prison governor and prison officers acting with the governor's authority.[164] A prisoner alleging that he has been confined in a manner ultra vires the Prison Rules may, however, seek a judicial review. But success does not affect the lawfulness of his detention.

14-37 Section 12(1), however, only operates as a defence against the prison governor or officers acting lawfully within his authority. A fellow inmate locking an inmate in some confined space enjoys no authority to interfere with the claimant's movements.[165] A prison officer subjecting a prisoner to what he knows to be unauthorised restraint commits both the torts of false imprisonment and misfeasance in a public office.[166] The officer, just like the fellow inmate, lacks the defence of s.12(1) in such circumstances.

14-38 **Intolerable conditions** The House of Lords in *R. v Deputy Governor of Parkhurst Prison, Ex p. Hague* rejected any suggestion in earlier judgments of the Court of Appeal[167] that an otherwise lawful imprisonment may be rendered unlawful by intolerable conditions of detention. To do so would be to "confuse conditions of detention with the nature of confinement".[168] A prisoner subjected to intolerable treatment is not, however, left remediless. In appropriate circumstances an action for assault and battery may lie. And where the claimant's health is imperilled by the conditions of his detention, he can sue in negligence.[169] Confining a prisoner in conditions injurious to his health may also constitute a breach of the custodian's duty of care,[170] and a breach of art.3 of the European Convention on Human Rights.[171]

(e) Limitations on police detention: conditions of detention

14-39 Parts IV and V of the Police and Criminal Evidence Act 1984 provide not only for limits on the duration of police detention but also rules for the treatment of detained persons. Sections 38 and 39 define the custody officer's responsibilities for

---

163 [1992] 1 A.C. 58 at 178, per Lord Jauncey. For serious doubt about the correctness of the decision in this case, see *R. (on the application of Munjaz) v Mersey Care NHS Trust* [2005] UKHL 58; [2006] 2 A.C. 148; [2006] Lloyd's Rep. Med. 1 at [42]–[43], per Lord Steyn (dissenting).

164 [1992] 1 A.C. 58 at 163, per Lord Bridge.

165 [1992] 1 A.C. 58 at 164, per Lord Bridge.

166 See *Racz v Home Office* [1994] 2 A.C. 45; *Karagozlu v Commissioner of Police of the Metropolis* [2006] EWCA Civ 1691; [2007] 1 W.L.R. 1881 (loss of "residual liberty" potentially actionable in misfeasance in public office) and see also para. 13-132.

167 e.g. *Middleweek v Chief Constable of Merseyside* (Note) [1992] 1 A.C. 179; *Weldon v Home Office* [1992] 1 A.C. 58.

168 *Weldon v Home Office* [1992] 1 A.C. 127, at 177. Presumably, similar analysis will apply to any action alleging "intolerable conditions" while held in police custody, too.

169 See *Racz v Home Office* [1994] 2 A.C. 45; *Brooks v Home Office* [1999] 2 F.L.R. 33.

170 But see *H v Home Office* (1992) 136 S.J.L.B. 140 (prisoner failed in action for negligence when he alleged that he had been placed in solitary confinement after other prisoners discovered he was a sex offender through the negligence of prison officials).

171 See *Keenan v UK (Application No.27229/95)* (2001) 33 E.H.R.R. 38; (2001) 10 B.H.R.C. 319; *Price v UK (Application No.33394/96)* (2002) 11 B.H.R.C. 401. Note, however, that a change of the conditions of confinement from open to closed conditions does not engage art.5: *Davies v Secretary of State for Justice* [2008] EWHC 397 (Admin).

persons in police custody. In the light of the judgment of the House of Lords in *R. v Deputy Governor of Parkhurst Prison Ex p. Hague*,[172] it is unlikely that an action for breach of statutory duty would succeed against a custody officer. Those provisions of Pt V which authorise physical contact with the person detained—for example, to conduct a search or take fingerprints—give rise to an action for battery where the conditions for lawful touching set out by the Act are not met.

Right to have someone informed or consult a solicitor Section 56 of the Police and Criminal Evidence Act 1984 provides that a person being held in custody at a police station shall be entitled, if he so requests, to have one friend or relative or other person who is known to him or is likely to take an interest in his welfare told of his detention, as soon as is practicable, except to the extent that delay is permitted by the section.[173] Section 57 provides for additional rights for juveniles[174] and s.58 confers an entitlement to consult a solicitor and provides for the circumstances in which police officers may delay access to legal advice.[175] No remedy for breach of these provisions is specified by the Act. However, in *Cullen v Chief Constable of the Royal Ulster Constabulary*[176] the House of Lords held that the failure to permit a person detained in custody to consult in private with a solicitor or to inform him of the reasons for delaying his access to a solicitor, contrary to a statutory right to the same does not render his continued detention unlawful, and so does not give rise to an action for false imprisonment.[177] The position might be different, however, if the breach was in bad faith, e.g. where the claimant was "detained in custody in order to keep him incommunicado or to prevent him from participating in political activities of which the authorities disapprove".[178] The only sanction for breach of ss.56-58 is to be found in the discretion to exclude evidence obtained by way of a confession in s.76 of the Act.[179] 14-40

(f) Responsibility for imprisonment committed through the instrumentality of officers of justice

Imprisonment by officers of justice The question of the responsibility of a defendant for a tort in which he has not personally participated, but which is alleged to have been committed by his authority, or by his employee in the course of his employment[180] is dealt with in Ch.6. There is however, a special kind of agency which it is convenient to consider here. An act amounting to a trespass may have been committed through the instrumentality of some officer or minister of the law, 14-41

172 [1992] 1 A.C. 58; see paras 8-14 and 8-18.

173 s.56(10) provides that "[n]othing in this section applies to a person arrested or detained under the terrorism provisions". S.65 defines the "terrorism provisions" as "section 41 of the Terrorism Act 2000, and any provision of Schedule 7 to that Act conferring a power of detention".

174 In the form of amendments to the Children and Young Persons Act 1933 s.34.

175 s.58(12) provides that "[n]othing in this section applies to a person arrested or detained under the terrorism provisions".

176 [2003] UKHL 39; [2003] 1 W.L.R. 1763.

177 Note, however, *Cadder v HM Advocate* [2010] UKSC 43; [2010] 1 W.L.R. 2601 in which Lord Hope held (at [60]) that a person who has been detained must have access to an enrolled solicitor before being questioned by the police unless, in the particular circumstances of the case, there are compelling reasons for restricting that right [breach of art.6 of the ECHR].

178 *Cadder v HM Advocate* [2010] UKSC 43; [2010] 1 W.L.R. 2601 at [61], per Lord Millett.

179 See *R. v Eric Smith* [1987] Crim. L.R. 579.

180 As to the liability of the chief officer of police, see Police Act 1996 s.88. See also para.6-18.

and it may be sought in consequence to charge a party as a principal because he initiated the proceedings under which the alleged wrong was inflicted.

14-42 **Ministerial and judicial proceedings** Legal proceedings may be either ministerial or judicial. In the case of the former, the party employs the machinery of law entirely at his own risk and is directly responsible for the consequences. In the case of the latter, he appeals to the discretion of a judge or magistrate, which is thus interposed so that the steps taken result immediately from the exercise of that discretion and not from the act of the party.[181] Under such circumstances the defendant may be liable in malicious prosecution if he has wrongfully set the law in motion, but he cannot be sued in trespass.[182] Equally, where a defendant is granted bail, is unable to provide the surety and thus remanded in custody, "although a judicial act precludes liability in false imprisonment, it does not relieve the prosecutor of liability in false imprisonment ... for the damage caused by his setting the prosecution in motion".[183]

14-43 **Arrests by ministerial officers** If the arrest or other trespass is effected by a purely ministerial officer and not under the authority of any court, the defendant must clearly be answerable if he in fact authorised the act in question. It is not necessary that he should in terms have made a request or demand; it is enough if he makes a charge on which it becomes the duty of the constable to act.[184] But it is quite a different thing if a party simply gives information, and the constable thereupon acts according to his own judgment. In such a case the informer incurs no responsibility in the tort of false imprisonment.[185] The critical test is whether the defendant was "responsible for the claimant's arrest by directing or requesting, or directly encouraging the officers to arrest the claimant; and in that respect did they go beyond laying information before police officers for them to take such action as they saw fit".[186] There is a distinction therefore between a mere witness (e.g. a member of hospital security staff) who simply gave information to the proper authority on which it could act or not, and someone who procured or directly requested or encouraged the police to arrest the claimant.[187] The former would not be liable for false imprisonment even if the information provided was incorrect. If a person signs the charge-sheet after an arrest has been made, this may be evidence that he has authorised the arrest by a ministerial officer, but it is only evidence and not conclusive.[188] Thus where a constable having taken the claimant into custody on his own judgment, requested the defendant to sign the charge-sheet and the

---

181 *Austin v Dowling* (1870) L.R. 5 C.P. 534 at 540, per Willes J. The distinction between a ministerial and judicial act is explained at para.5-101 and survives the introduction of the Human Rights Act 1998 (*Zenati v Commissioner of Police of the Metropolis* [2015] EWCA Civ 80; [2015] Q.B. 758).

182 *Lock v Ashton* (1848) 12 Q.B. 871; cf. *Diamond v Minter* [1941] 1 K.B. 656. Note, however, *Beckett v Walker* [1985] C.L.Y. 129 (magistrate's clerk liable for false imprisonment due to negligent issue of warrant without bail).

183 *Calix v Attorney General of Trinidad and Tobago* [2013] UKPC 15; [2013] 1 W.L.R. 3283 at [23] per Lord Kerr.

184 *Hopkins v Crowe* (1836) 4 A. & E. 774; *Roberts v Buster's Auto Towing Service Ltd* (1976) 70 D.L.R. (3d) 716 (BCSC).

185 *Gosden v Elphick* (1849) 4 Ex. 445; *Grinham v Willey* (1859) 4 H. & N. 496 at 499, per Pollock CB.

186 *Ahmed v Shafique* [2009] EWHC 618 (QB) at [87], per Sharp J. See also *Davidson v Chief Constable of North Wales* [1994] 2 All E.R. 597 (store detective not liable when she gave erroneous information causing police to arrest claimant).

187 *Ali v Heart of England NHS Foundation Trust* [2018] EWHC 591 (Ch).

188 In *Sewell v National Telephone Co* [1907] 1 K.B. 557, Collins MR said (at 560): "The act that was

defendant did so, it was held that there was no evidence to make him liable for the imprisonment.[189] But where the officer stated that he would not detain the claimant unless the defendant made a charge and signed the charge-sheet and the defendant thereupon signed the charge-sheet, this was held to be evidence of an imprisonment by the defendant.[190]

Judicial acts There is not only a distinction between the act of a ministerial officer such as a policeman and the act of a judicial officer such as a magistrate, but there is a distinction between the ministerial and judicial acts of courts of justice. A judicial act follows in the ordinary course of procedure from an order given by a judicial officer in the exercise of his functions. For such an act there is no remedy in trespass against the party initiating the proceedings. Even if the court acts altogether outside its competence, the party is still protected, for he has a right to state his case and leave it to the court to decide whether it has jurisdiction or not.[191] However, where there is an absence of jurisdiction the position is different: if the party, instead of leaving the orders of the court to be carried out in the ordinary way by its officers, personally intervenes, as by superintending the execution of process, he thereby makes himself a trespasser.[192] He only incurs this liability by participating in the very act itself; not by merely taking the necessary formal steps in accordance with the procedure of the court to set its officers in motion.[193] **14-44**

Ministerial act of court of justice Many proceedings are taken under the authority of courts of justice which are ministerial.[194] If the order of the court was altogether without jurisdiction there is no protection, and liability for trespass may lie.[195] If it was within the jurisdiction of the court, however irregular, it protects all proceedings duly taken in pursuance of it, until it is set aside.[196] **14-45**

Setting aside proceedings An order of a court may be set aside on the ground of error, as a matter of favour, or because it was irregularly obtained. There can only be error where there had been a judicial decision and anything done under a judicial decision cannot be a ground of trespass against a party, because it is not his act but the act of the court. It is obvious that, where an order is set aside as a matter of favour, the order is admitted to have been in itself a proper one, and it therefore gives validity to all proceedings taken while it was still in force. But an order obtained without judicial intervention and in an irregular or dishonest manner, when once set aside, is, so far as concerns the person thus obtaining it, as though it had never been made. It is for the party who seeks thus to deprive his adversary of the protection of the order to show on what ground it was annulled.[197] In *Williams v* **14-46**

---

done (signing the charge-sheet) was merely to provide a prosecutor and that does not let in liability to an action for false imprisonment unless the person who takes that step has taken on himself the responsibility of directing the imprisonment".

189 *Grinham v Willey* (1859) 4 H. & N. 496.

190 *Austin v Dowling* (1870) L.R. 5 C. & P. 534.

191 *West v Smallwood* (1838) 3 M. & W. 418; *Brown v Chapman* (1848) 6 C.B. 365. It would probably be otherwise if to the knowledge of the party the proceedings were altogether misconceived.

192 *Painter v Liverpool Gas Co* (1836) 3 A. & E. 433. See *West v Smallwood* (1838) 3 M. & W. 418.

193 *Cooper v Harding* (1845) 7 Q.B. 928.

194 For the distinction between ministerial and judicial acts, see para.5-101.

195 *Houlden v Smith* (1850) 14 Q.B. 841.

196 *Prentice v Harrison* (1843) 4 Q.B. 852.

197 *Williams v Smith* (1863) 14 C.B. (N.S.) 596.

Smith,[198] an attachment was obtained against the claimant on an affidavit of his disobedience to an order of the court. He had given an excuse for his conduct to the defendant, which was afterwards held good and the attachment was set aside. The defendant, not thinking the excuse to be material, had made no mention of it in his affidavit. It was held that an action of false imprisonment did not lie because "[i]n order to entitle the party against whom the process issues to maintain an action for any intermediate acts done under it, he must show that the process has been set aside by reason of some misconduct or at least some irregularity on the part of the person suing out".[199] The act of the court even if erroneous cannot be made the foundation of an action for damages. Both the party and his solicitor are answerable for what is done under a process improperly taken out and subsequently avoided.[200]

14-47 **Party personally intervening** Just as a party may make himself liable for what is done under process issued without jurisdiction by officiously intervening in its execution, so where the process is within the jurisdiction of the court, if he takes it on himself to give orders or directions to the officer entrusted with its execution, and in consequence a wrongful act is committed, he will be liable, since he will have made the officer his agent to do that wrong,[201] and this liability attaches by virtue of the principal- agent relationship.[202] On the other hand, where a person simply gives advice or information to the officer or urges him to do that which it is his duty to do, he does not thereby become responsible for the subsequent proceedings.[203]

14-48 **What is an intervention** It is not always very easy to draw a distinction between what is mere advice and what is a direction. The question is one of fact. In *Morris v Salberg*,[204] the claimant's goods had been seized under a writ directed against his son. The jury found that the sheriff seized the goods because he was misled by the address given to him. It was held that the jury had found in effect that the sheriff had acted under the direction of the defendant and that the question was one for them. The claimant accordingly recovered judgment. If the execution creditor positively affirms to the officer of the court that a certain individual is the person, or that certain goods are the property of the person against whom the process issues, that amounts to an authority to the officer, and the creditor is answerable for the consequences of obeying his direction.[205] If no previous authority has been given by him, a party does not become liable by subsequent ratification. A person can only validly ratify where the act has been done at the time in his name. But a ministerial officer of justice purports to act in the name of the court to which he belongs and not in the name of the suitor.[206]

---

198 (1863) 14 C.B. (N.S.) 596. See also *Clissold v Cratchley* [1910] 2 K.B. 244.
199 (1863) 14 C.B. (N.S.) 596 at 264.
200 *Barker v Braham* (1773) 3 Wils. 368; *Bates v Pilling* (1826) 6 B. & C. 38.
201 cf. *Sowell v Champion* (1837) 6 A. & E. 407.
202 *Morris v Salberg* (1889) 22 Q.B.D. 614.
203 *Cronshaw v Chapman* (1862) 7 H. & N. 911. See also *Davidson v Chief Constable of North Wales* [1994] 2 All E.R. 597.
204 (1889) 22 Q.B.D. 614.
205 *Walley v M'Connell* (1849) 13 Q.B. 903.
206 *Woollen v Wright* (1862) 1 H. & C. 554.

6. DEFENCES TO TRESPASS TO THE PERSON

In an action of trespass to the person, once the trespass is admitted or proved it is for the defendant to justify the trespass if he can,[207] to show he acted with lawful excuse.[208] So, for example, if the claimant proves that he was the victim of a battery or that he was imprisoned by the defendant the onus lies upon the defendant to show that he acted in self-defence (in the case of battery[209]) or some other defence in the case of an imprisonment.[210] A defendant may justify trespass to the person by establishing one of the following defences: **14-49**

(a) the defendant was acting in defence of his person or property;
(b) the defendant was using reasonable force in the prevention of crime[211];
(c) the defendant was preventing or stopping a breach of the peace;
(d) the defendant was effecting or assisting in the lawful arrest of offenders or suspected offenders or persons unlawfully at large[212];
(e) the defendant was exercising a statutory power of stop and search;
(f) the defendant was exercising special statutory powers deriving from anti-terrorism legislation;
(g) the defendant was assisting an officer of the law;
(h) the claimant consented to the interference;
(i) the claimant was mentally disordered and required treatment for his disorder under the Mental Health Act 1983;
(j) the claimant lacked the mental capacity to consent to other forms of medical treatment or care and required treatment in his best interests;
(k) the defendant was administering reasonable chastisement in the exercise of parental or other authority;
(l) the defendant was exercising the authority of a shipmaster or commander of an aircraft;
(m) there is a statutory defence in certain cases where there have been previous criminal proceedings[213];
(n) the defendant was detaining the claimant prior to deportation;
(o) the defendant was conducting an authorised strip search.

Trespass ab initio Where what is prima facie a wrongful act is committed under the authority of the law, and this authority is abused, it ceases to provide protection and the party is liable not merely in respect of the way in which he exceeds his lawful authority, but also for all that he did in exercise of the right. He is said to be a trespasser ab initio, on the assumption that his subsequent misconduct evidences an intention from the first to commit unlawful acts under the colour of a **14-50**

---

[207] See *Dumbell v Roberts* [1944] 1 All E.R. 326 at 331; *Dallison v Caffery* [1965] 1 Q.B. 348.
[208] *F v West Berkshire HA* [1990] 2 A.C. 1
[209] *Ashley v Chief Constable of Sussex* [2008] UKHL 25; [2008] 1 A.C. 962.
[210] *Kuchenmeister v Home Office* [1958] 1 Q.B. 496; *Kenlin v Gardiner* [1967] 2 Q.B. 510.
[211] Criminal Law Act 1967 s.3, which also provides that it shall replace the rules of the common law in relation to the purposes mentioned in the section. Note, too, that it has been suggested at first instance that a reasonable (albeit mistaken) belief on the part of the arresting officer that the force used was necessary (as required by the Police and Criminal Evidence Act 1984 s.117) will defeat a claim in battery by the arrested person: *Alleyne v Commissioner of Police of the Metropolis* [2012] EWHC 3955 (QB) at [130]–[135], per Seys-Llewellyn QC.
[212] Criminal Law Act 1967 s.3. See also Police and Criminal Evidence Act 1984 s.117.
[213] See paras 14-135 and 30-32.

lawful authority.[214] This ancient doctrine has been said to be obsolete,[215] but has never been overturned. But if A, being in lawful custody, is detained after he had acquired a right to his discharge, the detention is treated as a fresh imprisonment, and does not make the prior imprisonment unlawful, for it is said that in such a case unlawful prolongation cannot have been contemplated on the original arrest.[216]

(a) Self-defence

14-51 **Use of force in defence of person or property** The question of the lawfulness of the use of force in defence of person or property is considered elsewhere.[217]

(b) Preventing crime

14-52 The Criminal Law Act 1967 s.3(1), empowers any person to use such force as is reasonable in the circumstances "in the prevention of crime, or in effecting or assisting in the lawful arrest of an offender or of persons unlawfully at large".[218] Section 3(2) provides that subs.(1) replaces the rules of common law "on the question when force is used for a purpose mentioned in the subsection is justified by that purpose". Thus, that Act confers on every person, private citizen and constable, a general and public right to use force in the prevention of crime and the apprehension of offenders. If invoked as a defence to the commission of a crime, a mere honest belief that a crime is being committed is sufficient to entitle a defendant to rely on the defence under s.3.[219] Whether the defence will succeed then depends on whether the defendant used only reasonable force.[220] It is unclear, when s.3 is invoked as a defence to the commission of a tort, whether the defendant's belief that a crime was being committed must be *both* honest and reasonable. This is certainly the case when the defence of self-defence is relied on in the civil law (although for the criminal law a mere honest belief suffices).[221] Section 3(2) probably does not abolish any individual and private right at common law to act in self-defence or the defence of others. The private and public rights will usually be coterminous. But this is not necessarily so, as in the case where a man is attacked by a person not guilty of a crime by virtue of insanity, or by a child below the age of criminal responsibility. The Police and Criminal Evidence Act 1984 s.117, authorises constables to use reasonable force in the exercise of any of their powers under that Act.[222] Thus, for example, the power to use reasonable force applies not only to the execution of a lawful arrest, but also to the removal of persons who are attempting

---

214 *Six Carpenters' Case* (1610) 8 Rep. 146a; *Canadian Pacific Wine Co v Tuley* [1921] 2 A.C. 417.

215 Lord Denning MR suggested that the doctrine was obsolete in *Chic Fashions (West Wales) Ltd v Jones* [1968] 2 Q.B. 299 though he appeared to change his mind in *Cinnamond v British Airports Authority* [1980] 1 W.L.R. 582 at 588.

216 *Smith v Egginton* (1837) 7 A. & E. 167.

217 See generally paras 29-02 to 29-15. See also paras 3-156 to 3-159.

218 Here, a "crime" means a crime under English law only; not public international law: *R. v Jones* [2006] UKHL 16; [2007] 1 A.C. 136.

219 *R. v Morris* [2013] EWCA Crim 436; [2014] 1 W.L.R. 16 at [19], per Leveson LJ (s.3 relied on in relation to the offence of dangerous driving). But not if "entirely fanciful": *R. v Wilkinson* [2018] EWCA Crim 2154; [2019] R.T.R. 20.

220 *R. v Morris* [2013] EWCA Crim 436; [2014] 1 W.L.R. 16 at [20].

221 It is submitted that s.3, when invoked in connection with the commission of a tort, ought to require an honest *and* reasonable belief by analogy with the decision and reasoning in *Ashley v Chief Constable of Sussex Police* [2008] UKHL 25; [2008] 1 A.C. 962. See further para.29-03.

222 See *DPP v Meaden* [2003] EWHC 3005 (Admin); [2004] 1 W.L.R. 945.

to prevent or inhibit the execution of a lawful arrest.[223] It is s.3 of the Criminal Law Act 1967 which authorises the use of force by a private citizen effecting an arrest under the powers of arrest conferred on him by s.24A of the 1984 Act.[224] And other legislation grants specific powers in relation to the apprehension of offenders, in some cases to all members of the public, in others to persons holding specific offices, such as churchwardens, and in very many cases to police officers.

Reasonable force Should excessive or unreasonable force be used to effect a lawful arrest, the arrestor, albeit not liable for false imprisonment, may still be liable for assault and battery.[225] The degree of force reasonable must be judged in the light of the circumstances apparent to the arrestor; and he will not be found to have used unreasonable force because of a defect in the planning of the arrest or crime prevention operation which with hindsight can be seen to render the amount of force used unnecessary. A defence under s.3(1) is available only to the person actually using force to prevent a crime or effect an arrest; the crucial issue is therefore whether he and he alone acted unreasonably.[226] In appropriate circumstances the use of a properly trained police dog does not constitute an unreasonable use of force in effecting an arrest. If the dog deployed causes severe injury and permanent scarring to the person being arrested, the force used may still be judged reasonable in the circumstances.[227] On the other hand, the use of hooding during a forcible arrest will always amount to the use of unreasonable force since "it is likely to pose a risk to the detainee's physical or mental health by virtue of the force".[228] The question of what constitutes unreasonable *force* in making an arrest is a mixed question of fact and law and should generally be left to the jury.[229] Where, however, the issue is the reasonableness of an *imprisonment or detention*, this is a question of law for the judge alone to determine.[230] 14-53

(c) Preventing a breach of the peace

What is a breach of the peace? The most authoritative statement on the meaning of a breach of the peace derives from the decision of the House of Lords in *R. (on the application of Laporte) v Chief Constable of Gloucestershire*.[231] In that case, Lord Bingham said that: "[a] breach of the peace is not, as such, a criminal of- 14-54

223 See *Minio-Paluello v Metropolitan Police Commissioner* [2011] EWHC 3411 (QB); *Isaacs v Metropolitan Police Commissioner* [2013] EWHC 4157 (QB).

224 A constable exercising powers under statutes other than the Police and Criminal Evidence Act 1984 must similarly also rely on s.3 of the 1967 Act to authorise the use of force, unless the statute expressly confers that power.

225 *Allen v Metropolitan Police Commissioner* [1980] Crim. L.R. 441.

226 *Farrell v Secretary of State for Defence* [1980] 1 W.L.R. 172 (approved *NTC v Commissioner of Police of the Metropolis* [2015] EWHC 1432 (QB)); *R. v Owino* [1996] 2 Cr. App. R. 128.

227 See, e.g. *Roberts v Chief Constable of Kent* [2008] EWCA Civ 1588.

228 *R. (on the application of Equality and Human Rights Commission) v Prime Minister* [2011] EWHC 2401 (Admin); [2012] 1 W.L.R. 1389 at [83], per Sir Anthony May.

229 *Pollard v Chief Constable of West Yorkshire* [1999] P.I.Q.R. P219. For consideration of what constitutes reasonable force in the context of the criminal law see the Criminal Justice and Immigration Act 2008 s.76.

230 *Connor v Chief Constable of Merseyside* [2006] EWCA Civ 1549; [2007] H.R.LR. 6 at [70]–[71] (applying *Dallison v Caffery* [1965] 1 Q.B. 348).

231 [2006] UKHL 55; [2007] 2 A.C. 105.

fence, but founds an application to bind over."[232] By way of clarification, Lord Brown explained that a breach of the peace "involves actual harm done either to a person or to a person's property in his presence or some other form of violent disorder or disturbance and itself *necessarily involves a criminal offence*".[233] Accordingly, someone may be liable to be bound over for a breach of the peace if they act in a manner likely to provoke others to violence even though they have not themselves committed a breach of the peace. On the other hand, mere annoyance or insult to an individual stopping short of actual personal violence, is not a breach of the peace.[234] Nor will a civil trespass alone constitute a breach of the peace: there must be evidence that violence might reasonably be expected to result from that trespass.[235] A breach of the peace can take place on private premises since, although the involvement of the public at large is relevant to determine whether there has been a breach of the peace, it is not a prerequisite of such a breach.[236] As such, in exceptional circumstances even a purely domestic dispute may constitute a breach of the peace.[237] A breach of the peace is not a criminal offence within the meaning of s.34(1) of the Police and Criminal Evidence Act 1984; so arrest and detention for breach of the peace are not subject to the protections given to arrested persons in the 1984 Act, though it is good practice to treat any person detained for breach of the peace as if the relevant provisions of the Act were applicable.[238] Despite this, the law on breach of the peace complies with art.5 of the European Convention on Human Rights.[239]

14-55 **Common law powers to suppress breaches of the peace** The common law confers on all citizens the power to act to suppress breaches of the peace.[240] More particularly, the House of Lords in *Albert v Lavin* established that (a) the common law power to arrest participants in a breach of the peace extends, not simply to cases where a breach of the peace is continuing or to prevent its renewal,[241] but also to circumstances when a breach of the peace is imminent[242]; and (b) that, exceptionally, private citizens as well as constables may detain a person breaking or threatening to break the peace without making a formal arrest. The powers conferred at

232 [2006] UKHL 55; [2007] 2 A.C. 105 at [28].

233 [2006] UKHL 55; [2007] 2 A.C. 105 at [111] (emphasis added).

234 *Grant v Moser* (1843) 5 M. & G. 123 (persistently ringing a door-bell not a breach of the peace); cf. *Ingle v Bell* (1836) 1 M. & W. 516.

235 *Percy v DPP* [1995] 1 W.L.R. 1382. See also *Nicol v DPP* [1996] Crim. L.R. 318; (1996) 160 J.P. 155.

236 *McConnell v Chief Constable of Greater Manchester Police* [1990] 1 W.L.R. 364; *Chief Constable of Humberside Police v McQuade* [2001] EWCA Civ 1330; [2002] 1 W.L.R. 1347.

237 See *Addison v Chief Constable of the West Midlands Police* (1995) [2004] 1 W.L.R. 29.

238 *Williamson v Chief Constable of West Midlands Police* [2003] EWCA Civ 337; [2004] 1 W.L.R. 14 at [23].

239 *Steel v United Kingdom* (1999) 28 E.H.R.R. 603 (ECtHR). "The principle of proportionality ... is not only embedded in article 5 but is part of the common law relating to arrest for breach of the peace": *R. (on the application of Hicks) v Commissioner of Police of the Metropolis* [2017] UKSC 9; [2017] A.C. 256 at [30] per Lord Toulson.

240 *Albert v Lavin* [1982] A.C. 546 at 565. And for endorsement of the duty of citizens to seek to prevent breaches of the peace, see *R. (on the application of Laporte) v Chief Constable of Gloucestershire* [2006] UKHL 55; [2007] 2 A.C. 105 at [29] and [110]–[111], per Lords Bingham and Brown respectively.

241 *Timothy v Simpson* (1835) 1 Cr. M. & R. 757; *Baynes v Brewster* (1841) 2 Q.B. 357; and see *Williams* [1959] Crim. L.R. 578.

242 *Albert v Lavin* [1982] A.C. 546; *R. v Howell* [1982] Q.B. 416; *R. (on the application of Laporte) v Chief Constable of Gloucestershire* [2006] UKHL 55; [2007] 2 A.C. 105.

common law to intervene to stop or prevent a breach of the peace are considerable and are additional to statutory powers of arrest conferred by the Police and Criminal Evidence Act 1984 and subsequent legislation.[243]

Powers of intervention A private citizen intervening to stop or prevent a breach of the peace must himself be a witness to the relevant events; unlike a constable, he cannot act on information from others. Having intervened he must normally hand the prisoner over to a constable or take him before a magistrate.[244] A private person must, on request, assist the police in suppressing a breach of the peace.[245] Once the breach of the peace is over, with no danger of renewal, the right to intervene is gone.[246] Should the participants rush away they cannot without warrant or other authority be detained, however fresh the pursuit or immediate the capture. Where it is not clear who is the aggressor, the bystander intervening need not enquire who initiated a breach of the peace. He may detain either of them if it is reasonably necessary to do so to prevent an affray continuing.[247] **14-56**

Breach of the peace "imminent" Where no actual breach of the peace has taken place in the presence of the arrestor, a power of arrest to prevent an imminent breach of the peace must be based on evidence of a real and present threat that a breach of the peace is about to occur. Refusal to accept a constable's advice to leave the vicinity of an earlier disturbance did not of itself amount to sufficient evidence that the arrested person was about to commit a breach of the peace.[248] Where a person intervenes to stop an imminent breach of the peace he must have reasonable grounds for his belief that the person he detains is about to commit a breach of the peace. An honest but mistaken belief that a breach is imminent will not suffice. In determining whether the grounds for preventive action were reasonable, the immediacy of the threat will be considered. In one case, police were held to be entitled at common law to stop pickets in cars one and a half miles from a working mine when the banners and language of the pickets led them to believe a breach of the peace would ensue when the pickets reached their destination.[249] Such an action at a further geographical move would have been unlawful at common law.[250] Except in the presence of imminent danger,[251] no one may intervene to detain any person not committing a breach of the peace in order to protect that person from ap- **14-57**

---

243 See in particular the Public Order Act 1986 (s.40 of which expressly preserves all common law powers to deal with or prevent a breach of the peace) and the Criminal Justice and Public Order Act 1994.

244 *Williamson v Chief Constable of West Midlands Police* [2003] EWCA Civ 337; [2004] 1 W.L.R. 14. See para.14-78 onwards on the arrestor's duties after making an arrest.

245 *R. v Brown* (1841) C. & M. 314.

246 *Baynes v Brewster* (1841) 2 Q.B. 357.

247 *Timothy v Simpson* (1835) 1 G.M. & R. 757.

248 *Foulkes v Chief Constable of Merseyside Police* [1998] 3 All E.R. 705; *Bibby v Chief Constable of Essex* (2000) 164 J.P. 297. In *R. (on the application of Laporte) v Chief Constable of Gloucestershire Constabulary* [2006] UKHL 55; [2007] 2 A.C. 105 the House of Lords stressed that there is no power to take action short of arrest if it would not be lawful to make an arrest because a breach of the peace was not imminent. Moreover, the circumstances in which it would be appropriate to take action against wholly innocent individuals will be exceptional.

249 *Moss v Charles McLachlan* [1985] I.R.L.R. 76. Note, however, that in *R. (on the application of Laporte) v Chief Constable of Gloucestershire* [2006] UKHL 55; [2007] 2 A.C. 105 the House of Lords indicated that *Moss* took the notion of imminence to the furthermost of any acceptable understandings.

250 But note the much more extensive powers granted to police under the Criminal Justice and Public Order Act 1994 s.60 (powers to stop and search in anticipation of violence).

251 Even in case of imminent danger the existence and extent of the power of "protective arrest" of an

prehended violence.[252] The leading case is now *R. (on the application of Laporte) v Chief Constable of Gloucestershire*.[253] There, the House of Lords held that the police had acted unlawfully in preventing the claimant from travelling to an anti-war demonstration at an RAF base. Against the background of art.11 of the European Convention on Human Rights (providing for the right to freedom of peaceful assembly and to freedom of association with others), the decision of the police to stop and turn around three coaches of protestors 5km away from the demonstration on the basis that the police anticipated a breach of the peace at the demonstration was not proportionate because it was premature and indiscriminate since they were unable to identify at that stage which, if any, of the passengers appeared likely to go on to commit a breach of the peace.[254] The only possible exception envisaged was where "there was no other way of preventing an imminent breach of the peace".[255] (Imminence was considered essential because otherwise "it could be a recipe for officious and unjustified intervention in other people's affairs".[256]) Beyond this, however, Lord Brown also opined that *in exceptional circumstances* the police will be able take action against those whose conduct, although not itself breaching the peace, appears likely to provoke others to do so.[257] But there is no lawful basis for taking action short of arrest to prevent a breach of the peace which is not sufficiently imminent to justify arrest. If it would not be lawful to arrest the claimant, it will not be lawful to take action short of arrest.[258] His Lordship stressed that the reasonable apprehension of an imminent breach of the peace was "an important threshold requirement, which must exist before any form of preventive action is permissible at common law".[259]

14-58 **Powers of constables to deal with breaches of the peace** The Police and Criminal Evidence Act 1984 left unscathed constables' common law powers to intervene to prevent or stop breaches of the peace. A constable may arrest a person who commits a breach of the peace in his presence provided that he makes the ar-

innocent person remained unsettled, and there is no authority for extending this power to any person other than a magistrate or officer of the peace: see *Humphries v Connor* (1864) 17 Ir. C.L.R. 1; *Connors v Pearson* [1921] 2 Ir. R. 51.

252 *Connors v Pearson* [1921] 2 Ir. R. 51.

253 [2006] UKHL 55; [2007] 2 A.C. 105.

254 [2006] UKHL 55; [2007] 2 A.C. 105 at [53] and [152]–[153], per Lords Bingham and Mance respectively.

255 [2006] UKHL 55; [2007] 2 A.C. 105 at [84], per Lord Rodger.

256 [2006] UKHL 55; [2007] 2 A.C. 105 at [62]. For Lord Rodger (at [62]), imminence meant a breach of the peace must be likely to happen, but that a police officer need not be able to say that the breach is going to happen in the next few seconds or next few minutes, since that would impose an impossible standard. Lord Mance also accepted (at [141]) that "imminence" does not have to be judged in "absolute and purely temporal terms". Instead, he opined, it "has to be judged in the context under consideration, and the absence of any further opportunity to take preventive action may thus have relevance".

257 [2006] UKHL 55; [2007] 2 A.C. 105 at [120]. However, since his Lordship stressed (at [124]) that "the police's first duty is to protect the rights of the innocent rather than to compel the innocent to cease exercising them", it would seem to follow that the circumstances that would warrant the description "exceptional" will be very few and far between. It would also appear to follow from his analysis that far from having any right to arrest an individual not reasonably believed to be about to commit a breach of the peace, the police were actually under a duty to protect their right to engage in lawful protest under art.11 of the European Convention on Human Rights.

258 [2006] UKHL 55; [2007] 2 A.C. 105 at [50], [65]–[66] and [141], per Lords Bingham, Rodger and Mance respectively.

259 For application of this approach, see *Wright v Metropolitan Police Commissioner* [2013] EWHC 2739 (QB).

rest when or immediately after the offence is committed, or while there is a danger of its renewal[260] though it may be that he is not entitled to make an arrest at all if there is no danger of a further breach.[261] When a constable reasonably believes that a breach of the peace is about to take place he may take any reasonable measures necessary to prevent such a breach. He may arrest any person threatening the peace,[262] or in appropriate circumstances may temporarily restrain that person without arresting him.[263] Equally, a constable may act on the information and complaint of others. If he comes to a place where an affray is said to be in progress, and is led reasonably to believe that a breach of the peace has already occurred and is likely to be immediately renewed, he may apprehend the responsible parties for the preservation of the peace. In addition he may receive into his custody a person already apprehended by a bystander, provided he reasonably believes that the prisoner was apprehended while in the act of breaching the peace.[264] The leading case on constables' powers with respect to breaches of the peace is now *R. (on the application of Laporte) v Chief Constable of Gloucestershire*[265] where the House of Lords held that forcing demonstrators back onto coaches and escorting them back to London without any stops had been unlawful. Nor was there any justification for stopping those demonstrators who intended to carry out a peaceful protest from reaching their intended destination.

Powers of entry *McLeod v Commissioner of Police of the Metropolis*[266] confirms that at common law, police have the power to enter private premises to prevent a reasonably anticipated breach of the peace. That common law power is expressly preserved by s.17(6) of the Police and Criminal Evidence Act 1984. The power of entry is not limited to places where public meetings are taking place.[267] The police exercising such a power of entry into private premises must, however, have a genuine apprehension of a breach of the peace in the near future and any power to enter private premises against the will of the occupier must be exercised with "great care and discretion". In *McLeod v United Kingdom*,[268] the European Court of Human Rights held that the common law concept of breach of the peace and the powers granted to constables to prevent breaches of the peace and to enter property to do so did not in principle violate art.8 of the European Convention on Human Rights. But when so acting, a constable's action must be proportionate to the threat posed to public order. 14-59

Statutory powers in relation to disorderly or offensive behaviour The Public Order Act 1986 gives to constables extensive powers to intervene to stop disorderly behaviour. Section 4 makes it an offence for a person: 14-60

[260] See *North v Pullen* (1961) 106 S.J. 77; [1962] Crim. L.R. 97.

[261] See *R. v Walker* (1854) Dears 358; *R. v Light* (1857) 27 L.J.M.C. 1; *R. v Marsden* (1868) L.R. 1 C.C.R. 131. See also, per Alderson J in *Cook v Nethercote* (1835) 6 C. & P. 744. But cf. *R. v Light*, above, at 3, per Williams J.

[262] *R. v Howell* [1982] Q.B. 416.

[263] *Albert v Lavin* [1982] A.C. 546; *Joyce v Hertfordshire Constabulary* (1984) 80 Cr. App. R. 298 at 302. This power of restraint short of arrest is only available where a breach of the peace is occurring or imminent: *R. (on the application of Laporte) v Chief Constable of Gloucestershire* [2006] UKHL 55; [2007] 2 A.C. 105.

[264] *Timothy v Simpson* (1835) 1 C.M. & R. 757 at 761 and 763.

[265] [2006] UKHL 55; [2007] 2 A.C. 105. See the full discussion of this case at para.14-57.

[266] [1994] 4 All E.R. 553.

[267] *Thomas v Sawkins* [1935] 2 K.B. 249.

[268] (1999) 27 E.H.R.R. 493.

(a) to use towards another threatening, abusive or insulting words or behaviour[269]; or

(b) to distribute or display to another any writing, sign or other visible representation which is threatening, abusive or insulting,

with intent to cause that person to believe that immediate unlawful violence will be used against him or anyone else by any person, or to provoke the immediate use of unlawful violence by the person insulted or by anyone else, or whereby the person insulted is likely to believe that unlawful violence may be used or provoked.[270]

A related offence is created by s.4A of the 1986 Act in relation to the same kinds of words or behaviour being used so as to cause another harassment, alarm or distress. In both cases, the offences can be committed in either a public or private place, save that no offence will be committed where the words or behaviour are used (or the writing, sign or visible representation are displayed) by one person inside a dwelling[271] and the other person is also inside the dwelling. Nonetheless, if a constable has reasonable grounds to believe that an offence has been committed, he may still arrest anyone whom he has reasonable grounds to suspect of being guilty of it.[272]

14-61 Section 5 of the Public Order Act 1986 creates an additional and complementary offence of using threatening or abusive words or behaviour or disorderly behaviour, or displaying any writing, sign or other visible representation which is threatening or abusive, within the hearing or sight of a person likely to be caused harassment, alarm or distress thereby.[273] As with the offence created by s.4, an offence under s.5 may be committed in a public or private place subject to the same exception as regards dwellings.[274] A general power of arrest in relation to the commission of these offences exists under s.24 of the Police and Criminal Evidence Act 1984. Unlike the Public Order Act 1986 s.4A, under s.5 the prosecution does not have to prove any intention to cause harassment, alarm or distress.[275] The relevant mental element is set out in s.6(4), namely either an intention that the words or behaviour should be threatening or abusive, or an awareness that they may be threatening or abusive.

14-62 Police powers to deal with disorderly crowds, or groups who are believed to threaten disorder, were extended by the Criminal Justice and Public Order Act 1994.

---

[269] The person alleged to be threatened by the relevant behaviour must be present for an offence to be committed under s.4: *Atkin v DPP* (1989) 89 Cr. App. R. 199; and see *DPP v Clarke* (1992) 94 Cr. App. R. 359. See also *Simcock v Rhodes* (1977) 66 Cr. App. R. 192 (defining "insulting" for the purposes of s.5 of the Public Order Act 1936).

[270] Presumably case law interpreting the earlier legislation remains relevant in this context. To justify arrest on the grounds that violence may be provoked, it must be shown to be genuinely likely that provocation would trigger unlawful violence. Thus, where the sole witnesses of the insulting behaviour etc are police officers who would/should not be so provoked, arrest will not be justified. See, e.g. *Parkin v Norman* [1983] Q.B. 92; *Grant v Taylor* [1986] Crim. L.R. 252.

[271] s.4(2) and s.4(3) respectively. Communal landings outside self-contained flats do not constitute part of a dwelling: *Rukwira v DPP* [1993] Crim. L.R. 882.

[272] Police and Criminal Evidence Act 1984 s.24(2).

[273] As amended by the Crime and Courts Act 2013 s.57(2) which removed the "insulting" limb from s.5(1). See *DPP v Orum* [1989] 1 W.L.R. 88 (a constable may be the person subjected to alarm); and alarm may be on behalf of a third party and not necessarily personal alarm (*Lodge v DPP* [1989] C.O.D. 179).

[274] On the meaning of "dwelling" under s.5(2), see *DPP v D* [2017] EWHC 2244 (Admin); [2017] 4 W.L.R. 177.

[275] *DPP v Smith* [2017] EWHC 3193 (Admin).

The Act confers, inter alia, powers to stop and search persons and vehicles where senior officers have reason to believe incidents involving serious violence are imminent in their locality[276]; powers to remove trespassers from land in certain circumstances[277]; powers to act to prevent "raves"[278]; and powers to intervene to prevent trespassory assemblies.[279] These powers are reinforced by the general power of arrest under s.24 of the Police and Criminal Evidence Act 1984.

Degree of force lawful In suppressing breaches of the peace or in the prevention of crime generally it is only lawful to use such force as is reasonable in the circumstances.[280] In considering what is reasonable force the court will take into account all the circumstances including in particular the nature and degree of force used, the seriousness of the evil to be prevented and the possibility of preventing it by other means.[281] The justification for the use of force in suppressing breaches of the peace is no different in principle from that invoked to prevent crime generally and any difference is really only one of degree. If the military forces of the Crown are employed in suppressing a riot, their status is that of ordinary citizens. The fact that they possess special arms and organisation is simply a reason for not lightly employing them.[282] It is sometimes supposed that it is never lawful to fire at a mob until a magistrates' order has been given. This, however, is erroneous. It must frequently happen that in the suppression of a riot the innocent suffer along with the guilty. But if the force used is reasonable and proper under the circumstances, the person employing it is protected, though he may cause damage to one entirely guiltless of participation in the misconduct of the mob.[283] On the other hand, in modern circumstances, the position would have to be extreme indeed before it would be considered reasonable for anyone, police or military, to open fire on a crowd. **14-63**

Mass detention of a crowd In *Austin v Commissioner of Police of the Metropolis*[284] the House of Lords upheld the decision of the Court of Appeal that the police had acted lawfully in cordoning off Oxford Circus and detaining over a thousand people for a period of some seven hours. The police had been engaged in an especially difficult exercise in crowd control and their main aims had been, first, to avoid the occurrence of personal injuries and damage to property, and secondly, to disperse as quickly as possible a crowd, some of whom were intent on violence and impeding the police. Bearing these factors in mind, they held that the police had acted reasonably and proportionately in their endeavour to prevent serious public disorder and violence. This ruling was subsequently confirmed by the **14-64**

[276] Criminal Justice and Public Order Act 1994 s.60. For the application of s.60 in this context (and for confirmation that it is not irreconcilable with the right to liberty afforded by art.5 of the European Convention on Human Rights) see *R. (on the application of Roberts) v Commissioner of Police of the Metropolis* [2015] UKSC 79; [2016] 1 W.L.R. 210.

[277] Criminal Justice and Public Order Act 1994 ss.61–62D and ss.68–69.

[278] Criminal Justice and Public Order Act 1994 ss.63-66; and see ss.72–80 regarding squatters.

[279] Criminal Justice and Public Order Act 1994 ss.70-71 (inserting ss.14A–14C in the Public Order Act 1986).

[280] Criminal Law Act 1967 s.3. And see *Farrell v Secretary of State for Defence* [1980] 1 W.L.R. 172.

[281] For consideration of what constitutes reasonable force in the context of the criminal law see the Criminal Justice and Immigration Act 2008 s.76.

[282] *Report on the Featherstone Riots*, 1893; see also *R. v Pinney* (1832) 5 C. & P. 254.

[283] *Farrell v Secretary of State for Defence* [1980] 1 W.L.R. 172. For compensation for damage to property see the Riot Compensation Act 2016 (in force, from 6 April 2017).

[284] [2009] UKHL 5; [2009] 1 A.C. 564.

European Court of Human Rights where it was held that the practice of containing a crowd behind a police cordon did not involve a breach of art.5 ECHR provided that it was unavoidable and necessary in order to avert a real risk of serious injury or damage.[285] Curiously, while before the House of Lords, both the appellant and the respondent conceded that if there was no infringement of art.5, there was also no false imprisonment. But the idea that the tort of false imprisonment mirrors precisely the protection of liberty afforded by art.5 is, with respect, unfounded (even though just this proposition seemed to be accepted by their Lordships[286]). That art.5 clearly cannot be coextensive with the common law tort is plain from the fact that art.5 only binds state actors, not private citizens (who are, of course, caught by the tort). Equally, there is also a difference in the degree to which liberty must be restricted.[287] In *R. (on the application of Jalloh (formerly Jollah)) v Secretary of State for the Home Department*,[288] the Supreme Court unanimously rejected the argument that the concept of imprisonment for the purpose of the tort of false imprisonment should be aligned with the concept of deprivation of liberty within the meaning of art.5 ECHR. The multi-factorial approach of the latter was very different from the approach of the common law to imprisonment and any move to formally align them would be a "retrograde step".[289] It is, stated the Supreme Court, possible therefore for there to be imprisonment at common law without a deprivation of liberty under art.5, although it declined to decide whether the converse was true.[290]

(d) Lawful arrest

(i) When is arrest justified?

14-65 **Statutory powers of summary arrest** The Police and Criminal Evidence Act 1984, as originally drafted, both codified and extended the statutory powers of summary arrest granted to constables. Since then, the Act has been revised and simplified so that s.24 confers a general power of arrest in relation to the commission of "any offence wherever committed".

14-66 Section 26 of the Police and Criminal Evidence Act 1984 repealed all previous statutory provisions conferring summary powers of arrest on constables (save for those statutory powers expressly saved by Sch.2 to the Act). But this related only to powers of arrest granted exclusively to constables. Where a statute had conferred a power of arrest exercisable by constables or private citizens, s.26 did not apply, and a constable, as much as any private individual, could continue to exercise the

[285] *Austin v United Kingdom* (39692/09) (2012) 55 E.H.R.R. 14; see further para.13-103.

[286] See, e.g. the description of the background to the case (argued before their Lordships solely on the art.5 point) in the speech of Lord Hope, [2009] UKHL 5; [2009] 1 A.C. 564 at [11].

[287] See, e.g. *HL v United Kingdom* (2005) 40 E.H.R.R. 32; (2005) 17 B.H.R.C. 418 at [91]. In *Zenati v Commissioner of Police of the Metropolis* [2015] EWCA Civ 80; [2015] Q.B. 758, the Court of Appeal acknowledged the distinction between actions in respect of art.5 ECHR and in false imprisonment. See also *Walker v Commissioner of Police of the Metropolis* [2014] EWCA Civ 897; [2015] 1 W.L.R. 312.

[288] [2020] UKSC 4; [2020] 2 W.L.R. 418.

[289] [2020] UKSC 4; [2020] 2 W.L.R. 418 at [33].

[290] [2020] UKSC 4; [2020] 2 W.L.R. 418 at [34]; favouring the view of the Court of Appeal in *Austin v Commissioner of Police of the Metropolis* [2007] EWCA Civ 989; [2008] Q.B. 660.

relevant power of arrest.[291] As such, constables' powers of arrest under statutes predating the 1984 Act together with their powers of arrest and detention at common law were unaffected. Furthermore, the section did nothing to prevent the subsequent creation of other, ad hoc, powers of arrest (and these have been created from time to time[292]).

Arrest by a constable Section 24(1) of the Police and Criminal Evidence Act provides that a constable may arrest without a warrant: **14-67**

"(a) anyone who is about to commit an offence;
(b) anyone who is in the act of committing an offence;
(c) anyone whom he has reasonable grounds for suspecting to be about to commit an offence;
(d) anyone whom he has reasonable grounds for suspecting to be committing an offence."

If a constable has reasonable grounds for suspecting that an offence has been committed (even though it turns out that no such offence has been committed), he may arrest without a warrant anyone whom he has reasonable grounds to suspect of being guilty of it.[293] And if an offence has been committed, a constable may arrest without a warrant: (a) anyone who is guilty of the offence; and (b) anyone whom he has reasonable grounds for suspecting to be guilty of it.[294] These powers of summary arrest can only be exercised if the constable has reasonable grounds for believing that for any of the reasons mentioned in s.24(5) it is necessary to arrest the person in question.[295] The reasons are:

"(a) to enable the name of the person in question to be ascertained (in the case where the constable does not know, and cannot readily ascertain, the person's name, or has reasonable grounds for doubting whether a name given by the person as his name is his real name);
(b) correspondingly as regards the person's address;
(c) to prevent the person in question—
  (i) causing physical injury to himself or any other person;
  (ii) suffering physical injury;
  (iii) causing loss of or damage to property;
  (iv) committing an offence against public decency[296]; or
  (v) causing an unlawful obstruction of the highway;
(d) to protect a child or other vulnerable person from the person in question;
(e) to allow the prompt and effective investigation of the offence or of the conduct of the person in question;

---

291 *Gapper v Chief Constable of Avon and Somerset Constabulary* [2000] 1 Q.B. 29 at 32, per Swinton Thomas LJ.

292 See, e.g. Criminal Justice Act 2003 ss.24A and 24B —arrest for failing to comply with a conditional caution.

293 s.24(2).

294 s.24(3).

295 s.24(4). The fact that the arrest must be necessary impliedly requires a police officer to consider measures short of arrest for "if he does not do so he is open to challenge". On the other hand, "[t]o require of a policeman that he pass through particular thought processes each time he considers an arrest, and in all circumstances no matter what urgency or danger … is to impose an unrealistic and unattainable burden": *Hayes v Chief Constable of Merseyside Police* [2011] EWCA Civ 911; [2012] 1 W.L.R. 517 at [40]; applied in *Kandawala v Cambridgeshire Constabulary CBS* [2017] EWCA Civ 391; *Commissioner of Police of the Metropolis v MR* [2019] EWHC 888 (QB).

296 This provision applies only where members of the public going about their normal business cannot reasonably be expected to avoid the person in question: s.24(6).

(f) to prevent any prosecution for the offence from being hindered by the disappearance of the person in question."

14-68 **Arrest by a private citizen** Section 24A(1) provides that a person other than a constable may arrest without a warrant:

"(a) anyone who is in the act of committing an indictable offence;
(b) anyone whom he has reasonable grounds for suspecting to be committing an indictable offence."

Where an indictable offence has been committed, a private citizen may arrest:

"(a) anyone who is guilty of the offence;
(b) anyone whom he has reasonable grounds for suspecting to be guilty of it."[297]

These powers of summary arrest can only be exercised if the person has reasonable grounds for believing that for any of the reasons mentioned in s.24A(4) it is both necessary to arrest the person in question *and* it appears to the person making the arrest that it is not reasonably practicable for a constable to make it instead.[298] The reasons listed in s.24A(4) are to prevent the person in question:

"(a) causing physical injury to himself or any other person;
(b) suffering physical injury;
(c) causing loss of or damage to property; or
(d) making off before a constable can assume responsibility for him."

Section 24A preserves the marked difference in the powers of constables and private citizens to effect a lawful arrest. A private citizen may only arrest in the case of an indictable offence (whereas under s.24 a constable may arrest for any offence), and may only arrest where someone is in the act of committing the offence or where an offence has been committed and the person arrested is guilty of the offence or there were reasonable grounds for suspecting him to be guilty of the offence. A constable, by contrast, may arrest where an offence is about to be (or there are reasonable grounds for suspecting an offence is about to be) committed; and where a constable has reasonable grounds for suspecting that an offence has been committed (even if it turns out not to have been) he may arrest anyone whom he has reasonable grounds to suspect of being guilty of it, but the private individual cannot. Thus, a private citizen still acts at his peril in making the decision to arrest, given that his suspicions about whether an offence has actually been committed may turn out to be incorrect (assuming of course that he is sufficiently familiar with the criminal legal system that he knows which offences are indictable). In addition, a private citizen must also form the view that it is necessary to make the arrest and not reasonably practicable for a constable to make the arrest. Necessity involves the judgment that there may be physical injury or loss of or damage to property or that the person arrested is "making off" before a constable can assume responsibility for him.

14-69 **Reasonable grounds for suspicion** Where what is in issue is whether the arrestor had reasonable grounds for suspicion, it is for the judge to rule on whether there

[297] s.24A(2).
[298] s.24A(3).

were such reasonable grounds, as in an action for malicious prosecution,[299] but the burden of proof is different. Whereas in an action for malicious prosecution the claimant must establish absence of reasonable cause,[300] in an action for false imprisonment the burden lies on the defendant to justify the arrest. He must prove affirmatively that he acted on reasonable grounds.[301] Reasonable grounds for suspicion are not to be equated with prima facie proof of guilt, as the former may properly be based on matters which would not be admissible in evidence.[302] The Court of Appeal[303] disapproved any contention that reasonable grounds for suspicion must be based on "a good deal more" than "mere suspicion". The test is simply whether in all the circumstances the objective information available to the constable supports reasonable grounds for suspicion of guilt. A direct charge made by a third party may be sufficient to justify arrest unless there are surrounding facts to show that the charge is unreasonable.[304] There is no general or absolute rule that a constable must make all practicable inquiries to confirm or dispel his suspicions before making an arrest.[305] Indeed, the Court of Appeal has stated explicitly that "the threshold for the existence of 'reasonable grounds' for suspicion is low, meaning that the amount of material that is known to the arresting officer in order to found 'reasonable grounds' for suspicion may be small, even sparse".[306]

The constable arresting a person on suspicion of an offence must himself have reasonable grounds for his suspicions.[307] It is not enough that, with hindsight, the facts of the case indicate that there might have been such grounds.[308] On the other hand, as was pointed out in *Buckley v Chief Constable of Thames Valley Police*, "suspicion is a state of mind well short of belief and even further short of a belief in guilt or that guilt can be proved".[309] In other words, the threshold for showing reasonable grounds for suspicion is a low one and a briefing prior to an arrest *may* **14-70**

299 *Dallison v Caffery* [1965] 1 Q.B. 348; *Wiltshire v Barrett* [1966] 1 Q.B. 312.

300 See para.15-35.

301 *Holtham v Commissioner of Police for the Metropolis, The Times,* 28 November 1987; *Hanson v Waller* [1901] 1 K.B. 390.

302 *Hussein v Chong Fook Kam* [1970] A.C. 942; *Baker v Oxford* [1980] R.T.R. 315.

303 *Holtham v Commissioner of Police for the Metropolis, The Times,* 28 November 1987. Whether the officer had reasonable grounds for suspicion must be determined objectively on the basis of matters known to him at the time: see *Alford v Chief Constable of Cambridgeshire* [2009] EWCA Civ 100; and in similar vein, *Chief Constable of West Yorkshire v Armstrong* [2008] EWCA Civ 1582.

304 *Davidson v Chief Constable of South Wales* [1994] 2 All E.R. 597 (acting on information from store detective).

305 *Holtham v Commissioner of Police for the Metropolis, The Times,* 28 November 1987; *Castorina v Chief Constable of Surrey* (1988) 138 N.L.J. 180; cf. *Dumbell v Roberts* [1944] 1 All E.R. 326 at 329.

306 *Alanov v Chief Constable of Sussex* [2012] EWCA Civ 234 at [25], per Aikens LJ. See also *Mouncher v Chief Constable of South Wales* [2016] EWHC 1367 (QB) at [434], expressing doubt, however, at the treatment of the omission of relevant material in the briefing of the arresting officer in *Alford* fn.303 above (see [431]–[433]). The court in *Commissioner of Police of the Metropolis v MR* [2019] EWHC 888 (QB) confirmed at [31] that the test for establishing that there are reasonable grounds for suspicion is well established and the threshold for suspicion is low.

307 *O'Hara v Chief Constable of the Royal Ulster Constabulary* [1997] A.C. 286: not enough that the arresting officer was instructed to arrest C by a superior officer. See also *Parker v Chief Constable of Essex* [2018] EWCA Civ 2788; [2019] 1 W.L.R. 2238.

308 *Siddiqui v Swain* [1979] R.T.R. 454. But his subjective belief in the arrested person's guilt or otherwise is irrelevant: *Castorina v Chief Constable of Surrey* (1988) 138 N.L.J. 180; *Chapman v DPP* (1988) 89 Cr. App. R. 190.

309 [2009] EWCA Civ 356 at [9], per Hughes LJ.

suffice for these purposes.[310] In order to have reasonable suspicion, a constable need not have evidence amounting to a prima facie case. Hearsay information, including information from other officers, may suffice to create reasonable grounds to arrest. But that information must be within the knowledge of the arresting officer since the discretion to arrest vests in the constable, not his superior officers.

14-71 In *Jarrett v Chief Constable of West Midlands Police*[311] Potter LJ said that the reasonable grounds for suspicion: "can arise from information received from another, even if it subsequently proves to be false, provided that a reasonable man, having regard to all the circumstances, would regard them as reasonable grounds for suspicion". The subjective and objective strands of the test are inextricably intertwined, so that: "to seek to decide whether a police officer has objectively got reasonable grounds of suspicion that an offence has been committed ... without first determining ... whether the suspicion to which he speaks is genuine is highly undesirable". An entry in the police national computer is sufficient objective justification for an arrest, where the police officer believed that the claimant might be armed with a gun.[312] The fact that the entry was false was irrelevant. A police officer is entitled to base the grounds for his suspicion on information received from a police informant or from a member of the public, although if the situation was not urgent, the police officer may have to make additional enquiries before he would be treated as having reasonable grounds for suspicion. In some circumstances the mere fact that the person arrested had the opportunity to commit an offence may amount to reasonable grounds for suspicion.[313] Thus, where there are grounds to suspect six people of the offence of perverting the course of justice, where the likelihood is that it was only one or perhaps two of those six, the police were justified in arresting all of them.[314]

14-72 **Acting on reasonable suspicion** Once reasonable grounds for suspicion can be established, police officers, and presumably private citizens, have a discretion as to whether or not to exercise a power of arrest conferred on them by ss.24 or 24A.[315] Section 24 requires a police officer to conclude that the arrest was "necessary", but the reasons listed in s.24(5) and, indeed the decision that arrest was necessary, inevitably involves an exercise of discretion in the sense that there must be judgment exercised as to whether the conditions are satisfied. That discretion must be exercised in good faith but can only be challenged as unlawful if it can be shown to have been exercised "unreasonably" under the principles laid down in *Associated Picture Houses Ltd v Wednesbury*.[316] In *Mohammed-Holgate v Duke*,[317] the House of Lords accordingly held that an arrest motivated by a constable's belief that the arrested person would be more likely to confess if taken into custody was not

310 *O'Hara v Chief Constable of the Royal Ulster Constabulary* [1997] A.C. 286.
311 [2003] EWCA Civ 397 at [28].
312 *Hough v Chief Constable of Staffordshire* [2001] EWCA Civ 39.
313 *Cumming v Chief Constable of Northumbria Police* [2003] EWCA Civ 1844 at [41], per Latham LJ.
314 *Cumming v Chief Constable of Northumbria Police* [2003] EWCA Civ 1844 at [41], per Latham LJ.
315 *Mohammed-Holgate v Duke* [1984] A.C. 437; judgment rested on interpretation of s.2 of the Criminal Law Act 1967 but seems equally applicable to the 1984 Act.
316 [1948] 1 K.B. 223. Similarly, a default warrant issued by magistrates in respect of unpaid fines can be executed at the discretion of the police, but that discretion has to be exercised reasonably: *Henderson v Chief Constable of Cleveland* [2001] EWCA Civ 335; [2001] 1 W.L.R. 1103. Thus, it could be lawful for the police to delay the execution of the warrant until the conclusion of a criminal investigation.
317 [1984] A.C. 437.

unlawful. Arrest for the purpose of using the period of detention to confirm or dispel reasonable suspicion by questioning the suspect or seeking further evidence with his assistance was an act within the broad discretion of the arrestor. But a belief that a suspect will more readily answer questions does not of itself justify arrest; reasonable suspicion must be grounded prior to the arrest. Thus, any officer who carries out an arrest knowing that there is no possibility of a charge, acts unlawfully.[318] Similarly, a police officer must both consider whether it is necessary to arrest and have grounds, as per s.24(5) of the Police and Criminal Evidence Act 1984, for believing that it is necessary to do so at the time of the arrest.[319]

Executing a search warrant A warrant authorising the police to enter and search premises carries with it an implied authority to arrest persons on the premises if such detention is necessary to enable the search to be effective.[320] What is necessary is a matter of fact and degree but the burden on the police in justifying an interference with civil liberties will be a heavy one.[321] In addition, s.117 of the Police and Criminal Evidence Act 1984 may permit an officer executing a search warrant to detain someone, to prevent them walking around their own home while it is being searched.[322] The authority given by the warrant has to enable the search to be effective. 14-73

(ii) Duties when making an arrest

Duty of party arresting to inform of the fact of arrest Any interference with the liberty of the subject must be justified strictly, and if on an arrest the powers given by the law are exceeded, or the law's requirements are not complied with, the arrestor will be liable in an action for false imprisonment even where, had the arrest been carried out correctly, it could have been justified. These principles, derived from the decision of the House of Lords in *Christie v Leachinsky*,[323] were given statutory force by s.28 of the Police and Criminal Evidence Act 1984. Section 28, however, provides only a skeletal framework for the rules governing the manner of arrest, so that earlier case law fleshing out that skeleton remains relevant.[324] The Act provides that: (1) an arrested person must be informed of the fact of arrest[325]; and (2) that he must be informed of the ground for the arrest,[326] unless in either case it was not reasonably practicable for the arrested person to be so informed because 14-74

318 *Plange v Chief Constable of South Humberside Police* (1992) 156 L.G. Rev. 1024. It is lawful to arrest a suspect to impose bail conditions provided the police have reasonable grounds to believe that bail conditions were necessary to protect a witness from intimidation which might make the investigation substantially less effective, see *R. (on the application of L) v Chief Constable of Surrey* [2017] EWHC 129 (Admin); [2017] 1 W.L.R. 2047.

319 *Richardson v Chief Constable of West Midlands* [2011] EWHC 773 (QB); [2011] 2 Cr. App. R. 1.

320 *Connor v Chief Constable of Merseyside* [2006] EWCA Civ 1549; [2007] H.R.L.R. 6 (applying *Murray v Ministry of Defence* [1988] 1 W.L.R. 692 and *DPP v Meaden* [2003] EWHC 3005 (Admin); [2004] 1 W.L.R. 945). The prior decision in *Hepburn v Chief Constable of Thames Valley Police* [2002] EWCA Civ 1841, was effectively confined to its own peculiar facts in *Connor*.

321 *Connor v Chief Constable of Merseyside* [2006] EWCA Civ 1549; [2007] H.R.L.R. 6 at [65]–[66], per Hallett LJ.

322 *DPP v Meaden* [2003] EWHC 3005 (Admin); [2004] 1 W.L.R. 945; distinguishing *Hepburn v Chief Constable of Thames Valley Police*.

323 [1947] A.C. 573.

324 *Lewis v Chief Constable of South Wales* [1991] 1 All E.R. 206 at 208.

325 Police and Criminal Evidence Act 1984 s.28(1).

326 Police and Criminal Evidence Act 1984 s.28(3).

he escaped from the arrestor before the information could be given.[327] Whenever an arrest is effected other than by informing the arrested person that he is under arrest, "the arrest is not lawful unless the person arrested is informed that he is under arrest as soon as is practicable after his arrest".[328] It is the same for citizens and police officers. Thus, "where a police officer restrains a person, but does not at that time intend or purport to arrest him, then he is committing an assault, even if an arrest would have been justified".[329] But when an offender became trapped in a car by an automatic locking mechanism designed to ensnare intruders, his arrest was lawful, for officers informed him of the fact as soon as they arrived within minutes of the man's detention.[330] Where the arrestor is a constable, s.28(2) provides that the requirement to inform of the fact of arrest applies "regardless of whether the fact of the arrest is obvious". It must be made clear to the arrested person that he is now lawfully detained and compelled to submit to the arrestor. There is no single formula which must be used and which will always serve the purpose.[331] Where, for the purpose of assisting with an investigation, a person has attended a police station voluntarily or any other place where a constable is present, or accompanies a constable to a police station without having been arrested, he is entitled to leave at will unless placed under arrest, and if a decision is taken by a constable to prevent him from leaving at will he must be informed that he is under arrest.[332]

14-75 **Duty to inform of the grounds for arrest** Section 28(3) imposes the general duty to inform the arrested person why he is being arrested. The subsection provides "no arrest is lawful unless the person is informed of the ground of the arrest at the time of, or as soon as is practicable after, the arrest". In *DPP v Hawkins*,[333] the arrested man resisted arrest for some time. It was therefore impracticable to inform him immediately of the ground for his arrest. But when it became possible to do so, the arresting officers failed to inform him, thus making his continued detention unlawful. The Divisional Court held however that the later failure to explain the ground for the arrest when that became practicable did not retrospectively make the initial detention unlawful. Indeed, the constable had a duty to maintain the arrest until it was practicable to inform the arrested man of the ground for his arrest. Only the escape of the suspect before he can reasonably practicably be told of the reason for his arrest will excuse a failure by a constable to give the ground for the arrest.[334] It is also clear that the ground for the arrest must be the *true* ground[335] and it must be explained in sufficient detail and non-technical language to enable the person to

---

327 Police and Criminal Evidence Act 1984 s.28(5). See *DPP v Hawkins* [1988] 1 W.L.R. 1166.

328 Police and Criminal Evidence Act 1984 s.28(1).

329 *Wood v DPP* [2008] EWHC 1056 (Admin) at [7]. It is important, however, not to take these words out of their context and they do not support the proposition that the only circumstance in which a police officer can lay hands on a citizen is in the course of an arrest: *Metcalf v DPP* [2015] EWHC 1091 (Admin); [2015] 2 Cr. App. R. 25 at [10].

330 *Dawes v DPP* [1994] R.T.R. 209.

331 *Wheatley v Lodge* [1971] 1 W.L.R. 29; *Alderson v Booth* [1969] 2 Q.B. 216; *Adler v CPS* [2013] EWHC 1968 (Admin); [2014] Crim. L.R. 224.

332 Police and Criminal Evidence Act 1984 s.29. He must also be informed of the ground of arrest under s.28(3); see para.14-75.

333 [1988] 1 W.L.R. 1166.

334 Police and Criminal Evidence Act 1984 s.28(5); *Lewis v Chief Constable for South Wales* [1991] 1 All E.R. 206; s.28(4). The duty to provide reasons under this provision also applies to those arrests conducted in accordance with the Immigration Act 1971 Sch.2 para.17: *FS (Afghanistan) v Secretary of State for the Home Department* [2011] EWHC 1858 (QB).

335 *Wheatley v Lodge* [1971] 1 W.L.R. 29; *R. v Holah* [1973] 1 W.L.R. 127. In *R. v Chalkley* [1998] Q.B.

grasp the facts on which the arrest is founded. For example, telling a man he was arrested "for burglary" was held to be inadequate. He must be told where and when the alleged burglary occurred.[336] It is probably not necessary to specify what statutory power the arrestor relies on, or whether he is arresting the person on suspicion of an offence or by virtue of a warrant.[337] What is crucial is that the arrested man is given enough information to understand in substance why he is being deprived of his liberty.[338] So, in *Taylor v Chief Constable of Thames Valley Police*[339] the Court of Appeal held that for the purposes of the Police and Criminal Evidence Act 1984 s.28(3), the question to be determined was whether, having regard to all the circumstances of the particular case, the person arrested was told in simple, non-technical language that he could understand, the essential legal and factual grounds for his arrest.

A reasonable explanation What an arrestor says to a suspect at the time of the arrest must be examined in the light of all the circumstances surrounding an arrest, including any earlier conversation between the parties.[340] The test is whether the arresting officer has done what is reasonable in all the circumstances to explain the grounds for the arrest. If he has done all a reasonable person can be expected to do, the arrest is not unlawful simply because the arrested person failed to comprehend what he had been told. So, for example, if he were arresting a deaf person, there would no duty to speak so that the arrested man could lip-read.[341] Nor where an arrestor does not know that the arrested man cannot speak English need he summon an interpreter before arresting the suspect.[342] The provisions of s.28(1) and (3) might however be read as imposing a duty to take such steps as soon as "practicable", i.e. when the person is detained at the police station. 14-76

Other factors If a person is not informed of the fact or grounds of his arrest as soon as is practicable, that arrest is initially unlawful. However, arrest is a continuing act and once the suspect is subsequently informed of the facts and/or grounds of arrest, thereafter he is lawfully detained. But that initial period of detention, from the time of the arrest until he is given the requisite information, remains unlawful.[343] If A is arrested when he intervenes to attempt to prevent the arrest of B, and B's arrest turns out to be unlawful, so too is the purported arrest of A himself.[344] The duties imposed by s.28 to inform an arrested person of the fact of, and ground for, the 14-77

848, the Court of Appeal held that where an arrested person had been told a true ground for his arrest, that arrest did not become unlawful simply because police had a collateral motive: also wishing to investigate another more serious offence.

336 *R. v Telfer* [1976] Crim. L.R. 562.

337 *R. v Kulynycz* [1971] 1 Q.B. 367.

338 *Christie v Leachinsky* [1947] A.C. 573 at 587–588, per Viscount Simon. So, if a police officer informed a man who was wanted for murder that he was arresting him for murder, but by reason of diminished responsibility he was convicted of manslaughter, this would not render the arrest unlawful: *Shields v Chief Constable of Merseyside* [2010] EWCA Civ 1281; *The Times*, 3 March 2011 at [23], per Toulson LJ.

339 [2004] EWCA Civ 858; [2004] 1 W.L.R. 3155.

340 *Minio-Paluello v Commissioner of Police for the Metropolis* [2011] EWHC 3411 (QB).

341 *John Lewis & Co Ltd v Tims* [1951] 2 K.B. 459 at 467; [1952] A.C. 676 at 681; *Wheatley v Lodge* [1971] 1 W.L.R. 29.

342 *Wheatley v Lodge* [1971] 1 W.L.R. 29 at 34.

343 *Lewis v Chief Constable for South Wales* [1991] 1 All E.R. 206.

344 *Edwards v DPP* (1993) 97 Cr. App. R. 301. See also *Cumberbatch v Crown Prosecution Service*; *Ali v Department of Public Prosecutions* [2009] EWHC 3353 (Admin); [2010] M.H.L.R. 9.

arrest apply to the exercise of any power of arrest. It is also submitted that the common law rules requiring explanation of any lawful restraint or interference with the person demand that similar information be given to a person detained under common law powers to intervene to stop a breach of the peace,[345] and to the exercise of any other coercive power granted either by the Police and Criminal Evidence Act 1984 or other legislation.[346]

(iii) Duty after arrest complete

14-78 Whenever a person exercises a power of arrest, it is his duty to ensure that the arrested person is taken before a magistrate, or to a police station, as speedily as is reasonably possible.[347] Every power of summary arrest on a criminal charge is granted for the purpose of its further investigation by a magistrate, and no arrest can be justified which is not for this purpose.[348] A private citizen has no authority to question the suspect, or to detain him in his own custody while he gathers further evidence. However, evidence that the arrestor did not take the arrested man immediately to the police station or by the most direct route will not per se render his detention unlawful. So in *John Lewis & Co Ltd v Tims*,[349] the taking of a person arrested for shoplifting by store detectives to the manager's office so that the manager might decide whether to press charges and summon the police was held not to render the arrest illegal. Nor does an initially lawful arrest become unlawful if the arrestor relents and decides not to hand the suspect over to the police.[350] The issue in each and every case is whether there was an unreasonable delay in taking the arrested person to the police station. Whether there is evidence that the steps taken were unreasonable or the delay too great is a matter for the judge. Whether, if there is such evidence, the delay was in fact too great is for the jury.[351]

14-79 **Constables and private persons** In *Dallison v Caffery*,[352] it was held that at common law what amounts to reasonable conduct subsequent to arrest differed according to whether the arrestor was a private citizen or a constable. While a private citizen had no right to initiate an investigation by, for example, taking the person arrested on a detour to effect an identification,[353] constables' powers should be more liberally interpreted. Thus, a constable might reasonably take an arrested person back to his home to see if stolen property is there, or to some place where the arrested person alleges that there is evidence of an alibi.[354] This distinction is preserved by s.30 of the Police and Criminal Evidence Act 1984. Sections 30(1) and (1A) provide that whenever a person is arrested by a constable at a place other than

---

345 *Albert v Lavin* [1982] A.C. 569.

346 *Pedro v Diss* [1981] 2 All E.R. 59.

347 *John Lewis & Co Ltd v Tims* [1952] A.C. 676 at 691; *Dallison v Caffery* [1965] 1 Q.B. 348.

348 *Christie v Leachinsky* [1947] A.C. 573; *R. v Houghton* (1978) 68 Cr. App. R. 197 at 205; *R. v Holmes Ex p. Sherman* [1981] 2 All E.R. 612; (1981) 72 Cr. App. R. 266.

349 [1952] A.C. 676. Similarly, when a child was lawfully arrested, a detour to inform his father was found not to amount to an unreasonable and unlawful delay in taking the child to the police station: *R. v Brewin* [1976] Crim. L.R. 742.

350 *Wright v Court* (1825) 4 B. & C. 596.

351 *John Lewis & Co Ltd v Tims* [1952] A.C. 676.

352 [1965] 1 Q.B. 348.

353 *Hall v Booth* (1834) 3 N. & M. 316.

354 *Dallison v Caffery* [1965] 1 Q.B. 348. A refusal by a constable to make such a detour to confirm or deny an arrested person's alibi does not render the arrest and detention unlawful. He has discretion in the matter: *McCarrick v Oxford* [1983] R.T.R. 117.

a police station or taken into custody by a constable after arrest by some other person "the person must be taken by a constable to a police station as soon as practicable after the arrest". But s.30(10) preserves the common law rule from *Dallison v Caffery* to allow some latitude for preliminary inquiries by constables by providing that "[n]othing in subsection (1A) … prevents a constable delaying taking a person to a police station or releasing him under section 30A if the condition in subsection (10A) is satisfied". In turn, subsection (10A) makes clear that the condition is that "the presence of a person at a place (other than a police station) is necessary in order to carry out such investigations as it is reasonable to carry out immediately". In addition, specific statutory powers of arrest may prescribe a time period within which the arrested person must be brought before a magistrate.[355]

Section 30 of the 1984 Act further provides that, in general, arrested persons should be taken only to "designated police stations" which are properly equipped for the reception of prisoners. Once at the police station, the common law required that the arrested person be charged without delay and taken before a magistrate as soon as there was sufficient evidence on which to prefer a charge, or released if such evidence was not forthcoming.[356] Save under special statutory authority the police have no power to detain suspects for inquiries or questioning independent of their right of arrest. 14-80

Restraints on persons in custody No greater restraint may be placed on a person in lawful custody than is necessary to secure his detention. Arrest and imprisonment justify the removal of a person's liberty; his other civil rights over his body and to freedom from assault and battery remain unaffected except to the extent that infringement is necessary to restrain his escape. Thus, if there is a reasonable apprehension of escape or rescue the prisoner may be handcuffed, but not otherwise.[357] Section 32 of the 1984 Act authorises constables to search any person arrested other than at a police station where the constable has reasonable grounds to believe (inter alia) that the arrested person presents a danger to himself or to others, or has about him anything which he may use to escape or which constitutes evidence of a crime. The arrested person's dignity is protected by a prohibition of removal of other than outer clothing in public and the search must be limited to "the extent that is reasonably required" for the purpose[358] for which the power to search is exercised. Case law establishing constables' powers to search arrested persons at common law probably does not authorise search of an arrested person by a private arrestor. But if an arrestor believes on reasonable grounds that the arrested person has a weapon about him, searching and disarming him will be justified under s.3 of the Criminal Law Act 1967. 14-81

Once in custody it is unclear to what extent prisoners may be restrained or otherwise dealt with to prevent self-injury. The judgment in *Leigh v Gladstone*[359] that it was not an actionable assault to force-feed a prisoner because the authorities had a duty to do all that was necessary to preserve the prisoner's health is no longer good law. A prisoner of sound mind certainly retains the right to refuse medical treatment or food and drink and the prison authorities have no duty to take 14-82

355 *Wheeldon v Wheeldon* [1997] 3 F.C.R. 769.
356 *R. v Houghton* (1978) 68 Cr. App. R. 197 at 205–206.
357 *R. v Taylor* (1895) 59 J.P. 393.
358 Police and Criminal Evidence Act 1984 s.32(3); see *Lindley v Rutter* [1981] Q.B. 128 (unlawful to remove female prisoner's brassière simply because routine practice).
359 (1909) 26 T.L.R. 139.

coercive measures to prolong his life.[360] Equally, a prisoner whose conduct threatens others or constitutes a crime may be restrained with whatever degree of force is necessary and reasonable. Authority that a prisoner may be subjected to the use of force for his own good is more sparse.[361]

14-83 **Escape from custody** A person who has escaped from lawful custody is still considered theoretically a prisoner, and his recapture is but a continuance of his former imprisonment.[362] Recapture may therefore be effected without the restrictions as to time or place which may have been attached to the original execution of the process against him. A person privileged from arrest is not privileged from recapture.[363] In effecting a recapture, at any rate upon a fresh pursuit, it was probably lawful at common law to break open the outer door of a dwelling-house.[364] On this principle, it was held that where a party had been formally arrested by touching him through a broken window it was lawful thereupon to break into the house in order to effect his actual apprehension.[365] Section 17(1) of the Police and Criminal Evidence Act 1984 allows the police to enter and search any premises in order to recapture any person unlawfully at large and whom he is pursuing[366] as well as any person unlawfully at large who is liable to be detained.[367] Notably, in the case of those who are liable to be detained, there is no requirement that the arresting officer be in hot pursuit. A principal is always considered to be in the custody of his bail, and the bail may discharge himself at any time by making the custody actual and handing over his prisoner to the custody of the law. In so doing he has the same licence of procedure as in any other recapture.[368]

(e) Police powers of stop and search

14-84 Part I of the Police and Criminal Evidence Act 1984 grants constables power to stop and search persons and vehicles for stolen or prohibited articles; and these powers are additional to a range of existing statutory powers to stop and search.[369] Section 1(1) authorises stop and search in any place to which at the time a constable proposes to exercise those powers the public has access, and in any other place to

---

360 *Secretary of State for the Home Department v Robb* [1995] Fam. 127; *T (Adult: Refusal of Medical Treatment), Re* [1993] Fam. 95. See also *R. v Collins and Ashworth Hospital Authority Ex p. Brady* [2000] Lloyd's Rep. Med. 355 (where the prisoner was found to lack the relevant mental capacity).

361 *Connors v Pearson* [1921] 2 Ir. R. 51.

362 *Anon* (1704) 6 Mod. 231. See *R. v David Timmis* [1976] Crim. L.R. 129 (lawful custody starts after lawful arrest).

363 *Ex p. Lyne* (1822) 3 Stark. 132; *Foxall v Barnett* (1853) 23 L.J.Q.B. 7.

364 *Genner v Sparks* (1704) 6 Mod. 173.

365 *Sandon v Jervis* (1858) E.B. & E. 935 at 942; applied in *Hart v Chief Constable of Kent* [1983] R.T.R. 484; *Nichols v Bulman* [1985] R.T.R. 236. But a power of arrest does not imply a power of entry: *Morris v Beardmore* [1981] A.C. 446; *Clowser v Chaplin* [1981] 1 W.L.R. 837.

366 s.17(1)(d).

367 s.17(1)(cb). The section does not apply to a patient liable to be detained in a hospital under the Mental Health Act 1983 (see para.14-115). See further para.18-60 on s.17.

368 *Anon* (1704) 6 Mod. 231; *Ex p. Lyne* (1822) 3 Stark. 132.

369 See, e.g. the Criminal Justice and Public Order Act 1994 s.60 which grants extensive powers to authorise the stop and search of persons and vehicles. See also Terrorism Act 2000 ss.47A; Aviation Security Act 1982 s.24B (power of constables to stop and search at aerodromes); Violent Crime Reduction Act 2006 ss.45–47 (conferring powers on members of staff to search school pupils, further education students and persons in attendance centres for weapons).

which people have ready access, provided that place is not a dwelling.[370] In such places, a constable is empowered to search persons and vehicles, provided there are reasonable grounds for suspecting that stolen or prohibited articles may be found.[371] A constable finding such articles may seize them.[372] "Prohibited article" is defined as any offensive weapon[373] or any article made or adopted for use in the commission of certain offences of dishonesty.[374]

Conditions for exercise of power Section 2 sets out conditions for the exercise of powers of stop and search. A constable who has exercised his power to stop a person or vehicle by virtue of s.1 or any other enactment need not continue to conduct a search where to do so subsequently appears to be unnecessary or impracticable. His initial detention of the person to be searched does not become unlawful but, if continued after the constable has decided not to pursue a search, will be false imprisonment unless there are grounds for a lawful arrest and such an arrest has been effected.[375] A constable contemplating a search other than of an unattended vehicle in the exercise either of his powers under s.1 or under any other enactment save s.27(2) of the Aviation Security Act 1982, may conduct such a search lawfully only after (1) having established to the person to be searched that he is a constable[376]; and (2) having informed the person of his name, address and police station, the object of the search, the grounds for making the search and the person's rights under s.3 of the Act.[377] Section 2(9) prohibits a constable from requiring a person to remove any clothing in public other than an outer coat, jacket or gloves and prohibits constables not in uniform from stopping vehicles. Section 3 establishes detailed rules relating to making records of searches and for access to those records by persons subject to search under s.1 of the 1984 Act or other statutory powers. Failure to comply with the requirements to inform the suspected person of the constable's authority, the object and grounds for the search, and the suspected person's rights under s.3 will render the search and concurrent deten- 14-85

[370] This could extend to gardens, provided they are easy to enter. In such cases the Police and Criminal Evidence Act s.1(4)–(5) provides that a constable may not search a person or vehicle in a garden or yard occupied and used for the purpose of a dwelling unless he has reasonable grounds to believe that the person in question does not reside in the dwelling and is not in the garden or yard with the permission of the resident of the dwelling. Where the occupier of the dwelling does not agree to constables entering his premises to stop and search, entry must be authorised under s.17 of the Act. Quaere to what extent the occupier's permission may be implied: see *Robson v Hallett* [1967] 2 Q.B. 939; and *R. v Lamb* [1990] Crim. L.R. 58; *Wiltshire v DPP* [2014] EWHC 4659 (Admin). See further *Syed v DPP* [2010] EWHC 81 (Admin); [2010] 1 Cr. App. R. 34 on the power of entry under s.17(1)(e).

[371] Police and Criminal Evidence Act 1984 s.1(2), (3). As to reasonable suspicion see *King v Gardner* (1980) 71 Cr. App. R. 13.

[372] Police and Criminal Evidence Act 1984 s.1(6).

[373] Police and Criminal Evidence Act 1984 s.1(7), (9). "Offensive weapon" means any article made or adopted for use causing injury to persons or intended for such use.

[374] Police and Criminal Evidence Act 1984 s.1(7), (8). The relevant offences include burglary, theft, and offences under s.12 of the Theft Act 1968.

[375] The power to stop and detain probably embraces a power to detain for the purposes of asking such questions as are required to determine whether a search is necessary: *R. v Green* [1982] Crim. L.R. 604. Detention for questioning beyond that immediately necessary for the proper exercise of the power to search will be unlawful.

[376] If he is not in uniform he must provide documentary evidence that he is a constable: Police and Criminal Evidence Act 1984 s.2(2).

[377] Police and Criminal Evidence Act 1984 s.2(3). See *Browne v Commissioner of Police of the Metropolis* [2014] EWHC 3999 (QB): failure to comply with s.2 rendered use of force in the circumstances unlawful.

tion unlawful.[378] An initially lawful search probably does not become retrospectively unlawful by reason of a breach of the requirements of s.3 itself. Section 4 makes provision for road checks, and s.6 confers certain powers to stop and search vehicles on constables employed by statutory undertakers.

14-86 **Search after arrest** Section 32 authorises search of a person after his arrest at a place other than a police station and s.54 authorises search of persons detained at police stations. Section 32(1) provides that a constable may search a person arrested other than at a police station: (1) if he has reasonable grounds to believe that the arrested person may present a danger to himself or others[379]; and (2) if he has reasonable grounds to believe that the arrested person may have concealed on him anything which he might use to escape from lawful custody or which might be evidence in relation to an offence.[380] The power to search the arrested person for evidence is thus not limited to a power to search only for evidence relating to the offence for which the person was arrested, although the complementary power conferred by s.32(2)(b) to enter and search the premises where the person was arrested is so restricted.[381] The power to search is exercisable only to the extent that it is reasonably required for the purposes for which it is conferred,[382] nor is a constable authorised to require a person to remove in public more than his outer coat, jacket and gloves, but there is power to search a person's mouth.[383] Section 32 does not authorise routine searches of all arrested persons, or searches solely to establish identity.[384] Where the conditions imposed by s.32 are present there is power to search any arrested person. The search of a person is an infringement of his liberty over and above that necessarily resulting from arrest; he is therefore entitled to be informed of the grounds for the search, and it is submitted that failure to explain the grounds for the search will make that search unlawful.[385] Section 32(8) and (9) authorise seizure of anything found which the constable reasonably believes may be used to cause physical injury to the arrested person or another, or may be used to assist escape, or, save for items of legal privilege, is evidence of an offence, or has been obtained in consequence of the commission of an offence.

14-87 **Searches in custody** Subject to the statutory provisions applying to terrorism, the search of arrested persons in detention at police stations and intimate searches are lawful only if authorised by ss.54 and 55 of the Police and Criminal Evidence Act 1984. Section 54(1) imposes a duty on the custody officer at the police station to "ascertain … everything which a person has with him" when he is brought to the police station after arrest or when he is arrested at a police station.[386] Section 54(4) authorises the custody officer to seize any such thing save for clothes and personal

---

378 *Sobczak v Director of Public Prosecutions* [2012] EWHC 1319 (Admin); [2013] Crim. L.R. 515.

379 Police and Criminal Evidence Act 1984 s.32(1). The power conferred by s.32(1) is not subject to the conditions in s.32(3) and (5), but is subject to s.32(4).

380 Police and Criminal Evidence Act 1984 s.32(2)(a).

381 Although complementary to the power contained in s.32(1), there is no requirement for the purposes of s.32(2)(b) that the arrestee be reasonably perceived to be a danger to himself or others: *Hanningfield v Chief Constable of Essex* [2013] EWHC 243 (QB); [2013] 1 W.L.R. 3632.

382 Police and Criminal Evidence Act 1984 s.32(3), (5).

383 Police and Criminal Evidence Act 1984 s.32(4).

384 *R. v Eeet* [1983] Crim. L.R. 806; *Lindley v Rutter* [1981] Q.B. 128.

385 *Brazil v Chief Constable of Surrey* [1983] 1 W.L.R. 1155; *McBean v Parker* [1983] Crim. L.R. 399.

386 The custody officer may record or cause to be recorded all or any of the things which he ascertains under the Police and Criminal Evidence Act 1984 s.54(1): s.54(2).

effects. Clothes and personal effects may be taken only: (1) if the custody officer believes that the arrested person may use them either to injure himself or someone else or to damage property or to interfere with evidence or to assist him to escape[387]; or (2) if the custody officer has reasonable grounds for believing they may constitute evidence relating to any offence. Section 54(6) authorises a search of the arrested person if the custody officer considers it necessary[388] to enable him to carry out his duty under s.54(1). The search must not be an intimate search and must be performed by a constable of the same sex as the person to be searched.[389] Section 54(5) imposes a duty to explain the grounds for the seizure of any property unless the arrested person is violent or likely to become violent or is incapable of understanding what is said to him. The statute is silent about informing a person before exercising the power of search under s.54(6), but it is submitted that the common law rules requiring that reasons for the search be given remain relevant.[390] Section 54A authorises searches and examination to ascertain the identity of a person detained at a police station.

Intimate searches An intimate search, defined as a search which consists of physical examination of a person's body or orifices other than a person's mouth,[391] is unlawful and a battery unless authorised under s.55 of the 1984 Act. Such a search may be authorised only by an officer of the rank of inspector or above.[392] Authorisation may be given orally or in writing. The officer can lawfully authorise an intimate search only if he has reasonable grounds for believing that an arrested person in police detention has concealed on him either: (1) anything which he could use to cause physical injury to himself or another and might so use that thing while in police detention or the custody of the court; or (2) a Class A drug which he was in possession of with the appropriate criminal intent before his arrest. The officer must further have reasonable grounds to believe that only by means of an intimate search can the relevant object be discovered.[393] Failure to explain why an intimate search is proposed and to attempt to persuade the person to surrender any object voluntarily will render the search a battery, and possibly an indecent assault. Intimate searches to be carried out by a constable should always be carried out by a person of the same sex as the arrested person,[394] and intimate searches for drug offences should always be carried out by a registered medical practitioner or nurse[395] and where practicable such persons should perform all intimate searches.[396] Breach of either of these provisions renders the search a battery.[397] Finally, detailed provision is made for the keeping of records in relation to intimate searches. Provision is made in s.62 for the taking of intimate samples, that is, a sample of blood, semen or any other tissue fluid, saliva or pubic hair or swab taken from a person's **14-88**

---

387 See *D v Chief Constable of Merseyside* [2015] EWCA Civ 114; [2015] Crim L.R. 539.

388 There appears on the face of the statute to be no requirement that the custody officer establish that he had reasonable grounds for believing a search to be necessary.

389 Police and Criminal Evidence Act 1984 s.54(7),(9).

390 *Brazil v Chief Constable of Surrey* [1983] 1 W.L.R. 1155.

391 Police and Criminal Evidence Act 1984 s.65.

392 Police and Criminal Evidence Act 1984 s.55(1).

393 Police and Criminal Evidence Act 1984 s.55(2).

394 Police and Criminal Evidence Act 1984 s.55(7).

395 Police and Criminal Evidence Act 1984 s.55(4).

396 Police and Criminal Evidence Act 1984 s.55(5).

397 Where the search relates to a drug offence only, the effect of s.55(4) is that constables are not empowered to conduct such searches.

body orifice.[398] Such a sample may be taken only (1) if authorised by an officer of the rank of inspector or above; and (2) with the consent of the arrested person. Taking such a sample in the course of an intimate search, without establishing the conditions in s.62, will render the search a battery.

(f) Anti-terrorism legislation[399]

14-89 The Terrorism Act 2000 s.41(1), provides that a constable may arrest without warrant a person whom he reasonably suspects to be a terrorist. Just as with s.24 of the Police and Criminal Evidence Act, the constable's reasonable suspicion must be objectively grounded.[400] Where a person is arrested under this section a special regime in respect of detention (treatment, review and extension of detention) applies.[401] The Act also provides for stop and search where a constable reasonably suspects a person to be a terrorist (and for search of a person where he has been arrested under s.41) to discover whether he has in his possession anything which may constitute evidence that he is a terrorist.[402] The powers conferred by the Terrorism Act 2000 are in addition to powers which a constable has at common law or by virtue of any other enactment and do not affect those powers.[403] A constable may also use reasonable force for the purpose of exercising a power conferred on him by the Act.[404]

14-90 The Terrorism Prevention and Investigation Measures Act 2011 empowers the Secretary of State to impose specified "terrorism prevention and investigation measures" (TPIMs) on an individual[405] so long as certain conditions are met.[406] TPIMs may restrict, among other things, the individual's freedom to reside in, or visit, certain places as well as his or her freedom of movement within and beyond the UK.[407] In addition, the Act makes provision for the exercise by constables of an elaborate array of powers of entry, search, seizure and retention in connection with the imposition of TPIMs.[408] These powers are expressly conferred in addition

---

398 See Police and Criminal Evidence Act 1984 s.65. The taking of non-intimate samples is governed by s.63 of the same Act. This normally requires the written consent of the person from whom the sample is taken, but there is provision for taking non-intimate samples without consent in specified circumstances.

399 For a definition of terrorism see the Terrorism Act 2000 s.1; and for definition of a terrorist see s.40. For the definition of a "terrorism related activity", see the Terrorism Prevention and Investigation Measures Act 2011 s.4.

400 *Raissi v Commissioner of Police of the Metropolis* [2008] EWCA Civ 1237; [2009] Q.B. 564 at [9], per Sir Anthony Clarke MR

401 Terrorism Act 2000 s.41(2) and Sch.8. See *Ward v Police Service of Northern Ireland* [2007] UKHL 50; [2007] 1 W.L.R. 3013.

402 Terrorism Act 2000 s.43(1) and (2). There are also powers to stop and search vehicles, the drivers of, or passengers in, vehicles pedestrians: see ss.43A, 47A of, and Sch.6B to the Terrorism Act 2000.

403 Terrorism Act 2000 s.114(1).

404 Terrorism Act 2000 s.114(2).

405 s.2.

406 The conditions are that (i) the Secretary of State is satisfied on the balance of probabilities that the person has been involved in terrorism-related activity; (ii) some or all of the activity in question is new; (iii) the Secretary of State reasonably considers such a measure to be necessary to protect the public from a risk of terrorism; (iv) the Secretary of State reasonably considers it necessary to impose such a measure to prevent or restrict the individual's involvement in terrorism; (v) the Secretary of State receives such permission from the court or the case is one of such urgency that he may impose such a measure without first obtaining the court's permission: s.3.

407 Sch.1.

408 Sch.5.

to any other common law or statutory powers that constables possess.[409] The Counter-Terrorism and Border Security Act 2019 s.13 also confers a power on the police to enter and search the home address of a registered terrorist offender.[410] A justice of the peace in England and Wales[411] on application from a senior police officer (that is, a superintendent or above) of the relevant force, may issue a warrant to allow a constable to enter and search the home of the offender for the purposes of assessing the risks that he or she may pose to the community. The warrant must be executed by a constable of the police force in whose area the premises are located.

(g) Assisting an officer of the law

If a private individual acts to assist a police officer engaged in effecting an arrest or carrying out any other process of the law and the circumstances are such as to justify the conduct of the officer, the person assisting will also be justified, although he would not have been entitled to act by himself, for it cannot be unlawful to take part in a lawful act. And a person may be justified in initiating the process which leads to an arrest by a police officer which it would have been unlawful for him to effect personally. In *Davidson v Chief Constable of North Wales*,[412] a store detective mistakenly suspected the claimant of theft when in fact no theft had been committed. Had she arrested the claimant herself, the arrest would have been unlawful as private persons have no power of arrest where an offence has not been committed. She did not attempt an arrest but called the police who subsequently arrested the claimant. It was held that the police officers acted lawfully within s.24(6) of the Police and Criminal Evidence Act 1984. They had reasonable cause to believe that an offence had been committed. Nor was the store detective liable for unlawful arrest. She neither detained the claimant herself, nor in any sense directed or procured the arrest herself.[413] But if a private individual has procured an unlawful arrest,[414] or intervened to assist a police officer to effect such an arrest, then the private individual will be jointly liable with the police officer for false imprisonment.[415] The fact that the person intervening did not know that the arrest was unlawful is irrelevant since an honest belief that the arrest was lawful will not excuse a false imprisonment.[416] 14-91

Statutory protection The protection given by s.6 of the Constables Protection Act 1750 to constables and other officers executing invalid warrants of magistrates, and by s.126 of the County Courts Act 1984 to county court officers executing invalid process of the county court, includes private individuals acting by the order, and in aid, of such officers. The language would appear to point rather to the case 14-92

[409] Sch.5 para.2(a).
[410] Inserting s.56A into the Counter-Terrorism Act 2008.
[411] Sheriff in Scotland or magistrate in Northern Ireland.
[412] [1994] 2 All E.R. 597.
[413] On which see *Pike v Waldrum* [1952] 1 Lloyd's Rep. 431.
[414] *Ahmed v Shafique* [2009] EWHC 618 (QB).
[415] *Hepburn v Chief Constable of Thames Valley Police* [2002] EWCA Civ 1841 (the person intervening in this case was a fellow police officer).
[416] *Hepburn v Chief Constable of Thames Valley Police* [2002] EWCA Civ 1841 at [24], per Sedley LJ.

of persons who act in a subordinate capacity as mere assistants and who do not take it upon themselves to direct the proceedings.[417]

(h) Consent by the claimant

14-93 On one view, consent is not a true defence to an action for battery, in that the absence of consent is part and parcel of the tort itself. In *Freeman v Home Office (No.2)*,[418] McCowan J held that the claimant has the burden of proving the absence of consent,[419] an approach which effectively redefines battery to mean an "unconsented to interference with another's bodily integrity". The traditional view, however, is that consent operates as a defence, and accordingly it is for the defendant to prove that the claimant consented.[420] In Canada[421] and Australia[422] this is undoubtedly the case. It is suggested that this latter approach is also consistent with the basic principle that any direct interference with the person is unlawful and must be justified by the defendant. A claimant attacked in the street with a knife should not have to plead and prove that he did not consent to the attack (easy though that may be). By the same token, a competent patient cut by the surgeon's scalpel should not have to prove the absence of consent—it is a matter for the surgeon to justify by reference to the patient's consent.[423]

14-94 **The limits of consent** The victim's consent alone does not constitute a defence to a criminal charge of assault "if actual bodily harm is intended and/or caused".[424] Some lawful justification for the permission to do, or risk, harm must be present, as is the case where a person participates in a lawful game or sport or consents to surgery. It is not in the public interest that "people should try to cause, or should cause each other actual bodily harm, for no good reason"[425] and hence such conduct is prohibited by the criminal law. The House of Lords in *R. v Brown*,[426] holding that consensual sadomasochism could constitute criminal assault, found that it was irrelevant that the ensuing bodily harm was trifling or transient. Any degree of ascertainable bodily harm is justifiable only if "good reason" justifies the ac-

---

417 cf. *Painter v Liverpool Gas Co* (1836) 3 A. & E. 433. In *Nathan v Cohen* (1812) 3 Camp. 257, the defendant had caused a warrant to issue against the claimant, directed to three constables, had gone with them and pointed out the claimant as the person to be arrested. Lord Ellenborough held that he was within the protection of 21 Jac. 1, c.12, s.5 (1623), which speaks of certain officers and those who act "in their aid and assistance or by their commandment", the words being disjunctive. In the statutes referred to in the text, the act for which protection is claimed must have been by the order and also in aid of the officer.

418 [1984] Q.B. 524 at 539.

419 Note, however, that the correctness of this conclusion was questioned by Sir Anthony Clarke MR in *Ashley v Chief Constable of Sussex* [2006] EWCA Civ 1085; [2007] 1 W.L.R. 398 at [31].

420 See, e.g. *Collins v Wilcock* [1984] 1 W.L.R. 1172 at 1178, per Goff LJ; *F (Mental Patient: Sterilisation), Re* [1990] 2 A.C. 1 at 29; *R. v Brown* [1994] 1 A.C. 212 at 246–247, per Lord Jauncey; *T v T* [1988] Fam. 52.

421 *Reibl v Hughes* (1980) 114 D.L.R. (3d) 1 at 9.

422 *Secretary, Department of Health and Community Services v JWB (Marion's Case)* (1992) 106 A.L.R. 385 at 453, per McHugh J (but see now obiter comments in *White v Johnston* [2015] NSWCA 18).

423 For the general principles governing consent to medical treatment, see para.9-53 onwards.

424 *Att Gen's Reference (No.6 of 1980)* [1981] Q.B. 715 at 719; *R. v Coney* (1882) 8 Q.B.D. 534 (prize fighters were held guilty of assault despite mutual consent).

425 *Att Gen's Reference (No.6 of 1980)* [1981] Q.B. 715 at 719; *R. v Coney* (1882) 8 Q.B.D. 534

426 [1994] 1 A.C. 212. The European Court of Human Rights has ruled that the judgment in *R. v Brown* did not constitute a violation of art.8 of the Convention (respect for private life): *Jassard and Brown v United Kingdom* (1997) 24 E.H.R.R. 39.

cused's conduct.[427] In *R v BM*[428] the Court of Appeal ruled that body modification, such as the removal of an ear or nipple, or tongue splitting, performed on a consenting adult by a practitioner with no medical training or qualification, could not form an exception to the general rule in *R v Brown* that consent was no defence to causing actual bodily harm or wounding. Nonetheless, even though consent may not bar a prosecution, it is submitted that consent will constitute a good defence to a civil action in battery.[429] The claimant cannot claim compensation for the consequences of an act which he has freely invited, or in respect of which he has consented. The footballer cannot allege that a legitimate tackle is a battery[430]: consent to physical contact within the rules of the game may be implied.[431] Thus, when the defendant maintains that the claimant consented to the force used against him, the key question becomes whether that consent extended to the degree or type of force employed against him. The claimant's consent need not be specific to the alleged act of battery. He may consent to the general contact envisaged in a fight or in sport.[432] Moreover, when the act consented to constitutes a crime and the claimant is a participant in mutual criminal activity, a civil action between the parties may be barred on the grounds of ex turpi causa.[433] Contributory negligence is not a defence to trespass to the person, and therefore the claimant's conduct is relevant only in so far as it constitutes consent or the principle of ex turpi causa applies.[434]

Consent to proportionate force Whenever consent or ex turpi causa is pleaded as a defence to an action in battery, the force used by the defendant must be proportionate to the circumstances. Consent to the considerable degree of rough contact in rugby does not extend to savage blows and kicks. Players consent only to the use of force of the "kind reasonably expected to happen during a game".[435] Evidence of initial harassment and provocation will not excuse a fatal attack on the victim either on grounds of consent or ex turpi causa.[436] **14-95**

Consent induced by fraud A consent induced by fraud is invalid where the misapprehension of the consenting party goes to the root of the whole transaction **14-96**

---

427 *R. v Brown* was distinguished in *R. v Wilson (Alan Thomas)* [1997] Q.B. 47. In *R. v Dica* [2004] EWCA Crim 1103; [2004] Q.B. 1257 the Court of Appeal held that it was possible to consent to the risk of contracting a potentially fatal disease (HIV) through "ordinary" sexual intercourse (although if the defendant deliberately caused infection or spread HIV with intent to cause grievous bodily harm, the agreement of the participants provides no defence: [2004] EWCA Crim 1103; [2004] Q.B. 1257 at [58]).

428 [2018] EWCA Crim 560; [2019] Q.B. 1.

429 *Murphy v Culhane* [1977] Q.B. 94.

430 Although this is sometimes referred to as the defence of volenti non fit injuria, volenti is not appropriate. The players in a contact sport have consented to the contacts that, in a different context, would otherwise amount to a battery. They have not, however, assumed the risk of injury attributable to negligence by participants in the sport. See para.3-132.

431 cf. the position of those who work with children with special needs, who display violent tendencies, who do not impliedly consent to violence against them: *H v Crown Prosecution Service* [2010] EWHC 1374 (Admin); [2012] Q.B. 257.

432 *Blake v Galloway* [2004] EWCA Civ 814; [2004] 1 W.L.R. 2844 at [20].

433 *Murphy v Culhane* [1977] Q.B. 94. See further paras 3-02 onwards.

434 *Co–operative Group (CWS) Ltd v Pritchard* [2011] EWCA Civ 329; [2012] Q.B. 320; see para.3-68.

435 *R. v Billinghurst* [1978] Crim. L.R. 553.

436 *Lane v Holloway* [1968] 1 Q.B. 379.

and affects the nature and quality of the act done. In *R. v Dica*[437] the Court of Appeal held that a defendant who, knowing that he was HIV positive, recklessly transmitted the disease through consensual sexual intercourse could be guilty of inflicting grievous bodily harm, contrary to s.20 of the Offences against the Person Act 1861, and that consent to sexual intercourse could not be regarded as consent to the risk of the consequent disease (although if the victim did in fact consent to the risk that would be a defence). It is submitted that the logic of *R. v Dica* is equally applicable to actions in tort.

14-97 **Consent and fraud in the context of medical treatment** It has been said that if a patient's consent to medical treatment has been obtained by fraud or misrepresentation then it is not a valid consent,[438] though in *Sidaway v Bethlem Royal Hospital Governors*[439] Sir John Donaldson MR limited this to situations where there has been fraud or misrepresentation as to the nature of what is proposed to be done.[440] However, in the light of *R. v Dica* the position may have to be reconsidered. In *Appleton v Garrett*[441] a dentist was held liable in trespass to the person for carrying out unnecessary dental treatment, on a large scale, for profit. He withheld the information that the treatment was unnecessary because he knew that the claimants would not have consented had they known the true position. In such cases, arguably, what occurs is not strictly "medical treatment", so the consent must go not simply to the defendant's act (e.g. drilling a tooth), but also to the context in which the act takes place (i.e. providing bona fide, medical treatment that is appropriate). On the other hand, the failure by a dentist to tell patients that she had been struck off the dental register did not vitiate the patient's consent and thus render the accused criminally liable for assault as there was still bona fide treatment supplied and it merely related to the dentist's qualifications or attributes.[442] However, a fraudulent misrepresentation that the person administering Botox injections was a medical practitioner where administration by a medically qualified practitioner was for each woman a condition of giving consent would be regarded as deception capable of vitiating consent.[443]

14-98 **Consent obtained by duress** Consent affords no defence if the will of the consenting party was overpowered by force or the fear of violence. A claimant cannot give a real consent unless he has in fact the freedom to choose whether or not he should do so. A mistaken belief as to the authority of the defendant may destroy in substance the claimant's freedom to choose.[444] In *Freeman v Home Office*[445] the claimant contended that, as a prisoner, his relationship with prison medical staff was

---

437 [2004] EWCA Crim 1103; [2004] Q.B. 1257; *R. v Cort* [2003] EWCA Crim 2149; [2004] Q.B. 388: consent induced by fraud is not a defence to kidnapping (and, presumably, the tort of false imprisonment).

438 "Of course, if information is withheld in bad faith, the consent will be vitiated by fraud": *Chatterton v Gerson* [1981] Q.B. 432 at 443, per Bristow J.

439 [1984] Q.B. 493 at 511.

440 This approach is reflected in *Chatterton v Gerson* [1981] Q.B. 432 at 443 where Bristow J said: "once the patient is informed in broad terms of the nature of the procedure which is intended, and gives her consent, that consent is real". See also *Hills v Potter* [1984] 1 W.L.R. 641 at 653; [1983] 3 All E.R. 716 at 728; *Freeman v Home Office (No.2)* [1984] Q.B. 524 at 556, per Sir John Donaldson MR.

441 [1996] P.I.Q.R. P1; [1997] 8 Med. L.R. 75.

442 *R. v Richardson (Diane)* [1999] Q.B. 444. cf. *R. v Tabassum* [2000] Lloyd's Rep. Med. 404.

443 *R v Melin (Ozan)* [2019] EWCA Crim 557; [2019] Q.B. 1063.

444 See *T v T* [1964] P. 85 at 99 and 102; and see decisions on volenti by employees, para.3-126 onwards.

such that, as a matter of law, he could not give a free and effective consent to medical treatment proposed by the prison medical officer. The judge rejected that submission, holding each case must be looked at on its own facts to determine whether in the prison context and in the light of the medical officer's power to influence the prisoner's future, a valid consent was given. It was accepted that an abuse of authority by the defendants could vitiate an apparent consent even without evidence of the use or threat of physical force.

Consent or necessity Much of the debate on the boundaries of consent to battery has revolved around consent to medical treatment. Where the patient lacks capacity to consent, treatment may be justified on the basis of the principle of necessity, providing what is done is done in the patient's best interests.[446] The provisions of the Mental Capacity Act 2005 now provide a statutory regime which facilitates treatment for patients lacking mental capacity.[447] However, where a patient has been detained under the Mental Health Act 1983, the 1983 Act enjoys primacy, thereby ousting the facility to deprive a person of their liberty in accordance with the 2005 legislation.[448] In such cases, however, the inherent jurisdiction of the court can be invoked to obtain a declaration that treatment in accordance with a patient's best interests may proceed without incurring tortious liability.[449] 14-99

(i) Confinement and treatment for mental disorder under the Mental Health Act 1983

Detention under the Mental Health Act 1983 The detention, care and treatment of mentally disordered patients for their mental disorder[450] is governed by the Mental Health Act 1983 (based on the philosophy that, whenever possible, the admission to hospital and treatment of mentally disordered patients should be on a voluntary basis[451]). Part II of the Act makes provision for the compulsory admission to, and detention in, hospital of certain mentally disordered patients. It constitutes the sole ground on which mentally incapacitated persons may be compulsorily admitted to hospital for the purpose of assessment and treatment of their disorder.[452] The common law doctrine of necessity cannot be used as an 14-100

Note, however, that a conditional discharge from an hospital order under s.73 of the Mental Health Act 1983 which states that the patient "shall comply" with medication prescribed by a particular doctor does not amount to compulsion: *R. (on the application of H) v Mental Health Review Tribunal* [2007] EWHC 884 (Admin); (2007) 10 C.C.L. Rep. 306.

445 [1984] Q.B. 524.

446 *F v West Berkshire HA* [1990] 2 A.C. 1. See para.14-119 onwards.

447 See paras 14-124 to 14-128.

448 *An NHS Trust v A* [2013] EWHC 2442 (COP); [2014] Fam. 161.

449 *Great Western Hospitals NHS Foundation Trust v AA* [2014] EWHC 132 (Fam); [2014] 2 F.L.R. 1209.

450 The Mental Health Act 1983 does apply to treatment for physical ailments, even in respect of patients who are detained under the Act: *F v West Berkshire HA* [1990] 2 A.C. 1.

451 See Mental Health Act 1983 s.131(1). On the other hand, compulsory detention is possible, and although there is a Code of Practice dealing with seclusion of detained patients, it is not per se unlawful to depart from the Code. Properly used, seclusion does not violate arts 3, 5 or 8 of the European Convention on Human Rights: *R. (on the application of Munjaz) v Mersey Care NHS Trust* [2005] UKHL 58; [2006] 2 A.C. 148.

452 Note the concept of mental disorder is *not* synonymous with that of incapacity. As such, non-consensual treatment of a *competent* patient's disorder is possible under the 1983 Act.

alternative.[453] The key provisions here are s.2 providing for admission for assessment, s.3 providing for admission for treatment, and s.4 providing for "an emergency application". An application for admission for assessment must be founded on the written recommendation of two medical practitioners and must be made on the grounds that the patient:

(a) is suffering from mental disorder of a nature or degree which warrants detention in hospital for assessment (or for assessment followed by medical treatment) for at least a limited period; and
(b) ought to be so detained in the interests of his own health or safety or with a view to the protection of others.

Admission for assessment authorises the patient's detention for 28 days.[454] In cases of urgent necessity an emergency application for admission for assessment may be founded on the recommendation of one medical practitioner alone and will authorise the patient's detention for 72 hours.[455] Applications for admission for treatment must be made under s.3 of the Act on the grounds that:

> "(a) he [the patient] is suffering from mental disorder of a nature or degree which makes it appropriate for him to receive medical treatment in a hospital; and
> (c) it is necessary for the health or safety of the patient or for the protection of other persons that he should receive such treatment and it cannot be provided unless he is detained under this section; and
> (d) appropriate medical treatment is available for him."

Part IVA of the 1983 Act makes special provision for the treatment of community patients.[456] Of particular note is the fact that such patients may have their liberty curtailed to the extent that they may have to comply with certain conditions attached to the community treatment order, such as those requiring attendance at a certain place for treatment or periodic examination.[457] In *Welsh Ministers v PJ*[458] the Supreme Court warned that imposing conditions in a community treatment order which would amount to a deprivation of the patient's liberty would, however, breach art.5 ECHR. The fact that the purpose of the deprivation was to enhance rather than curtail the patient's freedom did not affect this assessment.

14-101 **Mental disorder** The powers under the 1983 Act are conferred in respect of those suffering from a mental disorder, which is defined in terms of "any disorder or disability of the mind".[459] This concept acts as the chief control device by which patients may be compulsorily detained under the Act. The Act does not permit the compulsory detention of patients "for their own good" or where their conduct has little detrimental effect on others. Thus, unusual or irrational thinking, or the holding of what some would consider to be "shocking views", are not per se evidence of mental disorder. Accordingly, the detention of a pregnant woman with pre-

---

[453] *R. (on the application of Sessay) v South London and Maudsley NHS Foundation Trust* [2011] EWHC 2617 (QB); [2012] Q.B. 760.
[454] Mental Health Act 1983 s.2(4).
[455] s.4(4).
[456] "Community patients" are those in respect of whom a community treatment order has been made under s.17A(7). These are patients who have been detained under the Mental Health Act 1983 but discharged by the responsible clinician under s.17A(1) subject to being liable to recall under s.17E.
[457] s.17B(2), (3).
[458] [2018] UKSC 66; [2019] 2 W.L.R. 82.
[459] s.1(2).

eclampsia who resisted hospitalisation, claiming that she would rather see her baby die than give up on a natural birth, was unlawful.[460] In order to ground a compulsory admission for treatment, it must be established that the patient is suffering from mental disorder, that such detention is necessary for the health and safety of the patient (or others) and that appropriate medical treatment will be available after his admission.[461] The medical treatment concerned need not be by way of medication or active therapy but may be simply nursing care and rehabilitation under supervision.[462] Subject to a patient having been released back into the community under the auspices of the supervised community treatment regime,[463] there is no power under the 1983 Act to require a patient's attendance at outpatient clinics. Nor, subject to the same caveat, is it lawful to admit a patient under s.3, administer medication, and then simply release him on licence until such time as he needs further medication. And, unless the patient is being dealt with on the basis of supervised community treatment, he cannot be compulsorily treated unless he also needs to be detained.[464]

Procedural safeguards Sections 11–15 of the 1983 Act make further provision for the procedure in relation to applications for assessment and treatment.[465] Applications should be made by the nearest relative or an approved mental health professional. When the application is made by an approved mental health professional he must take such steps as are practicable to inform the nearest relative that an application has been made and to explain the latter's power under s.23(2)(a) to apply for the patient's discharge.[466] Section 12 provides that the two medical recommendations required in support of an application for admission shall normally comprise (a) a recommendation from a specialist in mental disorder; and (b) a second recommendation from a medical practitioner who has previous acquaintance with the patient. In *Re S-C (Mental Patient: Habeas Corpus)*[467] Sir Thomas Bingham MR affirmed that compliance with the provisions of the Mental Health Act 1983 governing the detention of patients in hospital will be strictly enforced.[468] It followed that when a social worker obtained the patient's admission to hospital relying on the patient's mother's "consent" as nearest relative, when she was well aware that the father was the nearest relative as defined by s.26 of the Act (and that the father objected), the patient's admission to hospital was unlawful. Section 13(2) **14-102**

460 *St George's Healthcare NHS Trust v S* [1999] Fam. 26.

461 Mental Health Act 1983 s.3(2).

462 *R. v Mersey Mental Health Review Tribunal Ex p. D, The Times,* 13 April 1987.

463 Mental Health Act 1983 ss.17A–17G and Pt IVA.

464 *R. v Hallstrom Ex p. W (No.2)* [1986] Q.B. 1090; *R. v BHB Community Healthcare NHS Trust Ex p. Barker* [1999] Lloyd's Rep. Med. 101; [1999] 1 F.L.R. 106.

465 See, e.g. *TW v Enfield LBC* [2014] EWCA Civ 362; [2014] 1 W.L.R. 3665 (on s.11). The Act (ss.7–10) also authorises the reception of the patient into the guardianship of either local authorities or of some other private citizen. Only patients over 16 may be received into guardianship and the procedures for application for guardianship are broadly similar to those for application for detention.

466 For the power to apply to the court to direct that the function of the nearest relative be discharged by some other person on the grounds (inter alia) that he unreasonably objects to an application for admission for treatment or has acted without due regard to the welfare of the patient see s.29; and see *W v L (Mental Health Patient)* [1974] Q.B. 711 (objective test); *Whitbread v Kingston and District NHS Trust* (1998) 39 B.M.L.R. 94. See also *R. (on the application of Holloway) v Oxfordshire CC* [2007] EWHC 776 (Admin); [2007] B.L.G.R. 891 (on a "without notice" application to displace the "nearest relative").

467 [1996] Q.B. 599 at 603.

468 For subsequent endorsement of this strict approach see *TTM v Hackney LBC* [2011] EWCA Civ 4; [2011] 1 W.L.R. 2873.

of the Act further states that, prior to compulsory admission for treatment, a patient must be interviewed in a suitable manner in order to enable the approved mental health professional to satisfy himself that detention for treatment is necessary. Where, however, a patient is entirely uncooperative by virtue of his condition, it is sufficient for the doctor to observe the patient's conduct over a sufficient period of time in order to reach a conclusion on the necessity of admission for treatment.[469]

14-103 The period of detention authorised in pursuance of a successful application for admission for treatment is six months.[470] On the expiry of the first six months, authority to detain the patient may be renewed for a further six months and thereafter renewals are annual.[471] Such extensions may be obtained where a patient within two months of his or her discharge date is re-examined by a clinician who then furnishes evidence to the hospital managers that continued detention is warranted on grounds that reflect those justifying detention in the first place.[472] Any patient who has been detained under the Act, or made the subject of a community treatment order, or about whom a report suggesting further detention has been furnished, may apply to a First-tier Tribunal (or the Mental Health Review Tribunal in the case of Wales) for his discharge.[473]

14-104 Article 5(4) of the European Convention on Human Rights provides that: "Everyone who is deprived of his liberty by arrest or detention shall be entitled to take proceedings by which the lawfulness of his detention shall be decided speedily by a court and his release ordered if the detention is not lawful". This article has been invoked in a number of cases which have challenged the procedural safeguards contained in the Mental Health Act 1983.[474] In *R. (on the application of H) v Secretary of State for Health*[475] the House of Lords held that neither the 28-day detention under s.2, nor the extension of that period, under s.29(4) was incompatible with art.5(4) of the European Convention on Human Rights since they are capable of being operated in a manner which is consistent with the Convention.

14-105 **Consent to treatment** Part IV of the Mental Health Act 1983 provides detailed rules primarily relating to consent to treatment by patients suffering from mental disorders and detained in mental hospitals by virtue of that Act. Part IV also lays down rules which are applicable, in certain cases, to voluntary patients in hospital, and to persons afflicted by mental disorders who are not confined or resident in hospital at all.[476] Section 63 permits treatment without consent, or indeed notwithstanding the specific refusal of consent by a patient. And in *R. v Ashworth Hospital Authority Ex p. B*[477] the House of Lords clarified that s.63 can authorise treatment of a patient for any mental disorder from which he is suffering, irrespec-

---

469 *M v Queen Mary's Hospital Managers* [2008] EWHC 1959 (Admin); [2008] M.H.L.R. 303 at [12].
470 Mental Health Act 1983 s.20.
471 Mental Health Act 1983 s.20(2).
472 Mental Health Act 1983 s.20(3), (4).
473 Mental Health Act 1983 s.66, and see Pt V of the Act. Generally, patients under 16 and those admitted for assessment may apply to a Tribunal. See para.14-113.
474 See, e.g. *R. (on the application of C) v The Mental Health Review Tribunal, London and South West Region* [2001] EWCA Civ 1110; [2002] 1 W.L.R. 176.
475 [2005] UKHL 60; [2006] 1 A.C. 441; [2005] 4 All E.R. 1311. See, however, *MH v United Kingdom (11577/06)* (2014) 58 E.H.R.R. 35: special safeguards were needed for detained mental patients who lacked legal capacity to institute proceedings before judicial bodies.
476 e.g. to persons in prison: see *R. v Mental Health Commission Ex p. W, The Times*, 27 May 1988. And see Mental Health (Hospital, Guardianship and Treatment) (England) Regulations 2008 (SI 2008/1184).
477 [2005] UKHL 20; [2005] 2 A.C. 278. See also *R. (on the application of AL) v Secretary of State for*

tive of whether this falls within the form of disorder from which he was classified as suffering in the application, order or direction justifying his initial detention.

Section 63 deals with treatment for which no consent is required. It covers most, but not all, detained patients[478] as well as community patients who have been recalled to hospital. It does not dispense with the requirement for consent to treatment for the disorder on the part of a voluntary patient, or a mentally ill patient not in hospital (except those community patients who have been recalled). Nor does it authorise treatment, of any patient, for physical illness or disorder, for example, abortion or sterilisation of a mentally handicapped woman. Tube feeding a patient suffering from anorexia has, however, been held to constitute treatment for mental disorder.[479] **14-106**

Safeguards for certain forms of treatment Sections 57, 58 and 58A provide certain safeguards for patients. Section 57 applies to all patients in relation to any surgical operation to destroy brain tissue (or its functioning), and any "surgical implantation of hormones for the purpose of reducing male sexual drive".[480] Such treatment is prohibited unless two conditions are met: **14-107**

(1) the patient must consent; and
(2) an independent medical practitioner and two other persons who are not medical practitioners (appointed by the Care Quality Commission[481]) must certify in writing that:
    (a) the patient is capable of understanding the nature and purpose and likely effects of the treatment proposed and that he has consented to it; and
    (b) that the treatment is appropriate to be given.

Section 58 applies only to the administration of medicine to a detained patient; and then not until at least three months have elapsed since the first occasion during his period of detention when medicine was administered to him. As originally drafted s.58 covered electro-convulsive therapy (but this is now catered for by s.58A[482]). Now, under s.58(3), medicine cannot be given to a detained patient unless conditions (a) or (b) are satisfied. Section 58(3)(a) is the more straightforward and requires that the patient must have consented to the provision of the medicine and either the approved clinician or a registered medical practitioner appointed for this particular purpose has certified in writing that the patient is capable of understanding the nature of the treatment as well as its purpose and likely effects, and that he has consented to it. Under s.58(3)(b), in the absence of patient consent, medicine can only be administered where a registered medical practitioner ap- **14-108**

---

the Home Department [2005] EWCA Civ 2; [2006] 1 W.L.R. 88

[478] See Mental Health Act 1983 s.56, exempting certain detained patients from the operation of s.63.

[479] *B v Croydon HA* [1995] Fam. 133. The refusal to eat must be a manifestation of the mental disorder: *JK v A Local Health Board* [2019] EWHC 67 (Fam); (2020) 171 B.M.L.R. 184.

[480] The latter added by the Mental Health (Hospital, Guardianship and Treatment) (England) Regulations 2008 (SI 2008/1184) reg.27. To fall within s.57(2) the implant must be a hormone surgically inserted, and so the Mental Health Act Commission acted unlawfully in refusing permission for a prisoner to receive a drug to reduce sexual drive which was neither a hormone nor inserted surgically: *R. v Mental Health Act Commission Ex p. W*, *The Times*, 27 May 1988, Div Ct. Section 57(1) empowers the Secretary of State to bring further treatments within the scope of s.57.

[481] The Act makes reference to the regulatory authority, but the Health and Social Care Act 2008 Sch.3 para.13 explains that the regulatory authority is in fact the Care Quality Commission.

[482] This section applies both to detained patients and informal patients under the age of 18: s.56(5).

pointed for the purpose (not being the responsible clinician or the approved clinician in charge of the treatment) has certified in writing that the patient is not capable of understanding the nature, purpose and likely effects of the treatment or being so capable has not consented to it, but that it is appropriate for the treatment to be given. In relation to electro-convulsive therapy (and such other treatment as may be specified by regulations), s.58A makes a tripartite distinction between patients above 18 years of age and able to consent, those below 18 and able to consent, and patients unable to supply a valid consent. With regard to the first class, s.58A(3) requires that the patient must have consented to the treatment in question, and either the approved clinician in charge of it or a registered medical practitioner appointed under s.58(3) has certified in writing that the patient is capable of understanding the nature, purpose and likely effects of the treatment and has consented to it. With regard to those competent patients below 18 years of age, s.58A(4) stipulates that the patient must have consented to the treatment in question, and that a registered medical practitioner appointed under s.58(3) (not being the approved clinician in charge of the treatment) has certified in writing that the patient is capable of understanding the nature, purpose and likely effects of the treatment and has consented to it, and that it is appropriate for the treatment to be given. Finally, in the case of patients who lack the capacity to consent, s.58A(5) provides that electro-convulsive therapy can be given to such a patient so long as it has been properly certified that he is incapable of understanding the nature, purpose and likely effects of the treatment, but that it is nonetheless appropriate for the treatment to be given, and that giving the patient the treatment would not conflict with a valid and applicable advance decision made under the Mental Capacity Act 2005, or a decision made by a donee or deputy or by the Court of Protection.

14-109 **Emergency treatment** Section 62(1) provides that ss.57 and 58 (and therefore the protection for patients that they provide) do not apply, where such treatment is immediately necessary:

(a) to save the patient's life; or
(b) (not being irreversible) to prevent a serious deterioration of his condition; or
(c) (not being irreversible or hazardous) to alleviate serious suffering by the patient; or
(d) (not being irreversible or hazardous) represents the minimum interference necessary to prevent the patient behaving violently or being a danger to himself or others.

Section 58A (as it applies to electro-convulsive therapy) does not apply where treatment is immediately necessary and paragraphs (a) or (b) apply.[483] The effect of s.62 is to exempt medical staff in cases of dire emergency from the detailed provisions of ss.57, 58 and 58A in relation to the forms of treatment governed by those sections. It does not *of itself* authorise non-consensual treatment. In the case of a detained patient, any treatment normally within ss.57, 58 and 58A may be given to him without consent relying on the authority of s.63 of the Act, dispensing with the need for consent by a detained patient to treatment for his mental disorder. Non-consensual treatment can never under the Act be imposed on a voluntary patient.

[483] Mental Health Act 1983 s.62(1A). Where s.58A relates to "such other treatment as may be specified by regulations" (s.58A(1)(b)) then s.62(1B) provides that it does not apply where any of the paragraphs (a) to (d) of s.62(1) apply.

Only if the imposition of treatment could be justified at common law,[484] can such treatment be lawful.[485] Furthermore, the authority conferred on medical staff by s.63 of the Mental Health Act to compel detained patients to accept medication cannot be used to force a patient whose disorder does not warrant detention in hospital to accept medication. The device of admitting patients for one night to invoke compulsory treatment provisions and then releasing them on indefinite leave of absence was held to be ultra vires in *R. v Hallstrom Ex p. W*.[486] A patient admitted unlawfully and then subjected to forcible treatment entailing physical contact has a cause of action in battery.[487]

Relationship to the Human Rights Act All of the compulsory powers of treatment conferred by the Mental Health Act 1983 must be viewed in the light of the European Convention on Human Rights. In *Herczegfalvy v Austria* the European Court of Human Rights, considering whether compulsory medical treatment could amount to a breach of art.3 of the Convention, said that "the established principles of medicine are admittedly in principle decisive in such cases" so that "as a general rule, a method which is a therapeutic necessity cannot be regarded as inhuman or degrading. The court must nevertheless satisfy itself that the medical necessity has been convincingly shown to exist".[488] In *R. (on the application of W) v Broadmoor Hospital*, Hale LJ concluded that: "[o]ne can at least conclude from this that forcible measures inflicted upon an incapacitated patient which are *not* a medical necessity may indeed be inhuman or degrading. The same must apply to forcible measures inflicted upon a capacitated patient".[489] But the fact that there is a responsible body of medical opinion against the proposed treatment is not decisive to determine that medical necessity has not been convincingly shown.[490] The existence of a competing body of medical opinion is relevant to the question of whether treatment is in the patient's best interests or medically necessary, but it is no more than that.[491] The answer to the question whether medical necessity has been convincingly shown depends upon a number of questions, including: 14-110

"(a) how certain is it that the patient does suffer from a treatable mental disorder;
(b) how serious a disorder is it;
(c) how serious a risk is presented to others;
(d) how likely is it that, if the patient does suffer from such a disorder, the proposed treatment will alleviate the condition;
(e) how much alleviation is there likely to be;
(f) how likely is it that the treatment will have adverse consequences for the patient; and

---

484 Or under s.3 of the Criminal Law Act 1967.

485 In the case of treatments covered by s.57 it is difficult to see how psychosurgery or hormone implants could be immediately necessary and/or minimum interference.

486 [1986] Q.B. 824. Though note, now, the provision for community treatment orders under the Mental Health Act 1983 ss.17A–17G.

487 Quaere whether a patient who submits in an erroneous belief that the doctors are entitled to require him to accept treatment can sue.

488 (1993) 15 E.H.R.R. 437 at [82]. It has since been held that the test of therapeutic necessity is not reducible to any kind of precise science: *R. (on the application of B) v Haddock* [2006] EWCA Civ 961; [2006] Lloyd's Rep. Med. 433. However, where the therapeutic necessity of the treatment has been established in the best interests of the patient, it necessarily follows that there is no breach of the patient's Convention rights: *R. (on the application of B) v S (Responsible Medical Officer, Broadmoor Hospital)* [2006] EWCA Civ 28; [2006] 1 W.L.R. 810.

489 [2001] EWCA Civ 1545; [2002] 1 W.L.R. 419 at [79] (original emphasis).

490 *R. (on the application of N) v Dr M* [2002] EWCA Civ 1789; [2003] 1 W.L.R. 562.

491 *R. (on the application of N) v Dr M* [2002] EWCA Civ 1789; [2003] 1 W.L.R. 562 at [27]–[29].

(g) how severe may they be."[492]

The treatment of a competent detained patient with anti-psychotic medication under s.58(3)(b) of the Mental Health Act 1983, contrary to his religious beliefs, does not necessarily involve a breach of art.3 of the European Convention on Human Rights. In order to constitute a breach of art.3, the proposed treatment has to reach a minimum level of severity for ill-treatment, taking into account all the circumstances, including the positive and adverse mental and physical consequences, the nature and context of the treatment, the manner and method of its execution, its duration, and, if relevant, the sex, age and health of the patient.[493]

14-111 **Judicial review** On judicial review of a decision involving the forcible treatment of a detained patient, the test to be applied in determining the lawfulness of the decision is no longer *Wednesbury* unreasonableness. Rather there must be a "proportionality" review whereby the intensity of the review depends on the subject-matter.[494] However, since compulsory medical treatment potentially engages arts 2 (the right to life), 3 (protection against torture or inhuman or degrading treatment) and 8 (the right to respect for private and family life) of the European Convention on Human Rights, this effectively entails a full merits review, involving the finding of primary facts following oral evidence (if necessary), with the court reaching its own view as to whether the patient is competent to consent, and whether compulsory treatment is justified.[495]

14-112 **Discharge** An order for discharge may be made in respect of a patient who is for the time being liable to be detained or subject to guardianship.[496] The power of the nearest relative to order the discharge of the patient does not apply where the responsible clinician certifies that the patient, if discharged, would be likely to act in a manner dangerous to other persons or himself.[497]

14-113 **Discharge by a tribunal** There is provision for the discharge by a First-tier Tribunal (or the Mental Health Review Tribunal for Wales in the case of Wales) of a patient liable to be detained under the Act or a community patient on an application[498] by or in respect of the patient when the criteria set out in s.72 are satisfied.[499]

---

492 *R. (on the application of N) v Dr M* [2002] EWCA Civ 1789; [2003] 1 W.L.R. 562 at [19].

493 *R. (on the application of PS) v Responsible Medical Officer* [2003] EWHC 2335 (Admin); [2004] M.H.L.R. 1.

494 See *R. v Home Secretary Ex p. Daly* [2001] UKHL 26; [2001] 2 A.C. 532 at [27]–[28], per Lord Steyn.

495 *R. (on the application of W) v Broadmoor Hospital* [2001] EWCA Civ 1545; [2002] 1 W.L.R. 419. *R. (on the application of B) v Haddock* [2006] EWCA Civ 961; [2006] Lloyd's Rep. Med. 433; [2006] H.R.L.R. 40.

496 Mental Health Act 1983 s.23(1). A community patient will cease to be liable to recall, and the application for admission for treatment shall cease to have effect, if a discharge order is made: s.23(1A). The question of who can make the order for discharge varies with the status of the patient (but includes the responsible clinician, the managers of the hospital, and the "nearest relative"): see s.23(2).

497 Mental Health Act 1983 s.25.

498 Mental Health Act 1983 s.66(1), (4). Unreasonable delay in hearing an application to a tribunal by a detained patient can constitute a breach of art.5(4) of the European Convention on Human Rights which requires the lawfulness of a person's detention to be considered speedily by a court: *R. (on the application of C) v The Mental Health Review Tribunal, London and South West Region* [2001] EWCA Civ 1110; [2002] 1 W.L.R. 176; *R. (on the application of K) v Mental Health Review Tribunal*

In *R. v Canons Park Mental Health Review Tribunal Ex p. A*[500] the Court of Appeal held that the discharge criteria in s.72 of the Mental Health Act 1983 were not a "mirror image" of the compulsory admission criteria in s.3 of the Act. But in *R. v London South and South West Region Mental Health Review Tribunal Ex p. Moyle*[501] Latham J held that the reasoning of the majority in the *Canons Park* case could not stand with the decision of the House of Lords in the Scottish case of *Reid v Secretary of State for Scotland*[502] where it was held that the criteria for discharge were in fact meant to be mirror images of the admission criteria. Furthermore, it is unlikely that the decision in *Canons Park* would withstand a challenge under art.5 of the European Convention for the Protection of Human Rights. If the criteria for an initial compulsory detention are no longer satisfied, it is difficult to see how continued detention can be justified. Where a mental health review tribunal has discharged a patient, an application for compulsory admission cannot be made unless there is information not known to the tribunal which puts a significantly different complexion on the case as compared to that before the tribunal.[503]

Conditional discharge It is not uncommon for tribunals to impose conditions (e.g. as to appropriate supervision or accommodation) when ordering the discharge of a detained patient.[504] If conditions are imposed it may be difficult for a social services authority or health authority to meet those conditions, given limitations on their resources. But the failure of a social services authority or health authority to make the necessary arrangements to comply with the conditions attached to a conditional discharge, with the result that the patient remains detained, does not render the tribunal's decision unlawful, nor does it amount to a breach of art.5(1).[505] Section 117 of the Mental Health Act 1983 imposes a duty on the clinical commissioning group or local health board and the local social services authority to provide or arrange the provision of after-care services for patients who have ceased to be detained, but this is not an absolute obligation and there is no contravention of art.5 if, as a consequence of the failure to meet this statutory duty, the discharge cannot be put into effect.[506] Section 117 does not apply, however, to a patient on escorted leave of absence from a hospital.[507] In *R. (on the application of H) v Secretary of State for the Home Department*[508] Lord Bingham said that the duty of the health authority was simply to use its best endeavours to procure compliance with conditions laid down by a mental health review tribunal for the conditional discharge of 14-114

[2002] EWHC 639 (Admin); (2002) 5 C.C.L. Rep. 458; [2003] M.H.L.R. 1.

499 For these purposes, the tribunal should apply the civil standard of proof: *R. (on the application of AN) v Mental Health Review Tribunal (Northern Region)* [2005] EWCA Civ 1605; [2006] Q.B. 468.

500 [1995] Q.B. 60.

501 [2000] Lloyd's Rep. Med. 143.

502 [1999] 2 A.C. 512.

503 *R. (on the application of Von Brandenburg (aka Hanley)) v East London and the City Mental Health NHS Trust* [2003] UKHL 58; [2004] 2 A.C. 280.

504 Note that in relation to a conditionally discharged restricted patient, the Supreme Court has ruled that neither the tribunal nor the Secretary of State are permitted to impose conditions amounting to detention or a deprivation of liberty, even if the patient consents: *Secretary of State for Justice v MM* [2018] UKSC 60; [2019] A.C. 712.

505 *R. v Mental Health Review Tribunal Ex p. Hall* [2000] 1 W.L.R. 1323.

506 *R. (on the application of K) v Camden and Islington HA* [2001] EWCA Civ 240; [2002] Q.B. 198.

507 *R. (on the application of CXF) v Central Bedfordshire Council* [2018] EWCA Civ 2852; [2019] 1 W.L.R. 1862.

508 [2003] UKHL 59; [2004] 2 A.C. 253; [2004] 1 All E.R. 412 at [29]; applied in *R. (on the application of W) v Doncaster MBC* [2004] EWCA Civ 378; [2004] B.L.G.R. 743.

a patient. Where a tribunal considers that a patient can be satisfactorily treated and supervised in the community, if its conditions for discharge were met, the patient is not unlawfully detained if it proves impossible to meet those conditions with the result that the patient remains detained in hospital. Where the alternative, should the conditions prove impossible to meet, is not discharge, either absolutely or subject only to a condition of recall, but continued detention, the failure to meet the conditions does not render the patient's continued detention unlawful. It is only where there are no longer any grounds for detention that continued detention would be unlawful.[509]

14-115 **Retaking patients absent without leave** Powers are given for any approved mental health professional, officer on the staff of the hospital, constable, or any person authorised in writing by the managers of the hospital to take into custody and return to the hospital patients absent without leave.[510] While a detained patient absent without leave is deemed to be "unlawfully at large", a constable is not entitled to enter premises to arrest such a person in reliance on s.17(1)(d) of the Police and Criminal Evidence Act 1984 unless he is actually in hot pursuit of the absconding patient. It is not enough that the constable has reason to believe that the patient is to be found on those premises. He must be actively chasing after the patient, and the pursuit must be almost contemporaneous with entry into the premises. When it is desired to gain entry to premises where it is believed an absconding patient may be found, but there is no current pursuit of him, the proper course of action is to apply for a warrant to retake the patient under s.135(2) of the Mental Health Act 1983.[511]

14-116 **Protection against civil or criminal proceedings** Section 139(1) of the Mental Health Act 1983 provides that no person shall be liable whether on the ground of want of jurisdiction or any other ground to any civil or criminal proceedings in respect of any act done in pursuance of the Act unless such act was done in bad faith or without reasonable care. This provision does not, however, bar a challenge to the legality of acts allegedly done in compliance with the Act by way of an application for judicial review.[512] Section 139(2) places a procedural bar on actions by detained patients.[513] No civil proceedings may be brought by such a patient in respect of acts done in pursuance of the Act unless a High Court judge is satisfied that there are grounds for the contention that the person proceeded against acted in bad faith or without reasonable care.[514] For these purposes, "[t]he threshold under

509 [2003] UKHL 59; [2004] 2 A.C. 253; [2004] 1 All E.R. 412 at [28], per Lord Bingham.

510 Mental Health Act 1983 s.18. See also ss.35–36.

511 *D'Souza v DPP* [1992] 1 W.L.R. 1073. There is no requirement to identify named professionals who are to accompany a constable in the execution of a warrant under s.135 of the Mental Health Act 1983, and so the execution of such a warrant is not invalid simply because the approved social worker and the registered medical practitioner named in the warrant were not present: *Ward v Metropolitan Police Commissioner* [2005] UKHL 32; [2006] 1 A.C. 23.

512 *Waldron, Re* [1986] Q.B. 824 (also reported as *R. v Halstrom Ex p. W* [1985] 3 All E.R. 775).

513 The predecessor to s.139(2), s.141(2) of the Mental Health Act 1959, was held not to apply to the institution of proceedings by informal patients, since acts done to an informal patient are not done in pursuance of the Act: *R. v Runighian* [1977] Crim. L.R. 361.

514 A failure to obtain the leave of the High Court under s.139(2) renders the proceedings a nullity: *Seal v Chief Constable of South Wales Police* [2007] UKHL 31; [2007] 1 W.L.R. 1910. Since the failure renders the proceedings a nullity, it follows that if, by the time the procedural error has been discovered, the limitation period has expired the claimant cannot issue fresh proceedings with a view

s.139 is a low one".[515] It is arguable that a private law action brought under s.7 of the Human Rights Act 1998 would also require leave under s.139(2) of the Mental Health Act 1983.[516] However, s.139(4) provides that s.139 does not apply to proceedings against various institutional bodies of the NHS.[517] It is clear that s.139(2) does not apply (and therefore leave is not required for an action against these defendants) and the traditional view has also been that, irrespective of the substantive defence provided to a doctor by s.139(1), the hospital employing that doctor would be vicariously liable for his actions (e.g. in the tort of battery) even if the doctor was not liable because he acted in good faith and with reasonable care.[518] However, in *R. (on the application of W) v Broadmoor Hospital* Hale LJ suggested that a health authority or NHS Trust could only be held vicariously liable for those actions for which the doctors would themselves be liable, which would indirectly confer the benefit of s.139(1) on the employers. Brooke LJ went further and suggested, provisionally, that a hospital authority may not be vicariously liable at all for the actions of a responsible medical officer (RMO [now a "responsible clinician"]) in making treatment decisions under s.57 or 58 of the Act, since the Act vests the duty to carry out the specified functions in the RMO personally.[519] It was not the hospital, through the agency of one of its medical staff, in whom was vested the power to direct treatment without consent, but the RMO himself.

The decision of the Court of Appeal in *TTM v Hackney LBC*[520] appears to have important implications for the continued usefulness of s.139(1) of the Mental Health Act 1983 as a protection to defendants. In judicial review proceedings, a local authority was held to be vicariously liable both at common law and for breach of the claimant's art.5 rights under the European Convention on Human Rights for the action of an approved mental health professional who made an invalid application to detain the claimant under the Mental Health Act 1983, in breach of s.11(4) of the Act. This was notwithstanding the fact that it was common ground that the approved mental health professional had acted in good faith (an argument that she had acted without reasonable care was not ruled upon). It is clear that counsel for the Secretary of State for Health sought to avoid a declaration that s.139(1) was incompatible with art.5, and therefore submitted that if a breach of art.5 was found to have occurred s.139(1) should be read, in accordance with s.3 of the Human Rights Act 1998, so as to enable the claimant to recover compensation for the breach. In view of the fact that neither counsel for the local authority nor counsel for the Health Secretary disputed the claimant's argument that s.139(1) could be **14-117**

to obtaining leave. In *Seal v UK* (50330/07) (2012) 54 E.H.R.R. 6; [2011] M.H.L.R. 1 the European Court of Human Rights held that the requirement to obtain leave under s.139(2) did not involve a breach of the claimant's right of access to the court under art.6. As to the criteria governing an application for leave under s.139, see *Winch v Jones* [1986] Q.B. 296; *Johnston v Chief Constable of Merseyside* [2009] EWHC 2969 (QB); [2009] M.H.L.R. 343; and *Hewlett v Chief Constable of Hampshire* [2018] EWHC 3927 (QB) (permission to issue claim under s.139(2)).

515 *DD v Durham CC* [2013] EWCA Civ 96; [2013] M.H.L.R. 85 at [23] per Sir John Thomas P.

516 *R. (on the application of W) v Broadmoor Hospital* [2001] EWCA Civ 1545; [2002] 1 W.L.R. 419 at [54] and [61], per Brooke and Hale LJJ respectively.

517 Including the Secretary of State, the NHS Commissioning Board, a clinical commissioning group, a special health authority or a NHS Trust or NHS Foundation Trust.

518 *R. (on the application of W) v Broadmoor Hospital* [2001] EWCA Civ 1545; [2002] 1 W.L.R. 419 at [24] and [58], per Simon Brown and Hale LJJ respectively.

519 *R. (on the application of W) v Broadmoor Hospital* [2001] EWCA Civ 1545; [2002] 1 W.L.R. 419 at [42]–[43].

520 [2011] EWCA Civ 4; [2011] 1 W.L.R. 2873.

read in this way, Toulson LJ (with whom May and Jackson LJJ agreed) was "happy to proceed on the basis that it is open to the court to read s.139(1) in that way without further consideration of the matter".[521] The implication is thus that, in any case where the defendant's conduct amounts to a breach of the claimant's Convention rights, s.139(1) will no longer provide a defence. It remains to be seen whether, if on another occasion the defendant sought more robustly to rely on s.139(1), the court would be prepared to construe it in this way.

14-118 **Medical practitioners recommending compulsory admission** A medical practitioner signing a recommendation for compulsory admission owes a duty to the supposed mentally disordered person to act honestly and with reasonable care in giving his certificate, and for breach of that duty he is liable to an action for negligence[522] and damages can be recovered in this action for detention resulting from negligence in making the recommendation.[523] But where a Commissioner for Lunacy wrongly detained a person who had been temporarily released from a mental hospital and handed him back to the manager of the mental hospital with the result that he was confined in that and other mental hospitals for nine years it was held that his confinement was not the direct consequence of the detention by the Commissioner but in the circumstances of the case was the result of an independent act of the manager who exercised his own discretion in determining whether the person should be detained.[524]

(j) Treatment and care of patients lacking mental capacity (other than under the Mental Health Act 1983)

(i) Common law

14-119 **Treatment at common law** In *F v West Berkshire HA*[525] the House of Lords held that treatment of a person unable to consent[526] to medical treatment on his own behalf was justified under the common law principle of necessity. The test of what is necessary is the "best interests of the patient" and this is to be determined by the *Bolam* test, i.e. the treatment is necessary if a responsible body of professional opinion agree that it was in the best interests of the patient to have that treatment.[527] An operation or other treatment, said Lord Brandon, would be in the patient's best interests if, but only if, it is carried out to save the patient's life or ensure improvement or prevent deterioration in his physical or mental health.[528] Lord Goff made it clear that the defence of necessity was not one confined to medical and other

521 [2011] EWCA Civ 4; [2011] 1 W.L.R. 2873 at [66]. See also para.14-102.

522 *Hall v Semple* (1862) 3 F. & F. 337; *Everett v Griffiths* [1921] 1 A.C. 631; *Harnett v Fisher* [1927] A.C. 573; *De Freville v Dill* (1927) 96 L.J.K.B. 1056.

523 *Hall v Semple* (1862) 3 F. & F. 337; *Everett v Griffiths* [1921] 1 A.C. 631 at 667, per Viscount Finlay.

524 *Harnett v Bond* [1925] A.C. 669.

525 [1990] 2 A.C. 1.

526 On the common law idea of capacity to consent see: *Masterman-Lister v Brutton & Co and Jewell & Home Counties Dairies* [2002] EWCA Civ 1889; [2003] 1 W.L.R. 1511; and *MB, Re (Medical Treatment)* [1997] 2 F.L.R. 426.

527 *Bolam v Friern Hospital Management Committee* [1957] 1 W.L.R. 582; see para.9-76.

528 [1990] 2 A.C. 1 at 55. Logically there is only one best option, and the court must choose that option in making decisions in the patient's best interests rather than leaving the doctors to choose from the range of lawful options: *S (Adult Patient: Sterilisation), Re* [2001] Fam. 15. The court has the power to make an interim declaration authorising treatment that may become necessary to preserve life or avoid imminent risk of serious injury to the patient: *NHS Trust v T (Adult Patient: Refusal of*

health professionals.[529] If a person is lying unconscious in the street and a passer-by seeks to administer first-aid, or a mentally incapacitated person is endangering his own safety and a neighbour restrains him, no battery is committed. But officious intervention cannot be justified by the principle of necessity. For example, intervention cannot be justified when a more appropriate person is willing and available to act. In a case of temporary unconsciousness a doctor should do no more than is reasonably required in the patient's best interests before he recovers consciousness; nor may he proceed contrary to the known wishes of the patient, to the extent that he is rationally capable of forming such a wish.[530]

Advance statements about medical treatment It is possible for an individual, while competent, to give a statement in advance as to the forms of medical treatment that he will or will not accept, in anticipation of circumstances that may arise in which it would not be possible for him either to give a valid consent or to refuse consent to treatment.[531] A competent patient may even obtain an injunction restraining anyone from performing treatment in the future to which he objects.[532] Moreover, there is nothing in the European Convention on Human Rights which alters the right of a competent patient to make a statement refusing life-sustaining medical treatment in the future.[533] A decision to proceed with medical treatment in defiance of such an advance statement would give rise to an action for battery.[534] However, care must be taken to ensure that any advance directive made by the patient covers the particular circumstances that have arisen.[535] 14-120

Restraint at common law In *R. v Bournewood Community and Mental Health Services Trust Ex p. L*,[536] the House of Lords held that common law powers to detain mentally incapacitated patients on grounds of the necessity to safeguard their welfare survive, and exist in parallel with the Mental Health Act 1983. In that case, their Lordships had to tackle two questions: (1) was L (who had entered hospital as an informal patient) in fact detained, against his will, given that he was on an unlocked ward?; and (2) if he was so detained, did the hospital have lawful authority to justify that detention? On the issue of L's detention, their Lordships all agreed that there were periods when L was undoubtedly detained. The majority also agreed that, given his profound mental incapacity, any detention of L was lawful applying the common law principle of necessity developed in *F v West Berkshire HA*.[537] 14-121

Medical Treatment) [2004] EWHC 1279 (Fam); [2005] 1 All E.R. 387.

529 [1990] 2 A.C. 1 at 76.

530 [1990] 2 A.C. 1 per Lord Goff.

531 *Airedale NHS Trust v Bland* [1993] A.C. 789 at 857 and 864, per Lord Keith and Lord Goff respectively. The Mental Capacity Act 2005 now provides a statutory basis for advance decisions to refuse medical treatment. See para.14-124 onwards.

532 *C (Adult: Refusal of Treatment), Re* [1994] 1 W.L.R. 290, where Thorpe J granted an injunction restraining the amputation of the patient's gangrene-infected foot without express consent.

533 *AK (Adult Patient) (Medical Treatment: Consent), Re* [2001] 1 F.L.R. 129; *B (Adult: Refusal of Medical Treatment), Re* [2002] EWHC 429 (Fam); [2002] 2 All E.R. 449.

534 See *T (Adult: Refusal of Treatment), Re* [1993] Fam. 95 at 117 where Butler-Sloss LJ observed that doctors who treat a Jehovah's Witness against his known wishes "do so at their peril".

535 *T (Adult: Refusal of Treatment), Re* [1993] Fam. 95; *St George's Healthcare NHS Trust v S* [1999] Fam. 26. See also *HE v A Hospital NHS Trust* [2003] EWHC 1017 (Fam); [2003] 2 F.L.R. 408 on the courts' approach to the revocation of an advance statement about medical treatment.

536 [1999] 1 A.C. 458.

537 Such common law powers to provide mental health care to persons unable to consent to treatment

14-122 Subsequently, in *HL v UK*[538] the European Court of Human Rights held that although the common law defence of necessity could provide a legal basis for detention of a patient lacking capacity, it must be shown that the detention was not arbitrary. Necessity did not provide a set of procedural rules, so there was no provision for a review of the patient's detention. The contrast between the lack of any fixed procedural rules by which the admission and detention of compliant incapacitated persons was conducted, and the extensive procedural safeguards contained in the Mental Health Act 1983 was "striking".[539] This resulted in the patient's liberty being removed by the hospital's health care professionals solely on the basis of their own clinical assessments, completed as and when they considered fit. Neither habeas corpus nor any remedies available via judicial review were adequate as they did not allow for the resolution of complaints on the basis of incorrect diagnoses and judgments. Thus, L's detention contravened arts 5(1) and 5(4) of the European Convention on Human Rights, and it was irrelevant that he had not resisted his detention.[540] The court's decision in *HL v UK* would appear to undermine the common law defence of necessity, at least in so far as it relates to detention of a mentally ill claimant.[541] So, even if a mentally ill person is housed otherwise than in a care home or hospital pursuant to the Mental Health Act, and that person's living arrangements are relatively normal, those arrangements (insofar as they involve constant supervision and control) must be subject to periodic, independent checks in order not to comprise a deprivation of their liberty.[542] Procedural safeguards of this kind are contained in the amended Mental Capacity Act 2005.[543] The Court of Appeal has held, however, that in general there is no art.5 deprivation of liberty in the case of life-saving treatment of a person of unsound mind in the urgent or intensive care context where the mentally ill patient was receiving materially the same medical treatment as a person of sound mind.[544]

14-123 When a mentally disordered person is threatening violence to others, restraint may be justified[545] by the general principles of self-defence and defence of others, and entry on to premises may be authorised by s.17(1)(e) of the Police and Criminal

survive, and are inherent in, s.131(1) of the Mental Health Act. Section 131(1) of the Mental Health Act permits competent patients to consent to informal admission and allows informal admission of patients lacking mental capacity where such a mode of treatment is necessary for their welfare.

538 (Application No.45508/99) (2005) 40 E.H.R.R. 32; (2005) 17 B.H.R.C. 418.

539 (Application No.45508/99) (2005) 40 E.H.R.R. 32; (2005) 17 B.H.R.C. 418 at [120].

540 This point has been subsequently endorsed by the Supreme Court in *P v West Cheshire and Chester Council* [2014] UKSC 19; [2014] A.C. 896 at [55], per Lady Hale.

541 There is nothing, however, in the decision to suggest that the necessity principle cannot be invoked in connection with other forms of treatment.

542 *P v West Cheshire and Chester Council* [2014] UKSC 19; [2014] A.C. 896.

543 See Mental Capacity Act 2005 ss.4A, 4B and Sch.A1 (in relation to those detained in hospitals or care homes and the power of a court to authorise deprivations of liberty). In *P v West Cheshire and Chester Council* [2014] UKSC 19; [2014] A.C. 896, Lady Hale seemed to think (at [8]) that these amendments were a satisfactory response to the concerns raised in *HL v United Kingdom*.

544 *R. (on the application of Ferreira) v HM Senior Coroner for Inner South London* [2017] EWCA Civ 31; [2018] Q.B. 487, the Court of Appeal confining the *West Cheshire* case to the question of living arrangements for persons of unsound mind. The patient was, in the view of the Court, physically restricted by her illness and the treatment she received (which included sedation), but the root cause of any loss of liberty was her physical condition, not any restrictions imposed by the hospital.

545 *Brookshaw v Hopkins* (1772) Lofft. 240 at 243, per Lord Mansfield; *Re Greenwood* (1855) 24 L.J.Q.B. 148.

Evidence Act 1984 for the purpose of saving life or limb[546] or preventing serious damage to property.[547]

(ii) *Mental Capacity Act 2005*

The Mental Capacity Act 2005 enacts many of the Law Commission's recommendations for the treatment of mentally incapacitated adults. It covers most aspects of the lives of incapacitated adults, including the personal welfare and property and financial affairs, but in so far as it provides a statutory process to authorise medical treatment (or indeed, any form of care involving a touching of the incapacitated adult) the legislation supplies a defence to what would otherwise constitute battery. The Supreme Court has ruled that the question of whether that person has been deprived of his or her liberty for the purposes of s.64(5) of the Mental Capacity Act 2005, means that he or she "was under continuous supervision and control and was not free to leave".[548] **14-124**

Who lacks capacity? The Act provides for the first time a statutory definition of what constitutes incapacity. The starting point is that a person must be assumed to have capacity unless it is established that he lacks capacity.[549] The fact that he makes a foolish decision, or a decision that others (such as medical professionals) disagree with, does not establish that he lacks capacity.[550] A person lacks capacity in relation to a matter if at the material time he is unable to make a decision for himself[551] in relation to the matter because of an impairment of, or a disturbance in, the functioning of the mind or brain[552]; and it is irrelevant whether the impairment or disturbance is permanent or temporary.[553] A person is unable to make a decision for himself if he is unable: **14-125**

(a) to understand the information relevant to the decision[554];
(b) to retain that information;
(c) to use or weigh that information as part of the process of making the decision; or

[546] This can include protecting a person from himself: *Baker v Crown Prosecution Service* [2009] EWHC 299 (Admin); (2009) 173 J.P. 215. But this must involve "serious injury" and not merely "a concern for the welfare of someone within the premises": *Syed v DPP* [2010] EWHC 81 (Admin); [2010] 1 Cr. App. R. 34.

[547] See also s.136 of the Mental Health Act 1983 (as amended by the Policing and Crime Act 2017) which provides for the removal of mentally disordered persons to a place of safety without a warrant. It is important that before deciding to remove a person to, or to keep a person at, a place of safety under subsection (1), the constable must, if it is practicable to do so, consult (a) a registered medical practitioner; (b) a registered nurse; (c) an approved mental health professional; or (d) a person of a description specified in regulations made by the Secretary of State: s.136(1C).

[548] *P v Cheshire West and Chester Council* [2014] UKSC 19; [2014] A.C. 896 at [47], per Lady Hale.

[549] Mental Capacity Act 2005 s.1(2).

[550] "A person is not to be treated as unable to make a decision merely because he makes an unwise decision": Mental Capacity Act 2005 s.1(4).

[551] A person is not to be treated as unable to make a decision "unless all practicable steps to help him do so have been taken without success": Mental Capacity Act 2005 s.1(3).

[552] Mental Capacity Act 2005 s.2(1).

[553] Mental Capacity Act 2005 s.2(2).

[554] The information relevant to a decision includes "information about the reasonably foreseeable consequences of (a) deciding one way or another, or (b) failing to make the decision": Mental Capacity Act 2005 s.3(4).

(d) to communicate his decision (whether by talking, using sign language or any other means).[555]

The "fact that a person is able to retain the information relevant to a decision for a short period only does not prevent him from being regarded as able to make the decision".[556]

14-126 **Advance statements about medical treatment** The Mental Capacity Act 2005 gives statutory form to an "advance decision", which is defined as a decision made by an adult (P) when he has capacity to do so that if, at a later time, and in such circumstances as he may specify, a specified treatment is proposed to be carried out or continued by a person providing health care for him, and at that time he lacks capacity to consent to the carrying out or continuation of the treatment, the specified treatment is not to be carried out or continued.[557] The advance decision does not apply to treatment if at the material time P has capacity to give or refuse consent to it[558]; if the treatment is not the treatment specified in the advance decision; if any circumstances specified in the advance decision are absent; or if circumstances exist which were not anticipated at the time of the advance decision and which would have affected P's decision had he anticipated them.[559] A person who carries out or continues treatment in ignorance of a valid advance decision does not incur any liability.[560] Similarly, a person who withholds or withdraws treatment in the reasonable belief that a valid advance decision applies to the treatment is not liable for the consequences.[561] Where a court is asked to rule on whether a valid advance decision applies in the circumstances, then a person will be able to provide life-sustaining treatment or do anything reasonably believed to be necessary to prevent a serious deterioration in P's condition while the ruling is sought, notwithstanding the apparently valid advance decision.[562]

14-127 **Medical treatment of mentally incapacitated adults** The Mental Capacity Act 2005 changes, inter alia, the legal basis upon which any treatment or care can be provided for incapacitated patients, whether the incapacity is permanent or temporary. The provisions of the Act do not apply, however, to medical treatment for mental disorder where such treatment is governed by the Mental Health Act 1983 Pt IV.[563] The 2005 Act makes it lawful for any person (D) to do an act in connection with the care or treatment of another person (P), if D reasonably believes that P lacks capacity in relation to the matter in question and that it will be in P's

---

555 Mental Capacity Act 2005 s.3(1).

556 Mental Capacity Act 2005 s.3(3). This allows for those situations where the individual's competence fluctuates. Provided he has the relevant capacity at the time he makes the decision, the fact that at other times he lacks capacity is irrelevant to the validity of that decision.

557 Mental Capacity Act 2005 s.24(1). The treatment or circumstances may be expressed "in layman's terms": s.24(2). See also para.9-61.

558 Mental Capacity Act 2005 s.25(3).

559 Mental Capacity Act 2005 s.25(4). An advance decision will not apply to life-sustaining treatment unless P specified that it was to apply to that treatment even if life is at risk; and it is in writing and appropriately signed and witnessed: s.25(5) and (6).

560 Mental Capacity Act 2005 s.26(2).

561 Mental Capacity Act 2005 s.26(3).

562 Mental Capacity Act 2005 s.26(5). Where a "one-off" medical intervention will resolve the issue, there might be a temptation to apply to the court for a ruling in order to rely on the protection of s.26(5), thus presenting the patient with a fait accompli.

563 Mental Capacity Act 2005 s.28.

best interests for the act to be done.[564] Where D does an act that is intended to restrain P, s.5, however, is subject to two conditions.[565] First, D must reasonably believe that it is necessary to do the act in order to prevent harm to P.[566] So, when police officers restrained an autistic child with a strong aversion to being touched, the officers' honest belief that it was in the child's best interests to be so restrained was not regarded as a reasonable belief (as required by the statute) where it had been practicable and appropriate to consult the boy's carers before performing such restraint.[567] (It was also held necessary, under s.1(6) of the Act, for the police officers to have considered whether there was a less restrictive way of handling the matter before acting in the way that they did.) Secondly, the act must be a proportionate response to the likelihood of P suffering harm and the seriousness of that harm.[568] For the purpose of these provisions "restraint" means (a) the use of, or threats to use, force to secure the doing of an act which P resists; or (b) restriction of P's liberty of movement, whether or not P resists.[569] The Mental Capacity Act sets in place a complex scheme for determining when it will be lawful to deprive P of his liberty.[570]

A new Court of Protection has the power to make declarations as to whether a person has or lacks capacity to make decisions, and declarations as to the lawfulness of an act or omission, or course of conduct, in relation to that person.[571] The court also has the power to make decisions on behalf of the person lacking capacity (P) and to appoint a deputy to make decisions on P's behalf.[572] This includes the power to give or refuse consent to the carrying out or continuation of treatment by a person providing health care for P.[573] In relation to the withdrawal of clinically assisted nutrition and hydration which was keeping the patient with a prolonged disorder of consciousness alive, the Supreme Court in *An NHS Trust v Y*[574] indicated that, provided the relevant provisions of the Mental Capacity Act 2005 were followed, the relevant guidance observed and there was agreement on what was in the best interests of the patient, there would be no mandatory requirement for a court order to be obtained. It is also possible for an adult who has capacity to grant a "lasting power of attorney" to another adult, conferring on the donee authority to make decisions about the donor's (P's) personal welfare and property and affairs (or specified matters concerning personal welfare or property and affairs) which includes **14-128**

564 Mental Capacity Act 2005 s.5. The meaning of "best interests" is set out in s.4 and the decision as to what constitutes a patient's best interests is to be determined by the court rather than the patient and her relatives by systematically comparing the various pros and cons of treatment: *W v M* [2011] EWHC 2443 (Fam); [2012] 1 W.L.R. 1653.

565 Mental Capacity Act 2005 s.6(1).

566 Mental Capacity Act 2005 s.6(2).

567 *ZH v Commissioner of Police for the Metropolis* [2013] EWCA Civ 69; [2013] 1 W.L.R. 3021.

568 Mental Capacity Act 2005 s.6(3).

569 Mental Capacity Act 2005 s.6(4).

570 The key provisions are, ss 4A(3) and 4B. Other, more marginal provisions in relation to those detained in hospitals or care homes and the power of a court to authorise deprivations of liberty can be found in Sch.A1 and s.16A(1). The details fall beyond the scope of this work and reference should be made to specialist texts, but it should be noted that the Deprivation of Liberty Safeguards under the 2005 Act are due to be replaced from Spring 2022 by the Liberty Protection Safeguards (LPS): see Mental Capacity (Amendment) Act 2019.

571 Mental Capacity Act 2005 s.15.

572 Mental Capacity Act 2005 s.16. The power to make decisions is subject, among other things, to s.4, P's best interests. The powers of deputies are more restricted than the powers of the court: s.20.

573 Mental Capacity Act 2005 s.17(1)(d).

574 [2018] UKSC 46; [2019] A.C. 978.

authority to make such decisions when P no longer has capacity.[575] A lasting power of attorney has to be exercised in the best interests of P, and subject to any restrictions specified in the document itself. It cannot authorise the donee of the power to do an act that is intended to restrain P unless:

(1) P lacked, or the donee reasonably believed that P lacked, capacity in relation to the matter in question;
(2) the donee reasonably believed that it was necessary to do the act in order to prevent harm to P; and
(3) the act is a proportionate response to the likelihood of P suffering harm and the seriousness of that harm.[576]

Where a lasting power of attorney authorises the donee to make decisions about P's personal welfare, the authority:

(1) does not apply to such decisions unless P lacks, or the donee reasonably believes that he lacks, capacity;
(2) is subject to any valid advance decision of P to refuse treatment; and
(3) extends to the giving or refusing of consent to the carrying out or continuation of treatment by a person providing health care for P (except that this does not authorise the giving or refusing of consent to carrying out or continuing life-sustaining treatment unless the instrument contains an express provision to that effect and is also subject to any conditions or restrictions in the instrument).[577]

(k) Parental or other authority

14-129 **Parental responsibility** The Children Act 1989 abolished the common law notion of parental rights and replaced it with that of "parental responsibility". Even where parents are unmarried, the father is likely to have parental responsibility jointly with the mother (something he would gain as of right had they been married) since s.4 provides a host of very simple means by which this can be acquired, such as jointly registering the child's name. Non-parents may also acquire parental responsibility in a number of ways. A person appointed a guardian of a child has parental responsibility for her,[578] as do persons in whose favour a child arrangements order is made (for the duration of the order[579]). Local authorities acquire parental responsibility when a child is taken into care.[580]

14-130 **Discipline and control** A person with parental responsibility is authorised to do certain acts, and empower others to act, in a manner which might otherwise constitute a tort. Such a person has a right to control the child's movements whether this action is designed to protect the child from harm, or constitutes reasonable punishment for misbehaviour.[581] It would appear that the right to administer moder-

575 Mental Capacity Act 2005 s.9(1).
576 Mental Capacity Act 2005 s.11(1)–(4).
577 Mental Capacity Act 2005 s.11(7) and (8).
578 Children Act 1989 s.5(6).
579 Children Act 1989 s.12(2), as amended. See also s.12(2A) of the Children Act 1989.
580 Children Act 1989 s.33(3)(a).
581 *R. v Rahman* (1985) 81 Cr. App. R. 349 at 353.

ate and reasonable chastisement to a child survives at common law.[582] But this right must now be read subject to s.58 of the Children Act 2004.[583] Beyond this, any other person who has lawful control of the child has the authority to chastise the child, provided he is acting in loco parentis. So a child-minder may at common law smack a disobedient child, but an older sibling has no such authority unless formally left in charge of his brother or sister.[584] The power previously given to constables under s.30(6) of the Anti-social Behaviour Act 2003 in relation to minors has now been repealed.[585]

The Children Act 2004 s.58(3) provides that reasonable chastisement of a child which causes actual bodily harm is no defence to an action for battery.[586] In this context, "actual bodily harm" has the same meaning as it has for the purposes of s.47 of the Offences against the Person Act 1861.[587] **14-131**

Corporal punishment in schools Corporal punishment was finally prohibited in all schools by virtue of the Education Act 1996 s.548. And it makes no difference whether parents support such punishment.[588] On the other hand, a teacher who acts in order to avert an immediate danger of personal injury to any person (including the child himself) or damage to the property of any person commits no battery.[589] It is also the case that a teacher can invoke normal self-defence principles (or those applicable to the defence of others).[590] **14-132**

(l) Authority of shipmaster or commander of an aircraft

Master of a ship The master of a vessel on the high seas or in a foreign port[591] was at common law treated as standing in the position of the head of a family[592] and has disciplinary powers not only over the crew but also the passengers.[593] He is justified at common law in arresting and confining in a reasonable manner and for a reasonable time any sailor or other person on board his ship if he has reasonable cause to believe and does in fact believe that such arrest or confinement is necessary for the preservation of order and discipline, or for the safety of the vessel or **14-133**

---

582 *R. v Hopley* (1860) 2 F. & F. 202; *R. v Woods* (1921) 85 J.P. 272.

583 See para.14-131.

584 See *R. v Woods* (1921) 85 J.P. 272.

585 Repealed by Anti-social Behaviour, Crime and Policing Act 2014 Sch.11(1) para.41(c) on 20 October 2014. But see now s.35(7) of the 2014 Act: "If the constable reasonably believes that the person to whom the direction [excluding a person from an area] is given is under the age of 16, the constable may remove the person to a place where the person lives or a place of safety."

586 Nor is it a defence to criminal proceedings based on ss 18, 20 and 47 of the Offences against the Person Act 1861 or s.1 of the Children and Young Persons Act 1933. The Children (Abolition of Defence of Reasonable Punishment) (Wales) Act 2020 provides that, from 20 March 2022, all corporal punishment in Wales will not be capable of justification in any civil or criminal proceedings as reasonable punishment.

587 Children Act 2004 s.58(4). There is no statutory definition of actual bodily harm.

588 *R. v Secretary of State for Education and Employment Ex p. Williamson* [2005] UKHL 15; [2005] 2 A.C. 246.

589 Education Act 1996 s.548(5).

590 See also Education Act 1996 s.548(4): "Any reference to giving corporal punishment to a child is to doing anything for the purpose of punishing that child (whether or not there are other reasons for doing it) which, *apart from any justification*, would constitute battery" (emphasis added).

591 *Lamb v Burnett* (1831) 1 C. & J. 291.

592 *Murray v Moutrie* (1834) 6 C. & P. 471 at 473, per Tindal CJ.

593 *Aldworth v Stewart* (1866) 4 F. & F. 957. See also *Pike v Waldrum* [1952] 1 Lloyd's Rep. 431.

the persons or property on board.[594] The power is "based upon necessity and is limited to the preservation of necessary discipline and the safety of the ship"[595] or the persons or property on board.[596] The common law rule is largely replicated in the Merchant Shipping Act 1995 s.105: "The master of any United Kingdom ship may cause any person on board the ship to be put under restraint if and for so long as it appears to him necessary or expedient in the interest of safety or for the preservation of good order or discipline on board the ship". Clearly, the master of a vessel at sea may be compelled to act in a very decisive and severe manner if he is to maintain discipline and carry out his voyage, and therefore a licence was accorded to him that would not be tolerated in the case of a parent or schoolmaster.

14-134 **Commander of an aircraft** The Civil Aviation Act 1982 s.94, confers similar statutory powers on the commander of an aircraft in flight where a person has done or is about to do any act on the aircraft which jeopardises or may jeopardise the safety of the aircraft or of persons or property on board the aircraft, or good order and discipline on board the aircraft, or has done any act which in the opinion of the commander is a serious offence under any law in force in the country in which the aircraft is registered. The commander may take such measures, including restraint of the person, as may be necessary: (i) to protect the safety of the aircraft or of persons or property on board the aircraft; or (ii) to maintain good order and discipline on the aircraft; or (iii) to enable the commander to disembark or deliver that person.

(m) Previous criminal proceedings

14-135 Assault and battery are crimes as well as torts. The Offences against the Person Act 1861 ss.44–45, provide that in certain cases, summary criminal proceedings (whether they result in conviction or acquittal), shall operate as a bar to subsequent civil proceedings. In addition, where a civil action amounts to a collateral attack on the final decision of a criminal court of competent jurisdiction, the civil action will be treated as an abuse of the process of the court and struck out.[597] Section 329 of the Criminal Justice Act 2003 introduced a defence to a claim for trespass to the person where the claimant has been convicted of an imprisonable offence committed on the same occasion as the alleged trespass to the person. The defence applies where the defendant did the act amounting to trespass to the claimant's person only because: (a) he believed that the claimant: (i) was about to commit an offence; (ii) was in the course of committing an offence; or (iii) had committed an offence immediately beforehand; and (b) he believed that the act was necessary to: (i) defend himself or another person; (ii) protect or recover property; (iii) prevent the commission or continuation of an offence; or (iv) apprehend, or secure the conviction of, the claimant after he had committed an offence; or was necessary to assist in achieving any of those things.[598] However, the defendant's act must not have been grossly disproportionate in all the circumstances.[599] In such cases, a claimant must

---

[594] *Hook v Cunard S.S. Co Ltd* [1953] 1 W.L.R. 682.
[595] *Aldworth v Stewart* (1866) 4 F. & F. 957 at 961, per Channel B.
[596] cf. *Hook v Cunard S.S. Co* [1953] 1 W.L.R. 682.
[597] *Hunter v Chief Constable of the West Midlands* [1982] A.C. 529.
[598] Criminal Justice Act 2003 s.329(4)(a) and (5).
[599] Criminal Justice Act 2003 s.329(4)(b).

obtain the permission of the court if he wishes to bring civil proceedings[600]; yet proceedings brought without such permission are not null and void, and this procedural defect can be cured by application to the court.[601]

(n) Detention of persons prior to deportation

Detention of persons prior to deportation The Immigration Act 1971 Sch.3 para.2, provides that where a recommendation for deportation of an illegal immigrant has been made, and that person is not detained in pursuance of the sentence or order of any court, the immigrant shall be detained pending the making of a deportation order, unless (a) the court by which the recommendation is made grants bail to the person; or (b) the person is released on immigration bail under Sch.10 to the Immigration Act 2016.[602] Nonetheless, in such instances, there is an implied duty to undertake ongoing reviews of a detainee, so the Secretary of State will be liable for false imprisonment or a breach of art.5 of the European Convention on Human Rights if he fails to undertake such reviews while the making of a deportation order is still pending.[603] Equally, there are important limits on the power to recommend deportation in the first place. The leading case is *Lumba v Secretary of State for the Home Department*.[604] There, the claimants were foreign nationals who had been detained after completing sentences of imprisonment for various offences, pending deportation under the Immigration Act 1971. They alleged that they had been unlawfully detained because, although the Home Office had a published policy on the circumstances in which detention would be used, the Secretary of State had applied an unpublished policy involving almost blanket detention of all foreign national prisoners pending deportation. The claimants sought judicial review and damages for false imprisonment on the basis that the unpublished policy was unlawful in that it involved a breach of public law rendering their detention under that policy illegal. The defendant argued, inter alia, that the claimants would have been detained even if the decision to detain had been made in accordance with the published policy. The Supreme Court, by a majority, held that the unpublished policy was unlawful and that consequently the claimants had been falsely imprisoned by virtue of an unlawful exercise of the Secretary of State's power to detain.[605] It was no defence to prove that a lawful decision to detain the claimants 14-136

600 Criminal Justice Act 2003 s.329(2) and (3).

601 *Adorian v Commissioner of Police of the Metropolis* [2009] EWCA Civ 18; [2009] 1 W.L.R. 1859.

602 The ability to exercise the power to detain lawfully under the Act is a condition precedent to the exercise of the power to grant bail: *B (Algeria) v Secretary of State for the Home Department* [2018] UKSC 5; [2018] A.C. 418. Once a deportation order is given, a claimant may nevertheless be unlawfully detained and entitled to pursue a claim for damages for false imprisonment if the decision to deport is unlawful: *R. (on the application of DN (Rwanda) v Secretary of State for the Home Department* [2020] UKSC 7; [2020] 2 W.L.R. 611.

603 *Kambadzi v Secretary of State for the Home Department* [2011] UKSC 23; [2011] 1 W.L.R. 1299.

604 [2011] UKSC 12; [2012] 1 A.C. 245. See also *R. (on the application of O) v Secretary of State for the Home Department* [2016] UKSC 19; [2016] 1 W.L.R. 1717. Note also *Onos v Secretary of State for the Home Department* [2016] EWHC 59 (Admin); and *R. (on the application of FK) v Secretary of State for the Home Department* [2016] EWHC 56 (Admin) (Secretary of State not following own published policy). cf. *R. (on the application of Lee-Hirons) v Secretary of State for Justice* [2016] UKSC 46; [2017] A.C. 52.

605 Note, however, that not every breach of public law will give rise to a cause of action in false imprisonment. According to Lord Dyson ([2011] UKSC 12; [2012] 1 A.C. 245 at [68]), public law errors that do not bear upon the decision to detain will not do so.

could and would otherwise have been made.[606] On the other hand, a different majority of the Supreme Court also held that the causation test was relevant to the question of whether the claimants should be awarded substantive, as opposed to nominal, damages for the false imprisonment. Since the claimants were entitled to be placed in the position that they would have been in had the tort not been committed, and if the Secretary of State had applied the published policy the claimants would still have been detained, they had suffered no loss or damage from the false imprisonment and were entitled only to nominal damages to reflect the fact that they had been the victim of a tort.[607] In addition, the Secretary of State's decision to detain prior to deportation will be subject to judicial review if there is no prospect of effecting a deportation for reasons other than that the detainee is thwarting the process by failing to declare important personal information required by the authorities in the country to which he is due to be deported.[608] And a claim for false imprisonment will similarly be available where the Secretary of State either unreasonably prolongs a detention in the face of either serious mental health problems caused to the detainee by virtue of the detention where no immediate prospect of resolving the deportation issue exists,[609] or where there is a telling absence of any real chance of effecting a deportation.[610]

14-137 One particular problem that has troubled the courts is whether a potential deportee can continue to be detained where the legality of a proposed deportation is under review by the European Court of Human Rights. In *R. (on the application of Muqtaar) v Secretary of State for the Home Department*,[611] a Somali national had been detained pending deportation, but at that time the European Court of Human Rights was still considering the legality of deportation in an analogous case. The Strasbourg court issued a direction (known as a r.39 indication) that the deportation should not take place until it had resolved that other case. Pending the resolution of that case, the Somali immigrant remained imprisoned. In the instant case, the detainee argued that he should have been released. The Court of Appeal held otherwise. According to their Lordships, when the r.39 indication was received, there had been a realistic prospect that the Strasbourg proceedings would be resolved within a reasonable period of time. Equally, it had not been apparent that the Strasbourg Court's resolution of the other case would prevent the prisoner's

---

606 [2011] UKSC 12; [2012] 1 A.C. 245 at [62], [175], [221] and [239], per Lords Dyson, Hope, Collins and Kerr respectively.

607 In similar vein, see also *OM (Nigeria) v Secretary of State for the Home Department* [2011] EWCA Civ 909; and *R. (on the application of Moussaoui) v Secretary of State for the Home Department* [2012] EWHC 126 (Admin); [2012] A.C.D. 55. See further para.1-13.

608 *R. (on the application of MH) v Secretary of State for the Home Department* [2010] EWCA Civ 1112. See *R. (on the application of Z (Eritrea)) v Secretary of State for the Home Department* [2017] EWCA Civ 14: detention of a failed asylum seeker for 43 months pending deportation lawful where asylum seeker had caused his detention to be prolonged by his persistent failure to co-operate in obtaining an emergency travel document and by his repeated issue of judicial review proceedings.

609 *R. (on the application of Lamari) v Secretary of State for the Home Department* [2012] EWHC 1630 (Admin). cf. *R. (on the application of LE (Jamaica)) v Secretary of State for the Home Department* [2012] EWCA Civ 597 (the detainee's schizophrenia was capable of being satisfactorily managed within detention); and *R. (on the application of Moussaoui) v Secretary of State for the Home Department* [2012] EWHC 126 (Admin); [2012] A.C.D. 55 (the detainee's mental health was merely one, non-determinative consideration along with his conviction for many prior thefts).

610 *R. (on the application of Murad) v Secretary of State for the Home Department* [2012] EWHC 1112 (Admin); *R. (on the application of ZA (Iraq)) v Secretary of State for the Home Department* [2015] EWCA Civ 168.

611 [2012] EWCA Civ 1270; [2013] 1 W.L.R. 649.

deportation.[612] Accordingly, his continued detention was lawful (there being no requirement that the Secretary of State be able to identify a timescale within which removal could be effected). Equally, since the Secretary of State had a number of similar cases to consider, it was not unlawful for her to continue to detain the Somali national in this case even after the Strasbourg Court had decided (in the other case) that such deportations would be contrary to the Convention.[613] On the other hand, unreasonable delay in deciding whether or not to deport a detainee may give rise to liability for false imprisonment during that part of the detention attributable to the unreasonable delay in reaching a final decision about deportation.[614]

(o) Strip searches

In *Wainwright v United Kingdom*[615] the European Court of Human Rights held that although strip searches of visitors to a prison may be a legitimate measure for tackling an endemic drugs problem in the prison, the manner in which the searches are carried out must be proportionate to that legitimate aim. Analogous principles no doubt apply to those subjected to similar searches sometimes conducted at ports of entry into the country. **14-138**

7. DAMAGES

Damages in trespass Any trespass to the person, however slight, gives a right of action to recover at least nominal damages. The defendant may still be liable in trespass for all the consequences flowing from the tort whether or not those consequences are foreseeable.[616] Even where there has been no physical injury, substantial damages may be awarded for indignity, discomfort or inconvenience. Where liberty has been interfered with, damages are given to vindicate the claimant's rights even though no pecuniary damage has been suffered.[617] However, where a claimant has been falsely imprisoned by virtue of a breach by the defendant of public law principles, the claimant will be able to recover only nominal damages if, on the facts, proper compliance with public law would have resulted in the claimant's detention. In such circumstances, the claimant will have suffered no loss or damage as a result of the defendant's unlawful exercise of the power to detain.[618] Equally, in *Parker v Chief Constable of Essex*,[619] substantial damages would not be awarded for false imprisonment where the police could establish that, had the defendant acted lawfully, the claimant would have been detained in any event, because no harm would ultimately have been caused. The test is what would have happened had it been appreciated what the law required. The court held that "[l]y- **14-139**

612 cf. *R. (on the application of Abdi) v Secretary of State for the Home Department* [2011] EWCA Civ 242.

613 *R. (on the application of Abdi) v Secretary of State for the Home Department* [2011] EWCA Civ 242 at [36]–[39], per Richards LJ.

614 *Saleh v Secretary of State for the Home Department* [2013] EWCA Civ 1378.

615 (12350/04) (2007) 44 E.H.R.R. 40. Cf. *Yousif v Commissioner of Police of the Metropolis* [2016] EWCA Civ 364 (strip search while in police custody not in breach of arts 3 or 8 ECHR).

616 *Wilson v Pringle* [1987] Q.B. 237 at 247; *Williams v Humphrey, The Times,* 20 February 1975.

617 cf. *Kuchenmeister v Home Office* [1958] 1 Q.B. 496. See *Beckett v Walker* [1985] C.L.Y. 129 (£200 for 53 hours after negligent issue of warrant).

618 *Lumba v Secretary of State for the Home Department* [2011] UKSC 12; [2012] 1 A.C. 245; *Bostridge v Oxleas NHS Foundation Trust* [2015] EWCA Civ 79; [2015] Med L.R. 113 (in the context of detention under the Mental Health Act 1983).

619 [2018] EWCA Civ 2788; [2019] 1 W.L.R. 2238, allowing appeal against [2017] EWHC 2140 (QB).

ing behind the decision in *Lumba* therefore is the principle that although procedural failings are lamentable and render detention unlawful, they do not, of themselves, merit substantial damages … That is not to encourage sloppy practice but, rather, to reflect actual loss".[620] In contrast, in *R. (on the application of Hemmati) v Secretary of State for the Home Department*,[621] where the decision to detain the claimants was unlawful, the Supreme Court held that asylum seekers, detained pending their deportation to another EU Member State, were entitled to substantial damages for the tort of false imprisonment because the decision to detain them had been outside the discretionary power to detain contained in Sch.2 to the Immigration Act 1971. It was no answer to a claim for substantial damages for unlawful imprisonment that the detention would have been lawful had the *law* been different.[622]

14-140 Apart from any special damages alleged and proved, such as medical expenses, the damages are at large. The time, place and manner of the trespass and the conduct of the defendant may be taken into account and the court may award aggravated damages on these grounds.[623] In *W v Meah*,[624] an award of damages was made in respect of rape and vicious sexual assault. The issue of quantum in such cases had not previously been considered in England. Woolf J held that aggravated damages could be awarded. Since then, however, the appropriateness of aggravated damages has been questioned in *Richardson v Howie*.[625] There, the Court of Appeal considered that where the claimant was the subject of an attack constituting trespass to the person, compensatory damages should be awarded for injury to feelings, including the indignity, mental suffering, humiliation or distress as well as anger or indignation arising from the circumstances, but that the award should not be characterised as aggravated damages. Their Lordships felt it was no longer appropriate to describe the damages awarded for injury to feelings as aggravated damages. On the other hand, where the claimant has sustained psychiatric harm as a result of an assault or harassment, it may be better for the judge to make an assessment of damages in respect of that psychiatric harm separately from the damages awarded in respect of injury to feelings.[626] Certainly, the point was made in *Rowlands v Chief Constable of Merseyside* that there is a difference between psychiatric harm and "the humiliation and injury to pride and dignity that may fol-

---

620 [2018] EWCA Civ 2788; [2019] 1 W.L.R. 2238 at [104] and [108], per Sir Brian Leveson P.

621 [2019] UKSC 56; [2019] 3 W.L.R. 1156. It makes no difference if the loss of liberty is due to a lack of legal authority for the detention as a consequence of a failure to comply with domestic legislation or, as in this case, an EU regulation.

622 [2019] UKSC 56; [2019] 3 W.L.R. 1156 at [112]; distinguishing *Lumba v Secretary of State for the Home Department* [2011] UKSC 12; [2012] 1 A.C. 245; and *Parker v Chief Constable of Essex Police* [2018] EWCA Civ 2788; [2019] 1 W.L.R. 2238.

623 *Rookes v Barnard* [1964] A.C. 1129 at 1221–1233; *Broome v Cassell & Co Ltd* [1972] A.C. 1027. For consideration of the principles relevant to breach of the European Convention on Human Rights when patients detained under the Mental Health Act 1983 were denied speedy hearings to review their detention, contrary to art.5(4) of the Convention, see *R. (on the application of KB) v Mental Health Review Tribunal, Secretary of State for Health* [2003] EWHC 193 (Admin); [2004] Q.B. 936.

624 [1986] 1 All E.R. 935.

625 [2004] EWCA Civ 1127; [2005] P.I.Q.R. Q3. See also *CD v Catholic Child Welfare Society* [2016] EWHC 3335 (QB); and *R. (on the application of Diop) v Secretary of State for the Home Department* [2018] EWHC 3420 (Admin): better to make one global award of general damages which would reduce the risk of double counting. Aggravated damages were, however, awarded in *Mohidin v Commissioner of Police of the Metropolis* [2015] EWHC 2740 (QB): basic award did not provide adequate compensation for the racist humiliation inflicted on Mohidin.

626 *Martins v Choudhary* [2007] EWCA Civ 1379; [2008] 1 W.L.R. 617.

low from the particular circumstances of the [wrongful] arrest".[627] In such circumstances, the claimant is entitled to compensation for this, over and above any established psychiatric harm. By contrast, where the claimant is disabled and receives an award of damages for injury to feelings under the Disability Discrimination Act 1995, "the risk of overlap is such that an award of aggravated damages is inappropriate".[628]

Exemplary damages The circumstances in which an award of exemplary damages should be made against police officers liable for trespass to the person were considered by the Court of Appeal in *Holden v Chief Constable of Lancashire*.[629] It was held that for such damages to be awarded, the conduct of the constable need not have been malicious or violent. It is "unconstitutional" conduct by a police officer which brings that tort within the first category of exemplary damages established in *Rookes v Barnard*.[630] Their Lordships doubted, though, whether every act done by a constable without lawful authority, beyond the scope of his duty, can automatically be classified as "unconstitutional". All the circumstances of the incident, including "arrogant and abusive" conduct[631] as well as any provocation offered will be considered.[632] Where, however, an assault virtually amounted to "torture", a particularly high award of exemplary damages was thought justified.[633] In assessing damages for false imprisonment, the judge may consider as aggravating the damages any evidence that the defendant was persisting in the charge originally made in bringing about the false imprisonment and, in reduction of damages, any evidence showing that the defendant had withdrawn or apologised for the charge. In *Thompson v Commissioner of Police of the Metropolis*,[634] the Court of Appeal, setting out guidelines for juries on awards of damages in false imprisonment and malicious prosecution, suggested that any award of exemplary damages was unlikely to be less than £5,000 and might be as much as £25,000 with an absolute maximum of £50,000[635] in cases where officers of at least the rank of superintendent had been directly involved in the misconduct. The courts will, in exceptional cases, issue an injunction to restrain future assaults.[636] 14-141

Exemplary damages and vicarious liability The normal rule where there are joint defendants is that the court should only make one award of exemplary damages, and this should not be more than the sum that would be awarded against any 14-142

---

627 [2006] EWCA Civ 1773; [2007] 1 W.L.R. 1065 at [28].

628 *ZH v Commissioner of Police for the Metropolis* [2012] EWHC 604 (QB); [2012] Eq. L.R. 425 at [156], per Sir Robert Nelson (quantum of damages not challenged when unsuccessfully appealed: [2013] EWCA Civ 69; [2013] 1 W.L.R. 3021).

629 [1987] Q.B. 380. In *Kuddus v Chief Constable of Leicestershire Constabulary* [2001] UKHL 29; [2002] 2 A.C. 122 the House of Lords also opened up the possibility of such awards against the police in respect of other actions, e.g. misfeasance in public office.

630 [1964] A.C. 1129; see para.27-134.

631 See *Rowlands v Chief Constable of Merseyside* [2006] EWCA Civ 1773; [2007] 1 W.L.R. 1065 at [54], per Moore-Bick LJ.

632 *O'Connor v Hewitson* [1979] Crim. L.R. 46. But cf. *Reynolds v Metropolitan Police Commissioner* [1982] Crim. L.R. 600.

633 *Treadaway v Chief Constable of the West Midlands*, *The Times*, 25 October 1994 (£40,000).

634 [1998] Q.B. 498. See also *Clark v Chief Constable of Cleveland* [2000] C.P. Rep. 22; and para.27-134.

635 Awarded in *Rees v Commissioner of Police of the Metropolis* [2019] EWHC 2339 (QB) (appeal outstanding).

636 *Egan v Egan* [1975] Ch. 218; and see para.28-15.

individual defendant. So if exemplary damages would not be justified against one of the defendants, no award should be made, no matter how outrageous the behaviour of the other joint defendants, because joint defendants are severally liable to the claimant for the full amount of the damages, and it would be wrong that an "innocent" defendant might have to pay damages which were intended to punish someone else. In *Kuddus v Chief Constable of Leicestershire Constabulary*,[637] this led Lord Scott to doubt whether exemplary damages were ever appropriate in a case against an employer based on vicarious liability. However, since then (when the question as a matter of law was technically left open by their Lordships) it has been held by the Court of Appeal in *Rowlands v Chief Constable of Merseyside* that it is possible to make an award of exemplary damages against an employer (a chief constable in that case).[638]

14-143 **Compensation by the criminal courts** A person who suffers injury as a result of a criminal assault may be able to obtain compensation by virtue of the Powers of Criminal Courts (Sentencing) Act 2000 s.130(1) which provides that a court which has convicted a person of an offence may make a compensation order requiring the defendant to pay compensation for any personal injury, loss or damage resulting from that offence, or any other offence which is taken into consideration by the court in determining sentence, or to make payments for funeral expenses or bereavement in respect of a death resulting from any such offence, other than a death due to an accident arising out of the presence of a motor vehicle on a road. Compensation shall be such amount as the court considers appropriate, having regard to any evidence and to any representations that are made by or on behalf of the accused or the prosecutor,[639] and the court will have regard to the means of the accused in determining the amount payable under the order,[640] but the amount of compensation awarded is not assessed by the rules governing damages in tort.[641] Nor must the amount of compensation payable correlate with the degree of involvement in an offence committed by two or more persons.[642] Where the offence arises out of the presence of a motor vehicle on a road, a compensation order may only be made if it is in respect of damage treated by subs.130(5) as resulting from an offence under the Theft Act 1968 or Fraud Act 2006 (i.e. where stolen property is recovered but has been damaged, the damage is treated as arising out of the offence); and if the damage consists of injury, loss or damage in respect of which the offender is uninsured a compensation order cannot be made where compensation is payable under any of the Motor Insurers' Bureau (MIB) agreements.[643] The expectation is that such losses will be covered by motor insurance or the MIB agreements. Where a compensation order has been made and a civil claim for dam-

---

637 [2001] UKHL 29; [2002] 2 A.C. 122.

638 [2006] EWCA Civ 1773; [2007] 1 W.L.R. 1065 at [47]. See also para.6-18.

639 Powers of Criminal Courts (Sentencing) Act 2000 s.130(4). See also *R. v Sones* [2012] EWCA Crim 1377 at [13] per Hedley J.

640 s.130(11). See also *R. v Hobden* [2009] EWCA Crim 1584 at [8]. The fact that it will take D many years to make the payment required by the compensation order will not be a reason not to make such an order (see *R. v Ganyo* [2011] EWCA Crim 2491; [2012] 1 Cr. App. R. (S.) 108), although there must be sufficient material on which to conclude there were sound prospects of payment (*R. v Carrington* [2014] EWCA Crim 325; [2014] 2 Cr. App. R. (S.) 41) and the proposed period of repayment must be realistic (*R. v Hossain* [2016] EWCA Crim 1099).

641 *R. v Thomson Holidays Ltd* [1974] Q.B. 592, a decision on the Powers of Criminal Courts Act 1973.

642 *R. v Baker-Owens* [2013] EWCA Crim 2315.

643 Powers of Criminal Courts (Sentencing) Act 2000 s.130(6). Compensation can include the loss of a "no-claims bonus": s.130(7).

ages is made subsequently,[644] the damages in the civil claim should be assessed without regard to the compensation order, but the claimant may only recover the damages in excess of the compensation order and any sum equivalent to the portion of the compensation order which he has failed to recover.[645] There is provision to order the parents or guardian of a child or young person to pay a compensation order where the child or young person has been convicted of an offence where a compensation order could be made, unless it would be unreasonable having regard to the circumstances of the case.[646]

Criminal injuries compensation Claims for ex gratia payments of compensation may be made by a victim of a crime of violence to the Criminal Injuries Compensation Authority.[647] A claim will be entertained where the applicant or a deceased person (whose dependant is claiming), suffered personal injury directly attributable either to a criminal offence or to an arrest or attempted arrest of a suspected offender or to the prevention of crime or assisting a constable engaged in the above pursuits. The injury must occur in Great Britain or aboard a British vessel or aircraft. 14-144

Damages for related human rights breaches As noted at various points in this chapter, there is considerable overlap between the various torts involving trespass to the person and the European Convention on Human Rights. But cases involving detention by state authorities are worthy of special note from the perspective of damages since it is possible that the tort of false imprisonment may not have been committed, even though there has been a violation of the art.5(4) right to a speedy review of the continuing need for a prisoner's detention. Such was the case in *R. (on the application of Sturnham) v Parole Board*.[648] In that case, a prisoner was serving an indeterminate sentence. His imprisonment was prolonged because of delay on the part of the Parole Board in reviewing his case following the expiry of his tariff. Since his incarceration remained grounded in law until such time as the Board reviewed his case and sanctioned his release, he was unable to sue on the basis of either the tort of false imprisonment or under the Human Rights Act 1998 in respect of a violation of his art.5(1) right to liberty. On the other hand, there was a violation of his art.5(4) right to a speedy review of his case. In respect of such delays, the Supreme Court held that where, on the balance of probabilities, the prisoner would have enjoyed an earlier release but for the delay, he should be awarded compensatory damages. As to quantum in such cases, Lord Reed JSC. said that "the most reliable guidance as to the quantum of awards under section 8 will … be awards made by the European Court [of Human Rights] in comparable cases brought by applicants from the UK or other countries with a similar cost of living".[649] Modest damages were also said to be payable in cases where, even though it could not be shown that an earlier review would have resulted in an earlier 14-145

---

644 An applicant for a compensation order need not also establish civil liability towards him: *R. v Chappell* (1985) 80 Cr. App. R. 31.

645 Powers of Criminal Courts (Sentencing) Act 2000 s.134.

646 Powers of Criminal Courts (Sentencing) Act 2000 s.137.

647 See the Criminal Injuries Compensation Act 1995. Details of the scheme are available at the Criminal Injuries Compensation Authority website: *https://www.gov.uk/government/organisations/criminal-injuries-compensation-authority* [Accessed 28 July 2020].

648 [2013] UKSC 23; [2013] 2 A.C. 254. See further paras 13-128 and 13-129.

649 [2013] UKSC 23; [2013] 2 A.C. 254 at [39]

release, the breach of art.5(4) had demonstrably or presumptively caused the prisoner to suffer feelings of frustration and anxiety about his continued detention.[650]

In *Brown v Parole Board for Scotland*,[651] the Supreme Court (unanimously) took the opportunity to reconsider the approach adopted in *R. (on the application of Kaiyam) v Secretary of State for Justice*,[652] which had found an ancillary duty under art.5 ECHR to facilitate the rehabilitation and release of prisoners serving indeterminate sentences when in the post-tariff stage.[653] The Court held that more recent case law of the European Court of Human Rights, notably *Kaiyam v United Kingdom*,[654] had indicated that the approach in *Kaiyam* had been significantly different from, and more demanding than, the duty imposed by the Convention. It concluded on this basis that cases on breach of art.5.1(a) on account of a delay in access to rehabilitative courses would be rare. In particular, the ECtHR's approach does not entail an obligation under the Convention to secure the applicant's immediate release, as other remedies exist which can remedy the lack of opportunity for rehabilitation.

650 [2013] UKSC 23; [2013] 2 A.C. 254 at [13].
651 [2017] UKSC 69; [2018] A.C. 1.
652 [2014] UKSC 66; [2015] A.C. 1344.
653 [2014] UKSC 66; [2015] A.C. 1344 at [38].
654 (2016) 62 E.H.R.R. SE13: no appearance of a violation of art.5(1) ECHR —application inadmissible.

CHAPTER 15

MALICIOUS PROSECUTION

TABLE OF CONTENTS

1. INTRODUCTION

Malicious institution of proceedings[1] A claimant who has been subjected to legal proceedings improperly instituted against him will naturally be aggrieved by the institution of those proceedings, be they criminal or civil. Where the charge or claims against the claimant are unfounded, they may ultimately fail, but nonetheless cause injury to the claimant. He is put to the expense of defending himself. Damaging publicity may harm his reputation and cause him further financial loss. The trauma of litigation may injure his health. Other significant and potentially long-lasting implications may follow.[2] Until recently, the development of remedies in tort for malicious institution of proceedings was limited, and the general coverage of this chapter necessarily reflects this limitation. In particular, the House of Lords re-affirmed in 2000 that, in England and Wales, such a tort is limited to the malicious institution of criminal prosecutions and certain civil claims which constitute "special cases of abuse of legal process".[3] However, so far as civil claims **15-01**

[1] As to the foundation of the action, see *Mohamed Amin v Bannerjee* [1947] A.C. 322; and *Casey v Automobiles Renault Canada Ltd* (1995) 54 D.L.R. (2d) 600. Note also the discussion in *H v AB* [2009] EWCA Civ 1092; *The Times*, 8 October 2009 at [21]–[23]; and *Crawford Adjusters (Cayman) Ltd v Sagicor General Insurance (Cayman) Ltd* [2013] UKPC 17; [2014] A.C. 366 at [40]–[61] as to the origins of the tort and of its subsequent development.

[2] On the nature of the damage required for an action of malicious prosecution, see para.15-06 onwards. See also e.g. *Clifford v Chief Constable of Hertfordshire* [2011] EWHC 815 (QB): malicious prosecution of child pornography offences had a destructive effect on the claimant's feelings of self-worth and his relationships with his wife and family and business associates.

[3] *Gregory v Portsmouth City Council* [2000] 1 A.C. 419 HL. See below para.15-09.

are concerned, the position has now been reversed by decisions of the Privy Council and Supreme Court. The future shape of the tort is therefore likely to be quite different. In the course of this development, the courts have emphasised that the requirements of malice[4] and of absence of reasonable and probable cause[5] pose high hurdles, with the implication that this will control the circumstances in which actions will be brought. On the other hand, the much greater likelihood of being exposed to a malicious civil claim, given the public nature of today's criminal prosecution process, means that these developments have the potential to greatly expand the circumstances in which remedies for malicious prosecution may be sought.

15-02 **Extension to civil claims** In *Crawford Adjusters (Cayman) Ltd v Sagicor General Insurance (Cayman) Ltd*,[6] the Privy Council chose by a majority of 3–2 to depart from the position stated by the House of Lords in *Gregory v Portsmouth*,[7] arguing that the rationale for excluding a tort of malicious prosecution of civil proceedings was no longer valid. The status of the decision in *Crawford* was somewhat uncertain until the decision of the Supreme Court in *Willers v Joyce*.[8] As a decision of the Privy Council, *Crawford Adjusters* appeared to be of only persuasive authority, particularly given that it was subject to two strong dissenting judgments.[9] On the other hand, it was clearly based upon analysis of English law. In *Willers v Joyce*,[10] a panel of nine justices decided (again by a bare majority, of 5–4) that the tort of malicious prosecution extends in English law to civil actions generally. As noted by Lord Wilson, a member of the majority in both cases, it seems likely there will be more claims for malicious civil prosecution, than for malicious criminal prosecution, in modern conditions.[11] Indeed, Lord Sumption, dissenting in both decisions, regarded the tort of malicious prosecution as it applies to criminal proceedings, as virtually extinct, and saw it as ironic that the well-established restriction on the tort should be swept away and a potentially very wide tort created which would offer litigants an occasion for prolonging disputes by way of secondary litigation.[12] Making the same point in the minority in *Willers v Joyce*,

---

4 See para.15-57 onwards.

5 See para.15-35 onwards.

6 [2013] UKPC 17; [2014] A.C. 366. Commented on by T.K.C. Ng (2014) 130 L.Q.R. 43.

7 [2000] 1 A.C. 419 HL.

8 [2016] UKSC 43; [2018] A.C. 779.

9 Lords Neuberger and Sumption dissented.

10 [2016] UKSC 43; [2018] A.C. 779. Discussed by J. Sorabji (2017) 36 C.J.Q. 387.

11 "… in England and Wales, there is much less chance of being a victim of a criminal prosecution brought maliciously and without reasonable cause than of a civil action so brought. For most criminal prosecutions are brought at the direction of the Crown Prosecution Service, which, by its code, must first be satisfied that the evidence in support of it is such as to render the chance of a conviction greater than even": [2013] UKPC 17; [2014] A.C. 366 at [68].

12 [2013] UKPC 17; [2014] A.C. 366 at [144]–[148]. It is also ironic, perhaps, that after taking the litigation to the Supreme Court and establishing the general availability of an action for malicious civil prosecution, the claimant failed at trial: *Willers v Joyce* [2018] EWHC 3424 (Ch). The defendant could not be regarded as the prosecutor of the civil action against the claimant; there was clear reasonable and probable cause for the action; and it had not been established that the defendant's sense of embitterment towards the claimant was sufficient to constitute malice. Equally, there was no evidence of collateral or improper purpose sufficient for a claim in abuse of process (see para.15-68 et seq.). See further, paras 15-26 and 15-58. Underlining Lord Sumption's point about the extension of civil disputes, the claimant's solicitors were then pursued, unsuccessfully, for third party costs: *Willers v Joyce* [2019] EWHC 2183 (Ch); [2019] Costs L.R. 1351.

Lord Mance referred to the creation of an action for malicious civil prosecution as "necromancy".[13] It is suggested that it is an exaggeration to see the tort as applied to criminal proceedings as extinct, though the era of public prosecutions has certainly ensured that it is less widely used than it its heyday; but that it remains the case that the tort as it applies to civil proceedings has the potential to become much broader.

Policy balance A critical policy factor has restricted the ambit of the tort, but did not carry enough weight in the opinion of the majority Justices in *Crawford* and *Willers*[14] to prevent its expansion to civil proceedings. In relation to malicious prosecution, the interests of the claimant must inevitably be weighed against countervailing interests. First of these is the defendant's right to institute proceedings if he does so with the honest intention of protecting his own, or the public interest, or if the circumstances are such that whatever the defendant's own motives there are good grounds for instituting a prosecution. Associated with this is the need to avoid any "chilling" effect on law enforcement, whether through susceptibility of complainants or (now) claimants themselves to civil actions,[15] or (perhaps) through potential adverse influence on prosecutorial discretion whether of the police or of independent prosecutors.[16] As has been said in relation to malicious criminal proceedings: **15-03**

> "The tort of malicious prosecution is dominated by the problem of balancing two countervailing interests of high social importance: safeguarding the individual from being harassed by unjustifiable litigation and encouraging citizens to aid in law enforcement."[17]

Equally important is the need for finality in litigation, and the avoidance of satellite litigation or reopening of decisions. As Baroness Hale said in *Crawford Adjust-*

---

13 [2016] UKSC 43; [2018] A.C. 779 at [131].

14 See para.15-02.

15 *H v AB* [2009] EWCA Civ 1092; *The Times,* 28 October 2009.

16 See the decision of the Supreme Court of Canada, dismissing an action against a Crown prosecutor, in *Kvello v Miazga* [2009] SCC 51; [2010] 1 W.W.R. 45. In England and Wales malicious prosecution has not been successfully argued against Crown prosecutors as it has in exceptional cases in Canada: *Nelles v Ontario* [1989] 2 S.C.R. 170; *Proulx v Quebec* [2001] SCC 66; [2001] 3 S.C.R. 9. Note, however, the unsuccessful action against an officer of HM Customs and Excise in *Coudrat v Commissioners of Her Majesty's Revenue and Customs* [2005] EWCA Civ 616; [2005] S.T.C. 1006. Similar issues may arise in actions against police officers. In *Whitehouse v Chief Constable, Police Scotland* [2019] CSIH 52; 2019 S.L.T. 1269, the Inner House concluded that the Lord Advocate in Scotland does not enjoy an immunity against actions in malicious prosecution. The earlier decision in *Hester v McDonald* 1961 S.C. 370; 1961 S.L.T. 414 had been wrongly decided on this point. This fits well with the general approach in English courts, that immunities are only exceptionally appropriate and must be clearly justified.

17 J.D. Fleming, *The Law of Torts*, 9th edn (1992), p.609, quoted in *Martin v Watson* [1994] Q.B. 425 at 436 and 449 (now to be found in C. Sappideen and P. Vines (eds), *Fleming's The Law of Torts* 10th edn (2011) at [27.10]). The House of Lords in *Martin v Watson* [1996] 1 A.C. 74 took a different view of the policy balance in the particular case, but it is suggested that the facts of *Martin v Watson* make it an unusual case: more typical may be the facts in *H v AB* [2009] EWCA Civ 1092; *The Times,* 28 October 2009, where the policy issues were referred to at [44], [48]–[49], and [58]. As to the importance of the second consideration—as it applies to public prosecutors—in negativing any general duty of care *in negligence* in respect of the conduct of prosecution see *Elguzouli-Daf v Commissioner of Police for the Metropolis* [1995] Q.B. 335; para.15-63.

ers v Sagicor,[18] it would be "understandable if there were no such wrong at all". First, people should not be deterred from investigating charges or bringing lawsuits for fear of being sued; secondly, once proceedings are over, courts should not be "troubled with further claims".[19] However, Baroness Hale concluded that since such a wrong had been recognised for centuries, it should not be subject to unjustified restriction to criminal proceedings alone.

15-04 A constraining factor in relation to criminal proceedings arises from the evolution in criminal law and procedure. While the tort of malicious prosecution had its origins in a system of criminal law based on private prosecution,[20] in the modern criminal justice system private prosecutions are exceptional.[21] Leaving aside the role of the police as public prosecutors, the large majority of prosecutions since 1986 have been instituted by the Crown Prosecution Service which is the principal prosecuting authority in England and Wales and, to a lesser extent, by other independent prosecution agencies.[22] This development makes successful claims for malicious criminal prosecution far less likely. It is also inevitable that it will affect both the application of the principles, and to some extent their content.[23] This is an important source of tension in this tort, since the majority of authorities on the applicable principles were developed at a time when the context of criminal prosecution was entirely different.

15-05 **The Prosecution of Offences Act 1985** The Prosecution of Offences Act 1985 introduced an independent prosecution service, the Crown Prosecution Service (CPS), headed by the Director of Public Prosecutions.[24] The Director and under his directions Crown Prosecutors are charged with the duty of taking over the conduct of criminal proceedings instituted by the police.[25] The power of private prosecution is preserved by s.6 of the Act but the Director is empowered to take over such proceedings in order to discontinue them.[26] Significantly, since 2009 it has been the policy of the Director of Public Prosecutions to take over a private prosecution and to discontinue it unless, in his or her opinion, the evidence in support of it is such as to render the chance of a conviction greater than even.[27] Several questions relat-

---

18 [2013] UKPC 17; [2014] A.C. 366.

19 [2013] UKPC 17; [2014] A.C. 366 at [82].

20 See the collection by D. Hay and F.G. Snyder, *Policing and Prosecution in Britain 1750–1850* (Oxford, 1989), particularly the essay by D. Hay, "Prosecution and Power: Malicious Prosecution in the English Courts, 1750–1850", pp.343–396. Note also the analysis of Lord Sumption in *Crawford Adjusters v Sagicor* [2013] UKPC 17; [2014] A.C. 366 at [135]–[139].

21 The Director of Public Prosecutions has the power to discontinue private prosecutions (see para.15-05). For an example of a private prosecution (not raising issues of malicious prosecution), see *Scopelight v Chief Constable of Northumbria* [2009] EWCA Civ 1156; [2010] Q.B. 438. Here the CPS prosecution had been discontinued because important questions about the legality of the type of activity carried out by the defendant to the criminal action was being tested in another prosecution.

22 From December 2009, the Crown Prosecution Service was merged with the Revenue and Customs Prosecution Office, increasing further the proportion of prosecutions conducted by the Crown Prosecution Service.

23 See, e.g. the variation in the test for "reasonable and probable cause" as it applies to a Crown prosecutor in the Supreme Court of Canada in *Kvello v Miazga* [2009] SCC 51; [2010] 1 W.W.R. 45; and the discussion of the identity of an individual as the "prosecutor" where a public prosecutor conducts an investigation, in paras 15-20 to 15-25.

24 ss.1–3.

25 s.3(2).

26 See ss.6(2) and 23.

27 This policy has been held not to frustrate the purpose and objects underpinning the right to bring a

ing to the tort of malicious prosecution are posed by the Act and are touched on here. Other effects of the Act are explored in the following paragraphs of this chapter. When proceedings are instituted by the police and discontinued on the direction of the DPP after the claimant has been remanded in custody for a period by a magistrate, does an action in tort lie against those police officers who procured that remand if they acted without reasonable and probable cause and were motivated by malice? The claimant cannot sue in false imprisonment in respect of that period of detention authorised by the magistrates.[28] If he sues for malicious prosecution have the relevant proceedings terminated in his favour? It has been held in Canada[29] that discontinuance of the prosecution is sufficient. Alternatively, by analogy with the action for maliciously procuring a search warrant, the requirement that the proceedings terminate in the claimant's favour might be seen as unnecessary where the essence of the action becomes maliciously procuring a remand in custody. Should the DPP take over the prosecution, the question arises whether the police officers who initiated that prosecution and who supplied the information on which the DPP acts may still be sued for malicious prosecution. The DPP, taking over proceedings originally initiated by the police, exercises independent judgment. Nonetheless, it is clear that the test is whether the complainant is in substance the person responsible for the prosecution having been brought. While, given the modern role of the CPS, cases in which an action for malicious prosecution would lie following a decision by the CPS to prosecute would be rare, there may nevertheless be cases where it was unrealistic to expect the CPS to take a decision other than to prosecute.[30] On this basis, those undertaking the formal procedures necessary to begin the case against the claimant will remain the prosecutor.

2. Kinds of Damage Caused and Meaning of "Malicious Prosecution"

Nature of damage caused An abuse of the right to institute proceedings may of necessity be injurious, involving damage to character, or it may in any particular case bring about damage to person or property. Three sorts of damage to a claimant were identified by Holt CJ, any one of which is sufficient to support an action of malicious prosecution: 15-06

> "First, damage to his fame if the matter whereof he be accused be scandalous.[31] Secondly, to his person, whereby he is imprisoned.[32] Thirdly, to his property, whereby he is put to charges and expenses."[33]

private prosecution: *R. (on the application of Gujra) v Crown Prosecution Service* [2012] UKSC 52; [2013] 1 A.C. 484.

28 Detention subsequent to remand cannot give rise to an action for false imprisonment because of the intervention of the judicial process.

29 *Casey v Automobiles Renault of Canada Ltd* (1965) 54 D.L.R. (2d) 600.

30 See *Ministry of Justice v Scott* [2009] EWCA Civ 1215 (complaint had been made to the police in clear and strong terms by five prison officers, whose statements were consistent with each other and arguably it was virtually, in practical terms, impossible for the CPS to exercise independent discretion in the face of such evidence).

31 On "scandalous" as a synonym for "slanderous" see per Diplock J in *Berry v British Transport Commission* [1961] 1 Q.B. 149 at 161–163; [1962] 1 Q.B. 306 CA.

32 An action will lie for malicious arrest of a debtor, see at para.15-71.

33 *Savill v Roberts* (1698) 12 Mod. 208; considered in *Berry v British Transport Commission* [1961] 1 Q.B. 149; and *Gregory v Portsmouth* [2001] 1 A.C. 419 at 426, where Lord Steyn stated that "Damage is a necessary ingredient of the tort".

To these may be added the damage which someone suffers when his house is entered and his property seized.

15-07 In *Manley v Commissioner of Police for the Metropolis*,[34] the Court of Appeal endorsed the following statement by Roch LJ in *Clark v Chief Constable of Cleveland Police*,[35] setting out the three heads of compensation for malicious prosecution, but advised caution in the balance between them:

> "Compensation for malicious prosecution has three aspects. First, there is the damage to a person's reputation. The extent of that damage will depend upon the claimant's actual reputation and upon the gravity of the offence for which he has been maliciously prosecuted. The second aspect is the damage suffered by being put in danger of losing one's liberty or of losing property. Compensation is recoverable in respect of the risk of conviction. *McGregor on Damages* 16th Edition paragraph 1862 considers that an award under this head is basically for injury to feelings, unless there has been a conviction followed by imprisonment. The third aspect is pecuniary loss caused by the cost of defending the charge."

In *Manley*, it was pointed out that although a claimant of bad character[36] may not suffer damage to reputation to the same extent if prosecuted for an additional offence, there may be greater risk of punishment, and a risk of more severe punishment, should the prosecution succeed, all of which will cause stress and anxiety. The approach in *Manley* was applied in *Rees v Commissioner of Police of the Metropolis*.[37] In addition to a "basic award" for the harm (including mental distress and anxiety for the malicious prosecution for murder), there were additional awards for loss of liberty and for aggravated and exemplary damages. The "basic award" was broad enough to encompass loss of reputation and although this would be less for someone who "is already a criminal",[38] this depended on the gravity of the charge and the nature of previous criminality. In addition to the matters highlighted by Waller LJ in *Manley*, even a convicted criminal is bound to suffer additional notoriety and stigma from the accusation of murder. Antecedent history was relevant also to damages for loss of liberty (where this is not the first period of incarceration), and to aggravated damages, but the approach taken should be a balanced one.

15-08 In *Breeze v Chief Constable of Norfolk Constabulary*,[39] it was held that two directors who had been unsuccessfully prosecuted and expressly vindicated at trial could not succeed in their claim for the total loss of the share value in the company which resulted from their prosecution: the principle in *Johnson v Gore Wood*[40] applied, so that the appropriate claimant was the company itself. The directors' claim was framed in both malicious prosecution, and misfeasance in a public office. The company could not have pursued the claim in malicious prosecution, since it had

34 [2006] EWCA Civ 879; (2006) 150 S.J.L.B. 889 at [26].

35 [1999] EWCA Civ 1357; [2000] C.P. Rep 22.

36 Bad character should not be confused with living an "unconventional" lifestyle such as choosing to live away from society in squalid and unsanitary conditions which leads to a low level of social standing: *Calix v Attorney General of Trinidad and Tobago* [2013] UKPC 15; [2013] 1 W.L.R. 3283 at [10], "reputation has an objective value".

37 [2019] EWHC 2339 (QB). This was the quantum hearing following the decision of the Court of Appeal in *Rees v Commissioner of Police for the Metropolis* [2018] EWCA Civ 1587; para.15-52. The decision on quantum is subject to appeal.

38 [2019] EWHC 2339 (QB) at [18].

39 [2018] EWHC 485 (QB); [2018] 2 B.C.L.C. 638.

40 [2002] 2 A.C. 1.

not itself been prosecuted. However, it could in principle pursue the claim in misfeasance and thus was the appropriate party to seek to recover damages. However, the claimants were given the opportunity to plead that they fell within an exception to the *Johnson v Gore Wood* principle, in that the tort had deprived the company of all its value, effectively preventing it from pursuing its claim. This was a broad, but potentially arguable interpretation of the exception in *Giles v Rhind*.[41]

It was argued before the House of Lords in *Gregory v Portsmouth City Council*[42] that whenever a claimant can establish that he has suffered the relevant damage from the institution of criminal, civil or disciplinary proceedings against him, he should be afforded a remedy. While rejected in *Gregory*, the argument was broadly accepted in the extension of malicious prosecution to civil proceedings.[43] The claimant in *Gregory*, a local councillor, sought to sue the defendant council for maliciously instituting disciplinary proceedings against him. He contended that the disciplinary process had caused such injury to his reputation, and put him to such expense, as to fall within a general tort of abuse of process. He further argued that, even if a broad tort of malicious institution of civil proceeding were not recognised, disciplinary proceedings are quasi-criminal. Disciplinary proceedings involve, counsel suggested, severe penalties affecting the lives and livelihoods of individuals. Even if for the most part any remedy for malicious institution of proceedings is limited to criminal prosecutions, disciplinary processes should be regarded as quasi-prosecutions. The House of Lords dismissed both arguments. They found no case for a radical extension of the tort of malicious prosecution. The victim of improper disciplinary proceedings enjoyed a range of other potential remedies in tort,[44] in defamation, malicious falsehood,[45] conspiracy or misfeasance in public office. Lord Steyn saw no stronger case to extend the tort of malicious prosecution to disciplinary proceedings than to civil proceedings more generally: indeed, he thought that there was a slightly stronger case for extending to civil proceedings, than to disciplinary proceedings, since the latter covered such a wide diversity of non-judicial processes.[46] He rejected the traditional explanation[47] for refusing a remedy for malicious institution of civil proceedings that any injury to reputation is cured by the finding in the claimant's favour: 15-09

> "The traditional explanation for not extending the tort to civil proceedings generally is that in a civil case there is no damage, the fair name of the defendant is protected by the trial and judgment of the court. The theory that even a wholly unwarranted allegation of fraud in a civil case can be remedied entirely at trial may have had some validity in Victorian times when there was little publicity before the trial … However realistic this view may have been in its own time, it is no longer plausible. In modern times wide dissemination in the media of allegations in litigation deprive this particular reason for restricting the tort to a closed category of special cases of the support of logic or good sense."[48]

---

41 [2002] EWCA Civ 1428; [2003] Ch. 618.

42 [2000] 1 A.C. 419 HL. For analysis and criticism of *Gregory* see P. Cane (2000) 116 L.Q.R. 346.

43 See para.15-02.

44 [2000] 1 A.C. 419 at 431–432.

45 Where aggravated damages are now available to compensate injury to feelings; see *Khodoparast v Shad* [2000] 1 W.L.R. 618 CA; *Sallows v Griffiths* [2001] F.S.R. 15 CA.

46 [2000] 1 A.C. 419 at 432.

47 See *Quartz Hill Consolidated Gold Mining Co Ltd v Eyre* (1883) L.R. 11 Q.B.D. 674 at 689–690, per Bowen LJ.

48 *Gregory v Portsmouth City Council* [2000] 1 A.C. 419 at 427–428.

However, in England, unlike the US, the principle is that in civil proceedings the expense to which the defendant is put is remedied in the award of costs. The House of Lords also judged that sufficient alternative remedies exist to provide adequate protection to the claimant's interests where he is aggrieved by either improperly instituted civil or disciplinary proceedings, and that these remedies may be permitted to develop in future. Lord Steyn[49] (with whom all the other judges agreed) "… for essentially practical reasons [was] not persuaded that the general extension of the tort to civil proceedings has been shown to be necessary". He thought there was a better case for allowing the other torts mentioned above to be developed if the need should arise, rather than "embarking on a radical extension of the tort of malicious prosecution". By contrast, both the Privy Council in *Crawford Adjusters (Cayman) Ltd v Sagicor General Insurance (Cayman) Ltd*[50] and the Supreme Court in *Willers v Joyce* have concluded that the tort applies equally to civil proceedings, regarding remarks to the contrary in *Gregory* as obiter dicta. *Gregory* was thus distinguished as a decision that the tort of malicious prosecution did not extend to disciplinary proceedings.[51]

15-10 In *Crawford Adjusters v Sagicor*, a claim had been brought against a surveyor (P), two firms and contractors claiming damages, inter alia, for breach of contract, deceit, conspiracy to defraud and negligence. This had been instigated by the defendant's employee (D), who had stated that he intended to drive P out of business and destroy him professionally. The claim was withdrawn before trial and a counterclaim was brought for abuse of process and malicious prosecution of civil proceedings. The Privy Council rejected the claim for abuse of process,[52] but the majority accepted that the claim for malicious prosecution should succeed. It was argued that in such cases, a claimant should recover not only out-of-pocket expenses, but damages for all foreseeable economic loss (here special damages of Cayman $1.3 million had been claimed). In *Willers v Joyce*[53] the claimant had been the subject of proceedings for alleged breaches of contractual and fiduciary duties to a company of which he was director, by causing it to incur the costs of pursuing a claim which had been brought but abandoned. He brought his claim in malicious prosecution on the basis that the defendant had controlled the company and had instructed him to bring the proceedings; and that the claimant had suffered damage to his health, reputation and earnings, as well as suffering a loss in that his legal expenses in defending the action were higher than the amount recovered through a costs order. The whole claim was permitted to proceed to trial, the majority concluding that it would be unjust for someone injured by malicious prosecution of legal proceedings not to be compensated for the injury that had been injuriously caused.

15-11 **"Malicious prosecution"** This term, it was concluded in both *Crawford Adjusters* and *Willers v Joyce*, is capable of applying to any form of legal proceedings, be it civil or criminal, although it was conceded that historically the action on the case for malicious prosecution was usually brought in the wake of unsuccessful

---

[49] [2000] 1 A.C. 419 at 432. See also *Gizzonio v Chief Constable of Derbyshire, The Times*, 29 April 1998 CA (claim for malicious refusal of bail rejected).

[50] [2013] UKPC 17; [2014] A.C. 366.

[51] [2013] UKPC 17; [2014] A.C. 366 at [38], per Lord Wilson.

[52] See para.15-73.

[53] [2016] UKSC 43; [2018] A.C. 779.

criminal proceedings.[54] Thus it is the malicious preferring of an unreasonable criminal charge that has been the usual foundation for the form of action under consideration, and that is what is ordinarily understood by the familiar title of an action of malicious prosecution. It will be seen that it bears some analogy to an action of defamation[55] inasmuch as it is in the first place an action for the vindication of character, which is involved in a criminal charge,[56] and only in the second place for the damage shown to have arisen under the special circumstances of the case.[57] However, it has been emphasised that in other respects there is no close analogy between the torts, since malicious prosecution is concerned essentially with abuses of legal process, and will be arguable in many circumstances where statements are protected by absolute privilege for the purposes of a defamation action.[58]

Malicious institution of other proceedings Prior to the recent extension to civil proceedings in general, it was recognised that in addition to a remedy for malicious prosecution, a claim in tort would lie in a "few special cases of abuse of legal process".[59] These included malicious presentation of a winding up order or bankruptcy petition,[60] maliciously procuring a bench warrant[61] or search warrant,[62] and the malicious arrest of a ship.[63] The common feature of such claims was **15-12**

54 [2013] UKPC 17; [2014] A.C. 366 at [43], per Lord Wilson; citing Diplock J in *Berry v British Transport Commission* [1961] 1 Q.B. 149 at 159.

55 See, per Bowen LJ in *Quartz Hill Consolidated Gold Mining Co Ltd v Eyre* (1883) L.R. 11 Q.B.D. 674 at 692. J. Baker, *The Oxford History of the Law of England, Vol.VI: 1483–1558* (Oxford, 2003) explains the origin of the tort of malicious prosecution as arising from the prosecutor's qualified privilege in an action for slander. Baker argues that a new form of action on the case emerged in the sixteenth century and may have been modelled on the prosecutor's privilege. Here "the plaintiff anticipated a defence of lawful prosecution by alleging in his declaration the defendant's malice and the absence of reasonable cause" (at 797); cited by Sedley LJ in *H v AB* [2009] EWCA Civ 1092; *The Times,* 28 October 2009 at [21].

56 The impact on reputation of certain civil proceedings was part of the rationale for extension to civil claims. In *Willers v Joyce* [2016] UKSC 43; [2018] A.C. 779 at [38], Lord Wilson referred to the proceedings as part of "determined campaign to destroy a person's reputation".

57 See further the discussion in paras 15-06 to 15-09.

58 See para.15-78; *Taylor v Serious Fraud Office* [1999] 2 A.C. 177; *Westcott v Westcott* [2008] EWCA Civ 818; [2009] Q.B. 407.

59 *Gregory v Portsmouth City Council* [2000] 1 A.C. 419 HL at 427, per Lord Steyn. These special cases are discussed more fully at para.15-66 onwards and were described by Baroness Hale in the *Crawford Adjusters case* [2013] UKPC 17; [2014] A.C. 366 at [86] as a "rag bag" list of ex parte processes which do damage before they can be challenged.

60 *Quartz Hill Consolidated Gold Mining Co v Eyre* (1883) 11 Q.B.D. 674. In this case, the court made it clear that in no case can a person, who has maliciously and unreasonably set the law in motion, absolve himself from the consequences which he invited and brought to pass, by the suggestion that their immediate cause was a mistake on the part of the judge: (1883) 11 Q.B.D. 674 at 684, per Brett MR; cf. *Farley v Danks* (1855) 4 E. & B. 493 at 499; 119 E.R. 180 at 182. See also *Pike v Waldrum* [1952] 1 Lloyd's Rep. 431.

61 *Roy v Prior* [1971] A.C. 470 HL.

62 *Gibbs v Rea* [1998] A.C. 786 PC.

63 *The Walter D Wallet* [1893] P. 202. In *Congentra AG v Sixteen Thirteen Marine SA (The Nicholas M)* [2008] EWHC 1615 (Comm); [2009] 1 All E.R. (Comm) 479; [2008] 2 Lloyd's Rep. 602, Flaux J concluded that the facts could arguably fall within the category of "wrongful arrest" (of a ship) recognised in *Gregory v Portsmouth City Council* and that this case may be an example of its application in a modern context. Here the ship had been detained for repairs while chartered by the defendant, and the claimant argued that the delay (which had caused them to lose their next charter) was the product of a conspiracy. An action in respect of wrongful arrest of a ship requires the claimant to prove that the arrest has been made in bad faith or with "crass negligence": *The Evangelismos* (1858) 12 Moo P.C. 352; 14 E.R. 945; *The Volant* (1864) Br. & L. 321; 167 E.R. 385. A mere error

that the very institution of proceedings resting on an ex parte legal process may cause immediate and irreversible damage to the claimants. Lord Steyn in *Gregory v Portsmouth City Council*[64] suggested that such claims did not constitute a separate tort of malicious abuse of process but rather they resembled the parent tort of malicious prosecution too closely to warrant separate treatment.[65] The majority of the Privy Council in *Crawford Adjusters*, and of the Supreme Court in *Willers v Joyce*,[66] argued that these cases supported the existence of a general tort of malicious prosecution applying to both criminal and civil proceedings, as part of a rationalisation of the field. The majority justices, and particularly Lord Wilson JSC, regarded this as a return to a broader principle. In the minority however, Lord Neuberger pointed out that no case had been identified where a civil prosecution was the basis of a successful claim in malicious prosecution beyond those identified here[67]; and Lord Sumption considered it coherent to limit the tort to civil claims where a power is invoked ex parte and without adjudication.[68]

3. Malicious Prosecution

15-13 **Essentials of the tort of malicious prosecution** In an action for malicious prosecution the claimant must show first that he was prosecuted by the defendant, that is to say, that the law was set in motion against him by the defendant on a criminal charge or, now, via civil proceedings[69]; secondly, that the prosecution was determined in his favour[70]; thirdly, that it was without reasonable and probable cause; and fourthly, that it was malicious. The onus of proving every one of these is on the claimant. Evidence of malice of whatever degree cannot be invoked to dispense with or diminish the need to establish separately each of the first three elements of the tort.[71] Nor does the presence of malice affect the operation of the

---

of judgment in arresting the ship, in the absence of bad faith, is not sufficient: *The Strathnaver* (1875) L.R. 1 App. Cas. 58. A failure to exercise reasonable care to ascertain entitlement to arrest the vessel does not amount to "crass negligence". Rather this refers to those "cases in which objectively there is so little basis for the arrest that it may be inferred that the arresting party did not believe in his entitlement to arrest the vessel or acted without any serious regard to whether there were adequate grounds for the arrest of the vessel": *Centro Latino Americano de Commercio Exterior SA v Owners of the Kommunar (The Kommunar) (No.3)* [1997] 1 Lloyd's Rep. 22 at 30, per Colman J. Query whether art.1 of the First Protocol to the ECHR would now permit a ship owner to recover compensation for the wrongful arrest of a ship in the absence of bad faith or "crass negligence" by the defendant.

64 [2000] 1 A.C. 419 at 427.

65 This is distinct from the tort of "abuse of process" which originated in *Grainger v Hill* (1838) 4 Bing. N.C. 212; 132 E.R. 769, and which is not dependent on absence of reasonable and probable cause and malice: see para.15-68.

66 [2016] UKSC 43; [2018] A.C. 779.

67 [2016] UKSC 43; [2018] A.C. 779 at [152]

68 [2016] UKSC 43; [2018] A.C. 779 at [174].

69 *Crawford Adjusters (Cayman) Ltd v Sagicor General Insurance (Cayman) Ltd* [2013] UKPC 17; [2014] A.C. 366; *Willers v Joyce* [2016] UKSC 43; [2018] A.C. 779. Note that these decisions did not imply that any change was needed to the other three requirements for the tort.

70 *Bynoe v Bank of England* [1902] 1 K.B. 467; cf. per Crompton J in *Castrique v Behrens* (1861) 3 E. & E. 709 at 721; 121 E.R. 608 at 613; and per Byles J in *Basebé v Matthews* (1867) L.R. 2 C.P. 684 at 689; *Everett v Ribbands* [1952] 2 Q.B. 198 CA; *Dunlop v Customs & Excise Commissioners, The Times,* 17 March 1998; (1998) 142 S.J.L.B. 135 (limitation period runs from acquittal).

71 *Martin v Watson* [1994] Q.B. 425 CA.

defence of illegality, which may apply to defeat an action for malicious prosecution.[72]

(a) Prosecution

Prosecution Very many of the decided cases relate to criminal prosecutions prior to the introduction of the Crown Prosecution Service in the Prosecution of Offences Act 1985.[73] The term criminal charge includes "all indictments involving either scandal to reputation or the possible loss of liberty to the person".[74] There are, however, cases in which, though the proceedings follow the forms of the criminal law, they are substantially civil in their nature, for example conviction on an indictment for the non-repair of a highway[75]; in such cases, and in cases of minor offences carrying a monetary penalty only and to which no moral stigma involving injury to "fair fame"[76] attaches, an action of malicious prosecution was previously thought not to lie in the absence of proof of special damage.[77] Given the extension to civil prosecutions, this distinction may no longer apply so neatly; but damage to reputation remains a recognised head of damage for the purpose of this tort. A moral stigma will inevitably attach where the law visits an offence with imprisonment, but it may attach also where a fine only can be inflicted if the charge alleges dishonesty, as where proceedings were taken against a traveller for attempting to avoid payment of a tramway fare.[78] At the same time, there are many regulations which the state has laid down for the public convenience and of which the breach is punished by a fine, but which it has been thought could not give rise to an action for malicious prosecution on the ground of scandal to reputation; for instance, would someone's reputation suffer because he was proceeded against for laying a drain pipe in an improper manner?[79] However, criminal charges not actionable on grounds of scandal to reputation or possible loss of liberty to the person, for example a finable offence not involving any moral stigma, are actionable on the ground of damage if there has been reasonable expenditure incurred in the defence which is not recovered in an award of costs in the criminal trial. 15-14

[72] *Gujra v Roath* [2018] EWHC 854 (QB); [2018] 1 W.L.R. 3208.

[73] The impact of this Act is considered at para.15-05.

[74] *Quartz Hill Consolidated Gold Mining Co v Eyre* (1883) 11 Q.B.D. 674 at 691; cf. *Berry v British Transport Commission* [1961] 1 Q.B. 149; reversed in part [1962] 1 Q.B. 306 CA.

[75] Similarly, an order of attachment is something punitive in its nature and sometimes simply a means of enforcing obedience. In the one case it is criminal, in the other civil in its nature: *Freston, Re* (1883) 1 Q.B.D. 545; *Re Gent* (1888) 40 Ch. D. 190; *R. v Barnardo* (1889) 23 Q.B.D. 305 at 308; *Re Armstrong Ex p. Lindsay* [1892] 1 Q.B. 327. In the one case, therefore, it is apprehended an action might lie in respect of proceedings for an order of attachment, since they would necessarily be injurious to reputation; while in the other there would be no injury unless there were actual damage. cf. *Wellesley v Duke of Beaufort* (1831) 2 Russ. My. 639 at 665; 39 E.R. 538 at 548.

[76] At first instance in *Berry v British Transport Commission* [1961] 1 Q.B. 149 at 166, Diplock J suggested that the test was: was the charge one which necessarily and naturally is defamatory of the claimant?

[77] *Berry v British Transport Commission* [1962] 1 Q.B. 306 CA (in civil cases, however, extra costs incurred in excess of the sum allowed on taxation are not at present recoverable as damages).

[78] *Rayson v South London Tramways Co* [1893] 2 Q.B. 304 distinguished in *Wiffen v Bailey* [1951] 1 K.B. 600; *Berry v British Transport Commission* [1962] 1 Q.B. 306.

[79] *Wiffen v Bailey* [1951] 1 K.B. 600 (non-compliance with notice requiring abatement of nuisance); and see *Berry v British Transport Commission* [1962] 1 Q.B. 306.

15-15 **What is a prosecution?** In establishing the first essential element of the tort of malicious prosecution two key issues must be addressed, what constitutes a prosecution? And who is the prosecutor? To prosecute is to set the law in motion, and the law is only set in motion by an appeal to some person clothed with judicial authority in regard to the matter in question. In *CFC 26 Ltd v Brown Shipley & Co Ltd*,[80] a case of alleged malicious civil prosecution, this was the reason why service of an enforcement notice would be an insufficient basis for such an action. In *Barkhuysen v Hamilton*,[81] Warby J emphasised that nothing short of the malicious institution of proceedings before a judicial body would suffice: it was not sufficient that through the defendant's statements, the claimant had been subject to arrest and criminal investigation. In this case, a claim for false imprisonment was however made out, where the claimant had been imprisoned as a direct and inevitable result of the defendant's false accusations of serious criminal activity. In addition, to be liable for malicious prosecution a person must at least be actively instrumental in so setting the law in motion.[82] This involves "active steps" to ensure that a prosecution results.[83] So forensic scientists who prepared reports for the police and the DPP as a result of which the claimant was prosecuted for murder could not be liable for malicious prosecution for in no way did they initiate those proceedings. They merely provided information requested by those seeking to decide whether to set the law in motion.[84] For the same reason, it appears unlikely that a witness offering evidence in a civil trial could be the subject of an action in malicious prosecution; and it may be argued on the same basis that there can be no action for malicious defence of a civil claim. This point was not concluded in either *Crawford Adjusters* or *Willers v Joyce*, but in the latter case, Lord Toulson for the majority said that for an English court to recognise such an action would be "bold, to say the least"; and denied that recognition of a tort of malicious prosecution of civil proceedings "carries with it as a necessary counterpart that there should be liability for bad faith denial of a claim. There is an obvious distinction between the initiation of the legal process itself and later steps which may involve bad faith ... but do not go to the root of the institution of legal proceedings".[85]

15-16 The boundary between malicious prosecution and false imprisonment is not always easy to draw. In principle, directing a police constable to make an arrest might lead to liability in an action for false imprisonment, rather than malicious prosecution, on the ground that the defendant has directed the arrest and therefore

80 [2016] EWHC 3048 (Ch).

81 [2016] EWHC 2858 (QB); [2018] Q.B. 1015.

82 *Danby v Beardsley* (1880) 43 L.T. 603; *Martin v Watson* [1996] 1 A.C. 74. See generally G. Kodilinye (1987) 36 I.C.L.Q. 157. Active instrumentality will not be sufficient where it is alleged that the prosecution was instigated by a private individual rather than the prosecuting authority itself: see the discussion of *H v AB* [2009] EWCA Civ 1092; *The Times*, 28 October 2009; para.15-24.

83 *H v AB* [2009] EWCA Civ 1092; *The Times*, 28 October 2009 at [69], per Moore-Bick LJ.

84 *Evans v London Hospital Medical College (University of London)* [1981] 1 W.L.R. 184 at 188–189.

85 [2016] UKSC 43; [2018] A.C. 779 at [51]; Lord Mance thought that "logically", the extension to civil claims should also apply to "any individual application or step in the course of a civil action" (at [133]); but it is doubtful that this is the case given the need to "set the law in motion". Prior to *Willers v Joyce*, in *Energy Venture Partners v Malabu Oil & Gas Ltd* [2014] EWHC 1390 (Comm), Males J felt unable to rule out the existence of a tort of malicious defence of civil proceedings following the decision in *Sagicor*; but thought that the requirement of an extraneous motive was not, in any case, present in the case (at [15]). It is suggested that the comments of Lord Toulson make the existence of such a tort less likely.

the arrest is the defendant's own act and not the act of the law. However, simply supplying information to the police on the basis of which a police officer decides to make an arrest will not itself engage liability for false imprisonment.[86] In *Sallows v Griffiths*,[87] the Court of Appeal applied the reasoning of the House of Lords in *Martin v Watson*[88] to find the defendant liable in tort where he had falsely and maliciously given a police officer information that the claimant had been guilty of a criminal offence, thereby procuring his arrest. It appears that no distinction was drawn by the Court of Appeal on the facts between maliciously procuring an arrest and maliciously procuring a prosecution.[89]

If a party goes before a magistrate who thereupon issues a warrant for arrest and production before a magistrate's court,[90] then his liability, if any, is clearly for malicious prosecution: **15-17**

> "The party making the charge is not liable to an action for false imprisonment, because he does not set a ministerial officer in motion but a judicial officer. The opinion and judgment of a judicial officer are interposed between the charge and the imprisonment."[91]

A justice of the peace or justice's clerk can only take action on an information laid before him. If he thinks that it discloses grounds for believing that an offence has been committed, he either issues a warrant for the arrest of the incriminated party or a summons commanding his attendance.[92] The gist of the action for malicious prosecution is that the defendant set the magistrate in motion. It has been said that:

---

86 *Davidson v Chief Constable of North Wales* [1994] 2 All E.R. 597 CA. See also *Ahmad v Shafique* [2009] EWHC 618 (QB), applying *Davidson* and distinguishing between "false arrest" (effectively, false imprisonment) as in *Davidson*, and "malicious procurement of an arrest" (which was described as a form of malicious abuse of process akin to malicious prosecution), as in the case of *Sallows v Griffiths* [2001] F.S.R. 15. False imprisonment does not require malice or falsehood to be shown.

87 [2001] F.S.R. 15.

88 [1996] 1 A.C. 74; see para.15-20.

89 [2001] F.S.R. 15 at [19]. It may be that since more recent interpretations of the test set out in *Martin v Watson* [1996] 1 A.C. 74 (para.15-20), and particularly the need to show that the discretion of the police or other public prosecutor was overborne, lengthier consideration would be required before concluding that the defendant in such a case was responsible for the arrest or prosecution: *Ahmad v Shafique* [2009] EWHC 618 (QB) at [84].

90 This is now exceedingly rare, but in principle it is still a course open to a private party: Magistrates' Courts Act 1980 s.1(4). See now also s.1(4A): "Where a person who is not a relevant prosecutor authorised to issue requisitions lays an information before a justice of the peace in respect of an offence to which this subsection applies, no warrant shall be issued under this section without the consent of the Director of Public Prosecutions." This amendment, introduced by s.153 of the Police Reform and Social Responsibility Act 2011 and further amended by Sch.11 para.3(2) Criminal Justice and Courts Act 2015, deals with specific offences, such as war crimes under the Geneva Conventions Act 1957, alleged to have been committed outside the UK.

91 per Willes J in *Austin v Dowling* (1869-1870) L.R. 5 C.P. 534 at 540; cf. *Lock v Ashton* (1848) 12 Q.B. 871; *Sewell v National Telephone Co* [1907] 1 K.B. 557; cf. *Pike v Waldrum* [1952] 1 Lloyd's Rep. 431 at 454.

92 A new method of instituting proceedings was introduced by s.29 of the Criminal Justice Act 2003, as amended by s.46(3) of the Criminal Justice and Courts Act 2015. This allows public prosecutors including the police and Crown Prosecution Service to institute proceedings by issuing a written charge sent directly to the accused person.

"Laying the information before the magistrate would not be the commencement of the prosecution, because the magistrate might refuse to grant a summons, and if no summons, how could it be said that a prosecution against anyone ever commenced?"[93]

The Supreme Court of Canada has, however, not accepted this, holding that where a magistrate receives an information alleging matters within his jurisdiction and has heard and considered the allegations, a prosecution has commenced even though he took no further step to issue a summons or warrant and the information was later withdrawn at the request of the informant.[94] Once a summons is issued, the commencement of the prosecution certainly relates back to the laying of the information.[95] In principle, a prosecution may also be commenced by preferring a bill of indictment directly to the proper officer of the Crown Court, who shall sign it, and thereafter it becomes an indictment if the consent of a High Court judge has been obtained.[96] In *Mohamed Amin v Bannerjee*,[97] the respondents had filed a petition of complaint charging the appellant with cheating under s.120 of the Indian Penal Code, and the magistrate held an inquiry in open court (at which the appellant was present and represented by counsel) and announced that no criminal case of any kind had been made out; it was held that the appellant was entitled to damages for malicious prosecution. The court held that the test for prosecution is not whether the criminal proceedings have reached a stage at which they may be correctly described as a prosecution, but whether they have reached a stage at which damage to the claimant results.[98]

15-18 **Search warrant** The Court of Appeal held in *Reynolds v Commissioner of Police for the Metropolis*[99] that "to procure the issue of a search warrant without reasonable or probable cause and maliciously is an actionable wrong".[100] That such an action exists was confirmed by the Privy Council in *Gibbs v Rea*: "That it is an actionable wrong to procure the issue of a search warrant without reasonable cause and with malice has long been recognised though seldom successfully prosecuted."[101] A claim for malicious procuring of such a warrant requires, as with any action for malicious prosecution, that the claimant prove absence of reasonable and probable cause and malice.[102] The proceedings being by their nature ex parte they can-

---

[93] per Brett M.R. in *Yates v The Queen* (1885) 14 Q.B.D. 648 at 657; *Yates v The Queen* (1885) 14 Q.B.D. 648 per Cotton LJ at 661, per Patterson J in *Gregory v Derby* (1839) 8 C. & P. 749 at 750; 173 E.R. 701 at 702. See *King v Cole* (1796) 6 T.R. 640; 101 E.R. 747. As to the liability of an informant who deliberately deceives the magistrate see *Martin v Watson* [1996] 1 A.C. 74 HL, at paras 15-20, 15-21 and 15-29.

[94] *Casey v Automobiles Renault Canada Ltd* (1965) 54 D.L.R. (2d) 600. The Court noted that *Yates v The Queen* was not concerned with malicious prosecution; *Casey* was followed in *Reid v Webster* (1966) 59 D.L.R. (2d) 189; and see *Mohamed Amin v Bannerjee* [1947] A.C. 322 PC.

[95] *Thorpe v Priestnall* [1897] 1 Q.B. 159 at 162.

[96] This is exceptionally rare however, as it cuts out any form of challenge by the defence until proceedings have been commenced before the Crown Court.

[97] [1947] A.C. 322 PC; considered in *Casey v Automobiles Renault Canada Ltd* (1965) 54 D.L.R. (2d) 600.

[98] *Mohamed Amin v Bannerjee* [1947] A.C. 322 at 331.

[99] [1985] Q.B. 881; *Elsee v Smith* (1882) 1 D & R. 97; *Wyatt v White* (1860) 5 H & N. 371.

[100] *Reynolds v Commissioner of Police for the Metropolis* [1985] Q.B. 881 at 886, per Waller LJ, and at 891, per Slade LJ.

[101] [1998] A.C. 786 at 797.

[102] Negligence by the police, even in the absence of reasonable and probable cause for obtaining a search warrant, is not sufficient to establish malice: *Keegan v Chief Constable of Merseyside* [2003] EWCA

not terminate in the claimant's favour. The tort is committed on proof of intent to use the process of obtaining a warrant for purposes other than a lawful search. Damage will generally ensue from the execution of the warrant, but exceptionally, it may be established that the issue of the warrant itself caused harm.[103] In *Reynolds v Commissioner of Police for the Metropolis*,[104] an action was held to lie for maliciously procuring a warrant under s.16(1) of the Forgery Act 1913 without reasonable and probable cause to believe that the subject to the warrant had forged documents in his possession. However, on the facts the claimant failed to show such absence of reasonable and probable cause.[105] The police evidence established that there were sufficient grounds to seek the warrant, and the advice received by them from the office of the DPP was a relevant, although not conclusive, factor in establishing the necessary grounds to seek the warrant. It is submitted that an action now lies for maliciously procuring the issue of any search warrant from a judicial office-holder, whatever the specific statutory authority empowering the issue of the warrant.[106] For example, if a search warrant is obtained under ss.8–15 of the Police and Criminal Evidence Act 1984, and it is established that there were no sufficient grounds for the issue of the warrant under the section relied on by officers applying for that warrant and that the police officers acted maliciously, an action may lie.[107]

Warrants of further detention The Police and Criminal Evidence Act 1984 limits the period for which an arrested person may be detained in police custody without charge. Sections 43 and 44 of that Act empower magistrates to issue warrants of further detention and extensions of such warrants authorising detention for up to a maximum of 96 hours. A person alleging that he has been wrongly detained in custody and that there were no proper grounds for his continued detention cannot maintain an action in false imprisonment once the judicial process has intervened and his further detention is by virtue of the relevant warrant. Yet, if such a person can establish absence of reasonable and probable cause and malice on the part of the officers obtaining a warrant, there seems no reason why an action in tort should not lie akin to the established tort of maliciously procuring a search warrant.[108] **15-19**

Civ 936; [2003] 1 W.L.R. 2187. Kennedy LJ suggested at [33] that in future in such a case (a heavy-handed and frightening search of the claimants' home early in the morning), an action under the Human Rights Act 1998 may lie since ECHR art.8 is engaged. In *Keegan v UK* (28867/03) (2007) 44 E.H.R.R. 33, the European Court of Human Rights concluded that the police action violated art.8 ECHR and that the absence of a domestic remedy where there was no "malice" also violated ECHR art.13. Contrast, however, *Williams v Chief Constable of Dyfed and Powys* [2010] EWCA Civ 1627: search warrant was a necessary and proportionate interference in the claimants' art.8 rights and no breach of Human Rights Act 1998.

103 *Gibbs v Rea* [1998] A.C. 786.

104 [1985] Q.B. 881.

105 As did the claimant in *Wyatt v White* (1860) 5 H. & N. 371; 157 E.R. 1226.

106 Special provisions under successive Terrorism Acts do not require warrants of detention from magistrates.

107 See para.18 65.

108 And see *Roy v Prior* [1971] A.C. 470 (maliciously procuring a bench warrant), below at para.15-71. On ss.43 and 44 generally see para.14-35.

15-20 **Who is the prosecutor?** The decision of the House of Lords in *Martin v Watson*,[109] and some important subsequent decisions of the Court of Appeal, address the complex question of who should be held responsible for initiating a criminal prosecution when police and public prosecutors act on information offered or charges preferred by a private person. The judgment in *Martin v Watson* clearly establishes that the claimant must demonstrate that the defendant acted in such a manner as to be responsible directly for the initiation of proceedings. The responsibility for initiating the prosecution must be his or hers, not the result of a truly independent judgment to prosecute on the part of the police, or other third party.[110] In *Martin v Watson*, the parties had a long history of ill feeling. The defendant complained to the police that the claimant had indecently exposed himself to her. He was arrested and charged but ultimately the prosecution offered no evidence against him. It was found at first instance that the defendant had deliberately made a false allegation against the claimant intending that as a consequence of her allegation the police should launch a prosecution against him. Other separate complaints made by her to the police were not pursued by them. The majority of the Court of Appeal had concluded that the defendant was not the prosecutor. Deliberate deception of the police did not of itself constitute undertaking responsibility for the subsequent prosecution,[111] nor was the defendant vicariously liable[112] for the act of the police officers who decided on the basis of her information to prosecute the claimant on the charge of indecent exposure. There was no evidence[113] that the police officers concerned were only prepared to go ahead with the prosecution if the defendant formally accepted responsibility for that decision. The House of Lords unanimously reversed the decision of the Court of Appeal.

15-21 **Complainants as prosecutors** Their Lordships held that on the facts of *Martin v Watson*,[114] the defendant was responsible for initiating the prosecution. She, not the police, was the prosecutor. This does not mean that a person who merely gives information to the police on the basis of which a decision to prosecute is made by the police or the Crown Prosecution Service will be liable for malicious prosecution. The informant will *not* be the prosecutor. However, a complainant would be regarded as the prosecutor and liable for malicious prosecution if the following conditions are met:

(1) The defendant falsely and maliciously gave information about an alleged crime to a police officer stating a willingness to testify against the claimant and in such a manner as makes it proper to infer that the defendant desired and intended that a prosecution be brought against the claimant.
(2) The circumstances are such that the facts relating to the alleged crime are exclusively within the knowledge of the defendant so that it is virtually impossible for the police officer to exercise any independent discretion or judgment on the matter.
(3) The conduct of the defendant must be shown to be such that he makes it

---

109 [1996] 1 A.C. 74.
110 *Danby v Beardsley* (1884) 43 L.T. 603.
111 [1994] Q.B. 425 at 446–447, per Ralph Gibson LJ; at 442–463, per Hobhouse LJ but note McCowan LJ's vigorous dissent at 450.
112 [1994] Q.B. 425 at 461, per Hobhouse LJ.
113 As had been the case in *Malz v Rosen* [1966] 1 W.L.R. 1008.
114 [1996] 1 A.C. 74.

> virtually inevitable that a prosecution will result from the complaint. His conduct is of a nature that "… if a prosecution is instituted by the police officer the proper view of the matter is that the prosecution has been procured by the complainant".[115]

The Court of Appeal finding in the defendant's favour, despite her false witness, had been greatly influenced by policy considerations that to hold individuals liable in such cases would discourage members of the public from reporting criminal activity to the police. Victims of sexual offences which generally go unwitnessed by third parties would feel especially vulnerable. Priority should be given to the public interest in law enforcement. The House of Lords, finding against the defendant, responded that if such an argument of policy were to be conceded, the logical result:

> "would be to stultify completely the tort of malicious prosecution since the rationale would apply not only to those giving information which resulted in a police prosecution but also to those who themselves signed the charge sheet or laid the information."[116]

In the absence of a claim in malicious prosecution, victims of unfounded and malicious accusations would be denied any remedy and such a result "would constitute a serious denial of justice".[117]

Application of Martin v Watson Subsequent decisions of the Court of Appeal in *Mahon v Rahn (No.2)*,[118] *H v AB*,[119] and *Ministry of Justice (Sued as Home Office) v Scott*,[120] have sought to clarify how to apply the approach in *Martin v Watson*. These cases involved prosecutions by independent public prosecutors. They make it clear that the complainant will not be deemed to be the prosecutor where, in the circumstances of the case, the professional prosecutor is able to exercise an independent judgment in the matter.[121] It is a question, therefore, whether the complainant can be said to have actively "procured" the prosecution of the claimant.[122] This may be regarded as inherent in the second of the three points made in *Martin v Watson* and set out above: in effect, the prosecuting authority is unable to exercise its discretion. It has become clear that the range of cases in which this is the case will, however, be narrow because weighing the persuasiveness of evidence is a normal part of the public prosecutor's role and a normal step towards the exercise of their discretion.[123] It is also clear that if the complainant is not the 15-22

115 [1996] 1 A.C. 74 at 86–87.
116 [1996] 1 A.C. 74 at 87.
117 [1996] 1 A.C. 74 at 89.
118 [2000] 1 W.L.R. 2150.
119 [2009] EWCA Civ 1092; *The Times*, 28 October 2009.
120 [2009] EWCA Civ 1215.
121 An illustrative decision, applying the test in *Martin v Watson*, is *Kalma v African Minerals Ltd* [2018] EWHC 3506 (QB). The claim related to the potential liability of the defendant company where several forms of injury, loss, or damage were inflicted by the police during and after a protest at the company's site in Sierra Leone in 2010, and a strike in 2012. In respect of the claims for malicious prosecution, it was held that it was not in this instance "virtually impossible for the police to have exercised any independent discretion or judgment on the matter". Indeed, the police appeared in some instances to have been willing to proceed without evidence from any source. The claimants' appeals, founded on common design and duty of care in negligence, were also rejected by the Court of Appeal: *Kalma v African Minerals Ltd* [2020] EWCA Civ 144.
122 The courts citing with approval Richardson J in *Commercial Union Assurance of NZ Ltd v Lamont* [1989] 3 N.Z.L.R. 187 at 196.
123 See, however, the decision of the Court of Appeal in *Commissioner of Police of the Metropolis v*

prosecutor, then neither lack of truthfulness nor malice will be sufficient to ground an action.

15-23 In *Mahon v Rahn (No.2)*,[124] an unsuccessful prosecution was initiated by the Serious Fraud Office after intensive investigation. The claimant brought a civil action against the defendant bank, on the basis of a letter disclosed during the trial.[125] Brooke LJ drew a distinction between a "simple" case like the one in *Martin v Watson*, and "a more complex case" where the Crown Prosecution Service or other prosecuting authority (here the Serious Fraud Office) is in receipt of evidence from a variety of sources and has to decide in the exercise of its discretion whether it has sufficient evidence to set the law in motion. He suggested that although in a "simple" case "it may be possible to determine the issue" (who is the prosecutor) "quite easily" by asking the three questions derived from *Martin v Watson* and set out above, "in the more complex case it is likely to be more difficult to apply these tests".[126] He also noted that "it would be unwise to be over-prescriptive in setting out the circumstances in which a lay informant may properly be regarded as the prosecutor, or as one of the prosecutors, for the purposes of the tort of malicious prosecution".[127] Caution, in such circumstances, was needed. In this case, the Court of Appeal concluded that the claimants had no reasonable prospect of showing that the defendant bank was the prosecutor. The SFO was conducting wide investigations and exercising its own independent discretion as a skilled organisation set up to handle prosecutions involving serious fraud.

15-24 In *H v AB*,[128] *Mahon v Rahn (No.2)* was further interpreted. Sedley LJ said that the approach of Brooke LJ, with its division into simple and complex cases, should not be seen as introducing a "bright line" approach, but "attempts to recognise the reality of prosecutorial decision-making in a modern criminal justice system".[129] In *H v AB*, the defendant had been the complainant and key witness in a successful prosecution for rape. The claimant had served two years of a four year sentence before being released when new evidence came to light, such that the conviction was considered unsafe. In light of the time served, no retrial was ordered. The Court of Appeal held that, given that AB did nothing designed to promote the prosecution and had to be persuaded to give evidence,[130] she clearly could not be regarded as the prosecutor. However, even if she had gone directly to the authorities, she would not have been the prosecutor for these purposes. It would be necessary to show that she had deliberately manipulated the authorities into taking a course they would not otherwise have taken.[131] A prosecuting authority will generally assess the credibility of a complainant by reference to plausibility and any circumstantial evidence. The circumstances in which a complainant (even an untruthful one) can

Copeland [2014] EWCA Civ 1014; [2015] 3 All E.R. 391, discussed at para.15-25.

124 [2000] 1 W.L.R. 2150.

125 Defamation proceedings were also commenced; but the publication of the letter was held to be protected by absolute privilege, such that malice would be irrelevant.

126 [2000] 1 W.L.R. 2150 at [269]–[270]. This distinction was disapproved, however, by Moses LJ in *The Commissioner of the Police of the Metropolis v Copeland* [2014] EWCA Civ 1014; [2015] 3 All E.R. 391 at [32], who argued that it was over-complicated and that the same test should be applied in every case.

127 [2000] 1 W.L.R. 2150 at [267].

128 [2009] EWCA Civ 1092; *The Times,* 28 October 2009.

129 [2009] EWCA Civ 1092; *The Times,* 28 October 2009 at [37].

130 She had not contacted the police directly but confided in work colleagues, one of whom alerted the police.

131 [2009] EWCA Civ 1092; *The Times,* 28 October 2009 at [47], Sedley LJ, with the express agreement of Moore-Bick LJ at [84], and Wall LJ at [58].

be regarded as the prosecutor where an independent prosecuting authority investigates the complaint are therefore very limited, requiring manipulation of the authority in order to achieve the prosecution. Wall LJ stated that if the CPS makes an independent decision to prosecute, and its process is not "overborne or perverted" in some way by the complainant, the complainant is not the prosecutor. Successful cases will therefore be rare.[132] This is true whether or not the complainant told the truth, and malice per se does not remove the protection of this test. The starting point therefore is that the prosecuting authority is to be regarded as the prosecutor, and there must be compelling reasons for regarding the complainant as the "true" prosecutor. The consequences for any complainant of a serious crime of a finding to the contrary were noted by the Court of Appeal, reflecting the continued importance of policy considerations.[133]

In contrast, in *Ministry of Justice (Sued as Home Office) v Scott*,[134] the Court of Appeal declined to strike out an action for malicious prosecution brought by S, a serving prisoner, where the initial complainants had been prison officers. An incident had occurred in which S alleged that he had been assaulted by a prison guard, H. Following the incident, S had been prosecuted on charges of assaulting H and for affray, but had been acquitted on both charges. In an action for malicious prosecution, he claimed that five prison guards had given false evidence against him in a malicious prosecution. The Court of Appeal thought it arguable that the prison officers could be said to have "procured" the prosecution. While the role of the CPS in modern law would make it rare for individual complainants to be found to be the prosecutor where the CPS made a decision to proceed,[135] nevertheless in this case it was "unrealistic" to think that the CPS could make any decision other than to go forward with the prosecution where five prison guards gave evidence. It was arguably virtually impossible for the CPS to exercise any independent discretion in such a case. Notably, this was the case even though other potential evidence might be available,[136] but the strong terms in which five officers gave evidence was always likely to be decisive in the independent prosecutors' decision. It is suggested that this case is far removed from the typical case of an individual complainant as in *H v AB*, and that it is therefore not inconsistent with the approach to such cases taken there. Longmore LJ, in particular, emphasised in *Scott* that he could not be sure, for the purposes of striking out, that the CPS had been able to reach a judgment to prosecute which was independent of the "mere assertion of the potential witnesses for the prosecution".[137] He also implied that the ability to weigh the credibility of witness statements in the light of other evidence would make a difference to the conclusion about independent judgment. Also ap- **15-25**

132 [2009] EWCA Civ 1092; *The Times,* 28 October 2009 at [59].

133 "But who would willingly give evidence if they had to be warned that, should it come down to their word against that of the accused and the accused for whatever reason be acquitted, they could be sued as the prosecutor and made to pay heavy damages on the bare footing that the accused was telling the truth and they had therefore lied?": [2009] EWCA Civ 1092 at [49], per Sedley LJ. The importance of policy and impact on the conduct of criminal justice were also noted by the Supreme Court of Canada in *Kvello v Miazga* [2009] SCC 51; [2010] 1 W.W.R. 45.

134 [2009] EWCA Civ 1215. See also *The Commissioner of the Police of the Metropolis v Copeland* [2014] EWCA Civ 1014; [2015] 3 All E.R. 391.

135 Pill LJ [2009] EWCA Civ 1215 at [41], expressly endorsing comments to this effect in *H v AB* [2009] EWCA Civ 1092; *The Times,* 28 October 2009 at [58].

136 Pill LJ [2009] EWCA Civ 1215 at [41], with whom the other judges agreed, did not accept that "the right to bring an action for malicious prosecution is confined to cases in which there is a single prosecution witness with exclusive knowledge of the facts".

137 [2009] EWCA Civ 1215 at [50].

plying the approach of the authorities examined here is the decision of the Court of Appeal in *Rees v Commissioner of Police for the Metropolis*.[138] Here, a police officer had prompted evidence from an unreliable witness, and had concealed this fact from the CPS. The Court of Appeal concluded that the officer's conduct was such that the CPS "were deprived of their ability to exercise a truly independent judgment".[139] It should be asked what effect it would have had on their judgment if they had been told that the evidence of the eyewitness—who suffered from a personality disorder and was highly suggestible—had been improperly procured. It was accepted that the cases are "fact specific". Here, however, the investigating officer had presented to the independent prosecutor a case which he knew included an important feature procured through his own criminality. Applying the words of Wall LJ in *H v AB*, "There is nothing more likely to have 'overborne or perverted' the decision to prosecute".[140] A less nuanced approach appears to have been expressed in *Commissioner of Police for the Metropolis v Copeland*,[141] where a police officer who alleged he had been assaulted by the claimant was held to be the prosecutor, though he was not the prosecuting officer. Although there were other witnesses and other sources of evidence, the Court of Appeal held that the bad faith of the officer, as found by the civil jury, had vitiated the discretion of the prosecutors. It is suggested that the Court of Appeal's description of the authorities considered in this and the preceding paragraphs in terms of a "simple quest" to determine who was in substance responsible for the prosecution does not capture the restricted approach to defining witnesses as prosecutors to be found in those cases.

15-26 **Application to prosecution of civil claims** In *Willers v Joyce*,[142] Rose J observed that the question of who is the prosecutor may be more difficult to answer in relation to a malicious civil prosecution. As she explained:

> "There is clearly a difficulty … in transposing the test set out in the authorities arising from criminal prosecutions into a situation where the previous prosecution is of a civil claim … When the CPS brings a prosecution, it is relatively straightforward to identify who, outside the organisation, has provided the information which results in the decision to prosecute. Where a company decides to embark on a major piece of litigation there are many different individuals inside and outside the corporate structure who will have contributed their information and opinions."[143]

Nevertheless, the approach set out in *Martin v Watson* and later cases could be applied. In doing this, it was not enough to attempt to attribute the company's acts to its director, on the basis that he was the dominant personality and controlling mind behind the company. A more detailed approach to the decision to prosecute the action would be required: "in deciding whether an individual who generally has a position of influence within the company should have the company's actions attributed to him, I consider it is necessary to examine in detail his role in the particular decision taken, not simply to move from generalised expressions of his dominant—even terrifying—personality to an assumption that he took the deci-

138 [2018] EWCA Civ 1587.
139 [2018] EWCA Civ 1587 at [57].
140 [2018] EWCA Civ 1587 at [59].
141 [2014] EWCA Civ 1014; [2015] 3 All E.R. 391.
142 [2018] EWHC 3424 (Ch).
143 [2018] EWHC 3424 (Ch) at [192].

sion in question, at least where there is evidence about how the particular decision was actually taken." Applying the approach in the case law derived from *Martin v Watson*, Rose J accepted that Mr Gubay probably expressed his strong view that the Langstone Action should be commenced but did not accept that the directors did not exercise their independent judgment in coming to the conclusion that it was a proper case to bring. Mr Gubay was not the prosecutor of the Langstone Action on that basis.[144]

Relevance of untruthfulness and malice in identifying the complainant as prosecutor The approach in *H v AB* underlines that a defendant may be untruthful, yet not be considered the prosecutor. There was no evidence as to the defendant's untruthfulness, but this did not affect the conclusion that she could not be regarded as the prosecutor. There was equally no evidence as to malicious motive. Again, the defendant could not on the facts be considered to be the prosecutor, irrespective of her motive. Malicious *prosecution* is separate from bearing false witness, the latter being dealt with, if it can be established, by the criminal law. By contrast, where the defendant is shown *not* to be untruthful or malicious, this will be decisive in her favour. It is clear from the three-part test applied in *Martin v Watson*[145] that a complainant will be the prosecutor only if *both* untruthful *and* malicious.[146] The first of the three parts requires that the defendant "falsely and maliciously gave information" about an alleged crime. If it can be established on the civil balance that a complainant was truthful or lacking in malice, then they cannot be regarded as the prosecutor, no matter what part they played.[147] **15-27**

Where magistrate acts of his own motion A person who simply makes an honest and candid statement of facts to a magistrate, without formulating any charge, is not responsible for the consequences of any step which the magistrate may thereupon in the exercise of his discretion think fit to take. The magistrate acts of his own motion and not at the instigation of the person giving the information, who therefore is not to be considered as a prosecutor.[148] **15-28**

Where a charge made If an actual charge is made, though in an indefinite form and as a mere matter of suspicion and hearsay, a prosecution is instituted,[149] and the prosecutor is answerable for the ulterior consequences, and it is not open to him to say that they were due to the mistake or indiscretion of the tribunal which he has put in motion.[150] The distinction between cases where mere information is given and cases where a charge is made is fine. Where a defendant had laid an information **15-29**

144 [2018] EWHC 3424 (Ch) at [219].

145 [1996] 1 A.C. 74; the test is set out at para.15-21.

146 The separateness of these tests is explored in the following sections. In principle, someone may tell the truth for malicious reasons.

147 This approach was applied in *Quaquah v Group 4 Falck Global Solutions Ltd* [2003] EWHC 1504 (QB); [2004] Prison L.R. 1: the defendants were not untruthful, and therefore could not be prosecutors within the test in *Martin v Watson*.

148 *Cohen v Morgan* (1825) 6 D. & R. 8; per Lord Campbell CJ in *Farley v Danks* (1855) 4 E. & B. 493 at 499; 119 E.R. 180 at 182; per Erle CJ in *Steward v Gromett* (1859) 7 C.B. (N.S.) 191 at 204; 114 E.R. 788 at 793. See also *Evans v London Hospital Medical College (University of London)* [1981] 1 W.L.R. 184.

149 *Davis v Noake* (1816–17) 6 M. & S. 29; 105 E.R. 1153; *Elsee v Smith* (1822) 1 D. & R. 97; and *Wyatt v White* (1860) 5 H. & N. 371; 157 E.R. 1226.

150 See, per Brett MR in *Quartz Hill Consolidated Gold Mining Co v Eyre* (1883) 11 Q.B.D. 674 at 684, dissenting from a contrary expression of opinion by Martin B in *Johnson v Emerson* (1871) L.R. 6

before a magistrate that there was reasonable cause to suspect that the claimant was detaining a girl for immoral purposes, and the magistrate thereupon issued a search warrant, it was held that the defendant, not having in any way deceived the magistrate who decided that there was reasonable cause for suspicion, could not be held liable for the manner in which the latter had thought fit to exercise his discretion.[151] This decision turned to a great extent on the language of the statute in question, and was later followed in an action which was brought for maliciously procuring a search warrant to issue for goods alleged to be stolen.[152] In so far as those two cases may be cited as authority for a proposition that a person applying for a search warrant is *not* normally to be considered a prosecutor,[153] any such authority is cast into doubt by the decision of the Privy Council in *Gibbs v Rea*.[154] Albeit the issue of whether the defendant police officers were prosecutors in their application for a search warrant was not raised directly in the proceedings, the tenor of the speech delivered by Gault J on behalf of the majority of the Judicial Committee assumes that police officers applying for a warrant are normally to be regarded as prosecutors. It may be presumed that the magistrate will act properly in considering the application before him. He will conscientiously discharge his duty in dealing with evidence placed before him by the applicant for the warrant. But he has no control over or ability to establish the accuracy of facts presented to him by police officers.[155] Where the magistrate in granting a warrant acts, as he normally will, on charges and evidence placed before him by a party actively seeking a warrant, the applicant plays effectively the same role as a prosecutor pursuing a criminal charge. Naturally the magistrate acts judicially, but such is the case in all claims for malicious prosecutions. The essence of the claim is the improper and malicious procurement of a judicial act.

15-30 **Deceiving tribunal** There are older authorities holding that a defendant who makes a maliciously false statement which causes a judicial act like the issue of a search warrant or an order for arrest to the prejudice of the claimant will be liable to the claimant even though he may not technically have been a prosecutor on the above reasoning.[156] It would appear that, on the reasoning in *Martin v Watson*,[157] deception of a tribunal resulting in an arrest or search of the claimant's premises can amount to malicious abuse of process. Giving false evidence may not per se constitute a malicious abuse of process. What must be established is that the defendant set out to procure a warrant giving testimony as to matters exclusively within his knowledge and in a context where, in the light of his evidence, the grant of the warrant was almost inevitable.

Ex. 329 at 370–380; but cf. the opinion of Kelly C.B. and Cleasby B in that case.

151 *Hope v Evered* (1886) 17 Q.B.D. 338; *Lea v Charrington* (1889) 23 Q.B.D. 45.

152 *Utting v Berney* (1888) 5 T.L.R. 39 (no evidence of malice).

153 In any event, some of the language used in *Hope v Evered*, above (see, per Lord Coleridge CJ at 340), seems hardly consistent with the law as laid down in *Quartz Hill Consolidated Gold Mining Co v Eyre* (1883) 11 Q.B.D. 674. Great stress is laid on the fact that the magistrate in issuing a search warrant acts judicially, but in all actions of malicious prosecution the essence of the claimant's case is that he has been wronged by means of a judicial act.

154 [1998] A.C. 786 PC.

155 [1998] A.C. 786 at 798.

156 per Lord Campbell in *Farley v Danks* (1855) 4 E. & E. 493; 119 E.R. 180 HL (liability in an action for maliciously procuring an arrest). But compare *Hargreaves v Bretherton* [1959] 1 Q.B. 45 (no civil action against a witness for perjury); *Marrinan v Vibart* [1963] 1 Q.B. 528 CA (no civil action against a witness in respect of his evidence before a court). See para.15-78.

157 [1996] 1 A.C. 74.

Principal and agent A defendant may be liable in this as in other torts for acts done with his authority or subsequently ratified. If an agent institutes a prosecution within the scope of his employment and in pursuance of a general authority, any malice or unreasonableness which may actuate him in so doing is imputed to his principal.[158] If, however, a principal himself controls a prosecution and simply employs a ministerial agent to carry out the proceedings, the fact that the agent was malicious or had reason to know the prosecution ill-founded will not, it seems, affect his innocent principal.[159] In either case, if the state of mind of the agent is such as to make his participation in the unfounded proceedings wrongful, he is liable. That part of the judgment of the Court of Appeal in *Martin v Watson* holding that in no sense is a police officer, who decides to initiate a prosecution having considered information proffered to him by a private citizen, the agent of that citizen would appear to survive the judgment of the House of Lords.[160] A defendant may become liable by holding himself out as prosecutor or allowing himself to be considered as such, though in reality he is only acting as agent for others.[161] **15-31**

Maliciously continuing proceedings A malicious prosecution may consist in the wrongful continuance of proceedings already commenced by other persons. Such continuance, however, will not in itself amount to a ratification of the antecedent steps, and it may well be that in such circumstances there may be good cause for the continuance of a prosecution the initiation of which was wrongful.[162] It was said in *Tims v John Lewis & Co Ltd*[163] that a prosecutor who continues after discovering facts which show the prosecution to be groundless will, at any rate if he does not inform the court of these facts, be guilty of malice and will possibly have no reasonable or probable cause for continuing the prosecution. Similarly in *Rees v Commissioner of Police for the Metropolis*[164] Mitting J accepted that a prosecutor who continues a prosecution after he knows that it has become baseless may be liable for the tort of malicious prosecution; and that a police officer who deliberately suppresses information which would reveal to the CPS that a prosecution had become baseless might also be treated as a prosecutor; but this question did not arise on the facts of that case.[165] **15-32**

(b) Determination of prosecution

Determination of prosecution The reason why a claimant cannot as a rule succeed if a prosecution, of which he complains, terminates adversely to himself is that otherwise there might be a conflict between civil and criminal justice, and all the issues, the conclusive determination of which properly belongs to the criminal court, **15-33**

---

158 That the principal is a corporation is immaterial; *Edwards v Midland Ry* (1880) 6 Q.B.D. 287; *Cornford v Carlton Bank* [1900] 1 Q.B. 22; *Citizens' Life Assurance Co v Brown* [1904] A.C. 423; *Pratt v British Medical Association* [1919] 1 K.B. 244 at 280; and see para.5-74 onwards, where the matter is fully discussed.

159 *Stevens v Midland Counties Ry* (1854) 10 Ex. 352 at 356; 156 E.R. 480 at 482, per Platt B; *Johnson v Emerson* (1871) L.R. 6 Ex. 329; *Tims v John Lewis & Co Ltd* [1952] A.C. 676 HL.

160 *Martin v Watson* [1996] 1 A.C. 74 at 461; see para.15-20.

161 *Clements v Ohrly* (1847) 2 C. & K. 686; 175 E.R. 287; *Martin v Watson* [1994] Q.B. 425 CA at 458.

162 *West v Beeman* (1858) 27 L.J. Ex. 57; *Moon v Towers* (1860) 8 C.B. (N.S.) 611; 141 E.R. 1306.

163 [1951] 2 K.B. 459 at 472; reversed on another point, *John Lewis & Co Ltd v Tims* [1952] A.C. 676 HL.

164 [2017] EWHC 273 (QB) at [154]; see further para.15-60.

165 This point was not considered on appeal: [2018] EWCA Civ 1587; see further paras 15-52 and 15-55.

might be tried over again by a sort of informal appeal.[166] Extended to malicious civil proceedings, there remains a need to avoid collateral attack on decisions. It makes no difference that a conviction took place before some court of inferior jurisdiction against which no appeal lay to a higher court. The convicted person will not be allowed to do indirectly that which he cannot do directly.[167] Sometimes, however, from the circumstances of the case, it is impossible that the proceeding in question should have been determined in the claimant's favour. Thus, if his house is ransacked under a search warrant and nothing is found there to incriminate him, the matter goes no further, but it cannot be said to be decided in his favour. Yet in such a case he would have a right of action if malice and absence of reasonable cause were proved.[168]

15-34 **Determination need not be conclusive** So long as proceedings are pending no action lies on the ground that they have been wrongfully instituted. "It is a rule of law that no one shall be allowed to allege of a still depending suit that it is unjust."[169] It must appear that the proceedings were brought to a "legal end". Where the claimant alleged that he had been arrested on a false charge and subsequently discharged from imprisonment, it was held that he did not sufficiently show on the face of his declaration the termination of the proceedings.[170] The end, however, need not be a final and conclusive one. If a magistrate refuses to commit for trial a person charged before him,[171] the particular prosecution is concluded, although it may be lawful to institute a fresh prosecution for the same offence. It is not necessary for the claimant to prove that he was absolutely in the right, but rather that the matter of which he complains was so terminated as not to be inconsistent with his right to maintain his action.[172] *Craig v Hasell*[173] shows that it is enough if the proceeding was brought to an end by consent of the claimant and on terms. So, it is enough if the proceedings have been abandoned without being brought to a formal end, though this cannot often happen in a criminal prosecution.[174]

(c) Reasonable and probable cause

15-35 **Reasonable and probable cause** The question of reasonable and probable cause may create difficulties in the conduct of a trial: first, it involves the proof of a negative, and secondly, in dealing with it the judge has to take on himself a duty of an

---

166 per curiam, *Castrique v Behrens* (1861) 3 E. & E. 709 at 721; 121 E.R. 608 at 613; *Bynoe v Bank of England* [1902] 1 K.B. 467 at 470; *Everett v Ribbands* [1952] 2 Q.B. 198 at 202.

167 *Basebé v Matthews* (1867) L.R. 2 C.P. 684; *Bynoe v Bank of England* [1902] 1 K.B. 467; *Everett v Ribbands* [1952] 1 Q.B. 198.

168 *Wyatt v White* (1806) 5 H. & N. 371; *Everett v Ribbands* [1952] 2 Q.B. 198, per Denning LJ at 205; *Reynolds v Commissioner of Police for the Metropolis* [1985] Q.B. 881. See para.15-18.

169 per curiam, *Gilding v Eyre* (1861) 10 C.B. (N.S.) 592 at 604; 142 E.R. 584 at 589.

170 *Morgan v Hughes* (1788) 2 T.R. 225; 100 E.R. 123.

171 *Delegal v Highley* (1837) 3 Bing. N.C. 950; 132 E.R. 677.

172 This was approved by the High Court of Australia in *Beckett v NSW* [2013] HCA 17; (2013) 297 A.L.R. 206, which overturned its previous decision in *Davis v Gell* [1924] HCA 56; (1924) 35 C.L.R. 275 (which had held that where proceedings were terminated by the entry of a *nolle prosequi*, the claimant must prove his or her innocence to succeed in a subsequent action for malicious prosecution) as contrary to principle.

173 (1843) 4 Q.B. 481 at 492; 114 E.R. 980 at 984.

174 *Pierce v Street* (1832) 3 B. & Ad. 397; 110 E.R. 142; *Watkins v Lee* (1839) 5 M. & W. 270; 151 E.R. 115. Contrast *Arundell v Tregono*(1607) Yelv. 116; 80 E.R. 79; *Casey v Automobiles Renault Canada Ltd* (1995) 46 D.L.R. (2d) 600.

exceptional nature. The claimant has, in the first place, to give some evidence tending to establish an absence of reasonable and probable cause which is operating on the mind of the defendant.[175] To do this, the claimant must identify the circumstances in which the prosecution was instituted. It is not enough to prove that the real facts established no criminal liability against him, unless it also appears that those facts were within the personal knowledge of the defendant. If they were not, the claimant must show the nature of the information on which the defendant acted, which is sometimes done by putting in the depositions which were before the magistrate.[176] Where private prosecutors are concerned, sometimes a case may be made out, whatever the state of facts may be, by means of evidence that the defendant did not believe in the justice of his own prosecution, for if that is so, there is no reasonable and probable cause for *him*.[177] Presumably the same will apply to civil claimants whose actions are later the subject of proceedings for malicious civil prosecution. However, if an action is brought against a public prosecutor, the position should in principle be different for the reasons set out below. The question then arises as to what approach to "reasonable and probable cause" ought to apply to police officers as well as Crown prosecutors and other independent prosecution authorities.

In Canada, actions for malicious prosecution may succeed against Crown prosecutors in exceptional circumstances.[178] The Supreme Court of Canada has held that in such a case, "reasonable and probable cause" is not a question of subjective belief in the *guilt* of the claimant. As a public servant, the prosecutor must set aside personal views as to likely guilt and innocence and make a *professional* assessment of the legal strength of the case: "Given the burden of proof in a criminal trial, belief in 'probable' guilt therefore means that the prosecutor believes, based on the existing state of circumstances, that proof beyond reasonable doubt could be made out in a court of law."[179] To hold otherwise, and to require the prosecutor's decision to be based on personal views, would run counter to the "impartial and quasi-judicial role of the prosecutor", which is an important aspect of the proper administration of justice.[180] Indeed the Crown prosecutor with personal doubts as to guilt should not follow these in substitution for the threshold views of the judge or jury. **15-36**

While actions for malicious prosecution have not been successfully brought against Crown prosecutors in England and Wales,[181] actions against police officers in respect of their decision to charge or to submit files to the CPS for prosecution **15-37**

---

175 *Willians v Taylor* (1829) 6 Bing. 183; 130 E.R. 1250; *Abrath v North-Eastern Ry* (1886) 11 App. Cas. 247. See also *Stapeley v Annetts* [1970] 1 W.L.R. 20 (defendant does not have to furnish particulars of reasonable and probable cause).

176 *Walker v South Eastern Ry* (1870) L.R. 5 C.P. 640.

177 *Willians v Taylor* (1829) 6 Bing. 183; *Broad v Ham* (1839) 5 Bing. N.C. 722; 132 E.R. 1278; *Turner v Ambler* (1847) 10 Q.B. 252; 116 E.R. 98; *Johnson v Emerson* (1871) L.R. 6 Ex. 329; *Tempest v Snowden* [1952] 1 K.B. 130; *Leibo v Buckman* [1952] 2 All E.R. 1057; *Glinski v McIver* [1962] A.C. 726.

178 It has been authoritatively said that in light of the historical immunity enjoyed by Crown prosecutors in Canada, an "extremely high threshold" is justified for success in such an action: *Kvello v Miazga* [2009] SCC 51; [2010] 1 W.W.R. 45 at [43], citing the dissenting judgment of Vancise JA in the court below.

179 [2009] SCC 51 at [63].

180 *Kvello v Miazga* [2009] SCC 51; [2010] 1 W.W.R. 45 at [65] and [66].

181 See however *Rudall v CPS* [2016] EWHC 2884 (QB), where a claim against both CPS and police was considered arguable. The claimant alleged that the aim of pursuing a prosecution was to prevent him from practising as a solicitor. At trial, the claim failed on the facts since there was reasonable

may raise some of the same issues, with appropriate amendment.[182] There is some support for this in the House of Lords' decision in *Glinski v McIvor*,[183] although the opinions of their Lordships on this point were not consistently expressed. In *Coudrat v Commissioners of Her Majesty's Revenue and Customs*,[184] the Court of Appeal suggested that an officer of that authority was entitled to lay a charge if he was satisfied that there was "a case fit to be tried". He did not have to believe in the probability of conviction. The meaning of "reasonable and probable cause" and particularly of subjective belief in the case of a public prosecutor (whether police or independent prosecuting authority) is explored in para.15-52.

15-38 **Evidence** The issue of whether the defendant had reasonable and probable cause to institute a prosecution or procure a warrant will normally depend on resolving a conflict of evidence between the claimant and defendant. In *Gibbs v Rea*,[185] however, the defendants elected to give no evidence. The Privy Council (by a majority of three to two)[186] found that the silence of the defendant could afford evidence of absence of reasonable and probable cause. The defendants had procured a search warrant to search the claimant's premises in the Cayman Islands under misuse of drugs legislation. The claimant advanced evidence that there was nothing about his income or personal circumstances to indicate that he was trafficking in drugs. His testimony that there was no evidence to cause reasonable suspicion that he was involved in drug-related crime went unchallenged. The Privy Council upheld a judgment of the Court of Appeal in the Cayman Islands that the claimant's case that there was no reasonable and probable cause to apply for a search warrant demanded an answer. Absent any such answer, the claimant made out a good case.

(i) Role of judge and jury

15-39 **The province of judge and jury[187]** It is for the judge to say whether there is evidence to go to the jury, and if there is, it is for the defendant then to elect whether he will attempt to impeach, contradict, or supplement it. The question whether the defendant took care to inform himself of the facts before prosecuting ought not to be left to the jury unless there is evidence of his not having made reasonable inquiries, and the question whether the defendant honestly believed in the charge which he made ought not to be left to the jury unless there is some evidence of absence of that belief.[188] Where all the evidence is before the court, every disputed fact and every disputed inference of fact is for the jury to decide, but with one important

---

and probable cause for the prosecution, and no malice was established: *Rudall v CPS* [2018] EWHC 3287 (QB); [2019] Lloyd's Rep. F.C. 115; see paras 15-52 and 15-62.

[182] *Kearney v Chief Constable of Merseyside Police and CPS* 15/9/2006 (Birkenhead County Court) raised the issue of the extent to which the police can rely upon the advice of the CPS as indicating reasonable and probable cause, and the extent to which the CPS can rely upon the conduct of the case by counsel in its later stages as revealing reasonable and probable cause.

[183] [1962] A.C. 726.

[184] [2005] EWCA Civ 616; [2005] S.T.C. 1006 at [41]. The court relied upon dicta in *Glinski v McIver* [1962] A.C. 726.

[185] [1998] A.C. 786.

[186] Note the vigorous dissent of Lords Goff and Hope on this matter ([1998] A.C. 786 at 801-810).

[187] Juries are retained for trial of claims for malicious prosecution: s.69(1)(b) of the Senior Courts Act 1981; s.66(3)(b) of the County Courts Act 1984. For consideration of the circumstances in which it is appropriate to hear a claim for malicious prosecution without a jury see *Phillips v Commissioner of Police of the Metropolis* [2003] EWCA Civ 382; [2003] C.P. Rep. 48.

[188] *Bradshaw v Waterlow & Sons Ltd* [1915] 3 K.B. 527; *Cox v English, Scottish and Australian Bank*

exception: that the final inference as to the presence or absence of reasonable and probable cause is to be drawn by the judge alone.[189] The judge must accordingly make the jury find the facts and draw the subordinate inferences specially, or he must leave the whole case to them with a hypothetical direction that if they take such and such a view of the case there is reasonable and probable cause, and otherwise not. However numerous and complicated the facts may be, one or other of these courses has to be adopted.[190] In *Tempest v Snowden*,[191] Evershed MR said:

> "I think it desirable that where the question of honest belief is an issue in the case the form of the question should be: 'Did the defendant honestly believe in the [claimant's] guilt' or 'Did the defendant honestly believe in the charges he was preferring', and that it is better not to put into the question a reference to reasonable grounds."

The functions of judge and jury The question of the functions of the judge and jury in malicious prosecution was before the House of Lords in *Herniman v Smith*.[192] The House of Lords held that the function of the jury is to find any relevant facts which are in dispute. When the facts operating on the mind of the prosecutor are ascertained, it is for the judge to decide if they afford reasonable and probable cause for prosecuting: 15-40

> "If there is any evidence of lack of honest belief in the guilt of the accused on the part of the prosecutor, the fact whether he honestly believed or not is a disputed but essential fact on which the judge is to draw his conclusion and is a question for the jury. Questions may arise as to what the true facts are upon which the prosecutor acted ... If the evidence on which he acted for any cause reasonably apparent to him might be unreliable and incomplete, was he aware or should he in the circumstances of the particular case have been aware that there was other reliable evidence available? ... But to ask the general question whether the defendant took reasonable care to inform himself of the true state of the facts appears to me in many cases merely to ask the jury what the judge has to decide for himself."[193]

On this basis, the reasonableness of the accuser's belief in the existence of the facts on which he acted is not a question for the jury.[194] In *Glinski v McIver*,[195] the House of Lords reviewed the authorities on malicious prosecution and reaffirmed that although the question of honest belief in the guilt of the accused is relevant to the

[1905] A.C. 168; *Herniman v Smith* [1938] A.C. 305; and *Tempest v Snowden* [1952] 1 K.B. 130; *Leibo v Buckman* [1952] 2 All E.R. 1057; *Glinski v McIver* [1962] A.C. 726; *Reynolds v Commissioner of Police for the Metropolis* [1985] Q.B. 881 at 886.

189 *Herniman v Smith* [1938] A.C. 305; *Glinski v McIver* [1962] A.C. 726; *Dallison v Caffery* [1965] 1 Q.B. 348 CA.

190 *Panton v Williams* (1841) 2 Q.B. 169; *Lister v Perryman* (1870) L.R. 4 H.L. 521. A summary of the factors necessary to constitute a prima facie presumption of reasonable and probable cause can be found in the judgment of the Court of Appeal in *Hicks v Faulkner* (1882) 46 L.T. 127. cf. paras 15-42 to 15-49. See also *Brown v Hawkes* [1891] 2 Q.B. 718, where it was said (per Cave J), that absence of reasonable and probable cause is some evidence from which malice may be inferred, but if the finding is no malice, then the inference is negatived. There cannot be an absence of reasonable and probable cause when the Attorney General has granted his fiat for the prosecution on a fair representation of the facts: *Bradshaw v Waterlow & Sons Ltd* [1915] 3 K.B. 527.

191 [1952] 1 K.B. 130 at 137.

192 [1938] A.C. 305 (approving *Bradshaw v Waterlow & Sons Ltd* [1915] 3 K.B. 527).

193 [1938] A.C. 305 at 315 and 317, per Lord Atkin; approved in *Glinski v McIver* [1962] A.C. 726.

194 The House disapproving of the opinion of Hawkins J in *Hicks v Faulkner* (1878) 8 Q.B.D. 167 at 172.

195 [1962] A.C. 726; A.L. Goodhart (1963) 79 L.Q.R. 190 at 195; *Dallison v Caffery* [1965] 1 Q.B. 348 CA; *Reynolds v Commissioner of Police for the Metropolis* [1985] Q.B. 881 CA.

question of reasonable and probable cause it should not be submitted to the jury unless there is affirmative evidence of want of such belief; evidence which shows malice does not per se amount to evidence of lack of honest belief for a prosecutor actuated by malice may have an honest belief in the guilt of the accused. If the jury finds that the defendant honestly believed in the guilt of the claimant, it does not necessarily follow that there is reasonable and probable cause; it still remains for the judge to decide whether there were reasonable grounds for the honest belief imputed to the defendant.[196]

15-41 **Submission of questions of fact to the jury** The jury are to carry the induction of facts up to the stage at which an immediate inference can be drawn as to the presence or absence of reasonable and probable cause. But different minds may take different views as to what an immediate inference is, and some will proceed by one step to a conclusion at which others will only arrive by degrees. Thus sometimes, if the witnesses are unimpeached in character and do not contradict one another, nothing at all may be left to the jury[197]; at other times, they may have to decide almost in terms the issue itself. In *Quartz Hill Consolidated Gold Mining Co v Eyre*,[198] the question was whether the defendant had reasonable and probable cause for presenting a winding-up petition against the claimant company. This depended on whether he had reasonable ground at the time of the petition for supposing himself then a shareholder. He had held some shares which a fortnight previously he had directed his broker to sell, forwarding at the same time a transfer. He had been told by the broker that a sale would be impracticable, but the transfer had not been returned, and in fact the shares had been sold. It was held that it was for the jury to say whether under such circumstances he might reasonably consider himself a shareholder and therefore reasonably present the petition.

(ii) *Factors relevant to reasonable and probable cause*

15-42 **What is reasonable and probable cause** As has been already seen, reasonable and probable cause depends upon the information and, traditionally, the belief of the defendant. In the earlier case law, concerned largely with private prosecutors but also to some extent with police officers, belief in the guilt of the accused was often said to be central:

> "There must be a reasonable cause—such as would operate on the mind of a reasonable man; at all events such as would operate on the mind of the party making the charge; otherwise there is no probable cause for him: I cannot say that the defendant acted on probable cause, if the state of facts was such as to have no effect on his mind."[199]

In *Herniman v Smith*,[200] the House of Lords approved the definition of reasonable

[196] *Tempest v Snowden* [1952] 1 K.B. 130 at 138.

[197] *Davis v Hardy* (1827) 6 B. & C. 225; 108 E.R. 436; *Blachford v Dod* (1831) 2 B. & A. 179; 109 E.R. 1110.

[198] (1883) 111 Q.B.D. 674.

[199] per Tindal CJ in *Broad v Ham* (1839) 5 Bing. N.C. 722 at 725; 132 E.R. 1278; *Turner v Ambler* (1847) Q.B. 252; 116 E.R. 98.

[200] [1938] A.C. 305. See also *Glinski v McIver* [1962] A.C. 726; *Abbott v Refuge Assurance Co Ltd* [1962] 1 Q.B. 432.

and probable cause by Hawkins J in *Hicks v Faulkner*[201]:

> "An honest belief in the guilt of the accused based upon a full conviction, founded upon reasonable grounds, of the existence of a state of circumstances which, assuming them to be true, would reasonably lead any ordinary prudent and cautious man, placed in the position of the accuser, to the conclusion that the person charged was probably guilty of the crime imputed."

This test requires a finding as to the subjective state of mind of, in most cases, the police officer responsible (i.e. no honest belief), and an objective consideration of the adequacy of the evidence (i.e. the circumstances are such that they would lead an ordinary and prudent man to believe in the charge).[202] In *Moulton v Chief Constable of the West Midlands*,[203] the fact that the evidence contained inconsistencies did not necessarily signify the absence of reasonable and probable cause where the officers had an honest belief in the truth of the allegations and the evidence taken as a whole gave reasonable grounds for this belief. In contrast, a police officer who arrested and prosecuted the claimant for wilful obstruction of a constable in the execution of his duty was found to have initiated the prosecution without even having considered the reasons for, and circumstances of, the claimant's allegedly obstructive conduct. Consequently he had initiated the prosecution without reasonable and probable cause for he could not have reasonable grounds for believing that the obstruction was wilful as he had failed to address his mind to this crucial issue.[204] It is suggested that it is necessary to adjust the nature of the test in the case of a public prosecutor, given their role in the criminal justice system and that the relevant test for public prosecutors (including the police when charging, for example) must be understood in terms of applicable Codes of Practice.[205]

Knowledge of defendant With regard to the defendant's information it is immaterial to consider what the facts were unless they were in the knowledge of the defendant at the time of making the charge. In *Delegal v Highley*,[206] the defendant, in an action for malicious prosecution, pleaded facts which showed that the claimant was in fact guilty of the crime imputed, and it was held that the plea was bad for not alleging that the defendant was aware of those facts: **15-43**

> "The question of reasonable and probable cause depends in all cases not upon the actual existence, but upon the reasonable bona fide belief in the existence, of such a state of things as would amount to a justification of the course pursued in making the accusation complained of—no matter whether this belief arises out of the recollection and memory of the accuser or out of information furnished to him by others."[207]

On the other hand, it would be obviously absurd to make a defendant liable because matters of which he was not aware put a different complexion upon facts which in themselves appeared a good cause of prosecution. But neglect to make reasonable

201 (1878) 8 Q.B.D. 167 at 171. See also *Gibbs v Rea* [1998] A.C. 786 at 797.

202 *Moulton v Chief Constable of the West Midlands* [2010] EWCA Civ 524 at [25]; *Howarth v Chief Constable of Gwent Constabulary* [2011] EWHC 2836 (QB) at [12].

203 [2010] EWCA Civ 524.

204 *Wershof v Commissioner of Police for the Metropolis* [1978] 3 All E.R. 540 at 553.

205 This issue is explored in para.15-53.

206 (1837) 3 Bing. N.C. 950; 132 E.R. 677.

207 per Hawkins J in *Hicks v Faulkner* [1878] 8 Q.B.D. 167 at 173, per Lord Goddard CJ in *Tims v John Lewis & Co Ltd* [1951] 2 K.B. 459 at 474 (reversed on another ground, *John Lewis & Co Ltd v Tims* [1952] A.C. 676 HL).

use of the sources of information available before instituting proceedings may be evidence of want of reasonable and probable cause and also of malice.[208]

15-44 **Evidence showing prima facie case may be sufficient** A person is not bound before instituting proceedings to see that he has such evidence as will be legally sufficient to secure a conviction. In *Dawson v Vansandau*,[209] the defendant had preferred a charge of conspiracy against the claimant on the evidence of an alleged accomplice, and it was held that he might well have reasonable and probable cause. "An accomplice or tainted witness may give evidence sufficient to make out a prima facie case and warrant the preferring of a criminal charge, though it might not be sufficient evidence upon which to convict."[210] Neither is it necessary that the defendant should act only on legal evidence and inquire into everything at first hand. It is sufficient if he proceeds on such information as a prudent and cautious person may reasonably accept in the ordinary affairs of life[211]; and it is for the claimant to satisfy the jury that there was a want of proper care in testing that information.[212]

15-45 In *Coudrat v Revenue and Customs Commissioners*,[213] the Court of Appeal stated that when considering whether to charge a suspect there must be prima facie admissible evidence of each element of the offence. Plainly inadmissible evidence should be ignored, but it is not necessary or appropriate to consider the possibility that evidence might be excluded at the trial after full legal argument or in the exercise of the judge's discretion. Nor is it necessary to test the full strength of the defence: "An officer cannot be expected to investigate the truth of every assertion made by the suspect in interview."[214] A defendant is also entitled to rely on circumstantial evidence when deciding whether to charge a suspect: "It is very often the case that there is no direct evidence of guilty knowledge in fraud cases and the prosecutor relies on the drawing of inferences from circumstantial evidence."[215] In *A v State of New South Wales*[216] the High Court of Australia commented that:

> "It is clear that absence of reasonable and probable cause is not demonstrated by showing only that there were further inquiries that *could* have been made before a charge was laid. When a prosecutor acts on information given by others it will very often be the case that some further inquiry *could* be made."

Thus there is no:

> "general and inflexible rule, that a prosecutor acts without reasonable and probable cause in prosecuting a crime on the basis of only the uncorroborated statements of the person alleged to be the victim of the accused's conduct. ... The objective sufficiency of the mate-

208 See *Abrath v North-Eastern Ry* (1886) 11 App. Cas. 247; *Watters v Pacific Delivery Service Ltd* (1964) 42 D.L.R. (2d) 661.

209 (1863) 11 W.R. 516, *Glinski v McIver* [1962] A.C. 726.

210 *Dawson v Vansandou* (1863) 11 W.R. 516 at 518; cf. *Bradshaw v Waterlow & Sons Ltd* [1915] 3 K.B. 527 at 534.

211 *Lister v Perryman* (1870) L.R. 4 H.L. 521; *King v Henderson* [1898] A.C. 720; see *Chatfield v Comerford* (1866) 4 F. & F. 1008; 176 E.R. 886; *Glinski v McIver* [1962] A.C. 726.

212 *Abrath v North-Eastern Ry* (1883) 11 Q.B.D. 440. See also *Brown v Hawkes* [1891] 2 Q.B. 718.

213 [2005] EWCA Civ 616; [2005] S.T.C. 1006.

214 [2005] EWCA Civ 616; [2005] S.T.C. 1006 at [42].

215 [2005] EWCA Civ 616; [2005] S.T.C. 1006 at [46].

216 [2007] HCA 10; (2007) 81 A.L.J.R. 763 at [86].

rial considered by the prosecutor must be assessed in light of all of the facts of the particular case."[217]

Mere suspicion It is not justifiable to commence a prosecution on mere suspicion.[218] It is not a reasonable ground for a charge of forgery that the forged document resembles the handwriting of the party accused,[219] nor is possession of stolen goods a long time after their abstraction a reasonable ground for a charge of theft.[220] Historically, it has been held that evidence of the claimant's bad character has no bearing on the issue of reasonable and probable cause,[221] but under ss.98 and 101 of the Criminal Justice Act 2003, evidence as to the defendant's bad character is sometimes admissible; as such, in these circumstances it seems it will be relevant to "reasonable and probable cause", given the importance of evidence in the decision to prosecute.[222] **15-46**

Knowledge of evidence furnishing an answer to the charge It may sometimes be contended that a prosecution is unreasonable, not on the ground that the prosecutor had no substantial information before him pointing to the guilt of the claimant, but because he was also aware of countervailing evidence which afforded a good answer to the charge. A prosecutor has no right to pick and choose among the evidence before him, and act only upon such portions of it as show that he has good cause for proceeding; nor is he bound to assume that the theory put forward for the defence is sound (although, as explained below, he should take likely defences into account).[223] In *Herniman v Smith*, Lord Atkin said[224]: **15-47**

> "No doubt circumstances may exist in which it is right before charging a man with misconduct to ask him for an explanation. But certainly there can be no general rule laid down, and where a man is satisfied, or has apparently sufficient evidence, that in fact he has been cheated, there is no obligation to call on the cheat and ask for an explanation which may only have the effect of causing material evidence to disappear or be manufactured. It is not required of any prosecutor that he must have tested every possible relevant fact before he takes action. His duty is not to ascertain whether there is a defence but whether there is reasonable and probable cause for a prosecution."

However, the Code for Crown Prosecutors, issued under s.10 of the Prosecution of Offences Act 1985, requires prosecutors to take into account likely lines of defence when considering sufficiency of evidence for the purpose of bringing a prosecution. Police officers considering whether to charge must also take into account the provi-

---

[217] [2007] HCA 10; (2007) 81 A.L.J.R. 763 at [87].

[218] *Meering v Grahame White Aviation Co* (1919) 122 L.T. 44 at 56; as considered in *Tims v John Lewis & Co Ltd* [1951] 2. K.B. 459 at 474.

[219] *Clements v Ohrly* (1847) 2 C. & K. 686; 175 E.R. 287; cf. *Matin v Commissioner of Police of the Metropolis (No.2)* [2002] EWCA Civ 907, in which the Court of Appeal held that proceedings for malicious prosecution had no real prospects of success in circumstances where the statement of a handwriting expert had provided reasonable and probable cause for the prosecution.

[220] *Hogg v Ward* (1858) 3 H. & N. 417; 157 E.R. 533. This was a case of wrongful arrest by a policeman. But the question of reasonableness would appear to be the same as in the case of malicious prosecution, although the burden of proof is different.

[221] *Newsam v Carr* (1817) 2 Stark. 69; 171 E.R. 575.

[222] See para.15-52.

[223] cf. per Alderson B in *Musgrove v Newell* (1836) 1 M. & W. 582 at 585; 150 E.R. 567 at 568; per Alderson B in *Heslop v Chapman* (1853) 23 L.J.Q.B. 49 at 51; *Harrison v National Provincial Bank of England* (1885) 1 T.L.R. 355.

[224] [1938] A.C. 305 at 319. And see *Glinski v McIver* [1962] A.C. 726 at 745; and *Dallison v Caffery* [1965] 1 Q.B. 348 CA.

sions of the Code.

15-48 **Lapses of memory and judgment** A defendant is not necessarily to be considered as unreasonable because he might and ought to have known, had his memory and judgment of particular facts been perfectly accurate and sound, that he had no good ground for proceedings. Memory and judgment may play a person false in a particular instance, though in general he may have good reason for trusting them. If, for instance, he has made a mistake in the identification of stolen property and in consequence has prosecuted, it will be for the jury to say whether his mistake was an unreasonable one.[225] In *Hicks v Faulkner*,[226] the claimant had sworn in a county court action that he had given a certain key to the defendant; the defendant denied this and prosecuted the claimant for perjury. It was held that there might be good cause for the prosecution, even assuming the claimant to have spoken the truth, provided the defendant had an honest though mistaken trust in his own memory:

> "If a man has never seen reason to doubt, but on the contrary has ever had reason to trust, the general accuracy of his memory, and that memory presents to him a vivid apparent recollection that a particular occurrence took place in his presence within a recent period of time, is it not reasonable to believe in the existence of it?"[227]

15-49 **Mistakes of law** It has been said that no prosecutor can be made liable in an action simply on the ground that he is mistaken in his law[228]; the suggestion apparently being that the prosecutor is only answerable for the facts and the tribunal for the law. This, however, seems very questionable. If someone simply comes before a magistrate and states facts, facts susceptible to examination by the magistrate, but the magistrate thereupon takes a mistaken view, the informant is not responsible for what happens, because in such a case he may not be considered to be a prosecutor.[229] But, if he is a prosecutor, he cannot shelter himself under the mistakes of the magistrate, and his responsibility begins before the magistrate has an opportunity of intervening. If A were to take the goods of B under circumstances which showed a clear absence of intention to steal, and B knowing all the facts were to prosecute him for theft, it would be no defence in an action of malicious prosecution for B to say that he thought any taking was in law a theft. Nor if a police officer prosecutes for wilful obstruction of a constable in the execution of his duty, and has no grounds to believe that the obstruction was in fact wilful, can he escape liability by arguing that he did not appreciate that wilful obstruction required any guilty intention.[230] It is not evidence, however, of absence of reasonable and probable cause that a mistake has been made on a difficult and doubtful question of law.[231]

---

225 *Douglas v Corbett* (1856) 6 E. & B. 511; 119 E.R. 955.

226 (1878) 8 Q.B.D. 167.

227 (1878) 8 Q.B.D. 167 at 172–173.

228 per Bramwell B in *Johnson v Emerson* (1871) L.R. 6 Ex. 329 at 365. cf. the same learned judge in *Dicks v Brooks* (1880) 15 Ch. D. 22 at 40.

229 But see *Martin v Watson* [1996] 1 A.C. 74 HL, para.15-21.

230 *Wershof v Commissioner of Police for the Metropolis* [1978] 3 All E.R. 540 at 553.

231 *Phillips v Naylor* (1859) 4 H. & N. 565; 157 E.R. 962; cf. *Beechey v William Hill (Park Lane)* [1956] C.L.Y. 5442.

15-50 **Acting under legal or other competent advice**[232] It has been said that if a prosecutor fairly takes competent legal advice he is in all events justified in acting upon it.[233] The opinion of counsel however is better regarded as a potent factor which those concerned are entitled to take into account rather than as being conclusive.[234] Undoubtedly, if the prosecutor believes in the facts of the case and is advised by competent counsel before whom the facts have been fairly laid it will be difficult to show lack of reasonable and probable cause.[235] That the advice of the Director of Public Prosecutions has been sought has been said to be relevant but not conclusive, in negating any allegation of absence of reasonable and probable cause.[236] Clearly, given the increased role of the CPS in modern prosecution, this is particularly significant. That someone has taken pains to form an opinion, however, is no proof that the opinion is sound, though it may tend to show that it is honest and therefore have a bearing on the issue of malice. If a private citizen goes to the police, gives them an honest and accurate account of an event which has occurred, and is advised by a responsible police officer that the event constituted a particular offence, then, if he bona fide believes that advice, he had reasonable and probable cause for prosecution.[237] In *Hewlett v Crutchley*,[238] it was held to be no defence that counsel's opinion had been taken if the statement of facts was incorrect.

15-51 **Mixed grounds of prosecution** If there are sufficient grounds present to a prosecutor's mind for the commencement of proceedings, his defence in the action will not be impaired by the fact that he is acting also on considerations that may be unfounded or absurd. The goodness of some of his reasons will not be affected by the badness of others.[239]

15-52 **Absence of belief in merits of prosecution** Certain older authorities suggest that a prosecutor ought to be convinced, if not of the guilt of the accused, at least of the probability of his guilt. However, it has also been said that when the question of honest belief arises it is sufficient for the prosecutor to believe in his right to prosecute, or that the prosecution is justifiable, and it is not necessary that he should have a positive belief in the guilt of the accused.[240] This may be summarised as belief in the merits of the cause rather than belief in guilt, and this test seems more appropriate in an era of public prosecutions. This approach is also broadly compat-

232 As to prosecutions after the introduction of the Crown Prosecution Service, see para.15-05.

233 per Baily J in *Ravenga v Mackintosh* (1824) 2 B. & C. 693 at 697; 107 E.R. 541 at 542; *Abrath v North-Eastern Ry* (1883) 11 Q.B.D. 440 CA; *De Grouwe v Wytinck* [1952] 4 D.L.R. 326; *Glinski v McIver* [1962] A.C. 726 at 745, per Viscount Simonds and at 759, per Lord Denning, with Lords Radcliffe and Devlin more doubtful at 756 and 777; *Malz v Rosen* [1966] 1 W.L.R. 1008 at 1013; *Riches v DPP* [1973] 1 W.L.R. 1019 CA.

234 *Abbott v Refuge Assurance Co Ltd* [1962] 1 Q.B. 432.

235 See the quotation from *Hicks v Faulkner* cited in para.15-42.

236 *Reynolds v Commissioner of Police for the Metropolis* [1985] Q.B. 881 CA.

237 *Malz v Rosen* [1966] 1 W.L.R. 1008.

238 (1813) 5 Taunt. 277; 128 E.R. 696.

239 *Hailes v Marks* (1861) 7 H. & N. 56; 158 E.R. 391.

240 *Turner v Ambler* (1847) 10 Q.B. 252; 116 E.R. 98; *Haddrick v Heslop* (1848) 12 Q.B. 267; 116 E.R. 869; *Tempest v Snowden* [1952] 1 K.B. 130 at 139, per Denning LJ; *Leibo v Buckman* [1952] 2 All E.R. 1057 at 1069; *Hicks v Faulkner* (1878) 8 Q.B.D. 167 at 171; and where it is laid down that the defendant must have believed in the guilt of the accused, must now be read in the light of the above cases. And see *Glinski v McIver* [1962] A.C. 726, where Lord Denning at 759 expressed it as an honest belief that there is a case proper to be laid before the court, and Lord Devlin at 766-767 as cause for thinking that the claimant was probably guilty and that he had a good enough case to warrant a prosecution.

ible with the approach of the Supreme Court of Canada in *Kvello v Miazga*,[241] where it was suggested that a Crown prosecutor, at least, should set aside personal views and not allow these to substitute for those of the judge and jury. The question arises of whether others involved in the administration of justice are subject to a similar test, including the police in respect of some of their functions. The key English authority of *Glinski v McIver*[242] also provides some support but includes conflicting opinions on this point. The opinions of Lord Denning (a public prosecutor need not be convinced of the guilt of the accused; he need only be satisfied that there is a proper case to go before the court),[243] and Lord Devlin (the prosecutor is only concerned with the question whether there is a case fit to be tried) are broadly compatible with the approach in *Kvello*. The opinion of Lord Radcliffe (the test is honest belief in the truth of the charge) and to some extent the opinion of Viscount Simonds (the defendant's belief is relevant, though it is hard to say there is lack of reasonable and probable cause where the defendant has acted on competent advice), are less compatible with it. Lord Reid concurred with the less easily categorised conclusions of Viscount Simonds. In *Coudrat v Commissioners of Her Majesty's Revenue and Customs*,[244] the Court of Appeal referred to *Glinski v McIver* and derived from it a test based on whether a charging officer believed there was a case fit to be tried; and whether there was, objectively, evidence sufficient to justify such a belief. In *Rees v Commissioner of Police for the Metropolis*[245] McCombe LJ referred to the judgments of Lords Denning and Devlin in *Glinski v McIver* when addressing the question whether a prosecutor (in this case, a police officer) has subjective reasonable and probable cause for the prosecution where he presents a case heavily reliant on evidence which is highly likely to be ruled inadmissible because of his own misconduct. McCombe LJ concluded that the case presented by the officer to the CPS was not a "proper" one; nor was it "fit to be tried". There was no evidence that he had given any thought to the question whether there was a case fit to be laid before the court without the tainted evidence, and the officer could not be found to have "honestly believed" that there was a proper case to be laid before the court. Here, there may have been objectively sufficient evidence, without the witness whose evidence was likely to be inadmissible, to provide reasonable and probable cause to prosecute; but the officer could not be said to have *believed* that he had reasonable and probable cause.[246] In *Rudall v CPS*[247] the court emphasised that absence of subjective belief in the charge, in the sense above, was conclusive of absence of reasonable and probable cause even if objectively, such a cause existed. On the facts however, the prosecutor had a genuine belief in the charge.

15-53 It is suggested that in principle, the test for reasonable and probable cause should, as in *Coudrat*, be based on the guidance applying to public prosecutors in making charging decisions. However, the test of whether there is a case fit to be tried, used in *Coudrat*, is no longer the applicable test for public prosecutors. Current Guidance on Charging to Police Officers and Crown Prosecutors issued under s.37A of

---

241 [2009] SCC 51; [2010] 1 W.W.R. 45.
242 [1962] A.C. 726. The defendant was a police detective.
243 See particularly at 758: "Guilt or innocence is for the tribunal and not for him [the prosecutor]".
244 [2005] EWCA Civ 616; [2005] S.T.C. 1006.
245 [2018] EWCA Civ 1587 at [69]–[75].
246 [2018] EWCA Civ 1587 at [76].
247 [2018] EWHC 3287 (QB); [2019] Lloyd's Rep. F.C. 115.

the Police and Criminal Evidence Act 1984,[248] para.1 requires both the police and CPS to apply the principles in the Code for Crown Prosecutors when determining charges. The "Full Code" test (which is generally applicable and set out in the Code for Crown Prosecutors) requires the prosecutor to charge if there is enough evidence to provide a "realistic prospect of conviction", and if it is in the public interest to proceed. The "realistic prospect" is essentially a sufficient evidence test and involves determination of whether a fair minded tribunal properly applying the law would be more likely than not to convict. In some circumstances, a lower "Threshold Test" is applied, where the police do not wish to release on bail for prescribed reasons and where not all of the likely evidence is available as yet. This test requires there to be "at least reasonable suspicion", compatible with art.5 of the ECHR.[249] As such, it is clear that public prosecutors (police or independent prosecutor) deciding whether to charge cannot reach a decision to do so or not to do so on the basis of their own personal opinion as to guilt.[250] It is logical that the terms of the guidance ought to determine the content of "reasonable and probable cause", and this would be consistent both with *Coudrat*, and with the reasoning of the Supreme Court of Canada in *Kvello v Miazga*.[251]

Questioning the defendant's bona fides A claimant has no right to have the question of the defendant's belief submitted to the jury unless he gives some evidence to show that the latter was not acting bona fide.[252] It is obviously difficult in many cases to distinguish the consideration of honesty of belief and honesty of motive. The one is a question of reasonable and probable cause, the other of malice. From lack of honest belief it may well be inferred that there is a lack of honest motive[253]; but it by no means follows that the converse inference may be made: 15-54

> "It might be shown that although the defendant thought the claimant was guilty, yet in preferring the charge he was not acting upon that view but from some indirect motive. No such evidence has been pointed out to us and indeed its existence is negated by the finding of the jury as to the honest belief of the defendants."[254]

He who believed that there is no ground for a prosecution must be acting from some motive other than a desire to forward the ends of justice, so that lack of honesty of

---

[248] See *The Director's Guidance on Charging*, 5th edn (2013): *http://www.cps.gov.uk/publications/directors_guidance/dpp_guidance_5.html*. The Guidance splits responsibility between the Crown Prosecution Service and police. The police retain power to charge only for minor offences, but the Guidance applies to both.

[249] The Code for Crown Prosecutors (2013), paras 5.1 onwards.

[250] Notice the successful claim against the DPP for *failure* to prosecute in *R. (B) v DPP (Equality and Human Rights Commission Intervening)* [2009] EWHC 106 (Admin); [2009] 1 W.L.R. 2072. When applying the evidential test in para.5 of the Code for Crown Prosecutors, namely whether there was enough evidence to produce a realistic prospect of conviction, the prosecutor should not adopt a purely predictive approach but a merits-based approach to the evidence. The claimant (who had been the victim of an assault) ought to have been given the opportunity of appearing as a witness even if the prosecutor thought the jury would be unconvinced by his evidence. Depriving him of this opportunity was a breach of art.3 ECHR.

[251] [2009] SCC 51; [2010] 1 W.W.R. 45.

[252] *Bradshaw v Waterlow & Sons Ltd* [1915] 3 K.B. 527; *Herniman v Smith* [1938] A.C. 305 at 315; *Tempest v Snowden* [1952] 1 K.B. 130; *Leibo v Buckman* [1952] 2 All E.R. 1057; *Glinski v McIver* [1962] A.C. 726.

[253] *Brown v Hawkes* [1891] 2 Q.B. 718.

[254] *Brown v Hawkes* [1891] 2 Q.B. 718 at 726, per Lord Esher MR.

belief goes also to malice,[255] but it is perfectly possible that the most malicious motives may coexist with a genuine belief in the guilt of the accused. And if want of reasonable and probable cause is not proved by the claimant, the defect is not supplied by evidence of malice.[256] "From the most express malice the want of probable cause cannot be implied."[257] In *Heslop v Chapman*,[258] the defendant had prosecuted the claimant for perjury. There were facts before him which showed that the claimant had wilfully sworn what was false; but in answer to a third party who expressed belief in the claimant's innocence he said that he only indicted the claimant to close his mouth. It was held that this expression tended to show not only his motive but also his belief and therefore was evidence of lack of reasonable and probable cause.[259] It is to be remembered that if the defendant has an honest belief that prosecution is justifiable the claimant can still show lack of reasonable and probable cause by showing that there were no reasonable grounds for the belief.

15-55 **Guilt of claimant** It has been said[260] that if, in an action of malicious prosecution, it be found as a fact that the claimant was guilty of the offence charged, the absence of reasonable and probable cause is thereby negated even though the defendant did not believe him guilty. On the other hand, where the jury found in effect that the claimant had been guilty of obtaining money by false pretences, but that the defendant at the time when he prosecuted did not believe that the claimant had intended to defraud, the judge directed a verdict for the claimant.[261] Although this seems more in accordance with the principle that reasonable and probable cause depends, not on the actual facts, but upon the facts of which the prosecutor had knowledge or believed on reasonable grounds to exist, it is obvious that a claimant whom the jury considers really guilty, even if he is entitled to a bare verdict, cannot well be entitled to more. There has been some difficulty in cases where the prosecution resulted in a conviction at first instance which was quashed on appeal.[262] The better opinion is that this will be considered in the light of all the facts in determining whether there was reasonable and probable cause, and the fact that the first tribunal convicted will not settle as a matter of law that there was reasonable and probable cause for the prosecution.[263]

---

[255] cf. Denning LJ in *Tempest v Snowden* [1952] 1 K.B. 130 at 139; Lord Goddard CJ in *Tims v John Lewis & Co Ltd* [1951] 2 K.B. 459 at 472 (reversed on another ground in *John Lewis & Co Ltd v Tims* [1952] A.C. 676); *Glinski v McIver* [1962] A.C. 726.

[256] *Turner v Ambler* (1847) 10 Q.B. 252; 116 E.R. 98; *Tempest v Snowden* [1952] 1 K.B. 130 at 140, per Denning LJ.

[257] *Johnstone v Sutton* (1786) 1 T.R. 510; 99 E.R. 1215; *Glinski v McIver* [1962] A.C. 726 at 744, per Viscount Simonds.

[258] (1853) 23 L.J.Q.B. 49.

[259] See *Huntley v Simson* (1857) 2 H. & N. 600; 157 E.R. 247. See also *Willians v Taylor* (1829) 6 Bing. 183; 130 E.R. 1250; and *Nicholson v Coghill* (1825) 4 B. & C. 21; 107 E.R. 967.

[260] per Jervis CJ and Pollock CB in *Heslop v Chapman* (1853) 23 L.J.Q.B. 49 at 52; and Lindley J in *Shrosbery v Osmaston* (1877) 37 L.T. 792 at 794; *Glinski v McIver* [1962] A.C. 726 at 776, per Lord Devlin.

[261] per Wightman J, *Williams v Banks* (1859) 1 F. & F. 557; 175 E.R. 851.

[262] *Winfield and Jolowicz on Tort*, 19th edn (2014), para.20-008; P.H. Winfield 53 L.Q.R. 12.

[263] *Winfield and Jolowicz on Tort*, 19th edn (2014), para.20–008; *Herniman v Smith* [1938] A.C. 305; *Berry v British Transport Commission* [1960] 1 Q.B. 149; reversed in part [1962] 1 Q.B. 306 CA. See *Qema v News Group Newspapers Ltd* [2012] EWHC 1146 (QB): where conviction overturned in circumstances where there may have been material non-disclosure by the prosecution and/or the prosecution may have been an abuse of process, this does not signify that the defendant had no reasonable and probable cause for setting the prosecution in motion. On the facts, it was apparent

Divisible charge If a person is prosecuted on a charge which is divisible in its nature, as for instance, if the indictment is for perjury and contains several assignments, and he shows absence of reasonable and probable cause for one part of the charge, he is entitled so far to succeed, even though it appears that as to the residue, reasonable and probable cause existed.[264] In *Leibo v Buckman*,[265] where the defendant had charged the claimant with stealing £27 3s., the Court of Appeal, by a majority, held that even assuming there was reasonable and probable cause with respect to the stealing of £7 15s. out of the £27 3s., this would be no defence where there was no reasonable and probable cause with respect to the balance of £19 8s. Jenkins LJ said: 15-56

> "The question may, perhaps, resolve itself into one of degree. Where there is a charge of theft of 20s. and reasonable and probable cause is shown as regards 19s. of it, it may well be that the prosecutor, when sued for malicious prosecution, is entitled to succeed because he was in substance justified in making the charge, even though he did so maliciously. But the contrary must surely be the case if the figures are reversed and reasonable and probable cause is shown as to 1s. only out of the 20s."[266]

(d) Malice

Improper motives The Privy Council in *Williamson v Attorney General of Trinidad and Tobago*[267] made it clear that "[a]n improper and wrongful motive lies at the heart of the tort" and "must be the driving force behind the prosecution". "Malice in this context has the special meaning common to other torts and covers not only spite or ill-will but also improper motive."[268] The proper motive for a prosecution is, of course, a desire to secure the ends of justice.[269] If a claimant satisfies a jury, either negatively that this was not the true or predominant[270] motive of the defendant or affirmatively that something else was, he proves his case on the point. Mere absence of proper motive is generally evidenced by the absence of reasonable and probable cause.[271] The jury, however, are not bound to infer malice 15-57

---

that the defendant knew from personal observation sufficient facts to prove the criminal charges brought against the defendant.

264 *Reed v Taylor* (1812) 4 Taunt. 616; 128 E.R. 472; *Ellis v Abrahams* (1846) 8 Q.B. 709; 115 E.R. 1039; *Leibo v Buckman* [1952] 2 All E.R. 1057.

265 [1952] 2 All E.R. 1057 CA (Denning LJ dissenting); the case turned on the question whether there was evidence on which the jury could find a lack of honest belief in the claimant's guilt. See also *A v State of New South Wales* [2007] HCA 10; (2007) 81 A.L.J.R. 763 at [96] (claimant prosecuted for sexually assaulting two children entitled to succeed in malicious prosecution in relation to the charges relating to one of the children, though the action in respect of the other child failed).

266 [1952] 2 All E.R. 1057 at 1071. The Court of Appeal in *Moulton v Chief Constable of the West Midlands* [2010] EWCA Civ 524 rejected the argument that the threshold requirement for malice should be lowered in cases of malicious prosecution to comply with art.5(1)(c) ECHR on the basis that in reality it imposed a *lower* requirement on the defendant authority than the actual requirements of malicious prosecution.

267 [2014] UKPC 29 at [12].

268 *Gibbs v Rea* [1998] A.C. 786 at 797 PC; and see *Mitchell v Jenkins* (1833) 5 B. & Ad. 588 at 595; 110 E.R. 908 at 910 (see also para.21-206 onwards).

269 per Alderson B in *Stevens v Midland Counties Ry* (1854) 10 Ex. 352 at 356; 156 E.R. 480 at 482. See also *Wershof v Commissioner of Police for the Metropolis* [1978] 3 All E.R. 540.

270 cf. *Winfield and Jolowicz on Tort*, 19th cdn (2014), para.20-016, pointing out that motives are frequently mixed.

271 See *Gibbs v Rea* [1998] A.C. 786.

from unreasonableness[272]; and in considering what is unreasonable they are not bound to take the ruling of the judge:

> "Absence of reasonable cause, to be evidence of malice, must be absence of such cause in the opinion of the jury themselves, and I do not think they could be properly told to consider the opinion of the judge on this point if it differed from their own—as it possibly might and in some cases probably would—as evidence for their consideration in determining whether there was malice or not."[273]

The Privy Council in *Williamson*[274] confirmed that malice, though a separate requirement, "can be inferred from a lack of reasonable and probable cause". However, it was emphasised that the finding of malice is always dependent on the facts of the individual case. It may be concluded that lack of reasonable and probable cause is not always sufficient to show malice. The absence of belief in the defendant's mind as to the merits of the case (appropriately adjusted in light of the discussion of reasonable and probable cause, above) will probably afford strong evidence of malice[275]; so also any lack of good faith in his proceedings, any indication of a desire to concoct evidence or procure a conviction at any cost.[276] In *Rees v Commissioner of Police for the Metropolis*[277] it was concluded that honest belief in the guilt of the claimant does not negate the existence of malice. The judge had ruled that the senior investigating officer's preparation of the prosecution case was tainted by illegality of a serious kind (an intention to pervert the course of justice). This finding was sufficient to render him malicious: "He knowingly put before the decision-maker a case which he knew was significantly tainted by his own wrongdoing and which he knew could not be properly presented in that form to a court." To find that there was no malice in such a case would be "a negation of the rule of law". If someone, in spite of a warning that his action towards the claimant was illegal, takes legal advice and persists in his proceeding, his action may be not so much malicious as ignorant. He thought he was acting under good advice and relied on bad law.[278] A claimant may sometimes be able to show what the exact mo-

---

272 *Mitchell v Jenkins* (1833) 5 B. & Ad. 588; 110 E.R. 908; *Brown v Hawkes* [1891] 2 Q.B. 718; *Wershof v Commissioner of Police for the Metropolis* [1978] 3 All E.R. 540. However, the relationship between the absence of reasonable and probable cause for the prosecution and proof of malice can be difficult. "In particular, attempts to reduce that relationship to an aphorism—like, absence of reasonable cause is evidence of malice, but malice is never evidence of want of reasonable cause—may very well mislead. Proof of particular facts may supply evidence of both elements. For example, if the plaintiff demonstrates that a prosecution was launched on obviously insufficient material, the insufficiency of the material may support an inference of malice as well as demonstrate the absence of reasonable and probable cause. No universal rule relating proof of the separate elements can or should be stated": *A v State of New South Wales* [2007] HCA 10; (2007) 81 A.L.J.R. 763 at [90] (citations omitted).

273 *Hicks v Faulkner* (1878) 8 Q.B.D. 167 at 175; approved by Brett MR in *Quartz Hill Consolidated Gold Mining Co v Eyre* (1883) 11 Q.B.D. 674 at 687.

274 [2014] UKPC 29.

275 *Haddrick v Heslop* (1848) 12 Q.B. 267; 116 E.R. 869; cf. *Leibo v Buckman* [1952] 2 All E.R. 1057 at 1064, per Denning LJ (dissenting).

276 *Clarke v Postan* (1834) 6 C. & P. 423; 172 E.R. 1304; *Stevens v Midland Counties Ry* (1854) 10 Ex. 352; 156 E.R. 480; *Heath v Heape* (1856) 1 H. & N. 478; 156 E.R. 1289; *Busst v Gibbons* (1861) 30 L.J. Ex. 75.

277 [2018] EWCA Civ 1587.

278 *Snow v Allen* (1816) 1 Stark, 502; 171 E.R. 543; cf. *Pike v Waldrum* [1952] 1 Lloyd's Rep. 431 at 452.

tive was, as by proving expressions of spite or ill-will on the defendant's part[279]; or by showing that he had some collateral object to secure.[280] Thus, where the defendant had said that by indicting the claimant he would close his mouth in another legal proceeding then pending, it was held that this was good evidence of malice.[281] In *A v State of New South Wales*,[282] the police officer who charged the claimant with sexually abusing two young children said that if it was up to him he would not have charged the claimant, but that he had been under "pressure" to do so from superior officers who told him to lay the charges if there was a prima facie case, because the claimant was an employee of the Police Service. The High Court of Australia held that this "pressure" could constitute evidence of an improper motive, and therefore of malice, on the basis that the dominant purpose of the police officer was not to bring a wrongdoer to justice but to avoid criticism by, or perhaps even secure the favour of, his superiors.

Application to civil proceedings The meaning of malice should in principle be the same whether the proceedings in issue are civil or criminal. It was made clear in *Willers v Joyce*[283] that malice, and absence of reasonable and probable cause, are two separate requirements. No submissions were made to the Supreme Court in relation to malice in this case, but Lord Mance in the minority expressed concern that the test for malice as it stands could be too inclusive. In particular, Lord Mance thought it clear from the facts of *Crawford Adjusters* that malice can be established where the defendant's "dominant motive" is to injure, even if he also believes the claim to be well founded and intends to "injure" the claimant by pursuing it to judgment.[284] He would have preferred to confine malice to cases where there is actual appreciation on the part of the defendant that the original claim was unfounded. This however does not fit the existing authorities; and it may be added that the need to show absence of reasonable and probable cause provides an extra safeguard. Thus, a civil claimant who is motivated by ill-will, but whose genuine belief in the truth of the allegations is also reasonable, would not be the subject of a successful claim. In determining the trial of the claim in *Willers v Joyce*,[285] Rose J pointed out that: 15-58

> "It is difficult to transpose the element of malice or improper motive from the criminal case law to the civil context. Criminal prosecutions are brought in the public interest by an impartial Government agency which has no private interest in the outcome of the proceedings. In contrast, a claimant in a civil action does not need to show any reason why he is bringing the claim other than the desire to recover money to which he is entitled as a matter of law. The court does not generally inquire into whether the motive of a claimant bringing an action is proper or improper. Every judge of the Business & Property Courts has experience of presiding over cases arising out of the unreasoning hatred that is generated when former close friends and business partners fall out. Indeed, part of the function of the judicial process is to provide a non-violent course through which such bit-

---

279 See *Michell v Williams* (1843) 11 M. & W. 205; 152 E.R. 777.

280 *Stevens v Midland Counties Ry* (1854) 10 Ex. 352; 156 E.R. 480, but it is not malice when the defendant's motive was to recover his money and he had at that time first to prosecute, i.e. not malice to do something which the law said must be done before civil proceedings could be brought: *Abbott v Refuge Assurance Co Ltd* [1962] 1 Q.B. 432 CA.

281 *Haddrick v Heslop* (1848) 12 Q.B. 267; 116 E.R. 869.

282 [2007] HCA 10; (2007) 81 A.L.J.R. 763.

283 [2016] UKSC 43; [2018] A.C. 779 at [54].

284 [2016] UKSC 43; [2018] A.C. 779 at [139].

285 [2018] EWHC 3424 (Ch) at [280].

ter enmity can be channelled and, one hopes, resolved to some extent by the cathartic process of the trial and judgment. Another difference is that the CPS has only a limited discretion not to pursue a prosecution where there is a good prospect of a conviction. An individual claimant in a civil case (subject to any fiduciary duties as a director, liquidator or executor) has an unfettered discretion to forbear from pursuing a valuable civil claim if he does not want to upset a continuing good relationship with the potential defendant or simply if he does not want the hassle of court proceedings."

Rose J concluded that the question of what will constitute malice for the purpose of prosecution of a civil claim had not been resolved by the Supreme Court in *Willers v Joyce*[286]; and that it is even more entwined with the issue of lack of reasonable and probable cause than where the bringing of a criminal case is in issue. As she had found that Mr Gubay was not in fact the prosecutor of the action in question, and that there was reasonable and probable cause for that claim, she did not need to decide whether Mr Gubay's state of mind amounted to malice.

15-59 It is open to the defendant, with a view to rebutting malice and showing his good faith, to give in evidence all the facts and circumstances that were present to his mind at the time of instituting the proceedings.[287] Where a claimant advances unchallenged evidence that there appears to be no honest motive to suspect him of the offence alleged against him, the silence of the defendant may be sufficient to result in an inference of malice.[288] Note that if reasonable and probable cause is found, the question of malice or no malice is irrelevant.[289] "Even though a prosecutor is actuated by the most express malice, nevertheless he is not liable so long as there was reasonable and probable cause for the prosecution."[290]

15-60 Given that in *Martin v Watson*[291] the House of Lords ruled that where it is essentially the evidence of a private person which procures a prosecution by the police that person is to be considered a prosecutor, police whose information motivates the decision to proceed with a prosecution by the Crown Prosecution Service, as well as those who proceed with charges themselves, should be capable of being regarded as prosecutors for the purpose of this tort. Indeed it is arguable that they should be more likely to be regarded as prosecutors, since prosecutorial experience is less likely to permit the effective weighing of credibility of the police officers providing information and evidence, than the weighing of credibility of lay witnesses or complainants. However, even if police officers are still held to be prosecutors, when the evidence has been reviewed by lawyers in the Crown Prosecution Service and found sufficient to proceed, proof of absence of reasonable and probable cause may be exceptionally difficult.[292] But it seems it is not impossible. In *Clifford v Chief Constable of Hertfordshire Constabulary*,[293] at first instance, Cranston J accepted the claimant's argument that having launched the prosecution, the police in that case

---

286 [2016] UKSC 43; [2018] A.C. 779.

287 *Thomas v Russell* (1854) 9 Ex. 764; 156 E.R. 327.

288 *Gibbs v Rea* [1998] A.C. 786 PC.

289 *Turner v Ambler* (1847) 19 Q.B. 252; 116 E.R. 98; *Brown v Hawkes* [1891] 2 Q.B. 718; *Herniman v Smith* [1938] A.C. 305; *Moulton v Chief Constable of the West Midlands* [2010] EWCA Civ 524.

290 per Denning LJ in *Tempest v Snowden* [1952] 1 K.B. 130 at 140. See also *Glinski v McIver* [1962] A.C. 726 and para.15-40.

291 [1996] 1 A.C. 74. For a recent example concerning the police, see *The Commissioner of the Police of the Metropolis v Copeland* [2014] EWCA Civ 1014; [2015] 3 All E.R. 391 (correct question was whether the policeman was instrumental in bringing the prosecution or was, in substance, the person, or at the very least, a person responsible for the prosecution being brought).

292 See *Reynolds v Commissioner of Police for the Metropolis* [1985] Q.B. 881 CA.

293 [2008] EWHC 3154 (QB).

retained a duty to inform the CPS of matters that became known and that were relevant to the prosecution. As such, the police may still be regarded as "prosecuting" the offence for the purposes of tort liability even if the prosecution is transferred to an independent prosecutor. This applies whether it is the police, or the prosecutor, who lays the charges. The question will be whether the conduct of the police, in terms of what they have done or omitted to do in relation to the independent prosecutor, satisfies the components of the tort.[294] These aspects of the decision in *Clifford* were not followed by Mitting J in *Rees v Commissioner of Police of the Metropolis*,[295] on the basis that they were not consistent with decisions regarding witnesses and whether they could be treated as "the prosecutor".[296] Mitting J suggested that "it cannot be that the police become a prosecutor ... merely because after charge they fail to forward some non-trivial information to the CPS relevant to the prosecution".[297] It was possible that if the police deliberately suppress information which would reveal to the CPS that the prosecution had become baseless, that may suffice for the police to be treated as prosecutor; but that would need to be tested in a case where it arose. An appeal from the decision of Mitting J was upheld, but did not consider this point, since the police officer was considered to be "the prosecutor".[298] Nevertheless, absence of evidence as to subjective belief in the fitness of the case for trial on the part of the officer was sufficient to show absence of reasonable and probable cause. The decision of Mitting J in Rees was applied in *Coghlan v Chief Constable of Cheshire Police*,[299] expressing caution about the comments in Clifford and striking out a claim for malicious prosecution against police officers on the basis that they were not prosecutors.[300]

Whether the withholding of a report from the CPS (and indeed from the investigating officer) might in the right circumstances form the basis of an action for malicious prosecution was raised in the case of *Alford v Chief Constable of Cambridgeshire*,[301] but the Court of Appeal found it unnecessary to give an answer since there was in any event reasonable and probable cause for the prosecution, even if the second report had been available to the CPS. The appellant in this case was a police officer who had been charged with causing death by dangerous driving after driving a police vehicle in pursuit of a car which then crashed. An initial report prepared within the police service was highly critical of the appellant's driving and formed the basis of the charges made. A second report was apparently less critical, and was not released to the CPS, nor to the officer leading the investigation. A third expert report, from another police force, concluded that there was no case to answer against the appellant and his prosecution was therefore discontinued. The Court of Appeal determined that in the light of the contents of the second report, it would not have tipped the balance even if made known. There was no absence of reasonable and probable cause for the prosecution, and so malice did not need to be discussed. The action failed. **15-61**

294 [2008] EWHC 3154 (QB) at [48]–[50]. The decision of Cranston J was reversed on appeal, but not on this point: *Clifford v Chief Constable of Hertfordshire* [2009] EWCA Civ 1259 (the judge had rejected one account of events for reasons which were flawed). The claim of malicious prosecution was ultimately held to be made out at trial: [2011] EWHC 815 (QB).

295 [2017] EWHC 273 (QB).

296 See para.15-20 onwards.

297 [2017] EWHC 273 (QB) at [154].

298 [2018] EWCA Civ 1587.

299 [2018] EWHC 34 (QB).

300 Further, separate claims for malicious prosecution were also struck out in *Coghlan v Chief Constable of Greater Manchester* [2018] EWHC 1784 (QB).

301 [2009] EWCA Civ 100.

15-62 There is no general immunity in tort conferred on the Crown Prosecution Service or its officers.[302] In theory then, a Crown Prosecutor could be the subject on an action for malicious prosecution. In practice, even if absence of reasonable and probable cause is proved, malice is unlikely to be established on the part of the independent prosecutor. Incompetence cannot constitute malice.[303] In addition, the policy reasoning which has ensured that the liability of Crown prosecutors in Canada remains very restricted may discourage the success of any such actions in England and Wales.[304] However, in *Rudall v CPS*,[305] Phillips J held that there was an arguable claim for malicious prosecution against the CPS.[306] In this case, the claimant argued that the dominant motive for prosecution was to keep him under investigation and subject to prosecution and therefore unable to practice as a solicitor. The fact that the prosecution proceeded for several years without the CPS taking steps to obtain the evidence it was advised to seek could give rise to an inference of bad faith; and there were legitimate questions about motive which were properly resolvable at trial. At trial, however, Lambert J concluded that there was no evidence to undermine the honesty and integrity of the prosecutor, nor to suggest lack of honest belief in the charge.[307]

15-63 **Conduct of prosecutions** The Court of Appeal held in *Elguzouli-Daf v Commissioner of Police for the Metropolis*[308] that the Crown Prosecution Service owes no general duty of care in relation to the conduct of prosecutions. The claimant had been arrested, charged and remanded in custody in relation to a serious offence. Eventually, forensic examinations revealed that he could not have committed the offence, and after 22 days proceedings were discontinued. He alleged that the CPS acted negligently in not obtaining, processing or communicating the results of forensic tests with sufficient diligence. The Court of Appeal struck out the claim in negligence. A CPS prosecutor could be liable for malicious prosecution, or misfeasance in public office. To impose a general duty of care to accused persons in respect of the conduct of prosecutions would have an "inhibiting effect on the

302 See *Welsh v Chief Constable of Merseyside* [1993] 1 All E.R. 692; *Elguzouli-Daf v Commissioner of Police for the Metropolis* [1995] Q.B. 335 CA.

303 *Thacker v Crown Prosecution Service, The Times,* 29 December 1997. This was also clearly stated by the Supreme Court of Canada in *Kvello v Miazga* [2009] SCC 51; [2010] 1 W.W.R. 45.

304 Indeed it is not clear that the English courts would go so far, particularly given that Crown Prosecutors have duties to proceed with prosecutions also. The recognition of some prosecutorial liability in Canada should be seen in the context of recognition in that jurisdiction of negligence duties on the part of the police in respect of the investigation of crime which have been largely rejected in English law. This indicates that the policy balance has been regarded very differently in Canada, so that it is by no means clear that English law would follow the Canadian lead in recognising even exceptional malicious prosecution actions against independent prosecutors. While English courts have rejected proposed negligence duties owed to witnesses and potential victims of crime in respect of police investigations (paras 13-31 to 13-39), the Supreme Court of Canada has extended the range of duties owed to include a duty to *suspects*, explicitly noting that the protection offered by malicious prosecution is insufficient: *Hill v Hamilton-Wentworth Regional Police Services Board* [2007] 3 S.C.R. 129; (2007) 285 D.L.R. (4th) 620. For comment, see E. Chamberlain (2008) 124 L.Q.R. 205.

305 [2016] EWHC 2884 (QB).

306 Another original feature of the decisions is that, given the close and continuing involvement of the police in decision-making relating to the prosecutions, Phillips J also accepted it as arguable that the police were joint tortfeasors with the CPS.

307 *Rudall v CPS* [2018] EWHC 3287 (QB); [2019] Lloyd's Rep. F.C. 115.

308 [1995] Q.B. 335.

discharge by the CPS of its central function of prosecuting crime".[309] *Welsh v Chief Constable of Merseyside*[310] should be regarded as decided on its special facts. In that case the judge refused to strike out a claim in negligence against the CPS where it was alleged that the CPS failed to inform a magistrates' court from which the claimant was "on bail for two offences" that those offences had subsequently been taken into consideration by the Crown Court. The claimant was consequently arrested and detained. In *Elguzouli*, Steyn LJ[311] suggested that the judgment in *Welsh* is explicable on the grounds that in that case the CPS had assumed a particular responsibility to the claimant to keep the magistrates' court informed of the fact that the offences had already been dealt with elsewhere.

(e) Courts-martial and foreign courts

Malicious prosecution before courts-martial Whether an action will lie for a malicious prosecution before a court-martial or other malicious exercise of military authority remains doubtful. In *Johnstone v Sutton*,[312] the opinion was expressed[313] that it would not, on the ground that the existence of such a right of action would be mischievous and prejudicial to discipline. Since then, the weight of authority and opinion has supported this view.[314] Following the decision of the House of Lords in *Gregory v Portsmouth City Council*[315] the following questions may determine the matter. Were the relevant court martial proceedings essentially concerned with charges which are criminal in nature, or were they charges of misconduct constituting largely disciplinary offences? It was in part on this basis that the court in *Brooks v Ministry of Defence*,[316] refused to strike out a claim alleging malicious prosecution on the part of Army personnel. The court held that the defendant's argument 15-64

---

309 [1995] Q.B. 335 at 349. Where a claim for malicious prosecution is brought against the CPS, it must be shown that the relevant allegations do amount to more than mere claims of incompetence. *Thacker v Crown Prosecution Services, The Times,* 29 December 1997.

310 [1993] 1 All E.R. 692.

311 [1995] Q.B. 335 at 348-349. See also per Morritt LJ at 352-353. See also Arden LJ in *An Informer v Chief Constable* [2012] EWCA Civ 197; [2013] Q.B. 579 at [99]: "In *Welsh's* case Tudor Evans J held that there had been an express assumption of responsibility. *Welsh's* case therefore remains good law."

312 (1786) 1 T.R. 548 at 550; 99 E.R. 1215 at 1246.

313 By Lords Mansfield and Loughborough, contrary to the unanimous opinion of the Court of Exchequer. The defendant succeeded on the ground that reasonable and probable cause existed for the prosecution. This judgment was affirmed in the House of Lords on the same ground, their Lordships apparently disagreeing with the opinion that the action would not in any event lie: see, per Lawrence J in *Warden v Bailey* (1811) 4 Taunt. 67 at 75; 128 E.R. 253 at 256.

314 *Dawkins v Lord Rokeby* (1866) 4 F. & F. 806; 176 E.R. 800 (Assizes); *Dawkins v Lord Paulet* (1869) L.R. 5 Q.B. 94 (see, however, the dissenting judgment of Cockburn CJ); *Dawkins v Lord Rokeby* (1873) L.R. 8 Q.B. 255; affirmed in HL (1875) L.R. 7 H.L. 744 (but only on the ground that statements made by a witness before a military court of inquiry were absolutely privileged); *Marks v Frogley* [1898] 1 Q.B. 888 at 889 and 900; *R. v Army Council Ex p. Ravenscroft* [1917] 2 K.B. 504 (mandamus refused partly on ground that the court will not interfere in matters relating to military law prescribing rules for the guidance of officers); *Fraser v Hamilton* (1917) 33 T.L.R. 431 (an action will not lie against a superior official of the Army or Navy for maliciously causing the retirement of the claimant); *Heddon v Evans* (1919) 35 T.L.R. 642; and see *Fraser v Balfour* (1918) 87 L.J.K.B. 1116 at 1118: "That question is still open at all events in this House. It involves constitutional questions of the utmost gravity." It is of course different where a wrongful act is committed without jurisdiction under mere colour of military authority, but in such a case the injured party sues for the act itself and not for the malicious prosecution.

315 [2000] 1 A.C. 419 HL; see para.15-09.

316 2002 WL 347008 (QBD), 25 March 2002.

that the charge brought against the claimant (common assault) was not a criminal charge should be dealt with at trial.

15-65 **Malicious proceedings in foreign court** It would seem that malicious prosecutions in a foreign court may be actionable. The claimant can only succeed under the same conditions as would apply to an action brought in respect of the misuse of a domestic tribunal.[317]

4. MALICIOUS PROCEEDINGS IN BANKRUPTCY AND LIQUIDATION

15-66 **Malicious proceedings in bankruptcy and liquidation** Before the extension of malicious prosecution to civil proceedings, it was well recognised that an action lies in respect of the injury to reputation caused by maliciously and unreasonably commencing liquidation proceedings against a company or bankruptcy proceedings against an individual.[318] It is a serious matter to say of a trader that he is unable to pay his debts, and the endeavour to have someone declared bankrupt necessarily conveys this imputation in the most public manner possible. Ordinarily, it is not defamatory to impute insolvency to an individual who is not a trader, since insolvency does not touch him in his calling, and may be rather misfortune than fault. It may therefore be doubted whether an action lies without proof of special damage for the malicious prosecution of bankruptcy against a non-trader, inasmuch as such a prosecution is not necessarily productive of any legal damage.[319] It is necessary in this form of action, as in an ordinary case of malicious prosecution, to show that the proceedings which afford the ground of complaint terminated favourably to the claimant.[320] There must also be an absence of reasonable and probable cause.[321] As to what constitutes reasonable and probable cause, it was said by the Privy Council:

> "if there was reasonable and probable cause for the belief that the appellant was keeping out of the way in order to delay his creditors, then, although the truth may be otherwise and his innocence may be established, still the action will fail."[322]

The existence of this cause of action was, however, considered to provide support for the majority's argument in both *Crawford Adjusters (Cayman) Ltd v Sagicor*

---

[317] *Castrique v Behrens* (1861) 3 E. & E. 709; 121 E.R. 608; following *Bank of Australasia v Nias* (1851) 16 Q.B. 717; 117 E.R. 1055; *Taylor v Ford* (1873) 29 L.T. 392.

[318] Confirmed in *Gregory v Portsmouth City Council* [2000] 1 A.C. 419 HL at 427. See *Chapman v Pickersgill* (1762) 2 Wils. 145; 95 E.R. 734; *Kemp, Re* (1841) 1 Mont. D. & De. G. 657; *Farley v Danks* (1855) 4 E. & B. 493; 119 E.R. 180; *Johnson v Emerson* (1871) L.R. 6 Ex. 329; *Quartz Hill Consolidated Gold Mining v Eyre* (1883) 11 Q.B.D. 674; *Flame Bar-B-Q Ltd v Hour* (1980) 106 D.L.R. (3d) 438; *Business Computers International v Registrar of Companies* [1988] Ch. 229; [1987] 3 All E.R. 465 at 469; *Partizan Ltd v OJ Kilkenny & Co Ltd* [1998] 1 B.C.L.C. 157.

[319] See *Wyatt v Palmer* [1899] 2 Q.B. 106; and para.21-41.

[320] *Whitworth v Hall* (1831) 2 B. & Ad. 695; 109 E.R. 1302; *Metropolitan Bank v Pooley* (1885) 10 App. Cas. 210; *Beechey v William Hill (Park Lane)* [1956] C.L.Y. 5442. See also *Tibbs v Islington LBC* [2002] EWCA Civ 1682; [2003] B.P.I.R. 743 in which the proceedings failed in part on this ground where the defendant recovered a significant sum by way of the bankruptcy proceedings, although this was substantially less than the original claim.

[321] *Jacobs v Vockrodt* [2007] EWHC 2403 (QB); [2007] B.P.I.R. 1568: a bankruptcy petition is an abuse of process only where the petitioner knew or believed that the debt was the subject of a substantial dispute.

[322] *Cox v English Scottish and Australian Bank* [1905] A.C. 168 at 175.

General Insurance (Cayman) Ltd[323] and *Willers v Joyce*[324] that there was no principled justification for continuing to exclude a general action for malicious prosecution of civil proceedings. In both cases, false allegations made in civil proceedings were capable of leading to substantial damage to the claimant's reputation even if he or she had been vindicated at trial.[325] Rather than confining the action to a few disparate situations, it was argued that the courts should provide a remedy regardless of whether it was dealing with malicious prosecution of criminal or civil proceedings. The highest court has therefore extended the previous "'rag bag' or ... rational list of ex parte processes which do damage before they can be challenged"[326] to permit a general action for the malicious instigation of civil proceedings.

Defendant must instigate the bankruptcy proceedings In *Tibbs v Islington LBC*,[327] the Court of Appeal held that the action was only available when the defendant was the petitioning creditor. In *Tibbs* the defendant was only a supporting creditor and had not been substituted for the petitioning creditor. The Court of Appeal refused to extend the ambit of the tort to encompass a supporting creditor who had not instigated proceedings.[328] Previous authority[329] suggesting that the defendant presenting the bankruptcy petition must in some way have deceived the court has been held to be erroneous. Indeed, the presentation of the petition is of itself a good cause of action, even though it be immediately dismissed when it comes on for hearing: **15-67**

> "By proceedings in bankruptcy a man's fair name is injured ... because he is openly charged with insolvency before he can defend himself. It is not like an action charging a merchant with fraud, where the evil done by bringing the action is remedied at the same time that the mischief is published, namely, at the trial."[330]

5. ABUSE OF CIVIL PROCESS

Abuse of civil process Prior to the decision of the Privy Council in *Crawford Adjusters (Cayman) Ltd v Sagicor General Insurance (Cayman) Ltd*,[331] the House of Lords in *Gregory v Portsmouth City Council*[332] had seemed to make it clear beyond doubt that in England no *general* tort of maliciously instituting civil proceedings existed. Lord Steyn conceded that the justification often advanced to reject such a broad tort, that the judgment in the case brought against the claimant **15-68**

---

323 [2013] UKPC 17; [2014] A.C. 366.
324 [2016] UKSC 43; [2018] A.C. 779.
325 [2013] UKPC 17; [2014] A.C. 366 at [61], per Lord Wilson.
326 [2013] UKPC 17; [2014] A.C. 366 at [86], per Baroness Hale.
327 [2002] EWCA Civ 1682; [2003] B.P.I.R. 743.
328 The claimant also lost because the defendant actually recovered a significant amount (albeit substantially less than originally claimed) and as such the claimant could not assert that the proceedings complained of had been decided in his favour.
329 per Martin B in *Johnson v Emerson* (1871) L.R. 6 Ex. 329 at 379. The argument was that, if his affidavits were truthful, no injury could be done except through the mistake of the court itself for which he was not responsible.
330 *Quartz Hill Consolidated Gold Mining Co v Eyre* (1883) 11 Q.B.D. 674 at 684, per Brett MR.
331 [2013] UKPC 17; [2014] A.C. 366 (Lords Neuberger and Sumption dissenting). Commented on by TKC Ng (2014) 130 L.Q.R. 43.
332 [2000] 1 A.C. 419 HL. And see *Metall und Rohstoff AG v Donaldson Lufkin & Jenrette Inc* [1990] 1 Q.B. 391 CA at 471; *IKEA Ltd v Brown* [2009] EWHC 955 (Comm).

rectified any injury to reputation, no longer held good.[333] Nonetheless he considered that any injury to the claimant was remediable in other torts and, for "essentially practical reasons",[334] declined to extend the ambit of the tort beyond a closed category of special cases which resembled the parent action too much to warrant separate treatment.[335] The majority in *Crawford* argued for recognition of a general tort of malicious prosecution of civil proceedings, but did not, however, deny the existence of a distinct tort of abuse of the civil process.

15-69 **Scope of the tort: extortion under colour of process** Lord Wilson in *Crawford Adjusters* commented that: "It is hard not to regard abuse of process as a tort distinct from malicious prosecution if only because, apart from the need to establish a purpose not within the scope of the action (i.e. a 'collateral' or, more helpfully, an 'improper' purpose), abuse of process requires neither that the action should have been brought without reasonable cause nor that it should have terminated in favour of the alleged victim."[336] By contrast, Lord Toulson in *Willers v Joyce*[337] suggested that the leading case of *Grainger v Hill* should be seen as an instance of malicious prosecution, in which the existence of a collateral purpose was evidence of malice. He conceded however that it was not necessary to settle this point. It has long been established that a legal process, not itself devoid of foundation, may be maliciously employed for some collateral object of extortion or oppression, and in such cases the injured party may have a claim, although the proceedings of which he complains may not have been determined in his favour. Thus, in *Grainger v Hill*,[338] the claimant was arrested and under the duress of his imprisonment was compelled to give up the possession of certain papers. It was contended that he could not sue in respect of the malicious arrest, because it was not alleged to be without reasonable and probable cause, nor was the determination of the suit shown under which the arrest had taken place. It was held, however, that the objection could not prevail, inasmuch as the action was not for the malicious arrest, but for abusing the process of law to effect an object not within its proper scope. The Court of Appeal in *Speed Seal Products Ltd v Paddington*[339] also decided that *Grainger v Hill* provided "a basis for an arguable case" that there had been an actionable abuse of the process of the court.[340] The claimant must, however, establish that the defendant used the legal process for a predominant purpose "outside the ambit of

---

333 [2000] 1 A.C. 419 HL at 428; and see para.15-09.

334 [2000] 1 A.C. 419 HL at 432.

335 [2000] 1 A.C. 419 HL at 427. *Strickland v Hertfordshire CC* [2003] EWHC 287 (QB) —civil proceedings before magistrates under the Registered Homes Act 1984 s.11, in respect of the closure of a registered care home for the elderly, could not give rise to a claim for malicious prosecution (the Registered Homes Act 1984 was subsequently repealed by the Care Standards Act 2000). Note that there is authority that if anyone having no interest in the matter maliciously induces a pauper to bring an unfounded action, on the failure of which the defendant is unable to obtain his costs owing to the claimant's insolvency, legal damage flows directly from the wrongful conduct of the instigating party which affords a good ground of action: *Pechell v Watson* (1841) 8 M. & W. 691; 151 E.R. 1217. See also *Cotterell v Jones* (1851) 11 C.B. 713; 138 E.R. 655.

336 [2013] UKPC 17; [2014] A.C. 366 at [62].

337 [2016] UKSC 43; [2018] A.C. 799 at [25].

338 (1838) 4 Bing. N.C. 212; 132 E.R. 769. For restraining of vexatious actions, see para.15-76.

339 [1985] 1 W.L.R. 1327.

340 See also *Goldsmith v Sperrings Ltd* [1977] 1 W.L.R. 478; and *A Debtor (No.757 of 1954) Ex p. the Debtor v FA Dumont Ltd, Re* [1955] Ch. 600 at 623–624 (although not a claim in tort but of opposition to a receiving order).

the legal claim which the court is asked to adjudicate".[341] The Court of Appeal has indicated that such an action is compliant with art.6 ECHR.[342]

Malicious execution In *Gilding v Eyre*,[343] the defendant was a judgment creditor who had obtained a writ of *capias ad satisfaciendum*, directing the sheriff to arrest the debtor and unless he satisfied the judgment to produce him in court. The writ in *Gilding* had been endorsed with a direction to levy a sum substantially exceeding the true amount due. The debtor tendered the amount actually due, but refused to pay the balance. He was therefore arrested by the sheriff's officers and had to pay the balance to obtain his release. The court held: **15-70**

> "In the present case, the complaint is not that any undetermined proceeding was unjustly instituted. The alleged cause of action is, that the defendant has maliciously employed the process of the court in a terminated suit, in having by means of a regular writ of execution extorted money which he knew had been already paid and was no longer due on the judgment."[344]

Limits exist. If a person's goods are seized under a judgment irregularly or fraudulently signed, the proper remedy is to have the judgment set aside; then the seizure can be treated as not having been made under any legal process whatever and therefore as a mere trespass.[345] An action does not lie simply because an execution creditor acts with a malicious motive. If, however, part of judgment debt is paid and the creditor nevertheless maliciously takes out execution for the full amount, in such a case, the judgment being in itself unimpeachable, the remedy is for the unfair use of the power which it confers:

> "It would not be creditable to our jurisprudence if the debtor had no remedy by action where his person or goods have been taken in execution for a larger sum than remained due upon the judgment … the creditor well knowing that the sum for which execution is sued out is excessive, and his motive being to oppress or injure the debtor."[346]

If a judgment debt has been satisfied without the creditor's knowledge and he proceeds to levy execution, he may still be liable in trespass, though in the absence of malice he cannot be liable for malicious abuse of process.[347] From the nature of the case the claimant in an action of this kind cannot be required to prove the favourable determination of the proceeding of which he complains.[348]

---

341 *Metall und Rohstoff AG v Donaldson Lufkin & Jenrette Inc* [1990] 1 Q.B. 391 at 469–470.

342 See *Ali Daar v Chief Constable of Merseyside Police* [2005] EWCA Civ 1774. While art.6 protects the right of access to the courts, Laws LJ held (at [11]) that this right can be overridden by another constitutional interest: "The protection of the justice process against disrepute and manipulation will plainly be capable of providing such a higher interest".

343 (1861) 10 C.B. (N.S.) 592; 142 E.R. 584.

344 (1861) 10 C.B. (N.S.) 592 at 604 per Willes J.

345 *Bates v Pilling* (1826) 6 B. & C. 38; 108 E.R. 367; *Riddell v Pakeman* (1835) 2 C.M. & R. 30; 150 E.R. 13; *Brown v Jones* (1846) 15 M. & W. 191; 153 E.R. 817.

346 *Churchill v Siggers* (1854) 3 E. & B. 929 at 937–938; 118 E.R. 1389 at 1392-1393.

347 *Clissold v Cratchley* [1910] 2 K.B. 244.

348 *Gilding v Eyre* (1861) 10 C.B. (N.S.) 592; 142 E.R. 584. For other cases of abuse of civil process, see *Gibbs v Pike* (1842) 9 M. & W. 351; 152 E.R. 149 (maliciously registering a judgment); *Craig v Hasell* (1843) 4 Q.B. 481; 114 E.R. 980 (malicious issuing of an extent); *Redway v McAndrew* (1873) L.R. 9 Q.B. 74; *Horsley v Style* (1893) 69 L.T. 222 (registration of a document supposed to be a bill of sale); and for a claim for malicious arrest under emergency powers, see *Pike v Waldrum* [1952] 1 Lloyd's Rep. 431.

15-71 **Arrest under judge's order** The abolition of arrest in support of civil proceedings does limit, however, the scope of the tort of abuse of process. Debtors may now only be imprisoned for disobedience to a judge's order for payment made after judgment on satisfactory evidence of the debtor having adequate means, and only in severely restricted circumstances.[349] Arrest on civil process must therefore now always be a purely judicial act, and it will be rare for any cause of action to arise in respect of it. In *Daniels v Fielding*,[350] it was held that a claimant who sued in respect of an arrest under a judge's order must base his action, which was an action similar in character to an action for malicious prosecution, on some false charge or statement by the defendant by which the judge was misled. An action may also lie for a malicious detention as for a malicious arrest. In *Moore v Gardner*,[351] the claimant had been in custody under an attachment for non-payment of costs. He subsequently paid them to the solicitor on the other side, who, however, refused to give an order to the sheriff for his discharge and compelled him to go to the court. It was held that the claimant could not recover because the refusal was not alleged to be malicious, but it was not doubted that with proof of such an allegation the defendant might have been liable.

15-72 **Collateral or improper purpose for pursuing proceedings** In *Land Securities v Fladgate Fielder*,[352] the Court of Appeal recognised that although the concept of abuse of process was well known to the law, both in civil and criminal proceedings, it has rarely been treated as giving rise to a cause of action. Indeed, the action to date has only been successfully invoked in *Grainger v Hill*[353] itself (and, arguably, *Gilding v Eyre*[354]). In both cases, there had been a blatant misuse of a particular process, namely arrest and execution, within existing proceedings to achieve a collateral advantage. Reviewing all of the cases in which a tort of abuse of process had been discussed, the Court of Appeal observed, however, that there was no clearly accepted approach for identifying what is sufficiently collateral to establish the tort of abuse of process. Moore-Bick LJ found it helpful to consider whether the defendant's predominant purpose in bringing the proceedings was not to obtain the remedy that the law offers but to achieve some other object that lies outside the range of remedies that the law grants.[355] In the case itself, which involved judicial review proceedings, the court found such a claim unlikely to succeed. An action for judicial review may only be brought by first obtaining permission from the court to proceed and is subject to strict rules of standing. A defendant or interested party may thus challenge for abuse at this stage. Further, the public nature of such proceedings means that, although the defendant may be seeking to ensure that the public body compiles with the law, this does not mean that he or she is not seeking at the same time to serve a private interest of their own.

---

349 Debtors Act 1869 s.5, amended by Administration of Justice Act 1970 s.11. As to arresting persons who have been served with bankruptcy notices and who are about to abscond, see Insolvency Act 1986 s.364.

350 (1846) 16 M. & W. 200 at 207; 153 E.R. 1159 at 1162. cf. *Johnson v Emerson* (1871) L.R. 6 Ex. 329 at 379; *Roy v Prior* [1971] A.C. 470 HL.

351 (1847) 16 M. & W. 595; 153 E.R. 1327. See also *Crozer v Pilling* (1825) 4 B. & C. 26; 107 E.R. 969.

352 [2009] EWCA Civ 1402; [2010] Ch 467.

353 (1838) 4 Bing. N.C. 212; 132 E.R. 769, para.15-69.

354 *Gilding v Eyre* (1861) 10 C.B. (N.S.) 592; 142 E.R. 584 (*Grainger v Hill* was not, however, mentioned in this case).

355 [2009] EWCA Civ 1402; [2010] Ch 467 at [89].

The Court resolved, however, that it was not necessary on this appeal to define the precise limits of the tort of abuse of process.[356]

The Privy Council in *Crawford Adjusters (Cayman) Ltd v Sagicor General Insurance (Cayman) Ltd*[357] did seek, however, to clarify the nature of the relevant improper purpose in relation to a claim for abuse of process. In identifying a collateral (or perhaps more clearly an "improper") purpose for instigating proceedings, the court found a helpful metaphor in the concept of a stalking horse: "If the proceedings are merely a stalking horse to coerce the defendant in some way entirely outside the ambit of the legal claim upon which the court is asked to adjudicate they are regarded as an abuse of process for this purpose".[358] In *Crawford Adjusters* the court was in agreement that while the defendant's employee had intended to ruin the claimant, he had sought to achieve this through a victory in the civil proceedings themselves. The action was therefore not made out. Lord Wilson also considered the situation where the defendant has mixed motives, and doubted authority[359] suggesting that any legitimate purpose would negative the abuse even if the improper purpose was predominant. This is consistent with the view of Moore-Bick LJ in *Land Securities v Fladgate Fielder*. It should also be noted that motive and intention are irrelevant except where malice is in issue. As seen in *Crawford Adjusters* itself, the fact that a party who asserted a legal right was activated by feelings of personal animosity, vindictiveness or general antagonism was irrelevant.[360] 15-73

Economic loss "Charges and expenses", which are mentioned in *Savill v Roberts*,[361] as the third head of damage, were thought not to allow a cause of action based on the damage suffered as a result of the extra costs incurred in defending civil proceedings over and above the sum allowed on taxation.[362] However, in *Willers v Joyce*[363] the Supreme Court allowed the whole claim to proceed to trial, including a claim for excess of legal expenses in defending civil proceedings. In *Land Securities v Fladgate Fielder*[364] the Court of Appeal considered the action in *Grainger v Hill* to be confined to cases where the kinds of damage required for the tort of malicious prosecution were established[365]; and held that this could not extend to purely economic losses. To hold otherwise, said the Court, would be inconsist- 15-74

---

356 [2009] EWCA Civ 1402; [2010] Ch 467 at [67]–[68].

357 [2013] UKPC 17; [2014] A.C. 366.

358 [2013] UKPC 17; [2014] A.C. 366 at [63] and [152]; citing Isaacs J in *Varawa v Howard Smith Co Ltd* (1911) 13 C.L.R. 35 at 91 (High Court of Australia).

359 *JSC BTA Bank v Ablyazov* [2011] EWHC 1136 (Comm); [2011] 1 W.L.R. 2996.

360 *Broxton v McClelland* [1995] E.M.L.R. 485.

361 (1698) 12 Mod. 208; see para.15-06.

362 *Quartz Hill Consolidated Gold Mining Co v Eyre* (1883) 11 Q.B.D. 674 (paying extra costs is no legal damage); *Wiffen v Bailey and Romford UC* [1915] 1 K.B. 600 at 607 and 610. See, however, *Bradlaugh v Newdegate* (1883) 11 Q.B.D. 1 (where Lord Coleridge CJ thought the damages ought to be "the penalty and all costs"); and *Foxall v Barnett* (1853) 2 E. & B. 928; 118 E.R. 1014, although in this case the damages recovered arose directly from the act complained of, and damages were awarded for the expenses of quashing a coroner's inquisition. In *Berry v British Transport Commission* [1961] 1 Q.B. 149; [1962] 1 Q.B. 306 CA at 319–333, the rule was reviewed by Devlin LJ and the Court of Appeal refused to extend the civil rule to costs in criminal cases; see para.15-14.

363 [2013] UKPC 17; [2014] A.C. 366.

364 [2009] EWCA Civ 1402; [2010] Ch 467.

365 See para.15-06.

ent with the approach taken in *Quartz Hill*[366] and *Gregory v Portsmouth City Council*.[367] Lord Wilson in *Crawford Adjusters*[368] argued, however, that neither the tort of malicious prosecution nor the tort of abuse of process should be limited to the heads of damage described by Holt CJ in *Savill v Roberts* and that both torts should in future compensate for foreseeable economic losses suffered by the claimant as a consequence of civil proceedings. Reasonable expenditure incurred by the defence of a criminal charge which is not recovered by an award of costs in criminal proceedings has also been regarded as sufficient damage on which to base this cause of action.[369]

6. Vexatious Use of Process

15-75 **Vexatious use of process** It has been held that a process in itself perfectly well founded and proper may amount to a legal wrong if vexatiously and unnecessarily repeated. In *Heywood v Collinge*,[370] the defendant caused the claimant to be arrested (before arrest on mesne process was abolished) in an action commenced in the Exchequer; he did not proceed with that action and the claimant was consequently discharged. He then commenced fresh proceedings in the Queen's Bench in respect of the same cause of action, and again arrested the claimant. Under these circumstances, the court decided that an action might lie in respect of the second arrest without inquiring into the result of the proceedings:

> "If an action is not sustainable under such circumstances, we must be prepared to hold that the process of the court may be abused by a [claimant] for purposes however wanton or malicious. We may suppose the case of a party harassing the defendant under the forms of law by maliciously suing out three writs for the same cause on the same day and successively arresting the defendant on all three of them. In such a case the principle of the law allows an action, though in form it may have some novelty."[371]

So in the case of *Waterer v Freeman*,[372] an action was held to lie against a judgment creditor who, pending an execution, unnecessarily and maliciously seized his debtor's goods under a second writ.

15-76 **Vexatious litigants** Lord Bingham CJ in *Att Gen v Barker (Civil Proceedings Order)*[373] commented that:

> "The hallmark of a vexatious proceeding is in my judgment that it has little or no basis in law (or at least no discernible basis); that whatever the intention of the proceeding may be, its effect is to subject the defendant to inconvenience, harassment and expense out of all proportion to any gain likely to accrue to the claimant; and that it involves an abuse of the process of the court, meaning by that a use of the court process for a purpose or in a way which is significantly different from the ordinary and proper use of the court process."

If, on an application by the Attorney General, the High Court is satisfied that any

---

366 *Quartz Hill Consolidated Gold Mining Co v Eyre* (1883) 111 Q.B.D. 674.
367 [2000] 1 A.C. 419 HL. See para.15-09.
368 [2013] UKPC 17; [2014] A.C. 366 at [77].
369 *Berry v British Transport Commission* [1962] 1 Q.B. 306; and see *Hanrahan v Ainsworth* (1990) 22 N.S.W.L.R. 73 and para.15-14.
370 (1838) 9 A. & E. 268; 112 E.R. 1213.
371 (1838) 9 A. & E. 268; 112 E.R. 1213 at 274, per Coleridge J.
372 (1617) Hob. 205 at 266; 80 E.R. 352 and 412.
373 [2000] 1 F.L.R. 759 at [19].

person has habitually and persistently and without any reasonable ground instituted vexatious legal proceedings the court may order that no legal proceedings shall be instituted by that person in any court without the leave of the High Court and that any legal proceedings instituted by him in any court before the making of the order shall not be continued by him without such leave.[374]

Collusive proceedings in fraud of a third party A person may suffer damage by legal proceedings not immediately directed against him and to which he is not party. If such proceedings are not honest but undertaken with the view of injuring him, the guilty party will not escape his responsibility merely because he succeeded in using a process of law as the instrument of his fraud and malice. In *Smith v Tonstall*,[375] the claimant, a judgment creditor, alleged that the defendant had conspired with the judgment debtor and had seized and removed the goods of the latter under a sham judgment and execution, whereby the claimant had been prevented from obtaining satisfaction of his debts; and it was held that he had a good cause of action. In such a case it is immaterial how the proceedings complained of terminated, because they do not bind the claimant and he had no opportunity of intervening.[376] 15-77

No civil action for perjury It is said that "neither party, witness, counsel, jury or judge can be put to answer civilly or criminally for words spoken in office".[377] Thus there is absolute privilege in an action for defamation[378] and no civil action lies against a witness for perjury at the suit of the person damnified by the false evidence.[379] The immunity applies to most forms of civil action, for example conspiracy to defame,[380] and to a claim for misfeasance in public office.[381] It is, however, distinct from the question of malicious prosecution: "a remedy for malicious prosecution should remain available against those who would be entitled to the benefit of the absolute privilege but who have acted maliciously and without reasonable and probable cause during the investigation process. But that is a quite separate matter as it is the malicious abuse of process, not the making of the state- 15-78

374 Senior Courts Act 1981 s.42; see *Att Gen v Jones* [1990] 1 W.L.R. 859, CA. Once a person has been declared a vexatious litigant no court has power to discharge that order. However, an appeal against the order lies to the Court of Appeal: *Rohrberg v Charkin* (1985) 135 N.L.J. 185; *The Times*, 30 January 1985 CA. See also *Att Gen v Foley* [2000] 2 All E.R. 609; *Att Gen v Covey, Att Gen v Matthews, The Times*, 2 March 2001; *Perotti v Collyer-Bristow (A Firm)* [2004] EWCA Civ 639; [2004] 4 All E.R. 53. See also *Johnson v Perot Systems (Europe) Ltd* [2008] EWHC 3339 (QB): general civil restraint order imposed where J had persistently issued claims and made applications which were entirely without merit. Note also CPR r.3.11 (power of court to make civil restraint orders).

375 (1687) Carth. 3; 90 E.R. 607.

376 cf. *Castrique v Behrens* (1861) 3 E. & E. 709; 121 E.R. 608.

377 *R. v Skinner* (1772) Lofft 55 at 56; 98 E.R. 529 at 530, per Lord Mansfield.

378 See para.21-85. Threats to sue for slander to deter a potential witness from giving evidence may amount to an attempt to pervert the course of justice: *R. v Kellett* [1976] Q.B. 372 CA. In *Westcott v Westcott* [2008] EWCA Civ 818; [2009] Q.B. 407, the Court of Appeal held that absolute privilege for the purposes of a defamation action extended to a case where a potentially defamatory statement (here a complaint) is made to the police, and the statement is not subsequently used in civil or criminal proceedings. It is essential for the privilege to apply to this initial stage, so that complainants can have confidence that they will be immune from subsequent attack.

379 *Hargreaves v Bretherton* [1959] 1 Q.B. 528.

380 *Marrinan v Vibart* [1963] 1 Q.B. 528.

381 *Silcott v Commissioners of Police for the Metropolis* (1996) 8 Admin. L.R. 633 CA; *Gizzonio v Chief Constable of Derbyshire, The Times*, 29 April 1998 (no action for malicious denial of bail).

ment, which provides the cause of action."[382] A claimant unable to establish all the requisite elements to prove malicious prosecution cannot reframe his claim in the tort of misfeasance to bypass the operation of rules of witness immunity.

15-79 The immunity of witnesses in court is treated as necessary in the interests of the administration of justice and is based on public policy.[383] This immunity will extend to a prospective witness in giving proof of evidence before the commencement of the trial, since if the witness could be sued on the basis of his witness statement made before the trial this would undermine the basic immunity given to a witness for evidence given in court.[384] The immunity also extends to statements made out of court which could fairly be said to be part of the process of investigating a crime or a possible crime with a view to prosecution.[385] On the other hand, in *Darker v Chief Constable of West Midlands Police*[386] the House of Lords held that the immunity does not extend to the fabrication of evidence which was to be referred to in a statement of evidence. Although, said Lord Hope, there was force in the argument that for the purpose of the immunity there was no logical distinction between making witness statements and investigation and other preparatory conduct with a view to making the witness statements, the predominant requirement of public policy was that claimants who had suffered a wrong should have a right to a remedy. There was a distinction between what a witness says in court (including what a prospective witness states in a witness statement that he will say in court) and the fabrication of evidence. So, for example, the immunity would apply to a witness who falsely stated in the witness box that a suspect had made an oral confession to him, but would not apply to a witness who, in order to support the evidence he would give in court, fabricated a written note containing an admission that the suspect had not made.[387] The Court of Appeal in *Singh v Reading BC*[388] also indicated that the immunity would only extend to that necessary to prevent the core immunity in relation to the giving of evidence from being outflanked. Similarly, in *Daniels v Chief Constable of South Wales*[389] it was said that concealment and withholding of evidence would be treated in the same way as fabrication of evidence, and that the immunity was essentially a witness immunity which had been subject to certain "limited but necessary extensions".[390] In *Crawford v Jenkins*[391] the Court of Appeal said that there was a fundamental distinction between claims which involved an abuse of the process of a court, including both malicious prosecution

---

382 *Taylor v Serious Fraud Office* [1999] 2 A.C. 177 at 219, per Lord Hope.

383 *Darker v Chief Constable of West Midlands Police* [2001] 1 A.C. 435 at 445–446, per Lord Hope.

384 *Watson v M'Ewan* [1905] A.C. 480 at 487. It is irrelevant whether the witness actually gives evidence based on the witness statement: *Darker v Chief Constable of West Midlands Police* [2001] 1 A.C. 435 at 458.

385 *Taylor v Serious Fraud Office* [1999] 2 A.C. 177.

386 [2001] 1 A.C. 435.

387 [2001] 1 A.C. 435 at 469, per Lord Hutton. "The purpose of the immunity is to protect witnesses against claims made against them for something said or done in the course of giving or preparing to give evidence. It is not to be used to shield the police from action for things done while they are acting as law enforcers or investigators", per Lord Hope at [2001] 1 A.C. 435 at 448.

388 [2013] EWCA Civ 909; [2013] 1 W.L.R. 3052. In this case, it did not apply where the complaint related not to the content of the witness statement (which, it was alleged, had been obtained under pressure by the defendants), but the means by which it had been procured in an action for breach of the claimant's employment contract with the defendants. See also *Smart v The Forensic Science Service Ltd* [2013] EWCA Civ 783; [2013] P.N.L.R. 32 (allegations of deceit and negligence in handling and preparation of exhibits for use in criminal trial not struck out).

389 [2015] EWCA Civ 680.

390 [2015] EWCA Civ 680 at [42].

391 [2014] EWCA Civ 1035; [2016] Q.B. 231; [2015] 1 All E.R. 476.

and malicious procurement of a bench warrant[392]; and claims which involved no such abuse of process. It was right as a matter of both principle and policy that in the former category, where the court itself could not be the subject of an action, a claim should be available against the person who procures the misuse of the court's process. However, in a case in the latter category, where a complainant has procured an arrest without invoking a process of the court and where no prosecution follows, in principle the police who carry out the arrest may be liable and thus there is no reason to depart from the usual witness immunity rule. Thus, the defendant in this case, who made a complaint to the police against her former husband leading to his arrest, was protected by the witness immunity rule. In *Hersi & Co v Lord Chancellor*,[393] it was determined that withholding information in evidence is equivalent to giving misleading evidence, so that any such allegation also falls within the ambit of witness immunity.

There are now important exceptions to this general immunity in the tort of negligence for both advocates[394] and expert witnesses.[395] The court in *Jones v Kaney* believed that a clear distinction could be made between expert witnesses and ordinary witnesses of fact. Unlike the latter who may not even have volunteered to give evidence, a "friendly" expert witness will have assumed a duty to the claimant and this could, therefore, give rise to negligence liability.[396] The immunity of an expert witness from civil suit has also been held by the Court of Appeal not to extend to immunity from *fitness to practise* proceedings. Thus a paediatrician who had given expert evidence at the trial of a defendant charged with the murder of two of her children could be charged with serious professional misconduct before a fitness to practise panel in respect of this evidence, which had since been shown to be seriously flawed.[397] **15-80**

392 *Roy v Prior* [1971] A.C. 470.

393 [2018] EWHC 946 (QB) at [115].

394 *Arthur JS Hall & Co v Simons* [2002] 1 A.C. 615 (see para.9-137).

395 *Jones v Kaney* [2011] UKSC 13; [2011] 2 A.C. 398 (see para.9-42).

396 [2011] UKSC 13; [2011] 2 A.C. 398 at [18] per Lord Phillips PSC.

397 *Meadow v General Medical Council* [2006] EWCA Civ 1390; [2007] Q.B. 462. *Meadow* was discussed without disapproval by the Supreme Court in *Jones v Kaney* [2011] UKSC 13; [2011] 2 A.C. 398.

Roy v Prior [1971] A.C. 470.

[2018] EWHC [illegible] (QB) [illegible]

CHAPTER 16

WRONGFUL INTERFERENCE WITH GOODS

TABLE OF CONTENTS

1. Introduction

16-01 **Wrongful interference with goods** Despite some simplification, clarification and assimilation for procedural purposes by the Torts (Interference with Goods) Act 1977, the law concerning the protection of interests in chattels remains very complex. Some of its complexities stem from the interplay of principles of property, tort and contract,[1] for it is as much concerned with disputed title to chattels as with their loss, destruction or damage.[2] Much of its complexity, however, stems from history. English law never developed a single wrong of wrongful interference with goods: instead, it developed a congeries of different and often overlapping torts. Thus a defendant wrongfully interfering with a claimant's chattels may be liable for any of three torts[3]: conversion, trespass to chattels, and a tort which will be will be referred to here as "reversionary injury".[4] Before 1978 he could also be guilty of a fourth, detinue; but this was abolished by the Torts (Interference with Goods) Act

---

[1] For an excellent examination of this interplay see A. Weir, *Casebook on Tort*, 10th edn (London: Sweet & Maxwell, 2004), pp.483–487. See too G. Samuel, "Wrongful Interference with Goods" (1982) 31 I.C.L.Q. 357; P. Birks, "Personal Property: Proprietary Rights and Remedies" (2000) 11 K.C.L.J. 1, especially 1–10; P. Cane, *Tort Law and Economic Interests*, 2nd edn (Oxford: OUP, 1996), Ch.2; S. Green, "Understanding the wrongful interference actions" [2010] Conv. 15.

[2] This is because English law, unlike (say) German law (which laconically provides under BGB, art.985, that "the owner may demand the surrender of his property from the person in possession of it"), has no proprietary action equivalent to the Roman *vindicatio*—a point made by Lady Hale in *OBG Ltd v Allan* [2007] UKHL 21; [2008] 1 A.C. 1 at [308]. Instead an owner seeking to recover a chattel from a wrongful possessor who refuses to return it sues in tort for conversion; if he wins he receives either damages reckoned by the value of the goods or a court order for their return. See para.16-23 onwards.

[3] Not to mention negligence as well. A bailor may also have an action for breach of bailment, which arguably ought to be regarded as sui generis: see P. Winfield, *Province of the Law of Tort*, (Cambridge: CUP, 1931), Ch.5; Palmer, *Bailment*, 3rd edn, (London: Sweet & Maxwell, 2009), para.1-048 onwards. This matter of classification may be important: for if breach of bailment is not a tort, it is arguably unaffected by the Torts (Interference with Goods) Act 1977: see N. Palmer, "The Application of the Torts (Interference with Goods) Act 1977 to Actions in Bailment" (1978) 41 M.L.R. 629; and N. Palmer, "The Abolition of Detinue" [1981] Conv. 62; and *Scipion Active Trading Fund v Vallis Group Ltd* [2020] EWHC 1451 (Comm) at [102]–[114].

[4] There is a possible fourth: replevin. It is in desuetude in England (though active in other jurisdictions, e.g. Canada). It is arguably not a tort at all: more a remedy to allow a person to get back his property that has got into the wrong hands. Nevertheless it has some of the characteristics of a tort, including the availability of compensation for the claimant in certain cases. It is briefly noted at para.16-154.

1977.[5] In all these torts, moreover, liability may overlap. If D unlawfully vandalises P's car, he commits trespass; if he steals it, he commits both trespass and conversion. If the car had been let on hire purchase or conditional sale to P by a finance company X, D would in addition commit the tort of reversionary injury against X. Conversely, it may be possible for D to find a way of interfering with P's property without committing any of the above torts. If so, he escapes liability completely.[6] Before dealing with the law in detail, a brief overview is necessary of the various torts concerned, their history and the reforms wrought by the Torts (Interference with Goods) Act 1977.

The torts outlined We begin with trespass,[7] a remedy affording compensation for injury to a chattel in the claimant's possession. It lies for any direct and wrongful interference with possession, and is actionable per se (though the claimant can also recover any loss actually suffered). The essence of conversion, by contrast, lies in the unlawful appropriation of another's chattel. It is a wide tort, covering the deliberate taking, receipt, purchase, sale, disposal or consumption of another's property.[8] Thus, unlike trespass, it covers not merely an interference with the claimant's possessory interest in his chattels but also an injury to his right or title in them. It follows that, in many cases, trespass and conversion overlap: if D takes P's bottle of wine and drinks it, he commits both. But they remain distinct. If D merely moves the bottle from one shelf to another, he commits trespass but not conversion, since there is no appropriation. Conversely, if D is a bailee of the bottle and proceeds wrongfully to drink the contents he commits conversion but not trespass: he has consumed the wine, but has not interfered with P's possession (since P was not in possession at the relevant time). The third tort is reversionary injury.[9] The actions for trespass and conversion suffer from a major gap because they lie only at the suit of a person with possession of goods, or (in the case of conversion) an immediate right to possess them. This means that in certain cases an owner out of possession (say because he has leased his goods to a third party or let them out on hire purchase) cannot recover in either. As a result, he is given an action on the case which allows him to recover any actual loss suffered. This loss was often known as "damage to the reversion"; hence the name "reversionary injury" which is used in this book. 16-02

The former action of detinue, abolished by the Torts (Interference with Goods) Act 1977,[10] also needs a brief mention. It lay at the suit of a claimant having a right to immediate possession for the wrongful detention of his chattel. The wrongful detention was normally, though not invariably, evidenced by the defendant's refusal 16-03

---

[5] The 1977 Act purports to group all these torts together under the rubric "wrongful interference with goods" (see s.1): but this is a matter of nomenclature only. The substantive differences remain.

[6] e.g. *British Economical Lamp Co v Empire, Mile End* (1913) 29 T.L.R. 386 (refusal of landowner to allow claimant to collect property left there: no tort). Sed quaere whether this case is still good law: see para.16-23.

[7] See para.16-132 onwards.

[8] By statute, it has also been extended to encompass one case of inadvertent action, namely where a bailee in breach of duty causes the item bailed to him to be lost or destroyed (Torts (Interference with Goods) Act 1977 s.2(2)).

[9] See para.16-150 onwards.

[10] s.2(1), probably the shortest subsection on record, brusquely states "Detinue is abolished". The tort, however, remains of importance in other common law jurisdictions. For a résumé of the previous law see *Cullen v Barclay* (1881) 10 L.R. Ir. 224; *Fleming's Law of Torts*, 10th edn (Thomson Reuters: Australia, 2012), para.4.50.

to deliver it up on demand; the redress claimed was the return of the chattel or payment of its value, together with damages for its detention.[11] Normally detinue lay only against a defendant who was in possession,[12] but it also extended to make liable a bailee who in breach of his duty to the bailor had alienated or lost the bailed goods (this being on the basis that such a bailee could not invoke his own wrong in order evade his liability to restore his bailor's property[13]). But by 1977 the tort of conversion had expanded in scope to cover almost every case of detinue, save, it seems,[14] that of the bailee who had lost the goods. It merely remained for the 1977 Act to extend conversion to cover this case[15] and abolish detinue entirely.

16-04 **Statutory reform** The Law Reform Committee in 1971[16] recommended replacing detinue, conversion and trespass to chattels by a single new tort of "wrongful interference" to cover intentional acts, done without lawful justification, involving interference with chattels.[17] The proposed new tort would have had the common law characteristics of conversion, though with certain modifications. The resulting Torts (Interference with Goods) Act 1977,[18] however, gave only partial effect to the Committee's recommendations. It abolished detinue,[19] extended conversion to the case where a bailee in breach of duty to his bailor allowed goods to be lost or destroyed, and sought to eradicate some doubts and anomalies affecting conversion and trespass.[20] To facilitate common treatment with regard to remedies and also various procedural provisions,[21] it also by s.1 created the new name of "wrongful interference with goods" to cover: (a) conversion; (b) trespass to goods; (c) negligence so far as it resulted in damage to goods or to an interest in goods; and (d) "any other tort so far as it results in damage to goods or to an interest in goods". But it went no further.

16-05 Thus, contrary to the Law Reform Committee's recommendation no new tort was created apart from the one case of statutory conversion by bailees. However, was been one conceptual change in the character of conversion and of trespass from

---

11 *Rosenthal v Alderton & Sons Ltd* [1946] K.B. 374, citing *Viner's Abridgement*, Vol.8, p.40; Bullen Leake & Jacob's *Precedents of Pleading*, 12th edn (London: Sweet & Maxwell, 1975), pp.358–360.

12 Hence the action savoured as much of contract and property as of tort: see *Broadbent v Ledward* (1839) 11 A. & E. 209; *Gledstone v Hewitt* (1831) 1 C. & J. 565; *Bryant v Herbert* (1878) 3 C.P.D. 189 and 389.

13 *Reeve v Palmer* (1858) 5 C.B. (N.S.) 84 at 93; *Jones v Dowle* (1841) 9 M. & W. 19; *Ballet v Mingay* [1943] K.B. 281. For an action of detinue to succeed against a bailee whose bailment had determined a demand before action brought was essential in order to establish a wrongful withholding: *Cullen v Barclay* (1881) 10 L.R. Ir. 224.

14 The Law Reform Committee believed this to be so: 18th Report (1971) Cmnd.4774, s.8. In *Howard E Perry & Co Ltd v British Railways Board* [1980] 1 W.L.R. 1375 at 1380-1381, Megarry VC, who had incidentally been a signatory of that report, agreed.

15 Torts (Interference with Goods) Act 1977 s.2(2).

16 See its 18th Report on "*Conversion and Detinue*" (1971) Cmnd.4774.

17 Unintended acts involving such interference would be actionable, if at all, under the existing law of negligence.

18 For comments or summaries, see N. Palmer, "The Application of the Torts (Interference with Goods) Act 1977 to Actions in Bailment" (1978) 41 M.L.R. 629; and N. Palmer, "The Abolition of Detinue" [1981] Conv. 62; J. Thornely, "New Torts for Old?" [1977] C.L.J. 248-251; G. Samuel, "Wrongful Interference with Goods" (1982) 31 I.C.L.Q. 357.

19 s.2(1). See N. Palmer, "The Abolition of Detinue" [1981] Conv. 62.

20 ss.10, 11.

21 ss.4–9.

purely personal to quasi-proprietary actions. This results from the new availability, in actions for any form of "wrongful interference" where the defendant is in possession or control of the goods, of orders for specific restitution or for redelivery of the goods or payment of damages representing their value. Previously specific restitution had been exclusive to detinue, with the other torts giving rise to damages only.

2. CONVERSION[22]

History: conversion and trover Conversion (sometimes still referred to as "trover"[23]) arose as an action on the case to fill the gaps left by trespass and detinue.[24] The essence of the wrong was the unauthorised dealing with the claimant's chattel so as to question or deny his title to it.[25] 16-06

(a) Forms of conversion

Forms of conversion Apart from the case of a bailee who in breach of duty to his bailor allows the goods bailed to become lost or destroyed, which is now made conversion by s.2(2) of the 1977 Act, conversion is an act of deliberate dealing with a chattel in a manner inconsistent with another's right whereby that other is deprived of the use and possession of it.[26] As will appear,[27] the defendant need not intend to question or deny the claimant's rights; it is enough that his conduct is inconsistent with those rights. 16-07

It is not possible to categorise exhaustively all modes of conversion,[28] for while some acts are necessarily an absolute abrogation of the claimant's rights and deprive 16-08

---

[22] See generally S. Douglas, "The Nature of Conversion" [2009] C.L.J. 198; S. Green & J. Randall, *The Tort of Conversion* (2009).

[23] Because until the Common Law Procedure Act 1852 the claimant alleged a fictitious casual "finding" (Fr. *trouver*) by the defendant of his property and its subsequent appropriation. See *Glyn, Mills & Co v East & West India Dock Co* (1880) 6 Q.B.D. 475, 490 (Bramwell LJ).

[24] C. Fifoot, *History and Sources of the Common Law* (1949), Ch.6; Simpson, "The Introduction of the Action on the Case for Conversion" (1959) 75 L.Q.R. 364; J. Barton, "Remedies for Chattels" in E. Ives and A. Manchester (eds), *Law, Litigants and the Legal Profession* (1983), pp.30–38.

[25] Or, as Douglas puts it, the exclusion of the claimant from use or possession of his goods. See S. Douglas, "The Nature of Conversion" [2009] C.L.J. 198, 209.

[26] This was accepted by the Court of Appeal as accurately summarising the tort of conversion in *Kuwait Airways Corp v Iraqi Airways Co (Nos 4 & 5)* [2002] UKHL 19; [2002] 2 A.C. 883 at [414]–[438]. See too Lord Nicholls in the same case at [39]: "In general, the basic features of the tort are threefold. First, the defendant's conduct was inconsistent with the rights of the owner (or other person entitled to possession). Second, the conduct was deliberate, not accidental. Third, the conduct was so extensive an encroachment on the rights of the owner as to exclude him from use and possession of the goods." In addition, note the very careful judgment of Allsop P. in *Bunnings Group Ltd v CHEP Australia Ltd* [2011] NSWCA 342; (2012) 82 N.S.W.L.R. 420 at [124]: "The essential elements, or basic features, [of conversion] involve an intentional act or dealing with goods inconsistent with or repugnant to the rights of the owner, including possession and any right to possession. Such an act or dealing will amount to such an infringement of the possessory or proprietary rights of the owner if it is an intended act of dominion or assertion of rights over the goods".

[27] See para.16-75.

[28] "I have frequently stated that I never did understand with precision what was a conversion": Bramwell LJ in *Hiort v L & NWR* (1879) 4 Ex. D. 188 at 194. See too Lord Nicholls in *Kuwait Airways Corp v Iraqi Airways Co (Nos 4 & 5)* [2002] UKHL 19, [2002] 2 A.C. 883 at [39]: "Conversion of goods can occur in so many different circumstances that framing a precise definition of universal application is well nigh impossible."

him of the whole value of his interest in the goods, there may be others where the courts retain a degree of discretion in deciding whether those acts amount to a sufficient deprivation. Nevertheless the principal ways in which a conversion may take place can be set out under the following headings, dealt with more fully below:

(i) when property is wrongfully taken or received by someone not entitled to do so;
(ii) when it is wrongfully parted with;
(iii) when it is lost by a bailee in breach of his duty to the bailor;
(iv) when it is wrongfully sold, even without delivery, so as to pass good title to the buyer;
(v) when it is wrongfully retained;
(vi) when it is wrongfully misused or destroyed; and
(vii) when the defendant, without physically interfering with it, wrongfully denies access to it to the claimant.

Where a collection of individual items is alleged to have been converted by some act short of outright taking, the question of the defendant's liability should generally be answered in the light of his treatment of the items as a whole, rather than piecemeal in relation to each component part. Thus in *Kuwait Airways Corp v Iraqi Airways Co*[29] where the claimants' fleet of ten airliners was unlawfully expropriated by the defendants, it was held by the Court of Appeal that what was in issue was the defendants' actions in relation to the fleet generally rather than as regards individual aircraft.[30]

(i) Conversion by taking or receiving property

16-09 **Intention to exercise dominion** Anyone who without authority receives or takes possession of another's goods with the intention of asserting some right or dominion over them, or deals with them in a manner inconsistent with the right of the true owner is prima facie guilty of conversion; provided there is an intention on the part of the person so dealing with them to negative the right of the true owner or to assert a right inconsistent therewith.[31] A thief, therefore, commits conversion, as does a person purporting to exercise a lien he does not have[32]; not to mention a person who buys goods which turn out not to have belonged to the seller[33] and a seller of goods who, having dispatched them, wrongfully retakes them from the carrier (even temporarily).[34]

16-10 The taking must, however, be accompanied by an intention to exercise permanent or temporary dominion: if it is not, it may be a trespass, but is no conversion. Atkin LJ put the difference thus:

"An act of conversion differs from mere trespass inasmuch as the former must amount

---

29 [2001] 3 W.L.R. 1117; [2001] 1 Lloyd's Rep. 161.

30 This point was not challenged on a subsequent appeal to the House of Lords at [2002] UKHL 19; [2002] 2 A.C. 883.

31 *Lancashire & Yorkshire Ry Co v MacNicoll* (1919) 88 L.J.K.B. 601.

32 e.g. *Tear v Freebody* (1895) 4 C.B.N.S. 228.

33 cf. *The Saetta* [1993] 2 Lloyd's Rep. 268 (shipowner taking delivery from charterer of bunkers which in fact belonged to a third party). It is submitted that a person who takes goods on hire from a non-owner is in the same category: cf. *Saleh Farid v Theodorou* unreported 30 January 1992 CA, where this seems to have been assumed.

34 *The Playa Larga* [1983] 2 Lloyd's Rep. 171. cf. *Indian Herbs (UK) Ltd v Hadley & Ottoway Ltd*, unreported 21 January 1999 CA (seller wrongfully retaking under retention of title clause).

to a deprivation of possession to such an extent as to be inconsistent with the right of the owner and evidence of an intention to deprive him of that right, whereas the latter includes every direct forcible injury or act disturbing the possession of the owner, however slight the act may be."[35]

Thus in *Fouldes v Willoughby*[36] the claimant put two horses on a Mersey ferry and paid for their passage. Subsequently the ferryman wrongfully refused to carry them, took them from the claimant and turned them loose on the landing-place. A direction to the jury that this was a conversion was overturned, on the ground that the jury ought to have been asked to consider whether the defendant had intended merely to get rid of the horses from his boat, or alternatively to assert some right or dominion over them.[37] Again, it is submitted that the mere receipt of goods in good faith[38] for repair or storage will not, without more, amount to a conversion; there is no intent to exercise any form of dominion over them.[39] And there is much to be said for treating honest and trivial takings similarly, such as mistakenly removing the wrong hat from a rack.[40] But the distinction can be a narrow one. A case on the other side of the line is *Kuwait Airways Corp v Iraqi Airways Co (Nos 4 & 5)*.[41] Kuwaiti airliners abstracted at gunpoint by an invading Iraqi army were refurbished and repainted by the defendants and then flown as part of their own fleet. The House of Lords had little difficulty in holding that by so acting the defendants had converted the aircraft.[42] It should be noted, however, that the taking or receiving need not be with the intention of acquiring full ownership. It is enough if any interest is claimed, such as a lien,[43] which is inconsistent with the right of the person truly entitled.

Taking and using or interfering with goods A mere transitory exercise of **16-11**

35 *Sanderson v Marsden* (1922) 10 Ll. L. Rep. 467 at 472.

36 (1841) 8 M. & W. 540; see also *Sanderson v Marsden* (1922) 10 Ll. L. Rep. 467.

37 "It has never yet been held that the single act of removal of a chattel independent of any claim over it, either in favour of the party himself or anyone else, amounts to a conversion of a chattel. In the present case, therefore, the simple removal of the horses by the defendant for a purpose wholly unconnected with any least denial of the right of the plaintiff to the possession and enjoyment of them is no conversion." (Lord Abinger at (1841) 8 M. & W. 540, 547). See too *British Midland Tool Ltd v Midland International Tooling Ltd* [2003] EWHC 466 (Ch); [2003] 2 B.C.L.C. 523 (doubts expressed—rightly, it is suggested—whether borrowing and copying compact disc amounted to conversion).

38 Quaere where the receiver knows that the person delivering the goods is acting wrongfully as against the true owner, as where a dishonest garage repairs a car for a thief. It is apprehended that this would amount to conversion. The test of whether ancillary dealings with goods amount to conversion is whether they are "an interference with the property which would not, as against the true owner, be justified, or at least excused, in one who came lawfully into the possession of the goods" (Lord Blackburn in *Hollins v Fowler* (1875) L.R. 7 H.L. 757, 766; followed by Allsop P. in *Bunnings Group Ltd v CHEP Australia Ltd* [2011] NSWCA 342; (2012) 82 N.S.W.L.R. 420 at [149]). Repairs carried out on the orders of a known wrongdoer are neither justified nor excused.

39 See *Barclays Mercantile Finance Ltd v Sibec Developments Ltd* [1992] 1 W.L.R. 1253, 1257 onwards (Millett J).

40 This seems to be accepted in most American jurisprudence: see *Prosser on Torts*, 5th edn, (West Group, 1984) pp.94–95; and cases such as *Blackinton v Pillsbury*, 156 N.E. 895 (1927); and J. Fleming, *The Law of Torts* (10th edn) (Thomson Reuters, Australia), para.4.100.

41 [2002] UKHL 19; [2002] 2 A.C. 883. See A. Tettenborn, "English public policy internationalised - and conversion clarified too" [2002] C.L.J. 502.

42 See [2002] UKHL 19; [2002] 2 A.C. 883 at [39], per Lord Nicholls ("so extensive an encroachment on the rights of the owner as to exclude him from use and possession of the goods").

43 See *Tear v Freebody* (1858) 4 C.B. (N.S.) 228. A similar decision is *Brandeis Goldschmidt Ltd v Western Transport Ltd* [1981] Q.B. 864.

dominion, such as unlawfully "borrowing" or using goods, may still amount to conversion. "If a man takes my horse and rides it and then redelivers it to me nevertheless I may have an action against him, for this is a conversion, and the redelivery is no bar to the action but shall be merely a mitigation of damages."[44] Thus in *Kuwait Airways Corp v Iraqi Airways Co*[45] Iraqi forces unlawfully expropriated a number of Kuwaiti airliners and the defendants' pilots then ferried them from Kuwait to Iraq. This ferrying was assumed all along to amount to a conversion of the aircraft involved.[46] The same goes for taking a car for an unlawful joy-ride[47]; wrongfully removing cattle from a farmer in a misguided attempt to ensure their welfare[48]; and, it seems, for wrongfully sending an opponent's legal papers to one's solicitors for copying.[49] In short, any taking of a chattel for the use of the defendant or a third party potentially amounts to a conversion,[50] and the fact that the defendant did not intend permanently to deprive the owner of his property is of itself not conclusive.[51] It follows that, if a defendant wrongfully takes and uses the chattel of another, and without further default on his part it is lost or damaged before it can be returned to the owner, he is potentially liable for the whole damage.[52] In *384238 Ontario Ltd v R.*[53] the Canadian Federal Court of Appeal held that when the Crown detained stock under the mistaken belief that they had a lien over it, but gave it back three days later when they realised their mistake, they were

---

[44] *Rolle* Ab.tit. Action sur Case, p.5; *Lord Petrie v Heneage* (1701) 12 Mod. 519 at 520, per Holt CJ (unauthorised wearing of another's pearl); *Model Dairy Co Ltd v White* (1935) 41 Arg. L.R. 432; and *Milk Bottles Recovery Ltd v Camillo* [1948] V.L.R. 344 (use by defendants of others' milk bottles for delivery of their own milk). cf. *Penfolds Wines Pty Ltd v Elliot* (1946) 74 C.L.R. 204; and S. Douglas, "The Nature of Conversion" [2009] C.L.J. 189, 203. American authority may be different here, with frequent suggestions that a very transitory use is often said not to be conversion: see *Prosser on Torts*, 5th edn (West Group, 1984), 101; and, e.g. *Jeffries v Pankow*, 229 P. 963 (Ore 1928).

[45] [1995] 1 W.L.R. 1147, appealed to the House of Lords on other grounds: [2002] UKHL 19; [2002] 2 A.C. 883.

[46] In the event the defendants' acts in so doing were held protected by sovereign immunity. But subsequent acts done in relation to the aircraft, not cloaked by sovereign immunity, were held to amount to actionable conversion: *Kuwait Airways Corp v Iraqi Airways Co* [2002] UKHL 19; [2002] 2 A.C. 883.

[47] So held in New Zealand: see *Aitken Agencies Ltd v Richardson* [1967] N.Z.L.R. 65; approved by Allsop J in *Bunnings Group Ltd v CHEP Australia Ltd* [2011] NSWCA 342; (2012) 82 N.S.W.L.R. 420 at [138].

[48] *Tongue v RSPCA* [2017] EWHC 2508 (Ch); [2018] B.P.I.R. 229, especially at [93].

[49] See *White v Withers LLP* [2009] EWCA Civ 1122; [2009] 3 F.C.R. 435. In the Court of Appeal Wilson and Sedley LJJ at [73] and [84] suggested that if the evidence was ultimately admissible in the proceedings this should equally immunise the defendant against liability in tort; Ward LJ at [57]–[58] doubted whether this was so. In *Imerman v Tchenguiz* [2010] EWCA Civ 908; [2011] Fam. 116 at [36]–[53], [116]–[117], the Court of Appeal trenchantly, and it is suggested rightly, upheld Ward LJ's minority view.

[50] per Alderson B in *Fouldes v Willoughby* (1841) 8 M. & W. 540 at 548. See too, per Holt CJ in *Petre v Heneage* (1701) 12 Mod. 519 at 520; *Mulgrave v Ogden* (1590) Cro. Eliz. 219.

[51] *The Playa Larga* [1983] 2 Lloyd's Rep. 171 (person causing ship to sail away with claimant's sugar on board liable even though he took no part in subsequent sale of sugar to third party). The passage in the text (para.21-12 of the 15th edition) was quoted at p.181. See too *Brandeis Goldschmidt Ltd v Western Transport Ltd* [1981] Q.B. 864; and *Tongue v RSPCA* [2017] EWHC 2508 (Ch); [2018] B.P.I.R. 229, referred to above.

[52] This paragraph was approved by Mance J in *Kuwait Airways v Iraqi Airways Co* [1999] C.L.C. 31 (upheld without discussion of the point: [2002] UKHL 19; [2002] 2 A.C. 883).

[53] (1984) 8 D.L.R. (4th) 676. Note that this decision can be supported on an alternative ground: i.e. that the claimant was estopped from asserting his rights.

not liable in conversion. It is submitted, with respect, that this is wrong.[54] The essence of conversion lies in the exercise of dominion contrary to the owner's interest, and the fact that the defendant does not use what he keeps should be irrelevant.[55]

However, it is not every temporary intromission that amounts to conversion. The test is whether the defendant dealt with the goods "as if they were owned" by him[56]; hence if an act in relation to goods would be justified or excusable in a person who knew he was not dealing with his own property, it is not conversion.[57] Defendants exonerated on this basis have included a timber trader who mistakenly took part of someone else's cargo into store hard by a discharged vessel,[58] and a consignee of goods carried on another's pallets who kept the pallets for the time standard in the trade before returning them into circulation.[59] **16-12**

Receipt by way of pledge There was formerly some doubt whether a mere receipt by a pledgee of goods pledged by a wrongdoer was a conversion.[60] This was because a pledgee was regarded as exercising a right only against the pledgor, and not being concerned with the ownership of the goods as such. The 1977 Act now puts the matter beyond doubt by providing that "receipt of goods by way of pledge is conversion if the delivery of the goods is conversion".[61] **16-13**

Taking possession of premises Taking possession of premises in which someone else's goods are deposited is not necessarily a conversion: it is so only if the defendant evinced an intention thereby to exercise dominion over the goods. Thus in *Thorogood v Robinson*[62] the defendant had entered X's land under a writ of possession. He prevented the claimant's servants removing some lime belonging to the claimant. The claimant sued in trover. A decision for the defendant on the ground that the jury had found no intention to deprive the claimant of his property was upheld.[63] Similarly it has been held that a forcible taking possession of premises, under an assignment of a lease, and subsequent refusal to deliver up **16-14**

---

54 This passage was cited by Mance J, without disapproval, in *Kuwait Airways v Iraqi Airways* [1999] C.L.C. 31 (appealed on other grounds: [2002] UKHL 19; [2002] 2 A.C. 883).

55 cf. the position where goods are wrongfully retained after a demand for their return; here the question whether the defendant uses them is irrelevant. See, e.g. *Brandeis Goldschmidt Ltd v Western Transport Ltd* [1981] Q.B. 864.

56 See *ACN 116746859 v Lunapas Pty Ltd* [2017] NSWSC 1583 at [111] ("The mere detention or the mere handling of a plaintiff's goods will not necessarily amount to conversion by a defendant. But once the degree of use amounts to employing the goods as if they were owned, then a conversion is established.") (emphasis added).

57 Conversion must be "an interference with the property which would not, as against the true owner, be justified, or at least excused, in one who came lawfully into the possession of the goods" (Lord Blackburn in *Hollins v Fowler* (1875) L.R. 7 H.L. 757, 766; followed by Allsop P in *Bunnings Group Ltd v CHEP Australia Ltd* [2011] NSWCA 342; (2012) 82 N.S.W.L.R. 420 at [149]). Thus it has been said that mistakenly and momentarily taking the wrong hat from a rack is not conversion: J. Fleming, *The Law of Torts*, 10th edn (Thomson Reuters, 2011), para.4.100.

58 *Sanderson v Marsden* (1922) 10 Ll. L. Rep. 467.

59 *Bunnings Group Ltd v CHEP Australia Ltd* [2011] NSWCA 342; (2012) 82 N.S.W.L.R. 420.

60 *Spackman v Foster* (1883) 11 Q.B.D. 99 suggested it was not, as did the Victorian Court of Appeal in *Sell Your Gold Pty Ltd v Australian Diamond Trading Corporation Pty Ltd* [2018] VSCA 355: the earlier case of *M'Combie v Davies* (1805) 6 East 538 hinted that it was.

61 s.11(2), adopting the recommendation of the Law Reform Committee's 18th Report (1971) Cmnd.4774, para.43.

62 (1845) 6 Q.B. 769.

63 See too *Wilde v Waters* (1855) 24 L.J.C.P. 193; *Wansbrough v Maton* (1836) 4 A. & E. 884.

fixtures contained therein, does not amount to a conversion of the fixtures,[64] unless the defendant subsequently uses or deals with them.[65] Similar principles, it is suggested, apply to the defendant who takes possession of other property, such as a ship, containing chattels belonging to the claimant.[66]

16-15 **Taking by misrepresentation or duress** Procuring property by misrepresentation or fraud does not, it is submitted, amount to conversion unless the misrepresentation is such as to negative any intention to pass property.[67] So too with taking by threats. It is not enough if property is surrendered under a threat of unpleasant consequences. There must be such duress as to be equivalent to a forcible taking,[68] such as threats of violence[69] or possibly economic duress by the threat of a wrongful act.[70]

(ii) Conversion by transfer of property

16-16 **Conversion by delivery** Conversion does not lie for mere negligent loss or damage, even if the goods are in the defendant's hands.[71] However, a person who without authority actually delivers another's goods to a third party by way of sale or gift, or otherwise in a manner adverse to the right of the person really entitled,[72]

---

[64] *Longstaff v Meagoe* (1834) 2 A. & E. 167; cf. *British Economical Lamp Co v Empire, Mile End* (1913) 29 T.L.R. 386. But if there is the right to sever fixtures vested in the claimant, then, though he cannot sue for conversion, he has a special action against the defendant in possession who wrongfully prevents him from exercising his right: *London & Westminster Loan & Discount Co v Drake* (1859) 6 C.B. (N.S.) 798.

[65] *W Hanson (Harrow) Ltd v Rapid Civil Engineering Ltd* (1987) 38 B.L.R. 106. But a mortgagee taking over premises with fixtures in them is apparently under no duty to return them at all, since they simply become part of the realty and hence subject to the security: e.g. *Hobson v Gorringe* [1897] 1 Ch. 182; *Reynolds v Ashby* [1904] A.C. 467.

[66] cf. *The Saetta* [1993] 2 Lloyd's Rep. 268 (bunkers belonging to third party redelivered with chartered ship: here there was a clear intent to exercise dominion, and hence a conversion).

[67] This is implicit in the cheque transfer case of *Hounslow LBC v Jenkins* [2004] EWHC 315 (QB), holding that the transferor could equally not rely on any equitable interest arising out of the mistake. See too *Toronto-Dominion Bank v Carotenuto* (1998) 154 D.L.R. (4th) 627 (A dupes B into providing bank draft in favour of C: no action by B against C for conversion of draft). In *Mitsui OSK Lines (Thailand) Co Ltd v Jack Fair Pty Ltd* [2015] FCCA 558; [2015] Lloyd's Rep. Plus 55 at [66]–[72] the Australian Federal Court expressed the view that a receiver of goods presenting a copy of a bill of lading which, unknown to it, did not in fact authorise delivery to it committed conversion against the carrier. It is suggested that this is incorrect.

[68] *Powell v Hoyland* (1851) 6 Ex. 67. Presumably a taking as a result of a lawful threat is a fortiori not a conversion.

[69] Compare the New South Wales case of *Rosecell Pty Ltd v JP Haines Plumbing Pty Ltd* [2016] NSWCA 112 (purchaser of goods surrendered as a result of serious physical violence liable).

[70] See *Grainger v Hill* (1838) 4 Bing. N.C. 212 (defendants who obtained a ship's register from the claimant, under colour of a wrongful threat to levy execution, liable in conversion).

[71] "If a man finds my garments and suffereth them to be eaten with moths by the negligent keeping of them, no action lieth": *Walgrave v Ogden* (1590) Leon 224. See too *BMW Financial Services Ltd v Bhagwanani* [2007] EWCA Civ 1230 (not conversion negligently to crash car, causing it to be unavailable to owner); and *The Arpad* [1934] P. 189, 232 (Maugham LJ).

[72] This requirement is important. If the owner has in any way consented to the delivery it is not contary to his rights and hence there can be no conversion. For an example, see the Canadian decision in *Lloydminster Credit Union Ltd v 324007 Alberta Ltd* 2011 SKCA 93; (2011) 336 D.L.R. (4th) 699 (claimant authorised a possessor to dispose of goods on the basis that any proceeds to be paid over to it: even if monies not accounted for, no conversion).

is treated differently and is presumptively guilty of a conversion.[73] The same applies to a constructive delivery, as by a transfer on the books of a warehouseman or an endorsement of a document of title,[74] and also where a landowner on whose land chattels are placed excludes the true owner and allows someone else to remove them.[75] A similar analysis should obtain (it is submitted) in the case of a purported sale by a non-owner of goods already in the possession of the would-be buyer.[76] But there must be a delivery of some kind: a mere contract by A to sell B's goods to C is not a conversion unless its effect is ipso facto to deprive B of his title to them under some exception to *nemo dat quod non habet*.[77] So too, it is not conversion merely to allow someone with no title to goods to take them away where the defendant is not himself in possession of them.[78]

In order to be liable under this head, the defendant must take some active part in the delivery of the goods. Thus a broker, acting in good faith merely as a medium of communication between the parties, is unaffected by the lack of lawful authority in his principals to deal with the goods concerned[79]; and a manager of a company who merely processes a wrongful sale by a company is not necessarily liable for that reason alone.[80] But if the defendant does something more than make the contract, for instance if the goods themselves or documents representing them pass through his hands (as with an auctioneer[81]), then if that transfer is unlawful he becomes himself a wrongdoer.[82] The defendant on this assumption cannot be guilty of any wrong by merely giving a temporary custody to some servant or agent, since by so doing he does not alter his position[83]; the wrongful act is done when he purports to give to some stranger, along with the mere possession, some right over the property itself. **16-17**

---

73 *Martindale v Smith* (1841) 1 Q.B. 389.

74 *M'Combie v Davies* (1805) 6 East 538; *Hiort v Bott* (1875) L.R. 9 Ex. 86; *Van Oppen v Tredegars* (1921) 37 T.L.R. 504. And see *Union Credit Bank v Mersey Docks & Harbour Board* [1899] 2 Q.B. 205. cf. the Australian decision in *Toll Holdings Ltd v Stewart* [2016] FCA 256 (issuing electronic delivery orders addressed to bailee).

75 See *Smith (Administrator of Cosslett (Contractors) Ltd v Bridgend CC* [2001] UKHL 58; [2002] 1 A.C. 336, especially at [69]–[70] (contractor's plant and equipment subject to ineffective security in favour of landowner: landowner liable for allowing third party to remove them).

76 *Van Oppen v Tredegars Ltd* (1921) 37 T.L.R. 504; as explained by McNair J in *Douglas Valley Finance Ltd v Hughes* [1969] 1 Q.B. 738, 751.

77 *Lancashire Waggon Co v Fitzhugh* (1861) 6 H. & N. 502; *Consolidated Co v Curtis & Son* [1892] 1 Q.B. 495, 498 (Collins J).

78 Thus in *Ashby v Tolhurst* [1937] 2 K.B. 242, the owners of a car park (who were not bailees) were not guilty of conversion merely because the attendant allowed a thief to drive away a customer's car. The lack of possession in the defendant, it is submitted, distinguishes this case from *Smith (Administrator of Cosslett (Contractors) Ltd) v Bridgend CBC* [2001] UKHL 58; [2002] 1 A.C. 336, above.

79 *National Mercantile Bank v Rymill* (1881) 44 L.T. 767; doubted, but distinguished on the facts, in *RH Willis & Son v British Car Auctions Ltd* [1978] 1 W.L.R. 438. It is submitted, however, that a broker who knowingly arranges the sale of something his principal does not own will be liable to the true owner as a joint tortfeasor.

80 *Odone v Hawarden Services Ltd* [2014] EWHC 1694 (QB), especially at [71] (Norris J).

81 See *RH Willis & Son v British Car Auctions Ltd* [1978] 1 W.L.R. 438. See too cases such as *Delaney v Wallis* (1885) 14 L.R. Ir. 31; *Barker v Furlong* [1891] 2 Ch. 172; *Consolidated Co v Curtis & Son* [1892] 1 Q.B. 495; and *Union Transport Finance Ltd v British Car Auctions Ltd* [1978] 2 All E.R. 385.

82 See *Hollins v Fowler* (1874-75) L.R. 7 H.L. 757 (broker causing delivery of wrongfully-obtained cotton). It should be noted, however, that on the facts the defendant was held also to have taken possession of the goods as a principal, and hence would have been liable in any event).

83 *Canot v Hughes* (1836) 2 Bing. N.C. 448.

16-18 **Transfer conferring a special property** As the unauthorised taking of goods with the intent of thereby asserting a lien or special property is a conversion, so too if A hands over B's goods to C so as to purport to give C a special property in them.[84] Hence an unauthorised act such as pledging goods to a third party, creating a lien over them, or hiring them out to someone else,[85] is a conversion. "If a person take my horse to ride and leave him at an inn that is a conversion; for though I may have the horse on sending for him and paying for the keeping of him, yet it brings a charge on me."[86] But in many transactions there may be implicit consent to the creation of such interests. Thus in cases of long-term hire and hire-purchase, the owner impliedly authorises the hirer to create repairmen's liens, since these are reasonably incidental to the use contemplated[87]; and a carrier may equally be impliedly authorised to store, and thus create a warehouseman's lien over, uncollected goods.[88]

16-19 **Misdelivery by bailee** It is the duty of a bailee, such as a carrier or warehouseman, to deliver the goods with which he is entrusted to or to the order of his bailor. To deliver them to an impostor (e.g. a fraudster presenting a forged bill of lading)[89] or to anyone else[90] is prima facie a conversion. Moreover, the mere fact that delivery is to the owner will not protect the defendant, if the owner in fact had no right to receive the goods. So a carrier commits a conversion if, in breach of contract with his consignor, he delivers to the consignee and thus destroys the former's lien,[91] or if he delivers goods to the consignee without production of the bill of lading where the bill of lading has been pledged to a bank.[92] The duty, however is not absolute. It may in particular be qualified by statute,[93] or by the terms of the bailment; if the bailee acts in accordance with these, he is protected.[94] Thus a sea carrier issuing a bill of lading contracts to deliver to anyone who presents a duly

---

84 See Buller J in *Syeds v Hay* (1791) 4 T.R. 260, 264. Similarly it is a conversion by a carrier to deliver goods to another carrier unless the defendant is authorised to make a subcontract: *Garnham, Harris & Elton Ltd v Alfred W Ellis (Transport) Ltd* [1967] 1 W.L.R. 940.

85 *Hill v Reglon Pty Ltd* [2007] NSWCA 295.

86 Buller J in *Syeds v Hay* (1791) 4 T.R. 260, 264 (though note that an innkeeper no longer has a lien on a horse: Hotel Proprietors Act 1956 s.2(2)).

87 *Green v All Motors Ltd* [1917] 1 K.B. 625; *Bowmaker Ltd v Wycombe Motors Ltd* [1946] K.B. 505; *Tappenden v Artus* [1964] 2 Q.B. 185. Similar principles doubtless apply to conditional sales, but probably not to gratuitous bailments such as a simple loan: see *Tappenden v Artus* [1964] 2 Q.B. 185, 201 (Diplock LJ).

88 See Males J in *Sang Stone Hamoon Jonoub Co Ltd v Baoyue Shipping Co Ltd* [2015] EWHC 2288 (Comm); [2016] 1 Lloyd's Rep. 320 at [48]–[52] (uncollected iron ore stored in Chinese warehouse by sea carrier).

89 *Motis Exports Ltd v Dampskibsselskabet AF 1912, Aktieselskab* [1999] 1 Lloyd's Rep. 837 (affirmed on other grounds, [2001] 1 Lloyd's Rep. 211). For a more up-to-date example involving electronic delivery and the use of a hacked PIN number, see *Glencore International AG v MSC Mediterranean Shipping Co SA* [2017] EWCA Civ 365; [2017] 2 Lloyd's Rep. 186.

90 *Devereux v Barclay* (1819) 2 B. & A. 702; *Stephenson v Hart* (1828) 4 Bing. 476; *Hiort v London and North Western Ry* (1879) 4 Ex.D. 188. (See, however, the observations of Martin B in *Crouch v Great Northern Ry* (1856) 11 Ex. 742, 756–757.)

91 *Sze Hai Tong Bank v Rambler Cycle Co* [1959] A.C. 576. Similarly with delivery in breach of a valid order to stop in transit: e.g. *Litt v Cowley* (1816) 7 Taunt 169; *Reddell v Union Castle Ltd* (1914) 84 L.J.K.B. 360.

92 *The Stone Gemini* [1999] 2 Lloyd's Rep. 255.

93 e.g. a pawnbroker taking a pledge under a regulated agreement is protected if he surrenders the pawn to a person producing the pawn receipt, even if not entitled to the goods: Consumer Credit Act 1974 s.117(3).

94 *Heugh v London & North Western Ry Co* (1870) L.R. 5 Ex. 51; *M'Kean v M'Iver* (1870) L.R. 6 Ex.

endorsed copy of it; the mere fact that someone else with another copy may have a better right as against the consignor does not make the carrier liable in conversion unless he had notice of the competing claim.[95]

Sale in emergency or where bailor disappears A bailee has an implied power at common law to sell the bailor's goods in the case of real and urgent emergency, and will not be liable in conversion if he does.[96] But this arguably will not protect a bailee who sells goods merely to relieve himself of an unwelcome incumbrance, even if he cannot contact the owner.[97] However, subject to various safeguards, a bailee now has a statutory power to sell the goods (or apply to the court for their sale[98]) if his bailor fails to collect them or give directions for their delivery or cannot be contacted despite the bailee's reasonable efforts. The bailee is then accountable to the bailor for the proceeds of sale less the expenses of sale and any sum due to him from the bailor in respect of the goods.[99] In other cases, for example where goods remain in the hands of a carrier or warehouseman while other parties argue about them at leisure, the court can it seems at common law order sale.[100] 16-20

(iii) Conversion by loss: the case of the bailee

Goods lost or destroyed At common law there could be no conversion where there was no voluntary act. Therefore if a bailee in breach of his duty to his bailor[101] lost goods or allowed them to be destroyed, he could not be sued for conversion,[102] although he might be liable in contract, negligence, detinue or breach of 16-21

36. This may also explain the decision in *Maynegrain P/L v Compofina Bank* [1984] 1 N.S.W.L.R. 258; (1984) 58 A.L.J.R. 389 PC. Goods in a warehouse were pledged to X, who unknown to the warehouseman was acting on behalf of Y. With X's permission the warehouseman disposed of the goods: he was held not liable to Y. See F. Reynolds, "Attornment to agent of undisclosed principal" (1984) 4 O.J.L.S. 434-437.

95 *Glyn, Mills & Co v West India Dock Co* (1880-82) 7 App. Cas. 591.

96 See *Australasian SN Co v Morse* (1869) L.R. 4 P.C. 222; *The Winson* [1982] A.C. 939, 958; *Ridyard v Roberts* unreported 16 May 1980 CA (abandoned livestock).

97 *Sachs v Miklos* [1948] 2 K.B. 23 CA; *Anderson v Erlanger* [1980] C.L.Y. 133. Things may, however, be changing. In *Da Rocha-Afodu v Mortgage Express Ltd* [2014] EWCA Civ 454 and *Campbell v Redstone Mortgages Ltd* [2014] EWHC 3081 (Ch) it seems to have been accepted that a mortgagee taking possession could, as involuntary bailee, be justified in selling goods left behind on the premises on the basis that it had done all that was right and reasonable.

98 Torts (Interference with Goods) Act 1977 s.13.

99 See the Torts (Interference with Goods) Act 1977 ss.12, 13 and Sch.1. Under these provisions both *Sachs v Miklos*, above; and *Munro v Willmott* [1949] 1 K.B. 295 would now be differently decided. In *Taylor v Diamond* [2012] EWHC 2900 (Ch) at [106] Norris J thought it seriously doubtful whether an involuntary bailee could take advantage of this power. It is submitted, however, that his doubts were misplaced. Sections 12 and 13 of the Act refer simply to a "bailee", and why read them down so as to exclude an involuntary bailee, with the perverse effect of treating a person who had goods thrust upon him willy-nilly less favourably than one who has agreed to look after them?

100 See *D'Amico Shipping Italia SpA v Endofa DMCC*, unreported 28 August 2015 QBD (Comm Ct) (tanker stranded off German coast for three months while interested parties argued over whether cargo represented oil previously filched in West Africa).

101 This duty being to take reasonable care of the goods concerned, the bailee bearing the burden of proof of absence of fault. See, e.g. *Bullen v Swan Electric Engineering Co* (1907) 23 T.L.R. 258; *Houghland v RR Low (Luxury Coaches) Ltd* [1962] 1 Q.B. 694; *Port Swettenham Authority v TW Wu and Co (M) Sdn Bhd* [1979] A.C. 580. In addition a bailee misusing the goods or wrongfully failing to return them on time is liable as an insurer: *Mitchell v Ealing LBC* [1979] Q.B. 1.

102 See *The Arpad* [1934] P. 189, 232 (Maugham LJ).

bailment.[103] But under s.2(2) of the Torts (Interference with Goods) Act 1977, introduced to make up for the abolition of detinue as a separate tort, the bailee in such a situation is now liable to his bailor in conversion.[104]

(iv) *Conversion by wrongful but effective sale*

16-22 **Conversion by wrongful but effective sale** A delivery by way of sale on the part of a non-owner, even if ineffective to pass title to the buyer, is a conversion.[105] By contrast, a mere bargain and sale without delivery is not, even if the non-owner purports thereby to transfer title to the would-be buyer.[106] However, there is one exception to this latter rule. If the wrongful sale is effective, despite the absence of delivery, to transfer title to the buyer under one or other of the exceptions to the rule *nemo dat quod non habet*, then the seller does commit conversion vis-à-vis the true owner who is thus deprived of his title.[107] Examples of such sales include cases where the true owner is estopped from denying the possessor's power to pass a good title,[108] or where a hire purchaser sells a vehicle to a bona fide private purchaser.[109]

(v) *Conversion by keeping or refusal to return*

16-23 **Conversion by keeping: demand and refusal** The ordinary way of showing a conversion by unlawful retention of property is to prove that the defendant, having it in his possession,[110] refused to surrender it on demand.[111] Indeed, such a demand is generally a precondition of the right of action for detention[112]: the mere

---

[103] *Ross v Johnson* (1772) 5 Burr. 2825; see too *Heald v Carey* (1852) 11 C.B. 977; and *Volcafe Ltd v Cia Sud Americana de Vapores* [2018] UKSC 61; [2019] A.C. 358 at [9]–[10] (Lord Sumption). Before 1978 the bailee was also liable in detinue: see para.16-03.

[104] He may also be liable in negligence or for breach of bailment.

[105] See para.16-21.

[106] *Lancashire Waggon Co v Fitzhugh* (1861) 6 H. & N. 502; *Consolidated Co v Curtis & Son* [1892] 1 Q.B. 495, 498 (Collins J). A fortiori with a purported lease with no delivery: *Sadcas Pty Ltd v Business & Professional Finance Pty Ltd* [2011] NSWCA 267.

[107] See, e.g. *Delaney v Wallis* (1885) 14 L.R. Ir. 31, 36 (Dowse B) (actually concerning market overt, since abolished by the Sale of Goods (Amendment) Act 1994; but the principle remains).

[108] Sale of Goods Act 1979 s.21(1).

[109] Hire Purchase Act 1964 ss.27-29.

[110] Including possession through a bailee, at least one from whom the defendant is readily able to recover the goods, whether on payment of storage charges or otherwise: *Mainline Private Hire Ltd v Nolan* [2011] EWCA Civ 189; [2011] C.T.L.C. 145. The goods must, however, actually be in the possession of an agent or bailee in order for liability under this head to attach. Thus if a company possesses goods, it does not necessarily do so as agent of the sole shareholder; and if not, the latter cannot be sued for conversion even if he can, but does not, cause the company to deliver them up: *Thunder Air Ltd v Hilmarsson* [2008] EWHC 355 (Ch).

[111] Including deliberately failing to take steps, such as issuing a delivery order, that are necessary to enable the claimant to obtain the goods from an agent of his: *Trafigura Beheer BV v Mediterranean Shipping Co SA* [2007] EWHC 944 (Comm); [2007] 2 All E.R. (Comm) 149 (carrier, having been duped into putting goods at disposal of fraudster, refused to issue delivery order to true owner). The case was subsequently appealed (see [2007] EWCA Civ 794; [2008] 1 All E.R. (Comm) 385), but not on this point.

[112] *Clayton v Le Roy* [1911] 2 K.B. 1031. This was strictly speaking a detinue case, but the principle was stated to apply to conversion too: see at 1052 (Farwell LJ). Note too *General and Finance Facilities Ltd v Cooks Cars (Romford) Ltd* [1963] 1 W.L.R. 644, 649 (Diplock LJ). A letter sent, but not received, will not do: *King v Walsh* [1932] I.R. 178. In so far as demand and refusal is a prerequisite for liability in conversion, it obviously only applies to conversion by keeping: *Cuff v*

unpermitted possession of another's chattel is not as such a conversion of it.[113] Normally, though not exclusively, this form of conversion is used where an owner seeks to recover his goods or their value from a wrongful possessor, there being no proprietary action equivalent to that existing in other systems of law for this purpose.[114] For this reason this head of liability is wide. On principle, any detention clearly adverse to the rights of the owner, such as assertion of a lien that does not exist,[115] will suffice to establish it. It should be noted, however, that the defendant's obligation is normally only to allow the claimant to collect the goods, not to deliver them to him.[116] There is some old authority that where goods have been placed by the owner on the defendant's property the defendant does not commit conversion by merely refusing to allow the owner entry to collect them, provided he does nothing else inconsistent with the owner's rights.[117] But this must be open to some doubt, since otherwise the defendant would be entitled in effect to deprive the owner of the use of his property indefinitely without any right of redress. The better position, it is submitted, is that there should be liability here,[118] with the additional possibility of an injunction to compel the defendant to allow collection.[119]

Refusal to deliver by agent in charge of goods It is no answer for a person who unlawfully refuses to give up property in his custody to say that he was in possession merely as an agent or employee of someone else.[120] However, the potential harshness of this rule is mitigated because it is often the case that an employee or agent is not regarded as in possession of his principal's goods at all.[121] If so he cannot be sued in conversion when he refuses to give them up, though the principal on whose behalf he acts can.[122] **16-24**

Broadlands Finance Ltd [1987] 2 N.Z.L.R. 343.

113 See *Barclays Mercantile Finance Ltd v Sibec Developments Ltd* [1992] 1 W.L.R. 1253, 1257 onwards (Millett J, citing the passage in the text). So, it is submitted, the innocent repairer of a stolen car is not as such a converter.

114 e.g. German Civil Code art.985 ("the owner may demand the surrender of his property from the person in possession of it").

115 See, e.g. *Finlayson v Taylor, The Times,* 14 April 1983 (refusal of access to premises where property was, plus assertion of lien, deemed conversion); *Brandeis Goldschmidt Ltd v Western Transport Ltd* [1981] Q.B. 864.

116 *Capital Finance Co Ltd v Bray* [1964] 1 W.L.R. 323 (demand for return of claimants' car to place specified by claimants technically bad).

117 "Where an outgoing tenant leaves a picture hanging on a wall, the new tenant may refuse to admit the owner of the picture and take it, and may not choose to put himself to the trouble of giving it, but the picture is still the owner's chattel. The question in such a case would be whether the jury could infer from the refusal that the new tenant exercised any dominion over the chattel. If it appears that he had merely said, 'I don't want your chattel, but I shall not give myself any trouble about it,' that would not give the owner an action of trover." (Maule J in *Wilde v Waters* (1855) 24 L.J.C.P. 193). See too *British Economical Lamp Co v Empire, Mile End Ltd* (1913) 29 T.L.R. 386; and N. Palmer, "Title to Goods and Occupation of Land" (1980) 9 Ang-Am. L.R. 279, 281 onwards.

118 cf. *Thorogood v Robinson* (1845) 6 Q.B. 769.

119 Such an injunction was granted, without discussion of the cases mentioned in fn.117 above, in *Howard E Perry & Co Ltd v British Railways Board* [1980] 1 W.L.R. 1375 (steel stockholders get injunction telling defendants to allow them to enter strikebound premises to collect steel).

120 *Cranch v White* (1835) 1 Bing. N.C. 414; *Davies v Vernon* (1844) 6 Q.B. 443.

121 A servant may perhaps hold as a bailee if at such a distance from his master as to have virtual discretion as to how he discharges his duties: F. Pollock & R. Wright, *Possession in the Common Law*, pp.139–140.

122 *Mires v Solebay* (1678) 2 Mod. 242; explained in *Davies v Vernon* (1844) 6 Q.B. 443. See also

16-25 **Demand must be unconditional and specific, and refusal unequivocal** The demand should be unconditional in its terms, though a peremptory demand for the goods or their value will suffice.[123] If the demand is unclear or equivocal, for example because it is merely a request for "immediate commencement of the process to return" goods, it may not be enough.[124] The demand should also be for specific property: a demand for an unspecified part of a larger collection will not do.[125] The refusal must also be unconditional.[126] A person on whom a demand for goods is made may not have them immediately available even though they are under his control; he may be the agent of another, or he may be under the belief that he has himself some right or title to the property. In all these cases he cannot be required to act at a moment's notice, or refuse at his peril.[127] He is entitled to a reasonable time to get the goods into his own hands, and where necessary to consult his principal. So a warehouseman's employee is not liable in conversion if he refuses to give up goods while he checks with higher authority[128]; again, a person in possession of another's goods has the right to a reasonable opportunity to check whether the person asking for them really is entitled to them.[129] On the other hand, a refusal does not cease to be unconditional if the defendant, while admittedly in possession of goods and while not disputing the claimant's right, claims time to do something to the goods other than taking steps towards their return. Thus in *Secretary of State for Defence v Guardian Newspapers Ltd*[130] the defendants were held liable for conversion when they refused to hand over secret documents that had come into their possession before they had obliterated all marks that might identify their source.

16-26 **Delay in complying with demand** A bailee or person in possession of the goods of another must normally deliver them up forthwith on demand. Thus it has been held to be no defence to an action for conversion based on a demand and refusal that the defendant in possession of goods fears unpleasant consequences, such as

---

Alexander v Southey (1821) 5 B. & A. 247 (manager and keyholder of warehouse not a convertor merely because he refused to deliver up goods); *Marshall v Dibble* (1920) 39 N.Z.L.R. 497. But see *Stephens v Elwall* (1815) 4 M. & S. 259.

[123] *Thompson v Shirley* (1793) 1 Esp. 31.

[124] *Schwarzschild v Harrods Ltd* [2008] EWHC 521 (QB). In *Rushworth v Taylor* (1842) 3 Q.B. 699 a demand for the return in its original state of a gun known to have been damaged in the defendant's hands was held insufficiently peremptory: sed quaere.

[125] *Abington v Lipscombe* (1841) 1 Q.B. 766. Where the claimant makes a general demand for more goods than those he is entitled to, but expressly and specifically including those to which he is entitled, a general refusal may prove a conversion: *Greenslade v Evans* (1848) L.T. (O.S.) 124.

[126] *Mires v Solebay* (1678) 2 Mod. 242. In a suitable case refusal may be inferred from simple inactivity in the face of a claim, since otherwise a defendant in possession could stymie conversion proceedings by simply doing and saying nothing: see *R. (on the application of Atapattu) v Home Secretary* [2011] EWHC 1388 (Admin), especially at [60]–[92] (Home Office had unconditionally refused to return a foreign visitor's passport by stonewalling his demands for it). *Schwarzschild v Harrods Ltd* [2008] EWHC 521 (QB), suggesting to the contrary that mere inaction in the face of a demand could not be a refusal, must be regarded as very doubtful.

[127] *Alexander v Southey* (1821) 5 B. & A. 247; *Towne v Lewis* (1849) 7 C.B. 608; *Clark v Chamberlain* (1836) 2 M. & W. 78; *Clayton v Le Roy* [1911] 2 K.B. 1031, 1051.

[128] *Alexander v Southey* (1841) 5 B. & A. 247; cf. *Wilson v Anderton* (1830) 1 B. & A. 450, where the employee was held to have acted unreasonably and was liable. Note the judgment of Scrutton J in *Wetherman v London & Liverpool Bank of Commerce Ltd* (1914) 31 T.L.R. 20.

[129] As in *Clayton v Le Roy* [1911] 2 K.B. 1031. See too *Pillott v Wilkinson* (1864) 3 H. & C. 345.

[130] *The Times,* 16 December 1983, per Scott J; affirmed on different grounds, [1984] Ch. 156; [1985] A.C. 339.

industrial action, if he returns them.[131] Indeed, delay in complying with the demand will not only render the defendant liable in conversion, but will normally make him an insurer of the goods in respect of all subsequent damage on the basis that he is thereafter in breach of bailment. Thus in *Mitchell v Ealing LBC*[132] the defendant council had gratuitously agreed to store the claimant's furniture for a limited time. When the claimant later demanded it, a time and place for delivery were agreed but by mistake the defendants' representative failed to appear. A further date for delivery was arranged but meanwhile the furniture was stolen. It was held that, as a result of the delay in making delivery, the defendants were liable for the loss as insurers.[133]

However, the need for immediate delivery may be qualified in at least two cases. First, in the event of doubt as to the claimant's entitlement the defendant is entitled to a reasonable time to make enquiries. In *Pillott v Wilkinson*[134] the owner of warehoused wine demanded it; the warehouseman, faced with a notice of attachment from a third party, requested a brief delay, but the claimant issued proceedings forthwith. The Exchequer Chamber made it clear that if a defendant had a bona fide doubt as to the claimant's right he had a reasonable time[135] to clear it up.[136] This includes, where appropriate, a reasonable time to take court proceedings such as interpleader or, in the case of property in the hands of the police, proceedings under the Police (Property) Act 1897[137]; and possibly, where court proceedings are necessary to establish his right or discharge a relevant court order, to take those proceedings.[138] Secondly, there may be physical difficulties in delivery, as where the claimant's goods need to be sorted out from other goods to which he is not **16-27**

131 *Howard E Perry & Co Ltd v British Railways Board* [1980] 1 W.L.R. 1375 (threat of strike by carrier's employees). For criticism see N. Palmer, "Conversion off the Rails" (1981) 44 M.L.R. 87.

132 [1979] Q.B. 1. See too *Toor v Bassi* [1999] E.G.C.S. 9.

133 In order to invoke this rule, however, the claimant must positively prove that the goods were lost after the demand. If he cannot do so, strict liability will not apply: *Jerry Juhan Developments Ltd v Arco Tyres Ltd*, *The Times*, 15 January 1999.

134 (1864) 3 H. & C. 345; for other bailee cases, see *Vaughan v Watt* (1840) 6 M. & W. 492; and *Spencer v S Franses Ltd* [2011] EWHC 1269 (QB). See too *Lee v Bayes* (1856) 18 C.B. 599, 607 (Jervis CJ); also *Green v Dunn* (1811) 3 Camp. 215n (defendant unsure of claimant's identity at time of demand).

135 Measured from first serious demand, not necessarily from subsequent solicitor's letter: *Spencer v S Franses Ltd* [2011] EWHC 1269 (QB) (formal demand four years after first request: defendant held to have had ample time).

136 Where a debtor is insolvent, a creditor may be prevented from asserting a lien over his goods without the leave of the court: see s.11 of the Insolvency Act 1986. In such a case it has been suggested that, by analogy with the rule in the text, the creditor may nevertheless detain the goods concerned while he makes an application for leave; see *Bristol Airport v Powdrill* [1990] Ch. 744 at 767, per Woolf LJ. Staughton LJ at 711 left the point open. See too *Vaughan v Watt* (1840) 6 M. & W. 492; *Lee v Bayes* (1856) 18 C.B. 599.

137 *Gough v Chief Constable of the West Midlands* [2004] EWCA Civ 206; *The Times*, 4 March 2004. Similarly, if police have a discretion whether to allow seized goods to be used in evidence by a private prosecutor, they are entitled to a reasonable time to make up their mind: *Scopelight Ltd v Chief of Police for Northumbria* [2009] EWCA Civ 1156; [2010] Q.B. 438 at [54].

138 For example, where a debtor is in administration, a creditor may need court permission to assert a lien: see s.11 of the Insolvency Act 1986. In such a case it has been suggested that the creditor may delay while he applies for leave; see *Bristol Airport v Powdrill* [1990] Ch. 744, 767 (Woolf LJ) (Staughton LJ at 711 leaving the point open). In *Spencer v S Franses Ltd* [2011] EWHC 1269 (QB) at [306]–[312] Thirlwall J, encountering a defendant in possession of a mediaeval tapestry who faced proceedings in England for conversion by failing to surrender it and a US injunction (admittedly unenforceable in England) prohibiting him from parting with it, left it open whether he was entitled to a reasonable opportunity to try to discharge the US order. It is suggested that he should not be so entitled: once it is established that the foreign injunction is ineffective in England, there is no reason to give it any weight.

entitled: in such a case there is much to be said for giving a pro tanto defence.[139] But in any case, once the reasonable time has elapsed, the defendant must hand over the goods. If he does not do so he will be liable in conversion, and in addition the goods will be entirely at his risk thereafter.[140]

16-28 **Other evidence of unlawful keeping** A demand and refusal is not the only form of evidence of an unlawful keeping. There may be a conversion of a chattel by the use and enjoyment of it in a manner altogether inconsistent with the right of the owner. Thus if a person entrusted with the custody of wine in cask bottles it for his own consumption, it would seem there is some evidence of a conversion even though he does not actually drink or sell any of it.[141] In *Falk v Fletcher*[142] the claimant shipped cargo on board the defendant's vessel, but the master refused to give him bills of lading in his own name and sailed with the cargo, ultimately refusing to deliver it to the claimant's agent at the port of destination. It was held that there had been a conversion when the ship sailed. Similarly, it was held in *Kuwait Airways Corp v Iraqi Airways Co (Nos 4 & 5)*[143] that by keeping, painting and refurbishing aircraft belonging to the claimants with a view to future use the defendants had converted them.

16-29 **Refusal to attorn no conversion** A possessor is not liable in conversion merely because he refuses to attorn to the real owner or acknowledge his title. Thus, if a buyer purchases goods in a warehouse he can sue the warehouseman for refusal to deliver them, but not for a mere refusal to enter his name on the books of the warehouse.[144] This is really an aspect of the rule that denial of title is not, without more, a conversion.[145]

(vi) Conversion by destruction or misuse

16-30 **Conversion by destruction** It is conversion deliberately[146] to destroy another's goods without authority: for example, by drinking wine, grinding corn, or smash-

[139] See *Metall Market OOO v Vitorio Shipping Co Ltd* [2013] EWCA Civ 650; [2014] Q.B. 760 at [48]–[49] (Sir Bernard Rix) (steel coils stowed in vessel with many others, and not readily separable).
[140] *Burroughes v Bayne* (1860) 5 H. & N. 296. See too *Mitchell v Ealing LBC* [1979] Q.B. 1, above.
[141] *Philpott v Kelly* (1835) 3 A. & E. 106.
[142] (1865) 18 C.B. (N.S.) 403; *London Jewellers Ltd v Sutton* (1934) 50 T.L.R. 193. cf. *Jones v Hough* (1879) 5 Ex. D. 115, where the facts were the same as *Falk v Fletcher*, save that the goods were delivered to the claimant at the end of the voyage: held, no conversion, since no intent to exercise dominion. This latter case has considerable affinities with *Fouldes v Willoughby* (1841) 8 M. & W. 540, above.
[143] [2002] UKHL 19; [2002] 2 A.C. 883. See too *Tower Hamlets LBC v The London Borough of Bromley* [2015] EWHC 1954 (Ch); [2015] B.L.G.R. 622 (massive and very valuable Henry Moore sculpture, though property of LCC's successor, restored, repaired, remounted and insured by Tower Hamlets: held, sufficient acts of conversion to cause limitation to run in Tower Hamlets' favour).
[144] In *M'Combie v Davies* (1805) 6 East 538, the defendant's name appeared on the books of a bonded warehouse as the owner of certain tobacco. The claimant being the real owner called upon him to give a delivery order. The defendant refused. Lord Ellenborough held that this was no conversion, apparently considering it a mere neglect to acknowledge the claimant's title. The other judges more correctly treated the case as one of demand and refusal.
[145] See para.16-34.
[146] But not negligently, save in the case of the bailee's statutory liability under s.2(2) of the Torts (Interference with Goods) Act 1977, referred to at para.16-21.

ing up a surveillance camera.[147] So too where goods are dealt with so that their identity is destroyed,[148] as with applying a process of manufacture to raw material.[149] But provided the chattel continues to exist as such, any injury done to it, such as cutting planks,[150] may be a trespass but is nothing more.[151]

Use leading to loss The above paragraph dealt with deliberate destruction. There is, however, one authority suggesting that liability may go further, and that any use of a chattel in a way known to be likely to lead to its loss or destruction will amount to a conversion if it is in fact lost as a result. This is *Moorgate Mercantile Co Ltd v Finch*,[152] where the Court of Appeal held the hire-purchaser of a car liable in conversion to a finance company when it was confiscated after he was caught using it for smuggling. It was enough, said Danckwerts LJ, that he used the car in such a way that confiscation was likely, even if undesired.[153] It is submitted, however, that the result in *Finch* is open to some doubt. It is difficult to characterise the defendant's actions in *Finch* as other than negligence leading to loss, for which conversion does not lie at common law.[154] Indeed, in a later case, *BMW Financial Services Ltd v Bhagwanani*,[155] where a defendant borrowed a car belonging to a finance company, negligently crashed it abroad and left it at a garage for repair, the Court of Appeal was adamant that there had been no conversion. Although an attempt was made to distinguish *Finch*,[156] it seems difficult to see much difference between the cases. It is respectfully suggested that the latter is the better authority.[157] Of course, where (as in *Finch*) the defendant is a bailee and the claimant a bailor, such liability may now be predicated on the statutory cause of action in conversion against a bailee under s.2(2) of the Torts (Interference with Goods) Act 1977.[158] But where he is not, it is suggested that the better view is that there is no conversion. 16-31

(vii) Conversion by wrongful denial of access

Conversion by denial of the benefit of goods The forms of conversion outlined above all involve misdealings by someone who has, at one time or another, had possession of the goods concerned. But they are not exhaustive.[159] There may be a conversion of goods, even though the defendant has never been in possession of 16-32

---

147 *Pelletier v Collins* 2014 SKCA 130; (2014) 446 Sask. R. 303. See too the British Columbia case of *Insurance Corp. of British Columbia v Alexander* 2016 BCSC 1108 (trashing car in course of riot).

148 *Heald v Carey* (1852) 11 C.B. 977.

149 19a Com.Dig. Action Trover E. See too *Richardson v Atkinson* (1723) 1 Stra. 576 (watering wine).

150 *Simmons v Lillystone* (1853) 8 Ex. 431.

151 In *Naylor v Hutson* [1994] F.S.R. 63 it was suggested that it was conversion for the possessor of a car to strip it of its cherished registration number so that the number could be transferred to his own vehicle. But this, it is submitted, is doubtful. However great the loss caused by such operations, changing a vehicle's registration number hardly amounts to destroying it.

152 [1962] 1 Q.B. 701.

153 [1962] 1 Q.B. 701, 706.

154 e.g. *Rushworth v Taylor* (1843) 3 Q.B. 699; *The Arpad* [1934] P. 189 at 232, per Maugham LJ; *BMW Financial Services Ltd v Bhagwanani* [2007] EWCA Civ 1230. See too the ancient case of *Walgrave v Ogden* (1590) 1 Leon 224.

155 [2007] EWCA Civ 1230.

156 On the basis that in that case there had been a deliberate criminal use of the car, whereas in the *BMW* case there was mere negligent damage and a subsequent reasonable deposit for repair: see [2007] EWCA Civ 1230 at [17]–[19].

157 As suggested in S. Douglas, "The Nature of Conversion" [2009] C.L.J. 198, 217.

158 See para.16-21.

159 Megarry VC acknowledged the force of this observation in *Howard E Perry & Co Ltd v British*

them or physically handled them at all, if he has in some way dealt with them so as to deny the right of the owner, or assert a right inconsistent with it.[160] So it may be conversion for an occupier peremptorily to refuse access to a lessor of chattels brought onto the property by a now-bankrupt lessee,[161] or for a joint occupier to lock his co-occupier out, thereby depriving the latter of the use of his possessions.[162] Again, in *Oakley v Lyster*[163] the claimant owned hardcore deposited on X's land. When the defendant, who did not have possession of the land or the hardcore, prevented the claimant from collecting it, he was held liable in conversion. In *Kuwait Airways Corp v Iraqi Airways Co*,[164] the Iraqi army forcibly abstracted a fleet of aircraft from Kuwait and caused them to be flown to Iraq with a view to their transfer to the defendants. The defendants' actions in refurbishing the aircraft, repainting them in their own colours, and insuring and registering them in their own name were held by the House of Lords to amount to conversion. Indeed, in a subsequent case even less was found sufficient: in *Blue Sky One Ltd v Blue Airways LLC*[165] a mere change in an aircraft's registration was apparently regarded as sufficient interference.

16-33 However, this form of conversion is subject to limits. Merely preventing a claimant from using his chattel without interfering with access to it, or possession of it, is not enough. Thus in *Club Cruise Entertainment & Travelling Services Europe BV v Department for Transport*[166] an over-zealous official who detained a ship in port without any power to do so was held not to have converted the vessel: her owners remained in possession and retained unfettered access to her. It is true that some difficulty is caused in this connection by an earlier decision of McNair J[167] that a defendant was guilty of conversion of lorries when he surreptitiously caused them to be stripped of their haulage licences but otherwise did not interfere at all with the owner's rights to possess or drive them. But that case seems hard to reconcile with principle or with the result in *Club Cruise*[168]; and it is respectfully suggested that it should now be regarded as highly doubtful.

16-34 **Denial of title** All the above cases involved some dealing, or purported dealing, with the goods by the defendants. It was sometimes thought that the rule went further, and that a mere flat denial of the claimant's title could equally give rise to

Railways Board [1980] 1 W.L.R. 1375 at 1380B.

[160] *Hiort v Bott* (1875) L.R. 9 Ex. 86; *Van Oppen & Co Ltd v Tredegars Ltd* (1921) 37 T.L.R. 504; *Bryanston Leasings Ltd v Principality Finance Ltd* [1977] R.T.R. 45 (hirer's failure to return lost vehicle registration documents or co-operate in replacement held to be conversion of claimant's cars, because of consequent difficulties).

[161] *London Trocadero Ltd v Family Leisure Holdings Ltd* [2012] EWCA Civ 1037 at [36]–[40] (Davis LJ, approving the statement of the law in the present work).

[162] *BVC v EWF* [2019] EWHC 2506 (QB) at [216]–[217].

[163] [1931] 1 K.B. 148. But it may well be that a defendant cannot be liable under this head where he has no access to, or other control whatever over, the relevant land: see the Australian decision in *Black Diamond Group Pty Ltd v Manor of Maluka Pty Ltd* [2014] QSC 219; [2015] 1 Qd R. 180 at [44].

[164] [2002] UKHL 19; [2002] 2 A.C. 883.

[165] [2009] EWHC 3314 (Comm).

[166] [2008] EWHC 2794 (Comm); [2009] 1 Lloyd's Rep. 201.

[167] *Douglas Valley Finance Co Ltd v S Hughes (Hirers) Ltd* [1969] 1 Q.B. 738.

[168] Flaux J in *Club Cruise* purportedly distinguished the earlier case on the basis that there, there *had* been a "wrongful assumption of ownership by the defendants and a denial of the plaintiffs' right" (see [2008] EWHC 2794 (Comm); [2009] 1 Lloyd's Rep. 201 at [52]). With respect, this seems highly unconvincing.

liability.[169] However, s.11(3) of the Torts (Interference with Goods) Act 1977, stating succinctly that "denial of title is not of itself conversion", now puts the matter beyond argument. Mere denial of title, however absolute, is not of itself a conversion if unaccompanied by any other "dealing" with the goods.

(b) Subject matter of conversion

General At common law, conversion lies in respect of dealings with any corporeal personal property (including tickets,[170] papers[171] and title deeds[172]). The Torts (Interference with Goods) Act 1977, having introduced the concept of "wrongful interference with goods", defines "goods" in s.14 as including "all chattels personal other than things in action and money".[173] It is suggested, however, that this may not be an infallible guide as to the common law position on what kinds of property are amenable to conversion. 16-35

Tangible and intangible property Until recently it was not entirely clear whether conversion could be applied to intangible property as well as to chattels.[174] However, in *OBG Ltd v Allan*[175] a majority of the House of Lords settled the matter definitively, holding that there could as a matter of law be no conversion of incorporeal assets, and hence that defendants who had appropriated to themselves the benefits of certain contractual rights vested in the claimants could not be sued as converters. Similar reasoning has been applied in other cases to deny the convertibility of other intangible assets, such as copyright,[176] information,[177] and documents stored electronically on a computer's hard disk which are alleged to have derived from the claimants or been generated on an email account provided by them.[178] Nevertheless, it would seem that there is in some cases a sui generis ac- 16-36

[169] For the pre-1977 cases, which were not unanimous, see, e.g. *M'Combie v Davies* (1805) 6 East 538 (Lord Ellenborough); *Oakley v Lyster* [1931] 1 K.B. 148, 150 (Scrutton LJ); *England v Cowley* (1873) L.R. 8 Ex. 126; *Hartley v Moxham* (1842) 3 Q.B. 701; *Van Oppen v Tredegars* (1921) 37 T.L.R. 504. cf. *Wansbrough v Maton* (1836) 4 A. & E. 884, and generally N. Palmer, "Title to Goods and Occupation of Land: A Conflict of Interests" (1980) 9 Ang.-Am. L.R. 279.

[170] *Rugby Football Union v Viagogo Ltd* [2011] EWHC 764 (QB); [2011] N.P.C. 37 at [46] (upheld on other grounds: [2012] UKSC 55; [2012] 1 W.L.R. 3333) (ticket touts' activities concerning rugby match admission tickets could be conversion, even if paper on which tickets printed of negligible value).

[171] For example, cheques and other forms of commercial paper; see para.16-38.

[172] See para.16-40.

[173] As in the Sale of Goods Act 1979 s.61(1).

[174] This had been largely a matter of assumption in England, with some exiguous authority against the extension (e.g. *Stewart v Engel* [2000] B.C.C. 741). Australian authority was also sceptical: see *Hoath v Connect Internet Services Pty Ltd* [2006] NSWCA 158; (2006) 229 A.L.R. 566, 594 (domain name). American authority had been more equivocal, with some cases allowing suits for conversion of intangibles. One colourful example was *Kremen v Cohen*, 337 F.3d 1024 (2003) (fraudulent takeover of internet domain "*www.sex.com*" could amount to conversion).

[175] [2007] UKHL 21; [2008] 1 A.C. 1. This result is criticised in S. Green & J. Randall, *The Tort of Conversion* (2009), pp.128 onwards; and in S. Green, "Theft and conversion - tangibly different?" (2012) 128 L.Q.R. 564.

[176] *Stewart v Engel* [2000] B.C.C. 741. cf. *Environment Agency v Churngold Recycling Ltd* [2014] EWCA Civ 909; [2015] Env. L.R. 13 (copies of documents unlawfully taken).

[177] *Murphy v Electoral Commission* [2019] EWHC 2762 (QB); [2020] 1 W.L.R. 480 at [50].

[178] *Thunder Air Ltd v Hilmarsson* [2008] EWHC 355 (Ch); *Capita Plc v Darch* [2017] EWHC 1248 (Ch); [2017] I.R.L.R. 718 at [67]–[74] (emails written on employer's hardware, allegedly concerned with unlawful diversion of business). See too *Your Response Ltd v Datateam Business Media Ltd*

tion, distinct from conversion, for knowing misdealings with intangible assets of value which cause loss to those entitled to the benefit of those intangibles.[179]

16-37 **Money** It was often said that at common law conversion could never lie in respect of money unless it was "in a bag" or otherwise differentiated. But this was never entirely accurate.[180] The true rule is that no action lies for conversion in respect of dealings with money once either it has passed into currency or has been taken in good faith for value. In other cases there is no reason why conversion should not be available.[181] Thus where A steals B's cash and pays it to C, C cannot be sued in conversion.[182] A fortiori, if a person simply receives a sum to be repaid on request the property in it passes, and his only liability is for the debt. But a thief of cash is, it seems, liable to an action in conversion,[183] as is the finder of a lost banknote,[184] and the defendant who, having undertaken to return or hand over specific coins entrusted to him, converts them to his own use.[185] The reason, it is suggested, is that in none of these cases has the cash passed into general currency between the time it left the claimant's hands and its arrival in the defendant's. It is further suggested that with regard to the statutory definition of "goods" in the 1977 Act[186] the exclusion of "money" will be confined to money as currency in the above sense.[187] One further point ought to be added. Even where an action in conversion is barred because what the defendant handled was money that has passed into currency, the claimant may nevertheless have a valid action for money had and received in so far as he can trace his money into the defendant's hands, and the latter did not take it in good faith and for value.[188]

16-38 **Negotiable instruments and securities** Cheques, negotiable instruments and other securities, such as guarantees, insurance policies and bonds, considered as corporeal property, are simply pieces of paper. Their sole value is as choses in action, which cannot as such be converted.[189] If, however, such physical documents

[2014] EWCA Civ 281; [2015] Q.B. 41 (partly on basis that intangible material in database not subject to conversion, no possibility of having a lien over it).

179 See *Armstrong DLW GmbH v Winnington Networks Ltd* [2012] EWHC 10 (Ch); [2013] Ch. 156 (misappropriation of EUAs, an EUA being a form of intangible but very valuable EU licence to pollute). See L. Chambers & C. Buckingham, "Intangible Property and Proprietary Restitution in the High Court" [2013] L.M.C.L.Q. 296.

180 See the antique cases of *Hall v Dean* (1600) Cro. Eliz. 841; *Draycot v Piot* (1601) Cro. Eliz. 818; and *Kinaston v Moor* (1627) Cro. Car. 89.

181 See D. Fox, *Property Rights in Money* (2008), paras.9.03-9.12.

182 *Lipkin Gorman v Karpnale Ltd* [1991] 2 A.C. 548, 559 (Lord Templeman), and the authorities there cited.

183 *Hall v Dean* (1600) Cro. Eliz. 841; (semble) *Thomas v Whip* (1714) Buller N.P. 130a; cf. *Miller v Race* (1758) 1 Bur. 452 at 457.

184 *Burn v Morris* (1834) 2 Cr. & M. 579; and see *Miller v Race* (1758) 1 Bur. 452 at 457.

185 *Orton v Butler* (1822) 5 B. & A. 652.

186 s.14(1).

187 cf. *Moss v Hancock*, above where a £5 coin which was a coin of the realm was regarded as having been sold as a curio. As to foreign notes and coins, it is suggested that, in so far as they have been used as currency, they fall to be treated in the same way as sterling.

188 As in, e.g. *Lipkin Gorman v Karpnale Ltd* [1991] 2 A.C. 548. See too, e.g. *Clarke v Shee* (1774) 1 Cowp. 197; *Foster v Green* (1862) 7 H. & N. 881; *Wookey v Pole* (1820) 4 B. & A. 1, 7 (Best J). See generally D. Fox, *Property Rights in Money* (2008), Ch.8.

189 See, for example, *Bank of Montreal v Tourangean* (1980) 118 D.L.R. (3d) 293 (assignee of company's book-debts cannot sue for conversion of a cheque payable to the company, even though debt embodied in the cheque is a book-debt. The assignee may own the intangible book-debts: but

are unlawfully dealt with,[190] as where a cheque is stolen and paid into a bank account controlled by the thief, the person entitled to them may recover full damages based on their value as choses in action.[191] This principle extends to any document which is specially prepared in the ordinary course of business as evidence of a debt or obligation, thus including (for example) share certificates[192] and trading stamps.[193] Nevertheless, it applies only in so far as the document is, in fact, a valid security. Thus no substantial recovery is available in respect of a cheque which, when converted, had been avoided as a result of an unauthorised alteration.[194] The measure of damages is prima facie the value of the debt or obligation of which the document is evidence.[195] But it is suggested that this can only be a presumptive rule.[196]

Realty when severed There can be no conversion of land.[197] But if a portion of realty is severed and taken away, the owner, instead of suing in respect of the injury to be realty, may elect to treat the severed portion as his chattel and sue for its conversion. In this way a remedy may be obtained for coal wrongfully worked, 16-39

---

he is not the legal owner of the tangible cheque). True, in *Voyer v CICB* [1986] 1 W.W.R. 174, a bank was held liable in conversion when it wrongfully set a customer's credit balance off against an alleged indebtedness. It is submitted that this is wrong, and that it would have been more appropriate for the customer to sue for a declaration that his account had been wrongly debited

190 This raises some issues in regard to the modern practice of banks imaging cheques and then destroying them, rather than presenting them in paper form. It is thought, however, that a bank which took a cheque, imaged it and then presented the image for payment would remain liable for converting the original cheque.

191 e.g. *Alsager v Close* (1842) 10 M. & W. 576; *Waston v McLean* (1858) E.B. & E. 75; *Midland Bank Ltd v Eastcheap Dried Fruit Co* [1961] 2 Lloyd's Rep. 251; *Ernest Scragg & Sons v Perseverance Banking & Trust Co* [1973] 2 Lloyd's Rep. 101; *International Factors Ltd v Rodriguez* [1979] Q.B. 351. The claimant must of course prove his entitlement here as elsewhere: see *Surrey Asset Finance Ltd v National Westminster Bank Plc*, *The Times,* 30 November 2000 (drawer cannot sue for conversion of cheque once delivered to payee).

192 e.g. *MCC Realisations Ltd v Lehman Bros* [1998] 4 All E.R. 675 (share certificates: action failed for other reasons); *Malkins Nominees Ltd v Société Financière Mirelis SA* [2004] EWHC 2631 (Ch) (share certificate plus transfer form). See too the Singapore decision in *AAHG LLC v Hong Hin Kay Albert* [2016] SGHC 274.

193 cf. *Building and Civil Engineering Holidays Scheme Management Ltd v Post Office* [1966] 1 Q.B. 247 (statutory cause of action, but measure of damages face value as in tort). Similar principles no doubt extend to tickets and tokens of various kinds evidencing valuable rights other than debts (e.g. travel tickets, credit cards, club membership cards), although assessment of damages may be more difficult; see (1971) Cmnd.4774, paras 90-91.

194 *Smith v Lloyds TSB Bank Plc* [2001] Q.B. 541; Hare [2001] C.L.J. 35. The position is probably the same with forged cheques: see *Mathew v Sherwell* (1810) 2 Taunt. 439; and M. Brindle (ed.), *Law of Bank Payments*, 5th edn, (London: Sweet & Maxwell, 2017), para.6-137.

195 *Alsager v Close* (1842) 10 M. & W. 576, 584 (Abinger CB); *Bavins, Junr, & Sims v London & South Western Bank* [1900] 1 Q.B. 270, 275 (A.L. Smith LJ). See too *Malkins Nominees Ltd v Société Financière Mirelis SA* [2004] EWHC 2631 (Ch) (share certificates).

196 The true rule, it is submitted, is that the claimant may recover only in so far as, but for the conversion, there would have been a reasonable prospect of the instrument being actually paid or enforced. Conversion of a cheque for £1 million drawn by a pauper could hardly give rise to damages of £1 million at the suit of the payee. See generally M. Brindle (ed.), *Law of Bank Payments*, 5th edn, (London: Sweet & Maxwell, 2017), para.6-132 onwards.

197 e.g. *Plantation Holdings (FZ) LLC v Dubai Islamic Bank PJSC* [2017] EWHC 520 (Comm) at [252] (no possible claim for conversion of a leasehold interest by bank to which conditionally assigned) (where the text of this paragraph was approved). However, title deeds, though by a quirk of the law not regarded as personalty, can form the subject-matter of conversion: see *Plant v Cotterill* (1860) 5 H. & N. 430. But today, now that such deeds are of relatively minor importance in establishing rights, this is not of great significance.

timber wrongfully cut, fruit picked, or fixtures wrongfully removed.[198] However, there must be severance; while chattels remain fixed to the realty no action in conversion lies, even if (as in the case of tenant's fixtures) they are chattels which the claimant has a right to take away.[199]

16-40 **Animals** Animals and birds are subject to the law of conversion in the ordinary way. But conversion does not lie in respect of beasts, birds or fish in the wild, since they are *res nullius*. However, once such a creature has been reduced into possession, whether alive[200] or dead (for instance, by being caught, trapped or shot[201]) it is subject to the law of conversion. In such a case title will, it seems, automatically vest in the person on whose land it was taken,[202] whether or not he himself took it.[203] Hence a poacher, though not guilty of theft, can be sued for conversion of his bag.[204] Once reduced into possession, a wild animal does not become *res nullius* again so long as either it has an *animus revertendi*,[205] or its owner keeps it in sight and retains the desire and at least a potential ability to retake it.[206]

16-41 **Dead bodies**[207] It has been said that there is no property in a corpse.[208] However, it now seems clear that this exception, in so far as it remains at all, is a very nar-

[198] *Berry v Heard* (1637) Cro. Car. 242 (timber); *Wood v Morewood* (1841) 3 Q.B. 440n (coal); *Mills v Brooker* [1919] 1 K.B. 555 (fruit); *Gibson v F.K. Developments Ltd* 2017 BCSC 2153 (cutting down a tree); *Belgrave Nominees P/L v Berlin-Scott Air Conditioning P/L* [1984] V.R. 947 (fixture). For a colourful contemporary instance, see the outré decision in *Creative Foundation v Dreamland Leisure Ltd* [2015] EWHC 2556 (Ch); [2016] Ch. 253 (valuable graffiti by modish street artist peeled off).

[199] *Mackintosh v Trotter* (1838) 3 M. & W. 184. But there may, however, be a special action on the case if there be an interference with the exercise of the right of removal; see *London and Westminster Loan and Discount Co v Drake* (1859) 6 C. & B. (N.S.) 798.

[200] *Hamps v Darby* [1948] 2 K.B. 311 (homing pigeons). See too generally *Borwick Development Solutions Ltd v Clear Water Fisheries Ltd* [2020] EWCA Civ 578.

[201] As in *Blades v Higgs* (1865) 11 H.L.C. 622 (poacher's bag of shot rabbits). For what amounts to possession of fish in the process of being caught, see *Young v Hichens* (1844) 6 Q.B. 606.

[202] See *Blades v Higgs* (1865) 11 H.L.C. 622 (gamekeeper acting for landowner justified in seizing poacher's bag of rabbits). But note that the Crown retains prerogative rights in certain cases to swans, provided they be white and swimming in open and common waters, and also to fish royal (i.e. sturgeon, and by a blatant misclassification, whales). See generally the *Case of Swans* (1592) 7 Rep. 15b. These rights are preserved by the Wild Creatures and Forest Laws Act 1971 s.1. In any case, sale of a live or dead wild sturgeon or whale is an offence under s.9(5) of the Wildlife and Countryside Act 1981; similarly with possession of a live or dead wild swan (s.1(2)).

[203] Or, if different, the person who had the right to take it, for example by virtue of a grant of fishing or shooting rights. See, e.g. *Toome Eel Fishery v Cardwell* [1966] N.I. 1 at 29 (buyers of eels illegally caught in Lough Neagh liable in conversion to owners of fishing rights).

[204] *Blades v Higgs* (1865) 11 H.L.C. 622 (rabbits shot by poacher forcibly confiscated by landowner's servants: poacher's action dismissed). There is, however, authority that where game is started by A on B's land but killed on C's, the property vests in A: see *Churchward v Studdy* (1811) 14 East 249; and *Blades v Higgs* (1865) 11 H.L.C. 622 at 633, per Lord Westbury. But if so, this is very odd. A more rational view is that it should vest in C (as was observed by Lord Chelmsford in the latter case).

[205] *Hamps v Darby* [1948] 2 K.B. 311 at 320 (farmer liable for shooting homing pigeon).

[206] *Kearry v Pattinson* [1939] K.B. 471 (swarming bees). Note that if the animal is on someone else's land and that person lawfully refuses the erstwhile owner access to recapture it, the latter is regarded as having lost the ability to retake it: [1939] K.B. 471.

[207] R. Atherton, "Who owns your body?" (2003) 77 A.L.J. 178; J. Wall, "The legal status of body parts: a framework" (2011) 31 O.J.L.S. 783; N. Palmer & E. McKendrick (eds), *Interests in Goods*, 2nd edn (Informa Law, Routledge, 1998), Ch.2; S. Green & J. Randall, *The Tort of Conversion*, (Oxford: Hart, 2009) pp.115 onwards; S. Douglas & I. Goold, "Property in human biomaterials: a new methodology" [2016] C.L.J. 478; S. Walpole, "Property in human bodily products" (2019) 135 L.Q.R. 31.

row one. To begin with, there is venerable authority that once a body has undergone a process or other application of human skill, such as stuffing or embalming, it can be the subject of property in the ordinary way.[209] And the same goes for body parts: thus in the grisly case of *R. v Kelly*[210] robbers who abstracted and sold preserved anatomical specimens from the Royal College of Surgeons' collection were held rightly convicted of theft. Furthermore, in *Yearworth v North Bristol NHS Trust*[211] the Court of Appeal doubted whether there was even a need for the application of a process of human skill. It is suggested that these doubts were well-founded. Take the case of bodies and body parts which have not been subject to any such process, but are legitimately wanted for some other purpose, such as accident investigation or use as an exhibit in court. Despite the earlier suggestions to the contrary,[212] there seems no reason in principle why they should not be subject to property rights: it would certainly be odd if they could be purloined by any passer-by with impunity.[213] In so far as there can be property in corpses or parts thereof, presumably it will vest initially in the first possessor.[214] It should also be noted that, even if there is no property in a corpse, personal representatives or other persons charged with the duty of burying a body have certain rights to its custody and possession in the interim,[215] infringements of which are actionable.[216] But this right does not include a right to

---

208 See Blackstone, *Commentaries*, 15th edn (1809), Bk II, Ch.28, 429; *Handyside's case* (1749) 2 East P.C. 652 (unsuccessful claim in trover against doctor for bodies of Siamese twins); *R. v Sharpe* (1857) Dears. & B. 160 at 163; *Williams v Williams* (1882) 20 Ch. D. 659, 665; see too *Takamore v Clarke* [2012] NZSC 116; [2013] 2 N.Z.L.R. 733 at [70] (Elias CJ: no action in conversion by next-of-kin). In *Dobson v North Tyneside Health Authority* [1997] 1 W.L.R. 596 it was held that the next-of-kin had no property in a corpse or part of it: but that is a slightly different matter, and leaves open the issue of property as such.

209 *Doodeward v Spence* (1908) 6 C.L.R. 406 (grisly museum exhibit consisting of stillborn child with two heads: action in detinue succeeded). Hence it is submitted that conversion would lie for a skeleton or cadaver, or part of it, used for research or exhibition: cf. *Re Organ Retention Group Litigation* [2004] EWHC 644 (QB); [2005] Q.B. 506 at [148]; [2004] Fam. Law 501. And compare *Masson v Westside Cemeteries Ltd* (1996) 135 D.L.R. (4th) 361 (ashes deposited in vault: next-of-kin successfully sued cemetery as bailees when it lost them).

210 [1999] Q.B. 621.

211 [2009] EWCA Civ 37; [2010] Q.B. 1. See particularly at [45], per Lord Judge CJ. Also note the British Columbia case of *JCM v ANA* 2012 BCSC 584; (2012) 349 D.L.R. (4th) 471.

212 *Dobson v North Tyneside AHA* [1997] 1 W.L.R. 596 (deceased's brain pickled in paraffin for use at inquest, then disposed of: next-of-kin sue for conversion. Held: not equivalent to stuffing or embalming, and no property arose); and cf. in Australia *Re Cresswell* [2018] QSC 142 at [152]–[161]; and in New Zealand *Re Lee* [2017] NZHC 3263; [2018] 2 N.Z.L.R. 731. But Dobson could equally well have been decided on the basis that if property did arise, it was not vested in the next-of-kin anyway.

213 cf. *R. v Kelly* [1999] Q.B. 621 at 631, where Rose LJ thought it not unarguable that property would inhere. See generally S. Douglas & I. Goold, "Property in human biomaterials: a new methodology" [2016] C.L.J. 478.

214 The statement in the text was accepted by Gage J in *Re Organ Retention Group Litigation* [2004] EWHC 644 (QB); [2005] Q.B. 506 at [156] (parents have no right to sue in conversion or any analogous tort where organs removed for post-mortem purposes and then kept). Compare *Dobson v North Tyneside AHA* [1997] 1 W.L.R. 596.

215 *Takamore v Clarke* [2012] NZSC 116; [2013] 2 N.Z.L.R. 733 at [73] (Elias CJ). As to who has the right to bury, it seems that in the case of a child it is the parents (e.g. *R. v Vann* (1851) 2 Den. 325), and in the case of anyone else the executor or administrator: cf. *Smith v Tamworth City* (1997) 41 N.S.W.L.R. 680. If there is no such person it is the person with the best right to a grant of administration: *Burrows v HM Coroner for Preston* [2008] EWHC 1387; [2008] 2 F.L.R. 1225 (QB) at [13] (Cranston J). If matters are unclear it is the person in good faith de facto possession, but the decision of the person concerned is challengeable in court if wholly unreasonable: *Grandison v Nembhard* (1989) 4 B.M.L.R. 140, 143 (Vinelott J).

216 So held in Canada: *Edmunds v Armstrong Funeral Home Ltd* [1931] 1 D.L.R. 676. Similarly a New

the return of organs lawfully removed for post-mortem or similar purposes.[217] Also, by statute[218] relatives also have certain powers in relation to the use of a body for medical purposes.

16-42 **Human tissue**[219] A living person, and organs within him, cannot be owned or possessed.[220] It follows that the proper cause of action for unlawful removal of an organ is assault, rather than conversion.[221] However, substances produced by a living person are on principle subject to the ordinary rules of property. After some doubt, this was made clear by the Court of Appeal in *Yearworth v North Bristol NHS Trust*,[222] where donors of sperm samples were allowed to bring proceedings in breach of bailment against a hospital which negligently allowed them to spoil, thus causing them distress. On the other hand, it should be remembered that, even if there are rights of property in sensitive human productions such as sperm or organs, the owner's rights to deal with such material are severely limited under the Human Fertilisation and Embryology Act 1990 and the Human Tissue Act 2004. The removal of tissue from a dead person without relatives' consent may also raise issues of art.8 and on occasion art.3 of the ECHR.[223]

Zealand court has held the right enforceable by injunction: *Murdoch v Rhind* [1945] N.Z.L.R. 425 (prevention of burial outside family plot). cf. *Pollok v Workman* (1900) 2 F. 354; and *Hughes v Robertson*, 1913 S.C. 394. All these cases concerned unauthorised post-mortems. US authority is largely to the same effect: e.g. *Torres v State of New York*, 228 N.Y.S. 2d 1005 (1962). In *Re Organ Retention Group Litigation* [2004] EWHC 644 (QB); [2005] Q.B. 506, Gage J seemed willing provisionally to accept this conclusion.

217 *Re Organ Retention Group Litigation* [2004] EWHC 644 (QB); [2005] Q.B. 506. Note however *MacKenzie v Att-Gen* [2015] NZHC 191 at [68]–[75], where the holding in the *Organ Retention* case was doubted in New Zealand.

218 See Human Tissue Act 2004 Pt I.

219 See M. Brazier and E. Cave, *Medicine, Patients & the Law*, 6th edn (Penguin, 2016), Ch.19.

220 See *R. v Bentham* [2005] UKHL 18; [2005] 1 W.L.R. 1057 (person using fingers as make-believe gun could not be convicted of "possessing" imitation firearm); *Yearworth v North Bristol NHS Trust* [2009] EWCA Civ 37; [2010] Q.B. 1 at [30]. This is salutary, since otherwise the recipient of a transplanted organ would potentially be liable as a converter. See generally N. Palmer & E. McKendrick (eds), *Interests in Goods*, 2nd edn, Ch.2. It is also arguable that s.32 of the Human Tissue Act 2004, prohibiting commercial dealings in organs for transplant, shows a legislative intent to preclude claims for damages reckoned by their value.

221 cf. *Moore v Regents of the University of California*, 793 P.2d 479 (1990) (not conversion to use patient's excised spleen for profitable biotechnology development, though it was a breach of physician's fiduciary duty).

222 [2009] EWCA Civ 37; [2010] Q.B. 1; also *Bazley v Wesley Monash IVF Pty Ltd* [2010] QSC 118; [2011] 2 Qd R. 207 (though cf. *Re Edwards* [2011] NSWSC 478; (2011) 4 A.S.T.L.R. 392, where the court was regarded as having a discretion to allot the substance to whoever it thought just). See too *R. v Welsh* [1974] R.T.R. 478; and *R. v Rothery* [1976] R.T.R. 550 (alleged drunk drivers properly convicted of theft of samples of own urine); and generally L. Skene, "Property Interests in Human Bodily Material" (2012) 20 Med. L. Rev. 227.

223 See *Elberte v Latvia* (2015) 61 E.H.R.R. 7; and R. Neethu, "Elberte v Latvia: The to be or Not to be Question of Consent" (2017) 25 Med. L. Rev 484.

(c) Persons entitled to sue[224]

(i) Generally

16-43 **Claimant must have possession or immediate right to possession** A person has title to sue for conversion if and only if he himself[225] had, at the time of the conversion, either actual possession or the immediate right to possess the property concerned.[226] It is not necessary to prove ownership, and indeed even an owner may not sue unless he either possesses or has the immediate right to possess. Thus, for example, a purchaser of goods in whom the title is vested cannot sue for conversion until he pays or tenders the price and thus becomes entitled to possession.[227] A right to immediate possession continues to be able to ground an action for wrongful interference, however, even if its exercise is temporarily barred, as for example in the case of a company subject to administration.[228]

16-44 It is submitted that in this respect a person with a concurrent interest in goods may recover proportionately according to his interest:[229] a point of some importance, since bulk commodities such as oil and grain are frequently stored communally in tank farms or silos. If A's property is mixed with B's to form an undivided bulk, there is no reason why A should not as a co-owner maintain conversion in respect of his interest in the bulk, for instance if the possessor of the bulk refuses to deliver an amount proportionate to A's interest,[230] or if a third party interferes with A's rights.[231] Thus in *Re Stapylton Fletcher Ltd*[232] wines of a given type and vintage bought by several customers of an insolvent wine merchant were separated and stored separately from the merchant's own stock. It was held that each customer was

224 See the excellent N. Curwen, "Title to sue in conversion" [2004] Conv. 308.

225 It is submitted that the right must be in the claimant personally, and that (for example) the sole owner of a company cannot sue in respect of the company's right. Such a person was held in *Thunder Air Ltd v Hilmarsson* [2008] EWHC 355 (Ch) not to be a valid defendant in conversion proceedings; by parity of reasoning he should not be able to be a claimant either.

226 *Wilbraham v Snow* (1668) 2 Wms. Saund. 47a. Thus a *res nullius*, such as a wild bird or animal, cannot be the subject of an action for conversion. Nor can property previously disposed of by the claimant: see *Daebo Shipping Co Ltd v The Ship Go Star* [2012] FCAFC 156; (2012) 294 A.L.R. 635 (owner withdraws vessel under charter and appropriates bunkers: sub-charterer of vessel has no claim with regard to the bunkers since vessel previously sub-sub-chartered, with bunkers, to third party). And the same goes for abandoned property, unless and until appropriated by another: *Dean v Kotsopoulos* 2012 ONCA 143. Similar reasoning seems to underlie the statement in *Jones v Winkworth* (1658) Hard. 111 that there can be no conversion of an original legal record, being public property. Sed quaere in the latter case: why should the Crown not be entitled to possession/able to sue if it is stolen?

227 *Lord v Price* (1873) L.R. 9 Ex. 54. *Bolwell Fibreglass P/L v Foley* [1984] V.R. 97. See para.16-150, for reversionary injury.

228 See *Barclays Mercantile Business Finance Ltd v Sibec Developments Ltd* [1992] 1 W.L.R. 1253. The relevant legislation is the Insolvency Act 1986 Sch.B1 para.43(3), forbidding an owner-cum-creditor to repossess goods in the company's possession without the leave of the court.

229 cf. *Bloxham v Hubbard* (1804) 5 East 407. At common law the defendant could plead in abatement that the other co-owners ought to have been joined in the action: but this is not so today, since an action no longer falls to be defeated for want of parties.

230 See *Lupton v White* (1808) 15 Ves. 432; *Indian Oil Corp Ltd v Greenstone Shipping Co SA* [1988] Q.B. 345; *Mercer v Craven Grain Storage* unreported 12 February 1993 QBD (the case went to the House of Lords on an unrelated point: unreported 17 March 1994).

231 Compare *Devani v Republic of Kenya* [2015] EWHC 3535 (Admin), a case of embezzlement of oil in a Kenyan tank-farm, where the possibility of an action by the owner was accepted.

232 [1994] 1 W.L.R. 1181. The case arose out of a liquidator's application under s.35 of the Insolvency Act 1986; but if the customers were tenants in common, it follows that they could bring conversion.

a legal tenant in common of a proportionate share of the separated wine. Where the mixing is done wrongfully by B himself, it is up to B to prove how much of the bulk belongs to him.[233] On the same basis, it is suggested that a buyer of part of a bulk who obtains a concurrent interest under ss.20A and 20B of the Sale of Goods Act 1979 can also sue.[234] However, this is subject to two provisos. First, the right of a co-owner to sue his other co-owners is limited to cases of destruction, wrongful sale and disposals which pass good title to the disponee.[235] Secondly, where co-owners join in entrusting a chattel to a third party, no action lies for detention or refusal to return it unless all the co-owners concur in demanding its redelivery.[236]

16-45 **Time when claimant's right arose** The right on which a conversion claimant relies must have existed at the time of the alleged conversion.[237] A right to the goods obtained at some other time will not suffice. Thus in *The Future Express*[238] the buyer of a cargo of wheat agreed with his bank that bills of lading should be made out to the bank's order and put in its hands as soon as they arrived from the sellers. The buyer subsequently persuaded the carriers, with the assent of the sellers, to deliver direct to him. He took the cargo, sold it and decamped with the proceeds. Later still the sellers sent the bills of lading to the bank. The Court of Appeal held that the bank could not sue the carriers in conversion for delivering contrary to the terms of the bill of lading; at the time that delivery took place, the bank had had no right whatever in the goods, and the fact that they might later have obtained such a right was irrelevant. Conversely, on similar principles a person who had a right to possession in the past but has since lost it cannot recover.[239]

16-46 There is one real, and one apparent, exception to this principle. The genuine exception is the principle of relation back which gives, in certain circumstances, an action for a wrong committed prior to the time when the claimant was entitled to possession. In particular, a personal representative may sue for dealings with respect to goods between death and grant of probate or letters of administration, and a trustee in bankruptcy for dealings between the commencement of the bankruptcy and his appointment.[240] The apparent exception arises from the decision in *Bristol*

233 *Lupton v White* (1808) 15 Ves. 432; *Indian Oil Corp v Greenstone* [1988] Q.B. 345.

234 cf. L. Gullifer, "Constructive Possession after the Sale of Goods (Amendment) Act" [1999] L.M.C.L.Q. 93.

235 See Torts (Interference with Goods) Act 1977 s.10. Hence partial disposals, or wrongful pledges, are not covered.

236 *Atwood v Ernest* (1853) 13 C.B. 881. The reason is that "[w]here several joint owners of a chattel concur in delivering it to a third person he may detain it until all the joint owners require him to return it"—(1853) 13 C.B. 881 at 889, per Maule J. *Atwood v Ernest* was a detinue case, but a similar rule applies in conversion: *Harper v Godsell* (1870) L.R. 5 Q.B. 422.

237 See generally *Smith (Administrator of Cosslett (Contractors) Ltd) v Bridgend CBC* [2001] UKHL 58; [2002] 1 A.C. 336 (where, however, it was held that the claimant did have such a right).

238 [1993] 2 Lloyd's Rep. 542. Similarly see *The Cherry* [2002] SGCA 49; [2003] 1 Sing. L.R. 471; *Antariksa Logistics Pte Ltd v McTrans Cargo (Singapore) Pte Ltd* [2012] SGHC 154; [2013] 1 Lloyd's Rep. 117 at [44].

239 So decided by the Supreme Court of Canada: *373409 Alberta Ltd v CIBC* (2003) 220 D.L.R. (4th) 193 (cheque made out to one-man company fraudulently diverted into proprietor's bank account: bank not liable to company in conversion because act of proprietor act of company and hence effective to divest company of rights in cheque). See too the Australian decision in *Daebo Shipping Co Ltd v The Go Star* [2012] FCAFC 156; (2012) 294 A.L.R. 635 (no claim by sub-charterer for conversion of bunkers after transfer by him of his rights to sub-sub-charterer).

240 *Garland v Carlisle* (1837) 4 Cl. & F. 693.

& West of England Bank v Midland Ry Co.[241] There, goods were delivered to a buyer without production of the bill of lading, contrary to the rights of the then holder of the bill. After this wrongful delivery, the bill of lading holder endorsed it to the claimant, who sued the carriers for conversion. A plea that the claimant had no title to sue was rejected. Although this case can be read as saying that a purchaser of goods takes over pre-existing rights to sue for conversion,[242] the better view of this case today is that the defendants were being sued not as prior converters but as bailees who, having wrongfully disposed of the goods, were liable for failure to deliver them on demand to the claimants.[243]

(ii) Title to sue arising from possession

The rights of the possessor It has been already seen that in actions of conversion, the issue as to who has title to goods is not directly raised. What matters is possession or the immediate right to possession: even though most actions in conversion are brought by owners, the claimant does not have to prove his ownership.[244] Thus, a possessor, for example by finding, may deposit the goods with a depositee, and have an action if they are converted by the depositee or a stranger.[245] If a claimant proves that he has been once in possession, and the defendant cannot show that he has a better title, the claimant will normally succeed.[246] **16-47**

Moreover, for these purposes possession counts even if illegitimately gained; thus it has been said that "even wrongful possession, such as that acquired by a thief, will, in principle, be protected except against the owner of the thing stolen or someone acting lawfully on his behalf".[247] Although it might be thought odd, or **16-48**

---

241 [1891] 2 Q.B. 653. See too *London Joint Stock Bank v British Amsterdam Maritime Agency* (1910) 16 Com. Cas. 102.

242 And was so taken in a previous edition of this work (20th edn, para.17-46).

243 See in particular *Margarine Union GmbH v Cambay Prince Steamship Co Ltd* [1969] 1 Q.B. 219, 246-250 (Roskill J); *The Future Express* [1993] 2 Lloyd's Rep 542 at 548–549 (Lloyd LJ); and *The Cherry* [2002] SGCA 49; [2003] 1 Sing. L.R. 471, especially at [57]–[66].

244 *Armory v Delamirie* (1721) 1 Stra. 505; *Eastern Construction Co v National Trust Co* [1914] A.C. 197, 209; *Glenmorgan Farm Ltd v New Zealand Bloodstock Leasing Ltd* [2012] 1 N.Z.L.R. 555 at [26]–[28] (Harrison J); *Antariksa Logistics Pte Ltd v McTrans Cargo (S) Pte Ltd* [2012] SGHC 154; [2013] 1 Lloyd's Rep. 117 at [63] (ownership neither necessary nor sufficient criterion). At common law, indeed, the fact that a third party had a better right to the goods was entirely irrelevant. Today, however, it is open to the defendant to prove that a named third party has a better right than the claimant: Torts (Interference with Goods) Act 1977 s.8, and see para.16-87.

245 *Bourne v Fosbrooke* (1865) 18 C.B. (N.S.) 515. See too *Bansal Hemant Govindprasad v Central Bank of India* [2003] SGCA 3; [2003] 2 Sing. L.R. (R.) 33 (shipping documents negotiated to bank but later handed to customer: sufficient evidence of bank's right to sue third party for conversion).

246 *Burton v Hughes* (1824) 2 Bing. 173; *Jeffries v Great Western Railway* (1856) 5 E. & B. 802. For a less dated example, see *R. (on the application of Atapattu) v Home Secretary* [2011] EWHC 1388 (Admin) (claim by Sri Lankan visitor for unjustified detention of his passport not defeasible merely because passport technically the property of the Sri Lankan government, provided claimant in possession of it when deprived). Note, however, that this rule is it seems modified with wild creatures such as lake fish: *Borwick Development Solutions Ltd v Clear Water Fisheries Ltd* [2020] EWCA Civ 578.

247 P. Winfield, *Tort*, 9th edn (London: Sweet & Maxwell, 1971), pp.308–309. The current (20th) edition of *Winfield & Jolowicz on Tort* does not include this statement. See generally D. Fox, "Enforcing a Possessory Title to a Stolen Car" [2002] C.L.J. 27. A fortiori, the fact that some other wrong has been committed in relation to goods to which the claimant has an otherwise good title is irrelevant: see *Ecclestone v Khyami* [2014] EWHC 29 (QB) at [125]–[129] (Dingemans J) (car unlawfully taken, but true owner then transferred it to claimant).

even contrary to public policy,[248] that an admitted thief should be able to sue for conversion, the rule is now clearly cemented. Thus in *Gough v Chief Constable of the West Midlands*[249] police seized parts from a motor dealer that were fairly clearly stolen. It was held that as regards those parts where it was not clear who the true owner was, the dealer could demand their return. On the other hand, three points are worth noting. First, few thieves are likely in practice to court publicity by suing for their ill-gotten gains. Secondly, it is now always open to a defendant in an action for conversion to allege that some third party has a better title to the property concerned than the claimant.[250] Thirdly, it is arguable that, despite the authorities referred to above, an action by a thief for the return of stolen property would now be barred on the grounds that it is an offence under s.329 of the Proceeds of Crime Act 2002 for anyone knowingly to acquire or possess criminal property.[251]

16-49 **Finders** A person who finds and picks up something abandoned ipso facto becomes owner: title to a *res nullius* goes to the first person to take it.[252] But even where property has not been abandoned, a finder will get a possessory title sufficient to found an action in conversion against anyone who does not have a better right than he has. The point is illustrated in the classic case of *Armory v Delamirie*,[253] where a small boy who found a precious stone was held entitled to get it back from a jeweller he later entrusted it to; he had gained possession when he found it, and that sufficed. However, matters are not always as simple as this, because possession is a relative concept: and a question often arises as to whether the finder gets a better title than, say, the person on whose land the chattel was found. If at the time of the finding the latter was regarded in law as having possession of the thing found, he will prevail as against the finder[254] by virtue of his prior possessory right.

16-50 It seems clear that the owner or occupier of the land will be deemed to possess anything buried in, or attached to, the land, whether or not he knows about it, and hence will prevail over the finder.[255] However, a finder seems likely to prevail against the occupier if the thing found lies unattached on the land and unknown to

[248] In *Gough v Chief Constable of the West Midlands* [2004] EWCA Civ 206 Potter LJ, while applying the rule, confessed to finding it "rebarbative": see [2004] EWCA Civ 206 at [48]. Quaere whether s.329 of the Proceeds of Crime Act 2002, making it an offence per se to possess criminal property, might today change the result.

[249] [2004] EWCA Civ 206. See too *Costello v Chief Constable of Derbyshire* [2001] EWCA Civ 381; [2001] 1 W.L.R. 1437 (police detain stolen car but cannot show who true owner is: liable in conversion to alleged thief for full value). The decision in *Costello* was later approved by the Privy Council in *Jaroo v Att Gen of Trinidad* [2002] UKPC 5; [2002] 1 A.C. 871 where indeed the protection of a mere possessory title was held covered by a constitutional guarantee of the sanctity of property. Other illustrations include *Verrecchia v Metropolitan Police Commissioner* unreported 15 March 2001; *R. (Morgan) v Dyfed Powys Chief Constable* [2003] EWHC 1568 (Admin).

[250] Torts (Interference with Goods) Act 1977 s.8; see para.16-85 onwards.

[251] cf. however the doubts expressed on this point in *Webb v Chief Constable of Merseyside* [2000] Q.B. 427, 433 (May LJ), apparently approved in *Scopelight Ltd v Northumbria Chief Constable* [2009] EWCA Civ 1156; [2010] Q.B. 438 at [18].

[252] See *The Lusitania* [1986] Q.B. 384; and cf. *R. v White* (1912) 107 L.T. 528. On abandonment generally, see N. Palmer & E. McKendrick (eds), *Interests in Goods*, 2nd edn (1998), Ch.23. This is, of course, subject to specific rights such as the Crown's prerogative claim to wreck, treasure etc.

[253] (1721) 1 Stra. 505.

[254] Though not, of course, as against the true owner.

[255] *Waverley BC v Fletcher* [1996] Q.B. 334 (buried brooch found in park using metal-detector). For earlier cases see *Elwes v Brigg Gas Co* (1886) 33 Ch. D. 563 (prehistoric boat buried in soil); *South Staffordshire Water Co v Sharman* [1896] 2 Q.B. 44 (rings buried in mud); *City of London Corp v*

the occupier[256]; unless, perhaps, he is a trespasser on the land,[257] or unless the property was found on premises normally reserved by the occupier for his own private use, such as a private house or the back of a shop.[258] Thus *in Parker v British Airways Board*[259] a person finding a bracelet in the departure lounge at Heathrow Airport was held entitled to keep it.[260] Moreover, despite criticism, it is suggested that the distinction between things found on land and things buried in it has a good deal of sense behind it, if only because things found in land are much more likely to belong to the occupier or his predecessor than those merely lying on it.

Somewhat similar problems may arise where a chattel is sold or bailed and later found by the buyer or bailee to contain contents previously unknown to or forgotten by the seller or bailor. In the case of a sale the seller is likely to prevail on the ground that he did not intend to transfer his ownership or right to possession of the unknown or forgotten contents, unless it can be shown that the sale was, in effect, of the chattel "with any contents"[261]; a fortiori a bailor should prevail against his bailee.[262] **16-51**

There are others whose rights may override the finder's. Thus an employer will usually be entitled to things found on his premises, or in some larger chattel of his such as a ship or vehicle, by his employee in the course of the latter's employment, either because the employer already has sufficient de facto possession,[263] or because the employee is deemed to find for his employer.[264] Similarly, rights may be regulated by agreement, for example between building contractors and site own- **16-52**

Appleyard [1963] 1 W.L.R. 982 (money in hidden safe); *Webb v Ireland* [1988] I.R. 353 (buried treasure found with metal detector at national monument).

256 Quaere if the occupier does know of it? There is no authority: but it is submitted that even here the finder ought to prevail in the absence of some physical taking of possession by the occupier.

257 *Hibbert v McKiernan* [1948] 2 K.B. 142, where a trespassing finder of balls on golf course was convicted of stealing them from the golf club. Sed quaere. The case is not easily reconciled with *Bridges*' and *Hannah*'s cases, fn.259, unless perhaps possession has different meanings in civil and criminal law. See also *R. v Woodman* [1974] Q.B. 754; *Parker v British Airways Board* [1982] Q.B. 1004 at 1017.

258 That is, where the owner has "manifested an intention to exercise control over the building and the things that may be upon it or in it": *Parker v British Airways Board* [1982] Q.B. 1004 at 1018, per Donaldson LJ. cf. *Re Cohen (deceased), National Provincial Bank Ltd v Katz* [1953] Ch. 88.

259 [1982] Q.B. 1004. On this case, in which Donaldson LJ reviewed the authorities, see S. Roberts, "More lost than found" (1982) 45 M.L.R. 683; A. Tettenborn, "Gold discovered at Heathrow Airport" [1982] C.L.J. 242. Other cases: *Bridges v Hawkesworth* (1851) 15 Jur. 1079 (visiting salesman finding banknotes on floor of shop prevailed against shopkeeper because they "never were in the custody of the [shopkeeper], nor in the protection of his house before they were found"—per Patteson J); *Hannah v Peel* [1945] K.B. 509 (soldier occupying requisitioned house found brooch in window-frame and prevailed against house-owner); *Kowal v Ellis* (1977) 76 D.L.R. (3d) 546 (property lying on farmer's land).

260 In practice, regulations and byelaws may often require finders of chattels in such public places such as airports, railway stations or buses to deliver them to the appropriate authority or person in control of the premises or vehicle. But they will not usually affect the finders' title for the purposes of the civil law.

261 *Thomas v Greenslade* [1954] C.L.Y. 341; *The Times,* 6 November 1954; *Merry v Green* (1841) 7 M. & W. 623. See also *City of London Corp v Appleyard* [1963] 1 W.L.R. 982, where, for the purposes of the law of finding, McNair J held that the possessor of a safe also possessed its unknown contents.

262 See *Cartwright v Green* (1803) 8 Ves. 405.

263 *Grafstein v Holme and Freeman* (1958) 12 D.L.R. (2d) 727 (money found by employee in box in basement of employer's shop). *Sharman,* above might have been, but was not, decided on this ground.

264 *White v Alton-Lewis Ltd* (1974) 49 D.L.R. (3d) 189; and *Newman v Bourne & Hollingsworth Ltd* (1915) 31 T.L.R. 209, 210 (Atkin LJ) (both findings by shop assistants); *Willey v Synan* (1937) 57

ers as to what should happen to articles of rarity found in the course of carrying out the works concerned.[265] And it has been held that the Crown's right to bring proceedings to forfeit proceeds of crime applies as much to the finder's right as to anyone else's.[266]

16-53 **Finders: treasure trove and miscellaneous Crown rights** At common law, the Crown was absolutely entitled to treasure trove, namely gold and silver in coin, bullion or plate, which had been deliberately hidden (as against merely lost) and of which the owner was unknown.[267] This right has now been extended and consolidated by the Treasure Act 1996.[268] The Act extends considerably the category of property vested in the Crown (now defined simply as "treasure"),[269] and by s.4(1) provides that all such property when found vests ipso facto in the Crown, but subject to all prior rights.[270] Hence where an item of treasure is lost by X and found by Y, the Crown prevails as against Y, but not X.[271] The Secretary of State has a power, but no duty, to compensate the finder and/or the owner of the land where the treasure was found with a sum up to, but not more than, the value of the treasure.[272] Apart from treasure, the Crown has miscellaneous prerogative and other rights: for example, to estrays,[273] flotsam, jetsam and ligan, and wreck.[274] However, these matters presumably only affect disputes between the finder and the Crown. If the Crown is not party to the relevant proceedings, or chooses not to make a

---

C.L.R. 200, 216–217 (Dixon J) (boatswain found coins in ship); *Crinion v Minister of Justice* [1959] Ir. Jur. Rep. 15 (policeman on duty found money on public footpath); *Parker v British Airways Board* [1982] Q.B. 1004, 1017 (Donaldson LJ). But cf. *Byrne v Hoare* [1965] Qd. R. 135, where an Australian policeman on duty at cinema who found a gold nugget was held entitled to keep it.

265 e.g. *London Corp v Appleyard* [1963] 1 W.L.R. 982.

266 *Fletcher v Leicestershire Constabulary* [2013] EWHC 3357 (Admin); [2014] Lloyd's Rep. F.C. 60 (large wad of cash found and handed to police, who with some ingratitude promptly took proceedings to forfeit it as the proceeds of some unknown criminal conduct).

267 *Att Gen v Moore* [1893] 1 Ch. 676; *Att Gen for the Duchy of Lancaster v G E Overton (Farms) Ltd* [1981] Ch. 333; affirmed [1982] Ch. 277. For the old law, see N. Palmer, "Treasure Trove And The Protection Of Antiquities" (1981) 44 M.L.R. 178; R. Krys, "Treasure Trove under Anglo-American Law" (1982) 11 Ang.-Am. L.R. 214.

268 Applying to all findings after 24 September 1997 (SI 1997/1977).

269 Under s.1, as supplemented by the Treasure (Designation) Order 2002 (SI 2002/2666), "treasure" now means (a) any coin over 300 years old being comprised in a hoard of 10 or more; (b) any such coin forming part of a hoard of two or more, if containing at least 10 per cent gold or silver by weight; (c) any prehistoric metal object found with an item falling within (a) or (b); (d) any other artefact over 300 years old if containing 10 per cent gold or silver; (e) any prehistoric object with any gold or silver content; and (f) anything that would have amounted to treasure trove at common law. The result is potentially a rather wide definition. For example, a Carolean silver teaspoon mislaid by an unknown occupant of a modern house and later found by a buyer at the back of a cupboard would technically vest in the Crown immediately on discovery. It should be noted that under s.2 this definition may be added to or limited by statutory instrument: but the power of addition is confined to articles over 200 years old considered to have cultural importance. For a suggestions that the Act is too niggardly to scholarship and too generous to private individuals, see J. Bray, "The law on treasure from a land lawyer's perspective" [2013] Conv. 265.

270 Defined as rights existing when the treasure reached the place where it was eventually found: s.4(2).

271 Unless, presumably, X had abandoned it, in which case he would have no right to assert.

272 See s.10. Although any legal duty to pay compensation is expressly excluded, no doubt an irrational decision not to compensate would be challengeable by judicial review in an appropriate case.

273 i.e. beasts found wandering and apparently ownerless: *Halsbury's Laws*, 5th edn, Crown and Crown Proceedings, para.291.

274 As to these, see N. Palmer & E. McKendrick eds, *Interests in Goods*, 2nd edn (1998), Ch.7; Merchant Shipping Act 1995 ss.241 onwards, and Civil Aviation Act 1982 s.87.

claim, the relative rights of the finder and the landowner would fall to be decided under the general rules referred to above.

Bailees Just as a finder may rely on his possession to bring conversion against anyone other than the true owner, so also may a bailee. So an agent,[275] a pledgee,[276] a buyer under a reservation of title clause,[277] or even someone casually looking after goods for someone else,[278] is able to sue in conversion. Indeed, at common law this was true whether or not the bailee was liable over to his bailor for the loss of the goods, and whether or not the true owner's identity was known.[279] This remains true on principle: however, by s.8 of the Torts (Interference with Goods) Act 1977 it is now open to the defendant to allege that some named third party, such as the bailor, has a better right to the goods.[280] Recovery by, or settlement with, the bailee bars any subsequent action by the bailor.[281] 16-54

Bailee's right against bailor Certain bailments give an exclusive right of possession to the bailee. This is true, for instance, if goods are pledged or hired for a fixed period; and in such a case the bailee can, until his right be determined, sue the bailor himself[282] and resist any action by the latter for conversion. The bailee, however, may lose his right if he does any act altogether inconsistent with the terms on which he holds the goods; the right to immediate possession will then revert to the owner, who may thereupon sue the wrongdoer or anyone claiming under him.[283] In such a case the bailee's right to claim against the owner presumably disappears. Moreover, the contract of bailment may expressly provide that on the happening of a particular event the bailor's right of possession shall revive, in which case the same conclusion will follow. 16-55

Goods in the custody of employees An employee with mere custody of goods for his employer—for instance a porter moving pictures round a gallery or a librarian shelving books—is not regarded as possessing them. Possession here is in the employer: it follows that the employee cannot himself sue third parties in conversion.[284] However this rule is less significant than it may seem. It does not apply where the employer evinces an intent to make the employee a bailee of his 16-56

275 *Morrison v Gray* (1824) 2 Bing. 260 (factor).

276 *Sze Hai Tong Bank v Rambler Cycle Co* [1959] A.C. 576; *The Erin Schulte* [2014] EWCA Civ 1382; [2016] Q.B. 1 (both cases of pledgees of bills of lading).

277 *Indian Herbs (UK) Ltd v Hadley & Ottoway Ltd* unreported 21 January 1999 CA.

278 As in *National Crime Authority v Flack* [1998] A.L.R. 501.

279 See *The Winkfield* [1902] P. 42 (a negligence case, but the rule on title to sue is the same as in conversion).

280 See para.16-85.

281 See *O'Sullivan v Williams* [1992] 3 All E.R. 385; *The Endurance 1* [2000] 2 Sing. L.R. (R.) 120 at [38].

282 *Brierly v Kendall* (1852) 17 Q.B. 937; cf. *Massey v Sladen* (1868) L.R. 4 Ex. 13; *City Motors (1933) Pty Ltd v Southern Aerial Super Service Pty Ltd* (1961) 106 C.L.R. 477. Similarly with a buyer under a reservation of title clause before the period of credit has run out: *Indian Herbs (UK) Ltd v Hadley & Ottoway Ltd* unreported 21 January 1999 CA.

283 See *North General Wagon & Finance Co Ltd v Graham* [1950] 2 K.B. 7 CA; and *Union Transport Finance Ltd v British Car Auctions Ltd* [1978] 2 All E.R. 385 CA (damages recovered from auctioneer who sold car on instructions of a hire-purchaser); *Calor Gas Ltd v Homebase Ltd* [2007] EWHC 1173 (Ch) (breach of bailment with regard to gas bottles).

284 *Hopkinson v Gibson* (1805) 2 Smith 202; Pollock & Wright, *Possession in the Common Law* (1888), p.39. However, the authorities are not unanimous. Compare A.L. Smith LJ in *Meux v Great Eastern Ry Co* [1895] 2 Q.B. 387 at 394 (footman entrusted mistress's luggage to railway company, which

goods, and this in turn is likely to be the case where either the employee is allowed to use the goods for his own purposes (as with a company car),[285] or where he is otherwise given considerable discretion how to employ them,[286] It also appears that an employee who receives goods for his employer is a bailee, and thus a possessor, before he hands them over.[287] In short, the practical result seems to be that in most cases the servant will be able to sue. Moreover, it is submitted that this is no bad thing. The plea by a convertor that he has been sued by the wrong claimant is normally an unmeritorious one, particularly since under the Torts (Interference with Goods) Act 1977[288] he now has the right, if he does think someone else has a better right than the claimant, to insist on that person being joined.

16-57 **Lessees** A lessee[289] has possession of the demised premises and anything let with them (for example, furniture in a furnished letting). If the premises fall down, he thus has a special property in the materials to rebuild them[290]; again, if fixtures become detached it is suggested that the lessee retains his right of possession.[291] But if he unlawfully pulls the premises down, there is old authority that the right of possession of the materials at once passes to the landlord[292]; and similarly with the tenant who deliberately and wrongfully detaches fixtures.[293]

16-58 **Goods in transit: bills of lading** With goods in transit, it is submitted that for the purpose of suing in conversion the holder of a bill of lading is regarded as being in possession of the goods it relates to.[294] The position where no bill of lading is used, for instance where goods are carried under a sea waybill, air waybill or CMR consignment note, is referred to below.[295]

16-59 **Goods impounded under distress** Before s.71 of the Tribunals, Courts and Enforcement Act 2007 came into force in April 2014, the law with regard to goods impounded under distress was anomalous. Although in the actual possession of the

destroyed it: footman could have sued personally).

285 cf. *Wood Motors Ltd v McTavish* (1971) 21 D.L.R. (3d) 480.

286 cf. *Moor v Robinson* (1831) 2 B. & Ad. 817 (captain of a canal barge is bailee); as with (it is suggested) a delivery driver, a salesman provided with samples, or an employee entrusted with a computer for use on the employer's business.

287 F. Pollock & R. Wright, *Possession*, p.60.

288 s.8; see para.16-85 onwards.

289 Including, it is suggested, a licensee who has effective control of the premises.

290 *Herlakenden's Case* (1588) 4 Rep. 62a.

291 Some of the judges in *Farrant v Thompson* (1822) 5 B. & Ad. 826, suggested that fixtures in all cases of severance vest immediately in the owner of the fee. This, however, is contrary to the resolution in *Herlakenden's Case* (1588) 4 Rep. 62a.

292 per Holroyd J in *Farrant v Thompson* (1822) 5 B. & Ad. 826 at 829.

293 *Farrant v Thompson* (1822) 5 B. & Ad. 826 at 827. Sed quaere whether this should not be limited to the tenant's rights against the landlord. If the person who steals a car has possession sufficient to allow him to bring conversion against a third party (see para.16-48), why not a tenant who steals the bathroom fittings?

294 "But where goods were represented by documents the transfer of the documents did not change the possession of the goods, save for one exception … The one exception was the case of bills of lading, the transfer of which by the law merchant operated as a transfer of the possession of, as well as the property in, the goods." – Lord Wright in *Official Assignee of Madras v Mercantile Bank of India Ltd* [1935] A.C. 53 at 58. See too *Cro Travel Pty Ltd v Australia Capital Financial Management Pty Ltd* [2018] NSWCA 153. The technical absence of a necessary indorsement does not seem to affect the matter; see the latter case at [232]–[256], following the antique authority of *Meyer v Sharpe* (1813) 5 Taunt 79.

295 Para.16-66.

landlord or his agents, they were considered as being in the custody of the law, and therefore he could maintain no action for trespass or conversion, his only remedy being by the separate action of pound breach.[296] Under the 2007 Act, however, both distress for rent and pound-breach are abolished and replaced with a new procedure, with no special rule applicable to interference with goods subject to it.

(iii) Title to sue by virtue of immediate right to possession

Immediate right to possession Just as mere possession will found an action in conversion, so also will an immediate right to possession. Thus a bailor at will can sue his bailee in conversion if the latter refuses to return the goods, as can a lessor once the lease has expired, or a seller of goods who has validly exercised a right of stoppage in transit after ownership has passed to the buyer. For these purposes a derivative right suffices: thus a purchaser of goods in the hands of a third party can, if his seller had an immediate right to possession of them, sue the third party.[297] It seems that, if the claimant has a proprietary right to immediate possession, the mere fact that there is some legislative bar to enforcing it, such as the provisions of the insolvency legislation, will nevertheless not preclude an action in conversion.[298] **16-60**

There are nevertheless many ways in which a claimant may fail to show the necessary right. For example, if goods are let or pledged, the hirer or pledgee, as the case may be, has until the contract is determined the exclusive right to possess[299]; it follows that the owner, having no right of possession, cannot sue.[300] The same applies to goods subject to a lien; the owner's right is of necessity excluded, and the lienee is therefore the only person who can bring the action.[301] So too, if a chattel is mortgaged, the mortgagee cannot maintain trespass or conversion before default.[302] However, in all these cases, the bailor may have an action for reversionary injury: a matter dealt with in more detail below.[303] **16-61**

Claimant's right must be proprietary For these purposes, it seems that the immediate right to possession on which the owner relies must be a proprietary right[304]; **16-62**

---

296 See para.16-153.

297 See *Franklin v Neate* (1844) 13 M. & W. 481 (buyer of goods in hands of pawnbroker); *Pendragon Plc v Walon Ltd* [2005] EWHC 1082 (QB) (buyer of cars in hands of storageman). For the position of an enforcement officer under a writ of control see *365 Business Finance Ltd v Bellagio Hospitality WB Ltd* [2020] EWCA Civ 588.

298 *Barclays Mercantile Finance Ltd v Sibec Developments Ltd* [1992] 1 W.L.R. 1253 (see now Insolvency Act 1986 Sch.B1 para.43). Not so, however, if the statutory bar goes to the court's jurisdiction to hear the case at all: see *Re Leyland DAF Ltd* [1994] 2 B.C.L.C. 106.

299 Best CJ in *Burton v Hughes* (1824) 2 Bing. 173. cf. *The Erin Schulte* [2013] EWHC 808 (Comm); [2013] 2 Lloyd's Rep. 338 at [81] (Teare J) (decision upheld at [2014] EWCA Civ 1382; [2016] Q.B. 1).

300 *Gordon v Harper* (1796) 7 T.R. 9. It is suggested that a buyer from the owner can be in no better position: in so far as the owner has no immediate right to possession, he can pass no better right to the buyer.

301 *Milgate v Kebble* (1841) 3 M. & G. 100; *Legg v Evans* (1840) 6 M. & W. 36; *Lord v Price* (1874) L.R. 9 Ex. 54.

302 *Fenn v Bittleston* (1851) 7 Ex. 152. See, too, *Bradley v Copley* (1845) 1 C.B. 685; and *Jelks v Hayward* [1905] 2 K.B. 460. (Contra, *White v Morris* (1852) 11 C.B. 1015.)

303 See paras 16-150 onwards.

304 N. Curwen, "Title to sue in conversion" [2004] Conv. 308, 311. Contra, R. Goode, "The Right to Trace" (1976) 92 L.Q.R. 360, 364; and S. Green & J. Randall, *The Tort of Conversion*, pp.95 onwards.

a mere contractual right to be given possession will not do.[305] Thus in *Jarvis v Williams*[306] X sold bathroom fitments to Y and delivered them, at Y's request, to Z. By a later arrangement Y agreed to redeliver the fitments to X, but Z refused to let X collect them. It was held that X could not sue Z; the only right he had to possession of the goods was his contractual right against Y. Similarly, although a co-owner of part of an undivided bulk can sue,[307] the claimant's right must actually be proprietary: a mere contractual right to delivery of a stated proportion of goods in someone else's hands will not suffice.[308] On the other hand, where property is delivered to A as agent for B or in pursuance of some similar transaction, B does have a sufficient interest to sue in conversion. Thus in *International Factors Ltd v Rodriguez*[309] a company agreed to factor its debts and to hand over all cheques received in payment. A director of the company took four cheques and paid them into the company's own account. The Court of Appeal rejected a plea that the factoring company had no title to sue the director for conversion.

16-63 **Right to immediate possession: transferees** Where goods are in the hands of a person with a proprietary interest in them sufficient to defeat an action in conversion, it is suggested that that person's interest binds not only the owner himself, but anyone else to whom the owner may have transferred his rights. In so far as the owner before the transfer would not have had a right to possession sufficient to found an action in conversion against the possessor,[310] the transferee in turn can gain no better right than he had.[311] This seems clear as regards a pledgee,[312] and logically ought to be so with a lienee.[313] It is suggested that a similar rule applies to the more important case of leases (including finance leases) and hires for a fixed period. Admittedly it has been suggested that the lessee's or hirer's interest is not clearly proprietary, and hence a transferee from the owner can demand the return of the goods forthwith from the hirer, leaving the latter to his action in damages against the transferor.[314] However, this would be, to say the least, an unfortunate result,[315]

---

305 *Addison v Round* (1836) 4 A. & E. 799 (duty to deliver possession of books insufficient to ground trover as a remedy for refusal to deliver). Similarly, it would be odd if a would-be buyer of goods with neither ownership nor possession, but a mere right against the seller under the contract of sale, could bring conversion against the seller were the latter to refuse delivery, or against any transferee in the event of alienation. Cases such as *Mirabita v Imperial Ottoman Bank* (1877) L.R. 3 Ex. D. 164 certainly assume the contrary.

306 [1955] 1 W.L.R. 71 (strictly speaking a detinue case; but the principle was the same). On similar principles a cheque made out to A and endorsed by him to B gives the latter no right to sue in conversion unless and until delivered: see *Robinson v Midland Bank Ltd* (1925) 41 T.L.R. 402, 406.

307 See paras 16-44 and 16-123.

308 e.g. *South Australian Insurance Co v Randell* (1869) L.R. 3 P.C. 101; *Re Wait* [1927] 1 Ch. 606; *Re Goldcorp Exchange Ltd* [1995] 1 A.C. 74. But cf. *Re Stapylton Fletcher Ltd* [1994] 1 W.L.R. 1181.

309 [1979] Q.B. 351. (See also *Bute (Marquess) v Barclays Bank* [1955] 1 Q.B. 202.) In S. Green & J. Randall, *The Tort of Conversion*, pp.98-99, it is suggested that the claimants' right there can only have been contractual: sed quaere.

310 cf. *Gordon v Harper* (1796) 7 T.R. 9

311 cf. *Rich v Aldred* (1705) 6 Mod. 216, per Holt CJ: "If A bails goods to C, and after gives his whole right in them to B, B cannot maintain detinue for them against C, because the special property that C acquires by the bailment was not thereby transferred to B."

312 Thus in *Franklin v Neate* (1844) 13 M. & W. 481 it was accepted that a buyer of pawned goods could not recover them from the pawnee except on paying the amount due under the pledge.

313 Despite the apparent suggestion to the contrary in *Pendragon Plc v Walon Ltd* [2005] EWHC 1082 (QB) at [12], which (it is suggested) is heterodox and should not be followed.

314 See in particular W. Swadling in N. Palmer & E. McKendrick, *Interests in Goods*, 2nd edn (1998), Ch.20.

and the better view is that a lessee's right is a proprietary right[316] and hence opposable to a transferee suing in conversion.[317]

Bailment at will When there is a simple bailment at will of a chattel, as by loan or deposit, the bailee holds merely as agent for the bailor, and either may sue a stranger for a wrongful act.[318] In *Manders v Williams*,[319] the claimant sent casks of beer to a customer, on terms that the empty casks should be returned or paid for at invoice price at the claimant's option. The casks were subsequently seized under an execution against the customer. It was held that the claimant could maintain conversion against the sheriff, because directly the casks were emptied the claimant had had the right to demand their return, and hence the right of immediate possession. It should be noted that recovery by the bailor in such a case, or settlement with him by the defendant, bars any subsequent action by the bailee.[320] 16-64

Other bailments On the other hand, where the bailment is not a bailment at will, it has been stated above that the owner will not be able to bring conversion against third parties unless and until he has obtained, as against the bailee, the right to immediate possession of the goods. Thus if a pledgee sells or pledges the goods concerned to a third party before default is made, the pledgor is not entitled from that mere fact to bring an action for conversion, because he has no right of possession until he has tendered what is due upon the pledge[321] (though once he has done so his right to possession revives and he can sue[322]). On the other hand, the hirer's right to possession under a contract of hire or hire-purchase is normally terminated 16-65

---

315 It would mean, for instance, that whenever a leasing company became insolvent, all items out on lease for however long could be sold by the liquidator to a buyer who could then instantly recall them, leaving the lessees with a worthless right to prove in the insolvency. A similar course of action would be open to the liquidator of a finance company which had advanced money on a sale and lease-back of (say) plant and equipment. This would be, at the very least, remarkable.

316 As Robert Walker LJ suggested, in the context of a finance lease, in *On Demand Information Plc (in Administrative Receivership) v Michael Gerson (Finance) Plc* [2001] 1 W.L.R. 155 at 171: "Contractual rights which entitle the hirer to indefinite possession of chattels so long as the hire payments are duly made, and which qualify and limit the owner's general property in the chattels, cannot aptly be described as purely contractual rights." (The decision was later reversed in the House of Lords, but on unrelated grounds: *On Demand Information Plc (in Administrative Receivership) v Michael Gerson (Finance) Plc* [2002] UKHL 13; [2003] 1 A.C. 368).

317 See G. Watt, "The proprietary effect of a chattel lease" [2003] Conv. 61.

318 *Rooth v Wilson* (1817) 1 B. & A. 59; *Nicolls v Bastard* (1835) 2 C.M. & R. 659; *Calor Gas Ltd v Homebase Ltd* [2007] EWHC 1173 (Ch) (bailment at will of gas canisters). See too *East West Corp v DKBS 1912* [2003] EWCA Civ 83; [2003] Q.B. 1509 at [27] (Mance LJ); and *The Winkfield* [1902] P. 42. Note that the bailor at will does not have to prove ownership: *Jeddi v Sotheby's* [2018] EWHC 1491 (Comm).

319 (1849) 4 Ex. 339; and see *Jelks v Hayward* [1905] 2 K.B. 460. In *East West Corp v DKBS 1912* [2003] EWCA Civ 83; [2003] Q.B. 1509, Mance LJ doubted whether a person who delivered a bill of lading relating to goods to a bank to be held to his order could sue for conversion of the goods it represented. Sed quaere: this seems contrary to principle. See Baughen [2003] L.M.C.L.Q. 413.

320 See *O'Sullivan v Williams* [1992] 3 All E.R. 385; *The Endurance 1* [2000] 2 Sing. L.R. (R.) 120 at [38].

321 *Halliday v Holgate* (1868) L.R. 3 Ex. 299; *Donald v Suckling* (1866) L.R. 1 Q.B. 585: and see *Yungmann v Brieseman* (1892) 67 L.T. 642. However, it seems this does not apply to goods distrained. If taken from the distrainor the owner has an immediate right to possession sufficient to allow him to bring conversion: *Turner v Ford* (1846) 15 M. & W. 212.

322 cf. *Vaughan v Watt* (1840) 6 M & W 492. But note that this does not apply to a deposit by way of equitable mortgage, where the mortgagor must bring an action for redemption: *Bank of New South Wales v O'Connor* (1889) 14 App. Cas. 273.

if he purports to alienate the goods concerned; from which it follows that the owner in such a case can sue the purchaser in conversion.[323]

16-66 With goods in transit, it was suggested above[324] that for the purpose of suing in conversion the holder of a bill of lading was treated in possession. Where some other document is used, for instance a sea waybill, air waybill or CMR consignment note, it is suggested that there is no such automatic effect, such documents of themselves neither being documents of title nor carrying the right to delivery of the goods. In such a case the right to immediate delivery is, it is submitted, prima facie in the shipper as bailor, unless and until he transfers his proprietary rights to someone else.[325] If, however, the carrier retains a valid lien over the goods, for example for freight, then it is suggested that the result is different and the proprietor can sue only for damage to the reversion.

16-67 **Trust property: the position of the trustee** Where a cestui que trust is in possession in accordance with the provisions of the trust instrument, the trustee is deemed to have an immediate right to possession at common law sufficient to enable him to bring an action for substantial damages for conversion.[326] This may, moreover, include not simply the value of the thing converted, but all loss suffered by the trust estate.[327]

16-68 **Trust property: the position of the beneficiary**[328] A mere equitable proprietary right, such as the interest of a *cestui que trust* or an equitable pledgee, cannot without more found an action in conversion. Thus in *MCC Realisations Ltd v Lehman Bros*[329] A held share certificates in their possession on bare trust for B. A then pledged those same certificates to C. B's action against C for conversion failed in the Court of Appeal, on the basis that they had no legal proprietary interest. But, of course, if the holder of the equitable interest also has possession of the goods, then he may be able to succeed on the basis of that possession[330]; and similarly, if A receives property on trust for, and also as agent for, B, B will be able to sue.[331] It should also be noted that even if the equitable owner does not have a right to sue

---

323 See *Cooper v Willomatt* (1845) 1 C.B. 672; *North General Wagon and Finance Co v Graham* [1950] 2 K.B. 7 CA. cf. *Union Transport Finance Ltd v British Car Auctions* [1978] 2 All E.R. 385 CA (damages recovered from auctioneer who sold car on instructions of a hire-purchaser).

324 Para.16-58.

325 It is true that a right to delivery may be given to the consignee by legislation: see for example s.2 of the Carriage of Goods by Sea Act 1992 s.2(1)(b), in the case of sea waybills, or CMR, art.13.1 for CMR carriage. But such claims are not, it is submitted, proprietary claims and as such are incapable of founding a claim in conversion: see above, para.16-62.

326 *Barker v Furlong* [1891] 2 Ch. 172. Furthermore, this remains so even if under the terms of the trust the *cestui que trust* has the right to remain in possession as against the trustee: *White v Morris* (1852) 11 C.B. 1015.

327 *Malkins Nominees Ltd v Société Financière Mirelis SA* [2004] EWHC 2631 (Ch); see too *Chappell v Somers & Blake* [2003] EWHC 1644 (Ch); [2004] Ch. 19, especially at [27]–[28] (same for an executor).

328 A. Tettenborn, "Trust Property and Conversion: an Equitable Confusion" [1996] C.L.J. 36.

329 [1998] 4 All E.R. 675. See too *Hounslow LBC v Jenkins* [2004] EWHC 315 (QB) (equitable interest in cheque sent by mistake does not allow suit for conversion).

330 As happened in *Healey v Healey* [1915] 1 K.B. 938 (spouse in possession of goods the subject of marriage settlement). That this was the proper explanation was confirmed in the *MCC* case, above.

331 *International Factors v Rodriguez* [1979] Q.B. 351, as explained in the *MCC* case, above.

in conversion, he may well have a right to sue in equity on the basis of dishonest assistance in a breach of trust, or of knowing receipt of trust property.[332]

(d) Position of defendant

(i) Co-owners

Co-ownership: the position at common law If two or more people owned a chattel either jointly or in common, at common law one of them could not bring an action against the others merely for an interference with his right of possession,[333] for instance by using it in manufacture,[334] or pledging it,[335] or creating a lien over it.[336] An action would lie only if the defendant co-owner went further and destroyed the property, or passed a title good as against the other co-owners, or otherwise deprived the others of all possible use and enjoyment of the property, either in the present or the future.[337] In other cases the claimant's only recourse was to an action for reversionary injury.[338] 16-69

Co-owners under the Torts (Interference with Goods) Act 1977 Section 10(1) of the Torts (Interference with Goods) Act 1977 provides that co-ownership is no longer a defence where one co-owner: 16-70

> "(a) destroys the goods, or disposes of the goods in a way giving a good title to the entire property in the goods, or otherwise does anything equivalent to the destruction of the other's interest in the goods, or
> (b) purports to dispose of the goods in a way which would give a good title to the entire property in the goods if he was acting with the authority of all co-owners of the goods."

Section 10(1)(a) is effectively a restatement of the common law.[339] Section 10(1)(b), however, removes the old rule that a mere unauthorised sale of co-owned property was no conversion as against the other co-owners; thus such sales are now subject to the general law on conversion.[340] It should be noted, however, that the reform is not complete. Section 10(1)(b) is limited to dispositions purporting to alienate the entire interest in the goods: from which it seems to follow that co-ownership continues to be a defence in respect of lesser transactions—in particular, wrongful pledges.

Co-owners and buyers from a fixed bulk Under ss.20A and 20B of the Sale of 16-71

---

332 See Underhill & Hayton, *Law of Trusts and Trustees*, 19th edn (2016), Ch.24.
333 Co. Litt. 200a.
334 *Fennings v Granville (Lord)* (1808) 1 Taunt. 241; *Jacobs v Seward* (1872) L.R. 5 H.L. 464.
335 *Mayhew v Herrick* (1849) 7 C.B. 229. The unauthorised co-owner merely had an equitable duty to account, an unsatisfactory remedy if he were insolvent. See too *Monaco Motors Ltd v Halpin* [1985] N.Z. Recent Law 188; [1984] B.C.L. 1280.
336 *Jones v Brown* (1856) 25 L.J. Ex. 345.
337 *Barnardiston v Chapman* (1714) 4 East. 121n (*semble*); *Baker v Barclays Bank Ltd* [1955] 1 W.L.R. 822, 827 (Devlin J); *Morgan v Marquis* (1854) 9 Ex. 145 at 148.
338 See *Farrar v Beswick* (1836) 1 M. & W. 682; A. Tettenborn, "Reversionary Injury to Chattels" [1994] C.L.J. 326, 329. For the action for reversionary injury, see para.16-150 onwards.
339 s.10(3) of the Act indeed says as much.
340 Quaere whether the buyer from the errant co-owner now also becomes liable in conversion. At common law it seems he did not: cf. *Mayhew v Herrick* (1849) 7 C.B. 229. The 1977 Act does not in terms affect the situation, since it only applies to the disponent co-owner.

Goods Act 1979,[341] where a buyer pays for a quantity of goods forming part of a larger bulk, he prima facie becomes a proportionate co-owner of the goods then comprising that bulk, concurrently with the seller or other buyers, as the case may be. Accordingly, he thereby comes under the regime described above. Where the total quantity of goods in the bulk is insufficient to satisfy the demands of all the co-owners, the shares of each are reduced pari passu (see s.20A(4)). This causes problems where one buyer obtains delivery of his full contractual allocation and thus prevents another buyer getting his own aliquot share. On principle the short-changed buyer could bring an action in conversion against both the seller (for delivering the excess) and the buyer (for accepting it). This liability, however, is heavily qualified by statute. Section 20B(1)(a) protects the seller by deeming the buyer to have consented to deliveries to other buyers up to their contractual entitlements.[342] Moreover, the other buyer is also protected, since s.20B(3)(a) precludes any "obligation on a buyer of goods out of a bulk to compensate any other buyer of goods out of that bulk for any shortfall in the goods received by that buyer".[343] It must be noted, however, that ss.20A and 20B are limited to tortious liability: they explicitly state that contractual liability (for example, that of the seller for non-delivery) remains entirely unaffected.[344]

(ii) Conversion wrongful unless excused

16-72 A defendant deals with others' goods at his peril: unless he can invoke some specific defence he is potentially liable, however reasonable or well-intentioned his action.[345] Thus police have been held liable for retaining goods seized from an alleged thief where there was no indication who actually owned them and the police merely wished to deprive the latter of them[346]; on a similar basis it seems clear that the fact that papers abstracted from an opponent in litigation may be admissible in evidence does not excuse their being converted in the first place[347]; and again, prison

---

341 Inserted by the Sale of Goods (Amendment) Act 1995.

342 Even, apparently, if the seller knows of the shortfall; the section makes no reference to good faith or lack of knowledge.

343 Quaere, however, how far this goes. Would it apply to an action for restitution to recover the price received if the other buyer resold the goods, or to an action for return of the goods themselves? The section refers simply to a "duty to compensate", which does not in terms apply to either: but it is to be hoped that the courts would not apply such a narrow construction.

344 See ss.20B(3)(b), 20B(3)(c).

345 See, e.g. *Tongue v RSPCA* [2017] EWHC 2508 (Ch); [2018] B.P.I.R. 229, esp. at [92]–[93] (conversion for RSPCA to move cattle without permission from absent farmer's land to another farm where they could be better cared for). cf. *Imerman v Tchenguiz* [2010] EWCA Civ 908; [2011] Fam. 116 at [36]–[53], [116]–[117] (fact that documents purloined during litigation might be admissible in evidence irrelevant to liability in conversion).

346 *Costello v Chief Constable of Derbyshire* [2001] EWCA Civ 381; [2001] 1 W.L.R. 1437. See too *Scopelight Ltd v Chief Constable of Northumbria* [2009] EWHC 958 (QB); [2009] 2 Cr. App. R. 22 (police had no power to retain seized goods for private, as against public, prosecutors' benefit: hence order for return) (reversed on the matter of the right to retain at: [2009] EWCA Civ 1156; [2010] Q.B. 438).

347 *Imerman v Tchenguiz* [2010] EWCA Civ 908; [2011] Fam. 116 at [36]–[53], [16]–[117] (Lord Neuberger MR). See too *White v Withers LLP* [2009] EWCA Civ 1122; [2009] 3 F.C.R. 435 at [57]–[58] (Ward LJ) (though in that case Wilson and Sedley LJJ at [73] and [84] had inclined to the opposite view).

authorities have similarly been mulcted in damages for destroying contraband confiscated from prisoners rather than merely keeping it until it could be returned.[348]

(iii) Defendant's ignorance of claimant's right generally no defence

Defendant's ignorance of claimant's right generally irrelevant On principle a defendant is liable in conversion whether or not he knew, or had reason to know, that what he was doing infringed the claimant's rights.[349] The law on this point was succinctly expressed by Diplock LJ in *Marfani & Co Ltd v Midland Bank Ltd*[350]: 16-73

> "At common law one's duty to one's neighbour who is the owner, or entitled to possession, of any goods is to refrain from doing any voluntary act in relation to his goods which is a usurpation of his proprietary or possessory rights in them. Subject to some exceptions it matters not that the doer of the act of usurpation did not know, and could not by the exercise of any reasonable care have known of his neighbour's interest in the goods. This duty is absolute; he acts at his peril."

So prima facie anyone who, being a bailee, delivers goods to a non-owner or who receives property by sale, pledge[351] or gift from a non-owner commits conversion whether or not he knew or had reason to know of the latter's defect in title.[352] Again, a receiver interfering with goods under an invalid appointment,[353] or a pledgee taking goods under a void pledge,[354] is likely to find himself with no defence. Nevertheless, two qualifications need noting. First, the fact that he has acted in good faith may protect him by taking his act out of those capable of amounting to conversion at all.[355] Secondly, in connection with innocent receipt it must be remembered that a non-owner in possession is frequently able to confer a good title on an innocent

---

348 *R. (Coleman) v Governor of Wayland Prison* [2009] EWHC 1005 (Admin); *The Times*, 23 April 2009. The general principle remains, but the actual decision has been reversed by statute: see the Prison Act 1952 s.42A, inserted by the Prisons (Property) Act 2013.

349 *Lancashire & Yorkshire Ry Co v MacNicoll* (1918) 88 L.J.K.B. 601; *Voss v Suncorp-Metway Ltd* [2004] Qd. R. 214 (bank taking cheque paid into account in same name as person from whom stolen). Compare negligence. Where A reasonably thinks B is the owner of goods in fact belonging to C, A cannot, it seems, be sued in negligence by C if he damages them; cf. *The Pioneer Container* [1994] 2 A.C. 324.

350 [1968] 1 W.L.R. 956, 970–971. See too Cleasby B in *Fowler v Hollins* (1872) L.R. 7 Q.B. 616, 639: "persons deal with property in chattels or exercise dominion over them at their peril." In the difficult case of *Robot Arenas Ltd v Waterfield* [2010] EWHC 115 (QB), buyers of a property were exonerated when, having found it full of what they reasonably saw as abandoned junk (but was in fact neither abandoned nor junk), they trashed the contents. The reason was that, as involuntary bailees, they had acted honestly and reasonably. But with respect, and despite the tentative support of *Palmer on Bailment*, 3rd edn (London: Sweet & Maxwell, 2009) para.6-020, this is difficult to reconcile with the rule that defendants act at their peril. The decision must be regarded with some little scepticism.

351 At common law receipt by way of pledge was arguably not conversion; but this anomaly was removed by s.11(2) of the Torts (Interference with Goods) Act 1977.

352 "Certainly a man is guilty of a conversion who takes my property by assignment from another who has no authority to dispose of it; for what is that but assisting that other in carrying his wrongful act into effect": per Lord Ellenborough in *M'Combie v Davies* (1805) 6 East 538.

353 As in *OBG Ltd v Allan* [2007] UKHL 21; [2008] 1 A.C. 1.

354 *Wilson v Robertsons (London) Ltd* [2006] EWCA Civ 1088 (pledge under loan agreement invalidated by Consumer Credit Act 1974).

355 *Bunnings Group Ltd v CHEP Australia Ltd* [2011] NSWCA 342; (2012) 82 N.S.W.L.R. 420 at [138]; above, para.16-07.

third party: for instance, sales passing title by estoppel,[356] or which come within ss.24 and 25 of the Sale of Goods Act 1979, or transfers of a negotiable instrument to a holder in due course.[357] In such cases of exceptions to the rule *nemo dat quod non habet* the recipient is obviously under no liability.

16-74 **Innocent dealing by the defendant on behalf of another no defence** Moreover, the mere fact that the defendant acted as an agent for someone else, however innocently, is equally no defence to an action in conversion.[358] Thus where the defendant's employer had bought goods from a bankrupt and the defendant, not knowing of the bankruptcy, took delivery of the goods and forwarded them, it was held that he was liable in conversion to the assignees of the bankrupt[359]:

> "The clerk acted under an unavoidable ignorance and for his master's benefit when he sent the goods to his master; but nevertheless, his acts may amount to a conversion, for a person is guilty of conversion who intermeddles with my property and disposes of it, and it is no answer that he acted under authority from another who had himself no authority to dispose of it."[360]

So, if an auctioneer sells goods and hands over the proceeds to his principal without notice of any defect in his title, the true owner may recover from him the value over again.[361]

(iv) Exceptional cases where ignorance of claimant's title a defence

16-75 **Exceptions to strict liability** Notwithstanding the above, there are a considerable number of exceptions, both at common law and by statute, to the principle that a converter is liable notwithstanding any lack of knowledge on his part. To these we now turn.

16-76 **Agent not intending to alter property** If an agent intermeddles merely with the custody of a chattel in ignorance of his principal's lack of title, and also in ignorance that any alteration of property is intended, he is not guilty of a conversion:

> "The true proposition as to possession and detention and asportation seems to me to be, that a possession or detention which is a mere custody or mere asportation made without reference to the question of the property in goods or chattels is not a conversion".[362]

---

356 Sale of Goods Act 1979 s.21(1) (proviso).

357 Bills of Exchange Act 1882, ss.29(1), 38(2) (bills of exchange), 73 (cheques), 89 (promissory notes).

358 See *Winter v Bancks* (1901) 84 L.T. 504; *Scragg & Sons v Perseverance Banking & Trust Co Ltd* [1973] 2 Lloyd's Rep. 101.

359 *Stephens v Elwall* (1815) 4 M. & S. 259. Note that today he would no longer be so liable, since he would have a statutory defence under the Insolvency Act 1986, s.307(4). But the principle remains.

360 *Stephens v Elwall* (1815) 4 M. & S. 259, 261 (Lord Ellenborough).

361 e.g. *Cochrane v Rymill* (1879) 40 L.T. 744; *Consolidated Co v Curtis* [1892] 1 Q.B. 495; *Union Transport Finance Ltd v British Car Auctions Ltd* [1978] 2 All E.R. 385; *RH Willis & Son v British Car Auctions Ltd* [1978] 1 W.L.R. 438.

362 See *Fowler v Hollins* (1872) L.R. 7 Q.B. 616, 630 (Brett J). See too *Marcq v Christie Manson & Woods Ltd* [2003] EWCA Civ 731; [2004] Q.B. 286 at [14] (Tuckey LJ) ("possession of goods by an agent on the instructions of their apparent owner for the purpose of carrying out what have been described as ministerial acts such as storage or carriage does not amount to conversion"); also *Tat Seng Machine Movers Pte Ltd v Orix Leasing Singapore Ltd* [2009] SGCA 42; [2009] 4 Sing. L.R. 1101 at [58]; *Antariska Logistics Pte Ltd v McTrans Cargo Pte Ltd* [2012] SGHC 154; [2013] 1 Lloyd's Rep. 117 at [46].

On this principle a forwarding agent who packs and ships goods does not render himself liable because his employer had no title,[363] apparently because his act is so purely ministerial that, if performed in good faith and without notice, no presumption of a conversion can be raised therefrom.[364]

Unfortunately, finding a precise demarcation line between justifiable ministerial handling and conversion, especially where the agent knows a question of title may be involved, is not easy. Take the case of the auctioneer. If he receives goods for sale, and on selling them hands them over with the view of passing the property, he is more than a mere intermediary and will be liable in conversion if the vendor had no title.[365] But a defendant may act as a mere broker, confining himself to the negotiation of the sale, and leaving his principal to deliver possession, in which case his act is no conversion.[366] A case on one side of the line was *National Mercantile Bank v Rymill*.[367] An auctioneer received goods for sale from a non-owner; the latter then cancelled his instructions and arranged to sell the goods privately to a buyer to whom the auctioneer delivered them. The auctioneer escaped liability as a mere intermediary equivalent to a broker. By contrast, in *RH Willis and Son v British Car Auctions Ltd*[368] a car wrongfully sent by a hire-purchaser for auction failed to reach the reserve price, whereupon the auctioneers privately obtained the highest bidder's confirmation of his bid and with the hirer's agreement sold and delivered it to him. In this case, having actively participated in the sale arrangements, the auctioneers were held liable. **16-77**

Bailee acting on bailee's orders A bailee in possession of goods who, without notice[369] of any defect in his bailor's title, delivers goods to the bailor or to his order is protected from liability vis-à-vis the true owner. As Blackburn J put it in *Hollins v Fowler*[370]: **16-78**

"I cannot find it anywhere distinctly laid down, but I submit to your Lordships that on

363 *Greenway v Fisher* (1824) 1 C. & P. 190.

364 For the burden of proof, see *Tat Seng Machine Movers Pte Ltd v Orix Leasing Singapore Ltd* [2009] SGCA 42; [2009] 4 Sing. L.R. 1101 at [87], [94]: once the defendant raises a prima facie case of ministerial handling, the burden of proof shifts to the claimant.

365 *Consolidated Co v Curtis & Son* [1892] 1 Q.B. 495; *Cochrane v Rymill* (1879) 40 L.T. 744; *Barker v Furlong* [1891] 2 Ch. 172; *RH Willis & Son v British Car Auctions Ltd* [1978] 1 W.L.R. 438.

366 See the case put by Bramwell LJ in *Cochrane v Rymill* (1879) 40 L.T. 744, 746. If he knows that the sale he is procuring is wrongful and infringes the claimant's possessory rights, he may however be liable for procuring a conversion. Compare *Wolff v Trinity Logistics USA Inc* [2018] EWCA Civ 2765; [2019] 1 W.L.R. 3997 at [28].

367 (1881) 44 L.T. 307, 767. It is submitted that this is an aspect of the rule that a bailee who returns goods to his bailor or to the latter's order escapes liability if he acts innocently: para.16-80. On this case see too Brett J's remarks in *Hollins v Fowler* (1875) L.R. 7 H.L. 757, 779–785; Collins J in *Consolidated Co v Curtis & Son* [1892] 1 Q.B. 495, 501; and Scrutton LJ in *Underwood v Bank of Liverpool* [1924] 1 K.B. 775, 790–791.

368 [1978] 1 W.L.R. 438.

369 "Notice" here seems to mean actual knowledge of facts indicating a lack of right in the *soi-disant* owner. The Court of Appeal in *Marcq v Christie Manson & Woods Ltd* [2003] EWCA Civ 731; [2004] Q.B. 286 made it clear that a bailee in such a case (here an auctioneer) was under no duty to make enquiries as to title. Jack J in the same case at first instance ([2002] EWHC 2148 (QB); [2002] 4 All E.R. 1005) stated further at [59] that the defendant bailee bore the burden of proof that he did not have the relevant knowledge or notice; see too *Tat Seng Machine Movers Pte Ltd v Orix Leasing Singapore Ltd* [2009] SGCA 42; [2009] 4 Sing. L.R. 1101 at [86]–[89].

370 (1875) L.R. 7 H.L. 757 at 766–767. In *RH Willis and Son v British Car Auctions Ltd* [1978] 1 W.L.R. 438. Lord Denning MR held this statement of principle by Blackburn J to have been inferentially accepted by the House of Lords in the same case and therefore to be binding on the Court of Appeal. And see Cave J in *McEntire v Potter* (1889) 22 Q.B.D. 438 at 441.

principle, one who deals with goods at the request of the person who has the actual custody of them, in the bona fide belief that the custodier is the true owner, or has the authority of the true owner, should be excused for what he does if the act is of such a nature as would be excused if done by the authority of the person in possession, if he was a finder of the goods, or intrusted with their custody."

So there is no liability if, without knowledge of any defect in title, a garage repairs and returns a car, a remover moves furniture from one house to another, or a carrier carries goods and hands them over as instructed.[371] The same goes for an auctioneer who returns items that fail to sell to the person consigning them[372] and (it is submitted) a pledgee who returns goods to a non-owning pledgor.[373] And the Privy Council has reached a similar result in the case of a bailment by attornment to a non-owner.[374] Of course, in such a case, it equally goes without saying that, even of the bailor had no title, the bailee will escape liability in conversion if he hands over the goods to a person who is in fact entitled to possession of them.[375] This is a matter of particular practical importance in sea carriage where goods are delivered by a carrier to someone other than the bill of lading holder.[376]

16-79 On the other hand, this principle of non-liability is itself subject to two exceptions. First, it only protects a bailee who has no notice of his bailor's lack of title. Once the bailee has notice of the existence of competing claims to the goods, he delivers to either claimant at his peril. His only safe course is to interplead. Secondly, protection is limited to the bailee who delivers to his actual bailor (or to his order). A bailee who delivers, even without negligence, to an impostor, or to anyone else who is not in fact the bailor's representative, is liable in the ordinary way.[377] Thus in *Motis Exports Ltd v Dampskibsselskabet AF 1912*,[378] Rix J had no difficulty in attaching liability to a shipowner who parted with goods against a forged bill of lading, albeit he had acted innocently and without any negligence.

---

371 See *Sheridan v New Quay Co* (1858) 4 C.B. (N.S.) 618, 650 (Willes J); *Fowler v Hollins* (1872) L.R. 7 Q.B. 616, 632 (Martin B); *Glyn Mills Currie & Co v East & West India Dock Co* (1882) 7 App. Cas. 591.

372 *Marcq v Christie Manson & Woods Ltd* [2003] EWCA Civ 731; [2004] Q.B. 286, criticised in A. Hudson (2005) 10 *Art, Antiquity & Law* 201. The fact that the auctioneer had a lien over the goods was held irrelevant here. See too *Re Samuel* [1945] Ch. 408 (solicitor receiving jewellery on behalf of his client, an undischarged bankrupt, and handing it over to his client's agent with a view to sale: not liable to trustee in bankruptcy).

373 See Bigham J in *Union Credit Bank Ltd v Mersey Docks & Harbour Board* [1899] 2 Q.B. 205, 216.

374 See the Privy Council decision in *Maynegrain P/L v Campafina Bank* [1984] 1 N.S.W.L.R. 258 (bailee who attorned to X and then disposed of the property on X's instructions not guilty of conversion merely because X, in taking the attornment, had been acting for an undisclosed principal Y). And compare *The Pioneer Container* [1994] 2 A.C. 324 (bailee generally owes duty of care only to person he thinks is the owner, not to some third party of whose title he is entirely unaware). But see N. Palmer, "The Vindication of Commercial Security over Commodities" [1986] L.M.C.L.Q. 218.

375 See dicta in *Barclays Bank Ltd v Commissioners of Customs & Excise* [1963] 1 Lloyd's Rep. 81 at 88; *The Houda* [1994] 2 Lloyd's Rep. 541, 556 (Millett LJ).

376 For discussion, see *The Houda* [1994] 2 Lloyd's Rep. 541, 556 (Millett LJ).

377 As in, e.g. *Hiort v Bott* (1874) L.R. 9 Ex. 86. Note, however, that pawnbrokers now have a statutory protection in this regard: see Consumer Credit Act 1974 s.117, protecting them provided they hand over the goods in good faith to anyone presenting the pawn receipt.

378 [1999] 1 Lloyds Rep. 837 (affirmed on other grounds in the CA: [2000] 1 Lloyd's Rep. 211). See too *Glencore International AG v MSC Mediterranean Shipping Co SA* [2017] EWCA Civ 365; [2017] 2 Lloyd's Rep. 186. The former case is criticised in P. Todd, "Delivery against Forged Bill of Lading" [1999] L.M.C.L.Q. 449. See too *Helson v McKenzies (Cuba St) Ltd* [1950] N.Z.L.R. 878.

The involuntary bailee[379] Unlike an ordinary bailee, it seems an involuntary bailee who hands over goods to someone other than the true owner is entitled to further protection. He always has an escape if he can show that he acted innocently and with reasonable care in the circumstances, even if the person to whom he parted with the goods was not the bailor at all but an impostor. In *Elvin & Powell Ltd v Plummer Roddis*[380] a fraudster pretending to represent the defendants fraudulently ordered clothing to be sent to their premises by the claimants; he then telegraphed in the claimants' name saying it had been delivered in error, and asking for it to be given up to a person who turned out to be his accomplice. It was held that the defendants, having delivered to the accomplice in all innocence and without negligence, were not liable in conversion. Similarly, where a person has goods delivered to him which he thinks belong to him, but which in fact do not, Staughton J held in *AVX Ltd v EGM Solders Ltd*,[381] that his only duty was not to dispose of the goods without taking reasonable steps to ensure that they were his to dispose of. If he did take such care he was not liable in conversion: if he did not, he was. **16-80**

Miscellaneous statutory protections Commercial considerations necessitate some statutory mitigation of the normally strict liability of the converter. Four instances are particularly worth noting. First, in the case of cheques, a bank is strictly liable at common law if it collects a cheque for payment into its customer's account to which the customer in fact has no title.[382] However, s.4 of the Cheques Act 1957[383] now protects the bank provided it can show it acted in good faith and without negligence. The authorities on this section are legion and complex, and the reader is referred to specialist works on banking law for details.[384] Secondly, protection is now available in certain cases of insolvency. Thus ss.307(4) and 346(7) of the Insolvency Act 1986 shield a person who deals for value with a bankrupt's property not knowing of the bankruptcy, and hence in ignorance of the fact that property concerned will have ipso facto vested in the trustee in bankruptcy. And, perhaps more significantly, s.234(3) of the same Act provides that a liquidator, receiver or administrator who seizes what appears to be the company's property[385] is not liable in damages to the true owner unless he had reasonable grounds for believing he was not entitled to act as he did.[386] Thirdly, s.117 of the Consumer Credit Act 1974 now protects a pawnbroker from liability provided he hands over the pledge to someone producing the pawn receipt.[387] He need not concern himself with whether that person is in fact the true owner of the goods. Fourthly, under the Tribunals, Courts and Enforcement Act 2007 Pt 3, the enforcement agent is given **16-81**

---

379 See generally N. Palmer, *Bailment*, 3rd edn (London: Sweet & Maxwell, 2009), Ch.13.

380 (1933) 50 T.L.R. 158.

381 *The Times*, 7 July 1982. His Lordship also suggested (rightly, it is submitted) that there might be a right actually to dispose of the goods if they were noxious or dangerous.

382 e.g. *Capital & Counties Bank Ltd v Gordon* [1903] A.C. 240.

383 Replacing the slightly narrower s.82 of the Bills of Exchange Act 1882; see also s.80 of the same Act.

384 e.g. M. Brindle et al, *Law of Bank Payments*, 5th edn (2017, Sweet & Maxwell), para.6-155 onwards.

385 But apparently only tangible property: see *Welsh Development Agency v Export Finance* [1992] B.C.L.C. 148 at 171, 190.

386 On which see *Birdi v Price* [2018] EWHC 2943 (Ch); [2019] 3 All E.R. 250. Note the limitation to liability in damages: presumably this leaves intact his duty to account to the true owner. Damages for these purposes includes misfeasance proceedings: s.304(3) of the 1986 Act.

387 Even, apparently, if the pawnbroker knows of the lack of title. Presumably, however, the section refers to the actual receipt: a pawnbroker handing over the goods against a forgery, however undetectable, seemingly falls outside the umbrella of s.117 and is therefore strictly liable.

extensive protection from liability in respect of seizure of goods that seem to, but in fact do not, belong to the debtor.[388]

(e) Multiple claims: jus tertii, estoppel and double liability

16-82 **Former position at common law**[389] If the claimant makes out a good prima facie title by possession or otherwise, the defendant has always been able to escape if he can show a better right in himself or in some person under whose authority he is acting, or under whom he claims.[390] The common law, however, took a different attitude to attempts to oppose to the claimant's title that of some stranger who made no claim for himself (*jus tertii*). This plea was barred in cases where the claimant had possession of the goods in question, either personally[391] or through a bailee at will.[392] This was apparently so even if the defendant had meanwhile delivered up the converted goods, or paid their value, to the true owner.[393] Conversely, payment, even under a judgment, of the value of the goods to such a claimant gave the defendant no defence to a subsequent action by the true owner,[394] so the converter might incur double liability by having to surrender the goods or pay their full value to one claimant and also to pay their full value to another. In addition to this, at common law a bailee was generally estopped, in an action brought against him by his bailor, from denying that the latter bailor had a good title to the chattel bailed,[395] unless he had been actually evicted by title paramount,[396] or had acknowledged the

[388] See Sch.12 paras 63–68. On reasonable belief, on which many of the relevant protections rest, see *Rooftops South West Ltd v Ash Interiors (UK) Ltd* [2018] EWHC 2799 (QB). The statutory procedure under the 2007 Act replaces the previous proceeding of execution, and the enforcement agent the sheriff.

[389] For further consideration of the position at common law, see the 14th edn of this work, paras 1142–1149, and (1971) Cmnd.4774. This remains relevant in most Commonwealth jurisdictions, where there is no equivalent of the Torts (Interference with Goods) Act 1977.

[390] Examples of where this occurred include *Blades v Higgs* (1861) 11 H.L.C. 621; and *Buckley v Gross* (1863) 3 B. & S. 566. See too *Rogers v Lambert* [1891] 1 Q.B. 318, 323-324 (Lord Esher MR); also *The Jupiter (No.3)* [1927] P. 122, 250 (Hill J).

[391] *Jeffries v Great Western Ry* (1856) 5 E. & B. 802, especially at 805 (Lord Campbell CJ); *Bourne v Fosbrooke* (1865) 18 C.B. (N.S.) 515; *Wilson v Lombank Ltd* [1963] 1 W.L.R. 1294. For a recent example, see *Blue Sky One Ltd v Mahan Air* [2010] EWHC 631 (Comm) at [98]–[99], where Beatson J expressed the view that a mortgagor in possession of a chattel (an aircraft) could sue for its full value without giving credit for the mortgagee's interest.

[392] *Bourne v Fosbrooke* (1865) 18 C.B. (N.S.) 515. This use of the word "possession" is one of its many ambiguities of meaning. A man is said to be in actual possession when he has the immediate custody or control of a chattel. He is said to be in constructive possession, inter alia, when it is held by his bailee at will: see *USA v Dollfus Mieg et Cie SA* [1952] A.C. 582, 605 (Earl Jowitt).

[393] *Wilson v Lombank Ltd* [1963] 1 W.L.R. 1294 (a case of trespass, where a claimant with no title nevertheless recovered the full value of a car which the defendant had taken from the claimant's possession, although the defendant had meanwhile surrendered it to the true owner).

[394] *Attenborough v London & St Katharine's Dock Co* (1877) 3 C.P.D. 450, 454.

[395] See *Henderson v Williams* [1895] 1 Q.B. 521; *Kahler v Midland Bank Ltd* [1950] A.C. 24 at 38; *Rogers v Lambert* [1891] 1 Q.B. 318. It was similarly irrelevant that the claimant had unlawfully sub-bailed the goods to the defendant: *Anderson Group Pty Ltd v Tynan Motors Ltd* (2006) 65 N.S.W.L.R. 400 at 403. The rule was apparently considered commercially essential, to prevent a depositary of goods setting up the title of someone other than his bailor in order to keep the bailed goods for himself (e.g. *Cheesman v Exall* (1851) 6 Ex. 341 at 346, per Martin B). But this was never very convincing.

[396] *Shelbury v Scotsford* (1602) Yelv. 22. Aliter if the bailee promised to return at all events thus taking the risk of such eviction: *Ross v Edwards* (1895) 73 L.T. 100.

validity of the true owner's claim of title and defended the bailor's action by his authority.[397]

But a plea of *jus tertii* was allowed at common law in two cases. The first was where neither the claimant nor anyone through whom he claimed had ever had a possessory right in the goods.[398] The second was where any possessory right the claimant might have had had been voluntarily surrendered or taken away by operation of law.[399] In both these cases the defendant was saying not "you have a prima facie title but X has a better one", but "you have proved no title of any sort, and therefore you must fail *in limine*".[400] **16-83**

The position under the Torts (Interference with Goods) Act 1977 However, the common law position described above has been considerably changed by the Torts (Interference with Goods) Act 1977.[401] Effectively the Act permits the defendant to plead that a named third party[402] has a better right than the claimant, and to have all known competing claims determined simultaneously. **16-84**

(i) *Jus tertii: joinder of competing claimants*

Jus tertii: joinder of competing claimants Section 8(1) of the 1977 Act provides that: **16-85**

> "in any action for wrongful interference with goods[403] the defendant is entitled to show, in accordance with rules of court,[404] that a third party has a better right than the claimant as respect all or any part of the interest claimed by the claimant, or in right of which he sues, and any rule of law (sometimes called *jus tertii*) to the contrary is abolished."

This section materially changes the common law position.[405] First, as against a wrongdoer, possession is now tantamount to title only where no named third party

---

[397] *Biddle v Bond* (1865) 6 B. & S. 225; *The Jupiter (No.3)* [1927] P. 122 at 250; *Kahler v Midland Bank Ltd* [1950] A.C. 24 at 38. The true owner's authority to defend the action on his behalf was essential: *Rogers v Lambert* [1891] 1 Q.B. 318; *Russian Commercial and Industrial Bank v Comptoir D'Escompte de Mulhouse* [1925] A.C. 112.

[398] *Gadsden v Barrow* (1854) 9 Ex. 514; *Richards v Jenkins* (1886) 17 Q.B.D. 544; Pollock and Wright, *Possession in the Common Law* (1888), p.92.

[399] *Leake v Loveday* (1842) 4 M. & G. 972.

[400] There was some argument about a claimant who did not himself have possession, but derived his title from someone who did. Despite some suggestions that the plea of *jus tertii* was always available against non-possessing claimants, the better view is that here it was not open to the defendant. See C. Baker, "The ius tertii: a Restatement" (1990) 16 U.Qd.L.J. 46; A. Tettenborn, "Reversionary Damage to Chattels" [1994] C.L.J. 326, 335.

[401] Following the Law Reform Committee's 18th Report, (1971) Cmnd.4774. In this see generally paras 51–78; for particular recommendations, paras 62, 66, 70; and for summary, para.128(9).

[402] The third party must be named. It follows that where the defendant knows that the claimant is not the true owner but cannot say who is, the common law position remains. See, e.g. *Costello v Derbyshire Chief Constable* [2001] EWCA Civ 381; [2001] 1 W.L.R. 1437.

[403] Defined in s.1. Section 8 therefore applies to actions for forms of wrongful interference other than conversion, e.g. trespass and negligence or any other tort so far as it results in damage to goods or to an interest in goods. For the effect of the section on bailment claims, see *Scipion Active Trading Fund v Vallis Group Ltd* [2020] EWHC 1451 (Comm) at [102]–[114].

[404] See CPR 19.5A.

[405] On the question whether it leaves the common law exceptions intact, the better position seems to be that it does: N. Palmer, *Bailment*, 3rd edn (London: Sweet & Maxwell, 2009), para.4-061. But compare the doubts on this expressed in *De Franco v Met. Police Commr*, *The Times*, 8 May 1987.

is known to have a better right.[406] Secondly, since the defendant in any action for wrongful interference may apply for joinder of a named *tertius*, a bailee sued by his bailor is no longer estopped from denying that his bailor had a good title.[407] Thirdly, it modifies the rule in *The Winkfield*[408] that a bailee in possession could sue in his own name for the full amount of the loss of, or damage to, the goods, whether or not he was himself liable to his bailor; the defendant may now join the bailor, with damages no doubt being apportioned between bailor and bailee according to the values of their respective interests.[409] If for some reason the bailor cannot be joined (for example if he is untraceable), the bailee can it seems recover the full amount of the loss or damage, being then accountable for the excess beyond the value of his own interest.[410] In addition, procedural changes were made with a view to the reduction of multiple hearings. Under s.9 of the 1977 Act, proceedings for wrongful interference with the same goods may be consolidated whether or not founded on the same wrongful act, even if any of the claims relates additionally to other goods.

(ii) Double liability

16-86 At common law it was no defence to a claim for conversion merely to show that, in respect of the same wrongful act, the defendant had already surrendered the goods, or paid damages representing their full value, to some earlier claimant having a possessory title to them.[411] He might thus have to pay full damages twice over, yet have no right to reimbursement by the earlier claimant.[412] Section 7 of the 1977 Act therefore seeks to prevent this. It applies where either one of two or more rights of action for wrongful interference is founded on a possessory title, or the measure of damages in such an action founded on a proprietary title is, or includes, the entire value of the goods, although the interest is one of two or more interests in the goods.[413]

16-87 Where two or more claimants are parties to the same proceedings, the relief is

---

406 *Armory v Delamirie* (1722) 1 Str. 505, which established the principle, was such a case, since the true owner was unknown. For a more recent example, see *Costello v Chief Constable of Derbyshire* [2001] EWCA Civ 381; [2001] 1 W.L.R. 1437 (possessor of stolen goods succeeds where no indication whom they had been stolen from). Note that the named third party may be someone who has since disposed of his interest, provided he had it when the alleged conversion took place: *De Franco v Met. Police Commr*, *The Times*, 8 May 1987.

407 So reversing *Biddle v Bond* (1856) 6 B. & S. 225; and *Rogers, Son & Co v Lambert & Co* [1891] 1 Q.B. 318.

408 [1902] P. 42; *Eastern Construction Co Ltd v National Trust Co Ltd* [1914] A.C. 197 at 210. *The Winkfield* remains important, of course, in other jurisdictions where the 1977 Act is not in force. It was crucial in the Singapore case of *The Jag Shakti* [1986] A.C. 337.

409 s.7(2): the bailor would thereby avoid the risk of the bailee failing, through insolvency or otherwise, to account to him. For s.7, see para.16-86 onwards.

410 See s.7(3). If the bailee claims only the value of his own limited interest, the bailor, if not joined as a party under s.8, remains free to sue for damages to his reversionary interest, but the actions, if concurrent, might be heard together in the same court under s.9. See para. 16-85 onwards.

411 *Attenborough v London & St Katharine's Dock Co* (1877) 3 C.P.D. 450, 454 (Bramwell LJ); and see (1971) Cmnd.4774, paras 51–65. However, this does not seem to have applied as between bailor and bailee, where recovery by one automatically barred the other: see *O'Sullivan v Williams* [1992] 3 All E.R. 385.

412 *Marriot v Hampton* (1797) 7 T.R. 269.

413 1977 Act s.7(1). Quaere whether it is open to the defendant to such a claim for reimbursement to plead that he has spent the money or otherwise changed his position, on the basis that since *Lipkin Gorman v Karpnale Ltd* [1991] 2 A.C. 548 this plea is generally open to defendants to actions based

to be such as to avoid double liability.[414] This convenient process, however, is impracticable if the claims are not made concurrently. Thus, where only one claimant is involved, he may still obtain judgment for the full value of the goods, even if he has only a possessory title or a limited interest. However, on full or partial satisfaction of a claim for an amount greater than the claimant would have been awarded had other claimants been parties, the claimant becomes liable to account over to any other potential claimant to such extent as will avoid double liability.[415] Further, where, as the result of enforcement of a double liability, any claimant is unjustly enriched, he is liable to reimburse the wrongdoer to that extent.[416] Thus, if a converter of goods pays damages first to a finder of the goods, and then to their true owner, the finder is unjustly enriched unless he accounts over to the true owner under s.7(3); and then the true owner will be unjustly enriched and become liable to reimburse the converter of the goods under s.7(4).

(f) Illegality and public policy as bars to a claim in conversion

Situation where recognising claimant's title to goods illegal or contrary to public policy 16-88 It is a good defence in an action for conversion that the true owner is not entitled to immediate possession either because possession of the goods concerned is itself illegal, or because it is illegal for the defendant to give him possession.[417] It seems that a person may also have a defence to an action in conversion on the grounds of public policy where the return of goods is sought for an immediate and blatant criminal purpose, as where a would-be murderer or thief demands the return of a dagger or jemmy[418]; however, this defence is limited to immediately-contemplated crimes, and does not justify retention of property merely because the defendant reasonably suspects that the claimant may commit a crime with it.[419] In addition, it seems that in some cases the courts may have a discretion to refuse relief where recognising a claimant's title, while not directly conducing to illegality, would seriously contravene the policy of an Act of Parliament.[420]

On its own the fact that the goods of one person have got into the possession of 16-89

---

on restitution or unjust enrichment.

414 1977 Act s.7(2). As to joinder of claimants as parties, see para.16-85.

415 1977 Act s.7(3).

416 1977 Act s.7(4).

417 *Kahler v Midland Bank Ltd* [1950] A.C. 24 (deposit of securities with Czech bank, governed by Czech law; defence to detinue that Czech exchange control regulations prohibited transfer to claimant, and (per Lord Radcliffe at 55) the same would have applied in conversion). See too *Malone v Metropolitan Police Commissioner* [1980] Q.B. 49 (action for return of foreign currency at a time when possession was a criminal offence under the Exchange Control Act 1947). This may be important in connection with the fact that it is now an offence under s.329 of the Proceeds of Crime Act 2002 to knowingly possess any property which is the proceeds of any crime unless it has been obtained for adequate consideration.

418 *Guildford BC v Hein* [2005] EWCA Civ 979; [2005] B.L.G.R. 797 at [65] (Waller LJ); *Chief Constable of Merseyside v Owens* [2012] EWHC 1515 (Admin) at [30] (Thomas P).

419 *Chief Constable of Merseyside v Owens* [2012] EWHC 1515 (Admin) (police not entitled to retain video recording belonging to claimant because they thought he might use it to identify and take revenge on subject: showing of actual intent needed). The reason, as pointed out by Thomas P at [29], is that the opposite result would amount to condoning executive confiscation of property unsanctioned by Parliament.

420 *McCarthy v Northern Ireland Chief Constable* [2016] NICA 36; [2018] N.I. 158 (refusal to make any order with regard to seized psychoactive substances, since owner's possession, while not illegal, was contrary to purposes of the Psychoactive Substances Act 2016). With respect this arguably shows insufficient deference to the need to avoid extra-parliamentary confiscation: see the previous note.

another in consequence of some unlawful dealing, or that such dealing might in some way be furthered by allowing a conversion suit, is no reason to bar the right to sue as a matter of public policy.[421] Indeed, it was once thought that a claimant guilty of illegality who could nevertheless technically found his claim to possession without invoking it could never be met with a public policy defence.[422] But it is now clear that this goes too far,[423] and that in principle the illegality of the underlying transaction may bar a claim, provided that this would accord with the intention of the relevant legislation and not be a disproportionate penalty.[424] For example, it might well be that were a car to be lent for a major drug-smuggling operation, any action by the owner for its return, however impeccable his title, would be barred.

3. Remedies for Conversion

16-90 **Forms of relief available** Before the 1977 Act there were important differences between conversion and detinue with regard to remedies. Conversion lay only for damages (normally the value of the goods plus consequential loss[425]). Detinue, by contrast, could yield a judgment either for specific restitution[426] or for delivery up of the chattel or payment of its value as assessed at the date of judgment, together with damages for its detention. Under the 1977 Act, the situation has been rationalised. Detinue has been abolished,[427] and all the above remedies are now available in any action for wrongful interference, including conversion. Thus by s.3 of the Act, where the defendant is in possession or control of goods[428] relief may be given, so far as appropriate and subject to rules of court,[429] in any one, but not more,[430] of the following forms:

(a) an order for delivery of the goods, and for payment of any consequential damages; or
(b) an order for delivery of the goods, but giving the defendant the alternative of paying damages by reference to the value of the goods, together in either case with payment of any consequential damages; or
(c) damages simpliciter.[431]

Relief under the first head above is at the discretion of the court, whereas the claim-

---

421 *Belvoir Finance Ltd v Stapleton* [1971] 1 Q.B. 210 (hire purchase agreement in breach of credit controls); *Zabihi v Janzemini* [2008] EWHC 2910 (Ch) especially at [286] (smuggled goods).

422 *Bowmakers Ltd v Barnet Instruments Ltd* [1945] K.B. 65, esp. at 70–71 (du Parcq LJ); see too *Belvoir Finance Ltd v Stapleton* [1971] 1 Q.B. 210, 217–218 (Lord Denning MR); and cf. *Singh v Ali* [1960] A.C. 167.

423 *Patel v Mirza* [2016] UKSC 42; [2017] A.C. 467 at [110]–[115] (Lord Toulson).

424 *Patel v Mirza* [2016] UKSC 42; [2017] A.C. 467 at [101]–[109] (Lord Toulson).

425 See generally *General & Finance Facilities Ltd v Cooks Cars (Romford) Ltd* [1963] 1 W.L.R. 644, 649 (Diplock LJ).

426 A discretionary form of relief first made available under the Common Law Procedure Act 1854 s.78. Previously recourse to Chancery had been necessary; for an account of the history, see *General & Finance Facilities Ltd v Cooks Cars (Romford) Ltd* [1963] 1 W.L.R. 644, 650 (Diplock LJ).

427 s.2(1): see para.16-03.

428 If he is not, say because he has lost or destroyed the goods, then for obvious reasons the only relief can be damages.

429 See CPR r.12.4(1) and r.40.14.

430 1977 Act s.3(3)(a).

431 Including, as formerly, both the assessed value of the goods and any consequential loss.

ant may himself choose between the other two.[432] In addition to these forms of final judgment, orders for the delivery up of goods detained may be made by way of interlocutory relief.[433]

(a) Orders for delivery

(i) Judgment for specific delivery

Judgment for specific delivery and consequential damages Section 3(2)(a) allows the court to order specific delivery without allowing the defendant the alternative of paying their value as damages; in such a case the court may also order payment of damages for any consequential loss.[434] But such orders are discretionary[435] and relatively infrequent. They will not usually be made in respect of ordinary articles of commerce for which damages would provide adequate compensation,[436] save where the defendant is insolvent and so refusing specific relief would effectively expropriate the claimant.[437] But they are apt to be granted for unique or sentimental items,[438] articles of particular value to the claimant,[439] and things not easily or readily replaceable,[440] or whose replacement would take considerable time and effort.[441] Even here, however, the court retains a general discretion to refuse 16-91

---

432 1977 Act s.3(3)(b). This provision also is subject to rules of court; CPR r.40.14 provides that, notwithstanding anything in s.3(3), on a claim relating to detention of goods by a partial owner whose right of action is not founded on a possessory title the judgment or order shall be for the payment of damages only. This rule both preserves the rule that a person with no immediate right to possession is confined to damages limited to his reversionary interest in the goods, and also prevents a co-owner obtaining either specific delivery or the assessed value of the goods unless all the other co-owners have authorised him in writing to sue on their behalf.

433 1977 Act s.4.

434 Normally under such a judgment the only pecuniary redress possible is damages for consequential loss. If, however, it is shown to the satisfaction of the court that such an order for specific delivery has not been complied with, the court may revoke that order, or the relevant part of it, and instead order the payment of damages assessed by reference to the value of the goods. See s.3(4).

435 1977 Act s.3(3)(b).

436 See *Whiteley v Hilt* [1918] 2 K.B. 808, 819 (per Swinfen Eady MR); *Blue Sky One Ltd v Blue Airways LLC* [2009] EWHC 3314 (Comm) at [314]–[316] (Beatson J) (jumbo jets held for leasing out); *Tanks & Vessels Industries Ltd v Devon Cider Co Ltd* [2009] EWHC 1360 (Ch) at [55]–[56] (cider vats).

437 See *X-Fab Semiconductor Foundries AG v Plessey Semiconductors Ltd* [2014] EWHC 1574 (QB) at [32], following dicta of Beatson J in *Blue Sky One Ltd v PKF Finance US Inc* [2009] EWHC 3314 at [309]; also *Dawsonrentals Bus & Coaches Ltd v Geldards Coaches Ltd* [2015] EWHC 2596 (QB) (leased buses).

438 e.g. *García v De Aldama* [2002] EWHC 2087; [2003] E.C.D.R. CN1 (manuscript of poet Federico García Lorca: specific delivery would have been granted had claimant proved his case).

439 *Secretary of State for Defence v Guardian Newspapers Ltd, The Times,* 16 December 1983 (confidential memorandum) (affirmed on other grounds, [1985] A.C. 359).

440 e.g. *Howard E Perry Ltd v British Railways Board* [1980] 1 W.L.R. 1375 (steel otherwise unobtainable owing to strike); *Steel Linings Ltd v Bibby & Co* [1993] R.A. 27 (tools of trade); *X-Fab Semiconductor Foundries AG v Plessey Semiconductors Ltd* [2014] EWHC 1574 (QB) (highly specialised electronic equipment).

441 Neatly christened "commercially unique" by Beatson J: *Blue Sky One Ltd v Blue Airways LLC* [2009] EWHC 3314 (Comm) at [314]. The chattels in question there were Boeing 747 aircraft. See too *Pendragon Plc v Walon Ltd* [2005] EWHC 1082 (QB) (specific delivery of 114 Rover cars ordered in view of (a) claimants' urgent need for them; and (b) the bankruptcy of the manufacturers, which meant that equivalents would not be readily obtainable elsewhere).

relief where appropriate, for example to prevent prejudice to third party interests,[442] promote human or animal welfare,[443] or to safeguard human rights.[444]

16-92 Any such order may be subject to conditions; in particular, where damages by reference to the value of the goods would not be the whole of their value, the order may require an allowance to be made by the claimant to reflect the difference.[445] For example, where in a bailor's action against his bailee the measure of damages would not be the full value of the goods, the court may make it a condition of ordering specific delivery that the bailee should pay the bailor a sum reflecting that difference.[446] It seems, however, that the power to impose conditions does not justify ordinary delivery up of the goods, but only in some altered state: the defendant must be ordered to give them up as they are, or not at all.[447] Similarly, in cases where the defendant is entitled[448] to an allowance for improvement of the goods after the act of wrongful interference, the court may both assess that allowance and make its payment a condition of an order for specific delivery.[449] It is suggested that an order for specific delivery imposes a duty on the defendant to have the goods available for collection by the claimant, but does not oblige him to take them to him[450]; hence the expenses of delivery are prima facie for the claimant's account. It seems, however, that at least in the case of bulky goods not on the defendant's premises, the defendant must facilitate their collection by informing the claimant where they are and saying that they are at his disposal.[451]

---

442 *Dawsonrentals Bus and Coaches Ltd v Geldards Coaches Ltd* [2015] EWHC 2596 (QB) (specific return of leased buses used for school transport delayed for a week, to allow school authorities to find alternative transport).

443 For example, the county court case of *Probert v Society for the Welfare of Horses*, Pontypool County Court, reported in the *Daily Telegraph* for 1 February 1997. The owner of a horse was convicted of mistreating it and fined; the animal was later removed and unlawfully kept by the defendant charity. The judge refused an order for specific delivery against the charity, despite the claimant's impeccable title. See too *Sharma v Plumridge*, unreported 22 May 1991 CA (no specific delivery of pet dogs owing to passage of time).

444 See, e.g. *Capita Plc v Darch* [2017] EWHC 1248 (Ch); [2017] I.R.L.R. 718 at [67]–[74] (demand for handover of emails, even if sounding in conversion—which it did not—might well be met with an art.8 defence concerning privacy).

445 1977 Act s.3(6).

446 This example is given in s.3(6) itself: for other examples, see A. Manchester (1977) 127 New L.J. 1219.

447 *Secretary of State for Defence v Guardian Newspapers Ltd*, *The Times,* 16 December 1983, Scott J (This decision was upheld in the Court of Appeal ([1984] Ch. 156), and in the House of Lords [1985] A.C. 33. In the Court of Appeal, Slade LJ apparently agreed with Scott J on this point.) The case concerned a secret ministerial memorandum which the defendants were prepared to hand back, but only having mutilated it so as to conceal who had leaked it in the first place.

448 1977 Act s.6(1) and (2); see para.16-102 onwards.

449 1977 Act s.3(7). Alternatively a court may refuse specific restitution entirely against a defendant who has spent large sums in all innocence on the improvement of property: *Nash v Barnes* [1922] N.Z.L.R. 303.

450 It seems that this was the position in detinue: cf. *Capital Finance Co Ltd v Bray* [1964] 1 W.L.R. 323. Quaere whether ss.3(6) and s.4(3) now enable the court to require of the defendant an actual delivery (see A. Manchester (1977) 127 N.L.J. 1219). Megarry VC appeared to assume so in *Howard E Perry Ltd v British Railways Board* [1980] 1 W.L.R. 1375; sed quaere. If a defendant's legal duty is merely to let the claimant collect his goods (cf. *Capital Finance Co Ltd v Bray*, above), he should not be able to be forced by injunction to go any further.

451 cf. *Metals & Ropes Co Ltd v Tattersall* [1966] 1 W.L.R. 1500.

(ii) Judgment for delivery or damages at defendant's option

The court may, at the claimant's choice, make an order under s.3(2)(b) of the 1977 Act for delivery of the goods, but give the defendant the alternative of paying damages, together in either alternative with payment of any consequential damages. The defendant may satisfy the order by returning the goods at any time before execution of judgment, but without prejudice to his liability to pay consequential damages.[452] The provisions empowering the court to impose conditions, especially concerning allowances to be made to the defendant, on orders for specific delivery under s.3(2)(a) apply equally to orders for delivery or payment of damages under s.3(2)(b). **16-93**

(iii) Interlocutory orders for delivery up

Before considering the third form of final judgment in conversion, namely damages simpliciter under s.3(2)(c) of the 1977 Act, it is convenient to consider here the provisions of s.4 concerning interlocutory orders for delivery up. The court has power, on the application of any person, to make an order for the delivery up or safe custody of any goods which are or may become the subject-matter of subsequent proceedings for wrongful interference in the court, or as to which any question may arise in such proceedings.[453] The order may require delivery either to the claimant or to a person appointed by the court for the purpose, and on such terms and conditions as the order specifies.[454] The first such order was made in *Howard E Perry & Co Ltd v British Railways Board*.[455] There the defendants detained in their depots 500 tons of the claimants' steel, having been threatened with a ruinous strike if they allowed the owners to collect it. Megarry VC accepted that, like final orders for specific delivery without the option of paying damages,[456] interlocutory orders must be at the court's discretion, but nevertheless considered that the severe shortage of steel owing to the strike justified departure from the principle that specific delivery will not normally be granted of ordinary commercial goods.[457] **16-94**

---

452 1977 Act s.3(5). Where the claimant obtains judgment for damages simpliciter, the defendant cannot satisfy the judgment by returning the chattel, but he may well reduce the damages to a nominal figure.

453 1977 Act s.4(2); and see CPR 25.1(1)(c), 25.1(1)(e) (which, however, are narrower than s.4 of the Act in restricting applicants to parties in proceedings which are in being and pending. The power applies to actions for other forms of wrongful interference besides conversions. See, too, I. Topping, "Delivery up—the Forgotten Remedy" (1985) 36 N.I.L.Q. 236.). It has been suggested that, all other things being equal, the principle in *American Cyanamid Co v Ethicon Ltd* [1975] A.C. 396 concerning the award of interlocutory injunctions should apply here: *Infinity Health London Ltd v Tooth Clinic Ltd* [2014] EWHC 3007 (QB).

454 1977 Act s.4(3). Where appropriate an undertaking in damages analogous to that demanded in the case of interlocutory injunctions may be required: see, e.g. *VVB M&E Group Ltd v Optilan (UK) Ltd* [2020] EWHC 4 (TCC); 88 Con. L.R. 235 at [6]–[9].

455 [1980] 1 W.L.R. 1375.

456 1977 Act s.3(3)(b).

457 For other cases where such orders were made, see *Adventure Film Productions Ltd v Tully* (1982) [1993] E.M.L.R. 376; *Secretary of State for Defence v Guardian Newspapers Ltd* [1984] Ch. 156 (affirmed on other grounds, [1985] A.C. 339). cf. *Bear Necessities Daycare Ltd v Lancashire Fuels 4 U Ltd* [2015] EWHC 721 (QB) at [33] (such orders not lightly made in absence of threats of disposal or dissipation); and *Roandale v Metropolitan Police Commissioner* [1979] Crim. L.R. 254, where Park J refused as premature such an interlocutory order for delivery up of a large quantity of allegedly obscene publications seized by the police under s.3 of the Obscene Publications Act 1959

(b) Damages

(i) General rule: value of the goods[458]

16-95 **Damages for deprivation of goods** In theory, conversion is no different from any other tort: the measure of damages is simply the loss suffered by the claimant.[459] In practice, however, the measure of damages for deprivation of his goods is nearly always their market value.[460] To some extent this is an arbitrary rule, not dependent on the claimant's loss. Thus, for example, an owner of goods is entitled to recover their value even if the defendant proves that the claimant would have been deprived of his goods in any event, and hence that the claimant has, in some sense, suffered no loss at all—a rule which doubtless reflects considerations of simplicity and public policy as anything else.[461] So in *Kuwait Airways Corp v Iraqi Airways Co*[462] aircraft forcibly removed by Iraqi forces invading Kuwait were converted by the defendant airline. The House of Lords rebuffed a plea by the defendants that the claimants would in any case have been kept out of their property as a result of the activities of the Iraqi army. In addition the claimant is entitled to recover any special loss which flows naturally and directly from the wrong.[463] Where goods are repeatedly converted, prima facie each conversion is a separate tort carrying a separate liability.[464]

---

and detained for some three weeks without being brought before magistrates or a summons being issued.

458 See generally *McGregor on Damages*, 20th edn (London: Sweet & Maxwell, 2017), para.38-006 onwards; A. Tettenborn, "Damages in Conversion—The Exception or the Anomaly?" [1993] C.L.J. 128.

459 "The aim of the law, in respect of the wrongful interference with goods, is to provide a just remedy. Despite its proprietary base, this tort does not stand apart and command awards of damages measured by some special and artificial standard of its own .... The fundamental object of an award of damages in respect of this tort, as with all wrongs, is to award just compensation for loss suffered." (Lord Nicholls in *Kuwait Airways v Iraq Airways Co* [2002] UKHL 19; [2002] 2 A.C. 883 at [67]). See too *Brandeis Goldschmidt & Co Ltd v Western Transport Ltd* [1981] Q.B. 864 at 870, per Brandon LJ; *VFS Financial Services Ltd v Euro Auctions Ltd* [2007] EWHC 1492 (QB) at [102]; *Checkprice (UK) Ltd (in administration) v Revenue & Customs Commissioners* [2010] EWHC 682 (Admin); [2010] S.T.C. 1153 at [56] (Sales J); *Plantation Holdings (FZ) LLC v Dubai Islamic Bank PJSC* [2017] EWHC 520 (Comm) at [256] (Picken J).

460 "Normally ('prima facie') the measure of damages is the market value of the goods at the time the defendant expropriated them. This is the general rule, because generally this measure represents the amount of the basic loss suffered by the claimant owner. He has been dispossessed of his goods by the defendant." (Lord Nicholls in *Kuwait Airways v Iraq Airways Co* [2002] UKHL 19; [2002] 2 A.C. 883 at [67].) It has been said that departures from the value of the goods as the measure of damages, while entirely permissible, should be rare: see *Blue Sky One Ltd v Mahan Air* [2010] EWHC 631 (Comm) at [114] (Beatson J); and *Al-Khyami v El-Muderris* [2018] EWHC 24 (QB) at [75].

461 S. Douglas, "The Nature of Conversion" [2009] C.L.J. 198, 220, perceptively suggests as much. In any case the disregard of what would otherwise have happened to the goods applies only to value claims, and not (for example) to consequential losses, where causation must be proved in the ordinary way: see *Glenmorgan Farm Ltd v New Zealand Bloodstock Leasing Ltd* [2011] NZCA 672; [2012] 1 N.Z.L.R. 555.

462 [2002] UKHL 19; [2002] 2 A.C. 883. See too *Kuwait Airways Corp v Iraqi Airways Co (No.10)* [2002] EWHC 1626 (Comm).

463 *Re Simms* [1934] 1 Ch. 1. See para.16-110 onwards, for consequential damages.

464 cf. *RB Policies* at Lloyds v Butler [1950] 1 K.B. 76 (a limitation case). In *Middle Temple v Lloyds Bank Plc* [1999] All E.R. (Comm) 193; and *Linklaters v HSBC Bank Plc* [2003] EWHC 1113 (Comm); [2003] 2 Lloyd's Rep. 545 it was suggested, obiter, that there might be contribution between serial converters under s.1 of the Civil Liability (Contribution) Act 1978. Sed quaere. If the

Time of assessment of value At common law, a distinction was drawn in this connection between conversion and detinue. In detinue the value of the goods was assessed at the date of judgment, when their return would have been ordered, and not at the earlier time of refusal to return them.[465] In conversion, however, despite some contrary authority,[466] it appears to be established that the time of conversion[467] is normally the proper time for assessment of the value of the goods.[468] With the abolition of detinue and the extension to conversion of the former remedies in detinue it might have been expected that the 1977 Act would make the date of judgment the time of assessment. In fact, however, the Act is silent on the matter except for one neutral reference to time.[469] Presumably, therefore, the established rules as to time of assessment in conversion continue to apply. 16-96

Rise in value after conversion From what has been said above, it follows that where a claimant seeks damages for conversion in respect of goods that have since appreciated, he is prima facie limited[470] to their value at the time of conversion. However, this does not mean that the subsequent rise in value is necessarily out of account. First, there is no reason why such an appreciation should not—provided it is foreseeable—be recoverable as consequential damages. *The Playa Larga*[471] is a case neatly in point. A cargo of sugar was converted by the defendants when worth $206 a tonne; but later, and before the claimant had any chance to recover it, the price rose to $240-odd. It was held that the claimant could claim the latter figure; the rise in value represented a loss suffered by him that flowed directly from the original conversion. Alternatively, a court may reach much the same result on the basis that is not strictly bound to the time of conversion and may award the value at a later time, such as that of judgment, if that more truly represents the claimant's 16-97

two conversions took place on different occasions, were both defendants liable for the "same damage" as required by s.1(1) of that Act? It seems doubtful.

465 *Rosenthal v Alderton & Sons Ltd* [1946] K.B. 374.

466 e.g. *Greening v Wilkinson* (1825) 1 C. & P. 625 at 626 which concerned conversion of warrants for cotton which had risen in value between the date of conversion and trial. Abbott CJ held that the jury might award the value of the cotton "at the time of the conversion or at any subsequent time in their discretion, because the claimant might have had a good opportunity of selling the goods if they had not been detained." But the decision was doubted by Maule J in *Reid v Fairbanks* (1853) 13 C.B. 692, 728; and in *Caxton Publishing Co Ltd v Sutherland Publishing Co Ltd* [1939] A.C. 179, 203, Lord Porter was similarly sceptical as to whether the view of Abbott CJ could be supported.

467 Where there has been a series of different conversions, the claimant may rely on any of them: at least this seems to be the reasoning in cases like *Greenwood v Bennett* [1973] Q.B. 195. The suggestion to the contrary in *Highland Leasing v Paul Field* [1986] C.L.Y. 3224, that the claimant cannot rely on any act of conversion by the defendant except the first, is (it is submitted) heterodox and should not be followed.

468 *Mercer v Jones* (1813) 3 Camp. 477; *Henderson v Williams* [1895] Q.B. 521 CA at 530, 532; *Solloway v McLaughlin* [1938] A.C. 247 at 257; *Caxton Publishing Co v Sutherland Publishing Co* [1939] A.C. 179, 192, 203; *General & Finance Facilities v Cooks Cars (Romford) Ltd* [1963] 1 W.L.R. 644, 649; *Steinman v Steinman* (1983) 143 D.L.R. (3d) 396, 407. See too D. Gordon, "Anomalies in the Law of Conversion" (1955) 71 L.Q.R. 346.

469 s.6(1), concerning allowances to be made for improvements to the goods.

470 If the value of what is converted subsequently goes down, of course, the claimant gets a windfall: *Solloway v McLoughlin* [1938] A.C. 247 (shares wrongfully sold, then replaced by converter who had bought them back at a lower price: held, owner could claim value as at time of sale).

471 [1983] 2 Lloyd's Rep. 171. See too *Scheps v Fine Art Logistic Ltd* [2007] EWHC 541 (QB) (very abstract sculpture inadvertently disposed of as rubbish: recovery of value then, augmented by subsequent would-be appreciation). Presumably, however, the claimant in such a case must sue reasonably promptly: he can hardly be allowed to speculate indefinitely and for free against the defendant. See *Sachs v Miklos* [1949] 2 K.B. 23.

loss. So in *IBL v Coussens*[472] a company director wrongfully refused to return a couple of company cars then worth £62,000; but when judgment was given, they were worth a great deal more. In the absence of evidence that they would have sold the cars any earlier, the claimants recovered the latter figure.

16-98 However, each case will depend on its own facts; and where the loss to the claimant due to the subsequent rise is substantially his own fault, the result will be different. Thus in *Sachs v Miklos*[473] the defendant, having gratuitously stored the claimant's goods from 1940 to 1943, twice wrote asking him to take them away. Receiving no reply, he sold them for £15. In 1946 the claimant reappeared and demanded the goods, whereupon the defendant tendered the £15 but, the market value having risen to £115, the claimant sued in both detinue and conversion. The Court of Appeal remitted the case to the county court to determine whether the claimant had received the defendant's letters, in which case any loss due to subsequent increase in value of the goods would be irrecoverable as being attributable to his own failure to collect his goods; but otherwise the value should be assessed at the time when the claimant became aware of the conversion. It seems, however, that where the claimant relies not on a wrongful sale but on a destruction of the goods, their value of the goods is invariably reckoned as at the time of conversion even if the claimant has delayed unwarrantably in collecting them.[474]

16-99 **Decline in value after conversion** If the goods decline in value between the dates of conversion and of judgment, the claimant may recover damages assessed by reference to the value at the date of conversion,[475] so preventing the defendant from profiting from his own wrongdoing.[476] However, it is arguable that this will not apply where the only conversion proved is a refusal to return on demand and the claimant does eventually recover his property, so that essentially the claim is merely for temporary deprivation. In detinue, the claimant in such a case was limited to claiming the value as at the time of return,[477] and could only claim further damages if he could show actual loss (for example that he lost the opportunity, which he would have exercised, to sell the goods at an advantageous price).[478] And it now seems accepted that a similar principle applies where the action is in conversion. Despite the general rule allowing a claimant to claim the value of his property when

472 [1991] 2 All E.R. 133. See too *Trafigura Beheer BV v Mediterranean Shipping Co SA* [2007] EWCA Civ 794; [2008] 1 All E.R. (Comm) 385 ($1.5 million worth of copper wrongfully put at fraudsters' disposal by carriers and then immobilised in China because of litigation: recovery of value at date of judgment).

473 [1949] 2 K.B. 23. On similar facts today the defendant would have a right of sale under ss.12, 13 of, and Sch.1 to the 1977 Act.

474 *Irving v Keen* unreported 3 March 1995 (claimant ignored request to collect car in 1984: defendant disassembled it in 1988; damages as at higher, 1988, value). Sed quaere: why should there be a distinction between selling and destroying unwanted goods left on one's hands? The equities seem similar in both cases.

475 *Rhodes v Moules* [1895] 1 Ch. 236 at 254; *Solloway v McLaughlin* [1938] A.C. 247, where, on subsequently discovering that his stockbroker had sold his shares and repurchased the same number at a lower price, the claimant recovered the value as at the date of conversion less the value of the replacement shares when received, although he would probably not himself have sold them before the market price fell. See too *BBMM Finance (Hong Kong) Ltd v Eda Holdings Ltd* [1990] 1 W.L.R. 409; *Trailways Transport Ltd v Thomas* [1996] 2 N.Z.L.R. 443.

476 See *Kuwait Airways Corp v Iraqi Airways Co* [2002] UKHL 19; [2002] 2 A.C. 883 at [88] (Lord Nicholls), suggesting that damages of this sort were really gain-based damages awarded on the broad principles enunciated by him in *Att Gen v Blake* [2001] 1 A.C. 268, 278–280.

477 *Brandeis Goldschmidt & Co Ltd v Western Transport Ltd* [1981] Q.B. 864.

478 See *Williams v Archer* (1847) 5 C.B. 318; and *Williams v Peel River Land Co* (1886) 55 L.T. 689.

converted and ignore any subsequent depreciation, a mere temporary deprivation of itself gives rise to a right merely to damages for actual loss.[479] But if the goods converted had been held for resale on the spot market, then the claimant is entitled to the value as at the time of refusal to return to mark the fact that he has lost the chance of an advantageous sale.[480]

How is the value assessed? If there is a market price, the value of the goods is to be taken as that market price at the relevant time.[481] It may be that there is a difference between market prices for sellers and buyers.[482] If so, it is suggested that the relevant figure is prima facie the value for which the claimant could have disposed of it and not the replacement value,[483] unless he actually intends to replace it (or has already done so).[484] If there is no market,[485] the value of the goods to the claimant[486] must be determined by any available evidence, such as the price at which the goods have been bought, or sold under a subcontract.[487] For example, in **16-100**

[479] In *BBMM Finance (Hong Kong) Ltd v Eda Holdings Ltd* [1990] 1 W.L.R. 409, a conversion case, the Privy Council seem to have accepted that had the facts been similar to *Brandeis Goldschmidt & Co Ltd v Western Transport Ltd* [1981] Q.B. 864, the claimant would have been limited to nominal damages. See [1990] 1 W.L.R. 409, 413, approved in *Malkins Nominees Ltd v Société Financière Mirelis SA* [2004] EWHC 2631 (Ch) at [24]–[25] and [31]–[34].

[480] *Glenbrook Capital LP v Hamilton* [2014] EWHC 2297 (Comm) (failure on demand to return silver held for investment and sale: value at time of demand given, despite later 50 per cent decline in bullion market).

[481] See *J & E Hall Ltd v Barclay* [1937] 3 All E.R. 620; *Chubb Cash Ltd v John Crilley & Son* [1983] 1 W.L.R. 599. On the valuation of a chattel in a highly volatile market, see *Kuwait Airways v Iraq Airways Co* [2001] 3 W.L.R. 1117; [2001] 1 Lloyd's Rep. 161 at 262–263 (upheld without discussion of the point: [2002] UKHL 19; [2002] 2 A.C. 883). There the Court of Appeal held that aircraft wrongfully abstracted by the Iraqi army on its invasion of Kuwait fell to be valued on the "current market price" principle, taking into account a "base value" and then adjusting it according to the strength of the market for aircraft at the relevant time.

[482] For example, a custom-made machine tool is likely to be worth a great deal more to a buyer who needs one than to a seller hopefully trying to dispose of one.

[483] "What it would be worth to the owner"—see *Acatos v Burns* (1877-78) L.R. 3 Ex. D. 282, 288 (Bramwell LJ). See too the property damage case of *The Maersk Colombo* [2001] EWCA Civ 717; [2001] 2 Lloyd's Rep. 275 (sale value of crane claimants never intended to replace). But note the contrary decision in *Bird v Burgoine* unreported 8 December 1987 (conversion of classic car: CA award replacement value). In so far as tax payable on new items feeds through into the value of a secondhand one, the tax element may of course increase the latter: see *Martin v LCC* [1947] 1 K.B. 628 (purchase tax element in lost jewellery).

[484] As in, e.g. *J & E Hall Ltd v Barclay* [1937] 3 All E.R. 620. See too *Wilson v Robertsons (London) Ltd* [2006] EWCA Civ 1088 (ring with sentimental value wrongfully sold: since owner reasonably intended to buy replacement, recovered replacement cost).

[485] Or, it would seem, if the claimant is a dealer in the things converted, and already has in stock more than he can sell: *Johnson & Johnson Ltd v CP Security* (1986) 10 I.L.R.M. 559.

[486] See *VFS Financial Services Ltd v Euro Actions Ltd* [2007] EWHC 1492 (QB) at [92] (claimant recovers net price he would have got); and the carrier's case of *Sony Computer Entertainment UK Ltd v Cinram Logistics UK Ltd* [2008] EWCA Civ 955; [2009] 2 All E.R. (Comm) 65 (loss of goods costing claimants £56,000 to produce but sold by them for £290,000: recovery of latter sum). This sum may not be the same as the price at which a defendant sold them: see *Fairfax Gerrard Holdings Ltd v Capital Bank Plc* [2006] EWHC 3439 (Comm); [2007] 1 Lloyd's Rep. 171 (value of unique machine tool discounted by 40 per cent from wrongful sale price to reflect likely realisation difficulties). The case was later successfully appealed on liability: see [2007] EWCA Civ 1226; [2008] 1 Lloyd's Rep. 297.

[487] *The Arpad* [1934] P. 189; applied in *Heskell v Continental Express Ltd* [1950] 1 All E.R. 1033; *Ernest Scragg & Sons v Perseverance Banking and Trust Co* [1973] 2 Lloyd's Rep. 101. And see *J Sargent (Garages) Ltd v Motor Auctions (West Bromwich) Ltd* [1977] R.T.R. 121, where the claimant motor dealers were held entitled to the retail price at which they had expected to sell a car with several

France v Gaudet[488] the claimant had made a specially advantageous bargain for the sale of certain wine, which the defendant subsequently converted. The claimant, being unable to complete his contract owing to the fact that no wine of the like quality was procurable in the market, was allowed as damages the whole sum which he would have received from the purchaser. In the circumstances of that case, the price at which the goods had been resold was held to afford good evidence of their value.[489] Where the claimant himself had contemplated selling the goods, the defendant will generally be given credit for the cost of the putative sale, as that would have been incurred anyway.[490] In a suitable case replacement cost may be some guide as to value.[491] In one case, where goods had been wrongfully sold in the course of a voyage, the owner obtained as damages the cost price of the goods and the freight paid and it was held that this was in the circumstances a proper method of arriving at their value.[492] In another decision, where the claimant's timber was wrongfully intercepted in transit down river, he obtained the amount he would have realised at the port of destination, less the cost of conveying the timber to that market.[493] In effect these decisions support the proposition that generally speaking goods in the course of trade should be valued as at the place of conversion.

16-101 **Presumption of value against wrongdoer?** Where there is a doubt about the value of a chattel which has passed wrongfully into the possession of a defendant, there is some authority that he must either produce it or account for its non-production, or otherwise it will be assumed against him that it was of the highest possible value.[494] But the authority is somewhat dated, and it is suggested that the courts today are more likely to insist on proper proof of value by the claimant.[495] Thus where a Hatton Garden jeweller lost diamonds entrusted to him, but there was no clear evidence of their quality, Field J understandably declined to give the claimant an almost certain windfall by awarding damages on the assumption that all the diamonds had been "finest quality"(the highest grade in the diamond trade).[496] On the other hand, judicial time is limited, and where miscellaneous items of relatively low value are involved, courts may in practice award a fairly rough-and-ready figure without demanding meticulous proof.[497]

---

unusual features for which there was no market.

488 (1871) L.R. 6 Q.B. 199.

489 See comments on this case in *The Arpad* [1934] P. 189, where Greer LJ at 219 disapproved the reasons given by Mellor J, but the decision is explained by Maugham LJ at 234–236.

490 *Clarke v Nicholson* (1835) 1 C.M. & R. 724; *Whitmore v Black* (1844) 13 M. & W. 507. Aliter where no such sale was envisaged: *Glasspoole v Young* (1829) 9 B. & C. 696. A similar rule applied where the claimant sued a copyright infringer for statutory conversion under s.18 of the Copyright Act 1956 (now repealed): *Infabrics Ltd v Jaytex Ltd* [1982] A.C. 1.

491 *J & E Hall Ltd v Barclay* [1937] 3 All E.R. 620.

492 *Ewbank v Nutting* (1849) 7 C.B. 797.

493 *Burmah Trading Corp v Mirza Mohammed Ally Sherazee* (1878) L.R. 5 Ind. App. 130.

494 *Armory v Delamirie* (1721) 1 Stra. 505.

495 In the British Columbia decision in *Bangle v Lafreniere* 2012 BCSC 256; 214 A.C.W.S. (3d) 309 at [39], Sewell J said that the "maximum value" presumption applied "only in situations in which the wrongful conduct of the defendant makes it impracticable for the plaintiff to value the loss." cf. *Williamson v Phillips, Son & Neale*, unreported 29 July 1998 (presumption referred to in *Armory v Delamirie*, above, only applies, if at all, where other evidence entirely lacking).

496 *Colbeck v Diamanta (UK) Ltd* [2002] EWHC 616 (QB).

497 See the trespass to goods case of *Diaz v Karim* [2017] EWHC 595 (QB) (unlawful eviction of student from lodging: items of personal property thrown out and lost: round figure of £5,000 awarded).

Improvements made to converted chattel[498] At common law an owner could enjoy without payment an unwanted benefit resulting from another's unauthorised improvement of a chattel in his possession.[499] However, it was also established that if he sued to recover the chattel from someone else he could not profit from any increase in its value caused by its bona fide improvement by the defendant.[500] Thus, in *Munro v Willmott*[501] the defendant, unable to contact the owner of a car which had been left with him, sold it. The sale was in the event wrongful: nevertheless, he was held able, in both detinue and conversion, to deduct from the value of the car at the date of judgment his expenditure in repairing and repainting it. Moreover the rule, it seems, applied to actions not only against the improver but against any other bona fide possessor.[502] **16-102**

This latter rule has now received limited statutory recognition. Section 6(1) of the 1977 Act now provides as follows: **16-103**

> "If in proceedings for wrongful interference[503] against a person (the improver) who has improved the goods, it is shown that the improver acted in the mistaken but honest belief that he had a good title to them, an allowance shall be made for the extent to which, at the time at which the goods fall to be valued in assessing damages,[504] the value of the goods is attributable to the improvement."

A similar allowance must be made in such proceedings against a transferee of the goods by way of purchase, bailment or other disposition from the improver, if that transferee took in good faith, regardless of whether or not the improver himself had had any honest belief in his own title.[505] To achieve the same result where the court orders specific delivery, any order must be conditional on the claimant paying the defendant a sum equivalent to the value of the improvement.[506]

The Act does not say whether s.6 replaces, or adds to, the common law protec- **16-104**

---

498 For valuable comments on the cases prior to 1978 see G. Jones, "Restitutionary Claims for Services Rendered" (1977) 93 L.Q.R. 273, 288–295; J. Weir, "Doing Good by Mistake" [1973] C.L.J. 23; Law Reform Committee, *18th Report*, Cmnd.4774, c.89. For a commentary on s.6 of the 1977 Act see V. Sacks (1978) 41 M.L.R. 713, 717. The most controversial question is whether even a morally innocent tortfeasor should be allowed any increase in value beyond the amount actually expended on the improvement: see P. Matthews, "Freedom, unrequested improvements and Lord Denning" [1981] C.L.J. 340.

499 2 Bl. Comm. 404; cf. *Appleby v Myers* (1867) L.R. 2 C.P. 651 at 659–660, per Blackburn J. In *Greenwood v Bennett* [1973] Q.B. 195 at 202, 203, Lord Denning MR's readiness to hold that the improver should have an independent restitutionary action against the owner for the increase in value was dissented from by Cairns LJ and not supported by Phillimore LJ See Goff & Jones, *Law of Unjust Enrichment*, 9th edn (London: Sweet & Maxwell, 2016), paras 4-30, 5-41. But cf. *Thomas v Robinson* [1977] 1 N.Z.L.R. 385.

500 *Reid v Fairbanks* (1853) 13 C.B. 692 (defendant liable only for uncompleted value of claimant's half-built ship, which he converted and then completed); *Munro v Willmott* [1949] 1 K.B. 295; *Dean v J Thomas & Son Ltd* [1981] Qd. R. 62.

501 [1949] 1 K.B. 295.

502 *Greenwood v Bennett* [1973] Q.B. 195; also *McKeown v Cavalier Yachts Ltd* (1988) 13 N.S.W.L.R. 303. See J.A. Weir, "Doing Good by Mistake" [1973] C.L.J. 23.

503 It is thought that these words probably include interpleader proceedings such as those in *Greenwood v Bennett*, above. But they clearly do not cover the case where the owner simply recapts his goods extra-judicially.

504 This is the 1977 Act's only reference to time of assessment of value and so, as regards conversion, must presumably mean the time of conversion.

505 1977 Act s.6(2) and (4). If the transferee later sought to recover his money from his transferor on the basis of failure of consideration, the latter gets a similar allowance: see s.6(3), and the example given in s.6(2) itself.

506 1977 Act s.3(7). This provision may compel an impecunious claimant to opt for damages rather than

tion available to the defendant. This can be important: for example, the defendant in *Munro v Willmott*,[507] who was protected at common law, would not come under s.6 because he knew that the property he improved did not belong to him. In view of the eminent justice of protecting such defendants, it is respectfully suggested that s.6 and the common law protection are cumulative: that is, in so far as a defendant would have had the right to an allowance for improvement at common law, he continues to have one today.[508]

16-105 **Severed realty** Principles similar to, but not identical with, those applicable at common law to improvements to chattels apply where a portion of realty is severed and the party entitled elects to sue for it as a chattel rather than for trespass to land.[509] Thus, if minerals are unlawfully mined, the estate owner may take full advantage of the severance if he can recapt them. Otherwise, if the defendant's wrongdoing was deliberate, the expenses of raising the minerals to the pit's mouth, but not those of winning them from the soil, must be deducted from the value of the goods in assessing damages or must be paid to the wrongdoer as a condition of an order for delivery. Where, however, the defendant has acted in good faith, though mistakenly, the expenses of both severing and raising the minerals must be so deducted or paid.[510] It should be added that s.6 of the 1977 Act does not seem to apply here: that is limited to improvement to chattels, and at the time that the defendant "improved" the claimant's property it was not a chattel.

16-106 **Particular forms of property: securities and documents** The measure of damages for depriving the claimant of a cheque or other security for money is its value at the time of the wrongful act. A security will for these purposes be presumed good and worth its face value[511]; but this is only a presumptive rule.[512] If the security is in fact invalid, nothing is recoverable.[513] If, owing to the insolvency of a relevant party or otherwise, the security is depreciated, account will be taken of this[514]; where there is a relevant market, its value in that market will be taken. This reasoning ap-

the return of his chattel.

507 [1949] 1 K.B. 295.

508 This inference receives some support from the statement of M. Stewart QC, sitting in *Highland Leasing Ltd v Paul Field* [1986] C.L.Y. 3224, that s.6 did not change the common law in areas it left untouched.

509 Since severance of minerals from the soil makes them saleable rather than "improves" them, it is doubtful whether s.6 of the 1977 Act applies, so as to entitle a person honestly but mistakenly believing that he has a right to sever them to an allowance for the increase in their value (which, as at common law, would include the costs of both winning and raising the minerals).

510 See generally D. Gordon, "Anomalies in the Law of Conversion" (1955) 71 L.Q.R. 346; P. Matthews, "Freedom, Unrequested Benefits and Lord Denning" [1981] C.L.J. 340; and *Bilambil-Terranova P/L v Tweed Shire Council* [1980] 1 N.S.W.L.R. 465.

511 See *Morison v London County & Westminster Bank* [1914] 3 K.B. 356 at 365, where the authorities are collected; *International Factors Ltd v Rodriguez* [1979] Q.B. 351; *Prescott Meat Co Ltd v Northern Bank Ltd* [1981] N.I. 150. Obviously a defendant cannot plead a diminution of value which it may have suffered through his own wrongful conduct: see *Delegal v Naylor* (1831) 7 Bing. 460; *Alsager v Close* (1842) 10 M. & W. 576.

512 Which can perhaps be fairly easily inferred. Were a cheque for £1 million to be converted, no doubt a court would take some convincing that the drawer's account would indeed have been good for that sum before awarding it as damages.

513 See, e.g. *Smith v Lloyds TSB Bank Plc* [2001] Q.B. 541 (cheque unenforceable because of alteration); C. Hare, "Loss Allocation for Materially Altered Cheques" [2001] C.L.J. 35.

514 *Delegal v Naylor* (1831) 7 Bing. 460.

plies also to other documents with a transferable character or money value,[515] and to bearer share certificates and share transfer forms.[516] However, if a document is easily replaceable without loss, except the trivial cost of replacement, it would seem that the face value would be an inappropriate measure unless that loss has in fact been sustained.[517] In addition to any claim based on face value, the claimant can recover any other loss suffered as consequential loss.[518]

Particular forms of property: title deeds In respect of conversion of title-deeds it is said that a claimant is entitled prima facie to recover the value of the estate which they represent,[519] the damages being, of course, reducible to a nominal sum on their return. But today this seems highly doubtful. Modern developments in conveyancing and land registration now make it extremely unlikely that loss of title deeds will cause loss of the land they represent: and in this case the traditional measure of damages is obviously inappropriate.[520] Presumably the proper measure would be the value of the deeds (if any) as curiosities, plus any extra costs incurred by the claimant in proving and perfecting his title. **16-107**

(ii) Damages beyond value of goods: special damages

Damages are at large Damages for conversion are on principle at large. It follows that, apart from any claim for the value of the goods, the claimant can also recover damages for any further loss suffered as a result of the conversion. **16-108**

Aggravated and exemplary damages Aggravated damages may be awarded for the circumstances of a conversion if it is peculiarly high-handed or distressing.[521] Exemplary damages have never been awarded hitherto for conversion, but this is no doubt because of the belief that persisted until 2001 that they were unavailable in respect of any tort where they had not been awarded prior to the decision in *Rookes v Barnard*.[522] It is now clear, however, that such damages are available for any tort.[523] It follows that they are available in conversion as elsewhere, and subject to the same conditions.[524] **16-109**

---

515 e.g. a power of attorney over real estate: see the Canadian decision in *Kamal Holdings and Ventures Inc v Verma* 2016 ABQB 115. See too *Building & Civil Engineering Holiday Scheme Management Ltd v Post Office* [1960] 2 Q.B. 430 (trading stamps); also *Bavins, Junior & Sims v London and South Western Bank* [1900] 1 Q.B. 270, 275 (A.L. Smith LJ).

516 As in *MCC Realisations Ltd v Lehman Bros* [1998] 4 All E.R. 675 (share certificates); and *Malkins Nominees Ltd v Société Financière Mirelis SA* [2004] EWHC 2631 (Ch) (share certificate and stock transfer).

517 An example would be an ordinary share certificate. Presumably in such a case the damages would be the administrative costs of replacement.

518 cf. *Malkins Nominees Ltd v Société Financière Mirelis SA* [2004] EWHC 2631 (Ch) (share certificate converted when represented 10 per cent holding: diluted to 1 per cent and then returned: liability for loss).

519 per Alderson B in *Lossemore v Radford* (1842) 9 M. & W. 657 at 659. See too per curiam in *Williams v Archer* (1847) 5 C.B. 318 at 327–329; and see *Crossfield v Such* (1852) 8 Ex. 159 at 165, which, though a case of detinue, seems to raise the same point by implication.

520 *Chen v Gu* [2011] NSWSC 1622 at [141]–[154] (Rein J, following the statement in the text).

521 *Owen & Smith v Reo Motors (Britain) Ltd* [1934] All E.R. Rep. 734 (high-handed deprivation of car). See too *King v Gross* (2008) 443 A.R. 214 (obsessive dog-lover kidnapping, secreting and spaying breeder's prize Shih-Tzu).

522 [1964] A.C. 1129.

523 See *Kuddus v Chief Constable of Leicestershire* [2001] UKHL 29; [2002] 2 A.C. 122. Outside

16-110 **Consequential damage** The claimant may recover all such damages as are the natural and direct result of the conversion, for example the cost of seeking out the chattel converted,[525] or hiring a replacement for it,[526] litigation costs against third parties,[527] or (where appropriate) a rise in value between the time of conversion and the time of judgment.[528] In the case of conversion by refusal to hand over goods there may be a claim for deterioration and accruing storage charges.[529] In the case of conversion amounting to a public aspersion on the claimant's ownership or business integrity, damages may reflect that fact.[530] A defendant may, it seems, be liable for specific profits lost owing to the claimant being deprived of the chattel,[531] or for the loss of a contract for the purchase of it.[532] However, the mere abstract capacity for profitable use is normally reckoned as included in the capital value; where it is, the loss of such use is not a separate head of damage, since otherwise there would be double recovery.[533]

16-111 Consequential losses may in addition encompass non-pecuniary interests, such as inconvenience[534] and distress[535] at being deprived of one's property.[536]

16-112 **Consequential damage: limitations on recovery** To be recoverable a given head of consequential damage must have been caused by the conversion: consequential loss that would have been suffered anyway is not compensable.[537] In addition any such loss must have been reasonably foreseeable to the hypothetical converter at

England, where the *Rookes* limitation never applied, exemplary damages have been awarded for conversion. See, e.g. *Tufuga v Haddon* [1984] NZ Recent Law 285 (outrageous action by creditor in seizing goods); and cf. *Jamieson's Tow and Salvage Ltd v Murray* [1984] 2 N.Z.L.R. 144.

524 They were duly awarded against an inveterate large-scale thief in *Borders (UK) Ltd v Metropolitan Police Commissioner* [2005] EWCA Civ 197 (criticised in D. Campbell & J. Devenney, "Damages at the Borders of Legal Reasoning" [2006] C.L.J. 208).

525 *Aziz v Lim* [2012] EWHC 915 (QB) at [117] (diamonds wrongfully sold, ending up in the hands of Swiss buyers: owner can claim cost of seeking out, and attempting to recover possession of, diamonds in Geneva).

526 On which, see the negligence case of *Lagden v O'Connor* [2003] UKHL 64; [2004] 1 A.C. 1067 (if claimant's financial position such that he has to pay an increased rate of hire, he can claim the full amount).

527 As in *Trafigura Beheer BV v Mediterranean Shipping Co SA* [2007] EWHC 944 (Comm); [2007] 2 All E.R. (Comm) 149 (copper converted by carrier; costs of litigation with third parties recoverable). The point was not raised on appeal (see [2007] EWCA Civ 794; [2008] 1 All E.R. (Comm) 385).

528 See *The Playa Larga* [1983] 2 Lloyd's Rep. 171; para.16-97.

529 *Uzinterimpex JSC v Standard Bank Plc* [2008] EWCA Civ 819; [2008] 2 Lloyd's Rep. 456 (though the claim there failed on mitigation grounds).

530 *Ecclestone v Khyami* [2014] EWHC 29 (QB) at [152]–[160] (Dingemans J) (though the claim failed on the facts).

531 *Bodley v Reynolds* (1846) 8 Q.B. 779 (carpenter's tools: loss of employment).

532 *Williams v Peel River Land Co* (1886) 55 L.T. 689; *Oakley v Lyster* [1931] 1 K.B. 148. And see *Michael v Hart* [1901] 2 K.B. 867.

533 *Reid v Fairbanks* (1853) 13 C.B. 692; cf. *The Llanover* [1947] P. 80.

534 *Carlisle v Chief Constable, RUC* [1988] N.I. 307 (personal effects of person arrested wrongfully taken).

535 *Graham v Voigt* (1989) 89 A.L.R. 11 (distress of keen philatelist at loss of stamp collection); *King v Gross* (2008) 443 A.R. 214 (sentimental damages for kidnapping and sterilising prize dog). Compare the breach of bailment case in *Yearworth v North Bristol NHS Trust* [2009] EWCA Civ 37; [2010] Q.B. 1 (sperm donors can recover for distress at spoilage of seed in hospital's custody).

536 However, it seems that damage due to loss of reputation resulting from the abstraction of an embarrassing letter cannot be claimed: to recover this the claimant must sue in defamation: *Lonrho Plc v Fayed* (No.5) [1993] 1 W.L.R. 1489.

537 *Glenmorgan Farm Ltd v New Zealand Bloodstock Leasing Ltd* [2011] NZCA 672; [2012] 1 N.Z.L.R. 555 (wrongful seizure of racehorse: no claim for lost profits when clear horse would have been right-

the time of conversion,[538] except it seems where the converter knew he was acting wrongfully.[539] Furthermore, a claimant in conversion, as for any tort, must take reasonable steps to mitigate any consequential loss suffered, for example by agreeing to a sale of commercial goods the subject of a dispute which will otherwise deteriorate or incur undue storage charges.[540]

Loss of hire or use-value If a chattel would in fact have been let out on hire, there is no doubt that the claimant deprived of it can claim any hire payments lost, though of course he has to prove them[541]; and furthermore there may come a time when, in order to mitigate his damage, he is bound to obtain an alternative chattel to hire out.[542] Where a chattel detained is one which is normally let out on hire by the claimant, and where it is used by the defendant,[543] the claimant is entitled to a reasonable sum for the hire of the chattel during the period of its detention[544]; and this sum will not be affected by the actual benefit obtained from the chattel by the defendant during that period, nor by the fact that during some part of the time of wrongful detention the claimant would not have been able to find a hirer, nor (arguably) by the fact that the claimant has in fact been able to borrow equivalent goods from some third party.[545] Indeed, there is no rule that, in an appropriate case, damages for loss of hire may not exceed the capital value of the chattel itself.[546] But if the goods have been disposed of by the wrongdoer the hiring charge will cease at the time of such disposal, and the owner will get in addition damages for the loss he has sustained by the conversion, which is usually the value at the time of conversion.[547] **16-113**

A similar rule has been applied to property the claimant never intended to hire **16-114**

fully seized anyway).

538 *Saleslease Ltd v Davis* [1999] 1 W.L.R. 1664 (machine worth £5,000 converted: no claim for putative hire profits of £13,000 in absence of knowledge of relevant facts by defendant); *Rapid Roofing P/L v Natalize P/L* [2007] 2 Qd. R. 335 (similar); *Sandeman Coprimar SA v Transitos y Transportes Integrales SL* [2003] EWCA Civ 113; [2003] Q.B. 1270 (bailee lost seals on liquor showing that duty paid: no liability for owner being forced to pay duty again, since too remote); *Checkprice (UK) Ltd (in administration) v Revenue & Customs Commissioners* [2010] EWHC 682 (Admin); [2010] S.T.C. 1153 (wrongful retention of liquor: alleged lost profits from late return too remote).

539 *Kuwait Airways Corp v Iraqi Airways Co (Nos 4 and 5)* [2002] UKHL 19; [2002] 2 A.C. 883 at [99] onwards, per Lord Nicholls.

540 As in *Uzinterimpex JSC v Standard Bank Plc* [2008] EWCA Civ 819; [2008] 2 Lloyd's Rep. 456. See P. Morgan, "Mitigation and Conversion" [2010] L.M.C.L.Q. 220.

541 *Greer v Alstons Engineering Sales and Services Ltd* [2003] UKPC 46.

542 See *Greer v Alstons Engineering Ltd* [2003] UKPC 46 (mechanical digger unlawfully detained for some years: PC acquiesce in decision of Trinidad Court of Appeal that owner limited to two years' lost hire).

543 On which see the very careful and instructive judgments in *Gaba Formwork v Turner Corp* (1991) 32 N.S.W.L.R. 175.

544 *Strand Electric and Engineering Co Ltd v Brisford Entertainments Ltd* [1952] 2 Q.B. 246. See too *Inverugie Investments Ltd v Hackett* [1995] 1 W.L.R. 713, per Lord Lloyd; *Ministry of Defence v Ashman* [1993] 2 E.G.L.R. 102 (applying a similar principle to land).

545 The point was left open by Lord Mustill in the property damage case of *Giles v Thompson* [1994] 1 A.C. 142 at 166–167. See too *Dimond v Lovell* [2002] 1 A.C. 384. On principle, however, the case for recovery is strong. A person's right to damages for total loss of his car is unaffected by the fact that he has been given another outright: the same result should follow where his claim is for loss of use of his vehicle and the gift is of the use of another.

546 *Hillesden Securities Ltd v Ryjack Ltd* [1983] 1 W.L.R. 959.

547 *Strand Electric and Engineering Co Ltd v Brisford Entertainments Ltd* [1952] 2 Q.B. 246, above. (Damages on basis of hiring charge awarded for whole period of detention until judgment, the claim being one for detinue. In conversion, strictly no damages would be obtainable for loss of use after demand and refusal but, since the abolition of detinue, such loss should be recoverable as

out at all, where there was nevertheless a figure that might be called a reasonable hire charge, or something analogous. In the damages case of *The Mediana*,[548] for instance, it was held that a harbour authority deprived of the use of a lightship could claim the cost of keeping a replacement lightship, even though this was expense they would have incurred anyway because they always had a spare on hand. It can be argued that such liability is limited to where the defendant has used the chattel, or alternatively damaged it, and hence that it should not apply to a mere keeping.[549] It is suggested, however, that in so far as such damages are regarded as compensatory,[550] this is a difficult distinction to justify: in so far as something has a use value and the claimant has been deprived of the opportunity to use it, there seems no reason to deny substantial damages, whatever use the defendant may or may not have obtained for himself.[551]

16-115 It seems, however, that damages for loss of use are limited to the case where either the defendant returns the goods *in specie* to the claimant, or where damages are awarded to reflect the value of the goods at the time of judgment.[552] Where the damages are reckoned by reference to the goods' value at the time of the original conversion, it has been said that use-value damages are inappropriate. The reason is that the claimant's rights in the goods are regarded as essentially "bought out" at the time of conversion: if so, it is wrong on principle to compensate him in addition for events occurring after that time.[553]

16-116 **Position where chattel returned** Since damages for detention are intended to compensate the claimant for his loss and not to punish the defendant, the fall in value of property subsequently returned is only recoverable if such loss is proved, or can be inferred, to have been suffered in the particular circumstances, as with goods, scrip or stock acquired for resale, but otherwise only nominal damages are recoverable under this head.[554]

consequential damages.) See too *Saleh Farid v Theodorou*, unreported 30 January 1992 CA.

548 [1900] A.C. 113; *Greer v Alstons Engineering Ltd* [2003] UKPC 46. cf. *Birmingham Corp v Sowsbery* [1970] R.T.R. 84 (corporation bus); and *The West Wales* [1932] P. 165. Contra, however, *Blue Monkey Gaming Ltd v Hudson* unreported 16 June 2014 Ch D.

549 Compare *Brandeis Goldschmidt & Co Ltd v Western Transport Ltd* [1981] Q.B. 864 (nominal damages for detention of copper under non-existent lien); also *Black Diamond Group Pty Ltd v Manor of Maluka Pty Ltd* [2014] QSC 219; [2015] 1 Qd R. 180 at [48]–[56]. No doubt this is why such damages are sometimes referred to as restitutionary: see *McGregor on Damages*, 20th edn (Sweet & Maxwell, 2017), para.14-11; and e.g. *Tanks & Vessels Industries Ltd v Devon Cider Co Ltd* [2009] EWHC 1360 (Ch) at [64].

550 Which now seems established: *One Step (Support) Ltd v Morris-Garner* [2018] UKSC 20; [2019] A.C. 649 at [26] and [95] (Lord Reed) and [115]–[123] (Lord Sumption).

551 See the reasoning in *One Step (Support) Ltd v Morris-Garner* [2018] UKSC 20; [2019] A.C. 649 at [30] (Lord Reed). The question of liability was left open by Allsop P in the New South Wales decision in *Bunnings Group Ltd v CHEP Australia Ltd* [2011] NSWCA 342; (2012) 82 N.S.W.L.R. 420 at [175]–[179]. But his Honour (with whom Macfarlan JA agreed) seems to have inclined to the view that use was not necessary, since he categorised use damages as compensatory and not restitutionary, in contrast to Giles JA in the minority. The result in *Brandeis Goldschmidt & Co Ltd v Western Transport Ltd* [1981] Q.B. 864, above, can be reconciled with this reasoning on the basis that raw copper has no use value and hence in that case there was no basis for anything other than a nominal award.

552 On which, see para.16-96.

553 So held in *Tanks& Vessels Industries Ltd v Devon Cider Co Ltd* [2009] EWHC 1360 (Ch); see especially at [62]–[67].

554 *Barrow v Arnaud* (1846) 8 Q.B. 595 (corn); *Williams v Archer* (1847) 5 C.B. 318 (scrip); *Williams v Peel River Land Co* (1886) 55 L.T. 689 (stock); as explained in *Brandeis Goldschmidt & Co Ltd*

(iii) Nature of claimant's interest

Damages where claimant relies on possession At common law a claimant who relied on his actual possession in an action against a stranger having no interest in the goods was entitled to recover exactly the same measure of damages as if he were the absolute owner, on the ground that a wrongdoer was not to be heard to deny the title of the injured party.[555] The rule was finally established by the Court of Appeal in *The Winkfield*,[556] allowing the Post Office to recover from a third-party wrongdoer the full value of mails entrusted to it. Nor was this latter right of action limited to the amount of the liability over of a bailee to his bailor,[557] since it was incidental to the possession and not based on any potential liability. The possessor's right to claim full damages did, however, carry with it a duty to account to the owner for the excess beyond the value of his own interest on the basis of money had and received.[558] Since 1978, however, the difference between possession and a right to possess as the basis of a claimant's claim has been much reduced in importance by the 1977 Act's provisions abolishing restrictions on pleading the *jus tertii*, requiring identification by a claimant of any other claimant or interested party known to him, permitting defendants to apply for joinder of such persons as parties, and preventing double liability so far as practicable by, inter alia, apportioning damages between two or more claimants.[559] Yet the above rule remains and will be of importance where, as in cases of finding, the rival claimant or other interested person cannot be identified and joined. There the claimant may still recover the full value of the goods, but must account over to the true owner if and when later identified.[560] 16-117

Claimants with limited interest and similar cases in relation to reduction of damages A claimant in conversion can generally recover the value of the goods, whether or not this represents his actual loss. Thus he can claim the value of goods destroyed, notwithstanding the fact that they are subject to a mortgage or other 16-118

---

v Western Transport Ltd [1981] Q.B. 864 (claims for fall in value and for interest on bank overdraft rejected, and £5 nominal damages awarded, for wrongful detention of copper redelivered on summary judgment, as claimant had acquired it for use in manufacture and sale of resulting products at unspecified future time, possibly after period of detention and no loss was proved). Except for the first, these were actions for detinue. See A. Tettenborn (1982) 132 N.L.J. 154.

555 *Wilson v Lombank Ltd* [1963] 1 W.L.R. 1294, a case of trespass in which the full value of the chattel was recovered by the claimant. Such a decision was highly favourable to the claimant, for it allowed a claimant who had possession only, but not the right to possess, full conversion damages notwithstanding that he could sue only in trespass. The reason was said to be that otherwise there would be "an invitation to all the world to scramble for the possession:" see Lord Kenyon in *Webb v Fox* (1797) 7 T.R. 391 at 397.

556 [1902] P. 42, overruling *Claridge v South Staffordshire Tramway* [1892] 1 Q.B. 422. See also *Glenwood Lumber Co v Phillips* [1904] A.C. 405; *Eastern Construction Co v National Trust Co* [1914] A.C. 197; *The Joannis Vatis* [1922] P. 92.

557 In *The Winkfield* [1902] P. 42 there was no such liability, the claimant being the Post Office, which was statutorily insulated from responsibility.

558 *Tomlinson (A) (Hauliers) Ltd v Hepburn* [1966] A.C. 451 (bailee receiving insurance money must account for excess beyond sum required for his own indemnity). It is an open question whether he holds the excess on trust. He may well do so: cf. the analogous case of *Mathew v TM Sutton Ltd* [1994] 1 W.L.R. 1455 (pawnbroker selling goods to pay debt held to be trustee of excess received from buyer).

559 ss.7, 8.

560 s.7(3), (4).

security,[561] or that he has previously sold them to a third party to whom risk has passed, and that third party has actually paid him.[562] Again, a buyer whose seller wrongfully retakes the goods can recover in full, even though he may not have paid for them and by the retaking is relieved of the obligation to do so.[563] However, there are three major exceptions to this principle: first, the unpaid seller who remains in possession; secondly, the case where the claimant is regarded as only having a limited proprietary interest in the goods; and thirdly, co-owners.

16-119 **The unpaid seller in possession** A buyer who has obtained possession of goods from his seller can recover in full against the latter if he wrongfully retakes them, whether or not the buyer has actually paid for them.[564] But the same is not true where the unpaid vendor, having sold goods on credit, then wrongfully resells them without having delivered them at all. In such a case, in order to avoid what would otherwise be an outrageous result, the buyer must give credit for the price he would have had to pay the seller but now need not.[565]

16-120 **The claimant with limited proprietary interest** A claimant whose proprietary interest in goods is limited can, in an action against one of his co-proprietors, only recover to the extent of his limited interest. A co-owner is one example; but similar principles apply, for example to a mortgagor. Thus in *Brierly v Kendall*,[566] the claimant had assigned to the defendant certain chattels under a bill of sale, which gave the claimant exclusive right of possession until default. The defendant seized before default; nevertheless, it was held that the claimant could recover only what his right of possession against the defendant was worth. It should be noted, however, that this only applies to actions against co-proprietors: as against third parties the claimant recovers in full.[567]

16-121 **Hire-purchase** Similar reasoning, moreover, is now applied to property let on hire-purchase. As against the hirer and third parties alike, the owning finance company is regarded as having only a limited interest in the goods and hence as able

---

561 *Blue Sky One Ltd v Mahan Air* [2010] EWHC 631 (Comm), especially at [98]–[99] (Beatson J).

562 *The Charlotte* [1908] P. 206 (strictly speaking a negligence case; but the principle is the same). Compare more recently *The Baltic Strait* [2018] EWHC 629 (Comm); [2018] 2 Lloyd's Rep. 33 at [31]–[33] (Andrew Baker J).

563 *Gillard v Brittan* (1841) 8 M. & W. 575. See too *Johnson v Lancashire & Yorkshire Ry Co* (1878) 3 C.P.D. 499; *Page v Cowasjee Eduljee* (1866) L.R. 1 P.C. 127, 146–147. Since the creation in 1875 of the procedure by way of counterclaim, however, these cases are less important than they were.

564 As he can from a third party: *Center Optical (Hong Kong) Ltd v Jardine Transport Services (China) Ltd* [2001] 2 Lloyd's Rep. 678 (High Court of Hong Kong).

565 "A man cannot by merely changing the form of action entitle himself to recover damages greater than the amount to which he is in law entitled according to the true facts of the case and the real nature of the transaction." (Bramwell B in *Chinery v Viall* (1860) 5 H. & N. 288 at 295). For a more recent example, see the Australian decision in *Butler v Egg Marketing Board* (1966) 114 C.L.R. 185 (state monopoly buyer, when suing defendant for wrongful sale bypassing it, must give credit for price it would have paid). And cf. *Indian Herbs (UK) Ltd v Hadley & Ottoway Ltd*, unreported 21 January 1999, CA (conversion against seller for retaking goods under retention of title clause: accepted, credit to be given for unpaid portion of price).

566 (1852) 17 Q.B. 937. cf. *Johnson v Stear* (1863) 15 C.B. (N.S.) 330.

567 *Blue Sky One Ltd v Mahan Air* [2010] EWHC 631 (Comm), above, especially at [98]–[99] (mortgagor of aircraft could recover in full from a third party converter without reference to the fact that its own interest was burdened with that of a mortgagee).

only to sue for the unpaid hire instalments.[568] Thus in *Wickham Holdings Ltd v Brooke House Motors Ltd*[569] the claimants were entitled to recover as damages their loss on the wrongful sale of their car while on hire-purchase, not to recover the full value of the car without giving credit for money already received on the hire-purchase contract.[570] Presumably similar reasoning would apply to property on conditional sale,[571] though (oddly) not to property which had been the subject of an outright contract of sale.[572] What is sauce for the goose is sauce for the gander: where the hire-purchaser himself sues for conversion of the goods, he is similarly limited to the value of his interest.[573]

Lien In the case of an ordinary lien, however, there is no right in the holder of the goods who converts them[574] to deduct, in an action at the suit of the owner, the amount for which he had the lien from the value of the goods. The right conferred by the lien is only one of personal retention and is altogether forfeited by the unlawful act of conversion.[575] But it is otherwise where a pledgee wrongfully sells or repledges a chattel.[576] **16-122**

Co-owners Where only one of several co-owners sues for conversion,[577] by virtue of s.8(1) of the 1977 Act[578] he recovers only in respect of his proportionate interest in the goods.[579] **16-123**

Trustees A trustee can recover the full value of the goods converted which formed part of the trust estate,[580] together with any further loss suffered by the trust estate as a result of the conversion.[581] **16-124**

Recovery by bailor bars recovery by bailee and vice versa Although where **16-125**

---

[568] *Belsize Motor Supply Co v Cox* [1914] 1 K.B. 244; *Whiteley v Hilt* [1918] 2 K.B. 808.

[569] [1967] 1 W.L.R. 295; *Belvoir Finance Co Ltd v Stapleton* [1971] 1 Q.B. 210 CA, where the hire-purchase contract was illegal.

[570] Conversely, however, if lower than the outstanding instalments, the value may put a ceiling on recovery. In *Chubb Cash Ltd v John Crilley & Son* [1983] 1 W.L.R. 599, a cash-register let out on hire-purchase was wrongfully sold for £178, though the outstanding instalments were £1,200. Damages were limited by the Court of Appeal to £178, the value of the cash-register at the time of sale.

[571] Which is for practical purposes almost indistinguishable from hire-purchase.

[572] Because of the decision in *The Charlotte* [1908] P. 206.

[573] *Chartered Trust Plc v King* unreported 23 February 2001.

[574] e.g. by selling them without first going through the procedure as to notice etc required by s.12 of the 1977 Act.

[575] *Mulliner v Florence* (1878) 3 Q.B.D. 484. For two exceptional cases in which on moral grounds the claimant was refused the full value of his goods, see *Du Bost v Beresford* (1810) 2 Camp. 511; *Cameron v Wynch* (1846) 2 C. & K. 264. But most lienholders have statutory powers of sale, see: Innkeepers Act 1878 s.1, as limited by Hotel Proprietors Act 1956; Sale of Goods Act 1979 s.48; Torts (Interference with Goods) Act 1977 ss.12, 13 and Sch.1

[576] *Donald v Suckling* (1866) L.R. 1 Q.B. 585; *Halliday v Holgate* (1868) L.R. 3 Ex. 299.

[577] Which he can do in the case of destruction or sale under s.10(1) of the 1977 Act.

[578] Which allows the defendant to raise the point that others are entitled in addition to the claimant.

[579] The position at common law was probably the same (see *Bloxam v Hubbard* (1804) 5 East 407). For further discussion of the common law rules, see the 17th edn of this work, para.13-141 fn.73.

[580] *Barker v Furlong* [1891] 2 Ch. 172. Furthermore, this remains so even if under the terms of the trust the *cestui que trust* has the right to remain in possession as against the trustee: *White v Morris* (1852) 11 C.B. 1015.

[581] *Malkins Nominees Ltd v Société Financière Mirelis SA* [2004] EWHC 2631 (Ch): see too *Chappell v Somers & Blake* [2003] EWHC 1644 (Ch); [2004] Ch.19, especially at [26]–[27] (same for an executor).

both the bailee and the bailor have suffered damage by the wrongful act of a third party each may bring a separate action for the loss suffered by himself,[582] full recovery of the value of the chattel by either bars the other from suing the wrongdoer.[583] In order to prevent injustice where (for example) the bailee mishandles the suit or is not to be trusted with the proceeds, the 1977 Act requires a claimant to identify other potential claimants so as to permit the defendant to seek their joinder and thus allow the court, in giving damages, to apportion them between the various claimants.[584] However, when such joinder is impracticable, as where the bailor cannot be traced, or is not obtained, the common law continues to apply and the bailee may recover the full value subject to a duty to account over to his bailor.[585]

(iv) Return of chattel

16-126 When a chattel has been wrongfully taken, detained or otherwise converted, there is a vested cause of action which cannot be defeated merely by the fact that the claimant subsequently gets his goods again before judgment.[586] But after such redelivery the action is merely for consequential damage or deterioration in value, if any.[587] The position is the same if the claimant, after action brought, thinks proper to take the chattel back.[588] The court has, besides, power to stay any action on delivery of the chattel and payment of costs, if the circumstances are such as to show that the claimant thereby clearly obtains the full redress to which he is entitled.[589] If the claimant obtains judgment for the value of the chattel, or accepts at trial an offer to return the goods, judgment may be entered by consent for the value of the goods, to be reduced to a nominal sum on their redelivery.[590] Even though no such provision is made, yet, if, in fact, the claimant gets his property back, the court will treat this as pro tanto a satisfaction and reduce the award accordingly[591] and, on a similar principle, if certain of the chattels in question are given up, the action may be stayed in part,[592] provided the bulk is severable without

---

582 *Claridge v South Staffordshire Tramways Co* [1892] 1 Q.B. 422 at 424, per Hawkins J.

583 "The wrongdoer having once paid full damages to the bailee, has an answer to any action by the bailor." (Collins MR in *The Winkfield* [1902] P. 42 at 61). For the converse (recovery by bailor bars the bailee) see *O'Sullivan v Williams* [1992] 3 All E.R. 385.

584 s.7(2). This followed the *Law Reform Committee's recommendation*: (1971) Cmnd.4774, para.62.

585 See para.16-117.

586 A judgment for damages only under s.3(2)(c) of the 1977 Act cannot be satisfied by redelivery after judgment, but a judgment for delivery of the goods or payment of damages can be satisfied by redelivery before execution of judgment: s.3(5).

587 *Hiort v London and North Western Railway* (1879) 4 Ex. D. 188. Aliter, however, where the goods are returned in substantially altered form: *Irving v Keen*, unreported 3 March 1995 (defendant dismantles, and hence converts, claimant's car in 1988: liable to pay 1988 value, despite return of mouldering remnants in 1990).

588 *Moon v Raphael* (1835) 2 Bing. N.C. 310.

589 *Fisher v Prince* (1762) 3 Burr. 1363; *Pickering v Truste* (1796) 7 T.R. 53 (trespass); *Solloway v McLaughlin* [1938] A.C. 247 at 259 PC; *BBMM Finance v EDA Holdings Ltd* [1990] 1 W.L.R. 490; cf. *Tucker v Wright* (1826) 3 Bing. 601 (value of goods uncertain after prolonged detention: stay refused).

590 *M'Leod v M'Ghee* (1841) 2 M. & G. 326 at 328; *Wintle v Rudge* (1841) 5 Jur. 274.

591 *Plevin v Henshall* (1833) 10 Bing. 24.

592 *Earle v Holderness* (1828) 4 Bing. 462.

diminution of value.[593] The same rule applies to an unpaid seller who recovers a proportion of the money value of the goods sold.[594]

Transaction equivalent to return In some cases a transaction by which the claimant got the benefit of the property, though it never came back physically into his hands, has been treated as equivalent to a redelivery. In *Hiort v London & North Western Ry Co*[595] the defendants warehoused corn to the claimant's order. They wrongly delivered it to one G. The claimant afterwards sold the same corn and made out a delivery order to the purchaser. It was endorsed by him to G, and handed by G to the defendants. The court pointed out that the claimant had not been damnified, because he had an action for the price against his purchaser, and they held that what had occurred was the same thing as if the defendants had got back the corn from G, and afterwards delivered it under the claimant's order. In *Plevin v Henshall*[596] the claimant had obtained a verdict in conversion against the defendant. The goods in question in the action were lying in a house for the rent of which the claimant was liable, and the landlord distrained upon them. The defendant having paid the rent, the verdict was reduced by the amount of the distress, it being held that the parties were in the same situation as if, after the verdict, the defendant had gone and paid the claimant the sum in question. Otherwise the claimant would have had the benefit of the goods twice over, while the defendant, without getting the goods, would have paid their full value. **16-127**

But the mere fact that the claimant has received sums which he would not have received but for the conversion, and which directly or indirectly represent the proceeds of the property converted, will not of itself amount to satisfaction: it must be shown that they were received from the convertor specifically on account of his liability.[597] The principle was graphically illustrated by the Australian decision in *Hunter BNZ Finance Ltd v ANZ Banking Group*.[598] The claimant financiers provided X with a cheque made out to a supplier, which X was to use to buy goods on behalf of the claimants which the claimants would then lease back to X. X bought no goods, instead dishonestly paying the cheque into his own account with the defendant bank; then, having paid the claimants a few instalments on the phantom goods to allay suspicion, he vanished with the proceeds. The defendant bank was held liable in conversion of the cheque, and the instalments paid by X were held to be out of account; they might in fact go to reduce the claimants' loss, but they were not paid on account of any liability in conversion. **16-128**

(v) *Successive conversions and satisfaction*

The owner of a chattel who has been deprived of his possession may well have a remedy against more than one person. For example, A may have wrongfully taken it and B may afterwards have bought it, sold it or wrongfully detained it. A and B are here not joint tortfeasors; there is a perfectly independent right of action against **16-129**

[593] *Bunney v Poyntz* (1832) 4 B. & Ad. 568.
[594] *Kemp v Falk* (1882) 7 App. Cas. 573.
[595] (1879) 4 Ex. D. 188.
[596] (1833) 10 Bing. 24.
[597] *Edmundson v Nuttall* (1864) 17 C.B. (N.S.) 280 (goods converted: later taken in execution and sold to satisfy debt owed by claimant: no credit for discharge of debt).
[598] [1990] V.R. 41. See too *Lloyds Bank Ltd v Chartered Bank of India, Australia & China* [1929] 1 K.B. 40.

each.[599] Furthermore, judgment of itself does not affect ownership of a chattel or of any interest in it. But the 1977 Act, largely reaffirming the position at common law,[600] provides that, where damages for wrongful interference fall to be, assessed on the footing that the claimant is being compensated for the whole of his interest in the goods,[601] their payment or settlement extinguishes the claimant's title.[602] Hence the property is thereby changed as from the date of the wrongful act and vested in the defendant,[603] and the claimant will consequently lose all right of action against any other convertor. It should be noted, however, that this rule applies only to complete satisfaction. Recovery of less than the full value does not transmute the property or affect any other right of action.[604] On the other hand, the claimant cannot recover twice over, and therefore any damages which he may have actually received in one action will have to be taken into consideration in the other.[605]

(vi) *Contributory negligence*

16-130 There was formerly some doubt as to whether contributory negligence was a defence to conversion at common law.[606] The matter, however, has now been put beyond doubt by s.11(1) of the Torts (Interference with Goods) Act 1977, which provides that contributory negligence is irrelevant to a claim[607] for conversion or

---

599 *Winter v Bancks* (1901) 84 L.T. 504; and neither may escape liability on the ground that the claimant could alternatively have recovered against the other, or against some third party in contract: *International Factors Ltd v Rodriguez* [1979] Q.B. 351 CA.

600 See *Brinsmead v Harrison* (1871) L.R. 6 C. & P. 584.

601 Subject, where relevant, to a reduction for contributory negligence in the case of forms of wrongful interference other than conversion and intentional trespass, to which contributory negligence is by s.11(1) no defence.

602 1977 Act s.5(1), (2). This does not apply where the damages are so assessed but the damages actually paid are limited to some lesser amount by virtue of any enactment or rule of law: s.5(3); and the provisions of s.5 may be varied by agreement or by court order: s.5(5). The right of a third party to whom the claimant actually accounts over under s.7(3) for the whole value of that party's interest under all heads is similarly extinguished thereby: s.5(4). Where the claimant is simultaneously seeking to recover his goods in specie from someone other than the present defendant, and does not wish to lose his rights against that other by operation of s.5 if damages are paid, it may be appropriate to stay any assessment of damages for the time being: *Aziz v Lim* [2012] EWHC 915 (QB) at [117] (Hildyard J).

603 If the defendant has previously sold the chattel, then the title goes to whoever derives title from the defendant.

604 *Morris v Robinson* (1824) 3 B. & C. 196; *Ellis v Stenning* [1932] 2 Ch. 81. These were cases at common law: but it is suggested they are unaffected by the Act. The same applies, it seems, where the sum payable in respect of a conversion is limited by contract: see *Trafigura Beheer BV v Mediterranean Shipping Co SA* [2007] EWHC 944 (Comm); [2007] 2 All E.R. (Comm) 149 at [119]. The point did not feature on appeal (see [2007] EWCA Civ 794; [2008] 1 All E.R. (Comm) 385).

605 "If, indeed, the claimants were to recover the full value of the goods in each action, a Court of Equity would interfere to prevent them having double satisfaction": per Bayley J in *Morris v Robinson* (1824) 3 B. & C. 196, 205. The 1977 Act does not implement the Law Reform Committee's recommendation (*18th Report*, Cmnd.4774, para.96) that part satisfaction "should be taken into account at assessing the claimant's loss in any further proceedings between the parties"; but s.9 is in terms wide enough to permit two or more actions for wrongful interference with the same goods against successive wrongdoers to be heard together in the same court, provided they are concurrent.

606 In favour: *Lumsden v Trustee Savings Bank* [1971] 1 Lloyd's Rep. 114. Against: *Lloyds Bank Ltd v Savory* [1933] A.C. 201, 229 (Lord Wright); *Boma Mfg Co v CIBC* (1997) 140 D.L.R. (4th) 463. See too *Souhrada v Bank of NSW* [1976] 2 Lloyd's Rep. 444.

607 Note that what matters here is the facts pleaded by the claimant. If they disclose a conversion, then

intentional trespass to goods.[608] The only exception is also statutory: by s.47 of the Banking Act 1979, contributory negligence by the drawer remains a partial defence to an action against a bank for conversion of a cheque.

(vii) Limitation of actions[609]

The right of action and the title of any person in whose favour a cause of action for conversion of a chattel has accrued will normally be extinguished on the expiration of six years from the time of the conversion, unless he recovers possession within that period.[610] But if, before he recovers possession of it, the same chattel is again converted, whether by the same or another converter, the six-year limitation period runs from the date of the original conversion.[611] If, however, the defendant had deliberately concealed from the claimant any fact relevant to his right of action, the period does not begin to run, except in favour of a subsequent purchaser for value who was neither party to, nor actually or constructively aware of the concealment, until the claimant has, or should have, discovered the concealment.[612] Further, a person from whom a chattel is stolen or obtained by deception or blackmail, or anyone claiming through him, may sue without limit of time the obtainer or anyone who subsequently converts the chattel before he recovers possession. But as against a subsequent purchaser in good faith of the stolen chattel his title will be extinguished six years after the innocent purchase; yet even thereafter he may sue the thief or obtainer and any subsequent converter whose wrong preceded the innocent purchase.[613] 16-131

4. TRESPASS TO GOODS

(a) The nature of trespass to goods

The nature of trespass to goods The action of trespass to goods has always been concerned with the direct, immediate interference with the claimant's possession of a chattel. There is no need for a physical removal: any unpermitted physical intromission suffices, from deliberate damage[614] to lesser acts of interference[615]: for 16-132

---

whether or not conversion is pleaded *eo nomine* the claimant can pray in aid s.11(1) against a plea of contributory negligence. See *Yates v West Wilts DC*, unreported 11 March 1993, CA.

608 The results of this provision can be bizarre. If X's goods are stolen entirely owing to X's negligence and later pass through the hands of Y who acts innocently and reasonably, X nevertheless has the right to sue Y for the full value of the goods. Even more oddly, if X lends his car to Y, who is obviously drunk, and Y destroys it in a crash, X's damages will be reduced if he frames his action in negligence or breach of bailment, but he will recover in full if he claims for statutory conversion pursuant to s.2(2) of the 1977 Act!

609 See generally Ch.31. This section deals only with those rules of limitation of particular significance to conversion claims.

610 Limitation Act 1980 ss.2 and 3(2). But it seems that the effect of s.3(2) is limited to the goods originally converted, and does not apply to new goods made or emanating from those goods. See the Australian decision in *Grant v YYH Holdings Pty Ltd* [2012] NSWCA 360, interpreting analogous New South Wales legislative provisions (where rare-breed ewes converted, six-year limitation period extinguished title to those beasts, but not to their progeny born less than six years before action brought).

611 Limitation Act 1980 s.3(1). cf. *RB Policies at Lloyds Ltd v Butler* [1950] 1 K.B. 76.

612 Limitation Act 1980 s.32. cf. *Beaman v ARTS Ltd* [1949] 1 K.B. 550.

613 Limitation Act 1980 s.4.

614 As in *Sheldrick v Abery* (1793) 1 Esp. 55 (stabbing a horse); or *Fish & Fish Ltd v Sea Shepherd UK*

example, wheel-clamping a car,[616] physically manhandling animals,[617] interfering with vehicles,[618] handling papers beyond the extent justified under a search warrant,[619] or boarding a bus other than as a bona fide passenger.[620] The interference must, however, be of a direct nature and involve some kind of physical contact or affectation. "Thus, to lock the room in which the claimant has his goods is not a trespass to them."[621] Although no one ever doubted that a mere handling was enough for liability if physical damage was caused,[622] it was long unclear whether the same applied in the absence of damage.[623] The matter was settled, however, by Butterfield J in *Transco Plc v United Utilities Water Plc*.[624] Workmen repairing water mains mistakenly turned off an underground gas stopcock in the belief that it controlled a nearby water-pipe; despite the lack of any damage to the stopcock, they were held liable in trespass to the owners of the stopcock for the latter's expenses in compensating their customers for the resulting gas outage. It is suggested that this is correct, since otherwise objects such as pictures or other exhibits in a museum or art collection could be fingered or handled with impunity.

16-133 This does not mean, however, that all intentional touching of another's goods should amount to trespass. On the contrary, the theatregoer who moves someone else's coat in the cloakroom in order to retrieve his own should not be liable in trespass, nor should the pedestrian who picks up a dropped parcel on the pavement to return it to the owner, or brushes past a car parked in a crowded street,

---

[2013] EWCA Civ 544; [2013] 1 W.L.R. 3700 (appealed on other grounds, [2015] UKSC 10; [2015] A.C. 1229) (participation by environmental activists in the deliberate cutting of nets and fish cages at sea).

615 "The act of handling a man's goods without his permission is prima facie tortious."—Lord Diplock in *Inland Revenue Commissioners v Rossminster Ltd* [1980] A.C. 952 at 1011. A novel example might be where a defendant sends a voluminous fax message to the claimant's fax number knowing that the recipient does not wish to receive it. In *Chair King Inc v GTE Mobilnet, Inc*, 135 S.W.2d 365 (2004) a Texas court seems to have accepted that the sending of "junk faxes" might be a trespass, but in the event denied liability on the basis that trespass required physical harm and no harm had been done.

616 *Arthur v Anker* [1997] Q.B. 564

617 *Fitzwilliam Land Co v Cheesman* [2018] EWHC 3139 (QB) (anti-hunting protest).

618 *UK Oil and Gas Investments Plc v Persons Unknown* [2018] EWHC 2252 (Ch); [2019] J.P.L. 161 (anti-fracking demonstrators).

619 *Slaveski v Victoria* [2010] VSC 441 at [300] ("In the context of the execution of a search warrant, a police officer will commit a trespass to goods if he or she copies or transcribes information from documents found on the premises without the occupier's consent or a court order authorising him or her to use the documents for that purpose").

620 *Rugby Football Union v Viagogo Ltd* [2011] EWHC 764 (QB); [2011] N.P.C. 37 at [10] (Tugendhat J) (upheld on other grounds, [2012] UKSC 55; [2012] 1 W.L.R. 3333).

621 *Hartley v Moxham* (1842) 3 Q.B. 701. Similarly it has been said in Australia that while throwing poisoned bait to a dog might be trespass to it, merely leaving poison for it to eat would not be: *Hutchins v Maughan* [1947] V.L.R. 131, 134.

622 *Fouldes v Willoughby* (1841) 8 M. & W. 540, 549 (Alderson B: "Scratching the panel of a carriage would be a trespass."). Similarly, semble, with wheel-clamping a car: *Arthur v Anker* [1997] Q.B. 564 (where, however, the defendant was held protected by the terms of a warning notice).

623 Commonwealth authority was generally against liability: e.g. *Everitt v Martin* [1953] N.Z.L.R. 298, 302–303 (Adams J); *Wilson v Marshall* [1982] Tas. R. 287; *384238 Ontario Ltd v R.* (1984) 8 D.L.R. (4th) 67. The same went for the preponderance of US jurisprudence: Prosser & Keeton, *Torts*, 5th edn (West Group, 1984), p.90; *Restatement of Torts, Second*, para.218(b)–(d); and, e.g. *Thrifty-Tel, Inc v Bezenek* (1996) 46 Cal. App. 4th 1559, 1566; 54 Cal.Rptr.2d. 468, 473 (1996); and *Intel Corp v Hamidi*, 30 Cal. 4th 1342; 71 P.3d 296 (2003). But most English writers supported liability: see *Salmond & Heuston on the Law of Torts*, 21st edn (London: Sweet & Maxwell, 1996), p.95.

624 [2005] EWHC 2784 (QB).

perhaps causing inadvertent damage in the process.[625] It is submitted that an analogy should be drawn here with trespass to the person, where Goff LJ has said that there is not trespass where the actor has not in the circumstances "gone beyond generally acceptable standards of conduct".[626] The theatregoer and the pedestrian have not; and that is the ground on which they ought to be excused.

The character of the interference Apart from the requirement that the interference must be of a direct nature, there must be some blameworthy state of mind in the trespasser. An accidental interference of a non-negligent nature is not a trespass. In *National Coal Board v JE Evans & Co (Cardiff) Ltd*[627] contractors unwittingly and without negligence damaged an underground cable which the claimant's predecessors had laid in the ground without notification to the landowners. The Court of Appeal held that there was no liability in trespass, and that inevitable accident amounted to a good defence. On the other hand, to be liable the defendant need not appreciate that his interference is wrongful. If he uses a chattel deliberately, erroneously believing that it is his, that is a deliberate and direct act amounting to trespass, though it is accidental, as far as he is concerned, that the legal result is wrong. It is sufficient that he intended to do the act complained of, or was negligent in producing an injury; he need not foresee the legal consequence of his interference.[628] **16-134**

(b) Subject-matter of trespass to goods

Subject-matter of trespass At common law, it is submitted that trespass, like conversion, lies in respect of interference with any corporeal personal property,[629] and subject to the same limitations.[630] It should be noted for these purposes that physical mediums on which information is stored, such as computer disks or "smart cards", are of course corporeal property, from which it follows that the alteration or erasure of that data should be capable of amounting to a trespass.[631] **16-135**

---

625 Note that a well-established object of suing in trespass is to recover for damage resulting without having to prove negligence: cf. in the personal injury field, *Letang v Cooper* [1965] 1 Q.B. 232; and *Wilson v Pringle* [1987] Q.B. 237.

626 *Collins v Wilcock* [1984] 1 W.L.R. 1172 at 1178: applied by Croom-Johnson LJ in *Wilson v Pringle* [1987] Q.B. 237 at 250 onwards. It is submitted that it is better to regard this as a substantive defence to trespass, rather than to base this conclusion on some form of implied consent. See ibid. The passage in the text was discussed, with apparent approval, by Ward LJ in *White v Withers LLP* [2009] EWCA Civ 1122; [2009] 3 F.C.R. 435 (trespass, on principle, for wife to remove documents from husband's house to send to solicitors for copying and use in divorce proceedings. It was left open, however, how far the Family Division's condonation of minor infractions pursuant to *Hildebrand v Hildebrand* [1992] 1 F.L.R. 244 might provide a defence).

627 [1951] 2 K.B. 861. It is true that the claimant's property here had been placed by the claimant's predecessors in title in land where they had no right to put it, thus making the claimants trespassers with regard to the land where the defendant's excavation broke their cable. But it is hard to see that this matters.

628 *Wilson v Lombank Ltd* [1963] 1 W.L.R. 1294; *Colwill v Reeves* (1811) 2 Camp. 575; and see *Moore v Lambeth County Court Registrar (No.2)* [1970] 1 Q.B. 560 CA.

629 On which see para.16-35.

630 e.g. as to dead bodies, see para.16-43.

631 It has long been clear that such alteration or erasure amounts to criminal damage to "property" under the Criminal Damage Act 1971: *Cox v Riley* (1986) 83 Cr. App. R. 54. Logically this reasoning seems applicable to trespass too.

16-136 **"Cyber-trespass"**[632] While the definition of corporeal personal property may normally be straightforward, questions may nevertheless arise in a number of borderline cases, in particular in respect of electronic technology. For example, it is hard to see why a deliberate attempt through the internet unlawfully to manipulate data on a computer should not amount to a trespass to that computer. The configuration of a computer hard disk is a physical feature of it, and the defendant's act in altering or accessing it changes that configuration, at least temporarily. American courts have fairly consistently so held,[633] and it is suggested that English courts should do likewise.[634]

16-137 A more difficult question is whether accessing data rather than altering it ought to amount to trespass, for example where a defendant causes a search engine or "spider" to access and extract data in circumstances where the owner of the computer concerned has made it clear that he does not wish this to be done. Although the formal requirements of trespass are made out here,[635] it is suggested that the defendant should have a defence here analogous to that applicable in trespass to goods generally where the act complained of has not "gone beyond generally acceptable standards of conduct".[636] The use of such devices is generally accepted practice, and the law should recognise this fact.[637] A further, and still more difficult, issue is whether the sending of unsolicited email should be capable of amounting to a trespass to either the recipient's computer or the mainframe computer operated by his internet service provider. It is submitted that prima facie the "generally acceptable standards of conduct" defence should be applicable here; but the result may well be different where the email concerned: (a) is not sent for a bona fide purpose; (b) is so voluminous that it overwhelms the claimant's own machine[638]; or (c) where it is commercial "spam" whose transmission is prohibited under the Privacy and Electronic Communications (EC Directive) Regulations 2003.[639]

(c) The claimant's interest

16-138 **Need for interference with possession** Though the right to possession, without actual possession, may enable a claimant in conversion to maintain a claim, in trespass the claimant must be in possession at the time of the interference. "The

---

632 L. Quilter, "Regulating Conduct on the Internet: The Continuing Expansion of Cyberspace Trespass to Chattels" 17 Berkeley Tech. L.J. 421 (2002).

633 e.g. *Thrifty-Tel, Inc v Bezenek*, 46 Cal. App. 4th 1559; 54 Cal.Rptr.2d 468 (1996). In *Sotelo v Direct Revenue LLC*, 384 F.Supp.2d 1219 (Ill 2005) the surreptitious placing of spyware was similarly treated.

634 As Chadwick LJ seemingly did in *Taylor v Rive Droite Music Ltd* [2005] EWCA Civ 1300; [2006] E.M.L.R. 4. At [68], he apparently accepted that unlawfully deleting computer files from a hard disk amounted to trespass to goods (i.e. the disk drive).

635 Since the configuration of the mainframe or hard disk is necessarily altered, at least temporarily, by the access.

636 *Collins v Wilcock* [1984] 1 W.L.R. 1172, 1178; see para.16-133.

637 Though it must be admitted that American courts lean towards imposing liability here (e.g. *Register.com Inc v Verio, Inc*, 356 F.3d 393 (2001); *eBay Inc v Bidder's Edge Inc*, 100 F.Supp.2d 1058 (N.D. Cal. 2000).

638 cf. *CompuServe Inc v Cyber Promotions, Inc*, 962 F.Supp. 1015 (1997).

639 SI 2003/2426 reg.22. However, trespass liability is somewhat otiose here, since breach of the Regulations gives rise to civil liability anyway: SI 2003/2426 reg.30. In December 2005 a businessman incommoded by spam was apparently awarded an agreed £270 in the Colchester Small Claims Court on this basis (*The Guardian*, 28 December 2005).

distinction between the actions of trespass and trover is well settled: the former is founded on possession: the latter on property."[640] There are certain exceptions to this rule. First, a trustee not in possession may sue in trespass any third party notwithstanding that the chattels are in the hands of the beneficiary.[641] Secondly, an executor or administrator may sue in trespass anyone interfering with the chattels of the deceased before probate or letters of administration are granted. The representative's title relates back to the time of the trespass.[642] Thirdly, the owner of a franchise (for example to take wreck or treasure trove) can sue in trespass anyone taking the goods before he could seize them.[643] Fourthly, where a bailment is determinable at will, the bailor retains sufficient possession to entitle him to sue third parties;[644] and a fortiori, the same rule applies where the bailment has actually been determined.[645]

(d) Remedies for trespass to goods

The classification of trespass to goods along with conversion and negligence **16-139** resulting in damage to goods or to an interest in goods as variant forms of "wrongful interference with goods" diminishes neither the essential differences between the characteristics of these three torts nor the coincidences between trespass and conversion (as by a destruction or taking)[646] or trespass and negligence (as by negligent direct physical injury to goods).[647] But the Torts (Interference with Goods) Act 1977 does thereby subject trespass to the various procedural provisions already examined in relation to conversion. Thus, the traditional remedies of damages and/or injunction remain available,[648] but where the defendant is in possession or control of the goods the claimant in trespass, as in conversion, may now alternatively seek a final order for special delivery, or for delivery or damages,[649] or an interlocutory order for delivery up of the goods.[650] If the claimant has been deprived of his goods, the rules as to allowances for improvements,[651] avoidance of double liability[652] and joinder of other interested persons,[653] the hearing of concurrent actions in the same court,[654] the liability of co-owners to one another,[655] and the

---

640 See *Ward v Macauley* (1791) 4 T.R. 489 at 490, per Lord Kenyon. But this can be fairly generously applied. For instance, a husband is likely to be regarded as sufficiently in possession of documents of his contained in the matrimonial home to allow him to sue in trespass for their abstraction: *White v Withers LLP* [2009] EWCA Civ 1122; [2009] 3 F.C.R. 435 at [49], per Ward LJ.

641 *White v Morris* (1852) 11 C.B. 1015; *Barker v Furlong* [1891] 2 Ch. 172.

642 *Tharpe v Stallwood* (1843) 5 M. & G. 760; *Partridge v Equity Trustees Executors & Agency Co Ltd* (1947) 75 C.L.R. 149.

643 *Dunwich (Bailiffs) v Sterry* (1831) 1 B. & Ad. 831.

644 *Nicolls v Bastard* (1835) 2 C.M. & R. 659. In *USA v Dollfus Mieg et Cie SA* [1952] A.C. 582, 611 Lord Porter suggested that this might only apply where the bailment was gratuitous. But with respect, there seems little reason for any such limitation.

645 *Calor Gas Ltd v Homebase Ltd* [2007] EWHC 1173 (Ch) at [41] (Henderson J).

646 cf. *Wilson v Lombank Ltd* [1963] 1 W.L.R. 1294.

647 cf. *The Winkfield* [1902] P. 42.

648 s.3(2)(c), (8)(c).

649 s.3(1)–(3); see para.16-91 onwards.

650 s.4; see para.16-94.

651 s.6; see para.16-102 onwards.

652 s.7; see para.16-86 onwards.

653 s.8; see para.16-85 onwards.

654 s.9; see para.16-85 onwards.

655 s.10; see para.16-71.

extinction of title by satisfaction of a judgment for damages[656] are in general the same as for conversion.

16-140 **Damages** Trespass to goods is a tort actionable per se, and thus when proved entitles the claimant at least to a nominal award.[657] In the case of deprivation, the measure of damages for trespass is, it is suggested, similar to that in conversion.[658] Where goods are damaged or interfered with without the claimant being deprived of them, the claimant is entitled to damages representing the loss actually suffered as the direct result of the trespass,[659] plus any consequential losses.[660] In a suitable case (for example, wrongful eviction), a substantial award for trespass to goods can be made despite the lack of proved pecuniary damage.[661] Aggravated damages may be awarded where appropriate,[662] as may punitive damages.[663]

(e) Defences

16-141 **Consent and self-help** Trespass to goods may of course be justified by the express or implicit consent of the possessor. For example, where a landowner displays a prominent notice clearly telling visitors[664] that vehicles unlawfully parked will be clamped and a release fee charged, he has a defence at common law to any action in trespass arising out of the clamping,[665] at least where the charge is not unreasonable.[666] There is also a statutory power to detain livestock straying onto the defendant's land.[667] In addition, there may well be a right at common law to seize any other chattel on land by way of distress damage feasant,[668] provided that it is doing some appreciable harm to the land[669] or some other chattel on it.[670]

---

656 s.5; see para.16-129.

657 e.g. *Hogarth v Jennings* [1892] 1 Q.B. 907.

658 See para.16-95 onwards.

659 *Lamb v Wall* (1859) 1 F. & F. 503.

660 Such as the cost of putting up a bond where a ship is unlawfully detained: see the Irish decision in *Island Ferries Teoranta v Minister for Communications* [2015] IESC 95.

661 *Cleal v Thomas*, unreported 11 July 1983 CA.

662 *Young v Sprague* [2014] NSWCA 456.

663 As a result of the removal in *Kuddus v Leicestershire Chief Constable* [2001] UKHL 29; [2002] 2 A.C. 122 of any restrictions based on the cause of action. cf. *Jamieson's Tow & Salvage Ltd v Murray* [1985] 2 N.Z.L.R. 144; and the more recent *Canadian King v Gross* 2008 ABPC 94; (2008) 443 A.R. 214 (dog-lover kidnapping and spaying breeder's prize Shih-Tzu bitch: $6,000 punitive damages).

664 The notice must be clear and unequivocal: see *Vine v Waltham Forest London Borough Council* [2000] 1 W.L.R. 2383 (notice not sufficiently prominent).

665 *Arthur v Anker* [1997] Q.B. 564. Under s.54 of the Protection of Freedoms Act 2012, it is a criminal offence without lawful excuse to immobilise a vehicle on private land with a view to preventing its removal by the owner. Whether this would affect civil liability is unclear, but the statement in s.54(2) that legally-binding consent by the owner is not a lawful excuse suggests that it does not, since otherwise the reference to legally-binding consent would be otiose.

666 See the remark of Bingham MR in *Arthur v Anker* [1997] Q.B. 564, 573.

667 Animals Act 1971 s.7.

668 Such was seemingly accepted in *Arthur v Anker* [1997] Q.B. 564. See generally Sparkes [1986] Conv. 107. It is not clear whether s.54 of the Protection of Freedoms Act 2012, which makes it a criminal offence without lawful authority to clamp a vehicle on private land, takes away the common law right of distress damage feasant, but it is suggested that the better view is that it does not. This is because it requires the clamping to have been done without lawful authority; and while consent of the owner is said not to be not lawful authority, the section says nothing about other defences, which presumably remain applicable. The older common law authorities on distress damage feasant all concerned livestock, but any common law right in respect of any animal was abolished

Execution of process: events before 6 April 2014 Before the activation of Pt 3 of the Tribunals, Courts and Enforcement Act 2007 in April 2014, the execution of the process of the courts rested with a special class of ministerial officers: in the superior courts with their enforcement officers, and in the county courts with the district judges.[671] Unless some specific protection existed, the sheriff or other officer charged with the execution of process was liable, for any act not covered by the authority of the process, and which was otherwise a trespass or conversion.[672] For example, if there were two persons of the same name and judgment had been given against one of them, the sheriff or other officer acted at his peril. If he levied execution against the wrong person, he was liable to an action. But some protections were available. **16-142**

At common law an order of a superior court was in all cases a protection to the officer executing it so long as he did not exceed his mandate; he was not bound to take notice of any defect or irregularity attending the process, even if apparent.[673] This was not so, however, with the order of an inferior court. This protected the officer if good on its face,[674] but if it appeared on the face of it to be such as the court could not legally make, he was not justified in putting it into force.[675] As regards county court executions, there was also a further statutory protection whereby the authority of the court was sufficiently proved by the production of the warrant of the court,[676] and the officers were protected notwithstanding "any defect of jurisdiction or other irregularity in the warrant".[677] Furthermore, even if there had been a technically illegal entry into premises but goods subject to execution had been seized, the execution stood good in favour of the creditor.[678] **16-143**

At common law prima facie any chattel could be taken in execution, and also money, cheques and other securities.[679] But while growing crops were regarded as chattels, the permanent growth of the land, such as grass and fruit, could not be seized.[680] Necessary clothing and bedding[681] belonging to the judgment debtor or **16-144**

by s.7(1) of the Animals Act 1971.

669 The requirement of some appreciable harm was accepted by a majority of the Court of Appeal in *Arthur v Anker* [1997] Q.B. 564, see 574–575 (Bingham MR) and 579–580 (Neill LJ).

670 See *Boden v Roscoe* [1894] 1 Q.B. 608 (under common law rules, animal could be detained for damage done to other animals).

671 County Courts Act 1984 ss.85–111 and 118–127; Courts Act 2003 s.99 and Sch.7. Under the Tribunals, Courts and Enforcement Act 2007 Pt 3, these ministerial actors are replaced by a class of "enforcement officers", a class which includes those certificated under s.64 of the Act, together with a number of others exempt from the certification process, such as police officers.

672 *Jelks v Hayward* [1905] 2 K.B. 460; *Watson v Murray & Co* [1955] 2 Q.B. 1. The damages are also the same: ibid.

673 *Countess of Rutland's Case* (1605) 6 Rep. 53; *Brown v Watson* (1871) 23 L.T. 745; *Williams v Williams & Nathan* [1937] 2 All E.R. 559; *Barclays Bank Ltd v Roberts* [1954] 1 W.L.R. 1212, where the Court of Appeal left open the question of whether a sheriff and his officers would be liable if, while acting under a writ of possession, they received notice of facts showing that an occupier was protected by the Rent Acts but nevertheless evicted him.

674 Even though he may be aware that under the circumstances of the case it was illegally issued: see *Olliet v Bessey* (1682) Jones T. 214.

675 Since he is supposed to know the law, and, therefore, to be aware that the document is a mere nullity: see *Andrews v Morris* (1841) 1 Q.B. 3; and *Watson v Bodell* (1845) 14 M. & W. 57.

676 County Courts Act 1984 s.127.

677 County Courts Act 1984 s.126.

678 See *Percival v Stamp* (1854) 9 Ex. 167, 171–172 (Parke B).

679 Judgments Act 1838 s.12; County Courts Act 1984 s.89.

680 See *Evans v Roberts* (1826) 5 B. & C. 829, 832 (Bayley J).

681 On which, see *Davies v Harris* [1900] 1 Q.B. 729; *Rondeau Le Grand & Co v Marks* [1918] 1 K.B. 75.

his family, and the necessary tools and implements of his trade, were protected.[682] Those who levied execution were confined to seizing goods reasonably sufficient to satisfy the relevant indebtedness of the judgment debtor. A seizure that was excessive, even if in good faith, gave rise to liability in respect of any damage caused to the debtor.[683] If malice was proved there might be a claim for exemplary damages.[684]

16-145 Generally speaking only the property[685] of the debtor could be seized, but this included a present right of possession amounting to a special property, such as a pledgee's interest.[686] In certain cases, however, goods might be liable to execution after ceasing to be the property of the execution debtor. For example, if a debtor had disposed of goods at an undervalue the transaction could be set aside, thus enabling judgment creditors to have access to those assets.[687] Furthermore, since a writ of fieri facias directed the seizure of such goods as the debtor had at the time of its issue, it followed that at common law goods alienated subsequently to that date might be taken, though by statute the rights of a good faith purchaser were protected.[688]

16-146 **Events after 6 April 2014: the Tribunals, Courts and Enforcement Act 2007** Part 3 of the Tribunals, Courts and Enforcement Act 2007 puts the above matters on a simpler statutory footing. What were once writs of fieri facias and warrants of execution are now recast and known as writs (or warrants) of control.[689] Seizure of property under them is exclusively in the hands of "enforcement agents" certificated under s.64 of the Act, or those exempt from such certification.[690] All the property of the debtor, at the time the writ or warrant from the court is received by the person whose duty it is to endorse it, is regarded as "bound goods" and hence subject to seizure[691] on notice to the debtor.[692] Goods may be seized either at the debtor's usual residence or place of business, or on the highway[693]; alternatively, if they are at some other premises the court may issue a warrant to allow them to be seized there.[694] Certain categories of goods are exempt from seizure on the basis that they are reasonably required to satisfy the basic domestic needs of the debtor

---

682 Insolvency Act 1986 s.283; *Re Dawson* [1899] 2 Q.B. 54.

683 *Gawler v Chaplin* (1848) 2 Ex. 503; *Watson v Murray & Co* [1955] 2 Q.B. 1 (where no actual damage was suffered); *Moore v Lambeth County Court Registrar (No.2)* [1970] 1 Q.B. 560.

684 *Moore v Lambeth County Court Registrar (No.2)* [1970] 1 Q.B. 560 at 572.

685 Not including goods held in a representative capacity or on trust: if these are seized the owner may bring trespass or conversion. See *Farr v Newman* (1792) 4 T.R. 621; *Fenwick v Laycock* (1841) 2 Q.B. 108.

686 See *Legg v Evans* (1840) 6 M. & W. 36, 42 (Parke B).

687 See generally Insolvency Act 1986 ss.423–435. Bills of sale that fail to comply with certain of the requirements of the Bills of Sale Act 1878 or the Bills of Sale Act (1878) Amendment Act 1882 are void against the transferor, from which it follows that the goods subject to them may also be seized.

688 Courts Act 2003 Sch.7 para.8(2).

689 See Tribunals, Courts and Enforcement Act 2007 s.62(4) and Sch.12.

690 Sch.12 para.2(2).

691 Sch.12 para.4. There is protection for the good faith purchaser: para.5(2). Note that pending seizure or agreement by the debtor the enforcement agent has no right to sue in conversion: *365 Business Finance Ltd v Bellagio Hospitality WB Ltd* [2020] EWCA Civ 588.

692 Sch.12 para.7. The minimum period of notice is generally seven days discounting Sundays and bank holidays: Taking Control of Goods Regulations 2013 (SI 2013/1894) para.6 (made under the 2007 Act Sch.12 para.7).

693 Sch.12 para.9. The reference to the highway is no doubt directed at the seizure of ungaraged motor vehicles.

694 Sch.12 para.15.

and his family, such as the tools of his trade up to a value of £1,350, certain essential items of bedding, furniture and household equipment, pets, and vehicles carrying a blue badge and used for the transport of the disabled.[695] Furthermore, goods may not be seized from a child debtor, or from premises where no non-vulnerable adult is present.[696] All seizures must take place between 6am and 9pm.[697] The agent is prohibited from seizing goods that are not the debtor's,[698] which presumably means that he remains strictly liable in trespass in respect of such goods,[699] except apparently where he seizes a car or other property on a highway, in which case he is liable only if negligent.[700] In addition, the agent having seized goods has a power of sale[701]; here, in contrast to the position with regard to seizure, the agent who seizes goods that are not the debtor's is protected from liability except in so far as he had notice of the relevant third party's interest.[702] The existing protections for those acting under apparently valid orders of the High Court or a County Court apparently remain in force.

5. Negligence Resulting in Damage to Goods

Negligence as wrongful interference The general nature of liability in negligence as a nominate tort is fully considered elsewhere.[703] Various procedural provisions of the Torts (Interference with Goods) Act 1977[704] would consequently be likely, in an action for such wrongful interference, to modify the general law of negligence. By s.1(c) of the 1977 Act the third form of "wrongful interference with goods" is "negligence so far as it results in damage to goods or to an interest in goods". Whilst that provision clearly covers negligent damage to, or destruction of, goods, it is doubtful whether the words "damage to an interest in goods" cover financial loss which does not result from negligent infringement of some proprietary or possessory right.[705] **16-147**

The better view, therefore, appears to be that an action for wrongful interference will lie under s.1(d) for negligent damage to, or destruction of, goods and that **16-148**

695 Taking Control of Goods Regulations 2013 (SI 2013/1894) para.4 (made under the 2007 Act, Sch.12 para.3).

696 Taking Control of Goods Regulations 2013 (SI 2013/1894) para.10.

697 Taking Control of Goods Regulations 2013 (SI 2013/1894) para.13.

698 Sch.12 para.10.

699 The enforcement agent has extensive protections under Sch.12 paras 63 and 64, but these only apply to his actions in selling the goods or paying over the proceeds. They do not seem apt to protect him from liability for seizing them in the first place.

700 Sch.12 para.13(2). This provides that any liability arising out of his seizing goods on a highway is excluded, except to the extent that he acted without reasonable care: the wording seems wide enough to cover seizure of the wrong goods.

701 Sch.12 paras 38 onwards. For detailed regulations covering this, see Taking Control of Goods Regulations 2013 (SI 2013/1894) Part 3. The sale passes good title even if the goods are not the debtor's unless the buyer has notice of this, or an application to the court has already been made: Sch.12 para.51.

702 Sch.12 para.63.

703 See Ch.7.

704 e.g. ss.3 (remedies), 4 (interlocutory orders), 5 (extinction of title on payment of damages), 7 (double liability), 8 (pleading *jus tertii*) and 9 (concurrent actions).

705 The similarly restricted fourth head of "wrongful interference" in s.1(d)—"any other tort so far as it results in damage to goods or to an interest in goods"—clearly excludes the nominate torts of conversion, trespass and negligence specifically mentioned in s.1(a), (b) and (c), but appears apt to include at least some actions for reversionary injury (on which, see para.16-150).

in such an action the various procedural provisions of the Act may modify the ordinary procedure in negligence cases. It also seems clear that the provisions of the Act will cover actions for conversion against a bailee who negligently destroys or loses the goods.[706] It has been argued,[707] however, that a bailee's liability for breach of duty to his bailor is by no means necessarily synonymous or coextensive with tortious liability for negligence and that, by choosing to sue for breach of bailment or of some promissory undertaking rather than for wrongful interference, a bailor may evade various procedural provisions of the Act and so, for example, prevent the defendant pleading the *jus tertii* under s.8.

16-149 **Procedural consequences** The various procedural provisions of the 1977 Act are likely to have a limited impact on actions for wrongful interference by negligence. The usual remedies for negligence, namely damages and/or injunction, remain available whether or not the defendant possesses or controls the goods.[708] The orders of specific delivery, or for delivery or damages, which may now be made in any action for wrongful interference where the defendant is in possession or control of the goods,[709] will be unavailable in cases of negligent loss or partial damage[710] and unwanted for total destruction, where damages or a sum agreed in settlement or compromise will both be preferred and also, if paid, extinguish the claimant's title to the wreckage.[711] Nor is a defendant charged with negligence a likely candidate for an allowance for improving the goods.[712] However, such a defendant may claim reimbursement to avoid double liability if he has been obliged to pay damages to rival claimants to the goods,[713] and may wish to plead the *jus tertii* and by summons apply for directions as to joinder of named persons,[714] whilst the claimant, except in vehicle collision cases, may have to give particulars of his title and identify any other persons whom he knows to have, or to claim, any interest in the goods.[715] Further, where the goods are subject to two or more claims for wrongful interference (whether or not the claims are for the same wrongful act or any of them relates also to the other goods), the later claim or claims may be heard in the same court as the first claim, even if county court financial or territorial limits have to be waived for that purpose.[716]

6. REVERSIONARY INJURY[717]

16-150 **General** The origin of reversionary injury lay in two lacunae in the existing scheme of torts protecting personal property. The first was the inability, except in

---

[706] i.e. where the claimant takes advantage of s.2(2).

[707] See N. Palmer, "The Application of the Torts (Interference with Goods) Act 1977 to Actions in Bailment" (1978) 41 M.L.R. 629, where the subject-matter of this paragraph is more fully discussed.

[708] ss.3(2)(c), (8)(c).

[709] ss.3(1)–3(3).

[710] Since the defendant will not have possession or control of lost goods, and since the "damages by reference to the value of the goods" payable as an alternative to delivery under s.3(2)(b) must clearly represent their full value: see s.3(5). Claimants seeking discretionary specific restitution orders under s.3(2)(a) and (3)(b) for goods in the defendants' possession or control are more likely to found their actions in conversion than in negligence.

[711] s.5. If the defendant is the claimant's bailee, the claimant may prefer to found his action for loss or destruction in conversion under s.2(2) or on breach of bailment.

[712] s.6: see para.16-102 onwards.

[713] s.7: para.16-82 onwards.

[714] ss.8(1), 8(2)(c).

[715] ss.8(2)(a), (b).

[716] s.9.

[717] See generally A. Tettenborn, "Reversionary Damage to Chattels" [1994] C.L.J. 326.

rare circumstances, of a co-owner to sue his other co-owner or anyone claiming through him in conversion. The second was the problems faced by the owner of goods who had neither possession nor an immediate right to it, for example a bailor for a fixed term,[718] a person who bought goods for which he had not paid,[719] or a mortgagee before default, who could not sue in either conversion or trespass. Both categories were, in the course of the nineteenth century, given a special cause of action on the case in respect of actual loss suffered.[720] As for the co-owner, the action for reversionary injury is now of little interest since he can now sue in conversion anyway.[721] But the case of the non-possessing claimant remains important.

The action for reversionary injury lies, it is suggested, in respect of any act which would, but for the problem of the claimant's lack of title to sue, amount to trespass,[722] negligence[723] or conversion,[724] provided it has the effect of depriving him either temporarily or permanently of the benefit of his reversionary interest, whether because the goods are destroyed or seriously damaged[725] or because they are wrongfully disposed of by a transaction whereby the disponee acquires a good title, so preventing recovery of them. But actual damage is necessary: a mere wrongful taking or detention, which may not affect his reversionary interest if the goods are returned or released before he regains the right to immediate possession, will not suffice.[726] Similarly with a wrongful sale: except in so far as the claimant can prove it has destroyed his title or at the very least reduced his chances of recovering his goods, no damages are available.[727] There is no authority whether a purely possessory title, such as that of a finder, will suffice to found an action for reversionary injury. It is submitted, however, that the better view is that it will.[728] Except in the case where goods are physically damaged or the claimant's title to them is **16-151**

---

718 *Ward v Macauley* (1791) 4 T.R. 489 (trespass); *Gordon v Harper* (1796) 7 T.R. 9 (conversion). Aliter if the bailment is at will: *Manders v Williams* (1849) 4 Ex. 339.

719 *Lord v Price* (1874) L.R. 9 Ex. 54. For the unpaid seller's lien, see now Sale of Goods Act 1979 ss.41–43.

720 For the early authorities, see A. Tettenborn, "Reversionary Damage to Chattels" [1994] C.L.J. 326, 328.

721 Torts (Interference with Goods) Act 1977 s.10. But the old action may be significant in one case, namely where goods are wrongfully pledged by one co-owner. Section 10 only covers disposals purporting to deal with the whole interest in the goods, which a pledge does not.

722 There is no direct authority on this. But the analogous cause of action in the case of trespass to land is well-established: e.g. *Mayfair Property Co v Johnston* [1894] 1 Ch. 508.

723 *Hall v Pickard* (1812) 3 Camp. 187; *Mears v London & South Western Ry Co* (1862) 11 C.B. (N.S.) 850.

724 *Tancred v Allgood* (1859) 4 H. & N. 438. See also the Singapore decision in *AAHG LLC v Hong Hin Kay Albert* [2016] SGHC 274 (share certificates).

725 *Mears v London & South Western Ry Co* (1862) 11 C.B. (N.S.) 850. The question is whether "the thing complained of will continue indefinitely unless something is done about it": Steel J in *HSBC Rail (UK) Ltd v Network Rail Infrastructure Ltd* [2005] EWHC 403 (Comm); [2005] 1 All E.R. (Comm) 689 at [34]; upheld on appeal at [2005] EWCA Civ 1437; [2006] 1 W.L.R. 643.

726 See *Tancred v Allgood* (1859) 4 H. & N. 438; and *Mukibi v Bhavsar* [1967] E.A. 473, in both of which the claimant failed on this ground. Note that the claimant can recover whether or not he will in fact have to pay for the damage: see *Dee Trading v Baldwin* [1938] V.L.R. 173 (owner of car on hire purchase can recover from third party even though hirer bound by hire-purchase contract to repair it). But if the damage has actually been repaired at no cost to the bailor, then the latter has no cause of action: *HSBC Rail (UK) Ltd v Network Rail Infrastructure Ltd* [2005] EWHC 403 (Comm); [2005] 1 All E.R. (Comm) 689.

727 *Mukibi v Bhavsar* [1967] E.A. 473.

728 The reasons are complex, but broadly as follows: (1) at common law *jus tertii* could be defeated by a claimant who, while not in possession himself, derived his title from someone who had been: see para.16-84 onwards; (2) except where actual damage to goods or destruction of the claimant's title

destroyed, there is some doubt as to whether reversionary injury counts as "wrongful interference with goods" so as to attract the provisions of the Torts (Interference with Goods) Act 1977.[729]

7. Wrongful Interference by Other Torts

(a) Other torts generally

16-152 **Wrongful interference by other torts generally** After embracing individually the nominate torts of conversion, trespass and negligence the statutory definition of "wrongful interference with goods" goes on, in s.1(d) of the 1977 Act, to include "any other tort so far as it results in damage to goods or to an interest in goods". As with the similar wording concerning wrongful interference by negligence, the question arises whether the words "damage to an interest in goods" include the loss or destruction of the goods themselves. The scope of this residual category of wrongful interference is naturally imprecise. Whilst it would clearly cover claims for damage to chattels arising from torts such as nuisance[730] and the non-natural user of land under the rule in *Rylands v Fletcher*,[731] the provisions of the 1977 Act are likely to have little material application in such cases, where the defendant is unlikely to have possession or control of the claimant's goods and the claimant's claim may be for an injunction and/or for consequential loss rather than for damages measured by the value of the goods themselves. But a defendant might possibly wish to plead the *jus tertii* and seek to avoid possible double liability in such circumstances.[732] Actions on the case for injury to reversionary interests are dealt with above in this connection.[733]

(b) Rescous and pound breach

16-153 The torts of rescous and pound breach, though venerable, are essentially now superseded. Rescous lay when goods which had been distrained were rescued from the distrainor's actual possession before they had been impounded; once impounded, they were regarded as in the custody of the law and their removal was the wrong of pound breach.[734] At common law these remedies were available to any distrainor; but where goods were distrained for rent the wrongdoer was statutorily liable to the person aggrieved for treble damages.[735] To all intents and purposes, however, these wrongs have disappeared as a result of the activation in April 2014

is involved, a claim for reversionary injury is not a claim within s.1(d) of the 1977 Act for "any other tort so far as it results in damage to goods or to an interest in goods" and therefore not a claim for "wrongful interference with goods" under the statute; (3) it follows that s.8 of the 1977 Act, purporting to exclude *jus tertii*, does not affect the matter. For the detailed reasons for this view, and general discussion of the *jus tertii* point in connection with reversionary injury, see Tettenborn, op. cit. at 335.

[729] For discussion of the point see A. Tettenborn, "Reversionary Damage to Chattels" [1994] C.L.J. 326, 336.

[730] e.g. the vixens in *Hollywood Silver Farm Ltd v Emmett* [1936] 2 K.B. 468: see Ch.20. But in nuisance, unlike conversion, the claimant must own or occupy the land on which the damage occurs.

[731] (1868) L.R. 3 H.L. 330. See Ch.20.

[732] ss.7, 8; see para.16-82 onwards.

[733] See para.16-150 onwards.

[734] To be liable for pound breach, a person must realise that the goods have been impounded: *Abingdon RDC v O'Gorman* [1968] 2 Q.B. 811 (but see *Lavell & Co v O'Leary* [1933] 2 K.B. 200).

[735] Distress for Rent Act 1689 s.3 (now repealed). See *Eyland & Sons Ltd v TSL Turton* (2014) Ltd

of Pt 3 of the Tribunals, Courts and Enforcement Act 2007. Section 71 of the Act abolishes distress for rent, which was the main context in which they arose, in favour of a more limited statutory remedy and in addition abolishes the common law remedies for rescue where the new procedure applies, replacing them with a simple statutory liability for loss where a debtor wrongfully interferes with controlled goods.[736] But the disappearance may not be quite complete, in particular in respect of distress damage feasant. The Animals Act 1971 swept away this right as regards damage by animals, but left it extant as regards other property: and this residual right also seems unaffected by the 2007 Act. It therefore (it seems) remains subject to the common law, including the concomitant remedies of rescous and pound-breach.

(c) Replevin

The former remedy of replevin Replevin was a summary process by which a person deprived of possession of goods could obtain their return until the matter could be determined by a court of law.[737] The claimant either deposited a sum as security or entered into a bond to commence an action within a certain time, and to prosecute it without delay: if he succeeded he could recover in respect of any special damages sustained and also the value of the goods if not redelivered to him.[738] **16-154**

Replevin could only be brought when there had been a taking by trespass.[739] **16-155** Because the remedy was available where goods had been taken out of the claimant's possession, a bailee was entitled to replevy.[740] The ordinary use of replevin was in cases of distress for rent, but it was also employed by parties complaining of a seizure of their goods under process of an inferior court issued without jurisdiction.[741] There could, however, be no replevin against an execution of a superior court.[742] Although the common law did not allow replevin against a revenue seizure or distress for any Crown due,[743] the Crown Proceedings Act 1947 would appear of sufficient scope to allow it in other proceedings against government departments.[744] Since the activation of Pt 3 of the Tribunals, Courts and Enforcement Act 2007, however, replevin, like rescous and pound-breach, has effectively been a dead letter.

[2015] EWHC 3942 (QB).

736 See the Tribunals, Courts and Enforcement Act 2007 Sch.12 para.67.

737 For the detailed process, see County Courts Act 1984 s.144 and Sch.1.

738 *Gibbs v Cruikshank* (1873) L.R. 8 C. & P. 454; cf. *Sperry Inc v CIBC* (1985) 17 D.L.R. (4th) 236.

739 *Shannon v Shannon* (1804) 1 Sch. & Lef. 324; *Mellor v Leather* (1853) 1 E. & B. 619; *Mennie v Blake* (1856) 6 E. & B. 842.

740 *Smith v Mulcahy* [1934] 1 K.B. 608 at 635.

741 *R. v Burchett* (1722) 1 Str. 567; *George v Chambers* (1843) 11 M. & W. 149; *Allen v Sharp* (1848) 2 Ex. 352. For examples of its use in rating disputes, see *Governors of Bristol Poor v Wait* (1834) 1 A. & E. 264; *Mersey Docks & Harbour Board v Cameron* (1864–65) 11 H.L.C. 443; *Marshall v Pitman* (1833) 9 Bing. 595; *London & North Western Ry Co v Buckmaster* (1874) L.R. 10 Q.B. 444; *London CC v Hackney BC* [1928] 2 K.B. 588.

742 See *George v Chambers* (1843) 11 M. & W. 149 at 160, per Parke B.

743 *R. v Oliver* (1717) Bunb. 14: also *Cawthorne v Campbell* (1790) 1 Anst. 205 at 212, per Eyre CB.

744 See s.21 (relief against Crown allowed unless it would have some effect as injunction).

(e) Replevin

[65] [2015] EWHC 3442 (QB).

[68] Gibbs v Cruikshank (1873) L.R. 8 C.P. 454; cf. Spicer v Farr (1848) 17 L.J.Q.B. (4th) 236.

[70] Smith v Plomer (1934) 1 K.B. 608 at 655.
[71] R. v Burton (1724) 1 Str. 587; George v Chambers (1843) 11 M. & W. 149; Morris v Salberg (1889) 22 Q.B.D. 614; Bull v Price (1831) 7 Bing. 237; see also Lucas v Tarleton (1858) 3 H. & N. 116; Bentley v Eastern (1910) 2 K.B. 382. For examples of its use in rating disputes, see Governors of Bristol Poor v Wait (1834) 1 A. & E. 264; Warne v Rocke; Harbour Board v Cameron (1864-65) 11 H.L.C. 443; Marshall v Pitman (1833) 9 Bing. 595; Dayley & North Western Ry Co v Brandreth (1874) L.R. 10 Q.B. 112; London CC v Hackney BC [1928] 2 K.B. 588.

[73] ... v Rice (1777) Bunb. 14; also Commonwealth v Campbell (1990) 1 Aust. 20 at 212 per Evatt J.

Chapter 17

DECEIT

Table of Contents

1. Introduction[1]

Definition The modern development of the tort of deceit (sometimes called simply "fraud") dates from *Pasley v Freeman*[2] in 1789. There, the defendant falsely represented to the claimant that a third party was creditworthy when he knew he was not; the claimant suffered loss as a result of extending credit to him. The claimant was held to have an action.[3] The tort involves a perfectly general principle: where a defendant makes a false representation, knowing it to be untrue, or being reckless as to whether it is true, and intends that the claimant should act in reliance on it, then in so far as the latter does so and suffers loss[4] the defendant is liable.[5] Although most cases concern claimants duped into entering into commercial transactions, deceit extends well beyond this.[6] Where appropriate it can **17-01**

---

1. J. Murphy, "Misleading appearances in the tort of deceit" [2016] C.L.J. 301.
2. (1789) 3 T.R. 51.
3. Though note that today the representation, being one as to credit, would have to be in writing: Statute of Frauds Amendment Act 1828. See para.17-55 onwards.
4. Damage is of the gist of the action; see *Smith v Chadwick* (1884) 9 App. Cas. 187, 190 (Lord Blackburn).
5. See, e.g. *Derry v Peek* (1889) 14 App. Cas. 337, 374 (Lord Herschell); *Standard Chartered Bank v Pakistan National Shipping Corp* [1998] 1 Lloyd's Rep. 684, 704 (Cresswell J); *AIC Ltd v ITS Testing Services (UK) Ltd* [2006] EWCA Civ 1601; [2007] 1 Lloyd's Rep. 555 at [251] (Rix LJ); *Parna v G & S Properties Ltd* [1971] S.C.R. 306, 316 (Spence J); *McBride v Christie's Australia Pty Ltd* [2014] NSWSC 1729 at [335].
6. For a more esoteric application see *A v Att-Gen* [2018] NZHC 986; [2018] 3 N.Z.L.R. 439 (police search after presenting fake warrant: liability for loss caused). Another is paternity fraud: e.g. *P v B (Paternity: Damages for Deceit)* [2001] 1 F.L.R. 1041 (action by cohabitee against partner for

even encompass fraudulently obtaining a court judgment.[7] Each aspect of the tort is discussed in detail below.

17-02 **Deceit and other liability for misrepresentation** Damages may, of course, be awarded for a misrepresentation even if it is not fraudulent. If a representation is a term of a contract, damages are available if it is false without even proof of fault: again, since the decision of the House of Lords in *Hedley Byrne & Co Ltd v Heller & Partners Ltd*,[8] it has been clear that misrepresentation can give rise to liability in the tort of negligence at common law, at least where there is something that can be construed as an acceptance of responsibility for its truth. In addition, under the Misrepresentation Act 1967 s.2(1), a person who induces another to contract with him by misrepresentation is liable unless he proves he was not at fault. Very often a claimant is much better advised to sue on one of these bases, given that "fraud must be distinctly alleged and as distinctly proved",[9] and that there exist strict rules about when a lawyer is entitled to plead it on his client's behalf.[10] In addition, the defendant's liability insurance may exclude liability for fraud; the defendant in an action for deceit (but not in one for negligence) may on principle demand trial by jury[11]; and while summary judgment is available in fraud cases[12] it is not readily given. However, there may be advantages to suing for fraud. There is no need to show a special relationship or undertaking of responsibility (in contrast to *Hedley Byrne* liability)[13]; damages may not be reduced for contributory negligence[14] and may on occasion be more generous than elsewhere[15]; and s.32(1)(a) of the Limitation Act 1980 provides a more generous limitation regime, effectively

---

deceiving him that child was his and causing him to pay for its upkeep); see too *A v B* [2007] EWHC 1246 (QB); [2007] 2 F.L.R. 1051.

7 The judgment has, however, first to be overturned. For an example, see *Gentry v Miller* [2016] EWCA Civ 141; [2016] 1 W.L.R. 2696; and its sequel, *UK Insurance Ltd v Gentry* [2018] EWHC 37 (QB) (recovery in respect of insurance fraud arising out of bogus collision).

8 [1964] A.C. 465. Liability for negligent misstatements is dealt with in para.7-104 onwards.

9 See *Davy v Garrett* [1877] 7 Ch. D. 473 at 489, per Thesiger LJ. See also *Gardner Neptune Shipping v Occidental* [1990] 1 Lloyd's Rep. 330 (on which, R. Hooley, "Fraud and the Misrepresentation Act 1967" (1991) 107 L.Q.R. 31; *Haringey LBC v Hines* [2010] EWCA Civ 1111; [2011] H.L.R. 6, especially at [39]. On the pleading requirements see *Boyse (International) Ltd v Natwest Markets Plc* [2020] EWHC 1264 (Ch) at [35]–[37].

10 "The pleading of fraud or deceit is a serious step, with significance and reputational ramifications going well beyond the pleading of a claim in negligence": Sales LJ in *Playboy Club London Ltd v Banca Nazionale Del Lavoro SpA (No 2)* [2018] EWCA Civ 2025 at [46]; see too *Mason v Clarke* [1955] A.C. 778, 794 (Viscount Simonds). It is unethical for a member of the Bar to allege fraud without clear instructions and reasonably credible evidence: Bar Standards Board Handbook 4.3, Code of Conduct, Rule C9.c. But note that this evidence need not necessarily be admissible in court: thus in the wasted costs decision in *Medcalf v Mardell* [2002] UKHL 27; [2003] 1 A.C. 120 the House of Lords declined to castigate as improper the pleading of fraud on the basis of documents subject to legal professional privilege.

11 Senior Courts Act 1981 s.69; on which, see *Barclays Bank Ltd v Cole* [1967] 2 Q.B. 738; and cf. *Stafford Winfield & Cook Partners v Winfield* [1981] 1 W.L.R. 458.

12 For examples, see *Cheshire Building Society v Dunlop Haywards (DHL) Ltd* [2008] EWHC 51 (Comm); [2008] P.N.L.R. 19; and *Ticketus LLP v Whyte* [2013] EWHC 4069 (Ch). For a discussion of the point of principle see the Canadian decision in *Hryniak v Mauldin* 2014 SCC 7; (2014) 366 D.L.R. (4th) 641.

13 For a discussion of this see para.7-104 onwards.

14 See para.17-52.

15 See paras 17-48 to 17-50 (on causation and remoteness respectively).

preventing time from running at all until the claimant discovers the fraud[16] or could with reasonable diligence have discovered it.[17]

Limits on the ambit of liability In a few cases liability in deceit is curtailed for public policy reasons. For example, privilege in court proceedings extends as much to deceit as to any other liability.[18] In addition, it has been held that public policy limits on damages for the cost of bringing up a healthy child apply as much in deceit as elsewhere,[19] and that as between married parties in the course of divorce, claims in deceit for paternity fraud may be pre-empted by the provisions of the Matrimonial Causes Act 1973 on financial adjustment.[20] But these exceptions are narrow. Thus the courts have declined to introduce any general qualification of liability in respect of statements made within the family,[21] and the House of Lords have emphatically held that it is no defence that the defendant told lies merely in his capacity as the servant or agent of someone else.[22] 17-03

Standard of proof in deceit claims Despite early sporadic suggestions to the contrary,[23] the Court of Appeal made it clear in *Hornal v Neuberger Products Ltd*[24] that allegations of fraud need only be proved to civil standard of preponderance of 17-04

---

16 Note that the word "fraud" in s.32(1) of the Limitation Act 1980 is not confined to deceit or dishonesty in the sense in which it is used in this chapter: *Beaman v ARTS Ltd* [1949] 1 K.B. 550; *Kitchen v RAF Association* [1958] 1 W.L.R. 563. But this does not affect the point in the text.

17 Millett LJ explained the subsection in *Paragon Finance Plc v Thakerar & Co* [1999] 1 All E.R. 400, 418, saying that claimants "must establish that they could not have discovered the fraud without exceptional measures which they could not reasonably have been expected to take". See too *Biggs v Sotnicks (A Firm)* [2002] EWCA Civ 272; [2002] Lloyd's Rep. P.N. 331.

18 *Walsh v Staines* [2008] EWCA Civ 1324; [2009] C.P. Rep. 16. But the immunity is strictly limited. So the mere fact that a payment has been embodied in a consent order is no bar to proceedings in deceit to recover it: *Zurich Insurance Co Plc v Hayward* [2011] EWCA Civ 641; [2011] C.P. Rep. 39 (insurance payout to person now alleged to have been malingering; appealed on other grounds, [2016] UKSC 48; [2017] A.C. 142). In *Smart v Forensic Science Service Ltd* [2013] EWCA Civ 783; [2013] P.N.L.R. 32 the Court of Appeal refused to strike out a deceit claim by a criminal defendant against a laboratory said to have deliberately falsified evidence against him: sed quaere.

19 See the paternity fraud case of *A v B* [2007] EWHC 1246 (QB); [2007] 2 F.L.R. 1051 at [61]–[63].

20 So held in *FRB v DCA* [2019] EWHC 2816 (Fam); [2020] 1 F.C.R. 371.

21 See *P v B (Paternity: Damages for Deceit)* [2001] 1 F.L.R. 1041 (action by cohabitee against girlfriend for duping him into thinking a child was his and hence paying for its upkeep); and the similar *A v B* [2007] EWHC 1246 (QB); [2007] 2 F.L.R. 1051; and *AXB v BXA* [2018] EWHC 588 (QB) (claim based on lie that defendant pregnant by claimant). The existence of liability, it was said, would not tend to subvert intimate relationships, particularly since a claimant was unlikely to sue while the relationship was still on foot. But this is not uncontroversial: in *Magill v Magill* [2006] HCA 51; (2006) 81 A.L.J.R. 254 a majority in the High Court of Australia (Gummow, Kirby, Crennan, and Hayne JJ) seems to have thought that the tort of deceit should have little or no part to play in interspousal relations; and in *PP v DD* 2017 ONCA 180; (2017) 409 D.L.R. (4th) 691 the Ontario Court of Appeal regarded this as a reason to strike out a claim for deceit where a girlfriend, having falsely assured the plaintiff she was using contraception, fell pregnant by him. See generally N. Wikeley & L. Young, "Secrets and lies: no deceit down under for paternity fraud" (2008) 20 Child & Fam. L.Q. 81.

22 *Standard Chartered Bank v Pakistan National Shipping Corp (No.2)* [2002] UKHL 43; [2003] 1 A.C. 959 (on which, see Parker [2003] L.M.C.L.Q. 1); *Nitron Group BV (In Liquidation) v Barington Alliance LLP* [2020] EWHC 1244 (Comm). But there may be some incidental protection for a mere mouthpiece in this connection: see *GE Commercial Finance Ltd v Gee* [2005] EWHC 2056 (QB); [2006] 1 Lloyd's Rep. 337, referred to below at para.17-21 fn.122.

23 e.g. *Thurtell v Beaumont* (1823) 1 Bing. 339.

24 [1957] 1 Q.B. 247; followed in *Bromley v Att Gen* [1968] N.Z.L.R. 75. See too *Otkritie International Investment Management Ltd v Urumov* [2014] EWHC 191 (Comm) at [84]–[91] (Eder J).

probability and no more. Nevertheless, even if the standard is the civil standard, in practice more convincing evidence will often be required to establish fraud than other types of allegation.[25] The reason is the straightforward one given by Lord Nicholls in a later case: "When assessing the probabilities the court will have in mind as a factor, to whatever extent is appropriate in the particular case, that the more serious the allegation the less likely it is that the event occurred and, hence, the stronger should be the evidence before the court concludes that the allegation is established on the balance of probability. Fraud is usually less likely than negligence. ..."[26] Nevertheless, there is no bar in a suitable case to the grant of summary judgment against a defendant if the evidence is sufficiently overwhelming.[27] On a similar basis, the Court of Appeal will not hold a defendant guilty of fraud contrary to the view of the trial judge unless it is completely satisfied that the latter was wrong. Doubts, even grave doubts, on the correctness of the judge's finding will be insufficient to persuade an appellate court to reverse it.[28]

2. Requirements

(a) Representation

17-05 **Misrepresentation or misleading conduct required for liability** To found an action in deceit the claimant must show a misrepresentation of present fact or law (or, at the very least, something done which was aimed at inducing action on the basis of false information).[29] However, a representation may be either express or implied from conduct[30]; furthermore, adopting the representation of a third party can be sufficient.[31] Where an issue arises as to whether a representation is true or not, the

---

25 See *Smith New Court Securities Ltd v Citibank NA* [1997] A.C. 254, 274 (Lord Steyn); and *Dadourian Group International Inc v Simms* [2009] EWCA Civ 169; [2009] 1 Lloyd's Rep. 601 at [32] (Arden LJ).

26 See *Re H (Minors)* [1996] A.C. 563, 586–587; as explained in *Re S-B (Children)* [2009] UKSC 17; [2010] A.C. 678 at [13]–[18] (Lady Hale); and *UK Insurance Ltd v Gentry* [2018] EWHC 37 (QB) at [19]–[21] (Teare J).

27 *Cheshire Building Society v Dunlop Haywards (DHL) Ltd* [2008] EWHC 51 (Comm); [2008] P.N.L.R. 19 (complicity in mortgage fraud inferred from eightfold overvaluation coupled with evidence of bribery).

28 *Gross v Lewis Hillman Ltd* [1970] Ch. 445.

29 For example, the deceit may be practised, not on a person, but on a machine such as a computer: *Renault UK Ltd v Fleetpro Technical Services* [2007] EWHC 2541 (QB); [2008] Bus. L.R. D17 at [122]. In *IG Index Plc v Colley* [2013] EWHC 478 (QB) at [746]–[763] Stadlen J held defendants liable for fraud where, aided by a dishonest employee, they placed false bets with a spread-betting company; in addition, he explicitly stated that there was no requirement for any misrepresentation at all. But this is problematical, since if it is true it is not clear where the boundaries of fraud fall to be drawn. Furthermore, it must be arguable that there was at least an implicit (and untrue) representation there by the defendants that the bets placed by them represented bona fide transactions.

30 See para.17-06 onwards. See too *Whyfe v Michael Cullen & Partners* [1993] E.G.C.S. 193 (business lease very obscurely worded, with rent inevitably uneconomic and surrender an inevitability: Court of Appeal refuse to strike out action by lessees for deceit on basis that lease deliberately dressed up to look unremarkable when in fact not).

31 *Bradford Third Equitable Benefit Building Society v Borders* [1941] 2 All E.R. 204, 211 (Lord Maugham). (In fact fraud was held not established on the facts of the case.) In *Libyan Investment Authority v King* [2020] EWHC 440 (Ch) at [123]–[126] it was said that if a vendor of an interest in a joint property venture procured from valuers a valuation he knew might well be misleading, which was then sent to an investor, he would be guilty of deceit.

court normally looks to the reasonable meaning of what the defendant said[32]; indeed, this is often decisive.[33] Nevertheless, in strict law the issue in a deceit case is the meaning the representee was intended to put on what was said, even if this differs from the literal meaning of the words used:

> "If a person makes a representation of that which is true, if he intends that the party to whom the representation is made should not believe it to be true, that is a false representation."[34]

Conversely, if a statement is in terms untrue, but is not intended to be interpreted in its literal sense, it cannot be charged as a deceit.[35]

Misrepresentation and non-disclosure The general rule is that a positive act or representation is required: "mere silence, however morally wrong, will not support an action of deceit".[36] However, there are, as might be expected, a number of qualifications to this principle which greatly reduce its effect.[37] **17-06**

Half-truths A half-truth or fragmentary statement may amount to deceit if it is suggestive of a falsehood and intended so to be[38]: for example, where a defendant relays the favourable portion of a surveyor's report but omits the less encouraging part[39]; or where a joint venturer, knowing of a low valuation of the project, procures **17-07**

---

32 *Barley v Muir* [2018] EWHC 619 (QB) at [177] (Soole J). This may of course depend on context: see *Copthall Ltd v Scorched Earth Services Ltd* [2017] EWHC 1341 (QB) at [36]–[47] (representation that $1.4 million advanced by third party to business in which claimant asked to invest; clear from previous negotiations that this did not mean a pure cash injection).

33 *Property Alliance Group Ltd v Royal Bank of Scotland Plc* [2018] EWCA Civ 355; [2018] 1 W.L.R. 3529, esp. at [89]–[96], [101], [111] (meaning of "hedge" in financial context). Again, apparently imprecise words may be deceptive if it is clear that a reasonable representee would understand them in a particular way. See, e.g. *Burki v Seventy Thirty Ltd* [2018] EWHC 2151 (QB) (statement that dating agency had a "substantial" number of unattached available men held false, and actionable in deceit, when in fact it had at best 100).

34 See Alderson B in *Moens v Heyworth* (1842) 10 M. & W. 147 at 158.

35 See para.17-25.

36 See Lord Maugham in *Bradford Third Equitable Benefit Building Society v Borders* [1941] 2 All E.R. 205, 211. See also *Peek v Gurney* (1873) L.R. 6 H.L. 377, 403 (Lord Cairns); *Arkwright v Newbold* (1881) 17 Ch. D. 301, 318 (James LJ); and *J D Wetherspoon Plc v Van de Berg & Co Ltd* [2007] EWHC 1044 (Ch); [2007] P.N.L.R. 28 at [17] (Lewison J).

37 Not surprisingly, the principle itself is controversial. In *Wood v Balfour* [2011] NSWCA 382; (2011) 15 B.P.R. 29,773 a case of the sale of a house with hidden defects, a majority of the New South Wales Court of Appeal seemingly abandoned the need for a positive representation: see Giles JA at [6] (with whom Meagher JA agreed). Macfarlan JA at [50] suggested that the act of marketing a house of itself could count as a representation that there were no defects of which the seller knew, which (one suspects) in practice comes to much the same thing. In the event no guilty knowledge was proved in the seller, so the point was, as matters turned out, moot.

38 cf. *Mentmore Manufacturing Co Ltd v Fomento (Sterling Area) Ltd* (1955) 72 R.P.C. 157; also *William Sindell Plc v Cambridgeshire CC* [1994] 1 W.L.R. 1016 (statement that vendor not aware of a defect in title carried implied representation that it had taken reasonable steps to ascertain whether any existed). It has, indeed, been said that in practice the line between misrepresentation and non-disclosure is often imperceptible: see *Pan Atlantic Insurance Co Ltd v Pine Top Insurance Co Ltd* [1995] 1 A.C. 501, 549 (Lord Mustill).

39 The example is James LJ's: see *Arkwright v Newbold* (1881) L.R. 17 Ch. D. 301, 318. So too with a glowing reference to an art dealer's "impeccable reputation" that glosses over unresolved allegations by the Getty Museum of passing off fake works (*Mellor v Partridge* [2013] EWCA Civ 477); and an apparently independent recommendation of a tradesman not mentioning a close relationship with the recommender which makes it far from independent (*Sear v Kingfisher Builders (a firm)*

the provision of a much higher one and sends the latter but not the former to an investor.[40] As Lord Cairns stated in *Peek v Gurney*,[41] "there must ... be some active misstatement of fact, or, in all events, such a partial and fragmentary statement of fact, as that the withholding of that which is not stated makes that which is stated absolutely false".[42] Thus in that case a share prospectus was held deceptive when it mentioned a price supposedly payable for a business by the promoters, but said nothing of other collateral agreements which effectively meant the promoters would not in fact pay a penny for it. So too a statement of the profits of a business to an investor will readily carry the implication that those profits were bona fide and honestly earned.[43] A helpful test has been said to be "whether a reasonable representee would naturally assume that the true state of facts did not exist and that, had it existed, he would in all the circumstances necessarily have been informed of it."[44] However, it should be noted that what amounts to a half-truth for these purposes is highly fact-sensitive. Thus a literally true answer to a very specific question may exonerate the defendant even though the latter knows further facts that alter matters drastically and would have been revealed had a wider question been asked.[45]

17-08 **Active conduct or concealment** Active non-verbal conduct can amount to misrepresentation, and hence deceit, just as much as words can.[46] So, for instance, pledging goods knowing one has no title to them is deceit,[47] as is ordering goods on credit for someone known to be insolvent[48] or presenting company accounts to a buyer in the knowledge that they have been doctored.[49] No doubt the same would

---

(No.3) [2013] EWHC 21 (TCC), especially at [6]–[7]).

40 See *Libyan Investment Authority v King* [2020] EWHC 440 (Ch) at [127].

41 (1873) L.R. 6 H.L. 377.

42 (1873) L.R. 6 H.L. 377 at 403. See too Lord Steyn in *Smith New Court Securities Ltd v Scrimgeour Vickers (Asset Management) Ltd* [1997] A.C. 254, 274 ("a cocktail of truth, falsity and evasion is a more powerful instrument of deception than undiluted falsehood").

43 *Bennett Gould & Partners Ltd v O'Sullivan* [2018] EWHC 2450 (QB) at [91]. Presenting a loan proposal based on the EURIBOR rates index is similarly a representation that the lender is not itself fraudulently manipulating the index (though it does not imply that someone else is not doing so): *Marme Inversiones 2007 SL v NatWest Markets Plc* [2019] EWHC 366 (Comm) at [142].

44 *Geest Plc v Fyffes Plc* [1999] 1 All ER (Comm) 672, 683 (Colman J): approved in *Property Alliance Group Ltd v Royal Bank of Scotland Plc* [2016] EWHC 3342 (Ch), which was affirmed by the CA: [2018] EWCA Civ 355; [2018] 1 W.L.R. 3529 at [130].

45 *Thorp v Abbotts* [2015] EWHC 2142 (Ch) (vendors of very bourgeois house asked whether they had had communications or discussions affecting their property: negative answer justified, even though major development was planned on a *nearby* property and vendors had talked to neighbours about it and attended protest meetings).

46 See the old criminal case of *R. v Barnard* (1837) 7 C. & P. 784 (buyer donned university garb to which not entitled and thus induced seller to give him credit: held, rightly convicted of obtaining by false pretences). A more modern instance (in a claim brought under s.2(1) of the Misrepresentation Act 1967) is *Spice Girls Ltd v Aprilia World Service BV* [2002] EWCA Civ 15; [2002] E.M.L.R. 27 (representation by conduct: participating jointly in the filming of advertisements for the claimant constituted a representation that pop group did not contemplate breaking up during the term of the advertising contract).

47 See *Advanced Industrial Technology Corp Ltd v Bond Street Jewellers Ltd* [2006] EWCA Civ 923; also *FundingSecure Ltd v Green* [2019] EWHC 208 (Ch). See too the Canadian decision in *HSBC Bank Canada v Lourenco* 2012 ABQB 380; (2012) Alta. L.R. (5th) 1.

48 *Contex Drouzhba Ltd v Wiseman* [2007] EWCA Civ 1201; [2008] B.C.C. 301 (though complications may arise under the Statute of Frauds Amendment Act 1828: see para.17-55).

49 *Man Nützfahrzeuge AG v Freightliner Ltd* [2005] EWHC 2347 (Comm), esp. at [79] onwards. The point was not argued on appeal at [2007] EWCA Civ 910; [2008] P.N.L.R. 6.

apply to an agent knowingly contracting without authority to do so. Indeed, it seems that in a suitable case the mere doing of business with another may in itself carry a representation that the business is bona fide and in accordance with established practice.[50] Another straightforward example is positive steps taken to conceal defects in something being sold (as against merely keeping silent about them). So in *Gordon v Selico Ltd*,[51] the Court of Appeal awarded damages for deceit where a defendant fraudulently arranged to cover up infestations of dry rot in a flat before letting it. Similarly, in the antique case of *Schneider v Heath*[52] a seller of a ship was held liable when he deliberately floated it so as to hide sub-waterline defects when the buyer came to inspect it.

Duty to speak In certain cases, notably where there is a fiduciary relation between the parties, there may be a duty to reveal information so that (for example) non-disclosure will make any resulting transaction voidable. It now seems accepted that in such cases non-disclosure may equally be capable of amounting to fraud at common law. Thus in *Conlon v Simms*[53] a solicitor who in partnership negotiations failed to mention a number of shady dealings in which he had previously been involved was held liable in deceit to his co-partner. However, while this exception seems established in the case of fiduciary relations,[54] its extent to other situations is not entirely clear. Logically it should equally apply to contracts such as commercial insurance, where there may be a duty to speak under Pt 2 of the Insurance Act 2015.[55] But it seems clear that it does not, since Sch.1 to the 2015 Act gives an exhaustive list of remedies for non-disclosure that does not include damages.[56] **17-09**

50 *Lindsay v O'Loughnane* [2010] EWHC 529 (QB); [2012] B.C.C. 153 (controller of foreign exchange dealers booked deals knowing that, contrary to previous practice and business ethics, clients' sums not segregated but used immediately to pay pressing creditors; liable for deceit when dealers collapsed owing claimant over £500,000). Flaux J referred specifically to an implicit representation that the company was trading "properly and legitimately": see [100]–[119]). On the other hand, since charges for work done are often the subject of negotiation, the mere submission of an invoice is not necessarily a representation that the sum claimed is actually owing: see *Browne (J) Construction Co Ltd v Chapman Construction Services Ltd* [2016] EWHC 152 (QB); (2016) 165 Con. L.R. 175 at [70].

51 (1986) 18 H.L.R. 219.

52 (1813) 3 Camp 506. cf. *Reynell v Sprye* (1852) 1 De G.M. & G. 660; *Walters v Morgan* (1861) 3 De G.F. & J. 718 at 723; and see too *Abel v McDonald* (1964) 45 D.L.R. (2d) 198.

53 [2006] EWHC 401 (Ch); [2006] 2 All E.R. 1024. This aspect of the case was upheld by the Court of Appeal, though the appeal was allowed on other grounds (see [2006] EWCA Civ 1749; [2008] 1 W.L.R. 484; [2007] 3 All E.R. 802). See too *JD Wetherspoon Plc v Van De Berg & Co Ltd* [2007] EWHC 1044 (Ch); [2007] P.N.L.R. 28 (property acquisition agents, as fiduciaries, bound to inform principals of covert arrangements to divert real estate profits to their own: failure to do so capable of amounting to tortious deceit).

54 It was applied by Teare J in the company law context in *JSC BTA Bank v Ablyazov* [2013] EWHC 510 (Comm), where a senior bank officer, by failing to disclose his interest in a number of companies, procured the bank to make irrecoverable loans to them; see especially at [170].

55 Note that this only applies to commercial insurance. There has been no positive duty of disclosure in consumer insurance since the Consumer Insurance (Disclosure and Representations) Act 2012 came into force.

56 The same was the case at common law: *Banque Keyser Ullmann SA v Skandia (UK) Insurance Co Ltd* [1990] 1 Q.B. 665, 770 onwards (the point was not decided in the House of Lords: see *Banque Financière de la Cité SA v Westgate Insurance Co Ltd* [1991] 2 A.C. 249). This might still be relevant where it is the insurer who fails to make disclosure, since the Act only applies to disclosure by the assured and leaves the common law of *uberrima fides* in place as regards the insurer.

17-10 **Other qualifications** Four other qualifications are worth mentioning. First, statements of belief or opinion generally carry an implication that the belief or opinion is reasonably held.[57] It follows that a defendant who affirms a belief while failing to disclose information in his possession indicating it is not reasonably held is guilty of a misrepresentation, and may (if a suitable state of mind is shown) be guilty of deceit. Secondly, a defendant who has made a true statement is bound to correct it if, though true when made, it is later to his knowledge falsified by events. This is dealt with below.[58] Thirdly, a person may be liable in deceit as a joint tortfeasor if he is a knowing and active party to a scheme to defraud, even if he has not himself said anything and the actual representation has been made by someone else.[59] Fourthly, it is sometimes suggested that there is a duty to disclose, and hence that non-disclosure may amount to deceit, where the parties are dealing with a dangerous chattel (though this is more doubtful). This is discussed below.[60]

17-11 **Misrepresentation: promises and statements of intention** A representation as to the future will not as such found liability in deceit.[61] Nor will a broken promise, as such.[62] However, the limits of this principle must be borne in mind. It is clearly established that a representation of present intention, whether the intention be that of the representor or of a third party,[63] is a sufficient representation of an existing fact to form the foundation of an action for deceit.[64] "The state of a man's mind", said Bowen LJ, "is as much a fact as the state of his digestion. It is true that it is very difficult to prove what the state of a man's mind at a particular time is, but if it can be ascertained it is as much a fact as anything else."[65] Therefore, in *Edgington v Fitzmaurice*,[66] it was held that a prospectus was deceptive when it contained false statements of what the company intended to do with investors' money once it got it.[67] Again, where a defendant obtains property against a promise to pay an annu-

---

57 See para.17-13.

58 See para.17-18.

59 *Dadourian Group International Inc v Simms* [2009] EWCA Civ 169; [2009] 1 Lloyd's Rep. 601 at [72]–[94].

60 See para.17-17.

61 e.g. *Montpellier Estates Ltd v Leeds City Council* [2013] EWHC 166 (QB) (local authority's statements as to intent to develop land). See too the criminal cases of *R. v Sunair Holidays Ltd* [1973] 1 W.L.R. 1105; and *British Airways Board v Taylor* [1976] 1 W.L.R. 13 (prosecutions for "double-booking" failed: statement that customers would be accommodated in the future not as such statements of fact, the requirement of a false statement under the relevant consumer protection legislation being the same as that in deceit).

62 See *Beckett v Cohen* [1972] 1 W.L.R. 1593; and *R. v Sunair Holidays Ltd* [1973] 1 W.L.R. 1105 for a full discussion of the distinction between an implied statement of present fact which may form a promise and the breaking of a promise relating to future facts or conduct.

63 *R. v Gordon* (1889) 23 Q.B.D. 354 at 360, per Wills J; *Kettlewell v Refuge Assurance Co* [1908] 1 K.B. 545 (affirmed [1909] A.C. 243); and cf. *DPP v Ray* [1974] A.C. 370 (on "obtaining by deception" under the now-repealed Theft Act 1968 s.15).

64 *Edgington v Fitzmaurice* (1885) 29 Ch. D. 459.

65 (1885) 29 Ch. D. 459, 483.

66 (1885) 29 Ch. D. 459, 483.

67 The prospectus said the money was wanted for further investment in the business: in fact it was needed to pay off existing debts. See too *Al Khudairi v Abbey Brokers Ltd* [2010] EWHC 1486 (Ch); [2010] P.N.L.R. 32, especially at [124]–[126] (Newey J) (claimants' money deposited with company, misused and lost: fraudulent statements by company controller as to how he intended to handle claimants' money held to amount to deceit, thus allowing personal claim against controller on company's insolvency). Another example is *Khakshouri v Jimenez* [2017] EWHC 3392 (QB) (representation of intent not to sell asset unless with the benefit of a collateral land deal).

ity, he will be liable in deceit if in fact he intends to pay it only if and to the extent that it suits him to do so.[68]

Moreover, a statement as to the future will often imply a statement as to present intention; as Lord Herschell put it, "that which is in form a promise may be in another aspect a representation".[69] Thus a promisor generally represents by implication that he has at the moment of making the promise the intention of fulfilling the obligations that he is undertaking; and if it can be shown that no such intention existed in his mind at that moment, he is guilty of a misrepresentation.[70] Nevertheless, this principle cannot be taken too far. The mere fact that the intention which was represented to exist was not eventually carried into effect is little or no evidence of the original non-existence of the intention. The representor may have subsequently changed his mind[71]; and in such a case there is no misrepresentation at all. Furthermore, it should be noted that there is an exception where parties are in negotiation over price, in which case a misstatement as to the highest price which the one party has the intention to give, or the lowest price which the other has the intention to accept, will not afford a cause of action.[72] The law permits the seller some latitude in exaggerating the value of his goods and so the purchaser is not bound to disclose the highest price he chooses to give, but is "at liberty to do that as a purchaser which every seller in this town does every day, who tells every falsehood he can to induce a buyer to purchase".[73] 17-12

Misrepresentation: statements of opinion A mere statement that one thinks a given state of affairs exists is not a statement that it does in fact exist[74]: it follows that it cannot engender liability in deceit on that basis.[75] However, this is not a very important limitation in practice. A statement of opinion is invariably regarded as incorporating an assertion that the maker does actually hold that opinion[76]; hence 17-13

---

[68] *Watts v Watts* [2014] EWHC 3056 (Ch); [2014] W.T.L.R. 1781, esp. at [15].

[69] See *Clydesdale Bank Ltd v Paton* [1896] A.C. 381 at 394. Thus where a person orders goods on credit he states not only that he will pay for them but also that he intends to do so.

[70] *Re Shackleton* (1875) L.R. 10 Ch. 446; *Re Eastgate* [1905] 1 K.B. 465. See too *East v Maurer* [1991] 1 W.L.R. 461 (seller of business said he would not compete when he had every intention of doing so: accepted, liable in deceit).

[71] As in *Jordan v Money* (1854) 5 H.L.C. 185.

[72] *Vernon v Keys* (1810) 12 East. 632; affirmed (1812) 4 Taunt. 488. No doubt a similar principle applies to negotiations over other terms.

[73] per Mansfield CJ in *Vernon v Keys* (1812) 4 Taunt. 488 at 493. This quotation must be read in its context relating to the price the purchaser was prepared to give. As an exception it must not be carried too far: see *Haygarth v Wearing* (1871) L.R. 12 Eq. 320; and *Armstrong v Strain* [1951] 1 T.L.R. 856, 860 (Devlin J (affirmed, [1952] 1 K.B. 232)). cf. *Smith New Court Securities Ltd v Citibank NA* [1997] A.C. 254 (false statement that third party had offered a given sum for securities accepted as sufficient to found liability).

[74] See the contract case of *Bisset v Wilkinson* [1927] A.C. 177 (vendor's statement of opinion as to capacity of farm: even though wrong, no misrepresentation allowing rescission of contract).

[75] Indeed, it is possible to qualify possible liability by characterising what would otherwise be a statement as a mere unverified assertion of belief: see *Raiffeisen Zentralbank Österreich AG v Royal Bank of Scotland Plc* [2010] EWHC 1392 (Comm); [2011] 1 Lloyd's Rep 123 at [86] (Christopher Clarke J); and also *Cassa di Risparmio della Repubblica di San Marino SpA v Barclays Bank Ltd* [2011] EWHC 484 (Comm); [2011] 1 C.L.C. 701 at [222] (Hamblen J). But this will not, it is suggested, exonerate the representor if he actually knows the suggestion to be untrue: see below.

[76] "A representation of fact may be inherent in a statement of opinion and at any rate the existence of the opinion in the person stating it is a question of fact." (Lord Merrivale in *Bisset v Wilkinson* [1927] A.C. 177 at 182). See too Devlin J in *Armstrong v Strain* [1951] 1 T.L.R. 856 at 860 (affirmed [1952] 1 K.B. 232); and Lord Evershed MR in *Brown v Raphael* [1958] Ch. 636 at 641.

the expression of an opinion not honestly entertained and intended to be acted upon amounts to fraud.[77] And the same goes for projections as to the future: if a defendant says he expects an event to take place when he does not, he makes an untrue statement of fact.[78] The only obstacle in the way of maintaining an action for a false representation on this basis lies in the difficulty of proving what the defendant's real opinion was,[79] and in the difficulty of distinguishing a representation of the existence of an opinion from the representation of the existence of a fact on which that opinion is based.

17-14 Furthermore, at least where the facts are not equally well known to both sides, then a statement of opinion by one who knows the facts best will often carry with it a further implication of fact, namely that the representor by expressing that opinion impliedly states that he believes that facts exist which reasonably justify it.[80] If he does not actually believe in such facts, it follows that he will be liable in deceit.[81] In such a case, the test as to whether a statement of opinion involves such a further implied representation will involve a consideration of the meaning which is reasonably conveyed to the representee. The material facts of the transaction, the knowledge of the respective parties, their relative positions, the words of the representation and the actual condition of the subject-matter are all relevant to this issue.[82]

17-15 **Misrepresentation: statements of law** Throughout the nineteenth and twentieth centuries, propositions of law tended to be regarded as inherently non-factual.[83] Hence statements of law were treated as statements of opinion at most, demonstrable as false only by proof that the representor did not in fact entertain that view of

---

[77] See, e.g. *Commercial Banking Co of Sydney Ltd v RH Brown & Co* (1972) 126 C.L.R. 337 (opinion conveyed by bank as to client's financial standing not honestly held); also *Anderson v Pacific Insurance Co* (1872) L.R. 7 C. & P. 65, 69 (Willes J); also *Khambay v Nijhar (t/a Gravitas Consulting)* [2015] EWHC 190 (QB) at [76]; and *Vald. Nielsen Holding A/S, Newwatch Ltd v Baldorino* [2019] EWHC 1926 (Comm) at [133] (both approving the statement of the law in this paragraph). Hence characterising a statement as a mere assertion of belief will still not protect the maker if he does not in fact believe it to be true.

[78] See *Karberg's Case* [1892] 3 Ch. 1, 11.

[79] See, e.g. *Peek v Gurney* (1873) L.R. 6 H.L. 377, 404.

[80] *Barings Plc (In Liquidation) v Coopers & Lybrand (A Firm)* [2002] EWHC 461 (Ch); [2002] P.N.L.R. 39 at [48]–[52]; *BSkyB Ltd v HP Enterprise Services UK Ltd* [2010] EWHC 86 (TCC); [2010] B.L.R. 267; 129 Con. L.R. 147 (statement by contractor that it was capable of handling project when it knew it had no reasonable grounds for making it). See too the contract cases of *Smith v Land & House Property Corp* (1885) 28 Ch. D. 7, 15 (Bowen LJ); and *Brown v Raphael* [1958] Ch. 1636 (both concerned with the right to rescind, where the same requirement applies of a representation of fact, though not of a guilty state of mind). This paragraph was cited with approval in *Vald. Nielsen Holding A/S, Newwatch Ltd v Baldorino* [2019] EWHC 1926 (Comm) at [134].

[81] *Barings Plc (In Liquidation) v Coopers & Lybrand (A Firm)* [2002] EWHC 461 (Ch); [2002] P.N.L.R. 39 at [48]–[52]. In fact the representor there, a banking executive who signed a representation to accountants that there was nothing untoward, had the necessary bona fide belief and therefore there was no liability.

[82] *Bisset v Wilkinson* [1927] A.C. 183; *Smith v Chadwick* (1884) 9 App. Cas. 187; *Brown v Raphael* [1958] Ch. 1636; *Jaffray v Society of Lloyds* [2002] EWCA Civ 1101 at [58].

[83] Thus a contract could not be rescinded on the basis of a misrepresentation or mistake of law (*Eaglesfield v Londonderry (Marquis)* (1876-77) 4 Ch. D. 693) (though there were suggestions that fraudulent statements of law might be on a different footing (*West London Commercial Bank v Kitson* (1884) 13 Q.B.D. 360, 362–363)); nor was money thought to be recoverable if paid by mistake of law rather than fact (e.g. *Bilbie v Lumley* (1802) 2 East 469).

the law which he expressed.[84] However, the distinction between factual and legal statements was difficult to draw at the best of times,[85] and has now been discredited elsewhere in the law.[86] It is therefore submitted that in the law of deceit misstatements of law now fall to be treated on a similar footing to misstatements of fact,[87] though given the uncertainty inherent in case law development and statutory interpretation, proof that a defendant knowingly misrepresented the law is likely in practice to be hard to come by.

Mere puffs There is no misrepresentation in the case of mere exaggerated praise by a vendor of his wares; he is entitled to assume that his statement will be construed as mere puffing. But though a vendor may entertain "sanguine expectations" of the advantages to be derived from his goods, and may employ "high colouring and even exaggeration" in his description of them, he must make no misstatement of any material facts or circumstances.[88] 17-16

Misrepresentation: dangerous and defective chattels There is no doubt that a seller[89] of goods who states that they are sound when he knows they are not is liable to the buyer or anyone else who relies on his statement and suffers loss. So in the old case of *Langridge v Levy*[90] the seller of a shotgun who told the buyer that it was safe when he knew it was not was held liable in deceit to the buyer's son who relied on the assertion and was injured when the firearm exploded. In *Langridge's* case, however, there was it seems a positive representation by the defendant.[91] What is the position where there is no such representation, but merely a sale or circulation of a chattel known to be defective? It has been suggested that anyone who sells 17-17

---

84 See *Beattie v Ebury (Lord)* (1872) L.R. 7 Ch. 777 at 802, per Mellish LJ.

85 See the convoluted, and hardly informative, example given by Jessel MR in *Eaglesfield v Londonderry (Marquis)* (1876-77) 4 Ch. D. 693 at 702-703 (statement that a woman is married may be factual or legal according to the circumstances). Statements as to the legal effect of a document could be remarkably awkward in this connection. Compare *West London Commercial Bank v Kitson* (1884) 13 Q.B.D. 360 (whether Act of Parliament gave power to directors to sign for company matter of fact) with *Eaglesfield v Londonderry (Marquis)* (1876-77) 4 Ch. D. 693 (ranking of share issues inter se matter of law).

86 The leading case, *Kleinwort Benson Ltd v Lincoln City Council* [1999] 2 A.C. 349, reversed previous authorities and decided that money paid by mistake of law could be recovered on the same basis as if the mistake had been factual. *Pankhania v Hackney LBC* [2002] EWHC 2441 (Ch); [2002] N.P.C. 123 then decided that statements of law were misrepresentations under the Misrepresentation Act 1967. See too *Brennan v Bolt Burdon* [2004] EWCA Civ 1017; [2005] Q.B. 303 (legal mistakes as capable of impugning a contract as factual ones).

87 Even, it would seem, where the law is unexpectedly changed with retrospective effect by legal decision, as happened in *Kleinwort Benson Ltd v Lincoln City Council* [1999] 2 A.C. 34, above. But proof of a guilty state of mind in such a case. so as to establish liability in deceit, would be well-nigh impossible.

88 See Lord Chelmsford in *Central Ry Co of Venezuela v Kisch* (1857) L.R. 2 H.L. 99 at 113. It is suggested that the "mere puffs" principle is largely an outgrowth of the rule that statements of opinion are not as such statements of fact.

89 Doubtless the same principle applies to a lender or a person letting out goods on hire or otherwise making them available.

90 (1837) 2 M. & W. 519. cf. *Dobell v Stevens* (1825) 3 B. & C. 623; and the American *Patterson v Landsberg* (1905) 7 F. 675.

91 See (1837) 2 M. & W. 519 at 530, per Parke B. Admittedly, on the facts the evidence seems scanty: see the comments of Lord Atkin on *Langridge's* case in *Donoghue v Stevenson* [1932] A.C. 562 at 587–588.

a chattel he knows is likely to cause injury is potentially liable in fraud.[92] But this, it is suggested, is highly doubtful. In *Ward v Hobbs*[93] a farmer sold pigs that, to his knowledge, were diseased and which duly infected the buyer's own herd. Bramwell B clearly thought that the farmer was not liable in deceit in the absence of a positive representation over and above the marketing of the pigs.[94] Of course, it may be possible in some cases to construct a representation: if a car were sold without an engine, the seller might well be guilty of a misstatement in describing it as a car at all. But such cases aside, it is submitted that if there is to be liability for selling dangerous or defective goods, it is better regarded as liability in negligence[95] rather than in the tort of deceit.[96]

17-18 **Continuing representations** The tort of deceit is complete only when the representation is acted upon.[97] Where there is an interval between the time when the representation is made and the time when it is acted on, and the representation relates to an existing state of things, the representation is deemed to be repeated throughout the interval. Hence if it is false to the maker's knowledge at the time when it is relied on there will be a deceit at that time.[98] It also follows that if, during the time between the making of the representation and the claimant acting upon it,[99] the defendant discovers it to be false or circumstances change to his knowledge so that it is now untrue, liability may be incurred.[100] Again, in *Briess v Woolley*[101] a

---

92 "Knowledge of a dangerous defect in a product may provide a foundation for a case of fraud against a person who makes or circulates a dangerous product without warning of the danger of physical damage known to him."—*Hamble Fisheries Ltd v L Gardner & Sons Ltd* [1999] 2 Lloyd's Rep. 1, 9 (Mummery LJ). cf. *Bodger v Nichols* (1873) 28 L.T. 441.

93 (1877) 3 Q.B.D. 150. See too *Keates v Cadogan* (1851) 10 C.B. 591 at 600 (no liability in respect of known defects in real property: disponor must show "aggressive deceit").

94 See (1877) 3 Q.B.D. 150 at 157. The House of Lords upheld the decision on the basis that the pigs had been expressly sold unwarranted, leaving open whether Bramwell B's wide statement was correct: (1878) 4 App. Cas. 13. See too *Baglehole v Walters* (1811) 3 Camp. 154 (sale of ship "with all faults": seller not liable unless he used artifice to conceal the faults from buyer); *Hurley v Dyke* [1979] R.T.R. 265, esp. at 303.

95 Or, where appropriate, under s.14 of the Sale of Goods Act 1979, ss.9 and 10 of the Consumer Rights Act 2015, or the strict liability provisions of the Consumer Protection Act 1987.

96 Compare the cases concerned with the liability of bailors, which have normally been put on the basis of negligence rather than the specific tort of deceit: e.g. *Blakemore v Bristol etc Ry* (1858) 8 E. & B. 1035 at 1051. Similarly with donors: *Coughlin v Gillison* [1889] 1 Q.B. 145; *MacCarthy v Young* (1861) 6 H. & N. 329. It is instructive to note that a more recent case similar to *Ward v Hobbs* (1877) 3 Q.B.D. 150, involving the sale of a car known to be dangerous, was regarded by the House of Lords as essentially turning on negligence liability: *Hurley v Dyke* [1979] R.T.R. 265.

97 See *Briess v Woolley* [1954] A.C. 333 at 353, per Lord Tucker; *Northern Bank Finance Ltd v Charlton* [1979] I.R. 149, 166 (Finlay P).

98 *Briess v Woolley* [1954] A.C. 333 at 353-354, per Lord Tucker; *DPP v Ray* [1974] A.C. 370. Conversely, if a statement known to be false when made becomes true before it is acted on there will be no liability: see *Ship v Crosskill* (1870) L.R. 10 Eq. 73; and *Briess v Woolley* [1954] A.C. 333 at 353.

99 A time that can be remarkably delayed. In the Australian decision in *McBride v Christie's Australia Pty Ltd* [2014] NSWSC 1729 a painting was auctioned on terms that if it was found to be non-genuine within five years, the sale could be undone by the purchaser. Auctioneers made innocent representations as to its authenticity before the auction; shortly after the sale they discovered the truth but said nothing. They were held liable in deceit, the reliance lying in the fact that the buyers had thus been prevented from cancelling the sale.

100 e.g. *Slough Estates Plc v Welwyn-Hatfield DC* [1996] 2 P.L.R. 50 (statement of intent originally true: defendant guilty of deceit when changed mind but did not tell claimant). See too *Fitzroy Robinson Ltd v Mentmore Towers Ltd* [2009] EWHC 1552 (TCC); [2009] B.L.R. 505 (statement by architects

managing director fraudulently made a false representation to induce the sale of a business before his appointment as agent of the shareholders to negotiate the sale. Some time after his appointment as agent, the sale was effected as a result of the previous false representation. The shareholders were held liable for the fraud of the managing director as their agent; the representation was a continuing representation which they (through him) had fraudulently failed to correct after his appointment. However, this is not an invariable rule: it only applies to statements intended to be continuing representations. Whereas this inference will be readily drawn if the representation seeks to induce the claimant to enter into some transaction,[102] in other cases it may not be.[103]

(b) State of mind

(i) *The belief of the defendant*

The state of mind necessary for liability in deceit Although the decision in *Pasley v Freeman*[104] established the existence of a tort based on fraud, it did not make entirely clear what state of mind was required in the defendant in order to establish it. The leading case on this point is the later decision of the House of Lords in *Derry v Peek*.[105] There, Lord Herschell laid down the essentials of fraud in the following propositions: 17-19

> "First, in order to sustain an action of deceit, there must be proof of fraud and nothing short of that will suffice. Secondly, fraud is proved when it is shown that a false representation has been made (i) knowingly, (ii) without belief in its truth, or (iii) recklessly, careless[106] whether it be true or false. Although I have treated the second and third as distinct cases, I think the third is but an instance of the second, for one who makes a statement under such circumstances can have no real belief in the truth of what he states. To prevent a false statement from being fraudulent, there must, I think, always be an honest belief in its truth."[107]

It follows from this that a statement honestly believed to be true, however implausible it may be, is not capable of amounting to fraud.[108] Thus in *Niru Bat-*

---

that particular partner would manage project: liable in deceit when he resigned and firm did not tell client); *Concept Oil Services Ltd v EN-GIN Group LLP* [2013] EWHC 1897 (Comm), especially at [48] (Flaux J); also *Jones v Dumbrell* [1981] V.R. 199. cf. the contractual misrepresentation case of *With v O'Flanagan* [1936] Ch. 575; and also *Spice Girls Ltd v Aprilia World Service BV* [2002] EWCA Civ 15; [2002] E.M.L.R. 27 at [51] (Morritt VC) (a case decided under the Misrepresentation Act 1967, but still in point).

101 [1954] A.C. 333.

102 As, for example, in *Inter Export LLC v Townley* [2018] EWCA Civ 2068; see esp. at [30]–[32] (representation by director that buyer had funds to pay for commodity).

103 *Bank of Tokyo-Mitsubishi UFJ Ltd v Baskan Gida Sanayi VE Pazarlama AS* [2009] EWHC 1276 (Ch); [2010] Bus. L.R. D1 (bank's statement about person it later discovered to be fraudster not continuing).

104 (1789) 3 T.R. 51.

105 (1889) 14 App. Cas. 337.

106 In the sense of not caring.

107 (1889) 14 App. Cas. 337 at 376. See too Rix LJ in *AIC Ltd v ITS Testing Services (UK) Ltd* [2006] EWCA Civ 1601; [2007] 1 All E.R. (Comm) 667 at [256]–[259].

108 An attempt to argue that there could in addition be deceit liability where, even in the absence of knowledge or recklessness, conduct was such that any reasonable and honest person would regard it as dishonest, as held in a different context in *Ivey v Genting Casinos UK Ltd* [2017] UKSC 67;

tery Manufacturing Co v Milestone Trading Ltd[109] a bank presented a letter of credit to a buyer for payment, despite the fact that it was obvious to any reasonable person that no payment was due under it since the goods had never been shipped. But this fact was not in the mind of the relevant bank officer when he arranged the presentation: it followed that, however casual or naïve he might have been, no claim lay in deceit. Similarly, in *Derry v Peek*[110] itself a company prospectus stated that the company had certain parliamentary powers which in fact it did not possess. Shareholders who had bought shares on the faith of the statement in the prospectus sued the promoters in deceit when the company went into liquidation. Their action failed: it had not been proved that the directors lacked honest belief in what they had said.[111] Nevertheless, although the unreasonableness of the grounds of the belief will not of itself support an action for deceit, it will of course be evidence from which fraud may be inferred. As Lord Herschell has pointed out, there must be many cases:

> "where the fact that an alleged belief was destitute of all reasonable foundation would suffice of itself to convince the court that it was not really entertained, and that the representation was a fraudulent one."[112]

17-20 **Motive irrelevant** It should be noted that if the requisite degree of knowledge or recklessness is shown, the defendant's motive in making the representation is irrelevant: "If fraud be established it is immaterial that there was no intention to cheat or injure the person to whom the false statement was made."[113] The fact that the representor was not actually dishonest,[114] or acted with the aim of facilitating a bona fide business transaction,[115] is beside the point (though of course lack of

---

[2018] A.C. 391; was rightly rebuffed in *Glossop Cartons & Print Ltd v Contact (Print & Packaging) Ltd* [2019] EWHC 2314 (Ch) at [48]–[49].

109 [2003] EWCA Civ 1446; [2004] Q.B. 985; upholding [2002] EWHC 1425 (Comm); [2002] 2 All E.R. (Comm) 705. See too *Uzinterimpex JSC v Standard Bank Plc* [2008] EWCA Civ 819; [2008] 2 Lloyd's Rep. 456 (allegedly abusive demand by buyer on advance payment guarantee: no liability in deceit since on the evidence buyer did not in fact believe that conditions of guarantee were not satisfied).

110 (1889) 14 App. Cas. 337.

111 (1889) 14 App. Cas. 337, 376 (Lord Herschell). See too *Angus v Clifford* [1891] 2 Ch. 449 to the same effect. Note, however, that directors in the position of the defendants in *Derry v Peek* are under a statutory liability which does include negligence: see Financial Services and Markets Act 2000 s.90, re-enacting the Directors' Liability Act 1890, and para.17-57.

112 See *Derry v Peek* (1889) 14 App. Cas. 337 at 376; also *Gross v Lewis Hillman* [1970] Ch. 445 at 465, per Harman LJ

113 *Bradford Third Benefit Building Society v Borders* [1941] 2 All E.R. 205, 211 (Viscount Maugham); also *Polhill v Walter* (1832) 3 B. & Ad. 114; *Derry v Peek* (1889) 14 App. Cas. 337, 365 (Lord Herschell); *Watts v Spence* [1976] Ch. 165, 176 (Graham J); and *Ludsin Overseas Ltd v Eco3 Capital Ltd* [2013] EWCA Civ 413 at [77]–[78] (Jackson LJ).

114 "It is not necessary that the maker of the statement was 'dishonest' as that word is used in the criminal law. The relevant intention is that the false statement shall be acted upon by a person to whom it is addressed."—*Standard Chartered Bank v Pakistan National Shipping Corp (No.2)* [2000] 1 Lloyd's Rep. 218 at 224, per Evans LJ.

115 See *Standard Chartered Bank v Pakistan National Shipping Corp (No.2)* [2000] 1 Lloyd's Rep. 218, esp. at 224 (date of presentation of letter of credit falsified to speed up business deal: presenter still guilty of deceit. The case was reversed on other grounds at [2002] UKHL 43; [2003] 1 A.C. 959). A similar type of case is *Shinhan Bank Ltd v Sea Containers Ltd* [2000] 2 Lloyd's Rep. 406 (buyer signing receipts for undelivered goods to accommodate seller, knowing seller would then use them to obtain bank finance: buyer liable to bank for deceit); and see too *Brown Jenkinson and Co Ltd v Percy Dalton (London) Ltd* [1957] 2 Q.B. 631 (agreement to issue clean bills of lading for dam-

dishonest intent may be powerful evidence of a bona fide belief in the truth of the facts asserted by the defendant[116]).

Absence of belief in truth; recklessness If the defendant knows his statement to be untrue he will be responsible for any loss suffered as a result.[117] Little more need be said on this point. However, liability goes further than this. Even if the party making the representation may have had no knowledge of its falsehood, he will still be responsible if he had no belief in its truth and made it, "not caring whether it was true or false".[118] As Lord Herschell put it: 17-21

> "Any person making such a statement must always be aware that the person to whom it is made will understand, if not that he who makes it knows, yet at least that he believes it to be true. And if he has no such belief he is as much guilty of fraud as if he had made any other representation which he knew to be false, or did not believe to be true."[119]

This principle can have wide-ranging consequences. For example, it means that a seller who says a property is in good condition without having taken steps to check,[120] or an indolent surveyor who provides production-line valuations of numerous properties without bothering to appraise each individually,[121] may be liable in deceit. On the other hand, there are limitations to it. A defendant who is a mere mouthpiece or ministerial employee may well make a statement on behalf of his employer without any personal belief whatever as to its truth or otherwise. Although theoretically this might be said to amount to recklessness, it might be thought unjust to hold him liable in the absence of personal dishonesty, and there is some authority that in such a case he may have a defence.[122]

Timing: defendant forgetting facts once known Since the tort of deceit is committed at the time the claimant relies on the defendant's false statement, it is not enough to show that the defendant once knew facts contrary to the representation made by him, if at the time of making it he had honestly forgotten them. In an action of deceit it is essential that the defendant should be without honest belief in the truth of his statement at the time of making it[123] (though no doubt when it can be 17-22

---

aged goods deceitful and hence promise to indemnify shipowner for liability ineffective), and also *Ansbacher (Henry) & Co Ltd v Brinks Stern (A Firm)* [1998] P.N.L.R. 221.

116 *Barings Plc v Coopers & Lybrand (No.5)* [2002] EWHC 461 (Ch); [2002] P.N.L.R. 39.

117 *Pasley v Freeman* (1789) 3 T.R. 51. This was the first case in which fraud was held to give a cause of action between persons not parties to a contract.

118 See *Joliffe v Baker* (1883) 11 Q.B.D. 255 at 275, per Smith J.

119 per Lord Herschell in *Derry v Peek* (1889) 14 App. Cas. 337 at 368; see also (1889) 14 App. Cas. 337 at 361. See too *AIC Ltd v ITS Testing Services (UK) Ltd* [2005] EWHC 2122 (Comm); [2006] 1 Lloyd's Rep. 1 (defendants test cargo of petrol for quality and send results to buyers: when told of doubts as to correctness of results, repeat "we stand by that test" despite having no idea whether correct or not: held, liable to buyers in deceit). The decision was reversed by the Court of Appeal on the facts (see *AIC Ltd v ITS Testing Services (UK) Ltd* [2006] EWCA Civ 1601; [2007] 1 All E.R. (Comm) 667), but it is submitted that the principle remains.

120 *Francis v Knapper* [2016] EWHC 3093 (QB) at [60].

121 As happened in *Mortgage Express Ltd v Countrywide Surveyors Ltd* [2016] EWHC 224 (Ch).

122 See *GE Commercial Finance Ltd v Gee* [2005] EWHC 2056 (QB); [2006] 1 Lloyd's Rep. 337 (junior employee relayed fraudulent employer's falsehoods to factoring company: despite lack of direct knowledge of, or positive belief in, the truth of what he was saying, Tugendhat J thought, obiter, that "open to question" whether liable: see [2005] EWHC 2056 (QB); [2006] 1 Lloyd's Rep. 337 at [105]).

123 See *Derry v Peek* (1889) 14 App. Cas. 337, 343 (Lord Halsbury); *Angus v Clifford* [1891] 2 Ch. 449,

shown that the defendant has at one time known facts inconsistent with the truth of his statement, this will be strong evidence that he knew such facts at the time of making the statement).

17-23 **Timing: defendant's later knowledge** In the converse case, where the defendant does not acquire knowledge of the untruth of his statement until after it has been made, but becomes aware of it before the claimant has acted upon it, it follows from general principle that he is bound to communicate the truth and will be answerable in damages if he does not.[124]

17-24 **Timing: statement becoming untrue ex post facto** It may be that a statement was in fact true at the time when made, but before being acted upon by the party to whom it was made had been rendered untrue by reason of later events. In such a case, then if the defendant was aware of those events he may be liable in deceit.[125]

17-25 **Ambiguous representations** Where a statement is capable of being understood in more than one sense, it is essential to liability in deceit that the party making the statement should have intended it to be understood in its untrue sense, or at the very least that he should have deliberately used the ambiguity for the purpose of deceiving the claimant.[126] Even though the more natural and reasonable interpretation of the statement is that put upon it by the claimant, and though on that interpretation it is untrue to the knowledge of the defendant, that will not suffice if the defendant did not intend it to be so understood.[127] Thus in *Akerhielm v De Mare*[128] a buyer of shares who had relied on an ambiguous statement in a company prospectus failed in his action in deceit once it was shown that the defendants had honestly believed the statement to be true in the sense in which they had intended it to be read. Even if the claimant's interpretation was a proper one, they had not shown the requisite knowledge of falsity in the defendants. On the other hand, if the defendant alleges that he understood his statement in a way that a reasonable person would not have

471; *Bradford Third Benefit Building Society v Borders* [1941] 2 All E.R. 205, 220 (Lord Wright); *Armstrong v Strain* [1951] 1 T.L.R. 856, 870–871 (per Devlin J; affirmed [1952] 1 K.B. 232).

124 See (obiter) per Lord Blackburn in *Brownlie v Campbell* (1880) 5 App. Cas. 925, 950; cf. *Briess v Woolley* [1954] A.C. 333. In *Ansbacher (Henry) & Co Ltd v Brinks Stern (A Firm)* [1998] P.N.L.R. 221, the point was raised but it became unnecessary to decide it, though the court would have found it difficult to accept that the defendant continued to hold the honest belief he claimed to have had.

125 *Incledon v Watson* (1862) 2 F. & F. 841; *With v O'Flanagan* [1936] Ch. 575, 584; *Bradford Third Benefit Building Society v Borders* [1941] 2 All E.R. 205 at 220, per Lord Wright. This includes the case where a misrepresentation is made by one agent and it is another agent who fails to correct it: *Marme Inversiones 2007 SL v NatWest Markets Plc* [2019] EWHC 366 (Comm) at [260]–[261]. See R. Bigwood, "Pre-Contractual Misrepresentation and the Limits of the Principle in With v O'Flanagan" [2005] C.L.J. 94; and compare the reasoning in *Briess v Woolley* [1954] A.C. 333 (see para.17-18) on continuing representations.

126 See now *Whyfe v Michael Cullen & Partners* [1993] E.G.C.S. 193. Similarly, if the alleged deceit is contained in answers to a questionnaire which is itself ambiguous: *Cheltenham BC v Laird* [2009] EWHC 1253 (QB); [2009] I.R.L.R. 621 at [174].

127 *Hallows v Fernie* (1868) L.R. 3 Ch. App. 467, 476–477; *Arkwright v Newbold* (1881) 17 Ch. D. 301; (1884) 9 App. Cas. 187 at 201, per Lord Blackburn; *Low v Bouverie* [1891] 3 Ch. 82, 101–106; *Aaron's Reefs Ltd v Twiss* [1896] A.C. 273, 282; *Akerhielm v De Mare* [1959] A.C. 789 at 805–806; also *Gross v Lewis Hillman Ltd* [1970] Ch. 445.

128 [1959] A.C. 789. The case was applied by the Court of Appeal in *Ansbacher v Brinks Stern* [1998] P.N.L.R. 221. See also *Foster v Action Aviation Ltd* [2014] EWCA Civ 1368 and *Leni Gas & Oil Investments Ltd v Malta Oil Pty Ltd* [2014] EWHC 893 (Comm) at [5]–[9] (Males J).

understood it, then as a matter of evidence this may well weigh with the court in deciding whether he honestly understood it in that sense.[129]

(ii) *State of mind: vicarious liability*

Vicarious liability of employer[130] There is no doubt that a blameless employer may be vicariously liable for a deceit committed by a dishonest employee in the course of his employment,[131] in the same way as he can be liable for any other deliberate tort.[132] The events must of course be capable of giving rise to vicarious liability,[133] and in general the normal rules of vicarious liability apply.[134] However, there are two important limitations on the employer's potential liability in this connection. First, it has to be shown that the employee in the course of his employment not only acted dishonestly, but actually committed the principal act amounting to the tort of deceit. The point was neatly illustrated by *Crédit Lyonnais Nederland NV v Export Credits Guarantee Department*.[135] As part of a scheme to induce a bank to buy forged bills of exchange relating to bogus export transactions, a fraudster obtained certain guarantees from the defendants, which he had suborned X, a dishonest employee of theirs, to authorise on their behalf. The bank sued the defendants in deceit, arguing (correctly) that the employee was liable to them as an accessory of the fraudster, and that in issuing the guarantees to aid the fraudster he had acted within the scope of his employment. The House of Lords nevertheless held that the action failed. The essential elements of the tort of deceit had been committed by the fraudster and not by X, and the mere fact that X had abetted a tort in the course of his employment did not make the defendants liable for it as his employers. 17-26

Secondly, the rule that an act may be done in the course of employment even if 17-27

---

[129] [1959] A.C. 789 at 805.

[130] See Ch.6, for vicarious liability generally.

[131] e.g. *Lloyd v Grace, Smith and Co* [1912] A.C. 716 (solicitor's clerk defrauding client); *Barings Plc (In Liquidation) v Coopers & Lybrand (Issues Re Liability)* [2003] EWHC 1319 (Ch); [2003] P.N.L.R. 34 (lies told by unauthorised traders to company's auditors to cover up their trail: held, employers liable on principle to auditors on basis of vicarious liability). cf. *Barwick v English Joint Stock Bank* (1867) L.R. 2 Ex. 259, 265, per Willes J. Equally it does not matter for these purposes that the fraud was as much against the employer as the claimant: cf. *Kwei Tek Chao v British Traders & Shippers Ltd* [1954] 2 Q.B. 459, 470 (per Devlin J).

[132] See, e.g. *Morris v Martin* [1966] 1 Q.B. 716 (conversion by theft). For what amounts to "course of employment" in this connection, see generally *Lister v Hesley Hall Ltd* [2001] UKHL 22; [2002] 1 A.C. 215 and para.6-29 onwards.

[133] See, e.g. *Frederick v Positive Solutions (Financial Services) Ltd* [2018] EWCA Civ 431 (financial adviser persuaded claimants to remortgage homes to invest in fraudulent scheme of his own and submitted fraudulent mortgage applications through web portal of defendants, with whom associated; no liability in defendants, since they had done no more than provide the opportunity for the fraud, and in any case fraudster's activity had been a "recognisably independent business" from the defendants' and thus outside the scope of any employment).

[134] For example, as to seconded servants: see the Scots decision in *Royal Bank of Scotland Plc v Bannerman Johnstone MacLay* [2005] CSIH 39; 2005 1 S.C. 437; [2005] P.N.L.R. 43 (accountant seconded to company by firm tells lies to its bankers: arguable that still employed by firm and hence latter liable). Similarly, a representor may act for two people at the same time. See *Man Nützfahrzeuge AG v Freightliner Ltd* [2005] EWHC 2347 (Comm), esp. at [92] et seq. (financial manager of company presents falsified accounts to potential buyer of company: acting for both company and seller). The point was not argued on appeal: [2007] EWCA Civ 910; [2008] P.N.L.R. 6.

[135] [2000] 1 A.C. 486.

entirely unauthorised[136] is modified in the case of deceit. An employer will be vicariously liable for a statement made by his employee only if the employee had actual or ostensible authority to make it.[137] So in *Armagas Ltd v Mundogas SA*[138] an employee of the defendant shipping company, while negotiating on their behalf but without their authority, defrauded the claimants into thinking that the defendants were contracting to charter a ship for three years. The claimant's action for breach of contract having failed because the employee had no authority to contract on their behalf, the House of Lords held that their action in deceit on the basis of vicarious liability for their employee's deception was equally doomed: absent authority to make representations, there could be no liability in tort for unauthorised statements. It is, moreover, now clear that despite the relaxation elsewhere of the rules of vicarious liability in cases such as *Various Claimants v Institute of the Brothers of the Christian Schools*[139] and *Cox v Ministry of Justice*,[140] the requirement of authority in order to give rise to vicarious liability remains the law.[141]

17-28 **Knowledge and agency: the fraudulent agent** A principal is liable for torts committed by his agent acting within his authority.[142] It follows that where an agent makes a representation he knows to be false, and it was within his actual or ostensible authority to make that representation, the principal will be liable even if personally entirely innocent.[143] The innocent principal will equally be liable where the fraudulent agent passes on the representation indirectly, for example through another (innocent) agent of the same principal,[144] or for that matter by giving it to the principal himself who then in good faith transmits it to the claimant.[145] However, if he is himself an intended victim of the fraud he will not be vicariously liable to other victims of that fraud.[146] Furthermore, there is a pragmatic qualification to the rules of vicarious liability where the victim of the fraud himself owed a duty of care to the employer to detect the precise fraud in issue. An example is where a dishonest employee tells lies to a company auditor or stockbroker in order to hide his own

136 e.g. *Limpus v London General Omnibus Co* (1862) 1 H. & C. 862.

137 See *Lloyd v Grace, Smith & Co* [1912] A.C. 716, esp. at 736 (Lord Macnaghten); *Armagas Ltd v Mundogas SA* [1986] A.C. 717, below. For a case of actual authority giving rise to liability see *Khakshouri v Jimenez* [2017] EWHC 3392 (QB), esp. at [124]–[125] (one director giving other director carte blanche to negotiate on his behalf for loan to a struggling Charlton Athletic FC).

138 [1986] A.C. 717.

139 [2012] UKSC 56; [2013] 2 A.C. 1.

140 [2016] UKSC 10; [2016] A.C. 660.

141 See *Winter v Hockley Mint Ltd* [2018] EWCA Civ 2480; [2019] 1 W.L.R. 1617. See too dicta of Flaux LJ in *Frederick v Positive Solutions (Financial Services) Ltd* [2018] EWCA Civ 431 at [77]. Suggestions to the contrary in *Group Seven Ltd v Notable Services LLC* [2019] EWCA Civ 614; [2019] 3 W.L.R. 1011 at [145] should, it is suggested with respect, be regarded as doubtful.

142 See *Bowstead & Reynolds on Agency*, 21st edn (2017), para.8-177 onwards.

143 *Briess v Woolley* [1954] A.C. 333; cf. *Pearson v Dublin Corp* [1907] A.C. 351 (semble) and *Anglo-Scottish Beet Sugar Corp Ltd v Spalding Urban DC* [1937] 2 K.B. 607 at 621. If the principal is not innocent, he will of course be liable with the agent as a joint tortfeasor.

144 *London County Properties v Berkeley Property Co* [1936] 2 All E.R. 1039 CA, as interpreted by the Court of Appeal in *Armstrong v Strain* [1952] 1 K.B. 232; cf. *Anglo-Scottish Beet Sugar Corp v Spalding Urban DC* [1937] 2 K.B. 607.

145 *Pearson & Son Ltd v Dublin Corp* [1907] A.C. 351; *Anglo-Scottish Beet Sugar Corp v Spalding Urban DC* [1937] 2 K.B. 607, 619–620.

146 See *Kwei Tek Chao v British Traders and Shippers Ltd* [1954] 2 Q.B. 459 (forwarding agents acting for sellers of goods produce falsified bills of lading; sellers innocently present bills to buyers; sellers not liable for acts of forwarding agents). cf. *Bradford Third Benefit Building Society v Borders* [1941] 2 All E.R. 205, 223, 226 (Lords Wright and Porter).

fraud. In such a case, the defendant when sued for negligence by the company cannot cancel out his liability by bringing a cross-claim for deceit[147]: the duty to unmask the fraud takes precedence over liability in deceit.[148]

Knowledge and agency: other cases The previous paragraph deals with the fraudulent agent of a blameless principal. We now turn to the converse situation, namely where the agent who makes the representation believes it to be true but the principal knows facts which show that it is not. If the principal expressly authorises his agent to make a statement which he himself knows to be false, he is of course liable[149] (indeed, if the agent knows of the falsity as well, he will himself be a joint tortfeasor[150]). Equally, there will be fraud on the part of the principal if he deliberately employs an agent, from whom he conceals facts in the expectation that as a result of his ignorance the latter will give false information to some third party.[151] However, to render the principal liable in an action of deceit in such a case, it must it seems be proved that there was a fraudulent state of mind on his part[152]: that is, that he intended the claimant to be misled or at the very least was indifferent as to whether he might be. Where a false representation has been made innocently by an agent acting within his authority, the mere fact that the principal knows the facts which render the representation false will not make the latter liable if he has not expressly authorised the representation or deliberately concealed facts from the agent with a view to the claimant being misled.[153] So in *Armstrong v Strain*[154] estate agents with general authority to make representations about a house on their books innocently told a purchaser that it was sound when, as the owner knew, it was not. The Court of Appeal upheld a finding that the owner was not liable to the purchaser in deceit. 17-29

147 *Singularis Holdings Ltd (In Liquidation) v Daiwa Capital Markets Europe Ltd* [2019] UKSC 50; [2019] 3 W.L.R. 997; see too *Barings Plc (In Liquidation) v Coopers & Lybrand (A Firm) (Issues Re Liability)* [2003] EWHC 1319 (Ch); [2003] P.N.L.R. 34, esp. at [728].

148 See the *Barings* case [2003] EWHC 1319 (Ch); [2003] P.N.L.R. 34 at [740]. The other argument used in the case, that the cause of the auditor's liability was its own negligence rather than the deceit of the employee, is difficult to accept: not only is it question-begging, but if true it would prevent the auditor suing the fraudulent employee himself, which presumably was not the intention.

149 e.g. *London County Freehold Properties Ltd v Berkeley Property Co Ltd* [1936] 2 All E.R. 1039, as interpreted in *Armstrong v Strain* [1952] 1 K.B. 232 (seller of investment properties knowingly arms agents with false information as to state of rent roll for transmission to buyers: liable in deceit).

150 It was once doubted whether an agent who knowingly lied on the orders of a guilty principal was personally liable at all: but this heresy was scotched by the House of Lords in *Standard Chartered Bank v Pakistan National Shipping Corp (No.2)* [2002] UKHL 43; [2003] 1 A.C. 959 (and see too *International Media Advertising Ltd v Ministry of Culture and Tourism of the Republic of Turkey* [2018] EWHC 3285 (QB) at [275]–[283]). On the *Standard Chartered* case see B. Parker, "Fraudulent Bills of Lading and Bankers' Commercial Credits" [2003] L.M.C.L.Q. 1).

151 See *Standard Chartered Bank Ltd v Pakistan National Shipping Corp (No.2)* [2000] 1 Lloyd's Rep. 218, esp. at 225 (bank gave stale letter of credit to agent for presentation knowing agent would present it to issuing bank who did not know it was stale: bank guilty of fraud). See too *Cornfoot v Fowke* (1840) 6 M. & W. 358 at 373, per Parke B; *Ludgater v Love* (1881) 44 L.T. 694; *Armstrong v Strain* [1951] 1 T.L.R. 856 at 861. cf. *Bradford Third Benefit Building Society v Borders* [1941] 2 All E.R. 205, 220 (Lord Wright).

152 The claimant must "bring home fraud to the principal": *Cornfoot v Fowke* (1840) 6 M & W 358 at 370, per Rolfe B.

153 *Armstrong v Strain* [1952] 1 K.B. 232; *Cornfoot v Fowke* (1840) 6 M. & W. 358; *Gordon Hill Trust Ltd v Segall* [1941] 2 All E.R. 379.

154 [1952] 1 K.B. 232; see too *Greenridge Luton One Ltd v Kempton Investments Ltd* [2016] EWHC 91 (Ch) at [77]–[79] (Newey J); and cf. *Awaroa v Commercial Securities Ltd* [1976] 1 N.Z.L.R. 19.

17-30 **Partners** Under s.10 of the Partnership Act 1890, partners are liable for wrongful acts committed by any one of their number while "acting in the ordinary course of the business of the firm". This liability may of course include cases of fraud committed by a partner, provided the act of the errant partner is so closely connected to the business of the firm as to be within his actual or apparent authority, as where a partner in an accountancy firm forges share transfers and then fraudulently confirms their genuineness to stockbrokers.[155] But the limits of this liability should be noted: if no reasonable person would think the transaction was part of the firm's ordinary business, then the firm will not be liable.[156] Furthermore, the same restriction applies here as with vicarious liability: all the acts of the partner which were necessary to make him liable in deceit must have been committed in the course of the firm's business.[157] It should be noted, however, that partners will not be liable on this basis unless the partner making the statement himself had the requisite degree of knowledge. Although s.16 of the Partnership Act 1890 supposedly attributes all partners' knowledge to the firm, it has been held that this does not render the firm liable in deceit merely because one partner innocently makes a statement that another partner knows to be false.[158]

(c) Representation intended to be acted on by the claimant

17-31 **Representation must be intended to be acted on by claimant** In order to give a cause of action in deceit, not only must the statement complained of be untrue to the defendant's knowledge, but it must in addition be made with intent to deceive the claimant: with intent, that is to say, that it shall be acted upon by him.[159] It seems that intent, for these purposes, includes not only the case where the defendant actually desires the claimant to rely on what he says, but also where he appreciates that in the absence of some unforeseen intervention he will actually do so.[160] But if intent of one or other kind is not shown, then the claimant will fail. So where the defendant, a director of an oil company, untruly stated to a broker that the company had received no news of a major find, intending by this untruth to protect the company's interests and not to induce shareholders to sell their holdings, it was held that no

---

[155] *McHugh v Kerr* [2003] EWHC 2985 (Ch); see too *Goldberg v Miltiadous* [2010] EWHC 450 (QB) (accountancy firm liable for partner who duped investor into sinking money in dubious Cyprus real estate); and the Australian decision in *Crouch & Lyndon (A Firm) v IPG Finance Australia Pty Ltd* [2013] QCA 220; [2014] P.N.L.R. 3 (setting up bogus mortgage loans). cf. *Dubai Aluminium Co Ltd v Salaam* [2002] UKHL 48; [2003] 2 A.C. 366 (similar principles with regard to dishonest breach of fiduciary duty). So too under the Limited Liability Partnerships Act 2000 s.6.

[156] *Coughlan (JJ) Ltd v Ruparelia* [2003] EWCA Civ 1057; [2004] P.N.L.R. 4 (solicitor, supposedly acting in his capacity as partner, dishonestly puffs a fraudulent investment scheme promising implausible returns of 6,000 per cent per year: no liability, since cannot be said that "viewed fairly and properly, it is the kind of transaction which forms part of the ordinary business of a solicitor").

[157] *Dubai Aluminium Co Ltd v Salaam* [2002] UKHL 48; [2003] 2 A.C. 366 (actually concerning dishonest breach of fiduciary duty, but still in point).

[158] See the Scots decision in *Zurich GSG Ltd v Gray & Kellas* [2007] CSOH 91; 2007 S.L.T. 917; [2008] P.N.L.R. 1.

[159] *Peek v Gurney* (1873) L.R. 6 H.L. at 377, 411–413 (Lord Cairns); *Bradford Third Benefit Building Society v Borders* [1941] 2 All E.R. 205, 211; *Kitcher v Fordham* [1955] 2 Lloyd's Rep. 705, 707.

[160] *Shinhan Bank Ltd v Sea Containers Ltd* [2000] 2 Lloyd's Rep. 406 (buyer signing receipts for undelivered goods knowing seller would use then to obtain bank finance: liable to bank in deceit when seller collapsed). This criterion of "intent" is borrowed from criminal law: see *R. v Woollin* [1999] 1 A.C. 82. The passage at this footnote was approved in *Zagora Management Ltd v Zurich Insurance Plc* [2019] EWHC 140 (TCC); (2019) 182 Con. L.R. 180 at [743]–[745].

action for fraud lay at the suit of a shareholder.[161] However, provided the defendant intended the claimant to act on the representation, it is immaterial whether he intended him so to act in the precise way in which he did.[162]

Representation not made to claimant directly A representation made to the claimant directly causes no problems; so too with a statement made to someone known to be acting as agent for the claimant.[163] But a representation made to a third party with intent that it be passed on to the claimant to be acted on by him will equally suffice.[164] Thus in *Swift v Winterbotham*[165] a claimant who gave credit on the basis of a fraudulent banker's reference successfully sued the bank in deceit even though the reference had been sent not to him but to his own bank; similarly, in *OMV Petrom SA v Glencore International AG*[166] buyers of oil successfully recovered against dishonest traders who misdescribed their wares to a commission agent knowing full well that the latter would pass on the information. All that is required for these purposes is that the representation be intended, in one way or another, to reach the claimant in order to induce him to act on it.[167] Nor is it even necessary that the defendant know precisely who the statement is intended for, 17-32

161 *Tackey v McBain* [1912] A.C. 186. See too *Goose v Wilson Sandford & Co (No.2)* [2001] Lloyd's Rep. P.N. 189. More recently, see *Zagora Management Ltd v Zurich Insurance Plc* [2019] EWHC 140 (TCC); (2019) 182 Con. L.R. 180 (producer of fraudulent building regulations certificate for apartment block did not intend reliance by later buyer of freehold).

162 *Goose v Wilson Sandford & Co (No.2)* [2001] Lloyd's Rep. P.N. 189.

163 *OMV Petrom SA v Glencore International AG* [2015] EWHC 666 (Comm) (oil traders deliberately misdescribed oil to commission agent for the buyer) (not argued on appeal at [2016] EWCA Civ 778; [2017] 3 All E.R. 157).

164 "Every man must be held responsible for the consequences of a false representation made by him to another, upon which a third person acts, and so acting is damnified, provided it appear that such false representation was made with the intent that it should be acted upon by such third person in the manner that occasions the injury or loss" (Page Wood V-C in *Barry v Croskey* (1861) 2 J. & H. 1, 23). This case was approved by Lord Cairns in *Peek v Gurney* (1873) 6 H.L. 377 at 412. And see also *Brown Jenkinson & Co Ltd v Percy Dalton (London) Ltd* [1957] 2 Q.B. 621, 631 (Morris LJ); and *Libyan Investment Authority v King* [2020] EWHC 440 (Ch) at [123] (misleading valuation of joint venture given to intermediary who passed it on to investor).

165 (1873) L.R. 8 Q.B. 244 (appealed on other grounds, L.R. 9 Q.B. 301). A similar banker's reference case is *Commercial Banking of Sydney v RH Brown & Co* (1972) 126 C.L.R. 337. See also *Langridge v Levy* (1837) 2 M. & W. 519; 4 M. & W. 337 (untrue statement to buyer that shotgun was sound relayed to buyer's son, who was injured using it: son successfully recovered in deceit); *Pilmore v Hood* (1838) 5 Bing. N.C. 97 (false representations made to X regarding sale of business. P knew X passed on to P; D sold to P without correcting); *Renault UK Ltd v Fleetpro Technical Services Ltd* [2007] EWHC 2541 (QB); [2008] Bus. L.R. D17 (vehicle purchasers falsely told dealers they were entitled to importers' fleet discount: potentially liable to importers for deceit (though action failed for other reasons)).

166 [2015] EWHC 666 (Comm) (point not argued on appeal at [2016] EWCA Civ 778; [2017] 3 All E.R. 157).

167 "In order to enable a person injured by a false representation to sue for damages, it is not necessary that the representation should be made to the plaintiff directly; it is sufficient if the representation is made to a third person to be communicated to the plaintiff, or to be communicated to a class of persons of whom the plaintiff is one, or even if it is made to the public generally, with a view to its being acted on, and the plaintiff as one of the public acts on it and suffers damage thereby." (Quain J in *Swift v Winterbotham* (1873) L.R. 8 Q.B. 244 at 253, cited with approval by Blackburn J in *Richardson v Silvester* (1873) L.R. 9 Q.B. 34 at 36). See also *Pilmore v Hood* (1838) 5 Bing. N.C. 97 (D made false representations made to X regarding business knowing X would repeat them to P; liable when sold to P without correcting); *Schenk v Cook* [2017] EWHC 144 (QB) esp. at [84] (similar). See too *Barry v Croskey* (1861) 2 J. & H. 1, 23; *Brown Jenkinson & Co Ltd v Percy Dalton (London) Ltd* [1957] 2 Q.B. 621.

provided he intends it to be relied on by someone in the claimant's position[168]: thus in another banker's reference case a bank was held liable when it sent a fraudulent reference to another bank for the benefit of a customer of whose identity it was entirely unaware.[169] Indeed, in one case it was even held that an action for deceit could be based on a newspaper advertisement, provided the claimant showed that he was one of the class of persons at whom it was directed.[170]

17-33 Nevertheless, it must be shown that there was an actual intention to deceive the claimant in question, whether individually or by reference to a class to which he belongs; it will not be enough merely to show that the misstatement is reasonably calculated to deceive him. Thus the House of Lords in *Peek v Gurney*[171] held that promoters of a company, who issued a fraudulent prospectus as a prospectus and as nothing more, were not liable for so doing to persons who, not being original allottees of the company's shares, purchased their shares in the market; the reason being that the promoters had no object in making the false statements except to get the shares taken up; they had no intent to influence market dealings.[172] Again, in *Gross v Lewis Hillman Ltd*[173] sellers of commercial property made certain misrepresentations to the buyers about it: the buyers agreed to purchase it, but then assigned the benefit of the contract to the claimants. The claimants' claim in deceit failed: even if the representations had been fraudulent (which they had not) they had been made to the buyers and the claimants could not sue in respect of them.

17-34 It is obviously a question of fact whether in a particular case a person was intended to rely on a false statement. In practice, however, the test is often whether it was in the defendant's interest that he should do so. So where persons spread a false rumour for the purpose of raising the price of certain stock, they were not liable in damages to those who dealt with other persons on the faith of such rumour being true,[174] there being no intention to deceive any persons other than those who dealt with the defendants themselves, given the defendants had nothing to gain unless the investors dealt with themselves.[175]

---

168 See Cresswell J in *Standard Chartered Bank v Pakistan National Shipping Corp (No.2)* [1998] 1 Lloyd's Rep. 684 at 696: enough that claimant "within the class of persons within their contemplation as likely to be deceived".

169 *Commercial Banking Co of Sydney v RH Brown & Co* (1972) 126 C.L.R. at 337. cf. *Brown Jenkinson & Co Ltd v Percy Dalton (London) Ltd* [1957] 2 Q.B. 621 (carrier who knowingly issued false bills of lading liable to consignees in deceit, since he intended them to be relied on by any number of consignees, bankers and indorsees).

170 *Richardson v Silvester* (1873) L.R. 9 Q.B. 34 (false advertisement that farm for sale: would-be buyer can recover wasted expenses).

171 (1873) L.R. 6 H.L. 377. See too *Tackey v McBain* [1912] A.C. 186 (untrue denial of major find by oil company made to protect company's interests generally, not to influence market: no liability to shareholder who sold on faith of it); and also *Wetherspoon (JD) Plc v Van De Berg & Co Ltd* [2007] EWHC 1044; [2007] P.N.L.R. 28; *Group Seven Ltd v Nasir* [2017] EWHC 2466 (Ch); [2018] P.N.L.R. 6 at [516]–[521] (Morgan J) (varied on appeal on other grounds: *Group Seven Ltd v Notable Services LLC* [2019] EWCA Civ 614; [2020] Ch. 129).

172 cf. *Andrews v Mockford* [1896] 1 Q.B. 372, where there was an intent to boost the shares in the market generally, and hence a purchaser in that market successfully sued.

173 [1970] Ch. 445.

174 See *Barry v Croskey* (1861) 2 J. & H. 1 at 18, per Page Wood VC; also *Peek v Gurney* (1873) L.R. 6 H.L. 377 at 412, per Lord Cairns.

175 Note in *Langridge v Levy* (1837) 2 M. & W. 519; 4 M. & W. 337, the defendant having sold a gun to the claimant's father for the use of himself and his son and sold it as sound and secure when he knew it to be unsafe, was held liable in an action of deceit to the claimant, who was wounded by the bursting of the gun. There, the court upheld the verdict expressly upon the ground that the

(d) Claimant must have been influenced by the misrepresentation

The claimant must have been influenced by the misrepresentation[176] To entitle a claimant to succeed in an action in deceit, he must show that he[177] acted (or in a suitable case refrained from acting[178]) in reliance on the defendant's misrepresentation.[179] If he would have done the same thing even in the absence of it, he will fail.[180] What is relevant here is what the claimant would have done had no representation at all been made. In particular, if the making of the representation in fact influenced the claimant, it is not open to the defendant[181] to argue that the claimant might have acted in the same way had the representation been true.[182] It seems clear that the claimant must have acted himself to his detriment. If his loss results, not from his own reliance, but from that of third parties, the defendant may be liable for torts of unlawful interference with trade,[183] passing off or malicious falsehood, or even negligence[184]; but he will not be liable in deceit.[185] 17-35

declaration contained an averment that the gun was sold for the use of the purchaser and his son. Lord Atkin in *Donoghue v Stevenson* [1932] A.C. 562 at 587–588 referring to this case said: "User by the plaintiff was one of the acts contemplated by the fraudulent defendant." The case can hardly be regarded as having decided any principle of general application.

176 This formulation of the law was specifically approved by Lord Clarke in *Hayward v Zurich Insurance Co Plc* [2016] UKSC 48; [2017] A.C. 142 at [26].

177 Or a machine, such as a computer, under his control: see *Renault UK Ltd v Fleetpro Technical Services* [2007] EWHC 2541 (QB); [2008] Bus. L.R. D17 at [122] (defendants causing to be inserted into computer orders for cars with a fleet discount to which they knew they were not entitled).

178 An example of inaction as reliance can be seen in *McBride v Christie's Australia Pty Ltd* [2014] NSWSC 1729 (fraud by auctioneer after sale, with the result that the buyer did not take steps, as he was entitled to do, to annul the transaction: held, deceit lay).

179 See, e.g. *Holmes v Jones* (1907) 4 C.L.R. 1692; see too *Zagora Management Ltd v Zurich Insurance Plc* [2019] EWHC 140 (TCC); (2019) 182 Con. L.R. 180. The statement in this paragraph was approved by Lewison J in *Mellor v Partridge* [2013] EWCA Civ 477 at [20].

180 e.g. *Smith v Chadwick* (1883–84) 9 App. Cas. 187; *Nash v Calthorpe* [1905] 2 Ch. 237 (company prospectus cases: claimants failed to prove reliance); *Francis v Knapper* [2016] EWHC 3093 (QB) (sale of holiday park: buyer would have purchased anyway).

181 Oddly enough, it seems that there is nothing to prevent the claimant advancing as evidence of reliance an argument that he would have acted differently had the representation been true: see *Parabola Investments Ltd v Browallia CAL Ltd* [2009] EWHC 901 (Comm); [2009] 2 All E.R. (Comm) 589 at [105], per Flaux J (accepted on appeal: [2010] EWCA Civ 486; [2011] Q.B. 477).

182 See *Downs v Chappell* [1997] 1 W.L.R. 426 at 433; *Bank of Tokyo-Mitsubishi UFJ Ltd v Baskan Gida Sanayi VE Pazarlama AS* [2009] EWHC 1276 (Ch); [2010] Bus. L.R. D1 at [1005]; *OMV Petrom SA v Glencore International AG* [2016] EWCA Civ 778; [2017] 3 All E.R. 157 (Romanian state oil buyer deceived on an industrial scale with regard to what oil it was buying: nothing to the point, even if true, that it was so desperate for oil it would have bought in any case). Note, however, that the point was left studiedly open by Males J in *Leni Gas & Oil Investments Ltd v Malta Oil Pty Ltd* [2014] EWHC 893 (Comm) at [20].

183 In *National Phonograph Co v Edison-Bell* [1908] 1 Ch. 335, lies told to third parties in order to gain an economic advantage at the expense of the claimant were held to be unlawful means, though no action in deceit could have been brought by the third parties, who themselves were not harmed. *National Phonograph* has been accepted as correct on this point in *OBG Ltd v Allan* [2007] UKHL 21; [2008] 1 A.C. 1 at [49].

184 cf. *Ministry of Housing v Sharp* [1970] 2 Q.B. 223 (negligent statement by registrar to purchaser of house causing incumbrancer to lose charge).

185 See the Australian decision in *Larkins v Chelmer Holdings Ltd* [1965] Qd. R. 68 (architect misrepresented that work not completed; money as a result withheld from builder; no action in deceit). See generally J. Murphy, "Misleading appearances in the tort of deceit" [2016] C.L.J. 301.

17-36 **Joint inducement suffices** Although the claimant must show that he was induced to act as he did by the misrepresentation, it need not have been the sole cause. Provided it substantially contributed to deceiving him, that will be enough.[186] If the claimant's mind was partly influenced by the defendant's misstatements the defendant will not be any the less liable because the claimant was also partly influenced by a mistake of his own.[187] In such cases, moreover, the claimant has the benefit of a presumption that he was influenced at least to some extent by the deceptive statement.[188]

17-37 This is particularly significant where a claim is paid or settled, often for commercial reasons, despite suspicions that it might be fraudulent. Thus in *Hayward v Zurich Insurance Co Plc*[189] insurers were held able to rescind a personal injury settlement for fraud (and potentially recoup any payments made) even though they had suspected deceit all along.[190] But the limits of this must be noted. It has been held that if the claimant not only suspects, but actually knows, that what he hears is false, this pre-empts the matter. Here he cannot sue, for the simple reason that he was never taken in and hence cannot have been induced.[191]

17-38 **Ambiguity** An ambiguous statement, true in one sense but not in another, may be fraudulent if intended to be read in its untrue connotation.[192] Nevertheless, in such a case the claimant must of course show that he acted upon it in the sense in which it is false. In *Arkwright v Newbold*,[193] Cotton LJ said:

> "In my opinion it would not be right in an action of deceit to give a plaintiff relief on the ground that a particular statement, according to the construction put on it by the court, is false, when the plaintiff does not venture to swear that he understood the statement in the sense which the court puts on it."

17-39 **Carelessness of claimant in not discovering the untruth no defence** A person

---

186 *Parabola Investments Ltd v Browallia CAL Ltd* [2009] EWHC 901 (Comm); [2009] 2 All E.R. (Comm) 589 (unsuccessfully appealed on other grounds, [2010] EWCA Civ 486; [2011] Q.B. 477); *Leni Gas & Oil Investments Ltd v Malta Oil Pty Ltd* [2014] EWHC 893 (Comm) at [16] (Males J). See too *Australian Steel & Mining Corp Pty Ltd v Corben* [1974] 2 N.S.W.L.R. 202; *Paul & Vincent v O'Reilly* (1913) 49 Ir. L.T. 89. cf. the negligent misrepresentation case of *JEB Fasteners Ltd v Marks Bloom & Co* [1983] 1 All E.R. 583 at 589, per Stephenson LJ; *Khakshouri v Jimenez* [2017] EWHC 3392 (QB) at [20] (Green J); *BV Nederlandse Industrie Van Eiprodukten v Rembrandt Enterprises, Inc* [2019] EWCA Civ 596; [2019] 3 W.L.R. 1113 at [26]–[43]; and the very significant compromise case of *Hayward v Zurich Insurance Co Plc* [2016] UKSC 48; [2017] A.C. 142 referred to below.

187 See *Edgington v Fitzmaurice* (1885) 29 Ch. 459 at 483, per Bowen LJ; also *Peek v Derry* (1887) 37 Ch. D. 541. cf. *Tatton v Wade* (1856) 18 C.B. 371.

188 See *Dadourian Group International Inc v Simms* [2009] EWCA Civ 169; [2009] 1 Lloyd's Rep. 601 at [95]–[108]; following dicta in *Goose v Wilson Sandford & Co (No.2)* [2001] Lloyd's Rep. P.N. 189 at 200–201; *OMV Petrom SA v Glencore International AG* [2015] EWHC 666 (Comm) at [133]–[158] (Flaux J); *Hayward v Zurich Insurance Co Plc* [2016] UKSC 48; [2017] A.C. 142 at [36]. For a case where the presumption was held rebutted on the facts, see *Yukos Hydrocarbons Investments v Georgiades* [2020] EWHC 173 (Comm).

189 [2016] UKSC 48; [2017] A.C. 142.

190 On the Hayward case see K. Lindeman, "Unravelling settlements made with 'eyes wide open'" (2017) 36 C.J.Q. 273; R. Lee, "Proof of Inducement in the Law on Misrepresentation" (2017) L.M.C.L.Q. 151; and E. Bant, "Unravelling Fraud in the Wake of Hayward v Zurich Insurance" [2019] L.M.C.L.Q. 91.

191 See *Holyoake v Candy* [2017] EWHC 3397 (Ch) especially at [386]–[395] (Nugee J).

192 See para.17-25.

193 (1881) 17 Ch. D. 301 at 325.

to whom a misrepresentation is made is not deceived if he actually knows the truth.[194] But it is no answer to an action for deceit that the claimant might have discovered the falsity by the exercise of ordinary care: it does not lie in the mouth of a liar to argue that the claimant was foolish to take him at his word.[195] Thus, where a vendor of a public house was sued in deceit for misrepresenting the takings of the business, it was held to be no defence that the vendor's books were in the house at the time and would have disclosed the truth had the claimant chosen to look at them.[196] Nor can the representor escape liability on the ground that knowledge of the truth must be imputed to the representee; as, for example where the representee's agent knew the true facts.[197]

Reliance and materiality Since the reasonableness of the claimant's reliance is not relevant to liability in deceit, it is submitted that it equally follows that the materiality or otherwise of the defendant's statement is out of account. All that is required is reliance: once this is shown the fraudulent defendant should not be permitted to argue that what he said would not have induced a reasonable person to so act.[198] **17-40**

3. DAMAGES[199]

Proof of damage Deceit is not actionable per se: damage, in other words, is of the gist of the action.[200] Moreover, it is up to the claimant to prove his loss.[201] Nevertheless, there is authority that where a claimant proves that he has been deceived into expending money the burden shifts to the defendant if he wishes to argue that the expenditure did not in fact amount to a loss to the claimant.[202] **17-41**

---

194 *Renault UK Ltd v Fleetpro Technical Services* [2007] EWHC 2541 (QB); [2008] Bus. L.R. D17 at [130]. Note, however, that the mere fact that some other agent of the claimant knew of the untruth will not negative liability: see ibid. at [124], following dicta of Scrutton J in *Wells v Smith* [1914] 3 K.B. 722.

195 See Lord Chelmsford in *Venezuela Central Ry v Kisch* (1857) L.R. 2 H.L. 99 at 120; see also *Whyfe v Michael Cullen & Partners* [1993] E.G.C.S. 193 and *Commission for the New Towns v Cooper (Great Britain) Ltd* [1995] Ch. 259 CA (party to a contract can be bound by its induced mistake). Nor is the Law Reform (Contributory Negligence) Act 1945 available here to reduce the damages: see para.17-52.

196 *Dobell v Stevens* (1825) 3 B. & C. 623; and see *Pilmore v Hood* (1838) 5 Bing. N.C. 97. cf. too the contract case of *Redgrave v Hurd* (1881) 20 Ch. D. 1; and *Buxton v Birches Time Share Resort Ltd* [1991] 2 N.Z.L.R. 641 NZCA.

197 *Wells v Smith* [1914] 3 K.B. 722. See, however, *Strover v Harrington* [1988] Ch. 390, where the agents were purchaser's solicitors who by implication had actual authority to receive all relevant information on their client's behalf. *Wells v Smith* was distinguished as a case where the claimant's agent himself was a party to the defendant's fraud. Sed quaere.

198 Compare the contract decision in *Museprime Properties Ltd v Adhill Properties Ltd* (1990) 61 P. & C.R. 111.

199 G. Treitel, "Damages for Deceit" (1969) 32 M.L.R. 556; A. Tettenborn et al., *Law of Damages*, paras 17.64–17.87.

200 See *Smith v Chadwick* (1884) 9 App. Cas. 187 at 190, per Lord Blackburn; *Diamond v Bank of London & Montreal Ltd* [1979] Q.B. 333 at 349, per Stephenson LJ.

201 *Renault UK Ltd v Fleetpro Technical Services Ltd* [2007] EWHC 2541 (QB); [2008] Bus. L.R. D17 (car importers deceived into making price support payments to dealers by false statement that buyers entitled to fleet discount: but in the market conditions prevailing, no proof that cars could have been sold at list price anyway, so no loss suffered).

202 *Parallel Imports (Europe) Ltd v Radivan* [2007] EWCA Civ 1373.

17-42 **Types of loss recoverable** The damage recovered in deceit cases is normally pecuniary loss: but it may take the form of personal injury, loss of property, real inconvenience or discomfort, or substantial mental distress.[203]

17-43 **Measure of damages** The measure of damages in deceit is the loss directly flowing from the claimant's reliance on the defendant's statement[204]; that is, generally speaking, the sum that will put him in the same position as if he had not relied on it.[205] Credit must of course be given for any gains made by the claimant,[206] though to qualify for deduction such gains must be both tangible and relatively permanent.[207]

17-44 **Position if representation true irrelevant** Since the claimant's entitlement is to be put in the position he would have occupied had he not relied on the defendant's representation, it follows that no account is taken of what his position would have been had that representation been true.[208] It follows that if the claimant is duped into buying an asset, he is generally entitled to recover the difference between the price paid and the market value of the property he received in exchange, and not the difference between the market value and the amount the defendant said the property was worth.[209] Thus in *Doyle v Olby (Ironmongers) Ltd*,[210] where the claimant was deceived into buying a run-down and infructuous business, an award of the latter sum was overturned by the Court of Appeal. Again, if the claimant is deceived into

---

203 See para.17-49.

204 "The defendant is bound to make reparation for all the actual damages directly flowing from the fraudulent inducement."—Lord Denning MR in *Doyle v Olby* (Ironmongers) Ltd [1969] 2 Q.B. 158, 167. See too *Clark v Urquhart* [1930] A.C. 28, 67–68 (per Lord Atkin).

205 See *Doyle v Olby* (Ironmongers) Ltd [1969] 2 Q.B. 158, 167 (Lord Denning MR); *GE Commercial Finance Ltd v Gee* [2005] EWHC 2056 (QB); [2006] 1 Lloyd's Rep. 337 at [335], per Tugendhat J.

206 *Smith New Court Securities Ltd v Citibank NA* [1997] A.C. 254 at 267, per Lord Browne-Wilkinson. See, e.g. *Komerçni Banka AS v Stone & Rolls Ltd* [2002] EWHC 2263 (Comm); [2003] 1 Lloyd's Rep. 383 (bank deceived into paying out on fraudulent letter of credit: credit for fee received for issuing it). The defendant bears the burden of proving such benefits: *Midco Holdings Ltd v Piper* [2004] EWCA Civ 476; [2004] N.P.C. 59; and *Barker v Winter* [2018] EWHC 1785 (QB) at [28].

207 *Barker v Winter* [2018] EWHC 1785 (QB) at [28] (munificent transfers of money obtained from besotted lover: no credit for sensual pleasures of lavish lifestyle derived partly from monies given). In *Burki v Seventy Thirty Ltd* [2018] EWHC 2151 (QB) at [174]–[175] a court went further and suggested that no credit fell to be given for the value of services received: thus a claimant duped into paying for computer dating services recovered her entire membership fee without reference to what she got in return. It is suggested, however, that this must be limited to cases where what was supplied was of little or no value to the claimant. If A dupes B into buying, say, electricity from him at more than the going rate for a year, is it really open to B to sue A for all his money back and get, in effect, a year's free power? One hopes not.

208 See, e.g. *McConnell v Wright* [1903] 1 Ch. 546, 554 (Collins MR); *Doyle v Olby (Ironmongers) Ltd* [1969] 2 Q.B. 158, 166 (Lord Denning MR); *East v Maurer* [1991] 1 W.L.R. 461, 465 (Beldam LJ); *Smith New Court Securities Ltd v Citibank NA* [1997] A.C. 254, 281–282 (Lord Steyn); *Inter Export LLC v Townley* [2017] EWHC 530 (Ch) at [6]–[8] (Proudman J)(upheld on appeal at [2018] EWCA Civ 2068). The position in many American jurisdictions is different: e.g. *Midwest Home Distributor, Inc v Domco Industries, Ltd*, 585 NW.2d 735 at 738–742 (Iowa 1998).

209 Thus if a defendant fraudulently says the asset is worth £120 when it is in fact worth £90, and the claimant buys it for £110, damages in deceit are £20 and not £30. For statements of this principle, see, e.g. *Pearson v Wheeler* (1825) Ry. & M. 303 at 304; *Doyle v Olby (Ironmongers) Ltd* [1969] 2 Q.B. 158 at 166, per Lord Denning MR; *Saunders v Edwards* [1987] 1 W.L.R. 1116 at 1121, per Kerr LJ; *Smith New Court Securities Ltd v Citibank NA* [1997] A.C. 254 at 281–282, per Lord Steyn.

210 [1969] 2 Q.B. 158.

entering into a transaction by a statement as to the gains to be made from it, he can recover only the amount he loses as a result of relying on the representation and not the profit the defendant said he would make. So in *East v Maurer*,[211] where the seller of a business fraudulently overstated the profits available, the Court of Appeal reversed a judgment at first instance awarding the buyer the amount of those extra profits.[212] (Conversely, a seller deceived into delivering goods by a representation that payment is forthcoming recovers the entire market value of those goods without reference to the price).[213]

However, the loss flowing from reliance on the defendant's representation may, in an exceptional case, approximate to restoring his position had the statement been true. Thus in *BHP Billiton Petroleum Ltd v Dalmine SpA*[214] quality control employees of a subcontractor supplying pipes for an offshore oil project certified pipes as sound which they knew to be substandard. In due course the pipes leaked. The project owner sued the subcontractor in deceit. It was accepted that it was entitled to be put in the position it would have occupied had the pipes in fact been up to standard: the reason being that, had the subcontractor's employees not mis-certified the pipes concerned, they would have been rejected and sound pipes supplied in their stead without further charge. **17-45**

Claims for would-be profits Although the "reliance measure" outlined above precludes the recovery of stated profits as such, this does not necessarily mean that the claimant is limited to out-of-pocket losses, or that all claims reflecting lost profits are precluded. Suppose a claimant is deceived into entering into a transaction by a fraudulent statement as to the profits to be made, and can show in addition that if he had not relied on the defendant's statement he would have made some other gainful investment (or for that matter would have laid his money out at interest). In such a case it is clear that he can recover the would-be profits or interest, as the case may be, that he would have made from that other investment.[215] Indeed, an action may lie for deceit even in respect of a transaction which turned out highly gainful for the claimant, if by reason of the deceit he was prevented from investing his money elsewhere so as to turn an even greater profit.[216] It goes without saying that if the claimant's prospects of making those alternative profits would **17-46**

211 [1991] 1 W.L.R. 461. See too the negligence case of *Swingcastle Ltd v Alastair Gibson* [1991] 2 A.C. 223 (valuers misvalue property for mortgagees: mortgagors insolvent: no recovery for interest that mortgagors should have paid and which would have been recoupable from property if valuation correct).

212 Though it did award the claimant the profits she would have made had she bought another similar business.

213 *Inter Export LLC v Townley* [2018] EWCA Civ 2068, esp. at [58]–[68]; upholding the earlier *Smith Kline & French Laboratories Ltd v Long* [1989] 1 W.L.R. 1.

214 [2003] EWCA Civ 170; [2003] B.L.R. 271.

215 See, e.g. *East v Maurer* [1991] 1 W.L.R. 461 (purchaser duped into buying business by overstated profits: recovers profits she would have made from alternative business she would have bought); *Parabola Investments Ltd v Browallia Cal Ltd* [2010] EWCA Civ 486; [2011] Q.B. 477. See too *Clef Aquitaine SàrL v Laporte Minerals (Barrow) Ltd* [2001] Q.B. 488; and *4Eng Ltd v Harper* [2008] EWHC 915 (Ch); [2009] Ch. 91 (fraudster's victim can claim in respect of chance that he would have made other, highly profitable, investment of money he was swindled out of) (commented on in C. Mitchell, "Loss of chance in deceit" (2009) 125 L.Q.R. 12).

216 See *Clef Aquitaine SarL v Laporte Minerals (Barrow) Ltd* [2001] Q.B. 488 (misrepresentation to proposed distributor about prices that he could sell products for: distributorship in fact profitable, but damages for loss of opportunity to negotiate lower prices from manufacturer and make a bigger profit).

have depended on the hypothetical action of some third party, then recovery will be reckoned on the basis of the loss of a chance.[217]

17-47 **Timing** Prima facie damages in deceit are reckoned as at the time of reliance on the representation.[218] Thus where an asset is bought as a result of the defendant's fraud damages are generally the difference between price and value at the time of purchase,[219] without reference to the fact that the value has since risen[220] or fallen,[221] or that the ultimate profit made by a corporate buyer from a misdescribed commodity has not been appreciably reduced.[222] However, this is not a "strict and inflexible rule",[223] and on occasion some other date has been taken. First, where the claimant is effectively "locked in" to a transaction, or where, acting reasonably, he can only be expected to escape from it some time later, then damages will generally be reckoned as at that later time so as to allow the claimant to claim any extra losses suffered as a result.[224] Thus in *Doyle v Olby (Ironmongers) Ltd*,[225] a person tricked into buying a failing business recovered the difference between what he paid for it and the sum for which he later (and reasonably) disposed of it. Again, in *Smith New*

---

[217] See *Parabola Investments Ltd v Browallia Cal Ltd* [2010] EWCA Civ 486; [2011] Q.B. 477 at [23] (on the basis of the decision in *Allied Maples Group Ltd v Simmons & Simmons* [1995] 1 W.L.R. 1602).

[218] See the old cases on buyers of shares misled by optimistic prospectuses, where the claimant was invariably awarded the difference between price and value at the time of purchase: e.g. *Twycross v Grant* (1877) 2 C.P.D. 469; *Peek v Derry* (1887) 37 Ch. D. 541 (reversed on other grounds: see *Derry v Peek* (1889) 14 App. Cas. 337); *McConnell v Wright* [1903] 1 Ch. 546. That this was the prima facie measure of damages in deceit was confirmed by Lord Browne-Wilkinson in *Smith New Court Securities Ltd v Scrimgeour Vickers (Asset Management) Ltd* [1997] A.C. 254, 267; and in *Butler-Creagh v Hersham* [2011] EWHC 2525 (QB). The same goes where the seller complains of a deceit by the buyer causing a sale at an undervalue: *Vald. Nielsen Holding A/S, Newwatch Ltd v Baldorino* [2019] EWHC 1926 (Comm) at [484]–[488].

[219] See the cases referred to in the previous note; also *Waddell v Blockey* (1879) 4 Q.B.D. 678; and *Saunders v Edwards* [1987] 1 W.L.R. 1116, a case concerning the purchase of a flat, where the Court of Appeal held that the correct date for the quantification of the claimant's loss was the completion date, that being the date of actual loss.

[220] See, e.g. *Great Future International Ltd v Sealand Housing Corp* [2002] EWHC 2454 (Ch); *The Times,* 17 December 2002 (claimant deceived into buying shares: shares rose in value after purchase: no account of later rise in determining damages); *Butler-Creagh v Hersham* [2011] EWHC 2525 (QB) (same with regard to real estate).

[221] *Waddell v Blockley* (1879) 4 Q.B.D. 678. See too the example given by Cockburn CJ in *Twycross v Grant* (1877) 2 C.P.D. 469 at 544-545: if D dupes C into buying a racehorse which later dies from some unconnected cause, C must credit the value of the horse on purchase and cannot claim the whole price paid and since wasted.

[222] *OMV Petrom SA v Glencore International AG* [2016] EWCA Civ 778; [2017] 3 All E.R. 157 (misstatement as to technical grade, and hence value, of crude oil supplied: not open to defendant to argue that oil actually supplied was nearly as good for buyer's purposes of refining and onsale).

[223] *Smith New Court Securities Ltd v Scrimgeour Vickers (Asset Management) Ltd* [1997] A.C. 254 at 267, per Lord Browne-Wilkinson.

[224] See *Smith New Court Securities Ltd v Scrimgeour Vickers (Asset Management) Ltd* [1997] A.C. 254 at 266, per Lord Browne-Wilkinson; *Doyle v Olby (Ironmongers) Ltd* [1969] 2 Q.B. 158. But it does not seem that the defendant can use this as a means of reducing his liability: see *Great Future International Ltd v Sealand Housing Corp* [2002] EWHC 2454 (Ch); *The Times,* 17 December 2002, referred to above.

[225] [1969] 2 Q.B. 158. See too *Downs v Chappell* [1997] 1 W.L.R. 426 (a similar case); and *Standard Chartered Bank v Pakistan National Shipping Corp (Assessment of Damages)* [2001] EWCA Civ 55; [2001] 1 All E.R. (Comm) 822 (buyers deceived by false bills of lading into accepting substandard bitumen: damages reckoned on later resale price).

Court Securities Ltd v Scrimgeour Vickers (Asset Management) Ltd[226] stockjobbers were induced by fraud into buying a block of shares which later collapsed in value owing to a previously undiscovered fraud against the company. It was held by the House of Lords that they only had to credit the reduced amount they later received on resale: they could not have been expected to sell earlier. Put another way, it can be said that where the fraud still has an effect after discovery, so that the subsequent losses cannot be said to result from a positive decision of the claimant, those losses are recoverable.[227] Secondly, where an asset purchased by the claimant later drops in price as a result of the correction of a false market created by the defendant himself, then not surprisingly damages are reckoned by reference to the later, lower, price.[228] Where an asset is alleged to have been sold at an undervalue as a result of a deceit practised by the buyer, the starting-point is that the claimant recovers the market value of the asset less the price received: it has been said, however, that account should be taken in such a case of the fact that the asset might have been sold for less than its full value.[229]

Causation The claimant in deceit must, of course, show that his loss results from the defendant's misrepresentation[230] (though it should be noted that rules of causation are often manipulated in favour of deceit claimants[231]). The better position is that the claimant is not limited to such losses as are suffered in connection with the falsity of the representation, but can recover all losses directly resulting.[232] So if a buyer is deceived into buying bonds which he then chooses to retain as a business decision, and those bonds later decline in value, he cannot recover in respect of the subsequent decline: this is due to his own commercial choice, not to the original deceit.[233] Similarly, while there is some authority that a defendant who deceives the claimant into entering a business transaction is liable without reference to whether the claimant might otherwise have invested his money in some other unprofitable scheme,[234] this attitude is difficult to defend. If the claimant can increase his **17-48**

226 [1997] A.C. 254.

227 *Parabola Investments Ltd v Browallia Cal Ltd* [2010] EWCA Civ 486; [2011] Q.B. 477 at [32] onwards. See also *Khakshouri v Jimenez* [2017] EWHC 3392 (QB).

228 See *Broome v Speak* [1903] 1 Ch. 856 (affirmed *Shepheard v Broome* [1904] A.C. 342); *McConnell v Wright* [1903] 1 Ch. 546 (both misleading prospectus cases).

229 *Vald. Nielsen Holding A/S, Newwatch Ltd v Baldorino* [2019] EWHC 1926 (Comm) at [544]–[567] (Jacobs J). Sed quaere. It is arguable that such matters should be out of account. If an owner is deceived into selling an asset at an undervalue, should it be open to the defendant to argue that but for his fraud the claimant might have given away the asset to someone else?

230 In a suitable case it was accepted in *4 Eng Ltd v Harper* [2008] EWHC 915 (Ch); [2009] Ch. 91 that damages could be recovered for loss of a chance.

231 As admitted by Lord Hoffmann in *Smith New Court Securities Ltd v Scrimgeour Vickers (Asset Management) Ltd* [1997] A.C. 254: see at 280, 285.

232 See the Australian decision in *Copping v ANZ McCaughan Ltd* (1997) 67 S.A.S.R. 525, 539. The apparent contrary suggestion in *Glossop Cartons & Print Ltd v Contact (Print & Packaging) Ltd* [2019] EWHC 2314 (Ch) at [103] that losses due to ordinary commercial risks run by the buyer of property formed an exception to recovery seems, with respect, doubtful.

233 *Waddell v Blockley* (1879) 4 Q.B.D. 678. But if the choice is affected by the misrepresentation, or his choice is constrained by good business reasons, he will recover his whole loss: *Smith New Court Securities Ltd v Scrimgeour Vickers (Asset Management) Ltd* [1997] A.C. 254.

234 See *Slough Estates Ltd v Welwyn-Hatfield DC* [1996] 2 P.L.R. 50 (following dicta by Lord Steyn in *Smith New Court Securities Ltd v Scrimgeour Vickers (Asset Management) Ltd* [1997] A.C. 254, 281), the court declined to follow the contrary decision in *Downs v Chappell* [1997] 1 W.L.R. 426 on this point).

recovery by showing he would have invested his money profitably, by parity of reasoning the defendant ought to be able to reduce his exposure by showing that, but for his deceit, the claimant would have lost it in any case.[235]

17-49 **Consequential losses** Damages in deceit are at large and in principle are available to compensate the claimant for all his damage, including consequential losses.[236] Any damage directly flowing from the fraudulent inducement may be recovered[237] unless it is caused by the claimant behaving completely without prudence or common sense.[238] Thus in *Hornal v Neuberger Products Ltd*[239] a buyer recovered for seven weeks' downtime on a machine tool he had been defrauded into buying; and in *Archer v Brown*,[240] a person swindled into paying for shares he never received recovered interest on the money borrowed to finance the transaction.[241] A person deceived into buying real estate recovered stamp duty paid and maintenance costs on the property he did not want[242]; and a claimant bankrupted as a result of being defrauded recovered for the associated losses.[243] There is equally no bar to recovery in respect of property damage or personal injury: thus in an old case the seller of a shotgun falsely stated to be sound was liable for injury suffered when it exploded,[244] and on a similar basis the deceitful vendor of a plague-infested cow was held liable to the buyer for the loss of his herd which the beast infected.[245] Non-pecuniary damage is, it seems, recoverable for matters such as distress[246] or inconvenience.[247]

---

[235] See *Downs v Chappell* [1997] 1 W.L.R. 426, above; *Yam Seng Pte Ltd v International Trade Corp Ltd* [2013] EWHC 111 (QB); [2013] 1 Lloyd's Rep. 526 at [209]–[217] (Leggatt J).

[236] *St Paul Travelers Insurance Co Ltd v Okporuah* [2006] EWHC 2107 (Ch) (would-be buyer of house tells lies to lender as part of mortgage fraud in collaboration with seller: lender's loss later increased when, after loan drawdown, seller fails to give title to house at all: buyer liable for full loss to lender); *Greenridge Luton One Ltd v Kempton Investments Ltd* [2016] EWHC 91 (Ch) (even though contract induced by fraud rescinded before performance, recovery of expenses incurred in and about it). See too *Cemp Properties (UK) Ltd v Dentsply Research and Development Corp* [1991] 34 E.G. 62.

[237] An instructive example is *Nationwide Building Society v Dunlop Haywards (DHL) Ltd* [2009] EWHC 254 (Comm); [2010] 1 W.L.R. 258 (victim of large mortgage fraud recovered not only net advance, but also would-be interest on the sums lost; managerial and staff time spent in investigation; loss of business and extra borrowing costs caused by the claimants' loss of creditworthiness when the fraud was publicised; the cost of maintaining increased reserves demanded by the regulator; and extra interest that had to be offered to nervous investors). The costs of investigating fraud and fraudster were also recovered in *4Eng Ltd v Harper* [2008] EWHC 915 (Ch); [2009] Ch. 91; and in *Mellor v Partridge* [2013] EWCA Civ 477 (see especially at [45]).

[238] *Doyle v Olby (Ironmongers) Ltd* [1969] 2 Q.B. 158; *Banque Bruxelles Lambert SA v Eagle Star Insurance Co Ltd* [1997] A.C. 191; *Royscot Trust Ltd v Rogerson* [1991] 2 Q.B. 297. cf. *NZ Refrigerating Co Ltd v Scott* [1969] N.Z.L.R. 30.

[239] [1957] 1 Q.B. 247.

[240] [1985] Q.B. 401.

[241] See too *KBC Bank v Industrial Steels (UK) Ltd* [2001] 1 Lloyd's Rep. 370 (knowing presentation of false documents to bank under letter of credit: presenter liable inter alia for cost of litigation brought by bank against other banks in the chain before it discovered the falsity).

[242] *Butler-Creagh v Hersham* [2011] EWHC 2525 (QB).

[243] *Kinch v Rosling* [2009] EWHC 286 (QB).

[244] *Langridge v Levy* (1837) 2 M. & W. 519; 4 M. & W. 337. See too *Burrows v Rhodes* [1899] 1 Q.B. 816; *Banks v Cox* [2002] EWHC 2166 (QB) (buyer swindled into buying unprofitable nursing-home recovers for depressive illness caused thereby).

[245] *Mullett v Mason* (1866) L.R. 1 C. & P. 559. So also with damage to the thing fraudulently sold: see *Nicholls v Taylor* [1939] V.L.R. 119 (car damaged when tyre fraudulently misrepresented as new burst).

[246] £500 was given for distress in *Saunders v Edwards* [1987] 1 W.L.R. 1116; and also in *Shelley v Pad-*

Remoteness The claimant in deceit is entitled to recover all damage directly flowing from the defendant's tort.[248] In particular there is no requirement that the losses be foreseeable: "it does not lie in the mouth of the fraudulent person to say that they could not reasonably have been foreseen."[249] Thus it does not matter that the claimant's loss is increased by some entirely extraneous unanticipated event, such as a sudden downturn in the property market.[250] However, this does not mean that the claimant is under no duty to mitigate his loss in so far as he can reasonably do so. Thus the buyer of a business from a fraudulent seller is bound to extricate himself as soon as he reasonably can by selling it rather than allowing losses to accumulate further.[251] **17-50**

Aggravated and exemplary damages[252] There is little doubt that aggravated damages may be awarded to compensate the claimant for injury to his feelings arising from a blatant or callous exercise in deceit.[253] As for exemplary damages, since the decision in *Kuddus v Chief Constable of Leicestershire*[254] they are clearly available in principle, at least where the deceit was by a public authority or was calculated to make a profit over and above any damages received,[255] and possibly **17-51**

---

dock [1979] Q.B. 120 (affirmed [1980] Q.B. 348); and again in *Burki v Seventy Thirty Ltd* [2018] EWHC 2151 (QB) (lovelorn lady duped into joining computer dating club: see esp. at [175]–[181]). See too *Shaw v Sequence (UK) Ltd* [2004] EWHC 3249 (QB); [2004] All E.R. (D) 232 (Nov) (annoyance of clients deceived by their estate agent: £1,000 basic award plus £1,500 aggravated damages); *Kinch v Rosling* [2009] EWHC 286 (QB) (£10,000 for distress of victim bankrupted owing to fraud); and the colourful Canadian decision in *Beaulne v Ricketts* (1979) 96 D.L.R. (3d) 550 (claimant deceived into bigamous marriage). But one Canadian decision goes the other way: in *PP v DD* [2017] ONCA 180; (2017) 409 D.L.R. (4th) 69 a boyfriend failed to recover for distress at his girlfriend's falling pregnant following false statements as to her use of contraceptives.

247 *Mafo v Adams* [1970] 1 Q.B. 548 (loss of benefit of a regulated tenancy).

248 See *Doyle v Olby (Ironmongers) Ltd* [1969] 2 Q.B. 158 at 168, per Winn LJ; *Smith New Court Securities Ltd v Scrimgeour Vickers (Asset Management) Ltd* [1997] A.C. 254 at 284, per Lord Steyn. See para.17-49.

249 *Doyle v Olby (Ironmongers) Ltd* [1969] 2 Q.B. 158, 167 (per Lord Denning MR). See too *Smith New Court Securities Ltd v Scrimgeour Vickers (Asset Management) Ltd* [1997] A.C. 254, 264–267 (Lord Browne-Wilkinson), 281 (Lord Steyn); *Nationwide Building Society v Dunlop Haywards (DHL) Ltd* [2009] EWHC 254 (Comm); [2010] 1 W.L.R. 258 at [12].

250 *Slough Estates Ltd v Welwyn-Hatfield DC* [1996] 2 P.L.R. 50 (claimant bought into commercial development: defendant liable for increased loss due to property meltdown).

251 *Downs v Chappell* [1997] 1 W.L.R. 426 (duped buyer of business only recovered losses up to time he ought to have sold on); see too *Smith New Court Securities Ltd v Scrimgeour Vickers (Asset Management) Ltd* [1997] A.C. 254 at 266, per Lord Browne-Wilkinson.

252 See generally para.27-134 onwards.

253 *Archer v Brown* [1985] Q.B. 401. See also *Mafo v Adams* [1970] 1 Q.B. 548 at 558; *Saunders v Edwards* [1987] 1 W.L.R. 1116; *Shaw v Sequence (UK) Ltd* [2004] EWHC 3249 (QB); [2004] All E.R. (D) 232 (Nov) (deceit by estate agent: damages of £1,000 for vexation increased to £2,500 for over-contentious attitude and non-apology). In *Barker v Winter* [2018] EWHC 1785 (QB) at [28], where a lover duped his partner out of large sums, aggravated damages were refused because the lover suffered from a condition making him pathologically addicted to obtaining and spending money. Sed quaere. With respect this seems remarkably generous to the defendant, and more appropriate to criminal than civil proceedings.

254 [2001] UKHL 29; [2002] 2 A.C. 122: see para.27-143.

255 i.e. Lord Devlin's categories in *Rookes v Barnard* [1964] A.C. 1129; see para.27-136 onwards. For an example of an award of punitive damages for a deceit aimed at profit, see *Hassan v Cooper* [2015] EWHC 540 (QB); [2015] R.T.R. 26 (attempt to make a fraudulent claim arising out of a genuine car accident: award against the claims agents responsible related to the amount which they had attempted to extract from the defendant's insurers; smaller award against individual claimant).

even where it was not.[256] An instance where they were awarded on this basis was *Axa Insurance UK Plc v Financial Claims Solutions Ltd*,[257] involving repeated fraudulent claims against motor insurers. The Court of Appeal awarded £20,000 against the company responsible, and an additional £20,000 against each of the moving spirits behind it.[258]

4. Defences

17-52 **Contributory negligence and deceit** It is now clear that damages for deceit, which were never subject to any defence of contributory negligence at common law,[259] equally cannot be reduced under the Law Reform (Contributory Negligence) Act 1945.[260]

17-53 **Exclusion of liability by contract or notice** It is now clear that at common law a person cannot as a matter of public policy rely on a contract or notice to exclude liability for his own fraud.[261] But this absolute prohibition, it seems, applies only where the person seeking to protect is himself complicit in the fraudulent conduct. Thus there is no objection on principle to a suitably-worded clause excluding liability in respect of the fraud of an agent or employee for whose acts a person would otherwise be liable.[262] On the other hand, such a clause is, of course, subject to the

---

256 Lord Nicholls in *Kuddus v Chief Constable of Leicestershire* [2001] UKHL 29; [2002] 2 A.C. 122 at [66] doubted whether the "type of action" limitations that had previously constrained exemplary damages claims continued to survive. It remains to be seen whether this suggestion is followed.

257 [2018] EWCA Civ 1330; [2019] R.T.R. 1.

258 The requirement that the tort be committed with a view to gains outstripping losses the court held satisfied, perhaps surprisingly, by the fact that the defendants had hoped—vainly—not to be caught and hence to keep their gains for themselves. Although this proposition can pray in aid a dictum of Lord Hailsham in *Broome v Cassell* [1972] A.C. 1027, 1079 ("It is not necessary that the defendant calculates that the plaintiff's damages if he sues to judgment will be smaller than the defendant's profit"), it is nevertheless potentially far-reaching in that it opens up the prospect of an award of punitive damages in the case of almost any deliberate tort committed in the hope of lucre.

259 See Mummery J's analysis of the common law position in *Alliance & Leicester Building Society v Edgestop Ltd* [1993] 1 W.L.R. 1462 at 1474.

260 The point was put beyond doubt in *Standard Chartered Bank v Pakistan National Shipping Corp (Nos 2 and 4)* [2002] UKHL 43; [2003] 1 A.C. 959. See too the earlier decisions in *Alliance & Leicester Building Society v Edgestop Ltd* [1993] 1 W.L.R. 1462; and *Corporación Nacional del Cobre de Chile v Sogemin Metals Ltd* [1997] 1 W.L.R. 1396. The exclusion of contributory negligence as a partial defence is criticised in J. Murphy, "Misleading appearances in the tort of deceit" [2016] C.L.J. 301.

261 "There is no doubt that a party cannot contract that he shall not be liable for his own fraud."—Lord Hoffmann in *HIH Casualty & General Insurance Ltd v Chase Manhattan Bank* [2003] UKHL 6; [2003] 2 Lloyd's Rep. 61 at [76]. See too Lord Bingham at [16]; also *Pearson & Son Ltd v Dublin Corp* [1907] A.C. 351 at 353–354, per Lord Loreburn; at 356, per Lord Halsbury. Equally ineffective in this respect is an entire agreement clause (*Bonhams 1793 Ltd v Cavazzoni* [2014] EWHC 682 (QB) at [11] (Cooke J); following *FoodCo UK LLP v Henry Boot Developments Ltd* [2010] EWHC 358), a non-reliance clause (*Property Alliance Group Ltd v Royal Bank of Scotland Plc* [2016] EWHC 3342 (Ch) at [230]–[231] (Asplin J) (affirmed without reference to the point at [2018] EWCA Civ 355; [2018] 1 W.L.R. 3529), or a statement that information in fact known to be false is being transmitted by the defendant merely as the mouthpiece of another (*Francis v Knapper* [2016] EWHC 3093 (QB) at [16]–[20] (Andrew Baker J)).

262 See the judgment of the Court of Appeal in *HIH Casualty & General Insurance Ltd v Chase Manhattan Bank* [2001] EWCA Civ 1250; [2001] 2 Lloyd's Rep. 483 at [109]. The House of Lords left the point open ([2003] UKHL 6; [2003] 2 Lloyd's Rep. 61), though Lord Scott seemingly agreed with the Court of Appeal ([2003] UKHL 6 at [122]). In *Frans Maas (UK) Ltd v Samsung Electronics (UK)*

usual statutory limitations on exemption clauses.[263] Furthermore, there is a very strong presumption that exception clauses do not cover fraud,[264] and very specific wording is likely to be required in order to overcome it.[265]

Public policy defences to deceit liability Public policy usually demands that nobody be permitted to found an action on an illegal act.[266] So if the claimant suffers loss as a result of dealings with the defendant which are intrinsically illegal, he will not normally be able to recover damages for that loss even though his loss resulted from fraudulent misrepresentations made by the defendant.[267] However, as this is an issue of public policy, the nature and true quality of the illegality are important.[268] The mere fact that the deceit arose in connection with a contract itself unenforceable for illegality will not suffice.[269] Thus in *Saunders v Edwards*,[270] an action for fraudulent misrepresentation concerning the sale of a flat, it was established that both purchaser and vendor had grossly inflated the price of the fixtures to reduce the incidence of stamp duty. However, as the claimant purchaser was not seeking to sue on the contract,[271] the court allowed him to sue in deceit,[272] the claimant having an "unassailable" claim for damages.[273] In order to make out a defence based on public policy, the defendant must establish that the claimant's conduct is so clearly reprehensible as to justify its condemnation by the court and that the conduct is so much part of the claim against the defendant as to justify refusing any remedy to the claimant.[274] This can be difficult to show.[275] Thus in **17-54**

Ltd [2004] EWHC 1502 (Comm); [2004] 2 Lloyd's Rep. 251 Gross J was prepared to uphold a clause protecting an employer from liability for dishonest conduct by his employees; although that case involved theft, by parity of reasoning the principle presumably applies to deceit too.

263 In particular the Misrepresentation Act 1967 s.3; the Unfair Contract Terms Act 1977; and the Consumer Rights Act 2015.

264 They were held not to do so in *Pearson & Son Ltd v Dublin Corp* [1907] A.C. 351; and *HIH Casualty & General Insurance Ltd v Chase Manhattan Bank* [2003] UKHL 6; [2003] 2 Lloyd's Rep. 61.

265 "[I]t is in my opinion plain beyond argument that if a party to a written contract seeks to exclude the ordinary consequences of fraudulent or dishonest misrepresentation or deceit by his agent, acting as such, inducing the making of the contract, such intention must be expressed in clear and unmistakable terms on the face of the contract."—Lord Bingham in *HIH Casualty & General Insurance Ltd v Chase Manhattan Bank* [2003] UKHL 6; [2003] 2 Lloyd's Rep. 61 at [16].

266 *Holman v Johnson* (1775) 1 Cowp. 341 at 343; *Thackwell v Barclays Bank* [1986] 1 All E.R. 676.

267 The text here was approved by Gross J in *Colin Buchanan & Partners Ltd v Marcus de Berg* [2003] EWHC 839 (QB) at [112] (where, however, the defence was not made out on the facts).

268 See generally *Patel v Mirza* [2016] UKSC 42; [2017] A.C. 467.

269 e.g. *Dott v Brickwell* (1906) 23 T.L.R. 61 (unlicensed moneylender could not sue for repayment of loan but could sue borrower in fraud for deceiving him into lending). See too *The Siben (No.2)* [1996] 1 Lloyd's Rep. 35.

270 [1987] 1 W.L.R. 1116.

271 Whether he could have done so was left open by Kerr LJ: see [1987] 1 W.L.R. 116 at 125.

272 The vendor had lied that the flat he was selling included a roof terrace. A fortiori, when a claimant is fraudulently induced to enter into an illegal transaction by the defendants, and is unaware of the illegal nature of the transaction: *Shelley v Paddock* [1980] Q.B. 348; see also *Dott v Brickwell* (1906) 23 T.L.R. 61.

273 See the discussion of *Saunders v Edwards* by Lord Goff in *Tinsley v Milligan* [1994] 1 A.C. 340 at 360. In that case, Lord Browne-Wilkinson and Lord Goff disapproved of the "public conscience" test formulated in *Saunders* (whereby the court would have regard to the extent to which the public conscience would be affronted by recognising rights acquired by illegal transactions) but thought the actual decision to be correct.

274 See the judgment of Cresswell J in *Standard Chartered Bank v Pakistan National Shipping Corp (No.2)* [1998] 1 Lloyd's Rep. 684 at 705–6, upheld by Evans LJ on appeal as summarising the law "impeccably" (see [2000] 1 Lloyd's Rep. 218 at 226).

Standard Chartered Bank Plc v Pakistan National Shipping Corp (No.2)[276] a confirming bank induced to pay a letter of credit by presentation of falsified bills of lading successfully claimed from the presenters despite the fact that it had itself presented the documents to the issuing bank at a time when it knew the credit was stale.

5. MISREPRESENTATION AS TO CREDIT OF THIRD PERSONS

17-55 **The Statute of Frauds Amendment Act 1828** Under s.6 of the Statute of Frauds Amendment Act 1828[277]:

> "No action shall be brought whereby to charge any person upon or by reason of any representation or assurance made or given concerning or relating to the character, conduct, credit, ability, trade, or dealings of any other person, to the intent or purpose that such other person may obtain credit, money, or goods upon, unless such representation or assurance be made in writing, signed by the party to be charged therewith."

Despite the generality of its wording, it has been held that the Act applies to fraudulent misrepresentations only, and not to actions in contract[278] or for negligent misrepresentation.[279]

17-56 A representation as to credit is essentially one which relates to the ability of a person effectually to perform and satisfy the engagement of a pecuniary nature into which he has proposed to enter and upon the faith of which he is to obtain money, credit or goods.[280] A bank's assurance that brokers offering to sell sugar were respectable and reliable has been held to come within the Act in as far as it concerned the reliability of the brokers, but not otherwise[281]; similarly, a statement by a bank to a person requested to sign accommodation bills that the person primarily liable is fit to be accommodated is also covered.[282] However, the limits of the section, which tends to be narrowly construed,[283] must be noted. It only applies to cases where the subject of the representation seeks to obtain actual money or goods on credit: the obtaining of credit in abstracto, for example by postponing the calling-in of an existing debt, is not enough.[284] Again, it is doubtful whether it extends beyond representations as to the debtor's own creditworthiness so as to

---

275 Indeed, it seems that in no English case has the ex turpi causa defence been successfully raised in an action for deceit.

276 [2000] 1 Lloyd's Rep. 218 (appealed on other grounds: [2002] UKHL 43; [2003] 1 A.C. 959).

277 Alternatively known as Lord Tenterden's Act. For a useful analysis, see T. Henderson, "Section 6 of Lord Tenterden's Act: the unexpected shield against fraud" (2016) 11 J.I.B.F.L. 667.

278 *Banbury v Bank of Montreal* [1918] A.C. 626.

279 *WB Anderson & Sons Ltd v Rhodes (Liverpool) Ltd* [1967] 2 All E.R. 850; [1967] C.L.J. 155. But the Court of Appeal in *UBAF Ltd v European American Banking Corp* [1984] Q.B. 713 accepted that s.6 of the 1828 Act did apply to a claim brought under s.2(1) of the Misrepresentation Act 1967.

280 See *Lyde v Barnard* (1836) 1 M & W. 101 at 119, per Lord Abinger. The deceit involved in ordering goods on credit on behalf of someone known to be insolvent is within the Act: see *Contex Drouzhba Ltd v Wiseman* [2007] EWCA Civ 1201; [2008] B.C.C. 301 (though there the requirement of writing was satisfied, the defendant having signed on behalf of the company).

281 *Diamond v Bank of London & Montreal Ltd* [1979] Q.B. 333.

282 *Clydesdale Bank Ltd v Paton* [1896] A.C. 381 (decided under the Scottish equivalent of the 1828 Act s.6 of the Mercantile Law (Scotland) Amendment Act 1856).

283 For the obvious reason that, if held applicable, it provides an unattractive shield for undeserving fraudsters.

284 *Roder UK Ltd v West* [2011] EWCA Civ 1126; [2012] Q.B. 752 (oral assurances by officers of company that debt would be paid in due course; no bar on deceit claim when debtor later collapsed).

cover, for example, statements about his financial or managerial competence,[285] or about the value of property to be offered by him as security for a loan.[286] Where the representor is an individual, it has been held that the signature must be that of the defendant personally[287] in order to satisfy the Act: his agent's signature, even if authorised, will not suffice.[288] As regards companies, however, the position is different. Despite some earlier authority to the contrary,[289] the Court of Appeal in *UBAF Ltd v European American Banking Corp*[290] has made it clear that the signature of any duly authorised agent of the company satisfies the requirements of the 1828 Act.

6. Statutory Liability for Misstatements in a Prospectus

Company prospectuses: statutory liability of directors and others The law governing compensation for false or misleading particulars contained in a company prospectus is now largely contained in the Financial Services and Markets Act 2000. Section 90(1) of that Act renders the persons responsible for any listing particulars liable to pay compensation to anyone who has acquired any of the securities in question and has suffered loss in respect of them as a result of any untrue or misleading statement in the particulars. It should be noted that the grounds on which this liability can arise cover negligent misstatements as well as deceitful ones, the burden of proof as to lack of negligence lying on the defendant.[291] It should also be noted that the remedies in the 2000 Act are cumulative with those existing at common law.[292] **17-57**

7. The Action for Fraud Arising out of Bribery

Fraud and bribery When an agent is bribed to persuade his principal to enter into a transaction on terms disadvantageous to the latter, he may of course make himself liable in deceit: for example, if he untruthfully tells his principal that the terms are the best that can be obtained. But even if he does not, and merely deals on the principal's behalf, this event itself gives rise to a tortious liability[293] in both **17-58**

285 *Lindsay v O'Loughnane* [2010] EWHC 529 (QB); [2012] B.C.C. 153 (fraudulent statement by the controller of a company in difficulties that certain funds in fact misappropriated had been mislaid not within Act).

286 In *Lyde v Barnard* (1836) 1 M. & W. 101 the Court of Exchequer divided equally on the issue (the case concerned false statements as to property offered as security by an embarrassed aristocratic borrower). But it is difficult to see such statements as concerning the "character, conduct, credit, ability, trade, or dealings" of the would-be debtor; and it is submitted that the better view is that they are not caught by the Act.

287 On emails in this context, see *Lindsay v O'Loughnane* [2010] EWHC 529 (QB); [2012] B.C.C. 153 at [95] (Flaux J) (automatically-generated electronic signature suffices, as does signature typed by writer: but not mere presence of sender's name and details in header).

288 *Swift v Jewsbury* (1874) L.R. 9 Q.B. 301.

289 *Hirst v West Riding Union Banking Co* [1901] 2 K.B. 560.

290 [1984] Q.B. 713.

291 Financial Services and Markets Act 2000 Sch.10 para.1.

292 Financial Services and Markets Act 2000 s.90(6).

293 There is a parallel compensatory claim in equity against the agent for breaking his fiduciary duty, and against the briber for helping him break it (see *Royal Brunei Airlines Sdn Bhd v Tan* [1995] 2 A.C. 378). But in *Fyffes Group Ltd v Templeman* [2000] 2 Lloyd's Rep. 643 at 660 Toulson J pointed out that the measure of damages was the same under either head (save possibly for the availability of compound interest in an equitable claim).

himself and the briber to the principal for loss suffered by the latter.[294] This head of claim is somewhat confusingly known as "fraud",[295] and shares some,[296] though not all,[297] of the elements of the tort of deceit.[298]

17-59 The measure of damages under this head is the loss actually suffered by the principal.[299] There is a strong, though not conclusive,[300] presumption that the amount of the bribe represents a loss to the principal, on the pragmatic basis that he would otherwise have benefited from it by way of discount or otherwise.[301] In addition the principal can claim any further losses he may have suffered.[302] As with deceit properly so called, contributory negligence is no defence.[303] In addition to being liable in damages, both the errant agent and, it seems, the briber himself are liable

---

294 Examples are numerous. See, e.g. *Salford Corp v Lever* [1891] 1 Q.B. 168 CA; *Grant v Gold Exploration and Development Syndicate Ltd* [1900] 1 Q.B. 233; *Hovendon & Sons v Millhoff* (1900) 83 L.T. 41; *Arab Monetary Fund v Hashim* [1993] 1 Lloyd's Rep. 543 (employer paid contractor the full amount due under a contract which was induced by a bribe paid to the employer's agent: employer entitled to recover amount of the bribe from contractor on the basis that contractor received a greater sum than what was the true price).

295 "Bribery is … a specialist variety of fraud": HH Judge Pelling in *Chancery Client Partners Ltd v MRC 957 Ltd* [2016] EWHC 2142 (Ch); [2016] Lloyd's Rep. F.C. 578 at [23]. See too, for similar statements, *Conway v Prince Eze* [2019] EWCA Civ 88 at [106]; and *Motortrak Ltd v FCA Australia Pty Ltd (No 2)* [2018] EWHC 1464 (Comm) at [15] (Moulder J).

296 For example, the exacting standard of proof (see *Fyffes Group Ltd v Templeman* [2000] 2 Lloyd's Rep. 643 at 656), and the inapplicability of contributory negligence (see below).

297 For example, an employer can be vicariously liable under this head even for an act that was not within his employee's actual or ostensible authority, thus marking off this head of liability from deceit proper.

298 "[T]he claim based on bribery is not a species of deceit but a special form of fraud where there is no representation made to the principal of the agent let alone reliance."-Steel J in *Petrotrade Inc v Smith* [2000] 1 Lloyd's Rep. 486 at 490. For a useful summary of the ingredients of the cause of action, see *Otkritie International Investment Management Ltd v Urumov* [2014] EWHC 191 (Comm) at [66]–[73] (Eder J). On the other hand, a dishonest agent may also commit deceit by lying to his principal, in which case he is liable in the ordinary way: see, e.g. *Mahesan v Malaysia Government Officers Co-operative Housing Society Ltd* [1979] A.C. 374; and *Daraydan Holdings Ltd v Solland International Ltd* [2004] EWHC 622 (Ch); [2005] Ch. 119.

299 See *Mahesan v Malaysia Government Officers Co-operative Housing Society Ltd* [1979] A.C. 374 at 381. If none, for example if the attempt to bribe is unsuccessful, there is therefore no liability: *Chancery Client Partners Ltd v MRC 957 Ltd* [2016] EWHC 2142 (Ch); [2016] Lloyd's Rep. F.C. 578.

300 *Mahesan v Malaysia Government Officers Co-operative Housing Society Ltd* [1979] A.C. 374 at 383, per Lord Diplock. The statements in *Novoship (UK) Ltd v Mikhaylyuk* [2012] EWHC 3586 (Comm) at [108]; and *Motortrak Ltd v FCA Australia Pty Ltd* [2018] EWHC 990 (Comm) at [134]–[136] that there is an "irrebuttable" presumption of loss in the amount of the bribe should, it is suggested, be taken with some scepticism.

301 *Industries & General Mortgage Co Ltd v Lewis* [1949] 2 All E.R. 573; *Petrotrade Inc v Smith* [2000] 1 Lloyd's Rep. 486; *Fyffes Group Ltd v Templeman* [2000] 2 Lloyd's Rep. 643.

302 For example, if he can show a specific way in which the agreement negotiated by the corrupt agent is less advantageous to him than a contract negotiated at arm's length. See, e.g. *Fyffes Group Ltd v Templeman* [2000] 2 Lloyd's Rep. 643.

303 *Corporación National del Cobre de Chile v Sogemin Metals Ltd* [1997] 1 W.L.R. 1396.

to pay over the amount of the bribe to the principal[304] on the basis that they are regarded as having been unjustly enriched by the amount of it.[305] But the claims for damages and for recoupment of the amount of the bribe are alternative: the principal must elect which to exercise.[306]

---

304 Agent: see, e.g. *Boston Deep Sea Fishing Co v Ansell* (1888) 39 Ch. D. 339 and Briber: see *Fyffes Group Ltd v Templeman* [2000] 2 Lloyd's Rep. 643.

305 The agent because he should not have taken the bribe in the first place: the briber because he presumably gained at least to the extent of the bribe.

306 *Mahesan v Malaysia Government Officers Co-operative Housing Society Ltd* [1979] A.C. 374; see A. Tettenborn, "Bribery, Corruption and Restitution-The Strange Case of Mr Mahesan" (1979) 95 L.Q.R. 68; and C. Needham, "Recovering the Profits of Bribery" (1979) 95 L.Q.R. 532.

CHAPTER 18

TRESPASS TO LAND AND DISPOSSESSION

TABLE OF CONTENTS

1. THE NATURE OF TRESPASS

Definition of trespass Trespass to land consists of any unjustifiable intrusion by one person upon land in the possession of another. The slightest crossing of the boundary is sufficient. "If the defendant place a part of his foot on the plaintiff's land unlawfully, it is in law as much a trespass as if he had walked half a mile on it".[1] But though an actual or intending intruder may be enjoined, the courts cannot by injunction create an exclusion zone around the boundary.[2] 18-01

Examples of trespass It is a trespass to remove any part of the land in the possession of another or any part of a building (or other erection) which is attached to the soil so as to form part of the realty. So a landlord who removes the doors and windows of a house in the possession of his tenant commits a trespass,[3] but there is no trespass if he has the supply of gas and electricity cut off so as to compel the tenant to leave the house.[4] It is also a trespass to place anything on or in land in the 18-02

---

[1] *Ellis v Loftus Iron Co* (1874) L.R. 10 C. & P. 10 at 12.

[2] *Patel v Patel* [1988] 2 F.L.R. 179.

[3] *Lavender v Betts* [1942] 2 All E.R. 72.

[4] *Perera v Vandiyar* [1953] 1 W.L.R. 672. By the Protection from Eviction Act 1977 s.1 it is an offence unlawfully to evict or harass residential occupiers or to re-enter leasehold premises without court order. But breach of these duties does not give rise to an action for compensation: *McCall v Abelesz* [1976] Q.B. 585. Criminal compensation may be available: *R. v Bokhari* (1974) 59 Cr. App. R. 303. An injunction is available for breach of s.3 of the Act as a tort: *Warder v Cooper* [1970] Ch.

possession of another, such as fixing air conditioning equipment into his wall,[5] entering land below the surface by mining or otherwise,[6] or growing a creeper up his wall.[7] While dumping rubbish on another's land is trespass, causing land to become fouled by a discharge of oil into a navigable river is not.[8] Equally, one who has a right of entry upon another's land and acts in excess of his right[9] or after his right has expired, is a trespasser;[10] and a person who, without authorisation, enters an area that has been designated a safety zone by a public authority, is also a trespasser.[11] Every continuance of a trespass is a fresh trespass in respect of which a new cause of action arises from day to day as long as the trespass continues. So one who built on the claimant's land some buttresses to support a road and paid damages in an action for trespass was held liable in damages in a second action for not removing the buttresses after notice.[12]

18-03 **Trespass in the air-space above land** It may be a trespass to invade the air-space above land.[13] Intrusion into air-space at any height, is not automatically wrongful, but it is clear that it is a wrong where such air-space is necessary for the full use of land below.[14] The earlier authorities were reviewed in *Kelsen v Imperial Tobacco Co (of Great Britain and Ireland) Ltd*.[15] There, an advertising sign erected by the defendants projected some four inches into the air-space of a neighbouring occupier and McNair J held this to be a trespass, and not a nuisance,[16] granting a mandatory injunction for removal.[17] The limits of this decision should, however, be noted. So, although it is not a trespass to fly over private property at a reasonable and safe height,[18] this does not mean that *all* intrusions by low-flying aircraft are justifiable.

18-04 **Possession of air-space over leased land** Whether under a lease of the surface the possession of the air-space will pass, so as to render the lessee the proper person to sue for a trespass upon it, depends on the construction of the lease. In *Gifford v Dent*,[19] it was held that the tenant of the forecourt had possession so as to sue for a

495. The Housing Act 1988 ss.27–29, gives a prescribed measure of damages for unlawful eviction and extends the offence of harassment.

5 *Eaton Mansions (Westminster) Ltd v Stinger Compania de Inversion SA* [2011] EWCA Civ 607; [2011] H.L.R. 42.

6 See paras 18-16 and 18-71.

7 *Simpson v Weber* (1925) 41 T.L.R. 302.

8 *British Waterways Board v Severn Trent Water Ltd* [2001] EWCA Civ 276; [2002] Ch. 25. See paras 18-08 and 19-02 for the difference between trespass and nuisance.

9 e.g., unreasonable user of the highway: *Cambridge City Council v Traditional Cambridge Tours Ltd* [2018] EWHC 1304 (QB); [2018] L.L.R. 458.

10 *Hillen v ICI (Alkali) Ltd* [1936] A.C. 65.

11 *Sheffield City Council v Fairhall* [2017] EWHC 2121 (QB); [2018] R.T.R. 11; [2018] Env. L.R. 12 at [68].

12 *Holmes v Wilson* (1839) 10 A. & E. 503; *Konskier v Goodman Ltd* [1928] 1 K.B. 421.

13 See *Laiqat v Majid* [2005] EWHC 1305 (QB); [2005] N.P.C. 81.

14 *Anchor Brewhouse Developments Ltd v Berkley House (Docklands Developments) Ltd* (1987) 2 E.G.L.R. 173.

15 [1957] 2 Q.B. 334.

16 If damage and interference with user can be proved, the wrong may be an actionable nuisance.

17 cf. *Tollemache & Cobbold Breweries v Reynolds* (1983) 268 E.G. 52 (injunction to remove eaves refused, but declaration given that the complainant could carry out remedial work at his own cost).

18 *Bernstein v Skyviews and General Ltd* [1978] Q.B. 479.

19 [1926] W.N. 336.

trespass committed by the tenant of the second floor in hanging a sign which projected over the forecourt. And in *Kelsen v Imperial Tobacco Co (of Great Britain and Ireland) Ltd*, McNair J could "find nothing in this lease which displaces the prima facie conclusion which one would otherwise reach that the air-space above the demised premises is part of the premises conveyed".[20]

Aircraft Section 76(1) of the Civil Aviation Act 1982 provides that no action shall lie in respect of trespass by reason only of the flight of aircraft over any property at a height above the ground which, having regard to wind, weather and all the circumstances of the case, is reasonable, or of the ordinary incidents of such flight. Section 76(2) further provides that where material loss or damage[21] is caused to any person or property on land or water by, or by a person in, or an article or person falling from, an aircraft while in flight,[22] taking off[23] or landing, then unless the loss or damage was caused or contributed to by the negligence of the person by whom it was suffered, damages in respect of the loss or damage shall be recoverable without proof of negligence or intention or other cause of action as if the loss or damage had been caused by the wilful act, neglect or default of the owner of the aircraft. This part of the Act applies only to liability for civil (not military) aircraft.[24] **18-05**

Intention or negligence in the defendant It is no defence that the trespass was due to a mistake of law or fact, provided the physical act of entry was voluntary. Thus there will be liability where the boundary between the claimant's and the defendant's land is ill-defined and the defendant, in mowing his own grass by mistake mows some of the claimant's,[25] and when a master of hounds' pack enters prohibited ground where, knowing of the risk of entry, the master negligently failed to prevent an entry.[26] In short, as Aikenhead J has made clear, "a negligent incursion on to, and damage of, a claimant's land or property can in law be a trespass".[27] **18-06**

Entry without intention or negligence If the entry is involuntary—that is, if it is committed unintentionally and without negligence—no liability is incurred.[28] Thus, the High Court of Australia has held that falling onto railway tracks in an epileptic fit is no trespass.[29] **18-07**

20 [1957] 2 Q.B. 334 at 341. See also *Davies v Yadegar* (1990) 22 H.L.R. 232.

21 Which includes, in relation to persons, loss of life and personal injury: s.105.

22 "Flight" is not confined to lateral travel from one fixed point to another. It may refer to an aircraft that takes off, flies to a certain point (for, say, reconnaissance) and then returns to the same place from which it took off: *Peires v Bickerton's Aerodromes Ltd* [2017] EWCA Civ 273; [2017] 1 W.L.R. 2865 at [48]–[49].

23 This seems only to include that period after the aircraft has come to its take-off position: *Blankley v Godley* [1952] 1 All E.R. 436.

24 Civil Aviation Act 1982 Pt III.

25 *Basely v Clarkson* (1682) 3 Lev. 37.

26 *League Against Cruel Sports Ltd v Scott* [1986] Q.B. 240. A pack master is also liable vicariously for other members of the hunting party. However, if an owner does not prohibit entry, there may be an implied licence. See para.18-54 for licence coupled with interest, e.g. to kill and take deer.

27 *Network Rail Infrastructure Ltd v Conarken Group Ltd* [2010] EWHC 1852 (TCC); [2010] B.L.R. 601 at [67] (affirmed in relation to the negligence issue: [2011] EWCA Civ 644; [2011] B.L.R. 462).

28 *Smith v Stone* (1647) Style 65.

29 *Public Transport Commission of NSW v Perry* (1977) 14 A.L.R. 273.

18-08 **Trespass distinguished from nuisance** Trespass differs from nuisance in that it is a direct as opposed to a consequential infringement of another's right, and is actionable without proof of damage, whereas damage must be proved in nuisance.[30] Thus, if a defendant throws rubbish onto the land of another, or if he sends the stinking water in his yard into his neighbour's cellar,[31] these are acts of trespass. But if a defendant causes such material to pass on the claimant's land merely as the result of the exercise of his own rights of property, as where he fixes a spout on his roof, whereby the rain-water is discharged on to the claimant's land,[32] or allows the branches or roots of his trees to spread over his boundary,[33] or a game of cricket results in the escape of balls hit over the boundary,[34] these are acts of nuisance, not trespass. Equally, in *British Waterways Board v Severn Trent Water Ltd*[35] the Court of Appeal made it clear that a trespass action may be brought by the riparian right owner in respect of the direct fouling of a river, notwithstanding that an action would not lie in respect of the fouling of adjoining land, the crucial element being the directness of the invasion.

18-09 **Trespass lies without damage** To support an action of trespass it is not necessary that there should have been any actual damage.[36] The fact that trespass is actionable per se has enabled the action of trespass to be used for the purpose of settling title through actions of ejectment, though today such questions may also be decided by a declaratory judgment. The reason for this principle seems to be that acts of direct interference with another's possession are likely to lead to breaches of the peace and the policy of the law therefore demands that the claimant be relieved from the requirement of proving damage. So where the owners of an industrial enterprise anticipate the commission of trespass by environmental protestors they can be granted an interim injunction to prevent such trespass.[37] Where entry is merely threatened, a quia timet injunction is the appropriate remedy,[38] though in cases where the would-be protestors are persons unknown, such injunctions can only be granted with some caution on the part of the courts. Quite how much caution must be exercised is unclear. In one case in which various fracking companies reasonably anticipated that various protest groups would seek to disrupt their activities, the Court of Appeal was insistent that a quia timet injunction could only be obtained where its terms were very clear and precise so that a member of the public could, without having to seek legal advice, understand exactly what was prohibited. The court in so saying set very strict limits according to which an injunction could be issued against persons unknown.[39] Within months of that case being

---

30 See para.19-02. But if damage is caused, it may make no difference if the action is framed in trespass or nuisance: *Home Brewery Co v William Davis & Co (Loughborough) Ltd* [1987] Q.B. 339.

31 *Preston v Mercer* (1656) Hardr. 61.

32 *Reynolds v Clarke* (1725) 2 Ld. Ray. 1399.

33 *Smith v Giddy* [1904] 2 K.B. 448; *Lemmon v Webb* [1895] A.C. 1.

34 *Miller v Jackson* [1977] Q.B. 966.

35 [2001] EWCA Civ 276; [2002] Ch. 25.

36 See, e.g. *Anchor Brewhouse Developments v Berkley House (Docklands Developments) Ltd* (1987) 2 E.G.L.R. 173. Nor is the trifling nature of the trespass any defence: *Yelloly v Morley* (1910) 27 T.L.R. 20.

37 *Hampshire Waste Services Ltd v Intending Trespassers upon Chineham Incinerator* [2003] EWHC 1738 (Ch); [2004] Env. L.R. 9.

38 *Hampshire Waste Services Ltd v Intending Trespassers upon Chineham Incinerator* [2003] EWHC 1738 (Ch); [2004] Env. L.R. 9.

39 *Boyd v Ineos Upstream Ltd* [2019] EWCA Civ 515; [2019] 4 W.L.R. 100. The agreed judgment of

decided, however, a differently constituted Court of Appeal suggested (in another fracking case) that some relaxation of those limits was in order: specifically, contrary to what had been said in the first case, that: "although the court must be careful not to impose an injunction in wider terms than are necessary to do justice, the court is entitled to restrain conduct that is not in itself tortious or otherwise unlawful if it is satisfied that such a restriction is necessary in order to afford effective protection to the rights of the claimant in the particular case".[40] Where it is reasonable to anticipate a future trespass because protestors who have trespassed in the past have only modified the nature of their protests, injunctive relief for a prolonged period of time may be granted.[41] Equally, an interim injunction may be granted where travellers have set up camp (and caused damage to) various park and ride sites around a city in the past, and it is foreseeable that, if evicted from any given park and ride site, they will simply relocate to another.[42] Such injunctions may even be granted where the names of the travellers are unknown.[43] And where a potential threat is posed by something growing on the claimant's land which was planted there by the defendant, the claimant may seek a mandatory injunction to have the defendant remove it.[44]

2. Who May Sue for Trespass

Person in possession Trespass is actionable at the suit of the person in possession of land, or walkways over water (such as piers) which jut out from the land.[45] Such a person may claim damages or an injunction,[46] or both. A tenant in occupation can sue, but not a landlord, except in cases of injury to the reversion.[47] Similarly, a person in possession can sue although he is neither the owner nor derives title from the owner, and indeed may be in possession adverse to the owner. 18-10

Concurrent possession For the purposes of the tort of trespass to land, and for the purposes of possession, land and its subsoil and superstructures may be divided 18-11

the Court of Appeal set out (at [34]) six requirements: (1) a sufficiently real and imminent risk of trespass would have to exist; (2) it would have to be impossible to name the persons likely to commit the tort; (3) there would have to be the ability to give effective notice of the injunction (and for the method of such notice to be set out in the order); (4) the terms of the injunction would have to correspond to the threatened tort and not be so wide as to prohibit lawful conduct; (5) its terms would also have to be sufficiently clear and precise so as to enable persons potentially affected to know what they had not to do; (6) the injunction would have to have clear geographical and temporal limits.

40 *Cuadrilla Bowland Ltd v Persons Unkown* [2020] EWCA Civ 9; [2020] 4 W.L.R. 29 at [50], per Leggatt LJ (in an approved judgment of the entire court).

41 See *Wensley v Persons Unknown* [2014] EWHC 3702 (Ch) (granting a two-year injunction to restrain anti-fracking protestors from trespassing on rural land in Lancashire).

42 *Norfolk CC v Johnstone* [2020] EWHC 113 (QB).

43 *Kingston-Upon-Thames RLBC v Persons Unkown* [2019] EWHC 1903 (QB). But the terms of such injunctions must be proportionate to the threat posed and "the absence of any alternative sites … [is] a relevant factor in the proportionality exercise": *Bromley LBC v Persons Unknown* [2020] EWCA Civ 12; [2020] H.R.L.R. 6 at [69], per Coulson LJ.

44 *Nelson v Nicholson, The Independent,* 22 January 2001.

45 *Hounslow LBC v Devere* [2018] EWHC 1447 (Ch).

46 e.g. *John Trenberth v National Westminster Bank* (1980) 39 P. & C.R. 104. But the award of an injunction is subject to judicial discretion. cf. *Charrington v Simons & Co Ltd* [1971] 1 W.L.R. 598 at 603, per Russell LJ; *Patel v WH Smith (Eziot) Ltd* [1987] 1 W.L.R. 853. An injunction is prima facie available even if there is no damage.

47 See para.18-26.

in horizontal layers, as with apartment flats,[48] or where A possesses the pasturage on the surface while B possesses the peat beneath the surface.[49] A third person, C, could even be in possession of the minerals below the peat. Indeed, even this last possession may be sub-divided into separate possession of the upper and lower seams of the minerals.[50] Each of such parties will be entitled to sue in trespass or expel by force a stranger trespassing on the subject matter of his possession.[51] Anything attached to the soil, such as the herbage,[52] trees, underwood etc may be the subject of a separate possession, and the owner can maintain an action of trespass in respect of it. Movable fees are also known to the law of real property and freehold may exist subject to moving boundaries.[53] But the law of trespass is not confined to the protection of freehold and real property. Thus where statute has conferred exclusive rights over reserved burial plots and declared those rights to be personal estate, it has been held that an infringement of such a right is actionable as a trespass, including encroachments upon the surface of the plot in which there is such a right of property.[54]

18-12 **Owner of profit à prendre** The owner[55] of a profit à prendre can sue in trespass for any interference with the subject matter of his *profit*. So, the owner of an exclusive right of fishing can sue in trespass anyone who fishes in his fishery or otherwise interferes with it.[56] On the other hand, "an easement differs from a profit à prendre" and "although both may be classed under the head of servitudes, the owner of an easement cannot maintain trespass, the only remedies available to him for disturbance being by abatement or by an action for nuisance".[57]

18-13 **Evidence of possession** Possession means generally the occupation or physical control of land. The degree of physical control necessary to constitute possession may vary from one case to another, for "by possession is meant possession of that character of which the thing is capable".[58] "The type of conduct which indicates possession must vary with the type of land. In the case of vacant and unenclosed land which is not being cultivated there is little which can be done on the land to indicate possession".[59] In the case of a building, possession is evidenced by occupation, or, if the building is unoccupied, by possession of the key or other method of obtaining entry.[60] In the case of land without buildings, possession is shown by "acts

---

48 *Ramroop v Ishmael* [2010] UKPC 14.

49 *Wilson v Mackreth* (1766) 3 Bur. 1824.

50 As, e.g. in *Butterley Co v New Hucknall Colliery* [1910] A.C. 381.

51 *Cox v Glue* (1848) 5 C.B. 533.

52 *Richards v Davies* [1911] 1 Ch. 90. Note that cultivated crops are treated as mere chattels: *Evans v Roberts* (1826) 5 B.C. 829.

53 *Baxendale v Instow Parish Church* [1982] Ch. 14 (a moveable fee is an estate in land which from time to time changes its position, such as, in this case, the foreshore changed by recession or encroachment of sea).

54 *Reed v Madon* [1989] Ch. 408.

55 A possessory title probably suffices: *Mason v Clarke* [1955] A.C. 778 at 794, per Lord Simonds; but see at 806, per Lord Keith; and see *Lowe (Inspector of Taxes) v JW Ashmore* [1971] Ch. 545.

56 *Holford v Bailey* (1849) 13 Q.B. 426; *Nicholls v Ely Beet Sugar Factory* [1931] 2 Ch. 84.

57 *Paine & Co Ltd v St Neots Gas & Coke Co* [1939] 3 All E.R. 812 at 823, per Luxmoore LJ.

58 *Lord Advocate v Young* (1887) 12 App. Cas. 544 at 556, per Lord Fitzgerald.

59 *Wuta-Ofei v Mabel Danquah* [1961] 1 W.L.R. 1238 at 1243; *Ocean Estates v Norman Pinder* [1969] 2 A.C. 19.

60 *Jewish Maternity Society's Trustees v Garfinkle* (1926) 95 L.J.K.B. 766.

of enjoyment of the land itself",[61] such as building a wall upon it,[62] or taking grass from it.[63] The same is true where what is claimed is possession of the river bed or foreshore in tidal waters to which a boat has been moored, so long as the mooring can be shown to be sufficiently secure and that the boat would not float away by reason of wind or tide.[64] However, where there is a public right of way over the land in question, no adverse possession can be claimed (e.g. by stationing one's caravan and associated structures there for the requisite period of 12 years[65]). Evidence of possession of part of the land in question may be evidence of possession of the whole. "If you prove the cutting of timber in one part, I take that to be evidence to go to a jury to prove a right in the whole wood".[66]

In *Nata Lee Ltd v Abid*[67] the Court of Appeal emphasised the importance of a court taking a properly balanced approach to the assessment of whether a trespass has occurred. In this case, on the first day of the trial the judge had, by way of a case-management decision, excluded evidence garnered by the appellant's surveyor. He had done so largely for reasons associated with the late submission of this evidence. The question that arose was whether the decision to exclude the evidence fell within the case-management discretion enjoyed by first instance judges. In deciding that the decision to exclude the evidence fell outside this discretion, Briggs LJ did not dismiss as irrelevant the lateness of submission. Rather, he preferred to think in terms of the fact that, without this evidence, there was a "vitiating lack of balance in the judge's assessment" of evidence in the case such that "while the delay was serious and not satisfactorily explained, the balance ought to have come down in favour of admitting Mr Shattock's factual evidence".[68] This commitment to having proper evidence supplied by both parties on the question of whether a trespass has occurred, reflects closely the courts' commitment to hearing evidence from both sides on the often related question of whether a defendant has been in adverse possession.[69] 18-14

Proof of ownership is prima facie proof of possession.[70] That is, the presumption is that the person holding title to the land is in possession.[71] Yet even a long continued assertion of title, without proof of title, can be significant.[72] What is also of significance in this context is the facility within the Land Registration Act 2002[73] whereby a squatter may, after ten years adverse possession, apply to be registered as the legal proprietor of the land in question.[74] That said, if the squatter only secures 18-15

61 *Jones v Williams* (1837) 2 M. & W. 326 at 331.
62 *Every v Smith* (1857) 26 L.J. Ex. 344.
63 *Harper v Charlesworth* (1825) 1 B.C. 574.
64 *Port of London Authority v Ashmore* [2010] EWCA Civ 30; [2010] 1 All E.R. 1139 at [26], per Sir John Chadwick.
65 *R. (on the application of Smith) v Land Registry* [2010] EWCA Civ 200; [2011] Q.B. 413.
66 *Jones v Williams* (1837) 2 M. & W. 326 at 331, per Parke B. And see *Higgs v Nassauvian Ltd* [1975] A.C. 464.
67 [2014] EWCA Civ 1652; [2015] 2 P. & C.R. 3.
68 [2014] EWCA Civ 1652; [2015] 2 P. & C.R. 3 at [71].
69 See further, para.18-80.
70 *Hebbert v Thomas* (1835) 1 C.M. & R. 861 at 864, per Parke B.
71 *Jones v Chapman* (1847) 2 Ex. 803 at 821; *Lows v Telford* (1876) 1 App. Cas. 414 at 426.
72 *Fowley Marine (Emsworth) Ltd v Gafford* [1968] 2 Q.B. 618 at 849 and 853–854, per Russell and Willmer LJJ.
73 Sch.6 para.1(1).
74 Note that it is for the Land Registry, not the County Court, to decide in the first instance whether adverse possession has been acquired: *Swan Housing Association Ltd v Gill* [2012] EWHC 3129

such registration by virtue of a fraudulent application, or an application based on an innocent but erroneous claim about having satisfied the adverse possession requirements, then the register can be restored to its former state, once again recording the original proprietor's title.[75]

18-16 **Possession of minerals** Possession of the surface of land prima facie includes possession of the subjacent minerals also,[76] even though they be unopened, for possession of the surface prima facie operates to exclude others from access to the minerals. But that presumption is always liable to be rebutted by showing that the possession of the minerals is in fact in somebody else, for the minerals may be worked from the adjoining land, and apparently even a wrongdoer may, in the absence of fraud,[77] by driving levels through a whole seam of coal, acquire possession of the unworked coal within the limits to which the levels extend.[78] But the mere wrongful getting of neighbouring coal by a mine owner is not such a possession of the seam as to confer a title under the Statute of Limitations.[79]

18-17 **De facto possession** A person claiming as against the true owner cannot be said to have possession unless the true owner has been dispossessed.[80] In order to determine whether the acts of user do or do not amount to dispossession of the owner, the character of the land, the nature of the acts done on it and the intention of the squatter all fall to be considered.[81] Moreover, to found a claim in trespass, possession must be exclusive.[82] Accordingly, pasturing cattle on strips of grass at the side of a private road does not give the owner of the cattle possession of the strips, because the right of passage exercised by other persons prevents his possession from being exclusive.[83] In *Fowley Marine (Emsworth) Ltd v Gafford*,[84] the Court of Appeal held that the claimants had exclusive possession in a tidal creek and that the unpermitted acts of boat owners in mooring their craft in the creek did not amount to acts of concurrent possession, since those acts were not shown to be

(QB); [2013] 1 W.L.R. 1253 at [15], per Eady J.

75 *Baxter v Manion* [2011] EWCA Civ 120; [2011] 1 W.L.R. 1594. As to the power more broadly to rectify errors on the register, see Land Registration Act 2002 Sch.4.

76 *Smith v Lloyd* (1854) 9 Exch. 562 at 574, per Parke B. See *Bocardo SA v Star Energy UK Onshore Ltd* [2010] UKSC 35; [2011] 1 A.C. 380. Common law reserves to the Crown all gold and silver in mines: *The Case of Mines* (1567) 1 Plowd. 310.

77 *Bulli Coal Mining Co v Osborne* [1899] A.C. 351; *Oelkers v Ellis* [1914] 2 K.B. 139.

78 See *Ashton v Stock* (1877) 6 Ch. D. 719 at 726, per Hall VC.

79 *Ashton v Stock* (1877) 6 Ch. D. 719; *Thompson v Hickman* [1907] 1 Ch. 550.

80 See para.18-80.

81 *Buckinghamshire CC v Moran* [1990] Ch. 623. Slade LJ stressed that although the intention of the squatter is material to the question of dispossession, the intention of the owner as to future possible use is generally not material except to the extent that the squatter's knowledge of the owner's intention may bear on his *animus possidendi*: *Buckinghamshire CC v Moran* [1990] Ch. 623 at 639–640.

82 In *Marsden v Miller* (1992) 64 P.C.R. 239, the mere erection of a fence round an area of disputed land had failed to exclude all others from the land and was held not to give rise to such possession as was necessary to support an action for trespass.

83 *Coverdale v Charlton* (1878) 4 Q.B.D. 104. The same principle applies where the land in question is subject to a public right of way. The ongoing existence of this right of way will defeat any claim that the possession gained was exclusive: *R. (on the application of Smith) v Land Registry* [2010] EWCA Civ 200; [2011] Q.B. 413.

84 [1968] 2 Q.B. 618.

done with the intention to take possession.[85] In terms of understanding what is required by way of the trespasser's intention, the law was clarified by the decision of the House of Lords in *JA Pye (Oxford) Ltd v Graham*.[86] In that case, Lord Browne-Wilkinson indicated that possession requires two elements: factual possession and the intention to possess. In relation to the former he was clear that "an appropriate degree of physical control" suffices,[87] while with respect to the intention to possess he expressly approved[88] the dictum of Slade J in *Powell v McFarlane*[89] that there must be "intention, in one's own name and on one's own behalf, to exclude the world at large, including the owner with the paper title if he be not himself the possessor, so far as is reasonably practicable and so far as the processes of the law will allow".

Defence of jus tertii A de facto possession gives a right to retain the possession and undisturbed enjoyment as against all wrongdoers. It is not, however, sufficient as against the lawful owner. And one who alleged that he had an oral tenancy had, by virtue of s.40 of the Law of Property Act 1925[90] (which prevented him from proving his oral tenancy),[91] to respect the title of the owner. He who has such a possession may, just as may the lawful owner, use a reasonable degree of force in its defence.[92] He may sue in trespass anyone who disturbs his possession, and in such an action it is no answer for the defendant to show that the title and right to possession is in another person. *Jus tertii* is no defence to the action unless the defendant can show that the act complained of was done by the authority of the true owner.[93] Nor does it matter how recently the possession was acquired.[94] Where a trespass action is brought by a bare possessor, *jus tertii* cannot be raised to mitigate the damages payable. This is because possession is, as against a wrongdoer, prima facie evidence of title, and it cannot be displaced merely by showing that the possession was of recent origin and was not derived from any person who had title.[95] **18-18**

Trespasser A trespasser who enters and expels the person in possession does not obtain possession so as to enable him to maintain trespass against the evicted person seeking repossession unless the person expelled has submitted to the expulsion by delaying to re-expel the intruder within a reasonable time. In the absence of submis- **18-19**

85 [1968] 2 Q.B. 618 at 638, per Willmer LJ.

86 [2002] UKHL 30; [2003] 1 A.C. 419.

87 [2002] UKHL 30; [2003] 1 A.C. 419 at [41]. For these purposes, there is no fixed notion of an appropriate degree of control. Each case needs to be adjudged "bearing in mind the nature of the land": *Greenmanor Ltd v Laurence Pilford* [2012] EWCA Civ 756 at [27], per Etherton LJ; cf. *Chambers v Havering LBC* [2011] EWCA Civ 1576; [2012] 1 P. & C.R. 17.

88 [2002] UKHL 30; [2003] 1 A.C. 419 at [42].

89 (1979) 38 P. & C.R. 452.

90 See now the Law of Property (Miscellaneous Provisions) Act 1989 s.2.

91 *Delaney v TP Smith Ltd* [1946] 1 K.B. 393.

92 *Green v Goddard* (1704) 2 Salk. 641; *Weaver v Bush* (1798) 8 T.R. 78.

93 *Graham v Peat* (1801) 1 East 244; *Nicholls v Ely Beet Sugar Factory* [1931] 2 Ch. 84. In the case of Crown land *jus tertii* is available to intruders unless the claimant shows he is in occupation with the consent and privity of the Crown or that the title has passed to him by adverse possession: *Harper v Charlesworth* (1825) 4 B.C. 574 at 586–590.

94 *Catteris v Cowper* (1812) 4 Taunt. 547.

95 *Eastern Construction Co v National Trust Co* [1914] A.C. 197; *Glenwood Lumber Co v Phillips* [1904] A.C. 405. The possessor may have to account to the true owner for the damages recovered: *Eastern Construction Co v National Trust Co* [1914] A.C. 197 at 210.

sion and until the expiry of a reasonable time, expulsion by a mere trespasser does not divest the lawful occupier of possession.[96]

18-20 **Self-help by rightful owner** What will be considered to be without delay must depend upon all the circumstances of the case. In *Browne v Dawson*, a ten-day delay was considered to be a reasonable time. In *McPhail v Persons Unknown*,[97] it was said that "a trespasser may in any case be turned off land before he has gained possession, and he does not gain possession until there has been something like acquiescence in the physical fact of his occupation on the part of the rightful owner". But acquiescence may be inferred from delay, and self-help is a remedy to be safely employed only when the rightful owner acts as soon as he is aware of the wrongful intrusion.[98] One remedy, then, which a possessor has for an expulsion by a trespasser is at once to turn out the intruder and reinstate himself, but it is unlikely that the landowner may use force to this end.[99] He may break open the outer door, or use such force as is reasonably necessary (and not excessive) to effect an entry. Such an entry by the possessor is to be treated as if it were a forcible resistance of an intrusion upon a possession which he had never lost. But except in cases of emergency, the use of force will usually be inadvisable since legal process by order for possession is available with a minimum lapse of five days from service on unlawful occupiers, and in case of urgency a court may give leave for issue of an order within a lesser period of time.[100] One matter that requires clarification is whether art.8 of the European Convention on Human Rights has any bearing on applications by *private landowners* for possession orders. Clearly, squatters' living conditions, and therefore their private lives, will inevitably be affected by the grant of a possession order. In *Malik v Fassenfelt*,[101] it was simply assumed on appeal that art.8 was relevant. But since the point was not directly contested, Lord Toulson cautioned: "I do not think that it would be right in these circumstances to decide whether the judge was correct about the availability of article 8 as a potential defence to the claim [for a possession order]".[102] Lloyd LJ expressed a very similar view.[103]

---

[96] *Browne v Dawson* (1840) 12 A. & E. 624. In such a case the burden of proof is on the intruder to show that he is not a trespasser when the claimant asserts title and intention to resume possession: *Portland Managements Ltd v Harte* [1977] Q.B. 306.

[97] [1973] Ch. 447 at 456.

[98] cf. *Burton v Winters* [1993] 1 W.L.R. 1077 ("self-redress is a summary remedy which is justified only in clear and simple cases, or in an emergency": per Lloyd LJ at 1082). On the other hand, in cases where self-help would entail an act by the claimant that is prohibited by a restrictive covenant, the appropriate remedy is a mandatory injunction requiring the defendant to take the necessary remedial action: *Nelson v Nicholson*, *The Independent*, 22 January 2001.

[99] In *Malik v Fassenfelt* [2013] EWCA Civ 798; [2013] 3 E.G.L.R. 99 at [25] Sir Alan Ward noted, obiter, that "the landowner has the remedy of self-help but the Criminal Law Act 1977 has prevented the use of force to evict an occupier". As such, "[h]is opportunity to obtain immediate relief by resorting to self-help may be curtailed if the squatters refuse to leave without a fight."

[100] See the Civil Procedure Rules 1998 (SI 1998/3132) r.55. The position of an owner seeking to recover possession after expiration of a tenancy is very different. Generally he must proceed by court order. By the Protection from Eviction Act 1977 s.2, any right of re-entry or forfeiture can only be enforced by court order "while any person is lawfully residing in the premises or part of them".

[101] [2013] EWCA Civ 798; [2013] 3 E.G.L.R. 99.

[102] [2013] EWCA Civ 798; [2013] 3 E.G.L.R. 99 at [42].

[103] [2013] EWCA Civ 798; [2013] 3 E.G.L.R. 99 at [51].

Exclusive possession The leading case in this area is *Street v Mountford*.[104] Generally speaking, the intention of the parties to give exclusive possession to the occupant is evidenced by the terms of their agreement (unless the written agreement is a sham[105]) and such a letting of residential premises for a term of time, normally at a rent, ordinarily gives rise to a tenancy.[106] The question is not whether the parties or one of them were minded to give and take exclusive possession but whether the effect of their transaction is in fact the giving of exclusive possession.[107] The general effect of subsequent decisions of the House of Lords is that a tenancy is necessarily created where exclusive possession is in fact conferred, and the fact of such possession does not depend on what they say or how they describe the transaction but on the effect of their arrangement.[108] Where the agreement signed purports to evade the Rent Acts and avoids the language of "tenancy" the courts will simply look at whether, on its true construction, the agreement creates a right of exclusive possession.[109] An exception exists where access is reserved for genuine purposes, such as attendance or servicing.[110] A homeless person occupying temporary accommodation does not have exclusive occupation so as to give rise to a tenancy.[111] The same applies to hotel guests[112] and those who stay at a charitable almshouse: they are mere licensees whose occupation is a personal privilege as beneficiaries of the charity.[113] **18-21**

Lodgers and sub-tenants A lodger in a private house cannot sue in trespass, because possession remains in the landlord.[114] By contrast, a sub-tenant is one to whom rooms in a house are demised so that he becomes the actual tenant of those rooms. He therefore has possession and can sue in trespass.[115] The question of exclusive possession is one of fact to be decided according to the circumstances. Such factors as the access of the landlord's servants or the landlord's control of the outer door will be relevant. It is probable that the only practicable test is the exclusiveness of the occupier's possession. **18-22**

Licensees and third parties It would seem that exclusive possession as against the landlord is not conclusive of the tenant's possessory interest vis-à-vis third parties.[116] The terms of an occupational licence may give the licensee such control over access as to entitle him to the protection of the law of trespass against intruders. **18-23**

---

104 [1985] A.C. 809. The same principles apply to business premises: *London & Associated Investment Trust Plc v Calow* (1987) 53 P.C.R. 340.

105 See, e.g. *Skipton Building Society v Clayton* (1993) 66 P.C.R. 223.

106 The presumption of tenancy may be displaced by a declared intention not to create a legal relationship at all (see, e.g. *Colchester BC v Smith* [1991] Ch. 448; affirmed on other grounds: [1992] Ch. 421), or by circumstances, as where occupation is granted pursuant to a contract of employment (see, e.g. *Norris v Checksfield* [1991] 1 W.L.R. 1241).

107 *AG Securities v Vaughan; Antoniades v Villiers* [1990] 1 A.C. 417 at 458.

108 See *Bruton v London and Quadrant Housing Trust* [2000] 1 A.C. 406.

109 *Antoniades v Villiers* [1990] 1 A.C. 417; cf. *Mikeover Ltd v Brady* [1989] 3 All E.R. 618.

110 *AG Securities v Vaughan* [1990] 1 A.C. 417. See also *Stribling v Wickham* [1989] 27 E.G. 81.

111 *Westminster City Council v Clarke* [1992] 2 A.C. 288.

112 *Smith v Overseers of St Michael's, Cambridge* (1860) 3 E. & E. 383.

113 *Gray v Taylor* [1998] 1 W.L.R. 1093.

114 *Allan v Liverpool* (1874) L.R. 9 Q.B. 180 at 191, per Blackburn J; *Appah v Parncliffe Investments Ltd* [1964] 1 W.L.R. 1064.

115 *Lane v Dixon* (1847) 3 C.B. 776.

116 See para.18-57.

The typical lodger with non-exclusive possession has to be distinguished from the typical modern occupational licensee, since nowadays "a person who has no more than a licence may yet have possession of the land",[117] and the terms of the licence may confer a sufficient right of possession. In *Manchester Airport Plc v Dutton*,[118] the Court of Appeal held, by a majority, that the court had jurisdiction to grant a licensee an order for possession against trespassers even before the licensee was in de facto possession, if such an order was necessary to give effect to the licensee's right to occupy under the contract with the licensor.

18-24 **Servants** In the absence of an intention on the part of the owner to treat the occupier as a tenant, mere occupation of premises by those such as servants does not amount to possession even if their occupation is exclusive.[119] This presumption against exclusive possession by a servant may be compared with a bailee at will or a servant using his employer's movable property.[120] But it is only a presumption: an expression of contrary intention or the circumstances of the case may displace it.

18-25 **Public bodies** Whether public bodies authorised by commission or statute to construct and, from time to time, repair public works, or to control and regulate the repair of public highways, thereby acquire an interest in the soil of such works or highways, so as to entitle them to sue a trespasser causing physical damage thereto, is simply a question of intention to be deduced from the language of the commission or statute, as the case may be.[121]

18-26 **Reversioner** Although, in general, the only person who can sue for a trespass is the person who was in actual or constructive possession at the time the trespass was committed, an exception exists where the trespass has caused a permanent injury to the land affecting the reversionary interest. The reversioner may sue at once without waiting until his future estate falls into possession.[122] He may sue for any act involving a partial destruction of the freehold. But for an ordinary continuing trespass, even though committed under a claim of a right of way, the reversioner cannot sue.[123] He cannot sue for the erection of a temporary structure on his land, such as a hoarding erected to obstruct a window on his property for a year.[124] He can, however, sue for acts of trespass which, if acquiesced in, would result in the loss or gain of an easement.[125]

18-27 **Co-owners** One co-owner of land can only bring an action in trespass against the other if the latter has actually been ousted or dispossessed.[126] Each co-owner is

[117] *Hounslow LBC v Twickenham Garden Developments Ltd* [1971] Ch. 233 at 257, per Megarry J.
[118] [2000] Q.B. 133.
[119] *White v Bayley* (1861) 10 C. & B. (N.S.) 227; *Goudge v Broughton* [1929] 1 K.B. 103. See also para.18-92.
[120] See para.16-56 onwards.
[121] cf. *Duke of Newcastle v Clark* (1818) 8 Taunt. 602; with *Coverdale v Charlton* (1878) 4 Q.B.D. 104; and *Rolls v St George, Southwark* (1880) 14 Ch. D. 785.
[122] *Jones v Llanrwst Urban DC* [1911] 1 Ch. 393; *Mayfair Property Co v Johnston* [1894] 1 Ch. 508.
[123] *Baxter v Taylor* (1832) 4 B. & Ad. 72.
[124] *Cooper v Crabtree* (1828) 20 Ch. D. 589.
[125] See para.19-85.
[126] Though trespass depends on ouster by a co-owner, other illegitimate uses short of ouster may give rise to other liabilities, e.g. accounting for net profits received from a stranger.

entitled to possession of the whole land, so that if one turns the other off the land or part of it, it is a trespass.[127] If the common property or part of it is destroyed, there is an ouster. So, trespass lies by one co-owner against another who digs and carries away the soil.[128] It is not trespass, however, if one co-owner uses the land in the ordinary and natural way, as by cutting grass and making it into hay,[129] or working a coal mine.[130] In such a case the owner making the hay or working the mine must account for the profits. When there are co-owners of a wall, such as a party wall,[131] one owner can maintain trespass against the other if there is a simple destruction of the wall.[132] But if the wall has been destroyed with the intention of rebuilding it,[133] or the foundations have been temporarily removed with the object of replacing them,[134] there is no trespass. Trespass will only lie if one owner is ousted from possession of the wall, for example, if the wall is heightened and a building is placed so as to occupy the whole width of the top.[135] Special statutory procedures exist to facilitate the repair of party structures and the swift resolution of disputes relating to them.[136]

3. Trespass by Relation

Trespass by relation Historically, actual possession was for many purposes more highly favoured than property or the legal right to possession. Where, at the time of the commission of any trespass upon land, the owner happened to be out of possession, either by reason of his having been wrongfully ousted or by reason of his having neglected to enter into possession upon the accrual of his title, he was without remedy for such trespass. Over time, the injustice of not extending to the right to possession the remedies granted to those with bare possession were recognised, and a legal fiction was introduced whereby the party having the right to possession was, upon entry, deemed to have been in possession from the date when his right of entry accrued. This doctrine of possession by relation gradually achieved general application.[137] The courts, however, did not completely treat the right of possession as per se equivalent to possession; they still required that a claimant who sought to recover damages for a trespass committed while he was out of possession should, before the action was brought, go through the form of entry, or, of making a formal claim.[138] A claim for *mesne* profits—i.e. damages for wrongful occupancy of the land (usually assessed in terms of the reasonable rental value of the land)—being based on trespass by relation, also required an entry by the 18-28

127 *Murray v Hall* (1849) 7 C.B. 441; *Jacobs v Seward* (1872) L.R. 5 H.L. 464: putting a lock on a gate (not kept locked) is not enough.
128 *Wilkinson v Haygarth* (1846) 12 Q.B. 837.
129 *Jacobs v Seward* (1872) L.R. 5 H.L. 464; *Bull v Bull* [1955] 1 Q.B. 234 at 237.
130 *Job v Potton* (1875) L.R. 20 Eq. 84.
131 See Law of Property Act 1925 s.38 Sch.1 Pt V.
132 *Jones v Read* (1876) I.R. 10 C.L. 315.
133 *Cubitt v Porter* (1828) 8 B. & C. 257.
134 *Standard Bank of British South America v Stokes* (1878) 9 Ch. D. 68.
135 *Stedman v Smith* (1857) 8 E. & B. 1.
136 See the Party Wall etc. Act 1996 ss.3–5 and 10. The legislation does not apply to disputes about ownership.
137 Bl. Comm. 3 at 210; *Barnett v Earl of Guildford* (1855) 11 Exch. 19.
138 See *Dunlop v Macedo* (1891) 8 T.L.R. 43; *Southport Tramways v Gandy* [1897] 2 Q.B. 66.

claimant. However, this requirement does not now apply where the claim is joined with an action for the recovery of land.[139]

18-29 **Entry** A right to the immediate possession of land is converted into actual possession by entry upon any part of it, or by the making of a claim to it in its immediate neighbourhood. Merely putting a foot or any part of the person across the boundary is sufficient to constitute entry. Where the party entering does so under a right of entry, his entry upon any part of the land vests in him the possession of the whole of the land to which his title relates. He may thereafter sue the defendant for trespass. Alternatively, the party entitled to enter may simply make a claim for possession, and this will have the same effect. For it has been held that "the slightest acts by the person having title to the land ... indicating his intention to take possession, are sufficient to enable him to bring an action for trespass against a defendant".[140] Entry or claim by an agent is enough to vest the possession in the principal. The effect of this is that a person entitled to possession after entry, such as a mortgagee,[141] can sue for trespass committed at any time after his legal right of entry accrued, because he is deemed to have been in possession from that date and the wrongdoer becomes a trespasser by relation.[142] So, likewise, a landlord who is entitled to re-enter on the termination of a lease may after entry sue for any trespass committed after it came to an end.[143] By the Law of Property Act 1925 s.149(2), terms of years are "capable of taking effect at law or in equity" from the date fixed for the commencement of the term without entry. A mere agreement for a lease may entitle the tenant to sue in trespass in respect of an act committed after the agreed date for the start of the tenancy.[144]

18-30 **As between two persons in occupation title gives possession** The legal effect of entry by a person entitled is not in any way affected by the fact that another who, without title, was previously in possession persists in remaining upon the land concurrently with the true owner.[145] Thus, although two or more persons may be concurrently in possession as joint tenants or tenants in common, there can be no such thing as concurrent possession by two persons claiming adversely to one another.

4. JUSTIFICATION OF TRESPASS

18-31 **Justification of trespass** An entry is not a trespass if it is justifiable. Justification of the entry may be afforded either by operation of law, or by the act of the

---

139 See further para.18-74.

140 *Ocean Estates Ltd v Norman Pinder* [1969] 2 A.C. 19 at 25, per Lord Diplock.

141 *Citibank Trust Ltd v Ayivor* [1987] 1 W.L.R. 1157. By the Administration of Justice Act 1970 s.36, the court has a discretion to postpone possession by a mortgagee of a dwelling-house. Whether an equitable mortgagee has an inherent right to take possession is unclear, but such a mortgagee may be put into possession by court order: Law of Property Act 1925 s.90(1).

142 *Ocean Accident etc Co v Ilford Gas Co* [1905] 2 K.B. 493.

143 It has been held that to entitle the landlord in such circumstances the defendant must be in possession wrongfully and this is not the case where a tenant remains after breach of covenant, merely making the lease voidable, and before the landlord serves a writ or otherwise determines the lease: *Elliott v Boynton* [1924] 1 Ch. 236.

144 See *Walsh v Lonsdale* (1882) 21 Ch. D. 9 at 14; *Allhusen v Brooking* (1884) 26 Ch. D. 559 at 565.

145 *Jones v Chapman* (1847) 2 Exch. 803 at 821, per Maule J; approved in *Lows v Telford* (1876) 1 App. Cas. 414 at 426.

claimant or of his predecessors in title, where the entry is made under a right of easement[146] or of a profit à prendre, or under a licence, and a like rule applies where persons deviate on to private land because the owner of such land has obstructed a right of way adjacent thereto.[147] But at common law no right of entry or access to a neighbour's land or building exists for the purpose of repairing one's own property.[148] The legislature has now intervened, however, enabling the court to order access for preservation work on neighbouring land.[149]

(a) Licence to enter by law

Licence to enter given by law In certain cases the law gives a licence to enter against the consent of the possessor; as where someone enters by authority of the law.[150] Equally, a licence is given by law to go upon the adjoining land to abate a nuisance[151]; and an entry may be justified for the purpose of preventing the spread of fire.[152] If the claimant wrongfully deposits goods on the defendant's land, the defendant may lawfully go upon the claimant's land for the purpose of returning them.[153] A person cannot justify entering the land of another against his will for the purposes of sport,[154] or of following game straying from his own land over the boundary.[155] However, where a right to enter upon the claimant's land for certain legitimate purposes exists, and the defendant has abused that right by entering upon the land for other, illegitimate purposes, it is probable that the claimant will only be able to obtain an injunction in order to restrain the defendant from entering the land with a view to engaging in those illegitimate purposes.[156] **18-32**

Modern statutes Modern statutes have greatly added to those powers of entry recognised by the common law. Thus, by s.60 of the National Parks and Access to the Countryside Act 1949 a person exercising certain, statutory open-air recreation rights will not be treated as a trespasser. Equally, s.1(2) of the Access to Neighbouring Land Act 1992 is also of considerable importance since, following a successful application to the court, it allows "reasonably necessary repairs to one's own land" to be done if those repairs cannot be effected "without entry upon the servient land". Access is at the discretion of the court and subject to various safeguards and conditions.[157] The Party Wall etc. Act 1996 s.8, confers rights of entry in relation to the carrying out of work authorised under that Act. In *British Waterways Board v Severn Trent Water Ltd* it was recognised that a statute may **18-33**

146 There is no principle of law that an easement cannot be acquired by prescription where the use has been tolerated for the appropriate number of years by the landowner: *Mills v Silver* [1991] Ch. 271. cf. *Patel v WH Smith (Eziot) Ltd* [1987] 1 W.L.R. 853.

147 *Stacey v Sherrin* (1913) 29 T.L.R. 555.

148 *John Trenberth Ltd v National Westminster Bank Ltd* (1980) 39 P. & C.R. 104.

149 See the Access to Neighbouring Land Act 1992, para.18-33.

150 *Thomas v Sawkins* [1935] 2 K.B. 249.

151 See para.29-26.

152 *Cope v Sharpe* [1912] 1 K.B. 496.

153 *Rea v Sheward* (1837) 2 M. & W. 424.

154 *Paul v Summerhayes* (1878) 5 Q.B.D. 9; *League Against Cruel Sports Ltd v Scott* [1986] Q.B. 240; see para.18-06.

155 *Deane v Clayton* (1817) 7 Taunt. 489.

156 See the suggestion to this effect implicit in the judgment of Teare J in *RWE Npower Plc v Carrol* [2007] EWHC 947 (QB) at [25].

157 See s.2.

authorise certain acts that would otherwise constitute a trespass.[158] But whether a statute actually has this effect is ultimately a matter of statutory construction. By s.159 of the Water Industry Act 1991 the appellant had the power to "lay a relevant pipe ... in any land which is not in, under or over a street". The question was whether such a power carries with it the implied authority to discharge the contents of such a pipe. In the Court of Appeal, Peter Gibson LJ held that no such incidental power of discharge should be implied and that discharge into the respondent's canal required a licence from STW. There was nothing necessary about its discharge into the canal. Similarly, in another case where DEFRA performed statutory clean-up operations following an outbreak of foot and mouth disease but, in so doing, went beyond the limited powers granted to it under the Animal Health Act 1981, there was again an actionable trespass.[159] By contrast, there is no abuse of statutory power where a local authority enters land under s.178 of the Town and Country Planning Act 1990 in order to ensure compliance with an enforcement notice issued in connection with an unauthorised use of land.[160]

18-34 In *Manchester Ship Canal Co Ltd v United Utilities Water Plc*[161] the Supreme Court reaffirmed the principle recognised in *British Waterways Board v Severn Trent Water Ltd* that the Water Industry Act 1991 carried with it an implied right on the part of a sewerage undertaker to discharge surface water and certain treated effluents into private watercourses where the duties imposed under the Act could not be performed without continuing to discharge from existing outfalls. This did not mean, however, that the 1991 Act could be invoked in defence of discharges made through outfalls that had been constructed since the enactment of the statute.

18-35 **Police powers** The powers of entry held by the police are now contained in the Police and Criminal Evidence Act 1984, supplemented with a Code of Practice. Section 17 specifies the occasions on which a constable may enter premises to effect an arrest while s.18 details where entry to conduct a search after an arrest is permissible. But if the police search premises other than those belonging to the suspect, they will commit a trespass given that s.18 states that the premises in question must be "occupied or controlled by the person who is under arrest".[162] Section 32 allows entry to conduct a search upon arrest for an indictable offence and the Act also provides certain powers where premises are searched under authority of a warrant and lays down the conditions under which search warrants may be issued.

18-36 **Entry for recaption of goods at common law**[163] A person may, at common law, enter the claimant's land in order to recapture his goods if those goods were taken and put there by the wrongful act of the claimant himself.[164] But beyond this

158 [2001] EWCA Civ 276; [2002] Ch. 25.

159 *Secretary of State for the Environment, Food and Rural Affairs v Feakins* [2005] EWCA Civ 1513; [2007] B.C.C. 54. In similar vein see, *Manchester Ship Canal Co Ltd v United Utilities Water Plc* [2014] UKSC 40; [2014] 1 W.L.R. 2576.

160 *Challinor v Staffordshire CC* [2011] EWCA Civ 90.

161 [2014] UKSC 40; [2014] 1 W.L.R. 2576.

162 *Khan v Commissioner of Police of the Metropolis* [2008] EWCA Civ 723; (2008) 152(23) S.J.L.B. 31. See also *Cash v Chief Constable of Lancashire* [2008] EWHC 396 (Ch).

163 See para.29-14.

164 *Patrick v Colerick* (1838) 3 M. & W. 483.

proposition the common law is unclear. In *Anthony v Haney*,[165] Tindal CJ was of the opinion (obiter) that entry was permissible on the land of an innocent person where: (a) the goods came there by accident; (b) a thief took them to such land; or (c) the occupier refused to redeliver them. With regard to accidental presence, this would seem a reasonable allowance of law, but the justification would not extend to an owner of goods by whose wrong (for example, trespass) the goods came there. On the contrary, the occupier might detain pending compensation for any damage done. With regard to refusal to redeliver the Chief Justice thought that a positive refusal might be considered a conversion[166] "or at any rate the owner might in such case enter and take his property subject to the payment of any damage he might commit".[167] It is suggested that such a right can be asserted at least where the owner of goods is blameless with regard to their presence on the land and where he gives reasonable notice and an explanation of the facts before entering for recaption. But to enter without giving an opportunity for voluntary redelivery would be unjustifiable and therefore a trespass.

Rescue of chattels under statute The Tribunals, Courts and Enforcement Act 2007 came into force on 6 April 2014. Thereunder, the common law rules of rescuing goods have been replaced by a very limited statutory power to take goods in settlement of a debt[168]; but the Act does not operate retrospectively so that, in relation to goods distrained before the Act came into force, the common law applies.[169] The statute injects welcome clarity into this area of the law, but cuts back considerably a valuable self-help remedy. 18-37

Where original possession was lawfully acquired One cannot justify entering onto the claimant's land to retake goods, the original possession of which was lawfully acquired, merely because he converts them.[170] A tenant who has given up possession of premises cannot justify a subsequent entry for the purpose of removing a chattel which he had left behind.[171] He ought to have removed it while he had a right to the land; and indeed where the incoming tenant, or landlord merely declines to put himself to the trouble of delivering it, and refuses permission to its owner to enter and take it, it has been doubted whether the owner has any remedy, unless the refusal can be construed as a conversion.[172] The problem will not arise if the occupier by contract or licence permits the entry, though it should be noted that by the Consumer Credit Act 1974[173] such rights of entry and seizure are not permissible in contracts of hire purchase or conditional sale. 18-38

165 (1832) 8 Bing. 186.
166 By the Torts (Interference with Goods) Act 1977 s.11(3) denial of title is not of itself conversion, but denial and unconditional refusal to deliver remain evidence of conversion.
167 *Anthony v Haney* (1832) 8 Bing. 186 at 192–193.
168 Tribunals, Courts and Enforcement Act 2007 s.65(1), (2)(d); Sch.12 para.66.
169 Tribunals, Courts and Enforcement Act 2007 s.66.
170 Y.B. 9 Edw. 4, 35, pl.10.
171 *Wilde v Waters* (1855) 24 L.J.C.P. 193.
172 *Wilde v Waters* (1855) 24 L.J.C.P. 193 at 195. The refusal to permit entry is not of itself conversion, but the occupier may convert the goods by actually denying title or evincing a determination to retain permanently.
173 s.90(1).

18-39 **Trespass ab initio** Where a person having entered upon land under an authority given by law subsequently abuses that authority, he becomes a trespasser ab initio, his misconduct relating back so as to make his original entry tortious.[174] Where a person enters premises for a purpose partly lawful and partly unlawful, for example, in order to seize goods or documents some of which are lawfully removable and others not, he becomes a trespasser ab initio in respect of the unlawful seizure only.[175] A person only becomes a trespasser ab initio if he commits an act of positive misfeasance. Mere nonfeasance, such as omitting to pay his bill at an inn or refusing to deliver up a distress upon tender of the sum due,[176] is not enough. The doctrine of trespass ab initio has received some judicial disparagement but as yet stands unaffected by statutory abrogation[177] or judicial modification.[178] And with regard to the vastly increased number of powers of entry by public officials as well as the police powers of entry, it is thought that the doctrine has some considerable surviving utility.[179]

(b) Justification under right of way and easement

18-40 **Justification under right of way** The commonest case of justification is the exercise of a right of way. Any user of a way in excess of the right of the party using it will render him a trespasser; it is, therefore, material in each case to determine the extent of the right.[180] For example, the court may have to decide whether a right of way over residential property granted in favour of neighbouring business premises carries with it, not just a right of way in favour of the owner of the business premises, but also, by implication, a right of way in favour of his customers.[181] In *Mills v Silver*,[182] the defendants put down some 700 tons of stone along a rough track over which they were entitled to a right of way; they were held liable in trespass on the ground that converting the track into a stone road went well beyond mere repair and was accordingly inconsistent with the extent of the particular prescriptive right enjoyed.

18-41 **Private way** Private rights of way may be either general or limited. Where the right is created by express grant or by Act of Parliament, the extent of the right will depend upon the actual terms of the grant or Act. If the terms be general, the purposes for which the way may be used will be general. The user will not be

---

174 Bl. Comm., Vol.3, 213.

175 *Harvey v Pocock* (1843) 11 M. & W. 740; *Canadian Pacific Wine Co v Tulley* [1921] 2 A.C. 417.

176 *West v Nibbs* (1847) 4 C.B. 172. In the *Six Carpenters case* (1610) 8 Rep. 146a—in which the carpenters ordered then consumed wine they did not pay for—it was held (at 146b) that a mere omission does not give rise to a trespass ab initio: "not paying for the wine, the defendants shall not be trespassers, for the denying to pay for it is no trespass, and therefore they cannot be trespassers ab initio."

177 Although s.3(6) of the Access to Neighbouring Land Act 1992 prevents the doctrine from applying to persons entering by virtue of an access order made under that Act.

178 *Chic Fashions (West Wales) Ltd v Jones* [1968] 2 Q.B. 299. Lord Denning MR was of the opinion that "the *Six Carpenters'* Case was a by-product of the old forms of action. Now that they are buried, it can be interred with their bones". The doctrine has no application to burglary under the Theft Act 1968: *R. v Collins* [1972] 1 Q.B. 710.

179 See, e.g. *Cinnamond v British Airports Authority* [1980] 1 W.L.R. 582 at 588.

180 *Harris v Flower* (1905) 74 L.J. Ch. 127; *Evelyn v Isis Housing Co-operative* [2017] EWCA Civ 130.

181 *Greatorex v Newman* [2008] EWCA Civ 1318; [2008] N.P.C. 132.

182 [1991] Ch. 271. See also *Jobson v Record* [1997] N.P.C. 56.

restricted to access at the date of the grant.[183] And a successor in title to a grant holder may even, by operation of proprietary estoppel, take advantage of that right of way without fear of trespass liability where the relevant landowner acquiesces in a representation that such a right would be held by the successor.[184] The extent of the right depends on the construction of the grant, but it may be necessary to look at the surrounding circumstances to arrive at the true construction.[185] Where a right of way or other easement is claimed by prescription, the general rule is that the extent of the right is to be gathered from the user, but it will not necessarily be limited by the actual user proved. "You must generalise to some extent."[186] Proof of user for one class of purposes may be evidence of a right of user for another class of purposes not involving a substantially greater burden on the servient tenement.[187] A starting point and a finishing point are essential to the claim of a private way;[188] but if those points are clear, the intermediate track need not necessarily be defined.[189]

Public way According to long-standing authority the right of the public in respect of a highway was limited to the use of it for the purpose of passing and repassing and for such other reasonable purposes as it is usual to use the highway; if a member of the public used it for any other purpose than that of passing and repassing he would be a trespasser.[190] Thus, where the defendant was the owner of a grouse moor crossed by a highway, the soil of which was vested in him, and the claimant on the occasion of a grouse drive went upon the highway for the purpose of interfering with the defendant's right of shooting, it was held that the claimant was a trespasser.[191] **18-42**

Meetings on the highway The rights of the public on highways have undergone significant extension as a result of *DPP v Jones*,[192] in which the House of Lords held that it is not the case that a member of the public who uses the highway for a purpose other than that of passing and repassing, or any ancillary purpose, will necessarily thereby become a trespasser. In particular, it was held that the broad proposition that the public have no right of holding public meetings on the highway, no longer represents the law. The defendants had been convicted of taking part in a "trespassory assembly" contrary to ss.14A–14C of the Public Order Act 1986. Since liability under these provisions turns on exceeding "the limits of the public's **18-43**

183 *Watts v Kelson* (1870–71) L.R. 6 Ch. 166 at 169, per Romilly MR; *South Eastern Ry v Cooper* [1924] 1 Ch. 211.

184 *Valentine v Allen* [2003] EWCA Civ 915.

185 *Todrick v Western National Omnibus Co* [1934] 1 Ch. 190 at 205–207; rev'd on other grounds [1934] 1 Ch. 561. cf. *White v Grand Hotel, Eastbourne Ltd* [1913] 1 Ch. 113. On construing the grant against the buyer, see *St Edmundsbury Ipswich Diocesan Board of Finance v Clark (No.2)* [1975] 1 W.L.R. 468.

186 *Cowling v Higginson* (1838) 4 M. & W. 245 at 257. See further *London Tara Hotel Ltd v Kensington Close Hotel Ltd* [2011] EWCA Civ 1356; [2012] 2 All E.R. 554.

187 *Williams v James* (1867) L.R. 2 C. & P. 577 at 580; *Wimbledon etc v Dixon* (1875) 1 Ch. D. 362 at 371.

188 See *Todrick v Western National Omnibus Co* [1934] 1 Ch. 190.

189 *Wimbledon etc v Dixon* (1875) 1 Ch. D. 362 at 369.

190 *Iveagh v Martin* [1961] 1 Q.B. 232 at 273.

191 *Harrison v Duke of Rutland* [1893] 1 Q.B. 142; *Hickman v Maisey* [1900] 1 Q.B. 752. Cf. *Randall v Tarrant* [1955] 1 W.L.R. 255, where a motorist parked his car and then trespassed on an adjoining field, the Court of Appeal distinguished *Hickman v Maisey* and held that the trespass was not so closely bound up with the parking as to make the motorist a trespasser on the highway.

192 [1999] 2 A.C. 240.

right of access" the conviction necessarily depends upon the assumption that the defendants, who had participated in a peaceful and non-obstructive demonstration upon a highway, had thereby committed a trespass by using the highway for a purpose other than that of passing and repassing. The majority denied the validity of that assumption,[193] though certain members of the majority emphasised that not every reasonable, peaceful, and non-obstructive activity on the highway would henceforth be lawful. All the circumstances would need to be taken into account, including the predominant purpose of the participants.[194] Accordingly, although the decision in *DPP v Jones* represents a significant change of principle in relation to the use of a highway, the question whether or not a particular user exceeds the public right will inevitably remain predominantly a question of fact; and the rights of landowners may well turn out not to have been reduced substantially.[195] Misuse of the highway apart from the law of trespass may attract liability in public nuisance.[196] And if persons meet to picket premises by the highway, that may amount to a trespass, at least where the picket is not within the statutory immunity accorded to actions in furtherance of a trade dispute.[197]

18-44 **Water** There is no general right in the public to pass over the foreshore for the purpose of bathing in the sea.[198] There may however be an exception in relation to fishing and navigation in the sea that covers the foreshore at high tide.[199] Furthermore, an exclusive right to gather shellfish from the foreshore may be acquired by prescription, but that exclusive right will not extend to sandbanks that subsequently (and fairly suddenly) become attached to the foreshore when channels that had formerly separated those sandbanks from the foreshore silt up.[200] To allow the established prescriptive right to be extended over the sandbanks in this way would be tantamount to conferring an exclusive right over new territory by prescription without there being the requisite long-use that characterises such rights. It would, without proper legal foundation, eclipse overnight the right held by members of the public to take shellfish from those sandbanks.[201] There is no public right to enter the foreshore for the collection of sea-coal cast there from submarine outcrops.[202] There is no right to put down permanent moorings in tidal waters where the bed soil is privately owned.[203] Though public rights of navigation have been established from time immemorial over many navigable rivers, there is no public right at common law to tow on the banks of a navigable river,[204] and the public cannot acquire, by prescription, the statutory right to navigate a river.[205]

---

[193] [1999] 2 A.C. 240 at 257.
[194] [1999] 2 A.C. 240 at 257 at 281 and 286–7, per Lords Clyde and Hutton.
[195] There is no suggestion in *DPP v Jones* that the actual decisions in *Harrison v Duke of Rutland* and *Hickman v Maisey*, were wrong.
[196] See para.19-181 onwards.
[197] cf. *Hubbard v Pitt* [1976] Q.B. 142 (picket of estate agent's office as political protest).
[198] *Blundell v Catterall* (1821) 5 B. & A. 268.
[199] *Llandudno Urban DC v Woods* [1899] 2 Ch. 705.
[200] *Loose v Lynn Shellfish Ltd* [2016] UKSC 14; [2017] A.C. 599.
[201] *Loose v Lynn Shellfish Ltd* [2016] UKSC 14; [2017] A.C. 599 at [73].
[202] *Alfred F Beckett v Lyons* [1967] Ch. 449.
[203] *Fowley Marine (Emsworth) Ltd v Gafford* [1968] 2 Q.B. 618 (though there is a right to navigate and anchor temporarily). The same rules apply to tidal stretches of canals: see *Moore v British Waterways Board* [2013] EWCA Civ 73; [2013] Ch. 488.
[204] *Ball v Herbert* (1789) 3 T.R. 253.
[205] *Att Gen (ex rel. Yorkshire Derwent Trust Ltd) v Brotherton* [1992] 1 A.C. 425, construing s.31(1) of

Justification under easements of other descriptions There are also a variety of easements under which a person may have a right to do some act on the land of another other than that of merely passing across it, but short of giving him exclusive possession.[206] Thus, the owner of a house may have an easement to hang lines across his neighbour's yard for the purpose of drying linen.[207] Equally, the owner of a public house may have an easement to erect a signboard on the adjoining land,[208] or a fascia on the adjoining house.[209] And a statutory water undertaker may have an easement to maintain a water main beneath the land of the servient tenement,[210] while the right to park cars can also amount to an easement in some circumstances.[211] On the other hand, where what is claimed amounts to a right to exclusive and unrestricted possession, it cannot be an easement within s.62 of the Law of Property Act 1925. In *Hanina v Morland*,[212] the defendant's claim in respect of the use of the claimant's flat rooftop was effectively a claim to a right of unrestricted, exclusive possession which could never be an easement since it was inconsistent with any notion of a dominant and servient tenement. An owner with a right of support by a servient tenement may enter it "and take the necessary steps to ensure the support continues by effective repairs".[213] Similar ancillary rights attach to repairs of watercourses and drains,[214] even though on general principle a dominant owner has no duty to repair. Where the right is expressed in terms of a right to enter the claimant's land for the purposes of installing, repairing, renewing, maintaining, cleansing or repairing conduits laid across that land, they must be read restrictively. As such, if there is an existing pipe which functions only imperfectly, this does not mean that there is a right to lay an alternative pipe following a completely different course across the claimant's land in the hope that it would function better.[215] But if the owner of a plot of land sells part of it to a property developer, yet retains that part of the plot which lies between the land sold and a range of public utilities running beneath the main road, there will be an implied easement of necessity permitting the owner of the land sold for development to dig up part of the retained land in order to install connections to those utilities.[216] So far as the servient tenement owner is concerned, he may not do 18-45

the Highways Act 1980.

206 *Grigsby v Melville* [1972] 1 W.L.R. 1355 (exclusive occupation of cellar).

207 *Drewell v Towler* (1832) 3 B. & Ad. 735.

208 *Hoare v Metropolitan Board of Works* (1874) L.R. 9 Q.B. 296; *Moody v Steggles* (1879) 12 Ch. D. 261.

209 *Francis v Hayward* (1883) 22 Ch. D. 177.

210 *Bate v Affinity Water Ltd* [2019] EWHC 3425 (Ch).

211 *London and Blenheim Estates v Ladbroke Retail Parks* [1992] 1 W.L.R. 1278 at 1285–1288 (not considered on appeal in [1994] 1 W.L.R. 31).

212 (2000) 97(47) L.S. Gaz. 41.

213 *Bond v Nottingham Corp* [1940] Ch. 429 at 439. Easements of repair may also, occasionally, impose positive obligations—such as the duty to construct and maintain a boundary fence—on the part of the servient owner. But such easements will be rare, and in one case the Court of Appeal specifically left open the question of whether any such easement can be created by express grant in *Churston Golf Club Ltd v Haddock* [2019] EWCA Civ 544; [2019] 4 W.L.R. 60.

214 *Peter v Daniel* (1848) 5 C.B. 568; *Beeston v Weate* (1856) 5 E. & B. 986; but for the limits of ancillary rights see *White v Taylor (No.2)* [1969] 1 Ch. 150; and *Martin v Childs* [2002] EWCA Civ 283.

215 *Martin v Childs* [2002] EWCA Civ 283.

216 *Donovan v Rana* [2014] EWCA Civ 99; [2014] 1 P. & C.R. 23 at [33]–[34], per Vos LJ.

anything that interferes with the enjoyment of the easement without, himself, committing a trespass.[217]

(c) Justification under customary rights

18-46 **Justification under customary rights** By immemorial custom the inhabitants of a particular locality may be entitled to exercise a variety of rights, such as a right of fetching water from a spring,[218] or a right to dry fishing nets on a person's land,[219] or a right to use it for purposes of sports and recreation.[220] To be valid, a custom must be reasonable,[221] or at any rate not unreasonable (that is, it must not be inconsistent with some general principle as opposed to some particular rule or maxim of the common law[222]). The time for ascertaining whether or not a custom is reasonable is its inception.[223] The custom must also be definite as to the nature of the user and of the locality to which it applies.[224]

18-47 **Extent of custom** Although customs are usually confined to the inhabitants of a particular town, manor, or parish,[225] there is no rule of law requiring that the area of a custom should not be wider in extent, provided that the district be one known to and defined by the law, such as a hundred.[226] How wide the area may be is not clear, but it seems that it may be in exceptional cases at least as wide as a county.[227] On the other hand, a customary right in the nature of a profit à prendre to gather sea-coal on a certain foreshore cannot validly exist in favour of all the inhabitants of the county of Durham.[228] And a custom for the general public to go upon a common and stay there to witness horse races without payment is void,[229] though it is otherwise where the benefit of a custom is claimed only to be enjoyed on payment.[230]

(d) Justification by licence

18-48 **Justification by licence: bare licences** It is a defence to show that the defendant is on the land with the leave and licence (express or implied) of the owner.[231]

217 *Virdi v Chana* [2008] EWHC 2901 (Ch); [2008] N.P.C. 130.
218 *Race v Ward* (1855) E. & B. 702.
219 *Tyson v Smith* (1838) 9 A. & E. 406 at 421; *Mercer v Denne* [1904] 2 Ch. 534.
220 *Hall v Nottingham* (1875) 1 Ex. D. 1.
221 Bl. *Comm.*, Vol.1, p.77.
222 *Johnson v Clark* [1908] 1 Ch. 303 at 311, per Parker J.
223 *Mercer v Denne* [1904] 2 Ch. 434 at 557, per Farwell J.
224 *Beresford v Bacon* (1685) 2 Lut. 1317; *Mounsey v Ismay* (1863) 1 H. & C. 729.
225 A custom for the inhabitants of a locality to exercise rights over land outside their own locality is bad: *Edwards v Jenkins* [1896] 1 Ch. 308.
226 i.e. a group of townships, dating back to pre-Norman times.
227 Y.B. 8 Edw. 4; cited at length by Holroyd J in *Blundell v Catterall* (1821) 5 B. Al. 268 at 296; *Mercer v Denne* [1905] 2 Ch. 538.
228 *Beckett Ltd v Lyons* [1967] Ch. 449. Such a right can exist only by virtue of statutory grant or by a grant in trust for the benefit of persons within a defined locality as in *Goodman v Saltash Corp* (1882) 7 App. Cas. 633.
229 *Earl of Coventry v Willes* (1863) 9 L.T. (N.S.) 384. cf. *R. v Doncaster MBC Ex p. Braim* (1987) 85 L.G.R. 233.
230 *Tyson v Smith* (1838) 9 A. & E. 406.
231 Where land is in joint occupation, one occupier may have express or implied authority from the other to allow entries, but if he has not, then an entrant permitted by one occupier will be a trespasser vis-

A licensee has no proprietary interest in the land, and accordingly has no remedy against a third party who disturbs him in the exercise of his licence. So in *Hill v Tupper*, it was held that a person with the exclusive right to hire out boats on a canal had no right of action against another who, without any licence, also hired out boats on the canal.[232] Importantly, the courts have been prepared to infer contractual licences to protect persons in occupation under informal family arrangements.[233] But the mere fact of permitted occupancy does not produce an irrevocable licence if there is no reason to impute a contractual arrangement between the parties.[234]

Extent and construction of licence It is important to appreciate that the defendant's presence on the claimant's land, or his encroachment onto his neighbour's buildings or fixtures, is only justified to the extent granted by the licence.[235] If the defendant exceeds the permission granted, his acts will constitute a trespass. Thus, in *R. (on the application of JC Decaux UK Ltd) v Wandsworth LBC*,[236] where the defendant in possession of a licence to erect an advertising hoarding according to a particular method used a more intrusive method, he was held to be a trespasser.[237] But if the permission granted is very general in nature, referring to no more than a broad permission to construct an advertising hoarding, any consequential protrusion of it into the claimant's airspace will not be a trespass.[238] 18-49

Effect of revocation A licensee who remains on land after his licence expires or is properly revoked is a trespasser.[239] Furthermore, it will be of no avail to suggest, in any case where the licence has been revoked by a local authority, that the revocation constitutes a violation of the trespasser's art.8 right to respect for his or her private life.[240] A licensee whose licence has been revoked is, however, entitled to a reasonable time for "packing-up", in which to leave[241] and to remove his goods,[242] and until such reasonable time has elapsed he cannot be prevented from entering on the land for the purpose of removing his goods.[243] Equally, a local authority must follow all proper procedures, in accordance with the civil procedure rules, if it is to regain possession of a council house from someone who has flagrantly behaved in breach of the tenancy agreement.[244] And, a licence granted for a fixed period for valuable consideration cannot be revoked before the expiration of the period for which it is granted provided that it is specifically enforceable either by specific performance or injunction.[245] In such a case,[246] the licensee does not 18-50

à-vis the other: *Ferguson v Welsh* [1987] 1 W.L.R. 1553 at 1563.

232 (1863) 2 H. & C. 121.

233 *Chandler v Kerley* [1978] 1 W.L.R. 693 at 697, per Lord Scarman.

234 *Horrocks v Forray* [1976] 1 W.L.R. 230.

235 See, e.g. *Seeff v Ho* [2011] EWCA Civ 186.

236 [2009] EWHC 129 (Admin).

237 See also *British Waterways Board v Severn Trent Water Ltd* [2001] EWCA Civ 276; [2002] Ch. 25.

238 *Stadium Capital Holdings (No.2) Ltd v St Marylebone Properties Co Plc* [2009] EWHC 2942 (Ch); (reversed on quantum: [2010] EWCA Civ 952).

239 *Wood v Leadbitter* (1845) 13 M. & W. 838; *Thompson v Park* [1944] K.B. 408.

240 *Stokes v Brent LBC* [2009] EWHC 1426 (QB).

241 *Robson v Hallett* [1967] 2 Q.B. 939.

242 *Minister of Health v Bellotti* [1944] K.B. 298 at 306.

243 *Cornish v Stubbs* (1870) L.R. 5 C. & P. 334; *Canadian Pacific Ry v The King* [1931] A.C. 414.

244 *Cardiff CC v Lee* [2016] EWCA Civ 1034; [2017] 1 W.L.R. 1751.

245 *Hurst v Picture Theatres* [1915] 1 K.B. 1.

246 e.g. *Frogley v Earl of Lovelace* (1859) John 333.

become a trespasser if his licence is prematurely revoked, since he has a specific equitable right to remain on the land. On the other hand, a licensee seeking an equitable remedy may be refused one if his hands are "unclean" insofar as he is unwilling to carry out his part of the bargain. But not every sort of misconduct will raise a bar. In *Williams v Staite*,[247] the defendants in occupation of a cottage under an equitable licence behaved troublesomely towards the claimant, but "their conduct, however reprehensible, was not such as to justify revocation of their licence to occupy the cottage as their home".[248] Goff LJ said: "Excessive user or bad behaviour cannot bring the equity to an end or forfeit it. It may give rise to an action for damages ... but I see no ground on which the equity, once established, can be forfeited."[249]

18-51 Where a licence is revocable, the licensor in his notice of revocation is not obliged, unless contractually bound, to specify the time within which the licensee must remove himself and his goods.[250] The revocation will be good even if the time given is insufficient.[251] If the licensor revokes a contractual licence prematurely, an action for breach of contract will lie.[252] Also, if the licensor revokes a gratuitous licence without reasonable notice, he may be liable for damage sustained by the licensee.[253] Once a licence is revoked and the licensee's property removed from the land, the licensee, if he forcibly re-enters, becomes a trespasser and an interim injunction will be granted restraining further trespass and ordering him to remove his property from the land.[254]

18-52 **Revocability of contractual licences** A gratuitous licence can be revoked by notice so that if the licensee remains on the land after the revocation he is a trespasser. A licence granted for valuable consideration under a contract can only be revoked in accordance with the terms of the contract. If the contract is for the licensee to watch a spectacle, such as a performance at a theatre, the licence cannot, in the case of a well-behaved licensee, be revoked until after the spectacle is over[255] because it is an implied term in the contract that the licence shall not be revoked. An injunction can be obtained to prevent premature revocation of the licence.[256]

18-53 **Problems with revocation** Since the decision of the House of Lords in *Winter Garden Theatre (London) Ltd v Millennium Productions Ltd*,[257] it seems that the question of revocability must be determined by means of interpretation of the contract, and that, as between licensor and licensee, where the licensor expressly or impliedly promises by contract not to revoke, he may not, unless the licensee

247 [1979] Ch. 291.
248 [1979] Ch. 291 at 298.
249 [1979] Ch. 291 at 300.
250 *Australian Blue Metal Co Ltd v Hughes* [1963] A.C. 74. Whether there need be notice, and if so, whether it must be a "dated" notice or may be for a period of grace, are questions of construction upon individual contracts.
251 *Minister of Health v Bellotti* [1944] K.B. 298.
252 *Kerrison v Smith* [1897] 2 Q.B. 445.
253 *Aldin v Latimer Clark, Muirhead & Co* [1894] 2 Ch. 437.
254 *Thompson v Park* [1944] K.B. 408.
255 *Winter Garden Theatre (London) Ltd v Millennium Productions Ltd* [1948] A.C. 173 at 189.
256 See, e.g. *Hurst v Picture Theatres* [1915] 1 K.B. 1. See also *Butler v MS & L Ry* (1888) 21 Q.B.D. 207.
257 [1948] A.C. 173.

gives him just cause to withdraw his promise, revoke so as to turn the licensee into a trespasser. In connection with revocability of contractual licences the decision of the Court of Appeal in *Thompson v Park*[258] gave rise to difficulty, for the doctrine of revocability (subject to payment of damages) was there revived and an injunction awarded to exclude a contractual licensee. The decision has not been followed by the Court of Appeal. In *Verrall v Great Yarmouth BC* Lord Denning MR made an order for specific performance saying that, "since the *Winter Garden* case it is clear that once a man has entered under his contract of licence, he cannot be turned out". He added that: "On principle it is the same if it happens before he enters… [If] the licensor refuses to let him come in, then he can come to the court and in a proper case get an order for specific performance to allow him to come in".[259]

Licences coupled with interest A licence is also irrevocable if it is coupled with an interest (i.e. a grant of property). In such a case, the licence cannot be revoked so as to defeat the grant to which it is incident. Thus it has been said that "a licence to hunt in a man's park and carry away the deer killed to his own use, to cut down a tree in a man's ground, and to carry it away the next day after to his own use, are licences as to the acts of hunting and cutting down the tree, but as to the carrying away of the deer killed and tree cut down they are grants"[260] and as such are irrevocable. 18-54

Chattel interests The interest need not be an interest in realty, but may be purely a chattel interest. Thus, "if A sells to B felled timber lying on A's land on the terms that B may enter and carry it away, the licence conferred is an irrevocable licence because it is coupled with, and granted in aid of, the legal property in the timber which the contract for sale confers on B".[261] In *Wood v Manley*,[262] the claimant sold a rick of hay, which was then standing on his close, to the defendant, with the condition that it might remain there up to Lady Day, and that until that date the defendant might enter the close as often as occasion required for the purpose of removing portions of the stack. The licence was held to be irrevocable. 18-55

Validity of acts done before revocation A licence, even though gratuitous, is also irrevocable in the sense that a licensee cannot be compelled, after he has acted on or executed the licence, to undo what he has lawfully done.[263] A licensor cannot complain of that which he allows. On the other hand, when he properly and validly revokes the licence, he acquires a right to sue for any continuing or subsequent trespass. But it may be that "owing to some supervening equity the licence has become irrevocable".[264] So a licensor who induces the licensee to believe that the licence will not be revoked and allows him to spend money on works on the licensor's land may find himself restrained by injunction from revoking his 18-56

258 [1944] K.B. 408.
259 [1981] Q.B. 202 at 216.
260 *Thomas v Sorrell* (1674) Vaughan 330 at 351.
261 *Jones & Sons Ltd v Tankerville* [1909] 2 Ch. 440 at 442. See also, *Wood v Manley* (1839) 11 A. & E. 34.
262 (1839) 11 A. & E. 34.
263 *Feltham v Cartwright* (1839) 5 Bing. N.C. 569. See also *Armstrong v Sheppard & Short Ltd* [1959] 2 Q.B. 384 at 399.
264 *Plimmer v Mayor (etc.) of Wellington* (1884) 9 App. Cas. 699 at 714.

licence.[265] In order to be precluded from revoking, the licensor must have appreciated what his real rights were, since "the doctrine of acquiescence is founded upon conduct with a knowledge of your legal rights".[266] On the other hand, a licensor's permission is valid even if he is ignorant as to his title, and accordingly he cannot sue for trespass until he revokes his consent.[267]

18-57 **When licence binding on third parties** At common law a revocable licence was revoked where the licensor conveyed the land to another. Accordingly, the licensee became a trespasser if he remained on the land or entered it after the conveyance.[268] This was so even if the licensor's purchaser bought with express notice.[269] The Court of Appeal in *Clore v Theatrical Properties Ltd*[270] declined to recognise a valid equity against the purchaser with notice so as to bind him. The cases of those licences which are coupled with a validly created interest in the licensor's property stand apart, because it is clear that these are both irrevocable and assignable, and such licences are enforceable by and against successors in title of both the grantor and grantee. Apart from such cases, it was clear that a licence, even though reinforced by a contract not to revoke it, could not bind a purchaser with notice. But in *Errington v Errington and Woods*,[271] it was held that a contractual licence to occupy a dwelling-house bound the licensor's devisee. The court preferred to base its decision on the ground of a licence binding on the third party rather than on the more orthodox argument that the contract to convey the house on the completion of mortgage payments created an equitable interest in the property which would bind a third party. In *National Provincial Bank v Ainsworth*,[272] however, the House of Lords rejected the idea that this approach could be extended beyond the sphere of contractual licences. They held that a deserted wife has no proprietary interest in the matrimonial home to avail her against her husband's assignees.[273] In *Binions v Evans*,[274] where landlords agreed with the widow of a man who had worked for them all his life that she might continue to reside in the cottage for the rest of her life, and then sold to the claimants giving them notice of the agreement, the Court of Appeal held that the agreement was binding on the purchaser.[275] The reasoning in this case was more orthodox than in *Errington*, being based on the creation of a trust in favour of a widow. And the Court of Appeal has now re-established the proposition that a contractual licence per se does not create an interest in land binding on the licensor's purchaser even with notice. The Court will not impose a constructive trust unless it is satisfied that the conscience of the purchaser is affected.[276]

---

265 *Ramsden v Dyson* (1866) L.R. 1 H.L. 129.
266 *Willmott v Barber* (1880) 15 Ch. D. 96 at 105. On acquiescence as a defence, see *Jones v Stones* [1999] 1 W.L.R. 1739. See also *Armstrong v Sheppard & Short Ltd* [1959] 2 Q.B. 384.
267 *Willmott v Barber* (1880) 15 Ch. D. 96 at 105.
268 *Wallis v Harrison* (1838) 4 M. & W. 538.
269 *King v David Allen & Sons* [1916] 2 A.C. 54.
270 [1936] 3 All E.R. 483.
271 [1952] 1 K.B. 290.
272 [1965] A.C. 1175.
273 The Family Law Act 1996 provides protection against eviction or exclusion from the matrimonial home to a spouse not entitled to occupy it.
274 [1972] Ch. 359. And see *DHN Food Distributors Ltd v Tower Hamlets London Borough* [1976] 1 W.L.R. 852.
275 [1972] Ch. 359.
276 *Ashburn Anstalt v WJ Arnold & Co* [1989] Ch. 1.

Licensee as claimant in trespass Whatever the degree of protection a licensee may have against his licensor or his successors in title, while the licensee is in exclusive possession he has the right to sue in trespass any third party wrongfully interfering with that possession. "Exclusive" possession may be relative. Lord Upjohn in *National Provincial Bank v Ainsworth*[277] said that: 18-58

> "the wife's occupation is not exclusive against the deserting husband for [subject to court order] he can at any moment return and resume the role of occupier without the leave of the wife. Nevertheless, I cannot seriously doubt that in this case in truth and in fact the wife at all material times was and is in exclusive possession of the home. Until her husband returns she has the dominion over the house and she could clearly bring proceedings against trespassers."

In principle, the licensee in exclusive occupation under an unrevoked licence has the right to sue in trespass his licensor.[278] Yet, in *Hill v Tupper*[279] the claimant was unsuccessful in asserting trespass against third parties because, though he had the "exclusive" right contractually to put pleasure boats on the canal, he had no exclusive possession over the canal itself, and nor did he have a profit à prendre in the canal (for example, to fish).[280]

(e) Justification by necessity

Justification by necessity Trespass can be justified by showing that it was necessary to enter upon the land to preserve life or property.[281] The defendant bears the burden of showing that the necessity arose without negligence on his part.[282] The necessity depends on the state of things when the trespass takes place, and not upon the inference as to necessity to be drawn from the event.[283] What is necessary in the case of a person with property to protect might not be considered necessary in the case of a volunteer, such as someone helping to extinguish a fire with which the fire brigade are already coping.[284] It has been held that homelessness is no justification for unpermitted occupation of a dwelling-house, even if vacant.[285] Nor is entry on a neighbour's land to effect repairs to one's own property a justification.[286] The Court of Appeal has refused to allow necessity as a defence to a trespass carried out to uproot genetically modified crops which the defendants believed represented a threat to public safety.[287] And it has also been stated that a boundary fence which has moved because of settlement, so as to encroach by a matter of inches onto a neighbour's land, does not justify that neighbour in removing the entire fence by way of self help: there was no emergency.[288] 18-59

277 [1965] A.C. 1175 at 1232.

278 *Marcroft Wagons Ltd v Smith* [1951] 2 K.B. 496 at 501.

279 (1863) 2 H. & C. 121. See para.18-48.

280 See para.18-12.

281 *Maleverer v Spinke* (1538) Dyer 35b at 36b; *Cope v Sharpe* [1910] 1 K.B. 168. The defence of necessity is not favoured by the courts, especially where the defendant acted to protect a private rather than a public interest.

282 *Rigby v Chief Constable of Northamptonshire* [1985] 1 W.L.R. 1242.

283 *Cope v Sharpe (No.2)* [1912] 1 K.B. 496.

284 *Carter v Thomas* [1893] 1 Q.B. 673.

285 *Southwark LBC v Williams* [1971] Ch. 734 at 744.

286 But see now the Access to Neighbouring Land Act 1992, and para.18-33.

287 See *Monsanto Plc v Tilly* [2000] Env. L.R. 313.

288 *MacNab v Richardson* [2008] EWCA Civ 1631; [2009] 35 E.G. 108 at [34]–[35].

(f) Police powers of entry and search

18-60 **Entry to arrest and search** Section 17(5) of the Police and Criminal Evidence Act 1984 abolished all rules of common law empowering constables to enter premises without a warrant, save in relation to powers of entry to deal with or prevent a breach of the peace.[289] In their stead, ss.17, 18 and 32 confer extensive powers of entry on constables, and are without prejudice to any other enactment (so that earlier statutes conferring express powers of entry on constables for specific purposes remain in force[290]). Section 17 is broadly concerned with authorising entry in order to effect an arrest. By s.17(1), a constable is authorised to enter and search premises:

(a) to execute warrants of arrest in connection with or arising out of criminal proceedings and warrants of commitment issued under s.76 of the Magistrates' Courts Act 1980;
(b) to arrest a person for an indictable offence[291];
(c) to arrest a person for offences under the Public Order Acts of 1936 and 1986[292]; the Criminal Law Act 1977[293]; s.76 of the Criminal Justice and Public Order Act 1994[294]; s.4. or s.163 of the Road Traffic Act 1988; s.27 of the Transport and Works Act 1992; various provisions contained in ss.4–8 of the Animal Welfare Act 2006; s.61 of the Animal Health Act 1981; ss.97 and 144 of the Legal Aid, Sentencing and Punishment of Offenders Act 2012[295]; and various provisions of the Bail Act 1976;
(d) to recapture a person unlawfully at large and whom the constable is pursuing[296]; or to recapture a person unlawfully at large who is liable to be detained in a prison, young offender institution, secure training centre or secure college;
(e) to recapture any person who is, or is deemed for any purpose to be, unlawfully at large while liable to be detained in a prison, remand centre, young offender institution, secure training centre or secure college; or in pursuance of s.92 of the Powers of Criminal Courts (Sentencing) Act 2000[297];
(f) to arrest a child or young person who has absconded after having been

---

[289] s.17(5), (6); see also *McLeod v Commissioner of Police for the Metropolis* [1994] 4 All E.R. 553 (power of entry extends to private premises); *Mcleod v United Kingdom* (1999) 27 E.H.R.R. 493 ECHR.

[290] e.g. Misuse of Drugs Act 1971 s.23; Gambling Act 2005 s.306.

[291] Entry is authorised under s.17 not only into the premises occupied by the person sought but also into premises occupied by other persons where the constable has reasonable grounds to believe that the person sought is to be found: *Kynaston v DPP* (1988) 87 Cr. App. R. 200.

[292] Under s.1 of the 1936 Act (prohibition of political uniforms); and s.4 of the 1986 Act: see Sch.2 para.7 to that Act.

[293] Under ss.6–8 and 10 (offences relating to entering and remaining on property). A constable entering premises under these provisions must be in uniform: s.17(3) of the Police and Criminal Evidence Act 1984.

[294] Failure to comply with an interim possession order, see Sch.10 para.53. A constable entering premises under this provision must be in uniform: s.17(3) of the Police and Criminal Evidence Act 1984.

[295] A constable entering premises under s.144 of the Legal Aid, Sentencing and Punishing of Offenders Act 2012 must be in uniform: s.17(3) of the Police and Criminal Evidence Act 1984.

[296] The constable must be in hot pursuit of the escapee.

[297] Note: there is no need for the constable to be in hot pursuit of persons unlawfully at large but liable to be detained in any of the listed institutions.

remanded to local authority accommodation, a place of safety, or a place in which he has been accommodated following a remand under s.91 of the Legal Aid, Sentencing and Punishment of Offenders Act 2012, pursuant to s.32(1A) of the Children and Young Persons Act 1969; and

(g) to save life and limb or prevent serious damage to property.[298]

Section 17(2) seeks to control the exercise of the above powers of entry by providing that, except in the case of entry to preserve life or limb or prevent serious damage, powers of entry under s.17(1) are exercisable only when the constable has reasonable grounds for believing that the person he is seeking is on the premises and that the right to enter is limited in the case of premises comprising separate dwellings, such as a block of flats, to parts of the premises in common use and the specific dwelling where the constable reasonably suspects the person may be found.[299] Powers of search conferred by s.17(1) are limited to powers to search for the purpose for which the power of entry is conferred. A constable entering premises to recapture an escaped prisoner or quell a violent attack on an inhabitant of the premises cannot then, by virtue of s.17, search the premises for drugs or stolen goods.[300] Such a search would have to be authorised under s.18. A constable exercising a power of entry under s.17 must give his reasons for exercising that power unless those reasons are self-evident. In *O'Loughlin v Chief Constable of Essex*,[301] officers used force to break into a house after being refused entry by the claimant. They had demanded entry but had declined to give reasons why it was sought. The Court of Appeal held that in these circumstances s.17 provided no defence.

Section 18 provides for entry and search of premises occupied or controlled by a person under arrest for an indictable offence when a constable has reasonable grounds for suspecting that there is on the premises evidence (other than items of legal privilege) relating either to the offence in respect of which the person has been arrested or to "some other indictable offence which is connected with or similar to that offence".[302] And the power to search the relevant premises is limited to the extent that is reasonably required to discover such evidence. "Fishing expeditions" are not authorised by s.18.[303] The exercise of the power of entry and search conferred by s.18 is normally subject to a pre-condition that the entry and search be authorised in writing by an officer of the rank of inspector or above.[304] But a constable may conduct a search under s.18 before taking an arrested person to a police station and without authorisation "if the presence of that person at a place other than a police station is necessary for the effective investigation of the offence".[305] An immediate search of the arrested person's premises might thus be justified where it can be established that there was a significant risk that delay might result in necessary evidence being destroyed. 18-61

Entry on arrest Section 32(2)(b) empowers a constable, after arresting a person for an indictable offence at a place other than a police station, "to enter and search 18-62

[298] Property, for these purposes, includes animals (such as pet dogs that are in imminent danger of maltreatment): *Marzan v RSPCA* [2016] EWHC 993 (Admin).
[299] s.17(2)(b).
[300] s.17(4).
[301] [1998] 1 W.L.R. 364.
[302] s.18(1).
[303] s.18(3).
[304] s.18(4); *R. v Badham* [1987] Crim. L.R. 202.
[305] s.18(5); and see also s.30(10).

any premises in which [the arrested person] was when arrested or immediately before he was arrested for evidence relating to the offence for which he was arrested".[306] This power to search is limited to the extent that it exists only if the search is reasonably required to find anything that may assist the arrested person in escaping lawful custody or evidence relating to the offence.[307] And the officer must also have reasonable grounds to believe that such a thing or evidence is to be found on those premises.[308] Section 117 of the 1984 Act authorises the use of reasonable force, if necessary, to exercise the powers of entry conferred by that Act. When a constable exercises a power of entry conferred on him by other legislation, the use of force to effect entry must be justified either under the legislation authorising entry,[309] or because the circumstances also fall within s.17, or within the power conferred by s.3 of the Criminal Law Act 1967 to prevent crime.

18-63 Where a constable enters premises without lawful authority no defence of mere trivial interference protects him.[310] He is liable for trespass to land, unless he can rely on the implied permission of the occupier to be on those premises,[311] and if so, only until that implied permission is revoked.[312] However, revocation of a constable's implied permission to be on premises requires something more than mere vulgar abuse.[313]

18-64 **Search warrants** Section 8 of the Police and Criminal Evidence Act 1984 provides that a magistrate may issue a search warrant to enter and search premises on the application of a constable, when he (the magistrate) is satisfied that there are reasonable grounds for believing that the following conditions are met:

(1) an indictable offence has been committed;
(2) there is material on the premises likely to be of substantial value[314] to the investigation of the offence;
(3) that material is likely to be relevant[315] evidence;
(4) the material does not consist of items subject to legal privilege[316] or excluded material[317] or special procedure[318] material;
(5) access to the material cannot practicably be obtained without a warrant or

[306] It is a question of fact in every case whether the constable was genuinely seeking evidence relating to the offence for which the person has been detained: *R. v Beckford* (1991) 94 Cr. App. R. 43.
[307] For close analysis of the provision, see *Hanningfield v Chief Constable of Essex* [2013] EWHC 243 (QB); [2013] 1 W.L.R. 3632 at [9]–[12].
[308] s.32(3), (6). See also *R. v Badham* [1987] Crim. L.R. 202.
[309] Legislation conferring a right of entry without warrant may specifically prohibit the use of force without a warrant first having been obtained.
[310] *Morris v Beardmore* [1981] A.C. 446. But see *R. v Lamb* [1990] Crim. L.R. 58 (unwitting trespasser need not leave premises before intervening to prevent breach of the peace).
[311] Either by virtue of a general implied licence to enter and approach the front door of a dwelling; see *Robson v Hallett* [1967] 2 Q.B. 939; or a licence implied from the occupier's conduct: *Faulkner v Willets* [1982] R.T.R. 159. An invitation to enter may be given by one co-occupier alone and cannot be unilaterally revoked by another: *R. v Thornley* (1981) 72 Cr. App. R. 302.
[312] *Snook v Mannion* [1982] R.T.R. 321.
[313] *Snook v Mannion* [1982] R.T.R. 321.
[314] Whether by itself or together with other material: see s.8(1)(b).
[315] Evidence admissible at a trial for the offence: see s.8(4).
[316] As defined in s.10.
[317] Defined by ss.11–13. Excluded material basically consists of confidential personal records of a trade, business or profession, human tissue etc taken for medical purposes and "journalistic material" held in confidence.
[318] Defined by s.14. Confidential material not falling within the ambit of excluded material.

the purpose of the search will be frustrated unless the constable gains immediate entry to the premises.[319]

A constable entering premises under the authority of a search warrant granted under s.8 may seize and retain any evidence in respect of which the search was authorised.[320] The general power to issue search warrants to facilitate the investigation of crime granted by s.8 of the 1984 Act is without prejudice to, and additional to, other statutory powers to grant such warrants.[321] There is no general rule that a constable must first exhaust all other means of obtaining access to the relevant material before seeking the issue of a search warrant.[322] Nor is there any obligation to disclose to the party affected by the warrant the material upon which the magistrates had relied when deciding to grant the warrant. Instead, "all that is required is that ... [the magistrate] be satisfied, from the information contained in the constable's application and from the constable's answers on oath to any questions put, that 'there are reasonable grounds for believing' the matters set out in section 8(1)(a) to (e)".[323] And such warrants, according to the Supreme Court, can perfectly well be obtained on an ex parte basis.[324]

On the other hand, police officers are under a duty to disclose all material facts when making a without-notice application for a search warrant, including information which might undermine the application. And the duty to make such disclosure extends to disclosing facts which were not actually known, but which would have been known had the officer made proper inquiries.[325] A warrant to search premises does not of itself authorise the search of persons found there.[326] Moreover, it seems arguable that a warrant procured out of malice will not be valid.[327] Equally, even in the absence of bad faith, a warrant will be invalid if those responsible for drafting it "acted with patent and egregious disregard for, or indifference to, the constitutional safeguards within the statutory scheme".[328] And a search will not be lawful if the copy of the warrant the officer concerned is obliged to give to the occupier[329] fails to specify all those particulars contained in s.15(6) of the 1984 Act.[330] **18-65**

Section 16 enacts rules relating to the execution of search warrants and applies whether the relevant warrant is issued under s.8 of the 1984 Act or by virtue of some **18-66**

---

319 s.8(1)(e), (3).

320 s.8(2). But note the wider powers of seizure under s.19: see also para.5-129 onwards.

321 s.8(5). Several such powers continue to be relevant, e.g. Theft Act 1968 s.26(1) and (3) (to enter and search for stolen goods); Misuse of Drugs Act 1971 s.23(3) (to search for controlled drugs); Obscene Publications Act 1959 s.3.

322 *R. v Billericay JJ and Dobbyn Ex p. Frank Harris (Coaches)* [1991] Crim. L.R. 472.

323 *R. (on the application of Haralambous) v St Albans Crown Court* [2018] UKSC 1; [2018] A.C. 236 at [15].

324 *R. (on the application of Haralambous) v St Albans Crown Court* [2018] UKSC 1; [2018] A.C. 236 at [27].

325 *R. (on the application of Brook) v Preston Crown Court* [2018] EWHC 2024 (Admin); [2018] A.C.D. 95 at [16].

326 *Herman King v The Queen* [1969] 1 A.C. 304. But it may permit an officer executing the search warrant to detain someone, to prevent them walking around their own home, while it is being searched. The authority given by the warrant has to enable the search to be effective: *DPP v Meaden* [2003] EWHC 3005 (Admin); [2004] 1 W.L.R. 945.

327 See *Fitzpatrick v Commissioner of Police of the Metropolis* [2012] EWHC 12 (Admin); [2012] Lloyd's Rep. F.C. 361 at [144].

328 *R. (on the application of Chatwani) v National Crime Agency* [2015] EWHC 1283 (Admin); [2015] A.C.D. 110 at [141], per Hickinbottom J.

329 Police and Criminal Evidence Act 1984 s.16(5).

330 *R. (on the application of Bhatti) v Croydon Magistrates' Court* [2010] EWHC 522 (Admin); [2011] 1 W.L.R. 948.

other statutory power.[331] It provides inter alia that a warrant to enter and search premises may be executed by any constable, and may authorise persons to accompany any constable who is executing it. Entry and search under a warrant must be within one month from its date of issue and at a reasonable hour unless it appears to the constable executing it that the purposes of the search will be frustrated by entry at a reasonable hour. Provision is made for the constable to identify himself to the occupier if he is present and for the production of the warrant.[332] A search under warrant is limited to a search for the purposes for which the warrant is issued. Accordingly, searches conducted under warrants that are drawn too widely are unlawful. This may occur where the warrant fails to comply with the requirement in s.15(6)(b) to specify, "so far as practicable", the articles sought.[333] But the qualification "so far as practicable" is an important one since it will allow for some measure of latitude in the terms in which a warrant is constructed where a search of various different types of electronic devices may be necessary,[334] or where it is impossible to specify in advance the type of property sought because the property in question is bound up with, and likely to shed light on, money laundering activities.[335] On the other hand, a warrant will certainly be regarded as having been drawn too widely where it purports to permit seizure of material "deemed relevant" by the searching officers.[336] This is because such wording would effectively delegate to the officers concerned a task that, under the statute, falls to the justices. Any officer who seized material that turned out to be irrelevant could (inappropriately) seek subsequently to legitimise his entry and seizure simply by saying that he had deemed the material seized to be relevant at the time. The application for a search warrant must also specify which part of the premises is to be searched where police are aware that the premises comprise a number of individual dwellings.

5. Measure of Damages

(a) General

18-67 A claimant in trespass is entitled to recover damages, even though he has sustained no actual loss.[337] To recover substantial damages the claimant must show an interest in the land beyond an interest for a day or two, otherwise the damages

---

331 e.g. Protection from Harassment Act 1997 s.2B. See also s.15 of the 1984 Act in relation to procedural safeguards in this context; *R. v Reading JJ Ex p. South West Meats Ltd* [1992] Crim. L.R. 672. Note, however, that the safeguards contained in s.16 (as well as those contained in s.15) do not apply to post-arrest powers of search under s.18 or s.32 of PACE: *R. (on the application of Singh) v National Crime Agency* [2018] EWHC 1119 (Admin); [2018] 1 W.L.R. 5073.

332 If there is a dispute about whether there has been compliance with these requirements, the onus is on the police officer to show on the balance of probabilities that he identified himself and that he produced the warrant: *Alleyne v Commissioner of Police of the Metropolis* [2012] EWHC 3955 (QB) at [96]. See s.16(6)–(7) for the duty of a constable executing a warrant on premises in the absence of the occupier. *R. v Chief Constable of Lancashire Ex p. Parker* [1993] Q.B. 577.

333 *Van der Pijl v Kingston Crown Court* [2012] EWHC 2989 (Admin); [2013] 1 W.L.R. 2706.

334 *R. (on the application of Cabot Global Ltd) v Barkingside Magistrates' Court* [2015] EWHC 1458 (Admin); [2015] 2 Cr. App. R. 26.

335 *R. (on the application of Atwal) v Lewes Crown Court* [2015] EWHC 1783 (Admin).

336 *R. (on the application of Superior Import/Export Ltd) v Revenue and Customs Commissioners* [2017] EWHC 3172 (Admin); [2018] Lloyd's Rep. F.C. 115.

337 Such damages are likely to be nominal only: *Hanina v Morland* (2000) 97(47) L.S. Gaz. 41. Injunctions may also be obtained in such cases: *Patel v WH Smith (Eziot) Ltd* [1987] 1 W.L.R. 853.

will usually be nominal.[338] But whether the measure of damages must correspond precisely with the claimant's interest is not clear. According to a number of cases, one method of quantifying the damages is by reference to a hypothetical negotiation between the parties. The damages are fixed in accordance with the price the defendant would have had to pay to do the acts complained of had he negotiated for permission to do them. However, the so-called licence fee will be computed in line with the actual duration of the trespass rather than by reference to any longer period of time for which the defendant would probably have sought permission to do the thing complained of had the parties actually negotiated a licence.[339] The use of hypothetical contracts now rests on Supreme Court authority. In *Bocardo SA v Star Energy UK Onshore Ltd*,[340] the court used the hypothetical contract device, but was careful to be attentive to the background statutory (compulsory aquisition) scheme that would have impinged upon any negotiations between the parties.[341] Where the claimant has altogether been deprived of his land through a trespass, damages will amount at least to the value of his interest, but there appears to be no authority for the proposition that the value of his interest generally limits the measure of damages.[342] Indeed, it has been held that in wrongful eviction cases, the claimant may recover damages not merely for the letting value of the property for the full length of time that the right of occupation had existed, but also for the anxiety, inconvenience and stress involved in the loss of the home.[343] In cases of unauthorised parking, the court retains the freedom to compute for itself the damages payable where the defendant refuses to pay a penalty imposed by a private parking enforcement company. But, in deciding the quantum, where the parking enforcement company is a member of an accredited trade association (ATA), the court is likely to "be influenced … [on] quantum by the fact that the charges [levied by the company] had been approved in advance by the ATA".[344] When substantial damage has been caused, the measure of damages varies according to whether the trespass belongs to one or other of the three following classes.

(i) Trespass productive of benefit to the defendant without damage to the claimant First, the trespass may consist of a mere user of the soil by passing over it without doing any damage. In such cases the damages will be the price a reasonable man would pay for the right of user.[345] If the trespass consists in using a right of way which the defendant was not entitled to use, the measure of damages is the usual charge for wayleave in the district,[346] or where colliery spoil has been tipped, the measure is not only the loss of open ground but also the value of the site as a tip.[347] Again, where residential property has been occupied wrongfully the claim- 18-68

338 *Twyman v Knowles* (1853) 13 C.B. 222; *Rust v Victoria Graving Dock* (1887) 36 Ch. D. 113 at 119.

339 *Eaton Mansions (Westminster) Ltd v Stinger Compania de Inversion SA* [2013] EWCA Civ 1308; [2014] H.L.R. 4.

340 [2010] UKSC 35; [2011] 1 A.C. 380.

341 [2010] UKSC 35; [2011] 1 A.C. 380 at [91], per Lord Brown.

342 cf. the rule for bailee of goods in *The Winkfield* [1902] P. 42. See also para.16-85.

343 *Smith v Khan* [2018] EWCA Civ 1137; [2018] H.L.R. 31 at [39] and [45].

344 *R. (on the application of Duff) v Secretary of State for Transport* [2015] EWHC 1605 (Admin); [2015] R.T.R. 28 at [41], per Edis J.

345 See, e.g. *Sinclair v Gavaghan* [2007] EWHC 2256 (Ch).

346 *Jegon v Vivian* (1871) L.R. 6 Ch. 742; *Phillips v Homfray* (1871) L.R. 6 Ch. 770.

347 *Whitwham v Westminster Brymbo Coal Co* [1892] 2 Ch. 538.

ant may sue for the "ordinary letting value".[348] On the other hand, where the premises are the claimant's home rather than merely commercial residential premises, the court may add to the ordinary letting value a general damages sum to reflect the insult of the trespass, as occurred in *Davies v Ilieff*.[349] Finally, where there is an incursion into the airspace above the claimant's land by an advertising hoarding fixed to a structure on the defendant's land, the measure of damages is a complicated matter. In one case, the first instance judge suggested that the damages should equate to the totality of the earnings generated by adverts placed on the hoarding, but the Court of Appeal held that this was too simplistic an approach, and suggested various possible alternative bases of calculation.[350] Ultimately, the matter of quantum was remitted to be settled on a later date.[351]

18-69 **(ii) Physical damage to the land** Secondly, the trespass may involve actual physical damage to the land, as where a roadway is cut up by a constant use, or a bank is dug away.[352] The measure of damages in such a case is the amount by which the value of the land has been diminished, and not the cost of restoration. (But note that if the claimant is able to show that his or her chief concern is with the protection of property rights—rather than with the recovery of damages—then it may be possible to obtain a mandatory injunction requiring the defendant to make such restoration.[353]) In certain cases, as in the case of the road above, the diminution in value may be equal to the cost of restoration, but as a rule it will be less. As Lord Loreburn said in the case of a damaged road, the claimants' claim that "they were entitled to raise the road to the old level, cost what it might and whether it was more commodious to the public or not, will not, in my opinion, bear investigation. Such a rule might lead to a ruinous and wholly unnecessary outlay."[354] If it were otherwise "it would follow that a party who has let the sea in upon the land of another, the land itself being worth only £20, would have to pay, by way of damages, the expenses of excluding it again by extensive engineering operations".[355] Where, in widening a ditch, a strip of a field was cut and carried away, the measure of damages was the value to the owner of the land removed and not the cost of restoring it to its original condition.[356]

18-70 **Cost of reinstatement sometimes recoverable** The costs of repair and reinstatement exceeding diminution in value may sometimes be awarded, namely, where those expenditures are reasonable in all the circumstances.[357] So, in *Cooper v Ry*

---

348 *Swordheath Properties Ltd v Tabet* [1979] 1 W.L.R. 285 at 288, per Megaw LJ; cited with approval in *Inverugie Investments Ltd v Hackett* [1995] 1 W.L.R. 713; see also para.18-77.

349 (2000) unreported.

350 These included the expenses incurred by the defendant, the charging of a reasonable fee for the use of the airspace, and restitution of *part* of the profits generated by the adverts (bearing in mind the fact that only *part* of the hoarding was in the claimant's airspace).

351 *Stadium Capital Holdings v St Marylebone Properties Co Plc* [2010] EWCA Civ 952.

352 See, e.g. *Rochford v Essex CC* (1916) 85 L.J. Ch. 281.

353 *Udal v Dutton* [2007] EWHC 2862 (TCC); [2008] 1 P. & C.R. DG13. On the relevant criteria to be applied in applications for mandatory injunctions, see more generally para.28-14 onwards.

354 *Lodge Holes Colliery Co Ltd v Wednesbury Corp* [1980] A.C. 323 at 326; *Nalder v Ilford Corp* [1951] K.B. 822.

355 *Jones v Gooday* (1841) 8 M. & W. 146.

356 *Jones v Gooday* (1841) 8 M. & W. 146. In similar vein, see *Moss v Christchurch RDC* [1925] 2 K.B. 750.

357 *Bryant v Macklin* [2005] EWCA Civ 762 (but reinstatement has to be "reasonable reinstatement").

Executive,[358] where straying cattle derailed a train, the Railway Executive recovered the cost of repair of the train and the track. But such damages are only awarded where the claimant intends to do the work and make good the harm to his property.[359] Whether diminution in value or replacement costs are chosen depends on the overriding principle of putting the claimant in the position he had been in prior to the infliction of harm.[360]

(iii) Severance and removal of things attached to the soil Thirdly, the trespass may involve the severing and carrying away of things attached to the soil. Here, historically, a claimant could sue either in trespass for the damage to the land, or in trover for the value of the things severed qua chattels. Where the things severed were of a higher value before severance the claimant would, of course, elect to sue in trespass, and he was entitled to recover the diminution in the value of the land. Thus, in trespass, for taking fixtures, he could recover their value as fixtures,[361] though if he made the mistake of suing in trover he could only recover their lower value as chattels.[362] So, too, if a trespasser engages in the clandestine mining of coal,[363] or cuts down and removes ornamental timber, the owner may recover the value of the trees when standing. **18-71**

Damages in severance cases In principle the measure of damages applicable to the tortious taking of coal is equally applicable to the taking of other things which are increased in value by severance from the freehold, such as ripe crops or timber ready for cutting.[364] By s.6 of the Torts (Interference with Goods) Act 1977, the improver who acts in the honest but mistaken belief that he has title to the goods is to be allowed the value attributable to his improvement. Minerals and other materials severed from the freehold are goods, so if severing and raising constitute an "improvement" and the improver (or a purchaser in good faith from him) is sued for trespass or conversion, he may claim the value of improvement. It is not clear from the Act whether "improvement" includes any enhancement of value by beneficial work, and it may be that "improvement" is confined to physical additions of value. On such a view of the Act's scope, s.6 would not apply and the rights and liabilities of the wrongful taker would remain as at common law.[365] **18-72**

(b) Exemplary and aggravated damages

Exemplary damages may not be awarded, except where the wrong is an oppressive, arbitrary or unconstitutional action by servants of the government, or where the wrongdoer's conduct has been calculated to make a profit exceeding the **18-73**

358 [1953] 1 W.L.R. 223.

359 *Perry v Sidney Phillips & Son* [1982] 1 W.L.R. 1297. Compensation may be assessed not by reference to the time the damage was inflicted but by reference to the earliest time when repairs could be reasonably undertaken: *Dodd Properties (Kent) v Canterbury CC* [1980] 1 W.L.R. 433.

360 *Dominion Mosaics and Tile Co v Trafalgar Trucking Co* [1990] 2 All E.R. 246.

361 *Thompson v Pettitt* (1847) 10 Q.B. 101.

362 *Clarke v Holford* (1848) 2 C. & K. 540.

363 *Peruvian Guano Co v Dreyfus Brothers* [1892] A.C. 166. The penal rule would seem appropriate only to trespassers who have calculated making an illegitimate gain.

364 Canadian cases (e.g. *Wasson v California Standard Co* (1964) 47 D.L.R. (2d) 71) have extended the principle to timber trespasses. Also, in New Zealand, to shale: *Blenheim Borough and Wairan River Board v British Pavements (Canterbury) Ltd* [1940] N.Z.L.R. 564.

365 See para.16-103.

compensation payable to the claimant.[366] However, this latter category "is not confined to moneymaking in the strict sense". It "extends to cases in which the defendant is seeking to gain at the expense of the claimant some object—perhaps some property which he covets—which either he could not obtain at all or not obtain except at a price greater than what he wants to put down".[367] Whichever way the defendant seeks to profit, it is clear that his behaviour must be "sufficiently outrageous to merit punishment".[368] On the other hand, it is permissible to award "aggravated" damages, for coincidental injury to the claimant's proper pride and dignity, or where the trespass is accompanied by noise and disturbance.[369] But this will not occur where the defendant's trespass was accidental,[370] for there must be "high-handed, insulting or oppressive conduct"[371] by the defendant. Nor may such damages be claimed by a corporate claimant, for such claimants are incapable of suffering the requisite injury to dignity.[372]

6. ACTION FOR THE RECOVERY OF LAND

18-74 **Recovery of land and correction of Land Register** In the action for the recovery of land (sometimes called ejectment), the claimant is out of possession and claims immediate possession of the land. To do this he must recover "by the strength of his own title and not by the weakness of the defendant's".[373] He must therefore prove the links in his own title.[374] He may, for example, prove his title as a mortgagee and claim for possession if the mortgagor is in default.[375] The defendant, on the other hand, need only prove that he is in possession and need not prove any title.[376] Proof that the claimant was in possession before the defendant,[377] no matter for how short a time, is prima facie evidence of his having title, for such prior possession raises a presumption that he was seised in fee; and such presumption cannot be rebutted merely by showing that the claimant did not derive his possession from any person who had title.[378] Whether or not it may be rebutted by showing that the title is in fact in a third person is doubtful, though *Doe (dec'd) Carter v Barnard*[379] and *Nagle v Shea*[380] suggest that *jus tertii* is a defence. An important point to note in this context is that where A has defrauded B out of his title to land, and subsequently registered title in his own name, B will be able to seek rectifica-

---

366 *Rookes v Barnard* [1964] A.C. 1129.
367 [1964] A.C. 1129 at 1227; *Drane v Evangelou* [1978] 1 W.L.R. 455.
368 *Eaton Mansions (Westminster) Ltd v Stinger Compania de Inversion SA* [2012] EWHC 3354 (Ch); [2012] 49 E.G. 66 (C.S.) at [76], per Bartley Jones QC. (The question of exemplary damages was not pursued on appeal: [2013] EWCA Civ 1308; [2014] H.L.R. 4.)
369 *Chamberlain v Greenfield* (1772) 3 Wils. 292.
370 *Horsford v Bird* [2006] UKPC 3; [2006] 1 E.G.L.R. 75.
371 *Stanford International Bank Ltd v Austin Lapp* [2006] UKPC 50.
372 *Eaton Mansions (Westminster) Ltd v Stinger Compania de Inversion SA* [2013] EWCA Civ 1308; [2014] H.L.R. 4.
373 *Martin v Strachan* (1744) 5 T.R. 107n.
374 *Philips v Philips* (1878) 4 Q.B.D. 127.
375 *West Penwith Rural DC v Gunnell* [1968] 1 W.L.R. 1153.
376 *Danford v McAnulty* (1883) 8 App. Cas. 456 at 462, per Lord Blackburn.
377 For these purposes, a local authority is deemed to have possession of a public highway so that a possession order can be obtained against protestors occupying it and causing a public nuisance: *City of London Corp v Samede* [2012] EWHC 34 (QB); (2012) 109(5) L.S.G. 21.
378 *Doe (dec'd) Smith v Webber* (1834) 1 A. & E. 119; *Doe (dec'd) Hughes v Dyeball* (1829) Moo. M. 346.
379 (1849) 13 Q.B. 945.
380 (1874) Ir. Rep. 8 C.L. 224.

tion of the register. But B must do this within twelve years, since the effluxion of time from the moment that A took possession will count towards A's claiming adverse possession (and thereby being in a position to defeat a rectification of the register).[381]

Modern law *Doe (dec'd) Carter v Barnard* was doubted by Lord Macnaghten in *Perry v Clissold*[382] as it is difficult, if not impossible, to reconcile with *Asher v Whitlock*.[383] In *Asher v Whitlock*, a claimant with a better title than the defendant recovered possession although neither party had a title against the lord of the manor. Though the third party's title was not directly in issue, the case is the leading authority on the nature of the claimant's title in ejectment. This question was investigated by the High Court of Australia in *Allen v Roughley*,[384] where Dixon CJ and Fullagar J rejected Sir William Holdsworth's view that the claimant's title in ejectment depends on proof of an absolutely good title and that therefore *jus tertii* is pleadable. It is submitted that the law can now be expressed in the following propositions: 18-75

(a) In a case of ordinary trespass where the claimant in possession sues for interference with his possession of land, *jus tertii* is no defence.[385]
(b) If the claimant is not in possession and is suing an occupier for ejectment, he claims a right to possession based on the strength of his title, so he must show that title, for "possession is good against all the world except the person who can show a good title".[386]
(c) Since title to land is relative, the claimant may show a better title either:
    (i) by his prior possession previous to that of the defendant. In any such case, where the defendant has taken possession wrongfully from the claimant, the defendant cannot plead *jus tertii* and it is irrelevant that, as in *Asher v Whitlock*, some third person has a better right to possess than the claimant; or
    (ii) by his title, independently of prior possession, to own the land. In any such case, where the claimant produces a documentary or paper title the defendant may challenge it by pleading *jus tertii*, that is, that the claimant has no such title as alleged and that the title belongs to another person.

Estoppel between landlord and tenant A defendant in the action for recovery of land is estopped from denying the title of a claimant from whom he derived his interest. So were a landlord to sue his tenant, the tenant would be estopped from disputing his landlord's title,[387] and any attempt to do so will operate as a forfeiture 18-76

---

[381] *Rashid v Nasrullah* [2018] EWCA Civ 2685; [2020] Ch. 37. The previous Court of Appeal decision in *Parshall v Bryans* [2013] EWCA Civ 240; [2013] Ch. 568 was held to be inconsistent with the House of Lords' decision in *JA Pye (Oxford) Ltd v Graham* [2002] UKHL 30; [2003] 1 A.C. 419.
[382] [1907] A.C. 73.
[383] (1865) L.R. 1 Q.B. 1.
[384] (1955) 94 C.L.R. 98.
[385] See para.18-18.
[386] Cockburn CJ in *Asher v Whitlock* (1865) L.R. 1 Q.B. 1 at 5. When the claimant shows a good title and has an intention to regain possession, then the burden of proof is on the defendant to confess and avoid, e.g. by showing he has a valid tenancy: *Portland Managements Ltd v Harte* [1977] Q.B. 306.
[387] *Delaney v Fox* (1857) 2 C.B. (N.S.) 768.

of the lease.[388] But the tenant is always entitled to show that his landlord's title has expired in the interval, either by reason of his having assigned his reversion, or by reason of the landlord having been himself a tenant under a limited interest which has since been determined.[389] At common law, an entry was required before a lessee could sue for trespass; but this was not so in ejectment.[390] One co-owner can bring ejectment against another co-owner if he has been ousted from possession of the joint property.[391] Also, as a procedural matter, where a lessee seeks to eject a freeholder who has granted the lease but refuses to vacate the premises as per an order for possession, the lessee does so against a trespasser and under RSC Ord.113 r.7, he does not require the court's permission to issue the writ of possession.[392]

18-77 **Mesne profits** In an action for the recovery of possession of land the claimant may join a claim for mesne profits (i.e. damages for wrongful occupancy),[393] but he is entitled, too, to pursue an award of mesne profits in a subsequent action.[394] When the claimant sues for mesne profits alone, he must first enter to gain possession, and then the principle of trespass by relation[395] enables him to sue for former profits. But if recovery of land is time-barred by adverse possession, the right to recover mesne profits and rent is lost.[396] Mesne profits include compensation for the value of the use and occupation of the premises,[397] and also any damage which has been caused to the premises themselves,[398] for the term "mesne profits" is not confined to the profits which have accrued to the defendant, but extends to all loss that the claimant has sustained.[399] In considering the value of the use and occupation the net annual value must be taken.[400] In *Inverugie Investments Ltd v Hackett* the wrongfully dispossessed owner of a block of hotel apartments, which he had acquired for investment purposes, was able to recover a "reasonable rent" for each apartment for 365 days a year, notwithstanding that for much of the year partial occupancy at discounted prices was apparently all that could have been achieved.[401]

---

388 See *Warner v Sampson* [1959] 1 Q.B. 297, where the Court of Appeal considerably mitigated the rule of forfeiture in connection with pleadings: mere denial of title in the defence is insufficient to cause a forfeiture. *Warner v Sampson* was applied in *WG Clarke (Properties) Ltd v Dupre Properties Ltd* [1992] Ch. 297.

389 *England v Slade* (1792) 4 T.R. 682; *Doe (dec'd) Higginbotham v Barton* (1840) 11 A. & E. 307.

390 *Ryan v Clark* (1849) 14 Q.B. 65 at 73, per Patteson J; Law of Property Act 1925 s.149(2).

391 *Murray v Hall* (1849) 7 C. & B. 441.

392 *Pritchard v Teitelbaum* [2011] EWHC 1063 (Ch); [2011] N.P.C. 43. (The equivalent Civil Procedure Rule to RSC Ord.113 r.7 is CPR Part 55).

393 See para.18-28. On the measure of damages see *Ministry of Defence v Ashman* (1993) 66 P.C.R. 195; and *Ministry of Defence v Thompson* (1993) 66 P. & C.R. 195.

394 The subsequent action for mesne profits is not prevented by the doctrine of res judicata: *Farrar v Leongreen Ltd* [2017] EWCA Civ 2211; [2018] 1 P. & C.R. 17.

395 See para.18-28. But no entry is required after C's land interest ceases: *Southport Tramways v Gandy* [1897] 2 Q.B. 66.

396 *Mount Carmel Investments Ltd v Thurlow (Ltd)* [1988] 1 W.L.R. 1078; *Jolly, Re* [1900] 2 Ch. 616.

397 This is whether occupied by the defendant himself or by a tenant holding under him: *Doe v Harlow* (1840) 12 A. & E. 40.

398 *Dunn v Large* (1783) 3 Doug. 335.

399 *Goodtitle v Tombs* (1770) 3 Wils. 118 at 121. Note that mesne profits contain a combination of compensatory and restitutionary elements: *Inverugie Investments Ltd v Hackett* [1995] 1 W.L.R. 713 at 718, per Lord Lloyd.

400 Tax to which a claimant receiving rent would have been liable is to be deducted: *Hall & Co Ltd v Pearlberg* [1956] 1 W.L.R. 244.

401 *Inverugie Investments Ltd v Hackett* [1995] 1 W.L.R. 713 at 718, per Lord Lloyd.

In *Shepherd v Collect Investments Ltd*[402] the Court of Appeal had to grapple with the difficult question of quantifying the rental value of industrial land upon which the trespasser had tipped a certain amount of waste matter. The appellant had been a trespasser on the respondent's land for 51 months and had been ordered to pay damages equating to lost rent valued at £78,000 per annum. The appellant argued that this figure was too high because the expert valuation from which this figure was derived was not a genuine estimate of what would have been a reasonable rent for the land concerned. Instead, the expert valuer had based the amount on the average rental value of industrial land in that part of the country. The appellant's argument that the figure arrived at was too high was based on the fact that it failed to take account of the waste that he himself had tipped there and which would have reduced significantly the amount that could have been obtained by way of rent for that land. In a judgment with which the other members of the Court of Appeal signalled their agreement, David Richards LJ held that the valuation was a legitimate one and that the trespasser "could not rely on the poor condition of the land to justify a lower figure".[403]

Although mesne profits can be claimed up to the time when the possession is surrendered[404] the question of when surrender occurs may not be straightforward. In *Jones v Merton LBC*,[405] the appellant had formerly been a council flat tenant who had fallen behind on the payment of his rent and become a "tolerated trespasser".[406] He was later attacked in the flat, receiving a gun wound to the leg. Hoping to avoid a repeat episode, he left the flat and subsequently arranged for a friend to remove all his possessions from it. He did not notify the local authority that he had left, nor did he return the keys or give notice of having had his possessions removed some months later. The local authority later claimed rent arrears up until the time that they had become aware of his having left. The appellant contested his liability to pay, arguing that his possession of the flat had been surrendered at a much earlier date. The Court of Appeal had to determine just when possession had been surrendered. They found for the appellant: a tolerated trespasser loses his status as such upon giving up possession quite *regardless of notification* to a former landlord. The appellant had remained in factual possession until the date when his friend removed his personal possessions.[407] His retention of the keys was held to be immaterial.[408] **18-78**

Sometimes, the property in question may have been permanently appropriated by the defendant. In *Ramzan v Brookwide Ltd*,[409] a first floor store room belonging to property X (an Indian restaurant) was located above property Y. Initially, while property X was owned by the claimant's father, the store room could only be accessed via property X. But, while still under the father's ownership, certain work was done later whereby the store room became part of property Y and the store room was now only accessible via that property. This construction work meant that the upper floor of property X could no longer be used as a function room. Shortly thereafter, the claimant acquired ownership of property X. The question that arose on these complex facts was what measure of damages the claimant would be **18-79**

402 [2018] EWCA Civ 162.
403 [2018] EWCA Civ 162 at [29], per David Richards LJ.
404 *Southport Tramways v Gandy* [1897] 2 Q.B. 66.
405 [2008] EWCA Civ 660; [2009] 1 W.L.R. 1269.
406 See para.19-63.
407 [2008] EWCA Civ 660; [2009] 1 W.L.R. 1269 at [32], per Wilson LJ.
408 [2008] EWCA Civ 660; [2009] 1 W.L.R. 1269 at [33].
409 [2011] EWCA Civ 985; [2012] 1 All E.R. 903.

entitled to. The Court of Appeal held that the claimant's "only claim would be that the trespass had prevented him from re-establishing the earlier use of the first floor as a function room" and since restoring it would take about six months, "some deduction should be made for this".[410] Additionally, the Court of Appeal also made clear that no claim for mesne profits (based on the notional letting value of the store room) would lie since there was never any prospect of *both* using the store room in conjunction with the restaurant *and* letting it out to some third party. Thus, the claimant had to choose between the two heads of loss as they were alternative not cumulative claims; and this the claimant had done.[411] Finally, the misappropriation of the store room had a continuing effect on the life of the claimant which justified an award of exemplary damages.[412]

7. Statutes of Limitation

18-80 **Adverse possession and licensed possession** Adverse possession for a sufficient period of time extinguishes title[413] and in effect produces an involuntary loss of property by a proprietor who fails to challenge a squatter (or other adverse possessor),[414] within the period of time allowed by statute. Also, to interrupt the adverse possession, the title owner must meaningfully bring the adverse possessor's possession to an end.[415] Since the law on adverse possession (which has been held not to be undermined by the doctrine of illegality[416]) permits a successful squatter, even with knowledge of the true title, to expropriate without compensation, it is necessary to define closely the limits of his ability to acquire another's land by adverse possession. However, where there is no evidence as to who the true owner is, the Land Registry will be entitled to register the applicant squatter's possessory, not absolute, title based on his or her adverse possession.[417] The phrase "adverse possession" in the Limitation Act 1980,[418] means no more than that a person is in adverse possession in whose favour time can run under the statute. By necessary implication, "time cannot run … in favour of a licensee" whose possession has been granted or tolerated.[419] Happily the courts have elaborated upon the concept. The

410 [2011] EWCA Civ 985; [2012] 1 All E.R. 903 at [41], per Arden LJ.
411 [2011] EWCA Civ 985; [2012] 1 All E.R. 903 at [67], per Arden LJ.
412 [2011] EWCA Civ 985; [2012] 1 All E.R. 903 at [80], per Arden LJ.
413 Limitation Act 1980 ss.15 and 17 (subject to s.18 in the case of unregistered land; and subject to the Land Registration Act 2002 s.98(1) in the case of registered land). The same 12 year rule applies to loss of title by adverse possession in Northern Ireland by virtue of the Limitation (Northern Ireland) Order 1989 art.21(1): *O'Brien v Martin* [2017] NICh 20.
414 It is possible to enter into adverse possession without being a squatter. For example, one might acquire title to an unregistered stretch of a tidal river bed: see *Port of London Authority v Ashmore* [2010] EWCA Civ 30; [2010] 1 All E.R. 1139 (acknowledged to be correct in *Moore v British Waterways Board* [2013] EWCA Civ 73; [2013] Ch. 488 at [57], per Lewison LJ). Equally, one may have been the tenant of a company registered abroad whose land in this country, when the company is wound up, passes to the Crown as bona vacantia. In principle, one may acquire rights of adverse possession against the Crown in such circumstances since one's occupation has never been with the consent of the Crown: *Everitt v Zeital* [2018] EWHC 1316 (Ch).
415 *Zarb v Parry* [2011] EWCA Civ 1306; [2012] 1 W.L.R. 1240.
416 *Rashid v Nasrullah* [2018] EWCA Civ 2685; [2020] Ch. 37 at [68]–[72].
417 *R. (on the application of Truong Dia Diep) v Land Registry* [2010] EWHC 3315 (Admin).
418 Sch.1 Pt I para.8.
419 See, e.g. *Smart v Lambeth London Borough Council* [2013] EWCA Civ 1375; [2014] H.L.R. 7; *Smith v Molyneaux* [2016] UKPC 35; [2017] 1 P. & C.R. 7.

leading case is *JA Pye (Oxford) Ltd v Graham*.[420] There, the House of Lords insisted that the words of the Act were to be given their ordinary and plain meaning. Thus, upon satisfaction of the twin tests of factual possession and intention to possess, time would run against the true owner. Adverse possession, Lord Hope said, is not a complex notion but one "used as a convenient label only, in recognition simply of the fact that the possession is adverse to the interests of the paper owner".[421] On the other hand, the statutory provisions governing adverse possession have since been held by the European Court of Human Rights to support violations of art.1 of Protocol 1 of the ECHR which provides for the right to the peaceful enjoyment of one's property.[422] But the existing rules persist; and despite what Lord Hope said about the relative simplicity of the concept of adverse possession, it has since been established that the question of the requisite intention requires some clarification. In *Roberts v Swangrove Estates Ltd*,[423] the Court of Appeal held that intention to trespass had to be distinguished from intention to enter into possession and on this basis found that the defendants had been in adverse possession even though they never intended to trespass.[424] Since then, it has been further clarified that in order to satisfy the statutory requirement of having reasonable belief that the disputed land was actually owned by the person in adverse possession,[425] such belief is to be judged according to what the person in adverse possession believed *personally* rather than what it was (or would have been) reasonable for the solicitors acting on his behalf to believe.[426]

So far as factual possession is concerned, the person claiming adverse possession will satisfy this requirement if he is able to provide evidence of his user of the land.[427] One established example is that of paving an area of land with a permanent surface.[428] In deciding whether the defendant is entitled to mount a counterclaim based on his adverse possession, the judge is bound to take seriously the evidence of both parties, as the Court of Appeal made emphatically clear in *Weymont v Place*.[429] In *Best v Chief Land Registrar*,[430] the Court of Appeal also supplied some examples of the kinds of acts to which the claimant might advert in seeking to demonstrate his adverse possession. These included, not merely the act of squatting but also the act of maintaining the property itself, and even maintaining external structures, such as a boundary fence. In essence, as Morgan J put it in *Food Converters Ltd v Newell*,[431] "the concept of possession of land does not require a person to be physically present on the land for every moment of the 12 year **18-81**

[420] [2002] UKHL 30; [2003] 1 A.C. 419.

[421] [2002] UKHL 30; [2003] 1 A.C. 419 at [69].

[422] *JA Pye (Oxford) Ltd v United Kingdom* (2006) 43 E.H.R.R. 3.

[423] [2008] EWCA Civ 98; [2008] Ch. 439.

[424] [2008] EWCA Civ 98; [2008] Ch. 439 at [87]. However, where there has been a mistaken registration of both A and B as the registered owners of land, it is impossible for either party to enter into adverse possession vis-à-vis the other since anyone with registered title cannot possibly be in adverse possession relative to another. Adverse possession as between A and B only becomes possible after the mistake in the Register has been rectified: see *Parshall v Bryans* [2013] EWCA Civ 240; [2013] Ch. 568.

[425] Land Registration Act 2002 Sch.6 para.5(4)(c).

[426] *IAM Group Plc v Chowdrey* [2012] EWCA Civ 505; [2012] 2 P. & C.R. 13 at [27], per Etherington LJ.

[427] *Akhtar v Brewster* [2012] EWHC 3521 (Ch).

[428] *Thorpe v Frank* [2019] EWCA Civ 150; [2019] 1 W.L.R. 6217.

[429] [2015] EWCA Civ 289; [2015] C.P. Rep. 29.

[430] [2015] EWCA Civ 17; [2016] Q.B. 23.

[431] [2018] EWHC 926 (Ch) at [35].

period... [for it is enough] if the person claiming to be in possession for 12 years, without interruption, has had the requisite degree of control of the land throughout the relevant period of 12 years".

18-82 **Licence a matter of fact** The Law Reform Committee recommended that the finding of a licence should depend on findings of fact alone and the Limitation Act 1980 Sch.1 Pt I para.8(4) now provides that:

> "for the purpose of determining whether a person occupying any land is in adverse possession of the land it shall not be assumed by implication of law that his occupation is by permission of the person entitled to the land merely by virtue of the fact that his occupation is not inconsistent with the latter's present or future enjoyment of the land. This provision shall not be taken as prejudicing a finding to the effect that a person's occupation of any land is by implied permission of the person entitled to the land in any case where such a finding is justified on the actual facts of the case."

The giving of a licence is a matter of fact and does not depend on positive acceptance by the licensee. Thus, where an occupier in adverse possession received a letter of licence to continue her occupation, the Court of Appeal held that time stopped running in her favour because she had received it, notwithstanding that she made no response to it.[432] Her possession was not adverse because it was referable to a lawful title to possess conferred by the licence.[433] Similarly, in *Smith v Lawson*,[434] the Court of Appeal held that a representation that no further rent would be collected gave rise to a promissory estoppel which would have prevented the owner from claiming possession for non-payment of rent. It followed that the occupant was effectively a licensee and could not establish adverse possession. But in the absence of a licence stopping time running, a mere letter demanding possession does not stop it. Unless a squatter vacates or gives a written acknowledgment, the owner must issue his writ within the prescribed time.[435]

18-83 **Period of limitation** So far as an action for damages in trespass is concerned, the claimant must normally bring his case within six years from the accrual of the cause of action.[436] However, when recovering land from a squatter, two rather different limitation periods apply, depending on whether the land in question was unregistered or registered. For unregistered land, the Limitation Act 1980 stipulates that a claimant must bring an action within 12 years of the time at which the right to bring that action first accrued to him or to some person through whom he claims.[437] At the determination of this period, his right and title to the land is extinguished.[438] When the person bringing the action, or his predecessor in title, has been in possession but has been dispossessed or has discontinued his possession, the right of action accrues on the date of the dispossession or discontinuance of

[432] *BP Properties Ltd v Buckler* (1987) 2 E.G. 168. In order to evict, the licensor must revoke the licence.

[433] cf. *Colchester BC v Smith* [1992] Ch. 421, in which an occupier who might otherwise have acquired land by adverse possession was prevented by estoppel from raising the question of title.

[434] (1998) 75 P. & C.R. 466.

[435] *Mount Carmel Investments Ltd v Thurlow (Ltd)* [1988] 1 W.L.R. 1078. It seems that the owner out of possession can stop time running by giving permission to stay (see *BP Properties v Buckler* (1987) 2 E.G. 168) and an entry may stop time running.

[436] Limitation Act 1980 s.2. The usual extension in cases of disabilities applies. See further para.31-21.

[437] Limitation Act s.15(1). There are modifications of this period in the case of the Crown: Sch.1 Pt II.

[438] Limitation Act s.17; *Nicholson v England* [1926] 2 K.B. 93.

possession.[439] In the case of registered land, the Land Registration Act 2002 provides that a claimant in adverse possession may apply to become the registered proprietor of the land after only 10 years' adverse possession.[440] Upon becoming the registered proprietor, the original proprietor's right to recover the land is extinguished. Although a squatter who enters a residential property commits a criminal offence under s.144 of the Legal Aid, Sentencing and Punishment of Offenders Act 2012, this illegality does not prevent his conduct from qualifying as adverse possession under Sch.6 to the Land Registration Act 2002.[441] On the other hand, the fact that the squatter is committing such an offence will make it easier for the true owner to enlist the assistance of the police in removing him.

When right of action accrues The right of action to recover land does not accrue until there is adverse possession in some person in whose favour the period of limitation can run. Adverse possession depends essentially on the nature of the squatter's user and how far it is inconsistent with, or prejudicial to, the purposes of the persons entitled.[442] If there is no-one in adverse possession, the right of action does not accrue until adverse possession is taken.[443] An act which may be a trespass does not necessarily constitute a dispossession.[444] For example, trivial incursions, such as children playing on land next to their mother's bungalow,[445] do not count for this purpose. In each case the conduct (*corpus*) and the motive (*animus*)[446] of the trespasser are to be considered on the facts.[447] The intention, or *animus possidendi*, is simply intention to keep possession; it does not necessarily involve an intention to gain a title. The conduct or *corpus* is any act of possession. Thus in *Treloar v Nute*,[448] the Court of Appeal found that where defendants extended agricultural operations to an adjacent plot unused by the claimant, fenced it in, and finally began to build a bungalow, the initial acts of levelling the ground constituted adverse possession from which time began to run against the claimant. The fact that the owner makes no use of, and apparently has no use for, his land does not preclude adverse possession. Nor does the fact that he has no immediate use for the land yet has plans for its use at a later date.[449] 18-84

Action under a will or intestacy or otherwise In actions to recover the land of a deceased person, whether under a will or on intestacy, and the deceased person was on the date of his death in possession of the land, the right of action accrues 18-85

439 Limitation Act Sch.1 Pt I para.1. Dispossession is the squatter expelling the true owner; discontinuance, the departure of the true owner followed by entry of the squatter.

440 Land Registration Act 2002 Sch. 6 para.1.

441 *Best v Chief Land Registrar* [2015] EWCA Civ 17; [2016] Q.B. 23 at [71].

442 *Wallis's Cayton Bay Holiday Camp Ltd v Shell-Mex BP Ltd* [1975] Q.B. 94. In each case it is necessary to decide whether the squatter had held adverse possession. See para.18-17.

443 Limitation Act 1980 Sch.1 Pt I para.8.

444 *Williams Brothers Direct Supply Ltd v Raftery* [1958] 1 Q.B. 159. cf. *Buckinghamshire CC v Moran* [1990] Ch. 623.

445 *Tecbild Ltd v Chamberlain* (1969) 20 P. & C.R. 633.

446 Defined, *Powell v McFarlane* (1979) 38 P. & C.R. 452 at 471. See also *Buckinghamshire CC v Moran* [1990] Ch. 623 at 639-640; *Lambeth LBC v Blackburn* [2001] EWCA Civ 912; (2001) 33 H.L.R. 74 (making it clear that a squatter who changes the locks on the premises in which he is squatting may reasonably be taken to have formed the intention to exclude the world at large, including the true owner).

447 *Prudential Assurance Co Ltd v Waterloo Real Estate Inc* [1999] 2 E.G.L.R. 85.

448 [1976] 1 W.L.R. 1295; *Williams v Usherwood* (1983) 45 P. & C.R. 235.

449 *Buckinghamshire CC v Moran* [1990] Ch. 623.

on the date of his death.[450] When any person brings an action to recover land, being an estate or interest in possession assured otherwise than by will to him or to some person through whom he claims, by a person who, at the date when the assurance took effect was in possession of the land and no person has been in possession of the land by virtue of the assurance, the right of action accrues when the assurance took effect.[451]

18-86 **Occupation by successive trespassers** Where a succession of trespassers, deriving possession from each other, together occupy land for the period of limitation, the true owner is barred, although each individual trespasser may occupy the land for less than 12 years. This is because a trespasser in possession, as against everyone but the true owner, can devise or convey his interest in the land or transmit it by inheritance.[452] And a bar may be raised also by continuous adverse possession by successive trespassers each in turn dispossessing the earlier. If, however, before the right of action is barred, the land ceases to be in adverse possession, the right of action does not accrue until the land is again taken into adverse possession.[453] So, where a succession of independent trespassers, not deriving title from each other nor maintaining continuous adverse possession by a chain of dispossessions, occupy land for the period of limitation, the true owner is not barred.

18-87 **Freeholder** It was thought at one time that "the effect of the Act [was] to make a parliamentary conveyance of the land to the person in possession after that period of (twelve) years has elapsed"[454] but the right view is that "the operation of the statute in giving a title is merely negative; it extinguishes the right and title of the dispossessed owner, and leaves the occupant with a title gained by the fact of possession, and resting on the infirmity of the right of others to eject him".[455] So in *St Marylebone Property Co Ltd v Fairweather*,[456] where a squatter had barred by adverse possession the rights of a 99-year leaseholder, the question was whether a surrender by the leaseholder to his freehold reversioner entitled the freeholder to evict the squatter's successor in title. The House of Lords held that as the squatter had not acquired the leaseholder's estate or any of his rights, it followed that on surrender from the leaseholder, the freeholder gained a right of action to recover the land from the squatter, the freeholder's right to possess not being affected by the squatter's former immunity from attack by the leaseholder.

18-88 **Remainderman** In the case of future estates the right accrues at the time when the estate becomes an estate in possession. But if the owner of the particular estate was out of possession at the time when his interest determined, then the action can only be brought within 12 years after the owner of the particular estate ceased to

450 Limitation Act 1980 Sch.1 Pt I para.2.

451 Limitation Act 1980 Sch.1 Pt I para.3.

452 *Asher v Whitlock* (1865) L.R. 1 Q.B. 1; *Mount Carmel Investments Ltd v Thurlow (Ltd)* [1988] 1 W.L.R. 1078.

453 Limitation Act 1980 Sch.1 Pt I para.8(2); *Trustees, Executors etc v Short* (1888) 13 App. Cas. 793.

454 *Doe (dec'd) Jukes v Sumner* (1845) 14 M. & W. 39 at 42.

455 *Taylor v Twinberrow* [1930] 2 K.B. 16 at 23.

456 [1963] A.C. 510. For registered title, see *Spectrum Investment Co v Holmes* [1981] 1 W.L.R. 221. cf. *Central London Commercial Estates Ltd v Kato Kagaku Ltd* [1998] 4 All E.R. 948. The decision in *St Marylebone Property Co Ltd v Fairweather* does not apply to registration of a possessory title by a squatter. By the Land Registration Act 2002 s.97 and Sch.6, the squatter with 10 years' adverse title is entitled to be registered as the proprietor of the land. In connection with statutory tenancies see *Jessamine Investment Co v Schwartz* [1978] Q.B. 264.

be in possession, or within six years after the future estate falls into possession, whichever period is the longer. However, if the owner of the future estate is once barred, all persons claiming to be entitled to any subsequent estates under any deed, will, or settlement, executed or taking effect after the accrual of the right of action of the owner of the particular estate, are also barred.[457] Under the general rule, possession established by very long periods of adverse possession may be defeated upon the vesting of a future interest.

Reversioner Where land is let under a lease, time runs from the date when the lessor became entitled to an estate in possession, that is, from the expiration of the lease.[458] If he became entitled to possession by reason of any forfeiture or breach of condition, time runs from the forfeiture or breach[459]; but if the forfeiture is waived, time runs only from the date when the lessor became entitled to an estate in possession.[460] So, under a lease containing a proviso for re-entry on non-payment of rent where no rent had been paid for over 12 years, it was held that the lessor was not debarred from recovering possession, and that each non-payment of rent gave rise to a fresh right of re-entry from which time started to run.[461] In such a case, the lessor can only recover six years' arrears of rent.[462] But if the rent reserved by a lease in writing is more than £10 per annum, and the tenant not merely does not pay it to the landlord, but pays it wrongfully to a third person, then in such a case the statute runs not from the expiry of the lease but from the date of the first wrongful receipt of rent by such third person.[463] The receipt of rent by a person wrongfully claiming the land in reversion is deemed to be in adverse possession of the land.[464] **18-89**

Tenancies In the case of a tenancy from year to year under a lease not in writing, the statute runs from the end of the first year or from the last receipt of rent, whichever occurs later.[465] But where the tenancy is from year to year under a lease in writing, in the absence of something done by the tenant amounting to a repudiation of the landlord's title, it seems that the statute does not run until the landlord chooses to give a notice to quit.[466] In the case of possession under an agreement for a lease the statute does not run during the period of the intended term.[467] For tenancies at will, time runs in favour of the occupier till the tenancy has been actually determined. On actual determination, the tenancy becomes a tenancy at sufferance; in effect, adverse possession. Finally, where there are beneficial joint tenants who hold the land on trust for sale,[468] and one joint tenant is in sole possession of the land, no right of action accrues during his possession to a person entitled **18-90**

457 Limitation Act 1980 s.15(2), (3), (4).
458 Limitation Act 1980 Sch.1 Pt I para.4.
459 Limitation Act 1980 Sch.1 Pt I para.7(1).
460 Limitation Act 1980 Sch.1 Pt I para.7(2).
461 *Barratt v Richardson and Cresswell* [1930] 1 K.B. 686.
462 Limitation Act 1980 s.19; *Archbold v Scully* (1861) 9 H.L.C. 360.
463 Limitation Act 1980 Sch.1 Pt I para.6.
464 Limitation Act 1980 Sch.1 Pt I para.8(3)(b).
465 Limitation Act 1980 Sch.1 Pt I para.5; *Hayward v Chaloner* [1968] 1 Q.B. 107. Time runs against the landlord even if he is content that his tenant should not pay rent and does not bother to ask him for it. The tenant is in adverse possession once the period covered by the last payment of rent has expired.
466 See *Stagg v Wyatt* (1838) 2 Jur. 892, as to when a notice to quit is to be presumed.
467 *Warren v Murray* [1894] 2 Q.B. 648.
468 See the Law of Property Act 1925 s.36.

to a beneficial interest in the land or the proceeds of sale, because he is in possession as a trustee and beneficiary.[469]

18-91 **Beneficiary in possession** Under the Limitation Act 1980, time cannot run against trustees or co-beneficiaries unless the beneficiary in possession is solely and absolutely entitled.[470]

18-92 **Occupation by employees** Where an employee is permitted to occupy gratuitously premises belonging to his employer for the purpose of the more convenient discharge of his duties, he does not normally acquire any tenancy. Such occupation is treated solely as that of his employer.[471] This is so even if the employee is permitted under his employment contract to carry on an independent business on the premises.[472] Consequently, however long such occupation by the employee, it will never give him a good title against his master.

18-93 **Encroachment by tenants** A tenant who takes the opportunity afforded him by his tenancy to make encroachments upon the adjoining land of third persons, is presumed to have intended to make them for the benefit of his lessor, unless there be circumstances pointing to an intention to take the land for his own benefit exclusively.[473] And the assent of the lessor to the making of the enclosure makes no difference.[474] The tenant, therefore, in general cannot acquire a statutory title to the subject matter of the encroachment by possession and during the tenancy; the statute only begins to run in his favour after the tenancy has expired. But one who occupies, as his own, land belonging to another, and subsequently becomes tenant to the latter of land adjacent to the land so occupied, does not thereby change the character of his possession, but can, whilst he remains tenant of the adjacent land, acquire as against his landlord a title to the land so occupied by him, provided of course that he does not pay rent or otherwise act as tenant in respect of it.[475]

18-94 **Land in mortgage** When a mortgagee of land has been in possession of any of the mortgaged land for a period of 12 years, no action to redeem the land can be brought by the mortgagor.[476] An action by a mortgagee of land to recover his debt is barred on the expiration of 12 years after the right to receive the money accrued.[477] The right accrues on the date of any payment made in respect of the mortgage debt, whether of principal or interest.[478] The right to recover arrears of interest is barred on the expiration of six years from the date on which the interest became due.[479] The mortgagee's action to foreclose is an action to recover land and

469 Limitation Act 1980 Sch.1 Pt I para.9; *Landi, Re* [1939] Ch. 828; *Milking Pail Farm Trusts, Re* [1940] Ch. 996.

470 Limitation Act 1980 Sch.1 Pt I para.1 and para.8; *Bridges v Mees* [1957] Ch. 475.

471 *Bertie v Beaumont* (1812) 16 East 33; *National Steam Car Co v Barham* (1919) 122 L.T. 315; see also para.18-24.

472 *White v Bayley* (1861) 10 C.B. (N.S.) 227.

473 *Doe v Jones* (1846) 15 M. & W. 580.

474 *Whitmore v Humphries* (1871) L.R. 7 C. & P. 1.

475 *Dixon v Baty* (1866) L.R. 1 Ex. 259.

476 Limitation Act 1980 s.16.

477 Limitation Act 1980 s.20.

478 Limitation Act 1980 s.29(5).

479 Limitation Act 1980 s.20(5). But if interest is claimed in redemption proceedings, the mortgagor is liable to pay all arrears however old: *Holmes v Cowcher* [1970] 1 W.L.R. 834.

the period of 12 years applies, but each payment of interest constitutes an acknowledgment at which time (and not before) the right of action accrues.[480]

Extensions of time If at the time of the accrual of his right of action the party entitled is under a disability by reason of his being an infant, or of unsound mind, a further extension of time is allowed of six years from the termination of the disability, subject to this: that the action must be brought within 30 years after the accrual of the right.[481] When the action is based on the fraud of the defendant or his agent, or a right of action is concealed deliberately by the defendant or his agent, or the action is for relief from the consequences of a mistake, the limitation period does not begin to run until the claimant has discovered the fraud, concealment, or mistake, or could with reasonable diligence have done so.[482] With regard to concealment "deliberate commission of a breach of duty in circumstances in which it is unlikely to be discovered for some time amounts to deliberate concealment of the facts involved in that breach of duty".[483] But these provisions do not enable an action to recover property to be brought against a purchaser where the property has been resold for valuable consideration to an innocent third party. **18-95**

Acknowledgement Where there has accrued any right of action to recover land and the person in possession acknowledges the title of the person to whom the right of action has accrued, the right is deemed to have accrued on the date of the acknowledgment.[484] The acknowledgment must be in writing signed by the maker or his agent[485] and made to or for the account of the person whose claim is being acknowledged.[486] Such acknowledgements also serve to interrupt the continuity of adverse possession, and future claims based on adverse possession can only be based on possession since the date of the acknowledgement.[487] A current period of limitation may be repeatedly extended by acknowledgments, but a right of action once statutorily barred cannot be revived by a subsequent acknowledgment or payment.[488] **18-96**

8. WASTE

Waste The subject of injuries to reversionary interests in land caused by an act of trespass on the part of a stranger has already been dealt with.[489] What remains are those injuries to the reversion caused by a person in possession under a limited interest and which are known by the name of "waste". The action for waste is an action in tort.[490] Waste has been defined to be "the committing of any spoil or destruction in houses, land etc by tenants, to the damage of the heir, or of him in **18-97**

---

480 Limitation Act 1980 ss.20(2), 29(3).
481 Limitation Act 1980 s.28.
482 Limitation Act 1980 s.32. See *Sheldon v RHM Outhwaite (Underwriting Agencies) Ltd* [1996] 1 A.C. 102.
483 Limitation Act 1980 s.32(2).
484 Limitation Act 1980 s.29(2).
485 The agent's authority need not be express; acknowledgment given with general authority will suffice: *Wright v Pepin* [1954] 1 W.L.R. 635.
486 Limitation Act 1980 s.30.
487 *Ofulue v Bossert* [2009] UKHL 16; [2009] 1 A.C. 990 at [77], per Lord Neuberger.
488 Limitation Act 1980 s.29(7).
489 See para.18-26.
490 *Defries v Milne* [1913] 1 Ch. 98 at 108.

reversion or remainder".[491] Nominal damages cannot be recovered,[492] nor, unless the damage is substantial, will the court interfere by injunction.[493] It is essential to show that the building or other act complained of is an injury to the inheritance.[494] The breaking up of a permanent pasture and the working of mines unopened at the commencement of the tenancy is waste.[495] So also is the accumulation of large quantities of rubbish,[496] and the cutting of timber, except for the purpose of repairs. To this rule, however, there is apparently an exception in the case of what have been termed "timber estates": estates which are cultivated merely for the produce of saleable timber, and upon which the practice has been to cut the timber periodically, and treat the proceeds as part of the annual profits of the land.[497] Again, where a material and enduring alteration is made in the character of the land, even though such alteration may tend to enhance its value, it is waste, in respect of which a court will award substantial damages for the past wrong, and an injunction restraining future acts of a similar character.[498] In an action for waste, the measure of damages is (in the absence of any matter of aggravation) the diminution in the value of the reversion, less a discount for immediate payment.[499]

18-98 **Permissive waste** All the kinds of waste referred to above belong to the class known as "voluntary waste", which consists of acts of misfeasance. There is another class of waste known as "permissive waste", which consists of omission—i.e. neglecting to keep the premises in a state of repair—in cases in which a duty to repair exists. Such duties really only arise between landlord and tenant, and as such the action nearly always sounds in contract. Certainly, no action in tort will lie against a tenant for life for permissive waste,[500] even in the case of leaseholds,[501] unless by the terms of the limitation under which he holds, he is expressly required to keep the premises in repair.[502]

---

491 Bac. Abr., Vol.8, p.379.

492 *Doherty v Allman* (1878) 3 App. Cas. 709 at 733, per Lord Blackburn.

493 *Doherty v Allman* (1878) 3 App. Cas. 709 at 733, per Lord Blackburn.

494 *Jones v Chappell* (1875) L.R. 20 Eq. 539; *Meux v Cobley* [1892] 2 Ch. 253.

495 Co. Litt. p.53b.

496 *West Ham Charity Board v East London Waterworks Co* [1900] 1 Ch. 624.

497 *Dashwood v Magniac* [1891] 3 Ch. 306; *Honeywood v Honeywood* (1874) L.R. 18 Eq. 306 at 309.

498 *West Ham Central Charity Board v East London Waterworks Co* [1900] 1 Ch. 624; *Hyman v Rose* [1912] A.C. 623.

499 *Whitham v Kershaw* (1885–86) 16 Q.B.D. 613.

500 *Cartwright, Re* (1889) 41 Ch. D. 532.

501 *Parry and Hopkin, Re* [1900] 1 Ch. 160.

502 *Woodhouse v Walker* (1880) 5 Q.B.D. 404.

CHAPTER 19

NUISANCE AND RYLANDS V FLETCHER

TABLE OF CONTENTS

1. THE NATURE OF NUISANCE

(a) Role of nuisance

19-01 **Nuisance defined**[1] The essence of nuisance is a condition or activity which unduly interferes with the use or enjoyment of land. In ordinary speech, smells and smoke and a variety of different things may amount to a nuisance in fact but whether they are actionable as the tort of nuisance will depend upon a variety of considerations and a balancing of conflicting interests. An actionable nuisance is incapable of exact definition,[2] and it may overlap with some other heading of liability in tort such as negligence.[3] Furthermore, recent decisions of the House of

[1] See Murphy, *The Law of Nuisance* (2010); Buckley, *The Law of Negligence and Nuisance*, 6th edn (2017); Beever, *The Law of Private Nuisance* (2013); Steele, "Private Law and the Environment Nuisance in Context" (1995) 15 L.S. 236; Gearty, "The Place of Private Nuisance in a Modern Law of Torts" [1989] C.L.J. 214; Lee, "What is Private Nuisance?" (2003) 119 L.Q.R. 298.

[2] *Bamford v Turnley* (1860) 3 B. & S. 62 at 66, 79 and 83–88; *Harrison v Good* (1871) L.R. 11 Eq. 338 at 351; *Pwllbach Colliery Co Ltd v Woodman* [1915] A.C. 634 at 638–639.

[3] See, e.g. *Graff Brothers Estates Ltd v Rimrose Brook Joint Sewerage Board* [1953] 2 Q.B. 318 (a claim for damages for wrongfully removing the support of land and houses may cover claims in negligence, trespass and nuisance); *Southport Corp v Esso Petroleum Co Ltd, Esso Petroleum Co Ltd v Southport Corp* [1956] A.C. 218 (relation between nuisance, negligence and trespass discussed).

Lords have confirmed that the rule in *Rylands v Fletcher*,[4] sometimes treated as a separate head of liability, is to be regarded as coming under the nuisance umbrella.[5] Nuisance is an act or omission which is an interference with, disturbance of or annoyance to, a person in the exercise or enjoyment of: (a) a right belonging to him as a member of the public, when it is a public nuisance; or (b) his ownership or occupation of land or of some easement, profit, or other right used or enjoyed in connection with land, when it is a private nuisance. The rights conferred by the law of nuisance arise by virtue of the general common law, and are therefore not dependent for their coming into existence on the terms of any conveyance of the land in question.[6]

Nuisance and trespass The distinction between trespass and nuisance is the old distinction between trespass and case. Trespass is a direct entry on the land of another, and is actionable per se, without proof of special damage, but nuisance is the infringement of the claimant's interest in property without direct entry by the defendant, and generally actionable only on proof of special damage. For example, to build a wall partly on someone else's is a trespass, but to build on one's own land a wall which, through disrepair, falls on to another's land is a nuisance.[7] It is a trespass for A directly to discharge water on to B's land, but if water spills from A's land over intermediate land onto B's land this amounts to a nuisance.[8] Such a distinction may be on certain facts an exceedingly fine one.[9] But the distinction will not normally become vital to the claimant's claim where he can allege and prove special damage. If he cannot prove special damage, then he will have to show an entry by way of trespass. It is a nuisance and not a trespass if the branches of a tree, whether planted or self-sown, growing on the land of one man, overhang his neighbour's land,[10] or if the roots burrow into his land and damage his buildings.[11] 19-02

Public nuisance A public nuisance is a criminal offence: 19-03

> "A person is guilty of a public nuisance …, who (a) does an act not warranted by law, or (b) omits to discharge a legal duty, if the effect of the act or omission is to endanger the

[4] (1866) L.R. 1 Ex. 265; affirmed in (1886) L.R. 3 HL 330 HL.

[5] Until the nineteenth edition of this book the rule in *Rylands v Fletcher* was the subject of a separate chapter, but see now paras 19-44 to 19-62.

[6] See *Thornhill v Sita Metal Recycling Ltd* [2009] EWHC 2037 (QB); [2009] Env. L.R. 35.

[7] *St Anne's Well Brewery Co v Roberts* (1928) 140 L.T. 1; [1928] All E.R. Rep. 28, per Scrutton LJ; see also *Lemmon v Webb* [1895] A.C. 1; *Kine v Jolly* [1905] 1 Ch. 480 at 487, per Vaughan Williams LJ; *Mann v Saulnier* (1959) 19 D.L.R. (2d) 130 (top of fence leaning over neighbouring land not trespass); Hudson, "Trespass or Nuisance" (1960) 19 M.L.R. 188 at 190.

[8] *Nobilo v Waitemata County* [1961] N.Z.L.R. 1064.

[9] In *Southport Corp v Esso Petroleum Co Ltd* [1954] 2 Q.B. 182, where oil was discharged from a ship and carried by wind and water onto the claimant's foreshore, judicial opinion varied. See also, per Denning LJ at 195–196 (nuisance only); per Morris LJ at 204 (may be trespass). See [1956] A.C. 218 at 225, per Devlin J (both trespass and nuisance) and at 242 and 244, per Lords Radcliffe and Tucker (nuisance only). In *Home Brewery Plc v Davis & Co* [1987] Q.B. 339, it was held that the squeezing out of water from the defendants' land on to the claimant's was actionable and it made no difference in result whether the cause of action arose in trespass or in nuisance.

[10] *Lemmon v Webb* [1895] A.C. 1; *Smith v Giddy* [1904] 2 K.B. 448.

[11] *Butler v Standard Telephones and Cables Ltd* [1940] 1 K.B. 399; *Davey v Harrow Corp* [1958] 1 Q.B. 60 CA at 71–73; [1957] C.L.J. 137 at 140; and [1958] C.L.J. 32 at 34; *McCombe v Read* [1955] 2 Q.B. 429; *Mills v Smith (No.2)* [1964] 1 Q.B. 30.

life, health, property, morals, or comfort of the public, or to obstruct the public in the exercise or enjoyment of rights common to all Her Majesty's subjects."[12]

It is sufficient if it materially affects the reasonable comfort and convenience of a class of Her Majesty's subjects who come within the sphere or neighbourhood of its operation; it may affect some to a greater extent than others; it is not necessary to prove that every member of the class has been injuriously affected, and it is a question of fact whether the number of persons affected is sufficiently large to attract the description "public" to the nuisance.[13] It is only a civil wrong and actionable as such when a private individual has suffered particular damage over and above the general inconvenience and injury suffered by the public,[14] for example through the obstruction of a highway. It is quite possible for the same act to constitute both a public and a private nuisance; the two causes of action are not mutually exclusive, nor is a cause of action in private nuisance subsumed in one for public nuisance. In *Colour Quest Ltd v Total Downstream UK Plc*[15] a huge explosion for which the defendants were responsible endangered the health and comfort of the public over a wide area; a submission by the defendants that claimants who owned property within the affected area were confined to claims in private nuisance was rejected.

19-04 **Examples** In truth the concept of public nuisance is a historical survival which does not fit easily into modern law. As a crime it is unduly vague by contemporary standards, and as a tort it is apt to be a source of anomaly sitting, as it does, uneasily alongside the concepts of both negligence and private nuisance. Public nuisances at common law include such diverse activities as carrying on an offensive trade, exposing in the public streets a person suffering from an infectious disease,[16] selling food unfit for human consumption, obstructing the highway by rendering it dangerous and inconvenient to pass, allowing a house near the highway to be ruinous, making or selling fireworks or throwing them about the street, holding an "acid house" party,[17] keeping a disorderly house,[18] motor-racing[19] or obstructing a

---

[12] *Archbold: Criminal Pleading, Evidence and Practice* (2017), para.31-40. See generally Spencer, "Public Nuisance—A Critical Examination" [1989] C.L.J. 55; Neyers, "Reconceptualising the Tort of Public Nuisance" [2017] C.L.J. 87. The proposition that a common law offence of public nuisance continues to exist was confirmed by the House of Lords in *R. v Goldstein* [2005] UKHL 63; [2006] 1 A.C. 459 (rejecting a submission that the concept was too vague and imprecise to provide a basis for criminal liability).

[13] *Att Gen v PYA Quarries Ltd* [1957] 2 Q.B. 169 at 184, per Romer LJ; and at 190–191, per Denning LJ; *British Celanese Ltd v AH Hunt (Capacitors) Ltd* [1969] 1 W.L.R. 959 at 969, per Lawton J. See also *DPP v Fearon* [2010] EWHC 340 (Admin); [2010] 2 Cr. App. R. 22 at [8] per Elias LJ.

[14] See para.19-181. On the nature of the particular damage, see Kodilnye, "Public Nuisance and Particular Damage in the Modern Law" (1986) 6 L.S. 182. In *The Claimants appearing on the Register of the Corby Group Litigation v Corby BC* [2008] EWCA Civ 463; [2009] Q.B. 335 the Court of Appeal held that, until the House of Lords rules otherwise, it is still the law that damages for personal injury are recoverable in *public* (as distinct from private) nuisance; and the Court therefore refused to strike out such a claim.

[15] [2009] EWHC 540 (Comm); [2009] 2 Lloyd's Rep. 1; reversed in part, but not on this point: [2010] EWCA Civ 180; [2011] Q.B. 86.

[16] *R. v Vantandillo* (1815) 4 M. & S. 73; *Metropolitan Asylum District v Hill* (1881) 6 App. Cas. 193 at 204.

[17] *R. v Ruffell (David)* (1992) 13 Cr. App. R. (S.) 204 CA; *R. v Shorrock (Peter)* [1994] Q.B. 279 CA.

[18] Bl. Comm., iv. 167.

[19] *East Dorset DC v Eaglebeam* [2006] EWHC 2378 (QB); [2007] Env. L.R. D9; *Croydon LBC v*

navigable river by lowering its depth.[20] Various matters have been declared to be nuisances by statute, particularly by the Environmental Protection Act 1990 Pt III,[21] and the Clean Air Act 1993.[22] The Noise Act 1996 contains measures concerned with noise, including a new criminal offence relating to the emission of noise at night, subject to a resolution by the local authority adopting the Act's provisions. The Environmental Protection Act 1990 also contains wide-ranging provisions with respect to waste disposal and pollution control generally.[23]

Relevance of common law The element which all public nuisances, whether at common law or by statute, have in common with private nuisances is that of annoyance or inconvenience. The wide range of modern statutory regulation of environmental conditions has made the common law remedies less useful than in earlier times, but though in many respects reduced to a supportive or supplemental role in this area the common law of nuisance remains of use where the injured party requires compensatory damages or where the public agency is not prepared to take action.[24] It may be noted that where the word "nuisance" occurs in a statute, then unless it is otherwise expressly defined, it will bear its common law meaning.[25] 19-05

(b) Scope of private nuisance

Private nuisance Just as in issues of public nuisance, modern statutory control has had an effect in diminishing the role of private nuisance as a regulation of duties between neighbours. Refusal of planning permission may prevent many activities which would otherwise be a nuisance, but the tort of nuisance still provides sanctions against excessive interferences from activities which are not in themselves unlawful or unpermitted by public control over the use of property. The acts which constitute public nuisances are all of them unlawful acts. In private nuisance, on the other hand, the conduct of the defendant which results in the nuisance is, of itself, not necessarily or usually unlawful. A private nuisance may be and usually is caused by a person doing, on his own land, something which he is lawfully entitled to do. 19-06

Persons Unknown [2016] EWHC 3018 (QB).

20 *Tate & Lyle Industries Ltd v GLC* [1983] 2 A.C. 509. See also *Jan de Nul (UK) v NV Royal Belge* [2000] 2 Lloyd's Rep. 700; affirmed [2002] EWCA Civ 209; [2002] 1 Lloyd's Rep 583.

21 This restates the law relating to statutory nuisances, replacing Pt III of the Public Health Act 1936, and improves the summary procedures for dealing with them. Those procedures were considered by the House of Lords, in the context of the 1936 Act, in *Sandwell MBC v Bujok* [1990] 1 W.L.R. 1350. A conviction for statutory nuisance can, in appropriate cases, lead to a compensation order under the Powers of Criminal Courts (Sentencing) Act 2000 s.130: *Herbert v Lambeth LBC* (1991) 90 L.G.R. 310 DC. But an action for damages for breach of statutory duty is not available: *Issa v Hackney LBC* [1997] 1 W.L.R. 956.

22 Consolidating and amending the Clean Air Acts 1956 and 1968.

23 See Purdue, "Integrated Pollution Control in the Environmental Protection Act 1990: A Coming of Age of Environmental Law?" (1991) 54 M.L.R. 534. The whole statutory regime of environmental health law falls outside the scope of a treatise on torts. See generally *Encyclopaedia of Environmental Law and Practice*.

24 Enforcement of duties under relevant legislative provisions is, for the most part, the concern of local authorities and other public agencies, although occasionally provision may be made for private suit by a person aggrieved by the breach of a statutory duty. In certain cases the public authority may be under a duty compellable by mandatory order, e.g. *R. v Surrey CC Ex p. Send Parish Council* (1979) 40 P. & C.R. 390 (duty to prevent continued obstruction of public footpath).

25 See *National Coal Board v Neath BC* [1976] 2 All E.R. 478 DC.

His conduct only becomes a nuisance when the consequences of his act are not confined to his own land but extend to the land of his neighbour by:

(1) causing an encroachment on his neighbour's land, when it closely resembles trespass;
(2) causing physical damage to his neighbour's land or building or works or vegetation upon it; or
(3) unduly interfering with his neighbour in the comfortable and convenient enjoyment of his land.

It may be a nuisance when a person does something on his own property which interferes with his neighbour's ability to enjoy his property by putting it to profitable use. It is also a nuisance to interfere with some easement or profit or other right used or enjoyed with his neighbour's land. In referring to the breaking down of instances of private nuisance into the three categories referred to in this paragraph Sir Terence Etherton MR expressed himself as follows in *Network Rail Infrastructure Ltd v Williams*[26]:

> "The difficulty with any rigid categorisation is that it may not easily accommodate possible examples of nuisance in new social conditions or may undermine a proper analysis of factual situations which have aspects of more than one category but do not fall squarely within any one category, having regard to existing case law".

The instant case concerned the notorious "bamboo-like perennial plant" Japanese knotweed which had spread from the defendant's land on to that of the claimants. It involved both category (1), encroachment, and category (3), interference with enjoyment.

(i) Nuisance by encroachment or damage

19-07 **Examples** Nuisances of the first kind, in the nature of encroachments, occur when a man builds on to his own house a cornice which projects over his neighbour's garden so as to cause rainwater to flow thereon,[27] when his trees overhang his neighbour's land,[28] and when the roots of his trees grow into his neighbour's land.[29] Nuisances of the second kind, causing physical damage to land or to something erected or growing upon it, occur when a man allows a drain on his own land to become blocked or makes a concrete paved drive[30] so that the water overflows onto his neighbour's land,[31] maintains a mound of earth or other artificial erection on his own land so as to cause damp to enter his neighbour's land,[32] works the mines under his own land so as to cause the surface of his neighbour's land to subside, allows

---

26 See [2018] EWCA Civ 1514; [2019] Q.B. 601 at [41].

27 *Fay v Prentice* (1845) 1 C.B. 828.

28 *Smith v Giddy* [1904] 2 K.B. 448; *Lemmon v Webb* [1895] A.C. 1; *Earl of Lonsdale v Nelson* (1823) 2 B. & C. 302 at 311. For trees overhanging the highway, see para.19-100.

29 *Butler v Standard Telephones and Cables Ltd* [1940] 1 K.B. 399; *Davey v Harrow Corp* [1958] 1 Q.B. 60 CA. See also *Hilda's Montessori Nursery Ltd v Tesco Stores Ltd* [2006] EWHC 1054 (QB) (in which the causal processes by which tree-roots operate to cause subsidence are examined).

30 *Bennetts v Honroth* [1959] S.A.S.R. 171 (paved drive leading to private garage diverting storm waters to neighbouring land actionable). See Derham, "Interference with Surface Waters by Lower Landholders" (1958) 74 L.Q.R. 361 at 380.

31 *Sedleigh-Denfield v O'Callaghan* [1940] A.C. 880; considered and applied in *Pemberton v Bright* [1960] 1 W.L.R. 436.

32 *Hurdman v NE Ry* (1878) 3 C.P.D. 168; *Broder v Saillard* (1876) 2 Ch. D. 692; *Maberley v Peabody & Co* [1946] 2 All E.R. 192.

buildings upon his land to become dilapidated so that they, or parts of them, fall upon his neighbour's land,[33] sets up vibrations on his own land which cause damage to his neighbour's buildings,[34] or emits noxious fumes from his land which damage his neighbour's crops or trees.[35]

In the case of nuisance by encroachment or damage, liability is established by proving the encroachment or the damage to the land as the case may be. The situation of the land affected, the character of the neighbourhood and the surrounding circumstances are not matters to be taken into consideration: **19-08**

> "It is a very desirable thing to mark the difference between an action brought for a nuisance upon the ground that the alleged nuisance produces material injury to the property, and an action brought for a nuisance on the ground that the thing alleged to be a nuisance is productive of sensible personal discomfort. With regard to the latter ... whether that may or may not be denominated a nuisance must undoubtedly depend greatly on the circumstances of the place where the thing complained of actually occurs ... . But where an occupation is carried on by one person in the neighbourhood of another, and the result of that trade or occupation or business is a material injury to property, then there unquestionably arises a very different consideration."[36]

What Lord Westbury meant by "material injury to the property" includes visible physical deterioration, but he continued by referring to "sensible injury to the value of property". Whether a diminution in the selling value of land or buildings without physical damage falls within this category is doubtful[37]; it appears to be relevant to his second category where the character of the neighbourhood is to be taken into account.[38] The position is the same when the nuisance consists of the interference with an easement. In that case, the character of the neighbourhood and the circumstances of the place where the interference took place are not matters to be taken into account.[39]

---

33 *Wringe v Cohen* [1940] 1 K.B. 229; *Todd v Flight* (1860) 9 C.B. (N.S.) 337. It is not a nuisance if the defendant's house pulls the plaintiff's house on to the defendant's land: *Sack v Jones* [1925] Ch. 235.

34 *Grosvenor Hotel Co v Hamilton* [1894] 2 Q.B. 836; *Hoare & Co v McAlpine* [1923] 1 Ch. 167.

35 *St Helens Smelting Co v Tipping* (1865) 11 H.L.C. 642; *Salvin v North Brancepeth Coal Co* (1874) L.R. 9 Ch. 705; *Manchester Corp v Farnworth* [1930] A.C. 171.

36 *St Helens Smelting Co v Tipping* (1865) 11 H.L.C. 642 at 650, per Lord Westbury LC; *Halsey v Esso Petroleum Co Ltd* [1961] 1 W.L.R. 683 at 689–692. See also *Clift v Welsh Office* [1999] 1 W.L.R. 796 CA. cf. *Northumbrian Water Ltd v Sir Robert McAlpine Ltd* [2014] EWCA Civ 685; (2014) 154 Con. L.R. 26 in which *Clift's* case was distinguished (see further para.19-15).

37 cf. *Halsey v Esso Petroleum Co Ltd* [1961] 1 W.L.R. 683 where the nuisance injured goods in or near the plaintiff's house which itself was not materially affected. The locality test was not applied to that injury. Lord Westbury's statement may perhaps be seen as a mere presumption against judging by locality in damage cases: Buckley, *The Law of Negligence and Nuisance*, 6th edn (London: LexisNexis, 2017), Ch.11, para.11.09.

38 cf. *Smith v Inco Ltd* [2011] ONCA 628; (2011) 107 O.R. (3d) 321 in which the Ontario Court of Appeal held that a reduction in property values unaccompanied by actual physical damage, but caused by unjustified fears by the public about the possible health consequences of emissions from the defendants' refinery, did not constitute an actionable nuisance at all.

39 *Horton's Estate Ltd v James Beattie Ltd* [1927] 1 Ch. 75 (the standard of light in manufacturing districts is no different from that in the country).

(ii) *Nuisance by interference with enjoyment*

19-09 **Examples** Nuisances of the third kind, causing an interference with the enjoyment of land, are, for example creating smells by the carrying on of an offensive manufacture or otherwise,[40] causing smoke or noxious fumes to pass on to the claimant's property,[41] raising clouds of coal dust,[42] making unreasonable noises,[43] or vibration,[44] using a building as a hospital for infectious diseases whereby the adjoining owners live in perpetual dread of infection,[45] using a house for prostitution,[46] allowing travellers to gather to the detriment of the claimant's neighbouring property,[47] causing crowds to collect,[48] watching and besetting a man's house so as to compel him to act in a particular way,[49] causing excessive heat to pass into an adjacent tenement comprised in the same block of buildings[50] and abstracting heat and reducing premises to "arctic conditions".[51] Dicta in the House of Lords suggest that nuisances of this third kind "will generally arise from something *emanating* from the defendant's land",[52] and that the exceptional cases which do not

---

40 *Walter v Selfe* (1851) 4 De G. & Sm. 315; *Bamford v Turnley* (1860) 3 B. & S. 62 (brick-burning); *R. v Pierce* (1683) 2 Show. 327 (soap-boiling); *Crump v Lambert* (1867) L.R. 3 Eq. 409; *Att Gen v Squires* (1906) 5 L.G.R. 99 (factory chimney); *Aldred's Case* (1610) 9 Rep. 57b (keeping swine); *Rapier v London Tramway Co* [1893] 2 Ch. 588 (stables); *Att Gen v Tod Heatley* [1897] 1 Ch. 560 (rubbish); *Att Gen v Cole* [1901] 1 Ch. 205 (fat melting); *Adams v Ursell* [1913] 1 Ch. 269 (fried fish shop); *Wood v Conway Corp* [1914] 2 Ch. 47 (gas fumes); *Bainbridge v Chertsey Urban DC* (1915) 84 L.J. Ch. 626 (sewage farm).

41 *Crump v Lambert* (1867) L.R. 3 Eq. 409; *St Helens Smelting Co v Tipping* (1865) 11 H.L.C. 642; *Salvin v North Brancepeth Coal Co* (1874) L.R. 9 Ch. 705; *Manchester Corp v Farnworth* [1930] A.C. 171; Clean Air Act 1993.

42 *Pwllbach Colliery v Woodman* [1915] A.C. 634.

43 *Ball v Ray* (1873) L.R. 8 Ch. 467; *Broder v Saillard* (1876) 2 Ch. D. 692 (stables); *Inchbald v Robinson* (1869) L.R. 4 Ch. 388 (circus); *Soltau v De Held* (1851) 2 Sim. (N.S.) 133 (ringing bells); *Hawley v Steele* (1877) 6 Ch. D. 521 (rifle range); *Polsue and Alfieri v Rushmer* [1907] A.C. 121 (printing machinery); *Colwell v St Pancras BC* [1904] 1 Ch. 707 (electric station); *Vanderpant v Mayfair Hotel Co* [1930] 1 Ch. 138 (hotel kitchen); *Leeman v Montagu* [1936] 2 All E.R. 1677 (crowing of cockerels); *Metropolitan Properties Ltd v Jones* [1939] 2 All E.R. 202 (electric motor); *Newman v Real Estate Debenture Corp* [1940] 1 All E.R. 131 (banging of doors of lift); *Halsey v Esso Petroleum Co Ltd* [1961] 1 W.L.R. 683 at 696–702 (machinery and traffic); *Dunton v Dover DC* (1977) 76 L.G.R. 87 (playground noise). For statutory provisions relating to noise see the Noise Act 1996.

44 *Shelfer v City of London Electric Lighting Co* [1895] 1 Ch. 287; *Knight v Isle of Wight Electric Light Co* (1904) 73 L.J. Ch. 299; *De Keyser's Royal Hotel v Spicer* (1914) 30 T.L.R. 257; *Hoare v McAlpine* [1923] 1 Ch. 167.

45 *Metropolitan Asylum District v Hill* (1881) 6 App. Cas. 193; *Att Gen v Nottingham Corp* [1904] 1 Ch. 673. See also *Birmingham Development Co v Tyler* [2008] EWCA Civ 859; [2008] B.L.R. 445 (fear must be "*well-founded*: that is, that the property or activities are *actually* dangerous": per Rimer LJ at [55]; original emphasis).

46 *Thompson-Schwab v Costaki* [1956] 1 W.L.R. 335. See also *Laws v Florinplace* [1981] 1 All E.R. 659 (sex shop in residential area).

47 *Lippiatt v South Gloucestershire Council* [2000] Q.B. 51 CA.

48 *Walker v Brewster* (1867) L.R. 5 Eq. 25; *Bellamy v Wells* (1891) 39 W.R. 158; *Barber v Penley* [1893] 2 Ch. 447; *Chase v London CC* (1898) 62 J.P. 184; *Lyons, Son & Co v Gulliver* [1914] 1 Ch. 631.

49 *Church of Jesus Christ of Latter Day Saints v Price* [2004] EWHC 3245 (QB); cf. *Thomas v National Union of Mineworkers* [1986] Ch. 20.

50 *Sanders-Clark v Grosvenor Mansions Co* [1900] 2 Ch. 373; *Reinhardt v Mentasti* (1889) 42 Ch. D. 685 (heat from kitchen-stoves renders wine cellar unfit for its purpose).

51 *Dublin (South) City Market Co v McCabes Ltd* [1953] I.R. 283 at 311.

52 *Hunter v Canary Wharf Ltd* [1997] A.C. 655 at 685, per Lord Goff (emphasis added) (mere exist-

satisfy this requirement[53] "may go to the limit of the law of nuisance".[54] But the need for such a requirement is far from clear, and the mechanistic nature of the concept of emanation means that it would be unlikely to contribute to the principled resolution of disputes in so diverse an area of the law.

Question of degree In nuisance of the third kind, "the personal inconvenience and interference with one's enjoyment, one's quiet, one's personal freedom, anything that discomposes or injuriously affects the senses or the nerves",[55] there is no absolute standard to be applied. In *Barr v Biffa Waste Services*[56] the Court of Appeal reversed the trial judge who had denied that odours emanating from the defendant's waste-tipping site could constitute a common law nuisance unless they crossed a "threshold" of his own imposition relating to the frequency of the interference. It is therefore always a question of degree whether the interference with comfort or convenience is sufficiently serious to constitute a nuisance.[57] The acts complained of as constituting the nuisance, such as noise, smells or vibration, will usually be lawful acts which only become wrongful from the circumstances under which they are performed, such as the time, place, extent or the manner of performance. In organised society everyone must put up with a certain amount of discomfort and annoyance caused by the legitimate activities of his neighbours. Ordinary domestic use of premises therefore cannot constitute a nuisance, even though interference with the enjoyment of neighbouring premises is caused, if that interference results solely from construction defects for which the defendant is not responsible.[58] In attempting to fix the general standard of tolerance the vague maxim *sic utere tuo ut alienum non laedas*[59] has been constantly invoked. But the maxim is of no use in deciding what is the permissible limit in inconvenience and annoyance between neighbours, and the courts in deciding whether an interference can amount to an actionable nuisance have to strike a balance between the right of the defendant to use his property for his own lawful enjoyment and the right of the claimant to the undisturbed enjoyment of his property.[60] No precise or universal formula is possible, but a useful test is what is reasonable according to ordinary usages of mankind living in a particular society[61]: 19-10

> "Whether such an act does constitute a nuisance must be determined not merely by an

ence of defendants' building not a nuisance). See also *Anglian Water Services v Crawshaw Robbins & Co* [2001] B.L.R. 173 (doubting whether mere deprivation of domestic gas supply could constitute a nuisance).

53 See, e.g. *Bank of New Zealand v Greenwood* [1984] 1 N.Z.L.R. 525 (glass roof causing deflected sunlight to throw a dazzling glare on neighbouring premises). See also *Thompson-Schwab v Costaki* [1956] 1 W.L.R. 335 and *Laws v Florinplace* [1981] 1 All E.R. 659.

54 *Hunter v Canary Wharf Ltd* [1997] A.C. 655 at 700, per Lord Lloyd.

55 *St Helens Smelting Co v Tipping* (1865) 11 H.L.C. 642 at 650, per Lord Westbury.

56 [2012] EWCA Civ 312; [2013] Q.B. 455 especially at [36], per Carnwath LJ referring to this paragraph in the 20th edition of this work.

57 See, e.g. *Murdoch v Glacier Metal Co Ltd* [1998] Env. L.R. 732 CA (no liability for factory noise in view of the character of the neighbourhood).

58 See *Baxter v Camden LBC* [2001] Q.B. 1 CA ("owner-occupiers would not be liable one to the other if the party wall between their houses is not an adequate sound barrier so that ordinary noise from one house unreasonably interferes with the use and enjoyment of the other": per Tuckey LJ at 12).

59 i.e. "So use your own property as not to injure your neighbour's".

60 *Sedleigh-Denfield v O'Callaghan* [1940] A.C. 880 at 903, per Lord Wright.

61 *Sedleigh-Denfield v O'Callaghan* [1940] A.C. 880 at 903, per Lord Wright. The test of reasonableness is an objective one for the court and "does not turn on some overriding and free-ranging assessment by the court of the respective reasonableness of each party in the light of all the facts and circumstances": per Sir Terence Etherton MR in *Fearn v Board of Trustees of the Tate Gallery* [2020]

abstract consideration of the act itself, but by reference to all the circumstances of the particular case, including, for example, the time of the commission of the act complained of; the place of its commission; the manner of committing it, that is, whether it is done wantonly or in the reasonable exercise of rights; and the effect of its commission, that is, whether those effects are transitory or permanent, occasional or continuous; so that the question of nuisance or no nuisance is one of fact."[62]

19-11 **Standard of comfort** A nuisance of this kind, to be actionable, must be such as to be a real interference with the comfort or convenience of living according to the standards of the average man. An interference which alone causes harm to something of abnormal sensitiveness does not of itself constitute a nuisance.[63] A man cannot increase the liabilities of his neighbour by applying his own property to special uses, whether for business or for pleasure.[64] In practice the general application of the concepts of foreseeability and reasonable user may have rendered the notion of abnormal sensitivity less significant in modern law,[65] although it is submitted that it remains useful as a guideline when applying those broad concepts in particular cases. But once the nuisance is established, the remedies by way of damages or an injunction will extend to delicate and sensitive operations such as the growing of orchids.[66] When it is said that a householder is entitled to have the air in his house untainted and unpolluted by any acts of his neighbour, that means that he is entitled to have "not necessarily air as fresh, free and pure as at the time of building the plaintiff's house the atmosphere then was, but air not rendered to an important degree less compatible, or at least not rendered incompatible, with the physical comfort of human existence".[67] Moreover, the discomfort must be substantial not merely with reference to the claimant; it must be of such a degree that it would be substantial to any person occupying the claimant's premises, irrespective of his position in life, age, or state of health; it must be "an inconvenience materially interfering with the ordinary comfort physically of human existence, not merely according to elegant or dainty modes and habits of living, but according to plain and sober and simple notions among the English people".[68] Where a social practice is sufficiently general and widely practised, there is no reason why it should not be protected, though pursued for pleasure and not profit. Thus, to send regularly large volumes of heavy smoke over a field habitually used for sporting activities may well be accounted a nuisance. And normal horticulture is certainly protected.

EWCA Civ 104; [2020] 2 W.L.R. 1081 at [38] (emphasis added).

62 *Stone v Bolton* [1949] 1 All E.R. 237 at 238–239, per Oliver J (approved as to nuisance [1950] 2 K.B. 201 CA, and on other grounds [1951] A.C. 850).

63 *Robinson v Kilvert* (1889) 41 Ch. D. 88 (ordinary heating damaging brown paper—"exceptionally delicate trade"); *Bridlington Relay Ltd v Yorkshire Electricity Board* [1965] Ch. 436 (interference with special radio and television relay system)

64 *Eastern and South African Telegraph Co v Cape Town Tramways* [1902] A.C. 381 at 383; *Hoare & Co v McAlpine* [1923] 1 Ch. 167; *Whycer v Urry* [1956] J.P.L. 365 (Court of Appeal held practice of ophthalmic optician in a business area too specially delicate for protection); *Cooke v Forbes* (1867) L.R. 5 Eq. 166 (sulphuretted hydrogen damaged coconut matting by reason of delicate nature of its manufacture, injunction refused without prejudice to claim in damages).

65 See *National Rail Infrastructure Ltd v CJ Morris* [2004] EWCA Civ 172; [2004] Env. L.R. 41 at [33]–[35], per Buxton LJ.

66 See per Lord Simonds in *McKinnon Industries Ltd v Walker* [1951] 3 D.L.R. 577 at 581. See also per Sir Terence Etherton MR in *Fearn v Board of Trustees of the Tate Gallery* [2020] EWCA Civ 104; [2020] 2 W.L.R. 1081 at [99].

67 per Knight Bruce VC in *Walter v Selfe* (1851) 4 De G. & Sm. 315 at 322; affirmed 19 L.T. 308; *Polsue and Alfieri v Rushmer* [1907] A.C. 121.

68 *Walter v Selfe* (1851) 4 De G. & Sm. 315 at 322.

It is not necessary to prove injury to health.[69] Indeed, it seems that no regard should be had to the needs of insomniacs or invalids.[70]

Television reception The question whether interference with television reception is capable of constituting an actionable private nuisance was considered by the House of Lords in *Hunter v Canary Wharf Ltd*,[71] which arose out of the construction of Canary Wharf Tower in London's docklands. The House held unanimously that where the cause of the interference was the erection of a large building, which blocked the path of the television signal, the claimant would be without a remedy. The situation was treated as analogous to that of loss of a view or prospect, which has for centuries been accepted as giving rise to no cause of action.[72] This analogy was considered to be appropriate because just as uncertainty as to the degree of protection required renders a right of prospect incapable of acquisition as an easement, so not dissimilar factors applied in the present case: 19-12

"Radio and television signals … come from various directions over a wide area as they cross the developer's property … Their passage from one point to another is invisible. It would be difficult, if not impossible, for the developer to become aware of their existence before he puts up the new building. If he were to be restricted by an easement from putting up a building which interfered with these signals, he might not be able to put up any substantial structures at all. The interference with his freedom would be substantial. I do not think that it would be consistent with principle for such a wide and novel restriction to be recognised. If that is so for easements, then the same result must follow so far as a remedy in nuisance is concerned".[73]

This reasoning adopted by the House leaves open the possibility that interference caused in other ways, such as by electronic devices, might nowadays be held to be actionable.[74] A majority of their Lordships do indeed appear to have taken the view, obiter, that a remedy might be available in such circumstances.[75] It is submitted that this is in fact the law. The belief that interference with television reception could not ordinarily constitute a sufficient interference with ordinary beneficial enjoyment as to amount to a legal nuisance[76] now seems outdated.[77]

Character of neighbourhood In considering the standard of comfort or convenience of living of the average man, the character of the neighbourhood must be taken into account.[78] A person who lives in the heart of a large manufacturing town cannot reasonably expect the same purity of air or freedom from noise as in a secluded 19-13

---

69 *Crump v Lambert* (1867) L.R. 3 Eq. 409.

70 *Bloodworth v Cormack* [1949] N.Z.L.R. 1058 at 1064, per Callan J; *Murray v Laus* [1960] N.Z.L.R. 126 (noise).

71 [1997] A.C. 655.

72 See, e.g. *Aldred's Case* (1610) 9 Co. Rep. 57b at 58b, per Wray CJ. But cf. per Lord Cooke of Thorndon who preferred to base the decision on the ground that the erection of the tower was reasonable in the circumstances ("only a lawyer" would suggest "that the amenity of television reception is fairly comparable to a view of the surroundings": [1997] A.C. 655 at 719).

73 [1997] A.C. 655 at 727, per Lord Hope.

74 cf. *Bridlington Relay Ltd v Yorkshire Electricity Board* [1965] Ch. 436.

75 But cf. per Lord Lloyd in *Hunter v Canary Wharf Ltd* [1997] A.C. 655 at 699 ("interference with television reception is not capable of constituting an actionable private nuisance").

76 See *Bridlington Relay Ltd v Yorkshire Electricity Board* [1965] Ch. 436, per Buckley J, sed quaere.

77 cf. *Nor-Video Services v Ontario Hydro* (1978) 84 D.L.R. (3d) 221 Ont. H.C.J.

78 cf. per Lord Neuberger in *Coventry v Lawrence* [2014] UKSC 13; [2014] A.C. 822 at [60]: "the concept of 'the character' of the locality may be too monolithic in some cases, and a better descrip-

country district. In *Sturges v Bridgman*,[79] where the nuisance complained of was that of a noisy trade, Thesiger LJ laid it down that:

> "whether anything is a nuisance or not is a question to be determined, not merely by an abstract consideration of the thing itself, but in reference to its circumstances: what would be a nuisance in Belgrave Square would not necessarily be so in Bermondsey; and where a locality is devoted to a particular trade or manufacture carried on by the traders or manufacturers in a particular and established manner not constituting a public nuisance, judges and juries would be justified in finding, and may be trusted to find, that the trade or manufacture so carried on in that locality is not a private or actionable wrong."

In *Sturges v Bridgman*, the mortars and pestles of a confectioner created noise in an area consisting largely of consulting rooms of medical practitioners, and liability was established. The approach of Thesiger LJ does not mean, however, that a person who lives in, for example, a noisy neighbourhood can never complain of any additional noise. He can do so if an increased volume of noise is, judged by local standards, so substantial as considerably to detract from the standard of comfort previously prevailing.[80] Thus in *Thomas v Merthyr Tydfil Car Auction Ltd*[81] claimants who lived near the defendants' business were able to recover damages for nuisance by noise notwithstanding that they lived in an area where "there were business uses and busy roads nearby". Nevertheless the defendant is entitled to have the activities impugned by the claimant to be taken into account in assessing the nature of the locality, but only in so far as they are in fact *lawful*: i.e. to the extent that they do *not* constitute a nuisance. If they are unlawful "they should be notionally stripped out of the locality when assessing its character".[82]

19-14 **Relevance of planning permission** Prior to the decision in *Coventry v Lawrence*[83] the extent to which a grant of planning permission could be relied upon by defendants in nuisance cases was a source of some uncertainty. The Supreme Court has now confirmed authoritatively that the long-held view, which was initially put in question by a decision of the High Court in 1995,[84] remains good law. This is that the grant of planning permission cannot, in itself, authorise a nuisance. In *Coventry* the Supreme Court unanimously restored the decision of the trial judge who had held that noise from a motor-racing stadium constituted a nuisance, and reversed the decision of the Court of Appeal[85] which considered that planning permission granted to the defendants had had the effect of making motor-racing a dominant activity within the locality. Lord Neuberger disapproved a distinction drawn by the Court of Appeal, in this and previous cases,[86] between "strategic" planning permission for large-scale developments, which could change the nature of a locality for

tion may often be something like 'the established pattern of uses' in the locality." See generally S. Steel, "The locality principle in private nuisance" (2017) 76 C.L.J. 145.

79 (1879) 11 Ch. D. 852 at 856. See also *Ball v Ray* (1873) L.R. 8 Ch. 467 at 470–471.

80 *Crump v Lambert* (1867) L.R. 3 Eq. 409; *Polsue and Alfieri v Rushmer* [1906] 1 Ch. 234; *Bosworth-Smith v Gwynnes* (1920) 89 L.J. Ch. 368.

81 [2013] EWCA Civ 815; (2013) 149 Con. L.R. 105.

82 See *Coventry v Lawrence* [2014] UKSC 13; [2014] A.C. 822 at [65], per Lord Neuberger. The defendant's activities will be "lawful" for this purpose if they "have been held to be a nuisance by the court, but the court has then decided to refuse an injunction and award damages instead": per Lord Neuberger at [69].

83 [2014] UKSC 13; [2014] A.C. 822.

84 *Gillingham BC v Medway (Chatham) Dock Co Ltd* [1993] Q.B. 343.

85 *RDC Promotions v Lawrence* [2012] EWCA Civ 26; [2012] 1 W.L.R. 2127.

86 See, e.g. *Wheeler v JJ Saunders Ltd* [1996] Ch. 19 CA.

nuisance purposes, and permission more limited in its scope which could not have this effect.[87] Although Lord Carnwath disassociated himself from the rejection of this distinction,[88] at least two other Justices agreed with Lord Neuberger on this point,[89] and it is therefore submitted that the proposition that planning permission can have a direct effect upon the nature of a locality for nuisance purposes no longer represents the law. This is not is not to say, however, that a grant of planning permission will always be irrelevant in nuisance cases. In *Coventry v Lawrence* the Supreme Court indicated that it may sometimes be of assistance, albeit only as one factor, in determining the "reasonableness" of the defendant's activity[90]; and specific conditions attached to a grant of permission, such as limitations on the hours when it may be undertaken, may provide a useful "benchmark" for a court seeking to incorporate limitations of that kind in its own order.[91]

Demolition and rebuilding Noise and dust caused by demolition and rebuilding will not be actionable if the operations are reasonably carried on, and all reasonable and proper steps are taken to ensure that no undue inconvenience is caused to neighbours. In considering what is reasonable, account must be taken of modern methods. The damages awarded will only be in respect of losses caused by the acts of the defendants which are in excess of what is permissible[92]: **19-15**

> "A man who pulls down his house for the purpose of building a new one no doubt causes considerable inconvenience to his next-door neighbours during the process of demolition; but he is not responsible as for a nuisance if he uses all reasonable skill and care to avoid annoyance to his neighbour by the works of demolition. Nor is he liable to an action even though the noise and dust and the consequent annoyance be such as would constitute a nuisance if the same, instead of being created for the purpose of demolition of the house, had been created in sheer wantonness, or in the execution of works for a purpose involving a permanent continuance of the dust and noise. For the law, in judging what constitutes a nuisance, does take into consideration both the object and the duration of that which is said to constitute the nuisance."[93]

Nevertheless, the claimant merely has to establish that an actionable degree of interference has occurred, the burden is then on the defendant to prove that his actions were reasonable.[94] The principle that harm caused by temporary building work is not actionable is, however, confined to mere inconvenience and does not extend to physical damage to property.[95] Although even physical damage will not result in liability in the absence of negligence, providing it results only from an isolated act as distinct from a continuous occurrence, unless the rule in *Rylands v Fletcher* is applicable.[96]

Temporary interference The duration of an interference is an element in assess- **19-16**

---

[87] [2014] UKSC 13; [2014] A.C. 822 at [86]–[90].
[88] [2014] UKSC 13; [2014] A.C. 822 at [223].
[89] See especially, per Lord Mance [2014] UKSC 13; [2014] A.C. 822 at [165], declaring the distinction to be "unsustainable in principle and fairness"; see also per Lord Sumption at [156].
[90] [2014] UKSC 13; [2014] A.C. 822 at [156] (Lord Sumption) and [218] (Lord Carnwath).
[91] [2014] UKSC 13; [2014] A.C. 822 at [96] (Lord Neuberger) and [218] (Lord Carnwath).
[92] *Andreae v Selfridge & Co Ltd* [1938] Ch. 1.
[93] *Harrison v Southwark and Vauxhall Water Co* [1891] 2 Ch. 409 at 413, per Vaughan Williams LJ; *Phelps v City of London Corp* [1916] 2 Ch. 255; *Harper v GN Haden & Sons Ltd* [1933] Ch. 298.
[94] See *Andreae v Selfridge & Co Ltd* [1938] Ch. 1 at 9, per Sir Wilfred Greene MR; see also *Hiscox Syndicates Ltd v The Pinnacle Ltd* [2008] EWHC 145 (Ch) at [30].
[95] *Clift v Welsh Office* [1999] 1 W.L.R. 796 CA.
[96] See *Northumbrian Water Ltd v Sir Robert McAlpine Ltd* [2014] EWCA Civ 685; (2014) 154 Con.

ing its actionability, together with the character and quality of that interference, but it is not a decisive factor, for a temporary interference which is substantial will be an actionable nuisance.[97] Though the interference may be actionable even if of temporary or very short duration, it is often said that nuisance requires "a state of affairs".[98] This does not mean that the actual damage must be of a continuing character. As has been said, "Most nuisances do arise from a long continued condition; and many isolated happenings do not constitute a nuisance. It is, however, clear from the authorities that an isolated happening by itself can create an actionable nuisance."[99] Provided that the defendant's property was in a state which constituted a potential hazard to his neighbour, the neighbour has a cause of action on the first occasion of damage.

19-17 **Acts done with the intention of annoying** Acts done with the intention of annoying a neighbour and actually causing annoyance will be a nuisance, although the same amount of annoyance would not be a nuisance if done in the ordinary and reasonable use of property.[100] In *Hunter v Canary Wharf Ltd*[101] it was suggested, obiter, in the House of Lords that the "malicious erection of a structure for the purpose of interfering with television reception should be actionable in nuisance" in circumstances in which such interference would not be actionable in the absence of malice.[102] Thus although malicious abuse of rights is not in itself an actionable wrong,[103] malice in this context is an element—often a powerful element—in determining the reasonableness of the user.[104]

(iii) Nuisance by keeping animals

19-18 Where farm animals in the nature of "livestock" under the Animals Act 1971 stray and cause damage, an action may be brought under s.4 of that Act. But where there is no such straying and animals otherwise cause an unreasonable annoyance

L.R. 26. (On the rule in *Rylands v Fletcher* see below, para.19–44 onwards).

97 *Bamford v Turnley* (1860) 3 B. & S. 62 at 84, per Bramwell B; *Fritz v Hobson* (1880) 14 Ch. D. 542 at 556; *Knight v Isle of Wight Electric Co* (1904) 73 L.J. Ch. 299; *Colwell v St Pancras BC* [1904] 1 Ch. 707; *Metropolitan Properties Ltd v Jones* [1939] 2 All E.R. 202 (noise lasting three weeks an actionable nuisance); *Matania v National Provincial Bank Ltd* [1936] 2 All E.R. 633 CA (nuisance by temporary dust and noise caused by extensive building alterations sufficiently substantial to be actionable); *Crown River Cruises Ltd v Kimbolton Fireworks Ltd* [1996] 2 Lloyd's Rep. 533 (firework display which lasted for only 15 or 20 minutes held to be actionable in nuisance).

98 *Stone v Bolton* [1950] 1 K.B. 201 at 208, per Jenkins LJ: "the causing or permitting of a state of affairs from which damage is likely to result."

99 per Lawton J in *British Celanese Ltd v AH Hunt (Capacitors) Ltd* [1969] 1 W.L.R. 959 at 969. See also *Colour Quest Ltd v Total Downstream UK Plc* [2009] EWHC 540 (Comm); [2009] 2 Lloyd's Rep. 1 at [421], per Steel J. The decision of Steel J was subsequently reversed in part, but not on this point: [2010] EWCA Civ 180; [2011] Q.B. 86.

100 *Christie v Davey* [1893] 1 Ch. 316; *Hollywood Silver Fox Farm v Emmett* [1936] 2 K.B. 468 (deliberately firing guns to cause vixens to abort); distinguished in *Rattray v Daniels* (1959) 17 D.L.R. (2d) 134 (bulldozing close to mink farm in whelping season, no intention to harm, no negligence, no liability); *Grandel v Mason* [1953] 3 D.L.R. 65 (liable in nuisance and negligence because of knowledge of peculiar sensitivity of mink); distinguishing *Nova Mink v Trans-Canada Airlines* [1951] 2 D.L.R. 241.

101 [1997] A.C. 655.

102 [1997] A.C. 655, per Lord Cooke at 721.

103 See para.1-59.

104 See para.1-60.

to a neighbour, that may be treated as a nuisance at common law.[105] Smells caused by keeping horses[106] or pigs[107] may be a nuisance, and so may the noise caused by the crowing of large numbers of cockerels at a poultry farm.[108] With regard to actionable public nuisance a dog with a loose lead running about in the streets of London has been held to be a nuisance,[109] but a herd of cattle in the charge of a drover is not and neither is a stray animal on the highway though it would probably be a nuisance for animals in numbers to obstruct free passage.[110] "The stray horse on the road … is no more a nuisance in law merely because of its presence there than the fallen cart horse or its modern analogue the lorry which has temporarily broken down."[111] As for private nuisance, the cases distinguish between the introduction or collection of a stock of animals and the natural increase of wild animals on the defendant's land. In *Farrer v Nelson*,[112] the defendant reared a large number of pheasants and brought them to a wood near the claimant's land, where they damaged the crops. The defendant was held liable. In *Seligman v Docker*,[113] the defendant, who kept pheasants on land adjoining the claimant's land, was held not liable for damage attributable to their increase in numbers during a favourable season. It was also held that he was under no obligation to keep down the numbers by shooting.

Excessive or abnormal user The principal consideration is whether the increase in animal life was due to some excessive or abnormal user of the defendant's land. It has been held a nuisance to keep an excessively large quantity of manure, so that an excessive number of flies are bred in it and infest the neighbouring houses.[114] On the other hand, where a heap of bone manure, which attracted rats, was kept on the defendant's premises and the rats damaged the crops on a neighbouring farm, the defendant succeeded; the manure was held not to be unusual or excessive.[115] It may be open to question whether the law may not recognise a duty to cull or crop an excessively large animal population which is the result of natural increase in the wild. The denial of a duty to abate, as in *Seligman v Docker*, is now difficult to reconcile with the cases discussed in the next paragraph. **19-19**

(iv) Natural nuisances

Natural nuisances It used to be thought that harm originating in some natural condition of land and not the effect of human activity was not generally actionable as a nuisance, and certain older cases indicated that this indeed was the law.[116] But in the second half of the twentieth century the judges extended the boundaries **19-20**

[105] See, generally, P. North, *Civil Liability for Animals* (2012).

[106] *Ball v Ray* (1873) L.R. 8 Ch. 467; *Broder v Saillard* (1876) 2 Ch. D. 692; *Rapier v London Tramways Co* [1893] 2 Ch. 588; *Munro v Southern Dairies Ltd* [1955] V.L.R. 332.

[107] *Aldred's* Case (1610) 9 Rep. 57b; *R. v Wigg* (1705) 2 Ld. Ray. 1163.

[108] *Leeman v Montagu* [1936] 2 All E.R. 1677.

[109] *Pitcher v Martin* [1937] 3 All E.R. 918 (and negligence).

[110] *Ellis v Banyard* (1911) 106 L.T. 51; *Cunningham v Whelan* (1917) 52 Ir. L.T.R. 67; *Atkinson v Fleming* [1956] 5 D.L.R. 309 (liable in negligence). See *Searle v Wallbank* [1947] A.C. 341.

[111] *Searle v Wallbank* [1947] A.C. 341 at 361, per Lord du Parcq.

[112] (1885) 15 Q.B.D. 258.

[113] [1949] Ch. 53.

[114] *Bland v Yates* (1914) 58 S.J. 612 (he was doing much more in a market gardening district than was to be expected from a market gardener).

[115] *Stearn v Prentice Bros* [1919] 1 K.B. 394.

[116] *Giles v Walker* (1890) 24 Q.B.D. 656; *Pontardawe RDC v Moore-Gwyn* [1929] 1 Ch. 656; *Neath*

of nuisance to include such natural nuisances. In *Goldman v Hargrave*,[117] the Judicial Committee of the Privy Council held an occupier of land in Australia to be under a duty of care to abate a fire which had started by lightning striking a tree on his land and which spread to his neighbour's land. It was recognised that the law on this question was not static and that the decision represented a step in extending the responsibilities of landowners towards their neighbours, Lord Wilberforce saying, "[i]t is only in comparatively recent times that the law has recognised an occupier's duty as one of a more positive character than merely to abstain from creating, or adding to, a source of danger or annoyance."[118]

19-21 **Development of liability** The development of liability for natural nuisances was taken a large step further by the Court of Appeal in *Leakey v National Trust*.[119] The National Trust owed a natural hill in Somerset which by natural forces slipped so as to damage the claimant's contiguous property. It was argued for the Trust that there could be no liability for such accidents of nature, and also that if there was any liability it sounded only in negligence and not in nuisance. The statement of claim did not refer to "negligence" as such but alleged breach of duty to take reasonable care to prevent the defendant's land from falling onto the claimant's. Megaw LJ was prepared to regard that "as being properly described as a claim in nuisance".[120] On the issue of substance the court followed *Goldman v Hargrave* both as to the existence of the duty and as to its scope and content.[121] In *Bybrook Barn Centre v Kent CC*[122] the Court of Appeal applied *Leakey v National Trust* to hold a highway authority liable for flooding caused when a naturally occurring stream overflowed as it passed through a culvert owned by the defendant highway authority. The authority was aware that the culvert had become inadequate to carry the stream, but had failed to take remedial measures. *Goldman v Hargrave* and *Leakey v National Trust* were referred to in *Network Rail Infrastructure Ltd v Williams*[123] in which the Court of Appeal imposed liability on Network Rail for failing to prevent the spread of Japanese knotweed from their land.

19-22 **The duty** The duty in cases of nuisances caused by naturally occurring conditions is a duty of care, but not one shaped to the contours of the reasonable man at

---

RDC v Williams [1951] 1 K.B. 115. But the immunity did not extend to public nuisance and even within the field of private nuisance certain forms of harm caused by natural agencies have always been actionable, e.g. tree branches and roots, as in *Davey v Harrow Corp* [1958] 1 Q.B. 60; followed in *Morgan v Khyatt* [1964] 1 W.L.R. 475 PC; *Russell v Barnet LBC* (1984) 83 L.G.R. 152 (where the defendants had control over the trees causing subsidence, though they were rooted in soil presumptively belonging to the adjacent proprietor). The standard is one of reasonable care, as in the case of harm caused by trees to road users; see para.19-100, *British Road Services v Slater* [1964] 1 W.L.R. 498. The liability of a proprietor for falling trees is not necessarily affected by the right of a highway authority to cut back or remove the tree.

117 [1967] 1 A.C. 645.

118 [1967] 1 A.C. 645 at 661.

119 [1980] Q.B. 485 CA, noted by Markesinis in [1980] C.L.J. 259. See also Markesinis, "Negligence, Nuisance and Affirmative Duties of Action" (1989) 105 L.Q.R. 104 at 118–119, where *Sedleigh-Denfield v O'Callaghan*, *Goldman v Hargrave* and *Leakey v National Trust* are related to the House of Lords' judgments in *Smith v Littlewoods Ltd* [1987] 1 A.C. 241.

120 [1980] Q.B. 485 at 514.

121 See also *Holbeck Hall Hotel Ltd v Scarborough BC* [2000] Q.B. 836 CA (no liability for land slip which could not have been foreseen without extensive geological investigations).

122 [2001] B.L.R. 55; [2001] Env. L.R. 30.

123 [2018] EWCA Civ 1514; [2019] Q.B. 601.

large. The standard of care is to be measured by the personal capabilities and circumstances of the defendant. As Lord Wilberforce said in *Goldman v Hargrave*:

> "the owner of a small property where a hazard arises which threatens a neighbour with substantial interests should not have to do so much as one with large interests of his own at stake and greater resources to protect them: if the small owner does what he can and promptly calls on his neighbour to provide additional resources, he may be held to have done his duty: he should not be liable unless it is clearly proved that he could, and reasonably in his individual circumstances should, have done more."[124]

Though Shaw LJ confessed to "substantial misgivings" in the *Leakey* case, the result of these two decisions is to recognise a duty of care on the occupier to abate the source of a natural nuisance emanating or likely to emanate from his land, though under the important practical qualification that the circumstances of the parties may qualify the duty to act to the sharing of the cost of remedial work, and it is not impossible that in certain circumstances the standard of care may be no higher than that of giving warning and allowing the neighbour to enter and himself abate the source of the threatened or actual nuisance. In *Vernon Knight Associates Cornwall Council*[125] Jackson LJ summarised the effect of the authorities as follows:

(i) A landowner owes a measured duty in both negligence and nuisance to take reasonable steps to prevent natural occurrences on his land from causing damage to neighbouring properties.
(ii) In determining the content of the measured duty, the court must consider what is fair, just and reasonable as between the two neighbouring landowners. It must have regard to all the circumstances, including the extent of the foreseeable risk, the available preventive measures, the costs of such measures and the resources of both parties.
(iii) Where the defendant is a public authority with substantial resources, the court must take into account the competing demands on those resources and the public purposes for which they are held. It may not be fair, just or reasonable to require a public authority to expend those resources on infrastructure works in order to protect a few individuals against a modest risk of property damage.

In *Vernon Knight Associates* itself the Court of Appeal imposed liability upon a highway authority for failure to prevent foreseeable flood damage. Prevention would not have incurred the expenditure of substantial resources: a system already in place to prevent flooding had simply not been operated effectively.

Financial resources The principles relating to the responsibilities of neighbouring landowners faced with a common hazard were considered at some length by the Court of Appeal in the unusual case of *Abbahall Ltd v Smee*.[126] The claimant and defendant were the owners respectively of the lower and upper properties in one building. The roof of the building had fallen dangerously into disrepair threatening the defendant's lower property as well as the defendant's upper property. The defendant, who was of very limited means, had acquired the title to the upper property by adverse possession; there were no covenants between the parties and their relationship was therefore governed by the ordinary law of nuisance. The 19-23

124 [1967] 1 A.C. 645 at 663.
125 [2013] EWCA Civ 950; [2013] B.L.R. 519 at [49]. See further para.7-183.
126 [2002] EWCA Civ 1831; [2003] 1 W.L.R. 1472.

defendant accepted that she owed some duty at common law to the claimant to contribute to the cost of repairing the roof. She also contended, however, in reliance on the judgments in *Goldman v Hargrave* and *Leakey v National Trust*, that her relative poverty should be taken into account. In the court below her contribution had been assessed, on that basis, as limited to one-quarter of the cost. On appeal the Court of Appeal ordered that the two parties should each bear half the cost. Munby J, delivering the leading judgment in the Court of Appeal, said that the situations in the *Goldman* and *Leakey* cases were "far removed" from the instant case, and observed that neither case "went so far as to assert that the defendant's financial resources are always relevant, let alone determinative". He concluded as follows[127]:

> "The nature of the duties governing neighbours in a case such as this simply cannot depend on such transient matters as their means … Reasonableness between neighbours who choose to live together in the same building, sharing the same roof, requires that all share—and share equally—the cost of repairing and maintaining the roof".

Abbahall v Smee was, however, distinguished in *Coope v Ward*[128] in which the Court of Appeal declined, on the particular facts, to order that each neighbour should contribute equally to alleviation of the consequences of the collapse of a wall, which was close to both of their properties. In imposing the cost primarily on one of the neighbours, the Court emphasised that, as had indeed been acknowledged in *Abbahall* itself, any presumption in favour of equal sharing of the burden where the parties lived under the same roof did not apply in cases where they lived side by side.[129]

(v) Wrong to occupiers

19-24 **Nuisance primarily a wrong to occupiers of land** A private nuisance is primarily a wrong to the owner or the occupier of the land affected.[130] The correctness of this proposition was emphatically reaffirmed by the House of Lords in 1997 in *Hunter v Canary Wharf Ltd*.[131] In a fundamental review of the authorities the House upheld the traditional test of possession or occupation as laid down in a well-known case in which it was held that the wife of a tenant of land had no right to sue for damages in nuisance.[132] In reaching its decision the House of Lords, by a majority,[133] reversed the Court of Appeal which had held that residence in a property as a "home", without any legally protected interest, was sufficient to confer a right to sue.[134] Their Lordships accordingly refused to distinguish cases of direct physical damage to, or encroachment upon, a neighbour's land from situations involving mere interference with enjoyment or utility. A claimant has to have an interest

127 See [2002] EWCA Civ 1831; [2003] 1 W.L.R. 1472 at [57]–[61].

128 [2015] EWCA Civ 30; [2015] 1 W.L.R. 4081.

129 See [2015] EWCA Civ 30; [2015] 1 W.L.R. 4081 at [77], per Christopher Clarke LJ.

130 *Hunter v Canary Wharf Ltd* [1997] A.C. 655 HL. See also *Tate & Lyle Industries Ltd v GLC* [1983] 2 A.C. 509; *Sedleigh-Denfield v O'Callaghan* [1940] A.C. 880 at 908, per Lord Wright.

131 [1997] A.C. 655. See Kidner, "Nuisance and Rights of Property" [1998] Conv. 267.

132 *Malone v Laskey* [1907] 2 K.B. 141; overruled so far as it relates to negligence, without affecting this point, by *Billings & Sons Ltd v Riden* [1958] A.C. 240.

133 Lord Cooke of Thorndon dissenting.

134 See [1996] 2 W.L.R. 348. See also the majority decision of the Court of Appeal in *Khorasandjian v Bush* [1993] Q.B. 727, which was overruled by the House of Lords in *Hunter*'s case.

in land in the latter category as well as in the former.[135] Lord Goff of Chieveley considered that "any … departure from the established law on this subject" would cause uncertainty due to "the problem of defining the category of persons who would have the right to sue".[136] Nevertheless, a person who is merely "de facto in exclusive possession" can apparently claim.[137] But legislative provisions relating to spouses, such as the Family Law Act 1996,[138] will seemingly not be sufficient in themselves to confer a right to sue.[139]

Continuing nuisances In the case of continuing nuisances the traditional principle, that nuisance is a wrong to the owner or occupier, has been extended so as to enable claimants to recover damages for harm which originated in the time of their predecessors in title[140]: **19-25**

> "Where there is a continuing nuisance inflicting damage on premises, those who are in possession of the interest may recover losses which they have borne whether the loss began before the acquisition of the interest, or whether it began after the acquisition of the interest. The test is: what is the loss which the owner of the land has to meet in respect of the continuing nuisance affecting his land?"[141]

Thus, in *Delaware Mansions Ltd v Westminster City Council*,[142] the House of Lords held that defendants who had refused to take remedial action in respect of tree-roots were liable to the freehold owners of blocks of flats affected, notwithstanding that the claimants were not the owners of the freehold at the time when the physical damage caused by the tree-roots occurred.[143] The nature of the duty for a continuing nuisance caused by encroaching tree roots will necessarily be highly fact-specific; the reasonableness of the defendants' action or inaction depending in part on the extent of the parties' knowledge at any particular time.[144] The right to sue for nuisance is discussed more fully below.[145]

---

135 In *McKenna v British Aluminium Ltd* [2002] Env. L.R. 30; *The Times,* 25 April 2002 Neuberger J refused to strike out a contention that the requirement of a legally protected interest might need to be reconsidered in the light of the Human Rights Act 1998.

136 See [1997] A.C. 655 at 693.

137 See, per Lord Hoffmann in *Hunter v Canary Wharf Ltd* [1997] A.C. 655 at 704 (doubting the decision in *Metropolitan Properties Ltd v Jones* [1939] 2 All E.R. 202). See also *Tinseltime Ltd v Roberts* [2011] EWHC 1199 (TCC); [2011] B.L.R. 515 (successful claim by licensee entitled to exclusive possession).

138 See s.30.

139 See *Hunter v Canary Wharf Ltd* [1997] A.C. 655 at 708, per Lord Hoffmann (referring to the Matrimonial Homes Act 1983).

140 *Delaware Mansions Ltd v Westminster City Council* [2001] UKHL 55; [2002] 1 A.C. 321; *Masters v Brent LBC* [1978] Q.B. 841.

141 *Masters v Brent LBC* [1978] Q.B. 841 at 848, per Talbot J.

142 [2001] UKHL 55; [2002] 1 A.C. 321.

143 "… where there is a continuing nuisance of which the defendant knew or ought to have known, reasonable remedial expenditure may be recovered by the owner who has had to incur it": per Lord Cooke, [2001] UKHL 55; [2002] 1 A.C. 321 at [38]. *Constructive* notice of the problem by the defendant may be sufficient to enable the claimant to recover even if the latter did not formally notify the defendant prior to the carrying out of the remedial works: see *Kirk v Brent LBC* [2005] EWCA Civ 1701; [2006] Env. L.R. D7 at [18]–[30], per Lloyd LJ.

144 See *Berent v Family Mosaic Housing Association* [2011] EWHC 1353 (TCC); affirmed [2012] EWCA Civ 961; [2012] B.L.R. 488 (especially per Judge Wilcox in [2011] EWHC 1353 (TCC) at [101]).

145 See para.19-63.

(vi) *Necessity for damage*

19-26 **Necessity for damage** In nuisances of the second kind,[146] namely, those causing physical damage to land, actual, not merely prospective, damage is essential to a cause of action. Until damage is caused no nuisance exists, only the potentiality of a nuisance.[147] But an injunction of a *quia timet* nature can be obtained in the face of impending harm, though no actual damage has as yet occurred. If the impending damage is not imminent or at least very likely to occur in the near future, the court will not usually exercise its discretion in the issue of an injunction.[148] In *Network Rail Infrastructure Ltd v Williams*,[149] which concerned the potential of Japanese knotweed for causing harm, Sir Terence Etherton MR said, obiter:

> "It is usually said that there must be proof of imminent physical injury or harm for a quia timet injunction to be granted … It is possible, however, that that is too prescriptive and that what matters is the probability and likely gravity of damage rather than simply its imminence … Although the point has not been considered before in the cases I see no reason why, in appropriate circumstances, as in the present case, a claimant should not be able to obtain a final mandatory injunction where the amenity value of the land is diminished by the presence of roots even though there has not yet been any physical damage".

19-27 **Other cases** In other cases of nuisance, no actual financial or physical damage need be proved. Where the nuisance consists of an encroachment, the law will presume damage.[150] In a case where rain-water was caused to fall on the claimant's land by a cornice projecting from the defendant's building, it was said, "the mere fact of the defendant's cornice overhanging the plaintiff's land may be considered as a nuisance to him, importing a damage which the law can estimate".[151] Similarly, if the nuisance consists of interference with the amenities of living, such as is produced by noise or smells, no actual financial loss or injury to health[152] need be proved. The damage in such a case consists in the annoyance and discomfort caused to the occupier of the premises. The same rule applies to nuisances which consist of interference with easements:

> "Disturbance of easements and the like, as completely existing rights of use and enjoyment, is a wrong in the nature of trespass, and remediable by action without any allegation or proof of specific damage."[153]

---

146 See para.19-06.

147 *Sedleigh-Denfield v O'Callaghan* [1940] A.C. 880 at 896 and 919–920.

148 *Salvin v North Brancepeth Coal Co* (1874) L.R. 9 Ch. 705. "If some picturesque haven opens its arms to invite the commerce of the world, it is not for this court to forbid the embrace, although the fruit of it should be the sights, and sounds, and smells of a common seaport and shipbuilding town, which would drive the Dryads and their masters from their ancient solitude", per James LJ at 709–710.

149 See [2018] EWCA Civ 1514; [2019] Q.B. 601 at [71]–[72].

150 This proposition was confirmed by Sir Terence Etherton MR in *Network Rail Infrastructure Ltd v Williams* [2018] EWCA Civ 1514; [2019] Q.B. 601 at [42] (encroachment by Japanese knotweed).

151 *Fay v Prentice* (1845) 1 C.B. 828, per Coltman J. But where there is no original encroachment, damage must be proved, as for roots and branches of trees: *Lemmon v Webb* [1894] 3 Ch. 1 at 11, per Lindley LJ.

152 *Crump v Lambert* (1867) L.R. 3 Eq. 409. See also *Fearn v Board of Trustees of the Tate Gallery* [2020] EWCA Civ 104; [2020] 2 W.L.R. 1081 at [34], per Sir Terence Etherton MR.

153 per Lord Wright MR in *Nicholls v Ely Beet Sugar Factory Ltd* [1936] Ch. 343 at 349 (not necessary to prove damage in action by owner of a several fishery against a person who had discharged refuse into a stream).

A public nuisance is only actionable at the suit of a private person on proof of special damage.[154]

Damages The measure of damages for nuisance is the same as that for tort generally.[155] "The damages are whatever loss results to the injured party as a natural consequence of the wrongful act of the defendant."[156] Generally, where negligence is necessary to establish liability in nuisance, then if the kind of damage is not reasonably foreseeable, that kind of damage is too remote a consequence.[157] Even where liability is strict, the effect of the decision of the House of Lords in *Cambridge Water v Eastern Counties Leather*[158] is that only foreseeable, rather than all direct, consequences qualify for compensation. When damage to property has been caused, the general rule is that the measure of damages is the difference between the money value of the owner's interest in the property before and after the damage was done, and not the cost of repair.[159] Where the diminution in value has been caused by prolonged acts of harassment by a neighbouring occupier, the claimant will be entitled to damages even if the court also awards an injunction to restrain the harassment. It would be unreal to suppose that the injunction would restore the value of the property: future purchasers could still be influenced by the defendant's pattern of behaviour and the possibility of its revival despite the injunction.[160] **19-28**

Intangible loss Where an actionable nuisance interferes with the claimant's property and in addition damages his chattels, it seems that the claimant can recover such consequential damages.[161] Damages for personal injury, however, do not appear as such[162] to be recoverable in private nuisance.[163] It has always seemed unlikely that such damages could be recovered, given the focus of the tort upon property and its enjoyment. No reported English case appears to have given such an award, and dicta in the House of Lords now support the view that such recovery is not possible.[164] In cases involving interference with amenity and enjoyment of property the court must place a value on an intangible loss which "cannot be as- **19-29**

---

154 See para.19-181.

155 See Ch.27, "Damages".

156 per Lindley LJ in *Grosvenor Hotel Co v Hamilton* [1894] 2 Q.B. 836 at 840.

157 *Overseas Tankship (UK) Ltd v Miller SS Co Pty* [1967] 1 A.C. 617 PC.

158 [1994] 2 A.C. 264 HL. The decision itself concerned the rule in *Rylands v Fletcher* but the House saw that rule as essentially a branch of the law of nuisance (see below).

159 *Moss v Christchurch RDC* [1925] 2 K.B. 750. As to time at which damages should be assessed, see *Dodd Properties (Kent) Ltd v Canterbury CC* [1980] 1 W.L.R. 433 CA.

160 See *Raymond v Young* [2015] EWCA Civ 456; [2015] H.L.R. 41.

161 See *Hunter v Canary Wharf Ltd* [1997] A.C. 655 at 706, per Lord Hoffmann. See also *Midwood Co Ltd v Manchester Corp* [1905] 2 K.B. 597; *Halsey v Esso Petroleum Co Ltd* [1961] 1 W.L.R. 683.

162 Evidence of illness, for example, can no doubt be invoked to prove the gravity of a nuisance, provided the claimant is not hypersensitive.

163 Such damages are, however, still recoverable in public nuisance until the Supreme Court rules otherwise: see *The Claimants appearing on the Register of the Corby Group Litigation v Corby BC* [2008] EWCA Civ 463; [2009] Q.B. 335. cf. doubts expressed obiter by Lord Goff in *Hunter v Canary Wharf Ltd* who was inclined to the view that the appropriate remedy for personal injuries should now only "lie in our fully developed law of negligence, and that personal injury claims should be altogether excluded from the law of nuisance": see [1997] A.C. 655 at 692.

164 See especially, per Lord Lloyd in [1997] A.C. 655 at 696 and, per Lord Goff (previous note). But cf. per Lord Cooke (dissenting) in [1997] A.C. 655 at 718–719.

sessed mathematically".[165] The Court of Appeal once suggested that such damages could be assessed by analogy with damages for personal injury,[166] but this was disapproved by the House of Lords in *Hunter v Canary Wharf Ltd*.[167] Since only the owner, or the occupier with the right to exclusive possession, is entitled to sue for interference with enjoyment each member of a family does not have a separate cause of action, and "the quantum of damages does not depend on the number of those enjoying the land in question".[168] If, however, the defendant is a public authority an individual family member may have a cause of action under art.8 of the European Convention for the Protection of Human Rights, for interference with his private and family life.[169] If interference with amenity has been so great as to reduce the value of the claimant's property, a substantial award of damages for the reduction in value will normally be taken to include compensation for the loss of amenity itself: the claimant will therefore be unlikely to receive a separate award under that head.[170] In *Network Rail Infrastructure Ltd v Williams*[171] claimants onto whose land Japanese knotweed had spread were awarded substantial sums, based on the reduction in value of their properties, for the loss of enjoyment of their land.

19-30 **Source of the interference** Though nuisance requires the misuse of property, the interference need not emanate from the land of the defendant,[172] for a trespasser may be liable.[173] A public nuisance may emanate from a highway or a waterway, and an action for a private nuisance can be brought for an interference which emanates from land not occupied by the defendant, who may be a licensee or trespasser there.[174]

---

165 per Lord Lloyd in *Hunter v Canary Wharf Ltd* [1997] A.C. 655 at 696, citing *Ruxley Electronics and Construction Ltd v Forsyth* [1996] A.C. 344. See also, per Lord Hoffmann in *Hunter* 's case [1997] A.C. 655 at 706 (and, per Lord Cooke at 712); *Jan de Nul (UK) v NV Royal Belge* [2000] 2 Lloyd's Rep. 700 at 716 (the decision in this case was subsequently affirmed: see [2002] EWCA Civ 209; [2002] 1 Lloyd's Rep. 583). In an appropriate case damages for loss of amenity may be based on a percentage of the rental value of the property: see *Jafari v Tareem Ltd* [2019] EWHC 3119 (Ch).

166 See *Bone v Seale* [1975] 1 W.L.R. 797.

167 See per Lord Hoffmann in [1997] A.C. 655 at 706. The multiplicand/multiplier *method* of assessing general damages can nevertheless be conveniently deployed in nuisance cases where there is a loss of amenity: see *Anslow v Norton Aluminium Ltd* [2012] EWHC 2610 (QB) at [474].

168 per Lord Lloyd in *Hunter v Canary Wharf Ltd* [1997] A.C. 655 at 696.

169 See *Dobson v Thames Water Utilities* [2009] EWCA Civ 28; [2009] 3 All E.R. 319. For subsequent proceedings see [2011] EWHC 3253 (TCC); (2011) 140 Con. L.R. 135 (liability for breach of the Convention established but, on the facts, damages unnecessary to achieve "just satisfaction"). For a case in which the European Court of Human Rights imposed liability under art.8 for illness caused by pollution in the water supplied to the claimant's home see *Otgon v Moldova (22743/07)* (2016) 19 C.C.L. Rep. 618.

170 See *Raymond v Young* [2015] EWCA Civ 456; [2015] H.L.R. 41.

171 [2018] EWCA Civ 1514; [2019] Q.B. 601.

172 cf. *Dwr Cymru Cyfyngedig (Welsh Water) v Barratt Homes Ltd* [2013] EWCA Civ 233; [2013] 1 W.L.R. 3486, per Lloyd-Jones LJ, obiter, at [57]: "nuisance does not require a use by the defendant of *its* land" (original emphasis).

173 cf. *Lippiatt v South Gloucestershire Council* [2000] Q.B. 51 CA (nuisance caused by travellers trespassing on to the claimants' land from that of the defendants). See also para.19-70.

174 *Salmond and Heuston on the Law of Torts*, 21st edn (1996), p.56. In *Southport Corp v Esso Petroleum Co Ltd* [1956] A.C. 218 at 224–225; Devlin J said obiter: "I can see no reason why if the defendant as a licensee or trespasser misuses someone else's land, he should not be liable for a nuisance in the same way as an adjoining occupier would be." Lord Radcliffe at 242 agreed with Denning LJ [1954] 2 Q.B. 182 at 196–197, who took the contrary view. *Sedleigh-Denfield v O'Callaghan* [1940] A.C. 880 at 918; *Halsey v Esso Petroleum Co Ltd* [1961] 1 W.L.R. 683 at 699–700; *Fennell v Robson Excavations Pty Ltd* [1977] 2 N.S.W.L.R. 486. See also *Olympic Delivery*

2. NUISANCE AND THE STANDARD OF DUTY

(a) The problem

Nuisance and negligence It was said by Lord Wilberforce in *Goldman v Hargrave*[175] that "the tort of nuisance, uncertain in its boundary, may comprise a wide variety of situations, in some of which negligence plays no part, in others of which it is decisive" and he added, "the present case is one where liability, if it exists, rests upon negligence and nothing else; whether it falls within or overlaps the boundaries of nuisance is a question of classification which need not here be resolved". Because nuisance has this protean character,[176] the cases contain judicial statements some of which assert that the duty of an occupier towards his neighbour is strict[177] and some of which assert the duty to be based on reasonable foreseeability of harm, i.e. negligence. Such statements, if taken out of context and applied generally to nuisance as a whole, naturally produce contradiction and perhaps confusion, and in the light of such disparate statements the standard of duty has been considered a vexed and difficult question. But if, as Lord Wilberforce says, there is no single standard applicable to all situations covered by the tort of nuisance, it is illusory to seek a single answer to the question. Instead, attention should be directed towards identifying different kinds of situations and the appropriate standard of duty in each. Moreover, in approaching this task, it seems desirable to bear in mind that in modern times the general field of liability for negligence has been greatly expanded and the rule of strict liability in *Rylands v Fletcher* has been reduced in scope. This has had an inevitable effect upon the way in which the judges have handled the law of nuisance, and Lord Parker CJ[178] has said that "the present tendency of the law is not only to move further and further away from absolute liability but more and more to assimilate nuisance and negligence". It seems important therefore to be guided by the more recent cases,[179] and to treat with caution statements concerning the standard of duty to be found in the older cases. 19-31

Injunction cases Many cases of nuisance are concerned with the remedy of injunction. Indeed the availability of the injunction as a possible remedy has been taken as significant in drawing a line between nuisance and negligence.[180] In the cricket-ball case of *Miller v Jackson*,[181] Lord Denning MR said that: 19-32

"if the plaintiff seeks a remedy in damages for injury done to him or his property, he can

Authority v Persons Unknown [2012] EWHC 1012 (Ch).

175 [1967] 1 A.C. 645 at 657.

176 per Lord Wright in *Sedleigh-Denfield v O'Callaghan* [1940] A.C. 880 at 903: "The forms which nuisance may take are protean. Certain classifications are possible, but many reported cases are no more than illustrations of particular matters of fact which have been held to be nuisances."

177 e.g., per Lord Loreburn in *Pwyllbach Colliery Co Ltd v Woodman* [1915] A.C. 634 at 638: "their duty to their neighbours is not merely to take care so as to avoid causing a nuisance. Their duty is to abstain from causing one at all."

178 *British Road Services Ltd v Slater* [1964] 1 W.L.R. 498 at 504.

179 See, e.g. *Cambridge Water Co v Eastern Counties Leather* [1994] 2 A.C. 264 HL at 300, per Lord Goff.

180 The availability of the injunction as an identifying characteristic of the tort of nuisance should not be confused with its actual award in any given case. In *Coventry v Lawrence* [2014] UKSC 13; [2014] A.C. 822 the Supreme Court signalled that injunctions may not be granted as readily in nuisance cases as in the past.

181 [1977] Q.B. 966 at 980. See para.19-107.

lay his claim either in negligence or nuisance. But, if he seeks an injunction to stop the playing of cricket altogether, I think he must make his claim in nuisance. The books are full of cases where an injunction has been granted to restrain the continuance of a nuisance. But there is no case, as far as I know, where it has been granted so as to stop a man being negligent. At any rate in a case of this kind, where an occupier of a house or land seeks to restrain his neighbour from doing something on his own land, the only appropriate cause of action, on which to base the remedy of an injunction, is nuisance ... It is the very essence of a private nuisance that it is the unreasonable use by a man of his land to the detriment of his neighbour. He must have been guilty of the fault, not necessarily of negligence, but of the unreasonable user of the land ..."

Though the availability of an injunction may be a touchstone of nuisance, this passage again reiterates that nuisance and negligence are not synonymous.

19-33 **Existence of tort already established** Moreover, important as injunction is as a remedy characterising nuisance, the question of whether or not to issue an injunction only arises when it has been decided that there is an actual or imminent nuisance to stop or prevent, i.e. that the existence of the tort is already established. And where the court has reached the stage of ruling upon the remedy, "consideration of the strictness of the duty is then out of place".[182] In the 1993 case of *Cambridge Water Co Ltd v Eastern Counties Leather Plc*,[183] in which the House of Lords considered the role of foreseeability in nuisance at length, Lord Goff said that:

"It is, of course, axiomatic that in this field we must be on our guard, when considering liability for damages in nuisance, not to draw inapposite conclusions from cases concerned only with a claim for an injunction. This is because, where an injunction is claimed, its purpose is to restrain further action by the defendant which may interfere with the plaintiff's enjoyment of his land, and ex hypothesi the defendant must be aware, if and when an injunction is granted, that such interference may be caused by the act which he is restrained from committing. It follows that these cases provide no guidance on the question whether foreseeability of harm of the relevant type is a prerequisite of the recovery of damages for causing such harm to the plaintiff."

It should also be borne in mind that those cases in which an injunction has been refused do not, of course, necessarily signify that the court in all such cases found against tortious liability.

19-34 **Intermediate positions** A further complication in analysing liability in nuisance is that the choice of the court may not be simply between a duty of care to avoid foreseeable damage and a strict duty involving no need to prove negligence at all. The duty of care may be qualified or mitigated, as is the case with natural nuisances,[184] and between an ordinary duty of care and strict duty there are, in practice, intermediate positions. Lord Denning MR[185] once said that "in an action for public nuisance, once the nuisance is proved and the defendant is shown to have caused it, then the legal burden is shifted onto the defendant to justify or excuse himself". And in relation to private nuisance there seems no reason why the maxim res ipsa loquitur should not apply in appropriate cases to require the defendant to

---

[182] Law Commission, *Civil Liability for Dangerous Things and Activities* (2007), Law Com. No.32, p.25.

[183] [1994] 2 A.C. 264 at 300.

[184] See para.19-20 onwards.

[185] *Southport Corp v Esso Petroleum Ltd* [1954] 2 Q.B. 182 at 197.

show that he was not at fault and was not negligent. Another intermediate position is where the defendant has employed independent contractors and, contrary to the general rule of non-liability for the torts of such contractors, he has been held vicariously liable for nuisances caused by them.[186]

(b) Foreseeability and fault

Unreasonable user and foreseeability "The very essence of a private nuisance ... is the unreasonable user by a man of his land to the detriment of his neighbour."[187] But though actual or constructive knowledge of such detriment on the part of the defendant is one element in determining whether user is reasonable, the courts have habitually taken more into account when assessing reasonableness of user. In addition to the defendant's conduct and knowledge there are the considerations of the nature of the claimant's interest and a balancing of that interest against that of the defendant, the character of the interference and its duration, and indeed all material circumstances including the interests of third parties and those of the community as a whole.[188] Negligence, on the other hand, though requiring a consideration of circumstances as well as conduct, is rarely a question of degree. To be run down on the highway by a negligent driver is to be the victim of a tort and the claimant's task is only to show that a careful and competent driver would not have run him down. But the use of land to the detriment of a neighbour may involve some foreseeable harm which the court considers not excessive as between neighbours and to a degree which has to be tolerated under a principle "of give and take, or live and let live".[189] Reasonableness of user in nuisance therefore cannot be taken as solely determinable by reference to the character of the defendant's conduct, and this may be the source of the difficulty in understanding properly those judicial statements which speak of "fault" as distinguished from negligence as a requirement for nuisance.[190] 19-35

The Wagon Mound (No.2) An important general statement on the question is the speech of Lord Reid in delivering the opinion of the Judicial Committee of the Privy Council in *The Wagon Mound (No.2)*.[191] On the issue of nuisance by the discharge of inflammable oil into Sydney harbour, the trial judge had held that the damage to the claimant's ships by fire from the ignited oil was not reasonably foreseeable and so damages were not recoverable for negligence, but he held that the defendants were liable in nuisance, because in nuisance liability did not depend on foreseeability. The Judicial Committee decided that on the facts the damage was reasonably foreseeable and therefore the claimants were entitled to damages. 19-36

Fault On the question of nuisance Lord Reid acknowledged (at 639) that "[n]uisance is a term used to cover a wide variety of tortious acts or omissions and 19-37

186 See para.19-72.
187 per Lord Denning MR in *Miller v Jackson* [1977] Q.B. 966 at 980.
188 See, generally, *Coventry v Lawrence* [2014] UKSC 13; [2014] A.C. 822.
189 per Lawton LJ in *Kennaway v Thompson* [1981] Q.B. 88 at 94.
190 For a review of the authorities on the applicability of the notions of reasonable user and foreseeability in the law of nuisance see *Arscott v Coal Authority* [2004] EWCA Civ 892; [2005] Env. L.R. 6, CA. See also *Hughes v Riley* [2005] EWCA Civ 1129; [2006] 1 P. & C.R. 29.
191 *Overseas Tankship (UK) Ltd v Miller SS Co Pty* [1967] 1 A.C. 617 at 639–640. This was a case of public nuisance, but the Privy Council applied their rule as to damages both to public and private nuisance.

in many negligence in the narrow sense is not essential". But he continued, "although negligence may not be necessary, fault of some kind is almost always necessary and fault generally involves foreseeability ...". In the present case, discharge into navigable waters, foreseeability was a necessary element of liability. The judgment then continues (at 640):

> "It could not be right to discriminate between different cases of nuisance so as to make foreseeability a necessary element in determining damages in those cases where it is a necessary element in determining liability, but not in others. So the choice is between it being a necessary element in all cases or in none. In their Lordships' judgment the similarities between nuisance and other forms of tort ... far outweigh any differences, and they must therefore hold that the judgment appealed from is wrong on this branch of the case. It is not sufficient that the injury suffered by the respondent's vessels was the direct result of the nuisance if that injury was in the relevant sense unforeseeable."

19-38 **Cambridge Water** It appears that Lord Reid was focusing in the passage just quoted primarily upon the test for remoteness of damage in nuisance,[192] and was not seeking in any way to undermine the principle that a defendant whose continuing activities have interfered with the claimant's enjoyment of his land cannot be allowed to contend that that interference was unexpected or unanticipated, for many and perhaps most nuisances are deliberate interferences in which the defendant has miscalculated the amount of interference which the law allows as between neighbours. Thus, as Lord Goff emphasised in the House of Lords in *Cambridge Water Co Ltd v Eastern Counties Leather Plc*[193]:

> "It is still the law that the fact that the defendant has taken all reasonable care will not of itself exonerate him from liability, the relevant control mechanism being found within the principle of reasonable user."

However, Lord Goff then continued:

> "But it by no means follows that the defendant should be held liable for damage of a type which he could not reasonably foresee; and the development of the law of negligence in the past sixty years points strongly towards a requirement that such foreseeability should be a prerequisite of liability in damages for nuisance, as it is of liability in negligence. For if a plaintiff is in ordinary circumstances only able to claim damages in respect of personal injuries where he can prove such foreseeability on the part of the defendant, it is difficult to see why, in common justice, he should be in a stronger position to claim damages for interference with the enjoyment of his land where the defendant was unable to foresee such damage."

In the *Cambridge Water* case, the defendants escaped liability for pollution of the underground water supply caused by seepage into it of chemicals accidentally spilt during their leather tanning process, on the ground that that seepage had not been foreseeable.[194] The effect of Lord Goff's speech in this case, when combined with that of Lord Reid in *The Wagon Mound (No.2)*, has been to confirm the accuracy

---

192 See, per Lord Goff in *Cambridge Water Co Ltd v Eastern Counties Leather Plc* [1994] 2 A.C. 264 at 301. See also Dias, "Trouble on Oiled Waters: Problems of The Wagon Mound (No.2)" [1967] C.L.J. 62.

193 [1994] 2 A.C. 264 at 300.

194 The actual decision of the House of Lords turned upon the rule in *Rylands v Fletcher*, but nuisance was extensively considered. See also *Hamilton v Papakura DC* [2002] UKPC 9; *The Times,* 5 March 2002 PC.

of Lord Wright's statement, in the earlier House of Lords case of *Sedleigh-Denfield v O'Callaghan*,[195] that "[l]iability for nuisance is not, at least in modern law, a strict or absolute liability". While this statement does not apply to the rule in *Rylands v Fletcher*[196] nor, apparently, to public nuisances affecting the highway,[197] it succinctly summarises the general position in relation to private nuisance.

(c) Nature of defendant's conduct

Creating nuisances Three situations may be distinguished mainly with reference to the nature of the defendant's conduct[198]: 19-39

(a) If the defendant deliberately or recklessly uses his land in a way which he knows will cause harm to his neighbour, and that harm is considered by a judge to be an unreasonable infringement of his neighbour's interest in his property and therefore an unreasonable user by the defendant of his property, the defendant is liable for the foreseeable consequences. This proposition covers all those cases of obvious or "patent" nuisances, and they are peculiarly the cases which call for prevention or prohibition by injunction. It is no defence that the defendant believed that he was entitled to do as he did or that he took all possible steps to prevent his activity from amounting to a nuisance. In this sense, and in this context, it is correct to say that "at common law, if I am sued for nuisance, *and the nuisance is proved*, it is no defence on my part to say, and to prove, that I have taken all reasonable care to prevent it".[199] Similarly, Lord Simonds has said that "*if a man commits a legal nuisance* it is no answer to his injured neighbour that he took the utmost care not to commit it".[200]

(b) If the defendant knew or ought to have known that in consequence of his conduct harm to his neighbour was reasonably foreseeable, he is under a duty of care to prevent such consequences as are reasonably foreseeable. In such case the defendant is liable because he is considered negligent in relation to his neighbour, and here nuisance and negligence coincide. Whether his liability is described as falling under one legal rubric or the other would seem to be only a difference of words. 19-40

(c) If the defendant neither knows and intends harm nor is negligent with regard to the consequences of his conduct, then he may be nevertheless liable if the claimant can bring his case within the rule in *Rylands v Fletcher*,[201] and in that event there is strict liability. In those circumstances of non-natural user, followed by escape and consequent damage to the claimant, the defendant 19-41

---

[195] [1940] A.C. 880 at 904.

[196] See paras 19-44 to 19-62.

[197] See para.19-43.

[198] See Eekelaar, "Nuisance and Strict Liability (1973) 8 Ir. Jur. (N.S.) 191, upon which some of the following passages are based. For another analysis see Gearty, "The Place of Private Nuisance in a Modern Law of Torts" [1989] C.L.J. 214.

[199] per Lindley LJ in *Rapier v London Tramways* [1893] 2 Ch. 588 at 599 (emphasis supplied).

[200] *Read v Lyons* [1947] A.C. 157 at 183 (emphasis supplied). He continues, "There the liability is strict." This, it is submitted, is too broad a proposition if meant to apply to all kinds of nuisance. On the other hand, he may have had in mind the rule that deliberate infringement of a neighbour's interest carries liability which continues after the person creating the nuisance has ceased to occupy the premises and so no longer has the means of abating the nuisance he has created. See para.19-70.

[201] See para.19-44.

is held by law to be in effect the gratuitous insurer of his neighbour's safety, and it is immaterial that he failed to prevent the harm through his own negligence or that of his agents. But it is important to note that even here, as a result of the actual decision in the *Cambridge Water* case, the damage which occurred must have been foreseeable if liability is to be imposed.

19-42 **Adopting or continuing nuisances** It is clear that in cases where liability is sought to be imposed upon a defendant, not on the ground that he created the nuisance but on the ground that he permitted it to continue, proof of negligence at least is essential. As Lord Wright said in *Sedleigh-Denfield v O'Callaghan*[202]: "If the defendant did not create the nuisance he must, if he is to be held responsible, have continued it, which I think means simply that he neglected to remedy it when he became or should have become aware of it." In *Sedleigh-Denfield*, trespassers had interfered with the drainage system on the defendant's land, causing water to overflow onto that of the claimant. The defendants were held liable but only on the basis that, through one of their servants, they were taken to have knowledge of the interference and yet did nothing to remedy it. Lord Atkin observed that "The occupier or owner is not an insurer; there must be something more than the mere harm done to the neighbour's property to make the party responsible … some degree of personal responsibility is required…".[203] The general principles governing liability of an occupier for nuisances not created by him were considered more recently by the Supreme Court of Victoria in *City of Richmond v Scantelbury*.[204] If the occupier knows or ought to know of such a nuisance, and the possibility of damage occurring in consequence is a real risk, he must take such positive action as a reasonable person, in his position and circumstances, would consider necessary to eliminate the nuisance.[205] The principles governing liability for "adopting" or "continuing" nuisances cannot, however, be applied as between landlord and tenant so as to hold the former liable for water entering the latter's flat owing to defects in its construction which preceded the grant of the lease. In the absence of any covenant in the lease compelling the landlord to make good the defect the principle *caveat lessee* will apply.[206]

19-43 **Highway cases** Cases of nuisances connected with the highway have received special treatment by the judges, perhaps because of the public interest involved in the safe use of the highway. Ordinary highway collisions are actionable on proof of negligence, but in relation to obstructions on the highway amounting to a public nuisance and causing particular harm to the claimant it has been held that the defendant may be liable notwithstanding that there was no foreseeable danger. In *Dymond v Pearce*,[207] Stephenson LJ said that the unauthorised parking of a vehicle in obstruction of the highway:

> "in the present state of the authorities was prima facie a nuisance actionable at the suit of

[202] [1940] A.C. 880 at 905.

[203] [1940] A.C. 880 at 897. See also *Younger v Molesworth* [2006] EWHC 3088 (QB); [2006] N.P.C. 130 in which Langley J noted the difficult factual questions that can arise in determining whether the requisite degree of personal responsibility on the part of the defendant has been established.

[204] [1991] 2 V.R. 38 Aus. Ct.

[205] See also *Goldman v Hargrave* [1967] 1 A.C. 645.

[206] See *Jackson v JH Watson Property Investment Ltd* [2008] EWHC 14 (Ch); [2008] Env. L.R. 30; [2008] 11 E.G. 94.

[207] [1972] 1 Q.B. 496. See para.19-186 onwards.

the person injured by it (whether foreseeably dangerous or not at the time when it was created), because it was not justified by any right to park it there in the lorry driver as a user of the highway or as an occupier of adjoining premises or in any other capacity."[208]

Also, liability appears to be strict where artificial projections fall on to the highway.[209] The older decisions do, however, need to be treated with some caution, in so far as they involved damages claims, in view of the general trend away from strict liability for such claims in other nuisance contexts. Thus, in *Hunter v Canary Wharf Ltd*[210] Lord Goff of Chieveley expressed himself, obiter, as follows:

"... although, in the past, damages for personal injury have been recovered at least in actions of public nuisance, there is now developing a school of thought that the appropriate remedy for such claims as these should lie in our now fully developed law of negligence, and that personal injury claims should be altogether excluded from the domain of nuisance."[211]

If, therefore, strict liability continues to exist in highway cases it should probably be regarded as peculiar to that context and not as part of the general law of private nuisances occurring between neighbours. Denning LJ once emphasised the special nature of these public nuisances:

"In an action for private damage arising out of a public nuisance the court does not look at the conduct of the defendant and ask whether he was negligent. It looks at the actual state of affairs as it exists in or adjoining the highway, without regard to the merits or demerits of the defendant. If the state of affairs is such as to be a danger to persons using the highway ... it is a public nuisance. Once it is held to be a danger, the person who created it is liable unless he can show sufficient justification or excuse."[212]

3. THE RULE IN RYLANDS V FLETCHER

(a) Status of Rylands rule

Nature of the rule In *Rylands v Fletcher*,[213] Blackburn J said: **19-44**

"We think that the true rule of law is, that the person who for his own purposes brings on his lands and collects and keeps there anything likely to do mischief if it escapes must keep it in at his peril, and, if he does not do so, is prima facie answerable for all the damage which is the natural consequence of its escape."

In the House of Lords, Lord Cairns concurred in his judgment, but introduced an

[208] [1972] 1 Q.B. 496 at 508, agreeing with Sachs LJ. However, Edmund-Davies LJ, though agreeing that a causative connection between obstruction and injury had not been shown on the facts, differed on the law, holding (ibid. at 506) that "fault is essential to liability in the sense that it must appear that the reasonable man would be bound to realise the likelihood of risk to highway users from the presence of an obstructing vehicle on the road".

[209] See paras 19-101 and 19-189.

[210] See [1997] A.C. 655 at 692.

[211] But note that, until the Supreme Court rules differently, it is still the law that damages for personal injury can be recovered in public nuisance: see *The Claimants appearing on the Register of the Corby Group Litigation v Corby BC* [2008] EWCA Civ 463; [2009] Q.B. 335.

[212] *Morton v Wheeler*, *The Times*, 1 February 1956; quoted by Edmund-Davies LJ in *Dymond v Pearce* [1972] 1 Q.B. 496 at 506–507.

[213] (1866) L.R. 1 Ex. 265 at 279; affirmed in (1886) L.R. 3 HL 330 HL. See Murphy, "The Merits of Rylands v Fletcher" (2004) 24 O.J.L.S. 643; Nolan, "The Distinctiveness of Rylands v Fletcher" (2005) 121 L.Q.R. 421.

element of flexibility by restricting the rule to circumstances where the defendant had made "a non-natural use" of the land.[214] This is "strict liability", in the limited sense that it is unnecessary for a claimant to prove negligence in the defendant or his agents. Although it might once have developed as a separate branch of the law in its own right, the rule in *Rylands v Fletcher* is now perceived, as a result of three House of Lords decisions stretching across more than half a century,[215] to be simply a special sub-rule of the law of private nuisance dealing with damage caused by isolated escapes of dangerous substances from land.[216]

19-45 **Transco and Cambridge Water** This principle was taken up and applied by the later Victorian judges with a considerable degree of vigour, but increasingly in more recent times it has undergone dilution. The rule has attracted a large number of exceptions or defences to liability which have limited its general scope and force, and cases in which it has been applied have become infrequent. In *Transco v Stockport MBC*,[217] counsel for the defendant invited the House to hold that the rule was obsolete, and should be treated as having been absorbed by the tort of negligence. In rejecting this submission the House subjected the rule to a very wide-ranging examination, before concluding that the rule still has a part to play in English law. In so holding the House confirmed the approach which it had itself taken 10 years earlier in *Cambridge Water Co Ltd v Eastern Countries Leather Plc*,[218] another decision of major importance in this area. In that case the defendants were leather manufacturers who used a chemical solvent in their tanning process. Until 1971, when their manufacturing processes changed, small quantities of solvent spilled on to the concrete floor of their premises. From there it seeped through into the soil below and escaped into percolating channels of underground water which the claimant company used for the local public supply. The water was rendered unfit for human consumption as a result, but it was found as a fact that the seepage had been quite unforeseeable. The claimants attempted to hold the defendants liable under the rule in *Rylands v Fletcher*, but were unsuccessful. The actual claim in *Transco v Stockport MBC*, which arose out of the leakage of a large quantity of water from a pipe used to supply a block of flats, also failed on the facts.

19-46 **Restrictive approach** Although the House of Lords in the *Cambridge Water* case was opposed to undue narrowing of the scope of the rule by artificial invocation of the concept of natural user,[219] in other respects their Lordships adopted a restrictive approach to the doctrine. In so doing, they echoed the general approach of the House in its earlier examination of the scope of the rule, shortly after the end of the Second World War, in *Read v J Lyons & Co Ltd*.[220] The claimant had been employed in the defendants' munitions factory, and was injured there by the explosion of a shell. No allegation of negligence was made by her against the defendants. The

---

[214] (1866) L.R. 1 Ex. 265 at 338–340. *Porter (JP) Co Ltd v Bell* (1955) 1 D.L.R. 62 at 66, per Macdonald J.

[215] See *Transco v Stockport MBC* [2003] UKHL 61; [2004] 2 A.C. 1; *Cambridge Water Co Ltd v Eastern Counties Leather Plc* [1994] 2 A.C. 264; *Read v J Lyons & Co Ltd* [1947] A.C. 156.

[216] Isolated escapes *not* involving dangerous substances are not actionable in the absence of negligence: see, e.g. *Northumbrian Water Ltd v Sir Robert McAlpine Ltd* [2014] EWCA Civ 685; (2014) 154 Con. L.R. 26.

[217] [2003] UKHL 61; [2004] 2 A.C. 1.

[218] [1994] 2 A.C. 264.

[219] See para.19-54.

[220] [1947] A.C. 156.

basis of her claim was that the defendants carried on the manufacture of high-explosive shells knowing that they were dangerous things. The House of Lords held the defendants were not liable, on the ground that the rule in *Rylands v Fletcher* does not apply unless there has been an escape from the defendant's land, to a place outside his occupation or control, of something dangerous in the sense that, if it escapes, it will do damage.[221] That was the ratio of the decision, but the dicta accompanying the decision displayed a conservative or restrictive approach to the rule of strict liability. The speeches denied the existence of any general principle of strict liability for ultra-hazardous activities; in the absence of negligence, liability would only be found in certain defined situations.[222] In *Cambridge Water*, their Lordships took the view that in principle the rule should be seen as little more than "an extension of the law of nuisance to cases of isolated escapes",[223] and this view was subsequently endorsed by the House in *Transco v Stockport MBC*.[224]

Rule rejected in Australia Shortly after the House of Lords handed down its decision in *Cambridge Water*, the High Court of Australia, by a majority of five to two, held in *Burnie Port Authority v General Jones Pty Ltd*,[225] that the rule in *Rylands v Fletcher* no longer existed as an independent head of liability in that country but should instead be regarded "as absorbed by the principles of ordinary negligence".[226] In *Burnie*, the defendant building owners employed independent contractors to do certain reconstruction work which involved the use of highly flammable material. Owing to the gross negligence of the contractors a fire was started which spread to a part of the building occupied by the claimants under an agreement with the defendants. The claimants' property was destroyed and they sued the defendants. Although the action succeeded, and the defendants were held liable for the negligence of their contractors, this was not on the basis of the rule in *Rylands v Fletcher* but on the ground that "a person who takes advantage of his or her control of premises to introduce a dangerous substance, to carry on a dangerous activity, or to allow another to do one of these things" owes a "non-delegable" duty in the tort of negligence to those who suffer damage as a result. The majority regarded this approach as preferable "to the rule in *Rylands v Fletcher*, with all its difficulties, uncertainties, qualifications and exceptions".[227] The reasoning of the High Court of Australia in *Burnie's* case was analysed by Lord Walker of Gestingthorpe in his speech in *Transco v Stockport MBC*. He concluded that "the case for writing off *Rylands v Fletcher* as a dead letter" had not been made out,[228] but acknowledged the need for greater clarity in identifying the conditions for the application of the rule. He emphasised the disadvantages which abolition of the rule could have for claimants obliged to discharge the burden of proving negligence 19-47

[221] [1947] A.C. 156 at 176.

[222] There is no one common principle from which all cases of strict liability can be deduced: [1947] A.C. 156 at 167 and 181; *Rylands v Fletcher* does not lay down or reflect "an aspect of some wider principle applicable to dangerous businesses or dangerous things": per Lord Uthwatt at 186.

[223] [1994] 2 A.C. 264 at 306.

[224] [2003] UKHL 61; [2004] 2 A.C. 1. See, e.g. per Lord Bingham at [9] ("a sub-species of nuisance"); and per Lord Hobhouse at [52] ("an aspect of the law of private nuisance"); see also per Lord Hoffmann at [27].

[225] (1994) 120 A.L.R. 42. Mason CJ, Deane, Dawson, Toohey and Gaudron JJ, Brennan and McHugh JJ dissenting.

[226] (1994) 120 A.L.R. 42 at 67.

[227] (1994) 120 A.L.R. 42 at 67–68.

[228] [2003] UKHL 61; [2004] 2 A.C. 1 at [99].

against well-resourced corporate defendants.[229] The rule therefore remains part of the common law in England, and its various aspects accordingly still need to be explained.

(b) Activities subject to the Rylands rule

19-48 **Things to which the rule is applicable** The principle of *Rylands v Fletcher* applies, in Blackburn J's language, to "anything likely to do mischief if it escapes"; and accordingly, the basic idea is the escape from the defendant's control or containment of "things" which have a special potential to cause harm in such an event.

19-49 **"Dangerous things"** "Things" have been equated with "dangerous things"[230] and this has led to confusion with liability for negligence. If things within the defendant's control are likely to escape and do damage, any resulting damage constitutes liability in negligence. Strict liability is concerned with a thing that is likely to do mischief if it escapes, even though escape is not reasonably foreseeable. It is clear from the speeches in the House of Lords in *Transco v Stockport MBC*[231] that the requirement for the accumulation to have been a potential source of "danger", while necessarily dependent upon the facts of the particular case, will not be an easy threshold for a claimant to cross. Thus Lord Bingham of Cornhill said[232]:

> "I do not think the mischief or danger test should be at all easily satisfied. It must be shown that the defendant has done something which he recognised, or judged by the standards appropriate at the relevant place and time, he ought reasonably to have recognised, as giving rise to an *exceptionally high risk of danger or mischief* if there should be an escape, however unlikely an escape may have been thought to be."

In *Colour Quest Ltd v Total Downstream UK Plc*[233] liability under *Rylands v Fletcher* was conceded when a vapour cloud caused by the spillage of a large quantity of petrol stored on the defendants' site exploded, and caused damage to property over a wide area surrounding the site. While decisions from earlier periods cannot necessarily be regarded as still authoritative, the following examples can also usefully be noted. The principle has been applied to water (including sewage),[234] fire,[235] a motor vehicle, whether or not the tank contains petrol,[236] a blowlamp,[237] gas,[238] explosives,[239] electricity,[240] poison,[241] paraffin,[242] a roundabout known as a

---

[229] [2003] UKHL 61; [2004] 2 A.C. 1 at [110].

[230] See Stallybrass [1929] C.L.J. 376 at 397; *Northwestern Utilities Ltd v London Guarantee Co* [1936] A.C. 108 at 118; *Barker v Herbert* [1911] 2 K.B. 633 at 642; *Read v Lyons* [1947] A.C. 156 at 158–159 (argument of counsel).

[231] [2003] UKHL 61; [2004] 2 A.C. 1.

[232] [2003] UKHL 61; [2004] 2 A.C. 1 at [10] (emphasis added).

[233] [2009] EWHC 540 (Comm); [2009] 2 Lloyd's Rep. 1; reversed in part, but not on this point, in [2010] EWCA Civ 180; [2011] Q.B. 86.

[234] *Charing Cross Electricity Supply Co v Hydraulic Power Co* [1914] 3 K.B. 772; *Humphries v Cousins* (1877) 2 C.P.D. 239; *Smeaton v Ilford Corp* [1954] Ch. 450 (rule considered with reference to local authority performing statutory duties—disposal of sewage).

[235] *Jones v Ffestiniog Ry* (1868) L.R. 3 Q.B. 733.

[236] *Musgrove v Pandelis* [1919] 2 K.B. 43 CA; *Perry v Kendricks Transport Co* [1956] 1 W.L.R. 85 CA.

[237] *Balfour v Barty-King* [1957] 1 Q.B. 496 CA.

[238] *Goodbody v Poplar BC* (1915) 84 L.J.K.B. 1230; *Hanson v Wearmouth Coal Co* [1939] 3 All E.R. 47; *Federic v Perpetual Investments* (1968) 2 D.L.R. (3d) 50.

[239] *Rainham Chemical Works v Belvedere Fish Guano Co* [1921] 2 A.C. 465; and paras 19-174 and 19-175.

chair-o-plane[243]; to a quantity of colliery spoil tipped on the side of a steep hill without any provision for drainage, so that the spoil slid down the hill and did damage[244]; to vibrations set up by pile-driving[245]; and to the granting of licences to caravan dwellers to use a field, whereby a nuisance was caused to the neighbourhood.[246]

Principle inapplicable The principle has been held not to apply to the branch of a tree liable to fall on the highway,[247] an aeroplane,[248] an oilcan,[249] a boiler without a safety valve,[250] a cricket ball driven out of the ground,[251] and the tipping of "swarf" into barges.[252] **19-50**

Things naturally on land In respect of things naturally on land, the principle has no application. In respect of elements of nature in conditions unaffected by artificial work or alteration there was formerly a line of cases indicating immunity of the land owner from whose property an escape occurred. In the second half of the twentieth century, however, the courts introduced a qualified duty of care where the natural condition of land causes harm to a neighbour, but they fall far short of imposing any duty of a strict nature.[253] **19-51**

Natural user of land Again, a person who uses his land in the exercise of his ordinary rights incurs no strict liability if he injures his neighbour. A user of this kind is termed a natural user, and for damage caused by the natural or ordinary use of land there is no liability under the principle of *Rylands v Fletcher*.[254] The erection of a wall[255] or buildings[256] on land is a natural user of the land as is such activity as **19-52**

---

240 *National Telephone Co v Baker* [1893] 2 Ch. 186; and para.19-173.

241 *West v Bristol Tramways Co* [1908] 2 K.B. 14; *Halsey v Esso Petroleum Co Ltd* [1961] 1 W.L.R. 683 at 692 and 701 (sulphate in smuts or oily drops, but not petrol tankers).

242 *Mulholland and Tedd Ltd v Baker* [1939] 3 All E.R. 253.

243 *Hale v Jennings Bros* [1938] 1 All E.R. 579.

244 *Att Gen v Cory Bros* [1921] 1 A.C. 521.

245 *Hoare & Co v McAlpine* [1923] 1 Ch. 167. Not followed in *Barrette v Franki Compressed Pile Co of Canada* [1955] 2 D.L.R. 665 (vibrations a nuisance not within *Rylands v Fletcher*).

246 *Att Gen v Corke* [1933] Ch. 89. It is difficult to see how it can be said that the landowner was bound to keep the caravan dwellers on his land at his peril, or that he was liable for damage caused by their "escape". The case "could at least have been equally well decided on the basis that the landowner there was in possession of the property and was himself liable in nuisance for the acts of his licensees": per Pennycuick VC in *Smith v Scott* [1973] Ch. 314. In *Smith v Scott*, where the landlord was held not liable for unruly tenants, the lease provided expressly that no nuisance should be caused. But the landlord is liable for nuisance expressly or impliedly authorised in the letting or licensing of land: *Tetley v Chitty* [1986] 1 All E.R. 663. With regard to nuisances caused by trespassers on the defendant's property, see para.19-94.

247 *Noble v Harrison* [1926] 2 K.B. 332.

248 *Fosbroke-Hobbes v Airwork Ltd* [1937] 1 All E.R. 108.

249 *Wray v Essex CC* [1936] 3 All E.R. 97.

250 *Ball v London CC* [1949] 2 K.B. 159.

251 *Bolton v Stone* [1951] A.C. 850.

252 *Burley v Stepney Corp* [1947] 1 All E.R. 507.

253 See paras 19-20 to 19-23.

254 per Lord Cairns (1868) L.R. 3 HL 330 at 338; *Blake v Woolf* [1898] 2 Q.B. 426; *Rickards v Lothian* [1913] A.C. 263; *Bartlett v Tottenham* [1932] 1 Ch. 114 at 131.

255 *Ilford Urban DC v Beal* [1925] 1 K.B. 671; *St Anne's Well Brewery Co v Roberts* (1928) 140 L.T. 1; [1928] All E.R. Rep. 28 CA.

256 *Wilkins v Leighton* [1932] 2 Ch. 106.

painting a house or a bridge,[257] so that any liability in respect of these works must be based on trespass, nuisance or negligence. In any event, walls and buildings are not within the principle, as they are not things essentially dangerous in themselves.[258] The working of mines in the ordinary course of mining is a natural user of land,[259] and consequently damage caused by percolating water during such working gives no cause of action.[260] "The owner of one piece of land has a right to use it in the natural course of user, unless in doing so he interferes with some right created either by law or contract",[261] and by using it in this way he does not bring himself within *Rylands v Fletcher* even if he causes damage to his neighbour. The courts are, however, increasingly taking the view that the concepts of "natural" and "non-natural" use of land are actually unhelpful, and that an approach similar to the concept of "reasonable user" elsewhere in nuisance is more appropriate. In *Arscott v Coal Authority*[262] Laws LJ said:

> "While no doubt the rule in *Rylands v Fletcher* is alive and well, and what are plainly natural—perhaps 'ordinary' is a better word—uses of land will continue to be respected and allowed unless pursued excessively, still the importance of the distinction in our law between natural and non-natural uses is receding."

Moreover certain "natural" users may attract strict liability by virtue of another head of tort liability, for example the straying of livestock under s.4 of the Animals Act 1971.

19-53 **Non-natural use of land**[263] Blackburn J said the rule only applied to a thing "which was not naturally there"; in the House of Lords Lord Cairns added that the defendant is only liable if, in bringing it there, he is making "a non-natural use" of the land:

> "It is not every use to which land is put that brings into play that principle (*Rylands v Fletcher*). It must be some special use bringing with it increased danger to others, and must not merely be the ordinary use of land or such a use as is proper for the general benefit of the community."[264]

The test thus formulated was a flexible one which enabled the judges to take account of changes in industrial uses and indeed the usages of contemporary society. This approach was reflected in *Read v Lyons* in which Lord Porter said:

> "Each case seems to be a question of fact subject to a ruling of the judge as to whether … the particular use can be non-natural, and in deciding this question I think that all the circumstances of the time and place and produce of mankind must be taken into considera-

257 *Vaughan v Halifax-Dartmouth Bridge Commission* (1961) 29 D.L.R. (2d) 523.

258 *Barker v Herbert* [1911] 2 K.B. 633 at 642; *St Anne's Well Brewery Co v Roberts* (1928) 140 L.T. 1; [1928] All E.R. Rep. 28.

259 See *Willis v Derwentside DC* [2013] EWHC 738 (Ch); [2013] Env. L.R. 31, per Briggs J at [45]–[46] (referring to the twentieth edition of this work).

260 *Wilson v Waddell* (1876) 2 App. Cas. 95.

261 *Wilson v Waddell* (1876) 2 App. Cas. 95 at 99, per Lord Blackburn.

262 [2004] EWCA Civ 892; [2005] Env. L.R. 6 CA at [29].

263 See Stallybrass, "Dangerous Things and Non-Natural Use of Land" [1929] C.L.J. 376; Newark, "Non-Natural User and Rylands v Fletcher" (1961) 24 M.L.R. 557; Blackburn, "The Rule in Rylands v Fletcher" (1961) 4 Can. Bar J. 39; Williams, "Non-Natural Use of Land" [1973] C.L.J. 310.

264 per Lord Moulton in *Rickards v Lothian* [1913] A.C. 263 at 280, approved by Lord Simon in *Read v J Lyons & Co Ltd* [1947] A.C. 156 at 169. See the comment of Upjohn J on this in *Smeaton v Ilford Corp* [1954] Ch. 450 at 460 and 467–472.

> tion so that what might be regarded as … non-natural may vary according to those circumstances."[265]

Thus the storage of strips of metal foil used in the manufacture of electrical components was once held to be a natural user, because it was not a "special use bringing with it increased danger to others", when a quantity of the foil was blown into a nearby electricity sub-station and caused a power failure.[266] In Canada a nickel refinery, which emitted nickel particles for many years, has been held not to constitute non-natural user.[267]

Different approach after Cambridge Water In 1993, however, in *Cambridge Water Co Ltd v Eastern Counties Leather Plc*,[268] the House of Lords indicated that a markedly different approach would henceforth be adopted. The House took the view that the concept of natural or ordinary use of land had been unduly extended by courts anxious to restrict the incidence of the rule in *Rylands v Fletcher*. In the light of its own decision to the effect that liability under the rule would henceforth be restricted in any event by the need to establish foreseeability of harm of the relevant type, the House expressed the hope that "the courts may feel less pressure to extend the concept of natural use".[269] Opinions expressed on the point in earlier cases may therefore need to be reassessed. *Cambridge Water* itself concerned the storage, in an industrial village, of chemicals for use in the leather tanning industry. At first instance, Ian Kennedy J had held that this was not a non-natural use of land for the purpose of the rule but the House of Lords disagreed. Lord Goff expressed himself as follows[270]: **19-54**

> "I feel bound to say that the storage of substantial quantities of chemicals on industrial premises should be regarded as an almost classic case of non-natural use; and I find it very difficult to think that it should be thought objectionable to impose strict liability for damage caused in the event of their escape."

In particular Lord Goff indicated, in disagreement with the trial judge, that "the creation of employment as such, even in a small industrial complex" was not sufficient to constitute a particular use of land as natural or ordinary. It is therefore clear that the use of the land for the general benefit of the community is not enough to exclude the application of the rule,[271] and even before the *Cambridge Water* case *Rylands v Fletcher* had been applied, notwithstanding the wider view of the "natural user" defence, to gas companies,[272] water companies,[273] tram companies,[274] railway companies,[275] colliery companies,[276] and the manufacture of explosives in

265 [1947] A.C. 156 at 176. *Mackenzie v Sloss* [1959] N.Z.L.R. 533 at 536.
266 *British Celanese Ltd v AH Hunt (Capacitors) Ltd* [1969] 1 W.L.R. 959.
267 *Smith v Inco Ltd* [2011] ONCA 628; (2011) 107 O.R. (3d) 321 (Ontario CA).
268 [1994] 2 A.C. 264.
269 [1994] 2 A.C. 264 at 309.
270 [1994] 2 A.C. 264 at 309.
271 *Smeaton v Ilford Corp* [1954] Ch. 450 at 470–471, per Upjohn J. cf. Denning LJ in *Pride of Derby Angling Association v British Celanese* [1953] Ch. 149 at 189.
272 *Northwestern Utilities v London Guarantee and Accident Co* [1936] A.C. 108.
273 *Charing Cross Electricity Supply Co v Hydraulic Power Co* [1914] 3 K.B. 772.
274 *National Telephone Co v Baker* [1893] 2 Ch. 186; *West v Bristol Tramways* [1908] 2 K.B. 14.
275 *Jones v Ffestiniog Ry* (1868) L.R. 3 Q.B. 733.
276 *Rylands v Fletcher* (1868) L.R. 3 HL 330.

wartime.[277]

19-55 **Domestic activities unaffected** But although the storing of water, gas and electricity in bulk in mains and the like is within the rule, *Cambridge Water* has not affected the established proposition that ordinary domestic supplies of such things are not a "non-natural" user of land.[278] In *Transco v Stockport MBC*[279] the House of Lords held that the requirement of non-natural user would only be met by uses "shown to be extraordinary and unusual".[280] The requirement was held not to be met on the facts of the *Transco* case itself, in which a service pipe which supplied water to a block of flats fractured. Although it was necessarily very much larger than water pipes within individual premises, the pipe in question was not considered to constitute a non-natural use of land. There was "no evidence that it created a greater risk than is normally associated with domestic or commercial plumbing".[281] In *Ellison v Ministry of Defence* the carrying out of construction works on a disused airfield were considered to constitute an ordinary use of land, and hence not to be within the concept of non-natural user for the purposes of the rule.[282]

(c) Scope of liability

(i) Parties

19-56 **Who is liable under the rule?** In *Rylands v Fletcher*, water from the defendant's reservoir flowed into the claimant's mine, and the judgments accordingly deal with things brought or collected on land. The principle of the decision, however, is not limited to persons who keep or accumulate dangerous things on their own land.[283] The person liable is the owner or controller of the dangerous thing. If he brings or collects it on land, he is liable although he is not the owner or occupier of the land, but has merely a licence to use or enter upon it.[284] If he brings it on the highway,[285] and it escapes and causes damage he is similarly liable.[286] The occupier of the land from which it escapes is also liable if it is brought or collected on the land for his purposes or with his permission,[287] but not otherwise.[288] Whether an owner of land on which there is already a dangerous thing, for example a reservoir, remains li-

---

277 *Rainham Chemical Works v Belvedere Fish Guano Co* [1921] 2 A.C. 465. The House of Lords was inclined to take a different view on this point in *Read v J Lyons & Co Ltd* [1947] A.C. 156 at 169–170 and 173–174, but expressed no concluded opinion on it. cf. *Cambridge Water Co Ltd v Eastern Countries Leather Plc* [1994] 2 A.C. 264 at 308–309, per Lord Goff.

278 *Collingwood v Home & Colonial Stores Ltd* [1936] 3 All E.R. 200 CA.

279 [2003] UKHL 61; [2004] 2 A.C. 1.

280 See per Lord Bingham [2003] UKHL 61; [2004] 2 A.C. 1 at [11].

281 [2003] UKHL 61; [2004] 2 A.C. 1, per Lord Hoffmann at [49]; see also per Lord Bingham at [13].

282 (1996) 81 B.L.R. 101.

283 *Northwestern Utilities Ltd v London Guarantee and Accident Co* [1936] A.C. 108.

284 *Rainham Chemical Works v Belvedere Fish Guano Co* [1921] 2 A.C. 465 at 479; *National Telephone Co v Baker* [1893] 2 Ch. 186.

285 *Jones v Ffestiniog Ry* (1868) L.R. 3 Q.B. 733; *Powell v Fall* (1880) 5 Q.B.D. 597; *West v Bristol Tramways* [1908] 2 K.B. 14; *Rigby v Chief Constable of Northamptonshire* [1985] 1 W.L.R. 1242 at 1255. In *Rigby*'s case, Taylor J quoted the text of this section with approval down to this note, and added "I can see no difference in principle between allowing a man-eating tiger to escape from your land onto that of another and allowing it to escape from the back of your wagon parked on the highway."

286 Escapes from accumulations on vessels on navigable rivers would also appear to be within the rule: *Crown River Cruises Ltd v Kimbolton Fireworks Ltd* [1996] 2 Lloyd's Rep 533, per Potter J.

287 *Rainham Chemical Works v Belvedere Fish Guano Co* [1921] 2 A.C. 465.

able after he has let the land to a tenant is doubtful.[289] On principle it would seem that an owner not in occupation or control of land is not strictly liable unless he has expressly or impliedly authorised the accumulation. There seems to be no justification for treating a local authority differently merely because it is a local authority.[290] The words "for his own purposes" in the rule as stated by Blackburn J do not mean that the defendant is only liable when he is obtaining some personal benefit from collecting the mischievous thing. The proposition that local authorities are not exempt from the rule, merely because they act for the community at large rather than for their own benefit, is supported by the reasoning of the House of Lords in *Transco v Stockport MBC*.[291] A local authority which is required by statute to receive sewage into its sewer may be liable.[292]

To whom liability is owed? "Once there has been an escape … those damnified may claim. They need not be the occupiers of adjoining land or indeed of any land."[293] In Blackburn J's statement of the rule there is no requirement that the harm must be suffered by the adjacent owner into whose land the material escapes. It has therefore been held that the claimant may be a person suffering harm by an escape into the land of a third party.[294] It has also been held that a water company authorised by statute to carry water under the surface of the highway is liable for water from a broken main which damaged the cables of an electricity supply company also under the highway,[295] and that a gas company, whose mains were under the street, was liable for an escape of gas which caused an explosion in an hotel.[296] A railway company has been held liable for damage to stacks in a field caused by the emission of sparks from a railway engine,[297] and so has the owner of a traction engine driven along the highway for damage similarly caused.[298] The older cases on who can claim under the rule must, however, now be read in the light of the decision of the House of Lords in *Hunter v Canary Wharf Ltd*.[299] In that case it was held that a claimant for nuisance had to have an interest in the land affected. It would seem likely that the same principle now applies to claims under the rule, in view of the perception that *Rylands v Fletcher* is itself part of the tort of nuisance. This view is supported by observations in *Transco v Stockport MBC*.[300] Nevertheless, in one case the High Court declined to strike out a claim under the rule brought by claimants without an interest in land, holding that it was arguable that a more expansive 19-57

288 *Whitmores Ltd v Stanford* [1909] 1 Ch. 427.

289 Compare the opposing views of Atkin LJ in *Rainham Chemical Works v Belvedere Fish Guano Co* [1920] 2 K.B. 487 at 502; and Lord Buckmaster in [1921] 2 A.C. 465 at 476. Probably the courts will apply the analogous rules in nuisance.

290 per Upjohn J in *Smeaton v Ilford Corp* [1954] Ch. 450.

291 [2003] UKHL 61; [2004] 2 A.C. 1, see, especially, per Lord Walker at [105].

292 See *Smeaton v Ilford Corp* [1954] Ch. 450 at 469 and 472, per Upjohn J. But cf. *Dunne v North Western Gas Board* [1964] 2 Q.B. 806 (criticised by Lord Walker in *Transco v Stockport MBC*: see previous note).

293 *British Celanese Ltd v AH Hunt (Capacitors) Ltd* [1969] 1 W.L.R. 959 at 963, per Lawton J; *Halsey v Esso Petroleum Co Ltd* [1961] 1 W.L.R. 683 (damage to motorcar on the highway).

294 *British Celanese Ltd v AH Hunt (Capacitors) Ltd* [1969] 1 W.L.R. 959 at 964, per Lawton J.

295 *Charing Cross Electricity Supply Co v Hydraulic Power Co* [1914] 3 K.B. 772.

296 *Northwestern Utilities Ltd v London Guarantee and Accident Co* [1936] A.C. 108.

297 *Jones v Ffestiniog Ry* (1868) L.R. 3 Q.B. 733.

298 *Powell v Fall* (1880) 5 Q.B.D. 597; *Gunter v James* (1908) 24 T.L.R. 868; *Mansel v Webb* (1919) 88 L.J.K.B. 323.

299 [1997] A.C. 655.

300 See [2003] UKHL 61; [2004] 2 A.C. 1, per Lord Bingham at [9], per Lord Hoffmann at [35], and per Lord Hobhouse at [55].

view of those entitled to claim was now required by virtue of the European Convention on Human Rights.[301]

(ii) Types of damage

19-58 **Economic loss** Non-physical losses, such as pure pecuniary or economic loss, appear always to have been irrecoverable under the rule.[302] Where water leaked from the defendants' pipes and made the construction of a tunnel, which the claimant had contracted to do, a more expensive operation than the claimant had anticipated, it was held that the defendants were not liable.[303] In giving judgment, Blackburn J said:

> "If we did so [allow the action] we should establish an authority for saying that, in such a case as that of *Rylands v Fletcher*, the defendant would be liable, not only to an action by the owner of the drowned mine, and by such of his workmen as had their tools or clothes destroyed, but also to an action by every workman and person employed in the mine, who in consequence of its stoppage made less wages than he would otherwise have done."

A contractor upon inundated land cannot therefore recover for purely financial loss, nor can other non-occupiers.[304]

19-59 **Personal injuries** The question was raised in *Read v J Lyons & Co Ltd*,[305] whether damages for personal injuries can be recovered under the rule in *Rylands v Fletcher*. Until this case, no doubt had ever been expressed that they were recoverable. The Court of Appeal awarded such damages without question in *Miles v Forest Rock Granite Co*[306] and in *Hale v Jennings Bros*,[307] and Lord Parker CJ in the Court of Appeal said that it is not open to that court "to hold that the rule applies only to damage to adjoining land or to a proprietary interest in land and not to personal injury".[308] This view is, however, now very difficult to support in the light of the approach currently favoured by the House of Lords, towards the irrecoverablity of damages for personal injury at common law in the absence of negligence.[309] Indeed, although technically obiter, observations by the House in *Transco v Stockport MBC*[310] would seem effectively to have ended, and settled in

301 See *McKenna v British Aluminium Ltd* [2002] Env L.R. 30; *The Times*, 25 April 2002: art.8 of the Convention on Human Rights, and art.1 of the First Protocol respectively, refer in broad terms to protection of a person's "home" and "possessions".

302 See *Anglian Water Services Ltd v Crawshaw Robins Co Ltd* [2001] B.L.R. 173 at [149].

303 *Cattle v Stockton Waterworks* (1875) L.R. 10 Q.B. 453.

304 See *Weller v Foot and Mouth Disease Research Institute* [1966] 1 Q.B. 569. There seems to be no case actually deciding whether the *occupier* can recover for purely financial loss but in principle it seems doubtful that he can do so. cf. *Murphy v Brentwood DC* [1991] 1 A.C. 398.

305 [1947] A.C. 156 at 169 and 173. The cases on the point were cited by Lord Porter alone (at 178). He said the question "may some day require examination".

306 (1918) 34 T.L.R. 500; *Aldridge and O'Brien v Van Patter* [1952] 4 D.L.R. 93.

307 [1938] 1 All E.R. 579.

308 *Perry v Kendricks Transport Co* [1956] 1 W.L.R. 85 (licensee).

309 See, generally, dicta in *Cambridge Water Co Ltd v Eastern Counties Leather Plc* [1994] 2 A.C. 264; [1994] 1 All E.R. 53; and *Hunter v Canary Wharf Ltd* [1997] A.C. 655; [1997] 2 All E.R. 426.

310 See [2003] UKHL 61; [2004] 2 A.C. 1, per Lord Bingham at [9] ("… the claim cannot include a claim for death or personal injury"); and per Lord Hoffmann at [35] ("… damages for personal injury are not recoverable under the rule").

the negative, the long-standing debate about whether or not damages for personal injury are ever recoverable in actions based on the rule in *Rylands v Fletcher*.

(iii) Remoteness

Remoteness of damage Blackburn J said that the defendant liable under the rule of strict liability "is prima facie answerable for all the damage which is the natural consequence of its escape". Until recently, however, the modern cases have afforded little guidance on the question how far the liability may reach. In *The Wagon Mound (No.1)*,[311] the Judicial Committee of the Privy Council in giving its opinion on the question in relation to negligence declined to give an answer in relation to strict liability, nor did the opinion of the Judicial Committee in *The Wagon Mount (No.2)*[312] on public and private nuisance advert to the question. The matter has, however, now been authoritatively considered by the House of Lords in *Cambridge Water Co Ltd v Eastern Counties Leather Plc*. Lord Goff, with whose speech the other members of the House agreed, analysed the language of Blackburn J and concluded[313] that: 19-60

> "the general tenor of his statement of principle is … that knowledge, or at least foreseeability of the risk, is a prerequisite of the recovery of damages under the principle; but that the principle is one of strict liability in the sense that the defendant may be held liable notwithstanding that he has exercised all due care to prevent the escape from occurring."

In *Cambridge Water*, chemicals had escaped from the defendant's industrial premises and then seeped into the local water supply, rendering it unfit for human consumption. In exonerating the defendants from liability, Lord Goff succinctly expressed their Lordships' ratio decidendi as being that "foreseeability of damage of the relevant type should be regarded as a prerequisite of liability in damages under the rule".[314]

(iv) Escape

Escape There is no liability, however, unless the thing which does the damage "escapes from a place where the defendant has occupation or control over land to a place which is outside his occupation or control". Accordingly, when a worker in a munitions factory was injured by the explosion of a shell in the factory, it was held that without proof of negligence she could not recover.[315] The "escape" requirement was confirmed in *Transco v Stockport MBC*,[316] in which Lord Scott of Foscote actually based his decision adverse to the claimants by a reading of the facts which denied that the requirement had been satisfied in the *Transco* case itself.[317] Water which had leaked undetected, over a long period, from the defendants' pipe entered a disused railway embankment eventually causing it to collapse. Unfortunately the embankment supported a gas pipe owned by the claimants, leaving it dangerously 19-61

311 [1961] A.C. 388 at 426–427.
312 [1967] A.C. 617 at 639.
313 [1994] 2 A.C. 264 at 302.
314 [1994] 2 A.C. 264 at 306. See also *Hamilton v Papakura DC* [2002] UKPC 9; *The Times*, 5 March 2002; *Ellison v Ministry of Defence* (1996) 81 B.L.R.101.
315 *Read v J Lyons & Co Ltd* [1947] A.C. 156 at 168.
316 See [2003] UKHL 61; [2004] 2 A.C. 1, e.g. per Lord Hoffmann at [34].
317 See [2003] UKHL 61; [2004] 2 A.C. 1 at [77]–[80].

exposed; and the cost of the measures necessary to protect the pipe formed the basis of the *Rylands v Fletcher* claim. As it happened, however, the embankment itself was in the ownership of the defendants, which according to Lord Scott precluded liability. The other members of the House were, however, content to assume that the "escape" requirement had been satisfied and to decide the case, albeit adversely to the claimants, on the broader ground of absence of non-natural user. If there is an escape in the course of a non-natural user, the damage caused is actionable even if the material escaping and doing the damage was not the subject-matter of the accumulation or collected on his land by the defendant.[318]

(v) *Exceptions to the rule of strict liability*

19-62 **Exceptions** As Blackburn J indicated in his judgment in *Rylands v Fletcher*, there are some exceptions to the principle of "strict liability". They are:

(1) the act of God;
(2) the act or default of the claimant;
(3) the consent of the claimant;
(4) the independent act of a third party; and
(5) statutory authority.

These exceptions are considered within the general discussion of defences to nuisance later in this chapter.[319]

4. WHO CAN SUE FOR NUISANCE?

19-63 **Occupiers and residents**[320] The person in possession or occupation of the land affected can sue in private nuisance,[321] and such a person can also sue for a continuance of a nuisance which began before he became occupier.[322] Ownership of a timeshare giving a right to exclusive possession for only a week or two each year is apparently sufficient.[323] But, apart from rights arising from public nuisance,[324] persons with no proprietary interest are accorded no cause of action in this tort. Thus in *Malone v Lasky*,[325] the Court of Appeal held that the wife of the tenant of a house, as a mere licensee, had no right of action for injury caused by a tank falling on her

---

318 *Miles v Forest Rock Granite Co* (1918) 34 T.L.R. 500 (rock thrown by blasting of explosives).

319 See paras 19-85 to 19-105.

320 See Kodilinye, "Standing to Sue in Private Nuisance" (1989) 9 L.S. 284. See also para.19-24.

321 *Inchbold v Robinson* (1869) L.R. 4 Ch. 388 (yearly tenant); *Jones v Chappell* (1875) L.R. 20 Eq. 539 (weekly tenant). In *Tate & Lyle v GLC* [1983] 2 A.C. 509, though the claim succeeded for public nuisance, it failed as a private nuisance because it did not affect the claimant's riparian rights.

322 *Delaware Mansions Ltd v Westminster City Council* [2001] UKHL 55; [2002] 1 A.C. 321. *Thompson v Gibson* (1841) 7 M. & W. 456; *Masters v Brent LBC* [1978] Q.B. 841; *GUS Property Management Ltd v Littlewoods Mail Order Stores Ltd*, 1982 S.C. (H.L.) 157; 1982 S.L.T. 533 HL.

323 See *Regency Villas Title Ltd v Diamond Resorts (Europe) Ltd* [2015] EWHC 3564 (Ch); [2016] 4 W.L.R. 61 (subsequent proceedings in the Court of Appeal at [2017] EWCA Civ 238; [2017] Ch. 516, and the Supreme Court at [2018] UKSC 57; [2019] A.C. 553, did not affect the point in the text).

324 In *Hunter v Canary Wharf Ltd* the continued availability of damages for personal injury in public nuisance cases was doubted: see per Lord Goff in [1997] A.C. 655 at 692. But cf. *The Claimants appearing on the Register of the Corby Group Litigation v Corby BC* [2008] EWCA Civ 463; [2009] Q.B. 335 (Court of Appeal refused to strike out claim for damages for personal injury in public nuisance).

325 [1907] 2 K.B. 141 (overruled so far as it related to negligence, but without affecting this point, in *Billings & Sons Ltd v Riden* [1958] A.C. 240).

owing to vibrations set up by the defendant.[326] The correctness of the principle which this case embodies was confirmed by the House of Lords in 1997 in *Hunter v Canary Wharf Ltd*,[327] in which residents of properties who were not householders were held unable to sue for interference with the enjoyment of their homes caused by construction work in London's docklands. In so holding the House overruled a 1993 majority decision of the Court of Appeal in which an adult child living in her parents' home had been granted an injunction in private nuisance to protect her from pestering telephone calls by a former boyfriend.[328] The fact that the calls were made to her "home" had been considered sufficient to enable her to sue notwithstanding the absence of any legally protected interest in the property.[329] In reaffirming that such an interest remains an essential ingredient of a claim in private nuisance, the House of Lords in *Hunter*'s case contended that the passing of the Protection from Harassment Act 1997 had made it unnecessary to distort the law of private nuisance "merely as an expedient to fill a gap",[330] which the majority of the Court of Appeal were perceived to have done in the case which was overruled. If, however, the defendant is a public authority the Court of Appeal has held that residents who are unable to sue at common law for nuisance, due to the absence of any proprietary interest, may nevertheless seek damages under art.8 of the European Convention for the Protection of Human Rights for interference with their private and family life.[331] Although the enjoyment of exclusive possession is necessary to confer a right of action in nuisance itself, de facto possession can be sufficient.[332] In *Pemberton v Southwark LBC*[333] the Court of Appeal, distinguishing *Hunter v Canary Wharf Ltd*, held that where a claimant's tenancy has been terminated by an order for possession, but the execution of that order has been suspended, the claimant can sue in nuisance. Such a claimant has "the peculiar status of a 'tolerated trespasser'"[334] and, as such, his right to exclusive possession

---

326 But the injured person who is not an occupier may have a claim under the Defective Premises Act 1972 s.4.

327 [1997] A.C. 655.

328 *Khorasandjian v Bush* [1993] Q.B. 727.

329 [1993] Q.B. 727 at 734–735, per Dillon LJ; disapproved in *Hunter v Canary Wharf Ltd*: Lord Goff considered that settlement of claims could become more difficult if "anybody who lived in the relevant property as a home had the right to sue": see [1997] A.C. 655 at 693. But cf. per Lord Cooke of Thorndon, dissenting, [1993] Q.B. 727 at 718.

330 per Lord Hoffmann in [1997] A.C. 655 at 707.

331 See *Dobson v Thames Water Utilities* [2009] EWCA Civ 28; [2009] 3 All E.R. 319. Any award of damages for nuisance to the property owner may nevertheless be relevant to whether an award of damages under the Convention would be necessary in order to afford "just satisfaction" (under art.41 of the Convention) to the resident unable to sue at common law, *Dobson v Thames Water Utilities* [2009] EWCA Civ 28; [2009] 3 All E.R. 319. For subsequent proceedings see *Dobson v Thames Water Utilities* [2011] EWHC 3253 (TCC); (2011) 140 Con. L.R. 135 (breach of the Convention established but no damages awarded).

332 See *Hunter v Canary Wharf Ltd* [1997] A.C. 655 at 703–704, per Lord Hoffmann. See also *Foster v Warblington Urban DC* [1906] 1 K.B. 648; *Newcastle-under-Lyme Corp v Wolstanton Ltd* [1947] Ch. 427; *Tinseltime Ltd v Roberts* [2011] EWHC 1199 (TCC); [2011] B.L.R. 515.

333 [2000] 1 W.L.R. 1672.

334 per Sir Christopher Slade [2000] 1 W.L.R. at 1686. The terminology of "tolerated trespasser" was used by Lord Browne-Wilkinson in *Burrows v Brent LBC* [1996] 1 W.L.R. 1448 at 1455. But see also *Knowsley Housing Trust v White* [2008] UKHL 70; [2009] 1 A.C. 636, per Lord Walker at [3]–[4]: "Lord Browne-Wilkinson did not, as I read the authorities, invent the rather unfortunate phrase 'tolerated trespasser'. It seems to have been coined by counsel … . He did not wholly-heartedly endorse it. But it has since then become too firmly embedded to be dislodged."

prior to execution of the order entitles him to claim.[335] In *Austin v Mayor and Burgesses of the London Borough of Southwark*[336] Lady Hale, with the agreement of other members of the court, carried out a detailed review of the status of "tolerated trespasser". She pointed out that recent legislative developments[337] mean that the circumstances which gave rise to the status will not arise in the future, and that existing "tolerated trespassers" have been given "a new tenancy which is in most respects the same as the tenancy they would otherwise still have had".[338] As far as the law of nuisance is concerned, the effect would appear to be that while the confused terminology of "tolerated trespasser" will disappear the claimants who would formerly have needed to invoke that status will still be able to sue in nuisance but on a more regular basis.

19-64 **Co-owners** Where an occupier in sole possession has suffered harm by way of nuisance, he can sue notwithstanding that the defendant carrying out operations nearby is a co-owner and co-occupant with him in the area from which the nuisance emanates, for example where a co-owner excavates a track thereby causing damage to a nearby building occupied by the claimant.[339] But if the defendant has intruded upon the sole possession of the claimant where he causes damage, that is trespass.

19-65 **Reversioner** A reversioner can sue for injury done to the reversion, but not otherwise. It follows from this that the injury must be of a permanent nature, and not a mere temporary annoyance. Permanent in this connection means:

> "such as will continue indefinitely unless something is done to remove it. Thus, a building which infringes ancient lights is permanent within the rule, for, though it can be removed before the reversion falls into possession, still it will continue until it be removed. On the other hand, a noisy trade, and the exercise of an alleged right of way, are not in their nature permanent within the rule, for they cease of themselves, unless there be someone to continue them."[340]

Accordingly, a reversioner can sue for acts which tend either to destroy evidence of the fact that the adjoining land is burdened with a servitude in his favour, or to establish evidence against him that his land is burdened with a corresponding servitude in favour of the adjoining land. For example, he can sue in respect of the erection of a hoarding against his ancient lights,[341] the locking of a gate across a way to which he is entitled for his tenants,[342] the erection by the adjoining owner of a house with projecting eaves so that rain-water is discharged upon his land,[343] and the discharge of sewage from a drain.[344] So, too, where the claimant was entitled for his tenants to a right of access to his wharf and siding from the railway of the

[335] The House of Lords dismissed a petition for leave to appeal from the decision in *Pemberton's* case: see [2001] 1 W.L.R. 538.

[336] [2010] UKSC 28; [2011] 1 A.C. 355 at [44]–[56].

[337] See Sch.11 to the Housing and Regeneration Act 2008.

[338] [2010] UKSC 28; [2011] 1 A.C. 355 at [55].

[339] *Hooper v Rogers* [1975] Ch. 43 CA (injunction for probable future damage).

[340] *Jones v Llanrwst Urban DC (No.2)* [1911] 1 Ch. 393 at 404, per Parker J.

[341] *Shadwell v Hutchinson* (1829) M. & M. 350; *Metropolitan Association v Petch* (1858) 5 C.B. (N.S.) 504.

[342] *Kidgill v Moor* (1850) 9 C.B. 364.

[343] *Tucker v Newman* (1839) 11 A. & E. 40.

[344] *Jones v Llanrwst Urban DC (No.2)* [1911] 1 Ch. 393.

defendants, and the defendants, with the intention of preventing such access, left large quantities of rolling stock lying continually across the mouth of the siding, the obstruction thereby caused was considered sufficiently permanent to enable the claimant to sue for an injury to his reversionary interest.[345] Keeping vans an unreasonable time in the highway is not actionable at the suit of a reversioner, because the defendant cannot acquire a prescriptive right to commit a public nuisance.[346] Physical injury to the reversion, such as is caused by vibration calculated to destroy buildings on the land, gives a right of action to the reversioner.[347] In *Metropolitan Housing Trust Ltd v RMC FH Co Ltd*[348] Morgan J noted, in the context of *potential* loss of a right to light, that it was clear that a "reversioner can sue in relation to a nuisance where the nuisance will, or even might, continue to a time when the reversion falls into possession".

Temporary nuisances On the other hand, there is no right of action in respect of noise or smoke or other nuisance of a temporary nature,[349] even if it drives the tenants away or reduces the letting value of the property.[350] But if the owner cannot get a tenant because of the nuisance, he can himself, though not in occupation, bring an action for damage to shrubs by noxious fumes.[351] Moreover in *John Smith & Co (Edinburgh) Ltd v Hill*[352] Briggs J suggested that a temporary nuisance which would justify the tenant in refusing to pay rent, such as wrongfully leaving scaffolding attached to the premises, might enable the reversioner to sue since the loss of rent would constitute an irrecoverable loss to the reversion: **19-66**

"In my judgment it is at least well arguable that the supposed rule that a reversioner may not sue on a temporary nuisance is no more than a logical consequence, when applied to typical facts, of the true principle, which is that a reversioner may not sue in relation to a nuisance unless it causes injury to his reversion. If that is the true principle, then there may be unusual fact situations … in which a temporary nuisance does injure the reversion …"

Light Whether a reversioner can bring an action to prevent his land being burdened in favour of the defendants with a negative easement such as that of light has never been expressly decided. Under the Prescription Act 1832, the opening of new windows, and uninterrupted enjoyment for the statutory period confers an easement of light, and operates to restrict the adjoining owner's power of using his land for building purposes. But it would be very unjust that a reversioner of the adjoining land, who was unable to obtain the tenant's consent or planning permission to a physical obstruction of the defendant's window-lights, should be powerless to prevent the accrual of a right which might turn out to be most injurious to his property. The difficulty facing the owner is now resolved by statute, for the owner, **19-67**

[345] *Bell v Midland Ry* (1861) 10 C.B. (N.S.) 287. See also *John Smith & Co (Edinburgh) Ltd v Hill* [2010] EWHC 1016 (Ch); [2010] 2 B.C.L.C. 556 at [29] per Briggs J; and para.19-66.

[346] *Mott v Shoolbred* (1875) L.R. 20 Eq. 22.

[347] *Meux's Brewery Co v City of London Electric Lighting Co* [1895] 1 Ch. 287 at 317; *Colwell v St Pancras BC* [1904] 1 Ch. 707.

[348] See [2017] EWHC 2609 (Ch); [2018] Ch. 195 at [54].

[349] *Simpson v Savage* (1856) 1 C.B. (N.S.) 347; *Cooper v Crabtree* (1882) 20 Ch. D. 589.

[350] *Mumford v Oxford, Worcester etc Ry* (1856) 1 H. & N. 34; *Simpson v Savage* (1856) 1 C.B. (N.S.) 347. But cf. per Briggs J in *John Smith & Co (Edinburgh) Ltd v Hill* [2010] EWHC 1016 (Ch); [2010] 2 B.C.L.C. 556 at [27] suggesting that these cases might be distinguishable if a "temporary" nuisance is such as to provide the tenant with a right to redress against the landlord.

[351] *Wood v Conway Corp* [1914] 2 Ch. 47 at 58, per Buckley LJ.

[352] [2010] EWHC 1016 (Ch); [2010] 2 B.C.L.C. 556 at [30].

whether in possession or not, may take advantage of the Rights of Light Act 1959, under which a prospective servient owner is able to bring about the consequences which flow from the erection of a screen by registering a statutory notice against a prospective dominant building. The notice takes effect as if the access of light had been obstructed physically, and as if the obstruction had been known to and acquiesced in by all concerned. It remains effective for one year, unless earlier cancelled, and thus breaks the running of time in favour of the dominant building.[353]

19-68 **Owner of incorporeal hereditament** The owner of an easement, profit à prendre or other incorporeal right can sue for the disturbance of his right. The interference will be actionable if it is substantial, and it will not be substantial if it does not interfere with the reasonable use of the right of way or similar right in question.[354] If, therefore, the owner of an exclusive right of fishing in a particular place finds that the fish are being driven away or destroyed by the act of a person in fouling or disturbing the water, he may bring an action against the wrongdoer.[355] Because the object of such actions is essentially to vindicate a right of property claimed by the owner, it is only necessary for him to prove that his right has been infringed, and it is not necessary to prove actual damage.[356]

19-69 **Public nuisances** Public nuisances generally may be prosecuted under the criminal law. With regard to highway nuisances the remedy by indictment was abolished by the Highways Act 1959 s.59, and the present remedies are by service of a notice on the highway authority, or an action for damages by a claimant who has suffered particular damage,[357] or an injunction. For public nuisances an action for an injunction may be brought by the Attorney General on his own initiative or on the relation of some other person, for example a local authority, who may be joined as co-claimants in respect of any damage to their property.[358] Whether such an action shall be brought or not is generally in the discretion of the Attorney General.[359] But a local authority acting under the Local Government Act 1972 s.222, may sue without the concurrence of the Attorney General.[360] A local authority seeking an interlocutory injunction under s.222 will not necessarily be required to give

---

353 For Law Commission proposals recommending that the procedure whereby the acquisition of rights to light by prescription can be prevented should be simplified (including repeal of the Rights to Light Act 1959) see *Rights to Light* (2014), Law Com. No.356, Ch.2 and App.A.

354 *Celsteed Ltd v Alton House Holdings* [1985] 1 W.L.R. 204 at 216, per Scott J, granting injunction for protection of an equitable easement.

355 *Fitzgerald v Firbank* [1897] 2 Ch. 96; *Rawson v Peters* (1972) 225 E.G. 89; (1972) 116 S.J. 884 CA. But even if there is no easement, a possessory right may suffice to bring an action: *Newcastle-under-Lyme Corp v Wolstanton Ltd* [1947] Ch. 92, per Evershed J.

356 *Nicholls v Ely Beet Sugar Factory Ltd* [1936] 1 Ch. 343; *Weston v Lawrence Weaver Ltd* [1961] 1 Q.B. 402. See also *Clochfaen Estate Ltd v Bryn Blaen Wind Farm Ltd* [2019] EWHC 1562 (nominal damages for interference with sporting, shooting and fishing rights).

357 The Court of Appeal has held that exemplary damages cannot be awarded in public nuisance: see *Gibbons v South West Water Services Ltd* [1993] Q.B. 50. But the reasoning underlying this case (that such damages should actually have been held available in public nuisance prior to 1964) was overruled by the House of Lords in *Kuddus v Chief Constable of Leicestershire Constabulary* [2001] UKHL 29; [2002] 2 A.C. 122. Accordingly a claim for such damages might succeed provided it could be brought within one of the two broad categories identified in *Rookes v Barnard* [1964] A.C. 1129; see para.27-136.

358 *Att Gen v Logan* [1891] 2 Q.B. 100.

359 *London CC v Att Gen* [1902] A.C. 165.

360 *Solihull MBC v Maxfern Ltd* [1977] 1 W.L.R. 127; *Stoke-on-Trent City Council v B&Q (Retail) Ltd* [1984] A.C. 754; *Nottingham City Council v Zain* [2001] EWCA Civ 1248; [2002] 1 W.L.R. 607;

an undertaking in damages, the discretion of the court to exempt the Crown from the requirement to give such an undertaking extends also to local authorities when exercising a law enforcement function in the public interest.[361]

5. WHO CAN BE SUED FOR NUISANCE?[362]

(a) Wrongdoer

Liability of actual wrongdoer The person liable for a nuisance is the actual wrongdoer, whether or not he is in occupation of the land.[363] For example, where a building is erected so as to obstruct the claimant's ancient lights[364] or market,[365] the person who originally created the nuisance remains liable for all the damage flowing from its continuance, even though by reason of his not being in possession of the premises he is unable to prevent their continuance. "If a wrongdoer conveys his wrong over to another, whereby he puts it out of his power to redress it, he ought to answer for it."[366] Accordingly, he remains liable even if he has sold or leased the building.[367] In the same way, a contractor who is employed to erect a building on another's land is liable if the building is a nuisance.[368] When a piece of fat from a butcher's shop was on the pavement, either because it was brought out on the shoe of a customer or got out in some other way, and a person walking in the highway slipped on it and was injured, the butcher was held liable because he had created the nuisance.[369] 19-70

Authorising third parties The wrongdoer may create the nuisance either personally or by his servants or agents. He is liable on this ground if he authorises a licensee to burn bricks upon his land, thereby creating a nuisance,[370] or if he allows gypsies to camp on his land so as to be a nuisance from their noise and the insanitary conditions of the camp.[371] A mother has been held liable for a nuisance created by her daughter in a house in which she lived as her mother's licensee.[372] 19-71

Ealing LBC v Connors [2016] EWHC 1387 (QB); [2016] J.P.L. 1100. Proceedings for certain statutory nuisances may be promoted by individuals aggrieved: e.g. under s.82 of the Environmental Protection Act 1990.

361 *Kirklees MBC v Wickes Building Supplies Ltd* [1993] A.C. 227.

362 See on this generally, Friedman, "Incidence of Liability in Nuisance" (1943) 59 L.Q.R. 63.

363 *Jones (Insurance Brokers) Ltd v Portsmouth City Council* [2002] EWCA Civ 1723; [2003] 1 W.L.R. 427; *Hall v Beckenham Corp* [1949] 1 K.B. 716.

364 *Roswell v Prior* (1706) 12 Mod. 635.

365 *Thompson v Gibson* (1841) 7 M. & W. 456; and see *Wilcox v Steel* [1904] 1 Ch. 212.

366 *Roswell v Prior* (1706) 12 Mod. 635 at 639.

367 See *Roswell v Prior* (1706) 12 Mod. 635 at 639.

368 *Thompson v Gibson* (1841) 7 M. & W. 456.

369 *Dollman v Hillman Ltd* [1941] 1 All E.R. 355.

370 *White v Jameson* (1874) L.R. 18 Eq. 303.

371 *Att Gen v Stone* (1894) 2 T.L.R. 76; *Page Motors v Epsom & Ewell BC* (1981) 80 L.G.R. 337; (1981) 125 S.J. 590. See also *Lippiatt v South Gloucestershire Council* [2000] Q.B. 51. As to the incidence of liability, it has been said there is no difference between a claim for private nuisance and a claim for private damage resulting from a public nuisance. See *Sedleigh-Denfield v O'Callaghan* [1940] A.C. 880 at 905, 907 and 918. But prescription is no defence to an action based on public nuisance; and in private nuisance the claimant need not prove that the damage was peculiar to himself.

372 See *Cocking v Eacott* [2016] EWCA Civ 140; [2016] Q.B. 1080. But in other cases the particular facts might enable alleged licensors to benefit from the more favourable rules which apply to *landlords* when their *tenants* commit nuisances: see per Arden LJ *Cocking v Eacott* [2016] EWCA

An occupier is not liable, however, for a nuisance created by a trespasser without his knowledge or consent, unless he continues or adopts the nuisance so created.[373]

19-72 **Nuisance created by independent contractor**[374] Whether a person can be said to be a wrongdoer if the nuisance is created by his independent contractor depends on whether he could reasonably have foreseen that the work he had instructed the independent contractor to do was likely to result in a nuisance. In *Bower v Peate*,[375] Cockburn CJ said:

> "A man who orders work to be executed from which, in the natural course of things, injurious consequences to his neighbour must be expected to arise, unless means are adopted by which such consequences may be prevented, is bound to see to the doing of that which is necessary to prevent the mischief, and cannot relieve himself of his responsibility by employing someone else—whether it be the contractor employed to do the work from which the danger arises or some independent person—to do what is necessary to prevent the act he has ordered to be done from becoming wrongful."

19-73 **Scope of the principle** This principle applies to the creation of dangers in the highway,[376] and to interference with the right of support.[377] It has not been confined to public nuisances but also applied to cases of private nuisance where it appears the nature of the work involves inherent dangers, being itself "a dangerous operation". In *Matania v National Provincial Bank*,[378] the occupier of the first floor of a building employed contractors to carry out alterations to his premises. The work, by its noise and the dust it set up, was a nuisance to the occupier of the second and third floors and the person carrying out the alterations was held liable for the act of his contractors "just as … if they had let the floor down".[379] In *Spicer v Smee*[380] the occupier of a house, who had electric wiring installed which was inadequately protected so as to constitute a nuisance, was held liable for a fire which originated in her house and spread to the adjoining house as a result of this nuisance. In this case, it was said "that where danger is likely to arise unless the work is properly done, there is a duty to see that it is properly done". This statement would make the occupier liable in nuisance generally for any negligence by a contractor, but it is too widely expressed.[381] In *Salsbury v Woodland*,[382] the Court of Appeal made it clear that an occupier is not liable for the negligence of a contractor work-

---

Civ 140; [2016] Q.B. 1080 at [42] and Vos LJ at [29]. On the liability of landlords see para.19-81.

373 See para.19-94.

374 See *Woodland v Essex CC* [2013] UKSC 66; [2014] A.C. 537, per Lord Sumption at [8]–[10]. For a discussion of the cases see Atiyah, *Vicarious Liability in the Law of Torts* (1967), pp.351–357. See also para.19-163.

375 (1876) L.R. 1 Q.B.D. 321 at 326; quoted with approval by Atkinson J in *Spicer v Smee* [1946] 1 All E.R. 489 at 495. See the comment by Lord Blackburn in *Hughes v Percival* (1883) 8 App. Cas. 443 at 446.

376 See para.19-186.

377 See para.19-139.

378 [1936] 2 All E.R. 633. See also *Alcock (Douglas Alexander) v Wraith* (1991) 59 B.L.R. 20; *Fattahi v Charles Grosvenor Ltd* [2019] EWHC 3497 (QB).

379 per Romer LJ [1936] 2 All E.R. 633 at 649. See also *Tinseltime Ltd v Roberts* [2011] EWHC 1199 (TCC); [2011] B.L.R. 515.

380 [1946] 1 All E.R. 489. See also *Johnson v BJW Property Developments Ltd* [2002] EWHC 1131 (TCC); [2002] 3 All E.R. 574 (the judgment in this case contains a general review of the authorities on vicarious liability for nuisances caused by independent contractors, but one which now needs to be read in the light of subsequent developments: see *Willmott Dixon Construction Ltd v Robert West Consulting Ltd* [2016] EWHC 3291 (TCC); [2017] P.N.L.R. 17 at [17]).

381 cf. *Biffa Waste Service Ltd v Mashinenefabrik Ernst Hese GmbH* [2008] EWCA Civ 1257; [2009]

ing on his land merely because injury is caused to the user of an adjoining highway.[383] To impose on the occupier general vicarious liability for the contractor's negligence the work must involve some special risk or hazard to highway users or be in discharge of "some positive and continuing duty", for example as with artificial projections over the highway.

Collateral negligence Even when he is liable for a nuisance created by his independent contractor, an employer is not liable for his contractor's collateral negligence, that is, negligence not directly arising from what the contractor is employed to do. When a tool was placed on a window sill by a contractor's workman, and the window was caught by the wind, so that the tool fell and injured the claimant in the highway, the employer of the contractor was held not liable because it was collateral negligence.[384] Before an employer can be liable for the negligence of his subcontractor's employee it has to be shown that the subcontractor was employed to do work the nature of which, and not merely the performance of which, cast on the superior employer the duty of taking precautions.[385] 19-74

(b) Occupier

Continuance of nuisance The occupier of the land is liable for a nuisance, even though he has not created it, if he has continued it during the period of his occupancy.[386] A person who becomes the occupier of land with a nuisance already upon it is liable for the continuance of the nuisance, if he knows or ought to have known of its existence, for it was his "fault to contract for an interest in land on which there was a nuisance".[387] The rule that the incomer is not liable unless he knows or ought to know means that mere awareness of the existence of something which ultimately becomes a source of harm will not give rise to liability unless its propensity for causing harm was foreseeable.[388] 19-75

Continuing and adopting If the nuisance is created after he becomes the occupier, he is liable if he knows or, by the exercise of reasonable care should have known, of the nuisance.[389] He is also liable if he adopts it: 19-76

> "An occupier of land 'continues' a nuisance if with knowledge or presumed knowledge of its existence he fails to take any reasonable means to bring it to an end, though with ample time to do so. He 'adopts' it if he makes any use of the erection, building, bank or artificial contrivance which constitutes the nuisance."[390]

The occupier has been held liable for continuing the nuisance when a piece of

Q.B. 725 discussed in para.19-163. See also *Tinseltime Ltd v Roberts* [2011] EWHC 1199 (TCC); [2011] B.L.R. 515 at [49] per Judge Stephen Davies.

382 [1970] 1 Q.B. 324.

383 See also *Rowe v Herman* [1997] 1 W.L.R. 1390 CA.

384 *Padbury v Holliday and Greenwood Ltd* (1912) 28 T.L.R. 492.

385 per Fletcher Moulton LJ in *Padbury v Holliday* (1912) 28 T.L.R. 492 at 495.

386 *Coupland v Hardingham* (1813) 3 Camp. 398; *White v Jameson* (1874) L.R. 18 Eq. 303.

387 *Roswell v Prior* (1706) 12 Mod. 635; cf. *Broder v Saillard* (1876) 2 Ch. D. 692; *Ryppon v Bowles* (1615) Cro. Jac. 373; *Coupland v Hardingham* (1813) 3 Camp. 398.

388 *British Road Services Ltd v Slater* [1964] 1 W.L.R. 498.

389 *Barker v Herbert* [1911] 2 K.B. 633; *St Anne's Well Brewery Co v Roberts* (1928) 140 L.T. 1; [1928] All E.R. Rep. 28; *Wilkins v Leighton* [1932] 2 Ch. 106.

390 *Sedleigh-Denfield v O'Callaghan* [1940] A.C. 880 at 894, per Lord Maugham; applied in *Smeaton v Ilford Corp* [1954] Ch. 450; and in *Pemberton v Bright and the Devon CC* [1960] 1 W.L.R. 436

vacant land surrounded by a hoarding which was out of repair was made a receptacle for litter, refuse and other matter probably thrown there by inhabitants in the neighbourhood and was a public nuisance,[391] where a ditch was piped and, owing to the absence of a guard at the entrance to the pipe, the pipe became blocked and a flood was caused on the adjacent property,[392] where snow, which had fallen five days before, slid from the roof of a shop and injured a person on the highway,[393] and where a piece of glass fell from the window of a house damaged by enemy action three days after the damage[394]:

> "In order to establish liability for continuing a nuisance by failing to prevent it, one must necessarily prove that the person so failing must be in a position to take effective steps to that end."[395]

And this amounts to a duty to abate the nuisance, which is in the nature of a duty of care to neighbours. This duty now extends to the nuisance of omission, where the nuisance arises from a state of nature and the occupier unreasonably fails to prevent damage occurring to his neighbour.[396] But in this situation the standard of care is, exceptionally, measured subjectively with reference to the defendant's actual capacities and circumstances and not with reference to those of the "reasonable man".[397] Moreover, it now appears that this "subjective" duty will also extend to cases of continuation or adoption where the nuisance was originally created by human intervention rather than by an act of nature.[398] The adoption principle will not, however, apply in any event in favour of a tenant against his landlord if the source of the alleged nuisance pre-existed the creation of the tenancy and did not constitute a breach of covenant.[399]

19-77 **Statutory undertakers** The principle that an occupier of land can be liable for continuing a nuisance, which he has not created, cannot be applied without qualification to occupiers who are statutory undertakers. In such cases it will be necessary to consider whether the imposition of liability would be consistent with the statutory scheme. In *Marcic v Thames Water Utilities*[400] the House of Lords, reversing the Court of Appeal, held that the authorities favouring the imposition of

---

CA (culvert fixed without adequate protection by county council who along with the occupier were held liable); *Smith v GW Ry* (1926) 42 T.L.R. 391 (railway company not liable for escape of oil from tank wagon, they did not permit the continuance and took all reasonable means to prevent it). For consideration of the precise *level* of the duty on occupiers contemplated by the speeches in *Sedleigh-Denfield v O'Callaghan* see *Cocking v Eacott* [2016] EWCA Civ 140; [2016] Q.B. 1080 at [25] per Vos LJ.

391 *Att Gen v Tod Heatley* [1897] 1 Ch. 560.

392 *Sedleigh-Denfield v O'Callaghan* [1940] A.C. 880; overruling *Job Edwards Ltd v Birmingham Navigations* [1924] 1 K.B. 341. The dissenting judgment of Scrutton LJ was preferred.

393 *Slater v Worthington's Cash Stores Ltd* [1941] 1 K.B. 488.

394 *Leanse v Egerton* [1943] K.B. 323; cf. *Cushing v Walker & Sons* [1941] 2 All E.R. 693, see para.19-94, where the defendants succeeded.

395 per Upjohn J in *Smeaton v Ilford Corp* [1954] Ch. 450 at 462.

396 *Goldman v Hargrave* [1967] 1 A.C. 645; *Leakey v National Trust* [1980] Q.B. 485. See also *Holbeck Hall Hotel v Scarborough BC* [2000] Q.B. 836.

397 See cases cited in the previous note; see also para.19-22.

398 See dicta in *Anthony v Coal Authority* [2005] EWHC 1654 (QB); [2006] Env. L.R. 17 at [129]–[133], per Pitchford J (dealing with the liability of the creator of an originally unforeseeable nuisance, but the liability of an adopter or continuer is an a fortiori case).

399 See *Jackson v JH Watson Property Investment Ltd* [2008] EWHC 14 (Ch); [2008] Env. L.R. 30; [2008] 11 E.G. 94.

400 [2003] UKHL 66; [2004] 2 A.C. 42; [2004] 1 All E.R. 135.

liability for the "continuance" or "adoption" of nuisances had not impliedly overruled a separate line of authority relating to flooding caused by overloaded sewers. It is therefore still the law that water companies, which are obliged to permit all in their area to have access to the drainage system, will not be liable in nuisance simply because the sewers are no longer able to cope with the increased demand and flooding results. Where the underlying problem is the need for more resources to be allocated to improvement of the infrastructure, the statutory scheme contained in the Water Industry Act 1991 provided for that need to be evaluated by a Director General of Water Services; and the imposition of common law nuisance liability would be inconsistent with his role.[401] Lord Nicholls said that it was "abundantly clear that one important purpose of the enforcement scheme in the 1991 Act is that individual householders should not be able to launch proceedings in respect of failure to build sufficient sewers".[402] The principle in *Marcic's* case will not protect the defendants from liability at common law if the nuisance resulted not from a mere lack of capacity in the sewerage system but from a negligent failure at operational level adequately to discharge their statutory responsibilities to clean and maintain the sewers.[403] Statutory undertakers in breach of a statutory obligation will not thereby incur liability for any nuisance allegedly resulting unless the statute in question gives rise to liability for breach of statutory duty under the usual principles applicable to such claims.[404]

(c) Landlord and tenant

Nuisance by disrepair When premises become a nuisance through being allowed to fall into disrepair, there may be liability to third persons on the landlord or the tenant or both. Liability to persons who come on the premises and are there injured is discussed elsewhere.[405] 19-78

When landlord liable If a nuisance arises prior to a letting, the owner does not cease to be liable by virtue of parting with possession. If he knew of the potentially harmful condition of the property before letting, or ought to have known of it,[406] he remains liable for harm accruing after the letting.[407] It used to be thought that the landlord could exonerate himself by obtaining from his tenant a covenant to 19-79

401 See now the Water Industry Act 1991 s.1A (inserted by the Water Act 2003 s.34) which replaces the Director General of Water Services with the Water Services Regulation Authority, but this does not affect the point in the text.

402 [2003] UKHL 66; [2004] 2 A.C. 42; [2004] 1 All E.R. 135 at [35]. But cf. *Southern Gas Networks Plc v Thames Water Utilities Ltd* [2018] EWCA Civ 33; [2018] 1 W.L.R. 5977 at [81] per Hickinbottom LJ suggesting that the reasoning of Lord Nicholls on this point differed significantly from that of Lord Hoffmann, who apparently considered that the common law *itself* precluded an action when the sewers were inadequate because new ones had not been constructed.

403 See *Dobson v Thames Water Utilities* [2007] EWHC 2021 (TCC); [2008] 2 All E.R. 362, although this case was subsequently appealed (see [2009] EWCA Civ 28; [2009] 3 All E.R. 319) there was no appeal on this point. At the trial of the action liability for common law nuisance was imposed on the defendants: see *Dobson v Thames Water Utilities* [2011] EWHC 3253 (TCC); (2011) 140 Con. L.R. 135. cf. *Bell v Northumbrian Water Ltd* [2016] EWHC 133 (TCC); *Oldcorn v Southern Water Services Ltd* [2017] EWHC 62 (TCC); [2017] Env. L.R. 25.

404 See *Dwr Cymru Cyfyngedig (Welsh Water) v Barratt Homes Ltd* [2013] EWCA Civ 233; [2013] 1 W.L.R. 3486 (no liability for failure to permit access to sewers contrary to s.106 of the Water Industry Act 1991). For the action for breach of statutory duty see Ch.8.

405 See Ch.11.

406 *Gandy v Jubber* (1864) 5 B. & S. 78; *Bowen v Anderson* [1894] 1 Q.B. 164.

407 *Sampson v Hodson-Pressinger* [1981] 3 All E.R. 710 at 713–714, per Eveleigh LJ.

repair,[408] but this proposition had come under severe criticism,[409] and has been generally overturned by the Court of Appeal.[410] In the words of Sachs LJ (at 639), the landlord:

> "remains liable to third parties for the effects of a nuisance of which he has knowledge at the date of granting a lease unless excused by some further fact over and above taking a covenant to repair—although of course, he may have his remedy over against the tenant when that covenant is effective."

This knowledge includes presumed knowledge, that is, the case where the landlord should have known but did not.[411] Even if the landlord neither knew nor ought to have known of the disrepair or other dangerous condition at the time of letting, he may nevertheless be liable for such conditions at the time of letting, and he may nevertheless be liable for such conditions arising during the tenancy if he has retained a measure of control over the premises, and he is in no better position by virtue of having taken a covenant from his tenant. The landlord retains sufficient control either because he has a duty to repair, or a power. If the landlord himself undertakes to repair he is liable to a person injured through disrepair[412] whether he knew or ought to have known of the disrepair or not, unless the disrepair is due to the act of a trespasser or to a secret and unobservable operation of nature, such as a subsidence under or near the foundations, when he is only liable if he allows the disrepair to continue after he has knowledge or means of knowledge of its existence.[413]

19-80 **Covenants and rights of entry** A landlord's covenant may be implied by statute. Thus the Landlord and Tenant Act 1985 s.11, places on the landlord a duty of structural and exterior repair and the maintenance of certain services in tenancies of dwelling-houses for less than seven years.[414] Notice of the defect to the landlord is normally necessary for the triggering of the duty to repair.[415] If there is no covenant to repair on the part of the landlord, the landlord is still liable if he has reserved the right to enter and do any necessary repairs.[416] This is so even if the right to enter and do repairs is only implied, and it is usually implied when the premises are let on a weekly tenancy.[417] Where the landlord sells the reversion and the new landlord takes with notice of an existing nuisance, the new landlord becomes li-

---

408 *Pretty v Bickmore* (1873) L.R. 8 C. & P. 401.

409 e.g. per Denning LJ in *Mint v Good* [1951] 1 K.B. 517 at 528.

410 *Brew Bros Ltd v Snax (Ross) Ltd* [1970] 1 Q.B. 612. See also *Mistry v Thakor* [2005] EWCA Civ 953.

411 See *Mistry v Thakor* [2005] EWCA Civ 953 at [33], per Pill LJ.

412 *Payne v Rogers* (1794) 2 H.Bl. 350; *Nelson v Liverpool Brewery Co* (1877) 2 C.P.D. 311 at 313.

413 *Wringe v Cohen* [1940] 1 K.B. 229; *Spicer v Smee* [1946] 1 All E.R. 489.

414 See further Landlord and Tenant Act 1985 s.13(1A) (extending the application of s.11) and s.14 (exceptions). See also the Defective Premises Act 1972 s.4 which imposes a statutory liability on landlords under an obligation to repair for injury or damage caused by their failure to discharge that obligation.

415 See *Edwards v Kumarasdamy* [2016] UKSC 40; [2016] A.C. 1334 (reversing the Court of Appeal which had held that liability for damage caused by the disrepair had not depended on notice: see [2015] EWCA Civ 20; [2015] Ch. 484).

416 *Heap v Ind Coope and Allsopp Ltd* [1940] 2 K.B. 476; *Wilchick v Marks* [1934] 2 K.B. 56.

417 *Mint v Good* [1951] 1 K.B. 517 (boy in highway injured by fall off wall of the forecourt of a house owned by defendant and let to a weekly tenant—no right expressly reserved to enter and do repairs, but such a right was implied and the landlord was held liable); distinguished in *Sleafer v Lambeth BC* [1960] 1 Q.B. 43 CA at 56–57.

able,[418] notwithstanding the first landlord remains liable for the nuisance arising before the sale. The landlord is not liable where the condition giving rise to the nuisance occurs only after he has parted with possession to a tenant, and when he is under no obligation to repair and has retained no right or power of control. Here the tenant as occupier is exclusively liable.

Landlord's liability in other cases The owner is liable if he has let the premises to a tenant for the purpose of doing an act likely to cause a nuisance, for example burning lime,[419] if he has authorised his tenant to do an act which is likely to cause a nuisance,[420] or if he has let the premises with a nuisance on them.[421] On the other hand: 19-81

> "If a landlord lets premises, not in themselves a nuisance, but which may or may not be used by the tenant so as to become a nuisance, and it is entirely at the option of the tenant so to use them or not, and the landlord receives the same benefit whether they are used or not, the landlord cannot be made responsible for the acts of the tenant."[422]

The law was reviewed by the Supreme Court in *Coventry v Lawrence (No.2)*[423] which concerned the possible liability of landlords for a noise nuisance caused by their tenants while engaging in speedway racing and similar activities, at a stadium which the landlords had leased to them. Three points emerge from the leading judgment of Lord Neuberger.[424] First, the terms of the lease will not themselves give rise to liability unless they render the nuisance "inevitable, or nearly certain". Secondly, the presence or absence of generally worded covenants against nuisance will rarely be relevant in determining the scope of the substance of the lease. Thirdly, if the lease itself does not give rise to liability, the landlord can only be liable if he "actively" or "directly" participated in the commission of the nuisance.[425] This is inevitably a very fact-sensitive inquiry.[426] The Court of Appeal once struck out a claim in nuisance against a landlord for failing to prevent his tenants from subjecting the claimant to racial harassment.[427] Nevertheless, a landlord can be liable in nuisance if he allows "troublemakers to occupy his land and to use it as a base for

418 *Sampson v Hodson-Pressinger* [1981] 3 All E.R. 710 CA. The court emphasised that the new landlord was receiving rent and was in breach of the covenant for quiet enjoyment in favour of his tenant (the claimant). He could therefore be considered as authorising the continuation of the nuisance.

419 *Harris v James* (1876) 45 L.J.Q.B. 545; *Sampson v Hodson-Pressinger* [1981] 3 All E.R. 710 CA; *Tetley v Chitty* [1986] 1 All E.R. 663. cf. *Southwark LBC v Mills* [2001] 1 A.C. 1.

420 *Jenkins v Jackson* (1888) 40 Ch. D. 71. See comment by McNeill J in *Tetley v Chitty* [1986] 1 All E.R. 663 at 671, preferring to place the landlord's responsibility on objective foreseeability. It is clear that negligence in the letting with regard to potential nuisance is actionable. On the facts the case was within the principle in *Harris v James* (1876) 45 L.J.Q.B. 545.

421 *R. v Pedley* (1834) 1 A. & E. 822.

422 *Rich v Basterfield* (1847) 4 C.B. 783.

423 [2014] UKSC 46; [2015] A.C. 106.

424 See [2014] UKSC 46; [2015] A.C. 106 at [15]–[18].

425 This aspect of the case led to a division of opinion between the Justices as to the interpretation to be placed on the particular facts of the case (the majority exonerated the landlord whilst a minority would have imposed liability).

426 See, e.g. *Fouladi v Darout Ltd* [2018] EWHC 3501 (Ch) (landlord not liable).

427 See *Hussain v Lancaster City Council* [2000] Q.B. 1. See also *Smith v Scott* [1973] Ch. 314 (local authority held not liable for nuisance created by their tenants in annoying neighbours by noise and vandalism).

causing unlawful disturbance to his neighbours".[428] Thus in *Lippiatt v South Gloucestershire Council*,[429] in which the defendant failed to remove travellers who had encamped on its land and caused nuisances against neighbouring farmers, the Court of Appeal refused to strike out a claim against the defendant. Where the owner is liable, that does not relieve the occupier from liability.[430]

19-82 **No liability for ordinary use of premises** A landlord cannot be liable in nuisance on the basis of authorisation if the tenant's activities, however much they interfere with the claimant's enjoyment of land, are incapable in law of constituting an actionable nuisance. This is so even if the interference of which complaint is made is a consequence of defects in the structure of the premises which existed prior to the letting, provided the landlord was not himself responsible for those defects. In this sense it is still the case that "there is no law against letting a tumble-down house".[431] These propositions were confirmed and vividly illustrated by the House of Lords in 1999 in *Southwark BC v Mills*.[432] The claimant was a tenant of a local-authority flat, the sound-proofing of which was so inadequate that the ordinary, every-day activities of the occupants of neighbouring flats, including even washing and cleaning, created an intolerable level of noise. The flat had, however, complied with all applicable building regulations at the time of its construction. The claimant's attempt to hold the local authority liable as landlord, for letting the flat in a condition in which intolerable interference by noise was inevitable, failed.[433] The claimant was deemed to have taken the flat in the physical condition in which she found it, and she could not complain that her neighbour's activities constituted nuisances for which the landlord was responsible since ordinary domestic use of premises could not be actionable.[434] Moreover the principle confirmed in *Mill's* case is not confined to mere interference with enjoyment but applies also in situations in which the tenant suffers actual property damage as a result of a structural defect for which the landlord is not responsible.[435]

19-83 **When tenant liable** The tenant is liable as occupier, either on the basis of creating or continuing the nuisance. He does not escape liability because his landlord may be liable,[436] even if the landlord has positively covenanted with him to repair.[437]

19-84 **Sale of premises in state of disrepair** Liability for nuisance depends on creation of the harmful condition by misfeasance or on allowing it to continue. If a

---

[428] per Evans LJ in *Lippiatt v South Gloucestershire Council* [2000] Q.B. 51 at 61.

[429] [2000] Q.B. 51.

[430] *R. v Watts* (1703) 1 Salk. 357; *Att Gen v Roe* [1915] 1 Ch. 235.

[431] per Erle CJ in *Robbins v Jones* (1863) 15 C.B.N.S. 221 at 240.

[432] [2001] 1 A.C. 1.

[433] cf. *Sampson v Hodson-Pressinger* [1981] 3 All E.R. 710 CA (a case treated in *Southwark LBC v Mills* as having turned upon its own special facts).

[434] "The appellants say that the ordinary use of the flats by their neighbours would not have caused them inconvenience if they had been differently built. But that ... is a matter of which they cannot complain": per Lord Hoffmann in *Southwark LBC v Mills* [2001] 1 A.C. 1 at 16.

[435] *Jackson v JH Watson Property Investment Ltd* [2008] EWHC 14 (Ch); [2008] Env. L.R. 30; [2008] 11 E.G. 94.

[436] *Wilchick v Marks and Silverstone* [1934] 2 K.B. 56 at 68.

[437] *St Anne's Well Brewery Co v Roberts* (1928) 140 L.T. 1 at 8; [1928] All E.R. Rep. 28 at 34, per Lawrence LJ. The tenant can of course claim on the covenant.

vendor sells or a tenant assigns land on which a nuisance exists but which he has not created, then on principle liability ceases as he ceases to occupy.[438]

6. DEFENCES TO AN ACTION FOR NUISANCE

(a) Prescriptive right to commit nuisance

Prescriptive right to commit nuisance A right to commit a private nuisance may be acquired by prescription as an easement,[439] in those cases in which such a right is capable of being an easement.[440] Thus, a man may acquire a right to discharge rain-water from his eaves on to his neighbour's land,[441] to send smoke through flues in a party wall,[442] to discharge surface-water on to adjoining land,[443] and to extract water from a millpond.[444] But a man cannot acquire a prescriptive right for his trees to overhang or for the roots of his trees to grow into his neighbour's land, apparently on the ground that there is a perpetual change in the quantity of inconvenience caused.[445] In *Coventry v Lawrence*[446] Lord Neuberger said, resolving earlier doubts on the point,[447] "it appears to me that both principle and policy favour the conclusion that a right to create what would otherwise be a nuisance by *noise* to land *can* be an easement".[448] Moreover, even where the right claimed may be insufficiently precise to constitute an *easement*, it may nevertheless be capable of being acquired by prescription.[449] To acquire a prescriptive right to annoy your neighbour by means of smoke, smells, noise or vibration will seldom be straightforward in view of the need to establish that the interference continued for 20 years and *constituted a nuisance during that time*,[450] notwithstanding that it is likely to have varied in frequency and intensity. Nevertheless "these problems should not stand in the way 19-85

438 See *Att Gen v Tod Heatley* [1897] 1 Ch. 560, where the defendant's responsibility was transferred to the succeeding owner. There is little authority on this point. Doubtless the vendor who covenants to repair and ceases to occupy can nevertheless be held responsible for the duration of the covenant.

439 No easement to commit a private nuisance can be acquired by prescription unless the practice is *nec vi nec clam nec precario*; thus a secret and hidden practice can never found a prescriptive title, see e.g. *Liverpool Corp v Coghill* [1918] 1 Ch. 307.

440 In *Palmer v Bowman* [2000] 1 W.L.R. 842 the Court of Appeal held that no easement can be acquired for the drainage of naturally occurring water from higher to lower land in undefined channels, since such drainage is itself a natural process for which no easement is necessary.

441 *Thomas v Thomas* (1835) 2 C.M. & R. 34; *Fay v Prentice* (1845) 1 C.B. 828; *Harvey v Walters* (1873) L.R. 8 C. & P. 162.

442 *Jones v Pritchard* [1908] 1 Ch. 630.

443 *Att Gen v Copeland* [1902] 1 K.B. 690; *Longton v Winwick Asylum Board* (1911) 75 J.P. 348; appeal compromised 76 J.P. 113. cf. *Gardner v Davis* [1999] E.H.L.R. 13 CA (easement affording shared drainage into a septic tank no defence to an action in nuisance for discharging sewage onto the servient tenement itself).

444 *Cargill v Gotts* [1981] 1 W.L.R. 441; noted (1981) 97 L.Q.R. 382.

445 *Lemmon v Webb* [1894] 3 Ch. 1; [1895] A.C. 1; *Khyatt v Morgan* [1961] N.Z.L.R. 1020 at 1024, per Leicester J; affirmed [1962] N.Z.L.R. 791; *Morgan v Khyatt* [1964] 1 W.L.R. 475 PC.

446 [2014] UKSC 13; [2014] A.C. 822.

447 See, e.g. *Lawrence v Fen Tigers Ltd* [2011] EWHC 360 (QB) at [223], per Judge Richard Seymour QC (sitting as a Judge of the High Court at first instance in *Coventry v Lawrence* [2014] UKSC 13; [2014] A.C. 822).

448 [2014] UKSC 13; [2014] A.C. 822 at [34] (emphasis added). The other Justices, Lords Sumption, Mance, Clarke and Carnwath apparently agreed with Lord Neuberger on this point.

449 See *Pwllbach Colliery v Woodman* [1915] A.C. 634 at 649, per Lord Sumner (right to spread coal-dust over adjoining land); cited with approval by Lord Neuberger in *Coventry v Lawrence* [2014] UKSC 13; [2014] A.C. 822 at [32].

450 *Coventry v Lawrence* [2014] UKSC 13; [2014] A.C. 822 at [43]–[46]. The defence of prescription

of a continuing nuisance by noise being able to give rise to a prescriptive right to transmit sound waves over servient land."[451] A dominant owner who manages to succeed in establishing such a right by prescription will, however, not be allowed the degree of latitude accorded, for example, to those enjoying rights of way or drainage, in determining the level or frequency of noise which the exercise of that right permits.[452]

19-86 **No prescription for public nuisance or breach of statute** No right can be acquired by user, however long, to use one's premises in such a manner as to amount to a public nuisance,[453] nor where the right claimed is contrary to a statute can it be legalised by prescriptive user.

(b) Authorisation by statute

19-87 **Authorisation of nuisance by statute** Though statutory authority is a general defence to actions in tort, most of the cases have arisen in the field of nuisance.[454] The statutory authority to commit a nuisance must, in order to afford a defence to the parties committing it, be express or necessarily implied.[455] The early law on this question was formed in litigation upon the Victorian Acts of Parliament enabling the construction of railways. The courts construed these Acts favourably to railway companies, and it was established[456] that where a statute has authorised the doing of a particular act, or the user of land in a particular way, which act or user will inevitably involve a nuisance, any resulting harm is not actionable, providing every reasonable precaution consistent with the exercise of the statutory powers has been taken to prevent the nuisance occurring.[457] Thus statutory authorisation to construct an oil refinery was held by the House of Lords, in *Allen v Gulf Oil Refining Ltd*,[458] to authorise impliedly its operation even to the harm of neighbours, provided that there was no negligence in so doing.[459] The burden of proving that a nuisance is inevitable lies on the persons having statutory authority.[460] It is discharged by showing that all reasonable care and skill, according to the state of scientific knowledge at the time, has been taken.[461] In *Allen's* case the defendants had been authorised to acquire land near Milford Haven "for the construction of a refinery" but no

failed on this ground in *Coventry v Lawrence* itself: see [2014] UKSC 13; [2014] A.C. 822 at [143].

451 [2014] UKSC 13; [2014] A.C. 822 at [37], per Lord Neuberger.

452 [2014] UKSC 13; [2014] A.C. 822 at [39], per Lord Neuberger.

453 *R. v Cross* (1812) 3 Camp. 224; *Mott v Shoolbred* (1875) L.R. 20 Eq. 22.

454 See Kodilinye (1990) 19 An. Am. L.R. 72.

455 *Geddis v Proprietors of Bann Reservoir* (1878) 3 App. Cas. 430; *Quebec Ry v Vandry* [1920] A.C. 662. See also *The Manchester Ship Canal Co Ltd v United Utilities Water Plc* [2014] UKSC 40; [2014] 1 W.L.R. 2576 at [2], per Lord Sumption: "The implication must be more than convenient or reasonable. It must be necessary" (a case of trespass).

456 Davies, "Injurious Affection and Compensation" (1974) 90 L.Q.R. 361 at 362–365 discussing the provisions of the Land Compensation Act 1973; and see Craig, "Compensation in Public Law" (1980) 96 L.Q.R. 413.

457 *R. v Pease* (1832) 4 B. & Ad. 30; *Vaughan v Taff Ry* (1860) 5 H. & N. 679; *Hammersmith Ry v Brand* (1869) L.R. 4 H.L. 171; *London, Brighton etc Ry v Turman* (1885) 11 App. Cas. 45.

458 [1981] A.C. 1001.

459 *Allen v Gulf Oil Refining Ltd* [1981] A.C. 1001.

460 This is not only a burden of legal argument on the statutory undertaker to show that the statute must be construed in his favour, but a burden of proof on the facts, that is, that the injurious affection was an inevitable result of carrying out the authorised work.

461 *Manchester Corp v Farnworth* [1930] A.C. 171 at 183, per Lord Dunedin. See also per Lord Phillips MR delivering the judgment of the Court of Appeal in *Marcic v Thames Water Utilities Ltd*

express power had been given for the operation of the refinery in any particular way or indeed for the construction of any particular kind of refinery. The Court of Appeal held that the operation of the refinery to the detriment of neighbours was actionable and not clothed with statutory immunity. But the House of Lords[462] construed the statute differently. The Act by necessary implication authorised operation and use and the defendants could claim immunity if they could show that they had used all due diligence and that the resulting harm was the inevitable consequence of the authorised operations of the refinery. To that extent the House considered Parliament had manifested an intention to take away the private rights of the neighbours without otherwise providing for their compensation.[463] An important provision, s.158 of the Planning Act 2008, confers statutory authority "for the purpose of providing a defence in civil or criminal proceedings for nuisance" when an order granting development consent is made as part of a national infrastructure project.[464] Statutory authorisation should not be confused with the widespread regulation of much modern industrial activity: compliance with complex requirements which may be imposed by statutory regulatory bodies does not in itself enable defendants to resist common law nuisance claims.[465]

Limit of immunity If, however, due diligence or reasonable care is not taken, there will be liability even when the defendant acted under statutory authority. In *Tate & Lyle v Greater London Council*,[466] the defendants were liable in public nuisance when, acting with statutory authority, they constructed ferry terminals in the Thames. Their design and construction of these works were faulty and the ensuing siltation which prevented access to the claimants' jetties was actionable, the claimants recovering three-quarters of their dredging costs, the other quarter not being recoverable as the inevitable consequence of the defendant's work if it had been carefully performed under their statutory powers. **19-88**

Negligent exercise of statutory powers A defendant who creates a nuisance through the exercise of statutory powers will therefore normally be liable if he exercises those powers negligently.[467] Difficult questions on the boundary between public and private law may occasionally arise if the defendant contends that the **19-89**

[2002] EWCA Civ 64; [2002] Q.B. 929 at [86]; this point is not affected by the reversal of the decision of the Court of Appeal by the House of Lords in [2003] UKHL 66; [2004] 2 A.C. 42; [2004] 1 All E.R. 135.

462 [1981] A.C. 1001, Lord Keith dissenting. Lord Wilberforce pointed out that if the defendants were liable in nuisance for inevitable harm to neighbours the whole refinery might be closed down by injunction. There would doubtless be such a risk, though against that it may be said that injunctions, unlike damages, are discretionary.

463 While Parliament is alert to provide express compensation for persons whose land is compulsorily acquired, it may be doubted whether the interests of those injuriously affected receive the same degree of parliamentary consideration in fact. The Land Compensation Act 1973 does however give a right to compensation when public works produce injurious affection.

464 Section 152 of the Act provides for the award of compensation in such cases.

465 See *Barr v Biffa Waste Services* [2012] EWCA Civ 312; [2013] Q.B. 455 at [94], per Carnwath LJ (repudiating a suggestion by the trial judge that the common law should "march in step" with the legislation so that compliance with the regulations would negate "unreasonableness").

466 [1983] 2 A.C. 509.

467 See *Geddis v Proprietors of Bann Reservoir* (1878) 3 App. Cas. 430 at 455–456, per Lord Blackburn. But cf. per Lord Browne-Wilkinson in *X (Minors) v Bedfordshire CC* [1995] 2 A.C. 633 at 732–733. If the statute in question contains its own compensation scheme it will be a question of fact and construction whether even victims of negligence are confined to the statutory scheme or can bring a common law claim: see, e.g. *Hall v Environment Agency* [2017] EWHC 1309 (TCC); [2018] 1

context in which the power was exercised rendered that exercise "non-justiciable", or immune from liability, on grounds of general public interest[468] or because it concerned a "policy" rather than an "operational" matter.[469] These issues do, however, more commonly arise in relation to negligence liability as such,[470] when an attempt is made to use the statute as the foundation for a liability which would not otherwise exist, than in the context of the tort of nuisance.

19-90 **Statutory powers saving liability for nuisance** Statutory powers are frequently conferred with a proviso that the statutory undertakers are to be liable for nuisance. When liability for nuisance is thus preserved, and the project is to be performed not as a mandatory duty but under permissive statutory authority, the undertakers are liable for nuisances they themselves have created, whether or not they have been negligent.[471] If they have not created the nuisance but the nuisance is caused by the scope of some noxious thing, such as sewage, which they have statutory authority to bring on to land, they are only liable on proof of negligence.[472] If a local authority takes over a system of sewerage created by some previous authority it is not liable for a nuisance when these sewers are inadequate to carry the sewage of the district through its failure to exercise its statutory powers to enlarge them.[473] But if a local authority, with statutory authority preserving its liability for nuisance, itself actually commits a nuisance by discharging sewage into a river, it cannot escape liability by proving that it has statutory powers to enlarge its sewage disposal plant and has failed to exercise them. So, where the Derby Corporation constructed sewers which were adequate in 1901, when completed, but inadequate in 1953, owing to the increase of population, and they allowed sewage to be discharged into a river and caused a nuisance, it was held that the question of nonfeasance was irrelevant, because once it was proved there was a nuisance, the sole question was whether the nuisance was authorised by statute and, as it was not, the Corporation was held liable.[474]

19-91 **Statutory authority as a defence to the rule in Rylands v Fletcher** When a dangerous thing is used under statutory authority, it is generally necessary to prove negligence in order to establish liability.[475] The negligence of an independent

W.L.R. 1433; see also *Southern Gas Networks Plc v Thames Water Utilities Ltd* [2018] EWCA Civ 33; [2018] 1 W.L.R. 5977.

468 See *X (Minors) v Bedfordshire CC* [1995] 2 A.C. 633.

469 See *Barrett v Enfield LBC* [2001] 2 A.C. 550 HL, in which the House of Lords showed revived interest in the "policy/operational" distinction originally developed in *Anns v Merton LBC* [1978] A.C. 728 but questioned in *Rowling v Takaro Properties Ltd* [1988] A.C. 473.

470 See Ch.7. See also Buckley, *The Law of Negligence and Nuisance*, 6th edn (2017), Ch.15.

471 *Rapier v London Tramways* [1893] 2 Ch. 588; *Batcheller v Tunbridge Wells Gas Co* (1901) 84 L.T. 765; *Midwood v Manchester Corp* [1905] 2 K.B. 597; in *Pride of Derby etc v British Celanese Ltd* [1953] Ch. 149, negligence was not alleged.

472 *Smeaton v Ilford Corp* [1954] Ch. 450. See also *Dobson v Thames Water Utilities* [2007] EWHC 2021 (TCC); [2008] 2 All E.R. 362 (Ramsey J); [2009] EWCA Civ 28; [2009] 3 All E.R. 319 (for subsequent proceedings see *Dobson v Thames Water Utilities* [2011] EWHC 3253 (TCC); (2011) 140 Con. L.R. 135 in which liability for an odour nuisance caused by negligence was imposed).

473 See, generally, *Marcic v Thames Water Utilities* [2003] UKHL 66; [2004] 2 A.C. 42; [2004] 1 All E.R. 135 HL.

474 *Pride of Derby etc v British Celanese Ltd* [1953] Ch. 149.

475 *Geddis v Proprietors of Bann Reservoir* (1878) 3 App. Cas. 430; *Green v Chelsea Waterworks Co* (1894) 70 L.T. 547; *Dunne v North Western Gas Board* [1964] 2 Q.B. 806. See also *Transco v Stockport MBC* [2003] UKHL 61; [2004] 2 A.C. 1, per Lord Hoffmann at [30]–[31], and para.19-87.

contractor is sufficient.[476] To come within this exception, the statute must authorise the use of the dangerous thing either expressly or by necessary implication,[477] mere permission to use it is not enough.[478] If the statute saves liability for nuisance, it is sometimes unnecessary to prove negligence once nuisance is established.[479]

Summary of statutory authority as defence in cases of nuisance The following propositions have been approved by the House of Lords[480]: 19-92

(a) in the absence of negligence, a body is not liable for a nuisance which is attributable to the exercise by it of a duty imposed on it by statute;
(b) it is not liable in those circumstances even if by statute it is expressly made liable, or not exempted from liability, for nuisance;
(c) in the absence of negligence, a body is not liable for a nuisance which is attributable to the exercise by it of a power conferred by statute if, by statute, it is neither expressly made liable, nor expressly exempted from liability, for nuisance;
(d) a body is liable for a nuisance by it attributable to the exercise of a power conferred by statute even without negligence, if by statute it is expressly [either] made liable, [or not exempted from liability], for nuisance.[481]

(c) Act of God

Act of God as a defence to the rule in Rylands v Fletcher The act of God[482] is a recognised exception to the principle of *Rylands v Fletcher*.[483] Its meaning is an operation of natural forces "which no human foresight can provide against, and of which human pretence is not bound to recognise the possibility".[484] It is only a defence if it was impossible to provide against the occurrence, and it is not enough to show that it was not reasonably possible to provide against it. It is a question of 19-93

---

476 *Hardaker v Idle DC* [1896] 1 Q.B. 335.

477 *West v Bristol Tramways* [1908] 2 K.B. 14.

478 *Jones v Ffestiniog Ry* (1868) L.R. 3 Q.B. 733.

479 *Midwood v Manchester Corp* [1905] 2 K.B. 597; *Powell v Fall* (1880) 5 Q.B.D. 597; *Charing Cross Electricity Supply Co v Hydraulic Power Co* [1914] 3 K.B. 772; *Pride of Derby and Derbyshire Angling Association v British Celanese* [1953] Ch. 149. cf. *Smeaton v Ilford Corp* [1954] Ch. 450 at 475-477. The Court of Appeal reviewed the cases in *Dunne v North Western Gas Board* [1964] 2 Q.B. 806 and expressed the view that it was questionable whether the nationalised gas industry (as it then was) collected gas for its "own purposes" within the rule in *Rylands v Fletcher*. As the Gas Board had acted without negligence, they were protected from liability on a strict basis in the event of escape. See also the previous paragraph.

480 per Webster J in *Department of Transport v North West Water Authority* [1983] 3 W.L.R. 105 at 109, and approved by the House of Lords in [1984] A.C. 336 at 359.

481 It is respectfully submitted that the words in parenthesis, although approved by the House of Lords, should be omitted: otherwise proposition (d) appears partially to conflict with proposition (c). The true position would seem to be that a body may be liable without negligence for a nuisance attributable to the exercise of a statutory power but only if the statute expressly makes it liable for nuisance.

482 See Hall, "An Unsearchable Providence: the Lawyer's Concept of Act of God" (1993) 12 O.J.L.S. 227.

483 *Greenock Corp v Caledonian Ry* [1917] A.C. 556, where *Nichols v Marsland* (1876) 2 Ex. D. 1 is doubted. *Nichols v Marsland* appears to be the only case reported where act of God has afforded a defence, perhaps because the court felt unable to disturb the finding of fact by a jury: see para.19-126.

484 per Lord Westbury in *Tennant v Earl of Glasgow* (1864) 2 M. 22; followed in *Greenock Corp v Caledonian Ry* [1917] A.C. 556. cf. *Southern Water Authority v Pegrum* (1989) 153 J.P. 581.

fact whether an extraordinary violent rainfall[485] or an unusually high tide[486] or an exceptionally strong wind[487] is such that human foresight or prudence could not recognise the possibility of the occurrence. An escape caused by an act of God in this sense is not therefore within the rule in *Rylands v Fletcher*, but the courts have limited the scope of the exception so far that it can only apply in exceedingly rare circumstances. In theory it is doubtful whether act of God in any degree ought to afford a defence to a case of strict liability based on the creation of abnormal risks for neighbours and where culpability in the form of negligence is not material. Scrutton LJ believed that "the fact that an artificial danger escaped through natural causes was no excuse to the person who brought an artificial danger there".[488] The defence is not available in the statutory forms of strict liability for animal escapes,[489] and in the field of "natural nuisances" the operation of natural forces upon land in its natural condition does not now exonerate or prevent the imposition of a limited duty of care.[490] To the extent that act of God must be accepted as excepting from the rule in *Rylands v Fletcher* it will be in practice confined to such cataclysms of nature as earthquakes or inundations following tidal surges of unprecedented heights.

(d) Act of a trespasser

19-94 There is generally no liability upon an occupier for a nuisance caused by a trespasser:

> "An occupier is not prima facie responsible for a nuisance created without his knowledge and consent. If he is to be liable a further condition is necessary, namely, that he had knowledge or means of knowledge, that he knew or should have known of the nuisance in time to correct it and obviate its mischievous effects."[491]

Where a railing in an area adjoining the highway had been broken by a trespasser so as to create a nuisance, and a child fell into the area through the gap and was injured, it was held that the occupier was not liable for the nuisance created by the act of the trespasser, when he neither knew nor should have known of the nuisance.[492] Where the blast from an enemy bomb loosened a slate on the roof of a building and, in a high wind 18 days later, the slate was blown off and injured a person on the highway, it was held that the occupiers of the property were not liable on its being proved that reasonable inspection of the roof did not disclose that the slate had been loosened by the blast.[493] Where water flooded into the claimant's flat from vacant premises above where pipes had been broken by trespassers, she was unable to recover against her landlords either in nuisance or negligence.[494] Even if the acts of vandalising trespassers are frequent it may be difficult for such a claimant to establish that the defendant had effective means of control, thereby acquir-

---

485 *Greenock Corp v Caledonian Ry* [1917] A.C. 556; *Att Gen v Cory Bros* (1919) 35 T.L.R. 570 at 574, per Scrutton LJ; and [1921] 1 A.C. 521 at 536, per Lord Haldane.

486 *Greenwood Tileries Ltd v Clapson* [1937] 1 All E.R. 765.

487 *Cushing v Walker & Son* [1941] 2 All E.R. 693 at 695.

488 *Att Gen v Cory Bros* (1919) 35 T.L.R. 570 at 574.

489 See Ch.20.

490 See paras 19-20 and 19-21.

491 per Lord Wright, in *Sedleigh-Denfield v O'Callaghan* [1940] A.C. 880 at 904.

492 *Barker v Herbert* [1911] 2 K.B. 633 (the house was vacant at the time).

493 *Cushing v Peter Walker & Sons Ltd* [1941] 2 All E.R. 693 (enemy action was the act of a trespasser).

494 *King v Liverpool City Council* [1986] 1 W.L.R. 890 CA.

ing liability for the acts of third parties.[495] Generally, the law is slow to impose liability for omission to act,[496] though in particular cases a special relationship may be held to exist between the defendant and third parties, raising a duty of care to protect other persons from the misconduct of such third parties who trespass and cause fires or floods.

Continuance There will be liability if the nuisance created by the trespasser is continued after the occupier has knowledge or ought to have knowledge of its existence and is in a position to take effective steps to prevent it.[497] So, where a stream was culverted by a trespasser, but the occupier of the land knew of the culvert's existence and allowed it to remain, it was held that the occupier was liable for a flooding caused by a blockage of the culvert.[498] Similarly, where property was damaged by enemy action, but the occupier did not take prompt steps to make it safe towards persons passing along the highway, although he knew of the damage, the occupier was held liable.[499] Where an occupier is held responsible for continuance of a nuisance caused by a third party, such as a trespasser, or an act of nature, the "measured duty of care" which rests upon it will depend upon the particular circumstances of the case. In *Lambert v Barratt Homes Ltd*[500] the Court of Appeal held that where flooding which emanated from a local authority's land had been caused by a third party the authority was only under an obligation towards the victim actively to assist in finding a solution to the problem which caused the flooding, and to cooperate in its implementation, as distinct from being obliged itself to bear the full cost of implementation. 19-95

(e) Act of a third party as a defence to the rule in Rylands v Fletcher

Independent act of third party The owner of a dangerous thing is not liable under the rule in *Rylands v Fletcher* if the thing has escaped through the independent act of a third party, and there has been no negligence on his part.[501] In the absence of such a defence the rule would "make a householder liable for the consequences of an explosion caused by a burglar breaking into his house during the night and leaving a gas tap open".[502] If the defendant establishes that the escape was caused by the act of a third party, he avoids liability, unless the claimant can go on to show that the act was of the kind which the defendant could reasonably 19-96

---

495 In *Smith v Littlewoods Organisation Ltd* [1987] 1 A.C. 241, the House of Lords denied a duty of care where trespassers caused a fire in the defendant's vacant cinema which spread to the claimant's property. cf. *Goldman v Hargrave* [1967] 1 A.C. 645, see paras 19-20, 19-22, on duty to abate a fire known to be burning. In *Smith v Littlewoods Organisation Ltd* Lord Goff, at 279, explained *Goldman v Hargrave* as based on actual or presumed knowledge of the occupier who is "in exclusive control of the premises upon which the danger has arisen".

496 See *Stovin v Wise* [1996] A.C. 923 HL at 943–944, per Lord Hoffmann.

497 *Sedleigh-Denfield v O'Callaghan* [1940] A.C. 880 at 897; *Smeaton v Ilford Corp* [1954] Ch. 450 at 462; *Page Motors v Epsom & Ewell BC* (1982) 80 L.G.R. 337.

498 *Sedleigh-Denfield v O'Callaghan* [1940] A.C. 880; *Pemberton v Bright and the Devon CC* [1960] 1 W.L.R. 436. cf. *Lambert v Barratt Homes Ltd* [2010] EWCA Civ 681; [2010] B.L.R. 527.

499 *Leanse v Egerton* [1943] 1 K.B. 323 (presumed knowledge).

500 [2010] EWCA Civ 681; [2010] B.L.R. 527; see further para.7-183.

501 *Rickards v Lothian* [1913] A.C. 263 at 279; applied in *Perry v Kendricks Transport Ltd* [1956] 1 W.L.R. 85 CA; *Balfour v Barty-King etc* [1957] 1 Q.B. 496 CA.

502 *Rickards v Lothian* [1913] A.C. 263 at 282.

have foreseen and guarded against.[503] A stranger is a person over whose acts the defendant has no control,[504] and his act is such that the defendant ought not reasonably to have anticipated and guarded against it.[505] He is either a trespasser, or a licensee acting in a totally unpermitted and unforeseeable manner.[506] Thus, where the defendant's reservoir overflowed owing to the emptying of a third person's reservoir into the main drain above the defendant's premises, combined with an obstruction of the drain below, the defendants were held not liable because the overflow was "caused by a stranger over whom and at a spot where they had no control".[507] Similarly, the occupier of a lavatory on an upper floor was held not responsible for damage done by the malicious act of an unknown person who, by turning on the tap and plugging the wastepipe, caused the water to overflow on to a lower floor.[508] If, however, after knowing of the obstruction the occupier turns on the water he is liable for the resulting damage.[509]

19-97 **Relationship of the defence to negligence** The act of the third party must be deliberate or intentional, and not merely negligent, because against the negligence of third parties the owner of the dangerous thing is bound to guard other persons.[510] Accordingly, if water is stored in a cistern, constructed without negligence, the owner is not liable if a mischievous boy bores a hole in it thereby causing damage to others, because the act was a deliberate one.[511] Again, where the defendants negligently delivered by mistake to the claimants' premises a quantity of highly inflammable celluloid film scrap without giving any warning of its nature, and one of the claimants' typists negligently caused it to explode, thereby causing serious damage, it was held that the defendants were liable.[512] The court expressly drew a distinction between the negligence of the typist, which was something the defendants should have foreseen and for which they were liable, and her intentional act in setting fire to the material for which, had it been proved, the defendants would not have been liable. On the same principle, when a gas main was broken by the removal of support from underneath it by a local authority who were constructing new sewerage works, the gas company were held liable in negligence for damage caused by an explosion of the gas, because they knew of the works being carried out by the local authority and were negligent in failing to inspect their mains and

---

503 *Perry v Kendricks Transport Ltd* [1956] 1 W.L.R. 85 at 91 and 93, per Jenkins and Parker LJJ; *Hanson v Wearmouth Coal Co Ltd and Sunderland Gas Co* [1939] 3 All E.R. 47 at 53, per Goddard LJ.

504 An independent contractor employed by the occupier is not a stranger for this purpose: *Balfour v Barty-King etc* [1957] 1 Q.B. 496 at 505 (one has control of an independent contractor in that one chooses him, invites him to one's premises and can order him to leave); see also *Hobbs (Farms) v Baxenden Chemical Co* [1992] 1 Lloyd's Rep. 54. (In *Rylands v Fletcher* itself, the damage was caused by an independent contractor.)

505 *Perry v Kendricks Transport Ltd* [1956] 1 W.L.R. 85 CA (small boy throwing match into tank containing petrol vapour; held in the circumstances to be a stranger).

506 *Hale v Jennings Brothers* [1938] 1 All E.R. 579 CA; *H & N Emanuel v Greater London Council* [1971] 2 All E.R. 835 CA. Also a servant going where he is forbidden to go: *Stevens v Woodward* (1881) 6 Q.B.D. 318 at 321.

507 *Box v Jubb* (1879) 4 Ex. D. 76.

508 *Rickards v Lothian* [1913] A.C. 263.

509 *Harrison v GN Ry* (1864) 3 H. & C. 231.

510 See *Northwestern Utilities Ltd v London Guarantee and Accident Co* [1936] A.C. 108 at 119; *Sullivan v Creed* [1904] 2 Ir. R. 317; *Dixon v Bell* (1816) 5 M. & S. 198; *Williams v Eady* (1893) 10 T.L.R. 41; *Shiffman v Order of St John* [1936] 1 All E.R. 557.

511 per Bramwell B in *Nicholas v Marsland* (1876) 2 Ex. D. 1.

512 *Philco Radio Ltd v J Spurling Ltd* [1949] 2 K.B. 33.

to discover whether the bed on which their mains lay was being disturbed.[513] They should have anticipated that their mains might be disturbed and should have taken the necessary steps to guard against a disturbance. It has been said that once the escape has been proved to be the act of a stranger which the defendant ought to have foreseen, "one reaches the point where the claim based on *Rylands v Fletcher* merges into the claim in negligence".[514] Though it might appear somewhat paradoxical that the defendant should be held liable for negligence for acts of strangers "even though he escapes liability under the rule in *Rylands v Fletcher*",[515] it seems that the proper approach is based on burden of proof. The defendant can exonerate himself by showing the escape was caused by the deliberate act of a person not within his control. If he does so, the claimant is remitted to the more onerous task of showing that the defendant was negligent because of failure to guard effectively against such interference in circumstances where that interference and ensuing damage was reasonably foreseeable.

Impact of third party defence The policy of the law in allowing the defendant to avoid strict liability where escape has been caused by such human interferences is open to question. The exception is not allowed where strict liability for animals applies.[516] The defence seems founded on the theory that the defendant ought not to be answerable unless he has culpably failed to prevent the escape and that it is not culpable to fail to guard against interferences of strangers unless, indeed, such an interference could have been foreseen. In effect, the defendant's duty is reduced to one which, apart from the burden of proof, resembles a duty of care in negligence. A rule of truly strict liability, on the other hand, is concerned to impose liability on an occupier from whose control dangerous things escape even if he could not foresee an escape. The circumstances of the escape would, on that view, be immaterial; it would be enough to show a causal connection with the claimant's injury. This exception or defence, perhaps more than any other qualification to the rule in *Rylands v Fletcher*, has had the effect of restricting its scope, in many cases reducing the issue between the parties to the question whether sufficient care was taken to control the accumulation or other dangerous activity on the defendant's land.[517] Nevertheless, although the anomalous nature of the third party defence was highlighted by Lord Hoffmann in his speech in *Transco v Stockport MBC*,[518] the overall effect of the speeches in that case appears to be to confirm its continuing existence. 19-98

513 *Northwestern Utilities Ltd v London Guarantee and Accident Co* [1936] A.C. 108; applied in *Weisler v North Vancouver District, British Columbia and Christie* (1959) 17 D.L.R. (2d) 319.

514 *Perry v Kendricks Transport Ltd* [1956] 1 W.L.R. 95 at 90, per Jenkins LJ.

515 *Salmond and Heuston on the Law of Torts*, 21st edn (1996), p.317.

516 See Ch.20.

517 Some of the illustrations in the cases above concern intruders who deliberately leave taps running and similar instances where it is clear the defendant's user could not be considered "non-natural". Instead of contemplating cases which are not within the scope of the rule in the first place, it would seem more helpful to suppose cases clearly within the rule, e.g. an accumulation of explosive material such as gas, and consider whether, for example, an explosion caused by a gang of terrorists should exonerate the defendant. It is not obvious that the loss should lie where it fell. As the function of the rule is to provide protection in the nature of insurance, it would seem immaterial that the defendant neither caused the escape nor was negligent in allowing escape.

518 [2003] UKHL 61; [2004] 2 A.C. 1 at [32].

(f) Ignorance of the nuisance

19-99 As the general rule is that no one is liable for nuisance unless he either created it or continued it after knowledge or means of knowledge, it follows that it is a defence to prove ignorance of the facts constituting the nuisance, unless that ignorance is due to the omission to use reasonable care to discover the facts. In *Ilford Urban DC v Beal and Judd*,[519] the claimant built a wall on her land. This wall was in fact built over a sewer which was some eight or nine feet deep and became cracked by the wall. The defendant was held not liable on the ground that she was ignorant of the existence of the sewer and could not reasonably have been expected to know of it. In *St Anne's Well Brewery Co v Roberts*,[520] part of the ancient city wall of Exeter collapsed and damaged the claimant's inn which adjoined it. The cause of the collapse was obscure and the owners of the wall were held not liable, Scrutton LJ saying:

> "it appears to me that the cardinal thing which would have to be proved to establish any liability against anybody would be knowledge of the defect which ultimately resulted in the fall, or failure to acquire that knowledge because he had failed to use reasonable care to ascertain what he should have ascertained."

In *Wilkins v Leighton*,[521] a house built on the upper part of a slope caused a retaining wall to collapse and damage a house below. The owner and occupier of the upper house was held not liable, on the ground that she neither knew nor should have known that her house constituted a nuisance or hidden danger to the lower house. Cases which appear to conflict with this general proposition are probably to be regarded as falling within the principle of *Rylands v Fletcher*.[522]

19-100 **Trees** With regard to trees and other natural growth projecting over or into the highway, the duty of the occupier is based on reasonable foreseeability of harm. Thus, the occupier who employs independent contractors to fell a tree adjacent to the highway is not liable for the resulting damage unless there is some inherently dangerous or specially hazardous risk to highway users.[523] In *Noble v Harrison*[524] the branch of a tree growing on the defendants' land overhung the highway and owing to a latent defect, not discoverable on reasonable examination, it fell and damaged a coach which was being driven along the highway. The defendant was held not liable for a nuisance "caused by a secret and unobservable operation of nature".[525] In *Cunliffe v Bankes*,[526] a tree growing near the highway fell owing to its diseased condition, with the result that a motorist collided with it and was killed. The owner had taken all reasonable steps to ascertain the condition of the tree,

---

519 [1925] 1 K.B. 671; *Humphries v Cousins* (1877) 2 C.P.D. 239, decided the other way on somewhat similar facts, was distinguished on the ground that the defendant in that case must have known of the existence of the drain.

520 (1928) 140 L.T. 1 at 7; [1928] All E.R. Rep. 28 at 33.

521 [1932] 2 Ch. 106.

522 (1868) L.R. 3 H.L. 330; *Broder v Saillard* (1876) 2 Ch. D. 692; *Humphries v Cousins* (1877) 2 C.P.D. 239; see, per Lord Atkin in *Sedleigh-Denfield v O'Callaghan* [1940] A.C. 880 at 898.

523 *Salsbury v Woodland* [1970] 1 Q.B. 324 CA.

524 [1926] 2 K.B. 332; *Chapman v Barking and Dagenham LBC* [1997] 2 E.G.L.R. 141; [1997] N.P.C. 82; *Darroch v Carroll* [1955] N.Z.L.R. 997 (reviews the authorities).

525 [1926] 2 K.B. 332 at 341, per Wright J.

526 [1945] 1 All E.R. 459; *Caminer v Northern and London Investment Trust* [1951] A.C. 88; *Quinn v Scott* [1965] 1 W.L.R. 1004.

which he could not have realised was likely to fall, and was held not liable. In *Stagecoach South Western Trains Ltd v Hind*[527] the defendant landowner's tree collapsed as a result of undetected decay and damaged the claimant's train which was on a railway line running alongside the defendant's property. Coulson J reviewed the authorities on the duties of tree-owners and concluded that there is no duty on such owners "as a matter of course and without any trigger or warning sign, to pay for an arboriculturalist to carry out periodic inspections of the trees on his or her land".[528] However, there is a duty on the owner to carry out regular preliminary informal inspections themselves, "particularly where those trees may border a highway, a railway or the property of another".[529] On the facts of the case the landowner had not been in breach of duty. Where the defendant has inherited or acquired the property on which a defective tree overhangs the highway, the defendant is not liable unless he has become aware of the risk or should, with reasonable care, have become aware of the danger which it posed.[530] A highway authority can be liable for dangerous trees on the highway: adoption or dedication of the highway is sufficient to render the authority liable at common law in nuisance or negligence.[531]

Artificial structures With regard to artificial structures or projections over the highway the law as stated in *Wringe v Cohen* places a stricter duty on the occupier[532]: 19-101

> "If premises become dangerous as the result of something done by an occupier and they cause damage, the occupier is liable although he did not know of the danger and was not negligent in not knowing … On the other hand, if premises become dangerous, not by the occupier's act or neglect of duty, but as the result of the act of a third party, or of a latent defect, the occupier is not liable without proof of knowledge or means of knowledge and failure to abate it."

Though the decision in *Wringe v Cohen* has received some adverse comment, it has been taken as stating the rule for highway injuries from artificial projections on a basis of strict liability (secret operations of nature and acts of trespassers excepted). Nevertheless, it has been pointed out that "it can hardly be imagined that any damage caused neither by the act of a third person nor by a latent defect could be due to anything but knowledge or negligence of the occupier".[533] *Wringe v Cohen* may therefore represent an intermediate position between strict liability and negligence where the burden of disproving negligence lies on the occupier and where he is

---

527 [2014] EWHC 1891; [2014] 3 E.G.L.R. 59.

528 See [2014] EWHC 1891; [2014] 3 E.G.L.R. 59 at [71].

529 [2014] EWHC 1891; [2014] 3 E.G.L.R. 59 at [73]. See, e.g. *Witley Parish Council v Cavanagh* [2018] EWCA Civ 2232 (liability imposed).

530 *British Road Services v Slater* [1964] 1 W.L.R. 498, per Parker CJ.

531 *Hurst v Hampshire CC* [1997] 2 E.G.L.R. 164; (1997) 96 L.G.R. 27 CA (rejecting the contention that only the Highways Act 1980 s.96, could give rise to liability).

532 [1940] 1 K.B. 229 CA at 248. For detailed criticism of *Wringe's* case, see *O'Leary v Meltitides and Eastern Trust Co* (1960) 20 D.L.R. (2d) 258 at 266–268. "It is out of accord with current authority and requires reconsideration by a higher tribunal": per Isley CJ. The facts of *Wringe* had nothing to do with the highway and the statements by the Court of Appeal as to projections over the highway are therefore strictly obiter dicta.

533 Friedmann, "Nuisance, Negligence and the Overlapping of Torts" (1940) 3 M.L.R. 305 at 309 and further discussed in (1943) 59 L.Q.R. 305.

vicariously liable for the negligence of independent contractors.[534]

(g) Contributory negligence

19-102 Contributory negligence, subject to the apportionment provisions of the Law Reform (Contributory Negligence) Act 1945, is a defence to an action in nuisance save where the consequences were intended by the defendant.[535]

19-103 **Act or default of claimant as a defence to Rylands v Fletcher** If the damage is caused by the act or default of the claimant himself, he clearly has no remedy. This exception is expressly recognised by Blackburn J in his judgment in *Rylands v Fletcher*. Where the claimant worked his mine, which was under the defendant's canal, knowing that he would thereby cause the canal water to escape into his mine, he failed to recover when the water actually escaped and damaged his mine.[536] Similarly, in *Eastern and SA Telegraph Co Ltd v Cape Tramways Co Ltd*, when an escape of electricity injured a peculiarly sensitive apparatus on the claimant's land, he failed to recover, for "a man cannot increase the liabilities of his neighbour by applying his own property to special uses, whether for business or pleasure".[537] If the claimant's conduct, however, merely amounts to contributory negligence he will still be able to recover some damages, but the amount will be reduced by the amount of his blameworthiness.[538]

(h) Consent of claimant as a defence to Rylands v Fletcher

19-104 **Consent of claimant** A person who consents to the dangerous thing being brought to a place from which it may cause him injury if it escapes has no right of action unless he can prove negligence. Consent to the risk of accidental escapes may be implied when the dangerous thing is brought on premises for the common benefit of the claimant and the defendant, for example when one spout collects the drainage of several roofs or one cistern supplies water to several flats.[539] A further application of this principle is when a person enters into occupation of property in which a dangerous thing is installed, such as gas, water and electricity. Such a person cannot complain that the property was not constructed differently and has no right of action if, without negligence on the part of anyone, the dangerous thing escapes and causes damage.[540] The presence of negligence will, however, negate the

---

534 See *Salmond and Heuston on the Law of Torts*, 21st edn (1996), p.67 (where the rule of strict liability is questioned: "the owner of a tree adjoining a highway should be in no different position from the owner of a house adjoining the highway"). See also Buckley, *The Law of Negligence and Nuisance*, 6th edn (2017), Ch 14 para.14.26.

535 *Caswell v Powell Duffryn Associated Collieries Ltd* [1940] A.C. 152 at 165, per Lord Atkin; *Hicks v British Transport Commission* [1958] 1 W.L.R. 493 CA at 507; *Trevett v Lee* [1955] 1 W.L.R. 113 CA at 122.

536 *Dunn v Birmingham Canal Co* (1872) L.R. 7 Q.B. 244 at 246.

537 [1902] A.C. 381 PC at 393. See also para.19-11.

538 Law Reform (Contributory Negligence) Act 1945 s.1.

539 See para.19-135.

540 *Peters v Prince of Wales Theatre* [1943] K.B. 73 (fire-extinguishing apparatus burst without negligence and damaged the part of the building occupied by defendants—no liability. Common benefit is only an element in showing implied consent). It does not apply between consumers of gas and the commercial undertaking supplying them—*Northwestern Utilities Ltd v London Guarantee etc Co Ltd* [1936] A.C. 108; *Prosser & Sons Ltd v Levy* [1955] 1 W.L.R. 1224 CA (no implied

defence. In *Colour Quest Ltd v Total Downstream UK Plc*[541] an explosion occurred as a result of the spillage of petrol on the defendants' part of a large oil-storage site. Although the defendants conceded liability under *Rylands v Fletcher* to claimants altogether outside the site, they denied liability under the rule for damage suffered by claimants who occupied premises *inside* the perimeter of the site, who were also engaged in the business of oil-storage, on the ground that they had *consented* to the dangerous accumulation. Steel J rejected the defendants' submission holding that their negligence vitiated the consent, enabling the claims in *Rylands v Fletcher* to be maintained.

(i) Necessity as a defence to Rylands v Fletcher

Necessity In *Rigby v Chief Constable of Northamptonshire*,[542] the claimant's premises were set on fire when the police fired a canister of CS gas into them in order to flush out an intruder who was a dangerous psychopath. Taylor J was inclined to the view that such situation could not come within *Rylands v Fletcher*, as distinct from trespass, because the damage was direct rather than consequential.[543] His Lordship also observed, however, that "if one is to embrace cases of voluntary release or firing (such as this one) within the *Rylands v Fletcher* principle, it seems irresistibly logical that the defence of necessity must be open on the same basis as in trespass".[544] But in the more usual type of case, involving an involuntary escape, the defence of necessity would be inappropriate since, *ex hypothesi*, the escape would have occurred without any decision or choice by the defendant. Nevertheless, he might be able to "rely on the necessity of bringing the dangerous thing to the point at which it escaped".[545] **19-105**

(j) Ineffectual defences

Suitable place It is no defence that the activity giving rise to the nuisance is carried on at a convenient or suitable place[546]: **19-106**

> "The whole neighbourhood where these copper smelting works were carried on is a neighbourhood more or less devoted to manufacturing purposes of a similar kind, and therefore it is said that, as this copper smelting is carried on in what the appellant contends is a fit place, it may be carried on with impunity … I apprehend that this is not the meaning of the word 'suitable'… The word 'suitable' unquestionably cannot carry with it this

---

consent by claimant to presence of water pipe which was, unknown to him, defective).

541 [2009] EWHC 540 (Comm); [2009] 2 Lloyd's Rep. 1; reversed in part, but not on the point in the text: [2010] EWCA Civ 180; [2011] Q.B. 86.

542 [1985] 1 W.L.R. 1242.

543 But cf. per Potter J in *Crown River Cruises Ltd v Kimbolton Fireworks Ltd* [1996] 2 Lloyd's Rep. 533. His Lordship saw no good reason why intentional releases should not come within the rule, at least where the intentional release was not deliberately aimed at the claimant with the intention of causing damage to him.

544 per Taylor J in *Rigby v Chief Constable of Northamptonshire* [1985] 1 W.L.R. 1242 at 1255.

545 *Rigby v Chief Constable of Northamptonshire* [1985] 1 W.L.R. 1242 at 1255.

546 *Bamford v Turnley* (1860) 3 B. & S. 62; *Shotts Iron Co v Inglis* (1882) 7 App. Cas. 518; *Polsue and Alfieri v Rushmer* [1907] A.C. 121; *Crump v Lambert* (1867) L.R. 3 Eq. 409. Of course if the alleged nuisance is only interference with enjoyment the question whether the activity constituted a nuisance at all can involve consideration of the locality: see para.19-13.

consequence, that a trade may be carried on in a particular locality, the consequence of which trade may be injury and destruction to the neighbouring property."[547]

19-107 **Public interest** It is not in itself a defence to a claim for nuisance to show that the business or other activity in question is a useful one and one which is necessary or at least highly desirable in the public interest.[548] Nevertheless the Supreme Court has indicated that factors other than the interests of the parties themselves may be of great importance in determining whether an *injunction* should be awarded. In *Coventry v Lawrence*[549] that Court signalled a departure from the long-standing principles in *Shelfer v City of London Electric Lighting Co*[550] which appeared strictly to limit the circumstances in which an injunction should be refused.[551] According to the very different approach now favoured by the Supreme Court factors such as the closure of the defendant's business,[552] with consequent loss of their jobs by his employees, and consideration by planning authorities of the public benefit when granting planning permission for the defendant's activities,[553] can be put in the balance when deciding whether to refuse the claimant an injunction. In earlier cases the public interest in preserving a playing field,[554] and an RAF airfield[555] have been held to justify denying an injunction to claimants who had established liability in nuisance.

19-108 **Care and skill used** Although the trade or business is carried on with all due care and skill and every effort is made to prevent it from being a nuisance, yet if a nuisance is caused these matters afford no defence.[556] Where an action was brought against an hotel company for nuisance consisting of noise, Luxmoore J said:

> "the making or causing of such a noise as materially interferes with the comfort of a neighbour when judged by the standard to which I have just referred, constitutes an actionable nuisance, and it is no answer to say that the best-known means have been taken to reduce or prevent the noise complained of, or that the cause of the nuisance is the exercise of a business or trade in a reasonable and proper manner."[557]

19-109 **Coming to the nuisance** The Supreme Court has confirmed[558] that the fact that the claimant has come to the nuisance does not prevent him from establishing liability.[559] Thus, where a claimant bought an estate near a copper smelting works and found the fumes were damaging the trees on his land, he was held able to claim

---

547 per Lord Westbury in *St Helens Smelting Co v Tipping* (1865) 11 H.L.C. 642 at 651.

548 *St Helens Smelting Co v Tipping* (1865) 11 H.L.C. 642; *Bamford v Turnley* (1860) 3 B. & S. 62; *Adams v Ursell* [1913] 1 Ch. 269. See, generally, Lee, "The Public Interest in Private Nuisance" (2015) 74 C.L.J. 329.

549 [2014] UKSC 13; [2014] A.C. 822.

550 [1895] 1 Ch. 287.

551 See paras 19-152 and 28-11.

552 [2014] UKSC 13; [2014] A.C. 822 at [124], per Lord Neuberger.

553 [2014] UKSC 13; [2014] A.C. 822 at [125], per Lord Neuberger; see also per Lord Sumption at [161].

554 *Miller v Jackson* [1977] Q.B. 966.

555 *Dennis v Ministry of Defence* [2003] EWHC 793 (QB); [2003] Env. L.R. 34.

556 *Rapier v London Tramways Co* [1893] 2 Ch. 588; *Adams v Ursell* [1913] 1 Ch. 269 ("the defendant supplies fresh fish and has the most approved appliances"); *Farrell v John Mowlem & Co Ltd* [1954] 1 Lloyd's Rep. 437 at 440; *Bone v Seale* [1975] 1 W.L.R. 797.

557 *Vanderpant v Mayfair Hotel Co* [1930] 1 Ch. 138.

558 *Coventry v Lawrence* [2014] UKSC 13; [2014] A.C. 822.

559 *Elliotson v Feetham* (1835) 2 Bing. N.C. 134; *Bliss v Hall* (1838) 4 Bing. N.C. 183.

an injunction, though the works had been in operation when he acquired the estate.[560] But this proposition is subject to the general principle that in the case of nuisances which do not cause physical damage but interfere with comfort and amenity, the local character of the neighbourhood is relevant in determining liability.[561]

Limits In *Coventry v Lawrence*[562] Lord Neuberger suggested, obiter, that the proposition that it is no defence that the claimant came to the nuisance should not apply if the defendant's activity had not constituted a nuisance to the claimant's predecessors and only interfered with the claimant's enjoyment of his land because of changes in his usage of his own land made *after* the commencement of the defendant's criticised activity. In such circumstances the defendant's previous usage might be treated "as part of the character of the neighbourhood". Lord Neuberger said[563]: 19-110

> "... where a claimant builds on, or changes the use of, her land, I would suggest that it may well be wrong to hold that a defendant's pre-existing activity gives rise to a nuisance provided that (i) it can only be said to be a nuisance because it affects the senses of those on the claimant's land, (ii) it was not a nuisance before the building or change of use of the claimant's land, (iii) it is and has been, a reasonable and otherwise lawful use of the defendant's land, (iv) it is carried out in a reasonable way, and (v) it causes no greater nuisance than when the claimant first carried out the building or changed the use."

The proposition that it is no defence that the claimant came to the nuisance has no application in cases of landlord and tenant in respect of the state of the premises at the time of the demise, since the lessee is deemed to take the premises as they are.[564]

Nuisance one of many It is no defence to prove that the act of the defendant by itself is not a nuisance and only becomes a nuisance when combined with that of others.[565] The conduct of the defendant is not to be considered in isolation; the reasonableness of his conduct is assessable with reference to the conduct of others.[566] Where two rival proprietors of merry-go-rounds, each of which had an organ, carried on their businesses near to the claimant's house, an injunction was granted, Chitty J saying, "If the acts of two persons, each being aware of what the other is doing, amount in the aggregate to what is an actionable wrong, each is amenable to the remedy against the aggregate cause of complaint".[567] This is so, even if the act of one of them is enough of itself to amount to an actionable wrong, the other in that event being also liable, although his proportion of damages will be less: 19-111

---

560 *St Helens Smelting Co v Tipping* (1865) 11 H.L.C. 642.

561 See para.19-13.

562 [2014] UKSC 13; [2014] A.C. 822 at [53]–[55].

563 [2014] UKSC 13; [2014] A.C. 822 at [56].

564 *Baxter v Camden LBC* [2001] Q.B. 1 CA at 15, per Tuckey LJ and at 19, per Stuart-Smith LJ; affirmed [2001] 1 A.C. 1 HL. See also *Jackson v JH Watson Property Investment Ltd* [2008] EWHC 14 (Ch); [2008] Env. L.R. 30; [2008] 11 E.G. 94.

565 *Thorpe v Brumfit* (1873) L.R. 8 Ch. 650 at 656, per James LJ; *Blair and Sumner v Deakin* (1887) 57 L.T. 522; *Polsue and Alfieri v Rushmer* [1907] A.C. 121.

566 This important principle of the law of nuisance appears to have been overlooked in two decisions of the High Court in which defendants were exonerated, despite contributing materially to the harm suffered by the claimants, on the ground that "but for" the contribution of others their activities would not have amounted to a nuisance: see *Chetwynd v Tunmore* [2016] EWHC 156 (QB); [2017] Q.B. 188; and *Bell v Northumbrian Water Ltd* [2016] EWHC 133 (TCC), sed quaere.

567 *Lambton v Mellish* [1894] 3 Ch. 163.

> "I cannot believe that the law, while holding all of a number of defendants liable if none of them individually commits an actionable wrong, will relieve all the rest if the wrong of one of them is big enough to be by itself actionable."[568]

19-112 **Jus tertii** To plead that a third party has a better title than the claimant to land affected by a nuisance is not a defence. It has been so held in actions for interference with a servitude[569] and it would seem that this is so with regard to nuisances generally, since the wrong is an interference with the rights of the occupier as such.[570]

7. PARTICULAR TYPES OF NUISANCE

(a) Nuisance to water rights

19-113 **Water rights** Nuisance to a natural stream may consist in causing an alteration of (a) the quantity; or (b) the quality of the stream. "Every riparian proprietor is entitled to the water of his stream, in its natural flow, without sensible diminution or increase and without sensible alteration in its character or quality."[571] A riparian proprietor is the owner of land in actual contact with the stream, whether or not he owns the soil of the stream.[572] Riparian land, however, is not all land in the same occupation in contact with the stream, however far from the stream it may extend; it is only such land as is in reasonable proximity to the stream.[573] The abstraction of water, both surface and underground, is now regulated by statute by licence from river authorities,[574] and the landowner's rights and the rights of statutory undertakers in relation to water as set out below are now subject to licensing under statute.

(i) Taking water

19-114 **Water for riparian purposes** A riparian proprietor can take and use water from the stream for ordinary purposes connected with the riparian land, that is, for domestic purposes and the wants of his cattle, even to the exhaustion of the whole supply.[575] For extraordinary purposes, that is, for any other purposes connected with the riparian land, he may only take and use so much water as not sensibly to diminish the flow or alter the character of the water; even in such a case, the water must be used for a reasonable purpose connected with the riparian land and restored substantially undiminished in volume and unaltered in character.[576] Irrigation is an extraordinary purpose in this connection.[577] Thus, extraction from a river of over 10 per cent of the flow in order to spray crops etc has been prohibited by injunc-

---

568 per Harman J in *Pride of Derby v British Celanese* [1952] 1 All E.R. 1326 at 1333; affirmed on other grounds [1953] Ch. 149.

569 *Nicholls v Ely Beet Sugar Factory* [1931] 2 Ch. 84.

570 *Newcastle-under-Lyme Corp v Wolstanton* [1947] Ch. 92 at 109–110, per Evershed J; see also *Hunter v Canary Wharf Ltd* [1997] A.C. 655 at 688, per Lord Goff.

571 *Young v Bankier Distillery* [1893] A.C. 691 at 698, per Lord Macnaghten.

572 *Lyon v Fishmongers' Co* (1876) 1 App. Cas. 662.

573 *Attwood v Llay Main Collieries* [1926] Ch. 444.

574 Water Resources Act 1991 Pt II. See also *British Waterways Board v National Rivers Authority* [1992] N.P.C. 100 CA.

575 *Miner v Gilmour* (1858) 12 Moo. P.C. 131 at 156.

576 *McCartney v Londonderry Ry* [1904] A.C. 301; *Miner v Gilmour* (1858) 12 Moo. P.C. 131 at 156; *Baily v Morland* [1902] 1 Ch. 649.

577 *Embrey v Owen* (1851) 6 Ex. 353; *Swindon Waterworks Co v Wilts Canal Co* (1875) L.R. 7 HL 697.

tion at the instance of a lower riparian owner, but that injunction was not extended to the use of water collected by the defendant in a reservoir fed by surface drainage and not part of a watercourse.[578]

Water for non-riparian purposes For purposes unconnected with the riparian land, the riparian proprietor has no right to take any water from the stream. The abstraction of water to supply a town,[579] to fill boilers of locomotive engines,[580] and to work machinery at a colliery, have been restrained on this ground.[581] But the abstraction of water and its subsequent return, unpolluted and undiminished in volume, at a point above the claimant's land is not actionable.[582] 19-115

(ii) Interference with flow

Interference with the flow of a stream The riparian owner may sue for public nuisance where the depth of water is so reduced as to impede or obstruct the navigable use of a river to his particular disadvantage and damage. But as a matter of private nuisance he has no right to object to an alteration of the depth of the water which does not threaten to cause damage to his land or to interfere with his acknowledged riparian rights or to cause a nuisance to the occupier of the land. Thus where the defendants in *Tate & Lyle v Greater London Council*[583] reduced the depth of water in the Thames, they were held not liable for a private nuisance, because the interference was only with the use of the river, not with the use of the claimant's jetties.[584] With regard to his duties a riparian proprietor who interferes with the flow of a stream so as to increase the burden or diminish the benefit of the flow to another proprietor commits a nuisance.[585] The interference may consist in altering the bed of the stream,[586] erecting a mound of earth on his land so as to cause the stream in time of flood to be diverted from its ordinary flood channel and flow on to the land of another proprietor,[587] interrupting the regularity of the flow by penning back the water, or otherwise.[588] 19-116

Rights and duties of riparian owner A riparian owner, however, is entitled to heighten the banks on his land so as to prevent flood water from coming on to it, 19-117

There are special provisions as to spray irrigation in the Water Resources Act 1991 s.57.

578 *Rugby Joint Water Board v Walters* [1967] Ch. 397. An example of "abnormal agricultural use" would be converting part of a farm into a trout-hatchery: *Cargill v Gotts* [1981] 1 W.L.R. 441 at 451, per Lawton LJ.

579 *Swindon Waterworks Co v Wilts Canal Co* (1875) L.R. 7 HL 697; *Roberts v Gwyrfai RDC* [1899] 2 Ch. 608.

580 *McCartney v Londonderry Ry* [1904] A.C. 301.

581 *Attwood v Llay Main Collieries* [1926] Ch. 444. Other examples are: *Stollmeyer v Trinidad Lake Petroleum Co* [1918] A.C. 485; *Ormerod v Todmorden Mill Co* (1883) 11 Q.B.D. 155.

582 *Kensit v Great Eastern Ry* (1884) 27 Ch. D. 122.

583 [1983] 2 A.C. 509 HL.

584 It was held that the siltation did not interfere with the defendant's use and occupation of the jetties (sed quaere, on the facts, that reducing depth did not affect such use). The jetties were, in the circumstances of this case, not part of the claimant's realty and thus not a part of the river bank to which riparian rights attached. But physical damage to land by flooding or erosion could amount to a private nuisance.

585 *Orr-Ewing v Colquhoun* (1877) 2 App. Cas. 839.

586 *Fear v Vickers* (1911) 27 T.L.R. 558.

587 *Menzies v Breadalbane* (1828) 3 Bli. (N.S.) 414; *Bickett v Morris* (1866) L.R. 1 Sc. 47; *Marriage v E Norfolk Catchment Board* [1949] 2 K.B. 456.

588 *Sampson v Hoddinott* (1857) 1 C.B. (N.S.) 590; *Roberts v Gwyrfai RDC* [1899] 2 Ch. 60.

even though this has the effect of diverting the flood water on to the land of another.[589] When a public authority, in exercise of their duty as highway authority, inserted a new culvert in a stream, thereby altering the bed of the stream, with the result that the flow of water to a mill was diminished, it was held that they were liable unless they were able to prove that it was not practically feasible for them to perform their statutory duty without diminishing the flow of the stream.[590] A riparian proprietor may dam up the stream for the purpose of a mill, as long as he does not interfere with the rights of other proprietors, either above or below him; but if the dam forms a pond, he does not acquire the right to the exclusive use of the whole of the water in the pond.[591] A riparian proprietor may not place a weir impervious to fish across a non-navigable river, so as to obstruct the passage of fish up the river.[592] Similarly, the owner of land on which there is a spring forming the source of a natural stream has no right to diminish the flow of the stream by intercepting the water at the spring.[593] Moreover, a riparian proprietor is under a duty of care, as defined in *Leakey v National Trust*,[594] to keep the bed of the stream clear, by cutting weeds which have grown in the bed or by removing silt or stones which have accumulated. In *Bybrook Barn Centre v Kent CC*,[595] the Court of Appeal held that surrounding natural changes can turn an originally unobjectionable installation into a nuisance.[596]

(iii) Pollution

19-118 **Pollution of stream** A riparian proprietor may be restrained from altering the natural quality of the water in the stream by polluting it,[597] raising its temperature,[598] or changing it from soft water to hard.[599] It is not necessary to prove actual damage to a lower riparian proprietor.[600] When pollution occurs, it is no defence to show that the stream is also polluted by other persons.[601]

19-119 **Sewage** A local authority which discharges crude sewage from one of its sewers into a stream can be restrained by injunction from doing so on the action of a ripar-

589 *Gerrard v Crowe* [1921] 1 A.C. 395; *R. v Pagham, Sussex Sewers Comrs* (1828) 8 B. & C. 355; *Nield v L & NW Ry* (1874) L.R. 10 Ex. 4.

590 *Provender Millers (Winchester) v Southampton CC* [1940] Ch. 131.

591 *White v White* [1906] A.C. 72.

592 *Weld v Hornby* (1806) 7 East 195; *Leconfield v Lonsdale* (1870) L.R. 5 C. & P. 657.

593 *Mostyn v Atherton* [1899] 2 Ch. 360.

594 [1980] Q.B. 485, CA. See para.19-21 (overruling *Neath RDC v Williams* [1951] 1 K.B. 115: see per O'Connor J in *Leakey* at first instance [1978] Q.B. 849).

595 [2001] Env. L.R. 30; [2001] B.L.R. 55.

596 In the light of this decision the earlier case of *Radstock Co-operative and Industrial Society v Norton-Radstock Urban DC* [1968] Ch. 605, in which the Court of Appeal declined to impose liability when a sewer pipe became an obstruction due to natural changes in the flow of a river, would probably now be decided differently.

597 *Wood v Waud* (1849) 3 Exch. 748; *Sharp v Wilson Rotheray & Co* (1905) 93 L.T. 155; *Jones v Llanrwst Urban DC* [1911] 1 Ch. 393; *Pride of Derby v British Celanese Ltd* [1952] 2 All E.R. 1326; affirmed on other grounds [1953] Ch. 149.

598 *Mason v Hill* (1832) 5 B. & A. 1; *Ormerod v Todmorden Mill Co* (1883) 11 Q.B.D. 155; *Tipping v Eckersley* (1855) 2 K. & J. 264; *Pride of Derby v British Celanese* [1952] 2 All E.R. 1326.

599 *Young v Bankier Distillery* [1893] A.C. 691.

600 *Crossley & Sons Ltd v Lightowler* (1867) L.R. 2 Ch. 478; *Pennington v Brinsop Hall Coal Co* (1877) 5 Ch. D. 769.

601 *Wood v Waud* (1849) 3 Exch. 748; *Crossley & Sons Ltd v Lightowler* (1867) L.R. 2 Ch. 478; *Harrington v Derby Corp* [1905] 1 Ch. 205.

ian owner.[602] In *Dobson v Thames Water Utilities*[603] liability in damages was imposed upon the defendants for an odour nuisance caused by the negligent operation of their sewage treatment works. The pollution of rivers, including the discharge of sewage without a permit, will also attract criminal sanctions.[604]

(iv) Underground and artificial water flow

Underground water Water flowing underground in a defined channel is a natural stream to which the law of surface streams is applicable.[605] Water percolating underground in no defined channel or in a channel which, though defined, can only be ascertained by excavation is subject to a different rule.[606] It is not actionable to intercept or otherwise interfere with the percolation of such water, even though the benefit of the percolation has been enjoyed for the period of prescription.[607] Therefore, a person who sinks a well on his own land, with the consequence of diminishing the volume of a stream by intercepting the water which had formerly percolated into the stream, commits no actionable wrong.[608] Every person may appropriate the whole of the water percolating under his land, "even though the consequence may be that he takes not only the water which at first was under his property, but all the adjoining water which by natural force comes under his land when he has taken that which was there in the first instance".[609] Accordingly, it is not actionable to intercept the percolation of water into the claimant's well,[610] or to cause water which has already collected on the claimant's land, as in a well, to percolate away from it.[611] The motive with which the defendant so intercepts the water is immaterial. If a landowner sinks a tunnel on his land, the effect of which is to cut off the underground water supply from his neighbour, no action will lie, even though his object was not to benefit his own land but to extort money from his neighbour by forcing him to buy him out at his own price.[612] There is no right to have land or water supported by water.[613] Therefore to pump out percolating water from excavations and thereby to cause damage to a neighbour's building by ground subsidence is not actionable as a nuisance,[614] and this is so whether an 19-120

602 *Haigh v Deudraeth RDC* [1945] 2 All E.R. 661. On liability for nuisances caused by sewage see generally *Dobson v Thames Water Utilities* [2007] EWHC 2021 (TCC); [2008] 2 All E.R. 362, per Ramsey J; *Dobson v Thames Water Utilities* [2009] EWCA Civ 28; [2009] 3 All E.R. 319.

603 [2011] EWHC 3253 (TCC); (2011) 140 Con. L.R. 135.

604 See the Pollution Prevention and Control Act 1999 s.2; and the Environmental Permitting (England and Wales) Regulations 2016 (SI 2016/1154) regs 12(1) and 38.

605 *Chasemore v Richards* (1859) 7 H.L.C. 349.

606 *Bradford Corp v Ferrand* [1902] 2 Ch. 655; *Bleachers' Association v Chapel-en-le-Frith Urban DC* [1933] Ch. 356.

607 *Chasemore v Richards* (1859) 7 H.L.C. 349.

608 *Chasemore v Richards* (1859) 7 H.L.C. 349.

609 per Cotton LJ in *Ballard v Tomlinson* (1885) Ch. D. 115 at 123; *Hubbs v Prince Edward County* (1957) 8 D.L.R. (2d) 394 (liability in nuisance and negligence; defendants placed chemically treated sand on their land adjoining plaintiff's; it seeped into and contaminated claimant's well).

610 *Acton v Blundell* (1843) 12 M. & W. 324.

611 *New River Co v Johnson* (1860) 2 E. & E. 435; *Acton v Blundell* (1843) 12 M. & W. 324.

612 *Bradford Corp v Pickles* [1895] A.C. 587.

613 *Popplewell v Hodkinson* (1869) L.R. 4 Ex. 248; *Jordeson v Sutton etc Gas Co* [1899] 2 Ch. 217; *English v Metropolitan Water Board* [1907] 1 K.B. 588; *Chetwynd v Tunmore* [2016] EWHC 156 (QB); [2017] Q.B. 188.

614 *Langbrook Properties Ltd v Surrey CC* [1970] 1 W.L.R. 161. See para.19-141.

injured party claims in nuisance or in negligence. There is no duty of care to a neighbour, in abstracting percolating water, to avoid causing subsidence.[615]

19-121 **Percolation downhill** Where water percolates underground downhill the lower occupier cannot complain of the influx of that water from the upper and adjacent tenement. In *Palmer v Bowman*[616] the Court of Appeal held that since the drainage of naturally occurring water from higher to lower land, in undefined channels, is itself a process of nature, it follows that no easement is required to justify such drainage. In holding that the occupier of lower land cannot complain of such natural discharges of water, the Court of Appeal followed the reasoning of the High Court in *Home Brewery Plc v William Davis & Co (Loughborough) Ltd*.[617] In that case the High Court had also held, however, that the occupier of the lower land is under no obligation to receive the influx and may bar it or pen it back, even if this causes damage to the higher occupier, provided that the barring or rejection is not an unreasonable use of the lower land. Thus the infilling of claypits on lower land for the purpose of developing the site for residential dwellings was held a reasonable use and the consequent harm by impeding the natural drainage was not an actionable nuisance.[618] On the facts of *Palmer v Bowman*, however, it was unnecessary for the Court of Appeal to decide whether the actual decision in the *Home Brewery* case, to the effect that the occupier of the higher land nevertheless cannot complain if the lower occupier impedes the natural flow by making reasonable use of his own land, was correct. The court emphasised that it expressed no view on that question.[619]

19-122 **Fouling underground water supply** Although there can be no property in percolating water, an action will lie against one who fouls the water supply existing in the underground strata, so that the water reaches the claimant in an impure condition.[620] In *Cambridge Water Co Ltd v Eastern Counties Leather Plc*,[621] however, the House of Lords held that this liability is not strict but is based on foreseeability of the fouling occurring. The House therefore decided, reversing the Court of Appeal, that the accidental spillage of chemicals which eventually seeped, unforeseeably, through the floor of the defendant's premises and into percolating water beneath, did not give rise to liability.

19-123 **Artificial watercourses** The rights of riparian owners over the water of an artificial watercourse are based upon an agreement, express or presumed from the user, between them. To ascertain these rights there should be taken into account the character of the watercourse, whether it is temporary or permanent, the circumstances under which it was presumably created and the mode in which it has in fact

---

615 *Stephens v Anglian Water Authority* [1987] 1 W.L.R. 1381 CA. At 382, Slade LJ gives a summary of the law of subjacent support to the surface. See comment by Fleming in (1988) 104 L.Q.R. 183 citing American and Canadian cases and questioning the application of the rule on the loss of water to the case of causing loss of support. To abstract water to the claimant's loss is a different kind of injury from causing his land or buildings to collapse.

616 [2000] 1 W.L.R. 842.

617 [1987] Q.B. 339.

618 See also *Court v Van Dijk* [2016] EWCA Civ 483.

619 See per Rattee J, with whom Aldous and Auld LJJ agreed, in [2000] 1 W.L.R. 842 at 855.

620 *Womersley v Church* (1867) 17 L.T. 190; *Snow v Whitehead* (1884) 27 Ch. D. 588; *Ballard v Tomlinson* (1885) 29 Ch. D. 115.

621 [1994] 2 A.C. 264.

been used and enjoyed.[622] The proper inference from all the facts may be that the riparian owners have the rights that they would have had over the water of a natural watercourse.[623]

(b) Liability in respect of damage caused by escaping water

(i) Common law

Liability in respect of water Liability in respect of water depends on whether the water is naturally on the land or whether it is artificially accumulated or interfered with in some way.[624] The owner of land on a lower level cannot complain of water naturally flowing or percolating to his land from a higher level.[625] Nevertheless, the higher proprietor is liable if he deliberately drains his land on to his lower neighbour's land,[626] and this appears to be so if the water is caused to flow in a more concentrated form than it naturally would as the result of artificial alterations in the levels and contours of the higher land.[627] Nor is it permissible to drain water on to another's land so as to affect the quality as well as the quantity of the water in a way injurious to its use at the lower level.[628] But if rainwater happens to overflow on to the claimant's land, as a result of an obstruction on the defendant's land, there will be no liability providing that the obstruction did not constitute non-natural user and that what occurred had not been foreseeable.[629] **19-124**

Barriers Although the lower proprietor cannot complain of the natural unconcentrated flow of percolating water from a higher land: **19-125**

> "he may put up barriers and pen it back, notwithstanding that doing so damages the upper proprietor's land, at all events if he uses reasonable care and skill and does no more than is reasonably necessary to protect his enjoyment of his own land. But he must not act for the purposes of injuring his neighbour."[630]

Thus, where a lower proprietor filled in clay-pits for building houses on the site, thereby barring the natural drainage from the land of the higher proprietor, it was held that this was a reasonable user of the site and that the higher proprietor had

---

622 *Wood v Waud* (1849) 3 Exch. 748; *Baily v Clark* [1902] 1 Ch. 649.

623 *Sutcliffe v Booth* (1863) 32 L.J.Q.B. 136; *Maung Bya v Maung Kyi Nyo* (1925) L.R. 52 Ind. App. 385.

624 In the Australian case of *Gartner v Kidman* (1962) 36 A.L.J.R. 43; (1961-1962) 108 C.L.R. 12 there is a review of the cases on the flow of surface water, especially, per Windeyer J, 108 C.L.R. 12 at 23–24 and 47–49, on the flow of natural surface water, as contrasted with the flow of watercourses or of artificially accumulated water. But cf. *Ellison v Ministry of Defence* (1996) 81 B.L.R. 101 in which the actual decision in *Gartner v Kidman* was not applied.

625 *Palmer v Bowman* [2000] 1 W.L.R. 842; [2000] 1 All E.R. 22 CA.

626 *Thomas v Gower RDC* [1922] 2 K.B. 76; *Foster v Warblington Urban DC* [1906] 1 K.B. 648.

627 See para.19-131.

628 In *John Young & Co v The Bankier Distillery Co* [1893] A.C. 691, a colliery pumped hard water into a soft-water burn to the detriment of the distillery, and were subject to an interdict. (On riparian rights English and Scottish law is the same, per Lord Shand at 701.)

629 See *Arscott v Coal Authority* [2004] EWCA Civ 892; [2005] Env. L.R. 6 CA. For a case in which liability was imposed upon a highway authority for failure to prevent foreseeable flooding see *Vernon Knight Associates v Cornwall Council* [2013] EWCA Civ 950; [2013] B.L.R. 519 (paras 7-183 and 19-22). See also *Ellison v Ministry of Defence* (1996) 81 B.L.R. 101 (in which the authorities are examined).

630 per Windeyer J in *Gartner v Kidman* (1961-1962) 108 C.L.R. 12 at 48–49.

no cause of action for ensuing damage.[631]

19-126 **Diversion of natural stream** A person who diverts a natural stream does so at his peril, and is liable under the rule in *Rylands v Fletcher*, subject to the "defences" available to the rule, for any damage caused by the failure of his works to contain the diverted stream:

> "It is the duty of anyone who interferes with the course of a natural stream to see that the works which he substitutes for the channel provided by nature are adequate to carry off the water brought down even by extraordinary rainfall, and if damage results from the deficiency of the substitute which he had provided for the natural channel he will be liable."[632]

In *Greenock Corp v Caledonian Ry*,[633] the Greenock corporation, in laying out a park, altered the course of a natural stream so as to make a paddling pond for children. Owing to an extraordinary rainfall the stream overflowed at the pond and the accumulated water damaged the railway company's property. The corporation were held liable on the principle stated above. On the other hand, if there has been no diversion of the stream, but the stream has overflowed and the water has accumulated against a wall or other erection which bursts under the pressure of water and does damage, the owner of the wall is not liable.[634] If a natural stream is enclosed in a culvert, the owner of the culvert must maintain it so as to prevent the stream from damaging neighbouring property.[635] The owner of a wall fronting on a river is under no obligation to maintain the wall for the benefit of other landowners, and if he pulls it down so that the river in flood goes on the adjoining land he is not liable.[636]

19-127 **When liability will not be imposed** Even if a stream is diverted, there will be no liability if it can be shown that the injured party would have suffered the same damage if the stream had not been diverted.[637] Again, if the diversion has been "fortified by prescription", the person injured cannot allege that another state of things is the true state of nature.[638]

---

631 *Home Brewery Plc v William Davis & Co (Loughborough) Ltd* [1987] Q.B. 339, the judgment of Piers Ashworth QC containing a full discussion of the authorities. See also *Ryeford Homes v Sevenoaks DC* (1989) 16 Con. L.R. 75. But cf. *Palmer v Bowman* [2000] 1 W.L.R. 842; [2000] 1 All E.R. 22 and para.19-121.

632 per Lord Finlay LC in *Greenock Corp v Caledonian Ry* [1917] A.C. 566 at 572. Whether a diversion has actually caused any flooding alleged to have resulted from it can give rise to difficult questions of fact; see, e.g. *Davies v Campfield* [2017] EWHC 2746 (Ch).

633 [1917] A.C. 566; approving *Kerr v Earl of Orkney* (1857) 20 D. 298; and distinguishing *Nichols v Marsland* (1876) 2 Ex. D. 1, on the ground that it was based on a jury's finding of fact, with doubt whether the finding was correct (per Lord Parker at 581) and regarding the case as unsatisfactory (per Lord Shaw at 580). Scrutton LJ in *Att Gen v Cory Bros* (1919) 35 T.L.R. 570, thought *Nichols v Marsland* difficult to reconcile with *Rylands v Fletcher*.

634 *Tennent v Earl of Glasgow* (1864) 2 M. 22 HL.

635 *Booth v Thomas* [1926] Ch. 109, per Russell J; affirmed on other grounds [1926] Ch. 397; *Pemberton v Bright and the Devon CC* [1960] 1 W.L.R. 436 CA. See also *Bybrook Barn Centre v Kent CC* [2001] B.L.R. 55; [2001] Env. L.R. 30 CA.

636 *Thomas and Evans Ltd v Mid-Rhondda Co-operative Soc* [1941] 1 K.B. 381.

637 *Greenock Corp v Caledonian Ry* [1917] A.C. 556. *Workman v GN Ry* (1863) 32 L.J.Q.B. 279; *Nitro-Phosphate and Odam's Chemical Manure Co v London and St Katherine's Docks* (1878) 9 Ch. D. 503; *Baldwin's Ltd v Halifax Corp* (1916) 85 L.J.K.B. 1769 at 1774.

638 See previous note.

Water in mines In the case of adjoining mine-owners the owner of the mine on a lower level cannot complain of water which naturally gravitates into his mine from a mine at a higher level. In *Smith v Kenrick*,[639] where the claimant and the defendant were the owners of adjoining mines, the defendant worked a horizontal bar of coal which had the effect of causing a body of water which had naturally accumulated in his mine to go into the claimant's mine. The defendant was held not liable, on the ground that it was: 19-128

> "the natural right of each of the owners of two adjoining coal mines, neither being subject to any servitude to the other, to work his own in the manner most convenient and beneficial to himself, although the natural consequence may be that some prejudice will accrue to the owner of the adjoining mine, so long as that does not arise from the negligence or malicious conduct of the party."

The essence of *Smith v Kenrick* is that there was no artificial accumulation of the escaping water, only a reasonable user of land affecting the drainage flow underground.[640] On the other hand, a deliberate discharge of surplus water may incur liability[641] because there is an active interference, for example by pumping. The law as to operations on the surface is not different from that applicable to operations underground.[642]

Natural accumulation in rivers and streams There are cases[643] which hold that the owner of the bed of a river is under no obligation to dredge it, so that if it becomes choked with the natural growth of weeds and the accumulation of silt as a consequence of which it overflows, he is not liable for the damage. But it seems likely that the qualified duty of care recognised in *Leakey v National Trust*[644] now applies to natural water courses. There is no immunity for the owner and he has a duty of care to control overflows, the standard of care being measured by his individual capability and resources. 19-129

Accumulating water A person who accumulates water by way of non-natural user is bound to keep it from doing damage at his peril. The manner in which the water is accumulated is immaterial: whether it is collected in a reservoir, a pipe, a canal, a drain, or a mound of earth, the person collecting it is liable for its escape without any proof of negligence. In *Rylands v Fletcher*[645] itself the defendants caused a reservoir to be constructed on their land. The water so collected flowed into the claimants' mine and caused damage, and the defendants were held liable on the ground that they kept the water on their land at their peril. On the other hand, in *Transco v Stockport MBC*[646] the House of Lords held that the running of water through a large service pipe did *not* give rise to liability under the rule, even though the pipe was very much greater in size than an ordinary domestic water pipe. Liability was, however, imposed when a company laid hydraulic mains, which burst 19-130

---

639 (1849) 7 C.B. 515.

640 The judgment in the *Home Brewery case* [1987] Q.B. 339 at 642, sounds a note of caution about the principle in *Smith v Kenrick* "in its widest application". See para.19-20, for the changing attitude of the law to natural nuisances, and para.19-129.

641 *Baird v Williamson* (1863) 15 C.B. (N.S.) 376.

642 *Whalley v Lancashire and Yorkshire Ry* (1884) 13 Q.B.D. 131.

643 *Hodgson v York Corp* (1873) 28 L.T. 836; *Neath RDC v Williams* [1951] 1 K.B. 115.

644 [1980] Q.B. 485. See para.19-21.

645 (1868) L.R. 3 HL 330.

646 [2003] UKHL 61; [2004] 2 A.C. 1.

without any negligence on the part of the company, and damaged some electric cables.[647] Similarly, when a watercourse was constructed for the purpose of bringing water to a mill, and, owing to the shuttle which regulated the flow of water from the river into the watercourse getting out of repair, the watercourse overflowed and caused damage, the owner of the watercourse was held liable.[648] His liability was not affected by the fact that he had granted to the claimant a right to use the water for a mill belonging to the claimant.

19-131 **Construction work** Again, where a local authority constructed a road on the side of a hill so that it acted as a catch-water for rain from the upper slopes, and in a heavy rain the water flowed over the road into the valley beneath and damaged the claimant's mills, the local authority were held liable.[649] Where the occupier of land placed a quantity of earth against the wall of his building, so as to cause rainwater to percolate through the wall of his neighbour, he was held liable on the ground that, "if any one by artificial erection on his own land causes water, even though arising from natural rainfall only, to pass into his neighbour's land, and thus substantially to interfere with his enjoyment, he will be liable to an action at the suit of him who is so injured".[650] Also, when water came down the defendant's pipes and collected in his cellar, whence it percolated into the claimant's cellar, the defendant was held liable on the principle of *Rylands v Fletcher*.[651] Again, where the occupier of the upper floor of a building was engaged in the operation of washing cinematograph films, using for that purpose large quantities of circulating water, a boiler, a sink, and several containers, and the water escaped to the floor below, it was held that the case was within *Rylands v Fletcher* and the occupier of the upper floor was liable.[652]

(ii) Statutory undertakers

19-132 **Negligence and strict liability** Those bodies now concerned with water resources[653] operate under statutory powers, and at common law they are exempt from liability except on proof of negligence, unless the statute preserves their liability.[654] A very large exception to this general rule is now contained in the Water Industry Act 1991 s.209, which provides that "where an escape of water, however caused, from a pipe vested in a water undertaker causes loss or damage", then the undertaker is strictly liable.[655] It is a defence that the escape was wholly due to the claimant's fault, or that of his servant, agent or contractor, but act of God or

647 *Charing Cross Electricity Supply Co v Hydraulic Power Co* [1914] 3 K.B. 772.

648 *RH Buckley & Sons Ltd v N Buckley & Sons* [1898] 2 Q.B. 608.

649 *Baldwin's Ltd v Halifax Corp* (1916) 85 L.J.K.B. 1769. The same result would follow if an occupier of land dug a drain on his land and discharged the water, so collected, on to his neighbour's land in a concentrated flow.

650 *Hurdman v North Eastern Ry* (1878) 3 C.P.D. 168. *Broder v Saillard* (1876) 2 Ch. D. 692 is a somewhat similar case. cf. *Lambert v Barratt Homes Ltd* [2010] EWCA Civ 681; [2010] B.L.R. 527. See also *Sedleigh-Denfield v O'Callaghan* [1940] A.C. 880 (overflow from blocked culvert held to be a nuisance). *Simpson v Att Gen* [1959] N.Z.L.R. 546.

651 *Snow v Whitehead* (1884) 27 Ch. D. 588.

652 *Western Engraving Co v Film Laboratories Ltd* [1936] 1 All E.R. 106.

653 See the Water Industry Acts 1991 and 1999, and the Water Resources Act 1991.

654 *Green v Chelsea Waterworks Co* (1894) 70 L.T. 547; *Dunn v Birmingham Canal Co* (1872) L.R. 8 Q.B. 42. The Reservoirs Act 1975 s.28 Sch.2, preserves strict liability for the construction of reservoirs.

655 See also the related provision in s.82 of the New Roads and Street Works Act 1991 which similarly

independent act of a third party is no defence, and the statutory liability is therefore "far stricter than under the rule in *Rylands v Fletcher*".[656] The words "loss or damage" are, however, apparently confined to those heads of damage normally recoverable in negligence, so that the "purely non-physical is excluded from recovery",[657] and interruption with the domestic gas supply has been held to be outside the section.[658]

(iii) Sewers and drains

Rylands v Fletcher In *Jones v Llanrwst Urban DC*[659] Parker J said: 19-133

> "I think it clear that the principle of *Fletcher v Rylands* would apply to the owner of a sewer, whether he made his sewer or not. His duty at common law would be to see that the sewage in his sewer did not escape to the injury of others, and mere neglect of this duty would give any persons injured a good cause of action."

Accordingly, where the claimant and the defendant were the occupiers of adjoining houses, and a drain which commenced on the defendant's premises and, after collecting the sewage of several other houses, doubled back under the defendant's house, got out of repair so that the sewage escaped into the claimant's cellar, the defendant was held liable, although he did not know of the existence of the return drain.[660] Again, where the defendant maintained a drain on his land and the drain became choked, so that the adjoining land was flooded, he was held liable on the ground of nuisance.[661] When drains or sewers are constructed under statutory authority, there is no liability except on proof of negligence. The negligence may take place in the original construction of the works[662] or in their subsequent management.[663]

Statutory provisions When sewers are made or maintained under statutory provisions, an action will normally lie for damage caused by an overflow of the sewers, 19-134

---

imposes strict liability upon statutory undertakers in certain circumstances, but apparently does not preclude the imposition of negligence liability if the particular nature of the claimants' loss causes it to fall outside the strict liability scheme: see *Southern Gas Networks Plc v Thames Water Utilities Ltd* [2018] EWCA Civ 33; [2018] 1 W.L.R. 5977.

656 per Lord Hoffmann in *Transco v Stockport MBC* [2003] UKHL 61; [2004] 2 A.C. 1 at [42]. The Contributory Negligence Act 1945, the Fatal Accidents Act 1976, and the Limitation Act 1980 apply to the liability under the section.

657 per Stanley Burnton J *Anglian Water Services Ltd v Crawshaw Robins & Co Ltd* [2001] B.L.R. 173 at [149].

658 See *Anglian Water Services Ltd v Crawshaw Robins & Co Ltd* [2001] B.L.R. 173

659 [1911] 1 Ch. 393 at 405, cited with approval by Evershed MR in *Pride of Derby and Derbyshire Angling Association v British Celanese Ltd* [1953] Ch. 149. But though bulk sewage may attract strict liability it may well be doubted whether sewage in an ordinary domestic scale is within the rule of *Rylands v Fletcher*, on the analogy of domestic water supplies; para.19-135.

660 *Humphries v Cousins* (1877) 2 C.P.D. 239. In *Ilford Urban DC v Beal* [1925] 1 K.B. 671, Branson J pointed out that the defendant must have known that there was a drain carrying away his own sewage, although he may have been ignorant of the return drain. If he neither knew nor ought to have known the existence of the drain, he would not have been liable.

661 *Sedleigh-Denfield v O'Callaghan* [1940] A.C. 880; *Pemberton v Bright and the Devon CC* [1960] 1 W.L.R. 436 CA.

662 *Collins v Middle Level Commrs* (1869) L.R. 4 C. & P. 279; *Harrison v GN Ry* (1864) 3 H. & C. 231.

663 *Dixon v Metropolitan Board of Works* (1881) 7 Q.B.D. 418. (Flood caused by the opening of water-gate at outfall of sewer. Defendants not liable because gate was constructed to let out water in case of heavy rain.)

if the overflow was due to the original negligent construction of the sewers[664] or to a subsequent negligent act on the part of the sewage authority, as by sending sewage from one sewer into another already overcharged with sewage.[665] The omission to enlarge the capacity of the sewer to enable it to deal with an increase of population, so that a flood occurs, does not give rise to an action for negligence or nuisance at common law if the sewage authority has taken the sewers over from some predecessor.[666] This proposition was confirmed by the House of Lords in *Marcic v Thames Water Utilities*.[667] In a case of this nature, the appropriate remedy is instead complaint to the Water Services Regulation Authority pursuant to the Water Resources Act 2003.[668] If the sewage authority has itself constructed the sewers and has failed to enlarge them so as to meet the growing needs of their district, whether it is liable for the damage caused by an overflow depends on the true construction of the statute imposing the duty to sewer. The imposition of liability for negligent failure to operate a sewage works will not necessarily conflict with the statutory scheme for regulation by the Water Services Regulation Authority: whether it does so will depend upon the extent to which issues of policy or capital expenditure were involved.[669] Even if it is not liable in negligence the sewage authority may be liable in nuisance if it caused, continued or adopted the nuisance.[670] Liability for damages for breach of statutory duty will not, however, be imposed unless the usual requirements for such a claim are satisfied.[671] In *Dwr Cymru Cyfyngedig (Welsh Water) v Barratt Homes Ltd*[672] the Court of Appeal held that s.106 of the Water Industry Act 1991, which obliges water companies to permit access to its sewers, does not give rise to a claim for damages for breach of statutory duty if the company fails to comply with it. An occupier wrongfully denied access can, however, obtain redress in public law by an application to the court to compel it.[673]

---

664 *Fleming v Manchester Corp* (1881) 44 L.T. 517; *Brown v Sargent* (1858) 1 F. & F. 112.

665 *Dent v Bournemouth Corp* (1897) 66 L.J.Q.B. 395.

666 *Pride of Derby and Derbyshire Angling Association v British Celanese Ltd* [1953] Ch. 149; *Smeaton v Ilford Corp* [1954] Ch. 450; *Lawrysyn v Town of Kipling* (1965) 48 D.L.R. (2d) 660; affirmed in (1966) 55 D.L.R. (2d) 471.

667 [2003] UKHL 66; [2004] 2 A.C. 42. For an analysis of the relationship between statute and common law in the reasoning of the House of Lords in *Marcic v Thames Water Utilities see Southern Gas Networks Plc v Thames Water Utilities Ltd* [2018] EWCA Civ 33; [2018] 1 W.L.R. 5977 at [81], per Hickinbottom LJ. See also para.19-77.

668 The Water Services Regulation Authority replaced the former Director General of Water Services (see the Water Industry Act 1991 s.1A, inserted by the Water Act 2003 s.34). For cases on equivalent earlier statutory provisions see *Stretton's Derby Brewery Co v Derby Corp* [1894] 1 Ch. 431; *Robinson v Workington Corp* [1897] 1 Q.B. 619; *Hesketh v Birmingham Corp* [1924] 1 K.B. 260.

669 See *Dobson v Thames Water Utilities* [2007] EWHC 2021 (TCC); [2008] 2 All E.R. 362 (subsequently appealed: see [2009] EWCA Civ 28; [2009] 3 All E.R. 319, but there was no appeal on this point). For the trial of the action in this case see *Dobson v Thames Water Utilities* [2011] EWHC 3253 (TCC); (2011) 140 Con. L.R. 135 in which liability at common law for an odour nuisance was imposed.

670 *Smeaton v Ilford Corp* [1954] Ch. 450.

671 See Ch.8.

672 [2013] EWCA Civ 233; [2013] 1 W.L.R. 3486.

673 See *Barratt Homes Ltd v Dwr Cymru Cyfyngedig (Welsh Water)* [2009] UKSC 13; [2010] 1 All E.R. 965 (decided in earlier proceedings between the same parties).

(iv) *Storage and piping*

Escape of water collected on roof and in cisterns One of the exceptions to the principle of *Rylands v Fletcher* is when the water or other dangerous thing is collected or brought into existence with the consent of the claimant or for the common benefit of the claimant and the defendant.[674] The authorities on this topic were reviewed by the Court of Appeal in *Prosser & Sons Ltd v Levy*.[675] This exception prevents the occupier of a flat from recovering damages for loss he has sustained owing to defective gutters or spouts, or for leaks from cisterns or other parts of the ordinary domestic apparatus of a house, unless he can prove negligence. When a landlord lets a flat to a tenant, keeping the roof and gutters under his own control, he is not liable for flooding caused by the gutter or spout becoming blocked except on proof of negligence[676]; but if he omits to have the gutter or spout cleared within a reasonable time after notice he will be liable.[677] When a shop in an arcade was let to a tenant, and water from the roof of the arcade got into the shop owing to an accumulation of rubbish in the pipe by which the water was carried into the sewer, it was held that the landlord was not liable in the absence of negligence, as the arrangements for carrying the water from the glass roof to the sewer were for the joint benefit of the tenant and the landlord.[678] 19-135

Negligence in relation to cisterns If the landlord retains control of a cistern for the supply of water to flats in his building, he is not liable to his tenants for a burst in one of the water pipes,[679] or an escape of water from the cistern, unless he is negligent.[680] The occupier of the flat in which the cistern is kept is also free from liability in the absence of negligence. Where a water-closet in an upper floor got out of order, without any negligence on the part of the occupier of the upper floor, and flooded the lower floor, the occupier of the upper floor was held not liable to the occupier of the floor below.[681] If water from a burst pipe in one flat causes damage to another flat in the same building, the occupier of the first flat is not liable without negligence.[682] 19-136

674 *Att Gen v Cory Bros* [1921] 1 A.C. 521 at 539.

675 [1955] 1 W.L.R. 1224; *Gilson v Kerrier DC* [1976] 1 W.L.R. 904 at 912–914. See also *Colour Quest Ltd v Total Downstream UK Plc* [2009] EWHC 540 (Comm); [2009] 2 Lloyd's Rep. 1; reversed in part in [2010] EWCA Civ 180; [2011] Q.B. 86.

676 *Gill v Edouin* (1984) 71 L.T. 762; *Bishop v Consolidated London Properties* (1933) 102 L.J.K.B. 257, where a pigeon blocked an open gutter causing an overflow, and the landlord was held liable.

677 *Hargroves & Co v Hartopp* [1905] 1 K.B. 472; *Cockburn v Smith* [1924] 2 K.B. 119; cf. *Jackson v JH Watson Property Investment Ltd* [2008] EWHC 14 (Ch); [2008] Env. L.R. 30; [2008] 11 E.G. 94 (landlord not liable where the flooding of the tenant's property results from defective building work by the landlord's predecessor in title).

678 *Kiddle v City Business Properties Ltd* [1942] 1 K.B. 269 and 274. (This principle does not apply between adjoining owners whose holdings are entirely independent the one of the other, i.e. where there is no relation of landlord or tenant.)

679 *Anderson v Oppenheimer* (1880) 5 Q.B.D. 602.

680 *Carstairs v Taylor* (1871) L.R. 6 Ex. 217. See also *Gavin v Community Housing Association Ltd* [2013] EWCA Civ 580; [2013] 2 P. & C.R. 17.

681 *Ross v Fedden* (1872) L.R. 7 Q.B. 661.

682 *Tilley v Stevenson* [1939] 4 All E.R. 207.

19-137 **Construction of building** A person who enters into occupation of property takes it as it is and cannot complain that it was not constructed differently,[683] with the result that if he suffers damage from water accumulating without negligence on the part of anyone, as by a gutter or a pipe being blocked, he has no right of action.[684] When the claimant took a lease of part of a building, which included a theatre occupied by the defendants, in which was installed a sprinkler system which, during a severe frost, was damaged, so that water from it came into the claimant's premises and damaged his stock, it was held that the defendants were not liable in the absence of negligence.[685]

19-138 **Person liable for damage caused by water** When accumulated water escapes and does damage, the person liable is he who has accumulated the water or caused it to be accumulated. The employment of an independent contractor is no defence, as *Rylands v Fletcher* itself shows. If the water is accumulated on land the occupier is liable because it is his water which has escaped. The position of the owner is discussed above.[686] If water is accumulated on the land of one owner for the benefit of land belonging to an adjoining owner, as if a watercourse goes through A's land to work B's mill, an escape of the water would impose liability upon the adjoining owner B, and not on the owner of the land on which the water was accumulated.[687]

(c) Withdrawal of support

19-139 **Right to support** The owner of land has a right to the support of his land in its natural state from the adjacent and subjacent land of the neighbouring owners. This right is not an easement but a natural incident of his ownership.[688] There is no natural right of support for buildings,[689] but such a right may be acquired as an easement by grant, express or implied, or by prescription at common law or under the Prescription Act 1832.[690] An acquired right is similar in character to a natural

---

683 *Baxter v Camden LBC* [2001] Q.B. 1 CA.

684 See *Kiddle v City Business Properties Ltd* [1942] 1 K.B. 269. See also *Jackson v JH Watson Property Investment Ltd* [2008] EWHC 14 (Ch); [2008] Env. L.R. 30; [2008] 11 E.G. 94.

685 *Peters v Prince of Wales Theatre (Birmingham) Ltd* [1943] K.B. 73.

686 See para.19-56.

687 *Whitmores (Edenbridge) Ltd v Stanford* [1909] 1 Ch. 42 at 48, dictum, per Eve J. In this case the owner of the land (A) had not brought or accumulated the water on his land; the adjacent owner (B) had a prescriptive right to the flow of water. The touchstone of *Rylands v Fletcher* liability is that of control over the place and the accumulation.

688 *Humphries v Brogden* (1850) 12 Q.B. 739; *Dalton v Angus* (1881) 6 App. Cas. 740; *Backhouse v Bonomi* (1861) 9 H.L.C. 503. It is no objection to a claim for loss of support that the immediate cause of the loss was subsidence of land adjoining that of the claimant, if the defendants were in fact responsible for the subsidence of the intervening land: *Bell v Northumbrian Water Ltd* [2016] EWHC 133 (TCC) at [51]–[53].

689 *Dalton v Angus* (1881) 6 App. Cas. 740 at 792; *North Eastern Ry v Elliott* (1860) 1 John H. 145 at 153; *Rogers v Taylor* (1857) 2 H. & N. 828. In New Zealand, where there are no longer easements of support by prescription the Court of Appeal has laid down a duty of care in the support of adjacent buildings: *Bognuda v Upton Shearer Ltd* [1972] N.Z.L.R. 741.

690 *Dalton v Angus* (1881) 6 App. Cas. 740; *Lemaitre v Davis* (1881) 19 Ch. D. 281; *Lloyd's Bank Ltd v Dalton* [1942] Ch. 466 (knowledge that support is given by his building to the dominant tenement will be imputed to the owner of the servient tenement when he had a reasonable opportunity of acquiring that knowledge).

right.[691] If the adjacent or subjacent support is withdrawn so as to cause land to subside, and the subsidence has not been caused by the additional weight of the buildings or other erections upon the land, the landowner is entitled to recover, in addition to damages for the subsidence of his land, damages for the injury to his buildings or other erections although he has no acquired right of support in respect of them.[692]

Withdrawal of support When the ownership of the surface is severed from that of the underlying minerals, the owner of the minerals cannot let down the surface unless the right to do so is given to him by the instrument of severance or by legislation.[693] To exclude the right of support, the language used must unequivocally convey that intention either by express words or by necessary implication.[694] A mere right to compensation is not in any way inconsistent with the common law obligation and does not, of itself, exclude the right of support.[695] On the other hand, if the parties to the instrument of severance contemplated that the minerals would be worked and must have known that they could not be worked without infringing the right of support, then a right to let down the surface will arise by necessary implication[696]; but necessary implication is not established by showing that if profitable working of the mines is to be carried out the surface must be let down.[697] **19-140**

Water There is no right to have land supported by water, and such a right cannot be acquired by prescription. Therefore one who, by draining his own land, withdraws from an adjoining owner the support of water lying beneath the land of that owner, and thereby causes the surface of that land to subside, is not liable for the damage inflicted.[698] This rule does not apply to cases in which the withdrawal of support by the shrinkage of subjacent clay[699] or by the oozing out of wet sand, silt, or other partially liquid substance, results in a subsidence of the adjacent surface.[700] **19-141**

Damage The mere withdrawal of support is not of itself a nuisance; it only becomes wrongful if and when a subsidence occurs. Accordingly, the right of action does not accrue until actual damage is occasioned, and the Statute of Limitations does not run from the date of the excavation but from the date of the **19-142**

---

691 *Bonomi v Backhouse* (1859) E.B. & E. 646, per Willes J.

692 *Brown v Robins* (1859) 4 H. & N. 186; *Stroyan v Knowles* (1861) 6 H. & N. 454.

693 See para.19-146.

694 *Butterknowle Colliery Co v Bishop Auckland Co-operative Society* [1906] A.C. 305; *Hext v Gill* (1872) 7 Ch. App. 699; *Warwickshire Coal Co v Coventry Corp* [1934] 1 Ch. 488.

695 *New Sharlston Collieries v Westmorland* [1904] 2 Ch. 443n.

696 *Butterley Co v New Hucknall Colliery* [1910] A.C. 381; *Beard v Moira Colliery* [1915] 1 Ch. 257; *Weldon v Butterley Co* [1920] 1 Ch. 130; *Jones v Consolidated Anthracite Collieries* [1916] 1 K.B. 123.

697 *Warwickshire Coal Co v Coventry Corp* [1934] 1 Ch. 488; *Wath-upon-Dearne Urban DC v Brown & Co* [1936] 1 Ch. 172.

698 *Popplewell v Hodkinson* (1869) L.R. 4 Ex. 248; *English v Metropolitan Water Board* [1907] 1 K.B. 588; *Langbrook Properties Ltd v Surrey CC* [1970] 1 W.L.R. 161; see para.19-120.

699 *Brace v South East Regional Housing Association Ltd* [1984] 270 E.G. 1286 CA.

700 *Jordeson v Sutton etc Gas Co* [1899] 2 Ch. 217; *Trinidad Asphalt Co v Ambard* [1899] A.C. 594; *Fletcher v Birkenhead Corp* [1907] 1 K.B. 205; *Lotus v British Soda Co* [1972] Ch. 123 (liquefaction of mineral support).

damage.[701] Each successive subsidence gives rise to a fresh cause of action, even though there has been no new excavation.[702] Liability for the damage is on the person who made the excavation and not on the lessee or owner in possession at the date of the subsidence.[703] But if an excavation is made under land by one person and at a later date another excavation is made under the same land by another person and a subsidence is caused, the person making the second excavation will be liable for all the damage caused by the subsidence, even though there would have been no subsidence but for the first excavation.[704]

19-143 **Damages** The damages recoverable do not include the depreciation in market value of the property due to the risk of future subsidence, because in the event of a fresh subsidence a fresh right of action will arise.[705] If the condition of the land has been changed to a substantial extent by the withdrawal of support, an action may be brought without proof of pecuniary loss.[706] Damages for subsidence are frequently recoverable under the provisions of a conveyance of the surface, with a reservation of minerals, giving the owner of the minerals the right to let down the surface subject to a proviso for payment of compensation to the surface owner. Such a proviso is a covenant running with the surface and entitles the surface owner to recover compensation from the lessee of minerals as well as the owner.[707] Without an express assignment of the damages, the surface owner cannot recover compensation for damage caused before he became owner of the surface.[708]

19-144 **Injunction** Though damages cannot be claimed until subsidence has occurred, the claimant may seek an injunction to compel the defendant to preserve the claimant's land from future or further subsidence. Such injunction (whether mandatory or prohibitory) is a remedy within the discretion of the court. Generally an injunction is only obtainable where damages would not be an adequate or sufficient remedy for harm caused. A prohibitory injunction is proper where no harm has occurred but is purely prospective; a mandatory injunction where some harm has occurred and further grave damage is in prospect as a matter of very strong probability. Where a mandatory injunction is sought, the cost to the defendant of preventive or restorative work is to be taken into account, and where the defendant has acted wantonly or unreasonably he may be ordered to restore the status quo even if the cost is out of all proportion to the advantage thereby secured to the claimant. But where the defendant has acted reasonably, though in the event producing injurious harm to the claimant and the claimant has received compensation for that harm, the cost of preventive or restorative work as further protection may be a stronger factor against

701 *Backhouse v Bonomi* (1861) 9 H.L.C. 503 (applied in *Midland Bank Plc v Bardgrove Property Services Ltd* (1992) 65 P. & C.R. 153).

702 *Darley Main Colliery v Mitchell* (1866) 11 App. Cas. 127; cf. para.31-08.

703 *Greenwell v Low Beechburn Coal Co* [1897] 2 Q.B. 165; *Hall v Norfolk* [1900] 2 Ch. 493. An exception to this rule was the Coal Industry Nationalisation Act 1946 s.48(1). See now the Coal Mining Subsidence Act 1991 and the Coal Industry Act 1994 s.43(4).

704 *Manley v Burn* [1916] 2 K.B. 121.

705 *West Leigh Colliery Co v Tunnicliffe* [1908] A.C. 27.

706 *Att Gen v Conduit Colliery* [1895] 1 Q.B. 301.

707 *Dyson v Forster* [1909] A.C. 98; *Westhoughton Urban DC v Wigan Coal and Iron Co* [1919] 1 Ch. 159; *Aynsley v Dedlington Coal Co* (1918) 87 L.J.K.B. 1031.

708 *Snowdon v Ecclesiastical Commissioners* [1935] 1 Ch. 181.

the issue of a mandatory injunction. Where a defendant is enjoined to do restorative work, he is entitled to be told exactly what he must do.[709]

Support for buildings There is no natural right of support for buildings, and therefore a landowner may make an excavation on his own land notwithstanding that by so doing he may cause his neighbour's building to fall.[710] Also, if in pulling down his own house he removes the support of his neighbour's house, he is not bound to shore up his neighbour's house or take any other active steps for its protection.[711] But if his neighbour has an easement of support for his building from the adjoining buildings, he must not pull down his building so as to remove the support from his neighbour's building.[712] Nor may an owner in common of a track excavate or deepen it so as to threaten probable harm to his neighbour's house, and a mandatory injunction can be obtained even though the harm is not imminent but only a proven probability.[713] The employment of an independent contractor in such cases is no defence.[714] Where adjacent properties have rights of mutual support, the owner of a derelict property owes a duty to take reasonable measures of repair so as to support the adjacent building.[715] In *Rees v Skerrett*[716] the defendant's property was demolished, leaving the wall of the claimant's adjoining terraced house exposed. The Court of Appeal held that damage attributable to the suction effect of wind, to which the claimant's property had not formerly been subjected, was within the scope of the right of support. Moreover, in the light of the principle established in *Leakey v National Trust*, one owner may now owe a common law duty to take reasonable steps to protect the neighbouring property from foreseeable weather damage caused by demolition of his own property.[717] 19-145

Subsidence by coal mining The right of British Coal to withdraw support for land or buildings is now regulated by the Coal Mining Subsidence Act 1991, providing for compensation for such damage or with the owner's consent making good such damage to the reasonable satisfaction of the owner. 19-146

(d) Nuisance to light

Right to light There is no natural right to light. Such a right must always be acquired, either by grant or prescription, and when acquired by prescription must be in respect of a building,[718] and defined windows or other apertures in the nature 19-147

709 *Redland Bricks Ltd v Morris* [1970] A.C. 652.

710 *Wyatt v Harrison* (1832) 3 B. & Ad. 871; cf. *Brown v Robins* (1859) 4 H. & N. 186.

711 *Southwark and Vauxhall Water Co v Wandsworth Board of Works* [1898] 2 Ch. 603 at 612.

712 *Dalton v Angus* (1881) 6 App. Cas. 740.

713 *Hooper v Rogers* [1975] Ch. 43 CA.

714 *Hughes v Percival* (1883) 8 App. Cas. 443.

715 *Bradburn v Lindsay* [1983] 2 All E.R. 408. The decision departs from earlier cases which confined the duty to a duty not to withdraw support (*Bond v Nottingham Corp* [1940] Ch. 429 at 438-439, per Greene MR), whereas the decision imposes a duty of positive repair.

716 [2001] EWCA Civ 760; [2001] 1 W.L.R. 1541.

717 The well-known dictum of Lord Denning MR in *Phipps v Pears* [1965] 1 Q.B. 76 at 83 therefore no longer represents the law; Lord Denning said that: "Every man is entitled to pull down his house if he likes. If it exposes your house to the weather, that is your misfortune. It is no wrong on his part."

718 *Colls v Home & Colonial Stores Ltd* [1904] A.C. 179 at 205, per Lord Lindley; *Harris v de Pinna* (1886) 33 Ch. D. 238. In 2014 the Law Commission published its final report on *Rights to Light* (2014), Law Com. No.356 with a variety of recommendations intended to "simplify the law" so as

of windows in that building,[719] and not of openings not primarily intended to admit light, such as a doorway,[720] or of a piece of open ground.[721] The right, when acquired, is often called "ancient lights" and is the right to prevent the owner of the servient tenement from building or putting up any erection on his land in such a way as to deprive the owner of the dominant tenement of so much light as to constitute an actionable nuisance:

> "An owner of ancient lights is entitled to sufficient light, according to the ordinary notions of mankind, for the comfortable use and enjoyment of his house as a dwelling-house, if it is a dwelling-house, or for the beneficial use and occupation of the house, if it is warehouse, a shop, or other place of business."[722]

An owner acquires by prescription the right to light for his building as a whole, not for particular portions to it, so his right to sufficient light is not affected by internal rearrangement of his building.[723]

19-148 **Amount of light** An owner is entitled to sufficient light, so "the inquiry is directed not to the amount of light taken, but to the amount of light left".[724] The amount of light to which an occupier is entitled varies with the nature of the occupation. Thus in *Allen v Greenwood*,[725] the Court of Appeal held that the claimants had acquired, by prescription, the right to an amount of light necessary for the proper use of a greenhouse as a place for growing plants and not that amount needed merely for illumination. It was held as a matter of law that a right to a specifically high degree of light can be acquired by known enjoyment[726] of that specifically high degree for the full period of 20 years, just as such a right can be conferred by actual grant. As was said by Buckley LJ, it would be "ridiculous to say that a greenhouse had enough light because a man could read a newspaper there with reasonable comfort". The case was concerned with a common or garden greenhouse; different considerations would apply if an occupier was experimenting with solar heat or claiming an amount of light necessary for plants requiring more light than those usually raised in a greenhouse. Interference with a use of abnormal sensitiveness would not be a nuisance in the first place.[727]

19-149 **Locality and quantum** It has been asserted that locality is irrelevant, and that "the human eye requires as much light for comfortable reading or sewing in

---

to make "negotiation [between the parties] more efficient" (Executive Summary [1.1]).

719 *Tapling v Jones* (1865) 11 H.L.C. 290 at 305–306. cf. the greenhouse in *Allen v Greenwood* [1980] Ch. 119, at para.19-148, which was regarded as a building with windows rather than a garden under glass.

720 *Levet v Gas Light and Coke Co* [1919] 1 Ch. 24.

721 *Potts v Smith* (1868) L.R. 6 Eq. 311 at 318; *Roberts v Macord* (1832) 1 Moo. Rob. 230.

722 *Colls v Home & Colonial Stores Ltd* [1904] A.C. 179 at 208, per Lord Lindley. See also *Kelk v Pearson* (1871) L.R. 6 Ch. 809 at 811; *Charles Semon & Co v Bradford Corp* [1922] 2 Ch. 737; *Jolly v Kine* [1907] A.C. 1.

723 *Carr-Saunders v Dick McNeil Associates Ltd* [1986] 1 W.L.R. 922.

724 *Carr-Saunders v Dick McNeil Associates Ltd* [1986] 1 W.L.R. 922 at 928, per Millett J.

725 [1980] Ch. 119.

726 In this case the defendant's knowledge was clear because the user was completely obvious, but it may be more difficult to show sufficient knowledge where the user of special light occurs within a building internally.

727 See para.19-11. The reception of light for purposes of photography would seem to be a user on which an occupier could found a prescriptive right: *Allen v Greenwood* [1980] Ch. 119 at 133, per Goff LJ.

Darlington Street, Wolverhampton, as in Mayfair".[728] But the Court of Appeal has said that the general nature of the locality may be taken into account,[729] and further indicated that the higher standards expected for comfort in more modern times are also to be taken into account.[730] The amount of light is not measured by user in the past; it is measured by actual present user and any potential user which may be reasonably expected.[731] The courts have rejected mechanical rules in measuring quantum of sufficient light. There is no longer a "45 degrees rule" against obstructions so measured upwards from a room out of a window,[732] nor is there a rigid "50-50 rule" measuring one lumen of light against 50 per cent of the floor area of a room.[733] The guiding principle is simply such access of light as will leave premises adequately lit for the ordinary purposes for which they may reasonably be expected to be used.

Light from other sources In considering whether a right to light has been acquired, light coming to the dominant tenement from other sources must be taken into account, except light the enjoyment of which could be stopped by a third party without committing an actionable wrong.[734] The court is bound to take into account what other lights were enjoyed by the owner of the dominant tenement: (i) at the date of the action; and (ii) at the date of the commencement of the period of prescription, disregarding light not acquired by grant or prescription of which the dominant tenement may be deprived. If a building receives light from two sides through windows which are ancient lights, the owners of the land on either side can only build to such a height as, if a building of similar height were erected on the other side, would leave sufficient light for the dominant tenement so as not to constitute a nuisance.[735] If the dominant owner in such a case assents to the abstraction of his light from one side, it does not negative his right to the easement over the other side, although it cannot increase the burden of that easement.[736] In considering whether or not a nuisance has been committed, reflected or diffused light cannot be disregarded.[737] **19-150**

Alteration of dominant tenement The dominant owner does not lose his right to light by rebuilding or making structural alterations to the exterior of his property, but he cannot thereby increase the burden on the servient tenement beyond a reasonable amount of light. In every case the question to be determined is whether or not the erection on the servient tenement would have been a nuisance if the dominant **19-151**

---

[728] per Russell J in *Horton's Estate Ltd v James Beattie Ltd* [1927] 1 Ch. 75 at 78.

[729] *Fishenden v Higgs Hill Ltd* (1935) 153 L.T. 128; *Ough v King* [1967] 1 W.L.R. 1547.

[730] *Ough v King* [1967] 1 W.L.R. 1547.

[731] *Moore v Hall* (1878) 3 Q.B.D. 178 at 182, per Cockburn CJ; *Carr-Saunders v Dick McNeil Associates* [1986] 1 W.L.R. 922 at 928.

[732] *Colls v Home & Colonial Stores Ltd* [1904] A.C. 179 at 210.

[733] *Carr-Saunders v Dick McNeil Associates Ltd* [1986] 1 W.L.R. 922 at 927.

[734] *Colls v Home & Colonial Stores Ltd* [1904] A.C. 179; *Smith v Evangelization Society* [1933] 1 Ch. 515.

[735] *Sheffield Masonic Hall Co v Sheffield Corp* [1932] 2 Ch. 17. The claimant cannot invoke this principle if the prospect of the other land being built upon is "far-fetched and utterly remote": *Tamares (Vincent Square) Ltd v Fairpoint Properties (Vincent Square) Ltd* [2006] EWHC 3589 (Ch); [2007] 1 W.L.R. 2148 at [50].

[736] *WH & Bailey & Son v Holborn and Frascati* [1914] 1 Ch. 598.

[737] *Sheffield Masonic Hall Co v Sheffield Corp* [1932] 2 Ch. 17.

building had been unaltered[738]; it is not necessary to prove that the structural identity of the old windows has been preserved, or that the rooms within have remained unaltered.[739] If, however, windows in respect of which a right to light is claimed have, in fact, been boarded up throughout the prescription period the claimant cannot rely on the rule that alteration of the dominant property does not affect the existence of the right.[740] If the building on the servient tenement is altered, for example by heightening one portion and lowering another, so that the direction from which light is received is changed, no nuisance is committed as long as the dominant building continues to receive as much light as the smallest amount enjoyed within the last 20 years.[741]

19-152 **Injunction and damages** When once it is established that the interference with the claimant's light will produce substantial damage, the claimant will be prima facie entitled to an injunction.[742] The order will be in general terms without referring to the angle of incidence of the light, unless there is some special evidence justifying the insertion of such a clause.[743] An injunction, however, will *not* be granted if:

(1) the injury to the claimant's legal rights is small;
(2) the injury is capable of being estimated in money;
(3) the injury is one which can be compensated adequately by a small money payment; and
(4) it would be oppressive to the defendant to grant an injunction.[744]

Moreover, even if these criteria are not satisfied, it by no means follows that an injunction will be granted. In *Coventry v Lawrence*[745] the Supreme Court indicated that the tendency to treat failure to satisfy these criteria as effectively entitling the claimant to an injunction was no longer appropriate: the discretion to award or refuse an injunction should be unfettered, and the interests of third parties may justify refusal.[746] An injunction will not be granted if it would be a hardship on the owner of the servient tenement to prevent him from using his building site to its best

---

738 *Ankerson v Connelly* [1907] 1 Ch. 678; *News of the World Ltd v Allen Fairhead & Sons Ltd* [1931] 2 Ch. 402; *Smith v Evangelization Society* [1933] 1 Ch. 515.

739 *Carr-Saunders v Dick McNeil Associates Ltd* [1986] 1 W.L.R. 922.

740 *Tamares (Vincent Square) Ltd v Fairpoint Properties (Vincent Square) Ltd* [2006] EWHC 3589 (Ch); [2007] 1 W.L.R. 2148. See also *Smith v Baxter* [1900] 2 Ch. 138.

741 *Davis v Marrable* [1913] 2 Ch. 421.

742 "I would accept that the prima facie position is that an injunction should be granted, so the legal burden is on the defendant to show why it should not", per Lord Neuberger in *Coventry v Lawrence* [2014] UKSC 13; [2014] A.C. 822 at [121] (not a right to light case but the point is of general application). See also *Ottercroft Ltd v Scandia Care Ltd* [2016] EWCA Civ 867 (mandatory injunction granted for infringement of right to light). See, generally, paras 28-06 to 28-11.

743 *Parker v First Avenue Hotel Co* (1883) 24 Ch. D. 282; *Litchfield-Speer v Queen Anne's Gate Syndicate* [1919] 1 Ch. 407.

744 *Shelfer v City of London Electronic Lighting Co* [1894] 1 Ch. 287, but note that this case must now be read in the light of *Coventry v Lawrence* [2014] UKSC 13; [2014] A.C. 822 in which the Supreme Court indicated that it was "out of date" and should no longer be followed "slavishly": per Lord Sumption at [161].

745 [2014] UKSC 13; [2014] A.C. 822.

746 For a review of the authorities, including the right to light cases, see [2014] UKSC 13; [2014] A.C. 822, per Lord Neuberger at [100]–[126]. The Law Commission has recommended that there should be a new statutory provision requiring the court to deny an injunction if it "would be a disproportionate means of enforcing the claimant's right to light": see *Rights to Light* (2014), Law Com. No.356 (see cl.2 of the Rights to Light (Injunctions) Bill set out in App.B to the Report).

advantage, when no harm will be done to the dominant tenement beyond that for which damages would be an adequate compensation.[747] The measure of damages includes not only the diminution in value of the dominant tenement but also of the whole building site of which the tenement forms part,[748] even if part of that site is not immediately ripe for development.[749] Damages can be given for a threatened injury.[750]

Air and prospect It is not a nuisance to prevent the free access of air to another man's land, although it may cause him damage, for example by building so to cut off the winds from a windmill,[751] or causing his chimney to smoke.[752] On the other hand, a right to air through a defined passage or aperture may be acquired as an easement by grant or prescription, and an interference with that right will be actionable.[753] **19-153**

Prospects and privacy It is not a nuisance to interfere with a view or prospect[754] where the act complained of is otherwise lawful.[755] Similarly, it is not a nuisance for a man to erect a building on his own land which enables him to invade the privacy of his neighbour by looking through his windows or otherwise.[756] In *Fearn v Board of Trustees of the Tate Gallery*,[757] decided in 2020, the Court of Appeal emphatically reaffirmed that this position was still good law, notwithstanding suggestions in the court below, that a right to privacy might now be recognised by the common law of nuisance in certain circumstances.[758] Thus in the *Fearn* case, a complaint by the owners of flats which were overlooked by a public "viewing gallery", constructed on a nearby building occupied by the defendants, had no cause of action in private nuisance. Public law, in the field of town and country planning, is the appropriate medium for the resolution of such issues.[759] The continuing vitality of the old authorities denying that loss of a view or prospect is actionable in nuisance was reflected in the 1997 decision of the House of Lords in *Hunter v Canary Wharf Ltd*,[760] in which they were invoked by analogy to justify refusal of relief for interference with the path of television signals by the erection of a large building: **19-154**

"The house owner who has a fine view of the South Downs may find that his neighbour

---

747 *Slack v Leeds Industrial Co-operative Society* [1924] 2 Ch. 475. See, e.g. *Tamares (Vincent Square) Ltd v Fairpoint Properties (Vincent Square) Ltd* [2006] EWHC 3589 (Ch); [2007] 1 W.L.R. 2148.

748 *Griffith v Richard Clay & Sons* [1912] 2 Ch. 291.

749 *Wills v May* [1923] 1 Ch. 317.

750 *Leeds Industrial Co-operative Society v Slack* [1924] A.C. 851. Damages will not normally be awarded on a restitutionary basis: *Forsyth-Grant v Allen* [2008] EWCA Civ 505; [2008] 2 E.G.L.R. 16.

751 *Webb v Bird* (1862) 13 C.B. (N.S.) 841; *Chastey v Ackland* [1895] 2 Ch. 389.

752 *Bryant v Lefever* (1879) 4 C.P.D. 172.

753 *Bass v Gregory* (1890) 25 Q.B.D. 481; *Hall v Lichfield Brewery Co* (1880) 49 L.J. Ch. 655; *Cable v Bryant* [1908] 1 Ch. 259.

754 *William Aldred's Case* (1610) 9 Co. Rep. 57b at 58b; *Dalton v Angus* (1881) 6 App. Cas. 740 at 824, per Lord Blackburn.

755 *Campbell v Paddington Corp* [1911] 1 K.B. 869.

756 *Browne v Flower* [1911] 1 Ch. 219. See also *Victoria Park Racing Co v Taylor* (1937) 58 C.L.R. 479 (broadcasting horse-racing commentary from property adjacent to race-course).

757 [2020] EWCA Civ 104; [2020] 2 W.L.R. 1081.

758 See *Fearn v Board of Trustees of the Tate Gallery* [2019] EWHC 246 (Ch); [2019] Ch. 369.

759 See *Fearn v Board of Trustees of the Tate Gallery* [2020] EWCA Civ 104; [2020] 2 W.L.R. 1081 at [83].

760 [1997] A.C. 655.

has built so as to obscure his view. But there is no redress, unless, perchance, the neighbour's land was subject to a restrictive covenant in the house owner's favour. It would be a good example of what in law is called '*damnum absque injuria*': a loss which the house owner has undoubtedly suffered, but which gives rise to no infringement of his legal rights. In the absence of a restrictive covenant, there is no legal right to a view."[761]

(e) Fire

(i) Common law

19-155 **Danger from fire** Fire is a dangerous thing, and consequently the principle of *Rylands v Fletcher* applies to it.[762] In *Gore v Stannard (t/a Wyvern Tyres)*,[763] however, the Court of Appeal subjected the application of the rule in *Rylands v Fletcher* to fire cases to an extensive and far-reaching examination, and concluded that its scope in that context is significantly narrower than interpretations of the rule in previous cases appeared to suggest. An electrical fire started on the defendant's premises, without fault on his part, and ignited a stock of several thousand tyres which he kept as part of his business. The resulting conflagration destroyed the claimant's neighbouring premises. The trial judge held the defendant liable under the rule in *Rylands v Fletcher* but the Court of Appeal reversed his decision. Tyres are difficult to set alight, even though once ignited they are capable of burning fiercely; moreover their storage on the defendant's premises did not represent a "non-natural" use of land. These findings alone would have been sufficient to negate liability under the rule as conventionally understood in cases involving fire. This required inherently inflammable material, stored in the course of a non-natural use of land, to catch fire and the fire to spread. But the Court went on to disapprove this interpretation and apparently to hold that *Rylands v Fletcher* liability should only be imposed in fire cases when the defendant, in the course of non-natural user, had deliberately introduced on to his land, or ignited, the fire itself, which then spread to neighbouring land. In practice this would seem to reduce the scope for liability under the rule in fire cases to vanishing point since it is not easy to envisage circumstances in which a fire thus commenced could spread to neighbouring land without any negligence on the defendant's part. Nevertheless the fact that the rule has not been formally abrogated in this context means that claimants continue to enjoy the potential advantage of not having actually to prove negligence, which could be beneficial if the evidence necessary to do so has been lost in the fire.

(ii) Statutory exemption for fires accidentally beginning

19-156 **Fires Prevention (Metropolis) Act 1774** At common law if a fire started in the house or on the land of one man and spread to the land of another, the person from whose house or land the fire started had to make good the damage. His liability was

---

761 [1997] A.C. 655 at 699, per Lord Lloyd. For criticism of this position see Pontin, "A room with a view in English Nuisance Law" (2018) 38 L.S. 644.

762 *Jones v Ffestiniog Ry* (1868) L.R. 3 Q.B. 733; *Musgrove v Pandelis* [1919] 2 K.B. 43; see Ogus, "Vagaries in Liability for the Escape of Fire" [1969] C.L.J. 104. For a full review of the state of the law relating to liability for fire damage, under the rule in *Rylands v Fletcher* and also in negligence and nuisance, see *Johnson v BJW Property Developments Ltd* [2002] EWHC 1131 (TCC); [2002] 3 All E.R. 574. This review must, however, now be read in the light of the decision of the Court of Appeal in *Gore v Stannard (t/a Wyvern Tyres)* considered in the text (see next note).

763 [2012] EWCA Civ 1248; [2014] Q.B. 1.

not based on negligence, for he was liable for accidental fires,[764] and the only defences were those available under what later became the *Rylands* rule, such as an act of God which could not have been foreseen or guarded against,[765] or the independent act of a third party.[766] The common law liability still remains[767] (subject to later modifications such as those to the rule in *Rylands v Fletcher* considered in the previous paragraph) in all cases which are not covered by the Fires Prevention (Metropolis) Act 1774. Section 86 of the Act modified the common law liability by providing, "no action, suit or process whatever, shall be had, maintained or prosecuted against any person in whose house, chamber, stable, barn or other building, or on whose estate any fire shall … accidentally begin".[768] In spite of its title, the Act applies throughout the country and is not limited to the metropolis. The Act does not apply when the fire starts from the highway, and therefore it is not necessary to prove negligence to escape the statutory exemption.[769] The wording of the Act, which refers only to real property, would not seem apt to cover movable property not on the defendant's land, for example, a vehicle on the highway or a houseboat moored in a harbour. Special provisions relate to fires caused by sparks from steam railways.[770] The applicability of the Act to fire cases coming within the rule in *Rylands v Fletcher* was considered at length in *Gore v Stannard (t/a Wyvern Tyres)*.[771] The Court of Appeal was divided on the question whether the words "accidentally begin" have the effect of protecting defendants in *Rylands v Fletcher* fire cases from liability. Lewison LJ took the view that they do have this effect, and that only cases involving negligence should be outside the protection of the Act.[772] Etherton LJ expressed a forceful opinion to the opposite effect, upholding the orthodox view that fires falling within *Rylands v Fletcher* are outside the protection of the Act and can therefore give rise to liability.[773] Ward LJ in effect took the same view as Etherton LJ so that the existing law on this point, laid down in the difficult decision of the Court of Appeal in *Musgrove v Pandelis*,[774] remains unchanged.

764 Rolle's Abridgement, Action sur Case (B.), pur fewe 2; *Anon.* (1583) Cro. Eliz. 10; per Bankes LJ in *Musgrove v Pandelis* [1919] 2 K.B. 43 at 46; per Lord Wright in *Collingwood v Home & Colonial Stores Ltd* [1936] 3 All E.R. 200.

765 *Tuberville v Stamp* (1697) 1 Salk. 12, per Holt CJ: "If a sudden storm had arisen which he could not stop, it was matter of evidence, and he should have shown it."

766 *Beaulieu v Finglam* (1401) 2 Men. 4 at 18, pl. 6, per Markham J: "If a man outside my household against my will sets fire to the thatch of my house or does otherwise so that my house is burned and also the houses of my neighbours, I shall not be held to answer to them, because this cannot be said to be done by wrong on my part, but against my will."

767 But not in Australia: see *Burnie Port Authority v General Jones Pty Ltd* (1994) 120 A.L.R. 42, in which the High Court of Australia held that the so-called *ignis suus* rule was not part of the common law in that jurisdiction.

768 The section (which is still in force despite the repeal of most of the Act's other provisions) re-enacted earlier legislation: 1706 (6 Anne, c.31).

769 *Powell v Fall* (1880) 5 Q.B.D. 597; *Gunter v James* (1908) 24 T.L.R. 868; *Mansel v Webb* (1919) 88 L.J.K.B. 323.

770 See the Railway Fires Act 1905 and the Railway Fires Act (1905) Amendment Act 1923. cf. *Jones v Ffestiniog Ry* (1868) L.R. 3 Q.B. 733.

771 [2012] EWCA Civ 1248; [2014] Q.B. 1.

772 [2012] EWCA Civ 1248; [2014] Q.B. 1 at [89]–[96] and [147]–[170].

773 [2012] EWCA Civ 1248; [2014] Q.B. 1 at [69]–[72].

774 [1919] 2 K.B. 43. See para.19-159.

19-157 **Fire caused by intention or negligence** In *Filliter v Phippard*,[775] it was decided that the Act was no defence if the fire was caused by the negligence of the householder or of one of his servants, or was lit intentionally. The court held that the word "accidental" was not used in contradistinction to wilful but to negligent, and meant "a fire produced by mere chance, or incapable of being traced to any cause". In *Filliter v Phippard*, both these elements were present, as the fire was lit intentionally on the defendant's land for the purpose of burning weeds, and the negligence consisted in lighting the fire in the existing state of the wind and omitting to prevent it from spreading to the claimant's hedges. The result is that if the occupier of a house or land starts a fire either intentionally or by negligence, he is bound at his peril to keep it from doing damage to others,[776] subject only to the exceptions to the *Rylands* rule set out above. He is liable not only for his own acts or omissions but also for those of his servants, agents and independent contractors.[777] But unless it can be proved affirmatively that the origin of the fire was due to either of the causes just stated, the occupier is not liable. Defendants invoking the protection of the Act are not required to disprove negligence.[778] Accordingly, when a fire broke out in the basement of the defendant's grocery store and the cause was unknown, although it was thought to be some defect in the electrical wiring, the defendant was held not liable.[779]

19-158 **Liability as occupier** An occupier of premises may be liable for damage caused by the escape of fire from those premises, quite apart from his liability in negligence as the person whose negligent act started the fire. So in a case[780] where the defendant was insured against liability as "occupier" of premises, it was held that the defendant who lit a paraffin rag and negligently applied it to a sparrow's nest in the wall of his house was liable for the destruction by the ensuing fire of his neighbour's property and thus could claim under that provision of the insurance policy.

19-159 **Accidental fire continued by negligence** A fire, which has begun accidentally within the meaning of the Act, may be continued by the negligence of the householder and so render him liable. In *Musgrove v Pandelis*,[781] the servant of the defendant, in attempting to start a motorcar, caused the petrol in the carburettor to catch fire; the fire would have burnt itself out in a short time, but the servant omitted to turn off the tap from the petrol tank, with the result that the fire increased and

---

775 (1847) 11 Q.B. 347; *Richards v Easto* (1846) 15 M. & W. 244, per Parke B; *Williams v Owen* [1955] 1 W.L.R. 1293 (innkeeper not liable to a guest for damage caused to guest's car by accidental fire); *Canadian Forest Products Ltd v Hudson Lumber Co Ltd* (1960) 20 D.L.R. (2d) 712 (British Columbia Supreme Court held that neither nuisance nor the rule in *Rylands v Fletcher* can be invoked upon a logging operator for damage by fire to adjoining property without negligence, especially when the logging operations are carried on under conditions fixed by permit issued by forestry officials); *Mackenzie v Sloss* [1959] N.Z.L.R. 533 (spark from tractor constructing fire-break—no liability); *Edwards v Blue Mountains City Council* (1961) 78 W.N. (N.S.W.) 864, noted in (1962) 35 A.L.J. 392 (defendants burning garbage not liable under *Rylands v Fletcher* on account of statutory authority, but liable in nuisance and negligence).

776 *Mulholland and Tedd Ltd v Baker* [1939] 3 All E.R. 253 (the facts are set out at para.19-164).

777 *Black v Christchurch Finance Co* [1894] A.C. 48; *Balfour v Barty-King* [1957] 1 Q.B. 496 CA; *H & N Emanuel v Greater London Council* [1971] 2 All E.R. 835 CA; *Hobbs (Farms) v Baxenden Chemical Co* [1992] 1 Lloyd's Rep. 54.

778 *Mason v Levy Auto Parts of England Ltd* [1967] 2 Q.B. 530 at 538–539.

779 *Collingwood v Home & Colonial Stores Ltd* [1936] 3 All E.R. 200.

780 *Sturge v Hackett* [1962] 1 W.L.R. 1257 CA.

781 [1919] 2 K.B. 43.

burnt down the claimant's rooms over the garage. It was held that the Act was no defence because, assuming the fire to be accidental in its origin, the negligence of the defendant's servant was responsible for the continuance of the fire and the destruction of the claimant's property. If burning fuel accidentally falls out of a domestic grate and sets the carpet on fire and the householder is negligent in extinguishing the fire, so that damage is caused to the neighbouring property, the Act will be no defence.[782] Under such circumstances the householder is bound to take reasonable care to prevent the fire from spreading and if he omits to take such care he is liable. Moreover, an occupier is under a duty of care in relation to a fire accidentally started by natural forces. His duty to abate is now established by the decision of the Judicial Committee of the Privy Council in *Goldman v Hargrave*.[783] A redgum tree on the defendant's land was set on fire by lightning. After felling it, the defendant decided not to extinguish the fire with water but to let it burn out. A wind revived the fire which spread to the claimant's property. Liability was imposed.[784]

Scope of duty The duty to abate a fire, which is as a matter of reasonable foresight a danger, thus exists, but it will become necessary in future cases to decide how far the occupier need go to discharge the duty. The situation may require in certain circumstances no more than a summoning of the fire-brigade. It appears that the courts may be called on to examine the question with reference to the individual character of the occupier, for example "less must be expected of the infirm than of the able-bodied". Normally, in qualifying negligence the courts have referred the conduct of the defendant to the standard of "the reasonable man", but according to the judgment of the Judicial Committee "the reasonable man" in abating a fire hazard may take some of the physical and financial aspects of the occupier himself.[785] It may be that a more lenient approach to the defendant thus placed under a positive duty to act is to be justified by the consideration that the hazard is not of his making, and though in some circumstances he will be prompted to act by motives of self-interest, in other circumstances he may be required by the law to abate a fire of natural origin for the sole benefit of a neighbour. **19-160**

Fire in domestic grate The question has been discussed whether a fire caused by a piece of coal jumping from a domestic grate accidentally begins within the meaning of the Fires Prevention (Metropolis) Act, and on this question differing judicial opinions have been expressed.[786] No doubt the fire in the grate was an intentional and not an accidental fire, but this fire was intended to be controlled and rendered harmless by the grate. It would seem, therefore, that unless there was some negligence in the making of the fire or in leaving it in the grate unguarded or unat- **19-161**

---

782 per Lush J in *Musgrove v Pandelis* [1919] 1 K.B. 314 at 318; per Scrutton LJ in *Job Edwards Ltd v Birmingham Navigations* [1924] 1 K.B. 341 at 361.

783 [1967] 1 A.C. 645. The law is the same whether the question is identified as one of negligence or nuisance. This judgment substantially adopts the opinion of Scrutton LJ in *Job Edwards Ltd v Birmingham Navigations* [1924] 1 K.B. 341 at 357. For recent discussion of *Goldman v Hargrave* see *Gore v Stannard (t/a Wyvern Tyres)* [2012] EWCA Civ 1248; [2014] Q.B. 1 at [156]–[159] per Lewison LJ.

784 cf. *Leakey v National Trust* [1980] Q.B. 485.

785 [1967] 1 A.C. 645 at 663–664.

786 per Duke LJ in *Musgrove v Pandelis* [1919] 2 K.B. 43 at 51, thought that the Act was no protection; contra, per Scrutton LJ in *Job Edwards Ltd v Birmingham Navigations* [1924] 1 K.B. 341 at 361.

tended or in preventing the further spread of the fire, the Act in such a case will be a defence. In *Sochacki v Sas*,[787] a lodger who occupied a bed-sitting-room in a house left his room for two or three hours. The fire was burning, but there was no fireguard or fender. During his absence, a fire broke out and spread to the rest of the building doing considerable damage. It was held that neither the doctrine of *Rylands v Fletcher* nor the doctrine of res ipsa loquitur applied, and as there was no evidence that the fire was too large for the grate or any other evidence of negligence, the lodger was not liable.[788]

19-162 **"Dangerous thing"** In *Gore v Stannard (t/a Wyvern Tyres)*[789] the Court of Appeal confirmed, by a majority,[790] that a fire within the rule in *Rylands v Fletcher* does not begin accidentally for the purposes of s.86 of the Fire Prevention (Metropolis) Act 1774. Nevertheless earlier cases in which claims based on the rule for the escape of fire have succeeded now have to be read in the light of the reformulation of the *Rylands* rule itself in *Gore* as it applies in cases of fire. This seems to require the defendant to have been responsible for introducing the fire itself on to his or her land, in the course of a "non-natural" use, prior to its escape to the land of the claimant.[791] As a result, earlier decisions in which liability has been imposed under the rule (irrespective of negligence) where inflammable materials happen to have caught fire,[792] would now apparently be decided differently.

(iii) Responsibility for fire

19-163 **Vicarious liability for operations involving the creation of fire** In the difficult case of *Honeywill and Stein Ltd v Larkin Bros Ltd*,[793] the Court of Appeal held that a person who carries on himself or causes to be carried on by his servants, agents, or independent contractors any operation which involves the creation of fire is under a non-delegable duty to see that the fire is harmless to third parties. It followed that the occupier would be liable for the negligence of an independent contractor[794] notwithstanding the general principle that employers of independent contractors are not liable for the latter's negligence save in exceptional circumstances. In *Honeywill* a cinema company employed a firm of acoustic specialists to install a sound reproduction apparatus. The specialists, when the work was finished, employed photographers to photograph the apparatus. The photographers used flashlights which set fire to the theatre, and the specialists were held liable to the cinema company on the ground that (at 200):

---

[787] [1947] 1 All E.R. 344; *J Doltis Ltd v Isaac Braithwaite & Sons (Engineers) Ltd* [1957] 1 Lloyd's Rep. 522 (*Rylands v Fletcher* does not apply unless the fire in question has escaped from the premises of the occupier on whose premises it is lit; burning of paper in grate not negligent nor non-natural user; no liability for damage to occupier's premises for fire lit thereon by contractors); *Canadian Forest Products Ltd v Hudson Lumber Co* (1960) 20 D.L.R. (2d) 712 at 723–724, per Whittaker J.

[788] The judgment of Lord Goddard CJ in *Sochacki v Sas* was quoted from with approval by Lewison LJ in *Gore v Stannard (t/a Wyvern Tyres)* [2012] EWCA Civ 1248; [2014] Q.B. 1 at [151].

[789] [2012] EWCA Civ 1248; [2014] Q.B. 1.

[790] Ward and Etherton LJJ, Lewison LJ dissenting. See also *Musgrove v Pandelis* [1919] 1 K.B. 314; *Perry v Kendricks Transport Ltd* [1956] 1 W.L.R. 85 CA.

[791] See para.19-155.

[792] See, especially, *Mason v Levy Auto Parts of England Ltd* [1967] 2 Q.B. 530; and *LMS International Ltd v Styrene Packaging & Insulation Ltd* [2005] EWHC 2065 (TCC); [2006] T.C.L.R. 6.

[793] [1934] 1 K.B. 191. *The Pass of Ballater* [1942] P. 112 at 115–116. See also *Burnie Port Authority v General Jones Pty Ltd* (1994) 120 A.L.R. 42. cf. *Green v Fibreglass* [1958] 2 Q.B. 245.

[794] See, e.g. *Johnson v BJW Property Developments Ltd* [2002] EWHC 1131 (TCC); [2002] 3 All E.R. 574.

"to take the photograph in the cinema with a flashlight was … a dangerous operation in its intrinsic nature, involving the creation of fire and explosion on another person's premises … The appellants in procuring this work to be performed by their contractors … assumed an obligation to the cinema company which was, as we think, absolute,[795] but which was at least an obligation to use reasonable precautions to see that no damage resulted to the cinema company from these dangerous operations."

In *Biffa Waste Services Ltd v Maschinenfabrik Ernst Hese GmbH*[796] the Court of Appeal subjected its own controversial decision in *Honeywill and Stein Ltd v Larkin Bros Ltd*, and the criticisms to which it has been subjected, to an extensive analysis, and observed that it was "difficult to reconcile with the decision of the House of Lords in *Read v J Lyons & Co Ltd*[797] rejecting the contention that special rules of absolute liability apply to extra-hazardous acts".[798] The Court in *Biffa's* case, unable formally to depart from its own earlier decision, concluded that "the principle in *Honeywill* is anomalous" and that cases in which it could be applied would be "truly exceptional".[799] In particular, an activity should not be classified as "ultra-hazardous" without taking into account the existence of precautions which could have the effect of obviating any underlying danger. As a result the Court reversed the decision of the court below,[800] which had applied the *Honeywill* principle so as to impose vicarious liability for a fire. On the other hand, it has long been clear that the creation of fire is one of the exceptional situations in which an employer will be liable for the negligence of his independent contractor.[801] Vicarious liability was not imposed in the *Biffa Waste Services* case because the employers were entitled to assume that appropriate precautions would be taken to ensure that no fire would arise.

Operations involving the risks of fire Anyone who does anything likely to cause a fire is under a duty to take care that a fire is not caused. So, where carriers, by mistake, delivered highly inflammable celluloid film scrap to the claimants without giving any warning of its dangerous character, they were held liable for damage by a fire set up by one of the claimants' typists in thoughtlessly applying a lighted cigarette end to the scrap.[802] Again, where a boy of nine obtained petrol by falsely stating that his mother's motorcar was "stuck down the street", and used it to make a torch as a result of which he was severely burned, the suppliers were held liable on the ground that: 19-164

"to put a highly inflammable substance into the hands of a small boy is to subject him to

795 "Absolute" suggests liability in the absence of negligence on the part of anyone, but the sense is not consistent with the remainder of the sentence. It may be that a negative has been omitted. The liability indicated is that of vicarious liability for negligence by independent contractors. See Lord Denning MR in *H & N Emanuel Ltd v Greater London Council* [1971] 2 All E.R. 835 at 839.

796 [2008] EWCA Civ 1257; [2009] Q.B. 725.

797 [1947] A.C. 156.

798 [2008] EWCA Civ 1257; [2009] Q.B. 725 at [75].

799 [2008] EWCA Civ 1257; [2009] Q.B. 725 at [85].

800 See [2008] EWHC 6 (TCC); [2008] B.L.R. 155. The decision is equally applicable to both negligence and nuisance: see *Tinseltime Ltd v Roberts* [2011] EWHC 1199 (TCC); [2011] B.L.R. 515 at [49], per Judge Stephen Davies. See also *Lindsay v Berkeley Homes (Capital) Plc* [2018] EWHC 2042 (TCC).

801 See *Gore v Stannard (t/a Wyvern Tyres)* [2012] EWCA Civ 1248; [2014] Q.B. 1 at [34]–[35], per Ward LJ and [155], per Lewison LJ, and the cases there cited by both Lord Justices.

802 *Philco Radio v J Spurling Ltd* [1949] 2 K.B. 33. See also *LMS International v Skyrene Packaging* [2005] EWHC 2065 (TCC); [2006] T.C.L.R. 6.

temptation and the risk of injury and this is no less true if the boy has resorted to deceit in order to overcome the suppliers' scruples."[803]

In other cases the occupier of a motor garage was held liable for a fire caused by the act of his servant in smoking while filling a tin with benzol[804]; a person who was investigating an escape of gas by means of a naked light was held liable for an explosion caused by a lighted match struck by a friend who was assisting him[805]; the employer of a driver of a lorry was held liable for the act of the driver in throwing a lighted match on the floor of a garage while petrol was being transferred from his lorry to an underground tank, thereby causing a conflagration and an explosion[806]; a man who made a fire in his yard to smoke out a rat in a drain was held liable for the damage resulting from the fire spreading to a packaging case and exploding a drum of paraffin[807]; and an employer was held liable to his servant who was injured because highly combustible material was placed near a boiler, so that when the boiler was fired sparks were emitted and the material was set on fire.[808] In *Anthony v Coal Authority*[809] the defendants were held liable for a fire which broke out in their coal tip. The fire had started as a result of spontaneous combustion, but the defendants were held liable on the basis that the fire should have been foreseen, and could have been prevented by the taking of reasonable steps.

19-165 **Liability of occupier** Apart from liability for fire caused by his servants or independent contractors, an occupier of land is liable for fire caused by any person lawfully on his land with his consent, if he authorised the fire, but otherwise not.[810] It is possible, however, that a broad view of authorisation will be taken for this purpose.[811] He is not liable for fire caused by a trespasser or stranger,[812] unless by his negligence he allows it to continue. In *Ribee v Norrie*[813] the Court of Appeal held that a tenant is not a "stranger", and that the landlord will be liable for fires negligently caused by his tenants unless the latter's behaviour was wholly outside the terms of the tenancy. One of the defendant's tenants negligently dropped a cigarette, causing a fire which spread to the premises of the claimant. The Court, reversing the court below, held that this was sufficient to impose liability on the defendant. The Court emphasised that the defendant, who did not live on the premises, had done nothing to discourage smoking by his tenants, which was clearly foreseeable. Where the fire has started without human agency but by natural causes there is a duty to abate it, as described by the Judicial Committee in *Goldman v*

---

803 *Yachuk v Oliver Blais Ltd* [1949] A.C. 386.
804 *Jefferson v Derbyshire Farmers Ltd* [1921] 2 K.B. 281.
805 *Brooke v Bool* [1928] 2 K.B. 578.
806 *Century Insurance Co v Northern Ireland Road Transport Board* [1942] A.C. 509.
807 *Mulholland and Tedd Ltd v Baker* [1939] 3 All E.R. 253.
808 *D'Urso v Sanson* [1939] 4 All E.R. 26.
809 [2005] EWHC 1654 (QB); [2006] Env. L.R. 17.
810 *Whitmores (Edenbridge) Ltd v Stanford* [1909] 1 Ch. 427 at 438; *Sturge v Hackett* [1962] 1 W.L.R. 1257 CA; *H & N Emanuel v Greater London Council* [1971] 2 All E.R. 835 CA, and see para.19-157. But if the occupier asks a contractor to inspect land with a view to gorse burning, but makes no arrangement for the contractor to set the fire, the occupier is not responsible when the fire is started without authority or permission: *Erisksen v Clifton* [1963] N.Z.L.R. 705.
811 See *Ribee v Norrie* [2001] P.I.Q.R. P8, below.
812 *Job Edwards Ltd v Birmingham Navigations* [1924] 1 K.B. 341; *Balfour v Barty-King* [1956] 1 Q.B. 496 CA at 505.
813 [2001] P.I.Q.R. P8.

Hargrave.[814] An occupier of land who authorises, expressly or by implication, persons to enter on his land for the purposes of carrying on a dangerous operation which involves or may involve the creation of fire or of an act likely to cause fire on the land is liable for the damage caused to third parties.[815] On the other hand, he is not liable for fire caused by a dangerous operation carried out by persons lawfully on his land purely for their own purposes and outside any authority given to them.[816]

(iv) Claimants

Who can sue The duty is owed to anyone who suffers damage by the fire: **19-166**

> "The principle is that if a man does work on or near another's property which involves danger to that property unless proper care is taken, he is liable to the owners of the property for damage resulting to it from the failure to take proper care, and is equally liable if, instead of doing the work himself, he procures another whether agent, servant or otherwise to do it for him."[817]

Accordingly, not only the owners of any building damaged by fire, but also the owners of any chattels lawfully on the premises, may maintain an action against the person liable for the fire.

Firemen The occupier who negligently starts a fire is liable to a fireman injured in the course of fighting the fire, and this is so regardless of whether the injury is suffered as the result of exceptional or merely ordinary risks undertaken by the fireman.[818] A defence of volenti non fit injuria is clearly not available,[819] though the fireman's claim might be qualified by contributory negligence if, for example he contributed to his injury "by his foolhardy exposure to an unnecessary risk either of his own volition or acting under the orders of a senior fire officer". Generally, the standard of responsibility required of an occupier is the ordinary duty of care. The liability of a non-occupier negligently starting a fire is to be similarly assessed. A defendant is liable to those injured while fighting the fire whether as professional firemen or as amateur volunteers.[820] **19-167**

(f) Gas

Danger from gas Gas is a dangerous thing and, subject to any relevant statutory provisions, the duty of those who bring gas to any place is therefore that laid down in *Rylands v Fletcher*, that is, to keep it at their peril from doing harm.[821] **19-168**

Supply of gas under statutory powers The commercial supply of gas is **19-169**

---

814 [1967] 1 A.C. 645, and see para.19-159. See also *Gore v Stannard (t/a Wyvern Tyres)* [2012] EWCA Civ 1248; [2014] Q.B. 1 at [156]–[159], per Lewison LJ.

815 *Rainham Chemical Works v Belvedere Fish Guano Co Ltd* [1921] 2 A.C. 465.

816 See fn.810.

817 per Talbot J in *Brooke v Bool* [1928] 2 K.B. 578 at 587; *Sochacki v Sas* [1947] 1 All E.R. 344 at 345.

818 *Ogwo v Taylor* [1988] A.C. 431 HL, where the earlier cases are discussed in the speech of Lord Bridge of Harwich.

819 *Ogwo v Taylor* [1988] A.C. 431 at 447, per Lord Bridge: "would be utterly repugnant to our contemporary notions of justice." The House declined to follow the so-called "fireman's rule" negativing a duty of care, which has been adopted in certain American jurisdictions.

820 See *Russell v McCabe* [1962] N.Z.L.R. 392.

821 *Northwestern Utilities v London Guarantee and Accident Co* [1936] A.C. 108; *Goodbody v Poplar*

normally supplied by companies acting under statutory powers[822] and such companies are only liable when negligence is proved, unless statute preserves their strict liability as s.14 of the Gas Act 1965 does for underground storage. Where gas is supplied by the company in exercise of its statutory powers, "the 'wild beast' theory referred to in the well-known case of *Rylands v Fletcher* is inapplicable".[823] The negligence may consist in causing an escape of gas or omitting to remedy an escape caused without negligence on their part. For example, when a gas authority supplied a defective service pipe to a shop and a servant of a gas-fitter employed in another part of the shop tried to locate the leak by means of a lighted candle and caused an explosion, the gas authority was held liable.[824] Similarly, a gas authority was held liable for an explosion caused by their negligence in not effectively cutting off the supply of gas to a meter about to be disconnected. Lord Esher MR said that gas was so dangerous a thing that it required the greatest precaution.[825] An escape of gas from gas pipes is itself evidence of negligence.[826] Gas companies are bound to have a reasonable system of inspection of their mains and pipes so as to enable them to discover an escape of gas within a reasonable time of its occurrence, and a failure to detect an escape of gas within a reasonable time is negligence.[827] Accordingly, where a gas main was deprived of support, owing to excavations made in connection with a sewer, so that it became cracked by the weight of traffic above and the gas escaped for two or three days, accumulated, and then exploded, injuring the claimant as he was passing, the gas authority were held liable.[828] If the escape of gas has not been detected within a reasonable time, it is not necessary for the claimant to show the steps which ought to have been taken to detect it.[829] If a gas company knows that excavations are being made by others near its mains or pipes, they are under a duty of care to see that the excavations do not damage their mains or pipes, and they are under a further duty to have a system of inspection so as to learn within a reasonable time whether any such excavations are being made.[830] Also, if gas mains are laid, without any right of support being obtained, in an area where colliery subsidence is likely to occur, the gas company will be liable for an explosion caused through the breaking of its mains by subsidence, unless it has taken all reasonable precautions to prevent them from being broken.[831]

19-170 **Nuisance** A detailed statutory code regulates the rights and obligations of gas sup-

BC (1915) 84 L.J.K.B. 1230; *Parry v Smith* (1879) 4 C.P.D. 325; *Dominion Natural Gas Co v Collins* [1909] A.C. 640. The deliberate discharge of gas (e.g. by CS gas canister) into the claimant's property would seem a matter of trespass: *Rigby v Chief Constable of Northamptonshire* [1985] 1 W.L.R. 1242 at 1251.

822 The industry is regulated by the Gas Act 1986 as amended by the Gas Act 1995 and the Utilities Act 2000.

823 per Russell CJ in *Price v South Metropolitan Gas Co* (1895) 65 L.J.Q.B. 126; *Dunne v North Western Gas Board* [1964] 2 Q.B. 806.

824 *Burrows v March Gas and Coke Co* (1870) L.R. 5 Ex. 67.

825 *Patterson v Blackburn Corp* (1892) 9 T.L.R. 55.

826 *Hanson v Wearmouth Coal Co* [1939] 3 All E.R. 47 at 53; *Pearson v North West Gas Board* [1968] 2 All E.R. 669.

827 See Gas Act 1986, especially s.16 (standard of quality), and s.18 (safety regulations).

828 *Price v South Metropolitan Gas Co* (1895) 65 L.J.Q.B. 126.

829 *Manchester Corp v Markland* [1936] A.C. 360.

830 *Northwestern Utilities Ltd v London Guarantee and Accident Co* [1936] A.C. 108; *Shell-Mex BP Ltd v Belfast Corp* [1952] N.I. 72.

831 *Hanson v Wearmouth Coal Co* [1939] 3 All E.R. 47.

pliers and consumers,[832] and the number of reported cases concerning gas related incidents is relatively small. The Court of Appeal has nevertheless held that a supplier of gas subject to a statutory duty to supply cannot be liable in the absence of negligence, and therefore cannot be held strictly responsible either in nuisance or under *Rylands v Fletcher*.[833] Where the escape of gas can be held to constitute a nuisance, it is not necessary to show that the escape has continued for a substantial time.[834] But where the escape of gas is not the result of defective piping but is the result of the bursting of an adjacent water main with which the gas company had nothing to do, the company is not liable for injuries caused by the ensuing explosions and, similarly, a company escaped liability for an escape of gas caused by frost fracture, "a risk which is well known to exist but which, according to the evidence in this case, cannot be avoided by the exercise of reasonable care on the part of the defendants".[835] The nature of nuisance liability in respect of the supply of gas was considered, in somewhat unusual circumstances, in *Anglian Water Services Ltd v Crawshaw Robins Co Ltd*.[836] Instead of an escape of gas, the case was concerned with a situation in which the defendant third parties *disrupted* the supply of gas to domestic premises. Stanley Burnton J declined to impose liability for the inconvenience resulting from loss of cooking and heating facilities. He said[837]:

> "My conclusion is that the negligent interruption of a supply of gas by a third party is not actionable as a private nuisance. It does not involve an invasion of any substance or form of energy on to the claimant's land. It is not one of the exceptional cases of liability in nuisance without such an invasion. A home owner or tenant does not have a property right in the supply of gas. His or her protection lies in his or her rights against the gas supplier."

Escapes from gas pipes Gas companies are not liable for escapes of gas from pipes over which they have no control, as where a stop-cock inside a house was left on after the tenant had left and an explosion resulted,[838] or where a faulty pipe was laid inside a flat by the owner.[839] They are under no obligation to inspect gas service pipes, unless they receive warning of some defect or should otherwise have been aware of a defect.[840] If such pipes form part of the ordinary domestic installation of gas, the owner or occupier of the house is not liable to other occupiers of the house or of other floors in the house, except on proof of negligence, because they **19-171**

---

832 See the Gas Act 1986 Sch.2B (inserted by the Gas Act 1995).

833 *Dunne v North Western Gas Board* [1964] 2 Q.B. 806; *Pearson v North West Gas Board* [1968] 2 All E.R. 669. Quaere whether the subsequent "privatisation" of the gas industry should have any effect on the status of the decisions in these cases.

834 *Midwood v Manchester Corp* [1905] 2 K.B. 597; *Charing Cross Electricity Supply Co v Hydraulic Power Co* [1914] 3 K.B. 772, where the nuisance "consisted in streams of water suddenly issuing from a fracture in the pipe under a very high head". See also *Colour Quest Ltd v Total Downstream UK Plc* [2009] EWHC 540 (Comm); [2009] 2 Lloyd's Rep. 1; reversed in part in [2010] EWCA Civ 180; [2011] Q.B. 86.

835 *Pearson v North West Gas Board* [1968] 2 All E.R. 669 at 672. In this case the statutory exemption from strict liability resulted in the claimant receiving no compensation for the death of her husband, her own severe injuries, and the destruction of their home.

836 [2001] B.L.R. 173.

837 [2001] B.L.R. 173 at [143].

838 *Holden v Liverpool New Gas and Coke Co* (1846) 3 C.B. 1.

839 *Henderson v Newcastle and Gateshead Gas Co* (1893) 37 S.J. 403.

840 *Glennister v Condon and Eastern Gas Board* [1951] 2 Lloyd's Rep. 115; *Lloyde v West Midlands Gas Board* [1971] 1 W.L.R. 749 CA. See also the Gas Act 1986 Sch.2B (inserted by the Gas Act 1995).

must be taken to have consented to the presence of gas in the building.[841] Where, however, a strong smell of gas, never present before, persists on the premises for about eight hours and is followed by an explosion, the occupier of the premises, who has taken no steps in the matter, is liable for damage caused by the explosion.[842]

19-172 **Installing or interfering with gas** A person who installs gas or interferes with gas already installed is liable to anyone injured through an escape of gas, if the escape is due to his installation or interference. The installer owes a duty of care, and if the installation was recent and without opportunity for subsequent interference, the damage caused by an explosion may raise a presumption of fault in that res ipsa loquitur.[843] The employment of an independent contractor is no defence to those who install or interfere with an installation of gas.[844]

(g) Electricity

19-173 **Danger from electricity** It has been decided that the principle of *Rylands v Fletcher* applies to electricity,[845] and consequently the owners of wires or cables through which an electric current is passing must keep them innocuous at their peril. When electricity is used under statutory authority,[846] it is necessary to show negligence on the part of the electricity companies before an action will lie against them, unless the statute preserves their liability. Accordingly, when an electric current, which was used under statutory powers to work a tramway, interfered with telephone wires, it was held that no action lay in the absence of negligence.[847]

(h) Explosives

19-174 **Danger from explosives** A person who owns or manufactures explosives is under the strict liability of *Rylands v Fletcher* with regard to them. When quarry owners were engaged in blasting operations, as a result of which a person walking on the highway was struck by a piece of stone, they were held liable independently of any question of negligence because "the case was like that of the escape of a dangerous and mischievous animal".[848] In *Rainham Chemical Works v Belvedere Fish Guano Co*,[849] a fire occurred at the defendants' munitions factory during the First World War, causing an explosion. They were held liable on the principle of *Rylands v Fletcher* for: (1) storing explosives; and (2) carrying on the business of

841 See *Ross v Fedden* (1872) L.R. 7 Q.B. 661; *Peters v Prince of Wales Theatre* [1943] K.B. 73; and other cases dealing with escape of water, para.19-135, *Miller v Robert Addie & Sons' Collieries*, 1934 S.C. 150 (landlord not liable to tenant for escape of gas from service pipe leading to an adjoining house owned by him, without proof of negligence).

842 *Glennister v Condon and Eastern Gas Board* [1951] 2 Lloyd's Rep. 115.

843 *Lloyde v West Midlands Gas Board* [1971] 1 W.L.R. 749 CA. See also *Dominion Natural Gas Co v Collins* [1909] A.C. 640.

844 *Hardaker v Idle DC* [1896] 1 Q.B. 335.

845 *National Telephone Co v Baker* [1893] 2 Ch. 186; *Eastern and South African Telephone Co v Cape Town Tramways* [1902] A.C. 381; *Hillier v Air Ministry*, *The Times*, 8 December 1962; *Nor-Video Services v Ontario-Hydro* (1978) 84 D.L.R. (3d) 221.

846 See now the Electricity Act 1989 (which provided for the privatisation of the electricity industry) and the Utilities Act 2000.

847 *National Telephone Co v Baker* [1893] 2 Ch. 186.

848 *Miles v Rock Granite Co* (1918) 34 T.L.R. 500.

849 [1921] 2 A.C. 465.

manufacturing explosives without preventing damage to third parties.[850] The occupiers of the land on which the defendant company carried on its operations were also held liable, on the ground that they had permitted the company to operate on their land.

War and peace Doubts were subsequently expressed in the House of Lords in *Read v J Lyons & Co Ltd*, whether it is a non-natural user of land to manufacture explosives at government request in time of war,[851] and on the same occasion Lord Macmillan said he would "hesitate to hold that in these days and in an industrial community it was a non-natural use of land to build a factory on it and conduct there the manufacture of explosives".[852] But these remarks were obiter and, since the observations in the House of Lords in *Cambridge Water Co Ltd v Eastern Counties Leather Plc*,[853] it is certain that such operations and accumulations come within the scope of *Rylands v Fletcher*, at least in peacetime. Moreover, in *Transco v Stockport MBC*[854] Lord Bingham of Cornhill, referring to *Read v J Lyons & Co Ltd*, said: "I would question whether, *even in wartime*, the manufacture of explosives could ever be regarded as an ordinary user of land." The keeping of explosives is regulated by the criminal law[855] and may also amount to a public nuisance. 19-175

(i) Poisonous waste

Environmental Protection Act By s.73(6) of the Environmental Protection Act 1990, where any damage (including personal injuries) is caused by waste which has been deposited on land, any person who deposited it or caused or knowingly permitted it to be deposited may be liable in civil law for the damage. The substantive damage is that covered by ss.33 and 63(2) of the Act which relate to the Act's waste management licensing system. There are various defences[856] including the taking of "all reasonable precautions" and the exercise of "all due diligence".[857] Liability is also negated where the damage was wholly due to the fault of the person who suffered it,[858] or was suffered by a person who voluntarily accepted the risk thereof.[859] The Law Reform (Contributory Negligence) Act 1945 applies to civil liability arising under the Act.[860] The Act preserves all common law liabilities,[861] and does not therefore supersede liability under the rule in *Rylands v Fletcher*. In view of the decision of the House of Lords in *Cambridge Water v Eastern Counties Leather Plc*,[862] however, holding that foreseeability of damage is a prerequisite of 19-176

850 The substance which actually exploded, DNP, had never been known to explode before and it is possible that the case might now be differently decided on the grounds that what occurred had not been foreseeable: see the doubts expressed by Lord Goff in *Cambridge Water Co v Eastern Counties Leather Plc* [1994] 2 A.C. 264 at 303.

851 See per Viscount Simon [1947] A.C. 156 at 169-170.

852 [1947] A.C. 156 at 173-174.

853 [1994] 2 A.C. 264.

854 [2003] UKHL 61; [2004] 2 A.C. 1 at [11] (emphasis added).

855 See, e.g. the Fireworks Act 2003.

856 s.33(7).

857 s.33(7)(a).

858 s.73(6)(a).

859 s.73(6)(b).

860 s.73(9)(b).

861 s.73(6).

862 [1994] 2 A.C. 264.

liability in this area, knowledge of the poisonous nature of the substance will normally be required.[863]

(j) Nuclear installations

19-177 **Nuclear installations**[864] The dangers inherent in the setting up of nuclear installations—atomic energy, radioactive substances, the emission of ionising radiations, the use of radioisotopes for medical and industrial purposes, and the disposal of waste therefrom—created new problems of liability to which the common law, in the form of actions for negligence, nuisance, and under *Rylands v Fletcher* provided no satisfactory answer. The risk of damage is so widespread as to inflict losses of millions of pounds in the course of a single emission of ionising radiations. The ordinary periods of time under Limitation Acts were unsuitable and potentially unjust owing to the long period which might intervene between the impact of ionising radiations on the claimant and his suffering ascertainable damage.[865]

19-178 **Nuclear Installations Act 1965** By the Nuclear Installations Act 1965,[866] no person other than the United Kingdom Atomic Energy Authority shall use any site for the operation of nuclear plant unless a licence to do so has been granted in respect of that site by the Minister of Power. Liability arises only when there is a nuclear incident which occurs at, or in connection with, certain nuclear installations, or in the course of transport of nuclear substances; and it can arise only in connection with licensed nuclear sites.[867] Section 7(1) enacts[868]:

> "it shall be the duty of the licensee to secure that—
>
> (a) no such occurrence involving nuclear matter as is mentioned in subsection (2) of this section causes injury to any person or damage to any property of any person other than the licensee, being injury or damage arising out of or resulting from the radioactive properties, or a combination of those and any toxic, explosive or other hazardous properties, of that nuclear matter; and
>
> (b) no ionising radiations emitted during the period of the licensee's responsibility—
>
> (i) from anything caused or suffered by the licensee to be on the site which is not nuclear matter; or
>
> (ii) from any waste discharged (in whatever form) on or from the site,
>
> cause injury to any person or damage to any property of any person other than the licensee."[869]

---

863 See [1994] 2 A.C. 264 at 302–304, per Lord Goff; doubting *West v Bristol Tramways Co* [1908] 2 K.B. 14; and dicta in *Rainham Chemical Works v Belvedere Fish Guano Co* [1921] 2 A.C. 465 which appeared to provide authority to the contrary effect.

864 See, generally, Tromans, *Nuclear Law: The Law Applying to Nuclear Installations and Radioactive Substances* (2010); Cook, *The Law of Nuclear Energy*, Sweet & Maxwell (2013); Street and Frame, *Law Relating to Nuclear Energy* (1966).

865 Street and Frame, op. cit., p.38.

866 As amended by the Energy Act 1983 Pt II ss.27–34. The 1965 Act consolidated the law relating to nuclear installations, namely, the Nuclear Installations (Licensing and Insurance) Act 1959 and the Nuclear Installations (Amendment) Act 1965. And see further the Nuclear Installations Act 1969, and the Atomic Energy Authority Act 1971.

867 Street and Frame, *Law Relating to Nuclear Energy* (1966), p.47.

868 The Nuclear Installations (Liability for Damage) Order 2016 (SI 2016/562) (art.3), will, when brought into force, substitute a revised version of this provision.

869 For other occurrences liability is confined to nuclear matter which is not excepted matter. "Nuclear

Liability under the Act The liability of the licensee under s.7(1)(a), once damage within the Act is proved to have resulted, is a strict one; there is no need to prove negligence on the part of anyone.[870] Any person, other than the licensee, may sue, provided he can prove "injury" (which means "personal injury" and includes loss of life) or "damage to any property". Liability was imposed in *Blue Circle Industries Plc v Ministry of Defence*[871] in respect of radioactive contamination of the claimants' land, the topsoil of which had had to be removed before the property could be sold. The defendants contended that the very small amounts of radioactive material had not physically damaged the claimants' property. But the Court of Appeal held that the claimants had suffered damage to property within s.7(1)(a).[872] There is no need that the dangerous matter should "escape" from the site on which it was kept on to other land. The Act creates a statutory right of action for damages, where injury or damage has been caused in breach of a duty.[873] 19-179

8. Obstruction of the Highway

(a) Right of access

Right of access to highway 19-180

> "The owner of land adjoining a highway has a right of access to the highway from any part of his premises. This is so ... whether he is entitled to the whole or some interest in the ground subjacent to the highway or not. The rights of the public to pass along the highway are subject to this right of access: just as the right of access is subject to the rights of the public and must be exercised subject to the general obligations as to nuisance and the like imposed upon a person using the highway."[874]

This common law right of access remains in force, though nowadays qualified considerably by public law.[875] It is a private right, distinct from the right of the owner of that land to use the highway itself as one of the public.[876] It is not confined to access to the door of the house, but includes a right of access to the walls, for example for the purpose of displaying advertisements.[877] An interference with this right is actionable per se,[878] and, if it is such as to hinder customers from resorting

---

matter" and "excepted matter" are defined in s.26(1).

870 Street and Frame, *Law Relating to Nuclear Energy* (1966), p.52.

871 [1999] Ch. 289.

872 The Court distinguished the decision of Gatehouse J in *Merlin v British Nuclear Fuels* [1990] 2 Q.B. 557. In that case a mere increased risk of personal injury, or a reduction in the value of a house, due to raised radioactivity levels was held not to fall within the Act on the ground that only actual personal injury or property damage did so.

873 ss.12 and 16.

874 per Lord Atkin in *Marshall v Blackpool Corp* [1935] A.C. 16 at 22. Other cases to the same effect are: *St Mary, Newington v Jacobs* (1871) L.R. 7 Q.B. 47; *Tottenham Urban DC v Rowley* [1912] 2 Ch. 633; affirmed [1914] A.C. 95; cf. *Ching Garage Ltd v Chingford Corp* [1961] 1 W.L.R. 470 HL (Highways Act 1980 s.66); cf. *LCC v Cutts* [1961] 1 W.L.R. 292 DC.

875 e.g. Highways Act 1980 ss.126–131.

876 *Lyon v Fishmongers' Co* (1876) 1 App. Cas. 662; *Att Gen v Thames Conservators* (1862) 1 H. & M. 1; *Chaplin v Westminster Corp* [1901] 2 Ch. 329 at 333–335; *Ineos Upstream Ltd v Persons Unknown* [2017] EWHC 2945 (Ch) at [42].

877 *Cobb v Saxby* [1914] 3 K.B. 822.

878 *Walsh v Ervin* [1952] V.L.R. 361.

to the house for business purposes, damages for loss of business can be obtained.[879] An owner of land adjoining a navigable river has a similar private right of access to the river.[880] This private right ceases as soon as the highway is reached and any subsequent interference, for example with the right to carry goods from the premises to a van standing in the roadway, is a public nuisance if it is a nuisance at all.[881]

(b) Public nuisance by obstruction of highway

(i) Special damage

19-181 **Special damage** It is a public nuisance to obstruct[882] or hinder the free passage of the public along the highway by land[883] or water.[884] A private individual has a right of action in respect of a public nuisance if he can prove that he has sustained particular damage other than and beyond the general inconvenience and injury suffered by the public, and that the particular damage which he has sustained is direct and substantial.[885] An action for public nuisance of this type does not depend upon contiguity to the highway, but depends upon whether the claimant's property is sufficiently proximate to it to be affected by the nuisance on it.[886] In *Iveson v Moore*[887] where the claimant was prevented by the defendant's obstruction of the highway from using the way for carting coal from his colliery, and the coal was deteriorated by the delay, the special damage was held sufficient to support the action, it being the primary object of a public highway to afford free passage to the public.[888] Frontagers on a private road have a special interest, over and beyond that of the general public, in preventing damage to the road, as to entitle them to sue for damage to the road by the use of a skid pan on the wheel of a vehicle.[889] But mere personal inconvenience caused by the claimant being delayed by an obstruction in

---

879 *Fritz v Hobson* (1880) 14 Ch. D. 542 at 554–556.

880 *Lyon v Fishmongers' Co* (1876) 1 App. Cas. 662; *Chaplin v Westminster Corp* [1901] 2 Ch. 329.

881 *Chaplin v Westminster Corp* [1901] 2 Ch. 329. See also *Hiscox Syndicates Ltd v The Pinnacle Ltd* [2008] EWHC 1386 (QB); [2008] N.P.C. 71 at [14], per Akenhead J.

882 If the obstruction is caused by activities carried out pursuant to a statutory order redress can only be sought by way of judicial review to challenge the validity of the order, and not by a private law nuisance action: *Great House at Sonning Ltd v Berkshire CC* [1996] R.T.R. 407 CA.

883 See *East Hertfordshire DC v Isobel Hospice Trading Ltd* [2001] J.P.L. 597.

884 *Tate & Lyle v GLC* [1983] 1 A.C. 509 (siltation of navigable river by badly placed ferry terminals). In *Att Gen (ex rel. Yorkshire Derwent Trust) v Brotherton* [1991] 1 A.C. 425, the House of Lords held that s.31 of the Highways Act 1980 (formerly the Rights of Way Act 1932), which deals with the acquisition of public rights of way by long user, is not applicable to non-tidal rivers and is confined to land.

885 *Benjamin v Storr* (1874) L.R. 9 C. & P. 400; *Fritz v Hobson* (1880) 14 Ch. D. 542; *Vanderpant v Mayfair Hotel Co* [1930] 1 Ch. 138. For a recent application of the principle see *Jan de Nul (UK) v NV Royal Belge* [2000] 2 Lloyd's Rep. 700; affirmed [2002] EWCA Civ 209; [2002] 1 Lloyd's Rep. 583.

886 *Southport Corp v Esso Petroleum Co* [1956] A.C. 218 at 224–225, per Devlin J.

887 (1699) Ld. Ray. 486.

888 See also *Att Gen v Brighton and Hove Co-operative Supply Association* [1900] 1 Ch. 276 (in which the defendants had occupied half the highway for most of the day loading and unloading at their store); and *Rose v Miles* (1815) 4 M. & S. 101 (where the successful plaintiff, being prevented from navigating his barges on a public navigable creek, had been obliged to convey his goods overland at considerable expense). Several of the relevant cases are collected in the judgment of Erle CJ in *Ricket v Metropolitan Ry* (1864–1865) 5 B. & S. 149.

889 *Medcalf v Strawbridge* [1937] 2 K.B. 102.

the highway, without pecuniary damage, will not suffice[890]; nor is it enough that the claimant has been put to expense in exercising his right of abating the obstruction.[891] Particular damage is not limited to special damage, in the sense of actual pecuniary loss; it may consist of proved general damage, for example inconvenience and delay, provided that it is substantial and appreciably greater in degree than any suffered by the general public.[892]

Picketing It follows from the decision of the House of Lords in *Hunter v Canary Wharf Ltd*,[893] to the effect that an interest in land is necessary for a claim in private nuisance, that harassment on the highway by pickets, which does not constitute a public nuisance, cannot constitute a private nuisance. Any decisions to the contrary[894] must accordingly be regarded as incorrect. Such picketing might, however, now fall within the Protection from Harassment Act 1997. **19-182**

Trading losses Not only is unlawful interference with the claimant's use of the highway actionable on proof of particular damage, the principle has been extended to obstruction of the public with consequential harm to the claimant's trade on adjacent premises. It has been held to be actionable to keep vans constantly outside the claimant's coffee-shop, interfering with the light and obstructing the access to the shop and rendering it uncomfortable by smells,[895] to obstruct the access of customers to the claimant's shop by blocking up a passage,[896] allowing theatre queues to assemble,[897] or making a shop window so attractive as to draw crowds or people blocking up the claimant's shop door,[898] and to erect a stand without lawful authority in the street which obstructed the view of a procession from the claimant's house, as a result of which he lost the letting value of his rooms for that occasion,[899] and to picket a place of business by way of protest against the business practices of the claimant.[900] **19-183**

Prospective customers If a highway is obstructed as a result of which prospective customers are diverted from the claimant's shop, causing a loss of business to the claimant, there has been a difference of judicial opinion whether there is a right **19-184**

---

890 *Winterbottom v Lord Derby* (1867) L.R. 2 Ex. 316.

891 *Winterbottom v Lord Derby* (1867) L.R. 2 Ex. 316.

892 *Chaplin v Westminster Corp* [1901] 2 Ch. 329. For review of the cases, see *Walsh v Ervin* [1952] V.L.R. 361 at 368–371, per Scholl J; and the *Wagon Mound (No.2)* [1963] 1 Lloyd's Rep. 402 at 430–435, per Walsh J; Fridman, "The Definition of Particular Damage in Nuisance" (1953) 2 Annual L. Rev. at 490–503, Western Australia; Kodilnye, "Public Nuisance and Particular Damage in the Modern Law" (1986) 6 L.S. 182. For a different test of particular damage in Canada, see *Stein v Gonzales* (1985) 14 D.L.R. (4th) 263.

893 [1997] A.C. 655.

894 See, e.g. *Thomas v National Union of Mineworkers* [1986] Ch. 20. cf. Peter Gibson LJ, dissenting, in *Khorasandjian v Bush* [1993] Q.B. 727.

895 *Benjamin v Storr* (1874) L.R. 9 C. & P. 400.

896 *Fritz v Hobson* (1880) 14 Ch. D. 542. See also *Business Environment Group Ltd v Wendy Fair (Wembley) Ltd* [2005] EWCA Civ 1230.

897 *Barber v Penley* [1893] 2 Ch. 447; *Lyons v Gulliver* [1914] 1 Ch. 631. cf. *Dwyer v Mansfield* [1946] K.B. 437. See also *Fabbri v Morris* (1947) 176 L.T. 172 (statutory liability).

898 *Wagstaff v Edison Bell Phonograph Co* (1893) 10 T.L.R. 80.

899 *Campbell v Paddington Corp* [1911] 1 K.B. 869.

900 *Hubbard v Pitt* [1976] Q.B. 142. See also *Church of Jesus Christ of Latter Day Saints v Price* [2004] EWHC 3245 (QB).

of action.[901] On principle, it would appear that such a loss is a particular damage suffered by the claimant beyond that suffered by the general public,[902] and that there is no good reason for distinguishing the claimant's loss of custom from other forms of harm caused by a public nuisance on the highway.[903] For example, where a ferry is obstructed or hindered or where its service is unreasonably curtailed so that employees are hindered in going to work, it has been held that the employer can sue in public nuisance because he has suffered a particular damage.[904]

(ii) Obstruction

19-185 **Loading and unloading** The owner of premises abutting on a highway is entitled to make a reasonable use of that highway for the purpose of obtaining access to and of loading and unloading goods at his premises, notwithstanding that some inconvenience is caused to the public, provided that a serious obstruction is not caused.[905]

19-186 **Creation of dangers in highway** Anyone who creates a source of danger upon a highway, as by digging a trench across it, placing a log or a pile of stones in the middle of it, or driving piles into the bed of a navigable river, is liable to any member of the public who, while using the highway, suffers any injury by reason of the dangerous obstruction.[906] In *Trevett v Lee*, the defendant's house fronted on a quiet country road. In time of drought he laid a hosepipe of a half-inch diameter across the road to enable water to be brought by gravity from a supply tank on the other side. The claimant fell over the hosepipe in the road and was injured. The Court of Appeal held it did not constitute a nuisance, for in all the circumstances it was a reasonable user.[907] If he has authorised an independent contractor to do the act complained of, he is liable for his failure to warn the public or to take other

---

901 *Wilkes v Hungerford Market Co* (1835) 2 Bing. N.C. 281 decided that such an action was maintainable; in *Ricket v Metropolitan Ry* (1868) L.R. 2 HL 175 at 196, such damage was held to be too remote; Willes J in *Beckett v Midland Ry* (1867) L.R. 3 C. & P. 82 at 100, treated *Wilkes* as overruled; as did Kennedy J in *Martin v London CC* (1898) 14 T.L.R. 575; *Wilkes* was thought to be rightly decided by Greer and Scrutton LJJ in *Blundy, Clark & Co v London and North Eastern Ry* [1931] 2 K.B. 334 at 352 and 362; and by Lord Hanworth MR in *Harper v Haden & Sons Ltd* [1933] 1 Ch. 298 at 306.

902 See *Salmond and Heuston on the Law of Torts*, 21st edn (1996), pp.87–88.

903 "I conclude that there is long standing and consistent authority in support of the proposition that a claimant can recover damages in public nuisance where access to or from his premises is obstructed so as to occasion a loss of trade attributable to obstruction of his customers' use of the highway and liberty of access." per Steel J in *Colour Quest Ltd v Total Downstream UK Plc* [2009] EWHC 540 (Comm); [2009] 2 Lloyd's Rep. 1 at [459]. The decision of Steel J was subsequently reversed in part, but not on this point: [2010] EWCA Civ 180; [2011] Q.B. 86. See Neyers and Andrews, "Loss of Custom and Public Nuisance" [2016] L.M.C.L.Q. 135.

904 *Gravesham BC v British Railways Board* [1978] Ch. 379, especially at 870–871, per Slade J. cf. *Network Rail Infrastructure Ltd v Conarken Group Ltd* [2011] EWCA Civ 644; [2011] B.L.R. 462 (owner of railway bridge rendered unusable by defendants able to recover financial losses including contractual payments to compensate third parties entitled to use the bridge).

905 *Att Gen v Brighton and Hove Co-operative Association* [1900] 1 Ch. 276; *Att Gen v WH Smith & Son* (1910) 26 T.L.R. 482; *Vanderpant v Mayfair Hotel Co* [1930] 1 Ch. 138 at 154.

906 *Penny v Wimbledon Urban DC* [1899] 2 Q.B. 72 (unlighted heap of soil).

907 [1955] 1 W.L.R. 113 CA. Quaere whether a hosepipe laid across the road by one who was not a frontager would constitute a nuisance. *Clarke v Sugrue & Sons*, *The Times*, 29 May 1959 (no liability for piece of rope left on highway by independent contractor).

adequate precautions to protect the public from danger.[908] Accordingly, where the defendants, who were laying telephone wires in the street, employed a plumber to connect some tubes and the plumber dipped a lamp into a cauldron of molten solder, causing an explosion which injured the claimant, the defendants were held liable.[909] The defendant is therefore liable for independent contractors who perform work negligently in or upon the highway, though he is not vicariously liable for their work adjacent to the highway unless that work is inherently dangerous.[910] A thing may be a nuisance in the highway even though it does not prevent or impede the flow of traffic or the passage of pedestrians.[911] In *Wandsworth LBC v Railtrack Plc*[912] the Court of Appeal held that pigeon-droppings on the highway created a hazard to pedestrians and constituted a public nuisance.[913] It is a nuisance to leave an unlighted lorry at night obstructing the highway.[914]

Lighting obstructions in highway A person who, either by himself or his **19-187**
independent contractor, causes an obstruction to be placed in the highway is under a duty to take reasonable care to prevent it from being a danger to the public. This is usually performed by lighting it.[915] Local authorities, however, frequently have statutory powers to erect structures in the highway without any statutory obligation to light them and a question arises whether they are liable for collisions caused through the absence of light. When the authority has assumed a duty of lighting an obstruction it has been held liable for negligence for not fulfilling that duty on the ground that its conduct creates something in the nature of a trap. So, when a street refuge was inadequately lighted,[916] a bollard was unlit,[917] and the entrance to an air-raid shelter was unlit,[918] in each case the authority was held liable for negligence in performing its self-imposed duty of lighting. Where a bomb crater in the highway was railed off and red lamps put round, but the lamps were blown out by the wind, the authority was held liable when there was evidence that the attendant had not visited the lamps that night.[919] When the streets are lit, it may well be that the obstruction is no longer a danger, but when they are not, the local authority must take such steps as are open to them to prevent damage. When an air-raid shelter was erected in the roadway and was unlighted, with the result that a motorist in the dark collided with it, the local authority was held liable.[920]

---

908 *Penny v Wimbledon Urban DC* [1899] 2 Q.B. 72; *The Snark* [1899] P. 74; affirmed [1900] P. 105.

909 *Holliday v National Telephone Co* [1899] 2 Q.B. 392.

910 *Salsbury v Woodland* [1970] 1 Q.B. 324 CA (tree-felling; for artificial structures, see para.19-189).

911 See, e.g. *Pope v Fraser* (1939) 55 T.L.R. 324 (pool of acid); *Dollman v Hillman* [1941] 1 All E.R. 355 (fat from a butcher's shop); *Holling v Yorkshire Traction Co* [1948] 2 All E.R. 662 (smoke and steam). See also *Almeroth v Chivers & Sons Ltd* [1948] 1 All E.R. 53 (pile of slates). cf. *Harper v Haden & Sons Ltd* [1933] Ch. 298.

912 [2001] EWCA Civ 1236; [2002] Q.B. 756.

913 The defendants, owners of a bridge under which the pigeons roosted, were held liable since they had knowledge of the nuisance and had failed to take reasonable steps to abate it.

914 *Ware v Garston Haulage Co* [1944] K.B. 30; explained and distinguished in *Maitland v Raisbeck* [1944] K.B. 689; and see *Parish v Judd* [1960] 1 W.L.R. 867; *Moore v Maxwells of Emsworth* [1968] 1 W.L.R. 1077. Some evidence of negligence is required.

915 *Penny v Wimbledon* [1899] 2 Q.B. 72.

916 *Baldock v Westminster City Council* (1918) 88 L.J.K.B. 502.

917 *Polkington v Lambeth BC* [1938] 1 All E.R. 339.

918 *Knight v Sheffield Corp* [1942] 2 All E.R. 304.

919 *Foster v Gillingham Corp* [1942] 1 All E.R. 304.

920 *Fisher v Ruislip and Northwood Urban DC* [1945] K.B. 584, where the cases on this subject are exhaustively discussed; *Morris v Luton Corp* [1946] 1 K.B. 114.

19-188 **Traffic on the highway** Nuisance is not confined to obstructions in the strict sense of the word. Apart from obstruction, it is an actionable public nuisance to produce a danger to other road users. Thus a car parked on the road may be an obstruction without being a danger,[921] and conversely a vehicle may be a danger without being an obstruction. Those who place unmanageable vehicles upon the road,[922] or employ them in a manner injurious to other persons,[923] are guilty of nuisance. But the mere fact of skidding does not prove a vehicle to be so unmanageable as to bring it within this category.[924] The fact that the rear light of a vehicle on the highway is out, without any negligence on the part of those responsible for the vehicle, does not create a nuisance.[925]

19-189 **Buildings adjoining highway** There is an obligation on the occupier of land adjoining or proximate to a highway not to use his land, or to allow his land or any buildings upon it to get into such a condition, as to be a nuisance.[926] Thus, the occupier of a building was held liable for damage caused by a lamp which was suspended over a highway and fell upon the claimant as he was using the highway.[927] The fact that the fall was due to the negligence of an independent contractor in failing to discover the defect which caused the fall was no defence. It is a public nuisance to permit a house abutting on a highway to be ruinous and likely to fall down,[928] and should any portion of the house fall and injure a passer-by, an action lies. In such a case it is no defence for the owner or occupier to prove that he neither knew nor ought to have known of the danger:

> "If, owing to want of repair, premises on a highway become dangerous and, therefore, a nuisance, and a passer-by or an adjoining owner suffers damage by their collapse, the occupier, or the owner if he has undertaken the duty of repair, is answerable whether he knew or ought to have known of the danger or not."[929]

This only applies to dangers caused by want of repair.[930] If they are caused by the act of a trespasser or by a latent defect, knowledge of the danger on the part of the owner or occupier must be proved.[931] When a person in the highway was injured through the fall of a quantity of snow which had accumulated on the roof of the defendants' shop it was held that the defendants were liable because they had known for five days of the potential source of danger on their roof and had taken no steps

---

921 See *Dymond v Pearce* [1972] 1 Q.B. 496 CA at 502, per Sachs LJ.

922 *Wing v LGO Co* [1909] 2 K.B. 652 at 665, per Fletcher Moulton LJ.

923 *McKee v Malcolmson* [1925] N.I. 120 (motorcycle race).

924 *Wing v LGO Co* [1909] 2 K.B. 652; *Parker v LGO Co* (1909) 101 L.T. 623; *Laurie v Raglan Building Co Ltd* [1942] 1 K.B. 152. But contra Mackenna J in *Richley v Faull* [1965] 1 W.L.R. 1454.

925 *Maitland v Raisbeck* [1944] K.B. 689; *Parish v Judd* [1960] 1 W.L.R. 867.

926 But where an occupier allows his land to interfere with visibility on the highway, it does not follow that the highway authority can itself be held liable in damages to a third party for failing to exercise powers available to it to compel removal of the interference: *Stovin v Wise* [1996] A.C. 923.

927 *Tarry v Ashton* (1876) 1 Q.B.D. 314.

928 *R. v Watts* (1703) 1 Salk. 357; *Harrold v Watney* [1898] 2 Q.B. 320 (child injured in attempting to climb insecure fence adjoining highway); *Mullan v Forrester* [1921] 2 Ir. R. 412.

929 *Wringe v Cohen* [1940] 1 K.B. 229 at 233, per Atkinson J. See para.19-101. See also *Heap v Ind Coope and Allsopp Ltd* [1940] 2 K.B. 476 (passer-by on highway falls through cellar cover of an inn).

930 It does not apply to trees falling on the highway: *Cunliffe v Bankes* [1945] 1 All E.R. 459.

931 See, e.g. *Leanse v Egerton* [1943] K.B. 323 (presumed knowledge). cf. *Cushing v Walker & Sons* [1941] 2 All E.R. 693 (claim failed).

to remove it.[932]

Excavations and other dangers adjoining highway It is a nuisance to allow an excavation immediately adjacent to the highway to be unfenced so as to be dangerous to persons using the way.[933] The rule is not confined to excavations; it covers anything dangerous to users of the highway. For example, a golf course from which balls are habitually driven on to the highway may be a nuisance.[934] The use of barbed wire or spikes[935] as a fence to land so immediately adjoining a highway as to be likely to injure persons or animals lawfully using the highway is a nuisance.[936] A tree is not a nuisance merely because its branches overhang the highway,[937] but if the branches overhang so as to hinder or obstruct the reasonable use of the highway, it will be a nuisance.[938] 19-190

(c) Non-repair of highway

Nuisance arising from non-repair of highway To the general rule that an action will lie for any special damage caused by a nuisance in a highway there was at common law an exception where the nuisance arose from the non-repair of the highway.[939] There was no remedy for nonfeasance, except by indictment.[940] But in 1964, the legal position was substantially changed by statute, and the relevant provisions are now to be found in the Highways Act 1980. 19-191

Circumstances relating to the statutory duty The rule of law exempting the parish inhabitants and any other persons or their successors from liability for non-repair of highways has been abrogated, but s.58(1) of the Act provides that in an action against a highway authority in respect of damage resulting from their failure to maintain a highway maintainable at the public expense, it shall be a defence (without prejudice to any other defence or the law relating to contributory negligence) to prove that the authority had taken such care, as in all the circumstances was reasonably required, to secure that that part of the highway to which the action relates was not dangerous for traffic.[941] Subsection (2) directs the court in considering the defence to pay regard to the following circumstances: 19-192

---

932 *Slater v Worthington's Cash Stores Ltd* [1941] 1 K.B. 488. See also *Mistry v Thakor* [2005] EWCA Civ 953.

933 *Barnes v Ward* (1850) 9 C.B. 392 (unfenced area).

934 *Castle v St Augustine's Links* (1922) 38 T.L.R. 615; cf. *Bolton v Stone* [1951] A.C. 850, where a cricket ball, driven on to the highway, injured the claimant and the occupiers of the cricket ground were held not liable. The case was decided on negligence, but the issue of nuisance was raised. It was conceded that the case could only succeed on nuisance if negligence was established.

935 *Fenna v Clare & Co* [1895] 1 Q.B. 199; *Morrison v Sheffield Corp* [1917] 2 K.B. 866.

936 Highways Act 1980 s.166.

937 *Noble v Harrison* [1926] K.B. 332.

938 *Hale v Hants and Dorset Motor Services* [1947] 2 All E.R. 628.

939 *Russell v Men of Devon* (1788) 2 T.R. 667; *Cowley v Newmarket Local Board* [1892] A.C. 345.

940 Indictment was abolished by the Highways Act 1959 s.59, and the Highways Act 1980 s.56, provides for the service of a notice on the highway authority.

941 s.41 provides the statutory duty to maintain the highway. The section can give rise to concurrent liability when other undertakers, such as tramway operators, also have statutory responsibility for the state of the highway in addition to the highway authority itself: *Roe v Sheffield City Council* [2003] EWCA Civ 1; [2004] Q.B. 653 CA.

(a) the character of the highway, and the traffic which was reasonably to be expected to use it;
(b) the standard of maintenance appropriate for a highway of that character and used by such traffic;
(c) the state of repair in which a reasonable person would have expected to find the highway;
(d) whether the highway authority knew, or could reasonably have been expected to know, that the condition of the part of the highway to which the action relates was likely to cause danger to users of the highway;
(e) where the highway authority could not reasonably have been expected to repair that part of the highway before the cause of action arose, what warning notices of its condition had been displayed.[942]

The Act applies whether the claimant is suing for nuisance, negligence or breach of statutory duty,[943] and it binds the Crown, and thus extends the duty to road maintenance by the Minister of Transport. It is no defence for failure to remove a danger to the highway, in breach of the provision, that the removal "would harm the visual appearance of the highway", e.g. because it was an attractive tree.[944] The statutory duty does, however, only afford protection to those who suffer personal injury or damage to property. In *Wentworth v Wiltshire CC*,[945] the Court of Appeal held that a farmer who suffered loss of profit when the road which served his farm became unusable, due to danger resulting from failure to repair, was unable to recover damages for breach of statutory duty.

19-193 **Standard of care** The creation of a danger by a positive act and the creation of a danger by failure to repair remains a material difference. The placing of a thin metal plate over an excavated hole in the pavement and leaving it unlighted has attracted liability for negligence and breach of statutory duty,[946] but where failure to repair causes harm to a pedestrian the courts have been careful not to require too high a standard of care from highway authorities. It has been said that "a highway is not to be criticised by the standards of a bowling green",[947] and minute differences between flagstone levels are not evidence of lack of care in maintenance. Even if a danger exists, it will be open for the defendant to show that no complaints had been made and that satisfactory periodic inspection has been carried out,[948] or that the danger was not due to a failure to repair.[949] The statutory duty under s.41

[942] For the purpose of the defence it is not relevant to prove that the highway authority had arranged for a competent person to carry out or supervise the maintenance of that part of the highway to which the action relates unless it is further proved that proper instructions were given and carried out. This statutory provision confirms *Hardaker v Idle DC* [1896] 1 Q.B. 335.

[943] *Whiting v Hillingdon LBC* (1970) 68 L.G.R. 437; (1970) 114 S.J. 247; highway authority liable under the Act not additionally responsible as occupier under Occupiers' Liability Act 1957.

[944] See *R. (on the application of Dillner) v Sheffield City Council* [2016] EWHC 945 (Admin); [2016] Env. L.R. 31 at [29] per Gilbart J.

[945] [1993] Q.B. 654. cf. *Network Rail Infrastructure Ltd v Conarken Group Ltd* [2011] EWCA Civ 644; [2011] B.L.R. 462 (see para.19-184).

[946] *Pitman v Southern Electricity Board* [1978] 3 All E.R. 901 CA.

[947] *Littler v Liverpool Corp* [1968] 2 All E.R. 343n at 345. cf. *Pitman v Southern Electricity Board* [1978] 3 All E.R. 901 CA.

[948] *Pridham v Hemel Hempstead Corp* (1970) 69 L.G.R. 523 CA. Three-monthly inspection of minor residential road in the circumstances sufficient. cf. *Wilkinson v York City Council* [2011] EWCA Civ 207 (regime for inspecting a road once a year considered inadequate).

[949] *Burnside v Emerson* [1968] 1 W.L.R. 1490 CA. Flooding by rain-water.

of the Highways Act 1980 is to maintain the highway to a standard safe for ordinary users:

> "so that it is free of danger to all users who use the highway in the way normally to be expected of them ... Motorists who thus use the highway and to whom a duty is owed are not to be expected by the authority all to be model drivers ... The highway authority must provide not merely for model drivers but for the normal run of drivers."[950]

Though the highway authority need not provide a surface safe for motorists driving deliberately at excessive speeds, it must expect some normal drivers to be relatively inexperienced, just as it has been held that there is a duty to guard against injury to pedestrians not perfectly sighted.[951] The statutory duty has been held to include drainage.[952] A highway authority is not liable for ordinary puddles but it will be liable for a flood due to failure to drain.[953] Since 2003 highway authorities have also been under a statutory duty "to ensure, so far as is reasonably practicable, that safe passage along a highway is not endangered by snow or ice".[954] This provision will give rise to an action for damages for breach of statutory duty, but it is not retrospective. Moreover, since local authorities do not owe a common law duty of care to road users to remove snow and ice, the law of negligence will not come to the aid of those injured before it was enacted.[955] In *Gorringe v Calderdale MBC*[956] the House of Lords held that the statutory duty to maintain the highway under s.41 of the Highways Act 1980 does *not* extend to the painting of safety markings on the surface of the road.[957] Nor does it extend to the maintenance of street furniture.[958] Moreover, an authority will not normally be liable merely for failing to exercise its statutory power[959] to compel the removal, from land owned by third parties, of obstructions which restrict the view of users of the highway.[960] On the other hand, planting bushes and shrubs on the highway which create a hazard can give rise to liability.[961]

---

950 *Rider v Rider* [1973] 1 Q.B. 505 at 514 CA, per Sachs LJ, construing s.44 of the Highways Act 1959 (now Highways Act 1980 s.41).

951 *Haley v London Electricity Board* [1965] A.C. 778.

952 See *Thoburn v Northumberland CC* (1999) 1 L.G.L.R. 819 CA.

953 *Tarrant v Rowlands* [1979] R.T.R. 144.

954 See the Railways and Transport Safety Act 2003 s.111 inserting s.41(1A) into the Highways Act 1980 and reversing the decision of the House of Lords in *Goodes v East Sussex CC* [2000] 1 W.L.R. 1356.

955 See *Sandhar v Department of Transport Environment and the Regions* [2004] EWCA Civ 1440; [2005] 1 W.L.R. 1632.

956 [2004] UKHL 15; [2004] 1 W.L.R. 1057. See also *Ali City of Bradford* [2010] EWCA Civ 1282; [2012] 1 W.L.R. 161; *Valentine v Transport for London* [2010] EWCA Civ 1358; [2011] P.I.Q.R. P7.

957 Effectively overruling *Bird v Pearce and Somerset CC* [1979] R.T.R. 369; (1979) 77 L.G.R. 753 CA.

958 See *Shine v London Borough of Tower Hamlets* [2006] EWCA Civ 852 (loose bollard, common law negligence liability imposed).

959 Under the Highways Act 1980 s.79.

960 *Stovin v Wise* [1996] A.C. 923.

961 *Yetkin v Newham LBC* [2010] EWCA Civ 776; [2011] Q.B. 827. See also *Kane v New Forest DC* [2001] EWCA Civ 878; [2002] 1 W.L.R. 312. cf. *Sumner v Colborne and Denbighshire CC* [2018] EWCA Civ 1006; [2019] Q.B. 430 (no liability for view-obscuring vegetation merely adjacent to the highway).

See [illegible] [2006] EWCA Civ 852 (whose held no common law negligence liability imposed).

Chapter 20

ANIMALS

Table of Contents

1. Liability for Animals

Common law and statute The common law of tort included many special rules with reference to harm caused by animals.[1] Some of these categories, for example cattle-trespass, were of great antiquity, and the law relating to the peculiar[2] position of animals in relation to tort liability was adversely criticised in more modern times.[3] In 1967, the Law Commission issued their *Report on Civil Liability for Animals*[4] and on the basis of their recommendations and draft legislation, Parliament passed the Animals Act 1971 which now substantially embodies the law upon the subject.[5] An explanation of the present law is therefore largely a commentary upon the provisions of the Act. With the exception of the abolition of the rule in *Searle v Wallbank*,[6] the Act adopted the pattern of the common law and preserved the basic distinction of the *scienter* action between animals belonging to dangerous and non-dangerous species. General liability in tort is concurrent with liability under the Animals Act 1971. There still remains a separate body of law peculiar to animals, despite the fact that animals are, like other chattels, merely agents and instruments of damage, albeit animate and automotive. 20-01

---

1 The principal work on the older common law on liability for animals was Williams, *Liability for Animals* (1939), that on the modern law is P. North, *Civil Liability for Animals* (Oxford: Oxford University Press, 2012) (effectively a second edition of P. North, *The Modern Law of Animals* (1972)). For a review of the influences on the process of legal reform, exploring the reasons why the current law remains so complex, see R. Bagshaw, "The Animals Act 1971" in T.T. Arvind and J. Steele (eds), *Tort Law and the Legislature: Common Law, Statute and the Dynamics of Legal Change* (Oxford: Hart Publishing, 2013).

2 "The law of torts has grown up historically in separate compartments and … beasts have travelled in a compartment of their own." per Lord Simonds in *Read v Lyons* [1947] A.C. 156 at 182.

3 *Report of the Committee on the Law of Civil Liability for Damage done by Animals*, Cmnd. 8746 (1953), under the chairmanship of Lord Goddard.

4 Law Com. No.13.

5 Note that in Scotland, separate and differently worded legislation was enacted after a long period of deliberation: Animals (Scotland) Act 1987. The legislative history is set out in *Welsh v Brady* [2009] CSIH 60; 2009 S.L.T. 747.

6 [1947] A.C. 341.

20-02 **Other statutory provisions** In addition to the provisions of the Animals Act 1971, certain other statutes have been introduced to deal with harmful animals. The Guard Dogs Act 1975 provides for control and licensing of guard dogs but specifically excludes civil liability for breach of its provisions. The Dangerous Wild Animals Act 1976 contains a list of animals so classified and regulates the keeping of such animals; damage caused by such an animal would, it seems, be within s.2(1) of the Animals Act. The Dangerous Dogs Act 1991 was passed in response to public disquiet over the injuries inflicted by certain breeds of "fighting" dogs and provides for pit bull terriers and tosas to be subject to restrictions, imposes criminal penalties on those who fail to observe the statutory restrictions and provides for other breeds to be brought within these provisions in future.[7] The Act also creates criminal offences where a dog injures any person either in a public place or elsewhere if the dog is not kept under control. The Act is silent on the question of civil liability but it may yet be decided in the courts, in accordance with the usual principles of interpretation, that a civil remedy is available to a person injured by a dog of the relevant breed, where the owner or person in control is in breach of the statute.

2. THE ANIMALS ACT 1971[8]

(a) Strict liability for animals under Section 2

20-03 **Section 2(1): Liability for damage done by dangerous animals** The old *scienter* action was abolished[9] and replaced by the provisions of s.2 of the Act. Section 2(1) provides that "where any damage is caused by an animal which belongs to a dangerous species, any person who is a keeper of the animal is liable for the damage".[10] A basic feature of liability under s.2(1) is that it depends not on the dangerous nature of any individual animal but upon the animal belonging to a species defined by the Act as dangerous, so that if the animal belongs to a dangerous species it is irrelevant that the particular animal is tame. The Act does not define "an animal"[11] but does define a dangerous species as one "which is not commonly domesticated in the British Islands, and whose fully grown animals normally have such characteristics that they are likely, unless restrained, to cause severe damage or that any damage they may cause is likely to be severe".[12] This category is defined as a

---

7 The Dangerous Dogs (Designated Types) Order 1991 (SI 1991/1743) added Dogo Argentino and Fila Braziliero to the breeds within the Act. It may be argued that the 1991 Act puts the specified breeds into a category where liability would be strict as in the case of animals belonging to a dangerous species for the purposes of the Animals Act 1971.

8 A full commentary on the Act is contained in North, *Civil Liability for Animals* (2012).

9 s.1(1)(a).

10 In addition to civil liability for injury there is a regulatory scheme of licensing the keeping of certain kinds of animals under the Dangerous Wild Animals Act 1976.

11 P. North, *Civil Liability for Animals* (Oxford: Oxford University Press, 2012), para.2.04, suggests the inclusion of birds, reptiles and insects, but not bacteria. Bees are not statutory "livestock". Fish would clearly be included, e.g. a live shark. The listing in the schedule to the Dangerous Wild Animals Act 1976 would be strong evidence of its nature for the purpose of the 1971 Act. See *Winfield and Jolowicz on Tort*, 19th edn (2014), para.17-008 fn.31.

12 s.6(2). "Species" includes sub-species and variety: s.11. The language of s.6(2) is discussed in detail by North, *Civil Liability for Animals* (2012), paras 2.35–2.52. Note that s.6(2)(b) is expressed in the alternative. A species may be dangerous even if such animals are not likely to cause severe damage provided that if damage is caused it is likely to be severe. For example, an elephant may not be likely

matter of law, which means that it is a matter for the court, and expert evidence will not be decisive. It also follows that the keeper's ignorance that the animal belongs to a dangerous species is irrelevant. A species may be regarded as dangerous if it is not commonly domesticated in this country, even though it is domesticated abroad, e.g. a camel.[13] Damage caused by an animal of a dangerous species attracts strict liability,[14] though liability is not absolute, since the Act permits certain defences. Provided that there is a causal link, there is no requirement that the damage must be the product of the particular characteristic(s) which renders the species as a whole dangerous.[15] The keeper is liable for "any damage".[16]

Liability for animals of a non-dangerous species[17] The Act in s.2(2) lays down the conditions for liability where the animal does not fall within the category of a dangerous species. These are that: **20-04**

"(a) the damage is of a kind which the animal, unless restrained, was likely to cause or which, if caused by the animal, was likely to be severe[18]; and

(b) the likelihood of the damage or of its being severe was due to characteristics of the animal which are not normally found in animals of the same species or are not normally to be found except at particular times or in particular circumstances[19]; and

(c) those characteristics were known to that keeper or were at any time known to a person who at that time had charge of the animal as that keeper's servant or, where that keeper is the head of a household, were known to another keeper of the animal who is a member of that household and under the age of 16."

---

to cause damage, but if it does the damage will probably be serious.

13 *Tutin v Chipperfield Promotions Ltd* (1980) 130 N.L.J. 807.

14 Since liability is not based on negligence, recoverable damage would seem to depend on direct causation and not reasonable foreseeability: *Behrens v Bertram Mills Circus* [1957] 2 Q.B. 1 at 17, per Devlin J (*scienter*).

15 *Behrens v Bertram Mills Circus* [1957] 2 Q.B. 1 at 18, per Devlin J: "If a tiger is let loose in a funfair, it seems to me to be irrelevant whether a person is injured as the result of a direct attack or because on seeing it he runs away and falls over."

16 "Damage" would seem to include damage to property as well as personal injury, since s.2(1) makes the keeper liable for "any damage".

17 The Act does not define an "animal" but it can include a bird. A Northern Ireland court held that a bantam cockerel was deemed to be an animal (see *Kane v McKenna* unreported 30 November 1990). "Species" in the Act is defined in s.11 as including "sub-species and variety". In *Hunt v Wallis* (1991) [1994] P.I.Q.R. P128 a border collie ran behind the claimant and collided with her, causing her to fall and injure her leg. The court considered the propensity of the dog in question to behave in this way in relation to other dogs of the same breed, rather than to other dogs generally, thus equating breed with "species" for the purposes of s.2(2) of the Animals Act 1971. Pill J held that the dog had no characteristics of a kind not usually found in border collies and held that the defendants were not liable under the Act (nor in negligence).

18 There is no requirement that the damage should in the event be "severe". In both alternatives, the test is likelihood of damage. On the relationship between the two limbs of s.2(2)(a), see North, *Civil Liability for Animals* (2012), paras 2.64-2.69. "Damage" is defined in s.11 as including "the death of, or injury to, any person (including any disease and any impairment of physical or mental condition)", but since the definition is not exhaustive, damage to property, including other animals, is within the scope of s.2(2). In *Chauhan v Paul* [1998] C.L.Y. 3990, the Court of Appeal observed that there might be sufficient damage and causation if being chased by a dog caused a heart attack.

19 On this requirement see *Cummings v Grainger* [1977] Q.B. 397 CA. In *Chauhan v Paul* [1998] C.L.Y. 3990, the claimant, a postman, was chased by a dog, which caused him to fall and be injured. The court held that the dog was not "dangerous" and did not have a tendency to bark and chase persons on the premises.

In *Curtis v Betts*,[20] the Court of Appeal considered the "somewhat tortuous wording" of s.2(2) and upheld an award of damages under the Act to a young boy who had been bitten on the face by a bull mastiff defending its territory. Stuart-Smith LJ recommended a step-by-step approach to the subsection. Judges should "consider each part of the subsection in turn and satisfy themselves that the [claimant] has made out his case on one or other of the limbs of each part". More recently s.2(2) has been described as "oracular and opaque",[21] and "grotesque".[22] In *Turnbull v Warrener* the Court of Appeal went further and expressed doubts about the direction in which interpretation of the subsection has developed, suggesting that the resulting extension of strict liability has undermined the intentions behind the statute. In both *Turnbull v Warrener* and *Goldsmith v Patchcott* the defence in s.5(2)[23] was interpreted broadly, and in *Turnbull*, this was done with the express intention of balancing the wide liability created by s.2(2).[24]

20-05 **Section 2(2)(a): Likelihood of damage or its severity** In *Smith v Ainger*,[25] "likely" was held to mean "such as might well happen" or "where there is a material risk that it will happen", rather than "probable" or "more probable than not".[26] The claimant was knocked over and broke his leg when the defendant's dog attacked the claimant's dog. The Court characterised the kind of damage as "personal injury to a human being caused by the direct application of force". Where the personal injury was the result of an attack by a dog it was unrealistic to distinguish between a bite and the consequences of a knock. The defendant's dog had a history of attacking other dogs, and therefore it could be said that it was likely to attack another dog; if it did so there was a material risk that the owner of the other dog would intervene and would be bitten or knocked as a result, and accordingly the claimant's injury constituted damage of a kind which, unless restrained, the dog was likely to cause. It is only necessary to show that injury to people is likely given the animal's characteristics; it is not necessary to show that the animal itself has a vicious tendency to injure people.[27]

20-06 For the most part, subsequent courts have found the test in s.2(2)(a) to be easily

---

20 [1990] 1 W.L.R. 459 CA.

21 *Goldsmith v Patchcott* [2012] EWCA Civ 183; [2012] P.I.Q.R. P11 at [31].

22 *Turnbull v Warrener* [2012] EWCA Civ 412; [2012] P.I.Q.R. P16 at [4].

23 See para.20-16.

24 *Turnbull v Warrener* [2012] EWCA Civ 412; [2012] P.I.Q.R. P16 at [55].

25 *The Times*, 5 June 1990, CA.

26 Note that in *Mirvahedy v Henley* [2003] UKHL 16; [2003] 2 A.C. 491 at [97] and [98], Lord Scott in his dissenting speech, said that whilst he agreed with the rejection of a test of "probability" in *Smith*, he was "unable to agree that 'such as might happen', a phrase consistent with no more than possibility, can be right" and suggested a test of "reasonably to be expected". On the facts, he considered that the test was not satisfied as a horse loose on the highway does not usually result in damage to third parties, that if damage to third parties does result the damage is not usually severe, no more perhaps than a dent to a car, and that the cases in which serious injury or damage results are fortunately few and far between. He cited the Court of Appeal decision in *Jaundrill v Gillett, The Times,* 30 January 1996 in support of his conclusion but as the application of s.2(2)(a) had been conceded by the defendant, he proceeded on the assumption that the damage was likely. In *Williams v Hawkes* [2017] EWCA Civ 1846; [2018] R.T.R. 16 (see para.20-08), *Jaundrill v Gillett* was described as likely to be confined to its facts. Considerable caution should therefore be taken if citing it as an authority.

27 In *Wallace v Newton* [1982] 1 W.L.R. 375, a horse became out of control and crushed the claimant's arm. It was held that the claimant was not required to prove that the horse had a vicious propensity to attack people but only that it had characteristics not normally found in other horses, and the claimant recovered damages on proving that the horse had exhibited previously unpredictable and unreli-

satisfied. Indeed in *Goldsmith v Patchcott*,[28] a case where the claimant suffered serious injury through being thrown from a horse, Jackson LJ expressly said that s.2(2)(a) "will only eliminate a small number of cases". He added that "[m]ost animal-related damage which someone wishes to sue about" would fall into one of the categories in the subsection.[29] By contrast, the meaning of s.2(2)(a) was raised as a significant issue in *Turnbull v Warrener*,[30] and the Court was divided on the proper approach to take. Maurice Kay LJ was of the view—consistent with *Smith v Ainger* and intervening authorities such as *Freeman v Higher Park Farm*[31]—that there was no need to show that severe injury was statistically probable in order to fall within s.2(2)(a). Where a rider is thrown from a horse, as in this instance, severe injury was "reasonably to be expected". Lewison LJ, by contrast, was prepared to say that authorities such as *Freeman* were, in respect of s.2(2)(a), decisions of fact rather than principle, and that the statute had never been intended to apply to an "ordinary riding accident". It was not, in his Lordship's view, self-evident that a rider who falls from a rearing horse (or a cantering horse) "is likely to suffer severe injury", because many such accidents occur without severe injury being suffered, and was prepared to uphold the judge's decision that the test in s.2(2)(a) was not fulfilled. Since Stanley Burnton LJ agreed with the reasoning of Lewison LJ on this point, the likelihood is that a range of accidents previously treated as clearly within s.2, and particularly riding accidents, will now be questioned much more closely. It is suggested however that there is clearly no need to demonstrate statistical likelihood for the terms of s.2(2)(a) to be satisfied.[32] Illustrating this, s.2(2)(a) was held not to be satisfied, in circumstances where s.2(2)(b) and s.2(2)(c) would be so satisfied, in *Lynch v Ed Walker Racing Ltd*.[33] The claimant was a stable boy who had been thrown from a horse and rendered unconscious when the horse whipped around and fell. Following a trial of liability, the judge held that neither limb of s.2(2)(a) had been satisfied and dismissed the claim. On the basis of the witness evidence, which stated that injuries were rare as a result of a horse whipping around and that people rarely fell off a horse because it whipped, she held that it was unlikely that an injury would be caused (limb one) by a horse whipping around and that if an injury was caused, it was unlikely to be severe (limb two). Langstaff J conceded that, at first glance, it seemed that the judge might have erred. It appeared that she had looked at the first limb of s.2(2)(a) but not the second. But the evidence on the likelihood of injury and the severity of the injury overlapped. When the judge looked at the facts of the case and said that it was not common for there to be a fall of the instant type, she might have been addressing the severity, as if

able characteristics and that these were known to the defendant. See also *Welsh v Stokes* [2007] EWCA Civ 796; [2008] 1 W.L.R. 1224 (horse not likely to cause injury, but any injury it causes likely to be severe); and *Freeman v Higher Park Farm* [2008] EWCA Civ 1185; [2009] P.I.Q.R. P6 (horse bucked throwing its rider; s.2(2)(a) satisfied because if a horse causes physical injury, it is likely to be severe).

28 [2012] EWCA Civ 183; [2012] P.I.Q.R. P11.

29 [2012] EWCA Civ 183; [2012] P.I.Q.R. P11 at [33].

30 [2012] EWCA Civ 412; [2012] P.I.Q.R. P16.

31 [2008] EWCA Civ 1185; [2009] P.I.Q.R. P6.

32 All three judges in *Turnbull v Warrener* agreed, in any event, that the claim failed because it fell within the defence in s.5(2) (see para.20-16). For comparison see *Tapp v Trustees of the Blue Cross Society* unreported 15 May 2013 (Northampton County Court): s.2(2)(a) was satisfied because a bite by a horse was inherently likely to be severe given the size of the animal; the defence under s.5(2) failed because the claimant had not engaged with the animal, but entered a field where it approached her.

33 [2017] EWHC 2484 (QB).

an injury was unlikely at all then it was unlikely to be severe. The judge emphasised the speed, circumstances and seriousness; that went not only to the likelihood of an injury but its severity too. There was no basis for disturbing her decision.

20-07 **Section 2(2)(b): Characteristics of the animal** Section 2(2)(b) comprises two limbs. The first limb refers to characteristics "not normally found in animals of the same species" and the second limb refers to characteristics not normally found in animals of the same species "except at particular times or in particular circumstances". The first limb covers the abnormal animal case where animals of the species are normally docile but the particular animal is not. The second limb clearly covers characteristics which might not be normal for the species but which are triggered in the particular animal by particular circumstances such as the fear of farm machinery felt by a particular horse.[34] The difficulty with the second limb is whether it should be read as applicable to a characteristic which is normal for the species but only arises in a particular circumstance or whether it should be read subject to the first limb and not applicable to a normal characteristic.[35] In *Cummings v Grainger*[36] the Court of Appeal interpreted the second limb independently of the first, concluding that an Alsatian guard dog which attacked a trespasser was acting on a characteristic arising in particular circumstances even though this was normal behaviour for such dogs in such circumstances. But in *Breedon v Lampard*[37] the Court of Appeal interpreted the second limb as subject to the first limb, that is, as not applying to any characteristic which was normal for the species. Thus, it concluded that the characteristic of a horse to kick when approached too quickly from behind did not fall under the second limb as it was a normal characteristic of the species.[38]

20-08 In *Mirvahedy v Henley*[39] the majority of the House of Lords approved the *Cummings* rather than the *Breedon* interpretation. In *Mirvahedy* the claimant motorist suffered personal injuries when the car he was driving collided with the defendants' horse which had panicked and escaped with several others from its field. It was not clear what had frightened the horses in this way. The House of Lords held, by a majority of three to two, that the defendants were liable under s.2(2) as the behaviour of the horse fulfilled the requirements of the subsection. To bolt was a characteristic of the species which was normal "in particular circumstances", the circumstances here being some sort of fright or other external stimulus.[40] Giving the leading speech, Lord Nicholls conceded that on this interpretation:

> "it [wa]s not easy to conceive of circumstances where dangerous behaviour which is characteristic of a species will not satisfy requirement (b) [as] a normal but dangerous

---

34 *Flack v Hudson* [2001] Q.B. 698.

35 See North, *Civil Liability for Animals* (2012), paras 2.76 to 2.88.

36 [1997] Q.B. 397. See the similar interpretation in *Curtis v Betts* [1990] 1 W.L.R. 459: dog defending its own territory was acting from a characteristic arising in a particular circumstances but normal for the species.

37 [1985] C.A. transcript 1035. The *Breedon* interpretation was preferred by Pill LJ in *Gloster v Chief Constable of Greater Manchester Police* [2000] P.I.Q.R. P114.

38 Both Lloyd and Oliver LJJ adopted this interpretation but the claim failed principally on the ground that even if the characteristic requirement was satisfied, the keeper did not have the required knowledge of the characteristic.

39 [2003] UKHL 16; [2003] 2 A.C. 491.

40 See also *Tapp v Trustees of the Blue Cross Society* 15 May 2013 (Northampton County Court) above fn.32, where a horse which bit the claimant had adopted a herd mentality which was normal in the circumstances for horses which had escaped from a field, and s.2(2)(a) was satisfied.

characteristic of a species will usually be identifiable by reference to particular times or particular circumstances. [This] means that requirement (b) will be met in most cases where damage was caused by dangerous behaviour as described in requirement (a).”[41]

He justified the interpretation as according more easily with the statutory language. Lord Walker recognised that this interpretation would impose strict liability for behaviour which was entirely normal for that animal of his species and would make the keeper's liability depend on knowledge of something which was likely to be common knowledge among those who keep the animals. But as between the keeper, who could decide whether “to run the unavoidable risks involved in [keeping the animal and] whether or not to insure against those risks”, and the entirely innocent victim of the animal's behaviour, he could see “nothing unjust or unreasonable in the [keeper] having to bear the loss”.[42] The approach in *Mirvahedy v Henley* was followed in *Williams v Hawkes*.[43] Here, a Charolais steer had escaped from its field and found its way onto a major road after being “spooked”. It ran along the highway in a panic and collided with the claimant's car. The court found that s.2(2)(b) was satisfied, since expert evidence suggested that the likelihood of damage was due to characteristics of the steer not normally found in animals of the same species except at particular times or in particular circumstances, and was not simply due to the size and weight of the steer. There were no grounds for differentiating between this case and *Mirvahedy* on the basis that the steer had run into the claimant's car while the horse in *Mirvahedy* had remained static. In *Estacio v Honigsbaum*,[44] *Mirvahedy* was applied to a bite by a dog which had probably taken fright on being trapped in a tight space while its owner was seeking to get it into a car. As Deputy District Judge Tomlinson put it, biting is not something which dogs do ordinarily but it is something that dogs do at particular times and in particular circumstances and one of those particular times and circumstances is where a dog might feel itself threatened or a dog might find itself in a constrained space. Section 2(2)(b) was satisfied, as were the other limbs of s.2(2).

The Court of Appeal decision in *Freeman v Higher Park Farm*,[45] where a horse had bucked violently and thrown its rider, shows that despite the approach in **20-09**
Mirvahedy v Henley, not every normal but dangerous characteristic of an animal will come within s.2(2)(b). In respect of the first limb of s.2(2)(b), the Court of Appeal found that there was simply no evidence adduced which would suggest that bucking is not a normal characteristic of horses generally. Thus, the judge had been entitled to say that the first limb of s.2(2)(b) was not satisfied on the evidence.

---

41 [2003] UKHL 16; [2003] 2 A.C. 491 at [43]. Lord Nicholls at [46] argued that this did not empty requirement (b) of all content as it could operate to bar a claim in some cases of accidental damage:

> “Take a large and heavy domestic animal such as a mature cow. There is a real risk that if a cow happens to stumble and fall on someone, any damage will be severe. This would satisfy requirement (a). But a cow's dangerousness in this regard may not fall within requirement (b). This dangerousness is due to a characteristic normally found in cows at all times. The dangerousness results from their very size and weight. It is not due to a characteristic not normally found in cows except at particular times or in particular circumstances.”

42 [2003] UKHL 16; [2003] 2 A.C. 491 at [157]. This reasoning is, perhaps, less apposite in cases where the claimant has willingly participated in an activity with full knowledge of the usual risks inherent in it. Being bound by *Mirvahedy*, the Court of Appeal has turned toward restricting liability in such cases by means of the defence of assumption of risk: see para.20-16.

43 [2017] EWCA Civ 1846; [2018] R.T.R. 16.

44 (County Court, Clerkenwell) 18 May 2017.

45 [2008] EWCA Civ 1185; [2009] P.I.Q.R. P6.

Although the horse (Patty) was known to have a propensity to buck, it could not be said that the severity of the likely damage was due to a characteristic of the animal not normally found in animals of the same species. Turning to the second limb of s.2(2)(b), the Court of Appeal asked whether the likelihood of the severity of damage which caused s.2(2)(a) to be satisfied was due to a characteristic of Patty which is not normally found in animals of the same species "except at particular times or in particular circumstances". In this instance, it was known that Patty in particular was inclined to buck when beginning to canter, and that is what had happened during the incident in question. Although the House of Lords in *Mirvahedy* had said that "a normal but dangerous characteristic of a species will usually be identifiable by reference to particular times or particular circumstances",[46] this had to be a matter of evidence in every case. In this case, "there was no evidence whatever that horses usually buck at particular times or in particular circumstances." As such, the approach in *Mirvahedy* does not remove the need to adduce evidence of the characteristics of animals of the same species as referred to in s.2(2)(b). Despite this, in *Goldsmith v Patchcott*[47] the Court of Appeal accepted the truth of Lord Nicholls' observation in *Mirvahedy* that in most cases where s.2(2)(a) was satisfied, s.2(2)(b) would also be satisfied. This being the case, Jackson LJ declared that he was not sure what purpose was served by s.2(2)(b). In *Turnbull v Warrener*,[48] while concluding with express reluctance that the case (of a horse resisting control when first cantering with a bitless bridle) fell within the terms of s.2(2)(b), two members of the Court of Appeal described the subsection as having been virtually "emasculated" by its drafting. The remaining judge, Stanley Burnton LJ, appears to have been prepared to find, rather, that the case did not fall within the terms of s.2(2)(b), thereby giving the subsection more substance.

20-10 **Relationship between s.2(2)(a) and s.2(2)(b)** The interpretation of s.2(2)(b) and its relationship with s.2(2)(a) has been subject to scrutiny from the Court of Appeal in *Clarke v Bowlt*,[49] *Welsh v Stokes*,[50] and *McKenny v Foster*.[51] In *Clarke v Bowlt*, as the claimant drove past the defendant's horse, it moved from the verge into the road and collided with the car, causing damage. Neither claimant nor defendant was found to have been negligent. At trial the judge held the defendant liable on the ground that s.2(2)(a) was satisfied because the weight of the horse made it likely that any damage would be severe; and, applying *Mirvahedy*, s.2(2)(b) was satisfied because the movement into the road was due to a characteristic of horses found only at particular times and in particular circumstances. Giving the leading judgment of the Court of Appeal, Lord Phillips CJ reversed the decision on the ground that the judge had failed to apply the characteristic test of s.2(2)(b) to the likelihood identified under s.2(2)(a). The judge had identified severity of damage due to the weight of the horse as the relevant "likelihood" for s.2(2)(a) but had then identified the characteristic for s.2(2)(b) as being uncontrolled movement. The two findings did not match. If the weight of the horse was the basis of s.2(2)(a), then s.2(2)(b) could not be satisfied as weight was a normal characteristic of all horses at all times. If uncontrolled movement was taken as the basis of s.2(2)(b) then

[46] [2003] UKHL 16; [2003] 2 A.C. 491 at [43], per Lord Nicholls.
[47] [2012] EWCA Civ 183; [2012] P.I.Q.R. P11.
[48] [2012] EWCA Civ 412; [2012] P.I.Q.R. P16.
[49] [2006] EWCA Civ 978; [2007] P.I.Q.R. P12.
[50] [2007] EWCA Civ 796; [2008] 1 W.L.R. 1224.
[51] [2008] EWCA Civ 173.

s.2(2)(a) could not be satisfied as horses are generally likely to follow the direction of their rider rather than make uncontrolled movements. Sedley LJ commented that if the fact that horses were simply capable of causing damage was taken as satisfying s.2(2), then "there will be few, if any cases, of damage done by a domesticated animal which do not render the keeper liable-the very reverse of the situation which the 1971 Act was designed to bring about".[52] *Mirvahedy* was different as there the characteristic for s.2(2)(b) was bolting in response to a shock and that made damage likely for the purposes of s.2(2)(a).

In *Welsh v Stokes*, the relevant "particular circumstances" for the purposes of the second limb of s.2(2)(b) were that the horse that the claimant was riding did not want to go forward and had a rider who was unable to handle him and give him the confidence to deal with the situation. The horse reared up and the claimant fell off, the horse also falling and landing on her. The link between the damage referred to in s.2(2)(a) and the particular characteristic of the horse was "obvious" since the finding that the damage that was caused was likely to be severe and that the horse had the characteristic of rearing made it inevitable that the likelihood of the damage being severe would be held to be due to that characteristic.[53] For the purpose of s.2(2)(b): **20-11**

> "the core meaning of 'normal' is 'conforming to type'. If a characteristic of an animal is usual, then it will certainly be normal. The best evidence that a characteristic conforms to the type of animals of a species is that the characteristic is usually found in those animals."[54]

So a horse which did not have a normal characteristic of rearing up generally could satisfy the requirements of s.2(2)(b) in the particular circumstances of the case, since it was a normal characteristic of the horse to rear up in such circumstances given that rearing was a characteristic normally found in horses as a species in the particular circumstances (and the horse was conforming to type):

> "The relevant question was not whether [the horse] tended to rear generally, but whether he had the characteristic of rearing in the particular circumstances. I do not accept that the judge made inconsistent findings. When he said that [the horse] was not likely to rear up and that rearing up was not a normal characteristic 'for him', he was saying no more than that [the horse] had no track record of rearing. He was not saying that it was not normal for horses as a species to rear up in the particular circumstances."[55]

McKenny v Foster[56] required exploration of the meaning of s.2(2)(b) and of its interplay not only with s.2(2)(a) but also with s.2(2)(c). In *McKenny*, there was a collision between a car and a cow which had been standing in the road. It was dark and the car was travelling within the speed limit. The car's passenger was killed, as was the cow, and the driver of the car was injured. It was accepted that the cow **20-12**

---

52 [2006] EWCA Civ 978; [2007] P.I.Q.R. P12 at [21].

53 [2007] EWCA Civ 796; [2008] 1 W.L.R. 1224 at [40], per Dyson LJ. A contrasting case is *Kublin v Jane Allison Equestrian Limited* unreported 30 April 2013 (Oxford County Court): the horse (Olly) had a propensity to spook when another horse (Martha) spooked, and all horses are likely to turn and run away from something which startles them. However, the claimant was an experienced horsewoman who could be expected to control this behaviour, and the injury was caused by Olly slipping and falling onto her. It was the fall therefore that was likely to cause damage, and this was not a characteristic behaviour within s.2(2)(b).

54 [2007] EWCA Civ 796; [2008] 1 W.L.R. 1224 at [46].

55 [2007] EWCA Civ 796; [2008] 1 W.L.R. 1224 at [60], per Dyson LJ.

56 [2008] EWCA Civ 173.

must have escaped from her field in a state of extreme agitation at being separated from her calf, since she would have had to climb over a substantial fence and jump a 12 foot cattle grid in order to so. She had not been in such a state on being weaned from her previous two calves, nor had she shown agitation during the day. Such a state of agitation was said to be quite out of character both for her, and for her breed. Her ability to escape was exceptional. The Court of Appeal emphasised that in order to succeed under the second limb of s.2(2)(b), the claimants would have to define the relevant "causative characteristic" (the characteristic of the animal which caused the injury). This would have to be a characteristic only found at particular times and in particular circumstances, and the characteristic so defined would also have to be known to the defendants (s.2(2)(c)). Finally, the characteristic had to be a *dangerous* characteristic. Finding that strict liability within the Act was not established in this case, May LJ distinguished this case from the facts of *Mirvahedy* (horses are known to bolt when very frightened, but cows are not known to enter states of extreme agitation enabling them to climb fences and leap cattle grids on being weaned from their calves). Importantly, he also distinguished it from the example given by Lord Nicholls in *Mirvahedy* of an attack by a newly calved cow or a dog on guard duty, as fitting into the second limb of s.2(2)(b). The cow's behaviour in the present case was exceptional and not normal in any circumstances.[57] The strict liability claim failed because while simple agitation on being separated from a calf is a normal characteristic which occurs on specific occasions, it was neither dangerous, nor causative of the injury in this case. The behaviour that was both dangerous and causative was defined as "exceptional and exaggerated agitation resulting from her maternal instinct so that she was in the state of an excited, wild animal." This was neither normal, nor known to the defendants. It was also not characteristic of the cow or its breed—indeed it might not even be definable as a "characteristic" at all.[58]

20-13 **Proposed reform** In March 2009, the Department for Environment Food and Rural Affairs published a consultation document, seeking views on changes to the Animals Act 1971. The proposed change was to replace the existing wording of s.2(2)(b) with a new formulation referring to the damage being caused by "unusual or conditional" characteristics of the animal. For strict liability to apply in a case involving an unusual characteristic, the keeper must have known of the characteristic. For cases where damage was caused by a conditional characteristic, the keeper of the animal would have a defence if he or she could show that there was no particular reason to expect that the relevant circumstances that provoked the conditional characteristic would arise at the time. It was conceded that this might loosen the strictness of the liability recognised in *Mirvahedy*, but it was also commented that subsequent case law has in any event introduced uncertainty over the extent of the strictness of the liability defined in that case. The general results of the Consultation were announced in September 2009, but changes to the Act were not implemented.[59]

20-14 **Section 2(2)(c) Knowledge of the animal's propensities** The Act requires

[57] Thus, it was different from the behaviour of cows with calves which attacked a dog-walker in *McKaskie v Cameron*, unreported 1 July 2009, Preston County Court (see para.20-25): such attacks are not uncommon enough to be exceptional where the cows have calves with them.

[58] [2008] EWCA Civ 173 at [29]. For discussion of interpretations of s.2, see Compton and Hand, "The Animals Act 1971—Where are We Now?" [2009] J.P.I.L. 1.

[59] See North, *Civil Liability for Animals* (2012), paras 2.92–2.96.

knowledge of the animal's characteristics. As in the *scienter* action, knowledge may be acquired not merely by incidents of past damage or attempts by the animal, for example, to bite a human being, but by the apparent propensity of the animal to do the harm in fact caused. Generally, the required knowledge must be actual and present as a matter of fact.[60] As s.2(2)(c) makes plain, this knowledge is either that of the animal's keeper or the keeper's servant in charge of the animal or a member of the keeper's family under the age of 16 who can also be considered as a keeper of the animal. The limits of "imputed" knowledge are confined to the two categories mentioned. The first case is that of the "keeper's servant", that servant being one "who at that time[61] had charge of the animal as that keeper's servant".[62] The language is restrictive, for evidently a "servant" cannot include anyone temporarily in charge of the animal, so a person may be in charge on behalf of the keeper and servants may have that knowledge but their knowledge may not be imputed to their employer unless they are in charge of the animal.[63] In the second case, the knowledge of the minor is attributable to the head of the household only if the minor is also a "keeper". Thus, a child who acquires the relevant knowledge by, for example, taking his parents' dog out for a walk, does not as a matter of law transmit that knowledge to his parents. But he may of course do so as a matter of fact, in which event the parents as the keepers will have acquired actual knowledge.[64] Both kinds of imputed knowledge depend on the servant in charge or the minor as keeper having actual knowledge; it is not enough that such persons should have known but did not. In order to show that a keeper knew that the particular animal which caused the damage had the characteristics that satisfy s.2(2)(b) it does not have to be proved that the keeper knew that the particular animal had previously behaved in that way. It is sufficient to show that the keeper knew that that species of animal normally behave in that way in the particular circumstances.[65] Only a relevant characteristic which is both causative of the injury referred to in s.2(2)(a), and known to the defendant as required by s.2(2)(c), will be sufficient to establish strict liability under s.2.

The "keeper" of an animal Whether damage is caused by an animal of a dangerous species or an animal of a species that is not dangerous, s.2 of the Act places responsibility on the "keeper", who is defined in s.6(3) as one who "owns the animal **20-15**

---

60 "Knowledge" is not defined in the Act, and it appears that the principles of the *scienter* action may therefore be relevant on this question: *Glanville v Sutton & Co Ltd* [1928] 1 K.B. 571; *Brock v Richards* [1951] 1 K.B. 529.

61 This refers not to the time of the injury but to the time when knowledge of abnormal characteristics was acquired.

62 North, *Civil Liability for Animals* (2012), paras 2.110–2.114

63 North, *Civil Liability for Animals* (2012), para.2.112. In *Maclean v The Forestry Commission*, 1970 S.L.T. 265, one employee, not in charge, had knowledge of a dangerous characteristic of a horse, but the employee in charge lacked knowledge. per Lord Wheatley: "If each is to be regarded in his own way as the *alter ego* of the employers it seems to produce a schizophrenic legal persona, and I cannot imagine the law leads to such a result."

64 See North, *Civil Liability for Animals* (2012), paras 2.119–2.121, on the question how far such actual knowledge may be inferred as a matter of evidence.

65 *Welsh v Stokes* [2007] EWCA Civ 796; [2008] 1 W.L.R. 1224 (a general characteristic of horses to rear in particular circumstances; a keeper, if aware of that general characteristic, does not need to have some additional and more particular knowledge about the specific horse). And see *McKaskie v Cameron*, unreported 1 July 2009, Preston County Court, para.20-25: farmer who knew that cows with calves may attack dog-walkers had sufficient awareness under s.2(2)(c) though his cows had previously been docile. In respect of the interplay between the various parts of s.2, see the discussion of *McKenny v Foster* [2008] EWCA Civ 173 at para.20-12.

or has it in his possession; or he is the head of a household of which a member under the age of 16 owns the animal or has it in his possession". The subsection includes in the definition anyone who has ceased to own or possess the animal "until another person becomes a keeper thereof by virtue of those provisions".[66] Liability under the old *scienter* action depended on possession and control of the animal, and this is preserved by the Act. But ownership without possession appears to be a new ground of liability introduced by the Act.[67] Where a minor is a keeper by virtue of ownership or possession, the head of the household is also keeper though neither owning nor possessing the animal.[68] That part of the definition concerned with an escaped or an abandoned animal provides an injured person with recourse against the original keeper, even though injured after the escape or abandonment and without distinguishing circumstances, for example an indigenous wild animal reverting to life in the wild.[69] The original keeper is only relieved of liability when the animal comes into the ownership or possession of another person. There is nothing which prevents one keeper from bringing a claim against another keeper under the 1971 Act, subject to any defences provided in the Act.[70]

20-16 **Defences** The Act gives the following defences to the "keeper" under the Act:

(a) *Voluntary assumption of risk.* Section 5(2), which gives a defence based on the voluntary assumption of risk,[71] should be read in conjunction with s.6(5) that "where a person employed as a servant by a keeper of an animal incurs a risk incidental to his employment he shall not be treated as accepting it voluntarily". The defence to an action under s.2 is therefore not available to an employer as it was before the Act,[72] and it would seem that the defence is now totally inapplicable in an action by a servant against his employer even where he was employed expressly to assume hazardous duties.[73] In recent years the s.5(2) defence has been given a broad interpretation, in response to the courts' unease at the breadth of strict liability under s.2(2).

---

66 s.6(4) provides an exception to the definition for someone taking and keeping possession of an animal "for the purpose of preventing it from causing damage or of restoring it to its owner".

67 North, *Civil Liability for Animals* (2012), para.2.17, discusses some of the problems consequently arising, e.g. on sale of an animal with mischievous propensities unknown to the buyer, no one is liable for damage caused before the new owner acquires knowledge, because the vendor parting with title and possession ceases to be a "keeper" and the new "keeper" is not liable under s.2(2).

68 The Act does not define headship of a household or membership.

69 An escaped fox and an escaped tiger are not differentiated. Liability unlimited in time is reasonable for the tiger, but what about the fox?

70 *Flack v Hudson* [2001] Q.B. 698 CA.

71 See *Cummings v Grainger* [1977] Q.B. 397 CA, which held that a trespasser bitten by an Alsatian guard-dog had voluntarily assumed the risk. See also the Guard Dogs Act 1975. See further para.29-21 and para.3-122.

72 *Rands v McNeil* [1955] 1 Q.B. 253.

73 e.g. a snake handler, lion-tamer or zoo-keeper. In *Canterbury City Council v Howletts & Port Lympne* [1997] I.C.R. 925, where a zoo keeper was killed by a tiger and the owners encouraged "bonding" between animals and keepers, the personal representatives of the keeper were entitled to sue. North, *Civil Liability for Animals* (2012), para.2.137, discusses the question whether the wording of s.6(5) is apt to cover express and factual assumption of risk as contrasted with assumption to be inferred from the employee's conduct or behaviour in his work. The Law Commission, above, fn.4, at s.20 regarded the rationale of strict liability for a peculiarly dangerous activity to be "that the person carrying it on is in the best position to take precautions against or to mitigate the damage which may flow from the activity", and recommended that the burden should be on the employer to provide insurance cover.

In both *Goldsmith v Patchcott*[74] and *Turnbull v Warrener*[75] the Court of Appeal found that the claimants, who were experienced horsewomen, had accepted the risks ordinarily associated with horses, even to the extent that these satisfied s.2(2)(a) and (b). In both instances, as in *Freeman v Higher Park Farm*,[76] the Court emphasised that the defence is not to be imbued with the intricacies of "volenti non fit injuria" at common law—thus escaping the limitations of the common law defence. Rather, all that needs to be shown is that: (1) the claimant fully appreciated the risk; and (2) they exposed themselves to it. It is not necessary that the claimant could foresee the "precise degree of energy with which the animal will engage in its characteristic behaviour".[77] Thus, the defence will not defeat a claimant who was unaware of a dangerous propensity or characteristic of the animal which was known to the keeper, where that characteristic caused the harm. An example of this is *Flack v Hudson*,[78] where the horse's keeper, but not the claimant's wife, knew that the horse had a tendency to be frightened by agricultural machinery. However, *Flack* has been distinguished in later cases, where the dangerous characteristic is one common to horses generally in particular circumstances, and is considered to be within the claimant's knowledge. The claimants' experience with the animals has been a significant factor in these cases. So also is the voluntary nature of the exposure to the risk. In *Turnbull v Warrener*, this "realistic application" of s.5(2) was expressly related by Lewison LJ to the issues motivating the House of Lords' decision in *Tomlinson v Congleton BC*,[79] and he took the view that the claimant's fall should be seen as merely the result of "one of the risks inherent in riding horses".[80] These decisions therefore link certain claims under the Animals Act—where the claimant is participating in a leisure activity with an understanding of the ordinary risks—with other decisions regarding voluntarily assumed risks associated with leisure activities.

(b) *The claimant was a trespasser.* Section 5(3) provides a defence to an action under s.2, and is discussed in para.29-21.[81]

(c) *Fault of the claimant.* Section 5(1) provides a defence to an action under ss.2, 3 and 4, where the damage "is due wholly to the fault of the person suffering it".[82] Where the damage was due partly to his fault, the court may apportion blame under the Law Reform (Contributory Negligence) Act 1945.[83]

---

74 [2012] EWCA Civ 183; [2012] P.I.Q.R. P11.

75 [2012] EWCA Civ 412; [2012] P.I.Q.R. P16.

76 [2008] EWCA Civ 1185; [2009] P.I.Q.R. P6.

77 *Goldsmith v Patchcott* [2012] EWCA Civ 183; [2012] P.I.Q.R. P11 at [50].

78 [2001] Q.B. 698.

79 [2003] UKHL 47; [2004] 1 A.C. 46, see para.7-185.

80 [2012] EWCA Civ 412; [2012] P.I.Q.R. P16 at [55]–[56]. To similar effect is the decision in *Bodey v Hall* [2011] EWHC 2162 (QB); [2012] P.I.Q.R. P1, where the claimant was tipped out of a trap in which she was riding as a groom: the risk associated with the accident did not go beyond those of which the claimant would have been aware. In *Preskey v Sutcliffe*, unreported 18 February 2013 (Leeds County Court), Judge Belcher found that a claimant who had chosen to restrain a boxer dog had thereby voluntarily accepted the risk that the dog might feel threatened. He had exposed himself to the risk of being bitten and the defendants had the benefit of the statutory defences under both s.5(1) and (2).

81 See *Cummings v Grainger* [1977] Q.B. 397 CA for the effect on this defence of the Guard Dogs Act 1975.

82 *Preskey v Sutcliffe* (fn.80) is a case where the damage was found to be wholly the fault of the claim-

(d) *Common law defences no longer available.* Finally, there are certain defences which were probably available under the *scienter* action which have disappeared with that action and which are not revived in the Act. These are (i) act of God[84]; (ii) act of third party[85]; and (iii) the fact that there has been no escape from control.[86] At common law it was not clear whether it was open to the defendant to deny liability on the ground that there had been no failure of control or whether the claimant had to prove an escape. But the present law is clear under the Act. The keeper is responsible for the harm caused by the animal and there is nothing in the Act which indicates that as a necessary legal condition of liability the animal must have escaped or done the damage while out of control.[87]

(b) Strict liability for dogs under Section 3

20-17 **Liability for injury done by dogs to livestock** Section 3 provides that "where a dog causes damage by killing or injuring livestock, any person who is a keeper of the dog is liable for the damage, except as otherwise provided by this Act". It preserves the strict liability of the previous law and the principal feature of this category of liability is that there is no requirement of knowledge on the part of the keeper, as in s.2(2). If a dog injures livestock, there will therefore normally be no need to resort to the general statutory action under s.2(2), and indeed the claimant would be ill-advised to assume the additional onus of proving knowledge of the dog's propensity to attack livestock. It remains the law that a higher degree of protection is afforded to livestock than to human beings, since an attack on a human being is actionable only under s.2(2). The damage must be to "livestock"[88] and the person responsible is the "keeper" who is defined in the same way as for the

---

ant, who had elected to restrain a dog from following its owner despite the owner's requests to release the dog.

83 Applied by s.10 to actions under ss.2, 3 and 4 of the Act. "Fault" is defined by s.4 of the 1945 Act as "negligence, breach of statutory duty or other act or omission which gives rise to a liability in tort or would, apart from this Act, give rise to the defence of contributory negligence", and this definition is incorporated into the Act by s.11 of the Animals Act 1971.

84 At common law this largely rested on a dictum by Bramwell B. in *Nichols v Marsland* (1875) L.R. 10 Ex. 255 at 260 that "if a man kept a tiger, and lightning broke his chain, and he got loose and did mischief", he was by no means sure the keeper would not be liable. The Law Commission, see fn.4, at s.24 regarded it as a defence and recommended its abolition.

85 The Law Commission, see fn.4, decided to: "resolve any doubts which may remain in spite of the majority view in *Baker v Snell* ([1908] 2 K.B. 825) as to the availability of the defence of the act of a third party, by a clear rule that this defence is not available. In view of the rationale of strict liability for special risks it is our view that the act of a third party is one of the circumstances against which the person creating the risk should take precautions."

86 *Rands v McNeil* [1955] 1 Q.B. 253 at 257.

87 The Law Commission, see fn.4, at s.19. Failure of control is now only relevant in the factual sense that damage caused by an animal was not prevented by any restraint which the keeper insufficiently provided or failed to provide, and is now therefore only descriptive of a possible causal link between keeping and damage.

88 Defined in s.11 as "cattle, horses, sheep, pigs, goats and poultry, and also deer not in the wild state, and in sections 3 and 9, also, while in captivity, pheasants, partridges and grouse". A new definition of "horse", inserted by s.1(3)(a) of the Control of Horses Act 2015, includes "an ass, mule, or hinny" (previously included in the definition of "cattle"). A further definition of poultry is domestic varieties of "fowls, turkeys, geese, ducks, guinea-fowls, pigeons, peacocks and quails". The term "cattle" did not include rabbits kept for commercial purposes under the Dogs Act 1906 ss.1 and 7: *Tallents v Bell and Goddard* [1944] 2 All E.R. 474.

purpose of s.2.[89] The keeper's defences are that the person suffering damage did so wholly due to his own fault or that there was contributory negligence.[90] It is a defence[91] that "livestock was killed or injured on land to which it had strayed and either the dog belonged to the occupier or its presence on the land was authorised by the occupier". Where several dogs together cause damage and several keepers are liable, each may be sued for the whole damage.[92] But where each dog acts separately, each keeper is responsible only for the damage done by his dog.

(c) Strict liability for straying livestock under Section 4

Liability for damage and expenses due to trespassing livestock The old law of cattle-trespass having been abolished,[93] the Act, by s.4, introduced a new form of strict liability which is framed generally on the common law principles. It provides that: 20-18

> "where livestock belonging to any person[94] strays on to land in the ownership or occupation of another and
>
> (a) damage is done by the livestock to the land or to any property on it which is in the ownership or possession of the other person; or
>
> (b) any expenses are reasonably incurred by that other person in keeping the livestock while it cannot be restored to the person to whom it belongs or while it is detained in pursuance of section 7 of this Act, or in ascertaining to whom it belongs;"

the person to whom the livestock belongs is liable for the damage or expenses, except as otherwise provided by this Act.

Section 4 of the Control of Horses Act 2015 inserted a new s.4(3), providing that s.4 no longer applies to horses on land in England. Instead, a new s.4A applies a very similar provision to horses on land in England without lawful authority. New provisions, ss.7A and 7B, deal with powers to detain such horses. The statute, initially a Private Member's Bill with Government support, was designed to deal with the problem of "fly-grazing" on land in England.[95]

The definition of "livestock" The term "livestock", defined in s.11 in the Act, comprehends most ordinary farm animals.[96] As was the case in cattle trespass at 20-19

---

89 See para.20-15. This represents a change in that under the previous Acts the person liable was the dog's owner or the occupier of the place where the dog was kept. The owner without possession and the possessor without ownership are now both "keepers".

90 As under s.2. See ss.5(1), 10, and para.20-16.

91 s.5(4). The defences seem to be available to the occupier even if he was negligent in failing to keep out the livestock, but it is pointed out in North, *Civil Liability for Animals* (2012), para.7.14 that, if there has been a breach of duty to fence out, the occupier might be liable on that account for injury caused by his dog to straying livestock.

92 *Arneil v Paterson* [1931] A.C. 560. The keepers may apportion under the Civil Liability (Contribution) Act 1978 s.1.

93 s.1(1)(c).

94 s.4(2) provides that: "For the purposes of this section any livestock belongs to the person in whose possession it is". Similarly, s.4A(3) provides that "a horse belongs to the person in whose possession it is".

95 The Control of Horses (Wales) Act 2014 had already been enacted to deal with the problem in Wales. Neither the Animals Act 1971, nor the Control of Horses Act 2015, applies to Scotland or Northern Ireland.

96 See fn.88.

common law, dogs and cats are not included in the statutory definition of livestock.[97] The damage by livestock which is actionable under ss.4 and 4A is damage to land or other property, so no claim for personal injuries is possible.[98] Also the language of the section denies liability for purely financial loss.[99] Clearly, there must be some damage of the kind stated in ss.4 and 4A, and the statutory action is therefore, unlike cattle-trespass at common law, not actionable per se. Less clear is the question whether the livestock must have trespassed.[100] The Act refers to livestock which have "strayed", and therefore the position is unclear where animals have been depastured with permission and that permission has been withdrawn so that their continued presence constitutes a trespass: "it is difficult to see … how such livestock can be said to have strayed".[101] Probably a technical trespass is no longer necessary, and the courts will therefore have to decide in future cases what constitutes a "straying".[102]

20-20 **Parties and defences** The principal effect of s.4 has been to enable an action to be brought not only by one in possession of land but by anyone owning or occupying land. The owner can therefore sue for an injury to his reversionary interest.[103] The defendant must be someone in possession of the livestock. Though this will normally be the occupier of the place from which the livestock have strayed, the Act does not require this to be so, for example if A allows B to pasture livestock on A's land without A having any duty in relation to their care, and they stray, it appears that B, but not A, can be sued under s.4 for damage.

20-21 **Defences** The possessor of the offending livestock or horse(s) may have a defence in the following cases:

(i) Where any damage is wholly due to the fault of the person suffering it.[104] This is subject to the special rules relating to fencing, considered below.

---

97 Law Commission, see fn.4, at ss.60 and 64. Nor are bees included; such excluded species fall solely within s.2 and, for dogs, s.3. But the person in control of dogs, such as the master of foxhounds, may be liable for trespass to land at common law on the basis that persistent hunting close to prohibited land in circumstances where it is effectively impossible to prevent trespass by the hounds could provide evidence of an intention to trespass: *League Against Cruel Sports Ltd v Scott* [1986] Q.B. 240.

98 As was possible at common law: *Wormald v Cole* [1954] 1 Q.B. 614.

99 North, *Civil Liability for Animals* (2012), para.3.22, points out that infection or disease may result in damage to other livestock, but some such physical harm seems necessary. Where the loss caused is purely financial it is a question whether there is a common law duty of care and breach: see *Weller & Co v Foot and Mouth Research Institute* [1966] 1 Q.B. 569; and *D Pride & Partners (A Firm) v Institute for Animal Health* [2009] EWHC 685 (QB); [2009] N.P.C. 56 (considered at para.7-153). Financial loss to the occupier should be distinguished from the costs of detention expended by the occupier under these sections.

100 The heading to this section is borrowed from the side-note to s.4, but the text of s.4 makes no reference to trespass. The Law Commission at s.68 recommended that the new rule "should require a 'trespass' by the defendant's livestock upon the [claimant's] land and damage resulting therefrom". This was with the object of preventing any claim for "depasturing of chattels", as where chattels belonging to A were lawfully on B's land and are there damaged by B's cattle.

101 North, *Civil Liability for Animals* (2012), para.3.30; and see *Wiseman v Booker* (1878) 3 C.P.D. 184, there referred to, as a possible guide to the meaning of "straying".

102 It may be doubted whether *Ellis v Loftus Iron Co* (1874) L.R. 10 C. & P. 10 is still law.

103 Law Commission, see fn.4, at s.66. An example given is a cottage and garden let by a farmer for a short term to a holiday maker, but the Act is not confined to short lettings of this nature.

104 s.5(1).

(ii) Contributory negligence.[105]
(iii) Straying from the highway, when the livestock or horse was lawfully present on the highway.[106]
(iv) Failure to fence. The Act[107] provides that in determining liability under ss.4 and 4A the straying is not to be regarded as wholly the claimant's fault by reason only that it could have been prevented by fencing, and continues, "but a person is not liable under that section where it is proved that the straying of the livestock on to the land would not have occurred but for a breach by any other person, being a person having an interest in the land, of duty to fence".

Certain defences certainly or possibly applicable to cattle-trespass are not included in the Act and are therefore no longer available to a defendant under s.4. These are (i) act of God; (ii) volenti non fit injuria[108]; and (iii) act of third party.[109]

No duty on the occupier to fence out If, in the absence of obligation, the claimant could have fenced out but did not, and as a result the defendant's livestock stray onto his land, the claimant can claim under s.4. But there may be a particular duty to fence arising by contract, custom,[110] easement[111] or statute. If such an obligation is owed by the defendant to the claimant and is broken so that straying occurs, clearly the defendant must pay for damage under s.4, for the damage results directly from his own breach. The defence provided by the Act is concerned with the breach of obligation by any person other than the defendant, that person having an interest in the land on to which the defendant's livestock strayed. Clearly, where the claimant owes a duty to the defendant and a breach results in straying of the defendant's livestock, the defendant is exonerated. But certain further situations may be considered[112]: **20-22**

(a) The obligation may be owed by the claimant to a person other than the defendant whose livestock strayed, for example a tenant may covenant with his landlord to maintain fences without owing an obligation to his neighbours to fence out. The rule in cattle-trespass[113] was that a breach of such a covenant was not relevant to an action at common law. The defendant could not rely on a breach of an obligation owed to a third party. But the words of the Act are applicable to this case. The tenant had a duty to fence; he broke it and the defendant's livestock strayed. The defence therefore is available to the defendant.
(b) The obligation is owed by the claimant to a neighbour and as a result of

105 s.10, applying the Law Reform (Contributory Negligence) Act 1945.
106 s.5(5), enacting the rule in *Tillett v Ward* (1882) 10 Q.B.D. 17. Lawful use of the highway is that of passage. Thus where livestock have previously strayed on to the highway and are left to wander at will to graze the verges this does not amount to lawful user: *Matthews v Wicks*, *The Times*, 25 May 1987 CA. Section 5(5A) applies the same principle to a horse which strays from the highway when its presence there was a lawful use of the highway.
107 s.5(6).
108 Except in so far as covered by s.5(1).
109 As to straying, e.g. where a trespasser leaves a gate open. Semble, aliter if the third party drove the livestock onto the claimant's land, but the drover might well be liable for ordinary trespass at common law.
110 *Egerton v Harding* [1975] Q.B. 62 CA. Immemorial usage may found a presumption of lawful origin.
111 *Crow v Wood* [1971] 1 Q.B. 77 CA.
112 See the analysis in North, *Civil Liability for Animals* (2012), paras 4.19–4.41.
113 *Holgate v Bleazard* [1917] 1 K.B. 443.

breach, livestock not belonging to the neighbour stray from that land on to the claimant's. Again, it appears that the defendant to whom the livestock belongs can invoke the statutory defence. The claimant has an interest in the land and owes a fencing duty. The Act does not require him to owe that duty to the defendant.[114]

(c) The obligation is owed by a person other than the claimant, for example the landlord has covenanted with his neighbour and his tenant is the claimant. At common law the tenant was in no better position than his landlord[115] and the Act produces the same result. The landlord manifestly has an interest in the land, and the result is that his breach of covenant enables the defendant to invoke the defence against the tenant as claimant.

3. LIABILITY FOR ANIMALS ON THE HIGHWAY

20-23 **Animals straying on to the highway** At common law there was no duty of care to restrain animals from straying on to the public highway. This ancient immunity from liability developed before the emergence of modern traffic conditions, but was confirmed by the House of Lords in 1947 in *Searle v Wallbank*.[116] It was subject to a substantial body of adverse criticism[117] and the Law Commission in 1967 concluded that the case for changing the principle was overwhelming. Their recommendation for change was carried out by s.8 of the Act which provides that "so much of the rules of the common law relating to liability for negligence as excludes or restricts the duty which a person might owe to others to take such care as is reasonable to see that damage is not caused by animals straying on to a highway is hereby abolished". Subsection (2) provides that[118]:

> "where damage is caused by animals straying from unfenced land to the highway a person who placed them on the land shall not be regarded as having committed a breach of the duty to take care by reason only of placing them there if—
>
> (a) the land is common land, or is land situated in an area where fencing is not customary, or is a town or village green; and
> (b) he had a right to place the animals on that land."[119]

The change is concerned with straying on to the highway, not with straying off the highway on to adjoining land. Section 5(5) of the Act provides a defence to liability under s.4 in the latter situation. But the common law before the Act

[114] North, *Civil Liability for Animals* (2012) paras 4.28–4.29, considers the variant cases where the defendant's livestock was unlawfully on the neighbour's land. Can such a trespasser invoke the defence? At common law he had no defence and the Act does not deal with the case directly. But it seems unlikely that s.5(1) and (6) can be taken to equip a trespasser with such a defence. See also *Searle v Wallbank* [1947] A.C. 341.

[115] *Wiseman v Booker* (1878) 3 C.P.D. 184.

[116] [1947] A.C. 341.

[117] See generally the Law Commission, see fn.4.

[118] As originally proposed in the Law Commission's Draft Bill the matters to be taken into account were more numerous. The present subsection represents a compromise of interests by placing a presumption against breach of duty where land is unfenced in the circumstances set out. Fencing is defined in the Act s.11, which also provides that "common land" and "town or village green" shall have the same meanings as in the Commons Registration Act 1965.

[119] *Davies v Davies* [1975] Q.B. 172 CA. The licensee of a person having such a right has also "a right" to depasture animals and can invoke the defence, under this subsection.

recognised a duty of care to prevent straying off the highway,[120] and this remains the law. There is a duty of care in both situations, the only difference being that in straying on to the highway the duty is statutory in origin. Substantially, therefore, the liability for damage caused by animals straying on to or being driven on the highway[121] or from the highway to adjacent land is governed by a criterion of reasonable care.[122] Where livestock strays on to a highway, there may in certain circumstances be strict liability under s.4 of the Act.[123]

In *Hole v Ross-Skinner*[124] the claimant was injured when driving his car on the highway, by colliding with the defendant's horse which had escaped from the field where it was kept. At first instance, on hearing evidence that the state of the fences and gates of the defendant's land were "scruffy" and ill-maintained, the judge accepted that the defendant had a duty of care to keep the fencing secure and that that duty had been breached. On appeal, it was held that since the fence had been cut and the gate opened by an unknown third party, there was no evidence of breach of duty by the defendant. The poor condition of the gates and fences was not a basis for inferring negligence by the defendant. On the other hand, in *Donaldson v Wilson*[125] the Court of Appeal held that a farmer whose land was crossed by a frequently used right of way, which led to a public highway, was under a duty to take additional care to see that cattle on his land were properly secured and did not stray onto the highway. 20-24

4. COMMON LAW LIABILITIES

Common law liabilities The Act abolished the old *scienter* action and the even older action for cattle-trespass,[126] but outside the limits of that repeal it left other areas of common law liability for animals intact. Where, for example, animals are allowed to accumulate in numbers on the highway, that may be actionable public nuisance; the smell of a pig farm may constitute private nuisance or the sending of animals on to another's land may amount to trespass.[127] But more generally, the statutory liabilities do not displace wider liabilities at common law. Although a claimant may prefer to claim under a strict liability established by ss.2, 3 or 4, he may resort to an action based on negligence if he chooses: 20-25

> "It is also true that, quite apart from the liability imposed upon the owner of animals or the person having control of them by reason of knowledge of their propensities, there is the ordinary duty of a person to take care either that his animal or his chattel is not put to such a use as is likely to injure his neighbour—the ordinary duty to take care in the cases put upon negligence."[128]

[120] *Gayler and Pope Ltd v B Davies & Son Ltd* [1924] 2 K.B. 75.
[121] *Deen v Davies* [1935] 2 K.B. 282.
[122] Where the animal is deliberately driven off the highway on to adjoining premises, this is ordinary trespass to land.
[123] Not at the suit of an ordinary user, because he has no ownership or occupation of the land, but it appears that an occupier of land over which a public right of way passes might claim under s.4 for damage recoverable under that section.
[124] [2003] EWCA Civ 774.
[125] [2004] EWCA Civ 972; (2004) 148 S.J.L.B. 879.
[126] s.1(1).
[127] *League Against Cruel Sports Ltd v Scott* [1986] Q.B. 240.
[128] *Fardon v Harcourt-Rivington* (1932) 48 T.L.R. 215 at 217.

This remains the position since the Act,[129] and a claimant may also resort to a claim under the Occupiers' Liability Act 1957. Thus the "keeper" of the animal may be strictly liable under ss.2 or 3, but other persons may have been negligent in failing to avoid damage actionable under those sections and thus be liable at common law or under the Occupiers' Liability Act 1957 as well as, or instead of, the "keeper". In the Scottish case of *Hill v Lovett*,[130] the claimant suffered serious injury as a result of being bitten by one of two dogs, owned by her employer, when she entered his garden to clean the windows. Neither dog had attacked a stranger before, but they were known to be pugnacious and protective of their territory and to be "prone to nip". The claimant succeeded against her employer at common law, on the ground that he was in breach of duty in failing to provide her with a safe place of work, and against the employer and his wife under the Occupiers' Liability (Scotland) Act 1960. In *McKaskie v Cameron*,[131] a farmer was found liable under the Occupiers' Liability Act 1957 to a walker who had been seriously injured by cows when walking her dog along what she probably took to be the route of a public footpath.[132] The cows had their calves with them and attacks on walkers (particularly dog-walkers) by cows with calves are not uncommon, even if they are far from common, and even if these particular cows had previously been docile. Given expert evidence on the familiarity of such incidents, the judge concluded that it was a breach of the common duty of care under the 1957 Act to keep cows with their calves in a field crossed by a public footpath unless that footpath was fenced, particularly given that the cows could have grazed in other fields, leaving the fields crossed by public footpaths to be grazed by sheep.[133] The judge gave extended consideration to the question of implied consent to the use of a route across the field which was not that of the footpath, and concluded that the claimant did have the "right" to deviate from the path.[134] He did not, however, appear to have had the case of *Greenhalgh v British Railways Board*[135] drawn to his attention. There, it was held that s.2(6) of the Occupiers' Liability Act 1957 does not apply to a person lawfully exercising a public right of way.

20-26 It has been pointed out that for strict liability under s.2(2) some actual knowledge of abnormal characteristics must be attributable to the keeper or to one of those other persons mentioned in s.2(2)(c), but in the absence of such proven knowledge it is open to a claimant to show that damage was reasonably foreseeable, and if he established the general requirements of actionable negligence against a defendant, he may succeed on that account. In *Smith v Prendergast*[136] the owner of a scrapyard

---

129 *Draper v Hodder* [1972] 2 Q.B. 556 CA—the defendant was held liable for failing to take reasonable precautions against the foreseeable risk that a pack of terriers could attack a child, since it was known that terriers can be dangerous when roaming free in a pack.

130 1992 S.L.T. 994.

131 Unreported 1 July 2009, Preston County Court, Claim No.6NE04848.

132 The farmer had heard his cows bellowing and arrived at the field to see them "tossing something about": this proved to be the claimant.

133 The judge also held that there would have been liability under the Occupiers' Liability Act 1984 if Ms McKaskie should be thought to have been a trespasser, given that she had (probably mistakenly) not taken the exact route of the footpath across the field. He also held that there would have been liability under s.2 of the Animals Act 1971, since the propensity to attack was possessed by cows with calves where they are troubled by the presence of a dog, and this general propensity would be known to the farmer.

134 Transcript at [111].

135 [1969] 2 Q.B. 286. See para.11-21.

136 *The Times*, 18 October 1984, CA.

was held responsible for an attack by a stray Alsatian dog which had taken up residence in his yard three weeks earlier. The dog had not done anything in that time to indicate it might bite. The scrapyard owner was held to have been negligent in failing to supervise and control the dog for a reasonable period in order to observe whether it was docile.[137]

In *Whippey v Jones*,[138] the Court of Appeal emphasised in respect of liability in negligence that the duty of care will generally be breached only if a reasonable person in the defendant's position would "contemplate that injury is likely to follow" from his acts or omissions.[139] In this case, the defendant had acted as a reasonable dog-handler would do, and the judge had erred in finding the duty of care to have been breached where the injury was only foreseeable as a "possibility". The defendant, Mr Whippey, had taken his Great Dane, Hector, to a park for exercise. Hector was found by the judge to be "gentle". He did not jump up. However, he weighed around 12 and a half stone and was inclined to approach people in a manner that might appear to be aggressive. He was, therefore, intimidating. Mr Whippey unleashed Hector after satisfying himself that no other people were present. He did not see the claimant, Mr Jones, who was running along the footpath. Hector knocked the claimant causing him to slip towards a river and break his ankle. The judge found that the injury did not fall within s.2(2)(a) of the Animals Act 1971, since it had not been an injury the animal was *likely* to cause (nor that was likely to be severe). He did find, however, that the defendant was liable in negligence, since the injury was foreseeable "as a possibility". The Court of Appeal concluded that liability in negligence in these circumstances required foreseeability of injury as a likelihood, so that the "possibility" of injury as established on the facts was not enough. It should perhaps be noted that the relevant test was also explained by the Court in a more general and more orthodox way: "there must be a sufficient probability of injury to lead a reasonable person (in the position of the defendant) to anticipate it".[140] One approach is to regard *Whippey v Jones* as a case of reasonable risk-taking, like *Bolton v Stone*.[141] Consideration of likelihood is thus more easily understood as a relevant aspect of breach of duty. The defendant had (it was found) carefully checked for other adults, and Hector was not inclined to be aggressive rather than intimidating. As such, the defendant had acted reasonably in unleashing him. Although *Whippey v Jones* was cited in *Harris v Miller*,[142] the test applied appears more conventional. The claimant had, at the age of 14, been seriously injured falling from a horse owned by the defendant. It was found that the horse, a thoroughbred, was powerful and difficult to control. The defendant had limited experience of riding and the claimant had not previously ridden a horse, rather than a pony. The defendant's standard of care was to be assessed "by reference to that of the ordinary and reasonably prudent horse owner": such a person "would ensure that he or she is possessed of sufficient information about both horse **20-27**

---

137 See also *Pitcher v Martin* [1937] 3 All E.R. 918—owner liable in nuisance and negligence when dog escaped from his control and tripped claimant in the course of chasing a cat; *Birch v Mills* [1995] C.L.Y. 3683—defendant liable for an attack by a herd of cows upon the claimant while walking dogs on leads down a public road. If it was foreseeable that the cows would attack a dog it was foreseeable that a person attached to the dog was likely to get hurt.

138 [2009] EWCA Civ 452; (2009) 159 N.L.J. 598. See also *Addis v Campbell* [2011] EWCA Civ 906.

139 [2009] EWCA Civ 452; (2009) 159 N.L.J. 598 at [16].

140 [2009] EWCA Civ 452; (2009) 159 N.L.J. 598

141 [1951] A.C. 850; see para.7-176.

142 [2016] EWHC 2438 (QB) at [97].

and rider to be able to assess any risk from what is an inherently dangerous activity".[143] In this instance, the duty of care was breached.

20-28 Any defences available to a common law cause of action could apply where an animal is the cause of the damage. Thus, where a police dog bites a suspect in the course of assisting a police officer to arrest the suspect there will be a defence to an action for battery if the use of such force was reasonable in the circumstances under the Criminal Law Act 1967 s.3.[144]

143 [2016] EWHC 2438 (QB) at [150].

144 *Pollard v Chief Constable of West Yorkshire Police* [1999] P.I.Q.R. P219 CA.

CHAPTER 21

DEFAMATION

TABLE OF CONTENTS

1. GENERALLY

Action of defamation The law recognises the right of every person, during life,[1] to possession of a good name. A person who communicates to a third party matter which is untrue and likely in the course of things substantially to damage the reputation of a third person is, on the face of it, guilty of a legal wrong for which the remedy is a claim in tort for defamation.[2] Defamation is the tort which protects reputation and that is the core concern at the heart of defamation law: the deterring and remedying of unwarranted harm to reputation. The purpose of the law of defamation is to hold a balance between freedom of speech and the right to reputation.[3] There are other causes of action which may seem to overlap with defamation.[4] However, a claim brought relying upon other causes of action may be held to be an abuse of process if the purpose is to circumvent the rules of the tort of defamation[5] including those relating to the granting of interim injunctions.[6] It is, however, increasingly common for privacy, data protection or harassment claims to be brought alongside defamation claims.[7] **21-01**

Reputation as both a private and public good Reputation is both a private right and a public good. In *Reynolds v Times Newspapers Ltd*[8] Lord Nicholls said: **21-02**

> "Reputation is an integral and important part of the dignity of the individual. It also forms the basis of many decisions in a democratic society which are fundamental to its well-being: whom to employ or work for, whom to promote, whom to do business with or to vote for. Once besmirched by an unfounded allegation in a national newspaper, a reputation can be damaged forever, especially if there is no opportunity to vindicate one's reputation. When this happens, society as well as the individual is the loser. For it should not be supposed that protection of reputation is a matter of importance only to the af-

---

1 An action is not maintainable for defamation of a deceased person: *Broom v Ritchie* (1904) 6 F. 942; *Smith v Dha* [2013] EWHC 838 (QB) where the court held that the death of the claimant abates the action, even if the claim is in progress and a hearing has taken place.

2 Criminal libel has now been abolished in England, Wales and Northern Ireland. It remains on the statute book of some Commonwealth jurisdictions.

3 See, e.g. *Panday v Gordon* [2005] UKPC 36; [2006] 1 A.C. 427 at [12]–[15].

4 For examples of causes of action, see conspiracy (*Lonrho v Fayed (No.5)* [1993] 1 W.L.R. 1489 CA); breach of an implied duty not to damage trust between an employer and employee (*Malik v BBCI* [1995] 3 All E.R. 545 CA; *BCCI v Ali* [1999] 4 All E.R. 83); negligence (*Spring v Guardian Assurance* [1995] 2 A.C. 296, where the House of Lords granted a remedy to the claimant who sued his former employer for negligence in writing a derogatory reference in relation to him, though an action for libel would not have lain since the occasion was one of qualified privilege and malice could not be shown); harassment (e.g. *Georgallides v Etzin* [2005] EWHC 1790 (QB)); misuse of private information (*McKennitt v Ash* [2006] EWCA Civ 1714; [2008] Q.B. 73); and breach of statutory duty under the General Data Protection Regulation and the Data Protection Act 2018; and Human Rights Act 1998.

5 *Gulf Oil (Great Britain) Ltd v Page* [1987] 1 Ch. 327; *LNS (Terry) v Persons Unknown* [2010] EWHC 119 (QB); [2010] E.M.L.R. 16 at [85]–[88] where Tugendhat J explained, citing the judgment of Ralph Gibson LJ in *Gulf Oil*, that it is a matter for the court to decide whether the principle of free speech prevails or not, and that it does not depend solely upon the choice of the claimant as to his cause of action. The matter was also considered by the Court of Appeal in the context of misuse of private information in *McKennitt v Ash* [2006] EWCA Civ 1714; [2008] Q.B. 73. See the judgment of Buxton LJ (with whom Latham and Longmore LJJ agreed) at [79]–[80] and Longmore LJ at [85]–[87].

6 See para.21-252.

7 *Sunderland Housing Co Ltd v Baines* [2006] EWHC 2359 (QB).

8 [2001] 2 A.C. 127 at 201.

fected individual and his family. Protection of reputation is conducive to the public good. It is in the public interest that the reputation of public figures should not be debased falsely. In the political field, in order to make an informed, choice, the electorate needs to be able to identify the good as well as the bad. Consistently with these considerations, human rights conventions recognise that freedom of expression is not an absolute right. Its exercise may be subject to such restrictions as are prescribed by law and are necessary in a democratic society for the protection of the reputations of others."

21-03 **Defamation in the rights context** The Human Rights Act 1998 gave effect in the courts of the UK to rights and freedoms guaranteed under the European Convention on Human Rights including the right to a fair trial under art.6; the right to respect for a private life under art.8; and a right to freedom of expression under art.10. The effect of the Convention on defamation law has been considerable and continues. Defamation law was oft-criticised in this jurisdiction[9] as being too restrictive to free speech (hence, the decision in *Reynolds*, above, and other cases where attempts have been made to re-balance the law mostly with reference to art.10[10]). This was particularly so immediately before and after the passing of the Human Rights Act 1998.[11] Cases in Strasbourg[12] and England, however, have established that a right of reputation is one of the rights guaranteed by art.8 of the Convention. Whilst the issue remains controversial, the question has now been settled here, at least, by the decision of the Supreme Court in *Re Guardian News and Media Ltd*[13] in which the court concluded that where a claimant complains that the impact of publication on his reputation will seriously affect his private life, the publication will engage art.8. The effect upon defamation law by this and similar Strasbourg decisions can be seen in various places throughout this chapter, most importantly in respect of publications by public authorities.[14] Where both arts 8 and 10 are engaged, the courts are required to conduct a "balancing exercise" in determining which of the competing rights should prevail.[15] Where only one of the articles is engaged, the party said to have interfered with the right engaged must satisfy the court that the interference was proportionate and necessary to achieve a legitimate aim.[16]

---

9 e.g. May LJ in *Morrell v International Publishing Co* [1989] 3 All E.R. 733 at 734–735. See also the observations of Stuart-Smith LJ in *Williams v Mirror Group Newspapers, The Independent,* 12 February 1991 CA; and Neill LJ in *Rechem International Ltd v Express Newspapers Plc, The Times,* 19 June 1992 CA.

10 See, for instance, *Derbyshire County Council v Times Newspapers Ltd* [1993] A.C. 534 at 551; *Rantzen v Mirror Group Newspapers* [1994] Q.B. 670 at 691.

11 See *Reynolds v Times Newspapers Ltd* [2001] 2 A.C. 127.

12 *Chauvy v France* (2005) 41 E.H.R.R. 29 at [70]; *Radio France v France* (2005) 40 E.H.R.R. 29 ECtHR at [31]; *Cumpana and Mazare v Romania* (2005) 41 E.H.R.R. 14 ECtHR at [91]; *White v Sweden* (2008) 46 E.H.R.R. 3 ECtHR.

13 [2010] UKSC 1; [2010] 2 A.C. 697.

14 See, e.g. *Wood v Chief Constable of West Midlands Police* [2004] EWCA Civ 1638; [2005] E.M.L.R. 20; *Clift v Slough BC* [2010] EWCA Civ 1484; [2011] 1 W.L.R. 1774; *McLaughlin v Lambeth LBC* [2010] EWHC 2726 (QB); [2011] E.M.L.R. 8.

15 See for example *Re S (A Child) (Identification: Restrictions on Publication)* [2004] UKHL 47; [2005] 1 A.C. 593.

16 In *Clift v Slough BC* [2010] EWCA Civ 1484; [2011] 1 W.L.R. 1774 the Court of Appeal accepted that the act of a local authority in including a person on its violent persons register and emailing that information to various other departments was disproportionate and in breach of the individual's rights under art.8 of the Convention. As a result, the local authority did not have a defence of qualified privilege. The Court of Appeal recognised that the right to reputation is an aspect of the right to a private life protected under art.8, and that in cases involving public authorities, following the enact-

Defamation Reform: The Defamation Act 2013 The perceived need to rebalance defamation law to provide greater protection for freedom of expression, particularly from foreign claimants and in favour of academics and scientists, was the impetus leading up to the passing of the Defamation Act 2013. The Act came into force on 1 January 2014 along with the Defamation (Operators of Websites) Regulations 2013.[17] The main features are as follows: 21-04

(i) A new threshold test for determining whether a statement is defamatory. Section 1 provides that a statement is not defamatory unless its publication has caused or is likely to cause serious harm to reputation of the claimant. It creates a further threshold test for a body trading for profit, providing that harm to the reputation of such a body is not "serious harm" unless it has caused or is likely to cause serious financial loss.

(ii) A reversal of the presumption in favour of trial by jury, by virtue of s.69(1) of the Senior Courts Act 1981. The presumption now works the other way, so that trial by jury must be justified in accordance with a series of criteria, including that such a trial would be in the public interest or the interests of justice.[18]

(iii) A new public interest defence, which abolishes the common law defence of responsible journalism as set out in *Reynolds v Times Newspapers Ltd*.[19]

(iv) A defence of "truth", replacing the common law defence of justification.

(v) A defence of "honest opinion", replacing the common law defence of "fair comment" or "honest comment".

(vi) A defence for peer-reviewed statements in scientific or academic journals.

(vii) Wider scope is given to report-based absolute and qualified privilege, extending the ambit of absolute privilege to reports of court proceedings around the world (whereas it was previously limited to reports of UK courts, the European Court of Justice, the European Court of Human Rights and international tribunals set up by the Security Council of the United Nations). Qualified privilege is also extended to "summaries" in addition to copies or extracts of material produced by a range of bodies which includes more international bodies or organisations.

(viii) The "multiple publication" (or *Duke of Brunswick*[20]) rule, which entitled a claimant to bring an action more than one year after the original publication where the publication had been repeated is abolished. The "single publication rule" will apply to repeat publication of the same material by the same publisher, and prevent such an action being brought after the limitation period has expired in respect of the original publication (the limitation period being one year). This will mean that it will not be possible to bring an action over archive internet articles which are deemed under the *Duke of Brunswick* rule to be republished every day that they are accessible online.

---

ment of the Human Rights Act 1998, defences such as qualified privilege could only be applied in compliance with the art.8 right.

17 SI 2013/3027 and SI 2013/3028 respectively.

18 It seems that jury trials will now be extremely rare: *Yeo v Times Newspapers Ltd* [2014] EWHC 2853 (QB); [2015] 1 W.L.R. 971. There have been no jury libel trials since the Act came into force.

19 [2001] 2 A.C. 127.

20 *Duke of Brunswick v Harmer* (1849) 14 Q.B. 185.

(ix) New provisions aimed at dealing with "libel tourism".
(x) Further provisions deal with secondary responsibility, making it more difficult to bring actions against Internet Service Providers or the broadcasters of live programmes.

21-05 **Jurisdiction** The issue of jurisdiction has become increasingly relevant to defamation claims, in a European context[21] and in relation to international publications, especially in the light of increased means of communication and the advent of the internet and social media.[22] The Defamation Act 2013 introduces new provisions aimed at dealing with "libel tourism". Section 9 provides that the court does not have jurisdiction to hear and determine an action for defamation against a party who is not in the UK, another EU Member State or a state that is a contracting party to the Lugano Convention unless England and Wales is clearly the most appropriate place in which to bring an action in respect of the statement. From 31 December 2020 (the end of the Brexit transition period) this will change to remove references to other EU member and Lugano Convention states, such that s.9 will apply to any actions against a party who is not in the UK. In *Wright v Ver*[23] Nicklin J approached analysis of the provision in two stages: (1) assessment of the nature of the publication and its extent in each jurisdiction; and (2) assessment of the evidence of harm to reputation in the jurisdictions in which there has been publication. A challenge to jurisdiction under s.9 may be brought at any time, and CPR 11 does not apply as the CPR cannot confer jurisdiction where by statute the court does not have it.[24]

21-06 **Costs** The expense of a defamation action remains a concern and the 2013 Act does not address the rules on the recoverability of costs. The European Court of Human Rights has ruled that success fees sought as part of a conditional fee agreement are a disproportionate interference with the right to freedom of expression.[25] This issue remains controversial, and recently came before the Supreme Court.[26] The Justices found it unnecessary to decide whether there is a general rule that the funding arrangements breach publishers' art.10 rights, but found that even if there was such a rule, as the claimants had relied on an Act of Parliament, ruling that success fees and after the event insurance premiums were not recoverable in these cases would interfere with their Protocol 1 art.1 rights; and their arts 8 and 6 rights also may be infringed. The matter is one left to Parliament. From April 2013 s.58 of the Courts and Legal Services Act 1990 (as amended by s.44 of the Legal Aid, Sentencing and Punishment of Offenders Act 2012), abolished the recoverability of success fees from losing parties in civil proceedings generally. Such fees are payable out of, and limited by reference to, the damages recovered by the claimant. However, the provisions did not come into force in relation to defamation claims

---

21 See, e.g. *Shevill v Presse Alliance SA* [1995] 2 A.C. 18; and *eDate Advertising GmbH v X* [2012] Q.B. 654 (ECJ).

22 See, e.g. *Berezovsky v Michaels* [2000] 1 W.L.R. 1004; *King v Lewis* [2004] EWCA Civ 1329; [2005] E.M.L.R. 4; *Lord McAlpine of West Green v Bercow* [2013] EWHC 1342 (QB); *Monroe v Hopkins* [2017] EWHC 433 (QB); [2017] 4 W.L.R. 68.

23 [2019] EWHC 2094 (QB); affirmed [2020] EWCA Civ 672.

24 *Sadik v Sadik* [2019] EWHC 2717 (QB); [2020] E.M.L.R. 7, which also includes discussion of s.9 generally.

25 *MGN Ltd v United Kingdom* (39401/04) (2011) 53 E.H.R.R. 5 ECtHR.

26 *Times Newspapers Ltd v Flood, Miller v Associated Newspapers Ltd, Frost v MGN Ltd* [2017] UKSC 33; [2017] 1 W.L.R. 1415.

(and other privacy and publication claims) until 6 April 2019.[27] Success fees are no longer recoverable from the losing party in defamation claims, although after the event insurance premiums remain recoverable. Defamation claims are subject to the same budgeting rules pertaining to all civil claims.

Courts and Crimes Act 2013 The other important reform to the law in this area relates to the recommendations made by Lord Justice Leveson in his report into the culture, practices and ethics of the press. Throughout late 2011 and 2012 Leveson LJ conducted a detailed review of English media regulation, in light of the voicemail interception (or "phone hacking") scandal. The Leveson Report was published on 29 November 2012. Following discussions and negotiations between the main political parties, the decision was taken to seek to incorporate Leveson LJ's findings in a Royal Charter instead of via statutory underpinning and the Privy Council granted a royal charter on press regulation in October 2013. In November 2014 the Press Recognition Panel was established. It has responsibility for assessing whether self-regulatory bodies set up by the press which apply for recognition comply with the criteria set out in Sch.4 to the Royal Charter. In October 2016 IMPRESS was recognised by the Panel. At the time of writing IMPRESS has 136 members, many of them local publications. None of the major national newspapers are members. The majority are instead members of IPSO, the successor to the Press Complaints Commission which has not sought recognition. *The Guardian*, *Independent* and *Financial Times* newspaper publishers have instead made their own arrangements. The "carrot and stick" designed to lead publishers to sign up to the approved scheme can be found in ss.34–42 of the Crime and Courts Act 2013, where provision is made to allow the courts to take into account whether defendants are publishers of news-related material (as defined) when considering issues of aggravated and exemplary damages and costs. The aggravated and exemplary damages provisions under ss.34–39 of the Crime and Courts Act 2013 came into force on 3 November 2015. The extent to which the court will award exemplary or aggravated damages remains to be seen. In the case of exemplary damages the provisions allow the court to make an award where the defendant's conduct has shown a deliberate or reckless disregard of an outrageous nature for the claimant's rights, such that the court should punish the defendant for it and other remedies would not be adequate to do so. Aggravated damages may be awarded against the defendant only to compensate for mental distress and not for purposes of punishment. It was thought that the recognition of the first body by the Press Recognition Panel would trigger the coming into force of s.40 of the Act, which would allow costs to be awarded against a publisher even if they succeeded in defending a claim, unless they were a member of an approved regulator. However, the Government has instead held a public consultation on whether to bring that section into force, and has not yet done so. 21-07

2. The Cause of Action

Libel and slander Defamation consists of two torts—libel and slander.[28] Defamation in transitory form is usually slander, whereas defamation in permanent form 21-08

---

[27] Legal Aid, Sentencing and Punishment of Offenders Act 2012 (Commencement No.13) Order 2018 (SI 2018/1287).

[28] See Kaye, "Libel and Slander—two torts or one?" (1975) 91 L.Q.R. 524. Malicious falsehood is often discussed as a species of defamation.

is libel.[29] Libel generally indicates something printed or written, but it includes also anything in a more or less permanent form,[30] such as a painting or picture,[31] effigy,[32] caricature,[33] advertisement,[34] talking film,[35] or any disparaging object.[36] Reading out a defamatory document to a third party is the publication of a libel.[37] Dictating defamatory matter to a typist is clearly slander,[38] but if the dictated matter is turned into a letter and published to a third party the dictator may be liable for the publication of a libel through his agent.[39] With regard to matter recorded on a record, tape or some other recording instrument, it is submitted that the publication of the recorded matter would be a publication in permanent form, i.e. libel.[40] Section 166 of the Broadcasting Act 1990 provides that the publication of words in the course of any programme, including a programme service, shall be treated as a publication in permanent form. It applies to any programme included in a programme service (see ss.201 and 202).[41] Communications from an internet site would seem to come within s.201(b) and are therefore libel by statute. They have been treated as such by the courts.[42] The Theatres Act 1968 provides that the publication of words in the course of a performance of a play (other than certain performances excepted by s.7 of the Act) is to be treated as publication in permanent form.[43]

21-09 **Falsehood and malice** The publication[44] of defamatory matter with reference to the claimant will give rise to a cause of action in defamation. The claimant must in his statement of case be able to set out with reasonable certainty the alleged

---

29 For a detailed discussion of the differences between the two, *Gatley on Libel and Slander* (12th edn), paras 3.6–3.12.

30 See Broadcasting Act 1990 s.166(1); and *Kazir v Australian Broadcasting Commission* [1964] V.R. 702.

31 *Du Bost v Beresford* (1810) 2 Camp. 511; *Garbett v Hazell, Watson and Viney Ltd* [1943] 2 All E.R. 359; *Thaarup v Hulton Press Ltd* (1943) 169 L.T. 309.

32 *Monson v Tussauds* [1894] 1 Q.B. 671.

33 *Dunlop v Dunlop* [1920] 1 Ir. R. 280.

34 *Tolley v Fry* [1931] A.C. 333.

35 *Youssoupoff v MGM Pictures Ltd* (1934) 50 T.L.R. 581.

36 e.g. a gallows at the claimant's door; 5 Rep. 125a at 125b; *Carr v Hood* (1808) 1 Camp. 355n; *Eyre v Garlick* (1878) 42 J.P. 68. In *Jefferies v Duncombe* (1809) 11 East. 237, the claimant recovered damages against the defendant for keeping in front of the claimant's house a lamp burning during the daytime "thereby intending to mark out the dwelling of the claimant as a bawdy house". The action is described in the report as one of nuisance. It would seem in substance an action of libel.

37 *Forrester v Tyrrell* (1839) 9 T.L.R. 257; followed and preferred to dicta in *Osborn v Thomas Boulter & Son* [1930] 2 K.B. 226 at 231, 236, 237; in *Robinson v Chambers (No.2)* [1946] N.I. 148; cf. *Longdon-Griffiths v Smith* [1951] 1 K.B. 295.

38 But that publication may be protected by qualified privilege: *Osborn v Thomas Boulter & Son* [1930] 2 K.B. 226; *Bryanston Finance Ltd v de Vries* [1975] Q.B. 703; *Riddick v Thames Board Mills Ltd* [1977] Q.B. 881 CA.

39 Reading back defamatory matter to the person who has dictated it, or the submission of the letter to him is not publication by the typist: cf. *Eglantine Inn Ltd v Smith* [1948] N.I. 29 at 33; cf. *Osborn v Thomas Boulter & Son* [1930] 3 K.B. 226.

40 See *Gatley on Libel and Slander* (12th edn), paras 3.6–3.12.

41 See s.1. As to jurisdiction where a statement is broadcast from a station abroad and heard within the jurisdiction, see *Jenner v Sun Oil Co* [1952] 2 D.L.R. 526.

42 *Godfrey v Demon Internet Ltd* [2001] Q.B. 2001; see *Gatley on Libel and Slander* (12th edn) at 3.12. The authors consider that emails, SMSs and Tweets would be libels but telephonic communication via the internet is more likely to be treated as a slander.

43 Theatres Act 1968 ss.4(1) and 7.

44 For what is meant by publication, see para.21-55 onwards.

defamatory words,[45] their alleged meaning[46] and, if necessary, factors relied upon as identifying the claimant as the subject of the allegations. The claimant need not allege that the imputation published is false or that it has been published maliciously. Since it is not to be assumed that anyone is of bad character, defamation of an individual is taken to be false until it is proved to be true. Malice only becomes relevant if the defendant seeks to rely on a defence which may be defeated on proof of malice, such as qualified privilege.[47] It may also be relevant to any claim for aggravated or exemplary damages.[48] Since the coming into force of the Defamation Act 2013 the claimant must also set out the matters relied upon to show that publication of the words has caused or is likely to cause serious harm to the claimant's reputation.[49]

Motive immaterial The motive of the defendant is immaterial in determining his liability. "A man may be the publisher of a libel without a particle of malice or improper motive."[50] If, therefore, the defamatory matter would *reasonably*[51] be understood by members of the public who knew the claimant to refer to him, the defendant is liable, even though he may prove that the words, when written, were not and could not have been intended to apply to the claimant, and indeed, that he was not aware and had no reason to be aware of the claimant's existence.[52] It is for the publisher of the statement to describe the person he intends to refer to with sufficient clarity to ensure that no reasonable person would think the statement applied to anybody else.[53] **21-10**

Exceptions Whilst defamation remains a tort of strict liability, there are exceptions. Where a defence of qualified privilege is raised motive may be in issue. A mere distributor of a defamatory publication would not be liable at common law unless shown to be negligent.[54] Section 1 of the Defamation Act 1996 provides a defence for a person who is not an editor, author, or commercial publisher and can show he has taken reasonable care. Under s.10 of the Defamation Act 2013, it is not possible to bring an action in defamation against any person other than the author, editor or publisher of the statement complained of unless the court is satisfied that it is not reasonably practicable for an action to be brought against one of those primarily responsible persons. **21-11**

---

45 *Collins v Jones* [1955] 1 Q.B. 564.

46 CPR Pt 53 PD 2.3.

47 See para.21-206 onwards.

48 See para.21-226 onwards.

49 Defamation Act 2013 s.1.

50 per Lord Bramwell in *Abrath v NE Ry* (1886) 11 App. Cas. 247 at 253.

51 *Nevill v Fine Art and General Insurance Co* [1897] A.C. 68 at 78–79, per Lord Shaw; *Shaw v London Express Newspaper* (1925) 41 T.L.R. 475; *Hough v London Express Newspaper Ltd* [1940] 2 K.B. 507; *Bridgmont v Associated Newspapers Ltd* [1951] 2 K.B. 578; *Morgan v Odhams Press Ltd* [1971] 1 W.L.R. 1239 HL; *Hayward v Thompson* [1982] Q.B. 47 CA.

52 *Hulton & Co v Jones* [1910] A.C. 20.

53 *Newstead v London Express Newspaper* [1940] 1 K.B. 377 (Two persons of same name living in same district. Words published of, and true of, an existing person can be defamatory of another person of the same name if they might reasonably be understood as referring to him). Where complaint is made by an individual that he has been defamed and the publisher believes it was unintentional, the sensible course would be to make an offer of amends under ss.2–4 of the Defamation Act 1996 (see para.21-182) Considerations relating to the lack of an intention to defame may also properly be put forward in mitigation of damages: *Jones v Hulton & Co* [1909] 2 K.B. 444 at 479, 481.

54 *Goldsmith v Sperrings Ltd* [1977] 1 W.L.R. 478.

21-12 **Defamatory meaning** On the question of whether the words complained of have a defamatory meaning, liability is based on an objective test.[55] A defendant may be liable for words innocent on the face of them which are in fact defamatory of another person by reason of facts unknown to the author or publisher but known to the person to whom they are published.[56] Similarly a defendant may be liable for a defamatory statement that can reasonably be taken as referring to the claimant by persons with special knowledge, even though the defendant neither had nor could have had any knowledge of the facts that caused those persons with special knowledge to connect the claimant with the statement.[57] This is commonly referred to as an "innuendo" meaning.

21-13 **Reference to the claimant** The claimant must prove that he is referred to, but he may have been referred to by initials[58] or by asterisks[59] or by a fictitious name[60] or the name of somebody else[61] or by reasonable inference from a statement concerning another person[62] or by a statement true of another person which might reasonably be understood as referring to him.[63] The fact that the claimant has a common name is not sufficient of itself to negate reference to him.[64] In the case of a corporate claimant it is not necessary to prove that a publisher of words complained of knew its formal legal name.[65] The question whether the defamatory words refer to the claimant is determined by an objective test, and liability arises if the words are in fact defamatory of the claimant whether or not there has been an intention to refer to him, or negligence in relation to reference to him.[66] Evidence is admissible to prove that persons with special knowledge understood the claimant to be referred to in any of the above situations.[67] There is no rule that for a statement to be defama-

55 See, e.g. *Fullam v Newcastle Chronicle* [1977] 1 W.L.R. 651 at 654 CA ("The essence of libel is the publication of written words to a person or persons by whom they would be reasonably understood to be defamatory of the plaintiff"); *Charleston v News Group Newspapers Ltd* [1995] 2 A.C. 65; *Rothschild v Associated Newspapers Ltd* [2012] EWHC 177 (QB) at [23] (upheld on appeal: [2013] EWCA Civ 197; [2013] E.M.L.R. 18). Tugendhat J said "the court is not concerned with what the writer or publisher intended, nor with what any actual reader may have understood, still less with what the claimant understood. The meaning (or each of the meanings where there are multiple allegations) must be a single meaning, that is a meaning which the court finds would be understood by the hypothetical reasonable reader".

56 *Cassidy v Daily Mirror* [1929] 2 K.B. 331; *Hough v London Express Newspaper Ltd* [1940] 2 K.B. 507.

57 *Morgan v Odhams Press* [1971] 1 W.L.R. 1239 HL. The Court of Appeal in *Baturina v Times Newspapers Ltd* [2011] EWCA Civ 308; [2011] 1 W.L.R. 1526 confirmed that the rule is compliant with art.10.

58 *Roach v Garvan* (1742) 2 Atk. 469; *O'Brien v Clement* (1846) 16 M. & W. 159.

59 *Bourke v Warren* (1826) 2 C. & P. 307.

60 *R. v Clerk* (1728) 1 Barn. 304; *Youssoupoff v MGM Pictures Ltd* (1934) 50 T.L.R. 581.

61 *Levi v Milne* (1827) 4 Bing. 195.

62 *Cassidy v Daily Mirror* [1929] 2 K.B. 331 at 338; *Morgan v Odhams Press Ltd* [1971] 1 W.L.R. 1239 HL.

63 *Newstead v London Express Newspaper Ltd* [1940] 1 K.B. 377.

64 See *Jameel v Dow Jones & Co Inc* [2005] EWCA Civ 75; [2005] Q.B. 946.

65 *Euromoney Institutional Investor Plc v Aviation News Ltd* [2013] EWHC 1505 (QB) at [61]–[62] where Tugendhat J approved the test set out in *Duncan & Neill on Defamation* (3rd edn) at para.10.02.

66 See *Morgan v Odhams Press Ltd* [1971] 1 W.L.R. 1239; and see *Hyams v Peterson* [1991] 1 N.Z.L.R. 711.

67 *Bottomley v Bolton* (1970) 115 S.J. 61 CA.

tory of the claimant it must contain "some key or pointer"[68] indicating him or her. It is sufficient if a sensible person in the light of any special facts or knowledge proved, could reasonably have understood that the statement referred to the claimant.[69] The circumstances in which the statement was published will be relevant in ascertaining whether an inference that the claimant was referred to was reasonable. A person is not expected to read the daily newspaper with the same care as that of a businessman scrutinising a contract.[70] It is for the judge to decide whether the words complained of are capable of being taken as referring to the claimant, and a question of fact whether they were reasonably so understood.[71] Where the defamatory words do not clearly refer to the claimant (i.e. by name), the defendant is entitled to particulars of the material facts on which the claimant relies in support of his allegation that he has been referred to.[72] The general rule is that a person must be identified at the time of publication and not by reference to later material.[73] Whilst generally two or more publications by the same defendant cannot be aggregated to give rise to a cause of action in defamation, in certain limited circumstances, where there is a sufficient nexus between the earlier and later publications, this may be possible.[74]

Defamation of a class The question whether an individual can sue in respect of words which are directed against a group, or body, or class of persons generally, was considered by the House of Lords in *Knupffer v London Express Newspaper Ltd*,[75] and the law may be summarised as follows: **21-14**

(a) The crucial question remains whether or not the words are reasonably capable of referring to the claimant. What matters is whether the words were published "of the claimant" in the sense that he can be said to be personally pointed at[76] rather than the application of any arbitrary general rule subject to exceptions that liability cannot arise from words published of a

---

68 See *Morgan v Odhams Press Ltd* [1970] 1 W.L.R. 820 CA at 828. See also *Hyams v Peterson* [1991] 1 N.Z.L.R. 711.

69 *Morgan v Odhams Press Ltd* [1971] 1 W.L.R. 1239; distinguishing *Astaire v Campling* [1966] 1 W.L.R. 34; *Hayward v Thompson* [1982] Q.B. 47 CA; and see *Hyams v Peterson* [1991] 1 N.Z.L.R. 711.

70 *Morgan v Odhams Press Ltd* [1971] 1 W.L.R. 1239, per Lord Reid at 1245.

71 The jury's decision will not be overturned lightly: *Hayward v Thompson* [1982] Q.B. 47. Now that the jury has ceased to be the presumptive tribunal of fact in defamation cases (Defamation Act 2013 s.11), the issue of capability is likely to fall away and a judge will be able to determine reference and meaning at an early stage.

72 *Bruce v Odhams Press Ltd* [1936] 1 K.B. 697; cf. *Greenslade v Swaffer* [1955] 1 W.L.R. 1109; *Morgan v Odhams Press Ltd* [1971] 1 W.L.R. 1239.

73 *Grapelli v Derek Block (Holdings)* [1981] 1 W.L.R. 822 CA; but see *Hayward v Thompson* [1982] 1 Q.B. 47; and *Chase v News Group Newspapers Ltd* [2002] EWHC 2209 (QB) where Eady J declined to strike out a claim where the claimant sought to establish identification from subsequent publications indicating there is no bright line as to the circumstances when the general rule would not apply.

74 *Simon v Lyder* [2019] UKPC 38; [2019] 3 W.L.R. 537; referring to *Grapelli v Derek Block (Holdings)* [1981] 1 W.L.R. 822 CA; and *Hayward v Thompson* [1982] 1 Q.B. 47.

75 [1944] A.C. 116. Applied in *Schloimovitz v Clarendon Press, The Times,* 6 July 1973 (definition of "Jew"). See *Church of Scientology of Toronto v International News Distributing Co* (1974) 48 D.L.R. (3d) 176; *Booth v BCTV Broadcasting System* (1983) 139 D.L.R. (3d) 88; *Farrington v Leigh, The Times,* 10 December 1987 CA.

76 cf. *Braddock v Bevins* [1948] 1 K.B. 580 at 588–589.

class. In *Orme v Associated Newspapers Group Ltd*[77] it was held that as it was widely known that the claimant was the leader of the Unification Church (the "Moonies") in England, defamatory allegations against that organisation would be reasonably identified with the claimant personally by readers of the defendant newspaper. At the very least people would think that Mr Orme must have known of the alleged malpractices and so be part of them.

(b) Normally, where the defamatory statement is directed to a class of persons, no individual belonging to the class is entitled to say that the words were written or spoken of himself. "No doubt, it is true to say that a class cannot be defamed as a class, nor can an individual be defamed by a general reference to the class to which he belongs."[78] As Willes J said in *Eastwood v Holmes*: "If a man wrote that all lawyers were thieves, no particular lawyer could sue him unless there was something to point to the particular individual."[79]

(c) Words which appear to apply to a class may be actionable if there is something in the words, or the circumstances under which they were published, which indicates a particular claimant or claimants.[80]

(d) Again if the reference is to a limited class or group, for example trustees, members of a firm, tenants of a particular building, so that the words can be said to refer to each member, all will be able to sue.[81]

(e) Whether there is evidence on which the words can be regarded as capable of referring to the claimant is a matter of law for the judge. If there is such evidence, then it is a question of fact whether the words lead reasonable people who know the claimant to the conclusion that they do refer to him.[82]

In *Knupffer* the claimant was the representative of the British branch of the Young Russia Party. There were two thousand members of the party, with 24 members in Britain. A British newspaper accused the party of being pro-Hitler but there was no reference to any particular member in the article. The House of Lords upheld the Court of Appeal's decision that the article was not capable of referring to the claimant, as distinct from the party as a whole. In contrast is *Riches v News Group Newspapers Ltd*,[83] in which the *News of the World* made various allegations of misconduct against "Banbury CID", naming only one officer. There were 12 officers who made up Banbury CID, 10 of whom sued for libel. They succeeded in showing that the allegations would have been understood to refer to them.

3. WHAT IS DEFAMATORY?

21-15 **The defamatory imputation** The gist of the torts of libel and slander is the publication of matter conveying a defamatory imputation. In determining whether

[77] *The Times*, 4 February 1981.

[78] per Lord Porter in *Knupffer v London Express Newspaper Ltd* [1944] A.C. 116 at 124.

[79] (1858) 1 F. & F. 347 at 349. And see *EETPU v Times Newspapers Ltd* [1980] Q.B. 585.

[80] *Le Fanu v Malcomson* (1848) 1 H.L.C. 637; *Orme v Associated Newspapers Group Ltd*, *The Times*, 4 February 1981.

[81] *Browne v DC Thomson & Co*, 1912 S.C. 359; *Foxcroft v Lacy* (1613) Hob. 89. A Canadian court held that there could be no class action for defamation since each member of the class would suffer different damage. *Campbell v Toronto Star* (1990) 73 D.L.R. (4th) 190.

[82] But note what is said at para.21-13.

[83] [1986] Q.B. 256.

words are defamatory there are two stages, to decide what the words mean, and to decide whether those words are defamatory in that meaning.[84]

(a) The test

The test at common law A statement may be defamatory in relation to the claimant's personal character, office or vocation. In the former case the test usually applied was whether the matter complained of was calculated to hold the claimant up to "hatred, contempt, or ridicule".[85] This "ancient formula" was, however, insufficient in all cases, for a person's business reputation may be damaged in ways which nobody would connect with "hatred, ridicule or contempt", as, for instance, the imputation of a clever fraud which however much to be condemned morally and legally might yet not excite what a member of the jury might understand as hatred or contempt.[86] Lord Atkin in *Sim v Stretch*[87] applied the test, "would the words tend to lower the claimant in the estimation of right-thinking members of society generally". Or, in the words of Neill LJ in *Gillick v BBC*[88] would the words be "likely to affect a person adversely in the estimation of reasonable people generally". The alternative "or which would cause him to be shunned or avoided" must be added to cover such cases as an imputation of insanity.[89] What is defamatory in one era may not continue to be so in another. The most common direction given to juries in recent times was that a defamatory allegation is one that tends to make reasonable people think the worse of the claimant.[90] *Brown v Bower*[91] is a recent example of the potential for changing social mores to affect what is and is not defamatory. The court found the meaning of the words complained of to be that there were grounds to suspect that the claimant had paid young male prostitutes to subject him to consensual rough sex. The parties had agreed that the words complained of were defamatory at common law. Nicklin J was troubled by the possibility that they might not be, and considered whether, despite the parties' agreement, he ought to determine the issue, it being one of law.[92] He took the view that he should only do so if the argument that the meaning was not defamatory was overwhelming, which it was not. 21-16

84 The court may determine meaning at any time in a defamation case. Applications for a determination on meaning can be made at any time after the service of the particulars of claim, and are to be made promptly: CPR PD 53B 6.1. Thus the courts are showing a willingness to decide the actual meaning at an early stage: see *Lord McAlpine of West Green v Bercow* [2013] EWHC 1342 (QB). See *Johnston v League Publications Ltd* [2014] EWHC 874 (QB) at [1]. See paras 21-23 and 21-24.

85 per Parke B in *Parmiter v Coupland* (1840) 6 M. & W. 105 at 108; cf. *Capital and Counties Bank v Henty* (1882) 7 App. Cas. 741 at 762. The test laid down by Parke B is not exhaustive.

86 per Scrutton and Atkin LJJ in *Tournier v National Provincial Bank* [1924] 1 K.B. 461 at 477, 487.

87 (1936) 52 T.L.R. 669 at 671; followed by Scott LJ in *Holdsworth v Associated Newspapers Ltd* [1937] 3 All E.R. 872 at 880; cf. *Sim v HJ Heinz Co Ltd* [1959] 1 W.L.R. 313; and see *Skuse v Granada Television Ltd* [1996] E.M.L.R. 278 CA.

88 [1996] E.M.L.R. 267.

89 *Youssoupoff v MGM Pictures Ltd* (1934) 50 T.L.R. 581 at 587. Scrutton LJ preferred "a false statement about a man to his discredit" (1934) 50 T.L.R. 581 at 584. The sound track in *Youssoupoff* was held to be libellous. There seems to be no reason in principle why a visual representation in a film should not also be libellous.

90 *Sim v Stretch* [1936] 2 All E.R. 1237. Note that, under s.11 of the Defamation Act 2013 there is no longer a presumptive right to a jury.

91 [2017] EWHC 2637 (QB); [2017] 4 W.L.R. 197.

92 Applying *Monroe v Hopkins* [2017] EWHC 433 (QB); [2017] 4 W.L.R. 68.

21-17 **The threshold of seriousness at common law** In *Thornton v Telegraph Media Group Ltd*[93] Tugendhat J considered the test for whether words are defamatory, and undertook a thorough review and analysis of the test. He drew a distinction between personal defamation—imputations as to the character or attributes of an individual—and business or professional defamation: where the imputation is as to an attribute of an individual, a corporation or similar body, and that imputation is with regard to the way the profession or business is conducted. He acknowledged that the varieties are not mutually exclusive. With regard to personal defamation, he considered that this could be further sub-divided into three sub-categories: imputations as to what is sinful, mischievous or illegal; imputations that are not voluntary, or the result of the claimant's conscious act or choice, but rather a misfortune such as a disease; and imputations that ridicule the claimant. In relation to professional defamation, he recognised two sub-categories, namely imputations as to a person's goods or services being below the required standard and thus likely to cause adverse consequences to customers, and those allegations which could prevent investors from providing financial support, or dealing with the business or professional. The judge also identified that any definition of defamatory imputations must contain a threshold of seriousness, in that it should exclude trivial claims. This was required by the development of the law recognised in *Jameel v Dow Jones & Co Inc*[94] as arising from the passing of the Human Rights Act 1998: regard for art.10 of the European Convention on Human Rights and the principle of proportionality both required it.

21-18 **Defamation Act 2013** Section 1 of the Defamation Act 2013 now provides a statutory definition of the word "defamatory". The section requires a claimant to show that the publication of the defamatory statement "has caused or is likely to cause serious harm to the reputation of the claimant". Where the claimant is a "body that trades for profit", harm is not "serious harm" unless "it has caused or is likely to cause the body serious financial loss". The Explanatory Notes to the Act state that s.1 is intended to build on the consideration given by the courts in *Thornton* and the *Jameel* abuse cases to the question of what is sufficient to establish that a statement is defamatory. The notes do not state, and it was not suggested in Parliament, that the common law tests for what is a defamatory statement would be abolished. Indeed, some standard of opinion, for instance, "right thinking persons generally" is required. However, as will be seen, some of the old definitions, such as ridicule, may not survive under the new Act.

21-19 **Serious harm** The introduction of a serious harm threshold is one of the major changes introduced by the Defamation Act 2013. After a series of first instance decisions on the meaning of s.1(1) of the Act (which applies to claimants other than bodies trading for profit), the case of *Lachaux v Independent Print Ltd*[95] reached the Supreme Court. Approving the decision of Warby J at first instance, the Supreme Court found that the defamatory character of a statement no longer depends on the meaning of the words and their inherent tendency to do harm. The threshold has been raised and its application is to be determined by reference not just to the meaning of the words, but their actual impact on those to whom they were

93 [2010] EWHC 1414 (QB); [2011] 1 W.L.R. 1985.

94 [2005] EWCA Civ 75; [2005] Q.B. 946.

95 [2019] UKSC 27; [2020] A.C. 612.

communicated.[96] Inferences of fact as to the seriousness of the harm may be drawn from the material before the court.[97] Lord Sumption said of the change: "I do not accept that the result is a revolution in the law of defamation, any more than the lower thresholds of seriousness introduced by the decisions in *Jameel* and *Thornton* effected such a revolution."[98] If a claimant wishes to rely on particular facts to prove serious harm those facts must be pleaded.[99] The Supreme Court also confirmed that the "repetition rule" (which has "nothing to do with the threshold of seriousness") and the "rule in *Dingle*" (evidence of damage to reputation by earlier publications of substantially the same statement are irrelevant to the assessment of damage caused by the publication complained of) remain good law.[100]

The serious harm threshold cannot be overcome by aggregating the harm caused by a number of less serious defamatory imputations; multiple articles cannot be treated as a "statement" for the purposes of s.1.[101] Reference (i.e. the extent to which the claimant is identifiable from the publication) may be relevant to serious harm: if only a small number of individuals would understand the defamatory statement to refer to the claimant it may not cause serious harm to reputation. In *Alexander-Theodotou v Kounis*[102] the court found that only a small number of readers would have identified the claimants as those being referred to, and those individuals would already have formed an adverse opinion of the claimants' conduct in the relevant matter; as such no serious harm was caused, and the claim was dismissed. 21-20

Although the Court of Appeal warned against lengthy interim proceedings on the issue of serious harm in *Lachaux v Independent Print Ltd*,[103] it may be appropriate to order the matter be tried as a preliminary issue where the particular circumstances warrant it.[104] Allegations that imputed arrogance, greed and unreasonable behaviour in relation to the claimants' benefit claims were found to be defamatory at common law and statements of opinion, but did not to cross the serious harm threshold, in *Sube v News Group Newspapers Ltd*.[105] It was also found that where an imputation is an opinion that lessens its defamatory impact. On serious harm in slander cases see *Yavuz v Tesco Stores Ltd*.[106] 21-21

Serious financial loss In *Brett Wilson LLP v Persons Unknown*,[107] the court for the first time considered s.1(2) of the Defamation Act 2013, which requires a body which trades for profit to prove that the publication complained of has caused or is likely to cause serious financial loss. The claim was against persons unknown who had published accusations of misconduct against the firm on the "Solicitors from Hell" website. The claimant applied for default judgment. The claimant is a boutique law firm which attracted a considerable amount of work from the internet. It was able to show that one potential client had not instructed the firm because of the publication. It also relied on other factors such as the prominence of the publica- 21-22

96 [2019] UKSC 27; [2020] A.C. 612 at [12]–[15].
97 [2019] UKSC 27; [2020] A.C. 612 at [21].
98 [2019] UKSC 27; [2020] A.C. 612 at [17].
99 *Tinkler v Ferguson* [2019] EWHC 1501 (QB).
100 [2019] UKSC 27; [2020] A.C. 612 at [23]–[24].
101 *Sube v News Group Newspapers Ltd* [2018] EWHC 1961 (QB); [2018] 1 W.L.R. 5767.
102 [2019] EWHC 956 (QB).
103 [2017] EWCA Civ 1334; [2018] Q.B. 594.
104 *Hope Not Hate Ltd v Farage* [2017] EWHC 3275 (QB).
105 [2018] EWHC 1234 (QB).
106 [2019] EWHC 1971 (QB).
107 [2015] EWHC 2628 (QB); [2016] 4 W.L.R. 69.

tion complained of on an internet search for the firm's name, the inference that other individuals would have read the publication complained of but not notified the claimant and the claimant's belief that there had been a considerable drop-off in the conversion of enquiries to instructions since the publication complained of. On the basis of this the court found that there was sufficient evidence of serious financial loss. This suggests the court is taking a holistic approach to assessing whether serious financial loss has been or is likely to be caused. Once the serious harm threshold had been overcome, damages were considered to be at large.[108] In *Lachaux*, Lord Sumption confirmed that "serious financial loss is not the same as special damage."[109] Serious financial loss, like other forms of serious harm, is capable of inference from the evidence.[110]

21-23 **Defamatory meaning** In considering whether a statement has a defamatory meaning, the court should give to the material in question its "natural and ordinary meaning". Words are to be taken in the sense that is most natural and obvious, and in which those to whom they are spoken will be sure to understand them. The test of reasonableness guides and directs the court.[111] The principles to be applied when determining the natural and ordinary meaning of words were recently re-stated in *Koutsogiannis v The Random House Group Ltd*[112]:

(i) The governing principle is reasonableness.
(ii) The intention of the publisher is irrelevant.
(iii) The hypothetical reasonable reader is not naïve but he is not unduly suspicious. He can read between the lines. He can read in an implication more readily than a lawyer and may indulge in a certain amount of loose thinking but he must be treated as being a man who is not avid for scandal and someone who does not, and should not, select one bad meaning where other non-defamatory meanings are available. A reader who always adopts a bad meaning where a less serious or non-defamatory meaning is available is not reasonable: s/he is avid for scandal. But always to adopt the less derogatory meaning would also be unreasonable: it would be naïve.
(iv) Over-elaborate analysis should be avoided and the court should certainly not take a too literal approach to the task.
(v) Consequently, a judge providing written reasons for conclusions on meaning should not fall into the trap of conducting too detailed an analysis of the various passages relied on by the respective parties.

---

108 See also *Undre v London Borough of Harrow* [2016] EWHC 931 (QB); [2017] E.M.L.R. 3, where the court again considered the s.1(2) Defamation Act 2013 serious financial loss threshold. The second claimant failed to meet the threshold since the evidence relied upon did not show any loss to have been caused by the publication complained of.

109 *Lachaux v Independent Print Ltd* [2019] UKSC 27; [2020] A.C. 612 at [15] (albeit obiter dicta).

110 *Euroeco Fuels (Poland) Ltd v Szczecin and Swinoujscie Seaports Authority SA* [2018] EWHC 1081 (QB); [2018] 4 W.L.R. 133 at [71] (reversed on other grounds: [2019] EWCA Civ 1932; [2019] 4 W.L.R. 156); *Burki v Seventy Thirty Ltd* [2018] EWHC 2151 (QB); *Gubarev v Orbis Business Intelligence Ltd* [2019] EWHC 162 (QB); see also the cases cited earlier in this paragraph.

111 These principles derive from a long list of authorities and are repeated whenever meaning is determined. See *Lewis v Daily Telegraph Ltd* [1964] A.C. 234; *Skuse v Granada Television Ltd* [1996] E.M.L.R. 278; *Gillick v Brook Advisory Centres (No.1)* [2001] EWCA Civ 1263; *Jeynes v News Magazines Ltd* [2008] EWCA Civ 130.

112 [2019] EWHC 48 (QB); [2020] 4 W.L.R. 25 at [11], [12].

(vi) Any meaning that emerges as the produce of some strained, or forced, or utterly unreasonable interpretation should be rejected.

(vii) It follows that it is not enough to say that by some person or another the words might be understood in a defamatory sense.

(viii) The publication must be read as a whole, and any "bane and antidote" taken together. Sometimes, the context will clothe the words in a more serious defamatory meaning. In other cases, the context will weaken (even extinguish altogether) the defamatory meaning that the words would bear if they were read in isolation).

(ix) In order to determine the natural and ordinary meaning of the statement of which the claimant complains, it is necessary to take into account the context in which it appeared and the mode of publication.

(x) No evidence, beyond publication complained of, is admissible in determining the natural and ordinary meaning.

(xi) The hypothetical reader is taken to be representative of those who would read the publication in question. The court can take judicial notice of facts which are common knowledge, but should beware of reliance on impressionistic assessments of the characteristics of a publication's readership.

(xii) Judges should have regard to the impression the article has made upon them themselves in considering what impact it would have made on the hypothetical reasonable reader.

(xiii) In determining the single meaning, the court is free to choose the correct meaning; it is not bound by the meanings advanced by the parties (save that it cannot find a meaning that is more injurious than the claimant's pleaded meaning).

The classic exposition of the principles in *Jeynes v News Magazines Ltd*,[113] with the addition given in *Rufus v Elliott*,[114] was cited with approval by the Supreme Court in *Stocker v Stocker*.[115] Generally no evidence beyond the words themselves is admissible,[116] although as in *Greenstein v Campaign Against Anti-Semitism*[117] on occasion evidence proving the existence of contextual material can be admitted.[118] The court may determine meaning without a hearing.[119] In *Triplark Ltd v Northwood Hall (Freehold) Ltd* Warby J found meanings that went "slightly beyond" the pleaded meanings, stating "Within limits the claimant may choose, or not, to adopt any additional elements of meaning that I find".[120]

21-24 Where one or both parties seek a ruling on meaning the parties must apply for an order for it to be heard as a preliminary issue so as to enable the court to use its case management and, where appropriate, costs budgeting powers.[121] A ruling on meaning can be sought at any time after the Particulars of Claim. In *Morgan v As-*

113 [2008] EWCA Civ 130.
114 [2015] EWCA Civ 121; [2015] E.M.L.R. 17.
115 [2019] UKSC 17; [2019] 2 W.L.R. 1033 at [35], [36].
116 *Koutsogiannis v The Random House Group Ltd* [2019] EWHC 48 (QB); [2020] 4 W.L.R. 25.
117 [2019] EWHC 281 (QB).
118 See also *Yeo v Times Newspapers Ltd* [2014] EWHC 2853 (QB); [2015] 1 W.L.R. 971.
119 *Hewson v Times Newspapers Ltd* [2019] EWHC 650 (QB); *Hamilton v News Group Newspapers Ltd* [2020] EWHC 59 (QB).
120 [2019] EWHC 3494 (QB) at [31]. See also *Allen v Times Newspapers Ltd* [2019] EWHC 1235 (QB); *Ager v Career Development Finance Ltd* [2019] EWHC 2830 (QB) at [21].
121 *Bokova v Associated Newspapers Ltd* [2018] EWHC 320 (QB); see CPR PD 53B 6.1.

sociated Newspapers Ltd[122] Nicklin J noted that significant complication and cost would have been avoided had the court been asked to determine meaning (and the issue of fact/opinion) before a defence was filed. However, ruling on meaning as a preliminary issue will not always be appropriate if doing so would not be likely to save time and cost, and if meaning is not easily separable from other issues.[123] Once the court has determined the actual meaning of the words, it is not open to the defendant to seek to defend as true some other meaning.[124] Judicial determination of meaning as a preliminary issue does not necessarily establish the intensity of the sting, which may be a matter for trial. In some cases, the meaning of the words complained of and their defamatory sting will go together, but not always.[125] In *Sakho v WADA*[126] Steyn J also determined the meaning of republications which the claimant did not rely upon as separate causes of action, but instead sought damages in relation to the repetition via the republications as well as the original publications, and which were relied upon in relation to serious harm.

21-25 Whilst in the libel context there can be only one meaning that the court may find the words bear, it is worthy of note that in malicious falsehood[127] the single meaning rule does not apply, which could lead to a claimant failing in libel but succeeding in malicious falsehood. The Court of Appeal has considered such a potential outcome "bizarre".[128]

21-26 **Context** The context in which words are published is very important. In construing the meaning of an alleged libel, the whole publication is to be taken into account, provided that it all relates to the same defamatory allegation. This includes all of the text, even where spread across different pages, headlines, photographs and any text/insert boxes.[129] The claimant is not permitted to pick out this or that sentence which he may consider defamatory, for there may be other passages which will take away their sting. Bane and antidote may be found together. In the case of the internet, words may take on a different interpretation because of the way people treat and react to bulletin boards and blogs. It has been said that words published on bulletin boards and blogs may be more akin to slanders than libels.[130] Language which is not defamatory on its face may become so when the circumstances are taken into account. In *Lord McAlpine of West Green v Bercow*[131] an apparently innocuous question posted on Twitter was found to be defamatory to certain readers

---

[122] [2018] EWHC 3960 (QB).

[123] *Reay v Beaumont* [2018] EWHC 2172 (QB); *Dahlan v Middle East Eye Ltd* [2019] EWHC 2261 (QB).

[124] *Bokova v Associated Newspapers Ltd* [2018] EWHC 2032 (QB); [2019] Q.B. 861.

[125] *Simpson v MGN Ltd* [2016] EWCA Civ 772; [2016] E.M.L.R. 26.

[126] [2020] EWHC 251 (QB); [2020] E.M.L.R. 14.

[127] See Ch.22.

[128] *Cruddas v Calvert* [2015] EWCA Civ 171; [2015] E.M.L.R. 16.

[129] *Charleston v News Group Newspapers Ltd* [1995] 2 A.C. 65 HL. In *Dee v Telegraph Media Group Ltd* [2010] EWHC 924 (QB); [2010] E.M.L.R. 20 Sharp J ruled that in relation to newspaper articles on the same subject spread over a number of pages, the ordinary reasonable reader was to be taken to have turned over the pages and read what he was directed to on the continuation pages. In *Horan v Express Newspapers* [2015] EWHC 3550 (QB) the court considered the full context of the article complained of, including the text on both pages 1 and 5 of the newspaper, the photograph used, the headlines and insert box. But in *Telnikoff v Matusevitch* [1992] A.C. 343 the House of Lords decided that a letter, written by the defendant, had to be looked at on its own since the claimant's article, to which it was a response, would not necessarily have been read by those who read the letter.

[130] *Smith v ADVFN Plc* [2008] EWHC 1797 (QB).

[131] [2013] EWHC 1342 (QB).

who would have been aware of specific facts. The tweet was: "Why is Lord McAlpine trending? *innocent face*". The judge observed that the tweet was not a publication to the world at large, such as a daily newspaper or broadcast. It was a publication on Twitter and the hypothetical reader must be taken to be a reasonable representative of users of Twitter who followed the defendant. The circumstances which would be known to such readers were that there was extensive speculation regarding the identity of an unnamed "senior Tory politician" who was said to be guilty of child abuse. The claimant would have been known to have been a senior conservative politician. The court concluded that the words "innocent face" would be regarded as insincere and ironical, giving rise to the defamatory imputation that the claimant was the abuser. Particular care needs to be taken where the words are published in a political context, especially during election time. Whilst the rules of meaning require no adaptation where the individual said to be defamed is a political or civil servant, it is necessary to avoid an over-elaborate analysis.[132] The Supreme Court confirmed the importance of context in *Stocker v Stocker*,[133] in which the fact that publication was in a Facebook post was critical, as Facebook is a casual medium, where an ordinary reader would read a post quickly and move on. The first instance judge was wrong to consider the dictionary definition of words in determining meaning. The meaning of the words "He tried to strangle me" in a Facebook post was that the claimant had grasped the defendant by the throat and applied force to her neck rather than that he had tried to kill her; as such the defendant's justification defence succeeded. In *Bukovsky v Crown Prosecution Service*,[134] the words complained of were contained in a charging announcement published by the Crown Prosecution Service. In that context, the court upheld the judge's finding that the ordinary reasonable reader would not have understood that the claimant, having been charged with "making" indecent photographs of children, was present at the scene of the abuse and took the photographs himself. Rather, they would understand that words have special meanings when used in statutes, and would understand that the claimant had been charged with making indecent photographs of children contrary to the Protection of Children Act 1978 s.1. The Court of Appeal added that it would proceed cautiously when asked to substitute its view on meaning for that of the first instance judge and would only do so where it was satisfied that the judge was wrong. Whether any antidote in a piece will reduce the gravity of the meaning of a publication taken overall is highly dependent upon context.[135]

Material behind a hyperlink in online words complained of may need to be taken **21-27**
into account as part of the context when determining meaning.[136] In *Falter v*

[132] *Waterson v Lloyd* [2013] EWCA Civ 136; [2013] E.M.L.R. 17 at [66]; *Thompson v James* [2014] EWCA Civ 600; [2014] B.L.G.R. 664; *Mughal v Telegraph Media Group Ltd* [2014] EWHC 1371 (QB).

[133] [2019] UKSC 17; [2019] 2 W.L.R. 1033. See also *Banks v Cadwalladar* [2019] EWHC 3451 (QB) on the interpretation of language used on social media (and also more generally); and *Abdulrazaq v Hassan* [2019] EWHC 2930 (QB) applying the same to WhatsApp.

[134] [2017] EWCA Civ 1529; [2018] 4 W.L.R. 13.

[135] *Poroshenko v BBC* [2019] EWHC 213 (QB); *Zarb-Cousin v Association of British Bookmakers* [2018] EWHC 2240 (QB); *Kirekegaard v Smith* [2019] EWHC 3393 (QB).

[136] *Greenstein v Campaign Against Anti-Semitism* [2019] EWHC 281 (QB); *Monroe v Hopkins* [2017] EWHC 433 (QB); [2017] 4 W.L.R. 68; *Banks v Cadwalladar* [2019] EWHC 3451 (QB); *Kirekegaard v Smith* [2019] EWHC 3393 (QB); and as to the limits *Caine v Advertiser & Times Ltd (No. 2)* [2019] EWHC 2278 (QB); see also in a different context *R. (Chabloz) v CPS* [2019] EWHC 3094

Atzmon[137] although not purporting to make a hard and fast rule about the approach that the ordinary reasonable reader would take to hyperlinks, Nicklin J considered that at one extreme there might be a publication which consisted of little more than a hyperlink such that it would be necessary to click the link to make sense of the publication, and at the other a publication with a large number of links might be such that it would be unrealistic to expect more than a small minority of readers to look at them all. In *Poulter v Times Newspapers Ltd*[138] Nicklin J drew a distinction between the online and hard copy versions of articles in that in the hard copy the two articles complained of were on the same two pages separated by a photograph of the claimant, whereas the online articles were at separate URLs. Although one article was accessible from the other via a "related link", there was no exhortation or encouragement to readers to follow the link. In *Banks v Cadwalladar*[139] Saini J found that the ordinary reasonable reader would follow the exhortation in one of the Tweets in question to follow the hyperlink, and therefore the Tweet bore the same meaning at the publication it linked to.

21-28 **Defamatory matter published as hearsay—"the repetition rule"** Matter which is otherwise defamatory will not be the less actionable merely because it is rumour, hearsay, or supposition. If the rule were otherwise, every dealer in defamation would have free range provided that the libel or slander was preceded by some such preface to his libel as "I am informed", "I am of opinion".[140] In *Shah v Standard Chartered Bank*[141] the agent of the defendant had made statements to Bank of England representatives to the effect that the claimants' company had been guilty of money laundering. The claimants sued and the defendants alleged inter alia that they were merely repeating what had been rumoured. The Court of Appeal considered the cases of *Aspro Travel v Owners Abroad*[142] and *Stern v Piper*[143] and applied the "repetition rule" affirming that, in the words of Lord Devlin in *Lewis v Daily Telegraph Ltd*, "for the purposes of the law of libel a hearsay statement is the same as a direct statement and that is all there is to it". It is therefore not enough to justify the existence of a rumour; the publication of it would be justified only by showing objectively that the rumour was true. The rule on repetition was discussed in *Al-Fagih v HH Saudi Research and Marketing*[144] and in *Lukowiak v Unidad Editorial SA*,[145] in both of which the allegations made by the defendants consisted of "reportage" of allegations made by others and merely reported by the newspaper in question. The rule established in *Stern v Piper* and *Shah v Standard Chartered Bank* was confirmed, although the Court acknowledged the special difficulties connected with the duty of a free press to report disputes on matters of public interest.

(Admin); [2020] 1 Cr. App. R. 17.

137 [2018] EWHC 1728 (QB).

138 [2018] EWHC 3900 (QB).

139 [2019] EWHC 3451 (QB).

140 See *Harrison v Thornborough* (1713) 10 Mod. 196; *M'Pherson v Daniels* (1829) 10 B. & C. 263; *Watkin v Hall* (1868) L.R. 3 Q.B. 396; *Botterill v Whytehead* (1879) 41 L.T. 588; *Cadam v Beaverbrook Newspapers Ltd* [1959] 1 Q.B. 413; *Lewis v Daily Telegraph Ltd* [1964] A.C. 234; *Truth (NZ) Ltd v Holloway* [1960] 1 W.L.R. 997 PC.

141 [1999] Q.B. 241.

142 [1996] 1 W.L.R. 132.

143 [1997] Q.B. 123.

144 [2001] EWCA Civ 1634; [2002] E.M.L.R. 13.

145 [2001] E.M.L.R. 46.

Eady J in *Lukowiak* also considered the effect of *Thoma v Luxembourg*[146] where it was held that "a general requirement for journalists systematically to distance themselves from the content of a quotation that might insult or provoke others or damage their reputation was not reconcilable with the press's role" and would be an infringement of art.10. However, in the event, Eady J decided the issue of the reported allegations in the overall context of qualified privilege. In *Al-Fagih* the Court of Appeal confirmed that the question of reported allegations in the defendant's newspaper was to be viewed overall in the light of the defence of qualified privilege as stated in *Reynolds*.[147] In *Chase v News Group Newspapers Ltd*[148] the Court of Appeal upheld the decision of Eady J, to the effect that the "repetition rule" approved in *Stern* and *Shah* was correct and was not inconsistent with the requirements of the Human Rights Act 1998, as it was not an undue restraint on the defendant's rights under art.10 of the Convention. Where part of the publication complained of consists of hearsay statements, when assessing meaning the court should take the usual approach and view the publication as a whole.[149] In *Lachaux v Independent Print Ltd*[150] it was confirmed that the repetition rule survives the coming into force of the Defamation Act 2013. In *Hewson v Times Newspapers Ltd*[151] it was observed that words such as "alleged" or "claimed" are unlikely, of themselves, to shield a publisher from the effect of the repetition rule. Rather, it is the overall effect of the publication which matters.[152]

The innuendo If the language is defamatory on the face of it, the claimant has of course no further difficulty; it speaks for itself. An innuendo (sometimes referred to as a "true innuendo") is "a meaning alleged to be conveyed to some person by reason of knowing facts extraneous to the words complained of".[153] Extrinsic facts must be known to the persons understanding a statement innocent on its face as defamatory of the claimant at the time of the publication of that statement. When agents, without authority, booked concerts for the claimant and then had to cancel those concerts invoking as an excuse a spurious claim that the claimant was ill, later notices of concerts arranged by the claimant, which may have led people to believe that the earlier "illness" was a "put-up job" and that the claimant had deliberately lied, did not render the agents liable in defamation in respect of their own false but non-defamatory statements.[154] But when obviously defamatory allegations are made by the defendants concerning a person described but not expressly named, later publications by them, which solve the issue of his identity for those who have failed to guess it, may be used to support the evidence called to prove that the original al- **21-29**

---

146 (2003) 36 E.H.R.R. 21 ECtHR.

147 *Reynolds v Times Newspapers Ltd* [2001] 2 A.C. 127. See also *Roberts v Gable* [2007] EWCA Civ 721; [2008] Q.B. 502; see now s.4 of the Defamation Act 2013.

148 [2002] EWCA Civ 1772; [2003] E.M.L.R. 11. See also *Mark v Associated Newspapers* [2002] EWCA Civ 772; [2002] E.M.L.R. 38.

149 *Hiranandani-Vandrevala v Times Newspapers Ltd* [2016] EWHC 250 (QB); [2016] E.M.L.R. 16: the court took into account the denials included, the repeated uses of the word "alleged" and that the publisher had not adopted the allegations, and found the piece bore a meaning of "cogent grounds to suspect" guilt rather than guilt.

150 [2019] UKSC 27; [2020] A.C. 612.

151 [2019] EWHC 650 (QB).

152 *Poulter v Times Newspapers Ltd* [2018] EWHC 3900 (QB) at [43], [44]; and *Poroshenko v BBC* [2019] EWHC 213 (QB) at [28].

153 CPR PD 53 para.2.3(1)(b). See also *Lewis v Daily Telegraph Ltd* [1964] A.C. 234; and *Fox v Boulter* [2013] EWHC 1435 (QB).

154 *Grapelli v Derek Block (Holdings) Ltd* [1981] 2 Q.B. 157 CA.

legations did in fact refer to the claimant.[155] An innuendo constitutes a separate cause of action from any cause of action arising from the words in their ordinary meaning and requires particulars under CPR PD 53.[156] Such a special defamatory meaning may be alleged where words in their natural and ordinary meaning are innocent, in which case the innuendo meaning constitutes the sole cause of action, or where the words are defamatory in their ordinary meaning but the special facts or matters create a more serious imputation, in which case the ordinary meaning and the innuendo meaning constitute separate claims.[157] If the words are not defamatory in their ordinary meaning,[158] the claimant will fail unless he can prove the meaning alleged in the innuendo; it will not suffice to prove some lesser defamatory meaning not alleged.[159] The innuendo must be specific, averring a specific meaning which is actionable.[160] Words may be ironical and used in a sense exactly opposite from that which is natural.[161] They may, by hidden reference, convey an imputation that is altogether unconnected with their apparent meaning.[162] However, caution is now required since any innuendo meaning must be able to surmount the threshold of seriousness required by s.1 of the Defamation Act 2013. If a meaning is only understood by a few people to be defamatory of a claimant, it may not meet the serious harm to reputation test.

21-30 **Statements of case and innuendo** The claimant must set out the extraneous facts on which he relies as giving rise to the innuendo.[163] If the claimant pleads such an innuendo and the particulars do not support the special meaning alleged in the innuendo, it may be struck out. Although the whole of the publication is taken into account in determining the meaning of a part of it, the claimant may not plead part of an article as a libel and then plead another part of it as an extrinsic fact in support of an innuendo.[164] When an innuendo is pleaded and the defamatory inference arising from the defendant's words would be understood only by certain persons with special knowledge of the extrinsic facts, particulars must be given identifying those persons in addition to particulars of facts on which their knowledge is based.[165] A claimant may set out in his statement of case any natural and ordinary meaning which he contends is a reasonable implication to the ordinary person from the words themselves as published. Such a statement of an alleged natural and ordinary meaning, although it may be referred to as an "innuendo", is only part of the one cause of action arising from the natural and ordinary mean-

---

155 *Hayward v Thompson* [1982] Q.B. 47 CA; *Chase v News Group Newspapers Ltd* [2002] EWHC 2209 (QB).

156 CPR PD 53B 4.2(4)(b). See also *Watkins v Hall* (1868) L.R. 3 Q.B. 396 at 402; *Grubb v Bristol United Press Ltd* [1963] 1 Q.B. 309 CA; *Lewis v Daily Telegraph Ltd* [1964] A.C. 234; [1962] C.L.J. 158 at 160; [1963] C.L.J. 201. But see *Pedley v Cambridge Newspapers Ltd* [1964] 1 W.L.R. 988, as to the technicality of this.

157 *Lewis v Daily Telegraph Ltd* [1964] A.C. 234.

158 See para.21-23.

159 *"Truth" (NZ) Ltd v Holloway* [1960] 1 W.L.R. 997 PC.

160 *Cox v Cooper* (1863) 12 W.R. 75; *Jacobs v Schmaltz* (1890) 62 L.T. 121.

161 cf. *Cox v Cooper* (1863) 12 W.R. 75.

162 *Arne v Johnson* (1712) 10 Mod. 111.

163 CPR PD 53 para.2.3(2).

164 *Grubb v Bristol United Press Ltd* [1963] 1 Q.B. 309.

165 *Fullam v Newcastle Chronicle and Journal Ltd* [1977] 1 W.L.R. 651; *Grapelli v Derek Block (Holdings) Ltd* [1981] 1 W.L.R. 823 at 825 and 829 CA.

ing; it is not an innuendo in the legal sense[166] creating a separate cause of action and it does not require particulars under CPR PD 53.[167] The master or judge has authority to strike out statements or innuendoes which are rhetorical or nothing more than embellishments of the natural and ordinary meaning, but the pleading of distinct meanings can be helpful,[168] and may be required by the court.

"Lucas-Box meanings"[169] In *Lucas-Box v News Group Newspapers Ltd*[170] the Court of Appeal held that similarly, in the reverse situation, a defendant pleading justification (or truth) must unambiguously set out any meaning which he ascribes to the writing of which the claimant complains if that differs from the meaning or meanings pleaded by the claimant.[171] This requirement also applies where a defendant pleads honest opinion.[172] He is not entitled to take the claimant by surprise. Now that the presumption in favour of jury trials has been removed and judges are increasingly deciding meaning as a preliminary issue, meaning may be decided before a defence is pleaded, and where this happens, the defendant must plead to the meaning found by the court.[173] **21-31**

Consent If there is consent of the claimant to the publication of the statement which in its ordinary and natural meaning is true, a defamatory innuendo cannot be relied on.[174] "If you get a true statement and authority to publish the true statement it does not matter in the least what people will understand it to mean."[175] **21-32**

Judge and jury The 20th edition contained a section on the role of the jury, and in particular its role in determining whether words were capable of bearing a defamatory meaning.[176] Now that s.11 of the Defamation Act 2013 has removed the presumption in favour of juries, capability hearings have largely fallen away in favour of the judge deciding the actual meaning of the words complained of.[177] Given the central importance of meaning in any defamation action it is likely that meaning will be determined as a preliminary issue wherever possible. This is because it furthers the overriding objective to determine the actual meaning of the **21-33**

---

166 It is also described as a "false innuendo".

167 *Lewis v Daily Telegraph Ltd* [1963] 1 Q.B. 340, CA; [1964] A.C. 234; *Grubb v Bristol United Press Ltd* [1963] 1 Q.B. 309. As to possible restriction of the claimant to or by the meanings pleaded, see *Slim v Daily Telegraph Ltd* [1968] 2 Q.B. 157, CA.

168 *Grubb v Bristol United Press Ltd* [1963] 1 Q.B. 309; *Lewis v Daily Telegraph Ltd* [1964] A.C. 234. These cases also contain the history of prefatory averments.

169 See further para.21-69.

170 [1986] 1 W.L.R. 147 CA.

171 per Ackner LJ [1986] 1 W.L.R. 147 CA at 151–152. This requirement is now set out at CPR PD 53 para.2.5(1). It was recommended in *Armstrong v Times Newspapers Ltd* [2006] EWHC 1614 (QB) that where the defendant seeks to argue that the words bear a different meaning from that contended for by the claimant, the defendant should set out that alternative meaning in the defence, whether or not a defence of justification is raised.

172 CPR PD 53 para.2.6(1).

173 *Morgan v Associated Newspapers Ltd* [2018] EWHC 3960 (QB).

174 *Cookson v Harewood* [1932] 2 K.B. 478; cf. *Chapman v Ellesmere* [1932] 2 K.B. 431; *Russell v Duke of Norfolk* [1949] 1 All E.R. 109.

175 *Cookson v Harewood* [1932] 2 K.B. 478, per Scrutton LJ at 482. However, this may be considered too technical these days. See *Johnston v League Publications Ltd* [2014] EWHC 874 (QB).

176 Previous versions of the CPR Pt 53 contained the procedure for a judge to determine whether words complained of were capable of bearing the meaning contended for by a party.

177 CPR PD 53B 6.1.

words at as early a stage of the litigation as possible.[178] The court also has the power to determine as a preliminary issue whether the words complained of are allegations of fact or opinion.[179] Many of the first instance authorities on serious harm have emphasised the desirability of deciding both that issue and meaning at a preliminary stage.[180]

(b) Examples of defamatory allegations

21-34 **Allegations as to conduct and characteristics** An action was sustainable by a wife against a newspaper which published photographs of her husband with another woman described as his wife, as the publication was an aspersion on her moral character.[181] It remains defamatory of a man to allege that, by having an affair with another woman he had been unfaithful and had thereby humiliated his domestic partner, or to accuse someone of being a "homewrecker", i.e. having an affair with a person who he or she knows is in a stable relationship.[182] Changing mores may affect the question whether conduct, especially in the sphere of sexual matters, is defamatory,[183] particularly having regard to the serious harm threshold. It has been held not to be capable of being defamatory to say that an individual had changed her gender.[184] However, whilst public opinion has become more liberal in recent years where sexual activity is concerned, there are some types of sexual activity in respect of which public opinion has become less permissive.[185] The relevant time for the judgment is the time of publication. Hence in *Mitchell v Faber & Faber*[186] the claimant complained of a statement made in a book, published by the defendants, which he claimed was defamatory of him, in that it represented him as racist and intolerant because of his conduct towards non-white colleagues. The Court of Appeal held that the conduct described in the book should be viewed in the contemporary climate of opinion on publication and not, as the judge had held at first instance, in the context of the 1960s when it had taken place and when racist comments were said not have attracted such disapproval.

21-35 **Imputation of non-blameworthy conduct** An imputation of conduct not in itself blameworthy, however distasteful or objectionable the conduct may be according

---

178 *Bercow v Lord McAlpine of West Green (No.1)* [2013] EWHC 981 (QB); [2014] E.M.L.R. 3 at [40]. See also *Cruddas v Calvert* [2013] EWHC 1427 (QB); [2014] E.M.L.R. 4 at [100] (although the decision was reversed on appeal: see [2013] EWCA Civ 748; [2014] E.M.L.R. 5, the points made about meaning being tried as a preliminary issue were not affected); *RBOS Shareholders Action Group Ltd v News Group Newspapers Ltd* [2014] EWHC 130 (QB); [2014] E.M.L.R. 15 at [18]; and *Hamaizia v Commissioner of Police for the Metropolis* [2013] EWHC 848 (QB) at [54].

179 *British Chiropractic Association v Singh* [2010] EWCA Civ 350; [2011] 1 W.L.R. 133; *Cammish v Hughes* [2012] EWCA Civ 1655; [2013] E.M.L.R. 13; *Euromoney Institutional Investor Plc v Aviation News Ltd* [2013] EWHC 1505 (QB).

180 See, e.g. *Ames v The Spamhaus Project Ltd* [2015] EWHC 127 (QB); [2015] 1 W.L.R. 3409.

181 *Cassidy v Daily Mirror* [1920] 2 K.B. 331.

182 *Contostavlos v News Group Newspapers Ltd* [2014] EWHC 1339 (QB).

183 See the discussion in *Gatley on Libel and Slander* (12th edn) at 2.29; they are also matters on which the court acknowledges reasonable people may disagree: *Simpson v MGN Ltd* [2016] EWCA Civ 772; [2016] E.M.L.R. 26; *Brown v Bower* [2017] EWHC 2637 (QB); [2017] 4 W.L.R. 197.

184 *Krause v Newsquest Media Group Ltd* [2013] EWHC 3400 (QB).

185 *AVB v TDD* [2014] EWHC 1442 (QB) at [73]–[78] where, in the context of a privacy and harassment trial, Tugendhat J cited recent legislation designed to protect individuals from exploitative sexual conduct or where harm is caused to third parties as examples of sexual behaviour that would be seen to be defamatory.

186 [1998] E.M.L.R. 807.

to the notions of certain people, is not a legal injury.[187] There is a distinction between imputing what is merely a breach of professional etiquette and what is illegal, mischievous, or sinful; between, in fact, matters of taste and matters of crime.[188] In *Modi v Clarke*[189] the claimant, a cricket administrator, sued over the allegation that he was secretly plotting to destroy the structure of world cricket. The Court of Appeal held that it could not be considered disparaging to accuse someone of seeking to destroy the structure of cricket because it would not be considered by society at large to be defamatory. The Court also said that it was not disparaging of someone to say that he had gone to see someone in confidence and without telling others with the objective of doing a deal that might undermine the commercial position of another because it happens and is part of business life. However, it was held that the allegation about the claimant was capable of being defamatory of him because it imputed dishonourable conduct to him as he was accused of breaking the rules to which he had subscribed.[190] In *Rufus v Elliott*[191] a press release stated that the claimant had revealed the contents of a text message in which the defendant had used the "n" word. This revelation led to the defendant resigning from his role as a trustee of an anti-racism group. However, it did not mean that the claimant had acted disloyally. The conduct attributed to the claimant was not such as to lower him in the estimation of right-thinking members of society generally, who would not think less of someone for revealing that the defendant, as a trustee of an anti-racism organisation, had used an unacceptable racist term, even if in doing so he revealed the contents of a private text message.

Conduct objectionable to a particular class In *Mawe v Piggott*[192] the claimant had been attacked in the defendant's newspaper for certain denunciations of the Fenian conspirators which he was said to have made, and it was argued that he was exposed to hatred and contempt in the opinion of many people by being represented as an informer or prosecutor or otherwise aiding in the detection of crime. The judgment says: **21-36**

> "That is quite true but we cannot be called upon to adopt that standard. The very circumstance which will make a person be regarded with disfavour by the criminal classes will raise his character in the estimation of right-thinking men. We can only regard the estimation in which a man is held by society, generally."[193]

To say of a person that they have reported certain acts wrongful in law to the police

[187] In *Clay v Roberts* (1863) 8 L.T. 397 at 398 Pollock CB asked "Would it be libellous to write of a lady of fashion that she had been seen on the top of an omnibus, or of a nobleman that he was in the habit of burning tallow candles?"

[188] *Clay v Roberts* (1863) 8 L.T. 397 at 398. See also *Thornton v Telegraph Media Group Ltd* [2010] EWHC 1414 (QB); [2011] 1 W.L.R. 1985.

[189] [2011] EWCA Civ 937.

[190] [2011] EWCA Civ 937. See also *Angel v HH Bushell & Co Ltd* [1968] 1 Q.B. 813 at 825. Similarly, in *His Highness Prince Moulay Hicham Ben Abdullah Al Alaoui of Morocco v Elaph Publishing Ltd* [2015] EWHC 1084 (QB) Dingemans J stated that it is not defamatory to say of someone that they are working against the interests of a ruler. Whether a person would think less of such an individual depends on their political views. The article in question was however capable of bearing a meaning that the claimant had lied.

[191] [2015] EWCA Civ 121; [2015] E.M.L.R. 17.

[192] (1869) Ir. Rep. 4 C.L. 54. See *Berry v Irish Times* [1973] I.R. 368.

[193] (1869) Ir. Rep. 4 C.L. 54 at 62; cf. *Miller v David* (1984) L.R. 9 C. & P. 118; *Byrne v Deane* [1937] 1 K.B. 818; *Lawson v Thompson* (1969) 1 D.L.R. (3d) 270; see also *Rufus v Elliott* [2015] EWCA Civ 121.

is not defamatory.[194] Nor is it defamatory to allege that an individual was taking action designed to destroy the structure of world cricket because this was only disparaging to those who believed in the present structure.[195] Nevertheless, allegations of conduct particularly objectionable to certain classes of person may still be generally defamatory. In *Shah v Akram*[196] the defendant published a document attacking the claimant's standing as a devout Muslim and alleging that he had insulted Islam. The Court of Appeal held that the imputations made against the claimant were defamatory. It was not true that they would have no effect on the claimant's reputation with ordinary, right thinking persons but only with fellow Muslims. The ordinary non-Muslim, even if not himself religious, would think less of the claimant for deliberately insulting the faith of others. The Court of Appeal has emphasised the importance of context: "It will not be defamatory of itself to say that someone is working against the interests of an institution or a ruler ... However, it may be, depending on the particular words used and their context."[197] In that case the words used and their context were capable of bearing a meaning that the claimant had shown himself devious, underhand and disloyal.

21-37 **Ridicule** It is defamatory under the common law to expose someone to ridicule.[198] However, ridicule is likely to be the definition of defamatory meaning that dies as a result of s.1 of the Defamation Act 2013. There are unlikely to be many, if any, cases where an allegation of ridicule is considered harmful enough to overcome the new threshold test.[199]

21-38 **Criminal association** An imputation of a criminal offence or conviction or attempt to commit such an offence would usually be defamatory, unless it was a very minor case.[200] Allegations that an individual is suspected of a criminal offence are also defamatory,[201] but a headline "Licensing Prosecution: Prisoners Acquitted" was held not to be, as there was no allegation in it that the claimant had committed any offence, and, even if it were a misdescription to call him a prisoner, it was no libel, for a person might be a prisoner quite innocently.[202] An allegation that a man has

194 *Byrne v Deane* [1937] 1 K.B. 818.

195 *Modi v Clarke* [2011] EWCA Civ 937 at [30].

196 [1981] 79 L.S. Gaz. 814 CA.

197 *Prince Moulay Hicham Ben Abdallah Al Alaoui of Morocco v Elaph Publishing Ltd* [2017] EWCA Civ 29; [2017] 4 W.L.R. 28.

198 *Berkoff v Burchill* [1997] 4 All E.R. 1008.

199 See *Gatley on Libel and Slander* (12th edn) at 2.10. This does not mean that ridiculing an individual, particularly persistently, could not be the subject of a civil or criminal complaint but the more likely cause of action would be under the Protection from Harassment Act 1997. See *Trimingham v Associated Newspapers Ltd* [2012] EWHC 1296 (QB); [2012] 4 All E.R. 717.

200 See *Gatley on Libel and Slander* (12th edn) at 2.28.

201 *Monson v Tussauds* [1894] 1 Q.B. 671; In *Chase v News Group Newspapers Ltd* [2002] EWCA Civ 1772; [2003] E.M.L.R. 11 the Court of Appeal re-iterated at [45] that "The sting of a libel may be capable of meaning that a claimant has in fact committed some serious act, such as murder. Alternatively it may be suggested that the words mean that there are reasonable grounds to suspect that he/she has committed such an act. A third possibility is that they may mean that there are grounds for investigating whether he/she has been responsible for such an act." All tiers would be considered defamatory.

202 *Leon v Edinburgh Evening News*, 1909 S.C. 1014. The difficult question as to whether a true statement that a charge has been made or a writ issued can be defamatory was discussed in *Cadam v Beaverbrook Newspapers* [1959] 1 Q.B. 413; and see *Lewis v Daily Telegraph Ltd* [1963] 1 Q.B. 340, CA; affirmed [1964] A.C. 234 HL.

brought a blackmailing suit is defamatory[203] but an allegation that an action had been brought against someone for inducing a civil breach of contract would not necessarily be.[204] It is defamatory to accuse someone of knowingly having links to terrorists or that a bank negligently allowed itself to be used to facilitate terrorism but it would not be defamatory to say that someone merely provided services or accommodation to terrorists without any realisation of their role.[205] Where the defamatory allegation is that a person who is employed to perform a public duty takes a bribe to act corruptly in discharging that duty, it will be understood to mean that he committed a criminal offence.[206] It is defamatory to report that individuals were involved in the lead-up to a murder because even if that did not mean that the individuals were guilty of murder it was possible to be involved in a murder by being guilty of committing some lesser offence.[207] It is clearly defamatory to accuse someone of corruption[208] but in the political context absent a specific allegation to that effect care should be taken before concluding that the allegation is one of criminal corruption.[209] It is defamatory to say of a company, set up to pursue a legal claim that it is being used, or is strongly suspected of being used, by a director as a conduit for the fraudulent misappropriation of funds contributed by its members for his own personal benefit because it would deter third parties from being associated with it or dealing with it.[210]

Juxtaposition There may be a "defamation by juxtaposition", i.e. the circumstances in which the matter is exhibited may determine its defamatory nature, as is illustrated by the case of *Monson v Tussauds Ltd*[211] where a wax figure representing the claimant was placed at the entrance to the "Chamber of Horrors" at Madame Tussauds. In *Dwek v Macmillan*[212] the claimant sued for libel in respect of a book in which there was a photograph of the claimant sitting beside a known prostitute. It was held that the publication was capable of being defamatory. **21-39**

Imputation of insanity or disease As with ridicule, whilst an imputation of insanity may have been defamatory under the common law it is unlikely to meet the threshold of seriousness under s.1 of the Defamation Act 2013. In *Terry v Persons Unknown*, Tugendhat J considered the limited classes of cases where the law of privacy and defamation overlapped. The judge referred to cases where the information in the past would have been said to be defamatory even though it was involuntary, such as disease. He considered that there was always a difficulty in fitting such cases into the law of defamation but it was done because there was no **21-40**

[203] *Marks v Samuel* [1904] 2 K.B. 287.
[204] *Modi v Clarke* [2011] EWCA Civ 937 at [32].
[205] *Al Rahi Banking and Investment Corp v Wall Street Journal Europe SPRL* [2003] EWHC 1358 (QB), per Eady J at [25]. Although note that the claimant bank would now also need to overcome the serious financial loss threshold at s.1(2) of the Defamation Act 2013.
[206] *Flood v Times Newspapers Ltd* [2013] EWHC 2182 (QB) at [12].
[207] *Hamaizia v Commissioner of Police for the Metropolis* [2013] EWHC 848 (QB) at [50].
[208] *Broadcasting Corp of New Zealand v Crush* [1988] 2 N.Z.L.R. 234.
[209] See *Cruddas v Times Newspapers Ltd* [2013] EWCA Civ 748; [2014] E.M.L.R. 5.
[210] *RBOS Shareholders Action Group Ltd v News Group Newspapers Ltd* [2014] EWHC 130 (QB); [2014] E.M.L.R. 15 at [33]–[36].
[211] [1894] 1 Q.B. 671; cf. *Garbett v Hazell, Watson and Viney Ltd* [1943] 2 All E.R. 359 CA; *Wheeler v Somerfield* [1966] 2 Q.B. 94 CA.
[212] [1999] 12 C.L. 162.

alternative cause of action.[213] Now a claim could be brought for misuse of private information.[214] Hence, in *Ibrahim v Swansea University*[215] allegations that the claimant had "suffered with mental health difficulties" or from "chronic fatigue syndrome and anxiety" were held not to be capable of being defamatory, since no reasonable person would nowadays think the worse of someone who had suffered from either condition. The claim was accordingly struck out.

21-41 **Imputation of insolvency** There is nothing defamatory per se in an allegation that a person owes money. The same applies to an allegation that a creditor has unsuccessfully sought to obtain an account of what the claimant owes him, or that the creditor and debtor are due to meet to resolve a dispute over a debt.[216] Likewise, a bare statement that the claimant has had a judgment made against him is not defamatory, without an implication that he is unwilling or unable to pay.[217] However an imputation that a person is insolvent, whether or not he is a trader, is defamatory, even though it carries no moral blame.[218] Further, it has been held that to write of a solicitor holding public appointments that he is "cleaned out" may injure his reputation and credit,[219] and that "refer to drawer" written on a cheque is capable of being defamatory.[220] Nevertheless, the claimant will often rely on an imputation to the effect that the insolvency was caused by circumstances discreditable to him, so as to avoid a dispute over whether or not the statement is defamatory. In *Aspro Travel v Owners Abroad*[221] the Court of Appeal held that the statements "they are going bust" and "they will be bankrupt in a few days" could be defamatory as they might imply that the claimants were prepared to trade, knowing their company was insolvent and this would lower their standing in the eyes of the community. The difference between a meaning of actual insolvency or one of mere pecuniary difficulties may be important.[222]

21-42 **Defamation of someone in their profession or employment** Statements may be defamatory of a person with reference to his profession or employment on the grounds that they disparage him in that capacity.[223] Statements may be defamatory, though they are not necessarily so, if they tend to injure the claimant in his calling or office, even though they are not provocative of "hatred, ridicule or contempt".[224] To be defamatory, however, the words must involve a reflection on the personal character, or on the official, professional or trading reputation of the claimant.[225] It is not sufficient to show only that they injure him in his trade or business. For example it may not be defamatory to allege that a tradesman has

213 *Terry (previously "LNS") v Persons Unknown* [2010] EWHC 119 (QB); [2010] E.M.L.R. 16 at [96], per Tugendhat J. See also Tugendhat J's judgment in *Thornton v Telegraph Media Group Ltd* [2010] EWHC 1414 (QB); [2011] 1 W.L.R. 1985.

214 See, e.g. *Campbell v Mirror Group Newspapers Ltd* [2004] UKHL 22; [2004] 2 A.C. 457.

215 [2012] EWHC 290 (QB).

216 *McCutcheon v Can International*, unreported, 19 December 2001.

217 *Stubbs v Russell* [1913] A.C. 386.

218 *Kiam v Neil (No.2)* [1996] E.M.L.R. 493.

219 *AB v CD* (1904) 7 F. 22 at 25, per Lord MacLaren.

220 *Jayson v Midland Bank Ltd* [1968] 1 Lloyd's Rep. 409 CA.

221 [1996] 1 W.L.R. 132.

222 *FlyMeNow Ltd v Quick Air Jet Charter GmbH* [2016] EWHC 3197 (QB).

223 For a detailed discussion of business and professional defamation the starting point is now *Thornton v Telegraph Media Group Ltd* [2010] EWHC 1414 (QB); [2011] 1 W.L.R. 1985.

224 per Lord Blackburn in *Capital and Counties Bank v Henty* (1882) 7 App. Cas. 741 at 771.

225 *Gatley on Libel and Slander* (12th edn) at 2.35 et seq. It was doubted in *Drummond-Jackson v BMA*

ceased to carry on business, or that his business is suffering from increased competition.[226] Though such statements must clearly be injurious,[227] they do not reflect adversely on the tradesman in his conduct of the business. An imputation of insolvency[228] is defamatory if made with reference to the claimant's calling. No one can be defamed in respect of an office which he has ceased to fill or a vocation which he has ceased to follow, but imputations against a person in some particular relation may also affect him in his general character. If it is alleged of a retired solicitor that he was guilty of sharp practice in his profession, he is not libelled as a solicitor for he is no longer one, but he is libelled as a person since he is accused of dishonesty.[229] But if the imputation is that he was unskillful in his profession, then it may be questioned whether from any point of view such language is defamatory. It is defamatory to say of a local authority officer that he operates a "slush fund",[230] or to accuse a businessman of being a willing beneficiary of cronyism.[231]

Corporations—common law The Defamation Act 2013 has fundamentally impacted the common law position that corporate bodies did not have to prove special damage in order to sue for libel.[232] At common law, a trading corporation could be defamed by defamatory matter which related to its business or the conduct of its affairs. A company was said to have a "trading character which may be destroyed by libel".[233] So a trading corporation could sue in its corporate capacity for a defamatory statement disparaging its goods,[234] or imputing insolvency,[235] or any other matter calculated to injure it in the way of its business.[236] **21-43**

Corporations and the Defamation Act 2013 Section 1(1) provides that a statement is not defamatory unless its publication has caused or is likely to cause serious harm to the reputation of the claimant. Section 1(2) provides that harm to the reputation of a body that trades for profit is not serious harm unless it has caused or is likely to cause the body serious financial loss. The requirement that the body **21-44**

[1970] 1 W.L.R. 688 CA, whether a sound analogy can be drawn between a professional man's technique and a trader's goods (per Lord Pearson at 698) and it was suggested that an attack on a professional man's technique might necessarily imply an attack on his ability; cf. *Ratcliffe v Evans* [1892] 2 Q.B. 524.

226 *Stephenson v Donaldson & Sons* (1981) 262 E.G. 148.

227 *Ratcliffe v Evans* [1892] 2 Q.B. 524; such words will be actionable as malicious falsehood if the requisites of that tort are proved, see Ch.22.

228 *Read v Hudson* (1700) 1 Ld. Ray. 610; *Jones v Littler* (1841) 7 M. & W. 423. An imputation of insolvency is actionable if made against a trader though without reference to his trade: *Jones v Jones* [1916] 2 A.C. 481.

229 per Parke J in *Boydell v Jones* (1838) 4 M. & W. 446 at 450.

230 *Thompson v James* [2014] EWCA Civ 600.

231 *Miller v Associated Newspapers Ltd* [2014] EWCA Civ 39.

232 *Derbyshire County Council v Times Newspapers Ltd* [1993] A.C. 534 at 537, per Lord Keith. The House of Lords declined the invitation to rule that trading corporations should not be entitled to sue unless they could prove financial loss in *Jameel v Wall Street Journal Europe SPRL* [2006] UKHL 44; [2007] 1 A.C. 359.

233 per Kay LJ. *South Hetton Coal Co v North Eastern News Association* [1894] 1 Q.B. 133 at 147.

234 *British Empire Type Setting Co v Linotype Co* (1898) 79 L.T. 8 (affirmed (1899) 81 L.T. 331); or for slander of title of goods, cf. Ch.22.

235 *Metropolitan Saloon Omnibus Co v Hawkins* (1859) 4 H. & N. 87.

236 *JW Thorley's Cattle Food Co v Massam* (1880) 14 Ch. D. 763; *South Hetton Coal Co v North Eastern News Association* [1894] 1 Q.B. 133; *Irish People's Assurance Society v City of Dublin Assurance Co* [1929] Ir. R. 25; *D & L Caterers Ltd v D'Anjou* [1945] K.B. 364 (slander); *Sungravure Property v Middle East Airliban SAL* (1975) 49 A.J.L.R. 17 (innuendo alleged airline was especially susceptible to hijacking).

must trade for profit means that bodies such as charities are not required to prove serious financial loss. It is unclear what is meant by serious financial loss or what a company will have to prove and establish. The Act does not specify whether that phrase ("serious financial loss") means the same as special damage or whether it requires something less such as diminution in goodwill. In *Lachaux v Independent Print Ltd* Lord Sumption stated that serious financial loss "is not the same as special damage"[237] albeit that serious financial loss was not directly in issue in that case. However, the section is intended to make it more difficult for corporations to sue for libel and some evidence will be required to show that the publication caused or is likely to cause serious financial loss.[238] The corporation and the person controlling it may of course each have an action,[239] and this may be of increasing significance where the corporate claimant has difficulty establishing that it is likely to or has suffered serious financial loss.

21-45 **Other legal entities** Section 1(2) refers to a body that trades for profit. That excludes a number of entities that might be able to sue. However, Parliament considered that, at least in terms of public authorities, the position at common law was now clear. Before 1993, it was not clear whether a local authority could sue for defamation. In *Derbyshire CC v Times Newspapers Ltd*[240] the House of Lords held, affirming the decision of the Court of Appeal, that the claimant council could not sue for defamation in relation to its "governing reputation", since to allow a governmental body to sue for defamation would be an undesirable fetter on political criticism. The Court of Appeal based its decision on art.10 of the Convention. The House of Lords preferred to base its decision on the common law, but confirmed that to allow such an action would be an undesirable fetter on legitimate political criticism. The entity and the person controlling it may of course each have an action.[241] In the *Derbyshire* case it was relevant that the council leader, Mr Bookbinder, could bring an action for defamation against the newspaper.[242] It will not be every pubic authority or body that is funded by public money that will be caught by the *Derbyshire* principle.[243] The position of trade unions is unclear. By virtue of s.10(1) of the Trade Union and Labour Relations (Consolidation) Act 1992, a trade union is not, and cannot be treated as if it were, a body corporate, unless it is a "special register" body under the 1992 Act. The tort of defamation requires the

[237] [2019] UKSC 27; [2020] A.C. 612 at [15].

[238] The case law on s.1(2) so far is summarised at para.21-22 and the principles will become settled as further cases are considered.

[239] *Lewis v Daily Telegraph Ltd* [1963] 1 Q.B. 340 CA; affirmed [1964] A.C. 234.

[240] [1993] A.C. 534; and now see the Human Rights Act 1998.

[241] *Lewis v Daily Telegraph Ltd* [1963] 1 Q.B. 340, CA; affirmed [1964] A.C. 234.

[242] *Bookbinder v Tebbit* [1989] 1 W.L.R. 640. See also *McLaughlin v Lambeth LBC* [2010] EWHC 2726 (QB); [2011] E.M.L.R. 8, where the court refused to strike out a claim by the current and former head teachers of a school in the Lambeth local authority. The claimants sued for defamation after being accused (inter alia) of mistreating and failing to give proper supervision to newly qualified teachers. The defendants sought to strike out the action on the basis that the claim was an abuse of process, since it was an unlawful attempt to circumvent the rule in *Derbyshire CC v Times Newspapers Ltd* [1993] A.C. 534, which prevents governmental bodies from suing for defamation. However, the judge refused the application. In *Derbyshire* the House of Lords drew a distinction between governmental bodies and individuals employed by them: the right to sue of any individual carrying on the day to day functions of the governmental authority was not limited by the *Derbyshire* decision, provided they were referred to (or identifiable) from the publication.

[243] See *Gatley on Libel and Slander* (12th edn) at 8.20; and see *Duke v University of Salford* [2013] EWHC 196 (QB); [2013] E.L.R. 259 where Eady J held that a university could sue for libel.

possession of a legal personality which can be defamed. The legislation has been interpreted as depriving trade unions of the necessary personality and reducing them to mere unincorporated associations.[244] However, the modern view is that the position is wrong.[245] It was held in *Goldsmith v Bhoyrul*,[246] an action brought on behalf of the referendum party, that although the referendum party was registered as a company, its whole purpose was to function as a political party and a political party may not sue in defamation for damage to its reputation.

Libel on thing may be libel on person To attack the reputation of a thing may be to attack the reputation of a person.[247] An unfavourable review of a book may be a libel on the author, although he is not directly referred to; though in such a case in order to become actionable it must be shown that the unfavourable review exceeded the bounds of an honest opinion defence. To allege of a tradesman that he habitually sells worthless goods is an impeachment of the vendor as well as of what he sells, and is necessarily defamatory because injurious to him in his trade.[248] But it is not defamatory to assert that a particular article which he has in stock is worthless.[249] A statement that a certain ship is unseaworthy is directed against the character of the ship, not against the character of the owner, but if it be added that this unseaworthy vessel is advertised to carry passengers, the statement becomes defamatory, for it involves almost necessarily a charge of misconduct or mismanagement.[250] In *Patterson v ICN Photonics Ltd*[251] the Court of Appeal struck out a defamation claim brought by the manufacturer of a cosmetic laser treatment system over an allegation that it should only be used under medical supervision. It could not be inferred from the words used in this case that the manufacturer was responsible for its use without medical supervision. It has also been held contrary to art.10 to prevent criticism of products or services offered by traders, unless the allegation genuinely attacks the reputation of the producer.[252] 21-46

244 *EEPTU v Times Newspapers Ltd* [1980] Q.B. 585, decided under the Trade Union and Labour Relations Act 1974, the predecessor to the 1992 Act.

245 The *EEPTU* decision has been criticised, since the 1992 Act permits trade unions to sue and be sued in contract and tort, and this might suggest that they ought to be able to sue for defamation. See *Gatley on Libel and Slander* (12th edn) at 8.24 for a detailed critique. Lord Hope in the House of Lords in *Jameel v Wall Street Journal Europe SPRL* [2006] UKHL 44; [2007] 1 A.C. 359 at [96], [100], [101] seems to assume that a trade union could sue for defamation.

246 [1998] Q.B. 459.

247 *Australian Newspaper Co v Bennett* [1894] A.C. 284; see *Gatley on Libel and Slander* (12th edn) at 2.47.

248 cf. per Lord Esher MR in *South Hetton Coal Co v North Eastern News Association* [1894] 1 Q.B. 133 at 139; and see *Drummond-Jackson v BMA* [1970] 1 W.L.R. 688 CA (attack on dentist's technique).

249 *Evans v Harlow* (1844) 5 Q.B. 624; approved by Lord Herschell LC in *White v Mellin* [1895] A.C. 154 at 161; and see *Linotype Co v British Empire Type Setting Co* (1899) 81 L.T. 331 HL.

250 *Ingram v Lawson* (1840) 6 Bing. N.C. 212. So in *Burnet v Wells* (1700) 12 Mod. 420, it was held clearly actionable to say of a tradesman in the way of his trade, "[h]e hath nothing but rotten goods in his shop". But it was agreed that if the words were that he had rotten goods no action would lie. In *Watkin v Hall* (1868) L.R. 3 Q.B. 396 at 399, Blackburn J said it is actionable to say of a cattle dealer that he has disease among his cattle. But this seems doubtful. See also, *JW Thorley's Cattle Food Co v Massam* (1880) 14 Ch. D. 763; *Thomas v Williams* (1880) 14 Ch. D. 864. A claim may lie in malicious falsehood or slander of goods (see Ch.22).

251 [2003] EWCA Civ 343.

252 See also *Charterhouse Clinical Research Unit Ltd v Richmond Pharmacology Ltd* [2003] EWHC 1099 (QB).

4. Slander

21-47 **Slander distinguished from libel** Slander consists of a defamatory imputation in some non-permanent form by spoken words, or other sounds,[253] or by gestures.[254] The law recognises a distinction between libel and slander for historical reasons though not resting on any satisfactory principle.[255] In *Barkhuysen v Hamilton*[256] Warby J summarised the common law of defamation thus:

> "the tort of slander is committed by a person who (1) speaks to at least one person other than the claimant, words that (2) refer to the claimant, (3) bear a meaning or meanings defamatory of the claimant, and (4) cause the claimant special damage, or fall within one of the exceptions to the general rule that slander is not actionable without proof of special damage. The onus of proving all these matters lies on the claimant."

Until the passing of the Defamation Act 2013, whereas libel is always actionable without proof of any special damage, slander had, in order to be actionable without proof of special damage ("actionable per se"), to impute: (1) a criminal offence punishable by imprisonment; or (2) certain contagious diseases; or (3) in the case of a woman, unchastity; or (4) be likely to damage the claimant's reputation in relation to any office, profession, calling, trade or business held or carried on by him at the time of publication. However, s.14 of the Act has made two changes to the law of slander. Section 14(1) repeals the Slander of Women Act 1891. Section 14(2) provides that the publication of a statement that conveys the imputation that a person has a contagious or infectious disease does not give rise to a cause of action for slander unless the publication causes the person special damage. The position now is that slander is only actionable on proof of special damage unless the words impute a crime for which the claimant can be made to suffer physically by way of punishment and where the words are calculated to disparage the claimant in any office, profession, calling, trade or business held or carried on by him at the time of publication. It must also be remembered that by the Broadcasting Act 1990, words broadcast by radio or television, and, by s.4 of the Theatres Act 1968,[257] words used in the course of the public performance of a play, are to be treated as published in permanent form, i.e. as libel, and will thus be actionable without proof of special damage.

(a) Imputing a criminal offence

21-48 **The imputation of a criminal offence must be clear** Spoken words which convey a mere suspicion that the claimant has committed a crime punishable by imprisonment will not support an action without proof of special damage.[258] It will be necessary for the claimant to satisfy the court that in the circumstances such words were equivalent to an absolute affirmation of guilt.[259] But an allegation that

[253] The malicious hissing of an actor is a slander of him in the way of his profession: *Gregory v Brunswick* (1844) 6 M. & G. 953 at 959.
[254] per Lord Abinger in *Gutsole v Mathers* (1836) 1 M.& W. 495 at 501.
[255] per curiam, *Thorley v Lord Kerry* (1812) 4 Taunt. 355 at 364–365; cf. *Report of the Committee on the Law of Defamation*, Cmd.7536, para.38.
[256] [2016] EWHC 2858 (QB); [2018] Q.B. 1015 at [43].
[257] See para.21-08.
[258] cf. *Lewis v Daily Telegraph Ltd* [1963] 1 Q.B. 340 CA; affirmed [1964] A.C. 234 HL.
[259] *Tozer v Mashford* (1851) 6 Ex. 539; *Simmons v Mitchell* (1880) 6 App. Cas. 156.

a person has voted twice in one parliamentary division at an election,[260] or that he was a blackmailer,[261] satisfies the requirement. It is, moreover, not essential that the exact offence should be specified; words involving a general charge of criminality will suffice. Thus, "You have committed an act for which I can transport you", has been held an actionable expression.[262] The facts stated on which the imputation is based must of course constitute a crime,[263] though it is not necessary that the offence charged should be indictable, it may be punishable summarily.[264] The ground on which words imputing a criminal offence are actionable per se is the damage to the claimant's good name, not the fact that he is put in jeopardy of criminal proceedings.[265] So, to say of a person that he is "a convicted person" is actionable per se although he is no longer exposed to the danger of prosecution as he has already been tried.[266] If the offence imputed is punishable only by a fine, the slander is not actionable without proof of special damage,[267] even though the court would have been empowered to commit to prison in default of payment of the fine.[268] In Canada, it was held to be actionable to impute a crime committed out of the jurisdiction.[269] The point does not appear to have arisen in England.[270]

(b) Imputing disease

Imputing disease As noted above, this exception has been abolished by s.14(2) of the Defamation Act 2013, which provides that the publication of a statement that conveys the imputation that a person has a contagious or infectious disease does not give rise to a cause of action for slander unless the publication causes the person special damage. It is to be noted that there is now a cause of action for misuse of private information[271] and that is likely to be the route a claimant would take to deal with allegations of this kind. **21-49**

(c) Imputing unchastity to a woman

Imputing unchastity to a woman At common law an imputation by words upon the chastity of a woman was not actionable in itself, but by the Slander of Women Act 1891, "words spoken and published which impute unchastity or adultery to any woman or girl shall not require special damage to render them actionable". The Act **21-50**

260 *Kinnell v Walker* (1910) 27 T.L.R. 67.
261 *Marks v Samuel* [1904] 2 K.B. 287.
262 *Curtis v Curtis* (1834) 10 Bing. 477; see also *Francis v Roose* (1838) 3 M. & W. 191. Nor is it is necessary to plead any particular criminal offence, although doing so has been described as "helpful": *Barkhuysen v Hamilton* [2016] EWHC 2858 (QB); [2018] Q.B. 1015 at [149].
263 *Jackson v Adams* (1835) 2 Bing. N.C. 402.
264 *Webb v Beavan* (1883) 11 Q.B.D. 609. But it must be an offence punishable with at least imprisonment in the first instance.
265 *Gray v Jones* (1939) 55 T.L.R. 437.
266 *Gray v Jones* (1939) 55 T.L.R. 437; following *Fowler v Dowdney* (1838) 2 Moo. & R. 119 at 120, per Lord Denman CJ ("he is a returned convict").
267 *Webb v Beavan* (1883) 11 Q.B.D. 609; *Michael v Spiers and Pond* (1909) 101 L.T. 352; *Bedi v Karim* [2013] EWHC 4280 (QB) at [10].
268 *Hellwig v Mitchell* [1910] 1 K.B. 609; *Wiffen v Bailey* [1915] 1 K.B. 600 at 611, per Phillimore LJ; *Ormiston v GW Ry* [1917] 1 K.B. 598.
269 See *Gatley on Libel and Slander* (12th edn), para.4.6.
270 The Court of Appeal in *D & L Caterers v D'Ajou* [1945] K.B. 364, left open the point whether a slander imputing to a limited company the commission of a criminal offence, which when committed by an individual was punishable by imprisonment, was actionable per se.
271 See Ch.26.

has now been repealed by s.14(1) of the Defamation Act 2013 and a claimant would have to show that an oral allegation of this kind was defamatory (as defined by both the common law and under s.1 of the Defamation Act 2013) and caused special damage.

(d) Slander of a person in his profession, trade or employment

21-51 **Slander of a person in profession, trade or employment** Under the common law a person who pursues any office, profession, calling, trade or business may have an action if he is slandered in respect of it. Provided the office is lawful the perceived social ranking or status of the calling is irrelevant.[272] Thus a gamekeeper had a good cause of action against the defendant for saying that he had poisoned foxes,[273] and an engineer fitter for the statement that he was a grossly unskilled workman.[274] Similarly, to impute fraudulent conduct or lack of skill in the exercise of his profession to a professional person is actionable per se.[275] A person may conduct several professions simultaneously.[276] A claimant who alleges that he has been slandered in his calling must show that he held the office[277] or pursued the vocation at the time when the words complained of were published.[278] It has been held to be arguable that the position of chairman of a residents association is an office of the kind protected by this exception.[279]

21-52 **Defamation Act 1952 s.2: slander affecting official, professional or business reputation** The common law position was altered by s.2 of the Defamation Act 1952, which provides that:

> "In an action for slander in respect of words calculated to disparage the claimant in any office, profession, calling, trade or business held or carried on by him at the time of the publication, it shall not be necessary to allege or prove special damage, whether or not the words are spoken of the claimant in the way of his office, profession, calling, trade or business."

Where the defamatory words are spoken of the claimant in the way of his calling and disparage him therein they will be actionable per se under the old law. Following the extension of this category by the Defamation Act 1952, defamatory words

---

272 Old cases which decided that some occupations were not of sufficient dignity to support an action for slander must be regarded as no longer law, e.g. *Bell v Thatcher* (1676) 1 Vent. 275 (postman); *Wharton v Brook* (1669) 1 Vent. 21 (schoolmistress).

273 *Foulger v Newcombe* (1867) L.R. 2 Ex. 327.

274 *Slack v Barr* (1918) 82 J.P. 91.

275 *Boydell v Jones* (1838) 4 M. & W. 446 (solicitor); *Botterill v Whytehead* (1879) 41 L.T. 588 (architect); *Dakhyl v Labouchere* [1908] 2 K.B. 325n (physician); cf. *Turner v MGM Pictures Ltd* [1950] 1 All E.R. 449 (critic); *Greenslade v Swaffer* [1955] 1 W.L.R. 1109 (journalist).

276 *Bull v Vasquez* [1947] 1 All E.R. 334 (words spoken of the claimant in respect of his position as an army officer, notwithstanding that he was on an indefinite parliamentary leave to exercise his profession as a Member of Parliament).

277 In *Cleghorn v Sadler* [1945] K.B. 325, it was held that a duty to "fire-watch" imposed on citizens in war time was not an "office" within this category and therefore words spoken of the claimant in relation to that occupation were not actionable per se.

278 cf. Defamation Act 1952 s.2. In *Jones v Stevens* (1823) 11 Price 235, the claimant sued for a libel on himself "in the way of his profession and business of attorney". He was on the rolls but had not taken out a certificate, and it was held that he still retained his professional character and could be libelled in that character; cf. also, per Platt B in *Gallwey v Marshall* (1853) 9 Ex. 294 at 301.

279 *Bedi v Karim* [2013] EWHC 4280 (QB) at [10].

may now be actionable per se even though they are not spoken of the claimant directly concerning his office or profession provided that the particular imputation they convey is likely to disparage the claimant in that profession. If the defamatory imputation conveyed by the words is such that it will naturally tend to injure or prejudice the reputation of the claimant in his calling the words will be actionable per se.[280]

Distinction between profitable and honorary office Before the Defamation Act 1952, where defamatory words were spoken of a person in respect of an office held by him, the law drew a distinction between offices of profit and offices of an honorary nature. In the case of offices of profit,[281] words were actionable per se which alleged either dishonesty or incompetence. In the case of honorary officers[282] an imputation of dishonesty, corruption or criminal breach of duty sufficed,[283] whether or not the conduct charged would be ground for removal from the office,[284] but a mere imputation of unfitness for such an office through want of ability was not actionable per se, unless the charge, if true, would enable the claimant to be deprived of office.[285] Thus it was not actionable per se to say of a town councillor that he was a habitual drunkard,[286] but it was to accuse an alderman of using his office to put money into his own pocket.[287] This distinction, though hardly satisfactory,[288] was well established. After the enactment of the 1952 Act, it appeared, following *Robinson v Ward*,[289] that the distinction would be upheld. However in the case of *Maccaba v Lichtenstein*,[290] Gray J elected not to follow the decision of Diplock J in *Robinson*, stating that the wording of s.2 "is so clear that it does not permit any distinction to be drawn between offices of profit and offices of honour". Whilst these decisions are in conflict it is to be expected that the decision of Gray J will prevail. 21-53

[280] s.2 was passed to alter the law as laid down in such cases as *Jones v Jones* [1916] 2 A.C. 481; *Hopwood v Muirson* [1945] K.B. 313. As to the meaning of "calculated" in the phrase "calculated to disparage" cf. *Oxford English Dictionary*; *McDowell v Standard Oil* [1927] A.C. 632; Burrow's *Words and Phrases*, "calculated to deceive"; and for judicial usage cf. *Wilkinson v Downton* [1897] 2 Q.B. 57; *Willey v Peace* [1950] 2 All E.R. 724 at 725; *Greenslade v Swaffer* [1955] 1 W.L.R. 1109 at 1115. And see *Gatley on Libel and Slander* (12th edn) at 4.15–4.19.

[281] See, for the meaning of "profit", *Thomas v Moore* [1918] 1 K.B. 555; *Alexander v Jenkins* [1892] 1 Q.B. 797 at 800, 802, per Lord Herschell.

[282] Quaere, whether limited to public offices: *Thomas v Moore* [1918] 1 K.B. 555; and, per Lopes LJ in *Booth v Arnold* [1895] 1 Q.B. 571 at 577.

[283] *Booth v Arnold* [1895] 1 Q.B. 571. This seems to be the true ground of the decision, and not that the dishonesty imputed would have been ground for removal, though Lopes LJ relied on both; cf. *Onslow v Horne* (1771) 3 Wils. 177; *Adams v Meredew* (1829) 3 Y. & J. 219.

[284] *Booth v Arnold* [1895] 1 Q.B. 571.

[285] *How v Prinn* (1702) 2 Salk. 694; *Alexander v Jenkins* [1892] 1 Q.B. 797. Fire-watching in the 1939–1945 War was not an office of honour or credit but a compulsory duty and defamation in respect of that employment was not actionable per se, *Cleghorn v Sadler* [1945] 1 K.B. 325.

[286] *Alexander v Jenkins* [1892] 1 Q.B. 797.

[287] *Booth v Arnold* [1895] 1 Q.B. 571.

[288] per Lord Herschell in *Alexander v Jenkins* [1892] 1 Q.B. 797 at 801.

[289] *The Times*, 17 June 1958; 108 L.J. 491.

[290] [2004] EWHC 1580 (QB).

(e) Slander causing special damage

21-54 **Slander causing special damage** If the defamatory words spoken are not actionable per se they are actionable if they cause "special damage".[291] The term "special damage" is confusing. It is often used to describe a specific and quantifiable financial loss. In that sense it can be contrasted with a general loss of business or profits which is said to be general damage. However, a general loss of profits is considered sufficient damage which would entitle a claimant to bring a slander action, provided such loss was foreseeable.[292] The authorities are not entirely clear on the question of whether in such cases, when the special damage has been proved, damages may be recovered only for the special damage proved or in accordance with general principles. The balance of opinion appears to be that the damages are limited to the proved special damage.[293] The special damage must not be too remote, and in particular must not result from unauthorised repetition.[294]

5. PUBLICATION

21-55 **Publication** In order to succeed in an action for defamation a claimant must prove that the libel or slander has been published,[295] i.e. communicated to some person or persons other than the claimant himself. A husband and a wife are regarded as one to the extent that no publication can be made by a communication from one to the other respecting a third party.[296] But defamatory matter can be published to the husband or wife of the person who is the subject of the defamation.[297] A claimant has been able to rely on a publication to his own agent, and the fact that such agent invited and procured the publication has not affected the defendant's liability.[298] However, these days a publication of that kind or to a limited class of people is likely to be held to be either an abuse of process[299] or insufficiently serious to

---

[291] i.e. damage which is pecuniary or capable of being estimated in money: *Chamberlain v Boyd* (1883) 11 Q.B.D. 407 at 415. A mere threat of future loss is not sufficient: *Michael v Spiers and Pond* (1909) 101 L.T. 352; nor is illness: *Allsop v Allsop* (1860) 5 H. & N. 534; not followed *Rigby v Mirror Newspapers Ltd* (1963) 64 S.R. (N.S.W.) 34, which held that a claimant in an action for defamation is entitled to include a claim for pain of body and mind; but see *Wheeler v Somerfield* [1966] 2 Q.B. 94 at 104, where it was said that there has never been a case where damages have been recovered for injury to health; but the loss of a marriage is: *Speight v Gosnay* (1891) 60 L.J.Q.B. 231; or of consortium: *Lynch v Knight* (1861) 9 H.L.C. 577; cf. *Ward v Lewis* [1955] 1 W.L.R. 9 (allegation of conspiracy to defame failed because no nexus alleged between the slanders and the damage claimed).

[292] *Ratcliffe v Evans* [1892] 2 Q.B. 524.

[293] *Gatley on Libel and Slander* (12th edn) at 5.10; *Dixon v Smith* (1860) 5 H. & N. 450; 29 L.J. Ex. 125; *Ratcliffe v Evans* [1892] 2 Q.B. 524 at 530-532. And see Helmholz, "Damages in Actions for Slander at Common Law" (1987) 103 L.Q.R. 624.

[294] The law governing damage resulting from repetition is dealt with at paras 21-217 to 21-223, and that concerned with damages generally in defamation, at paras 21-224 to 21-248.

[295] *Hebditch v MacIlwaine* [1894] 2 Q.B. 54, CA at 58, 61, 64.

[296] *Wenhak v Morgan* (1888) 20 Q.B.D. 635; aliter, after divorce, cf. *Capal v Powell* (1864) 17 C.B. (N.S.) 743, or judicial separation; cf. *Cuenod v Leslie* [1901] 1 K.B. 880. And see *Robinson v Robinson* (1897) 13 T.L.R. 564, per Kennedy J.

[297] *Wenman v Ash* (1853) 13 C.B. 836; cf. *Praed v Graham* (1889) 24 Q.B.D. 53; cf. *Watt v Longsdon* [1930] 1 K.B. 130.

[298] *King v Waring* (1803) 5 Esp. 13; *Duke of Brunswick v Harmer* (1850) 14 Q.B. 185 at 189.

[299] *Jameel v Dow Jones & Co Inc* [2005] EWCA Civ 75; [2005] Q.B. 946, where publication was to the claimant's agents and only one or two others not connected with him, and his claim was struck out as an abuse of process. Consent may also be a defence: para.21-198.

overcome s.1 of the Defamation Act 2013.[300] A libel may be published by reading the contents of the writing to a third person or allowing him to read them for himself.[301]

Single publication rule At common law, each communication of the material is a separate publication and gives rise to a separate cause of action.[302] It has been held by Strasbourg that it is not an infringement of art.10 to allow a claimant to sue in respect of an article that remains accessible on a newspaper internet archive outside of the primary limitation period.[303] However, s.8 of the Defamation Act 2013 changed the law and introduced a single publication rule. The rule applies where a person publishes a statement to the public *and* subsequently publishes (whether or not to the public) that statement or a statement that is substantially the same. Only the person who published the first publication is covered by the provision. The section will not apply if the second statement is materially different.[304] It is arguable that the pre-Defamation Act 2013 law applied to all publications on a website which were accessed before 1 January 2014 (when the Act came into force)—i.e. each time the website was accessed constituted a new publication—and the first time the website was accessed on or after 1 January 2014 constituted a single publication under s.8, with time starting to run for limitation purposes from that date. However, in *Richardson v Facebook*[305] Warby J considered that there is room for debate on the application of s.8 in this context. 21-56

Defamation action based on documents disclosed in other legal proceedings Defamation claims are not permitted to proceed (or will be struck out as an abuse of process) where they are based on documents disclosed in separate legal proceedings. The position was formerly governed by the common law, which provided that there was an implied undertaking preventing the recipient of a document disclosed that he would not use it as the basis for other proceedings.[306] So far as civil proceedings are concerned, this rule is now enacted in CPR r.31.22. The restriction does not apply to documents which have been read to or by the court, or referred to, at a public hearing.[307] The rationale is that it is in the public interest and for the proper administration of justice that such action be prevented, so as to 21-57

---

300 The Defamation Act 2013 s.1 states that a statement is not defamatory unless its publication has caused or is likely to cause serious harm to the reputation of a claimant.

301 5 Rep. 125b (cf. *Hearne v Stowell* (1840) 12 A. & E. 719; *Smith v Wood* (1813) 3 Camp. 323); *Forrester v Tyrrell* (1893) 9 T.R.L. 257 CA, followed and preferred to dicta in *Osborn v Thomas Boulter & Son* [1930] 2 K.B. 226 at 231, 236, 237; in *Robinson v Chambers* [1946] N.I. 148; cf. *Longdon-Griffiths v Smith* [1951] 1 K.B. 295. The handing back by a printer to the author of a defamatory document printed in the course of business is not of itself a publication by the printer so as to make him liable; nor is the handing back to the employer by a clerk or typist of a document copied or made to the employer's order a publication by the clerk or typist. There is, of course, publication to the printer or clerk or typist by the author or employer in such cases when the document is handed to them: *Eglantine Inn Ltd v Smith* [1948] N.I. 29 at 33.

302 *Duke of Brunswick v Harmer* (1850) 14 Q.B. 185 at 189; *Berezovsky v Michaels* [2000] 1 W.L.R. 1004 at 1012 HL.

303 *Times Newspapers Ltd v United Kingdom* [2009] E.M.L.R. 14.

304 See *Gatley on Libel and Slander* (12th edn) at 6.6 to 6.8.

305 [2015] EWHC 3154 (QB); [2015] Info. T.L.R. 69.

306 *Riddick v Thames Board Mills Ltd* [1977] Q.B. 881 CA; and see *Hayward v Wegg-Prosser* (1978) 122 S.J. 792; *Home Office v Harman* [1981] Q.B. 534 CA; *ITC Film Distributors v Video Exchange Ltd* [1982] Ch. 436. The position is now governed specifically by CPR r.31.22.

307 CPR r.31.22(a). The restriction will also end if the court gives permission (r.31.22(b)) or the party who disclosed the document and the party to whom the document belongs agree (r.31.22(c)). Docu-

ensure that parties and others required to comply with disclosure obligations do so without fear of subsequent litigation. But in New Zealand it was held that an action for libel based on statements to the police would be permitted to continue and production of the statement was ordered by the Court of Appeal. The Court did not consider that the person making a statement to the police would be influenced or inhibited by the prospect of disclosure and consequently the public interest did not demand that discovery of the documents be refused.[308] In *Taylor v SFO*,[309] an SFO employee wrote to the Attorney General of the Isle of Man, proposing that the claimant, T, a solicitor, should be interviewed. T was shown the document by a suspect and sued the defendants for defamation. The House of Lords held that where documents have been prepared as part of a criminal investigation, the person preparing them is entitled to immunity from suit and they cannot therefore be used to ground a civil action (here defamation). However in *P v T Ltd*[310] an order was granted to the claimant directing disclosure of the identity of a complainant whose allegations had led to his dismissal from his employment. Sir Richard Scott VC granted the order on the ground that the interests of justice required that the claimant should be able to discover if the tort of defamation had been committed against him. In *Tufano v Vincenti*[311] the claimant brought defamation proceedings over an expert report prepared for the purposes of separate family proceedings. The family court had ordered the appointment of a guardian for the claimant's children and the ensuing psychiatric report made reference to the claimant. The court struck out the claim in accordance with the principles set out in *General Medical Council v Meadow*[312] in which it was held that immunity from suit extended to any civil proceedings brought against a defendant based on the evidence which the defendant gave to the court and that such immunity applied as much to experts as to any other witness.

21-58 **Prima facie evidence** It is by no means necessary for a claimant in all cases to prove directly that the defamatory matter was brought to the actual knowledge of anyone. If he makes it a matter of reasonable inference that such was the fact, he establishes a sufficient prima facie case. The posting of a letter is good evidence of a publication to the party to whom the letter was addressed.[313] The circulation by a lending library of copies of a book containing libellous matter is evidence of

ments read by the judge prior to a hearing and to which reference is made in the judgment will be deemed to have been referred to at a hearing held in public—see *SmithKline Beecham Biologicals SA v Connaught Laboratories Inc* [1999] 4 All E.R. 498 CA; and *Re Mobile Phone Voicemail Litigation* [2012] EWHC 397 (Ch); [2012] 1 W.L.R. 2545.

308 *Apperley v Tippene* [1978] Crim. L.R. 632; and cf. *Neilson v Laugharne* [1981] Q.B. 736 CA; *Hehir v Commissioner of Police for the Metropolis* [1982] 1 W.L.R. 715 (production of reports prepared in the course of an investigation of a complaint against a constable under s.49 of the Police Act 1964 refused). Yet in *Conerney v Jacklin* [1985] Crim. L.R. 234 CA, a constable was allowed to proceed with an action for libel based on allegations made by the defendant in a complaint lodged pursuant to s.49. The court distinguished statements made in the course of an investigation, which would be protected from discovery, from the initial complaint itself, which could not attract public interest immunity from an action in defamation. Complaints against the police now fall under Pt 2 of the Police Reform Act 2002. And see observations of Waite J in *X, Y and Z (Minors), Re; Wynne v Mail Newspapers* [1991] Fam. Law 318.

309 [1999] 2 A.C. 177.

310 [1997] 1 W.L.R. 1309. See also *Ashworth Hospital Authority v MGN Ltd* [2002] UKHL 29; [2002] 1 W.L.R. 2033 at [57].

311 [2006] EWHC 1496 (QB).

312 [2006] EWCA Civ 1390; [2007] Q.B. 462.

313 *Warren v Warren* (1834) 1 C.M. & R. 250.

publication to the subscribers.[314] The dispatch of a postcard[315] is good evidence of publication to the various post-office officials through whose hands it passes, for they have an opportunity of seeing the contents. So, ordinarily, the printing of a libel imports, in the first instance, a publication to the persons employed in the printing.[316] But in all these cases there is only a presumption which may be rebutted, if the person to whom publication is alleged denies that the defamatory matter came to his knowledge.[317] Thus, where libellous matter respecting an undesignated third party was written on a postcard and transmitted by post, the fact that the communications would not be understood by the persons through whose hands it passed as referring to the claimant was held to negative the presumption of publication during transmission.[318] Further, where a defamatory article was published on the internet but shown to have been read only by five persons, three of whom were agents or lawyers acting on behalf of the claimant, the action was struck out as an abuse of process.[319] On the internet, there is no presumption of publication merely because words complained of are posted. They must be shown to have been read by individuals, either by calling the individuals who read them or by pleading a platform of facts from which an inference can be drawn.[320]

Joint publication The publication of a libel may be a joint tort,[321] as where in pursuance of a common design one composes, another prints and another distributes a libel, or where an employee publishes a libel within the scope of his employment: **21-59**

> "Where defamatory matter is contained in a book, periodical, or newspaper there are normally a series of publications each of which constitutes a separate tort. First, there is publication by the author to the publisher for which the author is solely liable. Secondly, there is the publication by the author and publisher jointly to the printer, for which the author and publisher are jointly liable. Thirdly, there is the publication of the printed work to the trade and the public, for which the author, publisher and printer are jointly liable. It is normally in respect of this last publication that proceedings for libel are brought, although it is open to the claimant to sue in respect of the separate publications set out above."[322]

Slander may be a joint tort, as where one instigates another to utter the slander, or

---

314 *Vizetelly v Mudie's Select Library* [1900] 2 Q.B. 170.

315 *Sadgrove v Hole* [1901] 2 K.B. 1. But not a letter in an unclosed envelope: *Huth v Huth* [1915] 3 K.B. 32.

316 *Baldwin v Elphinston* (1774) 2 W. Bl. 1037 at 1038. See, however, *Watts v Fraser* (1837) 7 A. & E. 233 at 233; cf. *Eglantine Inn Ltd v Smith* [1948] N.I. 29.

317 *Clutterbuck v Chaffers* (1816) 1 Stark. 471; cf. *Huth v Huth* [1915] 3 K.B. 32 at 39. There are some dicta in *R. v Burdett* (1820) 4 B. & A. 95, which taken by themselves would seem to show that the posting of a letter is not merely evidence of publication but necessarily a publication. However, the real meaning appears to be that the posting is the commencement of the publication which becomes complete when the communication reaches the addressee. And see *Bata v Bata* [1948] W.N. 366 where *R. v Burdett* was considered.

318 *Sadgrove v Hole* [1901] 2 K.B. 1. But not a letter in an unclosed envelope: *Huth v Huth* [1915] 3 K.B. 32. For "posting" on the Internet see *Godfrey v Demon Internet* [2001] Q.B. 201.

319 *Jameel v Dow Jones & Co Inc* [2005] EWCA Civ 75; [2005] Q.B. 946. Also see *Al Amoudi v Brisard* [2006] EWHC 1062 (QB); [2007] 1 W.L.R. 113; *Carrie v Tolkien* [2009] EWHC 29 (QB); [2009] E.M.L.R. 9; and *Noorani v Calver* [2009] EWHC 561 (QB).

320 *Al Amoudi v Brisard* [2006] EWHC 1062 (QB); [2007] 1 W.L.R. 113; *Carrie v Tolkien* [2009] EWHC 29 (QB); [2009] E.M.L.R. 9; and *Noorani v Calver* [2009] EWHC 561 (QB).

321 As to joint tortfeasors, see para.4-03; and the *Report of the Committee on the Law of Defamation*, Cmd.7536, paras 116-137. See the Defamation Act 1952 s.11.

322 *Report of the Committee on the Law of Defamation*, Cmd.7563, para.116. And see *Cutler v McPhail* [1962] 2 Q.B. 292; and *Riddick v Thames Board Mills* [1977] Q.B. 881.

similarly in the case of employer and employee. But the publication of the same slander by different people cannot of itself constitute a joint tort.[323] Two or more persons who separately publish identical or similar slanders may, however, be jointly sued, subject to the power of the court to order separate trials of the different causes of action if a joint trial would be embarrassing.[324]

21-60 **Authorised repetition** In the case of either libel or slander a person may, without directly participating in the publication, make himself responsible for it. "Not only he who publishes the libel himself, but also he who procures another to do it is guilty of the publication."[325] Thus where, at a board of guardians, remarks defamatory of the claimant were made and the chairman expressed a hope that the press would take notice of them, it was held that he was liable for the publication in a newspaper of a fair report of what occurred.[326] And although it has been stated that a defendant is not generally liable for an unauthorised repetition or republication of defamatory matter,[327] if he publishes to a person who is under a moral obligation to repeat it to someone else, he causes and procures this second publication and is answerable for it.[328] He is also liable if the republication is reasonably foreseeable.[329]

21-61 **Publication by agent** The maxim of *respondeat superior*[330] applies, and if an employee acting within the scope of his employment publishes a libel the employer can be sued.[331] Section 1(4) of the Defamation Act 1996 provides that, for the purposes of the statutory defence under s.1:

> "Employees or agents of an author, editor or publisher are in the same position as their employer or principal to the extent that they are responsible for the content of the statement or the decision to publish it."

In *Monir v Wood*[332] the defendant, chairman of the local UKIP political party branch, was liable for a tweet posted by the vice-chairman, given that the task of tweeting had been delegated to the vice-chairman, and the defendant retained

---

323 *Chamberlain v White* (1623) Cro. Jac. 647; *Coryton v Lithebye* (1671) 2 Wm. Saund. 112.

324 *Thomas v Moore* [1918] 1 K.B. 555.

325 Bac. Ab. Libel B.2.

326 *Parkes v Prescott* (1869) L.R. 4 Ex. 169; para.21-220. But not where a speech is made without knowledge that it will be reported, *McWhirter v Manning, The Times,* 29 and 30 October 1954.

327 *Ward v Weeks* (1830) 7 Bing. 211; approved in *Clarke v Morgan* (1877) 38 L.T. 354; and in *Weld-Blundell v Stephens* [1920] A.C. 956; para.21-217 onwards.

328 *Derry v Handley* (1867) 16 L.T. 263. The rule probably extends to social and legal obligations as well. See *Riddick v Thames Board Mills Ltd* [1977] Q.B. 881, per Stephenson LJ at 900 and Waller LJ at 909 (where they disagree whether employees, who gave an account over the telephone about the claimant's work and dismissal, were responsible for the publication of a written report by the personnel officer with whom they spoke). See also *McManus v Beckham* [2002] EWCA Civ 939; [2002] 1 W.L.R. 2982; *Baturina v Times Newspapers Ltd* [2011] EWCA Civ 308; [2011] 1 W.L.R. 1526.

329 See *McManus v Beckham* [2002] EWCA Civ 939; [2002] 1 W.L.R. 2982; *Terluk v Berezovksy* [2011] EWCA Civ 1534 at [28]; and para.21-219.

330 "Let the superior answer."

331 *Citizens' Life Assurance Co v Brown* [1904] A.C. 423; *Finburgh v Moss Empires*, 1908 S.C. 928 (slander); *Neville v C & A Modes*, 1945 S.C. 175 (slander). For cases where the publication was held outside the scope of the employment, see *Glasgow Corp v Lorimer* [1911] A.C. 209 at 214, per Lord Loreburn LC; *Aiken v Caledonian Ry*, 1913 S.C. 66; *Mandelston v NB Ry*, 1917 S.C. 442. As to master and servant and scope of employment see para.6-06 onwards.

332 [2018] EWHC 3525 (QB).

control of the twitter account throughout. Having decided that the defendant was liable for publication by his agent, the court did not consider it necessary to decide whether he was vicariously liable for the tweet. In *Regan v Taylor*[333] the defendant was a solicitor representing a police officer in several libel actions. In an interview he described the magazine "Scallywag", of which the claimant was editor, in deeply unfavourable terms, without having any specific authority from his client. He claimed that his statement was covered by qualified privilege and the Court of Appeal upheld the decision of the court at first instance to enter summary judgment for him since there was no reasonable prospect of this defence being rebutted.

Intention or negligence Publication must be intentional or negligent. There is publication if the defendant, or somebody for whom he is responsible, has made known the matter, which is in fact defamatory, to a person other than the claimant unless he can show that the making known of the matter was not due to any want of due care. He may furthermore be responsible if his conduct shows approval or consent to the further display of defamatory matter even if he did not make the original publication as if, for example, he fails to remove defamatory matter displayed on his wall or notice board with knowledge that it is or may be defamatory.[334] If a person intends to issue the particular document or negligently allows it to fall into other hands, there is prima facie sufficient publication. A person other than the author, editor or publisher who seeks to avail himself of the statutory defence under s.1 of the Defamation Act 1996 must show that he took reasonable care and that he did not know and had no reason to believe that what he did caused or contributed to the publication of a defamatory statement.[335] Such a person may also rely on s.10 of the Defamation Act 2013, which provides that a court does not have jurisdiction to hear and determine an action for defamation brought against a person who was not the author, editor or publisher of the statement complained of unless the court is satisfied that it is not reasonably practicable for an action to be brought against the author, editor or publisher. The issuing of defamatory material by an automated process involving no human element, such as where an internet search engine produces results which include defamatory content, does not constitute publication by the search provider.[336] 21-62

Ignorance of contents of documents[337] If the defendant does not know, and has no reasonable means of knowing, and is under no legal obligation to know the nature of the document, though the matter published is libellous, he has not published the libel. Thus, the postman who delivers a libellous letter, although in one sense he shares in the publication, is not answerable; nor is anyone who is a mere vehicle of communication.[338] 21-63

Publication by mistake to wrong person A defendant who knows, or ought to know, that a statement is defamatory will be liable if he publishes that statement 21-64

333 [2000] E.M.L.R. 549; (2000) 150 N.L.J. 392.

334 *Byrne v Deane* [1937] 1 K.B. 818.

335 e.g. *Godfrey v Demon Internet* [2001] Q.B. 201.

336 See *Metropolitan International Schools Ltd v Designtechnica Corp* [2009] EWHC 1765 (QB); [2011] 1 W.L.R. 1743. Although the Supreme Court of South Australia has found Google to be liable as a publisher: *Google Inc v Duffy* [2017] SASFC 130.

337 *Gatley on Libel and Slander* (12th edn) at 6.18.

338 *Day v Bream* (1837) 2 Moo. & R. 54; cf. *Emmens v Pottle* (1885) 16 Q.B.D. 354 at 357. For the protection of the Post Office, see the Postal Services Act 2000 s.90.

to a third party even if he had not intended to issue the statement to anyone other than the person to whom the statement relates. Thus where the defendant, intending to send a libel to the plaintiff, sent it by mistake to a third person, it was held that this mistake did not affect the nature of his act.[339] A person who so issues libellous matter will be responsible even though he is under the mistaken impression that he is communicating it to a person to whom the communication is privileged. And this is so whether the mistake is as to the person to whom the communication is made, or as to the existence of facts which would give rise to a right or duty to make it. If the defendant writes a defamatory matter in a letter to A, but by mistake places it in an envelope addressed to B, who receives and reads it, he will be liable even though the publication of the letter to A would have been privileged.[340] He will equally be liable if, in sending it to the person to whom he intended to send it, he made a mistake in supposing that the person had any such interest or duty in the matter as would have made the communication privileged even if his mistake was both honest and reasonable.[341] In all such cases the defendant issues the libellous matter at his peril. But where a defendant published a letter on an occasion otherwise privileged, it was held that he was protected even though his possession of the letter had originally been obtained wrongfully.[342]

21-65 **Letter opened by third person** When a letter is addressed to a particular person the writer is not as a general rule responsible except for a publication to that person.[343] If it were stolen and published by a thief the writer would not be liable.[344] But if the sender knows or ought to know that the letter will probably be read by some person other than the addressee, as for instance a clerk in the latter's service, he will be responsible in the event of its being so read.[345] If he wants to protect himself he should write "private" on the envelope.[346] Where the defendant delivered a defamatory letter in an unstamped business envelope with a typed address, addressed to the plaintiff but not marked "private", and the letter was opened in error by the plaintiff's husband, the Court of Appeal held that a jury's verdict was not perverse where they found a publication in the particular circumstances on the basis that the defendant anticipated that someone other than the plaintiff would open and read the letter and that it was a natural and probable consequence of the defendant's writing and delivery of the letter that the plaintiff's husband would open and read it. They were properly directed that the issue of publication turned on whether the defendant knew or ought to have known or might have expected that the letter might be opened and read by someone other than the plaintiff.[347] If, however, the defendant has no knowledge of the possibility of such a publication he is not liable if it

---

339 *Fox v Broderick* (1864) 14 Ir. C.L.R. 453; and see *Powell v Gelston* [1916] 2 K.B. 615 (no publication by defendant).

340 This follows from the judgments in *Hebditch v MacIlwaine* [1894] 2 Q.B. 54; where the decision in *Thompson v Dashwood* (1883) 11 Q.B.D. 43, to the contrary was overruled.

341 *Hebditch v MacIlwaine* [1894] 2 Q.B. 54; *Beach v Freeson* [1972] 1 Q.B. 14. Also *Hynes-O'Sullivan v Driscoll* [1988] I.R. 436 (Irish Supreme Court).

342 *Thurston v Charles* (1905) 21 L. & T.R. 659.

343 *Keogh v Incorporated Dental Hospital of Ireland (No.2)* [1910] 2 Ir. R. 677.

344 *Pullman v Hill* [1891] 1 Q.B. 524 at 527.

345 *Pullman v Hill* [1891] 1 Q.B. 524 at 527; cf. *Gomersall v Davies* (1898) 14 T.L.R. 430. In the case of fax and electronic mail there is presumably an increased likelihood that the matter sent will be open to others than the recipient.

346 per Lopes LJ in *Pullman v Hill* [1891] 1 Q.B. 524 at 529.

347 *Theaker v Richardson* [1962] 1 W.L.R. 151 CA.

should take place.[348] Thus, where a libellous letter was addressed to the plaintiff at his office and in his absence was opened by his partner, it was held that the defendant was not liable for the publication, the jury having found that he did not know such a thing was possible.[349]

Responsibility for publication on the Internet The author of a publication online is liable as the publisher of the statement according to ordinary principles of liability. In *Bussey Law Firm PC v Page*[350] publication of a defamatory posting on Google Maps was found to have originated from the defendant's Google account. The court concluded that the account holder was responsible for publication, and that his argument that the account had been hacked was extremely improbable. Publication of tweets on Twitter have founded libel claims.[351] If a message on a publicly accessible website or social media page is intended to be private it is for the person writing to ensure it is sent privately. Taking part in an exchange on a public Facebook wall is akin to putting a comment on an office noticeboard accessible to anyone or sending a letter to a company and failing to mark it private, and so the author of comments on a person's Facebook "wall" was directly responsible for the publication of those comments to all of the person's Facebook "friends" who read them.[352] However, the author may not be worth suing or may not be identifiable. The issue that has exercised the courts and legislators is to what extent those who facilitate publication online are liable and that depends upon what role they play and their state of knowledge.[353] The cases to date are not easy to reconcile and nor is it always easy to distinguish between liability for publication and the defences that are available for those who publish on the internet or allow material to remain online.[354] Broadly speaking, where an internet intermediary knows or ought reasonably to be aware of the content of the article complained of, though not necessarily of its defamatory nature as a matter of law, and has a realistic ability to control publication of such content, the intermediary is a main or primary publisher of such content.[355] Where an internet intermediary merely "facilitates" access to websites provided by others by, for example, providing the computer systems through which communications happen to pass on their route from one computer to another, there is no publication.[356] Where an internet intermediary hosts a website and has not received notification of the defamatory material then it is 21-66

---

[348] *Sharpe v Skues* (1909) 25 T.L.R. 336; *Powell v Gelston* [1916] 2 K.B. 615.

[349] *Sharpe v Skues* (1909) 25 T.L.R. 336. Similarly, where the libel was sent in an unsealed envelope and the plaintiff's butler read it out of curiosity, it was held that there was no evidence of publication by the defendant, for there was no evidence that he knew of the likelihood of his letter being opened by the butler or anyone else but the claimant: *Huth v Huth* [1915] 3 K.B. 32; cf. also *R. v Adams* (1882) 22 Q.B.D. 66.

[350] [2015] EWHC 563 (QB).

[351] *Lord McAlpine of West Green v Bercow* [2013] EWHC 1342 (QB); *Monroe v Hopkins* [2017] EWHC 433 (QB); [2017] 4 W.L.R. 68.

[352] *Stocker v Stocker* [2019] UKSC 17; [2019] 2 W.L.R. 1033; the point on liability for Facebook posts was directly addressed in the first instance judgment at [2016] EWHC 474 (QB).

[353] See Gatley, on Libel and Slander (12th edn) Ch. 6.

[354] For defences see para.21-174 onwards.

[355] *Tamiz v Google Inc* [2013] EWCA Civ 68; [2013] 1 W.L.R. 2151; but see *Oriental Press Group Ltd v Fevaworks Solutions Ltd* [2013] HKFCA 47; and *Gatley on Libel and Slander* (12th edn), para.6.29, above ("the applicable principles for internet publications").

[356] *Bunt v Tilley* [2006] EWHC 407 (QB); [2007] 1 W.L.R. 1243.

neither the primary or secondary publisher of the material complained of.[357] Where an internet intermediary that hosts a website is notified of the defamatory postings, it is to be treated as a publisher if it fails to disable access to, or take down the material, once it has had reasonable time to do so.[358] However, all these points address whether a host or facilitator is prima facie liable. In addition to being able to avail themselves of all the general defences to a defamation claim, internet service providers gain additional protection from the Electronic Commerce (EC Directive) Regulations 2002, implementing an EU Directive,[359] s.1 of the Defamation Act 1996[360] and ss.5 and 10 of the Defamation Act 2013.[361] Though the Defamation Act 1996 s.1 and the Electronic Commerce (EC Directive) Regulations 2002 may also apply to an "operator of a website", the Defamation Act 2013 s.5, read together with the Defamation (Operators of Website Regulations) 2013, provides an additional defence where the operator can show that it was not the operator who posted the statement on the website.[362] Not imposing liability on the host of an internet forum for anonymous comments is not a breach of art.8 of the European Convention on Human Rights.[363]

6. DEFENCES

21-67 **Defences** When a claimant has proved against the defendant a publication of matter which is defamatory of him, and has overcome the "serious harm" test at s.1 of the Defamation Act 2013, he has established his case, and the burden of proof switches to the defendant to prove any defence which he has pleaded. The Defamation Act 2013 put common law defences of justification (i.e. truth), fair comment (now honest opinion) and *Reynolds* privilege on a statutory footing. It also extended the categories of privilege and added new defences relating to peer-reviewed journals and website operators. This section will deal with each defence, first the common law version and then the changes made by the Defamation Act 2013. The common law remains important in interpreting the statutory defences, despite the explicit abolition of those defences by the Act. The Act builds on the base of the common law, and the common law is likely to continue to be referred to by judges interpreting the new provisions. The Defamation Act 2013 also introduced a new defence relating to operators of websites (s.5). This will be dealt with, together with the defences under the Electronic Commerce (EC Directive) Regulations 2002 ("the E-Commerce Regulations") with which the s.5 defence overlaps. An overlap also exists between these defences and the question of whether a website operator can be considered to be a "publisher" of the defamatory material.[364] The main defences usually relied upon are: (1) justification (truth); (2) privilege which may be (a)

---

[357] *Tamiz v Google Inc* [2013] EWCA Civ 68; [2013] 1 W.L.R. 2151. As the editors of *Gatley on Libel and Slander* (12th edn) point out that this would appear to sweep away the common law rule that liability is strict and was rejected in the HKFCA in *Oriental Press Group Ltd v Fevaworks Solutions Ltd* [2013] HKFCA 47.

[358] *Tamiz v Google Inc* [2013] EWCA Civ 68; [2013] 1 W.L.R. 2151.

[359] See paras 21-176 to 21-179.

[360] See para.21-175.

[361] See paras 21-180 to 21-181.

[362] See paras 21-180 to 21-181.

[363] *Høiness v Norway* (Application no. 43624/14) (2019) 69 E.H.R.R. 19.

[364] See paras 21-66 and 21-174 to 21-180.

absolute; or (b) qualified; (3) publication on a matter of public interest (previously *Reynolds* privilege); (4) honest opinion.

(a) Justification/Truth

(i) *Justification under the common law*

Justification[365] It is a complete defence to an action for defamation for the defendant to plead justification, that is, that the statement is true. The defence is available in relation to both facts and opinions, where those opinions are capable of being said to be either true or false. The court must consider whether the meaning has been shown to be substantially true, bearing in mind the balance to be struck between free speech and private rights.[366] The burden of proof is on the defendant. Where evidence that would support a plea of justification comes to the defendant's knowledge well after the commencement of proceedings, he may be allowed to amend his defence to include such a plea, but his conduct in entering a plea of justification at a late stage will be subject to a careful investigation by the court,[367] and the more serious the nature of the allegation the more clearly satisfied the court must be that no prejudice is caused to the claimant which cannot be remedied by monetary compensation.[368] The court will balance the public interest in ensuring that it determines the proper issues and that the claimant is not given a false vindication against the stress, inconvenience and delay for a claimant in a defamation claim, faced by a late amendment. It has been said that a plea of justification should not be entered until the defendant has clear evidence to support such a defence.[369] However the court should not strike out a defence of justification except in cases where the defence clearly cannot be supported by the evidence.[370] Also, only in clear cases will an unsuccessful defendant be allowed to adduce fresh evidence to support a plea of justification when he has not attempted to obtain that evidence before the trial of the action.[371] 21-68

(1) Meaning to be proved true

The meaning that must be proved to be true The meaning of the defamatory statement is a theme which runs through the whole of defamation law and, in 21-69

[365] There is a general rule that no interlocutory injunction will be granted against a defendant who pleads justification unless the defence has no reasonable prospects of success. See *Greene v Associated Newspapers Ltd* [2004] EWCA Civ 1462; [2005] Q.B. 972; *Bonnard v Perryman* [1891] 2 Ch. 269; *Crest Homes v Ascott* [1980] F.S.R. 396 CA; *Herbage v Times Newspapers Ltd, The Times,* 1 May 1981 CA, and para.21-252.

[366] *Cruddas v Calvert* [2013] EWHC 2298 (QB) at [54]–[56].

[367] *Associated Leisure Ltd v Associated Newspapers Ltd* [1970] 2 Q.B. 450 CA; see also *London Computer Operators v BBC* [1973] 1 W.L.R. 424 CA (late amendment of particulars of justification); *Atkinson v Fitzwalter* [1987] 1 W.L.R. 201 CA; *Mackenzie v Business Magazines, The Times,* 5 March 1996; cited with approval in *Tancic v Times Newspapers Ltd, The Times,* 12 January 2000 CA. See also *Al Rajhi Banking and Investment Corp v Wall Street Journal Europe Sprl* [2003] EWHC 1358 (QB).

[368] *Atkinson v Fitzwalter* [1987] 1 W.L.R. 201.

[369] *Associated Leisure Ltd v Associated Newspapers Ltd* [1970] 2 Q.B. 450 at 456, per Lord Denning MR.

[370] *McDonald's Corp v Steel* [1995] 3 All E.R. 615.

[371] *Williams v Reason* [1988] 1 W.L.R. 96 CA. The rules in *Ladd v Marshall* [1954] 1 W.L.R. 1489 governing fresh evidence sought to be adduced on appeal will generally apply.

particular, the defence of truth/justification.[372] The fundamental principle is that the defence will not succeed if the meaning that is proved to be true is a materially less serious meaning than that which the words are held to bear. Defendants are free to plead so as to justify "any reasonable meaning of the words published which a jury, properly directed, might find to be the real meaning".[373] However, particulars of justification must indicate unambiguously the meaning, or meanings, which the defendant seeks to justify and give details of the matters on which he or she relies in support of that allegation.[374] The removal of the presumption of the right to a jury trial by s.11 of the Defamation Act 2013 allows a judge to make a determination on meaning at an early stage. This should mean that only defences of truth directed towards the actual meaning of the words complained of reach trial.[375] Judges have referred to the benefits of deciding meaning at an early stage in the cases which have been brought since the coming into force of the Defamation Act 2013.[376]

21-70 **Investigations: three tiers of meaning** In cases involving an investigation by the police or other authorities it has become common for the courts to define three levels of defamatory meaning of descending gravity which are referred to as "*Chase*" levels of meaning. A "level one" meaning is that the claimant is guilty of the misconduct that is the subject of the investigation. A "level two" meaning is that a person is reasonably suspected of being guilty of the misconduct. A "level three" meaning is that there are reasonable grounds to enquire or investigate whether a person is guilty of misconduct. In *Travel Insurance Facilities Plc (t/a Tifgroup) v Times Newspapers Plc* Jay J found what he called a level one and a half meaning.[377] If there is potential for a jury trial the judge should only exclude a meaning where it would be perverse for a jury to conclude that it was the meaning of the article.[378]

21-71 **"Grounds to suspect" meanings** In *Chase v News Group Newspapers Ltd*,[379] the claimant, a nurse, sued the defendants for allegations that health service officials had gone to the police and told them that she was suspected of having killed a number of seriously ill children in her care. The defendants pleaded justification and the court had to decide what was the "sting" of the words in question. The Court of Appeal gave a comprehensive summary of the rules relating to justification, especially where the allegation complained of amounts to a statement that a claim-

372 *Foley v Ashcroft* [2012] EWCA Civ 423; [2012] E.M.L.R. 25.

373 *Prager v Times Newspapers Ltd* [1988] 1 W.L.R. 77 at 86. The Court of Appeal in *Lucas-Box v Associated Newspaper Group* [1986] 1 W.L.R. 147 held that, whatever the previous practice, a defendant pleading justification "must make it clear to the claimant what is the case which he is seeking to set up". For examples of *Lucas-Box* meanings going beyond the meaning complained of by the defendant, see *Carlton Communications Group v News Group Newspapers Ltd; Cook v News Group Newspapers Ltd* [2001] EWCA Civ 1644; [2002] E.M.L.R. 16 CA.

374 CPR Pt 53 PD 11, *Lucas-Box v Associated Newspaper Group* [1986] 1 W.L.R. 147 at 153. See *Lim v Lawless*, *The Independent*, 23 August 1991 CA, but actions for libel should not depend on tactics: see *Polly Peck (Holdings) Plc v Trelford* [1986] Q.B. 1000 at 1021; *Control Risks Ltd v New English Library Ltd* [1990] 1 W.L.R. 183 CA.

375 This builds on a trend already apparent from the case law, for example *Lord McAlpine of West Green v Bercow* [2013] EWHC 1342 (QB). See para.21-31.

376 See for example *Ames v The Spamhaus Project Ltd* [2015] EWHC 127 (QB); [2015] 1 W.L.R. 3409; *Lachaux v Independent Print Ltd* [2015] EWHC 620 (QB).

377 [2019] EWHC 1337 (QB).

378 *Jameel v Wall Street Journal Europe SPRL* [2005] EWCA Civ 74; [2005] Q.B. 904 at [14].

379 [2002] EWCA Civ 1772; [2003] E.M.L.R. 11.

ant is suspected of serious crime, namely: (1) "the conduct rule"[380]—that where the defendant states that there are reasonable grounds for the suspicion, there must be some conduct of the defendant to give rise to that suspicion; (2) the "repetition rule"—that a suspicion based on hearsay will not, as a rule, be enough[381]; and (3) that a defendant cannot rely, by way of justification, on events occurring subsequently to the occasion when the reasonable suspicion was alleged. The Court of Appeal held that these rules are not incompatible with art.10 of the ECHR. However, it did qualify the strictness of the rules in two material ways. First, strong circumstantial evidence implicating a claimant may afford reasonable grounds to suspect[382] even if it does not directly focus on some conduct of the claimant, but the opinions of those who carried out an investigation into the claimant are not "circumstantial evidence" and no conclusion about the claimant's conduct could be inferred from their opinions.[383] Secondly, the admissibility of hearsay is now generally permitted under the Civil Evidence Act 1995.[384] Provided the defendant complies with the rules for the admission of hearsay evidence,[385] such evidence may be relied upon to establish a primary fact. The rules make life difficult for defendants in terms of the evidence they are allowed to adduce and the matters that can be put to a claimant in cross-examination. This has meant that whilst there are a number of interim disputes about whether a publication carries a guilt or reasonable grounds to suspect meaning, few cases reach trial where the only issue is whether it is true that there were reasonable grounds to suspect the claimant of the conduct alleged.[386]

Repetition of a defamatory statement A defendant may not rely on the fact that he is merely repeating a defamatory statement made by another in order to avoid liability. The defendant must prove the truth of the substance of the meaning of the underlying allegation, it is not sufficient to prove that the allegation was made by another.[387] Hearsay evidence is permitted,[388] but it must go to prove the truth of the primary facts.[389] Where part of the publication complained of consists of repeated statements which are protected by privilege (e.g. repetition of statements made in the course of parliamentary proceedings), the repetition rule is disapplied in determining the overall meaning of the publication.[390] **21-72**

General and specific allegations Difficulties can arise when determining whether **21-73**

380 On which see *King v Telegraph Group Ltd* [2003] EWHC 1312 (QB) (on appeal at [2004] EWCA Civ 613; [2005] 1 W.L.R. 2282), in which Eady J sets out what have become known as the "Musa King principles"; and *Miller v Associated Newspapers Ltd* [2014] EWCA Civ 39 in which the Court of Appeal affirmed the Musa King principles.

381 See para.21-72.

382 See *King v Telegraph Group Ltd* [2003] EWHC 1312 (QB).

383 *Miah v BBC* [2018] EWHC 1054 (QB).

384 For the use of hearsay evidence in the context of a reasonable grounds to suspect defence see *Miller v Associated Newspapers* [2014] EWCA Civ 39 at [31]–[40].

385 See under CPR Pt 33.

386 For a rare example of a "reasonable grounds to suspect" defence succeeding at trial, see *Rothschild v Associated Newspapers Ltd* [2013] EWCA Civ 197; [2013] E.M.L.R. 18. However, the defence was unsuccessful in *Miller v Associated Newspapers Ltd* [2014] EWCA Civ 39, which highlighted the evidential difficulties defendants may face in complying with the conduct rule.

387 *Stern v Piper* [1997] Q.B. 123; *Shah v Standard Chartered Bank* [1999] Q.B. 241 CA.

388 See para.21-71.

389 See further *Gatley on Libel & Slander* (12th edn), para.11.13.

390 *Curistan v Times Newspapers Ltd* [2008] EWCA Civ 432; [2009] Q.B. 231.

an allegation is of a general or specific nature. In *Bookbinder v Tebbit*[391] the defendant attacked the expenditure involved in the decision of the claimant to overprint "Derbyshire is a nuclear free zone" on Derbyshire County Council notepaper. The claimant was the Labour leader of the Council. In his justification defence, the defendant cited a large number of other examples of what he considered to be wasted expenditure on the part of the claimant unconnected with the particular allegation in relation to the notepaper. The Court of Appeal held that he would not be permitted to do so. The words were held to be incapable of bearing a general meaning that the claimant habitually wasted taxpayer's money and the defendant was therefore limited to proving the truth of the specific allegation concerning the notepaper.[392] *Williams v Reason*[393] was a case that went the other way. The claimant complained about an article in the Sunday Telegraph which suggested that he had infringed his status as an amateur rugby footballer by receiving cash payments, giving a number of examples. The defendants sought to prove the truth of other allegations of abuse of amateur status which had not been referred to in the article. The Court of Appeal held in this case that the words were capable of being understood as a general charge against the claimant to the effect that he was a "shamateur", i.e. someone who pretends to be an amateur. It followed that the justification defence could refer to any alleged examples of "shamateurism" in order to support the general charge. It is usually the defendant who seeks to allege that the words are capable of bearing a general meaning, particularly where he or she cannot prove the truth of the specific allegation. Where the defendant seeks to prove a general allegation he must prove the truth of a sufficient number of discreditable acts to justify the general charge. The Court of Appeal set out some general principles to be derived from the case law in *Rothschild v Associated Newspapers Ltd*[394]: (1) a justification defence will run if the defendant shows that what he has alleged is substantially true; (2) a libel cannot be justified by proof of misconduct on the claimant's part which is unconnected with the accusation complained of; (3) however a defendant is entitled to justify a common sting derived from parts of a publication, taken as a whole; (4) an instance of common sting justification arises where a general charge is justified by proved examples, even where the published example is unproved; but (5) in such a case the sting of the instance or instances which are proved must in essence be as sharp as the published, unproved libel. However, Eady J (concurring) expressed doubt as to whether principle (5) is necessary in exemplar cases.[395] In *Building Register Ltd v Weston*[396] the defendant's more general particulars of alleged mis-selling by the claimant did not engage with the precise sting of a specific allegation of "duping" the defendant into entering into an online contract by leading him to inadvertently click on a tab which was then claimed to be an electronic signature. Therefore, the general particulars could not justify the specific allegation.

391 [1989] 1 W.L.R. 640 CA.

392 In fact the claimant in his original statement of claim alleged that the words bore the general meaning that he wasted public funds. However he amended it to plead the specific allegation and then successfully struck out the defendant's plea to the general allegation.

393 [1988] 1 W.L.R. 96.

394 [2013] EWCA Civ 197; [2013] E.M.L.R. 18 at [24] per Laws LJ.

395 [2013] EWCA Civ 197; [2013] E.M.L.R. 18 at [56].

396 [2014] EWHC 2361 (QB).

(2) Facts to be proved substantially true

Facts alleged must be substantially true The general rule is that the defendant must prove the truth of the defamatory sting of the publication[397] but he need not prove the literal truth of every fact which he has stated. It is enough if he prove the substantial truth of every material fact. Where the charge against the claimant is general in its nature the defendant may give particulars of facts occurring within a reasonable time after the publication of the libel which go to show the existence of a tendency or character such as the claimant is alleged in the libel to possess, since the law will not allow a person to recover damages for injury to a character he is not in fact entitled to.[398] A defendant may justify an article as substantially true where the defendant cannot justify the specific meaning, but can justify the general meaning, as long as the words complained of are capable of carrying the broader imputation of misconduct.[399] 21-74

Interpretation of regulations or other documents Where the success or failure of a plea of justification turns on the interpretation of regulations or other legal documents it is for the judge to determine the true meaning of the regulations.[400] 21-75

Evidence of commission of a criminal offence Section 12 of the Defamation Act 1996 amended s.13 of the Civil Evidence Act 1968.[401] The rule is that where there is in issue whether or not the claimant committed any criminal offence, proof that the claimant has been convicted of the offence before a court in the UK[402] is to be conclusive evidence of commission of the offence. Section 13(2A)(b) of the Civil Evidence Act 1968, inserted by the Defamation Act 1996, states that in a case in which there is more than one claimant: 21-76

> "proof that any of the plaintiffs stands convicted of an offence shall be conclusive evidence that he committed the offence so far as that fact is relevant to any issue arising in relation to his cause of action or that of any other plaintiff."

Complaint of only certain parts of a statement When the claimant complains only of certain parts of an article or statement which contains in essence charges that are not clearly severable and distinct, the judge may look at the whole article to ascertain whether it is defamatory. In bringing forward evidence to prove the truth 21-77

---

397 cf. *Beevis v Dawson* [1957] 1 Q.B. 195; *Truth (NZ) Ltd v Holloway* [1960] 1 W.L.R. 997. As to the possibility of the claimant postponing giving evidence himself in rebuttal of the defendant's charges until after the defendant's evidence, and the discretion of the court in such cases, see *Beevis v Dawson* [1957] 1 Q.B. 195 CA.

398 See e.g.: *Maisel v Financial Times Ltd* [1915] 3 K.B. 336; *McGrath v Black* (1926) 95 L.J.K.B. 951. Note however that no such facts are admissible where the allegation sought to be justified is that there were grounds to suspect the claimant of any disreputable conduct—see discussion of the "conduct" rule at para.21-71.

399 See *Rothschild v Associated Newspapers Ltd* [2013] EWCA Civ 197; [2013] E.M.L.R. 18; and also *Warren v Random House Group Ltd* [2008] EWCA Civ 834; [2009] Q.B. 600.

400 Thus in *Williams v Reason* [1988] 1 W.L.R. 96, where the alleged libel was in essence a charge of "shamateurism" against a rugby player, the trial judge's failure to direct the jury conclusively on the interpretation of regulations of the Rugby Union prohibiting payments to amateurs, save in prescribed circumstances, constituted grounds for a new trial.

401 See *Levene v Roxhan* [1970] 1 W.L.R. 1323 CA (attempt to strike out statement of claim as an abuse of the process of the court where one of the allegations related to an offence of which the claimant had been convicted).

402 Or, in the case of a service offence, a conviction anywhere of that service offence.

of the statement the defendant will not be limited to the parts of which the claimant has chosen to complain.[403] The defendant will succeed if he can prove the truth of the meaning that the statement bears as a whole. The Court of Appeal offered the following guidance on when a defendant may be permitted to introduce evidence relating to allegations of which the claimant does not complain, in order to justify the "sting" of the libel in *Polly Peck (Holdings) Plc v Trelford*[404]:

(1) When the claimant complains not only of the ordinary meaning of selected parts of a statement of article but also seeks to establish further inferential meanings, i.e. a "false" innuendo:

> "the defendant is entitled to look at the whole publication in order to aver that in their context the words bear a meaning different to that alleged by the claimants. The defendants are entitled to plead that the words are true and give particulars of the facts and matters he relies on. ... It is fortuitous that some or all of those facts and matters are culled from parts of the publications of which the claimant has not chosen to complain."[405]

(2) When several defamatory allegations have a common sting so that they are not to be regarded as separate and distinct, the defendants are entitled to justify the sting with reference to parts of the publication not complained of by the defendant.

Identifying when the "sting" of a libel is such as to render allegations not separate and distinct but part and parcel of a common charge against the claimant is a difficult question of fact and degree.[406] Care must be taken that the defendant is not allowed to plead facts in partial justification only which do not meet the whole sting of the libel.[407] And the Court of Appeal has warned that it is:

> "the duty of the court to see that the defendant, in particularising a plea of justification or fair comment does not act oppressively. Whether the particularisation of the plea is oppressive depends not only on the facts of the case but also on the attitude of the claimant ... because a claimant can limit the extent and cost of the inquiry at trial by making timely admissions of fact."[408]

In *Cruise v Express Newspapers*[409] the claimants, well-known film actors, sued in respect of articles in the defendants' newspaper which contained damaging allegations about the claimants' private life. The defendants pleaded justification but the Court of Appeal held that where the claimants sued in respect of an article containing two separate and distinct stings and the claimants complained of one of the stings, the defendants could not by way of justification rely on pleas of fair comment and justification in relation to the other sting. On the other hand, in *Rothschild*

---

403 *S & K Holdings Ltd v Throgmorton Publications Ltd* [1972] 1 W.L.R. 1036 CA (see judgment of Edmund-Davies LJ on the difficulty of deciding if charges are severable), and see para.21-73.

404 [1986] Q.B. 1000; and see *Khashoggi v IPC Magazines Ltd* [1986] 1 W.L.R. 1412 CA; *Mintoff v Associated Newspapers Group Plc, The Times*, 26 April 1989 CA; *Kelly v Special Broadcasting Service* [1990] V.R. 69.

405 [1986] Q.B. 1000 at 1032.

406 The receipt of boot money was held to be evidence capable of justifying an allegation of "shamateurism" resting mainly on allegations relating to payments allegedly improperly received by an amateur sportsman for writing a book: *Williams v Reason* [1988] 1 W.L.R. 96 CA.

407 *Prager v Times Newspapers Ltd* [1988] 1 W.L.R. 77.

408 *Polly Peck (Holdings) Plc v Trelford* [1986] Q.B. 1000 at 1032, per O'Connor LJ.

409 [1999] 1 W.L.R. 327.

v Associated Newspapers Ltd[410] the court found the words complained of to bear both a general and a specific meaning. The defendant had proved facts which were exemplars of the general meaning, and although it could not prove the facts relating to the specific meaning (which was also an exemplar of the general meaning), this was sufficient for the justification defence to succeed, as the claimant had no more reputation to lose in relation to the specific incident referred to in the words complained of. The claimant in *Prince Al Saud v Forbes LLC*[411] was entitled to confine his claim to a narrow allegation that concerned defaulting on contractual payments, even though the article undoubtedly did also bear the wider meanings pleaded by the defendant.

(ii) Truth under s.2 of the Defamation Act 2013

Defamation Act 2013 s.2 The Defamation Act 2013 abolishes the defence of justification and creates a statutory defence of truth. It provides: 21-78

> "**2.** Truth
>
> (1) It is a defence to an action for defamation for the defendant to show that the imputation conveyed by the statement complained of is substantially true.
>
> (2) Subsection (3) applies in an action for defamation if the statement complained of conveys two or more distinct imputations.
>
> (3) If one or more of the imputations is not shown to be substantially true, the defence under this section does not fail if, having regard to the imputations which are shown to be substantially true, the imputations which are not shown to be substantially true do not seriously harm the claimant's reputation.
>
> (4) The common law defence of justification is abolished and, accordingly, section 5 of the Defamation Act 1952 (justification) is repealed."

The defence is intended to reflect in statutory language the pre-existing common law defence, whilst removing the potentially confusing terminology of "justification." The use of the word "imputation" rather than "words complained of" is also said by the Explanatory Notes to incorporate the repetition rule in statutory form. The thinking behind the Explanatory Notes would appear to be that the following two statements necessarily convey the same imputation: "X said Y is a murderer" and "Y is a murderer." That this is so will not always be clear.[412] In *Lachaux v Independent Print Ltd*[413] the Supreme Court confirmed that the repetition rule does indeed survive the coming into force of the Act. Subsections 2 and 3 are intended to replace s.5 of the Defamation Act 1952 and appear likely to continue the position as described at para.21-74, such that is it only necessary to prove the substantial truth of the implication (i.e. the meaning), rather than the truth of every fact cited in the publication complained of; and that a defence with multiple meanings will not fail if the truth defence does not succeed in relation to one or more of those meanings if those meanings taken alone do not cause serious harm to the claimant's reputation. Indeed, the Explanatory Notes cite *Chase v News Group Newspapers Ltd*[414] in this regard.

The abolition of justification Subsection 2(4) abolishes the common law defence 21-79

---

410 [2013] EWCA Civ 197; [2013] E.M.L.R. 18.
411 [2014] EWHC 3823 (QB).
412 See further para.21-28.
413 [2019] UKSC 27; [2020] A.C. 612.
414 [2002] EWCA Civ 1772; [2003] E.M.L.R. 11.

of justification. The scope of this abolition remains to be determined by the court, as some rules referred to above, might be said to be part of the law of justification, or alternatively, part of the law on meaning. Other rules which more clearly appear to be part of the law on justification—such as the conduct rule[415]—may be open to revisitation by the court. There is likely to be a degree of uncertainty for a period until matters come before the court. This applies to all the defences which have been abolished and re-constituted in statutory form. In *Lachaux v Independent Print Ltd*[416] Sir David Eady found that the principle in *Polly Peck (Holdings) Plc v Trelford*[417] survives the abolition of the common law defence of justification.

(iii) Rehabilitation of Offenders Act 1974

21-80 **The Rehabilitation of Offenders Act 1974** This Act provides that after a specified rehabilitation period, persons convicted of offences and sentenced, within the limits of s.5, shall become rehabilitated persons and for the purposes of the Act their convictions shall be spent. The effect of this provision is that generally a rehabilitated person must be treated for all purposes in law as a person who has not committed, or been charged with, or prosecuted for, or convicted of, or sentenced for the offence that was the subject of the spent conviction. There are a number of exceptions to this rule including an important modification in relation to actions for defamation concerning a spent conviction (s.8).

21-81 **Publication of matter imputing commission of an offence** When a rehabilitated person brings an action for defamation founded upon the publication of any matter imputing that the claimant has committed, or been charged with, or prosecuted for, or convicted of, or sentenced for an offence that was the subject of a spent conviction, the defendant will not be prevented by the Act from relying on any defence of justification or truth available to him or restricted in the matters he may establish in support of any such defence. However, if the claimant can prove that the publication was made with malice, the defendant will no longer be able to rely on justification/truth. Malice, in this context, is defined as proof that the defendant acted from "some spiteful, irrelevant or improper motive". The onus of establishing such malice rests on the claimant and an interim injunction will generally be refused unless the evidence of malice is so overwhelming that the judge is satisfied that no reasonable jury could be so perverse as to acquit the defendant of such malice.[418] In *KJO v XIM*[419] Eady J considered (obiter) what would be required to succeed in a claim for defamation based on the malicious disclosure of a spent conviction. Such a case in malice would generally be based not on the proposition that the defendant knew the allegations concerning the claimant to be false, but on the contrary, while knowing the words to be true, published them with the dominant motive of injuring the claimant's reputation. This was the alternative ground for advancing malice canvassed by Lord Diplock in *Horrocks v Lowe*.[420] The judge described this as "almost untrodden territory". The judge also considered whether disclosure of a spent conviction could amount to an infringement of the right to

415 See para.21-71.
416 [2015] EWHC 620 (QB).
417 [1986] Q.B. 1000.
418 *Herbage v Pressdram* [1984] 1 W.L.R. 1160 CA.
419 [2011] EWHC 1768 (QB).
420 [1975] A.C. 135.

privacy under art.8 ECHR, or a breach of the principles of the Data Protection Act 1998, observing that such a disclosure could arguably amount to a breach of confidentiality. The defendant will also be entitled to rely on the spent conviction to advance any defence of honest opinion or privilege open to him or to rebut allegations of malice[421] raised against a plea of qualified privilege. If an unsuccessful attempt is made to introduce evidence of a spent conviction, a report of that attempt will not enjoy the privilege otherwise attaching to such reports,[422] unless it is a report of judicial proceedings in a bona fide series of law reports, or published for bona fide educational purposes.[423]

The effect of the Defamation Act 2013 Section 16(1)–(3) of the Defamation Act 2013 amends the Rehabilitation of Offenders Act 1974 such that the references to "justification" are replaced with references to "a defence under section 2 of the Defamation Act 2013", and the reference to "fair comment" is replaced with a reference to "a defence under section 3 of the Defamation Act 2013".[424] Thus the effect of the Act remains the same in relation to the new statutory defences as it was in relation to the common law defences. 21-82

(b) Absolute privilege

Privilege generally The rationale behind the defence of privilege is the recognition that in certain circumstances persons should be free to speak their mind (and others to report on what they say) without fear of being sued, even if what they publish is false and defamatory. Privilege is of two kinds: (1) absolute, which is a complete defence to an action; and (2) qualified, which may be defeated if the claimant can show malice on the part of the defendant. Malice is a term of art meaning a dominant improper motive, and in order to establish it, it is generally necessary to demonstrate that the defendant published the statement knowing it to be false or without caring whether it was true or false, i.e. recklessly.[425] 21-83

Principle of absolute privilege Absolute privilege is given to statements which are judicial, parliamentary, or official. Litigation and public business cannot be carried on without the character of individuals being constantly called in question and to permit a legal remedy to a person who is injured by such statements would endanger freedom of communication in matters where it is vitally necessary. Accordingly, where an occasion is covered by absolute privilege, the law protects those who act in the honest discharge of their legal right or duty, but also those who abuse the opportunity with malicious motive and deliberate untruthfulness to malign others; it is impossible to devise a shield sufficiently broad to cover the former without also including the latter. In determining whether any particular tribunal should be entitled to the protection afforded by absolute privilege, conflicting public interests have to be balanced. A citizen defamed must normally have access to redress but witnesses before tribunals similar to courts of justice must be free to testify 21-84

---

421 As defined in the context of privilege; see para.21-206 onwards.
422 See para.21-127 onwards.
423 See in detail s.8(7); and note *Practice Direction (Crime: Spent Convictions)* [1975] 1 W.L.R. 1065.
424 On which see further para.21-162.
425 Malice is considered further at para.21-206 onwards.

uninhibited by anxiety that subsequent legal action may investigate their motives for performing their public duty.[426]

(i) *Judicial proceedings*

21-85 **Judicial proceedings** With regard to judicial proceedings "neither party, witness, counsel, jury or judge, can be put to answer civilly, or criminally, for words spoken in office".[427] The rule is not confined to actions of defamation but applies whatever cause of action is sought to be derived from what was said or done in judicial proceedings,[428] unless perhaps the gist of the action is an abuse of the process of the court arising from some act or statement in the proceedings,[429] or where the antecedent act was not within the immunity.[430] The authorities are clear, uniform, and conclusive, that no action of slander or libel lies whether against judges, counsel, witnesses, or parties, for words written or spoken in the ordinary course of any proceedings before any court or tribunal recognised by law.[431] This immunity extends to all tribunals exercising functions equivalent to those of an established court of justice and "applies wherever there is an authorised inquiry, which, though not before a court of justice, is before a tribunal which has similar attributes".[432] This doctrine has never been extended further than to courts of justice and to tribunals acting in a similar manner. There is no single test which can

---

426 *Trapp v Mackie* [1979] 1 W.L.R. 377 HL.

427 per Lord Mansfield CJ in *R. v Skinner* (1772) Lofft 55 at 56. As to counsel, see *Munster v Lamb* (1883) 11 Q.B.D. 588; dissenting at 608 from Lord Denman CJ in *Kendillon v Maltby* (1842) Car. & M. 402 at 408, that judges are liable for slanderous language not relevant to the cases before them. As to witnesses, see *Seaman v Netherclift* (1876) 2 C.P.D. 53; cf. *Hargreaves v Bretherton* [1959] 1 Q.B. 45 (no liability in tort for perjury by a witness); the protection of a witness in the box extends to statements made by him in the preparation of a "proof"; *Watson v Jones* [1905] A.C. 480; *Beresford v White* (1914) 30 T.L.R. 591; *Lincoln v Daniels* [1962] 1 Q.B. 237 CA; *Marrinan v Vibart* [1963] 1 Q.B. 528 CA; *Thompson v Turbott* [1962] N.Z.L.R. 298; but see *Roy v Prior* [1971] A.C. 470 HL (action for maliciously procuring an arrest and status of evidence given ex parte). As to fair comment on a statement by a witness in the witness-box, see *Green v Odhams Press Ltd* [1958] 2 Q.B. 275 CA; and see 21 M.L.R. 517.

428 *Marrinan v Vibart* [1963] 1 Q.B. 528 CA; *Hargreaves v Bretherton* [1959] 1 Q.B. 45. However, the immunity no longer applies to barristers *Hall v Simons* [2002] 1 A.C. 615 and expert witnesses: *Jones v Kaney* [2011] UKSC 13; [2011] 2 A.C. 398.

429 See *Roy v Prior* [1971] A.C. 470; *Gregory v Portsmouth City Council* [2000] 1 A.C. 419 at 427; *Iqbal v Mansoor* [2013] EWCA Civ 149; [2013] C.P. Rep. 27.

430 *Singh v Reading Borough Council* [2013] EWCA Civ 909; [2013] 1 W.L.R. 3052.

431 per Kelly CB in *Dawkins v Lord Rokeby* (1873) L.R. 8 Q.B. 255 at 263. The privilege extends to superior and inferior courts, e.g. county court (*Scott v Standfield* (1868) L.R. 3 Ex. 230); bankruptcy registrar (*Ryalls v Leader* (1866) L.R. 1 Ex. 296); coroner (*Thomas v Churton* (1862) 2 B. & S. 475); magistrates in petty sessions (*Law v Llewellyn* [1906] 1 K.B. 487; *Primrose v Waterson* (1902) 4 F. 783, Ct of Sess). *White v Southampton University Hospitals NHS Trust* [2011] EWHC 825 (QB); [2011] Med. L.R. 296 found that the General Medical Council's Fitness to Practise Directorate is a quasi-judicial body; a letter sent by a medical director to the General Medical Council raising concerns about a doctor's probity and conduct was protected by absolute privilege. In *Huda v Wells* [2017] EWHC 2553 (QB); [2018] E.M.L.R. 7 Nicklin J held that complaints to the General Osteopathic Council were protected by absolute privilege as that body is quasi-judicial in nature. In *Mayer v Hoar* [2012] EWHC 1805 (QB) words that had been used in a letter written by a barrister in response to a request for comment by the Bar Standards Board were protected by absolute privilege.

432 per Lord Esher in *Royal Aquarium Society Ltd v Parkinson* [1892] 1 Q.B. 431 at 442; approved *O'Connor v Waldron* [1935] A.C. 76 at 81; *Lincoln v Daniels* [1962] 1 Q.B. 237 (where the authorities are reviewed). Illustrations of such tribunals are: military courts of inquiry (*Dawkins v Lord Rokeby* (1873) L.R. 8 Q.B. 255; *Dawkins v Prince Edward of Saxe-Weimar* (1876) 1 Q.B.D. 499);

conclusively determine whether a particular tribunal does act in a manner sufficiently similar to a court in order to be afforded absolute privilege in respect of its proceedings. Neither the fact that one tribunal is not empowered to take a final decision on the issue within its jurisdiction,[433] nor the fact that another tribunal is directed to conduct its hearing in private,[434] will necessarily prevent either tribunal being entitled to the protection of absolute privilege. The characteristics which the tribunal does share with courts of justice must be examined and a decision made whether the tribunal shows sufficient similarity in its functions and procedures for it to be said that it was "acting ... in a manner as nearly as possible similar to that in which a Court of justice acts in respect of an inquiry before it".[435]

What are judicial proceedings? It is not merely with respect to the hearing in open court that there is absolute privilege, but also with regard to every step taken in the conduct of a judicial proceeding.[436] The privilege will attach to matters incidental to the proceedings which are necessary for the administration of justice—although the test is one of necessity not convenience.[437] For instance, an affidavit filed in support of an interim application,[438] and the report of an official receiver under the Companies Act 1948.[439] But where something is done as a mere preliminary to setting a court in motion there may be no more than a qualified privilege, which may be defeated by proof of malice.[440] In *Daniels v Griffiths*[441] a statement made by the defendant to the parole board about the claimant, a prisoner, was not absolutely privileged. The privilege does not extend to merely administra- **21-86**

---

the disciplinary committee constituted under s.46 of the Solicitors Act 1957 (*Addis v Crocker* [1961] 1 Q.B. 11; see also *Gray v Avadis* [2003] EWHC 1830 (QB); *The Times,* 19 August 2003—letters sent in connection with an investigation by the Office of Supervision of Solicitors); the General Medical Council under the Medical Act 1858 (*Leeson v General Council of Medical Education* (1889) 43 Ch. D. 366 at 379, 383, 386); the Benchers of an Inn of Court (*Lincoln v Daniels* [1962] 1 Q.B. 237 CA; *Marrinan v Vibart* [1963] 1 Q.B. 528 CA); but not the Bar Council for it is the Benchers of the Inns (now the Senate on transfer by the Inns, cf. *S (A Barrister), Re* [1970] 1 Q.B. 160), who exercise the judicial functions of adjudicating on the complaint (*Lincoln v Daniels* [1962] 1 Q.B. 237 CA; *R. v West Yorkshire Coroner Ex p. Smith* [1985] Q.B. 1096 DC). And see *Report of the Committee on the Law of Defamation*, Cmd.7536, para.94.

433 *Trapp v Mackie* [1979] 1 W.L.R. 377 HL (inquiry into the dismissal of a headmaster where the final decision lay not with the commissioner conducting the inquiry but the Secretary of State for Scotland. The House of Lords found that in practice the commissioner's decision would have a major influence on the final decision).

434 *Addis v Crocker* [1961] 1 Q.B. 11; *Lincoln v Daniels* [1962] 1 Q.B. 237.

435 *Royal Aquarium and Summer and Winter Garden Society Ltd v Parkinson* [1982] 1 Q.B. 431 at 432; and see *Trapp v Mackie* [1979] 1 W.L.R. 377 at 383, per Lord Diplock; and contrast *Att-Gen v BBC* [1981] A.C. 303 HL.

436 But see *Roy v Prior* [1971] A.C. 470 HL—the privilege does not prevent an action for malicious prosecution.

437 *Lincoln v Daniels* [1962] 1 Q.B. 237 CA, per Devlin LJ.

438 *Revis v Smith* (1856) 18 C.B. 126; *Henderson v Broomhead* (1859) 4 H. & N. 569; *Gompas v White* (1889) 54 J.P. 23.

439 *Bottomley v Brougham* [1908] 1 K.B. 584; *Burr v Smith* [1909] 2 K.B. 306.

440 *Bank of British North America v Strong* (1876) 1 App. Cas. 307 (notice served on a debtor requiring him to make an assignment of his estate). But a complaint to a constable in the course of giving the claimant in charge has been held absolutely privileged: *Johnson v Evans* (1799) 3 Esp. 32. And see *Szalatnay-Stacho v Fink* [1947] K.B. 1 CA; cf. *Lincoln v Daniels* [1962] 1 Q.B. 237 CA (quaere whether a letter of complaint addressed to the Benchers of an Inn of Court would have more than qualified privilege). The issue of a writ will be protected as far as the parties are concerned, but as to newspapers publishing the contents of a writ, see *Cadam v Beaverbrook Newspapers Ltd* [1959] 1 Q.B. 413; and *Lewis v Daily Telegraph Ltd* [1964] A.C. 234. And see *Roy v Prior* [1971] A.C. 470.

441 [1998] E.M.L.R. 489.

tive proceedings, for example a meeting of the London County Council for the grant of music and dancing licences,[442] or licensing justices,[443] or meetings of a local authority.[444] It makes no difference that the authority in question has power to administer oaths and to summon witnesses.[445] There can be no judicial proceeding where there is nothing before a court with which it has jurisdiction to deal.[446] If a judge while sitting upon the bench delivers a harangue on any topic which he conceives to be of public interest, he does so at his peril. If, however, any application is made which on the face of it is not unfit to be heard, the inquiry then instituted in order to see whether the court has jurisdiction is a judicial proceeding, though the result be to show that there is no jurisdiction to deal with the matter.[447] The absolute privilege will still attach even if there is some unintentional irregularity. Thus where an arrangement by consent was wrongly registered by the solicitor to one of the parties as a judgment of the court and was subsequently set aside, it was held that no action for libel would lie.[448]

21-87 **Consensual conciliation proceedings** Evidence adduced in the course of consensual conciliation proceedings was held not to be adduced in the course of judicial or quasi-judicial proceedings. The object of the proceedings was not to arrive at a judicial determination, so the procedure differed radically from that of a court of law and could not attract absolute privilege.[449] By contrast, a letter sent to the European Commission in connection with competition proceedings did attract such privilege. The procedure adopted by the Commission was admittedly more in the nature of administrative than judicial proceedings in the perception of a common lawyer. But the public interest that the Commission should not be hindered in carrying out its duty to enforce European competition laws outweighed the litigant's private interest in vindicating his reputation.[450]

21-88 **Communications between solicitor and client** Communications between solicitor and client with reference to matters upon which the client is seeking professional advice are, it seems, absolutely privileged provided that the conversation be such as is fairly referable to the relationship of solicitor and client. The mere fact

[442] *Royal Aquarium v Parkinson* [1892] 1 Q.B. 431; cf. *Proctor v Webster* (1885) 16 Q.B.D. 112 (complaint to Privy Council not in its judicial capacity).

[443] *Attwood v Chapman* [1914] 3 K.B. 275; *R. v East Riding Yorkshire QS* [1968] 1 Q.B. 32 CA.

[444] *Standen v South Essex Recorders* (1934) 50 T.L.R. 365. The factors to be considered in deciding whether a tribunal is quasi-judicial within the rule are discussed in *Co-partnership Farms v Harvey-Smith* [1918] 2 K.B. 405 (tribunal under Military Service Act 1916); *Collins v Whiteway* [1972] 2 K.B. 378 (Court of Referees under Unemployment Insurance Act 1920); *O'Connor v Waldron* [1935] A.C. 76; *Mason v Brewis Bros* [1938] 2 All E.R. 420 (letter written to labour exchange); *Addis v Crocker* [1961] 1 Q.B. 11; *Lincoln v Daniels* [1962] 1 Q.B. 237 CA; *Purdew v Seress-Smith* [1993] I.R.L.R. 77 (allegations made to social security officer).

[445] *O'Connor v Waldron* [1935] A.C. 76 PC. And see *Att Gen v BBC* [1981] A.C. 303 HL (status of a local valuation court).

[446] See, per curiam, *Lewis v Levy* (1858) E.B. & E. 537 at 555; *Paris v Levy* (1860) 9 C.B. (N.S.) 342.

[447] *R. v Bolton* (1841) 1 Q.B. 66; per Lord Coleridge CJ in *Usill v Hales* (1878) 3 C.P.D. 319 at 323; approved in *Kimber v Press Association* [1893] 1 Q.B. 65 CA.

[448] *MacCabe v Joynt* [1901] 2 Ir. R. 115; *Barratt v Kearns* [1905] 1 K.B. 504; cf. *Addis v Crocker* [1961] 1 Q.B. 11.

[449] *Tadd v Eastwood* [1985] I.C.R. 132; and see para.21-85.

[450] *Hasselblad (GB) Ltd v Orbinson* [1985] Q.B. 475 CA; *Hasselblad (GB) Ltd v Hodes* [1985] 3 C.M.L.R. 664.

that the person speaking is a solicitor and the person to whom he speaks is his client affords no protection.[451]

Relevancy In any proceeding in court, the judge, advocate, or other person who claims the privilege is protected while acting "in office". He may in the discharge of his function publish matter which is "uncalled for, immaterial, irrelevant, and impertinent",[452] or malicious,[453] and yet not be liable to answer for it. It would seem, however, that the language in order to be privileged, though irrelevant, ought to have some reference to the subject-matter of inquiry; but even this restriction has been treated as open to question: 21-89

> "Suppose, while the witness was in the box, a man were to come in at the door, and the witness were to exclaim, 'that man picked my pocket,' I can hardly think that would be privileged. I can scarcely think a witness would be protected for anything he might say in the witness-box, wantonly and without reference to the inquiry. I do not say he would not be protected. It might be held that it was better that everything a witness said as a witness should be protected, than that witnesses should be under the impression that what they said in the witness-box might subject them to an action."[454]

In *W v Westminster CC*[455] the question was whether absolute privilege applied to communications made in a child protection case conference, by which social workers exchanged information with interested parties concerning child welfare. The judge concluded that it did not, but in doing so also observed that even had absolute privilege been available, it would not have applied to communications which were "irrelevant to the occasion".[456] In *Iqbal v Mansoor*[457] the Court of Appeal confirmed that witness statements made in the course of legal proceedings are prima facie protected by absolute privilege and it is not enough for the defamatory allegations to be irrelevant to the matter in hand for it to fall outside the privilege; it has to have no reference at all to the subject-matter of the proceedings.

Reports of judicial proceedings under the Defamation Act 1996 Section 14 of the Defamation Act 1996, as amended by s.7 of the Defamation Act 2013, provides that absolute privilege applies to fair and accurate contemporaneous reports of court proceedings. This applies even where the defendant knows that what was said in the proceedings was untrue. It will also apply to reports of previous (i.e. non-contemporaneous) proceedings where to do so is necessary to give context to a report of a contemporaneous hearing.[458] The section applies to any UK court including "any tribunal or body exercising the judicial power of the State", any court established under the law of a foreign state and any court or tribunal established by the UN Security Council or by international agreement (including the Court of Justice of the European Union or any court attached to that court, and the European Court of Human Rights). 21-90

---

451 *More v Weaver* [1928] 2 K.B. 520 CA; although see *Clarke v Davey* [2002] EWHC 2342 (QB); *Minter v Priest* [1930] A.C. 558; *Hayward v Wegg-Prosser* (1978) 123 S.J. 792.

452 *Scott v Stansfield* (1868) L.R. 3 Ex. 230.

453 *Tughan v Craig* [1918] 1 Ir. R. 245.

454 per Bramwell LJ in *Seaman v Netherclift* (1876) 2 C.P.D. 53 at 60.

455 [2004] EWHC 2866 (QB); [2005] 1 F.C.R. 39.

456 See also *Taylor v Serious Fraud Office* [1999] 2 A.C. 177 at 214, per Lord Hoffmann.

457 [2013] EWCA Civ 149; [2013] C.P. Rep. 27.

458 *Crossley v Newsquest (Midlands South) Ltd* [2008] EWHC 3054 (QB).

(ii) Parliamentary proceedings

21-91 **Parliamentary proceedings** Everything published in the course of parliamentary proceedings is absolutely privileged.[459] Article 9 of the Bill of Rights states:

> "That the freedom of speech, and of debates or proceedings in Parliament ought not to be impeached or questioned in any court, or any place out of Parliament."

Hence no Member of Parliament could be called on to answer for anything which he says in his place,[460] nor could anything that he said in Parliament be used to support an allegation of malice to rebut the defence of fair comment to statements made outside Parliament.[461] The Houses of Parliament are for certain purposes courts of judicature, and all that passes on such occasions is as fully protected as the proceedings in an ordinary court of law.[462] They receive petitions and distribute among their members documents and papers and into such publications the courts cannot inquire.[463] In *Rost v Edwards*[464] the claimant sued for libel in respect of allegations that he had misused his position as a member of a House of Commons committee and had failed to disclose consultancies in the Register of Members' Interests. The claimant sought to adduce evidence that, as a result of the libel, he had been deselected from the standing committee on the Electricity Bill and had failed to gain the chairmanship of the Select Committee on Energy. It was held that such evidence was covered by parliamentary privilege as it would constitute a direct inquiry into the affairs of the House of Commons. A letter written by a Member of Parliament to the Speaker was similarly covered by parliamentary privilege. The defendants sought in justification to adduce evidence derived from the Register of Members' Interests. Popplewell J found that claims for privilege in respect of the Register of Members' Interests were not within the definition of "proceedings in Parliament". The Privy Council expressed doubt as to this decision in *Television New Zealand v Prebble*[465] where the claimant, a member of the New Zealand Parliament, sued the defendants for libel in a programme which accused him of corrupt or dishonourable conduct when in office. The defendants sought to raise, by way of justification, the claimant's own speeches in Parliament which, they maintained, showed his ministerial conduct to have been misleading and improper. The Privy Council held that art.9 of the Bill of Rights prevented these debates or speeches from be-

---

459 Statements made outside parliament may be covered by qualified privilege but will not enjoy absolute privilege, even if reference is made to earlier privileged statements. See *Jennings v Buchanan* [2004] UKPC 36; [2005] 1 A.C. 115.

460 1 Will. Mar. sess. 2, c.2 (Bill of Rights); *Ex p. Wason* (1869) L.R. 4 Q.B. 573; *Dillon v Balfour* (1887) 20 L.R. Ir. 600; *Dingle v Associated Newspapers* [1961] 2 Q.B. 162, CA; affirmed [1964] A.C. 371. As to a letter by an MP to a Minister as a proceeding in Parliament, see *Re Parliamentary Privilege Act 1770* [1958] A.C. 331, and, as to breach of parliamentary privilege by a threat of proceedings for libel against an MP for writing such a letter; [1958] L.J. 134; *Hansard*, HC Deb. Vol.591, ser.5, cols 208-346 (1957–58).

461 *Church of Scientology of California v Johnson-Smith* [1972] 1 Q.B. 523. Distinguished in *Hyams v Peterson* [1991] 1 N.Z.L.R. 711.

462 *Kane v Mulvaney* (1866) Ir. Rep. 2 C.L. 402 at 415; *Goffin v Donnelly* (1881) 6 Q.B.D. 307.

463 *Lake v King* (1668) 1 Wm. Saund. 120; *Stockdale v Hansard* (1839) 9 A. & E. 1; *Dingle v Associated Newspapers* [1964] A.C. 371; as to petitions, see para.21-144; for a communication not in any way connected with the proceedings of the House, see *Rivlin v Bilainkin* [1953] 1 Q.B. 485; *Church of Scientology of California v Johnson-Smith* [1972] 1 Q.B. 523; *British Railways Board v Pickin* [1974] A.C. 765 HL.

464 [1990] 2 Q.B. 460.

465 [1995] 1 A.C. 321.

ing raised in legal proceedings; the privilege, being absolute, could not be waived by Parliament and it made no difference that the Member of Parliament concerned was the claimant.[466]

Subsequent reference to parliamentary statement In *Makudi v Triesman*[467] the Court of Appeal held that art.9 of the Bill of Rights can protect speech outside Parliament which repeats speech made in Parliament. These instances will be rare, and are likely to occur when: (1) there is a public interest in the repetition of the parliamentary speech; and (2) there is so close a nexus between the occasions of the speaker speaking in, and then out of Parliament, that the prospect of his or her obligation (or expectation or promise) to speak on the second occasion is reasonably foreseeable at the time of the first, and the purpose of the speech is the same or very closely related on both occasions. **21-92**

Defamation Act 1996 s.13 The 21st edition contained a discussion of this provision, which has now been repealed by the Deregulation Act 2015 Sch.23 para.44. The section allowed an individual to waive parliamentary privilege, for example where he wished to sue on an allegation that he accepted cash in return for asking parliamentary questions.[468] The repeal was included in the section of the Deregulation Act dealing with "legislation no longer of practical use", although the issue was relevant, and the implications of the repeal discussed in *Yeo v Times Newspaper Ltd*.[469] **21-93**

The Parliamentary Papers Act At common law there is no parliamentary privilege for publishing defamatory matter to the outside world.[470] However, by the Parliamentary Papers Act 1840,[471] a defendant who is sued for the publication of any papers by the direction of either House or of any copies of such papers, may produce a certificate of his authority verified by affidavit to the court in which the action is proceeding, and thereupon the action shall be stayed.[472] **21-94**

(iii) Official communications

Official communications It is frequently the duty of public servants, both civil and military, to publish matter of a defamatory nature, especially in the confidential **21-95**

---

466 The Privy Council also held, overruling the New Zealand Court of Appeal, that, despite the fact that the defendant's case was damaged by the application of art.9, the proceedings by the claimant should not be stayed—to do so would deny the claimant any chance of vindicating his good name. There were other aspects of the case which did not depend on proof of parliamentary proceedings so the defendants were not deprived of every defence.

467 [2014] EWCA Civ 179; [2014] Q.B. 839.

468 *Hamilton v Al-Fayed (No.1)* [2001] 1 A.C. 395.

469 [2015] EWHC 2132 (QB); [2015] 4 Costs L.R. 687.

470 *R. v Creevy* (1813) 1 M. & S. 273; *Stockdale v Hansard* (1839) 9 A. & E. 1. There may be qualified privilege arising out of the relationship between the member and his constituents for the circulation by a member of his speech to his constituents bona fide for the information of his constituents: *Davison v Duncan* (1857) 7 E. & B. 239; *Wason v Walter* (1868) L.R. 4 Q.B. 73 at 95. As to privilege at elections, see Defamation Act 1952 s.10, para.21-143.

471 Giving absolute privilege and passed in consequence of the decision in *Stockdale v Hansard* (1839) 9 A. & E. 1. By s.3, however, extracts from such papers have only a qualified privilege; *Mangena v Lloyd* (1908) 98 L.T. 640; *Mangena v Wright* [1909] 2 K.B. 958; *Dingle v Associated Newspapers* [1964] A.C. 371.

472 For the common law qualified privilege attaching to reports of parliamentary debates see para.21-123.

reports which in the ordinary course of affairs must be furnished to their superiors. The privilege attaching to such communications is absolute. It has been held that an official report on one of his subordinates, furnished by a general to his superiors, is privileged, though made maliciously.[473] There were two grounds for this, one applying only to military and naval affairs, the other to the public service generally: (1) no one serving in Her Majesty's forces can, in respect of any matter of discipline or question affecting his military status, appeal to any other jurisdiction than that which is created by the military law to which he has voluntarily submitted himself[474]; (2) as a matter of public policy officers of the army, just as Ministers of the Crown, should make their official communications without any possible fear of consequences before them.[475] On this latter principle it has been held that communication made by a Secretary of State to his parliamentary Under-Secretary in the course of his official duty cannot be made the subject of an action for libel.[476] The fact that a communication relates to commercial matters does not of itself preclude it from being one relating to state matters and therefore absolutely privileged.[477] It has been doubted whether absolute privilege for communications between officers of state extends below communications on the ministerial level.[478] In *Hasselblad (GB) Ltd v Orbinson*[479] the Court of Appeal held that communications with the European Commission relating to the enforcement of competition proceedings should be afforded absolute privilege. In *Mahon v Rahn (No.2)*[480] absolute privilege was held to apply to a report which the defendant bankers had provided to the TSA in the course of their investigations into fraud and also to the SFO which had initiated an unsuccessful prosecution against the claimants for fraud.[481]In *Lonsdale v National Westminster Bank Plc*[482] Karen Steyn QC (sitting as a Deputy High Court Judge) held that absolute privilege did not to extend to a report by the defendant bank to the National Crime Agency, although qualified privilege was said to apply. This decision, however, appears not to have taken account of an earlier High Court case which considered similar issues in respect of a complaint to police, and in respect of which absolute privilege was held to apply.[483]

21-96 **Communications between foreign officials** It has been a matter of some dispute as to when, if at all, communications between officials of foreign governments

473 *Dawkins v Lord Paulet* (1869) L.R. 5 Q.B. 94.

474 See *Sutton v Johnstone* (1785) 1 T.R. 493; *Re Mansergh* (1861) 1 B. & S. 400; *Dawkins v Lord Rokeby* (1875) 7 H.L. 744.

475 per Mellor J, in *Dawkins v Lord Paulet* (1869) L.R. 5 Q.B. 94 at 117; *Adam v Ward* [1917] A.C. 309.

476 *Chatterton v Secretary of State for India* [1895] 2 Q.B. 189; *Grant v Secretary of State for India* (1877) 2 C.P.D. 445; *Fayed v Al-Tajir* [1988] Q.B. 712 CA.

477 *Isaacs v Cook* [1925] 2 K.B. 391 (official report by High Commissioner for Australia in UK to Prime Minister of Australia); *Peerless Bakery Ltd v Watts* [1955] N.Z.L.R. 339.

478 In first instance in *Szalatnay-Stacho v Fink* [1946] 1 All E.R. 303, per Henn Collins J (this point was not considered in the Court of Appeal. [1947] K.B. 1); and see *Richards v Naum* [1967] 1 Q.B. 620 CA; *Peerless Bakery Ltd v Watts* [1955] N.Z.L.R. 339. But see *Multigroup Bulgaria Holdings v Oxford Analytica Ltd* [2001] E.M.L.R. 28.

479 [1985] Q.B. 475 CA.

480 [2000] 1 W.L.R. 2150.

481 See also *Taylor v Director of the Serious Fraud Office* [1999] 2 A.C. 177; and *Westcott v Westcott* [2008] EWCA Civ 818; [2009] Q.B. 407.

482 [2018] EWHC 1843 (QB); [2019] Lloyd's Rep. F.C. 94.

483 See *Westcott v Westcott* [2008] EWCA Civ 818; [2009] Q.B. 407 and the cases cited earlier in this paragraph.

should be afforded absolute rather than qualified privilege. In *Fayed v Al-Tajir*[484] the Court of Appeal held that an inter-departmental memorandum, prepared by the defendant who was ambassador at his country's London embassy, and criticising the claimant, a national of that state, should be afforded absolute privilege. The public interest, arising from the comity of nations, that the UK should not meddle in the affairs of a foreign sovereign required the English court to refrain from investigating such a document. The privilege thus afforded was a consequence of separate and independent grounds of public policy related to international relations and based in part on the provisions in art.24 of the Vienna Convention on Diplomatic Relations requiring inviolability of embassy documents.[485] Hence communications between embassy officials of a subordinate rank might well be the subject of such privilege, when equivalent officials in the UK would be of too lowly a status to attract such protection.[486] Furthermore, the judgment in *Fayed v Al-Tajir* leaves uncertain the degree of privilege afforded to officers of a foreign power not serving as diplomats in an embassy in the UK. Communications between such officials, if they do not attract absolute privilege, will at least be protected by qualified privilege.[487]

Statutory absolute privilege A variety of statutory provisions confer absolute privilege on reports, statements etc of persons and bodies performing investigative or regulatory functions. The details and scope of such provisions vary.[488] One example is s.10(5) of the Parliamentary Commissioner Act 1967, which gives absolute privilege to reports by the Commissioner to either House of Parliament, and to the publication of various matters to and by the Commissioner, his officers, and Members of Parliament for the purposes of the Act. 21-97

(c) Qualified privilege

(i) Principles

Nature and definition The main difference between qualified privilege and absolute privilege is that if the privilege is qualified it may be defeated on proof of malice. The law recognises that the occasion of the communication is such as to warrant some protection from a claim in defamation, although the occasion is not such as to require the protection of absolute privilege. "Qualified privilege" has been defined by Lord Atkinson in *Adam v Ward*[489] as follows: 21-98

> "A privileged occasion is, in reference to qualified privilege, an occasion where the person who makes the communication has an interest or a duty, legal, social or moral, to make it to the person to whom it is made, and the person to whom it is so made has a corresponding interest or duty to receive it. This reciprocity is essential."

Unreasonable use of privileged occasion Once it is ruled that the occasion is privileged and that the matter complained of has reference to the occasion, the only 21-99

484 [1988] Q.B. 712.
485 *Fayed v Al-Tajir* [1988] Q.B. 712 at 732, 735.
486 *Fayed v Al-Tajir* [1988] Q.B. 712 at 732, although they would likely still attract qualified privilege.
487 *Purdew v Seress-Smith* [1993] I.R.L.R. 77. See also *Komarek v Ramco Energy Plc*, unreported 21 November 2002.
488 See *Gatley on Libel and Slander* (12th edn) at 13.50 for a list of such provisions as at June 2013.
489 [1917] A.C. 309 at 334.

remaining question for consideration is whether the occasion was used without malice.[490] In *Clark v Molyneux*[491] it was held that on the question of malice, the burden of proof lies with the claimant[492]:

> "I apprehend the moment the judge rules that the occasion is privileged, the burden of showing that the defendant did not act in respect of the reason of the privilege, but for some other and indirect reason, is thrown on the claimant."[493]

So a local councillor did not lose the privilege afforded him at a meeting of the council when he made defamatory statements concerning another councillor honestly believing that what he said was true, albeit that he spoke in immoderate terms and was strongly prejudiced against the claimant.[494] In *Fraser v Mirza*[495] the defender's statement, made on an occasion of qualified privilege, was intended to convey a defamatory allegation in the truth of which he did not believe. The House of Lords held that on a proper construction, the statement did not bear that defamatory meaning. Nevertheless if the statement were found to have a lesser (though still defamatory) meaning, the defence of qualified privilege was lost because the defendant had misused the occasion of the privilege.

21-100 **Extraneous statements** Where, however, extraneous statements are published which can have no reference to the privileged occasion, or the occasion has been wilfully misused,[496] it becomes the duty of the judge to rule that so far as they are concerned the occasion is not privileged. Where a defendant, having received a lawyer's letter written on behalf of the claimant, replied in terms of general abuse of the latter, it was held that there was no privilege at all.[497] Mere exaggeration of language, however, though it may be evidence of malice, will not necessarily destroy privilege where the latter exists.[498] In *Tuson v Evans*[499] the publication was held to be not privileged and the occasion exceeded by the violence of the language used. In *Fryer v Kinnersley*[500] the privilege was assumed but the language was held to exceed the occasion. In *Robertson v M'Dougall*[501] no malice was proved but the language used was held to exceed the latitude allowed for privileged communications. Inadvertence or careless blundering is not necessarily evidence of malice.[502]

21-101 **Functions of judge and jury** The 20th edition contained a section on the role of

[490] *Adam v Ward* [1917] A.C. 309; *Angel v HH Bushell & Co Ltd* [1968] 1 Q.B. 813.
[491] (1877) 3 Q.B.D. 237.
[492] per Lindley LJ in *Stuart v Bell* [1891] 2 Q.B. 341 at 351; cf. *Darby v Ousely* (1856) 1 H. & N. 1.
[493] *Clark v Molyneux* (1877) 3 Q.B.D. 237 at 247, per Brett LJ.
[494] *Horrocks v Lowe* [1975] A.C. 135.
[495] 1993 S.L.T. 527.
[496] *Nevill v Fine Art etc Co* [1895] 2 Q.B. 156 at 170, 171; *Adam v Ward* [1917] A.C. 309 at 321, 339, 340, 348; cf. *Angel v HH Bushell & Co Ltd* [1968] 1 Q.B. 813.
[497] *Huntley v Ward* (1859) 6 C.B. (N.S.) 514. See also *Godson v Home* (1819) 1 B. & B. 7; *Warren v Warren* (1834) 1 C.M. & R. 250.
[498] *Cooke v Wildes* (1855) 5 E. & B. 328; *Cowles v Potts* (1865) 34 L.J. Q.B. 247.
[499] (1840) 12 A. & E. 733; see also, per Willes J in *Huntley v Ward* (1859) 6 C.B. (N.S.) 514 and *Nevill v Fine Art etc Co* [1895] 2 Q.B. 156 at 170, per Lopes J.
[500] (1863) 15 C.B. (N.S.) 423.
[501] (1828) 4 Bing. 670.
[502] *Brett v Watson* (1872) 20 W.R. 723; *Clark v Molyneux* (1873) 3 Q.B.D. 237 at 249, per Cotton LJ; and see *Turner v MGM Pictures Ltd* [1950] 1 All E.R. 449 at 462, 463; *Horrocks v Lowe* [1975] A.C. 135 HL (indeed it is doubtful whether after this judgment they can amount to evidence of malice at all).

the jury. Now that s.11 of the Defamation Act 2013 has removed the presumption in favour of juries in most cases all matters will be left to the judge. With a jury trial the question of whether the defamatory communication is privileged is a matter for the judge. The existence of malice where the statement has been published on an occasion of qualified privilege is a question of fact and thus where there is a jury, this is a question for the jury. It is a matter of law for the judge to decide whether there is reasonable evidence of malice which may be left to the jury.[503] Judges and juries have been counselled to "be very slow to draw the inference that a defendant was so far actuated by improper motives as to deprive him of the protection of the privilege unless they are satisfied that he did not believe that what he said or wrote was true or that he was indifferent to its truth or falsity".[504]

Publication by agent Where a communication would be privileged if made by a particular person, the privilege will also protect an agent publishing it on his behalf.[505] Moreover, where principal and agent are jointly sued, proof of malice on the part of the principal will not destroy the privilege of the agent if the agent is innocent of malice.[506] The agent's malice will, however, render the principal liable on the ordinary principles of vicarious responsibility[507] unless the agent has nothing to do with the composition of the libel or approval of it, but merely in obedience to orders does the mechanical act of distributing it.[508] 21-102

Degree of publicity With regard to the publicity given, it has been said that a defendant will not lose his privilege because he goes somewhat beyond the strict necessities of the case.[509] There is also authority to show that where an occasion is otherwise privileged it will not lose its character by the fact of the casual presence of one,[510] or even of several uninterested bystanders,[511] and that such presence is material only on the question of malice. Some doubts arise as to the exact rule to be deduced from these cases. Of course, if a defendant has practically no opportunity of making his communication except in the presence of uninterested persons, it is right that his privilege should be unaffected. The case of *Pittard v Oliver*[512] seems to have been decided on this principle; there reporters were present at a meeting of a board of guardians. The passage in *Toogood v Spyring*,[513] which says that the business of life must be carried on, impliedly asserts the same doctrine. 21-103

503 *Alexander v Arts Council of Wales* [2001] EWCA Civ 514; [2001] 1 W.L.R. 1840.

504 *Horrocks v Lowe* [1975] A.C. 135 HL at 150, per Lord Diplock. And see *Korach v Moore* (1991) 76 D.L.R. (4th) 506.

505 *Baker v Carrick* [1894] 1 Q.B. 838; *Boxsius v Goblet Freres* [1894] 1 Q.B. 842; *Watts v Times Newspapers Ltd* [1997] Q.B. 650.

506 *Egger v Chelmsford* [1965] 1 Q.B. 248; *Gardiner v Moore* [1969] 1 Q.B. 55; *Sun Life Assurance of Canada v Dalrymple* (1965) 50 D.L.R. (2d) 217.

507 See *Citizens' Life Assurance Co v Brown* [1904] A.C. 423; *Finburgh v Moss's Empires Ltd*, 1908 S.C. 928; *Moore v Canadian Pacific S.S. Co* [1945] 1 All E.R. 128 at 134; *Birne v National Sporting League*, *The Times*, 12 April 1957. The fact that the principal is a corporation is immaterial: see para.5-74.

508 See *Adam v Ward* [1917] A.C. 309 at 341; *Birne v National Sporting League*, *The Times*, 12 April 1957.

509 See *Beach v Freeson* [1972] 1 Q.B. 14.

510 *Toogood v Spyring* (1834) 1 C.M. & R. 181 at 193, 194; *White v Stone (Lighting and Radio) Ltd* [1939] 2 K.B. 827.

511 *Davies v Sneed* (1870) L.R. 5 Q.B. 608.

512 [1891] 1 Q.B. 474 at 478, per Lord Esher MR.

513 (1834) 1 C.M. & R. 181 at 194.

21-104 **Publication to a third person** The principle seems to be that if the occasion is privileged, a publication by the person exercising the privilege to third persons is protected if it is reasonable and in the ordinary course of business.[514] It is on this ground that publication to clerks, typists or copyists is protected. The mere fact that such persons have no legitimate interest in the subject-matter will not destroy the privilege. So where a solicitor, acting on behalf of his client, sent a libellous letter to the claimant and in the ordinary course of business the letter was seen by the latter's clerk, it was held that this publication was protected.[515] The majority of the Court of Appeal in *Bryanston Finance Ltd v de Vries*[516] held that where in the normal course of business an employer dictated letters to a typist, or otherwise necessarily communicated them to an employee, such publications were protected by privilege. This privilege arises because of the common interest between employer and employee in the circumstances.

21-105 **Limit of protection** No privilege attaches unless the publication, whether to subordinates or third persons, is reasonably necessary and in the ordinary course of business.[517] There has been said to be no privilege, therefore, for a publication by postcard or telegram[518] or letter copied by a clerk, outside the ordinary course of business. A communication which is otherwise privileged so far as the recipient is concerned on grounds of common interest will lose its privilege if the writer intends it to be republished in a magazine mainly intended for persons with a common interest but also on sale to members of the public.[519] The matter is summed up in the judgment of the court in *Toogood v Spyring*[520]:

> "Where, indeed, an opportunity is sought for making such a charge before third persons, which might have been made in private, it would afford strong evidence of malicious intention and thus deprive it of that immunity which the law allows to such a statement when made with honesty of purpose; but the mere fact of a third person being present does not render the communication absolutely unauthorised, though it may be a circumstance to be left with others, including the style and character of the language used, to the consideration of the jury, who are to determine whether the defendant has acted bona fide in making the charge, or been influenced by malicious motive."

However, this restriction will need to be reconsidered in the light of the internet.

---

514 per Collins MR in *Edmondson v Birch* [1907] 1 K.B. 371 at 380.

515 *Boxsius v Goblet Freres* [1894] 1 Q.B. 842; cf. *Roff v British and French Chemical Co* [1918] 2 K.B. 677.

516 [1975] Q.B. 703 (note the dissent of Lord Diplock. Lord Denning MR's view of the nature of such privilege appears wider than that of Lawton LJ and may not be subject to the restriction that the publication must be to advance or protect the business. Nevertheless the view of Lawton LJ receives support from Lord Diplock who dissented on the facts of the case).

517 *Pullman v Hill* [1891] 1 Q.B. 524; *R. v Lancashire CC Police Authority Ex p. Hook* [1980] Q.B. 603, CA at 615; *Adam v Ward* [1917] A.C. 309.

518 *Williamson v Freer* (1874) L.R. 9 C. & P. 393; *Sadgrove v Hole* [1901] 2 K.B. 1. However, the principle in *Williamson* was considered to belong to a bygone era by Eady J in *Hewitt v Grunwald* [2004] EWHC 2959 (QB) at [73] when considering privilege on the internet.

519 *Cutler v McPhail* [1962] 2 Q.B. 292.

520 (1834) 1 C.M. & R. 181 at 194. As to privilege where the communication is to the person defamed in the presence of a third party see, however, *White v Stone* [1939] 2 K.B. 827; *Osborn v Thomas Boulter & Son* [1930] 2 K.B. 226; *Bryanston Finance Ltd v de Vries* [1975] Q.B. 703; *Lacarte v Board of Education Toronto* (1959) 17 D.L.R. (2d) 609; cf. also *Somerville v Hawkins* (1851) 10 C.B. 583; *Taylor v Hawkins* (1851) 16 Q.B. 308. See Goodhart, 56 L.Q.R. 262.

In *Hewitt v Grunwald*[521] the court did not consider communicating with British Jews about terrorism by means of the internet to be either "unnecessary" or "disproportionate".

Limits of the protection for public authorities In *Clift v Slough BC*[522] a local authority published the name of the claimant on a violent person's register. The claimant sued and the local authority pleaded a defence of qualified privilege, contending that those who received the communication (being officers, employees and some third party organisations who provided services on behalf of the local authority) had a duty or interest in receiving the information. The local authority lost the defence of qualified privilege because its disclosure of defamatory information to certain departments was disproportionate and could not be justified under art.8 ECHR. Under the Human Rights Act 1998 s.6, any public authority has a duty to act compatibly with Convention rights. The court found that ill-considered and indiscriminate disclosure of defamatory information was bound to be disproportionate and the local authority should have verified the information and limited its disclosure to those that truly needed to know it or who were reasonably thought to be at risk from the individual. The court balanced the duty of the local authority to warn employees of the risks posed by the claimant as against their duty to protect her reputation under art.8 and concluded that in the case of certain classes of employee who were unlikely to come into contact with the claimant, the duty to protect the claimant's reputation outweighed the duty to warn of any risk. A public authority will therefore not be able to rely on a defence of privilege unless it can establish that it has complied with its public law duties under the Human Rights Act. Where a public authority publishes information about someone which interferes with his or her rights under art.8(1) ECHR then unless it can show that publication was in accordance with the law, necessary and proportionate in a democratic society for one of the legitimate aims listed in art.8(2) that publication will be unlawful. 21-106

Charges against more than one person It has also been decided that, where there is an imputation against two persons jointly, so that the misconduct charged against one cannot well be explained without introducing the name of the other, if circumstances exist which make the communication privileged with regard to one person it will be privileged with regard to both.[523] 21-107

Lapse of time It is arguable that a defence of qualified privilege on the basis of a corresponding duty and interest can be lost due to lapse of time, particularly where the claimant has been given assurances that the information in question will not be retained after a particular time.[524] 21-108

---

521 [2004] EWHC 2959 (QB).

522 [2010] EWCA Civ 1484; [2011] 1 W.L.R. 1774; *McLaughlin v Lambeth LBC* [2010] EWHC 2726 (QB); [2011] E.M.L.R. 8; cf. *Thompson v James and Carmarthenshire County Council* [2014] EWCA Civ 600; [2014] B.L.G.R. 664.

523 *Manby v Witt* (1856) 18 C.B. 544; *Davies v Snead* (1870) L.R. 5 Q.B. 608 at 611, per Blackburn J.

524 *W v JH* [2008] EWHC 399 (QB); [2009] E.M.L.R. 11. The court also noted the relevance of the Data Protection Act 1998 and the claimant's art.8 ECHR rights in these circumstances. See now the Data Protection Act 2018.

(ii) *Grounds of qualified privilege*

21-109 **Types of qualified privilege** There are two broad categories of qualified privilege. These are:

(a) *Duty and interest* Where the maker of the statement has a legitimate duty or interest in making the statement and the recipient or recipients of the statement ("the publishees") have a legitimate duty or interest in receiving it. This is a common law defence.

(b) *Fair and accurate reports of certain proceedings, documents and statements* Section 15 of the 1996 Act provides that a long list of reports set out in Sch.1 to the Act are protected by qualified privilege. These reports are, in effect, a "B" list, compared with those reports referred to in s.14, which are of greater importance and therefore worthy of absolute privilege. Nevertheless, in practice, it is very rare to prove malice in relation to such reports. This list has been supplemented by the Defamation Act 2013, which also created, by s.6, a new qualified privilege for peer-reviewed statements in scientific or academic journals. Common law qualified privilege, notionally based on duty and interest, has always been available for reports of certain proceedings and documents. However, because of the wide protection given by statute, it is rare that a defendant would need to rely on the common law privilege for reports.

(1) Duty and interest

21-110 **Grounds of qualified privilege** A privileged communication may be made in the discharge of a duty, legal, social or moral[525] or in the pursuance of a right, or for both reasons. It may be in the interest of the person to whom it is addressed, or in the interest of the person making it or in their common interest. Where a communication is said to be in the public interest, a separate defence under s.4 of the Defamation Act 2013 may apply.[526] It is not always easy to determine under which of these heads a particular case may fall; indeed, privilege may frequently be put upon more than one ground.[527] A few illustrations are given here without any pretence to an exhaustively accurate classification. The duty or interest must exist in fact. Privilege depends not upon the belief in the defendant's own mind as to his right or duty, but on whether he was right or mistaken in that belief.[528] It was formerly supposed that persons who, in seeking redress, had applied to the wrong tribunal were protected if their error was a natural and not unreasonable one,[529] but the authorities upon which this doctrine was based have been explained and it is now clear that "there is no protection to the person who wrongly assumes the facts

---

525 *Stuart v Bell* [1891] 2 Q.B. 341 at 354, per Lopes LJ.

526 See para.21-147 onwards.

527 See, per Erle CJ in *Whitely v Adams* (1863) 15 C.B. (N.S.) 392 at 418. Also see for example *Kearns v General Council of the Bar* [2003] EWCA Civ 331; [2003] 1 W.L.R. 1357; para.21-121.

528 per Byles J in *Whiteley v Adams* (1863) 15 C.B. (N.S.) 392 at 412; *Stuart v Bell* [1891] 2 Q.B. 341 at 349, "the question is, what is the defendant's duty; not what he thinks to be his duty"; *Adam v Ward* [1917] A.C. 309 at 334; *Phelps v Kemsley* (1942) 168 L.T. 18 at 20; *Eyre v New Zealand Press Association Ltd* [1968] N.Z.L.R. 736.

529 *Fairman v Ives* (1823) 5 B. & A. 642; *Harrison v Bush* (1885) 5 E. & B. 344.

which constitute a privileged occasion".[530] "You cannot by making a mistake create the occasion for making the communication."[531] However, if a person makes inquiries of D purporting to be a potential employer (for example) and D replies in good faith, he will not lose the privilege.[532] If this were not so it would be impossible to reply to inquiries without undertaking extensive investigations.

Interest of person to whom communication addressed The commonest form of privileged communication is that which is made in the interest of the person to whom it is addressed. "Where a person is so situated that it becomes right in the interest of society that he should tell to a third person certain facts",[533] he is privileged in so doing. The facts must be important for the person in question to know; they must be for the guidance and regulation of his conduct.[534] If the communication cannot influence conduct there is no privilege.[535] The privilege will depend partly upon the nature of the communication, and partly upon the relation in which the parties stand to one another. Thus in *Chapman v Ellesmere*[536] an inquiry was held by the stewards of the Jockey Club concerning the "doping" of a racehorse. The decision of the inquiry contained the statement that the claimant, who was the trainer of the horse, had been warned off, and this was published in the *Racing Calendar*, *The Times*, and to the news agencies. The Court of Appeal held that, there being no evidence of malice, the publication in the *Racing Calendar* was privileged on the ground of the duty of the stewards to communicate their decision to the racing public who had a corresponding interest in receiving it; the claimant had moreover by the terms of his licence agreed that the *Racing Calendar* should be the means of the communication of such decisions. The publication to the news agencies and *The Times* was not privileged as the public at large did not have an "interest" in the technical sense; it was a publication of matters which concerned a section of the public only. 21-111

Reciprocity essential There must not only be an interest in the recipient of the communication but an interest or duty in the person making the communication to make the communication in question: 21-112

530 *Hebditch v MacIlwaine* [1894] 2 Q.B. 54; *James v Baird* 1916 S.C. (H.L.) 158; *sub nom. Baird v Wallace-James*, 85 L.J.P.C. 193; *Beach v Freeson* [1972] 1 Q.B. 14; *Blackshaw v Lord* [1984] Q.B. 1; and see *Gatley on Libel and Slander* (12th edn) at 14.20-14.21; cf. *Hynes-O'Sullivan v O'Driscoll* [1988] I.R. 436, Irish Supreme Court.

531 *Davidson v Barclays Bank Ltd* [1940] 1 All E.R. 316 (criticised by Black J in *Pyke v Hibernian Bank* [1950] I.R. 195 at 231-232).

532 *Gatley on Libel and Slander* (12th edn) at 14.25.

533 per Blackburn J in *Davies v Snead* (1870) L.R. 5 Q.B. 608 at 611; per Lindley LJ, in *Stuart v Bell* [1891] 2 Q.B. 341 at 351; *Hunt v Great Northern Ry* [1891] 2 Q.B. 189.

534 See *Bromage v Prosser* (1825) 4 B. & C. 247.

535 *Dickeson v Hilliard* (1874) L.R. 9 Ex. 79—where the agent of one side in a contested election wrote to the opposing agent after the close of the poll, accusing a voter of bribery, as any duty he might have had with reference to the election was entirely over at the time it reached him, he had no interest or authority in the matter, and there was no privilege.

536 [1932] 2 K.B. 431; followed *Russell v Duke of Norfolk* [1949] 1 All E.R. 109; cf. *Cookson v Harewood* [1932] 2 K.B. 478n. And see *Star Gems v Ford* [1980] C.L.Y. 1671 (publication of allegations of business malpractice in the "Retail Chemist").

"Except in the case of communications based on common interest, the principle is that either there must be an interest in the recipient and a duty to communicate in the speaker, or an interest to be protected in the speaker and a duty to protect it in the recipient."[537]

"It may be, of course, that the interest of the person receiving the communication is of such a character as by its very nature to create a social duty in another under the circumstances to make the communication that he does in fact make."[538]

A defendant may protect himself by showing either that he was in a position of confidence or intimacy with the person to whom he published the matter complained of, or that he acted in consequence of a request for information lawfully made, or that although as a mere volunteer he had such special means of knowledge as to impose a special obligation upon him. In *Hewitt v Grunwald*[539] the claimants were trustees of a charity accused on the defendant's website (the website of the Board of Deputies of British Jews) of being a terrorist organisation. The claimants applied to strike out a defence of qualified privilege based on duty-interest on the basis that by virtue of publication on the internet (and thereby to the world at large) there was no reciprocity of duty and interest. The judge refused to strike out the defence, accepting that there was a legitimate interest on the part of Jews in Great Britain in the subject matter of the allegations. The judge did not consider communicating with British Jews about terrorism by means of the internet to be either "unnecessary" or "disproportionate". Where the defendant treasurer of a union made an allegation of forgery against the claimant, who was a union member, but the defendant was not acting under the auspices of the union, the occasion was not privileged.[540] The defendant had made clear in the statement itself that he was acting in his personal capacity. The judge also considered that for the defence to apply, there had to be some relationship of proportionality between the defendant's duties, the common interest in play, and the nature of the publication made. Put another way, the statement had to be fairly warranted by the occasion.

21-113 **Positive duty** There are, of course, certain cases in which it is clearly a duty for one person to disclose all he knows to another. An employee or agent is bound to lay before his employer all the information which he possesses with regard to the interests entrusted to his care.[541] So, where two or more people are jointly entrusted with the protection of any interest or the conduct of any investigation, it is clearly proper that the confidential communication between them of all matters affecting the discharge of their duty should be free and unrestrained.[542] So also "to protect those who are not able to protect themselves is a duty which everyone owes to

---

537 *Watt v Longsdon* [1930] 1 K.B. 130 at 147, per Scrutton LJ; and see *Phelps v Kemsley* (1943) 168 L.T. 18. It is not sufficient that the defendant honestly believed that the recipient had an interest or duty in respect of the communication, such interest or duty must really exist: *Beach v Freeson* [1972] 1 Q.B. 14.

538 *Watt v Longsdon* [1930] 1 K.B. 130 at 152, per Greer LJ.

539 [2004] EWHC 2959 (QB).

540 *Umeyor v Nwakamma* [2015] EWHC 2980 (QB).

541 *Cooke v Wildes* (1855) 5 E. & B. 328; *Lawless v Anglo-Egyptian Cotton Co* (1869) L.R. 4 Q.B. 262; *Moore v Canadian Pacific S.S. Co* [1945] 1 All E.R. 128.

542 *Hopwood v Thorn* (1849) 8 C.B. 293; *Harris v Thompson* (1853) 13 C.B. 333; *Wallace v Carroll* (1860) 11 Ir. C.L.R. 485; *Beatson v Skene* (1860) 5 H. & N. 838; *Collins v Cooper* (1902) 19 T.L.R. 118 CA; *Keith v Lauder* (1905) 8 F. 356; cf. *Longdon-Griffiths v Smith* [1951] 1 K.B. 295.

society".[543] In *Wood v Chief Constable of the West Midlands Police*[544] a police officer circulated letters warning insurers of criminal proceedings being brought against the director of a salvage company for handling stolen goods. The Court of Appeal agreed with the trial judge that the police officer's general duties to detect and prevent crime entitled him to write these letters. Whilst the police had "a job to do", any disclosure of information about an individual's arrest and charge could only be disclosed if there was a specific public interest justification. "Ill-considered and indiscriminate disclosure" would not be likely to measure up to that standard.

Confidential relationship The doctrine of privilege arising out of a confidential relationship has been extended very widely beyond the ground of positive duty, and whenever one person stands on such a footing with another that he may reasonably and properly take upon himself to tender advice or information, he will be privileged in so doing. Thus, an employer may warn his servants against the character of a fellow employee.[545] A near relation of a woman may give his opinion of her suitor.[546] A solicitor may give warning to a client of any peril to his interests, though not professionally consulted.[547] The relationship of host and guest imposes upon the former a social and moral duty to inform the latter of suspicions which have fallen upon his employee.[548] A Member of Parliament may publicly give political advice and information to his or her constituents, and may make representations on their behalf to the appropriate bodies in respect of complaints from them about public or professional services that they have received.[549] Similarly a bishop may give ecclesiastical advice and information to his clergy, and if in so doing either publishes defamatory matter, it will be prima facie privileged.[550] A ratepayer is entitled to lay facts reported to him before the local authority for investigation even though the report constitutes a libel.[551] A member of the public may make a complaint about the conduct of a member of the Bar to the Bar Council.[552] A similar privilege has been held to apply to a police surgeon who in consequence of his incorrect diagnosis of the illness of a constable makes an unfounded charge about him to his superior officer.[553] Limits remain however. A parochial clergyman, it would seem, is not in ordinary circumstances privileged in publishing to his parishioners at large matters defamatory of any individual, although the imputa- 21-114

543 per Lord Macnaghten in *Jenoure v Delmege* [1891] A.C. 73 at 77.

544 [2004] EWCA Civ 1638; [2005] E.M.L.R. 20.

545 *Somerville v Hawkins* (1851) 10 C.B. 583; *Hunt v Great Northern Ry* [1891] 2 Q.B. 189; *AB v XY*, 1917 S.C. 15; *Cochrane v Young*, 1923 S.C. 696.

546 *Todd v Hawkins* (1837) 8 C. & P. 88.

547 *Davies v Reeves* (1855) 5 Ir. C.L.R. 79.

548 per Kay LJ in *Stuart v Bell* [1891] 2 Q.B. 341 at 359; cf. *Bridgman v Stockdale* [1953] 1 W.L.R. 704 (invigilator privileged in informing examination candidates of the conduct of a fellow candidate).

549 *Beach v Freeson* [1972] 1 Q.B. 14.

550 *Wason v Walter* (1868) L.R. 4 Q.B. 73 at 95; *Laughton v The Bishop of Sodor and Man* (1872) L.R. 4 P.C. 495; see *R. v Rule* [1937] 2 K.B. 375, for interest between constituent and Member of Parliament; and see *Beach v Freeson* [1972] 1 Q.B. 14.

551 *Couper v Lord Balfour of Burleigh*, 1913 S.C. 492; *Baird v Wallace-James* (1916) 85 L.J.P.C. 193 HL. As to interest between borough council and ratepayers, see *De Buse v McCarthy* [1942] 1 K.B. 156; *Cutler v McPhail* [1962] 2 Q.B. 292.

552 See *Lincoln v Daniels* [1962] 1 Q.B. 237 at 252 and 269 (Devlin LJ at 264 reserved his opinion on this).

553 *A v B*, 1907 S.C. 1154.

tions are such as it might be his duty to tell the individual privately.[554] Where persons have previously been brought into a confidential relationship on a certain subject-matter, later communications on the same topic are privileged. Thus, an employer who has given another a reference for an employee may afterwards correct and qualify his previous statements,[555] and a person who has employed someone with a reference, which he finds to be undeserved, is privileged in communicating his opinion to the former employer.[556]

21-115 **Statement in answer to reasonable request for information** Where a person is asked a question about a matter by or on behalf of someone who appears to have a legitimate interest in the knowing the answer, he or she is under a social or moral duty to give an answer and the occasion is privileged. Thus, if one trader makes inquiries of another with regard to the solvency of persons with whom he proposes to have dealings, the latter is protected in communicating the information which he possesses.[557] A like rule applies in cases where an association makes a communication to its members respecting the solvency of an individual, whether or not that communication be detrimental to the character of the person specified, provided the communication is made from the sense of duty.[558] Where, however, a trade protection society or mercantile agency supplies information as to the credit of traders for reward to anyone who chooses to subscribe to it, there is said to be no privilege.[559] The protection given to statements made from a bona fide sense of duty is not to be extended to "communications made from motives of self-interest by persons who trade for profit in the characters of other people".[560] Where inquiries are being made with a view to the detection of a criminal offence, any answer honestly given affords no grounds for action, though it involves a direct charge of a crime or affects

---

[554] *Gilpin v Fowler* (1854) 9 Ex. 615; *Magrath v Finn* (1877) Ir. R. 11 C.L. 152; *Botterill v Whytehead* (1879) 41 L.T. 588.

[555] *Gardner v Slade* (1849) 13 Q.B. 796.

[556] See *Child v Affleck* (1829) 9 B. & C. 403; *Wilson v Robinson* (1845) 7 Q.B. 68; cf. *Angel v HH Bushell & Co Ltd* [1968] 1 Q.B. 813. See, however, *Fryer v Kinnersley* (1863) 15 C.B. (N.S.) 423 at 429, per Erle CJ (a case of exceeding the occasion). See also *Spring v Guardian Assurance* [1995] 2 A.C. 296 HL.

[557] cf. *Davies v Snead* (1870) L.R. 5 Q.B. 608 at 611; *Robshaw v Smith* (1878) 39 L.T. 423 at 424, per Grove J; *Waller v Loch* (1881) 7 Q.B.D. 619 at 623.

[558] *London Association for Protection of Trade v Greenlands* [1916] 2 A.C. 15; no direct decision was given on the question of privilege, but *Macintosh v Dun* [1908] A.C. 390 (a case in the Privy Council), below, was distinguished (see, per Lord Buckmaster at 26–27, and per Lord Atkinson at 37) for the same reasons as those given by Bray J in his dissenting judgment in the Court of Appeal of *Greenlands v Wilmshurst* [1913] 3 K.B. 507 at 556 namely: (1) the defendants were not an association which had combined for their mutual protection but were the proprietors of a business which was not a mutual society in any sense of the word; (2) the business was carried on for profit; (3) was it for the welfare of society that protection given to communications made in legitimate self-defence or from a bona fide sense of duty should be extended to communications made from motives of self-interest by persons who trade for profit in the characters of other people? cf. *Keith v Lauder* (1905) 8 F. 356; *Elkington v London Association for Protection of Trade* (1911) 27 T.L.R. 329; *Barr v Musselburgh Merchants Association*, 1912 S.C. 174.

[559] *Macintosh v Dun* [1908] A.C. 390. But see, per Scrutton LJ in *Watt v Longsdon* [1930] 1 K.B. 130 at 148: "*Macintosh v Dun* is not to be relied on too strongly since *London Association for Protection of Trade v Greenlands.*" But see *Gillet v Nissen Volkswagen Ltd* [1975] 3 W.W.R. 520 (where the Supreme Court of Alberta applied *Macintosh v Dun*).

[560] *Macintosh v Dun* [1908] A.C. 390, per Lord Macnaghten at 400. In the USA such a communication is privileged when made to subscribers who have a special interest in the information: cf. *King v Patterson* (1887) 83 L.T.J. 408.

the character of a third person.[561] Answers to inquiries by the police, and the initial complaint, are protected by absolute privilege.[562]

References by employers This is the most familiar example of this type of privilege. However, a claimant may have other routes in respect of references. In *Spring v Guardian Assurance*[563] the defendant employers were held to be liable in negligence for giving a derogatory reference for the claimant. Had the action been in defamation, qualified privilege might have been proved and the defence would have succeeded unless the claimant could show malice. 21-116

Inquiry must be reasonable on the face of it The mere fact that a person is asked a question does not necessarily give him privilege. He ought to be reasonably satisfied that his questioner has some interest or duty in the matter. "It is no part of a man's duty to go into the confessional to every chance person who may choose to ask impertinent questions."[564] If a question is first invited and then answered by a defamatory statement, such statement is to be considered as purely voluntary.[565] So, if the defendant has defamed the claimant in circumstances where no privilege arises, and then on being challenged reaffirms what he stated before, he will not be privileged in doing so. If, however, the first statement is privileged the original publication and its repetition and vindication stand on the same footing.[566] 21-117

Volunteered communications The real test in relation to volunteered communications is whether, having regard to all the circumstances, it was the moral or social duty of the defendant to volunteer the communication. The intention of protecting the interests of the recipient is not enough, the interest must create a corresponding duty on the part of the defendant to protect it.[567] Cases of this sort often present difficulty as: 21-118

> "the reason for holding any occasion privileged is common convenience and welfare of society, and it is obvious that no definite line can be drawn so as to mark off with precision those occasions which are privileged and separate them from those which are not."[568]

Where there is a moral duty to make the communication Volunteered communications are not now considered to stand on any special footing, and the officiousness of the intervention is merely one matter to be considered among others. There may be a social or moral duty in particular circumstances to make an 21-119

---

561 *Johnson v Evans* (1799) 3 Esp. 32; *Fowler v Homer* (1812) 3 Camb. 294; *Cockayne v Hodgkisson* (1833) 5 C. & P. 543; *Kine v Sewell* (1838) 3 M. & W. 297 at 302; *Padmore v Lawrence* (1840) 11 A. & E. 380 at 382; *Amann v Damm* (1860) 8 C.B. (N.S.) 597; *Wing Lee v Jones* [1954] 1 D.L.R. 520 (communication to police); *Clarke v Austin* (1974) 51 D.L.R. (3d) 598 (allegation that the claimant had been shoplifting made by the defendant to her, the defendant's, employer).

562 *Taylor v Director of the Serious Fraud Office* [1999] 1 W.L.R. 184; *Westcott v Westcott* [2008] EWCA Civ 818; [2009] Q.B. 407.

563 [1995] 2 A.C. 296 HL.

564 *Force v Warren* (1864) 15 C.B. (N.S.) 806 at 808, per Erle CJ; *Waller v Loch* (1881) 7 Q.B.D. 619 at 621, per Jessel MR.

565 *Gardner v Slade* (1849) 13 Q.B. 796.

566 *Griffiths v Lewis* (1845) 7 Q.B. 61; *Taylor v Hawkins* (1851) 16 Q.B. 308.

567 *Adam v Ward* [1917] A.C. 309.

568 per Lindley LJ in *Stuart v Bell* [1891] 2 Q.B. 341 at 346. See also *Coxhead v Richards* (1846) 2 C.B. 569 for the difficulties of working out where the line should be drawn; and *Kearns v General Council of the Bar* [2003] EWCA Civ 331; [2003] 1 W.L.R. 1357.

unsolicited communication in relation to matters in which the recipient's interest is concerned. The guide suggested in *Stuart v Bell*[569] is "[w]ould the great mass of right-minded men in the position of the defendant have considered it their duty under the circumstances to make the communication?" An employee or a friend may properly convey information or give advice which would be impertinent on the part of a stranger. The latter is only entitled to interfere when he has some special means of information on a matter of practical importance. Thus, where the defendant has reason to believe himself robbed by the claimant, he was held to be discharging a social duty in giving information to the claimant's employer.[570]

21-120 **Communications between persons having a common interest** Communications between parties who are alike concerned in the condition of some property or the management of some undertaking are privileged on the ground of their common interest.[571] All those to whom the communication is made must share the common interest.[572] A common interest may exist even where the interests of the parties are quite different,[573] and the interest does not have to be financial.[574]

21-121 **Existing relationships** In *Kearns v General Council of the Bar*[575] the Court of Appeal expressed a preference for categorising qualified privilege cases according to whether they take place in an "existing relationship", which was said to be a more helpful categorisation than the traditional duty and interest approach. Simon Brown LJ, with whom the other members of the court agreed, considered it understandable and unsurprising that privilege would attach more readily to communications within an existing relationship, than to those between strangers. This approach has been followed in *W v Westminster CC*,[576] a case concerning defamatory allegations made in a report published to various persons concerned with the welfare of a child (S) in the care of the Westminster local authority. The report was published to the head of the local authority Child Protection Unit, S's School Nurse and Headteacher, and S's mother. Tugendhat J, in finding that qualified privilege arose in these circumstances, and after quoting extensively from *Kearns*, described this as a case of "an existing and established relationship, going back many years, between the mother's family and the Social Services Department of the Council". *Kearns* was also applied in *Cambridge v Makin*,[577] where the defence of qualified

569 [1891] 2 Q.B. 341 at 350, per Lindley LJ; approved *Watt v Longsdon* [1930] 1 K.B. 130 at 153, per Greer LJ; cf. *Phelps v Kemsley* (1942) 168 L.T. 18.

570 *Amann v Damm* (1860) 8 C.B. (N.S.) 597 at 601. And see *Clarke v Austin* (1974) 51 D.L.R. (3d) 598 (employee making allegations of shoplifting to her own employer).

571 e.g. *Barr v Musselburgh Merchants' Association*, 1912 S.C. 174; *Ware and De Freville v Motor Trade Association* [1912] 3 K.B. 40; *Chapman v Ellesmere* [1932] 2 K.B. 431; *Bridgman v Stockdale* [1953] 1 W.L.R. 704; *Boston v WS Bagshaw & Sons* [1966] 1 W.L.R. 1126 CA; *Pleau v Simpson Sears Ltd* (1977) 75 D.L.R. (3d) 747 (notice in bank to stop forged cheques); *Toogood v Spyring* (1834) 1 C.M. & R. 181 (tenant's complaint to landlord about person carrying out repairs on property); *Knight v Gibbs* (1834) 1 A. & E. 43 (complaint from tenant to landlord about lodgers).

572 *Watt v Longsdon* [1930] 1 K.B. 130.

573 e.g. *Aspro Travel v Owners Abroad Group* [1996] 1 W.L.R. 132 CA.

574 e.g. *Laughton v Bishop of Sodor and Man* (1872) L.R. 4 P.C. 495.

575 [2003] EWCA Civ 331; [2003] 1 W.L.R. 1357.

576 [2004] EWHC 2866 (QB); [2005] 1 F.C.R. 39.

577 [2012] EWCA Civ 85; [2012] E.M.L.R. 19.

privilege failed and the defendant was found to be malicious. In this case the court gave guidance as to the approach to follow where there is no existing relationship.[578]

Interest of person making the communication Qualified privilege also attaches to communications which a person makes in his own interest, in defence either of his property or his character. For example, where the defendant, having sold goods to the claimant on credit and subsequently learned that the latter had sold off his stock and was not to be found, gave notice to the auctioneer in whose hands were the proceeds of the claimant's sale not to pay them over to him on the ground that he had committed an act of bankruptcy, the communication was held to be privileged.[579] A defence of qualified privilege will also be available to a solicitor who makes defamatory statements acting in the interest of his client.[580] The privilege was not, however, found to be available to the police in *Bento v Chief Constable of Bedfordshire Police*[581] where the police were found to have no duty to discuss the merits of a charging decision by the Crown Prosecution Service. 21-122

Self-justification It is reasonable and therefore privileged that a man should explain his motives and conduct to those who have been brought into confidential relations with him in respect of the subject-matter of the communication. The case of *Whitely v Adams*[582] provides a remarkable illustration of privilege of this kind. The defendant was a clergyman and litigation had arisen between a member of his congregation and the claimant. He was invited by one of the clergy of the claimant's parish to arbitrate in the dispute. He declined to do so and in giving his reasons published matter defamatory of the claimant who commenced an action. A friend of both parties, tried to mediate and to conciliate between them. In communicating with her the defendant repeated his defamatory assertions and thereupon a second action was brought. It was decided in both cases that the action must fail, because the defendant had a right to explain to both his correspondents the motive of his conduct and the ground of belief upon which he proceeded.[583] 21-123

Reply to attack If a person's character is attacked, he is not merely entitled to vindicate himself, but may reply by raising against his assailant any charges which may impair the latter's credit in that particular matter which is in controversy.[584] But he is not entitled to indulge in mere recrimination, or to put forth one piece of defamation in revenge for another of an altogether different nature—the reply must be fairly relevant to the attack, but the defendant is allowed a degree of latitude in this respect.[585] Where relevant, he may also make defamatory statements about third 21-124

---

578 See also *Downtex v Flatley* [2003] EWCA Civ 1282.

579 *Blackham v Pugh* (1846) 2 C.B. 611; approved in *Baker v Carrick* [1894] 1 Q.B. 838; cf. per Littledale J in *Coward v Wellington* (1836) 7 C. & P. 531 at 586.

580 *Watts v Times Newspapers Ltd* [1997] Q.B. 650.

581 [2012] EWHC 1525 (QB).

582 (1863) 15 C.B. (N.S.) 392.

583 See *Laughton v Bishop of Sodor and Man* (1872) L.R. 4 C. & P. 495. See also *Maccaba v Lichtenstein* [2004] EWHC 1577 (QB); [2005] E.M.L.R. 9.

584 *Laughton v Bishop of Sodor and Man* (1872) L.R. 4 C. & P. 495; *O'Donoghue v Hussey* (1871) I.R. 5 C.L. 124; *Dwyer v Esmonde* (1878) 2 L.R. Ir. 243.

585 *Roberston v M'Dougal* (1828) 4 Bing. 670; *Tuson v Evans* (1840) 12 A. & E. 733; *Senior v Medland* (1858) 4 Jur. (N.S.) 1039; *Koenig v Ritchie* (1862) 3 F. & F. 413; *Hancock v Case* (1862) 2 F. & F. 711; *Murphy v Halpin* (1874) I.R. 8 C.L. 127; and see *Turner v MGM Pictures Ltd* [1950] 1 All E.R. 449 at 470, per Lord Oaksey; *Mallet v Clarke* (1968) 70 D.L.R. (2d) 67.

parties.[586] In *Mengi v Hermitage*[587] the privilege applied even though the defendant had issued more than one "reply". However, in *Henry v BBC*[588] the defendant's claim of privilege was rejected where the "reply" came too long after the attack (in that case, a year). The privilege also extends to statements made by persons who are agents,[589] relatives or close associates of the person who has been attacked.[590] If the claimant is attacked in an obscure local newspaper and retaliates by publishing defamatory matter in a leading London paper or retorts in excessively intemperate language—if, in other words, he exceeds the occasion—the privilege is lost.[591] It may sometimes be the case that a charge can only be repelled by shifting the blame onto the shoulders of someone else. Where the defendant, a tradesman, wrote to a customer who had complained of being charged with the price of goods not delivered and laid the blame on the dishonesty of the claimant, who was a servant of the customer, the vindication was held to be privileged.[592] It would seem rather hard that a man, in order to protect his own character, should be allowed to impugn the character of another, possibly as innocent as himself. It has, however, been held that privilege is not lost by introducing the names of any persons which are reasonably required to make the communication clear and complete.[593] In the Australian case of *Radio 2UE Sydney Pty v Parker*[594] it was held that a person, whose character or conduct had been the subject of an attack in the media, was entitled to answer that attack in the press, on radio or on television. Statements made by him in that answer were held to be subject to qualified privilege and that privilege also protected the proprietor of the newspaper or radio station where his statements were made. In *Fraser-Armstrong v Hadow*,[595] the Court of Appeal held that the defendant could not avail himself of the defence of qualified privilege in defending himself against an attack by the claimant, where he knew the attack was justified, as this would constitute malice.

21-125 **Pre-emptive reply to attack** It is not clear whether the privilege extends to statements in rebuttal of an anticipated attack. In *Bhatt v Chelsea Westminster Healthcare NHS Trust*[596] the defendants had ceased to refer patients to the claimant's clinic and the claimant sued them in defamation in respect of press releases which they had prepared in relation to their conduct of the matter but had not yet released to the press. It was held that these press releases were covered by qualified privilege since they were prepared in reasonable expectation of an attack on them, even though the attack might not be by B himself but by the media or others. This approach was doubted, however, in *Bento v Chief Constable of Bedfordshire Police*.[597] Bean J was doubtful that a pre-emptive attack was covered by the privilege, but stated that even if it were it is confined to defamatory statements which are both

---

586 *Watts v Times Newspapers Ltd* [1997] Q.B. 650.
587 [2012] EWHC 3445 (QB).
588 [2005] EWHC 2787 (QB).
589 [2005] EWHC 2787 (QB); and *Regan v Taylor* [2000] E.M.L.R. 549.
590 *Standen v South Essex Recorders* (1934) 50 T.L.R. 365.
591 *Cooke v Wildes* (1855) 5 E. & B. 328; *Huntley v Ward* (1859) 1 F. & F. 552; *Fryer v Kinnersley* (1863) 15 C.B. (N.S.) 423 at 429; *Simpson v Downs* (1867) 16 L.T. 391; *Jones v Williams* (1885) 1 T.L.R. 572; *Fraser-Armstrong v Hadow* [1995] E.M.L.R. 140.
592 *Coward v Wellington* (1836) 7 C. & P. 531.
593 See *Watts v Times Newspapers Ltd* [1997] Q.B. 650.
594 (1992) 29 N.S.W.L.R. 448 (NSWCA).
595 [1995] E.M.L.R. 140. See also *Watts v Times Newspapers Ltd* [1997] Q.B. 650.
596 [1998] I.C.R. 576; [1997] I.R.L.R. 660.
597 [2012] EWHC 1525 (QB).

(1) in reasonable anticipation of an imminent attack; and (2) limited to a proportionate rebuttal of the anticipated attack.

Complaints against public officials It is lawful in the public interest[598] to make charges and complaints against all public officials, but such communications ought to be addressed only to those who have power to punish the offender or otherwise to redress the grievance.[599] The right to make specific accusations to particular persons must not be confounded with the general right of the public to discuss and comment on public matters. Therefore charges of misconduct against a poor-law official are not to be broadcast through the press, though they might properly be laid before the appropriate local authority.[600] In *Harrison v Bush*[601] it was held to be privileged to make a charge of misconduct against a magistrate to the Home Secretary, although the matter lay more immediately within the province of the Lord Chancellor. **21-126**

(2) Reports

Reports The privilege afforded to reports applies to reports of proceedings in courts of law, proceedings in Parliament, proceedings of certain statutory bodies and proceedings of public meetings and bodies. The Defamation Act 1996, supplemented by the Defamation Act 2013, extends absolute privilege to contemporaneous reports of judicial proceedings in public and extends and rationalises the law relating to qualified privilege for other proceedings. **21-127**

OF JUDICIAL PROCEEDINGS

Reports of legal proceedings at common law The general right of reporting legal proceedings has long been recognised at common law. "When you once establish that a court is a public court a fair and bona fide report of all that passes there may be published."[602] The 20th edition included a more detailed discussion of the privilege at common law.[603] Today, whilst the common law privilege subsists, the privilege is generally found within the Defamation Acts 1996 and 2013. **21-128**

---

598 Perhaps this may be said to be rather a general right than a privilege.

599 *Blagg v Sturt* (1846) 10 Q.B.D. 899; *Harrison v Bush* (1865) 5 E. & B. 344; *Purchell v Sowler* (1877) 2 C.P.D. 215 at 231; *Proctor v Webster* (1885) 16 Q.B.D. 112; *Jenoure v Delmege* [1891] A.C. 73; *Hebditch v MacIlwaine* [1894] 2 Q.B. 54; cf. *James v Baird* 1916 S.C. (HL) 158; sub nom. *Baird v Wallace-James* (1916), 85 L.J.P.C. 193; *Truth (NZ) Ltd v Holloway* [1960] N.Z.L.R. 69 (affirmed [1960] 1 W.L.R. 997 PC). As to communication to an MP by a constituent, see *R. v Rule* [1937] 2 K.B. 375; *Rivlin v Bilainkin* [1953] 1 Q.B. 485; and to the Bar Council or to the Benches of his Inn of Court by a member of the public about the conduct of a member of the Bar, see *Lincoln v Daniels* [1962] 1 Q.B. 237 at 252, 263, 264, 269; *Beach v Freeson* [1972] 1 Q.B. 14.

600 *Purcell v Sowler*; *Pittard v Oliver* [1891] 1 Q.B. 474; *Truth (NZ) Ltd v Holloway* [1960] N.Z.L.R. 69 (affirmed [1960] 1 W.L.R. 997 PC). And see *R. v Lancashire CC Police Authority Ex p. Hook* [1980] Q.B. 603 CA.

601 (1856) 5 E. & B. 344; cf. *R. v Rule* [1937] 2 K.B. 375. See also *Beach v Freeson* [1972] 1 Q.B. 14.

602 per Bramwell B in *Ryalls v Leader* (1866) L.R. 1 Ex. 296 at 300; per curiam, *Wason v Walter* (1868) L.R. 4 Q.B. 73 at 94. And see *Burnett v Sheffield Telegraph* [1960] 1 W.L.R. 502. But publication during the course of the proceedings of any extraneous matter likely to prejudice the course of justice may be contempt of court: *R. v Border Television Ex p. Att Gen* (1978) 68 Cr. App. R. 375, DC; *Att Gen v Leveller Magazine Ltd* [1979] A.C. 420 HL, but both decisions must now be read in the light of the Contempt of Court Act 1981. And in relation to publication of documents disclosed on discovery, see *Home Office v Harman* [1981] Q.B. 534 CA.

603 For detail see para.22-146 of the 20th edn.

21-129 **What may be reported** What is reported must be fairly a part of the proceedings. There is no right to report the unauthorised observations of a bystander[604] or disparaging observations made by any other than one who had a duty to make them[605]; nor even what a judge or magistrate says, unless in office. However, if it is necessary to inquire into the facts in order to see whether or not the court has jurisdiction, a report of such an inquiry is protected.[606] In *Farmer v Hyde*,[607] a person sitting in court intervened and the intervention was reported in five newspapers. It was held that the application made by this person was made in the course of proceedings publicly heard before a court exercising judicial authority and it made no difference that in the course of the application defamatory matter was published.

21-130 **Reports to be regarded as a whole** The general rule is that a report should be a fair account of the proceedings as a whole.[608] It must give with substantial accuracy the general effect of all that passed. Details may be omitted or summarised:

> "You may either have it to the utmost possible extent the limits of the paper will allow it to be given or in the more condensed form of a summary or epitome, but you must have the report honest and fair."[609]

21-131 **Fragmentary reports** It is lawful under certain circumstances to publish fragmentary reports. Thus, for instance, where a trial goes on from day to day there can be no doubt that the proceedings of each day may be published separately at the time.[610] However, after the trial is over it is probably not lawful to pick out one particular portion of the proceedings and publish a report of it, as this would be unlikely to be "fair and accurate" and therefore privileged.[611]

21-132 **Mixed comment and report** There are a number of older authorities which suggest that a report of proceedings will not be privileged if it is mixed with comments on what took place; that such comment should be kept separate from the report.[612] For example, Lord Denning in *Associated Newspapers Ltd v Dingle* stated that the privilege in the whole piece is lost where the publisher, although publishing a story to the same effect as the parliamentary paper, add its own details and

---

604 *Lynam v Gowing* (1880) 6 L.R.Ir. 259; cf., however, *Hope v Leng* (1907) 23 T.L.R. 243 (observation made by a party not in the box); and see *Farmer v Hyde* [1937] 1 K.B. 728.

605 *Delegal v Highley* (1837) 3 Bing. N.C. 950 at 960. Lord Goddard CJ held in *Laski v Newark Advertiser Ltd, The Times,* 3 December 1946, that it was to the public interest that "heckling" at a public meeting should be reported.

606 *Usill v Hales* (1878) 3 C.P.D. 319.

607 [1937] 1 K.B. 728.

608 cf. *Mitchell v Hirst, Kidd and Rennie* [1936] 3 All E.R. 872 (reporter, by inattention, failed to hear withdrawal of alternative charge); *Cook v Alexander* [1974] Q.B. 279 CA (report of a parliamentary debate).

609 *Risk Allah Bey v Whitehurst* (1868) 18 L.T. 615 at 618; *Webb v Times Publishing Co Ltd* [1960] 2 Q.B. 535.

610 *Lewis v Levy* (1858) E.B. & E. 537 at 560; *Kimber v Press Association* [1893] 1 Q.B. 65 at 71.

611 See *Gatley on Libel and Slander* (12th edn) at 13.45. For the absolute privilege in reports of judicial proceedings, see para.21-85.

612 per Cockburn CJ in *Risk Allah Bey v Whitehurst* (1868) 18 L.T. 615 at 618; considered in *Webb v Times Publishing Co Ltd* [1960] 2 Q.B. 535; *Stiles v Nokes* (1806) 7 East. 493; *Boydell v Jones* (1838) 7 Dowl. 210; *Lewis v Levy* (1858) E.B. & E. 537 at 553; *Hibbins v Lee* (1864) 4 F. & F. 243; and see *R. v Parke* [1903] 2 K.B. 432; cf. *Dingle v Associated Newspapers* [1961] 2 Q.B. 162 CA; affirmed [1964] A.C. 371 HL.

"spice": "It has 'put meat on the bones' and must answer for the whole joint."[613] However, in *Curistan v Times Newspapers Ltd* the court found that the report element of the article was still privileged under s.15 of the Defamation Act 1996, where the article also contained comment, but this was distinguishable and not "excessive".[614] The defence of honest comment may be available for comment on matters contained in a fair and accurate report of a judicial proceeding.[615]

OF PARLIAMENTARY DEBATES

Parliamentary reports under the common law The right to report parliamentary debates stands upon the same footing as the right to report proceedings in courts of law.[616] The report must amount to a fair representation of what took place in Parliament. The proceedings need not be reported in full, and a précis of a parliamentary debate, albeit written in a humorous sketch form, will be protected by privilege providing the selection of material is not arbitrary and unfair and that the matters highlighted are in truth the issues of real public interest or concern raised in the debate.[617] A fragmentary report of part of a debate which did not give a fair view of what took place would probably still not be protected.[618] In *Curistan v Times Newspapers Ltd*[619] the defendant newspaper reported on defamatory allegations which had been made of the claimant in the course of parliamentary proceedings, but added further factual allegations discovered through its own investigations. The defendant relied on statutory qualified privilege under s.15 of the Defamation Act 1996 (Pt 1 of Sch.1) and the court was required to determine the question of qualified privilege as a preliminary issue. The question was whether passages in the article which reiterated the accusations made in Parliament were protected by qualified privilege as being a fair and accurate report of the proceedings, notwithstanding the inclusion in the article of the additional allegations. The court ruled that the words reflected what had been said about the claimant in Parliament and that there was a clear and real nexus between those statements and the further material; the privilege was not lost by virtue of the inclusion of additional material. 21-133

OF OTHER PROCEEDINGS AND MEETINGS

Reports of other proceedings and meetings Privilege has been held at common law to attach to reports of other proceedings and meetings where it is in the public interest to do so.[620] However, there appears to be no practical reason to rely upon the common law defence rather than the categories of statutory qualified privileged in the Defamation Act 1996 (as extended by the Defamation Act 2013) and there is no known case where a report has been held to be privileged at common law but failed to attract privilege under the Act. In *Qadir v Associated* 21-134

613 [1964] A.C. 371 at 411.
614 [2008] EWCA Civ 432; [2009] Q.B. 231.
615 See for example *Addis v Odhams Press* [1958] 1 Q.B. 310; affirmed [1958] 2 Q.B. 275 CA.
616 *Wason v Walter* (1868) L.R. 4 Q.B. 73 at 93–94; cf. *Perera v Peiris* [1949] A.C. 1 at 20–21.
617 *Cook v Alexander* [1974] Q.B. 279, CA (there is also a right to comment on a fair and accurate report of proceedings in Parliament).
618 *Wason v Walter* (1868) L.R. 4 Q.B. 73. As to privilege for information given by an MP to a constituent, see para.21-94 fn.470.
619 [2008] EWCA Civ 432; [2009] Q.B. 231.
620 *Macintosh v Dun* [1908] A.C. 390; *Perera v Peiris* [1949] A.C. 1 at 14; *Tsikata v Newspaper Publishing Plc* [1997] 1 All E.R. 655.

Newspapers Ltd[621] Tugendhat J expressed doubt as to whether this common law form of privilege remained necessary in the light of the existence of the *Reynolds* defence (publication on a matter of public interest).

(iii) Statements covered by statutory qualified privilege

(1) General

21-135 **Statements covered by qualified privilege under the Defamation Act 1996** Reports are divided into two categories under the Defamation Act 1996. Section 15 provides that qualified privilege applies to the publication of certain reports specified in Sch.1 to the Act. The first category (see Pt I of Sch.1) comprises statements privileged "without explanation or contradiction", the second category (see Pt II of Sch.1) comprises statements which are privileged "subject to explanation or contradiction". With regard to statements within the second category (i.e. covered by Pt II of Sch.1), s.15 provides that qualified privilege will not be a defence if it is proved that the defendant has been requested by the claimant to publish in a suitable manner a reasonable letter or statement by way of explanation or contradiction, and has refused or neglected to do so. "In a suitable manner" means "in the same manner as the publication complained of, or in a manner that is adequate or reasonable in the circumstances."[622] In *Khan v Ahmed*[623] it was held that a letter demanding a full apology in terms satisfactory to the claimant was not a request within the meaning of the section, as s.7(2) of the 1952 Act (similar in terms to s.15 of the 1996 Act) contemplated a special request that the defendant should publish an explanation or contradiction in the terms put forward by the person allegedly libelled.

21-136 **Public interest and public benefit** As originally enacted s.15 of the 1996 Act further provided in relation to both categories of statements privileged by statute that nothing in the section is to be construed as protecting the publication of any matter the publication of which is prohibited by law, or of any matter which is not of public concern and the publication of which is not for the public benefit.[624] The Defamation Act 2013 amended this test, removing "public concern" and replacing it with "public interest".[625] This is intended to ensure uniformity of terminology, though it seems unlikely that it will make any practical difference to the test. In applying this, all the circumstances of the case must be taken into account, but it obviously imposes on reports the responsibility of excluding all irrelevant matter of a defamatory nature which may be dragged into a public discussion.[626] In *Tsikata v Newspaper Publishing Plc*[627] the Court of Appeal held that the publication by the defendants of reports describing findings of a government inquiry conducted in the

---

621 [2012] EWHC 2606 (QB); [2013] E.M.L.R. 15 at [112].

622 Defamation Act 1996 s.15.

623 [1957] 2 Q.B. 149.

624 s.15(3); for similar wording under the Defamation Act 1952, see *Boston v WS Bagshaw & Sons* [1966] 1 W.L.R. 1126 CA (television broadcast by police, in order to find a criminal, of public concern, and for the public benefit and privileged within the Act). The impressions of a chairman of a company as to the guilt of a servant of the company are not a matter of public concern within the section: *Ponsford v Financial Times* (1900) 16 T.L.R. 62.

625 s.7(2).

626 cf. *Kelly v O'Malley* (1889) 6 T.L.R. 248.

627 [1997] 1 All E.R. 655; s.7(4). The common law principle by virtue of which qualified privilege arises

claimant's own country overseas and implicating him in a plot was not deprived of a prima facie defence of qualified privilege under s.7(3) of the Defamation Act 1952 on the grounds that it was "not of public concern and not for the public benefit". This was a question of fact and the court held that there was legitimate public concern about human rights in the Commonwealth and public benefit in receiving information about the proceedings since the claimant was a politician and a public figure and there was an approaching election in his country. Like s.7 of the Defamation Act 1952 the 1996 Act provides expressly that nothing in s.15 is to be construed as protecting the publication of matter the publication of which is prohibited by law or as limiting or abridging any privilege subsisting apart from this section.[628] In *Qadir v Associated Newspapers Ltd*[629] the court held that it was not for the public benefit to publish allegations without also including the fact that they had been denied or disputed.[630]

Defamation Act 2013—amendments to Schedule 1 of the 1996 Act The 2013 Act added to and extended the categories of privilege set out under the 1996 Act, the main effect of which is to "internationalise" them, extending them beyond proceedings in UK or the European Union. Further, various categories of privilege which previously only attached to fair and accurate "copies of or extracts from" the publication in question, are now extended to include "summaries" of the publication. An addition to the categories of privilege is reports of the proceedings of scientific or academic conferences. **21-137**

(2) Statements privileged without explanation or contradiction

Statements privileged without explanation or contradiction[631] Part I of Sch.1 to the Defamation Act 1996 specifies the following statements as having qualified privilege without explanation or contradiction. The Defamation Act 2013 made no change to Pt I: **21-138**

(1) A fair and accurate report of proceedings in public of a legislature anywhere in the world.
(2) A fair and accurate report of proceedings in public before a court anywhere in the world.
(3) A fair and accurate report of proceedings in public of a person appointed to hold a public inquiry by a government or legislature anywhere in the world.
(4) A fair and accurate report of proceedings in public anywhere in the world of an international organisation or an international conference.
(5) A fair and accurate copy of or extract from any register or other document required by law to be open to public inspection.
(6) A notice or advertisement published by or on the authority of a court, or of a judge or officer of a court, anywhere in the world.

---

may still apply in cases not covered by the statutory extensions: cf. *Toogood v Spyring* (1834) 1 C.M. & R. 181 at 193; *Purcell v Sowler* (1877) 2 C.P.D. 215; *London Association for the Protection of Trade v Greenlands* [1916] 2 A.C. 15 at 23; *Perera v Peiris* [1949] A.C. 1 at 19-31; Wade, 66 L.Q.R. 348 at 352–353; and see para.21-139.

628 See also *McCartan Turkington Breen v Times Newspapers Ltd* [2001] 2 A.C. 277 (decided under the Defamation Act (Northern Ireland) 1955 s.7, corresponding to s.15 of the Defamation Act 1996).

629 [2012] EWHC 2606 (QB); [2013] E.M.L.R. 15.

630 See further para.21-140.

631 See *Curistan v Times Newspapers Ltd* [2008] EWCA Civ 432; [2009] Q.B. 231.

(7) A fair and accurate copy of or extract from matter published by or on the authority of a government or legislature anywhere in the world.

(8) A fair and accurate copy of or extract from matter published anywhere in the world by an international organisation or an international conference.

21-139 **Tsikata v Newspaper Publishing** In *Tsikata v Newspaper Publishing*[632] the claimant sued in respect of a report in the defendants' newspaper which stated that the claimant had been implicated by a special inquiry, 10 years earlier, in Ghana, his native country, into the killing of several judges. The defendants pleaded qualified privilege under s.7(1) and para.5 of the Schedule to the Defamation Act 1952 in that the report was a fair and accurate report of proceedings in public of a person appointed to hold a public inquiry by the government or legislature of Ghana. The claimant denied that the report was privileged on a number of grounds, namely that this was not a report within the relevant enactment since it was published 10 years after the inquiry, that it was not fair and accurate since it did not refer to certain facts, especially that the claimant had not been prosecuted because of the lack of evidence against him, that the inquiry had not been a proceeding in public and that, because of the passage of time, the publication could no longer be said to be of public concern or for the public benefit. On the trial of a preliminary issue the judge held that the report was covered by qualified privilege. The Court of Appeal dismissed the claimant's appeal and upheld the finding that a prima facie defence of qualified privilege had been established. In relation to the report of the inquiry, the court held that on a purposive interpretation of the term, the report did not have to be contemporary and that the inquiry had been a proceeding in public.

21-140 In *Qadir v Associated Newspapers Ltd*[633] a newspaper published two articles about court proceedings, one referring to the particulars of claim which accused the claimant of being involved in an alleged dishonest business deal, and another reporting on a sentencing hearing in a criminal fraud claim. In the first, the defendant did not report that the claimant disputed the claim or the contents of his defence, which had been filed five weeks before the newspaper article was published. The court held that it was not for the public benefit to publish the allegations without the fact that they had been denied/disputed. Further, there was no public interest in publishing the false information that the claimant had "declined to comment". In the second article, which alleged that the claimant had been "intimately involved" in "Britain's biggest mortgage fraud", those comments had been made during a sentencing hearing by counsel, but the judge had rebuked counsel, stating that he could not determine the complicity of others. The judge's comments had not been reported by the newspaper. The court held that the report of the sentencing hearing was not a fair and accurate report of those proceedings. The omission of the judge's comments seriously unbalanced the report, to the extent that the defendant could not rely upon the privilege, whether absolute or qualified.

(3) Statements privileged subject to explanation or contradiction

---

[632] [1997] 1 All E.R. 655.

[633] [2012] EWHC 2606 (QB); [2013] E.M.L.R. 15.

Statements privileged subject to explanation or contradiction[634] Part II of the Schedule to the Defamation Act 1996, as extended by the Defamation Act 2013,[635] specifies the following statements as having qualified privilege subject to explanation or contradiction: **21-141**

"9.—(1) A fair and accurate copy of, extract from or summary of a notice or other matter issued for the information of the public by or on behalf of—

(a) a legislature or government anywhere in the world;

(b) an authority anywhere in the world performing governmental functions;

(c) an international organisation or international conference.

(2) In this paragraph "governmental functions" includes police functions.

10. A fair and accurate copy of, extract from or summary of a document made available by a court anywhere in the world or by a judge or officer of such a court.

11.—(1) A fair and accurate report of proceedings at any public meeting or sitting in the United Kingdom of—

(a) a local authority or local authority committee;

(aa) in the case of a local authority which are operating executive arrangements, the executive of that authority or a committee of that executive;

(b) a justice or justices of the peace acting otherwise than as a court exercising judicial authority;

(c) a commission, tribunal, committee or person appointed for the purposes of any inquiry by any statutory provision, by Her Majesty or by a Minister of the Crown, a member of the Scottish Executive, the Welsh Ministers or the Counsel General to the Welsh Assembly Government or a Northern Ireland Department.

(d) a person appointed by a local authority to hold a local inquiry in pursuance of any statutory provision;

(e) any other tribunal, board, committee or body constituted by or under, and exercising functions under, any statutory provisions.

(1A) In the case of a local authority which are operating executive arrangements, a fair and accurate record of any decision made by any member of the executive where that record is required to be made and available for public inspection by virtue of s.22 of the Local Government Act 2000 or of any provision in regulations made under that section.

(2) In sub-paragraph (1)(a), (1)(aa) and (1A)—

"local authority" means—

(a) in relation to England and Wales, a principal council within the meaning of the Local Government Act 1972, any body falling within any paragraph of section 100J(1) of that Act or an authority or body to which the Public Bodies (Admission to Meetings) Act 1960 applies,

(b) in relation to Scotland, a council constituted under section 2 of the Local Government etc. (Scotland) Act 1994 or an authority or body to which the Public Bodies (Admission to Meetings) Act 1960 applies.

(c) in relation to Northern Ireland, any authority or body to which sections 23 to 27 of the Local Government Act (Northern Ireland) 1972 apply; and

"local authority committee" means any committee of a local authority or of local authorities, and includes—

(a) any committee or sub-committee in relation to which sections 100A to 100D of the Local Government Act 1972 apply by virtue of section 100E of that Act (whether or not also by virtue of section 100J of that Act), and

(b) any committee or sub-committee in relation to which sections 50A to 50D of the Local Government (Scotland) Act 1973 apply by virtue of section 50E of that Act.

(2A) In sub-paragraphs (1) and (1A)—

"executive" and "executive arrangements" have the same meaning as in Part II of the Local Government Act 2000.

---

634 See *McCartan Turkington Breen v Times Newspapers Ltd* [2001] 2 A.C. 277.

635 See the 20th edition for the Schedule under the 1996 Act alone (i.e. as it applies to publications prior to 1 January 2014).

(3) A fair and accurate report of any corresponding proceedings in any of the Channel Islands or the Isle of Man or in another member State.

11A. A fair and accurate report of proceedings at a press conference held anywhere in the world for the discussion of a matter of public interest.

12.—(1) A fair and accurate report of proceedings at any public meeting held anywhere in the world.

(2) In this paragraph a "public meeting" means a meeting bona fide and lawfully held for a lawful purpose and for the furtherance or discussion of a matter of public interest, whether admission to the meeting is general or restricted.

13.—(1) A fair and accurate report of proceedings at a general meeting of a listed company.

(2) A fair and accurate copy of, extract from or summary of any document circulated to members of a listed company—

(a) by or with the authority of the board of directors of the company,

(b) by the auditors of the company, or

(c) by any member of the company in pursuance of a right conferred by any statutory provision.

(3) A fair and accurate copy or extract from or summary of any document circulated to members of a listed company which relates to the appointment, resignation, retirement or dismissal of directors of the company or its auditors.

(4) In this paragraph "listed company" has the same meaning as in Part 12 of the Corporation Tax Act 2009 (see section 1005 of that Act).

14. A fair and accurate report of any finding or decision of any of the following descriptions of association, formed anywhere in the world, or of any committee or governing body of such an association—

(a) an association formed for the purpose of promoting and encouraging the exercise of or interest in any art, science, religion or learning, and empowered by its constitution to exercise control over or adjudicate on matters of interest or concern to the association, or the actions or conduct of any person subject to such control or adjudication;

(b) an association formed for the purpose of promoting or safeguarding the interests of any trade, business, industry or profession, or of the persons carrying on or engaged in any trade, business, industry or profession, and empowered by its constitution to exercise control over or adjudicate upon matters connected with that trade, business, industry or profession, or the actions or conduct of those persons;

(c) an association formed for the purpose of promoting or safeguarding the interests of a game, sport or pastime to the playing or exercise of which members of the public are invited or admitted, and empowered by its constitution to exercise control over or adjudicate upon persons connected with or taking part in the game, sport or pastime;

(d) an association formed for the purpose of promoting charitable objects or other objects beneficial to the community and empowered by its constitution to exercise control over or to adjudicate on matters of interest or concern to the association, or the actions or conduct of any person subject to such control or adjudication.

14A. A fair and accurate—

(a) report of proceedings of a scientific or academic conference held anywhere in the world, or

(b) copy of, extract from or summary of matter published by such a conference.

15.—(1) A fair and accurate report or summary of, or copy of or extract from, any adjudication, report, statement or notice issued by a body, officer or other person designated for the purposes of this paragraph by order of the Lord Chancellor.

(2) An order under this paragraph shall be made by statutory instrument which shall be subject to annulment in pursuance of a resolution of either House of Parliament."

The list of statements subject to qualified privilege can be extended by the Lord Chancellor. The Broadcasting Act 1996 makes provisions for OFCOM to publish its findings in relation to complaints about fairness or standards in broadcasting, and for the publication to be protected by qualified privilege.[636]

[636] ss.119 and 121.

Extent of qualified privilege under s.15 In *Blackshaw v Lord*[637] the Court of Appeal indicated that while para.12 of the 1952 Act (now replaced by para.15 of the 1996 Act) covered more than written statements handed out by officials of government departments and included oral information given to journalists, information volunteered by the relevant department fell more within the spirit of the provision than information elicited by a journalist's interrogation of an official. Even if statements made in response to questioning fell within para.12, assumptions, inferences and speculation on the part of the journalist clearly did not. In *McCartan Turkington Breen v Times Newspapers Ltd*[638] the claimants raised, inter alia, the argument that the defendants' article had quoted from a press release which had not actually been read aloud at the press conference. The House of Lords refused to rule that this therefore fell outside the protection of qualified privilege—it could be regarded as common practice and part of the "proceedings" of the meeting. 21-142

(4) Other instances of statutory qualified privilege

Statement at election One occasion of qualified privilege which could once have arisen by virtue of duty and interest[639] has been limited by statute. Section 10 of the Defamation Act 1952 provides that: 21-143

> "A defamatory statement published by or on behalf of a candidate in any election to a local government authority, to the National Assembly for Wales, to the Scottish Parliament or to Parliament shall not be deemed to be published on a privileged occasion on the ground that it is material to a question in issue at the election, whether or not the person to whom it is published is qualified to vote at the election."[640]

However, in *Culnane v Morris*[641] Eady J read the provision down as required by s.3 of the Human Rights Act 1998, stating that an election candidate could rely on privilege, as could any other citizen, if all the other elements of qualified privilege were present. It would impinge on a litigant's rights under art.6 and art.10 of the European Convention on Human Rights if he or she was precluded by the provision from relying on qualified privilege.

Privilege of petition As has been already seen, the publication of a petition in Parliament is absolutely privileged,[642] provided that such publication takes place in the due order and course of parliamentary proceedings. There is also of necessity a publication involved in preparing petitions and procuring signatures.[643] The nature of the privilege attaching to such publication appears to be undetermined. It has 21-144

---

637 [1984] Q.B. 1.

638 [2001] 2 A.C. 277.

639 See *Braddock v Bevins* [1948] 1 K.B. 580 at 589–593.

640 This section has altered the law as laid down in *Braddock v Bevins*, on this point: *Plummer v Charman* [1962] 1 W.L.R. 1469 CA (the court were prepared to consider that there might be an exceptional case where there might be a duty or interest to make the communication irrespective of the election). See also *Greenaway v Poole* [2003] EWHC 1735 (QB); permission to appeal refused: [2004] EWCA Civ 210.

641 [2005] EWHC 2438 (QB); [2006] 1 W.L.R. 2880.

642 See para.21-91; and *Dunne v Anderson* (1825) 3 Bing. 88.

643 There is no right to make defamatory statements at a meeting assembled to petition Parliament: *Hearne v Stowell* (1840) 12 A. & E. 719. Nor is a letter to an MP privileged where the publication is not connected in any way with parliamentary proceedings, *Rivlin v Bilainkin* [1953] 1 Q.B. 485. As to a letter by an MP to a Minister, see para.21-91.

been stated that the privilege is only qualified, but this may be doubted.[644] A petition to the Crown in its legislative capacity would appear to stand on the same footing as a petition to one of the Houses of Parliament.[645] When a petition is addressed to the executive the privilege is only qualified.[646]

21-145 **Parliamentary papers** In order to protect individuals in the reasonable use, for the purposes of discussion and information, of extracts and abstracts of papers published by parliamentary authority, a qualified privilege is created by s.3 of the Parliamentary Papers Act 1840,[647] which enacts that in any proceedings for printing (and now broadcasting under the Broadcasting Act 1990)[648] any such extract or abstract, it shall be lawful:

> "to give in evidence such report, paper, votes, or proceedings, and to show that such extract or abstract was published bona fide and without malice; and if such shall be the opinion of the jury, a verdict of not guilty shall be entered ..."

There may also be a defence of honest opinion available for allegations made against a person in an extract thus protected, though the allegations may be untrue. Such comment if made in the form of a letter to the press by a public servant (and published in a newspaper) on the conduct of another taking part in public affairs is protected as the matter is one of public interest as to which the public are entitled to information.[649] In cases falling under the Parliamentary Papers Act 1840, the burden is on the defendant to prove bona fides. If a newspaper seeks to rely on the privilege attaching to a parliamentary paper it can print an extract from the parliamentary paper and make any fair comment on it, and can reasonably expect other newspapers to do the same. But if it prints not an extract from the parliamentary paper but a story or feature to the same effect as the parliamentary paper but separate and distinct from it and garnishes and embellishes it with additional matter it is not protected by the privilege and is subject to the general law.[650] The Joint Committee on Parliamentary Privilege has called for the Parliamentary Papers Act 1840 to be replaced by modern statutory provisions which would, amongst other things, place the burden of proving malice on the claimant.[651]

21-146 **Peer reviewed statements in scientific or academic journals** Section 6 of the Defamation Act 2013 provides qualified privilege for peer-reviewed statements

---

644 per Best J in *Fairman v Ives* (1823) 5 B. & A. 642 at 648.

645 *Hare and Mellers Case* (1586) 3 Leo. 163.

646 *Fairman v Ives* (1823) 5 B. & A. 642; *Proctor v Webster* (1885) 16 Q.B.D. 112 (letter addressed to the Privy Council).

647 cf. *Mangena v Lloyd* (1908) 98 L.T. 640 at 642 (the section must be taken to mean where he prints and publishes). The decision in *Mangena v Lloyd* was reversed on another ground: *Mangena v Lloyd* (1909) 99 L.T. 824 CA. The first instance decision in *Mangena v Lloyd* was followed in *Mangena v Wright* [1909] 2 K.B. 958; *Dingle v Associated Newspapers Ltd* [1961] 2 Q.B. 162 CA; affirmed [1964] A.C. 371.

648 See s.203 and Sch.20 para.1.

649 *Mangena v Wright* [1909] 2 K.B. 958. See also *Addis v Odhams Press Ltd* [1958] 2 Q.B. 275 at 285, for a similar ruling in relation to fair comment on a fair report of a judicial proceedings. *Mangena v Wright* was considered by the High Court of Australia in *Bailey v Truth and Sportsman Ltd* (1938) 60 C.L.R. 700.

650 *Dingle v Associated Newspapers Ltd* [1964] A.C. 371 at 411, per Lord Denning.

651 *Joint Committee on Parliamentary Privilege Report of Session* 2013–14, pp.195–196.

published in scientific or academic journals,[652] which will be defeated only by malice.[653] To fall under the privilege two conditions must be met: (1) the statement relates to "a scientific or academic matter"[654]; and (2) that before the statement was published in the journal "an independent review of the statement's scientific or academic merit was carried out by (a) the editor of the journal; and (b) one or more persons with expertise in the scientific or academic matter concerned".[655] Neither "scientific" nor "academic" are defined by the Act, and the degree of independence and expertise required to fulfil the provisions of the Act also remain open to question. The defence is fairly narrowly defined and would not have applied in any of the cases which prompted attention to the area of free speech in scientific and academic debate.[656] Where the publication of a statement is privileged under s.6, publication of a fair or accurate copy of, extract from or summary of the statement is also privileged.[657]

(d) Publication on a matter of public interest

(i) Reynolds defence/defence under s.4 of the Defamation Act 2013

Publication on matters of public interest—the Reynolds defence/section 4 defence 21-147 In *Reynolds v Times Newspapers Ltd*[658] the House of Lords reviewed the law relating to qualified privilege in respect of publications in the media, and established a new variant of qualified privilege in which less emphasis was placed on the traditional, reciprocal duty and interest test, and more on the question of whether the publication was on a matter of public interest and whether it was the product of responsible journalism. After *Reynolds* the defence twice came before the highest court again,[659] in cases in which the court emphasised the potential flexibility of the defence. Criticism remained, however, that judges had engaged in over-heavy scrutiny of journalistic practices[660] and that the defence had not been applied widely enough beyond the paradigm of investigative journalism.[661] The elements of the common law *Reynolds* defence were summarised in *Rai v Bholowasia*[662] as: (1) there being a real public interest in the matter about which the material is published; (2) it being reasonable to include the material complained of as part of the overall story; and (3) the steps taken to gather and publish the information must have been responsible and fair (i.e. responsible journalism). Section 4 of the Defamation Act 2013 not only placed the defence on a statutory footing but also

---

652 The privilege covers statements whether published in electronic form or otherwise (s.6(1)) and also covers assessments of the statement carried out by one of the persons who independently reviewed the statements and written in the course of that review if published in the same journal (s.6(4)).
653 s.6(2).
654 s.6(3).
655 s.6(3).
656 Such as *British Chiropractic Association v Singh* [2010] EWCA Civ 350; [2011] 1 W.L.R 133; and *El Naschie v MacMillan Publishers Ltd* [2012] EWHC 1809 (QB).
657 s.6(5).
658 [2001] 2 A.C. 127.
659 *Jameel v Wall Street Journal Europe SPRL* [2006] UKHL 44; [2007] 1 A.C. 359; and *Flood v Times Newspapers Ltd* [2012] UKSC 11; [2012] 2 A.C. 273.
660 *Jameel v Wall Street Journal Europe SPRL* [2006] UKHL 44; [2007] 1 A.C. 359 at [38], per Lord Hoffmann.
661 For example, Libel Reform Group report *Free Speech Is Not For Sale* (2009).
662 [2015] EWHC 382 (QB).

altered it, so that the focus is now on (1) whether the statement was on a matter of public interest; and (2) whether the defendant reasonably believed that publication was in the public interest.[663] Nonetheless, the s.4 defence is expressly stated in the Explanatory Notes to the Act to be intended to reflect the *Reynolds* defence as set out by the Supreme Court in *Flood v Times Newspapers Ltd*.[664] Whether it in fact does so or not, the *Reynolds* jurisprudence is likely to remain a useful guide when dealing with the statutory defence.

21-148 **Public interest** There must be a real public interest in the matter about which the statement in question is published. There is no one test of what constitutes public interest, although guidance can be drawn both from defamation cases and from cases in related areas such as copyright, breach of confidence and misuse of private information, all of which use the concept. Examples include: government and political conduct,[665] promotion of animal welfare,[666] protection of public health and safety,[667] involvement in serious criminal activity,[668] the conduct of the police,[669] cheating, corruption or pressure on athletes in sport,[670] breach of charitable fiduciary rules,[671] corporate malpractice,[672] and correction of prior statements or misrepresentations by others.[673] In *Reynolds* itself the Court of Appeal offered the following guidance on what was meant by matters of public interest:

> "matters relating to the public life of the community and those who take part in it, including ... activities such as the conduct of government and political life, elections ... and public administration ... [and] more widely ... the governance of public bodies, institutions and companies which give rise to a public interest in disclosure, but excluding matters which are personal and private, such that there is no public interest in disclosure."[674]

Section 4 of the 2013 Act does not define public interest, and the Explanatory Notes

---

663 s.4(1).

664 [2012] UKSC 11; [2012] 2 A.C. 273, see Explanatory Notes at [29].

665 *Al Fagih v HH Saudi Research and Marketing (UK) Ltd* [2001] EWCA Civ 1634; [2002] E.M.L.R. 13; *Henry v BBC* [2005] EWHC 2787 (QB); *Cook v Telegraph Media Group Ltd* [2011] EWHC 763 (QB).

666 *Imutran Ltd v Uncaged Campaigns Ltd* [2001] All E.R. 385.

667 *Hubbard v Vosper* [1972] 2 Q.B. 84; *McKeith v News Group Newspapers Ltd* [2005] EWHC 1162 (QB); [2005] E.M.L.R. 32; *W v Edgell* [1990] Ch. 359.

668 *Hunt v Times Newspapers Ltd* [2013] EWHC 1868 (QB); *Lukowiak v Unidad Editorial SA* [2001] E.M.L.R. 46; *Loutchansky v Times Newspapers Ltd (Nos 2-5)* [2001] EWCA Civ 1805; [2002] Q.B. 783; *Jameel v Wall Street Journal Sprl* [2006] UKHL 44; [2007] 1 A.C. 359.

669 *Flood v Times Newspapers Ltd* [2012] UKSC 11; [2012] 2 A.C. 273; *Charman v Orion Publishing Group Ltd* [2007] EWCA Civ 972; [2008] 1 All E.R. 750; *Miller v Associated Newspapers* [2003] EWHC 2799 (QB); [2004] E.M.L.R. 33; *Hunt v Times Newspapers Ltd* [2013] EWHC 1868 (QB).

670 *Jockey Club v Buffham* [2002] EWHC 1866 (QB); *Armstrong v Times Newspapers Ltd* [2005] EWCA Civ 1007; [2005] E.M.L.R. 33; *Grobbelaar v News Group Newspapers Ltd* [2001] EWCA Civ 33; [2001] E.M.L.R. 18 (reversed on appeal, but not on this point: [2002] UKHL 40; [2002] 1 W.L.R. 3024); *Spelman v Express Newspapers* [2012] EWHC 355 (QB).

671 *Seray-Wurie v Charity Commission of England and Wales* [2008] EWHC 870 (QB).

672 *Cream Holdings Ltd v Banerjee* [2004] UKHL 44; [2005] 1 A.C. 253; *Loutchansky v Times Newspapers Ltd (Nos 2-5)* [2001] EWCA Civ 1805; [2002] Q.B. 783; *KGM v News Group Newspapers Ltd* [2011] EWCA Civ 808; [2012] E.M.L.R. 2.

673 *Prince Radu of Hohenzollern v Houston* [2007] EWHC 2328 (QB); *Hyde Park Residence Ltd v Yelland* [1999] E.M.L.R. 654; *KGM v News Group Newspapers Ltd* [2011] EWCA Civ 808; [2012] E.M.L.R. 2; *Ferdinand v MGN Ltd* [2011] EWHC 2454 (QB).

674 [1998] 3 W.L.R. 862, 909.

state that the concept is "well-established in the English common law".[675] It is notable that under s.4 it is either the whole or part of the publication which must be on a matter of public interest, not necessarily the specific statement complained of. This reflects the importance given to editorial judgment under s.4 and the idea that editorial judgment may see some items included for journalistic reasons that might be said not to be strictly necessary for the public to learn. Some guidance on the public interest may also be found in "relevant privacy codes" such as the IPSO Editors' Code of Practice.

Responsible journalism An essential element of the defence at common law is whether "the steps taken to gather and publish the information were responsible and fair."[676] In *Reynolds* Lord Nicholls identified ten non-exhaustive criteria which the court should consider in determining whether the standards of responsible journalism have been met[677]: 21-149

"1. The seriousness of the allegation. The more serious the charge, the more the public is misinformed and the individual harmed, if the allegation is not true.
2. The nature of the information, and the extent to which the subject matter is in a matter of public concern.[678]
3. The source of the information. Some informants have no direct knowledge of the events. Some have their own axes to grind, or are being paid for their stories.[679]
4. Steps taken to verify the story. See above.[680]
5. The status of the information. The allegation may have already been the subject of an investigation which commands respect.
6. The urgency of the matter. News is often a perishable commodity.
7. Whether comment was sought from the [claimant]. He may have information others do not possess or have not disclosed. An approach to the [claimant] will not always be necessary.[681]
8. Whether the article contained the gist of the [claimant's] side of the story.
9. The tone of the article. A newspaper can raise queries or call for an investigation. It need not adopt allegations as statements of fact.
10. The circumstances of publication, including the timing.

The list is not exhaustive. The weight to be given to the various factors will vary from case to case. Any disputes of primary fact will be a matter for the jury, if there is one. The decision on whether, having regard to the admitted or proved facts, the publication was subject to qualified privilege is a matter for the judge. This is the established practice and seems sound. A balancing operation is better carried out by a judge in a reasoned judgment than by a jury. Over time, a valuable corpus of case law will be built up.

675 *Explanatory Notes to the Defamation Act* 2013 at [30].

676 *Jameel v Wall Street Journal Europe SPRL* [2006] UKHL 44; [2007] 1 A.C. 359 at [53].

677 [2001] 2 A.C. 127 at 205. In *James Gilbert Ltd v MGN Ltd* [2000] E.M.L.R. 680, Eady J stated that a judge who has not clearly applied these criteria to the facts of the case may be vulnerable to the contention on appeal that he has not addressed all relevant matters.

678 There is an apparent tension with point 1, the seriousness of the allegation. It will often be the case that the more serious the allegation, the more important it is that the public should know about it.

679 What is relevant is the apparent and not the actual reliability of the source. See *GKR Karate (UK) Ltd v Yorkshire Post Newspapers Ltd* [2000] 1 W.L.R. 2571.

680 The adequacy of the steps taken by the defendant to verify the story is to be judged objectively by the court. The issue is not whether the journalist believed that proper steps had been taken, although this may be relevant to malice. See *GKR Karate (UK) Ltd v Yorkshire Post Newspapers Ltd* [2000] 1 W.L.R. 2571.

681 Nevertheless, in the absence of good reason, the failure to make an approach to the claimant or publish the response will inevitably be a factor that weighs heavily against a defendant. See [2001] 2 A.C. 127 at 206.

In general, a newspaper's unwillingness to disclose the identity of its sources should not weigh against it. Further, it should always be remembered that journalists act without the benefit of the clear light of hindsight. Matters which are obvious in retrospect may have been far from clear in the heat of the moment. Above all, the court should have particular regard to the importance of freedom of expression. The press discharges vital functions as a bloodhound as well as a watchdog. The court should be slow to conclude that a publication was not in the public interest and, therefore, the public had no right to know, especially when the information is in the field of political discussion. Any lingering doubts should be resolved in favour of publication."[682]

Lord Nicholls recognised that the generality of this approach would inevitably give rise to uncertainty, but expected that a body of case law would build up.[683]

21-150 **Development of the Reynolds defence** The nature and ambit of the *Reynolds* defence has been explored in numerous subsequent cases. From these the following principles have emerged:

(1) In considering whether a journalist has a duty to publish, the court should not ask whether he would be "open to criticism" if he did not publish. That is too stringent a test. There will be occasions where one newspaper decides to publish an allegation and another does not. The issue is whether the newspaper that did publish acted reasonably and responsibly in doing so.[684] The court should give due deference to editorial discretion.[685]
(2) The court can only consider the information known to the journalist at the date of publication. Whether a journalist has behaved reasonably and responsibly depends on what information was available when he wrote the article.[686]
(3) The *Nicholls* factors must be approached practically and flexibly, they are not a series of hurdles to be negotiated in succession.[687]
(4) Where the newspaper unambiguously asserts that the claimant is guilty of a criminal offence, justification is likely to be the only available defence.[688]
(5) Where the publication conveys a more serious defamatory meaning than was intended by the journalist, the defence of qualified privilege may still be available if it was reasonable for the journalist to conclude that the publication bore the meaning which he intended it to have.[689]
(6) There is no generic privilege for the maintenance of an archive of past press publications, whether electronic or hard copy. If circumstances have changed since the article was originally published, qualified privilege may no longer be available where the newspaper does not modify the version of the article on its website.[690]

---

682 Although, giving the benefit of the doubt to the defendant is consistent with art.10 of the ECHR the burden of proof notionally remains on the defendant.
683 This is a feature of the cases of the European Court of Human Rights.
684 *Loutchansky v Times Newspapers Ltd* [2001] EWCA Civ 536; [2002] Q.B. 321.
685 *Jameel v Wall Street Journal Europe SPRL* [2006] UKHL 44; [2007] 1 A.C. 359.
686 *Loutchansky* [2001] EWCA Civ 536; [2002] Q.B. 321.
687 *Jameel v Wall Street Journal Europe SPRL* [2006] UKHL 44; [2007] 1 A.C. 359.
688 *Grobbelaar v News Group Newspapers Ltd* [2002] UKHL 40; [2002] 1 W.L.R. 3024.
689 *Bonnick v Morris* [2002] UKPC 31; [2003] 1 A.C. 300.
690 *Flood v Times Newspapers Ltd* [2012] UKSC 11; [2012] 2 A.C. 273; *Loutchansky v Times Newspapers Ltd* [2001] EWCA Civ 536; [2002] Q.B. 321; and *Times Newspapers Ltd v United Kingdom* (App. No.00023676/03) [2009] E.M.L.R. 14.

(7) Where claims are brought in the English courts in respect of foreign publications with a limited readership in England, the issue of reasonable and responsible journalism will be judged by the circumstances and professional standards that apply in the home country of the publication.[691] (This may be a less common circumstance now that s.9 of the Defamation Act 2013 is in force).

(8) There is no reason why the *Reynolds* defence cannot apply to publications made by any person and published in any medium (e.g. books, slander), provided the conditions of "responsible journalism" are satisfied.[692]

Application of responsible journalism test In *Jameel v Wall Street Journal (Europe) SPRL*[693] Lord Bingham, with whom Lord Hope agreed, considered the ground on which the judge and the Court of Appeal had rejected the *Reynolds* defence—namely the failure of the newspaper to allow sufficient time prior to publication for the respondents to comment on the allegations—to be too narrow, with the effect that the "liberalising effect" that was the intention of the *Reynolds* decision had been subverted. He considered the article in issue to be the sort of neutral investigative journalism which the *Reynolds* defence existed to protect. Lord Hoffmann said that responsible journalism was an objective test and no more vague than standards such as "reasonable care" used in other branches of the law. He reiterated that the *Reynolds* standard of responsible journalism needed to be applied in a practical and flexible manner. Baroness Hale said there was only a public right to know if: (1) there was a real public interest in conveying and receiving the information; and (2) the publisher had taken the care of a responsible publisher to verify the information published. Lord Hoffmann considered the steps taken to gather and publish the information. He considered the question to be whether the defendant had behaved fairly and responsibly in gathering and publishing the information. Lord Hoffmann paid particular attention to efforts made by the defendants to verify. His Lordship went on to consider what opportunity had been afforded to the claimant to comment on the allegations prior to publication. He pointed out that Lord Nicholls had not suggested that failure to report the claimant's explanation would always be fatal to the defence. He considered the stance adopted by the judge and the Court of Appeal on this issue to be unrealistic. The story had been confirmed by the US Treasury. Whilst Lord Nicholls had said in *Reynolds* that the importance of approaching the claimant was that he might have information others did not or would not have disclosed, that was not the case here. The claimant in this case would have had no knowledge of whether there was covert surveillance of his bank account. He could only say that he knew of no reason why there should be. While Lord Hoffmann accepted that it might have been better had the defendants delayed publication to give him time to comment, the failure did not deprive them of the defence. In *Yeo v Times Newspapers Ltd*[694] the investigation and conduct of the journalists in the lead up to publication was examined in detail. Warby J found that although the investigation and publication could have been carried out differently, the way it was done still amounted to responsible journalism. 21-151

[691] *Lukowiak v Unidad Editorial SA* [2001] E.M.L.R. 46; and *Al Misnad v Azzaman Ltd* [2003] EWHC 1783 (QB).

[692] *Charman v Orion Publishing Group Ltd* [2007] EWCA Civ 972; [2008] 1 All E.R. 750; *Seaga v Harper* [2008] UKPC 9; [2009] 1 A.C. 1.

[693] [2006] UKHL 44; [2007] 1 A.C. 359.

[694] [2015] EWHC 3375 (QB); [2017] E.M.L.R. 1.

The judge undertook an assessment of the process, which did not require perfection, and left room for editorial judgment in how things should be done—the importance of editorial judgment is now reflected in s.4 of the Defamation Act 2013. Detailed and subtle criticisms of journalistic conduct would only have a proper place in a *Reynolds* trial "if there was such an accumulation of reasonable points of this kind that they could be said, in the mass, to support an allegation of systematic bias or unfairness".[695]

21-152 **Verification and sources** The leading authority is now *Flood v Times Newspapers Ltd*.[696] Where a newspaper adopts an allegation, the steps taken by way of verification will assume central importance in ascertaining whether publication of the allegation was in the public interest. Where a source is unknown it will be harder to verify the information.[697] That is not so where the defendant relies on a reportage defence.[698] Investigative steps must be taken to verify whether the claimant is guilty of the type of misconduct alleged, general investigation into the subject matter is not sufficient.[699] *Flood* is the leading authority on the *Reynolds* defence generally and represents the state of the law prior to the coming into force of the Defamation Act 2013. The Explanatory Notes to that Act refer to *Flood* stating that s.4 is intended to reflect the common law as set out in *Flood* and the case will undoubtedly be seen as providing guidance to the judiciary when interpreting the defence under s.4. The Supreme Court made clear that in *Reynolds* cases much will depend upon what the journalist(s) knew at the time of publication. The key question, in the words of Lord Brown of Eaton under Heywood, is:

> "could whoever published the defamation, given whatever they knew (and did not know) and whatever they had done (and had not done) to guard so far as possible against the publication of untrue defamatory material, properly have considered the publication in question to be in the public interest?"[700]

Allowance should be made of editorial judgment; it is not for the court to second guess whether it was appropriate to include every detail that went into the article in question.

21-153 **Claimant's opportunity to respond** This is an extremely important factor. Basic fairness requires that the person about whom the publication in question makes allegations be given an opportunity to respond. Also, it will often be one of the best ways to seek to verify a story. The subject of the story should be given a reasonable opportunity to respond and put their side.[701] The failure to put the story to the claimant, or to make sufficient effort to do so, will generally count against the defendant. However, the failure to give the claimant an opportunity to respond will

---

695 [2015] EWHC 3375 (QB); [2017] E.M.L.R. 1 at [159].

696 [2012] UKSC 11; [2012] 2 A.C. 273.

697 [2012] UKSC 11; [2012] 2 A.C. 273 at [34]. See also *Hunt v Times Newspapers Ltd* [2012] EWHC 1220 (QB).

698 See para. 21-160.

699 *Pinard-Byrne v Linton* [2015] UKPC 41; [2016] E.M.L.R. 4.

700 [2012] UKSC 11; [2012] 2 A.C. 273 at [113].

701 *Cook v Telegraph Media Group Ltd* [2011] EWHC 763 (QB)—Tugendhat J refused to give summary judgment to the defendant (the defendant having argued that the claimant had no real prospect of defeating the defences put forward, including *Reynolds* privilege), because the claimant had only been given three hours to comment prior to publication and the sufficiency of the opportunity to comment was an issue which needed to be resolved at trial.

not automatically invalidate the defence,[702] what is required of the responsible journalist will depend on all the facts of the case.[703] If the defendant has the claimant's version of events but fails to include it in the published piece this will almost always count against the defendant.[704] Similarly, it will count against a publisher if they put parts of the story to the claimant, but not the key or most damaging allegation.[705]

Considering the defence as a preliminary issue In *GKR Karate (UK) Ltd v Yorkshire Post Newspapers Ltd*[706] Popplewell J decided that *Reynolds* privilege could be heard as a preliminary issue despite the claimants' objection that without a full hearing the test laid down in *Reynolds* could not be properly applied. The decision was upheld by the Court of Appeal which considered it was "fair, sensible and economic". In *Kneafsey v Independent Television News Ltd*[707] the court found that the claimants had no realistic prospect of success on several grounds, including there being no realistic prospect of defeating a *Reynolds* defence, even though at the time of the summary judgment application the defence had not yet been pleaded (although it had been canvassed in correspondence, and the defendant had put in evidence). In *Armstrong v Times Newspapers Ltd*[708] the Court of Appeal ruled on the position where a claimant applies to strike out the defence of *Reynolds* privilege. On a summary judgment application a judge had to be careful to ensure that he accepted the defendant's case as true unless there was no reasonable prospect that some or all of it would be accepted as true at trial. It was wrong on the facts of the case to deny the defendant newspaper the benefit of the trial process, and the judge had erred in making findings of fact at the hearing without having heard all the evidence. In particular, the detailed history of the article was a matter for witness statements and disclosure, not for summary disposal. A failure to put allegations to a claimant was not necessarily determinative of the defence of qualified privilege and the defence would be restored. 21-154

Responsible journalism and book publishing In *Charman v Orion Publishing Group Ltd*[709] the Court of Appeal, applying *Jameel*, held that the defence of privilege based on responsible journalism applied equally to books. However, because authors and publishers were not under the same pressure of time before going to press, greater care would be expected of them in demonstrating that they had acted responsibly. The judge at first instance had erred in focusing on the passages complained of rather than the book as a whole in determining whether the author had taken proper care. The book, on the whole, was carefully researched and sourced, and the judge had not afforded sufficient weight to that. He had also failed to take sufficiently into account the care with which the author had exercised his editorial judgment. Ward LJ commented: 21-155

"*Jameel* emphasises how important it is that weight be given to the professional judg-

---

702 *Reynolds v Times Newspapers Ltd* [2001] 2 A.C. 127; *GKR Karate (UK) Ltd v Yorkshire Post Newspapers Ltd (No.2)* [2000] E.M.L.R. 410; *Armstrong v Times Newspapers Ltd* [2005] EWCA Civ 1007; [2005] E.M.L.R. 33.

703 *Jameel v Wall Street Journal Europe SPRL* [2006] UKHL 44; [2007] 1 A.C. 359.

704 *Reynolds v Times Newspapers Ltd* [2001] 2 A.C. 127.

705 *Galloway v Telegraph Group Ltd* [2006] EWCA Civ 17; [2006] E.M.L.R. 11.

706 [2000] 1 W.L.R. 2571 CA.

707 [2013] EWHC 4046 (QB).

708 [2005] EWCA Civ 1007; [2005] E.M.L.R. 33.

709 [2007] EWCA Civ 972; [2008] 1 All E.R. 750.

ment of the journalist. Where opinions may reasonably differ over the details which are needed to convey the general message, then deference has to be paid to the editorial decisions of the author, journalist or editor. True it may be that the journalist has to subject the material, as the judge held, to 'critical analysis'. But it is *his* assessment of that evaluation which is important, not the judge's own evaluation of the material conducted with the benefit of hindsight and with the sharp eye of a trained lawyer."[710]

21-156 **Responsible journalism under the Defamation Act 2013** Although the responsible journalism test and Lord Nicholls' ten factors (or similar) were not (after debate in Parliament) included in s.4 of the Defamation Act 2013, the factors remain relevant to the defence, as the defendant must show that he or she "reasonably believed" that publication of the statement complained of was in the public interest. In determining whether the defendant's belief was "reasonable" the court will consider the same types of questions as were posed under *Reynolds*, such as the steps taken to verify the information, the status of the information and whether the allegations were put to the claimant. In interpreting the statutory defence the courts also need to balance the competing rights in play—art.8 right to reputation and art.10 right to freedom of expression.[711] Another important aspect of determining what is reasonable under the statutory defence is the allowance the court is required to give to editorial discretion by s.4(4).[712] This reflects the position as outlined in *Flood v Times Newspapers Ltd*,[713] and as made clear in the Explanatory Notes, applies to all defendants, not just those with traditional newsroom editorial set-ups. The defence has been considered by the Court of Appeal in *Economou v de Freitas*[714] and by the Supreme Court in *Serafin v Malkiewicz*.[715]

21-157 *Economou* was a case in which the defendant, Mr de Freitas, was a member of the public, and was sued personally, but media organisations who had published articles which were authored by or contained contributions from him were not sued. The defendant was the father of a woman who had made a complaint of rape against the claimant. The CPS did not charge the claimant, and he brought a private prosecution against Ms de Freitas for perverting the course of justice, which the CPS took over. Shortly before the trial Ms de Freitas, who suffered from bipolar affective disorder, killed herself. Mr de Freitas contributed to a number of publications relating to his daughter's death, criticising the CPS and calling for the coroner to investigate its role in her death. The court found two of the publications actionable with the most serious meaning being there were strong grounds to suspect that the claimant was guilty of rape and had falsely prosecuted Ms de Freitas for perverting the course of justice. There was no dispute that the subject matter of the articles was of public interest, so argument centred on whether the defendant reasonably believed that publication was in the public interest. The Court of Appeal, in affirming the first instance decision, confirmed that "the statement complained of" in s.4 means the actual words used, and that therefore the defendant's intended meaning could be relevant to whether his belief was objectively reasonable. As to whether Mr de Freitas was entitled to rely on the media organisations to carry out further

---

710 [2007] EWCA Civ 972; [2008] 1 All E.R. 750 at [75].

711 The balancing exercise to be undertaken by the court in such circumstances was set out by Lord Steyn in *Re S (A Child) (Identification: Restrictions on Publication)* [2004] UKHL 47; [2005] 1 A.C. 593 at [17].

712 "… the court must make such allowance for editorial judgment as it considers appropriate."

713 [2012] UKSC 11; [2012] 2 A.C. 273.

714 [2018] EWCA Civ 2591; [2019] E.M.L.R. 7.

715 [2020] UKSC 23; [2020] 1 W.L.R. 2455.

checks and enquiries, Sharp LJ acknowledged that the issue raised difficulties for both free speech and reputation. She made clear that whether the s.4 defence applies will depend upon all the facts of the particular case. The Court of Appeal affirmed that the *Reynolds* factors could continue to be relevant to a s.4 defence. However, they are not the only factors to be taken into account and their relevance and weight will differ in accordance with the particular circumstances. In the present case, whether Mr de Freitas' conduct fell below the standard set out in the *Reynolds* factors was not the key to determining whether his belief was reasonable. Warby J at first instance had not found that the defendant had left verification all to the media, but that he had some information and had made what, for a person in his position, were reasonable and responsible investigations into the merits of the case against his daughter. Further, in the particular circumstances of the case Warby J made no error in concluding that in a story aimed at the CPS, including the claimant's side of the story would make little sense, and that the defendant had limited room for manoeuvre in expressing his criticisms of the CPS without risking implying something defamatory about the claimant.

In *Serafin*, whilst ordering a re-trial, the Supreme Court took the opportunity to outline some general points about the s.4 defence. Despite what is said in the Explanatory Notes, the s.4 defence and the *Reynolds* defence are not to be equiparated.[716] In this regard Lord Wilson noted in particular that Lord Nicholls' list of 10 factors had been included in the draft bill, but removed before it became law. The section outlines a two-stage test which must be approached one stage at a time. The first stage focuses on the subject matter, not the publication itself, asking whether that subject matter is a matter of public interest. At the second stage, in determining whether the publisher reasonably believed publication was in the public interest, the matters that make up the *Reynolds* factors may well be relevant, but are not to be regarded or referred to as a checklist. Reference to acting "responsibly" was also said to be best avoided. Although there is no "requirement" to seek comment from the individual, failure to do so will always be under consideration when considering whether the publisher had a reasonable belief in the public interest of publishing and may even be decisive. The Supreme Court rejected criticism of the following comment from Waby J in *Economou*, approved by the Court of Appeal in that case: **21-158**

> "I would consider a belief to be reasonable for the purposes of section 4 only if it is one arrived at after conducting such inquiries and checks as it is reasonable to expect of the particular defendant in all the circumstances of the case."[717]

The s.4 defence failed in *Hourani v Thomson*,[718] where the court found that the defendants did not have a reasonable belief that publication was in the public interest and indeed had taken no steps to verify the material. The s.4 defence also failed in relation to an online article in *Burgon v News Group Newspapers Ltd*[719] because the defendant failed to include in the article relevant information given by the claimant. When the matter was put to him, Mr Burgon told the journalist that the stylised "S" on an album cover was not a reference to Nazi iconography but to a Black Sabbath album cover. Dingemans J found that including a reference to Black **21-159**

716 [2020] UKSC 23; [2020] 1 W.L.R. 2455 at [72].
717 [2016] EWHC 1853 (QB); [2017] E.M.L.R. 4 at [241]; [2018] EWCA Civ 2591; [2019] E.M.L.R. 7 at [101].
718 [2017] EWHC 432 (QB) in particular at [164]–[174].
719 [2019] EWHC 195 (QB).

Sabbath was necessary as a part of responsible journalism. The s.4 defence also failed in *Turley v Unite the Union*[720] where the failure to take sufficient steps to verify the allegation, and to give the claimant an adequate opportunity to respond were important factors. Nicklin J also commented (obiter) that it appears from the statutory language that where there are two or more defendants relying upon a s.4 defence each must separately establish its own "reasonable belief", but that it was "not hard to imagine" circumstances where one of the defendants had not given specific consideration to the issue.[721]

(ii) Reportage

21-160 **Reportage under the common law** Reportage has been described as "a special and relatively rare form of *Reynolds* privilege."[722] It is a general reporting privilege based on neutral reporting of disputes. In the case in which it was first applied, *Al Fagih v HH Saudi Research and Marketing(UK) Ltd*,[723] the Court of Appeal concluded that a political dispute was being conducted in the public arena and it was thus in the public interest to know what allegations were being made by one side of the other. Provided the defendant did not adopt the allegations as true, the defence of qualified privilege ought to be available. As a form of qualified privilege, reportage is said not to contradict the repetition rule.[724] Where a defendant fails to maintain a neutral stance he or she will lose the privilege for reportage, but may still be able to avail of the public interest defence more generally, by proving that their reporting was reasonably believed to be in the public interest.[725] The second particular test in reportage cases is the existence of an ongoing dispute, which the words complained of are reporting on. The case law is unclear as to whether this is always a requirement[726] or whether disinterested reporting of a unilateral libel may also be protected.[727] Lord Neuberger MR in *Flood v Times Newspapers Ltd*[728] stated that it would be going too far to allow the publication of details of allegations against a named claimant without that claimant having a right to sue in defamation, simply because the general subject matter of the story is in the public interest. When *Flood* came before the Supreme Court their Lordships did not directly address the issue of whether a dispute is necessary, but in defining reportage as a special kind of *Reynolds* privilege where the public interest lies not in the substance of the allegation, but in the fact that the allegation has been made,[729] did not make reference to the need for a dispute.

---

720 [2019] EWHC 3547 (QB).

721 [2019] EWHC 3547 (QB) at [140].

722 *Al Fagih v HH Saudi Research and Marketing (UK) Ltd* [2001] EWCA Civ 1634; [2002] E.M.L.R. 13.

723 *Al Fagih v HH Saudi Research and Marketing (UK) Ltd* [2001] EWCA Civ 1634; [2002] E.M.L.R. 13.

724 *Roberts v Gable* [2007] EWCA Civ 721; [2008] Q.B. 502. On the repetition rule generally see para.21-28.

725 *Charman v Orion Publishing Group Ltd* [2007] EWCA Civ 972; [2008] 1 All E.R. 750.

726 *Al Fagih v HH Saudi Research and Marketing (UK) Ltd* [2001] EWCA Civ 1634; [2002] E.M.L.R. 13.

727 *Charman v Orion Publishing Group Ltd* [2007] EWCA Civ 972; [2008] 1 All E.R. 750, see in particular [91].

728 [2010] EWCA Civ 804; [2011] 1 W.L.R. 153.

729 *Flood v Times Newspapers Ltd* [2012] UKSC 11; [2012] 2 A.C. 273 per Lord Philips at [77]. Lord Mance at [158] referred to reportage as the situation where "the mere fact of a statement is itself of, and is reported as being of, public interest."

Reportage under the Defamation Act 2013 Section 4(3) of the Defamation Act 2013 enacts a statutory version of the reportage defence, which makes the existence of a dispute a central feature of the defence. It provides: 21-161

> "If the statement complained of was, or formed part of, an accurate and impartial account of a dispute to which the claimant was a party, the court must in determining whether it was reasonable for the defendant to believe that publishing the statement was in the public interest disregard any omission of the defendant to take steps to verify the truth of the imputation conveyed by it."

The defence applies to statements of opinion as well as statements of fact,[730] and thus will overlap with the honest opinion defence in s.3 of the Act. The statutory defence is also clearly intended to apply more widely than the traditional news media defendants who were generally those who relied upon the *Reynolds* defence. Exactly what will constitute a "dispute" for the purposes of this subsection remains to be determined.

(e) Honest comment/opinion

Defence of honest opinion At common law, the defence of honest opinion, or as it has been variously known "fair comment" or "honest comment" protects statements of opinion on matters in the public interest. The common law defence was replaced by a statutory defence under s.3 of the Defamation Act 2013. Under the statutory defence it is no longer necessary that the opinion be on a matter of public interest. The rationale behind the defence is that everyone has the right to comment within the limits of fair comment/honest opinion whether he be writer, reporter, newspaper editor, or ordinary citizen in a letter to a friend or by way of spoken comment. 21-162

Fair or honest comment at common law—basic elements The modern authoritative statement of the previous common law defence is to be found in the Supreme Court judgment in *Joseph v Spiller*[731] which considered the previous case law, and in particular the judgment of Lord Nicholls in *Tse Wai Chun Paul v Albert Cheng*.[732] There were five key elements which the defendant had to prove: 21-163

(1) The subject matter of the comment must be of public interest.
(2) The statement must be recognisable as comment as distinct from fact.[733]
(3) The comment must be based on facts which are true or protected by privilege.
(4) The comment must indicate explicitly or implicitly, at least in general terms, the facts on which it is based.

---

[730] s.4(5).

[731] [2010] UKSC 53; [2011] 1 A.C. 852.

[732] [2001] E.M.L.R. 31 (Hong Kong CA). Eady J in *Branson v Bower (No.2)* [2002] Q.B. 737, acknowledged that *Cheng* is merely of persuasive authority but recognised its importance. He also applied it in the case of *Sugar v Associated Newspapers*, unreported 6 February 2001; and it cited with approval in *Keays v Guardian Newspapers Ltd* [2003] EWHC 1565 (QB).

[733] The "single meaning" doctrine applies to cases where the defence of fair comment is relied upon. See *Lowe v Times Newspapers Ltd* [2006] EWHC 320 (QB); [2007] Q.B. 580, where the court observed that it would be hopelessly impractical to judge the validity of the fair comment defence by reference to what the author of the words had intended, thought or hoped the words might convey. The first step is to identify the meaning of the words and then decide whether the defence of fair comment has been established.

(5) The comment must be one which an honest person could hold. This is an objective test, but should not be confused with reasonableness; if an honest person could have made the comment, however prejudiced, exaggerated or obstinate his or her views, this requirement will be fulfilled.

Where these are surmounted, the defence will succeed unless the claimant proves that the comment was maliciously published.[734] In *Joseph v Spiller*[735] the fourth requirement was revised. The court ruled that it was not a prerequisite of the defence of honest comment that the readers should be in a position to evaluate the comment for themselves, as suggested by Lord Nicholls in *Tse Wai Chun Paul*. With the number of comments made online today, it would often be impossible for readers to evaluate defamatory comments without detailed information about the facts which had given rise to the comments, so if Lord Nicholls' requirement were interpreted too strictly it would rob the defence of much of its efficacy.[736] All that was required was that the comment identified at least in general terms, the facts on which it was based. In *Yeo v Times Newspapers Ltd*[737] the judge emphasised that the objective test as to whether or not the statement was a comment which could have been made by an honest person was a generous one[738] even if the comment could only have been made honestly by a person who is prejudiced or holds exaggerated or obstinate views. In that case Warby J found the defence to be made out based on the facts found as part of the justification defence, and other extrinsic facts. It did not matter if not all of the facts in the article were true, so long as a sufficient amount were to make out the defence.

21-164 **Honest opinion under the Defamation Act 2013 s.3—basic elements** Section 3 provides as follows:

"(1) It is a defence to an action for defamation for the defendant to show that the following conditions are met.
(2) The first condition is that the statement complained of was a statement of opinion.
(3) The second condition is that the statement complained of indicated, whether in general or specific terms, the basis of the opinion.
(4) The third condition is that an honest person could have held the opinion on the basis of—
(a) any fact which existed at the time the statement complained of was published;
(b) anything asserted to be a fact in a privileged statement published before the statement complained of.
(5) The defence is defeated if the claimant shows that the defendant did not hold the opinion.
(6) Subsection (5) does not apply in a case where the statement complained of was published by the defendant but made by another person ("the author"); and in such a case the defence is defeated if the claimant shows that the defendant knew or ought to have known that the author did not hold the opinion.
(7) For the purposes of subsection (4)(b) a statement is a "privileged statement" if the person responsible for its publication would have one or more of the following defences if an action for defamation were brought in respect of it—
(a) a defence under section 4 (publication on matter of public interest);

---

734 Malice in this sense is addressed at paras 21-206 to 21-209.
735 [2010] UKSC 53; [2011] 1 A.C. 852.
736 [2010] UKSC 53; [2011] 1 A.C. 852 at [99].
737 [2015] EWHC 3375 (QB); [2017] E.M.L.R. 1.
738 Citing *Turner v Metro-Goldwyn-Mayer Pictures* [1950] 1 All E.R. 449.

(b) a defence under section 6 (peer-reviewed statement in scientific or academic journal);
(c) a defence under section 14 of the Defamation Act 1996 (reports of court proceedings protected by absolute privilege);
(d) a defence under section 15 of that Act (other reports protected by qualified privilege).

(8) The common law defence of fair comment is abolished and, accordingly, section 6 of the Defamation Act 1952 (fair comment) is repealed."

The first point of note is that this removes the requirement that the comment be on a matter of public interest. It also expands the forms of privileged statement on which an honest comment can be based; notably this now includes statements privileged under the new publication on a matter of public interest defence at s.4.[739] Further, the statutory defence allows a defendant to rely on any fact which existed at the time of publication, even if it was not known to the defendant. As with the defences under ss.2 and 4 of the Act, s.3(8) abolishes the common law defence. Whilst the Explanatory Notes to the Act state that it is intended to "broadly reflect the current law", all be it without the public interest requirement,[740] some judicial interpretation may be required before the contours of the new defence are fully understood.

(i) Comment not fact

Fact or comment Whether a statement is fact or comment can be a very difficult distinction, particularly because in many publications there is a mixture of both. There is no statutory definition of fact and comment, and ultimately the question is how the words would strike the ordinary reasonable reader.[741] This requirement is continued under s.3(2) of the Defamation Act 2013. A convenient and succinct summary of the basic principles the court will apply when determining whether a statement is one of fact or of opinion can be found in *Koutsogiannis v Random House Group Ltd*[742]: 21-165

(1) The statement must be recognisable as comment, as distinct from an imputation of fact.
(2) Opinion is something which is or can reasonably be inferred to be a deduction, inference, conclusion, criticism, remark, observation etc.
(3) The ultimate question is how the word would strike the ordinary reasonable reader. The subject matter and context of the words may be an important indicator of whether they are fact or opinion.
(4) Some statements which are, by their nature and appearance opinion, are nevertheless treated as statements of fact where, for instance, the opinion implies that a claimant has done something but does not indicate what that something is, i.e. the statement is a bare comment.
(5) Whether an allegation that someone has acted "dishonestly" or "criminally" is an allegation of fact or expression of opinion will very much depend upon

[739] On which see paras 21-156 to 21-161.
[740] *Explanatory Notes to the Defamation Act* 2013 at [19].
[741] *Grech v Odhams Press Ltd* [1958] 2 Q.B. 275, CA; *London Artists Ltd v Littler* [1969] 2 Q.B. 375 CA.
[742] [2019] EWHC 48 (QB); [2020] 4 W.L.R. 25 at [16], [17].

context. There is no fixed rule that a statement that someone has been dishonest must be treated as an allegation of fact.

21-166 Allegations that imputed arrogance, greed and unreasonable behaviour in relation to the claimants' benefit claims were found to be defamatory at common law and statements of opinion, but did not to cross the serious harm threshold, in *Sube v News Group Newspapers Ltd*.[743] Whilst such allegations could attract disapproval, the court found that they did not relate to the most important of societal norms and there were no allegations of dishonesty or unlawful behaviour. None of the factual allegations in the article were found to be defamatory. The court also found that where an imputation is an opinion, that mitigates its defamatory impact. However, in *Morgan v Associated Newspapers Ltd*[744] the decision in Sube was described as "a most unusual case on the facts". In *Greenstein v Campaign Against Antisemitism*[745] Nicklin J found allegations of anti-Semitism and of lying to be expressions of opinion in the context in which they were published. The importance of the imputation being clearly recognisable as comment has carried over from the common law defence to the statutory defence.[746] In certain recent cases the court has found elements of the meaning(s) it has found to be fact and other elements to be opinion.[747]

(ii) Sufficient factual basis

21-167 **A sufficient factual basis—common law** It has often been said said that a comment cannot exist "in thin air". The defendant at common law had to prove that the factual building blocks on which the comment was based were true, or sufficiently true, or protected by privilege. For example, an allegation that C has disclosed the identity of a source is the fact on which the opinion—that he is a disgrace to journalism—is based. If C did not, in fact, disclose the identity of a source then the comment and the defence collapse. By analogy, it cannot be fair comment to attack an author for something he has not written. In *Merivale v Carson*[748] the defendant published a review of the claimant's play which suggested that it had an evil tendency on the basis that it treated adultery cavalierly. In fact, there was no mention of adultery in the play and the defence of fair comment therefore failed. The following principles are relevant:

(1) The facts must be indicated, at least in general terms either explicitly or implicitly.[749] If there is a general public awareness of the subject matter, comment can be made without setting out in the article the facts on which

---

743 [2018] EWHC 1234 (QB).

744 [2018] EWHC 1725 (QB); [2018] E.M.L.R. 25.

745 [2019] EWHC 281 (QB).

746 *Butt v Secretary of State for the Home Department* [2019] EWCA Civ 933; [2019] E.M.L.R. 23; *Dyson v Associated Newspapers Ltd* [2020] EWHC 188 (QB); see also *Lord Sheikh v Associated Newspapers Ltd* [2019] EWHC 2947 (QB); [2020] 1 W.L.R. 2965 on avoiding over-elaborate analysis.

747 See, e.g. *Morgan v Associated Newspapers Ltd* [2018] EWHC 1850 (QB); *Triplark Ltd v Northwood Hall (Freehold) Ltd* [2019] EWHC 3494 (QB).

748 (1888) 20 Q.B.D. 275 CA.

749 *Joseph v Spiller* [2010] UKSC 53; [2011] 1 A.C. 852.

the comment is based, provided that the subject matter of the comment is plainly stated.[750]

(2) Where some of the facts stated in the publication are true and some are false the defence will succeed if the defendant would have been entitled to make the same comment solely on the basis of the true facts. Under the old law of fair/honest comment it was necessary to rely on s.6 of the Defamation Act 1952. This has been abolished in relation to cases under the Defamation Act 2013 (see Defamation Act 2013 s.3(8)), as it is incorporated within the defence itself by s.3(4). In *Lait v Evening Standard Ltd*,[751] a basic fact in the article was wrong: the claimant was accused of having had to pay back £25,000 in expenses, but in fact that had been another MP. Nevertheless, the defendant argued that the allegation was an honest comment since it could be based merely on the fact that, as an MP who had claimed under the old expenses system, it was inappropriate for her to seek to defend the old system. The claimant contended that such an argument was unreasonable. However, the court ruled that the inclusion of the false allegation concerning the £25,000 claim did not preclude the defendant from succeeding in the defence provided that the comment was "fair" in relation to the facts that had been accurately stated. Reasonableness was not the test. The comment defence was available because the claimant, by having taken advantage of the flawed expenses system, had "forfeited the right to be heeded" on the topic of expenses. That was an opinion that could be honestly held, and the defence succeeded.

(3) Section 6 refers to "facts alleged or referred to in the words complained of". However, the defence succeeds if the comment can be considered "fair" on the basis of any of the facts on which the defendant is entitled to rely and which are proved to be true.

(4) Where the supporting facts are protected by absolute or qualified privilege the defence will succeed even where they are untrue.[752]

(5) The omission of "truly exculpatory" facts will be as fatal as getting the stated facts wrong. If D states that C has been convicted of a crime and comments on this, without stating that the conviction was subsequently quashed, the comment will not be protected.[753] However, the omission of relevant facts will not necessarily be fatal, but might be relevant to the issue of honest belief.[754]

(6) Unlike in a truth defence, the defendant cannot rely on facts or matters taking place after the date of publication on which to base the comment.[755] Furthermore, there is some authority that the facts on which the defendant relies must also be known to him at the time. However, in *Cohen v Daily Telegraph Ltd* Lord Denning said, "[a] man may comment on existing facts without having them all in the forefront of his mind at the time".[756] This is generally held to be a preferable view.

750 *Lowe v Times Newspapers Ltd* [2006] EWHC 320 (QB); [2007] Q.B. 580.
751 [2011] EWCA Civ 859; [2011] 1 W.L.R. 2973.
752 *Mangena v Wright* [1909] 2 K.B. 958; *Wason v Walter* (1868) L.R. 4 Q.B. 73.
753 See *Branson v Bower (No.2)* [2002] Q.B. 737 at [37]–[39].
754 *Cook v Telegraph Media Group Ltd* [2011] EWHC 763 (QB).
755 *Cohen v Daily Telegraph Ltd* [1968] 1 W.L.R. 916.
756 *Cohen v Daily Telegraph Ltd* [1968] 1 W.L.R. 916 at 920.

21-168 **Factual basis under the Defamation Act 2013 s.3** Section 3(4) recasts the requirement that the comment must be based on facts which are known to be true or protected by privilege. It requires the defendant to show that "an honest person could have held the opinion on the basis of (a) any fact which existed at the time the statement complained of was published; (b) anything asserted to be a fact in a privileged statement published before the statement complained of". In *Morgan v Associated Newspapers Ltd*[757] Nicklin J analysed the case law on defamation and opinion, making clear that in order to avail of an honest opinion defence the statement of opinion must be based on true facts. Section 3(3) retains the requirement, as stated in *Joseph v Spiller*,[758] that the statement complained of indicated, whether in general or specific terms, the basis of the opinion. The extent to which s.3(4) changes the law remains to be interpreted by the courts. The Explanatory Notes state that the intention was to simplify the law whilst "retain[ing] the broad principles of the common law defence".[759] That the defence can be based on any facts existing at the time of publication, if interpreted widely, could be a far-reaching change to the law—a defendant who stated an opinion based on wholly false facts could succeed in his or her defence on the basis of facts of which he had no knowledge at the time of publication, potentially relating to a wholly different area of the claimant's life, provided that an honest person could have based the comment on those facts. In *Morgan v Associated Newspapers Ltd*[760] Nicklin J indicated (obiter) that s.3(4) means that there must be a nexus between the opinion and the subject upon which it is expressed.[761] On a proper construction of s.3 a defence would not succeed if every fact set out in the publication was wrong, but some other fact existed upon which the opinion could be based. This would be a radical departure from the previous law, not indicated in the Explanatory Notes to the Act. Where an honest opinion defence is pleaded the particulars must be sufficient and pleaded with proper particularity.[762] As the question under s.3 is whether an honest person could have held the opinion expressed based on facts existing at the time, other, potentially exculpatory facts, are not relevant to this objective assessment under s.3(4)(a). If the defendant was said to have known the exculpatory facts it might be relevant to s.3(5) whether they honestly held the opinion.[763]

21-169 **Factual basis under the Defamation Act 2013 s.3—privileged statements** Section 3(4)(b) requires the privileged statement on which the comment is based to have been published before the statement complained of. This could present a problem if a comment piece appeared in the same publication (for example a newspaper) as a privileged report (for example of a court judgment, or a press release). There would seem to be no reason of principle why such a comment should not be protected. It might be that the court will require the requirement that publication be "before" as a requirement that publication is "not after" i.e. "before, or contemporaneous with." The other potential difficulty for defendants seeking to rely on s.3(4)(b) is that the defendant may well be seeking to rely on privileged facts

757 [2018] EWHC 1725 (QB); [2018] E.M.L.R. 25.

758 [2010] UKSC 53; [2011] 1 A.C. 852.

759 Explanatory Notes to the Defamation Act 2013 at [22].

760 [2018] EWHC 1725 (QB); [2018] E.M.L.R. 25.

761 See also *Burki v Seventy Thirty Ltd* [2018] EWHC 2151 (QB).

762 *Morgan v Associated Newspapers Ltd* [2018] EWHC 3960 (QB); referring to *Ashcroft v Foley* [2012] EWCA Civ 423; [2012] E.M.L.R. 25; *Higginbotham v Leech* (1842) 10 M. & W. 361.

763 *Carruthers v Associated Newspapers Ltd* [2019] EWHC 33 (QB).

which were published by someone else. This is particularly likely to be the case for, for example, social media commentators. Should the facts subsequently prove false, proving the validity of privilege (which now includes the s.4 defence of publication on a matter of public interest) by proxy may be virtually impossible.[764]

(iii) Public interest

Basis of comment This requirement is only relevant to the common law defence. It plays no part in the defence under s.3 of the Defamation Act 2013. The 22nd edition of this work provided more detailed commentary on the public interest requirement, but it is no longer relevant to the statutory defence which now pertains.[765] **21-170**

(iv) Malice

Relevance of malice at common law Malice, when considered in the context of the common law defence of honest opinion/comment, effectively meant that the defendant did not honestly believe in the opinion he was expressing. Unlike malice in other contexts, an improper motive for publishing a defamatory opinion would not amount to malice, if the defendant honestly believed the opinion.[766] The burden of proof in respect of malice lay on the claimant. It follows that where the defendant satisfied the five key elements of the defence as set out at para.21-163 there was no added burden on him to prove that he did in fact honestly hold the opinion in question. It was for the claimant, if he chose, to raise the issue of whether the opinion was honestly held, by alleging malice. It was very rare for malice to be proved in comment cases. Before the issue could arise, the defendant would already have had to persuade the court that the facts on which the comment was based were true or sufficiently true and that the comment was one which an honest person could have held. If that were the case it was very difficult to show that the comment, which after all is a subjective matter, was not the honest expression of the author's opinion. In *Cook v Telegraph Media Group Ltd*[767] Tugendhat J equated the standard to an allegation of dishonesty. Where a publisher bona fide published the opinion of another (for example, a newspaper publishing a letter to the editor) the defence was not defeated if the publisher (for example the newspaper editor) did not share the opinion. This does not amount to malice.[768] Tugendhat J found malice in the context of honest opinion on the counter-claim in *Thompson v James*.[769] **21-171**

Relevance of malice under the Defamation Act 2013 s.3 Section 3 does not restate the malice requirement in terms, but it does provide that "the defence is defeated if the claimant shows that the defendant did not hold the opinion."[770] This amounts to malice as it applied under the common law. As under the common law, the statutory defence contains a caveat for those (such as newspapers publishing let- **21-172**

[764] This difficulty was recognised by the Government during the development of the Act—Ministry of Justice, *Government's Response to the Report of the Joint Committee on the Draft Defamation Bill* (Cm.8295, 2010) at [41].

[765] See 22nd edn (2018) at paras 22-167 to 22-171.

[766] See *Branson v Bower (No.2)* [2002] Q.B. 737 at [8], per Eady J; and *Tse Wai Chun Paul v Cheng* [2001] E.M.L.R. 31.

[767] [2011] EWHC 763 at [27].

[768] *Telnikoff v Matusevitch* [1992] 2 A.C. 343.

[769] [2013] EWHC 515 (QB) at [351]–[359].

[770] s.3(5).

ters) publishing the opinions of others. According to s.3(6), in those circumstances "the defence is defeated if the claimant shows that the defendant knew or ought to have known that the author did not hold the opinion".

(v) *Procedure*

21-173 **Specifying the meaning to be defended** The Practice Direction to Pt 53 of the CPR[771] provides that:

> "Where a defendant relies on the defence under section 3 of the Defamation Act 2013 that the statement complained of was a statement of honest opinion,[772] they must—
>
> (1) specify the imputation they seek to defend as honest opinion; and
> (2) set out the facts and matters relied on in support of their case that—
> (a) the statement complained of indicated, in general or specific terms, the basis of the opinion; and
> (b) an honest person could have held that opinion on the basis of any fact which existed at the time it was published or anything asserted to be a fact in a privileged statement published before the statement complained of."

The note to this paragraph of the Practice Direction in the *White Book* comments that the defendant is obliged, as with truth, to set out the meaning which he seeks to defend as honest opinion, rather than merely identifying the words in the publication which will be defended as comment.[773]

(f) Secondary responsibility: s.1 of the Defamation Act 1996 and internet-specific defences

21-174 **Responsibility for publication** The first line of defence for those who are not the primary author, editor or publisher, particularly those who provide online platforms on which others publish statements, is likely to be to deny that they are a publisher of the words complained of at all.[774] If the defendant is regarded as a publisher, there are a number of specific defences which may be available. These are discussed in turn below.

(i) *Defamation Act 1996 s.1*

21-175 **Statutory basis** Section 1(1) of the 1996 Act provides a defence to a person who is responsible for a defamatory publication if he was not the author, editor or publisher of the statement. The Act defines "author", "editor" and "publisher":

A person is not to be considered the author, editor or publisher of a statement if he is only involved in certain processes in relation to the statement in question. Sec-

---

771 CPR PD 53B 4.4.

772 A previous version of the rules said "fair comment on a matter of public interest".

773 The rule is said to stem from the decision in *Control Risks Ltd v New English Library Ltd* [1990] 1 W.L.R. 183, "the precise effect of which has been the subject of some controversy among practitioners". The debate has been over whether there is a requirement to set out the precise meaning of the words said to be comment or merely to identify which words will be defended as fair comment. The note says that the latter approach has prevailed under the Practice Direction, but that "it may be that the courts take a liberal view of practitioners adopting the former approach".

774 See para.21-66.

tion 1(5) of the 1996 Act provides that:

"(5) In determining for the purposes of this section whether a person took reasonable care, or had reason to believe that what he did caused or contributed to the publication of a defamatory statement, regard shall be had to—

(a) the extent of his responsibility for the content of the statement or the decision to publish it,

(b) the nature or circumstances of the publication, and

(c) the previous conduct or character of the author, editor or publisher."

(ii) Defences under the E-Commerce Regulations

The E-Commerce Regulations—general The Electronic Commerce (EC Directive) Regulations 2002 ("the E-Commerce Regulations") implement the Directive 2000/31/EC of the European Parliament and of the Council of 8 June 2000 on certain legal aspects of information society services, in particular electronic commerce, in the Internal Market into domestic law. The regulations provide defences to a claim in damages (or to a criminal charge), but not a claim for an injunction,[775] to "internet service societies"[776] as they are termed in the legislation. There are defences for mere conduits,[777] caching,[778] and hosting.[779] At the time of writing, although the UK has left the European Union, the Regulations remain in force. 21-176

Mere conduits This defence applies to providers of an information society service which consists of "the transmission in a communication network of information provided by a recipient of the service or the provision of access to a communication network", provided that they did not (a) initiate the transmission: (b) select its recipient; or (c) modify the information contained therein. The defence will continue to apply where the provider carries out automatic, intermediate and transient storage of the information, provided that this is (a) for the sole purpose of carrying out the transmission; and (b) is for no longer than is reasonably necessary to achieve this purpose. This would appear to apply to internet service providers who simply provide their customers with access to the internet, and those who provide email and other transient communications. It is a wide defence, as the knowledge of the defendant is irrelevant (i.e. the defence applies even if the defendant is aware of the defamatory material to which it is providing access). 21-177

Caching This defence is the mid-level defence between mere conduit and hosting. The defence applies where information (for example a web page) is stored by the information society service in order to make its retrieval more efficient, and that efficiency is the sole purpose of the storage. The service provider will not be liable in damages (or subject to criminal penalty) where it: 21-178

(i) does not modify the information;

[775] Regs 17(1), 18(1) and 19(1).

[776] Recital 17 of the Directive summarises this as meaning: "any service normally provided for remuneration, at a distance, by means of electronic equipment for the processing (including digital compression) and storage of data, and at the individual request of a recipient of a service." Remuneration would seem to include remuneration through advertising revenues (see Recital 18).

[777] reg.17.

[778] reg.18.

[779] reg.19.

(ii) complies with conditions on access to the information;
(iii) complies with any rules regarding the updating of the information, specified in a manner widely recognised and used by industry;
(iv) does not interfere with the lawful use of technology, widely recognised and used by industry, to obtain data on the use of the information; and
(v) acts expeditiously to remove or to disable access to the information he has stored upon obtaining actual knowledge of the fact that the information at the initial source of the transmission has been removed from the network, or access to it has been disabled, or that a court or an administrative authority has ordered such removal or disablement.

As with the defence under reg.17, knowledge of the defamatory material will not fix the defendant with liability. The service provider will only become liable in damages if it continues to cache the information after becoming aware that it has been removed, access disabled or that a court has ordered that it be removed or access disabled.

21-179 **Hosting** This defence applies where an internet service provider stores information (such as webpages) supplied by another. The defence applies not only to the host of a webpage, it may also apply to the host of a portion of a webpage—for example the comments section of a website, such as those under news articles.[780] The service provider will not be liable in damages (or subject to criminal penalty) where:

(a) the service provider—
 (i) does not have actual knowledge of unlawful activity or information and, where a claim for damages is made, is not aware of facts or circumstances from which it would have been apparent to the service provider that the activity or information was unlawful; or
 (ii) upon obtaining such knowledge or awareness, acts expeditiously to remove or to disable access to the information; and
(b) the recipient of the service was not acting under the authority or the control of the service provider.

Under this defence the service provider will be liable if he or she has knowledge of the unlawful nature of the material. The service provide may also be liable if, although not possessed of actual knowledge of the unlawful nature of the material, it is clear that he or she has actual knowledge of facts or circumstances from which its unlawful nature would have been apparent.[781] It is worthy of note that reg.19 refers to knowledge that the statement is "unlawful", in contrast to s.1 of the Defamation Act 1996 which refers to "defamatory". A statement may be defamatory even though there is a viable defence. It would appear that in order to have knowledge that the material is "unlawful" the service provider would need to have some knowledge about the strength or weakness of any potential defence.[782]

---

[780] *Kaschke v Gray* [2010] EWHC 690 (QB); [2011] 1 W.L.R. 452; *Karim v Newsquest Media Group Ltd* [2009] EWHC 3205 (QB).

[781] See *Google France SARL v Louis Vuitton Malletier SA* (C-236/08) [2011] All E.R. (EC) 411, in which the European Court of Justice considered reg.19 (in its original form as art.14 of the Directive), in a trade mark infringement case.

[782] See *Bunt v Tilley* [2006] EWHC 407 (QB); [2007] 1 W.L.R 1243; *Kaschke v Gray* [2010] EWHC 690 (QB); [2011] 1 W.L.R. 452; *L'Oreal SA v eBay International AG* (C-324/09) [2012] All E.R.

(iii) *Defamation Act 2013 s.5*

Section 5 defence for operators of websites Section 5 of the Defamation Act 2013 provides a defence for operators of websites in respect of defamatory statements posted on their websites by third parties. Where the third party who made the statement is identifiable, the website operator will have a complete defence unless the claimant can show that the operator acted with malice. The third party is only considered to be identifiable if the claimant has sufficient information to bring proceedings against him or her.[783] Where the third party is not identifiable, the website operator will have a defence (again subject to malice) if it can show that it complied with the procedure set out under the Defamation (Operators of Websites) Regulations 2013, made under s.5.[784] The aim of the defence is to ensure that the dispute is between the complainant and the primary author of the post, where possible. 21-180

The procedure under the Defamation (Operators of Website) Regulations 2013 The Regulations provide for a notice and take down procedure, fleshing out the framework laid out in s.5. A complainant must give notice of his or her complaint to the website operator in the form prescribed in reg.2. This includes a requirement to set out why the statement complained of is defamatory (which may be contrasted to the use of the word "unlawful" in the E-Commerce Regulations). If a notice is defective, the website operator need only inform the complainant of this and inform him or her what the requirements are; it need not specify in what respect the notice is defective or take any action in relation to the statement complained of. On receipt of a notice in the correct form, the website operator must, within 48 hours, ask the author (a) if they wish for the statement to remain on the website; (b) to provide their contact details; and (c) if they are willing for those contact details to be provided to the complainant. If the website operator has no means of contacting the author, in order to retain the defence, he must take down the statement from the online location(s) specified in the notice. Once contacted by the website operator the author has five days to respond. Depending on that response, to retain the protection of the defence the website operator must do the following: 21-181

(1) If the website operator receives no response after the five day period or receives an inadequate response,[785] the operator must take down the statement within 48 hours.
(2) If the author indicates that he or she willing for the post to be taken down, the operator must take down the statement within 48 hours.
(3) If author wants the statement to remain (whether or not they are willing to provide contact details), the operator must notify the complainant of this within 48 hours.

Importantly, if the author responds to the website operator but refuses to allow his or her contact details to be passed to the complainant, then the complainant would still need to obtain a court order in order to obtain this information from the website operator (as was the position prior to the coming into force of s.5). Section 5(12)

(EC) 501; [2012] E.M.L.R. 6.

783 s.5(4).

784 SI 2013/3028. The Regulations came into force on 1 January 2014, at the same time as the Act.

785 i.e. including all the information specified in reg.2(2).

makes clear that the defence is not defeated simply because a website operator moderates comments on their website. It remains an open question whether moderating constitutes assuming "too much" control over the website such that an operator will be denied the benefit of a defence under the E-Commerce Regulations.[786] The question of whether website operators will in fact seek to rely on this defence, or will prefer to continue to rely on existing defences under the E-Commerce Regulations, remains to be answered.

(g) Offers to make amends: Defamation Act 1996 s.2

(i) Statutory basis

21-182 **Statutory basis** Defamation is a tort of strict liability, i.e. absence of intent or negligence is not, of itself, a defence. This can create hardship for a defendant who has made an innocent mistake and finds himself embroiled in a libel claim. There has also been concern that some claimants seize on the error as a licence to seek damages. The purpose of the defence of offer of amends created by the 1996 Act is to allow defendants to extricate themselves from claims at an early stage, by offering to make appropriate amends. If the claimant accepts, the claim is settled and the defendant must make amends. If they refuse, the claim proceeds and the fact that the offer was made will be a defence unless the defendant published the defamatory statement either knowing or having reason to believe that it was false and defamatory of the claimant. It is therefore more akin to a damage limitation exercise than a substantive defence.

(ii) Offer of amends

21-183 **The offer** An offer to make amends is effectively an offer of settlement. If it is accepted, it brings an end to the claim, although the parties may have to seek the court's assistance to hammer out the precise terms. It follows that it only acts as a defence where the offer is refused. Section 2 of the 1996 Act sets out the necessary elements[787] of an offer:

(1) it must be in writing;
(2) it must be expressed to be an offer of amends under s.2 of the 1996 Act; and
(3) it must be made before service of the defence and can be made before proceedings are issued.

There is no requirement to identify the terms of the offer. They are provided for as a matter of law from making the offer and are set out in subs.2(4):

"An offer to make amends under this section is an offer—

(a) to make a suitable correction of the statement complained of and a sufficient apology to the aggrieved party,

---

[786] This was a cause for concern during the passage of the Bill, and led to the insertion of s.5(12). See *Delfi v Estonia* (Application No.64569/09) (2016) 62 E.H.R.R. 6 for an example of a court in another State finding that a website operator had indeed fallen outside the protection of the Directive through their actions.

[787] Care must be taken when making an offer of amends to ensure that it includes the elements provided for under the Act. A failure to specify the publications covered by the offer or to confirm that the defendant will pay the costs of the claimant might give rise to doubt as to whether the defendant intends to make a statutory offer of amends. See *SD Marine Ltd v Powell* [2006] EWHC 3095 (QB).

(b) to publish the correction and apology in a manner that is reasonable and practicable in the circumstances, and

(c) to pay to the aggrieved party such compensation (if any), and such costs, as may be agreed or determined to be payable.

The fact that the offer is accompanied by an offer to take specific steps does not affect the fact that an offer to make amends under this section is an offer to do all the things mentioned in paragraphs (a) to (c)."

These terms are very general. There remains considerable scope for dispute in relation to each head, which is considered below. However, in principle, it offers the claimant all that they could achieve from a defamation claim, subject to one proviso. The remedies do not specifically include an injunction against repetition, which in the case of a defendant of limited means may be the only reason for the claimant bringing proceedings. However a defendant who offers amends is unlikely to repeat the allegations, and would in most cases volunteer an undertaking. If not the court has a general power to grant an injunction.[788]

Qualified offers A qualified offer is an offer to make amends in relation to a specific defamatory meaning which the defendant accepts the statement conveys (s.2(2)).[789] This may arise where the claimant alleges that the statement conveys a meaning which the defendant did not intend it to, or where the defendant publishes two or more defamatory allegations of the claimant and subsequently realises that one of them is false. **21-184**

Withdrawal or substitution of the offer of amends Under s.2(6) of the Act it is open to a defendant to withdraw an offer of amends at any time before it is accepted. However, the defendant may not withdraw an offer once it has been accepted. Once accepted the claimant has a statutory right to enforce the offer under the Act. Holding the defendant to his or her offer has been found not to be contrary to art.10 or art.6 of the European Convention on Human Rights.[790] **21-185**

(iii) Acceptance of offer and damages

Acceptance of the offer Where the claimant accepts any offer of amends, general or qualified, the claim is stayed. If the offer is made before proceedings are issued he cannot bring proceedings. In both cases this is subject to recourse to the court in relation to the details and enforcement of the offer. If the parties can agree all aspects of the settlement, they may apply to court for a confirmatory consent order, and where appropriate, for permission to read a joint statement in open court.[791] However, because of the general nature of the offer, there remains considerable scope for dispute. The appropriate procedure where an offer of amends is ac- **21-186**

---

788 See s.37 of the Senior Courts Act 1981 (*White Book* Vol.2, para.9A-128).

789 A defendant cannot make an offer of amends while maintaining that the allegations complained of are not defamatory. An offer of amends has to contain an acceptance that the original statement refers to and is defamatory of the claimant. See *Club La Costa (UK) Ltd v Gebhard* [2008] EWHC 2552 (QB); *The Times,* 10 December 2008.

790 *Warren v Random House Group Ltd* [2008] EWCA Civ 834; [2009] Q.B. 600.

791 If the defendant objects to joining in the reading of a joint statement, the court may give permission for the claimant to make a unilateral statement in court. See *Winslet v Associated Newspapers Ltd* [2009] EWHC 2735 (QB); [2010] E.M.L.R. 11.

cepted is set out in CPR PD 53B 5. It should noted that the overriding objective set out in CPR Pt 1 will apply. Both sides should be (or at least be seen to be) reasonable and conciliatory or risk judicial displeasure when the matter comes to court.[792] In *Loughton Contracts Plc v Dun & Bradstreet Ltd*,[793] the defendants made an unqualified offer of amends. Their letter made it clear that the offer of amends was made only in respect of the general damages claim. The claimants argued that, following subsequent correspondence, the offer of amends had been accepted by them albeit that they would be entitled to claim special damages once they had obtained certain disclosure. The defendants contended that the correspondence indicated that the offer of amends had been rejected, and the court agreed. Relying on the decision in *Nail v News Group Newspapers Ltd*,[794] the judge determined that the claimant should not be allowed to widen the basis of the claim upon which the defendants had made the offer of amends. The judge nevertheless permitted the claimant to accept the offer out of time on the basis that throughout the correspondence they had always made it clear that they wished to accept the offer of amends in principle. This was coupled with the fact that to deny the claimant an opportunity to accept the offer now would lead to an unjust outcome: the claimants would be denied any compensation whatsoever since the defendants could, under s.4 of the Defamation Act 1996, rely on the failure to accept as a complete defence.

21-187 **Suitable correction and sufficient apology** Where the parties cannot agree the wording or publication of the apology and correction, the initiative lies entirely with the defendant. He may publish whatever apology or correction he feels is appropriate. He may seek the court's approval to make a statement in open court and give an undertaking to the court in relation to its publication.[795] The sanction for the defendant in not publishing a proper apology and correction, is a larger award of damages from the judge.[796] The judge, in assessing damages, will consider the proposals made by the defendant and any objections or counter-proposals made by the claimant.[797] If he feels that the defendant's apology and correction is inadequate, and the claimant was justified in refusing acceptance, the mitigating effect of the apology will be limited. In certain cases it may even aggravate the damages. If however, he feels that the apology and correction are acceptable and the claimant's demands are unreasonable, it will have the same mitigating effect as if it had been agreed. There is nothing that a claimant can do to compel a defendant to publish the apology that the claimant wants.

21-188 **Compensation** In the absence of agreement, compensation will be calculated by the judge on ordinary principles.[798] It follows from the wording of subs.2(4)(c) that

---

792 *Cleese v Associated Newspapers Ltd* [2003] EWHC 137 (QB); [2004] E.M.L.R. 3.

793 [2006] EWHC 1224 (QB).

794 [2004] EWCA Civ 1708; [2005] 1 All E.R. 1040.

795 See s.3(1)(4).

796 *Turner v News Group Newspapers Ltd* [2006] EWCA Civ 540; [2006] 1 W.L.R. 3469. See also *Veliu v Mazrekaj* [2006] EWHC 1710 (QB); [2007] 1 W.L.R. 495 where a discount of one third on the award of compensation was awarded where the defendants had not acted promptly or generously following the making of an offer of amends; *Barron v Collins* [2017] EWHC 162 (QB) where no correction or apology at all was made, which together with the subsequent behaviour of the defendant resulted in only a 10 per cent discount on the damages award.

797 See s.3(1)(5).

798 See s.3(1)(5). The principles governing the assessment of compensation are set out in para. 21-225 onwards.

it is open to the judge not to award any damages. In *Nail v News Group Newspapers Ltd*[799] the Court of Appeal specifically recognised the offer of amends would give rise to "substantial mitigation". For guidance on the procedure and directions which are likely to be made by the court where the parties are unable to agree on the level of compensation, see *Abu v MGN Ltd*,[800] *Cleese v Associated Newspapers Ltd*,[801] *Barron v Collins*[802] and *Lisle-Mainwaring v Associated Newspapers Ltd*.[803] In *Barron v Collins* Warby J sets out the legal principles to be applied as well as assessing the impact of unreasonable behaviour on the part of the defendant after the offer is made. In *Lisle-Mainwaring* HH Judge Parkes QC sets out an analysis of the approach to be taken to compensation awards under s.3(5). Judges will use their case management powers to prevent a disproportionate amount of time and costs being spent on the assessment of compensation. The allocation of resources will depend on the seriousness of the allegation and the extent of the damage caused. CPR PD 53B 5 requires any application to court to be made in accordance with the Pt 8 procedure.

Qualified offers—procedure In relation to a qualified offer, the award should, in principle, relate solely to the meaning which is the subject of the offer. Otherwise there is no real difference between a general and qualified offer and no incentive on the part of the defendant to make such an offer. However, the defendant should not be able to call evidence to prove the truth of any of the other defamatory meanings in the publication but may rely upon matters admissible as "directly relevant background context", to mitigate damage.[804] **21-189**

Non-acceptance Where the claimant does not accept a general offer the claim continues in the normal way. The fact that an offer has been made will be an absolute defence unless the claimant can show that the defendant should be disqualified from relying on it. This will arise where the defendant knew or had reason to believe that the statement was false and that it was defamatory of the claimant. The burden of proof is on the claimant. **21-190**

(iv) Disqualification

The test for disqualification Section 4(3) of the 1996 Act provides: **21-191**

> "**4.—**(3) There is no such defence if the person by whom the offer was made knew or had reason to believe that the statement complained of—
> (a) referred to the aggrieved party or was likely to be understood as referring to him, and
> (b) was both false and defamatory of that party.
>
> but it shall be presumed until the contrary is shown that he did not know and had no reason to believe that was the case."

799 [2004] EWCA Civ 1708; [2005] 1 All E.R. 1040.
800 [2002] EWHC 2345 (QB); [2003] 1 W.L.R. 2201.
801 [2003] EWHC 137 (QB); [2004] E.M.L.R. 3.
802 [2017] EWHC 162 (QB).
803 [2017] EWHC 543 (QB).
804 *Abu v MGN Ltd* [2002] EWHC 2345 (QB); [2003] 1 W.L.R. 2201; and *Burstein v Times Newspapers Ltd* [2001] 1 W.L.R. 579 CA.

Subsection 4(3) has three elements to it: identification, defamatory meaning and falsity. It must be shown that the defendant was aware of all three elements for the defence to be defeated. The relevant question is whether the defendant knew or had reason to believe that the allegation was false and defamatory in relation to the claimant. "Had reason to believe" in s.4(3) is equivalent to the recklessness or conscious indifference to the truth which amounts to malice for the purposes of qualified privilege.[805] In *Thornton v Telegraph Media Group Ltd*,[806] Tugendhat J accepted that the defence of an offer of amends was defeated by a successful plea of malice and concluded that the reviewer knew the allegations to be false or was recklessly indifferent to the veracity of the allegation. The judge also concluded that the malice finding justified an award of aggravated damages, as did the manner in which the newspaper dealt with the complaint and the manner of the claimant's cross-examination. An award of £65,000 damages was made.

21-192 **Non-acceptance of a qualified offer** In cases of qualified offers, the offer is solely a defence in relation to the particular defamatory meaning to which it relates (s.4(2)). In common with general offers, the defendant, if he chooses to rely on it, cannot rely on any other defence in relation to that meaning. The defendant should rely on another or other substantive defences in relation to any other defamatory allegations in the publication (s.4(4)).

(v) Rejection

21-193 **Rejection** There is no concept in the 1996 Act of "rejection" of an offer of amends by the claimant and no time limit within which to accept it. In *Rigg v Associated Newspapers Ltd*[807] the claimant brought proceedings for defamation and malicious falsehood over what she claimed were quotations falsely attributed to her in a *Daily Mail* article. She claimed aggravated damages on the basis that the journalist who interviewed her had acted in bad faith and that the article contained a number of deliberate falsehoods. The defendants made an offer of amends, alleging that they were satisfied that the journalist had not acted in bad faith, and that this was demonstrated by her contemporaneous notes. However they refused to allow access to the notes until after the claimant had accepted the offer of amends. The claimant successfully applied for disclosure of the notes. The judge accepted that they would have an important bearing on whether the defendants knew that the allegations complained of were false, and thereby on whether or not to accept the offer of amends. He ordered their disclosure pursuant to his general discretion under CPR Pt 31.

(vi) Joint liability

21-194 **Joint liability** There may be a number of people responsible for the dissemination of the defamatory material, who will be jointly liable. In common with the acceptance of a Pt 36 offer, the acceptance of an offer of amends made by one defendant does not affect any claim against another participant. However, the defendant who makes the offer cannot be made to make any contribution to another participant

---

[805] *Milne v Express Newspapers* [2004] EWCA Civ 664; [2005] 1 W.L.R. 772.
[806] [2011] EWHC 1884 (QB); [2012] E.M.L.R. 8.
[807] [2003] EWHC 710; [2004] E.M.L.R. 4.

in excess of the amount payable under the offer.[808] Where appropriate, he will be entitled to claim a contribution from another participant in respect of the damages which he pays pursuant to the offer.

(h) Miscellaneous defences

(i) *Limitation*

Limitation The main purpose of a defamation claim is to repair damage to a claimant's reputation. In order for it to be effective it must be done quickly. With this in mind, s.5 of the 1996 Act amended s.4A of the Limitation Act 1980 to reduce the limitation period for defamation from three years to one year. The limitation period for malicious falsehood was reduced from six years to one. These reductions do not apply to Scotland, which may encourage a claim being brought in Scotland solely to avoid a limitation defence. The time runs from the date of publication,[809] although the day of publication is excluded from the calculation making it in effect a year and a day.[810] A claim for contribution under the Civil Liability (Contribution) Act 1978 must be brought within two years of the date of judgment or settlement.[811] In order to minimise the harshness[812] of the one-year limitation, which is the shortest under the 1980 Act, the court is given a general equitable discretion to allow a claim to proceed notwithstanding that the limitation period has expired under s.32A Limitation Act 1980. **21-195**

The disapplication of the one-year limitation period is an exceptional step, the Court of Appeal held in *Bewry v Reed Elsevier (UK) Ltd*,[813] overturning the first instance decision to disapply the limitation period. The claimant had failed to provide a good reason for the delay which occurred both before and after the issue of proceedings. Ignorance of the limitation period will rarely, if ever, carry much weight given the sound policy reasons underlying the one-year period. In *Brady v Norman*[814] the Court of Appeal confirmed that, when considering the discretion to dis-apply the limitation period for defamation actions it was proper to take into account the respective prejudice to the parties. In a libel action, a direction under **21-196**

808 See *Veliu v Mazrekaj* [2006] EWHC 1710 (QB); [2007] 1 W.L.R. 495.

809 Where special damage is an essential element (such as certain claims in slander), the claim is not complete and time will not start to run until special damage accrues. Where the claimant lacks capacity because of a disability, time will not start to run until the claimant has ceased to be under the disability (Limitation Act 1980 s.28(4A)). The introduction of the serious harm threshold at s.1 of the Defamation Act 2013 does not affect the position that time starts to run at the date of publication: *Lachaux v Independent Print Ltd* [2019] UKSC 27; [2020] A.C. 612 at [18].

810 *Otuo v Watchtower Bible and Tract Society of Britain* [2017] EWCA Civ 136; [2017] E.M.L.R. 15.

811 Limitation Act 1980 s.10.

812 The cause of action for defamation accrues on publication. That is an objective question, nothing to do with the subjective knowledge of the defamed person, either of the fact of the defamation or the identity of the defamer. In *Edwards v Golding* [2007] EWCA Civ 416; *The Times*, 22 May 2007, the claimant had sought to add a party to proceedings for defamation some years after the publication of the allegedly defamatory material. He contended that the cause of action had not accrued for the purposes of the one year limitation period until such time as he, the claimant, had knowledge of the identity of the publisher and thus who to sue. The argument was rejected since, if it were correct, there would be no need for the discretionary provision to extend the time limit (under s.32A of the Limitation Act 1980) which takes account of factors such as the claimant's knowledge of the facts concerning the defamation.

813 [2014] EWCA Civ 1411; [2015] 1 W.L.R. 2565.

814 [2011] EWCA Civ 107; [2011] E.M.L.R. 16.

s.32A is always highly prejudicial to the defendant.[815] A claim, brought to protect one's reputation ought to be pursued with vigour, given the ephemeral nature of most media publications. In *Lokhova v Tymula*[816] unexplained delay in progressing proceedings, coupled with a weak substantive case, meant the balance of prejudice did not favour disapplying the limitation period. The defendant would be substantially more prejudiced by the disapplication of the limitation period than the claimant would be by its application. In *Economou v de Freitas*[817] the court refused a claimant permission to amend his claim to add a new claim in respect of which the one year limitation had expired. Warby J considered the appropriate course to take was to consider the general principles as to adding causes of action outside the limitation period in accordance with s.35(3) of the Limitation Act 1980. As the proposed new claim arose out of a different communication, albeit between the same parties, Warby J considered that since it did not arise out of the same or substantially the same facts as were already in issue, he had no power or discretion to permit the amendment. When considering s.32A of the Limitation Act, Warby J found that the application came too close to trial and the delay in raising the issue was not adequately explained, and so the defendant would suffer substantial prejudice if the limitation period were disapplied, whereas the claimant would suffer no serious prejudice given the claims he had already pleaded. He refused to disapply the limitation period.

21-197 In *Nugent v Willers*[818] when examining a provision of Isle of Man law almost identical in terms to s.32A of the Limitation Act, the Privy Council approved the principles in *Brady v Norman* and *Steedman v BBC*, summarising the position as follows[819]:

(1) It is for the claimant to make out a case for the disapplication of the normal limitation rule.
(2) The court is required to have regard to all of the circumstances and in particular the length of and reasons for the delay; the date when all or any of the facts relevant to the cause of action became known to the claimant and the extent to which he acted promptly and reasonably; and the extent to which, having regard to the delay, relevant evidence is likely to be unavailable or less cogent than it would have been if the claim had been brought within time.
(3) Allowing an action to proceed will always be prejudicial to a defendant but, conversely, the expiry of the limitation period will always be in some degree prejudicial to the claimant. Accordingly, in exercising its discretion, the court must consider the degrees of prejudice to the claimant and the defendant, all of the other circumstances to which attention is directed by the section and any other relevant circumstances of the particular case in issue.
(4) It was plainly the intention of Parliament that a claimant should assert and pursue his need for vindication speedily.

The Privy Council stated that the court is entitled to treat some periods of delay as more relevant than others, and that it is reasonable for a court to take the view

815 See also *Steedman v BBC* [2001] EWCA Civ 1534; [2002] E.M.L.R. 17.
816 [2016] EWHC 225 (QB).
817 [2016] EWHC 1218 (QB).
818 [2019] UKPC 1; [2019] E.M.L.R. 14.
819 [2019] UKPC 1; [2019] E.M.L.R. 14 at [17].

that the most relevant period of delay will be that after the relevant facts came to the claimant's attention.

(ii) *Consent to publication*

Consent (or assent) to publication It is a general defence to a tort that the claimant expressly or impliedly consented to the tortious act, which in the case of defamation is the publication of the defamatory statement. The defence is also known by the Latin maxim, "volenti non fit injuria". In defamation cases the defence is narrowly construed and will not be established in many situations where it might reasonably be said that the claimant bears some of the responsibility for the defamatory statement being published.[820] If the statement is sent to the person defamed in circumstances where he is under a duty to send it on to other persons, his part in so doing cannot be regarded as an assent to the publication.[821] Proof of consent must be clear and unequivocal and must relate to the publication complained of. In *Cook v Ward*,[822] the claimant at a private function told a humorous anecdote about himself which was subsequently accurately reported in a newspaper. It was held that he had not consented to the publication in the newspaper.[823] The same principle applies to an off-the-record interview—there can be no consent to its dissemination. Consent must relate to the actual libel published. A person who wishes to publicise a particular matter does not consent to every statement made as a result of his actions.[824] It is sometimes the case that the claimant procures the publication of the defamatory statement in order to create a claim. For example, the victim of a defamatory attack made by an MP under absolute privilege may challenge him to repeat the defamatory statement outside the House. The offer unsurprisingly is rarely taken up, but it may be difficult to establish consent in these circumstances.[825] Where the claimant becomes a member of an association he consents to its rules which may provide for the publication to members of certain material such as the decisions or findings of a committee of the association. He will therefore be held to have consented to such publication.[826] This principle has also been applied in respect of publications made as part of the process of disciplinary proceedings against an employee, where he has accepted the disciplinary code as part of his contract of employment.[827] This is not to be equated with the qualified privilege arising from the legitimate interests of members of an association or company in discussing its affairs, and which in contrast to consent, will be defeated by malice. 21-198

---

820 *Rigg v Associated Newspapers Ltd* [2003] EWHC 710 (QB); [2004] E.M.L.R. 4. See also *Howe v Burden* [2004] EWHC 196 (QB).

821 *Collerton v McLean* [1962] N.Z.L.R. 1045.

822 (1830) 4 Moo. & P. 99. See also *Marco Pierre White v New York Times Company*, unreported 31 March 2000, in which the defendant, who had misinterpreted an ambiguous extract from the claimant's autobiography, could not rely on the defence of consent.

823 In an appropriate case the defendant may be able to rely on the original statement as evidence of justification. See *Rigg v Associated Newspapers Ltd* [2003] EWHC 710 (QB); [2004] E.M.L.R. 4.

824 *Mihaka v Wellington Publishing* [1975] 1 N.Z.L.R. 10.

825 See for example *Duke of Brunswick v Harmer* (1849) 14 Q.B. 185, which today would be dismissed as an abuse of process under *Jameel* principles.

826 *Chapman v Ellesmere* [1932] 2 K.B. 431.

827 *Friend v Civil Aviation Authority* [1998] I.R.L.R. 253 CA.

(iii) Accord and satisfaction

21-199 **Accord and satisfaction—release** The fact that a claim has been settled by agreement constitutes a defence in the event that the claimant seeks to pursue his claim notwithstanding the agreement. The defence is commonly described as accord and satisfaction or release. It is a general defence available to all claims. Ordinary contractual principles apply, although there are particular considerations to be borne in mind with regard to defamation claims.[828] There must be consideration for any agreement. This is generally the publication of an apology and/or payment of damages and costs. However, the consideration need not reflect the seriousness of the defamation to be sufficient. There must be agreement between the parties in relation to the essential terms of settlement. An agreement to publish an apology, without agreeing its terms, may be insufficiently certain to be binding.[829] Where there is a breach of the agreement by the defendant it is a question of construction as to whether or not the claimant can resurrect the original claim or is limited to suing for the breach. If the discharge of liability is made conditional on the performance by the publisher of the settlement agreement, the claimant can choose either.

21-200 **Accord and satisfaction where there are joint tortfeasors** The basic rule is that where accord and satisfaction had been made with one tortfeasor it is a defence to an action against the other tortfeasors. However, a claimant can expressly or impliedly reserve his or her right of action against the other tortfeasors whilst agreeing to release one or more of them. For example, in *Ansari v Knowles*[830] the court held that settlement with one university joint tortfeasor did not dispose of the claims against his own employer university or a fellow lecturer. Whether an agreement releases only one, or multiple tortfeasors is a matter of interpreting the settlement agreement in its particular factual matrix.

(iv) Abuse of process

21-201 **Abuse of process—general** There are a number of heads of abuse which may result in a case or part of a case being struck out.[831] Those most relevant to defamation claims are dealt with below.

21-202 ***Jameel* and *Thornton* grounds** Attempts have been made to rely upon the Court of Appeal decision in *Jameel v Dow Jones & Co Inc*[832] to strike out cases as an abuse of process where "the game is not worth the candle." This will often be because there has been publication to a limited number of individuals, and/or because the publication does not constitute a real and substantial tort.[833] The defendant in such cases argues that the claim is trivial, and as such it would be disproportionate for the court to allow it to continue. The court will consider all the

---

828 *Marks v Conservative Newspaper* (1886) 3 T.L.R. 244; *British Russian Gazette v Associated Newspapers* [1933] 2 K.B. 616; *Watts v Aldington* (1993), [1999] L. & T.R. 578; *The Times*, 16 December 1993 CA; *Ansari v Knowles* [2012] EWHC 3137 (QB).

829 Under general contractual principles there can be no agreement unless the terms are sufficiently certain, see *G Scammell & Nephew Ltd v Ouston* [1941] A.C. 251.

830 [2012] EWHC 3137 (QB).

831 See *Abbey v Gilligan* [2012] EWHC 3217 (QB); [2013] E.M.L.R. 12, in particular at [126] onwards.

832 [2005] EWCA Civ 75; [2005] Q.B. 946.

833 *Thornton v Telegraph Media Group Ltd* [2010] EWHC 1414 (QB); [2011] 1 W.L.R. 1985.

circumstances of the case, including the seriousness of the libel, the numbers to whom it was published, the potential damages likely to be awarded should the claimant succeed and the cost of continuing proceedings. Applications of this nature have been made many times in recent years.[834] In assessing whether a libel claim is an abuse of process a court should consider what the claimant could achieve by way of vindication if the case went to trial, including matters which would go to the assessment of damages.[835] Where a claimant has been able to effectively restore their reputation through other means it may become an abuse of process on *Jameel* grounds to continue a libel claim.[836] Where a claimant has received vindication from one defendant but wishes to continue the case against another, the court should consider whether for practical purposes the claimant has obtained all he or she is going to obtain by way of redress such that contining the case would be futile,[837] whereas just because a claim against one defendant would amount to *Jameel* abuse, does not automatically mean that a claim against a second defendant will also be an abuse.[838]

Abuse of process and serious harm Most such cases are now likely to fail to overcome the serious harm threshold of s.1 of the Defamation Act 2013, which is explicitly stated to build on the previous case law including *Thornton* and *Jameel*.[839] In *Ames v The Spamhaus Project Ltd*[840] it was held that serious harm was best considered as a preliminary issue rather than an application under CPR Pts 3.4 or 24. It will be a rare case which has caused or is likely to cause serious harm but which is nonetheless an abuse of process on *Jameel* grounds. In *Stocker v Stocker*[841] the court refused to strike out a claim on *Jameel* grounds over an email sent to a single recipient. The defendant contended that the recipient did not believe the contents of the email, and that the claimant was indifferent to the recipient's view of his reputation. The court nevertheless refused to strike out the claim in respect of that email, since the *Jameel* jurisdiction was to be exercised exceptionally, was not a "numbers game" and was highly fact-specific (applying *Ames v The Spamhaus Project Ltd*). **21-203**

834 For example, and in addition to *Jameel* and *Thornton* themselves: *Mardas v New York Times* [2008] EWHC 3135 (QB); [2009] E.M.L.R. 8; *Adelson v Associated Newspapers Ltd* [2008] EWHC 278 (QB); [2009] E.M.L.R. 10; *Haji-Ioannou v Dixon* [2009] EWHC 178 (QB); *Carrie v Tolkien* [2009] EWHC 29 (QB); [2009] E.M.L.R. 9; *Lonzim Plc v Sprague* [2009] EWHC 2838 (QB); *Baturina v Times Newspapers Ltd* [2011] EWCA Civ 308; [2011] 1 W.L.R. 1526; *Kaschke v Osler* [2010] EWHC 1075 (QB); *Hays Plc v Hartley* [2010] EWHC 1068 (QB); *Kordowski v Hudson* [2011] EWHC 2667 (QB); *Tamiz v Google* [2013] EWCA Civ 68; [2013] 1 W.L.R. 2151; *Euromoney Institutional Investor Plc v Aviation News Ltd* [2013] EWHC 1505 (QB); *Tamiz v Guardian News & Media Ltd* [2013] EWHC 2339 (QB); *Ansari v Knowles* [2013] EWCA Civ 1448; [2014] C.P. Rep. 9; *Liberty Fashion Wears Ltd v Primark Stores Ltd* [2015] EWHC 415 (QB); *Alsaifi v Trinity Mirror Plc* [2018] EWHC 1954 (QB); [2019] E.M.L.R. 1.

835 *Weston v Bates and Leeds United Football Club* [2015] EWHC 3070 (QB).

836 *Sobrinho v Impresa Publishing SA* [2016] EWHC 66 (QB); [2016] E.M.L.R. 12.

837 *Ansari v Knowles* [2013] EWCA Civ 144, [2014] C.P. Rep. 9, where the Court of Appeal refused to strike out the claim.

838 *Alsaifi v Trinity Mirror Plc* [2018] EWHC 1954 (QB); [2019] E.M.L.R. 1.

839 See para.21-18.

840 [2015] EWHC 127 (QB); [2015] 1 W.L.R. 3409.

841 [2016] EWHC 147 (QB).

21-204 **Abuse of process — delay** A claim may also be struck out as an abuse of process where there is a delay in bringing the matter to trial. In *Adelson v Anderson*[842] proceedings were struck out after the claimant delayed seven years in pursuing the claim and failed to comply with court orders. The court inferred that he no longer sought vindication and that there was no basis for ordering an injunction since the defendants had shown no indication of repeating the allegations of which he complained. However, delay will not always be grounds for a strike out, particularly where there is a credible reason for the delay.[843] A long running libel case was struck out for abuse of process, with the court considering delay and what remained at stake in proceedings in *Weston v Bates and Leeds United Football Club*.[844] The court considered delay at various stages of proceedings, including by issuing/serving a claim form at the last minute. Unless there is a good reason for any significant delay in progressing proceedings, adverse inferences may be drawn from such conduct.

21-205 **Abuse of process—advancing matters already determined** It can also be an abuse of process to advance a truth or honest opinion defence using as particulars matters which have already been determined, or should have been determined, in previous court proceedings.[845] A determination on this type of *Henderson v Henderson*[846] abuse and the related doctrine of res judicata abuse of process will always be fact specific.[847] In *Building Register v Weston* Nicola Davies J rejected art.10 arguments, stating that the defendant was still permitted to defend the case but only on the basis of those matters which in the opinion of the court it was fair to try. Libel proceedings which are a collateral attack on the claimant's previous conviction and sentencing will also constitute an abuse of process.[848]

7. MALICE

(a) General

21-206 **Meaning of malice** The foregoing discussion of the law of defamation has very frequently involved the use of the word "malice", more particularly in connection with the defence of qualified privilege.[849] It is therefore necessary to examine in further detail what malice means in this context. In connection with defamation, "malice" is a legal term of art not necessarily to be equated with its popular meaning. In this context the expression means a dominant improper motive for publishing the statement complained of. The classic exposition of malice was given by Lord Diplock in *Horrocks v Lowe*[850] where, in summary, it was stated that malice can be shown either by proving that the defendant had an improper motive for publishing, or that the defendant did not have an honest belief that what he published was true. Whether these are separate heads of malice, or whether the absence of honest belief indicates a dominant improper motive is not entirely clear

842 [2011] EWHC 2497 (QB).
843 *Morrissey v McNicholas* [2011] EWHC 2738 (QB).
844 [2015] EWHC 3070 (QB).
845 *Building Register Ltd v Weston* [2014] EWHC 2361 (QB).
846 (1843) 3 Hare 100.
847 See also *Johnson v Gore Wood & Co* [2002] 2 A.C. 1.
848 *Richardson v Trinity Mirror (Merseyside) Ltd* [2016] EWHC 1927 (QB).
849 Malice when discussed in relation to honest opinion has a different meaning. See para.21-171.
850 [1975] A.C. 135 HL.

from the case law,[851] although the latter would appear to be the favoured view.[852] In any event, it is clear that showing either will prove the claimant's case on malice.

21-207 Where a defendant pleads qualified privilege the burden of proof will be on the claimant to prove malice in order to defeat the privilege.[853] The process of proving what lay in a person's mind can never be simple and in *Horrocks v Lowe*[854] Lord Diplock warned courts to be "very slow" in deciding that a defendant was totally actuated by improper motives on a privileged occasion. It has been said that honest belief does not necessarily negate malice; one might honestly believe the truth of the statement and yet publish it for improper reason or motive.[855] In practice, such cases are almost unheard of.[856]

21-208 **Abuse of occasion** The question always is—if the occasion is held to be privileged, has the defendant abused it? This question may well be bound up with that of whether the occasion is one of privilege in the first place, particularly where the form of privilege claimed is that of common law duty and interest.[857] In *Qadir v Associated Newspapers Ltd*,[858] it was held that where a defendant relied upon qualified privilege for a fair and accurate extract from a register or other document required by law to be open to public inspection, it was a good plea of malice to allege misuse of the privileged occasion, that is use of the occasion for a purpose other than that for which the privilege was accorded, as long as it was also pleaded that misuse of the occasion was the dominant purpose or motive of the defendant. However on the facts the journalist was held, in respect of the first article, to have been recklessly indifferent to the truth in continuing to state falsely that the claimant had made no comment about the allegations and with regard to the second article had deliberately produced an unfair report—from this the court could infer malice. But if a defendant makes a statement believing it to be true, he will not lose his privilege, though he has no reasonable ground for his belief.[859] Nor is it always absolute proof of malice for a defendant to state what he knows to be untrue for "he may believe it to be untrue, and yet be perfectly justified in publishing it to persons with whom he is in communication, and with whom it may be his duty to communicate freely on the subject of the information he has received".[860]

21-209 **Claimant to furnish particulars** By CPR PD 53B 4.8:

"(1) If the defendant contends that any of the statement complained of, or any part

---

851 In the Scottish case of *Fraser v Mirza* 1993 S.C. (H.L.) 27; 1993 S.L.T. 527 the House of Lords held that absence of belief in the truth of a defamatory allegation was usually conclusive evidence of improper motive amounting to malice, whereas other cases have suggested that the claimant can show either two varieties of malice: *Loutchansky v Times Newspapers Ltd (Nos 2-5)* [2001] EWCA Civ 1805; [2002] Q.B. 783; *Lille v Newcastle City Council* [2002] EWHC 1600 (QB).

852 See *Roberts v Bass* [2002] HCA 57; (2002) 12 C.L.R. 1, which argued that the alternative view is neither historically correct nor consistent with *Horrocks v Lowe*.

853 *Stuart v Bell* [1891] 2 Q.B. 341 at 351, per Lindley LJ. See *Beech v Freeson* [1972] 1 Q.B. 14.

854 [1975] A.C. 135 HL.

855 *Christie v Westcom Group* (1991) 75 D.L.R. (4th) 546.

856 In *Branson v Bower (No.2)* [2002] Q.B. 737 Eady J commented that he had never come across such a case.

857 See discussion in *Gatley on Libel and Slander* (12th edn) at 17.9, 14.63 and 14.64.

858 [2012] EWHC 2606 (QB); [2013] E.M.L.R. 15.

859 per Brett LJ *Fountain v Boodle* (1842) 3 Q.B. 5.

860 per Kelly CB in *Botterill v Whytehead* (1879) 41 L.T. 588 at 590; *Brine v Bazalgette* (1849) 3 Ex. 692. A more recent example is *W v Westminster CC* [2004] EWHC 2866 (QB); [2005] 1 F.C.R. 39. A scenario was also contemplated by Lord Diplock in *Horrocks v Lowe* [1975] A.C. 135, 151.

thereof, was honest opinion, or was published on a privileged occasion, and the claimant intends to allege that the defendant did not hold the opinion or acted with malice (as applicable), the claimant must serve a reply giving details of the facts or matters relied on."

(b) Examples of malice

21-210 **Violence of language** Strong or violent language may in some circumstances constitute evidence of malice.[861] Where, however, a person is acting in self-defence or in the vindication of his character somewhat greater licence is allowed and his language is not to be scrutinised with minuteness in order to raise an inference of malice. "The language in which a defamatory charge is repudiated is not to be weighed in nice scales."[862] In *Khader v Aziz*[863] a malice claim based on "grossly exaggerated language" was struck out, since there was no evidence that the defendant did not believe the publication to be true or was indifferent to its truth or falsity.

21-211 **Knowledge of falsity of charge** It is often said that honesty of belief is the touchstone of malice. If a defendant is proved to have knowingly made false allegations, that can be evidence of malice. Conversely, where a defendant honestly believes his statement to be true, he may not lose his privilege notwithstanding that he has no reasonable grounds for his belief,[864] and even though his belief is induced by "gross and unreasoning prejudice" with regard to the claimant.[865] It may sometimes happen that where a confidential relationship exists, one person may communicate to another rumours and reports not as matters which he himself states as fact, but as requiring attention and calling for investigation.[866] In *W v Westminster CC*[867] the defendants were social workers concerned with the welfare of a child. At a child protection case conference allegations that the claimant was grooming the child for paedophilia were disclosed by the social workers. At trial the judge found that notwithstanding the social workers had no belief in the truth of such allegations, they considered it in accordance with their duties under the Children Act 1989 to pass on the allegations to members of the case conference. Although in fact it was not within their duties to communicate such matters the judge found that they acted in good faith and that in the circumstances their absence of honest belief was not to be equated with malice. Such cases are, however, exceptional. No person has a general right or duty to make definite allegations in which he does not believe, and if he does so, this will generally be indicative of a dominant improper motive.[868]

21-212 If the defendant has spoken as if from his own knowledge, a prima facie case

[861] *Spill v Maule* (1869) L.R. 4 Ex. 232; *Coke v Wildes* (1855) 5 E. & B. 328; cf. *Fryer v Kinnersley* (1863) C.B. (N.S.) 423; *Nevill v Fine Arts and General Insurance Co Ltd* [1895] 2 Q.B. 156 at 172, per Lopes LJ.

[862] *Adam v Ward* [1917] A.C. 309, 330, 347; *Laughton v The Bishop of Sodor and Man* (1872) L.R. 4 P.C. 495.

[863] [2010] EWCA Civ 716; [2010] 1 W.L.R. 2673.

[864] *Clark v Molyneux* (1877) 3 Q.B.D. 237.

[865] *Horrocks v Lowe* [1975] A.C. 135 HL.

[866] per Kelly CB in *Botterill v Whytehead* (1879) 41 L.T. 588 at 590 (see para.21-211); per Bramwell LJ in *Clark v Molyneux* (1877) 3 Q.B.D. 237.

[867] [2004] EWHC 2866 (QB); [2005] 1 F.C.R. 39.

[868] per Lord Denman CJ in *Fountain v Boodle* (1842) 3 Q.B. 5 at 11; per Brett LJ in *Clark v Molyneux* (1877) 3 Q.B.D. 237 at 247; *Palmer v Hummerston* (1883) 1 Cab. & El. 36.

against him is made by evidence showing the charge to be untrue. For although the truth is not directly in issue, his knowledge is.[869] Although mere carelessness or negligence on a privileged occasion is not malice,[870] a reckless indifference to the truth or falsity of the charge is also evidence from which malice may be inferred.[871] In *Cambridge v Makin*[872] the court found the defendant to be malicious based on his wilful blindness to the truth or falsity of the statements published. Such recklessness is subjective recklessness, as one cannot be indifferent to a risk of which one is not conscious.[873] The sources of the defendant's information may be most material in determining whether he honestly believed his statement to be true. "The state of mind of the defendant when he published the alleged libel is a matter directly in issue."[874] If his informants were persons who could not possibly know anything about the matter in question, that might be cogent evidence of malice.[875]

Direct evidence of ill-will A claimant may be able to show from extrinsic facts that the defendant harboured feelings of spite and ill-will towards him, and it may be fairly inferred that the publication in question was prompted by such feelings and consequently not by a legitimate motive: 21-213

> "If the claimant can show any example of spite or indirect motive, whether before or after the publication, he would establish his case provided that the examples given are so connected with the state of mind of the defendant as to lead to the conclusion that he was malicious at the date when the libel was published."[876]

It by no means, however, follows that this inference must necessarily be drawn.[877]

The terms of the defamatory statement (intrinsic evidence) The claimant can rely on the terms of the defamatory publication itself as evidence of malice.[878] The inclusion of material which is in any way connected with the relevant duty or interest will be prima facie protected by qualified privilege. Where only marginally relevant matters are included it may provide some evidence that the defendant was using the occasion for an improper purpose, although the court should be "slow" to draw such an inference.[879] Where the defendant includes material that is wholly irrelevant it will not be privileged, and may constitute evidence of malice to defeat the privilege which attaches to the relevant parts of the statement.[880] However mere 21-214

---

869 *Brown v Houston* [1901] 2 K.B. 855 at 859, per Vaughan Williams LJ.

870 per Cotton LJ in *Capital and Counties Bank v Henty* (1880) 5 C.P.D. 514 at 538; cf. *Lyon v Daily Telegraph Ltd* [1943] K.B. 746 at 753.

871 *Royal Aquarium etc Society v Parkinson* [1892] 1 Q.B. 431; cf. *Horrocks v Lowe* [1975] A.C. 135.

872 [2012] EWCA Civ 85; [2012] E.M.L.R. 19.

873 Or "Cunningham recklessness" as it is known in the criminal law (after *R v Cunningham* [1957] 2 Q.B. 396).

874 *Plymouth Mutual Co-operative and Industrial Society Ltd v Traders' Publishing Association Ltd* [1906] 1 K.B. 403 at 418, per Fletcher Moulton LJ.

875 *Elliott v Garrett* [1902] 1 K.B. 870; *White & Co v Credit Reform Association Ltd* [1905] 1 K.B. 653; *Lyle-Samuel v Odhams Ltd* [1920] 1 K.B. 135; *Chapman v Leach* [1920] 1 K.B. 336.

876 *Turner v MGM Pictures Ltd* [1950] 1 All E.R. 449 at 455, per Lord Porter; and *Thompson v James* [2013] EWHC 515 (QB).

877 *Stevens v Sampson* (1879) 5 Ex. D. 53; *Horrocks v Lowe* [1975] A.C. 135 HL.

878 On violent language see para.21-210.

879 per Lord Diplock in *Horrocks v Lowe* [1975] A.C. 135 at 151H.

880 *Adam v Ward* [1917] A.C. 309; *Horrocks v Lowe* [1975] A.C. 135. The preferred view today is that irrelevant material is evidence of malice rather than a way in which publication may fall outside the privilege.

carelessness of expression in a defamatory statement is not a ground for inferring malice.[881]

21-215 **Previous defamation** "You may give in evidence any words as well as any act of the defendant to show with what state of mind he spoke the words which are the subject of the action."[882] Therefore defamatory language used towards the claimant by the defendant on other occasions, whether prior[883] or subsequent[884] to the cause of action, may be evidence of malice. It is not, however, admissible for a claimant to make requests for further information to a defendant for the purpose of eliciting from him previous defamatory statements.[885] In the case of slanderous words spoken subsequent to the cause of action, an ill-feeling first shown to exist after the date of the publication complained of may be consistent with the ill-feeling having a later origin rather than malice.[886]

21-216 **General want of good faith** Lesser evidence of malice will suffice in the case of an officious and purely voluntary communication.[887] Where the defendant, after appearing against the claimant in a county court, spontaneously sent a report of the proceedings to a newspaper, this was held sufficient to justify a finding of malice; the evidence of a bad motive was small, but the probability of a good motive was smaller.[888]

8. REPETITION

21-217 **Injury by repetition** Defamatory allegations are often repeated, causing greater damage. Online, republication may make a defamatory allegation accessible to a vast number of people, and the court has acknowledged the tendency for statements to "go viral."[889] The liability of a person who repeats a slander was stated thus by Lush J in *Watkin v Hall*[890]:

> "It is no justification to a person, in giving currency to that which is injurious to the character of another, for him to say that he heard the statement made by another person. If he justifies at all, he must show that he made the communication under circumstances that gave it a privileged character, that he was justified in making the communication or that the words themselves, when he spoke the words, were true. It is not enough for him to say that he heard it from some other person."

---

[881] *Oliver v Chief Constable of Northumbria Police* [2004] EWHC 790 (QB); following *Roberts v Bass* [2002] HCA 57; (2002) 12 C.L.R. 1.

[882] per Lord Ellenborough CJ in *Rustell v Macquister* (1807) 1 Camp. 49n.

[883] *Barrett v Long* (1851) 3 H.L.C. 395; *Darby v Ouseley* (1856) 1 H. & N. 1.

[884] *Mead v Daubigny* (1792) Peake 168; *Pearson v Lemaitre* (1843) 5 M. & G. 700; cf. *Bridgmont v Associated Newspapers* [1951] 2 K.B. 578.

[885] *Caryll v Daily Mail Publishing Co* (1904) 90 L.T. 307.

[886] *Hemmings v Gasson* (1858) E.B. & E. 346.

[887] *Pattison v Jones* (1828) 3 M. & Ry. 101; cf. *Gardner v Slade* (1849) 13 Q.B. 796; *Greenlands v Wilmshurst* [1913] 3 K.B. 507 at 535, per Hamilton LJ.

[888] *Stevens v Sampson* (1879) 5 Ex. D. 53.

[889] *Cairns v Modi* [2012] EWCA Civ 1382; [2013] 1 W.L.R. 1015.

[890] (1868) L.R. 3 Q.B. 396 at 403; cf. *Truth (NZ) Ltd v Holloway* [1960] 1 W.L.R. 997; *Dingle v Associated Newspapers* [1961] 2 Q.B. 162 CA; affirmed [1964] A.C. 371 HL; *Lewis v Daily Telegraph Ltd* [1963] 1 Q.B. 340 CA; affirmed [1964] A.C. 234 HL.

The "repetition rule" survives the coming into force of the Defamation Act 2013.[891]

Liability of original publisher Ordinarily the first publisher is not liable for the damage which ensues from its repetition, for the repetition is the voluntary act of a free agent over whom he has no control.[892] However, it is clear that the original publisher will be liable for the consequences of repetition where[893]: 21-218

(a) he authorised the repetition; or
(b) he made the original publication in such circumstances or in such a state of mind that the court finds as a fact that he intended the repetition; or
(c) there is a duty to repeat; or
(d) where the repetition is the natural and probable consequence of the original publication.[894] This is governed by the ordinary rules of causation, and reasonable foreseeability is sufficient to found liability.[895]

The Defamation Act 2013[896] has changed the law to limit the liability of secondary publishers, but this will not affect the liability of an original publisher for republication.

Foreseeability of republication In *McManus v Beckham*,[897] the proprietors of an autograph shop sued Mrs Beckham for slander over allegations made in the shop that autographs purportedly by her husband were not genuine and that she did not want people "being ripped off", which were reported extensively in the press. The proprietors alleged that Mrs Beckham was responsible for the allegations appearing in the press. The Court of Appeal concluded that it was open to the jury to find that the damage caused by the press publications had been caused by the initial slander. It is sufficient that the circumstances of the publication were such as to make republication reasonably foreseeable. In other words, a reasonable person in the position of the defendant should have anticipated that there was a significant risk that what the defendant said or wrote would be repeated. 21-219

Where repetition authorised or intended Where the repetition is authorised the original slanderer is responsible for the damage caused by the repetition, but this liability results not because the damage is not too remote from the original slander, but because the original slanderer is a party to the repetition and a joint tortfeasor with the person who repeats it. This situation may arise where a person submits material to a newspaper or broadcaster,[898] tells a reporter a story defamatory of the claimant,[899] makes statements at a press conference or issues a press release[900] or 21-220

---

[891] *Lachaux v Independent Print Ltd* [2019] UKSC 27; [2020] A.C. 612; see further paras 21-19 and 21-28.

[892] *Ward v Weeks* (1830) 7 Bing. 211 at 215; *Parkins v Scott* (1862) 1 H. & C. 153; *Bree v Marescaux* (1881) 7 Q.B.D. 434 at 437; *Ratcliffe v Evans* [1892] 2 Q.B. 524 at 530; *Weld-Blundell v Stephens* [1920] A.C. 956.

[893] *Speight v Gosnay* (1891) 60 L.J.Q.B. 231 at 232.

[894] In addition to *Speight v Gosnay* see *Ward v Lewis* [1955] 1 W.L.R. 9; *Cutler v McPhail* [1962] 2 Q.B. 292.

[895] *Slipper v BBC* [1991] 1 Q.B. 283, CA; *Terluk v Berezovsky* [2011] EWCA Civ 1534.

[896] Defamation Act 2013 ss.10 and 13.

[897] [2002] EWCA Civ 939; [2002] 1 W.L.R. 2982.

[898] *Slipper v BBC* [1991] 1 Q.B. 283, CA; *Economou v de Freitas* [2018] EWCA Civ 2591; [2019] E.M.L.R. 7.

[899] *Adams v Kelly* (1824) Ry. & M. 157; *Parkes v Prescott* (1869) L.R. 4 Ex. 169.

gives an interview apprehending that it will be broadcast within the UK,[901] in which case he will be liable for republication by the newspaper or broadcaster. In *Alsaifi v Secretary of State for Education* the court set out the principles to be applied when assessing the liability of the source of a quote in relation to a subsequent article which includes that quote.[902]

21-221 **Where there is a duty to repeat** Where the person to whom the original publication is made is under a duty to repeat it to others, whether that duty is legal, social or moral, the original publisher will be liable for the repetition, although he has not directly authorised it, provided that at the time of the original publication he is aware of the circumstances giving rise to the duty to repeat.[903] Determining whether in fact the original slanderer was aware of a duty to republish will not always be straightforward and will depend on the circumstances of the case.[904]

21-222 **Claims against secondary publishers: Defamation Act 2013 s.10** Section 10 provides that the court does not have jurisdiction to hear a defamation claim against "a person who was not the author, editor or publisher of the statement complained of unless the court is satisfied that it is not reasonably practical for an action to be brought against the author, editor or publisher. "Author", "editor" and "publisher" are given the same meaning as in s.1 of the Defamation Act 1996. No guidance is given as to what "reasonably practical" means. Questions are likely to arise where the primary author and/or publisher is insolvent, where they are located in a jurisdiction where a judgment obtained against them in this jurisdiction could not be enforced,[905] or where the publication has been published anonymously.

21-223 **Order to remove: Defamation Act 2013 s.13** Section 13 is the corollary of s.10, and was enacted in order to allow to court to make an order to prevent the continued dissemination of the material complained of by secondary publishers where an action was brought only against the primary publisher. It allows the court, where judgment has been given for a claimant in a defamation action, to order (a) the operator of a website on which the defamatory statement is posted to remove the statement; or (b) any person who was not the author, editor or publisher of the statement to stop distributing, selling or exhibiting material containing the statement.

---

900 *Kirby-Harris v Baxter* [1995] E.M.L.R 516 CA; *Sims v Wran* [1984] 1 N.S.W.L.R. 317; *Dato' Seri Tiong Sing v Datul Justine Jinggut* [2003] M.L.J. 433.

901 *Terluk v Berezovsky* [2011] EWCA Civ 1534.

902 [2019] EWHC 1413 (QB); [2020] E.L.R. 1 at [23].

903 See *Derry v Handley* (1867) 16 L.T. 263; *Speight v Gosney* (1891) 60 L.J.Q.B. 231, CA; *Gatley on Libel and Slander* (12th edn), para.6.55.

904 This question gave rise to dissent in the Court of Appeal in *Riddick v Thames Board Mills Ltd* [1977] Q.B. 881 where a personnel officer telephoned two employees and asked for an account of the claimant's conduct and the circumstances of his dismissal by the defendant company. In the course of conversation the employees slandered the claimant and these slanders were later incorporated in a report made by the personnel officer to the chief personnel manager. Stephenson LJ, (at 900) with whom Lord Denning MR appeared to agree, found that the employees must have expected that details of the conversation would be taken down and passed on to higher authority. Waller LJ (at 909) thought that mere proof of the conversation alone without evidence of the speakers' state of mind was, despite its purpose, insufficient to engage liability for the subsequent publications.

905 Such as the USA, courtesy of the Securing the Protection of our Enduring and Established Heritage (SPEECH) Act.

9. REMEDIES

(a) Damages—General

Damages in general Damages are the primary remedy in defamation claims. There is no general power to order a defendant to apologise or to publish a correction. The Defamation Act 2013 includes a new power to order the defendant to publish a summary of the court's judgment,[906] and an injunction may be available to prevent further publication of the statement complained of.[907] The purpose of damages is both to vindicate the claimant's reputation and to compensate for distress and loss flowing from the libel.[908] In actions for defamation (except in slanders not actionable per se[909]) no proof of actual damage is necessary, and damages are at large.[910] The claimant, therefore, need only lay before the court the words or writing of which he or she complains,[911] together with any evidence necessary to overcome the serious harm threshold at s.1 of the Defamation Act 2013. The claimant may, however, lay before the court evidence of the damage to reputation and the distress caused by the publication. Where the allegation is serious and a substantial degree of distress has been suffered, a damages award may be substantial.[912] The 20th edition contained an analysis of the system for jury awards of damages. Now that s.11 of the Defamation Act 2013 has removed the presumption in favour of juries, jury awards are unlikely. Where a there is a jury it is the jury which awards damages, having received some guidance.[913] The Court of Appeal has the power to alter an award of damages rather than ordering a new trial.[914] 21-224

Principles of damages awards in defamation Whilst general damages are at large, there are number of principles which can be drawn from the case law in relation to the assessment of damages[915]: 21-225

(1) Where the summary procedure under ss.8–10 of the Defamation Act 1996

---

[906] s.12, on which see para.21-250.

[907] On which see para.21-255.

[908] *John v MGN Ltd* [1997] Q.B. 586.

[909] See para.21-47 onwards.

[910] But there has never been a case in England where damages have been recovered for injury to health: *Wheeler v Somerfield* [1966] 2 Q.B. 94 at 104 (but see *Rigby v Mirror Newspapers Ltd* (1963) 64 S.R. (N.S.W.) 34, where it was held that a claimant could include a claim for pain of body and mind; and see *Mirror Newspapers v Jools* (1986) 65 A.L.R. 174 Fed Ct of Aust.). In an unprecedented case in 1991, a High Court jury found that the claimant had been libelled, but awarded him no damages (reported in *The Times*, 26 November 1991).

[911] *Tripp v Thomas* (1824) 3 B. & C. 427; *Malachy v Soper* (1836) 3 Bing. N.C. 371 at 382, per Tindal CJ; *Youssoupoff v MGM Pictures Ltd* (1934) 50 T.L.R. 581 at 584, per Scrutton LJ; *English and Scottish Co-operative Properties v Odhams* [1940] 1 K.B. 440 at 455, 461; as to general damage see *Dingle v Associated Newspapers* [1961] 2 Q.B. 162 CA; [1964] A.C. 371 HL. See *Rookes v Barnard* [1964] A.C. 1129; *Broome v Cassell & Co Ltd* [1972] A.C. 1027 HL, for an analysis of rules relating to damages, in particular to aggravated and exemplary damages.

[912] The maximum award at present is understood to be around £300,000 for the most serious and widely publicised allegations, an amount which tallies with the top awards in personal injury cases: *Raj v Bholowasia* [2015] EWHC 382 (QB).

[913] *Rantzen v Mirror Newspapers* [1994] Q.B. 670; *John v MGN Ltd* [1997] Q.B. 586.

[914] Courts and Legal Services Act 1990 s.8.

[915] A list of factors was suggested by Hirst LJ in *Jones v Pollard* [1996] EWCA Civ 1186; [1997] E.M.L.R 233; approved in *Gur v Avrupa Newspaper Ltd* [2008] EWCA Civ 594; [2009] E.M.L.R. 4.

applies, damages are capped at £10,000.[916] When awarding damages under the procedure the practice is for judges to state what the award of damages would have been were it not for the cap.[917]

(2) A reasoned judgment may provide a claimant with some vindication, but how much will depend on the circumstances of the case (for example whether the truth of the allegations have been tested), where judgment is granted in default the effect on damages is likely to be fairly marginal.[918]

(3) The extent of publication is an important factor. Where publication is online, the court is cognisant of the potential for statements to "go viral".[919]

(4) Matters peculiar to the claimant will be taken into account, including the claimant's conduct,[920] credibility,[921] position and standing,[922] and the subjective impact of the libel on the claimant.[923]

(5) The gravity of the libel, often considered the most important factor: "the more closely it touches the claimant's personal integrity, professional reputation, honour, courage, loyalty and the core attributes of his personality, the more serious it is likely to be."[924]

(6) The absence of or refusal to provide a retraction or apology,[925] and the conduct of the defendant generally from publication to judgment, including repetition of the libel, persisting in a defence of truth and the manner of the cross-examination of the claimant.[926]

(b) Aggravated damages

21-226 **Aggravation** General damages may be aggravated by evidence of the circumstances of the publication, of the motives and conduct of the defendant and of the effect which it has actually produced. These aggravated damages, however, are still compensatory and should be distinguished from exemplary damages,[927] the purpose of which is punitive.[928] Aggravated damages are awarded for added injury to feel-

---

916 Defamation Act 1996 s.9(1)(c).

917 See for example *Jon Richard Ltd v Gornall* [2013] EWHC 1357 (QB).

918 *Purnell v Business Magazine Ltd* [2007] EWCA Civ 744; [2008] 1 W.L.R. 1; *Al-Amoudi v Kifle* [2011] EWHC 2037 (QB); *Cairns v Modi* [2012] EWCA Civ 1382; [2013] 1 W.L.R.1015.

919 *Cairns v Modi* [2012] EWCA Civ 1382; [2013] 1 W.L.R. 1015.

920 *Burstein v Times Newspapers Ltd* [2001] 1 W.L.R. 579; *Trumm v Norman* [2008] EWHC 116 (QB).

921 *Morgan v Odhams Press Ltd* [1971] 1 W.L.R. 1239; *Farmer v Hyde* [1937] 1 Q.B. 728.

922 *Gorman v Mudd*, unreported 15 October 1992 QB; *Neeld v Western Broadcasting Co* (1976) 65 D.L.R. (3d) 574.

923 *Jones v Pollard* [1996] EWCA Civ 1186; *Cruddas v Adams* [2013] EWHC 145 (QB).

924 *John v MGN Ltd* [1997] Q.B. 586 at 607; see also *Lillie & Reed v Newcastle City Council* [2002] EWHC 1600 (QB); *Campbell-James v Guardian Media Group Plc* [2005] EWHC 893 (QB); [2005] E.M.L.R. 24; *Galloway v Telegraph Media Group Ltd* [2004] EWHC 2786 (QB); [2005] E.M.L.R. 7.

925 *Cruddas v Adams* [2013] EWHC 145 (QB).

926 See, e.g. *Cairns v Modi* [2012] EWCA Civ 1382; [2013] 1 W.L.R. 1015; *Cruddas v Calvert* [2013] EWHC 2298 (QB). This is relevant even where an offer of amends has been made: *Barron v Collins* [2017] EWHC 162 (QB).

927 *Sutcliffe v Pressdram Ltd* [1991] 1 Q.B. 153.

928 *Rookes v Barnard* [1964] A.C. 1129 at 1231; per Pearson LJ in *McCarey v Associated Newspapers Ltd* [1965] 2 Q.B. 86 at 103-105; *Fielding v Variety Inc* [1967] 2 Q.B. 841 CA; *Broome v Cassell & Co Ltd* [1972] A.C. 1027; *Hayward v Thompson* [1982] Q.B. 47 CA. See also *Williams v Mirror Group Newspapers, The Independent,* 12 February 1991 CA. See para.27-134 onwards.

ings and as such are not available to a corporate claimant.[929] In *Rantzen v Mirror Group Newspapers*, the Court of Appeal stated that there is an "undoubted rule" that persistence by the defendant in a plea of justification or honest opinion may increase the damages awarded to the claimant,[930] and robust cross-examination of the claimant where a plea of justification is persisted in may also serve to aggravate the damages.[931] The proper defence of a libel action is not to be taken into account as an aggravating factor. In *Garcia v Associated Newspapers Ltd*[932] Dingemans J considered that the defence and cross-examination in the case were carried out fairly and properly and therefore did not award any aggravated damages: "Any other approach would be an impermissible interference with the vital right of the free press to defend itself, and would therefore be wrong." Where a defendant does all he can to damage the claimant's reputation whilst seeking to hide behind online anonymity an aggravated damages award will be appropriate.[933]

State of mind of defendant material "The spirit and intention of the party publishing a libel are fit to be considered by a jury in estimating the injury done to the claimant."[934] It is more grievous to be defamed out of personal spite and ill-will than through mere lack of proper care and consideration. In the former case there is insult as well as injury. The malice which aggravates damages is not merely the absence of right motive as in the case of privilege but the presence of some bad motive. The court may take into consideration the whole conduct of the defendant subsequent to the publication—"from the time of publication down to the time the verdict is given"—as evidence of the spirit in which the publication was made.[935] It will be a matter of aggravation if the defendant has persistently and deliberately given publicity to the defamation complained of,[936] if he has on other occasions caused damage to the claimant's reputation, if he failed to make any or sufficient apology or withdrawal,[937] if in his conduct of the litigation he has shown a spirit of determined hostility (including through prolonged or hostile cross-examination of the claimant), or has persisted in unfounded imputations and introduced new ones.[938] The claimant is not precluded from giving other acts of the defendant in evidence to prove malice by the fact that they are in themselves causes of action, 21-227

929 *Collins Stewart Ltd v Financial Times Ltd (No.2)* [2005] EWHC 262 (QB); [2006] E.M.L.R. 5; *Oyston v Ragozzino* [2015] EWHC 3232 (QB); citing *Eaton Mansions (Westminster) Ltd v Stinger Compania de Inversion SA* [2013] EWCA Civ 1308; [2014] C.P. Rep. 12.

930 [1994] Q.B. 670. The Neill Committee proposed that exemplary damages should no longer be awarded for defamation. But see too Law Commission, *Report on Aggravated, Exemplary and Restitutionary Damages* (1997), Law Com. No.247.

931 *Cruddas v Calvert* [2013] EWHC 2298 (QB).

932 [2014] EWHC 3137 (QB) at [303].

933 *Johnson v Steele* unreported 29 October 2014.

934 *Pearson v Lemaitre* (1843) 5 M. & G. 700 at 720; *Bridgmont v Associated Newspapers* [1951] 2 K.B. 578; cf. *McCarey v Associated Newspapers Ltd* [1965] 2 Q.B. 86.

935 *Praed v Graham* (1889) 24 Q.B.D. 53; cf. *Youssoupoff v MGM Pictures Ltd* (1934) 50 T.L.R. 581 at 584, 585, per Scrutton LJ; *Fielding v Variety Inc* [1967] 2 Q.B. 841 CA; *Cornwell v Myskow* [1987] 1 W.L.R. 630 CA.

936 *Plunkett v Cobbett* (1804) 5 Esp. 136; *Delegall v Highley* (1837) 8 C. & P. 444; *Gilpin v Fowler* (1854) 9 Ex. 615; *Dingle v Associated Newspapers* [1964] A.C. 371 HL.

937 *Rantzen v Mirror Group Newspapers Ltd* [1994] Q.B. 670.

938 In *Cairns v Modi* [2012] EWHC 756 (QB) (affirmed on appeal [2012] EWCA Civ 1382; [2013] 1 W.L.R.1015), Bean J awarded an additional £20,000 in aggravated damages for a "sustained and aggressive assertion of the plea of justification." See also *Thompson v James* [2013] EWHC 515 (QB); *Darby v Ouseley* (1856) 1 H. & N. 1; per Cockburn CJ in *Risk Allah Bey v Whitehurst* (1868) 18 L.T. 615 at 620; per Cockburn CJ in *Blake v Stevens* (1864) 4 F. & F. 232 at 240; *Praed v Graham*

but these should be treated not as independent heads of damage but only as matters of aggravation. In *Oyston v Reed*[939] the court made an award of damages including aggravated damages of £30,000 where the defendant, although not having defended the claims, persisted in claiming the allegations were true until the day of the hearing, had written a scurrilous and unpleasant email to the claimant's wife, acted in a hostile manner during the hearing and wrote to the judge before judgment was handed down making further allegations. In *Henry v News Group Newspapers Ltd*[940] the judge observed that in a claim for aggravated damages, the state of mind of the defendant is relevant only insofar as it is known to the claimant. It is not relevant to enquire as to what is going on behind the scenes or what might have been in the minds of journalists when they prepared the story, except to the extent that such conduct affected the harm sustained by the claimant. Thus the claimant was confined to pleading her case on aggravated damages with reference only to her perception of the defendant's journalists' conduct and the impact that had on her feelings.

(c) Exemplary damages

21-228 **Exemplary or punitive damages** In a defamation action exemplary damages may be awarded in the following circumstances: (1) where the defendant has deliberately libelled or slandered the claimant for profit; or (2) where the defendant is a "government servant" and has acted "oppressively, arbitrarily or unconstitutionally". Exemplary or punitive damages are only recoverable where compensatory damages, after taking into account all the circumstances of aggravation, remain an insufficient "punishment" of the defendant.[941] In the case of deliberate defamation for profit it is not necessary to prove that the defendant's belief was based on an exact mathematical calculation.[942] An example of such a course of conduct is when a publisher produces a defamatory but sensational book in the hope and belief that sales will exceed any award of damages.[943] A further example would be a newspaper deliberately publishing a defamatory statement with a view to increasing its circulation.[944] This latter condition will not be fulfilled simply because it is published in a newspaper which is itself published for profit[945] but it will be fulfilled where a newspaper deliberately publishes a statement knowing it to be false or recklessly careless whether it be true or false, and on the calculated basis that the compensatory damages would be less than the profit from the publication.[946] It would follow that an award of exemplary damages is unlikely to be available in respect of a newspaper article published on the inside pages of the newspaper and not advertised by the newspaper on the front page or elsewhere.

21-229 **Conditions for the award of exemplary damages for defamation** In *John v*

(1889) 24 Q.B.D. 53; *Scott v Sampson* (1882) 8 Q.B.D. 491 at 496.

939 [2016] EWHC 1067 (QB).

940 [2011] EWHC 1058 (QB).

941 *Broome v Cassell & Co Ltd* [1972] A.C. 1027 HL. See Stone (1972) 35 M.L.R. 449; McGregor (1971) 34 M.L.R. 520; and para.27-134 onwards.

942 *Broome v Cassell & Co Ltd* [1972] A.C. 1027.

943 *Broome v Cassell & Co Ltd* [1972] A.C. 1027.

944 See *John v MGN Ltd* [1997] Q.B. 586.

945 *Broadway Approvals Ltd v Odhams Press Ltd (No.2)* [1965] 1 W.L.R. 805 at 819, 821–823; *Manson v Associated Newspapers Ltd* [1965] 1 W.L.R. 1038.

946 *Manson v Associated Newspapers Ltd* [1965] 1 W.L.R. 1038; *John v MGN Ltd* [1997] Q.B. 586.

MGN Ltd[947] the claimant at first instance recovered £275,000 exemplary damages which was reduced by the Court of Appeal to £5,000. Sir Thomas Bingham MR, giving the judgment of the court, discussed if and when exemplary damages should be awarded. Accepting the test laid down by the Court of Appeal in *Riches v News Group Newspapers Ltd*,[948] such damages should be awarded only where:

(a) At the time of publication the defendant knew that he was committing a tort or was reckless as to whether it was tortious or not and decided to publish because the prospects of material advantage outweighed the prospects of material loss.

(b) The publisher acted in the hope or expectation of material gain. Mere publication for profit does not satisfy this test; there has to be an element of calculation, e.g. that the gain from the publication will exceed the potential disadvantages, especially if the claimant may not sue.

The principles governing exemplary damages were also discussed by Lord Woolf in *Thompson v Commissioner of Police for the Metropolis*,[949] an action for false imprisonment and malicious prosecution, where it was suggested that in actions against the police the minimum exemplary award should be £5,000. The court also stated that £50,000 should be the "absolute maximum" by way of exemplary damages.[950]

Multiple claimants Where there are multiple claimants an award of exemplary damages may properly reflect the fact that the defendant has libelled more than one person. Nevertheless, the total amount by way of exemplary damages should not exceed the total which the defendant ought to be made to pay by way of punishment.[951] **21-230**

Exemplary and aggravated damages under the Crime and Courts Act 2013 Sections 34–42 of and Sch.15 to the Crime and Courts Act 2013 (not all of which are in force at the time of writing) were enacted following recommendations of Leveson LJ in *The Report of An Inquiry into the Culture, Practices and Ethics of the Press* relating to regulation of the press. They establish a new system covering exemplary damages, aggravated damages and costs, as well as defining who is a "relevant publisher" for the purpose of coming within the system.[952] Although IMPRESS has now been approved as a regulator, an action which it was thought would bring into force s.40 on exemplary damages, the government has instead consulted on whether to bring the section into force. It is not in force at the time of writing.[953] **21-231**

---

947 [1997] Q.B. 586.

948 [1986] Q.B. 256.

949 [1998] Q.B. 498.

950 See also *Kuddus v Chief Constable of Leicestershire Constabulary* [2001] UKHL 29; [2002] 2 A.C. 122.

951 *Riches v News Group Newspapers Ltd* [1986] Q.B. 256 CA; *R (on the application of Lumba) v Secretary of State for the Home Department* [2011] UKSC 12; [2012] 1 A.C. 245.

952 See para.21-07.

953 On when exemplary damages might be awarded under this system if it is brought into force see *Gatley on Libel and Slander*, 12th edn (2015) at 9.32-9.34.

(d) Actual and special damage

21-232 **Actual damage** A claimant is entitled to damages by reason of the mere probability that consequences injurious to him may ensue from the defamation, but he may strengthen his case by proving that such consequences have in fact ensued. If, for instance, he has been held up to ridicule in a newspaper, he may show that this has led to his being derided by particular persons.[954] Similarly, a tradesman, of whom a widely circulated libel has been published, may prove a general falling-off of custom, even though he does not allege it in his pleading.[955] But in such cases the claimant gives the evidence in question merely for the purpose of emphasising the fact that that has actually happened which the law would presume without proof. "It is not special damage, it is general damage resulting from the kind of injury he has sustained."[956] Under s.3 of the Defamation Act 1952,[957] actions for slander of title, slander of goods or other malicious falsehood within that section are governed by the same considerations so far as proof of damage is concerned.

21-233 **Special damage** The claimant may prove special or consequential damage, provided he claims it in his pleading, but not otherwise.[958] The special damage required in an action for slander not actionable per se must involve the loss of some specific thing or temporal advantage capable of being estimated at a money value, if it is not the loss of actual money itself.[959] In *Collins Stewart Ltd v Financial Times Ltd (No.1)*[960] the defendant newspaper applied to strike out part of a claim for damages brought by the claimant, a stockbroking firm. The claimant sought to recover alleged losses of £230 million based on the difference between their current market value and what they contended the market value would have been, but for the publication of the article. The judge struck out as lacking certainty and precision. Special damage is likely to take on a more significant role, particularly in relation to corporate claimants, following the enactment of s.1(2) of the Defamation Act 2013. If the continuing cost of removing repetitions of a libel from the internet is to be claimed it must be properly pleaded.[961]

21-234 **Negativing special damage** Where a claimant alleges that in consequence of being defamed by the defendant he has suffered special damage, it is always open to the latter to suggest that the damage in question is attributable to other causes. If a customer is called to prove that he has ceased to deal with the claimant in consequence of a defendant's imputations, he may be asked if he did not act also

954 *Cook v Ward* (1830) 6 Bing. 409 at 415, per Tindal CJ; *Goslin v Corry* (1844) 7 M. & G. 342.

955 *Harrison v Pearce* (1858) 1 F. & F. 567; *Black v Lovering* (1885) 1 T.L.R. 497; *Ratcliffe v Evans* [1892] 2 Q.B. 524; considered in *Dingle v Associated Newspapers Ltd* [1964] A.C. 371; *Lewis v Daily Telegraph Ltd* [1963] 1 Q.B. 340, CA ([1964] A.C. 234 on a different point) (if large sums are to be attributed to loss of business it is desirable that they should be pleaded, particularised, and so far as possible be supported by evidence).

956 per Pollock CB in *Harrison v Pearce* (1858) 1 F. & F. 567; considered in *Dingle v Associated Newspapers Ltd* [1964] A.C. 371.

957 See paras 22-16 and 22-17.

958 *Black v Lovering* (1885) 1 T.L.R. 497; cf. *Lewis v Daily Telegraph Ltd* [1964] A.C. 234.

959 *Chamberlain v Boyd* (1883) 11 Q.B.D. 407; *Ratcliffe v Evans* [1892] 2 Q.B. 524 at 532; cf. para.21-54.

960 [2004] EWHC 2337 (QB); [2005] E.M.L.R. 5.

961 *Lisle-Mainwaring v Associated Newspapers Ltd* [2017] EWHC 543 (QB).

on other reports which reached him and what those reports were.[962] If a claimant has suffered a general loss of custom and has been defamed in more than one quarter, the court must consider the probabilities of the case and make such apportionment of the loss as it can.[963] In *ReachLocal UK Ltd v Bennett*[964] special damages of £241,945 were awarded to the claimant company which had suffered a defamatory online campaign against it by a rival. This was made up of sums for business booked but not proceeded with, the costs of paying certain customers to encourage them to continue to do business with the claimant, and of paying a public relations consultant to seek to address the reputational damage caused. The judge applied a discount of 20 per cent to the special damages claimed by the claimant for loss of business to account for loss of business for reasons other than the loss of trust in the claimant due to the defamatory statements.

(e) Mitigation of damages

Mitigation of damages In the general law of tort and contract the term mitigation of damages is understood to refer to the duty on the part of the claimant to take reasonable steps to minimise the loss arising from the unlawful act. In defamation it has a wider meaning and is generally used to refer to any matter which reduces the damages from what might otherwise be appropriate. The following matters are commonly relied on in mitigation of damages: (1) partial justification; (2) directly relevant background context; (3) conduct of the claimant; (4) evidence of the claimant's bad reputation; (5) evidence showing that publication by the defendant was without malice[965]; (6) evidence that the claimant has already recovered damages for substantially the same libel; and (7) the making of an apology or offer of amends. **21-235**

(i) Partial justification

Partial justification Where a defence of truth/justification fails the court is entitled to take into account in assessing damages the elements of the defamatory statement that have been proved to be true.[966] The extent of any reduction in cases of partial justification depends on the relative gravity of the proved and unproved allegations. It is a matter of impression for the court. The closer that the defendant comes to winning the action by virtue of proving the substantial truth of the allegation, the greater the reduction. Where the defendant has only just failed in proving justification the damages may be reduced to "vanishing point", as was the case in *Pamplin v Express Newspapers (No.2)*[967] and in *Grobbelaar v News Group Newspapers Ltd*.[968] **21-236**

---

962 *King v Watts* (1838) 8 C. & P. 614. See also *Hopwood v Thorn* (1849) 8 C.B. 293.

963 *Harrison v Pearce* (1858) 1 F. & F. 567. It has been held that on a statement of special damage by loss of custom the customers themselves must be called: *Barnett v Allen* (1858) 1 F. & F. 125; cf. *Dingle v Associated Newspapers* [1961] 2 Q.B. 162 CA; affirmed [1964] A.C. 371 HL.

964 [2014] EWHC 3405 (QB); [2015] E.M.L.R. 7.

965 e.g. the severe mental disorder of the defendant, *Vaughan v Ford*, 1953 (4) S.A. 486; [1954] C.L.Y. 1855; and as to the circumstances in which a libel was published see now *Plato Films Ltd v Speidel* [1961] A.C. 1090; and *Dingle v Associated Newspapers Ltd* [1964] A.C. 371 HL.

966 *Pamplin v Express Newspapers (No.2)* [1988] 1 W.L.R. 116.

967 *Pamplin v Express Newspapers (No.2)* [1988] 1 W.L.R. 116.

968 [2002] UKHL 40; [2002] 1 W.L.R. 3024.

(ii) Background context

21-237 **Directly relevant background context** It is often the case that the "partly true" information is clearly insufficient to prove the substantial truth of the defamatory allegation. A defendant can only advance a defence of justification where he has a realistic prospect of winning the case. It cannot be used simply to mitigate damages.[969] For many years the so-called rule in *Scott v Sampson*[970] had been understood to act as a prohibition on allowing a defendant to rely on acts of misconduct, which do not form part of a defence of justification, solely in order to mitigate damages. However, the effect of the rule has been much reduced by the Court of Appeal decision in *Burstein v Times Newspapers Ltd*,[971] where it was said that the rule in *Scott v Samson* does not prevent a defendant from drawing the court's attention to directly relevant background material. It was wrong to assess damages "in blinkers". The extent to which background evidence is admissible was a case management decision for the judge, taking into account the factors outlined in the CPR's overriding objective, in particular, proportionality.

21-238 **Admissibility of *Burstein* evidence** The extent to which background evidence is admissible will generally be a debatable issue.[972] Clearly the greater the proximity of the material to the libel, the more likely its inclusion. In *Carpenter v Associated Newspapers Ltd*[973] the claimant was accused of having made embarrassing sexual advances to a married man. The court held that applying the *Burstein* principle the defendant should be permitted to adduce evidence of the claimant's previous relationship with another married man. In contrast, in *Ghannouchi v Houni Ltd*[974] the claimant was accused of having close links to a terrorist organisation. Initial defences of justification and qualified privilege were abandoned. However in mitigation of damages the defendants sought to rely on the following: public pronouncements by the claimant made 10 or more years previously, aspects of the history of a political movement headed by the claimant including allegations made by former leaders of the movement that he had "chosen to resort to violence", the claimant's connections with the Sudanese regime (which offered him a diplomatic passport shortly after providing asylum to Osama bin Laden) and his connections with another alleged terrorist. Permission to rely on these points was refused. The judge acknowledged that the claimant should not put himself before the jury in a "false light". However, he considered the issue to be whether the *Burstein* principle permitted the defendants to put forward "directly relevant background context" in circumstances where they had abandoned defences of justification and qualified privilege. They could not, because this would amount to allowing in aspects of the defence of justification "by the back door". Further, none of the particulars put forward could properly be described as directly relevant background—they had not

---

969 See *Prager v Times Newspapers Ltd* [1988] 1 W.L.R. 77.

970 (1882) 8 Q.B.D. 491.

971 [2001] 1 W.L.R. 579.

972 In *Warren v Random House Group Ltd* [2008] EWCA Civ 834; [2009] Q.B. 600 the defendant sought permission to introduce certain matters in mitigation under the *Burstein* principle following the making and acceptance of an offer of amends. Permission was refused because the particulars were an attempt to introduce by an indirect route material which amounted to a plea of justification. This was not permissible in a case where the defendant had made an offer of amends as well as a public apology to the claimant.

973 [2001] All E.R. (D) 445 (Nov) (QB).

974 [2003] EWHC 552 (QB).

been included in the article complained of, for example. In *Hunt v Evening Standard Ltd*[975] Tugendhat J refused to strike out a claim of general bad reputation in respect of the claimant, who was alleged to have such a reputation "for being the head of an organised crime group and for violent, criminal behaviour." The decision to allow such evidence was in part based on the fact that the claimant had in his particulars of claim made the allegation that he had a good reputation, which permitted the defence to challenge such a claim. This was also in line with the liberal approach proposed by the Court of Appeal in *Burstein*. Some general guidance on when *Burstein* evidence will be admissible was given by the Court of Appeal in *Turner v News Group Newspapers Ltd*.[976] In *Lisle-Mainwaring v Associated Newspapers Ltd*[977] the judge refused to take into account *Burstein* particulars which had no real connection to the allegations sued upon and which did not damage her reputation in the same sector of her life. Where the relevant background context includes convictions and/or other relevant legal findings these will be matters for the court to take into account.[978] Section 1 of the Defamation Act 2013 requires the claimant to show that the publication caused serious harm to his or her reputation in order to bring a claim, thus the claimant's reputation will be very much in play from the outset.

(iii) Conduct of the claimant

Conduct of the claimant The conduct of the claimant is a relevant factor in the assessment of damages.[979] Conduct in this context is limited to the claimant's acts and omissions at the time the material is published and in the course of the litigation. It follows from general principles that a claimant must take reasonable steps to minimise the loss from the unlawful act. Delay in making a complaint can contribute to the injury to reputation (and would also suggest that the claimant has not been injured by the publication). This is particularly a factor where the defendant agrees to apologise as soon as the matter is brought to his attention. There may be occasions where the claimant has to a certain extent provoked the defamatory statement but the strict requirements of the defence of consent are not met and the defendant cannot rely on a "reply to attack" qualified privilege. The claimant's conduct can nevertheless mitigate the damages. In *Gorman v Mudd*,[980] Russell LJ felt that the claimant took part of the blame for the "unseemly quarrel that developed between her and the defendant". In *Godfrey v Demon Internet Ltd*[981] the defendant sought to rely on allegedly inflammatory internet postings by the claimant which, it submitted, were intended to provoke people into libelling him. There must be a direct correlation between the provocation and the libel. In *Burstein*[982] the Court of Appeal rejected the defendant's primary submission that the claimant had provoked the libel. The claimant in *Trumm v Norman*[983] would have been awarded £15,000 in damages but for the fact that he had published on his website comments that were unnecessarily provocative and offensive and which led to the 21-239

975 [2011] EWHC 272 (QB).
976 [2006] EWCA Civ 540; [2006] 1 W.L.R. 3469.
977 [2017] EWHC 543 (QB).
978 *Undre v Harrow LBC* [2016] EWHC 2761 (QB); [2017] E.M.L.R. 8.
979 See *Cassell v Broome* [1972] A.C. 1027 at 1071H; and *John v MGN Ltd* [1997] Q.B. 586.
980 *Independent*, 16 October 1992 CA.
981 [2001] Q.B. 201.
982 [2001] 1 W.L.R. 579 at [24].
983 [2008] EWHC 116 (QB).

publication of the allegations of which he complained in the proceedings. Damages were reduced to £7,500. The fact that the allegations have been published previously and the claimant has not taken any action is not to be taken into account. This rule, known as "the rule in *Dingle*"[984] remains good law after the coming into force of the Defamation Act 2013.[985] Nor may a court take into account any omission by the claimant to complain about other defamatory parts of the publication in question.[986] In any event, the failure to complain may be the subject of cross-examination as to credit.[987]

21-240 **Misconduct in the course of the litigation** This is also admissible and where serious, can lead to a dramatic reduction on the damages awarded. In *Campbell v News Group Newspapers Ltd*[988] the Court of Appeal considered that it would be an "affront of justice" if a claimant's own disreputable conduct had to be ignored in assessing the damages. In that case, it was found at trial that the claimant had procured witnesses to make false statements; attacked the credibility of a wholly innocent witness, and accused one of the defendant's lawyers of the most serious professional misconduct. The Court of Appeal considered that the claimant had acted in this way specifically to improve the outcome of the litigation itself. In the circumstances a jury award of £350,000 was reduced to £30,000. In *Joseph v Spiller*[989] the court awarded nominal damages to members of a band who brought a defamation claim against their former promoter and booking company. This was because, notwithstanding their being successful on liability, it was proved at trial that one of claimants had attempted to deceive the court by fabricating part of a claim for special damages. The judge concluded that since the reputations of all the claimants were intertwined, they all suffered damage to their reputations by virtue of the fabrication, which gave rise to the nominal damages award.

(iv) Bad reputation of the claimant

21-241 **Bad reputation of claimant** A claimant who brings an action of defamation puts his reputation in issue and the defendant in mitigation of damages may give evidence that the claimant bears a bad character. If he has no reputation to lose, attacks on his character cannot really have injured him and cannot therefore entitle him to substantial damages.[990] The law distinguishes between a claimant's actual reputation and the events in his life which determine or ought to determine his reputation.[991] Subject to limited exceptions, only where the defendant establishes that the claimant has, in fact, a bad reputation will the damages be reduced from

---

984 *Associated Newspapers Ltd v Dingle* [1964] A.C. 371.

985 *Lachaux v Independent Print Ltd* [2019] UKSC 27; [2020] A.C. 612.

986 *Plato Films Ltd v Speidel* [1961] A.C. 1090; although where properly pleaded as justification, they may mitigate damages under the principles set out above.

987 Following *Burstein* it is arguable that these matters should be considered as directly relevant background context.

988 [2002] EWCA Civ 1143; [2002] E.M.L.R. 43.

989 [2012] EWHC 2958 (QB).

990 *Scott v Sampson* (1882) 8 Q.B.D. 491 at 503, per Cave J. Followed in *Leonhard v Sun Publishing Co* (1956) 4 D.L.R. (2d) 514 (newspaper clippings showing words now complained of previously published on which claimant took no action admissible to show bad general reputation; but see *Dingle v Associated Newspapers Ltd* [1961] 2 Q.B. 162 CA; affirmed [1964] A.C. 371).

991 per Devlin J in *Speidel v Plato Films Ltd* [1960] 3 W.L.R. 391 at 396; affirmed [1961] A.C. 1090 at 1128, per Lord Radcliffe; and see *Dingle v Associated Newspapers Ltd* [1961] 2 Q.B. 162 at 195–196; affirmed [1964] A.C. 371 at 398–399, 417–418; *Goody v Odhams Press Ltd* [1967] 1 Q.B. 333

what might otherwise have been awarded. It is not permissible to demonstrate that the claimant would have a bad reputation if his past conduct were generally known. It follows that in order to establish that the claimant has a bad reputation the defendant must call witnesses who are limited to stating that the claimant has a bad reputation. They cannot, generally, refer to the particular incidents in the claimant's life which have given rise to the bad reputation.[992] Furthermore, in order to mitigate damages the claimant's bad reputation must relate to the sphere of his life to which the defamation is directed.[993] In *Goody v Odhams Press Ltd*[994] the Court of Appeal recognised that criminal convictions are an exception to the general rule. "They are the raw material upon which bad reputation is built up. They have taken place in open court. They are matters of public knowledge. They are accepted by people generally as giving the best guide to his reputation and standing."[995] Criminal convictions are therefore specific acts of misconduct which can be relied on as evidence of general bad reputation. The conviction must be in the same sphere of the claimant's life as the defamatory statement and have taken place within a relevant period so as to affect his current reputation.[996] *Goody v Odhams Press Ltd* was applied in *King v Grundon*[997] where the claimant's previous convictions for conspiracy to unlawfully detain and possession of a firearm was such that he had no reputation to protect or vindicate in the current proceedings. The proceedings served no useful purpose and were accordingly an abuse of process.

(v) Evidence showing that publication was without malice

Evidence that publication was without malice A defendant may seek to mitigate damages by showing that publication was without malice on his or her part.[998] However, as a matter of logic, it is difficult to see how this can have any connection with the damage caused to the claimant. Where the defendant pleads truth the fact that he honestly and reasonably believed the allegations to be true will be of little assistance. Where truth is not pleaded, an attempt to mitigate on this basis can backfire, appearing to be a thinly veiled attempt to justify the allegations through the back door.[999] Much will depend on how the case is presented. 21-242

(vi) Relevance of other publications and damages already recovered

Publication of same libels elsewhere A defendant cannot mitigate the damages by producing evidence of other publications to the same effect as his, nor can the 21-243

CA.

992 *Scott v Sampson* (1882) 8 Q.B.D. 491; *Plato Films v Speidel* [1961] A.C. 1090.

993 *Pamplin v Express Newspapers Ltd (No.2)* [1988] 1 W.L.R. 116. In *Jones v Pollard* [1997] E.M.L.R. 233, the Court of Appeal stressed that the boundaries between different spheres of a claimant's life should not be drawn with excessive precision.

994 [1967] 1 Q.B. 333.

995 [1967] 1 Q.B. 333 at 340G, per Lord Denning MR.

996 *Mitchell v Evening Chronicle* [2003] EWHC 1281 (QB); [2003] All E.R. (D) 54; *Oyston v Ragozzino* [2015] EWHC 3232 (QB).

997 [2012] EWHC 2719 (QB).

998 *Pearson v Lemaitre* (1843) 5 M. & Gr. 700.

999 *Williams v Mirror Group Newspapers, The Independent,* 12 February 1991 CA.

damages be mitigated by the other prior or concurrent publications being in any way regarded as having tarnished or impaired the defendant's reputation.[1000]

21-244 **Damages recovered for similar libel** Section 12 of the Defamation Act 1952 provides:

> "In any action for libel or slander the defendant may give evidence in mitigation of damages that the claimant has recovered damages, or has brought actions for damages, for libel or slander in respect of the publication of words to the same effect as the words on which the action is founded, or has received or agreed to receive compensation in respect of any such publication."

In such cases, for example where the similar libels are published in two national newspapers on the same day, the court ought to:

> "consider how far the damage suffered by the claimants can reasonably be attributed solely to the libel with which they are concerned and how far it ought to be regarded as the joint result of the two libels, if they think that some part of the damage is the joint result of the two libels they should bear in mind that the claimant ought not to be compensated twice for the same loss."[1001]

(vii) Apology and offer of amends

21-245 **Apology and offer of amends** In any action for defamation the defendant may give evidence in mitigation of damages that he made or offered an apology.[1002] The sufficiency of a retraction of a libel, made without an apology, is a matter for the court but is unlikely to be sufficient mitigation of damages.[1003] An apology must not in itself be defamatory of a third party as was the case in *Watts v Times Newspapers Ltd*.[1004] Under s.2 of the Defamation Act 1996 an offer of amends includes an offer to publish a suitable correction and apology. Where an offer of amends has been made, this is likely to count as "substantial mitigation".[1005] Also under the summary procedure under ss.8 and 9 of the Defamation Act 1996 provision can be made for a suitable apology to be made by the defendant in a manner acceptable to the

---

[1000] *Dingle v Associated Newspapers Ltd* [1964] A.C. 371 (the trial judge had wrongly taken into account in assessing the damages the publication of the same libel on privileged occasions both in the report of a Select Committee and in the publication of extracts of it in other papers). As to mitigation of damages where the claimant has recovered damages for or brought actions for similar libels, see para.21-244. In *Williams v Mirror Group Newspapers*, *The Independent,* 12 February 1991 CA, this was also applied to articles published after the offending publication. See also *Rath v Guardian News and Media Ltd* [2008] EWHC 398 (QB).

[1001] *Lewis v Daily Telegraph Ltd* [1964] A.C. 234 at 261, per Lord Reid. See also *Lisle-Mainwaring v Associated Newspapers Ltd* [2017] EWHC 543 (QB) where damages were reduced where the claimant had recovered over substantially the same allegations from her stepson and his wife, who were the source of the newspaper story sued on.

[1002] In *Rantzen v Mirror Group Newspapers* [1994] Q.B. 670 CA Neill LJ stated that the relevance of the absence of an apology depends on the facts of the case. Although it is not proof of malice, it can increase the injury to the claimant's feelings; approving Lord Hailsham in *Broome v Cassell* [1972] A.C. 1027; and Nourse LJ in *Sutcliffe v Pressdram Ltd* [1991] 1 Q.B. 153.

[1003] *Pine v MacMillan*, *The Times,* 25 November 1987 CA.

[1004] [1997] Q.B. 650.

[1005] *Nail v Associated Newspapers Ltd* [2004] EWCA Civ 1708; [2005] 1 All E.R. 1040. See authorities cited at para.21-188 for the amount of discount on damages applied where an offer of amends is made.

parties. There is also provision under s.12 of the Defamation Act 2013 for the court to order the defendant to publish a summary of its judgment.[1006]

(f) Other damages issues

Overruling jury awards The 20th edition included a section on cases in which the Court of Appeal had overruled a jury's award of damages. The Court of Appeal would not overrule an award unless it was so excessive that no reasonable jury could have awarded it.[1007] Now that s.11 of the Defamation Act 2013 has removed the presumption in favour of juries, jury awards are unlikely. 21-246

Human Rights and damages in defamation The action for the tort of defamation raises particularly important issues of human rights. Article 10 of the European Convention on Human Rights provides that "[e]veryone has the right to freedom of expression"; this right is "subject to such formalities, conditions, restrictions or penalties as are prescribed by law and are necessary in a democratic society" and one of the examples of such restrictions in the article is the protection of reputation as protected by art.8 ECHR. The 20th edition contained discussion of the jurisprudence relating to whether jury awards of damages were sufficiently prescribed by law as to be compatible with the protection of the defendant's human rights. With guidance given on the size of awards and the oversight of the Court of Appeal it was found that they were. In *John v MGN Ltd*[1008] and in *Rantzen v Mirror Newspapers*[1009] the Court of Appeal confirmed that English law was consistent with art.10 ECHR. 21-247

Proportionality In *Steel and Morris v United Kingdom*,[1010] the ECtHR ruled that a damages award of £40,000 made against two impecunious litigants and in favour of the McDonalds corporation failed to strike the right balance between the right of the corporation to defend its reputation as against the defendants' art.10 rights. Referring to the requirement under the Convention for an award of damages to bear a reasonable relationship of proportionality to the injury to reputation suffered, the court ruled that the awards were very substantial when compared to the modest incomes and resources of the applicants. However, in the Court of Appeal in *Gur v Avrupa Newspaper Ltd*[1011] Dyson LJ said, obiter, that any change to the fundamental and long-standing principle that the means of a defendant are irrelevant to the assessment of damages for a tort, could only be made by the House of Lords (now Supreme Court). 21-248

(g) Relief under the summary procedure

The Defamation Act 1996 introduced a summary procedure which is designed to reduce the time, expense and inconvenience of defamation proceedings. Section 8 provides that the court in such proceedings may dispose summarily of the claim if it appears to the court that it has no realistic prospect of success and there 21-249

[1006] See para.21-250.
[1007] See, e.g. *Grobbelaar v News Group Newspapers Ltd* [2002] UKHL 40; [2002] 1 W.L.R. 3024.
[1008] [1997] Q.B. 586.
[1009] [1994] Q.B. 670.
[1010] [2005] E.M.L.R. 15; (2005) 41 E.H.R.R. 22.
[1011] [2008] EWCA Civ 594; [2009] E.M.L.R. 4.

is no reason why it should be tried; under s.8(3) the court may give judgment for the claimant and grant him summary relief if it appears that there is no defence to the claim which has a realistic chance of success and there is no reason for a trial. Summary relief is defined by s.9 and means any or all of the following:

(1) a declaration that the statement was false and defamatory of the claimant;
(2) an order that the defendant publish a suitable correction and apology;
(3) damages.

The maximum amount specified is £10,000. The court may grant the claimant summary relief if he requests it, but it is notable that the court has the power to order summary disposal without the request or consent of the parties, though the court is not to dispose of the action and grant summary relief without a request from the claimant, unless it is satisfied that summary relief will adequately compensate him for the wrong he has suffered.[1012] An application for summary disposal may be dealt with on the papers, as may an application for judgment in default: if such an application is made, the claimant should file a skeleton argument to assist the court.[1013]

(h) Publication of a summary of the court's judgment

21-250 **Defamation Act 2013 s.12** Section 12 allows the court to order the defendant to publish a summary of its judgment. This is a potentially important new discursive remedy for claimants. The wording of the summary and the time, form and manner of its publication are a matter for the parties to agree,[1014] but if they cannot agree, the court will settle the wording[1015] and give such directions as to time manner, form and place of publication as it considers reasonable and practicable in the circumstances.[1016] This provision builds on the (rarely used) power under the summary procedure[1017] to order that a summary of its judgment be published where the parties cannot agree a correction or apology. Exactly how far the court will go in terms of directions for placement, timing and manner of publication of the summary of its judgment remains to be seen.[1018] It is expected that claimants will now seek this remedy as standard. It may be that vindication in this manner will affect damages awards, however at present a reasoned judgment is treated as a fairly marginal factor in assessing damages.[1019] The power under s.12 was first used in *Rahman v ARY Network Ltd*[1020] where Sir David Eady ordered broadcaster ARY to broadcast a summary of his judgment. The court did not order this remedy in *Monir v Wood*[1021] where the publication complained of was a tweet, and there was no method by which the defendant could publish a summary of the judgment such that it would come to the attention of a significant number of those to whom the defamatory statement had been published. Nicklin J considered that the publicity that would likely be given to the judgment by other means would provide sufficient vindication.

1012 See for example *Milne v Telegraph Group Ltd* [2001] E.M.L.R. 30.
1013 *Charakida v Jackson* [2019] EWHC 858 (QB); [2019] 4 W.L.R. 66.
1014 s.12(2).
1015 s.12(3).
1016 s.12(4).
1017 Defamation Act 1996 ss.8–9.
1018 For example, will the court order that a newspaper run the summary on its front page if the story complained of was on the front page?
1019 *Purnell v Business Magazine Ltd* [2007] EWCA Civ 744; [2008] 1 W.L.R. 1
1020 [2016] EWHC 3570 (QB).
1021 [2018] EWHC 3525 (QB).

Statements in open court Where a claim is settled (whether under CPR Pt 36 or otherwise), the claimant may apply to make a statement in open court (CPR PD 53B 3). The procedure is also available where an offer of amends has been made and accepted.[1022] Such a statement may be joint, where the defendant agrees the statement, or unilateral where it does not. In *Murray v Associated Newspapers Ltd*[1023] the Court of Appeal dismissed the defendant's appeal against Tugendhat J's decision to allow the claimant to make a unilateral statement in open court in a particular form of words. The defendant had objected to the statement on the grounds that it mischaracterised the meaning of the words complained of, by stating that the newspaper article had alleged the claimant was "dishonest". The Court of Appeal stated that whilst a statement in open court must be fair, proportionate and must not misrepresent either a party's case or the nature of any settlement, the court would be unlikely to disallow such a statement in the absence of any substantial unfairness. It made clear that "nit-picking" was to be discouraged. What is fair and reasonable to be included in a statement will depend upon the facts of the case. 21-251

(i) Injunction

Injunction[1024] As a general principle the so-called rule against prior restraint (in *Bonnard v Perryman*[1025]) has provided that an interim injunction will not be granted in defamation proceedings where the defendant intends to rely on a substantive defence such as truth, honest opinion or qualified privilege.[1026] The claimant, to obtain an interim injunction, has been required to demonstrate practically that there is no defence to the claim with a realistic prospect of success. In *Greene v Associated Newspapers Ltd*[1027] the Court of Appeal re-affirmed the rule in *Bonnard v Perryman* and held that it was ECHR compliant. The claimant must now also overcome the hurdle of the serious harm requirement imposed by s.1 of the Defamation Act 2013. 21-252

Where the claimant succeeds in satisfying the requirements for an injunction under *Bonnard v Perryman*, an injunction should not be refused solely because primary publication has occurred if the injunction could effectively prevent further dissemination of the libel. However there must be an urgent need for the injunction, and where the defendant has indicated that it does not intend to publish the defamatory material, an injunction is likely to be refused.[1028] In *British Data Management Plc v Boxer Commercial Removals Plc*[1029] the Court of Appeal confirmed that a quia timet injunction may be issued to restrain the publication of a threatened libel in a case where there is reasonable certainty as to the words of the publication; the claimant is not required to set out verbatim the words complained of. The general rule in *Bonnard v Perryman* will be displaced when the 21-253

1022 *Winslet v Associated Newspapers Ltd* [2009] EWHC 2735 (QB); [2010] E.M.L.R. 11.

1023 [2015] EWCA Civ 488; [2015] E.M.L.R. 21.

1024 See generally Ch.28.

1025 [1891] 2 Ch. 269; discussed in *Femis-Bank (Anguilla) v Lazar* [1991] Ch. 391.

1026 See *Holley v Smyth* [1998] Q.B. 726. For an application of the rule in the context of comparative advertising, see *Boehringer Ingelheim Ltd v Vetplus Ltd* [2007] EWCA Civ 583; [2007] F.S.R. 29; [2007] H.R.L.R. 33.

1027 [2004] EWCA Civ 1462; [2005] Q.B. 972.

1028 See, e.g. *Martin v Channel Four Television Corp* [2009] EWHC 2788 (QB).

1029 [1996] 3 All E.R. 707.

Attorney General seeks and makes out a case to restrain further publication of the libel as a contempt of court.[1030]

21-254 In *Robins v Kordowski*[1031] the High Court granted an interim injunction with regard to defamatory allegations published about a solicitor. In addressing the rule in *Bonnard v Perryman* the court concluded that the words complained of were unarguably defamatory and there were no grounds for concluding that the statements might have been true. They were published by the defendant without any personal knowledge of their truth. The words "It is of my honest opinion" did not turn statements of fact into comment for the purposes of a defence of comment, and the defendant was not entitled to such a defence since he had no knowledge of the underlying facts. Nor was there any prospect of a defence of qualified privilege succeeding, in light of the defendant seeking to charge a removal fee in order to take down the publication from his website. That was not responsible journalism, and in any event, no steps were taken to verify the information prior to publication, there had been no urgency to publish and no comment had been sought from the claimant. Other Reynolds criteria were not made out. The court had regard to s.12(3) of the Human Rights Act 1998 and concluded that it was likely that a permanent injunction would be obtained at trial. In considering the balance of convenience, it was significant that the claimant maintained that the website entries were affecting the claimant's standing in the local community; there was also evidence that damages would be an inadequate remedy since the defendant lacked funds. Accordingly, an injunction was a practical necessity. It was appropriate to grant an interim injunction requiring the defendant to comply with the terms of a settlement order which, amongst other matters, stipulated that he would not post defamatory statements.[1032]

21-255 **Final injunctions** The court will grant a final injunction where it has given judgment in favour of the claimant, the words are injurious to the claimant, and there is reason to apprehend further publication on the part of the defendant.[1033] The court has jurisdiction to grant an injunction even where the claimant has not claimed such relief in his or her particulars of claim.[1034] In *ZAM v CFW*[1035] the court granted a permanent injunction protecting the claimant's anonymity where the defendant had blackmailed the claimant and was likely to use a public judgment to make further demands. The court granted a final injunction in *Oyston v Reed*[1036] where the judge found it clear that unless restrained the defendant would continue to publish allegations defamatory of the claimant. In the period before the hand-down of the judgment the defendant had written to the judge making further scurrilous allegations. Here the judge also made an order wide enough to cover acts of harassment against the claimant or his wife, even though there was no separate claim under the Protection from Harassment Act 1997. In *Sloutsker v Romanova*[1037] the court granted a final injunction in a case where default judgment had been entered. Although the defendant was situated outside England and Wales she was subject to the court's jurisdiction. Publication had continued and the judge was satisfied that there was a

[1030] *Att Gen v News Group Newspapers Ltd* [1987] Q.B. 1.
[1031] [2011] EWHC 981 (QB).
[1032] *Power Places Tours Inc v Free Spirit* [2015] EWHC 3886 (QB).
[1033] *Procter v Bayley* (1889) 42 Ch. D. 390, CA.
[1034] CPR r. 16.2(5).
[1035] [2013] EWHC 662 (QB); [2013] E.M.L.R. 27.
[1036] [2016] EWHC 1067 (QB).
[1037] [2015] EWHC 2053 (QB); [2015] E.M.L.R. 27.

real prospect of re-publication if an injunction was not granted. A court would not refuse to grant an injunction it would otherwise grant just because the person subject to it might disobey, as per Lord Bingham in *South Buckinghamshire DC v Porter*[1038] "there is not one law for the law-abiding and another for the lawless and truculent", although in the present case the defendant had said she had the utmost respect for the English court. The court can grant a defamation injunction against persons unknown, provided that those persons can be defined with sufficient precision, for example "persons unknown responsible for the operation and publication of the website".[1039] If the claimant seeks an injunction against an internet publisher, they must establish that England and Wales is the centre of their interests.[1040]

1038 [2003] UKHL 26; [2003] 2 A.C. 558 at [32].

1039 *Brett Wilson LLP v Person(s) Unknown* [2015] EWHC 2628 (QB); [2016] 4 W.L.R. 69; and *Smith v Unknown Defendant Pseudonym 'Likeicare'* [2016] EWHC 1775 (QB).

1040 *Bolagsupplysningen OÜ v Svensk Handel AB (C-194/16)* [2018] Q.B. 963; *Said v Groupe L'Express* [2018] EWHC 3593 (QB); [2019] E.M.L.R. 9; see also *BVC v EWF* [2018] EWHC 2674 (QB); [2019] I.L.Pr. 7.

CHAPTER 22

MALICIOUS FALSEHOOD

TABLE OF CONTENTS

1. MALICIOUS FALSEHOOD

Nomenclature This tort attracts different names. In part this is due to the possible range of falsehoods concerned.[1] It originated from "slander of title", false allegations calculated to hamper the disposal of land. However, it developed, by analogy, to encompass "slander of goods"[2] and eventually disparagements as to quality as well as title were included.[3] In *Ratcliffe v Evans*,[4] the Court of Appeal decided that the tort could apply to falsehoods calculated to cause and causing actual damage to a business. Thus, this tort can be labelled: 22-01

(a) injurious falsehood;
(b) trade libel;
(c) slander of title;
(d) slander of goods;
(e) disparagement of goods; or
(f) malicious falsehood.

The Defamation Act 1952 describes this wrong by the formula "action for slander of title, slander of goods or other malicious falsehood".[5]

The general principle The general principle for this action is contained in *Ratcliffe v Evans*: "an action will lie for written or oral falsehoods, not actionable per se, or even defamatory, where they are maliciously published, where they are calculated in the ordinary course of things to produce, and where they do produce, actual damage …".[6] The tort protects against the defendant's falsehood that causes economic harm to the claimant.[7] The need to prove malice severely limits this tort. 22-02

---

[1] The tort is, however, narrowed by its requirements of malice and damage. On which see paras 22-12 and 22-17. *Kerly's Law of Trade Marks and Trade Names*, 16th edn (2017) notes at 21-004 that modern judgments seem to use the name malicious falsehood more than any other.

[2] See especially *Wren v Weild* (1869) L.R. 4 Q.B. 730.

[3] *Western Counties Manure Co v Lawes Chemical Manure Co* (1874) L.R. 9 Ex. 218.

[4] [1892] 2 Q.B. 524.

[5] See para.22-16.

[6] *Ratcliffe v Evans* [1892] 2 Q.B. 524 at 532, per Bowen LJ. And see *Serville v Constance* [1954] 1

22-03 **Malicious falsehood and defamation compared** Although malicious falsehood and defamation have different origins, there are obvious similarities between the two actions and the same facts may constitute both torts. This relationship between the two was successfully exploited in *Joyce v Sengupta*.[8] The claimant alleged the defendants had written a "grossly defamatory" article about her. In order to claim legal aid, available at that time for malicious falsehood but not defamation proceedings, the claimant sued for malicious falsehood, not defamation.[9] The defendants' application to strike the claim out as an abuse of process (the "true" claim being for defamation) was rejected by the Court of Appeal. The claimant was not obliged to pursue the most appropriate remedy.[10] However, there are clear and substantial differences between the torts, the most basic of which is that defamation protects the claimant's reputation, while malicious falsehood protects the claimant's interest in his property or trade (or economic interests more generally).[11] Again, the Court of Appeal in *Ajinomoto Sweeteners Europe SAS v Asda Stores Ltd* held that the single meaning rule in defamation[12] was not to be applied to the tort of malicious falsehood. Where plural meanings could be applied to the relevant words they were all to be considered.[13] In *Cruddas v Calvert*[14] Longmore LJ stated with regard to malicious falsehood claims, "... the duty of the judge at trial is to indicate the reasonably available meanings, decide if a substantial number of persons would reasonably have understood the words to have such a meaning and then decide, in respect of a meaning which is in fact false and damaging, whether the author was actuated by malice".

W.L.R. 487; see also *Drummond-Jackson v B.M.A.* [1970] 1 W.L.R. 688 CA (attack on dentist's anaesthetic technique). Under s.4A of the Limitation Act 1980, (as amended by s.5(2) of the Defamation Act 1996) the limitation period is one year.

7 See para.22-09. There is some overlap, therefore, with passing off. However, whereas passing off does not require malice, it does require injury to goodwill. See para.25-01.

8 [1993] 1 W.L.R. 337 CA. An attack on the reputation of a thing may in fact be defamatory of a person. On the difference between business/professional libel and malicious falsehood, see *Thornton v Telegraph Media Group Ltd* [2010] EWHC 1414 (QB); [2011] 1 W.L.R. 1985, Tugendhat J.

9 Legal aid is no longer available for malicious falsehood. Note also that the presumption in favour of jury trial in defamation cases has been removed by s.11 of the Defamation Act 2013. A claim for malicious falsehood survives the death of either party.

10 In *Ajinomoto Sweeteners Europe SAS v Asda Stores Ltd* [2009] EWHC 781 (QB); [2009] F.S.R. 16 Sir Charles Gray, sitting as a High Court Judge, commented at [28]: "I cannot see that there can be any objection to a claimant electing to sue in malicious falsehood rather than defamation. It is a matter for the claimant and its legal advisers to decide whether it is advantageous to assume the twin burdens of proving falsity and malice."

11 There is no defence of qualified privilege as in defamation: per Mummery J in *CHC Software v Hopkins & Wood* [1993] F.S.R. 241 at 248. However, absolute privilege may apply as a defence: *Samuels v Coole & Haddock* [1997] C.L.Y. 4860 (statements in an affidavit came within the absolute privilege of witness immunity); *Apison v Dilnot* [2011] EWHC 869 (QB) Tugendhat J (statements made as part of a complaint to the Bar Standards Board were protected by absolute privilege). And see *Makudi v Triesman* [2014] EWCA Civ 179; [2014] Q.B. 839. In *Thornton v Telegraph Media Group Ltd* [2011] EWHC 159 (QB); [2011] E.M.L.R. 25 Tugendhat J held that a defence of honest comment did not apply to the tort of malicious falsehood.

12 i.e. where a single natural and ordinary meaning of the words used has to be determined.

13 [2010] EWCA Civ 609; [2011] Q.B. 497; overturning [2009] EWHC 1717 (QB); [2010] Q.B. 204 (but not [2009] EWHC 781 (QB), see fn.10). There had been conflicting judicial debate as to whether the rule applied.

14 [2013] EWCA Civ 748; [2014] E.M.L.R. 5 at [30]. The difference between the single meaning rule in defamation and the multiple meaning rule in malicious falsehood was discussed at [31]–[33]. See also *Cruddas v Calvert* [2015] EWCA Civ 171; [2015] E.M.L.R. 16; and *Tinkler v Ferguson* [2019] EWCA Civ 819 at [29].

Malicious falsehood and freedom of speech Article 10 on freedom of expression applies to commercial speech.[15] Tugendhat J in *Ajinomoto Sweeteners Europe SAS v Asda Stores Ltd*[16] referred to the control mechanisms contained within the tort of malicious falsehood that helped to support freedom of expression. These included the need to prove malice and either actual damage or a statement calculated to cause pecuniary damage. (The need to show malice as an important device to preserve legitimate free speech was a point stressed earlier by Lord Denning in *Drummond Jackson v BMA*).[17] In *Thornton v Telegraph Media Group Ltd* Tugendhat J noted that "… some malicious falsehood claims also involve art.8 rights, although less frequently than in defamation claims".[18] The case of *Kaye v Robertson*,[19] though decided before the establishment of privacy protection, would now appear to be one such example. 22-04

Interim injunctions A concern to protect free speech is reflected in the approach to interim injunctions in claims of malicious falsehood.[20] Where the words are not manifestly false (as they were in *Kaye v Robertson*)[21] and the defendant intends to justify a statement, the defamation rule (against prior restraint) contained in *Bonnard v Perryman*[22] is applied and no interim injunction will be awarded. This was confirmed by Oliver J in *Bestobell Paints Ltd v Bigg*.[23] The Court of Appeal in *Greene v Associated Newspapers Ltd*[24] held that this remains the rule following 22-05

---

15 However freedom of expression is subject to such formalities "… necessary in a democratic society … for the protection of the reputation or rights of others". As far as the granting of injunctions is concerned the test of necessity would appear to be less strict in relation to speech connected with commercial competition: *Markt Intern Verlag GmbH and Klaus Beerman v Germany* (1990) 12 E.H.R.R. 161 ECtHR.

16 [2009] EWHC 1717 (QB); [2010] Q.B. 204. He also stated that the single meaning rule would have this effect, but this was overturned by the Court of Appeal, see para.22-03.

17 [1970] 1 W.L.R. 688 at 694–695. Here the defendants published a scientific paper attacking the claimant's dental technique. The claimant succeeded in defamation but there was a strong dissent from Lord Denning who felt that such criticism might be in the public interest and as such the claimant should have been allowed only the protection of malicious falsehood, with the need to show malice and that it was untrue. Gray J in *Ferguson v Associated Newspapers Ltd* unreported 3 December 2001: "malice … remains an allegation which is not to be made lightly."

18 [2011] EWHC 159 (QB); [2011] E.M.L.R. 25 at [34].

19 [1991] F.S.R. 62 CA. The claimant was a well-known television actor who was photographed by journalists without consent, while recovering in hospital after a serious accident. The newspaper article that resulted from this was falsely represented to be with his authority. This was held to amount to the tort of malicious falsehood. The case involved false words about the claimant, published maliciously (the journalists knew he had been incapable of giving his consent) and were calculated to cause the claimant pecuniary damage as he had a valuable right to sell his story. It is likely that such a claimant would now rely successfully on the privacy action that is developing from the action for breach of confidence (discussed in Ch.26)

20 *Microdata v Rivendale Ltd* [1991] F.S.R. 681 at 689, per Griffiths LJ; *Macmillan Magazines Ltd v RCN Publishing Co Ltd* [1998] F.S.R. 9, per Neuberger J. Note the *Practice Guidance (HC Interim Non-Disclosure Orders)* [2012] 1 W.L.R. 1003 with regard to applications for interim non-disclosure orders in civil proceedings to restrain the publication of information. Such applications may be in respect inter alia of a threatened malicious falsehood (see further para.26-57).

21 [1991] F.S.R. 62 at 67.

22 [1891] 2 Ch. 269. An interim injunction will normally not be awarded in a contested defamation action where the claimant is unable to show that a defence of justification is likely to fail at trial.

23 [1975] F.S.R. 421, per Oliver J; and see *Easycare Inc v Bryan Lawrence & Co* [1995] F.S.R. 597 at 602, per Aldous J; *Macmillan Magazines Ltd v RCN Publishing Co Ltd* [1998] F.S.R. 9, Neuberger J.

24 [2004] EWCA Civ 1462; [2005] Q.B. 972.

the enactment of the Human Rights Act 1998.[25] In *Francotyp-Postalia Ltd v Mailing Room Ltd*[26] it was accepted that s.12(3) of the Human Rights Act 1998 did not change the rule in Bonnard v Perryman as it applies to malicious falsehood.

22-06 **"Threats" actions** It may be slander of title to allege of anyone that he is selling goods in infringement of a patent or copyright.[27] However, the difficulty in establishing the tort (particularly the need to show malice) led to the introduction of special statutory protection against "threats", not limited by malice and the need to prove their falsity and damage. This process continued throughout the twentieth century, so that legislation has created statutory torts where the defendant threatens proceedings and is unable to prove infringement of a patent,[28] registered design,[29] registered trade mark[30] or design right.[31] Such actions can be brought by a "person aggrieved".[32] Copyright has never been accorded this statutory protection, so only malicious falsehood is available in such a case. The Intellectual Property (Unjustified Threats) Act 2017 reformed and in effect harmonised this statutory protection against groundless infringement threats. The stated aim of the Law Commission in making the reform recommendations was to make it easier for rights holders to pursue legitimate disputes.[33] Certain threats are not actionable[34] and proceedings in respect of actionable threats may not be brought against a professional adviser acting on their client's instructions, identifying their client in communications.[35]

22-07 **Slander of title** If property of any kind is for sale, and anyone without lawful motive comes forward and falsely alleges that any charges or liabilities[36] exist with respect to it, or otherwise calls into question the right or capacity of the vendor to make a good conveyance and in consequence the bargain goes off, an action lies (commonly known under the name of "slander of title").[37] This was "not properly an action for words spoken or for libel written or published, but an action on the case for special damage sustained by reason of the speaking or publication of the

25 In *Boehringer Ingelheim Ltd v Vetplus Ltd* [2007] EWCA Civ 583 it was conceded that the rule in *Bonnard v Perryman* applied to malicious falsehood.

26 [2015] EWCA Civ 1167.

27 *Wren v Weild* (1869) L.R. 4 Q.B. 730; *Mentmore Manufacturing Co v Fomento (Sterling Area) Ltd* (1955) 72 R.P.C. 157.

28 Patents Act 1977 s.70.

29 Registered Designs Act 1949 s.26. And see the Community Design Regulations 2005 (SI 2005/2339).

30 Trade Marks Act 1994 s.21.

31 Copyright Designs and Patents Act 1988 s.253.

32 The claimant need not be the person to whom the threats were made, so long as he is hampered in his trade by the threats.

33 See Law Commission, *Patents, Trade Marks and Designs: Unjustified Threats*, Law Com 360 (Oct 2015); *Patents, Trade Marks and Design Rights: Groundless Threats Report*, Law Com 346 (April 2014).

34 Threats not actionable are, in effect, with reference to alleged primary acts of infringement or an implied threat contained in a "permitted communication" (e.g. giving notice that the IP right exists).

35 For more detailed consideration see *Kerly's Law of Trade Marks and Trade Names*, 16th edn (2017) Ch.21.

36 In *Green v Button* (1835) 2 C.M. & R. 707, the claimant had contracted for the purchase of certain wood, but he was unable to obtain delivery owing to the defendant falsely and maliciously alleging an agreement under which he had a lien on the goods for moneys advanced to the claimant, and it was held that there was a good cause of action for slander of title.

37 Although this expression no doubt originally applied to real property, it was from very early times applied to personalty also. *Halsey v Brotherhood* (1881) 19 Ch. D. 386 at 390, per Baggallay LJ.

slander of the [claimant's] title".[38] The actual language used is still, however, a material part of the cause of action and must be set out in the statement of claim as in defamation.[39]

Slandering quality of goods It may be actionable falsely and maliciously to disparage the quality of a claimant's goods and thereby prevent their sale.[40] However, no action will lie for mere trade puffery or mere self-commendation.[41] In *London Ferro-Concrete Co Ltd v Justicz*,[42] the defendant was held liable for the tort when he went beyond merely saying that his methods were better than the claimant's and asserted that the claimant's methods were inadequate. 22-08

Other false statements causing damage The tort protects against falsehoods that are calculated to cause economic harm to the claimant. In *Joyce v Sengupta* Nicholls VC commented that: "this cause of action embraces particular types of malicious falsehood such as slander of title and slander of goods, but is not confined to those headings."[43] Though cases often involve denigration or disparagement, neither are necessary for the tort to be established. So in *Ratcliffe v Evans*,[44] a false statement that the claimant had ceased to carry on business was capable of amounting to the tort. As the tort protects against pecuniary damage, it tends to protect commercial interests.[45] However, it extends beyond commercial interests. In the old case of *Sheperd v Wakeman*,[46] the claimant lost her marriage through the defendant falsely and maliciously alleging that she was already married, and it was held that she had a good cause of action. Indeed, the decisions in *Kaye v Robertson*[47] and *Joyce v Sengupta*[48] (in which the claimants were not traders) reveal that an attack on economic interests (rather than merely commercial interests) may be sufficient. So, in *Quinton v Peirce*[49] in a local election, the claimant sued in malicious falsehood over alleged untrue statements about the claimant in the defendant's election leaflet. 22-09

---

38 per curiam, *Malachy v Soper* (1836) 3 Bing. N.C. 371 at 384–385, cited by McCardie J in *British Railways Traffic etc Co v CRC Co* [1922] 2 K.B. 260 at 266. As to proof of special damage now see paras 22-16 to 22-17.

39 *Gutsole v Mathers* (1836) 1 M. & W. 495.

40 *Western Counties Manure Co v Lawes Chemical Manure Co* (1874) L.R. 9 Ex. 218. This principle seems to be assumed in *White v Mellin* [1895] A.C. 154, though upon another ground doubts are thrown upon the above-mentioned case; *Hubbuck v Wilkinson* [1899] 1 Q.B. 86; *Alcott v Millar's Karri and Jarrah Forests* (1904) 91 L.T. 722.

41 See para.22-18.

42 (1951) 68 R.P.C. 261 CA.

43 [1993] 1 W.L.R. 337 at 341.

44 [1892] 2 Q.B. 524.

45 In *Riding v Smith* (1876) 1 Ex. D. 91, the claimant, a shopkeeper, lost custom through a malicious and false allegation that his wife, who assisted in the business, had committed adultery on his premises and the court decided that the action was maintainable. The statement was of such a nature as to be calculated to prevent persons using the claimant's shop.

46 (1662) 1 Sid. 79.

47 [1991] F.S.R. 62 CA.

48 [1993] 1 W.L.R. 337 CA.

49 [2009] EWHC 912 (QB); [2009] F.S.R. 17, Eady J. Morland J in *O'Shea v MGN Ltd* [2001] E.M.L.R. 40 stated, obiter, that the deliberate use of a lookalike photograph in a defamatory setting would constitute malicious falsehood.

2. Essentials of the Action

22-10 **Essentials of the action** In *Royal Baking Powder Co v Wright, Crossley & Co, Crossley & Co* the essentials of the action[50] were defined as: false words which are maliciously published and which are calculated to cause (and do cause) the claimant pecuniary loss. However the tort is often defined as applying to falsehoods "about" the claimant.[51] For example, in *Kaye v Robertson*, Glidewell LJ defined the essentials as "… that the defendant has published about the [claimant] words which are false, that they were published maliciously and that special damage has followed as the direct and natural result of their publication".[52] As this would include a falsehood, for example, about the claimant's product,[53] or indeed as in *Riding v Smith*, the claimant's wife,[54] it might be more appropriate to state that the words should concern the claimant or his property or otherwise refer to the claimant's pecuniary interests.[55] There appears to be a special case of malicious falsehood, where the defendant makes an untrue claim to a title of any kind or to be an inventor or designer—this falsehood may be actionable by the legitimate owner of the title in question, though the claimant is not referred to by the defendant. In *Customglass v Salthouse*[56] the false statement that the defendant had designed the claimant's boat was malicious falsehood, while in *Serville v Constance*[57] Harman J held that the defendant's false claim to a boxing title in fact held by the claimant was capable of amounting to malicious falsehood.[58] The claimant must in the first place strictly set out and prove the words complained of as in an action for defamation.[59] He must prove that they are false,[60] and he must prove that they are

---

[50] *Royal Baking Powder Co v Wright, Crossley & Co, Crossley & Co* (1901) 18 R.P.C. 95 at 99, per Lord Davey: "To support such an action it is necessary for the [claimants] to prove (1) that the statements complained of were untrue; (2) that they were made maliciously—that is, without just cause or excuse; (3) that the [claimants] had suffered special damage thereby."

[51] In *Marathon Mutual Ltd v Waters* [2009] EWHC 1931 (QB); [2010] E.M.L.R. 3 at [9], Judge Moloney QC accepted the defendants' argument that there must be some reference to the claimant or his business, to comply with art.10 ECHR that a restriction on free speech must be prescribed by law and not disproportionate.

[52] *Kaye v Robertson* [1991] F.S.R. 62 at 67.

[53] *Ajinomoto Sweeteners Europe SAS v Asda Stores Ltd* [2010] EWCA Civ 609; [2011] Q.B. 497.

[54] (1876) 1 Ex. D. 91. The court also commented that malicious falsehood would lie where false allegations of infectious diseases affecting a claimant's workforce were made.

[55] In *Niche Products Ltd v MacDermid Offshore Solutions LLC* [2013] EWHC 3540 (IPEC); [2014] E.M.L.R. 9 Birss J refused to strike out a claim for malicious falsehood. The parties were trade rivals and the claimant had issued a report that the defendant had changed the formulation of its product. The defendant published a letter stating that the claimant's report was "misleading and erroneous". Birss J stated "if a statement is likely to cause pecuniary damage then there is a nexus between the alleged falsehood and the claimant's economic interests" (at [32]; application to stay proceedings rejected by CA: [2014] EWCA Civ 379).

[56] [1976] 1 N.Z.L.R. 36.

[57] [1954] 1 All E.R. 662 at 665.

[58] However, though these cases were referred to by Judge Maloney QC, sitting as a High Court Judge in *Marathon Mutual Ltd v Waters* [2009] EWHC 1931; [2010] E.M.L.R. 3 it is submitted that he was wrong not to strike out the claim in malicious falsehood from the claimant whose income was largely derived from the "target" of the alleged falsehood (cf. *Gatley on Libel and Slander*, 12th edn (2013), para.21.4; and Wadlow, *The Law of Passing Off: Unfair Competition by Misrepresentation*, 5th edn (2016) para.616).

[59] *Gutsole v Mathers* (1836) 1 M. & W. 495. In *Cornwall Gardens Ltd v Garrard & Co Ltd* [2001] EWCA Civ 699, the Court of Appeal endorsed Bar Council guidance on counsel's obligations before pleading fraud, and applied it to the tort of malicious falsehood. As to the meaning of "reasonably

malicious.[61] The falsehood must be published to persons other than the claimant. It would appear that republication which is the natural and probable consequence of the initial deliberate publication might render the defendant liable,[62] though Laws LJ in *McManus v Beckham*, preferred the test "it must … be demonstrated that D foresaw that the further publication would probably take place or that D (or a reasonable person in D's position) should have so foreseen and that in consequence increased damage to C would ensue".[63] He found the root question to be whether "D, who has slandered C, should justly be held responsible for damage which has been occasioned … by a further publication". Except in cases within s.3 of the Defamation Act 1952,[64] actual damage must be proved. An action for malicious falsehood, unlike an action for defamation, survives the death of the claimant.[65] In *Huda v Wells*[66] Nicklin J held that in malicious falsehood "publication" (as with defamation cases) takes place where the statement complained of is heard or read by the publishee. In a malicious falsehood claim, that claim had to be limited to alleged publications within England and Wales.[67]

(a) Published falsehoods

False statement concerning and calculated to harm the claimant or his property There must be a false statement of some sort. "If the statement is true, however malicious the defendant's intention might be, no action will lie."[68] As in deceit, the statement may be oral, written, implied[69] or emanate from conduct.[70] The meaning of the words may be in issue: if so, the proper meaning must be established, before their truth or falsity can be tested.[71] The false statement must concern the claimant or his property/economic interests. Lord Watson in *White v Mellin* (a slander of goods claim) stressed "… it must be shown that the defendant's representations were made of and concerning the [claimant's] goods".[72] For the 22-11

credible admissible evidence" before alleging fraud, see *Medcalf v Mardell* [2002] UKHL 27; [2003] 1 A.C. 120.

60 There is no presumption in favour of the goodness of a man's title to property or of the quality of his merchandise.

61 *Royal Baking Powder Co v Wright, Crossley & Co* (1901) 18 R.P.C. 95; *British Railway Traffic etc Co v CRC Co* [1922] 2 K.B. 260; *Shapiro v La Morta* (1924) 40 T.L.R. 39 at 201.

62 *Cellactite & British Uralite v HH Robertson Co* [1957] C.L.Y. 1989; *The Times*, 23 July 1957.

63 [2002] EWCA Civ 939; [2002] 1 W.L.R. 2982 at [43]. See also Waller LJ at [34].

64 See para.22-16.

65 *Hatchard v Mege* (1887) 18 Q.B.D. 771.

66 [2017] EWHC 2553 (QB); [2018] E.M.L.R. 7 at [10].

67 See *Berezovsky v Forbes Inc (No.1)* [2000] 1 W.L.R. 1004 HL, Lord Hope at 1032.

68 per Maule J in *Pater v Baker* (1847) 3 C.B. 831 at 868.

69 The false disparagement could be either direct or "by *innuendo*", per Whitford J in *McDonalds v Burgerking* [1986] F.S.R. 45 at 59.

70 Conduct may be statement: see *Wilts United Dairies v Robinson* [1957] R.P.C. 220; *Royal Baking Powder Co v Wright, Crossley & Co* (1901) 18 R.P.C. 95. In *Euromoney Institutional Investor Plc v Aviation News Ltd* [2013] EWHC 1505 (QB) Tugendhat J considered that a statement of opinion cannot be a falsehood for the purposes of a claim in malicious falsehood (unless the defendant does not in fact hold that opinion).

71 In *Ajinomoto Sweeteners Europe SAS v Asda Stores Ltd* [2009] EWHC 781 (QB); [2009] F.S.R. 16 Sir Charles Gray, sitting as a High Court Judge ordered a trial on the preliminary issue as to meaning.

72 [1895] A.C. 154 at 167. In *Cruddas v Calvert* [2013] EWHC 1096 (QB) the claimant sought permission inter alia to amend the particulars of claim in a malicious falsehood action to include an allegation that the defendant's intention in publishing the relevant articles was also to harm a third party (the Prime Minister). Nicol J held that, though the authorities were not decisive, there are decisions

defendant to tell lies about himself is not the tort,[73] unless that in some way implicates the claimant. As in defamation, the claimant does not have to be named as such.[74] As well as being false, the statement must be calculated to cause actual economic harm.[75] Stable J in *Wilts United Dairy v Robinson*[76] made it clear that this is a separate element to the need for malice. Where malice is present the defendant would be liable "provided it is clear from the nature of the falsehood that it is intrinsically injurious".

(b) Malice

22-12 **Malice and bona fide publication** Malice is the key ingredient in this tort[77] and the onus of proving it is on the claimant. In *Cruddas v Calvert* the Court of Appeal discussed the need to show malice (given that the single meaning rule does not apply to malicious falsehood). In assessing whether malice existed in relation to an incorrect and false meaning that might foreseeably be placed on a statement the test to be applied is subjective: "a defendant should only be liable for malicious falsehood if the falsehood represents one of the possible correct meanings of the defendant's words and the defendant intended to convey that falsehood".[78] If a journalist had to expressly disavow every foreseeable incorrect interpretation of what he wrote "it would have a chilling effect on free speech".[79] Good faith is always a defence even though the statement causes damage.[80] And it is no evidence of malice if a defendant persists in asserting his claim after he has been informed that it is groundless.[81] In the case of *Greers Ltd v Pearman and Corder Ltd*[82] Scrutton LJ said:

> "Honest belief in an unfounded claim is not malice; but the nature of the unfounded claim may be evidence that there was not an honest belief in it. It may be so unfounded that the particular fact that it is put forward may be evidence that it is not honestly believed."

---

which assume that the intention must be to injure the claimant (see at [16]) and the other elements of the tort (that the publication must concern the claimant's economic interests and have caused him economic harm) must clearly relate to the claimant. The court was not prepared to make the novel extension suggested by the claimant.

73 *Schulke Mayr UK v Alkapharm UK Ltd* [1999] F.S.R. 161.This case was distinguished in *Niche Products Ltd v MacDermid Offshore Solutions LLC* [2013] EWHC 3540 (IPEC); [2014] E.M.L.R. 9, Birss J.

74 In *Lyne v Nicholls* (1906) 23 T.L.R. 86, Swinfen Eady J, a false assertion that the defendant's newspaper had a circulation 20 times any other weekly paper in the district (there being only one such newspaper, the claimant's) was actionable (though the action failed as no damage was proved).

75 Glidewell LJ in *Kaye v Robertson* [1991] F.S.R. 62 at 67, necessary for the claimant to prove that the words were calculated to produce damage. And see discussion of the phrase "calculated to cause pecuniary damage" in s.3 of the Defamation Act 1952, para.22-16.

76 [1957] R.P.C. 220 at 237.

77 Reasserted by Whitford J in *McDonald's Hamburgers v Burgerking UK* [1986] F.S.R. 45 (decision appealed to the Court of Appeal on other grounds: [1987] F.S.R. 112).

78 [2015] EWCA Civ 171; [2015] E.M.L.R. 16 at [114], per Jackson LJ.

79 [2015] EWCA Civ 171; [2015] E.M.L.R. 16 at [112].

80 *Shapiro v La Morta* (1924) 40 T.L.R. 39 Div Ct, and 201 CA. In *Spring v Guardian Assurance Plc* [1995] 2 A.C. 296 HL, the defendant, as former employer, provided a highly critical reference for the claimant, referring to him as a man "of little or no integrity". However, the claimant was unable to prove malice. The House of Lords did hold, however, that a duty of care in negligence existed in such circumstances.

81 *Steward v Young* (1870) L.R. 5 C. & P. 122.

82 (1922) 39 R.P.C. 406 at 417; considered *Joyce v Motor Surveys Ltd* [1948] Ch. 252.

The problem of definition The Court of Appeal in *Spring v Guardian Assurance* accepted that the test of what constitutes malice is the same as the test in relation to the torts of libel and slander.[83] In *Khader v Aziz*[84] Eady J noted the "stringent test" for malice: "[it] is to be firmly distinguished from being emotional, misguided or uncritical. Nor is it sufficient to plead that the defendant 'ought to have known' certain facts or failed to make enquiries about them. Negligence is quite different from malice." On appeal the concept of malice was discussed by Sir Anthony May. He noted: "... grossly exaggerated language may be evidence of malice. However it is necessary that the evidence should raise the probability of malice, and be more consistent with its existence than its non-existence."[85] In *Quinton v Peirce*, Eady J referred to the "high hurdle" of establishing malice, noting that "dislike is not to be equated with malice" nor was the fact that the defendant was "partial, biased and hard-hitting" (in his election pamphlet) to be equated with malice.[86] A review of the case law reveals that malice can be proved in various ways: "either personal spite, or an intention to injure the [claimant] without just cause or excuse or knowledge of the falsity of what is said."[87] Thus malice involves known falsehoods or impermissible motives (in the sense of aiming to injure rather than further your own interests). In *White v Mellin*,[88] Lord Herschell LC said that by the word maliciously: 22-13

> "It may be intended to indicate that the object of the publication must be to injure another person and that the advertisement is not published bona fide merely to sell the advertiser's own goods or *at all events* that he published it with a knowledge of its falsity. One or other of these elements it seems to me must be intended by the addition of the word 'maliciously'."

Malice and knowledge of falsity "If a man says something he knows to be untrue, it is malicious ipso facto, because he has said something that is false and something that he knows to be false."[89] There is no need to show additionally that the defendant intended to harm the claimant. Thus, in *Wilts United Dairies v Robinson* Stable J found the defendants liable though "[the defendants] were not there to harm the [claimants] what they were out for was making a profit, to advantage themselves".[90] Recklessness as to falsity of the allegations is sufficient, on a par with the tort of deceit. In *Cellactite & British Uralite v HH Robertson Co*,[91] inaccuracies in a sales manual concerning the claimants' rival product were "reck- 22-14

---

83 [1993] 2 All E.R. 273; [1993] I.C.R. 412. The Court of Appeal adopted Lord Diplock's definition of malice from the defamation case, *Horrocks v Lowe* [1975] A.C. 135 at 150. Note, however, that on the issue of negligence the House of Lords overturned the decision of the Court of Appeal: [1995] 2 A.C. 296.

84 [2009] EWHC 2027 (QB) at [31]–[32].

85 *Khader v Aziz* [2010] EWCA Civ 716; [2010] 1 W.L.R. 2673 at [20]; see also [29]. Part of Eady J's judgment in the lower court was referred to at [10]. And see discussion by Swift J in *Al-Ko Kober Ltd v Sambhi* [2019] EWHC 2409 (QB) at [21].

86 [2009] EWHC 912 (QB); [2009] F.S.R. 17 at [82]–[83], per Eady J.

87 See Heydon, *Economic Torts*, 2nd edn (1978), p.83.

88 [1895] A.C. 154 at 160.

89 *Wilts United Dairies v Robinson* [1957] R.P.C. 220 at 235, per Stable J. It is the defendant's subjective understanding of the meaning which is relevant: *Cruddas v Calvert* [2013] EWHC 2298 (QB) at [206], Tugendhat J.

90 *Wilts United Dairies v Robinson* [1957] R.P.C. 220 at 237. Tugendhat J in *Cruddas v Calvert* [2013] EWHC 2298 (QB) at [205], knowledge of falsity generally conclusive of malice "other than in those exceptional cases where a person may be under an obligation to pass on information which he knows to be false or does not believe to be true".

91 [1957] C.L.Y. 1989; *The Times*, 23 July 1957.

less statements", amounting to malice. Glidewell LJ in *Kaye v Robertson* accepted that malice would be inferred if "the words were calculated to produce damage and … the defendant knew when he published the words that they were false or was reckless as to whether they were false or not".[92]

22-15 **Malice and improper motive or intent to harm without just cause** There is a line of cases defining the malice required to support this action as actual ill-will or intent to injure or some indirect or dishonest motive. In *Halsey v Brotherhood*,[93] Lord Coleridge CJ, basing his judgment on *Wren v Weild*,[94] said:

> "It appears to me that a statement made under such circumstances does not give a ground for action merely because it is untrue and injurious to the plaintiff; there must be also the element of mala fides and a distinct intention to injure the plaintiff apart from the honest defence of the defendant's own property."

Further, McCardie J in *British Railway Traffic etc Co v CRC Co*[95] held that "the mere absence of just cause or excuse is not of itself malice. Malice in its proper and accurate sense is a question of motive, intention or state of mind". And in *Greers Ltd v Pearman and Corder Ltd*,[96] Bankes LJ thought "'maliciously' for this purpose means with some indirect object". Mala fides may render the defendant liable, though he believes (wrongly) the statement to be true.[97]

(c) Damage[98]

22-16 **Where no proof of special damage required** Section 3 of the Defamation Act 1952 provides:

> "(1) In an action for slander of title, slander of goods or other malicious falsehood, it shall not be necessary to allege or prove special damage—
> (a) if the words[99] upon which the action is founded are calculated to cause pecuniary damage to the plaintiff and are published in writing or other permanent form[100]; or
> (b) if the said words are calculated to cause pecuniary damage to the plaintiff in

92 [1991] F.S.R. 62 at 67; *Horrocks v Lowe* [1975] A.C. 135 at 149, per Lord Diplock. Carelessness is not sufficient: *Thompson v James* [2013] EWHC 585 (QB) at [16] per Tugendhat J "… carelessness is not malice" (a defamation claim); Birss J in *Niche Products Ltd v MacDermid Offshore Solutions LLC* [2013] EWHC 3540 (IPEC); [2014] E.M.L.R. 9. *Burgon v News Group Newspapers Ltd* [2019] EWHC 195 (QB), Dingemans J at [112], necessary to show a lack of honesty.

93 (1881) 19 Ch. D. 386 at 389; and see *Pater v Baker* (1847) 3 C.B. 831.

94 (1869) L.R. 4 Q.B. 730.

95 [1922] 2 K.B. 260 at 269.

96 (1922) 39 R.P.C. 406 at 417; followed in *Balden v Shorter* [1933] Ch. 427, per Maugham J; *London Ferro-Concrete Co v Justicz* (1951) 68 R.P.C. 261 CA; *Joyce v Motor Surveys Ltd* [1948] Ch. 252; *Mentmore Manufacturing Co v Fomento (Sterling Area) Ltd* (1955) 72 R.P.C. 157 at 160.

97 *Wilts United Dairies v Robinson* [1957] R.P.C. 220 at 237; and see *IBM v Web-Sphere Ltd* [2004] EWHC 529 (Ch); [2004] F.S.R. 39, per Lewison J.

98 Under the Crime and Courts Acts 2013 ss.34–38, in relation inter alia to malicious falsehood claims, where defendants are "relevant publishers" (in essence the press) exemplary damages cannot be awarded against a publisher who is a member of an approved regulator (except in special circumstances). As for other "relevant publishers" a court may make an award of exemplary damages where it considers it appropriate. Thus far the only approved regulator is IMPRESS. Aggravated damages are covered by s.39.

99 Which includes pictures or any other representation made in permanent form: see *Khodaparast v Shad* [2000] 1 W.L.R. 618 CA.

100 Broadcasting for general reception within the Act is to be treated as publication in permanent form for this purpose.

respect of any office, profession, calling, trade or business held or carried on by him at the time of the publication."

In *IBM v Web-Sphere Ltd*,[101] Lewison J noted that the phrase "calculated to cause pecuniary damage" should be interpreted as meaning likely or probable in an objective sense, rather than a possibility, in line with art.10 of the ECHR which requires any restriction on the right of freedom of expression to be swiftly justified as necessary in a democratic society.[102] In *Cruddas v Calvert*[103] Tugendhat J adopted the meaning "more likely than not to cause pecuniary damage". In *Tesla Motors Ltd v BBC*[104] Moore-Bick LJ noted that since the claim was for general damages it was unnecessary for the claimant to identify the amount of pecuniary loss which it is said the falsehoods were calculated to cause. However, the nature of the loss had to be identified and the mechanism by which it was likely to be sustained. The claimant recovers damages for the probable money loss but not for injury to reputation, though it would appear he can recover[105] for injured feelings as aggravated damages. Where he has relied on s.3 he cannot give evidence of special damage without having pleaded it.[106] In *Joyce v Sengupta*, the Court of Appeal noted that a claimant who relies upon s.3 may recover substantial damages and is not limited to nominal damages.[107]

Where proof of special damage required At common law the action would not lie where actual damage did not result,[108] and apart from cases falling within s.3 of the Defamation Act 1952, actual damage must still be alleged and proved. By "actual damage" is to be understood nothing more than an actual or temporal loss which has in fact occurred. Thus, a general loss of custom as distinct from the loss of particular known customers is sufficient to support the action,[109] provided the words complained of were published in such circumstances as to prevent the claim for such damage from being open to the objection that the loss of the custom must have been due to unauthorised repetition of the slander and not to the defendant's publication. The damage must be shown to be the direct result of the slander.[110] Where actual malice and damage are proved, an injunction may be granted to restrain publication of further slanders.[111] Probably, also, an injunction will be 22-17

[101] [2004] EWHC 529 (Ch); [2004] F.S.R. 39.

[102] And see Gray J in *Ferguson v Associated Newspapers Ltd* (2001, unreported, available Westlaw).

[103] [2013] EWHC 2298 (QB) at [195]. This phrase was also used by the Court of Appeal in *Tesla Motors Ltd v BBC* [2013] EWCA Civ 152 at [27]. In *Fage UK Ltd v Chobani UK Ltd* [2013] EWHC 630 (Ch); [2013] F.S.R. 32 at [152] Briggs J considered the phrase in relation to an allegation (allegedly involving malicious falsehood) made to a regulatory body.

[104] [2013] EWCA Civ 152 at [37]. In *Niche Products Ltd v MacDermid Offshore Solutions LLC* [2013] EWHC 3540 (IPEC); [2014] E.M.L.R. 9 Birss J struck out wholly speculative and insubstantial claims ([40]). He also noted (at [37]) that the requirements for pecuniary damage had to be met at the stage when the court is enquiring into liability.

[105] See para.22-17.

[106] *Calvet v Tomkies* [1963] 1 W.L.R. 1397 CA.

[107] [1993] 1 W.L.R. 337 at 346.

[108] *Ratcliffe v Evans* [1892] 2 Q.B. 524; *White v Mellin* [1895] A.C. 154; *Barrett v Associated Newspapers Ltd* (1907) 23 T.L.R. 666.

[109] *Ratcliffe v Evans* [1892] 2 Q.B. 524 at 529 and 531, per Bowen LJ; *Worsley Co Ltd v Cooper* [1939] 1 All E.R. 290; *Lewis v Daily Telegraph Ltd* [1963] 1 Q.B. 340, CA; affirmed [1964] A.C. 234 HL.

[110] See *Haddon v Lott* (1854) 15 C.B. 411.

[111] *Citation Plc v Ellis Whittam Ltd* [2013] EWCA Civ 155. Application for a permanent injunction struck out where no reasonable risk of repetition of the alleged malicious falsehood. The falsehood

granted where the claimant is able to show that damage will necessarily follow further publication, though none has been actually incurred at the time of the application[112] (and presumably it may be granted in cases within s.3 of the Defamation Act 1952, above, without proof that damage has actually occurred). The accepted view had been that only pecuniary loss was recoverable. Thus damages for injury to reputation are not recoverable.[113] As for damages for injury to feelings, though Lord Denning in *Fielding v Variety Inc*[114] stated they were not available, the Court of Appeal in *Joyce v Sengupta* was unhappy with this view[115] and in *Khodaparast v Shad*,[116] the Court of Appeal awarded aggravated damages to take into account distress, anxiety and injury to feelings.[117] Lord Steyn in *Gregory v Portsmouth City Council*,[118] while expressing no firm view on this decision, noted the potential of this tort to develop.

3. RIVAL TRADERS

22-18 **Comparative advertising** Actions of this kind have in modern times arisen as between rival traders, in cases in which a dealer in a particular commodity has published a statement disparaging the quality of his rival's goods. However, the courts are concerned that they should not be turned "into a machinery for advertising rival productions by obtaining a judicial determination which of the two was the better".[119] Mere puffs are not actionable[120] nor is mere "self-commendation".[121] Thus a mere comparison of the defendant's goods with those of the claimant, to the disadvantage of the latter, is not actionable even though in fact misleading.[122] In *White v Mellin*,[123] Lord Watson said:

---

had been made by the defendant's employee to a prospective client: the defendant had subsequently issued written instructions to all their sales staff not to make any such statements about the claimant trade rival.

112 *Ajello v Worsley* [1898] Ch. 274; *White v Mellin* [1985] A.C. 154; *Dunlop etc Co v Maison Talbot* (1904) 20 T.L.R. 579; *British Railway Traffic etc Co v CRC Co* [1922] 2 K.B. 260 at 272. *cf.* also *Halsey v Brotherhood* (1880) 15 Ch. D. 514 at 520.

113 *Joyce v Sengupta* [1993] 1 W.L.R. 337 at 348, per Nicholls VC.

114 [1967] 2 Q.B. 841 at 850.

115 [1993] 1 W.L.R. 337 at 348 (Sir Donald Nicholls VC).

116 [2000] 1 W.L.R. 618, CA. Followed in *Smith v Stemler* [2001] C.L.Y. 2309 with damages awarded for injury to feelings (£15,000) as well as economic loss (derogatory reference leading to summary dismissal).

117 Lord Denning's *dictum* otherwise in *Fielding v Variety Inc* [1967] 2 Q.B. 841 was stated not to have universal application ([2000] 1 W.L.R. 618 at [40]). The power to award damages for distress etc applied whether on proof of special damage or under s.3 of the Defamation Act 1952.

118 [2000] 1 A.C. 419 HL. A claim brought in malicious prosecution.

119 per Lord Herschell in *White v Mellin* [1895] A.C. 154 at 165.

120 As to the possibility of criminal sanctions, see the Consumer Protection from Unfair Trading Regulations 2008 (SI 2008/1277); Business Protection from Misleading Marketing Regulations 2008 (SI 2008/1276).

121 Nor is "mere vulgar abuse", Jacob J in *British Airways Plc v Ryanair Ltd* [2001] E.T.M.R. 24.

122 *Hubbuck v Wilkinson* [1899] 1 Q.B. 86 CA; *White v Mellin* [1895] A.C. 154. *Euromoney Institutional Investor Plc v Aviation News Ltd* [2013] EWHC 1505 (QB) at [105] Tugendhat J: "... the claim about copying is not one that a reasonable man could take seriously in this case. The claim to be first is one that advertisers constantly make".

123 [1895] A.C. 154 at 166.

"The fact that the representations made by the defendant might be calculated to disparage the food manufactured by the [claimant] and to interfere with its sale can afford no cause of action. And a statement by a trader that his goods are superior to those of another trader, even if untrue and the cause of loss to another trader, gives no cause of action."

More recently Jacob J noted that where advertising is concerned "the public are used to the ways of advertisers and expect a certain amount of hyperbole. In particular the public are used to advertisers claiming the good points of a product and ignoring others".[124]

Nevertheless, a trader who publishes statements which a sensible person would understand to amount to a serious and specific claim that, in comparison with his goods, his rival's products are materially defective, may be liable in tort.[125] In *Western Counties v Lawes*,[126] a statement that the claimant's rival product was of low quality was held to be injurious falsehood and in *Thorleys Cattle Food v Alassam*,[127] an allegation that the claimant had foisted a fictitious article on the public different from that represented amounted to the tort. The most useful case on this point is the judgment of Walton J in *De Beers v International General Electric*.[128] Here the defendant issued an advertising pamphlet purporting to report scientific tests which compared their product to that of the claimants, to the latter's detriment. The defendant claimed that this report was simply an elaborate self-commendation. However, the falsehoods contained in the report were capable of amounting to malicious falsehood. Walton J suggested the following analysis as useful: "whether a reasonable man would take the claim being made as being a serious claim or not."[129] Of course, malice must also be shown (see earlier discussion). **22-19**

Damage directly flowing from untruth In order to succeed the claimant must be able to show that the damage suffered by him flowed directly from the untruth of the statements of which he complains. The damage complained of must be attributable to the falsehood.[130] This may depend on how the falsehood is interpreted. In *Rima Electric Ltd v Rolls Razor* alternative goods were offered to customers in response to their request for the claimant's goods. This system of "switch selling" **22-20**

---

124 *Vodafone Group Plc v Orange Personal Communications Services Ltd* [1997] F.S.R. 34 at 38–39.

125 *De Beers Abrasive Products Ltd v International General Electric Co of New York Ltd* [1975] 1 W.L.R. 972. In *DSG Retail Ltd v Comet Group Plc* [2002] EWHC 116, Owen J held inaccurate price comparisons to be actionable as more than "mere puffs". And note the view of Birss J in *Niche Products Ltd v MacDermid Offshore Solutions LLC* [2013] EWHC 3540 (IPEC); [2014] E.M.L.R. 9 (an application to strike out) concerning malicious falsehood and the defendant's rebuttal letter.

126 (1874) L.R. 9 Ex. 218.

127 (1880) 14 Ch. D. 763.

128 *De Beers Abrasive Products Ltd v International General Electric Co of New York Ltd* [1975] 1 W.L.R. 972.

129 *De Beers Abrasive Products Ltd v International General Electric Co of New York Ltd* [1975] 1 W.L.R. 972 at 978. See also *McDonalds v Burgerking* [1986] F.S.R. 45 at 46. Jacob J noted in *Vodafone Group Plc v Orange Personal Communications Services Ltd* [1997] F.S.R. 34 that the public are used to the ways of advertisers and are aware that they will stress the good points of a product and ignore others.

130 Sterling J *Ajello v Worsley* [1898] 1 Ch. 274 at 281. The defendant, a retail dealer, advertised that he had in stock pianos of the claimant's manufacture, which he offered for sale at wholesale prices. In fact, the claimant had refused to supply him because he habitually failed to charge the retail trade prices and thereby damaged the claimant's trade. It was held that as the cause of the damage was the offer for sale at wholesale prices, which was not unlawful, and not the false statement that the pianos were in the defendant's possession, the claimant had no remedy.

was held to be a malicious falsehood on the facts: the defendant had indicated that they were obtaining the claimant's goods at below the prices charged to ordinary stockists which was likely to cause those legitimate dealers in the claimant's goods to feel aggrieved and look elsewhere for the products in question.[131]

22-21 **Registered Trade Marks and Comparative Advertising** Where a claimant objects to a comparative advertisement that contains his registered mark, he may allege both malicious falsehood and infringement of the registered mark.[132] Jacob J in *Cable & Wireless Plc v BT Plc*[133] considered that in such cases the tort claim often added nothing (though it increased costs) given it is difficult to imagine a case where the tort would provide wider protection than the statutory provision.[134]

[131] [1965] R.P.C. 4, per Wilberforce J.

[132] *Macmillan Magazines Ltd v RCN Publishing Co Ltd* [1998] F.S.R. 9, per Neuberger J. On registered trade marks and comparative advertising see Ch.24.

[133] [1998] F.S.R. 383 at 385, per Jacob J.

[134] *Kingspan Group Plc v Rockwool Ltd* [2011] EWHC 250 (Ch) Kitchin J: comparative advertisement infringed Trade Marks Act 1994 but no liability for malicious falsehood. And see Jacob J *British Airways Plc v Ryanair Ltd* [2001] E.T.M.R. 24.

CHAPTER 23

ECONOMIC TORTS

TABLE OF CONTENTS

1. GENERAL

23-01 **The core economic torts** The torts of procuring a breach of contract, intimidation, causing loss by unlawful means and the two forms of conspiracy are generally described today as "the economic torts".[1] They form the core of the tort liabilities for intentional disruption of economic interests and the principles governing them are interrelated. The description "the economic torts" is useful, even if not strictly accurate when the liabilities involved can extend more widely than damage to "economic" interests.[2] The general patterns of liability contain "ramshackle" elements (for they have "lacked their Atkin"),[3] though it has also been suggested

---

[1] cf. Lord Neuberger in *Revenue & Customs Commissioners v Total Network SL* [2008] UKHL 19; [2008] 1 A.C. 1174 at [216]: "Unlawful means conspiracy is one of the so-called economic torts, which include procuring a breach of contract, unlawful interference, causing loss by unlawful means, intimidation and conspiracy to injure (or lawful means conspiracy). These torts present problems even if they are considered individually (and yet more problems if they are treated as a genus)." For a valuable critical analysis see H. Carty, *An Analysis of the Economic Torts*, 2nd edn (Oxford: OUP, 2010); see too S. Deakin, "Economic Relations" Ch.30 in Sappideen and Vines (eds), *Fleming's The Law of Torts*, 10th edn (Thomson Reuters: Australia, 2011) updating Fleming's own Ch.30 in the 9th edn (Thomson Reuters: Australia, 1998). Older but still valuable specialist texts are J. Heydon *Economic Torts*, 2nd edn (London: Sweet & Maxwell, 1978), P. Cane, *Tort Law and Economic Interests*, 2nd edn (Oxford: OUP, 1996); and T. Weir, *Economic Torts* (1997). In general tort texts see D. Howarth, M. Matthews, J. Morgan, J. O'Sullivan and S. Tofaris, *Hepple & Matthews Tort: Cases and Materials*, 7th edn (Oxford: OUP, 2015), Ch.15; S. Deakin and Z. Adams, *Markesinis and Deakin's Tort Law* 8th edn (Oxford: OUP, 2019), Ch.15; E. Peel and J. Goudkamp (eds), *Winfield and Jolowicz on Tort*, 19th edn (London: Sweet & Maxwell, 2014), Ch.19; C. Witting, *Street on Torts*, 15th edn (Oxford: OUP, 2018), Ch.15. See too R. Smith, "The Economic Torts: Their Impact on Real Property" (1977) 41 Conv. (N.S.) 318; R. Heuston and R. Buckley (eds), *Salmond and Heuston on the Law of Torts*, 21st edn (1996), Ch.16. For Commonwealth developments: on Australia: Barker et al, *The Law of Torts in Australia*, 5th edn (2012), Ch.6; on New Zealand: S. Todd et al, *Todd on Torts* (formerly, *Law of Torts in New Zealand*), 8th edn (2019), Ch.13; on Canada: Klar, *Tort Law*, 6th edn (2017), Ch.17.

[2] For example, procuring a breach of contract might lead to physical damage to property if the contract concerned was to protect property from physical damage.

[3] Wedderburn (1983) 46 M.L.R. 224 at 226. In *Revenue & Customs Commissioners v Total Network SL* [2008] UKHL 19; [2008] 1 A.C. 1174 at [224], Lord Neuberger apparently treated the ramshackle nature of the economic torts as a reason for not adopting a single consistent approach to what constitutes unlawful means in relation to the various torts. See generally H. Carty, "Intentional Violation of Economic Interests" (1988) 104 L.Q.R. 250; P. Sales and D. Stilitz, "Intentional Infliction of Harm by Unlawful Means" (1999) 115 L.Q.R. 411; Bagshaw (1998) 18 O.J.L.S. 729; H. Carty (1999) 19 L.S. 489 (joint tortfeasors and "accessory" liability for assistance); J. Eekalaar (1990) 106 L.Q.R. 223 (conspiracy); P. Loughlan (1989) 9 O.J.L.S. 260 (assisting breach of fiduciary duty); P.

that these torts "have no inherent unity" and that it is "a mistake" to group them together.[4] The term "economic tort" is also applied more widely to other torts, such as passing off, malicious falsehood, slander of title, and wrongs in respect of patents, trademarks or breach of copyright (often referred to as wrongs to "intellectual property")[5] with which the core economic torts are frequently contiguous. The core economic torts also exist in parallel with, and sometimes overlap with, equitable wrongs such as "knowing receipt" and "knowing assistance".[6] The nature and enforcement of the core economic torts raise controversial policy questions, not least because the torts limit the liberty of competitors, protestors, and participants in industrial disputes, and might potentially impinge on free speech and freedom of association, as recognised in the European Convention on Human Rights and given statutory recognition in the Human Rights Act 1998.[7] The key policy choice requires a balancing of the advantages of predictability and judicial legitimacy that come from narrow and sharply-defined liabilities (responding to obviously excessive behaviour) against the advantages of flexibility in enabling the judiciary to respond to new and contentious methods of disrupting economic interests. Consideration of the role of the core economic torts in labour relations requires special attention to the statutory developments since 1875 in respect of "trade disputes".[8]

A useful sketch of the development of the general economic torts can begin in the nineteenth century, when the courts relinquished the precept that a person commits a wrong if he deliberately or maliciously "hinders another in his trade or business".[9] At the turn of that century, the House of Lords confirmed a fundamental principle when, in *Allen v Flood*,[10] it held that "an act that is legal in itself will not be made illegal because the motive of the act may be bad".[11] The case recognised **23-02**

Sales [1990] C.L.J. 491 (conspiracy and secondary liability); P. Davies and P. Sales, "Intentional Harm, Accessories and Conspiracies" (2018) 134 L.Q.R. 69; A. Tettenborn [1982] C.L.J. 58; D. Freedman [1999] C.L.J. 288; cf. attitudes in USA: S. Perlman, "Interference with Contract and Other Economic Expectations" (1982) 49 Univ. Chi. L.R. 61; and the classic article: Sayre, "Inducing Breach of Contract" (1923) 36 Harv. L.R. 663.

4 R. Stevens, *Torts and Rights* (Oxford: OUP, 2007) at 297; Both of these observations were quoted by Lord Neuberger in *Revenue & Customs Commissioners v Total Network SL* [2008] UKHL 19; [2008] 1 A.C. 1174 at [224].

5 See Chs 22, 24 and 25.

6 See *Lewin on Trusts*, 20th edn (2020) Chs 42 and 43.

7 See, per Neill LJ in *Middlebrook Mushrooms Ltd v TGWU* [1993] I.C.R. 612 at 620 CA (on the European Convention of Human Rights and free speech); compare Lord Denning MR in *Associated Newspapers Group v Wade* [1979] I.C.R. 664 at 690, who appears to go too far in treating interference with free speech and the freedom of the press as per se unlawful means.

8 See para.23-130 onwards.

9 *Keeble v Hickeringill* (1707) 11 East 574n. at 575, per Holt CJ. A different line of authority had already rejected mere competition as tortious: *The Schoolmasters of Gloucester Case* (1410) Y.B. 11, Hen. IV, f. 47, pl.21.

10 [1898] A.C. 1, HL.

11 This is how Lord Dunedin summarised the effect of *Allen v Flood* in *Sorrell v Smith* [1925] A.C. 700 at 718–719. The proposition was expressly and succinctly stated by Lord Macnaghten in *Allen v Flood*, at 154: "if there has been no violation of any right, malice by itself is not a cause of action." This was expressly denied by the minority Law Lords: see Lord Halsbury LC at 83–84. Although *Allen v Flood* has remained a foundational authority for more than a century it has also attracted unusually hostile criticism, both from judges and from some commentators: see, e.g. Lord Devlin, *Samples of Law Making* (1962) especially at pp.10–14; and *Rookes v Barnard* [1964] A.C. 1129 HL at 1216; and especially *Salmond & Heuston on the Law of Torts*, 21st edn (1996), pp.344–347, in effect harking back to the principles on the liability of workmen and trade unions in Sir W. Erle,

two grounds of liability: knowingly inducing a person "to commit an actionable wrong"[12] and intentionally causing loss by using unlawful means to interfere with the claimant's valuable relationship with another person.[13] Shortly after *Allen v Flood*, in *Quinn v Leathem*,[14] the House of Lords confirmed that defendants might also be held liable for economic harm, on a broader basis, where they had conspired to cause such harm to a claimant. In the absence of conspiracy, however, it remains "heresy" to aver that malicious interference with another's trade is per se actionable even when no unlawful means are employed or threatened.[15] And just as malice is insufficient, so too is "unfair conduct"; the common law has refused to embrace a tort of "unfair competition", even where one person has intentionally harmed his rival's economic interests.[16] If the results of competition, "the driving force for the success of the capitalist world", are said to be "unfair", the judge responds with "my nanny's great nursery proposition: 'The world is a very unfair place and the sooner you get to know it the better'."[17]

23-03 The progression of the economic torts through the central decades of the twentieth century saw a gradual expansion of liability for interference with contracts, or even with "business" or "trade", particularly where the defendants were the officials of trade unions,[18] alongside shrinkage of the conspiracy torts, which were frequently described as "anomalous".[19] But after half a century of case law that corresponded to no apparent masterplan, the House of Lords' decisions in

---

Memorandum: Royal Commission 11th Report on Trade Unions 1867–69 (C. 4123). Fleming found the reasoning in *Allen v Flood* [1898] A.C. 1 HL "rather glib", *The Law of Torts*, 9th edn (1998) p.766, a comment neither explained nor merited.

12 Lord Herschell spoke of there being a "chasm" between procuring a "violation of a legal right", such as by procuring a person to break a contract with a claimant, and inducing a person to do a lawful act which would cause the claimant loss: *Allen v Flood* [1898] A.C. 1 at 121.

13 per Lord Watson in *Allen v Flood* [1898] A.C. 1 at 96. In *OBG Ltd v Allan* [2007] UKHL 21; [2008] 1 A.C. 1, the House of Lords restored the distinction between these two grounds of liability: see Lord Hoffmann at [9] "The Law Lords who formed the majority in *Allen v Flood* [1898] A.C. 1 showed a clear recognition that *Lumley v Gye* (1853) 2 El. & Bl. 216 [the tort of procuring a breach of contract] and causing loss by unlawful means are separate torts, each with its own conditions for liability" and [38] "it is time for the unnatural union between the *Lumley v Gye* tort and the tort of causing loss by unlawful means to be dissolved. They should be restored to the independence which they enjoyed at the time of *Allen v Flood*."

14 [1901] A.C. 495 HL(I).

15 Lord Dunedin in *Sorrell v Smith* [1925] A.C. 700 at 719. *Allen v Flood* [1898] A.C. 1 HL, prevented the emergence of a cause of action, much desired by some judges, to the effect that, even if the means used were lawful, liability arose whenever one person did damage to another wilfully and intentionally without just cause and excuse, as held by Bowen LJ in *Mogul S.S. Co v McGregor Gow Ltd* (1889) 23 Q.B.D. 598 at 613, affirmed on other grounds [1892] A.C. 25 HL.

16 On competition, see *Warnink (Erven) BV v Townend & Sons (Hull) Ltd* [1979] A.C. 731 HL; *Cadbury Schweppes Pty Ltd v Pub Squash Pty Ltd* [1981] 1 W.L.R. 193 PC; *Reckitt & Colman (Products) Ltd v Borden* [1990] 1 W.L.R. 491 HL; *L'Oreal SA v Bellure NV* [2007] EWCA Civ 968; [2008] E.T.M.R. 1 at [135]–[161]. But fair dealing may be imposed by statute: e.g. Consumer Credit Act 1974; Unfair Contract Terms Act 1977; Competition Act 1998; Consumer Rights Act 2015.

17 per Harman J in *Swedac Ltd v Magnet & Southerns* [1989] F.S.R. 243 at 249: since *Bradford Corp v Pickles* [1895] A.C. 587 HL, the "unattractive nature of the motive does not make actionable that which is not actionable in itself"; see too *Cadbury-Schweppes Ltd v Pub Squash Co Ltd* [1981] 1 W.L.R. 193.

18 See, for example, *DC Thomson & Co Ltd v Deakin* [1952] Ch. 646; *Rookes v Barnard* [1964] A.C. 1129 HL; *Stratford & Sons Ltd v Lindley* [1965] A.C. 269 HL; *Torquay Hotel Co v Cousins* [1969] 2 Ch. 106 CA; *Merkur Island Shipping Corp v Laughton* [1983] 2 A.C. 570.

19 See, for example, *Crofter Hand Woven Harris Tweed v Veitch* [1942] A.C. 435 HL; *Lonrho Ltd v Shell Petroleum Ltd (No.2)* [1982] A.C. 173 at 189, per Lord Diplock.

OBG Ltd v Allan and *Revenue & Customs Commissioners v Total Network SL* redefined some of the elements of and boundaries between the economic torts for the twenty-first century.[20] Neither decision, however, pointed towards the courts developing extensive new means for judicial regulation of economic competition, nor extensive new protection for economic interests in other spheres; indeed *OBG Ltd v Allan* supplied a relatively restrictive restatement of the torts of procuring a breach of contract and causing loss by unlawful means. But a more flexible spirit appealed to the House of Lords in the *Total Network* case, where the court identified reasons for adopting a more interventionist approach when clarifying the scope of the tort of unlawful means conspiracy, a choice of direction that was subsequently confirmed by the Supreme Court in *JSC BTA Bank v Ablyazov (No.14)*.[21] The friction between these two approaches is responsible for some of the modern law's complexity.[22]

Procuring a breach of contract Half a century before *Allen v Flood*, the seminal decision in *Lumley v Gye* in 1853,[23] arising from a procurement of breach of a contract for services, established a general liability for intentionally inducing the breach of a contract between the claimant and a third party. Specific liabilities had existed more narrowly long before that case, relating to the master's right to sue for interference with, or enticement of, the servant or *per quod servitium amisit*.[24] The more generalised liability was imposed wherever a defendant induced the breach of a contract, first a contract for service or services, and later a contract of any kind, "maliciously". The defendant's liability, it was now said, arose wherever he procured "an actionable wrong or a breach of contract".[25] Later, the need for "malice" was dropped, and liability was defined as "knowingly and intentionally" procuring the breach of a contract without justification.[26] This definition formed the **23-04**

20 *OBG Ltd v Allan* [2007] UKHL 21; [2008] 1 A.C. 1; *Revenue & Customs Commissioners v Total Network SL* [2008] UKHL 19; [2008] 1 A.C. 1174. See H. Carty "The Economic Torts in the Twenty First Century" (2008) 124 L.Q.R. 641; S. Deakin & J. Randall "Rethinking the Economic Torts" (2009) 72 M.L.R. 519; P. Davies and P. Sales, "Intentional Harm, Accessories and Conspiracies" (2018) 134 L.Q.R. 69. For a critical assessment of developments across the main common law jurisdictions following the decisions see H. Carty "The Modern Functions of the Economic Torts; Reviewing the English, Canadian, Australian and New Zealand Positions" (2015) 74 C.L.J. 261.

21 [2018] UKSC 19; [2018] 2 W.L.R. 1125 at [6].

22 See, H. Carty "The Economic Torts in the Twenty First Century" (2008) 124 L.Q.R. 641 at 642, "the *Total* decision has arguably undermined the prospect for clarity that *OBG* represented, and thrown the economic torts back into the mess in which they were before *OBG*."

23 (1853) 2 El. & Bl. 216. See *Allen v Flood* [1898] A.C. 1, per Lord Herschell at 121: "A study of the case of *Lumley v Gye* has satisfied me that in that case the majority of the Court regarded the circumstance that what the defendant procured was a breach of contract as the essence of the cause of action." The decision in *Lumley v Gye* was an "enormous extension" of liability which added a "new chapter" to English law on civil liability: W. Holdsworth, *History of English Law*, 3rd edn (1945), Vol. IV, pp.384-385.

24 The phrase translates as "through which he has lost [the servant's] services". On the relationship of these actions to the Statute of Labourers, see G.H. Jones, "Per Quod Servitium Amisit" (1958) 74 L.Q.R. 39; Dixon CJ in *Att Gen (NSW) v Perpetual Trustee Co Ltd* (1952) 85 C.L.R. 237 at 242–248, affirmed [1955] A.C. 457 PC.

25 *Lumley v Gye* (1853) 2 El. & Bl. 216 at 233, per Erle J; at 231, per Crompton J and at 238, per Wightman J. See too Lord Woolf MR in *Credit Lyonnais Bank Nederland NV v Export Credits Guarantee Dept* [2000] 1 A.C. 486 at 496.

26 See para.23-16 onwards; per Lord Macnaghten in *Quinn v Leathem* [1901] A.C. 495 at 510; and *South Wales Miners' Federation v Glamorgan Coal Co* [1905] A.C. 239 at 246; *Lonrho v Fayed* [1992] 2 Q.B. 479 at 494, per Woolf LJ (affirmed on other grounds: [1992] 1 A.C. 448 HL).

foundation for the modern restatement of the tort in *OBG Ltd v Allan*,[27] where the House of Lords emphasised that it imposes a form of liability that is "secondary" to the primary liability of the procured party for breaking his or her contract with the claimant.[28]

23-05 Before the modern restatement, it was common to see the tort presented as a specific instance of a more general principle of liability for "knowing violation" of a legal right. A firm foundation for this understanding could be found in a dictum of Lord Macnaghten in *Quinn v Leathem*: "a violation of a legal right committed knowingly is a cause of action and it is a violation of a legal right to interfere with contractual relations recognised by law if there be no justification for the interference."[29] The approach facilitated the extension of the tort in two directions. First, a series of cases developed and refined liability for forms of "interference" with contractual relations beyond the procuring of breaches of contract. Secondly, liability was imposed for procuring a breach of obligations other than contracts. Thus in the "Docks Dispute" case in 1989, Butler-Sloss LJ described the general tort as the "interference with rights" or "direct invasion of legal rights" tort, and held that liability had been "extended to inducing breach of statutory duty … and inducing breach of equitable obligation".[30] Shortly afterwards, it was said that the four "necessary ingredients" of such a tort were: existence of the legal right; knowledge of the right and intention to interfere with it; direct and unjustifiable interference with the right (as "a necessary consequence of the defendant's actions"); and finally damage.[31]

23-06 Today, however, the reasoning in many of these cases is incompatible with the modern restatement of the tort of procuring breach of contract in *OBG Ltd v Allan*[32]:

[27] *OBG Ltd v Allan* [2007] UKHL 21; [2008] 1 A.C. 1.

[28] The liability of a defendant who procures another to commit a tort is generally imposed through joint tortfeasance, but, for obvious reasons, a person who procures another to break a contract cannot be held to have *jointly* broken the contract. On joint tortfeasors, see Ch.4. Joint tortfeasance makes it easy to understand why there appears to be no separate tort of "procuring a tort"; *Smith v Pywell* (1959) 178 E.G. 1009; *The Times,* 29 April 1959; H. Carty, "Joint Tortfeasance and Assistance Liability" (1999) L.S. 489. But there may be other obligations that a procurer cannot jointly breach because they are only imposed on the party procured, for example certain statutory and certain equitable obligations: see para.23-23; or infringement of copyright or database rights: *CBS Songs Ltd v Amstrad Consumer Electronics Plc* [1988] A.C. 1013 HL; cf. Mustill LJ in *Unilever v Gillette* [1989] R.P.C. 583; and Chadwick LJ in *MCA Records Inc v Charly Records Ltd* [2001] EWCA Civ 1441; [2002] F.S.R. 26, who both left this point open; *Football Dataco Ltd v Stan James Plc* [2013] EWCA Civ 27; [2013] Bus. L.R. 837 at [100]: "Once a party has procured an act which amounts to infringement by another he has effectively made it his own act … . This is not a case of secondary liability but one of primary liability along with another."

[29] per Lord Macnaghten in *Quinn v Leathem* [1901] A.C. 495 at 510. The passage is quoted and analysed by Lord Hoffmann in *OBG Ltd v Allan* [2007] UKHL 21; [2008] 1 A.C. 1 at [15]–[16].

[30] per Butler-Sloss LJ in *Associated British Ports v TGWU* [1989] 1 W.L.R. 939 at 959 CA (reversed other grounds, [1989] 1 W.L.R. 939 HL). So too, Neill LJ: the inducement of a breach of statutory duty is "akin to the inducement of a breach of contract" and it is necessary for the claimant to show a legal or equitable right "capable of forming the basis of a cause of action" (at 952). On equitable and fiduciary duties see para.23-23. For examples of these torts parallel to *Lumley v Gye* (1853) 2 El. & Bl. 216 see also *Barretts & Baird (Wholesale) Ltd v IPCS* [1987] I.R.L.R. 3 (statutory duty); *Meade v Haringey Council* [1979] 1 W.L.R. 637, CA (statutory duty); *Prudential Assurance v Lorenz* (1971) 11 K.I.R. 71 (equitable obligation to account), see paras 23-21 onwards.

[31] per Stuart-Smith LJ in *F v Wirral MBC* [1991] Fam. 69 at 115. This statement was obiter dicta in a judgment delivered in May 1990; the primary conclusion in the case was that there was no tort of unjustifiable violation or interference with parental rights.

[32] *OBG Ltd v Allan* [2007] UKHL 21; [2008] 1 A.C. 1.

there is no longer any economic tort based on knowing *interference* with contractual relations, but only liability for procuring a breach of contract *or* for intentionally causing loss by unlawful means.[33] Moreover, any tort liability for procuring breach of non-contractual obligations, such as statutory duties, that may exist in parallel to the tort in *Lumley v Gye* must follow the pattern of being accessory or secondary liability.

Conspiracy The tort of lawful means conspiracy, which was frequently called "conspiracy to injure",[34] is the primary exception to the modern position that the general economic torts are built around two prototypes: procuring another to commit a breach of contract, or similar actionable wrong, and intentionally causing loss by unlawful means. Conspiracy as a tort is a recent phenomenon. The early writ of conspiracy was largely restricted to abuse of legal procedure and merged into the modern tort of malicious prosecution.[35] As a crime, conspiracy was well known to the common law, extending in the late nineteenth century to persons organising a strike to the "unjustifiable annoyance and interference with the masters in the conduct of their trade". When statutory protection against that form of criminal conspiracy was provided in 1875, if the acts were done in contemplation or furtherance of a trade dispute, the courts created a parallel form of civil liability, which became known as "conspiracy to injure",[36] and now as "lawful means conspiracy". There, liability arises merely from the combination and its objects, without any independent illegality. Whereas the crime inhered in the agreement alone, the tort naturally required actual or threatened damage.[37] **23-07**

This lawful means conspiracy tort is "a modern invention altogether ... of use primarily when the act which causes damage would not be actionable if done by one alone".[38] As confirmed by the House of Lords in the *Crofter* case in 1942, lawful means conspiracy allows a claimant to succeed by reason of damage flowing from a combination alone, without proof of further illegality, provided the courts regard the object of the combination as illegitimate by reason of a predominant purpose to injure the claimant.[39] As a tort it is "anomalous" because acts done by two traders, such as "one street corner grocer in concert with a second", are not necessarily more oppressive today (if they ever were) than the same acts done by a large company or "multinational conglomerate". But the tort is too well established to be discarded.[40] **23-08**

---

33 *OBG Ltd v Allan* [2007] UKHL 21; [2008] 1 A.C. 1 at [38].

34 In *JSC BTA Bank v Ablyazov (No.14)* [2018] UKSC 19; [2018] 2 W.L.R. 1125 at [8], Lords Sumption and Lloyd-Jones identified "lawful means conspiracy" as a more satisfactory label for the tort than "conspiracy to injure" since "all actionable conspiracies are conspiracies to injure, although the intent required may take a variety of different forms".

35 Winfield, *History of Conspiracy and Abuse of Legal Procedure* (1921). On malicious prosecution today: *Martin v Watson* [1996] 1 A.C. 74 HL. See Ch.15.

36 per Oliver J in *Midland Bank Trust Co Ltd v Green (No.3)* [1979] Ch. 496 at 510–524; affirmed [1982] Ch. 529 CA; see *Quinn v Leathem* [1901] A.C. 495 HL.

37 Once pecuniary loss is proved, damages are at large; but damages for injury to reputation are not recoverable: *Lonrho Plc v Fayed (No.5)* [1993] 1 W.L.R. 1489 CA.

38 per Lord Denning in *Midland Bank Trust Co Ltd v Green* [1982] Ch. 529 at 538–539.

39 *Crofter Hand Woven Harris Tweed v Veitch* [1942] A.C. 435 HL; *Sorrell v Smith* [1925] A.C. 700 HL. See para.23-122.

40 per Lord Diplock in *Lonrho Ltd v Shell Petroleum Ltd (No.2)* [1982] A.C. 173 at 189; per Lord Bridge in *Lonrho Plc v Fayed* [1992] 1 A.C. 448 at 463; compare *Canada Cement LaFarge v British Columbia Lightweight* (1983) 145 D.L.R. (3d) 385 at 396–400.

23-09 Where two or more parties combine to cause harm by committing a tort, for example by procuring others to breach their contracts with the claimant, there may also be an actionable conspiracy, but in this case it is a conspiracy to use unlawful means.[41] The modern view is that this tort is separate from the "well-established principle that, where two or more parties join together in some way with a view to assisting or enabling one or more of them to commit a tort, all are liable for the tort as joint tortfeasors."[42] This separation is confirmed by the fact that the tort of unlawful means conspiracy can be established even when the "unlawful means" used did not themselves constitute an actionable wrong to the claimant.[43] Moreover, the conspiracy tort—but not the basis for joint tortfeasance—requires proof that the conspirators intended to cause loss to the claimant.[44] But whilst unlawful means conspiracy is an independent tort, centred on the wrongfulness of agreeing to act together in order to harm a claimant, the courts remain astute to prevent claimants from evading established limits on the ordinary principles of liability or gaining undue procedural advantages merely by pleading conspiracy.[45]

23-10 **Causing loss by unlawful means and intimidation** In *OBG v Allan* the House of Lords rejected the earlier rationalisation of the case law put forward by Lord Diplock in *Merkur Island Shipping Corp v Laughton* to the effect that procuring a breach of contract was a species of the genus liability of interfering with the trade or business of another by doing unlawful acts.[46] The Law Lords were agreed on the separate identity of the *Lumley v Gye* tort and a tort based on the intentional causing of loss by using unlawful means to disrupt a claimant's economic relations with third parties, in Lord Hoffmann's terminology "the tort of causing loss by unlawful means". Only a bare majority, however, supported the further point, that the type of "unlawful means" necessary to commit causing loss by unlawful means should extend no further than "actionable civil wrongs".[47] As a result of this new

---

41 As in *British Motor Trade v Salvadori* [1949] Ch. 556, and see para.23-105 (explained sociologically by Weir as an "anti-post War-spiv decision", and also "wrong": *Economic Torts* (1997), at p.36).

42 The quoted phrase is from Lord Neuberger's speech in *Revenue & Customs Commissioners v Total Network SL* [2008] UKHL 19; [2008] 1 A.C. 1174 at [225]. The well-established principle is commonly associated with *The Koursk* [1924] P. 140, CA at 155, per Scrutton LJ, and exemplified by the imposition of liability in *Brooke v Bool* [1928] 2 K.B. 578. See also, *JSC BTA Bank v Ablyazov (No.14)* [2018] UKSC 19; [2018] 2 W.L.R. 1125 at [9]: "the tort of conspiracy is not simply a particular form of joint tortfeasance."

43 *Revenue & Customs Commissioners v Total Network SL* [2008] UKHL 19; [2008] 1 A.C. 1174; *JSC BTA Bank v Ablyazov (No.14)* [2018] UKSC 19; [2018] 2 W.L.R. 1125 at [13]: "both lawful means and unlawful means conspiracies are torts of intent. But the nature of the intent required differs as between the two."

44 *JSC BTA Bank v Ablyazov (No.14)* [2018] UKSC 19; [2018] 2 W.L.R. 1125 at [12].

45 *Hesperides Hotels v Aegean Hotels* [1979] A.C. 508 HL (no action in respect of trespass on foreign land); *Ward v Lewis* [1955] 1 W.L.R. 9 at 10, per Denning LJ; *Nomart Management Ltd v West Hill Redevelopment Co* (1998) 155 D.L.R. (4th) 627 (Ont. CA); and on the relationship to joint tortfeasors: *Credit Lyonnais Bank Nederland NV v Export Credits Guarantee Dept* [1998] 1 Lloyd's Rep. 19 CA; [2000] 1 A.C. 486 HL at 490 and 498–499 (where conspiracy was not relied upon in the House of Lords).

46 *Merkur Island Shipping Corp v Laughton* [1983] 2 A.C. 570 at 609–610. cf. *Johnson v BFI Canada Inc* 2010 MBCA 101; (2010) 326 D.L.R. (4th) 497 at [40] and [45] where it was held that it would be wrong to decide the case on a basis other than that on which it had been argued, which in that case was inducing breach of contract; the liability on which the judge based his decision, "interference with economic or contractual relations" was a separate and admittedly broader tort per *OBG Ltd v Allan* [2007] UKHL 21; [2008] 1 A.C. 1.

47 *OBG Ltd v Allan* [2007] UKHL 21; [2008] 1 A.C. 1. The definition of "unlawful means" that gained

rationalisation, it seems likely that the previously-recognised tort of three-party intimidation will in future be treated as a nominate sub-species of the more general causing loss by unlawful means tort.[48] But as a result of the reasoning used in the cases which have subsequently expanded the tort of unlawful means conspiracy, support for the minority's opinion as to the definition of "unlawful means" has not evaporated.[49] Moreover, uncertainty persists as to the appropriate definition of "intention to cause loss", and there are doubts as to the scope of the tort of two-party intimidation.

The framework The connections between the different economic torts, the boundaries between them and even the levels of liability within them, are by no means all finally fixed. This is illustrated by the variations in the nature of the constituents required in the torts of knowingly and intentionally procuring a breach of contract, intimidation, causing loss by unlawful means and the two forms of conspiracy. The primary problems relate, first, to the true test of the defendant's "*intention*" and, second, to the range of what is accepted as "*unlawful means*". As already noted, the early decisions on procuring breach of contract, for example, began with a demand for "malice",[50] but after 1901 that was replaced by the need for an act of inducement or procurement effected "intentionally and knowingly"[51]; "malice" in the lay sense of "spite", is no longer required.[52] Even the requirement of "knowledge" has sometimes been applied to include "Nelsonian" knowledge, by turning a blind eye, while intention has on some occasions been extended to include recklessness, but in others limited to conduct intended to damage persons who were "targeted" directly, to the exclusion of those "incidentally" damaged, even if the damage to them was foreseeable.[53] Although *OBG Ltd v Allan* has helped to clarify 23-11

majority support is set out by Lord Hoffmann at [49].

48 See below para.23-62.

49 See P. Davies and P. Sales, "Intentional Harm, Accessories and Conspiracies" (2018) 134 L.Q.R. 69 at 74: "We suggest that the map of the law in this area needs to be revisited to make better sense of the authorities and the normative underpinning of tort liability. … [W]e suggest it would be desirable to favour the approach of Lord Nicholls in *OBG* to that of Lord Hoffmann, on the grounds that it provides a better fit with other authorities and a more coherent and principled account of tort liability in this field."

50 *Lumley v Gye* (1853) 2 El. & Bl. 216 at 224, 233–4; *Bowen v Hall* (1881) 6 Q.B.D. 333, 337; even Lord Devlin refers to the need for "malice" in *Rookes v Barnard* [1964] A.C. 1129, but "in the legal sense, that is, an intention to cause the breach and to injure the [claimant] thereby …", at 1212. The anomalous tort of "conspiracy to injure", now usually called lawful means conspiracy, based on a predominant purpose to injure (see para.23-122) contrasts understandably with the tort of conspiracy to use unlawful means, where an intention to injure is not necessarily dominant, but is required: *Lonrho Plc v Fayed* [1992] 1 A.C. 448 HL.

51 Lords Macnaghten and Lindley, *Quinn v Leathem* [1901] A.C. 495 at 510, 535.

52 *Hill v First National Finance Corp* [1989] 1 W.L.R. 225 CA at 233–4; *Pritchard v Briggs* [1980] Ch. 338 CA at 424, 431.

53 Contrast *Emerald Construction v Lowthian* [1966] 1 W.L.R. 691 CA; and *Stratford & Sons Ltd v Lindley* [1965] A.C. 269 HL; with *Timeplan Education Group v NUT* [1997] I.R.L.R. 457 CA; *Mercedes Benz v Clydesdale Bank*, 1997 S.L.T. 905 (OH); *Van Camp Chocolates v Aulsebrooks* [1994] 1 N.Z.L.R. 354 at 360; *Millar v Bassey* [1994] E.M.L.R. 44 CA, per Beldam LJ (intention to interfere with third party's contract with X inferred where defendant knew that would be the inevitable result of her breach of a contract with X); overruled by *OBG Ltd v Allan* [2007] UKHL 21; [2008] 1 A.C. 1; cf. the extended discussion of the different meanings of intention in *Douglas v Hello! Ltd (No.6)* [2005] EWCA Civ 595; [2006] Q.B. 125 at [174]–[225] and Lord Hoffmann's criticism of this analysis in *OBG Ltd v Allan* [2007] UKHL 21; [2008] 1 A.C. 1 at [135]. See P. Cane, *Tort Law and Economic Interests*, 2nd edn (1996), 118-120, and 148-149 on policy.

matters, not least by emphasising that in the context of the tort of procuring a breach of contract the necessary intention relates to the *procuring of the breach*, and not any subsequent damage to the claimant, uncertainties remain with respect to how to deal with defendants who fail to make reasonable inquiries, make mistakes about the law, or choose to take risk.[54] In the tort of causing loss by unlawful means, the question of the intention required is likewise not without difficulty.[55] *OBG Ltd v Allan* made clear that in this tort (which in Lord Hoffmann's analysis includes intimidation) the defendant must intend to cause loss to the claimant, and provided a clear account of that concept in terms of "ends" and "means",[56] but uncertainty has arisen in situations where the defendant intends to use unlawful means to make a gain but does not know who will shoulder the corresponding loss.[57] Moreover, whilst most cases have assumed that the tort of unlawful means conspiracy will employ the same notion of "intention to cause loss to the claimant", a loose citation in the recent case of *JSC BTA Bank v Ablyazov (No.14)*[58] has cast a shadow over what was thought to be clear.

23-12 Under causing loss by unlawful means, intimidation and unlawful means conspiracy, tensions remain as to the definition of "unlawful means", not least because different choices were made in *OBG Ltd v Allan* and the *Total Network* case as to whether crimes might fall within this category.[59] Even where the scope of "unlawful means" coincides across these torts, however, there are uncertainties with respect to the status of breach of contract and breach of equitable obligations,[60] and inconsistent answers have been given to the question of whether a defendant can be liable for a tort that requires use of "unlawful means" if he does not appreciate that the means that he uses are unlawful.[61]

---

54 *Allen v Pollock* [2020] EWCA Civ 258; [2020] Q.B. 781.

55 Compare *Barretts & Baird (Wholesale) Ltd v Institution of Professional Civil Servants* [1987] I.R.L.R. 3; *Lonrho v Fayed* [1989] 2 Q.B. 479 at 491, 494 (upheld on other grounds, *Lonrho Plc v Fayed* [1992] 1 A.C. 448 HL); *OBG Ltd v Allan* [2007] UKHL 21; [2008] 1 A.C. 1; see para.23-79.

56 *OBG Ltd v Allan* [2007] UKHL 21; [2008] 1 A.C. 1 at [164], per Lord Nicholls, and see at [62] per Lord Hoffmann.

57 *W.H. Newson Holding Ltd v IMI Plc* [2013] EWCA Civ 1377; [2014] Bus. L.R. 156; *Emerald Supplies Ltd v British Airways Plc (Nos 1 & 2)* [2015] EWCA Civ 1024; [2016] Bus. L.R. 145; *Media-Saturn Holding Gmbh v Toshiba Information Systems (UK) Ltd* [2019] EWHC 1095 (Ch); [2019] 5 C.M.L.R. 7; see para.23-81.

58 In *JSC BTA Bank v Ablyazov (No.14)* [2018] UKSC 19; [2018] 2 W.L.R. 1125 at [13], Lords Sumption and Lloyd-Jones cite a passage from a Canadian case that uses a different account of "intention" (*Canada Cement La Farge Ltd v British Columbia Lightweight Aggregate Ltd* (1983) 145 D.L.R. (3d) 385 at 388–391 (SCC)); discussed at para.23-107. Cases where it had been accepted that the necessary "intention" to cause loss to the claimant is the same in the tort of intentionally causing loss by the use of unlawful means and in unlawful means conspiracy include: *Meretz Investments NV v ACP Ltd* [2007] EWCA Civ 1303; [2008] Ch. 244 at [146]; *Digicel (St Lucia) Ltd v Cable & Wireless Plc* [2010] EWHC 774 (Ch) at Annex I, [84]; *Emerald Supplies Ltd v British Airways Plc (Nos 1 & 2)* [2015] EWCA Civ 1024; [2016] Bus. L.R. 145 at [133]; *Palmer Birch (a partnership) v Lloyd* [2018] EWHC 2316 (TCC); [2018] 4 W.L.R. 164 at [220]; *Media-Saturn Holding Gmbh v Toshiba Information Systems (UK) Ltd* [2019] EWHC 1095 (Ch); [2019] 5 C.M.L.R. 7 at [226].

59 *Compare OBG Ltd v Allan* [2007] UKHL 21; [2008] 1 A.C. 1 at [49]; with *Revenue & Customs Commissioners v Total Network SL* [2008] UKHL 19; [2008] 1 A.C. 1174 at [94].

60 See the problems deriving from *Rookes v Barnard* [1964] A.C. 1129 HL, para.23-71, and para.23-87, and on whether a breach of contract can count as unlawful means for the purposes of a claim for unlawful means conspiracy, see para.23-116. On equitable duties, see para.23-87 and para.23-117.

61 This issue has been raised expressly in several recent cases involving unlawful means conspiracy.

Three broad factors may be highly influential in determining the framework of the economic torts in the future. The first is whether the courts rise to the challenge of rationalising accessory liability across different areas of private law.[62] Currently, the position of some accessories in tort, for instance those who aid or abet, or assist,[63] is different from how they might be treated in criminal law, perhaps because of concerns about the imposition of vicarious liability. Limits on the tort liability of those who assist tortfeasors are currently paralleled by limits on when a defendant can be held to have *procured* a breach of contract, but such limits create pressure to the scope of the unlawful means conspiracy tort and equitable doctrines such as "knowing assistance".[64] **23-13**

The second broad factor is the key choice, already mentioned, between narrow and sharply-defined liabilities, which will enhance certainty and judicial legitimacy, and a more flexible, interventionist approach. The inconsistency between the approaches taken in *OBG Ltd v Allan* and the *Total Network* case has impeded attempts to identify a coherent framework for the economic torts,[65] and generated controversial questions such as those that ask about the existence and scope of two-party intimidation and a two-party form of causing loss by unlawful means. Importantly, the primary context where the economic torts operate appears to have changed in the last 40 years. When Lord Diplock provided a rationalisation of the "genus of torts" committed by "interfering with the trade or business of another person by doing unlawful acts" in 1983,[66] it was plausible to treat these torts as primarily of importance in regulating industrial conflict; today, however, most industrial cases turn on interpretation of the statutory conditions relating to ballots and notice, whilst the majority of cases involving issues relating to substantive features of the torts arise in commercial contexts. **23-14**

The third broad factor is the influence of procedural concerns. In most of the industrial relations litigation, the claimant's primary objective was to obtain an interim ("interlocutory") injunction, an order "until trial", an event which rarely ensued in such cases, and consequently the claimant's burden was merely to prove a "serious question to be tried",[67] or an "arguable" or "serious" case. The judgments in such cases frequently included principles which infused into the law generally, often expanding the tort liabilities, even though they had been found to be merely arguable.[68] By contrast, the modern commercial cases frequently involve full trials where facts are fiercely contested and substantial sums are at stake. Here, questions such as the precise meaning of "knowledge" or "intention", how to deal **23-15**

See, for example, *The Racing Partnership Ltd v Done Brothers (Cash Betting) Ltd* [2019] EWHC 1156 (Ch); [2020] Ch. 289; para.23-120.

62 See generally, P.S. Davies, *Accessory Liability* (2015).

63 *Credit Lyonnais Bank Nederland NV v Export Credit Guarantee Department* [2000] 1 A.C. 486 HL.

64 See now *Royal Brunei Airlines v Tan* [1995] 2 A.C. 378 PC; para.23-24; compare *Prudential Assurance v Lorenz* (1971) 11 K.I.R. 78; para.23-25; Carty (1999) 19 L.S. 489 at 507, 511.

65 *OBG Ltd v Allan* [2007] UKHL 21; [2008] 1 A.C. 1; *Revenue & Customs Commissioners v Total Network SL* [2008] UKHL 19; [2008] 1 A.C. 1174. Most academic writing recommends revising the conclusions reached in one or the other of these cases. See, for example, H. Carty "The Economic Torts in the Twenty First Century" (2008) 124 L.Q.R. 641; S. Deakin & J. Randall "Rethinking the Economic Torts" (2009) 72 M.L.R. 519; P. Davies and P. Sales, "Intentional Harm, Accessories and Conspiracies" (2018) 134 L.Q.R. 69.

66 *Merkur Island Shipping Corp v Laughton* [1983] 2 A.C. 570 at 609–610.

67 *American Cyanamid Co v Ethicon* [1975] A.C. 396 HL; see para.23-181

68 For example, *Stratford & Sons Ltd v Lindley* [1965] A.C. 269 HL; *Torquay Hotel Co v Cousins* [1969] 2 Ch. 106 CA.

with those who make mistakes and take risks, and who bears the burden of proof on such matters, have inevitably become more prominent.

2. Procuring a Breach of Contract

23-16 Knowingly and intentionally to procure or, as it is often put, to induce a third party to break his contract to the damage of the other contracting party without reasonable justification or excuse is a tort.[69] Such a tort was recognised in *Lumley v Gye*[70] by a majority in the Queen's Bench with respect to contracts for personal services, and later by the Court of Appeal.[71] It has now been held to apply to contracts of all kinds.[72] The ingredients of the tort were restated by the House of Lords in *OBG Ltd v Allan* with a view to drawing a clear line between this, the *Lumley v Gye* tort, and the tort of intentionally causing loss by unlawful means.[73]

(a) Breach

(i) *Breach of a valid and subsisting contract*

23-17 In *Allen v Flood* Lord Herschell declared "a breach of contract" to be "the essence" of the cause of action,[74] and in *OBG Ltd v Allan*[75] the House of Lords reiterated this fundamental proposition: "one cannot be liable for inducing a breach unless there has been a breach. No secondary liability without primary liability." Thus the court expressly rejected the view that had become orthodox between these two cases, that the tort could be committed by deliberate and direct interference with the performance of a contract without causing any breach.[76] This view, which had

---

69 *OBG Ltd v Allan* [2007] UKHL 21; [2008] 1 A.C. 1. Subsequently, the elements of this tort have been discussed by the Court of Appeal in *Meretz Investments NV v ACP Ltd* [2007] EWCA Civ 1303; [2008] Ch. 244; and *Allen v Pollock* [2020] EWCA Civ 258; [2020] Q.B. 781. In *Global Resources Group Ltd v Mackay* [2008] CSOH 148; 2009 S.L.T. 104 Lord Hodge having noted at [6] the parties' agreement that there were no material differences between the laws of Scotland and England in relation to this delict or tort, observed at [9] that Scots judges had drawn extensively on English law in defining this delict; but as he pointed out, cf. their views on recklessness, para.23-35. For a critique of the tort see Howarth (2005) 68 M.L.R. 195.

70 (1853) 2 El. & Bl. 216. An account of the litigation in its historical context is provided by S. Waddams, "Johanna Wagner and the Rival Opera Houses" (2001) 117 L.Q.R. 431.

71 *Bowen v Hall* (1881) 6 Q.B.D. 333 CA; *Temperton v Russell* [1893] 1 Q.B. 715, where the dicta must not be given a scope wider than the text indicates: *Allen v Flood* [1898] A.C. 1; *Crofter Hand Woven Harris Tweed Co v Veitch* [1942] A.C. 435 at 466.

72 See *Jasperson v Dominion Tobacco Co* [1923] A.C. 709 PC at 713; *DC Thomson & Co Ltd v Deakin* [1952] Ch. 646 at 677, per Evershed MR, and at 693, per Jenkins LJ. As to its application to contracts affecting land, see *Pritchard v Briggs* [1980] Ch. 338 CA, discussed para.23-47.

73 *OBG Ltd v Allan* [2007] UKHL 21; [2008] 1 A.C. 1, per Lord Hoffmann at [8] and [39]–[44]; per Lord Nicholls at [168]–[193]. cf. the analysis of the tort in terms of eight essential elements in *Sar Petroleum Inc v Peace Hills Trust Co* 2010 NBCA 22; (2010) 318 D.L.R. (4th) 70 at [40]. Compare the summary of five essential elements in *Daebo Shipping Co Ltd v Ship Go Star* [2012] FCAFC 156; (2012) 207 F.C.R. 220; (2012) 294 A.L.R. 635 at [88]; *TSG Franchise Management Pty Ltd v Cigarette & Gift Warehouse (Franchising) Pty Ltd (No.2)* [2016] FCA 674; (2017) 340 A.L.R. 230 at [57].

74 [1898] A.C. 1 at 121: "an unlawful act—namely, a breach of contract—was regarded as the gist of the action", at 123.

75 *OBG Ltd v Allan* [2007] UKHL 21; [2008] 1 A.C. 1 at [44], per Lord Hoffmann; see also [189], per Lord Nicholls, [264], per Lord Walker, [302] per Baroness Hale, and [319] per Lord Brown.

76 This view, now rejected, was clearly expressed by Lord Denning MR in *Torquay Hotel Co Ltd v*

treated acts of direct (and indirect) interference with the performance of contracts as tortious by way of an extension of the *Lumley v Gye* tort, was replaced in the *OBG* case by a restatement that confines this tort to situations where a *breach* of contract has been intentionally procured; tort liability will only be imposed for instances of interference with contractual performance (falling short of breach) when these fall within the scope of the separate tort of intentionally causing loss by the use of unlawful means. Consequently, the tort of procuring a breach of contract cannot be committed by persuading a person not to enter a contract. Similarly, where a defendant induces a party to exercise a right to terminate a contract the *Lumley v Gye* tort is not committed.[77] However, an injunction will lie even if no contract exists if the defendant has made it clear by his threats that he will, if one is concluded, procure its breach.[78]

In *Allen v Pollock*, Lewison LJ stated: "It seems to me to be clear that in order for a person to be liable in tort for inducing a breach of contract, the contract in question must be a binding and enforceable contract."[79] Thus, if the contract is void, for example, on grounds of incapacity,[80] no tort is committed by procuring a "breach" of it.[81] Nor is it tortious to induce a breach of a contract which is unlawful as being in unreasonable restraint of trade, although if the contract is severable, liability may arise for procuring breach of the remaining lawful terms of it, such as an outstanding negative covenant.[82] Where the contract is determinable, the defendant incurs no liability merely by inducing the contracting party to determine the contract lawfully, for there is then no breach.[83] It must follow therefore that it **23-18**

Cousins [1969] 2 Ch. 106; and approved by the House of Lords in *Merkur Island Shipping Corpn v Laughton* [1983] 2 A.C. 570, at 608, per Lord Diplock.

77 In *Sanders v Snell* [1998] HCA 64; (1998) 196 C.L.R. 329; (1998) 157 A.L.R. 491 at [23], the High Court of Australia stated that "To persuade or direct a contracting party to terminate the contract lawfully is not to procure a breach of the contract", citing *Sid Ross Agency v Actors and Announcers Equity Association* [1971] 1 N.S.W.L.R. 760 at 765, per Jacobs JA; *DC Thomson & Co Ltd v Deakin* [1952] Ch. 646 at 702, per Morris LJ; *Greig v Insole* [1978] 1 W.L.R. 302 at 333, per Slade J; *Cutsforth v Mansfield Inns Ltd* [1986] 1 W.L.R. 558 at 563, per Sir Neil Lawson.

78 See *Torquay Hotel Co Ltd v Cousins* [1969] 2 Ch. 106 CA (defendants intended to procure non-performance of "existing contracts by Esso and future contracts by Alternative Fuels so as to prevent those companies supplying oil to the Imperial Hotel": per Lord Denning MR at 141; no contract subsisted with Alternative Fuels; defendants liable to injunction in respect of both; see also Winn LJ at 146); and see *Union Traffic Ltd v TGWU* [1989] I.C.R. 98 at 105–106, per Bingham LJ and at 111–113, per Lloyd LJ.

79 *Allen v Pollock* [2020] EWCA Civ 258; [2020] Q.B. 781 at [25].

80 *De Francesco v Barnum* (1890) 45 Ch. D. 430; and later proceedings between different parties, 63 L.T. 514. There is no rule that a minor cannot commit the tort of procuring a breach of a contract: *Take-Two Interactive Software Inc v James* [2020] EWHC 179 (Pat) at [34], though the point does not seem to have been argued.

81 So too now a contract not made in writing for the sale of an interest in land: s.2 of the Law of Property (Miscellaneous Provisions) Act 1989, despite *Yaxley v Gotts* [2000] Ch. 162, CA. For some other statutory exceptions see the Contracts (Rights of Third Parties) Act 1999.

82 *Rickless v United Artists Corp* [1988] Q.B. 40 CA at 59, per Bingham LJ; *British Motor Trade Association v Gray*, 1951 S.C. 586; *Northern Messenger (Calgary) Ltd v Frost* (1966) 57 D.L.R. (2d) 456.

83 per Slesser LJ in *McManus v Bowes* [1938] 1 K.B. 98 at 127. In *Torquay Hotel Co Ltd v Cousins* [1969] 2 Ch. 106 at 117 Stamp J doubted the correctness of the dicta of Slesser LJ in *McManus v Bowes*; but the Court of Appeal did not repeat those doubts, and it is submitted that the text represents the law, despite the dicta of Diplock LJ in *Emerald Construction Co Ltd v Lowthian* [1966] 1 W.L.R. 691 at 703–704; see now *Cutsforth v Mansfield Inns* [1986] 1 W.L.R. 558 at 563, which supports the text. See too, per Morris LJ in *DC Thomson & Co Ltd v Deakin* [1952] Ch. 646 at 702 (where contract "lawfully terminated, there is no violation"); per Lord James in *Denaby and Cadeby Main*

is no tort to procure the breach of a voidable contract, at least where the person induced is the party who enjoys the right to rescind.[84] It is uncertain whether the tort is committed by procuring breach of a contract which is merely unenforceable by action.[85] There is, however, authority for the view that in order to establish his claim the claimant must show that he is able and willing to perform the contract.[86]

23-19 The view that the breach must be one that goes to the root of the contract has not survived into the modern law.[87] It is enough if the breach is of the only remaining obligation of a contract otherwise fulfilled (such as a valid covenant not to compete by an employee who has long ago left the employment).[88] Some cases have apparently misunderstood Lord Diplock's reference to "prevention of due performance of a *primary* obligation under a contract"[89] as meaning that certain terms in the contract may be insufficiently important to be "primary obligations".[90] But Lord Diplock was seeking to explain why a defendant might be liable for procuring a breach of a performance obligation even if the contract includes an exemption

---

Collieries Ltd v Yorkshire Miners' Association [1906] A.C. 384 at 406; *Posluns v Toronto Stock Exchange* (1964) 46 D.L.R. (2d) 210; affirmed (1968) 67 D.L.R. (2d) 165; *White v Riley* [1921] 1 Ch. 1 at 15, 26 and 32; and per Stuart-Smith LJ in *Associated British Ports v TGWU* [1989] 1 W.L.R. 939 at 970.

84 *Proform Sports Management Ltd v Proactive Sports Management Ltd* [2006] EWHC 2903 (Ch); [2007] 1 All E.R. 542 at [33], where it was held that there can be no liability for procuring breach of a voidable contract with a minor, on the facts a representation agreement between the claimant and the professional footballer Wayne Rooney: "[i]t does not matter whether the contract has already been avoided" (per Judge Hodge QC, [2006] EWHC 2903 (Ch); [2007] 1 All E.R. 542). The old case of *Keene v Boycott* (1795) 2 H.Bl. 511, to the contrary is not, it is submitted, now good law. Quaere where the contract is an "unconscionable bargain" or procured by economic duress; see Siopsis (1984) 100 L.Q.R. 523; but see as to the former, *Alec Lobb (Garages) Ltd v Total Oil (Great Britain) Ltd* [1985] 1 W.L.R. 173 CA.

85 e.g. formerly under s.5 of the Financial Services Act 1986 (cf. Lawson [1988] J.B.L. 281); see now s.20 of the Financial Services and Markets Act 2000; or formerly s.40 of the Law of Property Act 1925, now repealed by s.2 of the Law of Property (Miscellaneous Provisions) Act 1989. It has been held in Canada that procuring breach of such a contract is not tortious: *Brown v Spamberger and Bunting* (1959) 21 D.L.R. (2d) 630. *Smith v Morrison* [1974] 1 W.L.R. 659, suggests that the same answer should be given in England, especially if it is desired to exclude the tort from the area of land law (see R.J. Smith (1977) 41 Conv. (N.S.) 318). But contrast *Austin v Olsen* (1868) L.R. 3 Q.B. 208 at 211, per Mellor J; and *Unident Ltd v Delong* (1982) 131 D.L.R. (3d) 225 (technical unenforceability through lack of signature; tort action lies). On illegal employment contracts, see Jefferson (1996) 25 I.L.J. 234.

86 *Long v Smithson* (1918) 88 L.J.K.B. 223. cf. the case law on when workers taking industrial action short of a strike can pursue claims in contract against their employers: *Chappell v Times Newspapers Ltd* [1975] I.C.R. 145 at 174–5; *Henthorn v Central Electricity Generating Board* [1980] I.R.L.R. 361 CA; *Miles v Wakefield MDC* [1987] A.C. 539 HL; *Wiluszynski v Tower Hamlets LBC* [1989] I.C.R. 493 CA; *British Telecommunications Plc v Ticehurst* [1992] I.C.R. 383 CA especially at 399–405, per Ralph Gibson LJ; cf. *Bond v CAV Ltd* [1983] I.R.L.R. 360. See too *Kenny v An Post* [1988] I.R. 285 (rest break practice, not contractual right).

87 See Evershed MR in *DC Thomson & Co Ltd v Deakin* [1952] Ch. 646 at 689–690, doubting that view put by Porter J in *De Jetley, Marks v Greenwood* [1936] 1 All E.R. 863 at 872. It has received no support in any of the leading modern authorities.

88 Bingham LJ in *Rickless v United Artists Corp* [1988] Q.B. 40 CA at 58–59.

89 per Lord Diplock in *Merkur Island Shipping Corp v Laughton* [1983] 2 A.C. 570 at 608 (emphasis added); and *Dimbleby & Sons Ltd v NUJ* [1984] 1 W.L.R. 427 at 434–435 ("primary obligations to publish advertisements"). cf. Peter Gibson LJ in *OBG Ltd v Allan* [2005] EWCA Civ 106; [2005] Q.B. 762 at [47] stressing the need for the alleged tortfeasor having intended to prevent the performance of a primary obligation under the contract.

90 For example, Stuart-Smith J in *News Group Newspapers Ltd v SOGAT (No.2)* [1987] I.C.R. 181 at 209 ("it is doubtful if this is a primary obligation of the contract").

clause, excusing a party from liability in damages; the idea being that the breach of the primary obligation to perform remains, even though the secondary obligation, to pay damages on breach, has been removed.[91] In *Torquay Hotel Co Ltd v Cousins*,[92] an injunction was granted against defendants who were taking action in a labour dispute calculated to cause a supplier to stop supplies under a standing contract, even though a clause in the contract stated: "neither party shall be liable for any failure to fulfil any term of this agreement if fulfilment is delayed, hindered or prevented by any circumstance whatever which is not within their immediate control including … labour disputes." But it was important that the clause turned out on construction to be "an exception from liability for non-performance rather than an exception from obligation to perform".[93] Had it been the latter no liability for inducing any breach could have arisen.[94] In *OBG Ltd v Allan*,[95] while the House of Lords rejected Lord Denning MR's suggested extension of the *Lumley v Gye* tort to include interference short of breach, the importance of this construction of the exclusion clause in the reasoning of the majority of the Court of Appeal in the *Torquay Hotel* case appears to have been overlooked by both Lord Hoffmann and Lord Nicholls. There can be no liability, however, for procuring a person to refrain from doing something that he was at liberty not to do. Thus it cannot be a tort to induce a party to abstain from performance of a contract that is "not a synallagmatic contract at all but a mere unilateral or 'if' contract without any obligations on the part of [the claimant] as to its duration".[96] Similarly, it is not a tort to induce a person *to* perform his contractual obligations.[97]

---

91 See Lord Diplock in *Merkur Island Shipping Corp v Laughton* [1983] 2 A.C. 570 at 608; and per Neill LJ and per Stuart-Smith LJ in *Associated British Ports v TGWU* [1989] 1 W.L.R. 939 at 952 and 963 (reversed on other grounds, [1989] 1 W.L.R. 939 HL).

92 [1969] 2 Ch. 106; Lord Denning MR also thought that the defendants could not rely upon events of which they were themselves the cause, but the example which he gave involves the use of unlawful means: [1969] 2 Ch. 106 at 137–138. The general principle he enunciated was relied upon in *Falconer v ASLEF* [1986] I.R.L.R. 331 at 334, but was disapproved as erroneous in *Cheall v APEX* [1983] 2 A.C. 180 HL.

93 per Russell LJ [1969] 2 Ch. 106 at 143; see also, per Winn LJ at 146–147. This [illegible] accepted in *Associated British Ports v TGWU* [1989] 1 W.L.R. 939 at 952 (reversed on [illegible]unds, [1989] 1 W.L.R. 939, HL), per Neill LJ: "the primary obligation to make delive[illegible] the contract … remained even though the oil company was relieved from its second[illegible] to make monetary compensation for breach"; so too, Butler-Sloss LJ at 959 (no liab[illegible] absence of any cause of action" under the contract). See on this distinction *Photo* [illegible] *v Securicor Transport Ltd* [1980] A.C. 827 HL, which supports it (see especiall[illegible]ck at 849); on the construction of exemption clauses see Treitel, *Law of Contr*[illegible] (5) paras 7-014 to 7-033. See the clauses in *Merkur Island Shipping Corp v* [illegible] 2 A.C. 570, HL at 607; and in *Falconer v ASLEF* [1986] I.R.L.R. 331 at [illegible] ing that B.R. "may withdraw any service"; passenger recovers damages a[illegible] ere whether there was any obligation left to perform or merely a statemen[illegible] also the Unfair Contract Terms Act 1977 (a defendant could not benefit fro[illegible] hat statute; cf. Treitel, *The Law of Contract*, (2015), paras 7-051 to 7-094[illegible] Act 2015; and Treitel, *The Law of Contract*, (2015), paras 7-095 to 7-[illegible]

94 Sed quaere whether a [illegible] ho could not know the exact character of the clause, might be liable f[illegible] ch: consider Diplock LJ in *Emerald Construction v Lowthian* [196[illegible]

95 [2007] UK[illegible] *NUJ* [1984] 1 W.L.R. 427 at 434.

96 Lord D[illegible] *Government of Saskatchewan* (1979) 88 D.L.R. (3d) 609 SCC at [illegible] tted even if the obligations of one party are fully performed: *Rick*-

97 *Ce*[illegible] 988] Q.B. 40.

(ii) *Bare interference without breach*

23-20 The extension of the *Lumley v Gye* tort suggested by Lord Denning MR in *Torquay Hotel Co Ltd v Cousins*[98] and seemingly endorsed by the House of Lords in *Merkur Island Shipping Corp v Laughton*[99] to include "interference" with the performance of a contract which does not cause any breach, was rejected by the House of Lords in *OBG Ltd v Allan* where the leading speeches of both Lord Hoffmann and Lord Nicholls expressly confined the *Lumley v Gye* tort to inducing *breach* of a contract.[100] Any liability for interference with the performance of a contract short of causing its breach can only arise under the separate tort of intentionally causing loss by the use of unlawful means.[101] Once unlawful means and an intention to harm the claimant are present, consequential damage deliberately caused may be actionable; the intentional harm tort is available whether or not the non-performance of any contract involved a breach of it,[102] and even if the loss results simply from contractual performance becoming less valuable to the claimant.

(iii) *Breach of other obligations*

23-21 The civil liability bequeathed by *Lumley v Gye*, is not restricted to procuring breach of a contract. In *OBG Ltd v Allan* Lord Nicholls explained how the tort in *Lumley v Gye* developed as an emanation of a general principle of liability for procuring actionable wrongs.[103] But whilst this general principle clearly exists,[104] it is doubtful whether cases involving the specific tort of procuring breach should be treated as direct authorities as to its scope; it might be argued, for instance, that the rules that determine when a defendant will be liable for having procured another to commit a wrong that is actionable under the general law, such as battery or trespass to land, may not be the same as those that determine whether a defendant should be liable for having procured another to act in a way that is only wrongful because the other has made a contract that obliges him not to act in this way.[105] Nonetheless, there are several situations where the actionable wrongs procured by

98 [1969] 2 C
optional mod
99 [1983] 2 A.C. 137–138. See too Winn LJ at 147, suggesting that inducing a party to use an
[1987] I.C.R. 18 *rmance* which is allowed by the contract could be tortious.
100 [2007] UKHL 21; [607, per Lord Diplock. See also *News Group Newspapers Ltd v SOGAT*
2010 ONCA 557; (20 *ASLEF* [1986] I.R.L.R. 331.
contract was not sufficie at [44] and [189] respectively. In *Alleslev-Krofchak v Valcom Ltd*
101 See para.23-78 onwards. (4th) 193 (Ont CA) at [92] it was held that frustration of the
interference without breach
102 See *Dimbleby & Sons Ltd v Nu* the extension of the *Lumley v Gye* tort to cover bare
the "primary obligation" analysis of this work paras 25-31 to 25-35.
103 [2007] UKHL 21; [2008] 1 A.C. 1 at 427 HL. It has been suggested persuasively that
Erle J; *Allen v Flood* [1898] A.C. 1 at
104 *Fish & Fish Ltd v Sea Shepherd UK* [20 my: see Carty (1988) 104 L.Q.R. 257.
incur joint liability by procuring the comm *v Gye* (1853) 2 El. & Bl. 216 at 232, per
citing *CBS Songs Ltd v Amstrad Consume*
Templeman. A.C. 1229 at [19], "A defendant may
105 This distinction may explain the emphasis on kno ment, incitement or persuasion":
v Gye tort, on which see below para.23-29, and perh A.C. 1013, 1058, per Lord
tion, on which see below para.23-57.
e context of the *Lumley*
defence of justifica-

defendants seem very similar to breaches of contract, so the potential liability has been treated as associated with the tort in *Lumley v Gye*.

Statutory duties So, it is a tort knowingly and intentionally to induce a breach of statutory duty[106]—at least where the statutory provision affords a right to the claimant because the contravention is, on the true construction of the statute, actionable by him.[107] This tort of inducing a breach of statutory duty requires "a cause of action between obligor and obligee",[108] so the claimant must show "that on its true construction the statute which imposed the prohibition gave rise to a civil remedy".[109] Whilst the existence of the liability is clear, there are grounds for doubting whether this is truly an extension of the *Lumley v Gye* tort, as opposed to a situation where a procurer can be held jointly liable for the tort of breach of statutory duty.[110] The strongest arguments for the former view may be that a defendant can be liable for procuring a breach of a statutory duty that he could not himself have breached, as is the case with respect to procuring a breach of contract, and in some circumstances, particularly involving the public sector, a statute may impose obligations which are substantively similar to the sorts of obligations that are commonly created by contract in the private sector. 23-22

Equitable obligations The question whether those who procure others to break their equitable obligations commit an extended form of the *Lumley v Gye* tort is not straightforward. Two features combine to make matters complicated. First, in many circumstances equitable obligations run parallel to contractual obligations; indeed, frequently it will be possible to "imply" a contractual term corresponding to the equitable obligation. Secondly, however, equity has developed its own, separate, principles of accessory liability, particularly with respect to "knowing receipt" and "dishonest assistance". So far as these principles reflect a careful balancing of the competing interests, they provide a strong reason for not striving to develop an overlapping, but potentially inconsistent, regime based on the *Lumley v Gye* tort. 23-23

The equitable principles governing the position of third parties divide between "recipients" and "accessories"; they have been authoritatively established by Lord Nicholls in the *Royal Brunei Airlines* decision,[111] where a company holding money 23-24

---

[106] *F v Wirrall MBC* [1991] Fam. 69 at 114–115, per Stuart-Smith LJ. This may severely restrict, if not effectively remove, the right to take industrial action from workers who are subject to statutory duties since it will generally be tortious for a trade union to call on its members to take such action as an inducement to breach these duties: see *Ministry of Justice v Prison Officers' Association* [2017] EWHC 1839 (QB); [2018] I.C.R. 181.

[107] *Lonrho Ltd v Shell Petroleum (No.2)* [1982] A.C. 173 HL; *Meade v Haringey LBC* [1979] 1 W.L.R. 637 CA; *Cutler v Wandsworth Stadium Ltd* [1949] A.C. 398 HL; *Lonrho Plc v Fayed* [1992] 2 Q.B. 479 at 488, per Dillon LJ (affirmed on different grounds [1992] 1 A.C. 448 HL); *BBC Enterprises v Hi-Tech Xtravision* [1991] 2 A.C. 327 HL.

[108] per Butler-Sloss LJ in *Associated British Ports v TGWU* [1989] 1 W.L.R. 939 at 959; *Lonrho Ltd v Shell Petroleum (No.2)* [1982] A.C. 173 HL.

[109] per Dillon LJ in *Lonrho Plc v Fayed* [1990] 2 Q.B. 479 at 488 (affirmed on other grounds [1992] 1 A.C. 448 HL).

[110] In *OBG Ltd v Allan* [2007] UKHL 21; [2008] 1 A.C. 1 at [189], Lord Nicholls chose to "leave open the question of how far the *Lumley v Gye* principle applies equally to inducing a breach of other actionable obligations such as statutory duties or equitable or fiduciary obligations." P.S. Davies, *Accessory Liability* (2015), 184, treats the liability as an example of accessory liability for a tort and "based on general common law principles".

[111] *Royal Brunei Airlines v Tan* [1995] 2 A.C. 378 PC, reviewing the English and Commonwealth decisions and commentary, and settling the meaning of the leading authority *Barnes v Addy* (1874) L.R.

on trust for the airline used it, as the defendant its managing director arranged, to relieve its own cash-flow problems. He was held liable as an "accessory" to the breach of trust (and the company was liable too, because his knowledge was the company's knowledge). "Knowing assistance" arises when the third party had, as here, assisted and procured the breach of duty; he was liable to account if he had acted dishonestly, i.e. not as an honest person would in all the circumstances (not quite the test of "knowingly and intentionally" in the parallel tort liability). Without a finding of dishonesty, this limb of liability cannot extend to a party who participates by releasing confidential information (which may be the "trust property").[112] But if "knowing receipt" is alleged, i.e. that he had "knowingly received" trust property or assets resulting from it, the claimant must prove that he knew or ought to have known that it was traceable to the breach of duty.[113] The existence of the equitable principles explains why, in 1990, the Court of Appeal held that "procuring a breach of trust" was not tortious; such a tort was not needed given equity's traditional remedies against third parties.[114] Similarly, it appears that there is no general *tort* of "procuring a breach of fiduciary duty".[115]

23-25 There are cases, however, where a claimant has successfully relied on a tort that alleges the procuring of a breach of an equitable obligation. For example, an employer has been permitted to sue defendants who induced agents to break duties to account which could be regarded either as in the terms in their contracts[116]

---

9 Ch. App. 244 at 251–252; liability for "knowing receipt" by a third party requires proof that he had such knowledge that his receipt was traceable to a breach of trust or fiduciary duty as to make it unconscionable for him to retain the benefit and must be distinguished from liability for "assisting breach" of trust or fiduciary duty, which requires proof of dishonesty.

[112] *Satnam Investments v Dunlop Haywood Ltd* [1999] 3 All E.R. 652 CA (trade competitor did not participate in others' breach of fiduciary duty owed to S by publishing confidential information; nor did it act dishonestly, even when it took advantage of the commercial opportunity for itself). On "knowing receipt" see Lord Nicholls Ch.15 in Cornish, et al., *Restitution: Past, Present and Future* and Harpum, also in Cornish et al. Ch.16, pp.247–250.

[113] *Royal Brunei Airlines v Tan* [1995] 2 A.C. 378 PC; *El Ajou v Dollar Land Holdings* [1994] 2 All E.R. 685 at 700, Hoffmann J; *Bank of Credit and Commerce International SA v Ali (No.2)* [2001] UKHL 8; [2002] 1 A.C. 251; *Citadel General Assurance v Lloyd's Bank of Canada* (1998) 152 D.L.R. (4th) 411 (SCC: bank liable for knowing receipt, not procurement or assistance); *BCCI v Akindele* [2001] Ch. 437 CA; *Walker v Stones* [2001] Q.B. 902 CA; *Trustor AB v Smallbone (No.3)* [2001] 1 W.L.R. 1177; Nolan [2000] C.L.J. 447 (knowing receipt); *Casio Computer Co Ltd v Sayo* [2001] EWCA Civ 661 (knowing assistance).

[114] *Metall und Rohstoff AG v Donaldson, Lufkin & Jenrette Inc* [1990] 1 Q.B. 391 CA at 473–481 (overruled on other matters: *Lonrho v Fayed* [1992] A.C. 448).

[115] In *FM Capital Partners Ltd v Marino* [2018] EWHC 1768 (Comm) at [82], Cockerill J summarised the conditions for liability for dishonestly assisting a breach of fiduciary duty, noting that they were not seriously in issue in the case: this liability is potentially both broader than liability for procuring a breach of contract—in that it can cover acts that assist, induce or procure a breach—and narrower—in that the defendant must have acted dishonestly in providing the assistance. (An appeal on a different point was dismissed: [2020] EWCA Civ 245; [2020] 3 W.L.R. 109.) See also Loughlan (1989) 9 O.J.L.S. 260; also Carty (1999) 19 L.S. 489 at 510–514; cf. Sales [1990] C.L.J. 491. See also *Iranian Offshore Engineering & Construction Co v Dean Investment Holdings SA* [2019] EWHC 472 (Comm). In some circumstances it may be possible to formulate a claim as being one for the tort of conspiracy to cause harm by the use of unlawful means—those means being a breach of fiduciary duty—as a way of avoiding the need to prove dishonesty; but this approach will require proof that the conspirators shared a common intention of causing harm to the claimant.

[116] *Boulting v Association of Cinematograph and Allied Technicians* [1963] 2 Q.B. 606 (directors induced to break fiduciary—alternatively contractual—duties owed to company); *Associated British Ports v TGWU* [1989] 1 W.L.R. 939 CA (reversed on different grounds); *Bent's Brewery v Hogan* [1945] 2 All E.R. 570 (employee's duty of confidence in equity or as implied term in contract); see

or as equitable obligations, by relying on the latter, when the former was protected from action.[117] It must be noted that the contract of employment as such does not import a "fiduciary duty".[118] But the cases cited where an employer could rely on equitable obligations are essentially situations where the equitable and common law wrongs are recognised as having some "correspondence", as with the duty to account which is parallel to the duty of "loyalty and fidelity" in an employment contract, with equitable remedies as its "counterpart".[119]

Judgments In *Marex Financial Ltd v Sevilleja*[120] Knowles J held that there was a "good arguable case" that it was a tort to procure a company not to pay a judgment debt. There are also cases where a third party has been ordered not to behave in a way that would undermine an equitable remedy that has been granted: for example, after granting an injunction to prevent a breach of contract the court may extend the order against further parties who have knowledge of the breach where that is necessary to make the injunction effective.[121] But no tort will be committed by a defendant who intentionally procures another to take steps that will reduce the effectiveness of any remedy that a claimant may subsequently obtain. Thus, where A, a party to a covenant made with the claimant (B) prohibiting transfer of certain property, passes that property to a third party (C), the transferee C may be liable for knowingly procuring the breach and incur liability to a "secondary remedy", **23-26**

too, overlapping duties in whole or part, *Norbrook Ltd v King and Sands* [1984] I.R.L.R. 200 at 206; *Hivac v Park Royal Scientific Instruments Co* [1946] Ch. 169; compare *Faccenda Chicken v Fowler* [1987] Ch. 117 CA; Smith (1999) 115 L.Q.R. 245. On bribes see *Att Gen of Hong Kong v Reid* [1994] 1 A.C. 324 PC. On the wrong of inducing a breach of a common carrier's duties. *James v Commonwealth* (1988) 62 C.L.R. 364 at 370.

117 *Prudential Assurance v Lorenz* (1971) 11 K.I.R. 78 (agents in dispute with employer induced not to render an account of monies). See too *Dixon v Dixon* [1904] 1 Ch. 161 (right of receiver in equity to stop ex-partner encouraging employees to leave). The choice of terminology ("breach of contractual term" or "equitable wrong") may be very important where a trade union or workers have a statutory protection against such torts as inducing breach of contract in furtherance of a trade dispute: see TULRCA 1992 s.219.

118 *Nottingham University v Fishel* [2000] I.C.R. 1462: but the contract or part of it may create such a duty to act solely in the interests of the employer; the duty of "loyalty" does not extend that far: Elias J at 1490ff. (See Sims (2001) 30 I.L.J. 101). But see Buckley LJ in *Secretary of State for Employment v ASLEF (No.2)* [1972] I.C.R. 19 at 62. See too *Symbian Ltd v Christensen* [2001] I.R.L.R. 77 (duty of fidelity). For Commonwealth discussions of fiduciary duty and the contract of employment see R. McCallum and A. Stewart "Employee Loyalty in Australia" (1999) 20 Comp. Lab. Law and Policy Jo. 155, 160; and J. Oakley "Employee Duty of Loyalty—a Canadian Perspective" (1999) 20 Comp. Lab. Law and Policy Jo 185, 190–194.

119 *Coulthard v Disco Mix Club Ltd* [2000] 1 W.L.R. 707 (an incisive analysis by Jules Sher QC on limitation periods); followed in *CIA de Seguros Imperio v Heath REBX Ltd* [2001] 1 W.L.R. 112 CA (limitation in equitable claims); see too, analogies with tort on duties to account in *Nationwide Building Society v Various Solicitors (No.3)* [1999] P.N.L.R. 606.

120 *Marex Financial Ltd v Sevilleja* [2017] EWHC 918 (Comm); [2017] 4 W.L.R. 105. The separate question raised as to whether any part of the claim was precluded by the "No Reflective Loss Rule" was discussed further on appeal, and eventually decided in the claimant's favour by the Supreme Court: [2020] UKSC 31; [2020] 3 W.L.R. 255.

121 *Sefton v Tophams (No.2)* [1965] Ch. 1140 (possibly even if there is no tort by the third party, a matter not discussed in HL: [1967] A.C. 50); applying *Manchester Ship Canal v Manchester Racecourse* [1901] 2 Ch. 37 (treated as an ordinary inducing breach of contract case in *Pritchard v Briggs* [1980] Ch. 338 at 392–394, per Goff LJ); the extension against a further party may rest on the enforcement in rem of rights inherent in the contract: Kitto J, *Att Gen (South Wales) v Perpetual Trustee Ltd* (1952) 85 C.L.R. 237 at 297 (see [1955] A.C. 457 PC); Tettenborn [1982] C.L.J. 58, 81-85; Cohen-Grabelsky (1982) 45 M.L.R. 241, 264; and *RCA Corp v Pollard* [1983] Ch. 135.

such as an injunction ordering re-transfer of the property to B. But if C transfers the property to a fourth party (D) *before* any such remedy is sought by B, then D is not liable in tort, being a lawful transferee in the "onward transfer", even if all parties have full knowledge of the facts and even if it is assumed that D procured the transfer by C.[122]

23-27 **Breach of confidence**[123] Despite some doubts about its nature as a species of tortious liability,[124] breach of the duty not to disclose confidential information now appears to be a genus permitting several different types of actionable wrong.[125] Whatever the correct characterisation of breach of confidence as a cause of action, third parties who receive confidential information may be liable for failing to respect its confidential character. The circumstances in which it is received may be such that this liability is analogous to that for inducing breach of contract.

(b) Knowledge and intention

23-28 "An act of inducement is not by itself actionable."[126] The procurer must act with the requisite knowledge of the existence of the contract and intention to procure a breach.[127] It is not enough for a claimant to prove that a breach of contract was the natural consequence of the defendant's conduct[128]; he must show that the breach was an end in itself or the means to an end.[129]

---

[122] *Law Debenture Trust Corp v Ural Caspian Oil Corp* [1995] Ch. 152 CA, reversing Hoffmann J (even if C and D are companies in the same group and no attempt is made to "pierce the corporate veils", per Bingham MR at 165; but see the doubts of Saville LJ at 172–173, and Beldam LJ at 168–170; procurement was assumed in the Court of Appeal and conspiracy was not pleaded). Contrast liability for an act amounting to contempt because it interferes with the rights of a party who *has already obtained* an injunction: *Acrow (Automation) Ltd v Rex Chainbelt Inc* [1971] 1 W.L.R. 1676 CA, a form of "unlawful interference".

[123] See W. Cornish, D. Llewellyn and T. Aplin, *Intellectual Property: Patents, Copyright, Trade Marks and Allied Rights*, 9th edn (2019), Ch.8.

[124] See *Van Camp Chocolates v Aulsebrookes* [1984] 1 N.Z.L.R. 354, where Cooke J doubted whether it was a tort based on "unlawful means" even if it caused intended damage (which was not the case there); the claimant would have a cause of action under the equitable "principles relating to breach of confidence" at 360. See generally Ch.26.

[125] See Ch.26; Cornish, Llewellyn & Aplin, *Intellectual Property: Patents, Copyright, Trade Marks and Allied Rights*, 9th edn (2019), Ch.8; cf. Meagher, Gummow, Lehane, *Equity: Doctrines and Remedies*, 5th edn (2014), Ch.41.

[126] per Lord Devlin in *Rookes v Barnard* [1964] A.C. 1129 at 1212. Nor is an act facilitating breach without more: *Credit Lyonnais Bank Nederland NV v Export Credits Guarantee Department* [2000] 1 A.C. 486 HL at 496 and 500.

[127] *OBG Ltd v Allan* [2007] UKHL 21; [2008] 1 A.C. 1, per Lord Hoffmann at [39]–[41] and Lord Nicholls at [192]. cf. *Qantas Airways v Transport Workers Union of Australia* [2011] FCA 470; (2011) 280 A.L.R. 503 at [442]–[444] noting the view that although the requirement of knowledge was sometimes expressed as separate, it was in fact an aspect of intention; sufficient knowledge meant sufficient to ground an intention to interfere with contractual rights: *Allstate Life Insurance Co v Australia and New Zealand Banking Group Ltd* (1995) 130 A.L.R. 469. There may be some advantage in treating the two elements as distinct, since a defendant may avoid liability either by establishing that he did not know of the contractual terms concerned or by establishing that he did not intend his actions to bring about a breach of the terms by the party concerned.

[128] *Stott v Gamble* [1916] 2 K.B. 504; *Rickless v United Artists Corp* [1986] F.S.R. 507 at 518–524; affirmed [1988] Q.B. 40 CA; *DC Thomson & Co Ltd v Deakin* [1952] Ch. 646 at 663 and 698; *Central Canada Potash Co Ltd v Govt of Saskatchewan* (1979) 88 D.L.R. (3d) 609 SCC at 641–642.

[129] *OBG Ltd v Allan* [2007] UKHL 21; [2008] 1 A.C.1 at [42]–[43], per Lord Hoffmann; see too *Sar Petroleum Inc v Peace Hills Trust Co* 2010 NBCA 22; (2010) 318 D.L.R. (4th) 70 at [51]–[55] where

Knowledge The defendant must be shown to have had knowledge[130] of the existence of the contract that it is alleged that he has procured a party to break. In *JT Stratford & Sons Ltd v Lindley*,[131] Lord Pearce stated that it would be no answer to a claim for a defendant to assert that they "did not know with exactitude all the terms"; the relevant question was whether they had "sufficient knowledge of the terms to know that they were inducing a breach of contract." In some circumstances a court will be willing to infer that knowledge. For example, in the *JT Stratford* case,[132] the claimant's business was to let barges out on hire and to repair barges belonging to others, and the defendants, two trade union officials, had instructed the union's members, most of the watermen in London, to refuse to man or tow the claimant's barges and to refuse to man or tow any barge to the claimant's repair yard. In considering whether to grant an interlocutory injunction in respect of this embargo the House of Lords found that the defendants "knew that barges were always returned promptly on the completion of the job for which they had been hired, and it must have been obvious to them that this was done under contracts between the [claimant] and the barge hirers", which was sufficient in the circumstances to support an inference that they knew that their interference would involve the hirers breaking their contracts with the claimant.[133] The court accepted, however, that the evidence was less strong with regard to the defendants' knowledge of the terms of the contract to repair barges that existed between the claimant and Port of London Authority.[134] Similarly, in *Middlebrook Mushrooms Ltd v TGWU*[135] one of the reasons why a claim failed was because the claimant did not establish "even a shadowy case that the union know of the existence or terms" of the contracts between a mushroom supplier and supermarkets that it was alleged to be procuring the supermarkets to breach. 23-29

Where a defendant suspects that a contract might exist that binds the party he intends to induce to act in a way that might be a breach, has the means to confirm whether this is the case or not, and "deliberately disregards" this possibility, then he can be held to know of the contract.[136] But merely having the means to discover 23-30

it was said that the Supreme Court of Canada's decision in *Jones v Fabbi* [1973] S.C.R. 42 was to the same effect.

[130] Knowledge "is an essential ingredient of the cause of action", per Lord Russell of Killowen in *British Industrial Plastics Ltd v Ferguson* [1940] 1 All E.R. 479 at 483; *OBG Ltd v Allan* [2007] UKHL 21; [2008] 1 A.C. 1, per Lord Hoffmann at [39]–[41], and Lord Nicholls at [192].

[131] [1965] A.C. 269 at 332.

[132] [1965] A.C. 269.

[133] *Stratford & Son Ltd v Lindley* [1965] A.C. 269 at 323–324, per Lord Reid.

[134] *Stratford & Son Ltd v Lindley* [1965] A.C. 269 at 325, 328, 334, 338, and 342.

[135] per Neill LJ in *Middlebrook Mushrooms Ltd v TGWU* [1993] I.C.R. 612 at 621, and per Hoffmann LJ at 622 (there may be "common knowledge that the trade involves contracts that would be disrupted by the defendant's acts", citing *Union Traffic Ltd v TGWU* [1989] I.C.R. 98 at 104); *Wolff v Trinity Logistics USA Inc* [2018] EWCA Civ 2765; [2019] 1 W.L.R. 3997 at [46]–[52]; cf. *Century 21 Canada Limited Partnership v Rogers* 2011 BCSC 1196; (2011) 338 D.L.R. (4th) 32 at [348]–[350]: knowledge included situations where the defendant had the means of knowledge.

[136] *Emerald Construction Co Ltd v Lowthian* [1966] 1 W.L.R. 691 CA, per Lord Denning MR at 700–701; cited with approval in *OBG Ltd v Allan* [2007] UKHL 21; [2008] 1 A.C. 1, per Lord Hoffmann at [40]–[41], see also Lord Nicholls at [192]. See too *Diver v Loktronic Industries Ltd* [2012] NZCA 131; [2012] 2 N.Z.L.R. 388 where it was held that since this was an intentional tort, a subjective rather than an objective inquiry was required to establish whether the defendant had sufficient knowledge of the contract. Where actual knowledge was not proved, it had to be shown that the defendant had a suspicion of sufficient strength that a contract existed and made a deliberate choice not to make inquiries. It was not sufficient that the existence of a contract must have been obvious.

the existence of a contract is insufficient to establish knowledge. Thus in *Unique Pub Properties v Beer Barrels & Minerals (Wales) Ltd*[137] the claimants had sent to the defendants lists of 4,000 pubs which had contractually agreed to purchase some types of supplies exclusively from the claimants, but the Court of Appeal held that this was insufficient to establish that the defendants knew that one of the listed pubs was "tied" when they provided supplies to it without checking the list; the claimants had only met the publican's order after asking him if the pub was "tied" and receiving a negative answer, and their reason for not checking the list before accepting each order was the burden of doing so rather than a deliberate choice not to confirm something that they already suspected.[138] A defendant cannot be held to have known of a contract simply because he failed to draw the inferences that a reasonable person would have drawn; so-called "blind-eye knowledge" requires a "conscious decision not to inquire".[139] So, a defendant will avoid liability if he considered whether there was a contract and concluded that there was not, even if his honest mistake was "muddle-headed and illogical".[140] Good faith as such is no defence if knowledge and intention are proved.[141] But if the defendant is in "honest doubt" about the contract, he may escape liability provided that he did not make a "conscious decision not to inquire".[142]

23-31 In *Allen v Pollock*[143] the Court of Appeal considered a case where the defendants "knew that there was what appeared to be a contract; but were advised that the relevant term was probably unenforceable." Thus the case involved a conscious decision by the defendants to take a risk that they might be procuring a breach, having received equivocal advice, as opposed to a conscious decision not to inquire. Lewison LJ, with whose judgment the other two members of the Court agreed, stated that he found it "difficult to find a principled distinction between (a) a case in which the defendant does not know that there is a contract; (b) a case in which the defendant knows that there is a contract but does not know that the act that he induces will be a breach of contract; (c) a case where the defendant has an honest doubt about whether a contract as a whole is binding or enforceable; and (d) a case in which the defendant knows that there is a contract but believes that it is probable that the relevant term of the contract is unenforceable with the consequence

---

137 [2004] EWCA Civ 586; [2005] 1 All E.R. (Comm) 181.

138 [2004] EWCA Civ 586; [2005] 1 All E.R. (Comm) 181 at [31]–[38].

139 *OBG Ltd v Allan* [2007] UKHL 21; [2008] 1 A.C. 1, per Lord Hoffmann at [41].

140 *OBG Ltd v Allan* [2007] UKHL 21; [2008] 1 A.C. 1, per Lord Nicholls at [202], describing the mistake made by the defendant in *British Industrial Plastics Ltd v Ferguson* [1940] 1 All E.R. 479 HL. The same authority was relied on by Lord Hoffmann, at [41], who also highlighted, at [37], MacKinnon LJ's comment that the trial judge had "vindicated the honesty of Ferguson at the expense of his intelligence": [1938] 4 All E.R. 504 CA, at 513. MacKinnon LJ refused to overturn the trial judge's finding of fact, but noted: "A priori, I should find it difficult to imagine that anyone could be so stupid."

141 *Pritchard v Briggs* [1980] Ch. 338 at 410–415, per Goff LJ, at 424, per Stephenson LJ; *Greig v Insole* [1978] 1 W.L.R. 302 at 337–338 and 343–344. On knowledge in corporate defendants see, per Hoffmann J in *Law Debenture Trust Corp v Ural Caspian Oil Corp Ltd* [1993] 1 W.L.R. 138 at 148 (reversed on other grounds: [1995] 2 Ch. 152 CA). *Meridian Global Funds Management Asia Ltd v Securities Commrs* [1995] 2 A.C. 500 PC; Grantham (1996) 59 M.L.R. 732; on how a corporation can forget: Wedderburn (1984) 47 M.L.R. 345.

142 *OBG Ltd v Allan* [2007] UKHL 21; [2008] 1 A.C. 1 per Lord Hoffmann at [40]–[41]. See also *Sealed Air Australia Pty Ltd v Aus-Lid Enterprises Pty Ltd* [2020] FCA 29; [2020] 375 A.L.R. 324 per Kenny J at [217].

143 *Allen v Pollock* [2020] EWCA Civ 258; [2020] Q.B. 781 at [26].

that the act he proposes to procure will not amount to a breach."[144] Since (a) and (b) clearly fall outside the tort, and there is also authority suggesting that (c) does, the lack of a "principled distinction" supported his conclusion that (d) should also be insufficient for liability; a conclusion that he found to be in accordance with the policy that "people should be able to act on legal advice, responsibly sought, even if the advice turns out to be wrong".[145] The Court left open the question whether a defendant could be liable for procuring a breach if it pressed ahead having received only advice that "it is arguable that no breach will be committed".[146]

Before *OBG Ltd v Allan*[147] renovated the structure of the economic torts, and re-emphasised the importance of establishing that the defendant both knew of the contract and intended to procure its breach, there were cases where courts appeared to infer the requisite knowledge from a thin evidential foundation. So in *Associated Newspapers Group Ltd v Wade*, Lawton LJ said that an experienced trade union official in a printing union "must know" that advertisements are placed well in advance and that industrial action to interfere with them will interfere with contractual relations.[148] Similarly, in *Merkur Island Shipping v Laughton*, officials of a union were "deemed to have known of the almost certain existence of contracts of carriage" for a flag of convenience ship that was blacked by port workers as part of the union's efforts to improve the employment conditions of the crew.[149] It may be significant to note, however, that the cases where defendants were "deemed" to have known about contractual arrangements were interlocutory appeals; indeed in *Associated Newspapers Group Ltd v Wade* Lawton LJ expressly accepted that: "At the trial the defendant may be able to raise a doubt about his knowledge of relevant contractual arrangements", though he thought this unlikely.[150] Moreover, the cases involved the question of the defendants' knowledge of contracts that they were alleged to be indirectly interfering with, and subsequent to *OBG Ltd v Allan* these situations will fall outside the scope of the *Lumley v Gye* tort altogether. **23-32**

Intention Knowledge and intention are, of course, intimately connected; but their problems are not coterminous. Thus, affirmative proof that the defendants did not intend to induce any breach can rescue them even if all other constituents of liability are present.[151] In *OBG Ltd v Allan* the House of Lords re-emphasised that: "In the *Lumley v Gye* tort there must be an intention to procure a breach of **23-33**

144 *Allen v Pollock* [2020] EWCA Civ 258; [2020] Q.B. 781 at [33].

145 *Allen v Pollock* [2020] EWCA Civ 258; [2020] Q.B. 781 at [34]. This policy requires (d) to be outside tortious liability because, as Lewison LJ continued: "everyone knows, lawyers rarely give unequivocal advice; and even if they do the client must appreciate that there is always a risk (or in [counsel for the claimant's] word, 'a chance') that the advice will turn out to be wrong."

146 *Allen v Pollock* [2020] EWCA Civ 258; [2020] Q.B. 781 at [36].

147 [2007] UKHL 21; [2008] 1 A.C. 1.

148 *Associated Newspapers Group v Wade* [1979] I.C.R. 664 at 699, per Lawton LJ.

149 *Merkur Island Shipping Corp v Laughton* [1983] 2 A.C. 570 at 608–609, per Lord Diplock adopting Donaldson MR at 591; (overruled on other grounds in *OBG Ltd v Allan* [2007] UKHL 21; [2008] 1 A.C. 1); cf. Wedderburn (1983) 46 M.L.R. 632.

150 *Associated Newspapers Group v Wade* [1979] I.C.R. 664 at 699, per Lawton LJ. In interlocutory proceedings where the claimant needs to show no more than an arguable case, proof of knowledge is rarely difficult: see *Torquay Hotel Co Ltd v Cousins* [1969] 2 Ch. 106 at 138 and 146; *Solihull MBC v NUT* [1985] I.R.L.R. 211. But cf. *Middlebrook Mushrooms Ltd v TGWU* [1993] I.C.R. 612 CA; and *Timeplan Education Group Ltd v NUT* [1997] I.R.L.R. 457 CA.

151 *White v Riley* [1921] 1 Ch. 1 CA; *Timeplan Education Group Ltd v NUT* [1997] I.R.L.R. 457 CA.

contract."[152] Lord Hoffmann explained the meaning of "intention" in this context in terms of "ends, means and consequences".[153] Thus, a person will be held to have intended to procure a breach of contract if procuring a breach of contract was the end that he was seeking to achieve when he acted. Further, he will be held to have intended to procure a breach of contract if that was the means that he had chosen to achieve some further end, such as to make a gain for himself, and this conclusion cannot be negated by establishing that he would have preferred a different means to have been available; as Lord Hoffmann noted, "Mr Gye would very likely have preferred to be able to obtain Miss Wagner's services without her having to break her contract."[154] By contrast, a defendant will not be held to have intended to procure a breach of contract if such a breach was "neither an end in itself nor a means to an end, but merely a foreseeable consequence" of the defendant's actions.[155] Thus, if a defendant breaks a contract with a third party, and knows that this will very probably lead to the third party breaking a contract with a claimant, this will not be sufficient to establish that the defendant intended to procure the third party's breach.[156] Importantly, however, a defendant cannot describe an occurrence as "merely a foreseeable consequence" if it was actually an essential part of what he intended to achieve, what Lord Hoffmann refers to as "simply the other side of the same coin".[157] Thus, if the defendant in *Lumley v Gye* had known that Miss Wagner had made a contract with the claimant to sing exclusively in the claimant's theatre then he could not have established that his only intention was to persuade her to sing in his theatre and her breach of her exclusive-performance contract with the claimant a mere foreseeable consequence; in the circumstances, the defendant would be held to have intended to procure Miss Wagner to break her contract to sing exclusively at the claimant's theatre, since this would be the obverse of achieving his goal of having her sing at his theatre.

23-34 If a defendant is shown to have intended to procure a breach, it is no defence for them to show that they were not malicious or spiteful, or that their motive was not to cause damage to the claimant.[158] In this tort the requisite knowledge and inten-

---

152 [2007] UKHL 21; [2008] 1 A.C. 1 at [62], per Lord Hoffmann.

153 [2007] UKHL 21; [2008] 1 A.C. 1 at [42], per Lord Hoffmann.

154 [2007] UKHL 21; [2008] 1 A.C. 1 at [42], per Lord Hoffmann. The reference is to the foundational case of *Lumley v Gye*.

155 [2007] UKHL 21; [2008] 1 A.C. 1 at [43], per Lord Hoffmann.

156 Lord Hoffmann illustrated this proposition by referring to the facts of *Millar v Bassey* [1994] E.M.L.R. 44 CA, which involved Dame Shirley Bassey, the singer, breaking a contract with Dreamspace, a record production company, to take part in making an album, which led to Dreamspace breaking the contracts that it had made with a producer and musicians. Lord Hoffmann expressed the opinion that the majority of the Court of Appeal was "wrong" to have allowed claims to proceed by the musicians against Miss Bassey for procuring Dreamspace to break its contracts with them, since although those breaches were a foreseeable consequence of her action "those breaches of contract were neither an end desired by Miss Bassey nor a means of achieving that end": [2007] UKHL 21; [2008] 1 A.C. 1 at [43]. See also at [264], per Lord Walker. Lord Nicholls, at [166], similarly criticises the Court of Appeal's conclusions as to intention in *Millar v Bassey*, but does so in the context of a discussion of whether Miss Bassey intended to injure the claimants, rather than whether she intended to procure Dreamspace to break its contracts with them.

157 [2007] UKHL 21; [2008] 1 A.C. 1 at [134], per Lord Hoffmann, and see also [167], per Lord Nicholls. Both Lord Hoffmann and Lord Nicholls introduce this element of what a defendant will be held to have intended in the context of considering whether a defendant should be held to have intended to cause a loss that is the "obverse side" of the gain that he undoubtedly intended to make, but there is no reason to think that it is not a general part of their understanding of intention.

158 *South Wales Miners' Federation v Glamorgan Coal Co* [1905] A.C. 239; *Pritchard v Briggs* [1980]

tion to procure a breach do not require a "desire to injure".[159] A clear distinction has now been made between the nature of the defendant's intention that has to be proved in order to establish liability for inducing breach of contract and that required for liability under the tort of intentionally causing loss by unlawful means. In the latter "the defendant must have intended to cause damage to the claimant ... under *Lumley v Gye* on the other hand, an intention to cause a breach of contract is both necessary and sufficient".[160]

Recklessness Before *OBG Ltd v Allan*,[161] it was strongly arguable that a defendant could be held liable for having procured a breach of contract even if he was only reckless as to whether his actions would procure a breach.[162] In *Emerald Construction Co Ltd v Lowthian*,[163] officials of a bricklayers' trade union called upon building contractors to end their system of "labour only" subcontracts whereby the claimant firm supplied workers to them. The defendant officials knew of the contracts, but learned only during the proceedings of their terms, one of which gave the building contractors an option to cancel. The Court of Appeal upheld the claim for an interlocutory injunction, finding that the requirements of both knowledge and intention were satisfied. As to knowledge Lord Denning MR said: 23-35

> "Even if they did not know of the actual terms of the contract, but had the means of knowledge—which they deliberately disregarded—that would be enough. Like the man who turns a blind eye."[164]

To this point, his analysis is consistent with the account of "blind-eye knowledge" presented above, and in *OBG Ltd v Allan*,[165] Lord Hoffmann treated the case as authority on this point. Lord Denning MR continued, however:

Ch. 338 at 411–415 and 424.

159 *Hill v First National Finance Corp* [1989] 1 W.L.R. 225 at 233–234, per Stuart-Smith LJ; *DC Thomson & Co Ltd v Deakin* [1952] Ch. 646 at 696–697, per Jenkins LJ. See too *Walsh v Nicholls* (2004) 241 D.L.R. (4th) 643 (NBCA) at [58]; cf. *Meretz Investments NV v ACP Ltd* [2007] EWCA Civ 1303; [2008] Ch. 244 at [126]–[127], per Arden LJ: while "the mere fact that by injuring a third party a person intends to further his own business interests does not mean that he does not have the intent to injure that party", that proposition did not apply "where the causative act is something which the party believes he has a contractual right to do as against the relevant person, notwithstanding that the act would coincidentally cause that person detriment or loss". Thus no intention to induce breach of a leaseback option was established where the defendants believed on the basis of legal advice that the exercise of a power of sale would overreach this right. cf. *Century 21 Canada Limited Partnership v Rogers Communications Inc* 2011 BCSC 1196; (2011) 338 D.L.R. (4th) 32 at [352] where it was said that it was necessary to prove that the defendant acted with the *desire to cause breach of contrac*t with the substantial certainty that breach of contract would result from the defendant's conduct or indifference to whether the contract would be breached. cf. *TSG Franchise Management Pty Ltd v Cigarette & Gift Warehouse (Franchising) Pty Ltd (No.2)* [2016] FCA 674; (2017) 340 A.L.R. 230 at [58]; citing *Sanders v Snell* [1998] HCA 64; (1998) 196 C.L.R. 329: something more than an uncommunicated desire that the contract be breached had to be shown.

160 *OBG Ltd v Allan* [2007] UKHL 21; [2008] 1 A.C. 1 at [8], per Lord Hoffmann. In *Stocznia Gdanska SA v Latvia Shipping Co (No.3)* [2002] EWCA Civ 889; [2002] 2 All E.R. (Comm) 768 proof of intention was established where the primary objective of a decision not to fund the contract between a subsidiary company and the claimant was to prevent performance of the contract.

161 [2007] UKHL 21; [2008] 1 A.C. 1.

162 The 22nd edition of this work stated that "recklessness may also import intention under the modern authorities", para.24-18.

163 [1966] 1 W.L.R. 691.

164 [1966] 1 W.L.R. 691 at 700.

165 [2007] UKHL 21; [2008] 1 A.C. 1 at [41].

> "So here, if the officers deliberately sought to get this contract terminated, heedless of its terms, regardless whether it was terminated by breach or not, they would do wrong. For it is unlawful for a third person to procure a breach of contract knowingly, or recklessly, indifferent whether it is a breach or not."[166]

This part of Lord Denning MR's reasoning, with its reference to recklessness and indifference, was also quoted by Lord Hoffmann, and referred to by him without disapproval, though not in the course of his primary discussion of "intention to procure a breach of contract".[167] In *Emerald Construction* Diplock LJ expressed his opinion in different terms:

> "The element of intent needed to constitute the tort of unlawful procurement of a breach of contract is, in my view, sufficiently established if it be proved that the defendants intended the party procured to bring the contract to an end by breach of it if there were no way of bringing it to an end lawfully."[168]

Diplock LJ's opinion is consistent with the proposition that if a defendant intends to achieve a particular end by means of procuring a third party to act in a particular way, knows that what he is procuring the third party to do *may* be a breach of contract, and intends the third party to act in the same way regardless, then the defendant can be held to have intended to procure a breach. One way of explaining this would be to say that the defendant has manifested a conditional intention to procure a breach: the defendant intends to procure the third party's breach of contract so far as that is necessary, and in the circumstances it has proved to be necessary. Indeed this probably aligns with Lord Denning MR's approach, where the defendants could be held liable because their goal was to get the contract terminated and they were recklessly indifferent—did not care—as to whether this would involve a breach. Neither approach, however, should be treated as making a defendant liable for bringing about a breach that was a foreseen consequence of their project simply because they were indifferent to the possibility of that consequence. Moreover, both approaches must be read alongside the conclusion of the Court of Appeal in *Allen v Pollock* that a defendant will not be liable if he has

---

166 [1966] 1 W.L.R. 691 at 700–701. cf. *Torquay Hotel Co Ltd v Cousins* [1969] 2 Ch. 106, per Winn LJ at 146: "without regard to whether and without investigating whether" a contract existed. See too *Solihull MBC v NUT* [1985] I.R.L.R. 211 at 214 where Warner J held that since there was a serious issue to be tried as to whether the non-teaching activities which the defendant union called on its members to boycott were contractual, a sufficient case had been made out for an interlocutory (interim) injunction. "Reckless indifference or wilful blindness could amount to knowledge": *TSG Franchise Management Pty Ltd v Cigarette & Gift Warehouse (Franchising) Pty Ltd (No.2)* [2016] FCA 674; (2017) 340 A.L.R. 230 at [59]. cf. where there was no evidence of the existence or terms of the contracts of which the defendants were alleged to have induced breach: *Middlebrook Mushrooms Ltd v TGWU* [1993] I.C.R. 612 at 621, per Neill LJ allowing the defendants' appeal against an interlocutory injunction granted ex parte.

167 [2007] UKHL 21; [2008] 1 A.C. 1, quoted at [40] and referred to at [69]–[70]. Lord Hoffmann's main discussion of "intention to procure a breach of contract" is at [42]–[43].

168 [1966] 1 W.L.R. 691 at 703, per Diplock LJ. In *Mainstream Properties Ltd v Young* [2005] EWCA Civ 861; [2005] I.R.L.R. 964, Arden LJ took the view that only Lord Denning clearly thought that recklessness would suffice, with Diplock LJ treating it as a factor from which the court could infer intention and Russell LJ deciding the case on other grounds. An appeal against this decision was one of the three cases dealt with by the House of Lords in *OBG Ltd v Allan* [2007] UKHL 21; [2008] 1 A.C. 1; the appeal was dismissed. cf. the view of Jenkins LJ in *DC Thomson & Co Ltd v Deakin* [1952] Ch. 646 at 698, to the effect that it is not actionable "to advocate objects which can be achieved by lawful means because they can also be achieved by unlawful means".

received legal advice that his actions will probably not involve the procuring of a breach of contract.[169] There is an important distinction between pushing ahead with knowledge of the risk that you might be procuring a breach of contract and seeking to achieve a particular goal recklessly indifferent as to whether this will require a breach of contract: a useful rule of thumb in distinguishing the two states of mind is to ask "would the defendant have acted differently *if* it had become clear to him that he was definitely procuring a breach?"

(c) The wrongful procurement

One of the main effects of the House of Lords' decision in *OBG Ltd v Allan* was to reduce the range of acts which can amount to wrongful procurement falling within the *Lumley v Gye* tort by excluding those which more properly fall within the tort of intentionally causing loss by unlawful means as there defined in the speeches of Lords Hoffmann and Nicholls.[170] In *DC Thomson & Co Ltd v Deakin*,[171] it had been established that there were three distinct forms of wrongful interference which could give rise to liability for procuring breach of contract: (1) direct inducement; (2) other direct intervention; and (3) indirect procurement. The form of behaviour which most obviously falls within the bounds of "direct inducement" is a defendant, by himself or his agent, *persuading* a party to a contract to break that contract. This remains the core instance of behaviour that can give rise to liability under the *Lumley v Gye* tort. The category of "indirect procurement", by contrast, was developed to deal with situations where a defendant brought about a breach of contract, or at least non-performance of a primary contractual obligation, by using unlawful means to deny a party to the contract the means necessary to perform it, such as by persuading the party's employees to break their contracts of employment and to refuse to undertake the tasks necessary for their employer to perform a contract with a claimant. Thus, in *DC Thomson & Co Ltd v Deakin* one of the allegations was that the defendant had induced employees of B to break their contracts of employment, and to refuse to drive delivery-lorries to take paper to DC Thomson & Co Ltd, thereby bringing about a breach by B of its contract with DC Thomson & Co Ltd; had these facts been established then they would have amounted to an instance of indirect procurement, since the defendant would not have persuaded B to break its contract, instead he would have indirectly *prevented* B from performing, by denying it the workforce necessary to perform the contract. Similarly, the defendant would have been treated as having *indirectly* procured a breach (or at least non-performance) if he had *destroyed* the paper that B was going to deliver, or *immobilised* the lorries that B needed in order to deliver it. These indirect means of bringing about a breach (or non-performance) now clearly fall 23-36

---

169 *Allen v Pollock* [2020] EWCA Civ 258; [2020] Q.B. 781.

170 *OBG Ltd v Allan* [2007] UKHL 21; [2008] 1 A.C. 1 at [39]–[44] and [169]–[183] respectively. In *Meretz Investments NV v ACP Ltd* [2007] EWCA Civ 1303; [2008] Ch. 244 at [129]–[140] Arden LJ applied the analyses of inducement by Lords Hoffmann and Nicholls, which were not seen to be different and seen to have the agreement of the other Law Lords in *OBG Ltd v Allan*, in deciding that there was no inducement of ACP's failure to perform a contractual leaseback option where it was disabled from doing so by the exercise of a power of sale by its parent company, First Penthouse; nor was there any tortious liability for preventing performance of the leaseback option since the means used to prevent performance, First Penthouse's exercise of its power of sale, were not "independently unlawful".

171 [1952] Ch. 646 at 681–682, per Lord Evershed MR; and at 694–697, per Jenkins LJ.

outside the scope of the *Lumley v Gye* tort, and a party standing in a position similar to that of DC Thomson & Co Ltd will only be able to hold a defendant liable for such indirect interference if it can establish that it has committed the tort of intentionally causing loss by the use of unlawful means.

23-37 Between these core instances of *persuading* a party to break a contract and indirectly *preventing* performance of a contract there are a variety of forms of behaviour which can directly play a role in causing a breach of contract. Before *OBG Ltd v Allan*, it seemed as if the law attached great significance to whether the defendant's acts interfered with the contract directly or indirectly; now, however, this distinction has been rejected as "unsatisfactory".[172] Behaviour that prevents performance of a contract should now be regarded as only potentially falling within the unlawful means tort, and not within the *Lumley v Gye* tort, even if it appears to have operated "directly".[173] Thus such behaviour will only amount to an economic tort if it involves the use of unlawful means to intentionally cause loss. There may, however, be some forms of behaviour that assist or facilitate a breach, as opposed to preventing performance, and which are consequently better evaluated as possible forms of direct inducement that it may be appropriate to treat as sufficient to establish liability for the *Lumley v Gye* tort.

(i) *Direct inducement*

23-38 The most obvious form of direct inducement is active persuasion or enticement of the contracting party himself.[174] In such a situation, it matters not whether it was the inducer or the inducee who spoke the first word.[175] In addition to persuasion, procurement or inducement of the contract breaker, dealings inconsistent with the contract have also been recognised as a form of direct inducement.[176] It is not enough for actions of the defendant to have an "influence" on the mind of someone to whom they were not directed; the persuasion has to be directed at one of the par-

---

172 *OBG Ltd v Allan* [2007] UKHL 21; [2008] 1 A.C. 1 at [38], per Lord Hoffmann. See also at [181]–[188], per Lord Nicholls.

173 This is clearly indicated in the criticism of the reasoning of Lord Hewart LCJ in *GWK Ltd v Dunlop Rubber Co Ltd* (1926) 42 T.L.R. 376 by both Lord Hoffmann and Lord Nicholls in *OBG Ltd v Allan* [2007] UKHL 21; [2008] 1 A.C. 1 at [22]–[25] and [176]–[178] respectively.

174 As in *Lumley v Gye* (1853) 2 El. & Bl. 216 itself.

175 *British Motor Trade Association v Salvadori* [1949] Ch. 556; *Sefton v Tophams Ltd* [1964] 1 W.L.R. 1408, per Stamp J; [1965] Ch. 1140, per Sellers and Harman LJJ (reversed on other grounds [1967] A.C. 50); *Wolff v Trinity Logistics USA Inc* [2018] EWCA Civ 2765; [2019] 1 W.L.R. 3997 at [43].

176 See Neill LJ in *Middlebrook Mushrooms Ltd v TGWU* [1993] I.C.R. 612 at 618-619; in this passage, however, he adopted the four categories of direct interference identified by Jenkins LJ in *DC Thomson & Co Ltd v Deakin* [1952] Ch. 646 at 694–695; and in *OBG Ltd v Allan* [2007] UKHL 21; [2008] 1 A.C. 1 the House of Lords decided that the third and fourth categories, direct intervention against the contract or a party to it, and imposition of physical restraint on a party, should now be considered as forms of the intentional harm tort; see paras 23-42 and 23-78 onwards. See also Lord Hodge in *Global Resources Group Ltd v Mackay* [2008] CSOH 148; 2009 S.L.T. 104 at [13]: "A must induce B to break his contract with C by persuading, encouraging or assisting him to do so … the tort or delict … can also be committed where A has dealings with B which A knows are inconsistent with the contract between B and C." In *Lictor Anstalt v Mir Steel UK Ltd* [2011] EWHC 3310 (Ch); [2012] 1 All E.R. (Comm) 592 at [47]–[53] David Richards J rejected a submission that inducement required "actual persuasion and inducement" and held that an agreement to buy the parts used in construction of a "hot strip mill", which the seller had acquired from the claimant on terms that they remained the property of the supplier, for a very considerable price, was sufficient for there to be an arguable case of inducing breach of contract (appeal on other grounds dismissed [2012] EWCA Civ 1397; [2013] 2 All E.R. (Comm) 54).

ties to the contract. Thus where leaflets are distributed to the public urging them not to buy the produce of suppliers who had dismissed employees, it was held that there had been no direct interference with any contracts made by the suppliers with the nearby supermarkets.[177] A direct communication from one person to another, for example in the form of an ultimatum[178] or instructions[179] will of course suffice. This is still the case where the communication is made through the instrumentality or agency of a third person. Thus where a federation of retailers sent out communications to its members asking them to transmit them to wholesalers, the federation was held to have effected direct persuasion of the wholesalers on the basis that the members were used as a kind of post box.[180] What is needed is a persuasive communication; the mere presence of a silent persuader (a picket) has been held to be sufficient.[181]

Establishing whether or not a case is one of direct inducement can give rise to particular difficulties first where the alleged inducer is an employee of the contracting party which is in breach, and secondly where either the alleged inducer or the contracting party which is the object of the inducement is a company or some other corporate body. An employee acting bona fide and within the scope of his authority is not liable for procuring a breach of contract made between his employer and a third party for he is treated as the alter ego of his employer.[182] A director or of- **23-39**

177 *Middlebrook Mushrooms Ltd v TGWU* [1993] I.C.R. 612 CA.

178 As in *Emerald Construction Co Ltd v Lowthian* [1966] 1 W.L.R. 691.

179 As in *Dimbleby and Sons Ltd v NUJ* [1984] 1 W.L.R. 427 HL; cf. *Express Newspapers Ltd v Keys* [1980] I.R.L.R. 247 at 249, per Griffiths J, an "incitement".

180 *Daily Mirror Newspapers Ltd v Gardner* [1968] 2 Q.B. 762. Lord Denning MR later revised the view he expressed in that case, [1968] 2 Q.B. 762 at 781, that there was no difference between direct and indirect interference: see *Torquay Hotel Co Ltd v Cousins* [1969] 2 Ch. 106 at 138–139 where he said that the *Daily Mirror* case was one of direct interference.

181 *Union Traffic Ltd v TGWU* [1989] I.C.R. 98 CA at 106, per Bingham LJ (implicit persuasion). cf. *Lomar Global Risks Ltd v West* [2010] EWHC 2878; [2011] I.R.L.R. 138 at [220] per Hickinbottom J: "As a matter of law I am sure that even silence in certain circumstances can be persuasive in encouraging breach of contract and can intend to do so." Hickinbottom J's opinion on this point was followed and applied in *Premier Model Management Ltd v Bruce* [2012] EWHC 3509 (QB), where Simon Crookenden QC (sitting as a deputy High Court judge) held that a defendant intentionally encouraged a breach of contract by his receipt, even if silent, of confidential information that his partner breached a contract by sending.

182 *Said v Butt* [1920] 3 K.B. 497; see, per Evershed MR in *DC Thomson & Co Ltd v Deakin* [1952] Ch. 646 at 680–681. Contrary to the usual doctrine, any such servant of the company here counts as its alter ego: see [1960] C.L.J. 14 at 16. But if the servant or agent goes outside his authority, he can personally be an inducer, per Evershed MR in *DC Thomson & Co Ltd v Deakin*. See too *ADGA Systems International Ltd v Valcom Ltd* (1999) 168 D.L.R. (4th) 351 (Ont. CA); *Root Quality Pty Ltd v Root Control Technologies Pty Ltd* (2000) 177 A.L.R. 231 Fed. Ct of Aus; *Ontario Ltd v Magna International Inc* (2001) 200 D.L.R. (4th) 521 (Ont. CA); *Kay Aviation b.v. v Rofe* (2002) 202 D.L.R. (4th) 683 (Pr. Ed. Is. CA); *Walsh v Nicholls* (2004) 241 D.L.R. (4th) 643 (NBCA) at [66]. In *XY Inc v International Newtech Development Inc* 2013 BCCA 352; (2013) 366 D.L.R. (4th) 443, [58]–[66] it was emphasised that the "*Said v Butt* exception only applied where the individuals were performing their functions as corporate officers". The Singapore Court of Appeal carried out a detailed analysis of the rationale and limits of the *Said v Butt* exception in *PT Sandipala Arthaputra v ST Microelectronics Asia Pacific Pte Ltd* [2018] SGCA 17; [2018] 1 S.L.R. 818. This was cited and relied on by Lane J in *Antuzis v DJ Houghton Catching Services Ltd* [2019] EWHC 843 (QB); [2019] Bus. L.R. 1532, where he held that the question whether an employee or director had acted bona fide (so as to avoid liability for having induced a company to breach a contract) was one directed at the employee's or director's conduct and intention in relation to his duties towards the company—not towards the claimant (at [114]). On the facts, he concluded that two defendants, respectively the sole director of a company and its company secretary, were liable for having induced

ficer of the company may be personally liable if he has assumed a clear personal responsibility for what has been done by or for the company[183] or is manifestly a separate joint participant with the company.[184] A company is not liable vicariously for acts done by an officer or agent even where they are done in the course of his employment where those acts, though done to harm the claimant, lack one of the constituent elements of the tort.[185] In *Credit Lyonnais Bank Nederland v Export Credit Guarantee Department* the House of Lords rejected the argument, founded on Erle J's judgment in *Lumley v Gye* that procuring violation of a legal right is a tort, that intention to harm could make up for the missing ingredient.[186] Where directors of a company in a board meeting cause a breach of contract by the company they normally cannot be sued in tort for procuring the breach,[187] but the directors could be held liable for a conspiracy before the meeting to induce the board as a whole to break the contract.[188] Moreover, if a director has ordered or procured the breach by the company he may be liable in tort given that he possesses the requisite knowledge and intention.[189] On the other hand, a company can be directly induced into a breach only by an approach made to a director, or like officer, who has authority to act for the company,[190] and who is for this purpose to be treated as its alter

---

the company's breach of its contracts with the claimants, who were employed by the company to catch chickens.

183 *Williams v Natural Life Health Foods* [1998] 1 W.L.R. 830 HL at 835–837, per Lord Steyn; Grantham and Rickett (1999) 62 M.L.R.133; S. Griffin (1999) 115 L.Q.R. 36; this approach supports the corporate "veil" and also limited liability: J. Payne [1999] C.L.J. 456.

184 *AGDA Systems v Valcom Ltd* (1999) 168 D.L.R. (4th) 521 (Ont. CA) at 356–365, per Carthy JA. The company is not usually the director's undisclosed principal: *Yukong Line Ltd v Rendsberg Investments Corp* [1998] 1 W.L.R. 249; cf. *Nomart Management v West Hill Redevelopment Co* (1998) 155 D.L.R. (4th) 627 (Ont CA).

185 *Credit Lyonnais Bank Nederland v Export Credit Guarantee Department* [2000] 1 A.C. 486 at 495 "to make the employer responsible for that tort the conduct necessary to establish the employer's liability must have occurred in the course of the employment", per Lord Woolf MR.

186 *Credit Lyonnais Bank Nederland v Export Credit Guarantee Department* [2000] 1 A.C. 486 at 496–497. This proposition may be thought to cast doubt on the Court of Appeal decision in *Associated British Ports v TGWU* [1989] 1 W.L.R. 939 (reversed on other grounds, [1989] 1 W.L.R. 939).

187 *Scammell & Nephew Ltd v Hurley* [1929] 1 K.B. 419; *Imperial Oil Ltd v CG Holdings* (1990) 62 D.L.R. (4th) 261 (Nfd CA). In *Ontario Store Fixtures v Mmmuffins* (1989) 70 O.R. (2d) 42 it was said that there had to be separate identities of interest in this situation to give rise to a claim for inducing breach of contract; see too *1044807 Alberta Ltd v Brae Centre Ltd* 2008 ABCA 397; (2008) 302 D.L.R. (4th) 252 at [21]–[25] where it was said that there was general agreement that a director acting bona fide within the scope of his authority and in the best interests of the company would not be personally liable in tort for inducing breach of contract by the company; something more had to be proved to establish liability as for example where directors acted in their own interests in making payments from the company for the purpose of defeating the plaintiff's claim in *Gainers Inc v Pocklington Holdings Inc* 2000 ABCA 307; (2000) 194 D.L.R. (4th) 109.

188 *De Jetley, Marks v Greenwood* [1936] 1 All E.R. 863 at 872–873; and see *Belmont Finance Corp v Williams Furnishing Ltd (No.2)* [1980] 1 All E.R. 393 especially at 404, per Buckley LJ. cf. *Belmont Finance Corp v Williams* [1979] Ch. 250. Where the company is the victim, it can be the claimant in an action for conspiracy: [1979] Ch. 250.

189 *Meridian Global Funds v Securities Commission* [1995] 2 A.C. 500 PC; (1996) 17 Co Law. 99; *Evans & Sons Ltd v Spritebrand Ltd* [1985] 1 W.L.R. 317 CA (procuring breach of copyright); cf. *Mancetter Developments Ltd v Garmanson Ltd* [1986] Q.B. 1212 CA.

190 per Evershed MR in *DC Thomson & Co Ltd v Deakin* [1952] Ch. 646 at 681–682. The "directing mind and will" of a company may rest in different persons for different purposes; see para.23-103 on conspiracy. cf. *Mutual Finance Ltd v John Wetton & Sons Ltd* [1937] 2 K.B. 389 (undue influence on a company).

ego.[191] An approach to a mere servant of the company cannot be said to be a direct approach to the company itself.[192]

In *DC Thomson & Co Ltd v Deakin*,[193] the defendants were trade union officials, who had exhorted trade unionists in the printing and paper trades to bring pressure to bear on the claimants, a firm of publishers who refused to employ union labour, with the consequence that the claimant's paper suppliers, in order to avoid any dispute with their own employees, refused to carry out their contract with the claimants. In upholding the judge's refusal to grant interlocutory injunctions (on the ground that the evidence did not establish any direct procurement by the defendants of wrongful acts by the employees of the paper suppliers or that any wrongful act had been committed by those employees, and also on the ground that there was no evidence that the defendants knew of any contract between the paper suppliers and the claimants), the Court of Appeal found that there was no evidence that the officials had directly induced the suppliers, and that the employees of the suppliers had not broken their contracts of employment, because the supplying company anticipated any dispute by its refusal to make supplies. In these circumstances they held that there was no liability.[194] **23-40**

But in *JT Stratford & Son v Lindley*, a different result emerged,[195] the defendants being held liable for procuring breaches of the contracts to hire barges. The majority of their Lordships treated the case as one of indirect procurement, since the trade union officials had achieved their end by means of instructions issued to their members[196]; but a minority took the view that it was a case of direct procurement by reason of a letter sent to the trade association to which the hirers of barges belonged. That letter "made it clear to the Association of Master Lightermen, which in effect represented the hirers ... that the hirers could not return the barges to the customers". The letter was, it is true, couched in terms of mere information about the embargo and not of persuasive inducement; but "the fact that an inducement to break a contract is couched as an irresistible embargo rather than in terms of seduction does not make it any the less an inducement".[197] The fact that the communication was sent via the association did not prevent it being a direct inducement any **23-41**

---

191 On the alter ego doctrine generally see *Lennard's Carrying Co Ltd v Asiatic Petroleum Ltd* [1915] A.C. 705; and now *Meridian Global Funds v Securities Commission* [1995] 2 A.C. 500 PC; *El Ajou v Dollar Land Holdings Plc* [1994] 2 All E.R. 685 CA. The director must be acting in that capacity when he receives the knowledge: cf. *Bloor v Liverpool Derricking Co* [1936] 3 All E.R. 399; *Canadian Dredge and Dock v R.* (1985) 19 D.L.R. (4th) 314 (SCC). But the alter ego doctrine (the "directing mind or will") is not relevant where statute imposes a strict duty: *R. v Gateway Food Markets Ltd* [1997] I.C.R. 382 CA. Quaere when does a company forget knowledge once acquired? (See Wedderburn (1984) 47 M.L.R. 345). Compare *Fairline Shipping Corp v Adamson* [1975] Q.B. 180 (personal liability of director); *Trevor Ivory Ltd v Anderson* [1992] 2 N.Z.L.R. 217 (NZCA).

192 per Evershed MR in *DC Thomson & Co Ltd v Deakin* [1952] Ch. 646 at 681–682.

193 [1952] Ch. 646.

194 The claimants had conceded that there was no actionable conspiracy; and the absence of "wrongful acts" arose from the fact that there had been no breaches of employment contracts; contrast *Hadmor Productions Ltd v Hamilton* [1983] 1 A.C. 191 at 228–229, per Lord Diplock.

195 [1965] A.C. 269, HL. For the facts, see para.23-29.

196 As noted above, see para.23-20, after *OBG Ltd v Allan* [2007] UKHL 21; [2008] 1 A.C. 1, instances of indirect interference with a contract—which covers cases where performance has been *prevented*—can no longer give rise to liability under the *Lumley v Gye* tort, and if the defendant is to be liable it will be because it has committed the tort of intentionally causing loss by unlawful means, on which see para.23-78 onwards.

197 per Lord Pearce [1965] A.C. 269 at 333, with whom Lord Donovan appears to have agreed, at 342; see too *The Nadezhda Krupskaya* [1997] 2 Lloyd's Rep. 35 at 39.

more than did its transmission through the post.[198] In such a case, it is to be noticed that the inducement is held to be a "continuing" one, so that the constituents of the tort may be completed by the receipt of knowledge of the contract on the part of the defendants at a date subsequent to the commencement of the embargo, as where the claimant gives him notice of its terms.[199]

23-42 In the light of the decision in *OBG Ltd v Allan* these differing perceptions of defendants' acts which involve action by third parties to effect breach of contract may be of increased importance since cases which had hitherto been treated as indirect procurement of breach of contract appear now to be properly analysed as falling within the tort of intentionally causing loss by unlawful means,.[200] In *Middlebrook Mushrooms Ltd v TGWU* Neill LJ saw *Thomson v Deakin* as a case of indirect procurement because the "direct pressure [was] brought to bear on strangers to the contract" (the drivers).[201] By contrast Hoffmann LJ held that a procurement is direct if the defendant is "responsible" for the effective pressure; on this analysis *Stratford v Lindley* was therefore a case of direct procurement because the union members taking action were "instruments for whose action the defendant union officials were responsible. They and the union officials are often referred to interchangeably as 'the union'."[202] This new approach, radically extending the scope of "direct" inducement, would mean that the effect of *OBG Ltd v Allan* in apparently transferring tort liability for indirect procurement of breach of contract to the unlawful interference tort would be less than it appears to be on the face of it. If "direct" procurement extends to any action for which the defendant can be said to be in some sense responsible, the scope of the tort may prove to be little changed and, as Lord Hoffmann expressly acknowledged[203] the same acts may give rise to liability for both the inducing breach of contract and the unlawful interference torts.

23-43 **Information and advice** Direct inducement must be distinguished from other types of statement, for example the communication of mere information or

---

198 cf. *Daily Mirror Newspapers Ltd v Gardner* [1968] 2 Q.B. 762.

199 See *Merkur Island Shipping Corp v Laughton* [1983] 2 A.C. 570 HL; *Emerald Construction Co Ltd v Lowthian* [1966] 1 W.L.R. 691. See too the cases on "inconsistent transactions", para.23-45. In *Middlebrook Mushrooms Ltd v TGWU* [1993] 1 W.L.R. 612 at 620, Neill LJ saw the *Thomson* case as an indirect procurement because the "direct pressure [was] brought to bear on strangers to the contract" (the drivers). But Hoffmann LJ held that a procurement is direct if the defendant is "responsible" for the effective pressure; therefore, *Stratford* was a case of direct procurement because the union members taking action were "instruments for whose actions the defendant union officials were responsible". They and the officials are often referred to interchangeably as "the union": [1993] 1 W.L.R. 612 at 625. Sed quaere: the officials were not vicariously liable for the actions of the members (and would not be today even under s.20 of TULRCA 1992); and in 1965 the union was not liable in tort (s.4 of the Trade Disputes Act 1906, repealed by s.15 of the Employment Act 1982). It is difficult, therefore, to accept that the defendants' communications led to a direct procurement in *Stratford* because it was made by someone "immediately responsible for bringing the pressure or inducement to bear" (at 624, per Hoffmann LJ). This approach would radically extend the scope of "direct" interventions, especially in labour relations.

200 *OBG Ltd v Allan* [2007] UKHL 21; [2008] 1 A.C. 1; see per Lord Hoffmann at [34]–[38]; while he accepted that the same act could give rise to liability in both torts, his equivocation as to the continued authority of *Thomson v Deakin* leaves an element of uncertainty concerning the relationship between the two torts; cf. Lord Nicholls at [174]–[180].

201 [1993] I.C.R. 612 at 620.

202 [1993] I.C.R. 612 at 625. But neither the union nor the officials were then—and the union would not be today under TULRCA 1992 s.20—vicariously liable for the actions of the members.

203 *OBG Ltd v Allan* [2007] UKHL 21; [2008] 1 A.C. 1 at [37].

advice.[204] A "mere statement of, or drawing of the attention of the party addressed to, the state of facts as they are" is not an inducement but only transmission of information; and before it becomes an inducement giving rise to liability it must contain some element of "pressure, persuasion or procuration".[205] Without that element, transmission of "information" is not an inducement by itself, even if the defendant knew certain consequences might follow and, indeed, desired that they should.[206] Similarly, persuasion must be distinguished from advice—even advice which warns a person of the consequences of his action[207]: but advice which is intended to have persuasive effects is not distinguishable from an inducement.[208] Furthermore, inquiries made to elicit confidential information may be an effective inducement to break a contractual obligation not to disclose such details.[209] Advice has been held to extend to warnings which draw the attention of a contracting party to a state of facts and its dangers for him.[210] But in industrial decisions the courts have tended more readily to find a persuasive element in such communications.[211]

In labour disputes in particular it has become extremely difficult for those taking part to know when they have crossed the line between information and persuasion.[212] On the one hand in *Torquay Hotel Co Ltd v Cousins*[213] union of- **23-44**

---

204 Although Coleridge J, dissenting, thought it "practically impossible" to draw such a line in *Lumley v Gye* (1853) 2 El. & Bl. 216, itself. "This is a matter for the casuist rather than the jurist; still less is it for the juryman", at 252. cf. *Qantas Airways v Transport Workers Union of Australia* [2011] FCA 470; (2011) 280 A.L.R. 503 at [438].

205 per Evershed MR in *DC Thomson & Co Ltd v Deakin* [1952] Ch. 646 at 686. (The effect of an approach made by union officials to the paper suppliers in that case, informing them of the dispute and making it clear to them that their employees might refuse to carry supplies to the claimants, was held to be merely a transmission of information and not a procurement.) See also *South Wales Miners' Federation v Glamorgan Coal Co* [1905] A.C. 239; Hoffmann LJ in *Middlebrook Mushrooms Ltd v TGWU* [1993] I.C.R. 612 at 626; and Rix LJ in *Stocznia Gdanska SA v Latvian Shipping Co (No.3)* [2002] EWCA Civ 889; [2002] 2 All E.R. (Comm) 768 at 797–8, doubting whether a mere request could amount to the requisite persuasion or inducement.

206 *Camellia Tanker Ltd v ITWF* [1976] I.C.R. 274 at 295–297, per Megaw LJ, but see the later industrial cases, para.23-44. cf. *Woolley v Dunford* (1972) 3 S.A.S.R. 243.

207 See *Cutsforth v Mansfield Inns Ltd* [1986] 1 W.L.R. 558.

208 per Simonds J in *Camden Nominees Ltd v Forcey* [1940] Ch. 352 at 366. See too *Communications, Electrical, Electronic, Energy, Information, Postal, Plumbing and Allied Services Union of Australia ("CEPU") v Corke Instrument Engineering Australia Pty Ltd* [2005] FCA 799; (2006) 223 A.L.R. 480 Fed. Ct of Australia, where Corke and CEPU had agreed that they would enter further agreements on the conditions of employment of workers on construction sites where Corke was engaged to provide services. Corke was subsequently awarded a contract by Siemens for work on the construction of a power station but was unable to start this work because no further agreement with CEPU had been made. Finkelstein J held, at [19], that by insisting on Corke performing its obligations under the agreement between them CEPU "had created an inducement for Corke to breach its contractual obligations to Siemens". In *Qantas Airways v Transport Workers Union of Australia* [2011] FCA 470; (2011) 280 A.L.R. 503 at [447]–[450] Moore J said that it was tolerably clear that Finkelstein J was there adopting the distinction between persuasion and advice in *Thomson v Deakin*; the dichotomy between advice, which appeared to be a fairly broad concept, and persuasion or procuration was, per Moore J, relevant to an assessment of whether any of the defendant union officials had committed the tort.

209 *Bent's Brewery Co Ltd v Hogan* [1945] 2 All E.R. 570.

210 per Evershed MR in *DC Thomson & Co Ltd v Deakin* [1952] Ch. 646 at 686; *White v Riley* [1921] 1 Ch. 1.

211 See, e.g. Lord Pearce in *Stratford & Son Ltd v Lindley* [1965] A.C. 269 at 333. See paras 23-29 and 23-41.

212 See *Woolley v Dunford* (1972) 3 S.A.S.R. 243 at 290.

213 [1969] 2 Ch. 106 CA; cf. Winn LJ's dictum at 147: a father who tells his daughter that her fiancé has been convicted of indecent exposure induces her, in the ordinary meaning of language, to break

ficials who informed members in other sections of the union and at other places of work about a particular dispute with an employer were held to have engaged in inducement and it has been said that, since the statement made must always be construed in the context of the relative positions of the parties, even a "suggestion" contained within such information amounts to inducement if the defendant was "desperately anxious" to achieve the result of coercing the claimant.[214] On the other hand a distinction between inducement and the provision of information has sometimes been drawn[215] and it has been said that "the fact that the defendant has communicated to the contracting party the information that consequences will follow if he does not break his contract does not necessarily mean that the communication is the cause of the contract being broken".[216] Since in order to retain the statutory protection against liability in trade disputes for some economic torts, including inducing breach of contract, a trade union is now required to hold a postal ballot of members likely to participate before any call for members to take part in, or authorisation or endorsement of industrial action, in such cases the tortious inducement is likely to coincide with the call, authorisation or endorsement.[217] In other contexts there is authority for the view that it is an inducement to "facilitate" a breach, at least where some active step has been taken[218]; but this runs counter to the normal rule that a party is not liable if all he does is "facilitate" a tort.[219] Many statutes define "procurement" or "inducement" for their own purposes.[220] In copyright cases it has been held that the mere provision of the means for breaking a duty, even if careless, does not amount to an inducement, in the absence of a common design.[221] The sale of tape recorders known to be commonly used to record material in breach of copyright did not make the vendors liable for procuring, inciting or authorising the wrongdoing, there being no "common design" between the vendors and buyers.[222] The fact that the contractor was willing to be induced is no

her engagement; and a man who tells his mother-in-law that his central heating has broken down may thereby induce her to cancel an intended visit. Quaere what language he should adopt if he merely wishes to give good paternal advice or information?

214 per Lord Milligan in *Square Grip Reinforcement Ltd v Macdonald*, 1968 S.L.T. 65 at 72–73.

215 *Camellia Tanker Ltd SA v ITF* [1976] I.C.R. 274 CA.

216 per Hoffmann LJ in *Middlebrook Mushrooms Ltd v TGWU* [1993] 1 W.L.R. 612 at 626; cf. Neill LJ (with whom Mann LJ agreed) [1993] 1 W.L.R. 612 at 620: "if the case is to fall within the category of *Lumley v Gye* the persuasion has to be directed at one of the parties to the contract. It is therefore necessary in every case to examine the form and nature of the communication on which a plaintiff relies."

217 On industrial action ballots see para.23-162 onwards.

218 *British Motor Trade v Salvadori* [1949] Ch. 556 at 565; see, per Bingham LJ in *Rickless v United Artists Corp* [1985] 1 W.L.R. 317 CA.

219 See *Credit Lyonnais Nederland Bank v Export Credits Guarantee Dept* [2000] 1 A.C. 486; [1999] 2 W.L.R. 540 HL at 549–551; *CBS Songs Ltd v Amstrad Consumer Electronics Plc* [1988] A.C. 1013 HL. But where the party "facilitated" a transaction knowingly for the purpose of committing a tort he will be liable if he and the other party are acting in furtherance of a common design (as joint tortfeasors): *Paterson Zochonis v Merfarken Packaging* [1986] 3 All E.R. 522 CA. Quaere whether the facilitator and an active partner are guilty of conspiracy to use unlawful means? See para.23-105 onwards.

220 See, e.g. Race Relations Act 1976 s.31; see *Commission for Racial Equality v Imperial Soc of Teachers of Dancing* [1983] I.C.R. 473 at 476–477; *Anyanwu v South Bank Students' Union* [2001] UKHL 14; [2001] 1 W.L.R. 638; see now Equality Act 2010 s.111.

221 *Paterson Zochonis Co Ltd v Merfarken Packaging Ltd* [1986] 3 All E.R. 522 at 531, per Oliver LJ; at 534, per Fox LJ; and at 540–541, per Goff LJ.

222 *CBS Songs Ltd v Amstrad Consumer Electronics Plc* [1988] A.C. 1013 HL at 1057–1059, per Lord Templeman, rejecting the argument based on *Lumley v Gye* (1853) 2 El. & Bl. 216 at 232: "Gener-

defence if inducement has taken place.[223] But if he has already decided not to perform, the inducement should not give rise to liability.[224]

Inconsistent transactions In his exposition of the elements of the tort in *Thomson v Deakin* Jenkins LJ said that, where a third person with knowledge of a contract "has dealings with the contract breaker which the third party knows to be inconsistent with the contract, he has committed an actionable interference".[225] So, where the claimants agreed with third parties not to resell cars except as provided in their covenants and the defendants induced those parties to resell the cars to them in breach of the covenants in order to make a profit for themselves they committed the tort.[226] But it has been held that merely accepting the benefit of an inconsistent contract at the proposal of the contractor did not amount to tortious conduct.[227] Nor was the acquisition of property from an associated company actionable as this tort even though that company was known to have procured breaches of covenants concerning the property and therefore to be at risk of an injunction at the suit of the claimant, and the transfer of the property to the defendant provided an "easy escape from the salutary remedy" of a mandatory injunction to retransfer the property.[228] Still less does liability arise for "facilitating" a breach without any common design or intentional procurement of a breach.[229] While it has been suggested that in *OBG Ltd v Allan* the House of Lords "reaffirmed that a positive act of inducement or 23-45

---

ally speaking inducement, incitement or persuasion to infringe [copyright] must be by a defendant to an individual infringer and must identifiably procure a particular infringement in order to make the defendant liable as a joint infringer."

223 per Jenkins LJ in *DC Thomson & Co Ltd v Deakin* [1952] Ch. 646 at 694; *British Motor Trade Association v Salvadori* [1949] Ch. 556; *Sefton v Tophams Ltd* [1965] Ch. 1140 (reversed on other grounds [1967] 2 A.C. 50); *Aviva Insurance Ltd v Oliver* [2019] EWHC 2824 (Comm).

224 See, per Hobhouse J in *Rickless v United Artists* [1986] F.S.R. 502 at 517–524 (affirmed [1988] Q.B. 40 CA); cf. *Board of Broadview School Unit No.18 v Saskatchewan Teachers Federation* (1972) 32 D.L.R. (3d) 33. Inferentially, ss.62(6) and 226(4) of TULRCA 1992 (see para.23-136 onwards) appear to concur that "ineffective" inducements have no effect at common law; that is why they do not require explicit protection against liability for inducing breach of contract under s.219 of the TULRCA 1992.

225 *DC Thomson & Co Ltd v Deakin* [1952] Ch. 646 at 694, citing *British Industrial Plastics Ltd v Ferguson* [1940] 1 All E.R. 479 HL; see too Neill LJ in *Middlebrook Mushrooms Ltd v TGWU* [1993] I.C.R. 612 at 618. The second contract is probably not void unless the parties know of its inconsistent effect: *British Homophone Ltd v Kunz* (1935) 152 L.T. 589 at 593. In *The Beans Group Ltd v Myunidays Ltd* [2019] EWHC 320 (Comm), the defendant accepted that the quoted dictum from Jenkins LJ remains the law, despite the suggestion that it is inconsistent with the House of Lords' definitive reconsideration of the tort in *OBG Ltd v Allan* [2007] UKHL 21; [2008] 1 A.C. 1, perhaps because of a preference for winning the "case at first instance, if at all, on the facts, rather than attempting an ambitious argument of law which might be more vulnerable to appeal" (at [100]). See also *Aviva Insurance Ltd v Oliver* [2019] EWHC 2824 (Comm).

226 *British Motor Trade Association v Salvadori* [1949] Ch. 556; cf. Weir's unhistorical objection to this decision: *Economic Torts* (1997), 36n.

227 *Batts Combe Quarry Ltd v Ford* [1943] Ch. 51 CA; cf. *Long v Smithson* (1918) 88 L.J.K.B. 223.

228 *Law Debenture Trust Corp v Ural Caspian Oil Corp Ltd* [1995] Ch. 152 CA at 164, per Bingham MR.

229 See *Credit Lyonnais Bank Nederland v Export Credits Guarantee Dept* [2000] 1 A.C. 486 HL at 499–500, per Lord Woolf MR (tort law does not follow the wider liabilities of the criminal law); *Paterson Zochonis Ltd v Merfarken Packaging Ltd* [1986] 3 All E.R. 522 CA at 530–534 and 539–542; *CBS Songs v Amstrad Consumer Electronics Plc* [1988] A.C. 1013 HL; *British Telecommunications Plc v One in a Million* [1999] 1 W.L.R. 903; [1998] 4 All E.R. 476 at 487. See too *Harry Winton Investments Ltd v CIBC Development Corp* (2001) 199 D.L.R. (4th) 709 (Ont CA).

procurement is essential to the wrong",[230] none of the speeches in that decision directly addressed the issue of whether inconsistent transactions should still be seen as a form of direct inducement of breach.[231]

23-46 Unless and until this matter is clarified a number of issues arise concerning the circumstances in which inconsistent dealings may give rise to liability for directly inducing breach of contract. In his exposition of this form of the tort in *DC Thomson & Co Ltd v Deakin* Jenkins LJ said that "inconsistent dealing ... may, indeed, be commenced without knowledge by the third party of the contract thus broken; but if it is continued after the third party has notice of the contract, an actionable interference has been committed by him".[232] Such a principle requires the "continuance" of the effective inconsistent dealing[233]; and it has been held that if no damage can be proved by the claimant, the inconsistent dealing is not actionable.[234]

---

[230] *Calor Gas Ltd v Express Fuels (Scotland) Ltd* [2008] CSOH 13; 2008 S.L.T 123 at [47]. In that case it was held that no liability arose for inducing breach of a contractual obligation to return empty gas cylinders to a dealer authorised by the pursuer when cylinders were returned to dealers who had changed their suppliers from the pursuer to the defenders.

[231] In *Palmer Birch (a partnership) v Lloyd* [2018] EWHC 2316 (TCC); [2018] 4 W.L.R. 164, the court held that a defendant had committed the tort by "diverting" funds away from a contracting party with the intention of inducing it to breach a building contract, even though he was not under a legal obligation to provide the party with further funds. HH Judge Russen QC, explained, at [361]: "If the fine dividing line in this case between prevention and inducement turns upon the ability to categorise [the defendant's] actions as a diversion of funds away from [the contracting party] then, on the particular facts of this case and even in the absence of any unperformed contractual obligation to fund [the contracting party], he was guilty of that. Although those funds did not reach [the contracting party's] bank account, they could and should have done so. Whereas a simple finding that [the defendant] could have made the funds available to [the contracting party], but simply chose not to, might arguably leave [the claimants] on the wrong side of that fine line, my further conclusion that he should in the circumstances have done so sustains their claim ...". That decision may appear surprising since refusing to provide a contracting party with the funds that it needs to perform a contract cannot be equated with persuading the party to breach its contract. But the court was satisfied that by altering his plans with regard to the funding of the contracting party, and doing so with the intention of bringing about a breach of contract at a particular point in time, the defendant had gone further than simply "preventing" further performance of the contract. Where a defendant's diversion of funds away from a company is a wrong to the company, a claim by a creditor of the company for inducing a breach by means of such diversion will not fall foul of the principle against claims for "reflective loss": *Sevilleja v Marex Financial Ltd* [2020] UKSC 31; [2020] 3 W.L.R. 255 (reversing [2018] EWCA Civ 1468; [2019] Q.B. 173).

[232] [1952] Ch. 646 at 694, citing *De Francesco v Barnum* (1890) 45 Ch. D. 430. Many cases of this kind have concerned the old action for the "harbouring" of another's servant: *Fred Wilkins Ltd v Weaver* [1915] 2 Ch. 322. (The action was abolished by Administration of Justice Act 1982 s.2(c)(iii)). See Browne-Wilkinson J in *Swiss Bank Corp v Lloyds Bank Ltd* [1979] Ch. 548 at 572–574 (reversed on other grounds [1982] A.C. 584 HL). See Cohen-Grabelsky (1982) 45 M.L.R. 241; Tettenborn [1982] C.L.J. 58; Carty (1988) 104 L.Q.R. 250. In *The Beans Group Ltd v Myunidays Ltd* [2019] EWHC 320 (Comm), the defendant did not commit the tort when it initially entered a contract with a third party that was inconsistent with that party's contract with the claimant (which demanded exclusivity) because, at that time, the defendant honestly believed that the third party was at liberty to enter such a contract. The judge held, however, that the defendant committed the tort when it continued to supply services to the third party after being informed of the terms of the claimant's inconsistent contract, since the third party would have gone back to receiving such services from the claimant if the defendant had not continued its "inconsistent dealing".

[233] *Denaby and Cadeby Main Colliers v Yorkshire Miners' Association* [1906] A.C. 384 HL (when the union's strike pay was authorised "the unlawful acts had been committed, all the contracts of employment were terminated": per Lord James at 406); cf. *Smithies v National Association of Operative Plasterers* [1909] 1 K.B. 310 at 335, per Buckley LJ.

[234] *Jones Bros (Hunstanton) Ltd v Stevens* [1955] 1 Q.B. 275 (no damage where servant unwilling to return to first employer).

Where an inconsistent transaction[235] is continued knowingly and actively, and damage is proved, liability arises.[236] But where company C bought shares from B, an associated company, knowing that B had induced X to sell them to it in breach of a covenant with the claimant, thereby putting it out of his power to obtain an injunction for retransfer, the claimant's action against C failed; no injunction having actually been obtained, the transfer by B to C was lawful.[237] Where a party has actually obtained an injunction, however, an act which deliberately interferes with it will amount to contempt of court and an unlawful interference with that party's rights.[238]

Where an order for specific performance can be obtained this will normally leave no room for any remedy based upon inducement of any breach of the contract. The owner of a registered option to buy land can enforce it specifically in priority to an earlier right of pre-emption which is not binding as an "interest in land"; and in such a case, specific performance may well mean that "no question of damages ... arises".[239] But if further loss is proved, damages can be awarded for the tort.[240] Whether inconsistent dealing amounts to an actionable inducement frequently turns on whether damage has been caused or (in a quia timet action) is threatened.[241] In cases where the tort claim overlaps with a claim based on equitable proprietary rights the defendant's knowledge of these rights will be crucial.[242] However, it must be questioned whether the absence of a right to demand specific performance of an obligation necessarily means that inconsistent dealings are not actionable in tort. This is clearly not the case where, as for example in relation to contracts of employment, equitable remedies are not normally available.[243] In general equitable concepts do not necessarily define the area of liability in tort, any more than the tort of inducing breach of contract delimits equitable principles relating to such matters as **23-47**

---

235 Where rights of property are concerned, the question whether there is an "inconsistency" may be critical; see the analysis by the Court of Appeal in *Pritchard v Briggs* [1980] Ch. 338. The transactions may not in themselves be inconsistent (see per Stephenson LJ at 423), but steps to execute the one may cause breach of the other.

236 This may be the proper basis on which to explain cases where third parties who acquire property with notice of a condition attached can be liable for inducing its breach: see Hoffmann J in *Law Debenture Trust Corp v Ural Caspian Oil Corp Ltd* [1993] 1 W.L.R. 138 at 147–149 (reversed on other grounds [1995] Ch. 152 CA).

237 *Law Debenture Trust Corp v Ural Caspian Oil Corp* [1995] Ch. 152 CA; until an order is made, a debtor can dissipate his property to make himself judgment-proof: see at 165, per Bingham MR, at 169–170, per Beldam LJ, and at 172–173, per Saville LJ, distinguishing *Esso Petroleum Co Ltd v Kingswood Motors (Addlestone) Co Ltd* [1974] Q.B. 142 on the ground that there an injunction had already been granted; see para.23-55.

238 *Acrow (Automation) Ltd v Rex Chainbelt Inc* [1971] 1 W.L.R. 1676 CA; per Beldam LJ in *Law Debenture Trust Corp v Ural Caspian Oil Corp* [1995] Ch. 152 at 169–170.

239 *Pritchard v Briggs* [1980] Ch. 338 at 421, per Templeman LJ; and at 423, per Stephenson LJ.

240 per Goff LJ, *Pritchard v Briggs* [1980] Ch. 338 at 409–417 (conspiracy to interfere with contractual rights); and at 424, per Stephenson LJ For the possible impact upon the priorities laid down by land law, see R.J. Smith (1977) 41 Conv. (N.S.) 318; Wade (1980) 96 L.Q.R. 488.

241 *Sefton v Tophams Ltd* [1965] Ch. 1140 (reversed on other grounds [1967] 1 A.C. 50); *Jones Bros (Hunstanton) Ltd v Stevens* [1955] 1 Q.B. 275.

242 See *Swiss Banking Corp v Lloyds Bank Ltd* [1982] A.C. 584 HL (restriction to repay loan out of sale of securities not an equitable charge capable of defeating a later equitable charge granted to bank, which had actual knowledge of the covenant only after taking its charge). See the concession made on "actual" knowledge in [1979] Ch. 548 at 570; and the judgment of Browne-Wilkinson J at 569–575, where he based liability for the "tort of knowing interference" with the claimant's contractual rights upon the bank's knowledge acquired after the inconsistent transaction.

243 See per Jenkins LJ in *DC Thomson & Co Ltd v Deakin* [1952] Ch. 646 CA at 694.

breach of "confidence".[244] Where inconsistent transactions give rise to a prima facie case of liability for the tort of procuring breach of contract, it seems that the defence of justification is open to a party to the first contract who induces a breach of the second for example where he procures the breach in order to protect an "equal or superior right", even though the method of so doing is of commercial advantage.[245]

(ii) Indirect procurement

23-48 In *OBG Ltd v Allan* the House of Lords' attempt to rationalise and clarify the boundary between the torts of procuring a breach of contract and intentionally causing harm by the use of unlawful means rejected the inclusion of cases where the defendant directly intervenes by some wrongful act to prevent performance of a contract within the scope of the tort of procuring breach of contract. These cases should now be regarded as falling within the intentional harm tort.[246]

23-49 It is less clear how far the decision in *OBG Ltd v Allan* has affected the general standing of the Court of Appeal decision in *Thomson v Deakin* which had hitherto been regarded as an authoritative exposition of the ingredients of the tort of procuring breach of contract. In particular it cast doubt on the existence of liability falling within the *Lumley v Gye* tort for indirect procurement of breach of contract by unlawful means. As formulated by Jenkins LJ in *Thomson v Deakin* this form of the tort required the claimant to establish that the defendant knew of the claimant's contract, intended its breach and to this end used unlawful means—typically in a labour dispute "definitely and unequivocally persuaded, induced or procured employees to break their contracts of employment"—and that the breach of the contract forming the subject of the alleged interference ensued as a *necessary* consequence of these unlawful means.[247]

23-50 In *OBG Ltd v Allan*, while recognising the hitherto authoritative status of *Thomson v Deakin*, Lord Hoffmann expressed the view that it would have been preferable to subsume liability for indirect procurement of breach of contract by

---

[244] On the uncertain boundaries between the tort and other equitable concepts, including "constructive trusteeship" see *Binions v Evans* [1972] Ch. 359 CA at 368 and 371; *Belmont Finance Corp v Williams Furniture Ltd (No.2)* [1980] 1 All E.R. 393 CA; *Canada Safeway Ltd v Thomson* [1951] 3 D.L.R. 295; and the rejection of "inducing breach of trust" as a tort: *Metall und Rohstoff AG v Donaldson Lufkin & Jenrette Inc* [1990] 1 Q.B. 391 CA at 418; *Royal Brunei Airlines v Tan* [1995] 2 A.C. 378 PC; Carty (1988) 104 L.Q.R. 250, 282-284 (inconsistent dealing should be left to equitable remedies).

[245] See *Hill v First National Finance Corp* [1989] 1 W.L.R. 225, CA, discussed at para.23-58; *Smithies v National Association of Operative Plasterers* [1909] 1 K.B. 310 at 337 and 341. Goff LJ saw *Pritchard v Briggs* [1980] Ch. 338 at 415, as "the converse of that in the *Smithies* case", on his view of the facts. In *The Beans Group Ltd v Myunidays Ltd* [2019] EWHC 320 (Comm), the Court did not address the possibility that the defendant, which had initially entered a contract with a third party with the honest belief that the third party was at liberty to enter such a contract, could rely on this contract to justify continuing to deal with the third party in a way that was inconsistent with the third party's previous contract with the claimant; the possibility would rely on the idea that the defendant's contract with the third party, although inconsistent with the third party's contract with the claimant, nonetheless supplied *the defendant* with an equal contractual right.

[246] This is clearly indicated in both Lord Hoffmann's and Lord Nicholls' criticism of the reasoning of Lord Hewart LCJ in *GWK Ltd v Dunlop Rubber Co Ltd* (1926) 42 T.L.R. 376; see [2007] UKHL 21; [2008] 1 A.C. 1 at [22]–[25] and [176]–[178] respectively; see *Global Resources Group Ltd v Mackay* [2008] CSOH 148; 2009 S.L.T. 104 at [16]. On this form of the tort see para.25-53 of the 19th edition of this work.

[247] *DC Thomson & Co Ltd v Deakin* [1952] Ch. 646 at 697.

unlawful means within the tort of "causing loss by unlawful means of which there was an inadequate appreciation at that time of the scope, possibly even the existence".[248] Notwithstanding this view, Lord Hoffmann concluded that he "would not expect your Lordships to reject the unified theory adopted in *DC Thomson & Co Ltd v Deakin* unless it has serious disadvantages".[249] However he followed this reservation with a reasoned rejection of any distinction between "direct and indirect interference"[250] developing the doubts that he expressed in *Middlebrook Mushrooms Ltd v TGWU* concerning this distinction as expressed by Lord Denning MR in *Torquay Hotel Co Ltd v Cousins*.[251] The distinction was, Lord Hoffmann said, "irrelevant and misleading" and he formulated the question that had to be asked in relation to *Lumley v Gye* as "did the defendant's acts of encouragement, threat, persuasion and so forth have a sufficient causal connection with the breach of the contracting party to attract accessory liability".[252] This approach may be seen as a logical development of the view he expressed in *Middlebrook Mushrooms Ltd v TGWU* that an inducement should be seen as direct whenever the defendant or someone for whom he was legally responsible caused the breach of contract by bringing pressure to bear.[253]

While the speeches in *OBG Ltd v Allan* disclose a consensus on subsuming liability for acts which indirectly effect a breach of contract between the claimant and a third party within the tort of intentionally causing loss by unlawful means, if Lord Hoffmann's speech is taken to represent the views of the House on this point, this shift in the law will come at the expense of an expansion of the scope of direct inducement or procurement of uncertain extent. In labour disputes in particular, issues could well arise over the existence of "a sufficient connection" between the acts of the defendant unions or union officials and disruption of performance of employers' commercial contracts by actual or threatened industrial action.[254] **23-51**

Notwithstanding Lord Hoffmann's reservation over "rejecting" the unified theory adopted in *Thomson v Deakin*, his subsequent analysis of the elements of the *Lumley v Gye* tort refers only to "knowledge" of the defendant that he is procuring an act which is a breach of contract, "intention" to procure breach and "breach of contract".[255] This seems to be clearly intended to supersede the hitherto authoritative status of the analysis of the tort in *Thomson v Deakin* and not just that decision's inclusion of indirect procurement of breach of contract by unlawful means within this tort.[256] The status of that decision must now be uncertain as it does not analyse **23-52**

---

248 *OBG Ltd v Allan* [2007] UKHL 21; [2008] 1 A.C. 1 at [28].

249 *OBG Ltd v Allan* [2007] UKHL 21; [2008] 1 A.C. 1 at [33].

250 *OBG Ltd v Allan* [2007] UKHL 21; [2008] 1 A.C. 1 at [34]–[38].

251 [1969] 2 Ch. 106 at 138-139; see Hoffmann LJ in *Middlebrook Mushrooms Ltd v TGWU* [1993] I.C.R 612 at 620–626.

252 *OBG Ltd v Allan* [2007 UKHL 21; [2008] 1 A.C. 1 at [36]. See also, to similar effect, *Palmer Birch (a partnership) v Lloyd* [2018] EWHC 2316 (TCC); [2018] 4 W.L.R. 164 at [59]: "the necessary ingredient of a breach of contract in the inducement tort means that the liability of the alleged tortfeasor rests ... upon a degree of participation in the breach of contract which satisfies the general requirements of accessory liability for the wrongful act of another person."

253 [1993] I.C.R 612 at 624.

254 In proceedings for an interim (interlocutory) injunction any doubts over this issue would be likely to be resolved against the defendants.

255 [2007] UKHL 21; [2008] 1 A.C. 1 at [39]–[44].

256 It is, however, submitted that the statement in endnote 3 to [97] of the decision of the Ontario Court of Appeal in *Correla v Canac Kitchens* (2008) 294 D.L.R. (4th) 525 that the House of Lords in *OBG Ltd v Allan* held that *Thomson v Deakin* and *Torquay Hotel Co Ltd v Cousins* (where the majority

the tort of procuring a breach of contract in terms that are consistent with the scope of the tort as defined in *OBG Ltd v Allan*.[257]

(d) Damage

23-53 The claimant must prove not only the procuring but also that he has been damaged by the breach of contract.[258] If the breach, which has been procured by the defendant, has been such as must in the ordinary course of business inflict damage upon the claimant, it is unnecessary for him to prove particular damage.[259] Where the defendant continued to employ a servant after notice that he was still contractually bound to serve the claimants, no action was maintainable on proof that the servant would in no circumstances return to the claimants' service, and that therefore they had suffered no damage caused by the defendant.[260] When damage can be proved, or inferred, the claimant is entitled to recover in respect of that damage which was intended[261] or, whether intended or not, was a consequence of the tort which is not too remote.[262] Thus, the claimant may recover in respect of loss of business caused by non-performance of contracts other than that of which the defend-

reasoning differed from that of Lord Denning MR) as well as *Merkur Island Shipping* and *Millar v Bassey* were wrongly decided, is incorrect.

[257] The other leading speech, by Lord Nicholls, makes only one reference to *Thomson v Deakin* on the specific point that lawful acts by a third party cannot constitute an actionable interference with contractual rights: [2007] UKHL 21; [2008] 1 A.C. 1 at [179]. Lady Hale and Lord Brown's expressed agreement with Lord Hoffmann where his views differ from those of Lord Nicholls does not provide an unambiguous endorsement for Lord Hoffmann's restatement of the tort.

[258] *Exchange Telegraph Co v Gregory* [1896] 1 Q.B. 147; *Sefton v Tophams Ltd* [1965] Ch. 1140 (reversed on other grounds [1967] 1 A.C. 50); *British Industrial Plastics v Ferguson* [1938] 4 All E.R. 504; *Jones Bros (Hunstanton) Ltd v Stevens* [1955] 1 Q.B. 275. On the place where damage is suffered and service out of the jurisdiction: *Metall und Rohstoff AG v Donaldson, Lufkin & Jenrette Inc* [1990] 1 Q.B. 391, CA at 435–449 (overruled on other matters, *Lonrho Plc v Fayed* [1992] A.C. 448 HL); see also the Private International Law (Miscellaneous Provisions) Act 1995.

[259] *Exchange Telegraph Co v Gregory* [1896] 1 Q.B. 147; *Goldsoll v Goldman* [1914] 2 Ch. 603 at 615; *British Motor Trade Association v Salvadori* [1949] Ch. 556; *Nauru Local Govt Council v New Zealand Seamen's Union* [1986] 1 N.Z.L.R. 466 (NZCA): (loss of profit-making opportunity allowed); cf. *Lonrho Plc v Fayed (No.5)* [1993] 1 W.L.R. 1489 CA (no damages for loss of reputation); but see *Joyce v Sengupta* [1993] 1 W.L.R. 337 at 348–349 and 351.

[260] *Jones Bros (Hunstanton) Ltd v Stevens* [1955] 1 Q.B. 275.

[261] *Lumley v Gye* (1853) 2 El. & Bl. 216 at 233–234, per Erle J; *Quinn v Leathem* [1901] A.C. 495 at 537, per Lord Lindley.

[262] *British Motor Trade Association v Salvadori* [1949] Ch. 556 at 568–569; *Boxfoldia Ltd v N.G.A.* [1988] I.C.R. 752 (damage reasonably foreseeable). See, too, on measure of damages, *Posluns v Toronto Stock Exchange* (1964) 46 D.L.R. (2d) 210; affirmed (1968) 67 D.L.R. (2d) 165; Brodie (1998) 27 I.L.J. 79. Quaere whether *Pratt v BMA* [1919] 1 K.B. 244 is authority for allowing recovery for non-pecuniary loss; cf. *McGregor on Damages*, 20th edn (2017), para.48-008, or whether this is merely part of arriving at "a round sum based on the pecuniary loss proved", per Lord Devlin in *Rookes v Barnard* [1964] A.C. 1129 at 1221 ("leaving aside" aggravated damages). In *Walsh v Nicholls* (2004) 214 D.L.R. (4th) 643 (NBCA) at [84] it was said that punitive damages "are not excluded from the arsenal of proper judicial responses to intentional procurement of breach of contract"; cf. *Delphinium Ltée c 512842 NB Inc* 2008 NBCA 56; (2008) 296 D.L.R. (4th) 694 (NBCA) in which the defendant's appeal against punitive damages was allowed where the essence of the deliberate business decision to procure breach was "nothing more than what is referred to in the jurisprudence as an 'efficient breach'" which "exacted a sufficiently stiff price" in compensatory damages.

ant induced a breach, where such loss is foreseeable; but not for losses caused to his business which were not foreseeable or intended by the defendant.[263]

(e) Remedies

Interim injunction Where the claimant claims an interim ("interlocutory") injunction against the continuance or threat of the tort under discussion, he must persuade the court to exercise its discretion in his favour (and even in interlocutory proceedings, where the evidence is likely to be on affidavit and unsatisfactory, that normally means the discretion of the judge not of the appellate courts).[264] To do so he must, under the ordinary principles applicable to such cases, show that the damage which he is likely to suffer is such that the balance of convenience favours the granting of the remedy.[265] In industrial disputes, this burden is easily discharged by employers who seek injunctions against trade union defendants.[266] In 1979,[267] the House of Lords took account of "the realities" of such cases (which are usually interlocutory), accepting that the employer's claim to maintain the "status quo" before the strike and his demonstration that he will suffer great harm if it is not stopped, has to be balanced against the trade unionist defendants' need to "strike while the iron is hot" and the fact (as it is in nearly all such cases) that an interim ("interlocutory") injunction will decide the case, since the employer will not normally go on to trial.[268] However in 1984 Lord Diplock explained his remarks 23-54

---

[263] *Jones v Fabbi* (1973) 37 D.L.R. (3d) 27, applying *The Wagon Mound (No.1)* [1961] A.C. 388; and *McGregor on Damages*, 20th edn (2017), para.48-006. See also, *Jones v Fabbi* (1975) 49 D.L.R. (3d) 316 (on mitigation of damage). On difficulties in restoring the claimant to his original position: *Lakefield v Black* (1999) 166 D.L.R. (4th) 96 (Ont CA). On loss of a chance caused by inducement of breach of contract see *McGill v Sports and Entertainment Media Group* [2016] EWCA Civ 1063; [2017] 1 W.L.R. 989 at [57] et seq.

[264] *Duport Steels Ltd v Sirs* [1980] 1 W.L.R. 144, HL at 160–161, 165, 166 and 171; *Mercury Communications Ltd v Scott-Garner* [1984] Ch. 37 CA (judge's discretion overturned on fresh evidence and error of law); *Associated British Ports v TGWU* [1989] 1 W.L.R. 939 CA (judge's discretion overturned; need to consider "public interest"; reversed by HL on other grounds: ibid.).

[265] *Emerald Construction Co Ltd v Lowthian* [1966] 1 W.L.R. 691 CA.

[266] In cases of "labour injunctions" against trade unions and their officials, the material interests of the employer have counted for more than the rather intangible industrial interests of the union side. See, e.g. the approach in *Emerald Construction Co Ltd v Lowthian* [1966] 1 W.L.R. 691; *Solihull MB v NUT* [1985] I.R.L.R. 211; *University College NHS Trust v UNISON* [1999] I.C.R. 204 CA (see J. Hendy (2000) 29 I.L.J. 53); *Shipping Co Uniform Inc v ITF* [1985] I.R.L.R. 71; *Boston Deep Sea Fisheries Ltd v TGWU, The Times,* 13 March 14, 17, 18, 20, 21 and 9 April 1970; Wedderburn, *The Worker and the Law*, 3rd edn (1986), pp.688–705.

[267] *NWL Ltd v Woods* [1979] 1 W.L.R. 1294 HL, per Lord Diplock at 1305–1306; per Lord Fraser at 1310; and per Lord Scarman at 1314–1315. However the court retained a residual discretion to grant an injunction, see per Lord Diplock at 1307, and per Lord Scarman in *Express Newspapers Ltd v McShane* [1980] A.C. 672 at 695 (as corrected in [1980] 1 W.L.R. 147n). On the interrelation between the "balance of convenience" and s.17(2) of the Trade Union and Labour Relations Act 1974 (now s.221(2) of TULRCA 1992) see para.23-182.

[268] *NWL Ltd v Woods* [1979] 1 W.L.R. 1294 HL, per Lord Diplock at 1305–1307. Yet some judges continue to approach the interim remedy as if there will be a trial: see, e.g. Lawton LJ in *Associated Newspapers Group Ltd v Wade* [1979] I.C.R. 696 at 701; *Mercury Communications Ltd v Scott-Garner* [1984] Ch. 37 at 99, per Dillon LJ. In such cases the rule that no interlocutory injunction will be granted if it finally disposes of the action (*Cayne v Global Natural Resources* [1984] 1 All E.R. 225 CA) is not applied because the defendant is, at least in legal theory, still able to defend at final trial: *Thomas v NUM (South Wales Area)* [1986] Ch. 20.

in the *NWL* case as applying only to the period before 1982, when trade unions could not be sued in tort and actions were brought against officials only.[269]

23-55 If an injunction is granted, it will not necessarily be limited to the contracts affected by the defendant's past acts; and the courts have in many cases adopted the form proposed by Lord Upjohn in *Stratford v Lindley* restraining the defendant from "doing any act which causes or procures a breach or breaches by customers of the [claimant] of contracts *made now or hereafter*".[270] Thus, a claimant has succeeded in obtaining an injunction restraining a defendant from inducing breach of certain types of contracts not yet made, where the cause of action rested solely upon a finding that the latter intended to cause a breach of any such contracts made by the claimant.[271] Where necessary, the court will grant a mandatory injunction, especially where that is needed to restore property improperly acquired by the tortious acts[272]; but it should be slow to do so in industrial disputes.[273] So, too, where an injunction lies to prevent a breach of contract, it may be that the court will grant an injunction against a third party if that is necessary to make the first injunction effective, even though the third party is not strictly guilty of the tort.[274]

23-56 **Serious question** Until 1975, a claimant who sought an interlocutory injunction had to prove "a prima facie case of some breach of duty to him" (by the defendant).[275] But in *American Cyanamid Co v Ethicon Ltd*,[276] the House of Lords departed from that long-established test, in favour of a different principle less onerous to the claimant, namely that he must convince the court that "the claim is not frivolous or vexatious; in other words, that there is a serious question to be tried".[277]

---

269 *Dimbleby and Sons Ltd v NUJ* [1984] 1 W.L.R. 427 at 431–432; on the liability of trade unions in tort see now ss.20 and 21 of TULRCA 1992; see para.23-134.

270 [1965] A.C. 269 at 339 (emphasis added). See, e.g. *Emerald Construction Co Ltd v Lowthian* [1966] 1 W.L.R. 691. But the injunction should not be in unreasonably wide terms: *New Zealand Bakery Trades Union v General Foods Corp Ltd* [1985] 2 N.Z.L.R. 110 (NZCA); for an injunction in such terms see *Macmillan Bloedel Ltd v Simpson* (1995) 118 D.L.R. (4th) 1 (BCCA): (to defendants (Greenpeace), "John Doe and Jane Doe, and all persons having notice of this order"); upheld (1997) 137 D.L.R. (4th) 637 (SCC); but English courts do not follow this practice.

271 This was one ground of the decision in *Torquay Hotel Co v Cousins* [1969] 2 Ch. 106 at 111 (injunction restrained the union, directly or indirectly, from causing a breach by any supplier of oil under contracts with the complainant). See also Kloss (1971) 34 M.L.R. 690 at 691.

272 *Esso Petroleum Ltd v Kingswood Motors (Addlestone) Ltd* [1974] Q.B. 142.

273 See *Harold Stephen Ltd v Post Office* [1977] 1 W.L.R. 1172 CA (a principle not always observed): see para.23-136 onwards; see the authoritative article by Davies and Anderman (1973) 2 I.L.J. 213; S. Deakin and G. Morris, *Labour Law*, 6th edn (2012), pp.1090-1096; Wedderburn, "The Injunction and the Sovereignty of Parliament" in *Employment Rights in Britain and Europe* (1991), Ch.7; O'Regan (1991) 54 M.L.R. 385.

274 *Sefton v Tophams Ltd* [1965] Ch. 1140 (reversed on other grounds [1967] 1 A.C. 50); and *Manchester Ship Canal Co v Manchester Racecourse Co* [1901] 2 Ch. 37 CA (which may well be a case where the tort was established). See para.23-45 on inconsistent transactions; and see now *Warren v Mendy* [1989] I.C.R. 525 CA. Compare the developments in liability for contempt of court by third parties: *Att Gen v Newspaper Publishing Plc* [1992] 1 A.C. 191 HL, especially, per Lord Ackner at 215–216. See also the penetrating review by Lightman [1987] C.L.P. 25 at 45. On contempt of court and breach of confidence see *Ashworth v MGN Ltd* [2002] UKHL 29; [2002] 1 W.L.R. 2033. On third parties and contempt of court see *Att Gen v Punch Ltd* [2002] UKHL 50; [2003] 1 A.C. 1046.

275 *Stratford & Son Ltd v Lindley* [1965] A.C. 269 at 338, per Lord Upjohn.

276 [1975] A.C. 396 HL (a patent case). See Simpson (1984) 47 M.L.R. 578 at 581; Wedderburn, *The Worker and the Law*, 3rd edn (1986), pp.690–705.

277 [1975] A.C. 396 HL, per Lord Diplock at 407. Lord Diplock later claimed this new principle was not new, because it was only part of the overall "balance of convenience": *NWL Ltd v Woods* [1979] 1 W.L.R. 1294 at 1306–1307, where Lord Fraser shows how that has always been the case in

Concern was expressed that where the balance of convenience was heavily in favour of the claimant, he might obtain from the court an injunction based only upon a "serious question" and not a prima facie case of tortious conduct by the defendant.[278] Particular concern was expressed in relation to industrial disputes on that score, where usually the interlocutory remedy effectively decides the case.[279] It was therefore felt necessary to legislate on this matter in respect of trade disputes.[280] Finally, in the area of the economic torts where social and economic interests clash, it is important to note that the House of Lords has reserved to the courts an ultimate discretion to grant an injunction where the consequences of not doing so might be "disastrous" to an employer, a third party, the public or "perhaps the nation itself", unless there is a high probability that the defence will succeed.[281] The Court of Appeal has insisted that the trial judge must take account of "the public interest" in a manner which is bound to weigh in favour of the granting of an injunction in the case of industrial action of any scale.[282]

(f) Defence of justification

Intentionally procuring a breach of contract is actionable independently of the motive or reason for so doing since the action depends upon breach of the claimant's right and is not based on the spite, desire to injure or ill will of the defendant.[283] To this principle some exception has been made on the ground of justification but it has been recognised that "it would be extremely difficult, even if it were possible, to give a complete and satisfactory definition of what is 'sufficient justification'".[284] 23-57

Scotland: at 1308–1310. That was not the common understanding in England after the *Ethicon* decision (CA). The decision caused a change in procedure: *Thomas Marshall (Exports) Ltd v Guinle* [1979] Ch. 227; see further below, at para.23-180 onwards.

278 See *Hubbard v Pitt* [1976] Q.B. 142 at 178, per Lord Denning MR.

279 See, e.g. the subsequent proceedings in *Stratford & Son Ltd v Lindley (No.2)* [1969] 1 W.L.R. 1547 CA, where the "temporary" injunction had governed the relations of the parties for years. It is, of course, no answer to a claim for a quia timet injunction to plead that the attempt to induce a breach of contract is unlikely to succeed; the claimant need prove only that the attempt, if successful, is likely to cause him more than nominal damage. The need remains to prove a contract: *Crazy Prices (Northern Ireland) Ltd v Hewitt* [1980] I.R.L.R. 396 NICA. But proof of the contract is often meagre in interlocutory proceedings; cf. *Dimbleby and Sons Ltd v NUJ* [1984] 1 W.L.R. 427 HL; sometimes even too uncertain, see *Middlebrook Mushrooms Ltd v TGWU* [1993] I.C.R. 612 CA.

280 See s.17(2) of the Trade Union and Labour Relations Act 1974 (inserted by the Employment Protection Act 1975 Sch.16, Pt III, para.6, a few months after the *Ethicon* case); now s.221(2) of TULRCA 1992, see para.23-181; see Lord Fraser in *NWL Ltd v Woods* [1979] 1 W.L.R. 1294 at 1308; Wedderburn, *The Worker and the Law*, 3rd edn (1986), pp.681-748; Deakin and Morris, *Labour Law*, 6th edn (2012), 1091-1094. See too, per Lord Diplock and Lord Scarman in *NWL Ltd v Woods* [1979] 1 W.L.R. 1294; and per Lords Diplock, Fraser, Keith and Scarman in *Duport Steels Ltd v Sirs* [1980] 1 W.L.R. 142 HL; *Dimbleby and Sons Ltd v NUJ* [1984] 1 W.L.R. 427 HL at 430–436; and *Newham LBC v NALGO* [1993] I.C.R. 189 CA (no arguable case).

281 See, per Lord Diplock in *NWL Ltd v Woods* [1979] 1 W.L.R. 1294 at 1307 (as revised in [1980] 1 W.L.R. 147n); per Lord Scarman in *Express Newspapers Ltd v McShane* [1980] A.C. 672 at 694-695. See also *Duport Steels Ltd v Sirs* [1980] 1 W.L.R. 142 HL; Simpson (1980) 43 M.L.R. 327; Wedderburn (1980) 43 M.L.R. 319.

282 *Associated British Ports v TGWU* [1989] 1 W.L.R. 939 at 957, per Neill LJ, at 962, per Butler-Sloss LJ, and at 968–969, per Stuart-Smith LJ (reversed on other grounds [1989] 1 W.L.R. 939 HL).

283 *Read v Friendly Society of Stonemasons* [1902] 2 K.B. 732 CA; *South Wales Miners Federation v Glamorgan Coal Co* [1905] A.C.239 at 246, per Lord Macnaghten; *DC Thomson & Co Ltd v Deakin* [1952] Ch. 646 at 676, per Lord Evershed MR; *Edwin Hill & Partners v First National Finance Corp Plc* [1989] 1 W.L.R.225 at 234, per Stuart-Smith LJ.

284 *Glamorgan Coal Co v South Wales Miners Federation* [1903] 2 K.B. 545 at 573 CA, per Romer LJ;

Regard may be had "to the nature of the contract broken; the position of the parties to the contract; the grounds for the breach; the means used to procure the breach; the relation of the person procuring the breach to the person who breaks the contract; and ... the object of the person in procuring the breach;" but it is for "the good sense of the tribunal which [has] to decide ... to analyse the circumstances and discover on which side of the line each case" falls.[285] The utility of this guidance as to when the courts might find an inducement to break a contract to be justified was called into question by the Australian High Court in *Zhu v Treasurer of New South Wales* where it was observed that Romer LJ's dictum "might be relevant at a high level of generality but never appeared to be decisive of the outcome in any particular case".[286]

23-58 The defence has been held to be available in circumstances where the defendant acted in furtherance of a moral obligation as when representatives of an actors' association were held to owe a sufficient duty to their calling and the association's members to justify inducing a theatre proprietor to break a contract with an impresario who paid chorus girls wages which were so low that they were compelled to resort to prostitution.[287] But it is no justification to show that a trade union has only pursued its duty of obtaining better wages or of enforcing collective agreements or statutory procedures for the benefit of its members.[288] However, where a defendant possesses an "equal or superior right" he is justified in taking reasonable steps to protect it even though he knows that they will cause a breach of the claimant's contract. Thus in *Edwin Hill & Partners v First National Finance Corp Plc* the defendant had provided a loan to a property developer to enable it to acquire a site for development for which the plaintiffs were then engaged by the developer as architects. When developments in the property market made it impossible for the developer to proceed with its plans, the defendant was held to be justified in requiring the engagement of a prestigious firm of architects in place of the plaintiffs to enable the defendant to develop the site itself, rather than call in the

---

cf. Stirling LJ [1903] 2 K.B. 545 at 577 doubting whether it would be possible to lay down "a general rule ... which would determine in which cases such a justification exists." For a fuller analysis of the law see Stuart-Smith LJ in *Edwin Hill & Partners v First National Finance Corp Plc* [1989] 1 W.L.R. 225 at 228–233. On justification generally see Heydon (1970) Univ. Toronto L.J. 139. In *Whittaker v Child Support Registrar* [2010] FCA 43; (2010) 264 A.L.R. 473 at [203] it was held that where the defendant acted with statutory authority this provided a "short answer" to a claim for interference with contractual relations. On statutory authority as a defence to tort liability see Ch.3, paras 3-162 to 3-164.

[285] per Romer LJ in *Glamorgan Coal Co v South Wales Miners Federation* [1903] 2 K.B. 545 at 574, endorsing Bowen LJ in *Mogul Steamship Co v McGregor Gow* (1889) 23 Q.B.D. 598 at 618; applied by Goff LJ in *Pritchard v Briggs* [1980] Ch.338 at 416–417. See too Slade J in *Greig v Insole* [1978] 1 W.L.R. 302 at 340–341.

[286] [2004] HCA 56; (2004) 211 A.L.R. 159 at [117]. The judgment in this case includes a comprehensive analysis of the justification defence at [105]–[174].

[287] *Brimelow v Casson* [1924] 1 Ch. 302. While this decision was regarded as "isolated" in *Camden Nominees Ltd v Forcey* [1940] Ch. 352 at 366 it was approved by Lord Porter in *Crofter Hand Woven Harris Tweed v Veitch* [1942] A.C. 435 at 495–496, by Goff LJ in *Pritchard v Briggs* [1980] Ch. 338 at 416 as "based on a duty, albeit a moral one, and the facts were very strong indeed"; and by Stuart-Smith LJ in *Hill v First National Finance Corp Plc* [1989] 1 W.L.R. 225 at 230 as "a duty to their calling and its members".

[288] *South Wales Miners Federation v Glamorgan Coal Co Ltd* [1905] A.C. 239; *Timeplan Education Group v NUT* [1997] I.R.L.R. 457 CA (statutory scheme for regulating employment conditions); cf. Lord Hodge in *Global Resources Group Ltd v Mackay* [2008] CSOH 148; 2009 S.L.T. 104 at [14] "[the defender's] pursuit of his own economic advantage is not of itself justification".

loan.[289] It has been suggested that this decision made clear that justification was not restricted to cases where a high moral purpose was involved. Thus although the Insolvency Act 1986 contained no provisions enabling an administrator to sell assets free from contractual restrictions, since it did permit him to apply to the court to enable him to deal with the company's assets free from proprietary rights it was said that "[t]he proper balancing of competing interests involved in administration as an insolvency process may well be achieved by providing a defence of justification to a claim in tort in respect of a sale by an administrator in circumstances where there is a purely contractual restriction on sale".[290]

Although the English case law suggests that justification has a fairly restricted ambit, the defence has been the subject of more extensive consideration, perhaps affording it greater importance, in other common law jurisdictions. Where the litigation arises out of an industrial dispute, legislation on industrial relations has sometimes been influential. Thus in one New Zealand case the blacking of a barge which was being unloaded by workers who were neither seamen nor watersiders, as legislation required, was justified since it was "a shield to prevent industrial discord which the union was entitled not to be involved in and was only provoked by the conduct of the plaintiff".[291] By contrast an interim injunction against a union restraining it from blacking supplies of oil to a hydrofoil for which the respondent, after the blacking began, had obtained a temporary licence but the union still disputed the adequacy of the crewing arrangements, was upheld by the New Zealand Court of Appeal, albeit the court conceded that in the event of a court hearing on proceedings for a permanent injunction it would be possible to take account of the moral duty on a union to protect the interests of its members.[292] **23-59**

There has been considerable deliberation on justification in the Canadian case law.[293] Consistent with English authority it has been held that the defence is applicable where the defendant caused the breach of contract while acting under a duty imposed by law.[294] While some more recent decisions reflect the narrow scope of the defence,[295] others suggest that it might have a wider remit such that for instance **23-60**

---

289 [1989] 1 W.L.R. 225 at 233, per Stuart-Smith LJ: "it would be undesirable if the law were to insist that a mortgagee in [the position of the defendant] should exercise his strict legal rights if he is to be justified in interference with contracts between the mortgagor and third parties and could not be justified if he reached some sensible and reasonable accommodation which may be to the benefit of both himself and the mortgagor but which has the same effect on the third parties' contract".

290 *Lictor Anstalt v Mir Steel UK Ltd* [2011] EWHC 3310 (Ch); [2012] 1 All E.R. (Comm) 592 at [54]–[61] where on the facts the defence was held to be not so clearly made out as to entitle the defendant to summary judgment (upheld on appeal on other grounds [2012] EWCA Civ 1397; [2013] 2 All E.R. (Comm) 54).

291 *Pete's Towing Services Ltd v Northern Industrial Union of Workers* [1970] N.Z.L.R. 32, at 51; see generally 48-55.

292 *Northern Road Transport etc Union of Workers v Kawan Island Ferries Ltd* [1974] 2 N.Z.L.R. 617 (NZCA) at 623–624; see Hanson (1975) 38 M.L.R. 217.

293 A concise summary of the then state of English law was provided in *Posluns v Toronto Stock Exchange* (1964) 46 D.L.R. (2d) 210 at 270–1, per Gale J (Ont H.C.)

294 *Gainers v Pocklington Holdings Inc* (2001) 194 D.L.R. (4th) 109 (Alta CA); applying *De Jetley Marks v Greenwood* [1936] 1 All E.R. 863 at 873 where Porter J said that "justification must … involve action taken as a duty not the mere protection of the defendant's own interests."

295 *Drouillard v Cogeco Cable Inc* (2007) 282 D.L.R. (4th) 644 at [39]–[40] (Ont CA); and *512842 N.B. Inc v Delphinium Ltee* 2008 NBCA 56; (2008) 296 D.L.R. (4th) 694 where it was held that a defendant could only rely on its financial interests as justification for inducing breach of contract where this was done in exercise of a legal right. A desire to minimise financial risk could not therefore justify the defendant procuring breach of a contract for the sale of a fishing business by instructing

it could apply where a director considered that the company's best interests would be served by breaking its contractual commitments.[296] A more radical development of the law was suggested in *Sar Petroleum Inc v Peace Hills Trust Co* where, having noted that in the review of the extent of the *Lumley v Gye* and intentional harm torts by the House of Lords in *OBG Ltd v Allan* there was only one brief reference to the justification defence to inducing breach of contract, Robertson JA concluded that justification as applied by the Court of Appeal in *Edwin Hill v First National Finance Corporation* had effectively been incorporated by the House of Lords' decision in the test of intention; if the defendant was acting for a proper purpose the intention necessary for liability for inducing breach of contract would not exist.[297]

23-61 There are good reasons for not accepting the suggestion that being held to have acted for a proper purpose is inconsistent with being held to have acted with the intention of procuring a breach of contract; acceptance of the suggestion would be inconsistent with the long-established position, noted above, that a trade union will, absent statutory protection, be liable for having procured its members to break their contracts of employment even if it was only pursuing its duty of obtaining better wages or of enforcing collective agreements or statutory procedures for the benefit of its members.[298] A particular problem arises, however, where a defendant mistakenly believes that the nature of his purpose is sufficient to grant him a *legal* entitlement to procure a breach. As noted above, the courts in England and Wales have held that a defendant who honestly, but mistakenly, believes that his actions will not bring about a breach of contract at all *cannot* be held liable for having intentionally procured a breach of contract[299]; it is difficult to see why a defendant who had made an honest mistake about when he would be legally entitled to procure a breach should be treated less favourably, and in *Meretz Investments NV v ACP Ltd*[300] the Court of Appeal held that defendants who had received firm legal advice that they were entitled to cause another party to breach a contract could not be held to have acted with the intention of causing a breach.[301] From here, it would clearly

---

the seller to discontinue legal proceedings to compel the holder of the licence which was required to carry on the business to transfer it to the plaintiff.

[296] *1044807 Alberta Ltd v Brae Centre Ltd* 2008 ABCA 397; (2008) 302 D.L.R. (4th) 252 at [33]–[38]; even where this was not the case, a director would only be liable for inducing breach of contract where there was affirmative proof that the dominant purpose of his acts was depriving the plaintiff of the benefits of the contract.

[297] *Sar Petroleum Inc v Peace Hills Trust Co* 2010 NBCA 22; (2010) 318 D.L.R. (4th) 70 at [73]. Similar observations to the effect that in most cases justification appeared to be subsumed in another element of the tort were made in *Johnson v BFI Canada Inc* 2010 MBCA 101; (2010) 326 D.L.R. (4th) 497, but on the facts there it was held that justification was a defence where the defendant offered new contractual terms to a third party before the existing contract between them had expired but after the third party had entered into a new contract for the same service with the plaintiff.

[298] *South Wales Miners Federation v Glamorgan Coal Co Ltd* [1905] A.C. 239; *Timeplan Education Group v NUT* [1997] I.R.L.R. 457 CA (statutory scheme for regulating employment conditions); cf. Lord Hodge in *Global Resources Group Ltd v Mackay* [2008] CSOH 148; 2009 S.L.T. 104 at [14] "[the defender's] pursuit of his own economic advantage is not of itself justification."

[299] *British Industrial Plastics Ltd v Ferguson* [1940] 1 All E.R. 479 HL. The decision was approved in *OBG Ltd v Allan* [2007] UKHL 21; [2008] 1 A.C. 1 Lord Hoffmann at [41], per Lord Nicholls at [202]. See also *Allen v Pollock* [2020] EWCA Civ 258; [2020] Q.B. 781.

[300] *Meretz Investments NV v ACP Ltd* [2007] EWCA Civ 1303; [2008] Ch. 244.

[301] *Meretz Investments NV v ACP Ltd* [2007] EWCA Civ 1303; [2008] Ch. 244 at [124]–[127], per Arden LJ, [181]–[182], per Pill LJ. See also the treatment of *Meretz* by Lewison LJ, who had been the trial judge in the case, in *Allen v Pollock* [2020] EWCA Civ 258; [2020] Q.B. 781 at [21]. (The

be only a short step to hold that a defendant's honest belief that his actions were covered by a defence of justification could negate the possibility of liability; but this step has not yet been taken.

3. INTIMIDATION

The tort of intimidation[302] In *Rookes v Barnard*,[303] Lord Devlin accepted that there are two forms of the tort of intimidation. The first form, often called "two-party intimidation" will be committed by a defendant who intentionally causes loss to a claimant by making a threat that could be phrased "unless you act in this way (that will cause you loss), I will carry out this threat", with the result that the claimant acts in the required way and suffers loss. There are very few authorities discussing this form of the tort; indeed the textbook relied on by Lord Devlin claimed that, at that time, there was none,[304] but, as discussed below, the existence of this form of the tort means that it is necessary to consider the difficult question of what sorts of threats will be sufficient to found a claim. *Rookes v Barnard* itself involved the second form, often called "three-party intimidation". A defendant will commit this form of the tort if, with the intention of causing loss to the claimant, he delivers a threat to B that he will commit an act, or use means, unlawful as against B, as a result of which B does or refrains from doing some act which he is entitled to do, thereby causing loss to the claimant.[305] The name "intimidation" was attached to this liability by the House of Lords in 1964.[306] The tort is one of intention and the claimant must be a person whom the defendant intended to injure.[307] Doubts about the 23-62

authority of the relevant passage in *Meretz* is somewhat damaged by the fact that it treats the tort in *Lumley v Gye* as requiring proof of an "intention to cause harm", see [127], whilst the correct position is that it requires an "intention to procure a breach of contract", see above para.23-33, but the general principle that honest mistakes about legal entitlements ought to preclude liability remains clear.)

302 The use of the word "intimidation" in the law of tort must be understood to be limited to the meaning given to it in this section. It should not be confused with its use in other contexts, e.g. the crime of "intimidation" in s.241(1)(a) of TULRA 1992 (formerly s.7(1) of the Conspiracy and Protection of Property Act 1875) where the offence is limited to putting persons in fear by violence or threat of violence: *Gibson v Lawson* [1891] 2 Q.B. 545 (though it is now decided that there is no crime unless the act is tortious, at least for the crime of "watching" or "besetting" now in s.241(1)(d) of TULRA 1992: per Scott J in *Thomas v NUM (South Wales Area)* [1986] Ch. 20 at 56–65).

303 *Rookes v Barnard* [1964] A.C. 1129 HL at 1205.

304 Lord Devlin relied on the law as set out in *Salmond on the Law of Torts*, 13th edn (1961), p.697. The same passage appeared in Salmond's first edition (1907) at pp.439–440.

305 *Rookes v Barnard* [1964] A.C. 1129 HL. See also *Morgan v Fry* [1968] 2 Q.B. 710 at 724, where Lord Denning MR set out the "essential ingredients" of the tort, cited with approval by Longmore LJ in *Berezovsky v Abramovich* [2011] EWCA Civ 153; [2011] 1 W.L.R. 2290 at [5]; *Central Canada Potash Co Ltd v Government of Saskatchewan* (1977) 88 D.L.R. (3d) 609 at 635–642 (SCC).

306 *Hadmor Productions Ltd v Hamilton* [1983] 1 A.C. 191 at 229, per Lord Diplock; see also *News Group Newspapers Ltd v SOGAT (No.2)* [1987] I.C.R. 181 at 204, per Stuart-Smith J.

307 See Lord Devlin [1964] A.C. 1129 at 1208: "It must be proved that A's object is to injure C through the instrumentality of B": per Lord Evershed at 1183: "where the intention and effect of the threat is to injure such third party" (i.e. the claimant). cf. the passage in *Salmond on the Law of Torts*, 13th edn, p.697, approved by Lord Devlin at 1205, which refers only to whether the defendant intended to compel the person to whom the threat was addressed. The intent to injure is central to the tort: *Cheticamp Fisheries Co-op v Canada* (1995) 123 D.L.R. (4th) 121 at 137, per Chipman JA. Lord Hodson at 1202 in *Rookes*, above, spoke of intimidation as being actionable "if it is likely to harm the appellant and is followed by reasonably foreseeable damage" (adopting Sachs J [1963] 1 Q.B. 623 at 634). But this dictum seems to go only to the question of remoteness of damage, e.g. where A intends C to suffer damage of one type, but C in fact suffers damage of a different, though foresee-

existence of this tort were set at rest by *Rookes v Barnard*,[308] where the appellant, an employee of B.O.A.C., resigned from his trade union which had an informal agreement with B.O.A.C. that all employees at that place of work should be union members. Of the three respondents, B and F were lay officials of the union employed by B.O.A.C. and S was a full-time official employed by the union. These three, in accordance with the terms of a resolution passed at a meeting of union members, threatened B.O.A.C. that a strike of all the employees would take place within three days if the appellant non-unionist was not removed. In consequence, B.O.A.C. suspended and later (lawfully and with due notice) dismissed the appellant. In a collective agreement between the union and B.O.A.C. the union had agreed that employees would not strike.[309] The strike would have been a breach of contract by employees as against B.O.A.C. The House of Lords, reversing the Court of Appeal, held that the claimant succeeded in an action against B, F and S, based upon a conspiracy to commit the tort of intimidation against him.[310]

23-63 The continued existence of three-party intimidation as a separate tort must be called into question by the House of Lords' decision in *OBG Ltd v Allan*.[311] It seems clear that Lord Hoffmann, who gave one of the two leading speeches, intended that the liability found by the House of Lords to have been committed in *Rookes v Barnard* should be classified as an instance of liability for the tort which he called "intentionally causing loss by unlawful means".[312] None of the other speeches made any reference to this matter.[313] Since no doubt was expressed as to the correctness of the decision in *Rookes v Barnard*, and, in any case, Lord Hoffmann made no attempt to re-classify two-party intimidation, it is still appropriate to consider the elements of intimidation as a separate tort, notwithstanding the possibility that facts which give rise to liability for three-party intimidation may also satisfy the require-

---

able, character. If A threatens B without having C in mind at all, it is submitted that (unless the law of negligence imposes a duty of care) C cannot sue, even if A's threat is "likely" to cause him damage. Quaere where A threatens B but is reckless as to its effect upon C? Semble, A is not liable. cf. *Central Canada Potash Co Ltd v Government of Saskatchewan* (1979) 88 D.L.R. (3d) 609 at 642 (SCC). A threat that is ineffective is not actionable: cf. *Becton Dickinson v Lee* [1973] I.R. 1 at 31.

308 [1964] A.C. 1129 HL. For some of the many comments see: Hamson [1964] C.L.J. 159, continuing [1961] C.L.J. 189; Wedderburn (1964) 27 M.L.R. 257, continuing (1962) 25 M.L.R. 513 and (1961) 24 M.L.R. 572; Hoffmann (1965) 81 L.Q.R. 116; Weir [1964] C.L.J. 225; Kahn-Freund (1964) 14 Federation News (G.F.T.U.) 30; Christie (1964) 42 Can. B.R. 464; Elias and Ewing [1982] C.L.J. 334-341; Simpson (1982) 45 M.L.R. 447-450; Napier [1983] C.L.J. 43; G. Jones [1983] C.L.J. 47; Atiyah (1983) 99 L.Q.R. 353; Wedderburn, *The Worker and the Law*, 3rd edn (1986), pp.38-46 and 617-623; Carty (1988) 104 L.Q.R. 250 at 260; Cane, *Tort Law and Economic Interests*, 2nd edn (1996) pp.118-119 and 152; Murphy (2014) 77 M.L.R. 33. On trade dispute legislation: see para.23-130 onwards.

309 It was conceded by counsel that this clause became a term in each employee's employment contract. As to incorporation of such clauses into individual contracts, see now s.180 of TULRCA 1992.

310 As to the position of S in relation to liability for conspiracy see para.23-104, and on the trade dispute defences see para.23-140.

311 [2007] UKHL 21; [2008] 1 A.C. 1.

312 [2007] UKHL 21; [2008] 1 A.C. 1 at [7], "Salmond's tort of intimidation is therefore only one variant of a broader tort, usually called for short 'causing loss by unlawful means'". The longer name "intentionally causing loss by unlawful means" is used by Lord Hoffmann at [24], but elsewhere in his speech he predominantly uses the shorter form; cf. Lord Nicholls' use of the former label for this liability "interference with the claimant's business by unlawful means" at [141].

313 While Lady Hale and Lord Brown endorsed the views of Lord Hoffmann where they differed from those of Lord Nicholls, the question of the appropriate label for the tort at issue in *Rookes v Barnard* was not an issue on which Lord Nicholls expressed any opinion.

ments of the wider unlawful means tort.[314] Moreover, in *Construction, Forestry, Mining and Engineering Union v 321 Boral Resources (Vic) Pty Ltd* the Victoria Supreme Court rejected a submission that, following the decision in *OBG Ltd v Allan*, the tort of intimidation could no longer be considered part of Australian law; it was held that the fact that in English law three-party intimidation might now be considered part of a broader tort did not invalidate causes of action established in earlier Australian cases.[315]

(a) The threat

The word "threat", together with other words such as "coercion" or even "intimidation", has often been applied to utterances which are quite lawful and give rise to no liability.[316] A threat, for our purposes, is something which puts pressure on the person to whom it is addressed to take a particular course of action,[317] something by means of which that person is "improperly coerced".[318] A threat is an intimation by one to another that unless the latter does or does not do something the former will do something which the latter will not like.[319] The threat must be coercive,[320] it must be of the "or else" kind.[321] It must be capable of being effective, to produce the desired result,[322] and be more than "idle abuse", something to be taken seriously.[323] Furthermore, the concept is not limited to express threats; for there may be acts from which a threat can be implied, for example a strike begun without previous negotiation where the implication is clear that unless the employer does certain things the strike will be continued.[324] So too, keeping a person as "virtu- **23-64**

314 A different view is expressed in J. Murphy, "Understanding Intimidation" (2014) 77 M.L.R. 33, where the author argues, at 34–35, that there are no "sound juridical reasons to treat three-party intimidation as a discrete cause of action" and it has "disappeared as a tort in its own right", so the residual tort of intimidation only covers two-party situations.

315 [2014] VSCA 348; (2015) 318 A.L.R. 107. The submission was made on the ground that as defined in *Sid Ross Agency Ltd v Actors and Announcers Equity Association of Australia* [1971] 1 N.S.W.L.R. 760 intimidation depended entirely on the decision in *Rookes v Barnard* [1964] A.C. 1129, and that the tort articulated there had been subsumed in the broader tort of interference with business by the House of Lords' decision in *OBG Ltd v Allan* 2007 UKHL 21; [2008] 1 A.C. 1. In the Victoria Supreme Court decision it was noted that in *Northern Territory v Mengel* (1995) 185 C.L.R. 307 the Australian High Court had overruled its earlier decision that a separate cause of action existed where a person suffered loss as a result of the unlawful and intentional or positive act of another, and in *Sanders v Snell* [1998] HCA 64; (1998) 196 C.L.R. 329 it had declined to rule on whether the broader tort of intentionally causing loss to the plaintiff's business by unlawful means was part of Australian law.

316 *Crofter Hand Woven Harris Tweed Co v Veitch* [1942] A.C. 435 at 466–467, per Lord Wright. But as to "economic duress" and "coercive acts" see Lord Scarman in *Pao On v Lau Yiu Long* [1980] A.C. 614 PC at 635–636.

317 *Allen v Flood* [1898] A.C. 1 at 129, per Lord Herschell.

318 *Rookes v Barnard* [1964] A.C. 1129 at 1209, per Lord Devlin.

319 *Hodges v Webb* [1920] 2 Ch. 70 at 89, per Peterson J.

320 e.g. to make an employer "come to his senses": per Templeman J in *Camellia Tanker Ltd v ITWF* [1976] I.C.R. 274 at 284 (affirmed on other grounds, ibid. CA).

321 *Huljich v Hall* [1973] 2 N.Z.L.R. 279 at 288, per Turner P.

322 *Becton Dickinson Ltd v Lee* [1973] I.R. 1 at 31, per Walsh J. The effect must be causative of damage: *Hadmor Productions Ltd v Hamilton* [1983] 1 A.C. 191 at 229, per Lord Diplock.

323 *News Group Newspapers Ltd v SOGAT (No.2)* [1987] I.C.R. 181 at 204, per Stuart-Smith J.

324 *Rookes v Barnard* [1964] A.C. 1129 at 1208–1209, per Lord Devlin; at 1188, per Lord Evershed. Contrast *Stratford & Son Ltd v Lindley* [1965] A.C. 269 at 340; cf. *RCA Corp v Pollard* [1983] Ch. 135 at 144; Wedderburn (1983) 46 M.L.R. 229. In *Berezovsky v Abramovich* [2011] EWCA Civ 153; [2011] 1 W.L.R. 229 at [81]–[83], having stated that a threat could be implied as well as express,

ally a slave", in conditions of coercion as a "domestic drudge", has been regarded as "intimidation", perhaps because of the "implied threats of further assaults".[325] It may be noted that it is also possible that conduct amounting to a threat which is potentially actionable in the tort of intimidation could also be tortious either in the tort known as *Wilkinson v Downton* or under the Protection from Harassment Act 1997. Where that is the case the latter in particular may provide a simpler route to an effective remedy.[326]

23-65 **Warnings** The need for some coercive element is the basis for the distinction between a "threat"[327] and a "warning",[328] a distinction which is difficult to apply[329] but which is well founded on authority.[330] Thus, in *Rookes v Barnard*, it was noted that what had been said was a threat and not "merely informing B.O.A.C. that the men would strike if their terms were not accepted".[331] If all that a union official does is to inform an employer that men will or may strike, that is not intimidation.[332] It has been suggested that "there is now no necessity to be careful to distinguish between a threat and a warning on the basis that one is a threat to do an illegal act and the other a warning to do something lawful"; but this may overlook the legality of a threat to do something which is lawful.[333] Close inspection of the words may

---

depending on the context, Longmore LJ added that it was sufficient for the claimant to allege that the defendant threatened some act, such as (on the facts) expropriation would occur since this carried the implication that the defendant would do what he could to ensure that this would happen if the claimant did not comply with his wishes—on the facts by disposing of his interests in a particular company at a supposed undervalue. As to combinations which may constitute conspiracy to intimidate impliedly see per Fullagar J in *Williams v Hursey* (1959) 103 C.L.R. 30 at 80–83.

[325] *Godwin v Uzoigwe* [1993] Fam. Law 65; *The Times,* 18 June 1992 CA, per Stuart-Smith LJ (transcript, p.10).

[326] See paras 14-19 to 14-22. cf. *Great Canadian Railtour Co v Teamsters Local* 31 2012 BCCA 238; (2012) 350 D.L.R. (4th) 364 where in the absence of any such legislation but where the defendant union had accepted that harassing conduct by pickets could form part of the tort of intimidation, it was held that an injunction could restrain not only conduct which amounted to the tort but also conduct which formed part of or contributed to the commission of that tort.

[327] "A pre-intimation of proposed action of some sort. The action must be either per se a legal action or an illegal, i.e. a tortious action" per Lord Dunedin in *Sorrell v Smith* [1925] A.C. 700 at 730 where the words "i.e. a tortious" can no longer be accepted as defining "illegal"; see para.23-71.

[328] See *Stratford & Son Ltd v Lindley* [1965] A.C. 269 at 283–284, per Lord Denning MR; and at 292, per Pearson LJ (unaffected by reversal in the House of Lords on other grounds) and at 340–341, per Lord Donovan; *Pete's Towing Services Ltd v Northern Industrial Union of Workers* [1970] N.Z.L.R. 32 at 44 and 45.

[329] *Hodges v Webb* [1920] 2 Ch. 70 at 87 (the judgment by Peterson J which Lord Wright called an "admirable discussion" of these problems in the *Crofter* case [1942] A.C. 435 at 467).

[330] *Allen v Flood* [1898] A.C. 1 at 129; *Quinn v Leathem* [1901] A.C. 495 at 538; *Conway v Wade* [1909] A.C. 506 at 510, per Lord Loreburn; at 514, per Lord James; *Gaskell v Lancashire and Cheshire Miners Federation* (1912) 28 T.L.R. 518; *Santen v Busnach* (1913) 29 T.L.R. 214, CA; *Pratt v British Medical Association* [1919] 1 K.B. 244 at 261. In *Rookes v Barnard*, the argument that the distinction between threat and warning was relevant was not pursued; and Sachs J instructed the jury to "assume therefore that a resolution [to strike] was a threat": *The Times,* 5 May 1961.

[331] per Lord Reid [1964] A.C. 1129 at 1166. The jury had found that there was "a conspiracy to threaten strike action": [1961] 2 All E.R. 825 at 830.

[332] *Huntley v Thornton* [1957] 1 W.L.R. 321 at 344. Lord Donovan in *Stratford & Son Ltd v Lindley* [1965] A.C. 269 at 340: he does not incur liability "merely because he mentioned to an employer the possible alternative of a strike". cf. "If you go down that road, I will close you down" in *Beaverbrook Newspapers Ltd v Keys* [1978] I.C.R. 582 at 584; *News Group Newspapers Ltd v SOGAT (No.2)* [1987] I.C.R. 181 at 205.

[333] *Rookes v Barnard* [1964] A.C. 1129 at 1199, per Lord Hodson. Some early cases contained the "leading heresy" that threats might be actionable even if the act threatened was lawful: see paras 23-02

reveal that they fall into the category of neither "threat" nor "warning". Thus one interpretation of a notice given by a union official that workers would, from a certain date, not work with non-unionists but would carry out their duties as far as possible without associating with them, was that this was an offer made on behalf of the workers to continue working as from that date on changed terms of employment.[334]

(b) Unlawful act

It was at one time thought that a threat could amount to intimidation even if the act threatened was itself lawful.[335] But in the first half of the twentieth century, Lord Dunedin castigated that notion as "the leading heresy"[336] and in the *Crofter* case Lord Wright declared: **23-66**

> "There is nothing unlawful in giving a warning or intimation that if the party addressed pursues a certain line of conduct, others may act in a manner which he will not like and which will be prejudicial to his interests so long as nothing unlawful is threatened or done."[337]

This approach was confirmed in *Rookes v Barnard* where Lord Reid said:

> "So long as the defendant only threatens to do what he has a legal right to do he is on safe ground. At least if there is no conspiracy,[338] he would not be liable to anyone for doing the act, whatever his motive might be, and it would be absurd to make him liable for threatening to do it but not for doing it. But I agree with Lord Herschell (*Allen v Flood*)[339] that there is a chasm between doing what you have a legal right to do and doing what you have no legal right to do, and there seems to me to be the same chasm between threatening to do what you have a legal right to do and threatening to do what you have no legal right to do."[340]

Consequently, it is important to determine what is meant by "unlawful" or "what

---

and 23-66. The distinction between threat and warning is parallel to the equally difficult distinction drawn between on the one hand "advice" or mere "information" and on the other hand inducement in regard to the tort of procuring breach of contract; see para.23-43.

334 *Morgan v Fry* [1968] 2 Q.B. 710 at 731–732, per Davies LJ: "In a sense this does amount to a termination of the existing contract and an offer to continue on different terms. In the present case this was accepted by [the employer]."

335 *Quinn v Leathem* [1901] A.C. 495 at 537–538, per Lord Lindley; *Giblan v National Amalgamated Labourers' Union* [1903] 2 K.B. 600 at 619, per Romer LJ; *Pratt v British Medical Association* [1919] 1 K.B. 244 at 260–261, per McCardie J; *Valentine v Hyde* [1919] 2 Ch. 129 (a line of authority, it is submitted, no longer of authority on this point).

336 *Sorrell v Smith* [1925] A.C. 700 at 719.

337 *Crofter Hand Woven Harris Tweed Co v Veitch* [1942] A.C. 435 at 467. See also *Ware and De Freville v Motor Trades Association* [1921] 3 K.B. 40 at 84–91, per Atkin LJ; at 66–71, per Scrutton LJ; and Evershed MR in *DC Thomson & Co Ltd v Deakin* [1952] Ch. 646 at 676.

338 See para.23-98.

339 [1898] A.C. 1 at 121.

340 [1964] A.C. 1129 at 1168–1169. See also, per Lord Pearce at 1234; *Hadmor Productions Ltd v Hamilton* [1983] 1 A.C. 191 at 224, 225 and 229, per Lord Diplock. In the light of this very clear line of authority, the parties' agreement in *Berezovsky v Abramovich* [2011] EWCA Civ 153; [2011] 1 W.L.R. 2290 at [5] that "for the purposes of these interlocutory proceedings, … it is arguable that the means to be used need not necessarily be unlawful, if they can be categorised as 'illegitimate'" seems to be inconsistent with established authority.

you have no legal right to do" in this context—just as it is in the cognate torts of causing loss by unlawful means,[341] and of unlawful means conspiracy.[342]

23-67 The current state of the authorities, however, does not support a consistent definition of "unlawful means" across the economic torts. As the Supreme Court cautioned in *JSC BTA Bank v Ablyazov (No.14)*[343] "Some of the elements of the torts, notably intention and unlawful means are common to more than one of them. But it is dangerous to assume that they have the same content in each context." The most obvious reason for this comment is the decision of the House of Lords in *Revenue and Customs Commissioners v Total Network SL*,[344] where the court chose not to apply to the tort of unlawful means conspiracy the limits on what could constitute "unlawful means" that they had recently accepted in the context of the tort of causing loss by unlawful means, namely that those acts should be actionable at the suit of the third party. Where a claim in intimidation is based on a threat made against a third party, as in *Rookes v Barnard*,[345] it is strongly arguable that this narrower definition of "unlawful means"—requiring a threat of an act that would be actionable by that party if it were committed—is applicable.[346] As noted above, in *OBG v Allan*, the case that had established the narrower definition of "unlawful means" for the tort of causing loss by unlawful means, Lord Hoffmann treated the tort committed in *Rookes v Barnard* as an instance of that tort.[347]

23-68 But there are two reasons for hesitating before accepting that the "unlawful act" element of the tort of intimidation aligns precisely with the narrower definition of unlawful means employed by the tort of causing loss by unlawful means. The first reason is that this tort, at least as elaborated in the case of *OBG v Allan*, always requires three parties: the defendant must intentionally cause loss to the claimant by using unlawful means to restrict the freedom of a third party to deal with the claimant. By contrast, it is clear that a two-party form of the tort of intimidation exists, where the defendant intentionally causes harm to the claimant by making a threat to him or her directly. In *OBG v Allan*, Lord Hoffmann expressly warned that "two party intimidation" would raise "altogether different issues",[348] and in *Revenue & Customs Commissioners v Total Network SL*,[349] the House of Lords linked this comment to their view that a narrow definition of "unlawful means" was *only* required in *OBG v Allan* because the intentionally causing loss tort involved inflicting loss on a claimant through the medium of a third party. Thus, two-party intimidation, where a threat is made directly to a claimant as a means of causing

---

341 See para.23-78.

342 See para.23-105.

343 [2018] UKSC 19; [2018] 2 W.L.R. 1125 at [6].

344 [2008] UKHL 19; [2008] 1 A.C. 1174.

345 *Rookes v Barnard* [1964] A.C. 1129 HL.

346 *OBG Ltd v Allan* [2007] UKHL 21; [2008] 1 A.C. 1 at [61].

347 [2007] UKHL 21; [2008] 1 A.C. 1 at [7] and [47]; see also [29], where he described "primary liability for intentionally causing loss by unlawfully interfering with the liberty of a third party" as based on a principle "derived from" the foundational three-party intimidation cases of *Tarleton v McGawley* (1793) 1 Peake 270; and *Garret v Taylor* (1620) Cro. Jac. 567.

348 [2007] UKHL 21; [2008] 1 A.C. 1 at [61].

349 *Revenue & Customs Commissioners v Total Network SL* [2008] UKHL 19; [2008] 1 A.C. 1174 at [43], per Lord Hope, at [99], per Lord Walker, at [124], per Lord Mance, at [223], per Lord Neuberger. See also *JSC BTA Bank v Ablyazov (No.14)* [2018] UKSC 19; [2018] 2 W.L.R. 1125 at [12].

loss, might use the broader definition of "unlawful means" that has been developed in the tort of unlawful means conspiracy, and extends to at least some crimes.[350]

The second reason for hesitation is the development since *Rookes v Barnard*[351] of the doctrine of economic duress and, in particular, the notion that the remedies associated with that doctrine can follow "illegitimate pressure", a concept that is broader than threats of unlawful acts. Whilst the better view appears to be that economic duress does not itself amount to a tort,[352] the fact that it responds to a wider range of forms of pressure than "threats of unlawful means" has created pressure to expand the tort of two-party intimidation; if the tort does not expand, then a claimant may be unable to obtain a useful remedy in circumstances where he has lost the right to avoid a contract that he entered as a result of economic duress.[353] **23-69**

Violence and torts Intimidation as a tort has its origins in threats of violence and was, until relatively recently, regarded as "a rare and peculiar cause of action".[354] Thus, in a case which for over a century excited little interest[355] and in which the captain of a trading vessel off the coast of Africa fired guns to frighten potential customers in canoes and deter them from trading with a rival ship, it was held that an action lay at the suit of that ship's owners.[356] In all those early cases "you find there was either violence or the threat of violence, obstruction of the highway, or the access to the [claimant's] premises, nuisance or other unlawful acts done to the damage of the [claimant]".[357] It thus came to be said that a threat to commit any tort was a threat to use unlawful means[358]; and that unlawful means for this present **23-70**

350 See below, para.23-109, for discussion of which crimes can be "unlawful means" for the tort of unlawful means conspiracy. In *Berezovsky v Abramovich* [2011] EWCA Civ 153; [2011] 1 W.L.R. 2290, a claim involving two-party intimidation, the parties agreed (at [5]) that "for the purposes of these interlocutory proceedings, … it is arguable that the means to be used need not necessarily be unlawful, if they can be categorised as 'illegitimate'."

351 [1964] A.C. 1129 HL.

352 Different opinions were expressed on this issue by Lord Diplock and Lord Scarman in *Universe Tankships Inc of Monrovia v International Transport Workers Federation, "The Universe Sentinel"* [1983] 1 A.C. 366 at 385 and 400. The issue was discussed in detail by Leggatt LJ in *Al Nehayan v Kent* [2018] EWHC 333 (Comm); [2018] 1 C.L.C. 216 at [222]–[224], where he concluded that: "conduct amounting to duress will not necessarily give rise to liability in tort." See also the opinion of Sales J in *Investec Bank (Channel Islands) Ltd v The Retail Group plc* [2009] EWHC 476 (Ch) at [122], quoted by Leggatt LJ, that: "The primary object of a plea of economic duress in relation to a contract is to avoid the contract, which is a legal consequence significantly different from establishing a cause of action in damages."

353 This argument is made in *Chitty on Contracts* (33rd edn, 2018), vol. 1 at para.8-057, and was noted by Leggatt LJ in *Al Nehayan v Kent* [2018] EWHC 333 (Comm); [2018] 1 C.L.C. 216 at [223]. See also *Morley v Royal Bank of Scotland Plc* [2020] EWHC 88 (Ch), where Kerr J considered issues of economic duress and the tort of two-party intimidation, but was able to dismiss the intimidation claim on its facts without deciding whether the tort could be committed by use of "illegitimate pressure".

354 *Rookes v Barnard* [1963] 1 Q.B. 623 at 688, per Pearson LJ, reviewing the older authorities at 689–694, and, per Lord Hodson [1964] A.C. 1129 at 1198.

355 See *Allen v Flood* [1898] A.C. 1 at 66–67, per Wright J.

356 *Tarleton v McGawley* (1793) 1 Peake 270; so too threats of violence: *Garret v Taylor* (1620) Cro. Jac. 567; per Holt CJ in *Keeble v Hickeringill* (1705) 11 East 574n; cf. actual coercion impliedly threatening to continue it: *Godwin v Ozoigwe* [1993] Fam. Law 65; *The Times*, 18 June 1992 CA.

357 *Allen v Flood* [1898] A.C. 1 at 173–174, per Lord Davey; and at 135–137, per Lord Herschell; these cases also involved wrongful acts.

358 *Rookes v Barnard* [1964] A.C. 1129 at 1167, per Lord Reid; *Associated Newspapers Group Ltd v Wade* [1979] 1 W.L.R. 697 at 715 and 719 CA; *Morgan v Fry* [1968] 2 Q.B. 710 CA.

purpose included all acts which "are criminal or tortious in character".[359] Therefore, threats which involve the use of fraud are actionable.[360]

23-71 **Breach of contract** Until 1964 it was uncertain whether a threat of breach of contract ranked as unlawful means. In *Rookes v Barnard*, the Court of Appeal held that it did not.[361] To extend the tort to threats of breach of contract:

> "[w]ould overturn or outflank some elementary principles of contract law. If A breaks his contract with B, A is liable in damages to B, but he is not liable to C for damage caused to him by that breach of contract, even if such damage was foreseeable or even intended by A ... (it) seems inherently absurd to say that a mere threat to do something is actionable when the actual doing of it is not ..."[362]

The House of Lords, however, unanimously reversed this decision, although they appeared still to accept that "only parties to a contract can sue for breaches of that contract, notwithstanding that some third party may be damnified by the breach and intentionally so damnified".[363] Their Lordships felt that to threaten "a breach of contract may be a much more coercive weapon than threatening a tort", and saw "no difference in principle between a threat to break a contract and a threat to commit a tort".[364] "That a breach of contract is unlawful in the sense that it involves the

---

359 per Lord Evershed, in *Rookes v Barnard* [1964] A.C. 1129 at 1182. See also Lord Devlin at 1206: "It is not of course disputed that if the act threatened is a crime, the threat is unlawful". If, however, the definition of "unlawful means" in the tort of intimidation is to be aligned with the definition used in the intentionally causing loss tort after *OBG Ltd v Allan* [2007] UKHL 21; [2008] 1 A.C. 1, then threats to commit crimes will be insufficient as a foundation for the tort of intimidation (at least in its three-party form) unless the crime concerned, if committed, could give rise to a private law claim by the person threatened. And as to statutory criminal offences, see below para.23-72. See also *Hargreaves v Bretherton* [1959] 1 Q.B. 45 (use of perjury to damage claimant; no cause of action); *Roberts v Stone Ltd* (1945) 172 L.T. 240 at 242.

360 See, per Lord Wright in the *Crofter* case [1942] A.C. 435 at 476–477; per Kennedy LJ in *National Phonograph Co v Edison-Bell Consolidated Phonograph Co* [1908] 1 Ch. 335 at 368; compare *Lonrho v Fayed* [1990] 2 Q.B. 479, CA (affirmed on other grounds [1992] 1 A.C. 448 HL); but liability turns on the direct and intentional injury: *RCA Corp v Pollard* [1983] Ch. 135 at 153–154, per Oliver LJ. In *Conway v Wade* [1909] A.C. 506 HL, the defendant had, in effect, made a threat which entailed fraudulent misrepresentation as to his authority: see, per Lord James at 513; see *Rookes v Barnard* [1964] A.C. 1129 at 1176, per Lord Reid; and *Armagas Ltd v Mundogas SA* [1986] A.C. 717 at 781, per Lord Keith; *Mahesan S/O v Malaysian Govt Officers' Co-op Housing Soc* [1979] A.C. 374 PC (tort action against briber of agent). Nothing said in *Lonrho Ltd v Shell Petroleum Co Ltd (No.2)* [1982] A.C. 173 HL, doubts the proposition that fraud against a third person is capable of being unlawful means; cf. *Bradford etc Building Society v Borders* [1941] 2 All E.R. 205 at 220, per Lord Wright, to use the fraud of another to one's profit is actionable; the *National Phonograph Co* case, above; *Lonrho Plc v Fayed* [1990] 2 Q.B. 479 CA; [1992] 1 A.C. 448 HL; see also *Adams v R.* [1995] 1 W.L.R. 52 PC.

361 [1963] 1 Q.B. 623. Issues of "privity of contract" are here at stake; per Henry J in *Barretts & Baird (Wholesale) Ltd v IPCS* [1987] I.R.L.R. 3 at 8. Although it may be said that C sues on A's threat, not on the contract between A and B (see, per Lord Devlin [1964] A.C. at 1208), C is still a third party to the contractual obligations, breach of which is essential to his cause of action. In the same way, an action by B against A for anticipatory breach of contract is based upon the threat and not the breach. See now the Contracts (Rights of Third Parties) Act 1999, which does not affect the general argument; see C. Macmillan (2000) 63 M.L.R. 721.

362 [1963] 1 Q.B. 623, at 695–696, per Pearson LJ.

363 [1964] A.C. 1129 at 1187, per Lord Evershed. See below, para.23-87, on the tort of causing loss by unlawful means for the difficulties inherent in this proposition.

364 [1964] A.C. 1129 at 1169 and 1168 respectively, per Lord Reid; cf. *Riordan v Butler* [1940] Ir. R. 347; *Cooper v Millea* [1938] Ir. R. 749.

violation of a legal right there can be no doubt"[365]; and "to draw the line ... between contract and tort seems to me inconsistent with the principle that underlies *Lumley v Gye*".[366] Lord Devlin could find "nothing to differentiate a threat of a breach of contract from a threat of physical violence or any other illegal threat".[367] The two causes of action (for breach of contract—actual or anticipatory—and for intimidation) are "in law quite independent"; so that "in no circumstances does C sue on B's contract. The cause of action arises not because B's contract is broken but because it is not broken; it arises because of the action which B has taken to avert the breach."[368]

Breach of statute Coercive threats of torts or breach of contract appear, therefore, to contrast with the position of breaches of penal statutes after the House of Lords' decisions in *Lonrho Ltd v Shell Petroleum Co Ltd*[369] and *Gouriet v Union of Post Office Workers*.[370] Neither of those, however, was a case of coercive threat. Lonrho, moreover, failed in its action against defendants who had (it was assumed) committed criminal acts in pursuit of their own business interests and not with the predominant purpose "to injure those of Lonrho".[371] It may be questioned whether the result would be the same had Shell, before illegally supplying the rebels in Rhodesia with oil, told Lonrho: "if you do not conduct your trade in the conventional way rather than your present unconventional, though lawful, manner, we will supply Rhodesia with oil through other routes (illegally) and shut down your pipeline for years." Could they then have added: "We have only threatened a crime, so you cannot sue us?"[372] Decisions after Lonrho suggest that they could.[373] To hold otherwise would lead to the apparent absurdity that they would be liable 23-72

365 [1964] A.C. 1129 at 1201, per Lord Hodson.

366 [1964] A.C. 1129 at 1234, per Lord Pearce.

367 [1964] A.C. 1129 at 1209, adopting the arguments of Hamson [1961] C.L.J. 189 at 191. It should be noted that, here and at 1206, Lord Devlin clearly included threats to do any criminal act as within the scope of the tort. As noted above, however, if the definition of "unlawful means" in the tort of intimidation is to be aligned with the definition used in the intentionally causing loss tort after *OBG Ltd v Allan* [2007] UKHL 21; [2008] 1 A.C. 1, then threats to commit crimes will be insufficient as a foundation for the tort of intimidation (at least in its three-party form).

368 [1964] A.C. 1129 at 1207 and 1208. See Wedderburn (1964) 27 M.L.R. 257 at 263–267; Hoffmann (1965) 81 L.Q.R. 116; Carty (1988) 104 L.Q.R. 250 at 260–262. Compare Weir, *Economic Torts* (1997), pp.37–39; *Winfield and Jolowicz on Tort*, 19th edn (2014), para.19-24; and W. Van Gerven et al, *Tort Law: Scope of Protection* (1988), p.257. In *Metropolitan Conference Centre Inc v Hunter*, 2016 ABCA 83; (2016) 399 D.L.R. (4th) 687, the court rejected the submission that a threat of breach of contract—to "close down" the hiring of the Centre unless the respondents paid additional fees (which they did)—made on the day before the event for which it had been hired, was not serious enough to amount to intimidation.

369 [1982] A.C. 173 HL. Lonrho Ltd had failed in their allegation that Shell were in breach of their contract with them: [1982] A.C. 173 HL at 183 and 186. Remarkably, on the principle of *Rookes* [1964] A.C. 1129 HL, it seems that Lonrho might, however, have had an action against Shell if the latter's criminal activity had involved some coercive breach of contract made with a third party.

370 [1978] A.C. 435 HL.

371 Lonrho [1982] A.C. 173 at 188–189, per Lord Diplock; this was the "assumption" made for the conspiracy claim; but nothing suggests that it did not apply also to the claim for damage done by the "unlawful acts", which was dubbed "foreseeable loss": at 183. As to conspiracy, see para.23-108; *Lonrho Plc v Fayed* [1992] 1 A.C. 448 HL.

372 See, per Lord Denning MR in *Ex p. Island Records Ltd* [1978] Ch. 122 at 136, rejecting the argument: "It is a crime, and so you cannot sue me."

373 *RCA Corp v Pollard* [1983] Ch. 135 CA; *CBS Songs Ltd v Amstrad Consumer Electronics Plc* [1988] 1 Ch. 61 CA at 71–78, per Nicholls LJ (affirmed on other grounds: [1988] A.C. 1013 HL).

if they threatened, but not liable if they deliberately inflicted the damage by the same illegal means. It must be noted, however, that the doctrine of economic duress and the crime of blackmail, which also deal with threats, have both developed in such a way that they can respond to threats of committing acts that it would not have been unlawful to carry out, when those threats were coupled with particular types of demand; at least in the context of two-party intimidation, a strong argument can be made for drawing an analogy with these doctrines.

23-73 **Blackmail and illegitimate pressure** In *Al Nehayan v Kent*,[374] which included a claim for two-party intimidation, Leggatt LJ expressed the opinion that blackmail should be covered by the tort of intimidation, noting that: "Conduct which amounts to blackmail is plainly both coercive and unlawful, even if what the blackmailer has threatened to do is not."[375] The likelihood of this view becoming the law, however, has been somewhat reduced by the Court of Appeal's subsequent rejection of the further, related, suggestion made by Leggatt LJ in *Al Nehayan v Kent* of aligning economic duress and the crime of blackmail.[376] Nonetheless, it remains the case that the courts are willing to find economic duress even where a defendant has threatened to do something lawful, at least where the defendant was seeking to achieve a result that it did not believe, in good faith, that it was entitled to achieve.[377] But whilst that may provide a reason for extending the scope of the tort of two-party intimidation, the reason is not irresistible: "In principle, … the circumstances in which a contract may be rescinded and the defendant required to restore a benefit received from the claimant may not coincide with those in which the claimant is entitled to recover damages for loss caused by a wrongful act of the defendant."[378] Thus, despite the importance that the law attaches to preserving the reliability of commercial contracts, parties may be permitted to rescind agreements in circumstances where the law of torts can detect no wrongdoing. It is likely, however, that pressure to extend the tort of two-party intimidation in parallel with the doctrine of economic duress will continue, and where such submissions are made it will become important to consider whether the defendant honestly believed that he was entitled to persuade the claimant to act in the way that caused the claimant's loss.[379]

---

374 *Al Nehayan v Kent* [2018] EWHC 333 (Comm); [2018] 1 C.L.C. 216.

375 *Al Nehayan v Kent* [2018] EWHC 333 (Comm); [2018] 1 C.L.C. 216 at [227]–[231], passage quoted from [230]. See also the older case of *Microdata Information Services Ltd v Rivendale Ltd* [1991] F.S.R. 681 CA (decided in 1984), where the Court of Appeal upheld the grant of an injunction against a defendant who had threatened to inform a claimant's potential client about a dispute as to the claimant's right to license use of software unless the claimant met various demands: Griffiths LJ, at 689, expressly alluded to the parallel with blackmail.

376 See *Times Travel (UK) Ltd v Pakistan International Airlines Corpn* [2019] EWCA Civ 828; [2020] Ch. 98 at [104]–[105].

377 *Times Travel (UK) Ltd v Pakistan International Airlines Corpn* [2019] EWCA Civ 828; [2020] Ch. 98; *Morley v Royal Bank of Scotland Plc* [2020] EWHC 88 (Ch) at [236].

378 *Al Nehayan v Kent* [2018] EWHC 333 (Comm); [2018] 1 C.L.C. 216 at [224], per Leggatt LJ.

379 In *Morley v Royal Bank of Scotland Plc* [2020] EWHC 88 (Ch), Kerr J's finding that the defendant had not made any threat in "bad faith", at [237], relieved him of the need to decide how far the tort of intimidation parallels the doctrine of "lawful act economic duress". The defendant submitted that it remains the law that it is not a tort to threaten an act the defendant is legally entitled to do: *Rookes v Barnard* [1964] A.C. 1129, per Lord Reid at 1168–1169.

(c) Submission to threat

In the tort of intimidation, "it is essential to the cause of action that the person threatened should comply with the demand".[380] If A says to B: "I will hit you unless you give me £5", and B resists saying: "you can do your worst. I am not going to pay you £5", at that point B has no cause of action for damages. Similarly, if A threatens to hit B unless he dismisses his cook or gives up dealing with his butcher, and B resists, neither the cook nor the butcher can sue, for "they have suffered no damage by the threat".[381] If A threatens to hit B, the latter can sue for assault; or he can, without waiting for the event, sue for an injunction to prevent the threat being carried out.[382] It is the same if A makes a "bare threat", such as "I am going to hit you when I get you alone". In such cases the cause of action rests upon the impending tort of assault, not upon intimidation.[383] The tort of intimidation is not complete "unless the person threatened succumbs to the threat and damage is suffered"; but injunctive relief can be given to restrain both the unlawful act and the threat to commit it.[384] In the tort of intimidation, there must be a "coercive threat ... coupled with a demand. It must be intended to coerce a person into doing something that he is unwilling to do or not doing something that he wishes to do".[385] This approach was shared by the majority of the Law Lords in *Rookes v Barnard*.[386] If A threatens to use violence against B unless B acts to the detriment of C, C cannot sue where B resists, because he will suffer no harm in such a case. Whereas, if B complies with the threat, B cannot sue[387]; but "C will be able to sue because through B's compliance he has been injured", said Lord Devlin. He added, however: 23-74

380 *Stratford & Son Ltd v Lindley* [1965] A.C. 269 at 283, per Lord Denning MR. See also *Huljich v Hall* [1973] 2 N.Z.L.R. 279 at 285–286.

381 *Stratford & Son Ltd v Lindley* [1965] A.C. 269 at 302, per Salmon LJ. See also, per Lord Denning MR in *Morgan v Fry* [1968] 2 Q.B. 710 at 724: "the person so threatened must comply with a demand." As to compliance with the demand and contemplation of a trade dispute, see s.244(4) of TULRCA 1992; and para.23-195.

382 Or without waiting for the implied threat to continue or to be executed: *Godwin v Uzoigwe* [1993] Fam. Law 65; *The Times*, 18 June 1992 CA; compare *Khorasandjian v Bush* [1993] Q.B. 727 (harassment with threats of violence; quia timet injunction to prevent assault).

383 The claimant, for example, may obtain an injunction quia timet against threatened procurement of breach of both existing and future contracts: see *Stratford & Son Ltd v Lindley* [1965] A.C. 269; *Torquay Hotel Co v Cousins* [1969] Ch. 106. Sed quaere where A says: "I am going to break my contract with C when I feel like ruining you (B), as I know the breach will do"; cf. *Central Canada Potash Co Ltd v Government of Saskatchewan* (1979) 88 D.L.R. (3d) 609 at 641–642 (SCC); *Roehl v Houlehan* (1991) 74 D.L.R. (4th) 562 (Ont. CA).

384 per Stuart-Smith J in *News Group Newspapers Ltd v SOGAT (No.2)* [1987] I.C.R. 181 at 204.

385 per Lord Denning MR in *Stratford & Son Ltd v Lindley* [1965] A.C. 269 at 283–284. (Quaere whether these passages provide support for the view of Russell LJ in *Morgan v Fry* [1968] 2 Q.B. 710 at 737–739; and on causation, see Salmon LJ [1965] A.C. 269 at 306.) The coercive threat of illegal acts and the intent to injure must be the cause of the conduct: *Lonrho Plc v Fayed* [1990] 2 Q.B. 479 CA (upheld on other grounds: [1992] A.C. 448 HL); compare *Barretts & Baird (Wholesale) Ltd v IPCS* [1987] I.R.L.R. 3 at 10, per Henry J, approving *Van Camp Chocolates Ltd v Aulsebrooks* [1984] 1 N.Z.L.R. 354 at 360, per Cooke CJ (NZCA). Compare on intention: *Associated British Ports v TGWU* [1989] 1 W.L.R. 939, CA (reversed on other grounds, [1989] 1 W.L.R. 939 HL).

386 [1964] A.C. 1129 at 1187–1188, per Lord Evershed; at 1200–1201, per Lord Hodson; at 1207–1208, per Lord Devlin. Neither Lord Reid (at 1168–1169) nor Lord Pearce (at 1234–1235) dealt with the problem of resistance by B.

387 Quaere where submission, in face of a threat to take unlawful steps, would also damage B.

"The only case in which B and C are both likely to sue is if they both sue for the tort of intimidation in a case in which B has harmed himself by also harming C."[388]

(d) Two party intimidation

23-75 Some doubts have been expressed as to whether the same principles apply where A intimidates B to the damage of B ("two-party" intimidation) as apply to a case where A intimidates B to the damage of C ("three-party" intimidation).[389] In the first place, it may be thought odd that "two-party" intimidation should exist at all; for in so far as he claims damages, it might be said that B's own submission had caused the loss; and if he claims an injunction, that would rest upon the wrongdoing which was threatened without any need of a separate tort. Nevertheless, authority clearly supports the existence of "two-party" intimidation as well as the "three-party" tort.[390] As noted above, however, there are arguments available for allowing the two-party tort to use a broader range of "unlawful threats"[391] partly as a result of the influence of the doctrine of "economic duress".[392] A special problem arises in the

[388] [1964] A.C. 1129 at 1207–1208. Lord Devlin also claimed: "There is no anomaly about this and if one substitutes 'breach of contract' for 'physical violence' the position is the same." But it may be doubted whether this is so when the act threatened is only a breach of contract, and when B resists it. See para.23-87; and see *Williams v Hursey* (1959) 103 C.L.R. 30 at 122–124.

[389] per Lord Reid *Stratford & Son Ltd v Lindley* [1965] A.C. 269 at 325: A two-party and a three-party case are "not necessarily in pari casu and [the former] may involve questions which cannot arise when there is intimidation of a third person". The dicta of Lord Pearce at 336 are directed not to this problem, but to the ambit of Trade Disputes Act 1906 s.3, the predecessor of TULRCA 1992 s.219(1). See below. There is no reason to confine this tort to a "three-party" form: *Cellular Rental Systems v Bell Mobility* (1994) 116 D.L.R. (4th) 514 (Ont.).

[390] per Lord Devlin in *Rookes v Barnard* [1964] A.C. 1129 at 1205, adopting *Salmond on Torts* (13th ed.), p.697, "for example an action [for intimidation] will doubtless lie at the suit of a trader who has been compelled to discontinue his business by means of threats of personal violence made against him by the defendant with that intention." See also at 1209, per Lord Devlin; and, per Lord Denning MR in *Stratford & Son Ltd v Lindley* [1965] A.C. 269 at 285; per Salmon LJ, [1965] A.C. 269 at 302; per Stuart-Smith J in *News Group Newspapers Ltd v SOGAT (No.2)* [1987] I.C.R. 181 at 204–205 (especially note the seventh claimant able to sue for intimidatory threats). So, too, *Pete's Towing Services Ltd v Northern Industrial Union of Workers* [1970] N.Z.L.R. 32 at 41-43; *Mintuck v Valley River Band 63A* (1977) 75 D.L.R. (3d) 589 at 605–606. But see the doubt in *Central Canada Potash Co Ltd v Government of Saskatchewan* (1979) 88 D.L.R. (3d) 609 at 640 (a doubt clearly caused by the Supreme Court's preference not to make a breach of contract into an "illegal act" for the purposes of the tort: see at 641–642). In *Berezovsky v Abramovich* [2011] EWCA Civ 153; [2011] 1 W.L.R. 2290 both the outline of the essential ingredients of the tort (at [5]) and discussion of the adequacy of the claimant's pleading (at [80]–[86]) clearly contemplated the possibility of liability in the "two party" form of the tort.

[391] In summary, it is arguable that the narrowing of "unlawful threats" to threats of actionable civil wrongs in *OBG Ltd v Allan* [2007] UKHL 21; [2008] 1 A.C. 1 need not be extended to situations where the defendant causes harm to the claimant directly, rather than through using unlawful means to restrict a third party's freedom to deal with the claimant. Indeed, in *OBG Ltd* at [61] Lord Hoffmann expressly excluded cases of "two party intimidation", where a claimant was compelled by unlawful intimidation to act to his own detriment, from his discussion of "unlawful means", since he said that such cases raised "altogether different issues".

[392] *Universe Tankships Inc of Monrovia v ITF* [1983] 1 A.C. 366 HL; per Kerr LJ in *Occidental Worldwide Investment Corp v Skibs A/S Avanti* [1976] 1 Lloyd's Rep. 293 at 335–336; *B & S Contracts & Design Ltd v Victor Green Publications Ltd* [1984] I.C.R. 419 CA; *Atlas Express Ltd v Kafco Ltd* [1989] 1 Q.B. 833; *Dimskal Shipping SA v ITWF* [1992] 2 A.C. 152 HL; *CTN Cash and Carry Ltd v Gallaher Ltd* [1994] 4 All E.R. 714 CA; *Times Travel (UK) Ltd v Pakistan International Airlines Corpn* [2019] EWCA Civ 828; [2020] Ch. 98; *Morley v Royal Bank of Scotland Plc* [2020] EWHC 88 (Ch). See R. Bigwood "Economic Duress by (Threatened) Breach of Contract" (2001)

context of "two-party" intimidation as a result of the acceptance of breach of contract as an "unlawful act".[393] Once that extension is made, it becomes arguable that "two-party" intimidation extends to a threat of breach of contract, despite the fact that B may also have an action against A for anticipatory breach of contract. Thus, a threat by a landlord, intent on damaging his tenant's business, that he will commit breaches of the covenant for quiet enjoyment unless his tenant submits to him, or by a patentee that he will unlawfully withdraw a licence to exploit the patent from a trader, can both be the basis of an action for intimidation by the person threatened, just as if the landlord or patentee had threatened a personal assault.[394] Also, the threat by a debtor to pay nothing if his creditor does not submit to the offer of a lesser sum is capable of being intimidation.[395] Such a case gives colour to the notion that two-party intimidation adds to the claimant's remedies; for, apart from the possibility of higher damages[396] and, in some cases perhaps, a more extended availability of the remedy of injunction,[397] the action for intimidation may lie even if the threat does not amount to anticipatory breach of contract.[398]

---

117 L.Q.R. 376. cf. *Kolmar Group AG v Traxpo Enterprises Pvt Ltd* [2010] EWHC 113 (Comm); [2010] 2 Lloyd's Rep. 653 where the definition and ingredients of this tort in the 19th edition of this work were cited with approval (at [119]) and on the facts the claimants were held to be entitled to succeed on the basis of claims for either restitution of sums paid under economic duress or damages for intimidation; see [118] and [121].

393 The "acute difficulties" felt by some commentators about two-party intimidation stem wholly from the extension of unlawful means to breach of contract. See: Hoffmann (1965) 81 L.Q.R. 116 at 127–128; Hamson [1964] C.L.J. 159 at 168; Carty (1988) 104 L.Q.R. 250 at 261–262 (who prefers to use economic duress to fill any "gap"); Wedderburn (1965) 28 M.L.R. 205 at 210 (to allow a third party to sue on a coercive threat to break a contract but then deny an equivalent action to a damaged contracting party would be to pile "an absurd Pelion on an odd Ossa").

394 [1964] A.C. 1129 at 1187, per Lord Evershed. (These examples again illustrate the novelty of extending intimidation into the realm of threats to break contracts. The problem for example, in *Kenny v Preen* [1963] 1 Q.B. 499, CA, might have been solved by one sharp blow of the doctrine of intimidation.)

395 *D & C Builders v Rees* [1966] 2 Q.B. 617 at 625, per Lord Denning MR.

396 *The Heron II; Koufos v Czarnikow* [1969] 1 A.C. 350 HL; *NCB v Galley* [1958] 1 W.L.R. 16 CA. See Treitel, *The Law of Contract*, 14th edn (2015), Ch.20.

397 Quaere whether, in the case of a personal contract, an injunction might lie to restrain the tort even though the court would not normally grant such a remedy for breach of the contract. Lord Devlin adumbrates, but does not answer this question: [1964] A.C. 1129 at 1207–1208. Semble: it would not, at least in the case of a contract of employment: TULRCA 1992 s.236; per Henry J in *Barretts & Baird (Wholesale) Ltd v IPCS* [1987] I.R.L.R. 3 at 10; cf. *Warren v Mendy* [1989] 1 W.L.R. 853 CA.

398 See [1964] A.C. 1129 at 1206–1207, per Lord Devlin:

> "It was said that B.O.A.C. could not have sued for an anticipatory breach unless they first elected to rescind which they never did. I dare say that is right, but I do not think it matters at all whether B.O.A.C. could sue or not. The two causes of action—B.O.A.C.'s and the appellant's—are in law quite independent; and in fact they are virtually alternative because it is difficult to visualise (except in one case) a set of facts on which both could sue."

Quaere: if B.O.A.C. had chosen to affirm the contracts, might they still have had a remedy for damage flowing from the threats on the basis of "two-party" intimidation? There seems to be no authority on the question whether affirmation "cures" the tort in the way in which it affects the anticipatory breach. But if C agrees with B to rescind the contract which B has threatened to break in order to coerce A, there appears to be no basis left for any "illegal means" and none therefore for the tort; compare *Central Canada Potash Co Ltd v Govt of Saskatchewan* (1979) 38 D.L.R. (3d) 609 SCC at 636–640.

(e) Justification

23-76 Somewhat surprisingly, there may be a doctrine of justification whereby a defendant who has committed the tort of intimidation can excuse himself from liability. Lord Devlin suggested in *Rookes v Barnard* that such a defence might exist, but said that it was not in issue in that case.[399] The unusual feature of allowing justification here is the fact that, *ex hypothesi*, the defendant has been guilty of a threat of unlawful acts; and the analogous, but narrow, defence of justification in the tort of procuring breach of contract was commonly thought not to apply if the defendant there had made use of illegal means.[400] Lord Denning MR, while not expressing a final view as to the place, if any, of this defence, has suggested that union officials "might well be justified" in intimidating an employer in order to remove persons who were "really troublemakers who fomented discord in the docks, without lawful cause or excuse".[401] In 1973, he went even further and suggested that a worker who refused to join a trade union might be justified if he "conscientiously objected" but not if he did it "out of malice and with intent to injure". He was prepared to hold that justification was a defence to intimidatory threats by the union if the worker had "abused" his rights, acted simply "maliciously with intent to injure the union", or was a "troublemaker" who "brought everything upon himself by his own eccentric conduct".[402] Such an extension of the defence would be quite novel. In more moderate vein, Lord Devlin posed an example of one party threatening a breach of contract in response to a breach by the other side—for example, where A agrees to deliver goods to B in monthly instalments without making payment for the first a condition precedent to delivery of the second instalment. If B fails to pay and A threatens not to deliver the second instalment, is that intimidation? "I doubt it. But the case introduces questions not in issue here—whether a threat in such circumstances would be justifiable and whether it is intimidation to try to force a man into doing what the law, if invoked, would compel him to do."[403]

---

399 [1964] A.C. 1129 at 1206 and 1209. See Heydon (1970) 20 Univ. Toronto L.J. 139 at 178–182.

400 But this might not have been the law: compare Nagle CJ in *Latham v Singleton* [1981] 2 N.S.W.L.R. 843 at 869; and see the helpful survey in Creighton, Ford and Mitchell, *Labour Law: Text and Materials*, 2nd edn (1993), pp.1212–1221, citing *Ranger Uranium Mines v Federated Misc Workers' Union* (1987) 54 N.T.R. 6 (justification pleaded). After *OBG Ltd v Allan* [2007] UKHL 21; [2008] 1 A.C. 1 cases where the defendant is alleged to have used unlawful means to interfere with a contract will fall to be considered as potentially tortious under the tort of causing loss by unlawful means rather than the tort of inducing breach of contract; see para.23-78.

401 *Morgan v Fry* [1968] 2 Q.B. 710 at 729. It is noteworthy that, in the court below, Widgery J had been unable to see any ground which could justify use of unlawful means against the claimant: [1968] 1 Q.B. 521.

402 *Cory Lighterage Ltd v TGWU* [1973] I.C.R. 339 at 356–357. In suggesting that the worker "brought everything upon himself", Lord Denning seems almost to advert to a defence of volenti non fit injuria. But he regards the defence as one of justification. Moreover, he went further. The claimants were the employers who alleged, inter alia, that the union had threatened the unlawful act of inducing the other workers to break their employment contracts if the non-unionist were not removed. Lord Denning held that if the non-unionist could not have sued for intimidation by reason of the justification, the employers could have no cause of action either: "After all, the … intimidation was aimed at him, not the employers. If he cannot sue, how can they?" [1973] I.C.R. 339 at 357.

403 [1964] A.C. 1129 at 1209.

(f) Damage

The damage which a claimant can rely on as a foundation for his claim can clearly be pure economic loss, including damage to economic expectations.[404] In *Rookes v Barnard*, where the effect of the intimidation was that the claimant was dismissed from his job, Lord Devlin maintained that the claimant was not limited to claiming for pecuniary loss that he could specifically prove, nor by what he would have been awarded had he established a claim for wrongful dismissal against his employer, and even that he could properly "invite the jury to look at all the circumstances, the inconveniences caused to him by the change of job and the unhappiness maybe by a change in livelihood".[405] In the case of *Godwin v Uzoigwe*[406] a claimant who had been intimidated into working "excessively long hours at menial tasks" and into not going outside or making social connections was awarded £20,000 without any overt reference to her economic expectations; the case starkly raises the question whether a claim must always be based on damage to a claimant's economic position. An attractive answer to this might be that a claimant should be able to base a claim on any form of damage commonly recognised as actionable by the law of torts where the defendant has intentionally caused such damage by means of intimidation.[407] **23-77**

4. Causing Loss by Unlawful Means

In *OBG Ltd v Allan* the House of Lords both confirmed the existence of a tort of hitherto uncertain ambit which consists of one person using unlawful means with the intention and effect of causing damage to another and clarified some aspects of the liability.[408] While recognition of the existence of this tort can be traced back to **23-78**

---

404 *OBG Ltd v Allan* [2007] UKHL 21; [2008] 1 A.C. 1 at [8].

405 [1964] A.C. 1129 at 1221.

406 *Godwin v Uzoigwe* [1993] Fam. Law 65; *The Times*, 18 June 1992 CA.

407 cf. Murphy (2014) 77 M.L.R. 33, 45, who goes so far as to argue that two-party intimidation "has nothing especially to do with the protection of economic interests" and is "a wrong committed against human autonomy".

408 *OBG Ltd v Allan* [2007] UKHL 21; [2008] 1 A.C. 1; see in particular Lord Hoffmann at [46]–[64] and Lord Nicholls at [141]–[167]. Where they disagreed Lady Hale at [302] and Lord Brown at [319] expressed agreement with Lord Hoffmann. One issue that remains unresolved is that of the appropriate name by which this tort should be known, as the Canadian Supreme Court observed in *Bram Enterprises Ltd v A.I. Enterprises Ltd* 2014 SCC 12; (2014) 266 D.L.R. (4th) 573, where the single judgment of Cromwell J refers variously to both Lord Hoffmann's terminology and—more simply—"the unlawful means tort": 2014 SCC 12; (2014) 266 D.L.R. (4th) 573 at [2]. In most contexts, we follow Lord Hoffmann in using the label "causing loss by unlawful means", or—when emphasising the requirement for intentional harm—"intentionally causing loss by unlawful means". These labels have the advantage of avoiding the word "interference", which seems tainted by the—now discredited—idea that there is a tort of "unlawful interference with contractual relations". In *OBG Ltd v Allan* Lord Hoffmann referred to the tort discussed in this section, at [6], as "the tort of causing loss by unlawful means" or, at [24] as "intentionally causing loss by unlawful means", while Lord Nicholls, at [141], used the more familiar label of "interference with business by unlawful means"; in *JSC BTA Bank v Ablyazov (No.14)* [2018] UKSC 19; [2018] 2 W.L.R. 1125 Lords Lloyd-Jones and Sumption referred to it, at [6], as "unlawful interference with economic and other interests (sometimes called the 'intentional harm' tort)" and, at [12], as "the tort of intentionally harming the claimant by unlawful acts against third parties"; cf. the earlier formulations by Lord Diplock delivering the only substantive speech in *Hadmor Productions Ltd v Hamilton* [1983] 1 A.C. 191 at 228–229; *Merkur Island Shipping Corp v Laughton* [1983] 2 A.C. 570 at 609; and *Dimbleby & Sons Ltd v NUJ* [1984] 1 W.L.R. 427 at 429–30. For post-*OBG Ltd v Allan* formulations see Arden LJ in

Allen v Flood, nearly 90 years later it could still be described as "relatively undeveloped".[409] In *JT Stratford & Son Ltd v Lindley* two of the Law Lords gave as an alternative to procuring breach of contract as the ground for their decision, the fact that the respondents had used unlawful means to interfere with the business of the appellants.[410] Such intentional causing of loss by "interference with business" does not require that existing contracts have been broken, or, indeed, that any *contractual* relationship has been disrupted; indeed it may be doubted whether there is any *necessity* for damage to be done to a business interest.[411] But, at least in situations where three parties are involved, the claimant must suffer damage which the defendant has intentionally brought about through using unlawful means to affect the third party's freedom to deal with the claimant.[412] The distinct identities of this unlawful means tort and the tort of procuring breach of contract was one of the main points to emerge from the review of the ambit of both torts undertaken by the House of Lords in *OBG Ltd v Allan*. Earlier characterisations of the unlawful means tort as a "genus" of which procuring breach of contract was a "species" were there rejected. The key conditions of liability for causing loss by unlawful means, at least

---

Meretz Investments NV v ACP Ltd [2007] EWCA Civ 1303; [2008] Ch. 244 at [115]; *Global Resources Group Ltd v Mackay* [2008] CSOH 148; 2009 S.L.T. 104 at [17]; and *Correia v Canac Kitchens* (2008) 294 D.L.R. (4th) 525 (Ont. CA) where the tort is referred to as both "the intentional interference action" at [95] and "causing loss by unlawful means" at [100]. In *Future Investments SA v Federation Internationale De Football Association* [2010] EWHC 1019 (Ch), where part of the claim was for "causing harm by unlawful means", Floyd J stated the law at [19]–[25] in the same terms as Lord Hoffmann in *OBG Ltd v Allan*. In *Qantas Airways v Transport Workers Union of Australia* [2011] FCA 470; (2011) 280 A.L.R. 503 at [425]–[426] Moore J concluded that since the High Court in *Sanders v Snell* [1998] HCA 64; (1998) 196 C.L.R. 329 at [35]–[36] had found it unnecessary to decide whether this tort should be recognised in Australia, it had yet to be declared part of Australian law. On the recognition and development of the tort generally across common law jurisdictions see *Bram Enterprises Ltd v A.I. Enterprises Ltd* 2014 SCC 12; (2014) 366 D.L.R. (4th) 573 at [50]–[76]; and H. Carty "The Modern Functions of the Economic Torts; Reviewing the English, Canadian, Australian and New Zealand positions" (2015) 74 C.L.J. 261.

409 *Barretts & Baird (Wholesale) Ltd v IPCS* [1987] I.R.L.R. 3 at 10, per Henry J; cf. Lord Herschell in *Allen v Flood* [1898] A.C. 1 at 136–137.

410 [1965] A.C. 269 at 324, per Lord Reid and 328–329, per Viscount Radcliffe: "the defendants have inflicted injury on the plaintiffs in the context of their business and have resorted to unlawful means to bring this about."

411 The question whether the tort can extend to protect interests that are not associated with "business" has rarely been raised, but in *Chalfont St Peter Parish Council v Holy Cross Sisters Trustees Inc* [2019] EWHC 1128 (QB), Swift J stated, at [99], that there was "no authority for the proposition that a claimant's interests protected by the unlawful means tort extend beyond economic interests, and I can see no reason in principle which would justify such conclusion." With respect, one of the things that the tort protects claimants against is the use of unlawful means to prevent others from performing contracts with them, and there is no good reason for confining the tort to protecting the benefit of "business" contracts. Similarly, it is doubtful that there is any good reason for confining the tort so that it can be of no assistance where a defendant uses unlawful means with the intention of disrupting a claimant's access to a public service, such as medical care or education.

412 *OBG Ltd v Allan* [2007] UKHL 21; [2008] 1 A.C. 1 at [51], per Lord Hoffmann; see also [306] per Baroness Hale, [319]–[320] per Lord Brown, and [270] per Lord Walker. The significance of limiting the tort to behaviour interfering with a third party's liberty to deal with the claimant was underlined by the Court of Appeal in *Secretary of State for Health v Servier Laboratories Ltd* [2019] EWCA Civ 1160; [2019] 3 W.L.R. 938, where the Court analysed the status of *OBG* as a binding precedent on the point *and* expressed the opinion that the limit was appropriate as a matter of principle. By contrast, the Canadian Supreme Court refused to import into Canadian law Lord Hoffmann's requirement that the unlawful means must interfere with the third party's freedom to deal with the claimant: *Bram Enterprises Ltd v A.I. Enterprises Ltd* 2014 SCC 12; (2014) 266 D.L.R. (4th) 573 at [87].

in situations where three parties are involved,[413] are: (i) an intention to cause loss to the claimant, (ii) use of "unlawful means" against a third party; and (iii) interference with that third party's freedom to deal with the claimant. While it has been said that the defence of justification which applies to the tort of procuring breach of contract is "not usually regarded as a defence to this tort",[414] the existence of some form of justificatory defence has been suggested.[415]

(a) Intention to cause loss

23-79 In *OBG Ltd v Allan* the House of Lords confirmed that: "In the unlawful means tort, there must be an intention to cause loss."[416] "Because damage to economic expectations is sufficient to found a claim, there need not have been any intention to cause a breach of contract or interfere with contractual rights."[417] A simple example of the tort might involve a defendant using unlawful means against a claimant's customers with the intention of harming the claimant's business, and in such a case the intended harm might be a reduction in the number of new contracts made rather than any breach of existing contracts. Similarly, where A perpetrates deceit upon B intending B to act in a way which will cause damage to C, he is liable to C whether or not damage is also suffered by B since the unlawful means were in their nature actionable even if B's cause of action was not complete because he suffered no damage.[418] By contrast, where a defendant union brought its members out on strike in breach of employment contracts in a dispute with the employer who was consequently unable to fulfil functions under statute to the damage of the claimant abattoir owners, they could not sue the union because the damage, though an unavoidable by-product of the strike, was not the consequence of any intention to injure them.[419] But while the "purpose or intention of inflicting injury on the [claimant]" is an essential element of the tort,[420] it is not necessary to prove that this was the defendant's predominant purpose; it is sufficient that the unlawful act was "in some sense directed against … or intended to harm the [claimant]".[421]

---

413 For the question whether a two-party version of the tort of causing loss by the use of unlawful means exists, see below para.23-94.

414 *Johnson v BFI Canada Inc* 2010 MBCA 101; (2010) 326 D.L.R. (4th) 497 at [55].

415 *A.I. Enterprises Ltd v Bram Enterprises Ltd* 2012 NBCA 33; (2012) 350 D.L.R. (4th) 601 at [56] as one of the "essential tenets of the unlawful means tort"; (reversed on appeal without reference to this issue: 2014 SCC 12; (2014) 366 D.L.R. (4th) 573).

416 [2007] UKHL 21; [2008] 1 A.C. 1 per Lord Hoffmann at [62]; see also at [47], [51] and [135]–[136], per Lord Hoffmann; *Emerald Supplies Ltd v British Airways Plc (Nos 1 & 2)* [2015] EWCA Civ 1024; [2016] Bus. L.R. 145 at [130]: "the defendant must intend to injure the claimant". cf. *OBG* at [141] per Lord Nicholls: "The defendant must have intended to inflict the harm of which complaint is made." Lord Nicholls reverts to the more orthodox formulation of "intention to harm the claimant" at [164], and it seems clear from the cases before *OBG* that must now be interpreted as instances of this tort that a defendant who intends to cause harm to a claimant by using unlawful means to prevent its customers from trading with it or to prevent it from receiving essential supplies will be liable even if he has not identified precisely what harm these methods will cause.

417 [2007] UKHL 21; [2008] 1 A.C. 1, per Lord Hoffmann at [8].

418 *Lonrho v Fayed* [1990] 2 Q.B. 479 CA; affirmed on other grounds [1992] 1 A.C. 448 HL; *National Phonograph Co Ltd v Edison Bell Consolidated Phonograph Co Ltd* [1908] 1 Ch. 355 CA.

419 *Barretts & Baird (Wholesale) Ltd v IPCS* [1987] I.R.L.R 3 at 7 and 10.

420 *Copyright Agency Ltd v Haines* (1982) 40 A.L.R. 264 at 275; *Pacific Western Airlines v British Columbia Federation of Labour* (1986) 26 D.L.R. (4th) 87 at 91–95.

421 *Lonrho v Fayed* [1990] 2 Q.B. 479 at 488-489 per Dillon LJ; and see Ralph Gibson LJ at 494 and

23-80 In *OBG Ltd v Allan* both Lord Hoffmann and Lord Nicholls elaborated on the concept of intention to cause loss by referring to ends and means:

> "A defendant may intend to harm the claimant's business either as an end in itself or as a means to an end. A defendant may intend to harm the claimant as an end in itself where, for instance, he has a grudge against the claimant. More usually a defendant intentionally inflicts harm on a claimant's business as a means to an end. He inflicts damage as the means whereby to protect or promote his own economic interests."[422]

They distinguished a defendant's ends and chosen means, both of which he would be held to intend, from any foreseeable, or even likely, consequences of his acts, which he could properly deny that he intended: "a defendant's foresight that his unlawful conduct may or will probably damage the claimant cannot be equated with intention for this purpose".[423] They emphasised, however, that a defendant could not avoid the conclusion that he had acted with the intention of causing loss simply by establishing that the he would have preferred the world to have been different, so that he could have achieved his ends without having to harm the claimant.[424]

23-81 Both Lord Hoffmann and Lord Nicholls also discussed the position of a defendant who intended to make a gain which he knew would be at the expense of a claimant:

> "Take a case where a defendant seeks to advance his own business by pursuing a course of conduct which he knows will, in the very nature of things, necessarily be injurious to the claimant. In other words, a case where loss to the claimant is the obverse side of the coin from gain to the defendant. The defendant's gain and the claimant's loss are, to the defendant's knowledge, inseparably linked. The defendant cannot obtain the one without bringing about the other. If the defendant goes ahead in such a case in order to obtain the gain he seeks, his state of mind will satisfy the mental ingredient of the unlawful interference tort."[425]

Woolf LJ at 494 ("desire" to injure not required); affirmed on other grounds [1992] 1 A.C. 448 HL. See also *OBG Ltd v Allan* [2007] UKHL 21; [2008] 1 A.C. 1, per Lord Hoffmann at [62]: "In the unlawful means tort, there must be an intention to cause loss. … [I]t is necessary to distinguish between ends, means and consequences. One intends to cause loss even though it is the means by which one achieved the end of enriching oneself. On the other hand, one is not liable for loss which is neither a desired end nor a means of attaining it but merely a foreseeable consequence of one's actions." See too *Reach MD Inc v Pharmaceutical Manufacturers Association of Canada* (2003) 227 D.L.R. (4th) 458 (Ont. CA) at 471–472: "The first element of this tort will be met so long as [the defendant's] unlawful act was in some measure directed against [the claimant]. That is so even if … [the defendant's] predominant purpose was to advance its own interests and those of its members." cf. *Print N'Promotion (Canada) Ltd v Kovachis* 2011 ONCA 23; (2011) 329 D.L.R. (4th) 421 where the landlord's termination of the head lease because of the tenant's failure to pay the rent was not actionable in tort by a sub-tenant who was thereby prevented from using a wall of the premises for advertising purposes as an "intentional interference with contractual relations and economic interests" inter alia because no intention to damage the sub-tenant was established.

422 *OBG Ltd v Allan* [2007] UKHL 21; [2008] 1 A.C. 1 at [164], per Lord Nicholls, and see at [62] per Lord Hoffmann.

423 *OBG Ltd v Allan* [2007] UKHL 21; [2008] 1 A.C. 1 at [166], per Lord Nicholls, and see at [62] per Lord Hoffmann. See also *Barretts & Baird (Wholesale) Ltd v IPCS* [1987] I.R.L.R. 3; expressly endorsed by Lord Hoffmann in *OBG* at [64]: "The damage to the abattoir owners was neither the purpose of the strike nor the means of achieving that purpose which was to put pressure on the government." *Van Camp Chocolates Ltd v Aulsebrooks Ltd* [1984] N.Z.L.R. 354 (NZCA).

424 *OBG Ltd v Allan* [2007] UKHL 21; [2008] 1 A.C. 1 at [63], per Lord Hoffmann and [165] per Lord Nicholls.

425 *OBG Ltd v Allan* [2007] UKHL 21; [2008] 1 A.C. 1 at [167], per Lord Nicholls, and see at [134]

A series of recent cases have raised the question whether this reasoning can be relied on to impose liability on a defendant who used unlawful means to raise the prices that it could charge its customers, but was unsure and indifferent as to whether those customers would incur a loss as a result or be able to pass the extra costs on.[426] On this point the current position appears to be that a defendant who intends to profit by obtaining a higher price will only be held to have intended to cause loss to whoever pays the extra amount if it was "inherent in the nature of the arrangements" that the defendant's gain would be at the claimant's expense.[427]

(b) Unlawful means

This tort is based on the deliberate use of unlawful means; it differs therefore from both inducing breach of contract (where liability stems from persuading another to commit a legal wrong) and from the anomalous tort of lawful means conspiracy (where the liability stems from the predominant purpose of two or more parties acting in combination being to cause loss to the claimant).[428] The need for the claimant to establish that the defendant used unlawful means is central to ensuring that this economic tort imposes a liability that is consistent with the fundamental principle established in *Allen v Flood* that, lawful means conspiracy apart, acts that are otherwise lawful are not rendered unlawful by the bad motive of the person who performs them.[429] But not every unlawful act or means can be relied on as the foundation for a claim in this tort, even if damage is intended and caused. **23-82**

In *OBG Ltd v Allan* the House of Lords was divided by the issue of the breadth of unlawful means for the purposes of this tort.[430] Lord Nicholls endorsed the "wider interpretation" of Lords Reid and Devlin in *Rookes v Barnard* that it embraced "all acts a defendant is not permitted to do, whether by the civil law or criminal law". Recognising the potential which this approach contains for giving the tort a very wide remit, he added the qualification that liability should be limited to situations where "the claimant is harmed through the instrumentality of a third party".[431] This was, however, a minority view as Lady Hale and Lord Brown endorsed the narrower opinion of Lord Hoffmann on this issue. His conclusion on the ambit of "unlawful means" was that: **23-83**

---

per Lord Hoffmann.

426 *W.H. Newson Holding Ltd v IMI Plc* [2013] EWCA Civ 1377; [2014] Bus. L.R. 156; *Emerald Supplies Ltd v British Airways Plc (Nos 1 & 2)* [2015] EWCA Civ 1024; [2016] Bus. L.R. 145; *Media-Saturn Holding Gmbh v Toshiba Information Systems (UK) Ltd* [2019] EWHC 1095 (Ch); [2019] 5 C.M.L.R. 7.

427 *Emerald Supplies Ltd v British Airways Plc (Nos 1 & 2)* [2015] EWCA Civ 1024; [2016] Bus. L.R. 145 at [170]; *Media-Saturn Holding Gmbh v Toshiba Information Systems (UK) Ltd* [2019] EWHC 1095 (Ch); [2019] 5 C.M.L.R. 7 at [235]. In the *Emerald Supplies Ltd* case (at [168]–[169]) the Court of Appeal was inclined to accept that a claimant could establish the requisite intention if the defendant's intended gain would necessarily be at the expense of a member of a limited and identifiable class, and the claimant was a member of that class, but expressly rejected the suggestion that a claimant could establish an intention to injure it by relying on the fact that the defendant's gain would necessarily fall on someone linked to the defendant by a chain of contracts, since this would involve "an unknown and unknowable range of potential claimants".

428 See paras 23-16 and 23-122.

429 [1898] A.C. 1; see para.23-02.

430 On the related issue of the scope of unlawful means for the purposes of the tort of unlawful means conspiracy; see para.23-108. Importantly, it is now clear that the scope of unlawful means is different in the two contexts.

431 [2007] UKHL 21; [2008] 1 A.C. 1 at [162] and [159] respectively.

> "subject to one qualification, acts against a third party count as unlawful means only if they are actionable by that third party. The qualification is that they will also be unlawful means if the only reason why they are not actionable is because the third party has suffered no loss."[432]

Those acts against a third party that are actionable by that third party are predominantly civil wrongs, that is torts and breaches of contract; so acts that are only unlawful in some other sense, such as because they are crimes or regulatory infractions, will not, following *OBG*, count as "unlawful means" for the purposes of this tort.

23-84 In *Bram Enterprises Ltd v A.I. Enterprises Ltd*,[433] the Supreme Court of Canada followed the majority in OBG and concluded: "in order for conduct to constitute 'unlawful means' for this tort, the conduct must give rise to a civil cause of action by the third party or would do so if the third party had suffered loss as a result of that conduct."[434] The court highlighted several aspects of tort law's approach to regulating economic activity which pointed to a narrow scope for the unlawful means tort. These included a concern not to undermine certainty in commercial affairs by unduly expanding tort liability and a traditional reluctance to develop rules to enforce fair competition. The Court also, however, identified a rationale for the tort that was consistent with this narrow definition of unlawful means: the tort is "liability stretching", in the sense that it extends the right to sue from an immediate victim of a civil wrong to another party whom the defendant intended to target.[435] The Supreme Court therefore rejected the reasoning of the New Brunswick Court of Appeal which had held that the independent actionability requirement should be flexible and allow for exceptions which were principled and did not attract the criticism of ad hoc decision making.[436]

432 [2007] UKHL 21; [2008] 1 A.C. 1 at [49], endorsed by Lady Hale at [302] and by Lord Brown at [319]–[320]. The same majority also endorsed a further requirement, discussed below at para.23-90, that the unlawful means must interfere with the third party's freedom to deal with the claimant. Lord Walker, at [266] and [268], noted the difference of opinion between Lord Hoffmann and Lord Nicholls, and suggested, at [269], that "neither is likely to be the last word on this difficult and important area of the law".

433 2014 SCC 12; (2014) 366 D.L.R. (4th) 573 judgment of Cromwell J, with which the rest of the court concurred, at [26]–[49]. See P.-W. Lee "The Unlawful Means Tort in Canada" (2014) 130 L.Q.R. 559.

434 2014 SCC 12; (2014) 366 D.L.R. (4th) 573 at [76]. In a review of the jurisprudence of other common law jurisdictions the Court noted that while the Australian High Court had left the existence of the tort in Australian law open in *Sanders v Snell* [1998] HCA 64; (1998) 157 A.L.R. 491, the New Zealand Court of Appeal had adopted Lord Hoffmann's analysis of unlawful means in *Diver v Loktronic Industries Ltd* [2012] NZCA 131; [2012] 2 N.Z.L.R. 388.

435 See the application of this approach in *Grand Financial Management Inc v Solemio Transportation Inc*, 2016 ONCA 173; (2016) 395 D.L.R. (4th) 529 at [64]–[74].

436 2010 NBCA 33; (2012) 350 D.L.R. (4th) 601 at [5] and [80]–[81]. The Supreme Court also departed from earlier case law in the Ontario Court of Appeal: *Reach MD Inc v Pharmaceutical Manufacturers Association of Canada* (2003) 227 D.L.R. (4th) 458 at 471–2 preferring the broader view of unlawful means of Lord Denning MR in *Torquay Hotel Co Ltd v Cousins* [1969] 2 Ch. 106 ("an act which he is not at liberty to commit") in deciding that a ruling by a committee of the defendant association which it had no authority to make amounted to the use of unlawful means; cf. *Drouillard v Cogeco Cable Inc* 2007 ONCA 322; (2007) 282 D.L.R. (4th) 644: inappropriate to extend the tort to include breach of a company's internal policies as unlawful means; and *Correia v Canac Kitchens* 2008 ONCA 506; (2008) 294 D.L.R. (4th) 525 at [104] noting the differing approaches in the two earlier decisions.

Torts Where a defendant commits a tort against a third party with the intention of causing harm to a claimant by interfering with the third party's freedom to deal with the claimant then this will amount to a straightforward instance of the tort of causing loss by unlawful means. Thus in *DC Thomson & Co Ltd v Deakin*[437] Sir Raymond Evershed MR considered a situation where a defendant "by some other act, tortious in itself, prevents the contracting party from performing the bargain. … for example, physically detains the contracting party so that the contracting party is rendered unable by the detention to perform the contract." His conclusion was that the tort of procuring a breach of contract could be extended to cover this situation; but in *OBG* Lord Hoffmann commended an alternative analysis: the defendant incurs "not accessory liability under the principle in *Lumley v Gye*" but "primary liability for intentionally causing loss by unlawfully interfering with the liberty of a third party".[438] The advantages of the alternative analysis, which made it appropriate to disavow the extension of procuring breach of contract, were that the unlawful means tort does not depend on disruption of a *contractual* relationship—indeed, it "is indifferent as to the nature of the interest which is damaged"[439] —and does not require a troublesome distinction to be maintained between direct and indirect forms of interference.[440] Thus situations where a defendant prevents a third party from dealing with a claimant by torts against the third party such as procuring the third party's employees to break their contracts of employment, are now to be treated as falling within the scope of the causing loss by unlawful means tort. 23-85

Deceit As it is a tort, deceit can clearly be unlawful means.[441] If a defendant can commit the tort by tortiously destroying a third party's tools to prevent him from performing a valuable task for the claimant, then there is no obvious reason why he should not equally commit the tort if he deceives the third party into believing that his tools have been destroyed so as to achieve the same result. So far as there are doubts about whether the tort of causing loss by unlawful means can be committed by means of deceit they tend to flow from the separate question, considered below, of when a defendant's tort can be said to have restricted the third party's freedom to trade with the claimant.[442] 23-86

---

437 *DC Thomson & Co Ltd v Deakin* [1952] Ch. 646, CA at 678.

438 *OBG Ltd v Allan* [2007] UKHL 21; [2008] 1 A.C. 1 at [29], per Lord Hoffmann.

439 *OBG Ltd v Allan* [2007] UKHL 21; [2008] 1 A.C. 1 at [32], per Lord Hoffmann.

440 Before *OBG*, the cases relied on a distinction between indirect forms of interference, when unlawful means would be required, and direct forms, when they would not be required. In *OBG* at [34]–[38], Lord Hoffmann explained why this distinction was impossible to identify in any satisfactory way, frequently irrelevant, and misleading, in that it tended to suggest that the same set of facts could not involve the simultaneous commission of the torts of procuring a breach of contract and intentionally causing loss by the use of unlawful means.

441 *National Phonograph Co Ltd v Edison-Bell Consolidated Phonograph Co Ltd* [1908] 1 Ch. 335, as explained by Lord Hoffmann in *OBG Ltd v Allan* [2007] UKHL 21; [2008] 1 A.C. 1 at [49].

442 In *Secretary of State for Health v Servier Laboratories Ltd* [2019] EWCA Civ 1160; [2019] 3 W.L.R. 938, the defendants were alleged to have caused loss to the claimant by making false statements to the European Patent Office and the English courts, which led to a patent being obtained, and prevented the claimant from being able to purchase cheaper, generic drugs: the Court of Appeal upheld Roth J's decision that this situation could not give rise to a claim for intentionally causing loss by unlawful means because the (alleged) unlawful means had not restricted the freedom of the European Patent Office or the English courts to deal with the claimant.

23-87 **Breach of contract as unlawful means** What is the position where A commits a breach of his contract with B with the intention of harming C by limiting B's freedom to deal with C? Consider the examples, above, of A tortiously destroying B's tools so as to prevent B from performing a valuable task for C, and A deceiving B into believing that he has destroyed the tools; what if, instead, A breaks a contract to supply the required tools to B with the intention of harming C? Three arguments point in favour of a breach of contract potentially amounting to "unlawful means" for the purposes of the tort. First, A's breach of a contract with B is an actionable civil wrong by A against B, and thus falls within the basic definition of "unlawful means" that was accepted by the majority in *OBG Ltd v Allan*. Secondly, it seems clear that if a defendant uses the tort of procuring a breach of contract against B as a method of inflicting harm on C by limiting B's freedom to deal with C, then this can amount to the unlawful means tort,[443] and it would be odd if procuring a breach of contract could be "unlawful means" but actually breaking a contract could not be. Thirdly, *Rookes v Barnard*[444] established that a coercive *threat* to break a contract with a third party so as to persuade that third party to act to a claimant's detriment was actionable as an instance of the tort of intimidation and, as discussed above, after *OBG Ltd v Allan* it may be appropriate to regard liability for three-party intimidation as but one form of the wider unlawful means tort.[445] Two related arguments, however, point in the other direction, and offer some support for the proposition that a breach of contract should not be classed as "unlawful means" for the purposes of the intentional harm tort. First, treating such a breach as "unlawful means" could be described as "surprising" because it would lead to "large inroads into the doctrine of privity of contract"[446] : C would be able to bring a claim as a result of a contract between A and B, provided that he could establish that A's breach of his contractual obligation to B was *intended* to cause harm to him (C), and his claim would not be limited to any loss that B had suffered, or by any contractual terms of limitation agreed between A and B. Secondly, and relatedly, as the Supreme Court noted in the unlawful means conspiracy case of *JSC BTA Bank v Ablyazov (No.14)*,[447] contractual obligations are not general in the same way as the obligation to obey the criminal law is, and are only owed to specific parties: if A refuses to supply B with the tools that B needs in order to perform a valuable task for C, it is unclear why C's position should depend entirely on whether A had contractually promised B that he would supply the tools or B merely hoped or expected to

443 In *OBG Ltd v Allan* [2007] UKHL 21; [2008] 1 A.C. 1 at [47], Lord Hoffmann treats *Stratford & Son Ltd v Lindley* [1965] A.C. 269 as illustrating this point, and supporting the proposition, at [48]: "In principle, the cases establish that intentionally causing someone loss by interfering with the liberty of action of a third party in breach of a contract with him is unlawful."

444 *Rookes v Barnard* [1964] A.C. 1129 HL.

445 On intimidation, see para.23-62.

446 per Henry J in *Barretts & Baird (Wholesale) Ltd v IPCS* [1987] I.R.L.R. 3 at 8–9; see too the concern of Peter Gibson LJ dissenting in *Millar v Bassey* [1994] E.M.L.R. 44 CA (majority decision overruled in *OBG Ltd v Allan* [2007] UKHL 21; [2008] 1 A.C. 1); cf. *Stocznia Gdanska SA v Latvian Shipping Co* [2002] EWCA Civ 889; [2002] 2 All E.R. (Comm) 768, where it appears to have been accepted without argument that breach of contract amounted to unlawful means for the purposes of liability for indirect procurement of breach of contract, a form of economic tort liability which after *OBG Ltd v Allan* would fall under the unlawful interference tort. See too *Global Resources Group v Mackay Ltd* [2008] CSOH 148; 2009 S.L.T. 104 at [21]. Compare Lord Devlin's willingness to accept that unlawful means could differ in scope as between the different economic torts: *Rookes v Barnard* [1964] A.C. 1129 at 1210.

447 *JSC BTA Bank v Ablyazov (No.14)* [2018] UKSC 19; [2018] 2 W.L.R. 1125.

be able to obtain them from A. While it might be argued that there is an analogy between allowing C to rely on a tort by A against B as unlawful means, since A's tortious act would also ostensibly only be a wrong *to B*, there remains a distinction between these two scenarios: the duty not to commit torts is fixed by law while contractual duties are fixed by the parties who can agree to rescind them, and, to some extent, agree what should happen in the event of a breach. This said, if B agreed to release A from his contractual obligation to deliver the tools then there would be no tort to C since there would be no "unlawful means". On balance, it is suggested that a breach of contract ought to be held to constitute "unlawful means" for the purposes of the tort of causing loss by the use of unlawful means.[448] Until it is clear how breaches of contract will be treated in this context, it will be difficult to address the further question whether an equitable wrong can constitute unlawful means for the purposes of this tort; many equitable obligations exist as a result of a particular type of contractual relationship between the parties, and such obligations tend to share the characteristic of being a product of past dealings between specific parties rather than part of the general law.

The legislature recognised the problems that arise in industrial disputes if breach of contract can be "unlawful means" for the purposes of the economic torts generally when in 1974 it expressly provided that not only a threat of breach but also an actual breach of contract in trade disputes should not be regarded as "an unlawful act or the use of unlawful means".[449] But this provision was repealed in 1980 when policy on statutory protection against economic tort liability in trade disputes changed.[450] 23-88

Crimes and breaches of statutes The majority opinion in *OBG Ltd v Allan* —that acts against a third party can only constitute unlawful means if they are actionable by the third party, or would be actionable but for the fact that the third party suffered no loss[451]—was intended to settle uncertainties as to whether a crime or breach of a statute could be unlawful means, and a majority of the House of Lords in *Revenue & Customs Commissioners v Total Network SL*[452] treated the *OBG* case as having decided, at least for cases where a defendant caused harm to a claim- 23-89

---

448 A parallel issue concerns whether breaches of contract can constitute "unlawful means" for the purposes of the tort of conspiracy to cause harm by the use of unlawful means. Authorities relevant to this issue were discussed in *Palmer Birch (a partnership) v Lloyd* [2018] EWHC 2316 (TCC); [2018] 4 W.L.R. 164 at [228]–[234], and Judge Russen QC decided to proceed on the basis that a conspiracy to breach contracts can be tortious. The matter is controversial, however, and in the subsequent case of *The Racing Partnership Ltd v Done Brothers (Cash Betting) Ltd* [2019] EWHC 1156 (Ch); [2020] Ch. 289 Zacaroli J held, at [252], that the breach of a contract that existed between one of the conspirators and a third party could not amount to "unlawful means" for the purposes of the unlawful means conspiracy tort, since in the circumstances it was irrelevant to the claimants whether the harmful act followed a breach of contract or was done as a result of the third party accepting a fee to release the conspirator from his contractual obligation: see para.23-115.

449 Trade Union and Labour Relations Act 1974 s.13(3)(b), enacted "for the avoidance of doubt" although that was not logically its status. See Wedderburn (1974) 37 M.L.R. 525 at 540–543.

450 Employment Act 1980 s.17(8). In *Hadmor Productions Ltd v Hamilton* [1983] 1 A.C. 191 at 231 Lord Diplock said that s.13(3) had become "otiose" by 1980, but that was true only of s.13(3)(a), not of (b): see Simpson (1982) 45 M.L.R. 447, 451-453; Wedderburn, *The Worker and the Law*, 3rd edn (1986) 635–638; Henry J in *Barretts & Baird (Wholesale) Ltd v IPCS* [1987] I.R.L.R. 3 at 9.

451 *OBG Ltd v Allan* [2007] UKHL 21; [2008] 1 A.C. 1 at [49], per Lord Hoffmann with the express agreement of Lady Hale at [302] and Lord Brown at [320].

452 [2008] UKHL 19; [2008] 1 A.C. 1174 at [67], per Lord Walker (with whom Lord Scott agreed, see [47]), [123] per Lord Mance and [220] per Lord Neuberger.

ant by using the means against a third party, that a crime will not amount to unlawful means. The basic rule in relation to contravention of a statute is that a person will have a cause of action in tort for breach of statutory duty only where the statute on its proper construction so allows.[453] As a result, where a breach of statute *is actionable* by the third party then this can be treated as unlawful means, since it will amount to a tort against the third party, but otherwise "it is not for the courts to create a cause of action out of a regulatory or criminal statute which Parliament did not intend to be actionable in private law".[454]

(c) Interference with a third party's freedom

23-90 In *OBG Ltd v Allan*[455] Lord Hoffmann stated that:

> "Unlawful means therefore consists of acts intended to cause loss to the claimant by interfering with the freedom of a third party in a way which is unlawful as against that third party and which is intended to cause loss to the claimant. It does not in my opinion include acts which may be unlawful against a third party but which do not affect his freedom to deal with the claimant."

The main function of making the effect of the unlawful means on a third party's freedom into a condition of liability is to exclude from the scope of the tort situations where a defendant's wrong to a third party may have reduced a claimant's economic prospects in some other way. As an example of the sort of case that he intended to exclude from the scope of the tort Lord Hoffmann pointed to *RCA Corpn v Pollard*,[456] where the defendant had sold bootleg recordings and thereby reduced the value of the claimant's exclusive right to exploit records made by Elvis Presley; the defendant's activities infringed s.1 of the Dramatic and Musical Performers' Protection Act 1958, and in the opinion of Lord Hoffmann could have given rise to a civil claim by the Presley estate, but such unlawful means did not interfere with the freedom of the estate to perform its contract with the claimant

---

453 *Cutler v Wandsworth Stadium Ltd* [1948] A.C. 398 HL; see Ch.8. Similar rules provided for when a claimant could base a private law claim for compensation on breach of a directly applicable provision of European Community law (see, *Foster v British Gas* [1991] 2 A.C. 306 HL; [1991] I.C.R. 84 ECJ; *Griffin v South West Water Services* [1995] I.R.L.R. 15; and the review of the case law by Hirst LJ in *Three Rivers DC v Bank of England* [2003] 2 A.C. 1 HL) and these may remain relevant in establishing whether such a breach amounted to unlawful means in any case arising from facts that occurred before the United Kingdom's withdrawal from the European Union: the European Union (Withdrawal) Act 2018 Sch.1 para.4, "provides that the right to claim damages against the state for breaches of EU law (Francovich damages) will not be available after exit." (Explanatory Notes, para.214), but this is subject to transitional provisions.

454 *OBG Ltd v Allan* [2007] UKHL 21; [2008] 1 A.C. 1 at [57], per Lord Hoffmann. See also *Gouriet v Union of Post Office Workers* [1978] A.C. 435 HL; and *Lonrho Ltd v Shell Petroleum Co Ltd* [1982] A.C. 173 HL. In *Bram Enterprises Ltd v A.I. Enterprises Ltd* 2014 SCC 12; (2014) 366 D.L.R. (4th) 573 at [74], Cromwell J identified one of the advantages of adopting the narrow definition of "unlawful means" for the interference tort as being that such an approach would "not risk 'tortifying' conduct rendered illegal by statute for reasons remote from civil liability".

455 *OBG Ltd v Allan* [2007] UKHL 21; [2008] 1 A.C. 1 at [51], per Lord Hoffmann, with the agreement of Lady Hale at [302] and Lord Brown at [320].

456 [1983] Ch. 135 CA. Lord Hoffmann ([2007] UKHL 21; [2008] 1 A.C. 1 at [54]–[55]) identified *Isaac Oren v Red Box Toy Factory Ltd* [1999] F.S.R. 785; and *Lonrho Ltd v Shell Petroleum Co Ltd (No. 2)* [1982] A.C. 173 HL as further examples of cases where the unlawful behaviour of defendants had not interfered with any third parties' freedom to deal with the claimants in each case.

(since this required no more than not authorising anyone else to exploit the recordings) or to deal with the claimant in any other way.

Lord Hoffmann's primary reason for emphasising the "interference with freedom" limit on the scope of the tort was to preserve a distinction between more obviously unacceptable behaviour, such as using civil wrongs to prevent or impede third parties, such as customers, suppliers, contractors or employees, from dealing with the claimant, and behaviour that was "wrongful only in the irrelevant sense that a third party has a right to complain if he chooses to do so".[457] He also, however, suggested that the limit would reduce the risk of judges expanding the civil law effects of statutory wrongs beyond what Parliament had authorised, or undermining Parliament's specification of limited and exhaustive methods for enforcing statutory duties.[458] **23-91**

The limit has attracted criticism, partly because it allows the tort to prohibit defendants from using force or threats to impede third parties' dealings with a claimant, but prevents it from reaching defendants who lure away third parties with unlawfully attractive offers.[459] In *Bram Enterprises Ltd v A.I. Enterprises Ltd*, the Canadian Supreme Court decided that it was unnecessary to recognise a similar limit on the tort in Canadian law; that Court believed that the combination of a restricted definition of unlawful means and a narrow form of intention—the defendant having "aimed at" or "targeted" the claimant—would be sufficient to confine the tort within "proper bounds".[460] But in *Secretary of State for Health v Servier Laboratories Ltd*[461] the Court of Appeal concluded that the *OBG* case stood as a binding precedent for the "interference with freedom" limit on the scope of the tort and went on to express the opinion that even if the matter had not been covered by authority, the limit was appropriate as a matter of principle. **23-92**

(d) Justification

It was noted above that Lord Devlin suggested in *Rookes v Barnard* that such a defence might exist to the tort of intimidation,[462] and, given that the three-party form of this tort is now to be treated as a sub-variety of the unlawful means tort, any such defence may extend to this tort too. Any defence of justification is likely to focus on two inter-related elements: the defendant's reasons for causing harm to the claimant and the defendant's understanding of the means that he has used. Cases involving other economic torts suggest that the courts are reluctant to impose liability on a defendant who has mistakenly concluded either that the means that he plans to use are not unlawful or that in the circumstances he has a legal entitlement to use such means; in such cases they sometimes explain the absence of liability by describing the defendant as having a defence of justification.[463] **23-93**

---

457 *OBG Ltd v Allan* [2007] UKHL 21; [2008] 1 A.C. 1 at [56], per Lord Hoffmann.

458 *OBG Ltd v Allan* [2007] UKHL 21; [2008] 1 A.C. 1 at [56]–[58], per Lord Hoffmann.

459 See further R. Bagshaw, "Lord Hoffmann and the Economic Torts", Ch.5 in P.S. Davies and J. Pila (eds), *The Jurisprudence of Lord Hoffmann* (Oxford: Hart, 2015), pp.64–70.

460 *Bram Enterprises Ltd v A.I. Enterprises Ltd* 2014 SCC 12; (2014) 266 D.L.R. (4th) 573 at [87].

461 [2019] EWCA Civ 1160; [2019] 3 W.L.R. 938.

462 [1964] A.C. 1129 at 1206 and 1209. See Heydon (1970) 20 Univ. Toronto L.J. 139 at 178–182.

463 See, e.g. *Meretz Investments NV v ACP Ltd* [2007] EWCA Civ 1303; [2008] Ch. 244 at [174], per Toulson LJ (unlawful means conspiracy).

(e) Two-party causing loss by unlawful means

23-94 So far, the tort of causing loss by unlawful means has been discussed as it applies to cases involving three parties, that is where a defendant has used unlawful means on a third party in order to cause loss to a claimant by restricting the third party's freedom to deal with the claimant. Pivotal elements of the tort as described to this point, such as the requirement that the unlawful means must be "actionable" by the third party,[464] assume that the tort *only* operates in three-party contexts, and a two-party variant does not exist. The premise for this assumption is that where a defendant uses "actionable" unlawful means directly against a claimant with the intention of causing loss, the claimant will be able to base any action that he chooses to bring on the actionable wrong; so a two-party tort of causing loss by unlawful means would be tautologous. There are two situations, however, where a two-party tort of causing loss by unlawful means could be useful: the first relies on the exception to the requirement that the unlawful means must be actionable that allows the tort to cover threats and other means that could have been actionable but for the absence of actionable damage, whilst the second depends on the possibility that unlawful means could be defined more broadly for the purposes of a two-party tort.

23-95 The first potential situation where a two-party tort of causing loss by unlawful means might be useful is where a defendant threatens to commit a civil wrong to a claimant with the intention of coercing the claimant into acting in some way that will cause loss to himself. Such behaviour has been recognised to be tortious, being commonly described as "two-party intimidation".[465] Just as the tort of three-party intimidation can now be treated as a special, nominate form of the three-party tort of causing loss by unlawful means, similarly two-party intimidation could be classed as *a form* of causing loss by unlawful means that operates in a two-party setting. This classification might, however, be thought to be pointless if *all* the instances of causing loss by unlawful means that involve two parties are two-party intimidation cases: there would be no obvious advantage in redescribing the conditions of liability for two-party intimidation in more general terms.

23-96 The second potential situation where a two-party tort of causing loss by unlawful means could avoid redundancy depends on unlawful means being defined more broadly for the purposes of the two-party tort. At first sight, the idea of using different definitions of unlawful means for two-party and three-party forms of a tort might seem counter-intuitive and unattractively complex. But in *Revenue & Customs Commissioners v Total Network SL*,[466] when explaining why a broader definition of unlawful means could be used as an element in the definition of the tort of unlawful means conspiracy, the House of Lords suggested that a narrower definition was only required in *OBG v Allan* because the tort in that case involved causing loss to a claimant through the medium of a third party. In practical terms,

---

[464] See above para.23-83. *OBG Ltd v Allan* [2007] UKHL 21; [2008] 1 A.C. 1 at [49], endorsed by Lady Hale at [302]; and by Lord Brown at [319]–[320]. See also the requirement, discussed above at para.23-90, that the unlawful means must interfere with the third party's freedom to deal with the claimant.

[465] For discussion of this tort see above para.23-75.

[466] *Revenue & Customs Commissioners v Total Network SL* [2008] UKHL 19; [2008] 1 A.C. 1174 at [99], per Lord Walker, at [124], per Lord Mance, at [223], per Lord Neuberger. See also *JSC BTA Bank v Ablyazov (No.14)* [2018] UKSC 19; [2018] 2 W.L.R. 1125 at [12].

a two-party tort with a broader definition of unlawful means would allow a court to assist a "claimant whose economic interests had been deliberately injured by a crime committed against him by the defendant".[467] The objections to extending tort liability in this way, however, would include that such an extension would allow statutes to have consequences beyond those intended by Parliament and might require the development of a complex jurisprudence as to *which* crimes and statutory wrongs a claimant could invoke as the foundation for a two-party civil claim.[468] Moreover, the recognition of the extended two-party tort would indirectly undermine the limit imposed on unlawful means for the purposes of the three-party tort: a claimant in a three-party case could claim that the "actionable civil wrong" that the defendant committed to a third party was the extended two-party tort.

(f) Related statutory torts

Finally, the Employment Act 1982 created two new species of tort liability for unlawful interference with commercial interests.[469] Where a person refuses to enter into contracts or to consider tenders, or terminates a contract relating to the supply of goods or services he commits a tort if one of his objects is to ensure that persons who are (or are not) members of a trade union should do the relevant work[470] or if one of his reasons is that the person excluded does not, or is not likely to, recognise, negotiate or consult with a trade union.[471] It is not a tort if he so acts to exclude a person who does recognise a trade union. Proceedings for this statutory tort can be brought by the person excluded or by "any other person who may be adversely affected" by a contravention of the statute.[472] These torts have their greatest impact in the parallel removal of protection in tort from trade unions in trade disputes.[473] Their further treatment is therefore postponed to that section of this chapter.[474] 23-97

[467] In *OBG Ltd v Allan* [2007] UKHL 21; [2008] 1 A.C. 1, Lord Nicholls, who dissented from the majority's opinion as to the limits on what could constitute unlawful means in a three party cases also stated, at [161], that he was "far from satisfied that, in a two-party situation, the courts would decline to give relief to a claimant whose economic interests had been deliberately injured by a crime committed against him by the defendant."

[468] See below, at para.23-109 onwards, for discussion of cases dealing with a parallel question within the tort of unlawful means conspiracy.

[469] Employment Act 1982 ss.12, 13, 14, now TULRCA 1992 ss.144–145, 186–187, 222, 225; *Messenger Newspapers Ltd v NGA* [1984] I.R.L.R. 397.

[470] TULRCA 1992 ss.144, 145(1)–(4).

[471] TULRCA 1992 ss.186, 187(1), (2).

[472] TULRCA 1992 ss.145(5), 187(3).

[473] TULRCA 1992 ss.222(3), 225(1), (2); cf. Lewis and Simpson (1982) 11 I.L.J. 227; Wedderburn, *The Worker and the Law*, 3rd edn (1986), pp.606-611; Evans and Lewis (1988) 17 I.L.J. 209 at 223–226.

[474] See para.23-130 onwards. See also the liability under s.235A of TULRCA 1992 for interruption of goods or services: see para.23-173.

5. Conspiracy

(a) General

23-98 **The nature of conspiracy**[475] "A conspiracy consists … in the agreement of two or more to do an unlawful act, or to do a lawful act by unlawful means."[476] The principles were developed largely in the course of the twentieth century.[477] Conspiracy may be a crime[478]; but the historical links between the crime and the tort have now been greatly weakened.[479] The crime inheres in the agreement to act unlawfully[480]; but the tort arises when damage is caused (or, for a quia timet injunction, threatened) by the combination.[481] As a tort:

---

475 See *Crofter Hand Woven Harris Tweed Co v Veitch* [1942] A.C. 435 at 439–445, per Viscount Simon LC; and at 461-472, per Lord Wright; the monumental judgment of Evatt J in Australia in *McKernan v Fraser* (1931) 46 C.L.R. 343 at 363–412; *Lonrho Plc v Fayed* [1992] 1 A.C. 448 at 463–466, per Lord Bridge; *Revenue & Customs Commissioners v Total Network SL* [2008] UKHL 19; [2008] 1 A.C. 1174 at [65]–[78], per Lord Walker; *JSC BTA Bank v Ablyazov (No.14)* [2018] UKSC 19; [2018] 2 W.L.R. 1125; *Canada Cement La Farge v British Columbia Lightweight Aggregate Ltd* (1983) 145 D.L.R. (3d) 385 SCC at 396–400. For a critical appraisal see Carty "The Tort of Conspiracy as a Can of Worms", Ch.13 in Pitel et al (eds) *Tort Law: Challenging Orthodoxy* (Oxford: Hart, 2013). For a critique of judicial development of tortious liability for conspiracy which argues that if Lord Nicholls' analysis of the tort of causing loss by unlawful means in *OBG Ltd v Allan* [2007] UKHL 21; [2008] 1 A.C. 1 is preferred to that of Lord Hoffmann (see para.23-83), there is neither need nor justification for a separate tort of conspiracy in either of its forms, see P.S. Davies and Sir Philip Sales, "Intentional Harm, Accessories and Conspiracies" (2018) 134 L.Q.R. 69.

476 *Mulcahy v R.* (1868) L.R. 3 H.L. 306 at 317, per Wiles J; *Baxendale-Walker v Middleton* [2011] EWHC 998 (QB) at [59]–[60].

477 *Crofter Hand Woven Harris Tweed Co v Veitch* [1942] A.C. 435 at 461, per Lord Wright. The tort is "a modern invention": per Lord Denning MR in *Midland Bank Trust Co Ltd v Green (No.3)* [1982] Ch. 529 at 539. cf. *JSC BTA Bank v Ablyazov (No.14)* [2018] UKSC 19; [2018] 2 W.L.R. 1125 at [6], per Lords Sumption and Lloyd-Jones: "of all the economic torts it is the one whose boundaries are perhaps the hardest to define in principled terms."

478 See Criminal Law Act 1977 ss.1 and 5 abolishing the crime of conspiracy except for conspiracy to defraud (*Scott v Metropolitan Police Commissioner* [1975] A.C. 819 HL); conspiracy to corrupt public morals (*Shaw v DPP* [1962] A.C. 220 HL); conspiracy to outrage public decency (*R. v Knuller* [1973] A.C. 435 HL). The crime of conspiracy otherwise rests upon the agreement to pursue conduct which involves the commission of a criminal offence. See Smith and Hogan, *Criminal Law*, 15th edn (2018), ch.11.3.

479 Although "both the crime and the tort grew from a common root" there is "no good logical or historical reason" for "slavishly applying in the law of tort" rules applicable to the crime: per Oliver J in *Midland Bank Trust Co Ltd v Green (No.3)* [1979] Ch. 496 at 522 and 525; affirmed [1982] Ch. 529 CA where Fox LJ said at 540 that although "the crime and the tort shared the same definition … [which] suggests some considerable affinity between the two … the affinity is not … in fact very close at all". See too *JSC BTA Bank v Ablyazov (No.14)* [2018] UKSC 19; [2018] 2 W.L.R. 1125 at [9] per Lords Sumption and Lloyd-Jones: while "the essence of the crime is the agreement or understanding that the parties will act unlawfully, whether or not it is implemented … a tortious conspiracy, like most tortious acts, must have caused loss to the claimant or the cause of action will be incomplete. It follows that a conspiracy must necessarily have been acted on. But there is no more to it than that. The critical point is that the tort of conspiracy is not simply a particular form of joint tortfeasance." It is actionable as a distinct tort once it is established that a conspiracy has caused loss and it is not a form of secondary liability but a primary liability: per Lord Wright in *Crofter Handwoven Harris Tweed Co v Veitch* [1942] A.C. 435 at 462: "it is in the fact of conspiracy that the unlawfulness resides," reaffirmed in *Revenue & Customs Commissioners v Total Network SL* [2008] UKHL 19; [2008] 1 A.C. 1174.

480 *Mulcahy v R.* (1868) L.R. 3 H.L. 306 at 317. *Phillips v News Group Newspapers Ltd* [2012] UKSC 28; [2013] 1 A.C. 1 at [43]–[45] per Lord Walker; the offence of conspiracy was complete when the agreement was made, and the conspirators could be prosecuted even though no performance had taken place.

481 *Midland Bank Trust Co Ltd v Green (No.3)* [1979] Ch. 496 at 523–524, per Oliver J; affirmed [1982]

"very little is heard of it until the nineteenth century, when it was brought into prominence as a result of the legislature having, in 1875, enacted that combination in furtherance of trade disputes should not be indictable as conspiracies in any case where the act, if committed by one person, would not be a crime."[482]

It is now clear that a "conspiracy to injure might give rise to civil liability even though the end were brought about by conduct and acts which by themselves, and apart from the element of combination or concerted action, could not be regarded as a legal wrong".[483]

The two forms The tort of conspiracy takes two forms: conspiracy to use unlawful means, and lawful means conspiracy, which is sometimes called "conspiracy to injure".[484] The latter does, but the former does not, require a predominant purpose to injure.[485] Today, "it matters not" whether "the two types of actionable conspiracy" are treated "as different torts" or as "species of the same tort".[486] Liability for lawful means conspiracy, where the acts would without combination be lawful, forms a qualification to the general rule that the mere agreement of many persons to act in concert cannot make the act of any one or more wrongful, if it would not be wrongful when done by each alone independently.[487] Indeed: "Why should an act which causes economic loss to A but is not actionable at his suit if done by B alone become actionable because B did it pursuant to an agreement between B and C?"[488] The conventional reply (made particularly in the cases against trade unions or their officials after 1875) was that "numbers may annoy and coerce where one may 23-99

Ch. 529 CA, per Fox LJ at 541. Intentional, not merely foreseeable, damage is essential to the tort: *Crofter Hand Woven Harris Tweed Co Ltd v Veitch* [1942] A.C. 435 at 461, per Lord Wright; it is "the gist" of the cause of action, per Lord Diplock in *Lonrho Ltd v Shell Petroleum Co Ltd (No.2)* [1982] A.C. 173 at 188. Parallels between the tort and the crime must now be drawn with great caution. See *Kuwait Oil Tanker Co SAK v Al-Bader* [2000] 2 All E.R. (Comm) 271 at 312.

482 *Midland Bank Trust Co Ltd v Green (No.3)* [1979] Ch. 496 at 523, per Oliver J; the Conspiracy and Protection of Property Act 1875 s.3 gave this protection after *R. v Bunn* (1872) 12 Cox 316, had extended the crime of conspiracy in relation to organising strikes. That section was replaced by the Criminal Law Act 1977 ss.1 and 3. Similar protection against liability for the tort of conspiracy was provided by the Trade Disputes Act 1906 s.1; now TULRCA 1992 s.219(2); see para.23-154.

483 *Quinn v Leathem* [1901] A.C. 495 at 510, per Lord Macnaghten, approved in Crofter [1942] A.C. 435, per Viscount Maugham at 448, per Lord Wright at 461. cf. *JSC BTA Bank v Ablyazov (No.14)* [2018] UKSC 19; [2018] 2 W.L.R. 1125 at [10] where "the absence of just cause or excuse" for the combination was said to be "a more useful concept" in explaining what made a conspiracy tortious than either "a predominant purpose of injuring the claimant" in the case of lawful means conspiracy or "the use of unlawful means" in the case of the other form of conspiracy. "In either case there is no just cause or excuse *for the combination*" (emphasis in the original).

484 In *JSC BTA Bank v Ablyazov (No.14)* [2018] UKSC 19; [2018] 2 W.L.R. 1125 at [8], Lords Sumption and Lloyd-Jones identified "lawful means conspiracy" as more satisfactory than the rival label—"conspiracy to injure"—since "all actionable conspiracies are conspiracies to injure, although the intent required may take a variety of different forms".

485 *Lonrho Plc v Fayed* [1992] 1 A.C. 448, HL at 463–468, per Lord Bridge; *Paragon Finance v Thaktra* [1999] 1 All E.R. 400; *JSC BTA Bank v Ablyazov (No.14)* [2018] UKSC 19; [2018] 2 W.L.R. 1125 at [8]; *MX1 Ltd v Farahzad* [2018] EWHC 1041 (Ch); [2018] 1 W.L.R. 5553 at [22].

486 per Nourse LJ (judgment of the court) *Kuwait Oil Tanker Co SAK v Al-Bader* [2000] 2 All E.R. (Comm) 271 at 311. In the unlawful means type of conspiracy, where the unlawful means alleged were themselves a tort, the conspiracy claim did not merge with that tort so as to preclude the claimant from suing for conspiracy, [2000] 2 All E.R. (Comm) 271 at 319.

487 *Ware and De Freville v Motor Trade Association* [1921] 3 K.B. 40 at 70, per Scrutton LJ.

488 *Lonrho Ltd v Shell Petroleum Co Ltd (No.2)* [1982] A.C. 173 at 188, per Lord Diplock.

not"[489] and that a combination could make oppressive what in a single person was not.[490] This reasoning has been doubted, in that it is unrealistic:

> "to suggest today that acts done by one street-corner grocer in concert with a second are more oppressive and dangerous to a competitor than the same acts done by a string of supermarkets under a single ownership or that a multinational conglomerate … does not exercise greater power than any combination of small businesses."[491]

But the fact that not every gang is more dangerous than every individual does not provide a conclusive reason for thinking it absurd to impose special limits on those who are minded to participate in gangs with the purpose of causing harm to others. And the lawful means form of the tort, although arguably "anomalous", is too well-established to be "discarded".[492]

23-100 **The combination** The tort requires an agreement, combination, understanding, or concert to injure, involving two or more persons. Of the various words used to describe a conspiracy, "combination" has been preferred to "agreement" on the ground that "agreement" might be thought to require some agreement of a contractual kind, whereas all that is needed is a combination and common intention.[493] The tort has also been said to require "concerted action taken pursuant to agreement"[494]; but this is only because "a tortious conspiracy, like most other tortious acts, must have caused loss to the claimant, or the cause of action will be incomplete."[495] Because: "It is a rare case where there is evidence of an agree-

489 per Lord Lindley in *Quinn v Leathem* [1901] A.C. 495 at 538: "Annoyance and coercion by many may be so intolerable as to become actionable, and produce a result which one alone could not produce." Seeing strikes, as he did, as "a form of coercion, intimidation, molestation or annoyance" to employers and to workers willing to work, judges imposed the then new liability for conspiracy on this basis.

490 See *Mogul S.S. Co v McGregor Gow* (1889) 23 Q.B.D. 598 at 616, per Bowen LJ; affirmed at [1892] A.C. 25 HL. cf. Lord Walker in *Revenue & Customs Commissioners v Total Network SL* [2008] UKHL 19; [2008] 1 A.C. 1174 at [77] who regarded Bowen LJ's second reason, that "the very fact of the combination may shew that the object is simply to do harm, and not to exercise one's own just rights", as "more principled". Lord Walker identified a third, largely unarticulated reason influencing judges at the end of the 19th century, namely the deep suspicion by the governing class of collective action in the political and economic spheres as potential threats to the constitution and framework of society, [2008] UKHL 19; [2008] 1 A.C. 1174 at [78]; See also *JSC BTA Bank v Ablyazov (No.14)* [2018] UKSC 19; [2018] 2 W.L.R. 1125 at [7].

491 *Lonrho Ltd v Shell Petroleum Co Ltd (No.2)* [1982] A.C. 173 at 189, per Lord Diplock.

492 *Lonrho Ltd v Shell Petroleum Co Ltd (No.2)* [1982] A.C. 173 at 188–189, per Lord Diplock; *JSC BTA Bank v Ablyazov (No.14)* [2018] UKSC 19; [2018] 2 W.L.R. 1125 at [7], "the tort of conspiracy has an established place in the law of tort"; cf. *Lonrho Plc v Fayed* [1992] 1 A.C. 448 HL; *Canada Cement La Farge v British Columbia Lightweight Aggregate* (1983) 145 D.L.R. (3d) 385, SCC.

493 *Belmont Finance Corp v Williams Furniture Ltd (No.2)* [1980] 1 All E.R. 393 at 404, per Buckley LJ; cf. *Crofter Hand Woven Harris Tweed Co Ltd v Veitch* [1942] A.C.435 at 439–440 and 461, per Viscount Simon and Lord Wright. cf. *Douglas v Hello! Ltd (No.3)* [2003] EWHC 786; [2003] 3 All E.R. 996 where conspiracy allegations failed, inter alia, because there was "no common plan or intent" between those said to be involved. cf. *Phillips v News Group Newspapers Ltd* [2010] UKSC 28; [2013] 1 A.C. 1 at [44] where Lord Walker said that the crime of conspiracy "involved an agreement, express or implied." See also *Energy Renewals Ltd v Borg* [2014] EWHC 2166 (Ch); [2014] I.R.L.R. 73 at [61]–[62]; and *JSC BTA Bank v Ablyazov (No.14)* [2018] UKSC 19; [2018] 2 W.L.R. 1125.

494 *Lonrho Ltd v Shell Petroleum Co Ltd (No.2)* [1982] A.C. 173 at 188, per Lord Diplock.

495 *JSC BTA Bank v Ablyazov (No.14)* [2018] UKSC 19; [2018] 2 W.L.R. 1125 at [9].

ment", in most cases, "it will be necessary to scrutinise the acts relied upon in order to see what inferences can be drawn as to the existence or otherwise of the alleged conspiracy or combination".[496] Neither form of conspiracy is simply a variety of joint tortfeasance, though there may clearly be situations where a defendant will have simultaneously committed the conspiracy tort and acted so as to be jointly liable for a separate tort as a result of participation in a "common design" to commit it[497]; both forms of conspiracy tort impose primary liability for a wrong that imposes liability for having combined with another to injure the claimant without a just cause or excuse.[498] The previous edition of this work suggested that "the question whether a person is a party to a combination constituting a conspiracy is essentially the same as whether he is liable as a joint tortfeasor in procuring a wrong, by reason of a common design".[499] Recent cases, however, have tended to deny any association with joint tortfeasance and to emphasise that participation in an actionable conspiracy is a form of *primary* wrongdoing. Moreover, there are two further reasons why it may be appropriate not to rely too closely on authorities relating to joint tortfeasance through "common design" when seeking to determine whether a defendant's alliance with another amounts to a "combination": in instances of lawful means conspiracy there need not be any civil wrong that the conspirators could have jointly committed and, in any case, the requirements for establishing joint tortfeasance vary depending on the nature of the tort that is alleged to have been committed pursuant to a "common design".[500]

23-101 Husband and wife were once thought to be one person in the eyes of the common law and, therefore, to be incapable of conspiring together.[501] This is still the case in criminal conspiracy, indeed in this context the anomaly has been extended to civil partners, though it ceases to apply if the combination includes a third

---

496 *The Racing Partnership Ltd v Done Brothers (Cash Betting) Ltd* [2019] EWHC 1156 (Ch); [2020] Ch. 289 at [257]; quoting *Kuwait Oil Tanker Company SAK v Al-Bader* [2000] 2 All E.R. (Comm) 271 CA at [112].

497 Liability for a tort as a result of participation in a common design is discussed above, para.4-03.

498 *JSC BTA Bank v Ablyazov (No.14)* [2018] UKSC 19; [2018] 2 W.L.R. 1125 at [10] (emphasis in the original): "A person has a right to advance his own interests by lawful means even if the foreseeable consequence is to damage the interests of others. The existence of that right affords a just cause or excuse. Where, on the other hand, he seeks to advance his interests by unlawful means he has no such right. The position is the same where the means used are lawful but the predominant intention of the defendant was to injure the claimant rather than to further some legitimate interest of his own. ... In either case, there is no just cause or excuse *for the combination*."

499 22nd edn (2018) at para.24-97. This approach reflected the frequency with which judgments, particularly before the decision of the House of Lords in *Revenue & Customs Commissioners v Total Network SL* [2008] UKHL 19; [2008] 1 A.C. 1174, intermingled principles associated with conspiracy and joint tortfeasance.

500 In *Vestergaard Frandsen A/S v Bestnet Europe Ltd* [2013] UKSC 31; [2013] 1 W.L.R. 1556 at [34], Lord Neuberger adopted a proposition advanced by Lord Sumption in argument, to the effect that "in order for a defendant to be party to a common design, she must share with the other party, or parties, to the design, each of the features of the design which make it wrongful." Later in his judgment, at [36]–[37], he treated this as importing that a party can be party to a common design to commit a strict liability wrong, such as patent infringement, without knowing that the acts are wrongful, but can only be liable for a common design to commit a conscience-based wrong, such as misuse of a trade secret, if she knows that a conscience-based wrong is to be committed. The question whether a defendant can commit the tort of unlawful means conspiracy without knowing that the means are unlawful has become controversial, and is discussed below at para.23-120.

501 *DPP v Blady* [1912] 2 K.B. 89 at 92 (Lush J, dissenting on other matters); *Mawji v R.* [1957] A.C. 126 (polygamous marriage; the point was conceded).

person.[502] But it has been held that, in the absence of binding authority, and of a compelling rationale or public policy, the primitive maxim that spouses are one person should not be imported into the tort of conspiracy.[503]

23-102 It is not clear whether a trade union can be party to a conspiracy. In *EETPU v Times Newspapers Ltd* O'Connor J held that a union had no separate "personality" because what is now s.10(2) of TULRCA 1992 states that "a trade union shall not be, or be treated as if it were, a body corporate".[504] While that suggests that it cannot be party to a conspiracy, later decisions making a trade union liable in tort suggest that it can be a party.[505]

23-103 It seems to be the better view that an employer is not ordinarily "in combination" with his employees and that no charge of conspiracy can be brought when the latter merely go about his business.[506] A company, being a separate legal person, can conspire with its directors[507]; and the knowledge of the company may be found in the person (usually a director) who has management or control (as its "alter ego") for the transaction or act in question.[508] It has been held that a criminal conspiracy

---

502 s.2(2)(a) of the Criminal Law Act 1977. See also *R. v Lovick (Sylvia)* [1993] Crim. L.R. 890 (CA (Crim Div)).

503 *Midland Bank Trust Co Ltd v Green (No.3)* [1979] Ch. 496 at 527, per Oliver J; affirmed [1982] Ch. 529 CA at 538, per Lord Denning MR, and at 541, per Fox LJ.

504 [1980] Q.B. 585. The relevant statutory provision was then TULRA 1974 s.2(1).

505 e.g. *Dimbleby & Sons Ltd v NUJ* [1984] 1 W.L.R. 427 HL. On international and foreign "persons" see *International Tin Council, Re* [1990] 2 A.C. 418 HL; *Arab Monetary Fund v Hashim (No.3)* [1991] 2 A.C. 114 HL; Foreign Corporations Act 1991. On the Crown see *Folland v Ontario* (2003) 225 D.L.R. (4th) 50 (Ont. CA), where the court refused to strike out a claim for conspiracy to injure against the Crown, rejecting the submission that an action for malicious prosecution was the only possible claim against the Crown for prosecutorial misconduct.

506 per Lord Wright in *Crofter Hand Woven Harris Tweed Co v Veitch* [1942] A.C. 435 at 468; (Viscount Simon LC seems to take the opposite view at 441, but it is suggested that Lord Wright's view is more consistent with cases such as *Said v Butt* [1920] 3 K.B. 497); *Williams v Natural Life Health* [1998] 1 W.L.R. 830, HL; *Credit Lyonnais Bank of Nederland v Export Credits Guarantee Dept* [2000] 1 A.C. 486; Grantham and Rickett (1999) 62 M.L.R. 133, discussed at para.23-39.

507 *Belmont Finance Corp v Williams Furniture Ltd (No.2)* [1980] 1 All E.R. 393 CA; *Prudential Assurance Co Ltd v Newman Industries Ltd (No.2)* [1982] Ch. 204 CA (in both of which the knowledge of directors was imputed to their companies); *Digicel (St Lucia) Ltd v Cable & Wireless Plc* [2010] EWHC 774 (Ch) at Annex I, [77].

508 The "directing mind and will" of the company may be found in different persons for different purposes as its "alter ego": *El Ajou v Dollar Land Holdings Plc* [1994] 2 All E.R. 685 CA, especially, per Nourse LJ at 693–698, per Rose and Hoffmann LJJ at 699 and 705–706 (seeking out the person having de facto control); *Meridian Global Funds Ltd v Securities Commission* [1995] 2 A.C. 500 HL; cf. *Tesco Supermarkets Ltd v Nattrass* [1972] A.C. 153 HL (distinguished in *Supply of Ready Mixed Concrete (No.2), Re* [1995] 1 A.C. 456 HL). In *Belmont Finance Corp v Williams Furniture Ltd (No.2)* [1980] 1 All E.R. 393 at 404, Buckley LJ stated that a company has imputed to it the knowledge of a director under a duty to disclose to the company; but where the director would disclose his own breach of duty in disclosing the information, the company is not in possession of it: *Houghton v Nothard* [1928] A.C. 1 HL; cf. Wedderburn (1984) 47 M.L.R. 345 (how does a company forget?). So, too, where directors acquire information in another, private capacity and do not disclose it: *Lagunas Nitrate Co v Lagunas Syndicate* [1899] 2 Ch. 392 at 431, per Lindley LJ. Similarly, the knowledge of an agent is not necessarily that of the principal: *El Ajou v Dollar Land Holdings Plc* [1994] 2 All E.R. 685 CA at 702–703, per Hoffmann LJ; *David Payne & Co Ltd, Re* [1904] 2 Ch. 608 CA. In *The Dolphina* [2011] SGHC 273; [2012] 1 Lloyd's Rep. 304 (on the basis that the purpose of the tort of conspiracy "seems to lie in the law's concern to prevent harmful combinations": *Revenue & Customs Commissioners v Total Network SL* [2008] UKHL 19; [2008] 1 A.C. 1174, per Lord Hope at [44] and Lord Walker at [77]) it was held that for this purpose a company should be identified with the person or persons who could cause it to combine with others so as to harm the plaintiff, which in the first place would be its board of directors. On the facts,

between a "one-man" company and its sole controller is an impossibility because it is not possible to find an agreement between two minds.[509] This might not be the case in a civil action where the controller had used the corporate machinery in what was alleged to be a conspiracy to damage the claimant.[510]

The conspirators need not all join in at the same time, nor need they have exactly the same aim in mind; but the possession of a separate aim may be evidence that the party concerned has not participated in the combination at all, at any rate if he acted throughout in ignorance of the true facts.[511] The question is how far the defendant was aware of the plan and then "joined in the execution" of it.[512] A person may be a party to a combination to use unlawful means, even though he himself cannot commit the unlawful acts in question, for example a person who joins parties to a contract in making threats that they will break that contract, thereby constituting a conspiracy to intimidate.[513] **23-104**

(b) Unlawful means conspiracy

This form of the tort is committed where two or more persons combine and take action which is unlawful in itself with the intention of causing damage to a third party who does incur the intended damage.[514] It is not necessary for the injured party to prove that causing him damage was the main or predominant purpose of the combination but that purpose must be part of the combiners' intentions. The main issues raised by this form of the tort are: first, the degree of intention required, **23-105**

---

the defendant company's knowledge was held to include knowledge which one of its directors gained as a director of another company.

509 *R. v McDonnell* [1966] 1 Q.B. 233.

510 Sufficiently arguable: *Raja v McMillan* [2020] EWHC 951 (Ch). Such a controller can make a binding contract with his company: *Lee v Lee's Air Farming Ltd* [1961] A.C. 12 PC; and a combination of two or three wholly controlled companies would seem sufficient: cf. (1966) 82 L.Q.R. 151 at 153. In *Taylor v Smith* [1991] I.R. 142 (Ir. Supreme Court) such liability was favoured: see especially at 162–165.

511 See, per Harman J in *Huntley v Thornton* [1957] 1 W.L.R. 321 at 343; per Evatt J in *McKernan v Fraser* (1931) 46 C.L.R. 343 at 401 and 407; *Bird v O'Neal* [1960] A.C. 907 at 920-921, PC; *PTY Homes Ltd v Shand* [1968] N.Z.L.R. 105 at 110. On disparity of objects, see para.23-127. The combination has been said to need "an assenting mind" not "mere words"; per Rand J in *R. v O'Brien* [1955] 2 D.L.R. 311 at 315.

512 per Gatehouse J in *Metall und Rohstoff AG v Donaldson, Lufkin & Jenrette Inc* [1990] 1 Q.B. 391 ("a factual issue": reversed on other grounds, [1990] 1 Q.B. 391 CA; overruled in relation to those grounds *Lonrho Plc v Fayed* [1992] 1 A.C. 448 HL); *The Dolphina* [2011] SGHC 273; [2012] 1 Lloyd's Rep. 304 at [282]: "A conspirator need not know all of the details of the plot so long as he is aware of the common objective and what his role in bringing it about involves." *XY Inc v International Newtech Developments Inc* 2013 BCCA 352; (2013) 366 D.L.R. (4th) 443 at [54]–[55] where the personal defendants were part of a team which acted in concert to carry out unlawful acts that would injure the plaintiff.

513 This was the position of Silverthorne in *Rookes v Barnard* [1964] A.C. 1129. So too, the position of Captain Stafford in *Kuwait Oil Tanker Company SAK v Al-Bader* [2000] 2 All E.R. (Comm) 271 CA.

514 *Baxendale-Walker v Middleton* [2011] EWHC 998 at [60]; cf. *Pell Frischmann Engineering Ltd v Bow Valley Iran Ltd* [2009] UKPC 45; [2011] 1 W.L.R. 2370 at [55]. However the view of some commentators that unlawful means conspiracy was only a form of secondary liability for acts which were themselves an actionable civil wrong was rejected by the House of Lords in *Revenue & Customs Commissioners v Total Network SL* [2008] UKHL 19; [2008] 1 A.C. 1174 per Lord Walker at [101]–[104], Lord Mance at [116] and Lord Neuberger at [225]. On the overlap of liability for conspiracy and inducing breach of contract see *Tree Savers International v Savoy* (1992) 87 D.L.R. (4th) 202 at 206–207 (Alta. CA).

secondly what forms of behaviour will count as unlawful means, thirdly whether the unlawful means were "indeed the means" by which damage was caused, and fourthly whether the defendants must know that their means are unlawful.

(i) Intention

23-106 As in the other economic torts, difficulty has arisen over the degree of intention required for liability for unlawful means conspiracy. In 1982, the House of Lords appeared to decide in *Lonrho Ltd v Shell Petroleum Co (No.2)* that, even if unlawful means were involved, liability for conspiracy only arose where the defendants acted with "injury to the [claimant] and not the self-interest of the defendants ... [as] the predominant purpose of the agreement".[515] But a decade later, in *Lonrho Plc v Fayed*, the House of Lords rejected this interpretation of the law, which in the interim had not in fact been acceptable to other jurisdictions.[516] When conspirators use unlawful means to injure the claimant, the Law Lords decided, "it is no defence for them to show that their primary purpose was to further or protect their own interests; it is sufficient to make their action tortious that the means used were unlawful"; in such cases "an intention to injure the claimant", rather than a predominant purpose to injure, is enough.[517]

23-107 It was noted above, that a defendant can only be held liable for the tort of causing loss by unlawful means if he or she acted with an "intention to cause loss" to the claimant.[518] Since injury to the claimant does not have to be the "predominant purpose" of an unlawful means conspiracy, a common meaning for "intention" could have been adopted across both the economic tort liabilities that are based on the use of unlawful means. Indeed, many modern cases have assumed that the torts of causing loss by unlawful means and unlawful means conspiracy define "intention to injure" in the same way.[519] For the purposes of the causing loss by unlaw-

---

515 *Lonrho Ltd v Shell Petroleum Co Ltd (No.2)* [1982] A.C. 173, per Lord Diplock delivering the decision of the House of Lords ("Lonrho 1982"); cf. *Revenue & Customs Commissioners v Total Network SL* [2008] UKHL 19; [2008] 1 A.C. 1174 at [82], per Lord Walker: "Lord Diplock uncharacteristically failed to make a clear distinction between the requirement of predominant purpose under one variety of the tort of conspiracy and the lower requirement of intentional injury needed for the other variety."

516 See *Canada Cement La Farge Ltd v British Columbia Lightweight Aggregate Ltd* (1983) 145 D.L.R. (3d) 385 (SCC); *SSC B Lintas NZ v Murphy* [1986] 2 N.Z.L.R. 436; *Taylor v Smyth* [1991] 1 I.R. 142 Ir. S.C.

517 *Lonrho Plc v Fayed* [1992] 1 A.C. 448 at 466 and 468, per Lord Bridge. See too *WH Newson Holdings Ltd v IMI Inc* [2013] EWCA Civ 1377; [2014] 1 All E.R. 1132 at [32] onwards. cf. *Wagner v Gill* [2014] NZCA 336; [2015] 3 N.Z.L.R. 157 at [89]–[107] where French J, giving the judgment of the court, said that the House of Lords decision in *Total Network* did not endorse a broad view of intention in conspiracy cases, and on balance the court preferred to retain the requirement that the defendant's conduct had to be directed at the plaintiff.

518 See para.23-79.

519 Cases where it has been accepted that the necessary "intention" to cause loss to the claimant is the same in the tort of intentionally causing loss by the use of unlawful means and in unlawful means conspiracy include: *Meretz Investments NV v ACP Ltd* [2007] EWCA Civ 1303; [2008] Ch. 244 at [146]; *Digicel (St Lucia) Ltd v Cable & Wireless Plc* [2010] EWHC 774 (Ch) at Annex I, [84]; *Emerald Supplies Ltd v British Airways Plc (Nos 1 & 2)* [2015] EWCA Civ 1024; [2016] Bus. L.R. 145 at [133]; *Palmer Birch (a partnership) v Lloyd* [2018] EWHC 2316 (TCC); [2018] 4 W.L.R. 164 at [220]; *Media-Saturn Holding Gmbh v Toshiba Information Systems (UK) Ltd* [2019] EWHC 1095 (Ch); [2019] 5 C.M.L.R. 7 at [226]. Similarly, in *Recovery Partners GB Ltd v Rukhadze* [2018] EWHC 2918 (Comm); [2019] Bus. L.R. 1166 at [446](iv), Cockerill J applied dicta from *OBG Ltd v Allan* [2007] UKHL 21; [2008] 1 A.C. 1 on "intention" for the purposes of the tort of causing loss

ful means tort, a defendant will be held to have intended to cause loss to a claimant if this was the defendant's goal, or the means that the defendant had selected to achieve some goal, or the necessary corollary of the defendant's goal or means, in the sense of being simply "the other side of the same coin",[520] and this definition has been employed regularly in cases involving unlawful means conspiracy.[521] However, when providing a summary of the unlawful means conspiracy tort in *JSC BTA Bank v Ablyazov (No.14)*, Lords Sumption and Lloyd-Jones incorporated a different account of intention, relying on a Canadian case,[522] which suggested that a "constructive intent" can be sufficient, and will be found where conspirators have "directed" their unlawful conduct at a claimant and ought to have known that this would be likely to cause injury to the claimant.[523] "Constructive intent" is far easier to establish than a true intention, since the mere fact that a consequence is known to be likely does not mean that it is truly intended, and in the quotation cited by Lords Sumption and Lloyd-Jones the scope of the concept is extended still further by the insistence that it is enough that a party "ought to have known". But the suggestion that "constructive intent" is sufficient seems to be undercut by the requirement for the unlawful means to be "directed towards" the claimant. One way of understanding when *unlawful means* have been "directed at" a claimant would be that it is the case when those means are being used in order to cause loss to the claimant. To put the same point another way, it is not clear how a defendant who merely "ought to have known" that his unlawful acts would harm the claimant can be said to have "directed" those acts at the claimant. Given these uncertainties, and the absence of any strong indication that the Supreme Court in *JSC BTA Bank v Ablyazov (No.14)* intended to depart from the account of "intention to harm" that has been consistently used by the courts since *OBG Ltd*, it may be best to overlook the reference to "constructive intent".[524]

(ii) Unlawful means

The previous edition of this work observed that there is no good reason why the ambit of "unlawful means" in this form of conspiracy should not be coterminous with its scope in the other economic torts[525]; this, however, is not the current law: a broader range of unlawful acts can constitute "unlawful means" for the purposes of the unlawful means conspiracy tort as against those which can be relied on to establish liability for the tort of causing loss by unlawful means. It was noted above that a defendant will not be liable for committing the unlawful means tort in a three-party situation unless the means used (to cause loss to a claimant by restricting a **23-108**

by unlawful means in order to hold defendants liable for unlawful means conspiracy.

520 See para.23-81.

521 See cases cited above, fn.519.

522 *Canada Cement La Farge Ltd v British Columbia Lightweight Aggregate Ltd* (1983) 145 D.L.R. (3d) 385 at 388–391 (SCC) (if unlawful means used, liability in conspiracy if conduct directed at claimant and defendants knew this was likely to result in injury).

523 *JSC BTA Bank v Ablyazov (No.14)* [2018] UKSC 19; [2018] 2 W.L.R. 1125 at [13].

524 The uncertainty caused by the Supreme Court's discussion of "intention" in *JSC BTA Bank v Ablyazov (No.14)* [2018] UKSC 19; [2018] 2 W.L.R. 1125 at [13]–[14] is reflected in the divergent views of commentators. In contrast to the view expressed above, Grant and Mumford, *Civil Fraud*, 1st edn (London: Sweet & Maxwell, 2018), para.2-086, treat the case as having re-established the need for a "highly specific intention" which "targets" the claimant.

525 22nd edn (2018) at para.24-101.

third party's liberty to deal with him) could have been actionable at the suit of the third party.[526] But liability for participating in an unlawful means conspiracy can be established in situations where other forms of unlawful means have been used. It has been held that whenever the means used involves the commission of a tort, or torts, against the claimant, a combination to inflict harm using those means will be a tortious conspiracy.[527] Thus a combination to cause damage to the claimant by means of intimidatory threats to break contracts[528] or by way of procurement of breaches of contracts[529] or by violence or fraud[530] is actionable. But a claim can also be based on a conspiracy to cause loss by means of acts that are criminal, but not tortious. In *JSC BTA Bank v Ablyazov (No.14)*[531] the Supreme Court summarised the position: "a criminal offence could be a sufficient unlawful means for the purpose of the law of conspiracy, provided that it was objectively directed against the claimant."[532] The Court, however, left open the actionability of a combination to cause loss by means of "breaches of civil statutory duties, or torts actionable at the suit of third parties, or breaches of contract or fiduciary duty."[533] Lords Sumption and Lloyd-Jones identified these wrongs as "liable to raise more complex problems"; in the case of torts actionable at the suit of third parties, or breaches of contract or fiduciary duty, this was because: "Compliance with the criminal law is a universal obligation. By comparison, legal duties in tort or equity will com-

---

526 The position was summarised in *JSC BTA Bank v Ablyazov (No.14)* [2018] UKSC 19; [2018] 2 W.L.R. 1125 at [12]: in *Revenue & Customs Commissioners v Total Network SL* [2008] UKHL 19; [2008] 1 A.C. 1174 "the House declined to apply to unlawful means conspiracies the condition which it had held in *OBG Ltd v Allan* [2008] 1 A.C. 1 to apply to the tort of intentionally harming the claimant by unlawful acts against third parties, namely that those acts should be actionable at the suit of the third party. They held that the means were unlawful for the purpose of founding an action in conspiracy, whether they were actionable or not." cf. *Pro-Sys Consultants Ltd v Microsoft Corp* 2014 BCSC 1280; (2014) 376 D.L.R. (4th) 302 at [38]–[45] where the submission that the Supreme Court decision in *Bram Enterprises Ltd v A.I. Enterprises Ltd* 2014 SCC 12; (2014) 366 D.L.R. (4th) 573 had changed the law on what constituted unlawful means for the purposes of unlawful means conspiracy was rejected. In *Bram* Cromwell J had held that it was not necessary to seek identical treatment for "unlawful means" for all the torts where it was a requirement and he expressly limited his reasoning to the unlawful means tort and distinguished the approach to unlawful means in the torts of conspiracy and intimidation; see *Pro-Sys v Microsoft* at [67] and [69]. In *Reisinger v J.C. Akin Architect Ltd* 2017 SKCA 11; (2017) 411 D.L.R. (4th) 687 it was noted that in *Bram Enterprises Ltd v A.I. Enterprises Ltd* 2014 SCC 12; (2014) 266 D.L.R. (4th) 573 the Canadian Supreme Court had observed that unlawful means conspiracy might require a broader definition of unlawful means than that which was appropriate for the unlawful means tort because of the existence of "the so-called predominant purpose conspiracy tort." It was not necessary for the unlawful means or acts required for conspiracy to be actionable torts if they were otherwise unlawful.

527 *Crofter* [1942] A.C. 435 at 462, per Lord Wright; *Sorrell v Smith* [1925] A.C. 700 at 723, 729–730, per Lord Dunedin and at 712 and 714, per Viscount Cave LC.

528 *Rookes v Barnard* [1964] A.C. 1129. See also *Messenger Group Newspapers Ltd v NGA* [1984] I.R.L.R. 397 (intimidation, nuisance and other torts).

529 *Stratford & Son Ltd v Lindley* [1965] A.C. 269 HL; *Pritchard v Briggs* [1980] Ch. 338 at 410–418, per Goff LJ; *Norbrook Laboratories Ltd v King* [1984] I.R.L.R. 200 CA (NI) (interference with contract by unlawful means as well as nuisance and trespass). The suggestion made by Porter J in *De Jetley Marks v Greenwood* [1936] 1 All E.R. 863 at 872, that a conspiracy to induce a breach of contract is actionable only after the breach has been effected, does not seem to have survived the modern cases.

530 *Crofter* [1942] A.C. 435 at 462, per Lord Wright; *Metall und Rohstoff AG v Donaldson, Lufkin & Jenrette Inc* [1990] 1 Q.B. 391 CA at 481.

531 *JSC BTA Bank v Ablyazov (No.14)* [2018] UKSC 19; [2018] 2 W.L.R. 1125 at [11].

532 The Supreme Court treated this as having been decided by the House of Lords in *Revenue & Customs Commissioners v Total Network SL* [2008] UKHL 19; [2008] 1 A.C. 1174.

533 *JSC BTA Bank v Ablyazov (No.14)* [2018] UKSC 19; [2018] 2 W.L.R. 1125 at [15].

monly and contractual duties will always be specific to particular relationships."[534] This feature of such duties generates complexity because it means that the unlawful means employed by the conspirators may be wrongful only in relation to some person *other than* the claimant.[535] For example, in *The Racing Partnership Ltd v Done Brothers (Cash Betting) Ltd*[536] one of the unlawful methods by which the conspirators were alleged to have caused harm to the claimant was by using information from two online betting exchanges in breach of contracts with those exchanges that precluded use for commercial purposes, but, as Zacaroli J pointed out, from the claimant's point of view it was "irrelevant" whether the conspirators used the prices in breach of contract or by agreement, having paid the exchanges a fee.[537] In the case of breaches of civil statutory duties there is a further source of complexity: "Their relevance may depend on the purpose of the relevant statutory provision, which may or may not be consistent with its deployment as an element in the tort of conspiracy."[538]

Crimes In *Revenue & Customs Commissioners v Total Network SL*[539] the House of Lords held that unlawful means for the purposes of unlawful means conspiracy could include crimes whether or not the conspirators' criminal acts were otherwise actionable by the claimant. Lord Walker derived from the authorities "a general assumption, too obvious to need discussion, that criminal conduct engaged in by conspirators as a means of inflicting harm on the claimant is actionable as the tort of conspiracy, whether or not that conduct, on the part of a single individual, would be actionable as some other tort."[540] While Lord Scott agreed with Lord Walker,[541] the opinions of the other Law Lords on this point were expressed in more qualified terms. In Lord Neuberger's opinion, since a "claim in conspiracy to injure can be established even where no unlawful means, let alone any other actionable tort, is involved ... it would be anomalous if an unlawful means conspiracy could not found a cause of action where, as here, the means 'merely' involved a crime ... [which] had as its purpose the protection of the victim of the conspiracy".[542] Lord Hope similarly concluded that where, as on the facts, the case was virtually indistinguishable from the tort of lawful means conspiracy, the fact that the unlaw- 23-109

[534] *JSC BTA Bank v Ablyazov (No.14)* [2018] UKSC 19; [2018] 2 W.L.R. 1125 at [15].

[535] Some care is required here. The "complex problem" arises where conspirators, D1 and D2, cause loss to a claimant, C, by using means that are "unlawful" because they amount to a wrong to a third party, T. But in some cases, where the harm to C results from a wrong to T limiting T's freedom to deal with C, one or more of the conspirators may have committed the tort of causing loss by unlawful means *to C*, and the "complex problem" can be side-stepped by using *this tort to C* (instead of the wrong to T) as the "unlawful means" required to establish an unlawful means conspiracy.

[536] *The Racing Partnership Ltd v Done Brothers (Cash Betting) Ltd* [2019] EWHC 1156 (Ch); [2020] Ch. 289. Zacaroli J held, at [252], that the breach of the exchanges' terms and conditions could not amount to "unlawful means" for the purposes of the conspiracy tort: this reasoning is discussed further below, at para.23-115.

[537] *The Racing Partnership Ltd v Done Brothers (Cash Betting) Ltd* [2019] EWHC 1156 (Ch); [2020] Ch. 289 at [251].

[538] *JSC BTA Bank v Ablyazov (No.14)* [2018] UKSC 19; [2018] 2 W.L.R. 1125 at [15].

[539] [2008] UKHL 19; [2008] 1 A.C. 1174; reversing [2007] EWCA Civ 39; reported in [2008] 1 A.C. 1174 at 1178–1203, where, at [78] the Court of Appeal felt bound to follow its earlier decision in *Powell v Boldaz* [1998] Lloyd's Rep. Med. 116 at 126 that "the unlawful act relied on must be actionable at the suit of the plaintiff".

[540] [2008] UKHL 19; [2008] 1 A.C. 1174 at [94]; see generally [93]–[95].

[541] [2008] UKHL 19; [2008] 1 A.C. 1174 at [47].

[542] [2008] UKHL 19; [2008] 1 A.C. 1174 at [221].

ful means were not in themselves actionable did not seem to be "significant".[543] Lord Mance agreed with Lords Walker and Neuberger that "the history and jurisprudence of unlawful means conspiracy pointed clearly to the conclusion that at least some criminal acts, not amounting to torts, might suffice to ground the tort", but "not every criminal act committed in order to injure can or should give rise to tortious liability even where the element of conspiracy is present".[544]

23-110 In *JSC BTA Bank v Ablyazov (No.14)*[545] the Supreme Court held that a criminal contempt of court (albeit punishable in civil proceedings) could amount to unlawful means for the purposes of this form of the tort of conspiracy, at least where the claimant was a bank and the contempt involved serial breaches of a freezing order and receivership order, that had been made on the application of the bank. The single judgment of Lords Sumption and Lloyd-Jones provided further general guidance:

> "Conspiracy being a tort of primary liability, the question what constitute unlawful means cannot depend on whether their use would give rise to a different cause of action independent of conspiracy. The real test is whether there is a just cause or excuse for combining to use unlawful means. That depends on (i) the nature of the unlawfulness, and (ii) its relationship with the resultant damage of the claimant."[546]

The suggestion that whether acts constitute "unlawful means" depends on an evaluation of the conspirators' reasons for combining to use those means ("just cause or excuse") is not straightforward; the primary difficulty is that the *other* form of conspiracy—lawful means conspiracy—depends on the predominant object of the conspirators being objectionable, whilst this form, by contrast, depends on the unlawfulness of the means used: to suggest that whether the means are "unlawful" *turns on* the justness of the defendants' cause confusingly blends the two forms of the tort. Moreover, the two factors that are identified as relevant to whether the defendants have a "just cause of excuse"—"(i) the nature of the unlawfulness, and (ii) its relationship with the resultant damage of the claimant"—do not refer to the *cause* of the defendants' behaviour or to any possible *excuse* for it. With respect, there is a strong case for treating the attempt to unify the two forms of conspiracy in terms of an absence of "just cause or excuse" as unnecessarily ambitious, and beyond the ratio of the case; but rejection of the unifying explanation in terms of "just cause or excuse" casts no doubt on the significance of "(i) the nature of the unlawfulness, and (ii) its relationship with the resultant damage of the claimant" to the question whether particular means are sufficient to ground liability for "unlawful means conspiracy".[547]

---

[543] [2008] UKHL 19; [2008] 1 A.C. 1174 at [44].

[544] [2008] UKHL 19; [2008] 1 A.C. 1174 at [116] and [119]. cf. *Agribrands Purina Canada Inc v Kasamekas* 2011 ONCA 460; (2011) 334 D.L.R. (4th) 714 at [27]–[38] where Lord Walker's speech in the *Total Network* decision was cited in support of the need to recognise that the torts of intentional interference with economic relations and unlawful means conspiracy had each developed its own concept of unlawful conduct: "what is required therefore to meet the 'unlawful conduct' element of the conspiracy tort is that the defendants engage in concert in acts that are wrong in law, whether actionable in private law or not." See also *XY Inc v International Newtech Development Inc* 2013 BCCA 352; (2013) 366 D.L.R. (4th) 443 at [49]–[50]: presentation of false reports and breach of confidence held to satisfy the unlawful means requirement. cf. para.23-117.

[545] [2018] UKSC 19; [2018] 2 W.L.R. 1125.

[546] [2018] UKSC 19; [2018] 2 W.L.R. 1125 at [11].

[547] In *Palmer Birch (a partnership) v Lloyd* [2018] EWHC 2316 (TCC); [2018] 4 W.L.R. 164 at [189],

The identification of "the nature of the unlawfulness" as a factor that ought to influence whether a crime is held to be "unlawful means" can be linked to Lord Neuberger's suggestion in the *Total Network* case that it may be relevant whether the crime "had as its purpose the protection of the victim of the conspiracy".[548] Above, it was noted that Lords Sumption and Lloyd-Jones were hesitant about allowing claims for unlawful means conspiracy to be based on means that are wrongful only in relation to some person *other than* the claimant, and whilst they also described criminal law as imposing a "universal obligation",[549] it seems plausible that some behaviour may have been prohibited by the criminal law for reasons wholly unrelated to extending the range of acts that a claimant can legitimately object to a gang deploying against him or her in the course of economic competition. The matter is far from clear, however, and Lords Sumption and Lloyd-Jones may instead have been intending to refer to Lord Walker's acceptance in the *Total Network* case that "the sort of considerations relevant to determining whether a breach of statutory duty is actionable in a civil suit (*Cutler v Wandsworth Stadium Ltd*[550]) may well overlap, or even occasionally coincide with, the issue of unlawful means in the tort of conspiracy".[551] Lord Walker's comment is somewhat opaque; "the sort of considerations relevant to determining whether a breach of statutory duty is actionable in a civil suit" are those considerations which tend to indicate whether Parliament intended the duty it was imposing to create private law entitlements, and it is not clear that Parliament's intentions can be a direct guide to what forms of behaviour will count as "unlawful means" for the purposes of the conspiracy tort. 23-111

The second factor, the relationship between any crime committed by the conspirators and the resultant damage to the claimant, seems to be strongly related to the insistence that an unlawful means conspiracy can only be based on criminal behaviour where this was "indeed the means" or the "instrumentality" by which harm was intentionally inflicted.[552] It is submitted that this second factor is relevant in a broader range of cases than those based on crimes, and consequently it will be discussed separately below.[553] 23-112

Breach of statute Some earlier authorities suggested that breach of a criminal statute (or other crime) must always amount to unlawful means for the purposes of tort liability for conspiracy.[554] Subsequent to the *Total Network* and *JSC BTA Bank* 23-113

HH Judge Russen QC took the quoted passage to mean that "there may be categories of unlawfulness which a combiner may be excused from agreeing to perpetrate either because of the classification of the unlawful act (identified by reference to the purpose or duty which it subverts) or because it is too incidental to the claimant's position to be actionable".

548 [2008] UKHL 19; [2008] 1 A.C. 1174 at [221].

549 *JSC BTA Bank v Ablyazov (No.14)* [2018] UKSC 19; [2018] 2 W.L.R. 1125 at [15].

550 *Cutler v Wandsworth Stadium Ltd* [1949] A.C. 398.

551 [2008] UKHL 19; [2008] 1 A.C. 1174 at [96].

552 The phrase "indeed the means" comes from Lord Walker's speech in *Revenue & Customs Commissioners v Total Network SL* [2008] UKHL 19; [2008] 1 A.C. 1174 at [95], where he also equated the phrase with the concept of "instrumentality" used by Lord Nicholls in *OBG Ltd v Allen* [2008] 1 A.C. 1 at [159]. Lord Walker's analysis of this issue is cited with approval in *JSC BTA Bank v Ablyazov (No.14)* [2018] UKSC 19; [2018] 2 W.L.R. 1125 at [14].

553 See para.23-119.

554 *Sorrell v Smith* [1925] A.C. 700 at 714, per Viscount Cave LC and 719, per Lord Dunedin; and per Lord Wright in *Crofter* [1942] A.C. 435 at 461–462, including breach of s.7 of the Conspiracy and Protection of Property Act 1875 (now TULRCA 1992 s.241), but after the careful analysis of Scott

cases, it is clear that this was too bold, and whether a claim can be based on a particular statutory *crime* will depend on application of the general approach outlined in the previous six paragraphs. In the *JSC BTA Bank* case the Supreme Court stated that whether, or when, breach of a civil statutory duty would constitute "unlawful means" was "liable to raise more complex problems": "Their relevance may depend on the purpose of the relevant statutory provision, which may or may not be consistent with its deployment as an element in the tort of conspiracy."[555] Where a statutory provision is one that can be enforced by a claimant making a civil claim for the tort of breach of statutory duty, there is no obvious reason why its breach should not equally amount to "unlawful means" for the purposes of a claim for unlawful means conspiracy by the claimant: the claimant's position will be equivalent to having been the victim of a combination to commit an actionable tort.[556] But a broader range of breaches of non-criminal statutes may also be sufficient to complete the conspiracy tort.[557] It is submitted that the question from the *JSC BTA Bank* case of whether the "purpose of the relevant statutory provision" was "consistent with its deployment as an element in the tort of conspiracy" could be treated as asking both (i) whether the statutory provision had as its purpose the protection of the victim of the conspiracy (by analogy with the position in relations to crimes); and (ii) whether use of the statutory provision to extend the scope of the tort of unlawful means conspiracy would be in tension with the policy behind the statute; it may also be necessary to determine (again, by analogy with the position in relations to crimes) whether breach of the statutory provision was "indeed the means" by which harm was intentionally inflicted.[558] Similar principles to those applicable in deciding when breach of statute can constitute unlawful means were previously applied to determine when breach of directly applicable provisions of European Community law could amount to the use of unlawful means.[559]

23-114 **Acts that the defendants were not at liberty to commit** The *Total Network* and *JSC BTA Bank* cases have expanded the scope of "unlawful means" in the context of conspiracy, but do not appear to have gone so far as to re-instate the former "general" approach, which found unlawful means whenever defendants had done acts which they were not at liberty to commit.[560] Such an approach would risk

J in *Thomas v NUM (South Wales Area)* [1986] Ch. 20 at 54–65, no independent tort liability can be based on that section.

555 *JSC BTA Bank v Ablyazov (No.14)* [2018] UKSC 19; [2018] 2 W.L.R. 1125 at [15].

556 This view is also put forward in Grant and Mumford, *Civil Fraud*, 1st edn (London: Sweet & Maxwell, 2018), para.2-058.

557 For example, *Brent LBC v Davies* [2018] EWHC 2214 (Ch) raises the question whether a conspiracy of public officials to cause harm to a public authority by acting in ways that were contrary to the statutes that governed their powers might be actionable; in the actual case Zacaroli J did not have to confront such questions since he found that there had not been a pre-conceived plan to harm the claimant, and the conspirators were unaware that their actions were unlawful. In *Digicel (St Lucia) Ltd v Cable & Wireless Plc* [2010] EWHC 774 (Ch), at App.I at [62], Morgan J held that a non-actionable breach of a non-criminal statute would not be "unlawful means" for the purposes of unlawful means conspiracy, and a similar view was expressed by HH Judge Hodge QC, sitting as a judge of the High Court, in *Chiang v Mishcon de Reya* [2015] EWHC 164 (Ch) at [49]–[50].

558 On the requirement that the unlawful means must be "indeed the means", see para.23-119.

559 *Garden Cottage Food Ltd v Milk Marketing Board* [1984] A.C. 130 HL; *Barretts & Baird (Wholesale) Ltd v IPCS* [1987] I.R.L.R. 3; *R. v Secretary of State for Transport Ex p. Factortame* [2001] 1 W.L.R. 942; *Three Rivers DC v Bank of England (No.3)* [2003] 2 A.C. 1; Fox [2001] C.L.J. 33.

560 *Torquay Hotel Co Ltd v Cousins* [1969] 2 Ch. 106 at 139, per Lord Denning MR; an approach ap-

"tortifying" too many forms of behaviour that are prohibited for reasons very different from those that should determine the scope of protection in the economic sphere, would undercut the high requirement for a "predominant purpose" of causing injury that is a condition of liability for lawful means conspiracy, and would further magnify the contentious difference between the scope of the tortious liability of individuals acting alone and in combination with others.

Breach of contract Further difficulty arises in relation to a combination to commit a breach of contract as a form of unlawful means conspiracy. Where there is a combination to threaten a breach, this might amount to conspiracy to intimidate such as was found to have occurred by the House of Lords in *Rookes v Barnard*. But since in that case the House of Lords held that a breach of contract was an "illegal act" for the purposes of the tort of intimidation, there might not seem to be any reason for excluding it from the scope of unlawful means for the purposes of unlawful means conspiracy.[561] Yet Lord Devlin (alone of the Law Lords in *Rookes v Barnard*) went out of his way to leave this point open.[562] Notwithstanding this reservation, in several subsequent cases it was stated, albeit only in obiter dicta, that a person could be liable for conspiracy to break a contract to which he was not party where he merely combined, with a common design, together with the party or parties committing the breach.[563] Further, as a matter of justice it seems correct that defendants should be liable for committing unlawful means conspiracy if they combine so as to co-ordinate their breaking of their contracts with the claimant so as to amplify the loss caused. As noted above, however, in the *JSC BTA Bank* case Lords Sumption and Lloyd-Jones highlighted that there might be a reason for not treating a breach of contract as "unlawful means" in situations where the claimant was not a party to the broken contract, so that its breach could not be described as unlawful as between the defendants and him or her. This reasoning was followed in *The Racing Partnership Ltd v Done Brothers (Cash Betting) Ltd*,[564] where one of the unlawful methods by which the conspirators were alleged to have caused harm to the claimant was by using information that a contract with a third party prohibited them from using for commercial purposes; as Zacaroli J pointed out, from the claimant's point of view it was "irrelevant" whether the conspirators used the information in breach of contract or by agreement, after paying a fee. This reasoning, however, does not preclude the possibility that in some circumstances a breach of a contract with a third party might be relevant to a claimant's position; for example, if the claimant had supplied the information to the third party under a contract which provided that the third party should not allow anyone else to use it 23-115

proved in *Associated British Ports v TGWU* [1989] 1 W.L.R. 939 CA (reversed on other grounds [1989] 1 W.L.R. 939 HL).

561 The "Donovan" Report of the Royal Commission on Trade Unions (1968) Cmnd.3623 accepted the need to protect against this liability in trade disputes, see para.854, and the Trade Union and Labour Relations Act 1974 s.13(3) did so until its repeal by the Employment Act 1980 s.17(8).

562 [1964] A.C. 1129 at 1210: "I am not saying that a conspiracy to commit a breach of contract amounts to the tort of conspiracy; that point remains to be decided."

563 *Barretts & Baird (Wholesale) Ltd v IPCS* [1987] I.R.L.R. 3 at 8–10, per Henry J; and see Lord Denning MR in *Midland Bank Trust Co Ltd v Green (No.3)* [1982] Ch. 529 at 539. This is also consonant with the reasoning of the Court of Appeal in *Associated British Ports v TGWU* [1989] 1 W.L.R. 939 CA (reversed on other grounds, [1989] 1 W.L.R. 939 HL).

564 *The Racing Partnership Ltd v Done Brothers (Cash Betting) Ltd* [2019] EWHC 1156 (Ch); [2020] Ch. 289. Zacaroli J held, at [252], that the breach of the exchanges' terms and conditions could not amount to "unlawful means" for the purposes of the conspiracy tort.

commercially, then the inclusion of such a term in the third party's contract with the defendants might have been intended to secure the claimant's position.

23-116 It is submitted that the difficult question when a breach of contract can constitute "unlawful means" for the purposes of the tort of unlawful means conspiracy should be answered by distinguishing between three situations: (i) where defendants combine to break a contract (or contracts) between them and the claimant; (ii) where defendants combine to break a contract (or contracts) between them and a third party; and (iii) where defendants combine to break a contract and by doing so also commit some other tort to the claimant, such as intimidation. In the first of these situations, the breach of contract will be an actionable civil wrong to the claimant, so there seems little scope for conspirators to argue that they should be left at liberty to combine to use such a method of intentionally inflicting harm on the claimant. Indeed, where several defendants combine to co-ordinate the breaking of contracts that they have with the claimant in order to amplify the harm inflicted, the case for allowing the claimant to sue for unlawful means conspiracy seems strong. So far as there is any basis for hesitation in cases falling within the first situation, it might be that a court should be cautious before finding that a defendant has joined a conspiracy to break a contract where (i) that defendant was not itself a party to any contract broken; *and* (ii) that defendant would not have been held to have procured any breach of contract. Such hesitation would be particularly appropriate if it appeared that a claim was formulated as being for an unlawful means conspiracy primarily to circumvent obstacles to a finding that the defendant had committed the tort of procuring a breach of contract. With respect to the second situation, where defendants combine to inflict loss on a claimant by breaking a contract (or contracts) between them and a third party, it is submitted that such behaviour should not normally be classified as "unlawful means", since, as noted above, such behaviour will only ordinarily be wrongful vis-à-vis the third party. The possibility of liability in the third situation, however, will play an important role in reducing the significance of the presumption against liability in the second situation. Thus a combination to cause loss to a claimant by breaking a contract with a third party *in order to prevent* that third party from dealing with the claimant can be treated as a conspiracy to commit the tort of causing loss by the use of unlawful means, and a combination to cause loss to a claimant by threatening to break a contract with a third party *in order to persuade* that third party to cease dealing with the claimant can be treated as a conspiracy to commit the tort of intimidation: in such cases the claims can be built on the combination being pursued by means of committing an economic tort to the claimant, rather than directly on any breach of contract.

23-117 **Breach of fiduciary duties and equitable wrongs** It was noted above that in *JSC BTA Bank v Ablyazov (No.14)* the Supreme Court left open the actionability of a combination to cause loss by means of breach of fiduciary duty because of the "complex problems" that stem from the fact that such duties are specific to particular relationships.[565] In such cases there is also the risk of liability for the conspiracy tort being inconsistent with the principles under which third parties can be held liable in equity for "knowing receipt" or "knowing assistance".[566] Recent

---

[565] *JSC BTA Bank v Ablyazov (No.14)* [2018] UKSC 19; [2018] 2 W.L.R. 1125 at [15]. See above, para.23-108.

[566] See *Lewin on Trusts*, 20th edn (2020) Chs 42 and 43.

cases have proceeded on the basis, however, that a breach of fiduciary duty can amount to "unlawful means" for the purposes of the conspiracy tort.[567]

Justification The question whether a defendant can rely on a defence of justification to avoid liability for unlawful means conspiracy is not straightforward. Two obstacles face the submission that such a defence should be recognised: it would only have logical space to operate in cases where whatever justification the defendant invoked was both insufficient to prevent the means being categorised as unlawful and insufficient to permit a finding that the defendant never intended to harm the claimant. In *Palmer Birch (a partnership) v Lloyd*[568] HH Judge Russen QC expressly rejected the possibility of justification being a defence "to an otherwise established unlawful means conspiracy". However, an apparently contrary position was adopted by Toulson LJ in *Meretz Investments NV v ACP Ltd* where the three alleged conspirators had acted so as to: (i) lawfully exercise a power of sale of a lease, granted as security for the loan of money to carry out property development; which (ii) prevented the borrower from performing its contractual promise to leaseback the premises to the claimant. Despite the fact that the transaction brought about a breach of contract by the borrower, Toulson LJ reasoned that because the purchaser of the lease "had a perfectly legitimate reason for acting as he did [i]t would therefore be wrong to classify such conduct as founding an action for unlawful means conspiracy".[569] It is submitted that the *Meretz* case reveals that where a claim alleges a *conspiracy* to breach a contract it may be appropriate to recognise a defence of justification of a breadth equivalent to the potential defence of justification for *procuring* a breach of contract.[570] Otherwise, a party who could rely on his "equal or superior right" as a justification for procuring a breach could nonetheless end up liable—as a conspirator—for having combined with the party in breach to cause loss to the claimant by means of the breach. 23-118

(iii) "Indeed the means"

In the *Total Network* case, Lord Walker counter-balanced the extension of the concept of "unlawful means" to cover acts that would not be actionable if performed by a solitary defendant, such as some crimes, by insisting that to form the basis for a conspiracy claim such acts must have been "indeed the means ... of intentionally inflicting harm",[571] and this approach was endorsed by Lords Sumption and 23-119

---

[567] See, e.g. *Aerostar Maintenance International Ltd v Wilson* [2010] EWHC 2032 (Ch) at [170]–[172], where Morgan J expressly raised the concern about the overlap with secondary liability in equity; *Keymed (Medical & Industrial Equipment) Ltd v Hillman* [2019] EWHC 485 (Ch) at [122]. In *FM Capital Partners Ltd v Marino* [2018] EWHC 1768 (Comm) at [455]–[456] it was conceded that "knowing receipt" or "knowing assistance" could themselves amount to unlawful means for the purposes of an a unlawful means conspiracy (appeal dismissed without reference to this point: [2020] EWCA Civ 245; [2020] 3 W.L.R. 109); *Iranian Offshore Engineering & Construction Co v Dean Investment Holdings SA* [2019] EWHC 472 (Comm) at [172].

[568] [2018] EWHC 2316 (TCC); [2018] 4 W.L.R. 164 at [193].

[569] [2007] EWCA Civ 1303; [2008] Ch. 244 at [170], per Toulson LJ.

[570] See paras 23-57 to 23-61.

[571] *Revenue & Customs Commissioners v Total Network SL* [2008] UKHL 19; [2008] 1 A.C. 1174 at [95], per Lord Walker. He equated this requirement with one proposed by Lord Nicholls in *OBG Ltd v Allen* [2008] 1 A.C. 1 at [159], using the wording that the unlawful means must be the "instrumentality".

Lloyd-Jones in *JSC BTA Bank v Ablyazov (No.14)*.[572] Their elaboration of the "indeed the means" requirement, however, linked it to the conspirators' intentions: thus situations where it was the combination's predominant purpose or "constructive intention" to cause harm to the claimant were "contrasted with a situation in which the harm to the claimant was purely incidental because the unlawful means were not the means by which the defendant intended the harm to the claimant".[573] With respect, this contrast is problematic: the question whether the defendant intended to inflict *the harm suffered by the claimant*, as opposed to this harm being "purely incidental", is not the same as the question whether the defendants intended *particular means* to be "the instrument" by which harm would be inflicted. The difference can be seen by analysing a hypothetical case that has been frequently discussed: a defendant business—perhaps a courier or a pizza company—gains an advantage over its rival by instructing its delivery drivers to drive faster than the speed limit. Lord Nicholls' explanation for the *absence* of liability in such a situation does not claim that the defendant business had no intention to cause loss to its rival by luring away its potential (but impatient) customers, but that the "criminal conduct is not an offence committed against the rival company in any realistic sense of that expression".[574] And the claim that where unlawful means are not "indeed the means" then any harm inflicted on the claimant will have been unintended is equally absent from Lord Walker's discussion of the requirement in the *Total Network* case. Lord Walker is clear that it is *the means* that will have been "merely incidental" to the (intended) harm:

> "But all the statements of general principle in the classic cases seem to me to be consistent with the proposition that unlawful means, both in the intentional harm tort and in the tort of conspiracy, include both crimes and torts (whether or not they include conduct lower on the scale of blameworthiness) provided that they are indeed the means by which harm is intentionally inflicted on the claimant (rather than being merely incidental to it)."[575]

The nature of the requirement that Lord Nicholls and Lord Walker sought to identify may be illuminated by considering a variation on the delivery hypothetical, where a pizza delivery business knowingly employs illegal workers as delivery drivers, thereby committing a criminal offence.[576] In such a situation the business owner may well intend to take a portion of a rival business's trade, thereby inflicting a loss, but the unlawful means will not be "the instrument"; the work of the (illegally-employed) delivery drivers will be how the owner advances his or her business, but their *immigration status* will not be what encourages customers to stop ordering their pizzas from the rival.

---

[572] [2018] UKSC 19; [2018] 2 W.L.R. 1125 at [14].

[573] [2018] UKSC 19; [2018] 2 W.L.R. 1125 at [14].

[574] *OBG Ltd v Allen* [2008] 1 A.C. 1 at [160].

[575] *Revenue & Customs Commissioners v Total Network SL* [2008] UKHL 19; [2008] 1 A.C. 1174 at [93]. Similarly, in Lord Walker's explanation of the absence of liability in the *Lonrho v Shell* case, at [95], he does not treat the harm as unintended: "In *Lonrho Ltd v Shell Petroleum Co Ltd (No 2)* [1982] A.C. 173 the sanctions order against Southern Rhodesia was part of the story, but it was not the instrument for the intentional infliction of harm."

[576] Immigration, Asylum and Nationality Act 2006 s.21(1) (as amended).

(iv) *Knowledge of the unlawfulness of the means*

Recent litigation has raised the question whether defendants can have committed an unlawful means conspiracy if they did not know that the means that they used to inflict harm on the claimant were unlawful. In *Stobart Group Ltd v Tinkler*,[577] HH Judge Russen QC, sitting as a judge of the High Court, held himself bound by the decision of the Court of Appeal in *Belmont Finance Corporation v Williams Furniture (No.2)*[578] to conclude that: "The fact that the conspirator did not know that his actions were unlawful is no defence to liability. In order for him to be liable, it is enough to show that he had sufficient knowledge of the essential facts, that acts which were unlawful were to be carried out so as to implicate him in liability for them." He also, however, offered arguments in support of the view that this was the *right* answer.[579] He pointed to the practical problems that might be caused for claimants by having to inquire into each conspirator's legal knowledge in a case where, as in the one he was considering, the unlawfulness—breach of a director's fiduciary duties to the company—depended on law that was complicated and contestable; moreover, in such a case he believed it might be too easy for defendants to manufacture legal advice sufficient to negate any suggestion that a scheme was *known* to be unlawful; and he noted the knock-on legal issues that might arise with regard to "the standard of knowledge (or suspicion) required" and the legal burden of proof.[580] But in *The Racing Partnership Ltd v Done Brothers*[581] Zacaroli J reached a different conclusion. In this case it was alleged that one of the conspirators had committed the wrong of breach of confidence, though they honestly believed that they were at liberty to supply the information concerned, and the recipient was found to have been aware of a risk that the information could not be provided lawfully, but not to have *known* of the illegality, despite turning a blind eye to the risk.[582] On the question whether proof of knowledge of the unlawfulness was required, Zacaroli J held that it was: the decision of the Court of Appeal in *Belmont Finance*, which Judge Russen QC had held himself bound by, was held to have been decided **23-120**

---

577 *Stobart Group Ltd v Tinkler* [2019] EWHC 258 (Comm) at [573]. Norris J reached a similar conclusion in *First Subsea Ltd v Baltec Ltd* [2014] EWHC 866 (Ch) at [150]–[157].

578 [1980] 1 All E.R. 393 CA.

579 *Stobart Group Ltd v Tinkler* [2019] EWHC 258 (Comm) at [555]–[556].

580 Burden of proof was mentioned as an issue because in *Meretz Investments NV v ACP Ltd* [2007] EWCA Civ 1303; [2008] Ch. 244 at [174], Toulson LJ suggested that lack of knowledge of unlawfulness might take effect as part of a *defence* of justification. But the passage in Toulson LJ's judgment is problematic, since he claims to be agreeing with a proposition made by Arden LJ, whilst the passage in her judgment that he cites is one which adopts a different approach: she holds that the defendants' belief as to the lawfulness of their behaviour was inconsistent with them having had an intention to injure the claimant.

581 *The Racing Partnership Ltd v Done Brothers (Cash Betting) Ltd* [2019] EWHC 1156 (Ch); [2020] Ch. 289. The same conclusion had been common ground between the parties in a case previously tried by Zacaroli J: *Brent LBC v Davies* [2018] EWHC 2214 (Ch) at [284]. Morgan J had previously held that a defendant who genuinely believed that acts were lawful would not be liable for unlawful means conspiracy, but reached this conclusion by following the opinion of Toulson LJ, discussed in the previous footnote: *Digicel (St Lucia) Ltd v Cable & Wireless Plc* [2010] EWHC 774 (Ch), at App.I at [117]–[118].

582 *The Racing Partnership Ltd v Done Brothers (Cash Betting) Ltd* [2019] EWHC 1156 (Ch); [2020] Ch. 289 at [200]: "there is in my judgment an important distinction between recklessness as to whether conduct is unlawful, turning a blind-eye to suspicions to the contrary, and believing conduct is lawful but recognising the risk that someone affected by it might take a different view, and even seek to vindicate that view by taking legal proceedings."

per incuriam the earlier, contrary, decision of the Court of Appeal in *British Industrial Plastics Ltd v Ferguson*.[583] Significantly, however, Zacaroli J also disagreed with HH Judge Russen QC as to the merits of making knowledge a condition of liability: "I consider that to find a person liable, where that person knows that a (non-predominant) purpose of the combination is to injure the claimant but honestly believes, for example, that on its true construction the contract between the claimant and one of the conspirators does not prohibit the relevant action, would risk trespassing on legitimate competitive business practices."[584] Thus whilst HH Judge Russen QC emphasised the practical problems of proving knowledge about points of law, Zacaroli J focused directly on the question whether tort law ought to prohibit a defendant from combining with others—with the intention of causing loss—if the defendant *honestly* believed that the combination's methods would be lawful. He also doubted, however, whether Judge Russen QC's preferred inquiry into whether a defendant "had sufficient knowledge of the essential facts, that acts which were unlawful were to be carried out" would prove to be simpler in practice than an inquiry into knowledge of the law.[585]

23-121 Given the different opinions expressed, and the unsatisfactory state of the appellate authorities,[586] it is likely that further litigation will be required to settle the question. From the perspective of first principles, it might seem obvious that where the unlawful means relied on is a breach of contract it would be convenient for liability for unlawful means conspiracy to run in parallel with liability for procuring a breach of contract, where knowledge of the relevant contract is required, since this will reduce any temptation to allege conspiracy in order to circumvent the limits on the procuring tort. But the case for such consistency must not be exaggerated, particularly since it appears that knowledge of the illegality is not a general requirement for liability in the parallel field of joint tortfeasorship.[587] Indeed, the modern trend with regard to both forms of the conspiracy tort has been to emphasise that the act of joining a combination with the intention of inflicting loss on a claimant is *in itself* a significant part of what makes a defendant's behaviour tortious, whilst the modern account of the procuring tort is built around the idea of the defendant having done enough to be liable as an accessory to breach of a contract that he was

---

583 [1938] 4 All E.R. 504 CA. The House of Lords dismissed an appeal, at [1940] 1 All E.R. 479, but without making any reference to the unlawful means conspiracy claim.

584 *The Racing Partnership Ltd v Done Brothers (Cash Betting) Ltd* [2019] EWHC 1156 (Ch); [2020] Ch. 289 at [284].

585 Thus he raised the question whether knowledge that information was subject to an obligation of confidentiality was a question about "essential facts" or about a point of law.

586 To summarise: the opinion of Toulson LJ in *Meretz Investments NV v ACP Ltd* [2007] EWCA Civ 1303; [2008] Ch. 244 at [174], is obiter, and states that it coincides with an opinion of Arden LJ that she did not express in the paragraph that is cited; *Belmont Finance Corporation v Williams Furniture (No.2)* [1980] 1 All E.R. 393 CA, was decided without reference to *Ferguson*; and, in *British Industrial Plastics v Ferguson* [1938] 4 All E.R. 504 CA, the point is only expressly addressed by Finlay LJ, at 515, with MacKinnon LJ going no further than to say, at 513, that "the same considerations" applied in the conspiracy claim as in the claim for procuring breach of contract, and Slesser LJ relying on a different argument, at 512.

587 *Digicel (St Lucia) Ltd v Cable & Wireless Plc* [2010] EWHC 774 (Ch), at App.I at [93]: "If the principal tortfeasor commits a tort and that tortfeasor's belief as to the lawfulness of his action is not material to his liability then the established rules as to the liability of a joint tortfeasor do not require any investigation into the state of the joint tortfeasor's belief as to the lawfulness of his action." In this case Morgan J surveyed the case law in detail, at [94]–[119], and concluded that a conspirator who honestly believed that the means used by the combination were lawful should avoid liability.

not a party to. Moreover, where a defendant has joined a combination with the intention of inflicting loss on a claimant and knows what methods will be employed to achieve this, it is arguable that his or her eccentric beliefs as to the legality of such methods should not prevent liability, particularly where the methods are prohibited by the general criminal law.[588]

(c) Lawful means conspiracy

We now turn to combinations which employ no acts or means that are in themselves unlawful, commonly known as "lawful means conspiracies", or, sometimes, "simple conspiracies" or "conspiracies to injure".[589] Everything here turns on the distinction "between the case where the object is the legitimate benefit of the combiners and the case where the object is deliberate damage without any ... just cause".[590] Earlier cases must now be read in the light of this principle clearly established by the House of Lords in *Crofter Hand Woven Harris Tweed Co v Veitch*.[591] **23-122**

"Lord Cave L.C. in *Sorrel v Smith*[592] when what he called 'the famous trilogy of cases ...'[593] were submitted to a close examination ... formulated as a result two propositions of law which he stated as follows:

(1) A combination of two or more persons wilfully to injure a man in his trade is unlawful and, if it results in damage to him, is actionable.

(2) If the real purpose of the combination is, not to injure another, but to forward or

588 In the tort of intentionally causing loss by the use of unlawful means, where the unlawful means has to be a potentially actionable civil wrong, there is no authority suggesting that the defendant must have identified the means as being unlawful; but, there have been few cases, and none where the defendant expressly invoked his or her mistaken belief that the methods that he used were lawful.

589 The 22nd edition of this work used the label "conspiracy to injure", but the joint judgment of Lords Sumption and Lloyd-Jones in *JSC BTA Bank v Ablyazov (No.14)* [2018] UKSC 19; [2018] 2 W.L.R. 1125 at [8], expressed a preference for "lawful means conspiracy" because "all actionable conspiracies are conspiracies to injure, although the intent required may take a variety of different forms".

590 *Crofter Hand Woven Harris Tweed Co v Veitch* [1942] A.C. 435 at 469, per Lord Wright. Lord Wright identified the word "object" as preferable to other possibilities such as "purpose", "motive" etc: [1942] A.C. 435 at 469; but Viscount Simon LC was equally happy with "purpose", though not "motive" at 444–445, and "purpose" seems to have become the orthodox term: see, e.g. *Lonrho Ltd v Shell Petroleum Co Ltd* [1973] A.C. 173 at 188–189, per Lord Diplock; *Lonrho plc v Fayed* [1992] 1 A.C. 448 at 465–466, per Lord Bridge: "Where conspirators act with the predominant purpose of injuring the plaintiff and in fact inflict damage on him, but do nothing which would have been actionable if done by an individual acting alone, it is in the fact of their concerted action for that illegitimate purpose that the law, however anomalous it may now seem, finds a sufficient ground to condemn their action as illegal and tortious." The joint judgment of Lords Sumption and Lloyd-Jones in *JSC BTA Bank v Ablyazov (No.14)* [2018] UKSC 19; [2018] 2 W.L.R. 1125, uses "purpose" and "intention" interchangeably; and in *MX1 Ltd v Farahzad* [2018] EWHC 1041 (Ch); [2018] 1 W.L.R. 5553, Marcus Smith J uses "purpose" and "object" interchangeably in the paragraph where he provides a detailed analysis of the law, [22].

591 [1942] A.C. 435 HL.

592 [1925] A.C. 700 at 711–712.

593 *Mogul S.S. Co v McGregor, Gow Co* [1892] A.C. 25; *Allen v Flood* [1898] A.C. 1 (discussed at paras 23-02 and 23-78); and *Quinn v Leathem* [1901] A.C. 495 (in which this tort was invented; it has subsequently sometimes been called "the *Quinn v Leathem* type": per Lord Devlin in *Rookes v Barnard* [1964] A.C. 1129 at 1204; per Lord Bridge in *Lonrho Plc v Fayed* [1992] 1 A.C. 448 at 463; cf. per Lord Walker in *Revenue and Customs Commissioners v Total Network SL* [2008] UKHL 19; [2008] 1 A.C. 1174 at [73]: "*Quinn v Leathem* can ... be recognised as a case of 'unlawful object' (or 'lawful means') conspiracy.")

> defend the trade of those who enter into it, then no wrong is committed and no action will lie, although damage to another ensues."[594]

Thus a defendant who has combined with others to further "some legitimate interest of his own" will not be liable, but if a defendant joins with others with "the predominant purpose not of advancing his own interests but of injuring the claimant" then he will commit the tort because a conspirator whose predominant purpose is to injure the claimant will not be able to identify any "just cause or excuse" for combining with others to inflict harm in this way.[595]

23-123 **Legitimate and illegitimate objects** As Lord Cave suggested, pursuit of business or other similar gain is regarded as a legitimate object. Thus, in *Mogul*[596] the defendants, an association of shipowners, combined to reduce freights to an unremunerative level to drive the claimants (shipowners trading to the same ports) out of the trade. Their action, taken to protect their own trade interests, and not merely to injure the claimants, was held to be lawful. Similarly, at common law a trade association has been held entitled to enforce restrictions on retail prices by blacklisting traders,[597] to threaten to cut off supplies from a wholesaler if he continued to supply a particular retailer[598] and even to demand money from the offenders as an alternative to blacklisting.[599] So in *Crofter* itself, a combination between trade union officials and employers to prevent (without unlawful acts on anyone's part) the handling by dockers in the union of supplies for the employers' trade competitors was held to be legitimate. All the parties were pursuing their legitimate trade interests. Their Lordships did not finally define "legitimate interests", but the case shows that they include pursuit by companies of business profits and by trade unions of higher wages, wider membership and better collective bargaining procedures.[600] Indeed, as early as 1924 it was accepted that such objectives, together with exclusion from the industry of non-unionists, were

---

594 per Viscount Simon LC in *Crofter Hand Woven Harris Tweed Co v Veitch* [1942] A.C. 435 at 441-442, emphasising that the principles were formulated with reference to the facts of that case; similar principles apply outside the area of "trade". See also, per Viscount Maugham at 445–449; per Lord Wright at 469-470; per Lord Porter at 492; and *Canada Cement La Farge Ltd v British Columbia Lightweight Aggregate Ltd* (1983) 145 D.L.R. (3d) 385 SCC.

595 This formulation adopts the language used in the joint judgment of Lords Sumption and Lloyd-Jones in *JSC BTA Bank v Ablyazov (No.14)* [2018] UKSC 19; [2018] 2 W.L.R. 1125 at [10]. In that paragraph their Lordships link the question whether a defendant is acting with the predominant purpose of injuring the claimant to the question whether the defendant can establish any "just cause or excuse *for the combination*" (emphasis in the original).

596 *Mogul S.S. Co v McGregor, Gow Co* [1892] A.C. 25 HL; *Allen v Flood* [1898] A.C. 1 at 140, per Lord Herschell.

597 *Ware and De Freville v Motor Trade Association* [1921] 3 K.B. 40. But on this issue statute has gradually overtaken the common law: Competition Act 1998, repealing and replacing most of the Fair Trading Act 1973 and the Restrictive Trade Practices Acts 1976 and 1977.

598 *Sorrell v Smith* [1925] A.C. 700; cf. *Jenkinson v Nield* (1892) 8 T.L.R. 540; *Bulcock v St Anne's Master Builders' Federation* (1902) 19 T.L.R. 27; *Trollope & Sons v London Building Trades Fedn* (1895) 72 L.T. 342.

599 *Thorne v Motor Trade Association* [1937] A.C. 797. cf. *The Dolphina* [2011] SGHC 273; [2012] 1 Lloyd's Rep. 304 at [210]: predominant purpose of damaging the plaintiff bank not made out where purpose of one of the defendants was to secure payment due under a contract with one of the bank's customers.

600 [1942] A.C. 435 at 446–447, per Viscount Simon LC; at 456, per Viscount Maugham and at 478–480 per Lord Wright. See too *Byrne v Kinematograph Renters Soc Ltd* [1958] 1 W.L.R. 762.

legitimate.[601] Moreover, a genuine belief that such objectives are the object and likely result of the combination is now enough to validate it.[602] It is worthy of note that in some cases trade union officials have escaped liability for lawful means conspiracy by reason of the fact that they acted in order "to forward what they believed to be the interests of the union and fundamental trade union principle".[603] That genuinely held belief is sufficient to establish pursuit of a legitimate interest,[604] even if damage to the employer is known to be inevitable and is even intended.[605]

The action taken should not exceed what is necessary for the protection of such legitimate interest[606]; and although liability is not to be determined by asking whether the damage inflicted is disproportionate to the objective, "this may throw doubts on the bona fides of the avowed purpose".[607] To be legitimate, it is not necessary that the interests should be material in that they can be exchanged for cash; it was, therefore, legitimate for trade union officers to organise a boycott of a dance-hall which applied a "colour bar", thereby pursuing an object which, although it brought no financial benefits to members, was genuinely thought by them and their members to be in the interests of the union.[608] **23-124**

On the other hand, *Quinn v Leathem* shows that a combination is wrongful if the real object is to injure, and not to advance some legitimate interest of the conspirators.[609] On this ground, Leathem succeeded in that case against trade union officials who had intervened to prevent a customer of his from dealing further with him. Similarly, if the object is to injure the claimant by way of punishing him, or **23-125**

---

601 *Reynolds v Shipping Federation* [1924] 1 Ch. 28; see also *White v Riley* [1921] 1 Ch. 1 CA. cf. now ss.222 and 225 of TULRCA 1992.

602 [1942] A.C. 435 at 477–478, per Lord Wright. Such a belief is not enough to exclude liability for a conspiracy to use unlawful means: *Lonrho Plc v Fayed* [1992] 1 A.C. 448 HL.

603 *Stratford & Son Ltd v Lindley* [1965] A.C. 269 at 323, per Lord Reid (a case in which the House of Lords so held despite the fact that they also held that the defendants were not acting in furtherance of a "trade dispute"); *Deane v Craik, The Times,* 16 March 1962; *PTY Homes Ltd v Shand* [1968] N.Z.L.R. 105; *McKernan v Fraser* (1931) 46 C.L.R. 343 at 398–400, per Evatt J.

604 *Stratford & Son Ltd v Lindley* [1965] A.C. 269; see too *Rookes v Barnard* [1964] A.C. 1129 at 1232, per Lord Devlin; *Bowles v Lindley* [1965] 1 Lloyd's Rep. 207.

605 See *Hadmor Productions Ltd v Hamilton* [1983] 1 A.C. 191 at 228, per Lord Diplock.

606 *Trollope & Sons v London Building Trades Association* (1895) 72 L.T. 342.

607 *Crofter* [1942] A.C. 435 at 447, per Viscount Simon LC.

608 *Scala Ballroom (Wolverhampton) Ltd v Ratcliffe* [1958] 1 W.L.R. 1057 at 1061 (note that the union had black members and that the court accepted that the removal of the bar was important because it is "impossible for musicians to insulate themselves from their audience"). Had the defendants induced or threatened to induce their members to break their employment contracts they could have been prima facie liable under the *Lumley v Gye* or intimidation torts, but since racial discrimination is now unlawful under the Equality Act 2010, replacing similar provisions in the Race Relations Act 1976, it might follow that in such a case the defence of justification would be applicable to a claim for inducing breach of contract, and that this would similarly prevent a threat to induce a breach from being an unlawful threat for the purposes of a claim based on intimidation; alternatively, a court might refuse to allow a claimant to sue for intimidation where a threat had been used solely to persuade a claimant to comply with the law.

609 [1901] A.C. 495 HL. The case must be understood to turn upon the finding of fact that this intention was paramount: see *Crofter* [1942] A.C. 435 at 474, per Lord Wright. So too an equivalent finding must explain *Pratt v British Medical Association* [1919] 1 K.B. 244, in the light of *Thompson v BMA (NSW) Branch* [1924] A.C. 764. See also *Pacific Western Airlines v British Columbia Federation of Labour* (1986) 26 D.L.R. (4th) 87 ("hot declarations" in inter union support; no predominant intent to injure).

by way of compelling him to pay a debt, it is an actionable conspiracy.[610] Where a workman in a dispute with his local union committee was hounded by that committee from every job which he obtained in the district, the members of the committee were held liable for conspiracy because they had ceased to act in the interests of their union and were out to damage the claimant, thinking only of their own "ruffled dignity"; but two union officials who were ignorant of the true facts, but who had assisted the committee, were held not liable because their object was proved to be still the furtherance of union interests.[611] Similarly where employees refused to work alongside the claimants, who had once broken the agreed National Working Rules in the industry but had ceased to be in breach of them at the relevant time, an injunction was granted on grounds of a conspiracy to injure since the court could see no possible justification for continuation of the embargo.[612] Action taken to demonstrate the power of the combiners is illegitimate[613]; and where action is taken for reasons which are proscribed by legislation on discrimination, for example on racial grounds, it must be regarded as pursuit of an illegitimate object.[614] In the case of action taken against a claimant because of his views or opinions which fall outside the territory covered by this legislation, it is possible that genuine belief in the promotion of the combiners' own interests could suffice to preclude liability for conspiracy to injure. Similarly action taken in pursuit of political goals (other than those which are proscribed by legislation) might possibly be seen as pursuit of a legitimate objective.[615] It is doubtful whether it is lawful to combine to coerce another into taking action of a charitable nature in which none of the parties is materially interested.[616] Pursuit of family interests or duties may be a legitimate object[617]; a sale of property for full consideration to another probably cannot be improper.[618]

---

610 *Giblan v National Amalgamated Labourers Union* [1903] 2 K.B. 600; cf. *White v Riley* [1921] 1 Ch. 1, where, per Warrington LJ at 25, the object of the combination was not to injure the claimant but ensure that he joined a particular union.

611 *Huntley v Thornton* [1957] 1 W.L.R. 321.

612 *Hutchinson v Aitchison* (1970) 9 K.I.R. 69; sed quaere whether this decision paid insufficient attention to whether the defendant employees genuinely believed that they were acting in their own legitimate interests. Any trade dispute, it was held had ceased to exist.

613 *Crofter* [1942] A.C. 435 at 445–446, per Viscount Simon LC; at 449, per Viscount Maugham. Similarly action "which would undermine principles of commercial or moral conduct": at 439, per Viscount Simon LC.

614 cf. *Crofter* [1942] A.C. 435 at 451, per Viscount Maugham; and see *Boots v Grundy* (1900) 82 L.T. 769 at 773, per Phillimore J. Legislation currently proscribes discrimination on grounds of race, sex, disability, religion or belief, sexual orientation and age: see now the (largely consolidating) Equality Act 2010.

615 See especially Morris LJ in *Scala Ballroom (Wolverhampton) Ltd v Ratcliffe* [1958] 1 W.L.R. 1057 at 1063, whose dicta allow for legitimate "political" strikes. (For a more restrictive interpretation see Kahn-Freund (1959) 22 M.L.R. 71.) On "political" strikes in relation to the quite separate question of contemplation or furtherance of a "trade dispute", see para.23-193.

616 per Lord Porter in *Crofter* [1942] A.C. 435 at 493; and compare his dicta at 489.

617 It has even been suggested that such a duty can justify procurement of breach of contract: per Viscount Simon LC in *Crofter* [1942] A.C. 435 at 442–443; *Midland Bank Trust Co Ltd v Green* [1980] Ch. 590 at 633 (reversed on other grounds [1981] A.C. 513 HL); cf. *Pritchard v Briggs* [1980] Ch. 338 at 415–417, per Goff LJ.

618 *Midland Bank Trust Co Ltd v Green* [1980] Ch. 590 at 626, per Eveleigh LJ; but possibly not if the consideration is "wholly inadequate"; ibid. at 627; and see, per Lord Denning MR at 625. Compare the parallel principle on "justification" for inducing breach of contract: *Hill v First National Finance Corp Plc* [1989] 1 W.L.R. 225 CA at 235, per Nourse LJ; see para.23-58.

Mixed objectives and predominant purpose It is plain that a combination may have more than one object or purpose. If so: 23-126

> "liability must depend on ascertaining the predominant purpose. If that predominant purpose is to damage another person and damage results that is tortious conspiracy.[619] If the predominant purpose is the lawful protection or promotion of any lawful interests of the combiners (no illegal means being employed) it is not a tortious conspiracy even though it causes damage to another person."[620]

In ascertaining that predominant purpose the court can have regard to both the short and the long-term objectives of the combiners.[621]

Disparity of interests and objects To be legitimate there need not be "a complete identity of interest between parties to a combination"; but there must be "sufficient identity of object though the advantage to be derived from that same object may not be the same".[622] Thus, in the *Crofter* case[623] a sufficient community of interest was established between two different sections of the union, and between the union and the employers, even though it amounted only to a desire for a prosperous industry for different reasons. It has been said, however, that if a conspiracy be once established, "the actions of any one of them (i.e. the conspirators) in furtherance of the objects of their conspiracy will be treated as the actions of all of them".[624] But where the aims or objects of the combiners are distinct, and certainly where their knowledge of the facts differs, the court does not adopt that approach to the extent of imputing the motives of one conspirator to all the others.[625] A party 23-127

---

619 As in *Quinn v Leathem*, above. However the defendants' interests may still be legitimate even if their purpose includes a deterrent or even a punitive element: *Eastham v Newcastle Utd FC Ltd* [1964] Ch. 413.

620 per Viscount Simon LC in *Crofter* [1942] A.C. 435 at 445. See also, per Lord Wright at 473 and 478; per Viscount Maugham at 452; per Lord Porter at 490. See also, *Lonrho Ltd v Shell Petroleum Co Ltd (No.2)* [1982] A.C. 173 HL at 188–189; *Lonrho Plc v Fayed* [1992] 1 A.C. 448 HL; *Canada Cement La Farge v British Columbia Lightweight Aggregate Ltd* (1983) 145 D.L.R. (3d) 386 (SCC) (aliter if unlawful means employed).

621 *Crofter* [1942] A.C. 435 at 469, per Lord Wright; at 486, per Lord Porter; see also, per Evatt J in *McKernan v Fraser* (1931) 46 C.L.R. 343 at 400. Quaere where there are "two equal concurrent purposes", one legitimate and one not, a point undecided by Sachs J in *Rookes v Barnard* [1963] 1 Q.B. 623 at 638, and not discussed on appeal. Note that in *Crofter* at 445 Viscount Simon LC carefully stipulated "no illegal means being employed".

622 *Crofter* [1942] A.C. 435 at 479, per Lord Wright; and Viscount Maugham believed, [1942] A.C. 435 at 453, that "reasonable self interest in trade or business is a 'just cause or excuse' for those combining even though each of them has his own axe to grind". Lord Porter thought that a "desire for prosperity or peace in the industry" was enough to justify the combination: [1942] A.C. 435 at 495. See also, per Lord Thankerton at 460.

623 [1942] A.C. 435 HL. See also for two applied but different trade interests: per Harman J in *Byrne v Kinematograph Renters Soc Ltd* [1958] 1 W.L.R. 762 at 776; *Reynolds v Shipping Federation* [1924] Ch. 28.

624 *DC Thomson & Co Ltd v Deakin* [1952] Ch. 646 at 674, per Evershed MR.

625 See, e.g. *Huntley v Thornton* [1957] 1 W.L.R. 321 at 343 (where Harman J would not encumber the two ignorant officials with liability for the committee's motives); and, per Evatt J in *McKernan v Fraser* (1931) 46 C.L.R. 343 at 401 and 408. Differences of knowledge and of purpose may be relevant in deciding the primary question of "combination". That is clearly the approach suggested by the Privy Council in *Bird v O'Neal* [1960] A.C. 907 at 920–921; and by the adoption in *Pritchard v Briggs* [1980] Ch. 338 at 414 and 424 of Viscount Dilhorne's test as to knowledge in *Churchill v Walton* [1967] 2 A.C. 224 at 237; *Belmont Finance Corp Ltd v Williams Furniture Ltd* [1979] Ch. 250 at 261 and 271.

to a combination who had a separate and predominantly vindictive or mercenary interest of his own, other than trade interests, might not be protected[626]; but, in such a case, if the other parties have predominantly lawful objects of their own he will, even though malicious, incur no liability at all.[627] If, however, the other parties know of and countenance his vindictive purpose, they will, it is submitted, be jointly responsible with him for wrongful conspiracy.[628]

23-128 **Onus of proof** The burden of proving both the combination and the purpose of damaging the claimant is normally on the claimant himself.[629] In so far as the cases talk of a need for "just excuse" or "justification"[630] those words seem to be no more than a description of the need for evidence (as to his trade or other legitimate interests) which a defendant can put in to meet the claimant's case when the latter has adduced evidence of apparent intention to injure on the defendant's part,[631] and do not alter the primary burden of proof. By contrast it has been held that where the claimant can prove acts unlawful in themselves, done in pursuance of the conspiracy, that is the other form of the tort, unlawful means conspiracy, the burden of justifying such acts passes to the defendant.[632]

626 See, per Lord Thankerton in *Crofter* [1942] A.C. 435 at 460; per Viscount Maugham at 453; per Lord Wright at 480. Nor are mere "busybodies" protected, per Lord Porter at 491.

627 *Allen v Flood* [1898] A.C. 1; and see, per Evatt J in *McKernan v Fraser* (1931) 46 C.L.R. 343 at 401–410. There will be no actionable lawful means conspiracy, and malice alone is not a cause of action.

628 A proposition hesitantly supported by Lord Porter in *Crofter* [1942] A.C. 435 at 495. In *MX1 Ltd v Farahzad* [2018] EWHC 1041 (Ch); [2018] 1 W.L.R. 5553 at [22](5), Marcus Smith J stated that it was "an open question whether a party to the combination, who knows of and countenances the unlawful object of the other parties, can be said him or herself to have an unlawful object in mind." He noted the opinion in this text that such a party would be liable, then continued: "In my judgment, provided that party lacks another legitimate object, the inference that he or she is adopting the unlawful object of the others must be hard to resist." Compare *CBS Songs Ltd v Amstrad Consumer Electronics Plc* [1988] A.C. 1013 at 1057–1059 (common design and liability as joint tortfeasor); *Paterson Zochonis Ltd v Merfarken Packaging Ltd* [1986] 3 All E.R. 522, CA at 530, 534 and 538–541; cf. *Kuwait Oil Tanker Co SAK v Al-Bader* [2000] 2 All E.R. (Comm) 271 CA.

629 *Crofter* [1942] A.C. 435; per Lord Wright at 471–472; per Lord Porter at 495; per Lord Thankerton at 459; and *Sorrell v Smith* [1925] A.C. 700 at 726, per Lord Dunedin and at 748, per Lord Buckmaster. See also *Allen v Flood* [1898] A.C. 1 at 139, per Lord Herschell.

630 e.g. *Sorrell v Smith* [1925] A.C. 700 at 712, per Lord Cave LC.

631 Viscount Maugham in *Crofter* [1942] A.C. 435 at 449–450, did not, it is suggested, mean to say more than this; cf. *Metall und Rohstoff AG v Donaldson, Lufkin & Jenrette Inc* [1990] 1 Q.B. 371 CA at 454-460 and 467 (overruled on other grounds: *Lonrho Plc v Fayed* [1992] 1 A.C. 448 HL at 464). But some earlier judgments do suggest that the burden is on the defendant, e.g. per Bowen LJ in *Mogul S.S. Co v McGregor, Gow Co* (1889) 23 Q.B.D. 598 CA at 613; per Bankes LJ in *Ware and De Freville v Motor Trade Association* [1921] 3 K.B. 40 at 61 (Scrutton and Atkin LJJ disagreed at 70 and 79).

632 *Crofter* [1942] A.C. 435 at 495–496, per Lord Porter; and see *Lonrho Plc v Fayed* [1992] 1 A.C. 448 HL. For the question whether there is a defence of justification available in a case of unlawful means conspiracy, see para.23-118.

(d) Damage

Damage is an essential element of both forms of the tort of conspiracy,[633] the gist of the cause of action.[634] It has been held that the damage constituted by the expense incurred by claimants in exposing and resisting the wrongful activities of the defendants can be awarded to them as damage directly caused by the conspiracy.[635] Damages for injury to feelings or to reputation, however, cannot be recovered in an action based upon either a lawful means conspiracy[636] or an unlawful means conspiracy.[637] The special limitations surrounding the granting of injunctions against publication of allegedly defamatory material may, however, be displaced if a lawful means conspiracy is proved.[638] **23-129**

6. TRADE DISPUTES

(a) General

Trade disputes and the economic torts In the sphere of industrial conflict, the impact of the common law discussed in the preceding sections was greatly affected by the Trade Disputes Act 1906. That statute was the first to give protection against some of the liabilities described above in respect of acts done in contemplation or furtherance of a "trade dispute".[639] Had no such statute been enacted the modern system of trade unions and collective bargaining could not have emerged without constant risk of illegality.[640] The current provisions are mainly found in the Trade Union and Labour Relations (Consolidation) Act 1992 (TULRCA 1992) as **23-130**

---

633 *Crofter* [1942] A.C 435 at 440, per Viscount Simon LC. cf. *Ward v Lewis* [1955] 1 W.L.R. 9; *Lonrho Ltd v Shell Petroleum Co Ltd (No.2)* [1982] A.C. 173 HL; *Lonrho Plc v Fayed (No.5)* [1993] 1 W.L.R. 1489 CA at 1501, per Stuart-Smith LJ.

634 *Crofter* [1942] A.C. 435 at 461, per Lord Wright; per Lord Diplock in *Lonrho v Shell* [1982] A.C. 173 at 188; per Oliver J in *Midland Bank Trust Co Ltd v Green (No.3)* [1979] Ch. 496 at 524; cf. Holdsworth, *History of English Law*, 2nd edn (1937), Vol.VIII, pp.393–394.

635 *British Motor Trade Association v Salvadori* [1949] Ch. 556. Damages appear to be at large: *McGregor on Damages*, 20th edn (2017), para.48-020. On the remedy of interim (interlocutory) injunction see paras 23-180 to 23-183.

636 *Lonrho Plc v Fayed (No.5)* [1993] 1 W.L.R. 1489 CA, at least in the absence of proof of pecuniary loss, since that would allow the claimant "to circumvent the requirements of a defamation action … without the defendants being able to plead justification", per Dillon LJ at 1493. As to the place of such a claim for damages "parasitically", or as part of damages at large, see the differing formulations of Dillon LJ, [1993] 1 W.L.R. 1489 CA at 1494–1497, Stuart-Smith LJ at 1501 and 1504–1505, and Evans LJ at 1509. cf. *Joyce v Sengupta* [1993] 1 W.L.R. 337 CA (malicious falsehood and damage to reputation).

637 *Mbasogo v Logo Ltd* [2006] EWCA Civ 1370; [2007] Q.B. 846.

638 See *Gulf Oil (GB) Ltd v Page* [1987] Ch. 327 CA, limiting the practice based upon *Bonnard v Perryman* [1891] 2 Ch. 269, CA.

639 Described as "a golden formula which became the bedrock" after 1906 of the liberty to strike: Wedderburn, *The Worker and the Law* (1965), p.222, 3rd edn (1986), pp.520–521.

640 For detailed consideration see Kahn-Freund, *Labour and the Law*, 3rd edn (1983), Davies and Freedland (eds), Ch.8; Deakin and Morris, *Labour Law*, 6th edn (2012), Ch.11; Morris and Archer, *Collective Labour Law* (2000) Ch.6; Barrow, *Industrial Relations Law*, 2nd edn (2002), Chs 13-17; Wedderburn, *The Worker and the Law*, 3rd edn (1986) Chs 7 and 8; and (1989) 18 I.L.J. 1; Smith, Baker and Warnock, *Smith & Wood's, Employment Law*, 14th edn (2019), Ch.10; Wedderburn, *Employment Rights in Britain and Europe* (1991); and *Labour Law and Freedom* (1995), Chs 2 and 4; Simpson (1991) 54 M.L.R. 418; Carty (1991) 20 I.L.J. 1; Morris (1993) 22 I.L.J. 194; Simpson (1993) 22 I.L.J. 287.

amended by the Trade Union Reform and Employment Rights Act 1993 (TURERA 1993), the Employment Relations Act 1999 (ERA 1999), the Employment Relations Act 2004 (ERA 2004) and the Trade Union Act 2016. At common law, effective industrial action is invariably tortious, and the "immunities" enacted by Parliament necessarily (in the absence of positive rights to take such action) take the form of special defences against common law liability, while in the structure of industrial relations they are the method of establishing liberties which in other systems of law often derive from constitutional guarantees.[641] The "immunities" enjoyed in trade disputes:

> "are not simply legal privileges which could be abolished outright. Without some legal protection—however circumscribed—it would be impossible for trade unions or individuals to organise industrial action without risk of civil proceedings and the ultimate safeguard of a collective withdrawal of labour would be effectively nullified."[642]

That risk arises mainly from the core "economic torts". In recent decades policy behind the enactments has varied widely.[643] In 1979 Lord Scarman could say: "Briefly put, the law is now what Parliament had intended when it enacted the Act of 1906—but stronger and clearer than it was then."[644] The resurrection of the 1906 policy, often dubbed "collective laissez faire"[645] endured, however, only for a short time and extensive legislation in 1980–93 radically restricted the range of protection against the liabilities for common law economic torts. More recently, the ERA 1999 and ERA 2004 made some amendments to, but did not fundamentally change, this new, restrictive structure. By contrast the Trade Union Act 2016 (TUA 2016) has both reinforced and extended the restrictive character of this body of law. The present legislation can be fully understood only in the context of these divergent legal and social policies. A submission that the legislation should be strictly construed against defendant unions since they were seeking to take advantage of

[641] On "immunities" and "rights": Wedderburn (1980) 9 I.L.J. 65; *Employment Rights in Britain and Europe* (1991), Chs 3, 5 and 10. For a judicial perspective on the "so-called right to strike", see, per Henry J in *Barretts & Baird (Wholesale) Ltd v IPCS* [1987] I.R.L.R. 3 at 8–10. On "rights" and international labour standards: O'Higgins in Lewis (ed.), *Labour Law in Britain* (1986), Ch.20; Gibbons, *International Labour Rights* (1998); Ewing, *Britain and the ILO*, 2nd edn (1994); Wedderburn, *Labour Law and Freedom* (1995) at pp.387–409 (ILO and EC standards).

[642] *Trade Union Immunities* (1981) Cmnd.8218, para.384. Compare the "Donovan" Report of the Royal Commission on Trade Unions and Employers' Associations (1968) Cmnd.3623, Ch.XIV. Contrast the judicial persistence in regarding them as "privileges": per Lord Keith in *Duport Steels Ltd v Sirs* [1980] 1 W.L.R. 142 at 167; *Express Newspapers Ltd v McShane* [1980] A.C. 672 at 698, per Lord Salmon, and at 687, per Lord Diplock. But cf. per Millett LJ in *London Underground Ltd v RMT* [1996] I.C.R. 170 at 181: "first conferred by Parliament in 1906 ... [the immunities are] today recognised as encompassing a fundamental human right."

[643] The Industrial Relations Act 1971 repealed most of the earlier statutes in an attempt to create an overarching framework of labour law; but it was itself repealed by the Trade Union and Labour Relations Act 1974 which, as amended in 1976, restored protection in tort for trade unions, and for their officials in trade disputes, as a modernised form of the 1906 Act. Legislation from the Employment Act 1980 to TURERA 1993 introduced limitations on the extent and qualifications to the availability of these protections which are now contained in TULRCA 1992 ss.219–235A as subsequently amended by TURERA 1993, the Employment Relations Acts 1999 and 2004 and the Trade Union Act 2016.

[644] *NWL v Woods* [1979] 1 W.L.R. 1294 at 1312; see Wedderburn, "Industrial Relations and the Courts" (1980) 9 I.L.J. 65.

[645] See O. Kahn-Freund, "Labour Law" in Ginsberg (ed.), *Law and Opinion in the 20th Century* (1959), p.215 at p.224.

an immunity was rejected by the Court of Appeal in *London & Birmingham Railway Ltd v ASLEF* where Elias LJ endorsed the approach suggested by Lord Bingham in *P v NASUWT* that the legislation should be given a "likely and workable construction".[646]

It is necessary to examine in particular, therefore, the impact of these statutes upon the torts of procuring breach of contract, intimidation, intentionally causing loss by unlawful means, and conspiracy.[647] In the first period, after the decision in 1901 that a registered trade union could be made a defendant in an action in tort,[648] the Act of 1906 declared that no court should entertain an action against a trade union "in respect of any tortious act".[649] The reason for the section was the conviction that common law liability in tort could emasculate trade unions. The Trade Union and Labour Relations Act 1974 enacted a similar protection providing that "no action in tort shall lie in respect of any act" done by or on behalf of a trade union, or threatened so to be done, against a trade union or against an unincorporated employers' association.[650] This protection was removed in 1982.[651] A trade union has since that year had available the defences previously enjoyed by others (such as its officials) in respect of certain economic torts for acts done in contemplation or furtherance of "trade disputes". Much therefore depended on the definition of a trade dispute which was amended in the same year.[652] The availability of the union as a defendant in tort actions reopened the prospect of liability for contempt of court by a union whose agents fail to carry out the terms of an injunction.[653] Since the subject has acquired some technicality in legislation which is of great importance to those who have to take decisions "in circumstances of urgency" but is "most regrettably lacking in the requisite clarity",[654] it may be useful to outline some of the main developments. Parliament afforded immunity in 1906 for acts **23-131**

---

646 [2011] EWCA Civ 226; [2011] I.C.R. 848 at [9], concluding a concise account of the history and context of the legislation at [2]–[9], by endorsing Lord Bingham's approach in *P v NASUWT* [2003] UKHL 8; [2003] I.C.R. 386 at [7]. That approach was also expressly adopted in *London Underground Ltd v ASLEF* [2011] EWHC 3506 (QB); [2012] I.R.L.R, 196 by Eder J at [14], in *Balfour Beatty Engineering Services Ltd v Unite* [2012] EWHC 267 (QB); [2012] I.C.R. 822 by Eady J at [8]; and in *Royal Mail Group Ltd v Communication Workers Union* [2019] EWCA Civ 2150; [2020] I.C.R. 940 by Males LJ at [22].

647 See below. On the doubts as to whether the tort of intimidation retains its independent identity after the House of Lords decision in *OBG Ltd v Allan* [2007] UKHL 21; [2008] 1 A.C. 1, see para.23-63.

648 *Taff Vale Ry Co v ASRS* [1901] A.C. 426 HL.

649 s.4(1) of the Trade Disputes Act 1906.

650 See s.14(1); but liability was retained in respect of negligence and certain other torts committed other than in trade disputes, s.14(2). For the current definitions of "trade union" and "employers association": see ss.1 and 122 of TULRCA 1992 respectively.

651 Employment Act 1982 s.15, which also enacted a code of vicarious liability which, under ss.20 and 21 of TULRCA 1992, now applies to a trade union's liability for most of the economic torts; see para.23-134.

652 See now s.244 of TULRCA 1992 as amended; para.23-180 onwards.

653 See *Express and Star Ltd v NGA* [1986] I.C.R. 589; *Austin Rover Group Ltd v AUEW (TASS)* [1985] I.R.L.R. 162; see Lightman [1987] C.L.P. 25; Wedderburn, *The Worker and the Law*, 3rd edn (1986), pp.709–717 and 739–751; O'Regan (1991) 54 M.L.R. 385. On liability for contempt through acts of agents and employees see *Supply of Ready Mixed Concrete (No.2), Re* [1995] 1 A.C. 456 HL (employer liable when employees acted in breach of instructions: compare *Heatons Transport (St. Helens) Ltd v TGWU* [1973] A.C. 15 HL). On third parties and contempt of court see *Att Gen v Punch Ltd* [2002] UKHL 50; [2003] 1 A.C. 1046.

654 per Lord Diplock in *Merkur Island Shipping Corp v Laughton* [1983] 2 A.C. 570 at 612.

done "in contemplation or furtherance of a trade dispute"[655] to the following liabilities: simple conspiracy, "interference" with trade, business or employment and inducing a breach of a contract of employment.[656] It also provided that attending at or near any place merely for the purpose of peaceful communication of information or peaceful persuasion (picketing) "shall be lawful".[657] Following the innovative decision of *Rookes v Barnard* in 1964,[658] the Trade Disputes Act 1965 enacted protection for threats to break contracts of employment in trade disputes. On the repeal of the Industrial Relations Act 1971, the Trade Union and Labour Relations Act 1974 (TULRA 1974) set out an updated version of the earlier legislation. Immunity was afforded to individuals, most obviously, but not limited to, union officials in six areas for acts done "in contemplation or furtherance of a trade dispute".

23-132 First, liability for simple conspiracy to injure was excluded so long as the combination had not done, or procured the doing of, any act that was "actionable in tort".[659] Secondly, picketing was made "lawful" near any place (other than a residence) for the purpose only of obtaining or communicating information or peacefully persuading any person to work or not to work.[660] Thirdly, "for the avoidance of doubt" it was declared that "interference with the trade, business or employment of another" was not to be actionable in tort.[661] Fourthly, by reason of the extension of breach of contract into the category of "unlawful means" after *Rookes v Barnard*,[662] it was also declared "for the avoidance of doubt" that it did not constitute unlawful means for liability in tort.[663] Fifthly, limits were placed upon the granting of an interim (previously known as an interlocutory) injunction.[664] Last, the 1974 Act protected inducement to break a contract of employment and threats either to induce such breach or to break it (intimidation).[665] Since the cases had already demonstrated that liability could arise from inducement to break a commercial contract, it may at first sight be difficult to "fathom" why a parallel extension of immunity was not enacted in 1974.[666] The explanation lay in the political history, for at that date there was a minority government unable to pass the legislation in that form.[667] By 1976 its majority enabled it to pass an amending Act which provided protection in respect of:

(i) inducing breach of *any* contract;
(ii) interference or inducing interference with the performance of, *any* contract;

---

655 See para.23-180 onwards.
656 Respectively in Trade Disputes Act 1906 ss.1, 3, limb (2), and s.3 limb (1).
657 Trade Disputes Act 1906 s.2.
658 [1964] A.C. 1129 HL; see para.23-62.
659 TULRA 1974 s.13(4); now s.219(2) of TULRCA 1992; see para.23-154 onwards.
660 TULRA 1974 s.15; now s.220 of TULRCA 1992; see para.23-174.
661 TULRA 1974 s.13(2); repealed by s.19 of the Employment Act 1982; see para.23-139.
662 [1964] A.C. 1129 HL; see para.23-62.
663 TULRA 1974 s.13(3)(b); repealed by s.17(8) of the Employment Act 1980; see para.23-159.
664 TULRA s.17(1), (2), amended in 1975 and now s.221 of TULRCA 1992; see para.23-180. It must be repeated that these immunities applied only to acts done in contemplation or furtherance of trade disputes: see para.23-184 onwards.
665 TULRA s.13(1); see now s.219(1) of TULRCA 1992; see paras 23-136 to 23-141.
666 *Hadmor Productions Ltd v Hamilton* [1983] 1 A.C. 191 at 230, per Lord Diplock.
667 Wedderburn (1974) 37 M.L.R. 525; England and Rees (1976) 39 M.L.R. 698. On the other hand, it is not possible to say why in 1906, when this liability might have been foreseen, the Trade Disputes Act s.3, was confined to contracts of employment: Donovan *Report of the Royal Commission on Trade Unions and Employers' Associations, Cmnd.3623* (1968), para.887.

(iii) threats to do any such acts;
(iv) threats that a contract would be broken (intimidation).[668]

It is manifest from that history that by 1976, Parliament was attempting to provide immunity in trade disputes in respect of all the types of arguable tort liability connected with breach of a contract or interference with its performance.[669]

Restriction of immunities The policy of legislation from 1980 to 1993, which the Trade Union Act 2016 has revived, was to restrict the extent of these immunities, both those relating to the economic torts generally and those relating to picketing in particular, together with a narrowing of the definition of a "trade dispute".[670] The restrictions disapply protection for the economic torts (i.e. in what is now s.219(1) and (2) of TULRCA 1992).[671] The most important of these removes immunity from industrial action authorised by a trade union for inducing a breach of any contract (or interfering with its performance) and for conspiracy, without the support of a ballot.[672] So too, all protection under s.219 (the basic trade dispute protections) is now lost for picketing otherwise than at a worker's own place of work,[673] and for acts which interfere with the supply of goods and services by inducing breach of, or by interference with, or by inducing interference with, a contract of employment for the purpose of, inter alia, inducing an employer's supplier to recognise or negotiate with a union.[674] The same consequence now follows action aimed at sustaining any form of closed shop arrangement.[675] Some parts of the current legislation create obligations not strictly based on the law of tort but closely linked with these issues, for example the right of a member to challenge a trade union which aims to call industrial action without the support of a ballot,[676] and the right of an individual to obtain an order from the court against certain industrial action affecting the supply of goods or services.[677] But in other respects, the new legislation carries forward the form which created problems in the earlier statutes, for example by including in the liabilities for which protection is given in trade disputes "interference with a contract", which was inserted in the 1974 Act in case 23-133

---

[668] s.13(1)(a), (b) of TULRA 1974, as amended; by TULRA (Amendment) Act 1976 s.3(2); see now s.219(1) of TULRCA 1992; para.23-136.

[669] But the 1974 Act as amended did not extend protection to all types of unlawful means (e.g. violence). Parliament in 1976 had in mind what was "arguable" since that was the level a claimant needed to reach to obtain an interlocutory injunction; see para.23-180 onwards. What Parliament "intends" by such legislation must be judged by "what Parliament might reasonably have thought" the common law to be at that time (per Lord Devlin in *Rookes v Barnard* [1964] A.C. 1129 at 1216), not what it eventually turns out to be; see too para.23-139.

[670] Now s.244 of TULRCA; see para.23-180 onwards. This policy was not changed by the legislation of 1999 and 2004 and it re-emerged in the Trade Union Act 2016.

[671] Effectively covering inducing breach of contract, threats to break or induce breach of contracts and conspiracy.

[672] Now s.219(4) and ss.226–235 of TULRCA 1992, as amended by ss.17–21 of the TURERA 1993, Sch.3 to the ERA 1999, ss.22–26 of the ERA 2004 and ss.2–10 of the Trade Union Act 2016; see para.23-162 onwards.

[673] Now ss.219(3), 220 and 220A of TULRCA 1992 as amended by s.10 of the Trade Union Act 2016; see para.23-174 and on union officials, see para.23-179.

[674] Now ss.222 and 225 of TULRCA 1992; see paras 23-97 and 23-146.

[675] See s.222 of TULRCA 1992; para.23-148.

[676] See TULRCA 1992 s.62; para.23-162 onwards.

[677] See TULRCA 1992 s.235A, inserted by TURERA 1993 s.22; see *P v NASUWT* [2003] UKHL 8; [2003] 2 A.C. 663, and para.23-173.

bare interference turned out after all to be tortious.[678] The immunity against a wider liability for "interference" with trade or employment generally was, for similar reasons, inserted in the earlier legislation in case the common law should "go one way" in favour of liability for mere interference, which was then uncertain.[679] Mere interference—"*Quinn v Leathem* without the conspiracy"[680]—is not actionable save where harm has been intentionally caused by the use of unlawful means.[681] This wider protection, whether it was needed or not, was in any event repealed in 1982.[682]

23-134 This structure led the courts to analyse trade dispute cases by asking questions in three "stages":

> Stage 1: Have the claimants a cause of action at common law?
> Stage 2: Is any liability protected by the Act of 1974 (as amended in 1976) in a trade dispute? (now ss.219 and 220 of TULRCA 1992)
> Stage 3: Is the cause of action restored by the legislation of 1980–2016 (now ss.222–234A of TULRCA 1992 as amended)?[683]

A statutory code governing the vicarious liability of a trade union for the acts of persons taking part in industrial action, is now applied to a trade union in respect of the core economic tort liability set out in s.20 of TULRCA 1992 (broadly, inducing breach of contract, interference with contract, threats to commit these torts, threats to break contracts and conspiracy to use means actionable on these grounds[684]). In addition to the acts of (i) the principal executive committee, the president and the general secretary; and (ii) other persons acting within their authority under the rules, the union is now liable for acts of; (iii) all its officials and committees, notwithstanding limitations on their authority in the union rules.[685] Further, if an official was a "member" at the "material time" of a group of persons of which one purpose was the organising or co-ordination of industrial action, the union is liable for acts done or authorised by *any* other member of that group, whether or not the persons involved were members of the union.[686] Acting through persons falling within categories (i) and (ii), the union can repudiate the acts of other officials, for example authorising industrial action; but this must be done as soon as reason-

---

[678] See now *OBG Ltd v Allan* [2007] UKHL 21; [2008] 1 A.C. 1; above para.23-20.

[679] See Lord Reid in *Rookes v Barnard* [1964] A.C. 1129 at 1177: s.3 limb (2) of the Trade Disputes Act 1906 on interference was "necessary to achieve [Parliament's] object if the law should go one way but unnecessary if it went the other way"; it was re-enacted as s.13(2) of the 1974 Act; see para.23-139.

[680] See Lord Devlin in *Rookes v Barnard* [1964] A.C. 1129 at 1216.

[681] See para.23-20.

[682] By the Employment Act 1982 s.19; the reasons for the repeal are still relevant to the modern law; see para.23-139.

[683] per Lord Diplock in *Merkur Island Shipping Corp v Laughton* [1983] 2 A.C. 570 at 604–612; Henry J in *Barretts & Baird (Wholesale) Ltd v IPCS* [1987] I.R.L.R. 3 at 5–6. In *London & Birmingham Railway Ltd v ASLEF* [2011] EWCA Civ 226; [2011] I.C.R. 848 the Court of Appeal rejected a submission that since unions were seeking to take advantage of an immunity from common law liability the legislative protection in TULRCA s.219 should be construed strictly against them: "The statutory immunities are simply the form which the law in this country takes to carve out the ability for unions to take lawful strike action", per Elias LJ at [9].

[684] Technically the words of s.20 are based on the doctrine qui facit per alium facit per se (see s.20(1) "... taken to have been done by the union") rather than vicarious liability, but nothing seems to turn upon this.

[685] See TULRCA 1992 s.20(4), and for definition of the rules, s.20(7). It is arguable that the union is liable even if the executive committee is not quorate under the rules.

[686] s.20(3)(b). The "material time" appears to mean when the industrial action was under discussion.

ably practicable and in conformity with strict, statutory requirements.[687] The union must give written notice to the official concerned and do its best to give notices to each relevant member (in the precise words of the statutory disclaimer)[688] and to each employer of every member who might take part in the action.[689] The repudiation is invalidated if at any later time any persons within category (i) behave in a manner inconsistent with it, and this is deemed to be the case if the union fails to confirm the repudiation to parties to relevant commercial contracts who have not received a notice but who make inquiries within three months after it.[690] Where, however, the proceedings are in respect of a tort not falling within TULRCA 1992 s.20, the common law principles apply,[691] as in the case of liability for the tort of nuisance committed by pickets.[692] Provision is now also made for the statutory code to apply to contempt of court in cases where it applies to liability,[693] including the question whether the union is liable for not having satisfied the requirements concerning a ballot of members to support industrial action.[694]

Awards of damages against unions Further provision was made in 1982 in respect of union liability in tort. The amount of damages which can be awarded against a union is limited according to the size of its membership,[695] unless the proceedings are for negligence, nuisance, breach of duty causing personal injury, product liability under Pt I of the Consumer Protection Act 1987 or breach of duty in connection with ownership, possession or use of property, real or personal.[696] This limitation applies only to each set of "proceedings"; but no amount awarded as damages, costs or expenses may be recovered from certain "protected" funds, essentially funds held by union (or branch)[697] trustees on trusts other than for the union or its members as a whole, or in a political or "provident benefits" fund where that 23-135

687 See s.21(1)(4).

688 Including a statement that the members will, if dismissed when taking unofficial industrial action, "have no right to complain of unfair dismissal": s.21(3) (by reason of s.237).

689 TULRCA 1992 s.21(2).

690 TULRCA 1992 s.21(5), (6), (7).

691 See the common law principles of vicarious liability applied in *Heatons Transport Ltd v TGWU* [1973] A.C. 15, HL; compare *General Aviation Services (UK) Ltd v TWGU* [1985] I.C.R. 615 HL.

692 Either vicariously liable (*Thomas v NUM (South Wales Area)* [1986] Ch. 20) or on principles derived from "continuing or adopting" a private nuisance (*News Group Newspapers Ltd v SOGAT (No.2)* [1987] I.C.R. 181 at 217–218, per Stuart-Smith J). Quaere: where there is a "mixed" claim, based on some torts within, and others not within TULRCA 1992 s.20(1)? Semble the statutory code in s.20 applies unless the claimant proves only torts not within that area (*Thomas v NUM (South Wales Area)* [1986] Ch. 20).

693 See TULRCA 1992 s.20(6), reversing the effect of *Express and Star Ltd v NGA* [1986] I.C.R. 589 CA. On contempt of court, see Lightman (1987) C.L.P. 25; O'Regan (1991) 54 M.L.R. 385; Wedderburn, *Employment Rights in Britain and Europe* (1991), Ch.7; and on the expanded liabilities of third parties for contempt: *Att Gen v Times Newspapers Ltd* [1992] 1 A.C. 191 HL; Auerbach (1988) 17 I.L.J. 227; Wedderburn (1992) 21 I.L.J. 51.

694 TULRCA 1992 s.234A(9) (see para.23-162 onwards). The statutory code also applies to both liability and contempt where a member seeks an order in the absence of a ballot in support of official union action (s.62(5)) and where an individual seeks the statutory remedy for inducing unlawful industrial action affecting the supply of goods or services: TULRCA 1992 s.235A(6).

695 If less than 5,000 members, limited to £10,000 damages; if 5,000 but less than 25,000 members, to £50,000; if 25,000 but less than 100,000 members, to £125,000; and if 100,000 or more members, to £250,000: s.22(2) of TULRCA 1992. The Secretary of State may vary the amounts: s.22(3). The members of unions in a federation count as members of the federation: s.118(3).

696 See s.22 of TULRCA 1992, which extends the formula in the repealed s.14(2) of the Trade Union and Labour Relations Act 1974, not being limited to acts outside trade disputes as that was.

697 See *News Group Newspapers Ltd v SOGAT* [1986] I.C.R. 716 CA; cf. *Cope v Crossingham* [1909]

is not available under the rules (at the time of the proceedings) for financing industrial action.[698] The overall structure of liability in damages of a trade union after 1982 has made it easier for the court to exercise its discretion in favour of granting an injunction against a union, compared with the earlier period when the nominal defendant was an official,[699] especially where a claimant employer alleges that damages cannot be an "adequate" remedy.

(b) Trade disputes and procuring breach of contract

23-136 TULRCA 1992 provides in s.219(1):

> **"Protection from certain tort liabilities.**
>
> **219.—**(1) …
>
> (b) that it consists in his threatening that a contract (whether one to which he is a party or not) will be broken or its performance interfered with, or that he will induce another person to break a contract or interfere with its performance.
>
> An act done by a person in contemplation or furtherance of a trade dispute shall not be actionable in tort on the ground only:
>
> (a) that it induces another person to break a contract or interferes or induces another person to interfere with its performance."

Although these words do not set out all the constituents of the tort (such as "knowingly" and "intentionally") it is clear that they provide a protection in respect of the tort of inducing breach of contract,[700] and that that protection extends to all remedies, whether damages or an injunction.[701] Both when originally enacted in 1906[702] and when re-enacted on the repeal of the Industrial Relations Act 1971 in 1974 the protection was limited to inducing or procuring breaches of contracts of employment and did not extend to other contracts, for example commercial contracts or even contracts for personal services rendered by a person not *stricto sensu* a "servant".[703] Further, because of the word "only" no protection was provided where some other wrong had been committed, such as an inducement to break an

2 Ch. 148 CA; *Burnley Nelson Rossendale Textile Workers Union v NATWU* [1987] I.C.R. 69.

698 See s.23 of TULRCA 1992. None of the protections or limitations applies to a fine or other penalty imposed for contempt of court.

699 *Dimbleby & Sons Ltd v NUJ* [1984] 1 W.L.R. 427 at 432, per Lord Diplock, on his opinion in *NWL v Woods* [1979] 1 W.L.R. 1294; Simpson (1984) 47 M.L.R. 577 at 578–579.

700 *Rookes v Barnard* [1964] A.C. 1129 at 1172, per Lord Reid; at 1213–1214, per Lord Devlin; at 1237, per Lord Pearce. Unless he terminates his employment, the employee who takes industrial action commits a breach of his contract of employment: *Boddington v Lawton* [1994] I.C.R. 478 at 486–487; *Simmons v Hoover Ltd* [1977] Q.B. 284; *Boxfoldia Ltd v NGA* [1988] I.C.R. 752; and cf. *Haddow v ILEA* [1979] I.C.R. 202 at 206 (explaining a "suspension" of the contract as a case where the employer does not choose to put an end to it); *Miles v Wakefield MDC* [1987] A.C. 539 HL; *Seaboard World Airlines, Inc v TGWU* [1973] I.C.R. 458 at 460, per Donaldson P. (refusal to work voluntary overtime the only exception to breach of contract).

701 *Camden Exhibition and Display Ltd v Lynott* [1966] 1 Q.B. 555.

702 The origin was the "first limb" of the Trade Disputes Act 1906 s.3. It appears to have been thought in 1906 that the risk of liability arose only in respect of inducing breach of employment contracts, see Donovan Report (1968) Cmnd.3623, para.887; and the Green Paper *Trade Union Immunities* (1981) Cmnd.8128, paras 15 and 72. On the origins of the 1906 Act, see Kidner (1982) 2 L.S. 34; Wedderburn, *The Worker and the Law*, 3rd edn (1986), pp.16–47 and 585–587; Deakin and Morris *Labour Law*, 6th edn (2012) pp.9–10.

703 Crown employees are deemed to have contracts of employment for these purposes: s.245 of TULRCA 1992.

equitable duty to account,[704] or some other tort.[705] In the mid-1970s the state of the law, and in particular uncertainty concerning liability for indirect procurement of breach[706] and possibly bare interference[707] outflanked the protection provided in trade disputes by the 1906 and 1974 Acts. The 1974 Act was therefore amended in 1976 to include "interference with performance" and to cover all contracts of any kind and not just contracts of employment,[708] putting the law into a form which had been earlier proposed, but not enacted.[709] The legislative purpose was to "sweep away … the restraints of judicial review which the courts have been fashioning one way or another since the enactment of the Trade Disputes Act 1906".[710] In s.219, TULRCA 1992 still displays the remnants of that policy but the rest of Pt V of the Act makes the weakened protection available now only on satisfaction of many conditions.[711]

The basic modern protection therefore, now consolidated in s.219(1) of TULRCA 1992, attaches to liability for acts done in contemplation or furtherance of a trade dispute for inducing breach of, or interference with or inducing others to interfere with, the performance of any contract. This core immunity has been preserved, subject to many conditions.[712] Protection against a possible liability for bare interference with performance of a contract (short of breach) was clearly included to guard against the adoption by other judges of the liability advocated by Lord Denning MR **23-137**

---

704 *Prudential Assurance Co Ltd v Lorenz* (1971) 11 K.I.R. 78 (the duty, it was held, not arising exclusively from the employment contract and see para.23-25); cf. *Associated British Ports v TGWU* [1989] 1 W.L.R. 939 HL (statutory rules effective as contractual duties); cf. *Nottingham University v Fishel* [2000] I.C.R. 1452.

705 *Cunard S.S. v Stacey* [1955] 2 Lloyd's Rep. 247; *Royal London etc Soc Ltd v Williamson* (1921) 37 T.L.R. 742 (conversion); *Conway v Wade* [1909] A.C. 506 at 511–512, per Lord Loreburn; cf. *Norbrook Laboratories Ltd v King* [1984] I.R.L.R. 200 CA (NI) at 208–209, and on other torts committed by pickets see para.23-174. Semble: where liability for "economic duress" in a trade dispute is coterminous with liability for an economic tort protected by an immunity, the defendants are not liable under that doctrine: *Universe Tankships Inc of Monrovia v ITF* [1983] 1 A.C. 366 HL; but Lord Brandon dubitante, and the point was conceded; on the effects of restricting the immunities see *Dimskal Shipping SA v ITWF* [1992] 2 A.C. 152 HL (Lord Templeman dissenting).

706 See, e.g. *Stratford v Lindley* [1965] A.C. 269 HL.

707 *Torquay Hotel Co Ltd v Cousins* [1969] 2 Ch. 106, CA at 137–138.

708 See the recommendation of the Donovan Report, Cmnd.3623 (1968) that immunity should be extended to cover inducing breach of all contracts: paras 800–804 and 893–894 (per the majority, with qualifications).

709 In *Hadmor Productions Ltd v Hamilton* [1983] 1 A.C. 191 at 230, Lord Diplock was "unable to fathom" why in 1974 "a Labour Government … reverted" to the narrow formula of contracts of employment. The explanation was that it was a minority government whose proposals to include all contracts failed to pass through Parliament (see Wedderburn (1974) 37 M.L.R. 539 at 543); but by 1976 it had a sufficient majority to enact the wider immunity (England and Rees (1976) 39 M.L.R. 698 at 703).

710 per Lord Scarman in *NWL v Woods* [1979] 1 W.L.R. 1294 at 1312. Compare Lord Diplock and Lord Scarman on the history of the immunities also in *Express Newspapers Ltd v McShane* [1980] A.C. 672 at 686–688 and 693–694; Wedderburn (1980) 9 I.L.J. 65; Simpson (1980) 43 M.L.R. 327 at 334–336.

711 Representing the policy of the Acts of 1980 to 2016. On the main themes, see Kidner (1984) 13 I.L.J. 193; Lewis and Simpson (1982) 11 I.L.J. 227; Deakin (1990) 19 I.L.J. 1; Simpson (1991) 54 M.L.R. 418; Carty (1991) 20 I.L.J. 1; Wedderburn (1989) 18 I.L.J. 1; Ewing (1986) 15 I.L.J. 1; Wedderburn, "Laws About Strikes: A European Standard?" in McCarthy, *Legal Interventions in Industrial Relations: Gains and Losses* (1992), Ch.4; Ewing (1993) 22 I.L.J. 165; Morris (1991) 20 I.L.J. 89 and (1993) 22 I.L.J. 194. On ballots, see para.23-162 onwards.

712 On the requirements imposed on trade unions for ballots and notices to employers, see para.23-162.

in 1969,[713] but which has not occurred.[714] The clarification of the scope and essential requirements of the tort of inducing breach of contract by the House of Lords in *OBG Ltd v Allan* has underlined the point that the references to "interference" with the performance of a contract in s.219(1) of the Trade Union and Labour Relations (Consolidation) Act 1992 afford protection against a form of liability that does not currently exist at least as a form of the *Lumley v Gye* tort.[715]

23-138 **Meaning of this immunity** Some judges in decisions on the Acts of 1906 and 1974, notably Lord Pearce, expressed the view that the words "shall not be actionable in tort" meant that the act was not actionable by the employer whose workers were parties to the trade dispute, but that third parties might still use the inducement of breach of contract as unlawful means.[716] Some support for this interpretation was legitimately drawn from the analysis that such trade dispute protections did not alter the character of the acts done which were "in their nature" unlawful.[717] But the House of Lords subsequently declared this view to be "wrong".[718] Once given this protection from being actionable, "the act of inducing a breach of contract is a lawful act which is not actionable at the suit of anyone".[719] The legislature must be taken to have caused the act to become one which was not in its nature unlawful. This point remains of relevance in view of the importance of "unlawful means" in the modern law.

23-139 **Bare interference** It is of importance to note also that protection from liability was once given to acts done in contemplation or furtherance of a trade dispute on the ground only of a bare "interference with the trade, business or employment of another person". This was first enacted in 1906 and then carried over "for the avoidance of doubt" into the Act of 1974,[720] but it would not have been effective against most modern forms of *unlawful* interference, even if it had not been repealed, as it was in 1982.[721] It was inserted by Parliament at a time when there was doubt about the liability for bare threats or coercion (without unlawful means), often represented

---

713 *Torquay Hotel Co Ltd v Cousins* [1969] 2 Ch. 106 at 137–138.

714 See para.23-20; as Lord Devlin pointed out in *Rookes v Barnard* [1964] A.C. 1129 at 1216, such legislation cannot begin conditionally ("If it be held that interference is unlawful"); it has to assume the possibility of liability and risk being otiose if the common law is not in the end judicially extended.

715 [2007] UKHL 21; [2008] 1 A.C. 1. Such interference may amount to the tort of causing loss by unlawful means as defined by the House of Lords in that case. See para.23-78.

716 *Stratford & Son Ltd v Lindley* [1965] A.C. 269 at 336, per Lord Pearce. cf. *Morgan v Fry* [1968] 1 Q.B. 521; [1968] 2 Q.B. 710 at 728, per Lord Denning MR; *Torquay Hotel Co Ltd v Cousins* [1969] 2 Ch. 106 at 119, per Stamp J; at 139, per Lord Denning MR; and at 147, per Winn LJ All these cases involved primarily s.3 of the Trade Disputes Act 1906.

717 See the analysis of the 1906 Act by Lord Devlin in *Rookes v Barnard* [1964] A.C. 1129 at 1204 on s.3 and 1211 on s.1.

718 *Hadmor Productions Ltd v Hamilton* [1983] 1 A.C. 191 HL at 231, per Lord Diplock, speaking for the House. See also, per Templeman J in *Camellia Tanker Ltd v ITWF* [1976] I.C.R. 274 at 288–289 (affirmed on other grounds, [1976] I.C.R. 274 CA).

719 per Salmon LJ in *Stratford & Son Ltd v Lindley* [1965] A.C. 269 at 303. See the relevance to unlawful means: para.23-157 onwards.

720 Trade Disputes Act 1906 s.3 (second limb); and s.13(2) of the Trade Union and Labour Relations Act 1974.

721 Employment Act 1982 s.19. For a detailed consideration of the developments on "interference", see the 16th edition of this work, pp.899–902.

in Lord Devlin's phrase as "*Quinn v Leathem* without the conspiracy".[722] In Lord Reid's words, it appeared to have been inserted in a form where it "would be necessary to achieve their object if the law should go one way, but unnecessary if it went the other way".[723] The House of Lords decided that the statutory protection in 1906 of "interference" (which did not specify that unlawful forms of interference, such as violence, slander or deceit, were to be protected),[724] now that it was clear liability did not arise for bare threats or coercion, was "otiose but harmless" or "pointless".[725] It is of importance that these propositions formed part of the ratio of the *Rookes v Barnard* decision.[726] Two other views on the "interference" protection, however, had been advanced. Lord Evershed suggested it might apply not to a given liability but to a case where the damage suffered in a trade dispute related only to trade, business or employment.[727] Despite receiving some uncertain support,[728] this remains a minority opinion in the English courts. Secondly, Lord Diplock was of the view that statutory protection against liability for interference would have been given only where the means used were unlawful, for only then would the defendant need protection.[729] This, however, was very wide (even embracing violence) and was directly contrary to the reasoning of the majority of the House of Lords in *Rookes v Barnard*.[730] Neither Parliament nor the courts have

---

722 *Rookes v Barnard* [1964] A.C. 1129 at 1216.

723 *Rookes v Barnard* [1964] A.C. 1129 at 1177, i.e. necessary if the judges' common law was developed in the direction of making "*Quinn v Leathem* without the conspiracy" into a tort. See Lord Devlin's idiosyncratic doubt on that point, at pp.1215–1218.

724 *Rookes v Barnard* [1964] A.C. 1129, per Lord Reid at 1173; per Lord Devlin at 1214-1218; per Lord Hodson at 1202–1203 (no protection if unlawful "threats or violence"); and, per Lord Evershed at 1190–1196.

725 *Rookes v Barnard* [1964] A.C. 1129, per Lord Devlin at 1216; per Lord Reid at 1172–1178; per Lord Pearce at 1236; Lord Evershed said this interpretation made the enactment "nugatory", at 1192; see, per Lord Loreburn in *Conway v Wade* [1909] A.C. 506 at 511–512. See also, per Evershed MR in *DC Thomson & Co v Deakin* [1952] Ch. 646 at 689; per Lord Milligan in *Square Grip Reinforcement Ltd v Macdonald*, 1968 S.L.T. 65 at 74; *Mahon v Dunne* (1964) 99 I.L.T.R. 45.

726 [1964] A.C. 1129 HL at 1172–1177, 1192, 1203, 1216, 1218 and 1236; the defendants claimed that "interference with employment or business" was all they had done; but protection under the 1906 Act (s.3, limb (2)) was rejected because their interference took the form of tortious intimidation by an "unlawful" threat: see para.23-62 onwards. Stress was laid by all Law Lords on the phrase "on the ground only" in the statute.

727 [1964] A.C. 1129 HL at 1190–1196.

728 By the Court of Session in *Shell (UK) v McGillivray*, 1991 S.L.T. 667 OH; but see *Plessey Co Plc v Wilson* [1982] I.R.L.R. 198 (sit-in; Court of Session relying upon Lord Diplock's interpretation in *Hadmor Productions Ltd v Hamilton* [1983] 1 A.C. 191: "the tort of interference by the use of unlawful means committed in furtherance of a trade dispute will not be actionable … unlawful acts may attract immunity where the only consequences … are interferences with the trade or business": at 199–200).

729 *Hadmor Productions Ltd v Hamilton* [1983] 1 A.C. 191 at 229–231 (he found this to be a meaning "too plain and unambiguous to resort to legislative history": at 229). So too, in *Merkur Island Shipping Corp v Laughton* [1983] 2 A.C. 570 at 609–610, where ironically the analysis is central to Lord Diplock's understanding of the "genus" tort, see para.23-10; see also, per Dillon LJ at 586. See *Plessey Co Plc v Wilson* [1982] I.R.L.R. 198 (Ct Sess.: trespass in sit-in); *Phestos Shipping v Kurmiawan*, 1983 S.L.T. 389; Miller (1982) 11 I.L.J. 115; Brodie (1982) 11 I.L.J. 170 (on special features of Scottish law); Ewing [1981] J.L.S.S. 422. On the increased criminality of certain trespasses in England, see Criminal Justice and Public Order Act 1994, especially ss.61, 68 and 70 but note *DPP v Jones* [1999] 2 A.C. 240, HL; *DPP v Ziegler* [2019] EWHC 71 (Admin); [2020] Q.B. 253; para.23-174 onwards.

730 [1964] A.C. 1129; Lord Evershed did not formally dissent but he retained doubts as to the majority view, at 1192.

done anything to clarify these different approaches to the statutes since the repeal of s.13(2) of the 1974 Act in 1982.[731]

(c) Trade disputes and intimidation

23-140 The response of the legislature to *Rookes v Barnard*[732] was to match its new area of liability with an immunity in trade disputes.[733] Today, therefore, s.219(1) of TULRCA 1992 provides that an act done in contemplation or furtherance of a trade dispute is not actionable against a person on the ground only:

> "(b) that it consists in his threatening that a contract (whether one to which he is a party or not) will be broken or its performance interfered with, or that he will induce another person to break a contract or to interfere with its performance."[734]

Without some such protection, the burgeoning economic torts of the common law appeared to offer an open road to outflank the traditional "immunities" in trade disputes.[735] The litigation since 1976, in which claims based upon "intimidation" have been made, has not revealed substantial problems concerning the interpretation of the terms of s.219(1)(b) in its predecessor sections in the 1974 and 1976 Acts, other than those already discussed above.[736] So, where union officials in furtherance of a trade dispute threatened to induce union members employed by Thames TV to break their employment contracts, their threats were protected and their action (not being actionable) could not be relied upon as unlawful means by the claimants, a company whose contracts for sale of the "blacked" programmes to the network were in consequence not performed.[737]

23-141 **Economic duress?** The trade dispute immunities protect acts on the ground only that they are actionable in tort. But a claimant may choose to rely upon a threat to

---

[731] As some had hoped: Ewing (1982) 11 I.L.J. 209 (affirming that the repeal gave the House of Lords "the opportunity to sort out the mess", at 214). This issue is relevant also to problems related to "unlawful means" and the repeal of s.13(3) of the Trade Union and Labour Relations Act 1974 by s.17(8) of the Employment Act 1980; *Barretts & Baird (Wholesale) Ltd v IPCS* [1987] I.R.L.R. 3 at 8–10, per Henry J; see para.23-157 onwards.

[732] [1964] A.C. 1129. In the area of trade disputes, this decision was seen, in the words of the most eminent labour lawyer, as "a frontal attack upon the right to strike"; Kahn-Freund, *Federation News (GFTU)* (1964), Vol.14, p.30. cf. *Trade Union Immunities*, Cmnd.8128 (1981), p.18, para.68; Wedderburn, *The Worker and the Law*, 3rd edn (1986), pp.29–47 and 617–623. A strike or other industrial action normally involves a breach of employment contracts and frequently aims at interference with other contracts. A notice to take such action will, therefore, very often amount to intimidation at common law, as a threat to break contracts, para.23-62.

[733] The initial statutory response provided a trade dispute immunity only for threats to break contracts of employment: Trade Disputes Act 1965; the expansion to cover all contracts emerged in 1976, parallel to the history of the main immunity; para.23-140.

[734] On threats that a contract to which another person is a party will be broken, see para.23-154; unless the threatener means to induce a breach by that person, such a statement seems more likely to be a "warning" that that person will break it; see para.23-65.

[735] After *Rookes v Barnard* [1964] A.C. 1129; see especially *Stratford v Lindley* [1965] A.C. 269 CA and HL; *Morgan v Fry* [1968] 2 Q.B. 710 CA; *Torquay Hotel Co Ltd v Cousins* [1969] 2 Ch. 106 CA; *Cory Lighterage Ltd v TGWU* [1973] I.C.R. 339 CA; *Camellia Tanker Ltd v ITWF* [1976] I.C.R. 274 at 285 and 299–300; see also *Merkur Island Shipping Corp v Laughton* [1983] 2 A.C. 570 HL.

[736] cf. *Associated Newspapers Group Ltd v Wade* [1979] I.C.R. 664 CA.

[737] *Hadmor Productions Ltd v Hamilton* [1983] 1 A.C. 191 HL; Simpson (1982) 45 M.L.R. 447.

break, or to induce breaches of, contracts made in furtherance of a trade dispute as "economic duress" for the purpose of seeking restitutionary remedies.[738] The legislation provides no immunity against that liability. In *Universe Tankships*,[739] a majority of the Law Lords was prepared to accept the argument that where what is now s.219(1)(a) or (b) protected the inducement or the threat expressed as a tort, no such liability for coterminous economic duress would be permitted; but that view was based upon concessions by the claimant in that case. But now that the limitation of actionable duress to duress to the person has been "discarded",[740] and the scope of trade dispute protections reduced, this doctrine extends the range of remedies available to employers, especially in disputes with a transnational element, as where industrial action by way of blockade was taken against a ship in a foreign port lawfully under the local law, to enforce proper standards for the crew, but by reason of that "duress" the employer was able to recover from the union in England money paid by him under an agreement to end the blockade, even if no action in tort were available, for there are no statutory protections in England for economic duress.[741] It may be noted that greater reluctance has marked the introduction of duress to relieve an employee from oppressive contractual employment obligations.[742]

(d) Specific limitations on the protection against liability

Secondary action As s.219(4) makes clear, the protections afforded by s.219(1) and (2) of TULRCA 1992 are displaced by ss.222–225, which relate to two issues, the first of which is secondary action. Under s.224 of TULRCA 1992 an act is **23-142**

---

[738] See paras 23-73 and 23-75, on the relevance of this doctrine to the economic torts.

[739] *Universe Tankships of Monrovia Inc v ITWF* [1983] 1 A.C. 366 HL; see the positive doubt of Lord Brandon, at 407; and as to the reliability of the decision, see Wedderburn (1982) 45 M.L.R. 556; Sterling (1982) 11 I.L.J. 156. Lord Scarman suggested in *Universe Tankships*, at 400, that economic duress is now a tort; contra Lord Diplock at 385, expressing the majority view: quaere therefore whether the will of the corporate shipowner in Universe Tankships above was (as was conceded) overborne without proof of an approach to a senior director as its alter ego: *Mutual Finance Co v Wetton & Sons* [1937] 2 K.B. 389; *DC Thomson & Co Ltd v Deakin* [1952] Ch. 646 at 681–682; *El Ajou v Dollar Land Holdings Plc* [1994] 2 All E.R. 685 CA; see para.23-39.

[740] *Dimskal Shipping Co SA v ITWF* [1992] 2 A.C. 152 at 165, per Lord Goff.

[741] *Dimskal Shipping Co SA v ITWF* [1992] 2 A.C. 152 HL at 165 (Lord Templeman vigorously dissenting: "The contents of a bottle cannot be changed by altering the label", at 162). It appears to have been conceded that the blockade was duress. The formal application of the principles of restitution to such a case had earlier been given support in Goff and Jones, *Law of Restitution*, 5th edn (Jones, 1998), pp.321–332 (see now 9th edn, sub nom *Goff and Jones: The Law of Unjust Enrichment* (2016), Ch.10); compare on this extension, Wedderburn, *The Worker and the Law*, 3rd edn (1986), pp.648–654; *Williams v Roffey Bros & Nicholls* [1991] 1 Q.B. 1 CA; *Atlas Express Ltd v Kafco Ltd* [1989] 1 Q.B. 833. The English law may be contrasted with the position in Canada where in *Manalaysay v The "Oriental Victory"* [1978] 1 F.C. 440 at 446–447 it was said by Walsh J:

> "I believe that it must be said that accepted principles for setting aside contracts made under duress cannot be strictly applied in connection with agreements made by an employer with a union. All such contracts are entered into under considerable pressure often accompanied by strikes, threats of strikes or boycotts, or as a result of lockouts by the employer, and when a contract is signed after such industrial conflicts as a result of protracted negotiations it should not be set aside on grounds that it was entered into by one party or the other as the result of duress."

[742] *Hennessy v Craigmyle & Co Ltd* [1986] I.C.R. 461 CA (employee had alternative of social security if he lost his job; economic duress arises only when the "will is overborne"); compare the economic position of the shipowners in *Universe Tankships and Dimskal; and Stott v Merit Investment Corp* (1988) 48 D.L.R. (4th) 288 (Ont. CA); cf. *Credit Lyonnais Bank Nederland v Burch* [1997] 1 All E.R. 144 CA (undue influence and employment relationships); contrast Brodie (1996) 25 I.L.J. 121.

deprived of the protection of s.219 if one of the facts relied on for establishing liability is that there has been secondary action (other than lawful picketing).[743] Secondary action is defined as occurring "in relation to a trade dispute" only when:

(i) a person (a) induces another to break a contract of employment, or interferes or induces another to interfere with its performance; or (b) threatens either that he will do any of those acts or that a contract of employment under which he or another person is employed will be interfered with or broken; and

(ii) the employer under the contract of employment is not a party to the trade dispute.[744]

Industrial action is therefore secondary action where "the means of interference with the performance of a [commercial] contract is to procure employees of an employer who is not a party to a trade dispute to break their contracts of employment with that employer".[745] That is the target of the section. Moreover, "contract of employment" is here defined as including contracts for services[746] widening the scope of the limitation beyond contracts of "employees" *stricto sensu*.[747] The section operates by displacing the protection that might otherwise be provided by s.219; consequently, a defendant will only be liable to a party that suffers loss as a result of secondary action if the defendant has committed a tort in relation to that party, and this will require proof of the state of mind required to constitute whatever tort is alleged.[748]

23-143 It is less clear, however, what s.224(1) means by "in relation to a trade dispute". This is a critical phrase, because secondary action arises only if the employer is not a party to "the trade dispute".[749] If, for example, an official organises sympathetic strike action to support other union members in dispute with an employer party to

---

743 Lawful picketing is defined in s.224(3) as picketing that is declared lawful by s.220. Section 220A, inserted by the Trade Union Act 2016, adds to the conditions that must be fulfilled before picketing can be lawful.

744 s.224(2). On the difficult question of who is a "party" to a trade dispute, see paras 23-186 to 23-187. Until 1990, where the employer was a member of an employers' association party to a trade dispute, he was for the purposes of secondary action by statute regarded as a party to it, if he was "represented in the dispute by the association but not otherwise": Employment Act 1980 s.17(7); but this provision was repealed in 1990 and makes no appearance in TULRCA 1992 s.224 (compare *Dimbleby & Sons Ltd v NUJ* [1984] 1 W.L.R. 427 HL: groups of companies; subsidiaries separate parties to disputes). Even so, an employers' association may on the facts act for and on behalf of its members, just as a trade union normally does for its members: see, per Millett J in *Associated British Ports v TGWU* [1989] I.R.L.R. 291 at 300 (upheld on other grounds, [1989] 1 W.L.R. 939 HL).

745 per Lord Diplock in *Merkur Island Shipping Corp v Laughton* [1983] 2 A.C. 570 at 610: the "obvious [claimant]" is the employer party to the dispute, but either employer may sue, at 611.

746 s.224(6). Like s.235 (which defines a "contract of employment" for the part of the Act governing ballots) this subsection includes all contracts for services, apparently even of professional services which are normally excluded from the definition even of "worker": see s.296(1)(b). But this works to the disadvantage of workers taking action under s.224, since it enlarges the ambit of the contracts of "employment" within the section: s.224(1). In s.224(4), "worker" is defined in terms of s.244, the definition in the context of a trade dispute, see para.23-186.

747 cf. *Thomas v NUM (South Wales Area)* [1986] Ch. 20 at 79, per Scott J; *Hadmor Productions Ltd v Hamilton* [1983] 1 A.C. 191 HL; *Shipping Co Uniform Inc v ITF* [1985] I.C.R. 245 at 251 (self-employed ships' pilots; but see now s.4 of the Pilotage Act 1987).

748 See para.23-16 on inducing breach of contract (which also requires proof of knowledge of the contract), para.23-62 on intimidation, and para.23-78 on causing loss by unlawful means.

749 Referred to below as the "secondary employer".

a trade dispute with his union,[750] but the sympathetic strike has the effect of assisting the employees of a third employer who are engaged upon a separate trade dispute, does the sympathetic strike also become "secondary action" in relation to the other dispute? The Act deliberately—and understandably[751]—does not use the time-honoured golden formula "in contemplation or furtherance of a trade dispute". At this stage, therefore, the state of mind of the defendant in regard to the trade dispute does not appear to be central to the "relation" of his action to a trade dispute. But, it is suggested, before the third employer can bring an action for the torts in question the general principles of these torts require that he must be able to show that the defendant intended to cause him damage.

This approach is supported by definitions introduced in 1990 into what is now s.224. First, for the purposes of this section, an employer is not to be treated as party to a dispute between another employer and his workers.[752] Secondly, where more than one employer is in dispute with his workers the dispute between each employer and his workers "shall be treated as a separate dispute".[753] Thirdly, action undertaken in contemplation or furtherance of a trade dispute, which is "primary action" in relation to that dispute, may not be relied on as secondary action in relation to another dispute.[754] What then is "primary action"? The statute replies that it is "such action as is mentioned in [s.224(2)] where the employer under the contract of employment is the employer party to the dispute".[755] But the removal of the immunity does not take effect under s.224(1) unless the claimant's claim relates to liability (normally involving a commercial contract)[756] which is such that "one of the facts relied upon for the purpose of establishing liability" is the secondary action.[757] The statute is here describing a situation which involves an alleged liability (normally an indirect interference with performance of a contract which is not an employment contract, usually now dubbed a "commercial" contract), by unlawful means which include actual or threatened inducement of breach of an employment contract. So, where a union induced tug workers, in breach of their contracts, to refuse to service a ship, in pursuit of a boycott of flag of convenience vessels whose crews enjoyed poor conditions of employment, in order to keep it in port and unavailable for its charter, the shipowners were the party to the trade dispute enabled to sue by reason of the secondary action, the tug workers being employed 23-144

---

[750] Referred to below as the "primary employer". See now the similar question as to which action a ballot on industrial action "relates" where different groups of workers take action: s.233(3)(a) of TULRCA 1992; *Newham LBC v NALGO* [1993] I.C.R. 189 CA at 197. On ballots, see para.23-162 onwards.

[751] Understandably because the purpose of the Act is to limit the formula in the light of the meaning of "furtherance" (i.e. that it requires only a subjective and honest belief), confirmed in *Express Newspapers Ltd v McShane* [1980] A.C. 672 HL; see para.23-196.

[752] See s.224(4). This has the effect, of course, of finally blocking any tactics the workers might seek to adopt that could make an outside employer into a party.

[753] See s.224(4) In a group of companies this confirms the approach of treating each dispute with a subsidiary company as a separate dispute: see *Dimbleby & Sons Ltd v NUJ* [1983] 2 A.C. 427 HL.

[754] See s.224(5).

[755] s.224(5), semble this means "trade dispute".

[756] The torts in issue, from which the protection of s.219(1) (2) is removed (by ss.219(4) and 224), relate not only to actual or threatened breach or procurement of breach of contract (s.219(1)) but also to conspiracy to injure (s.219(2)); see Employment Act 1990 s.4, which removed the requirement that the liability must relate to a commercial contract (in Employment Act 1980 s.17(1)).

[757] See s.224(1). Threats are not separately dealt with below; and, unless specified, inducement of breach of contract includes, in what follows, threats to break, to induce breach, or to interfere with performance.

by the tug owners.[758] This is the typical case, a form of indirect interference with the commercial contracts by unlawful means which after the House of Lords' decision in *OBG Ltd v Allan* must be an instance of the causing loss by unlawful means tort.[759] It is assumed in all this by s.224 that the "employer" who is the primary party to the dispute can easily be identified; but where statute intervenes to allocate various powers or functions to diverse bodies as against the employees, the application of the section becomes problematical.[760]

23-145 The wording of s.224 of TULRCA 1992 contains a further difficulty. Secondary action requires an actual or threatened inducement to break, or to interfere with performance of, a contract of employment, or an interference with its performance, or a threat to break it. As for "interference", Lord Diplock equated that in *Merkur Island* (as far as the employment contracts were concerned) to actionable interference by inducing breach.[761] Consequently, if it be the case that a breach of a contract can itself constitute unlawful means for the purpose of the causing loss by unlawful means tort,[762] there is a gap; such a breach per se would not appear to be sufficient to constitute secondary action (although by reason of the words "threatens that a contract of employment ... will be broken", the section does appear to include a threat to break a contract).[763]

23-146 **Action to extend negotiation or union membership** The Employment Act 1982 introduced in ss.12 and 13 two new species of commercial torts (now found in TULRCA 1992 ss.145 and 187).[764] Each is defined by reference to a particular prohibited "ground" of action in the course of commercial practices. In the first, s.145 provides that where A determines not to enter into a contract with B, or fails to put him on a list of suppliers, or excludes him from tendering or terminates a contract with him (albeit lawfully, in other respects), he commits a tort if *one* of his "grounds" is that members (or non-members) of trade unions, or of a particular trade

---

758 *Merkur Island Shipping Corp v Laughton* [1983] 2 A.C. 570 HL; see too *Marina Shipping Ltd v Laughton* [1982] Q.B. 1127 CA; *Shipping Co Uniform Inc v ITF* [1985] I.C.R. 245 at 251 and 256, per Staughton J.

759 See para.23-78; cf. the previous law where this was seen as a form of the procuring breach of contract tort, per Jenkins LJ in *DC Thomson & Co Ltd v Deakin* [1952] Ch. 646 at 697; as adopted in *Merkur Island Shipping Corp v Laughton* [1983] 2 A.C. 570 at 607–610.

760 See Freedland (1989) 18 I.L.J. 231, 232 (teachers' employers under the Education (Modification of Enactments Relating to Employment) Order 1989 (SI 1989/901)). See now the Education (Modification of Enactments Relating to Employment) (England) Order 2003 (SI 2003/1964) art.5; cf. *Wandsworth LBC v NASUWT* [1994] I.C.R. 81 CA.

761 See [1983] 2 A.C. 570 unequivocally at 607 and 608 ("substituting 'interference with performance' for 'breach' except in relation to the breaking by the employees of their own contracts of employment") at 609 and 610 ("*break* their contracts of employment" [emphasis added]). So, too, per Staughton J in *Shipping Co Uniform Inc v ITF* [1985] I.C.R. 245 at 251–255; cf. *Marina Shipping Ltd v Laughton* [1982] I.C.R. 215 at 225, per Brightman LJ, dismissing the "interference" words as merely "refinements" of inducing another person "to break a contract of employment".

762 See paras 23-71, 23-87 and 23-115.

763 See *Barretts & Baird (Wholesale) Ltd v IPCS* [1987] I.R.L.R. 3 at 8–10, per Henry J; considering *Rookes v Barnard* [1964] A.C. 1129 HL. A lightning strike by employees might involve mere breach of contracts of employment, without inducement or threat by an outside party; sed quaere whether a threat would be implied, para.23-64. And the strikers may induce one another. A conspiracy to break such contracts simpliciter may retain protection under TULRCA 1992 s.219(2), since the subsection protects save where the combination does an act "actionable in tort"; sed quaere: see para.23-155; *Rookes v Barnard* [1964] A.C. 1129 at 1210, per Lord Devlin.

764 See para.23-97; ss.144 and 186 TULRCA 1992 also made void similar terms in contracts to supply goods or services. The provisions replaced the repealed s.18 of the Employment Act 1980, which prohibited certain acts to compel union membership after the *Leggatt Report* (1980), Cmnd.7706.

union, should do the work involved.[765] The tort is actionable at the suit not only of such suppliers and other commercial parties, but also "any other person who may be adversely affected" by a contravention of the section.[766] Section 222(3) of the 1992 Act proceeds to remove the trade dispute immunity in s.219 from a person who induces, or attempts to induce, another "to contravene section 145", i.e. to engage in any of these tortious practices.[767] To some extent the purpose of these sections in relation to industrial relations law is also accomplished more generally by s.222(1) of TULRCA 1992.[768]

Section 187(1) of TULRCA 1992 creates a second statutory tort. It is committed where a person engages in any of the commercial dealings falling within the section on the ground, this time, of "union exclusion": that is to say, where *any one* of his reasons for this action is that the supplier does not, or is not likely to, recognise, negotiate or consult with a trade union.[769] All forms of negotiation and consultation appear to be included.[770] This tort is actionable at the suit of the person against whom the action is aimed and, as before, also "any other person who may be adversely affected".[771] Once again, the protections of s.219 are removed (by s.225(1)(b)) from a person who attempts to induce another to contravene this section.[772] Section 225(2) then goes further. It applies where an act interferes, or can reasonably be expected to interfere, with the supply of goods or services (whether under a contract or not) and liability is based upon inducing a breach of an employment contract (or on interference, or an inducement to interfere, with it, or a threat **23-147**

765 TULRCA 1992 s.145(1)–(4); a term in a contract for supply of goods or services providing for such a practice is void: s.144. For the background, see Evans and Lewis (1988) 17 I.L.J. 88.

766 TULRCA 1992 s.145(5) which applies all "defences and other incidents" applying to actions for breach of statutory duty. On which see Ch.8.

767 Quaere whether this removal of immunity was needed if the person inducing another to commit the statutory tort were liable as a joint tortfeasor or conspirator who would enjoy no immunity in furtherance of the trade dispute for that tort. The phrase "attempted inducement" makes doubly certain that the trade dispute immunity will be excluded. But the removal of immunity is necessary only if joint liability for the statutory tort is unavailable; cf. *Credit Lyonnais Bank Nederland v Export Credits Guarantee Dept* [2000] 1 A.C. 486 HL.

768 As will be seen, ss.222(1) and 225 sweep away immunity from action to support closed shop and union preference practices; para.23-147. Nevertheless, ss.145 and 187 still cover wider purposes, e.g. control of local authorities' preferences for a unionised workforce in their suppliers or contractors (Lewis and Simpson (1982) 11 I.L.J. 228 at 232).

769 "Recognise" means recognise to any extent for the purposes of collective bargaining: s.178(3) of TULRCA 1992. Commercial pressure to ensure that any employer should not recognise a union remains unaffected. Quaere whether liability arises from acts causing breach of the "method by which [the parties] are to conduct collective bargaining" specified by the Central Arbitration Committee under para.31 of Sch.A1 to TULRCA 1992. See the Trade Union Recognition (Method of Collective Bargaining) Order 2000 (SI 2000/1300).

770 Including even cases where the supplier is under a legal duty to consult with, e.g. safety representatives (Health and Safety at Work Act 1974 s.2 and Health and Safety (Consultation with Employees) Regulations 1996 (SI 1996/1513)) or workers' representatives on collective dismissals (TULRCA 1992 s.188 as amended by SI 1995/2587 and SI 1999/1925) or transfers of undertakings (Transfer of Undertakings (Protection of Employment) Regulations 2006 (SI 2006/246) reg.13).

771 s.187(3) of TULRCA 1992. This must presumably include a worker not a member of a union (or of a particular union), who suffers any adverse consequences from the pressure to consult with a union (or a different union).

772 An inducement to incorporate in a contract for supply of goods or services a term for the recognition of, or negotiation or consultation with a trade union—which term would be void: s.186—is also deprived of the protection of s.219: see below, s.225(1)(a). TURERA 1993 Sch.7 para.23, added to the list of prohibited acts by way of refusing to deal on the ground of "union exclusion" (i.e. exclusion from a tender list, refusal to receive tenders, refusal to enter into a contract) the act of terminating a contract with the supplier (now s.187(2)(c)).

that it will be broken); then protection is removed by s.225(2) if *one* of the reasons for the act is the fact or belief that the supplier (being a person other than the employer under the employment contract) does not, or "might not", recognise, negotiate or consult with a trade union.[773] The removal of immunity is thus wider than the tort in respect of a breach of s.187.

23-148 None of these sections justified the description that they made the closed shop "unlawful"[774]; but they made it virtually impossible to use commercial or industrial pressure to operate such an arrangement lawfully. It was—and remains—the case that a "union membership agreement or arrangement" is per se lawful.[775] But s.222(1) and (2), first introduced in 1988, added a new dimension. The trade dispute immunity of s.219 of TULRCA 1992 is now disapplied, where *one* of the reasons for the defendant's act is the fact or belief that an employer employs, has employed, or "might employ", a person who is not a member of any union, a particular union, one of a number of unions or a particular branch or section of a union.[776] So, too, the immunity is lost if the fact or belief supporting the act is that an employer is failing "or might fail" to discriminate against any such worker.[777] It may be noted that if a union calls or threatens industrial action to prevent a non-member being engaged by an employer, it may be joined as a respondent in the non-member's claim for compensation before an employment tribunal; but no liability in tort arises.[778] Lastly, TULRCA 1992 ss.144 and 186, make any term in a contract for the supply of goods or services "void" in so far as it either requires work to be done by persons who are (or are not) members of trade unions or a particular union, or requires a party to recognise, negotiate or consult with a trade union (whether or not specified in the contract). Sections 222(3)(a) and 225(1)(a) proceed to withdraw the protection of s.219 from an act whereby a person induces, or attempts to induce, another to insert such a term in a contract.

---

[773] As first introduced in s.14(3) of the Employment Act 1982, the test was: "does not or is not likely to" (being changed to "might not" in para.4 of Sch.3 to the Employment Act 1988). This example illustrates the point that it is often necessary to look at the antecedent statutes which frequently made such changes step by step, gradually lessening the range of the trade dispute protection, between 1980 and 1993. See the Table of Derivations TULRCA 1992, p.169.

[774] *Messenger Newspapers Group Ltd v NGA* [1984] I.R.L.R. 397 at 399, per Caulfield J.

[775] The provisions enabling an employer to enforce a closed shop by way of dismissal were repealed finally by the Employment Act 1988 s.11 and Sch.4.

[776] TULRCA 1992 s.222(1)(5).

[777] TULRCA 1992 s.222(1)(b). Discrimination arises if the employer engages in conduct, in relation to persons employed by him, or who apply or are considered for employment, or in relation to provision of employment generally, which is different in some or all cases according to whether persons are not members of a union (or a particular union etc), and that conduct is more favourable to those who are members: s.222(2). In *Birmingham CC v Unite the Union* [2019] EWHC 478 (QB); [2019] I.R.L.R. 423, Freedman J held that the union did not lose its immunity under s.222(1)(b) where it was seeking parity for its members, rather than advantageous treatment. Acts done in furtherance of a trade dispute to induce the employer to hire or favour non-union workers appear to retain protection; but see the restrictions in s.137 (hiring), ss.145A and 145B (inducements), s.146 (detriment) and s.152 (dismissal). Ss.145A and 145B were inserted by the ERA 2004 and s.146 was amended by the ERA 1999 and ERA 2004 to counter the effects of *Associated British Ports v Palmer and Associated Newspapers Ltd v Wilson* [1995] 2 A.C. 454 HL, and to remedy the failure of the law to comply with art.11 of the ECHR identified by the European Court of Human Rights in *Wilson v United Kingdom* [2002] I.R.L.R. 568. See Wedderburn (2000) 29 I.L.J. 1, 18-20; Ewing (2003) 32 I.L.J. 1, 5–15.

[778] See TULRCA 1992 ss.137, 142 and 143(4) ("no other legal liability arises", save liability to pay such compensation). This would appear to exclude the remedy of injunction in the High Court, even on the reasoning in *Associated British Ports v TGWU* [1989] 1 W.L.R. 939 CA (reversed on other grounds, [1989] 1 W.L.R. 939 HL).

The structure of these sections of TULRCA 1992 suggests that the liability of a trade union which attempts to induce breaches of the code of commercial dealing laid down, whether it be in order to have a void clause incorporated in a contract or to have the employers unlawfully exclude suppliers who are, or may be, non-union enterprises, or who refuse to consult with trade unions, is to be judged by the normal common law principles about liability for the economic torts. This may explain the extent to which the trade dispute immunities are excluded by s.222(3) and, especially, s.225(2) which applies to interference with any supply of goods or services where *one* of the reasons is a belief that the employer might not consult. It would not necessarily follow that a union which attempted to induce an employer not to contract with a supplier who might refrain from consulting a trade union in respect of his employees would itself become a joint tortfeasor, or conspirator, with the guilty employer, so that the statutory tort (under s.145 or s.187) could be deployed against it.[779] Those sections expressly refrain from laying any duty upon third parties.[780] If the union were jointly liable for the statutory torts, removal of the immunities in trade disputes by ss.222 and 225 would be unnecessary. The point is most likely to arise in relation to the range of claimants. In extending that range to any person "adversely affected"[781] the new statutory code on commercial dealing goes wider than the common law, to such an extent that it would be wrong to impose that range of liability upon persons not expressly subjected to the statutory tort itself.[782] **23-149**

(e) Dismissals and immunities

When the law on unfair dismissal was first enacted in 1971 it was expressly provided that the dismissal of an employee who was taking part in a strike or irregular action short of a strike was not unfair unless other employees who took part were not dismissed and the reason for the dismissal of the employee was his exercising his statutory right to belong to or take part in the activities of a trade union.[783] After the re-enactment of the law on unfair dismissal in 1974, this was amended in 1975 to a general exclusion from the right to complain of unfair dismissal of employees who at the time of their dismissal were taking part in a strike or other industrial action except where there was "victimisation" in the sense that some workers who took part in the action were dismissed while others who took part were not. In "victimisation" situations the dismissed workers could make unfair dismissal **23-150**

[779] By analogy with Silverthorne in *Rookes v Barnard* [1964] A.C. 1129 HL; see para.23-155, and the "common design" cases, *CBS Songs Ltd v Amstrad Consumer Electronics Plc* [1988] A.C. 1013 HL. cf. per Lord Woolf MR *Credit Lyonnais Bank Nederland v Export Credits Guarantee Dept* [2000] 1 A.C. 486; [1999] 2 W.L.R. 540 HL at 550–551.

[780] Compare the principles for determining whether a breach of statutory duty gives rise to a cause of action approved in *Lonrho Ltd v Shell Petroleum (No.2)* [1982] A.C. 173 HL; see para.23-89. Indirect inducement to break the obligations in ss.145 and 187 of TULRCA 1992 would require extraneous unlawful means to be potentially actionable as an instance of the tort of causing loss by unlawful means: see para.23-78 onwards; *Barretts & Baird (Wholesale) Ltd v IPCS* [1987] I.R.L.R. 3 at 10.

[781] See ss.145(5) and 187(3) of TULRCA 1992.

[782] On the range of claimants at common law see *DC Thomson & Co Ltd v Deakin* [1952] Ch. 646 CA, especially, per Jenkins LJ at 696-698; *Van Camp Chocolates Ltd v Aulsebrooks Ltd* [1984] 1 N.Z.L.R. 354 (on the need to find causative intention: at 359–361); and see *Thomas v NUM (South Wales Area)* [1986] Ch. 20 at 54 (claimants restricted to breach of duty by pickets at their own pit); *Timeplan Education Group v NUT* [1997] I.R.L.R. 457 CA; but compare *Falconer v ASLEF* [1986] I.R.L.R. 331 (County Court).

[783] See Industrial Relations Act 1971 s.26.

claims.[784] In 1982 the "victimisation exception" was narrowed to situations where there were employees at the same "establishment" as the dismissed employee who were still taking part in the industrial action at the time of his dismissal who were not dismissed or, if other dismissed employees were offered re-engagement within three months of the dismissal but no such offer of re-engagement was made to the claimant employee.[785] The "victimisation" provision, now consolidated as s.238 of TULRCA, goes to employment tribunals' jurisdiction, so that where it applies to permit claims to be made, tribunals have to decide whether the dismissal was fair or unfair in accordance with the normal criteria laid down in the law on unfair dismissal.[786] Section 238 of TULRCA does not apply however to dismissals which fall within s.237, originally enacted as s.9 of the Employment Act 1990 or s.238A which was inserted by the Employment Relations Act 1999 and amended by the Employment Relations Act 2004.[787] Section 237 removes the right to complain of unfair dismissal from employees who were taking part in "unofficial action" at the time of their dismissal. Section 238A by contrast makes an explicit link between the law on unfair dismissal and the immunities against liability for the economic torts by introducing the concept of "protected" industrial action. Where an employee is induced to commit acts—going on strike or taking other industrial action—by an act which is not actionable by virtue of the immunities in s.219 and is dismissed for that reason, s.238A makes the dismissal automatically unfair in specified circumstances. What may be identified as the original provision in the law on unfair dismissal and industrial action, now in s.238, has thus become in effect a residual provision applicable only where neither s.237 (unofficial action) nor s.238A (protected action) applies.[788]

23-151 Under s.238A, two conditions have to be satisfied for a dismissal to be automatically unfair. The reason or principal reason for the dismissal must be that the employee had taken "protected industrial action" and the dismissal must take place within the "protected period".[789] Industrial action is "protected" where its inducement still enjoys the basic protection of s.219 of TULRCA 1992 (i.e. against liability for inducing breach of contract etc).[790] In the case of action organised by a trade union, or for which it is vicariously liable under s.20 of TULRCA 1992 this means that the action enjoys the support of a ballot within the meaning of the Act.[791] As modified by the Employment Relations Act 2004, the "protected period" is 12 weeks beginning on the first day that the employee started to take protected action, extended where necessary by the number of days during that period on which

---

784 Trade Union and Labour Relations Act 1974 Sch.1 para.7 as substituted by Employment Protection Act 1975 Sch.16 Pt III para.13, consolidated as Employment Protection (Consolidation) Act 1978 s.62.

785 Employment Protection (Consolidation) Act 1978 s.62 as amended by Employment Act 1982 s.9. *Power Packing Casemakers Ltd v Faust* [1983] Q.B. 471 CA; *Express & Star Ltd v Bunday* [1988] I.C.R. 379 CA; *Bigham v GKN Kwikform Ltd* [1992] I.C.R. 113; *Highland Fabricators v McLoughlin* [1985] I.C.R. 183; *Coates v Modern Methods* [1982] I.C.R. 763 CA; *Hindle Gears v McGinty* [1985] I.C.R. 111; *Manifold Industries v Sims* [1991] I.C.R. 504.

786 Employment Rights Act 1996 s.98. cf. s.107 on which see *Ford v Hudson* [1978] I.C.R. 482.

787 See ERA 1999 Sch.5 para.3; ERA 2004 ss.26-28.

788 See TULRCA ss.237(1), 238(2B).

789 TULRCA 1992 s.238A(2), (3) as amended.

790 TULRCA 1992 s.238A(1).

791 s.238A(1). On the requirements on ballots, see para.23-162 onwards. The employer has the burden of proving the reason or principal reason (Employment Rights Act 1996 s.98). In practice it may be difficult for the employee to prove that the employer's reason was the industrial action.

the employee was locked out by the employer.[792] A dismissal after the end of the protected period may also be unfair if the employee had stopped taking action before the end of that period.[793] Moreover, if the employee continued taking action after the end of the protected period, the dismissal may still be unfair if the employer had not taken reasonable procedural steps to resolve the dispute.[794]

By contrast under s.237 a dismissed employee "has no right to complain of unfair dismissal if at the time of the dismissal he was taking part in an unofficial strike or other unofficial action" whether or not the employer victimises him by selective dismissal.[795] Action is "unofficial" unless the employee taking part is a member of a trade union and that union has authorised the action, or where he is not a member of a union, there are among those taking part members of a union which has authorised it.[796] The provisions of s.20 of TULRCA 1992 on the vicarious liability of trade unions are applied to determine whether or not a trade union has authorised industrial action.[797] The arbitrary or even capricious consequences of these provisions are illustrated by *Balfour Kilpatrick Ltd v Acheson*[798] where workers on a construction site were dismissed when they took industrial action over working conditions. Some of the workers belonged to the AEEU whose shop steward had authorised the action within the terms of TULRCA 1992 s.20, others belonged on the TGWU, none of whose officials had been involved, and some were non-members. Since the dismissals occurred on the day before repudiation of the action by the AEEU took effect, dismissed AEEU members and non-members—but not members of the TGWU—were able to pursue their unfair dismissal claims. **23-152**

Section 237 is not without problems. There are, for example, established rights for an employee not to be disciplined or dismissed on the ground that he left the workplace, or refused to return, in circumstances of danger which he reasonably believed to be "serious and imminent".[799] If employees are dismissed in such a situation, the question arises whether the reason for the dismissal was the stoppage or the dangerous conditions of work.[800] Secondly, there may be some difficulty in knowing when unofficial industrial action less than a strike has ended (a go slow, working without enthusiasm or a "thinking strike"[801] for example) and therefore whether the employer has dismissed workers who were at the time of their dismissal **23-153**

---

792 TULRCA 1992 s.238A(3), (7A)-(7D) as amended by ERA 2004 s.26.

793 TULRCA 1992 s.238A(4).

794 In determining this issue regard must be had to whether the employer or union has failed to respond to an offer to resume negotiations or unreasonably failed to use available conciliation or mediation services: ss.238A(5) (6) and 238B as amended and inserted by ERA 2004 s.28.

795 TULRCA 1992 s.237(1).

796 TULRCA 1992 s.237(2). If an employee taking part is a member at the commencement of the action, he or she is treated as a member throughout whether or not membership has ceased, e.g. by resignation; but membership of a union "unconnected with the employment in question" is disregarded: s.237(6).

797 TULRCA 1992 s.237(3). If no members at all are involved it cannot be unofficial action: s.237(2). cf. *Nottinghamshire Healthcare NHS Trust v Prison Officers Association* [2003] I.C.R. 1192 EAT on the powers of a trade union to act on behalf of its members.

798 [2003] I.R.L.R. 683 EAT.

799 See Employment Rights Act 1996 ss.44 and 100.

800 In *Balfour Kilpatrick Ltd v Acheson* [2003] I.R.L.R. 683 the EAT rejected the argument that the workers leaving the site where bad weather and inadequate facilities meant that clothing and footwear were permanently wet was not an appropriate way of exercising the right in s.100(1)(c) of bringing to the employer's attention circumstances which they reasonably believed were harmful or potentially harmful to health and safety. A dispute between workers and their employer relating to physical conditions of work qualifies as a trade dispute: TULRCA s.244(1)(a); see para.23-189.

801 A form of action whereby employees (especially skilled staff) stop making suggestions to improve

"taking part" in industrial action.[802] Thirdly, the withdrawal of protection under s.219 from the acts of those organising action (for example, protest action) depends by virtue of s.223 on one of their reasons for their doing that act being the fact or belief that the employer has dismissed employees who have no right to complain by reason of s.237. The test here turns on the reasons of those organising the industrial action, unlike s.237 where the test is chronological (i.e. whether the employee was taking part in unofficial action *at the time* of the dismissal). Argument may therefore occur as to the reasons for union officials (or others) organising the action.[803] However, unlike an employer's liability for unfair dismissal of an employee on grounds of trade union membership or activity, which is automatically unfair only where it is the "principal reason",[804] it need only be "one of the reasons" for loss of protection to occur under s.223. That still leaves open the precise meaning of "fact or belief". If a union, for example, calls industrial action to protect members whom the employer has dismissed in circumstances which all the parties believe do not fall within s.237, it is open to question whether the employer will be able to rely on s.223 to obtain an injunction against the union to stop protest action if he subsequently discovers that s.237 did after all apply.[805]

(f) Trade disputes and conspiracy

23-154 Criminal conspiracy to "molest" or "annoy" an employer was protected in 1875[806] in respect of acts done in contemplation or furtherance of a trade dispute.[807] But subsequent decisions showed that the new tort of lawful means conspiracy as a civil liability was unaffected.[808] In consequence, protection was provided against this liability by the 1906 Act,[809] and is now similarly provided by TULRCA 1992 s.219(2):

"An agreement or combination by two or more persons to do or procure the doing of an

---

the business, which they have customarily made.

802 See para.23-150. The workers participating in what has become "unofficial" action, because the union repudiated it, may be unaware of the union's repudiation and therefore of their increased risk of dismissal, because they may not have received the notice from their union under s.21 in time; the union is obliged to give written notice, also, to the employer (s.21(2)(b)(ii)). Such an employer may not feel confident in his selective dismissals of unofficial strikers as he cannot be wholly certain that a repudiation is valid until the three months have passed during which the union is obliged to confirm the repudiation in response to inquiries from relevant employers (s.21(6)) and see para.23-134, though this is unlikely to deter those who wish to use such powers of dismissal. cf. *Balfour Kilpatrick v Acheson* [2003] I.R.L.R. 683 EAT.

803 The union officials, not the workers, because the "act" which needs protection under s.219 is the inducement of the workers to break their contracts of employment: see para.23-136; s.219 does not protect the breach of a contract of employment as such. It is submitted, therefore that the reasons in the minds of workers who take action (e.g. a desire to protest against the employer because of the dismissal of allegedly unofficial strikers) are irrelevant to the operation of s.223.

804 TULRCA s.152(1).

805 Where, for example, it was not clear at the time of the dismissals whether the employees had ceased to take industrial action short of a strike.

806 Conspiracy and Protection of Property Act 1875 s.3 protecting against the liability found in *R. v Bunn* (1872) 12 Cox 316. This protection-and crime-was overtaken by the Criminal Law Act 1977 ss.1 and 5 (as amended by the Criminal Attempts Act 1981 s.1 and Sch.).

807 "Trade dispute" in s.3 of the 1875 Act had broadly the same meaning as in the Act of 1974; TULRA 1974 Sch.3. On the current definition in TULRCA s.242, see para.23-184 onwards.

808 e.g. *Quinn v Leathem* [1901] A.C. 495 HL and see para.23-122 onwards.

809 Trade Disputes Act 1906 s.1; after its repeal in 1971 see Industrial Relations Act 1971 s.132(2) and (4), thereafter up to 1992 s.13(4) of TULRA 1974.

act in contemplation or furtherance of a trade dispute is not actionable in tort if the act is one which, if done without any such agreement or combination, would not be actionable in tort."

A mere breach of contract, without more, does not displace the protection because s.219(2) provides that, for the protection to be lost, the act must be one which, if done by an individual, would be actionable in tort.[810] But a combination to induce a breach of contract is an actionable conspiracy unless the inducement is protected by s.219(1)(a).[811] The tort of lawful means conspiracy requires a predominant intention to injure; but when unlawful means are used liability requires not that subjective element, but only an intention to injure.[812] But the requirement that the act done must be actionable in tort before the defendants lose the immunity of s.219(2) appears to mean that a combination to injure by means of a "mere" criminal offence[813] is not actionable as a conspiracy in respect of acts done in contemplation or furtherance of a trade dispute. There remains a difficulty, however, concerning the precise meaning of "actionable in tort". In *Rookes v Barnard*, it had been suggested that the claimant must prove that the act done or procured to be done would be in the full sense "actionable" if done by an individual, i.e. that a threat by one of the conspirators would have been sufficiently coercive to cause damage to the claimant.[814] But two different reasons were given in the House of Lords for rejecting that interpretation. Lord Reid said:

> "The section[815] cannot reasonably be held to mean that no action can be brought unless the precise act complained of could have been done by an individual without previous agreement or combination. In my view the section requires us to find the nearest equivalent act which could have been so done and see whether it would be actionable."[816]

But neither s.1 of the 1906 Act nor s.13(4) of the 1974 Act said anything about "nearest equivalent acts", and it is submitted that this dictum is not good law.

Secondly, Lord Devlin argued that the section meant "that the nature of the act must be such as to make it actionable even if done without any agreement or combination".[817] This "nature" remains the same whether or not damage would have been caused; therefore, in that case, for this purpose, it was sufficient that the threat, if done by one person, would have been intimidatory; and it was so because intimidation is a tort which "is of its nature actionable if done without agreement 23-155

[810] The subsection thus enacted the recommendation of the *Donovan Royal Commission Report*, Cmnd.3623, paras 853–854. The final words "in tort" were not in s.1 of the 1906 Act. Quaere whether a breach of contract without more can be unlawful means for the purposes of the tort of causing loss by unlawful means; the conspiracy might be expressed as a combination to effect the causing loss by unlawful means tort (*Barretts & Baird (Wholesale) Ltd v IPCS* [1987] I.R.L.R. 3 at 8–10; see para.23-87).

[811] So, too, a combination to threaten such inducement unless protected by s.219(1)(b).

[812] *Lonrho Plc v Fayed* [1992] 1 A.C. 448 HL; *Kuwait Oil Tanker Co SAK v Al-Bader* [2000] 2 All E.R. (Comm) 271 CA.

[813] See para.23-109.

[814] A threat by one worker in *Rookes v Barnard* [1964] A.C. 1129 at 1216 would probably not have been sufficient to coerce BOAC into dismissing the claimant: per Sellers LJ [1963] 1 Q.B. 623 at 662 and 674. But that goes to causation, not to the ambit of the tort.

[815] Trade Disputes Act 1906 s.1. That section required the act to be "actionable", whereas TULRCA 1992 s.219(2), requires it to be "actionable in tort". It is not apparent, however, whether this difference would affect the argument on the point under discussion.

[816] *Rookes v Barnard* [1964] A.C. 1129 at 1171.

[817] *Rookes v Barnard* [1964] A.C. 1129 at 1211. It may be that Lord Evershed, at 1189, Lord Pearce, at 1235, and Lord Hodson, at 1202, held the same view, though none of them stated it so precisely.

or combination". So, Lord Devlin concluded, the section "does not prevent the claimant from suing the doer of the act and the conspirators, if any, as well".[818] Although he could not threaten to break such a contract of employment (for he had none), Silverthorne was made liable in *Rookes* on this basis as a conspirator.[819] Since *Rookes*, protection has been afforded in trade disputes for this form of intimidation by threats to break employment contracts; but, if it is correct, this approach of Lord Devlin would apply equally to other torts not protected by s.219 of TULRCA 1992. The analysis which centres upon the "nature" of an act is congruent, too, with the way in which an act, wrongful in itself, may be "unlawful means" in the law of tort, even if the cause of action is incomplete because no damage has been suffered.[820]

23-156 So, too, where some among a group of persons commit acts which are tortious in nature, the combination appears to be one which is not protected by s.219(2) even in a trade dispute, if one or more of the group is left vulnerable to an action in tort. If such persons are pickets doing acts which are not lawful under s.220 of TULRCA 1992, the protection of s.219(2) is expressly removed from the conspiracy.[821] Other statutes since 1980 have employed an even more direct approach. Thus, removal of immunity by reason that no proper ballot has been held by a trade union,[822] or because defendants have induced one of the statutory torts connected with union membership or recognition,[823] or where they act against an employer because they believe he is employing non-unionists,[824] entails loss of the protection of s.219(2) along with the rest of the section. The more ready acceptance of trade union objectives as "legitimate" in the modern cases on lawful means conspiracy[825] has rendered s.219(2) of less importance than it was when first introduced in 1906. It is true that the question whether trade union defendants have pursued "legitimate" objects is frequently coterminous with the question whether those defendants were "furthering a trade dispute".[826] But this is not always so,[827] and the two questions are to be kept distinct.

---

818 *Rookes v Barnard* [1964] A.C. 1129 at 1211. cf. per Lord Denning MR in *Morgan v Fry* [1968] 2 Q.B. 710 at 729. But see also *Central Canada Potash Co Ltd v Governmental of Saskatchewan* (1979) 88 D.L.R. (3d) 609 (SCC).

819 It is now established that acts rendered not "actionable" by s.219 do not retain a residual "unlawful" character: *Hadmor Productions Ltd v Hamilton* [1983] 1 A.C. 191 HL at 231; see below, para.23-159.

820 See *Lonrho Plc v Fayed* [1990] 2 Q.B. 479 CA (fraud practised on a third party aimed at the claimant: especially, per Dillon LJ at 489; per Ralph Gibson LJ at 492).

821 By s.219(4).

822 Now TULRCA 1992 ss.219(4) and 226; see para.23-162 onwards.

823 TULRCA 1992 ss.145, 187, 222(3) and 225(1); see para.23-146 onwards.

824 TULRCA 1992 s.222(1).

825 cf. *Reynolds v Shipping Federation* [1924] 1 Ch. 28; and *Crofter Hand Woven Harris Tweed v Veitch* [1942] A.C. 435.

826 *Huntley v Thornton* [1957] 1 W.L.R. 321.

827 *Stratford & Son Ltd v Lindley* [1965] A.C. 269 HL is an illustration of the contours of the two questions not being the same; for, although not acting in furtherance of a trade dispute, the defendants were not liable for lawful means conspiracy because they were furthering genuine trade union objectives. So too, the defendants had "nothing to fear" from the tort of conspiracy in *Hadmor Productions Ltd v Hamilton* [1983] 1 A.C. 191 at 228, per Lord Diplock, even though they may have committed acts that were tortious (meaning nothing to fear from lawful means conspiracy: see *Lonrho Plc v Fayed* [1992] 1 A.C. 448 HL).

(g) Trade disputes and causing loss by unlawful means

There are additional complexities attendant upon the liability for the tort of causing loss by unlawful means arising in a trade dispute.[828] One difficulty was confronted by the Trade Union and Labour Relations Act 1974 in s.13(3) (which was not amended in 1976). The problem may be divided into two parts. First, if procuring the breach of one contract is the means of preventing performance of another, is it protected (now under s.219(1) of TULRCA 1992)? For example, if breach of a commercial contract is indirectly achieved by inducing a breach of an employment contract in furtherance of a trade dispute, has the breach of the commercial contract been brought about by "unlawful means" (so that liability ensues, after *OBG Ltd v Allan*[829] in the causing loss by unlawful means tort) even though the inducement of a breach of the employment contract is not "actionable" by reason of what is now s.219(1)? The better view before 1974 was that the act rendered "not actionable" could not amount to "unlawful means"[830] but there were dicta (especially those of Lord Pearce) suggesting the opposite.[831] After 1974, in relation to a different but parallel point (i.e. whether the act protected ceases to be "actionable" only in respect of a suit brought by the employer, and remains "actionable in tort" for another person who relies upon it as part of his cause of action) the view was judicially expressed that, although under the 1906 Act the dicta in favour of the narrow view were the stronger, the wider interpretation must be given to the statutory protection where "the words 'actionable in tort' mean exactly what they say without any addition and without any subtraction".[832] The question was settled in *Hadmor*, in 1983, when the House of Lords declared that Lord Pearce's view was "wrong" in relation both to the 1906 Act s.3, and the 1974 Act s.13(1).[833] That decision is determinant of the same point on s.219(1) of TULRCA 1992. An act made not actionable by statute is not unlawful, whoever the claimant may be. 23-157

Breach of contract Secondly, though, it was said (even before *Rookes v Barnard*)[834] that even if the inducement is not actionable as a tort, the breach itself of the employment contract remains an actionable breach of contract. That breach is an unlawful act. It was, therefore, arguable that a defendant who had made use of such a breach, whether by a protected inducement or not, had made use of "unlawful means" in securing indirectly the breach of the commercial contract.[835] To resolve all these difficulties, s.13(3) of the 1974 Act provided: 23-158

---

828 On the construction of the trade dispute defence which was originally in limb 2 of s.3 of the Trade Disputes Act 1906 and then re-enacted as TULRA 1974 s.13(2), which effectively deprived it of any utility, see para.23-139. TULRA 1974 s.13(2) was repealed by the Employment Act 1982 s.19(1).

829 [2007] UKHL 21; [2008] 1 A.C. 1; see para.23-78 onwards.

830 *Morgan v Fry* [1968] 2 Q.B. 710 at 728–729, per Denning MR; *Torquay Hotel Co Ltd v Cousins* [1969] 2 Ch. 106 at 139–140, per Lord Denning MR; *Stratford & Son Ltd v Lindley* [1965] A.C. 269 at 285 and 303–305, per Lord Denning MR and Salmon LJ. Support was also to be found in the meaning ascribed by Lord Devlin to "actionable" (i.e. "in its nature actionable") in *Rookes v Barnard* [1964] A.C. 1129 at 1211.

831 *Stratford & Son Ltd v Lindley* [1965] A.C. 269 at 336, per Lord Pearce and at 293, per Pearson LJ; in *Torquay Hotel Co Ltd v Cousins* [1969] 2 Ch. 106 at 147, per Winn LJ.

832 *Camellia Tanker Ltd SA v ITWF* [1976] I.C.R. 274 at 290, per Templeman J, reviewing the authorities at 285–288 (affirmed by the Court of Appeal, ibid. on other grounds).

833 *Hadmor Productions Ltd v Hamilton* [1983] 1 A.C. 191 at 231 (Lord Diplock speaking with the agreement of Lord Fraser, Lord Scarman, Lord Bridge and Lord Brandon).

834 [1964] A.C. 1129 HL.

835 *DC Thomson & Co Ltd v Deakin* [1952] Ch. 646 at 687, per Evershed MR; see Grabiner (1969) 32

"For the avoidance of doubt it is hereby declared that—
(a) an act which by reason of subsection (1) or (2) above[836] is itself not actionable;
(b) a breach of contract in contemplation or furtherance of a trade dispute;
shall not be regarded as the doing of an unlawful act or as the use of unlawful means for the purpose of establishing liability in tort."

Subparagraph (a) merely anticipated the decision of the House of Lords in 1983: that which is by statute not "actionable" is not unlawful.[837]

23-159 But s.13(3)(b) was different. The legislature presumably took the view that there was a risk of a breach of contract per se being seen as "unlawful means" in trade dispute cases,[838] in which case it might be possible for a claimant to couch his action not in the traditional terms of the protections since 1906 (say, procuring a breach of an employment contract) but in the language of intentionally causing harm by unlawful means or unlawful means conspiracy, alleging that the very breach was the unlawful means on which he relied. It was indeed stated that: "The intention of that subsection appears to be to ensure that the absolution given to the tort of inducing another person to break a contract was not out-manoeuvred by calling the tort another name."[839] The Employment Act 1980, however, included within the section dealing with "secondary action"[840] the provision: "Subsection (3) of section 13 of the 1974 Act shall cease to have effect": s.17(8). The effect of this subsection, which, unlike the rest of s.17, is not limited in its effect to "secondary action", was uncertain. The majority of the Court of Appeal in *Hadmor* took the view that the repeal of s.13(3) could not have been intended "to throw us back into the era of doubt which had existed before 1974; so that we should have to decide whether Lord Pearce was right or wrong in *Stratford v Lindley*".[841] But they went on, to decide that acts which s.13(3) of the 1974 Act had stated were "not to be regarded as unlawful" must now read, on the repeal of the subsection by the 1980 Act, "be regarded as unlawful" once again. The remarkable conclusion seemed to be that the immunity for inducing breach in trade disputes could be set aside by the semantic device of relying upon the breach itself as the unlawful means.

23-160 The House of Lords in *Hadmor* decisively rejected that view.[842] Lord Diplock

---

M.L.R. 435 at 437; *Barretts & Baird (Wholesale) Ltd v IPCS* [1987] I.R.L.R. 3 at 8–10, per Henry J; interpreting *Rookes v Barnard* [1964] A.C. 1129 HL.

[836] These subsections dealt with inducing a breach of contract and "interference with trade, business or employment": see para.23-139.

[837] See *Hadmor Productions Ltd v Hamilton* [1983] 1 A.C. 191 at 230–231, per Lord Diplock.

[838] As it was in *Barretts & Baird (Wholesale) Ltd v IPCS* [1987] I.R.L.R. 3. The limitation of "secondary action" to contracts of work or services and the wide range of s.13(3), are a major obstacle to the view that the subsection became unnecessary when secondary action was removed from protection by s.17 of the 1980 Act (now s.224 of TULRCA 1992; see para.23-142): see per Lord Diplock in *Hadmor Productions Ltd v Hamilton* [1983] 1 A.C. 191 at 231–232; and *Auerbach Legislating for Conflict* (1991), Chs 2–4.

[839] *Camellia Tanker Ltd SA v ITWF* [1976] I.C.R. 274 at 285, per Templeman J, discussing s.13(3) of the 1974 Act.

[840] Now TULRCA 1992 s.224; see para.23-142 onwards.

[841] *Hadmor Productions Ltd v Hamilton* [1981] 2 All E.R. 724 at 733, per Lord Denning MR "The provisions of s.17(8) of the Employment Act effectively destroyed the immunity which s.13(3) of the 1974 Act created. It is once again an actionable wrong to behave as the defendants did" (union officials threatening to call industrial action): per Watkins LJ at 736.

[842] *Hadmor Productions Ltd v Hamilton* [1983] 1 A.C. 191 HL: "quite impossible to ascribe to subsection (8) a meaning which … would make subsections (3) (4) and (5) (the old 'gateways' to legality

held that Lord Pearce had indeed been "wrong" in *Stratford v Lindley* in his belief that an act made not "actionable" might still remain unlawful. Moreover, the Law Lords found it hard to believe the legislature would have bothered to enact the complicated rules in s.17(1)-(7) on secondary action, if all the claimant needed for victory was a breach of any contract. But Lord Diplock also expressed the view that by the time the 1980 Act came to repeal it, s.13(3) of the 1974 Act had become "entirely otiose" by reason of the extensions of s.13(1) in 1976.[843] That was undoubtedly the case in respect of s.13(3)(a), confirming that nothing protected by s.13(1) or (2) could be unlawful means (the enactment in that respect was indeed for "the avoidance of doubt"). But Lord Diplock did not regard s.13(3)(b) as different; yet it had attempted to change the law—or provide against a possible interpretation of the law after 1964. The only provision that rendered a breach of contract itself free from the status of "unlawful means" in trade disputes had now been repealed. After 1983, the courts were, therefore, left with the task of interpreting the repeal of this provision which purported to be for the "avoidance of doubt",[844] without assistance from the Law Lords in *Hadmor*. "Philosophers may delight at the implications …" said Henry J in 1987, "but there is no pleasure for those who must grapple with doubt reborn".[845] The result appears to be that a breach of contract is arguably "unlawful means" and may be used by a claimant as part of an arguably good cause of action even in a trade dispute—and that is all he requires in order to seek an interim injunction—even if the defendants may have a good defence by having done no more than induce a breach of contract in a primary dispute with a proper ballot, as the law now requires.[846] The same principle underlay Lord Devlin's acknowledgement that breach of contract simpliciter might amount to unlawful means for the tort of conspiracy.[847] If that is correct, the law is in a surprising condition, and suffers from yet another illogicality that stems from the decision in 1964 to treat breach of contract as unlawful means in tort.[848]

---

under the 1980 Act version) wholly ineffectual, since it would impose liability in tort for all secondary action": per Lord Diplock at 232 (which is what the legislature did in 1990, see now TULRCA 1992 s.224: see para.23-142 onwards). The defendant union officials in consequence retained immunity under s.13(1)(b) (now s.219(1)(b) of TULRCA 1992) their wrongdoing (if any) being threats to induce breaches of the employment contracts; cf. *Merkur Island Shipping Corp v Laughton* [1983] 2 A.C. 570 HL at 609–610; Simpson (1982) 45 M.L.R. 447.

843 *Hadmor Productions Ltd v Hamilton* [1983] 1 A.C. 191 HL at 230–231.

844 See *Barretts & Baird (Wholesale) Ltd v IPCS* [1987] I.R.L.R. 3 at 9–10, per Henry J, approving the analysis of the statutory and common law developments in Wedderburn, *The Worker and the Law*, 3rd edn (1986), p.637.

845 *Barretts & Baird (Wholesale) Ltd v IPCS* [1987] I.R.L.R. 3 at 9.

846 *Barretts & Baird (Wholesale) Ltd v IPCS* [1987] I.R.L.R. 3 at 8; Henry J adverts to whether the striking workers might be liable for use of these unlawful means; but their liability in damages would sound in contract (not extending to higher damages for conspiracy or other tort: cf. *NCB v Galley* [1958] 1 W.L.R. 16 CA) and, as he makes clear at 10, no injunction should be granted to enforce the employment contracts, because of what is now s.236 of TULRCA 1992. But if the breaches of contract were unlawful means there could be, as he also held, an arguable cause of action for third parties in interlocutory proceedings for an injunction against the officials for the unprotected tort of interference by unlawful means. On the consequential widespread and undesirable consequences, acknowledged by Henry J, see Simpson (1987) 50 M.L.R. 506 at 508-515; compare S. Auerbach, *Legislating for Conflict* (1991). On the requirements for ballots, see para.23-162 onwards.

847 Although he refused to decide the point: *Rookes v Barnard* [1964] A.C. 1129 HL at 1210; see paras 23-115 onwards.

848 *Rookes v Barnard* [1964] A.C. 1129 HL.

23-161 **Concurrent torts** A different problem has received less attention. If in the course of furthering a trade dispute the defendant commits a tort which is not protected (such as defamation or trespass), it goes without saying that he will be liable to the claimant.[849] But if he induces a breach of contract as well in furtherance of the dispute, is the trade dispute immunity for that inducement lost by reason of the presence of the unprotected tort? A positive answer to that question may be implicit in some of the judgments, which have placed emphasis on the fact that s.3 of the Trade Disputes Act 1906 and s.13(1) of the 1974 Act (now s.219(1) of TULRCA 1992) provided immunity for the act done "on the ground only" of its being actionable in respect of the protected torts.[850] On the other hand, the opposite view has been expressed, i.e. that the liability of the defendant in such a case is for the unprotected tort alone,[851] while the lawful act of inducing the strike remains lawful, at any rate if the other tort is "independent of the inducement", even if "associated" with it, and is not part of the "unlawful means adopted to achieve the breach".[852] The better view is probably found in the latter approach, whereby the inducement or threat will remain protected as the "only" ground of action in respect of the industrial action, unless the extraneous, unprotected tort is the "unlawful means", the weapon used to make the inducement or threat effective.[853] This may affect the damages available to the claimant.

(h) Trade disputes and ballots

23-162 Part II of the Trade Union Act 1984 introduced provisions whereby the act of a trade union to induce a person to break or interfere with the performance of his contract of employment lost protection in a trade dispute if it did not have the support of a ballot.[854] These provisions have stolen the limelight from questions still

---

849 *Royal London Mutual Insurance Ltd v Williamson* (1921) 37 T.L.R. 742.

850 e.g. per Lord Reid in *Rookes v Barnard* [1964] A.C. 1129 at 1172–1173; so too, per Lord Devlin at 1214. But Sachs J put it to the jury on the basis of a "conspiracy" to "threaten strike action" by intimidation, and left open the position where there were "two equal concurrent" purposes—one lawful, the other unlawful: [1961] 2 All E.R. 825 at 830 and 835; and the appellate courts did not return to that issue: Wedderburn (1961) 24 M.L.R. 572, and (1964) 27 M.L.R. 257; so too, Hoffmann (1965) 81 L.Q.R. 116, 129. Nor does the question arise where the unprotected breach of duty that is induced is coterminous with the breach of contract: *Prudential Assurance Co v Lorenz* (1971) 11 K.I.R. 78, para.23-25; but see, per Stuart-Smith J in *News Group Newspapers Ltd v SOGAT (No.2)* [1987] I.C.R. 181 at 211–212.

851 See *Rookes v Barnard* [1964] A.C. 1129 at 1203, per Lord Hodson ("the intimidation is actionable, and the claimant is entitled to sue on that ground, not 'on the ground only' that his employment has been interfered with"). Quaere, per Lord Evershed, ibid. at 1185–1190; cf. per Russell J in *Brimelow v Casson* [1924] 1 Ch. 302 at 314; *Cunard S.S. v Stacey* [1955] 2 Lloyd's Rep. 247 CA; *Sheriff v McMullen* [1952] I.R. 236 at 254.

852 See *Norbrook Laboratories Ltd v King* [1984] I.R.L.R. 200 CA (NI) at 208–209, per Gibson LJ (trespass and nuisance by official inducing industrial action; damages to be assessed for these torts separately; inducing breach of contract protected by trade dispute immunity should be disregarded in damages for other torts); but see, per Lowry LCJ at 205.

853 If in furtherance of a trade dispute a union official induces breaches of contract with immunity by addressing union members lawfully as they leave the workplace, it is submitted that the immunity is not lost if he commits a trespass by stepping into the workplace, unless the latter was part of the means necessary to make the inducements effective. His liability for the trespass is a separate issue on a separate act. This result is also favoured by the arrangement of the provisions on picketing in TULRCA 1992 ss.219(3), 220, 220A, 224(3). The point has some practical importance in the light of possible claims to damages against a trade union: see TULRCA 1992 s.22; see para.23-135.

854 By s.10(1). (See now TULRCA 1992 s.226.)

unanswered in the principles of the law of tort discussed above. A similar requirement is made today, after extensive amendment in the Acts of 1988 and 1990, by TULRCA 1992 ss.226–235; these sections were further amended by TURERA 1993, the Employment Relations Acts 1999 and 2004 and the Trade Union Act 2016, so that the law is now somewhat complex.[855] The protection of s.219(1) and (2) is now displaced by s.226 where the act done by a trade union[856] induces a person "to take part, or continue to take part, in industrial action" without the support of a ballot.[857] Prior to March 2017, when the amendments made by the Trade Union Act 2016 came into force, this requirement was satisfied where a simple majority of those who voted were in favour of strike action and/or action short of a strike.[858] Two amendments to the TULRCA 1992 made by the 2016 Act have made the balloting obligation significantly more onerous. Section 2 of the 2016 Act has added the requirement that in all cases at least 50 per cent of those union members entitled to vote must do so.[859] Section 3 has inserted subsections (2A)–(2F) into s.226 of the 1992 Act; these subsections provide that in specified "Important Public Services" there is the additional requirement that at least 40 per cent of those entitled to vote voted in favour of strike action and/or industrial action short of a strike as the case may be.[860] This substantial addition to the law on trade disputes which began in 1984 by speaking of liability for inducing breach of contract as the defining factor, now relates to facts which may or may not import liability, since "inducing a person to take part in industrial action" is not per se a tort or otherwise unlawful.[861] The statute therefore is able to include within its scope

[855] Citation below refers to TULRCA 1992 as amended by TURERA 1993 (chiefly by ss.17–21 and Sch.8), ERA 1999 Sch.3, ERA 2004 ss.22–25 and TUA 2016 ss.2–9. For a concise summary of the law as it was before the amendments made by the 2016 Act see Elias LJ in *London & Birmingham Railway Ltd v ASLEF* [2011] EWCA Civ 226; [2011] I.C.R. 848 at [15]–[30].

[856] Since it will invariably be an act inducing a breach of employment contracts, the act will be taken to be "done" by the union where it is done or authorised by one of the persons for whom the union is liable under s.20 of the 1992 Act: see para.23-134. This makes its responsibility wider than the common law tests (see *General Aviation Services (UK) v TGWU* (1976) [1985] I.C.R. 615 HL; distinguishing *Heatons Transport (St Helens) Ltd v TGWU* [1973] A.C. 15 HL) especially given the hurdles concerning repudiation by the union in s.21 of the Act.

[857] TULRCA 1992 s.226(1)(a). Where a dispute involves more than one union, each union ballots its own members. Special provision is made for balloting overseas members of a union and for merchant seamen: TULRCA 1992 ss.232 and 230(2A) (2B), as amended (2B), as amended respectively.

[858] TULRCA 1992 s.226(2)(a)(iii).

[859] TULRCA 1992 s.226(2)(a)(iia).

[860] See the Important Public Services (Health) Regulations 2017 (SI 2017/132); Important Public Services (Education) Regulations 2017 (SI 2017/133); Important Public Services (Fire) Regulations 2017 (SI 2017/134); Important Public Services (Transport) Regulations 2017 (SI 2017/135); Important Public Services (Border Security) Regulations 2017 (SI 2017/136). No regulations have yet been made in respect of the remaining category of important public services specified in the amendments to s.226 of the 1992 Act by s.3 of the Trade Union Act 2016, namely decommissioning of nuclear installations and management of radioactive waste and spent fuel: s.226(2E)(e).

[861] That is, the inducement might relate to action which is not in breach of contract as to which see *Power Packing Casemakers v Faust* [1983] Q.B. 471 CA; and, per Donaldson P in *Seaboard Airlines Inc v TGWU* [1973] I.C.R. 458 at 460; but in interlocutory proceedings the lack of a valid ballot before industrial action will in practice make more difficult a defendant union's plea that it is arguable that the action induced would not involve breach of contract; cf. *Solihull MBC v NUT* [1985] I.R.L.R. 211; see para.23-182 onwards. The liability in TULRCA 1992 s.235A (inserted by TURERA 1993 s.22) by making the union's liability to members in s.62, of the Act available to any individual claimant as an unlawful act, (s.235A(2)(b)) comes close to making "official" union industrial action unlawful in itself if no ballot has been held, whether or not any tortious act is involved.

inducements to take action which are "ineffective" (whether by reason of the members being unwilling to be influenced or "for any other reason").[862] It has been stressed judicially that the reason for the introduction of a "secret ballot" was Parliament's desire to protect, not employers and the public, but the union's own members; "to ensure that [industrial] action should have the genuine support of the members who are called upon to take part",[863] which is "collective action", not individual action. So too, the sections relating to ballots do not put a new restriction on s.219, and once the union has obtained the support of a ballot, it may well be able to call on other persons to take action in support of it.[864] The statute does not in fact define for these purposes "industrial action" and the definition of "strike"—"any concerted stoppage of work"—goes much wider than industrial disputes.[865] Inevitably the legislator is driven to specify the legal nature of various types of industrial action.[866] The absence of a ballot altogether will mean loss of protection; but, as will be seen, failure to satisfy some only of the detailed requirements which go to make up that "support", especially those which since 1993 concern notification to employers, raises more complex questions which can be addressed only after the provisions have been examined.[867] These are summarised below in relation to:

---

862 TULRCA 1992 s.226(4). In addition to members who reject the union's call this provision seems to provide for such cases as communications sent to members which do not arrive or an official addressing members who are deaf. But the same does not apply to inducements founding tort liability, where the inducement must be effective. For a case where members were "too polite" to act on an inducement: *Secretary of State for Scotland v Prison Officers Association* [1991] I.R.L.R. 371 (Court of Session, OH: what is now TULRCA 1992 s.233, replaced the earlier, and different, statutory provisions applicable in that case).

863 *London Underground Ltd v RMT* [1996] I.C.R. 170, per Millett LJ at 180. This interpretation is consistent with the policy stated in the *Green Paper Democracy in Trade Unions* (1983) Cmnd.8778, Ch.3, which preceded the Trade Union Act 1984 in which the industrial action ballots provisions were first enacted. Millett LJ's judgment is helpful in identifying what has to receive the "support of a ballot" before the union can call on members to take action: collective action by persons within the ambit of s.219, [1996] I.C.R. 170 at 181 (see s.233). cf. *RJB Mining (UK) Ltd v NUM* [1997] I.R.L.R. 621 (no valid ballot as the law then stood). But see the qualification to Millett LJ's view by Lloyd LJ in *Metrobus Ltd v Unite* [2009] EWCA Civ 829; [2010] I.C.R. 173 at [40] relying on the amendments made by the Employment Relations Act 1999 to support the conclusion that the balloting obligations did require the employer's interests to be taken into account. See also *Royal Mail Group Ltd v Communication Workers Union* [2019] EWCA Civ 2150; [2020] I.C.R. 940 at [52], describing the purpose of s.230 as being "to ensure fair dealing between the employer and the union and to ensure a fair, open and democratic ballot so that industrial action is seen to have the genuine support of the union's members."

864 See *London Underground Ltd v RMT* [1996] I.C.R. 170 at 180, per Millett LJ. This important interpretation manifestly assumes that the inducement of other persons is in furtherance of the same trade dispute: see para.23-180 onwards.

865 TULRCA 1992 s.246. This definition of "strike" could include stoppages which would not, in lay terms, be called a strike, e.g. if no pressure was put on the employer. The courts are not bound by, but will take cognisance of the definition of strike for the purposes of computing continuity of employment in s.235(5) of the Employment Rights Act 1996; there coercion of the employer is the central feature. In what follows "taking action" includes both strike action and industrial action short of a strike. Industrial action is defined in TULRCA s.62(6) for the purposes of the union member's right to a ballot under that section as "a strike or other industrial action by persons employed under contracts of employment".

866 For example, ERA 1999 Sch.3 para.6, inserting TULRCA s.229(2A) and amending TULRCA s.246, defines the legal character of overtime bans and call-out bans as actions short of a strike for the purposes of ballot papers (reversing *Connex SE Ltd v RMT* [1999] I.R.L.R. 249 CA).

867 See para.23-149 onwards, especially 23-155.

(i) the requirement of a postal ballot;
(ii) entitlement to vote;
(iii) the need for separate ballots at each workplace;
(iv) the role of the scrutineer;
(v) the ballot paper and conduct of the ballot;
(vi) the duties to notify employers;
(vii) the effects of various failures to comply; and
(viii) the period of effectiveness of the ballot.[868]

It may be noted that after the original balloting provisions were enacted in 1984 as a qualification to the availability of statutory defences to certain economic tort liabilities, a parallel right for a union member to require the union to hold a ballot before calling for industrial action was introduced by the Employment Act 1988. This provision, now s.62 of TULRCA 1992, gives a member of a union the right to apply to the court for an order requiring the union to take steps for ensuring that no inducement to take action and no action occurs where no ballot satisfying the requirements of ss.226B–234 has been held. The same ballot can satisfy both statutory provisions.[869]

Postal ballots Since 1993, the ballot has been required to be fully postal. So far as is reasonably practicable, a voting paper must be sent to the member's home address giving him a convenient opportunity to vote by post.[870] The courts had earlier acknowledged that changes of address and the like will often make it impossible for a union to guarantee to reach each relevant member by post.[871] In response to pressures to permit electronic voting, in particular to facilitate the union's meeting **23-163**

868 On the correct approach to construction of the provisions on industrial action ballots in TULRCA ss.226–235 see *P v NASUWT* [2003] UKHL 8; [2003] 2 A.C. 663, per Lord Bingham at [7]: "The House must attempt to give the provisions a likely and workable construction." See too Elias LJ in *London & Birmingham Railway Ltd v ASLEF* [2011] EWCA Civ 226; [2011] I.C.R. 848 at [9]: "the legislation should simply be construed in the normal way without presumptions one way or the other", with Lord Bingham's "likely and workable construction" as the starting point. In *Balfour Beatty Engineering Services Ltd v Unite* [2012] EWHC 267 (QB); [2012] I.C.R. 822 at [8] Eady J added to these two approaches recognition "since the advent of the Human Rights Act 1998 at least that it is appropriate to construe the relevant statutory provisions in a way that is compatible with rights enshrined in the European Convention on Human Rights and Fundamental Freedoms ... the approach at Strasbourg has been to recognise the right to strike as part and parcel of the right to freedom of association conferred under Article 11(1)". The Code of Practice (Industrial Action Ballots and Notice to Employers: revised in 2017) is taken into account for interpretation: s.207(3); but it "puts a gloss on the law", warning unions they are "at risk of legal action" even where it would not be "successful": per Lord Inglewood, Parl. Deb. HL, 29 June 1995, col.914: Simpson (1993) 22 I.L.J. 297. On the 2005 revision of the Code of Practice see Simpson (2005) 34 I.L.J. 331. A revised version of the Code which takes account of the changes made to the law by the Trade Union Act 2016 was issued in March 2017.

869 TULRCA s.62(9). Lack of a ballot may also lead to an injunction at the instance of a member if the union is not observing its own rules by not holding a ballot before calling for industrial action, but in such a case the liability is for breach of contract; see e.g. *Taylor & Foulstone v NUM (Yorkshire Area)* [1984] I.R.L.R. 445.

870 TULRCA 1992 s.230(2) as substituted by TURERA 1993 s.17. Under s.230(2A)–(2C) as further substituted by ERA 1999 Sch.3 para.7, merchant seaman may be permitted to vote on board ship, or at a place where the ship is, if that is reasonably practicable. In *Royal Mail Group Ltd v Communication Workers Union* [2019] EWCA Civ 2150; [2020] I.C.R. 940, the Court of Appeal upheld a finding that a trade union representing postal workers had breached s.230(2) by encouraging its members to remove the voting papers that had been addressed to them from the "frame" where the mail was being sorted rather than waiting for them to be delivered their homes.

871 *British Railways Board v NUR* [1989] I.C.R. 678 CA at 684, per Lord Donaldson MR; but see now

the requirement for a minimum to 50 per cent of the members balloted to actually vote in a ballot, s.4 of the Trade Union Act 2016 required the Secretary of State to commission an independent review of the delivery of secure methods of electronic voting in industrial action ballots.[872] The obligation to hold such a ballot now arises whether the members to be induced to take action are employees or persons under a contract by virtue of which they personally perform services for another.[873]

23-164 **Entitlement to vote** As amended in 2004, s.227(1) provides that entitlement to vote must be accorded equally to all those members who it is reasonable for the union to believe at the time of the ballot will be induced by the union to take part in the action, and to no others.[874] This has been held to entitle a union to ballot workers who were not being induced by the union to take industrial action on a particular day but whom the union believed would be induced to take part in the industrial action.[875] After the 1999 and 2004 amendments the court may excuse failure to comply with the rule about entitlement (as well as a failure to comply with the posting rules) if the failures are accidental and unlikely to affect the result.[876] But, since 1999, if a person, being a member at the time of the ballot, is not accorded an

---

s.232A, para.23-164. In *Balfour Beatty Engineering Services Ltd v Unite* [2012] EWHC 267 (QB); [2012] I.C.R. 822 at [12] Eady J cited Lord Walker in *P v NASUWT* [2003] UKHL8; [2003] 2 A.C. 663 at [65]: "it is a fact of life that no trade union of any size can keep completely full and accurate records of the names and addresses of its ever changing body of members, still less their current places of work, trade categories and pay grades" as highlighting the need to make due allowance for these realities in deciding whether the union had conducted the ballot in accordance with s.230.

872 Such a review was conducted by Sir Ken Knight, and reported in December 2017. It recommended that e-balloting be tested in the context of non-statutory balloting over a reasonable period—to be decided by the Secretary of State—to examine its reliability, in particular its capacity to withstand attack by those motivated by a desire to disrupt.

873 TULRCA 1992 s.235; this seems to include even those who provide professional services and therefore fall outside the definition of worker in s.296, which applies for the purposes of the definition of a trade dispute in s.244; see para.23-189.

874 Thus where the union issued ballot papers to members who were shortly to leave employment with the employer, having accepted voluntary redundancy, it was held that the union had not satisfied this requirement: *British Airways Plc v Unite* [2009] EWHC 3541 (QB); [2010] I.R.L.R. 423. It was also held on these facts that the union could not establish a reasonable belief that they were entitled to vote so as to fall within the "small accidental failures" disregard in s.232B. In *United Closures and Plastics Ltd v Unite* [2011] CSOH 114; 2011 S.L.T. 1105 at [49]–[52] the court rejected a submission that a ballot on industrial action in a dispute over changes to working conditions had to be limited to workers who would be directly affected by these changes: ss.226A(2H) and 234A(5C), which define the "persons concerned" for the purposes of notices of an industrial action ballot and industrial action after a ballot in which the majority supported industrial action, refer respectively to those employees whom the union "reasonably believes" will be entitled to vote (s.226A) and induced by the union to take industrial action (s.234A).

875 *London Underground Ltd v ASLEF* [2011] EWHC 3506 (QB); [2012] I.R.L.R.196 at [47] where Eder J emphasised that s.227(1) referred to members who would be induced to "take part in" not "take" industrial action. Thus a ballot of drivers in a dispute over working on Boxing Day was not invalid because it was not limited to members who had been rostered to work on Boxing Day (whose identity was not, in any event, known at the time when ballot papers were sent out because the rosters for Boxing Day had not then been posted); moreover the union was considering calling for further industrial action on other days in the New Year.

876 TULRCA 1992 s.232B inserted by ERA 1999 Sch.3 para.9 and amended by ERA 2004 s.24(1). See *Balfour Beatty Engineering Services Ltd v Unite* [2012] EWHC 267; [2012] I.C.R. 822 at [18] where it was noted that since the duty was to provide those entitled to vote with a voting paper sent by post and a convenient opportunity to vote by post "so far as is reasonably practicable" the disregard of small accidental failures by the union in s.232B was an additional qualification to this duty on the union. It may be noted that before the 2004 amendment it had been held that the reference to s.230(2A) in s.232B was an error for s.230(2B): *P v NASUWT* [2001] EWCA Civ 652; [2001] I.C.R.

entitlement to vote, and is induced by the union to take part—and it is reasonable for the trade union to believe he would be induced to take part—the industrial action is not supported by the ballot.[877] This requirement is not met if a member is denied entitlement to vote and is induced to take part.[878] But to fail inadvertently to give a member the opportunity of voting is not the same as denying his entitlement to vote.[879] The phrase "and to no others" creates a difficulty where the employer engages new employees after a successful ballot who, being members of

1241 at [62] (upheld on appeal [2003] UKHL 8; [2003] 2 A.C. 663). In *London & Birmingham Railway Ltd v ASLEF* [2011] EWCA Civ 226; [2011] I.C.R. 848, Elias LJ cited the reasoning of the House of Lords in *P v NASUWT* in support of his conclusion that the accidental erroneous inclusion of two members who worked for another employer in the list of those entitled to vote was an error falling within the provision on entitlement to vote in s.230(2) so that the union could rely on the small accidental failures disregard in s.232B. cf. *Govia Thameslink Railway Ltd v ASLEF* [2016] EWHC 1320 (QB); [2016] I.R.L.R. 686 where it was held that this provision did not cover the inclusion of drivers employed by Govia who were unaffected by the introduction of driver only trains on the Gatwick Express, which was the issue in dispute; sed quaere they could still be called on to take industrial action in furtherance of the trade dispute between Govia and those drivers who were affected by the change to driver only trains.

877 TULRCA s.232A, subject to the permitted disregard of small accidental failures to comply with the provisions on entitlement to vote in s.227(1): s.232B as amended by the ERA 2004 s.24. While ss.232A and 232B, as amended, make the ballot easier for the union to handle, given the complexity of the legislative drafting, it is remarkable how few union ballots have been found lacking, where challenged. But persons (e.g. officials) for whom the union is responsible under the new sections are not, it seems, determined by s.20 because that code of vicarious liability applies to cases where proceedings in tort (based on an economic tort such as inducing breach of contract) are brought against the union, or where the statute states s.20 must be used in other situations, e.g. s.62(5), s.235A(6) and s.234A(8)(9). A union cannot excuse a failure to comply by pointing to problems arising from its own structure (e.g. a federal structure) *RJB (Mining) Ltd v NUM* [1997] I.R.L.R. 621 at 624 (though it might not be asked for "100 per cent perfection").

878 TULRCA 1992 s.227(1). In *P v NASUWT* [2001] EWCA Civ 652; [2001] I.C.R. 1241, Waller LJ endorsed the reasoning of Millett LJ in *London Underground Ltd v RMT* [1996] I.C.R. 170 at 178 to the effect that the words "at the time of the ballot" in that section mean the time when the ballot papers were sent out. For the "date of the ballot" see s.246.

879 *British Railways Board v NUR* [1989] I.C.R. 678, CA (some 200 members lacking opportunity to vote in a ballot with 64,000 voting). The duty to provide voting papers is qualified by "so far as reasonably practicable": s.230(2). In *P v NASUWT* [2001] EWCA Civ 652; [2001] I.C.R. 1241 it was held that although the provision in s.232B for small accidental failures to be disregarded did not then expressly apply to a small accidental failure to comply with s.232A (which was inserted in 1999 in place of the former s.227(2) and deprives industrial action of the support of a ballot where a member at the time of the ballot was induced by the union to take part in the action but had not been accorded entitlement to vote in the ballot), there was no such failure where a failure to comply with s.227(1) (which then required the union to ballot all and only those who it was reasonable at the time of the ballot would be called on to take industrial action) was accidental and unlikely to affect the result of the ballot. The House of Lords ([2003] UKHL 8; [2003] 2 A.C. 663) endorsed the Court of Appeal's reasoning on this point for reasons which, per Lord Hoffmann, with whom all the other Law Lords agreed, were "substantially the same as those given by Waller LJ"(who gave the judgment of the Court of Appeal). The 2004 amendments to the legislation have now made this explicit. Contrast *Midland Main Line Ltd v RMT* [2001] EWCA Civ 1206; [2001] I.R.L.R. 813, where Schiemann LJ said at 816 that there would be a failure to comply with s.227(1) where members who had not been balloted or called on to take industrial action were "induced to take industrial action by their own feelings that this is appropriate" or "in the knowledge that many of their colleagues will expect them to take industrial action, will do so", a conclusion "any reasonably worldly-wise judge would reach ... independently of any evidence". The amendment to s.227(1) made by s.23 of ERA 2004 which limits those who have to be balloted to those who it reasonable for the union to believe will be induced "by the union" to take industrial action effectively reverses this aspect of the decision. In *London & Birmingham Railway Ltd v ASLEF* [2011] EWCA Civ 226; [2011] I.C.R. 848 at [78]–[87] Elias LJ concluded that the de minimis principle in the *British Railways Board v NUR* case still applied. It was consistent with the reasoning of Lord Bingham in

the union, respond to the union's call for industrial action. It was suggested that, since the union could not ballot these members before they became employees, a call for industrial action should be limited to the members who were employees at that time.[880] But a closer look revealed that once the union had obtained support from a proper ballot for the collective industrial action, it was free to induce other persons, such as those who had become members after the ballot or even non-members, to support them in their dispute by withdrawing labour (in furtherance of the trade dispute). The new sections on ballots had not withdrawn the protections of s.219 so long as a ballot protected the union's industrial action.[881]

23-165 **Separate workplace ballots** The Employment Relations Act 1999 retained the principle of earlier measures that there should be a separate ballot at each workplace for members who are entitled to vote.[882] Whether the ballot satisfies all the statutory requirements must then be assessed in relation to each workplace separately. But this requirement is subject to three exceptions when one aggregate vote is still permissible. The first is where there is at least one member at each of the different workplaces who is "affected" by the dispute.[883] This is a widely drawn exception by reason of the definition of "affected" in s.228A(5); the essence is that the dispute relates "wholly or partly" to certain matters included in the definition of a trade dispute in s.244(1).[884] The second exception is where the union reasonably believes that all members have the same occupation or occupations and are employed by one or more employers with whom the union is in dispute.[885] The third exception is where entitlement to vote is accorded only to members employed by a particular employer with whom the union is in dispute.[886] Few separate workplace ballots were recorded under the law before 1999 and after the 1999 changes there are likely to be even less. The changes avoid difficulties under the previous provisions, for

P v NASUWT [2003] UKHL 8; [2003] 2 A.C. 663; and also Smith LJ's judgment in *British Airways Plc v Unite* [2010] EWCA Civ 669; [2010] I.C.R. 1316 that "substantial compliance" was sufficient in relation to the duty in s.231 to inform members of the result of the ballot. See too *United Closures & Plastics Ltd v Unite* [2011] CSOH 114; 2011 S.L.T. 1105 at [15].

880 Unless the number involved attracts the de minimis principle: per Lord Donaldson MR in *Post Office v UCW* [1990] I.C.R. 258 at 267–268. Since hiring is the function of the employer, this would mean the union would then be obliged to seek out new employees and retract any inducement to them.

881 Millett LJ in *London Underground v RMT* [1996] I.C.R. 170 at 181–182: the immunity of s.219 is still available; nothing in ss.226-235 curtails a union's long-accepted "right to induce non-members to support the industrial action ... by breaking their own contracts of employment". This crucial reinterpretation of the sections preserves the right to industrial action which had been under threat by interpretation of the new requirements about ballots.

882 TULRCA 1992 ss.228 and 228A as substituted by ERA 1999 Sch.3 para.5. A workplace is the premises where or from which the employee works, or the premises with which his employment has the closest connection: s.228(4).

883 s.228A(2).

884 The matters are: s.244(1)(d) discipline; (e) union membership or non-membership; (f) facilities for union officials, and any "decision" which the union reasonably believes the employer has made or will make affecting members within s.244(1)(a), (b) or (c), that is terms and conditions or physical conditions of employment, engagement or non-engagement or allocation of work or duties. Oddly a dispute relating to machinery for negotiation, consultation or other procedures relating to any of these matters, which is a trade dispute within s.244(1)(g), is not included.

885 s.228A(3). cf. *University of Central England v NALGO* [1993] I.R.L.R. 81 on the equivalent provision before the 1999 amendments.

886 s.228A(4).

instance where some workers return to work for short periods to provide safety cover.[887]

Appointment of scrutineer Thirdly, the union must (unless the total number of members entitled to vote does not exceed 50)[888] appoint an independent scrutineer for the ballot from among persons qualified to act by the regulations,[889] and the name of that scrutineer must appear on the voting paper.[890] The terms of appointment must require him to take steps to report to the union within four weeks after the date of the ballot[891]; the union must ensure that he carries out his functions without interference by its members, employees or officials, and comply with his reasonable requests.[892] The report must state whether he has been able to carry out his functions, if any reasonable grounds exist for believing a contravention has occurred and whether arrangements for handling voting papers and counting were satisfactory; and any person entitled to vote and his employer shall, on request within six months after the date of the ballot, be provided with a copy.[893] Fulfilling these requirements is a condition necessary for a valid ballot.[894] **23-166**

The ballot paper and calling for action Further, detailed provisions concerning the voting paper may be summarised as follows: the paper must contain the address and date for return and the name of the scrutineer[895] and the "specified person",[896] by name or description, who is authorised, in the event of a vote in favour (but not before) to call upon members to take part. He or she need not be authorised under the union rules, but they must fall within the scope of the statu- **23-167**

---

[887] See para.30 of the 2017 revision of the Code of Practice on Industrial Action Ballots and Notices to Employers which notes that it is possible for a union to hold more than one ballot on a dispute at a single workplace and that some of these ballots may include members at other workplaces. cf. *Partington v NALGO* [1981] I.R.L.R. 537 (union not allowed to apply rules on discipline where agreement made with employers not to call out safety workers). See now on "unjustifiable discipline" of members who refuse to join in industrial action, TULRCA s.64, but that wrong cannot amount to unlawful means in tort: s.64(4). Where, as is common, a union intends that safety personnel should carry out essential services during industrial action, s.228 would seem to be satisfied if it calls upon all the relevant workers to take part but then suspends the action by safety personnel at various workplaces for limited periods for safety work, making it clear that these suspensions are not terminations of their action: *Post Office v UCW* [1990] I.C.R. 258 CA; distinguishing *Monsanto Plc v TGWU* [1987] I.C.R. 269 CA.

[888] TULRCA 1992 s.226C; the Code of Practice 2005 states that where 50 or fewer members are entitled to vote, the union may want to consider whether the appointment of a scrutineer would still be of benefit in enabling the union to demonstrate compliance with the statutory requirements more easily (para.13). See now para.13 of the 2017 Code of Practice to the same effect; para.12 of this Code suggests that giving the scrutineer additional functions relating to the production and distribution of voting papers, being the person to whom the ballot papers are returned and retaining custody of the ballot papers after the ballot result, "may help to ensure adequate standards for the conduct of the ballot or simplify the balloting process".

[889] TULRCA 1992 s.226B(1)(2) inserted by TURERA 1993 s.20; the Trade Union Ballots and Elections (Independent Scrutineer Qualifications) Order 1993 (SI 1993/1909) as amended by SI 2002/2267 authorises a choice between four named bodies or a qualified solicitor or accountant, so long as they have not recently been employed by or been a member of the union.

[890] TULRCA 1992 s.229(1A).

[891] TULRCA 1992 s.226B(1)(b); on date of the ballot: s.246.

[892] TULRCA 1992 s.226B (3), (4); this scrutineer has no specific statutory right to inspect the register of members (contrast scrutineers in election of officials: s.49(5A), and see (7)).

[893] TULRCA 1992 s.231B, for a reasonable fee.

[894] See ss.226(2)(a)(i) and (b)(i) and s.62(2)(a)(i) and (b)(i), "so far as applicable".

[895] TULRCA 1992 s.229(1A).

[896] TULRCA 1992 ss.229(3), 233(1).

tory code on union vicarious responsibility.[897] A specified person may leave the calling of action to subordinate officials in specified conditions, such as when it should begin if current negotiations break down; but that person may not delegate the decision completely.[898] Before the date of the ballot the union may campaign for a "yes" vote; that by itself will not be regarded as a "call" for industrial action, as the union is not required to be neutral.[899] If action is called for by someone other than the specified person or his lawful delegate, and no specified person makes such a call, the union will be unprotected from liability if the first person is an official or other person for whom the statutory rules impose vicarious liability for the core economic torts.[900] The voting paper must contain the following statutory statement about breach of employment contract, without qualification or amendment:

> "If you take part in a strike or other industrial action, you may be in breach of your contract of employment. However if you are dismissed for taking part in a strike or other industrial action which is called officially, the dismissal will be unfair if it takes place fewer than twelve weeks after you started taking part in the action and depending on the circumstances may be unfair if it takes place later."[901]

23-168 **Content of the ballot paper** Difficulty has arisen about the nexus between the ballot paper, associated statements and the scope of action protected. This prompted two approaches. It has been held that the union must show that the members have not been asked to participate in a ballot "by reference to issues other than a trade dispute".[902] In *University College Hospital NHS Trust v Unison*,[903] it was even declared that, inspecting the "different strands of the ballot paper", the court found

---

897 TULRCA 1992 ss.229(3), 233(1), (2); on vicarious responsibility see s.20; para.23-134.

898 See *Tanks and Drums Ltd v TGWU* [1992] I.C.R. 1, CA ("it would be impracticable to leave matters so that there was no possibility for the exercise of judgment on the ground": per Neill LJ at 18).

899 *Newham LBC v NALGO* [1993] I.C.R. 189 CA. cf. the position where a union informs the employer that a proposed change in working practices is unacceptable and that it intends to ballot its members on industrial action. In *Govia Thameslink Railways Ltd v ASLEF* 2016 EWHC 1320 (QB); [2016] I.R.L.R. 686 at [61]–[70] Supperstone J held that communications from both ASLEF's General Secretary and its Executive Committee with both Govia and the union's members before the date of the ballot, which made clear that ASLEF did not agree to Govia's introduction of Driver Only (DOO) Trains on the Gatwick Express, constituted an infringement of the condition then in TULRCA s.233(2)(a)—now s.233(1)(b) after amendments made by the Trade Union Act 2016 s.22, Sch.4 para.13—that there must be no call for industrial action before the date of the ballot. In earlier, separate proceedings Christopher Clarke LJ had upheld Langstaff J's decision that there was a serious issue to be tried as to whether statements by ASLEF before the ballot amounted to inducements to members to refuse to drive DOO trains.

900 See para.23-134; ss.20 and 21 of TULRCA 1992 (see especially for the wide reach of s.20(3)(b)). The specified person can "endorse" industrial action already taken: s.233(3)(a). A person may make a "call" if they fall within s.20, TULRCA 1992 s.233(4).

901 TULRCA 1992 s.229(4). The second sentence was added by the ERA 1999 Sch.3 para.6 and amended by the ERA 2004 Sch.1 para.13. The union may comment but only on a separate document. On accompanying documents being equated with the paper, see *Blue Circle v TGWU* unreported 7 July 1989, per Alliott J (union therefore limited to 24-hour strike specifically mentioned); see Simpson (1989) 18 I.L.J. 234.

902 *London Underground Ltd v NUR (No.1)* [1989] I.R.L.R. 341 at 343, per Simon Brown J (four issues mentioned on the ballot paper; only one clearly within the definition of trade dispute); cf. *London Underground Ltd v NUR (No.2)* [1989] I.R.L.R. 343.

903 [1999] I.C.R. 204 CA. The feature in the ballot unacceptable to the Court of Appeal was the demand by the union that the employers should guarantee the conditions for employees of employers who were at that time unknown, but who would come into the scheme perhaps 30 years in the future. On the question whether this was furtherance of a trade dispute under TULRCA 1992 s.244, see para.23-190.

that references to the terms of employment of staff who might be employed many years in the future, made it "impossible to identify the motives of those who voted in favour of strike action … it follows that this nullifies the ballot which took place. In addition the ballot paper is very persuasive evidence as to what is the proposed purpose of the strike." The terms of the ballot paper showed that it "was for many purposes, one of which is clearly flawed".[904] Alternatively, it has been pointed out that "no express requirement to this effect is to be found in the statute"; it is, of course, necessary to "identify the strike which is called with the strike which was voted for. But that is a matter of evidence."[905] That the latter view is correct is suggested by the fact that the same ballot can suffice under these provisions and also under those affording a member a right to apply to the court, where no issue arises on trade disputes.[906] The union will of course become liable to an injunction if it is calling action which is not in contemplation or furtherance of a trade dispute, but that is not a reason to hold that the requisite ballot support was not obtained.[907] The paper must include one or both of the permitted questions (however framed): one asking if the members are prepared to take part in a strike, the other if they are prepared to take part in action short of a strike.[908] The two questions must be put and answered separately; no "rolled up" question is allowed.[909] In view of the difficulties surrounding the definition of "strike" and "industrial action short of a strike",[910] trade unions appear in practice to need to put both questions in many situations to be sure they are covered in subsequent events. Where both questions are put and one (for example for a strike) receives a majority, but the other (for action short of a strike) does not, that is nevertheless enough to support the strike as each

---

904 [1999] I.C.R. 204 CA, per Lord Woolf MR at 215. The terms of the ballot paper may well be evidence as to the nature and purpose of the threat to strike; but it is submitted that this had little or nothing to do with the "motives" of those involved, nor is that a matter the court is called upon to investigate in regard to the "furtherance" of the trade dispute.

905 *Associated British Ports v TGWU* [1989] I.R.L.R. 291 at 301, per Millett J (affirmed on other grounds [1989] 1 W.L.R. 939 HL): "What matters is that a majority supported strike action; it does not matter why they did so." The nature of the dispute may be revealed through the question on the ballot paper: *Wandsworth LBC v NAS/UWT* [1994] I.C.R. 81 at 96, per Neill LJ. If there is no trade dispute the union will, of course, have little chance of avoiding an injunction against its inducement of the action.

906 See TULRCA 1992 s.62(9). Also, a ballot may "relate" (s.233(3)(a)) to future industrial action by workers without "relating" to others already called on to take action: *Newham LBC v NALGO* [1993] I.C.R. 189 CA.

907 It is suggested that Woolf LJ went no further than this in *Newham LBC v NALGO* [1993] I.C.R. 189 at 198–200, in saying that the continuance of a "live dispute" on issues presented on the ballot paper depended on a party having an honest and genuine belief that the dispute continued; see the overlapping test of "furtherance" of a dispute, paras 23-195 to 23-196; see *Express Newspapers Ltd v McShane* [1980] A.C. 672 HL.

908 TULRCA 1992 s.229(2); on the definition of "strike" in s.246, and lack of definition of industrial action, para.23-162. See further on the lack of precision about the nature of industrial action the special provision designating overtime and call-out bans as action short of a strike: TULRCA 1992 s.229(2A) inserted by ERA 1999 Sch.3 para.6 (reversing the decision in *Connex SE v RMT* [1999] I.R.L.R. 249 CA).

909 *Post Office v UCW* [1990] I.C.R. 258 CA.

910 See para.23-162; a stoppage for five minutes every hour can be seen as a "concerted stoppage of work", but in ordinary language it would be called action short of a strike: Wedderburn, *Employment Rights in Britain and Europe* (1991), Ch.10. But a ballot on strike action alone was not invalidated by the inaccurate statement in accompanying information that in law all action was regarded as strike action: *British Telecommunications Plc v Communication Workers Union* [2003] EWHC 937 (QB); [2004] I.R.L.R. 58.

question must be considered separately.[911] Section 5 of the Trade Union Act 2016 has made three significant additions to the provisions in TULRCA s.229 on the content of the ballot paper. First, it must contain a summary of the matter(s) in issue in the trade dispute to which the proposed industrial action relates.[912] Secondly, where it contains a question on action short of a strike, the type or types of action must be specified; thirdly, it must state the period or periods within which each type of action is expected to take place.[913] The voting must be by marking a paper, as far as reasonably practicable in secret and without any costs to the voters[914]; members must be allowed to vote without interference or constraint imposed by the union, its members, officials or employees.[915] The union must ensure that votes are honestly and accurately counted[916]; and as soon as reasonably practicable it must provide those entitled to vote with what is now detailed information about the result.[917] The extent of the obligations now imposed on a trade union in drafting the ballot paper will depend on the courts' interpretation of the additional requirements introduced by the 2016 Act. Two central issues are raised by these amendments. The first is the legal effect of the way in which the ballot paper identifies the substance of the trade dispute; it is not clear whether a general reference to, for example, "pay", "working time" or "overtime working" will be sufficient. Secondly, it is especially unclear whether a statement of intended action such as "a

---

911 *West Midlands Travel Ltd v TGWU* [1994] I.C.R. 978 CA (reversing Schiemann J; 1256 for a strike, against 1225; but 1059 for and 1156 against action short of a strike); TULRCA 1992 s.226(2)(a)(iii), "the majority voting in the ballot" had "answered 'yes' to the question applicable".

912 In *Argos Ltd v Unite the Union* [2017] EWHC 1959 (QB) at [33], in refusing to grant an interim injunction, Dingemans J held that the claimants were not likely to be able to prove at trial that a summary on the ballot paper was inadequate: he held that the meaning of the summary should be assessed by reference to a hypothetical reasonable member of the union receiving the ballot paper.

913 TULRCA 1992 s.229(2B)–(2D). In *Thomas Cook Airlines Ltd v British Airline Pilots Association* [2017] EWHC 2253 (QB); [2017] I.R.L.R. 1137, in refusing an interim injunction against a strike, Lavender J expressed the view that a court was not more likely than not to interpret s.229(2D) as requiring more detail about the expected period of industrial action than "discontinuous industrial action in the form of strike action on dates to be announced over the period from 8th September 2017 to 18th February 2018."

914 The cost of postage may fall to be borne both ways by the union: cf. *Paul v NALGO* [1987] I.R.L.R. 83 CA (union internal election). The scheme for refunding union costs of secret postal ballots for certain purposes (TULRCA 1992 s.115) ceased in 1996.

915 This does not mean that the union is prohibited from being "partisan" in the campaign for the ballot: *Newham LBC v NALGO* [1993] I.C.R. 189. In *Royal Mail Group Ltd v Communication Workers Union* [2019] EWCA Civ 2150; [2020] I.C.R. 940, the Court of Appeal upheld the conclusion that there had been interference by a union which implemented (see [46]) "a plan pursuant to which it told its members to intercept ballot papers at their place of work, to open them immediately and to vote at the workplace, and to take part in filmed 'mass posting' events, rather than allowing the ballot papers to be delivered in the ordinary course of post to their home addresses." Males LJ offered the following guidance on the interpretation of "interference", at [49]: "it is directed to conduct, whether by words or action, which has the effect of preventing or hindering the ordinary course of events with which the section is concerned, that is to say, the process of voting in a ballot for industrial action. It is not in my judgment limited to conduct which amounts to intimidation, coercion, fraud or the like." See also Simler LJ at [76] and Sir Patrick Elias at [86]. Dissemination of false information might be interference, albeit innocent: *RJB Mining v NUM* [1997] I.R.L.R. 621 at 623 (but not prohibited if the employer is the guilty party).

916 Accidental inaccuracies are disregarded if they cannot affect the result: TULRCA 1992 s.230(4).

917 TULRCA 1992 s.231; as amended by s.6 of the Trade Union Act 2016 this information must now include the number of persons entitled to vote; whether or not the number of votes cast was at least 50 per cent of those entitled to vote, thus satisfying the minimum turnout requirement in s.226(2)(a)(iia) (inserted by s.2 of the 2016 Act) and, where the support of at least 40 per cent of those entitled to vote is required under the amendments made by s.3 of the 2016 Act, whether or not it has been achieved.

ban on overtime working at weekends" would limit the legality of a union's call for action such that a call for a ban on overtime working on other days or for other action short of a strike, would lack the required support of a ballot notwithstanding a majority vote and compliance with all the other conditions in the ballot in support of action short of a strike.

Notices to employers Not later than the seventh day before the opening of the ballot, the union must take reasonable steps to ensure that notice of the ballot (including its dates) is received by those it has reason to think are employers of members entitled to vote[918]—the first of the four notices which the union must give employers. In *London & Birmingham Railway Ltd v ASLEF* the Court of Appeal rejected the judge's finding that the purpose of the obligation to provide notices was to enable the employer to decide whether to take legal proceedings or not.[919] After the amendments made by the Employment Relations Act 2004 the notice must contain "lists" of the categories to which the employees who will be entitled to vote belong and of their workplaces, and "figures" showing the total numbers of affected employees, the numbers affected in each category[920] and at each workplace. The union is also required to provide an explanation of how these figures were arrived at.[921] Where the employer makes deductions from wages which are paid to the union (that is union subscriptions are paid by the "check off", see TULRCA 1992 ss.68 and 68A) the union may instead provide such information as will enable the employer to deduce the numbers affected in each category and at each workplace. The information so provided must be as accurate as is reasonably practicable in the light of the information in possession of the union; this is expressly stated to include information held for union purposes in electronic or other form which is in the possession or under the control of an officer or employee of the union.[922] But the union is not required to take steps to obtain the information from its members; the duty 23-169

918 TULRCA 1992 s.226A(1)(a); the opening is the day when a member is first sent a voting paper: s.226A(4). Under provisions such as these each corporate employer is treated by the courts as a separate employer: *Dimbleby & Sons Ltd v NUJ* [1984] 1 W.L.R. 67 HL.

919 [2011] EWCA Civ 226; [2011] I.C.R. 848 at [118]–[120] per Elias LJ (with whom Mummery and Etherton LJJ agreed); nor was it necessary for the union to explain "who did what and when" in compiling the figures or to explain a discrepancy with figures provided in earlier ballots, though it might be wise for the union to respond to a request for the latter.

920 In *British Airways Plc v British Airline Pilots' Association* [2019] EWCA Civ 1663; [2020] I.R.L.R. 43, the Court of Appeal confirmed that a union was not obliged to adopt any particular scheme for categorising the employees concerned, be that by occupation, grade or pay band, and, in particular it was not obliged to use whatever approach would best assist the employer in planning for industrial action; but a union might fail to fulfil its obligation if it selected categories that were "too uncertain or imprecise", at [63] per Simler LJ.

921 In *London & Birmingham Railway Ltd v ASLEF* [2011] EWCA Civ 226; [2011] I.C.R. 848 at [92] Elias LJ concluded that, consistently with the Code of Practice (see fn.868 at para.23-162) this required the union to state the sources of its data and identify any potential weaknesses in its records highlighting any potential inaccuracies of which it was aware; "the duty on the union is not an onerous one", [2011] EWCA Civ 226; [2011] I.C.R. 848 at [95].

922 TULRCA 1992 s.226A(2E) inserted by the Employment Relations Act 2004 s.22 in place of earlier amendments by the Employment Relations Act 1999, both intended to remove the duty on the union to give the employer the names of the employees involved which the original provisions had been held to impose (see *Blackpool and Fylde College v NATFHE* [1994] I.C.R. 648 CA). Like the earlier amendments (on which see *London Underground Ltd v RMT* [2001] EWCA Civ 211; [2001] I.C.R. 647; Wedderburn (2001) 30 I.L.J. 206) it still broadly requires the union to identify the workers involved. Submissions alleging the incompatibility of these provisions with art.11 of the European Convention on Human Rights were rejected by the Court of Appeal in *Metrobus Ltd v Unite* [2009] EWCA Civ 829; [2010] I.C.R.173. See too *British Telecommunications Plc v CWU* [2003] EWHC

is limited to providing information actually held by the union at the time it is provided.[923]

23-170 The second "notice" which the union must give to employers is a sample ballot paper, which must be received not later that the third day before the ballot.[924] Thirdly, every "relevant employer" whom it is reasonable for the union to believe was at the time of the ballot an employer of anyone entitled to vote must be informed of the result of the ballot "as soon as is reasonably practicable after the holding of the ballot."[925] Fourthly, after notifying the employer of the result and where the result was in favour of industrial action and the union decides to go ahead, it must send the employer notice of industrial action under TULRCA s.234A which gives the employer equivalent information to that required by s.226A in the notice of ballot.[926] As amended by s.8 of the Trade Union Act 2016 this s.234A notice must be given at least 14 days before the day specified in the notice for the commencement of the action, unless the employer and union agree that notice given seven days before the starting date is sufficient. It must state whether the action is intended to be continuous from the day specified or discontinuous when the "intended dates" for any of the affected workers to take part must be given.[927] While it has been recognised that it is possible for industrial action to be suspended, typi-

---

937 (QB); [2004] I.R.L.R. 58, where the union's notice failed to comply with the now replaced 1999 amendments since, although 90 per cent of the workforce were union members, it was possible that in some areas it was less than that and it would arguably have assisted the employers to make plans if it had been given information about the number of members at each workplace.

[923] *London & Birmingham Railway Ltd v ASLEF* [2011] EWCA Civ 226; [2011] I.C.R. 848 per Elias LJ at [60]–[77]; both the limitation of the duty by reference to information in possession of the union and the fact that unions would normally have this information available supported limiting the duty to provide figures from information actually held by the union at the time they were provided. This approach was followed in *United Closures & Plastics Ltd v Unite* [2011] CSOH 114; 2011 S.L.T. 1105 at [46]–[47]; cf. *EDF Energy Powerlink Ltd v RMT* [2009] EWHC 2852 (QB); [2010] I.R.L.R. 114, which seems to be inconsistent with this construction and *Metroline Travel Ltd v Unite* [2012] EWHC 1778 (QB); [2012] I.R.L.R. 749 where the information provided was held to be inadequate to enable the employer to "readily deduce" the numbers, categories and workplaces of those concerned as s.226A(2C) requires. cf. para.24 of the 2017 revision of the Code of Practice which suggests that "in order to reduce the likelihood of a dispute" the union "may wish to invite an opinion from the relevant employer" whether its conclusion on entitlement to vote complies with these statutory requirements; sed quaere.

[924] TULRCA 1992 s.226A(1)(b), (2F).

[925] TULRCA 1992 s.231A, providing the numbers of votes cast, "yes" and "no" votes, and spoiled papers. If separate workplace ballots are required it appears that the information should be provided for each workplace. In *Metrobus Ltd v Unite* [2009] EWCA Civ 829; [2010] I.C.R.173 it was said that this obligation had to be complied with in all cases, even where the union did not decide to call for industrial action after securing majority support in the ballot, although it is hard to see what sanction there could be for failing to do so if no industrial action took place. On the facts in that case it was held that the union had failed to discharge this obligation where the scrutineer's report was not actually received by the union's head office until the day after the ballot had closed and the employer was not informed of the result until the day after that when notice of when the action would begin was given. See Dukes (2010) 39 I.L.J. 82.

[926] TULRCA 1992 s.234A. As in the earlier notice under s.226A, the information in the union's possession is limited for these purposes to information held in a document whether in electronic or other form, in the possession or under the control of an officer or employee of the union: s.234A(3E). cf. the wide interpretation given to information possessed by the union under the now repealed 1999 amendments in *London Underground Ltd v RMT* [2001] EWCA Civ 211; [2001] I.C.R. 647 at [57]–[59]; see Wedderburn (2001) 30 I.L.J. 206. On obligatory information as to the "categories" of affected workers see *Westminster City Council v UNISON* [2001] EWCA Civ 443; [2001] I.C.R. 1046 at [78], per Buxton LJ: "a very broad word and not to be either exclusively or narrowly defined … It means no more than a reference to the general type of workers."

[927] TULRCA 1992 s.234A(3)(b). A union intends action to be discontinuous if it is to take place only

cally for negotiations over the issues in dispute, and then resumed without the need for a further notice,[928] that situation has to be distinguished from one where the union's authorisation or endorsement of the action ceases, but is later re-established, when a fresh notice of industrial action under s.234A must then be given.[929]

Effects of non-compliance In addition to those small accidental failures which are disregarded as a result of s.232B, noted above,[930] there are other limits on the effects of non-compliance with the prescriptive detail of these provisions. A failure to surmount each of the hurdles described above does not necessarily cause the union to lose the protection of s.219 against every type of claimant, although it cannot of course know at the time of the decision to ballot who will be the claimant or applicant in subsequent proceedings.[931] To rely on any ballot as support for the industrial action, the union must be able to show not only that a "yes" vote was obtained but that the basic provisions have been satisfied: i.e. the provisions concerning the appointment and report of the scrutineer (where applicable), entitlements to vote, separate workplace majorities (where applicable), voting papers and conduct of the ballot, information to members of the result and notification to all relevant employers of the result, as well as compliance with the rules about "calling" on members to take action.[932] The duty to provide a notice of the forthcoming ballot and a sample ballot paper[933] looks only to that employer in the dispute: it is specifically provided that if it fails in this, the union's act is "not protected as respects" that employer.[934] Others cannot rely upon it. Lastly and similarly, inducement of a person[935] by the union to take action is "not protected as respects his employer" if it does not send to that employer the required notice about the forthcoming industrial action, with information about the categories and numbers of members it intends to call out, specifying whether the stoppage will be continuous or discontinuous, plus the "lists" and "figures" relating to the affected 23-171

on some days; otherwise it is continuous: s.234A(6).

928 *Monsanto Plc v TGWU* [1987] I.C.R. 269 CA. See now TULRCA 1992 s.234A(7B).

929 TULRCA 1992 s.234A(7). This provision does not apply where industrial action ceased to be authorised or endorsed by the union in order to comply with a court order or undertaking (s.234A(7A)) nor where action is suspended by agreement with the employer but then later resumed (s.234A(7B)).

930 See para.23-164.

931 This distinction was introduced by the TURERA 1993. Under the 1984 Act and later amendments, the failure to hold a ballot or to satisfy any of the requirements led to wholesale loss of protection against liability for inducing breach of or interference with a contract of employment or inducing breach of or interfering with a commercial contract by the unlawful means of inducing breach of or interfering with the performance with contracts of employment: see *Solihull MB v NUT* [1985] I.R.L.R. 211; *Express and Star v NGA* [1986] I.C.R. 589 CA; *Austin Rover Group Ltd v AUEW (TASS)* [1985] I.R.L.R. 162; *Falconer v ASLEF* [1986] I.R.L.R. 331; Hutton (1985) 14 I.L.J. 255.

932 TULRCA 1992 s.226(2)(a), (b) and (c), and s.62(2): provisions in: ss.229(2), 226B, 227, 228, 229, 230, 231, 231A, 231B, and 233.

933 TULRCA 1992 s.226A.

934 TULRCA 1992 s.226(1)(b), contrasting this case with the basic provisions in (a) where non-compliance means the act is "not protected" generally.

935 Here, as elsewhere, it is no defence for the union if the person induced turns out to be a non-member; but such a person cannot vote in the ballot: s.227. Yet, bargaining for benefits for members only, under threat of taking industrial action, is also now unlawful for the union by way of removal of protection by s.222 and see para.23-148.

employees.[936] In addition, the failure to fulfil any of the listed requirements can also be the ground on which an individual can bring an action where industrial action affects supply of goods and services, under s.235A.[937]

23-172 **Duration of ballot protection** Under the provisions on industrial action ballots as originally enacted in 1984, a favourable ballot ceased to be effective at the end of four weeks beginning with the date of the ballot.[938] During the passage of the 1990 Bill, the issue arose of cases where a union was subjected to interim injunctions while litigation extended, especially in appeals, beyond the four week period, which meant that even if it won in court, the union would need to reballot its members.[939] The 1990 Act therefore amended the law so that where during the four week period a court order prohibited the union from calling for industrial action but the order subsequently lapsed or was discharged, recalled or set aside, the union could apply to the court for an order that the period during which the earlier order prohibited the calling of industrial action should not count towards the four week period within which a call for industrial action could be made.[940] A further amendment in 1999 enabled the period within which the ballot remained effective to be extended from four weeks to up to eight weeks by agreement between the union and the employer.[941] Section 9 of the Trade Union Act 2016 has further extended the period for which a ballot remains effective to six months or a longer period up to nine months by agreement between the union and the employer.[942] This extension of the period for which a union can rely on the support of a ballot is likely to cover most cases in which a court order prohibiting the union from calling for industrial action is reversed on appeal. The right of a union to apply for an order that the period during which an earlier court order prohibiting the union from calling for industrial action was in force, shall not count towards these new longer periods for which a ballot remains effective, is however retained.[943] So too is the provision forbidding the court from making an order if it appears likely that either the result of the ballot no longer represents the views of the members or an event is likely to occur as a result of which these members would be likely to vote against industrial action if another ballot were to be held.[944]

---

936 TULRCA 1992 s.234A as amended by ERA 1999 Sch.3 para.11 and ERA 2004 s.25.

937 Inserted by TURERA 1993 s.22; see para.23-173.

938 Trade Union Act 1984 s.10(3)(c), consolidated in TULRCA s.234(1). On the date of the ballot see now TULRCA 1992 s.246.

939 As in *Associated British Ports v TGWU* [1989] I.R.L.R.291 at 301, Millet J and [1989] 1 W.L.R. 939 CA and HL (union successful at first instance, not in the Court of Appeal but successful in the House of Lords; new ballot required for national dock strike); see also *Barretts & Baird (Wholesale) Ltd v IPCS* [1987] I.R.L.R. 3 (delay before inter partes hearing after ex parte injunction).

940 Employment Act 1990 s.8, consolidated in TULRCA 1992 s.234(2).

941 TULRCA 1992 s.234(1), as substituted by the Employment Relations Act 1999 s.4, Sch.3 paras 1 and 10.

942 TULRCA 1992 s.234(1A), as substituted by the Trade Union Act 2016 s.9(1).

943 TULRCA 1992 s.234(2).

944 TULRCA 1992 s.234(4). It is submitted that the courts would require objective evidence that such a change or event is reasonably probable.

(i) The statutory right of action

23-173 In 1993, a new right of action was given to individuals which, although not strictly an action in tort, is closely related to these issues.[945] An individual[946] who can show that an unlawful act done by any person (including a trade union)[947] induced, or is likely to induce, another to take part in industrial action with the effect of preventing or delaying the supply of goods or services, or reducing their quality, to that individual, may apply for an order of the court to require such persons to ensure that no new inducement is effected and no further steps are taken as a result of the original inducement.[948] Nor is the individual required to show that he or she is entitled to be supplied with the goods or services, by contract or otherwise.[949] Action under this section is "unlawful" where (a) it is actionable in tort by any person; or (b) in the case only of the act of a trade union, it could be the basis of an application by a member on the ground that industrial action has been or will be induced without the support of a valid ballot.[950] This is a double extension of liabilities: the scope of claimants is enlarged where the act is tortious against any person whatever, and in the absence of a ballot the union is liable at the suit of any individual in reliance on a right previously extended by statute only to its members.[951] In most cases involving a union, this section will raise the issue, therefore, of whether there has been a valid ballot, because alternative (b) allows the applicant to succeed even if the union's inducement is "ineffective".[952]

(j) Picketing and trade disputes

23-174 One of the acts which can render industrial action unlawful is picketing. It is not the case, however, that "everyone must have somewhere where he can effectively picket".[953] At common law picketing is not in itself wrongful, except possibly as a trespass to the highway,[954] unless it constitutes an obstruction in the nature of a

---

945 See TULRCA 1992 s.235A (TURERA 1993 s.22); G. Morris (1993) 22 I.L.J. 194. See the unsuccessful application in *P v NAS/UWT* [2003] UKHL 8; [2003] 2 A.C. 663.

946 In this context, the new right of action appears not to be intended to include corporate bodies, not least because the new action "derives from … the Government's Citizen's Charter", per Viscount Ullswater, Parl. Deb., HL, 1 March 1993, col.425; per Mrs G. Shepherd (Secretary of State), Parl. Deb., HC, 17 November 1992, col.175 (distinguishing "companies" from the "individual citizen" as a "customer" who is part of the "general public").

947 TULRCA 1992 s.235A(6) applies the provisions of s.20 for determining whether an act is authorised or endorsed by a trade union.

948 TULRCA 1992 s.235A(4); where the court finds the complaint well-founded it must make an order. Applications for interim relief fall within the section: s.235A(5). The defendant can be obliged to ensure that "no person engages in conduct" by virtue of the inducement. Semble, the court's "other powers" do not include power to grant damages.

949 TULRCA 1992 s.235A(3). But where the complaint goes to a "reduction in quality", it is submitted that there must here be some "nexus" or expectation linking the applicant to a particular standard or quality which might have been expected by him.

950 TULRCA 1992 s.235A(2); on the right of a member to apply in the absence of a ballot see s.62.

951 Semble: where the rules of the union provide for a ballot on industrial action, the contractual right of the members cannot be relied on by an applicant under this section, unless perhaps the breach of contract under the rules is deliberate and is therefore regarded as actionable in tort by way of being the use of "unlawful means"; see paras 23-87 and 23-115.

952 See s.62(6). Although s.226(4) also includes "ineffective" inducements, that section does not impose liability in tort for such inducements that have no effect.

953 per Bingham LJ in *Union Traffic Ltd v TGWU* [1989] I.C.R. 98 at 109.

954 See *News Group Newspapers Ltd v SOGAT (No.2)* [1987] I.C.R. 181 at 202–203 (marches lawful

nuisance.[955] A series of legislative provisions in the nineteenth century aimed at protecting peaceful picketing from liabilities for "molestation", "obstruction" or nuisance, proved to be ineffective.[956] Finally, the liberty to picket peacefully in trade disputes was thought to be established in 1906[957] and continued until restricted in 1980, notably to picketing a worker's own place of work.[958] Now s.220 of TULRCA 1992 declares: "It is lawful" in contemplation or furtherance of a trade dispute for a person to attend "at or near his own place of work" or, in the case of a union official accompanying a member whom he represents, at or near the place of work of that member "for the purpose only of peacefully obtaining or communicating information, or peacefully persuading any person to work or abstain from working".

23-175 Although the right to picket peacefully is expressed as a right—s.220 of TULRCA 1992 which is headed "Peaceful picketing" begins with the words "[i]t is lawful"—it has long been treated as another trade dispute immunity. TULRCA 1992 maintains this tradition by depriving an act "done in the course of picketing"[959] from the protections of s.219(1) and (2) against economic tort liability unless it is done in the course of attendance declared to be "lawful" by s.220.[960] The Trade Union Act 2016 has added a further requirement that where s.220A—which it has inserted into TULRCA 1992—applies, the provisions of that section must also be complied with.[961] The new s.220A introduces a set of additional conditions which must be satisfied in order for "any picketing that a trade union organises or encour-

---

until unreasonable obstruction of highway); *Harrison v Duke of Rutland* [1893] 1 Q.B. 142 at 146 (action for owner of the sub-soil); *Thomas v NUM (South Wales Area)* [1986] Ch. 20 at 56–65, per Scott J; *Norbrook Laboratories Ltd v King* [1984] I.R.L.R. 200 CA (NI); see now *DPP v Jones* [1999] 2 A.C. 240 HL, according a new width of rights for those using the highway for reasonable purposes without causing obstruction; and *DPP v Ziegler* [2019] EWHC 71 (Admin); [2020] Q.B. 253. On trespass to land see Ch.18.

955 *Lyons v Wilkins (No.1)* [1896] 1 Ch. 811 CA; (No.2) [1899] 1 Ch. 255 CA; interpreted in *Thomas v NUM (South Wales Area)* [1986] Ch. 20 at 59–65, per Scott J; *News Group Newspapers Ltd v SOGAT (No.2)* [1987] I.C.R. 181 at 202–204, per Stuart-Smith J; cf. *Thomson-Schwab v Costaki* [1956] 1 W.L.R. 335. But see *DPP v Fidler* [1992] 1 W.L.R. 91 (anti-abortion pickets, relaxing the principles in *Lyons v Wilkins* [1896] 1 Ch. 811 CA; [1899] 1 Ch. 255 CA). In *Ward Lock & Co v OPAS* (1906) 22 T.L.R. 327, the Court of Appeal held picketing to be lawful at common law as there had been no "annoyance or molestation" and "a complete absence of anything in the nature of picketing or besetting which could constitute a nuisance": see, per Fletcher Moulton LJ at 329–330. The facts in *Ward Lock* were, however, very special: see *Hubbard v Pitt* [1976] Q.B. 142 at 174–176.

956 For a summary of these provisions, relevant to decisions between 1825 and 1907, see Wedderburn, *Cases and Materials on Labour Law* (1967), pp.384-385; e.g. the Molestation of Workmen Act 1859 gave protection only if there was no breach of employment contracts: Orth, *Combination and Conspiracy* (1991), Ch.5.

957 Trade Disputes Act 1906 s.2, continued in a modified form by the Industrial Relations Act 1971, s.134, then re-enacted by the Trade Union and Labour Relations Act 1974 s.15. The major difference was that s.15 in 1974 did not protect, as s.2 of the 1906 Act had done, picketing of a mere residence, i.e. a home which is not also a place of work; see now TULRCA 1992 s.220.

958 Employment Act 1980 s.16(1); but the cases before 1980 remain authorities on other points in the text.

959 There is no statutory definition of "picketing". It is generally considered to be attendance in the course of an industrial dispute seeking to persuade workers not to work: see *Code of Practice on Picketing* (2017), para.10. The Code was revised in 2017 to take account of the amendments made to the law by the Trade Union Act 2016 which came into force in March 2017. This persuasion is sometimes assumed to induce them to break their contracts, even if no words are said: *Union Traffic Ltd v TGWU* [1989] I.C.R. 98, CA at 106, per Bingham LJ ("presence alone at the site" of the pickets was enough). Further on definitions of "picketing": Bercusson (1977) 40 M.L.R. 265 at 271.

960 TULRCA 1992 s.219(3). cf. s.224(1)(3) which maintain this protection in s.220 even where acts of lawful picketing are also within the definition of secondary action in s.224.

961 TULRCA 1992 s.219(3) as amended by the Trade Union Act 2016 s.10(1); s.220A.

ages its members to take part in" to have the benefit of the provisions on peaceful picketing in s.220. These new provisions require the union to appoint a "picket supervisor" who must be familiar with the provisions of the Code of Practice on picketing.[962] Reasonable steps must be taken by either the union or the supervisor to tell the police who the supervisor is, where the picketing is to take place and how the supervisor can be contacted. The supervisor must be provided with a letter from the union stating that the picketing is approved by the union, an ambiguous obligation given the wide range of incidents that can occur on a picket line; it is not clear whether the approval could of itself give rise to liability on the part of the union for any unlawful conduct by the pickets. The letter must be shown to the employer or someone acting on the employer's behalf as soon as is reasonably practicable. The supervisor must either be present while the picketing is taking place or readily contactable by the union and able to attend at short notice. The ambiguity which is inherent in some of these provisions could facilitate applications for interim relief on grounds which could include economic tort liability where a union's compliance with them is disputed.[963] Where it applies the statutory protection appears to legalise a mere trespass to the highway by pickets pursuing a trade dispute[964]; but it does not protect a trespass on the premises, only attendance "at or near".[965] Nor did it apply where it was held that a trial court would probably find that the defendant union official was deliberately threatening the claimant employer with "intimidating noisy protest" by people with no pre-existing connection with the workers on strike, with the object of harassing the employer and embarrassing it into conceding the union's demands.[966]

Crimes such as "trespassory assembly",[967] can prohibit assemblies which go beyond the limits of the public's right of access to the highway. But the majority in *DPP v Jones*[968] extended the right to "peaceful assemblies" on the highway, i.e. gatherings which are, on a decision providing an analogue in criminal law to the **23-176**

[962] See para.23-178.

[963] TULRCA 1992 s.224(1), (3). Quaere if non-compliance with any of the new statutory obligations could amount to unlawful means for the purposes of economic tort liability.

[964] *News Group Newspapers Ltd v SOGAT (No.2)* [1987] I.C.R. 181; *Ferguson v O'Gorman* [1937] I.R. 620 at 630–631. Where, individuals are made defendants as representing branches or other groups in the union, the courts have shown a tendency to extend the range of possible defendants by leave to mount representative proceedings: *Michaels (Furriers) Ltd v Askew, The Times,* 25 June 1983 CA; *UK Nirex v Barton, The Times,* 14 October 1986; but see *News Group Newspapers Ltd v SOGAT (No.2)* [1987] I.C.R. 181 at 222–224; Auerbach (1987) 16 I.L.J. 227.

[965] *Galt v Philp* [1984] I.R.L.R. 156; *Rayware Ltd v TGWU* [1989] I.C.R. 457 CA (nearest point on highway to workplace inside a large industrial estate is still "at or near"); *Timex Electronics Corp v AEEU*, 1994 S.L.T. 438; *Goulding v Lawrence Bolger* [1977] I.R. 211 (but for the modern law on picketing in Ireland, see *Westman Holdings v McCormack* [1992] 1 I.R. 151; Irish Industrial Relations Act 1991 s.11).

[966] *Thames Cleaning & Support Services Ltd v United Voices of the World* [2016] EWHC 1310 (QB); [2016] I.R.L.R. 695 per Warby J at [47]; apart from trespass to land, he said that encouraging demonstrators with the aim of intimidating workers, scaring them away from work, might amount to unlawful means conspiracy: [2016] EWHC 1310 (QB); [2016] I.R.L.R. 695 at [45].

[967] Under the Public Order Act 1986 s.14A (inserted by Criminal Justice and Public Order Act 1994 s.70) an order can prohibit a trespassory assembly.

[968] [1999] 2 A.C. 240 HL (Lords Slynn and Hope dissenting): per Lord Irvine LC: extended access to any reasonable use of the highway consistent with the primary right of passage (otherwise the right of peaceful assembly in art.11 of the ECHR would be "denied"); per Lords Hutton and Clyde: peaceful assembly on the highway may be permitted where it is reasonable and not an obstruction; see Pickford (1999) 149 N.L.J. 927. More recently, the Divisional Court in *DPP v Ziegler* [2019] EWHC 71 (Admin); [2020] Q.B. 253 at [76] suggested that the decision in *Jones* might need to be "treated with some caution" in light of the "constitutional shift" brought about by the Human Rights Act

"right to picket", inherent in s.220, where the objections have usually arisen in the torts of nuisance or trespass. Moreover, the purposes must be only those stated in the section,[969] so that the section will not protect those who commit an offence which takes them outside those purposes.[970] But "watching" or "besetting" or intimidation within TULRCA 1992 s.241 (which re-enacts s.7 of the Conspiracy and Protection of Property Act 1875),[971] does not cause picketing to be unlawful unless it is in itself unreasonable and so, for example, creates liability for the tort of nuisance.[972] This is even more clear since the reinterpretation of the section to remove from its ambit mere "persuasion".[973] The protection does not cover crimes, such as obstruction of a police officer in the execution of his duty.[974] Similarly, picketing which involves those participating in conduct which is tortious, is actionable at common law.[975] So, the critical questions are how far statute protects acts which amount to one of the economic torts—procuring a breach of contract, intimidation, or a conspiracy to injure; or which would at common law be a trespass or an obstruction in the nature of nuisance. As far as economic tort liability is concerned s.220 adds little to the defences provided in s.219. As already noted it is provided in s.224 that lawful picketing—that is picketing declared lawful by s.220—is excluded from the scope of secondary action from which s.224 removes the statutory defences in s.219. To that extent s.220 reinforces the policy underlying the trade dispute defences of excluding economic tort liability (to the extent provided in s.219) from industrial action taken in contemplation or furtherance of

---

1998, and held that an obstruction of the highway might not be criminal under s.137 Highways Act 1980 where criminalisation would be a disproportionate restriction on the Convention rights of free expression (art.10 ECHR) and free assembly (art.11 ECHR): the Supreme Court has given permission to appeal in this case: [2020] 1 W.L.R. 730.

969 The Trade Disputes Act 1906 s.2, said "merely" for these same purposes, but nothing appears to turn on that difference of wording. That section deleted the proviso to s.7 of the Conspiracy and Protection of Property Act 1875.

970 *British Airports Authority v Ashton* [1983] 1 W.L.R. 1079. Self-help against unlawful picketing is to be discouraged: *R. v Chief Constable of Devon and Cornwall* [1982] Q.B. 458 at 473, per Lord Denning MR.

971 As amended by the Public Order Act 1986; constable can arrest without warrant, s.241(3). On the 1875 Act, see *R. v Wall* (1907) 21 Cox C.C. 401; *Lyons v Wilkins (No.1)* [1896] 1 Ch. 811 CA; (No.2) [1899] 1 Ch. 255, CA; *R. v Jones* [1974] I.C.R. 310 CA; *Galt v Philp* [1984] I.R.L.R. 156 (Scot.); and see *Elsey v Smith* [1983] I.R.L.R. 292.

972 See, per Scott J in *Thomas v NUM (South Wales Area)* [1986] Ch. 20 at 56–65: in order to be an offence under s.7 the conduct must be tortious. On the narrow locus standi for claimants in private nuisance, see *Hunter v Canary Wharf* [1997] A.C. 655 HL. There is greater doubt about Scott J's view that there is a tort of "unreasonable harassment" at 64: per Stuart-Smith J in *News Group Newspapers Ltd v SOGAT (No.2)* [1987] I.C.R. 181 at 205–206 (nuisance); on the Protection from Harassment Act 1997, see paras 14-19 to 14-22.

973 See the remarkable decision in *DPP v Fidler* [1992] 1 W.L.R. 91, on what is now s.241 of TULRCA 1992: the Court of Appeal relied upon the amendment of the proviso to s.7 of the 1875 Act by s.2 of the 1906 Act, so as to depart from the meaning ascribed to it by *Lyons v Wilkins* [1896] 1 Ch. 811 CA; [1899] 1 Ch. 255 CA, and long followed since, that persuasion by itself could not amount to "compulsion" within the section (this interpretation was adopted by consent, with the agreement of the DPP; anti-abortion pickets who aimed to "embarrass and shock and shame those concerned" held not guilty). cf. *Att Gen Ontario v Dielman* (1994) 117 D.L.R. (4th) 449 (Ont.).

974 *Piddington v Bates* [1961] 1 W.L.R. 162; *Kavanagh v Hiscock* [1974] I.C.R. 282 DC; see, also *Messenger Newspapers Ltd v NGA* [1984] I.R.L.R. 397; affirmed at [1984] I.C.R. 345 CA; *Moss v McLachlan* [1985] I.R.L.R. 76 DC.

975 See, e.g. *News Group Newspapers Ltd v SOGAT (No.2)* [1987] I.C.R. 181; intimidation or defamation is not protected from liability: *Ryan v Cooke* [1938] I.R. 512; nor inducing breach of contract otherwise than in furtherance of a trade dispute: *Torquay Hotel Ltd v Cousins* [1969] 2 Ch. 106 CA; cf. *Middlebrook Mushrooms Ltd v TGWU* [1993] I.C.R. 612 CA, where no tort was committed.

a trade dispute. The situation in relation to other liability, civil or criminal, is arguably less supportive of any right of peaceful picketing.

Pickets and obstructions In *Tynan v Balmer*,[976] the defendant was the leader of about 40 pickets walking in a continuous circle outside a factory. The court decided that the picketing was an unreasonable user of the highway and a nuisance at common law, just as much as if the pickets had been "carrying banners advertising some patent medicine or advocating some political reform". The House of Lords adopted a similar approach in *Broome v DPP*.[977] There a picket approached a lorry entering a building site picketed in a trade dispute. After failing to persuade the lorry driver to turn back, the picket stood in front of the lorry and refused to move. No violent acts or threats were made; the picket obstructed the lorry for about nine minutes, after which he was arrested for wilful obstruction of the highway without lawful authority or excuse.[978] The House of Lords affirmed that he was guilty of this charge and swept aside the argument that, in modern times, a right of peaceful picketing to persuade a person not to work must import a right to argue with him, which meant a right to stop him for a reasonable period. Lord Reid said: 23-177

> "One is familiar with persons at the side of a road signalling to a driver requesting him to stop. It is then for the driver to decide whether he will stop or not. That, in my view, a picket is entitled to do. If the driver stops, the picket can talk to him but only for so long as the driver is willing to listen."[979]

Viscount Dilhorne could see no reason to give the statutory provision the wide interpretation for which the picket contended, even if it was otherwise a "meaningless" provision.[980] Mass picketing to seal off the entry to premises is a nuisance and, therefore, unprotected[981]; so too, picketing accompanied by unlawful threats and similar tortious acts.[982]

Thus, the traditional protection of "peaceful picketing" has never been one of any 23-178

---

976 [1967] 1 Q.B. 91 DC; so too, in *Messenger Newspapers Ltd v NGA* [1984] I.R.L.R. 397; affirmed [1984] I.C.R. 345 CA.

977 [1974] A.C. 587 HL. The statutory protection here was the Industrial Relations Act 1971 s.134; but the same reasoning would apply to TULRCA 1992 s.220. That section (which expressly referred to acts being neither a crime under s.7 of the 1875 Act nor a tort) was taken to give some protection for pickets against criminal liability; per Lord Salmon at 603, and see, per Viscount Dilhorne at 600. Contrast the *Code of Practice on Picketing* (2017) paras 46–49.

978 Contrary to the Highways Act 1959 s.121(1), which may be seen as a criminal equivalent to civil liability for nuisance; now s.137 of the Highways Act 1980; compare *Department of Transport v Williams*, *The Times*, 7 December 1993 CA, where contravention of s.303 of the Highways Act 1980, was held to be unlawful means in tort as well as a crime. On diverse meanings of "obstruction" in various criminal offences on the highway, see *Carey v Chief Constable of Avon and Somerset* [1995] R.T.R. 405 CA.

979 [1974] A.C. 587 at 597, per Lord Reid.

980 [1974] A.C. 587 at 600; cf. *Union Traffic Ltd v TGWU* [1989] I.C.R. 98 CA. Compare the differing approaches of the majority to the right of the public to use the highway in *DPP v Jones* [1999] 2 A.C. 240 HL; *DPP v Ziegler* [2019] EWHC 71 (Admin); [2020] Q.B. 253.

981 *Thomas v NUM (South Wales Area)* [1986] Ch. 20 at 76, per Scott J; cf. *Hunt v Broome* [1974] A.C. 587 at 603–604, per Lord Salmon.

982 *News Group Newspapers Ltd v SOGAT (No.2)* [1987] I.C.R. 181; *Thomas v NUM (South Wales Area)* [1986] Ch. 20; cf. *Read (Transport Ltd) v NUM (South Wales Area)* [1985] I.R.L.R. 67; *Thames Cleaning & Support Services Ltd v United Voices of the World* [2016] EWHC 1310 (QB); [2016] I.R.L.R. 695.

great width.[983] Under the current law, incorporating the new limitations introduced in 1980, in order to obtain protection against the causes of action mentioned in s.219(1) and (2), the picket acting in furtherance of a trade dispute must (unless he is within an exception or is a trade union official) attend only "at or near his own place of work".[984] The "place of work" does not move merely because the employer unilaterally moves the work to a new place, without moving the workers; it is a "geographical location" where the worker actually works under his employment contract.[985] The exception relates to a person who "works or normally works otherwise than at any one place",[986] or where it is "impracticable"[987] to attend for the purpose of picketing. A person within the exception may attend at or near "any premises of his employer from which he works or from which his work is administered". The Code of Practice (2017) recommends (as did earlier versions) that "in general" the number of pickets at any entrance should not exceed six, a provision of which the courts (and the police) have made extensive use.[988] Further, persons who are unemployed but who attend near the place where their employment was terminated in connection with a trade dispute or where that termination was one of the circumstances giving rise to the dispute, may attend near that place.[989] But where drivers dismissed as redundant picketed depots other than their main depot (which had been closed down) they were not protected, even though

983 Where threatening behaviour or violence occurs a variety of criminal liabilities may arise, e.g. "intimidation" or other crimes of public order; see *Moss v McLachlan* [1985] I.R.L.R. 76; Public Order Act 1986 ss.2 (violent disorder), 5 and 6 (harassment), Pt II (processions and assemblies), Sch.2 para.1 (amending s.7 of the 1875 Act, now TULRCA 1992 s.241); see also Morris (1985) 14 I.L.J. 149. With the enactment of the Criminal Justice and Public Order Act 1994 attendance at, near or on land or premises encounters new criminal liabilities in certain situations, e.g. ss.61 (removal of trespassers), 68 (aggravated trespass), 70, 71 (trespassory assemblies: new ss.14A, 14B, 14C of the Public Order Act 1986), 73 (squatters), 77 (residing in vehicles), although it is not anticipated that s.63 (raves) will normally be relevant to pickets. But see the liberal approaches of the majority in *DPP v Jones* [1999] 2 A.C. 240 HL; and of the Divisional Court in *DPP v Ziegler* [2019] EWHC 71 (Admin); [2020] Q.B. 253.

984 TULRCA 1992 ss.220 and 219(3). For the definition of "official": s.119. See *Code of Practice on Picketing* (2017) paras 21–23: "attendance at, or near, an entrance to or exit from the factory, site or office at which the picket works" (para.22); "even if those working at another place of work are employed by the same employer or are covered by the same collective bargaining agreements as the picket" (para.23).

985 *News Group Newspapers Ltd v SOGAT (No.2)* [1987] I.C.R. 181 at 213; compare the definition of "place of work" for the purpose of separate strike ballots in TULRCA 1992 s.228(4).

986 TULRCA 1992 s.220(2)(a).

987 TULRCA 1992 s.220(2)(b); semble including workers who work at a place where it would be contrary to an enactment, or dangerous to picket (e.g. some building sites or an oil rig) or possibly a workplace many miles into a private estate.

988 See *Code of Practice on Picketing* (2017) para.56, retaining the wording of earlier versions of the Code. *Thomas v NUM (South Wales Area)* [1986] Ch. 20 at 70–72; *News Group Newspapers Ltd v SOGAT (No.2)* [1987] I.C.R. 181 at 231; see generally Lewis (ed.), *Labour Law in Britain* (1986), Ch.7; Wedderburn, *The Worker and the Law*, 3rd edn (1986), pp.540-553. cf. Canadian doctrines on picketing "quasi-public" places: S. Robinson (1999) Jo. Can. Lab. E.L.J. 391 (with texts) and see the important decision of the Canadian Supreme Court in *Pepsi-Cola Beverages (West) Ltd v Retail, Wholesale and Development Store Union Local 558* [2002] 1 S.C.R. 156 that "secondary picketing", that is picketing by persons other than workers at their own place of work, is not per se unlawful, but is lawful unless it involves conduct that is independently criminal or tortious. The decision was expressly intended to align the law with the fundamental freedoms of association and expression set out in the Canadian Charter of Rights and Freedoms.

989 TULRCA 1992 s.220(3). The last category is generally said to include only workers who are not in employment, that is not those who have taken jobs at another place of work: Code of Practice, para.20; sed quaere whether a part-time job or entering a training scheme where the worker technically became an "employee", would always have this effect?

those other depots had been "ports of call" and it was now futile to picket the closed depot.[990]

Trade union officials Special provision is made for the trade union official. He may attend at or near the place of work of a worker if: 23-179

(i) the worker is a member of his union;
(ii) he is accompanying that member[991];
(iii) he represents that member; and
(iv) the worker is attending at or near his own place of work (or a permitted substitute, if he is within the exception).[992]

He "represents" a member only if he was elected or appointed to be a representative of some of the members and the member is one of that group, or, as in the case of national officers, all the members.[993] If a person attends at or near a place in a trade dispute and does not fall within one of the exceptions, he is not protected, even if his purpose is only the communication of information about industrial action. Moreover, the protection attaches to his acts "done in the course of picketing"; despite the lack of definition of the word "picketing", the tendency to define it as equivalent to the "attendance" permitted by the statute in contemplation or furtherance of a trade dispute, is fortified by the manner in which, for the purposes of the exemption from the effects of secondary action, "lawful picketing means acts done in the course of such attendance as is declared lawful by section 220".[994] But the precept that an act done in the course of picketing is protected only if done while attending at the right place of work, does not extend to other acts concerning picketing, for example inducing a union to organise picketing.[995] The union may be liable for acts done by pickets either vicariously[996] or on the ground that it organises action over which it has sufficient control and which it ought to have known would be likely to give rise to the tortious action.[997] When, however, pickets who are "lawful" in their attendance actively associate with others from whom protection is removed by s.219(3) (for example, because that is not their place of work), the ques-

990 *Union Traffic Ltd v TGWU* [1989] I.C.R. 98 CA; but a dismissed worker may picket only his last (main) place of work: ibid. In such cases, when the employer has transferred the business to another person, the dismissed worker may find also that he is unable to show that he is acting in furtherance of a trade dispute by picketing at that place: *Kenny v TGWU, The Times,* 15 June 1989. On trade disputes, see TULRCA 1992 s.244, and para.23-184 onwards.

991 So if all members leave the picket line the official is unprotected, even if he is the "picket supervisor": Code of Practice (2017), paras 27 and 28.

992 TULRCA 1992 s.220(1)(b); see also s.224(3)(b) making provision for secondary action.

993 TULRCA 1992 s.220(4) and Code of Practice paras 27 and 28. Thus "a branch official" may attend "only where members of his branch are lawfully picketing" (para.28); "he must represent and be responsible for them in the normal course of his union duties". Quaere: the meaning of being "responsible" for members in this context. Quaere: where members of two trade unions elect an official, directly or indirectly, to act for them, e.g. a convenor of shop stewards?

994 TULRCA 1992 s.224(3). See also, per Stuart-Smith J in *News Group Newspapers Ltd v SOGAT (No.2)* [1987] I.C.R. 181 at 213–214.

995 per Scott J in *Thomas v NUM (South Wales Area)* [1986] Ch. 20 at 78–80.

996 Either by reason of TULRCA 1992 s.20 or under common law principles, whichever is applicable: see paras 23-134 and 23-135.

997 The principle applicable to nuisance—adopting or continuing the nuisance—(see *Sedleigh-Denfield v O'Callaghan* [1940] A.C. 880 HL) and applied to picketing as tortious nuisance: *News Group Newspapers Ltd v SOGAT (No.2)* [1987] I.C.R. 181.

tion of liability for a conspiracy to use "unlawful means" arises.[998]

(k) Contemplation or furtherance of a trade dispute

23-180 **Labour injunctions** The statutory protections discussed above all apply only to acts done "in contemplation or furtherance of a trade dispute". That once golden formula appears in certain procedural, as well as substantive, provisions of the legislation. Indeed, when the great majority of cases in trade dispute matters take the form of interlocutory proceedings, procedure is here at least as important as substantive law. The 1974 Act attempted to curb the courts' power to grant ex parte "labour injunctions".[999] Where an application is made for an injunction ex parte, and the defendant claims, or in the opinion of the court would be likely to claim, that he acted in contemplation or furtherance of a trade dispute, the court:

> "shall not grant the injunction ... unless satisfied that all steps which in the circumstances were reasonable have been taken with a view to securing that notice of the application and an opportunity of being heard with respect to the application have been given to that party."[1000]

This provision, now s.221(1) of TULRCA 1992, appears to have been enacted in order that ex parte injunctions should not be granted without regard to defences arising from the immunities in trade dispute cases, where the balance of convenience will almost always appear to lie with the claimant.[1001] The court may, of course, at this stage encounter difficulty where it has to form its own "opinion" as to the likelihood of the defendant's claiming that he acted in contemplation or furtherance of

[998] Presumably that is why a "picket organiser" should "ensure that pickets understand the law and are aware of the provisions of this Code" and "ensure that workers from other places of work do not join the picket line and that any offers of support on the picket line from outsiders are refused": Code of Practice, para.61. Sed quaere whether lawful pickets need go that far in order to refute an allegation of "combination" with illicit pickets.

[999] See Davies and Anderman (1973) 2 I.L.J. 213; Wedderburn, (1989) 23 *Law Teacher* 3; O'Regan (1991) 54 M.L.R. 385. On the limited value of the cross-undertaking in damages to the defendant in such cases: *Barretts & Baird (Wholesale) Ltd v IPCS* [1987] I.R.L.R. 3; *Air Express v Ansett Air* (1982) 146 C.L.R. 249; see generally Zuckerman [1994] C.L.J. 546. On awards of damages: *Parker v Rasalingham, The Times,* 25 July 2000.

[1000] TULRA 1974 s.17(1), now TULRCA 1992 s.221(1). Quaere the effect in practice of this provision when the court has a discretion to act in cases of urgency? In *Barretts & Baird (Wholesale) Ltd v IPCS* [1987] I.R.L.R. 3, an injunction had first been granted ex parte by a judge on a Sunday over the telephone where the facts suggested that the defendant union would plainly raise the issue of acting in a trade dispute (which is all that subs.(1) requires); the injunctions were discharged some three weeks later because the claimants could show no arguable case (see Simpson (1987) 50 M.L.R. 506). Quaere whether these provisions and the general discretion of the court apply to s.235A of TULRCA 1992, where the court "shall" make an appropriate order if the individual's claim is "well-founded"? See para.23-173. This provision does not apply to an application for an interim declaration. The principles which should be applied in deciding such applications were set out in the judgment of Aikens LJ in *Rolls Royce Plc v Unite the Union* [2009] EWCA Civ 387; [2010] 1 W.L.R. 318 at [20]. See *Secretary of State for Education v NUT* [2016] EWHC 812 (QB); [2016] I.R.L.R. 512 at [22]–[30] where Kerr J said, inter alia, that the public interest lay in the court determining the issues as best it could within the time constraints, taking account of the evidence even though that might be incomplete. Although TULRCA 1992 s.221 did not by its terms apply to an application for an interim declaration, the courts should give proper weight to the likelihood of the defendant establishing a trade dispute defence: ibid. at [39].

[1001] See *NWL Ltd v Woods* [1979] 1 W.L.R. 1294 at 1308, per Lord Fraser of Tullybelton; at 1305–1307, per Lord Diplock.

a trade dispute.[1002]

Soon after the decision in *American Cyanamid Co v Ethicon*,[1003] Parliament added a further subsection, now s.221(2) of TULRCA 1992, to deal with interlocutory injunctions more generally inter partes, specifying that where a defendant facing an application for an interlocutory injunction claims that he has a defence because he acted in contemplation or furtherance of a trade dispute: **23-181**

> "the court shall, in exercising its discretion whether or not to grant the injunction, have regard to the likelihood of that party's succeeding at the trial of the action in establishing any matter which would afford a defence to the action under section 219 or section 220."[1004]

In the *Ethicon* case, the test used in previous cases[1005] whereby the claimant seeking an interlocutory injunction was required to prove not only that the "balance of convenience" lay in his favour but also that there was "a prima facie case of some breach of duty to him", was rejected, Lord Diplock stating there was no such rule as the "supposed rule" that he must show a "prima facie case", and that he need show only that "the claim is not frivolous or vexatious; in other words that there is a serious question to be tried".[1006] In such interim injunction cases, this test appeared to make it significantly easier for the claimant to succeed.[1007] Because of the permanent effect of most (theoretically interim) interlocutory injunctions in trade dispute cases, s.221(2) requires the courts specifically to "have regard" to the strength of the defendant's case at the interlocutory stage in respect of the matters which would provide him with a defence by reason of acting in contemplation or furtherance of a trade dispute.[1008]

After 1975, however, the courts displayed varying approaches to the section. **23-182**

1002 See the differing views in *Gouriet v Union of Post Office Workers* [1978] A.C. 435 at 484, per Lord Wilberforce; at 516–517, per Lord Edmund-Davies; at 525, per Lord Fraser of Tullybelton, and at 487, per Viscount Dilhorne.

1003 [1975] A.C. 396 HL.

1004 The provision is set out in its modern form in TULRCA 1992 s.221(2). It does not apply to Scotland: ibid.; see, per Lord Fraser of Tullybelton in *NWL Ltd v Woods* [1979] 1 W.L.R. 1294 at 1309–1310, who shows that the practice in Scotland is different from the *Ethicon* test. As "a matter of chronology" it was enacted nine months after the *Ethicon* decision, on which see *BBC v Hearn* [1977] 1 W.L.R. 1004 at 1016, per Roskill LJ (which leaves little doubt as to its paternity).

1005 per Lord Upjohn in *Stratford & Son Ltd v Lindley* [1965] A.C. 269 at 338. The case was not cited in the *Ethicon* decision: per Sir John Pennycuick in *Fellowes & Son v Fisher* [1976] Q.B. 122 at 140.

1006 *American Cyanamid Co v Ethicon Ltd* [1975] A.C. 396 at 407, per Lord Diplock (in addition to the requirement of the balance of convenience). As to whether damages are an adequate remedy, see *Express Newspapers Ltd v Keys* [1980] I.R.L.R. 247; *Mercury Communications Ltd v Scott-Garner* [1984] Ch. 37 at 92–93, per May LJ (damages may be inadequate because of the limit placed on award against trade unions by what is now TULRCA 1992 s.22); at 83, per Donaldson MR. On the claimant's need to have "clean hands": *News Group Newspapers Ltd v SOGAT (No.2)* [1987] I.C.R. 181 at 228–230 (moral reprehensibility not unclean hands); *Curust Financial Services Ltd v Loewe-Lack-Werk* [1994] 1 I.R. 450 (Sup. Ct: "element of turpitude" in doctrine of clean hands; mere breach of contract is not sufficient). On the need for an applicant for interlocutory relief to identify the legal, equitable or statutory rights which are to be determined at trial and in respect of which interlocutory relief is being sought see *Australian Broadcasting Commission v Lenah Game Meats Pty Ltd* (2001) 208 C.L.R. 119 Aus. HC; cf. *Daitchi Pharmaceuticals UK Ltd v Stop Huntingdon Animal Cruelty* [2003] EWHC 2337 (QB); [2004] 1 W.L.R. 1503 where media reports of the defendants' support for unlawful activities were held to be a relevant consideration, but so too were the defendants' rights to freedom of assembly and expression under the Human Rights Act 1998.

1007 See the discussion in *Hubbard v Pitt* [1979] Q.B. 142 at 174–178, per Lord Denning MR; *Fellowes & Son v Fisher* [1976] Q.B. 122 at 130–138, per Lord Denning MR and Browne LJ.

1008 Couched necessarily in the semantics of "the likelihood" of his success "at the trial": see *Mercury*

First, in a number of decisions now either overruled or of doubtful authority, the section was given little attention, especially where the Court of Appeal decided there was no "serious possibility" of the defence succeeding and replaced the discretion of the trial judge with its own.[1009] In interim proceedings the discretion properly belongs to the judge, not to the appellate courts.[1010] But if he errs in law or fails to take proper factors into account, such as "the public interest", the discretion of the appeal court may replace his.[1011] Secondly, the courts have recognised that the section was intended to affect the application of the *Ethicon* decision in trade dispute cases,[1012] and regarded the proper test now as being three-fold:

(a) has the claimant proved a "serious question to be tried";
(b) is the balance of convenience in his favour; and
(c) has the defendant satisfied the section?[1013]

Under s.221(2) of TULRCA 1992 the defendant should succeed "in most cases" if the "balance of probabilities" indicates that there is a "real likelihood" of the defence succeeding.[1014] The third approach subsumes the problems of the section under the broad heading of "the balance of convenience",[1015] making the "likelihood" of the defendant's success at trial, both under the 1992 Act and generally, one

---

Communications Ltd v Scott-Garner [1984] Ch. 37 at 99, per Dillon LJ (injunction, even though union "may succeed at trial"; but it would be "a close run thing"); *Associated British Ports v TGWU* [1989] 1 W.L.R. 939 at 955–957, per Neill LJ (reversed on other grounds, [1989] 1 W.L.R. 939 HL). In labour injunction cases, "the grant or refusal of an interlocutory injunction generally disposes finally of the action; in practice actions of this type seldom if ever come to actual trial", per Lord Diplock in *NWL Ltd v Woods* [1979] 1 W.L.R. 1294 at 1305; *Stratford v Lindley (No.2)* [1969] 1 W.L.R. 1547 CA. But see now the different approach to the "practical realities" of Lord Diplock in *Dimbleby and Sons Ltd v NUJ* [1984] 1 W.L.R. 427 at 431–432. Compare the position under the Irish Industrial Relations Act 1991: *Westman Holdings Ltd v McCormack* [1992] 1 I.R. 151; *Boyle v An Post* [1992] 2 I.R. 437.

1009 *United Biscuits Ltd v Fall* [1979] I.R.L.R. 110; *PBDS (National Carriers) Ltd v Filkins* [1979] I.R.L.R. 356 CA (both deprived of authority after *NWL v Woods* [1979] 1 W.L.R. 1294; and *Express Newspapers Ltd v McShane* [1980] A.C. 672 HL).

1010 *Duport Steels Ltd v Sirs* [1980] 1 W.L.R. 142 HL; *Hadmor Productions Ltd v Hamilton* [1983] 1 A.C. 191 at 223–224, per Lord Diplock; *London & Birmingham Railway Ltd v ASLEF* [2011] EWCA Civ 226; [2011] I.C.R. 848 at [10]–[14] per Elias LJ; but see *Mercury Communications Ltd v Scott-Garner* [1984] Ch. 37 (Court of Appeal exercised discretion where error of law below and fresh evidence); *Associated British Ports v TGWU* [1989] 1 W.L.R. 939 at 962–963, per Butler-Sloss LJ; at 967–970, per Stuart-Smith LJ (reversed on other grounds, [1989] 1 W.L.R. 939 HL); cf. *Shipping Co Uniform Inc v ITF* [1985] I.C.R. 245 at 256–257.

1011 See *Associated British Ports v TGWU* [1989] 1 W.L.R. 939 at 968–969, per Stuart-Smith LJ.

1012 *Associated Newspapers Group Ltd v Wade* [1979] I.C.R. 664 at 701, per Geoffrey Lane LJ.

1013 *NWL Ltd v Woods* [1979] 1 W.L.R. 1294 at 1314–1315, per Lord Scarman; *BBC v Hearn* [1977] 1 W.L.R. 1004 at 1016–1017; (1978) 41 M.L.R. 80. cf. *Examite Ltd (Cleveland Crane Hire) v Whittaker* [1977] I.R.L.R. 312 CA; *Porr v Shaw, Johnson & Holden* [1979] 2 Lloyd's Rep. 331 CA.

1014 *BBC v Hearn* [1977] 1 W.L.R. 1004 at 1016, per Lord Scarman; "sufficient probability", per Roskill LJ; but s.221 does not deprive the court of its discretion: *Duport Steels Ltd v Sirs* [1980] 1 W.L.R. 142. On the "likelihood" test for injunctions and the impact of the Human Rights Act 1998, see *Imutran Ltd v Uncaged Campaigns Ltd* [2001] 2 All E.R. 385 (freedom of expression).

1015 A test which has the advantage of making the practice in England and in Scotland the same: per Lord Fraser of Tullybelton in *NWL Ltd v Woods* [1979] 1 W.L.R. 1294 at 1309–1311; a result which Parliament must have intended when it enacted in (now) s.221(2) that that subsection does not apply to Scotland: per Lord Diplock at 1307. See *United Closures & Plastics Ltd v Unite* [2011] CSOH 114; 2011 S.L.T. 1105 at [41]–[44] where it was accepted by the petitioner that the correct approach to the balance of convenience was that described by Elias LJ in *London & Birmingham Railway Ltd v ASLEF* [2011] EWCA Civ 226; [2011] I.C.R. 848 at [10]–[12]; and Lord Fraser's opinion in *NWL Ltd v Woods* [1979] 1 W.L.R. 1294 at 1309–1311. It appears that in Northern Ireland practice is the same under the *Ethicon* test, even in the absence of such a section: *Crazy Prices (Northern Ireland)* of the factors to be weighed in the balance.[1016] The section has, however, been seen as merely "reminding the judges" that, in labour injunction cases where the balance appears to lie with the claimant and the action is prima facie tortious, they should take account of the likelihood of establishing a defence and of "the realities" (including the fact that grant or refusal of the injunction will "in effect, dispose of the action finally") in this "unique" or "exceptional" kind of case.[1017] This last test currently has most judicial support.[1018]

The mere fact that the case is unlikely to come to trial will not normally prevent the granting of an interlocutory injunction[1019]; and the reintroduction of tort liability for trade unions has even been seen as a factor changing the "practical realities" in a way that makes the exercise of discretion to grant an injunction easier (as the claimant is more likely to pursue the union than a mere official for damages).[1020] A feeling of unease "as to its effect on the shop floor and or industrial relations" is not a ground for refusing the injunction where the statutory requirements, for **23-183**

Ltd v Hewitt [1980] I.R.L.R. 396 CA (NI). The tendency in some other areas of employment law to move away from a strict adherence to the *Ethicon* test (*Lansing Linde Ltd v Kerr* [1991] 1 W.L.R. 251 CA; *Cambridge Nutrition Ltd v BBC* [1990] 3 All E.R. 523 CA; *Longley v NUJ* [1987] I.R.L.R. 109 CA) has not yet appeared in cases on trade disputes.

1016 The greater the likelihood of establishing a trade dispute defence, the greater the weight attached to it: per Lord Diplock in *Hadmor Productions Ltd v Hamilton* [1983] 2 A.C. 191 at 224. See too *Balfour Beatty Engineering Services Ltd v Unite* [2012] EWHC 267 (QB); [2012] I.C.R. 822 at [3]–[4], per Eady J: while a defendant trade union's establishing the likelihood of it having a trade dispute defence did not conclude the interim injunction issue in its favour, it would be exceptional for a court having reached that conclusion to grant relief; to similar effect, *Birmingham CC v Unite the Union* [2019] EWHC 478 (QB); [2019] I.R.L.R. 423; *British Airways plc v British Airline Pilots' Association* [2019] EWCA Civ 1663; [2020] I.R.L.R. 43 at [10].

1017 per Lord Diplock in *NWL Ltd v Woods* [1979] 1 W.L.R. 1294 at 1305–1307. He explains the *Ethicon* decision, when "properly understood", as not involving a change in practice, because the court always takes account of "practical realities" in determining the balance of convenience. But in *Ethicon*, he wholly rejected the "supposed rule" that the court must be satisfied at the interlocutory stage that the claimant has a "prima facie case" (as Lord Upjohn required in *Stratford & Son Ltd v Lindley* [1965] A.C. 269 at 338), adding only that the circumstances concerning balance of convenience would "vary from case to case" and, if the damage to both parties in that balance appeared to be similar, "it may not be improper to take into account in tipping the balance" the strength of each party's case; but even then only where on affidavit evidence "there is no credible dispute" as to the strength of one party's case being "disproportionate"; for there must not be "anything like a trial of the action on conflicting affidavits": [1975] A.C. at 407–409. Lord Diplock in 1979 treated trade dispute cases as "exceptional" or even "unique" in *NWL Ltd v Woods* [1979] 1 W.L.R. 1294 at 1306–1307, in the light of the "practical realities", especially the fact that the interim proceedings generally dispose finally of the action: at 1305.

1018 *NWL Ltd v Woods* [1979] 1 W.L.R. 1294 at 1305–1307, per Lord Diplock, and at 1308–1310, per Lord Fraser of Tullybelton; *Duport Steels Ltd v Sirs* [1980] 1 W.L.R. 142 HL; *Health Computing v Meek* [1981] I.C.R. 24 at 34; cf. *Crazy Prices (Northern Ireland) Ltd v Hewitt* [1980] I.R.L.R. 396 CA (NI). The importance of adopting an approach which does not deprive a union's members of an "effective right to withhold their labour" was expressly recognised in *British Airways Plc v Unite* [2010] EWCA Civ 669; [2010] I.C.R. 1316 by Smith LJ at [109] and [153]; and *London Underground Ltd v ASLEF* [2011] EWHC 3506 (QB); [2012] I.R.L.R. 196 by Eder J at [10]–[12]. Where a union's actions are likely to be held to be tortious because of "interference" with the conduct of the ballot, the fact that its members would have probably voted in the same way without the interference, and granted an "overwhelming" mandate for industrial action, is not a good reason to refuse an interim injunction; a new ballot should be conducted: *Royal Mail Group Ltd v Communication Workers Union* [2019] EWCA Civ 2150; [2020] I.C.R. 940.

1019 *Thomas v NUM (South Wales Area)* [1986] Ch. 20 at 68–74, per Scott J; *News Group Newspapers v SOGAT (No.2)* [1987] I.C.R. 181 at 224–226, per Stuart-Smith J.

1020 *Dimbleby & Sons Ltd v NUJ* [1984] 1 W.L.R. 427 at 431–432, per Lord Diplock; but see *Barretts & Baird (Wholesale) Ltd v IPCS* [1987] I.R.L.R. 3 at 10.

example on a ballot, have been contravened.[1021] The changes in definition of a trade dispute have made it easier to obtain a labour injunction[1022]; the burden remains on the defendant at "stage 2" to show he acted in furtherance of a trade dispute, and then on the claimant at "stage 3" to show it is displaced.[1023] Where there is a conflict of evidence requiring discovery and cross-examination, the court may grant the injunction where the balance of convenience so indicates.[1024] Finally, the courts reserve to themselves the right to grant an interim injunction, even where there is a high probability that the defendant's defence in a trade dispute will succeed, where the consequences of his action to the employer, third parties, the public or the nation would be sufficiently disastrous.[1025] The Court of Appeal has now gone even further by requiring that the trial judge must consider the "public interest".[1026] The court will also take into account freedom of expression where that is relevant.[1027]

23-184 **Elements of a trade dispute** Four distinct elements may be distinguished in the trade dispute formula itself. The defendant must be able to prove:

(a) a dispute;
(b) between the required parties;
(c) with the required relationship to a specified content; and
(d) action in contemplation or furtherance of that dispute.

(i) The dispute

23-185 The test of the existence of a trade dispute is objective.[1028] If there is no dispute[1029] at all between the parties, or if there has been a dispute in the past but it has died

[1021] *Blackpool and The Fylde College v NATFHE* [1994] I.C.R. 648 at 655, per Bingham MR.
[1022] See paras 23-186 and 23-188. But see *Wandsworth LBC v NALGO* [1994] I.C.R. 81 CA.
[1023] See *Merkur Island Shipping Corp v ITF* [1983] 2 A.C. 570 at 604, per Lord Diplock.
[1024] *Solihull MB v NUT* [1985] I.R.L.R. 211. Although it is available with leave cross examination is scarcely ever encountered in such cases. The only modern case appears to be *Associated British Ports v TGWU* [1989] I.R.L.R. 291 (affirmed [1989] 1 W.L.R. 939 HL), where the officials of the defendant union were called for cross examination. The claimant claimed that the trade dispute alleged by the union was not genuine and was a mere cover for a political dispute: "Having seen [them] in the witness box, it is right that I should record my finding that this serious calumny is wholly without substance", per Millett J at 299.
[1025] *NWL Ltd v Woods* [1979] 1 W.L.R. 1294 at 1307, per Lord Diplock (as corrected in [1980] 1 W.L.R. 147, note); *Express Newspapers Ltd v McShane* [1980] A.C. 627 at 694–695, per Lord Scarman (but see, per Lord Wilberforce dubitante at 685); *Duport Steels Ltd v Sirs* [1980] 1 W.L.R. 142 at 166, per Lord Fraser of Tullybelton ("immediate serious danger to public safety or health and if no other means" seemed available to avert the danger in time). But this would require "an altogether exceptional case": per Lord Scarman at 171. Semble, this principle cannot assist a claimant who enjoys no "private right" even if disastrous loss to the public is thereby threatened: *Gouriet v Union of Post Office Workers* [1978] A.C. 435 HL at 499, per Lord Diplock. cf. Simpson (1980) 43 M.L.R. 327; Wedderburn (1980) 43 M.L.R. 319 at 326. cf. Morris, *Strikes in Essential Services* (1986), pp.28–35.
[1026] In *Associated British Ports v TGWU* [1989] 1 W.L.R. 939 at 957, 962 and 968–969 (reversed on other grounds [1989] 1 W.L.R. 939 HL); the Court of Appeal insisted that the "public interest" must be expressly taken into account. Sed quaere whether this does not turn every such conflict between private parties into a public issue, and one which will invariably be won by one side if strikes are equated with "public inconvenience".
[1027] See *Middlebrook Mushrooms Ltd v TGWU* [1993] I.C.R. 612 CA at 620, per Neill LJ; *Microdata Information Services v Rivendale and Cryne* [1991] F.S.R. 681 CA; and see, per Lord Scarman in *Express Newspapers Ltd v McShane* [1980] A.C. 672 at 695.
[1028] *Express Newspapers Ltd v McShane* [1980] A.C. 672 at 686, per Lord Diplock; *NWL Ltd v Woods* [1979] 1 W.L.R. 1294 HL.

out, the protections do not apply.[1030] To some extent this heading overlaps with heading (d) "contemplation or furtherance" even though the test there is subjective, because where one party honestly claims to be still in dispute, the dispute continues.[1031] But once a dispute is over, the protections will not apply to action taken in consequence or as a result of it.[1032] So, too, in order to reverse a dictum which had it otherwise,[1033] the 1974 Act provided that where an act, threat or demand is made by a person or organisation against another which, if resisted, would have led to a trade dispute, then, notwithstanding that no actual dispute arises because that other submits to the act, threat or demand, it shall be treated as having been done or made in contemplation of a trade dispute with him.[1034] It has been suggested that one test is whether employees are in dispute with their employer about their rights under their "current contracts of employment"[1035]; but in the ordinary case, such as a wage claim, employees will be demanding that the terms of their current contracts should be changed.[1036] A dispute may also come into actual existence "long before the parties have become locked in combat" and it is "sufficient that they should be sparring for an opening".[1037] Furthermore, a "dispute" is not confined to disputes within Britain; it may relate "to matters occurring outside the United Kingdom" so long as the persons whose actions are in contemplation or furtherance of such a dispute are likely to be affected by the outcome of that dispute in relation to the required content.[1038]

1029 *Conway v Wade* [1909] A.C. 306 HL; as explained by Lord Wilberforce in *Express Newspapers Ltd v McShane* [1980] A.C. 672 at 684; see also, per Lord Diplock in *NWL Ltd v Woods* [1979] 1 W.L.R. 1294 at 1304; cf. per Lord Scarman at 1313–1314. cf. *Crazy Prices (Northern Ireland) Ltd v Hewitt* [1980] I.R.L.R. 396 CA (NI).

1030 *Stratford & Son Ltd v Lindley* [1965] A.C. 269 at 323, per Lord Reid; at 334, per Lord Pearce; at 341, per Lord Donovan. The dispute must be with a party with whom the defendant has a genuine issue: *Torquay Hotel Co Ltd v Cousins* [1969] 2 Ch. 106 CA; *Health Computing Ltd v Meek* [1981] I.C.R. 24.

1031 *Newham LBC v NALGO* [1993] I.C.R. 189 CA; cf. *Southwest Trains Ltd v RMT*, 25 October 1999, Turner J (holding at [35] that a union's perception that a dispute was continuing was "wrong" and "based on a misunderstanding"); on the subjective test of furtherance of actual, or of contemplation of imminent disputes: see para.23-195.

1032 *Hutchison v Aitchison* (1970) 9 K.I.R. 69 at 76; *Stewart v AUEW* [1973] I.C.R. 128; *Beaverbrook Newspapers Ltd v Keys* [1978] I.C.R. 582 CA. Where there is more than one dispute to which action may "relate" (cf. *Newham LBC v NALGO* [1993] I.C.R. 189 CA) one may continue even if the other ends.

1033 *Cory Lighterage v TGWU* [1973] I.C.R. 339 at 362, per Buckley LJ.

1034 TULRCA 1992 s.244(4). This solution must be considered when approaching the opinions of Lord Loreburn in *Conway v Wade* [1909] A.C. 506 at 509–510, and Lord Shaw at 522; *Hadmor Productions Ltd v Hamilton* [1983] 1 A.C. 191 HL.

1035 per Lord Diplock in *Dimbleby & Sons Ltd v NUJ* [1984] 1 W.L.R. 427 at 433 ("and it is only their current contracts that can be relevant"); Simpson (1984) 47 M.L.R. 577 at 582; Carty (1984) 100 L.Q.R. 342; Andrews [1984] C.L.J. 250 at 251 ("surely wrong"); compare (c), para.23-188.

1036 See para.23-190, on demands about future working conditions.

1037 *Beetham v Trinidad Cement Ltd* [1960] A.C. 132 at 143 PC, per Lord Denning. (The fact that the definition under consideration there included the words "difference or dispute" does not, it is suggested, weaken the authority of that dictum.)

1038 TULRCA 1992 s.244(3) (strictly speaking those "persons" are the organisers of the industrial action; but it is submitted that the court will consider whether the workers will be so "affected" even though their acts attract no immunity for their breaches of employment contracts). On transnational labour disputes, see Wedderburn, *Labour Law and Freedom* (1995), Chs 7 and 10.

(ii) Parties

23-186 Trade dispute "means a dispute between workers and their employer".[1039] Before 1982—indeed, since 1906—a trade dispute could exist between workers and any employer, or even between "workers and workers"; but that is no longer the case. The dispute must now be between workers and their employer to fall within TULRCA s.244(1). The 1982 Act made further amendments. For the purposes of the definition of a trade dispute, a "worker" is now defined as:

(a) a worker employed by the employer; or
(b) a person who has ceased to be so employed where the termination of his employment was effected in connection with, or was one of the reasons for, the dispute.[1040]

It has been held that the new definition of "worker" applies throughout the provision.[1041] A dispute to which a trade union or an employers' association is a party may be treated as a dispute to which workers, or as the case may be employers, who are members are parties[1042]; but the provision in the 1974 Act which provided that this was necessarily the case was repealed in 1982. A union official can, if he has their authority, act on behalf of workers "unofficially" and, thereby, as their agent make them parties to the dispute.[1043] And by voting in a strike ballot or by striking, the members may show they have "endorsed and adopted the actions taken by the union on their behalf".[1044] Although the courts have been unwilling to "pierce the corporate veil" in this area,[1045] the facts may equally reveal that

---

[1039] TULRCA 1992 s.244(1). There can be no trade dispute between workers and a potential unknown future employer: *University College Hospitals NHS Trust v UNISON* [1999] I.C.R. 204 CA; Hendy (2000) 29 I.L.J. 53. On the position where the employer is one of a number of associated bodies (e.g. companies in a group) see *Examite (Cleveland Crane) Hire v Whittaker* [1977] I.R.L.R. 312 CA; and cf. *Porr v Shaw Johnson & Holden* [1979] 2 Lloyd's Rep. 331 CA (dispute with flag of convenience shipowners' agents also dispute with owners); but compare *Dimbleby & Sons Ltd v NUJ* [1984] 1 W.L.R. 427 HL (group of companies, each a separate employer).

[1040] Now s.244(5) of TULRCA 1992. Employment is still defined to include any relationship whereby one person personally does work or performs services for another, TULRCA s.244(5).

[1041] *Dimbleby & Sons Ltd v NUJ* [1984] 1 W.L.R. 427 HL at 433–434; cf. *Kenny v TGWU*, *The Times*, 15 June 1989.

[1042] TULRA 1974 s.29(4) (which made provision for this to be the case) was repealed by s.18(5) Employment Act 1982. The courts accepted that this could be the result on normal agency principles before 1974, when the union could act on behalf of workers to start or pursue a dispute: per Viscount Radcliffe in *Stratford & Son Ltd v Lindley* [1965] A.C. 269 at 326; and Lord Diplock's assertion that before s.29(4) a union could not be a party to a dispute must be read in that context; *NWL Ltd v Woods* [1979] 1 W.L.R. 1294 at 1304.

[1043] As in *Camden Exhibition and Display Ltd v Lynott* [1966] 1 Q.B. 555 CA. Compare the issue of authority of shop stewards in *Heatons Transport (St Helens) Ltd v TGWU* [1973] A.C. 15 HL; and *General Aviation Services (UK) Ltd v TGWU* [1975] I.C.R. 276 CA (affirmed on other grounds (1976) [1985] I.C.R. 615 HL); decisions given under the Industrial Relations Act 1971, which survive its repeal in so far as they deal with the common law question of extent of authority: see Davies (1973) 36 M.L.R. 78. But compare the strict proof of authority required if the union purports to give notice terminating the individual employment contracts of members: *Boxfoldia Ltd v NGA* [1988] I.C.R. 752; compare *Morris v Bailey* [1969] 2 Lloyd's Rep. 215; *Gibbons v Associated British Ports* [1985] I.R.L.R. 376.

[1044] *Associated British Ports v TGWU* [1989] I.R.L.R. 291 at 300, per Millett J (affirmed on other grounds, [1989] 1 W.L.R. 939 HL): applying *R. v NAT Ex p. Keable Press Ltd* [1943] 2 All E.R. 633.

[1045] *Dimbleby & Sons Ltd v NUJ* [1984] 1 W.L.R. 427 at 433–444, per Lord Diplock.

an association or other agent was acting as agent for the employer, so rendering him a party.[1046]

Where workers are in dispute with their employer and he transfers the undertaking to a transferee, and they are dismissed by him (whether or not it is an unfair dismissal because it is effected by reason of the transfer),[1047] the question arises whether the dispute passes to the transferee. Under the "TUPE" Regulations which implement Directive 2001/23, he will now normally become their employer to whom pass the rights, powers, duties and liabilities under and in connection with the contracts of employment, with the status of "employer".[1048] It is submitted that, if the dismissals are unfair because the transfer is the principal reason, their rights to pursue the trade dispute as workers should continue so as to bind the transferee. Finally, a dispute between workers and a Minister of the Crown is to be treated as a trade dispute between those workers and their employer, if the dispute relates to matters which have been referred to a joint body on which the Minister is represented (such as a Joint Whitley Council) or to matters which cannot be settled without him exercising a power conferred on him by statute.[1049] There will be other cases in which the Crown may become a party, especially where statute deems Crown employees to have contracts of employment, even if in law they otherwise do not, for the purpose of liability of third parties (notably trade unions) who induce them to break their obligations.[1050] **23-187**

(iii) The content

Until 1982, a dispute had to be "connected with" one or more of the items set out in s.29(1) of the 1974 Act. The Employment Act 1982 replaced that wide test with the requirement, now in s.244(1) of TULRCA 1992, that the dispute "relates wholly or mainly to" such an item.[1051] These items are set out now in s.244(1) as follows: **23-188**

1046 *Porr v Shaw Johnson & Holden* [1979] 2 Lloyd's Rep. 331 CA.

1047 After *Wilson v St Helens BC* [1999] 2 A.C. 52 HL it has become clear that a dismissal is effective as a dismissal even if it is within the range of a "transfer" of the employer's undertaking and would otherwise have passed liability to the transferee: McMullen (1999) 28 I.L.J. 76; Hendy (2000) 29 I.L.J. 53, 59–60.

1048 reg.4 of the Transfer of Undertakings (Protection of Employment) Regulations 2006 (SI 2006/246) ("TUPE"); this is also the position on collective agreements and recognition of trade unions which pass to the transferee under regs 5 and 6 but the transferee will normally be free to cancel these because they are not legally binding (save under TULRCA 1992 Sch.A1). Quaere whether the court would see a trade dispute as arising "under or in connection with" the contract of employment: a negative inference may be drawn from *Angus Jowett Ltd v NUTGW* [1985] I.C.R. 646 (protective award); but contra, *Kerry Foods Ltd v Creber* [2000] I.C.R. 556 at 566, per Morrison J.

1049 See TULRCA 1992 s.244(2); see *Wandsworth LBC v NASUWT* [1994] I.C.R. 81 CA; *Secretary of State for Education v NUT* [2016] EWHC 812 (QB); [2016] I.R.L.R. 512 at [49]–[74]. The dispute still has to relate wholly or mainly to one of the issues set out in TULRCA s.244(1) and in that case it was held that it was more likely than not that the union would be able to establish that its demand for increased funding for sixth form colleges to enable them to improve teachers' pay and conditions was part of its strategy for the protection of members' jobs and conditions.

1050 TULRCA 1992 s.245 (this deems the relationship to be a "contract for the purposes of … the law relating to liability in tort" for inducing breach of contract etc; it is submitted this must include the legal position of the parties in circumstances where protection against that liability is afforded).

1051 Employment Act 1982 s.18(2)(c). Before 1982, the formula could include even a general strike in appropriate circumstances. See on the law under the 1906 Act, Goodhart (1927) 36 Yale L.J. 464; Ch.11, *Essays in Jurisprudence and the Common Law*; Citrine, *Trade Union Law*, 3rd edn (1967), pp.614-616, exposing the fallacies in *National Sailors and Firemen's Union v Reed* [1926] Ch. 536 at 539–540, per Astbury J. See this approach confirmed in *NWL Ltd v Woods* [1979] 1 W.L.R. 1294

"(a) terms and conditions of employment or the physical conditions in which any workers are required to work;
(b) engagement or non-engagement, or termination or suspension of employment or the duties of employment, of one or more workers;
(c) allocation of work or the duties of employment as between workers or groups of workers;
(d) matters of discipline;
(e) a worker's membership or non-membership of a trade union;
(f) facilities for officials of trade unions; and
(g) machinery for negotiation or consultation, and other procedures, relating to any of the above matters, including the recognition by employers or employers' associations of the right of a trade union to represent workers in any such negotiation or consultation or in the carrying out of such procedures."

23-189 The "workers" referred to (in paras (a), (b), (c), (e) and (g)) are now limited to workers employed by the employer in dispute with them; the "allocation of work" is now confined, therefore, to "demarcation issues" between groups of workers employed by that employer only.[1052] But workers can be party to a trade dispute even where they would not be personally affected by a proposed change in terms and conditions of employment.[1053] "Employment" in this section includes any "relationship whereby one person personally does work or performs services for another".[1054] Terms and conditions of employment can include hours of work, overtime pay, claims for promotion and regrading, and the like.[1055] Further, the word "conditions" is not confined to the contractual relationship but includes conditions

HL; *Express Newspapers Ltd v McShane* [1980] A.C. 672 HL. But contrast the narrow majority interpretation in *Universe Tankships Inc of Monrovia v ITF* [1983] 1 A.C. 366 HL at 387, 390, 392 and 397 (payment to seamen's welfare fund not "connected with conditions of employment"; but compare the minority view at 403 and 408; Wedderburn (1982) 45 M.L.R. 556 at 560–563; Sterling (1982) 11 I.L.J. 156). In *NWL Ltd v Woods* [1984] 1 W.L.R. 1294 at 1304–1305, Lord Diplock's extravagant example included cases where "the predominant object was to bring down the fabric of the present economic system by raising wages to unrealistic levels", as being "connected with" employment conditions; not so after 1982.

[1052] per Lord Diplock in *Dimbleby & Sons Ltd v NUJ* [1984] 1 W.L.R. 427 at 433–434. Semble: paras (d) and (f) must relate to issues concerning the same workers.

[1053] *British Telecommunications Plc v Communication Workers Union* [2003] EWHC 937 (QB); [2004] I.R.L.R. 58.

[1054] TULRCA 1992 s.244(5). So, it is not restricted to a situation where a contract of employment exists.

[1055] *Wandsworth LBC v NAS/UWT* [1994] I.C.R. 81 CA (dispute over extra working hours of teachers); *Camden Exhibition and Display Ltd v Lynott* [1966] 1 Q.B. 555 CA; *Express Newspapers Ltd v McShane* [1980] A.C. 672 HL; *Brendon Dunne Ltd v Fitzpatrick* [1958] I.R. 29; cf. also *R. v Industrial Disputes Tribunal Ex p. Queen Mary College* [1957] 2 Q.B. 488. See too *P v NASUWT* [2001] EWCA Civ 652; [2001] I.C.R. 1241; [2003] UKHL 8; [2003] 2 A.C. 663 (dispute as to reasonableness of employer's instruction to teach pupil in classroom). In the House of Lords, Lord Bingham rejected the appellant's submission that the definition covered nothing other than a dispute about terms and conditions of employment, broadly construed. Per Lord Hoffmann, with whom all the other Law Lords agreed, "a dispute about what the workers are obliged to do or how the employer is obliged to remunerate them at any level of particularity or generality is about terms and conditions of employment": [2003] UKHL 8; [2003] 2 A.C. 663 at [28]. In *ISS Mediclean Ltd v GMB* [2014] EWHC 4208 (QB); [2015] I.R.L.R. 96 at [21]–[22], in rejecting the claimant's submission that there was no trade dispute between the parties because it concerned a national collective agreement which was not a matter within its control, it was held that it was perfectly possible for an employer to be in dispute with its workers about pay even where funding for it came from another source.

applied in practice or "habitually" outside that area.[1056] Physical conditions includes safety at the place of work in respect of which employees now have statutory rights not to be disciplined or dismissed if they leave in face of serious and imminent dangers.[1057] The better view appears to be that the reference to "matters of discipline" means disciplinary questions arising out of the employment as between the employer and a worker.[1058] The suspension not merely of employment but of the "duties of employment" makes it clear that disputes which relate mainly to a lay-off of workers or the suspension of a worker on full pay are included within the formula.[1059]

So, too, fears about redundancy or job security can provide the required connection with "termination" or "non-engagement" objectively, even though "an impartial observer" might not regard the apprehensions as firmly based.[1060] But after 1982, these fears must be the matter to which the dispute wholly or mainly relates. So, where employees and their union feared for job security in changes being brought about by liberalisation and privatisation of the employer, BT, their industrial action was held to relate mainly to "the political decisions to liberalise the industry and to privatise BT", taken by the Government[1061]; but where teachers objected to the excessive workload imposed as a consequence of the introduction of the national curriculum the dispute was held to relate mainly to the extra working time it required.[1062] A new dimension to the problems relating to the content of (and to **23-190**

[1056] per Lord Diplock in *Hadmor Productions Ltd v Hamilton* [1983] 1 A.C. 191 at 227; per Lord Denning MR in *BBC v Hearn* [1977] 1 W.L.R. 1004 at 1010; cf. per Lord Scarman in *Universe Tankships Inc of Monrovia v ITF* [1983] 1 A.C. 366 at 402 (dissenting; also see, per Lord Brandon at 407); but see, per Lord Diplock (for the majority) at 386.

[1057] See Employment Rights Act 1996 ss.44 and 100, which implement the EC "Framework Directive" 89/391. In *P v NASUWT* [2001] EWCA Civ 652; [2001] I.C.R. 1241 Waller LJ was "less certain" than the trial judge that a dispute over the head teacher's instruction to teach an allegedly disruptive pupil did not relate to "the physical conditions in which the teachers were required to work".

[1058] And not, e.g. questions of "discipline" between a trade union and the worker in his capacity as union member.

[1059] Contrast the difficulties under Industrial Relations Act 1971 s.167(1); per Lord Denning MR in *Cory Lighterage Ltd v TGWU* [1973] I.C.R. 339 at 357–358.

[1060] per Lord Diplock in *Hadmor Productions Ltd v Hamilton* [1983] 1 A.C. 191 at 226 ("a classic instance" of a trade dispute under the earlier law); *General Aviation Services (UK) Ltd v TGWU* [1975] I.C.R. 276 CA (a decision on the words: "relates wholly or mainly to", in s.167(1) of the Industrial Relations Act 1971; affirmed on other grounds, (1976) [1985] I.C.R. 615 HL); and *Silver Tassie Co Ltd v Cleary* (1958) 92 I.L.T.R. 27 (misplaced belief of victimisation; sufficient for trade dispute).

[1061] *Mercury Communications Ltd v Scott-Garner* [1984] Ch. 37 CA at 81, per Donaldson MR; at 92, per May LJ ("in substantial degree a political and ideological campaign"); and at 98–99, per Dillon LJ; see Ewing and Rees (1984) 13 I.L.J. 60. But where there is proposed legislation, there may be a political dispute with the government and a genuine industrial dispute with employers about negotiations on future conditions of employment: *Associated British Ports v TGWU* [1989] I.R.L.R. 291 at 300–301 (affirmed on other grounds, [1989] 1 W.L.R. 939 HL; dock strike following proposed repeal of the Dock Workers Employment Scheme 1967).

[1062] *Wandsworth LBC v NAS/UWT* [1994] I.C.R. 81 (criticism "on educational grounds" but the main concern was the "excessive and unnecessary workload" in the extra time teachers had to work: per Neill LJ at 96). See too *Westminster City Council v UNISON* [2001] EWCA Civ 443; [2001] I.C.R. 1046 where, although the union "made no bones about their opposition to the privatisation of the assessment and advice unit, on no view was the threat of a strike used to further that opposition. The judge ... appears to assume that the workers ... must have been swayed by [the union's] political or policy arguments about the theory of privatisation when he had specific evidence given at some length that that was not the case", per Buxton LJ at 1062–1063. The uncontroverted evidence was that the dispute was solely about the identity of the employer and was, therefore, a trade dispute.

some extent, the parties to) a trade dispute within s.244 arose in *University College London Hospitals NHS Trust v UNISON*.[1063] A Hospital Trust was negotiating with a consortium which included various unidentified companies, over a scheme for them to build and eventually run a new hospital. Some of the employees would be transferred to the consortium. Their union, UNISON opposed the scheme on principle, but it called also on the claimant Trust to make a contract with the consortium to guarantee over the 30 years of the scheme that all transferred employees and all future and subcontracted employees of the consortium would receive equivalent terms and conditions to those enjoyed by employees who were not transferred. The Trust refused, and after a ballot approved by a large majority, UNISON called for strike action. The Court of Appeal, granting an injunction, held that, while this could no doubt be an industrial dispute, it could not be a trade dispute within s.244, since it referred to action over the terms of employment of staff who had not yet been employed. Even in regard to existing employees, who might gain additional security, the dispute was mainly concerned with their employment with unidentified future employers and could not fall within the definition in the section. As Judge LJ put it:

> "… although protection from liability in tort extends to disputes between workers and their current employers about future terms and conditions, … (s.244) is not apt to cover the terms and conditions of a non-existent contract of employment with a potential employer."[1064]

This is not likely to be the last of a problem which will accelerate in a world of global enterprise where change in the nature of the employers will increase during the life of employment contracts and of collective agreements. Where an employer wishes to limit the extent of his commitments, it may prove possible to commit himself, or part of an enterprise, to work over a limited period, leaving open the right to transfer the work involved to future, but presently unknown future employers, perhaps a fellow subsidiary company in a group.[1065] The express mention of "the right of a trade union to represent workers" resolves any doubt whether a "recognition dispute" is included.[1066] Inclusion of disputes about union membership (which comprises the issue of which union a worker should join) reaffirms the position under the 1906 Act, but with the important addition after 1982 that the workers in question must all be, or have been, employed by the employer in dispute.[1067]

23-191 On the other hand, extraneous factors not falling within the items listed have

[1063] [1999] I.C.R. 204 CA; see above on parties, para.23-186. The European Court of Human Rights rejected the union's complaint that this decision was incompatible with art.11 of the European Convention on Human Rights as inadmissible: *UNISON v United Kingdom* [2002] I.R.L.R. 497.

[1064] [1999] I.C.R. 204 CA at 216; so too Lord Woolf MR at 209–215. The Union considered that such a guarantee would be superior to any rights that could be acquired under the TUPE Regulations on transfer of undertakings (SI 1981/1794, now replaced by SI 2006/246 as amended by SI 2014/16).

[1065] The law protects the inherent prerogative of the employer to dispose of the business: *Newns v British Airways Plc* [1992] I.R.L.R. 575 CA.

[1066] Sed quaere whether this would lead to a different result in *Stratford & Son Ltd v Lindley* [1965] A.C. 269 HL, in the light of the facts found by the Law Lords that there was no trade dispute under the 1906 Act definition.

[1067] Now s.244(1)(e) of TULRCA 1992; as to workers dismissed in connection with the dispute, see above, (a); on the 1906 Act, cf. *White v Riley* [1921] 1 Ch. 1 CA; *Hodges v Webb* [1920] 2 Ch. 70 at 82. To this extent a dispute involving "inter-union rivalry" was, and still is, included within the formula. But any attempt by the union to take action to secure benefits for members only runs the risk that protection will be lost: TULRCA 1992 s.222, and para.23-148.

caused a dispute which looks like a trade dispute to turn out, on further inspection, not to be one because it lacks the necessary statutory content. The mere existence of strong personal feelings or of malevolent spite is not sufficient to have that effect.[1068] But where the defendant has been pursuing a personal feud or a grudge,[1069] even though it be in a context of matters relating to employment, or where he pursues a dispute out of sheer fury or anger with the claimant,[1070] there is no trade dispute since the matter is, or has become, essentially a personal quarrel. So, too, where trade union officials claimed to be furthering a recognition dispute with employers, but were found to be pursuing the union's prestige for reasons of "inter-union rivalry", it was held that, if there were a dispute, it could not be a trade dispute.[1071] Such cases were concerned with assertions of a "trade dispute" which were not "genuine", or a "sham", a "pretext" or "specious cover" for other matters, so lacking the required content.[1072]

In *BBC v Hearn*,[1073] trade union officials, as part of the campaign, which the union supported, against racial discrimination, asked the BBC for an assurance that their members would not have to work broadcasting the F.A. Cup Final to South Africa for television, in the absence of which they would ask their members not to work on the programme. When the BBC refused, the defendant claimed that a dispute about the requirement that his members carry out employment duties contrary to "national and international" policy was a trade dispute; but it was held that the dispute was concerned with objections to apartheid and that the union's action was coercive interference with the performance of employment contracts; it was not a trade dispute. That was a decision before 1982; but the position now is even clearer, for the dispute did not relate "wholly or mainly" to the required content and could not therefore be a trade dispute. Yet it has been said that the dispute "could readily have been turned into one"[1074] by the union demanding to renegotiate the contracts of employment so as to include the required condition.[1075] The classic trade dispute is, after all, a dispute about a demand for new employment conditions, such as a wage claim. 23-192

"Political" disputes Disputes which are about political matters only will not attract protection.[1076] But if, as Lord Denning MR put it, the union said to the 23-193

1068 *Dallimore v Williams* (1914) 30 T.L.R. 432 CA; (1912) 29 T.L.R. 67 CA; *Deane v Craik*, *The Times*, 16 March 1962; *Associated British Ports v TGWU* [1989] I.R.L.R. 291 at 300, per Millett J.

1069 per Lord Loreburn in *Conway v Wade* [1909] A.C. 506 at 509–510; *Huntley v Thornton* [1957] 1 W.L.R. 321 at 349–350 (beyond a certain point in the dispute the defendant union officials were held to have acted in pursuance of their own "grudge" and protection of their "ruffled dignity"). cf. *Hutchison v Aitchinson* (1970) 9 K.I.R. 68.

1070 *Torquay Hotel Co Ltd v Cousins* [1969] 2 Ch. 106 CA.

1071 *Stratford & Son Ltd v Lindley* [1965] A.C. 269 at 323, 335 and 342.

1072 *NWL Ltd v Woods* [1979] 1 W.L.R. 1294 at 1313, per Lord Scarman, on *Conway v Wade* [1909] A.C. 506; *Huntley v Thornton* [1957] 1 W.L.R. 321; and *Stratford & Son Ltd v Lindley* [1965] A.C. 269.

1073 [1977] 1 W.L.R. 1004 CA; approved in *NWL Ltd v Woods* [1979] 1 W.L.R. at 1304, per Lord Diplock; and at 1314, per Lord Scarman; *Express Newspapers Ltd v McShane* [1980] A.C. 672 at 682, per Lord Wilberforce; and at 694, per Lord Scarman.

1074 *NWL Ltd v Woods* [1979] 1 W.L.R. 1294 at 1304, per Lord Diplock.

1075 Pain J in *BBC v Hearn* [1977] I.R.L.R. 269 at 272 had held that such a demand had been made, but the Court of Appeal took a different view of the evidence: [1977] 1 W.L.R. 1004 at 1015, per Roskill LJ.

1076 *Assoc Newspapers Group v Flynn* (1971) 10 K.I.R. 71 (strike against Industrial Relations Bill); *Express Newspapers v Keys* [1980] I.R.L.R. 247; *BBC v Hearn* [1977] 1 W.L.R. 1004; *Mercury Communications Ltd v Scott-Gurner* [1984] Ch. 37 CA.

employer: "We would like you to consider putting a clause in the contract by which our members are not bound to take part in any broadcast which may be viewed in South Africa", and the employer refused, that could be a trade dispute[1077] (so long as the dispute related mainly to that issue concerning the conditions of employment). This logical conclusion, which in itself is largely unaffected by the amendments of 1982, may appear to be threatened by dicta in cases after *BBC v Hearn*. It has, for example, been said that the dispute must be based on the employees' "current" contracts of employment,[1078] and that it cannot extend to terms regulating the employer's relationship with a third party.[1079] Such tests are, a simple illustration suggests, difficult to justify. A dispute which related wholly to a claim by workers that their conditions should be changed so that they would have the right not to work on the premises of a particular customer of the employer, would surely (subject to the general law, including that on discrimination) be a trade dispute. But it has also been said:

> "A trade union cannot turn a dispute which in reality has no connection with terms and conditions of employment into a [trade dispute] ... by insisting that the employer inserts appropriate terms into the contracts of employment."[1080]

But that was in a context of (what the defendants had conceded to be) "economic duress",[1081] where the majority of the Law Lords refused to see a payment demanded by the union from flag-of-convenience employers into a world-wide fund for seamen (in addition to the back pay for the ship's crew), as having "the legal characteristics of a term or condition of employment", saying it had "nothing whatever" to do with the crew's conditions. Indeed, they likened it to a demand for a contribution to "a fund to assist the guerrillas in El Salvador".[1082] Moreover, what is legitimately within the scope of contractual conditions is for the parties, not for the court, to determine, just as it is for the parties to decide whether a dispute over those conditions has come to an end.[1083] If workers demanded of their employer that part of moneys that might come to them be paid into a fund for refugees from an earthquake in El Salvador and the employer refused, it is submitted that there would be a trade dispute. But where a union induced members to take action for a political campaign mainly relating to government policies on privatisation, there was no trade dispute.[1084]

1077 *BBC v Hearn* [1977] 1 W.L.R. 1004 at 1011, per Lord Denning MR, cited with approval by Lord Diplock in *Hadmor Productions Ltd v Hamilton* [1983] 1 A.C. 191 at 227.

1078 *Dimbleby & Sons Ltd v NUJ* [1984] 1 W.L.R. 427 at 433, per Lord Diplock.

1079 *Universe Tankships Inc of Monrovia v ITF* [1983] 1 A.C. 366 at 386, per Lord Diplock.

1080 *Universe Tankships Inc of Monrovia v ITF* [1983] 1 A.C. 366, at 392, per Lord Cross; see also, per Lord Diplock at 387; but contrast the dissent of Lord Scarman at 402–403; and Lord Brandon at 408–409; cf. Wedderburn (1982) 45 M.L.R. 556 at 562–563.

1081 See para.23-141; and *Dimskal Shipping SA v ITWF* [1992] 2 A.C. 152 HL (money paid abroad to release ship from industrial action wholly lawful in that country, recoverable in England for economic duress).

1082 *Universe Tankships Inc of Monrovia v ITF* [1983] 1 A.C. 366 at 387–389, per Lord Diplock; per Lord Cross at 391–393; per Lord Russell at 395. See Sterling (1982) 11 I.L.J. 156 at 165. But the demands in that case were made "on behalf of the crew"; the views of the minority, Lord Scarman and Lord Brandon, it is submitted, are to be preferred.

1083 *Newham LBC v NALGO* [1993] I.C.R. 189 CA.

1084 *Mercury Communications Ltd v Scott-Garner* [1983] Ch. 37 CA; cf. *Westminster City Council v Unison* [2001] EWCA Civ 443; [2001] I.C.R. 1046 where the union's campaign against privatisation of the Council's (housing) assessment and advice unit was distinguished from the dispute in the

Some of the earlier decisions were thought to import into this area of the law a test used in regard to lawful means conspiracy where motives are mixed, namely the ascertainment of the "predominant" motive.[1085] That was incorrect in the law before 1982 concerning content (as opposed to "contemplation or furtherance", dealt with below). Where union officials blacked a flag-of-convenience ship pursuant to demands for decent conditions for the crew but also in pursuit of an international campaign against all such ships, the House of Lords in *NWL Ltd v Woods*[1086] held in 1979 that a trade dispute existed. Once the dispute was (as the law was then) "connected with" a specified content, the predominant purpose was irrelevant and the only limitation was that it must be a real and not "ostensible" connection.[1087] After 1982 the link is more tightly defined, and the dispute must "relate wholly or mainly" to the content.[1088] But the test is whether the dispute so relates; it would be possible still for the dispute to relate mainly to one of the specified items and remain a trade dispute, even though some or all of the participants harboured a wish to inflict injury or political damage upon an opposing party. Where that question of purpose would normally have its effect would be, not upon the objective question of content, but on the subjective issue of "contemplation or furtherance".[1089] **23-194**

(iv) Contemplation or furtherance

A defendant may "further" an existing dispute. Or he may "contemplate" a dispute which either is imminent or is at least sufficiently probable for him to have acted with it in view and to have considered it as such.[1090] The 1982 Act made express provision that its amendments did not affect the question whether an act done by a person is done in contemplation or furtherance of a dispute "whether he is a party to the dispute or not".[1091] But the problem of when a dispute may be properly said to be "in contemplation" has caused acute difficulties[1092]; and the **23-195**

case about the identity of the employer once the unit had been privatised.

1085 e.g. *Conway v Wade* [1909] A.C. 506; *Huntley v Thornton* [1957] 1 W.L.R. 321; *Stratford & Son Ltd v Lindley* [1965] A.C. 269.

1086 [1979] 1 W.L.R. 1294 HL; especially, per Lord Diplock at 1304–1305, with whom Lord Fraser of Tullybelton agreed at 1308; per Lord Scarman at 1313–1314 (overruling *Star Sea Transport of Monrovia v Slater* [1978] I.R.L.R. 507 CA). See also *Hadmor Productions Ltd v Hamilton* [1983] 1 A.C. 191 HL.

1087 *NWL Ltd v Woods* [1979] 1 W.L.R. 1294 at 1314, per Lord Scarman.

1088 Now TULRCA 1992 s.244(1); *Mercury Communications Ltd v Scott-Garner* [1984] Ch. 37 CA; *Dimbleby & Sons Ltd v NUJ* [1984] 1 W.L.R. 427 HL.

1089 cf. *Huntley v Thornton* [1957] 1 W.L.R. 321.

1090 See *Conway v Wade* [1909] A.C. 506 at 512, per Lord Loreburn LC; at 522, per Lord Shaw; and at 517–518, per Lord Atkinson; *Express Newspapers Ltd v McShane* [1980] A.C. 672 at 691, per Lord Keith of Kinkel; at 694, per Lord Scarman. As to whether a dispute has come to an end see *ISS Mediclean Ltd v GMB* [2014] EWHC 4208 (QB); [2015] I.R.L.R. 96 where the claimant submitted that the correct approach was to ask whether the average, reasonable union member looking at the matter at or shortly after any interruption in the action would say that it had come to an end, citing Lord Donaldson MR in *Post Office v Union of Communication Workers* [1990] I.C.R. 258 at 267 with reference to the separate issue of whether the resumed industrial action had the support of a ballot. The point was not decided as the court held that on the facts in *ISS Mediclean* the dispute had not come to an end and the union's action was taken in furtherance of it.

1091 Employment Act 1982 s.18(7). This provision is not reproduced in TULRCA 1992; but it may be saved by the operation of Sch.3 para.2(3).

1092 See the different views in *Stratford & Son Ltd v Lindley* [1965] A.C. 269 at 323, per Lord Reid ("No statute makes express provision in this respect in connection with threats or demands to which the other party to an imminent dispute accedes.[1093] But the mere apprehension of or preparation for a dispute, or mere consideration of a dispute which is no more than a possibility, will not suffice.[1094] Nor does the intention to create a dispute.[1095] A dispute may be "contemplated" when a person has in mind some objective situation,[1096] or where it is reasonable to foresee a dispute.[1097]

23-196 But it will not suffice if the defendant proves that a trade dispute exists with one party but it is then shown that his action was not taken in furtherance of that dispute, for example where he deliberately causes damage to someone not in law involved in or connected with the dispute.[1098] But if the defendant genuinely believes that his action will help one or other party to an existing dispute, he acts "in furtherance" of it. Attempts to insert an "objective" element into the concept of "furtherance" are wrong,[1099] except in so far as it may go to show that no reasonable person could have thought that the act was capable of helping one side to achieve its objectives (but that, too, goes to honesty of purpose alone, not to the reasonableness of the act).[1100] So in *Express Newspapers Ltd v McShane*,[1101] trade union officials, in

---

doubt they acted in contemplation of a dispute"); per Viscount Radcliffe at 327 (not acting "even in contemplation of trade dispute"); per Lord Pearce at 335 (had the action not been "a specious cover for inter-union rivalry, the defendants' conduct would, I think, in spite of its oblique incidence constitute conduct in contemplation of a trade dispute"); per Lord Denning MR at 281 (acts done were "clearly in contemplation of such a dispute").

1093 TULRCA 1992 s.244(4): "An act threat or demand ... which, if resisted, would have led to a trade dispute ... [is] treated as done or made in contemplation or furtherance of a trade dispute notwithstanding that because [the person against whom it was made] accedes to the demand no dispute arises".

1094 *Bent's Brewery Co Ltd v Hogan* [1945] 2 All E.R. 570; *John Milligan & Co Ltd v Ayr Harbour Trustees*, 1915 S.C. 937.

1095 *Conway v Wade* [1909] A.C. 506 HL; *Esplanade Pharmacy Ltd v Larkin* [1957] I.R. 285.

1096 *Express Newspapers Ltd v McShane* [1980] A.C. 672 at 694, per Lord Scarman; *Conway v Wade* [1909] A.C. 506 at 522, per Lord Shaw; so too genuine fears of redundancies: *Hadmor Productions Ltd v Hamilton* [1983] 1 A.C. 191 HL.

1097 *Health Computing Ltd v Meek* [1981] I.C.R. 24 at 32, per Goulding J. cf. per Lord Wilberforce (dissenting on this point) in *Express Newspapers Ltd v McShane* [1980] A.C. 672 at 683 ("an actual or emerging trade dispute").

1098 *Torquay Hotel Co Ltd v Cousins* [1969] 2 Ch. 106, per Lord Denning MR, the acts were taken by the defendants "in furtherance of the anger which they felt toward" the claimants who had commented adversely on the union which had a trade dispute with another hotel in Torquay. Quaere what the result in that case would have been if the trade dispute had been established with the Hotels Association of which both hotels were members? Semble: after *Express Newspapers Ltd v McShane* [1980] A.C. 672 HL, the defendants would have acted in furtherance of the trade dispute if they had proved that, even if angry, they genuinely believed that action against the claimants would promote their trade dispute (so long as it is not overtaken by an "ulterior purpose such as revenge", per Lord Diplock: [1980] A.C. 672 at 687). But now under TULRCA 1992 s.244, they would need to show that the dispute remained one which *mainly* related to recognition: see para.23-188.

1099 See the earlier decisions which, giving "furtherance" an objective sense, cannot be relied upon in respect of their interpretation of "furtherance": e.g. *Beaverbrook Newspapers Ltd v Keys* [1978] I.C.R. 582 CA; *PBDS (National Carriers) Ltd v Filkins* [1979] I.R.L.R. 356 CA; *Associated Newspapers Group Ltd v Wade* [1979] I.C.R. 664 CA.

1100 *Express Newspapers Ltd v McShane* [1980] A.C. 672 HL (Lord Wilberforce dissenting on the law); see on the objective floor of evidence required for proof of a genuine and honest purpose, per Lord Diplock at 687–688, per Lord Keith of Kinkel at 692, per Lord Scarman at 693–694. Compare the subjective test on whether a dispute survives or continues: *Newham LBC v NALGO* [1993] I.C.R. 189 CA.

1101 [1980] A.C. 672 Lord Wilberforce dissenting; and see Lord Salmon requiring that the defendant "must honestly and reasonably believe" that his act may further the trade dispute, not acting out of pursuit of a trade dispute with provincial newspaper proprietors, called upon its members at the Press Association to strike and instructed members working on the national newspapers to refuse to work on Press Association copy. The House of Lords held that the acts had been done in furtherance of the trade dispute, because the subjective state of mind of the union officials was one of honest and genuine purpose to promote the dispute in the provincial papers.[1102] The test is subjective as in some earlier decisions on the Act of 1906 which excluded "furtherance" because the defendant did not have an honest purpose but acted predominantly out of "spite" or some such ulterior motive.[1103] "The presence of an improper motive is relevant if it is so overriding that it negatives any genuine intention to promote or advance the dispute."[1104] The subjective test of "furtherance" was the proper approach under the Acts of 1875 and 1906[1105] and a fortiori remains the right approach under the legislation consolidated in TULRCA 1992.[1106]

"spite" or to show his "muscle" or wholly unreasonably as "an embittered fanatic", at 689–690.

1102 cf. *Conway v Wade* [1909] A.C. 506 at 522, per Lord Shaw (the term "furtherance" means "for the purpose of promoting the interests of either or both parties" to the dispute).

1103 Such as *Conway v Wade* [1906] A.C. 506; *Huntley v Thornton* [1957] 1 W.L.R. 321.

1104 *Associated British Ports v TGWU* [1989] I.R.L.R. 291 at 300, per Millett J (affirmed on other grounds, [1989] 1 W.L.R. 939 HL); citing *Dallimore v Williams* (1912) 29 T.L.R. 67 CA; (1914) 30 T.L.R. 432 CA; *Norbrook Laboratories v King* [1984] I.R.L.R. 200 CA (NI). But compare the effect given by the Court of Appeal to an "intent to injure" in respect of liability in tort not protected by any immunity: [1989] 1 W.L.R. 939 (reversed on other grounds, [1989] 1 W.L.R. 939 HL).

1105 *Conway v Wade* [1909] A.C. 506 at 512, per Lord Loreburn; at 517, per Lord Atkinson; *Milligan v Ayr Harbour Trustees*, 1915 S.C. 937 at 950, per Lord Dundas.

1106 See *Express Newspapers Ltd v McShane* [1980] A.C. 672 at 694, per Lord Scarman ("It would need very clear statutory language to persuade me that Parliament intended to allow the courts to act as some sort of backseat driver in trade disputes"). The new form of s.244 leaves the answer to that question more uncertain. cf. s.13 of the Irish Industrial Relations Act 1990 which uses the wording "in the reasonable belief that the act was done in contemplation or furtherance of a trade dispute" to qualify similar statutory defences in Irish law and was described in *Dublin City Council v Technical Engineering and Electrical Union* [2010] IEHC 289; [2010] 4 I.R. 667 at [48] as a via media between the subjective test of furtherance upheld by a majority of the House of Lords in the *McShane* case and the objective test adopted by Lord Wilberforce in that case and Lord Denning MR in *Associated Newspaper Group Ltd v Wade* [1979] I.C.R. 664 CA.

Chapter 24

STATUTORY AND EU-DERIVED INTELLECTUAL PROPERTY RIGHTS

Table of Contents

1. Introduction

Intellectual property "Intellectual property" is the collective name often given to the branch of law that deals with such intangible rights as copyright, database 24-01 right, artist's resale right, moral rights, rights in performances, rights in designs, trade marks, passing off, patents and confidential information. This chapter deals with the main intellectual property rights which derive from UK statutes or EU legislation or both.[1] Most, but not all, of the rights covered in this chapter are proprietary in nature and can be dealt with by assignment or licence.[2] Owners of these rights may sue for infringement of them. The tort of "passing off" and the protection given by the courts to confidential information are (with a few exceptions[3]) creatures of the common law and equity respectively and are dealt with elsewhere.[4] This chapter aims to summarise the main principles governing subsistence and infringement of the statutory and EU-derived rights. Readers are referred to the specialist works mentioned for further reference.

24-02 **Nature of statutory intellectual property rights** Infringement of these rights has generally been recognised to be tortious in nature even though it involves the breach of statutory rights and is not a tort at common law.[5] It is not necessary for a claimant to prove actual damage to maintain an action for infringement. Nor is it necessary to prove intention to infringe. But there are many cases where knowledge is a pre-requisite of liability: for example, under the Copyright Act 1988 ss.22–24, liability for dealing with infringing copies only arises when a person knows or has reason to believe that they are infringing copies. Although innocence or ignorance of the rights can affect the relief granted, in general, a defendant cannot escape liability for infringement by saying that he did not intend to infringe or that he did not know he was infringing.[6]

24-03 **European influence on intellectual property rights** Each intellectual property right described below has been subject to the influence of European Union legislation to a greater or lesser extent. There has also been a partial approximation of the

---

1 References to the relevant specialist texts are given at the start of each section.

2 The rights which are property rights and can be assigned and licensed are: copyright (Copyright, Designs and Patents Act 1988 ("the Copyright Act 1988" or "CDPA 1988") ss.1(1) and 90); database right (Copyright and Rights in Databases Regulations 1997 (SI 1997/3032) regs 13 and 23); performers' property rights (Copyright Act 1988 ss.191A and 191B); UK unregistered design right (Copyright Act 1988 ss.213 and 222); Community designs (Council Regulation 6/2002 arts 27, 28, 32); UK registered designs (Registered Designs Act 1949 ("RDA 1949")); UK registered trade marks (Trade Marks Act 1994 s.22); EU registered trade marks (arts 16, 17 and 22 of Council Regulation (EC) 207/2009); and patents (Patents Act 1977 s.30(1). Artist's resale right may be transmitted to a trustee and is transmissible on death (Artist's Resale Right Regulations 2006, SI 2006/346 regs 9, 11). Moral rights may not be assigned but most pass on death (CDPA 1988 ss.94, 95, 205L, 205M). Performers' non-property rights are only transmissible on death (CDPA 1988 s.192A). Recording rights are not transmissible (CDPA 1988 s.192B). Infringements of performers' non-property rights and recording rights are actionable as breach of statutory duty (CDPA 1988 ss.194, 193).

3 For example, certain statutes that impose duties of confidence; see "breach of confidence" in Ch.26. See also Bently, Johnson, Malynicz and Aplin, Gurry on *Breach of Confidence—The Protection of Confidential Information*, 2nd edn (Oxford: Oxford University Press, 2012); and Directive (EU) 2016/943 on Trade Secrets.

4 See Chs 25 and 26.

5 See, e.g. *Fish & Fish Ltd v Sea Shepherd UK* [2015] UKSC 10; [2015] A.C. 1229 at [38], [40], [41] (copyright); *L'Oreal SA v eBay International AG* [2009] EWHC 1094 (Ch) [2009] E.T.M.R. 53 at [346] (trade marks); and *Grimme Landmaschinenfabrik GmbH & Co KG v Scott (t/a Scotts Potato Machinery)* [2010] EWCA Civ 1110; [2011] F.S.R. 7 at [88] (patents). The precise nature of the rights conferred is rarely a matter of practical importance.

6 *Gillette UK Ltd v Edenwest Ltd* [1994] R.P.C. 279 (authorities reviewed—innocence no defence to damages for trade mark infringement).

enforcement of intellectual property rights with the aim of establishing a high level of protection for the rights.[7] Copyright, rights in databases and rights in performances have been the subject of approximation of national laws by means of a series of Directives adopted over the period since 1986.[8] There is no European Union copyright code to replace national laws, but the Court of Justice of the European Union ("CJEU") has steadily built up a European copyright jurisprudence on the interpretation of the Directives.[9] Moral rights have not been the subject of EU legislation. By contrast, designs and trade marks have been almost entirely harmonised within the European Union and EU-wide rights are available in addition to or in substitution for national trade marks and designs (although UK unregistered design right[10] remains in place).[11] Both EU Trade Marks (CTMs) and Registered Community Designs (RCDs) are administered at the European Intellectual Property Office (EUIPO), located at Alicante, Spain.[12] Until recently, there has been no European Union instrument governing patent law, which has instead

---

[7] See Directive 2004/48/EC of 24 April 2004, on the Enforcement of Intellectual Property Rights and in particular Recital 10. This Directive has been implemented but few of its provisions were thought to require changes to the law. Specifically in relation to copyright, see also Directive 2001/29/EC of 22 May 2001, on the harmonisation of certain aspects of copyright and related rights in the information society, art.8. The most significant change resulting from these provisions has been the introduction of injunctions against intermediary service providers whose services have been used for infringement. See below para.24-53.

[8] The Directives, some of which are codified replacements of earlier Directives as amended, are as follows: Council Directive 87/54/EEC of 16 December 1986, on the legal protection of topographies of semiconductor products; Council Directive 93/83/EEC of 27 September 1993, on the coordination of certain rules concerning copyright and rights related to copyright applicable to satellite broadcasting and cable retransmission; Directive 96/9/EC of 11 March 1996, on the legal protection of databases; Directive 2001/29/EC of 22 May 2001, on the harmonisation of certain aspects of copyright and related rights in the information society; Directive 2001/84/EC of 27 September 2001, on the resale right for the benefit of the author of an original work of art; Directive 2006/115/EC of 12 December 2006, on rental right and lending right and on certain rights related to copyright in the field of intellectual property; Directive 2006/116/EC of 12 December 2006, on the term of protection of copyright and certain related rights (which was amended by Directive 2011/77/EU of 27 September 2011); Directive 2009/24/EC of 23 April 2009 on the legal protection of computer programs; Directive 2012/28/EU of 25 October 2012 on certain permitted uses of orphan works; Directive 2014/26/EU of 26 February 2014 on collective management of copyright and related rights and multi-territorial licensing of rights in musical works for online use in the internal market; and Directive 2017/1564 EU of 13 September 2017 on permitted uses for the print disabled. Directive 2019/790 of 17 April 2019 on Copyright in the Digital Single Market will not be implemented in the UK.

[9] This case law is binding on national courts. Concepts embodied in the Directives on copyright and related rights must be interpreted in a manner consistent with relevant international conventions: the Berne Convention, the WIPO Copyright Treaty (WCT), the WIPO Performances and Phonograms Treaty (WPPT) and the TRIPs Agreement. Terms of a provision of EU law must be given an autonomous and uniform interpretation throughout the European Union, in the interest of uniform application of EU law and the principle of equality. See *Levola Hengelo BV v Smilde Foods BV* (C-310/17) EU:C:2018:899; [2018] Bus. L.R. 2442; [2019] E.C.D.R. 2 at [33], [38] and [39]; and *Sociedade de Vestuario SA v G-Star Raw CV* (C-683/17) EU:C:2019:721 at [29] and [41].

[10] Conferred by CDPA 1988 Pt III.

[11] There is a significant EU jurisprudence on designs and an immense EU jurisprudence on trade marks with decisions being made both by CJEU and by the General Court.

[12] The relevant EU legislation in respect of designs comprises Directive 98/71/EC of 13 October 1998 on the legal protection of designs and Council Regulation 6/2002 of 12 December 2001 on community designs. For trade marks, see Council Regulation 40/94/EEC, codified by Council Regulation (EC) 207/2009 and now amended by Regulation (EU) 2015/2424. The latest harmonising directive is Directive 2015/2436/EC.

been a matter of national law and/or the provisions of the European Patent Convention. However, following 30 years of negotiation and an international agreement adopted in 2013, the EU stands on the brink of a unitary patent administered by a Unified Patents Court.[13]

24-04 **Brexit** At the time of writing, the UK has left the EU but there will be no change in the law prior to the end of the Brexit implementation period (which is presently fixed for 31 December 2020). At this point, there will be significant changes to the law.[14] In the field of copyright, subject to any agreement about the UK's future trading relationship with the EU, the changes will affect copyright clearances for satellite broadcasting, portability of online services, orphan works, accessible copies, collective rights management, cable retransmission and satellite decoder cards.[15] There will also be changes to database right.[16] Qualification for UK unregistered designs will be limited while Community designs will cease to apply in the UK and will be replaced by equivalent UK rights.[17] The EU wide exhaustion of rights scheme will also change.[18]

2. Copyright, Artist's Resale Right and Database Right

(a) Scope of protection

(i) Copyright

24-05 **Copyright, Designs and Patents Act 1988[19]** Copyright[20] is an exclusively statutory right arising under the Copyright, Designs and Patents Act 1988[21] ("the

[13] See para.24-127.

[14] A useful summary is at: *https://www.gov.uk/government/news/intellectual-property-and-the-transition-period* and linked pages [Accessed 28 March 2020].

[15] See the Intellectual Property (Copyright and Related Rights) (Amendment) (EU Exit) Regulations 2019 (SI 2019/605).

[16] See the Intellectual Property (Copyright and Related Rights) (Amendment) (EU Exit) Regulations 2019 (SI 2019/605).

[17] See the Designs and International Trade Marks (Amendment etc.) (EU Exit) Regulations 2019 (SI 2019/638).

[18] *https://www.gov.uk/guidance/exhaustion-of-ip-rights-and-parallel-trade-after-the-transition-period* [Accessed 28 March 2020].

[19] Since the Copyright Act 1988 entered into force it has been amended frequently, mainly to implement the EU Directives referred to in para.24-03. Other substantial amendments were made by the Broadcasting Acts 1990 and 1996. In addition, the Copyright Act 1988 has been amended to make provision for so-called "orphan works" and "extended collective licensing", to regulate "collective management organisations" and to modify and extend the acts which may be done without infringing ("permitted acts" or "exceptions"). On copyright, see generally *Copinger and Skone James on Copyright*, various editors, 17th edn (London: Sweet & Maxwell, 2016); and Laddie, Prescott and Vitoria, *The Modern Law of Copyright and Designs*, various editors, 5th edn (London: LexisNexis, 2018).

[20] What follows applies equally to "publication right", a right which is conferred on a person who, after the expiry of copyright protection, publishes a previously unpublished work: see the Copyright and Related Rights Regulations 1996 (SI 1996/2967), regs 16–17B.

[21] The Copyright Act replaced the Copyright Act 1956, which in turn replaced the Copyright Act 1911. The transitional provisions are contained in Sch.1. In general, the provisions of the 1988 Act apply to pre-existing works. There are special provisions concerning industrial designs (see below). First ownership of copyright is determined in accordance with the law in force when the work was made. The provisions of the 1956 Act will continue to be relevant for many years and some works dating

Copyright Act 1988" or "CDPA 1988"). Under Pt 1 of the Copyright Act 1988, the owner of the copyright in a copyright work has the exclusive right to do and to prohibit others from doing certain acts in relation to the work, which are referred to in the Act as "the acts restricted by the copyright". These "restricted" acts include copying and are dealt with below.[22] The author and in the case of a film, the director, of a work is also given certain "moral rights".[23] Part II of the Act is concerned with the rights that performers and others have in their performances.[24] Part III is concerned with UK unregistered design right (which was introduced by the Act)[25] and Pt IV amended the law in relation to registered designs.[26] Copyright arises automatically, upon creation of the work[27]: there are no formalities. It is limited in duration (see below). Copyright does not confer an absolute monopoly. Mere similarity of two works does not of itself constitute infringement, but may lead to the inference that one was copied from the other.

Scope of copyright protection: general Recent CJEU case law[28] has made clear that copyright only protects subject-matter which can be classed as a "work" within the meaning of the EU Information Society Directive (2001/29). For these purposes, two cumulative conditions must be satisfied. First, the subject-matter must be original in the sense that it is its author's own intellectual creation.[29] Secondly, it must be the *expression* of the author's own intellectual creation. Accordingly, ideas, procedures, methods of operation and mathematical concepts are not protected by copyright as such.[30] Furthermore, the subject-matter must be expressed in a manner which makes it identifiable with sufficient precision and objectivity (although not necessarily in permanent form). As was made clear in earlier UK case law, no clear principle is or could be laid down in the cases in order to tell whether what is sought to be protected is on the ideas side of the dividing line, or on the expression side.[31] The recent EU case law appears to be consistent with previous statements in the UK case law to the effect that copyright does not extend to clothing information, facts, ideas, theories and themes with exclusive property rights, so as **24-06**

from before the 1911 Act may still have copyright or fail to have it only because of incidents peculiar to the earlier law. For the earlier law, reference should be made to earlier editions of this work or earlier editions of the standard texts.

22 See para.24-32 onwards.

23 See para.24-59 onwards.

24 See para.24-70 onwards.

25 See para.24-76 onwards.

26 See para.24-98 onwards.

27 Compare patents, registered trade marks and registered designs for which application must be made. UK unregistered design right also arises automatically, if it arises at all.

28 *Levola Hengelo BV v Smilde Foods BV* (C-310/17) EU:C:2018:899; [2018] Bus. L.R. 2442; and *Sociedade de Vestuario SA v G-Star Raw CV* (C-683/17) EU:C:2019:721.

29 See para.24-22.

30 This does not involve a significant departure from previous UK case law. See *SAS Institute v World Programming Ltd* [2013] EWCA Civ 1482; [2015] E.C.D.R. 17; [2014] R.P.C. 8 at [20]; *Ladbroke (Football) Ltd v William Hill (Football) Ltd* [1980] R.P.C. 539 at 546, per Lord Denning MR; [1964] 1 W.L.R. 273 HL; *LB Plastics Ltd v Swish Products Ltd* [1979] R.P.C. 611 HL; *Elanco Products Ltd v Mandops (Agrochemical Specialists) Ltd* [1980] R.P.C. 213; cf. *Bauman v Fussell* [1978] R.P.C. 485; *Kleeneze Ltd v DRG (UK) Ltd* [1984] F.S.R. 399; *Designers' Guild Ltd v Russell Williams (Textiles) Ltd* [2000] 1 W.L.R. 2416; *Baigent and Leigh v The Random House Group Ltd* [2007] EWCA Civ 247; [2008] E.M.L.R. 7.

31 *Baigent and Leigh v The Random House Group Ltd* [2007] EWCA Civ 247; [2008] E.M.L.R. 7 at [5], [147], [101]. See *Kogan v Martin* [2019] EWCA Civ 1645; [2020] E.M.L.R. 4 at [34].

to enable a claimant to monopolise historical research or knowledge and prevent the legitimate use of historical and biographical material, theories propounded, general arguments deployed, or general hypotheses suggested (whether they are sound or not) or general themes written about.[32]

24-07 **Term of copyright protection** The period of copyright in a literary, dramatic, musical or artistic work is 70 years from the year of the death of the author or, if the work is of unknown authorship, from first publication or similar disclosure.[33] The term of protection of other types of work is dealt with below.[34]

24-08 **Subjects of copyright: general** Copyright is afforded by Pt I of the Copyright Act 1988 to a "closed list" "works" of specified types[35]: original[36] literary, dramatic, musical and artistic works; of sound recordings; films; broadcasts; and the typographical arrangement of published editions. It now seems clear that so far as literary, dramatic, musical or artistic works is concerned, the existence of this "closed list" of categories of protectable work is incompatible with the EU case law referred to in the previous paragraph.[37] Where a work satisfies the criteria laid down by that EU case law but falls outside the categories laid down by the Copyright Act 1988, the UK courts will have to decide, in accordance with the *Marleasing* case,[38] whether a conforming interpretation of the Copyright Act 1988 can be adopted.[39] The account of the works protected under the Copyright Act 1988 which follows must be read in light of this.

24-09 **"Works" and subsistence of copyright** The different types of work in which copyright may subsist are summarised below. Frequently, more than one copyright will subsist in a particular work. As a result, a particular act restricted by copyright may be governed by several copyrights, which may have different owners. For example, playing a recording of music in public is an act restricted by the copyright both in the recording, of which the producer is the author, and in the original music, of which the composer is the author. The performers of the music may also have relevant rights which would be infringed by acts of that kind. Similarly,

---

32 *Baigent and Leigh v The Random House Group Ltd* [2007] EWCA Civ 247; [2008] E.M.L.R. 7 at [156], [101].

33 CDPA 1988 s.12. Directive 93/98 (now codified as Directive 2006/116/EC as amended) required Member States to enact legislation extending the term of copyright in literary and artistic works to 70 years from the end of the calendar year in which the author died. The previous term was 50 years and there are transitional provisions relating to revived copyright etc. There are special rules for works of "co-authorship" (i.e. collaborative musical compositions with words—see CDPA 1988 s.10A) and joint authorship (see CDPA 1988 s.12(8)). As an author allows each part of a text to move on from one stage to the next he or she creates a new work in which copyright subsists. Earlier drafts can be separate copyright works: *Sweeney v Macmillan Publishers Ltd* [2002] R.P.C. 35; *Kogan v Martin* [2019] EWCA Civ 1645; [2020] E.M.L.R. 4 at [80].

34 See the paragraphs describing the relevant types of work.

35 CDPA 1988 s.1.

36 As to originality, see para.24-22.

37 See *Response Clothing Ltd v The Edinburgh Woollen Mill Ltd* [2020] EWHC 148 (IPEC); [2020] F.S.R. 25 at [55]–[63].

38 *Marleasing SA v La Comerciál Internacional de Alimentación SA* (C-106/89) EU:C:1990:395; [1990] ECR I-4135; [1992] 1 C.M.L.R. 305.

39 See *Response Clothing Ltd v The Edinburgh Woollen Mill Ltd* [2020] EWHC 148 (IPEC); [2020] F.S.R. 25 at [63].

unauthorised reproduction of a magazine may involve infringement of copyright in both text and photographs—which copyright may be owned by different people.

Literary works The definition of "literary work" is a wide one.[40] The authorities conflict as to whether it is wide enough to encompass any ordered information, for example, circuit diagrams.[41] There is no requirement for literary style or merit, although a single word or a title of a book or broadcast will not count as a literary work.[42] Comparatively little by way of originality has traditionally been required in order for a literary work to attract copyright. However, EU case law has introduced a requirement that the work be the author's own intellectual creation and this may have raised the hurdle.[43] Nevertheless, an extract of a larger work comprising as few as 11 words will be a protected work if it contains an element of the work which, as such, expresses the author's own intellectual creation.[44] **24-10**

Compilations, databases and typographical arrangement Most (if not all) "compilations" are now "databases", as defined in the EU Database Directive, because they are collections of independent materials arranged in a systematic or methodical way and accessible by electronic or other means.[45] The effect of the Directive as implemented is that if such a compilation was created after 27 March 1996 it will only be protected by copyright if by reason of the selection or arrangement of its contents, the compilation is its author's own intellectual creation.[46] If it does not meet that standard, it may nevertheless be protected by database right.[47] Compilations created on or before 27 March 1996 which were protected by copyright as at 31 December 1997 remain protected for the full term of copyright **24-11**

---

40 "any work, other than a dramatic or musical work, which is written, spoken or sung": CDPA 1988 s.3(1). It "accordingly includes (a) a table or compilation other than a database, (b) a computer program, (c) preparatory design material for a computer program, and (d) a database". "Writing" includes any form of notation or code regardless of the method by which or medium in or on which it is recorded and "written" is construed accordingly: CDPA 1988 s.178.

41 *Anacon Corp Ltd v Environmental Research Technology Ltd* [1994] F.S.R. 659. cf. *Electronic Techniques (Anglia) Ltd v Critchley Components Ltd* [1997] F.S.R. 401; *Sandman v Panasonic UK Ltd* [1998] F.S.R. 651.

42 *Exxon Corp v Exxon Insurance Consultants International Ltd* [1982] R.P.C. 69; *Green v Broadcasting Corp of New Zealand* [1989] 2 All E.R. 1056; see also *Dicks v Yates* (1881) 18 Ch. D. 76; cf. *Broemel v Meyer* (1913) 29 T.L.R. 148.

43 See *Infopaq International A/S v Danske Daglades Forening* (C-5/08) EU:C:2009:465; [2009] E.C.D.R. 16 as interpreted in *SAS Institute Inc v World Programming Ltd* [2013] EWCA Civ 1482; [2014] R.P.C. 8.

44 *Infopaq International A/S v Danske Dagblades Forening* (C-5/08) EU:C:2009:465; [2009] E.C.D.R. 16 at [48].

45 See the definition in Directive 96/9/EC art.1(2). Examples of cases involving databases can be found in *Forensic Telecommunications Services Ltd v Chief Constable of West Yorkshire Police* [2011] EWHC 2892 (Ch); [2012] F.S.R. 15; *Technomed Ltd v Bluecrest Health Screening Ltd* [2017] EWHC 2142 (Ch); [2018] F.S.R. 8; *Freistaat Bayern v Verlag Esterbauer GmbH* (C-490/14) EU:C:2015:735; [2016] E.C.D.R. 6 (topographic map); *Keystone Healthcare Ltd v Parr* [2017] EWHC 309; and *Racing Partnership Ltd v Done Brothers (Cash Betting) Ltd* [2019] EWHC 1156 (Ch); [2019] 3 W.L.R. 779; [2019] E.C.D.R. 17.

46 CDPA 1988, s.3(2), inserted by the Copyright and Rights in Database Regulations 1997 (SI 1997/3032), with effect from 1 January 1998. See also reg.29. In *Football Dataco Ltd v Yahoo! UK Ltd* (C-604/10) EU:C:2012:115; [2012] E.C.D.R. 10, the CJEU held that the copyright protection for a database concerns the "structure" rather than its "contents". Accordingly, intellectual effort in creating the data or in setting up the database cannot justify protection if it does not express any originality in the selection or arrangement of the data.

47 See para.24-20.

if they satisfy the previous test for originality.[48] If such a work, though composed entirely of existing materials, is arranged and combined in a novel form that may be sufficient.[49] Works of this period may be protected if their production has involved the labour of collecting common facts, for example, directories.[50] Protection is also provided for the typographical arrangement of published editions.[51]

24-12 **Computer programs** The boundary between what is and is not protected is not always easy to draw. The Software Directive[52] gives protection to the expression in any form of a computer program,[53] such as the source code and the object code, which permits reproduction in different computer languages.[54] However, neither the functionality of a computer program nor the programming language nor the format of data files used in the program in order to exploit certain of its functions constitute a form of expression of that program protected by copyright under the Directive.[55] Important exceptions to copyright in computer programs are dealt with below.[56]

24-13 **Dramatic works and TV formats** The expression "dramatic work" includes a work of dance or mime if written or otherwise recorded.[57] It includes films,[58] although films considered as first fixations are also dealt with separately, but not scenic effects by themselves.[59] Where a musical work requires action and scenery for its proper performance the music may be protected as a musical work and the whole as a dramatic work.[60] It is at least arguable as a matter of concept that the format of a television game or quiz show can be protected as a dramatic work. Such protection will not subsist unless at least (i) there are a number of clearly identified features which, taken together, distinguish the show from other shows; and (ii)

---

48 Copyright and Rights in Database Regulations 1997 (SI 1997/3032) reg.29.

49 *Ladbroke (Football) Ltd v William Hill (Football) Ltd* [1964] 1 W.L.R. 273 (football pool coupons); *Elanco Products Ltd v Mandops (Agrochemical Specialists) Ltd* [1980] R.P.C. 213 (leaflet giving particulars of the efficacy of a herbicide). For originality requirements see *Macmillan & Co Ltd v K & J Cooper* (1923) 93 L.J.P.C. 113 and *Cramp & Sons v Smythson Ltd* [1944] A.C. 329.

50 *Kelly v Morris* (1866) L.R. 1 Eq. 697; *Lamb v Evans* [1893] 1 Ch. 218; *Exchange Telegraph Co v Gregory* [1896] 1 Q.B. 147 at 157; *Kelly's Directories v Gavin* [1902] 1 Ch. 631; and see *Cambridge University Press v University Tutorial Press Ltd* (1928) 45 R.P.C. 335. See also *Nisbet v Golf Agency* (1907) 23 T.L.R. 370 (biographical notes resulting from questionnaires); *Collis v Cater* (1898) 78 L.T. 613 (tradesman's catalogues); *Independent Television Publications Ltd v Time Out Ltd* [1984] F.S.R. 64 (programme listings); *Waterlow Directories Ltd v Reed Information Services Ltd* [1992] F.S.R. 409 (lists of solicitors and barristers).

51 CDPA 1988 s.8. Protection is limited to making a facsimile copy of the arrangement, s.17(5). See *Newspaper Licensing Agency Ltd v Marks & Spencer Plc* [2001] UKHL 38; [2003] 1 A.C. 551.

52 Directive 2009/24/EC.

53 This includes preparatory design work leading to the development of a program if that work is such that a program can result from it at a later stage: see Recital 8 to the Directive.

54 See *Bezpečnostní softwarová asociace – Svaz softwarové ochrany v Ministerstvo kultury* (C-393/09) EU:C:2010:816; [2011] E.C.D.R. 3 at [35].

55 *SAS Institute Inc v World Programming Ltd* (C-406/10) EU:C:2012:259 [2012] E.C.D.R 22; [2012] R.P.C. 31. For the subsequent decision of the England and Wales Court of Appeal, see [2013] EWCA Civ 1482; [2014] R.P.C. 8. However, original data formats may be protected as literary works: *Technomed Ltd v Bluecrest Health Screening* [2017] EWHC 2142 (Ch); [2018] F.S.R. 8.

56 See para.24-48(j).

57 CDPA 1988 s.3.

58 See *Norowzian v Arks Ltd (No.2)* [2000] F.S.R. 363.

59 *Tate v Thomas* [1921] 2 Ch. 503. For the type of input into a film screenplay which may be protected, see *Kogan v Martin* [2019] EWCA Civ 1645; [2020] E.M.L.R. 4 at [42].

60 *Fuller v Blackpool Winter Gardens* [1895] 2 Q.B. 429.

those features are connected with each other in a coherent framework which can be repeatedly applied so as to enable the show to be reproduced in recognisable form.[61]

Musical works This paragraph deals with musical compositions. Sound recordings have a separate copyright and are dealt with below.[62] A musical work is a work consisting of music, exclusive of any words or action intended to be sung, spoken or performed with the music.[63] What is protected is not only the notes but other elements which make some contribution to the sound. Comparatively little by way of originality has traditionally been required in order for a musical work to attract copyright.[64] However, as indicated below,[65] the hurdle for originality may have been raised. **24-14**

Artistic works Artistic works[66] comprise graphic works (paintings, drawings,[67] diagrams,[68] maps, charts, plans, engravings, etchings, lithographs, woodcuts or similar works), photographs,[69] sculpture (including casts or models made for the purpose of sculpture)[70] and collage, all irrespective of artistic quality; works of **24-15**

---

61 *Banner Universal Motion Pictures Ltd v Endemol Shine Group Ltd* [2017] EWHC 2600 (Ch); [2018] E.C.D.R. 2 at [43]–[44].

62 See para.24-16.

63 CDPA 1988 s.3(1).

64 For example, in *Sawkins v Hyperion Records Ltd* [2005] EWCA Civ 565; [2005] 1 W.L.R. 3281 the Court of Appeal upheld a finding that an editor of a performing edition of a work by Lalande, who died some 280 years ago, was entitled to copyright. The editor had expended considerable skill and labour based on his expertise in editing the music in preparing the score, which was used by the defendant for making a recording of the works in question.

65 See para.24-22.

66 CDPA 1988 s.4. As to how little of what might be thought of as artistic activity has traditionally been needed to constitute an "artistic work", see *Walker v British Picker Co* [1961] R.P.C. 57; *British Northrop Ltd v Texteam (Blackburn) Ltd* [1974] R.P.C. 344; *Karo Step Trade Mark, Re* [1977] R.P.C. 255; cf. *Merchandising Corp of America Inc v Harpbond Ltd* [1983] F.S.R. 32; *Entec (Pollution Control) Ltd v Abacus Mouldings* [1992] F.S.R. 332. However, the new test of "author's own intellectual creation" laid down by the CJEU may have raised the hurdle. See para.24-22.

67 Including mechanical drawings with no artistic merit: *Saltman Engineering Co v Campbell Engineering Co* [1963] 3 All E.R. 413 (Note); (1948) 65 R.P.C. 203; *Dorling v Honnor* [1964] Ch. 560; [1965] Ch. 1 CA; *British Northrop Ltd v Texteam (Blackburn) Ltd* [1974] R.P.C. 344; *Wham-O-Manufacturing Co v Lincoln Industries Ltd* [1985] R.P.C. 127 NZCA; *Billhofer Maschinenfabrik GmbH v TH Dixon Co Ltd* [1990] F.S.R. 105; *Johnstone Safety Ltd v Peter Cook (International) Plc* [1990] F.S.R. 161; *Drayton Controls v Honeywell Control Systems* [1992] F.S.R. 245; *Entec (Pollution Control) Ltd v Abacus Mouldings* [1992] F.S.R. 332. It is not an infringement of copyright to make articles to an industrial design embodied in a copyright drawing, but such acts might constitute infringement of UK unregistered design right: see below.

68 See *Technomed Ltd v Bluecrest Health Screening Ltd* [2017] EWHC 2142 (Ch); [2018] F.S.R. 8; and (for circuit diagrams) *Sandman v Panasonic UK Ltd* [1998] F.S.R. 651.

69 In the case of a photograph, there can be sufficient originality for copyright to subsist in the selection of the position of the objects photographed, the angle and the lighting: *Antiquesportfolio.com Plc v Rodney Fitch & Co Ltd* [2001] F.S.R. 23. For the EU standard of originality see *Painer v Standard Verlags GmbH* (C-145/10) EU:C:2011:798; [2012] E.C.D.R. 6. However, the Directive permits Member States to protect "other photographs". Accordingly, a lower standard of originality may prevail in the UK.

70 See *Metix (UK) Ltd v GH Maughan (Plastics) Ltd* [1997] F.S.R. 718. In *Lucasfilm Ltd v Ainsworth* [2009] EWCA Civ 1328; [2010] Ch. 503, the Court of Appeal upheld a decision that armour and helmets used in a science fiction film were not "sculpture" because their purpose was functional and they were not created primarily for their visual appeal. A contention at first instance that they were works of artistic craftsmanship was not renewed in the Court of Appeal. The Court of Appeal's deci-

architecture, being buildings or models for buildings; and works of artistic craftsmanship.[71]

24-16 **Sound recordings** A sound recording is defined as a recording of sounds, from which the sounds may be reproduced, or a recording of the whole or any part of a literary, dramatic or musical work, from which sounds reproducing the work or part may be produced, regardless of the medium on which the recording is made or the method by which the sounds are reproduced or produced.[72] If the recording was lawfully published or otherwise made available within 50 years of its being made, the period of copyright is 70 years from the end of the year in which the recording was first published or made available. Otherwise, the period is 50 years from the end of the year in which the recording was made.[73]

24-17 **Films** A film is defined as a recording on any medium from which a moving image may by any means be produced.[74] The sound track accompanying a film is treated as part of the film. The period of copyright is 70 years from the end of the year of death of the last to die of the principal director, screenplay author, dialogue author or film music composer.[75]

24-18 **Broadcasts** A broadcast is defined[76] as an electronic transmission of visual images, sounds or other information which is either (i) transmitted for simultaneous reception by members of the public and capable of being lawfully received by them; or (ii) transmitted at a time determined solely by the person making the transmission for presentation to members of the public. An internet transmission is expressly excluded from this definition unless (a) it takes place simultaneously on the internet and by other means (so-called simulcasts); (b) it is a concurrent transmission of a live event; or (c) it is a transmission of recorded moving images or sounds forming part of a programme service offered by the person responsible for making the transmission, being a service in which programmes are transmitted at scheduled times determined by that person.[77] With some exceptions, the period of copyright

---

sion on "sculpture" was upheld by the Supreme Court: [2011] UKSC 39; [2012] 1 A.C. 208.

[71] As to the uncertain meaning of which, see *George Hensher Ltd v Restawile Upholstery (Lancs) Ltd* [1976] A.C. 64; *Lucasfilm Ltd v Ainsworth* [2008] EWHC 1878 (Ch); [2008] E.C.D.R. 17. In *Vermaat and Powell v Boncrest Ltd* [2001] F.S.R. 5, it was held that the author of a work of artistic craftsmanship had to be both a craftsman and an artist and that the patchwork in question, while pleasing to the eye, was not sufficiently artistic to qualify as such. In *Response Clothing Ltd v The Edinburgh Woollen Mill Ltd* [2020] EWHC 148 (IPEC); [2020] F.S.R. 25 at [64] the Judge adopted a broad definition with a view to achieving a conforming interpretation.

[72] Defined in CDPA 1988 ss.5A and 5B. The definition of sound recording excludes copies taken from a previous recording.

[73] CDPA 1988 s.13A as amended by the Copyright and Duration of Rights in Performances Regulations 2013 (SI 2013/1782), which came into force on 1 November 2013.

[74] CDPA 1988 s.5B. The definition excludes a copy taken from a previous film. For consideration of the exact nature of film copyright, see *Dramatico Entertainment Ltd v British Sky Broadcasting Ltd* [2012] EWHC 268 (Ch); [2012] E.C.D.R. 14 at [63]; *Football Association Premier League Ltd v QC Leisure* [2012] EWHC 108 (Ch); [2012] F.S.R. 12 at [69]; and *England and Wales Cricket Board Ltd v Tixdaq Ltd* [2016] EWHC 575 (Ch); [2017] E.C.D.R. 2 at [58].

[75] CDPA 1988 s.13B.

[76] CDPA 1988 s.6(1). It only covers encrypted transmissions if decoding equipment has been made available by or with the authority of the person making the transmission or providing the contents of the transmission: s.6(2).

[77] CDPA 1988 s.6(1A). See *England and Wales Cricket Board Ltd v Tixdaq Ltd* [2016] EWHC 575

in a broadcast is 50 years from the end of calendar year in which the broadcast was made.[78]

(ii) *Artist's resale right*

Artist's resale right In 2006, living British artists were granted the right to receive a royalty on the resale of their works following the first transfer of ownership by means of regulations implementing EC Directive 2001/84/EC.[79] A specified art-market professional is made jointly and severally liable with the seller to pay the royalty.[80] With effect from 1 January 2012, artists' heirs and beneficiaries are entitled to a resale royalty when a deceased artist's work is sold through an auction house, gallery or dealer. The right applies to any work of graphic or plastic art in which copyright subsists.[81] 24-19

(iii) *Database right*

Database right Database right was introduced by Directive 96/9/EC, which was implemented in the UK by the Copyright and Rights in Databases Regulations.[82] This legislation gives the maker of a qualifying database which has been the product of substantial investment the right to prevent unauthorised "extraction" or "re-utilisation" of the whole or a substantial part (qualitatively or quantitatively) of the contents of the database.[83] In *British Horseracing Board Ltd v William Hill Organisation Ltd*[84] the CJEU held that investment in the creation of horse race fixture data was not a relevant form of investment for these purposes. However, it adopted a fairly wide approach to the acts that constitute extraction and re-utilisation, which (it held) included any unauthorised act of appropriation and distribution to the public of the whole or a part of the contents of a database.[85] Direct access is not required for there to be infringement. The relatively general guid- 24-20

(Ch); [2017] E.C.D.R. 2 at [96].

78 CDPA 1988 s.14(2). The exceptions are in s.14(3).

79 The Artist's Resale Right Regulations 2006 (SI 2006/346), as amended by the Artist's Resale Right (Amendment) Regulations 2011 (SI 2011/2873). For further details of the scope and application of this right, see the specialist texts on copyright and Stokes, *Art and Copyright*, 2nd edn (Hart Publishing, 2012). In *Fundación Gala-Salvador Dali Visual, Entidad de Gestión de Artistas Plásticos (VEGAP) v Société des auteurs dans les arts graphiques et plastiques (ADAGP)* (C-518/08) EU:C:2010:191; [2010] E.C.D.R. 13; [2011] F.S.R. 4 the CJEU handed down a judgment on the subject of the persons entitled to receive royalties after the death of the artist, holding that only the artist's legal heirs may benefit, to the exclusion of testamentary legatees.

80 Artist's Resale Right Regulations 2006 reg.13.

81 Artist's Resale Right Regulations 2006 regs 3 and 4.

82 SI 1997/3032.

83 There are certain, rather limited, fair dealing and other exceptions, which are dealt with below, para.24-51.

84 (C-203/02) [2005] R.P.C. 13.

85 In *Football Dataco Ltd v Sportradar GMBH* (C-173/11) EU:C:2012:642; [2013] 1 C.M.L.R. 29 the CJEU held that the sending by one person, by means of a web server located in Member State A, of data previously uploaded by that person from a protected database to the computer of another person located in Member State B, at that person's request, for the purpose of storage in that computer's memory and display on its screen, constitutes an act of re-utilisation of the data by the person sending it. That act takes place, at least, in Member State B, where there is evidence from which it may be concluded that the act discloses an intention on the part of the person performing the act to target members of the public in Member State B; such intention is for the national court to assess.

ance given by the CJEU as to what constitutes a "substantial part" of the contents of the database means that the domestic courts will need to work out the principles in future cases.[86] As indicated above, copyright may subsist in databases which, by reason of the selection or arrangement of their contents, constitute the author's own intellectual creation.[87]

(b) Subsistence, authorship and ownership

(i) Copyright

24-21 **Qualification for protection: copyright** In broad terms, a work may qualify for UK copyright by reference to its author or by reference to its country of first publication. Copyright will subsist in the work if the author was a suitably qualifying or qualified person (within the meaning of the Copyright Act in force at the time the work was made) at the time specified in the relevant Act. An author who is an individual qualifies if, essentially, he or she was a British citizen or domiciled or resident in the UK or another country to which the relevant provisions of the legislation extend or have been applied. Analogous provisions apply to corporate authors.[88] Copyright will also subsist if the work was first published in the UK or another country to which the relevant provisions of the legislation extend or have been applied.[89] In practice, most works qualify for UK copyright under these provisions.[90]

---

[86] Extended discussion is beyond the scope of this work. See the judgment of the CJEU in *The British Horseracing Board Ltd v William Hill Organization Ltd* (C-203/02) EU:C:2004:695; [2005] 1 C.M.L.R. 15; [2005] R.P.C. 13 and the specialist copyright texts. With regard to what amounts to a "substantial part" of a database see judgments of the CJEU in *Directmedia Publishing GmbH v Albert-Ludwigs-Universität Freiburg* (C-304/07) EU:C:2008:552; [2008] E.C.R. I-7565; [2009] R.P.C. 10; *Apis-Hristovich EOOD v Lakorda AD* (C-545/07) EU:C:2009:132; [2009] E.C.R. I-1627; [2009] C.M.L.R. 3; and *Football Dataco Ltd v Stan James (Abingdon) Ltd* [2013] EWCA Civ 27; [2013] 2 C.M.L.R. 36 at [84], where it was held that the test of "substantial part" "depends on the scale of investment in obtaining verification of presentation of what was extracted. Even if only a small part is taken it can be qualitatively a substantial part if it represents significant investment".

[87] See para.24-11.

[88] CDPA 1988 s.154. Under CDPA 1988 s.159(1) to (3), the copyright part of the Act applies to citizens and corporations of countries which are parties to certain international copyright conventions or agreements to which the UK is also a party as it applies to UK citizens and corporations. The conventions are: the Berne Convention or the World Trade Organisation (for literary, dramatic, musical and artistic works, films and typographical arrangements), the Rome Convention (for sound recordings and broadcasts) and the WIPO Performances and Phonograms Treaty (for sound recordings). Section 159(4) provides that the application of subsections (1) to (3) to a particular country may be restricted or that their application may be extended to other countries by Order in Council. The Copyright and Performances (Application to Other Countries) Order 2016 (SI 2016/1219), contains numerous such provisions.

[89] CDPA 1988 s.155. Again, s.159 applies. There are special provisions governing the subsistence of copyright in broadcasts—in essence, these depend upon the country from which it was transmitted or sent: CDPA 1988 s.156.

[90] However, where the country of origin of a work is not an EEA state the term of copyright may be limited to that provided for in the country of origin: CDPA 1988 s.12(6); there are often limitations on the protection of foreign sound recordings; particular care must be taken with pre-1957 US works. See the specialist copyright texts.

Originality of literary, dramatic, musical or artistic works: traditional UK approach To be the subject of copyright, a literary, dramatic, musical or artistic work must be "original".[91] There is no requirement of originality for sound recordings, films considered as first fixations, broadcasts or typographical arrangement. In the UK, the requirement for originality has traditionally been interpreted as meaning that the work must originate from the author and not be copied, rather than that it must be novel or have literary, dramatic, musical or artistic merit (as the case may be).[92] Nevertheless, it was said that there was no originality in simply copying a previous work with only very minor changes, even though the redrawing involved a substantial amount of work; there must in addition be some element of material alteration or embellishment which, having regard to the quality rather than the quantity of the addition, sufficed to make the totality of the work original.[93] **24-22**

Originality of literary, dramatic, musical or artistic works: EU approach The test for originality is now determined by EU case law. A number of EU Directives specify that to benefit from protection a work must be original in the sense that it contains elements of the author's own intellectual creation. The CJEU has confirmed that this applies to all authors' works (i.e. to all works within the meaning of the Berne Convention at least).[94] Subsequent decisions of the CJEU in relation to particular types of work appear to require that the work be stamped with the author's "personal touch" or reflect his or her "personality".[95] More recently, it has been held both "necessary and sufficient that the subject matter reflects the personality of its author, as an expression of his free and creative choices".[96] Where the realisation of the subject matter has been dictated by technical considerations, rules **24-23**

91 CDPA 1988 s.1(1).

92 *University of London Press v University Tutorial Press* [1916] 2 Ch. 601 at 608–609, i.e. it must be "the product of the author's work and labour": *LB (Plastics) Ltd v Swish Products Ltd* [1979] R.P.C. 551 at 617, per Lord Wilberforce. It may still be original even if in part it is copied from an earlier work: *James Arnold & Co Ltd v Miafern Ltd* [1980] R.P.C. 397; *Autospin (Oil Seals) Ltd v Beehive Spinning* [1995] R.P.C. 683. Provided the requirement of originality is satisfied, there can be copyright in a work that is itself an infringement of copyright: *Warwick Film Production Ltd v Eisinger* [1969] 1 Ch. 508. See also *Hyperion Records Ltd v Sawkins* [2005] EWCA Civ 565; [2005] 1 W.L.R. 3281; [2005] R.P.C. 32, where Mummery LJ stated (at [31]) that a work need only be "original" in the limited sense that the author originated it by his efforts rather than "slavishly" copying it from the work produced by the efforts of another person.

93 *Interlego AG v Tyco Industries Inc* [1989] A.C. 217. See also *Walter v Lane* [1900] A.C. 539 where the House of Lords held that copyright subsisted in shorthand writers' reports of public speeches as "original literary" works on the basis that they had spent skill and time in writing up their reports of speeches that they themselves had not written. In *Sawkins v Hyperion Records Ltd* [2005] EWCA Civ 565; [2005] 1 W.L.R. 3281 at [31], Mummery LJ said: "The policy of copyright protection and its limited scope explain why the threshold requirement of an 'original' work has been interpreted as not imposing objective standards of novelty, usefulness, inventiveness, aesthetic merit, quality or value. A work may be complete rubbish and utterly worthless, but copyright protection may be available for it, just as it is for the great masterpieces of imaginative literature, art and music."

94 *Infopaq International A/S v Danske Daglades Forening* (C-5/08) EU:C:2009:465; [2009] E.C.D.R. 16. See *Levola Hengelo BV v Smilde Foods BV* (C-310/17) EU:C:2018:899; [2018] Bus. L.R. 2442 at [36]; and *Sociedade de Vestuario SA v G-Star Raw CV* (C-683/17) EU:C:2019:721 at [30].

95 See *Painer v Standard Verlags GmbH* (C-145/10) EU:C:2011:798; [2012] E.C.D.R. 6 at [92] (photographs); and *Football Dataco Ltd v Yahoo! UK Ltd* (C-604/10) EU:C:2012:115; [2012] E.C.D.R. 10 at [38] (databases).

96 *Land Nordrhein-Westfalen v Renckhoff* (C-161/17) EU:C:2018:634; [2018] E.C.D.R. 21 at [14] (photograph); *Sociedade de Vestuario SA v G-Star Raw CV* (C-683/17) EU:C:2019:721 at [30] (clothing designs).

or other constraints, which have left no room for creative freedom, the subject matters will not be original.[97] Purely informative reports whose content was essentially determined by the information they contained such that the information and its expression were indissociable and the reports were "entirely characterised by their technical function" would not be considered original.[98] It remains unclear whether the standard now applied by the CJEU is different from the traditional UK standard but if it is, it has raised the hurdle for protection.[99]

24-24 **Authorship** Authorship plays an important role in the law of copyright, both in relation to qualification for protection and because, in general, the author is the first owner of the copyright in the work. The author of a literary, artistic, musical or dramatic work is the person who creates it.[100] If such a work is computer-generated, the author is taken to be the person by whom the arrangements necessary for the making of the work were undertaken.[101] For other types of works, the Copyright Act 1988 provides for deemed authorship.[102] For sound recordings it is the producer (defined in s.178 as the person who undertakes the arrangements necessary for the making of the recording); for films, the producer (defined in the same way) and the principal director; for broadcasts, the maker of the broadcast; and for typographic arrangement, the publisher. A work will be one of joint authorship where the contribution of each author is not distinct from that of the other author or authors.[103]

24-25 **Ownership of copyright** As indicated in the previous paragraph, the general rule is that the author of a work is the first owner of copyright in it, but there are important exceptions, particularly for works made by employees in the course of their employment. In respect of these works, the employer is the first owner of copyright absent agreement to the contrary.[104] Although a person commissioning a

---

97 *Sociedade de Vestuario SA v G-Star Raw CV* (C-683/17) EU:C:2019:721 at [30] (clothing designs).

98 *Funke Medien NRW GmbH v Bundesrepublik Deutschland* (C-469/17) EU:C:2019:623; [2020] 1 C.M.L.R. 13; [2019] E.C.D.R. 25 at [24].

99 *SAS Institute Inc v World Programming Ltd* [2013] EWCA Civ 1482; [2014] R.P.C. 8 at [36]–[37]. Pre-22 December 2002 works may, however, only need to satisfy the UK standard: see art.10 of the Information Society Directive.

100 CDPA 1988 s.9(1).

101 CDPA 1988 s.9(3).

102 CDPA 1988 s.9(2).

103 CDPA 1988 s.10. It includes broadcasts made by more than one person. In *Kogan v Martin* [2019] EWCA Civ 1645; [2020] E.M.L.R. 4 at [53], the Court of Appeal summarised the criteria for a successful joint authorship claim. The work must be the product of a collaboration. There will be collaboration where the contributors undertake jointly to create the work with a common design as to its general outline, and share the labour of working it out. Derivative works do not qualify. Contributions limited to editorial corrections, critique or ad hoc suggestions of phrases or ideas to not qualify. In the literary or artistic context it is never enough to ask who did the writing. For example there may be joint authorship if one person creates the plot and another writes the text. Joint authors must have contributed a significant amount of the skill that went into the work. Authorship includes all those who created, selected, or gathered the detailed concepts or emotions which the words have fixed in writing and who have contributed elements which express their own intellectual creation (in the *Infopaq* sense). There is no need for a subjective intention to create a work of joint authorship. The fact that one author has the final say on what goes into the work does not preclude the other being a joint author but may affect the size of the parties' respective shares.

104 CDPA 1988 s.11. For when a work will be considered to have been created in the course of employment, see *Mei Fields Designs Ltd v Saffron Cards and Gifts Ltd* [2018] EWHC 1332 (IPEC); [2018] F.S.R. 33 at [36]–[42].

copyright work will not usually be entitled to the legal title to the copyright in it (absent agreement), in many circumstances the court will be prepared to imply terms to the effect that the person commissioning the work will be treated as the equitable owner of the copyright in it with the right to call for an assignment of the copyright.[105] There are special provisions governing Crown Copyright and Parliamentary Copyright and copyright vesting in certain international organisations.[106]

Assignment and disposition of copyright Copyright is transmissible (by assignment, testamentary disposition or operation of law) as personal property.[107] There are special provisions for the assignment of future copyright.[108] Copyright does not ordinarily pass by mere change of ownership of the original work.[109] 24-26

Foreign works Most although not all foreign works (including Commonwealth works) are entitled to UK copyright. The detail of the subsistence of copyright in these works is a complex subject and reference should be made to specialist texts.[110] 24-27

---

105 Such situations include, for example, where an advertising agency makes a work on behalf of a client and it is clear that the client was to have title to the copyright in the work, even though that was not expressly provided for in the contract between them: see *Griggs Group Ltd v Evans* [2005] EWCA Civ 11; [2005] F.S.R. 31, which outlines the main principles. By contrast, in *Clearsprings Management Ltd v Businesslinx Ltd* [2005] EWHC 1487 (Ch); [2006] F.S.R. 3, the court held that there was no need to imply anything more than a perpetual licence in a contract for the design of bespoke property management software.

106 CDPA 1988 ss.163–168.

107 CDPA 1988 s.90(1). An effective legal assignment must be in writing signed by or on behalf of the assignor: CDPA 1988 s.90(3). Even if the formalities required for a legal assignment are not satisfied, the assignment may take effect in equity. An equitable assignment may be defeated by a bona fide purchaser for value without notice of the equitable rights. See *Wah Sang Industrial Co v Takmay Industrial Co Ltd* [1980] F.S.R. 303 HKCA; *Ward, Lock & Co Ltd v Long* [1906] 2 Ch. 550. An assignment may be partial or for only part of the period of the copyright, or of some only of the assignor's rights under the copyright. See also *Cross-town Music Co 1 LLC v Rive Droite Music Ltd* [2010] EWCA Civ 1222; [2012] Ch. 68 where the Court of Appeal held that a provision in an assignment of copyright allowing automatic reverter of the rights to the assignor on a future event, namely an unremedied material breach of contract by the assignee, was a valid partial assignment within CDPA s.90(2).

108 CDPA 1988 s.90(1). See *Performing Right Society Ltd v B4U Network (Europe) Ltd* [2013] EWCA Civ 1236; [2014] F.S.R. 17. Extended and revived copyright can be assigned by a prospective owner: see Duration of Copyright and Rights in Performances Regulations 1995 (SI 1995/3297) reg.20.

109 Thus purchase of a picture does not by itself entitle the purchaser to reproduce it: *Marshall v Bull* (1901) 17 T.L.R. 684. But where the manuscript of an unpublished literary, dramatic or musical work, or an unpublished artistic work, sound recording or film, passes under a bequest made by the will of a testator who owned the copyright dying after May 1957, then unless a contrary intention appears, the bequest includes the copyright in the work: Copyright Act 1956 s.38; CDPA 1988 s.93.

110 The entitlement to copyright in foreign works is based on a series of international conventions and bilateral, reciprocal agreements entitling UK works to copyright in the foreign country concerned. See the Copyright and Performances (Application to Other Countries) Order 2016 (SI 2016/1219). The period of copyright in foreign works is in certain cases limited by reference to the length of copyright given to British works by the foreign country concerned; whilst in most cases there are special limitations upon the copyright in sound recordings. See generally CDPA 1988 ss.157-162 and the specialist copyright texts. Particular care must be taken with pre-1957 US works.

(ii) Artist's resale right

24-28 **Qualification for protection** The right subsists in a work so long as UK copyright subsists in it.[111] The right can only be exercised where (a) the author is living at the date of the sale and a national of an EEA state or a state which permits resale right protection for authors from EEA states and their successors; or (b) the author is dead at the date of sale and at the date of death was such a national.[112]

24-29 **Ownership** The right belongs to the author.[113] In the case of a work created by two or more authors, the right belongs to the authors as owners in common and shall be held in equal shares unless the authors agree otherwise in writing.[114] The right is not assignable except to a "qualifying body", that is a charity.[115] It may be transmitted by testamentary disposition or on intestacy and may vest in the personal representatives of a deceased person; a person who receives it in this way may transfer it further but only to a natural person or a qualifying body.[116]

(iii) Database right

24-30 **Qualification for protection** The right only subsists where there has been substantial investment in obtaining, verifying or presenting the contents of the database.[117] The focus is on the "maker", that is the person who takes the initiative in and assumes the risk of investing in the obtaining, verifying or presenting.[118] The right will not subsist unless at the "material time", the maker was an EEA national or habitual resident, a body or partnership formed in an EEA state which satisfied certain conditions or was connected with the Isle of Man in specified ways.[119] The "material time" is the time when the database was made or, if its making extended over a period, a substantial part of that period.[120]

24-31 **Ownership** The maker is the first owner. Where the database was "made jointly", all the makers are the owner. A database is "made jointly" if two or more persons, acting together in collaboration, take the initiative in and assume the risk in obtain-

[111] Artist's Resale Right Regulations 2006 (SI 2006/346) reg.3(1), (2) and see the definition of "copyright" in reg.2. The Regulations implement Directive 2001/84/EC on the resale right for the benefit of the author of an original work of art.

[112] Artist's Resale Right Regulations 2006 (SI 2006/346) reg.10.

[113] Artist's Resale Right Regulations 2006 (SI 2006/346) reg.3(1).

[114] Artist's Resale Right Regulations 2006 (SI 2006/346) reg.5. Works of two or more authors are described as "works of joint authorship" but the meaning of that expression is different to its meaning in the copyright context.

[115] Artist's Resale Right Regulations 2006 (SI 2006/346) reg.7. It can however be transferred to a trustee: reg.11.

[116] Artist's Resale Right Regulations 2006 (SI 2006/346) reg.9.

[117] Copyright and Rights in Databases Regulations 1997 (SI 1997/3032) reg.13(1). The Regulations implement Council Directive No.96/9/EC on the legal protection of databases. As to the kind of evidence which will satisfy a court that investment has been "substantial", see *Health & Case Management Ltd v The Physiotherapy Networks Ltd* [2018] EWHC 869 (QB) at [90]–[93].

[118] Copyright and Rights in Databases Regulations 1997 (SI 1997/3032) reg.14(1). As with copyright, databases made by an employee in the course of his or her employment vest in the employer and there are special provisions for Crown and Parliamentary copyright: reg.14(2)–(4).

[119] Copyright and Rights in Databases Regulations 1997 (SI 1997/3032) reg.18.

[120] Copyright and Rights in Databases Regulations 1997 (SI 1997/3032) reg.18(4)(b).

ing, verifying or presenting the contents.[121] Database right may be dealt with in the same way as copyright.[122]

(c) Infringement of copyright and database right

(i) Copyright

General Copyright is infringed by anyone who (not being the owner of the copyright, and without the owner's licence—express or implied)[123] does or authorises[124] another person to do any act restricted by the copyright.[125] Such infringement is generally termed "primary infringement" and knowledge or reason to believe that the activity is an infringement is not a prerequisite for liability. In addition, certain dealings in "infringing copies"[126] are themselves infringements if carried out with knowledge or reason to believe that they are infringing. These are termed "secondary" infringements.[127] There are a number of statutory exceptions to copyright infringement.[128] 24-32

121 Copyright and Rights in Databases Regulations 1997 (SI 1997/3032) regs 15, 14(5) and (6).

122 Copyright and Rights in Databases Regulations 1997 (SI 1997/3032) reg.23.

123 No formality is required to grant a licence but the defendant must establish the existence and extent of the alleged licence: *Noah v Shuba* [1991] F.S.R. 14. See generally as to the criteria for implication of a licence: *Robin Ray v Classic FM Plc* [1998] F.S.R. 622; and *Griggs Group v Evans* [2005] EWCA Civ 11; [2005] F.S.R. 31. The test of whether a licence was granted is objective: *Redwood Music Ltd v Chappell* [1982] R.P.C. 109. Where an architect only charges a nominal fee for preparing plans for obtaining planning permission, there is no implied licence to use the plans for the erection of the building; *Stovin-Bradford v Volpoint Properties Ltd* [1971] Ch. 1007; cf. *Blair v Tomkins* [1971] 2 Q.B. 78. While the courts will only imply a licence to manufacture spare parts in infringement of copyright in appropriate cases, they will not permit the manufacturer of goods to derogate from his grant by preventing the manufacture of spare parts: *British Leyland Motor Corp Ltd v Armstrong Patents Co Ltd* [1986] A.C. 577. cf. *Cannon Kabushiki Kaisha v Green Cartridge Co* [1997] A.C. 728. Such cases will depend on their facts: thus a licence has been implied where the repair of a mechanical device involved the reproduction of copyright drawings owned by the supplier (*Solar Thomson Engineering Co Ltd v Barton* [1977] R.P.C. 537) but not to establish a right to copy file layouts for a file transfer program (*Ibcos Computers Ltd v Barclays Mercantile Finance Ltd* [1994] F.S.R. 275). See also *Dyson Ltd v Qualtex (UK) Ltd* [2004] EWHC 2981 (Ch); [2005] R.P.C. 19. It is possible that the effect of *Soulier v Premier ministre* (C-301/15) C:2016:878; [2017] 2 C.M.L.R. 9; [2017] E.C.D.R. 23 is that the conditions for the existence of an implied licence are a matter of EU law involving stricter requirements than those laid down in the UK case law.

124 "Authorises" means to grant or purport to grant the right to do the act complained of and an authorisation can only come from someone having or purporting to have authority. An act is not authorised by someone who merely enables or possibly assists or even encourages another to do that act but does not purport to have any authority which he can grant to justify the doing of the act: *CBS Inc v Ames Records and Tapes Ltd* [1981] R.P.C. 407; and *CBS Songs Ltd v Amstrad Consumer Products* [1988] A.C. 1013. See also *Ibcos Computers Ltd v Barclays Mercantile Highland Finance Ltd* [1994] F.S.R. 275 (seller of computer program normally authorises purchaser to use it); *Performing Right Society v Mitchell and Booker* [1924] 1 K.B. 762; *Falcon v Famous Player's Film Co* [1926] 2 K.B. 474; *RCA Corp v John Fairfax & Sons Ltd* [1982] R.P.C. 91; *Standen Engineering Ltd v A Spalding & Sons Ltd* [1984] F.S.R. 554; and *Twentieth Century Fox Film Corporation v Newzbin Ltd* [2010] EWHC 608 (Ch); [2010] F.S.R. 21 ("file sharing"). The multi-factorial approach adopted in that case has been frequently followed: see, e.g. *Warner Music UK Ltd v Tunein Inc* [2019] EWHC 2923 (Ch), [197] "Authorising" can include commissioning another to produce an article to a particular design: *Pensher Security Doors Co Ltd v Sunderland CC* [2000] R.P.C. 249.

125 For the acts restricted by copyright, see para.24-33 and CDPA 1988 ss.16–21.

126 See below para.24-45 for the meaning of this expression.

127 See paras 24-45 to 24-46.

128 See para.24-48.

24-33 **Copying** The most significant act of infringement of copyright is copying the work or a "substantial part" of it or (in the case of a literary, dramatic or musical work), the making or copying of an adaptation of the work or of a substantial part of the work.[129] A number of general rules are laid down in s.17 of the Copyright Act 1988. Copying in relation to a literary, dramatic, musical or artistic work means reproducing the work in any material form and includes storing the work by electronic means. In relation to an artistic work, copying includes the making of a copy of a two-dimensional work in three dimensions and vice versa. Copying in relation to a film or broadcast includes making a photograph of the whole or any substantial part of any image forming part of it.[130] Copying in relation to the typographical arrangement of a published edition means making a facsimile copy of the arrangement. Finally, copying includes the making of copies which are transient or incidental to some other use of the work.[131]

24-34 **Proof of copying** In cases where the original and the alleged infringement are, on their face, two different works, there may be difficulty in deciding whether there has been copying. To constitute copying there must be both a sufficient objective similarity between the two works and some causal connection between them such as would make it proper to infer derivation of the one from the other.[132] The difficulty in establishing a causal derivation is particularly great where an adaptation is concerned (as where a novel must be compared with a play or film), or where the works concerned are compilations of material not in itself original; but it may exist in every class of case.[133] If subconscious copying is to be established the court will require strong evidence of the alleged infringer's familiarity with the original work.[134] A description can be so detailed that following it results in infringement by the reproduction of a substantial part of an artistic work.[135]

24-35 **Substantial part** Even if copying is established, there will only be infringement if what has been taken amounts to a "substantial part". In respect of literary,

---

129 CDPA 1988 ss.16, 17 and 21. See *Warwick Film Productions Ltd v Eisinger* [1969] 1 Ch. 508; *Ravenscroft v Herbert* [1980] R.P.C. 193; *Davis (Holdings) Ltd v Wright Health Group Ltd* [1988] R.P.C. 403.

130 A photograph is defined as a recording of light or other radiation on any medium on which an image is produced or from which an image may by any means be produced, and which is not part of a film: CDPA 1988 s.4(2).

131 In *Football Association Premier League Ltd v QC Leisure* and *Murphy v Media Protection Services Ltd* (C-403/08 and C-429/08) EU:C:2011:631; [2012] 1 C.M.L.R. 29; [2012] C.E.C. 242; [2012] E.C.D.R. 8 the CJEU held that the reproduction right extends to transient fragments of the works within the memory of a satellite decoder and on a television screen, provided that those fragments contain elements which are the expression of the authors' own intellectual creation. The unit composed of the fragments reproduced simultaneously must be examined in order to determine whether it contains such elements. See also *R. v Gilham* [2009] EWCA Crim 2293; [2010] E.C.D.R. 5. However, such copies may be within the temporary copying exception referred to in para.24-48(a).

132 *LB Plastics Ltd v Swish Products Ltd* [1979] R.P.C. 611 HL.

133 Such a connection may be inferred in a suitable case even when the alleged infringement has been produced by an independent designer working to instructions: *Solar Thomson Engineering Co Ltd v Barton* [1977] R.P.C. 537 at 560; *Weir Pumps Ltd v CML Pumps Ltd* [1984] F.S.R. 33.

134 *Francis Day and Hunter Ltd v Bron* [1963] Ch. 587 (no infringement found); *EMI Music Publishing Ltd v Papathanasiou* [1993] E.M.L.R. 306 (no infringement found).

135 *Plix Products Ltd v FM Winstone (Merchants) Ltd* [1986] F.S.R. 608, a decision of the New Zealand Court of Appeal, where the defendant had followed the course usually recommended for the avoidance of infringement but where infringement was nevertheless found.

dramatic, musical and artistic works, the purpose of the copyright is to protect the author's creativity. Accordingly, the question is whether what has been copied contains elements which are the expression of the intellectual creation of the author of the work.[136] Even an extract of 11 words may be sufficient if it satisfies that test.[137] The CJEU has recently held that copyright in a sound recording may be infringed by the reproduction of very short samples provided they are recognisable to the ear in the allegedly infringing recording.[138] Since copyrights in films considered as first fixations and broadcasts (so-called "signal" copyrights) are entrepreneurial rights the purpose of which is to protect the investment of the film producer or the broadcaster, the UK courts have held that the correct approach was to consider the degree of reproduction both quantitatively and qualitatively, having regard to the extent to which the reproduction exploited the investment made by the broadcaster or producer.[139] However, in the light of the CJEU's recent ruling on sound recordings (which are also entrepreneurial rights) it is not clear that this is correct. It seems that where a series of fragments have been taken, a "rolling" approach is inappropriate and it is necessary to ask whether each fragment itself amounts to a substantial part.[140]

Earlier statements on "substantial part" The following statements of principle predate the developments referred to in the previous paragraph but are probably still applicable, at least when read in the light of the new principles. First, "When it comes to a question of quantity it must be very vague. One writer might take all the vital parts of another's book, though it might be but a small proportion of the 24-36

136 *SAS Institute Inc v World Programming Ltd* [2013] EWCA Civ 1482; [2015] E.C.D.R. 17 at [38] applying *Infopaq International A/S v Danske Daglades Forening* (C-5/08) EU:C:2009:465; [2009] E.C.D.R. 16; *England and Wales Cricket Board Ltd v Tixdaq Ltd* [2016] EWHC 575 (Ch); [2017] E.C.D.R. 2 at [61].

137 *Infopaq International A/S v Danske Daglades Forening* (C-5/08) EU:C:2009:465; [2009] E.C.D.R. 16. See also *Newspaper Licensing Agency Ltd v Meltwater Holding BV* [2011] EWCA Civ 890; [2012] R.P.C. 1 (newspaper articles and headlines) but note that no specific examples were considered in this case and that the Court of Appeal assumed that the originality test remained the same after *Infopaq*. In the later case of *SAS Institute Inc v World Programming Ltd* [2013] EWCA Civ 1482; [2015] E.C.D.R. 17 the Court of Appeal stated that if the Information Society Directive had changed the test, it had raised the hurdle.

138 *Pelham GmbH v Hütter* (C-476/17) EU:C:2019:624; [2019] Bus. L.R. 2159. This decision was reached under the Information Society Directive (which, so far as sound recordings are concerned, only grants a reproduction and communication to the public right). However, the CJEU referred to "the exclusive right granted to a phonogram producer to reproduce *and distribute* his or her phonograph" (emphasis added). The CJEU was also asked to consider the position under the Rental and Lending Directive (2006/115/EEC), which provides a right to distribute hard copies of phonograms. It held that this right is only infringed where all or a substantial part of the phonogram is reproduced. In practice, the rights engaged are unlikely to be limited to those under the Rental and Lending Directive and so the applicable test will be that laid down by the CJEU under the Information Society Directive.

139 *England and Wales Cricket Board Ltd v Tixdaq Ltd* [2016] EWHC 575 (Ch); [2017] E.C.D.R. 2 at [66]. The director's creative input into a film is protected by the copyright in the dramatic work: see at [61].

140 See, e.g. *ITV Broadcasting Ltd v TV Catchup Ltd* [2011] EWHC 2977 (Pat); [2012] E.C.D.R. 5. In *Football Association Premier League Ltd v British Telecommunications Plc* [2017] EWHC 480; [2017] E.C.C. 17 at [31] it was held that a substantial part of a film was copied on the user's computer when unlicensed copies of films were streamed. In *Stichting Brein v Wullems* (C-527/15) EU:C:2017:300; [2017] Bus. L.R. 1816; [2017] E.C.D.R. 14 the CJEU rejected an argument that such copying was within the temporary copying exception (as to which see para.24–48(a)).

book in quantity. It is not only quantity but value that is always looked to."[141] Secondly, two drawings on a single sheet may be considered together and words used on drawings may be taken into account.[142] Thirdly, the copied features must be a substantial part of the copyright work but not necessarily of the defendant's work. The question to be asked is whether the defendant's work incorporates a substantial part of the claimant's work. Finally, in general, if a defendant's work is sufficiently similar to give rise to the inference that there has been copying what has been taken will be treated as sufficiently "substantial" to infringe.[143]

24-37 **Change of form** In order for a play to be a reproduction of a novel, it is not necessary that any of the actual words of the novel should be taken: there may be an infringement though no single sentence in the play is similar to any sentence in the novel.[144] On the other hand, it has been said that mere copying of a plot is not enough and there must be substantially a reproduction of the incidents of the novel in something like their original order.[145] A play which, from the commonplace character of its incidents, happens to resemble another previously produced, will not easily be held an infringement; both may well be derived from the common stock of dramatic ideas.[146] More generally, the courts recognise that there is freedom to make use of the common stock of ideas[147] up to a point. In doubtful cases, similarity between two works will be treated as establishing a prima facie case of infringement, which the alleged infringer may explain away if he can.[148]

---

141 *Bramwell v Halcomb* (1836) 3 My. & Cr. 737 at 738, per Lord Cottenham; cf. *Tinsley v Lacy* (1863) 1 H. & M. 747; *Ladbroke (Football) Ltd v William Hill (Football) Ltd* [1964] 1 W.L.R. 273; *Industrial Furnaces Ltd v Reaves* [1970] R.P.C. 605; *Antocks Lairn v I Bloohn Ltd* [1972] R.P.C. 219; *Fernald v Jay Lewis Productions* [1975] F.S.R. 499; *Sillitoe v McGraw-Hill Book Co (UK) Ltd* [1983] F.S.R. 545; *Independent Television Publications Ltd v Time Out Ltd* [1984] F.S.R. 64; *Geographia Ltd v Penguin Books Ltd* [1985] F.S.R. 208. Abridgments may be infringements: "I am not aware that one man has a right to abridge the works of another": per Knight Bruce VC in *Dickens v Lee* (1844) 8 Jur. 183 at 184. See also *Tinsley v Lacy* (1863) 1 H. & M. 747 at 754, per Page Wood VC See *Baigent v Random House Group Ltd* [2007] EWCA Civ 247; [2008] E.M.L.R. 7; [2007] F.S.R. 24 as to what constitutes reproduction of a sufficiently substantial part in the context of a literary work; and in the context of artistic works *Nova Productions Ltd v Mazooma Games Ltd* [2007] EWCA Civ 219; [2007] R.P.C. 25; and *Designers Guild Ltd v Russell Williams (Textiles) Ltd* [2000] 1 W.L.R. 2416; [2001] F.S.R. 11 (combination of flowers and stripes differently disposed was held to infringe by the House of Lords which restored the judge's finding). Note, however, that all these cases predate *Infopaq International A/S v Danske Daglades Forening* (C-5/08) EU:C:2009:465; [2009] E.C.D.R. 16.

142 *Temple Instruments v Kollis Heels* [1973] R.P.C. 15.

143 *Designers Guild Ltd v Russell Williams (Textiles) Ltd* [2000] 1 W.L.R. 2416; [2001] F.S.R. 11. See also, in connection with non-textual copying: *Navitaire Inc v Easyjet Airline Co* [2004] EWHC 1725 (Ch); [2005] E.C.C. 30; [2005] E.C.D.R. 17.

144 *Corelli v Gray* (1913) 30 T.L.R. 116.

145 *Rees v Melville* (1914) Mac. C.C. (1911-16) 168. However, in *Kogan v Martin* [2019] EWCA Civ 1645; [2020] E.M.L.R. 4 at [35], the Court of Appeal was prepared to assume that "copyright protection can extend to the plot of a literary work, even where the precise words are not taken". It is not sufficient merely to reproduce the style or technique: *Norowzian v Arks Ltd (No.2)* [2000] F.S.R. 363.

146 *Robl v Palace Theatre* (1911) 28 T.L.R. 69.

147 As to copyright in architectural drawings and the right to use the common stock of architectural ideas, see *Jones v London Borough of Tower Hamlets* [2001] R.P.C. 23. cf. *Cala Homes (South) Ltd v Alfred McAlpine Homes East Ltd* [1995] F.S.R. 818.

148 See, e.g. *Vane v Famous Players* (1928) Mac. C.C. (1928-35) 6; *King Features Synd v Kleeman* [1941] A.C. 417. For the sort of circumstances in which such similarity can be explained away see *Bauman v Fussell* [1978] R.P.C. 485; *Geographia Ltd v Penguin Books Ltd* [1985] F.S.R. 208.

Relevance of intention Infringement may be found irrespective of the alleged wrongdoer's intention.[149] Thus, it is possible for a defendant to infringe the copyright in a work of whose existence he is unaware or where he believes (wrongly) that he had a licence to use it.[150] A defendant's motive and intention may well be relevant to the question whether copying has taken place but are no longer considered relevant to whether a substantial part has been taken.[151] In an appropriate case, evidence of previous copying will be admitted by way of similar fact evidence.[152] 24-38

Burlesques, parody etc The general rules apply in considering whether works of this type infringe. However, since 1 October 2014 there has been a defence of fair dealing for the purposes of parody, caricature or pastiche.[153] In deciding whether the use is "fair", the court has to strike a fair balance between the rights of the copyright owner and those of the alleged infringer.[154] 24-39

Other primary infringements The other restricted acts which give rise to primary liability if committed in respect of a substantial part of a work without the requisite licence are: issuing copies to the public; renting or lending the work to the public; performing, showing or playing the work in public; communicating the work to the public; and making an adaptation or doing any of these acts in relation to an adaptation.[155] Issuing copies to the public means putting them into circulation for the first time and does not extend to any subsequent distribution, or other dealing.[156] Once a copy has been placed on the market in the EEA with the copyright owner's consent, the copyright is said to be "exhausted" and the copyright owner cannot seek to control any further distribution of the copy.[157] Lending includes mak- 24-40

---

149 *Lee v Simpson* (1847) 3 C.B. 871. cf. *Mansell v Valley Printing Co* [1908] 2 Ch. 441.

150 *Reade v Conquest* (1861) 11 C.B. (N.S.) 479. cf. also *Bryne v Statist Co* [1914] 1 K.B. 622. The relief that can be given against him may be limited; see below. A bona fide, but false, belief that a licence has been granted by the copyright owner is no defence to infringement.

151 *Baigent v The Random House Group Ltd* [2007 EWCA Civ 247; [2007] F.S.R. 24.

152 *Mood Music Publishing Co Ltd v De Wolfe Ltd* [1976] Ch. 119; [1976] F.S.R. 149.

153 CDPA 1988 s.30A.

154 *Deckmyn v Vandersteen* (C-201/13) EU:C:2014:2132; [2014] E.C.D.R. 21.

155 CDPA 1988 ss.18–21.

156 CJEU decisions on the "distribution right" provided for in the Information Society Directive have accorded the term "distribution" a much wider meaning which encompasses activities which in UK law would be considered to be secondary infringements (e.g. offering for sale) and thus require proof of knowledge or reason to believe as a condition of liability. See *Peek & Cloppenburg AG v Cassina SpA* (C-456/06) EU:C:2008:232; [2009] E.C.D.R. 9; *Donner* (C-5/11) EU:C:2012:370 [2015] E.C.D.R. 22; *Blomqvist v Rolex SA* (C-98/13) EU:C:2014:55; [2014] E.C.D.R. 10; *Dimensione Direct Sales Srl v Knoll International SpA* (C-516/13) EU:C:2015:315; [2015] E.C.D.R. 12; and *Syed* (C-572/17) EU:C:2018:1033 [2019] E.C.D.R 4. It seems unlikely that these activities are now primary infringements within the meaning of s.18 CDPA 1988 such that knowledge or reason to believe no longer needs to be proved. For the position where there is a chain of distribution, see *Response Clothing Ltd v The Edinburgh Woollen Mill Ltd* [2020] EWHC 148 (IPEC); [2020] F.S.R. 25 at [78]–[88].

157 For discussion, see *Art & Allposters International BV v Stichting Pictoright* (C-419/13) EU:C:2015:27; [2015] E.C.D.R. 8. Analogous principles apply to software which is made available for an unlimited period: *UsedSoft GmbH v Oracle International Corp* (C-128/11) EU:C:2012:407; [2012] E.C.D.R 19. Where the original material medium of the copy has been damaged, destroyed or lost, the licensee may not rely on this principle to provide a back-up copy without the authorisation of the rightholder: *Ranks* (C-166/15); EU:C:2016:762; [2017] Bus. L.R. 290.

ing an electronic copy of a work available in such a way that it is only available for a limited period.[158]

24-41 **Communication to the public** In the UK, the expression "communication to the public" means "communication to the public by electronic transmission" and includes both broadcasting and the making available of a work to the public by electronic transmission in such a way that members of the public may access it from a place and at a time individually chosen by them.[159] In deciding whether there has been a communication to the public, the court must take account of several complementary criteria.[160] There must be an act of "communication" to a "public". A "communication" is any act of making available, irrespective of the technical means or process used: as a rule every transmission which uses a specific technical means must be individually authorised, regardless of whether the work is actually accessed.[161] A "public" is an indeterminate but fairly large number of persons.[162] It is relevant to know how many persons have access at the same time as well as in succession.[163] It is necessary that the alleged infringer should have intervened, in full knowledge of the consequences of his or her action, to give access to the copyright work to his or her customers where they would not otherwise be able to access it.[164] The mere provision of physical facilities for making or receiving a communication is not itself a communication.[165] It is relevant to consider whether the communication is of a profit-making nature (although this is not determinative).[166] UK law, which (permissibly[167]) goes beyond what is required by EU law, provides for a general communication to the public right for broadcasters, which includes the simultaneous retransmission of a terrestrial broadcast.[168]

---

158 *Vereniging Openbare Biblioteken v Stichting Leenrecht* (C-174/15) EU:C:2016:856; [2016] E.C.D.R. 24.

159 CDPA 1988 s.20.

160 *Reha Training Gesellschaft v GEMA* (C-117/15) EU:C:2016:379; [2017] E.C.D.R. 1 at [35]; *Stichting Brein v Ziggo BV* (C-610/15) EU:C:2017:456; [2017] Bus. L.R. 1899 at [25]; *SGAE v Rafael Hoteles SA* (C-306/05) EU:C:2006:764; [2007] E.C.D.R. 2.

161 *Reha Training Gesellschaft v GEMA* (C-117/15) EU:C:2016:379; [2017] E.C.D.R. 1 at [38]–[39].

162 *Reha Training Gesellschaft v GEMA* (C-117/15) EU:C:2016:379; [2017] E.C.D.R. 1 at [41]. "Indeterminate" connotes "persons in general" as opposed to specific individuals belonging to a private group while the requirement of a "fairly large number" excludes groups of persons which are too small, or insignificant: *Reha Training Gesellschaft v GEMA* (C-117/15) EU:C:2016:379; [2017] E.C.D.R. 1 at [43]. See also *Stichting Brein v Ziggo BV* (C-610/15) EU:C:2017:456; [2017] Bus. L.R. 1899 at [41].

163 *Reha Training Gesellschaft v GEMA* (C-117/15) EU:C:2016:379; [2017] E.C.D.R. 1 at [44]; *Stichting Brein v Ziggo BV* (C-610/15) EU:C:2017:456; [2017] Bus. L.R. 1899 at [41].

164 *Reha Training Gesellschaft v GEMA* (C-117/15) EU:C:2016:379; [2017] E.C.D.R. 1 at [46]; *Stichting Brein v Ziggo BV* (C-610/15) EU:C:2017:456; [2017] Bus. L.R. 1899 at [34].

165 Recital 27 to Directive 2001/29; *Stichting Brein v Wullems* (C-527/15) EU:C:2017:300; [2017] Bus. L.R. 1816; [2017] E.C.D.R. 14 at [41]; *Stichting Brein v Ziggo BV* (C-610/15) EU:C:2017:456; [2017] Bus. L.R. 1899 at [38].

166 *GS Media BV v Sanoma Media Netherlands BV* (C-160/15) EU:C:2016:644; [2016] E.C.D.R. 25; *Reha Training Gesellschaft v GEMA* (C-117/15) EU:C:2016:379; [2017] E.C.D.R. 1 at [49]; *Stichting Brein v Ziggo BV* (C-610/15) EU:C:2017:456; [2017] Bus. L.R. 1899 at [46].

167 See *C More Entertainment AB v Sandberg* (C-279/13) EU:C:2015:199; [2015] E.C.D.R. 15.

168 CDPA 1988 s.20(1)(c). See *ITV Broadcasting Ltd v TV Catchup Ltd* [2011] EWHC 1874 (Pat); [2011] F.S.R. 40 at [49], [79]; *ITV Broadcasting Ltd v TVCatchup Ltd* (C-607/11) EU:C:2013:147; [2013] E.C.D.R. 9.

Position where original communication authorised Where the allegedly infringing communication involves a further communication of an original authorised communication (e.g. by hyperlinking to a publicly available web-page)[169] one of two alternative requirements must be satisfied before there can be a communication to the public. The first is that the communication is to a "new" public. A public is "new" if it was not taken into account by the rightholder when he or she authorised the original communication.[170] If the public is not "new" in this sense, there will still be a communication to the public if the transmission is by a different technical means to that adopted by the rightholder for the original communication.[171] 24-42

Examples of communication to the public The law is developing rapidly but the following activities have been held to amount to a communication to the public: the presentation by a publican of broadcasts on a television screen in a public house[172]; the reception of a broadcast signal by a hotel operator and its transmission to the rooms and common parts of the hotel[173]; the provision of hyperlinks to unlicensed content by a person who knows or ought to know that the content is unlicensed[174]; the operation of a website which indexed, categorised and kept up to date Torrent files identifying unlicensed copies for "sharing"[175]; the operation of various forms of streaming services[176]; the sale of media players containing links to infringing material[177]; making available on a website a photograph which had been copied from another freely available website[178]; recording terrestrial television programmes pursuant to users' online requests and transmitting the recordings to cloud storage[179]; and operating a website which collated and linked to online radio stations.[180] 24-43

---

169 *Warner Music UK Ltd v Tunein Inc.* [2019] EWHC 2923 (Ch) at [98].

170 *Reha Training Gesellschaft v GEMA* (C-117/15) EU:C:2016:379; [2017] E.C.D.R. 1 at [45]; *Stichting Brein v Ziggo BV* (C-610/15) EU:C:2017:456; [2017] Bus. L.R. 1899 at [44].

171 *GS Media BV v Sanoma Media Netherlands BV* (C-160/15) EU:C:2016:644; [2016] E.C.D.R. 25 at [37]. However, there was no mention of this requirement in *AKM v Zürs.net Betriebs GmbH* (C-138/16) EU:C:2017:218; [2017] E.C.D.R. 15.

172 *Football Association Premier League Ltd v QC Leisure* and *Murphy v Media Protection Services Ltd* (C-403/08 and C-429/08) EU:C:2011:631; [2012] 1 C.M.L.R. 29; [2012] C.E.C. 242; [2012] E.C.D.R. 8. There is an overlap with the public performance right in this respect.

173 *SGAE v Rafael Hoteles SL* (C-306/05) [2007] E.C.D.R. 2; *Phonographic Performance (Ireland) Ltd v Ireland* (C-162/10) [2012] E.C.D.R. 15. The same applied to the provision of television facilities to users of a spa (*OSA v Lecebne lazne Marianske Lazne as* (C-351/12) [2014] E.C.D.R. 25) and a rehabilitation centre (*Reha Training Gesellschaft v GEMA* (C-117/15) [2017] E.C.D.R. 1).

174 *GS Media BV v Sanoma Media Netherlands BV* (C-160/15) [2016] E.C.D.R. 25. A commercial operator will be presumed to have the relevant state of mind; by contrast a non-commercial operator will not. The sale of media players with embedded hyperlinks linking to unlicensed streaming sites was held to be a communication to the public in *Stichting Brein v Wullems* (C-527/15) EU:C:2017:300; [2017] Bus. L.R. 1816; [2017] E.C.D.R. 14.

175 *Stichting Brein v Ziggo BV* (C-610/15) [2017] Bus. L.R. 1899.

176 *ITV Broadcasting Ltd v TV Catchup Ltd* [2011] EWHC 1874 (Pat); *ITV Broadcasting Ltd v TVCatchup Ltd* (C-607/11) EU:C:2013:147; [2013] E.C.D.R. 9; *Football Association Premier League v British Telecommunications Plc* [2017] EWHC 480; [2017] E.C.C. 17; *Union Associations Européenes de Football v British Telecommunications Plc* [2017] EWHC 3414 (Ch).

177 *Stichting Brein v Wullems* (C-527/15) EU:C:2017:300; [2017] Bus. L.R. 1816; [2017] E.C.D.R. 14.

178 *Land Nordrhein-Westfalen v Renckhoff* (C-161/17) EU:C:2018:634; [2018] E.C.D.R. 21.

179 *VCAST Ltd v RTI SpA* (C-256/16) EU:C:2017:913; [2018] E.C.D.R. 5.

180 *Warner Music UK Ltd v Tunein Inc* [2019] EWHC 2923 (Ch). By aggregating the links it proved the service went beyond that of a conventional search engine or a simple hyperlinker: see at [121]–[131].

24-44 **Acts which do not amount to communication to the public** Acts which have been held not to amount to a communication to the public include a public performance by live performers[181]; the playing of sound recordings at a dentist's whose patient list is small[182]; and the provision of hyperlinks to lawfully available content.[183]

24-45 **Dealing with infringing copies and other secondary infringements** Copyright is infringed by the commission of certain acts in respect of an article which is or which the infringer knows or has reason to believe is an infringing copy. An article is an "infringing copy" of a work if its making constituted an infringement of the copyright in the work in question.[184] The acts are: possession in the course of business, sale, letting for hire, offer or exposure for sale or hire, exhibition in public, distribution in the course of a business, or distribution otherwise than in the course of a business to such an extent as to affect prejudicially the owner of the copyright.[185] Copyright is also infringed by: dealing in an article specifically designed or adapted for making copies of a work, knowing or having reason to believe it is to be used for making infringing copies[186]; permitting a place of public entertainment to be used for an infringing public performance of a literary, dramatic or musical work (unless the grantor of the permission believed on reasonable grounds that the performance would not infringe copyright)[187]; supplying apparatus, sound recordings or films, knowing or having reason to believe that they will be used so as to infringe copyright[188]; and transmitting a work by means of a telecommunications system, otherwise than by communication to the public, knowing or having reason to believe that infringing copies of the work will be made by means of the reception of the transmission in the UK or elsewhere.[189]

24-46 **Importation of infringing copies** Copyright is also infringed by importation, without licence, into the UK, otherwise than for the private and domestic use of the importer, of any article the making of which the importer knew or had reason to believe, constituted an infringement of the copyright or would have constituted such an infringement if it had been made in the UK.[190]

---

181 *Circul Globus Bucaresti* (C-283/10) EU:C:2011:772; [2011] E.C.R. I-12031.

182 *SCF v Del Corso* (C-135/10) EU:C:2012:140; [2012] E.C.D.R. 16. The patients were a determinate circle, the use was unlikely to affect the dentist's income and the patients were exposed to the music without exercising any choice in the matter. See the analysis of this case in *Reha Training Gesellschaft v GEMA* (C-117/15) EU:C:2016:379; [2017] E.C.D.R. 1 at [48], [50], [52].

183 *Svensson v Retriever Sverige AB* (C-466/12) EU:C:2014:76; [2014] E.C.D.R. 9 (same technical means and no new public).

184 CDPA 1988 s.27(2). For a relevant presumption, see s.27(4). There are special rules in relation to imported copies: see the next paragraph.

185 CDPA 1988 s.23. As to "knowledge" and "reason to believe" see notes to previous paragraph.

186 CDPA 1988 s.24(1).

187 CDPA 1988 s.25(1). See, as to "permit", *Performing Rights Society v Ciryl Syndicate* [1924] 1 K.B. 1.

188 CDPA 1988 s.26.

189 CDPA 1988 s.24(2).

190 CDPA 1988 ss.22 and 27. The reference to works which "constituted an infringement" is because the Act extends to certain regions under British dominion which are outside the UK, so that infringing copies made there infringe UK copyright. In general, the important clause is the alternative, "would have constituted such an infringement if ..." As to "knowledge" see *Infabrics Ltd v Jaytex Shirt Co Ltd* [1982] A.C. 1; *Hoover v George Hulme (Stockport) Ltd* [1982] F.S.R. 565; *Arrowin Ltd v Trimguard (UK) Ltd* [1984] R.P.C. 581. As to whether there would have been an infringement if

Reason to believe "Reason to believe" involves the concept of knowledge of facts from which a reasonable person would arrive at the relevant belief.[191] Facts from which a reasonable person might suspect the relevant conclusions do not amount to reason to believe. The courts will permit an innocent person a reasonable period to investigate the facts once put on formal notice that he or she is dealing with infringing copies.[192] 24-47

Exceptions to infringement: general The Information Society Directive provides for an exhaustive,[193] closed list of permitted exceptions to certain restricted acts, including the reproduction right. All the exceptions other than the temporary copying exception are optional but all must comply with the so-called "three-step-test"[194] and (where relevant) be applied in such a way as to effect a fair balance between the rights of the rightholder and the right to freedom of expression of the user.[195] The exceptions adopted by the UK are specified in detail in the Copyright Act 1988, where they are described as "acts permitted in relation to copyright works".[196] The exceptions are frequently very specific and close attention needs to be paid to their precise terms. In many cases the exceptions override contractual terms to the contrary. Provision is made for circumstances where the benefit of the exception is removed by technological protection measures.[197] There is no exception for "private" or "personal" use in the UK. The exceptions are as follows: 24-48

(a) Making a temporary copy (i) which is transient or incidental; (ii) which is an integral and essential part of a technological process; (iii) the sole purpose of which is to enable either a transmission of the work in a network between third parties by an intermediary or a lawful use of the work; and

---

the item complained of had been manufactured in the UK see *CBS United Kingdom Ltd v Charmdale Record Distributors Ltd* [1981] Ch. 91; *Polydor Ltd v Harlequin Record Shops Ltd* [1980] F.S.R. 194; [1980] F.S.R. 362 CA; and (C-270/80) [1982] C.M.L.R. 677; cf. *Barson Computers (NZ) Ltd v John Gilbert Co Ltd* [1985] F.S.R. 489.

191 *Linpac Mouldings Ltd v Eagleton Direct Export Ltd* [1994] F.S.R. 545 CA; and *LA Gear Inc v Hi-Tec Sports Ltd* [1992] F.S.R. 121. In *Cantel Medical (UK) Ltd v ARC Medical Design Ltd* [2018] EWHC 345 (Pat) at [246]–[252] the defendant was held not to have reason to believe where he knew nothing of the existence of the (design) rights in question. It is unclear whether this decision is correct. The case law was reviewed in *FBT Productions LLC v Let Them Eat Vinyl Distribution Ltd* [2019] EWHC 829 (IPEC); [2019] E.C.D.R. 10 at [35]–[41].

192 *Monsoon v India Imports* [1993] F.S.R. 486.

193 See *Pelham GmbH v Hütter* (C-476/17) EU:C:2019:624; [2019] Bus. L.R. 2159 at [56]–[65]; *Spiegel Online GmbH v Beck* (C-516/17) EU:C:2019:625; [2019] Bus. L.R. 2787; [2019] E.C.D.R. 24 at [40]–[49]; and *Funke Medien NRW GmbH v Bundesrepublik Deutschland* (C-469/17) EU:C:2019:623; [2020] 1 C.M.L.R. 13; [2019] E.C.D.R. 25 at [55]–[64].

194 Directive 2001/29/EC art.5(5). The test derives from art.9(2) of the Berne Convention for the Protection of Literary and Artistic Works, to which the UK is party, which only permits exceptions to the exclusive right of reproduction (i) in certain special cases; and (ii) provided (a) the permitted reproduction does not conflict with a normal exploitation of the work; and (b) does not unreasonably prejudice the legitimate interests of the author. For an analysis of this test, see *England and Wales Cricket Board Ltd v Tixdaq Ltd* [2016] EWHC 575 (Ch); [2017] E.C.D.R. 2.

195 Directive 2001/29/EC Recital 31. *England and Wales Cricket Board Ltd v Tixdaq Ltd* [2016] EWHC 575 (Ch); [2017] E.C.D.R. 2 at [73]. As to Member States' discretion, see also *Spiegel Online GmbH v Beck* (C-516/17) EU:C:2019:625; [2019] Bus. L.R. 2787; [2019] E.C.D.R. 24; and *Funke Medien NRW GmbH v Bundesrepublik Deutschland* (C-469/17) EU:C:2019:623; [2020] 1 C.M.L.R. 13; [2019] E.C.D.R. 25 at [39]–[54] and [65]–[76].

196 Sections 28–76A.

197 CDPA 1988 s.296ZE. For protection of such measures, see ss.296–296ZF.

(iv) which has no independent economic significance.[198] The aim is to prevent the reproduction right being used to interfere with the proper functioning of electronic networks and the Internet. Consistently with this, the making of copies on the screen and in a computer's cache in the ordinary course of browsing the Internet are within the scope of the permitted act.[199]

(b) Fair dealing[200] with a work for the purposes of research for a non-commercial purpose (if accompanied by a sufficient acknowledgement) or for private study.[201]

(c) Fair dealing for a group of related and potentially overlapping purposes: (i) fair dealing with a work which has been made available to the public[202] for the purpose of criticism or review; (ii) the use of a quotation[203] from a work which has been made available to the public (provided the use is fair dealing and the extent no more than required by the purpose); and (iii) fair dealing with a work other than a photograph for the purpose of reporting current events.[204] In each case the use must be accompanied by sufficient acknowledgement (unless this is impossible).[205]

---

[198] CDPA 1988 s.28A, implementing art.5(1) of the Information Society Directive. See *Football Association Premier League Ltd v QC Leisure* and *Murphy v Media Protection Services Ltd* (C-403/08 and C-429/08) EU:C:2011:631; [2012] 1 C.M.L.R. 29; [2012] C.E.C. 242; [2012] E.C.D.R. 8. See also *Infopaq International A/S v Danske Daglades Forening* (C-5/08) EU:C:2009:465; [2009] E.C.D.R. 16: the exception must be interpreted strictly because it is a derogation from the general principle that the right holder shall authorise any reproduction of a protected work. Thus in order to come within the exception, acts of reproduction carried out during a "data capture" process must not "enable the generation of an additional profit" for the user or lead to "a modification of" the work.

[199] *Public Relations Consultants Association Ltd v The Newspaper Licensing Agency Ltd* (C-360/13) EU:C:2014:1195; [2014] A.C. 1438. See also the Supreme Court's decision to refer this issue to the CJEU: [2013] UKSC 18; [2013] 2 All E.R. 852. However, the making of copies in a user' computer in the course of streaming unlicensed films was not within the exception: *Stichting Brein v Wullems* (C-527/15) EU:C:2017:300; [2017] Bus. L.R. 1816; [2017] E.C.D.R. 14.

[200] For a review of the law on "fair" dealing, see *England and Wales Cricket Board Ltd v Tixdaq Ltd* [2016] EWHC 575 (Ch); [2017] E.C.D.R. 2.

[201] CDPA 1988 s.29. Research for ultimately commercial purposes is not within the s.29 exception: *HM Stationery Office v Green Amps Ltd* [2007] EWHC 2755 (Ch). For the position of persons other than the researcher or student, such as librarians, see s.29(3). Separate provision is made for copies made for text and data analysis for non-commercial research: see s.29A.

[202] For these purposes it will be sufficient that the work has been made available in accordance with a non-contractual licence or a statutory authorisation: *Spiegel Online GmbH v Beck* (C-516/17) EU:C:2019:625; [2019] Bus. L.R. 2787; [2019] E.C.D.R. 24 at [85]–[95].

[203] The quotation must be recognisable in the allegedly infringing work in order for this exception to apply: *Pelham GmbH v Hütter* (C-476/17) EU:C:2019:624; [2019] Bus. L.R. 2159 at [66]–[74]. The quotation may be by way of hyperlink to an independent file: *Spiegel Online GmbH v Beck* (C-516/17) EU:C:2019:625; [2019] Bus. L.R. 2787; [2019] E.C.D.R. 24 at [75]–[84].

[204] CDPA 1988 s.30. For the reporting exception, see *Spiegel Online GmbH v Beck* (C-516/17) EU:C:2019:625; [2019] Bus. L.R. 2787; [2019] E.C.D.R. 24 at [60]–[74]. "Criticism or review" and "reporting current events" are expressions of wide and indefinite scope which should be interpreted liberally. The subjective intentions of the defendant are of limited importance in assessing whether the use of the work was for those purposes: *Pro Sieben Media AG v Carlton UK Television Ltd* [1999] 1 W.L.R. 605 CA. Examples of cases falling on the different sides of the line of fair dealing are: *IPC Media Ltd v News Group Newspapers* [2005] EWHC 317 (Ch); [2005] F.S.R. 35 (prominent use for comparative advertising was not fair dealing); *Fraser-Woodward Ltd v BBC* [2005] EWHC 472 (Ch); [2005] F.S.R. 36 (inclusion in broadcast of celebrity pictures was fair dealing); *HRH Prince of Wales v Associated Newspapers Ltd* [2006] EWCA Civ 1776; [2008] Ch. 57 (publication of substantial extracts of a journal was not fair dealing); and *England and Wales Cricket Board Ltd v Tixdaq Ltd* [2016] EWHC 575 (Ch); [2017] E.C.D.R. 2 (use of highlights was not reporting but if it had been would not have been fair). In the last of these cases it was emphasised that UK deci-

(d) Fair dealing for the purposes of caricature, parody or pastiche.[206]

(e) Incidental inclusion of copyright material in an artistic work, sound recording, film or broadcast.[207]

(f) The making and certain uses of "accessible copies" for the personal use of disabled persons.[208] The Act permits the making in the prescribed circumstances of copies both by a disabled person and by an "authorised body", that is an educational establishment or a body which is not conducted for profit.[209]

(g) A variety of uses in the educational context including: fair dealing for the purposes of illustration; the inclusion of short passages in anthologies; the performance of a literary, dramatic or musical work in the course of the activities of an educational establishment; and various acts of educational establishments including the recording of broadcasts, the copying and use of extracts and the lending of copies.[210]

(h) A variety of uses by libraries, archives, museums and educational establishments including: lending of books and e-books (public libraries); making works available through dedicated terminals (all such institutions); supply by one library of copies to other libraries; the making of copies to preserve or replace existing copies (libraries, museums and archives); the supply of single copies for non-commercial research or private study (libraries and archives); and the copying of works from the internet (deposit libraries).[211]

(i) Certain uses of so-called "orphan works" by certain institutions. An orphan work is a work in respect of which the rightholder cannot be identified or if identified cannot be found. The institutions are publicly accessible libraries, educational establishments and museums, film or audio heritage organisations and public service broadcasting organisations. The permitted uses are making the copy available to the public and reproducing the

---

sions prior to the implementation of the Information Society Directive in 2003 need to be treated with caution. As to reporting, see also CDPA 1988 s.58.

205 As to sufficient acknowledgement see CDPA 1988 s.178. In the case of reporting the dispensation from the need to provide an acknowledgement only applies to reporting by means of a sound recording, film or broadcast.

206 See *Deckmyn v Vandersteen* (C-201/13) EU:C:2014:2132; [2014] E.C.D.R. 21, where it is emphasised that in considering fairness, a fair balance has to be struck between the rights of the copyright owner and those of the user.

207 CDPA 1988 s.31. As to what constitutes incidental use of a copyright work see *The Football Association Premier League Ltd v Panini UK Ltd* [2003] EWCA Civ 995; [2004] 1 W.L.R. 1147 (photographs of footballers including reproductions of club logo not incidental inclusion of the logo). See also *FAPL v QC Leisure* [2008] EWHC 1411 (Ch); [2008] F.S.R. 32; and *Fraser-Woodward v BBC* [2005] EWHC 472 (Ch); [2005] E.M.L.R. 22.

208 CDPA 1988 ss.31A–31F.

209 "Educational establishment" is defined in CDPA 1988 s.174.

210 CDPA 1988 ss.32–36A. Not all of these exceptions apply to all types of work. Some of them only apply where licences are not otherwise available.

211 CDPA 1988 ss.40A–44A.The terms "library", "museum" and "conducted for profit" are defined in CDPA 1988 s.43A. "Educational establishment" is defined in CDPA 1988 s.174. Again, the exceptions are very specific and close attention needs to be paid to their terms. For digital lending, see *Vereniging Openbare Biblioteken v Stichting Leenrecht* (C-174/15) EU:C:2016:856; [2016] E.C.D.R. 24. Section 44 permits the making of copies of articles which need to be deposited in libraries or archives as a condition of an export licence.

work for this and related purposes. This exception is part of a pan-EU scheme.[212]

(j) Certain uses in connection with public administration[213]: "anything done for the purposes of" parliamentary or judicial proceedings, or the proceedings of Royal Commissions or statutory inquiries or for reporting such proceedings[214]; certain types of copying of material open to public inspection or on a statutory register; the copying by the Crown of works communicated to it by or with the licence of the copyright owner in the course of public business; the copying of public records; and the doing of particular acts under statutory authority.[215]

(k) Certain uses by lawful users of computer programs: the making of necessary back-up copies; certain forms of decompilation; the observation, studying and testing of the functioning of the program; and copying and adapting which is necessary for lawful use and not prohibited by the licence agreement.[216]

(l) Certain uses by lawful users of databases.[217]

(m) The making of articles to a design for anything other than an artistic work or a typeface. This will not infringe the copyright in a design model or document recording or embodying the design.[218] In broad terms, industrial products are not protected by copyright and attract the shorter terms of protection afforded by the various rights which protect designs. However, original design drawings for such products may be protected by copyright as artistic works. The object of this provision is to prevent the owner of the copyright in such drawings from using them to prevent such products being made.[219] A related provision, s.52 of the CDPA 1988, which limited the term of copyright in industrially applied artistic works to 25 years, has been repealed.

(n) A variety of miscellaneous exceptions.[220] The following is a selection only: use of a typeface in the ordinary course of printing[221]; use for public read-

---

212 CDPA 1988 s.44B and Sch.ZA, implementing Directive 2012/28/EU on certain permitted uses of orphan works.

213 CDPA 1988 ss.45–50.

214 CDPA 1988 ss.45 and 46. "Judicial proceedings" seemingly include arbitration proceedings: *London & Leeds Estates v Paribas Ltd (No. 2)* [1995] 1 E.G.L.R. 102. In New Zealand it has been held that the equivalent exception only applies to proceedings which are actually on foot: *Auckland Medical Aid Trust v Commissioner of Police* [1976] 1 N.Z.L.R. 485. The question whether this is so remains open in the UK but it has been held at least arguable that proceedings need not yet be in existence: *A v B* [2000] E.M.L.R. 1006. Implied licences may also come into play.

215 The need for the last of these exceptions (CDPA 1988 s.56) is unclear since there would in any event be a defence of statutory authority. The reference in s.56 to "a particular act" is designed to exclude cases where a general activity is authorised by Parliament.

216 CDPA 1988 ss.50A-50C, implementing what is now Directive 2009/24/EC on the legal protection of computer programs. As to back-ups, see *Sony Computer Entertainment v Owen* [2002] EWHC 45 (Ch). As to observing, studying and testing, see *SAS Institute Inc v World Programming Ltd* (C-406/10) [2013] Bus. L.R. 941 and (in the Court of Appeal) [2013] EWCA Civ 1482; [2015] E.C.D.R. 17.

217 CDPA 1988 s.50.

218 CDPA 1988 s.51.

219 See generally the specialist copyright texts.

220 CDPA 1988 ss.53–76.

221 CDPA 1988 s.54. See also s.55, limiting the term of typeface copyright.

ings and recitations[222]; the copying of scientific or technical abstracts[223]; the recording of folksongs and supplying copies for the purposes of non-commercial research or private study[224]; making a graphic work, photograph or film, or broadcasting an image of a building, sculpture, model for a building, or work of artistic craftsmanship if permanently situated in a public place or in premises open to the public[225]; advertising an artistic work for sale[226]; the making of subsequent works by the same artist provided he does not repeat the design of the earlier work[227]; the reconstruction of copyright buildings[228]; and various acts in relation to broadcasts including the right to record a broadcast in domestic premises for private and domestic use for the purposes of "time-shifting".[229]

Other defences There is a limited "public interest" defence,[230] which presumably has now to be applied in accordance with EU law. Intermediary service providers in the online sector may be able to rely on the "mere conduit", "caching" and "hosting defences provided for by the E-Commerce Directive".[231] As with other intellectual property rights, copyright may be unenforceable if what lies behind the enforcement is an attempt to partition the EU market contrary to the provisions on free movement. There must be a sufficient nexus between the exercise of the right and the alleged breach of EU rules.[232] 24-49

(ii) Database right

Infringement of database right Database right is infringed by the extraction or re-utilisation of a substantial part of the contents of the database without the consent of the owner of the right.[233] Repeated and systematic extraction or re-utilisation of insubstantial parts may amount to the extraction or re-utilisation of a substantial part.[234] For these purposes, "extraction" means the permanent or temporary transfer of the contents to another medium; "re-utilisation" means making the contents available to the public.[235] Where the creator of a database makes the content of the 24-50

222 CDPA 1988 s.59. Also the recording or communication of the same to the public provided that mainly non-copyright material is used.

223 CDPA 1988 s.60. This does not apply if a licensing scheme is in force.

224 CDPA 1988 s.61.

225 CDPA 1988 s.62.

226 CDPA 1988 s.63.

227 CDPA 1988 s.64.

228 CDPA 1988 s.65.

229 CDPA 1988 ss.68–72 and 75.

230 *Ashdown v Telegraph Group Ltd* 2001] EWCA Civ 1142; [2002] Ch. 149; *Hyde Park Residence Ltd v Yelland* [2001] Ch. 143; [2000] E.M.L.R. 363 CA; and *Imutran v Uncaged Campaigns Ltd* [2001] 2 All E.R. 385 (V-C). See also *HRH The Prince of Wales v Associated Newspapers Ltd* [2006] EWHC 522 (Ch); [2008] E.M.L.R. 3; [2006] E.C.D.R. 20; and *Unilever Plc v Griffin* [2010] EWHC 899 (Ch); [2010] F.S.R. 33.

231 Directive 2000/31/EC arts 12, 13 and 14; Electronic Commerce (EC Directive) Regulations 2002 (SI 2002/2013).

232 See, e.g. *Football Association Premier League Ltd v Luxton* [2016] EWCA Civ 1097; [2017] E.C.D.R. 7, where the defence failed.

233 See reg.16(1) of the Copyright and Rights in Databases Regulations (SI 1997/3032), implementing Directive 96/9/EC on the legal protection of databases.

234 See reg.16(2) of the Copyright and Rights in Databases Regulations (SI 1997/3032).

235 See reg.12 of the Copyright and Rights in Databases Regulations (SI 1997/3032). See generally *The*

database accessible to the public, the consultation of that database does not, by itself, constitute an infringement.[236]

24-51 **Exceptions to database right** The exceptions to database right are much more limited than those to copyright. There are exceptions in respect of public administration which substantially mirror those applicable to copyright.[237] In addition, database right is not infringed by fair dealing with the contents of the database by a lawful user for the purpose of teaching or research and for a non-commercial purpose[238]; or by the copying by a deposit library of a work from the internet.[239]

(d) Remedies for infringement of copyright and database right[240]

24-52 **Civil remedies** Infringements of copyright and database right are actionable at the suit of the owner or an exclusive licensee of the right or both.[241] When, however, there are concurrent rights the one may not (without leave of the court) proceed unless the other is joined as claimant or added as defendant, save for obtaining interim relief.[242] Certain infringements are actionable by a non-exclusive licensee.[243] Interim relief may be granted to an equitable owner.[244] If a copyright is jointly owned, either may sue: in particular, one may sue the other for reproducing the work without his or her consent.[245] Copyright infringement is a tort and the general rules as to joint

---

British Horseracing Board Ltd and Others v William Hill Organization Ltd (C-203/02) EU:C:2004:695; [2005] 1 C.M.L.R. 15; [2005] R.P.C. 13; *Directmedia Publishing GmbH v Albert-Ludwigs-Universität Freiburg* (C-304/07) EU:C:2008:552; [2008] E.C.R. I-7565; [2009] R.P.C. 10; *Football Dataco Ltd v Sportradar GMBH* (C-173/11) EU:C:2012:642; [2013] 1 C.M.L.R. 29; *Innoweb BV v ICT Media* (C-202/12) [2014] Bus. L.R. 308; and *Freistaat Bayern v Verlag Esterbauer GmbH* (C-490/14) EU:C:2015:735; [2016] E.C.D.R. 6.

236 *The British Horseracing Board Ltd v William Hill Organization Ltd* (C-203/02) EU:C:2004:695; [2005] 1 C.M.L.R. 15; [2005] R.P.C. 13 at [54]–[55]. The cases are reviewed in *77M Ltd v Ordnance Survey Ltd* [2019] EWHC 3007 (Ch) at [266]–[269].

237 See reg.20(2) of and Sch.1 to the Copyright and Rights in Databases Regulations (SI 1997/3032). For these exceptions so far as applicable to copyright, see para.24-48(i). For the exceptions in para.3 (headed "Material open to public inspection or on official register"), see *77M Ltd v Ordnance Survey Ltd* [2019] EWHC 3007 (Ch) at [296]–[314].

238 See reg.20(1) of the Copyright and Rights in Databases Regulations (SI 1997/3032).

239 See reg.20A of the Copyright and Rights in Databases Regulations (SI 1997/3032).

240 Remedies for infringement of copyright are set out in CDPA 1988 Ch.VI ss.96-115. Sections 96-102 are applied to database right by reg.23 of the Copyright and Rights in Databases Regulations (SI 1997/3032). In applying these remedies, the Court must comply with Directive 2004/48/EC on the enforcement of intellectual property rights. See also see *Hollister Inc v Medik Ostomy Supplies Ltd* [2012] EWCA Civ 1419; [2013] Bus. L.R. 428; [2013] F.S.R. 24; and *Merck KGaA v Merck Sharp & Doehme Corp* [2017] EWCA Civ 1834; [2018] E.T.M.R. 10.

241 CDPA 1988 ss.96(1) and 101. In the High Court, matters relating to copyright are assigned to the Chancery Division: see Senior Courts Act 1981 s.61 and Sch.1 para.1; and *APAC Rowena Ltd v Norpol Packaging* [1991] 4 All E.R. 516. Shorter claims may be brought in the Intellectual Property Enterprise Court, which is a specialist list of the Chancery Division. Copyright actions may also be brought in the County Court.

242 CDPA 1988 s.102. If added as a defendant he or she will not be liable for costs unless he or she takes part in the proceedings. In cases where claimants disagree, the name of one of them may be struck out and brought in as a defendant on suitable terms: *Warwick Film Productions Ltd v Eisinger* [1963] 1 W.L.R. 756.

243 CDPA 1988 s.101A.

244 *Merchant Adventurers v Grew* [1972] 1 Ch. 242.

245 *Cesinsky v Routledge* [1916] 2 K.B. 325. For the case of two similar publications by the same author for rival publishers, see *Education Co of Ireland v Fallon* [1919] Ir. R. 62. See above as to when a

tortfeasorship apply.[246] The claimant may claim all the usual relief for the infringement of a property right.[247] There are numerous statutory rebuttable presumptions as to authorship and publication.[248] It is possible to bring proceedings in the English courts in respect of infringements of the copyright laws of other countries, provided that the defendant is otherwise amenable to the jurisdiction.[249]

Injunction The primary remedy for infringement is an injunction.[250] Although this is a discretionary remedy, it will rarely be refused if the defendant threatens, expressly or impliedly, to repeat the infringements.[251] A claimant will not invariably be obliged to accept an undertaking by the defendant to commit no further infringement.[252] He need not prove any damage[253] but there must at least be a likelihood of future damage.[254] Interim injunctions, search and seizure (*Anton Piller*) orders etc are granted on the usual principles, as are orders requiring identification of the source of infringing goods.[255] If an infringing copy in respect of which the copyright owner would be entitled to an order for delivery up[256] is exposed for sale or hire it can be seized and detained by him or by a person authorised by him. Conditions include informing the police in advance and using no force.[257] The provision is aimed at street traders and the like. The High Court has power to grant an injunction against an intermediary (which may include a tenant of a market which sublets market stalls[258]), where the intermediary has actual knowledge of another person using their service to infringe copyright.[259] This power has been used 24-53

work is of joint authorship.

246 See *Fish & Fish Ltd v Sea Shepherd UK* [2015] UKSC 10; [2015] A.C. 1229. For the liability of company directors, see *MCA Records Inc v Charly Records Ltd* [2001] EWCA Civ 1441; [2002] F.S.R. 26 CA.

247 CDPA 1988 s.96(2).

248 See CDPA 1988 ss.104–106.

249 *Lucasfilm Ltd v Ainsworth* [2011] UKSC 39; [2012] 1 A.C. 208. Local law applies.

250 Interim injunctions are available on ordinary principles.

251 See the summary of the case law in *Stretchline Intellectual Properties Ltd v H&M Hennes & Mauritz UK Ltd* [2016] EWHC 162 (Pat); [2016] R.P.C. 15 at [6]–[12]. Copyright Act 1956 s.17(4) made an exception whereby an architect could not get an injunction once a building had been commenced. This provision has been repealed and has not been re-enacted, but an injunction is an equitable remedy which could be refused in such circumstances. See *Hunter v Fitzroy Robinson & Partners* [1978] F.S.R. 167. An injunction was refused to restrain an architect's client from substituting other plans for part of the work: *Barnett v Cape Town Foreshore Board* [1978] F.S.R. 176 SA. The equitable remedy of an injunction may be withheld where it is in the public interest that copyright material should be published (*Lion Laboratories Ltd v Evans* [1985] Q.B. 526; *Hyde Park Residence Ltd v Yelland* [2001] Ch. 143; *Ashdown v Telegraph Group Ltd* [2001] Ch. 685).

252 *Savory Ltd v World of Golf* [1914] 2 Ch. 566; *Performing Rights Society v Ciryl Syndicate* [1923] 2 K.B. 146; reversed in part [1924] 1 K.B. 1.

253 *Smith v Johnson* (1863) 22 L.R. Ch. 137.

254 *Borthwick v Evening Post* (1888) 37 Ch. D. 449. In general, infringement is inherently damaging, involving the doing of something by an infringer that the owner might have done himself (*Sutherland Publishing Co Ltd v Caxton Publishing Co Ltd* [1936] Ch. 323) or licensed the infringer to do for reward.

255 See Ch.28.

256 CDPA 1988 s.99.

257 CDPA 1988 s.100(2) and (3). There is no definition of a regular place of business, which would presumably cover, for instance, a market stall trading in the same place every week.

258 *Tommy Hilfiger Licensing LLC v DELTA CENTER a.s.* (C-494/15) EU:C:2016:528; [2017] E.T.M.R. 5.

259 CDPA 1988 s.97A implementing art.8(3) of the Information Society Directive (Directive 2001/29/EC).

extensively to order internet service providers to block access to websites and servers which are unlawfully communicating copyright material to the public.[260]

24-54 **Delivery up** The court has an inherent jurisdiction to order delivery up of infringing copies[261] for destruction in aid of an injunction. There is also a statutory right to the delivery up of infringing copies and articles which the defendant knows to be designed or adapted for making copies of a particular copyright work,[262] but no order may normally be made after the end of a period of six years from the date on which the infringing copy or article was made.[263] The court may alternatively order the destruction or sale of the copy or article with an order for division of the proceeds.[264]

24-55 **Damages or account of profits** A successful claimant is entitled to an inquiry as to damages[265] or, in the alternative, may choose an account of an infringer's profits.[266] As to damages, where a defendant competes with the claimant, the claimant will be entitled to his loss of profit on sales which would have been made by him but where the claimant exploits the work by licensing, he will be entitled to recover a royalty based on what a willing licensor and willing licensee would have agreed.[267] Loss of profits must be proved and it will not necessarily be assumed that

---

[260] The applicable principles were succinctly summarised in *Nintendo Co Ltd v Sky UK Ltd* [2019] EWHC 2376 (Ch); [2019] Bus. L.R. 2773. The case concerned trade marks and technological protection measures but the principles apply to all intellectual property cases. The rightholder will be obliged to bear the cost of compliance: *Cartier International AG v British Telecommunications Plc* [2018] UKSC 28; [2018] 1 W.L.R. 3259. For the CJEU's jurisprudence, see *UPC Telekabel Wien GmbH v Constantin Film Verleih GmbH, Wega Filmproduktionsesellschaft mbH* (C-314/12) EU:C:2014:192; [2014] E.C.D.R. 12. See also *McFadden v Sony Music Entertainment Germany GmbH* (C-484/14) EU:C:2016:689; [2016] E.C.D.R. 26: it may be permissible for a court to require an operator of a public wireless network which has been used to download infringing copies to require users to identify themselves as a condition of getting access. For the standing of exclusive licensees, see *Queensberry Promotions Ltd v British Telecommunications Plc* [2018] EWHC 3273 (Ch); [2019] E.C.D.R. 13.

[261] This expression is defined by CDPA 1988 s.27.

[262] CDPA 1988 s.99. If the copyright is the subject of an exclusive licence, the copyright owner must inform the licensee of his intention to exercise this right: s.102(5).

[263] CDPA 1988 s.113. The exceptions are where the copyright owner was under a disability and in cases of fraud and concealment.

[264] CDPA 1988 s.114. Such orders may be made by a county court where the value of the infringing copies or articles in question does not exceed the court's limit for actions in tort: s.115.

[265] *Glyn v Weston Feature Film Co* [1916] 1 Ch. 261. The tort test of remoteness applies to damages for copyright infringement: *Claydon Architectural Metalwork Ltd v DJ Higgins & Sons Ltd* [1997] F.S.R. 475. See also Enforcement Directive (2004/48/EC) art.13. As matters stand, the only real change wrought by this provision is to include provision for recovery of "unfair profits" and damages for "moral prejudice" in cases of knowing infringement. Awards of "unfair profits" will be rare: *Ghias v Grill'O Xpress Ltd* [2018] EWHC 3445 (IPEC). The meaning of "moral prejudice" is not clear. See *Liffers v Producciones Mandarina SL* (C-99/15) EU:C:2016:173; [2016] E.C.D.R. 22; and *Henderson v All Around the World Recordings Ltd* [2014] EWHC 3087 (IPEC).

[266] *Pike v Nicholas* (1870) L.R. 5 Ch. 251 at 260. See also *Potton Ltd v Yorkclose Ltd* [1990] F.S.R. 11. For when the infringer can deduct general overheads, see *OOO Abbott v Design and Display Ltd* [2016] EWCA Civ 98; [2016] F.S.R. 27; *Jack Wills Ltd v House of Fraser (Stores) Ltd* [2016] EWHC 626 (Ch). The claimant is entitled to sufficient information to make an informed choice between damages and profits before electing: *Island Records Inc v Tring International Plc* [1996] 1 W.L.R. 1256; *Brugger v Medicaid Ltd* [1996] F.S.R. 362.

[267] *General Tire and Rubber Co v Firestone Tyre and Rubber Co* [1975] 1 W.L.R. 819.

every sale made by a defendant would have been made by the claimant.[268] In cases in which the claimant does not exploit the work, the court will be left to make a crude estimate of a reasonable royalty or lump sum.[269] Damages will sometimes be based on the diminished value of the copyright in the claimant's hands.[270] There is a general discretion to award "additional" damages. The discretion is unfettered but relevant considerations are whether the infringement is flagrant and any benefit accruing to the defendant from it.[271] Where copyright is subject to an exclusive licence, the terms of the licence are taken into account in assessing damages and there is provision for securing that the copyright owner and exclusive licensee do not between them recover double damages.[272] Damages must be attributable to the infringement so where the damage is caused by the use of the ideas in a copied work rather than the text of the work itself, substantial damages will not arise. However, a fairly substantial sum may be awarded for the right to use the work.[273] There is no provision in the Copyright Act to provide a remedy in respect of groundless threats to bring legal proceedings for copyright infringement.[274]

Innocent infringers Innocent infringers have very limited protection against damages for infringement. If a defendant proves that at the date of the infringement he was not aware, and had no reasonable ground for suspecting, that copyright subsisted in the work, the claimant is not entitled to damages, although he is still entitled to claim an injunction, an account of profits, and delivery up of infringing copies.[275] A mistake as to the ownership of copyright is not enough to bring the **24-56**

268 *Columbia Pictures v Robinson* [1988] F.S.R. 531. The court will not require certainty of proof and will often adopt the maxim omnia praesumuntur contra spoliatorem ("all things are presumed against a wrongdoer"): see *Infabrics Ltd v Jaytex Ltd* [1985] F.S.R. 75.

269 For a review of the case law, see *Reformation Publishing Company Ltd v Cruiseco Ltd* [2018] EWHC 2761 (Ch); [2019] Bus. L.R. 78.

270 For discussion see *Sutherland Publishing Co Ltd v Caxton Publishing Co Ltd* [1936] Ch. 323; *Fenning Film Service v Wolverhampton etc Cinemas* [1914] 3 K.B. 1171; *Birn Bros Ltd v Keene & Co Ltd* [1918] 2 Ch. 281; *Ash v Dickie* [1936] Ch. 655.

271 CDPA 1988 s.97(2). Such a claim must be pleaded and grounds given. The following points arise from *Phonographic Performance Ltd v Ellis* [2018] EWCA Civ 2812; [2019] F.S.R. 15: additional damages may be partly or wholly punitive (at [37]); they are consistent with the Enforcement Directive but (having regard to the CJEU's decision *Stowarzyszenie 'Oławska Telewizja Kablowa' v Stowarzyszenie Filmowców Polskich* (C-367/15) EU:C:2017:36; [2017] E.C.D.R. 16) a particularly egregious award of exemplary damages may be an abuse of rights (at [42]); an infringement which is also a contempt of court will usually be flagrant (at [60]); flagrancy implies scandalous conduct or deceit (at [61]). Additional damages can be important where compensatory damages are small, as in *Nottinghamshire Healthcare NHS Trust v News Group Newspapers Ltd* [2002] EWHC 409 (Ch); [2002] E.M.L.R. 33. Often a "mark up" on ordinary damages is awarded: see, e.g. *Peninsular Business Service Ltd v Citation Plc* [2004] F.S.R. 17 (100 per cent mark up). Insulting behaviour may well give rise to additional damages under the section: *Beloff v Pressdram Ltd* [1973] 1 All E.R. 241. So will deceitful and treacherous conduct; *Nichols Advanced Vehicle Systems Inc v Rees* [1979] R.P.C. 127; *ZYX Music v King* [1995] 3 All E.R. 1; cf. *Ravenscroft v Herbert* [1980] R.P.C. 193. There can be no claim for additional damages where the claimant has elected an account of profits: *Redrow Homes Ltd v Betts Brothers Plc* [1999] 1 A.C. 197 HL.

272 CDPA 1988 s.102(4).

273 *USP Plc v London General Holdings Ltd* [2005] EWCA Civ 931; [2006] F.S.R. 6.

274 There is, however, provision for threats actions in respect of unregistered UK design right: s.253. Nor was there any provision under the 1956 Act but nevertheless an interlocutory injunction was granted in *Jaybeam Ltd v Abru Aluminium Ltd* [1976] R.P.C. 308. However, an action claiming damages for inducing a breach of contract by threats of bringing a copyright infringement action was struck out: *Granby Marketing Services Ltd v Interlego AG* [1984] R.P.C. 209.

275 CDPA 1988 s.97(1). Knowledge is a prerequisite for the establishment of secondary infringement:

defendant within the protection of this provision; he must have had no reasonable grounds for suspecting that any copyright existed in the work.[276]

24-57 **Prohibition of importation of copies—customs powers** There are two independent regimes under which a copyright owner may seek to prevent the importation of infringing copies. The most commonly used is that provided for by EU legislation. It applies to goods suspected of infringing intellectual property rights including copyright but not to goods of a non-commercial nature contained in travellers' personal luggage, goods manufactured with the consent of the right holder or overruns.[277] The rightholder may apply to the customs authorities for a "decision" pursuant to which they will detain goods which are the subject matter of the decision. The authorities can also detain goods on their own initiative. If the goods are detained, then unless the rightholder and the declarant or holder of the goods consent (or are deemed to have consented) to their destruction the copyright owner must commence court proceedings failing which the goods will be released.[278] As well as the EU regime, the Copyright Act provides that the owner of a copyright in a published literary, dramatic, or musical work may give notice to the customs authorities requiring prohibition of the importation of printed copies of the work into the UK for a specified period that shall not exceed five years or extend beyond the period in which the copyright subsists. The owner of the copyright in a sound recording or film may give similar notice by stating that infringing copies are expected to arrive in the UK at a specified time and place. In either case the importation of such copies, except for private and domestic use, then becomes prohibited, and any copies imported in contravention of the prohibition are liable to forfeiture.[279] Unlike the EU regime, this regime applies to goods made outside the EEA under a local licence (providing they are infringing copies[280]) and to overruns, provided in each case that the goods arrive from outside the EEA or arrive from within the EEA but have not been entered for free circulation.[281]

24-58 **Criminal sanctions** Most forms of infringement of copyright, when committed knowingly, are offences which can be tried summarily or on indictment; so are the manufacture or possession of articles specifically designed or adapted for making copies of a particular copyright work.[282] Local weights and measures authorities are

CDPA 1988 ss.22-26 but this is a different point, as there, lack of knowledge avoids infringement altogether. For innocence as a defence to damages see *Nichols Advanced Vehicle Systems Inc v Rees, Oliver* [1979] R.P.C. 127; *Infabrics v Jaytex Shirt Co* [1982] A.C. 1; *Sillitoe v McGraw-Hill Book Company (UK) Ltd* [1983] F.S.R. 545; *Wham-O Manufacturing Co v Lincoln Industries Ltd* [1985] R.P.C. 127 NZCA; *Smith v Greenfield* [1985] F.S.R. 9.

[276] *Byrne v Statist Co* [1914] 1 K.B. 622; *Lane v Associated Newspapers* [1936] 1 K.B. 715. See also *Smythson v Cramp* [1943] Ch. 133 at 139; but cf. [1944] A.C. 329 at 338. If a tradesman fails to make reasonable enquiries to find out whether a work is free of copyright this will not avail him: *Infabrics v Jaytex Shirt Co* [1982] A.C. 1.

[277] See Council Regulation (EC) No. 608/13 art.1(4), (5) and Customs Notice 34.

[278] Council Regulation (EC) No. 608/13 arts 17–23.

[279] CDPA 1988 ss.111–112.

[280] As defined by CDPA 1988 s.27(3).

[281] CDPA 1988, s.111(3A). See Customs Notice 34 para.8.1.

[282] CDPA 1988 s.107. Criminal proceedings are not as widely employed as the civil remedies but the criminal courts treat counterfeiting in particular as a serious offence of dishonesty meriting custodial sentences. See, e.g. *R. v Carter* (1992) 13 Cr. App. R. (S.) 576; [1993] F.S.R. 303; *R. v Evans* [2017] EWCA Crim 139; [2018] 4 W.L.R. 140.

charged with the enforcement of such sanctions within their area.[283] The normal standard of proof for criminal cases applies and the presumptions stipulated for civil cases do not apply.[284] In cases of illegal distribution of infringing articles, an immediate custodial sentence is likely unless the offending is very amateur, minor or short-lived, or there is compelling mitigation or other exceptional circumstances.[285] A court before which criminal proceedings are brought may make an order for delivery up of infringing copies[286] and in connection with such proceedings the civil presumptions do apply.[287] The court may make such an order of its own motion or on the prosecution's application but the person to whom the infringing copy is delivered up must retain it until an order is made, or a decision not to make an order under the Act is taken.[288] Criminal proceedings will not necessarily be stayed pending the outcome of parallel civil proceedings.[289]

3. Moral Rights

The nature of moral rights The concept of moral rights introduced by the Copyright Act 1988 was new in the UK, though it had long existed in the laws of other countries. Some of the rights already existed but were not so named.[290] Moral rights are concerned with protecting the personality and reputation of authors and deal with the following matters: the right to be identified as author or director; the right to object to derogatory treatment of a work; false attribution; and the right to privacy of certain photographs and films. All the rights subsist for the full copyright period save that of false attribution, which subsists until 20 years after a person's death.[291] None of the rights is infringed if the person entitled to it has consented[292] and they may be waived but only by an instrument in writing which may be conditional, subject to revocation and relate to existing or future works.[293] In contrast to the economic rights granted to copyright owners, moral rights are not assignable[294] and all (save false attribution) pass on death by testamentary disposition or with the copyright if no separate disposition is made; failing either of these **24-59**

283 CDPA 1988 s.107A. Private prosecutions are also brought. For the duties of the private prosecutor see *R. (on the application of Haigh) v City of Westminster Magistrates' Court* [2017] EWHC 232 (Admin); [2017] Lloyd's Rep. F.C. 193.

284 CDPA 1988 s.107(6).

285 *R. v Evans* [2017] EWCA Crim 139; [2018] 4 W.L.R. 140 at [22(7)].

286 CDPA 1988 s.108.

287 CDPA 1988 s.107(6).

288 The court may not make an order after the time stipulated in s.113 or if it is unlikely that an order will be made under s.114.

289 *Thames & Hudson Ltd v DACS Ltd* [1995] F.S.R. 153.

290 For example, false attribution of authorship was prohibited by Copyright Act 1956 s.43 and the position of a person commissioning the taking of photographs was already protected at common law. Chapter IV of the CDPA 1988 (ss.77-89) reflects art.6 bis of the Berne Convention for the Protection of Literary and Artistic Works (1886) (as revised). For more in-depth discussions of moral rights, see the standard texts; Ricketson and Ginsburg, *International Copyright and Neighbouring Rights, The Berne Convention and Beyond*, 2nd edn (Oxford: Oxford University Press, 2006); Adeney, *The Moral Rights of Authors and Performers—An International and Comparative Analysis* (Oxford: Oxford University Press, 2006); and Davies and Garnett, *Moral Rights*, 2nd edn (Sweet and Maxwell, 2016).

291 CDPA 1988 s.86.

292 CDPA 1988 s.87(1).

293 CDPA 1988 s.87(2), (3), (4).

294 CDPA 1988 s.94. Thus, if the copyright owner sells the copyright in the work, he will retain his moral rights.

things, they are exercisable by the deceased's personal representatives.[295] An infringement of a moral right is actionable as a breach of statutory duty owed to the person entitled to the right without proof of damage.[296] The remedies available are much the same as those available for copyright infringement.

24-60 **Right to be identified as author or director** The author of a copyright literary, dramatic, musical or artistic work, and the director of a copyright film has the right to be identified as such[297] in a manner appropriate to the kind of work in question[298] and in a sufficiently clear way.[299] If the author or director uses a pseudonym or some other form of identification, that is to be used.[300] In respect of works of joint authorship or directorship, each author or director has the right.[301] The right applies in respect of the whole or any substantial part of the work.[302] However, the right is only infringed if it has been asserted either generally or in relation to any specified act or description of acts by the terms of an assignment of the copyright in the work or by an instrument in writing signed by the author or director,[303] and the persons concerned are bound by the right, for instance by having notice of the assertion.[304] In an infringement action, any delay in asserting the right is to be taken into account.[305]

24-61 The right is subject to exceptions.[306] It does not apply to: a computer program; the design of a typeface; any computer-generated work; anything done by a copyright owner who acquired it as employer of the author or director[307]; in certain circumstances where the copyright in the work would not be infringed[308]; in relation to any work made for the purpose of reporting current events; in relation to publication in a periodical or a collective work of reference or a work made for the purpose of such a publication or made available with the consent of the author for the purpose of such a publication; nor to works subject to Crown or parliamentary copyright or to copyright vested in an international organisation unless the author or director has previously been identified as such in published copies of work.

24-62 **Right to object to derogatory treatment of work** The author of a copyright literary, dramatic, musical or artistic work, and the director of a copyright film has the

295 CDPA 1988 s.95.
296 CDPA 1988 s.103(1); and see *Clark v Associated Newspapers Ltd* [1998] 1 All E.R. 959.
297 CDPA 1988 s.77(1).
298 CDPA 1988 s.77(2)–(6).
299 CDPA 1988 s.77(7). The identification must in each case be not only clear but reasonably prominent.
300 CDPA 1988 s.77(8).
301 CDPA 1988 s.88(1), (3), (5).
302 CDPA 1988 s.89(1). Note that under s.89(1) the right to be identified as author and director and the right to privacy of certain photographs and films apply in relation to the whole or *any substantial part* of a work, whereas the right to object to derogatory treatment of a work and false attribution apply in relation to the whole or *any part* of a work [emphasis added].
303 CDPA 1988 s.78(1), (2).
304 CDPA 1988 s.78(3).
305 CDPA 1988 s.78(5).
306 CDPA 1988 s.79.
307 CDPA 1988 under s.11(2) or s.9(2)(a).
308 CDPA 1988 s.79(4), (4A), i.e. fair dealing with a sound recording, film or broadcast for the purposes of reporting current events (s.30), incidental inclusion (s.31), use in examination questions, use for the purposes of parliamentary or judicial proceedings, Royal Commissions and statutory inquiries (ss.45, 46), use of design documents and models (s.51), or use on the assumption of the expiry of the copyright in an anonymous or pseudonymous work (s.57).

right not to have his work subjected to derogatory treatment[309] consisting of an addition, deletion, alteration or adaptation which amounts to distortion or mutilation of the work or is otherwise prejudicial to the honour or reputation of the author or director.[310] The right is infringed by anybody who commits the kind of acts in respect of a derogatory treatment of the work (other than copying) which would normally infringe copyright in the work, if done without consent.[311] Where the infringement arises in respect of possessing or dealing with an article in the course of business, the moral right is only infringed where the person concerned knows or has reason to believe it is an infringing article.[312] The right extends to parts of a work if they are attributed to, or likely to be regarded as the work of, the author or director,[313] and to the whole or any part of the work.[314] There is a special provision for buildings; if the author of such a work is identified on it and it is subject to derogatory treatment he only has the right to have the identification removed.[315]

Exceptions There are a number of exceptions. The right does not apply to[316]: computer programs or any computer-generated work; works made for the purpose of reporting current events; publication in a periodical or collective work for reference or work made for the purposes of such publication or made available with the consent of the author for the purposes of such a publication, nor to the subsequent exploitation of such a work if not modified; anonymous or pseudonymous works where the copyright is assumed to have expired[317]; anything done for the purpose of avoiding the commission of an offence or complying with a statutory duty; and, in the case of the BBC, avoiding the broadcasting of indecent or offensive matter or matter likely to encourage crime or disorder. The two latter exceptions are subject to the proviso that there has to be a sufficient disclaimer if the author or director is identified. Where copyright in a work vests in an author's or director's employer,[318] or is the subject of Crown or parliamentary copyright, or where the copyright vests in an international organisation,[319] the right does not apply to anything done by or with the authority of the copyright owner unless the author has been identified; and where in such a case the right does apply, it is not infringed if there is a sufficient disclaimer.[320] 24-63

False attribution of authorship A person has the right not to have a work falsely 24-64

---

309 The following are excluded from "treatment": translation of a literary or dramatic work or an arrangement or transposition of a musical work involving no more than a change in key or register: CDPA 1988 s.80(2)(a). But such "treatments" may infringe copyright. As to what may constitute derogatory treatment, see: *Morrison Leahy Music Ltd v Lightbond Ltd* [1993] E.M.L.R. 144. For examples from other jurisdictions see Adeney, *The Moral Rights of Authors and Performers—An International and Comparative Analysis* (Oxford: OUP, 2006); Davies and Garnett, *Moral Rights*, 2nd edn (London: Sweet & Maxwell, 2016).

310 CDPA 1988 s.80(1), (2).

311 These acts are set out in full, CDPA 1988 s.80(3), (4) and (6), s.83.

312 CDPA 1988 s.83.

313 CDPA 1988 s.80(7).

314 CDPA 1988 s.89(2).

315 CDPA 1988 s.80(5).

316 CDPA 1988 s.81.

317 CDPA 1988 s.57.

318 CDPA 1988 under s.11(2) or 9(2)(a).

319 CDPA 1988 s.168.

320 CDPA 1988 s.82.

attributed to him as author or director.[321] The right applies in relation to the whole or any part of a work.[322] As with the rights previously discussed, this right is generally infringed by anyone who commits the kind of acts (other than copying) in respect of a falsely attributed work which would normally infringe copyright if done without consent, but there is again a defence of innocence available to those dealing with falsely attributed works in the course of business. It also applies where a literary, dramatic or musical work is falsely represented as being an adaptation of the work of a person or where a copy of an artistic work is falsely represented as having been made by the artist.

24-65 **Right to privacy in certain photographs and films** A person who for private and domestic purposes commissions the taking of a photograph or the making of a film has the right not to have copies issued to the public, or the work publicly exhibited or communicated to the public.[323] Where a work is jointly commissioned, a right exists for each person commissioning it.[324] The right applies in relation to the whole or any substantial part of a work.[325] This right is not, however, infringed by any of the following uses which would not infringe copyright in the work: the incidental inclusion in an artistic work, film or broadcast; use for the purposes of parliamentary or judicial proceedings, Royal Commissions or statutory inquiries; acts done with statutory authority; and acts done in relation to anonymous or pseudonymous works on the presumed expiry of copyright.[326]

4. Collective Management, Control of Licensing and Competition

24-66 **Collective management of copyright** Collective management of copyright has long been a feature of the media and entertainment market. Right holders (e.g. record companies) authorise collective management organisations (CMOs) to grant so-called "blanket" licences to users (e.g. night club operators). In general this has obvious benefits for both rightholder and user.[327] In some instances, the Copyright Act 1988 itself provides for compulsory collective management of aspects of copyright and rights in performances or encourages such management by providing for a permitted act to be displaced if collective licences are available. In 2014, regulations were introduced to permit the Comptroller of Patents to grant licences for the use of so-called orphan works[328] and to authorise licensing bodies to oper-

[321] CDPA 1988 s.84, or as a joint author or director: s.88(4), (5). In deciding whether the work in question contained a false attribution, the court must determine what was the single meaning conveyed by it to the notional reasonable reader: see *Clark v Associated Newspapers Ltd* [1998] 1 W.L.R. 1558 (action in respect of parody diaries succeeded where the claimant was well known as a diarist). See also *Moore v News of the World* [1972] 1 Q.B. 441 (decided under Copyright Act 1956); *Noah v Shuba* [1991] F.S.R. 14.

[322] CDPA 1988 s.89(2).

[323] CPDA 1988 s.85(1)

[324] CDPA 1988 s.88(6).

[325] CDPA 1988 s.89(1).

[326] CDPA 1988 s.85(2).

[327] At present more than twelve CMOs representing various right owners operate in the UK. See the standard copyright texts. They include the Performing Right Society (controlling musical works) and Phonographic Performance Limited (controlling sound recordings), who grant licences through a joint venture PPL PRS Ltd.

[328] The Copyright and Rights in Performances (Licensing of Orphan Works) Regulations 2014 (SI 2014/2863). A "work" is defined as an orphan work where the right owner or right owners cannot be identi-

ate extended collective licensing schemes in respect of works the copyright in which is not owned by the body or person on whose behalf the licensing body acts.[329]

Regulation of CMOs CMOs are often in a de facto monopoly position and accordingly it has been considered necessary to regulate them. Until relatively recently, CMOs in the UK were self-governing, subject to oversight by the Copyright Tribunal.[330] In 2013, the Government amended the Copyright Act so as to enable it to intervene if a collecting society's self-regulatory code of practice did not comply with the minimum standards laid down in regulations and, where a collecting society had not adopted a compliant code of practice, the Secretary of State might direct it to do so.[331] Regulations were made in 2014.[332] However, in 2014, the EU adopted a Directive on collective management.[333] Its aim is to improve the standards of governance and transparency of collecting societies and to facilitate multi-territorial licensing by such societies of author's rights in musical works for the provision of online services. The Directive was implemented in the UK by the Collective Management of Copyright (EU Directive) Regulations 2016,[334] which revoked the 2014 regulations on the grounds that they had been superseded. 24-67

Copyright Tribunal—control of licensing and competition The Copyright Tribunal[335] is a statutory tribunal consisting of a legally qualified chairman and two deputy chairmen appointed by the Lord Chancellor and up to eight ordinary members appointed by the Secretary of State. Its principal role is to exercise competition law constraints on certain types of copyright licensing in the media and entertainment industries,[336] and persons requiring licences under those rights, but it extends to licensing schemes for the rental of films or computer programs; reprographic copying; recordings made for educational purposes; licences relating to sound recordings, films or broadcasts, which include any entertainment or other event; payments in respect of retransmission; applications to settle royalties payable in respect of the rental of sound recordings, films and computer programs; applications for settling licences of right; and other minor rights.[337] References to the Tribunal are mainly of three sorts: those concerned with the reasonableness or otherwise of licence schemes maintained by the licensing bodies; claims for a licence by persons refused licences under a scheme; and claims for licences, or for 24-68

fied or located. Take up so far has been limited. Libraries, museums and similar bodies can benefit from the EU orphan works scheme, at least until the end of 2020: CDPA 1988 Sch.ZA1.

329 The Copyright and Rights in Performances (Extended Collective Licensing) Regulations 2014 (SI 2014/2588). At the time of writing there has been no take up.

330 See para.24-68.

331 CDPA 1988 Sch.A1, introduced by the Enterprise and Regulatory Reform Act 2013 Sch.22(1) para.1, with effect from 25 April 2013.

332 Copyright (Regulation of Relevant Licensing Bodies) Regulations 2012 (SI 2014/898).

333 Directive 2014/26/EU.

334 SI 2016/221.

335 CDPA 1988 s.145.

336 CPDA 1988 ss.145–146 and s.152 (on appeals from the tribunal). See the standard copyright texts for further details.

337 CPDA 1988 ss.130, 131, 132, 133, 134, 135A–135H, 142, 144, 144A and 149. The Broadcasting Act 1990 expanded the jurisdiction of the Copyright Tribunal to settle terms of payment for the right to reproduce programme listing information: see *News Group Newspapers Ltd v Independent Television Publications Ltd* [1993] R.P.C. 178. The Tribunal has the power to rule on the terms on which acts restricted by non-UK copyrights are licensed if the licensing scheme treats such acts as commercially indivisible from acts restricted by UK copyrights: *British Broadcasting Corp v Sky UK Ltd* [2018] EWHC 2931 (Ch); [2019] F.S.R. 12 at [105]–[115].

more favourable licences, by persons outside any existing scheme.[338] Participation in a licensing scheme avoids infringement.[339] The Tribunal has determined numerous issues in relation to licensing schemes.[340] An appeal from the Tribunal lies to the High Court but only on a point of law.[341]

24-69 **Competition law** Refusals to grant licences under a copyright (or indeed any of the rights considered in this chapter) can, in very special circumstances, be contrary to competition law, especially applying art.102 of the Treaty on the Functioning of the European Union (TFEU) or the Competition Act 1998.[342] Agreements between right holders and other practices may be prohibited by art.101 TFEU or under the Competition Act 1998. Conduct by CMOs may engage art.102.[343] Readers are referred to specialist texts for details.[344]

5. Rights in Performances[345]

24-70 **Rights in performances** With respect to performances a number of rights are conferred on performers and on persons having recording rights.[346] A performer's[347] consent[348] is required for the exploitation of his or her performances. A person having recording rights in relation to a performance has rights in relation to recordings made without his or her consent or that of the performer. These rights are contained in Pt II of the Copyright, Designs and Patents Act 1988, which also creates offences in relation to dealing with or using illicit recordings and certain other related acts.[349] "Performance" means a dramatic performance (which includes dance and mime), a musical performance, a reading or recitation of a literary work, or a performance of a variety act or any similar presentation, which is, or so far as it is,

---

338 The Copyright Tribunal has jurisdiction in other special cases: e.g. educational use (CDPA 1988 s.139).

339 CDPA 1988 ss.123(2), (5), 128(1) and 136.

340 See its website *https://www.gov.uk/government/publications/copyright-tribunal-decisions-and-orders* [Accessed 29 March 2020].

341 CDPA 1988 s.152.

342 See *Volvo v Veng* [1989] 4 C.M.L.R. 122; *CIRCA v Renault* [1990] 4 C.M.L.R. 265; *RTE v EC Commission* [1995] I-E.C.R. 743; *Chiron Corp v Murex Diagnostics Ltd (No.2)* [1994] F.S.R. 187; *IMS Health GmbH v NDC Health GmbH & Co KG* [2004] C.M.L.R. 28, CJEU.

343 See *Autortiesibu un Komunicesanas Konsultaciju Agentura-Latvijas Autoru Apvieniba v Konkurences Padome* (C-177/16) EU:C:2017:689; [2018] E.C.D.R. 11 (alleged abusive pricing).

344 See the standard copyright texts.

345 See Arnold, *Performers' Rights*, 5th edn (London: Sweet & Maxwell, 2015).

346 CDPA 1988 Pt II s.180. This area of the law has been substantially amended since the adoption of the CDPA 1988, first by the Copyright and Related Rights Regulations 2003 (SI 2003/2498), and subsequently by the Performances (Moral Rights etc) Regulations 2006 (SI 2006/18).

347 Either the performer or the performance has to be "qualified" (CDPA 1988 s.181), which will be the case if the performer is a qualifying individual (i.e. a citizen, subject or resident of a qualifying country) or the performance takes place in a qualifying country. Qualifying countries are: the UK; the other EEA states; the Channel Islands; the Isle of Man; Gibraltar; any country which is a party to the Rome Convention on Performers, Producers of Phonograms and Broadcasting Organisations (1961); or a country designated as having reciprocal protection under the Copyright and Performances (Application to Other Countries) Order 2016 (SI 2016/1219) (CDPA 1988 ss.206 and 208). SI 2016/1219 also restricts the scope of UK protection in respect of performances qualifying by reference to other countries where protection is restricted.

348 For "consent" see CDPA 1988 s.193.

349 CDPA 1988 s.198.

a live performance given by one or more individuals.[350] A recording, in relation to a performance, means a film or sound recording made directly from the live performance, made from a broadcast of the performance, or made, directly or indirectly, from another recording of the performance.[351] There is an extensive list of permitted acts which do not infringe the rights of performers or the recording rights in the performance; these broadly correspond to those excepted from the infringement of copyright.[352] The rights conferred by Pt II of the Act are independent of any copyright in, or moral rights relating to, any work performed or any film or sound recording of, or broadcast including the performance.[353]

Performers' rights Performers' rights are infringed by a person who, without consent,[354] makes a recording of the whole or of a substantial part of a performance directly from the live performance, broadcasts such a performance live, or makes a recording of it directly from a broadcast of the live performance.[355] A performer's rights are also infringed by a person who, without consent, makes a copy of a recording of the whole or any substantial part of a qualifying performance; this includes making a copy which is transient or is incidental to some other use of the original recording. In such a case, it is immaterial whether the copy is made directly or indirectly. This right to authorise or prohibit the making of such copies is referred to as "the reproduction right".[356] The performer also has the right to authorise or prohibit the issuing to the public of copies of a recording of the whole or any substantial part of a qualifying performance. This right is referred to as "the distribution right".[357] In addition, performers have the right to authorise or prohibit the following: the rental or lending of copies to the public (the rental right)[358]; and the making available to the public of a recording of a performance by electronic transmission in such a way that members of the public may access the recording from a place and at a time individually chosen by them (the making available right).[359] Performers also have a right to receive equitable remuneration from the owner of the copyright in the sound recording for the exploitation of sound recordings which are played in public or communicated to the public. This right may not be assigned by the performer except to a collecting society for the purpose of enabling it to enforce the right on his or her behalf.[360] Finally, a performer's rights are also infringed by a person who, without his or her consent, makes use of a recording made without consent by means of showing or playing it in public or communicating it to the public, imports it (otherwise than for private and domestic 24-71

[350] For a discussion about performances involving animals, see *Heythrop Zoological Gardens Ltd v Captive Animals Protection Society* [2016] EWHC 1370 (Ch); [2017] F.S.R. 10.

[351] CPDA 1988 s.180(2).

[352] CDPA 1988 s.189 and Sch.2.

[353] CPDA 1988 s.180(4).

[354] As to consent, see *Stansfield v Sovereign Music Ltd* [1994] E.M.L.R. 224; *Mad Hat Music Ltd v Pulse 8 Records Ltd* [1993] E.M.L.R. 172; *Bassey v Icon Entertainment Plc* [1995] E.M.L.R. 596; *Henderson v All Around the World Recordings Ltd* [2013] EWPCC 7.

[355] CDPA 1988 s.182(1).

[356] CDPA 1988 s.182A.

[357] CDPA 1988 s.182B. Note that "the issue to the public of copies of a recording" means the act of putting into circulation in the EEA copies not previously put into circulation by or with the consent of the performer or putting such copies into circulation outside the EEA.

[358] CDPA 1988 s.182C.

[359] CDPA 1988 s.182CA.

[360] CDPA 1988 s.182D.

use)[361] or, in the course of business possesses, sells or lets for hire, offers or exposes for sale or hire, or distributes an illicit recording[362] of a qualifying performance.[363] The rights subsist for a minimum of 50 years from the end of the calendar year in which the performance takes place. If during that period of 50 years, a sound recording of the performance is released, they subsist for 70 years from the end of the calendar year in which the recording is released. If during that period of 50 years a recording other than a sound recording of the performance is released, the rights subsist for 50 years from the end of the calendar year in which the recording is released.[364]

24-72 **Performers' property rights and non-property rights** The performer's reproduction right, distribution right, rental and lending right and making available rights are known as performers' property rights.[365] These rights are transmissible by assignment, by testamentary disposition or by operation of law, as personal or moveable property.[366] The usual remedies for infringement are available, with special provisions as to delivery up or disposal of illicit recordings.[367] Performers' property rights are treated similarly to copyright.[368] The other rights referred to in this section (other than performers' moral rights)[369] are known as performers' "non-property rights" and are not assignable or transmissible except on death.[370] An infringement of a performer's non-property rights is actionable by the person entitled to the right as a breach of statutory duty.[371]

24-73 **Recording rights** A person having the benefit of an exclusive recording contract[372] in relation to a performance has rights with regard to film or sound recordings made without his consent[373] or that of the performer, whether such recordings are made directly from the live performance, from a broadcast of the performance, or directly or indirectly from another recording.[374] This right is intended to protect recording companies against bootlegging. The rights are infringed by anyone who makes a recording of the whole or any substantial part of

---

[361] CDPA 1988 s.183.

[362] For these purposes, an "illicit recording" is defined (broadly speaking) as a recording of the whole or any substantial part of a performance made otherwise than for private purposes without the performer's consent: CDPA 1988 s.197(2).

[363] CDPA 1988 s.184.

[364] CDPA 1988 s.191. The word "released" is defined in subs.(3) and special provision is made in subss.(4) and (5) in respect of the duration of rights where the performer is not a national of an EEA state.

[365] CDPA 1988 s.191A.

[366] CDPA 1988 s.191B.

[367] CDPA 1988 ss.194, 195, 197, 203, 204 and 205. A right of seizure is provided, similar to that available in respect of articles that infringe copyright: CDPA 1988 ss.196 and 197.

[368] CDPA 1988 ss.191A-191M. cf. non-property rights: ss.192A–192B.

[369] See para.24-75.

[370] CDPA 1988 s.192A. Pursuant to s.192A(2), on the death of a person entitled to such a right, it passes to such person as he or she may by testamentary disposition specifically direct; to the extent that there is no direction, the right is exercisable by his or her personal representatives.

[371] CDPA 1988 s.194.

[372] CDPA 1988 s.185. The person with the benefit of the contract must be a qualifying person. If he or she is not, the right vests in any person licensed by that person to make recordings of the performance with a view to their commercial exploitation: s.185(3).

[373] For "consent" see CDPA 1988 s.193.

[374] See the definition of "recording" in CDPA 1988 s.180(2).

the performance,[375] shows or plays it in public, communicates it to the public,[376] imports an illicit recording otherwise than for his private and domestic use or deals with an illicit recording[377] by way of business.[378] The right subsists for the same period as the performer's right.[379] It is not assignable as such, but passes with the benefit of the exclusive recording contract.[380] The remedies for infringement are the same as for infringement of rights in performances.

Criminal sanctions The making without consent and certain dealings without consent in illicit recordings are criminal offences.[381] 24-74

Performers' moral rights Performers have the following moral rights in relation to qualifying performances: the right to be identified as a performer,[382] subject to the requirement that the right has been asserted,[383] and the right to object to derogatory treatment of a performance.[384] The right to be identified arises when a qualifying performance is given in public or broadcast live or when a sound recording of such a performance is communicated or issued to the public. The right does not apply where it is not reasonably practicable to identify the performer or where the performance has been given for the purpose of reporting current events or advertising goods or services. News reporting, the incidental inclusion of a performance or a recording etc are also permitted.[385] There will be a derogatory treatment if a performance is broadcast live or communicated to the public by means of a sound recording, with any distortion, mutilation or other modification that is prejudicial to the reputation of the performer. This right does not apply with respect to modifications made to a performance which are consistent with normal editorial or production practice.[386] This right is also infringed by possessing or dealing with an infringing article.[387] A performer's moral rights subsist so long as that performer's other rights subsist, including such rights when vested in a successor of the performer.[388] Moral rights are not assignable[389] but they may be waived[390] and they are transmissible by testamentary disposition.[391] An infringement of a moral 24-75

---

375 CDPA 1988 s.186.

376 CDPA 1988 s.187.

377 For these purposes, an "illicit recording" is defined (broadly speaking) as a recording of the whole or any substantial part of a performance subject to the exclusive recording contract made otherwise than for private purposes without the consent of the person with recording rights or of the performer: CDPA 1988, s.197(3).

378 CDPA 1988 s.188(1). See the list of dealings in subs.(1)(a).

379 CDPA 1988 s.191.

380 CDPA 1988 s.192B.

381 CDPA 1988 s.198. See as to remedies, requirements for the offence and related matters: ss.199–202.

382 CDPA 1988 s.205C.

383 CDPA 1988 s.205D. The right is normally asserted in writing by or on behalf of the performer. In an action for infringement the court shall, in considering remedies, take into account any delay in asserting the right.

384 CDPA 1988 s.205F.

385 CDPA 1988 s.205E.

386 CDPA 1988 s.205G.

387 CDPA 1988 s.205H.

388 CDPA 1988 s.205I.

389 CDPA 1988 s.205L.

390 CDPA 1988 s.205J.

391 CDPA 1988 s.205M. In the absence of a testamentary disposition they pass to any person to whom

right is actionable as a breach of statutory duty owed to the person entitled to the right.[392]

6. Unregistered Designs[393]

(a) Overview

24-76 **Forms of design protection—UK and EU** Four types of rights in respect of designs are available in the UK: UK unregistered design right, unregistered Community designs, UK registered designs and registered Community designs. UK unregistered design right is a "home grown" right which is provided for in Pt III of the Copyright Act 1988, where it is called "design right". It arises without the need for registration and can be used to prevent the copying of designs for the shape or configuration of articles.[394] It lasts for 15 years from the end of the year in which the design was recorded or an article was first made to the design. If, however, articles were first marketed within five years from the end of that year, it lasts for ten years from the end of the year in which they were first marketed.[395] The other three rights are much broader in scope, protecting the design of "the appearance of the whole or part of a product resulting from the features of, in particular, the lines, contours, colours, shape, texture or materials of the product or its ornamentation". An unregistered Community design applies throughout the EU and can be relied on to prevent copying during the three years from the date when the design was first made available to the public within the EU.[396] The UK and EU registered rights apply throughout the UK and the EU respectively and provide a monopoly right for up to 25 years provided registration is renewed.[397]

(b) UK unregistered design right

24-77 **Background** Before August 1989, when the Copyright Act 1988 came into force, it was an infringement of the copyright in engineering and similar drawings to reproduce them either directly or more commonly by copying an article made from them. Industrial designs were thus protected by the law of copyright. This gave an extensive and lengthy right, which was widely considered to be too broad. The Copyright Act 1988 s.51 removed that copyright protection by providing that it is not an infringement of any copyright in a design document[398] or model recording

---

the performer's property rights in the performance pass. Otherwise the rights are exercisable by the personal representatives.

392 CDPA 1988 s.205N.

393 See: *Russell-Clarke and Howe on Industrial Designs*, 9th edn (2016); Stone, *European Union Design Law*, 2nd edn (2016); *Copinger and Skone James on Copyright*, 17th edn (2016), Ch.13.

394 CDPA 1988 s.213(2).

395 CDPA 1988 s.216.

396 Council Regulation 6/2002 on Community designs, art.11(1). In *Beverly Hills Teddy Bear Company v PMS International Group Plc* [2019] EWHC 2419 (IPEC); [2020] F.S.R. 11 the Court referred to the CJEU the question whether for these purposes the event of first making available must take place within the geographical confines of the Community, or whether it was sufficient that the event, wherever it took place, was such that, in the normal course of business, the event could reasonably have become known to the circles specialised in the sector concerned, operating within the Community.

397 Registered Designs Act 1949 s.8. Council Regulation 6/2002 on Community designs art.12.

398 "Design document" means any record of a design, whether in the form of a drawing, a written

or embodying a design[399] for anything other than an artistic work or a typeface to make an article to the design or to copy an article made to the design.[400] It is also not an infringement of copyright to deal in articles which do not themselves infringe by reason of this exception.[401] This exception does not extend to the copying of the design documents themselves; nor does it cover typefaces, surface decoration or artistic works.[402] It remains an infringement of copyright to copy them. Further, because the exception does not exclude, for example, drawings *for* artistic works, it continues to be an infringement of copyright to reproduce the drawing for a sculpture by making a sculpture to that design—because the sculpture is itself an artistic work. In contrast, it is not an infringement of the copyright in a drawing for a functional object to make an object in the form depicted in the drawing, because the object itself is not an artistic work. In view of a CJEU decision from 2011, the status of s.51 is a matter of debate.[403] Section 52 of the Copyright Act 1988 significantly restricted the term of copyright protection afforded to artistic works that had been industrially exploited by or with the licence of the copyright owner by making copies of the work by an industrial process and then marketing such copies in the UK or elsewhere. However, this has now been repealed.[404]

UK unregistered design right This right is created by Copyright Act 1988 s.213, which provides as follows: **24-78**

"(1) Design right is a property right which subsists in accordance with this Part in an original design.

(2) In this Part design means the design of[405] the shape or configuration (whether internal or external) of the whole or part of an article.

(3) Design right does not subsist in—

---

description, a photograph, data stored in a computer or otherwise: CDPA 1988 s.51(3).

399 "Design" means the design of the shape or configuration (whether internal or external) of the whole or part of an article, other than surface decoration: CDPA 1988 s.51(3).

400 CDPA 1988 s.51(1). It is an exception of considerable importance and (arguably) leaves a gap in protection for "flat" designs such as certain designs for articles of clothing: see *Lambretta Clothing Co Ltd v Teddy Smith (UK) Ltd* [2004] EWCA Civ 886; [2005] R.P.C. 6. It may increase the importance of reliance on Community designs. In *Lucasfilm Ltd v Ainsworth* [2011] UKSC 39; [2012] 1 A.C. 208 the Supreme Court upheld the Court of Appeal's decision ([2009] EWCA Civ 1328; [2010] Ch. 503) that the helmets and armour forming part of the "Storm Trooper" costumes in the *Star Wars* films were not sculptures and hence did not qualify as artistic works which would be excluded from the operation of s.51 (the first instance decision that they were not works of artistic craftsmanship was not appealed).

401 CDPA 1988 s.51(2).

402 See *Metix (UK) Ltd v GH Maughan (Plastics) Ltd* [1997] F.S.R. 718.

403 The decision is *Flos SpA v Semeraro Casa e Famiglia SpA* (C-168/09) EU:C:2011:29; [2011] E.C.D.R. 8; [2011] R.P.C. 10, referring to the requirement for "cumulation" of copyright and Community designs stipulated for by art.17 of Council Directive 98/71/EC (the Designs Directive) and art.96(2) of Council Regulation 6/2002 (which are in identical terms). See the standard texts.

404 With effect from 28 July 2016 with a transitional period until 28 January 2017: Enterprise and Regulatory Reform Act 2013 (Commencement No.10 and Saving Provisions) Order 2016 (SI 2016/593). See the Government's Guidance at: *https://www.gov.uk/government/uploads/system/uploads/attachment_data/file/585718/160408_guidance_s52_final_web_accessible.pdf* [Accessed 29 March 2020].

405 Prior to 1 October 2014 the words "any aspect of" appeared between "the design of" and "the shape or configuration". The change, which applies to acts of infringement which are alleged to have been committed on or after 1 October 2014, precludes claims in respect of disembodied features, arbitrarily selected, which are not, in design terms, parts of the design: *Neptune (Europe) Ltd v Devol Kitchens Ltd* [2017] EWHC 2172 (Pat); [2017] E.C.D.R. 25 at [33], [42]. See also *DKH Retail Ltd*

(a) a method or principle of construction,
(b) features of shape or configuration of an article which—
(i) enable the article to be connected to, or placed in, around or against, another article so that either article may perform its function, or
(ii) are dependent upon the appearance of another article of which the article is intended by the designer to form an integral part, or
(c) surface decoration.

(4) A design is not 'original' for purposes of this Part if it is commonplace in a qualifying country[406] in the design field in question at the time of its creation; and 'qualifying country' has the meaning given in s.217(3).

(5) Design right subsists in a design only if the design qualifies for design right protection by reference to—
(a) the designer or the person by whom the design was commissioned or the designer employed (see sections 218 and 219), or
(b) the person by whom and country in which articles made to the design were first marketed (see section 220),

or in accordance with any Order under section 221 (power to make further provision with respect to qualification)."

24-79 **Meaning of "design"; exclusions** The design is only capable of being protected if it is the design of the shape or configuration of an article or a part of an article. A "part" of an article is an actual, but not abstract part which can be identified as such and which is not a trivial feature.[407] The "configuration" of an article includes the relative arrangement of its parts or elements.[408] Design right does not subsist in "a method or principle of construction", that is a process or operation by which a shape is produced, as opposed to the shape itself. This is to avoid giving the owner rights in a method or principle of construction as opposed to one particular individual and specific appearance. If it is possible to get several different appearances, which all embody the general features claimed, then those features are too general and amount to a method or principle of construction.[409] The so-called "must fit" exception in s.213(2)(a) is widely drafted to exclude all features satisfying the interface criteria, even if they have another purpose or are attractive.[410] The purpose of subs.(b)(i) is to prevent there being a right in, for example, a particular configuration of plug required to fit a socket or moulding required to fit into a groove. The so-called "must match" exclusion in subs.(b)(ii) would, for example, cover a decorative body part for a car. A car door panel would appear to fall within both

---

v H. Young (Operations) Ltd [2014] EWHC 4034 (IPEC); [2015] F.S.R. 21 at [10]; *Whitby Specialist Vehicles Ltd v Yorkshire Specialist Vehicles Ltd* [2014] EWHC 4242 (Pat); [2015] E.C.D.R. 11 at [41]; *Action Storage Systems Ltd v G-Force Europe.Com Ltd* [2016] EWHC 3151 (IPEC); [2017] F.S.R. 18 at [12]–[16].

406 The words "in a qualifying country" were added with effect from 1 August 2014 so as to ensure that the area of prior art under consideration corresponded with the catchment area for qualification. Qualification is dealt with below, para.24-81.

407 *Shnuggle Ltd v Munchkin Inc.* [2019] EWHC 3149 (IPEC); [2020] F.S.R. 22 at [92].

408 This is settled law at first instance but the question whether "configuration" adds anything to "shape" is open for argument in the Court of Appeal: *CliniSupplies Ltd v Park* [2012] EWHC 3453 (Ch); [2013] F.S.R. 27 at [53].

409 *Landor & Hawa International Ltd v Azure Designs Ltd* [2006] EWCA Civ 1285; [2007] F.S.R. 9 at [13].

410 See *Dyson Ltd v Qualtex (UK) Ltd* [2004] EWHC 2981 (Ch); [2005] R.P.C. 19.

exclusions.[411] Surface decoration is excluded from design right protection as is the colouring of articles.[412]

Meaning of "original", "commonplace" It is unclear whether a design is original if it is simply not copied (the old copyright test) or whether there is also a need for creativity (in line with CJEU case law on copyright).[413] The better view would appear to be that the EU copyright test is irrelevant and that a design is original if it is not copied and not commonplace. Even simple designs can qualify for protection but the simpler they are the more likely that they will be commonplace.[414] As to what is commonplace, the law and practice has been usefully summarised as follows[415] (citations omitted): **24-80**

"(1) A defendant alleging that a design is commonplace should plead the significant features of the design as he contends them to be, the prior art relied on in which those features are said to be found and the date from which each cited item of prior art was available to designers in the relevant design field.

(2) Prior art which renders a design commonplace will not be obscure. The evidential burden rests on the defendant to show that it is not.

(3) A design will be commonplace if it is shown to have been current in the thinking of designers in the field in question at the time of creation of the design.[416] Another way of looking at this is that a commonplace design will be one which is trite, trivial, common-or-garden, hackneyed or of the type which would excite no particular attention in those in the relevant design field.[417] A third way of characterising a commonplace design is that it will be ready to hand, not matter that has to be hunted for and found at the last minute.[418]

(4) The design field in question is that with which a notional designer of the article in issue is familiar.[419]

(5) A design made up of features which individually are commonplace is not neces-

---

[411] During the parliamentary debates on the Bill, these were referred to as "must fit" and "must match" provisions. They were said to give statutory effect to the decision of the House of Lords in *British Leyland Motor Corp v Armstrong Patents Co Ltd* [1986] A.C. 577, excluding spare parts from the ambit of copyright protection.

[412] *Lambretta Clothing Co Ltd v Teddy Smith (UK) Ltd* [2004] EWCA Civ 886; [2005] R.P.C. 6. Thus, design right protection was denied to the design comprising the colouring of a track top. Because of the effect of s.51 of the CDPA 1988, it was also not possible to rely on copyright protection to restrain reproductions of the work leading to a potential "gap" in protection.

[413] In *Whitby Specialist Vehicles Ltd v Yorkshire Specialist Vehicles Ltd* [2014] EWHC 4242 (Pat); [2015] E.C.D.R. 11 at [43], Arnold J assumed without deciding that some creativity was required.

[414] *Sales v Stromberg* [2005] EWHC 1624 (Ch); [2006] F.S.R. 7.

[415] By HH Judge Hacon in *Action Storage Systems Ltd v G-Force Europe.Com Ltd* [2016] EWHC 3151 (IPEC); [2017] F.S.R. 18 at [37].

[416] Applying *Lambretta Clothing Co Ltd v Teddy Smith (UK) Ltd* [2004] EWCA Civ 886; [2005] R.P.C. 6 at [56].

[417] This definition comes from *Ocular Sciences Ltd v Aspect Vision Care Ltd* [1997] R.P.C. 289, at p.429, approved in *Farmers Build Ltd v Carier Bulk Materials Handling Ltd* [1999] R.P.C. 13 at pp. 477 and 479. See also *Dyson Ltd v Qualtex (UK) Ltd* [2004] EWHC 2981 (Ch); [2005] R.P.C. 19 where it is noted that commonplace is a "far from easy concept".

[418] Applying *Ultraframe (UK) Ltd v Eurocell Building Plastics Ltd* [2005] EWCA Civ 761; [2005] R.P.C. 36 at [60].

[419] *Lambretta Clothing Co Ltd v Teddy Smith (UK) Ltd* [2004] EWCA Civ 886; [2005] R.P.C. 6 at [45]. In the case of designs created on or before 1 October 2014 it remains unclear whether the relevant design field is confined to that in the UK, or some other limited territory, or whether there is no geographical limit. For designs created after that date the issue is whether the design was "commonplace in a qualifying country in the design field in question", see the amendment to s.213(4) effected by s.1(3)(a) of the Intellectual Property Act 2014, which applies to designs created after 1 October 2014, see s.1(4) and SI 2014/2330. For what is a qualifying country, see para.24-81.

sarily itself commonplace. A new combination of run-of-the-mill features may not be commonplace.[420]

(6) If the designer of the accused article has expended sufficient skill and labour to make his design original (in the copyright sense) over a single piece of commonplace prior art, he is liable also to have succeeded in creating a design that is not rendered commonplace by that prior art."

24-81 **Qualification** A design may qualify for protection if the designer is a qualifying person and did not create it in the course of employment; if the person by whom the designer was employed is a qualifying person; or (if it does not otherwise qualify) if the first marketing was by a qualifying person or took place in the UK, another country to which Pt III of the Act extends[421] or another member state of the EEC.[422] A qualifying person is an individual who is habitually resident in a qualifying country or a body corporate which was formed under the law of a qualifying country or has a substantial place of business in such a country.[423] The following are qualifying countries: the UK, a country to which Pt III extends,[424] another EEC member state; or another country designated as having reciprocal protection.[425] Design right does not subsist in a design unless and until it has been recorded in a design document or an article has been made to the design.[426]

24-82 **First owner and transfer of title** The first owner of the right is the designer unless it is created by an employee in the course of his employment, in which case it belongs to the employer.[427] To be effective, any assignment of design right must be in writing signed by or on behalf of the assignor. Design right may pass under a will or by operation of law.[428] An exclusive licence must be in writing and signed by or on behalf of the design right owner.[429]

24-83 **Design right infringement—remedies** Design right is infringed by any person

[420] *Ocular Sciences Ltd v Aspect Vision Care Ltd* [1997] R.P.C. 289 at p.429, approved by the Court of Appeal in *Farmers Build Ltd v Carier Bulk Materials Handling Ltd* [1999] R.P.C. 13 at p.476 and in *Ultraframe (UK) Ltd v Eurocell Building Plastics Ltd* [2005] EWCA Civ 761; [2005] R.P.C. 36 at [64].

[421] Pt III can be extended under s.255 of the CDPA 1988. At the time of writing it has not been so extended.

[422] CDPA 1988 ss.218–220. Designs created before 1 October 2014 may also qualify for protection if they were commissioned by a qualifying person. See Intellectual Property Act 2014 s.2(3), which provides that the repeal of this provision does not apply to designs created before commencement of that section on 1 October 2014 (see Intellectual Property Act 2014 (Commencement No.3 and Transitional Provisions) Order 2014 (SI 2014/2330)).

[423] CDPA 1988 s.217(2).

[424] Pt III can be extended under s.255 of the CDPA 1988. At the time of writing it has not been so extended.

[425] CDPA 1988 s.217(3). A country may be designated in this way under s.256 of the CDPA 1988. At present 16 countries have been so designated, most of them commonwealth or former commonwealth countries: see Design Right (Reciprocal Protection) (No. 2) Order 1989 (SI 1989/1294). Noteworthy exceptions include the USA, China and Japan.

[426] CDPA 1988 s.213(6).

[427] CDPA 1988 s.215. A similar provision in relation to commissioned designs was repealed with effect from 1 October 2014 but without affecting title to designs created before that date. See Intellectual Property Act 2014 s.2(3), which commenced on 1 October 2014 (see Intellectual Property Act 2014 (Commencement No.3 and Transitional Provisions) Order 2014 (SI 2014/2330).

[428] CDPA 1988 s.222. Prospective ownership may also be assigned: s.223. Where rights subsist simultaneously in a design right and in a registered design, assignment of the latter will generally be held to include the former: s.224.

[429] CDPA 1988 s.225.

who, for commercial purposes and without a licence: makes an article exactly or substantially to that design; makes a design document recording it for the purpose of enabling such articles to be made; or imports into the UK infringing articles, has them in his possession or trades in them, when he knows or has reason to believe that they are infringing articles.[430] There is an exception from liability for private acts, experiments and teaching.[431] It is a requirement of liability for design right infringement that the defendant has copied the claimant's design. However where the defendant's design is sufficiently similar to the claimant's the burden may shift to the defendant to disprove copying.[432] For the latter class of infringement (secondary infringement) there is a defence of innocence.[433] In *Rolawn Ltd v Turfmech Machinery Ltd*, Mann J held that there was no infringement of design right under s.226 where some overall ideas had been copied, but the actual design had not: "what is protected from copying ... is the design, meaning the physical manifestation. It is not some underlying abstraction."[434]

Relief The usual forms of relief can be given together with additional damages in cases of flagrant infringement or where the infringer derives some special benefit,[435] but where an infringer does not know or have reason to believe that design right subsists, the entitlement to damages is removed altogether in cases of primary infringement and is limited to a reasonable royalty in cases of secondary infringement where the articles in question were innocently acquired.[436] It is also possible to apply to the courts for a declaration that a particular product does not infringe.[437] Orders for delivery up may be made, both of infringing articles and of anything which the defendant knows to be specially designed or adapted for making infringing articles.[438] An exclusive licensee has the same rights as the owner (except against him); where both have rights and the other is not a co-claimant he must normally be joined as a defendant.[439] Where copyright and design right subsist **24-84**

---

[430] CDPA 1988 ss.226 and 227. As to the meaning of copying the design so as to produce "articles exactly or substantially to the design", see *C & H Engineering v F Klucznik & Sons Ltd* [1992] F.S.R. 421; *Mark Wilkinson Furniture Ltd v Woodcraft Designs (Radcliffe) Ltd* [1998] F.S.R. 63 (copying surface decoration not an infringement of design right). See also *Red Spider Technology v Omega Completions Technology* [2010] EWHC 59 (Ch). As to the meaning of infringing article see s.228.

[431] CDPA 1988 s.244A.

[432] *A. Fulton & Co Ltd v Grant Barnett & Co Ltd* [2001] R.P.C. 16. In *Albert Packaging Ltd v Nampak Cartons & Healthcare Ltd* [2011] EWPCC 15; [2011] F.S.R. 32 it was held that the similarities between the design and the alleged infringement were due to common derivation from an independent source. For the significance of copying in the context of an application for summary judgment, see *Dahlia Fashion Co Ltd v Broadcast Session Ltd* [2012] EWPCC 23.

[433] CDPA 1988 s.227.

[434] [2008] EWHC 989 (Pat); [2008] E.C.D.R. 13 at [81].

[435] CDPA 1988 s.229. Additional damages were awarded in *Pendle Metalwares Ltd v Walter Page (Safeway's) Ltd* [2014] EWHC 1140 (Ch) to compensate for flagrant infringement which had put the rights-holder to significant expense.

[436] CDPA 1988 s.233. As there is a defence of innocence anyhow in respect of secondary infringement, it is hard to see how the latter protection arises, save where a secondary infringer acquires articles innocently and then goes on trading in them, knowing that they infringe.

[437] See, e.g. *Samsung Electronics (UK) Ltd v Apple Inc* [2012] EWHC 889 (Ch); [2013] F.S.R. 7; and [2012] EWCA Civ 729; [2013] F.S.R. 8.

[438] CDPA 1988 s.230. An order may not be made after six years from the date the infringing article was made unless the claimant was under a disability or in cases of fraud. The court may alternatively make an order for destruction or otherwise as it thinks fit: s.231. A county court has jurisdiction within the financial limits of actions in tort: s.232.

[439] CDPA 1988 ss.234 and 235.

in a work simultaneously it is not an infringement of the design right to do anything which infringes the copyright.[440]

24-85 **Compulsory licences** Licences of right are available in the last five years of the design right term.[441] If the Competition and Markets Authority reports that the conditions of a licence or the refusal to grant licences on reasonable terms operate against the public interest, the powers available are to cancel or modify the offending conditions and to provide for licences of right.[442] Where an infringement action is brought when a licence of right is available and the defendant undertakes to take such a licence, no injunction or order for delivery up will be made and damages will be limited to twice what would have been payable under a licence.[443] A person who has a licence of right may not claim a connection with the design right owner.[444] There are, in addition, wide powers to use design rights for the services of the Crown, which includes the health service.[445]

24-86 **Jurisdiction of the Comptroller and the court** The Comptroller has exclusive jurisdiction over the questions of the subsistence of a design right, its term, and the identity of the person in whom it first vested, save that the court has jurisdiction over these matters on appeal from the Comptroller, where they arise incidentally in infringement proceedings, where both parties agree to bring them before the court, or where the Comptroller gives leave.[446] The Comptroller also has jurisdiction to settle the terms of licences of right.[447] The court has exclusive jurisdiction in disputes over Crown use.[448] Infringement actions are brought in the court, frequently in the Intellectual Property Enterprise Court (IPEC). This may reflect the fact that the IPEC is arguably better suited than the Patents Court (or general Chancery Division) to determine what are often lower-value disputes requiring a straightforward, pragmatic approach.

24-87 **Unjustified threats of legal proceedings** A remedy exists, as with patents and registered designs, where unjustified threats of legal proceedings are made in respect of the alleged infringement of a design right.[449]

(c) Unregistered Community design

24-88 **Scope of protection** An unregistered Community design[450] protects a design for the appearance of a product or part of a product resulting from "the features of, in

---

440 CDPA 1988 s.236.

441 CDPA 1988 s.237. In default of agreement, the terms are settled by the comptroller. The Secretary of State may, by order, exclude certain designs from the operation of s.237(1).

442 CDPA 1988 s.238.

443 CDPA 1988 s.239.

444 CDPA 1988 s.254.

445 CDPA 1988 ss.240–244.

446 CDPA 1988 ss.246 and 251.

447 CDPA 1988 ss.237, 238, 247 and 248. Proceedings may not be brought earlier than one year before the earliest date on which the licence may take effect. An appeal lies to a person appointed under s.27A of the Registered Designs Act 1949: s.249.

448 CDPA 1988 s.252.

449 CDPA 1988 ss.253–253A.

450 See the summary of the law in the Community registered designs context in *Whitby Specialist Vehicles Ltd v Yorkshire Specialist Vehicles Ltd* [2014] EWHC 4242 (Pat); [2015] E.C.D.R. 11 at [20]–[30].

particular, the lines, contours, colours, shape, texture or materials of the product itself and/or its ornamentation".[451] A Community design may not subsist in features of appearance dictated solely by their technical function[452] or which permit the article to be connected to or placed around, in or against another product so that either may perform its function.[453] Protection does not extend to component parts which are not visible during normal use of the product.[454] To qualify for protection, a design must be "new" and have "individual character".[455] The scope of and conditions for protection for registered Community designs are by and large the same (apart from the requirement for registration). Accordingly, registered design cases are referred to in the following paragraphs.

Novelty The test for novelty is whether the design differs "only in immaterial details"[456] from designs made available to the public before the design itself was first made available to the public.[457] A design is made available if it is published, exhibited, used in trade or otherwise disclosed except where these events could not reasonably have become known in the normal course of business to the circles specialised in the sector concerned, operating within the Community.[458] Prior designs for any type of product can be taken into account. However, there is no **24-89**

451 Regulation 6/2002/EC art.3(a).

452 Regulation 6/2002/EC art.8(1). Protection is excluded where the need to fulfil a technical function is the only factor determining the choice of a feature and considerations of another nature, in particular those related to the product's visual aspect, have not played a role: *DOCERAM GmbH v CeramTec GmbH* (C-395/16) EU:C:2018:172; [2018] E.C.D.R. 13 (*Doceram*) at [26]. Protection will be excluded even if other designs fulfilling the same function exist: *Doceram* at [31]. In determining whether the technical function exclusion applies, the court must take account of all relevant objective circumstances which may be indicative of the reasons which dictated the choice of the feature in issue together with information on the use of the product concerned and the existence of alternative designs which fulfil the same technical function. There is no need to base the decision on the perception of an "objective observer": *Doceram* at [35]–[38].

453 Regulation 6/2002/EC art.8(2). See for example *Camatic Pty Ltd v Bluecube Ltd* [2012] E.C.D.R. 12, in which a Community registered design was held invalid under this so-called "must-fit" exception. Designs "serving the purpose of allowing the multiple assembly or connection of mutually interchangeable products within a modular system" are not excepted: art.8(3).

454 Regulation 6/2002/EC art.4(1) and Recital 12; *Groupe Nivelles v OHIM* (T-15/13) EU:T:2015:281; [2016] E.C.D.R. 11 at [37].

455 Regulation 6/2002/EC art.4. In *Beverly Hills Teddy Bear Company v PMS International Group Plc* [2019] EWHC 2419 (IPEC); [2020] F.S.R. 11 the Court referred to the CJEU the question whether the relevant date for assessing novelty was the date when the design came into being pursuant to art.11 of the Regulation or the date on which (within the meaning of art.7(1)) the relevant event of disclosure of the design could have become known to the relevant specialised circles. A design applied to or incorporated in a product which becomes a component part in a complex product is only to be considered new or of individual character if it remains visible during normal use by the end user, and to the extent that the visible parts of that product are new and have individual character. See, e.g. *Kwang Yang Motor Co., Ltd v OHIM* (T-11/08) EU:T:2015:831; [2012] E.C.D.R. 2, General Court.

456 "Immaterial details" means "only minor and trivial in nature, not affecting overall appearance". This is an objective test. The design must be considered as a whole. It will be new if some part of it differs from any earlier design in some material respect, even if some or all of the design features, if considered individually, would not be: *Shnuggle Ltd v Munchkin Inc* [2019] EWHC 3149 (IPEC); [2020] F.S.R. 22 at [26].

457 Regulation 6/2002/EC art.5.

458 art.7(1). Disclosures only made in confidence are ignored (art.7(1)). The question whether the events could reasonably have become known (etc) is one of fact in each case and events occurring outside the Community are not excluded from consideration if they could reasonably have become known etc: *Senz Technologies BV v OHIM* (T-22/13 and 23/13) EU:T:2015:310 [2015] E.C.D.R. 19 at [27].

requirement to prove that the informed user would know the product in which the earlier design is incorporated or to which it is applied.[459]

24-90 **Individual character: general** The test for individual character is whether the overall impression the design produces on the "informed user" differs from the overall impression produced by any design which has been made available to the public before the design for which protection is claimed was itself first made available to the public (as to which see the previous paragraph). For these purposes, it is not relevant to compare the design for which protection is sought with a combination of features taken from a number of earlier designs. The comparison is between the design sought to be protected and one or more earlier designs taken individually.[460] While it is permissible to consider individual similarities and differences, what matters is the overall impression.[461]

24-91 **The "informed user"** This person lies somewhere between the average consumer in trade mark law, who need not have any specific knowledge, and the sectoral expert with detailed technical expertise.[462] He or she is a user of the product in which the design is intended to be incorporated; is particularly observant; has knowledge of the design corpus and of the design features normally included in the designs existing in the sector concerned[463]; is interested in the products concerned and shows a relatively high degree of attention when using them; conducts a direct comparison unless this is impracticable or uncommon; and neither perceives the designs as a whole nor observes minimal differences in detail.[464] The appropriate level of generality is that which would be adopted by the informed user.[465]

24-92 **Relevant factors** In general, what is important is what the design and the prior art look like.[466] Account should be taken of the nature of the product to which the

---

459 *Easy Sanitary Solutions v Groupe Nivelles* (C-361/15 P) EU:C:2017:720; [2018] E.C.D.R. 4 at [104], [134], [135]. *L'Oreal Societe Anonyme v RN Ventures Ltd* [2018] EWHC 173 (Pat); [2018] E.C.D.R. 14 at [152].

460 *Karen Millen Fashions Ltd v Dunnes Stores* (C-345/13) [2016] E.C.D.R. 13; *Whitby Specialist Vehicles Ltd v Yorkshire Specialist Vehicles Ltd* [2014] EWHC 4242 (Pat); [2015] E.C.D.R. 11 at [25]. See also *Pulseon OY v Garmin (Europe) Ltd* [2019] EWCA Civ 138; [2019] E.C.D.R. 8 at [19]–[21].

461 *Samsung Electronics (UK) Ltd v Apple Inc* [2012] EWCA Civ 1339; [2013] E.C.D.R. 2 at [27]–[29]; *Whitby Specialist Vehicles Ltd v Yorkshire Specialist Vehicles Ltd* [2014] EWHC 4242 (Pat); [2015] E.C.D.R. 11 at [30].

462 *PepsiCo, Inc v Grupo Promer Mon Graphic SA* (C-281/10) EU:C:2011:679 [2012] F.S.R. 5 at [53]; *Senz Technologies BV v OHIM* (T-22/13 and 23/13) EU:T:2015:310 [2015] E.C.D.R. 19 at [50]–[51].

463 The informed user's knowledge of the prior art is not apparently comprehensive: see *Whitby Specialist Vehicles Ltd v Yorkshire Specialist Vehicles Ltd* [2014] EWHC 4242 (Pat); [2015] E.C.D.R. 11 at [22]–[23] referring to dicta of the General Court to the effect that the informed user has "some awareness of the state of the prior art" or "a certain degree of knowledge with regard to the features which [earlier] designs would normally include".

464 *Samsung Electronics (UK) Ltd v Apple Inc* [2012] EWHC 1882 (Pat); [2013] E.C.D.R. 1, summarising the EU case law, especially *PepsiCo, Inc v Grupo Promer Mon Graphic SA* (C-281/10) EU:C:2011:679 [2012] F.S.R. 5 at [53]–[59]. This summary was approved on appeal ([2012] EWCA Civ 1339; [2013] F.S.R. 9); and adopted in *Pulseon OY v Garmin (Europe) Ltd* [2019] EWCA Civ 138; [2019] E.C.D.R. 8 at [16].

465 *Rolawn Ltd v Turfmech Machinery Ltd* [2008] EWHC 989 (Pat); [2008] R.P.C. 27.

466 *Procter & Gamble Co v Reckitt Benckiser (UK) Ltd* [2007] EWCA Civ 936; [2008] E.C.D.R. 3 at [3].

design is applied or in which it is incorporated,[467] the industrial sector to which it belongs and the degree of freedom of the designer in developing the design.[468] The greater the designer's freedom in developing a design, the less likely it is that minor differences between the designs in issue will be sufficient to produce different overall impressions on the informed user. The converse is also true.[469] The degree of design freedom is limited by the constraints imposed by the technical function of the product, by statutory requirements applicable to the product,[470] by the need to incorporate features common to such products and by economic considerations.[471] Those constraints result in a standardisation of certain features which will thus be common to the designs applied to the product concerned.[472] Constraints imposed by the need to follow general trends are not relevant.[473]

Proprietorship The author of the design is the proprietor unless the design was created by an employee in the course of his employment, in which case it belongs to the employer.[474] 24-93

Infringement The proprietor has the exclusive right to "use" the design for products whose overall impression on the informed user does not differ from the design. However, there can be no infringement of an unregistered Community design without copying. If that is established, infringement involves very much the same questions as arise in connection with whether the design relied on has individual character. All other things being equal, a design should receive a broader scope of protection where the designer had a greater degree of freedom and vice versa[475]; while a design which is markedly different from the design corpus should receive a broader scope of protection than one which differs only slightly from the design corpus.[476] "Using" the design includes the making, offering, putting on the 24-94

---

467 And the way in which the product is used: *H&M Hennes & Mauritz BV & Co. KG v OHIM* (T-525/13) [2015] E.C.D.R. 20 at [39].

468 *H&M Hennes & Mauritz BV & Co. KG v OHIM* (T-525/13) EU:T:2015:617; [2015] E.C.D.R. 20 at [21] referring to Recital 14 to the Regulation.

469 *H&M Hennes & Mauritz BV & Co. KG v OHIM* (T-525/13) EU:T:2015:617; [2015] E.C.D.R. 20 at [29]; *Senz Technologies BV v OHIM* (T-22/13 and 23/13) EU:T:2015:310 [2015] E.C.D.R. 19 at [57].

470 *H&M Hennes & Mauritz BV & Co. KG v OHIM* (T-525/13) EU:T:2015:617; [2015] E.C.D.R. 20 at [28].

471 *Whitby Specialist Vehicles Ltd v Yorkshire Specialist Vehicles Ltd* [2014] EWHC 4242 (Pat); [2015] E.C.D.R. 11 at [24].

472 *Senz Technologies BV v OHIM* (T-22/13 and 23/13) EU:T:2015:310 [2015] E.C.D.R. 19 at [56].

473 *Shenzhen Taiden Industrial Co Ltd v OHIM* (T-153/08) EU:T:2010:248 at [58]; *Pulseon OY v Garmin (Europe) Ltd* [2019] EWCA Civ 138; [2019] E.C.D.R. 8 at [22]–[23].

474 Regulation 6/2002/EC Art.14.

475 *Whitby Specialist Vehicles Ltd v Yorkshire Specialist Vehicles Ltd* [2014] EWHC 4242 (Pat); [2015] E.C.D.R. 11 at [26]: (applying art.9(2) of the Designs Directive, which is in the same terms as art.10(2) of Regulation 6/2002/EC). However this does not apply where the striking elements of the design are those where there is little design freedom, in particular because of technical requirements: see at [29]. See also *L'Oreal Societe Anonyme v RN Ventures Ltd* [2018] EWHC 173 (Pat); [2018] E.C.D.R. 14 at [155].

476 *Whitby Specialist Vehicles Ltd v Yorkshire Specialist Vehicles Ltd* [2014] EWHC 4242 (Pat); [2015] E.C.D.R. 11 at [27]–[28]: (referring to Recital 13 to the Designs Directive, which is in the same terms as Recital 14 to Regulation 6/2002/EC). However this does not apply where the striking elements of the design are those where there is little design freedom, in particular because of technical requirements: see at [29].

market, importing, exporting or using of a product, or stocking a product for those purposes.[477]

24-95 **Defences** Article 110 of Regulation 6/2002 excludes protection for designs which constitute a component part of a complex product used for the purpose of the repair of that complex product so as to restore its original appearance. It is not necessary in order for the defence to operate that the protected design should be dependent on the appearance of the complex product.[478] However, the replacement part must have an identical visual appearance to that of the part which was originally incorporated into the complex product when it was placed on the market.[479] Moreover, in order to come within the defence, the manufacturer or seller of the allegedly infringing part is under a duty of diligence as regards compliance by downstream users with the conditions laid down in art.110. This duty is onerous.[480] Additional defences are provided for in art.20 for acts done privately and for non-commercial purposes, acts done for experimental purposes and acts for the purpose of making citations or teaching. The citation and teaching defences apply in a commercial context and are capable of extending to the display of images of a product protected by a design in advertisements for other products intended to be used as accessories. However, art.20(c) makes clear that the defence only applies if the display is compatible with fair trade practice, does not unduly prejudice the normal exploitation of the design and mentions the source.[481]

24-96 **Stay of proceedings** Article 91 of Regulation 6/2002 requires a stay of proceedings in most design disputes where the validity of the design in question is already in issue before another community design court. Where the claim is for a declaration of non-infringement and the counterclaim is for infringement, only the counterclaim need be stayed.[482]

24-97 **Remedies** The proprietor of a design which has been found to be infringed is entitled to substantially the same relief as is given to the proprietor of any other intellectual property right in similar circumstances. Injunctive relief in respect of Community designs can be far-reaching—for example, a Community-wide injunction was obtained by Apple Inc against Samsung Electronics in the Düsseldorf District Court in Germany in August 2011, in respect of tablet computers said to infringe Apple's iPad registered design.[483] Unjustified threats to sue for infringement are actionable.[484]

---

477 Regulation 6/2002/EC art.19.

478 See *Acacia Srl v Pneusgarda Srl* (C-397/16 and 435/16) EU:C:2017:992; [2018] Bus. L.R. 927 (Acacia) at [29]–[54].

479 See *Acacia* at [55]–[78].

480 See *Acacia* at [85]–[88].

481 See *Nintendo Co Ltd v Bigben Interactive GmbH* (C-24/16) EU:C:2017:724; [2018] E.C.D.R. 3 at [77]–[85].

482 *Samsung Electronics (UK) Ltd v Apple Inc* [2012] EWCA Civ 729; [2013] F.S.R. 8. However, a stay is not automatic, and was refused in *D. Jacobsen & Sons v Crocs Inc* [2014] EWHC 987 (Ch); [2014] E.C.C. 16. Contrast *Regent University v Regent's University London* [2013] EWPCC 39.

483 For an example of an interim injunction see *Utopia Tableware Ltd v BBP Marketing Ltd* [2013] EWPCC 15. The court can order publication of a finding of infringement where necessary to deter further infringement and to contribute to the awareness of the public at large. It can also order publication of a finding that a product does not infringe if there is a real need to dispel commercial uncertainty: *Samsung Electronics (UK) Ltd v Apple Inc* [2012] EWCA Civ 1339; [2013] F.S.R. 9 at

7. Registered Designs

Registered designs: general UK rights in registered designs are obtained by registration under the Registered Designs Act 1949 (RDA 1949). Alternatively, registration under Community Regulation 6/2002/EC provides a registered Community design. The RDA 1949 has been heavily amended to harmonise UK registered designs with Community law.[485] As a result, in broad terms, the provisions in relation to validity and infringement of unregistered Community designs apply also to UK and Community registered designs.[486] **24-98**

Registration The registrar of UK registered designs is the Comptroller-General of Patents, and the register is kept at the Intellectual Property Office. Registered Community designs are registered at the European Intellectual Property Office (formerly OHIM). Both registers may be searched online.[487] The date for considering whether a design is novel or has individual character is the date of filing of the application for registration or the date of priority if priority is claimed.[488] Disclosures by the designer, his successor in title or a third person as a result of information provided or action taken by the designer or his successor in title during the 12 month period prior to the date of filing or the date of priority are ignored.[489] Provision is made for registered designs to be invalidated if they do not satisfy the requirements for registration and on certain other grounds.[490] A registered design expires five years after registration unless renewed. Renewal may take place for up to four further five-year periods.[491] **24-99**

The scope of the registration The extent of the protection afforded by a particular registered design ultimately depends on the proper interpretation of the registration in issue and in particular of the images included in that registration.[492] The applicant is entitled to choose the level of generality at which the design is to be considered. If the applicant chooses too general a level, the design may be invalidated by the prior art. If the applicant chooses too specific a level, he or she may not be protected against similar designs.[493] The EUIPO has issued guidance as to the manner in which designs should be represented and the conventions to be **24-100**

---

[71], [75]. For some of the jurisdiction issues which may arise in infringement proceedings, see *Bayerische Motoren Werke AG v Acacia Srl* (C-433/16) EU:C:2017:550; [2017] E.C.D.R. 18; and *Nintendo Co Ltd v Bigben Interactive GmbH* (C-24/16) EU:C:2017:724; [2018] E.C.D.R. 3.

484 Community Design Regulations 2005 (SI 2005/2339) regs 2–2F.

485 Readers are referred to specialist texts for the complex transitional provisions arising from this harmonisation.

486 See paras 24-88 to 24-92.

487 See *https://euipo.europa.eu/ohimportal/en/databases* [Accessed 30 March 2020] and *https://www.gov.uk/search-registered-design* [Accessed 30 March 2020].

488 Council Regulation 6/2002/EC arts 5(1)(b) and 6(1)(b); RDA 1949 s.1B(2), (3), (7). Priority may be claimed where an application for a design right or utility model has been filed in or for any State Party to the Paris Convention for the Protection of Industrial Property or the Agreement establishing the World Trade Organisation or certain other States: Council Regulation 6/2002 art.41(1), (5); RDA 1949 s.14. Article 44 of the Council Regulation provides for exhibition priority.

489 Council Regulation 6/2002/EC art.7(2); RDA 1949 s.1B(5)(b), (6)(c)–(e).

490 Council Regulation 6/2002/EC arts 24–26; RDA ss.11ZA–11ZF.

491 Council Regulation 6/2002/EC art.12. RDA 1949 s.8.

492 *Magmatic Ltd v PMS International Ltd* [2016] UKSC 12; [2016] 4 All E.R. 1027 at [30]. For the importance of clear representations, see *Mast-Jägermeister SE v EUIPO* (C-217/17 P) EU:C:2018:534; [2018] E.C.D.R. 20 at [55].

493 See per Lewison J in *Procter & Gamble Co v Reckitt Benckiser (UK) Ltd* [2006] EWHC 3154 (Ch);

used, for example to indicate what is and is not part of the design.[494] In general, where a design is shown in colours, the colours are claimed; if it is shown in monochrome, it covers all colours.[495] However, a monochrome CAD drawing depicting a shape part of which is in grey and part of which is in black has been held to amount to a claim for a shape in two contrasting colours.[496] It seems that absence of decoration can be a feature of a registered design if that is what the images, properly interpreted, show.[497]

24-101 **Rectification of register** A registration may be cancelled or declared invalid, by the court, or by the Comptroller or EUIPO as the case may be, upon any ground on which registration might have been refused: that is, that the design was not "new" or possessing of "individual character", or the applicant for registration was not the proprietor of the design.[498] A counterclaim for cancellation is the proper procedure for raising the question of validity of the registration in proceedings for infringement.

24-102 **Proprietorship** The author of the design is the proprietor unless the design was created by an employee in the course of his employment, in which case it belongs to the employer.[499]

24-103 **Infringement** The same acts amount to infringement of a registered design as amount to infringement of an unregistered Community design.[500] In this case, however, it is not necessary to show copying. A central issue in many infringe-

---

[2007] E.C.D.R. 4 at [48]; referred to with approval in *Magmatic Ltd v PMS International Ltd* [2016] UKSC 12; [2016] 4 All E.R. 1027 at [30].

494 See *https://www.gov.uk/government/publications/designs-practice-notice-dpn-116/dpn-116-guidance-on-use-of-representations-when-filing-registered-design-applications* [Accessed 30 March 2020] and *https://euipo.europa.eu/ohimportal/en/design-guidelines* [Accessed 30 March 2020]. See also Schlöteburg *The Community Design: First Experience with Registrations* [2003] E.I.P.R. 383, which was relied on by the Supreme Court in *Magmatic Ltd v PMS International Ltd* [2016] UKSC 12; [2016] 4 All E.R. 1027 at [31].

495 *Magmatic Ltd v PMS International Ltd* [2016] UKSC 12; [2016] 4 All E.R. 1027 at [34].

496 *Magmatic Ltd v PMS International Ltd* [2016] UKSC 12; [2016] 4 All E.R. 1027 at [53].

497 *Magmatic Ltd v PMS International Ltd* [2016] UKSC 12; [2016] 4 All E.R. 1027 at [40]–[50] (obiter).

498 RDA 1949 ss.11 and 20 as amended by the Copyright Act 1956 s.46; Council Regulation 6/2002 arts 24 and 25. For an example of an ownership dispute, see *Ifejika v Ifejika* [2010] EWCA Civ 563; [2010] F.S.R. 29.

499 Council Regulation 6/2002/EC art.14(3). RDA 1949 s.2. Prior to 1 October 2014 s.2(1A) provided that commissioned designs belonged to the commissioner. This provision was repealed by the Intellectual Property Act 2014 s.6(1) but the old rule applies to designs created before that date or pursuant to a commission in a contract entered into before that date: see Intellectual Property Act 2014 (Commencement No.3 and Transitional Provisions) Order 2014 (SI 2014/2330) art.4. A dispute over ownership resulted in cancellation of the registration in *Ifejika v Ifejika* [2010] EWPCC 31; [2012] F.S.R. 6.

500 See para.24-94. For guidance as to the conduct of infringement proceedings, see *Spin Master Ltd v PMS International Group* [2017] EWHC 1477 (Pat); [2017] F.S.R. 44. For the sequence in which the issues should be determined, see *Pulseon OY v Garmin (Europe) Ltd* [2018] EWHC 47 (Ch) at [17]. For the correct approach to comparing a registered Community design with an alleged infringement, see *Cantel Medical (UK) Ltd v ARC Medical Design Ltd* [2018] EWHC 345 (Pat) at [181]–[182].

ment cases is the scope of the design as evidenced by the representations filed.[501] There is a defence of "prior use".[502]

Licence terms Following an adverse report by the Competition Commission,[503] the terms of a licence can be settled, in the absence of agreement, by the registrar. There are also provisions for Crown use.[504] 24-104

Coexistence of patent and registered design A patent right in an article and a registration of the design of the same article may coexist with the two rights protecting different aspects of the product. 24-105

Remedies for infringement All such relief by way of damages, injunctions, accounts or otherwise is available to the holder of registered design as is available in respect of the infringement of any other property right.[505] It is now a criminal offence knowingly to copy a UK registered design in the course of a business.[506] 24-106

Unjustified threats of legal proceedings A remedy exists, as with patents and design rights, where unjustified threats of legal proceedings are made in respect of alleged infringements of registered design.[507] 24-107

8. Registered Trade Marks

(a) Introduction

Trade mark infringement and passing off In addition to the common law right to prevent passing off,[508] it is possible, by registering a trade mark under the provisions of the Trade Marks Act 1994, to obtain statutory rights to prevent others using in the course of trade the same mark or a mark confusingly similar to it by others (subject to certain conditions about the identity or similarity of the goods or services in question, and subject to various defences to infringement which may be available). It is a negative right (restricting what others may do) rather than a positive right to use a particular mark.[509] 24-108

The Trade Marks Act 1994[510] The Trade Marks Act 1994 (TMA 1994), which 24-109

[501] See para.24-100.

[502] RDA 1949 s.7B; Council Regulation 6/2002 art.22.

[503] RDA 1949 s.11A.

[504] RDA 1949 s.12 and Sch.1.

[505] The Community Design Regulations 2005 (SI 2005/2339) reg.1A(2). RDA 1949 s.24A(1). Damages may not be awarded against a person who proves that at the time of the infringement he did not know and had no reason to supposing that the design was registered: Community Design Regulations 2005 (SI 2005/2339) reg.1A(3). RDA 1949 s.24A(2). The usual provision is made for delivery up.

[506] RDA 1949 s.35ZA.

[507] RDA 1949 ss.26–26F.

[508] For passing off, see Ch.25.

[509] *R. (on the application of British American Tobacco UK Ltd) v Secretary of State for Health* [2016] EWCA Civ 1182; [2018] Q.B. 149 (plain packaging for cigarettes).

[510] See Mellor et al, *Kerly's Law of Trade Marks and Trade Names*, 16th edn (Sweet & Maxwell, 2017) and Morcom et al, *The Modern Law of Trade Marks*, 5th edn (Butterworth, 2016). There is only scope in this work to provide a short outline of the law and reference to the leading cases. Note that there is a parallel system of European Union Trade Marks, established by Council Regulation 40/

came into force on 31 October 1994, superseded the Trade Marks Act 1938.[511] The 1994 Act was enacted to implement Council Directive 89/104[512] to approximate the laws of the Member States relating to trade marks[513] and the CJEU has given considerable guidance on interpretation of its terms.[514] European Union Trade Marks (EUTMs) are governed by the Trade Mark Regulation[515]; EUTMs replace what were formerly called Community Trade Marks, or CTMs. The law relating to validity and infringement is the same for both regimes. The 1994 Act effected significant changes in the law relating to registered trade marks but it does not affect the law relating to passing off.[516] There are transitional provisions which are now of limited if any importance.[517]

24-110 **The meaning of "trade mark"** In the 1994 Act, a "trade mark" is widely defined as any sign capable of being represented graphically which is capable of distinguishing goods or services of one undertaking from those of other

---

94/EEC, which was codified by Council Regulation (EC) 207/2009 and has now been amended by Regulation (EU) 2015/2424 (see fn.515) to which similar principles apply thanks to harmonising directives, the latest of which is Directive 2015/2436/EC (see fn.512). Such EUTMs have effect throughout the European Union, and may be obtained by application to the European Intellectual Property Office (formerly the Office for the Harmonization of the Internal Market (OHIM)) in Alicante, Spain. The EUIPO website contains comprehensive explanations of the types of intellectual property protection available: *https://euipo.europa.eu/ohimportal/en/home* [Accessed 3 April 2020]. Further discussion of this and international applications are beyond the scope of this work. For procedure generally, see Trade Marks Rules 2008 and CPR Pt 63 PD—Intellectual Property Claims, and the trade marks section of the UKIPO's website: *https://www.gov.uk/topic/intellectual-property/trade-marks* [Accessed 3 April 2020].

511 For the law under the Trade Marks Act 1938, see previous editions of this work and Blanco White and Jacob, *Kerly's Law of Trade Marks and Trade Names*, 12th edn (1986) and supplement (1994).

512 A consolidated revision of the directive was issued in 2008: Directive 2008/95/EC (the Directive). The Directive has now been superseded by Directive 2015/2436/EC and was repealed with effect from 15 January 2019; Member States were required to give effect to the bulk of the provisions of the new Directive by 14 January 2019 (see art.54(1)). The intention behind the new Directive is to make national law and procedures more accessible, efficient and more consistent with the new EUTM system.

513 [1989] OJ L40/1.

514 The UK courts are required to interpret provisions of national law, whether introduced to implement the Directive or not, in the light of the wording and purpose of the Directive. *Hansard* is of limited value in interpreting the Act: *British Sugar Plc v James Robertson Son Ltd* [1996] R.P.C. 281. See also *Wagamama Ltd v City Centre Restaurants Plc* [1995] F.S.R. 713. In *Budejovicky Budvar Narodni Podnik v Anheuser-Busch Inc* [2009] EWCA Civ 1022; [2010] R.P.C. 7, Jacob LJ stated: "Although the Judge below used the provisions of the UK Trade Marks Act 1994, it is common ground that those provisions not only are intended to implement the Directive but have the same meaning. … So, as I think should be the standard practice at all levels, I will use just the language of the Directive."

515 Council Regulation (EC) No.207/2009 on the European Union Trade Mark; the Regulation has been substantially amended by Regulation (EU) 2015/2424, which came into force on 23 March 2016. The direct effect of the new Regulation has been implemented in the UK by the European Union Trade Mark Regulations 2016 (SI 2016/299), which introduced various amendments to the TMA 1994 and the Community Trade Marks Regulations 2006 with effect from 6 April 2016.

516 TMA 1994 s.2(2). It should be noted that it is no defence to an action for passing off that the mark used by the defendant is a registered trade mark of his.

517 TMA 1994 Sch.3 ss.3, 10, 16, 17 and 18: these are dealt with under the old law. Reference should be made to the Act for the other transitional provisions governing, inter alia, delivery up of infringing goods, rights and remedies of licensees or registered users, co-ownership of registered marks, assignment and licensing of registered marks, priority, duration and renewal, certification trade marks and Sheffield marks.

undertakings.[518] A trade mark may, in particular, consist of words (including personal names), designs, letters, numerals or the shape of goods or their packaging. It may also consist of smells or sounds.[519]

(b) Registration

Registration of trade marks and applications for registration of trade marks An application for registration of a trade mark is made to the registrar[520] who examines whether the application for registration of a trade mark satisfies the requirements of the Act.[521] 24-111

(a) *Distinctiveness.* The chief purpose of a registered trade mark is to identify the goods on which it is used with its proprietor. It must therefore be distinctive. Of the restrictions on registrability, the most important relate to the distinctiveness of the proposed mark.[522] Marks which are not capable of distinguishing or which are "devoid of any distinctive character" may not

518 TMA 1994 s.1(1). There are special provisions governing "collective marks" (s.49), "certification marks" (s.50) and European Union Trade Marks (ss.51 and 52). The requirement that the mark be capable of graphical representation is removed by the new Regulation with effect from 1 October 2017. The Court of Justice has held that the representation of the layout of a retail store (such as an Apple "flagship" store) may be registered as a trade mark, provided that it is capable of distinguishing the goods and services of one undertaking from another: *Apple Inc v Deutsches Patent und Markenamt* (C-421/13) [2014] Bus. L.R. 962; [2014] E.T.M.R. 48.

519 In *L'Oréal SA v Bellure* [2007] EWCA Civ 968; [2008] E.T.M.R. 1 at [127] Jacob LJ, obiter, doubted whether a fragrance can be registered as a trade mark. A chocolate company was not entitled to register a shade of purple as "the predominant colour applied to the whole of the visible surface … of the packaging of the goods", since the proposed "sign" in fact lacked clarity, precision, self-containment, durability and objectivity: *Société Des Produits Nestlé SA v Cadbury UK Ltd* [2013] EWCA Civ 1174; [2014] 1 All E.R. 1079, and the offending wording was not allowed to be deleted from the registration, since it was a single mark rather than a series mark, and so the mark as a whole was invalid: *Cadbury UK Ltd v Comptroller General of Patents Designs and Trade Marks* [2016] EWHC 796 (Ch); [2017] F.S.R. 2; appeal dismissed: [2018] EWCA Civ 2715; [2019] F.S.R. 7. The same principles were applied in finding a trade mark for purple inhalers invalid in *Glaxo Wellcome UK Ltd (t/a Allen & Hanburys) v Sandoz Ltd* [2017] EWCA Civ 335; [2017] F.S.R. 33. Likewise in *Red Bull GmbH v European Union Intellectual Property Office* (C-124/18 P) EU:C:2019:641; [2019] E.T.M.R. 57, in which protection was claimed for the juxtaposition of the colours blue and silver in approximately equal proportions, but without specifying their form; and *Fromageries Bel SA v J Sainsbury Plc* [2019] EWHC 3454 (Ch); [2020] E.T.M.R. 14—lack of precision in "the colour red" for a 3D mark for cheeses.

520 TMA 1994 s.32, which sets out the requirements of an application. The website of the UK Intellectual Property Office is helpful: *https://www.gov.uk/topic/intellectual-property/trade-marks*. There are provisions in the Act concerning claims to priority from applications for protection of a trade mark in a Convention country and other overseas applications (CDPA 1988 ss.35 and 36). As to the meaning of "Convention country", see TMA 1994 s.55(1)(b).

521 TMA 1994 s.37. The registrar must permit the applicant to amend the application if it appears that the requirements for registrations are not met. Sections 62 to 74 of the Act govern the registrar and the Trade Marks Rules 2008 (SI 2008/1797, as amended) govern procedure before the registrar. Appeals from the registrar lie either to an appointed person or to the court: s.76(1). In *Koninklijke Philips Electronics NV v Remington Consumer Products Ltd* [2006] EWCA Civ 16; [2006] F.S.R. 30, the Court of Appeal upheld Rimer J's finding of invalidity of shape marks on the grounds that they consisted exclusively of the shape which was necessary to obtain a technical result but, reversing the judge, held that certain logo marks depicting the shape were distinctive and not excluded from registration. Applicants must identify the goods and services for which the protection of a trade mark is sought with sufficient clarity and precision to enable the competent authorities and economic operators to determine the extent of the protection conferred by the trade mark: *Chartered Institute of Patent Attorneys v Registrar of Trade Marks* (C-307/10) EU:C:2012:361; [2013] R.P.C. 11.

522 TMA 1994 s.3(1). Reference should be made to the section for the precise grounds for refusal. There

be registered. The same applies to signs which are descriptive of the goods or services for which they are sought to be registered.[523] Signs which consist exclusively of the shape which results from the nature of the goods themselves or the shape of the goods which is necessary to obtain a technical result or the shape which gives substantial value to the goods are also not capable of registration.[524] Marks may acquire distinctive character through use.[525]

---

is extensive jurisprudence both from the UK courts and from the Court of First Instance on the requirements for distinctiveness. See for general guidance: *Philips Electronics NV v Remington Consumer Products Ltd* [1999] R.P.C. 809 CA and the judgment of the CJEU in *Philips Electronics NV v Remington Consumer Products Ltd* (C-299/99) EU:C:2002:377 [2002] E.T.M.R. 81. See also *32Red Plc v WHG (International) Ltd* [2011] EWHC 62 (Ch); [2011] E.T.M.R. 21, with this point upheld on appeal: [2012] EWCA Civ 19; [2012] E.T.M.R. 14. In *JW Spear & Sons Ltd v Zynga Inc* [2012] EWHC 3345 (Ch); [2013] F.S.R. 28 (affirmed: [2013] EWCA Civ 1175; [2014] 1 All E.R. 1093) the claimant's "tile mark" was found to encompass an infinite number of permutations and combinations of letters and numbers on a tile, and was held to lack distinctive character. The mark "NOW TV" in *Starbucks (HK) Ltd v British Sky Broadcasting Group Plc* [2012] EWHC 3074 (Ch); [2013] F.S.R. 29 (affirmed: [2013] EWCA Civ 1465; [2014] F.S.R. 20) was held to be either a characteristic of the television service in question, or else devoid of distinctive character. As to distinctiveness in the case of unusual trade marks such as shapes of goods, see the discussion in *Bongrain SA's TM Application* [2004] EWCA Civ 1690; [2005] R.P.C. 14 (shape of cheese—mark refused). See also *Coca-Cola Co v Office for Harmonisation in the Internal Market (Trade Marks and Designs) (OHIM)* (T-411/14) [2016] E.T.M.R. 25, in which the shape of a bottle without fluting was held to lack distinctive character; *London Taxi Corp Ltd (t/a London Taxi Co) v Fraser-Nash Research Ltd* [2016] EWHC 52 (Ch); [2016] E.T.M.R. 18—shape marks for models of taxi cab lacked distinctive character. This was upheld on appeal: see [2017] EWCA Civ 1729; [2018] F.S.R. 7. The new Regulation and Directive use the broader form of words "shape or another characteristic" in setting out the exclusions corresponding to s.3(2) of the TMA 1994; this change has effect as of 23 March 2016. Distinctiveness and shape marks were discussed in *Mondelez UK Holdings & Services Ltd v EUIPO / Société des produits Nestlé SA* (T-112/13) (General Court) [2017] E.T.M.R. 13.

523 A mark having a single descriptive meaning is taken to be descriptive even if there are other, non-descriptive, meanings of the mark: *OHIM v Wm Wrigley Jnr Co ('DOUBLEMINT')* (C-191/01) EU:C:2003:579; [2004] 1 W.L.R. 1728. The CJEU has ruled that the exclusion for descriptiveness applies to a word mark which comprises the juxtaposition of a descriptive word combination plus a letter sequence which is not in itself descriptive, but which the public will readily perceive as being an abbreviation consisting simply of the first letters of the word combination—see *Alfred Strigl* (Joined cases C-90/11 and C-91/11). The marks in question were "Multi Markets Fund MMF" and "NAI—der Natur-Aktien-Index". In *Fine & Country Ltd v Okotoks Ltd* [2013] EWCA Civ 672; [2014] F.S.R. 11 the mark "FINE AND COUNTRY" was held to be not merely laudatory or descriptive. Contrast *British Shorinji Kempo Federation's Trade Mark Application* [2014] EWHC 285 (Ch), in which the words "shorinji kempo" were held to be generic identifiers of a particular martial art. The prohibition on descriptiveness also extends to indications of geographical origin. Contrast *Luen Fat Metal and Plastic Manufactory Ltd v Jacobs and Turner Ltd (t/a Trespass)* [2019] EWHC 118 (IPEC) in which it was said that the question was whether there was a sufficiently direct and specific link between the sign in issue and the goods, to enable the average consumer immediately to perceive, without further thought, a description of those goods or of one of their characteristics. In *Moreno Marin v Abadia Retuerta SA* (C-139/16), EU:C:2017:518; [2018] Bus. L.R. 431, the sign "la Milla de Oro" did not constitute an indication of geographical origin, since it was not accompanied by a geographical name designating the actual physical location where the product could be found—contrast *J Portugal Ramos Vinhos SA v Adega Cooperativa de Borba CRL* (C-629/17) EU:C:2018:988; [2019] E.T.M.R. 14. A similar challenge to the validity of the mark "Sivec" for quarried marble failed in *Mermeren Kombinat AD v Fox Marble Holdings Plc* [2017] EWHC 1408 (IPEC); [2018] F.S.R. 1. The mark had acquired distinctiveness as a trade mark by the time of its registration, whereas its parallel status as the name of a geographical location was too obscure to invalidate the registration.

524 TMA 1994 s.3(2). See *Philips Electronics NV v Remington Consumer Products Ltd* [1999] R.P.C.

(b) *Other restrictions on registration.* There are other restrictions on registrability where the trade mark is of such a nature as to deceive the public or is contrary to public policy or accepted principles of morality.[526] Certain protected emblems (such as Royal Arms) may only be registered in special circumstances.[527] A trade mark may not be registered if or to the extent that the application is made in bad faith.[528]

---

809 CA, which resulted in a reference to the CJEU. Subsequently in *Koninklijke Philips NV v Remington Consumer Products Ltd* [2006] EWCA Civ 16; [2006] F.S.R. 30, the Court of Appeal upheld Rimer J's finding of invalidity of shape marks on the grounds that they consisted exclusively of the shape which was necessary to obtain a technical result but, reversing the judge, held that certain logo marks depicting the shape were distinctive and not excluded from registration. In relation to the technical result exclusion, see *Lego Juris A/S v Office for Harmonisation in the Internal Market (Trade Marks and Designs) (OHIM)* (C-48/09 P) EU:C:2010:516; [2010] E.T.M.R. 63. "Technical result" must be interpreted as referring only to the manner in which the goods function, not the way they are manufactured: *Société des Produits Nestlé SA v Cadbury UK Ltd* (C-215/14) [2015] E.T.M.R. 50; [2016] F.S.R. 8. In *Rubik's Brand Ltd v EUIPO* (T-601/17) (General Court) [2020] E.T.M.R. 11 the surface lines depicted in the image of a Rubik's cube fell foul of the provision, notwithstanding that other elements (e.g. colour) were also required to fulfil the technical result of the product. See also *Novartis AG v EUIPO* (T-44/16) EU:T:2018:48 (shape of a plaster—invalid); and *Flamagas SA v EUIPO* (T-580/15), EU:T:2017:433; [2017] E.T.M.R. 33 (shape of cigarette lighter—invalid). The shape of London taxi cabs was held to add substantial value to the goods in *London Taxi Corp Ltd (t/a London Taxi Co) v Frazer-Nash Research Ltd* [2017] EWCA Civ 1729; [2018] F.S.R. 7. The issue of whether the notion of "shape" is limited to the three-dimensional properties of the goods, such as their contours, measurements and volume, or whether it can include other, non-three dimensional properties of the goods such as their colour (in particular red soles for luxury shoes), was referred to the CJEU in *Louboutin v Van Haren Schoenen BV* (C-163/16) EU:C:2018:423, [2018] E.T.M.R. 31: the Court held such a sign does not consist exclusively of a shape and as such could not fall foul of the exclusion..

525 The High Court referred certain questions to the CJEU on the issue of acquired distinctiveness in relation to the shape of the Kit-Kat four-finger chocolate bar—see *Société des Produits Nestlé SA v Cadbury UK Ltd* [2014] EWHC 16 (Ch); [2014] E.T.M.R. 17. Reflecting the CJEU's ruling, the Court held that in order to demonstrate acquired distinctiveness, it is necessary to show that a significant proportion of the relevant consumers perceive the goods or services as originating from a particular undertaking because of the shape in question, not just that they recognised the shape and associated it with the undertaking: *Société des Produits Nestlé SA v Cadbury UK Ltd* [2016] EWHC 50 (Ch); [2016] 4 All E.R. 1081 (an appeal against this was dismissed: [2017] EWCA Civ 358; [2018] 2 All E.R. 39). See now the latest ruling in *Mondelez UK Holdings & Services Ltd v EUIPO / Société des produits Nestlé SA* (T-112/13) EU:T:2016:735; [2017] E.T.M.R. 13 (a shape mark may acquire distinctiveness even if used in combination with a word or figurative mark)—upheld on appeal to the CJEU (C-84/17 P) [2018] Bus. L.R. 1848; [2019] F.S.R. 6. The same principles were applied in upholding a finding of no acquired distinctiveness in the shapes of London taxi cabs: *London Taxi Corp Ltd (t/a London Taxi Co) v Frazer-Nash Research Ltd* [2017] EWCA Civ 1729; [2018] F.S.R. 7. A longstanding shape mark for Tic Tac boxes was held to have only weak distinctive character in *BMB sp z oo v European Union Intellectual Property Office (EUIPO)* (T-695/15) EU:T:2017:684; [2018] E.T.M.R. 2.

526 TMA 1994 s.3(3). See on likely to deceive: *"Swiss Miss" TM* [1998] R.P.C. 889. An application for the mark "Canary Wharf" was refused because it was held to designate geographical origin: *Canary Wharf Group Plc v Comptroller General of Patents, Designs and Trade Marks* [2015] EWHC 1588 (Ch); [2015] F.S.R. 34.

527 TMA 1994 ss.3(3), 3(4) and 4.

528 TMA 1994 s.3(6). "Bad faith" is hard to define but includes dishonesty and some dealings which fall short of the standards of acceptable commercial behaviour observed by reasonable and experienced men. This has been described as whether the applicant knew his behaviour was unacceptable by the standards of reasonable men of business, i.e. it contains a significant objective component. See *Gromax Plasticulture Ltd v Don & Low Nonwovens Ltd* [1999] R.P.C. 367; *Ajit Weekly TM* [2006] R.P.C. 25; and *Hotel Cipriani Srl v Cipriani (Grosvenor Street) Ltd* [2010] EWCA Civ 110; [2010] R.P.C. 16. In *Chocoladefabriken Lindt & Sprungli v Franz Hauswirth* (C-529/07)

(c) *Earlier rights.* There are provisions to prevent registration of trade marks which conflict with earlier trade marks and earlier rights, with exceptions in the case of honest concurrent use[529] and consent. Marks may be registered subject to disclaimer or limitations with correspondingly limited effect.[530]

EU:C:2009:361; [2009] E.T.M.R. 56 the Court held that consideration *must* be given to the applicant's subjective intention identifying similar relevant types of knowledge that would be relevant as the English courts had identified in the cases referred to earlier. This principle was applied by Henderson J, finding bad faith, in *32Red Plc v WHG (International) Ltd* [2011] EWHC 62 (Ch); [2011] E.T.M.R. 21 (and not doubted on appeal: [2012] EWCA Civ 19; [2012] E.T.M.R. 14). Additional general guidance was provided by Henry Carr J in *Trump International Ltd v DTTM Operations LLC* [2019] EWHC 769 (Ch); [2019] F.S.R. 28. Applying for a mark with no intention of using it, but with the intention of using the mark as a basis for obtaining a top-level .eu domain name could amount to bad faith within the meaning of the relevant domain name regulation (Regulation 874/2004): *Internetportal und Marketing GmbH v Schlicht* (C-569/08) EU:C:2010:311; [2010] E.T.M.R. 48. Bad faith is an autonomous concept of EU law which should have uniform interpretation across the Community: *Malaysia Dairy Industries Pte Ltd v Ankenaevnet for Patenter og Varemaerker* (C-320/12) EU:C:2013:435; [2013] E.T.M.R. 36; that case also held that a finding of bad faith does not follow simply because an applicant was aware of an earlier registration of the same mark in a foreign country. There is no requirement in the EU Trade Mark Regulation that the applicant must intend to use the mark, thus the lack of such intention does not on its own amount to bad faith (at least in respect of EU trade marks): *Jaguar Land Rover Ltd v Bombardier Recreational Products Inc* [2016] EWHC 3266 (Ch); [2017] F.S.R. 20. On a reference from the UK court in *Sky Plc v Skykick UK Ltd* [2018] EWHC 943 (Ch); [2018] R.P.C. 12, the CJEU has held that s.32(3) TMA 1994 (which requires a declaration of use or bona fide intent to use) is incompatible with the Directive (C-371/18) EU:C:2020:45; [2020] E.T.M.R. 24.

529 TMA 1994 ss.5–8. Note that the holder of the earlier mark may be required to prove genuine use—see para.24-114. See, on the right to prevent registration under s.5(4) where use of the mark applied for would constitute passing off: *"Wild Child" TM* [1998] R.P.C. 455. Unregistered rights were held to invalidate a registration in *Jaguar Land Rover Ltd v Twisted Automotive Ltd* [2018] EWHC 3536 (Ch); [2019] R.T.R. 27. National rights in "extended form" passing off were also applicable in this context in *Tilda Riceland Private Ltd v OHIM* (T-304/09) [2012] E.T.M.R. 15, General Court, concerning the term "basmati". The Court of Appeal considered the effect of TMA 1994 s.5(4)(a) and earlier unregistered rights in *Caspian Pizza Ltd v Shah* [2017] EWCA Civ 1874; [2018] F.S.R. 12. The defendant's earlier rights, although in a different geographical area to that in which the claimant operated, were sufficient basis to invalidate a national trade mark registration. There was no equivalent to TMA 1994 ss.47(5) and (6) allowing for a declaration of only partial validity on the basis of a geographically limited earlier right. See Ch.25 for further discussion of extended passing off. A rice-related trade mark was also invalid against earlier unregistered UK rights in *Tresplain Investments Ltd v OHIM* (C-76/11 P) EU:C:2011:790; [2012] E.T.M.R. 22. The CJEU has given its views on the notion of "honest concurrent use" in *Budejovicky Budvar Narodni Podnik v Anheuser-Busch Inc* (C-482/09) EU:C:2011:605; [2012] E.T.M.R. 2. It ruled that the provisions of the Directive 2008/95/EC and Regulation (EC) 207/2009 do not allow a trade mark proprietor to prevent the use of an identical mark where there has been long concurrent use such that there is not likely to be any damage to the "essential function" of the earlier mark. Note that the case turned on its specific and rather unusual facts. The Court also ruled on the meaning of "acquiescence" as a concept of Community law. In *IPC Media Ltd v Media 10 Ltd* [2014] EWCA Civ 1439; [2015] F.S.R. 12 the Court of Appeal again found that the long period of honest concurrent use meant that the lower court was entitled to dismiss a claim for infringement. The honesty of concurrent use may change over time: *Bentley 1962 Ltd v Bentley Motors Ltd* [2019] EWHC 2925 (Ch); [2020] E.T.M.R. 8. Consensual use does not altogether preclude a trade mark owner from subsequently withdrawing consent and enforcing its rights against a former co-user of the mark: *Martin y Paz Diffusion SA v Depuydt* (C-661/11) EU:C:2013:577; [2014] E.T.M.R. 6. Peaceful co-existence of marks in two Member States need not rule out a likelihood of confusion in other Member States of the EU: *Ornua Co-operative Ltd v Tindale & Stanton Ltd Espana SL* (C-93/16) EU:C:2017:571; [2017] E.T.M.R. 37. For an examination of the effects of a coexistence agreement on later trade mark use, see *Merck KGaA v Merck Sharp & Dohme Corp* [2017] EWCA Civ 1834; [2018] E.T.M.R. 10.

530 TMA 1994 s.13. See *Paton Calvert Cordon Bleu TM* [1996] R.P.C. 94.

Opposition to registration When an application for registration has been accepted, the application is published and any person may give notice of opposition to the registration or may make observations as to whether the trade mark should be registered.[531] If no notice of opposition is given or the opposition proceedings are withdrawn or decided in favour of the applicant, the trade mark will be registered.[532] The role of expert evidence for the purposes of evaluating the likelihood of confusion has been examined by the Court of Appeal in *esure Insurance Ltd v Direct Line Insurance Plc*[533]: such evidence is usually inappropriate unless the market is one with which the judge is particularly unfamiliar. Similarly where the parties wish to make use of consumer survey evidence, directions as to the scope and methodology of the survey should be obtained prior to carrying it out. **24-112**

Duration of registration A trade mark is registered for a period of 10 years from the date of registration and may be renewed for further periods of 10 years upon payment of the appropriate fee.[534] **24-113**

Revocation for non-use etc and invalidity of registration The registration of a trade mark may be revoked on the grounds of non-use or suspension of use for five years without proper reason or because, by reason of the acts or inactivity of the proprietor, the mark has become the common name in the trade for the product or service for which it is registered or that, in consequence of the use made of it by the proprietor or with his consent, it is liable to mislead the public.[535] In addition, the registration of a trade mark may be declared invalid on the ground that the trade mark was not a registrable mark at the date of registration but if, in consequence of use made of it after registration, the mark has acquired a distinctive character, it **24-114**

---

531 TMA 1994 s.38.

532 TMA 1994 s.40.

533 [2008] EWCA Civ 842; [2008] E.T.M.R. 77; [2008] R.P.C. 34.

534 TMA 1994 ss.42 and 43.

535 TMA 1994 s.46. See also the "use conditions" introduced into TMA 1994 ss.6A and 47 by the Trade Marks (Proof of Use) Regulations 2004 (SI 2004/946). See s.46(2),(3) as to what constitutes "use" for the purpose of s.46. As to the type of evidence required to show "use" see *Moo Juice Trade Mark* [2005] EWHC 2584; [2006] R.P.C. 18. The CJEU has handed down a detailed decision on "use": see *Anheuser-Busch Inc v Budejovicky Budvar Narodni Podnik* (C-96/09 P) EU:C:2011:189; [2011] E.T.M.R. 31. Article 15(1) of Regulation 207/2009 requires that the territorial borders of the Member States of the Community be disregarded for the purposes of assessing whether a trade mark has been put to genuine use—*Leno Merken BV v Hagelkruis Beheer BV* (C-149/11) EU:C:2012:816; [2013] E.T.M.R. 16. Provisions of national law are irrelevant to the operation and scope of Regulation 207/2009 in relation to genuine use: *Rivella International AG v OHIM* (T-170/11) [2013] E.T.M.R. 4; General Court, appeal dismissed: [2014] E.T.M.R. 20. Genuine use may be satisfied for a registered trade mark which has become distinctive as a result of use as part of a composite mark with other elements, even where it has only ever been used as part of that composite: *Colloseum Holding AG v Levi Strauss & Co* (C-12/12) EU:C:2013:253; [2013] E.T.M.R. 34; cf. *Fruit of the Loom Inc v OHIM* (T-514/10) [2012] E.T.M.R. 44, General Court. A wordless EUTM may be genuinely used even where it has been used only in conjunction with another word EUTM superimposed over it and the combination of those two marks was itself registered as an EUTM: *Specsavers International Healthcare Ltd v Asda Stores Ltd* (C-252/12) [2014] F.S.R. 4, CJEU; the Court of Appeal consequently allowed the claimant's appeal: [2014] EWCA Civ 1294; [2015] F.S.R. 8. For discussion on proof of use see *Claridge's Hotel Ltd v Claridge Candles Ltd* [2019] EWHC 2003 (IPEC); [2019] E.T.M.R. 54. Use of marks on cruise ships that had entered UK territorial waters and docked at Southampton was held to be insufficient in *Johnny Rockets Licensing Corp v Eddie Rockets (Ireland) Ltd* [2016] E.T.M.R. 37; [2017] F.S.R. 9. In *Aiwa Co Ltd v Aiwa Corp* [2019] EWHC 3468 (Ch); [2020] E.T.M.R. 12 there was held to be no genuine use where the only sale of branded goods was on the second-hand market by third parties rather than by the proprietor of the mark.

will not be declared invalid.[536] The registration of a trade mark may also be declared invalid on the ground that it conflicts with an earlier mark or right.[537] An application for revocation or a declaration of invalidity may be made by any person[538] and there is provision for partial revocation or declaration of invalidity in relation to only some of the goods or services in respect of which the trade mark is registered.[539] Where the registration of a trade mark is declared invalid to any extent, the registration shall to that extent be deemed never to have been made.[540] There are provisions concerning rectification and correction of the register of trade marks and the procedure and evidence before the registrar of trade marks.[541] A registered trade mark may be surrendered.[542] As to the question of whether a mark has become a common name, this must be assessed by reference to the perception of both trade users and end consumers, although it is the perception of the end consumer that will generally be decisive.[543] The court in *Sky Plc v Skykick UK Ltd*[544] referred to the CJEU the question of whether an EU trade mark or a national trade mark registered in a Member State can be declared wholly or partially invalid on the ground that some or all of the terms in the specification of goods and services are lacking in sufficient clarity and precision to enable the competent authorities and third parties to determine on the basis of those terms alone the extent of the protection conferred by the trade mark. This issue arose following the ruling of the CJEU in *Chartered Institute of Patent Attorneys v Registrar of Trade Marks*.[545] The CJEU has answered in the negative.[546]

24-115 **Licensing and assignment of registered trade marks**[547] A registered trade mark is personal property[548] and may be assigned, licensed etc.[549] A licence to use a registered trade mark may be general or limited (for example to some but not all

---

536 TMA 1994 s.47(1).

537 TMA 1994 s.47(2).

538 There is a special exception in the case of five years' acquiescence by the proprietor of an earlier trade mark or other earlier right, TMA 1994 s.48(1). Questions have been referred to the CJEU about the scope of this acquiescence provision: see *Budejovicky Budvar Narodni Podnik v Anheuser-Busch Inc* [2009] EWCA Civ 1022; [2010] R.P.C. 7.

539 TMA 1994 ss.46(4) and 46(5) as well as ss.47(4) and 47(5). See for example the partial revocation in *Comic Enterprises Ltd v Twentieth Century Fox Film Corp* [2014] EWHC 185 (Ch); [2014] F.S.R. 35 ("Glee Club") (not disturbed on appeal: [2016] EWCA Civ 41; [2016] E.T.M.R. 22).

540 TMA 1994 s.47(6). This does not affect transactions past and closed.

541 TMA 1994 ss.64 (rectification or correction of the register), 66 (forms), 68 (costs), 69 (evidence), 76 (appeals from the registrar). Application may be made to the UK Intellectual Property Office or to the High Court. As to the latter, see CPR Pt 63. If the former procedure is used, cause of action and/or issue estoppel may operate if the party seeking revocation attempts to run the same arguments in subsequent court proceedings: *Evans v Focal Point Fires Plc* [2009] EWHC 2784 (Ch); [2010] R.P.C. 15. This case is to be contrasted with the Court of Appeal decision in *Special Effects Ltd v L'Oréal SA* [2007] EWCA Civ 1; [2007] R.P.C. 15.

542 TMA 1994 s.45.

543 *Backaldrin Osterreich the Kornspitz Co v Pfahnl Backmittel* (C-409/12) EU:C:2014:130; [2014] Bus. L.R. 320; [2014] E.T.M.R. 30.

544 [2018] EWHC 943 (Ch); [2018] R.P.C. 12.

545 (C-307/10) EU:C:2012:361; [2013] R.P.C. 11, as to which see fn.521.

546 (C-371/18) EU:C:2020:45; [2020] E.T.M.R. 24.

547 For the transitional provisions, see TMA 1994 Sch.3 ss.6-9.

548 TMA 1994 s.22. There are provisions governing co-ownership of registered trade marks and the rights of co-owners inter se: s.23.

549 TMA 1994 s.24. Under s.25, prescribed particulars of registrable transactions of trade marks, such as assignments and licences must be registered (by application to the registrar). Until an application has been made for registration of the prescribed particulars of a registrable transaction, (a) the

the goods or services for which the mark is registered or to use in a particular locality).[550] A licence must be in writing signed by or on behalf of the licensor.[551] A licensee has the right to call upon the proprietor to take infringement proceedings in respect of any matter which affects his interests. If the proprietor refuses to do so or fails to do so within two months of being called upon, the licensee may take proceedings in his own name.[552] An exclusive licence[553] may provide that the licensee shall have, to such extent as may be provided by the licence, the same rights and remedies in respect of matters occurring after the grant of the licence and remedies in respect of matters occurring after the grant of the licence as if the licence had been an assignment. An exclusive licensee is to that extent entitled to bring infringement proceedings in his own name against anyone other than the proprietor.[554] The courts will generally uphold, in the face of a restraint of trade or competition law attack, a bona fide agreement (usually known as a delimitation agreement) which resolves national or global trade mark disputes by restricting the parties' respective use of trade marks in specified ways or in specified territories.[555]

(c) Infringement of trade mark

Infringement of registered trade mark[556] There are three ways in which a registered trade mark may be infringed, and there are also ancillary torts relating to the affixation of trade marks in certain circumstances without consent: 24-116

(a) A person infringes a registered trade mark under s.10(1) if he uses[557] in the

---

transaction is ineffective as against a person acquiring a conflicting interest in or under the registered trade mark in ignorance of it and (b) a person claiming to be a licensee by virtue of the transaction does not have the protection of s.30 or 31 of the 1994 Act (rights and remedies of licensee in relation to infringement). The provisions relating to registered trade marks as objects of property apply also to applications for registered trade marks with minor modifications: s.27.

550 TMA 1994 s.28.

551 TMA 1994 s.28(2). For the contrast between this and the requirements of the Community Trade Mark Regulation (EC) 40/94 (codified in Regulation 207/2009 as amended by Regulation (EU) 2015/2424), see *Jean Christian Perfumes Ltd v Thakrar (t/a Brand Distributor and/or Brand Distributors Ltd)* [2011] EWHC 1383 (Ch); [2011] F.S.R. 34: an oral licence was a sufficient basis for bringing an action.

552 TMA 1994 s.30. The licence may exclude this right: s.30(3). The licensee must join the proprietor or obtain the leave of the court to proceed but may obtain interlocutory relief without so doing: s.30(4). There are provisions as to the liability for costs of a proprietor so joined: s.30(5).

553 An exclusive licence is a licence authorising the licensee to the exclusion of all other persons, including the person granting the licence, to use a registered trade mark in the manner authorised by the licence: TMA 1994 s.29(1).

554 TMA 1994 s.31(1). The right, which is concurrent to that of the proprietor, is subject to a number of conditions: see s.31.

555 See, e.g. *WWF World Wide Fund for Nature v World Wrestling Federation Entertainment Inc* [2002] EWCA Civ 196; [2002] F.S.R. 33.

556 There is an extensive jurisprudence on what constitutes infringement of a trade mark and the scope of the defences. The footnotes in the following paragraphs merely provide pointers to the key authorities.

557 A person uses a sign if, in particular, he:
- (a) affixes it to goods or the packaging thereof;
- (b) offers or exposes goods for sale, puts them on the market or stocks them for those purposes under the sign, or offers or supplies services under the sign;
- (c) imports or exports goods under the sign; of;
- (d) uses the sign on business papers or in advertising: see TMA 1994 s.10(4).

Use "in the course of trade" may include use by a non-profit organisation such as an NHS trust: *APT* course of trade a sign which is identical with[558] the trade mark in relation to goods or services which are identical with those for which it is registered.[559]

(b) A person infringes a registered trade mark under s.10(2) if he uses in the course of trade a sign where because (i) the sign is identical with the trade mark and is used in relation to goods or services similar to those for which the trade mark is registered; or (ii) the sign is similar to the trade mark and is used in relation to goods or services identical with or similar to those for which the trade mark is registered, there exists a likelihood of confusion on the part of the public, which includes the likelihood of association with the trade mark.[560]

(c) It is also an infringement of a registered trade mark under s.10(3) if a person uses in the course of trade a sign which is identical with or similar to the trade mark and is used in relation to goods or services which are not similar to those for which the trade mark is registered where the trade mark has a reputation in the UK and the use of the sign, being without due cause, takes unfair advantage of or is detrimental to the distinctive character or the repute of the trade mark. The High Court considered the principles applicable to identifying the extent of a mark's reputation within the EU in *Burgerista Operations GmbH v Burgista Bros Ltd*.[561] This can include for example "cybersquatting".[562] The CJEU has ruled in *Intel Corp Inc v CPM UK Ltd*[563]

Training and Consultancy Ltd v Birmingham and Solihull Mental Health NHS Trust [2019] EWHC 19 (IPEC); [2019] E.T.M.R. 22.

558 Identity is assessed strictly: see *Koninklijke Philips NV v Remington Consumer Products Ltd* [2004] EWHC 2327 (Ch); [2005] F.S.R. 17 and *LTJ Diffusion SA v Sadas Vertbaudet SA* (C-291/00) EU:C:2003:169; [2002] E.T.M.R. 40. An earlier black and white mark later used in colour is not identical to the same mark in colour unless the differences in colour are insignificant. An earlier mark in greyscale is not identical to the same mark in colour or in black and white unless the differences in colour or in contrast of shades are insignificant: see European Trade Mark and Design Network, *Common Communication on the Common Practice of the Scope of Protection of Black and White ("B&W") Marks*, 15 April 2014, p.2. "Insignificant" means a difference that only a reasonably observant consumer will perceive on a side-by-side comparison of the marks.

559 TMA 1994 s.10(1). As to the meaning of "use in relation to goods", see *Trebor Bassett Ltd v The Football Association* [1997] F.S.R. 211 (use of England logo on shirts of players photographed for football cards, not use in relation to the cards).

560 TMA 1994 s.10(2). See para.24-119.

561 [2018] EWHC 35 (IPEC); [2018] E.T.M.R. 16.

562 TMA 1994 s.10(3). On this concept see, *British Telecommunications Plc v One in a Million* [1999] 1 W.L.R. 903 where the Court of Appeal suggested obiter that, in an action based on s.10(3), it is not necessary to prove that the use complained of be trade mark use nor that it be confusing use. See also *Global Projects Management Ltd v Citigroup Inc* [2005] EWHC 2663 (Ch); [2006] F.S.R. 39. *One in a Million* held it to be infringement of trade marks and passing off to register Internet domain names incorporating the trade marks of famous companies and threaten to use them or sell them to others. The law was surveyed in *Victoria Plum Ltd (t/a Victoria Plumb) v Victorian Plumbing Ltd* [2016] EWHC 2911 (Ch); [2017] F.S.R. 17. See also on the effect of s.10(3), *Pfizer Ltd v Eurofood Link (UK) Ltd* [2000] E.T.M.R. 896; [2001] F.S.R. 3 (VIAGRA registered for anti-impotence tablets could prevent use of VIAGRENE for aphrodisiac drink under s.10(2) or s.10(3) as an alternative); *General Motors Corp v Yplon* [2000] R.P.C. 572. The scope of a s.10(3) claim extends to the situation where the goods are similar: *Adidas-Salomon AG v Fitnessworld Trading Ltd* (C-408/01) EU:C:2003:582; [2004] Ch. 120.

563 [2009] E.T.M.R. 13. The relevant principles were considered and applied in *Maier v ASOS* [2013] EWHC 2831 (Ch); [2014] F.S.R. 16 at [126]–[135], although the conclusion reached by the judge on the facts of the case was reversed by the Court of Appeal: [2015] EWCA Civ 220; [2016] 2 All E.R. 738.

that detriment to distinctive character requires proof of at least a serious likelihood of change in the economic behaviour of the consumer. The CJEU in *L'Oréal v Bellure*[564] held that taking unfair advantage of a trade mark's reputation does not require confusion or a likelihood of detriment to the distinctive character of the mark but rather only that the advantage to the infringer is one taken unfairly such that they seek to "ride on the coat tails" of the mark's reputation so as to benefit from its power of attraction. For a recent discussion see, e.g. *Claridge's Hotel Ltd v Claridge Candles Ltd*.[565]

(d) A person who applies a registered trade mark to material intended to be used for labelling or packaging goods, as a business paper, or for advertising goods or services, is treated as a party to any use of the material which infringes the registered trade mark, if when he applied the mark he knew or had reason to believe that the application of the mark was not duly authorised by the proprietor or a licensee.[566]

The nature and effect of the use The question of whether the use must be "trade mark use" (i.e. use so as to denote origin) to infringe has a long history.[567] An illustration of the difficulty of some of the issues may be found in *Arsenal Football Club Plc v Reed*,[568] in which the question was whether it was an infringement of a football club's trade mark for its name to sell scarves bearing that name. The High Court referred to the CJEU the question whether the cause of action for infringement required the defendant's use to be use as a trade mark. The defendant said that the sign "Arsenal" was intended to indicate allegiance to the team, not the trade origin of the clothing. The CJEU said that to constitute infringement the offending use must be such as to affect or be liable to affect the functions of the trade mark, **24-117**

564 (C-487/07) EU:C:2009:378; [2009] E.T.M.R. 55. See also the Court of Appeal's judgment following the CJEU verdict: [2010] EWCA Civ 535; [2010] E.T.M.R. 47. Unfair advantage was also considered in depth in *Red Bull GmbH v Sun Mark Ltd* [2012] EWHC 1929 (Ch); [2013] E.T.M.R. 53, in which Arnold J held that the strapline "NO BULL IN THIS CAN" infringed the claimant's "RED BULL" mark for energy drinks. See also the discussion of unfair advantage in *Jack Wills Ltd v House of Fraser (Stores) Ltd* [2014] EWHC 110; [2014] E.T.M.R. 28; *Hearst Holdings Inc v AVELA Inc* [2014] EWHC 439 (Ch) (IPEC); and the successful appeal against a finding of no unfair advantage in *Lonsdale Sports Ltd v Erol* [2013] EWHC 2956 (Pat); [2013] E.C.C. 33.

565 *Claridge's Hotel Ltd v Claridge Candles Ltd* [2019] EWHC 2003 (IPEC); [2019] E.T.M.R. 54. Also: *Red Bull GmbH v Big Horn UK Ltd* [2020] EWHC 124 (Ch); [2020] E.T.M.R. 27.

566 TMA 1994 s.10(5).

567 See *Celine Sarl v Celine SA* (C-17/06) EU:C:2007:497; [2007] E.T.M.R. 80 on the use of a trade mark in the context of infringement. As to use not constituting trade mark use see also: *Rugby Football Union v Cotton Traders Ltd* [2002] EWHC 467 (Ch); [2002] E.T.M.R. 76 (no infringement by use of English team rose emblem on rugby shirts); see *Unilever Plc v Griffin* [2010] EWHC 899 (Ch); [2010] F.S.R. 33, in which Arnold J was sceptical about whether the inclusion of the trade mark "MARMITE" in a party political broadcast constituted use in the course of trade. See also for circumstances in which use of a trade mark in a descriptive sense may not infringe: *Holterhoff v Freiesleben* (C-2/00) EU:C:2002:287; [2002] E.T.M.R. 79. The CJEU has ruled that merely filling a package supplied by a customer does not amount to "use" of the marks borne on that package, but it does create the conditions for use to occur—see *Frisdranken Industrie Winters BV v Red Bull GmbH* (C-119/10) EU:C:2011:837; [2012] E.T.M.R. 16. As to infringement by use on a foreign website, see *Euromarket Designs Inc v Peters and Crate Barrel Ltd* [2001] F.S.R. 20; and *800 Flowers Trade Mark* [2001] EWCA Civ 721; [2002] F.S.R. 12.

568 *Arsenal Football Club Plc v Reed* [2001] E.T.M.R. 77; CJEU judgment (C-206/01) EU:C:2002:651; [2003] E.T.M.R.19; and judgment of the Court of Appeal [2003] EWCA Civ 96; [2003] 3 All E.R. 865. See also the guidance given by the CJEU in *Anheuser-Busch v Budéjoveicky Budvar, národni podnik* (C-245/02) EU:C:2004:717; [2005] E.T.M.R. 27 at [59]–[64]; applied by *Julius Sämaan Ltd v Tetrosyl Ltd* [2006] EWHC 529; [2006] F.S.R. 42.

and in particular its essential function of guaranteeing to consumers the origin of the goods. This will be the case, in particular, where the use complained of is such as to create the impression that there is a material link in the course of trade between the third party's goods and the undertaking from which they originate. The claim succeeded.[569] Subsequent rulings of the CJEU have extended the notion of infringement to cover use which affects the mark's "investment function" (the proprietor's use of a mark to acquire or preserve a reputation capable of attracting customers and retaining their loyalty)[570] or "advertising function" (the proprietor's use of the mark for advertising purposes designed to inform and persuade customers).[571]

24-118 **Use on internet marketplaces** A large number of questions have been referred to the CJEU concerning trade mark use during searches on websites such as eBay and Google. The CJEU has given judgments in a number of cases, to which the reader should refer for full details. In the *Google France* cases,[572] the CJEU ruled that Google itself did not infringe trade marks by allowing advertisers to purchase "keywords" that are also trade marks, but that advertisers who used such keywords *would* infringe if internet users could not readily ascertain the trade origin of the goods so advertised. These important developments were usefully summarised by Arnold J in *Interflora*,[573] in which he held that the use of "Interflora" as a keyword by Marks & Spencer did infringe, since consumers were not able to tell, or could tell only with difficulty, that Marks & Spencer was not part of Interflora's network; however, the use of the mark did not take unfair advantage and was not without due cause. The use of trade marks in the context of an online marketplace was further considered in *Cosmetic Warriors v Amazon*,[574] where the court found that the claimant's "LUSH" mark had been infringed.

24-119 **Likelihood of confusion** In assessing the likelihood of confusion for the purposes of s.10(2), there is an interdependence between the similarity of the marks and the similarity of the goods or services, and the reputation or level of distinctiveness of the registered trade mark.[575] The likelihood of confusion must be appreciated globally, taking account of all factors relevant to the circumstances of the case. That

---

[569] [2003] EWCA Civ 696; [2003] R.P.C. 39.

[570] *Interflora Inc v Marks & Spencer plc* (C-323/09) EU:C:2011:604; [2012] F.S.R. 3.

[571] *Google France Sarl v Louis Vuitton Malletier SA* (C-236/08) EU:C:2010:159; [2010] E.T.M.R. 30.

[572] *Google France Sarl v Louis Vuitton Malletier SA* (C-236/08) EU:C:2010:159; [2010] E.T.M.R. 30 and two other joined cases: (C-238/08) and (C-237/08) [2010] E.T.M.R. 30. See also *Portakabin Ltd v Primakabin BV* (C-558/08) EU:C:2010:416; [2010] E.T.M.R. 52; and *Die BergSpechte Outdoor Reisen und Alpinschule Edi Koblmuller GmbH v Guni* (C-278/08) EU:C:2010:163; [2010] E.T.M.R. 33. In *L'Oréal v eBay International AG* (C-324/09) EU:C:2011:474; [2011] R.P.C 27, the court confirmed the approach of the *Google France* cases, and went into detail on the role of the online marketplace in infringement.

[573] [2013] EWHC 1291 (Ch); [2013] E.T.M.R. 35. The Court of Appeal in *Interflora Inc v Marks & Spencer Plc* [2014] EWCA Civ 1403; [2015] E.T.M.R. 5 has clarified that the burden of proof is on the claimant to demonstrate infringement. Note that the essential function of a trade mark may be damaged by online sales of counterfeits even if the vendor makes clear that the goods are replica, since there will still be a risk of post-sale confusion: *Cartier International AG v British Sky Broadcasting Ltd* [2014] EWHC 3354 (Ch); [2015] 1 All E.R. 949 (this did not form part of the subsequent appeal: [2016] EWCA Civ 658; [2017] 1 All E.R. 700).

[574] *Cosmetic Warriors Ltd v Amazon.co.uk Ltd* [2014] EWHC 181 (Ch); [2014] F.S.R. 31. "Use" can also include the importing of goods under the sign, even if dispatched to consumers in the EU from outside that territory: *Blomqvist v Rolex SA* (C-98/13) EU:C:2014:55; [2014] E.T.M.R. 25.

[575] *Canon Kabushiki Kaisha v Metro-Goldwyn-Mayer Inc* (C-39/97) EU:C:1998:442; [1998] F.S.R. 332. The concept of respective goods or services being "complementary" (and thus more prone to confu-

global appreciation of the visual, aural or conceptual similarities of the marks in question must be based on the overall impression given by the marks, bearing in mind in particular their distinctive and dominant components; confusion must be assessed on the totality of the evidence from the perspective of the average consumer, who is assumed to be reasonably well informed and reasonably observant and circumspect.[576] A thorough summary of the law was provided by Arnold J in *Och-Ziff*.[577] Note that evidence that the defendant has been "living dangerously" (trying to get as close to the claimant's mark as it believes it safely can) can make a finding of trademark infringement more likely.[578] The question of the average consumer was addressed (among other issues of infringement) in *Jack Wills*.[579] The Court of Appeal has given detailed guidance on the use of survey evidence of likelihood of confusion in two decisions in *Interflora v Marks & Spencer*; survey evidence should not be admitted unless it is of real utility in the claim, and in such a way that justifies the cost of obtaining it.[580]

---

sion) has been characterised as "closely connected in the sense that one is indispensable or important for the use of the other in such a way that consumers may think that the same undertaking is responsible for manufacturing those goods or for providing those services": *Kampol v OHIM* (T-382/12) O.J. C 253, 4 August 2014, 26 at [40].

576 *Sabel BV v Puma AG* (C-251/95) EU:C:1997:528; [1998] R.P.C. 199; and *Lloyd Schuhfabrik Meyer & Co GmbH v Klijsen Handel BV* (C-342/97) EU:C:1999:323; [2000] F.S.R. 77. See also *The European Ltd v The Economist Newspaper Ltd* [1998] F.S.R. 283. The Court of Appeal has made clear that evidence of "wrong way round" confusion is admissible as evidence of a likelihood of confusion, i.e. evidence showing that consumers familiar with the alleged infringing mark were confused upon seeing the mark alleged to be infringed: *Comic Enterprises Ltd v Twentieth Century Fox Film Corp* [2016] EWCA Civ 41; [2016] E.T.M.R. 22.

577 *Och-Ziff Management Europe Ltd v Och Capital LLP* [2010] EWHC 2599 (Ch); [2011] E.T.M.R. 1; [2011] F.S.R. 11 at [72] et seq. For discussions of issues surrounding infringement, see *32Red Plc v WHG (International) Ltd* [2011] EWHC 62 (Ch); [2011] E.T.M.R. 21; and on appeal [2012] EWCA Civ 19; [2012] E.T.M.R. 14; *Kingspan Group Plc v Rockwool Ltd* [2011] EWHC 250 (Ch); *Samuel Smith Old Brewery (Tadcaster) v Lee (t/a Cropton Brewery)* [2011] EWHC 1879 (Ch); [2012] F.S.R. 7; *Maier v ASOS Plc* [2015] EWCA Civ 220; [2016] 2 All E.R. 738; and *JW Spear & Sons Ltd v Zynga Inc* [2013] EWHC 3348 (Ch); [2014] F.S.R. 19 (SCRABBLE /SCRAMBLE—no infringement, upheld on appeal: [2015] EWCA Civ 290; [2016] 1 All E.R. 226). For contrasting decisions about whether re-using a trade-marked product can give rise to infringement see *Schutz (UK) Ltd v Delta Containers Ltd* [2011] EWHC 1712 (Ch) (in which infringement was found); and *Viking Gas A/S v Kosan Gas A/S* (C-46/10) EU:C:2011:485; [2011] E.T.M.R. 58 (no infringement, on the basis of exhaustion—see para.24-120(d)). Use of abbreviations on social media (e.g. LDNR for Londoner) was considered in *Frank Industries Pty Ltd v Nike Retail BV* [2018] EWHC 1893 (Ch); [2018] F.S.R. 35.

578 *Specsavers International Healthcare Ltd v Asda Stores Ltd* [2010] EWHC 2035 (Ch); [2011] F.S.R. 1. The Court of Appeal in *Specsavers*[2012] EWCA Civ 24; [2012] F.S.R. 19 allowed (in part) an appeal on certain issues of infringement, and referred a question to the CJEU about the scope of s.10(2) (i.e. art.9(1)(b) of Regulation (EC) 207/2009) where a mark is registered without reference to colour but has in practice been used almost exclusively with a particular shade (in this case green for "Specsavers" word marks and overlapping ovals). The CJEU ruled that the parties' use of colour will form part of the assessment of likelihood of confusion: (C-252/12) EU:C:2013:497; [2014] F.S.R. 4 (and see fn.535 in relation to genuine use). The Court of Appeal consequently allowed the claimant's appeal: [2014] EWCA Civ 1294; [2015] F.S.R. 8.

579 *Jack Wills Ltd v House of Fraser (Stores) Ltd* [2014] EWHC 110; [2014] E.T.M.R. 28.

580 *Interflora Inc v Marks & Spencer Plc* [2012] EWCA Civ 1501; [2013] 2 All E.R. 663; and [2013] EWCA Civ 319; [2013] F.S.R. 26. Lawyers preparing survey evidence should be careful not to mischaracterise the raw data—as to which see the judicial comment in *A&E Television Networks LLC v Discovery Communications Europe Ltd* [2013] EWHC 109 (Ch); [2013] E.T.M.R. 32. Applying *Interflora*, survey evidence was excluded in *Zee Entertainment Enterprises Ltd v Zeebox Ltd* [2013] EWHC 1644 (Ch); [2014] F.S.R. 10 (upheld on appeal: [2014] EWCA Civ 82; [2014] F.S.R.

Limitations on the effect of a registered trade mark

24-120 (a) *Reference to the proprietor's own goods—comparative advertising.* The 1994 Act does not prevent the use of a registered trade mark by any person for the purpose of identifying goods or services as those of the proprietor or of a licensee, but any such use otherwise than in accordance with honest practices in industrial or commercial matters[581] is treated as infringing the registered trade mark if the use without due cause takes unfair advantage of, or is detrimental to, the distinctive character or repute of the trade mark. Honest comparative advertising is thereby permitted.[582] The Court of Appeal referred questions to the CJEU on whether the defendant's indicative use of the claimant's registered trade mark may constitute infringement in the cases of *L'Oreal SA v Bellure*[583] and *O2 Holdings Ltd v Hutchison 3G UK Ltd*.[584] In *O2 Holdings Ltd*[585] the CJEU confined its judgment to Council Directive 89/104

---

26); and in *Cosmetic Warriors Ltd v Amazon.co.uk Ltd* [2013] EWHC 2470 (Ch); [2014] F.S.R. 15. Permission for survey evidence was given in *TJX UK v SportsDirect.com Retail Ltd* [2019] EWHC 3246 (Ch).

581 In *Barclays Bank Plc v RBS Advanta* [1996] R.P.C. 307, Laddie J said that the test was objective and depended on whether the use would be considered honest by members of a reasonable audience.

582 TMA 1994 s.10(6). See *Barclays Bank Plc v RBS Advanta* [1996] R.P.C. 307. There are several decisions on the application of s.10(6) to comparative advertising. Their effect is summarised by Jacob J in *Cable & Wireless Plc v British Telecommunications Plc* [1998] F.S.R. 383. See also *O2 Holdings Ltd v Hutchison 3G Ltd* [2006] EWCA Civ 1656; [2007] 2 C.M.L.R. 15; [2007] R.P.C. 16. As long as the use of the competitor's mark is honest, it will be permitted. The test is objective: would a reasonable reader be likely to say, upon being given the full facts, that the advertisement was not honest? A significantly misleading advertisement will fail that test. The provisions of s.10(6) are independent of the provisions of the Comparative Advertising Directive 2006/114/EC. Vulgar abuse making use of a trade mark, is protected by s.10(6) and is not actionable: *British Airways Plc v Ryanair Ltd* [2001] F.S.R. 32 ("Expensive BA ______ DS" with price comparison: claim failed). Section 10(6) falls to be interpreted narrowly and restricted to cases in which the use of the mark is not on the proprietor's own goods: *Levi Strauss & Co v Tesco Stores Ltd* [2002] EWHC 1625 (Ch); [2002] 3 C.M.L.R. 11; [2003] R.P.C. 18. Where a competitor uses a trade mark proprietor's product numbers, that may constitute comparative advertising, but the competitor will only be liable for trade mark infringement, if the effect of the reference to them is to create in the mind of the persons at whom the advertising is directed an association between the manufacturer whose products are identified and the competing supplier: *Toshiba Europe GmbH v Katun Germany GmbH* (C-112/99) EU:C:2001:566; [2002] F.S.R. 39. Sometimes an action for malicious falsehood can be more effective than reliance on trade mark rights. See, e.g. *DSG Retail v Comet Group Plc* [2002] EWHC 116 (QB); [2002] F.S.R. 58; but contrast the decision in *Kingspan Group Plc v Rockwool Ltd* [2011] EWHC 250 (Ch), in which a claim for malicious falsehood failed, while the claim for infringement based on comparative advertising succeeded. The court will not grant an interlocutory injunction in a comparative advertising case where the defendant has an arguable case and to do so would interfere with the right to free speech: *Macmillan Magazines Ltd v RCN Publishing Co Ltd* [1998] F.S.R. 9. See also *Boehringer Ingelheim Ltd v Vetplus* [2007] EWCA Civ 583; [2007] F.S.R. 29 (no interim injunction was granted to prevent comparative advertising). Section 10(6) does not only protect comparative advertising but prevents a claim arising from other kinds of genuine reference to the claimant's goods or services: *Wolters Kluwer (UK) Ltd v Reed Elsevier (UK) Ltd* [2005] EWHC 2053 (Ch); [2006] F.S.R. 28. The CJEU has ruled that the definition of "advertising" in the Directive extends to the use of a domain name and metatags, but not to the mere registration of a domain name: *Belgian Electronic Sorting Technology NV v Peelaers* (C-657/11) EU:C:2013:516; [2013] E.T.M.R. 45.

583 [2007] EWCA Civ 968; [2008] E.T.M.R. 1.

584 [2006] EWCA Civ 1656; [2007] 2 C.M.L.R. 15.

585 (C-533/06) [2008] 3 C.M.L.R. 14.

art.5(1)(b) (TMA 1994 s.10(2)). However, in *L'Oreal*[586] the CJEU stated that where a defendant used a claimant's mark and explicitly states that his product is an imitation of the claimant's, the advantage so gained must be considered to be one taken unfairly of the mark's reputation within the meaning of art.3a(1)(g) of Directive 2006/114/EC on comparative advertising.

(b) *Descriptive use, use of own name, ancillary use etc.* There is no infringement by:

(i) the use by a person of his own name or address[587];

(ii) the use of indications concerning the kind, quality, quantity, intended purpose, value, geographical origin, the time of production of goods or of rendering of services or other characteristics of goods or services; or

(iii) the use of the trade mark where it is necessary to indicate the intended purpose of a product or service (in particular, as accessories or spare parts) provided the use is in accordance with honest practices in industrial or commercial matters.[588]

(c) *Other exceptions to infringement.* There are a number of other exceptions to infringement, including situations where there are earlier rights.[589]

(d) *Exhaustion of rights.* A registered trade mark is not infringed by the use of the trade mark in relation to goods which have been put on the market in the European Economic Area (EEA) under that trade mark by the proprietor or with his consent[590] except where there are legitimate reasons for the proprie-

---

586 *L'Oréal SA v Bellure* NV (C-487/07) EU:C:2009:378; [2009] E.T.M.R. 55.

587 s.11(2). However honest a defendant's subjective intentions were, any use of his own name which amounted to passing off would not be in accordance with honest practices in industrial or commercial matters and the "own name" defence would not apply in such circumstances: *Asprey and Garrard Ltd v WRA (Guns) Ltd* [2001] EWCA Civ 1499; [2002] F.S.R. 31. It is possible to rely on the defence unless significant deception is shown to result: *Reed Executive Plc v Reed Business Information Ltd* [2004] EWCA Civ 159; [2004] E.T.M.R. 56. In relation to Community trade marks (Regulation 207/2009), a company may rely on its trading name as well as its corporate name, depending on the circumstances: *Hotel Cipriani Srl v Cipriani (Grosvenor Street) Ltd* [2010] EWCA Civ 110; [2010] R.P.C. 16; it is submitted that the same would apply in relation to s.11(2). For an example of a defendant choosing its company name with no good reason (and thereby having no defence to infringement) see *Smithkline Beecham Ltd v GSKline Ltd* [2011] EWHC 169 (Ch). The own-name defence was upheld in *Stichting BDO v BDO Unibank Inc* [2013] EWHC 418 (Ch); [2013] E.T.M.R. 31; and also in *A&E Television Networks LLC v Discovery Communications Europe Ltd* [2013] EWHC 109 (Ch); [2013] E.T.M.R. 32, in which "DISCOVERY HISTORY" did not infringe "THE HISTORY CHANNEL". An own-name defence failed as regards past acts but was upheld in relation to ongoing dealings in *Property Renaissance Ltd (t/a Titanic Spa) v Stanley Dock Hotel Ltd (t/a Titanic Hotel)* [2016] EWHC 3103 (Ch); [2017] E.T.M.R. 12.

588 TMA 1994 s.11(2). In *Hearst Holdings Inc v AVELA* [2014] EWHC 439 (Ch); [2014] F.S.R. 36 the court rejected the argument that the defendant was simply using pictures of the cartoon character "Betty Boop" in a descriptive manner (see [179]–[189]). The "repair clause" found in art.14 of the Design Directive 98/71/EC does not afford a defence to trade mark infringement: *Ford Motor Company v Wheeltrims srl* (C-500/14) EU:C:2015:680; [2016] E.C.D.R. 14 (marketing of spare-part wheel covers for cars). For use held not to be an honest indication of the kind of goods, see *Hasbro Inc v 123 Nahrmittel GmbH* [2011] EWHC 199 (Ch); [2011] E.T.M.R. 25 (product described as "play-dough"; claimant owned registered trade mark "PLAY-DOH"). The "indication of kind" defence was also rejected in *Bayerische Motoren Werke AG v Round & Metal Ltd* [2012] EWHC 2099; [2013] F.S.R. 18.

589 TMA 1994 s.11(3). Note that in general, estoppel and/or acquiescence cannot be relied on to provide a defence to trade mark infringement: *Coreix Ltd v Coretx Holdings Plc* [2017] EWHC 1695 (IPEC); [2018] F.S.R. 6.

590 The CJEU has given a restrictive interpretation of the concept of "consent" for the purpose of exhaustion of rights holding that consent to goods being placed on the market in the EEA could not be

tor to oppose further dealings in the goods.[591] The conditions set by the CJEU for parallel importers who repackaged or re-labelled trade marked goods in *Bristol Myers Squibb Co v Paranova A/S*,[592] were subsequently elaborated upon by the CJEU in its second reference for *Boehringer Ingelheim KG v Swingward Ltd*;[593] this was then applied by the Court of Appeal[594] in its resumed hearing. The Court of Appeal held that though the CJEU in its second reference had said that partial de-branding in principle damaged the trade mark, it was a question of fact. Co-branding did not automatically lead to the damage and de-branding was not an infringement of the trade mark. A registered trade mark owner's rights are not exhausted by placing the goods on the market outside the EEA[595]; only express consent to subsequent marketing in the EEA is likely to suffice to exhaust the proprietor's registered trade mark rights. In *Oracle v M-Tech*, the way in which the claimant marketed its goods was designed to make it difficult to tell if goods had first been marketed within the EEA; the Court of Appeal held that it was arguable that this was contrary to Community law on free movement of goods, but this was reversed by the Supreme Court.[596] The rights of a trade mark proprietor also appear to extend to preventing third parties from first marketing in the EEA goods that the proprietor has already sold under the mark outside the EEA but from which

---

inferred from the fact that the proprietor has not communicated the opposition to marketing, that no warning was given or that no contractual reservations were made at the time of sale—see joined *Zino Davidoff SA v A Imports Ltd* (C-414/99 to C-416/99) EU:C:2001:617; [2002] E.T.M.R. 9. The CJEU in *Schweppes SA v Red Paralela SL & Ors* (C-291/16) EU:C:2017:990; [2018] E.T.M.R. 13 has ruled that the proprietor of a mark is to be prohibited from opposing the import of identical goods bearing the same mark originating in another Member State when that mark initially belonged to the proprietor and was assigned to a third party with whom the proprietor remains economically linked or continues to coordinate its trade mark strategy in order to exercise joint control over the trade mark.

591 In particular, where the condition of the goods has been changed or impaired after they have been put on the market: TMA 1994 s.12. This section gives effect to the principle of exhaustion of rights within the EEA. The principles are reviewed in *Bristol Myers Squibb v Paranova* (C-427/93, C-429/93 and C-436/93) EU:C:1996:282; [1997] F.S.R. 102. See also *Mastercigars Direct Ltd v Hunters & Frankau Ltd* [2007] EWCA Civ 176; [2007] R.P.C. 24. For an example of a successful opposition to such remarketing, concerning disassembled components for charm bracelets, see *Nomination Di Antonio e Paolo Gensini snc v Brealey (t/a JSC Jewellery)* [2019] EWHC 599 (IPEC); [2019] F.S.R. 23; upheld on appeal: [2020] EWCA Civ 103. See also *Junek Europ-Vertrieb GmbH v Lohmann & Rauscher International GmbH & Co KG* (C-642/16) EU:C:2018:322 (no legitimate reasons for opposing), distinguished by Birss J in *Dansac A/S v Salts Healthcare Ltd* [2019] EWHC 104 (Ch); [2019] E.T.M.R. 25. The onus is on the defendant in an infringement action to put forward a defence of exhaustion: *Honda Motor Co Ltd v David Silver Spares Ltd* [2010] EWHC 1973 (Ch); [2010] F.S.R. 40.

592 [2003] Ch. 75.

593 (C-348/04) EU:C:2007:249; [2007] E.T.M.R. 71.

594 [2008] EWCA Civ 83; [2008] E.T.M.R. 55; [2008] E.T.M.R. 36. In *Speciality European Pharma Ltd v Doncaster Pharmaceuticals Group Ltd* [2015] EWCA Civ 54; [2015] 3 All E.R. 504 the Court of Appeal held that rebranding by a parallel importer went no further than was necessary to overcome artificial barriers to effective market access. The use of a small-print disclaimer to state that the parallel-imported goods are not made or marketed by the entity which owns the trade mark is not a defence to infringement: *Flynn Pharma Ltd v Drugsrus Ltd* [2015] EWHC 2759 (Ch); [2016] E.T.M.R. 4 (appeal subsequently dismissed: [2017] EWCA Civ 226; [2017] E.T.M.R. 25).

595 *Silhouette International Schmied GmbH & Co KG v Handelsgesellschaft mbH* (C-355/96) EU:C:1998:374; [1998] F.S.R. 729. See also *Coty Prestige Lancaster Group GmbH v Simex Trading AG* (C-127/09) EU:C:2010:313; [2010] E.T.M.R. 41.

596 *Oracle America Inc v M-Tech Data Ltd* [2010] EWCA Civ 997; [2010] E.T.M.R. 64; Supreme Court: [2012] UKSC 27; [2012] 1 W.L.R. 2026

the proprietor's marks have been stripped prior to EEA marketing by the third party.[597] Damage done to the reputation of the trade mark is a legitimate reason for objecting to further commercialisation within the meaning of s.12. However, where a proprietor uses a trade mark for bringing the public's attention to the further commercialisation of the goods, the proprietor must show that the use of the trade mark for this purpose seriously damages the reputation of the trade mark.[598] Similarly, if a licensee acts in contravention of the terms of its licence, but where the proprietor is taken to have given permission for the goods to be placed on the market, sale of the goods can only be prevented where the sale damages the reputation of the mark (e.g. its reputation for luxury).[599] The CJEU held in *Viking Gas v Kosan Gas* that the proprietor of a shape mark for gas canisters had exhausted its rights in that mark by placing the product on the market in the EEA, and could not prevent customers exchanging empty canisters for ones refilled by a third party, absent any proper reason for objecting under art.7(2) of Directive (EC) 207/2009.[600]

In all legal proceedings relating to a registered trade mark, the registration of a person as proprietor of a trade mark shall be prima facie evidence of the validity of the original registration and of any subsequent assignment or other transmission of it.[601]

(d) Proceedings

Proceedings for trade mark infringement and remedies Infringement of registered trade mark is actionable by the proprietor of the trade mark.[602] All such relief by way of damages injunctions, accounts or otherwise is available to him as is available in respect of the infringement of any other proprietary right[603] and orders may be made for the erasure, removal or obliteration of offending signs or the **24-121**

---

597 *Mitsubishi Shoji Kaisha Ltd v Duma Forklifts NV* (C-129/17) EU:C:2018:594; [2018] E.T.M.R. 37.

598 *Parfums Christian Dior SA v Evora BV* (C-337/95) EU:C:1997:517; [1998] R.P.C. 166.

599 *Copad SA v Christian Dior Couture SA* (C-59/08) EU:C:2009:260; [2009] E.T.M.R. 40.

600 *Viking Gas A/S v Kosan Gas A/S* (C-46/10) EU:C:2011:485; [2011] E.T.M.R. 58.

601 TMA 1994 s.72.

602 TMA 1994 s.14. In certain circumstances, infringement may be actionable at the suit of a licensee: see ss.30 and 31. No infringement proceedings may be begun before the date on which the trade mark is in fact registered: s.9(3). The fact that the mark alleged to infringe is itself registered is no bar to a finding of infringement, and the proprietor of the earlier mark need not first obtain a finding of invalidity against the later mark: *Fédération Cynologique Internationale v Federación Canina Internacional de Perros de Pura Raza* (C-561/11) EU:C:2013:91; [2013] E.T.M.R. 23. This presents an apparent conflict with s.11(1) TMA 1994, which may have to be resolved in due course.

603 TMA 1994 s.14(2). There are limitations on the right of persons who have not registered relevant transactions in due time: see s.25. Proof of infringement entitles a claimant to nominal damages but the burden is on the claimant to prove any actual damage. For a detailed consideration of the deduction and offset of overheads in calculating an account of profits, see *Jack Wills Ltd v House of Fraser (Stores) Ltd* [2016] EWHC 626 (Ch). The High Court (approved by the Court of Appeal) has established the availability of "blocking injunctions" to require internet service providers to block subscriber access to websites that are advertising and selling counterfeit goods: *Cartier International AG v British Sky Broadcasting Ltd* [2016] EWCA Civ 658; [2017] 1 All E.R. 700. The Supreme Court overturned the Court of Appeal's view that the ISPs should bear the costs of implementing such blocks ([2018] UKSC 28; [2018] 1 W.L.R. 3259). The "user" principle of applying a royalty was considered and applied in *32Red Plc v WHG (International) Ltd* [2013] EWHC 815 (Ch). An account of profits was assessed in *Woolley v UP Global Sourcing UK Ltd* [2014] EWHC 493 (Ch); [2014] F.S.R. 37; loss of profits was used to quantify damages in *Link Up Mitaka Ltd v Language Empire Ltd* [2018] EWHC 2633 (IPEC). On the approach to summary assessment of damages in a

destruction of infringing goods, and blocking injunctions are available against internet service providers in respect of websites selling infringing goods.[604] Damages may include any loss of trade actually suffered by the claimant either directly from the acts complained of or properly attributable to the injury to the claimant's reputation, business or goodwill, including the cost of corrective advertisements.[605] In some cases it may be appropriate to award a somewhat arbitrary capital sum to reflect the expropriation against the claimant's wishes of the monopoly right to use the mark.[606] There is no presumption that the claimant would have made the sales made by the defendant.[607] When conducting an account of profits it is not appropriate simply to allocate a proportion of the infringer's general overheads to the infringing activity; the infringer must show what costs are properly attributable to the infringements[608]. The liability of individual joint tortfeasors does not necessarily extend to the profits of a company with which they are jointly liable.[609] Orders may also be made for delivery up or disposal of infringing material goods or articles.[610] Interlocutory injunctions are granted on the usual principles.[611] Trade mark infringement can be amenable to summary judgment.[612]

case in which there was user of a trade mark on a website, resulting in some benefit to the claimant see *Roadtech Computer Systems Ltd v Mandata Ltd* [2000] E.T.M.R. 970. Innocence is no defence to damages (*Gillette UK Ltd v Edenwest Ltd* [1994] R.P.C. 279) but may be a defence to an account of profits.

604 TMA 1994 ss.14(2) and 15. For discussion of blocking injunctions see *Cartier International v British Telecommunications Plc* [2018] UKSC 28; [2018] 1 W.L.R. 3259, which held that trade mark owners must indemnify ISPs against the cost of complying with such injunctions. See also *Nintendo Co Ltd v Sky UK Ltd* [2019] EWHC 2376 (Ch); [2019] E.T.M.R. 60: an injunction may be available for circumvention of copyright protection measures contrary to CDPA 1988 ss.296 or 296ZD.

605 *Spalding v Gamage* (1918) 35 R.P.C. 101; *Manus v Fullwood* (1954) 71 R.P.C. 243.

606 *Duracell v Ever Ready* [1989] 1 F.S.R. 71.

607 *Draper v Trist* (1939) 56 R.P.C. 429; *Leather Cloth v Hirschfield* (1865) L.R. 1 Eq. 299.

608 *Hollister Inc v Medik Ostomy Supplies Ltd* [2012] EWCA Civ 1419; [2013] F.S.R. 24. For another example of account of profits see *Champagne Louis Roederer (CLR) v J. Garcia Carrion S.A.* [2017] EWHC 289 (Ch).

609 *Lifestyle Equities CV v Santa Monica Polo Club Ltd* [2020] EWHC 688 (Ch); [2020] E.T.M.R. 33.

610 TMA 1994 ss.16 and 19. See s.17 for the meaning of "infringing goods", "infringing material" and "infringing articles". There are time limits after which the remedy of delivery up is not available: s.18.

611 *American Cyanamid Co v Ethicon Ltd* [1975] A.C. 386; *Series 5 Software Ltd v Clarke* [1996] 1 All E.R. 853. A factor to be taken into account in deciding whether to grant an interim injunction is that the defendant's proposed operations might "swamp" the claimant's goodwill: *Elan Digital Systems Ltd v Elan Computer Ltd* [1984] F.S.R. 373 at 385. Often, an order for a speedy trial will be more appropriate. Trade mark infringement (and passing off) proceedings present a special difficulty: a defendant who has been enjoined and adopted a new mark as a result will often be unable to return to the mark in issue. In such a case, the interlocutory injunction application will, in practice, determine the whole action. For a detailed decision concerning calculation of damages resulting from a cross-undertaking in the context of a trade mark claim see *Lilly Icos LLC v 8PM Chemists Ltd* [2009] EWHC 1905 (Ch); [2010] F.S.R. 4. An injunction was refused in *Cowshed Products Ltd v Island Origins Ltd* [2010] EWHC 3357 (Ch); [2011] E.T.M.R. 42, after a detailed evaluation based on that same set of principles. Note that an injunction against infringement of an EUTM will, as a rule, extend to the entire European Union: *DHL Express France SAS v Chronopost SA* (C-235/09) EU:C:2011:238; [2011] E.T.M.R. 33. An injunction was also refused in *Protomed Ltd v Medication Systems Ltd* [2012] EWHC 3726 (Ch), where it was held that the claimant did not have a good arguable case on infringement; affirmed on appeal: [2013] EWCA Civ 1205. The principles relating to prohibitory and mandatory injunctions were considered in detail by the Court of Appeal in *Frank Industries Pty UK v Nike Retail BV* [2018] EWCA Civ 497; [2018] F.S.R. 24.

612 *British Sky Broadcasting Group Plc v Digital Satellite Warranty Cover Ltd (In Liquidation)* [2011] EWHC 2662 (Ch); [2012] F.S.R. 14. That case concerned s.10(1). Arnold J also considered database

Criminal offences and customs powers There are criminal sanctions for the unauthorised use of trade marks in relation to goods.[613] Offences include falsification of the register,[614] and falsely representing trade marks as registered.[615] The proprietor of a registered trade mark or a licensee may give notice in writing to the Commissioners of Customs and Excise requesting the Commissioners to treat infringing goods, material or article as prohibited goods. Where such a notice is in force, the importation of the goods to which the notice relates is prohibited, otherwise than by a person for his private and domestic use.[616] **24-122**

Special protection for well-known trade marks Under s.56 of the Trade Marks Act 1994, a proprietor of a trade mark which is entitled to protection under the Paris Convention as a well-known trade mark is entitled (with certain limits) to restrain by injunction the use in the UK of a trade mark which, or the essential part of which, is identical or similar to his mark, in relation to identical or similar goods or services, where the use is likely to cause confusion. This is only so where the mark in question is well known in the UK as being the mark of a person who is a national of a Paris Convention country or who is domiciled or has a real and effective industrial or commercial establishment in a Convention country whether or not that person carries on business or has any goodwill in the UK. A summary of the law relating to well-known trade marks under s.56 is provided by Arnold J in *Hotel Cipriani SRL v Cipriani (Grosvenor Street) Ltd*.[617] There is special protection against certain unauthorised uses of the Olympic symbol, pursuant to the Olympic Symbol etc Protection Act 1995. **24-123**

Unjustified threats of trade mark infringement proceedings It is an actionable wrong to threaten any person with proceedings for trade mark infringement unless the threat can be justified, other than in respect of: **24-124**

right and passing off. For summary judgment on s.10(2) infringement see *Lewis v Client Connection Ltd* [2011] EWHC 1627 (Ch); [2012] E.T.M.R. 6; and *United Airlines Inc v United Airways Ltd* [2011] EWHC 2411 (Ch).

613 TMA 1994 s.92. The House of Lords addressed criminal liability under s.92 in *R. v Johnstone* [2003] UKHL 28; [2003] 1 W.L.R. 1736. A criminal defendant should only be liable where his actions would have amounted to a civil infringement of the trade mark. The court may make a confiscation order under the Proceeds of Crime Act 2002 in relation to trade mark offences: *R. v Ghori* [2012] EWCA Crim 1115. In a separate decision the Court of Appeal rejected arguments that such an order was oppressive: *R. v Beazley* [2013] EWCA Crim 567; [2013] 1 W.L.R. 3331. Offences under TMA s.92(1) apply not only to counterfeit goods but also to "grey goods"—i.e. ones manufactured with the permission of the trade mark proprietor but not authorised for sale: *R. v C, R. v T, R. v M* [2017] UKSC 58; [2017] 1 W.L.R. 3006.

614 TMA 1994 s.94.

615 TMA 1994 s.95. It is also an offence to make unauthorised use of Royal arms etc s.99.

616 TMA 1994 s.89. As to the meaning of "counterfeit" in this context, Kitchin J held in *Nokia Corp v Revenue and Customs Commissioners* [2009] EWHC 1903 (Ch); [2009] E.T.M.R. 59 that the goods in question had to infringe someone's trade marks in the relevant territory. The CJEU has ruled that goods brought into the EU customs area under a suspensive procedure (rather than being actually sold or advertised) cannot be classified as counterfeit or pirated goods: *Koninklijke Philips Electronics NV v Lucheng Meijing Industrial Co Ltd* (C-446/09) EU:C:2011:796; [2012] E.T.M.R. 13. Contrast *Blomqvist v Rolex SA* (C-98/13) EU:C:2014:55; [2014] E.T.M.R. 25, in which the CJEU held that mere acquisition of goods through an online sales website was enough to justify seizure under the customs Regulation, even without an offer for sale or advertisement targeting consumers in the State where the seizure took place. As to what constitutes targeting UK consumers on the internet, see *Argos Ltd v Argos Systems Inc* [2018] EWCA Civ 2211; [2019] F.S.R. 3.

617 [2008] EWHC 3032 (Ch); [2009] R.P.C. 9 at [235]–[240]; affirmed at [2010] EWCA Civ 110; [2010] R.P.C. 16.

(a) applying, or causing another person to apply, a sign to goods or their packaging;
(b) importing, for disposal, goods to which or to the packaging of which a sign has been applied; or
(c) supplying services under a mark.[618]

"Any person" aggrieved may bring proceedings for a declaration that the threats are unjustifiable, an injunction against the continuance of the threats and damages in respect of any loss sustained by the threats.[619] The test is whether a reasonable person in the position of a recipient would understand from the communication that the trade mark exists, and a person intends to bring infringement proceedings against another person in respect of acts done (or to be done) in the UK.[620] Merely giving notice that a trade mark exists is one of the "permitted acts" under s.21B, i.e. it is not actionable. This is a similar provision to that relating to patents, where the principles are well-established (see below). It is a defence to an action for threats to prove that "the acts in respect of which proceedings were threatened constitutes (or if done would constitute) an infringement of the trade mark".[621]

9. Patents

(a) Introduction

24-125 **Patents—scope of section** This section outlines the law of patents. There are several well-regarded practitioners' books on the law of patents, to which reference should be made for the required detail.[622]

---

618 TMA 1994 ss.21–21E; as with patents (see para.24-148), the unjustified threats provisions in respect of trade marks were amended by the Intellectual Property (Unjustified Threats) Act 2017, replacing the old TMA 1994 s.21. Various detailed exceptions and conditions apply to the new provisions (such as for permitted communications, and professional advisers), and the reader is advised to consult the statute.

619 TMA 1994 s.21C(1).

620 TMA 1994 s.21(1). Under the old s.21 implied threats were actionable: *Scandecor Development AB v Scandecor Marketing AB* [1999] F.S.R. 26 CA; as were "veiled and muffled" threats: *L'Oréal (UK) Ltd v Johnson & Johnson* [2000] F.S.R. 686. cf. *Nvidia Corp v Hardware Labs Performance Systems Inc* [2016] EWHC 3135 (Ch); [2017] Bus. L.R. 549. A Community-wide mark could found an action for threats of infringement proceedings under the old provisions, but only if the threat was in relation to proceedings within the UK: *Best Buy Co Inc v Worldwide Sales Corp España SL* [2011] EWCA Civ 618; [2011] F.S.R. 30. See also *Data Marketing & Secretarial Ltd v S & S Enterprises Ltd* [2014] EWHC 1499 (IPEC); [2015] F.S.R. 1.

621 TMA 1994 s.21C(2).

622 See R. Miller, G. Burkhill, C. Birss and D. Campbell, *Terrell on the Law of Patents*, 18th edn (Sweet & Maxwell, 2016; 19th edn estimated June 2020); P. Cole et al, *CIPA Guide to the Patents Acts*, 9th edn (Sweet & Maxwell, 2019); G. Hamer et al, *Encyclopedia of United Kingdom and European Patent Law* (Sweet & Maxwell, two releases per year). For procedure in infringement etc before the courts, including the England and Wales Intellectual Property Enterprise Court (IPEC) (formerly the Patents County Court (PCC)) see Civil Procedure Rules (CPR) Pt.63, "Patents and Other Intellectual Property Claims". Detailed information on the work of IPEC is set out in the *Intellectual Property Enterprise Court Guide* (amended 5 August 2019) at: *https://www.gov.uk/government/publications/intellectual-property-enterprise-court-guide* [Accessed 3 April 2020] and the associated *Intellectual Property Enterprise Court: A Guide to Small Claims*, published 12 February 2018 and available on the same web page. See also A. Fox, *The Intellectual Property Enterprise Court: Practice and Procedure*, 2nd edn (Sweet & Maxwell, 2016). The small claims track is for low value intellectual property disputes, with a value capped at £10,000. The PCC was renamed with effect from 1 October 2013, to clarify its jurisdiction, which covers all areas of intellectual property, not

Introduction—the statutory framework Patents are purely statutory. The principal Act is the Patents Act 1977 (PA 1977), which brought UK law in line with the European Patent Convention 1973 (revised 2000) (EPC). Until the coming into force of that Act, somewhat different rules applied to the validity of patents under the Patents Act 1949—in particular that patents could be challenged on somewhat wider grounds. Some of the principles from the older cases are still of importance. Later laws, including the Copyright, Designs and Patents Act 1988, the Regulatory Reform (Patents Act) Order 2004, and the Patent Act 2004 have changed the 1977 Act.[623] **24-126**

The Unified Patent Court Until recently, there has been no European Union instrument governing patent law, although certain connected rights, such as Supplementary Protection Certificates, are governed by EU law.[624] Following an agreement reached in December 2012 by the European Parliament and 25 EU Member States (all Member States except Croatia (which subsequently joined the Union) Italy and Spain) concluding more than 30 years of negotiations, a patent package consisting of two Regulations and an international Agreement was adopted early in 2013, laying the foundations for the creation of unitary patent protection in the European Union. The Regulations implement enhanced co-operation in the area of unitary patent protection and the applicable translation requirements for such protection respectively. The Regulations entered into force on 20 January 2013. The third instrument, the Agreement on a Unified Patent Court (UPC), which would have exclusive jurisdiction relating to litigation concerning unitary patents, was signed by all Member States except Poland and Spain on 19 February 2013. These three instruments would apply once the international Agreement entered into force following ratification by 13 contracting states (now exceeded, but see below), including France, Germany and the UK.[625] Following the UK referendum vote in June 2016 there was substantial uncertainty about the future of the UPC, given the **24-127**

just patents. For procedure before the Intellectual Property Office (IPO, formerly the Patent Office), see the Patents Rules 2007 (SI 2007/3291), and Patent (Fees) Rules 2007 (SI 2007/3292), as amended to 6 April 2018, and The Manual of Patent Practice (updated 1 April 2020), all of which are available at: *http://www.gov.uk/topic/intellectual-property/patents* [Accessed 3 April 2020].

623 The most recent amendments came into effect on 1 October 2017 (relating to unjustified threats). An unofficial consolidation of the Patents Act 1977 (as amended up to and including 1 October 2017) is available on the Intellectual Property Office website: *https://www.gov.uk/government/publications/the-patents-act-1977* [Accessed 3 April 2020]. See also the Patents (Convention Countries) Order 2007 (SI 2007/276), (as amended by the Patents (Convention Countries) (Amendment) Order 2013 (SI 2013/538)) for the protection afforded to foreign nationals pursuant to the international obligations of the UK as a member of the EPC, PCT, Paris Convention for the Protection of Industrial Property and the World Trade Organisation (WTO).

624 The new unitary patent system does not provide for unitary Supplementary Protection Certificates (SPCs). The current EU SPC Regulation would allow national SPCs to be granted based on a unitary patent. The Commission is currently considering the creation of a unitary SPC. On SPCs generally, see para.24-131.

625 Regulation (EU) No.1257/2012 of the European Parliament and of the Council of 17 December 2012, implementing enhanced cooperation in the area of the creation of unitary patent protection; Council regulation (EU) No.1260/2012 of 17 December 2012, implementing enhanced cooperation in the area of the creation of unitary patent protection with regard to the applicable translation arrangements. The Agreement on a Unified Patent Court (UPC) was signed on 19 February 2013. This instrument is an international agreement concluded outside the EU institutional framework. Part 2 of the Intellectual Property Act 2014 implements a number of changes to patent law, including provisions enabling the UK to bring the Unitary Patent and Unified Patent Court into effect. More detailed amendments to PA 1977 are contained in the Patents (European Patent with Unitary Effect and Unified Patent Court) Order 2016 (SI 2016/388), which will give effect to the legislation on the

UK's intended role as a key signatory and one of the host countries for the court; however, in November 2016 the UK Government confirmed that it was proceeding with preparations to ratify the UPC Agreement, and ratified the Agreement on 26 April 2018. A "sunrise" period in which unitary patents would become available, but with an opt-out for applicants for European patents, had been scheduled to begin in September 2017. However, preliminary operations of the UPC could not begin pending the resolution of a complaint about the German national implementing legislation, which was before the country's Constitutional Court. That court decided on 13 February 2020 that the complaint was admissible and that the legislation had not received the required two-thirds majority approval in the Bundestag. This alone was a major setback for the UPC, but then on 27 February 2020 the UK government confirmed that it was withdrawing from the UPC. These two events together mean that the future of the court is now in real doubt.[626]

24-128 **European Patent Convention 1973** However, these latest EU developments had long been preceded by the European Patent Convention 1973 (amended in 2000 and referred to as the EPC) and build on the existing structure of the EPC. The EPC harmonised certain standard rules governing substantive patent law in Europe with the result that the patent laws in all EPC signatory States are intended to be in conformity with the EPC.[627] The EPC is not an EU instrument and its membership is not identical to that of the European Union. It establishes a single procedure for the examination of European patent applications and for the grant of European patents by the European Patent Office (EPO), based in Munich.[628] That said, a European patent as such is not a true pan-national intellectual property right as is a Community Trade Mark, but rather it creates a bundle of national patents which confer on its proprietor the same rights as would be conferred by national patents granted in the States designated in the patent with effect from the date that the mention of its grant is published in the European Patent Bulletin.[629] EU unitary patents will be granted and administered by the existing European Patent Office (EPO) alongside European patents. Thus, the new EU patent regime will allow unitary patents to be granted by the European Patent Office (EPO) for the 27 EU Member States on the basis of a single application. Once the system is in force, the Unified Patent Court will also have jurisdiction for existing and future traditional European bundle patents granted by the EPO to nationals of all EPO Member States including the EU Member States.

24-129 **Rights conferred by a patent** A patent or application for a patent is personal property.[630] A patent, if valid, gives the proprietor (and, in appropriate circumstances, an exclusive licensee thereof) the right to prevent others from making, sell-

unitary patent and UPC; the order comes into force on the date of entry into force of the Agreement on a Unified Patent Court: see art.1(2).

626 For updates and further information see the website of the Unified Patent Court at: *https://www.unified-patent-court.org* [Accessed 3 April 2020].

627 All Member States of the European Union are contracting states to the EPC, but the EPC also has 10 additional contracting states: Albania, Iceland, Liechtenstein, Monaco, Norway, Former Yugoslav Republic of Macedonia, Serbia, San Marino, Switzerland and Turkey.

628 The EPO's website may be viewed at: *http://www.epo.org* [Accessed 3 April 2020].

629 EPC art.64(1).

630 PA 1977 s.30.

ing or using the invention and the right to claim damages or an account of profits for infringement of that monopoly right.[631]

Application for a patent—priority date Essentially, there are three ways of obtaining a patent effective in the UK: **24-130**

(1) to apply to the UK Intellectual Property Office for a national patent[632];
(2) to apply to the European Patent Office for a European patent;
(3) to make an international application under the Patent Cooperation Treaty (PCT).[633]

By adopting the second route, it is possible to obtain patents in the Contracting States of the European Patent Convention with a single central application. The grant of a European patent may be opposed in the European Patent Office at any time during the nine months after its grant.[634] In addition, such patents may be challenged at any time after grant in the national courts (and patent offices) for each of the countries designated, where such patents are treated as national patents.[635] An important date in the law of patents is the so-called "priority date" which is usually the date of filing of the application.[636] The state of the art, for the purposes of determining matters such as novelty and obviousness, is assessed as at the priority date.

Term of patent The maximum term of a patent is 20 years from the date of fil- **24-131**

---

631 PA 1977 ss.60–71.

632 See PA 1977 ss.14–24 for procedure.

633 There is also the possibility of filing an international application with effect in several states under the Patent Cooperation Treaty (PCT) 1970, which is administered by the World Intellectual Property Organization (WIPO), in Geneva. The PCT provides a unified procedure for obtaining patent protection in 148 countries worldwide on the basis of a single application. National patents may be obtained in PCT Contracting States as well as regional patents such as those granted by the EPO. The international PCT phase includes a formalities check, an international search and the option of a preliminary examination. Readers are referred to the above-mentioned specialist works for details and the WIPO website (*https://www.wipo.int/pct/en* [Accessed 3 April 2020]).

634 EPC art.99. Oppositions frequently take several years to resolve. For a case on the principles to be applied in exercising the court's discretion, see *IPCom GmbH & Co KG v HTC Europe Co Ltd* [2013] EWCA Civ 1496; [2014] R.P.C. 12, where the Court of Appeal held that the default position should be to award a stay.

635 Whilst the PA 1977 recognises a granted European patent as if it were a national UK patent, this does not create a "jurisdictional" link. Thus, UK courts have no power to review the validity (or otherwise) of patents granted by the EPO on grounds not specified in the EPC, such as procedural errors which may have occurred during the examination and grant procedure: *Virgin Atlantic Airways Ltd v Jet Airways (India) Ltd* [2013] EWCA Civ 1713; [2014] R.P.C. 18.

636 PA 1977 s.5. EPC art.87. It is possible to obtain an earlier priority date relying on a similar earlier application filed not more than 12 months previously in the UK or a Contracting State of the Paris Convention for the Protection of Industrial Property or the World Trade Organisation (WTO). The law of priority is complex and the reader is referred to specialist works on the subject. For analysis, see *Edwards Lifesciences AG v Cook Biotech Inc* [2009] EWHC 1304 (Pat); [2009] F.S.R. 27; and *Novartis AG v Johnson & Johnson Medical Ltd* [2009] EWHC 1671 (Pat), per Kitchin J, affirmed by the Court of Appeal: [2010] EWCA Civ 1039; [2011] E.C.C. 10; (2011) B.M.L.R. 15. The question of "partial priority"—whereby only part of a given claim may be entitled to an earlier priority date—and the standard of disclosure required in order to claim priority generally have been revised by the Enlarged Board of Appeal of the European Patent Office in case G01/15; the UK courts should try to follow the EPO's interpretation of the EPC: see *Actavis UK Ltd v Merck & Co Inc* [2008] EWCA Civ 444; [2008] R.P.C. 26, per Jacob LJ at [48]. Case G01/15 has also dealt with the issue of so-called poisonous priority, which was raised in *Nicocigs Ltd v Fontem Holdings 1 BV* [2016] EWHC 2161 (Pat).

ing of the application, provided that the renewal fees are paid.[637] There is provision to extend the effective term of pharmaceutical and agrochemical patent protection by way of Supplementary Protection Certificates (SPCs) to compensate for the time lost in obtaining marketing approval. This is a complex subject in its own right, entailing the overlap of patent and regulatory regimes, and it has its own extensive case law.[638]

24-132 **Ownership, entitlement, licensing and employee inventions** A patent is personal property (without being a thing in action)[639] which may be assigned or transferred by operation of law in the same way as other personal property.[640] A patent may be co-owned, in which case any of the owners may bring proceedings for infringement but must join the other co-owners.[641] There are provisions for determining disputes as to entitlement to a patent before[642] and after grant.[643]

637 PA 1977 s.25. There is provision for renewing lapsed patents: ss.25 and 28. In *Re Bending Light Ltd* [2009] EWHC 59 (Pat), Kitchin J refused to allow an appeal against a decision not to renew a lapsed patent under s.28 because the applicant failed to show that his non-payment of the renewal fees at a time of financial difficulties occurred in circumstances where he had taken reasonable care to ensure their payment. A mere assertion that non-payment was unintentional is insufficient for the Comptroller to be "satisfied" within the meaning of s.28(3): *Matsushita Electrical Industrial Co v Comptroller General of Patents* [2008] EWHC 2071 (Pat); [2008] R.P.C. 35.

638 See PA 1977 s.128B to which the EU Regulations 1768/92 (medicinal products) and 1610/96 (plant protection products) are scheduled. The CJEU handed down three judgments on SPCs in 2011. Two established the principle that an application for an SPC must relate to a medicament (human or veterinary) "product" that: is protected by a patent; has been subject to an administrative authorisation procedure; and has not been placed on the market anywhere in the EEA as a medicinal product prior to being subject to safety and efficacy testing and a regulatory review (see *Generics (UK) Ltd v Synaptech Inc* (C-427/09) EU:C:2011:520; [2012] R.P.C. 4; and *Synthon BV v Merz Pharma GmbH & Co KGaA* (C-195/09) EU:C:2011:518; [2012] R.P.C. 3). In the third case, the CJEU held that the competent industrial property office of a Member State is precluded from granting a supplementary protection certificate relating to active ingredients which are not specified in the wording of the claims of the basic patent relied on. A certificate may be granted, however, for a combination of two active ingredients where the medicinal product in question contains not only that combination but also other active ingredients (*Medeva BV v Comptroller General of Patents, Designs and Trade Marks* (C-322/10) EU:C:2011:773; [2012] R.P.C. 25). See also the subsequent decision of the Court of Appeal [2012] EWCA Civ 523; [2012] 3 C.M.L.R. 9. Supplementary protection is only available when the marketing authorisation granted for the product is the first for that product. However, the CJEU in *Neurim Pharmaceuticals (1991) Ltd v Comptroller-General of Patents* (C-130/11) EU:C:2012:489; [2013] R.P.C. 23 held that the mere existence of an earlier marketing authorisation obtained for a veterinary medicinal product does not preclude the grant of a Supplementary Protection Certificate for a different application of the same product for human use for which a marketing authorisation has been granted. Thus, products relating to additional or second medical uses of an active ingredient are now eligible for supplementary protection. In *Teva UK Ltd v Gilead Sciences Inc* [2019] EWCA Civ 2272 an SPC was declared invalid because the product it protected was not covered by the patent.

639 PA 1977 s.30(1).

640 Certain transactions, such as assignments or mortgages, must be in writing signed by or on behalf of the parties to the transaction: PA 1977 s.30(6).

641 PA 1977 s.66. Each co-owner may work the invention without accounting to the other but may not grant licences, assign or mortgage it without the other's consent: s.36.

642 PA 1977 ss.8 and 9. For the approach to determining who is entitled to a patent in the absence of agreement between the parties see the House of Lords decision in *Rhone-Poulenc Rorer International Holdings Inc v Yeda Research & Development Co* [2007] UKHL 43; [2008] 1 All E.R. 425: claims to entitlement under s.7 of the PA 1977 require no reliance upon "some other rule of law" such as breach of contract or confidence, but rely merely on being able to fulfil the criteria in s.7. The issue of entitlement was decided in *BDI Holding GmbH v Argent Energy Ltd* [2019] EWHC 765 (IPEC); [2019] F.S.R. 25.

Licences, exclusive and non-exclusive, may be granted under a patent.[644] An exclusive licensee under a patent has the same right to sue for infringement as the proprietor, but must join the proprietor.[645] Patents made by employees belong to the employer in certain special circumstances—notably where the invention was made in the course of the employees' normal duties or those specifically assigned to him and the circumstances are such that an invention might reasonably be expected to result from the carrying out of those duties.[646] There are provisions entitling employees who make inventions which give rise to a patent to claim compensation from their employers in certain, rather limited, circumstances.[647]

The specification—description and claims Patent specifications fall into two parts: the description of the invention and the claims. The claims must define the matter for which the applicant seeks protection, be clear and concise, be supported by the description and must relate to one invention or to a group of inventions which are so linked as to form a single inventive concept.[648] The court is often asked to construe the claims of a patent, mainly for the purpose of determining whether there is infringement and whether prior art anticipates any given claim. An invention is taken to be that specified in the claims, as interpreted by the description and any drawings contained in the specification.[649] The Protocol on the Interpretation of art.69 of the European Patent Convention applies to the construction of 1977 Act patents. This provides that: **24-133**

> "Article 69 should not be interpreted as meaning that the extent of the protection conferred by a European patent is to be understood as that defined by the strict, literal meaning of the wording used in the claims, the description and drawings being employed only for the purpose of resolving an ambiguity found in the claims. Nor should it be taken to mean that the claims serve only as a guideline and that the actual protection conferred may extend to what, from a consideration of the description and drawings by a person skilled

643 PA 1977 ss.37 and 38.

644 There are provisions of EU competition law (especially art.101 of the Treaty on the Functioning of the European Union (TFEU) (ex art.81) and the Technology Transfer block exemption) which affect the terms that may be included in patent licences. The reader should consult specialist texts on EU competition law for details.

645 PA 1977 s.67. There are restrictions on the recovery of damages if the exclusive licence is not registered in due time: s.68.

646 PA 1977 s.39(1). They also belong to the employer where at the time of making the invention, because of the nature of the employee's duties and the particular responsibilities arising from the nature of the duties he had a special obligation to further the interests of the employer's undertaking: s.39(2). *LIFFE v Pinkava* [2007] EWCA Civ 217; [2007] 4 All E.R. 981—with regard to employee inventions, the Chancellor Sir Andrew Morritt noted at [56] that contractual duties can evolve over time: "The actions of employee and employer in performance of the contract may give rise to an expansion or contraction of the duties initially undertaken by a continuous process of subtle variation. I do not think that any extra or different duties so undertaken should be regarded only as duties 'specifically assigned'. It is quite possible for them, in the course of time, to have become 'normal'."

647 PA 1977 ss.40 and 41. See *Memco-Med Ltd's Patent* [1992] R.P.C. 403; *GEC Avionics Ltd's Patent* [1992] R.P.C. 107; *British Steel Plc's Patent* [1992] R.P.C. 117. The Patents Act 2004 somewhat increased the scope for employees obtaining compensation for certain inventions: Patents Act 2004, s.10 amending PA 1977 s.40. It is not possible for an employer to contract out of the rights conferred on the employee: s.42. In *Kelly v GE Healthcare Ltd* [2009] EWHC 181 (Pat); [2009] R.P.C. 12 Floyd J construed the unamended ss.40 and 41 rights in detail before awarding the claimants substantial sums for their invention. In *Shanks v Unilever Plc* [2019] UKSC 45; [2019] 1 W.L.R. 5997 the Supreme Court clarified when the courts would make and award of compensation, and vindicated the inventor's claim (which had been dismissed at all stages prior to the Supreme Court).

648 PA 1977 s.14(5).

649 PA 1977 s.125.

in the art, the patent proprietor has contemplated. On the contrary, it is to be interpreted as defining a position between these extremes which combines a fair protection for the patent proprietor with a reasonable degree of legal certainty for third parties."

Guidance has been provided by the English courts on the approach to construction, especially in the context of infringement actions in numerous cases. The law was comprehensively reviewed by the House of Lords in *Kirin-Amgen Inc v Hoechst-Marion Roussel Ltd*, and later by the Court of Appeal in *Virgin Atlantic Airways Ltd v Premium Aircraft Interiors Group*.[650] However, those authorities are now to be read in light of the guidance of the Supreme Court in *Actavis UK Ltd v Eli Lilly & Co*,[651] which considered the proper approach to the interpretation of claims, and in particular the requirement of the European Patent Convention 2000 to take account of "equivalents" to what is covered by the literal meaning of the claims. It concluded that the court must ask not just what is the "normal interpretation" of the claims, but also whether the alleged infringements represent variants on the claimed invention that differ only in an "immaterial" way. In order to answer that second question, the court reformulated the so-called *Improver* questions.[652] As to the "normal interpretation" of the claims, it appears that this is simply the same as the "purposive" (as opposed to rigidly literal) construction well known from the older authorities.[653]

(b) Validity

24-134 **Validity** The validity of a patent may be challenged on a number of grounds, the most important of which is that the patent does not claim a patentable invention.[654] This is a compendious term. An invention is only a patentable invention under the 1977 Act if it satisfies all the following conditions:

(a) *Novelty*. The invention must be new.[655]

---

650 *Kirin-Amgen Inc v Hoechst-Marion Roussel Ltd* [2004] UKHL 46; [2005] 1 All E.R. 667; [2005] R.P.C. 9 at [71]; *Virgin Atlantic Airways Ltd v Premium Aircraft Interiors Group* [2009] EWCA Civ 1062; [2010] R.P.C. 8 at [5]–[22]. *Virgin Atlantic* also makes clear that when reading the patent, the skilled addressee is assumed to have some knowledge of patent law in order to understand the relevance of different parts of the patent. See also on the approach to construction: *Improver Corp v Remington Consumer Products Ltd* [1989] R.P.C. 69. The court often applies the *Catnic* test when considering the ambit of a patent claim under the 1977 Act, although as noted in *Kirin Amgen Inc v Hoechst Marion Roussel Ltd* [2004] UKHL 46; [2005] 1 All E.R. 667 the formulations in the *Improver* case of the *Catnic* principles are only guidelines.

651 *Actavis UK Ltd v Eli Lilly & Co* [2017] UKSC 48; [2018] 1 All E.R. 171; [2017] R.P.C. 21. The Supreme Court also indicated that there are only limited circumstances in which it will be relevant to refer to the prosecution history of a patent for the purposes of assisting with construction.

652 This new approach to the "doctrine of equivalents" is discussed below at paras 24-140 and 24-141.

653 See Arnold J's interpretation of *Actavis* in *Generics (UK) Ltd (t/a Mylan) v Yeda Research and Development Co Ltd* [2017] EWHC 2629 (Pat); [2018] R.P.C. 2.

654 Note what is claimed must be an "invention". Thus it may be an objection to validity that the patent does not claim an invention at all: see *Genentech's Patent* [1989] R.P.C. 147.

655 An invention is taken to be novel if it does not form part of the state of the art which comprises all matter which has been made available to the public whether in the UK or elsewhere before the priority date of the invention: PA 1977 s.2(2). The court in *Unwired Planet International Ltd v Huawei Technologies Co Ltd* [2015] EWHC 3366 (Pat); [2016] Bus. L.R. 435 held that "before the priority date" is to be judged by reference to the time zone in which the filing took place, i.e. the 24-hour period beginning at midnight in that time zone; this was upheld on appeal: [2017] EWCA Civ 266; [2018] R.P.C. 6. Anticipation requires prior disclosure of subject matter which, if performed, must necessarily infringe the patent: *Synthon BV v Smithkline Beecham Plc* [2005] UKHL 59; [2006] 1

(b) *Not obvious.* The invention must involve an inventive step (i.e. it must not be obvious to a person skilled in the art).[656]

All E.R. 685, per Lord Hoffmann. The disclosure must also be enabling (ibid). Where the disclosure is in a document, the antecedent statement must be such that a person of ordinary knowledge of the subject would at once perceive and understand and be practically able to apply the discovery without the necessity of making further experiments and the information given by the prior publication must, for the purposes of practical utility, be equal to that given by the patent: *Hill v Evans* (1860) 31 L.J. Ch. 457. To anticipate the patentee's claim, the prior publication must contain clear and unmistakable directions to do what the patentee claims to have invented—it must "plant the flag" in the invention: *General Tire & Rubber Co v Firestone Tyre & Rubber Co Ltd* [1972] R.P.C. 457, but it is not essential that the disclosure be express, as long as the skilled person would inevitably infer the relevant teaching: *Edwards Lifesciences LLC v Boston Scientific Scimed Inc* [2017] EWHC 405 (Pat), affirmed on appeal: [2018] EWCA Civ 673; [2018] F.S.R. 29. Where a number of options are presented in a piece of prior art, each of these will generally be capable of anticipating. In contrast, a broad generic disclosure will not necessarily take away the novelty of a more specific one, such as a precise set of parameter ranges that fall within much broader ranges disclosed in the prior art: *Jushi Group Co Ltd v OCV Intellectual Capital LLC* [2018] EWCA Civ 1416; [2019] R.P.C. 1. Description of the same invention in a prior art document using different words may be sufficient to render the invention non-novel: *Belvac Production Machinery Inc v Carnaudmetalbox Engineering Ltd* [2009] EWHC 292 (Ch). Where there has been prior use of a product, the question is what the disclosure of the product was and whether it had made the product available to the public (see *Merrell Dow Pharmaceuticals Inc v Norton & Co Ltd* [1995] R.P.C. 233. The appeal to the House of Lords was dismissed [1996] R.P.C. 76). The information must have been made available to at least one member of the public who was free in law and equity to use it. Prior secret user will not render a patent invalid for lack of novelty under the 1977 Act. Disclosures in breach of confidence or at international exhibitions are disregarded if made within six months before the date of filing the application for the patent and there are other special exceptions (PA 1977 s.2(4)(c)) and there are provisions for including in the state of the art anticipatory patent applications published after the priority date (PA 1977 s.2(3)). Since *Actavis* (see para.24-133), Arnold J has indicated in *Generics (UK) Ltd (t/a Mylan) v Yeda Research and Development Co Ltd* [2017] EWHC 2629 (Pat); [2018] R.P.C. 2 that it is no longer the law that a claim will lack novelty if the prior art discloses subject matter that, if performed, would necessarily infringe the claim, since the potential scope of infringement has been broadened by *Actavis*. Arnold J held that a claim would only lack novelty if the prior art disclosed subject matter that fell within the claim on its "proper interpretation"—that is, the narrower scope of the purposive construction of the claim—it is not sufficient that the subject matter would infringe the claim applying the doctrine of equivalents.

656 PA 1977 s.3. The most up-to-date and authoritative guidance on obviousness was given by the Supreme Court in *Actavis Group PTC EHF v ICOS Corp* [2019] UKSC 15; [2020] 1 All E.R. 213; [2019] R.P.C. 9; see also *Allergan Inc v Aspire Pharma Ltd* [2019] EWHC 1085 (Pat) for subsequent application of those principles. In order to identify whether the invention is obvious the court will often adopt the "*Pozzoli*" approach, formulated by the Court of Appeal in *Pozzoli SpA v BDMO SA* [2007] EWCA Civ 588; [2007] F.S.R. 37. First, the court identifies: (a) the notional "person skilled in the art"; and (b) the relevant common general knowledge of that person; next it identifies the inventive concept of the claim in question or if that cannot readily be done, it construes it; thirdly, the court identifies what, if any, differences exist between the matter cited as forming part of the "state of the art" and the inventive concept of the claim or the claim as construed; and finally, it decides whether viewed without any knowledge of the alleged invention as claimed, those differences constitute steps which would have been obvious to the person skilled in the art or whether they require any degree of invention. However, this (like the "problem-and-solution" approach preferred by the European Patent Office) remains a gloss on the statutory test, and should not be applied mechanistically—see *Actavis v ICOS*. An ex post facto analysis is to be avoided: *Non-drip Measure Co Ltd v Strangers Ltd* (1943) 60 R.P.C. 135. In *Conor Medsystems Inc v Angiotech Pharmaceuticals Inc* [2008] UKHL 49; [2008] 4 All E.R. 621; [2008] R.P.C. 28, Lord Hoffmann held that the inventive concept should be determined by reference to the claim and not to some vague paraphrase based on the disclosure in the description (see particularly at [19]). A patent might be obvious due to being "obvious to try" —see *Actavis v ICOS*. A patent may also be held obvious because it makes no real technical advance: *Takeda UK Ltd v F Hoffman-La Roche AG* [2019] EWHC 1911 (Pat); [2019] Bus. L.R. 2681. Findings on obviousness are rarely overturned on appeal—see *Biogen v Medeva*

(c) *Capable of industrial application.* The invention must be capable of industrial application.[657]

(d) *Not specifically excluded.* None of the special reasons in ss.1(2) and 1(3) of the Patents Act 1977 for excluding patentability apply. Section 1(2) provides that the following (amongst other things) are not inventions for the purpose of the Patents Act 1977, namely, anything which consists of:
   (i) a discovery, scientific theory or mathematical method;
   (ii) a literary, dramatic, musical or artistic work or any other aesthetic creation whatsoever;
   (iii) a scheme, rule or method of performing a mental act, playing a game or doing business, or a programme for a computer[658]; or
   (iv) the presentation of information.

Section 1(3) excludes the grant of a patent for an invention the commercial exploitation of which would be contrary to public policy or morality.[659] If a patent

---

[1997] R.P.C. 1 45 HL. For guidance on what constitutes common general knowledge, see *General Tire & Rubber Co v Firestone Tyre & Rubber Co Ltd* [1972] R.P.C. 457 at 482–483; and *Beloit Technologies Inc v Valmet Paper Machinery Inc* [1997] R.P.C. 489 at 494–495. The approach to permission to appeal in patent cases was revised in *Teva UK Ltd v Boehringer Ingelheim Pharma GmbH & Co KG* [2016] EWCA Civ 1296; [2017] 4 All E.R. 976.

657 By which is meant that it can be made or used in any kind of industry including agriculture: PA 1977 s.4. See *Chiron Corp v Murex Diagnostics* [1996] F.S.R. 153. A method of treatment of the human or animal body by surgery or therapy or of diagnosis practised on the human or animal body shall not be taken to be capable of industrial application but that does not prevent a substance or composition being capable of industrial application merely because it is invented for use in any such method (PA 1977 s.4A). See as to second medical use of pharmaceutical substances: *Wyeth's Application* [1985] R.P.C. 545. For claims which do not accord with generally accepted scientific principles, see *Blacklight Power Inc v Comptroller-General of Patents* [2008] EWHC 2763 (Pat); [2009] R.P.C. 6. A helpful summary of the law relating to industrial applicability is provided by Kitchin J in *Eli Lilly & Co v Human Genome Sciences Inc* [2008] EWHC 1903 (Pat); [2008] R.P.C. 29 at [178]–[227] and by Jacob LJ on appeal in the same case: [2010] EWCA Civ 33; [2010] R.P.C. 14; (2010) 112 B.M.L.R. 161 at [50]–[112]. See also the decision of the Supreme Court in *Human Genome Sciences Inc v Eli Lilly & Co* [2011] UKSC 51; [2012] 1 All E.R. 1154.

658 IPO practice on the patentability of mental acts is set out in a Practice Notice dated 17 October 2011. Its practice on patenting computer-implemented inventions (software patents) is based on *Aerotel Ltd v Telco Holdings and Macrossan's Application* [2006] EWCA Civ 1371; [2007] 1 All E.R. 225; and *Symbian Ltd's Application* [2008] EWCA Civ 1066; [2009] R.P.C. 1 (see Practice Notice of 8 December 2008, which should be read with Practice Notices dated 2 November 2006 and 7 February 2008 on patentable subject-matter. For EPO practice on this subject, see the EPO Enlarged Board of Appeal decision, G3/08 of 12 May 2010 (OJ EPO 1/2011, 10). Note that the provision prevents anything from being treated as an invention for the purposes of the Act only to the extent that a patent or application for a patent relates to that thing as such (as to which see *Gale's Patent Application* [1991] R.P.C. 305). As to the test for patentability, the UK approach is that this is determined by the technical contribution of the invention (see *Aerotel Ltd v Telco Holdings Ltd* [2006] EWCA Civ 1371; [2007] 1 All E.R. 225; [2007] R.P.C. 7 and the interpretation of *Aerotel* in *Symbian Ltd v Comptroller General of Patents* [2008] EWCA Civ 1066; [2009] R.P.C. 1. See also, *HTC Europe Co Ltd v Apple Inc* [2013] EWCA Civ 451; [2013] R.P.C. 30 (*Symbian* followed); and *Lantana Ltd v Comptroller-General of Patents* [2014] EWCA Civ 1463; [2015] R.P.C. 16.

659 PA 1977 also prevents the grant of patents for inventions the publication or exploitation of which would be generally expected to encourage offensive, immoral or anti-social behaviour. Plant and animal varieties and essentially biological processes (not being microbiological processes or the products thereof) are excluded, PA 1977 s.1(3). A patent may also not be granted for methods of treatment or diagnosis, PA 1977 s.4A. European Directive 98/44/EC on the patentability of biotechnological inventions has been implemented into UK law by amendment to the PA 1977 s.76A and Sch.A2. Paragraph 3 of the Schedule provides that the following also are not patentable inventions: the human body, at the various stages of its formation and development, and the simple discovery of one

does not claim a patentable invention, it may be revoked by the court or the comptroller on the application of any person.[660] In practice, lack of novelty and obviousness are the most frequently invoked bases for challenging a patent.

Other grounds upon which a patent may be revoked As well as the objection that the invention is not a patentable invention,[661] a patent may be revoked on any of the following grounds, of which in practice (after lack of novelty and obviousness) insufficiency and added matter are the most frequently invoked. 24-135

(a) *Not entitled to the patent.* The patent was granted to person who was not entitled to be granted that patent.[662]
(b) *Insufficiency.* The specification does not disclose the invention clearly enough and completely enough for it to be performed by a person skilled in the art.[663] This attack is at its most powerful where the patentee has failed to give

of its elements, including the sequence or partial sequence of a gene; processes for cloning human beings; processes for modifying germ line genetic identity of human beings; uses of human embryos for industrial or commercial purposes and processes for modifying the genetic identity of animals which are likely to cause them suffering without any substantial medical benefit to man or animal, and animals resulting from such processes. In 2011 the CJEU delivered a judgment on the definition of the term "human embryo", *Brüstle v Greenpeace eV* (C-34/10) EU:C:2011:669; [2012] 1 C.M.L.R. 41. A new reference to the CJEU for a preliminary ruling on the definition of human embryos and seeking clarification of the CJEU's decision in *Brüstle* was made by the Patent Court in *International Stem Cell Corp v Comptroller General of Patents* (C-364/13) EU:C:2014:2451; [2015] R.P.C. 19. The CJEU ruled that "an unfertilised human ovum whose division and further development have been stimulated by parthenogenesis does not constitute a 'human embryo'". Following that decision, on 25 March 2015, the IPO published statutory guidance on inventions involving human embryonic stem cells replacing and updating previous practice notices on the subject.

660 PA 1977 s.72. It is not an abuse of process to claim for revocation of a patent even if the claimant has no commercial interest in the patent: *TNS Group Holdings Ltd v Nielsen Media Research Inc* [2009] EWHC 1160 (Pat); [2009] F.S.R. 23.

661 See para.24-134 for a discussion on the objections to validity.

662 PA 1977 s.72(1)(b). An application on this ground may only be made by a person entitled to be granted that patent or to be granted a patent for part of the matter comprised in the specification of the patent sought to be revoked and there are limits on the time in which such an application may be made: PA 1977 s.72(2).

663 PA 1977 s.72(1)(c). The Court of Appeal has summarised the principles relating to insufficiency in *Regeneron Pharmaceuticals Inc v Kymab Ltd* [2018] EWCA Civ 671; [2018] R.P.C. 14. Disclosure of an invention does not have to be complete in every detail so that anyone, whether skilled or not, can perform it. Since the specification is addressed to the skilled man it is sufficient if the addressee can understand the invention as described and can then perform it. The hypothetical addressee is not a person of exceptional skill and he is not expected to exercise any invention or any prolonged research, inquiry or experiment. In *Glaxo Group Ltd v Vectura Ltd* [2018] EWHC 3414 (Pat) five European patents were held invalid for insufficiency, since their specifications did not enable the skilled person, without undue effort, to determine whether a process or product was within the scope of the claims. The skilled person must, however, be prepared to display a reasonable degree of skill and common knowledge of the art in making trials and to correct obvious errors in the specification, if a means of correcting them can readily be found: *Mentor Corp v Hollister Inc* [1993] R.P.C. 7. The disclosure must be sufficient to enable the whole width of the claimed invention to be performed. What will suffice to satisfy this criterion will vary depending upon the nature of the claim that has been made: *Biogen Inc v Medeva Plc* [1997] R.P.C. 1. See also *Kirin-Amgen Inc v Hoechst Marion Roussel Ltd* [2004] UKHL 46; [2005] 1 All E.R. 667 where the House of Lords emphasised the need to analyse what the invention was before determining whether the specification of the patent enabled it. Older cases on the test of sufficiency continue to be of relevance. See for example: *R. v Arkwright* (1785) 1 W.P.C. 64; *Edison and Swan Electric Co v Holland* (1889) 6 R.P.C. 243; *Gold Ore v Golden Horseshoe* (1919) 36 R.P.C. 95; *IG Farbenindustrie AG's Patents* (1930) 47 R.P.C. 289 (sufficiency of selection patent); *British Thomson-Houston Co Ltd v Corona Lamp Works Ltd* (1922) 39 R.P.C. 49; *No-Fume v Pitchford & Co* (1935) 52 R.P.C. 231; *Valensi v*

adequate guidance as to how to make or perform the claimed subject-matter of the patent but in *Biogen Inc v Medeva Plc*,[664] the House of Lords gave guidance as to the scope for challenge to a patent under this head where the claims of the patent were over-broad, exceeding the patentee's technical contribution to the art. The House of Lords in *Generics (UK) Ltd v H Lundbeck A/S*[665] has clarified the law on sufficiency in the situation where a product is claimed as the result of an inventive process. Provided at least one method of making the product is adequately described in the specification the product claim is not insufficient. In *Conor Medsystems Inc v Angiotech Pharmaceuticals Inc*[666] Lord Hoffmann held that where the description exceeds the threshold of making the invention plausible it need not offer further explanation as to how or why the invention works provided that it will work as described.[667] Conversely, a patent's specification must disclose some plausible basis for believing that what is in the claim is in fact effective.[668] The Court of Appeal has also made it clear that a patent may be insufficient where it does not enable the skilled person to determine the limit of the invention.[669]

(c) *Added matter.* The matter disclosed in the specification of the patent extends beyond that disclosed in the application as filed.[670] The nub of the objection under this head is that the patentee has added a significant technical disclosure after he filed the patent.

British Radio Corp [1973] R.P.C. 337; *Genentech's Patent* [1989] R.P.C. 147. The question of sufficiency of the specification of a patent under the 1977 Act must be addressed by reference to the state of the art at the date of the application: *Biogen Inc v Medeva Plc* [1997] R.P.C. 1. The Court of Appeal has emphasised that the assertion that an invention must work across the scope of the claim must be plausible and credible: *Generics (UK) Ltd (t/a Mylan) v Warner-Lambert Co LLC* [2016] EWCA Civ 1006; [2017] R.P.C. 1; an appeal to the Supreme Court on the issue of insufficiency was dismissed (Lords Hodge and Mance dissenting): [2018] UKSC 56; [2019] 3 All E.R. 95.

664 [1997] R.P.C. 1.

665 [2009] UKHL 12; [2009] 2 All E.R. 955; [2009] R.P.C. 13.

666 [2008] UKHL 49; [2008] 4 All E.R. 621; [2008] R.P.C. 28, see particularly at [37]–[39]. See also *Regeneron Pharmaceuticals Inc v Genentech Inc* [2013] EWCA Civ 93; [2013] R.P.C. 28.

667 See also *Regeneron Pharmaceuticals Inc v Genentech Inc* [2013] EWCA Civ 93; [2013] R.P.C. 28; and *Actavis Group PTC EHF v Eli Lilly & Co* [2015] EWHC 3294 (Pat); [2016] R.P.C. 12.

668 *Generics (UK) Ltd (t/a Mylan) v Warner-Lambert Co LLC* [2018] UKSC 56; [2019] 3 All E.R. 95; *Eli Lilly and Co v Genentech Inc* [2019] EWHC 387 (Pat).

669 *Anan Kasei Co Ltd v Neo Chemicals and Oxides Ltd (formerly Molycorp Chemicals and Oxides Ltd)* [2019] EWCA Civ 1646; [2020] F.S.R. 8.

670 Or in certain earlier applications: PA 1977 s.72(1)(d). The decision as to whether there is an extension of disclosure must be made by a comparison of the two documents (application as filed and patent as granted) read through the eyes of a skilled addressee. The task of the court is threefold:

(a) to ascertain through the eyes of the skilled addressee what is disclosed, both explicitly and implicitly in the application;
(b) to do the same in respect of the patent as granted;
(c) to compare the two disclosures and decide whether any subject-matter relevant to the invention has been added whether by deletion or addition.

The comparison is strict in the sense that subject-matter will be added unless such subject-matter is clearly and unambiguously disclosed in the application, either explicitly or implicitly: *Bonzel (T) v Intervention (No.3)* [1991] R.P.C. 553; *Molnlycke AB v Proctor & Gamble Ltd (No.5)* [1994] R.P.C. 49; *A.P. Racing Ltd v Alcon Components Ltd* [2014] EWCA Civ 40; [2014] R.P.C. 27. The authorities on added matter were reviewed in *Conversant Wireless Licensing SARL v Huawei Technologies Co Ltd* [2019] EWHC 1687 (Pat). Amending a claim to include variations on embodiments that do not affect the way the invention works may avoid an added matter objection: *IPCOM GmbH and Co KG v HTC Europe Co Ltd* [2017] EWCA Civ 90.

(d) *Wrongful extension of protection by amendment.* The protection conferred by the patent has been extended by an amendment which should not have been allowed.[671]

Revocation proceedings and other challenges to validity The validity of a patent is most commonly put in issue by way of defence and/or counterclaim for revocation in proceedings for infringement of patent[672] or by way of a separate application for revocation.[673] Where validity is challenged, an order may be made for the unconditional revocation of the patent or, where the patent is only partially invalid, an order that the patent be revoked unless within a limited time the specification is satisfactorily amended.[674] An application for revocation of a patent may be made[675] in the High Court (Patents Court) in the Intellectual Property Enterprise Court (IPEC) (formerly the Patents County Court) or before the Comptroller.[676] A patentee may at any time offer to surrender his patent by notice to the comptroller, thereby avoiding the costs of revocation proceedings.[677] **24-136**

Amendment A patent may be amended, whether before or after grant, provided that the amendments comply with the requirements of the Act. The Act essentially prevents extending the protection conferred by the patent[678] (after grant) and prevents the adding of matter to the patent[679] (whether before or after grant). The court and comptroller retain a discretion to refuse an amendment (with the result **24-137**

---

671 PA 1977 s.72(1)(e). See para.24-137, "Amendment" on what amendments are allowable.

672 See PA 1977 s.74(1)(a).

673 PA 1977 s.74(1)(d). Note that s.74 of the 1977 Act limits the proceedings in which the validity of a patent may be put in issue. In summary there are:
- (a) proceedings for infringement;
- (b) threats actions under s.70;
- (c) declarations of non-infringement under s.71;
- (d) proceedings for revocation under s.72; and
- (e) disputes as to Crown use under s.58.

674 PA 1977 s.72(4).

675 An application for revocation may also be made by way of counterclaim in an action for infringement of patent. For procedure, see CPR Pt 63 PD—Intellectual Property Claims.

676 For procedure, see Patents Rules 2007 rr.76-84. Note that it is also possible to oppose a European patent which takes effect in the UK within nine months of the publication of the mention of its grant (European Patent Convention arts 99–105). If the opposition succeeds the patent will be revoked (European Patent Convention art.101(2)). Where opposition proceedings are ongoing at the EPO, applications for revocation made in the UK are normally stayed until the EPO proceedings are completed. See guidelines of the Court of Appeal indicating that a stay should be the default option: *IPCom GmbH v HTC Europe Co Ltd* [2013] EWCA Civ 1496; [2014] R.P.C. 12.

677 PA 1977 s.29(1). The offer will be advertised so that interested persons, such as licensees, may oppose the surrender.

678 PA 1977 s.76(3). See further *Vector Corp v Glatt Air Technologies* [2007] EWCA Civ 805; [2008] R.P.C. 10.

679 "... disclosing matter extending beyond that disclosed in the application as filed", PA 1977 s.76(2). In assessing whether matter has been added, the task of the court is threefold:
- (a) to ascertain through the eyes of the skilled addressee what is disclosed, both explicitly and implicitly in the application;
- (b) to do the same in respect of the patent as granted; and;
- (c) to compare the two disclosures and decide whether any subject-matter relevant to the invention has been added whether by deletion or addition.

The comparison is strict in the sense that subject matter will be added unless such subject matter is clearly and unambiguously disclosed in the application, either explicitly or implicitly: *Bonzel (T) v Intervention (No.3)* [1991] R.P.C. 553.

that the patent may be invalid) where there has been, for example, culpable delay or covetousness.[680] Application to amend may be made to the Comptroller[681] or the court.[682]

(c) Infringement

24-138 **Infringement** Section 60 of the 1977 Act specifically defines which acts do and do not constitute infringement:

(a) *Primary infringement.* Under s.60(1), a person infringes a patent if, but only if, while the patent is in force, he does any of the following things in the UK in relation to the invention[683] without the consent of the proprietor of the patent:
  (i) where the invention is a product, he makes, disposes of,[684] offers to dispose of,[685] uses[686] or imports the product[687] or keeps[688] it whether for disposal or otherwise;
  (ii) where the invention is a process, he uses the process or he offers it for use in the UK when he knows, or it is obvious to a reasonable person in the circumstances, that its use there without the consent of the proprietor would be an infringement of the patent;
  (iii) where the invention is a process, he disposes of, offers to dispose of, uses or imports any product obtained directly[689] by means of that process or keeps any such product whether for disposal or otherwise.

(b) *Supply of means essential.* Under s.60(2), a person also infringes a patent if, while the patent is in force and without the consent of the proprietor, he supplies or offers to supply in the UK a person other than a licensee or other person entitled to work the invention with any of the means, relating to an essential element of the invention, for putting the invention into effect when he knows, or it is obvious to a reasonable person in the circumstances, that those means are suitable for putting, and are intended to put, the invention

---

680 *Kimberly-Clark Worldwide Inc v Procter & Gamble Ltd (No.1)* [2000] R.P.C. 422 CA. Amendment will be refused if there has been culpable delay: *Instance v CCL Label Inc* [2002] F.S.R. 27. But see the Patents Act 2004 s.2 amending PA 1977 s.27 to provide that in considering whether to allow amendment after grant the comptroller shall have regard to the principles applicable under the EPC.

681 PA 1977 s.19 (before grant); s.27 (after grant). Proposed amendments to a granted patent are commonly advertised. An amendment may not be made by the comptroller where proceedings are pending in which validity may be put in issue (PA 1977 s.27(2)).

682 PA 1977 s.75. For procedure, see CPR Pt 63; Practice Direction—Intellectual Property Claims.

683 Whether the act is done "in relation to the invention" depends on whether the alleged infringement falls within the claims properly construed—see para.24-133, concerning construction of claims.

684 The disposal must be in the UK: *BASF v Hickson* (1906) 23 R.P.C. 149; *Morton Norwich Products Inc v Intercen Ltd* [1978] R.P.C. 501. As to what constitutes an offer for sale, see *Tamglass Ltd OY v Luoyang North Glass Technology Co Ltd* [2006] EWHC 65 (Pat); [2006] F.S.R. 32.

685 The offer must be an offer within the jurisdiction to dispose of infringing articles within the jurisdiction: *Kalman v PCL Packaging (UK) Ltd* [1982] F.S.R. 406.

686 See *Neilson v Betts* (1871) L.R. 5 H.L. 1.

687 As to who is the "importer", see *Sabaf SpA v MFI Furniture Centres Ltd* [2004] UKHL 45; [2005] R.P.C. 10 HL.

688 See *Smith Kline & French v Harbottle* [1980] R.P.C. 363 (warehouseman does not infringe by keeping).

689 See for meaning of "directly": *Pioneer Electronics Capital Inc v Warner Manufacturing Europe GmbH* [1995] R.P.C. 487.

into effect in the UK. This does not apply to the supply or offer of a staple commercial product unless the supply or the offer is made for the purpose of inducing the person supplied or, as the case may be, the person to whom the offer is made to do an act which constitutes an infringement of the patent by virtue of s.60(1).

Acts not constituting infringement[690] The following do not constitute infringement. 24-139

- (a) acts done privately and for purposes which are not commercial;
- (b) acts done for experimental purposes[691] relating to the subject-matter of the invention; or
- (c) acts consisting of the extemporaneous preparation in a pharmacy of a medicine for an individual in accordance with a prescription given by a registered medical or dental practitioner or consists of dealing with a medicine so prepared.[692]

It is also not an infringement to repair an existing patented product but it is infringement to make a new one under the guise of repair.[693]

Variants on the claimed invention[694] It is often the case that an action is brought in respect of a product not falling squarely within the wording of the claims but which is a variant on the claimed invention, delivering the same or similar benefits. The correct approach to the application of the so-called "doctrine of equivalents" has now been clarified by the Supreme Court in *Actavis UK Ltd v Eli Lilly & Co*.[695] The first step when considering infringement is to ask whether the accused product or process falls within the claim as a matter of "normal interpretation", i.e. the usual "purposive" construction of the claim.[696] If the answer to that first question is "no", then the court must ask whether the variant differs from the subject matter of the claim in only an immaterial way. As to what is "immaterial", the Supreme Court 24-140

690 See also para.24-143: "Defences".

691 See *Monsanto Co v Stauffer Chemical Co* [1985] R.P.C. 515. Field trials as to a product's efficacy do not qualify for this exclusion: *Corevalve Inc v Edwards Lifesciences AG* [2009] EWHC 6 (Pat); [2009] F.S.R. 8.

692 PA 1977 s.60(5). There are certain other exceptions for acts done for the needs of certain foreign ships, hovercraft, aircraft or vehicles which have entered the UK (PA 1977 s.60(5)(d)-(f)) and for use by a farmer of the product of his harvest for propagation or multiplication and of animal or animal reproductive material for an agricultural purpose where there has been a sale of plant propagating material or of breeding stock or other animal reproductive material by the proprietor of the patent or with his consent (PA 1977 s.60(5)(g) and (h)). An exception also applies to acts done in conducting a study, test or trial necessary for and conducted with a view to the application of certain provisions of EU Directives 2001/82/EC (as amended) and 2001/83/EC (as amended) concerning respectively veterinary medical products and medicinal products for human use (PA 1977 s.60(5)(i)).

693 *United Wire Ltd v Screen Repart Services (Scotland) Ltd* [2000] 4 All E.R. 353; [2001] F.S.R. 24, HL; *Schutz (UK) Ltd v Werit (UK) Ltd* [2013] UKSC 16; [2013] R.P.C. 16; applied in *Parainen Pearl Shipping Ltd v Kristian Gerhard Jebsen Skipsrederi AS* [2018] EWHC 2628 (Pat); [2019] R.P.C. 8.

694 See para.24-133, on construction.

695 [2017] UKSC 48; [2018] 1 All E.R. 171; [2017] R.P.C. 21. The *Actavis* principles have since been analysed in detail by Kitchin LJ in *Icescape Ltd v Ice-world International BV* [2018] EWCA Civ 2219; [2019] F.S.R. 5. The inventive concept or core of the invention was characterised in *Regen Lab SA v Estar Medical Ltd* [2019] EWHC 63 (Pat); [2019] R.P.C. 7 as "the new technical insight conveyed by the invention—the clever bit—as would be perceived by the skilled person".

696 See para.24-133.

said that it is appropriate to answer this by reference to a slightly reformulated version of the three-step test set out in *Improver* (and as before treating it as a guide, not a strict rule).[697] The updated set of questions is as follows:

(1) Notwithstanding that it is not within the literal meaning of the relevant claim(s) of the patent, does the variant achieve substantially the same result in substantially the same way as the invention?
(2) Would it be obvious to the person skilled in the art, reading the patent at the priority date, but knowing that the variant achieved substantially the same result as the invention, that it did so in substantially the same way as the invention?
(3) Would such a reader of the patent have concluded that the patentee nonetheless intended that strict compliance with the literal meaning of the relevant claim(s) of the patent was an essential requirement of the invention?

If the answers to those questions are "yes", "yes" and "no", then the alleged infringement is likely to be an immaterial variant that thus falls within the scope of protection of the claim. A German defence to infringement by equivalents, known as the *Formstein* defence, was raised in *Technetix BV v Teleste Ltd*,[698] whereby if the equivalent would have lacked novelty or inventive step as at the priority date, it would be held to fall outside the claim; the judge noted that the defence did not exist in English law, but did not rule out the possibility that it might be introduced.

24-141 The introduction of this updated approach to infringement by equivalents has given rise to what might seem some surprising outcomes in infringement proceedings, whereby a claim may be held infringed despite the alleged infringement lacking one or more apparently non-trivial integers of that claim. For example, in *E Mishan and Sons v Hozelock Ltd*[699] a garden hose product was held to infringe a claim that required the inner and outer hoses of the product to be "unattached" except at the couplings at their end points. The inner and outer hoses of the alleged infringement had attachment points that were not right at the ends, so were not literally "unattached" in the way the claim specified, but nonetheless the product was held to be an equivalent (although the patent was held invalid). In *Excel-Eucan Ltd v Source Vagabond Systems Ltd*[700] the allegedly infringing ammunition bag was held to be an infringing equivalent despite lacking "an openable closure extending substantially [the length of the bag]". It is instructive to read these and

---

697 Prior to *Actavis*, the courts' approach to alleged infringing variants was often based on the principles outlined in *Catnic Components Ltd v Hill Smith Ltd* [1983] F.S.R. 512 and the three-step test formulated in *Improver Corp v Remington Consumer Products* [1990] F.S.R. 181, per Hoffmann J, often known as the "Improver questions". Earlier cases must be read in light of *Actavis* but may still have some relevance: see *Daily v Etablissements Fernand Berchet* [1993] R.P.C. 357; *Lux Traffic v Pike Signals* [1993] R.P.C. 107; *Société Technique de Pulverisation Step v Emson Europe Ltd* [1993] R.P.C. 513 (despite the purposive construction, an integer cannot be treated as struck out despite the fact that it does not appear to make any difference to the inventive concept); *Rockwater Ltd v Technip France SA* [2004] EWCA Civ 381; [2004] R.P.C. 46.

698 *Technetix BV v Teleste Ltd* [2019] EWHC 126 (IPEC); [2019] F.S.R. 19.

699 *E Mishan and Sons Inc (t/a Emson) v Hozelock Ltd* [2019] EWHC 991 (Pat); affirmed [2020] EWCA Civ 871.

700 *Excel-Eucan Ltd v Source Vagabond Systems Ltd* [2019] EWHC 3175 (Pat). See also: *L'Oreal (UK) Ltd v Liqwd Inc* [2018] EWHC 1394 (Pat), upheld on appeal [2019] EWCA Civ 1943; *L'oréal Société Anonyme, L'oréal (UK) Ltd v RN Ventures Ltd* [2018] EWHC 173 (Pat); [2018] E.C.D.R. 14; *Illumina Inc v Premaitha Health Plc* [2017] EWHC 2930 (Pat); and *Regen Lab SA v Estar Medical Ltd* [2019] EWHC 1981 (Pat).

other examples where the courts have had to decide whether an "equivalent" infringes or not[701] in order better to understand the landscape post-*Actavis*.

Persons liable for infringement as joint tortfeasors The general rule in tort cases[702] that persons will be liable as joint tortfeasors when their respective shares in the commission of the tort are done in furtherance of a common design applies equally to patent cases.[703] It is a question of fact in each case what constitutes sufficient involvement in the commission of the tort to constitute common design.[704] 24-142

Defences The following are the most common defences to a claim for infringement[705]: 24-143

(a) *Act is not an infringing act.* What are and are not infringing acts are discussed at paras 24-139 and 24-140.
(b) *Product is outside the claims.* On the true construction of the claims, the product or process is not within them. See paras 24-133, 24-140 and 24-141.
(c) *Licence (express or implied) or exhaustion of rights.* It is only infringement to do the specified acts without the consent of the proprietor of the patent. If a person is licensed, expressly or impliedly, there will be no infringement.[706] Where an article protected by a patent is manufactured or sold by or with the consent of the patentee, a purchaser of that article is entitled, in the absence of notice to the contrary,[707] to exercise in relation to that article all the rights of an owner, including that of reselling the article and of passing with it the same right to deal with it.[708] Once a patented article has been put on the market in any EC country by the patentee or a licensee, the doctrine of "exhaustion of rights" applies and the patent in any

701 See fn.697.

702 See *The Koursk* [1924] P. 140.

703 See, e.g. *Unilever Plc v Gillette (UK) Ltd* [1989] R.P.C. 583.

704 For example, it has been held that a parent could be liable as a joint tortfeasor with its subsidiary where there was a meeting of minds between the parent and subsidiary with a view to furthering the sale of infringing products in the UK (*Unilever Plc v Gillette (UK) Ltd* [1989] R.P.C. 583). Equally, where a joint marketing agreement between a foreign supplier and its domestic customer was operated, the foreign supplier was liable as a joint tortfeasor (*Puschner v Tom Parker (Scotland)* [1989] R.P.C. 430). The general rule in patent cases is that the sale of an article which is intended for use in infringing a patent is not, ipso facto, sufficient to constitute infringement of that patent: *Townsend v Haworth* (1878) 48 L.J. Ch. 770 at 772; *Dunlop Pneumatic Tyre v Moseley* [1904] 1 Ch. 164 and 612. In very limited circumstances company directors may be liable for the infringing acts of their companies: *Evans & Son Ltd v Spritebrand Ltd* [1983] Q.B. 310; see also *MCA Records v Charly Records* [2001] EWCA Civ 1441; [2002] F.S.R. 26.

705 In addition, there are special defences to certain types of relief claimed—these are discussed in para.24-144. Note also that the Supreme Court has held that the grant of a patent gives rise to private rights, the infringement of which does not engage the public interest so as to give rise to the ex turpi causa defence. The paradigm case of turpitude is a criminal act but includes quasi-criminal acts (*Les Laboratoires Servier v Apotex Inc* [2014] UKSC 55; [2015] A.C. 430). A more rarely pleaded defence is experimental use: see s.60(5)(b) PA 1977 and *British Gas Trading Ltd v Vanclare SE LLC* [2016] EWHC 2278 (Pat).

706 The general defences of acquiescence and estoppel are available in actions for infringement: see, for the principle, *Habib Bank Ltd v Habib Bank AG* [1981] 1 W.L.R. 1265 (a passing off case).

707 *Gilette v Bernstein* (1941) 58 R.P.C. 271 at 282; *Roussel Uclaf SA v Hockley International Ltd* [1996] R.P.C. 441.

708 *Betts v Wilmott* (1871) L.R. 6 Ch. 239 at 244.

country may not be used to prevent goods entering another Member State.[709] The implied licence extends to "fair repair" of the article concerned, but not to the production of a new article under the cloak of making a repair.[710]

(d) *Patent invalid.* See para.24-134 onwards. This is a very common defence. If the patent is invalid, there can be no infringement[711] but relief may be granted for infringement of a partially valid patent.[712]

(e) *Prior user.* There is provision to allow persons who in good faith were doing (or making serious and effective preparations to do) acts before the priority date of the patent which would have infringed the patent had it been in force to continue to do such acts, such acts not constituting infringement.[713]

(f) *Competition law defences.* It was formerly a defence to proceedings for infringement to prove that at the time of the infringement there was in force a contract made by or with the consent of the patentee containing a term which is rendered void by the Patents Act s.44, but this has been removed by the Competition Act 1998.[714] In exceptional circumstances, the enforcement of a patent may constitute an abuse of dominant position, contrary to art.102 on the Functioning of the European Union (TFEU) (formerly art.82 of the Treaty of Rome).[715] Related to this area are what are known as "FRAND" defences; patentees in certain fields of industry (notably mobile telecommunications) will often undertake to license their patents on FRAND (fair, reasonable and non-discriminatory) terms as part of a quid pro quo for the invention in the patent being incorporated into an important industry standard (it is then said to be "essential" to the standard). The idea is to prevent patentees from blocking others from working the standard. Such FRAND obligations by the patentee may then give rise to a defence

---

709 This is a well-established principle of EU law: *Centrafarm v Sterling Drug* [1974] E.C.R. 1147. See for a comprehensive review of EU exhaustion principles: *Merck & Co Inc v Primecrown Ltd* (C-267/95 and C-268/95) EU:C:1996:468; [1997] F.S.R. 23.

710 *Sirdar Rubber Co Ltd v Wallington, Weston & Co* (1907) 24 R.P.C. 539 at 543; *British Leyland Motor Corp v Armstrong Patents Co* [1986] A.C. 577; *Dellareed Ltd v Delkin Developments* [1988] F.S.R. 329.

711 A convenient short cut in an infringement action is the so-called "Gillette Defence" (from *Gillette Safety Razor Co v Anglo-American Trading Ltd* (1913) 30 R.P.C. 465); if the alleged infringement was itself an obvious thing to do or to make at the priority date of the relevant claims, then the claims must be bad as covering something obvious. This defence must be strictly proved: *Hickman v Andrews* [1983] R.P.C. 147.

712 PA 1977 s.63.

713 PA 1977 s.64. They may not licence others to do such acts. The defence applies where a person was making "effective and serious preparations": see *Helitune Ltd v Stewart Hughes Ltd* [1991] F.S.R. 171 and *Lubrizol Corp v Esso Petroleum Corp Ltd* [1998] R.P.C. 727.

714 PA 1977 s.44 (repealed).

715 See *Parke Davis v Probel* [1968] E.C.R. 55, CJEU; *Volvo v Erik Veng* [1988] E.C.R. 6211; [1989] 4 C.M.L.R. 122, CJEU; *Pitney-Bowes v Francotyp-Postlia GmbH* [1991] F.S.R. 72 (authorities reviewed); *Chiron Corp v Murex Diagnostics Ltd* [1994] F.S.R. 187; [1996] F.S.R. 153, CA. The mere fact of securing the benefit of an exclusive right is not an abuse. Nor is it an abuse to refuse to licence as such. The exercise of a patent right may be prohibited if it gives rise to abusive conduct such as an arbitrary refusal to supply repairers: *Philips Electronics NV v Ingman Ltd* [1999] F.S.R. 112. See for a case where a competition law defence was not struck out and the court contemplated an inquiry into the patentee's licensing practices: *Intel Corp v Via Technologies Inc* [2002] EWCA Civ 1905; [2003] F.S.R. 33.

to any claim for an injunction, i.e. the defendant will try to negotiate a FRAND licence instead.[716]

(g) *No defence of innocence.* It is not a defence that a defendant did not know he was infringing (but innocence may affect the claim for damages: see below).

Action for infringement, relief and remedies[717] A patentee (or exclusive licensee) who succeeds in an action for infringement is entitled (subject to the provisions mentioned below) to damages or an account of profits, at his option.[718] If, however, a patent changes hands or if an exclusive licence is granted there can be no award of damages or account of profits unless the change is registered within six months or as soon as practicable thereafter.[719] A successful claimant is also entitled to an injunction against further infringement (subject to the overriding discretion of the court to refuse)[720] and to delivery up[721] of infringing articles. The existence of FRAND obligations and associated defences[722] has in turn led some claimants to seek a so-called "FRAND injunction", a remedy in which a defendant who has been held to infringe a standards-essential patent is subject to an injunction unless they enter a FRAND licence, with the terms of that licence to be determined by the court if not agreed. This is based on the approach taken by the High Court in *Unwired Planet v Huawei*,[723] in which Birss J determined the FRAND licence terms that the losing defendant would be subject to, and the form of injunction to which the claimant was entitled. Interlocutory injunctions may be 24-144

[716] The CJEU has set out certain steps a patentee may take in order to avoid abuse of a dominant position in the context of FRAND negotiations: *Huawei Technologies Co Ltd v ZTE Corp* (C-170/13) EU:C:2015:477; [2016] R.P.C. 4.

[717] For procedure in an infringement action, see CPR Pt 63 PD—Intellectual Property Claims. Particulars of infringement must be served with the claim form. If the defendant puts validity of the patent in issue, the statement of case must have a separate document attached to it headed "Grounds of Invalidity" (PD paras 4.1–4.6). There are provisions for case management, disclosure and inspection, experiments, use of models of apparatus etc. Remedies are provided for in PA 1977, s.61(1). These are the only remedies: see *Union Carbide Corp v BP Chemicals Ltd* [1998] F.S.R. 1.

[718] PA 1977 s.61(2). Opting for an account of profits does not have the effect of franking the infringing goods so as to condone future infringements: *Codex Corp v Racal-Milgo Ltd* [1984] F.S.R. 87. A successful patentee will also be entitled to a declaration that the patent is valid and has been infringed: s.61(1)(e). A certificate of contested validity may be made which puts the patentee in a stronger position as to recovery of costs against a subsequent challenger to validity: s.65. For a useful summary of the case law applicable to accounts of profits and enquiries as to damages in the UK, see *OOO Abbott and Chasmer v Design and Display Ltd and Eureka Display Ltd* [2014] EWHC 2924 (IPEC) and [2016] EWCA Civ 98; [2016] F.S.R. 27.

[719] PA 1977 s.68.

[720] See *Chiron Corp v Organon Teknika Ltd (No.10)* [1995] F.S.R. 325 (authorities reviewed). As to the scope of an injunction, see *Coflexip SA v Stolt Comex Seaway MS Ltd* [2001] R.P.C. 9.

[721] Delivery up may be effected by removal and delivery up of certain components to render a device non-infringing: *Codex Corp v Racal-Milgo Ltd* [1984] F.S.R. 87.

[722] See para.24-143(f) above.

[723] *Unwired Planet International Ltd v Huawei Technologies Co Ltd* [2017] EWHC 711 (Pat); [2019] 4 C.M.L.R. 7 and [2017] EWHC 1304 (Pat); [2017] R.P.C. 20. The court's finding that a global (not just UK) licence would be FRAND was upheld on appeal: [2018] EWCA Civ 2344; [2018] R.P.C. 20 (a Supreme Court appeal is currently outstanding). The Court of Appeal in *Huawei Technologies Co Ltd v Conversant Wireless Licensing SARL* [2019] EWCA Civ 38; [2019] R.P.C. 6 upheld the lower court's finding that the UK was the appropriate forum for litigating the patentee's UK patents, despite the defendants being Chinese and the possible outcome of the litigation being a FRAND licence of global scope (i.e. including China); this decision too is currently on appeal to the Supreme Court.

granted on the usual principles.[724] Orders may be made compelling a person who facilitated the infringement to give discovery of the names of infringers.[725]

24-145 **Damages** The measure of damages depends upon whether the patentee exploits his monopoly by licensing others to make and sell his invention, or by manufacturing or selling himself. In the first case, the normal measure of damages is the amount of royalties he has lost by reason of the infringer's failure to take a licence before making or selling the invention. Where the patentee himself manufactures or sells, and the defendant cannot show that he could have had a licence, the measure of damages is the amount the patentee has lost by reason of the defendant's obtaining orders for the patented article that would ordinarily have gone to the patentee.[726] Prima facie, it may be supposed that each act of infringement represents business diverted from the patentee, unless it is shown that this was not so; and it is irrelevant that the defendant could have done as much damage without infringing.[727] Damages are not recoverable if the defendant proves that at the date of the infringement he was not aware, and had no reasonable ground for supposing, that the patent existed.[728] Also, if the specification of the invention has been amended since the infringement was committed[729] or if the patent is found only partially valid[730] damages will only be awarded if the specification as originally published was framed in good faith and with reasonable skill and knowledge.

24-146 **Action for infringement of patent** Proceedings for infringement of patent are brought in the Chancery Division of the High Court,[731] the Intellectual Property Enterprise Court (formerly the Patents County Court) or (by agreement) before the

---

[724] *American Cyanamid v Ethicon* [1975] A.C. 396; [1975] R.P.C. 513; *Series 5 Software Ltd v Clarke* [1996] 1 All E.R. 853; [1996] F.S.R. 273. Interlocutory relief will be refused if, for example, the claimant can be adequately compensated in damages: *Polaroid Corp v Eastman Kodak* [1977] R.P.C. 379. See for a helpful review of some of the factors commonly taken into account: *Quantel Ltd v Shima Seiki Europe Ltd* [1990] R.P.C. 436. There has been a trend for there to be orders for speedy trials in addition to or instead of interim injunctions. See, e.g. *SmithKline Beecham Plc v Apotex Europe Ltd* [2003] EWCA Civ 137; [2003] F.S.R. 31. *Wake Forest University Health Sciences v Smith & Nephew Plc* [2009] EWHC 45 (Pat); [2009] F.S.R. 11 provides a further example. *Les Laboratoires Servier v Apotex Inc* [2008] EWHC 2347 (Ch); [2009] F.S.R. 3 provides an example of the risk in obtaining an interim injunction: the defendant was awarded £17.5 million for lost sales and market share during the period before the interim injunction was discharged. An application for an interim FRAND injunction was refused in *Ipcom GmbH and Co KG v Xiaomi Technology UK Ltd* [2019] EWHC 3074 (Pat).

[725] *Norwich Pharmacal Co v Commissioners of Customs and Excise* [1974] A.C. 133.

[726] *General Tire and Rubber Co v Firestone Tyre and Rubber Co Ltd* [1975] 1 W.L.R. 819. See also *Gerber Garment Technology Inc v Lectra Systems Ltd* [1997] R.P.C. 443. For an application of the principles for the quantification of damages see *Ultraframe (UK) Ltd v Eurocell Building Plastics Ltd* [2006] EWHC 1344 (Pat). It is standard practice to allow a successful claimant to raise further alleged infringements at an inquiry as to damages or account of profits: *AP Racing Ltd v Alcon Components Ltd* [2016] EWHC 815 (Ch); [2016] F.S.R. 28.

[727] *Meters Ltd v Metropolitan Meters Ltd* (1911) 28 R.P.C. 157; *Catnic Components Ltd v Hill Smith Ltd* [1983] F.S.R. 512.

[728] PA 1977 s.62(1). See *Benmax v Austin Motor Co* (1953) 70 R.P.C. 143, for discussion of these words; *Khawam v Chellaram & Sons (Nig)* [1964] 1 W.L.R. 711 (failure to investigate).

[729] PA 1977 s.62(3). See *Ronson Products Ltd v A Lewis & Co (Westminster) Ltd* [1963] R.P.C. 103; *Codex Corp v Racal-Milgo Ltd* [1983] R.P.C. 369 (does not affect account of profits).

[730] PA 1977 s.63(2) and (4).

[731] Actions for infringement must be brought in the Patents Court of the Chancery Division. Procedure is governed by CPR Pt 63 PD—Intellectual Property Claims.

comptroller.[732] An action can only be brought after a patent has been granted but the claimant can recover in respect of all acts of infringements between publication and grant provided these acts would have infringed the patent as published as well as in the form granted.[733] There are also provisions whereby the Intellectual Property Office can be asked to give a non-binding opinion on infringement and validity.[734]

Declaratory relief A person doing or proposing to do an act may seek a declaration from the court that the act is not or would not be an infringement of a patent.[735] The person must have applied in writing to the patentee for an acknowledgement that the act does not or would not infringe and must have furnished the patentee with full particulars in writing of the act in question. Only after the patentee has refused or failed to give such acknowledgement may such a declaration be made. It is also possible to obtain similar protection by seeking a declaration that a particular act would be anticipated and/or obvious as at a particular date, so that to the extent the act or product may be alleged to be patented, the patent too would be anticipated and/or obvious to the same extent.[736] Relief may also be granted in the form of an "Arrow declaration", named after *Arrow Generics Ltd v Merck & Co Inc*.[737] This takes the form of a declaration that a product or process was not novel, or was obvious, as at a particular date. It is typically sought where a defendant's case is that its product or process was either not new at the priority date of the patent or else that it was so close to the prior art that if the patent is broad enough to catch the product or process, then the patent must be invalid for lack of novelty or obviousness. The principles governing the grant of Arrow declarations were considered in detail in *Glaxo Group Ltd v Vectura Ltd*[738] and *Fujifilm Kyowa Kirin Biologics Co Ltd v Abbvie Biotechnology Ltd*.[739] 24-147

Unjustified threats of infringement proceedings It is an actionable wrong to threaten any person (other than in respect of the manufacture of goods, or the import of goods for disposal, or the use of a process, and subject to certain other excepted acts and "permitted communications" under ss.70A and 70B of the 1977 Act) with proceedings for infringement of patents unless the threat can be justified.[740] There are also exceptions for professional advisers under s.70D. "Any person" aggrieved by such a threat may sue the person making it for a declaration that the threat is unjustified, for an injunction to restrain repetition of the threat and for dam- 24-148

---

732 PA 1977 s.61. Procedure is governed by the Patent Rules 2007 (as amended) rr.73–91.

733 PA 1977 s.69.

734 PA 1977 ss.74A–74B.

735 PA 1977 s.71. A person may also seek a declaration under the inherent jurisdiction of the court provided that the patentee has asserted his right.

736 See, e.g. *Fujifilm Kyowa Kirin Biologics Co Ltd v Abbvie Biotechnology Ltd* [2017] EWHC 395 (Pat); [2018] R.P.C. 1.

737 [2007] EWHC 1900 (Pat); [2008] Bus. L.R. 487.

738 [2018] EWCA Civ 1496; [2019] Bus. L.R. 648. Arrow declarations were also granted in *Glaxo Group Ltd v Vectura Ltd* [2018] EWHC 3414 (Pat). An Arrow declaration may be refused where the patentee de-designates the UK from the protection of the patent: *Pfizer Ltd v F Hoffmann-La Roche AG* [2019] EWHC 1520 (Pat); [2019] R.P.C. 14.

739 [2017] EWHC 395 (Pat); [2018] R.P.C. 1.

740 PA 1977 ss.70–70E, as amended by the Intellectual Property (Unjustified Threats) Act 2017. The old s.70 was considered by the Court of Appeal in *Icescape Ltd v Ice-world International BV* [2018] EWCA Civ 2219; [2019] F.S.R. 5. It is suggested that the older cases referred to later in this paragraph will remain relevant to the application of the amended provisions.

ages,[741] so a person may be aggrieved although the threat is not against him. Indeed, the form of threat that is most damaging to a manufacturer is a threat against his customers, which may cause them to take their custom elsewhere, or a communication to a third party in the hope of so influencing customers.[742] Under the old s.70, the essence of a threat was an intimation that someone has patent rights and intends to enforce them against another[743]; the statutory test is now whether a reasonable person in the position of a recipient would understand from the communication that the patent exists, and a person intends to bring infringement proceedings against another person in respect of acts done (or to be done) in the UK. Merely giving notice that a patent exists is a permitted act, i.e. not actionable.[744] It is a defence to an action for threats to prove that "the acts in respect of which proceedings were threatened constitutes (or, if done, would constitute) an infringement of a patent".[745]

(d) Special regimes

Compulsory licences, licences of right and Crown use

24-149 (a) *Compulsory licences* There are provisions[746] for the grant of compulsory licences to ensure that a patentee does not abuse the patent monopoly and to protect the public interest. The main circumstances in which a compulsory licence may be granted are as follows:

(i) Where there is a failure to meet demand for a patented product on reasonable terms.

(ii) Where by reason of the refusal to grant a licence on reasonable terms, an export market is not fulfilled, the working of another significant patented invention is prevented or hindered or the establishment or development of commercial or industrial activities is unfairly prejudiced or hindered.

(iii) Where by reason of conditions imposed by the proprietor, the manufacture, use or disposal of non-patented materials or the establishment of industrial or commercial activities in the UK is unfairly prejudiced.[747] An application for a compulsory licence is made to the comptroller.[748]

(b) *Licences of right* A patentee may apply to the comptroller for an entry to be made in the register that licences under the patent are available as of right on terms to be agreed with him or, in default of agreement, settled by the comptroller.[749] A patentee can thereby reduce the renewal fees he has to pay.

---

741 PA 1977 s.70C. Loss of business is recoverable as damages: *Skinner v Perry* (1894) 11 R.P.C. 406; [1894] 2 Ch. 581.

742 See *Olin Mathieson Chemical Corp v Biorex Laboratories Ltd* [1970] R.P.C. 157.

743 See *Luna Advertising Co v Burnham* (1928) 45 R.P.C. 258; *Bowden Controls v Acco Cable Controls Ltd* [1990] R.P.C. 427 (threat can be veiled or implied just as much as it can be explicit).

744 PA 1977 s.70B(2)(a).

745 PA 1977 s.70C(3). Under the old s.70 see *FNM Corp Ltd v Drammock International Ltd* [2009] EWHC 1294 (Pat), Arnold J.

746 PA 1977 s.48 onwards. Sections 48A and 48B contain special provisions affecting patents belonging to WTO proprietors and non-WTO proprietors to take account of the obligations of the TRIPs agreement.

747 See s.48A. These are the main grounds applying to WTO proprietors. The grounds applying to others are somewhat different and wider.

748 PA 1977 s.48 and Patents Rules 2007 r.43.

749 PA 1977 s.46. A patentee can also apply to have such a voluntary endorsement cancelled at a later

(c) *Crown use* There are provisions which give any government department and any person authorised in writing by a government department a right to do for the services of the Crown certain acts which would otherwise constitute infringement.[750] The patentee has a right to be remunerated.

Plant breeders rights There is a special system of protection, akin to patent protection, for new plant varieties ("plant breeders rights"). These rights are governed by the Plant Varieties Act 1997, which implements in the UK the 1991 International Convention for the Protection of New Varieties of Plants (UPOV). The 1997 Act also brings the UK law on this subject into line with EU Regulation 2100/94,[751] which established the European Union Plant Variety Right. The right granted primarily allows the holder to prevent others from producing, reproducing, using, conditioning or selling the protected variety. The grant of EU rights gives protection throughout the EU and it should be noted that EU rights and UK rights cannot operate simultaneously.[752] **24-150**

date: PA 1977 s.37. The comptroller may also endorse a patent licence of right in consequence of an unfavourable Competition Commission report: s.51.

750 PA 1977 s.55. Use by the National Health Service of pharmaceutical products for treating patients falls within the scope of "for the services of the Crown": *Pfizer v Minister of Health* [1965] A.C. 512. A Crown use defence was successfully made out in *IPCom GmbH & Co KG v Vodafone Group Plc* [2020] EWHC 132 (Pat); [2020] Bus. L.R. 514.

751 [1995] OJ L227/1.

752 The UK and EU systems of plant breeders' rights are administered by the UK Plant Variety Office and the EU Plant Variety Office, respectively. For further information, see the UK Plant Variety Rights Office and Seeds Division of Defra. For further information see *https://www.gov.uk/guidance/plant-breeders-rights* [Accessed 3 April 2020].

[illegible] under PA 1977 s.37. [illegible] of an infringing [illegible] Commission report, § 51.

Chapter 25

PASSING OFF

Table of Contents

1. General Principles

General principles[1] It is an actionable wrong for a trader[2] so to conduct his business as to lead to the belief that his goods, services or business are the goods, services or business of the claimant. The claimant must establish a goodwill[3] attached to the goods or services which he supplies. That goodwill may arise from a brand name,[4] features of labelling or packaging, or descriptive material.[5] Secondly, he must demonstrate a material misrepresentation by the defendant to the public (whether or not intentional) leading to or likely to lead to the public believing that the goods or services offered by him are the goods or services of the claimant.[6] Thirdly, he must demonstrate that he suffers/is likely to suffer damage by reason of the erroneous belief engendered by the defendant's misrepresentation that the source of the defendant's goods or services is the same as the source of those offered by the claimant. This proposition describes the common form of passing off—where the defendant misrepresents that his own goods or services are the claimant's. Beyond this common form, however, the tort can apply to a variety of situations **25-01**

1 For a more detailed consideration of the tort see Wadlow, *The Law of Passing Off: Unfair Competition by Misrepresentation*, 5th edn (2016); and *Kerly's Law of Trade Marks and Trade Names*, 16th edn (2017). Actions for passing off and registered trade mark infringement often arise out of the same facts: see para.25-25.

2 The concept of a trader is wide for the purposes of the tort: see para.25-09.

3 For the definition of goodwill see para.25-05.

4 The claimant must show brand name recognition *HFC Bank Plc v Midland Bank Plc* [2000] F.S.R. 176, per Lloyd J.

5 Lord Scarman in *Cadbury Schweppes Pty Ltd v Pub Squash Co Pty Ltd (Pub Squash)* [1981] 1 W.L.R. 193; [1981] R.P.C. 429 at 490—the misrepresentation could involve descriptive material "such as slogans or visual images, which radio, television or newspaper advertising campaigns can lead the market to associate with the plaintiff's product, provided always that such descriptive material has become part of the goodwill of the product". The test is whether "the product has derived from the advertising a distinctive character which the market recognises". See also *Elida-Gibbs v Colgate-Palmolive* [1983] F.S.R. 95.

6 The need for the misrepresentation to be "material" was stressed by the Court of Appeal in *Fenty v Arcadia Group Brands Ltd (t/a Topshop)* [2015] EWCA Civ 3; [2015] 1 W.L.R. 3291 at [45].

and some misrepresentations concerning the quality of goods are actionable as passing off.[7]

25-02 **Evolving nature of the action** It is not possible to provide an exhaustive statement of the circumstances in which an action for passing off will succeed and the above summary cannot capture all of them: this cause of action is still evolving "to meet changes in methods of trade and communication as it had in the past".[8] Indeed Aldous LJ in *Arsenal FC Plc v Reed*[9] asserted that the tort could "perhaps best [be] referred to as unfair competition" and that the traditional form of passing off "is no longer definitive of the ambit of the cause of action". However the Court of Appeal in *L'Oreal SA v Bellure*[10] noted that though these dicta from Aldous LJ.[11] were far from clear, if he was suggesting a tort of unfair competition it was not open to the courts to legislate in this way. Sir John Mummery in *Starbucks (HK) Ltd v British Sky Broadcasting Group Plc*[12] noted the policy balance that needed to be borne in mind when pressure is put on the tort to evolve, while in *Starbucks (HK) Ltd v British Sky Broadcasting Group Plc* Lord Neuberger noted the balancing exercise underlying the law of passing off; the perceived need to protect success without unduly restricting competition.[13] As yet, therefore, there is no tort of copying or of competition as such[14]: goodwill, misrepresentation[15] and damage—the so-called "classical trinity"[16]—are essential to any passing off action. The three elements are interlinked: the misrepresentation made by the defendant must be such as to cause damage to the claimant's goodwill. The "cement" of these three elements is customer reliance.

25-03 **The classical trinity and Lord Diplock's test** The basis of the action is the classical trinity of:

"(1) a reputation (or goodwill) acquired by the [claimant] in his goods, name, mark, etc.

(2) a misrepresentation by the defendant leading to confusion (or deception) causing

---

7 See paras 25-17 and 25-18.

8 Aldous LJ in *British Telecommunications Plc v One In A Million Ltd* [1999] 1 W.L.R. 903 CA. Laddie J in *Irvine v Talksport Ltd* [2002] EWHC 367; [2002] 1 W.L.R. 2355 noted that old cases "do not illustrate more recent developments". *National Association of Software and Service Companies v Sood* [2005] F.S.R. 38 HC India. The defendant had engaged in "phishing" on the internet, an interim injunction was awarded, such activity amounting to passing off.

9 [2003] EWCA Civ 696; [2003] 3 All E.R. 865.

10 [2007] EWCA Civ 968; [2008] E.T.M.R. 1.

11 Both in *British Telecommunications Plc v One in a Million Ltd* [1999] 1 W.L.R. 903; and *Arsenal FC v Reed* [2003] EWCA Civ 696; [2003] 3 All E.R. 865.

12 [2013] EWCA Civ 1465; [2014] F.S.R. 20 at [11]; [90].

13 [2015] UKSC 31; [2015] 1 W.L.R. 2628 (see in particular [61]–[62]). The Court of Appeal in *Fenty v Arcadia Group Brands Ltd (t/a Topshop)* [2015] EWCA Civ 3; [2015] 1 W.L.R. 3291 stressed that there is no image right as such (see Kitchin LJ at [29]).

14 Jacob J in *Hodgkinson & Corby Ltd v Wards Mobility Services Ltd* [1994] 1 W.L.R. 1564 "there is no tort of making use of another's goodwill as such".

15 In *Mars UK Ltd v Burgess Group Plc* [2004] EWHC 1912 (Ch) Lloyd J. rejected as "not seriously arguable" the claimants' argument that the tort of passing off does not always require proof of misrepresentation; and see *L'Oreal SA v Bellure* [2007] EWCA Civ 968; [2008] E.T.M.R. 1 at [140]–[141].

16 See the speeches of Lord Oliver of Aylmerton and Lord Jauncey of Tullichettle in *Reckitt & Colman Products Ltd v Borden Inc* [1990] 1 W.L.R. 491; [1990] R.P.C. 341 at 406 and 417; and para.25-03.

(3) damage to the [claimant]."[17]

In *Erven Warnink BV v J Townend & Sons (Hull) Ltd (Advocaat)*,[18] Lord Diplock set out the essential five requirements of the tort as follows:

"(1) a misrepresentation
(2) made by a trader in the course of trade,
(3) to prospective customers of his or ultimate consumers of goods or services supplied by him,
(4) which is calculated to injure the business or goodwill of another trader (in the sense that this is a reasonably foreseeable consequence) and
(5) which causes actual damage to the business or goodwill of the trader by whom the action is brought."[19]

However, although this is of the highest authority it has been said that it does not give "the same degree of assistance in analysis and decision as the classical trinity".[20]

Instruments of deception A manufacturer must not only beware of deceiving his own customers; he must not put into their hands that which may become an instrument of deception towards others, i.e. goods which are inherently likely to deceive the ultimate purchasers or consumers.[21] This version of the tort is complete when the defendant disposes of the goods complained of to the middleman. However, the doctrine appeared to have been widened in the Court of Appeal decision in *British Telecommunications Plc v One In A Million*. There the defendants by registering the claimants' company names as domain names as part of a scam to gain money from the legitimate owners, were held liable for passing off, threatened passing off and instruments of deception. Aldous LJ discerned a jurisdiction to grant injunctive relief where the defendant is equipped with or intending to equip another with an instrument of deception. That included the registration of a name, even one that is not inherently deceptive.[22] However, in *L'Oreal SA v Bellure*[23] what the claimants complained of—the defendant produced non-confusing "smellalikes" of the **25-04**

[17] *Consorzio del Prosciutto di Parma v Marks & Spencer Plc* [1991] R.P.C. 351, per Nourse LJ.

[18] [1979] A.C. 731.

[19] See also the speech of Lord Fraser in that case.

[20] *Consorzio del Prosciutto di Parma v Marks & Spencer Plc* [1991] R.P.C. 351 at 368, per Nourse LJ. Note however that the tests suggested in *Advocaat* are the ones that tend to be preferred in extended passing off cases, see e.g. *Fage UK Ltd v Chobani UK Ltd* [2014] EWCA Civ 5; [2014] E.T.M.R. 26 at [69] (Kitchin LJ).

[21] *Johnston v Orr-Ewing* (1882) 7 App. Cas. 219; *Draper v Trist* (1939) 56 R.P.C. 429 at 434 and 436; *John Walker & Sons Ltd v Henry Ost Co Ltd* [1970] R.P.C. 489; *White Gorse Distillers Ltd v Gregson Associates Ltd* [1984] R.P.C. 61. But as to the deliberate fraud of a retailer, see *Payton v Snelling* [1901] A.C. 308 at 311; *Cadbury-Schweppes Pty Ltd v Pub Squash Co Ltd* [1981] 1 W.L.R. 193; [1981] R.P.C. 429. See the discussion in Wadlow, *The Law of Passing Off: Unfair Competition by Misrepresentation*, 5th edn (2016), 5-137 to 5-171. The relationship between this doctrine and that of joint tortfeasance may at times be unclear. Joint tortfeasance liability in passing off was discussed in *Glaxo Wellcome UK Ltd (t/a Allen v Hanburys) v Sandoz Ltd* [2017] EWCA Civ 227; [2017] F.S.R. 32.

[22] [1999] 1 W.L.R. 903. See also *EasyJet Co Ltd v Dainty* [2002] F.S.R. 6; *Phones4u Ltd v phone4u.co.uk* [2005] EWHC 334 (Ch); *SmithKline Beecham Ltd v GSKline Ltd* [2011] EWHC 169 (Ch) at [23] Arnold J. In *Vertical Leisure Ltd v Poleplus* [2014] EWHC 2077 (IPEC) HH Judge Hacon stated that the law set out in *British Telecommunications Plc v One In A Million* [1999] 1 W.L.R. 903 remains good law with regard to passing off and instruments of deception where domain name registration is concerned. cf. on the facts, *Argos Ltd v Argos Systems Inc* [2017] EWHC 231 (Ch); [2017] E.T.M.R. 19, Richard Spearman QC, sitting as Deputy Judge (the subsequent appeal

claimants' perfumes, with similar packaging to the relevant goods of the claimants—did not inherently tell a lie, and "if a third party down the line says something dishonest about a product honest in itself, the vendor of the honest product is not liable in passing off".[24]

2. REQUIREMENTS

(a) Goodwill

25-05 **Goodwill** The tort of passing off does not protect the mark, get-up etc as such. A passing off action protects a proprietary interest in goodwill.[25] Goodwill has been defined as[26] "the benefit and advantage of the good name, reputation[27] and connection of a business. It is the attractive force which brings in custom". The goodwill, however, need not be extensive.[28] A small business is as much entitled to protection as is a large one.[29] Goodwill in the sense of reputation may be acquired by famous personalities who trade on their reputation by commercialising their image and that valuable reputation will be protected by the tort against unlicensed use by other parties.[30] The damage that must be shown (as actual or prospective) is damage to the integrity of the claimant's goodwill.[31]

25-06 **Generation of goodwill; dissipation of goodwill** Goodwill must exist at the time

[2018] EWCA Civ 2211; [2019] F.S.R. 3 related to registered trade mark use).

23 [2007] EWCA Civ 968; [2008] E.T.M.R. 1. *L'Oreal SA v Bellure* was the subject of a further hearing by the Court of Appeal ([2010] EWCA Civ 535; [2010] R.P.C. 23), but only with regard to the registered trade mark claim.

24 The views of Aldous LJ in *British Telecommunications Plc v One in a Million Ltd* [1999] 1 W.L.R. 903 were "explained": [2007] EWCA Civ 968 at [130]–[132].

25 "A passing off action is a remedy for the invasion of a right of property not in the mark, name or get-up improperly used but in the business or goodwill likely to be injured by the misrepresentation …", per Lord Diplock in *Star Industrial Co Ltd v Yap Kwee Kor* [1976] F.S.R. 256. And see Sir John Mummery in *Starbucks (HK) Ltd v British Sky Broadcasting Group Plc* [2013] EWCA Civ 1465; [2014] F.S.R. 20 at [102]. In *Nuanti Ltd v Google Inc* [2019] E.T.M.R. 5, Phillip Johnson, Appointed Person, held that an open source project (where software developers give up their time without payment) can attract goodwill. The goodwill is in relation to attracting the provision of software developer services.

26 Lord Macnaghten in *IRC v Muller* [1901] A.C. 217 at 223–224.

27 Though reputation is referred to by Nourse LJ in *Consorzio del Prosciutto di Parma v Marks and Spencer Plc* [1991] R.P.C. 351 CA, reputation alone is not sufficient: goodwill means actual customer connection or experience. See *Anheuser-Busch Inc v Budejovicky Budvar NP (the Budweiser case)* [1984] F.S.R. 413; and see para.25-07.

28 *Knight v Beyond Properties Pty Ltd* [2007] EWHC 1251 (Ch); [2007] F.S.R. 34, per David Richards J. Reputation on a small scale could attract the protection of the tort of passing off but the size of goodwill had to be more than a reasonable person would consider to be trivial.

29 *Chelsea Man Menswear Ltd v Chelsea Girl Ltd* [1985] F.S.R. 567; [1987] R.P.C. 189 CA. In *Student Union Lettings Ltd v Essex Student Lets Ltd* [2018] EWHC 419 (IPEC); [2018] E.T.M.R. 21 at [50]–[53] Recorder Amanda Michaels discusses nationwide versus localised goodwill (in the context of Trade Marks Act 1994 s.11(3)).

30 In *Irvine v Talksport Ltd* [2002] EWHC 367 (Ch); [2002] 1 W.L.R. 2355, Laddie J stressed the "substantial reputation" of the claimant who had a property right in his goodwill which he could protect from unlicensed appropriation consisting of a false claim or suggestion of endorsement of a third party's goods or business; and see *Fenty v Arcadia Group Brands Ltd* [2015] EWCA Civ 3; [2015] 1 W.L.R. 3291 where it was held that unauthorised merchandising of the celebrity image may deceive the public into believing it is approved merchandise.

31 Acts done abroad may damage the claimant's UK goodwill: *Mecklermedia Corp v DC Congress Gesellschaft mbH* [1998] Ch. 40; [1997] F.S.R. 627.

of the passing off. A short period of trading will not always be sufficient to generate goodwill.[32] However, extensive pre-launch publicity may mean that goodwill is rapidly acquired once the product is launched.[33] Some cases raise the possibility that promotional activities and advertising alone may be sufficient to generate goodwill.[34] In *Starbucks (HK) Ltd v British Sky Broadcasting Group Plc* Lord Neuberger left open the question whether pre-launch goodwill is possible.[35] Where the claimant was formerly in trade but the trade has ceased, no action will lie[36] unless a residual goodwill remains.[37] It is a question of fact whether goodwill has been dissipated through non-use or whether there remains any residual goodwill[38]; the issue would appear to be whether the original customer connection continues to exist.[39] However, where goodwill has been abandoned, it is lost immediately. The concept of abandonment of goodwill was accepted by Lord Diplock in *Star Industrial Co Ltd v Yap Kwee Kor*.[40] He highlighted both non-use and a lack of intention to resume the former trade.

Goodwill and foreign undertakings In *Starbucks (HK) Ltd v British Sky Broadcasting Group Plc*[41] the Supreme Court reiterated that goodwill is territorial in nature, it must exist within the jurisdiction; mere reputation within the jurisdiction is insufficient. However the Supreme Court also accepted that it was not necessary for a claimant to have an office/establishment in the jurisdiction. Foreign undertakings[42] have sometimes been held to possess sufficient goodwill in the UK to maintain an action for passing off.[43] The question is whether the claimant has generated goodwill within the jurisdiction: "does the claimant have customers 25-07

32 e.g. *County Sound Plc v Ocean Sound Ltd* [1991] F.S.R. 367; cf. *Stannard v Reay* [1967] F.S.R. 140.

33 *Allen (WH) & Co v Brown Watson Ltd* [1965] R.P.C. 191.

34 *BBC v Talbot Motor Co Ltd* [1981] F.S.R. 228; *Elida Gibbs v Colgate-Palmolive* [1983] F.S.R. 95, per Goulding J. The majority of the Court of Appeal in *Marcus Publishing Plc v Hutton-Wild Communications Ltd* [1990] R.P.C. 576 at 585 refused an injunction on the basis that the product was not yet on the market, but Staughton LJ commented: "it may be … that it is now possible to create goodwill for a future product by lavish hospitality or advertising of some other kind and that a competitor ought not to be allowed to appropriate to himself the goodwill so engendered."

35 [2015] UKSC 31; [2015] 1 W.L.R. 2628 at [66].

36 *Norman Kark Publications Ltd v Odhams Press Ltd* [1962] 1 W.L.R. 380; [1962] 1 All E.R. 636.

37 *Ad-Lib Club v Granville* [1971] 2 All E.R. 300; [1972] R.P.C. 673; *Maslyukov v Diageo Distilling Ltd* [2010] EWHC 443 (Ch); [2010] E.T.M.R. 37, Arnold J; *Sutherland v V2 Music Ltd* [2002] EWHC 14 (Ch); [2002] E.M.L.R. 28, residual goodwill in a pop group's name existed and could be protected. However in such cases where there may have been fluctuating band membership the issue of ownership of goodwill can still be unclear: *Byford v Oliver* [2003] EWHC 295 (Ch); [2003] E.M.L.R. 20, per Laddie J.

38 See, e.g. *Pennycuick VC in Ad Lib Club Ltd v Granville* [1972] R.P.C. 673 at 677.

39 Iain Purvis QC in *WS Foster & Son Ltd v Brooks Brothers UK Ltd* [2013] EWPCC 18: the "acid test" for determining whether residual goodwill remains after a period of non-use is whether "there still the attractive force that brings in business, something on which customers would place reliance as to source or quality rather than a lingering association".

40 [1976] F.S.R. 256. In *Ultraframe v Fielding* [2005] EWHC 1638 (Ch); [2006] F.S.R. 17 Lewison J referred to a common case in which abandonment is held to have taken place, as "where a business is discontinued, with no prospect of restarting, and its assets are broken up and sold" (at [1878]).

41 [2015] UKSC 31; [2015] 1 W.L.R. 2628.

42 Note that under the Trade Marks Act 1994 s.56 a proprietor of a trade mark which is entitled to protection under the Paris Convention as a well-known trade mark is entitled to restrain by injunction the use in the UK of a trade mark which or the essential part of which is identical or similar to his mark, in relation to identical or similar goods or services, where the use is likely to cause confusion, whether or not that person carries on business or has any goodwill in the UK. See para.24-123.

43 *SA des Anciens Etablissements Panhard et Levassor v Panhard Levassor Motor Co* [1901] 2 Ch. 513

here",[44] as opposed to "people in the jurisdiction who happen to be customers elsewhere",[45] (as was the case on the facts of *Starbucks (HK) Ltd v British Sky Broadcasting Group Plc* itself).[46] The Supreme Court in *Starbucks (HK) Ltd v British Sky Broadcasting Group Plc* considered the position of a foreign service business and approved the decision of the Court of Appeal in *Hotel Cipriani SRL v Cipriani (Grosvenor Street) Ltd*. Here the claimant's business was located in Italy, but goodwill was present in the UK. Though the service was provided overseas, the Court of Appeal held that goodwill existed given "it had a substantial reputation in England and a substantial body of customers from England …".[47] The Court of Appeal discussed generally the issue of whether an overseas service had to be booked by customers from within this jurisdiction in order for there to be the requisite goodwill.[48] Lloyd LJ noted that: "in the circumstances of the present day, with many establishments worldwide featuring on their own or shared websites, through which their services and facilities can be booked directly (or their goods can be ordered directly) from anywhere in the world, the test of direct bookings may be increasingly outmoded. It would be salutary for the test to be reviewed in an appropriate case."[49] However, in view of the Court of Appeal decision in *Anheuser-Busch Inc*

(England one of claimant's markets).

44 *Athletes Foot Associates v Cobra Sports Ltd* [1980] R.P.C. 343 at 357, per Walton J. The claimant may have licensed the use of his name or mark on products which are sold here: *Globelegance v Sarkissian* [1974] R.P.C. 603. In *Jian Tools Inc v Roderick Manhattan Group Ltd* [1995] F.S.R. 924, Knox J, sales from the American claimant to a small number of English customers "transatlantically inspired" by magazines and recommendations by foreign residents were sufficient to create goodwill. The Supreme Court of Ireland in *C&A Modes Ltd v C&A Waterford Ltd* [1978] F.S.R. 126, held that there may be customers in the jurisdiction, though they travel abroad to obtain the claimant's goods or services. (*Alain Bernadin Cie v Pavilion Properties Ltd* [1967] R.P.C. 581 appeared to demand that the claimant have a trading base within the jurisdiction).

45 *Starbucks (HK) Ltd v British Sky Broadcasting Group Plc* [2015] UKSC 31; [2015] 1 W.L.R. 2628 (Lord Neuberger at [52]).

46 *Starbucks (HK) Ltd v British Sky Broadcasting Group Plc* [2015] UKSC 31; [2015] 1 W.L.R. 2628 at [52]. The claimant had substantial goodwill in Hong Kong for its internet subscription service. Chinese speaking English residents could gain free access to some of this service via the internet. Merely accessing a foreign service on the internet did not make people in this jurisdiction "customers" within the UK. In the Court of Appeal ([2013] EWCA Civ 1465; [2014] F.S.R. 20 at [104]), Sir John Mummery stated: "generating a goodwill for service delivery generally involves making, or at least attempting to make, some kind of connection with customers in the market with a view to transacting business and repeat business with them", adding that the claimant's customers are those who at the very least are targeted for projected business transactions.

47 [2010] EWCA Civ 110; [2010] R.P.C. 16, per Lloyd LJ at [118]; Sir Stanley Burnton LJ at [126]. See also *Sheraton Corp of America v Sheraton Motels Ltd* [1964] R.P.C. 202; *Alain Bernardin et Cie v Pavilion Properties Ltd* [1967] R.P.C. 581.

48 Citing the discussion in Wadlow, *The Law of Passing Off: Unfair Competition by Misrepresentation*, 3rd edn (2004), para.3-80 that service businesses were of several different kinds so that the same test may not be appropriate for each kind of service, e.g. with hotels the service will be provided at the premises of the supplier, whereas other services may be supplied at the customer's premises, and others simply at a suitable location (now see *Wadlow*, 5th edn (2016), para.3–99 to 3–100).

49 [2010] EWCA Civ 110; [2010] R.P.C. 16 at [124]. In the lower court, obiter, Arnold J [2008] EWHC 3032 (Ch); [2009] R.P.C. 9 at [215]–[221]; agreed with the view of Browne-Wilkinson VC in *Pete Waterman Ltd v CBS UK Ltd* [1993] E.M.L.R. 27 that it would be sufficient to find goodwill if the foreign service provider had customers here. In *Starbucks (HK) Ltd v British Sky Broadcasting Group Plc* [2015] UKSC 31; [2015] 1 W.L.R. 2628 Lord Neuberger noted that it could be enough if the claimant could show that there were people in the jurisdiction who by booking with or purchasing from an entity in this country obtained a right to receive the claimant's service abroad. Such an entity would not have to be part of the claimant; someone acting for/on behalf of the claimant would be sufficient.

v Budejovicky Budvar NP,[50] where goodwill in *goods* rather than services was concerned, there was no goodwill here if the claimant's goods are not available for sale to the public here, at least where the goods are "ordinary retail goods for domestic consumption".[51] However, Lloyd LJ noted that *Anheuser-Busch* had been the subject of criticism by commentators and judges in some other common law jurisdictions.[52] In *Yell Ltd v Giboin*[53] the defendant was the owner and controller of a website outside the UK but the services he advertised could be purchased in the UK. The alleged passing off was within the jurisdiction of the court. However, in *Plentyoffish Media Inc v Plenty More LLP* the claimant had a foreign-based dating website which had attracted visits or "hits" from UK visitors, but there was no evidence any of them had become members. The concept of customers in the jurisdiction required more than visiting a website; nor could the claimant equate visitors with customers simply because the "hits" generated revenue from advertisers.[54] In *Banner Universal Motion Pictures Ltd v Endemol Shine Group Ltd*[55] Snowden J held that it is not sufficient to establish goodwill in the jurisdiction that the claimant's website is accessed here, applying *Starbucks (HK) Ltd v British Sky Broadcasting Group Plc*.[56]

Ownership of goodwill The owner of the goodwill will be the person the market identifies the character or quality of the goods with.[57] The relevant market will often be the public but it may, for example, be retailers[58] rather than the ultimate customers. Ownership may be in issue where there is an overseas supplier and a UK distributor.[59] Joint ownership of goodwill is possible,[60] as is concurrent ownership.[61] **25-08**

---

50 [1984] F.S.R. 413.

51 [2010] EWCA Civ 110; [2010] R.P.C. 16 at [38]; "customers among the general public in the UK for those products" at [106], per Lloyd LJ. See *Wadlow*, 5th edn (2016), para.3–98: "there may be goodwill in England if there are customers here prepared to take whatever trouble is necessary to obtain the claimant's goods from abroad".

52 [2010] EWCA Civ 110; [2010] R.P.C. 16 at [107].

53 [2011] EWPCC 9, HH Judge Birss QC.

54 [2011] EWHC 2568 (Ch); [2012] R.P.C. 5, H.H. Judge Birss QC (sitting as a judge of the High Court).

55 [2017] EWHC 2600 (Ch); [2018] E.C.C. 4 at [81]–[85].

56 [2015] UKSC 31; [2015] 1 W.L.R. 2628.

57 *Dental Manufacturing Co v C de Trey & Co* [1912] 3 K.B. 76 at 88, per Buckley LJ. See also *Nishika Corp v Goodchild* [1990] F.S.R. 371; *Woolley v Ultimate Products Ltd* [2012] EWCA Civ 1038; *Group Lotus Plc v 1 Malaysia Racing Team SDN BHD* [2011] EWHC 1366 (Ch); [2011] E.T.M.R. 62 at [153], Peter Smith J: ownership where more than one company is involved in generating goodwill is a question of fact. In *Frost Products Ltd v FC Frost Ltd* [2013] EWPCC 34; [2013] E.T.M.R. 44, Vos J held that the fact that the company sold its products by using architects to specify its products, thereby forcing contractors to buy its products, did not deprive it of goodwill. *Bhayani v Taylor Bracewell LLP* [2016] EWHC 3360 (IPEC); [2017] E.T.M.R. 14, HH Judge Hacon: goodwill generated by the acts of a partner normally vests in the partnership.

58 *Perkins v Shone* [2004] EWHC 2249 (Ch).

59 See, e.g. *Scandecor Development AB v Scandecor Marketing AB* [1999] F.S.R. 26 CA (the UK distributor was also a former subsidiary); *Medgen Inc v Passion for Life Products Ltd* [2001] F.S.R. 30, per Keith Garnett QC (sitting as a judge of the High Court).

60 *Sir Robert McAlpine Ltd v Alfred McAlpine Ltd* [2004] EWHC 630 (Ch); [2004] R.P.C. 36.

61 *Daimler Chrysler AG v Alavi (t/a Merc)* [2001] E.T.M.R. 98. For partnerships with changing membership, see *Powell v Turner* [2013] EWHC 3242 (IPEC); *Byford v Oliver* [2003] EWHC 295 (Ch); [2003] E.M.L.R. 20, per Laddie J. On goodwill and members of an unincorporated association: *Artistic Upholstery Ltd v Art Forma (Furniture) Ltd* [1999] 4 All E.R. 277.

In the case of extended passing off[62] where a distinctive product has gained a reputation in the market, the members of the class entitled to share in the goodwill are "all those traders who have supplied and still supply to the English market a product which possesses those recognisable and distinctive qualities".[63] In *Fine & Country Ltd v Okotoks Ltd* it was held that a franchisor (providing a marketing umbrella for various independent estate agents) was capable of attracting goodwill, that goodwill being the ability to attract licence fees.[64]

25-09 **Traders** Goodwill is acquired through trading, hence only traders can rely on the tort of passing off. However case law shows that the concept of trader extends beyond commercial activities in the narrowest sense: thus protection has been given to the names of professional associations of sufficient standing,[65] to the names of charitable institutions[66] and to authors[67] and others involved in a professional, artistic or literary occupation. But the claimant in an action for passing off must establish that he is in some sense carrying on a business, with which the trade or public will be led to associate the defendant's activities.[68] This may involve the "business" of commercialising personality as in *Irvine v Talksport Ltd*.[69] Note that the Court of Appeal in *Chocosuisse Union des Fabricants Suisses de Chocolat v Cadbury Ltd*[70] held that a trade association which did not itself trade, lacked locus

62 See para.25-18.

63 Lord Diplock, *Erven Warnink BV v J. Townend & Sons (Hull) Ltd* [1979] A.C. 731 at 747. And see Kitchin LJ in *Fage UK Ltd v Chobani UK Ltd* [2014] EWCA Civ 5; [2014] E.T.M.R. 26 at [68]–[69].

64 [2013] EWCA Civ 672; [2014] F.S.R. 11, see [56]–[58].

65 See, e.g. *Society of Accountants and Auditors v Goodway and London Association of Accountants Ltd* [1907] 1 Ch. 489; *Institute of Electrical Engineers v Emerson* (1950) 67 R.P.C. 167; *British Medical Association v Marsh* (1931) 48 R.P.C. 565; *Law Society of England & Wales v Society of Lawyers* [1996] F.S.R. 739.

66 *British Legion v British Legion Club (Street)* (1931) 48 R.P.C. 565; Walker J in *British Diabetic Association v The Diabetic Society* [1995] 4 All E.R. 812; [1996] F.S.R. 1 accepted that a passing off action could be brought by one charity against another, at least where the charities are involved in trading type activities by fund-raising.

67 *Byron v Johnson* (1816) 35 E.R. 851; *Clark v Associated Newspapers* [1998] 1 W.L.R. 1558. However, this protection would seem to apply only to authors in their trade as authors: *Kaye v Robertson* [1991] F.S.R. 62 at 69 the claimant actor was not a trader in relation to his interest in his story about his accident and recovery.

68 In *Kean v McGiven* [1982] F.S.R. 119, CA, where the name "Social Democratic Party" was claimed by two political parties, an action for passing off would not lie. However this case was distinguished by the Court of Appeal in *Burge v Haycock* [2001] EWCA Civ 900; [2002] R.P.C. 28 (Countryside Alliance had goodwill in its name) as ex tempore and a decision on its facts. The claimant does not have to aim to trade at a profit and may be a public body, e.g. *BBC v Talbot Motor Co Ltd* [1981] F.S.R. 228. In *Cranford Community College v Cranford College Ltd* [2014] EWHC 2999; [2015] E.T.M.R. 7 (IPEC) HH Judge Hacon stated that goodwill could be acquired by a school in the state sector (however, here there was no goodwill established). This was applied in *Comptroller-General of Patents Designs and Trade Marks v Intellectual Property Agency Ltd* [2015] EWHC 3256 (IPEC) HH Judge Hacon (a government department/executive agency was entitled to the goodwill generated by its services and by its website and helpline).

69 [2002] EWHC 367; [2002] 1 W.L.R. 2355, per Laddie J. (The Court of Appeal upheld Laddie J's judgment on passing off but overruled him on quantum: [2003] EWCA Civ 423; [2003] 2 All E.R. 881). And see *Fenty v Arcadia Group Brands Ltd* [2015] EWCA Civ 3; [2015] 1 W.L.R. 3291. See para.25-17

70 [1999] R.P.C. 826. cf. *Consorzio del Prosciutto di Parma v Marks and Spencer Plc* [1991] R.P.C. 351 CA, where the claimants' capacity to sue was accepted without argument.

standi (whether in its own right or as a representative) to sue in passing off, since it lacked a legitimate business interest to sue.[71]

Use of mark in different field Where a claimant and a defendant use a common or very similar mark for different goods or services, it is a question of fact whether or not the claimant's goodwill in the mark extends to the field in which the defendant is using the mark and whether the use by the defendant will be such as to involve a misrepresentation. Where the respective fields of use of the claimant and defendant are different, it is difficult, but not impossible, to establish passing off.[72] **25-10**

Distinctiveness A claimant generates goodwill by the use of a distinctive name, mark, description or get up in relation to his goods, services or business. If the mark etc the claimant is using is not distinctive of him, no actionable misrepresentation will arise by the defendant's use of it.[73] It is not necessary for the claimant to show that he is himself known to the public by name. All that is necessary is to show that the trade, or the public, recognise the mark in question as denoting the goods of a particular manufacturer, so that a substantial proportion of the public, buying under the mark in question, would be likely to expect to get his goods.[74] Nor is there any need for actual experience of claimant's product: it is sufficient that it is the claimant's product that the customers want.[75] **25-11**

Distinctiveness and invented or fancy[76] words Some marks—in particular invented or fancy words—can easily become distinctive of a particular trader's goods, and the burden of showing that use of one of these will lead to deception is a comparatively light one. However, an invented word may come to be merely descriptive[77] ("generic") and the common property of everybody rightfully selling the class of goods which it describes. Where a word originally used only by one trader is employed by others in the same line of business, the test to decide whether the word has become generic is "whether it may still have the effect of inducing **25-12**

71 However, such an association may be able to sue where there is a false representation that the defendant is a member of that association.

72 *Eastman Photographic Materials Co Ltd v Griffiths Cycle Corp Ltd* (1898) 15 R.P.C. 105 (cameras/bicycles—relief granted); *Harrods Ltd v R Harrod Ltd* (1924) 41 R.P.C. 74 (bank/moneylender—relief granted); *Annabel's (Berkeley Square) Ltd v Shock* [1972] R.P.C. 838 (nightclub/escort agency—relief granted); *Lego System Aktieselskab v Lego M Lemelstrich* [1983] F.S.R. 155 (children's coloured plastic construction kits/coloured gardening equipment—relief granted upon strong evidence of likely confusion); *Fortnum Mason Plc v Fortnam Ltd* [1994] F.S.R. 438 (well-known retail store, "Fortnum Mason"/importer of cheap merchandise "Fortnam"—relief refused).

73 If a claimant fails to prove that the name or mark sued upon denotes him, he will fail: *Oertli v Bowman* [1957] R.P.C. 388; affirmed [1959] R.P.C. 1 HL.

74 *Birmingham Vinegar Brewery Co v Powell* [1897] A.C. 710: the words "Yorkshire Relish" had become known as meaning sauce of a particular manufacturer, although purchasers did not in fact know the claimant's name in connection with the sauce; *Hoffman-La Roche Co AG v DDSA Pharmaceuticals Ltd* [1972] R.P.C. 1.

75 *Copydex Ltd v Noso Products Ltd* (1952) 69 R.P.C. 38; see also *Sales Affiliates Ltd v Le Jean* [1947] Ch. 295, per Evershed J: claimants marketed perms under the name "Jamal". The defendants were using other perms in treating hair of customers who had asked for a Jamal perm.

76 i.e. bearing no relation to the type or quality of the goods etc.

77 e.g. linoleum: *Linoleum Manufacturing Co v Nairn* (1878) 7 Ch. D. 834.

the public to buy goods not made by the original owner of the trade mark as if they were his goods".[78]

25-13 **Descriptive expressions** It is not easy to establish goodwill (as to source)[79] in a name which consists of descriptive words and the law is reluctant to allow ordinary descriptive words in the English language to be fenced off so as to become the private preserve of one particular trader.[80] A trader who wishes to maintain an action for passing off in an expression prima facie descriptive of his goods or services[81] must show that the expression has lost its primary descriptive meaning and has acquired a so-called secondary meaning, as a term distinctive of his goods or services.[82] Although the action may succeed,[83] the court will not readily assume that the use of descriptive words is likely to cause confusion and will easily accept small but real differences as adequate to avoid it.[84] In *Phones 4U Ltd v Phone4U.co.uk Internet Ltd* Jacob LJ categorised cases involving very descriptive marks as cases attracting a "tolerated level of deception", where "a certain amount of deception is to be tolerated for policy reasons".[85] The court is especially reluctant to grant relief where the claimant has enjoyed a monopoly in the manufacture of the goods to which the expression relates and his use of the descriptive term has been unique for that reason.[86]

---

78 per Mellish LJ in *Ford v Foster* (1872) L.R. 7 Ch. App. 611 at 628. A word may become ambiguous in meaning, denoting to the majority of people goods of the claimant's manufacture, but to others merely goods of a certain size or shape: *Havana Cigar and Tobacco Factories v Oddenino* [1924] 1 Ch. 179.

79 With the "extended" form of passing off (see para.25-18) descriptive names such as "advocaat" or "Swiss chocolate" are, of course, protected. However in *BBC v Talksport Ltd* [2001] F.S.R. 6, there was held to be no goodwill in the phrase "live sports broadcasting" as this was merely descriptive of the service provided by the claimant.

80 *Marcus Publishing Plc v Hutton-Wild Communications Ltd* [1990] R.P.C. 576, per Dillon LJ. See Peter Smith J in *A&E Television Networks LLC v Discovery Communications Europe Ltd* [2013] EWHC 109 (Ch); [2013] E.T.M.R. 32 at [21]–[23]. See also *Evegate Publishing Ltd v Newsquest Media (Southern) Ltd* [2013] EWHC 1975 (Ch) Asplin J at [174]–[176]. On what does not constitute a descriptive phrase see *British Sky Broadcasting Group Plc v Microsoft Corp* [2013] EWHC 1826 (Ch), Asplin J (especially at [247]).

81 The fact that a word makes a skilful allusion to the character of goods does not make it descriptive: *Thermawear Ltd v Vedonis Ltd* [1982] R.P.C. 44; *Antec International Ltd v South-Western Chicks (Warren) Ltd* [1998] F.S.R. 738.

82 *Reddaway v Banham* [1896] A.C. 199. cf. the result in *Cellular Clothing Co v Maxton & Murray* [1899] A.C. 326. In *Ukelele Orchestra of Great Britain v Clausen* [2015] EWHC 1772 (IPEC); [2015] E.T.M.R. 40, HH Judge Hacon, the claimant's descriptive name had acquired secondary meaning; the defendant's use of the trade name The UK Ukelele Orchestra amounted to a misrepresentation causing damage to the claimant's goodwill.

83 The "Yorkshire Relish" case, *Birmingham Vinegar Brewery Co v Powell* [1897] A.C. 710; *Reddaway v Banham* [1896] A.C. 199; are examples. And see *Asian Business Publications Ltd v British Asian Achievers Awards Ltd* [2019] EWHC 1094 (IPEC), Recorder Amanda Michaels.

84 per Lord Simmonds in *Office Cleaning Services Ltd v Westminster etc Cleaners Ltd* (1946) 63 R.P.C. 39 at 42 (trade name case); *Furnitureland Ltd v Harris* [1989] 1 F.S.R. 536.

85 [2006] EWCA Civ 244; [2007] R.P.C. 5 at [21]. In *British Sky Broadcasting Group Plc v Sky Home Services Ltd* [2006] EWHC 3165 (Ch); [2007] 3 All E.R. 1066; [2007] F.S.R. 14, Briggs J held that an intention to mislead may lead to a disapplication of the principle that where a descriptive name is used, a small difference in name will suffice to distinguish the defendant's mark from that of an established competitor (Lord Simonds, *Office Cleaning Services Ltd v Westminster Window and General Cleaners Ltd* (1946) 63 R.P.C. 39 at 42–43: "the policy ... must not operate to reward someone who sets out to deceive").

86 *Canadian Shredded Wheat v Kellogg* (1938) 55 R.P.C. 125 ("Shredded Wheat"); *Parsons v Gillespie*

Get-up It is possible for the "get-up" of goods—the shape, colour and decoration of the packaging etc by means of which goods or business premises are identified[87]—to become well enough known as indicating those of a particular trader, for use of that get-up by others to amount to passing off.[88] Passing off cases based on the shape or nature of the goods themselves alone have seldom succeeded[89]: both distinctiveness and the likelihood of a misrepresentation are hard to prove in such cases. However, in *Numatic International Ltd v Qualtex UK Ltd*[90] it was held that the shape of the claimant's vacuum cleaner (the "Henry") had acquired secondary meaning and the defendant's replica product constituted passing off. Similarity in get-up will seldom give a cause of action, if the names or trade marks of the traders concerned are given reasonable prominence upon the goods.[91] An action based on the colouring of packets to identify products of different specifications may fail if the court considers that the granting of relief would effectively give a monopoly in the use of certain colours for coding purposes.[92] However, in cases where the consequences of any confusion arising would be serious, such as those concerned with medicines, the courts may be willing to grant relief.[93] 25-14

Business names The court will interfere to prevent the use of deceptive business names as it will to prevent the use of deceptive trade marks.[94] The name which it is sought to protect need not be the claimant's own[95]: a nom-de-plume has been protected.[96] An unregistered company may be granted an injunction to restrain the registration of a company under a deceptive name.[97] As in the case of trade descriptions generally, it is very difficult for a claimant to prevent the imitation by other 25-15

[1898] A.C. 239; *British Vacuum Cleaner v New Vacuum Cleaner* (1907) 24 R.P.C. 641.

87 See for cases involving business premises: *My Kinda Town Ltd v Soll* [1983] R.P.C. 407.

88 *Reckitt & Colman (Products) Ltd v Borden Inc* [1990] 1 W.L.R. 491, HL ("Jif Lemon"); *Edge v Niccolls* [1911] A.C. 693. cf. *Williams v Bronnley* (1909) 26 R.P.C. 765; *British American Glass Co Ltd v Winton Products (Blackpool) Ltd* [1962] R.P.C. 230; *Fage UK Ltd v Chobani UK* [2014] EWCA Civ 5; [2014] E.T.M.R. 26 at [124], per Lewison LJ.

89 See for a summary of the principles: *Hodgkinson and Corby Ltd v Wards Mobility Services* [1994] 1 W.L.R. 1564; see also *British American Glass v Winton* [1962] R.P.C. 230. In *L'Oreal SA v Bellure* [2006] EWHC 235 (Ch); [2007] R.P.C. 14 at [164] Lewison J noted that the smell of a perfume was not capable of being protected by the tort of passing off: "the law of passing off is not designed to protect a trader against others selling the same goods or copied goods." On appeal his discussion of the tort of passing off was upheld by Jacob LJ: [2007] EWCA Civ 968; [2008] E.T.M.R. 1. And see *London Taxi Corp. Ltd v Frazer-Nash Research Ltd* [2017] EWCA Civ 1729; [2018] E.T.M.R. 7 at [98]–[99].

90 [2010] EWHC 1237 (Ch); [2010] R.P.C. 25, Floyd J.

91 *GMG Radio Holdings Ltd v Tokyo Project Ltd* [2005] EWHC 2188 (Ch); [2006] F.S.R. 15, per Kitchin J—proposed artwork on defendants' product, though original, similar stylistically to that on claimants' product. However, no passing off as defendant used own brand name on product.

92 *Rizla Ltd v Bryant & May Ltd* [1986] R.P.C. 389.

93 *Hoffman-La Roche Co AG v DDSA Pharmaceuticals Ltd* [1972] R.P.C. 1. See, however, *GlaxoWellcome UK Ltd v Sandoz Ltd* [2019] EWHC 2545 (Ch) Arnold LJ.

94 *Office Cleaning Services Ltd v Westminster etc Cleaners Ltd* (1946) 63 R.P.C. 39 at 42.

95 *Ewing v Buttercup Margarine Co Ltd* [1917] 2 Ch. 1.

96 *Marengo v Daily Sketch* (1948) 65 R.P.C. 242; *Sykes v John Fairfax* [1978] F.S.R. 312 (Australia).

97 *Hendriks v Montagu* (1881) 17 Ch. D. 638. Companies Act 2006 ss.66–68 deals with issues around the similarity to other names on the registrar's index giving the Secretary of State power to require a change of name if in fact a new company is allowed a name "too like" that of an old one. By ss.69–74 objection may be made to a company's registered name because of similarity to another name in which the objector has goodwill. The complaint is made to the Company Names Adjudicator.

traders of business names which are largely descriptive.[98] But it is not impossible, especially when the name complained of incorporates the whole of the claimant's name.[99] Where there are two rival businesses, not only the name but the whole "package" will be examined, and relief may be granted having regard to the whole even where the parts of the package taken individually may be unobjectionable.[100]

(b) Misrepresentation

25-16 **Misrepresentation**[101] There must be a misrepresentation,[102] which is a question of fact.[103] In *British Telecommunications Plc v One in a Million Ltd*[104] Aldous LJ held that the mere registration of a domain name containing a well-known name or mark was in itself a misrepresentation (to persons who consult the register of domain names).[105] The misrepresentation must be likely to damage the claimant's goodwill.[106] Passing off may involve misrepresentations made only to suppliers.[107] It is no defence to say that the description used is literally true if, in fact, it misleads.

---

98 *British Vacuum Cleaner Co Ltd v New Vacuum Cleaner Co Ltd* [1907] 2 Ch. 312; *Office Cleaning Services Ltd v Westminster Window and General Cleaners Ltd* (1946) 63 R.P.C. 39.

99 *North Cheshire and Manchester Brewery Co Ltd v Manchester Brewery Co Ltd* [1899] A.C. 83; *Effluent Disposal Ltd v Midlands Effluent Disposal Ltd* [1970] R.P.C. 238.

100 *My Kinda Town Ltd v Soll* [1983] R.P.C. 15; reversed by the Court of Appeal on the facts, but not affecting this point: [1983] R.P.C. 407.

101 "It would … be impossible to enumerate or classify all the possible ways in which a man may make the false representation relied on", per Lord Parker in *Spalding (AG) & Bros v AW Gamage Ltd* (1915) 84 L.J. Ch. 449; 32 R.P.C. 273 HL.

102 Stressed by Jacob LJ in *Boehringer Ingelheim KG v Swingward Ltd* [2004] EWCA Civ 129; [2004] 3 C.M.L.R. 3. A defendant may use a mark so as to denote that his goods are suitable for use with the claimant's goods without thereby representing that the defendants' goods are of the claimant's manufacture, e.g. in *Gledhill v British Perforated Toilet Paper Co* (1911) 28 R.P.C. 714, the term "Gledhill coil" had come to mean "coils suitable for use with Gledhill till" and not "coils manufactured by Gledhill". See also *Cellular Clothing v White* (1953) 70 R.P.C. 9; *Singer v Wilson* (1875) 2 Ch. D. 434; 3 App. Cas. 376; *Singer Manufacturing Co v Loog* (1880) L.R. 18 Ch. D. 395; affirmed at (1882–83) L.R. 8 App. Cas. 15 (HL). In *National Guild of Removers & Storers Ltd v Bee Moved Ltd* [2018] EWCA Civ 1302 the defendant had formerly been a member of the claimant trade association. On ceasing membership, the defendant deleted reference to his former membership of that trade association from a house moving website. However, due to IT difficulties involving that website reference to the membership of the trade association was re-instated without the knowledge of the defendant. Held, the defendant had not "made" the misrepresentation (concerning membership) of which the claimant complained.

103 Where goods are sold in specialised markets, evidence of persons accustomed to dealing in those markets as to the likelihood of confusion and deception is essential: *International Business Machines Corp v Phoenix International (Computers) Ltd* [1994] R.P.C. 251; citing *GE Trade Mark* [1972] 1 W.L.R. 729 HL.

104 [1999] 1 W.L.R. 903. By analogy Patten J in *Reality Group Ltd v Chance* [2002] F.S.R. 13 refused to strike out the claim that the defendant's application to register the name "Reality" as a CTM was in itself passing off. *Bayerische Motoren Werke AG v BMW Telecommunications Ltd* [2019] EWHC 411 (IPEC), HH Judge Hacon. The principle applying to domain name registration is also applicable to company name registration.

105 However, as the Court of Appeal noted in *Media Agency Group Ltd v Space Media Agency Ltd* [2019] EWCA Civ 712; [2019] F.S.R. 27 there is still a need to show reputation and goodwill in the name or mark relied upon.

106 *Schulke Mayr UK v Alkapharm UK Ltd* [1999] F.S.R. 161 (misrepresentation did not refer to claimant).

107 *Woolworth (FW) & Co v Woolworths (Australasia) Ltd* (1930) 47 R.P.C. 337; *Waterford Wedgewood Plc v David Nagli Ltd* [1998] F.S.R. 92.

The false representation may be made expressly[108] or impliedly.[109] Since the cause of action depends upon the defendant making a misrepresentation, a trader who uses another's trade mark, but in conjunction with additional matter making it clear to all concerned that the goods are not those of the owner of the mark, will not pass off thereby although if the mark is a registered trade mark he may infringe. Making the distinction clear is not always possible, however; in particular, if the public know the claimant's goods but not his name.[110] A disclaimer is not appropriate where it is unlikely to come to the attention of the reader or may confuse him more if it does.[111] "[T]he qualification must be 'up front' and must be perfectly clear and unambiguous. There may be cases where it is impossible to disclaim adequately."[112] It is sometimes stated that for the tort of passing off, deception, rather than "mere confusion", is required.[113] However, in *Phones 4U Ltd v Phone4U.co.uk Internet Ltd*,[114] Jacob LJ reiterated his view that this distinction can be "elusive". Rather than focusing on the "causative effect", "a more complete test would be whether what is said to be deception rather than mere confusion is really likely to be damaging to the claimant's goodwill or divert trade from him".

Misrepresentations actionable as passing off The general rule is that any misrepresentation[115] calculated to harm the goodwill of another will suffice. The classic case of passing off is that of the defendant misrepresenting goods to be those 25-17

[108] Or some such act as supplying another's goods in response to an order for the claimant's.

[109] *Mornay Ltd v Ball & Rogers (1975) Ltd* [1978] F.S.R. 91, per Goulding J: the defendants marketed a gift package containing the claimants' bathfoam and an unidentified scent, not of the claimants' manufacture. The court accepted that there was arguably a representation that the claimant had authorised the (inferior) scent to be sold in conjunction with its product. See *British Sky Broadcasting Group Plc v Sky Home Services Ltd* [2006] EWHC 3165 (Ch); [2007] 3 All E.R. 1066; [2007] F.S.R. 14, Briggs J, where the misrepresentation was held to be, inter alia, that during telemarketing the defendant's employees failed to correct customer confusion as to the approval of the claimant.

[110] As in the "Yorkshire Relish" case, *Birmingham Vinegar Brewery Co v Powell* [1897] A.C. 710. See, on the difficulties of adequate disclaimer in such cases, *Parker-Knoll v Knoll International* [1962] R.P.C. 243; and [1962] R.P.C. 265 HL.

[111] *Associated Newspapers v Insert Media* [1991] 1 W.L.R. 571; need to be "massive and omnipresent": *Asprey & Garrard v WRA (Guns) Ltd* [2002] F.S.R. 30, Jacob J. On appeal in *Asprey & Garrard* Gibson LJ noted that: " … the judge was entitled to draw on his considerable experience in this field to say that such disclaimers hardly ever work": [2001] EWCA Civ 1499; [2002] E.T.M.R. 47; [2002] F.S.R. 31 at [37].

[112] Jacob LJ in *IN Newman Ltd v Adlem* [2005] EWCA Civ 741; [2006] F.S.R. 16 at [44]–[45].

[113] *Barnsley Brewery Co Ltd v RBNB* [1997] F.S.R. 462 at 467, per Robert Walker J; *Fine & Country Ltd v Okotoks Ltd* [2013] EWCA Civ 672; [2014] F.S.R. 11 at [55], per Lewison LJ: " … the essence of the action is not confusion, but misrepresentation". Indeed, the Court of Appeal in *Bristol Conservatories Ltd v Conservatories Custom Built Ltd* [1989] R.P.C. 455 noted that there may be passing off without confusion. In *Comic Enterprises Ltd v Twentieth Century Fox Film Corp* [2016] EWCA Civ 41; [2016] E.T.M.R. 22 evidence of customer confusion did not necessarily establish an actionable misrepresentation on the part of the defendant. Kitchin LJ said "the scope of protection conferred by the law of passing off is not the same as that afforded by a registered trade mark" (at [159]).

[114] [2006] EWCA Civ 244; [2007] R.P.C. 5 at [16], [19], Jacob LJ. And see *Henry Martinez (trading as Prick) v Prick Me Baby One More Time Ltd (trading as Prick)* [2018] EWHC 776 (IPEC); [2018] E.T.M.R. 27, Judge Melissa Clarke at [22]–[24].

[115] How the courts will allow the tort to develop is unclear. In *Matthew Gloag & Son Ltd v Welsh Distillers Ltd* [1998] F.S.R. 718, Laddie J refused to strike out an action where Scotch whisky was flavoured with herbs and sold by the defendants as "Welsh Whisky". The claimants, as scotch whisky producers, alleged that this was some sort of actionable product misdescription and the harm alleged was that the defendants were "diluting" the reputation of scotch whisky by using its quality to sell their own product.

of the claimant. A misrepresentation by the defendant that his and the claimant's business or goods are in some way connected[116] may also be an actionable passing off. So a trader may be restrained from falsely representing that he is a manufacturer's authorised dealer.[117] Persons selling unauthorised character merchandise have been restrained on the basis that members of the public would believe the defendant's goods to be authorised by those responsible for creating the characters.[118] False celebrity endorsement has been held to be an actionable misrepresentation. In *Irvine v Talksport Ltd*[119] the defendant's advertising brochure included a photograph of the claimant, the famous Formula One driver. This photograph had been manipulated to remove the mobile phone that the claimant had in his hand and replace it with the image of a portable radio to which the name of the defendant radio station had been added. Laddie J held that there was an implicit representation of endorsement and that this false representation rendered the defendant liable in passing off. Though Laddie J was keen to distinguish between endorsement cases and "mere" merchandising cases, where the famous image is on memorabilia rather than as recommendation/endorsement of the product, in *Fenty v Arcadia Group Brands Ltd* the Court of Appeal held that unauthorised merchandising of the celebrity image may deceive the public into believing it is approved merchandise and that false belief would be material to their decision to buy the product.[120] It is also passing off to misrepresent inferior lines of goods as higher

116 The exact nature of the mis-connection that must be shown by the claimant is not clear. In *Harrods Ltd v Harrodian School* [1996] R.P.C. 697, Millett LJ held that the relevant connection must be one by which the claimants would be taken by the public to have made themselves responsible for the quality of the defendants' goods or services (cited by Briggs J in *British Sky Broadcasting Group Plc v Sky Home Services Ltd* [2006] EWHC 3165 (Ch); [2007] 3 All E.R. 1066; and by Birss J in *Fenty v Arcadia Group Brands Ltd* [2013] EWHC 2310 (Ch); [2014] F.S.R. 5). However, Sir Michael Kerr in *Harrods Ltd*, dissenting, took a much wider view: provided the public assumed that the claimants were somehow "mixed up" with the defendants' business or goods that would be sufficient (echoing *Ewing v Buttercup Margarine Co Ltd* [1917] 2 Ch. 1). See also Proudman J in *Future Publishing Ltd v Edge Interactive Media Inc* [2011] EWHC 1489 (Ch); [2011] E.T.M.R. 50 at [71]: statements leading the public to believe the defendant's product "in some way approved or authorised" by the claimant. See *Victoria Plum (t/a Victoria Plumb) v Victorian Plumbing Ltd* [2016] EWHC 2911; [2017] E.T.M.R. 8 (Ch), Henry Carr J with regard to passing off and keyword advertising. In *Jadebay Ltd v Clarke-Coles Ltd* [2017] EWHC 1400 (IPEC); [2017] E.T.M.R. 34, Judge Melissa Clarke, it was held on the facts that the defendants' use of the claimants' Amazon listing was a misrepresentation.

117 *Sony KK v Saray Electronics (London) Ltd* [1983] F.S.R. 302. *International Scientific v Pattison* [1979] F.S.R. 429; *Kimberley-Clark Ltd v Fort Sterling Ltd* [1997] F.S.R. 877; *Musical Fidelity Ltd v Vickers* [2002] EWCA Civ 1989; [2003] F.S.R. 50. And see *Primark Stores Ltd v Lollypop Clothing Ltd* [2001] F.S.R. 37, identical clothes but manufactured without authorisation.

118 *Mirage Studios v Counter-Feat Clothing Co Ltd* [1991] F.S.R.; *Hearst Holdings Inc v AVELA Inc* [2014] EWHC 439 (Ch); [2014] E.T.M.R. 34, Birss J, especially at [107]. However, compare the views of Laddie J and the Court of Appeal in *Elvis Presley Trade Mark* [1997] R.P.C. 543 at 554; and [1999] R.P.C. 567; and *BBC Worldwide Ltd v Pally Screen Printing Ltd* [1998] F.S.R. 665 at 674.

119 [2002] EWHC 367; [2002] 1 W.L.R. 2355, per Laddie J. (The Court of Appeal upheld Laddie J's judgment on passing off but overruled him on quantum: [2003] EWCA Civ 423; [2003] 2 All E.R. 881). *McCulloch v Lewis A May* [1947] 2 All E.R. 845 rejected; *Henderson v Radio Corp Pty Ltd* [1969] R.P.C. 218 (a decision of the High Court of New South Wales, sitting in its appellate jurisdiction) preferred. Note the false brand endorsement claim in *Unilever Plc v Griffin* [2010] EWHC 899 (Ch); [2010] F.S.R. 33, Arnold J.

120 [2015] EWCA Civ 3; [2015] 1 W.L.R. 3291. It was accepted that mere sales of T-shirts with the celebrity image would not per se be passing off.

quality goods of the same manufacturer,[121] or to misrepresent second-hand, altered or deteriorated goods as new.[122] It would also appear to be passing off for the defendant to claim that the claimant's goods are his goods or that the claimant's quality (as evidenced by samples, commendations or testimonials)[123] is his quality.[124] This has been termed "inverse passing off".[125] If the defendant supplies a competing product when the customer had requested the claimant's product, there is passing off.[126] Initial interest confusion may result from a misrepresentation but involves customers not remaining confused at the time of any sale. It is not established whether such initial interest confusion may be sufficient to constitute passing off.[127] However, Wadlow contends that "switch selling"—often by advertising the claimant's goods so as to attract customers in order to persuade them to purchase other goods—may be capable of constituting actionable passing off.[128] Courts in this country have rejected claims based on post-sale confusion as improbable.[129]

---

121 *Spalding (AG) & Bros v AW Gamage Ltd* (1915) 84 L.J. Ch. 449; 32 R.P.C. 273; *Colgate-Palmolive v Markwell Finance Ltd* [1989] R.P.C. 497 and cases cited there.

122 *Standard Motor Co v Grantchester Garage* [1960] R.P.C. 211 and cases cited there; *Wilts United Dairies v Robinson* [1953] R.P.C. 94 (also malicious falsehood); *International Business Machines Corp v Phoenix International (Computers) Ltd* [1994] R.P.C. 251.

123 *Bristol Conservatories Ltd v Conservatories Custom Built Ltd* [1989] R.P.C. 455—defendant misrepresented that the claimant's goods/services were the defendant's, thereby appropriating the goodwill of the claimant; *Tallerman v Dowsing* [1900] 1 Ch. 1; *Copydex Ltd v Noso Products Ltd* (1952) 69 R.P.C. 38. In *Orvec International Ltd v Linfoots Ltd* [2014] EWHC 1970 (IPEC) HH Judge Hacon at [36] commented on inverse passing off: "the courts have not since disagreed with the principle expressed in *Bristol Conservatories* and it has become accepted that where a defendant represents the claimant's article as being the product of his own effort and skill, this may be an actionable misrepresentation."

124 cf. cases involving "product equivalence" misrepresentations, where the defendants are liable for incorrectly alleging that their goods are "equivalent to" or "the same as" the claimants: *Masson Seeley & Co v Embossotype Mfg Co* (1924) 41 R.P.C. 160, per Tomlin J; *Combe International Ltd v Scholl (UK) Ltd* [1980] R.P.C. 1, per Fox J.

125 In *Matthew Gloag & Son Ltd v Welsh Distillers Ltd* [1998] F.S.R. 718, Laddie J accepted the legitimacy of an allegation of inverse passing off as did the Court of Appeal of the Republic of Singapore in *John Robert Powers School Inc v Denyse Bernadette Tessensohn* [1995] F.S.R. 947. In *Doosan Power Systems Ltd v Babcock International Group Plc* [2013] EWHC 1364 (Ch); [2013] E.T.M.R. 40 at [174] Henderson J held there to be a "subtle" misrepresentation that the claimant's expertise was that of the defendant (rather than a source misrepresentation). However in *Woolley v Ultimate Products Ltd* [2012] EWCA Civ 1038 Arden LJ at [6] rejects "reverse passing off" in the sense of a misrepresentation that confuses the public into thinking that the goods of the claimant are the goods of the defendant.

126 *Bovril v Bodega* (1916) 33 R.P.C. 153.

127 *Wadlow*, 5th edn (2016), para.7-53 onwards contends that *Doosan Power Systems Ltd v Babcock International Group Plc* [2013] EWHC 1364 (Ch); [2013] E.T.M.R. 40, (see [178] per Henderson J) was in fact a case of inverse passing off and that *Och-Ziff Management Europe Ltd v Och Capital LLP* [2010] EWHC 2599 (Ch); [2011] F.S.R. 11 (where Arnold J appeared to accept initial interest confusion at [155]–[157]) was an "ordinary" case of passing off in which damage was inferred. See also HH Judge Hacon in *Moroccanoil Israel Ltd v Aldi Stores Ltd* [2014] EWHC 1686 (IPEC) at [21]–[28]. However, in *Property Renaissance Ltd v Stanley Dock Hotel Ltd* [2016] EWHC 3103 (Ch); [2017] E.T.M.R. 12, Henry Carr J (citing Kerly) stated at [130]: "initial interest deception, which is dispelled before the moment of purchase, may … be actionable if it is really likely to be damaging to the claimant's goodwill or to divest trade".

128 See *Wadlow*, 5th edn (2016) at para.7–53 onwards.

129 *Bostick Tld v Sellotape GB Ltd* [1994] R.P.C. 556; *Hodgkinson & Corby Ltd v Wards Mobility Ltd* [1994] 1 W.L.R. 1564 at 1577 (Jacob J), cf. NZ: *Levi Strauss & Co v Kimbyr Investments Ltd* [1994] F.S.R. 335.

25-18 **"Extended passing off": product misdescription** In *Advocaat*,[130] the House of Lords accepted that a misdescription concerning a distinctive product[131] (rather than a distinctive claimant)[132] could be passing off. This has been termed the "extended form of passing off".[133] It is, for example, passing off to use a partly descriptive term in which goodwill subsists, such as "champagne", in relation to a product which is not champagne. Such conduct is actionable by persons properly entitled to use such a term to describe their product, as it is the claimant's own goodwill in the product that is at stake.[134] In the *Parma Ham* case,[135] the Court of Appeal noted that the claimant must show a difference in kind, not merely one of degree. The Court of Appeal in *Diageo NA Inc v Intercontinental Brands* (ICB) Ltd[136] accepted that the extended form of passing off was not limited to products with "cachet". In *Chocosuisse Union des Fabricants Suisses de Chocolat v Cadbury Ltd*[137] Chadwick LJ explained that "Swiss Chocolate" though descriptive in nature had come to mean to a significant part of the public a class of products having a distinctive reputation.[138] In *Fage UK Ltd v Chobani UK Ltd*[139] the question was whether "Greek yoghurt" was a distinctive product for the purposes of extended passing off. The claimant contended that the term "Greek yoghurt", a thick and creamy yoghurt, could only be applied to strained yoghurt from Greece. Thick and creamy yoghurt could also be produced by the use of thickening agent, such yoghurt being sold as "Greek style yoghurt". The defendant produced strained yoghurt but not from Greece and called it "Greek yoghurt". It was held that Greek yoghurt was a distinctive product. A substantial proportion of UK purchasers of Greek yoghurt thought

---

130 *Erven Warnink BV v J Townend & Sons (Hull) Ltd* [1979] A.C. 731. It was first recognised and applied by Danckwerts J in *Bollinger v Costa Brava Wine Co* [1960] R.P.C. 16.

131 Lord Diplock in *Advocaat* [1979] A.C. 731 at 747: "if one can define with reasonable precision the type of product that has acquired the reputation, one can identify the members of the class entitled to share in the goodwill"; Laddie J in *Chocosuisse Union des Fabricants Suisses de Chocolat v Cadbury Ltd* [1998] R.P.C. 117: there must be a "defined class of goods with a distinctive reputation" (appeal on passing off dismissed: [1999] R.P.C. 826 CA). Designation of origin or geographical indications for agricultural products/foodstuffs may be covered by Reg (EU) 1151/2012. In *Fage UK Ltd v Chobani UK* [2014] EWCA Civ 5; [2014] E.T.M.R. 26 it was held that the EU law does not preclude the application of national rules for the protection of geographical denomination which do not fall within the scope of the 2012 Regulation (see Kitchin LJ at [88]).

132 Jacob J in *Hodgkinson & Corby Ltd v Wards Mobility* [1994] 1 W.L.R. 1564 at 1570 notes that in *Combe International Ltd v Scholl (UK) Ltd* [1980] R.P.C. 1, the deception is that the defendants' goods are the same as those of the claimant; whereas in *Advocaat* the deception is that the defendants' goods are the same as the goods sold by a class of persons of which the claimant is a member.

133 So termed by Laddie J in *Chocosuisse Union des Fabricants Suisses de Chocolat v Cadbury Ltd* [1998] R.P.C. 117. *Fage UK Ltd v Chobani UK Ltd* [2014] EWCA Civ 5; [2014] E.T.M.R. 26 " … so called extended passing off is no different in principle from conventional passing off … in each case the claimant must establish that the name he is seeking to protect has acquired a goodwill that is to say an attractive power …", per Kitchin LJ at [65].

134 *Erven Warnink BV v J Townend & Sons (Hull) Ltd* [1979] A.C. 731 ("*Advocaat*"); *Tattinger SA v Allbev Ltd* [1994] 4 All E.R. 75 ("champagne"/"elderflower champagne"); *John Walker & Sons Ltd v Henry Ost Co Ltd* [1970] 1 W.L.R. 917; [1970] R.P.C. 489 ("scotch whisky"—passing off abroad)

135 *Consorzio del Prosciutto di Parma v Marks and Spencer Plc* [1991] R.P.C. 351 CA.

136 [2010] EWCA Civ 920; [2011] 1 All E.R. 242 (vodka/vodkat). However, in *Fage UK Ltd v Chobani UK* [2014] EWCA Civ 5; [2014] E.T.M.R. 26 at [148] Lewison LJ shared the same concerns as Rix LJ in *Diageo* "that this form of passing off risks stifling healthy competition in relatively low cost generic goods" (and see Kitchin LJ at [69]).

137 [1999] R.P.C. 826.

138 However, the Court of Appeal decided that the trade association lacked locus standi. On the descriptive/distinctive distinction, see Kitchin LJ in *Fage UK Ltd v Chobani UK* [2014] EWCA Civ 5; [2014] E.T.M.R. 26 at [63].

139 [2014] EWCA Civ 5; [2014] E.T.M.R. 26.

it was made in Greece and this mattered to them, even though they might not know of the specification to which Greek yoghurt was made. For extended passing off the claimant must show "that the name has come to denote a particular kind of product which has recognisable characteristics which distinguish it from other products and that the public are motivated to buy the product by reason of those characteristics".[140] Lewison LJ approved of the passage from Laddie J's judgment in *Chocosuisse Union des Fabricants Suisses de Chocolat v Cadbury Ltd* that even if there is no difference in the quality and ingredients between goods sold by reference to the distinctive term and competing goods, that would not prevent a successful passing off action.[141] In deciding on the critical issues of distinctiveness and goodwill reference was also made to market practice; the unwritten labelling convention (limiting the description Greek yoghurt only to creamy strained yoghurt made in Greece); the evidence of trade witnesses and the premium price commanded by a Greek yoghurt product (as opposed to a Greek style yogurt). In *Military Mutual Ltd v Police Mutual Assurance Society Ltd*[142] it was noted, obiter, that though previous "extended passing off" cases have involved a name associated with a type of product, there was no reason why the tort should not similarly protect goodwill associated with the name of a type of service or perhaps goodwill associated with a name given to a type of organisation.

Proof of deception and confusion It is sufficient that the defendant misrepresents his goods in such a way that it is a reasonably foreseeable consequence that the claimant's business or goodwill will be damaged. In *Lumos Skincare Ltd v Sweet Squared Ltd*[143] the Court of Appeal noted that it was important, in assessing who the claimant must show has been or would be misled by the defendant's representation, to identify the market of each party and how the respective parties' products are used and sold. Proof of an intention to deceive is not essential.[144] However, if the object of the defendant is to deceive, the court is ready to infer that deception has occurred or is likely to do so.[145] Often a claimant will prove misrepresentation by calling evidence that members of the relevant public were in fact confused but a claimant may succeed although no deception has actually yet taken place.[146] The issue is whether there was a misrepresentation calculated to deceive. For the Court of Appeal in *Neutrogena Corp v Golden Ltd*,[147] the correct legal test on the issue of deception was whether on the balance of probabilities a substantial number of 25-19

140 [2014] EWCA Civ 5; [2014] E.T.M.R. 26 at [68], per Kitchin LJ. He reviewed the leading cases at [38]–[61].

141 [2014] EWCA Civ 5; [2014] E.T.M.R. 26 at [128].

142 [2018] EWHC 1575 (IPEC); [2018] E.T.M.R. 33 at [67], HH Judge Hacon.

143 [2013] EWCA Civ 590. And see *Evegate Publishing Ltd v Newsquest Media (Southern) Ltd* [2013] EWHC 1975 (Ch), Asplin J.

144 per Lord Cairns LC in *Singer Machine Manufacturers v Wilson* (1877) 3 App. Cas. 376 at 391; *Spalding* (AG) & Bros v AW Gamage Ltd (1915) 84 L.J. Ch. 449; 32 R.P.C. 273.

145 Lindley LJ *Slazenger & Sons v Feltham & Co* (1889) 6 R.P.C. 531 at 538. The defendant's conscious decision to "live dangerously" would be relevant, see Robert Walker J in *United Biscuits (UK) Ltd v Asda Stores Ltd* [1997] R.P.C. 513. at 531; though see Mann J in *Specsavers International Healthcare Ltd v Asda Stores Ltd* [2010] EWHC 2035 (Ch); [2011] F.S.R. 1 at [193] (there was an appeal on the registered trade mark issues only: [2012] EWCA Civ 24; [2012] F.S.R. 19).

146 *Reddaway v Bentham* [1892] 2 Q.B. 639; *Spalding (AG) & Bros v AW Gamage Ltd* (1915) 84 L.J. Ch. 449; 32 R.P.C. 273. On the "relevant public/consumer" see *Gama Healthcare Ltd v Pal International Ltd* [2016] EWHC 75 (IPEC) deputy Enterprise Judge Michaels (at [51]).

147 [1996] R.P.C. 473.

members of the public[148] would be misled into purchasing the defendants' product in the belief it was the claimants'.[149] In *Enterprise Holdings Inc v Europcar Group UK Ltd* Arnold J commented: "[the tort] requires the court to consider whether ordinary customers who purchase with ordinary caution and who know what is fairly common to the trade are likely to be misled".[150] It is the overall impact of the evidence that is important.[151] Where the conduct complained of has been going on for some time the court may well find, in the absence of proof of actual deception, that no deception is likely to occur.[152] A trade description is calculated to deceive if it is sent forth attached to or impressed on the goods in a manner likely to mislead those members of the public who may ultimately become purchasers. It is no answer to a complaint of misrepresentation to say that an observant person who made a careful examination, or who compared them side by side, would not be misled. The test is the impression likely to be produced on the likely customer taking into account a customer's "imperfect recollection".[153] The level of perspicacity of the relevant customers may depend on the transaction contemplated.[154]

(c) Damage

25-20 **Damage** Once a claimant has established that there has been a misrepresentation, it is usually easy to show that damage to goodwill will result. Some damage will often be assumed once it has been established that there is a misrepresentation so proof of actual damage is not essential to establishing liability.[155] Commonly damage in this tort involves diversion of sales or the risk of devaluation of

---

148 *Sofa Workshop Ltd v Sofaworks Ltd* [2015] EWHC 1773 (IPEC) HH Judge Hacon: the proportion of the relevant public to which the defendant's trade name must constitute a misrepresentation had to be "sufficient to cause material damage" to the claimant's goodwill (at [121]).

149 See the argument raised unsuccessfully by the defendant in *Fage UK Ltd v Chobani UK* [2014] EWCA Civ 5; [2014] E.T.M.R. 26 that a higher standard is required where a case involves cross-border trade. Readers are referred to specialist texts for details of the rules governing the admissibility of trade evidence and survey evidence in passing off cases. For a summary of the requirements for surveys, see *Imperial Group v Philip Morris* [1984] R.P.C. 293, endorsed by the Court of Appeal in *Marks and Spencer Plc v Interflora Inc* [2012] EWCA Civ 1501; [2013] 2 All E.R. 663 (Lewison LJ); and *Interflora Inc v Marks and Spencer Plc* [2013] EWCA Civ 319; [2013] F.S.R. 26 (in the context of registered trade mark infringement: survey evidence not to be admitted unless of real utility and costs justified). In *A&E Television Networks LLC v Discovery Communications Europe Ltd* [2013] EWHC 109 (Ch); [2013] E.T.M.R. 32 at [129] Peter Smith J adopted Lewison LJ's observations in *Marks and Spencer Plc v Interflora Inc* in a passing off action. And see *Zee Entertainment Enterprises Ltd v Zeebox Ltd* [2014] EWCA Civ 82; *GlaxoWellcome UK Ltd. v Sandoz Ltd.* [2019] EWHC 2545 (Ch) Arnold LJ. On the extent to which evidence of trade practice and consumer perception was expert evidence, see the appeal in *Fenty v Arcadia Group Brands Ltd (t/a Topshop)* [2015] EWCA Civ 3; [2015] 1 W.L.R. 3291 at [54]–[61].

150 [2015] EWHC 17 (Ch); [2015] E.T.M.R. 16 at [158].

151 Courts in this country have rejected claims based on post-sale confusion (after any disclaimers or distinguishing labels at the point of sale had been removed) as improbable: see para.25-17.

152 See *Payton v Snelling* [1901] A.C. 308 at 309.

153 See *Singer Manufacturing Co v Loog* (1882) 8 App. Cas. 15 at 18; *Saville Perfumery Ltd v June Perfect Ltd* (1941) 58 R.P.C. 147 at 175; cf. *Hookham v Pottage* (1872) L.R. 8 Ch. App. 91; *Civil Service Supply Association v Dean* (1879) 13 Ch. D. 512.

154 *HFC Bank Plc v Midland Bank Plc* [2000] F.S.R. 176, Lloyd J.

155 *Procea v Evans* (1951) 68 R.P.C. 210. In *British Sky Broadcasting Group Plc v Microsoft Corp* [2013] EWHC 1826 (Ch) at [250], Asplin J noted "damage is inherently likely where frequently the customers of a business wrongly connect it to another".

reputation/injurious association.[156] Lost licensing fees may be recovered if licensing is part of the claimant's goodwill[157] and loss of reputation control may also be recoverable (as in *Fenty v Arcadia Group Brands Ltd*).[158] Dilution (loss of distinctiveness) is also a head of recoverable damage.[159] In *Woolley v Ultimate Products Ltd*[160] Arden LJ noted that the heads of damage for the tort include "an erosion or diminution in the value of goodwill". But no cause of action arises for mere dilution of goodwill where there is no relevant misrepresentation that causes it. In *Student Union Lettings Ltd v Essex Student Lets Ltd*[161] there was no direct loss of sales caused by the defendants' misrepresentation. However harm could potentially arise through inadequacies in the defendants' services and the restriction of the claimants' intended expansion of its activities.

3. REMEDIES

Remedies The remedies in an action for passing off are similar to those available in an action for the infringement of a registered trade mark, principally damages[162] or an account of profits,[163] and an injunction. As with the infringement of a registered trade mark, the mere fact of actionable passing off gives a right at least 25-21

[156] As to loss of sales, see *Draper v Trist* [1939] 3 All E.R. 513; (1939) 56 R.P.C. 429 CA. With regard to injurious association see, e.g. *Annabel's (Berkeley Square) Ltd v Schock (Trading as Annabel's Escort Agency)* [1972] F.S.R. 261 CA. In *Associated Newspapers Ltd v Express Newspapers* [2003] EWHC 1322 (Ch); [2003] F.S.R. 51, Laddie J, the defendants were restrained from using a similar title for their newspaper to that used by the claimants' paper as there was a likelihood that the claimants would "lose control of its personality". The defendants' newspapers included adverts for adult chat lines and massage parlours, services which would not be acceptable in the claimants' papers. And see *Unilever Plc v Griffin* [2010] EWHC 899 (Ch); [2010] F.S.R. 33, Arnold J.

[157] *Fine & Country Ltd v Okotoks Ltd* [2013] EWCA Civ 672; [2014] F.S.R. 11. In relation to harm to expansion potential see *Alfred Dunhill Ltd v Sunoptic SA* [1979] F.S.R. 337 CA.

[158] *Fenty v Arcadia Group Brands Ltd (t/a Topshop)* [2015] EWCA Civ 3; [2015] 1 W.L.R. 3291. In *Comptroller-General of Patents Designs and Trade Marks v Intellectual Property Agency Ltd* [2015] EWHC 3256 (IPEC) HH Judge Hacon, the defendants were involved in a renewal scam on IP right holders, requesting higher fees than those they ultimately passed on to the claimant, the UK IPO. Though the claimant did in fact receive the appropriate renewal fees, inactivity on the part of the claimant in preventing the scam would be likely to harm its reputation; passing off was established. See also *Ukelele Orchestra of Great Britain v Clausen* [2015] EWHC 1772 (IPEC); [2015] E.T.M.R. 40, HH Judge Hacon: the use by the defendants of a confusingly similar trade name caused damage to the claimant's goodwill by their loss of control over their reputation as performers.

[159] Especially in cases of extended passing off, see, e.g. *Fage UK Ltd v Chobani UK Ltd* [2014] EWCA Civ 5; [2014] E.T.M.R. 26 at [67], per Kitchin LJ. On dilution and substitution see: *Och–Ziff Management Europe Ltd v Och Capital LLP* [2010] EWHC 2599 (Ch); [2011] F.S.R. 11, Arnold J at [158]–[160].

[160] [2012] EWCA Civ 1038 at [7].

[161] [2018] EWHC 419 (IPEC); [2018] E.T.M.R. 21, Recorder Amanda Michaels.

[162] In *Irvine v Talksport Ltd (Damages)* [2003] EWCA Civ 423; [2003] 2 All E.R. 881, the Court of Appeal awarded the claimant damages based on a reasonable royalty, consequent on the false endorsement. In *Harman v Burge* [2014] EWHC 2836 (IPEC), [15], H.H. Judge Hacon discussed the principles applicable to an inquiry as to damages.

[163] See generally on account of profits: *Weingarten v Bayer* [1904–07] All E.R. 877; 22 R.P.C. 341 HL. There is a useful discussion of this remedy as applied to passing off cases in *Hotel Cipriani SRL v Cipriani Ltd* [2010] EWHC 628 (Ch), per Briggs J. And see Judge Pelling QC in *Woolley v UP Global Sourcing UK Ltd* [2014] EWHC 493 (Ch); see *McCambridge Ltd v Joseph Brennan Bakeries* [2014] IEHC 269, [2015] F.S.R. 3 for discussion of the approach to an account of profits adjudication where unintentional passing off was involved.

to nominal damages,[164] and the damages recoverable on proper proof[165] may include damage caused by loss of sales and damage to the claimant's trade reputation.[166] Innocence of the defendant is no defence to the recovery of damages against him.[167]

25-22 **Injunctions** Final injunctions are commonly granted in passing off cases.[168] An appropriate form of injunction may be limited to restraining the defendant from using the mark in question "without sufficiently distinguishing his goods from those of the claimant".[169] Orders may be made for the obliteration of the offending mark upon the defendant's goods. Delivery up is only ordered as ancillary to an injunction and, especially where the defendant's goods can be sold without passing off (for example in foreign markets where the claimant's mark may be unknown), delivery up may not be appropriate. Interim injunctions are granted in passing off cases on the usual *American Cyanamid* principles,[170] unless the defendant's exercise of his ECHR art.10 freedom of expression is in issue. In such a case, where interim injunctions are sought s.12(3) of the Human Rights Act 1998 imposes a threshold test which has to be satisfied before a court may grant interim relief. Publication before trial is not to be restrained unless the court is satisfied that the applicant is likely to establish that publication should not be allowed.[171] In suitable cases, a search order[172] may be made to prevent the defendant concealing or destroying evidence as well as orders to compel disclosure of the names of other potential tortfeasors, such as suppliers of the offending goods.[173]

---

164 *Procea Products Ltd v Evans* (1951) 68 R.P.C. 210 at 219; explaining *Draper v Trist* (1939) 56 R.P.C. 429. An inquiry as to damages may be refused if it would be futile: *McDonalds Hamburgers Ltd v Burger King (UK) Ltd* [1987] F.S.R. 112 (inquiry ordered).

165 Only profits made as a result of passing off are recoverable, not profits due to competition itself: *My Kinda Town Ltd v Soll* [1983] R.P.C. 15 (reversed on the facts, but not affecting this point: [1983] R.P.C. 407 CA); *Baume v Moore* (1954) 71 R.P.C. 243.

166 As to loss of goodwill, see *Spalding (AG) & Bros v AW Gamage Ltd* (1915) 84 L.J. Ch. 449; 32 R.P.C. 273; *Unik Time Co Ltd v Unik Time Ltd* [1983] F.S.R. 121.

167 *Gillette UK Ltd v Edenwest Ltd* [1994] R.P.C. 279 (authorities reviewed). Different considerations may arise with an account of profits [1994] R.P.C. 279 at 290.

168 An injunction will not be limited to a particular geographical area where wider relief is appropriate: *Chelsea Man Menswear Ltd v Chelsea Girl Ltd* [1987] R.P.C. 189. An injunction will not be granted where the result would be a position prohibited by any of arts 30, 81 or 82 of the Treaty of Rome (now arts 36, 101 and 102 respectively of the Treaty on the Functioning of the EU).

169 See *Montgomery v Thompson* [1891] A.C. 217; *Havana Cigar & Tobacco v Oddenino* [1924] 1 Ch. 179; 41 R.P.C. 47; *cf. Magnolia Metal Co v Atlas Metal Co* [1897] 2 Ch. 371; (1897) 14 R.P.C. 389.

170 *American Cyanamid v Ethicon* [1975] A.C. 396; [1975] R.P.C. 513; *County Sound Plc v Ocean Sound Ltd* [1991] F.S.R. 367. In *Cowshed Products Ltd v Island Origins Ltd* [2010] EWHC 3357 (Ch); [2011] E.T.M.R. 42 at [54], H.H. Judge Birss QC, the court assessed the issue of unquantifiable harm and the balance of convenience.

171 See *Blandford Goldsmith & Co Ltd v Prime UK Properties Ltd* [2003] EWHC 326 (Ch), per Lewison J. For a more detailed consideration see para.26-33. In *Unilever Plc v Griffin* [2010] EWHC 899 (Ch); [2010] F.S.R. 33, Arnold J noted (applying *Cream Holdings Ltd v Bannerjee* [2004] UKHL 44; [2005] 1 A.C. 253) that in appropriate circumstances a lower degree of likelihood is acceptable.

172 CPR r.25, 1(1)(h) (formerly *Anton Piller* order).

173 The court may order the disclosure of information to enable the claimant to identify tortfeasors and trace the source of the offending goods: *RCA Corp of America v Reddingtons Rare Records* [1974] 1 W.L.R. 1445; [1975] 1 All E.R. 38. *Norwich Pharmacal Co v Commissioners of Customs and Excise* [1974] A.C. 133; *Coca-Cola Co v British Telecommunications Plc* [1999] F.S.R. 518, Neuberger J.

4. DEFENCES[174]

Honest concurrent use and use of own name Where confusion does arise, it may be a defence that the defendant is making honest concurrent use of the same name. With honest concurrent use (which may arise, e.g. where there has been a break up of a company structure)[175] there is no liability as any goodwill is shared between the parties. Though in theory any person may trade in his own name, or use it as part of his business name, provided he does so bona fide[176] Jacob LJ in *Reed Executive Plc v Reed Business Information Ltd*[177] stressed that this defence was "very narrow" adding "because the test is honesty, I do not see how any man who is in fact causing deception and knows that to be so can possibly have a defence to passing off". The question in each case is whether the use of the name is calculated to deceive the public unless precautions are taken.[178] Thus, it may be proper to restrain a man from trading under any name of which his surname forms part, without clearly distinguishing his goods from those of some other trader.[179] 25-23

Unconscionability The defences of acquiescence and estoppel apply to the tort of passing off.[180] No relief will be granted if it would be unconscionable to do so on the grounds that the claimant has acquiesced in the use complained of. The defendant must show that he has altered his position on the basis of an act, omis- 25-24

---

174 For a more detailed discussion see Wadlow, *The Law of Passing Off: Unfair Competition by Misrepresentation*, 5th edn (2016), Ch.9.

175 See, e.g. *Habib Bank Ltd v Habib Bank AG Zurich* [1981] 1 W.L.R. 1265 at 1278–1279, per Oliver LJ; *Scandecor Development AB v Scandecor Marketing AB* [1998] F.S.R. 500. However in a joint venture the licence given to the defendant to use the claimant's name was revoked when the defendant was no longer part of that joint venture: *Dawnay Day & Co Ltd v Cantor Fitzgerald Int* [2000] R.P.C. 669 CA. Note also *Daimler Chrysler AG v Alavi (t/a Merc)* [2001] E.T.M.R. 98, Pumfry J noted at [67] that there must come a time after which the court would not interfere with a continued course of trading which might have involved passing off at the inception but no longer did so.

176 *Turton v Turton* (1889) 42 Ch. D. 128; *Massam v Thorley's Cattle Food Co* (1880) 14 Ch. D. 748; *Rael-Brook Ltd v Head Shirts Ltd* [1963] R.P.C. 6. But, cf. *Parker-Knoll v Knoll International* [1962] R.P.C. 265. And this exception does not extend to nicknames: *Biba Group Ltd v Biba Boutique* [1980] R.P.C. 413; *NAD Electronics Inc v NAD Computer Systems Ltd* [1997] F.S.R. 380.

177 [2004] EWCA Civ 159; [2004] R.P.C. 40. In *Asprey & Garrard Ltd v WRA (Guns) Ltd* [2002] F.S.R. 30 Jacob J had noted that the own name defence was a "tricky area of passing off law" but that it did not apply to new company names "otherwise a route to piracy would be obvious".

178 *Allen v Original Samuel Allen & Sons Ltd* (1915) 32 R.P.C. 33. A trader cannot have any exclusive right to a mere address: *Street v Union Bank of Spain* (1885) L.R. 30 Ch. D. 156; but imitation of another trader's address may be an element in passing off: *Pullman v Pullman* (1919) 36 R.P.C. 240. Where, however, the name of a well-known city is included as part of a company's name, the onus resting on the claimant in establishing the right to a monopoly in that name is a heavy one; *Bristol-Myers Co v Bristol Pharmaceutical Co Ltd* [1968] R.P.C. 259; and a trader who carries on business at an address that includes the claimant's trade name will not be restrained from using that address, provided that he bona fide conducts his business from the place and not merely as an excuse for using the claimant's trade name: *Banbury Buildings Ltd v Sectional Concrete Buildings Ltd* [1970] R.P.C. 463.

179 *Wright, Layman and Umney Ltd v Wright* (1949) 66 R.P.C. 149; *Parker-Knoll v Parker-Knoll International* [1962] R.P.C. 265; *Boswell-Wilkie Circus* (Pty) Ltd v Brian Boswell Circus (Pty) Ltd [1986] F.S.R. 479; *Sir Robert McAlpine Ltd v Alfred McAlpine Plc* [2004] EWHC 630 (Ch); [2004] R.P.C. 36, per Mann J.

180 See *Coreix Ltd v Coretx Holdings Plc* [2017] EWHC 1695 (IPEC); [2018] F.S.R. 6, Recorder Douglas Campbell QC. In Easy *Rent a Car Ltd v Easygroup Ltd* [2019] EWCA Civ 477; [2019] 1 W.L.R. 4630 it was noted that consent is not the same as estoppel or acquiescence (David Richards LJ at [36]).

sion or representation of the claimant.[181] Delay alone will not bar the right but may have an effect on, for example, whether an injunction will be granted.[182] The courts give limited effect to the clean hands doctrine. Thus, no one can claim to be protected in the use of a trade mark, name, or description, which is a fraud on the right of another trader, or a deception on the public, or used as an instrument of dishonest trading. EU law had little impact on the law of passing off.[183] This is chiefly because of the difficulty in persuading any English court that any part of the Treaty on the Functioning of the EU permits a person to mislead likely purchasers as to the nature or quality of his goods.[184]

5. Relationship to Other Rights

25-25 **Relationship to Trade Marks Act 1994**[185] The most common cases of passing off are those in which the defendant uses or imitates a trade mark under which the claimant's goods have become known to the public. If the trade mark is registered for the goods concerned, any passing off is likely to involve infringement of the rights given by registration also. There may, however, be a successful action for passing off although the trade mark concerned is not registered. In a passing off action, the court looks to see whether there is a misrepresentation, whereas a registered trade mark will be infringed even though no misrepresentation actually takes place.[186] There are conceptually different criteria for establishing registered trade

---

181 See *Habib Bank Ltd v Habib Bank AG Zurich* [1981] 1 W.L.R. 1265 (claimant assisted defendant in setting up in business).

182 Peter Smith J noted in *A&E Television Networks LLC v Discovery Communications Europe Ltd* [2013] EWHC 109 (Ch); [2013] E.T.M.R. 32 that the lack of complaint for seven years was strong evidence for the defendant.

183 See, e.g. Wadlow, *The Law of Passing-Off: Unfair Competition by Misrepresentation*, 5th edn (2016) for a full discussion. There is, of course, a large body of EC jurisprudence dealing with registered trade marks.

184 In *Fage UK Ltd v Chobani UK Ltd* [2014] EWCA Civ 5; [2014] E.T.M.R. 26 Kitchin LJ noted, at [10], that as the law of passing off operates to prevent confusion and deception of the public, it operated compliantly with arts 34–36 of the Treaty on the Functioning of the EU. Where goodwill has been assigned to different trading entities so as to divide up the European Community, an argument based on art.101 TFEU may have some chance of success: see *Sirena SRL v Eda SRL* [1971] E.C.R. 69; [1971] C.M.L.R. 260; *IHT Internationale Heitztechnik GmbH v Ideal Standard GmbH* [1995] F.S.R. 59; [1994] 3 C.M.L.R. 857.

185 The Trade Marks Act 1994 does not affect the law relating to passing off: Trade Marks Act 1994 s.2(2). By s.5(4)(a) of the Trade Marks Act 1994, a trade mark shall not be registered if its use in the UK is liable to be prevented, inter alia, by the law of passing off. The issue of passing off should be assessed at the date upon which the application for registration was made *Dixy Fried Chickens (Euro) Ltd v Dixy Fried Chickens (Stratford) Ltd* [2003] EWHC 2902 (Ch), per Laddie J. In *Caspian Pizza Ltd v Shah* [2017] EWCA Civ 1874; [2018] E.T.M.R. 8 in opposition proceedings under the Trade Marks Act 1994 s.5(4)(a) it was held that the opponent could rely on local goodwill to invalidate the claimant's trade mark. Patten LJ said, at [23]: "goodwill which is established in a particular locality will be capable of preventing registration of a countrywide mark". In *Maier v ASOS Plc* [2015] EWCA Civ 220; [2015] F.S.R. 20 [165], with reference to art.8(4) of Regulation 207/2009 CTMR, the CTM equivalent of s.5(4)(a), Kitchin LJ discussed the relevant date for determining whether a claimant has established the necessary reputation or goodwill. On the relationship to CTM registration see: *Pinterest Inc v Premium Interest Ltd* [2015] EWHC 738 (Ch); [2015] F.S.R. 27 Arnold J.

186 *Fisons Plc v Norton Healthcare Ltd* [1994] F.S.R. 745 at 751. Equally, there is no need to prove any actual goodwill in the registered trade mark in order to succeed in an action for infringement although if the mark is not in fact distinctive of the goods or service in question it may be vulnerable to cancellation. In *Inter Lotto (UK) Ltd v Camelot Group Plc* [2003] EWCA Civ 1132; [2003] 4 All

mark infringement and for establishing passing off.[187] In *Interflora Inc v Marks & Spencer Plc* it was noted that the "average consumer" in trade mark infringement cases is conceptually different from "a substantial proportion of the public", the test used in passing off cases.[188]

Relationship to other statutory intellectual property rights The publisher of a work of literature, whose copyright is not infringed, may be protected against the sale of a work on the same subject put forward in such a form as to simulate his own.[189] Although copyright may be held not to exist in a mere title, it may be passing off to use or imitate a title already in use by another.[190] Conversely, the use of a person's logo or packaging design may be actionable as infringement of copyright. Under the Copyright, Designs and Patents Act 1988 it is actionable to affix anyone's name to a literary, dramatic, musical or artistic work of which he is not the author, so as to imply that the work is his or adapted from a work of his[191]; and where the person concerned is an author of established reputation such an implication will be actionable as passing off without actual use of his name.[192] An action for design right or registered design infringement may arise from the imitation of the product itself. **25-26**

E.R. 575, the Court of Appeal noted the potential conflict between the rights of the registered trade mark owner (with registration having retrospective effect) and the rights of a party with the right of action for passing off, gained by use.

187 Though in relation to establishing confusion Jacob LJ in *Reed Executive Plc v Reed Business Information Ltd* [2004] EWCA Civ 159; [2004] R.P.C. 40 at [82] commented "in the end I think they come to the same thing". And see Arnold J in *Enterprise Holdings Inc v Europcar Group UK Ltd* [2015] EWHC 17 (Ch); [2015] E.T.M.R. 16 at [158]–[159].

188 [2012] EWCA Civ 1501; [2013] 2 All E.R. 663. And see Kitchin LJ in *Comic Enterprises Ltd v Twentieth Century Fox Film Corp* [2016] EWCA Civ 41; [2016] E.T.M.R. 22 at [159]: "the scope of protection conferred by the law of passing off is not the same as that afforded by a registered trade mark".

189 *Metzler v Wood* (1878) L.R. 8 Ch. D. 606.

190 *Weldon v Dicks* (1878) L.R. 10 Ch. D. 247; *Dicks v Yates* (1881) L.R. 18 Ch. D. 76; see *Borthwick v Evening Post* (1888) L.R. 37 Ch. D. 449; *Ridgeway v Hutchison* (1923) 40 R.P.C. 335; *WH Allen & Co v Brown Watson Ltd* [1965] R.P.C. 191.

191 s.84. The action is for breach of statutory duty (false attribution of authorship) not for passing off: *Moore v News of the World* [1972] 1 Q.B. 441.

192 *Samuelson v Producers Distributing Co Ltd* [1932] 1 Ch. 201 (representing film as a cinematograph version of a sketch of established reputation).

Chapter 26

BREACH OF CONFIDENCE AND PRIVACY

Table of Contents

1. General Introduction

The traditional action for breach of confidence[1] The jurisdiction to provide remedies for breach of confidence is well established in English law.[2] Lord Goff noted that as a broad general principle, a duty of confidence arises when confidential information comes to the knowledge of a person, in circumstances where he has notice, or is held to have agreed, that the information is confidential, with the effect that it would be just in all the circumstances that he should be precluded from disclosing the information to others.[3] And traditionally there has been no limit in principle to the kind of information which might be the subject of a claim for breach of confidence, the four main classes of information which the courts have traditionally protected by this action[4] being: personal confidences, trade secrets,[5] artistic and literary confidences[6] and state secrets.[7] **26-01**

---

1 For more detailed consideration see Gurry, *Breach of Confidence*, 2nd edn (2012); Law Commission Report No.110, *Breach of Confidence* (1981), Cmnd.8388.

2 For the nineteenth century origins of the modern law, see *Prince Albert v Strange* (1849) 2 De. G & Sm. 652; *Morrison v Moat* (1851) 9 Hare 241; (1852) 21 L.J. Rep. (N.S.) Ch. 248 (medical formula).

3 *Att Gen v Guardian Newspapers Ltd (No.2)* [1990] 1 A.C. 109.

4 Simon Brown LJ in *R. v Department for Health Ex p. Source Informatics* [2001] Q.B. 424.

5 As well as classic trade secrets such as manufacturing formulae and methods, the law will protect a wide range of information useful in trade including customer lists (*Robb v Green* [1895] 2 Q.B. 315); possibly management techniques (*Stephenson Jordan & Harrison v McDonald & Evans* (1951) 68 R.P.C. 190; (1952) 69 R.P.C. 10); market reports (*PCR Ltd v Dow Jones Telerate Ltd* [1998] F.S.R. 170—claim in confidence failed on facts). The UK is bound by the TRIPs Agreement to protect com-

26-02 **Modern developments and the protection of privacy** However, this action continues to develop "to reflect changes in society, technology and business practice".[8] Moreover, the European Convention on Human Rights and the Human Rights Act 1998 have had an important impact on this action, given the right to respect for private life and to freedom of expression contained in arts 8 and 10 of the ECHR, respectively.[9] This has particularly shaped the modern development of the action where considerations of private confidential information are raised. After the House of Lords' decision in *Campbell v MGN Ltd*[10] where private information is in issue there is now an action for misuse of private information. Indeed in *OBG Ltd v Allan*[11] Lord Nicholls asserted that the action "now covers two distinct causes of action, protecting two different interests: privacy, and secret ('confidential') information. It is important to keep these two distinct." In *Vidal-Hall v Google Inc* Lord Dyson MR noted that: "there are problems with an analysis which fails to distinguish between a breach of confidentiality and an infringement of privacy rights under article 8, not least because the concepts of confidence and privacy are not the same and protect different interests."[12] It is now apparent that two different frameworks of liability have emerged: one for breach of confidence and one for misuse of private information/privacy (though it should be noted that some claimants seeking to protect privacy have pleaded both breach of confidence and misuse of private information).[13] Hence this chapter will deal separately with these two distinct forms of liability.

26-03 **Two distinct forms of liability** The two forms of liability have differences in framework and approach. At the same time the public domain limiting principle does not have the same force in cases of private information, Lord Nicholls noting in *OBG Ltd v Allan*:

> "... information may be in the public domain and not qualify for protection as confidential, and yet qualify for protection on the grounds of privacy. Privacy can be invaded by further publication of information or photographs already disclosed to the public."[14]

Where privacy interests are involved intrusive photographs are viewed with

---

mercial secrets used in a manner contrary to honest commercial practices. Also see Trade Secrets (Enforcement, etc.) Regulations 2018 (SI 2018/597), para.26-05.

6 Ideas for TV series (*Fraser v Thames Television* [1984] Q.B. 44); confidential film set designs (*Shelley Films Ltd v Rex Features Ltd* [1994] E.M.L.R. 134).

7 e.g. *Att Gen v Guardian Newspapers (No.2)* [1990] 1 A.C. 109.

8 Keene LJ in *Douglas v Hello! Ltd* [2001] Q.B. 967 at 1011.

9 See paras 26-29, 26-37, 26-39. In *Fearn v Board of Trustees of the Tate Gallery* [2020] EWCA Civ 104; [2020] 2 W.L.R. 1081 the Court of Appeal was critical of the trial judge's analysis that the tort of nuisance is capable, as a matter of principle, or protecting privacy rights (see [87] onwards).

10 [2004] UKHL 22; [2004] 2 A.C. 457.

11 [2007] UKHL 21; [2008] 1 A.C. 1 at [255] (*Douglas v Hello!* was one of three conjoined appeals heard by the House of Lords reported under the name *OBG Ltd v Allan*).

12 [2015] EWCA Civ 311; [2016] Q.B. 1003 at [21].

13 See, e.g. *Axon v Ministry of Defence* [2016] EWHC 787 (QB); [2016] E.M.L.R. 20, Nicol J; *PJS v News Group Newspapers Ltd* [2016] UKSC 26; [2016] A.C. 1081 (noted in detail, below). On the relationship of the action for breach of confidence and the action for misuse of private information see Lord Neuberger in *Imerman v Tchenguiz* [2010] EWCA Civ 908; [2011] Fam. 116 at [67]–[68].

14 [2007] UKHL 21; [2008] 1 A.C. 1 at [255].

particular concern,[15] the argument that the information is "trivial" carries less weight,[16] harm (probably) need not be proved[17] and damages for distress are available. However, that said, information concerning commercial or business activities might still involve a privacy claim: in *Browne v Associated Newspapers Ltd* it was noted that business information passed by a company director to his sexual partner might attract a reasonable expectation of privacy,[18] while in *McKennitt v Ash*[19] it was accepted that private information could encompass even information about the claimant's contractual dealings. On the facts a reasonable expectation of privacy arose, given the claimant was in a relationship of confidence with the contracting party.[20] Conversely, private information could also involve commercial confidentiality. Lord Phillips MR, in *Douglas v Hello! Ltd (No.3)* accepted that information could be both personal and commercially exploitable,[21] there being:

> "no reason in principle why equity should not protect the opportunity to profit from confidential information about oneself in the same circumstances that it protects the opportunity to profit from confidential information in the nature of a trade secret."

Juridical basis of the action There has been long-standing uncertainty as to how this action should be categorised. Courts are reluctant to categorise confidential information as property.[22] It should be noted that the Supreme Court in *Phillips v News Group Newspapers Ltd*[23] held that commercial (but not private) confidential information obtained through phone hacking came within the definition of "commercial information" and "intellectual property" for the purposes of s.72(5) of the Senior Courts Act 1981 (so as to prevent the defendant from relying on the privilege against self-incrimination). However though he determined it was not inappropriate to include commercial confidential information as an aspect of intellectual 26-04

15 See para.26-47.

16 *OBG Ltd v Allan* [2008] 1 A.C. 1 at [291], per Lord Walker.

17 *Att Gen v Guardian Newspapers Ltd (No.2)* [1990] 1 A.C. 109 at 255–256, per Lord Keith.

18 [2007] EWCA Civ 295; [2008] Q.B. 103 at [34], per Sir Anthony Clarke MR. Note in *LNS v Persons Unknown* [2010] EWHC 119 (QB); [2010] E.M.L.R. 16 where there was an attempt to restrain the publication of details of an alleged extra-marital affair on the basis of misuse of private information/breach of confidence, Tugendhat J (on the facts) found that the real basis of the action was to protect the claimant's business reputation and that damages would be adequate.

19 [2006] EWCA Civ 1714; [2008] Q.B. 73.

20 [2006] EWCA Civ 1714; [2008] Q.B. 73 at [24], per Buxton LJ.

21 [2005] EWCA Civ 595; [2006] Q.B. 125 at [118]; and in *OBG Ltd v Allan* [2007] UKHL 21; [2008] 1 A.C. 1 at [118] Lord Hoffmann; Lord Nicholls at [255] (he noted "in some instances information may qualify for protection both on the grounds of privacy and confidentiality").

22 *Boardman v Phipps* [1967] 2 A.C. 46, per Lord Upjohn, though compare *Att Gen v Guardian Newspapers* [1987] 1 W.L.R. 1248 at 1264. See Lord Phillips MR in *Douglas v Hello! Ltd (No.3)* [2005] EWCA Civ 595; [2006] Q.B. 125 at [126]–[137]. In *OBG Ltd v Allan* [2007] UKHL 21; [2008] 1 A.C. 1 at [275] Lord Walker noted "... information, even if it is confidential, cannot properly be regarded as a form of property" (though it should be noted that OK! strongly disclaimed any reliance on information as property). In *Veolia ES Nottinghamshire Ltd v Notts CC* [2010] EWCA Civ 1214; [2011] Env. L.R. 12 Rix LJ asserted (at [111]): "... confidential information is a well recognised species of property, protected by the common law ..." and see [121]. However, in *Force India Formula One Team Ltd v 1 Malaysia Racing Team Sdn Bhd* [2012] EWHC 616 (Ch); [2012] R.P.C. 29 Arnold J noted: "confidential information is not property" (at [376], commenting on the view of Rix LJ, above, at [417]). The Court of Appeal upheld the actual decision in this case: [2013] EWCA Civ 780; [2013] R.P.C. 36.

23 [2012] UKSC 28; [2013] 1 A.C. 1.

property, Lord Walker did acknowledge that "the prevailing current view is that confidential information is not strictly property".[24] Where the obligation of confidence arises (either expressly or impliedly) in a contractual relationship, the breach of confidence may be categorised as a breach of contract. However, the obligation can arise in a non-contractual setting. Here, the most favoured basis for the action to date is that of an equitable principle of good faith.[25] As far as commercial confidences are concerned, Evans LJ held that claims for breach of confidence "do not arise in tort" in *Kitechnology BV v Unicor GmbH*.[26] (It should be noted that the Supreme Court of Canada in *Cadbury Schweppes Inc v FBI Foods Ltd*[27] viewed the action as sui generis, while the Court of Appeal in *Douglas v Hello! (No.3)*[28] found the suggestion that a claim for breach of confidence fell to be "categorised as a restitutionary claim for unjust enrichment" persuasive). However there is growing judicial support for the recognition of the action for misuse of private information as a tort.[29]

2. ACTION FOR BREACH OF CONFIDENCE

26-05 **Action for breach of confidence** This section explores the action for breach of confidence. Confidential information in its commercial context includes trade secrets,[30] artistic and literary confidences and state secrets. However, it should be

---

24 See the discussion by Lord Walker [2012] UKSC 28; [2013] 1 A.C. 1 at [24]–[39]. Mummery LJ in *Fairstar Heavy Transport N.V. v Adkins* [2013] EWCA Civ 886; [2014] F.S.R. 8 at [47]–[48], though refusing to be drawn into the controversy, noted "some kinds of information, such as non-patentable know-how, are more akin to property in their specificity and exclusivity than say, personal information about private life".

25 In *Seager v Copydex Ltd* [1967] 1 W.L.R. 923, Lord Denning said: "The law on this subject does not depend on any implied contract. It depends on the broad principle of equity that he who has received information in confidence shall not take unfair advantage of it." *Vestergaard Frandsen A/S v Bestnet Europe Ltd* [2013] UKSC 31; [2013] 1 W.L.R. 1556 at [22], Lord Neuberger: "an action in breach of confidence is based ultimately on conscience".

26 [1995] F.S.R. 765. And see *Vidal-Hall v Google Inc* [2014] EWHC 13 (QB); [2014] 1 W.L.R. 4155, Tugendhat J; though cf. *Walsh v Shanahan* [2013] EWCA Civ 411 at [55], Rimer LJ. Common design could be invoked against a defendant in a claim based on breach of confidence, *Vestergaard Frandsen A/S v Bestnet Europe Ltd* [2013] UKSC 31; [2013] 1 W.L.R. 1556, Lord Neuberger (discussed below, especially at para.26-18).

27 [2000] F.S.R. 491. And see Lord Phillips MR in *Douglas v Hello! Ltd (No.3)* [2005] EWCA Civ 595; [2006] Q.B. 125 at [96].

28 *Douglas v Hello! Ltd (No.3)* [2005] EWCA Civ 595; [2006] Q.B. 125 at [97], per Lord Phillips MR.

29 See Lord Woolf in *A v B* [2002] EWCA Civ 337; [2003] Q.B. 195 at [4]; Lord Nicholls in *Campbell v MGN Ltd* [2004] UKHL 22; [2004] 2 A.C. 457 at [14]; Buxton LJ in *McKennitt v Ash* [2006] EWCA Civ 1714; [2008] Q.B. 73 at [8]; Lord Neuberger MR in *Imerman v Tchenguiz* [2010] EWCA Civ 908; [2011] Fam. 116 at [65]. In *Mosley v News Group Newspapers Ltd* [2008] EWHC 1777 (QB); [2008] E.M.L.R. 20 at [181]–[184] Eady J reviewed the debate as to whether or not this action is a tort; and note Tugendhat J in *Vidal-Hall v Google Inc* [2014] EWHC 13 (QB); [2014] 1 W.L.R. 4155 at [68]–[70]. In *Vidal-Hall v Google Inc* [2015] EWCA Civ 311; [2016] Q.B. 1003 at [43], Lord Dyson MR commented: "We cannot find any satisfactory or principled answer to the question why misuse of private information should not be characterised as a tort for the purposes of service out of the jurisdiction". And see *Ahuja v Politika Novine I Magazini Doo* [2015] EWHC 3380 (QB); [2016] 1 W.L.R. 1414, Tugendhat J; *Axon v Ministry of Defence* [2016] EWHC 787 (QB); [2016] E.M.L.R. 20 at [72], Nicol J, "the tort or remedy for misuse of private information". On service out of the jurisdiction see amendments to Practice Direction 6B and gateway 21 which covers claims for "breach of confidence or misuse of private information".

30 The Trade Secrets Directive 2016/943 (on the protection of undisclosed know-how and business information (trade secrets) against their unlawful acquisition, use and disclosure) which involves

noted that with state secrets[31] the trivia exception[32] may not apply[33] and the state needs to show there is a public interest in preventing the disclosure of the information.[34] The application of the Official Secrets Act 1989 should also be noted. In *OBG Ltd v Allan* the House of Lords characterised the action for breach of confidence as "moving forward rather than drawing back".[35] However, notwithstanding this, the continued requirement for confidentiality in this action is accepted.[36] Where trade secrets are concerned it should be noted that the Trade Secrets Directive 2016/943 (on the protection of undisclosed know-how and business information (trade secrets) against their unlawful acquisition, use and disclosure) was incorporated into domestic law by the Trade Secrets (Enforcement, etc.) Regulations 2018.[37]

Requirements Traditionally, there are three requirements for liability for breach of confidence. These principles are derived from *Coco v AN Clark (Engineers) Ltd*, per Megarry J.[38] First, the information in respect of which relief is sought must have the "necessary quality of confidence about it".[39] Secondly, the information must have been imparted in circumstances importing an obligation of confidence. The use of the word "imparted", however, is now clearly too limited for the modern action, it now being established that there is no need for an initial confidential relationship.[40] Thirdly, there must be an unauthorised use or disclosure of that information.[41] It is an open question whether detriment to the claimant is an es- 26-06

minimum protection that States must provide for the unlawful acquisition, use or disclosure of trade secrets, was incorporated into domestic law by the Trade Secrets (Enforcement, etc.) Regulations 2018 (SI 2018/597), in force 9 June 2018.

31 In an appropriate case, the Attorney General may sue on behalf of the Crown, e.g. *Att Gen v Guardian Newspapers (No.2)* [1990] 1 A.C. 109. In Scotland, the Lord Advocate is the appropriate claimant.

32 See para.26-10.

33 *Lord Advocate v Scotsman Publications Ltd* [1990] 1 A.C. 812; Lord Griffiths in *Att Gen v Guardian Newspapers (No.2)* [1990] A.C. 109 at 269.

34 Lord Keith in *Att Gen v Guardian Newspapers (No.2)* [1990] A.C. 109 at 260. Lord Goff at 282 said "that publication would be to its 'detriment' in the sense that the public interest requires that it should not be published".

35 Baroness Hale in *OBG Ltd v Allan* [2007] UKHL 21; [2008] 1 A.C. 1 at [307].

36 On the relationship between breach of confidence and defamation see *Viagogo Ltd v Myles* [2012] EWHC 433 (Ch), Hildyard J at [25]; [35]. For the relationship between misuse of private information/privacy and defamation see para.26-41.

37 SI 2018/597. See fn.30. There is a statutory definition of trade secret in Regulation 2. The IPO Explanatory Memorandum (*http://www.legislation.gov.uk/uksi/2018/597/memorandum* [Accessed 12 June 2020]) notes the existing protection based on inter alia the action for breach of confidence and states that the SI "addresses those areas where gaps occur or where the implementation of the provisions of the Directive will ensure legal certainty...". On the relationship of the Regulations and the action for breach of confidence see reg.3.

38 [1969] R.P.C. 41 at 47. In *OBG Ltd v Allan* [2007] UKHL 21; [2008] 1 A.C. 1, Lord Hoffmann applied Megarry J's framework for the action as set out in *Coco v AN Clark (Engineers) Ltd* [1969] R.P.C. 41.

39 per Lord Greene MR in *Saltman Engineering Co Ltd v Campbell Engineering Co Ltd* (1948) 65 R.P.C. 203 at 215.

40 See para.26-12.

41 *Wade v British Sky Broadcasting Ltd* [2016] EWCA Civ 1214: as in a claim for copyright infringement, the evidential burden of proof might shift to the defendant once the claimant showed sufficient similarities and opportunity so as to raise an inference of breach.

sential ingredient of the cause of action for breach of confidence[42] but a claimant must at least show apprehended damage in future, if an injunction is to be granted.[43]

26-07 **Limiting principles** In *Att Gen v Guardian Newspapers (No.2)* Lord Goff identified three limiting principles on the duty of confidence.[44] First, the principle of confidentiality only applies to information to the extent that it remains confidential. Once it has entered the public domain (which means no more than that the information in question is so generally accessible that in all the circumstances, it cannot be regarded as confidential) then the principle of confidentiality can have no application to it.[45] Secondly, the duty of confidence applies neither to useless information nor to trivia.[46] Thirdly, the public interest that confidence should be preserved may be outweighed by some other countervailing public interest, which favours use or disclosure, either to the world at large or, at least, to appropriate authorities.[47] That may require the court to carry out a balancing operation, weighing the public interest in maintaining confidence against the public interest favouring use or disclosure.[48] Where free speech issues are concerned, the impact of art.10 of the ECHR will have to be addressed[49] so that the issue becomes whether restraining disclosure of the confidential information is a justifiable interference with the art.10 right to freedom of expression.

26-08 **Parties** Only the party to whom the duty of confidence is owed has a right of action to protect it.[50] The claimant is usually the owner[51] of the confidential material or one whose confidential communications are otherwise protected by the law. However the majority of the House of Lords in *OBG Ltd v Allan*[52] determined that on the facts an obligation of confidence was also owed to an exclusive licensee of the information concerned. This case involved Hello! magazine's publication of unauthorised photographs of Michael Douglas and Catherine Zeta-Jones's wedding reception. The celebrity magazine OK! had contracted with the couple for "exclusive" rights over approved wedding photographs. The photographs were

---

42 See para.26-25

43 See para.26-33. With personal confidences, there is probably no need to show detriment, per Lord Keith in *Att Gen v Guardian Newspapers* [1990] A.C. 109 at 256.

44 *Att Gen v Guardian Newspapers (No.2)* [1990] 1 A.C. 109, 280. In *OBG Ltd v Allan* [2007] UKHL 21; [2008] 1 A.C. 1 Lord Walker (in his minority judgment) also stressed the limiting principles outlined by Lord Goff.

45 But see para.26-09.

46 See para.26-10.

47 As to the public interest in disclosure of confidential information, see paras 26-27 to 26-32.

48 These principles are distilled from the speeches of their Lordships in *Att Gen v Guardian Newspapers (No.2)* [1990] 1 A.C. 109 especially at 281–282, per Lord Goff.

49 See para.26-29; Lindsay J in *Douglas v Hello! (No.3)* [2003] EWHC 786 (Ch); [2003] 3 All E.R. 996: given ECHR art.10(2) there could be a conflict between art.10(1), freedom of expression and the rights under the law of confidence even where privacy rights under art.8 not involved, *HML PM Ltd v Canary Riverside Estate Management Ltd* [2019] EWHC 3496 (QB) Nicol J at [60].

50 *Fraser v Evans* [1969] 1 Q.B. 349 ("the party complaining must be the person who is entitled to the confidence and to have it respected"). In *Jones v IOS (RUK) Ltd* [2012] EWHC 348 (Ch) (HH Judge Hodge QC) it was held that the claimant had to have "sufficient interest in the information" (see [40]). And see *Abbey v Gilligan* [2012] EWHC 3217 (QB); [2013] E.M.L.R. 12 Tugendhat J at [40]–[41].

51 It is common to speak of the "owner" of the information but, because the courts have not held that information is property as traditionally conceived, use of the term "person to whom the duty is owed" is perhaps less controversial.

52 [2007] UKHL 21; [2008] 1 A.C. 1.

taken on a private occasion where there had been an express prohibition by the couple on unauthorised photography. In the Court of Appeal the Douglases' breach of confidence claim (which contained both privacy and commercial aspects) succeeded[53] but OK!'s claims failed. OK!'s appeal to the House of Lords was based inter alia on the alleged duty of confidence owed to them in the photographic images of the wedding. Unlike the Court of Appeal, the majority of the House of Lords—Lords Hoffmann, Brown and Baroness Hale held that the obligation of confidence extended to OK!, as exclusive licensee, because "everyone knew that the obligation of confidence was imposed for the benefit of OK! as well as the Douglases" and "they paid or the benefit of the obligation of confidence imposed on all those present".[54] The minority—Lords Nicholls and Walker—found no duty owed to OK! in respect of the unauthorised pictures.[55] As far as defendants are concerned, the position of those receiving information innocently is considered below, as is the position of indirect recipients and those on whom it is sought to impose secondary liability.[56] In *Warwickshire CC v Matalia*[57] the claimant county council had commissioned test papers from a university (which retained copyright) for use in local schools. The same paper was to be used for different sittings of the test. After the first sitting the defendant published details of the test—obtained from pupils who had sat the test—on his website. The county council had locus standi to bring a claim for breach of confidence: "As the provider and administrator of the tests the Council had a substantial and legitimate interest in the maintenance of confidentiality".[58] The defendant owed a duty of confidence to the claimant. The confidential character of the information was obvious to the defendant "whether or not the children who supplied the information to him were themselves under any duty of confidence".[59]

(a) Information in respect of which an action for breach of confidence may arise

The quality of confidence An action for breach of confidence will only arise if the information in question has the necessary quality of confidence about it.[60] There 26-09

53 *Douglas v Hello (No.3)* [2005] EWCA Civ 595; [2006] Q.B. 125.

54 Lord Hoffmann in *OBG Ltd v Allan* [2007] UKHL 21; [2008] 1 A.C. 1 at [114] and [117].

55 Lord Walker contended that "OK! no more had a monopoly in any possible photographs of the spectacle than it had in the spectacle itself": [2007] UKHL 21; [2008] 1 A.C. 1 at [296], citing the High Court of Australia in Victoria Park Racing and Recreation Grounds Ltd v Taylor (1937) 58 C.L.R. 479 in support.

56 Lord Griffiths, *Att Gen v Guardian Newspapers (No.2)* [1990] 1 A.C. 109 at 268: "the duty of confidence is, as a general rule, also imposed on a third party who is in possession of information which he knows is subject to an obligation of confidence." See generally paras 26-17 to 26-18. As for vicarious liability, see Lord Neuberger in *Vestergaard Fransden S/A v Bestnet Europe Ltd* [2013] UKSC 31; [2013] 1 W.L.R. 1556.

57 [2017] EWCA Civ 991; [2017] E.C.C. 25.

58 [2017] EWCA Civ 991; [2017] E.C.C. 25 at [30], per David Richards LJ.

59 See the discussion [2017] EWCA Civ 991; [2017] E.C.C. 25 at [46]–[47].

60 per Lord Greene MR in *Saltman Engineering Co Ltd v Campbell Engineering Co* (1948) 65 R.P.C. 203 at 215. The authors of Gurry on *Breach of Confidence*, 2nd edn (2012) note at para.5–14 that "the basic attribute which information must possess before it can be considered confidential is inaccessibility". Zacaroli J in *The Racing Partnership Ltd v Done Brothers (Cash Betting) Ltd* [2019] EWHC 1156 (Ch); [2019] 3 W.L.R. 779 stressed on the facts the ability to control commercially valuable information.

can be relative secrecy[61] but the information must not be "public property and public knowledge",[62] not "so generally accessible that, in all the circumstances, it cannot be regarded as confidential".[63] Even where the circumstances of communication involve confidentiality there can be no breach of confidence in revealing to others something which is already common knowledge.[64] However, limited or only partial dissemination may not amount to accessibility while matters which the public could find out about if they made the effort, or did the necessary work, may not necessarily be regarded as being in the public domain and therefore incapable of being protected.[65] In *Barclays Bank Plc v Guardian News and Media Ltd*[66] confidential documents (published in whole) appeared for four hours on defendant's website, with reference to these documents also made in the defendant's newspaper. Confidentiality continued to exist in the documents: though "generic" availability of material on the internet would mean that it was likely it had lost its confidential character " … very limited dissemination and only partial dissemination, perhaps in some remote or expert site that is generally not available to the public without a great deal of effort, may not result in such loss of confidentiality".[67] Something that has been constructed solely from materials in the public domain may possess the necessary quality of confidentiality. In *Saltman v Campbell*, it was said that what makes certain information confidential "is the fact that the maker of the document has used his brain and then produced a result which can only be produced by someone who goes through the same process".[68] Thus, manufacturing information may be confidential even if is possible to "reverse engineer" an article from materials in the public domain but to do so would take much longer without knowledge

---

61 "It is a question of degree": Sir John Donaldson MR in *Att Gen v Guardian (No.2)* [1990] A.C. 109 at 177. See also *Shelley Films Ltd v Rex Features Ltd* [1994] E.M.L.R. 134 at 148–149; *Creation Records Ltd v News Group Newspapers Ltd* [1997] E.M.L.R. 444 at 461–464.

62 per Lord Greene MR in *Saltman Engineering Co Ltd v Campbell Engineering Co Ltd* (1948) 65 R.P.C. 203. The majority of the Court of Appeal in *Schering Chemicals Ltd v Falkman Ltd* [1982] Q.B. 1 awarded an interlocutory injunction although the information was already in the public domain, as the defendant had revived the memory of matters prejudicial to the claimant (see Shaw LJ at [28] and Templeman LJ at [37]). However, the majority view was criticised by Lord Oliver in *Att Gen v Guardian Newspapers* [1987] 1 W.L.R. 1248 at 1319; and doubted in *BBC v HarperCollins Publishers Ltd* [2010] EWHC 2424 (Ch); [2011] E.M.L.R. 6, Morgan J.

63 *Lord Goff Att Gen v Guardian (No.2)* [1990] A.C. 109 at 282. It is submitted that the better view is that information disclosed in breach of confidence still enters the public domain thereby (see para.26-35, but cf. the view in *Speed Seal Products v Paddington* [1985] 1 W.L.R. 1327).

64 cf. the position where private confidences are involved, para.26-43. It should also be noted that in *Douglas v Hello!* though the authorised and unauthorised photographs portrayed basically the same information the majority did not find that the photographic images of the wedding were in the public domain even when the authorised photographs were published by OK!. Each photograph was protected as "the secret consists no less of each and every visual image of the wedding than of the wedding as a whole" (per Lord Brown [2007] UKHL 21; [2008] 1 A.C. 1 at [329]). This interpretation of the facts enabled the majority to impose an obligation of confidence, owed to the exclusive licensee. Lords Walker and Nicholls dissented on this point.

65 See *Coco v AN Clark (Engineers)* [1969] R.P.C. 41. And see also the discussion of the "springboard" doctrine, para.26-35.

66 [2009] EWHC 591 (QB), per Blake J.

67 [2009] EWHC 591 (QB) at [22]. Blake J also noted (at [26]) that it was "unattractive" for the defendant to rely on the publication by others if that publication was caused by their own wrongful publication on their website. On "theoretical accessibility" see *Venables v News Group Newspapers Ltd* [2001] Fam. 430 (Butler-Sloss P.).

68 *Saltman Engineering Co v Campbell Engineering Co* (1948) 65 R.P.C. 203.

of the information.[69] However, Jacob J in *Mars UK Ltd v Teknowledge*[70] held that the mere fact information was encrypted in a freely available product did not impose an obligation of confidence (especially as the product did not warn that such encryption was involved). Circumventing such encryption was not analogous to eavesdropping or the use of long-lens photography.

Information protected by the action The confidential information need not be complex to attract protection: "the simpler the idea, the more likely it is to require protection."[71] So, in *Fraser v Thames Television*[72] the idea for a television series was held to be capable of protection. The mere fact that the confidential information is not embodied in a document but may be carried away (for example by an ex-employee) in his head is not of itself a reason against restraining misuse.[73] However, Lord Goff stated that neither "useless" information nor "trivia" will be protected,[74] though what exactly is meant by the latter concept is not clear.[75] Nor will "vague aspirations or concepts" be protected, at least where entertainment ideas are in issue.[76] Hirst J in *Fraser v Thames Television*[77] noted that "the content of the idea [must be] clearly identifiable, original, of potential commercial attractiveness and capable of being realised in actuality". In *OBG Ltd v Allan*[78] the photographic images were held to be information. It should also be noted that Megarry J, in *Coco v AN Clark (Engineers) Ltd*[79] stated that the secret must represent "in some considerable degree [the confider's] independent efforts". A non-selective list of materials in the public domain will not be treated as confidential, even if putting it together involved some time and effort.[80] Evidence as to whether information should be regarded as confidential may be provided by the reasonable belief in this fact by the original possessor of that information.[81] Whether information should be treated as confidential will be judged in the light of the usage and practices of the particular industry concerned. Thus, the knowledge of the existence of a patent, which is a published document, may provide the basis for an action.[82] 26-10

69 See also *Alfa Laval Cheese Systems Ltd v Wincanton Engineering Systems Ltd* [1990] F.S.R. 583.

70 [2000] F.S.R. 138. cf. *Volkswagen AG v Garcia* [2013] EWHC 1832 (Ch); [2014] F.S.R. 12 Birss J, which also involved reverse engineering but where the confidential information had been obtained from an illegitimate source.

71 *Coco v AN Clark (Engineers) Ltd* [1969] R.P.C. 41

72 [1984] Q.B. 44.

73 *Printers Finishers Ltd v Holloway* [1965] 1 W.L.R. 1. See below on the position of ex-employees.

74 *Att Gen v Guardian Newspapers (No.2)* [1990] 1 A.C. 109 at 282.

75 Lord Walker in his dissenting judgment in *OBG Ltd v Allan* viewed this as an important limitation: [2007] UKHL 21; [2008] 1 A.C. 1 at [294]. "Tittle-tattle" will not be protected, per Megarry J in *Coco v AN Clark (Engineers) Ltd* [1969] R.P.C. 41 at 48.

76 *De Maudsley v Palumbo* [1996] F.S.R. 447. This concept was also applied to a design idea for a decorative pendant in *Sales v Stomberg* [2005] EWHC 1624 (Ch); [2006] F.S.R. 7.

77 [1984] Q.B. 44 at [65]–[66]. In *Bailey v Graham* [2011] EWHC 3098 (Ch) at [104], Judge Pelling QC, questioned whether a recipe for sauce was sufficiently certain to have the necessary quality of confidence, citing *De Maudsley v Palumbo* [1996] F.S.R. 447 that the material relied upon must be capable of being realised as an actuality (judgment upheld—on the issue of witness and parties' credibility—in [2012] EWCA Civ 1469).

78 [2007] UKHL 21; [2008] 1 A.C. 1.

79 [1969] R.P.C.41 at [47]–[48].

80 *Ocular Sciences Ltd v Aspect Vision Care Ltd* [1997] R.P.C. 289 at 375, Laddie J demanding that "there must be some product of the skill of the human brain".

81 *Faccenda Chicken Ltd v Fowler* [1987] Ch. 117; *Thomas Marshall (Exports) Ltd v Guinle* [1979] Ch. 227.

82 *Cranleigh Precision Engineering v Bryant* [1965] 1 W.L.R. 1293.

26-11 **Need for identification of the confidential information** The confidential information sought to be protected must generally be identified and particularised in the statement of case.[83] This is particularly important if an injunction is sought—a fortiori, an interim injunction[84]—when the court will require a claimant to identify with precision the information in respect of which relief is sought.[85] The courts are familiar with employers or manufacturers who are of the opinion that they have legitimate ground for complaint based merely on the belief that someone (usually an ex-employee) may be using something of theirs that has not been published.[86] This is not enough, and many motions for interim relief based on such tenuous grounds have failed.[87]

(b) Where an obligation of confidence arises

26-12 **Circumstances giving rise to an obligation of confidence** It must be proved that the defendant was under a legal obligation of confidence. Lord Goff in *AG v Guardian Newspapers (No.2)*[88] referred to the "broad general principle" that a duty of confidence arises when confidential information comes to the knowledge of a person in circumstances where he has notice that the information is confidential "with the effect that it would be just ... that he should be precluded from disclosing the information to others".[89] A wide range of circumstances can give rise to an obligation of confidence. They have in common that the person receiving the information was or should have been aware of the confidence attaching to the information.[90] Knowledge can include circumstances where the confidant has

---

83 *Ocular Sciences Ltd v Aspect Vision Care Ltd* [1997] R.P.C. 289. Applied, *Bains v Moore* [2017] EWHC 242 (QB); [2017] E.M.L.R. 20, Tugendhat J.

84 *PA Thomas & Co v Mould* [1968] 2 Q.B. 913.

85 *CMI-Centers for Medical Innovation GmbH v Phytopharm Plc* [1999] F.S.R. 235, interim injunctive relief is unlikely to be granted where no attempt has been made to disentangle material which is confidential from that which is not.

86 If the claimant fails to give proper particulars the court may infer that the true purpose of the action was harassment and the action will be struck out as an abuse of process, see Laddie J in *Ocular Sciences Ltd v Aspect Vision Care Ltd* [1997] R.P.C. 289.

87 See, for example, *Lock International Plc v Beswick* [1989] 1 W.L.R. 1268, where Hoffmann J drew attention to the need for critical scrutiny of that which was claimed to be confidential.

88 [1990] 1 A.C. 190 at 281.

89 An obligation of confidence can be imposed after the information has been communicated provided the information remains outside the public domain: *Surface Technology Plc v Young* [2002] F.S.R. 25. In *Abbey v Gilligan* [2012] EWHC 3217 (QB); [2013] E.M.L.R. 12 at [63] Tugendhat J, with regard to the law of confidentiality and leaks to journalists, noted that "a journalist considering whether or not to publish information must, in many cases, have an opportunity to read the information to make that decision. It cannot be right that the court should in such cases too readily find that the obtaining or reading of the information is a breach of confidence".

90 See *Coco v AN Clark (Engineers) Ltd* [1969] R.P.C. 41. In *Carflow Products v Linwood Securities* [1996] F.S.R. 424 Jacob J in determining whether a disclosure was made in confidence preferred the subjective approach to the objective approach. But note constructive knowledge accepted by Lord Goff *Att Gen v Guardian Newspapers Ltd (No.2)* [1990] 1 A.C. 109 at 281; Lord Hoffmann in *Campbell v MGN Ltd* [2004] UKHL 22; [2004] 2 A.C. 457 at 48; Lord Neuberger in *Vestergaard Frandsen A/S v Bestnet Europe Ltd* [2013] UKSC 31; [2013] 1 W.L.R. 1556 at [23]. He noted, at [25], liability for breach of confidence could also arise where a defendant learns of a trade secret in circumstances where she reasonably does not appreciate that it is confidential, but subsequently appreciates that it is in fact confidential. And see Arnold J in *Primary Group (UK) Ltd v The Royal Bank of Scotland Plc* [2014] EWHC 1082 (Ch); [2014] R.P.C. 26 at [210]–[223].

deliberately closed his eyes to the obvious.[91] In the vast majority of cases the duty of confidence will arise from a transaction or relationship between the parties.[92] However, it has become clear (especially since the judgment of Lord Goff in *Att Gen v Guardian Newspapers Ltd (No.2)*[93] that a duty of confidentiality may arise independently of any pre-existing relationship. The scope of the duty may also be in issue. In *R v Department of Health Ex p Source Infomatics (No.1)*[94] Simon Brown LJ noted that the touchstone by which to judge the scope of the confidant's duty and whether it had been breached was "his own conscience". The position of indirect recipients of information disclosed by a person owing an obligation of confidence and the issue of secondary liability are discussed below.[95]

Confidences arising from specific contractual provision or a relationship An obligation to treat certain information as being confidential is frequently expressly imposed by contract.[96] Examples include terms in agreements licensing industrial know-how and contracts of employment.[97] It may be that the express obligation of confidence does not survive the repudiation of the contract by the party seeking to enforce such an express contractual provision.[98] In the absence of express provision, the courts have been willing to imply a term of confidentiality in circumstances where this is clearly called for in the context of the relationship existing between the parties.[99] There are a number of distinct cases where the courts have held that an obligation of confidence arises. These include commercial relationships. So where, for instance, two parties enter into an agreement to exploit an industrial process or invention[100] a relationship of confidentiality is readily inferred. Likewise, when apparatus,[101] drawings or specifications[102] or other ideas[103] are provided for 26-13

---

91 *Att Gen v Guardian Newspapers (No.2)* [1990] 1 A.C. 109 at 281B. Note the discussion of secondary liability in para.26-18.

92 Reviewed in paras 26-13 to 26-15.

93 [1990] 1 A.C. 109.

94 [2001] Q.B. 424 at [31].

95 Paras 26-17 to 26-18.

96 The Court of Appeal in *Campbell v Frisbee* [2002] EWCA Civ 1374; [2003] I.C.R. 141 at [22] stated that it was arguable that "a duty of confidentiality that has been expressly assumed under contract carries more weight, when balanced against the restriction of the right of freedom of expression, than a duty that is not buttressed by express agreement"; and see *Associated Newspapers Ltd v HRH Prince of Wales* [2006] EWCA Civ 1776; [2008] Ch. 57 (para.26-50), commented upon by Sharp LJ in *Mionis v Democratic Press SA* [2017] EWCA Civ 1194; [2018] Q.B. 662 at [69]. However, cf. the observations of Walker LJ in *London Regional Transport v Mayor of London* [2001] EWCA Civ 1491; [2003] E.M.L.R. 4 at [46].

97 See, e.g. *Peter Pan Manufacturing Corporation v Corsets Silhouette Ltd* [1964] 1 W.L.R. 96; *Att Gen v Barker* [1990] 3 All E.R. 257.

98 Applying the principle in *General Billposting v Atkinson* [1909] A.C. 118 HL (a restraint clause in an employment contract lapsed when the employee was wrongfully dismissed). However, the Court of Appeal in *Campbell v Frisbee* [2002] EWCA Civ 1374; [2003] I.C.R. 141 at [16]–[22] raised the possibility that an obligation of confidence could survive the repudiation of the contract (though this involved private confidences).

99 *Saltman Engineering Co Ltd v Campbell Engineering Co* (1948) 65 R.P.C. 203 at [211]; *Ackroyds (London) Ltd v Islington Plastics Ltd* [1962] R.P.C. 97; *Coco v AN Clark (Engineers) Ltd* [1969] R.P.C. 41.

100 *Gallay Ltd's Application* [1959] R.P.C. 141; *James Industries Ltd's Patent* [1987] R.P.C. 235; cf. *Strachan and Henshaw Ltd v Pakcel Ltd* (1949) 66 R.P.C. 49; *Fomento Industrial SA v Mentmore Manufacturing* [1956] R.P.C. 87.

101 *Ackroyds (London) Ltd v Islington Plastics Ltd* [1962] R.P.C. 97.

102 *Saltman Engineering Co Ltd v Campbell Engineering Co Ltd* (1948) 65 R.P.C. 203; *Seager v*

use for a specific purpose, their use for any other purpose will be restrained. A confidential relationship may also arise by trade custom.[104] Again, a director may have a fiduciary relationship with his company[105] or a partner with his co-partners,[106] which will give rise to a duty of confidence. And where professional advisors such as lawyers,[107] bankers[108] and accountants[109] are involved it is usual if not inevitable that confidential matters will be disclosed, so that such advisors will be restrained from divulging and making use of confidential information.[110] (Lawyers are in a special position, in that their clients can invoke the law relating to professional privilege[111]). While these categories provide useful guidance as to the approach of the courts, there is no reason to believe that the obligation is limited to these particular categories.[112] A duty of confidence often survives the termination of the relationship which gave rise to it.[113] In *CF Partners (UK) LLP v Barclays Bank Plc*,[114] Hildyard J noted that "whilst it will not usually be unconscionable to

---

Copydex Ltd [1967] 1 W.L.R. 923; *Coco v AN Clark (Engineers) Ltd* [1969] R.P.C. 41; *Prince Albert v Strange* (1869) 2 De G. & Sm. 652; (1869) 1 Mac. G. 25.

103 *Fraser v Thames Television Ltd* [1984] Q.B. 44 (idea for television series). The Supreme Court of Canada in *Cadbury Schweppes Inc v FBI Foods Ltd* [2000] F.S.R. 491 held that the recipe for a tomato juice and clam broth drink was confidential although "nothing special"; cf. *Bailey v Graham* [2011] EWHC 3098 (Ch), Judge Pelling QC.

104 *Lac Minerals Ltd v International Corona Resources Ltd* [1990] F.S.R. 441 Sup. Ct of Canada.

105 *Nordenfelt v Maxim Nordenfelt Guns & Ammunition Co Ltd* [1894] A.C. 535; *Cranleigh Precision Engineering Ltd v Bryant* [1965] 1 W.L.R. 1293; *Thomas Marshall v Guinle* [1979] Ch. 227; *Electro Cad Australia Pty Ltd v Mejati* [1995] F.S.R. 291 (High Court Malaysia): director's fiduciary duties stronger than those owed by ordinary employee and could extend to period after resignation.

106 *Aas v Benham* [1891] 2 Ch. 244. But a duty of confidence does not necessarily give rise to a fiduciary relationship: *Arklow Investments Ltd v Maclean* [2000] 1 W.L.R. 594.

107 *A Firm of Solicitors, Re* [1997] Ch. 1. In *Ratiu v Conway* [2005] EWCA Civ 1302; [2006] 1 All E.R. 571. Auld LJ compared the fiduciary duty owed by a solicitor with the duty of confidentiality owed by a solicitor to a client. The latter is a separate obligation which can outlast the solicitor/client relationship—see Lord Millett in *Bolkiah v KPMG* [1999] 2 A.C. 222 at 235. In *Lillicrap v Nadler & Son* [1993] 1 W.L.R. 94 the Court of Appeal held that where a client sued his solicitor he waived his claim to confidence relating to matters relevant to the issue of the claim.

108 *Tournier v National Provincial* [1924] 1 K.B. 461 (discussed in *Primary Group (UK) Ltd v The Royal Bank of Scotland Plc* [2014] EWHC 1082 (Ch); [2014] R.P.C. 26 at [180], Arnold J); *XAG v A Bank* [1983] 2 All E.R. 464.

109 *Prince Jefri Bolkiah v KPMG* [1999] 2 A.C. 222.

110 Professional advisors such as solicitors or accountants owe a strict duty of confidence requiring more than merely taking all reasonable steps to keep relevant information confidential: *Prince Jefri Bolkiah v KPMG* [1999] 2 A.C. 222. Other professional advisors such as doctors (*X v Y* [1988] 2 All E.R. 648); hospitals (*Ashworth Hospital Authority v MGN Ltd* [2002] UKHL 29; [2002] 1 W.L.R. 2033) may receive confidential information of course but given the information they receive is likely to be of a personal nature their duty will be subject to the approach which has now evolved for such confidences.

111 On the distinction between legal professional privilege and the duty of confidence see *Webster v James Chapman & Co* [1989] 3 All E.R. 939. And on patent agents in respect of civil proceedings see Copyright Designs and Patents Act 1988 s.280. In *Kousouros v O'Halloran* [2014] EWHC 2294 (Ch); [2015] W.T.L.R. 1023 at [65] Simon J stated that once a privileged document comes into the hands of an opposing party, the law of confidence comes into play.

112 The class of persons who may come under an obligation of confidence is not closed: a TV company has been held to come under a duty of confidence in respect of protecting the identity of a supergrass in the course of filming, *Nicholls v BBC* [1999] E.M.L.R. 791.

113 See, e.g. the life-long duty of confidence to the Crown owed by former members of the S.I.S.: *Att Gen v Guardian Newspapers Ltd (No.2)* [1990] 1 A.C. 109; *Att Gen v Blake* [1998] Ch. 439.

114 [2014] EWHC 3049 (Ch) at [133], citing Lord Neuberger's emphasis on conscience in *Vestergaard Frandsen A/S v Bestnet Europe Ltd* [2013] UKSC 31; [2013] 1 W.L.R. 1556. Further "there may be equitable reasons for declining to regard the equitable obligation as confined by a contractual restriction" (at [134]).

use information in conformity with, or in a manner that does not offend, the terms consensually agreed, and the contract will shape the commitment, contract does not necessarily assuage conscience, and equity may yet give force to conscience."

Rights against employees An express duty of confidence may be imposed by a contract of employment.[115] In other cases, the courts have found a term to be implied.[116] Implied in a contract of employment is an undertaking by the employee to serve the employer with "good faith and fidelity".[117] The right of an employer to restrain an employee from divulging confidential information to others[118] or from making use of it for his own benefit[119] or that of a subsequent employer is well established.[120] The result can occasionally be to put an employee in a worse position than the rest of the world, which may acquire and be at liberty to use the information in legitimate ways. Many kinds of confidential information in the possession of employees have been protected. For example, an employee may not copy,[121] take away with him or use confidential documents such as lists of customers,[122] technical specifications,[123] particulars of secret processes[124] or materials supplied for his employer's use.[125] An employee will be restrained from making use of a secret even if he carries it in his head, especially if he deliberately commits it to memory.[126] But if the employer has already published a trade secret, the employee will not be restrained from further publishing it.[127] He may also work for another employer in his spare time, provided that such employment does not involve the disclosure or use of trade secrets, or is such as to inflict great harm on his 26-14

115 *Wessex Dairies v Smith* [1935] 2 K.B. 80; *Att Gen v Barker* [1990] 3 All E.R. 257; *Thomas Marshall v Guinle* [1979] Ch. 227. But see discussion of the rights of "whistleblowers" in the Public Interest Disclosure Act 1998 in para.26-32: any agreement that purports to preclude a worker from making a "protected disclosure" is void (PIDA 1998 s.1, inserting new s.43J into the Employment Rights Act 1996).

116 *Robb v Green* [1895] 2 Q.B. 315; *Hivac Ltd v Park Royal Scientific Instruments Ltd* [1946] Ch. 169; *Faccenda Chicken Ltd v Fowler* [1987] Ch. 117. In *Vestergaard Frandsen A/S v Bestnet Europe Ltd* [2013] UKSC 31; [2013] 1 W.L.R. 1556 at [30]–[31], Lord Neuberger refused to imply strict liability into the confidentiality clause.

117 *Robb v Green* [1895] 2 Q.B. 315, per Smith LJ. The general principles were reviewed in *Lancashire Fires Ltd v SA Lyons & Co Ltd* [1997] I.R.L.R. 113; [1996] F.S.R. 629. More senior employees may owe a fiduciary duty: *Crowson Fabrics Ltd v Rider* [2007] EWHC 2942 (Ch); [2008] F.S.R. 17 at [77]–[85].

118 *Saltri III Ltd v MD Mezzanine SA* [2012] EWHC 1270 (Comm) Hamblen J: where an employee was seconded to another employer, the documents produced during the secondment were prima facie confidential to the company to whom he had been seconded.

119 *Normalec Ltd v Britton* [1983] F.S.R. 318; *Att Gen v Guardian Newspapers Ltd* [1990] 1 A.C. 109.

120 *Morrison v Moat* (1851) 9 Hare 241.

121 *Louis v Smellie* (1895) 73 L.T. 226.

122 *Robb v Green* [1895] 2 Q.B. 315; *Faccenda Chicken Ltd v Fowler* [1987] Ch. 117; *Roger Bullivant Ltd v Ellis* [1987] I.C.R. 464.

123 *Merryweather v Moore* [1892] 2 Ch. 518. *Johnson & Bloy (Holdings) Ltd v Wolstenholme Rink Plc* [1989] F.S.R. 135.

124 *Lamb v Evans* [1893] 1 Ch. 218.

125 *Lamb v Evans* [1893] 1 Ch. 218.

126 *Faccenda Chicken Ltd v Fowler* [1987] Ch. 117; *Johnson & Bloy (Holdings) Ltd v Wolstenholme Rink Plc* [1989] F.S.R. 135; and *Lansing Linde Ltd v Kerr* [1991] 1 W.L.R. 251.

127 *Mustad v Dosen* [1964] 1 W.L.R. 109 (Note); [1963] R.P.C. 41; *Cranleigh Precision Engineering v Bryant* [1965] 1 W.L.R. 1293. As to the statutory protection for a "whistle-blowing" employee, see para.26-32.

employer.[128] Likewise, inventions made by an employee in his spare time belong to him and not to his employer, provided that he is not employed to invent.[129]

26-15 **Rights against ex-employees** The duty of confidentiality is highest while the employment is continuing.[130] In general, an employee may compete with his ex-employer after leaving his employment; and although he may not use information properly classed as trade secrets or their equivalent,[131] imparted to him in the course of his employment, he may use his general knowledge and skills so acquired.[132] This may include, for example, detailed knowledge of machinery and processes,[133] even though it might have been a breach of confidence to have disclosed such matters while still employed.[134] In *Faccenda Chicken Ltd v Fowler*[135] the Court of Appeal considered the scope of those obligations implied in the post-employment situation. Four factors were relevant in deciding whether information constituted a trade secret (or its equivalent) for these purposes: the nature of the employment; the nature of the information; whether the employer impressed upon the employee the confidentiality of the information and whether the information could be easily isolated from the other information which the employee is free to use or disclose. A restrictive covenant not to compete with a former employer or with the purchaser of a business[136] will be enforced provided that it protects the employer's legitimate business interests (whether trade secrets, goodwill or trade connection) and is reasonable in extent and in duration.[137] There is authority for the proposition that

[128] *Hivac Ltd v Park Royal Scientific Instruments Ltd* [1946] Ch. 169. As to what spare time work is not permissible for a technical employee, see *Lancashire Fires Ltd v SA Lyons & Co Ltd* [1997] I.R.L.R. 113; [1996] F.S.R. 629.

[129] *Electrolux Ltd v Hudson* [1977] F.S.R. 312; *Prout v British Gas Plc* [1992] F.S.R. 478 (employee suggestion scheme).

[130] *Normalec Ltd v Britton* [1983] F.S.R. 318. Where trade secrets are concerned it should be noted that the Trade Secrets Directive 2016/943 (on the protection of undisclosed know-how and business information (trade secrets) against their unlawful acquisition, use and disclosure) was incorporated into domestic law by the Trade Secrets (Enforcement, etc.) Regulations 2018 (SI 2018/597).

[131] "Information of a sufficiently high degree of confidentiality as to amount to a trade secret", Neill LJ, *Faccenda Chicken Ltd v Fowler* [1987] Ch. 117 at 136. It is arguable that an ex-employee who proposes to disclose rather than use confidential information (in its wider sense) may be bound by the duty of confidentiality: *Faccenda Chicken Ltd v Fowler* [1987] Ch. 117 at 136–138.

[132] *Mason v Provident Clothing & Supply Co Ltd* [1913] A.C. 724; *Hivac Ltd v Park Royal Scientific Instruments Ltd* [1946] Ch. 169; *Stephenson, Jordan and Harrison v Macdonald and Evans* (1952) 69 R.P.C. 10; *Faccenda Chicken Ltd v Fowler* [1987] Ch. 117; cf. *Thomas Marshall v Guinle* [1979] Ch. 227; *Lancashire Fires Ltd v SA Lyons & Co Ltd* [1997] I.R.L.R. 113. However, note *Force India Formula One Team Ltd v 1 Malaysia Racing Team Sdn Bhd* [2013] EWCA Civ 780; [2013] R.P.C. 36 at [67], information does not cease to be confidential simply because memorable.

[133] *Printers Finishers v Holloway* [1965] 1 W.L.R. 1; *Balston Ltd v Headline Filters Ltd* [1987] F.S.R. 330.

[134] In *Vestergaard Frandsen A/S v Bestnet Europe Ltd* [2013] UKSC 31; [2013] 1 W.L.R. 1556 at [44]–[45], the Supreme Court underlined the need for the law to "maintain a realistic and fair balance" between protecting trade secrets and not inhibiting competition. Goulding J in *Faccenda Chicken Ltd v Fowler* [1987] Ch. 117 divided information into three classes: trivial/easily accessible from public sources; confidential during employment but once learned, necessarily becomes part of the employee's skill and knowledge; "specified trade secrets, so confidential that … they cannot lawfully be used for anyone's benefit but the master's".

[135] [1987] Ch. 117.

[136] *Nordenfelt v Maxim Nordenfelt* [1894] A.C. 535; cf. *Herbert Morris Ltd v Saxelby* [1916] 1 A.C. 688.

[137] *Faccenda Chicken Ltd v Fowler* [1987] Ch. 117 at [137]; *FSS Travel & Leisure Systems Ltd v Johnson* [1998] I.R.L.R. 382 and see Silber J in *CEF Holdings Ltd v Munday* [2012] EWHC 1524 (QB); [2012] F.S.R. 35. In *Force India Formula One Team Ltd v 1 Malaysia Racing Team Sdn Bhd*

it may be possible to protect by a suitably limited express covenant, confidential information which is not protectable by an implied term of the contract of employment.[138] As to relief, the court will attempt to avoid generating a "new form of industrial slavery" by granting injunctive relief in terms which effectively prevents the employee from working for anyone except the claimant.[139] If the employer wrongfully repudiates the contract *General Billposting Co Ltd v Atkinson*[140] indicates that he will be unable to enforce a restrictive covenant contained within it against the employee.

Confidentiality independent of a pre-existing relationship Where a person obtains obviously confidential information, either deliberately or accidentally, an obligation of confidence may arise. Lord Goff in *Att Gen v Guardian Newspapers Ltd (No.2)*[141] said that "a duty of confidence arises when confidential information comes to the knowledge of a person ... in circumstances where he has notice ... that the information is confidential, with the effect that he should be precluded from disclosing the information to others". He instanced an obviously confidential document being wafted by an electric fan out of a window into a crowded street. An example of such chance possession of an obviously confidential document can be found in the facts of *English & American Insurance Co Ltd v Herbert Smith*.[142] The obligation can therefore attach to "strangers". Examples include: discovery of a private diary dropped in a public place[143]; taping confidential material said in a 26-16

[2013] EWCA Civ 780; [2013] R.P.C. 36 at [66]–[67] Lewison LJ discusses the distinction between information and skill/expertise. "Garden leave" arrangements—where the worker is still employed but not required to attend for work—would not as such be subject to restraint of trade principles, though arguably an excessive period might be, see the comment Dillon LJ in *Provident Financial Group Plc v Hayward* [1989] I.C.R. 160; [1989] 3 All E.R. 298. *D v P* [2016] EWCA Civ 87; [2016] I.C.R. 688: the starting point in the consideration of a claim by an employer to enforce an employee's negative covenant is that the ordinary remedy is an injunction. The Supreme Court in *Tillman v Egon Zehnder Ltd* [2019] UKSC 32; [2020] A.C. 154 considered the issue when, where part of a post-employment covenant was in restraint of trade, the circumstances in which the court should seek to remove it so as to leave the ex-employee bound by the remainder.

138 *Balston Ltd v Headline Filters Ltd* [1987] F.S.R. 330, per Scott J In *Force India Formula One Team Ltd v 1 Malaysia Racing Team Sdn Bhd* [2013] EWCA Civ 780; [2013] R.P.C. 36 at [60] Lewison LJ agreed with Scott J in declining to read Faccenda as holding that confidential information not protected by the implied term could not be protected by an express term. (See also *Lancashire Fires Ltd v SA Lyons & Co Ltd* [1997] I.R.L.R. 113). *Invista Textiles UK Ltd v Botes* [2019] EWHC 58 (Ch); [2019] I.R.L.R. 977 at [46]–[48], Birss J, contains a useful review of case law on restrictive covenants.

139 See, per Templeman LJ in *GD Searle & Co Ltd v Celltech Ltd* [1982] F.S.R. 92.

140 [1909] A.C. 118 (cf. if the breach did not constitute a repudiation or was not accepted by the employee: *Rock Refrigeration Ltd v Jones* [1997] I.C.R. 938; [1997] 1 All E.R. 1 CA). However, in *Campbell v Frisbee* [2002] EWCA Civ 1374; [2003] I.C.R. 141 (a case concerning personal information) Lord Phillips MR noted (at [22]) "we do not believe that the effect on duties of confidence assumed under contract when the contract in question is wrongly repudiated is clearly established"; and note Gurry, *Breach of Confidence*, 2nd edn (2012), para.12.149.

141 [1990] 1 A.C. 109 at [281]–[282], referred to by Lord Neuberger MR in *Tchenguiz v Imerman* [2010] EWCA Civ 908; [2011] Fam. 116 at [64]: "the law of confidence was authoritatively extended to apply to cases where the defendant had come by the information without the consent of the claimant."

142 [1988] F.S.R. 232, per Jacob J in *Mars UK Ltd v Teknowledge Ltd* [2000] F.S.R. 138 at [35]. The court will also restrain the use of privileged documents handed over by mistake in disclosure, if the mistake would have been obvious to a reasonable solicitor: *Derby & Co Ltd v Weldon (No.8)* [1991] 1 W.L.R. 73; *IBM Corp v Phoenix International (Computers) Ltd* [1995] 1 All E.R. 413.

143 obiter, per Lord Goff in *Att Gen v Guardian Newspapers (No.2)* [1990] A.C. 109 at 281.

private telephone conversation[144]; taking a photograph of a closed and secret film set.[145] In such cases, though the court sometimes highlights improper behaviour on the part of the defendant, the duty of confidence arises from knowledge that the information is confidential.[146]

26-17 **Indirect recipients of confidential information**[147] A third party to whom confidential information is relayed by a party under an obligation of confidence may also owe an obligation of confidence to the claimant not to use or disclose that information. That is certainly the case where the third party is aware[148] of the confidentiality attaching to the information, even if that awareness arises subsequently to the receipt of that information.[149] Even bona fide purchasers without notice of the information might be bound by any confidentiality attaching to the information, once they know of its status. However in such cases the court may decide to award an injunction rather than damages In *Valeo Vision SA v Flexible Lamps*, Aldous J said "although the court may step in to grant injunctive relief ... only in cases where the conscience of the defendant is bound would it be appropriate to grant relief by way of damages".[150] The test for knowledge—as with direct recipients—would appear to be an objective one viz would a reasonable person have appreciated that the information was confidential.[151]

26-18 **Secondary or accessory liability** The issue of secondary or accessory liability (assisting in a misuse of confidential information by another) was raised in *Vestergaard Frandsen A/S v Bestnet Europe Ltd*.[152] Lord Neuberger noted that "while a recipient of confidential information may be said to be primarily liable in a case of its misuse, a person who assists her in the misuse can be liable, in a secondary sense ... [though] she would normally have to know that the recipient

[144] *Francome v Mirror Group Newspapers Ltd* [1984] 1 W.L.R. 892.

[145] *Shelley Films Ltd v Rex Features Ltd* [1994] E.M.L.R. 134. The newspaper was enjoined on the basis that it ought, as a reasonable person, to know that the claimant intended the information to be kept confidential. Lord Walker in *OBG Ltd v Allan* [2007] UKHL 21; [2008] 1 A.C. 1 at [289]–[290], though supporting the decision in *Shelley Films Ltd v Rex Features Ltd* [1994] E.M.L.R. 134, cast doubt on the decision in *Creation Records Ltd v News Group Newspapers Ltd* [1997] E.M.L.R. 444.

[146] Either per se, or because it has been clearly "fenced off" as confidential/secret.

[147] Of course if the third party induced a breach of contract in order to obtain the information he would be liable for the tort of that name, *British Industrial Plastics v Ferguson* [1940] 1 All E.R. 479.

[148] *Lord Keith Att Gen v Guardian Newspapers (No.2)* [1990] 1 A.C. 109 at 260: " ... a third party who comes into possession of confidential information which he knows to be such, may come under a duty not to pass it on to anyone else." In *Primary Group (UK) Ltd v The Royal Bank of Scotland Plc* [2014] EWHC 1082 (Ch); [2014] R.P.C. 26 at [223] Arnold J said that an objective reasonable person test with regard to knowledge should to be used here also.

[149] *Valeo Vision SA v Flexible Lamps Ltd* [1995] R.P.C. 205 referring to the judgment of Sir John Donaldson MR in *Att Gen v Guardian Newspapers (No.2)* [1990] 1 A.C. 109.

[150] [1995] R.P.C. 205 at 228. However, note Lord Neuberger MR in *Tchenguiz v Imerman* [2010] EWCA Civ 908; [2011] Fam. 116 at [74]: "here the confidential information has been passed by the defendant to a third party, the claimant's rights will prevail as against the third party, unless he was a bona fide purchaser of the information without notice of its confidential nature." See Jones "Restitution of Benefits Obtained in Breach of Another's Confidence" (1970) 86 L.Q.R. 463; Law Commission, *Report on Breach of Confidence* (1981), Cmnd.8388.

[151] See, e.g. Lord Neuberger in *Vestergaard Frandsen S/A v Bestnet Europe Ltd* [2013] UKSC 31; [2013] 1 W.L.R. 1556 at [25]; Arnold J in *Primary Group (UK) Ltd v The Royal Bank of Scotland Plc* [2014] EWHC 1082 (Ch); [2014] R.P.C. 26 at [238].

[152] [2013] UKSC 31; [2013] 1 W.L.R. 1556.

was abusing confidential information".[153] Knowledge in this context would include "blind-eye knowledge" or a reckless disregard of others' possible rights (see Lord Nicholls in *Royal Brunei Airlines Sdn Bhd v Tan*).[154] The defendant, a former employee of the claimant company, had established a competing company unaware that this new company's product had been developed using the claimant's confidential information. The defendant was honestly unaware that there had been a misuse: an allegation that she was "playing with fire" or "taking a risk" did not as such suffice, though the fact that she took a risk might render it easier to hold that she was dishonest. On the issue of knowing assistance see also the earlier Court of Appeal decision in *Thomas v Pearce*.[155] Although Lord Neuberger noted the approach of equity "in this area" he also accepted that in principle the doctrine of common design applied to this action. Here the defendant's conscience must have been touched by knowledge of the misuse and the defendant would have to share with the others "each of the features of the design which make it unlawful". On the facts the defendant had neither received the trade secrets nor did she know they had been misused.[156]

Statutory obligations/public bodies Statutes may prohibit the communication of confidential information.[157] Most provide for criminal sanctions but some also found civil causes of action. As to state secrets, the principal general statute is the Official Secrets Act 1989.[158] Certain public bodies are under a duty to keep confidential information and documents that come to their attention in the course of their duties.[159] Whether they breach such an obligation by releasing such information may depend on whether such release is in the public interest and/or whether **26-19**

---

153 [2013] UKSC 31; [2013] 1 W.L.R. 1556 at [26].

154 [1995] 2 A.C. 378 PC, especially at 390F–391D.

155 [2000] F.S.R. 718, "more is required than merely careless, naive or stupid behaviour". In *Primary Group (UK) Ltd v The Royal Bank of Scotland Plc* [2014] EWHC 1082 (Ch); [2014] R.P.C. 26 at [234] Arnold J commented that *Thomas v Pearce* may be good law on the correct test for accessory liability but is no longer good law on the question of the test for imposing an equitable obligation of confidence.

156 [2013] UKSC 31; [2013] 1 W.L.R. 1556 at [34]. (And see *Marathon Asset Management LLP v Seddon* [2017] EWHC 300 (Comm); [2017] I.C.R. 791, Leggatt J, at [132]). *Unilever Plc v Gillette Ltd* [1989] R.P.C. 583, CA, a patent case, was distinguished as not applying to confidential information and involving possible strict liability, see [36]–[37]; cf. *Lancashire Fires Ltd v SA Lyons & Co* [1996] F.S.R. 629 where it had been conceded that the principle in *Unilever* applied to confidential information cases. See Lord Neuberger in *Vestergaard* [2013] UKSC 31; [2013] 1 W.L.R. 1556 at [38]–[39].

157 The principal general statute regulating the use of personal data—some of which is not necessarily confidential—is the Data Protection Act 2018; see further para.26-54.

158 The Attorney General may obtain an injunction to restrain breach of the Act and may also obtain an injunction to prevent a defendant from obtaining payment or other benefit from a breach of the duties of confidence imposed by it: *Att Gen v Blake* [1998] Ch. 439 CA.

159 The mere fact that information has been collected by a public body subject to public law obligations does not, ipso facto, make it confidential: see *Elliott v Chief Constable of Wiltshire*, *The Times*, 5 December 1996. In *Marcel v Commissioner of Police of the Metropolis* [1992] Ch. 225 a duty of confidence was owed in respect of information obtained by the police under the Police and Criminal Evidence Act 1984. See also *R. (on application of Ingenious Media Holdings Plc) v Revenue and Customs Commissioners* [2016] UKSC 54; [2016] 1 W.L.R. 4164; the discussion by Tugendhat J in *Mitchell v News Group Newspapers Ltd* [2014] EWHC 879 (QB) (application in defamation proceedings for non-party disclosure of witness evidence obtained by the Metropolitan Police Commissioner in the course of an investigation under the Police Reform Act 2002).

the purpose for which they received such information was being served.[160] For example, a photograph[161] taken by the police of a suspect under compulsion or a statement taken under caution[162] is confidential, but the police may make reasonable use of material so obtained for the purposes of the prevention and detection of crime.[163] It is necessary to consider what the legislation contemplated as the purposes for which the information could be used. The Copyright Designs and Patents Act 1988 contains specific provisions concerning photographs taken for private and domestic purposes.[164]

(c) Breach

26-20 **Use and disclosure** It is a breach of confidence to use[165] or disclose the information without the consent of the person to whom the duty is owed.[166] (However, a co-owner of confidential information cannot prevent another co-owner from making use of it in the absence of a contractual, fiduciary or other special relationship.[167]) The defendant might be liable even though he has only disclosed the substance of the information.[168] Lord Neuberger MR in *Tchenguiz v Imerman*[169] said that it is a breach of confidence for a defendant without authority "to examine, or to make, retain or supply copies to a third party of a document, whose contents are, and were (or ought to have been) appreciated by the defendant to be,

---

160 See paras 26-30 and 26-31.

161 *Hellewell v Chief Constable of Derbyshire* [1995] 1 W.L.R. 804.

162 *Taylor v Serious Fraud Office* [1999] 2 A.C. 177; *Woolgar v Chief Constable of the Sussex Police* [2000] 1 W.L.R. 25; *Bunn v BBC* [1998] 3 All E.R. 552.

163 *Hellewell v Chief Constable of Derbyshire* [1995] 1 W.L.R. 804. See also *Malone v Metropolitan Police Commissioner* [1979] Ch. 344; and *R. v Chief Constable of the North Wales Police Ex p. AB* [1999] Q.B. 396. However it should be noted that now in certain cases art.8 ECHR will be engaged and where public bodies are involved that will have direct effect.

164 s.85, one of the moral rights. Other statutes provide for circumstances in which information may be disclosed: see Contempt of Court Act 1981 s.10.

165 As to whether being galvanised into action by information constitutes misuse see *Arklow Investments Ltd v Maclean* [2000] 1 W.L.R. 594. In *CF Partners (UK) LLP v Barclays Bank Plc* [2014] EWHC 3049 at [984] Hildyard J commented that: "misuse may be inferred from the fact that the defendant, having obtained the confidential information, is influenced by it (whilst it retains its quality of confidentiality) in determining and then embarking on a course of conduct otherwise than for the purposes for which it was provided".

166 Under the Freedom of Information Act 2000 public authorities are under a duty to disclose information; however s.40 provides an exemption for "personal data" under the Data Protection Act 2018 and s.41 for information provided in confidence. And see the Environmental Information Regulations 2004 (SI 2004/3391) reg.12(5)(e): confidentiality to be preserved to protect a legitimate economic interest. The majority of the Supreme Court in *Kennedy v The Charity Commission* [2014] UKSC 20; [2015] A.C. 455 considered that art.10 ECHR does not impose on public authorities a general duty of disclosure of information.

167 *Murray v Yorkshire Fund Managers Ltd* [1998] 1 W.L.R. 951; cf. *Orr-Adams v Bailey* [2013] EWPCC 30, Recorder Amanda Michaels.

168 *Prince Albert v Strange* (1849) 2 De. G & Sm. 652 (the description in the catalogue of the claimant's etchings).

169 [2010] EWCA Civ 908; [2011] Fam. 116 at [69] and [72]. And see *Primary Group (UK) Ltd v The Royal Bank of Scotland Plc* [2014] EWHC 1082 (Ch); [2014] R.P.C. 26 at [243] per Arnold J. See also *Warwickshire CC v Matalia* [2018] EWHC 1340 (Ch), HH Judge Simon Barker QC (for the background facts see para.26-08): the defendant by continuing to seek to obtain and actually obtaining the confidential information without authority was in breach of confidence, even without the dissemination or publication of that information (citing *Tchenguiz v Imerman* [2010] EWCA Civ 908; [2011] Fam. 116).

confidential to the claimant". Though this was a case involving private information, this would also apply to commercial information, given that it was stressed that such unauthorised acts might jeopardise the confidentiality of the information.

Involuntary or accidental use Involuntary or accidental use of confidential information may still result in breach. Information may be communicated in confidence to a recipient who may not even particularly wish to receive it but who subsequently makes use of it unconsciously, not deliberately intending plagiarism (circumstances which have a parallel in the subconscious copying of copyright material). In such a case the court has granted relief.[170] Such a case should be distinguished from one where the defendant never attracted a duty of confidence.[171] Another example of inadvertent use arises in connection with inadequate "Chinese walls". The court will grant relief to prevent a professional firm in possession of a claimant's confidential information from acting against him, unless the defendant establishes that there is no risk of information being misused.[172] **26-21**

Negligent disclosure The recipient of information communicated in confidence owes a duty of care to preserve its confidentiality. It follows that, if he releases it negligently, he may be liable for the consequences of its disclosure, but only to the extent that these are themselves actionable and can reasonably be foreseen, in accordance with the general principles of liability in tort.[173] **26-22**

Disclosure of information improperly obtained Information may come into a party's hands not by being communicated directly to him but by dishonest means or a trick.[174] The use of information improperly obtained will be restrained even where, for instance, a document might be relevant in legal proceedings.[175] That is **26-23**

---

170 *Seager v Copydex* [1967] 1 W.L.R. 923. *Paymaster (Jamaica) Ltd v Grace Kennedy Remittance Services Ltd* [2017] UKPC 40; [2018] Bus. L.R. 492 at [41]: conscious plagiarism not a necessary component for a claim for breach of confidence.

171 *Thomas v Pearce* [2000] F.S.R. 718; *Vestergaard Frandsen A/S v Bestnet Europe Ltd* [2013] UKSC 31; [2013] 1 W.L.R. 1556 at [24], per Lord Neuberger MR, with reference to *Seager v Copydex*: "once it was found that they had received the information in confidence, their state of mind when using the information was irrelevant to the question of whether they had abused the confidence".

172 *Prince Jefri Bolkiah v KPMG* [1999] 2 A.C. 222. There is a heavy evidential burden in showing that there is no risk of information passing through a Chinese wall. *Marks & Spencer Plc v Freshfields Bruckhaus Deringer* [2004] EWCA Civ 741; [2005] P.N.L.R. 4: the principle in *Bolkiah* not confined to "same transaction" cases; rather applies where there is a real risk of a conflict of interest. And see *Georgian American Alloys Inc v White & Case LLP* [2014] EWHC 94 (Comm); [2014] 1 C.L.C. 86, Field J. An attempt to extend the "Bolkiah" principle and barring-out relief to cover ordinary employees was rejected in *Caterpillar Logistics Services (UK)Ltd v Huesca de Crean* [2012] EWCA Civ 156; [2012] 3 All E.R. 129 at [49]; whether the principle also applied to a former in-house litigator led to an obiter difference of views in the Court of Appeal in *Generics (UK) Ltd v Yeda Research & Development Co Ltd* [2012] EWCA Civ 726; [2013] F.S.R. 13.

173 *Weld-Blundell v Stephens* [1920] A.C. 956; *Furniss v Fitchett* [1958] N.Z.L.R. 396. *Lady Archer v Williams* [2003] EWHC 1670 (QB); [2003] E.M.L.R. 38; the defendant was liable for a newspaper's publication of some of the private information she had released to others in breach of confidence. It must have been obvious that there was a substantial risk that the information she was disclosing to various parties would find its way into the newspapers.

174 *ITC Film Distributors v Video Exchange Ltd* [1982] Ch. 431 (the defendant had obtained possession of his opponents' papers, including privileged material, by a trick).

175 *Lord Ashburton v Pape* [1913] 2 Ch. 469; *ITC Film Distributors v Video Exchange Ltd* [1982] Ch. 431. It may be, however, that *Ashburton v Pape* had to be understood as based on privilege, not just on confidentiality, see Lloyd J in *A v B (Copyright: Diary Pages)* [2000] E.M.L.R. 1007; and *Lord*

so even if the information has passed to another[176] who originally received it innocently.[177]

26-24 **Use by regulatory authorities[178] and for legal proceedings** Documents which are confidential may nonetheless be disclosable in legal proceedings, unless covered by public policy[179] or on one of the established grounds of privilege.[180] However, the courts have developed means of ensuring that particularly confidential disclosure documents receive due protection.[181]

26-25 **The issue of detriment** There is some debate as to whether the claimant must also prove harm or detriment where other than personal confidential information is involved. See for example Megarry J in *Coco v AN Clark (Engineers) Ltd*[182] who expressly kept open the possibility that detriment was not after all required and Lord Goff in *Att Gen v Guardian Newspapers (No.2)*[183] who wished "to keep open the question whether detriment to the plaintiff is an essential ingredient of an action for breach of confidence". In the case of state secrets, however, it should be recalled that the Crown must show a public interest in restraining disclosure. Where private

---

Neuberger MR in Tchenguiz v Imerman [2010] EWCA Civ 908; [2011] Fam. 116 at [61]; *Brake v Guy* [2019] EWHC 3332 (Ch), John Jarvis QC, sitting as Judge of the High Court. And see *DSM SFG Group Holdings Ltd v Kelly* [2019] EWCA Civ 2256; [2020] E.M.L.R. 10.

[176] *Prince Albert v Strange* (1849) 1 De G. & Sm. 652; 64 E.R. 293; (1849) 1 Mac. G. 25; 41 E.R. 1171 (on appeal); *Liquid Veneer Co Ltd v Scott* (1912) 29 R.P.C. 639; *Argyll v Argyll* [1967] Ch. 302; *Att Gen v Guardian Newspapers Ltd* [1990] 1 A.C. 109.

[177] *Printers & Finishers Ltd v Holloway* [1965] 1 W.L.R. 1; *Butler v Board of Trade* [1971] Ch. 680 at 690; *Derby & Co v Weldon (No.8)* [1991] 1 W.L.R. 73. Usually, there will be constructive notice of impropriety. Where there is not, the use of confidential information may perhaps not be restrained until after notice has been received: *Malone v Commissioner of Police of the Metropolis (No.2)* [1979] Ch. 344 at 361.

[178] As to regulatory authorities, see para.26-30. Under the Investigatory Powers Act 2016 UK intelligence/law enforcement agencies were granted new powers to intercept communications and powers of bulk communications data acquisition. In *R. (on the application of NCCL) v Secretary of State for the Home Department* [2018] EWHC 975 (Admin); [2019] Q.B. 481 the Investigatory Powers Act 2016 Pt 4 (on the retention of data) was held to be incompatible with fundamental rights in EU law. In *Big Brother Watch v United Kingdom (58170/13)*, *The Times*, 23 November 2018, ECtHR, the right to intercept internet communications in bulk under s.8(4) of the Regulation of Investigatory Powers Act 2000 was held to have breached art.8.

[179] *Att Gen v Clough* [1963] 1 Q.B. 773; *Att Gen v Mulholland* [1963] 2 Q.B. 477; *D v NSPCC* [1978] A.C. 171; *British Steel Corp v Granada Television Ltd* [1981] A.C. 1096. *Smithkline Beecham Plc v Generics (UK) Ltd* [2003] EWCA Civ 1109; [2004] 1 W.L.R. 1479 (whether confidential documents, disclosed in settled patent proceedings could be used in parallel proceedings). In general, medical records are not protected against disclosure in court proceedings for which they are relevant unless the public interest in preserving confidentiality outweighs the public interest in the administration of justice: see *D v NSPCC* [1978] A.C. 171. And note *Re A (A Child) Disclosure of Third Party Information* [2012] UKSC 60; [2013] 2 A.C. 66: Local Authority should disclose in contact proceedings allegations made in confidence of sexual abuse made against the child's father by a third party.

[180] *Wheeler v Le Marchant* (1881) L.R. 17 Ch. D. 675. And the courts will restrain the use of professionally privileged confidential information that has come into a party's hands accidentally where the mistake was obvious; *Derby & Co Ltd v Weldon (No.8)* [1991] 1 W.L.R. 73; *IBM v Phoenix International (Computers) Ltd* [1995] 1 All E.R. 413.

[181] For example, by means of confidentiality clubs of persons able to see disclosure documents.

[182] [1969] R.P.C. 41 at 48.

[183] [1990] 1 A.C. 109 at 282. Mummery LJ in *Federal Bank of the Middle East Ltd v Hadkinson* [2000] 2 All E.R. 395, 413 suggested that if detriment were required the diversion of business opportunities could suffice.

information is concerned it seems likely that the invasion of privacy per se suffices.[184]

(d) Defences

(i) Cessation of obligations

Cessation of obligations That the obligation to maintain confidence has ceased is a defence to a breach of confidence action. This may arise in a number of circumstances, by agreement or release,[185] for instance. Or the information may have entered the public domain. A person is not under a duty to maintain confidentiality of information which has ceased to be confidential.[186] The information may indeed cease to be confidential through effluxion of time.[187] Sometimes information is acquired confidentially which could have been independently ascertained by due inquiry. Although a person in possession of such information will be restrained from making use of it as a short cut to compete with its owner, there must come a time when such an advantage no longer obtains. So, a trader who has received information in confidence for a limited purpose, and who has not made use of it during the period of the confidential relationship between the parties, will not subsequently be restrained from using it when it is no longer secret.[188] When the owner of confidential information himself makes it public, for instance by publishing it in a patent specification, he cannot then be heard to say that it is still confidential.[189] It is unclear what the position is where someone other than the "owner" makes the information public.[190] **26-26**

(ii) Public interest

Public interest—general There are, broadly speaking, two aspects to the public interest defence. The first encompasses the disclosure of matters of real public concern;[191] though it should be noted that interference with freedom of expression has to be justified even where there is no public interest in a particular publication.[192] The second applies to the use or disclosure of the information in question for other public purposes.[193] **26-27**

Disclosure of matters of real public concern[194] There is a clearly established defence of disclosure of matters of public interest in the action for breach of **26-28**

184 *Att Gen v Guardian Newspapers (No.2)* [1990] A.C. 109 at 256, per Lord Keith.

185 *Ackroyds (London) Ltd v Islington Plastics Ltd* [1962] R.P.C. 97.

186 See, e.g. *Att Gen v Blake* [1998] Ch. 439 CA. Information may cease to be confidential by being read to or by the court in open court: see *Bunn v BBC* [1998] 3 All E.R. 552.

187 See *Arklow Investments Ltd v Maclean* [2000] 1 W.L.R. 594 Privy Council (NZ).

188 *Peter Pan Manufacturing Corporation v Corsets Silhouette Ltd* [1964] 1 W.L.R. 96.

189 *Mustad v Dosen* [1964] 1 W.L.R. 109 (Note); [1963] R.P.C. 41.

190 See para.26-35. In *Cranleigh Precision Engineering Ltd v Bryant* [1965] 1 W.L.R. 1293 a former director was restrained from making use of a patent specification which he learned about through his fiduciary relationship with his former company, from which he had not been released. However this decision may be coloured by the breach of fiduciary duty.

191 See para.26-28.

192 See para.26-29.

193 See paras 26-30 to 26-31.

194 In cases where there is a clear public interest that information should be more widely known, the

confidence. The much quoted dictum: "The true doctrine is that there is no equity in the disclosure of iniquity"[195] is merely an example of the broader principle that the disclosure of confidential information will not be restrained when there is a just cause or excuse for disclosing it.[196] The defence of public interest certainly covers "matters carried out or contemplated in breach of the country's security, or in breach of the law, including statutory duty, fraud, or otherwise destructive of the country or its people, including matters medically dangerous to the public: and doubtless other misdeeds of similar gravity"[197] but it is not limited to these categories.[198] The general principle is that disclosure should be made to one who has a proper interest in receiving the information.[199] The question is whether the information is such that it ought to be disclosed to a competent authority,[200] or whether it ought to be made available to the public at large through the media.[201] In the following cases (all prior to the Human Rights Act 1998) the information concerned was of "real public concern" and disclosure permitted: unreliability of intoximeters used in the course of testing the breath of drivers, disclosed by employees to newspaper[202]; medical practices alleged to be dangerous[203]; accountants disclosing information about their client, a collapsed bank, to a Bank of England inquiry.[204] In all these cases there is a conflict between two public interests: that of maintaining confidentiality and that of making matters or public interest known to those with a proper interest. A balancing act has to be performed.[205] It has been the case in the past that in undertaking this balancing act the courts have acknowledged the relevance of freedom of expression. However, this consideration is now enhanced by the Human Rights Act 1998.[206] This should be borne in mind when reviewing cases on the public interest defence that pre-date the Human Rights Act 1998.[207] In

---

court will not hold a defendant to a specific undertaking not to disclose it: *Hubbard v Vosper* [1972] 2 Q.B. 84.

195 *Gartside v Outram* (1857) 26 L.J. Ch. 113.

196 It does not extend only to the detection or prevention of wrongdoing: *Lion Laboratories Ltd v Evans* [1985] Q.B. 526. The burden lies on the defendant to justify the defence: see *Att Gen v Guardian Newspapers (No.2)* [1990] 1 A.C. 109.

197 See *Beloff v Pressdram Ltd* [1973] 1 All E.R. 241; *British Steel v Granada Television Ltd* [1981] A.C. 1096.

198 See *Lion Laboratories Ltd v Evans* [1985] Q.B. 526, per Stephenson LJ. See also the categories of information mentioned in the Public Interest Disclosure Act 1998, para.26-32, though the House of Lords made clear in *Cream Holdings Ltd v Banerjee* [2004] UKHL 44; [2005] 1 A.C. 253 that these "whistleblower" provisions added protection to employees; they were not intended to cut down the circumstances where public interest might apply to the publication of private information. There is a public interest in correcting misleading public statements: *Viagogo Ltd v Myles* [2012] EWHC 433 (Ch), Hildyard J.

199 See, e.g. *Initial Services v Putterill* [1968] 1 Q.B. 396; *Francome v Mirror Group Newspapers Ltd* [1984] 1 W.L.R. 892 (only limited disclosure required).

200 *Re A Company's Application* [1989] Ch. 477 (no injunction granted to prohibit disclosure of financial affairs to regulatory body).

201 *Initial Services Ltd v Putterill* [1968] 1 Q.B. 396; *Hubbard v Vosper* [1972] 2 Q.B. 84; *Lion Laboratories Ltd v Evans* [1985] Q.B. 526.

202 *Lion Laboratories Ltd v Evans* [1985] Q.B. 526.

203 *Hubbard v Vosper* [1972] 2 Q.B. 84.

204 *Price Waterhouse v BCCI Holdings (Luxembourg) SA* [1992] B.C.L.C. 583, principles reviewed and restated by Millett J.

205 *Lion Laboratories Ltd v Evans* [1985] Q.B. 526; *Att Gen v Guardian Newspapers (No.2)* [1990] 1 A.C. 109.

206 The issue of public interest/art.10 and privacy is discussed in para.26-49.

207 For cases post-Human Rights Act 1998 see *London Regional Transport v Mayor of London* [2001]

Brevan Howard Asset Management LLP v Reuters Ltd[208] the defendant claimed that the public interest applied. The judge, with whom the Court of Appeal agreed, held that *HRH Prince of Wales v Associated Newspapers Ltd*[209] applied in a commercial confidence case. There is an important public interest in the observance of duties of confidence; it is not enough to justify publication that the information is a matter of public interest. Sir Terence Etherton MR said that "the fact that information relates to information received in confidence is a factor that art.10(2) recognises as of itself justifying restrictions on freedom of expression".[210] There was nothing inconsistent between the application of the *Prince of Wales* case and the jurisprudence of the ECtHR.[211]

The effect of the Human Rights Act 1998 Article 10 of the Convention for the Protection of Human Rights and Fundamental Freedoms provides: **26-29**

> "(1) Everyone has the right to freedom of expression. This right shall include freedom to hold opinions and to receive and impart information and ideas without interference by public authority and regardless of frontiers …
>
> (2) The exercise of these freedoms, since it carries with it duties and responsibilities may be subject to such formalities, conditions, restrictions or penalties as are prescribed by law and are necessary in a democratic society … for the protection of the reputation or rights of others, for preventing the disclosure of information received in confidence …"

Thus art.10 recognises that preventing breach of confidence may be an exception to the right to freedom of expression. However, s.12 of the Human Rights Act 1998, provides that in considering whether to grant relief[212] which might affect the exercise of the Convention right to freedom of expression, the court must have particular regard to the importance[213] of that right and certain other factors.[214] Lord Woolf in *A v B Plc* noted that "even where there is no public interest in a particular publication interference with freedom of expression has to be justified".[215] At issue is whether there is a compelling social need to prevent disclosure in order to protect the confidential information; any restriction imposed on the art.10 right by a court must be rational, fair and not arbitrary and the right must be impaired no

---

EWCA Civ 1491; [2003] E.M.L.R. 4; *Jockey Club v Buffham* [2002] EWHC 1866 (QB); [2003] Q.B. 462.

208 [2017] EWCA Civ 950; [2017] E.M.L.R. 28.

209 [2006] EWCA Civ 1776; [2008] Ch. 57.

210 [2017] EWCA Civ 950; [2017] E.M.L.R. 28 at [62].

211 [2017] EWCA Civ 950; [2017] E.M.L.R. 28 at [66]. The difference in outcomes in *London Regional Transport v Mayor of London* [2001] EWCA Civ 1491; [2003] E.M.L.R. 4; and *Northern Rock Plc v The Financial Times Ltd* [2007] EWHC 2677 (QB) was explained (at [71]–[72]). Non-disclosure agreements and the public interest were discussed in *ABC v Telegraph Media Group Ltd* [2018] EWCA Civ 2329; [2019] 2 All E.R. 684. The Court of Appeal stressed the public interest in upholding contractual bargains (see *Mionis v Democratic Press SA* [2017] EWCA Civ 1194; [2018] Q.B. 662). See also *Linklaters LLP v Mellish* [2019] EWHC 177 (QB) Warby J. And see para.26-50.

212 This clearly applies to injunctions (and indeed s.12(3) deals specifically with prior restraints). However a claim for damages would also appear to be included: Lindsay J in *Douglas v Hello! Ltd (No.3)* [2003] EWHC 786 (Ch); [2003] 3 All E.R. 996 at [203].

213 The European Court of Human Rights has stated that the pressing social need for the restriction on freedom of expression must be "convincingly established" (*Handyside v United Kingdom* (1976) 1 E.H.R.R. 737). As to the impact of the Convention on cases of disclosure of state confidences, see *Observer v United Kingdom* (1991) 14 E.H.R.R. 153.

214 Human Rights Act 1998 s.12. And see *Viagogo Ltd v Myles* [2012] EWHC 433 (Ch), Hildyard J.

215 [2002] EWCA Civ 337; [2003] Q.B. 195.

more than is necessary. Where journalistic disclosure is involved[216] the journalist should be given sufficient latitude to allow disclosure necessary to add credibility to a legitimate story.[217] In a case not involving private information, where the defendant raised press freedom of speech, *Barclays Bank Plc v Guardian News and Media Ltd*,[218] Blake J considered the application of s.12(4) of the Human Rights Act 1998. He noted that though on the facts the defendant could use the contents of and selectively quote from the claimants' confidential documents to stimulate public debate, that did not necessarily give them complete freedom to publish in full that confidential information. Where the claimant alleges a misuse of private information the matter becomes more complex.[219]

26-30 **Use and disclosure for other public purposes** There are several cases in which the courts have permitted a public body to assist another regulatory body to perform public functions by passing certain confidential information to appropriate recipients.[220] In *Hellewell v Chief Constable of Derbyshire*[221] the police were held to be entitled to make reasonable use of a photograph, taken under compulsion, for the purposes of the prevention and detection of crime, the investigation of alleged offences and the apprehension of suspects or persons unlawfully at large. And in *Woolgar v Chief Constable of the Sussex Police*[222] the police were held entitled to disclose contents of a police interview of a nurse to the professional nursing body. The doctrine is limited: for example, the police are not entitled to disclose seized documents to a third party for use in civil litigation.[223]

---

[216] s.12(4) where the proceedings "relate to material which the respondent claims, or which appears to the court, to be journalistic, literary or artistic material (or to conduct connected with such material)", the court must also have particular regard to "(a) the extent to which (i) the material has, or is about to become, available to the public; or (ii) it is, or would be, in the public interest for the material to be published; (b) any relevant privacy code". Stewart J in *AMM v News Group Newspapers* [2014] EWHC 4063 (QB) noted that the relevant privacy code referred to in s.12(4)(b) was the IPSO Editors Code of Practice. Note that IPSO is not recognised under the Royal Charter: to date only IMPRESS is an approved regulator.

[217] See *Campbell v MGN Ltd* [2004] UKHL 22; [2004] 2 A.C. 457 (Lord Hope cites *Jersild v Denmark* (1994) 19 E.H.R.R. 1 at [31]: freedom of the press to exercise its own judgment in the presentation of journalistic material). In *Heythrop Zoological Gardens Ltd v Captive Animals Protection Society* [2016] EWHC 1370 (IPEC); [2017] F.S.R. 10 at [60] Birss J noted that "today campaigning organisations carry out an important journalistic function".

[218] [2009] EWHC 591 (QB) at [27]–[32]. See also *BBC v HarperCollins Publishers Ltd* [2010] EWHC 2424 (Ch); [2011] E.M.L.R. 6, with reference to s.12(3).

[219] See para.26-49.

[220] See also *R. v Chief Constable of the North Wales Police Ex p. AB* [1999] Q.B. 396 DC and CA (police held entitled to provide information to local site owner concerning persons with criminal record of paedophilia if there was a "pressing need" and, if possible, after providing opportunity to comment on proposed disclosure). The European Court of Human Rights has held that it is not a breach of the Convention right to respect for private life for medical records to be disclosed to a social security office for assessment of a compensation claim: *MS v Sweden* (1997) 3 B.H.R.C. 248, noting that there were "relevant and sufficient reasons for the communication ... and the measure was not disproportionate to the aim pursued". As to the position of information imparted during the course of family proceedings in chambers see *S v S (Judgment in Chambers: Disclosure)* [1997] 1 W.L.R. 1621.

[221] [1995] 1 W.L.R. 804.

[222] [2000] 1 W.L.R. 25 CA.

[223] *Marcel v Commissioner of Police of the Metropolis* [1992] Ch. 225 (information obtained by the police under Police and Criminal Evidence Act 1984 disclosed to third party who was bringing a civil claim). *R. (on application of Ingenious Media Holdings plc) v Revenue and Customs Commissioners* [2016] UKSC 54; [2016] 1 W.L.R. 4164: Lord Toulson summarised the "Marcel principle"

Use of confidential product approval data There is, in general, a public interest in freeing the use of confidential information submitted in the course of a statutory regulatory process for making medicines available to the public In *R. v Licensing Authority Ex p. Smith Kline & French Laboratories* the licensing authority was entitled to use the confidential information provided by SKF to assess applications by generic producers but this does not apply to data submitted pursuant to a voluntary industry scheme.[224] **26-31**

Public Interest Disclosure Act 1998 This Act amends the Employment Rights Act 1996 and protects workers who disclose certain kinds of information from suffering detriment,[225] including dismissal. The Act protects workers in respect of "qualifying disclosures"[226] to certain specified persons or institutions, including the employer where the disclosure is reasonably believed by the worker to be in the public interest.[227] There are special provisions for disclosures of "exceptionally serious failure".[228] Qualifying disclosures are disclosures which in the reasonable belief of the worker making the disclosure tend to show, for example, that a criminal offence has been committed, that legal obligations are not being complied with, that a miscarriage of justice has occurred or that health, safety or the environment are endangered. **26-32**

(e) Remedies[229]

Injunction Injunctions are usually sought and are regularly granted but may be limited in duration where the basis of relief lies in the "springboard doctrine".[230] An **26-33**

at [17]. In *Mitchell v News Group Newspapers Ltd* [2014] EWHC 879 (QB) at [16]–[18] Tugendhat J discussed the competing public interests in cases where a civil party sought to make use of statements made to the police in the course of a criminal investigation (see also his discussion of *Frankson v Home Office* [2003] EWCA Civ 655; [2003] 1 W.L.R. 1952). Note in *Hoechst UK Ltd v Chemiculture Ltd* [1993] F.S.R. 270 the broad statutory purposes meant that there was no impropriety in disclosure by a public authority to a person for whom, given the purposes of the statute, the information was of mutual interest and concern). For more detailed consideration see Gurry, *Breach of Confidence*, 2nd edn (2012), Ch.13. Where personal information is involved note the application of Human Rights Act 1998 and Data Protection Act 2018.

224 *R. v Licensing Authority Ex p. Smith Kline & French Laboratories* [1990] 1 A.C. 64 ("right and duty of licensing authority to make use of all the information supplied ... in considering whether to grant or reject any other application"); cf. use of such information submitted under non-statutory scheme: *R. v MAFF Ex p. Portman Agrochemicals Ltd* [1994] 3 C.M.L.R. 18 at [39], Brooke J. A number of EU Directives provide limitations on the use that regulatory authorities may make of confidential data in granting product approval to competitor's products.

225 By s.47B of the Employment Rights Act 1996. This section does not apply where the worker is an employee and the detriment amounts to a dismissal: s.47B(2)—this is governed by s.103A of the Employment Rights Act 1996.

226 Employment Rights Act 1996 s.43B.

227 Employment Rights Act 1996 s.43C–43G. The Enterprise and Regulatory Reform Act 2013 ss.17 to 20, made changes to these provisions, in particular amending s.43B by inserting the need for a reasonable belief that the disclosure is in the public interest.

228 Employment Rights Act 1996 s.43H.

229 It is unclear whether the Enforcement Directive 2004/48 (see Intellectual Property (Enforcement etc) Regulations 2006 (SI 2006/1028)) which concerns the enforcement of "intellectual property rights" (art.1) applies to a breach of confidence claim. Lewison LJ in *Force India Formula One Team Ltd v 1 Malaysia Racing Team Sdn Bhd* [2013] EWCA Civ 780; [2013] R.P.C. 36 at [108] was sceptical that it applied (it had been accepted by the parties in *Vestergaard Frandsen A/S v BestNet Europe Ltd* [2011] EWCA Civ 424 at [56] that the Directive applied to a claim for misuse of trade secrets).

injunction may be qualified so as to permit disclosure of the information to proper authorities to receive it in the public interest[231] and may be refused altogether when the court takes the view that damages are the only appropriate remedy.[232] Where art.10, freedom of expression, is not involved, interim injunctions are generally granted on the usual principles[233] but may be refused where, for example, the result would be to stop a plant from working entirely.[234] Section 12 of the Human Rights Act 1998 makes special provision where the court is considering relief which, if granted, might affect the exercise of the Convention right to freedom of expression. Where interim injunctions are sought, s.12(3) imposes a threshold test which has to be satisfied before a court may grant interim relief: publication before trial is not to be restrained unless the court is satisfied that the applicant is *likely to establish* that publication should not be allowed. The House of Lords in *Cream Holdings Ltd v Banerjee*[235] considered the meaning and application of the word "likely" in this provision. "Likely" was held to be a varying standard, dependent on the circumstances of the case. As the principal purpose of s.12(3) of the Human Rights Act 1998 was the protection of free speech at the interim stage the general approach was that the applicant should satisfy the court that it was more likely than not that he would succeed at trail (i.e. a higher level than the *American Cyanamid* one). However, the court might apply a lower standard "where the circumstances so required". Instances of such circumstances included potential grave effects of disclosure or where the court required a short-lived injunction to give a proper consideration to the application for the interim injunction. Declaratory relief may be available on the usual principles.[236] An injunction will be refused if it is futile because (say) the relevant material is in the public domain already and no further damage will be done.[237] In *Northern Rock Plc v Financial Times Ltd*[238] the defendant had posted the entire contents of ten pages of the claimants' confidential and commercially sensitive memorandum on its website. Information derived from this was included in various media reports of the commercial difficulties experienced by the claimant. The court refused an injunction to restrain republication of the extracts that had already appeared as this would be futile but granted an interim injunction to restrain publication of the information—"extensive word for word

As to the burden of proof: as in copyright claims, the evidential burden may pass to the defendant where similarities and an opportunity to copy existed: *Wade v British Sky Broadcasting Ltd* [2016] EWCA Civ 1214.

230 *Roger Bullivant Ltd v Ellis* [1987] I.C.R. 464. (See para.26-35).

231 *Initial Services v Putterill* [1968] 1 Q.B. 396; *A Company's Application, Re* [1989] Ch. 477.

232 For circumstances in which an injunction will be granted or refused and the acts that the injunction will be tailored to prohibit, see *Ocular Sciences Ltd v Aspect Vision Care Ltd* [1997] R.P.C. 289 at [395]–[416]. See also *Saltman Engineering Co Ltd v Campbell Engineering Co Ltd* (1948) 65 R.P.C. 203; *Seager v Copydex (No.2)* [1969] 1 W.L.R. 809 (public and private information combined); *Potters-Ballotini Ltd v Weston-Baker* [1977] R.P.C. 202.

233 *American Cyanamid v Ethicon* [1975] A.C. 396. In appropriate cases, they will be granted to restrain a defendant from fulfilling orders already made: *PSM International Ltd v Whitehouse* [1992] F.S.R. 489. In exceptional cases, where the claimant lacks means, the court may relax the requirement to provide a cross-undertaking: *Bunn v BBC* [1998] 3 All E.R. 552 at [558].

234 *Potter-Ballotini Ltd v Weston-Baker* [1977] R.P.C. 202. In restraint of trade cases *American Cyanamid* may not be applied if not appropriate on the facts, see *Lansing Linde Ltd v Kerr* [1991] 1 W.L.R. 251 CA.

235 [2004] UKHL 44; [2005] 1 A.C. 253. And see *Heythrop Zoological Gardens Ltd v Captive Animals Protection Society* [2016] EWHC 1370 (IPEC); [2017] F.S.R. 10, Birss J.

236 But is rarely sought or granted, see *Seager v Copydex (No.2)* [1969] 1 W.L.R. 809.

237 *Att Gen v Guardian Newspapers (No.2)* [1990] 1 A.C. 109.

238 [2007] EWHC 2677 (QB), per Tugendhat J.

copying"—that had only appeared on the website, further publication of which might cause further harm (the website attracting only a limited readership). Relief may be refused when a claimant has not come to the court with "clean hands".[239]

Damages or account of profits[240] The purpose of damages in a confidential information case is to put the claimant in the position he would have been in if the defendant had not wrongly obtained and used the claimant's confidential information.[241] Awards of damages are often calculated on the basis of the capitalisation of an appropriate royalty for the use of the information or a willing buyer/willing seller basis, or, if the information would have been available from an appropriate consultant, what such a consultant would charge for it, but each case will have to be considered on its facts.[242] The court can award damages on the basis of the claimant's loss of manufacturing profit where such loss is proved.[243] The court may award damages even where an injunction is inappropriate because the information has been disclosed through the defendant's wrongful act.[244] The Court of Appeal in *Vestergaard Frandsen A/S (now called MVF 3 APS) v Bestnet Europe Ltd* considered the approach to damages in respect of derived products which do not themselves constitute a misuse of confidential information. Floyd LJ noted "... one must seek to determine ... what recoverable harm can be traced back to the initial 26-34

239 *Hubbard v Vosper* [1972] 2 Q.B. 84. For discussion of confidence actions brought to circumvent *Bonnard v Perryman* where the real purpose was to protect business reputation see *Tillery Valley Foods v Channel 4 Television* [2004] EWHC 1075 (Ch), Mann J (at [21]); *Viagogo v Myles* [2012] EWHC 433 (Ch), Hildyard J at [80]–[81].

240 Sales J applied *Wrotham Park* damages rules to a contractual breach of confidence case in *Vercoe v Rutland Fund Management Ltd* [2010] EWHC 424 (Ch). Note Lord Reed in *Morris-Garner v One Step (Support) Ltd* [2018] UKSC 20; [2019] A.C. 649 preferred the expression "negotiating damages" to the term "*Wrotham Park* damages" and at [84] commented on *Vercoe*: "in effect the court awarded damages based on the commercial value of the information which the defendants misused". In the absence of a contractual obligation, there is uncertainty as to the theoretical basis of an award of damages. See Gurry, *Breach of Confidence*, 2nd edn (2012), Ch.19.

241 *Dowson & Mason Ltd v Potter* [1986] 1 W.L.R. 1419. And see *Vestergaard Frandsen A/S (now called MVF 3 Aps) v Bestnet Europe Ltd* [2016] EWCA Civ 541; [2017] F.S.R. 5 at [79]–[84]. There is no English decision whether exemplary damages are available though note Lindsay J in *Douglas v Hello! Ltd (No.3)* [2003] EWHC 786 (Ch); [2003] 3 All E.R. 996 at [273]: "I am content to assume, without deciding, that exemplary damages re available in respect of breach of confidence." And note the Australian decision *Harris v Digital Pulse Pty* [2003] NSWCA 10; (2003) 56 N.S.W.L.R. 298; (2003) 197 A.L.R. 626. On exemplary damages and publishers of news-related material see discussion of ss.34–38 of the Crime and Courts Act 2013 (see para.26-60). Relevant claims include claims for breach of confidence; misuse of private information. Aggravated damages are dealt with in s.39.

242 *Seager v Copydex (No.2)* [1969] 1 W.L.R. 809 at 813 (Lord Denning MR); *Gorne v Scales* [2006] EWCA Civ 311 at [74], the market value of the information on a willing seller/buyer basis; *Force India Formula One Team Ltd v 1 Malaysia Racing Team Sdn Bhd* [2013] EWCA Civ 780; [2013] R.P.C. 36 at [103] Lewison LJ, consultant's fee measure of damages where "that is an alternative means of obtaining an equivalent benefit from an alternative source"; *Talbot v General Television Corp Pty* [1981] R.P.C. 1 (Supreme Court of Victoria) (diminished value of television concept in claimant's hands after the breach of confidence had occurred). In *Cadbury Schweppes Inc v FBI Foods Ltd* [2000] F.S.R. 491 the Supreme Court of Canada awarded loss of profits, the assessment of which was tailored to give a broadly equitable result, without mathematical exactitude.

243 *Dowson & Mason Ltd v Potter* [1986] 1 W.L.R. 1419 (employer's loss of profit); *Vercoe v Rutland Fund Management Ltd* [2010] EWHC 424 (Ch) Sales J at [344]; *Vestergaard Frandsen A/S (now called MVF 3 Aps) v Bestnet Europe Ltd* [2016] EWCA Civ 541; [2017] F.S.R. 5 [66]–[67], Floyd LJ.

244 *Creation Records v News Group Newspapers Ltd* [1997] E.M.L.R. 444.

wrongful use of the confidential information in order to develop the product".[245] Damages are normally assessed in an inquiry as to damages although the court has jurisdiction to refuse an inquiry where either that would be fruitless (*McDonald's Hamburgers Ltd v Burgerking (UK) Ltd*)[246] or the defendant acted innocently (*Valeo Vision SA v Flexible Lamps*).[247] In the alternative, the court may order an account of profits.[248] In exceptional cases, in which the defendant has promised not to disclose information but does so to his profit, it may be possible to obtain restitutionary damages for breach of an agreement to keep the confidence.[249] Where valuable property was acquired as a result of the misuse of confidential information, the Canadian court imposed a constructive trust in *Lac Minerals Ltd v International Corona Resources Ltd*.[250]

26-35 **The "springboard doctrine"** Very often, part of the confidential information is in the public domain and part is not[251]; or the complete package of confidential information, as such, is not in the public domain but could be arrived at by diligent enquiry or routine research.[252] Where the owner of the confidential information has himself made it public, for instance by publishing it in a patent specification, no difficulty arises: relief will be refused.[253] But where a material amount of work would have to be done to arrive at it, the position is different.[254] It is here that the springboard doctrine arises. The courts will not permit someone who has come into possession of such information to take a short cut and make use of it in order to steal a march on his competitors or to compete with the person from whom he obtained

245 [2016] EWCA Civ 541; [2017] F.S.R. 5 at [87]. And see [86]: "it is a matter of degree whether the extent and importance of the use of the confidential information is such that continued exploitation of the derived matter should be viewed as continued use of the information". On the facts, an award based on quasi-consultancy fees was upheld and there was no "accelerated entry". See also the earlier striking out application in this case, *Vestergaard Frandsen A/S v Bestnet Europe Ltd* [2013] EWCA Civ 428 at [21]–[23] for the discussion on the difference between lost profits/royalty/market value awards. On the concept of a derived product see Laddie J in *Ocular Sciences Ltd v Aspect Vision Care Ltd (No.2)* [1997] R.P.C. 289 at 396.

246 [1987] F.S.R. 112.

247 [1995] R.P.C. 205.

248 In *Marathon Asset Management LLP v Seddon* [2017] EWHC 300 (Comm); [2017] I.C.R. 791 Leggatt J discussed the difference between licence fee damages and an account of profits (see [223]–[239]).

249 *Att Gen v Blake* [1998] Ch. 439. See Birks, "The Remedies for Abuse of Confidential Information" [1990] L.M.C.L.Q. 460.

250 [1990] F.S.R. 441 Sup. Ct of Canada; considered in *Ocular Sciences v Aspect Vision Care* [1997] R.P.C. 289 (Laddie J, not "an easy topic", at [412]). In *Lac Minerals* the misuse was central to the acquisition of the property. However in *United Pan Europe Communications NV v Deutsche Bank AG* [2000] 2 B.C.L.C. 461 Morritt LJ noted that the mere relevance of the misuse might be sufficient (for more detailed consideration see Gurry, *Breach of Confidence*, 2nd edn (2012) 20.20). There is some authority for the proposition that, in special circumstances, all the defendant's fruits of a breach of confidence belong in equity to the claimant: *Att Gen v Guardian Newspapers Ltd (No.2)* [1990] 1 A.C. 109. The principle must be applied with care: *Ocular Sciences v Aspect Vision Care*, above.

251 See, e.g. *Seager v Copydex* [1967] 1 W.L.R. 923; *House of Spring Gardens Ltd v Point Blank Ltd* [1985] F.S.R. 327 (Ir.).

252 *Terrapin Ltd v Builders Supply Co (Hayes) Ltd* [1967] R.P.C. 375.

253 *Mustad v Dosen* [1964] 1 W.L.R. 109 (Note); [1963] R.P.C. 41; *Franchi v Franchi* [1967] R.P.C. 149.

254 *Cranleigh Precision Engineering Ltd v Bryant* [1965] 1 W.L.R. 1293; [1966] R.P.C. 81 at [87]; cf. *Mustad v Dosen* [1964] 1 W.L.R. 109 (Note); *Speed Seal Products Ltd v Paddington* [1985] 1 W.L.R. 1327.

it in confidence.[255] Thus, one who has obtained possession of such a package will not be permitted to make use of it unless he obtains it independently from a legitimate source.[256] But such a disability will not be continued indefinitely; an injunction will only be granted over the period during which the unfair advantage continues.[257] However, though this is a legally difficult area,[258] the springboard doctrine does not as such extend the duty of confidence even after the information has entered the public domain: once the information ceases to be confidential Lord Goff contended "the subject matter is gone: the obligation is therefore also gone".[259] And that will be so if the information becomes public knowledge not only by the confider's act but also that of a third party and, indeed, arguably even where the confidentiality is destroyed by the act of the confidant. Laddie J in *Ocular Sciences Ltd v Aspect Vision Care Ltd* was "attracted" by Lord Goff's analysis. He noted "if a continuing activity of the defendant does not constitute a breach of confidence then it ought not to be injuncted even if it produces an unfair benefit to the defendant", though the defendant would still be liable in damages and an account of profits could include profits accruing to him from any subsequent exploitation of the information.[260] However, it may be that in the circumstances the information at issue retains a limited degree of confidentiality even after some disclosure, in which case an injunction may be granted but only for a limited time.[261]

Delivery up or destruction upon oath An order to effect delivery up of infringing items or their modification so as not to infringe is used in patent actions and is equally appropriate in actions based on breach of confidence. The return of 26-36

---

[255] *Terrapin Ltd v Builders Supply Co (Hayes) Ltd* [1967] R.P.C. 375; *Cranleigh Precision Engineering Ltd v Bryant* [1965] 1 W.L.R. 1293. In *QBE Management Services (UK) Ltd v Dymoke* [2012] EWHC 80 (QB); [2012] I.R.L.R. 458 at [8] Haddon-Cave J provides a summary of principles governing the grant of springboard relief. And see *Force India Formula One Team Ltd v 1 Malaysia Racing Team Sdn Bhd* [2013] EWCA Civ 780; [2013] R.P.C. 36 at [72]–[76].

[256] *Lamb v Evans* [1893] 1 Ch. 218. Or works it out again from scratch: *Northern Office Micro Computers (Pty) v Rosenstein* [1982] F.S.R. 124 Sup. Ct of SA.

[257] *Peter Pan Manufacturing Co v Corsets Silhouette Ltd* [1964] 1 W.L.R. 96; *Potters-Ballotini v Weston-Baker* [1977] R.P.C. 202; *Roger Bullivant Ltd v Ellis* [1987] I.C.R. 464. Simler J in *Devere Holding Co Ltd v Belgravia Wealth Management Europe Kft* [2014] EWHC 3189 (QB) at [39]: "the claimants must show that the defendants have gained an unfair competitive advantage over the claimants and that that advantage still exists and will continue to have that effect unless the relief sought is granted". The court should be concerned that it does not, in granting an injunction, give the injured party more protection than he realistically needs, and in particular, discourage or prohibit what in the course of time becomes quite legitimate competition.

[258] The Court of Appeal in *EPI Environmental Technologies Inc v Symphony Plastic Technologies Plc* [2006] EWCA Civ 3; [2006] 1 W.L.R. 495 at [73].

[259] Lord Goff in *AG v Guardian Newspapers (No.2)* [1990] 1 A.C. 190 at 287. He commented that the reasoning contra in *Speed Seal Products Ltd v Paddington* [1985] 1 W.L.R. 1327 "cannot to my mind be supported".

[260] [1997] R.P.C. 289 at 401. And in *Vestergaard Frandsen A/S v BestNet Europe Ltd* [2009] EWHC 1456 (Ch); [2010] F.S.R. 2, Arnold J at [42]–[96] reviewing the authorities noted that no injunction should be granted to restrain continued misuse of confidential information once the information had ceased to be confidential, whether the information had been published by the confidant, a stranger or the confider himself.

[261] As the law stands, it is not clear whether an injunction can be granted to prevent a defendant from benefiting from a past misuse of confidential information. In *BBC v HarperCollins Publishers Ltd* [2010] EWHC 2424 (Ch); [2011] E.M.L.R. 6 at [60] Morgan J held that an injunction was not to be awarded to punish the defendant or deprive him of a benefit, as opposed to protecting the claimant against further harm, unlawfully caused, and *Schering Chemicals Ltd v Falkman Ltd* [1982] Q.B. 1 was not to be relied upon as establishing that a court can award an injunction even after the material in question is no longer confidential.

confidential documents presents no difficulties,[262] but the courts are understandably reluctant to order the destruction of machinery, and the usual order is for modification to take out that part which makes use of information obtained in breach of confidence.[263] An order may, however, be made for the delivery up of offending goods.[264]

3. THE ACTION FOR MISUSE OF PRIVATE INFORMATION/PRIVACY

26-37 **The action for misuse of private information acknowledged** In recent years the action for breach of confidence has been developed to protect privacy interests.[265] This has been influenced by the incorporation of the ECHR by the Human Rights Act 1998 and, in particular, the Convention right to respect for private life, contained in art.8. This provides:

> "(1) Everyone has the right to respect for his private and family life, his home and his correspondence.
>
> (2) There shall be no interference by a public authority with the exercise of this right except such as is in accordance with the law and is necessary in a democratic society in the interests of national security, public safety or the economic well-being of the country, for the prevention of disorder or crime, for the protection of health or morals, or for the protection of the rights or freedoms of others."[266]

An important landmark in this process is the House of Lords' decision in *Campbell v MGN Ltd*.[267] Here Lord Hoffmann noted that "English law has adapted the action for breach of confidence to provide a remedy for the unauthorised disclosure of personal information ... this development has been mediated by the analogy of the right to disentitle them to a reasonable expectation of privacy article 8 of the European Convention on Human Rights".[268] In that case the defendant newspaper published the fact of the claimant's drug addiction and treatment. It also published details of that treatment, together with a covertly taken photograph of the claimant attending for treatment. The claimant, a celebrity model, accepted that as she had lied about her addiction, the truth about her addiction and the fact of seeking treatment was not protected. The majority of the House of Lords (Baroness Hale, Lords Hope and Carswell) however held that the *details* of the treatment and the accompanying photograph linked to the treatment went too far. This was private information, over and above setting the record straight, the disclosure of which was

---

[262] *Alperton Rubber Co v Manning* (1917) 86 L.J. Ch. 377; *Saltman Engineering Co Ltd v Campbell Engineering Co Ltd* (1948) 65 R.P.C. 203.

[263] *Saltman Engineering Co Ltd v Campbell Engineering Co Ltd* (1948) 65 R.P.C. 203; *Ocular Sciences Ltd v Aspect Vision Care Ltd* [1997] R.P.C. 289.

[264] *Reid and Sigrist Ltd v Moss* (1932) 49 R.P.C. 461; *Peter Pan Manufacturing Corp v Corsets Silhouette Ltd* [1964] 1 W.L.R. 96.

[265] See for example, Sedley LJ in *Douglas v Hello! Ltd* [2001] Q.B. 967 at 1002: "the law has to protect not only those people whose trust has been abused but those who simply find themselves subjected to an unwanted intrusion into their personal lives." There is a statutory right to privacy in photographs taken for private or domestic purposes: s.85 of the Copyright, Designs and Patents Act 1988.

[266] The notion of necessity implies that an interference corresponds to a pressing social need and that it is proportionate to the legitimate aim pursued: *Olsson v Sweden* (1988) 11 E.H.R.R. 259. Article 10, freedom of expression, may also afford privacy protection as certain kinds of surveillance may interfere with rights of freedom of expression under art.10: see *Halford v UK* (1997) 24 E.H.R.R. 523; [1997] I.R.L.R. 471, where the point was argued but not decided in the light of the finding of a violation of art.8.

[267] [2004] UKHL 22; [2004] 2 A.C. 457.

[268] [2004] UKHL 22; [2004] 2 A.C. 457 at [118].

distressing and put the treatment at risk. On the facts the claimant's art.8 right outweighed the defendant newspaper's right to freedom of expression, under art.10 of the ECHR. The House of Lords acknowledged that art.8 of the ECHR has reshaped the action for breach of confidence so that it now protects against the "misuse of private information".[269] In *Secretary of State for the Home Department v TLU*[270] Gross LJ referred to "evolving legal policy in this area" citing *R. (on the application of Catt) v Association of Chief Police Officers*[271] and Lord Sumption JSC's "illuminating thumbnail sketch of the development of the Law's protection of privacy". In the case itself there had been an accidental publication on the government website of the personal data of a failed asylum seeker: liability for misuse of private information also extended to unnamed family members, given that their identity and location could be inferred.

Potential scope of the action In *Campbell v MGN Ltd*[272] the House of Lords did not find there to be a new privacy right, reflecting the earlier views expressed in the House of Lords' decision in *Secretary of State for the Home Department v Wainwright*.[273] Buxton LJ in *McKennitt v Ash* accepted that there is no tort of privacy, so that a right to protect private information had to be "shoehorned" into the action for breach of confidence.[274] However, it has been acknowledged that the action is not limited to informational privacy. In *Campbell* Lord Nicholls himself noted that privacy can be invaded in other ways,[275] and acknowledged that the protection of "various aspects of privacy" is "a fast developing area of the law", while Lord Phillips MR in *Douglas v Hello! Ltd (No.3)*[276] noted the obligation on Member States to protect individuals from intrusion into their private domain. In *PJS v News Group Newspapers Ltd*[277] Lords Mance and Neuberger acknowledged that an art.8 claim could protect beyond secrecy or information, highlighting the protection from intrusion that can be involved in privacy claims. Moreover, the jurisprudence of the European Court of Human Rights reveals that the protection **26-38**

[269] Lord Nicholls at [14]: "information about an individual's private life would not, in ordinary usage, be called 'confidential'. The more natural description today is that such information is private. The essence of the tort is better encapsulated now as misuse of private information." As to what constitutes "misuse" see Lord Neuberger in *Tchenguiz v Imerman* [2010] EWCA Civ 908; [2011] Fam. 116 at [69].

[270] [2018] EWCA Civ 2217; [2018] 4 W.L.R. 101 at [29].

[271] [2015] UKSC 9; [2015] A.C. 1065.

[272] [2004] UKHL 22; [2004] 2 A.C. 457 at [11]; and see Baroness Hale at [133].

[273] [2003] UKHL 53; [2004] 2 A.C. 406 at [28]–[35]. And see *Fearn v Board of Trustees of the Tate Gallery* [2020] EWCA Civ 104; [2020] 2 W.L.R. 1081 at [33]: no common law tort of invasion of privacy.

[274] [2006] EWCA Civ 1714; [2008] Q.B. 73 at [53]. It should be noted, however, that in *PJS v News Group Newspapers Ltd* [2016] UKSC 26; [2016] A.C. 1081 at [25], [32] Lord Mance referred to the tort of "invasion of privacy".

[275] e.g. strip searches [2004] UKHL 22; [2004] 2 A.C. 457 at [15] but concluded "the extent to which the common law … protects other forms of invasion of privacy is not a matter arising in this present case".

[276] [2005] EWCA Civ 595; [2006] Q.B. 125 at [47]–[54].

[277] [2016] UKSC 26; [2016] A.C. 1081, Lord Mance [25]–[32]; Lord Neuberger [58]–[62]. He supported two core elements at [58], "unwanted access to private information and unwanted access to … one's personal space". The views of Eady J and Tugendhat J in *CTB v News Group Newspapers Ltd* at [2011] EWHC 1326 and [2011] EWHC 1334 respectively were approved. See also the views of Tugendhat J in *Goodwin v News Group Newspapers Ltd* [2011] EWHC 1437 (QB); [2011] E.M.L.R. 27; and Laws LJ in *R. (Wood) v Commissioner of Police of the Metropolis* [2009] EWCA Civ 414; [2010] 1 W.L.R. 123 at [20]–[22]. See P. Wragg, "Recognising a privacy-invasion tort: the conceptual unity of informational and intrusion claims" (2019) 78 C.L.J. 409.

provided by art.8 is wider than simply protecting against the misuse of private information. It should also be noted that private life for the purposes of art.8 does not necessarily exclude business or professional activities.[278]

26-39 **European Court of Human Rights jurisprudence and the developing action** Whether the common law has developed an adequate response to the requirements of art.8 depends on the interpretation of the jurisprudence of the European Court of Human Rights.[279] Indeed, the European Court of Human Rights' decision in *Wainwright v United Kingdom*[280] was that strip searches of prison visitors which failed to strictly comply with safeguards to protect the dignity of those searched were in breach of art.8 of the ECHR. And, given the decision of the House of Lords, the lack of redress in the national courts meant there had also been a violation of art.13. Again in *Von Hannover v Germany*[281] the European Court of Human Rights, with its acknowledgment that art.8 protection of private life extends to aspects relating to personal identity such as a person's name[282] or picture and includes a person's "physical and psychological integrity", arguably took a wider interpretation of private life than that taken by the House of Lords in *Campbell*. In *Von Hannover* photographs of Princess Caroline of Monaco going about her daily life in public places[283] was protected by art.8. The court held there was a "zone of interaction of a person with others even if in a public context, which may fall into the scope of private life".[284] There was held to be no legitimate interest in the details of her private life, the published articles and photographs making no contribution to a debate of public interest.[285] In *McKennitt v Ash* Buxton LJ queried whether the House of Lords in *Campbell v MGN* would have found for Von Hannover at the time of the judgment in *Campbell*.[286] It is clear, therefore, that there will be pressure on the common law to extend the range of this action in order to encompass wider privacy concerns. In *Mosley v United Kingdom* the European Court of Human Rights rejected the claim that the UK Government were obliged to introduce

---

278 See *Niemietz v Germany* (1993) 16 E.H.R.R. 97 at [29]–[31] and the discussion by Nicol J in *Axon v Ministry of Defence* [2016] EWHC 787 (QB); [2016] E.M.L.R. 20 at [41]–[49].

279 In the event of a conflict however between a decision of the House of Lords and a later decision of the European Court of Human Rights, lower courts must follow the former: *Kay v Lambeth LBC* [2006] UKHL 10; [2006] 2 A.C. 465.

280 (2007) 44 E.H.R.R. 40.

281 (2005) 40 E.H.R.R. 1; [2004] E.M.L.R. 21.

282 *Burghartz v Switzerland* (1994) 18 E.H.R.R. 101.

283 These "scenes from her daily life" included practising sport, leaving her Paris home and being on holiday. The German courts had held that these places were not sufficiently secluded.

284 (2005) 40 E.H.R.R. 1; [2004] E.M.L.R. 21 at [50] and [61], "activities of a purely private nature". And see *PG and JH v UK* App No.44787/98, 25 September 2001. In *Sciacca v Italy* (2006) 43 E.H.R.R. 20 there was held to be a violation of art.8 where police released photographs of a suspect to the press, the court noting that where a private figure was involved the zone of interaction which fell within the area of private life was enlarged. However cf. *Von Hannover v Germany (No.2)* [2012] E.M.L.R. 16 where the photographs and the articles they accompanied contributed to a public debate.

285 (2005) 40 E.H.R.R. 1; [2004] E.M.L.R. 21 at [65].

286 (2005) 40 E.H.R.R. 1; [2004] E.M.L.R. 21 at [39]. And see Sir Anthony Clarke MR in *Murray v Express Newspapers Plc* [2008] EWCA Civ 446; [2009] Ch. 481 at [60]. In *Re Att Gen's Ref (No.3 of 1999)* [2009] UKHL 34; [2010] 1 A.C. 145 at [19] Lord Phillips noted the suggestion that the European Court of Human Rights in *Von Hannover* took a wider view of what falls within an individual's private life than did the House of Lords in *Campbell*. It was not necessary to resolve this issue for the case in hand.

a pre-notification duty in privacy cases involving intimate or sexual details of private life.[287]

The correct approach As *Campbell v MGN Ltd*[288] established, where private information is concerned the modern approach of the courts is to reflect the privacy issues that may be raised, in line with art.8 of the ECHR.[289] The correct approach for the action has been consistently applied.[290] The court has first to decide two issues, which should be kept separate. First, whether the information was private, in the sense that it is protected by art.8. This means applying the objective "reasonable expectation of privacy" test (which is a question of fact).[291] If, applying this, art.8 is engaged, the court then has to consider whether there was an infringement. This will require the application of art.8(2), and when freedom of expression is involved, the court must undertake "the balancing exercise" to decide whether "in all the circumstances must the interests of the owner of the private information yield to the right to freedom of expression conferred on the publisher by Art.10".[292] The approach of the court for this exercise was highlighted by Lord Steyn in *Re S (A Child) (Identification: Restrictions on Publication)*. In this balancing exercise neither Article has precedence over the other, the court has to undertake an "intense focus" on the comparative importance of the specific rights being claimed, taking into account the justifications for interfering with or restricting each right and applying the proportionality test to each.[293] Lord Dyson in *Weller v Associated* **26-40**

287 (48009/08) [2011] ECHR 774; [2012] E.M.L.R. 1.

288 [2004] UKHL 22; [2004] 2 A.C. 457. Though Lord Phillips in *Douglas v Hello! (No.3)* [2005] EWCA Civ 595; [2006] Q.B. 125 appeared to hint at an emerging publicity or image right, Lord Hoffmann was adamant that "there is no question of creating an 'image right' ": *OBG Ltd v Allan* [2007] UKHL 21; [2008] 1 A.C. 1 at [124]. Where private information is involved Sir Anthony Clarke MR in *Murray v Express Newspapers Plc* [2008] EWCA Civ 446; [2009] Ch. 481 at [54], did not accept that should the claimant ultimately succeed in his claim the courts would have created an image right as the focus of the protection was not on the taking of the photograph in the street but on its publication.

289 *McKennitt v Ash* [2006] EWCA Civ 1714; [2008] Q.B. 73 at [4]. Buxton LJ provided (at [8] onwards) a "taxonomy of the law of privacy and confidence".

290 See, e.g. Ward LJ in *ETK v News Group Newspapers Ltd* [2011] EWCA Civ 439; [2011] 1 W.L.R. 1827 at [10].

291 That the reasonable expectation test is a question of fact was confirmed by the Court of Appeal in *Murray v Express Newspapers Plc* [2008] EWCA Civ 446; [2009] Ch. 481 at [41]. *Napier v Pressdram Ltd* [2009] EWCA Civ 443; [2009] E.M.L.R. 21 at [42], affirmed that the test for privacy is objective. See the analysis by N.A. Moreham, "Unpacking the reasonable expectation of privacy test" (2018) 134 L.Q.R. 651.

292 *McKennitt v Ash* [2006] EWCA Civ 1714; [2008] Q.B. 73 at [11], per Buxton LJ: "those articles are now the very content of the domestic tort that the English court has to enforce." In *HRH Prince of Wales v Associated Newspapers Ltd* [2006] EWCA Civ 1776; [2008] Ch. 57 at [67] it was noted that "a significant element to be weighed in the balance is the importance in a democratic society of upholding duties of confidence that are created between individuals".

293 *S (A Child) (Identification: Restrictions on Publication), Re* [2004] UKHL 47; [2005] 1 A.C. 593, per Lord Steyn at [17], noting that these four propositions emerged from the House of Lords' decision in *Campbell*. That this was the correct methodology was confirmed in subsequent cases, most recently by the Supreme Court in *PJS v News Group Newspapers Ltd* [2016] UKSC 26; [2016] A.C. 1081 (see [20]; Lord Mance noting that this balancing exercise will not readily attract appellate intervention). In *Murray v Express Newspapers Plc* [2008] EWCA Civ 446; [2009] Ch. 481, Sir Anthony Clarke MR reviewed the relevant decisions and confirmed the two-stage process; consideration of whether the publication was "highly offensive" may or may not be relevant to the consideration of the balance to be struck between arts 8 and 10.

Newspapers Ltd[294] stressed the difficulty any appellant would have in overturning the trial judge's decision whether a reasonable expectation of privacy was established and in overturning the trial judge's decision subsequent to the balancing process. Where an infringement of the Convention right to respect for private life is committed by a public authority, a claim may arise under s.7 of the Human Rights Act 1998 which provides for a claim by a victim of the unlawful act against a public authority if it acts in a way incompatible with a Convention right.[295] The nature of the direct claim brought against a public authority under s.7 of the Human Rights Act 1998 was discussed in *H v Tomlinson*.[296]

26-41 **The relationship between privacy and defamation claims** It is clear that the action for misuse of private information/privacy can also apply in "false privacy" cases—where the defendant seeks to publish false information concerning the claimant. Longmore LJ noted in *McKennitt v Ash* "the question in a case of misuse of private information is whether information is private, not whether it is true or false".[297] In *LNS v Persons Unknown* Tugendhat J stated that the relationship between defamation and the new cause of action for misuse of private information "was not yet clear" and considered the "limited classes of cases" where the law of privacy gives rise to an overlap with the law of defamation.[298] In *Hannon v News Group Newspapers Ltd* any claim in defamation was statute barred and the claimant sought to rely on breach of confidence and privacy. The defendant claimed that reputation could only be protected by a claim in defamation. On the point of principle Mann J was not satisfied that "it is necessary or appropriate, or even in some cases practically possible, to draw a hard line between the element of privacy or confidence claims which go into what might be called the realms of reputation and other elements".[299]

---

294 [2015] EWCA Civ 1176; [2016] 1 W.L.R. 1541 at [57].

295 Article 8 of the Convention provides constraints on the circumstances in which the state may lawfully invade a person's privacy, for example by surveillance: see *Kopp v Switzerland* (1999) 27 E.H.R.R. 91; *Malone v United Kingdom* (1984) 7 E.H.R.R. 14. On the issue of public authority's liability under art.8 in *Wainwright* [2003] UKHL 53; [2004] 2 A.C. 406 at [51] Lord Hoffmann noted that though art.8 may justify a monetary remedy for an intentional invasion of privacy where distress is the only damage suffered, "it does not follow that a merely negligent act should, contrary to general principle, give rise to a claim for damages for distress because it affects privacy rather than some other interest like bodily safety". Note under art.8 the police had a duty to inform an individual that they had been the victim of phone hacking: *R. (on the application of Bryant) v Metropolitan Police Commissioner* [2011] EWHC 1314 (Admin); [2011] H.R.L.R. 27, Foskett J. As for the protection of employee confidentiality: in light of art.8 of the ECHR an employee of a "public authority" may have the right not to have his private communications while at work interfered with, at least not without good reason—see *Halford v United Kingdom* (1997) 24 E.H.R.R. 523; [1997] I.R.L.R. 471, European Court of Human Rights. It is also arguable that intercepting an employee's private correspondence might constitute an interference with the employee's art.10 rights of freedom of expression.

296 [2008] EWCA Civ 1258; [2009] E.L.R. 14. At [20] it was noted that there were two aspects to the claim for breach of art.8, invasion of privacy and damage to reputation.

297 [2006] EWCA Civ 1714; [2008] Q.B. 73 at [86]

298 [2010] EWHC 119 (QB); [2010] E.M.L.R. 16 at [78] and [96]. He commented that the rule in *Bonnard v Perryman* and the Human Rights Act 1998 may not always be compatible (at [81]). See the comments of Mann J in *Hannon v News Group Newspapers Ltd* [2014] EWHC 1580 (Ch); [2015] E.M.L.R. 1. at [53].

299 [2014] EWHC 1580 (Ch); [2015] E.M.L.R. 1 at [29]. On the facts, Mann J held that the confidence/privacy claims were not de minimis and the reality of the claims could not be said to be damage to reputation only (*LNS (or Terry) v Persons Unknown* [2010] EWHC 119 (QB); [2010] E.M.L.R. 16

(a) The reasonable expectation of privacy

The reasonable expectation of privacy[300] "[I]nstead of the cause of action being based on the duty of good faith applicable to confidential personal information and trade secrets alike, it focuses on the protection of human autonomy and dignity—the right to control the dissemination of information about one's private life and the right to the esteem and respect of other people".[301] Certain information is obviously private[302]: information about health[303]; personal relationships[304] and finances. Where the information does not fall within such categories of obviously private, the test suggested in *Campbell*[305] is whether "in respect of the disclosed facts the person in question had a reasonable expectation of privacy".[306] The ques- **26-42**

considered, see especially at [53]). *Hannon* was applied in *ERY v Associated Newspapers Ltd* [2016] EWHC 2760 (QB); [2017] E.M.L.R. 9, Nicol J. See also para.26-58.

300 In *R. v Broadcasting Standards Commission Ex p. BBC (Dixons)* [2001] Q.B. 885 at 900, Lord Mustill found it difficult to see that privacy could apply to an "impersonal corporate body". And see *Abbey v Gilligan* [2012] EWHC 3217 (QB); [2013] E.M.L.R. 12, Tugendhat J—where the information concerned a company and was not personal to the claimant there was no reasonable expectation of privacy—and *Viagogo Ltd v Myers* [2012] EWHC 433 (Ch), Hildyard J at [34]. In relation to unauthorised or "purloined" information, Buxton LJ noted in *McKennitt v Ash* [2006] EWCA Civ 1714; [2008] Q.B. 73 at [15] that (in line with Campbell, Douglas and the European Court of Human Rights' decision in *Von Hannover v Germany* (2005) 40 E.H.R.R. 1; [2004] E.M.L.R. 21) the primary focus is on the nature of the information "because it is the recipient's perception of its confidential nature that imposes the obligation on him". In *Tchenguiz v Imerman* [2010] EWCA Civ 908; [2011] Fam. 116 at [66] Lord Neuberger MR noted that the "reasonable expectation of privacy" test in *Campbell v MGN Ltd* [2004] UKHL 22; [2004] 2 A.C. 457 "chimes well with the test suggested in classic commercial confidence cases, by Megarry J in *Coco v AN Clark (Engineers) Ltd* [1969] R.P.C. 41 at 47". He also noted that taking steps to obtain information in which there was a reasonable expectation of privacy would amount to a breach of confidence (at [68]).

301 Lord Hoffmann in *Campbell v MGN Ltd* [2004] UKHL 22; [2004] 2 A.C. 457 at [51]. It is worth noting that the NZ Court of Appeal in *Hosking v Runting* [2004] NZCA 34; [2005] 1 N.Z.L.R. 1 (referred to by the House of Lords in *Campbell*) disliked the English approach: they preferred the development of two distinct heads of liability, the one to protect confidentiality, the other a tort of wrongful publicity given to private lives.

302 See Baroness Hale in *Campbell v MGN Ltd* [2004] UKHL 22; [2004] 2 A.C. 457 at [136], drawing on the speech of Gleeson CJ in *ABC v Lenah Game Meats Pty Ltd* (2001) 185 A.L.R. 1. And see *Tchenguiz v Imerman* [2010] EWCA Civ 908; [2011] Fam. 116 at [76] per Lord Neuberger MR.

303 e.g. details of medical condition, medical treatment or indeed non-medical therapy as in *Campbell* itself. See also *Z v Finland* (1997) 25 E.H.R.R. 371 (medical data).

304 See para.26-48 and *Dudgeon v United Kingdom* (1981) 4 E.H.R.R. 149 (information relating to sexuality). The court may have to consider the extent to which the relationship in question has been conducted in secrecy. In *Ntuli v Donald* [2010] EWCA Civ 1276; [2011] 1 W.L.R. 294 the claimant had been unable to demonstrate that the relationship had not been conducted openly. And note *Ferdinand v MGN Ltd* [2011] EWHC 2454 (QB) at [58], Nicol J.

305 [2004] UKHL 22; [2004] 2 A.C. 457. Lord Nicholls and Baroness Hale rejected the phrase "highly offensive" contained in the privacy provision of the *Restatement (Second) of Torts*, §652D (referred to in the judgment of Gleeson CJ in the High Court of Australia decision, *ABC Corp v Lenah Game Meats Pty Ltd* (2002) 185 A.L.R. 1) as this suggested a stricter test of private information; Lord Hope, however, did refer to this test where the nature of the information was unclear. Consideration of whether the publication was "highly offensive" may or may not be relevant to the consideration of the balance to be struck between arts 8 and 10 (the NZ Court of Appeal case of *Hosking v Runting* [2004] NZCA 34; [2005] 1 N.Z.L.R. 1 applied the "highly offensive" test to the first stage. And see *X v Persons Unknown* [2006] EWHC 2783 (QB); [2007] E.M.L.R. 10, per Eady J).

306 [2004] UKHL 22; [2004] 2 A.C. 457 at [21], per Lord Nicholls. Baroness Hale at [134] said that it arises where "the person publishing the information knows or ought to know that there is a reasonable expectation that the information in question will be kept confidential" (echoing Lord Woolf CJ in *A v B Plc* [2002] EWCA Civ 337; [2003] Q.B. 195 at [11](ix)). The standard to be set is based

tion is what a reasonable person of ordinary sensibilities[307] would feel if [s]he was placed in the same position as the claimant and faced with the same publicity.[308] In *Re JR38's Application for Judicial Review*, Lord Clarke noted: "the concept of reasonable expectation is a broad objective concept and the court is not concerned with the subjective expectations of the person concerned ...".[309] In *Axon v Ministry of Defence* Nicol J noted that "the notion of 'private life' is not limitless".[310] In *Richard v BBC*[311] Mann J held that a police suspect prima facie (though not invariably) has a reasonable expectation of privacy in relation to a police investigation and police search; that expectation is not lost merely because the information has reached the media.

26-43 **Factors indicating a reasonable expectation of privacy** In *Murray v Express Newspapers Plc*[312] Sir Anthony Clarke MR noted that the question of a presence of a reasonable expectation of privacy was an objective question with a need to consider all the circumstances of the case, including

> "the attributes of the claimant, the nature of the activity in which the claimant was engaged, the place at which it was happening, the nature and purpose of the intrusion, the absence of consent and whether it was known or could be inferred, the effect on the claimant and the circumstances in which and the purposes for which the information came into the hands of the publisher".[313]

---

not on the recipient of the disclosure but on the reasonable person whose private information is threatened: *Campbell v MGN Ltd* [2004] UKHL 22; [2004] 2 A.C. 457.

[307] Lord Hope [2004] UKHL 22; [2004] 2 A.C. 457 at [94]: "the law of privacy is not intended for the protection of the unduly sensitive."

[308] Lord Hope [2004] UKHL 22; [2004] 2 A.C. 457 at [99]. In *Von Hannover v Germany* (2005) 40 E.H.R.R. 1; [2004] E.M.L.R. 21 the European Court of Human Rights appeared to set a lower threshold for determining whether information was to be deemed private. There, publication of photographs of Princess Caroline of Monaco in her daily life were held to fall within the scope of her private life.

[309] [2015] UKSC 42; [2016] A.C. 1131 at [109]. The majority of the Supreme Court held that a reasonable expectation of privacy was the touchstone for an allegation of art.8 violation. However Lords Kerr and Wilson dissented, Lord Kerr supporting a "more nuanced approach", at [55]–[66]. Lord Clarke suggested, at [110], that in the light of the present state of Strasbourg jurisprudence he would not go so far as to say that it was impossible that absent a reasonable expectation of privacy there was no relevant interference with personal autonomy. In *R. (Catt) v Association of Chief Officers of Police of England, Wales and Northern Ireland* [2015] UKSC 9; [2015] A.C. 1065 at [4] Lord Sumption JSC. said the test must extend to "every occasion on which a person has a reasonable expectation that there will be no interference with the broader right of personal autonomy recognised in the case law of the Strasbourg Court".

[310] [2016] EWHC 787 (QB); [2016] E.M.L.R. 20 at [41] (reviewing the case law at [41]–[49]) and at [64] Nicol J stated: "misconduct is not just relevant to the balance of interests under Articles 8 and 10 ... but is also material as to whether the claimant has a reasonable expectation of privacy in the information about that conduct".

[311] [2018] EWHC 1837 (Ch); [2019] Ch. 169. And see *ZXC v Bloomberg LP* [2020] EWCA Civ 611: reasonable expectation of privacy in information relating to a criminal investigation into claimant's activities; *ERY v Associated Newspapers* [2016] EWHC 2760 (QB). In *NT1 v Google LLC* [2018] EWHC 799 (QB); [2019] Q.B. 344, Warby J (a case on the "right to be forgotten") it was noted that with the passage of time a conviction may become part of an individual's private life (at [48] onwards). In *Khuja v Times Newspapers Ltd* [2017] UKSC 49; [2019] A.C. 161: on the facts, no reasonable expectation of privacy in relation to proceedings in open court. *Sutherland HM Advocate for Scotland* [2020] UKSC 32: no reasonable expectation re sexually explicit communication with intended child recipient.

[312] [2008] EWCA Civ 446; [2009] Ch. 481.

[313] [2008] EWCA Civ 446; [2009] Ch. 481 at [36]. No reasonable expectation of privacy in *Mahmood*

Lord Walker in *M v Secretary of State for Work and Pensions*[314] noted that the interference with private life had to be of some seriousness before art.8 was engaged. In *HRH Prince of Wales v Associated Newspapers Ltd*,[315] the Court of Appeal held that the information in the Prince of Wales' journal divulged by one of his employees to a newspaper was obviously of a private nature, it being particularly relevant that the disclosure by the employee had been in breach of a confidential relationship.[316] Even if the information had previously been available to the public there may be a good reason, based on privacy, to prevent further publicity or dissemination.[317] As for information posted on the internet, in *CC v AB*[318] some comments on the secret adulterous relationship between the claimant and the defendant's wife had been posted on the internet by the defendant but it was held that the information had not become generally accessible. In *WXY v Gewanter*[319] Slade J commented that even where there has been publication in one forum, publication in another forum can be restrained, noting the difference between internet websites and the print media. In *Weller v Associated Newspapers Ltd*[320] the photographs, though published in England had been taken in California, where such activity was lawful. However this was not determinative of the issue whether there was a reasonable expectation of privacy. In *Ali v Channel 5 Broadcast Ltd*,[321] the defendant broadcast scenes of the claimant and his wife being evicted from their home. On the facts there was a reasonable expectation of privacy: inter alia the broadcast showed them in a state of distress and it was foreseeable that the broadcast would have an adverse effect on their children.[322] The mere fact that some of the events took place in the street did not mean there was no reasonable expectation of privacy.[323] In *Arthurs v News Group Newspapers*[324] the claimant (who was 18 at the time) had taken part in a television talent show. The defendant newspaper disclosed that his father was a convicted IRA terrorist. It was held that there was no reasonable expectation of privacy: he had voluntarily put himself in the public eye and the father's convictions were in the public domain.

---

v Galloway [2006] EWHC 1286 (QB); [2006] E.M.L.R. 26. *Murray* was considered in *Weller v Associated Newspapers Ltd* [2014] EWHC 1163 (QB); [2014] E.M.L.R. 24.

314 [2006] UKHL 11; [2006] 2 A.C. 91 at [83].

315 [2006] EWCA Civ 1776; [2008] Ch. 57.

316 [2006] EWCA Civ 1776; [2008] Ch. 57 at [69]: "the nature of the relationship that gives rise to the duty of confidence may be important." And see *McKennitt v Ash* [2006] EWCA Civ 1714; [2008] Q.B. 73, nature of the pre-existing relationship between the parties; *Browne v Associated Newspapers Ltd* [2007] EWCA Civ 295; [2008] Q.B. 103 at [33].

317 See also *Mills v News Group Newspapers Ltd* [2001] E.M.L.R. 41 at [25] per Lawrence Collins J: the information could still be confidential even if "it has previously been very widely available.... In such cases restraining further dissemination of the confidential material may be justified to prevent harm." And see *Douglas v Hello! Ltd (No.3)* [2005] EWCA Civ 595; [2006] Q.B. 125 at [84], [105]–[106].

318 [2006] EWHC 3083 (QB); [2007] E.M.L.R. 11

319 [2012] EWHC 1601 (QB). She also noted, at [95], that "There is utility in restraining the publishing of information which, even if once known is likely to have faded from memory because of the passage of time". And see the discussion at para.26-56 of the Supreme Court decision *PJS v News Group Newspapers Ltd* [2016] UKSC 26; [2016] A.C. 1081.

320 [2015] EWCA Civ 1176; [2016] 1 W.L.R. 1541 ([70]–[71]).

321 [2018] EWHC 298 (Ch); [2018] E.M.L.R. 17, Arnold J; on appeal the finding of a reasonable expectation of privacy was not challenged: [2019] EWCA Civ 677.

322 [2018] EWHC 298 (Ch); [2018] E.M.L.R. 17 at [169].

323 See also para.26-47, and *Peck v UK* (2003) 36 E.H.R.R. 41; [2003] E.M.L.R. 15).

324 [2017] NICA 70; [2018] E.M.L.R. 11.

26-44 **Case law reviewed** In *Tchenguiz v Imerman*[325] Lord Neuberger MR held that each spouse has a right of confidence against the other in regard to that part of their life which was separate and distinct from their shared married life. However, the fact that the parties live together, especially if married, civil partners or lovers, may affect the question of whether information is confidential as between them. Further dissemination of personal information already in the public domain could still be a fresh intrusion of privacy especially where photographs are involved.[326] Though a reasonable expectation of privacy may arise from a relationship,[327] the mere fact that the information is imparted in the course of a relationship of confidence does not as such create an expectation of privacy.[328] In *Author of a Blog v Times Newspapers Ltd*[329] it was held that the identity of an anonymous blogger, revealed by detective work on the part of the defendant, did not have the necessary quality of confidence nor was it information in respect of which the claimant had a reasonable expectation of privacy, blogging being "essentially a public rather than a private activity". In *Hutcheson (formerly KGM) v News Group Newspapers Ltd*[330] the claimant had maintained that once art.8 was engaged (the information here relating to family life), there was automatically a reasonable expectation of privacy. However, it was held that such a reasonable expectation did not necessarily follow.[331] And there is a series of cases where the court has distinguished between the reasonable expectation of keeping the *details* of a relationship private and the (less likely) reasonable expectation of keeping the *fact* of a relationship private.[332] In *AB v Sunday Newspapers*[333] it was held that an informer had a reasonable expectation that his confidential relationship with the police would not be disclosed. In *Hannon v News Group Newspapers Ltd*[334] Mann J discussed whether there was a reasonable expectation of privacy in respect of an arrest and the circumstances

[325] [2010] EWCA Civ 908; [2011] Fam. 116 at [84] and [87]. In the case itself, a wife in ancillary relief proceedings had to return confidential financial documents unlawfully extracted from her husband's computer: the so-called "Hildebrand" rules had no legal basis.

[326] *Douglas v Hello! (No.3)* [2005] EWCA Civ 595; [2006] Q.B. 125 at [105], Lord Phillips. See *Trimingham v Associated Newspapers Ltd* [2012] EWHC 1296 (QB); [2012] 4 All E.R. 717 at [316] per Tugendhat J; and *Ferdinand v MGN Ltd* [2011] EWHC 2454 (QB) at [101]–[102] per Nicol J, noting both the unacceptable intrusion into privacy that they may represent but also the need for an "intense focus" on the competing rights even if the photograph is of a private occasion. See also *Contostavlos v Mendahum* [2012] EWHC 850 (QB) Tugendhat J concerning a "sex tape" involving the claimant.

[327] *Browne v Associated Newspapers Ltd* [2007] EWCA Civ. 295; [2008] Q.B. 103 at [25]–[26], per Clarke MR, the nature of any relationship between the relevant parties "is of considerable importance".

[328] *Browne v Associated Newspapers Ltd* [2007] EWCA Civ. 295; [2008] Q.B. 103 at [29].

[329] [2009] EWHC 1358 (QB); [2009] E.M.L.R. 22 at [9]–[11], per Eady J.

[330] [2011] EWCA Civ 808; [2012] E.M.L.R. 2.

[331] Gross LJ ([2011] EWCA Civ 808; [2012] E.M.L.R. at [24]) noted the views of Laws LJ in *R. (on the application of Wood) v CPM* [2009] EWCA Civ 414; [2010] 1 W.L.R. 123 at [22], that however "protean" art.8 may be it is important it should not be read so widely "that its claims become unreal and unreasonable". The views of Tugendhat J in *LNS v Persons Unknown* [2010] EWHC 119 (QB); [2010] E.M.L.R. 16—emphasising the importance of public discussion and the freedom to criticise—were described as "powerful" ([2011] EWCA Civ 808; [2012] E.M.L.R. 2 at [29]).

[332] See *Browne v Associated Newspapers Ltd* [2007] EWCA Civ 295; [2008] Q.B. 103; *Ntuli v Donald* [2010] EWCA Civ 1276; [2011] 1 W.L.R. 294; *Goodwin v News Group Newspapers Ltd* [2011] EWHC 1437 (QB); [2011] E.M.L.R. 27; *Trimingham v Associated Newspapers Ltd* [2012] EWHC 1296 (QB); [2012] 4 All E.R. 717 Tugendhat J; *SKA v CRH* [2012] EWHC 766 (QB) Tugendhat J.

[333] [2014] NICA 58; [2016] N.I. 179.

[334] [2014] EWHC 1580 (Ch); [2015] E.M.L.R. 1. *Axel Springer AG v Germany* (2012) 55 E.H.R.R. 6 was considered. And see cases in fn.311.

surrounding that arrest (alleged wrongful disclosure of information by police to newspapers).

Children and the reasonable expectation of privacy In *Murray v Express Newspapers Plc*[335] the position of a child was accepted to be somewhat different from that of an adult. It was at least arguable that as a child of "ordinary" parents could reasonably expect the press not to target him and publish photographs of him, so too could the child of famous parents. So in the case itself the infant claimant might have had a reasonable expectation of privacy in circumstances in which his famous mother might not. It all depended on the circumstances.[336] In *Weller v Associated Newspapers Ltd* Lord Dyson MR reviewed the judicial discussion of the reasonable expectation of privacy and children. He noted that "although the broad approach that must be adopted in answering the question whether there is a reasonable expectation of privacy is the same for children and adults, there are several considerations which are relevant to children (but not to adults) which may mean that in a particular case a child has a reasonable expectation of privacy where an adult does not".[337] He noted the factors concerning reasonable expectation of privacy listed in *Murray v Express Newspapers Plc*[338] He also noted that "children should be protected from the risk of embarrassment and bullying and potentially more serious threats to their safety".[339] 26-45

Public figures and the reasonable expectation of privacy As for public figures, Buxton LJ in *McKennitt v Ash*[340] commented that the European Court of Human Rights had in *Von Hannover v Germany*[341] "restated" what previously was thought to be the rights and expectations of public figures in respect of their private lives, 26-46

[335] See [2008] EWCA Civ 446; [2009] Ch. 481 at [37] and [46].

[336] On the facts of this case the family expedition to the cafe was at least arguably "part of each member of the family's recreation time intended to be enjoyed by them and such that publicity of it is intrusive and such as to adversely affect such activities in the future". (cf. NZCA in *Hosking v Runting* [2004] NZCA 34; [2005] N.Z.L.R. 1). But see *AAA v Associated Newspapers Ltd* [2013] EWCA Civ 554: in evaluating the strength of the child claimant's reasonable expectation of privacy the judge was entitled to take into account any relevant conduct of the parent(s).

[337] [2015] EWCA Civ 1176; [2016] 1 W.L.R. 1541 at [29]. He reviewed *Re JR38's Application for Judicial Review* [2015] UKSC 42; [2016] A.C. 1131; *Murray v Express Newspapers Plc* (at both High Court [2007] EWHC 1908 (Ch); [2007] E.M.L.R. 22 and Court of Appeal [2008] EWCA Civ 446; [2009] Ch. 481 levels) and the ECtHR decision in *Reklos v Greece* [2009] E.M.L.R. 16.

[338] [2008] EWCA Civ 446; [2009] Ch. 481. The factors listed in *Murray* at [36] were considered in relation to children by Lord Dyson M.R. in *Weller* [2015] EWCA Civ 1176; [2016] 1 W.L.R. 1541at [31]–[38].

[339] [2015] EWCA Civ 1176; [2016] 1 W.L.R. 1541 at [64]. In *O v A* [2014] EWCA Civ 1277; [2015] E.M.L.R. 4 a claim was brought by an 11-year-old claimant for (inter alia) misuse of private information. He sought to restrain the publication of his father's autobiography, alleging that details of the book would have an adverse effect on his psychological health. The Court of Appeal upheld the trial judge's decision that there was no cause of action for misuse of private information as the information was about the father/defendant and not the claimant himself (see [45]). The appeal to the Supreme Court ([2015] UKSC 32; [2016] A.C. 219) concerned the applicability of the tort in *Wilkinson v Downton*; held not to apply. Lord Neuberger (at [94]) commented that "publication of the defendant's book would plainly not have given rise to a cause of action in [the claimant's] favour".

[340] [2006] EWCA Civ 1714; [2008] Q.B. 73 at [64]. In *Axon v Ministry of Defence* [2016] EWHC 787 (QB); [2016] E.M.L.R. 20, Nicol J, the claimant, a commanding officer of a Royal Naval ship, had no reasonable expectation of privacy in relation to the details concerning his removal from command (despite the security markings on the relevant documents).

[341] (2005) 40 E.H.R.R. 1; [2004] E.M.L.R. 21 where at [69] the European Court of Human Rights noted that "anyone, even if they are known to the general public, must be able to enjoy a 'legitimate

and he noted that Lord Woolf's views in *A v B Plc*[342] on public figures and role models were not to be read as any sort of binding authority on arts 8 and 10. Eady J in *X v Persons Unknown*[343] noted that well-known people were entitled to a private life. In *HRH Prince of Wales v Associated Newspapers Ltd* it was noted that the fact that the claimant was an important public figure meant that disclosure "can be particularly intrusive".[344] However if the claimant was a "public figure" there may be a public interest involved in disclosing the private information.[345] In *Richard v BBC*[346] Mann J stated: "A public figure is not, by virtue of that quality, necessarily deprived of his or her legitimate expectations of privacy… it may be that a given public figure waives at least a degree of privacy by courting publicity, or adopting a public stance which would be at odds with the privacy rights claimed…".[347]

26-47 **Reasonable expectation of privacy in a public place**[348] It is possible to have a reasonable expectation of privacy in a public space. So in *Peck v UK*[349] the applicant appeared on a local authority's CCTV cameras attempting to commit suicide. The footage of the recognisable applicant was released to newspapers and broadcasters. This was held by the European Court of Human Rights to be a breach of art.8 of the ECHR as, though it took place in public, it was not foreseeable that the CCTV footage would receive such widespread dissemination. Lord Hoffmann (in *Campbell v MGN Ltd*)[350] in discussing whether the publication of a photograph could infringe a person's privacy gave as an example of such infringement the widespread publication of a photograph of someone in a humiliating or severely embarrassing situation, as in *Peck v UK*. Even a public person in a public place may have a reasonable expectation of privacy. In *Campbell v MGN Ltd* the fact that the photograph of the celebrity claimant attending a meeting for her drug addiction was taken in a public place did not alter its intrusiveness. Publicising the content of the photograph[351] was offensive especially as it was taken deliberately, in secret[352] and with a view to publishing it in conjunction with the article about details of her

---

expectation' of protection and respect for private life" (the German courts had rejected her claim partly because she was a "figure of contemporary society par excellence").

342 [2002] EWCA Civ 337; [2003] Q.B. 195.

343 [2006] EWHC 2783 (QB); [2007] E.M.L.R. 10 at [27].

344 [2006] EWCA Civ 1776; [2008] Ch. 57 at [70].

345 See the discussion at para.26–51. In *Goodwin v News Group Newspapers Ltd* [2011] EWHC 1437 (QB); [2011] E.M.L.R. 27 at [64] Tugendhat J noted "in the law of privacy there has been some recognition in the authorities of the concept of a public figure, defined as those who exercise public or official functions". In the case itself, the chief executive of one of the largest publicly quoted companies was a public figure. At [103] Tugendhat J noted sportsmen and celebrities do not come within that definition "but even in the case of sportsmen, there may be a public interest if the sexual relationship gives rise to conflicts with professional interests or duties, for example to his team".

346 [2018] EWHC 1837 (Ch); [2019] Ch. 169.

347 [2018] EWHC 1837 (Ch); [2019] Ch. 169 at [256]. See also the discussion at [284]–[287].

348 See Moreham, "Privacy in Public Spaces" [2006] C.L.J. 606.

349 (2003) 36 E.H.R.R. 41; [2003] E.M.L.R. 15. Note the obiter remarks of Lord Hope on the reasonable expectation of privacy in a public space in *Kinloch v HM Advocate* [2012] UKSC 62; [2013] 2 A.C. 93 at [19]–[21].

350 [2004] UKHL 22; [2004] 2 A.C. 457 at [74]–[75].

351 There is a distinction between the mere taking of a photograph and its publication, Lord Hoffmann, *Campbell v MGN* [2004] UKHL 22 at [74]. In a judicial review appeal, *Wood v Commissioner of Police for the Metropolis* [2009] EWCA Civ 414; [2010] 1 W.L.R. 123, it was noted obiter, that the mere overt taking of a photograph is not of itself capable of engaging art.8 unless there are aggravating circumstances, but cf. the State taking and keeping photographs of an individual going about his lawful business ("This action is a good deal more than the snapping of the shutter. The police are a state authority": at [45]); the European Court of Human Rights' decision in *S v UK*, 48 E.H.R.R. 50

treatment. However as Von Hannover shows, the protection in a public space is not limited to humiliating or embarrassing publications. Nor, it would seem, is harassment a necessary ingredient.[353] In *Murray v Express Newspapers Plc*[354] the defendant took a covert photograph of the claimant, the 19-month-old son of the well-known children's author J.K. Rowling, being pushed in a buggy by his parents in an Edinburgh street on a family outing to a local cafe. This was subsequently published. The claimant did not allege distress or harassment but claimed an infringement of his right to respect for his privacy under art.8 of the ECHR. The Court of Appeal upheld the claimant's appeal against an order striking the action out. It was arguable that art.8 was engaged (and that the balance between arts 8 and 10 was in favour of the claimant).[355] It all depended on the circumstances. Though the mere fact of being photographed in public without consent would not per se be actionable as an invasion of privacy—there being no right to one's image—"the real issue is whether publicising the content of the photographs would be offensive".[356] However the Court of Appeal rejected the High Court judge's distinction between a child (or adult) involved in family or sporting activities and more mundane activities such as walking down a street or the visit to the grocer's to buy milk. Though the Court of Appeal agreed that this distinction—between publicity of "activity... clearly part of a person's private recreation time intended to be enjoyed in the company of family and friends" which is intrusive and other public activity of a more routine type—was the basis of the European Court of Human Rights' approach in *Von Hannover*, they disagreed that it was possible to draw a clear distinction in principle between the two different kinds of activity.[357] It is unclear, therefore, whether publishing a photograph of a celebrity "popping out for milk"[358] would engage art.8. In *Weller v Associated Newspapers Ltd* (where it was held that

considered (the indefinite retention of fingerprints and DNA samples of unconvicted persons without consent a violation of art.8 rights).

352 And note *Douglas v Hello! Ltd (No.3)* [2005] EWCA Civ 595; [2006] Q.B. 125 at [107]: "unauthorised photos taken on a private occasion objectionable" (Lord Phillips MR).

353 There are references in the *Von Hannover* judgment to the fact that photographs in the tabloid press often being taken in a climate of "continual harassment" (2005) 40 E.H.R.R. 1; [2004] E.M.L.R. 21 at [59] and at [68] of the fact that "harassment" endured by public figures in their daily lives. However, Buxton LJ in *McKennitt v Ash* [2006] EWCA Civ 1714; [2008] Q.B. 73 at [41], stated that *Von Hannover* was not limited to situations involving a campaign of media intrusion. The European Court of Human Rights in *Sciacca v Italy* (2005) 43 E.H.R.R. 400 applied *Von Hannover* without intrusion.

354 [2008] EWCA Civ 446; [2009] Ch. 481.

355 The Court of Appeal were referred to the NZ decision in *Hosking v Runting* [2004] NZCA 34; [2005] 1 N.Z.L.R. 1 where on similar facts no privacy invasion was held to have arisen. However it was noted that in that case the court adopted the "highly offensive" standard for determining the expectation of privacy, a test rejected by the House of Lords in *Campbell v MGN*.

356 per Lord Hope in *Campbell v MGN* [2004] UKHL 22; [2004] 2 A.C. 457 at [122]; per Baroness Hale at [154]: "the activity photographed must be private." Lord Walker in *OBG v Allan* [2007] UKHL 21; [2008] 1 A.C. 1 at [293]. See *A v Newham LBC*, 2001 (available on Westlaw) where the defendant council used a photograph of the child claimant without consent in an AIDS leaflet.

357 [2008] EWCA Civ 446; [2009] Ch. 481 at [55]. Hence on the facts of this case the family expedition to the cafe was at least arguably "part of each member of the family's recreation time intended to be enjoyed by them and such that publicity of it is intrusive and such as to adversely affect such activities in the future".

358 Baroness Hale, *Campbell v MGN* [2004] UKHL 22 at [154]; cf. Lord Walker in *OBG v Allan* [2007] UKHL 21; [2008] 1 A.C. 1 at [293]. In *John v Associated Newspapers Ltd* [2006] EWHC 1611 (QB); [2006] E.M.L.R. 27 Eady J refused an injunction (inter alia) because there was no element of harassment, the contents of the photograph being "akin to 'popping out for a pint of milk'" (at [15]).

the child claimants had a reasonable expectation of privacy when taking part in a family trip with their celebrity father in a public place) Lord Dyson MR stated:

> "The essential point is that it was a family activity which belongs to that part of life which is protected by the broader right of personal autonomy recognised in the case law of the Strasbourg court … The family element of the activity distinguishes it from Naomi Campbell's popping out to the shops for a bottle of milk and Sir Elton John standing with his driver in a London street, outside the gate to his home wearing a baseball cap and tracksuit…".[359]

Again it is unclear whether simply publishing the photograph of a private person in a public place would be within the action.[360]

26-48 **Family and personal relationships** A pre-existing relationship between the parties will be relevant to whether there is a reasonable expectation of privacy.[361] In particular the courts will restrain the disclosure of information imparted in confidence between spouses[362] and, as the Court of Appeal acknowledged in *A v B Plc*[363] the courts will also recognise the extensive range of relationships beyond marriage that now exist, in order to restrain the disclosure of details of a sexual relationship.[364] The more stable the relationship the greater will be the significance attached to it by the court. However, though in some "kiss and tell" cases (where newspapers obtain intimate details from the other party in a transient sexual relationship) the courts had been reluctant to restrain the disclosure of intimate details, acknowledging the art.10 rights of the discloser,[365] this has been criticised as a "less generous view" than that which would be applied by the European Court of Human Rights.[366] In *CC v AB*, Eady J held that even an adulterous relationship could attract a legitimate expectation of privacy, noting: "it may yet be the case that a fleeting one-night encounter will attract less protection, if any, than a long-term relationship. This is an uncertain area, because it is by no means fully determined how appropriate it is for individual judges to apply moral evaluations to such encounters".[367] In *YXB v TNO*[368] Warby J held that, given a relationship that did not involve any form of intimacy other than sexual, the interference with privacy that the publication involved was correspondingly limited. In *Mosley v News Group Newspapers Ltd*, he doubted whether the concept of "no confidence in iniquity" can be applied to sexual activity between consensual adults in private, noting that the modern approach to privacy and sexual preferences and practices was "very differ-

---

359 [2015] EWCA Civ 1176; [2016] 1 W.L.R. 1541 at [61]. See *John v Associated Newspapers Ltd* [2006] EWHC 1611 (QB); [2006] E.M.L.R. 27.

360 *Aubry v Editions Vice-Versa Inc* [1998] 1 S.C.R. 591, Canadian SC, the private person was the main subject of the photograph. In *Murray* the Court of Appeal noted the wishes of the parents (on behalf of their child) to protect the child's freedom to live a normal life without the constraint of media intrusion.

361 *McKennitt v Ash* [2006] EWCA Civ 1714; [2008] Q.B. 73 at [15] and [24].

362 *Argyll v Argyll* [1967] Ch. 302.

363 [2002] EWCA Civ 337; [2003] Q.B. 195.

364 *Stevens v Avery* [1988] Ch. 449; *Barrymore v News Group Newspapers Ltd* [1997] F.S.R. 600.

365 See *Theakston v MGN Ltd* [2002] EWHC 137 (QB); [2002] E.M.L.R. 22, per Ouseley J; *A v B Plc* [2002] EWCA Civ 337; [2003] Q.B. 195.

366 *Douglas v Hello! Ltd (No.3)* [2005] EWCA Civ 595; [2006] Q.B. 125, per Lord Phillips MR at [73].

367 [2006] EWHC 3083 (QB); [2007] E.M.L.R. 11 at [22].

368 [2015] EWHC 826 (QB) (see at [61] for the factors taken into account).

ent from that of past generations.[369] In *AXB v BXA*,[370] Sir David Eady commented that: "the mere fact that a person wishes to publish an account of her own life ... does not provide a sufficient entitlement where to do so would engage the Article 8 rights of some other person(s) whose consent is not forthcoming".[371]

(b) Competing interests

Balancing art.8 and art.10 If art.8 is engaged (i.e. there is a reasonable expectation of privacy) the court must decide whether the interference with that right is justified.[372] Eady J in *Mosley v News Group Newspapers Ltd* noted "the judge will often have to ask whether the intrusion, or perhaps the degree of intrusion, into the claimant's privacy was proportionate to the public interest supposedly being served by it".[373] Where the defendant's right to freedom of expression under art.10 is involved, then, as *Campbell* makes clear, the two rights must be weighed together and any interference with either right must be proportionate and necessary. In effect the protection of one must be weighed against the harmful impact on the other.[374] Tugendhat J in *LNS v Persons Unknown* commented that: "freedom to live as one chooses is one of the most valuable freedoms. But so is the freedom to criticise (within the limits of the law) the conduct of other members of society as being socially harmful or wrong."[375] In *PJS v News Group Newspapers Ltd*[376] the Supreme Court were critical of the Court of Appeal's view in that case that s.12 of the Human Rights Act 1998 "enhanced" the weight which art.10 carried in the balancing exercise. This was noted to be contrary to considerable authority. 26-49

Relevant considerations in the balancing process Relevant considerations in this process include: how the information was obtained[377]; the potential of the 26-50

[369] [2008] EWHC 1777 (QB); [2008] E.M.L.R. 20 at [125]. However note *AVB v TDD* [2014] EWHC 1442 (QB), Tugendhat J. See para.26-51 with regard to "kiss and tell" scenarios.

[370] [2018] EWHC 588 (QB) at [56]. See below for the balancing process.

[371] See discussion below of "competing interests".

[372] See the earlier discussion at para.26-40. See *PNM v Times Newspapers Ltd* [2014] EWCA Civ 1132; [2014] E.M.L.R. 30 (information of claimant's arrest already extensively referred to in other court proceedings); and *ZXC v Bloomberg LP* [2017] EWHC 328 (QB); [2017] E.M.L.R. 21, Garnham J (information concerning law enforcement agency's investigation of claimant) where legitimate journalistic decisions to publish were held to be justified. However, now note *ZXC v Bloomberg LP* [2020] EWCA Civ 611.

[373] [2008] EWHC 1777 (QB); [2008] E.M.L.R. 20 at [14]. He doubted whether it would be justified, e.g. to install a camera in someone's house in order to catch them "smoking a spliff" (at [112]). Earlier cases on the public interest defence such as *X v Y* [1988] 2 All E.R. 648 (personal medical history disclosed) will still be relevant. And see *Lancashire CC v E* [2020] EWHC 182 (Fam); [2020] 1 F.L.R. 1071: a duty of religious confidentiality weighed against the public interest in protecting child from sexual abuse.

[374] Lord Steyn summarised the interplay between arts 8 and 10 in *S (A Child) (Identification: Restrictions on Publication), Re* [2004] UKHL 47; [2005] 1 A.C. 593. And see the discussion in *Att Gen's Ref (No.3 of 1999)* [2009] UKHL 34; [2010] 1 A.C. 145. Considerations of proportionality are of prime importance here. In *Goodwin v News Group Newspapers Ltd* [2011] EWHC 1437 (QB); [2011] E.M.L.R. 27 at [62] Tugendhat J provides a useful summary of the approach on this balancing exercise.

[375] [2010] EWHC 119 (QB); [2010] E.M.L.R. 16 at [104].

[376] [2016] UKSC 26; [2016] A.C. 1081. The Court of Appeal decision is at [2016] EWCA Civ 393.

[377] The use of unlawful means to obtain the information could well be a "compelling factor": per Lord Woolf in *A v B Plc* [2002] EWCA Civ 337; [2003] Q.B. 195 (however it must be confidential information that is involved: see *ABC v Lenah Game Meats Pty Ltd* (2001) 185 A.L.R. 1) or indeed

disclosure to cause harm and distress[378]; the extent of the intrusiveness[379]; the purpose of the disclosure;[380] the impact on the claimant's family life[381] and indeed the nature of the information at issue.[382] An evaluation of the use to which the defendant has put or intends to put his freedom of expression is relevant. Relief is more readily granted in respect of intrusive photographs (especially if covert).[383] A relationship of confidence was held to be a significant factor by Lord Phillips in *HRH Prince of Wales v Associated Newspapers Ltd*,[384] and it was held arguable in *Campbell v Frisbee* that an express contractual duty of confidence may carry more weight than a duty not so based when weighed against the right to freedom of expression.[385] Non-disclosure agreements and the public interest were discussed in

---

the use of covert or surreptitious means: see *Campbell v MGN Ltd* [2004] UKHL 22; [2004] 2 A.C. 457.

378 In *Campbell v MGN Ltd* [2004] UKHL 22; [2004] 2 A.C. 457 at [153] Baroness Hale noted the sense of betrayal likely and the potential to undermine the claimant's therapy was also noted.

379 The fact that the claimant is not a public figure may well be relevant: *A v Newham LBC* (2001), Garland J unreported, available Westlaw (photograph of child used without consent by defendant in their Aids and crime leaflets).

380 See *Von Hannover v Germany* (2005) 40 E.H.R.R. 1; [2004] E.M.L.R. 21; *Green Corns Ltd v Claverley Group Ltd* [2005] EWHC 958(QB); [2005] E.M.L.R. 31. However, in *Ferdinand v MGN Ltd* [2011] EWHC 2454 (QB) at [84] Nicol J stated that though the article was a "kiss and tell story" "stories may be in the public interest even if the reasons behind the informant providing the information are less than noble". In *CC v AB* [2006] EWHC 3083 (QB); [2007] E.M.L.R. 11 it was noted that the purpose for which the defendant sought to exercise his freedom of speech might be relevant (here, profit and revenge seemed to be the motivation).

381 *CC v AB* [2006] EWHC 3083 (QB); [2007] E.M.L.R. 11; *ETK v News Group Newspapers Ltd* [2011] EWCA Civ 439; [2011] 1 W.L.R. 1827; *SKA v CRH* [2012] EWHC 766 (QB) at [24] Tugendhat J: the court must have regard to the art.8 rights of non-parties but he noted "such persons should, if practicable, speak for themselves"; and see *Hutcheson (formerly KGM) v News Group Newspapers Ltd* [2011] EWCA Civ 808; [2012] E.M.L.R. 2 at [26].

382 Baroness Hale notes in *Campbell v MGN Ltd* [2004] UKHL 22; [2004] 2 A.C. 457 at [148] that there are different types of speech "some of which are more deserving of protection in a democratic society than others", highlighting the importance of political speech, intellectual and educational speech and artistic speech (and note the views of the European Court of Human Rights in *Von Hannover v Germany* (2005) 40 E.H.R.R. 1; [2004] E.M.L.R. 21). In *LNS v Persons Unknown* [2010] EWHC 119 (QB); [2010] E.M.L.R. 16 at [99] Tugendhat J rejected the submission that the conduct of the claimant in private must be unlawful before the defendant was permitted to criticise it in public. In *Bull v Desporte* [2019] EWHC 1650 (QB) Knowles J noted "in conducting that balancing exercise, where the information concerns private sexual activity, the right to this kind of expression is at the bottom end of the spectrum of importance of issues protected by Article 10 …".

383 *Theakston v MGN Ltd* [2002] EWHC 137 (QB); [2002] E.M.L.R. 22; *Campbell v MGN Ltd* [2004] UKHL 22; [2004] 2 A.C. 457. In *Douglas v Hello! Ltd* [2001] Q.B. 967 (unauthorised pictures of wedding taken surreptitiously) the defendant had argued that the guests lawfully there could have relayed the same information subsequently by word (or drawing). However Keene LJ at 1011 observed that "a picture is worth a thousand words". And note also *D v L* [2003] EWCA Civ 1169; [2004] E.M.L.R. 1 (secret recordings of private conversations could have more impact and cause more distress than an account of the conversations themselves). In *Von Hannover* (2005) 40 E.H.R.R. 1; [2004] E.M.L.R. 21 it was noted (at [59]) that the publication of photographs was an area where the protection of the rights of others was of particular importance. Lord Walker in *OBG v Allan* [2007] UKHL 21; [2008] 1 A.C. 1 at [288] commented that "if a photograph is a blatant and obviously unjustifiable invasion of personal privacy, its publication by the perpetrator will not give him a 'public domain' defence for further publication". And see *Mosley v News Group Newspapers Ltd* [2008] EWHC 1777 (QB); [2008] E.M.L.R. 20, Eady J at [15]–[16].

384 [2006] EWCA Civ 1776; [2008] Ch. 57.

385 [2002] EWCA Civ 1374; [2003] I.C.R. 141 at [22]. cf. observations of Walker LJ in *London Regional Transport v Mayor of London* [2001] EWCA Civ 1491; [2003] E.M.L.R. 4 at [46].

ABC v Telegraph Media Group Ltd,[386] where the Court of Appeal stressed the public interest in upholding the contractual bargain. However, the issue is whether in all the circumstances it is in the public interest that the confidence should be breached. Earlier public interest defence cases may still have relevance in this context,[387] though as Lord Nicholls warned in *Campbell v MGN Ltd*, arts 8 and 10 "call for a more explicit analysis of competing considerations."[388] In *Ali v Channel 5 Broadcast Ltd*[389] Arnold J held that though the broadcast did contribute to a debate of public interest, it went beyond what was justified for that purpose. On appeal it was held that this assessment could not be said to be wrong, though Irwin LJ noted that "where there was a rational view by which public interest can justify publication, particularly giving full weight to editorial knowledge and discretion, then the court should be slow to interfere".[390] In *Richard v BBC*[391] Mann J held the BBC liable to the celebrity claimant for infringement of his privacy. They had broadcast the fact that he was the subject of a police investigation and that his property had been searched. The claimant was never arrested or charged. The criteria provided in the *Axel Springer*[392] case were discussed, including: whether the disclosure contributed to a debate of public interest; the public status of the claimant; the method of obtaining the information; and the content, form and consequences of the publication. The judge noted that the BBC decided on an invasion of the claimant's privacy rights "in a big way"[393] and that the relevant privacy code for s.12(4)(b) was the BBC's own editorial guidelines. It was noted that a journalist's right of freedom of expression was subject to the proviso, inter alia, that the journalist be acting in good faith.[394]

Relevant considerations: public figures/celebrities Disclosure of details of the private life of public figures is only justifiable where it adds to the political or public debate.[395] There has been a long-standing view that what is interesting to the public **26-51**

---

386 [2018] EWCA Civ 2329; [2019] 2 All E.R. 684.

387 So, e.g. earlier cases on medical confidentiality might still be useful, e.g. *X v Y* [1988] 2 All E.R. 648; cf. *W v Egdell* [1990] Ch. 359. See also *Secretary of State for the Home Department v Central Broadcasting Ltd* [1993] E.M.L.R. 253; *R. v Chief Constable of the North Wales Police Ex p. AB* [1999] Q.B. 396 (criminal record of paedophilia disclosable if "pressing need" and, if possible, after providing opportunity to comment).

388 *Campbell v MGN Ltd* [2004] UKHL 22; [2004] 2 A.C. 457 at [19].

389 [2018] EWHC 298 (Ch); [2018] E.M.L.R. 17 (see para.26-43).

390 [2019] EWCA Civ 677 at [83].

391 [2018] EWHC 1837 (Ch); [2019] Ch. 169.

392 *Axel Springer AG v Germany (39954/08)* [2012] E.M.L.R. 15 (ECtHR).

393 [2018] EWHC 1837 (Ch); [2019] Ch. 169 at [301].

394 [2018] EWHC 1837 (Ch); [2019] Ch. 169 at [288].

395 *Von Hannover v Germany* (2005) 40 E.H.R.R. 1; [2004] E.M.L.R. 21 at [58]. The decisive issue was whether the photographs contributed to a debate of general interest (at [63]–[65]; [76]). Baroness Hale in *Campbell* noted that discussion of public information concerning public figures might be "relevant to their participation in public life" ([2004] UKHL 22; [2004] 2 A.C. 457 at [148]); and see *Couderc v France* [2016] E.M.L.R. 19 [100]–[101]. And note the "responsible journalism" analogy with defamation cases drawn by Eady J in *Mosley v News Group Newspapers Ltd* [2008] EWHC 1777 (QB); [2008] E.M.L.R. 20 at [140]. In *AAA v Associated Newspapers Ltd* [2013] EWCA Civ 554 the child claimant was associated with a public figure, being the result of that public figure's extra-marital affair. There was a public interest in the story as on the facts it raised issues concerning the fitness of that public figure for public office; and see *Trimingham v Associated Newspapers Ltd* [2012] EWHC 1296 (QB); [2012] 4 All E.R. 717 Tugendhat J. Note Lord Mance in *PJS v News Group Newspapers Ltd* [2016] UKSC 26; [2016] A.C. 1081 at [24].

is not necessarily in the public interest in relation to disclosure.[396] In *PJS v News Group Newspapers Ltd* the mere fact that the claimant and his partner were the subject of public and media attention did not justify the disclosure of alleged sexual infidelity which was of no real public interest. Lord Mance noted: "… criticism of supposed infidelity cannot be the guise under which the media can disclose kiss and tell stories of no public interest".[397] Indeed, Lord Mance after reviewing leading ECHR jurisprudence, noted "it may be that the mere reporting of sexual encounters of someone like the appellant, however well known to the public, with a view to criticising them does not even fall within the concept of freedom of expression under article 10 at all".[398] In *AMC v News Group Newspapers Ltd*[399] the claimant was a professional sportsman who had held positions of responsibility in his sport. The defendant claimed an art.10 right to reveal the claimant's clandestine sexual relationship, inter alia, on the basis the claimant was a role model. However it was noted that though a role model for sport "his position does not turn him into an example in every sphere of his existence". However, if the sexual relationship gives rise to conflicts with public duties or professional interests/duties there may be a public interest involved in disclosing the private information.[400] It was necessary to distinguish between being in the public eye and being a publicity seeker.[401] Where a public figure deliberately presents a false image or chooses to make untrue pronouncements about their life then the courts may take the view that the press are entitled to put the record straight.[402] Conversely, in *McKennitt v Ash*[403] it was relevant to the action that the claimant had guarded her privacy. In *Weller v Associated Newspapers*[404] Lord Dyson referred to the five criteria to be addressed in undertaking the balancing exercise, as referenced by the ECtHR in *Von Hannover*

---

396 See *McKennitt v Ash* [2006] EWCA Civ 1714; [2008] Q.B. 73 at [66] per Buxton LJ; a view also expressed by Baroness Hale in the defamation case, *Jameel v Wall Street Journal SPRL (No.3)* [2006] UKHL 44; [2007] 1 A.C. 359 at [147]; and Lord Phillips in *HRH Prince of Wales v Associated Newspapers Ltd* [2006] EWCA Civ 1776; [2008] Ch. 57. This is difficult to reconcile with Lord Woolf's comment in *A v B Plc* [2002] EWCA Civ 337; [2003] Q.B. 195 that weight must be given to the commercial interests of newspapers in publishing information that interested the public.

397 [2016] UKSC 26; [2016] A.C. 1081 at [22].

398 [2016] UKSC 26; [2016] A.C. 1081 at [24]

399 [2015] EWHC 2361 (QB), Laing J at [20].

400 *Goodwin v News Group Newspapers Ltd* [2011] EWHC 1437 (QB); [2011] E.M.L.R. 27 at [103] where Tugendhat J noted "… even in the case of sportsmen, there may be a public interest, for example to his team"; and see *McClaren v News Group Newspapers Ltd* [2012] EWHC 2466 (QB) Lindblom J: the public could reasonably expect a higher standard of conduct from a prominent public figure.

401 *X v Persons Unknown* [2006] EWHC 2783 (QB); [2007] E.M.L.R. 10 at [27]. Injunction granted in favour of famous model who wished to prevent unknown friends from contacting newspapers with information relating to her marriage.

402 *Theakston v MGN Ltd* [2002] EWHC 137 (QB); [2002] E.M.L.R. 22; Lord Woolf, *A v B Plc* [2002] EWCA Civ 337; [2003] Q.B. 195 at [11](xii).; *Campbell v MGN Ltd* [2004] UKHL 22; [2004] 2 A.C. 457; *Campbell v Frisbee* [2002] EWCA Civ 1374; [2003] I.C.R. 141 the court noted that if the claimant had painted a false picture there was an arguable case that the disclosure otherwise was in the public interest; Eady J in *KGM v News Group Newspapers Ltd* [2010] EWHC 3145 (QB) at [39]; and on this "false image" point see *Ferdinand v MGN Ltd* [2011] EWHC 2454 (QB) Nicol J at [65]. For an earlier case in this area see *Woodward v Hutchins* [1977] 1 W.L.R. 760, though Buxton LJ in *McKennitt v Ash* [2006] EWCA Civ 1714; [2008] Q.B. 73 at [33] asserted that this case dated back "to an era when the Convention had not invaded the consciousness of English lawyers".

403 [2006] EWCA Civ 1714; [2008] Q.B. 73. Comparison made with the claimants in *Woodward v Hutchins* [1977] 1 W.L.R. 760 at [36].

404 [2015] EWCA Civ 1176; [2016] 1 W.L.R. 1541 at [72]–[76].

v Germany (No.2)[405] viz. what is the contribution to the public interest debate; how well known is the person concerned and what is the subject of the report; the prior conduct of the person concerned; the content, form and consequences of the publication and the circumstances in which the photographs were taken.

Relevant considerations: children In *Murray v Express Newspapers Plc*[406] it was noted that where a child was involved, how his private life had been conducted by those responsible for his welfare and upbringing might be important. It should be noted that the interests of children do not automatically take precedence over the Convention rights of others.[407] However, Lord Dyson in *Weller v Associated Newspapers*[408] noted that "although a child's right is not a trump card in the balancing exercise, the primacy of the best interests of a child means that, where a child's interests would be adversely affected, they must be given considerable weight. It might require very powerful art.10 rights (for example, exceptional reasons in the public interest) to outweigh a child's art.8 rights where publication would be harmful to the child".[409] 26-52

Human Rights Act 1998 s.12(4) According to s.12(4) of the Human Rights Act 1998, the court must have particular regard to the importance of art.10 and where the proceedings "relate to material which the respondent claims, or which appears to the court, to be journalistic, literary or artistic material (or to conduct connected with such material)", to: "(a) the extent to which (i) the material has, or is about to become, available to the public; or (ii) it is, or would be, in the public interest for the material to be published; (b) any relevant privacy code."[410] In *Att Gen's Ref (No.3 of 1999)*[411] (which involved personal information), Lord Hope noted of s.12(4) that "the freedom of the press to exercise its own judgment in the presentation of journalistic material has been emphasised by Strasbourg". He cited *Jersild v Denmark*[412] and *Fressoz v France*.[413] Though at times a more restrictive ap- 26-53

---

405 (2012) 55 E.H.R.R. 15.

406 [2008] EWCA Civ 446; [2009] Ch. 481. Sir Anthony Clarke MR noted (at [38]) that if, e.g. the parents had courted publicity, the position might be different from where the parents had taken care to keep their children from the public gaze. In the case itself the important circumstances were the clandestine taking and subsequent publication of a series of photographs taken for the purposes of sale; that no consent was asked for; and the concern that such publication would create the risk of further intrusive photographic activity (at [18]).

407 *K v News Group Newspapers Ltd* [2011] EWCA Civ 439; [2011] 1 W.L.R. 1827 at [19], per Ward LJ. In *Spelman v Express Newspapers* [2012] EWHC 355 (QB) Tugendhat J, an injunction was refused where the child was 17 with a personality and public profile of his own.

408 [2015] EWCA Civ 1176; [2016] 1 W.L.R. 1541 at [39]–[42], particularly [40].

409 On the interests of children likely to be affected by the publication of private information about the claimant, see also Lord Mance and Lady Hale in *PJS v News Group Newspapers Ltd* [2016] UKSC 26; [2016] A.C. 1081 at [36]–[37] where Lord Mance noted s.12 of the Human Rights Act 1998 concerning "any relevant privacy code" and the requirements of the IPSO Code of Practice on the interests of children under 16; and Lady Hale at [72]–[74], who also noted that the child would have independent privacy interests of their own.

410 The newspaper industry has established a new press regulator, the Independent Press Standards Organisation. However note also the Royal Charter on the self-regulation of the press: so far the only approved regulator is IMPRESS. On s.12 generally see *Middleton v Persons Unknown* [2016] EWHC 2354 (QB), Whipple J. And see *ABC v Telegraph Media Group Ltd* [2018] EWCA Civ 2329; [2019] 2 All E.R. 684.

411 [2009] UKHL 34; [2010] 1 A.C. 145 at [25].

412 (1994) 19 E.H.R.R. 1 at [31].

413 (1999) 31 E.H.R.R. 28 at [54]. The issue whether the court had to have regard to the reasonable belief

proach is evident,[414] some cases have emphasised the importance of public discussion. In *Ferdinand v MGN Ltd*[415] Nicol J noted that the court's assessment of whether there is a public interest in the publication "must acknowledge that in a plural society there will be a range of views as to what matters or is of significance". Tugendhat J expressed similar sentiments on pluralism and the freedom to criticise in *LNS v Persons Unknown*.[416] In *Hutcheson (formerly KGM) v NGN Ltd*[417] the Court of Appeal also stressed "the general public interest in having a thriving and vigorous newspaper industry, representing all legitimate opinions". The Grand Chamber of the European Court of Human Rights in *Von Hannover v Germany (No.2)*[418] and *Axel Springer AG v Germany*[419] discussed the balancing exercise that needed to be undertaken when considering the private life of public figures and the essential role the press played in a democratic society. In *PJS v News Group Newspapers Ltd*[420] the requirement in s.12(4)(a)(i) to have regard to the extent to which the material has or is about to become available to the public was discussed in relation to material available on the internet.

(c) Relevant statutory provisions

26-54 **Data Protection Act 2018** Personal information is also protected by data protection law. Previously the principal general statute regulating the use of personal data was the Data Protection Act 1998. This implemented Directive 95/46/EEC. The EU adopted a directly effective General Data Protection Regulation (EU 2016/679) which came into force on 25 May 2018. This applies if the data controller, data processor or data subject is based in the EU (see art.3). This overhauls and harmonises the law on data protection and replaces the 1995 Directive. Personal data may include pseudonymised personal data. The GDPR (art.2) does not apply to the processing of personal data by an individual "in the course of a purely personal or household activity". The Regulation (art.5) sets out seven key principles relating to the processing of personal data: "Lawfulness, fairness and transparency"; "Purpose limitation"; "Data minimisation"; "Accuracy"; "Storage limitation"; "Integrity and confidentiality"; and "Accountability". Processing is only law-

---

of the person threatening to make the publication in the media was debated by Tugendhat J in *LNS v Persons Unknown* [2010] EWHC 119 (QB); [2010] E.M.L.R. 16 at [70]–[73], noting that under the public interest defence contained in s.32 of the Data Protection Act 1998 the court did have to have regard to the reasonable belief of the journalist so that it would be anomalous if the same was not also true for the public interest defence under the general law.

414 e.g. Ward LJ in *ETK v News Group Newspapers Ltd* [2011] EWCA Civ 439; [2011] 1 W.L.R. 1827 at [21] ("The intellectual, artistic or personal development of members of society is not stunted by ignorance of the sexual frolics of figures known to the public"); Eady J in *CDE v MGN Ltd* [2010] EWHC 3308 (QB); [2011] 1 F.L.R. 1524 at [73]. And see para.26-51.

415 [2011] EWHC 2454 (QB) at [64].

416 [2010] EWHC 119 (QB); [2010] E.M.L.R. 16, described as "powerful" by the Court of Appeal in *Hutcheson (formerly KGM) v NGN Ltd* [2011] EWCA Civ 808; [2012] E.M.L.R. 2 at [29].

417 [2011] EWCA Civ 808; [2012] E.M.L.R. 2 at [34]. Tugendhat J in *Goodwin v NGN Ltd* [2011] EWHC 1437 (QB); [2011] E.M.L.R. 27 at [133] stated "the public interest cannot be confined to exposing matters which are improper only by existing standards and laws and not by standards as they ought to be, or which people can reasonably contend that they ought to be". On leaks to journalists see *Abbey v Gilligan* [2012] EWHC 3217 (QB); [2013] E.M.L.R. 12 at [49]–[50] Tugendhat J. And see fnn.372 and 395 on the balance between arts 8 and 10 where private information is revealed as part of a legitimate journalistic decision.

418 [2012] E.M.L.R. 16.

419 [2012] E.M.L.R. 15.

420 [2016] UKSC 26; [2016] A.C. 1081 especially at [34]–[35].

ful if it complies with the requirements of the regulation (see art.6; there are also "special categories" of personal data under art.9: these attract additional requirements). Chapter 3 contains the rights of the data subject including (in art.17) a right to erasure (the "right to be forgotten"). Responsibilities/obligations of data controllers and data processors are contained in Ch.4. The Data Protection Act 2018 came into force on 25 May 2018. This replaced the Data Protection Act 1998. It enacts the GDPR into UK law and also adds to and tailors its provisions. The general processing regime is contained in Pt 2 cl.1 s.4(2)(b) stating: this chapter "supplements, and must be read with, the GDPR". (Part 2 cl.3 adds an equivalent regime to certain processing to which the GDPR does not apply.) As before, there are exemptions to the right afforded.

Protection from Harassment Act 1997 The Protection from Harassment Act 1997 may provide redress where there is an element of continued intrusion or harassment.[421] By s.1 a person must not pursue a course of conduct which he knows or ought to know amounts to harassment of another.[422] By s.3 the victim of harassment may bring a civil action and damages may be awarded for inter alia any anxiety caused by the harassment and any financial loss resulting from the harassment. There have been a number of privacy cases where the application of this Act to intrusive behaviour by the defendant (involving publications in newspapers rather than "door-stepping") has been discussed.[423] In *APW v WPA*[424] Tugendhat J noted that sending distressing text messages was arguably a course of conduct amounting to harassment within the Protection from Harassment Act 1997. In *WXY v Gewanter*[425] Slade J, obiter, stated that it is no defence under the Protection from Harassment Act 1997 to argue that the material is already in the public domain. It is appropriate to make a single award of damages for harassment and distress caused by misuse of confidential information, where the harassment consisted of that misuse of information.[426] 26-55

(d) Remedies

Injunction[427] In *Mosley v News Group Newspapers Ltd*[428] an injunction was not awarded as there was no reasonable expectation of privacy in respect of images 26-56

[421] It was reported that the paparazzi photograph agency Big Pictures (UK) Ltd agreed to pay damages and not to "doorstop" or pursue the actress Sienna Miller in settlement of the claim she brought against them under the Protection from Harassment Act 1997 (*The Times*, 22 November 2008).

[422] There are provisos in s.1(3) including that "in the particular circumstances" the conduct was reasonable.

[423] *AMP v Persons Unknown* [2011] EWHC 3454 (TCC) Ramsay J; AM v News Group Newspapers Ltd [2012] EWHC 308 (QB) Tugendhat J; *Trimingham v Associated Newspapers Ltd* [2012] EWHC 1296 (QB); [2012] 4 All E.R. 717, Tugendhat J.

[424] [2012] EWHC 3151 (QB) at [43]. However, the context in which they were sent was significant. As the 1997 Act also created a criminal offence "the conduct in question must be serious enough to attract the sanction of the criminal law" (at [12]).

[425] [2012] EWHC 1601 (QB) at [100].

[426] *WXY v Gewanter* [2013] EWHC 589 (QB); [2013] Info. T.L.R. 281 on assessment of damages, Tugendhat J. He noted that the Court of Appeal gave guidance on damages for harassment in *Vento v CC of West Yorkshire Police* [2002] EWCA Civ 1871; [2003] I.C.R. 318.

[427] Institutions could be the proper claimants in relation to the rights of those troubled children entrusted to their care: *Green Corns Ltd v Claverley Group Ltd* [2005] EWHC 958 (QB); [2005] E.M.L.R. 31 (defendant newspaper restrained from publishing addresses of care homes operated by the claimant (*Ashworth Hospital Authority v MGN Ltd* [2002] UKHL 29; [2002] 1 W.L.R. 2033, applied).

[428] [2008] EWHC 687 (QB); damages awarded by Eady J. [2008] EWHC 1777 (QB); [2008] E.M.L.R. 20.

already widely available, though subsequently damages were awarded. In *Venables v News Group Newspapers Ltd*[429] an injunction was awarded against the world, preventing disclosure of information about the claimant child murderers which might reveal their true identity or address after release from detention, principally on the basis of their rights to life, such being in danger. There have been subsequent cases brought by convicted criminals seeking to protect their new identities where art.8 was successfully invoked (even though the court accepted that there was no direct risk to the lives of those convicted).[430] Where interim injunctions are sought and such relief might affect the exercise of the Convention right to freedom of expression, s.12(3) of the Human Rights Act 1998 applies.[431] In *Douglas v Hello! Ltd (No.3)*[432] the Court of Appeal noted that the interim injunction should not have been discharged as the damages for mental distress did not provide an adequate remedy in respect of the intrusion into the claimants' private life, nor did it represent any real deterrent to media intrusion.[433] *PJS v News Group Newspapers Ltd*[434] is an important decision on privacy injunctions in the internet age. The Court of Appeal had awarded an injunction[435] to a celebrity with a young family, restraining publication of alleged extra-marital sexual activity by that celebrity. The celebrity had relied on both confidentiality and misuse of private information. Subsequently to the grant of that interim injunction the identity of the celebrity and details of the alleged extra-marital activity had been published overseas and on the internet (on numerous websites). In light of this, the Court of Appeal set aside the interim injunction it had awarded.[436] However by a majority (Lord Toulson dissenting) the Supreme Court granted the appeal and the interim injunction was continued until trial or further order. The court stressed that without the injunction there would be further unrestricted and extensive coverage in hard copy and other media in England and Wales. The defendant's purpose in applying to set aside the interim injunction would be to add extensively and in a qualitatively different medium to the existing invasions of the claimant's privacy and the privacy of his family. Unlike the ac-

---

429 [2001] Fam. 430.

430 *X (formerly known as Mary Bell) v SO* [2003] EWHC 1101 (QB); [2003] E.M.L.R. 37; *Carr v News Group Newspapers Ltd* [2005] EWHC 971 (QB). In *OPQ v BJM* [2011] EWHC 1059 (QB); [2011] E.M.L.R. 23 at [18], Eady J … noted this remedy is available, wherever necessary and proportionate, for the protection of Convention rights whether of children or adults. And see *A (A Protected Party) v Persons Unknown* [2016] EWHC 3295 (Ch); [2017] E.M.L.R. 11, Sir Geoffrey Vos C.

431 See *Browne v Associated Newspapers Ltd* [2007] EWCA Civ 295; [2008] Q.B. 103, especially at [23] and [40]–[44]; the Supreme Court in *PJS v News Group Newspapers Ltd* [2016] UKSC 26; [2016] A.C. 1081. And see para.26–33, especially the discussion of *Cream Holdings v Banerjee* [2004] UKHL 44; [2005] 1 A.C. 253; applied by Eady J in *CC v AB* [2006] EWHC 3083 (QB); [2007] E.M.L.R. 11 (interim injunction should not be granted unless the claimant was likely to obtain an order in similar terms).

432 [2005] EWCA Civ 595; [2006] Q.B. 125. The notional licence fee was held to be an inadequate basis for compensation.

433 *Douglas v Hello! (No.3)* [2005] EWCA Civ 595; [2006] Q.B. 125 at [256]–[257] per Lord Phillips: "the refusal of an interlocutory injunction in a case such as this represents a strong potential disincentive to respect for aspects of private life which the Convention intends should be respected." Compare *Spelman v Express Newspapers* [2012] EWHC 355 (QB) at [110]–[111], where Tugendhat J noted that though it was often a strong argument that damages were not an adequate remedy where the main interest was in keeping a secret, the position was less clear where the main issue was intrusion.

434 [2016] UKSC 26; [2016] A.C. 1081.

435 [2016] EWCA Civ 100; [2016] E.M.L.R. 17.

436 [2016] EWCA Civ 393.

tion for breach of confidence, the action for privacy/misuse of private information could protect against repetition that may involve further distress/invasiveness. No genuine public interest in the publication had been shown and the purpose of any trial would be largely undermined should the interim injunction not be awarded.[437]

Privacy injunctions and open justice The fact that there was a public interest in open justice and that the public had art.10 rights was noted by Lord Neuberger MR in *JIH v News Group Newspapers Ltd*.[438] The *Practice Guidance* in relation to applications for interim non-disclosure orders in civil proceedings to restrain the publication of information[439] refers to *JIH v News Group Newspapers Ltd* as providing the "proper approach". The Practice Guidance contains reference to leading case law and states that open justice is a fundamental principle and derogations from this principle can only be justified in exceptional cases.[440] The parties must ensure that the interference with the art.10 rights of third parties is kept to as short a time as possible.[441] Case law had already established: that the onus is on the applicant to show that derogation from the general principle of open justice is *strictly necessary*[442]; that any application to derogate from the general principle must be the subject of "intense scrutiny" by the court[443]; that derogations must be kept to an absolute minimum[444]; the court should ask whether a less drastic course of action could be adopted[445]; that the decision is case sensitive[446]; that the parties themselves could not agree to derogate, rather it is for the court to decide whether such a derogation from open justice is necessary.[447] In *TUV v Person or Persons Unknown* Eady J, noted that it would not always be proportionate to require a claimant to give prior notice of the application for an injunction to all non-party media organisations. 26-57

[437] Lord Neuberger, however, acknowledged that "the court must … be ready to consider changing their approach when it is clear that that approach has become unrealistic in practical terms or out of touch with the standards of contemporary society": [2016] UKSC 26; [2016] A.C. 1081 at [70]. And see *Bull v Desporte* [2019] EWHC 1650 (QB), Knowles J at [158], [166]; *BVC v EWF* [2019] EWHC 2506 (QB), Judge Parkes QC.

[438] [2011] EWCA Civ 42; [2011] 1 W.L.R. 1645 at [21(7)]. It should be noted that the practice and procedure of anonymity orders were discussed by the Supreme Court in two cases in 2010 (neither involving the action for breach of confidence but both raising art.8 vs art.10 issues): *Re Guardian News and Media* [2010] UKSC 1; [2010] 2 A.C. 697 at [63]–[64]; and *Secretary of State for Home Dept v AP (No.2)* [2010] UKSC 26; [2010] 1 W.L.R. 1652.

[439] *(HC Interim Non-Disclosure Orders)* [2012] 1 W.L.R. 1003. An application for such an order might be in relation e.g. to holding the proceedings in private; withholding the names of parties; access to documents on the court file being restricted or even prohibiting disclosure of the existence of the proceedings or order (the so-called "super-injunction").

[440] On the approach to be taken to post-settlement anonymity see *JIH v News Group Newspapers Ltd* [2012] EWHC 2179 (QB), Tugendhat J, based on the guidance of Lord Neuberger MR in *Hutcheson v Popdog Ltd* [2011] EWCA Civ 1580; [2012] 1 W.L.R. 782. And see *ABK v KDT* [2013] EWHC 1192 (QB) Tugendhat J: all undertakings in the Practice Guidance's Model Interim Non-Disclosure Order to be included.

[441] And see *Giggs (formerly known as CTB) v News Group Newspapers Ltd* [2012] EWHC 431 (QB); [2013] E.M.L.R. 5 at [111], Tugendhat J.

[442] See Kay LJ in *Ntuli v Donald* [2010] EWCA Civ 1276; [2011] 1 W.L.R. 294 at [52]–[54]; and see Tugendhat J in *Gray v UVW* [2010] EWHC 2367 (QB) at [55]–[56], no more than is "necessary and proportionate".

[443] See *LNS v Persons Unknown* [2010] EWHC 119 (QB); [2010] E.M.L.R. 16, Tugendhat J at [108]; *JIH v News Group Newspapers Ltd* [2011] EWCA Civ 42; [2011] 1 W.L.R. 1645, Lord Neuberger MR at [21(4)].

[444] See *Ntuli v Donald* [2010] EWCA Civ 1276; [2011] 1 W.L.R. 294 at [54].

[445] *Ambrosiadou v Coward* [2011] EWCA Civ 409; [2011] E.M.L.R. 21 at [52].

[446] *Ntuli v Donald* [2010] EWCA Civ 1276; [2011] 1 W.L.R. 294 at [54], Maurice Kay LJ.

[447] See *Goldsmith v BCD* [2011] EWHC 674 (QB), Tugendhat J at [64].

Rather "the law should only impose an obligation to notify those who are already believed to have shown some interest in publishing".[448] In *Goldsmith v BCD*[449] concern for the mental health of the defendant led to the anonymisation of that party. Concern over the impact on the parties' respective children may be significant.[450] It is also the policy of the law to protect those alleging they are the victim of a blackmailer.[451] Anonymisation was ordered in *JIH v News Group Newspapers Ltd*[452] with a view to reducing the risk of jigsaw identification, but in *Goodwin v New Group Newspapers Ltd*[453] Tugendhat J held that though revealing the name of the colleague with whom the claimant had had a sexual relationship would be an intrusion on her art.8 rights, her job description could be revealed as an important feature of the defendant's article. In *CTB v News Group Newspapers Ltd*[454] Eady J refused to vary an order for anonymity despite widespread coverage of the claimant's name on the internet, and in *CTB v News Group Newspapers Ltd*[455] Tugendhat J refused to remove an anonymity order although the claimant's name had been revealed on the internet and by an MP in Parliament.[456] The general approach to a request for a "super-injunction" (to prohibit the reporting of the fact that an injunction existed) was considered by Maurice Kay LJ in *Ntuli v Donald*.[457] Sometimes a super-injunction for a short period may be strictly necessary, e.g. to prevent "tipping off". This is echoed in the Practice Guidance.

26-58 **Injunctions and the relationship between privacy and defamation claims** If the nub of the claim was a complaint of the falsity of the allegation and the use of the action for breach of confidence or misuse of private information/privacy was in order to avoid the rules of the tort of defamation (including the restrictions on the grant of an interim injunction) then objections could be raised that there was an abuse of process.[458] In *LNS v Persons Unknown*[459] Tugendhat J stated that the relationship between defamation and the new cause of action for misuse of private

---

448 [2010] EWHC 853 (QB); [2010] E.M.L.R. 19 at [26].

449 [2011] EWHC 674 (QB) Tugendhat J.

450 *Ntuli v Donald* [2010] EWCA Civ 1276; [2011] 1 W.L.R. 294 Kay LJ at [24]; *ETK v News Group Newspapers* [2011] EWCA Civ 439; [2011] 1.W.L.R. 1827 Ward LJ at [19]; cf. adult children: *KGM v News Group Newspapers Ltd* [2010] EWHC 3145 (QB) Eady J at [28].

451 *POI v Lina* [2011] EWHC 25 (QB) Tugendhat J at [8]; *N v Ryan* [2013] EWHC 637 (QB) Sharp J. But Tugendhat J in *SKA v CRH* [2012] EWHC 766 (QB) at [74] did not accept that the alleged blackmailer forfeited his art.10 rights, it remaining necessary for the court "to consider the value of the speech that would be made if the defendants were permitted to make the disclosure they threaten to make". *PML v Persons Unknown* [2018] EWHC 838 (QB) Nicklin J (blackmail threat from hacker to publish data stolen from claimant; interim non-disclosure order without notice on the defendant); *LJY v Persons Unknown* [2017] EWHC 3230; [2018] E.M.L.R. 19 (QB) at [29] Warby J (blackmail allegation: "… blackmail represents a misuse of free speech rights. Such conduct will considerably reduce the weight to be attached to free speech and correspondingly increase the weight of the argument in favour of restraint"). See also *NPV v QEL* [2018] EWHC 703 (QB); [2018] E.M.L.R. 20, Nicklin J.

452 [2011] EWCA Civ 42; [2011] 1 W.L.R. 1645 at [40].

453 [2011] EWHC 1437 (QB); [2011] E.M.L.R. 27.

454 [2011] EWHC 1326 (QB); see also *KGM v News Group Newspapers Ltd* [2010] EWHC 3145 (QB) at [30], Eady J, with reference to protection for information available on the internet.

455 [2011] EWHC 1334 (QB). He noted, at [3]: "in so far as its purpose is to prevent intrusion or harassment, it has not failed."

456 In relation to information published previously on the internet, see *PJS v News Group Newspapers Ltd* [2016] UKSC 26; [2016] A.C. 1081, discussed at para.26-56.

457 [2010] EWCA Civ 1276; [2011] 1 W.L.R. 294, especially [46]–[54].

458 Buxton LJ in *McKennitt v Ash* [2006] EWCA Civ 1714; [2008] Q.B. 73 at [79]; Eady J in *Browne v Associated Newspapers Ltd* [2007] EWHC 202 (QB); [2007] E.M.L.R. 19 at [29] (not raised on

information "was not yet clear" but that the courts will have regard to an attempt to circumvent or avoid the rule under *Bonnard v Perryman* in defamation: "It is a matter for the court to decide whether the principle of free speech prevails or not and that does not depend solely upon the choice of the claimant as to his cause of action."[460] In *Spelman v Express Newspapers*[461] Tugendhat J referred to the uncertain issue of principle raised by the defendant "whether, and if so when, a court should refuse an injunction on the basis of *Bonnard v Perryman* when it is sought by a claimant who advances his case only on the basis of privacy".[462]

Damages[463] Damages for injury to a claimant's feelings or mental distress may be awarded (including aggravated damages).[464] In *Mosley v News Group Newspapers Ltd*[465] Eady J debated the nature of compensatory damages in privacy cases, noting that the law is concerned to protect such matters as personal dignity, autonomy and integrity although unlike the tort of defamation it was not as such concerned with injury to reputation. It was reasonable to suppose that damages for an intrusion into a person's sexual tastes would include distress, hurt feelings and loss of dignity.[466] However, Mann J in *Richard v BBC*[467] stated: "it is ... quite plain that the protection of reputation is part of the function of the law of privacy as well as the function of the law of defamation" and that this should "be reflected in the right of the court to give damages which relate to loss of reputation".[468] The Court 26-59

appeal). And see *RST v UVW* [2009] EWHC 2448 (QB); [2010] E.M.L.R. 13, Tugendhat J at [33].

459 [2010] EWHC 119 (QB); [2010] E.M.L.R. 16 at [78]. He noted (at [81]) that the rule in *Bonnard v Perryman* [1891] 2 Ch. 269 and the Human Rights Act 1998 may not always be compatible, though the harshness of the rule—that the defendant is free to say anything that is true, however distressing even if there is no public interest, "has been tempered by the recent developments of the law of harassment" (at [80]–[81]).

460 [2010] EWHC 119 (QB); [2010] E.M.L.R. 16 at [90]. Moreover, that point had more force (as was noted by Buxton LJ in *McKennitt v Ash*) "if the claimant admitted the truth of the allegations and was attempting to protect an undeserved reputation by recourse to the cause of action in misuse of private information, at least where there was a public interest in her not doing so". And see *Hannon v News Group Newspapers Ltd* [2014] EWHC 1580 (Ch); [2015] E.M.L.R. 1, Mann J; and Gurry, *Breach of Confidence*, 2nd edn (2012), para.18.43.

461 [2012] EWHC 355 (QB) at [65].

462 At [96] Tugendhat J identified classes of cases where there may be an overlap between misuse of private information and defamation. See the comments of Mann J in *Hannon v News Group Newspapers Ltd* [2014] EWHC 1580 (Ch); [2015] E.M.L.R. 1. at [53]. Note also Gurry, *Breach of Confidence*, 2nd edn (2012), para.18.44. And see para.26–41.

463 On damages see: *Cornelius v De Taranto* [2001] E.M.L.R. 12 (not appealed on this point; though a contractual duty was involved in that case; Morland J held that the proper protection of the art.8 right had to be given). In *A v Newham LBC*, unreported 2001, a settlement of £5,000 was agreed. The approach to privacy damages was summarised by Warby J in *Reid v Price* [2020] EWHC 594 (QB) at [50]–[51].

464 In *WXY v Gewanter* [2013] EWHC 589 (QB); [2013] Info. T.L.R. 281 aggravated damages of £5,000 were awarded given that the defendant's threats were to put pressure on the claimant for financial gain. On aggravated damages see Crime and Courts Act 2013 s.39. And see the discussion in *Bull v Desporte* [2019] EWHC 1650 (QB), Knowles J, at [146] onwards. In *Richard v BBC* [2018] EWHC 1837 (Ch); [2019] Ch. 169 Mann J awarded aggravated damages given that the BBC had submitted the offending broadcast for an award.

465 [2008] EWHC 1777 (QB); [2008] E.M.L.R. 20.

466 [2008] EWHC 1777 (QB); [2008] E.M.L.R. 20 at [212]–[231]. He noted that it may be appropriate to take into account aggravating conduct. He awarded £60,000 to Mosley.

467 [2018] EWHC 1837 (Ch); [2019] Ch. 169.

468 [2018] EWHC 1837 (Ch); [2019] Ch. 169 at [345]. He notes that loss of reputation has an impact on the feelings of the claimant. He states that the preponderance of speeches in *Khuja v Times*

of Appeal in *Gulati v MGN Ltd*[469] accepted that awards in privacy cases are not limited to damages for distress. According to Arden LJ "the essential principle is that, by misusing their private information ... [the appellants] ... deprived the respondents of their right to control the use of private information". Such damages were not the same as vindicatory damages. However, it was accepted that the assessment of compensation may be affected if the information would have become public knowledge anyway.[470] It has been said that such damages should be kept to a modest level, well below the level of general damages for serious physical or psychological injury.[471] However, in *Spelman v Express Newspapers*[472] Tugendhat J, discussing damages in relation to intrusion, commented: "if a remedy in damages is to be an effective remedy, then the amount that the court may award must not be subject to too severe a limitation." The approach of Mann J in *Gulati v MGN Ltd*[473] was followed by Arnold J in *Ali v Channel 5 Broadcast Ltd*.[474] On appeal the Court of Appeal upheld the level of damages awarded, commenting that "it is important that an appeal court should be slow to interfere with an assessment of damage in such a case as this, where the measure of damage is necessarily general and cannot be calculated mathematically".[475]

26-60 **Guidance on the measure of damages** Guidance on the measure of damages was provided by the Court of Appeal in *Gulati v MGN Ltd*[476] adopting the general approach set out by Mann J in the lower court.[477] This litigation comprised a series of cases involving invasions of privacy on a grand scale by the defendant newspaper publishers (including multiple interception of voicemails) where Mann J in awards ranging from £72,500 to £260,250, awarded compensation under three elements: damages for each publication; damages for hacking that did not result in publication; and damages for distress. On the general approach accepted by the Court of Appeal note the following. The appropriate compensation will depend on the nature of the information, its significance as private information, and the effect on the victim of its disclosure. A short-lived effect based on embarrassment will attract less compensation than a life-changing intrusion. The effect of repeated intrusions by publication can be cumulative, though possibly the cumulative effect will mean that additional distress is less rather than increased as a result of repeat disclosures. The extent of the damage may be claimant-specific: those with a thin skin may be caused

---

Newspapers Ltd [2017] UKSC 49; [2019] A.C. 161 acknowledges that the protection of reputation was part of the function of the law of privacy (at [343]). And see Mann J in *Hannon v News Group Newspapers* [2014] EWHC 1580 (Ch); [2015] E.M.L.R. 1 at [70]–[71]. In *ZXC v Bloomberg Plc* [2019] EWHC 970 (QB); [2019] E.M.L.R. 20, Nicklin J stated that in a misuse of private information claim, the claimant could not be awarded compensation for harm to reputation caused by the publication of a defamatory statement unless the defendant had been given the opportunity to defend as true. On appeal ([2020] EWCA Civ 611) no point was taken about the level of damages.

469 [2015] EWCA Civ 1291; [2017] Q.B. 149. And see *Lloyd v Google* [2019] EWCA Civ 1599; [2020] E.M.L.R. 2 at [54]: damages could be awarded for mere intrusion into a person's privacy, independent of any distress caused.

470 [2015] EWCA Civ 1291; [2017] Q.B. 149 at [45].

471 *Archer v Williams* [2003] EWHC 1670 (QB); [2003] E.M.L.R. 38, per Jackson J.

472 [2012] EWHC 355 (QB) at [114].

473 [2015] EWHC 1482; [2016] F.S.R. 12. See para.26-60.

474 [2018] EWHC 298 (Ch); [2018] E.M.L.R. 17.

475 [2019] EWCA Civ 677 at [118], Irwin LJ.

476 [2015] EWCA Civ 1291; [2017] Q.B. 149 at [74]

477 See [2015] EWHC 1482 at [229] of his judgment which (with one small qualification) was adopted by the Court of Appeal. And see discussion in *Bull v Desporte* [2019] EWHC 1650 (QB), Knowles J.

more distress (and receive more compensation) than those with a thick skin.[478] Whether or not to make a global award or separate awards for invasions of privacy was a matter for the exercise of judicial discretion. On the submission that where more than one injury has been inflicted the judge should perform an overall review at the end of the assessment of damages the Court of Appeal commented: "It might be appropriate to have an overall review if there were mitigating circumstances, such as the repeated misuse of information where there was some genuine mistake for instance as to its source, or timely apologies".[479] On the argument that the awards were disproportionate compared with awards by the ECtHR, Arden LJ said: "The court, when making an award for misuse of private information is not proceeding under either s.8 of the Human Rights Act 1998 or art.41 of the Convention. The question of the measure of damages is more naturally a question for English domestic law".[480] Finally, though there should be some reasonable relationship between the awards in personal injury and misuse of private information cases, "taking account of personal injury compensation does not mean that the outcome in this field has to be exactly the same".[481] In *Cooper v Turrell*[482] Tugendhat J held that the misuse of private medical information was of a high level of seriousness and there were aggravating circumstances: there had been an internet campaign against the claimant; the defendant knew the information was false and had targeted the release of the information to people whose good opinion was important to the claimant.

[478] In *Burrell v Clifford* [2016] EWHC 294 (Ch); [2017] E.M.L.R. 2 at [142], Spearman QC, sitting as Deputy Judge Chancery Division noted uneasiness about applying the eggshell skull rule to misuse of private information cases.

[479] [2015] EWCA Civ 1291; [2017] Q.B. 149 at [105]. (There were no such mitigating circumstances on the facts of the case itself).

[480] [2015] EWCA Civ 1291; [2017] Q.B. 149 at [89].

[481] [2015] EWCA Civ 1291; [2017] Q.B. 149 at [62]). Note *TLT v Secretary of State for the Home Department* [2016] EWHC 2217 (QB), Mitting J. Assessment of damages where the Home Office accidentally published asylum applicants' personal data: given that they were shocked and put in fear the cases were closer to those involving psychiatric injury. Liability (which was upheld) but not damages award appealed: [2018] EWCA Civ 2217; [2018] 4 W.L.R. 101.

[482] [2011] EWHC 3269 (QB).

26-61 **The issue of exemplary damages** In *Mosley v News Group Newspapers Ltd*[483] Eady J debated whether exemplary damages are admissible in a claim for infringement of privacy, contending that they should not be, due to the lack of authority and the fact that it would fail the tests of necessity and proportionality.[484] However, in *PJS v News Group Newspapers Ltd*[485] both Lord Mance and Lord Toulson contended that the contrary view on exemplary damages in privacy cases remains open to argument at higher levels.[486] Lord Mance further noted that whether an account of profits might be claimed is likewise an open question.[487]

483 [2008] EWHC 1777 (QB); [2008] E.M.L.R. 20.

484 [2008] EWHC 1777 (QB); [2008] E.M.L.R. 20 at [197]. See also *Weller v Associated Newspapers Ltd* [2014] EWHC 1163 (QB); [2014] E.M.L.R. 24. In *Aquaculture Corp v NZ Green Mussel Co Ltd* [1990] 3 N.Z.L.R. 299 at [301], Cooke P saw no difficulty in such an extension, but cf. *Giller v Procopets* [2008] VSCA 236.

485 [2016] UKSC 26; [2016] A.C. 1081 at [42] and [92] respectively.

486 Note also that under the Crime and Courts Act 2013 ss.34–38, in relation inter alia to breach of confidence and misuse of private information claims, where defendants are "relevant publishers" (in effect the Press but not broadcasters) exemplary damages cannot be awarded against a publisher which is a member of an approved regulator (except in special cases). As for other "relevant publishers" a court can make an award of exemplary damages where it considers it appropriate. So far the only approved regulator is IMPRESS.

487 In *Mirror Group Newspapers Ltd v United Kingdom* (39401/04) (2011) 53 E.H.R.R. 5 the ECtHR commented that substantial success fees were likely to violate art.10 freedom, particularly in privacy and defamation cases. This area was discussed by the Supreme Court in *Times Newspapers Ltd v Flood* [2017] UKSC 33; [2017] 1 W.L.R. 1415. Conditional fee agreement success fees are no longer recoverable in privacy proceedings (Legal Aid, Sentencing and Punishment of Offenders Act (Commencement No.13) Order 2018 (SI 2018/1287)).

CHAPTER 27

DAMAGES

TABLE OF CONTENTS

1. INTRODUCTION

27-01 **Scope of chapter** This chapter is primarily concerned with the principles governing the types of loss, or heads of damage, for which compensatory damages are payable and the method of assessing such damages.[1] As such it assumes that the logically prior question of the defendant's liability in tort has already been determined. This distinction between "liability" principles and "quantification" principles is a convenient one and it is also necessary for certain procedural[2] rules, but is not entirely free from difficulty as there are certain matters which may be classified under either category. This is particularly true of causation and remoteness of damage. Typically the courts have formulated the relevant principles in the context of liability issues, notably within the law of negligence, and for this reason, save for a brief account of their relevance to the assessment process,[3] they have been

---

[1] For specialist works see: Edelman, *McGregor on Damages*, 20th edn (2017); Burrows, *Remedies for Torts, Breach of Contract and Equitable Wrongs*, 4th edn (2019), Chs 2–18; Tettenborn, Wilby and Bennett, *The Law of Damages*, 2nd edn (2010).

[2] e.g. under CPR rr.14.7, 25.7. The distinction used to be relevant to the conflict of laws (the measure of damages was regarded as procedural and governed by the *lex fori*, while liability issues were regarded as substantive and governed by the *lex causae*: see, e.g., *Harding v Wealands* [2006] UKHL 32; [2007] 2 A.C. 1; *Cox v Ergo Versicherung AG* [2014] UKSC 22; [2014] A.C. 1379. But in the context of the applicable law for a tort, the effect of the Private International Law (Miscellaneous Provisions) Act 1995 s.15A is that that distinction is no longer important.

[3] See para.27-08.

dealt with in an earlier chapter.[4] What follows is an account of the general law of damages.[5] Some earlier chapters have dealt with the damages relevant to the tort or torts in question. So in this chapter, there will be no specific consideration of, for example, damages for defamation,[6] trespass to land[7] and trespass to the person,[8] malicious prosecution,[9] misrepresentation,[10] pure economic loss caused by negligence,[11] economic torts,[12] and interference with rights in chattels.[13] Damages for breach by a public authority of a victim's convention right under the Human Rights Act 1998 have also been considered in an earlier chapter.[14]

2. General Principles

(a) Form of damages

Generally damages are awarded in the form of a lump sum, providing a once and for all assessment of the losses flowing from the tort.[15] However, interim payments can be ordered in proceedings relating to personal injury and death claims,[16] and there is provision for the award of provisional damages in certain personal injury cases.[17] Moreover, a radical break from the lump sum approach was made 27-02

---

4 Ch.2.

5 The general principles considered must be read subject to the fact that the parties themselves may have validly limited damages (whether by contract or non-contractual notice) or exceptionally there may be a statutory provision limiting damages, e.g. s.185 of the Merchant Shipping Act 1995.

6 See paras 21-186, 21-224 onwards.

7 See para.18-67 onwards.

8 See para.14-139 onwards.

9 See para.15-06 onwards. But for consideration of costs as damages, see paras 27-126 to 27-127.

10 See para.17-41 onwards.

11 See para.2-182 onwards and paras 9-157, 9-195, 9-219, 9-239, 9-261. That includes the particularly important decision in *South Australia Asset Management Corp v York Montague Ltd* [1997] A.C. 191 HL; for detailed criticism of the reasoning in that case see Burrows, *Remedies for Torts, Breach of Contract, and Equitable Wrongs*, 4th edn (2019), pp.117–127.

12 See Ch.23.

13 See para.16-95 onwards. We also do not discuss in this chapter "loss of management time", on which see, e.g. *Admiral Management Services Ltd v Para-Protect Ltd* [2002] EWHC 233 (Ch); [2002] 1 W.L.R. 2722 (loss of revenue and damages for management time); *Aerospace Publishing Ltd v Thames Water Utilities Ltd* [2007] EWCA Civ 3; [2007] N.P.C. 5 (damages recoverable for payments made to staff to deal with the consequences of a flood caused by the defendant's breach of statutory duty).

14 See para.13-126 onwards. See also *Damages under the Human Rights Act 1998*, Law Commission No.266 (2000); *R. (on the application of KB) v Mental Health Review Tribunal* [2003] EWHC 193 (Admin); [2004] Q.B. 936; *Anufrijeva v London Borough of Southwark* [2003] EWCA Civ 1406; [2004] Q.B. 1124; *R. v Secretary of State for the Home Department Ex p. Greenfield* [2005] UKHL 14; [2005] 1 W.L.R. 673; *Van Colle v Hertfordshire Police* [2007] EWCA Civ 325; [2007] 1 W.L.R. 1821 (overturned on liability without discussing damages by the House of Lords [2008] UKHL 50; [2009] 1 A.C. 225); *Rabone v Pennine Care NHS Foundation Trust* [2012] UKSC 2; [2012] 2 A.C. 72; *R. (on the application of Faulkner) v Secretary of State for Justice* [2013] UKSC 23; [2013] 2 A.C. 254; *DSD v Commissioner of Police for the Metropolis* [2014] EWHC 2493 (QB); [2015] 1 W.L.R. 1833; *Alseran v Ministry of Defence* [2017] EWHC 3289 (QB); [2019] Q.B. 1251 (this decision of Leggatt J turns the approach of *Greenfield* on its head by treating the domestic scale for non-pecuniary loss as being of primary importance and relegating the Strasbourg level to being a secondary cross-check). For criticism of the *Greenfield* case, see Burrows, "Damages and Rights" in Nolan and Robertson (eds), *Rights and Private Law* (Oxford: Hart Publishing, 2012), pp.275, 290–303.

15 See para.30-15.

16 See para.27-71.

17 See para.27-72.

by ss.100–101 of the Courts Act 2003 (amending the Damages Act 1996) and the Damages (Variation of Periodical Payments) Order 2005.[18] From 1 April 2005, these provisions, which build on the out-of-court development of "structured settlements",[19] have allowed the courts for the first time[20] to award (reviewable) periodical payments for future pecuniary loss in cases of personal injury and death, even if both parties do not consent to this.[21]

27-03 As a general rule the damages award must be unconditional: the court cannot direct that the claimant must first act in a particular way (for example, return property to the defendant),[22] nor can it impose any control on the moneys in the hands of the claimant.[23] There are two exceptions to this. First, where the damages are received by a person who lacks capacity, viz. a minor or a person who lacks mental capacity, the court can issue directions relating to the investment or other dealings with the money.[24] Secondly, in some personal injury cases involving assistance rendered by a third party, damages have been awarded on the condition that the claimant pays them over to, or holds them on trust for, the third party.[25]

27-04 The old rule that damages must be expressed in sterling was abrogated in 1975.[26] Now if the claimant proves that his operations are conducted in a foreign currency and that that currency was used in a normal manner to meet the expenditure for which he claims—whether the expenditure was actually incurred in that currency or not—or that his loss can only be appropriately measured in that currency, then he is entitled to judgment in that currency.[27]

(b) General and special damages

27-05 The distinction between "general" and "special" damages is important not only for the purpose of the form of an award but also in relation to pleading and proof.[28] In a sense which is not relevant to this chapter the phrase "special damage" is used to signify that damage which the claimant must prove in certain cases as part of his cause of action. For the present purposes, the distinction is between "general damage" which the law presumes to flow from the wrong complained of and which need not be specially pleaded (though it should be averred that such damage has been

---

18 SI 2005/841.

19 See paras 27-73 to 27-75.

20 For the traditional denial of any power to award judgment in the form of periodical payments, see *Fournier v Canadian National Ry* [1927] A.C. 167.

21 See paras 27-76 and 27-77.

22 *Banbury v Bank of Montreal* [1918] A.C. 626.

23 *Lim Poh Choo v Camden and Islington AHA* [1980] A.C. 174 at 191, per Lord Scarman.

24 CPR r.21.11.

25 *Dennis v London Passenger Transport Board* [1948] 1 All E.R. 779; *Schneider v Eisovitch* [1960] 2 Q.B. 430; *Cunningham v Harrison* [1973] Q.B. 942 at 952, per Lord Denning MR; *Hunt v Severs* [1994] 2 A.C. 350 HL. See paras 27-26 to 27-28.

26 *Miliangos v George Frank (Textiles) Ltd* [1976] A.C. 443.

27 *The Despina R.* [1979] A.C. 685. See also *Shay v Wallace Arnold Tours* [1977] C.L.Y. 778; *The Lash Atlantico* [1987] 2 Lloyd's Rep. 114 CA; *The Transoceanica Francesca and Nicos V* [1987] 2 Lloyd's Rep. 15. But non-pecuniary loss, such as pain, suffering, and loss of amenity in a personal injury action should be expressed in sterling: *Hoffman v Sofaer* [1982] 1 W.L.R. 1350.

28 *Ratcliffe v Evans* [1892] 2 Q.B. 524 at 528, per Bowen LJ; *Stroms Bruks Aktie Bolag v John and Peter Hutchison* [1905] A.C. 515 at 525, per Lord Macnaghten. See Street, *Principles of the Law of Damages*, pp.18-22; Edelman, *McGregor on Damages*, 20th edn (2017), paras 3-001 to 3-006, 52-010 to 52-018; Jolowicz, "The Changing Use of 'Special Damage' and its Effect on the Law" [1960] C.L.J. 214.

suffered[29]) and "special damage" which means "the particular damage (beyond the general damage), which results from the particular circumstances of the case, and of the [claimant's] claim to be compensated, for which he ought to give warning in his pleadings in order that there may be no surprise at the trial".[30] So, for example, in *Domsalla v Barr*[31] it was held that if the claimant proposes to allege in an action for damages for personal injury that there are special circumstances which will cause him to suffer losses over and above those that would reasonably be expected to flow from his injury, such as that he lost the opportunity of setting up in business on his own account in the future, such circumstances must be pleaded.

The application of this principle, in the words of Lord Donovan, is "not dictated by any preconceived notion of what is general or special damage but by the circumstances of the particular case".[32] Nevertheless, the traditional practice has been that "special damages" refer to losses that are capable of substantially exact calculation, i.e. pre-trial pecuniary loss, whereas "general damages" refer to non-pecuniary loss and future pecuniary loss.[33] However, in respect of personal injury claims, the relevant pleading rule under the Civil Procedure Rules makes no reference to special damages. Rather it simply states, "[t]he claimant must attach to his particulars of claim a schedule of details of any past and future expenses and losses which he claims".[34] **27-06**

(c) General principle of compensation

The general object of an award of damages is to compensate the claimant for the losses, pecuniary and non-pecuniary, sustained as a result of the defendant's tort. The general principle is, in the oft-quoted words of Lord Blackburn, that the court should award "that sum of money which will put the party who has been injured, or who has suffered, in the same position as he would have been in if he had not sustained the wrong for which he is now getting his compensation or reparation".[35] The principle can readily be applied to losses which are capable of reasonably precise calculation in money terms, but in cases of personal injury, where damages are claimed for pain and suffering and the like, or in cases of defamation, the concept of restoration is clearly inappropriate.[36] Here compensation can be understood in a different sense, that of providing the claimant with some solace for his misfortunes.[37] As such the guiding principle can be expressed only in such vague **27-07**

---

29 *Admiralty Commissioners v S.S. Susquehanna* [1926] A.C. 655 at 661, per Viscount Dunedin.

30 *Ratcliffe v Evans* [1892] 2 Q.B. 524 at 528, per Bowen LJ.

31 [1969] 1 W.L.R. 630.

32 *Perestrello e Companhia Limitada v United Paint Co Ltd* [1969] 1 W.L.R. 570 at 579; *Calabar Properties Ltd v Stitcher* [1984] 1 W.L.R. 287.

33 See, e.g. *Jefford v Gee* [1970] 2 Q.B. 130 CA. But in *R. v Secretary of State for the Home Department Ex p. Greenfield* [2005] UKHL 14; [2005] 1 W.L.R. 673 at [11]–[12] Lord Bingham equated "special damages" with pecuniary loss and "general damages" with non-pecuniary loss.

34 CPR r.16.4(1)(e), 16 PD 4.2.

35 *Livingstone v Rawyards Coal Co* (1880) 5 App. Cas. 25 at 39. For examples of restatements see: *Admiralty Commissioners v S.S. Valeria* [1922] 2 A.C. 242 at 248, per Viscount Dunedin; *Liesbosch Dredger (Owners) v S.S. Edison (Owners)* [1933] A.C. 449 at 463, per Lord Wright; *Lim Poh Choo v Camden and Islington AHA* [1980] A.C. 174 at 187, per Lord Scarman; *Knauer v Ministry of Justice* [2016] UKSC 9; [2016] A.C. 908 at [1].

36 *British Transport Commission v Gourley* [1956] A.C. 185 at 197, per Earl Jowitt; *H West & Son v Shephard* [1964] A.C. 326 at 346, per Lord Morris.

37 *Warren v King* [1964] 1 W.L.R. 1 at 10, per Harman LJ and see Ogus, "Damages for Lost Amenities:

terms as awarding what is "fair reasonable and just".[38] However, some consistency between awards for non-pecuniary loss is attainable. The courts have shown themselves anxious to ensure such consistency not only by adhering to a judicial "tariff" system for assessing non-pecuniary loss in personal injury cases;[39] but also by laying down that the awards for non-pecuniary loss in a phone-hacking breach of privacy case should bear a "reasonable relationship" to the scale of damages for non-pecuniary loss in personal injury cases,[40] by permitting juries in defamation and other cases to be told of the scale of awards for non-pecuniary loss in personal injury cases[41] and by the Court of Appeal's laying down of some guideline figures for juries on quantum in false imprisonment and malicious prosecution claims against the police.[42] Even where restoration is possible, as with damaged property, the courts will not always award the cost of restoring the property to its original state; they may instead assess the damages on the diminished value of the asset.[43] It should be noted that in some exceptional cases exemplary damages may be awarded, the object of which is to punish the defendant rather than to compensate the claimant.[44] Restitutionary damages concerned to reverse the defendant's wrongful enrichment, rather than to compensate the claimant, may also sometimes be awarded.[45]

(d) Causation and remoteness

27-08 The loss for which compensation is claimed must be caused by, and not be too remote a consequence of, the defendant's tort. These matters straddle the distinction between liability and assessment of damages and have been fully dealt with in an earlier chapter.[46] With regard to the test of causation and the effect of overlap-

---

for a finger, a feeling or a function?" (1972) 35 M.L.R. 1.

38 *Rowley v London and North Western Ry Co* (1873) L.R. 8 Exch. 221 at 231; *Pickett v British Rail Engineering Ltd* [1980] A.C. 136 at 168, per Lord Scarman; *Lim Poh Choo v Camden and Islington AHA* [1980] A.C. 174 at 187; *Heil v Rankin* [2001] Q.B. 272 CA.

39 See para.27-57.

40 *Gulati v MGN Ltd* [2015] EWCA Civ 1291; [2017] Q.B. 149 at [63]. The damages were to compensate for the mental distress and the infringement of the right to privacy itself (and aggravated damages might also be awarded). Perhaps surprisingly, the damages actually awarded by the judge at first instance, admittedly for many different infringements of privacy suffered by each of several claimants, were held not to be wholly out of line with the scale of damages for personal injury. See further paras 26-59 to 26-60.

41 *John v MGN Ltd* [1997] Q.B. 586, CA (defamation); *Thompson v Commissioner of Police for the Metropolis* [1998] Q.B. 498 CA (false imprisonment and malicious prosecution). Though note that the right to a jury trial in defamation actions has been removed by s.11 of the Defamation Act 2013. See also para.27-152.

42 *Thompson v Commissioner of Police for the Metropolis* [1998] Q.B. 498 CA. See para.27-138 fn.703.

43 See para.27-120.

44 See paras 27-134 to 27-149.

45 See paras 27-150 to 27-151. Nominal damages may be awarded for torts actionable per se; see Edelman, *McGregor on Damages*, 20th edn (2017), Ch.12; Burrows, *Remedies for Torts, Breach of Contract, and Equitable Wrongs*, 4th edn, Ch.25. See, e.g. *R. (Lumba) v Secretary of State for the Home Department* [2011] UKSC 12; [2012] 1 A.C. 245 (false imprisonment, but would have been imprisoned in any event had correct procedures been followed). In *Grobbelaar v News Group Newspapers Ltd* [2002] UKHL 40; [2002] 1 W.L.R. 3024 (where damages of £1 were awarded and were described as nominal but are probably better viewed as contemptuous in that they recognised that the claimant's rights had been infringed while admonishing the claimant for his own conduct).

46 See Ch.2.

ping, concurrent and cumulative causes, the same principles operate both to establish a cause of action and to measure the amount of damages payable, and no further discussion is required here. In relation to remoteness the position is not so clear. In cases involving injury to the person or property, initial liability, the cause of action, is established by showing that that kind of injury was a reasonably foreseeable consequence of the defendant's conduct. However, the foreseeability principle is not the appropriate test for determining the extent of the recoverable losses which flow from the injury. As Eveleigh J said in *Wieland v Cyril Lord Carpets*,[47] "in determining liability for ... possible consequences [of an injury], it is not necessary to show that each was within the foreseeable extent or foreseeable scope of the original injury in the same way that the possibility of injury must be foreseen when determining whether or not the defendant's conduct gives a claim in negligence". Thus for the purposes of a typical personal injury claim the defendant must reasonably have foreseen that his conduct would inflict a physical injury on the claimant but he need not have foreseen the impact that injury would have on the claimant in relation to his health or his income.[48]

(e) Mitigation

The claimant is under a duty[49] to mitigate the losses resulting from the defendant's tort.[50] Damages are not recoverable for such losses as the claimant has avoided by taking action subsequent to the tort[51]: the general principle of compensa- **27-09**

---

[47] [1969] 3 All E.R. 1006 at 1009–1010.

[48] *Smith v Leech Brain & Co Ltd* [1962] 2 Q.B. 405; *Burke v John Paul & Co* [1967] I.R. 277; *Malcolm v Broadhurst* [1970] 3 All E.R. 508; *Brice v Brown* [1984] 1 All E.R. 997 (psychiatric harm). For damage to property, see, e.g. *The Arpad* [1934] P. 189 at 202, per Scrutton LJ; *Vacwell Engineering Co Ltd v BDH Chemical Ltd* [1971] 1 Q.B. 111; *Muirhead v Industrial Tank Specialities Ltd* [1986] Q.B. 507.

[49] Though this is not, strictly speaking, a legal duty, since it cannot be enforced as such. Failure to fulfil it simply entails a reduction in the damages awarded. See *Darbishire v Warran* [1963] 1 W.L.R. 1067 at 1075, per Pearson LJ.

[50] *British Westinghouse Co Ltd v Underground Railways Ltd* [1912] A.C. 673; *Jamal v Moolla, Dawood Co* [1916] A.C. 175 at 179. See also *Macrae v HG Swindells (trading as West View Garage Co)* [1954] 1 W.L.R. 597; *Darbishire v Warran* [1963] 1 W.L.R. 1067; *Canadian Imperial Bank of Commerce v Doucette* (1968) 70 D.L.R. (2d) 657; *Luker v Chapman* (1970) 114 S.J. 788; *Bellingham v Dhillon* [1973] 1 Q.B. 304; *Uzinterimpex JSC v Standard Bank Plc* [2008] EWCA Civ 819; [2008] 2 Lloyd's Rep. 456 (tort of conversion).

[51] It is a question of fact in each case whether a particular benefit which has accrued to the claimant as a result of his action relates sufficiently closely to a particular head of damage so as to justify a deduction: *Nadreph Ltd v Willmott & Co (A Firm)* [1978] 1 W.L.R. 1537 at 1543. Steps taken before the tort to offset the loss (e.g. an insurance policy) will generally constitute a benefit which is collateral to the defendant's liability and will thus not affect it: see the detailed discussion below, paras 27-45 to 27-54. But a failure to take precautionary action to reduce the risk of physical injury may give rise to a successful plea of contributory negligence: *O'Connell v Jackson* [1972] 1 Q.B. 270. On the somewhat unclear relationship between contributory negligence and mitigation see: Williams, *Joint Torts and Contributory Negligence* (1951), Ch.11; Street, *Principles of the Law of Damages*, pp.37–39. Note that there is also a potential inter-relationship between remoteness of damage and mitigation. In *Morris v Richards* [2003] EWCA Civ 232; [2004] P.I.Q.R. Q3 at [14] Schiemann LJ said that he was "reluctant to embark upon an analysis at a high level of abstraction of the circumstances in which action or inaction by a claimant is properly characterised as a failure to mitigate rather than as producing a situation in which the damage suffered by the claimant is characterised as too remote". Counsel had argued that the difference was significant in terms of who bore the burden of proof as to whether the claimant's conduct (in resigning from a job) was reasonable, the burden of proving that damage is not too remote being the claimant's, but the burden of

tion implies that he can claim only for losses actually sustained.[52] So if the claimant has lost his employment as the result of an actionable injury, damages for loss of earnings must take account of any earnings in an alternative employment. Further, he will not be allowed to recover for any losses which, though he did sustain, he might reasonably have avoided. In the example given, a deduction may be made where an injured claimant unreasonably declines to accept an offer of alternative employment or refuses medical care which, if successful, would have rendered him fit to resume his employment.[53] Where a claimant obtained alternative employment, but then resigned the defendant was held responsible for the continuing loss of earnings following the resignation, on the basis that the claimant was not at fault in losing the new job (though it would be different if she were at fault in losing the new job).[54] The owner of a damaged car might recover only the cost of purchasing a near equivalent on the market where this was cheaper than having his own model repaired.[55] The onus is on the defendant to show that the claimant failed to mitigate[56] and much will depend on what the court regards, in the circumstances, as being "reasonable".[57] Judges are reluctant to impose excessive demands on claimants.[58] While an injured person must reasonably seek medical care, he need not submit himself to a surgical operation involving some substantial

proving that the claimant had failed to mitigate her loss being the defendant's.

52 *Bellingham v Dhillon* [1973] 1 Q.B. 304.

53 *McAuley v London Transport Executive* [1957] 2 Lloyd's Rep. 500 CA; *Morgan v T Wallis* [1974] 1 Lloyd's Rep. 165.

54 *Morris v Richards* [2003] EWCA Civ 232; [2004] P.I.Q.R. Q3 at [21], per Keene LJ: "The liability of a tortfeasor is not to be reduced because the injured party, having lost employment because of the injury, takes a different job in an attempt to mitigate his or her damage but loses that job because it is beyond his or her capabilities."

55 *Darbishire v Warran* [1963] 1 W.L.R. 1067. But see *Coles v Hetherton* [2013] EWCA Civ 1704; [2015] 1 W.L.R. 160 in which it was reasoned that the duty to mitigate has no application to the reasonable cost of repairs where that is the diminution in value of the car and is therefore the direct, rather than a consequential, loss. In *Copley v Lawn* [2009] EWCA Civ 580; [2009] P.I.Q.R. P21 it was held that claimants, whose cars have been negligently damaged and have been supplied with temporary replacement cars by their insurers, do not fail in their duty to mitigate by refusing or ignoring the offer of replacement cars from the defendants' insurers where the cost of hire of those cars was not made clear. Even if this did constitute a failure in their duty to mitigate, they would still be entitled as damages to the cost of hire of those replacement cars. As emerges from *Sayce v TNT (UK) Ltd* [2011] EWCA Civ 1583; [2012] 1 W.L.R. 1261, some of the reasoning in *Copley v Lawn* is controversial.

56 *Roper v Johnson* (1873) L.R. 8 C. & P. 167; *Yetton v Eastwoods Froy* [1967] 1 W.L.R. 104 at 115; *Garnac Grain Co Inc v Faure & Fairclough Ltd* [1968] A.C. 1130; *London and South of England Building Society v Stone* [1983] 1 W.L.R. 1242 CA; *Gebrüder Metelmann GmbH & Co KG v NBR (London) Ltd* [1984] 1 Lloyd's Rep. 614; *Geest Plc v Lansiquot* [2002] 1 W.L.R. 3111 PC (disapproving *Selvanayagam v University of West Indies* [1983] 1 W.L.R. 585); *LE Jones (Insurance Brokers) Ltd v Portsmouth City Council* [2002] EWCA Civ 1723; [2003] 1 W.L.R. 427 at [26].

57 *Payzu Ltd v Saunders* [1919] 2 K.B. 581, per Bankes LJ at 588, per Scrutton LJ at 589.

58 *Banco de Portugal v Waterlow & Sons Ltd* [1932] A.C. 452 at 506, per Lord Macmillan; *London and South of England Building Society v Stone* [1983] 1 W.L.R. 1242: the claimant's "conduct in not taking steps to reduce the loss will not be weighed in nice scales at the instance of the party who has occasioned the loss", per Stephenson LJ at 1263; *Morris v Richards* [2003] EWCA Civ 232; [2004] P.I.Q.R. Q3 at [16]: the question of whether the claimant was at fault in losing her new job should be resolved "bearing in mind that it was the wrongful act of the defendant which put the claimant in the position of having to find a new job and that therefore she should not be judged too harshly"; *LE Jones (Insurance Brokers) Ltd v Portsmouth City Council* [2002] EWCA Civ 1723; [2003] 1 W.L.R. 427 at [26].

risk or of which the outcome is uncertain.[59] He should not be expected to start uncertain litigation against a third party,[60] nor to risk capital in a speculative venture,[61] nor to destroy his own property,[62] nor to put his good public relations at risk.[63]

In *Lagden v O'Connor*[64] the House of Lords made clear that, contrary to the apparent rule laid down in *The Liesbosch*,[65] damages can be awarded for a loss that flows from the claimant's impecuniosity. The majority of their Lordships (Lord Nicholls, Slynn and Hope) went on to hold that where a claimant, whose car has been tortiously damaged, reasonably wishes to hire a replacement car but, because of lack of funds, has no real choice other than to hire through an accident-hire scheme, he or she can recover the costs incurred in so doing. This is so even though those costs are higher (and include incidental benefits) than the normal costs of hiring a replacement car. In other words, viewed as an aspect of the duty to mitigate, an impecunious claimant will be acting reasonably in incurring the higher costs of an accident-hire scheme; whereas an affluent claimant will be acting unreasonably in incurring such high costs and will instead be compensated only for the normal hiring costs. In practice one would expect that defendants will find it difficult to challenge a claim for the higher costs of an accident-hire scheme that have been (or will be incurred) by the claimant. But Lord Nicholls suggested that insurers and credit hire companies should be able to agree on standard inquiries to assess a claimant's impecuniosity. And as a test of impecuniosity, he suggested "[an] inability to pay car hire charges without making sacrifices the plaintiff could not reasonably be expected to make".[66] **27-10**

A claimant may not increase the damages claimed by his own unnecessary act subsequent to the tort.[67] In *Admiralty Commissioners v S.S. Amerika*[68] one of His Majesty's submarines was sunk by the fault of the defendants, and the crew were drowned. The Commissioners claimed as an item of damage the capitalised amount of the pensions payable by them to the relatives of the crew. It was held that this could not be recovered, the pensions being voluntary payments in the nature of compassionate allowances. Again, in an action for trespass to the person, a claimant, who had been wrongfully removed from a railway carriage, was denied damages for the loss of his race glasses which he had carelessly left behind.[69] But where **27-11**

59 *Savage v Wallis* [1966] 1 Lloyd's Rep. 357; *Selvanayagam v University of West Indies* [1983] 1 W.L.R. 585. In *Emeh v Kensington AHA* [1985] Q.B. 1012 it was held that a mother's refusal to have an abortion did not constitute a failure to mitigate so as to bar or reduce damages in a claim for "wrongful birth"; see para.27-60.

60 *Pilkington v Wood* [1953] Ch. 770.

61 *Jewelowski v Propp* [1944] K.B. 510.

62 *Elliott Steam Tug Co v Shipping Controller* [1922] 1 K.B. 127 at 140.

63 *London and South of England Building Society v Stone* [1983] 1 W.L.R. 1242.

64 [2003] UKHL 64; [2004] 1 A.C. 1067, para.2-180. See also *Alcoa Minerals of Jamaica Inc v Herbert Broderick* [2002] 1 A.C. 371 PC. *Lagden v O'Connor* was applied in *W v Veolia Environment Services (UK) Plc* [2011] EWHC 2020 (QB); [2012] 1 All E.R. (Comm) 667 in holding that total hire fees of more than £138,000 to hire a replacement Bentley, while the claimant's Bentley was being repaired, were recoverable.

65 [1933] A.C. 449 HL.

66 [2003] UKHL 64 at [9].

67 In this situation the courts are just as likely to use the language of causation as they are mitigation. See also *The Calliope* [1970] P. 172 (contributory negligence).

68 [1917] A.C. 38. cf. *The San Onofre* [1922] P. 243.

69 *Glover v L & SW Ry* (1867) L.R. 3 Q.B. 25.

an act is reasonably done with a view to minimising any possible future damage and is not "extraneous or extrinsic"[70] any expenses appear to be recoverable. So, the expense of raising a ketch sunk by the defendant's negligence and obstructing navigation was recoverable.[71] And, on the basis that the Crown had an action for loss of services for injury to members of the Royal Air Force, the Crown was held entitled to recover the amount of the wages and rations of injured airmen during their incapacity, and of their treatment in a Royal Air Force hospital, since that amount could have been recovered by the airmen from the defendant as additional damages if the expense had not been reasonably borne by the Crown.[72]

(f) Certainty

27-12 There remains to consider the extent to which the losses pleaded must be certain and how account is taken of future contingencies.[73] A distinction must first be drawn between the question of the degree of proof required in relation to the losses pleaded in the statement of case and the question whether losses which depend on future contingencies may be pleaded and how they are to be assessed. With regard to the former, the general principle was stated by Bowen LJ in *Ratcliffe v Evans*[74]: "the character of the acts themselves which produce the damage, and the circumstances under which these acts are done must regulate the degree of certainty and particularity with which the damage done ought to be stated and proved. As much certainty and particularity must be insisted on … as is reasonable, having regard to the circumstances and to the nature of the acts themselves by which the damage is done." Clearly, special damages such as expenses and the loss on particular contracts must be pleaded and proved exactly.[75] Some elements in general damages, particularly non-pecuniary losses such as pain and suffering, are inferred or presumed and little is required by way of evidence.[76] Financial elements in the general damages will not normally be presumed,[77] and thus should be supported by evidence. In personal injury claims, the claimant must attach to his particulars of claim a schedule of details of any past and future expenses and losses which he claims.[78]

27-13 The problem of dealing with losses whose existence or amount are speculative

70 *The Oropesa* [1943] P. 32; and see the discussion of the cases therein.

71 *Dee Conservancy Board v McConnell* [1928] 2 K.B. 159.

72 *Att Gen v Valle-Jones* [1935] 2 K.B. 209; cf. *Metropolitan Police District (Receiver) v Tatum* [1948] 2 K.B. 68; not followed in *R. v Richardson and Adams* [1947] 4 D.L.R. 401. The action for loss of services was abolished by the Administration of Justice Act 1982. In any event *Valle-Jones* is no longer good law on the point that an action for loss of services will lie in such a case: *Att Gen (NSW) v Perpetual Trustee Co Ltd* [1955] A.C. 457.

73 Edelman, *McGregor on Damages*, 20th edn (2017), Ch.10; Burrows, *Remedies for Torts, Breach of Contract, and Equitable Wrongs*, 4th edn (2019), Ch.5.

74 [1892] 2 Q.B. 525 at 532–533.

75 See paras 27-05 to 27-06.

76 Edelman, *McGregor on Damages*, 20th edn (2017), 52-008.

77 *Domsalla v Barr* [1969] 1 W.L.R. 630. The same is true of business losses at least where the loss is consequent on a physical injury to property: e.g. *The Risoluto* (1883) 8 P. & D. 109 and see para.27-122. Where however the tort constitutes a direct invasion of a business interest (e.g. passing off, injurious falsehood, inducement of breach of contract) loss of profits is generally presumed: *Goldsoll v Goldman* [1914] 2 Ch. 603 at 615; *Draper v Trist* [1939] 3 All E.R. 513 at 526. Even so, it is often advisable to produce evidence of the loss, as the amount presumed might be small or even nominal: cf. *Hayward v Hayward* (1887) 34 Ch. D. 198.

78 See para.27-06.

because they depend on future or hypothetical events (including the actions of a third party) is a difficult one. Yet, except where provisional damages and periodical payments can be awarded,[79] there is no escape from it because many damage claims (particularly those for personal injuries) involve a substantial degree of prophesy. It has been reiterated many times that mere difficulty of assessment is not a bar to recovery.[80] This is necessarily subject to the de minimis principle; no account is to be taken of possibilities which are in actuarial terms small, speculative or fanciful.[81] As it was colourfully put by Erle CJ in 1860, "supposing a lady to have been injured and disfigured in a railway accident, she could not say that she ought to recover damages because she was prevented from going to a ball, at which she might have met a rich husband".[82]

Once it has been established that the chance of loss is not too small to be ignored under this principle, damages are assessed in proportion to that chance. The normal balance of probabilities standard is here inappropriate so that, for example, a claimant will not be awarded 100 per cent damages if the chance of his loss is assessed at 51 per cent.[83] A good example of uncertainty as to how an injury will adversely affect the claimant's future is provided by *Moeliker v Reyrolle & Co Ltd*[84] where, although the claimant had not yet suffered any loss of earnings, damages were awarded for his disadvantage in the labour market. Browne LJ said the following: **27-14**

> "The consideration of this head of damages should be made in two stages. 1. Is there a 'substantial' or 'real' risk that a [claimant] will lose his present job at some time before the estimated end of his working life? 2. If there is (but not otherwise), the court must assess and quantify the present value of the risk of the financial damage which the [claimant] will suffer if that risk materialises, having regard to the degree of the risk, the time when it may materialise, and the factors, both favourable and unfavourable, which in a particular case will, or may, affect the [claimant's] chances of getting a job at all, or an equally well paid job."[85]

---

79 See paras 27-72 and 27-76 to 27-77.

80 The classic statement is that of Vaughan Williams LJ in *Chaplin v Hicks* [1911] 2 K.B. 786 at 792. See also *The Mediana* [1900] A.C. 113 at 116-117; *Otter v Church, Adams Tatham Co* [1953] Ch. 280 at 290; *Moeliker v A Reyrolle & Co Ltd* [1977] 1 W.L.R. 132 at 141.

81 *Davies v Taylor* [1974] A.C. 207 at 212 and 220.

82 *Priestley v Maclean* (1860) 2 F. & F. 288 at 289.

83 The classic breach of contract case awarding damages for loss of a chance is *Chaplin v Hicks* [1911] 2 K.B. 786. For such damages in personal injury and death cases, see, e.g. *Mallett v McMonagle* [1970] A.C. 166; *Davies v Taylor* [1974] A.C. 207 at 212–213, 219–220; *Doyle v Wallace* [1998] P.I.Q.R. Q146 CA; *Langford v Hebran* [2001] EWCA Civ 361; [2001] P.I.Q.R. Q160; *Herring v Ministry of Defence* [2003] EWCA Civ 528; [2004] 1 All E.R. 44; *Brown v Ministry of Defence* [2006] EWCA Civ 546; [2006] P.I.Q.R. Q9; *Collett v Smith* [2008] EWHC 1962 (QB). For such damages in professional negligence claims see the important case of *Allied Maples Group Ltd v Simmons & Simmons* [1995] 1 W.L.R. 1602; and, e.g. *Hall v Meyrick* [1957] 2 Q.B. 455 (reversed on other grounds); *Kitchen v Royal Air Force Association* [1958] 1 W.L.R. 563; *First Interstate Bank of California v Cohen Arnold* [1996] P.N.L.R.; *Hartle v Laceys* [1999] Lloyd's Rep P.N. 315 CA; *Sharif v Garrett & Co* [2001] EWCA Civ 1269; [2002] 1 W.L.R. 3118; *John D Wood & Co Ltd v Knatchbull* [2002] EWHC 2822 (QB); [2003] P.N.L.R. 17; [2003] 8 E.G. 131; *Normans Bay Ltd v Coudert Brothers* [2004] EWCA Civ 215; *The Times,* 24 March 2004; *Dixon v Clement Jones* [2004] EWCA Civ 1005; [2005] P.N.L.R. 6; *Dudarec v Andrews* [2006] EWCA Civ 256; [2006] 1 W.L.R. 3002. See also *Malec v JC Hutton Pty Ltd* (1990) 92 A.L.R. 545; *Sellars v Adelaide Petroleum NL* (1994) 120 A.L.R. 16; *Chappel v Hart* [1998] HCA 55; (1998) 156 A.L.R. 517. See generally Burrows, "Uncertainty about Uncertainty: Damages for Loss of a Chance" [2008] J.P.I.L. 31.

84 [1977] 1 W.L.R. 132.

85 [1977] 1 W.L.R. 132 at 142.

27-15 Uncertainty may prevail not only on the question of how an injury will adversely affect the claimant's future, but also on the question of what would have been his prospects if the injury had not occurred. An example is provided by *Barry v British Transport Commission*.[86] Before the accident for which the defendants were liable, the claimant had been employed for a short period on work for which he was paid double his normal earnings. On the evidence there was a bare probability, but no more, that if he had not been injured, he would have continued to earn at the higher rate. The court awarded damages for lost earnings on the basis of about 60 per cent of the higher rate.

27-16 Uncertain events may operate to diminish as well as to increase the claimant's loss and the assessment process should take account of this. Thus in a personal injury claim, the court may make a deduction for the possibility that the claimant may recover earlier than anticipated[87] or that a surgical operation might have been unsuccessful even if performed at the right time.[88] A deduction is also appropriate for the possibility that part of the future loss would have been sustained even if the tort had not been committed. It is for this reason that the courts typically make a small deduction from personal injury damages for the fact that earnings might have been affected by contingencies such as unemployment or illness.[89]

27-17 It should be emphasised that the approach of awarding damages in proportion to the chance of loss is only applicable where the assessment is necessarily speculative because it depends on future or hypothetical events. When, on the other hand, the uncertainty revolves around past facts, the courts apply the usual civil standard of proof so that the facts are assumed true if the claimant can prove them on a balance of probabilities but are assumed untrue if that standard cannot be met. Accordingly, in *Hotson v East Berkshire AHA*,[90] the claimant was refused any damages because he had merely shown that there was a 25 per cent chance that, on arrival at hospital, his hip was in a condition whereby speedy medical treatment could have avoided the development of a permanent hip injury; the necessary causal link between the admitted negligence of the medical staff in initially failing to diagnose his injury correctly and the claimant's permanent disability had therefore not been established. As Lord Mackay said[91]:

> "the fundamental question of fact to be answered in this case related to a point in time before the negligent failure to treat began. It must, therefore, be a matter of past fact. It did not raise any question of what might have been the situation in a hypothetical state of facts. To this problem the words of Lord Diplock in *Mallett v McMonagle*[92] apply: 'In determining what did happen in the past a court decides on the balance of probabilities. Anything that is more probable than not it treats as certain'."

27-18 This area of the law was reviewed by the House of Lords in the difficult case of

---

86 [1954] 1 Lloyd's Rep. 372.

87 *Winkworth v Hubbard* [1960] 1 Lloyd's Rep. 150.

88 *Clark v MacLennan* [1983] 1 All E.R. 416.

89 *Mitchell v Mulholland (No.2)* [1972] 1 Q.B. 65 at 75. In *Herring v Ministry of Defence* [2003] EWCA Civ 528; [2004] 1 All E.R. 44 Potter LJ said that the level of reduction for contingencies traditionally applied by the judiciary has been too high.

90 [1987] A.C. 750. See also para.2-87 onwards.

91 *Hotson v East Berkshire AHA* [1987] A.C. 750 at 785. See also Lord Bridge at 782 and Lord Ackner at 792.

92 [1970] A.C. 166 at 176.

Gregg v Scott.[93] A doctor negligently diagnosed a lump under the claimant's left arm as benign when it was in fact cancerous. This led to a delay of nine months in the claimant receiving proper treatment. It was found that, on the balance of probabilities, the claimant would not have been "cured" of cancer (with "cure" meaning surviving for more than 10 years) even if there had been no delay. It was also found that the delay had reduced the claimant's chances of cure from 42 per cent to 25 per cent. The majority of the House of Lords (Lord Hoffmann, Lord Phillips and Baroness Hale) refused to award the claimant damages for the reduction in the chances of cure. Despite this, it remains to be seen whether a loss of chance approach can ever be appropriate in medical negligence cases, where the negligence has reduced the claimant's chances of cure. The case also left some other difficulties unresolved. Two linked uncertainties are particularly troubling. The first is that no clear justification was given for why a loss of the chance approach is thought appropriate—as many past cases have established that it is[94]—for professional negligence cases causing pure economic loss but not for medical negligence. The second is that, while receiving some apparent support from Lord Hoffmann[95] (and from Lord Nicholls dissenting),[96] the precise status of Stuart-Smith LJ's influential judgment in *Allied Maples Group Ltd v Simmons & Simmons*[97] was left unclear. Stuart-Smith LJ had there attempted to rationalise the law on hypothetical events by laying down that a loss of chance approach was appropriate where the uncertainty was as to the hypothetical conduct of third parties, but not the hypothetical conduct of the claimant who could be expected to prove, on the balance of probabilities, one way or the other, what he would have done had there been no breach of duty by the defendant. However, that particular uncertainty has subsequently been resolved by the support of the Supreme Court in *Perry v Raleys Solicitors*[98] for the distinction drawn in the *Allied Maples* case.

A further twist is that in *Barker v Corus (UK) Plc*,[99] the House of Lords, by a majority, treated the relevant damage in question (in applying the exception to normal causation recognised in *Fairchild v Glenhaven Funeral Services Ltd*)[100] as the material increase of risk of contracting mesothelioma. But it was stressed that this applied only because the outcome was known, i.e. the relevant disease (mesothelioma) had been contracted. Their Lordships did not, therefore, see themselves as opening the door to the recovery of damages simply because a defendant had negligently materially increased the risk of a claimant suffering a particular disease or injury. **27-19**

93 [2005] UKHL 2; [2005] 2 A.C. 176. See paras 2-89 to 2-99.
94 See para.27-14 fn.83.
95 [2005] UKHL 2 at [82]–[83].
96 [2005] UKHL 2 at [19].
97 [1995] 1 W.L.R. 1602.
98 [2019] UKSC 5; [2020] A.C. 352; see para.2-80.
99 [2005] UKHL 20; [2006] 2 A.C. 572. *Barker* has been statutorily reversed in mesothelioma cases by the Compensation Act 2006, s.3. See also *Sienkiewicz v Greif (UK) Ltd* [2011] UKSC 10; [2011] 2 A.C. 229; and the highly critical analysis of *Barker* in *Durham v BAI (Run off) Ltd* [2012] UKSC 14; [2012] 1 W.L.R. 867. In *Zurich Insurance Plc UK Branch v International Energy Group Ltd* [2015] UKSC 33; [2016] A.C. 509 the Supreme Court has made clear that, despite all the difficulties created by it, at common law *Barker* remains good law. See further para.2-72 onwards.
100 [2002] UKHL 22; [2003] 1 A.C. 32. See paras 2-53 onwards.

3. DAMAGES FOR PERSONAL INJURIES

(a) Itemisation of awards

27-20 In all but a few exceptional cases the victim of personal injury suffers two distinct kinds of loss which may be classed respectively as pecuniary and non-pecuniary. Pecuniary loss is that which is susceptible of direct translation into money terms and includes such matters as loss of earnings, actual and prospective, and out-of-pocket expenses, while non-pecuniary loss includes such immeasurable elements as pain and suffering and loss of amenity or enjoyment of life. In respect of the former, it is submitted, the court should and usually does seek to achieve precise compensation, while for the latter it seeks to award "fair compensation".[101] This distinction between pecuniary and non-pecuniary damage does not correspond to the traditional pleading distinction between "special" and "general" damages, which refers respectively to pre-trial pecuniary loss and to all other loss, whether pecuniary or non-pecuniary.[102] The practice of restricting any itemisation to that between special and general damages, which was for a long time defended by the judiciary,[103] was a major obstacle to precision in the assessment process since it rendered difficult both scrutiny by an appellate court and comparison with other cases.[104]

27-21 In the 1970s three factors combined to bring about an almost complete reversal by the courts of their former practice. First, growing realisation of the need for consistency in the interests of justice, and thus for comparability of awards of damages, led the full Court of Appeal to put an end to a period of uncertainty[105] and rule that juries should no longer be used for the assessment of damages save in exceptional cases.[106] Secondly, a change in the law concerning interest on awards of damages[107] compelled the courts to accept the inevitability of some form of itemisation, and in *Jefford v Gee*[108] the Court of Appeal held that judges must now assess separately the special damages (i.e. the damages payable for accrued pecuniary loss), the damages for non-pecuniary loss and the damages for future pecuniary loss. Thirdly, the Court of Appeal at last came to the conclusion that the parties themselves had a right to know how the judge arrived at his final figure. In *George v Pinnock*[109] Sachs LJ, with the concurrence of Orr and Buckley LJJ, referred to the "considerable body of judicial opinion which held that [claimant] and defendant alike are entitled to know what is the sum assessed for each relevant head of damage and thus to be able on appeal to challenge any error in the assessments. In my judgment, this court should be slow to emasculate that right of litigants". The

---

101 See para.27-07.

102 See paras 27-05 to 27-06.

103 *Watson v Powles* [1968] 1 Q.B. 596; *Fletcher v Autocar and Transporters Ltd* [1968] 2 Q.B. 322 at 326.

104 *George v Pinnock* [1973] 1 W.L.R. 118 at 126, per Sachs LJ.

105 *Hope v GW Ry* [1937] 2 K.B. 130; *Hennell v Ranaboldo* [1963] 1 W.L.R. 1391; *Sims v William Howard Son Ltd* [1964] 2 Q.B. 409.

106 *Ward v James* [1966] 1 Q.B. 273. cf. *Hodges v Harland and Wolff Ltd* [1965] 1 W.L.R. 523. In *H v Ministry of Defence* [1991] 2 Q.B. 103 the already heavy presumption against jury trial was held to have been made even stronger by s.69(3) of the Senior Courts Act 1981.

107 See para.27-67.

108 [1970] 2 Q.B. 130.

109 [1973] 1 W.L.R. 118 at 126. See also *Smith v Manchester Corp* (1974) 17 K.I.R. 1 at 7, per Edmund Davies LJ; and *Nicholls v National Coal Board* [1976] I.C.R. 266 at 272, per Browne LJ.

practice of itemisation has thus become well-established,[110] and indeed the courts very commonly go further and itemise pecuniary loss beyond the two main heads of pre-trial and future pecuniary loss.[111]

An award will not be overturned simply on the ground that the total amount of damages is too high: rather, one or more of the component items of the damages must be shown to be wrong.[112] Included as an error is where one head of loss overlaps another so as to overcompensate the claimant.[113] In *Harris v Harris*,[114] for example, damages had been awarded to a 12-year-old girl in respect of both her loss of marriage prospects and her future loss of earnings, but in assessing the latter the trial judge had failed to take into account the fact that, had she not been injured, the claimant might have married and given up paid employment; her damages were accordingly reduced by the Court of Appeal. Similarly, if a judge makes separate assessments for loss of future earnings and for loss of earning capacity,[115] he should take care not to duplicate the same loss.[116] Again, to award full loss of earnings plus the full cost of residential care will overcompensate the claimant since the cost of roof and board included in the latter would have been met from the claimant's earnings but for the injury.[117] Whether or not there may be an overlap between pecuniary losses and non-pecuniary losses is less clear. In *Fletcher v Autocar and Transporters Ltd*,[118] the Court of Appeal held that it may be wrong to award a claimant the full amount of his future loss of earnings as well as full compensation for loss of amenities if the hobbies which he enjoyed before his injury were expensive and paid for out of his earnings. In *Lim Poh Choo v Camden and Islington AHA*,[119] the House of Lords was not called upon to decide the issue since the amount awarded for loss of amenities was modest and was not based on any expensive pleasures or pursuits as postulated in the *Fletcher* case, but, with the concurrence of his judicial brethren, Lord Scarman doubted whether there was any overlap between pecuniary and non-pecuniary losses.[120] **27-22**

---

[110] *Pickett v British Rail Engineering Ltd* [1980] A.C. 136 at 167, per Lord Scarman; *Jamil bin Harun v Yang Kamsiah* [1984] A.C. 529.

[111] e.g. *Lim Poh Choo v Camden and Islington AHA* [1980] A.C. 174 at 197; *Housecroft v Burnett* [1986] 1 All E.R. 332 at 334. In *Bennett v Chemical Construction GB Ltd* [1971] 1 W.L.R. 1571 Edmund Davies LJ said: "Where in personal injury cases figures have been agreed between the parties regarding any of the items of damage, it is helpful that counsel should state to the court the basis of their calculation so that it may be recorded and embodied in the judgment."

[112] *Lim Poh Choo v Camden and Islington AHA* [1980] A.C. 174 at 188.

[113] *Fletcher v Autocar and Transporters Ltd* [1968] 2 Q.B. 322 at 326, 341; *Smith v Central Asbestos Co Ltd* [1972] 1 Q.B. 244 at 262; *Taylor v Bristol Omnibus Co* [1975] 1 W.L.R. 1054 at 1057; *Lim Poh Choo v Camden and Islington AHA* [1980] A.C. 174 at 190–191.

[114] [1973] 1 Lloyd's Rep. 445 CA.

[115] See para.27-37.

[116] *Clarke v Rotax Aircraft Equipment Ltd* [1975] 1 W.L.R. 1570.

[117] *Croke v Wiseman* [1982] 1 W.L.R. 71 at 83, per Griffiths LJ. cf. *Shearman v Folland* [1950] 2 K.B. 43; *Lim Poh Choo v Camden and Islington AHA* [1980] A.C. 174.

[118] [1968] 2 Q.B. 322 at 336–337 and 342–344. See also *Smith v Central Asbestos Co Ltd* [1972] 1 Q.B. 244 at 262, where Lord Denning MR suggested that it must be a "comfort" to the claimant "to know that he is getting full compensation for loss of future earnings ... To that extent the award for loss of amenities may be reduced."

[119] [1980] A.C. 174.

[120] [1980] A.C. 192. See also *Damages for Personal Injury: Non-Pecuniary Loss*, Law Commission Report No.257 (1999), paras 2.65–2.68; Edelman, *McGregor on Damages*, 20th edn (2017), paras 40-059 to 40-061.

(b) Medical and other expenses

27-23 The claimant may recover any medical or related expenses, such as hospital, nursing or special accommodation costs,[121] that he has reasonably[122] incurred or will reasonably incur[123] as a result of his injury.[124] He cannot recover as damages the capital cost of acquiring special accommodation for he retains the capital in question in the form of the accommodation[125]; but he may recover a sum for the cost of the capital.[126] Where the claimant has been deprived of her womb because of the defendant's negligence and therefore cannot have children, the costs of surrogacy may be recoverable, whether or not the child would be genetically linked to the claimant (i.e. even if neither the baby nor the pregnancy would be hers).[127] The Law

---

121 *Shearman v Folland* [1950] 2 K.B. 43; *Cutts v Chumley* [1967] 1 W.L.R. 742; *George v Pinnock* [1973] 1 W.L.R. 118.

122 *Winkworth v Hubbard* [1960] 1 Lloyd's Rep. 150 (medical treatment in New York held reasonable); *Rialas v Mitchell* (1984) 128 S.J. 704 CA (reasonable to be treated at home even if care in a private institution would be substantially cheaper); *Sowden v Lodge* [2004] EWCA Civ 1370; [2005] 1 W.L.R. 2129 (test is one of reasonableness not one of what is in the claimant's best interests: but, even if unreasonable for the claimant to live in her own home, rather than in local authority residential accommodation, it might be workable and reasonable to have extra services in such accommodation thereby requiring a "top-up-fee" paid for by the defendant); *Godbold v Mahmood* [2005] EWHC 1002; [2006] P.I.Q.R. Q5 (defendant had not shown that the claimant's proposed option of a privately-funded care home was unreasonable). In *Peters v East Midlands SHA* [2009] EWCA Civ 145; [2010] Q.B. 48 the disabled claimant would, on the balance of probabilities, be cared for and accommodated by a local authority in a residential home. It was held that she was entitled as of right to damages for the cost of self-funding that residential care even though the local authority would provide it for free if she did not self-fund. It was decided-with respect, controversially-that the duty to mitigate had no role to play here but that, even if it did, the claimant's preference to be self-funded, and not to be reliant on the state, was reasonable. It was thought that there was here no risk of double recovery (i.e. being awarded damages for self-funding and then being provided with free residential care) because the claimant's affairs were controlled by the Court of Protection. *R. (on the application of Tinsley) v Manchester City Council* [2017] EWCA Civ 1704; [2018] Q.B. 767 concerned a claimant who had been so severely injured in a road accident caused by another's negligence that he had been compulsorily detained in hospital under the Mental Health Act 1983. The relevant local authority refused to fund post-detention care services for the claimant on the ground that he had been awarded tort damages for future care and could therefore afford to pay for the care out of the damages. In judicial review proceedings, this refusal was held to be unlawful: the statute required such after-care services to be provided free of charge.

123 As with future loss of earnings, future expenses are generally calculated using a "multiplier" method, and there will normally be no adjustment for a higher rate of tax payable on the income from investing the damages. See paras 27-29 to 27-36.

124 See, generally, *Damages for Personal Injury: Medical, Nursing and Other Expenses; Collateral Benefits*, Law Commission Report No.262 (1999), s.A.

125 *George v Pinnock* [1973] 1 W.L.R. 118; *Cunningham v Harrison* [1973] Q.B. 942; *Roberts v Johnstone* [1989] Q.B. 878.

126 In *Wells v Wells* [1999] 1 A.C. 345 HL, it was laid down, inter alia, that the discount rate used in calculating the cost of the capital, for the purposes of applying *Roberts v Johnstone*, is the interest rate on index-linked government stock (ILGS), which was for the time being treated as being three per cent. However, the appropriate discount rate in assessing future pecuniary loss has subsequently been reduced to minus 0.25% by the Lord Chancellor, acting under the powers conferred by the Damages Act 1996 s.A1: see para.27-33. The effect of this negative discount rate on a *Roberts v Johnstone* award for the cost of the capital is unclear but it can be powerfully argued that the logical consequence is that there should now be no sum payable as the cost of the capital under *Roberts v Johnstone*. On the question of whether there should be a deduction for betterment, see *Roberts v Johnstone* [1989] Q.B. 878 at 893.

127 *Whittington Hospital NHS Trust v XX* [2020] UKSC 14; [2020] 2 W.L.R. 972. This includes the reasonable costs of undertaking surrogacy arrangements abroad even if those arrangements would

Reform (Personal Injuries) Act 1948 s.2(4), lays down that the possibility of avoiding expenses or part of them by making use of the facilities of the National Health Service is to be disregarded. However, if advantage is in fact taken of those facilities the claimant is not entitled to recover what he would have had to pay if he had contracted for them privately.[128] Similarly, if it appears to the court to be likely that the claimant will be unable to obtain privately all the nursing services he will need, so that he will eventually have to enter a National Health Hospital, an appropriate deduction shall be made.[129] Account should also be taken of the fact that a person who is dependent on institutional care saves on domestic expenses which otherwise would have been incurred: so, in the case of private care, a deduction will be made from the damages awarded for the cost of care,[130] while by the Administration of Justice Act 1982 s.5, "any saving which is attributable to his maintenance wholly or partly at public expense in a hospital, nursing home or other institution shall be set off against any income lost by him as a result of his injuries".[131]

In principle, the claimant should be able to recover for all other non-remote expenses that have been or will be reasonably incurred as a result of the injury. So, as recognised in *Daly v General Steam Navigation Ltd*,[132] a housewife is entitled to the cost of employing domestic help. On the other hand, in *Pritchard v JH Cobden Ltd*[133] the Court of Appeal refused to follow its earlier decision in *Jones v* **27-24**

---

be contrary to the Surrogacy Arrangements Act 1985 in the UK (declining to follow *Briody v St Helens and Knowsley HA* [2001] EWCA Civ 1010; [2002] Q.B. 856 on the ground that public policy in relation to surrogacy had moved on since that decision).

128 *Harris v Brights Asphalt Contractors Ltd* [1953] 1 Q.B. 617 at 635, per Slade J; *Cunningham v Harrison* [1973] Q.B. 942 at 957, per Lawton LJ; *Lim Poh Choo v Camden and Islington AHA* [1980] A.C. 174 at 188, per Lord Scarman; *Woodrup v Nicol* [1993] P.I.Q.R. Q104 at Q114, per Russell LJ.

129 *Cunningham v Harrison* [1973] Q.B. 942; *Lim Poh Choo v Camden and Islington AHA* [1980] A.C. 174; *Woodrup v Nicol* [1993] P.I.Q.R. Q104 CA; *Eagle v Chambers* [2004] EWCA Civ 1033; [2004] 1 W.L.R. 3081 (the same factual test should be applied to services provided by social services as to services provided by the NHS; and where a private care regime is needed, the burden of proving that services will be provided by the NHS or social services lies on the defendant); *Walton v Calderdale Healthcare NHS Trust* [2005] EWHC 1053 (QB); [2006] P.I.Q.R. Q3; *Freeman v Lockett* [2006] EWHC 102 (QB); [2006] Lloyd's Rep. Med. 151. Applying the basic principle that benefits should be deducted from damages (see *Hodgson v Trapp* [1989] A.C. 807; see para.27-41) where a court finds that a claimant will receive direct payments from a local authority for care, they must be taken into account (i.e. deducted) in assessing damages for the cost of care: *Crofton v NHS Litigation Authority* [2007] EWCA Civ 71; [2007] 1 W.L.R. 923.

130 *Shearman v Folland* [1950] 2 K.B. 43; *Lim Poh Choo v Camden and Islington AHA* [1980] A.C. 174.

131 This provision overruled *Daish v Wauton* [1972] 2 Q.B. 262 on this point. The claimant will be left overcompensated to the extent that he has suffered no loss of income or a loss of income lower than the expense saved. In *O'Brien v Independent Assessor* [2007] UKHL 10; [2007] 2 A.C. 312 the same approach was applied in the different context of the statutory compensation scheme for those whose conviction has been quashed for a miscarriage of justice: the saved cost of food, clothing and accommodation while in prison was held to be deductible from the compensation for loss of earnings.

132 [1981] 1 W.L.R. 120. See also *Hoffman v Sofaer* [1982] 1 W.L.R. 1350 at 1355-1356 (recovery in respect of "do-it-yourself" work around the home; *Kroeker v Jansen* (1995) 123 D.L.R. (4th) 652 (British Columbia CA); *Lowe v Guise* [2002] EWCA Civ 197; [2002] Q.B. 1369 (recovery for the fact that the injury prevented the claimant carrying out as many hours of gratuitous care for his disabled brother as previously, the difference being made up by his mother). For criticism of the inconsistency in the treatment of past and future loss in the *Daly* case, see *Damages for Personal Injury: Medical, Nursing and Other Expenses; Collateral Benefits, Law Commission Report No.262* (1999), paras 3.87–3.93.

133 [1988] Fam. 22. See, generally, *Damages for Personal Injury: Medical, Nursing and Other Expenses; Collateral Benefits, Law Commission Report No.262* (1999), Pt IV.

Jones[134] and held that, even though a divorce has foreseeably resulted from the injury, pecuniary loss on that divorce is irrecoverable. To have regard to the financial consequences of a divorce would create difficulties since divorce orders may not be made until several years after the trial of the personal injury action; recognition of such a claim would produce a "vicious circle" because divorce orders take into account any claims for damages that a party may have; and it is in any event inapt to talk of loss in this context because divorce orders merely redistribute the assets of the spouses. Damages were also denied to a claimant in respect of the compensation payable by him to the victims of his sexual attacks in a case where the injury tortiously inflicted by the defendant had changed the claimant's personality rendering him liable to attack women.[135] Such a loss was regarded as too remote and it was thought contrary to public policy to indemnify a claimant for the consequences of his crimes.

27-25 **Claimant's needs supplied by a third party** It may occur that a third party, either relative or friend, incurs some financial loss or expense in coming to the assistance of an injured person or in seeing that he is provided with necessary medical or nursing services. In such cases the third party has no claim in his own right against the tortfeasor responsible for the injury, as against him there will have been no tort, and the question arises, therefore, whether the injured person himself may recover damages with which to reimburse his benefactor. In *Roach v Yates*,[136] where the claimant's wife and sister-in-law both gave up their employment in order to nurse him, the Court of Appeal found no difficulty in awarding damages to the claimant because "he would naturally feel that he ought to compensate them for what they have lost". This decision was, however, overlooked and for a number of years the courts hesitated to award damages in respect of services rendered by a third party in the absence of a legal obligation on the claimant to pay for them.[137] But in a series of decisions it has now been clearly established that the claimant can recover in respect of the services rendered, irrespective of any legal obligation to pay for them.[138]

27-26 In *Cunningham v Harrison*[139] Lord Denning considered that the claimant should hold the damages recovered in respect of the third party's services on trust for the third party to whom he was therefore legally bound to pay them.[140] This approach rested on the view that the loss in question was the third party's, albeit that the action was brought by the injured claimant. A day later, in *Donnelly v Joyce*[141] a different approach was preferred by a differently constituted Court of Appeal which treated the loss as the claimant's and comprised the existence of the need for the

134 [1985] Q.B. 704.
135 *Meah v McCreamer (No.2)* [1986] 1 All E.R. 943.
136 [1938] 1 K.B. 256.
137 *Gage v King* [1961] 1 Q.B. 188; *Haggar v De Placido* [1972] 1 W.L.R. 716. For less restrictive views, see, e.g. *Schneider v Eisovitch* [1960] 2 Q.B. 430; and *Wattson v Port of London Authority* [1969] 1 Lloyd's Rep. 95.
138 *Cunningham v Harrison* [1973] Q.B. 942; *Donnelly v Joyce* [1974] Q.B. 454; *Housecroft v Burnett* [1986] 1 All E.R. 332; *Hunt v Severs* [1994] 2 A.C. 350 HL. Provided it is more than *de minimis*, there is no lower threshold of seriousness that needs to be crossed before gratuitous nursing care can be compensated: see *Giambrone v JMC Holidays Ltd (No.2)* [2004] EWCA Civ 158; [2004] 2 All E.R. 891.
139 [1973] Q.B. 942 at 952.
140 cf. *Dennis v LPTB* (1948) 64 T.L.R. 269; *Schneider v Eisovitch* [1960] 2 Q.B. 430; para.27-03.
141 [1974] Q.B. 454.

nursing services. The damages were to be assessed by reference to the proper and reasonable cost of meeting that need and the claimant was under no legal obligation to reimburse the third party. This was followed in *Housecroft v Burnett*[142] in which it was held that in assessing the proper and reasonable cost of supplying the claimant's needs, the ceiling should be the commercial rate and sufficient should be awarded to enable the claimant to make reasonable recompense to the third party, including making up for any loss incurred by giving up gainful employment.

The leading case is *Hunt v Severs*[143] in which the question at issue was whether the claimant could still claim the cost of nursing services (and expenses incurred in hospital visits) where they had been rendered gratuitously by the *defendant tortfeasor* who, on the facts, was the claimant's husband. The House of Lords answered this in the negative on the ground that the loss was the "third party's" and, on the facts, the defendant would thereby be paying damages for his own loss. Lord Denning's view in *Cunningham v Harrison* that the damages should be held in trust by the claimant for the third party was approved and the reasoning in *Donnelly v Joyce* disapproved. In Pt III of its Report, *Damages for Personal Injury: Medical, Nursing and Other Expenses; Collateral Benefits*,[144] the Law Commission recommended the legislative reversal of the actual decision in *Hunt v Severs*, while approving most of the central reasoning of their Lordships in that case (in particular, that the loss was the third party's rather than the claimant's). The principle established in *Hunt v Severs*, that a claimant can recover damages for the loss incurred by a third party in gratuitously caring for the claimant, was applied in *Drake v Foster Wheeler Ltd*[145] so as to allow the cost of care provided by a charitable hospice to be compensated. The claimant was the estate of the deceased who had been cared for, prior to his death, by the hospice. As the damages awarded for that care were subject to a trust in favour of the hospice, it was ordered that the tortfeasor should pay the damages direct to the hospice. **27-27**

[142] [1986] 1 All E.R. 332 CA. On quantum (but prior to *Hunt v Severs* [1994] 2 A.C. 350) see also, e.g. *Nash v Southmead HA* [1993] P.I.Q.R. Q156; *Fairhurst v St Helens and Knowsley HA* [1995] P.I.Q.R. Q1.

[143] [1994] 2 A.C. 350 HL. See Matthews and Lunney (1995) 58 M.L.R. 395; Hoyano [1995] Tort. L.R. 63; *Damages for Personal Injury: Medical, Nursing and Other Expenses; Collateral Benefits*, Law Commission Report No.262 (1999), paras 3.44–3.86. The High Court of Australia in *Kars v Kars* (1996) 71 A.J.L.R. 107 refused to follow *Hunt v Severs*, preferring the approach in *Donnelly v Joyce*. In *Hardwick v Hudson* [1999] 1 W.L.R. 1770 CA, *Hunt v Severs* was distinguished, and no damages were awarded, in respect of gratuitous clerical services provided to his business by the injured claimant's wife. The policy considerations favouring recompense for a voluntary carer (e.g. encouraging effective and economical care) did not apply to the provision of these services.

[144] Law Commission Report No.262 (1999).

[145] [2010] EWHC 2004 (QB); [2011] 1 All E.R. 63.

(c) Loss of earnings

27-28 The loss of earnings[146] for which damages can be recovered[147] includes all classes of earnings such as wages, salaries, professional fees,[148] a share in company or partnership profits,[149] prize-money,[150] or perquisites, such as a company car.[151] Income tax,[152] national insurance contributions[153] and compulsory contributions to an occupational pension scheme[154] that would have been paid from the earnings are deducted so as to avoid overcompensating the claimant. In principle the expenses involved in earning which have been saved (for example, the costs of travelling to work) should be deducted, although in general this appears not to be the practice.[155] Loss of earnings accrued down to the date of trial can normally be calculated by reference to the claimant's pre-accident earnings and the period of disability, but such a calculation depends upon the assumption that, but for the accident, the claimant would have continued to earn at the same rate. If this assumption is not justified, then allowance must be made accordingly.[156] It is also, of course, necessary that the claimant's inability to work be attributable to the defendant's tort. In *James v Woodall Duckham Construction Co Ltd*[157] the claimant was physically fit to return to work about three months after his injury but was unable to do so because of a neurosis for which there was no physical cause and which would disappear once his claim for damages was settled. The Court of Appeal accepted that he was entitled to damages for such loss of earnings as was due to this neurosis, but the claimant had delayed in issuing his writ and it was therefore, held that he could only recover damages in respect of the period between the date of his injury and the date when his action would have come on for trial if it had been pursued with ordinary diligence.

---

146 Analogous and also recoverable are a loss of pension rights; see, e.g. *Auty v National Coal Board* [1985] 1 W.L.R. 784; *West v Versil Ltd, The Times,* 31 August 1996 CA; *Longden v British Coal Corp* [1998] A.C. 653 HL. Also recoverable by a widow is the diminution in value of her dependency right under the Fatal Accidents Act 1976 as a result of the defendant having negligently injured, or caused a disease to, the widow, which reduces her life expectancy (and hence reduces the damages she can recover for loss of dependency under the 1976 Act on the tortious death of her husband): *Haxton v Philips Electronics UK Ltd* [2014] EWCA Civ 4; [2014] 1 W.L.R. 2721.

147 But illegality bars damages for loss of earnings if the claimant lied to his employers in order to obtain the employment: *Hewison v Meridian Shipping PTE* [2002] EWCA Civ 1821; [2003] I.C.R. 766, see para.3-48 (and see, analogously, para.27-94 fn.480); cf. *Major v Ministry of Defence* [2003] EWCA Civ 1433; (2003) 147 S.J.L.B. 1206, at para.3-50. Note that "collateral illegality" does not preclude a claim for loss of earnings: see para.3-51.

148 *Phillips v L & SW Ry* (1879) 5 C.P.D. 280.

149 *Lee v Sheard* [1956] 1 Q.B. 192; *Bellingham v Dhillon* [1973] 1 Q.B. 304; *Kent v British Railways Board* [1995] P.I.Q.R. Q42 CA; *Ward v Newalls Insulation Co Ltd* [1998] 1 W.L.R. 1722 CA.

150 *Mulvaine v Joseph* (1968) 112 S.J. 927.

151 *Kennedy v Bryan, The Times,* 3 May 1984.

152 *British Transport Commission v Gourley* [1956] A.C. 185. See paras 27-38 to 27-40.

153 *Cooper v Firth Brown Ltd* [1963] 1 W.L.R. 418.

154 *Dews v National Coal Board* [1988] A.C. 1; Anderson (1987) 50 M.L.R. 963.

155 *Dews v National Coal Board* [1988] A.C. 1 at 12-13. cf. *Eagle v Chambers* [2004] EWCA Civ 1033; [2004] 1 W.L.R. 3081 at [66]–[68].

156 *Phillips v L & SW Ry* (1879) 5 C.P.D. 280 at 291, per Brett LJ; *Rouse v PLA* [1953] 2 Lloyd's Rep. 179 at 184.

157 [1969] 1 W.L.R. 903.

(i) The "multiplier method"[158]

The assessment of damages for prospective loss of earnings is inevitably less precise than that for accrued loss by reason of the additional elements of uncertainty which enter into the calculation, such as the period of the claimant's future incapacity, his future employment prospects and the normal hazards of life.[159] The standard method of assessment (the so-called "multiplier" method) is to multiply the assessed net annual loss by the number of years for which it will last.[160] The starting point for calculating the multiplicand (the net annual loss) is what the claimant would have been earning at the time of trial.[161] This figure is then adjusted to reflect the claimant's prospects of promotion and thus of an increase in the real value of his earnings.[162] Where the claimant's working capacity has not been totally destroyed an allowance must be made for such income as he is likely to earn in the future.[163] In the case of a child claimant, it has been held acceptable to take the national average earnings during early working years as the basis of the multiplicand.[164] **27-29**

The starting point for the multiplier is the number of years during which the loss, represented by the multiplicand, is likely to endure and thus, typically, this is the remaining period of the claimant's working life.[165] This figure is then reduced to account not only for the elements of uncertainty contained in the prediction (for example, unemployment, redundancy, sickness), but more importantly also for the fact that the claimant receives a lump sum which he is expected to invest.[166] The basis of the award is, then, that the total sum will be exhausted at the end of the period contemplated and that during the period the claimant will draw upon both the income derived from the investment of the sum awarded and the capital itself. Low multipliers are used in respect of young children because they might never have become wage earners and because the capital sum is being awarded well in **27-30**

---

[158] Note that the multiplier method is appropriate for calculating all forms of prospective pecuniary loss, including medical and other expenses, not simply loss of earnings. Where, however, there is high level of uncertainty involved in the calculation, the court will award a lump sum on an "impressionistic" basis to compensate for the loss: *Chase International Express Ltd v McRae* [2003] EWCA Civ 505; [2004] P.I.Q.R. P21 (little or no evidence of the claimant's pre-accident employment history; use of multiplier method wrong in principle). See also para.27-37 on loss of "earning capacity".

[159] cf. paras 27-12 to 27-19.

[160] Edelman, *McGregor on Damages*, 20th edn (2017), paras 40-066 to 40-148; Burrows, *Remedies for Torts, Breach of Contract and Equitable Wrongs*, 4th edn (2019), pp.244–247.

[161] Rather than at the time of the injury: *Cookson v Knowles* [1979] A.C. 556 at 569 and 575. The case involved a claim under the Fatal Accidents Act, but the principle must apply equally to personal injury actions. It seems to have been so applied in *Lim Poh Choo v Camden and Islington AHA* [1979] Q.B. 196 at 204, 232, and this aspect of the decision was not questioned on appeal to the House of Lords: [1980] A.C. 174.

[162] *Roach v Yates* [1938] 1 K.B. 256 at 269; *Mitchell v Mulholland (No.2)* [1972] 1 Q.B. 65. No account should be taken of the speculative possibility that increased national prosperity will lead to a general rise in the real value of earnings: [1972] 1 Q.B. 65 at 83–84.

[163] *Billingham v Hughes* [1949] 1 K.B. 634; *Daniels v Sir Robert McAlpine and Sons* (1971) 11 K.I.R. 141.

[164] *Croke v Wiseman* [1982] 1 W.L.R. 71.

[165] Regard may be had to the possibility that the claimant would have continued to work beyond the normal age of retirement; *Jenkinson v Eagle International Freight Ltd, The Times,* 28 January 1983 CA.

[166] *Taylor v O'Connor* [1971] A.C. 115; *Wells v Wells* [1999] 1 A.C. 345 HL. See para.27-32.

advance of when there would have been any earnings.[167] Lower multipliers have sometimes been applied to young women compared to young men to take account of the workless years bringing up a family that the claimant would otherwise have had.[168] But this is then largely balanced out by an award for loss of marriage prospects as a pecuniary loss, i.e. the loss of the economic support of a husband during child-bearing years.[169] As such, an alternative approach favoured in *Hughes v McKeown*[170] is to make no deduction from the multiplier while not adding on elsewhere for loss of marriage prospects as a pecuniary loss; rather, one can regard a woman who is raising a family as working, albeit in a different capacity, and receiving the economic benefit of her husband's support. However this alternative approach is inappropriate when there is no rough-and-ready correlation between the loss of earnings and the lost support of a husband, for example, where the woman was a particularly high earner.[171]

(ii) The "lost years"

27-31 Where the injury has reduced the claimant's life expectancy, the multiplier is calculated according to his pre-accident working life expectancy, with a deduction for the living expenses that he would have incurred during those "lost years" which he will no longer live through.[172] As laid down in *Harris v Empress Motors Ltd*,[173] the living expenses deducted are what the claimant spends on maintaining himself at the standard of life appropriate to his case and includes a pro rata amount of any family expenditure on housing, heating, lighting etc. This contrasts with the living expenses that are deducted in calculating loss of dependency in a claim under the Fatal Accidents Act 1976.[174] The difference rests on the theory that lost years damages compensate a claimant for his own loss and not that of the dependants. In the

---

167 *Croke v Wiseman* [1982] 1 W.L.R. 71 (Lord Denning, dissenting, thought that a young child should not be awarded any damages for future loss of earnings).

168 *Harris v Harris* [1973] 1 Lloyd's Rep. 445; *Moriarty v McCarthy* [1978] 1 W.L.R. 155.

169 *Harris v Harris* [1973] 1 Lloyd's Rep. 445.

170 [1985] 1 W.L.R. 963.

171 *Housecroft v Burnett* [1986] 1 All E.R. 332 at 345.

172 *Pickett v British Rail Engineering Ltd* [1980] A.C. 136; overruling *Oliver v Ashman* [1962] 2 Q.B. 210. The calculation of the income lost should distinguish between income which is lost on death and income which survives death: *Head v Culver Heating Co Ltd* [2019] EWHC 1217 (QB); [2020] P.I.Q.R. Q2 at [66], [70]; so that income derived from capital which will survive the death should be ignored: *Adsett v West* [1983] Q.B. 826.

173 [1984] 1 W.L.R. 212. The Court of Appeal expressly rejected two alternative approaches adopted in earlier cases: the Fatal Accidents Act solution adopted in, e.g. *Benson v Biggs Wall & Co* [1983] 1 W.L.R. 72; *Harris v Empress Motors* [1983] 1 W.L.R. 65 (at first instance); and *Clay v Pooler* [1982] 3 All E.R. 570; and the "savings only" solution favoured in *Sullivan v West Yorkshire Passenger Transport Executive* (1980) unreported. But it approved the "available surplus" approach put forward in *White v London Transport Executive* [1982] Q.B. 489 where at 499 Webster J explained that the loss in question is of "the amenity of earning more than is needed to live a reasonably satisfying and potentially enjoyable life, taking into account in each case the particular circumstances of life of the particular [claimant]." See Evans and Stanton, "Valuing the Lost Years" (1984) 134 N.L.J. 515.

174 See para.27-100. The starting point for assessing the deduction of living expenses in the lost years is 50 per cent, though this can be displaced by evidence: *Head v Culver Heating Co Ltd* [2019] EWHC 1217 (QB); [2020] P.I.Q.R. Q2 at [53].

case of a child, the courts are reluctant to make an award for the lost years on the ground that generally the assessment is too speculative.[175]

(iii) The "discount" rate

The leading case on multipliers for future pecuniary loss in personal injury cases is *Wells v Wells*.[176] The House of Lords there laid down that the appropriate discount rate (for receiving the capital sum of damages, which can be invested, earlier than the lost income) is the rate of return on index-linked government stock (ILGS). At the time of the decision this was taken to be three per cent (net of basic rate tax)[177] which contrasted with the traditional basing of multipliers on four and one-half per cent interest (which is the rate of return traditionally expected from investing in equities and gilts). Their Lordships' preference for the ILGS rate was based on three main strands of reasoning. First, and most importantly, personal injury victims should not be regarded as being in the same position as ordinary prudent investors. This is because they have to rely on the investment fund to pay for their everyday needs. Therefore where the fund has fallen in value the personal injury victim cannot choose to leave it largely untouched in the expectation that its value will recover over time. Lord Lloyd of Berwick said: **27-32**

> "While ... I agree with the Court of Appeal that, in calculating the lump sum, courts are entitled to assume that the [claimant] will behave prudently I do not agree that what is prudent for the ordinary investor is necessarily prudent for the [claimant]. Indeed the opposite may be the case. What the prudent [claimant] needs is an investment which will buy him the income he requires without the risks inherent in the equity market; which brings us back to ILGS."[178]

Secondly, although there was at the time no ILGS maturing later than 2030, ILGS was thought to be the most accurate means of calculating future loss precisely because it is inflation-proof.[179] As Lord Lloyd said, "[t]he court now has at its disposal a tool for calculating damages which enables it to assume a stable currency until at least 2030".[180] Thirdly, even if true (which was contradicted by research carried out by the Law Commission),[181] it was thought to be irrelevant that the majority of claimants (or the particular claimant) are likely to invest the dam-

---

175 *Gammell v Wilson* [1982] A.C. 27 at 40; *Connolly v Camden and Islington AHA* [1981] 3 All E.R. 250; *Croke v Wiseman* [1982] 1 W.L.R. 71 (Griffiths LJ emphasised the futility of an award for the "lost years" where there will be no dependants because of the injury to the child; but this assumes that the "lost years" damages are to compensate the dependants and not the claimant); *Iqbal v Whipps Cross University Hospital NHS Trust* [2007] EWCA Civ 1190; [2008] P.I.Q.R. P9.

176 [1999] 1 A.C. 345 HL.

177 Higher rate tax, payable on the income from investing the damages for future pecuniary loss, should normally be ignored: *Hodgson v Trapp* [1998] A.C. 807 HL; *Wells v Wells* [1999] 1 A.C. 345 HL.

178 [1999] 1 A.C. 345 at 367.

179 Traditionally, courts have assessed damages without any adjustment for the risk of future inflation: *Mallett v McMonagle* [1970] A.C. 166; *Taylor v O'Connor* [1971] A.C. 115; *Mitchell v Mulholland (No.2)* [1972] 1 Q.B. 65; *Young v Percival* [1975] 1 W.L.R. 17; *Cookson v Knowles* [1979] A.C. 556; *Lim Poh Choo v Camden and Islington AHA* [1980] A.C. 174; *Auty v National Coal Board* [1985] 1 W.L.R. 784; *Robertson v Lestrange* [1985] 1 All E.R. 950. For criticism of this traditional approach see the 17th edition of this work, para.27-14.

180 [1999] 1 A.C. 345 at 367.

181 *Personal Injury Compensation: How Much is Enough? Law Commission Report No.225* (1994), Ch.10.

ages in equities or gilts. The important question is rather whether the claimant is entitled to have his damages calculated on the basis that he will not take the risk of investing in equities and gilts. Their Lordships further pointed out that the views of the Ogden Working Party,[182] the Law Commission[183] and of David Kemp QC,[184] who all favoured the ILGS rate, were entitled to great weight.

27-33 But while *Wells v Wells* set out the relevant principles applied by the courts in fixing the discount rate, it has been superseded by the Lord Chancellor fixing the discount rate under the powers conferred by s.1(1) of the Damages Act 1996. That subsection provides that: "in determining the return to be expected from the investment of a sum awarded as damages for future pecuniary loss … the court shall … take into account such rate of return (if any) as may from time to time be prescribed by an order made by the Lord Chancellor". By the Damages (Personal Injury) Order 2017[185] the Lord Chancellor set a discount rate of minus 0.75 per cent as from 20 March 2017.[186] The rate was increased to minus 0.25 per cent as from 5 August 2019.[187] The courts are bound by the rate set unless, applying s.A1(2) of the Damages Act 1996,[188] any party to the proceedings shows that a different rate of interest is "more appropriate in the case in question". The important issue has therefore now turned to the scope of s.1(2). In *Warriner v Warriner*[189] it was said that, in the interests of certainty, a departure from the rate set would probably be rare. In the instant case, there was nothing unusual justifying a lower rate than that set by the Lord Chancellor (which at that time was 2.5 per cent). In *Cooke v United Bristol Health Care*[190] the Court of Appeal rejected a different line of attack by the claimant on the conventional method for assessing future pecuniary loss. The claimants wanted to adduce evidence that the cost of care, and indeed earnings, had increased, and could be expected to increase, at a substantially higher rate than the retail prices index. Claimants, it was argued, are therefore being under-compensated by the conventional method, especially where there are high future costs of care. The claimants sought to argue that, to prevent such under-compensation, there should be adjustments to the multiplicands. But the Court of Appeal refused to allow such evidence to be adduced on the basis that, in reality, the claimants were arguing for a departure from the discount rate for multipliers set by the Lord Chancellor; and in line with *Warriner v Warriner* such a departure was thought to be unjustified.

---

182 *Actuarial Tables for Use in Personal Injury and Fatal Accident Cases*, 3rd edn (1998); (now 8th edn, July 2020), available at: *https://www.gov.uk/government/publications/ogden-tables-actuarial-compensation-tables-for-injury-and-death* [Accessed 21 July 2020].

183 *Structural Settlements and Interim and Provisional Damages*, Law Com No.224 (1994), paras 2.24-2.36.

184 Kemp and Kemp, *The Quantum of Damages*, Vol.1, Ch.7; Kemp, "Discounting Compensation for Future Loss" (1985) 101 L.Q.R. 556; Kemp, "Discounting Damages for Future Loss" (1997) 113 L.Q.R. 195.

185 SI 2017/206.

186 In *Simon v Helmot* [2012] UKPC 5; [2012] Med. L.R. 394, on an appeal from Guernsey, where there is no legislation governing the discount rate so that the courts must decide that rate, it was held that on the then present economic evidence a "negative discount rate" of minus 1.5 per cent should be applied in assessing damages for loss of future earnings (i.e. in calculating the multiplier, there should be an addition to, rather than a deduction from, the number of years during which the loss would be suffered).

187 Damages (Personal Injury) Order 2019 (SI 2019/1126); see para.27-34 below.

188 Inserted by the Civil Liability Act 2018 s.10.

189 [2002] EWCA Civ 81; [2002] 1 W.L.R. 1703.

190 [2003] EWCA Civ 1370; [2004] 1 W.L.R. 251.

Although not mentioned by the Court of Appeal, it is perhaps worth adding, as a further reason for rejecting the claimants' arguments that, in adopting the ILGS rate in *Wells v Wells*, the House of Lords assumed that it is the retail prices index that is the correct measure of inflation and this is also the index used for updating awards for non-pecuniary loss in personal injury cases.

There has continued to be considerable controversy as to whether the ILGS rates are the best way of assessing the discount rate and hence arriving at the correct amount of compensation. Those representing the interests of defendant insurers argued that the negative discount rate of minus 0.75 per cent over-compensated claimants because they can readily invest to obtain higher returns. Those representing personal injury victims counter-argued that one should not be treating personal injury victims as normal investors and that, in any event, empirical historical evidence shows that personal injury victims have not been overcompensated. The Ministry of Justice, following a consultation exercise, proposed[191] that, while full compensation should remain the aim of damages, the discount rate should not be set on what it considered to be the unrealistic basis that claimants will invest in ILGS. Rather it should be assumed that, while claimants are low-risk investors, they will invest (and would be professionally advised to invest) in a mixed portfolio which will enable them to achieve higher rates of return. It also proposed that, while the Lord Chancellor should set the rate, they should be advised by an independent expert panel; and that there should be a review of the discount rate at least once every three years. These proposals (but substituting five years for three years) were carried through into the Civil Liability Act 2018 (inserting a new Sch.A1 into the Damages Act 1996). It was following the first review of the rate, applying Sch.A1 paras 1(2) and 2, that the discount rate was increased from minus 0.75 per cent to minus 0.25 per cent.[192] 27-34

Costs of investment advice Closely linked to the discount rate is the question of whether damages can be recovered for the costs of investment advice. Logically if the assumption is ILGS investment, such costs should not be recoverable because that sort of investment is straightforward and does not require the sort of advice that investing in gilts and equities would do. This logic was accepted in *Page v Plymouth Hospital NHS Trust*.[193] There a claim for damages for the costs of investment advice and fund management charges was rejected as inconsistent with the assumption of ILGS investment and as being another attempt indirectly to depart from the (then) 2.5 per cent discount rate. In *Eagle v Chambers*,[194] the Court of Appeal approved the reasoning in *Page* and held that the same approach applied where the claimant was a patient subject to the Court of Protection. So just as the cost of investment advice was irrecoverable generally, so the cost of a Court of Protection's panel broker's fees was irrecoverable in respect of a patient of the Court of Protection. The discount rate assumed standard investment in ILGS without the need for invest- 27-35

---

191 *The Personal Injury Discount Rate: How it should be set in Future* (Draft Legislation, Ministry of Justice, September 2017, Cmnd.9500).

192 Damages (Personal Injury) Order 2019 (SI 2019/1126). Following a review, the Scottish government maintained the rate of minus 0.75 per cent for personal injury actions in Scotland: Government Actuary's Department, The Personal Injury Discount Rate, 27 September 2019 (available at *https://www.gov.uk/government/publications/the-personal-injury-discount-rate-review-and-determination-of-the-rate-in-scotland-by-the-government-actuary* [Accessed 21 July 2020]).

193 [2004] EWHC 1154; [2004] 3 All E.R. 367.

194 [2004] EWCA Civ 1033; [2004] 1 W.L.R. 3081.

ment advice. Claimants, including patients through the agency of the Court of Protection, were free to invest more broadly for higher returns. But to avoid overcompensation, those investment fees must be set off against the higher gains made.

27-36 **Ogden Tables** The decision in *Wells* was also important because of their Lordships' willingness to apply the Ogden Tables[195] as giving the appropriate multiplier for a particular rate of discount.[196] In Lord Lloyd's words:

> "I do not suggest that the judge should be a slave to the tables. There may well be special factors in particular cases. But the tables should now be regarded as the starting-point, rather than a check. A judge should be slow to depart from the relevant actuarial multiplier on impressionistic grounds, or by reference to 'a spread of multipliers in comparable cases' especially when the multipliers were fixed before actuarial tables were widely used."[197]

(iv) Loss of earning capacity

27-37 Instead of talking of loss of earnings, it would seem that one could equally well talk of loss of earning capacity.[198] Indeed this appears to be the preferred terminology in some jurisdictions.[199] But in England the tradition has been to talk of loss of earnings, whether past or prospective, rather than loss of earning capacity. However, the terminology of loss of earning capacity has come to be favoured where the loss of prospective earnings that the courts wish to compensate cannot be proved and calculated according to any actual loss of earnings at trial. This occurs in three main situations. The first is where the claimant's injury means that he may find it difficult to find another equally well paid job if he loses his present position.[200] The second is where the claimant is too young to have earned

---

[195] *Actuarial Tables for Use in Personal Injury and Fatal Accident Cases*, 8th edn (2020), available at *https://www.gov.uk/government/publications/ogden-tables-actuarial-compensation-tables-for-injury-and-death* [Accessed 21 July 2020].

[196] This contrasts with the traditional judicial scepticism shown towards actuarial evidence: *Watson v Powles* [1968] 1 Q.B. 396; *S v Distillers Co (Biochemicals) Ltd* [1970] 1 W.L.R. 114; *Taylor v O'Connor* [1971] A.C. 115; *Mitchell v Mulholland (No.2)* [1972] 1 Q.B. 65; *Auty v National Coal Board* [1985] 1 W.L.R. 784; *Spiers v Halliday, The Times,* 30 June 1984; *Hunt v Severs* [1994] 2 A.C. 350, 365. For criticism of this traditional scepticism, see the 17th edition of this work, para.27-14.

[197] [1999] 1 A.C. 345 at 379. This has rendered it unnecessary to bring into force s.10 of the Civil Evidence Act 1995 which provides that the Ogden Tables are admissible in evidence and may be proved by production of a Queen's Printer's copy.

[198] cf. *Street, Principles of the Law of Damages*, pp.44–55; Law Commission Report No.56, s.204; Pearson Commission (1978) Cmnd.7054, s.338.

[199] e.g. Australia; see Luntz, *Assessment of Damages for Personal Injury and Death*, 4th edn (2002), Ch.5.

[200] The terminology of "*Smith v Manchester Corp* damages" or damages for "handicap in the labour market" is here commonly used rather than loss of earning capacity. *Smith v Manchester Corp* (1974) 17 K.I.R. 1, CA; *Moeliker v A Reyrolle & Co Ltd* [1977] 1 W.L.R. 132; *Foster v Tyne and Wear CC* [1986] 1 All E.R. 567; *Robson v Liverpool CC* [1993] P.I.Q.R. Q78, CA; *Brown v Ministry of Defence* [2006] EWCA Civ 546; [2006] P.I.Q.R. Q9; *Ronan v Sainsbury's Supermarkets Ltd* [2006] EWCA Civ 1074; *Billett v Ministry of Defence* [2015] EWCA Civ 773; [2016] P.I.Q.R. Q1 (while in some cases it would be appropriate to use a multiplicand and multiplier and the Ogden Tables to assess "*Smith v Manchester Corp* damages" that was not an appropriate approach where, as on the facts of this case, the disability was of a minor kind that was causing the claimant no present loss of earnings; instead a relatively broad brush approach should be taken and, applying that approach,

anything.[201] The third is where there are so many uncertainties about the claimant's potential earnings that applying a conventional multiplicand/multiplier approach is thought inappropriate.[202] In these situations the courts, in line with their preference for loss of earning capacity terminology, have generally preferred to make an educated impressionistic guess at the overall loss of prospective earnings rather than adopting a multiplier approach.[203] But a conventional sum is not to be awarded: rather the risks and chances in all the circumstances of the particular case must be weighed up.[204] As the difference between loss of earnings and loss of earning capacity appears to be purely a matter of terminology, nothing of substance should turn on it.[205]

(v) *Effect of taxation*

27-38 In the leading case of *British Transport Commission v Gourley*[206] the House of Lords held that the claimant's liability to tax on the earnings for the loss of which he claims compensation is not *res inter alios acta* and must be taken into account in assessing the damages payable by the defendant: the compensatory principle required that he pay only the net loss suffered. Similarly, in an action of trespass, an award of damages in lieu of rent should be reduced by the amount the claimant would have paid in tax if he had actually received the rent,[207] and in an action for libel, if the damages include an element of loss of profits, the same principle will apply so that the claimant's tax position must be taken into account.[208] The principle also applies to special damages claims for past earnings, so that the claimant must account for savings on tax, including rebates.[209]

27-39 In calculating the claimant's liability to tax for the purpose of assessing damages, the rate of tax to be taken must be the effective rate of income tax which

---

the judge's assessment of these damages at £99,062 using the Ogden Tables was reduced by the Court of Appeal to £45,000).

201 *S v Distillers (Biochemicals) Ltd* [1970] 1 W.L.R. 114 at 125-126; *Joyce v Yeomans* [1981] 1 W.L.R. 549; *Mitchell v Liverpool AHA, The Independent,* 17 June 1985; *Cronin v Redbridge LBC, The Independent,* 20 May 1987.

202 *Blamire v South Cumbria HA* [1993] P.I.Q.R. Q1 CA; *Ward v Allies & Morrison Architects* [2012] EWCA Civ 1287; [2013] P.I.Q.R. Q1; *Irani v Duchon* [2019] EWCA Civ 1846; [2020] P.I.Q.R. P4.

203 e.g. *Joyce v Yeomans* [1981] 1 W.L.R. 549; *Mitchell v Liverpool AHA, The Times,* 17 June 1985; cf. *Croke v Wiseman* [1982] 1 W.L.R. 71.

204 *Foster v Tyne and Wear CC* [1986] 1 All E.R. 567 at 570.

205 A good illustration was formerly provided by *Foster v Tyne and Wear CC* [1986] 1 All E.R. 567, in which it was held that "loss of earnings" within s.2(1) of the Law Reform (Personal Injuries) Act 1948, which dealt with the half deduction from damages for loss of earnings of certain social security benefits, included loss of earning capacity. The subsection has since been repealed and this point no longer arises.

206 [1956] A.C. 185. See, generally, Edelman, *McGregor on Damages*, 20th edn (2017), Ch.18; Bishop and Kay, "Taxation and Damages: The Rule in Gourley's case" (1987) 104 L.Q.R. 211, advocating legislation making all damages awards taxable; Dawes, "Tax and Damages" (1998) 148 N.L.J. 337; Maugham and Peacock, "Taxing Damages Awards" (2000) 150 N.L.J. 1153. *Gourley* has not been followed in Canada or New Zealand: *R. v Jennings* (1966) 57 D.L.R. (2d) 644; *North Island Wholesale Groceries Ltd v Hewin* [1982] 2 N.Z.L.R. 176. In Australia, *Atlas Tiles v Briers* (1978) 144 C.L.R. 202, which had rejected *Gourley*, was overturned by *Cullen v Trappell* (1980) 146 C.L.R. 1.

207 *Hall & Co v Pearlberg* [1956] 1 W.L.R. 244. cf. *Sykes v Midland Bank Executor and Trustee Co Ltd* [1969] 2 Q.B. 518 at 536–537. (The point did not arise on appeal: [1971] 1 Q.B. 113.)

208 *Lewis v Daily Telegraph Ltd on appeal* at [1964] A.C. 234.

209 *Hartley v Sandholme Iron Co Ltd* [1975] Q.B. 600; *Brayson v Wilmot-Breeders* [1976] C.L.Y. 682.

would have been applicable to the sums in question, treated as the top part of the claimant's income,[210] if they had been earned, and this will depend upon several factors which may vary in each case such as allowances, reduced rates, other income of the claimant and his wife, charges or reliefs.[211] On the other hand, in relation to future loss, the court should not attempt to speculate on future rates of taxation, but should deal with it as matters are at the date of trial.[212]

27-40 In *Gourley* itself it was regarded as a pre-condition for the deduction of tax that the damages awarded are themselves not subject to tax.[213] If they are so subject, or even if it is doubtful whether they are so subject,[214] the defendant should pay the full amount of the claimant's gross loss.[215] But this approach has created particular difficulties in wrongful dismissal actions where awards of less than a certain amount are exempt from income tax and awards over that amount are taxable. In *Shove v Downs Surgical Plc*[216] Sheen J therefore preferred to estimate the net amount which would have been received by the claimant after deduction of income tax and to add to this an amount equivalent to the estimated tax liability on the damages awarded. A similar move towards greater accuracy, in preference to the application of a blunt rule of there being no *Gourley* deduction if the damages are themselves taxable, was taken in *Amstrad Plc v Seagate Technology Inc*.[217] Contractual damages were being awarded for loss of profits from the sale of some 67,500 computers. The corporation tax on the damages when received would be at a rate of 31 per cent. But the corporation tax on the profits, had they been received at the proper time, would have been at rates of 33–35 per cent. A *Gourley* deduction was made so as to ensure that the claimants were not overcompensated by the lowering of the tax rate. Although the difference in rates was small in percentage terms, in real terms the difference was some £3.4 million. That is, the damages were subject to £3.4 million less tax than the lost profits would have been.

(vi) Receipt of social security benefits

27-41 In respect of damages for personal injury the law is contained in the Social Security (Recovery of Benefits) Act 1997, accompanied by the Social Security (Recovery of Benefits) Regulations 1997.[218] The Act builds on, but significantly

---

210 *Lyndale Fashion Manufacturers v Rich* [1973] 1 W.L.R. 73. Expenses which the claimant would have incurred in earning the income had it not been lost may be deducted, as may also the appropriate proportion of earned income relief: [1973] 1 W.L.R. 73.

211 *British Transport Commission v Gourley* [1956] A.C. 185, per Lord Goddard at 208. Particulars of the claimant's income from all sources and of assessments to tax made upon him will be ordered, but should be limited to what is necessary to enable the party seeking them to know what case he has to meet: *Phipps v Orthodox Unit Trusts Ltd* [1958] 1 Q.B. 314.

212 *British Transport Commission v Gourley* [1956] A.C. 185 at 209, per Lord Goddard.

213 It is for this reason that the courts have generally not taken account of capital gains tax liability: Edelman, *McGregor on Damages*, 20th edn (2017) paras 18-061 to 18-071. For an example of damages being subject to tax, see *Deeny v Gooda Walker Ltd (No.2)* [1996] 1 W.L.R. 426 HL.

214 *Hall & Co v Pearlberg* [1956] 1 W.L.R. 244; *Stoke-on-Trent City Council v Wood Mitchell & Co Ltd* [1980] 1 W.L.R. 254.

215 *Morahan v Archer and Belfast Corp* [1957] N.I. 61; *Herring v British Transport Commission* [1958] T.R. 401; *Diamond v Campbell-Jones* [1961] Ch. 22 at 37; *Pryce v Elwood* (1964) 108 S.J. 583.

216 [1984] 1 All E.R. 7.

217 (1997) 86 B.L.R. 34.

218 SI 1997/2205. There have been subsequent amendments to the Act and to the Regulations (e.g. relating to lump sum payments made under state compensation schemes in respect of certain diseases)

modifies, the state recoupment scheme first introduced in 1989. The following points are intended as a guide to the main aspects of the 1997 Act[219]:

(1) The tortfeasor (the "compensator") must reimburse the state for the total amount of listed social security benefits received by the claimant during the "relevant period" in respect of the injury or disease.[220]

(2) The "relevant period" is five years or, if shorter, the period to a final settlement payment from the day following the accrual of the cause of action (or, in the case of disease, from the claimant's first claim for a listed benefit).[221]

(3) The listed social security benefits are: universal credit, disablement pension payable under s.103 of the Social Security Contributions and Benefits Act 1992, employment and support allowance, incapacity benefit, income support, invalidity pension and allowance, jobseeker's allowance, reduced earnings allowance, severe disablement allowance, sickness benefit, statutory sick pay, unemployability supplement, unemployment benefit, attendance allowance, daily living component of personal independence payment, care component of disability living allowance, disablement pension increase payable under s.104 or s.105 of the Social Security Contributions and Benefits Act 1992, mobility allowance, mobility component of personal independence payment, mobility component of disability living allowance.[222]

(4) Subject to significant limitations, the compensator may deduct the amount of the listed benefits, for which he must reimburse the state, from the compensation payable to the claimant.[223] The significant limitations are as follows. First, a benefit can only be deducted "like for like"; that is, against an equivalent head of compensation.[224] For example, a benefit listed as be-

but these do not affect the overall scheme outlined in this paragraph.

219 See, generally, R. Lewis, *Deducting Benefits from Damages for Personal Injury* (1999), Pt II; A. Dismore, "Social Security (Recovery of Benefits) Act 1997 and Regulations" [1998] J.P.I.L. 14. Analogously the Health and Social Care (Community Health and Standards) Act 2003 Pt 3, allows the state to recover from the tortfeasor some of the costs incurred by the NHS in treating the victim of a wrongfully caused personal injury.

220 Social Security (Recovery of Benefits) Act 1997 s.6. This applies, without any reduction, even if the claimant was contributorily negligent: see s.1(2)(a) referring to "liable to any extent". Payments under the Fatal Accidents Act 1976 are exempted from the statutory scheme: reg.2(2)(a) of the Social Security (Recovery of Benefits) Regulations 1997.

221 Social Security (Recovery of Benefits) Act 1997 s.3.

222 Social Security (Recovery of Benefits) Act 1997 s.29 and Sch.2. With regard to relevant social security benefits not listed in the 1997 Act the common law will apply to determine whether there should be deduction or not. *Hodgson v Trapp* [1989] A.C. 807 HL, suggests that there should be deduction of such benefits from damages. This is supported by *Clenshaw v Tanner* [2002] EWCA Civ 1848 in which housing benefit (which is not listed in the 1997 Act) was deducted from the claimant's loss of earnings. See also *Ballantine v Newalls Insulation Co Ltd* [2001] I.C.R. 25 CA (payment made under Pneumoconiosis etc (Workers' Compensation) Act 1979 deducted in full from damages for personal injury, applying *Hodgson v Trapp*).

223 Social Security (Recovery of Benefits) Act 1997 s.8. The deduction is from the compensation payable even if that compensation has already been reduced for contributory negligence (or because of other factors). But the compensation payable (and hence the amount from which there can be a deduction) includes interest awarded on the damages: *Griffiths v British Coal Corp* [2001] EWCA Civ 336; [2001] 1 W.L.R. 1493 CA.

224 Social Security (Recovery of Benefits) Act 1997 s.8 and Sch.2. But the Compensation Recovery Unit does not break down a payment of universal credit into its constituent parts on the certificate of recoverable benefits, with the result that compensators and claimants are, in practice, paying back some benefits which are completely unrelated to the claimant's injuries: see Challis, "A sting in the

ing paid in respect of lost earnings can only be deducted from compensation for lost earnings and not from compensation for cost of care. Secondly, the heads of compensation from which there can be deduction are loss of earnings (during the "relevant period"), cost of care (during the "relevant period") and loss of mobility (during the "relevant period").[225] There can therefore be no deduction from damages for pain, suffering, and loss of amenity. These limitations mean that, in contrast to the earlier recoupment scheme, a compensator is liable to reimburse the state in respect of a social security benefit even though that benefit may not be deductible from the damages payable.

(5) A central feature of the administration of the scheme is a certificate of recoverable benefits furnished to the compensator by the Secretary of State (i.e. by the Compensation Recovery Unit).[226]

(6) The compensator is not liable to reimburse the state for listed benefits payable after five years: such benefits are not to be deducted from damages.[227]

(7) In contrast to the earlier recoupment scheme, there is no exclusion for "small payments".[228] There is provision for regulations to be made for the disregarding of small payments[229] but no such regulations have yet been made (nor appear likely to be made).

27-42 Under the earlier recoupment scheme, there was a specific provision[230] to the effect that, in assessing the amount of interest payable on damages, the relevant sum of damages was to be reduced by the amount of the recoupable social security benefits. This was in line with principle in ensuring that the claimant was awarded interest only in respect of his loss (or put another way, in respect of those damages which he had been kept out of). But that specific provision was not re-enacted in the 1997 Act and this led the House of Lords in *Wadey v Surrey CC*[231] to decide that interest should be payable on the whole amount of damages irrespective of the deduction of social security benefits.

27-43 In *McCafferey v Datta*[232] it was held that, in determining whether an award of damages exceeds a payment into court, it was irrelevant that some or all of the damages were to be paid by the defendant to the Compensation Recovery Unit, rather than to the claimant. On the facts, therefore, a payment in of £2,500 did not beat an award of £22,373.33 the whole of which was payable to the CRU. Although this was a decision on the earlier recoupment scheme, there is nothing to suggest that the position is any different under the 1997 Act.[233]

27-44 In *Hassall v Secretary of State for Social Security*[234] it was decided by the Court of Appeal that the former recoupment scheme applied (and the same can be said of

tail?" (2019) 169 N.L.J. (7848), 20.

225 Social Security (Recovery of Benefits) Act 1997 s.8 and Sch.2.

226 Social Security (Recovery of Benefits) Act 1997 ss.4–5.

227 Social Security (Recovery of Benefits) Act 1997 ss.3, 17.

228 The half-deduction for five years of certain social security benefits laid down in s.2(1) of the Law Reform (Personal Injuries) Act 1948 no longer has any application, even to damages of £2,500 or less, having been repealed by s.33 of and Sch.3 to the 1997 Act.

229 Social Security (Recovery of Benefits) Act 1997 Pt II of Sch.1.

230 Social Security Administration Act 1992 s.103.

231 [2000] 1 W.L.R. 820 HL.

232 [1997] 1 W.L.R. 870 CA. See further *Williams v Devon CC* [2003] EWCA Civ 365; [2003] P.I.Q.R. Q68; *Crooks v Hendricks Lovell Ltd* [2016] EWCA Civ 8; [2016] 1 Costs L.O. 103.

233 See also CPR r.36.15.

234 [1995] 1 W.L.R. 812 CA.

the 1997 Act), even though the claimant was receiving approximately the same amount of social security benefits prior to the accident. This was because the benefits paid after the accident were paid on the different basis that the claimant was no longer fit for work and were therefore clearly paid in consequence of the accident. The fact that the claimant would be left undercompensated was regarded as flowing not from a defect in the recoupment scheme but from his failure to claim damages for the loss of the non-recoupable benefits. Following this, damages for loss of non-recoupable benefits have been awarded.[235] But under the 1997 Act, it is no longer possible to deduct benefits from damages for non-pecuniary loss, and as a result there is now much less scope for such an award.[236]

(vii) *Other collateral benefits*

The receipt of other benefits where no statute applies is governed by common law principles.[237] The primary principle is undoubtedly that of compensation: the object of the damages award is not to punish the defendant and therefore, in general, the claimant should recover no more than he has actually lost.[238] *Prima facie* the defendant's liability should be reduced where the claimant's loss has been diminished in whole or in part by a benefit received from a collateral source. As Lord Bridge said in *Hussain v New Taplow Paper Mills Ltd*,[239] "prima facie the only recoverable loss is the net loss". However, this must be qualified by several exceptions. First, the collateral benefit to be deducted, must be causally related to the loss for which the claimant seeks compensation.[240] For example, the fact that the claimant gains a windfall from the football pools in the weeks following his injury is obviously irrelevant to the defendant's liability. In the past, judges often attempted to determine the deductibility of benefits solely by reference to the character of the causal relationship between the benefit and the injury. They would thus ask whether the benefit was too "remote"[241] or whether the injury was a *causa causans* rather than merely a *causa sine qua non* of the receipt of benefit.[242] In *Parry v Cleaver*[243] this approach was discredited by some judges in the House of Lords. Such distinctions were too vague and unreliable to account for the different treatment of different categories of benefit. As Lord Pearce remarked, "each is certainly a *causa sine qua non* and probably each is entitled to be called a *causa causans*. Strict causation seems to provide no satisfactory line of demarcation."[244] 27-45

A second qualification to the principle of net compensation has regard to the source of the collateral benefit. If, it is said, the benefit results from the claimant's 27-46

[235] *Neal v Bingle* [1998] Q.B. 466 CA.

[236] R. Lewis, *Deducting Benefits from Damages for Personal Injury* (1999), pp.219–222.

[237] See generally Edelman, *McGregor on Damages*, 20th edn (2017), paras 40-149 to 40-182; *Damages for Personal Injury: Medical, Nursing and Other Expenses; Collateral Benefits*, Law Commission Report No.262 (1999).

[238] *British Transport Commission v Gourley* [1956] A.C. 185 at 202, per Earl Jowitt; *Parry v Cleaver* [1970] A.C. 1, per Lord Morris at 30, per Lord Pearson at 47; *Hussain v New Taplow Mills Ltd* [1988] A.C. 514 at 527; *Hunt v Severs* [1994] 2 A.C. 350 at 357–358.

[239] [1988] A.C. 514 at 527.

[240] *Redpath v Belfast and County Down Ry* [1947] N.I. 167 at 175; and see the contract case *Jebson v East and West India Dock Co* (1875) L.R. 10 C. & P. 300.

[241] e.g. *British Transport Commission v Gourley* [1956] A.C. 185 at 199, per Earl Jowitt.

[242] e.g. *Payne v Railway Executive* [1952] 1 K.B. 26 at 36, per Cohen LJ.

[243] [1970] A.C. 1, per Lord Reid at 15 at 33–34, per Lord Pearce; cf. Lord Wilberforce at 39 and Lord Pearson at 49.

[244] [1970] A.C. 1 at 34.

own resources and his sense of responsibility a deduction should not be made. This is generally the argument employed to justify the long-standing rule that the proceeds of personal accident insurance should be ignored[245]: "it would be unjust and unreasonable to hold that the money which he prudently spent on premiums and the benefit from it should enure to the benefit of the tortfeasor."[246]

27-47 The third qualification to the net compensation principle is that which has regard to the nature and purpose of the benefit.[247] "Surely", said Lord Reid in *Parry v Cleaver*,[248] "the distinction between receipts which must be brought into account and those which must not must depend not on their source but on their intrinsic nature". The crucial question is whether those conferring the benefit intended that the recipient should enjoy the proceeds whether or not he had an independent right of reimbursement against a tortfeasor. The matter was so expressed by Sir Owen Dixon CJ in the Australian case of *National Insurance Co of New Zealand Ltd v Espagne*.[249] He referred to benefits having:

> "this distinguishing characteristic, namely that they are conferred on him [the injured claimant] not only independently of the existence in him of a right of redress against others but so that they may be enjoyed by him although he may enforce that right: they are the product of a disposition in his favour intended for his enjoyment and not provided in relief of any liability in others fully to compensate him."

The purpose, so defined, of certain collateral benefits such as acts of benevolence or charity, may be almost self-evident.[250] In an oft-quoted passage Lord Reid said that "it would be revolting to the ordinary man's sense of justice, and therefore contrary to public policy, that the sufferer should have his damages reduced so that he would gain nothing from the benevolence of his friends or relations or the public at large, and that the only gainer would be the wrongdoer".[251]

27-48 The application of the primary principle and its qualifications means that all but two main categories of collateral benefits are deducted. The two categories are first, insurance payments and the like, and secondly, gratuitous payments and the like. As Lord Bridge said in *Hunt v Severs*[252]:

> "The starting point for any inquiry into the measure of damages which an injured [claimant] is entitled to recover is the recognition that damages in the tort of negligence are purely compensatory. He should recover from the tortfeasor no more and no less than he has lost. Difficult questions may arise when the [claimant's] injuries attract benefits from third parties. According to their nature these may or may not be taken into account as reducing the tortfeasor's liability. The two well-established categories of receipt which are to be ignored in assessing damages are the fruits of insurance which the [claimant] has himself provided against the contingency causing his injuries … and the fruits of the benevolence of third parties motivated by sympathy for the [claimant's] misfortune."

27-49 **Accident insurance** That the proceeds of a personal accident insurance policy

---

245 *Bradburn v Great Western Ry Co* (1874) L.R. 10 Ex. 1. See para.27-49.
246 *Parry v Cleaver* [1970] A.C. 1 at 14, per Lord Reid.
247 cf. Cooper, "A Collateral Benefits Principle" (1971) 49 Can. Bar Rev. 501.
248 [1970] A.C. 1 at 15.
249 (1961) 105 C.L.R. 569 at 573-574.
250 cf. paras 27-49 to 27-51.
251 *Parry v Cleaver* [1970] A.C. 1 at 14.
252 [1994] 2 A.C. 350 at 357–358. See also his earlier similar comments in *Hussain v New Taplow Paper Mills Ltd* [1988] A.C. 514 at 527.

will not be deducted from the damages award has been settled law since 1874.[253] This is usually justified on the ground that the source of the benefit is the claimant's thrift and foresight in using his own resources to provide compensation,[254] but it can perhaps also be argued that the purpose of accident insurance (in contrast to property and other indemnity insurance) is to provide the insured person with money on the occurrence of the insured risk over and above anything he receives by way of compensation from a third party.[255] After some conflict of judicial opinion,[256] the House of Lords in *Parry v Cleaver*[257] held by a majority that an occupational disability pension was sufficiently analogous to an accident insurance benefit for it to be treated in the same way, and for this purpose it was irrelevant whether the pension was contributory or non-contributory[258] or whether its payment was discretionary or obligatory.[259] Over 20 years later the House of Lords in *Smoker v London Fire and Civil Defence Authority*[260] held that the non-deduction principle of *Parry v Cleaver* remained good law, and was applicable even where the employer operating the disablement pension scheme was the tortfeasor, because the claimant had still "bought" it.

It should be noted, however, that though *Parry v Cleaver* principally established that the ill-health pension was not to be set off against damages for lost wages, it also laid down that the pension was to be taken into account in assessing the loss of a full occupational retirement pension to which the claimant's continued service would have entitled him. This aspect of *Parry v Cleaver* was followed by the House of Lords in *Longden v British Coal Corp*[261] in deciding that the claimant was entitled to damages for his net loss of pension after normal retirement age (i.e. one should deduct from the retirement pension he would have received after normal retirement age the disability pension that he would now receive after normal retirement age). The defendants' argument that, in calculating the loss of pension, one should also deduct the disability pension received prior to normal retirement age was rejected as inconsistent with the principal decision in *Parry v Cleaver*. 27-50

Charitable donations That payments gratuitously made to the claimant from a private source, out of motives of charity or sympathy, are not to be taken into account was laid down in the Northern Ireland case of *Redpath v Belfast and County* 27-51

---

[253] *Bradburn v Great Western Ry Co* (1874) L.R. 10 Ex. 1; approved by the House of Lords in *Parry v Cleaver* [1970] A.C. 1; and *Hussain v New Taplow Paper Mills Ltd* [1988] A.C. 514.

[254] e.g. *Parry v Cleaver* [1970] A.C. 1, per Lord Reid at 14 and per Lord Morris at 31.

[255] e.g. *Browning v War Office* [1973] 1 Q.B. 750 at 769, per Diplock LJ; *National Insurance Co of New Zealand v Espagne* (1961) 105 C.L.R. 569 at 575, per Sir Owen Dixon CJ.

[256] *Payne v Ry Executive* [1952] 1 K.B. 26 (no deduction); *Browning v War Office* [1973] 1 Q.B. 750 (deduction). The cases were usually reconciled on the ground that in the former payment of the pension was discretionary, whereas in the latter the claimant was entitled as of right: see, e.g. *Carroll v Hooper* [1964] 1 W.L.R. 345; *Elstob v Robinson* [1964] 1 W.L.R. 726. The distinction was discredited in *Parry v Cleaver* [1970] A.C. 1.

[257] [1970] A.C. 1, Lords Morris and Pearson dissenting.

[258] [1970] A.C. 1, per Lord Pearce at 36, per Lord Wilberforce at 42.

[259] [1970] A.C. 1, per Lord Reid at 20, per Lord Pearce at 36.

[260] [1991] 2 A.C. 502. In *Hopkins v Norcross Plc* [1994] I.C.R. 11, the same principles were applied by the Court of Appeal in holding that a retirement pension was not to be deducted in assessing damages for a wrongful dismissal.

[261] [1998] A.C. 653. See also *Auty v National Coal Board* [1985] 1 W.L.R. 784 CA; *West v Versil Ltd*, *The Times*, 31 August 1996 CA.

Down Ry[262] which has since been approved by the House of Lords.[263] Invariably the donor, it is to be assumed, wishes the injured party and not the tortfeasor to benefit from the act of benevolence, and the courts do not wish to discourage benevolence. But these justifications would suggest that gratuitous payments *made by the tortfeasor* should normally be deducted. This was accepted by the Court of Appeal in *Williams v BOC Gases Ltd*,[264] where the defendant employer had made an ex gratia payment to its employee, the claimant, which was expressed to be "an advance against damages that may be awarded to you in respect of any claim you may have against the company." In *Williams*, the apparently contrary decision of the Court of Appeal in *McCamley v Cammell Laird Shipbuilders Ltd*[265]—where money from an accident insurance policy taken out by the defendant employer for employees was held non-deductible on the supposed application of the benevolence exception—was said to be a case that should be confined to its own facts.

27-52 Subsequently, the Court of Appeal in *Gaca v Pirelli General Plc*[266] approved *Williams* and, in an enlightened decision, took the opportunity formally to overrule *McCamley* on the ground that it was inconsistent with, for example, Lord Bridge's reasoning in *Hussain v New Taplow Paper Mills*.[267] In *Gaca* the claimant was seriously injured at work in an accident for which the defendant employers were responsible. The defendants paid him an ill-health gratuity and he also received disability payments under the defendants' group accident insurance policy. The Court of Appeal held that the benevolence exception to the "net loss" principle did not apply to either of those two types of payment because they were provided by the tortfeasor (and the tortfeasor had not spelt out explicitly that ex gratia payments were not to be deducted from any damages). They should therefore be deducted in assessing damages. Not to deduct gratuitous payments where made by the tortfeasor would tend to discourage benevolence by the tortfeasor, which would be contrary to the purpose of the exception. In any event, the payments made under the group insurance policy were not paid out of benevolence. The exception was concerned with payments made out of sympathy or charity whereas these payments were arranged, and made, in order to promote good working relations between the employers and employees. This decision constitutes a long overdue and welcome clarification on the law on the benevolence exception generally and on benevolence provided by tortfeasors specifically.

27-53 **Employment benefits** If, under his contract of employment the claimant is entitled to sick pay, sickness benefit or the continuation of wages, a deduction must be made for the value of such receipts in assessing damages for loss of earnings.[268] The purpose of the payment is directly to reduce the loss and not to allow the injured party a bonus in addition to compensation received from the tortfeasor for that loss. As Lord Morris has remarked: "if he receives part of his pay ... he cannot assert that

262 [1947] N.I. 167.
263 *Parry v Cleaver* [1970] A.C. 1; *Hussain v New Taplow Paper Mills Ltd* [1988] A.C. 514.
264 [2000] I.C.R. 1181; [2000] P.I.Q.R. Q253. Obiter dicta to this effect of Lloyd LJ in *Hussain v New Taplow Paper Mills Ltd* [1987] 1 W.L.R. 336 at 351 were approved.
265 [1990] 1 W.L.R. 963.
266 [2004] EWCA Civ 373; [2004] 1 W.L.R. 2683.
267 [1988] A.C. 514.
268 *Hussain v New Taplow Paper Mills* [1988] A.C. 514; *Turner v Ministry of Defence* (1969) 113 S.J. 585 CA. See also *Parry v Cleaver* [1970] A.C. 1, per Lord Reid at 16, per Lord Morris at 34.

he has lost all his pay."[269] Again, in *Hussain v New Taplow Paper Mills Ltd*[270] Lord Bridge said the following: "It positively offends my sense of justice that a [claimant], who has certainly paid no insurance premiums as such, should receive full wages during a period of incapacity to work from two different sources, her employer and the tortfeasor. It would seem to me still more unjust and anomalous where, as here, the employer and the tortfeasor are one and the same." The same approach was taken in *Page v Sheerness Steel Plc*,[271] where the claimant was entitled to half pay for life under a permanent health insurance policy taken out and paid for by his employers. This was deducted in assessing his loss of earnings. Similarly in *Gaca v Pirelli General Plc*[272] the Court of Appeal held that the payments made to the injured employee under the employers' group personal accident insurance policy did not fall within the "insurance exception" to the general principle of deducting compensating advantages because the premiums were paid by the employers and not by the claimant employee. Also, where the claimant has been made redundant because of his injuries and has received a redundancy payment (including an inducement to take voluntary redundancy) that payment should be deducted.[273]

Third party can recover The discussion so far has assumed that the source of the collateral benefit is unable to recover its value either from the defendant or the claimant (out of his award of damages). If, exceptionally, this assumption is not true, then the question of deduction or non-deduction is easily resolved.[274] The circumstances in which a third party can sue the tortfeasor for reimbursement of his financial loss sustained as a result of the tort are, for reasons explored elsewhere,[275] very rare. Where they do exist, the benefit must be deducted.[276] Conversely, if the claimant is under a legal obligation to restore the benefit to the third party (who is not the tortfeasor) out of his damages award, then it is obviously inappropriate for a deduction to be made.[277] A clear example is where an employee is under a contractual obligation to refund sick pay to his employer if he succeeds in a damages claim, or where the employer provides sick pay in the form of a loan, repayable if damages are awarded.[278] In *Berriello v Felixstowe Dock & Ry Co*[279] an Italian seaman, injured in England, was paid (or was to be paid) two sums from the *Cassa Marittima Meridionale*, an Italian state welfare fund for Italian seamen. The Court of Appeal (Stocker LJ dissenting on liability) held that while these sums would normally be deducted from the claimant's damages they should not be deducted on these facts because, under Italian law, the *Cassa Marittima* had the right to recover the sums paid from the claimant should he recover damages cover- 27-54

[269] *Parry v Cleaver* [1970] A.C. 1.
[270] [1988] A.C. 514 at 532.
[271] [1999] 1 A.C. 345 HL.
[272] [2004] EWCA Civ 373; [2004] 1 W.L.R. 2683.
[273] *Colledge v Bass Mitchells & Butlers Ltd* [1988] I.C.R. 125; *Wilson v National Coal Board*, 1981 S.L.T.(S.) 67; cf. *Mills v Hassall* [1983] I.C.R. 330.
[274] cf. Fleming, *International Encyclopaedia of Comparative Law*, Vol.XI, Ch.11, pp.16-46; Cooper, "A Collateral Benefits Principle" (1971) 49 Can. Bar Rev. 501 at 521–533.
[275] See paras 7-103 onwards.
[276] cf. Street, *Principles of Law of Damages*, pp.104–107. This is in effect the approach applied to social security benefits; paras 27-41 to 27-44.
[277] *Inland Revenue Commissioners v Hambrook* [1956] 2 Q.B. 641 at 656-657, per Lord Goddard CJ. See also *Cunningham v Harrison* [1973] Q.B. 942; para.27-26.
[278] cf. Pearson Royal Commission (1978) Cmnd.7054, paras 502-505.
[279] [1989] 1 W.L.R. 695.

ing the same losses from a defendant. There would therefore be no question here of the claimant being overcompensated by non-deduction of the collateral benefits in assessing the damages.

(d) Non-pecuniary loss

27-55 Non-pecuniary losses[280] are different from pecuniary losses in that the sum awarded as compensation cannot be precisely equivalent to the loss: damages cannot restore a lost limb or happiness.[281] While there is some disagreement as to the function of damages for non-pecuniary loss,[282] many would agree with the Royal Commission's suggestions that they serve as a palliative, or provide the claimant with the means to purchase alternative forms of happiness, or help to meet hidden expenses caused by the injury.[283] While the practice of the courts is not to subdivide non-pecuniary damages under specific heads,[284] nevertheless proper consideration cannot be given to the claim without taking into account the various types of loss the claimant has suffered. Moreover, a number of cases each presenting some unusual feature has compelled the courts to deal individually with some of them. With the warning, then, that it may be found that these heads of damage overlap with one another in particular cases, the law concerning them will be described.

(i) Pain and suffering

27-56 The claimant is entitled to compensation for the pain and suffering, both actual and prospective,[285] which is attributable to his injury and its consequences. Injury includes disease and physical or mental[286] illness. Mental anguish must be compensated for as well as actual physical pain. So, for example, there must be compensation for a severely incapacitated person's realisation of the condition to which he has been reduced[287] or for the embarrassment of disfigurement[288] and, by s.1(1)(b) of the Administration of Justice Act 1982, "if the injured person's expecta-

---

280 See, generally, *Damages for Personal Injury: Non-Pecuniary Loss, Law Commission Report No.257* (1999).

281 per Lord Morris in *H West & Son v Shephard* [1964] A.C. 326 at 346; and *Parry v Cleaver* [1970] A.C. 1 at 22. Where a cause of action in negligence for personal injury has vested in the injured party's trustee in bankruptcy, the trustee in bankruptcy holds any damages recovered for non-pecuniary loss (but not for pecuniary loss) on constructive trust for the injured party: *Ord v Upton* [2000] Ch. 352.

282 Ogus, "Damages for Lost Amenities: for a Foot, a Feeling or a Function?" (1972) 35 M.L.R. 1; *Damages for Personal Injury: Non-Pecuniary Loss, Law Commission Report No.257* (1999), paras 2.4–2.7.

283 Pearson Royal Commission (1978) Cmnd.7054, para.360. See also *H West & Son v Shephard* [1964] A.C. 326 at 357–363, per Lord Devlin; *Skelton v Collins* (1966) 115 C.L.R. 94 at 130–133, per Windeyer J; *Andrews v Grand & Toy Alberta Ltd* (1978) 83 D.L.R. (3d) 452.

284 cf. *Watson v Powles* [1968] 1 Q.B. 596.

285 *Heaps v Perrite Ltd* [1937] 2 All E.R. 60; *H West & Son Ltd v Shephard* [1964] A.C. 326.

286 e.g. compensation neurosis, *James v Woodall Duckham Construction Co Ltd* [1969] 1 W.L.R. 903, para.27-28; anxiety neurosis, *Lucy v Mariehamms Rederi* [1971] 2 Lloyd's Rep. 314: morbid depression, *Hinz v Berry* [1970] 2 Q.B. 40; depression and personality change, *McLoughlin v O'Brian* [1983] A.C. 410; post-traumatic stress disorder, *Alcock v Chief Constable of South Yorkshire Police* [1992] 1 A.C. 310; *Frost v Chief Constable of Yorkshire Police* [1998] Q.B. 254; nervous breakdown consequent on workplace stress, *Walker v Northumberland CC* [1995] 1 All E.R. 737; *Barber v Somerset CC* [2004] UKHL 13; [2004] 1 W.L.R. 1089; chronic fatigue syndrome, *Page v Smith* [1996] A.C. 155.

287 *H West & Son Ltd v Shephard* [1964] A.C. 326; *Cutts v Chumley* [1967] 1 W.L.R. 742; *Povey v*

tion of life has been reduced by the injuries, the court, in assessing damages in respect of pain and suffering caused by the injuries, shall take account of any suffering caused or likely to be caused to him by awareness that his expectation of life has been so reduced".[289] On the other hand, if the claimant suffered no pain or mental anguish because, for example, he was rendered permanently unconscious, then, no matter how serious the injury, no damages may be recovered under this head.[290] By parity of reasoning it would seem to be clear that if the claimant's suffering is effectively reduced by the use of pain-killing drugs, the damages for pain and suffering will be accordingly smaller than they otherwise would have been.

(ii) *Loss of faculty and loss of amenity*

Usually the judges make a single award to cover pain and suffering and loss of amenities. It seems clear, however, that the major element in this is the compensation to represent the injury itself (often called the loss of faculty[291]) and the consequences that injury has on the claimant's way of life and therefore for his loss of happiness.[292] In the majority of cases, and especially when the injury is serious, it is unnecessary to distinguish between the consequences of the injury and the injury itself. Damages are awarded so as to cover both and, in any case, as Lord Reid has pointed out,[293] the normal man is usually more concerned about the dislocation of his life than about his actual physical injury. Nevertheless, it may be appropriate to consider the physical injury itself independently for two reasons. First, a minor but permanent impairment of bodily integrity may have no substantial effect on the claimant's enjoyment of life but he may recover a sum simply for the injury itself.[294] Secondly, and perhaps more importantly, the judges in assessing damages for loss of amenities tend to proceed according to the gravity of the physical disability.[295] In other words, they attribute an assumed loss of enjoyment of life to flow from different categories of injury. As will be seen, this prima facie figure may then be revised to take account of the special features of the claimant's case, but it necessarily provides a starting point which is convenient both because it obviates too close an investigation on such subjective matters as the claimant's inner feelings,[296] and because it renders damages awards more uniform and therefore **27-57**

Governors of Rydal School [1970] 1 All E.R. 841.

288 *Taylor v Chuck (RV) (Transport)* (1963) 107 S.J. 910.

289 This appears to be merely declaratory of the previous law—see, e.g. *Flint v Lovell* [1935] 1 K.B. 354 at 366–367, per Roche LJ; *Forrest v Sharp* (1963) 107 S.J. 536—but it assumes particular importance because of s.1(1)(a) of the Administration of Justice Act 1982 which abolished the separate head of damages for loss of expectation of life.

290 *Wise v Kaye* [1962] 1 Q.B. 638; *H West & Son Ltd v Shephard* [1964] A.C. 326; *Andrews v Freeborough* [1967] 1 Q.B. 1.

291 cf. *Andrews v Freeborough* [1967] 1 Q.B. 1 at 18, per Davies LJ.

292 cf. *H West & Son Ltd v Shephard* [1964] A.C. 326 at 355, per Lord Devlin.

293 *H West & Son Ltd v Shephard* [1964] A.C. 326 at 341.

294 e.g. *Forster v Pugh* [1955] C.L.Y. 741 (loss of spleen); *Dryden v Johnson Matthey plc* [2018] UKSC 18; [2019] A.C. 403 (platinum sensitisation—see para.7-05); but cf. *Hamilton v Burdon* [1962] C.L.Y. 859; *Grieves v FT Everard & Sons* [2007] UKHL 39; [2008] 1 A.C. 281 (pleural plaques).

295 *Wise v Kaye* [1962] 1 Q.B. 638 at 652, per Sellers LJ; *H West & Son Ltd v Shephard* [1964] A.C. 326, per Lord Pearce at 366; *Fletcher v Autocar and Transporters Ltd* [1968] 2 Q.B. 322 at 340, per Diplock LJ.

296 *Wise v Kaye* [1962] 1 Q.B. 638, per Sellers LJ at 649; *H West & Son v Shephard* [1964] A.C. 326, per Lord Pearce at 368–369.

predictable.[297] The conventional sums awarded for different types of injury are derived from the general experience of judges as manifested in previous comparable cases,[298] and represent the judiciary's perception of what is fair, just and reasonable compensation.[299] The figures emerging are not, of course, fixed for all time: it has been stressed that in having regard to them the judges should take account of changes in the retail prices index.[300] Moreover, in *Heil v Rankin*,[301] acting on the recommendation of the Law Commission, the Court of Appeal increased damages for non-pecuniary loss because awards had fallen behind what was regarded as "fair, just and reasonable". In an attempt to produce greater consistency in awards, the Judicial Studies Board in 1992 produced a report entitled *Guidelines for the Assessment of General Damages in Personal Injury Cases* which sets out the brackets for various injuries based on, but without mentioning the names of, cases.[302] The 15th edition of the *Guidelines for the Assessment of General Damages in Personal Injury Cases* was published in December 2019.[303] From 1 April 2013, when the legislative changes to the costs regime recommended by Sir Rupert Jackson came into force, damages for pain, suffering and loss of amenity (and indeed all awards of damages for non-pecuniary loss) were increased by 10 per cent. This uplift was essentially designed to compensate claimants, who are funding litigation under a conditional fee agreement, for the loss of their right to recover the success fee from the defendant so that the uplift does not apply where such a success fee is ordered under s.44(6) of the Legal Aid, Sentencing and Punishment of Offenders Act 2012).[304]

27-58 The starting figure derived from these sources may then be adjusted to take account of the special features of the claimant's case. The court therefore examines the circumstances of his life prior to the accident to see whether he was engaged in any special activities which he is now prevented from pursuing.[305] "If, for instance, the [claimant's] main interest in life was some sport or hobby from which he will in future be debarred, that too increases the assessment."[306] Thus the deprivation of sexual pleasures,[307] the loss of a holiday,[308] the loss of the comfort and

---

[297] *Ward v James* [1966] 1 Q.B. 273 at 300, per Lord Denning MR. See also *Hennell v Ranaboldo* [1963] 1 W.L.R. 1391.

[298] Collections of personal injury awards are available in Kemp and Kemp, *The Quantum of Damages; Current Law* and Halsbury, *Laws of England: Monthly Review*. On the other hand there are some kinds of injury for which there is no established pattern of awards. See *Hawkins v New Mendip Engineering Ltd* [1966] 1 W.L.R. 1341; and *Parry v English Electric Co Ltd* [1971] 1 W.L.R. 664. This was the justification given in *Hodges v Harland and Wolff Ltd* [1965] 1 W.L.R. 523, for the exceptional ordering of a jury trial. For an approach to multiple injuries, see *Dureau v Evans* [1996] P.I.Q.R. Q18.

[299] See para.27-07.

[300] *Walker v McLean (John) & Sons* [1979] 1 W.L.R. 760; *Wright v British Railways Board* [1983] 2 A.C. 773; *Heil v Rankin* [2001] Q.B. 272 CA.

[301] [2001] Q.B. 272 CA.

[302] The status of the Judicial Studies Board's Guidelines was considered in *Arafa v Potter* [1994] P.I.Q.R. Q73; and *Reed v Sunderland HA, The Times,* 16 October 1998. They are now widely used.

[303] Note that the Civil Liability Act 2018 Pt 1 (not yet in force) allows for regulations imposing a low fixed tariff of damages for pain, suffering and loss of amenity in respect of whiplash injuries, with a duration of up to two years, caused by negligent driving. The purpose of this is to crack down on fraudulent whiplash claims thereby reducing motor insurance premiums.

[304] *Simmons v Castle* [2012] EWCA 1039; [2012] EWCA Civ 1288; [2013] 1 W.L.R. 1239.

[305] *Heaps v Perrite Ltd* [1937] 2 All E.R. 60.

[306] *H West & Son v Shephard* [1964] A.C. 326 at 365, per Lord Pearce.

[307] *Cook v JL Kier & Co* [1970] 1 W.L.R. 774.

companionship of marriage[309] and even the fact that the claimant has had to give up employment which he clearly enjoyed[310] have justified a higher award.[311]

If such subjective factors are relevant to increase the sum awarded, it might seem logical to reduce the prima facie figure where the claimant is rendered unconscious or is unable to appreciate the loss. However, in *Wise v Kaye*,[312] the Court of Appeal held by a majority that though this fact justified making no award for pain and suffering, it had no bearing on the damages for loss of amenities. Two years later this decision was confirmed by the majority of the House of Lords in the similar case of *H West & Son Ltd v Shephard*,[313] which itself was followed by the House of Lords in *Lim Poh Choo v Camden and Islington AHA*.[314] So although the High Court of Australia has declined to follow *West v Shephard* on this point,[315] and while there has occasionally been a reluctance to do so by English judges,[316] it is settled that so far as English law is concerned it is the objective loss of amenities in respect of which damages are awarded. As Lord Morris said: 27-59

> "The fact of unconsciousness is … relevant in respect of and will eliminate those heads or elements of damage which can exist only by being felt or thought or experienced. The fact of unconsciousness does not, however, eliminate the actuality of the deprivations of the ordinary experiences and amenities of life which may be the inevitable result of some physical injury."[317]

There can be no separate award, over and above damages for pain, suffering and loss of amenity, for "loss of autonomy" where there has been medical negligence comprising a failure to obtain the patient's consent.[318]

(e) Damages for wrongful birth[319]

"Wrongful birth"[320] occurs where a doctor's or a health authority's negligence (or breach of contract) in connection with, for example, a sterilisation, vasectomy or abortion operation has resulted in an (originally) unwanted child being born. When first recognised, the trend in the English cases was to compensate all pecuniary and 27-60

308 *Ichard v Frangoulis* [1977] 1 W.L.R. 566.

309 *Hughes v McKeown* [1985] 1 W.L.R. 963; cf. *Lampert v Eastern National Omnibus Co* [1954] 1 W.L.R. 1047.

310 *Hearnshaw v English Steel Corp* (1971) 11 K.I.R. 306 CA.

311 *Meah v McCreamer* [1985] 1 All E.R. 367 (cf. *Meah v McCreamer (No.2)* [1986] 1 All E.R. 943), in which a substantial sum for non-pecuniary loss was awarded for a severe personality change, which led to the claimant being imprisoned for sexual offences on women, can no longer be regarded as good law as the claim should have been barred by illegality: *Clunis v Camden and Islington HA* [1998] Q.B. 978; *Gray v Thames Trains* [2009] UKHL 33; [2009] 1 A.C. 1339.

312 [1962] 1 Q.B. 638 (Diplock LJ dissenting).

313 [1964] A.C. 326 (Lords Reid and Devlin dissenting).

314 [1980] A.C. 174.

315 *Skelton v Collins* (1966) 39 A.L.J. 480.

316 *Andrews v Freeborough* [1967] 1 Q.B. 1, per Willmer LJ at 12, per Davies LJ at 18, per Winn LJ at 20.

317 [1964] A.C. 326 at 349.

318 *Shaw v Kovac* [2017] EWCA Civ 1028; [2017] 1 W.L.R. 4773.

319 See generally, Taylor (1985) 15 Fam. Law 147; Symmons (1987) 50 M.L.R. 269; Stewart (1995) 40 J.L.S.S. 298. "Wrongful birth" includes what is sometimes sub-categorised as "wrongful conception".

320 A claim by an infant for "wrongful life" has been rejected: *McKay v Essex AHA* [1982] Q.B. 1166. See Teff (1985) 34 I.C.L.Q. 423; Fortin [1987] J.S.W.L. 306; Scott, "Reconsidering 'Wrongful Life' in England after 30 Years" [2013] C.L.J. 115.

non-pecuniary loss suffered by the parents as a result of the wrongful birth, subject to the usual restrictions like remoteness and mitigation. So, for example, in *Emeh v Kensington AHA*,[321] where a sterilisation operation had been performed negligently, the mother was awarded damages for the past and future pain and suffering and loss of amenity of having and looking after the child, who had congenital abnormalities, plus loss of earnings and the past and future cost of maintaining the child. The Court of Appeal rejected both the argument that the claimant had failed in her duty to mitigate her loss by not having had an abortion and the argument that there were reasons of public policy for refusing such an award. Again in *Salih v Enfield HA*[322] the defendant negligently failed to warn the claimants of the risk that their child would be born handicapped by rubella syndrome, as turned out to be the case. In assessing damages for the unwanted birth (the mother would have had an abortion had she been properly warned) it was held by the Court of Appeal that the basic (as opposed to special) cost of maintaining the handicapped child was irrecoverable because, on the balance of probabilities, if the claimants had not had that child they would have had another and this they had now decided not to do because of the strain of looking after the handicapped child. In *Fish v Wilcox*,[323] the Court of Appeal held that a mother could not recover both her loss of earnings and the value of the nursing care provided by her to her handicapped child. That would amount to double compensation as the claimant could not carry on in her original employment and look after her child at the same time.

(i) The healthy child

27-61 **McFarlane v Tayside Health Board** The law on "wrongful birth" claims was reviewed, and the scope of the damages recoverable for the birth of at least a healthy child considerably restricted, by the House of Lords in *McFarlane v Tayside Health Board*.[324] This was a failed vasectomy case in which a surgeon had negligently advised a husband and wife that the vasectomy had rendered the husband infertile. The couple ceased to use contraceptives and the wife became pregnant giving birth to a healthy child. The House of Lords (Lord Millett dissenting on this point) held that the mother's non-pecuniary and pecuniary losses consequent on the pregnancy or child-birth were equivalent to personal injury losses and recoverable. But all their Lordships were in agreement that the parents could not recover for their economic loss in maintaining the child, which was regarded as pure economic loss. Three of their Lordships (Lords Slynn, Steyn and Hope) saw the issue as one of liability, rather than the extent of liability, and held that there was no duty of care owed to the parents with regard to the pure economic loss because, in line with the standard approach to that sort of loss, it was not fair just and reasonable for there to be such a duty. Lord Steyn, in particular, relied on what he termed considerations of distribu-

---

[321] [1985] Q.B. 1012; overruling *Udale v Bloomsbury AHA* [1983] 1 W.L.R. 1098. In addition to the cases discussed in the text, see, e.g. *Thake v Maurice* [1986] Q.B. 644; *Benarr v Kettering HA* (1988) 138 N.L.J. 179 (father entitled, inter alia, to the future cost of privately educating the child); *Allen v Bloomsbury HA* [1993] 1 All E.R. 651. In each of these cases, a healthy child was born so that the decisions on tort damages have been implicitly overruled by *McFarlane v Tayside Health Board* [2000] 2 A.C. 59 discussed in paras 27-61 to 27-66.

[322] [1991] 3 All E.R. 400; criticised by Glazebrook [1992] C.L.J. 226.

[323] (1993) 13 B.M.L.R. 134.

[324] [2000] 2 A.C. 59. By a four-three majority, the High Court of Australia in *Cattanach v Melchior* (2003) 77 A.J.L.R. 1312 went the other way from *McFarlane* and awarded the costs of maintaining the child.

tive, rather than corrective, justice[325]; that is, he relied on his view of popular morality in drawing the parameters of tort liability. Although a Scottish case, their Lordships made clear that, on this issue, the same law should apply in both England and Scotland.[326]

Two main matters were left unresolved by *McFarlane*. The first was what the position would be if the parents could sue for breach of contract. Lord Steyn expressly confined his views to claims in delict or tort; and certainly in respect of breach of contract one could not regard the issue as going to liability rather than the extent of liability.[327] Arguably the same basic policy approach to wrongful birth claims should apply whether the claim is brought in tort or for breach of contract. That point has subsequently been affirmed in the context of the breach of a strict contractual obligation in *ARB v IVF Hammersmith*.[328] A private IVF clinic acted in breach of its contract with the claimant by thawing and implanting embryos, created with the claimant's gametes, into his ex-girlfriend without his consent. This ultimately resulted in the birth of a healthy daughter. The claimant sought damages for that breach of contract to cover the costs of bringing up the daughter. It was held by the Court of Appeal that, applying *McFarlane*, such damages were not recoverable on policy grounds and that it did not matter that the claim was for breach of contract (comprising the breach of a strict duty) rather than the tort of negligence. The second unresolved issue from *McFarlane* was whether the position would be any different if the unwanted child was disabled. The previously leading case of *Emeh v Kensington AHA*[329] concerned a child with congenital abnormalities. That decision was not expressly overruled and Lord Steyn specifically left open what the position would be in such a case. 27-62

(ii) The disabled child

Parkinson v St James and Seacroft University Hospital NHS Trust It was not long before the question of the disabled child came before the appellate courts. In *Parkinson v St James and Seacroft University Hospital NHS Trust*,[330] a negligent sterilisation operation led to the birth of a disabled child. The Court of Appeal took 27-63

[325] For further discussion of these terms, see paras 1-15 to 1-16.

[326] In *Greenfield v Irwin (A Firm)* [2001] EWCA Civ 113; [2001] 1 W.L.R. 1279, the Court of Appeal applied *McFarlane* to dismiss a claim for loss of earnings by a mother in giving up her work to look after a healthy child born as a result of the defendant's negligence; and dismissed an argument that *McFarlane* infringed a mother's rights under art.8 of the ECHR.

[327] In *McFarlane* Lord Slynn commented that if a client wants to be able to recover the economic costs of raising a healthy child, they must do so by "an appropriate contract", but he did not specify what an appropriate contract might consist of: [2000] 2 A.C. 59 at 76. Patients treated under the NHS do not enter into a contractual relationship with their doctor. See also *Reynolds v The Health First Medical Group* [2000] Lloyd's Rep. Med. 240 (county court) where the claimant's attempt to put a failed sterilisation claim on a contractual basis in order to avoid the effect of *McFarlane* was rejected.

[328] [2018] EWCA Civ 2803; [2020] Q.B. 93.

[329] [1985] Q.B. 1012, CA: para.27-60.

[330] [2001] EWCA Civ 530; [2002] Q.B. 266. See also *Rand v East Dorset HA* (2000) 50 B.M.L.R. 39; *Hardman v Amin* [2000] Lloyd's Med. Rep. 448; *Lee v Taunton and Somerset NHS Trust* [2001] 1 F.L.R. 419; *Groom v Selby* [2001] EWCA Civ 1522; [2002] P.I.Q.R. P18; Quick, "Damages for Wrongful Conception" [2002] Tort L. Rev. 5. In *Khan v Meadows* [2019] EWCA Civ 152; [2019] 4 W.L.R. 26 the claimant would have had an abortion had she received the proper advice from the defendant about the risks of her child being born with haemophilia. As it was, her child was born and suffered from both haemophilia and autism. It was held that, applying the difficult decision of *South Australia Asset Management Corp v York Montague Ltd* [1997] A.C. 191, only the extra costs of bringing up a child with haemophilia—and not the extra costs of bringing up a child with autism—

a mid-position. The mother was awarded damages for the upbringing costs attributable to the disability. It was held that such damages had not been ruled out by *McFarlane*. On the other hand, damages for the costs which would be incurred in bringing up any child (healthy or disabled) were disallowed. Those damages, it was held, had been ruled out by *McFarlane* and to this extent, *Emeh*, in which all the costs of bringing up a disabled child were held recoverable, had been impliedly overruled by *McFarlane*.

(iii) The disabled parent

27-64 **Rees v Darlington Memorial Hospital NHS Trust** A further factual twist—the birth of a healthy child, following a negligently conducted sterilisation operation, to a disabled mother—brought the whole question back to a seven-judge House of Lords in *Rees v Darlington Memorial Hospital NHS Trust*.[331] All their Lordships decided that *McFarlane* had been correctly decided and should basically be followed. By a four-three majority (Lords Bingham, Nicholls, Millett and Scott in the majority, Lords Steyn, Hope and Hutton dissenting) it was then decided that the majority of the Court of Appeal in *Rees*[332] had been incorrect, as being inconsistent with *McFarlane*, to award damages to the mother for the additional upbringing costs attributable to the mother's disability.[333] On the other hand, a "gloss" (as it was termed by Lords Bingham and Nicholls)[334] was placed on *McFarlane* by the majority in holding that a conventional sum of £15,000 should be awarded to the mother (or jointly to the parents) where there has been an unwanted birth attributable to a civil wrong. Such a conventional sum is to be awarded irrespective of whether the child or the parents are healthy or disabled. Although Lord Bingham at one point said that this conventional award "would not be, and would not be intended to be, compensatory",[335] he had earlier spoken of "the real loss ... [of being] denied ... the opportunity to live her life in the way that she wished and planned" and of "a conventional award to mark the injury and loss".[336] In Lord Millett's words, "[t]he parents have lost the opportunity to live their lives in the way that they wished and planned to do. The loss of this opportunity, whether characterised as a right or a freedom, is a proper subject for compensation by way of damages".[337] Similarly, Lord Scott referred to *Farley v Skinner*[338]—a leading contractual case on mental distress—and spoke of the award as compensating the mother for being deprived of her expected benefit. It is submitted, therefore, that the conventional sum is best viewed as an award to compensate for non-pecuniary loss, namely a mother's mental distress consequent on having her lifestyle plans disrupted. Admittedly, a *fixed* conventional award—as opposed to a bracket of awards—for non-pecuniary loss is unusual but it is the approach used for bereave-

were recoverable; see para.2-139.

331 [2003] UKHL 52; [2004] 1 A.C. 309.

332 [2002] EWCA Civ 88; [2003] Q.B. 20.

333 In a powerful dissenting judgment Waller LJ pointed to some of the anomalies that might be thought to arise from "picking out" the disabled mother; e.g. the contrast between the rich, very well assisted, disabled mother and the poor, unassisted, healthy mother: [2002] EWCA Civ 88; [2003] Q.B. 20 at [53]-[54].

334 [2003] UKHL 52; [2004] 1 A.C. 309 at [7] and [17].

335 [2003] UKHL 52; [2004] 1 A.C. 309 at [8].

336 [2003] UKHL 52; [2004] 1 A.C. 309 at [8].

337 [2003] UKHL 52; [2004] 1 A.C. 309 at [123].

338 [2001] UKHL 49; [2002] 2 A.C. 732.

ment damages under the Fatal Accidents Act 1976 and it is the approach that used to be applied to the award of damages for (non-pecuniary) loss of expectation of life.

Although three of the majority would have overruled *Parkinson*, Lord Millett explicitly left open the question whether *Parkinson* had been correctly decided.[339] Without a majority for or against that decision, it technically remains good law.[340] Applying the majority's approach, therefore, in a wrongful birth case, a mother is entitled to all pecuniary and non-pecuniary loss directly attributable to the pregnancy and giving birth *and* the parents are entitled to a conventional sum of £15,000 for disruption of planned lifestyle. In so far as *Parkinson* remains good law, where the child is disabled, a mother will additionally be entitled to the upbringing costs attributable to the disability. **27-65**

In conclusion, the approach of the majority of their Lordships in *Rees* has much to commend it. It represents a fair and relatively clear answer to an intractable problem, albeit that it is unfortunate that there was no majority either way on *Parkinson*. Moreover, it should be appreciated—as Lord Hope explained with great clarity in his dissenting speech—that the conventional award is unique because, in contrast to damages for personal injury and death, it compensates mental distress in a situation where, for reasons of legal policy, the courts have decided that pecuniary loss is non-compensatable.[341] To place non-pecuniary loss above pecuniary loss is certainly odd. To that extent, it is clear that the majority have adopted a pragmatic compromise rather than a principled solution.[342] **27-66**

(f) Interest on damages

By the Senior Courts Act 1981 s.35A, and the County Courts Act 1984 s.69, a court *may* include in any sum for which judgment is given simple interest[343] on all or any part of the damages for which judgment is given or for which payment is made before judgment[344]; and, in the case of a judgment for damages for personal injuries[345] or death exceeding £200, such interest *shall* be included unless the court **27-67**

339 [2003] UKHL 52; [2004] 1 A.C. 309 at [112].

340 In *Farraj v King's Healthcare NHS Trust* [2006] EWHC 1228; [2006] P.I.Q.R. P29 at [39] Swift J said as much: "for the present, the decision in *Parkinson* represents the law."

341 [2003] UKHL 52; [2004] 1 A.C. 309 at [73].

342 For further discussion of the assessment of damages in respect of the unwanted birth of a child see M.A. Jones, *Medical Negligence*, 5th edn (Sweet & Maxwell, 2018), paras 12-134 to 12-158.

343 Interest, including compound interest, may now be awarded as damages at common law: *Sempra Metals Ltd v IRC* [2007] UKHL 34; [2008] 1 A.C. 561. But claimants in respect of damages for personal injury and death are unlikely to be able to prove more than a loss of simple interest so that simple interest will continue to be awarded under the statute.

344 Even where such payment is for the whole of the damages claimed; *Edmunds v Lloyds Italico* [1986] 1 W.L.R. 492. But s.35A does not empower an award of interest if the payment (whether in respect of a claim for a debt or damages) was made before proceedings had commenced: *President of India v La Pintada Cia Navegacion SA* [1985] A.C. 104 HL; *IM Properties Ltd v Cape & Dalgleish* [1999] Q.B. 297 CA. However, the House of Lords in *Sempra Metals Ltd v IRC* [2007] UKHL 34; [2008] 1 A.C. 561 awarded restitution for the benefit of having had the use of money (i.e. compound interest as restitution); and it was also accepted that damages for loss of use of money (i.e. interest as damages) can be awarded and that the *La Pintada* case should now be regarded as incorrect.

345 This includes damages awarded in respect of injury to a person other than the claimant. "Judgment" includes summary judgment obtained under CPR Pt 24: *Gardner Steel Ltd v Sheffield Bros* [1978] 1 W.L.R. 916. In *Thomas v Bunn* [1991] 1 A.C. 362 HL, it was held that where, e.g. there is a split trial, the judgment debt rate of interest runs from the damages judgment and not from the liability judgment.

is satisfied that there are special reasons to the contrary.[346] The courts have the discretion to fix the period for which interest is payable, within the limits of the date when the cause of action arose and the date of judgment or, in the case of a sum paid before judgment, the date of that payment. The rate of interest is also at the discretion of the courts. By the Civil Procedure Rules r.36.3(3), a Pt 36 offer (an offer to settle) is taken to include any interest payable, unless the contrary is indicated. While the defendant is not bound to make this addition, he will be at risk regarding costs if he fails to do so and an award of interest is eventually made.

27-68 The principles applied by the courts for the award of interest on damages in personal injury cases were formulated by the Court of Appeal in *Jefford v Gee*,[347] though they have been somewhat amended by subsequent decisions. The rate of interest to be adopted is the rate payable on the special account[348]; where this rate varies during the period in respect of which interest is payable an average rate should be taken. So far as the special damages for pecuniary losses accrued at the date of trial are concerned, interest should, in principle, be calculated from week to week because these losses will have accrued over the period between the injury and the trial. In practice, however, such minute attention to detail is not required and in all ordinary cases interest at half of the appropriate rate should be awarded on the total amount of the special damages.[349] But in exceptional circumstances, for example, where all, or virtually all, of the losses covered by special damages were incurred at the date of the accident, the claimant may be awarded the full rate.[350] However, if this is what the claimant wants, he should specify it in the pleadings and should set out the special circumstances relied on.[351] No interest is payable on the damages for loss of future earnings since, by definition, these are not paid in respect of an accrued loss.[352]

27-69 **Interest on damages for non-pecuniary losses** On the basis that interest is awarded for the claimant being kept out of his money, the court in *Jefford v Gee* also held that it should be paid for non-pecuniary losses from the date on which such compensation should have been recovered from the defendant.[353] This is normally the date of the service of the claim form, but may in some cases be the date of the

---

346 Unreasonable delay by the claimant in making a claim might be a special reason, but inflation which has a general impact cannot be: *Pickett v British Rail Engineering Ltd* [1980] A.C. 136 at 173, per Lord Scarman. See also *Spittle v Bunney* [1988] 1 W.L.R. 847; *Corbett v Barking, Havering Brentwood HA* [1991] 2 Q.B. 408; *Eagle v Chambers* [2004] EWCA Civ 1033; [2004] 1 W.L.R. 3081 at [161]–[162].

347 [1970] 2 Q.B. 130.

348 See Court Funds Rules 2011 (SI 2011/1734) rr.11. The rate is fixed from time to time by the Lord Chancellor. Since 1 July 2009, the special account rate has been 0.5 per cent.

349 *Jefford v Gee* [1970] 2 Q.B. 130 at 146; *Cookson v Knowles* [1979] A.C. 556; *Dexter v Courtaulds Ltd* [1984] 1 W.L.R. 372. See also Pearson Report, Cmnd.7054 (1978), paras 741–742.

350 *Ichard v Frangoulis* [1977] 1 W.L.R. 556; *Dodd v Rediffusion (West Midlands)* [1980] 3 C.L.Y. 635; *Prokop v DHSS* [1985] C.L.Y. 1037; *Dexter v Courtaulds Ltd* [1984] 1 W.L.R. 372; *Hobin v Douglas, The Independent*, 26 October 1998 CA. See generally *Damages for Personal Injury: Medical, Nursing and Other Expenses; Collateral Benefits* Law Commission Report No.262 (1999), paras 2.63–2.69, 7.1–7.16.

351 *Dexter v Courtaulds Ltd* [1984] 1 W.L.R. 372 at 377–378.

352 *Jefford v Gee* [1970] 2 Q.B. 130 at 146–147, approved in *Cookson v Knowles* [1979] A.C. 556. The same applies to damages for loss of earning capacity, where that term is being used, as it usually is (see para.27-37), to refer to future consequences: *Clarke v Rotax Aircraft Equipment* [1975] 1 W.L.R. 1570.

353 [1970] 2 Q.B. 130 at 147–148. See generally *Damages for Personal Injury: Non-Pecuniary Loss,*

letter before action, or, in an exceptional case, as where the defendant has fraudulently concealed the existence of the cause of the action, even earlier.[354] In *Cookson v Knowles*,[355] the Court of Appeal revised its view on non-pecuniary losses, holding that because of inflation no interest on the sums awarded should be ordered. It was argued that since the courts assess the lump sum award on the "scale" for figures current at the date of trial, a scale which in consequence of inflation is higher than that current at the date of injury or the date of writ, the claimant stands to gain by delay in bringing the case to trial. The fallacy in this reasoning was exposed by the House of Lords in *Pickett v British Rail Engineering Ltd*[356]: the claimant may receive more money by delaying his claim but in real terms he will not gain, as the scale of damages is increased only in line with inflation. It was held therefore that interest should be awarded on damages for non-pecuniary losses. But in *Birkett v Hayes*[357] the Court of Appeal emphasised that there was still some validity in the inflation argument in the sense that interest rates contain an inflationary element so that it would overcompensate the claimant to award damages, which take into account the need for preserving the value of money, plus interest at the full rate. It was therefore decided that, while some interest should be payable in line with the *Pickett* case, the rate should be merely 2 per cent as representing the "real" rate of interest at the time. This approach was confirmed by the House of Lords in *Wright v British Railways Board*[358] and the figure of 2 per cent was approved at least "for the time being".[359] Although the rate for awarding interest was not in issue in *Wells v Wells*,[360] it is arguable that their Lordships' preference for the rate of return on Index Linked Government Stock (ILGS), as the most accurate indicator of the rate of interest on a low-risk investment, means that the ILGS rate (for the time being taken to be three per cent in *Wells v Wells*) should be the rate of interest applied to damages for non-pecuniary loss. However, this argument was rejected by the Court of Appeal in *Lawrence v Chief Constable of Staffordshire*.[361]

Interest in fatal accident claims With regard to fatal accident claims, *Jefford v Gee* did not, as with personal injury cases, distinguish between losses which had accrued before the date of trial and those accruing after that time. In this respect it was criticised by the Law Commission[362] and in *Cookson v Knowles*[363] the House of Lords ruled that henceforth damages in fatal accident claims should be divided 27-70

Law Commission Report No.257 (1999), paras 2.29–2.58. Interest is payable up to the date of judgment even if the action is adjourned at the claimant's request: *May v AG Bassett & Sons* (1970) 114 S.J. 269.

354 *Chadwick v Parsons* [1971] 2 Lloyd's Rep. 49 (for proceedings on appeal, where this point was not discussed, see [1971] 2 Lloyd's Rep. 322). Where a second defendant is joined after service upon him of a third party notice by the first defendant, interest will be payable by him only from the date of service of the notice at the earliest: *Slater v Hughes* [1971] 1 W.L.R. 1438.

355 [1977] Q.B. 913. This was obiter and was not considered by the House of Lords on appeal: [1979] A.C. 556.

356 [1980] A.C. 136 at 151, per Lord Wilberforce; at 164, per Lord Edmund-Davies; at 173, per Lord Scarman.

357 [1982] 1 W.L.R. 816. See also Pearson Report, paras 744–747.

358 [1983] 2 A.C. 773. But outside the realm of personal injury and death, no interest will be awarded on damages for non-pecuniary loss: *Saunders v Edwards* [1987] 1 W.L.R. 1116 (deceit); *Holtham v Metropolitan Police Commissioner*, *The Times,* 28 November 1987 (trespass to the person).

359 [1983] 2 A.C. 773 at 785.

360 [1999] 1 A.C. 345 HL.

361 [2000] P.I.Q.R. Q349.

362 Report No.56, paras 278–279.

363 [1979] A.C. 556.

between the period before and the period after trial. Interest, calculated as for accrued losses in personal injury actions, should be awarded for the first but not for the second period.

(g) Interim payments[364]

27-71 In accordance with Rules of Court[365] and the Senior Courts Act 1981 s.32, and the County Courts Act 1984 s.50, the claimant may apply for an interim payment of the damages which the defendant may be held liable to pay him or for his benefit. The court may order an interim payment of such amount as it thinks just, not exceeding a reasonable proportion of the damages[366] which it considers are likely to be recovered by the claimant,[367] after taking into account any contributory negligence and any counterclaim. Before making an order, however, the court must be satisfied that one of the three following conditions is fulfilled:

(i) that the defendant has admitted liability;
(ii) that the claimant has obtained judgment against the defendant for damages to be assessed[368];
(iii) that if the action proceeded to trial the claimant would obtain judgment against the defendant[369] for substantial damages.[370]

By CPR r.25.9, the fact that an order for an interim payment has been made must not be disclosed to the court at trial until all questions of liability and quantum of damages have been determined, unless the defendant agrees. By CPR r.25.8, in giving final judgment the court may make any order with respect to the interim payment that proves to be necessary by way of adjustment and in particular, if the

---

[364] See *Structured Settlements and Interim and Provisional Damages, Law Commission Report No.224* (1994), Pt IV. Although originally confined to cases of personal injury and death, interim payments may now be made in any type of case.

[365] CPR rr.25.6–25.9.

[366] In *Eeles v Cobham Hire Services Ltd* [2009] EWCA Civ 204; [2010] 1 W.L.R. 409, it was held that the damages likely to be recovered by the claimant are, for these purposes, the damages payable as a lump sum and do not include damages which may be payable as a periodical payment order.

[367] This involves an estimate of the damages that are likely to be recovered. But the court's investigation should not turn into a long investigation of the issues in dispute; rather a broad approach should be taken: *Newport (Essex) Engineering Co v Press and Shear Machinery Co Ltd* (1984) 24 B.L.R. 71 CA.

[368] An interim payment can be ordered even though an appeal is pending: *Halvanon Insurance Co v Central Reinsurance Corp* [1984] 2 Lloyd's Rep. 420.

[369] Or, where there is more than one defendant, against at least one of the defendants (even if the court has not yet determined which of them is liable) provided all the defendants are insured in respect of the claim; or the defendants' liability will be met by an insurer under s.151 of the Road Traffic Act 1988 or by an insurer acting under the Motor Insurers Bureau Agreement, or by the Motor Insurers Bureau where it is acting itself; or all the defendants are public bodies. Interim payments comprising different fractions of the total amount thought to be "just" may be ordered against the different defendants provided the claimant does not overall recover more than the just amount (which, in the case of damages, cannot exceed a reasonable proportion of the damages likely to be recovered): *Schott Kem Ltd v Bentley* [1991] 1 Q.B. 61 CA.

[370] The court must be satisfied of this applying the civil standard of proof; *Shearson Lehman Brothers Inc v Maclaine, Watson & Co Ltd* [1987] 1 W.L.R. 480 CA at 489. The necessary standard is not met—and hence no interim payment can be awarded—where summary judgment has been refused and *unconditional* leave to defend has been given; *British and Commonwealth Holdings Plc v Quadrex Holdings Inc* [1989] Q.B. 842 CA; *Andrews v Schooling* [1991] 1 W.L.R. 783 CA.

interim payment exceeds the amount for which the defendant is held liable, may order repayment of the appropriate amount, plus interest,[371] by the claimant.

(h) Provisional damages[372]

By s.32A of the Senior Courts Act 1981[373] and the Civil Procedure Rules Pt 41, the High Court has power to award provisional damages in actions "for damages for personal injuries in which there is proved or admitted to be a chance that at some definite or indefinite time in the future the injured person will, as the result of the act or omission which gave rise to the cause of action, develop some serious disease or suffer some serious deterioration in his physical or mental condition".[374] In such a case the court is able to assess the damages on the assumption that the injured person will not develop the disease or suffer the deterioration but then to award further damages at a future date if the risk should in fact materialise.[375] However, the power can only be used if the particulars of claim include a claim for provisional damages.[376] The provisional order must specify the disease or type of deterioration as to which an application for further damages may be made and will normally specify the period within which such application must be made, although the period may be extended on an application by the claimant.[377] Only one application for further damages may be entertained in relation to each disease or type of deterioration specified in the provisional order.[378] In *Willson v Ministry of Defence*[379] provisional damages were refused on the ground that "serious deterioration" refers to a clear and severable event rather than an ordinary continuing deterioration, as in a typical osteo-arthritic case. It was further said by Scott Baker J that s.32A is concerned with a measurable rather than a fanciful chance. In awarding provisional damages in *Chewings v Williams*[380] it was held that a two per cent risk of an ankle amputation was more than fanciful. **27-72**

[371] *Mercers Co v New Hampshire Insurance Co* [1991] 1 W.L.R. 1173. But the decision that the interim sum should be repaid was reversed on appeal: [1992] 1 W.L.R. 792 CA. Interest (or other profit) gained from the use of the interim payment is to be ignored in deciding on the final judgment applying the principle that it is irrelevant what the claimant does with his "damages": *Parry v North West Surrey HA*, *The Times*, 5 January 2000.

[372] See Law Commission Report No.224 (1994) *Structured Settlements and Interim and Provisional Damages*, Pt V.

[373] Inserted by the Administration of Justice Act 1982 s.6(1). The same provisions apply to the county courts under the County Courts Act 1984 s.51.

[374] Senior Courts Act 1981 s.32A(1).

[375] Senior Courts Act 1981 s.32A(2).

[376] CPR r.41.2. Examples have so far been rare: but see *Cronin v Redbridge London BC*, *The Independent*, 20 May 1987; *Chewings v Williams* [2009] EWHC 2490 (QB); [2010] P.I.Q.R. Q1.

[377] CPR r.41.2. For provisional damages ordered without trial (i.e. following a settlement), see also *Hurditch v Sheffield HA* [1989] Q.B. 562.

[378] CPR r.41.3.

[379] [1991] 1 All E.R. 638. Provisional damages do not cover a potential improvement in the claimant's condition (which could have resulted in higher expenditure for the claimant's special needs in the community): *Adan v Securicor Custodial Services Ltd* [2004] EWHC 394 (QB); [2005] P.I.Q.R. P6.

[380] [2009] EWHC 2490 (QB); [2010] P.I.Q.R. Q1.

(i) Structured settlements[381]

27-73 Although a development in relation to out-of-court settlements of personal injury and death cases, rather than awards made by the courts, it is appropriate here to mention structured settlements. If the defendant's insurer purchased an annuity for the claimant it was accepted by the Inland Revenue in the late 1980s that the payments received by the claimant from the annuity were tax free (i.e. they were treated as capital not income). The defendant therefore had to pay less to produce the same (or a greater) stream of money for the claimant (the rate of discount, which presumably included the defendant's insurer's costs as well as the tax saving, appeared to run at 10 to 15 per cent). Such a settlement was also in the interests of claimants, who were guaranteed a stream of "income", and of the state, which was saved having to support those who squander lump sums of damages. A structured settlement was also more true to the aim of compensation than a lump sum. Self-financing structured settlements (that is, not involving insurers) were also entered into by public sector defendants, such as NHS trusts.

27-74 Structured settlements related to future pecuniary loss only: non-pecuniary loss and past pecuniary loss was paid in the usual form of a lump sum. Flexibility was possible in the sense that part of the future pecuniary loss could be paid in a lump sum or into a contingency fund to deal with unforeseen events; and more than one annuity could be bought depending on the claimant's likely future needs. Most annuities were index-linked and precise estimation of the claimant's life expectancy was not necessary; but otherwise structured settlements were as prone to inaccuracy as a lump sum for they were not reviewable. Although an annuity would normally cease on the claimant's death, it was usual to incorporate a guaranteed minimum time period of payments so that, as under the lump sum system, dependants would be guaranteed a (windfall) sum in the event of the claimant's unexpected death.

27-75 Structured settlements could not be imposed by the courts, although court approval was sometimes required because of, for example, the claimant's disability of infancy.[382] Since 1 April 2005, structured settlements have been absorbed within the wider concept of (reviewable) periodical payments and the Damages Act 1996, as amended by the Courts Act 2003, no longer refers to structured settlements. Structured settlements were therefore the forerunners of the new system of (reviewable) periodical payments.

(j) (Reviewable) periodical payments[383]

27-76 On 1 April 2005 a fundamental departure from lump sums was introduced by the Courts Act 2003 ss.100–101 (amending the Damages Act 1996), the Damages

---

[381] See generally Lewis, *Structured Settlements: The Law and Practice* (1993); Law Commission Report No.224 (1994) *Structured Settlements and Interim and Provisional Damages*, Pt III; Bevan and Gregory, "Structured Settlements" (2004) 154 N.L.J. 1280, 1388, 1658. For the impact of structured settlements on a claimant's entitlement to social security benefits, see Lewis, "Structured Settlements and State Benefits" (2001) 151 N.L.J. 1066.

[382] As in *Kelly v Dawes*, *The Times*, 27 September 1990.

[383] See, generally, Bevan and Gregory, "Periodical Payments" (2005) 155 N.L.J. 565, 907, 980; Lewis, "The Politics and Economics of Tort Law: Judicially Imposed Periodical Payments of Damages" (2006) 69 M.L.R. 418.

(Variation of Periodical Payments) Order 2005[384] and accompanying Civil Procedure Rules.[385] In the case of damages for future pecuniary loss in respect of personal injury or death, the courts are empowered (and are required to consider whether) to make an order that the damages are to take the form of periodical payments.[386] By s.2(8) of the Damages Act 1996, a periodical payments order (PPO) shall be updated by reference to the retail prices index unless, under s.2(9), the court making the PPO specifies that a different index should be used (such as an average earnings index for future care costs).[387] Moreover, the periodical payments order may be made variable so that it can be reviewed by the courts.[388] These provisions, therefore, give the courts the power to order (reviewable) periodical payments. This regime followed a consultation paper issued by the Lord Chancellor's Department in March 2002, which set out the arguments for and against (reviewable) periodical payments. It is clear that a particularly influential "political" factor was that, in respect of litigation against the National Health Service, periodical payments are more attractive to the NHS (at least in the short term) than having to find large capital sums.[389] However, before such an order can be made, a court has to be satisfied that the continuity of payment is reasonably secure.[390] Other than in respect of public sector defendants, this will essentially be so where the defendant's insurer purchases an annuity as under a structured settlement. Protection for claimants in the event of an insurer's insolvency or a public body's non-existence is provided by the Damages Act 1996 ss.4 and 6, as amended by the Courts Act 2003 s.101.

Of particular interest are the provisions that enable the variation of periodical payments.[391] The extent to which periodical payments can be reviewed is the most difficult and controversial aspect of this reform. The reviewability provisions closely match those on "provisional damages". The original court can make a variable order but only to deal with the development of some serious disease or the suffering of some serious deterioration or significant improvement in the claimant's condition. Moreover, only one application to vary a variable order can be made in respect of each specified disease or type of deterioration or improvement. **27-77**

384 SI 2005/841.

385 CPR r.41.4–41.10.

386 Damages Act 1996 s.2(1), as substituted by the Courts Act 2003 s.100. In *Godbold v Mahmood* [2005] EWHC 1002; [2006] P.I.Q.R. Q5, a periodical payments order was made in respect of future care costs but not future lost earnings.

387 *Tameside and Glossop Acute Services NHS Trust v Thompstone* [2008] EWCA Civ 5; [2008] 1 W.L.R. 2207 (updating future care costs by reference to the Annual Survey of Hours and Earnings, "ASHE 6115", was approved in this case). See also *Flora v Wakom (Heathrow) Ltd* [2006] EWCA Civ 1103; [2007] 1 W.L.R. 482. See generally, Trusted, "Periodical Payments after the Court of Appeal decision in Thompstone" [2008] J.P.I.L. 44; Lewis, "The indexation of periodical payments of damages in tort: the future assured?" (2010) 30 L.S. 391.

388 Damages Act 1996 s.2B, as substituted by the Courts Act 2003 s.100; and Damages (Variation of Periodical Payments) Order 2005 (SI 2005/841).

389 The Explanatory Notes to the Act make this clear.

390 Damages Act 1996 s.2(3). See, e.g. *YM v Gloucester Hospitals NHS Foundation Trust* [2006] EWHC 820; [2006] P.I.Q.R. P27.

391 Damages (Variation of Periodical Payments) Order 2005, authorised under Damages Act 1996 s.2B.

4. DEATH: SURVIVAL OF CAUSES OF ACTION

27-78 **Common law** At common law, by reason of the rule which is often expressed in the maxim *actio personalis moritur cum persona*, most actions in tort[392] died with the person, whether the person dying was the injured person or the wrongdoer. The main exception to this common law rule was that an action could be sustained against a deceased person's personal representatives in respect of property which had been appropriated by the deceased and added to his estate.[393]

(a) Law Reform (Miscellaneous Provisions) Act 1934

27-79 The old common law rule has been almost entirely reversed by s.1(1) of the Law Reform (Miscellaneous Provisions) Act 1934 which provides in general terms that on the death of any person all causes of action subsisting against or vested in him shall survive against, or, as the case may be, for the benefit of, his estate.[394] The only exceptions are that causes of action for defamation still die with either the wrongdoer or the injured person,[395] and that the right to claim bereavement damages under s.1A of the Fatal Accidents Act 1976[396] does not survive for the benefit of the estate.[397] To deal with cases in which damage is the gist of the action and the wrongdoer dies before (or at the same time as) the damage occurs, the Act provides that, where damage has been suffered by reason of any act or omission in respect of which a cause of action would have subsisted against any person if that person had not died before or at the same time as the damage was suffered, there is deemed to have been subsisting against him before his death such cause of action in respect of that act or omission as would have subsisted if he had died after the damage was suffered.[398]

27-80 **Time for bringing action** Special rules once applied to the limitation of actions

---

[392] As laid down in *Ronex Properties Ltd v John Laing Construction Ltd* [1983] Q.B. 398 the rule does not apply to the statutory right to claim contribution under the Civil Liability (Contribution) Act 1978 because that right is not based upon a breach of a tortious obligation owed by the defendant to the claimant. It therefore passes to his estate under the usual law of succession.

[393] For the earlier law, see the 8th edn of this work, pp.45–47, 50–51. For injuries to the personal property of the deceased after his death the executor or administrator can sue, whether the injury occurred prior to the grant of probate or letters of administration or not, provided in the case of an executor that he has obtained probate before production of the probate becomes necessary, and, in the case of an administrator, that he has obtained letters before commencing the action: Williams, Mortimer and Sunnucks, *Executors, Administrators and Probate*, 21st edn (2018).

[394] Claims for compensation for discrimination contrary to the Equality Act 2010 are causes of action within s.1(1) of the Law Reform (Miscellaneous Provisions) Act 1934 and therefore survive for the benefit of the victim's estate: *Harris v Lewisham and Guy's Mental Health Trust* [2000] 3 All E.R. 769 CA.

[395] There is persuasive authority for the view that if the party dies at the conclusion of the trial but before judgment, then judgment should be given to take effect as at the conclusion of the argument: *Hubert v DeCamillis* (1963) 41 D.L.R. (2d) 495.

[396] See para.27-93.

[397] Law Reform (Miscellaneous Provisions) Act 1934 s.1(1A), as inserted by s.4(1) of the Administration of Justice Act 1982. *Claims for Wrongful Death*, Law Commission Report No.263 (1999), paras 6.63–6.65, rejected reform of this rule.

[398] s.1(4). By virtue of this subsection a claim for contribution under the Civil Liability (Contribution) Act 1978 can be brought against a deceased tortfeasor's personal representatives, despite the fact that the claimant's cause of action for contribution does not come into existence until he has himself been held liable to the injured person and may, therefore, not subsist against the deceased at his death: *Harvey v RG O'Dell Ltd* [1958] 2 Q.B. 78.

brought against the estates of deceased persons, but now these rules have been abolished,[399] and the period of limitation runs from the accrual of the cause of action[400] and is unaffected by the death of the tortfeasor. Rules of the court[401] enable proceedings to be started against the estate of a deceased person even though there has been no grant of probate or letters of administration and also enable proceedings which purport to have been started against a person who has died (previously null and void)[402] to be treated as having been brought against the estate. The ordinary rules of limitation govern actions brought on behalf of the estate of deceased persons, but where the deceased person had suffered personal injuries as a result of negligence, nuisance or breach of duty,[403] a fresh period of limitation applying to the cause of action surviving for the benefit of the estate arises. The action must be brought within three years of the death, or of the date of the personal representative's knowledge of the relevant facts supporting the bringing of an action against the defendant.[404]

Effect of insolvency In the event of the insolvency of an estate against which proceedings are maintainable by virtue of the Act of 1934, any liability in respect of the cause of action in respect of which the proceedings are maintainable is deemed to be a debt provable in the administration of the estate, notwithstanding that it is a demand in the nature of unliquidated damages arising otherwise than by a contract, promise or breach of trust.[405] 27-81

Rights are additional By s.1(5) of the Act of 1934 the rights conferred by it are in addition to and not in derogation of any rights conferred by the Fatal Accidents Act 1976,[406] which provides a remedy where death is caused by the wrongful act, neglect or default of another, or the Carriage by Air Act 1961, which provides a remedy where a passenger by air is killed owing to accident. 27-82

(b) Assessing damages under the Law Reform Act

As one is here concerned with the survival rather than the creation of a cause of action, the same principles generally govern the measure of damages in the survival claim as in the action that the deceased would have had against the tortfeasor or that the injured person would have had against the deceased tortfeasor. Therefore, in a personal injury action surviving for the benefit of the deceased's estate the estate can recover damages for all the pecuniary loss and all the pain and suffering and loss of amenity that the deceased suffered prior to his death.[407] However, by s.1(2) of the 1934 Act the damages recoverable for the benefit of the deceased's estate 27-83

[399] Proceedings Against Estates Act 1970 s.1.
[400] See generally on limitation of actions, Ch.31.
[401] CPR r.19.8.
[402] *Dawson (Bradford) Ltd v Dove* [1971] 1 Q.B. 330.
[403] Limitation Act 1980 s.11(1).
[404] Limitation Act 1980 s.11(5), (6), (7).
[405] s.1(6). This was designed to exclude the operation of the Bankruptcy Act 1914 s.30(1) but it is now superfluous as s.30(1) has been repealed and, by s.382(1) and (2) of the Insolvency Act 1986, unliquidated tort claims are provable in bankruptcy or in the winding-up of an insolvent company.
[406] See para.27-89; see also para.27-108.
[407] *Rose v Ford* [1937] A.C. 826; *Andrews v Freeborough* [1967] 1 Q.B. 1; *Murray v Shuter* [1976] Q.B. 972. In *Whitehead v Searle* [2008] EWCA Civ 285; [2009] 1 W.L.R. 549 it was held that the survival to the estate of a deceased mother's loss of a chance claim for negligence by solicitors, in respect of their delay in pursuing her wrongful birth claim against a health authority, should not be allowed

shall not include any exemplary damages.[408] Also excluded are any damages for loss of income in respect of any period after the deceased's death; that is, the "lost years" claim[409] does not survive for the estate's benefit.[410] It is also laid down in s.1(2) that, where the deceased's death has been caused by the act or omission which gives rise to the cause of action, the damages recoverable for the benefit of the deceased's estate "shall be calculated without reference to any loss or gain consequent on his death except that a sum in respect of funeral expenses may be included".[411] The main part of this is intended to emphasise that, even where the tortfeasor has been responsible for the death, the estate can recover only what the deceased himself could have recovered. Thus if the deceased was a tenant for life of a valuable property, the loss of the life interest would be excluded in calculating the damages.[412] Similarly, neither the loss of an annuity ceasing on death nor the gain arising from policies of life insurance which become payable on death is of any relevance.[413] On the other hand, where the tortfeasor has been responsible for the death the provision goes on to empower the courts to award damages for the funeral expenses incurred on behalf of the estate.[414] This is exceptional in that it does not represent the survival of a claim the deceased would have had.[415]

27-84 **Provisional damages** Where provisional damages have been awarded under s.32A of the Senior Courts Act 1981,[416] does the right of the injured claimant to return to court for further damages survive for the benefit of his estate? And is it caught by the "lost years" bar? Dicta in *Middleton v Elliott Turbomachinery Ltd*[417] suggest that the claim is treated as if it was a judgment for damages to be assessed. Consequently in assessing those damages the court would be able to take account of the worsening of the claimant's condition, including death caused by that

to outflank the fact that the estate could not have recovered for the deceased mother's *future loss* had that wrongful birth claim survived.

408 s.1(2)(a)(i). For proposed reform of this rule, see *Aggravated, Exemplary and Restitutionary Damages*, Law Commission Report No.247 (1997), paras 5.274–5.275.

409 See para.27-31.

410 s.1(2)(a)(ii), as inserted by s.4(2) of the Administration of Justice Act 1982. See Cane and Harris (1983) 46 M.L.R. 478.

411 Law Reform (Miscellaneous Provisions) Act 1934 s.1(2)(c).

412 *Rose v Ford* [1936] 1 K.B. 90, per Greene LJ at 110.

413 *Rose v Ford* [1937] A.C. 826, per Lord Wright at 842; *Harris v Brights Asphalt Contractors* [1953] 1 Q.B. 617 at 634.

414 Funeral expenses may include the cost of having the body embalmed: *Hart v Griffiths-Jones* [1948] 2 All E.R. 729. In the same case, the sum of £225 claimed for the cost of a monument to be erected over the grave was held to be irrecoverable. It appears, however, that this was because the sum was excessive, not because the cost of a monument can never be recovered: *Stanton v Ewart F Youlden Ltd* [1960] 1 W.L.R. 543. "The legal position is, that a stone over a grave may properly be considered as part of the funeral expenses if it is a reasonable expenditure for the person in the position of the deceased and of the relatives who are responsible for the actual ordering of the stone; but in so far as it is merely a memorial set up as a sign of love and affection, then it should not be included": per McNair J at 546. And see *Gammell v Wilson* [1980] 3 W.L.R. 591 CA; affirmed, without appeal on this point [1982] A.C. 27 HL (award of £595 for gravestone upheld although on the facts the claim was very near the borderline between a tombstone and a memorial). Funeral expenses do not include the cost of a wake: *Grant v Secretary of State for Transport* [2017] EWHC 1663 (QB); *Blake v Mad Max Ltd* [2018] EWHC 2134 (QB); [2019] P.I.Q.R. Q1.

415 The decision in *Otter v Church, Adams, Tatham Co* [1953] Ch. 280 may be regarded as establishing another exception: there a personal representative recovered substantial damages even though the deceased in his lifetime could have recovered only nominal damages.

416 See para.27-72.

417 *The Times*, 29 October 1990 CA.

condition. Section 3 of the Damages Act 1996 implicitly accepts that the claim for further damages does survive. But by s.3(4) no award of further damages made after the death is to include any amount for loss of income in respect of any period after the death (i.e. the "lost years" bar applies).

(c) Instantaneous death

Some difficulty may be thought to arise in cases where the deceased has been killed on the spot, since it may be said that there was no interval of time in which the cause of action could vest before death. This is what happened in *Morgan v Scoulding*[418] and this was the argument for the defence. But that argument was rejected by Lewis J and it is submitted that the true view is that the cause of action is completed by the injuries[419] and is vested in the deceased at the moment of death. In *Morgan v Scoulding* this meant that damages could be claimed on behalf of the estate for the loss of expectation of life of the deceased. But now that that head of loss has been abolished,[420] and now that claims for loss of income in the "lost years" no longer survive for the benefit of the estate,[421] no recoverable loss survives for the benefit of the estate (unless there has been property damage) where the deceased has died instantaneously.[422] **27-85**

5. Death as a Cause of Action[423]

Rule in Baker v Bolton It is a rule of the common law, known as the rule in *Baker v Bolton*, that no one can recover damages in tort for the death of another. "In a civil court the death of a human being cannot be complained of as an injury."[424] The rule has been said to be based on the historical ground that the common law did not allow an action for trespass on facts which constituted a felony,[425] and, however this may be,[426] it was affirmed by the House of Lords in *Admiralty Commissioners v S.S. Amerika*.[427] So, at common law, a husband cannot recover **27-86**

---

418 [1938] 1 K.B. 786.

419 See *Rose v Ford* [1937] A.C. 826, per Lord Roche at 856.

420 See para.27-56 fn.289.

421 See para.27-83.

422 In *Hicks v Chief Constable of South Yorkshire Police* [1992] 1 All E.R. 690 CA; affirmed [1992] 2 All E.R. 65 HL, it was held that where injury, pain and suffering are in reality part of the death itself, albeit endured for a very short time before death, no damages are recoverable.

423 See, generally, *Claims for Wrongful Death*, Law Commission Report No.263 (1999). Note that there are some special statutory provisions which in particular circumstances qualify or override the law applicable under the Fatal Accidents Act 1976: see, e.g. s.32(1) of the Coal-Mining Subsidence Act 1991; the Carriage by Air Act 1961; the Merchant Shipping Act 1995, the Merchant Shipping (Carriage of Passengers by Sea) Regulations, 2012 (SI 2012/3152), and the Merchant Shipping (Convention Relating to the Carriage of Passengers and their Luggage by Sea) Order 2014 (SI 2014/1361); the Railways (Convention on International Carriage by Rail) Regulations 2005 (SI 2005/2092), and the Rail Passengers' Rights and Obligations Regulations 2010 (SI 2010/1504). For the previous law on some of these special statutory provisions, see the 20th edition of this work at paras 28-114 to 28-118.

424 *Baker v Bolton* (1808) 1 Camp. 493, per Lord Ellenborough; *Higgins v Butcher* (1606) Yelv. 89; *Osborn v Gillett* (1873) L.R. 8 Ex. 88; *Admiralty Commissioners v S.S. Amerika* [1917] A.C. 38.

425 *Admiralty Commissioners v S.S. Amerika* [1917] A.C. 38 at 44–47, per Lord Parker; [1917] A.C. 38 at 56–60, per Lord Sumner. cf. *Rose v Ford* [1937] A.C. 826 at 834, per Lord Atkin.

426 See Holdsworth, *History of English Law*, Vol.III, 331–336, 676–677.

427 [1917] A.C. 38.

damages for the death of his wife,[428] nor a parent for that of his child,[429] nor a master for that of his servant.[430] The common law position has, however, been substantially altered by statute, principally by the Fatal Accidents Act 1976.[431]

(a) Fatal Accidents Act 1976

27-87 Section 1 of the Fatal Accidents Act 1976 provides that an action may be brought for the benefit of the dependants of any deceased person[432] against a person who wrongfully caused the death. By s.1(1):

> "If death is caused by any wrongful act, neglect or default which is such as would (if death had not ensued) have entitled the person injured[433] to maintain an action and recover damages in respect thereof, the person who would have been liable if death had not ensued shall be liable to an action for damages, notwithstanding the death of the person injured."

The action, although brought for the benefit of the deceased's dependants, must be brought by and in the name of the executor or administrator of the deceased.[434] An executor's title to sue exists from the time of death, but an administrator's title exists only from the grant to him of letters of administration. If the claimant has not yet obtained a proper grant when he begins proceedings the old law was that the action was a nullity,[435] but the court now has power to allow an amendment of a statement of case to accord with a new capacity that the party has since acquired.[436] If there is no executor or administrator of the deceased, or no action is brought within six months of the death by and in the name of an executor or administrator, then the action may be brought by and in the name of all or any of the persons for whose benefit an executor or administrator could have brought it.[437] Only one action may be brought in respect of the death.[438] Therefore the claimant, be he executor, administrator, or dependant, must deliver to the defendant full particulars of all

---

428 *Baker v Bolton* (1808) 1 Camp. 493; *Higgins v Butcher* (1606) Yelv. 89; *Burgess v Florence Nightingale Hospital for Gentlewomen* [1955] 1 Q.B. 349.

429 *Clark v London General Omnibus Co* [1906] 2 K.B. 648.

430 *Osborn v Gillett* (1873) L.R. 8 Ex. 88.

431 ss.1–4 of the Fatal Accidents Act 1976 were inserted in a substantially amended form by s.3(1) of the Administration of Justice Act 1982.

432 Including dependants of a deceased foreigner: *Davidson v Hill* [1901] 2 K.B. 606; *The Esso Malaysia* [1975] Q.B. 198.

433 Injury includes any disease and any impairment of a person's physical or mental condition; see s.1(5).

434 s.2(1).

435 *Ingall v Moran* [1944] K.B. 160 (a case under the Law Reform (Miscellaneous Provisions) Act 1934); *Hilton v Sutton Steam Laundry* [1946] K.B. 65; *Burns v Campbell* [1952] 1 K.B. 15; *Finnegan v Cementation Co Ltd* [1953] 1 Q.B. 688.

436 CPR r.17.4(4).

437 s.2(2). Where there is no executor or administrator the dependants need not wait six months to see if an administrator is appointed: *Holleran v Bagnell* (1879) 4 L.R. Ir. 740. So in two cases where a widow purported to sue as administratrix before she had received letters of administration the action was saved in that the court found that as a dependant she would, in the absence of a properly appointed administrator, have been entitled to bring the action in that capacity: *Stebbings v Holst & Co Ltd* [1953] 1 W.L.R. 603; Bowler v John Mowlem & Co Ltd [1954] 1 W.L.R. 1445.

438 s.2(3). "Action" under s.2(3) of the 1976 Act is, by the Human Rights Act 1998 ss.3(1) and 6(1), to be interpreted as "served process", so that the existence of a previous unserved claim form does not bar a new claim brought within the limitation period: *Cachia v Faluyi* [2001] EWCA Civ 998; [2001] 1 W.L.R. 1966 CA.

the persons on behalf of whom the action is brought.[439] He is also under a duty to take all reasonable steps to inform dependants of the action and, if they wish to claim, to ensure that they are named as persons on behalf of whom the action is brought.[440] A dependant not named in the proceedings cannot be considered, but may apply before judgment to be brought into the proceedings.[441] Where an action on behalf of an infant had been settled and the action stayed it was held that the stay could be lifted to enable the deceased's widow to be added.[442] After judgment dependants excluded from the action have no remedy against the defendant but may be able to proceed against the executor, administrator or dependant who brought the action.[443]

(b) Dependants

The action under the Fatal Accidents Act is for the benefit of the dependants of the deceased, subject to a narrower restriction on who can be awarded bereavement damages.[444] The meaning of "dependant" is statutorily laid down in a list that has been enlarged on several occasions. By s.1(3) the list now comprises the spouse or civil partner or former spouse or former civil partner of the deceased, including a person whose marriage or civil partnership has been annulled or declared void[445]; any person who was living as the husband or wife or civil partner[446] of the deceased in the same household immediately before the date of the death and had been so living for at least two years before the death[447]; any parent or other ascendant of the deceased; any person who was treated by the deceased as his parent; any child or **27-88**

439 s.2(4). Particulars of the nature of the claim in respect of which damages are sought to be recovered must also be delivered: ibid. But it is sufficient if these particulars are shown on the statement of case: *Stebbings v Holst & Co Ltd* [1953] 1 W.L.R. 603.

440 *Cooper v Williams* [1963] 2 Q.B. 567, per Lord Denning MR at 581.

441 *Avery v L & NE Ry* [1938] A.C. 606 at 613, per Lord Atkin.

442 *Cooper v Williams* [1963] 2 Q.B. 567.

443 *Avery v L & NE Ry* [1938] A.C. 606. And he may also have a remedy against the solicitor advising the claimant if there is evidence that the solicitor was negligent in his performance of his duties in respect of the action: see *White v Jones* [1995] 2 A.C. 207 HL.

444 s.1(2). For bereavement damages, see para.27-93.

445 s.1(4)–(4A). As a result of the Marriage (Same Sex Couples) Act 2013 and Sch.3, references in the Fatal Accidents Act 1976 to marriage and its effects (e.g. "wife or husband") must now be read as including a same-sex marriage.

446 This therefore meets the long-standing criticism of the previous law that same-sex partners were excluded. Even if not a civil partner, the same-sex partner is included because he or she is living "as a civil partner".

447 In *Pounder v London Underground Ltd* [1995] P.I.Q.R. P217, it was held that a brief absence from the home during the two-year period prior to death did not give rise to a break in continuity in the context of a 10-year relationship. For a restrictive interpretation of the two-year requirement, see *Kotke v Saffarini* [2005] EWCA Civ 221; [2005] P.I.Q.R. P26. In *Swift v Secretary of State for Justice* [2013] EWCA Civ 193; [2014] Q.B. 373 the claimant's partner, with whom she had been living for about six months, was killed as a result of an admitted tort. While their son, who was born after that death, had a claim for pecuniary loss under the Fatal Accidents Act 1976, the claimant did not. This was because she had not been living with the deceased for two years prior to the death. She argued unsuccessfully that, in denying her a claim, the 1976 Act was incompatible with her right to family life under art.8 of the ECHR as protected by the Human Rights Act 1998. Note however that a claimant who, as a victim of an infringement of the right to life under art.2 of the ECHR, has a claim under the Human Rights Act 1998 may conceivably outflank the restrictive definition of dependants under the Fatal Accidents Act 1976: *Rabone v Pennine Care NHS Foundation Trust* [2012] UKSC 2; [2012] 2 A.C. 72; see para.27-93.

other descendant of the deceased[448]; any person who had been treated by the deceased as a child of the family in relation to any marriage or civil partnership of the deceased; and any person who is, or is the issue of, a brother, sister, uncle or aunt of the deceased.[449] A relationship by marriage or civil partnership is treated as a relationship by consanguinity, a relationship of the half-blood as a relationship of the whole blood and the stepchild of any person as his child.[450] An illegitimate person is to be treated as the legitimate child of his mother and reputed father,[451] or, in the case of a person who has a female parent by virtue of s.43 of the Human Fertilisation and Embryology Act 2008, the legitimate child of his mother and that female parent.[452] Although the list of dependants is now a wide one, it is still capable of causing hardship, which calls into question the need for a restriction beyond financial dependency. For example, the financially dependent friend and companion of the deceased remains excluded. These criticisms are reflected in the Court of Appeal's judgment in *Shepherd v The Post Office*[453] where it was said that a simpler approach would be a provision to the effect that any person who could show a relationship of dependence on the deceased should be entitled to make a claim. In similar vein, the Law Commission in its report, *Claims for Wrongful Death*,[454] has recommended that there should be added to the present list a generally-worded class of claimant whereby any other individual who "was being wholly or partly maintained by the deceased immediately before the death or who would, but for the death, have been so maintained" would be able to bring an action.

(c) Nature of Fatal Accidents Act claim

27-89 The cause of action under the Fatal Accidents Act is entirely separate from that which the deceased himself would have had if he had not died, and which now survives for the benefit of his estate. It is "new in its species, new in its quality, new in its principle, in every way new".[455] But it is a condition of the existence of the cause of action under the Act that the wrongful act, neglect or default which caused the death must have been such as would have entitled the deceased to sue had he not died.[456] A hypothetical question must be asked, the time taken being the moment of death, but the fiction maintained that death did not take place.[457] Only if at that moment the deceased could have maintained an action does a cause of action under the Fatal Accidents Act even exist. In *Corr v IBC Vehicles Ltd*[458] it was held that the deceased's suicide, consequent on an injury to him and subsequent depres-

---

448 Including a child *en ventre sa mère*: *The George and Richard* (1871) L.R. 3 A. & E. 466; *Lindley v Sharp* (1974) 4 Fam. Law 90; Edelman, *McGregor on Damages*, 20th edn (2017), para.41-006. Adopted children are treated as the children of their adoptive parents and no one else: Adoption Act 1976 s.39.

449 Quaere, does this mean children only, or all descendants.

450 s.1(5)(a).

451 s.1(5)(b)(i).

452 s.1(5)(b)(ii). This amendment was made by the Marriage (Same Sex Couples) Act 2013 (Consequential and Contrary Provisions and Scotland) Order 2014 (SI 2014/560).

453 *The Times*, 15 June 1995.

454 *Law Commission Report No.263* (1999), para.7.7 and Draft Bill, cl.1.

455 *The Vera Cruz* (1884) 10 App. Cas. 59, per Lord Blackburn at 70; *Pym v Great Northern Ry* (1862) 2 B. & S. 760, per Cockburn CJ at 767; *British Electric Ry v Gentile* [1914] A.C. 1034.

456 Fatal Accidents Act 1976 s.1(1).

457 *British Electric Ry v Gentile* [1914] A.C. 1034 at 1041, per Lord Dunedin; *Pym v Great Northern Ry* (1862) 2 B. & S. 760 at 767, per Cockburn CJ.

458 [2008] UKHL 13; [2008] 1 A.C. 884. See also *Pigney v Pointer's Transport Services Ltd* [1957] 1

sion caused by the defendant's negligence or breach of statutory duty, was actionable by his widow under the Fatal Accidents Act 1976. The suicide was reasonably foreseeable because it was of the same kind of harm as the depression; and taking into account that suicide was no longer a crime the chain of causation, as a matter of fairness, was not broken. Similarly, in the earlier case of *Reeves v Commissioner of Police of the Metropolis*,[459] it was held by the House of Lords that an action under the Fatal Accidents Act 1976 (and the Law Reform (Miscellaneous Provisions) Act 1934), in respect of the negligence of the police in failing to prevent the deceased's suicide, was not barred by the defences of volenti non fit injuria or novus actus interveniens. But in contrast to the *Corr* case, where the majority of their Lordships thought it inappropriate to reduce damages for contributory negligence because it had not been considered by the lower courts,[460] the damages in *Reeves* were reduced by 50 per cent for the contributory negligence of the deceased, who was of sound mind.

But if for any reason the deceased could not have maintained an action at the moment of his death, even though death results from a wrongful act, neglect or default, no cause of action under the Act can be maintained on behalf of the dependants. So if the deceased's right of action in respect of the wrong which eventually causes his death is statute-barred, no action under the Fatal Accidents Act can be brought.[461] With the exception of an award of provisional damages,[462] when the deceased has himself obtained judgment against the defendant or settled his claim no further action can be maintained on behalf of the dependants for their loss if his injuries later lead to his death.[463] In all these examples there has ceased to be a wrongful act, **27-90**

W.L.R. 1121; cf. *Farmer v Rash* [1969] 1 W.L.R. 160; *Swami v Lo* (1979) 105 D.L.R. (3d) 451.

459 [2000] 1 A.C. 360. See also *Kirkham v Chief Constable of Manchester* [1990] 2 Q.B. 283 CA.

460 Lord Scott dissented on this point and, in principle, Lords Mance and Neuberger thought that such a deduction might have been made had their Lordships had the benefit of full evidence and argument on the point.

461 Limitation Act 1980 s.12(1). And see *Williams v Mersey Docks and Harbour Board* [1905] 1 K.B. 804. But if the period of limitation applicable to the deceased's cause of action has not expired by the day of his death an action under the Fatal Accidents Act may be brought subject to its own fresh period of limitation; see Limitation Act 1980 s.12(2); and see *British Electric Ry v Gentile* [1914] A.C. 1034; *Venn v Tedesco* [1926] 2 K.B. 227.

462 Damages Act 1996 s.3: para.27-92. See also para.27-84.

463 This statement was assumed and accepted as probably correct by the House of Lords in *Pickett v British Rail Engineering Ltd* [1980] A.C. 136, per Lord Wilberforce at 146–147 and at 152, per Lord Salmon, although there is no House of Lords authority directly in point. On judgment see *Murray v Shuter* [1972] 1 Lloyd's Rep. 6; *McCann v Shepherd* [1973] 1 W.L.R. 540. For accord and satisfaction see *Read v Great Eastern Ry* (1868) L.R. 3 Q.B. 555; *Thompson v Arnold* [2007] EWHC 1875 (QB); [2008] P.I.Q.R. P1 (deceased's settlement of a claim prior to her death precluded a subsequent action by her dependants under the Fatal Accidents Act 1976). In *Jameson v Central Electricity Generating Board* [2000] 1 A.C. 455 HL, a settlement, satisfying a claim against one joint and several tortfeasor, on its true interpretation extinguished the cause of action (so that no action could be brought under the Fatal Accidents Act 1976) against the other joint and several tortfeasor. For exclusion of liability to the deceased by contract see *Griffiths v Earl of Dudley* (1882) 9 Q.B.D. 357; *Haigh v Royal Main Steam Packet Co Ltd* (1883) 52 L.J.Q.B. 640; *The Stella* [1900] P. 161; but such contracts would now be subject to the statutory control of exemption clauses under, e.g. the Unfair Contract Terms Act 1977 s.2(1) and the Consumer Rights Act 2015. cf. *Phillips v Rafia* [2007] EWCA Civ 74; [2007] 1 W.L.R. 1351 in which it was held that on its true construction the exclusion of liability in the Motor Insurers' Bureau (Uninsured Drivers) Agreement 1999, where "the claimant" was knowingly being driven by an uninsured driver, did not exclude the MIB's liability where the claim was being brought under the Fatal Accidents Act 1976. The deceased was not "the claimant" under the 1976 Act and the claim under the 1976 Act was not a survival of the deceased's claim.

neglect or default entitling the deceased to sue were he still alive.[464] And if the deceased's own conduct was such as to give rise to a defence of ex turpi causa or volenti non fit injuria against him had he lived to sue, these defences remain valid against his dependants. So in *Murphy v Culhane*,[465] where the deceased was killed in the course of criminal affray apparently started by him, the Court of Appeal refused to give judgment on pleadings admitting that the defendant killed the deceased and had in fact been convicted of his manslaughter. They ordered the case to go to trial to determine whether in view of the possible defences open to the defendant the deceased himself could have sued in respect of the injuries causing his death.

27-91 Before 1945 the deceased's contributory negligence would have defeated altogether a claim on behalf of his dependants. The Fatal Accidents Act 1976[466] provides that now their damages shall be proportionately reduced.[467] In *Dodds v Dodds*[468] it was held that the fact that the widow was responsible for the death of her husband should not affect the validity of her son's claim as a dependant of her deceased husband. The claim of each dependant is personal and individual. Therefore contributory negligence on the part of one dependant may reduce his damages against the defendant, but the damages awarded to other dependants will be unaffected.[469] The defendant may be able to recover contribution from the negligent dependant towards the whole sum of damages which he is ordered to pay under the Civil Liability (Contribution) Act 1978.[470] A contract by the deceased limiting the amount of damages (as opposed to excluding liability) which he personally might have received will lead to no reduction in the damages payable to the dependants[471] because all that s.1 of the Act requires is that the deceased could hypothetically have maintained an action.

27-92 By s.3 of the Damages Act 1996, an award of provisional damages does not operate as a bar to an action in respect of the injured person's death under the Fatal Accidents Act 1976; but such part of the provisional damages or further damages awarded before the injured person's death, as was intended to compensate him for pecuniary loss in a period which in the event falls after his death, shall be taken into account in assessing the amount of any loss of support suffered by dependants.

---

[464] In contrast, in *Reader v Molesworth Bright Clegg* [2007] EWCA Civ 169; [2007] 1 W.L.R. 1082 it was held that, where the deceased's action in negligence for personal injury, which had subsequently resulted in his death (from suicide), had been (negligently) discontinued after his death by his solicitors, that was not a bar to an action under the Fatal Accidents Act 1976. *At the date of the death* the deceased could still have maintained an action. The position would have been different (and governed by the cases cited in the previous footnote) had the action been discontinued prior to the death.

[465] [1977] Q.B. 94.

[466] s.5; as slightly amended by s.3(2) of the Administration of Justice Act 1982. From 1945 until 1976 the same result applied by virtue of the Law Reform (Contributory Negligence) Act 1945 s.1(4). See *Hurt v Murphy* [1971] R.T.R. 186.

[467] See, e.g. *Reeves v Commissioner of Police of the Metropolis* [2000] 1 A.C. 360 discussed in para.27-89.

[468] [1978] Q.B. 543.

[469] For Commonwealth decisions to this effect, see *Trueman v Hydro Electric Power Commission of Ontario* [1924] 1 D.L.R. 406; *Benjamin v Currie* [1958] V.R. 259; *Mulholland v McCrea* [1961] N.I. 135.

[470] See para.4-13 onwards.

[471] *Nunan v Southern Ry* [1924] 1 K.B. 223. Such a term might now be invalid vis-à-vis the deceased under, e.g. the Consumer Rights Act 2015.

(d) Damages for bereavement

By s.1A of the Fatal Accidents Act 1976, an action under the Act may now consist of or include a claim for damages for bereavement.[472] This is a novel departure for English law which previously set its face firmly against claims for solatium.[473] However, the persons entitled to claim damages for bereavement are limited to the spouse or civil partner of the deceased and, where the deceased was a child under 18[474] who was never married or a civil partner, his or her parents (or the mother only if such a child was illegitimate).[475] A fixed sum of damages, £15,120 from 1 May 2020, is to be awarded, although the Minister for Justice has power to vary the sum.[476] In the case of a claim by both parents, the fixed sum to be awarded is divided equally between them.[477] 27-93

(e) Assessment of Fatal Accident Act damages

(i) *Loss of pecuniary benefit*

Apart from bereavement damages, damages recoverable under the Act are to compensate for the pecuniary loss suffered by the dependants as a result of the death. By s.3(1), such damages may be awarded "as are proportioned to the injury resulting from the death to the dependants respectively" and by s.3(2), after deducting the costs not recovered from the defendant, any amount recovered "shall be divided among the dependants in such shares as may be directed". While the dependants can recover funeral expenses incurred in respect of the deceased,[478] by far the most important pecuniary loss is that of a pecuniary advantage, which is 27-94

---

472 See, generally, *Claims for Wrongful Death, Law Commission Report No.263* (1999), paras 2.65–2.74 and Pt VI. The Law Commission recommended, among other reforms, that the list of those who can claim bereavement damages should be widened and that the level of the award should be increased.

473 *Blake v Midland Ry* (1852) 18 Q.B. 93; *Franklin v SE Ry* (1858) 3 H. & N. 211, per Pollock CB at 214; *Davies v Powell Duffryn Collieries Associated Ltd* [1942] A.C. 601; *Pevec v Brown* (1964) 108 S.J. 219; *Mallett v McMonagle* [1970] A.C. 166 HL.

474 No bereavement damages can be awarded if the unmarried child died over the age of 18 even though the injuries causing his death were sustained when he was under 18: *Doleman v Deakin, The Times*, 30 January 1990.

475 s.1A(2). In *Rabone v Pennine Care NHS Foundation Trust* [2012] UKSC 2; [2012] 2 A.C. 72 the claimant parents of a deceased adult, who had committed suicide while on home release from hospital, were held to be entitled to damages, and were awarded £5,000, under the Human Rights Act 1998 as victims of the infringement of the right to life under art.2 ECHR. In this respect, a claim under the Human Rights Act 1998 may be regarded as outflanking the Fatal Accidents Act 1976 because the parents would have had no claim for bereavement damages under the 1976 Act: see A. Tettenborn, "Wrongful Death, Human Rights and the Fatal Accidents Act" (2012) 128 L.Q.R. 327. But, in answering a slightly different question, it was held by the Court of Appeal in *Smith v Lancashire Teaching Hospitals NHS Foundation Trust* [2017] EWCA Civ 1916; [2018] Q.B. 804 that the exclusion from the limited list of those who can claim bereavement damages, under s.1A(2)(a) of the 1976 Act, of a cohabitee who had been living with the deceased for two years as his wife (and the same reasoning applies to a cohabitee living as the deceased's husband or civil partner) infringed the cohabitee's art.8 and art.14 Convention rights under the Human Rights Act 1998. A declaration of incompatibility was made under the 1998 Act s.4.

476 s.1A(3), (5). The sum was raised from £12,980 to £15,120 by the Damages for Bereavement (Variation of Sum) (England and Wales) Order 2020 (SI 2020/316).

477 s.1A(4).

478 s.3(5); but not the cost of the wake: *Grant v Secretary of State for Transport* [2017] EWHC 1663 (QB); *Blake v Mad Max Ltd* [2018] EWHC 2134 (QB); [2019] P.I.Q.R. Q1.

often referred to as the loss of dependency.[479] Although it is not necessary for the dependants to prove that any pecuniary advantage had been derived from the deceased before his death, they must establish "a reasonable expectation of pecuniary benefit, as of right, or otherwise,[480] from the continuance of life".[481] In *Kandalla v British Airways Board*[482] the elderly parents of two young women doctors killed in an air disaster recovered damages on proof that they intended to flee from Iraq to England where their daughters, had they lived, would have supported them from their earnings. The parents of an intelligent girl of 16 who had almost completed her apprenticeship as a dressmaker received damages in *Taff Vale Ry Co v Jenkins*[483] notwithstanding that she had before her death earned nothing and conferred on them as yet no pecuniary benefit. The inference from the facts that she would have done so in the future was reasonable, and that was sufficient. In *Davies v Taylor*,[484] on the other hand, the claimant widow had deserted her husband five weeks before his death and had committed adultery on a number of occasions. Shortly before his death her husband had started divorce proceedings and it was found as a fact that there was no significant prospect of a reconciliation. The widow's claim for damages therefore failed. It was held in the House of Lords, however, that, while it is for a widow who has forfeited her right to maintenance to prove that, at the date of her husband's death, there had been a significant prospect of a reconciliation and not just a mere speculative possibility, the question is not one to be answered simply on a balance of probabilities. If a significant prospect of reconciliation is proved, that prospect must be evaluated and an award made of the appropriate proportion of the damages that would have been payable had the marriage been a stable one.

27-95 The pecuniary advantage lost need not be money which the dependants received or reasonably expected to receive. It also includes the loss of gratuitous services rendered by the deceased.[485] Thus a husband will be awarded damages in respect of his wife's services in the home, and children will be compensated for the loss

---

479 But occasionally "loss of dependency" has been used to refer to only some of the lost benefit: see *Taylor v O'Connor* [1971] A.C. 115 at 128, per Lord Reid.

480 As long as the expectation of pecuniary benefit does not result from professional crime or other cause sufficient to defeat the claim as being a benefit arising ex turpi causa: *Burns v Edman* [1970] 2 Q.B. 541; *Hunter v Butler* [1996] R.T.R. 396 CA.

481 *Franklin v SE Ry* (1858) 3 H. & N. 211, per Pollock CB at 214; *Dalton v SE Ry* (1858) 4 C.B. (N.C.) 296; *Pym v GN Ry* (1862) 2 B. & S. 759 at 768, per Cockburn CJ; *Hetherington v NE Ry* (1882) 9 Q.B.D. 160; *Barnett v Cohen* [1921] 2 K.B. 461 at 471–472; *Kassam v Kampala Aerated Water Co* [1965] 1 W.L.R. 668, per Lord Guest at 672. Loss of dependency can include a loss of, or reduction in, state benefits because of the death: *Cox v Hockenhull* [2000] 1 W.L.R. 750 CA. It can also include the loss of a future contribution to a child's purchase of a first home or the cost of a wedding: *AB v KL* [2019] EWHC 611 (QB); [2020] P.I.Q.R. Q1.

482 [1981] Q.B. 158.

483 [1913] A.C. 1; *Price v Glynea and Castle Coal and Brick Co* (1915) 85 L.J.K.B. 1278; *Wathen v Vernon* [1970] R.T.R. 471 CA.

484 [1974] A.C. 207; *Barnett v Cohen* [1921] 2 K.B. 461; *CC v TD* [2018] EWHC 1240 (QB); [2018] P.I.Q.R. P17 (no significant prospect of reconciliation following separation; wife's loss of dependency limited to what she would have received by way of maintenance payments).

485 Providing they can be translated into money's worth: *Franklin v SE Ry* (1853) 3 H. & N. 211; *Berry v Humm & Co* [1915] 1 K.B. 627; cf. *Sykes v NE Ry* (1875) 44 L.J.C.P. 191 (where the deceased had worked for his father for a full wage. Although the father had lost his son's services, he had suffered no pecuniary loss because he had always paid for them). The courts have not yet considered the impact of *Hunt v Severs* [1994] 2 A.C. 350, HL, a personal injury case, on claims under the Fatal Accidents Act 1976 where a third party has gratuitously provided services for a dependant. See *Claims for Wrongful Death, Law Commission Report No.263* (1999), paras 5.47–5.55.

of their mother's daily care and work on their behalf. In *Hay v Hughes*,[486] on the death of their parents, two young boys were taken into their grandmother's home and there is little doubt that she intended to care for them as a mother entirely free of charge. In determining the pecuniary value of the services of which their mother's death deprived the children, the Court of Appeal took into account in so far as it could be assessed in money's worth the whole of a good mother's care of her family, and not just the everyday physical tasks undertaken. And in *Regan v Williamson*,[487] in assessing the damages payable to a father and his children on the death of the wife, compensation was given to cover not just the cost of the aunt who came in daily to keep house and mind the children, but to cover the loss of the mother's care by night and at weekends. A wife and mother is no longer for the purposes of the Fatal Accidents Act regarded as a mere housekeeper.[488] Dependants cannot be compensated for loss of love and affection but will recover for losses of identifiable benefits calculable in monetary terms.[489] In some cases, an extra sum for lost services has been awarded to reflect the fact that those services would have been performed by a family member rather than, less conveniently, by a commercial provider (in other words, the awards reflected the fact that the services provided by a family member were, in that sense, more valuable than those provided by a commercial provider).[490]

27-96 The pecuniary advantage lost must result from the relationship between the dependant and the deceased. In *Burgess v Florence Nightingale Hospital for Gentlewomen*[491] a husband claimed in respect of the death of his wife who was also his professional dancing partner. Devlin J held that, although he could recover damages for pecuniary loss due to the death of his wife, he could not recover for the loss of earnings as a dancing partnership caused by her death, for that loss resulted from their professional and not their marital relationship.[492] But in *Malyon v Plummer*[493] the claimant had been employed in her husband's "one-man" company at a salary of between £600 and £800 a year and lost this income on his death as the company was unable to carry on business without him. The Court of Appeal valued her services to the company at £200, and awarded her damages in respect of the balance of her salary as a pecuniary advantage deriving from the marital relationship and lost as a result of her husband's death.

---

486 [1975] Q.B. 790; see also *Spittle v Bunney* [1988] 1 W.L.R. 847; para.27-101.

487 [1976] 1 W.L.R. 305.

488 [1976] 1 W.L.R. 305 at 308. This approach was followed in *Abrams v Cook, The Times*, 26 November 1987 where the claim was by a disabled wife for the loss of her husband's care; damages were not to be limited to the commercial cost of a nurse.

489 *Hay v Hughes* [1975] Q.B. 790; *Regan v Williamson* [1976] 1 W.L.R. 305; *Mehmet v Perry* [1977] 2 All E.R. 529 (where it was held that the children's precarious health justified the *father* giving up his employment to care for them himself rather than engaging a housekeeper); *Spittle v Bunney* [1988] 1 W.L.R. 847. As shown in *Clay v Pooler* [1982] 3 All E.R. 570, a wife and children can be compensated for loss of a husband's and father's services as a handyman around the house.

490 *Beesley v New Century Group Ltd* [2008] EWHC 3033 (QB); *Wolstenholme v Leach's of Shudehill Ltd* [2016] EWHC 588 (QB).

491 [1955] 1 Q.B. 349; and see *Sykes v NE Ry* (1875) 44 L.J.C.P. 191.

492 But he could and did recover a sum to represent her contribution from her share of the earnings to the household expenses, [1955] 1 Q.B. 349 at 361–362.

493 [1964] 1 Q.B. 330. In *Davies v Whiteways Cyder Co Ltd* [1975] Q.B. 262 the deceased had made substantial gifts to his dependants before his death. Because he was killed less than seven years after making the gifts estate duty became payable and it was held by O'Connor J that the amount of his duty, less a sum to cover the possibility that the deceased might in any event have died within the seven years period, could be recovered as damages under the Fatal Accidents Acts 1846–1959.

(ii) Assessing dependants' prospects

27-97 As damages are awarded for the loss of an expectation of pecuniary benefit, it follows that the dependants' future prospects and actual circumstances[494] after the death of the deceased must be taken into account. In an action by a widow, for example, her own expectation of life is a material factor and accordingly evidence of her state of health is admissible[495]; if she has actually died before the trial, damages must be awarded (to her estate) for the period of her survival only, not upon the basis of her expectation of life as it might have been supposed to be when her husband was killed.[496] Similarly, where a child has lost its mother and father as a result of the defendant's tort, but is subsequently adopted, damages for loss of dependency are confined to the difference between the pecuniary support that his natural father (as bread-winner) would have provided and that provided by his adoptive father: in contrast it would be improper to attempt to evaluate any potential difference in care between a natural and an adoptive mother.[497] Again, if a mother remarries and the children are accepted as members of the family by their stepfather, he incurs a legal obligation to support them[498] and this means that their damages should not be assessed on the basis that they have lost the support of a father but only so as to compensate them for the risk of loss in the future.[499]

27-98 It follows that in assessing the damages payable to a child in respect of the death of its father the court is bound to take into account the fact or the prospects of the mother's remarriage[500] and an equivalent rule applies to the assessment of the damages payable to a widower in respect of the death of his wife.[501] Section 3(3) of the Fatal Accidents Act 1976 provides, however, that in assessing the damages payable to a widow in respect of the death of her husband "there shall not be taken into account the remarriage of the widow or her prospects of remarriage". This statu-

---

494 Subject to s.4 of the Fatal Accidents Act 1976 which excludes the dependants' pecuniary gains: paras 27-108 to 27-113.

495 *Williamson v John I Thornycroft & Co Ltd* [1940] 1 K.B. 658 at 660, per Du Parcq LJ; *Whittome v Coates* [1965] 1 W.L.R. 1284; *Baugh v Delta Water Fittings Ltd* [1971] 1 W.L.R. 1295. Nevertheless in Baugh Lawson J held that the court will not stay an action by a widow on the ground that she refuses to submit to a medical examination save, perhaps, where there are genuine and substantial reasons for the defendant's application.

496 *Williamson v John I Thornycroft & Co Ltd* [1940] 1 K.B. 658; *Voller v Dairy Produce Packers Ltd* [1962] 1 W.L.R. 960. Although the damages must be assessed as at the date of the death of the deceased, the court is entitled to inform its mind of subsequent events throwing light on the realities, for it should never speculate where it knows: *Curwen v James* [1963] 1 W.L.R. 748 at 753, per Harman LJ.

497 *Watson v Willmott* [1991] 1 Q.B. 140. There was no discussion of s.4 of the 1976 Act: paras 27-108 to 27-113.

498 *Reincke v Gray* [1964] 1 W.L.R. 832 at 835 per Sellers LJ. The obligation derives from the Matrimonial Proceedings (Children) Act 1958 s.1(1) (repealed and replaced by the Matrimonial Causes Act 1973 ss.27 and 52) and the Matrimonial Proceedings (Magistrates' Courts) Act 1960 s.16 (repealed and replaced by Domestic Proceedings and Magistrates' Courts Act 1978 ss.1 and 88(1)).

499 *Reincke v Gray* [1964] 1 W.L.R. 832.

500 *Thompson v Price* [1973] 1 Q.B. 838; *Clay v Pooler* [1982] 3 All E.R. 570 at 578. But note reservations expressed to this view by Lord Edmund-Davies in *Hay v Hughes* [1975] Q.B. 790 at 806. Stepfather may never accept the child as a member of his family and so incur no legal obligation to support him. Test should be how likely it is that the mother will remarry *and* that her new husband will accept the child as a child of his family. See also *Benson v Biggs, Wall and Co Ltd* [1983] 1 W.L.R. 72; cf. *Stanley v Saddique* [1992] Q.B. 1: paras 27-108 to 27-113.

501 *Collins v Noma Electric Co* (1962) 106 S.J. 431; *Mehmet v Perry* [1977] 2 All E.R. 529 at 539; *Regan v Williamson* [1976] 1 W.L.R. 305.

tory reversal of a well-established common law rule,[502] which was itself strictly in accordance with the principle that damages under the Fatal Accidents Act are awarded for actual pecuniary loss, was decided upon because of the invidious character of the task of assessing a widow's prospects of remarriage which the judges were formerly required to perform.[503] Nevertheless the Act creates the anomaly that a widow who has actually remarried and who is supported by her second husband receives damages for the continuing loss of the support of her first husband[504] and it also creates the secondary anomalies that the claims of widows and widowers are no longer treated alike and that even a widow's prospects of remarriage must still be considered when the claims of children are in issue.[505] The Law Commission has recommended that s.3(3) should be repealed and that actual or predicted changes in the marital status (or analogous personal circumstances) of the dependant (or the deceased) should be dealt with in a number of new statutory provisions which would treat consistently the claims of widowers and widows.[506]

(iii) Assessing dependants' loss—the "multiplier method"

In contrast with a case in which the court has to decide, on a balance of probabilities, what in truth took place in the past, in assessing damages under the Fatal Accidents Act the court has to base its conclusion upon what it considers will happen and what, but for the death of the deceased, would have happened in the future, estimating what are the chances that a particular event will or would have occurred and reflecting those chances in the amount of damages it awards.[507] There are thus, inevitably, many imponderables which the court must take into account and, while arithmetical calculations are unavoidable and, indeed, essential, much of the calculation is bound to be in the realm of hypothesis where "arithmetic is a good servant but a bad master".[508] **27-99**

As with the assessment of damages for future loss of earnings in a personal injury action, the usual method of assessment[509] is the "multiplier method" by which the assessed net annual loss of dependency (multiplicand) is multiplied by a number **27-100**

---

502 Originally effected by the Law Reform (Miscellaneous Provisions) Act 1971 s.1(4); for the common law see cases cited in the 13th edn of this work and see *Wilson v Dagnall* [1972] 1 Q.B. 509.

503 See *Buckley v John Allen and Ford (Oxford) Ltd* [1967] 2 Q.B. 637 at 644–645. cf. *Goodburn v Thomas Cotton Ltd* [1968] 1 Q.B. 845.

504 *Thompson v Price* [1973] 1 Q.B. 838; *Gavin v Wilmot Breeden Ltd* [1973] 1 W.L.R. 1117.

505 *Thompson v Price* [1973] 1 Q.B. 838. The court may be unlikely to attach much weight to a widow's prospects of remarriage in an action brought by her in respect of the death of a son or daughter who had been supporting her but, theoretically, those prospects should not be ignored for s.3(3) covers only damages payable in respect of the death of a husband. If the widow had actually remarried by the date of the trial, this fact would certainly have to be taken into account. Where the claim is being brought by a cohabitee (under the definition of dependants: see para.27-88) her prospects of marriage are to be taken into account.

506 *Claims for Wrongful Death*, Law Commission Report No.263 (1999), paras 4.27-4.71; Draft Bill cl.4. See also *De Sales v Ingrilli* [2002] HCA 52; (2002) 212 C.L.R. 338 High Court of Australia.

507 *Mallett v McMonagle* [1970] A.C. 166 at 176, per Lord Diplock.

508 *Daniels v Jones* [1961] 1 W.L.R. 1103, per Holroyd Pearce LJ at 1110; *Kassam v Kampala Aerated Water Co Ltd* [1965] 1 W.L.R. 668, per Lord Guest at 674; *Hay v Hughes* [1975] Q.B. 790 at 810. cf. *Whittome v Coates* [1965] 1 W.L.R. 1285, per Lord Diplock LJ at 1293. In *Miller v British Road Services Ltd* [1967] 1 W.L.R. 443, Waller J declined to set out his precise method of arriving at a final figure; but in *Rawlinson v Babcock and Wilcox Ltd* [1967] 1 W.L.R. 481 at 489, where there was an unusually large number of imponderables, Chapman J apparently regretted that he was not "a stockbroker or merchant banker or a computer, or even a psychiatrist".

509 The multiplier method is not always appropriate; for example, where there has been no depend-

of years purchase. In a simple case, the starting point for assessing the multiplicand is to deduct from the annual wages earned by the deceased the estimated amount of his own living expenses, i.e. what he would have spent exclusively on himself.[510] The figure arrived at is then adjusted to take account, for example, of the variations in the deceased's rate of earning which might have occurred.[511]

27-101 But while this simple approach is appropriate where the action is brought on behalf of a widow, or of a widow and children in respect of the death of the breadwinner of the family, it clearly cannot be used where the pecuniary benefit was provided in kind and not in cash.[512] Thus, for example, where a wife and mother has been killed, the basic principle adopted is to consider how her position in the home can be *reasonably* replaced by someone else and what that will cost. The current cost of a nanny or housekeeper may therefore be used as a guideline in this exercise,[513] but some further compensation be made for those duties undertaken by a mother which a paid nanny or housekeeper will not replace as she, unlike a mother, will get free time and holidays.[514] On the other hand, the damages awarded must reflect the fact that older children do not require the same looking-after as young children and that a valuation according to the cost of a hired nanny thereby becomes less and less appropriate.[515] Moreover, lower damages should be awarded if the mother was unreliable and unlikely to have looked after the child properly.[516] When a father chooses to seek help from a relative known to his bereaved children he will not be denied the cost of paying for her services and/or keep even if outside help might work out slightly cheaper overall.[517] In *Cresswell v Eaton*[518] the value of a mother's services was based on the wages given up by the children's aunt to look after them (even though she herself had no dependency claim) with a modest discount for the fact that the mother (who was divorced from the father) had worked full-time. In *Mehmet v Perry*[519] the father gave up his own employment to care for his children himself on advice that the exceptionally precarious health of his two

ency because the deceased was not yet a wage-earner, as in *Taff Vale Ry v Jenkins* [1913] A.C. 1; or where the loss comprises a lower inheritance, as in *Taylor v O'Connor* [1971] A.C. 115; cf. *Singapore Bus Service (1978) Ltd v Lim Soon Young* [1985] 1 W.L.R. 1075.

510 *Davies v Powell Duffryn Associated Collieries Ltd* [1942] A.C. 601 at 617, per Lord Wright; *Harris v Empress Motors Ltd* [1984] 1 W.L.R. 212 at 217, per O'Connor LJ, who also pointed out that the modern practice is to deduct fixed percentages for the deceased's living expenses; *Crabtree v Wilson* [1993] P.I.Q.R. Q24.

511 But a widow is not entitled to claim for an increased award based on the prospect and desire of the deceased and herself to start a family which would have resulted in her increased dependency on her husband: *Malone v Rowan* [1984] 3 All E.R. 402; following *Higgs v Drinkwater*, CA, transcript 128A. For an adjustment because the deceased was saving money, see *Gavin v Wilmot Breedon Ltd* [1973] 1 W.L.R. 1117; cf. *Taylor v O'Connor* [1971] A.C. 115, where the deceased's savings would not have been used up in his lifetime.

512 It is also generally inappropriate where the deceased was the child of the dependant; see, e.g. *Dolbey v Goodwin* [1955] 1 W.L.R. 553.

513 *Hay v Hughes* [1975] 1 Q.B. 790. Ormrod LJ at 819 questioned whether the cost of the children's keep in a foster home might be a more reliable guide, but this was rejected in *Spittle v Bunney* [1988] 1 W.L.R. 847. In the latter case, the "cost" of a notional nanny was assessed according to the net wages a nanny would receive, rather than the expense of engaging her.

514 *Regan v Williamson* [1976] 1 W.L.R. 305; and see *Hurt v Murphy* [1971] R.T.R. 186 (father entitled to cost of daily help, even though residential help would have been cheaper, because his house was too small to accommodate another adult).

515 *Spittle v Bunney* [1988] 1 W.L.R. 847.

516 *Stanley v Saddique* [1992] Q.B. 1.

517 *Regan v Williamson* [1976] 1 W.L.R. 305.

518 [1991] 1 W.L.R. 1113.

519 [1977] 2 All E.R. 529.

younger children meant that no stranger could substitute for the dead mother as well as the surviving parent. It was held that in these circumstances his damages should be assessed on the basis of his own loss of earnings.

The multiplier The sum arrived at for the annual loss of dependency must then be capitalised by the application of an appropriate multiplier. The starting point for this is the number of years from the date of death during which the dependants would have received a pecuniary benefit from the deceased, and this depends on the judge's estimate of such uncertain factors as the expectation of working life left to the deceased at the date of his death[520] and the life expectancy of an adult dependant.[521] In the case of child dependants, the court must estimate whether the dependency would have ceased at the usual school-leaving age of 16[522] or would have continued during further education until 18 or beyond.[523] It might appear that the decision on this matter sometimes depends more on the ability and station in life of the deceased parent than on any attempt to assess the individual child's aptitude for further education. Where there is a claim by a cohabitee, a further factor to be taken into account, presumably in deciding the period of dependency, is "the fact that the dependant had no enforceable right to financial support by the deceased as a result of their living together".[524] In addition, the prospects of a divorce between a widow and the deceased are to be taken into account in assessing the widow's damages.[525] **27-102**

The figure arrived at for the duration of the dependency must then be adjusted. For example, the dependant's future prospects after the death should be taken into account.[526] Most importantly, the multiplier must be such that the capital sum awarded, together with the income earned by its investment, will be exhausted by the end of the period intended to be covered.[527] This means that the calculation must be made on the supposition that the dependants will spend each year a part of the capital as well as the whole of the income which they receive from so much of the capital as remains.[528] It follows that the number of years purchase taken as the multiplier will be considerably less than the number of years taken as the duration of the dependency. **27-103**

---

520 In *Gilbertson v Harland and Wolff Ltd* [1966] 2 Lloyd's Rep. 190, the deceased was an active man of 70 and damages were assessed on the basis that he would have gone on working until the age of 75, but normally it will be assumed, in the absence of evidence to the contrary, that a man would have retired at 65. See, e.g. *Whittome v Coates* [1965] 1 W.L.R. 1285 at 1288, per Sellers LJ.

521 *Grzelak v Harefield and Northwood Hospital Management Committee* (1968) 112 S.J. 195 (dependants included parents of deceased aged 77 and 80. Three years' purchase used for the assessment of their loss).

522 *K v JMP Co Ltd* [1976] Q.B. 85 CA (father not married to mother and worked as a labourer).

523 *Hay v Hughes* [1975] Q.B. 790 CA (parents had bought own house: father doing well and standing a good chance of promotion with the National Coal Board); *Dodds v Dodds* [1978] Q.B. 543 (father assistant service manager in company with good prospects of further promotion, but note account taken of I.Q. tests of child in this case).

524 Fatal Accidents Act 1976 s.3(4).

525 *Owen v Martin* [1992] P.I.Q.R. Q151. But mere statistics as to the prevailing divorce rate should not to be taken into account where the evidence is that the claimant and the deceased were happily married: *Wheatley v Cunningham* [1992] P.I.Q.R. Q100.

526 See para.27-98.

527 *Taylor v O'Connor* [1971] A.C. 115. Higher rate tax, payable on the income from investing the damages for future pecuniary loss, should normally be ignored: *Hodgson v Trapp* [1998] A.C. 807 HL; *Wells v Wells* [1999] 1 A.C. 345 HL.

528 See the sample calculations set out by Lord Pearson in *Taylor v O'Connor* [1971] A.C. 115 at 144.

27-104 **The discount rate** The leading case on multipliers for future pecuniary loss—which, albeit directly concerned with personal injury cases, must apply also to claims under the Fatal Accidents Act 1976—is *Wells v Wells*.[529] Their Lordships laid down that the appropriate discount rate is the rate of return on index-linked government stock (ILGS) which, at the time of the decision, was taken to be 3 per cent. Subsequently, the Lord Chancellor has set a discount rate of minus 0.25 per cent under the power conferred by s.A1 of the Damages Act 1996.[530] That rate applies to fatal accident as well as personal injury cases.

27-105 In the context of fatal accident claims, it was previously the law that, in contrast to personal injury claims, the multiplier was used to assess all the pecuniary loss and not merely the post-trial pecuniary loss. The leading case was *Cookson v Knowles*[531] in which the House of Lords laid down that the dependants' pecuniary loss prior to trial should be assessed separately from that after the trial. This was essentially because the former was less speculative and because no interest was to be paid on the future loss but was payable on the pre-trial loss, normally from the date of death until the time of trial at half the average rate on the special account over that period.[532] In *Graham v Dodds*[533] it was clarified that that itemisation did not mean that the multiplier method should be abandoned for pre-trial loss. Rather the multiplier should continue to be calculated from the date of death (rather than from the date of trial) on the basis that, in contrast to a personal injury case, there could be no certainty even that the deceased would have survived until trial. So if, for example, the multiplier was 14, and four years had elapsed between death and trial, the pre-trial loss was calculated using a multiplier of four and the post-trial loss, using a multiplier of 10. But a separate pre-trial and post-trial *multiplicand* was generally appropriate to take account of facts known at trial: e.g. the rate of wages for the job that the deceased had.[534]

27-106 In the light of the House of Lords' decision in *Wells v Wells*,[535] it was argued in previous editions of this work that, contrary to the approach in *Cookson v Knowles* and *Graham v Dodds*, the multiplier should be calculated from the date of trial. Although *Wells v Wells* was itself a personal injury case, it was clear that its approach was intended to apply to fatal accident claims as well. Their Lordships indicated that a sound actuarial approach should be taken using the Ogden Tables as a starting point. But as the Law Commission pointed out, it was difficult to see how the Ogden Tables could be properly used where one was calculating a multiplier from the date of death rather than from trial.[536] Subsequent editions of the Ogden Tables were produced with this criticism by the Law Commission in mind.[537] The Ogden Working Party argued that, in the light of *Wells v Wells*, multipliers for post-trial pecuniary loss should be calculated from the date of trial. In contrast, pre-trial loss should be calculated in much the same straightforward way as in personal injury cases, with the qualification that there would need to be a

---

529 [1999] 1 A.C. 345 HL. See para.27-33.
530 See para.27-34.
531 [1979] A.C. 556.
532 *Jefford v Gee* [1970] 2 Q.B. 130: see para.27-68.
533 [1983] 1 W.L.R. 808.
534 See especially Lord Fraser's speech in *Cookson v Knowles* [1979] A.C. 556 at 575–576.
535 [1999] 1 A.C. 345.
536 *Claims for Wrongful Death*, Law Com No.263 (1999) paras 4.1–4.23.
537 The Ogden Tables, *Actuarial Tables for Use in Personal Injury and Fatal Accident Cases*, are now in their 8th edn (2020), available at *https://www.gov.uk/government/publications/ogden-tables-actuarial-compensation-tables-for-injury-and-death* [Accessed 21 July 2020].

general discount for the uncertainty as to whether the deceased would have lived to trial. Those criticisms were accepted by the Supreme Court in *Knauer v Ministry of Justice*[538] which finally took the opportunity, applying the 1966 Practice Direction, to overrule *Cookson v Knowles* and *Graham v Dodds*. It is therefore now the law that the multiplier (for post-trial loss) in death cases is to be calculated from the date of trial not the date of death. The problem with not doing this is that the calculation of damages requires the courts to ignore facts known at trial and is therefore less accurate than it should be; and there should only be a discount for the early receipt of damages in respect of post-trial, not pre-trial, loss. According to the correct approach, therefore, as established by *Knauer*, post-trial pecuniary loss should be assessed using a multiplier calculated from the date of trial; whereas pre-trial losses should be calculated in much the same straightforward way as in personal injury cases (taking as the "multiplier" the number of years between the date of death and the trial) albeit with the qualification that there may need to be a discount for the uncertainty as to whether the deceased would have lived to trial.

It has already been pointed out that only one action may be brought in respect of the same death,[539] and it has also been held that it is of no concern to the defendant how the sum recovered from him is apportioned between the dependants.[540] Nevertheless, no question of group compensation arises, the quantum of damages of any one person whose claim is before the court is not to be regarded as being a proportion of a limited sum,[541] and each dependant's claim calls for separate consideration.[542] On the other hand, especially in cases in which the deceased leaves a widow and children who are still living at home, it is common practice for the court first of all to determine a total figure for the defendant's liability and then to divide the damages between the dependants.[543] Usually comparatively modest sums are awarded to the children and the remainder to the widow, but the basis for this is that their support through infancy and school-days is her legal obligation which she can be trusted to fulfil out of the money allocated to her. If there is any doubt as to her continued ability and willingness to do so, separate assessments should be made for the children.[544] Where the widow died 17 months after the death of her husband, leaving a daughter of 14, a separate assessment was made not only of the daughter's damages after her mother's death, but also in respect of the preceding 17 months.[545] There is no reason why the support of young children whose mother has died should be more sparingly estimated than if she had survived; it may be that the absence of a frugal mother will lead to a more expensive household budget.[546] 27-107

---

538 [2016] UKSC 9; [2016] A.C. 908.

539 See para.27-87.

540 *Eifert v Holt's Transport Co Ltd* [1951] 1 W.N. 467. A defendant may pay a single sum into court without specifying how it is to be allocated between the dependants: Fatal Accidents Act 1976 s.3(6).

541 *Avery v L & NE Ry* [1938] A.C. 606, per Lord Atkin at 612.

542 *Dietz v Lennig Chemicals Ltd* [1969] 1 A.C. 170 at 183, per Lord Morris. See, e.g. *Williamson v John I Thornycroft & Co Ltd* [1940] 2 K.B. 658; *Voller v Dairy Produce Packers Ltd* [1962] 1 W.L.R. 960; *Rawlinson v Babcock and Wilcox Ltd* [1967] 1 W.L.R. 481; *K v JMP Co Ltd* [1976] Q.B. 85.

543 *Bishop v Cunard White Star Co Ltd* [1950] P. 240 at 248, per Hodson J. This has been said to be the more usual method: *Kassam v Kampala Aerated Water Co Ltd* [1965] 1 W.L.R. 668 at 672, per Lord Guest; *Rawlinson v Babcock and Wilcox Ltd* [1967] 1 W.L.R. 481, per Chapman J at 483; *Thompson v Price* [1973] Q.B. 838 at 842, per Boreham J.

544 *Rawlinson v Babcock and Wilcox Ltd* [1967] 1 W.L.R. 481 at 483, per Chapman J.

545 *Rawlinson v Babcock and Wilcox Ltd* [1967] 1 W.L.R. 481; *Williamson v John I Thornycroft & Co Ltd* [1940] 2 K.B. 658; *Voller v Dairy Produce Packers Ltd* [1962] 1 W.L.R. 960.

546 *Kassam v Kampala Aerated Co Ltd* [1965] 1 W.L.R. 668 at 673, per Lord Guest.

(iv) *Pecuniary gains*

27-108 At common law the general rule, as stated by Lord Macmillan in *Davies v Powell Duffryn Associated Collieries Ltd*,[547] was that the "damages awarded to a dependant of a deceased person under the Fatal Accidents Act must take into account any pecuniary benefit accruing to that dependant in consequence of the death of the deceased". Over the years that rule was made subject to various statutory exceptions and s.4 of the Fatal Accidents Act 1976[548] now provides, "[i]n assessing damages in respect of a person's death in an action under this Act, benefits which have accrued or will or may accrue to any person from his estate or otherwise as a result of his death shall be disregarded".[549] Under the former s.4(1) any benefit—defined to mean social security benefit, or payment by a trade union or friendly society—insurance money, pension or gratuity was not to be deducted. The amended section therefore means that, in addition, the acceleration and certainty of the inheritance of the deceased's property[550] and awards under the Law Reform (Miscellaneous Provisions) Act 1934 are not deducted. With regard to the latter, however, the risk of serious overcompensation of the dependants was removed by the abolition of the survival for the estate of the lost years claim.[551]

27-109 In *Harland & Wolff Plc v McIntyre*,[552] retirement payments that had accrued to the deceased and, on his death, were paid by his employers to his estate, were non-deductible, by reason of s.4, in a claim brought for loss of retirement benefits under the Fatal Accidents Act 1976. The Court of Appeal reasoned that the possibility of such double recovery was inherent in s.4. Similarly in *Arnup v White Ltd*,[553] payments under the defendant employer's death-in-service and life insurance schemes were held to be benefits accruing as a result of the death of the employee within s.4 and therefore non-deductible in assessing damages under the Fatal Accidents Act 1976.[554]

27-110 It would seem that the words "benefit [accruing] … as a result of his death" in

---

547 [1942] A.C. 601 at 609.

548 As inserted by s.3(1) of the Administration of Justice Act 1982. For a straightforward decision applying s.4 see *Pidduck v Eastern Scottish Omnibuses Ltd* [1990] 1 W.L.R. 993 CA (widow's pension not deducted). Payments under the Fatal Accidents Act are exempted from the scheme operating under the Social Security (Recovery of Benefits) Act 1997: para.27-41 fn.220.

549 The Law Commission has recommended reform of s.4 in its Report, No.263 (1999) *Claims for Wrongful Death*, Pt V, Draft Bill cl.5.

550 In *Wood v Bentall Simplex Ltd* [1992] P.I.Q.R. P332, it was held that applying s.4, no deduction should be made for the claimant's inheritance of the deceased's share of the assets of a farming partnership. It was accepted, however, that there would be cases where the dependency so clearly rests on the very thing inherited (e.g. where a man living off investment income alone is killed and his widow inherits the investments) that the dependant suffers no loss and hence s.4 would be irrelevant.

551 See para.27-83.

552 [2006] EWCA Civ 287; [2006] 1 W.L.R. 2577.

553 [2008] EWCA Civ 447; [2008] I.C.R. 1064.

554 But in what, with respect, was an odd twist of reasoning that would make a nonsense of treating s.4 as an exception to deductibility, Smith LJ thought that whether the death caused the benefit was totally irrelevant under the Fatal Accidents Act 1976. This was said to be because, even if the benefit did not accrue as a result of the death under s.4, it could still not be deducted because it was irrelevant to offsetting the loss "resulting from the death" under s.3(1). It is submitted that this is an incorrect interpretation of s.3(1) and is out of line with many cases in the past which have held that benefits should be deducted under s.3(1) if not accruing as a result of the death under s.4.

s.4 must be narrowly construed[555] if they are not to include, for example,[556] remarriage by a dependant or a dependant's parent after the death, voluntary payments or services rendered to dependants after the death, or the earning capacity of a dependant after the death. Remarriage has already been considered[557]; the authorities state that voluntary services are in any event to be disregarded[558]; and there is conflict in the authorities as to whether earning capacity should be disregarded or not.[559] Consistent with a narrow interpretation of s.4 is the decision in *Hayden v Hayden*[560] in which the majority of the Court of Appeal (McCowan LJ dissenting) held that, where the tortfeasor was the father of the infant claimant and had given up his paid work to look after the claimant, the value of his services was not a benefit accruing as a result of the death under s.4 and was to be deducted in assessing the claimant's damages for the death of her mother. However, in the earlier and apparently contradictory decision in *Stanley v Saddique*[561] the Court of Appeal (Ralph Gibson LJ *dubitante*) reasoned that s.4 should not be given a narrow interpretation. It was therefore held that, in assessing a child's damages for the death of his mother, the benefits accruing to the child from the father's marriage to a woman who provided excellent motherly services to the child (and better care than the child's natural mother would have provided had she lived) were to be disregarded by reason of s.4.

Stanley v Saddique was followed in *R. v Criminal Injuries Compensation Board Ex p. K*,[562] where the question was what compensation should be payable to children under the old Criminal Injuries Compensation Scheme where their mother had been murdered, but the children had been well looked after by their uncle and aunt. On a judicial review application, the Divisional Court held that, following *Stanley v Saddique*, the gratuitous services of the uncle and aunt should be disregarded under s.4 of the 1976 Act. The children's compensation should not therefore have been reduced from £35,000 to £9,000. *Hayden v Hayden* was distinguished as a case on its special facts, namely that the provider of the gratuitous services was the tortfeasor and indeed was carrying out his parental duty. 27-111

Stanley v Saddique was also applied but with an important additional qualification in *H v S*.[563] The mother of infant children had been killed. Their father, who was not the tortfeasor, and had not previously provided them with any care or support, cared for them thereafter. The Court of Appeal held that the father's care and support was a benefit accruing as a result of the death and that, applying s.4 of the 1976 Act, it should therefore be disregarded in assessing damages. However, it was 27-112

555 See Law Commission Report No.56, ss.254–256; *Pearson Commission Report* (1978), Cmnd.7054, paras 537–539; 428 HL Official Report, Ser.5, col.28.

556 See also *Cameron v Vinters Defence Systems Ltd* [2007] EWHC 2267 (QB); [2008] P.I.Q.R. P5 (payment made to the dependant of the deceased under the Pneumoconiosis etc (Worker's Compensation) Act 1979 held not to be a benefit within s.4 of the Fatal Accidents Act 1976 and should therefore be deducted in assessing the dependant's damages: but this resulted from a purposive construction of s.4 and was designed to ensure that dependants did not gain by tactically delaying the commencement of proceedings under the 1976 Act until after payments had been made under the 1979 Act).

557 See para.27-98.

558 *Peacock v Amusement Equipment Co Ltd* [1954] 2 Q.B. 347; *Hay v Hughes* [1975] Q.B. 790.

559 *Howitt v Heads* [1973] Q.B. 64; *Cookson v Knowles* [1977] Q.B. 913 CA; affirmed, without discussion of this point [1979] A.C. 556; *Dodds v Dodds* [1978] Q.B. 543.

560 [1992] 1 W.L.R. 986 CA.

561 [1992] Q.B. 1.

562 [1999] Q.B. 1131.

563 [2002] EWCA Civ 792; [2003] Q.B. 965.

also held that *Hunt v Severs*[564]—the leading personal injury case on gratuitous services—should be applied to this Fatal Accidents Act claim. The Fatal Accident Act damages in respect of the lost gratuitous services were therefore here given only on the basis that they would be used to reimburse the voluntary carer (the father) for his services; and they were therefore to be held on a trust for the carer, which the court could enforce.

27-113 In addition to recommending the integration of the central reasoning in *Hunt v Severs* into the Fatal Accidents Act regime[565]—along the lines now applied in *H v S*—the Law Commission has recommended the replacement of s.4 by a new provision making clearer which benefits are, and are not, to be deducted.[566]

(f) Settlement of Fatal Accident Act claims

27-114 An executor or administrator, although the nominal claimant in the action, cannot validly agree with the defendant to accept a lump sum to cover all the dependants unless: (a) each of the dependants who is sui juris and desires to claim has approved the agreement; and (b) the court has sanctioned the agreement as being one for the benefit of each of the dependants who are infants.[567] Moreover, an agreement between the parties made "subject to the approval of the court" which is intended to include a settlement of the claim of an infant, is not a binding agreement which will only cease to be binding if the approval of the court is not forthcoming: a binding agreement only comes into existence for the first time when the court's approval is given.[568] This does not mean, however, that a dependant who is sui juris cannot settle his claim against the defendant without the approval of the court if there are other dependants who are under disability. The nominal claimant can, with the approval of a dependant who wishes to settle his claim, agree with the defendant that he shall pay to that dependant a sum of money in satisfaction of his claim, and the dependant is then as much bound by the agreement as if he had personally entered into it himself.[569] In assessing the damages to be paid to those dependants who have not settled their claims, the court will not take into account the sums paid by the defendant to other dependants unless they are such as to affect the losses suffered by those who are before the court. But if the widow's claim has been settled and the court considers the amount paid to her to have been inadequate, the result is likely to be an increased award to the infants: the ability of their mother to support them may be affected by the fact that she has too small a capital sum at her disposal, and this increases the loss that they have suffered in consequence of their father's death.[570]

(g) Relationship between Law Reform Act and Fatal Accidents Act claims

27-115 It is helpful to clarify this relationship because, where the defendant's tort has caused the death, an action may be brought under both the Law Reform (Miscel-

564 [1994] 2 A.C. 350: para.27-27.
565 *Claims for Wrongful Death*, Law Commission Report No.263 (1999), paras 5.47–5.55; Draft Bill, cl.3.
566 *Claims for Wrongful Death*, Law Commission Report No.263 (1999), paras 5.21–5.46; Draft Bill, cl.5.
567 *Jeffrey v Kent CC* [1958] 1 W.L.R. 927.
568 *Dietz v Lennig Chemicals Ltd* [1969] 1 A.C. 170.
569 *Jeffrey v Kent CC* [1958] 1 W.L.R. 927 at 930, per Paull J.
570 *Jeffrey v Kent CC* [1958] 1 W.L.R. 927 at 930, 932–933, per Paull J.

laneous Provisions) Act 1934 and the Fatal Accidents Act 1976 and the two are commonly combined. The former is for the benefit of those entitled to the estate, whereas the latter is for the benefit of the dependants (or, in the case of bereavement damages, only certain of the dependants) but these persons are very often the same. Where this was the case, it was formerly the law that both sets of damages could not be awarded in full. Awards under the 1934 Act (other than for pre-trial pecuniary loss)[571] were to be deducted from the Fatal Accidents Act award,[572] although by virtue of s.1(5) of the 1934 Act[573] there would be no deduction vice versa. The amended s.4 of the 1976 Act[574] reverses this so that no such deduction should be made from the Fatal Accidents Act damages. However, the risk of serious duplication of damages has at the same time been removed by the abolition of the survival of the "lost years" claim for the benefit of the estate.[575]

So where the death is not instantaneous, the survival action enables recovery on behalf of the estate of damages for the deceased's pre-death losses, both pecuniary and non-pecuniary, while the Fatal Accidents Act action enables dependants to recover their pecuniary loss and a spouse or parent to recover damages for bereavement. Funeral expenses may be recovered in either action (although clearly they would not be awarded twice over). On the other hand, where the death is instantaneous, and there has been no property damage, no damages can be recovered under the 1934 Act, apart from where the estate has incurred the funeral expenses.[576] **27-116**

6. Destruction of or Damage to Goods[577]

(a) Destruction of goods

Where goods are destroyed by the wrongful act of the defendant, the normal rule is that the claimant[578] is entitled to the sum of money which he would have to pay in the market for identical or essentially similar goods (i.e. the replacement cost),[579] plus in a proper case damages for the loss of use during the period before replacement.[580] In other words, in the case of profit-earning chattels, what has to be assessed is the value of the chattel to its owner as a going concern at the time and **27-117**

[571] *Murray v Shuter* [1976] Q.B. 972.

[572] *Davies v Powell Duffryn Associated Collieries Ltd* [1942] A.C. 601.

[573] See para.27-82.

[574] See para.27-108.

[575] See para.27-83.

[576] See para.27-85.

[577] The rules have mostly been worked out in cases involving ships, but they are of general application: *The Kingsway* [1918] P. 344 at 356, per Pickford LJ; *The Susquehanna* [1926] A.C. 655, per Lord Dunedin at 661; *The Hebridean Coast* [1961] A.C. 545, per Devlin LJ at 562; *Darbishire v Warran* [1963] 1 W.L.R. 1067, per Harman LJ at 1071; *Beechwood Birmingham Ltd v Hoyer Group UK Ltd* [2010] EWCA Civ 647; [2011] Q.B. 357, per Sir Mark Potter P at [47]. Interest can be awarded on the damages: *Metal Box Ltd v Currys Ltd* [1988] 1 W.L.R. 175; para.27-67.

[578] In accordance with the Torts (Interference with Goods) Act 1977 ss.7–8, a claimant with only a limited interest in the goods will normally not be allowed to recover more than the value of that interest: paras 16-85 and 16-95 onwards.

[579] *Clyde Navigation Trustees v Bowring* (1929) 34 Ll. L.R. 319; *Thatcher v Littlejohn* [1978] R.T.R. 369; *Dominion Mosaics and Tile Co Ltd v Trafalgar Trucking Co Ltd* [1990] 2 All E.R. 246 (paternoster machines). In *Bacon v Cooper (Metals) Ltd* [1982] 1 All E.R. 397, a contract case, the claimant was awarded the hire-purchase cost of a replacement chattel. Allowance must always be made for any salvage value of the article destroyed: *Thatcher v Littlejohn* [1978] R.T.R. 369 at 370.

[580] *Moore v DER Ltd* [1971] 1 W.L.R. 1476; *Stone v Fulleylove* [1985] C.L.Y. 929. See paras 27-123

place of the loss, and this means, at least in the case of ships, that regard must be had to existing and pending engagements.[581] In the leading case of *Liesbosch Dredger v S.S. Edison*,[582] where the claimants' dredger was sunk while engaged under contract in dredging operations in Patras harbour; the claimants were held entitled not only to the cost of a comparable dredger and of its adaptation and transport to Patras but also to compensation for disturbance and loss in carrying out the contract over the period of delay between the loss of the dredger and the time at which the substituted dredger could reasonably have been made available.

27-118 In *The Maersk Colombo*[583] the claimants' crane had been demolished by the defendants' negligence. It was decided that, contrary to the normal rule, the claimants were entitled as damages only to the resale value of the crane (£665,000) and not its replacement value (£2,359,484). The replacement value was so much higher because a second-hand crane would have had to be modified in, and transported from, the US to Southampton. The crucial factor in determining that that higher sum should not be awarded was that the claimants, prior to the accident, had already ordered a larger crane to replace the one damaged and therefore had no intention, after the accident, of buying another crane to replace the damaged one. In an excellent leading judgment, Clarke LJ analysed the main contract and tort cases on the question of whether damages should be based on difference in value or cost of replacement/reinstatement and explained that, in deciding between them, the important factors included reasonableness and intention. In rejecting an argument that there are distinct rules applying to tortious destruction of goods, he said[584]: "In my opinion a similar approach applies to the measure of damages for the tortious destruction of chattels as it applies to the measure of damages for both the tortious destruction of real property and for breach of contract in circumstances such as those in *Ruxley*."[585]

27-119 Where damages for loss of use are claimed, care must be taken to avoid duplication. If the market value of a ship reflects the fact that it is in any case virtually certain of profitable employment, then nothing can be added to that value in respect of charters actually lost,[586] for to do so would be pro tanto to compensate the claimant twice over. On the other hand, if the ship is valued without reference to its actual future engagements and only in the light of its profit-earning potential, then it may be necessary to add to the value thus assessed the anticipated profit on

---

to 27-124.

581 *Liesbosch Dredger v S.S. Edison* [1933] A.C. 449 at 464, per Lord Wright; *Jones v Port of London Authority* [1954] 1 Lloyd's Rep. 489.

582 [1933] A.C. 449. But what was said in *The Liesbosch* about loss flowing from impecuniosity being irrecoverable was departed from in *Lagden v O'Connor* [2003] UKHL 64; [2004] 1 A.C. 1067. See paras 2-180 and 27-10.

583 [2001] EWCA Civ 717; [2001] 2 Lloyd's Rep. 275. This was followed in *Ali Reza-Delta Transport Co Ltd v United Arab Shipping Co* [2003] EWCA Civ 684; [2003] 2 Lloyd's Rep 450 in which damages were based on the market selling price (of similar goods in Saudi Arabia where they had been tortiously destroyed) rather than the replacement costs; there was no evidence that the claimants had replaced, or would replace, the destroyed goods. In *Aerospace Publishing Ltd v Thames Water Utilities* [2007] EWCA Civ 3; [2007] N.P.C. 5 the principles in *The Maersk Colombo* were applied, albeit that a different conclusion was reached, in holding that, following the destruction of a photographic archive by flood water, damages should be awarded based on the cost of reinstating the archive rather than its diminution in value.

584 [2001] EWCA Civ 717; [2001] 2 Lloyd's Rep. 275 at [43].

585 *Ruxley Electronics & Construction Ltd v Forsyth* [1996] A.C. 334 HL.

586 *The Llanover* [1947] P. 80.

a charter or other engagement which it was unable to fulfil.[587] What the court has to ascertain in each case is the "capitalised value of the vessel as a profit-earning machine, not in the abstract but in view of the actual circumstances",[588] without, of course, taking into account considerations which were too remote at the time of the loss.[589]

(b) Damage to goods

The basic rule in the case of damage to goods is that the claimant is entitled to recover damages to the extent to which the value of the chattel has been reduced: this will usually be ascertained by reference to the cost of repair.[590] The cost will be ascertained as at the time when it was reasonable in the particular circumstances of the case for the claimant to have the chattel repaired.[591] It does not matter that the repairs have not been carried out at the date of the trial[592] or even that they are never carried out at all, for example if the damaged goods are lost before repair.[593] Nor is it a bar to damages being recoverable for the cost of repairs that the claimant has no legal liability to pay the repair costs because they are covered by a consumer credit agreement that is unenforceable against the claimant.[594] In *Coles v Hetherton*[595] it was held that, where it is reasonable to repair a damaged car, a claimant is entitled to damages for the reasonable cost of repairing the car even though the actual cost of the repairs, whether incurred by the claimant or his insurer, are lower. The Court of Appeal reasoned that the reasonable cost of repair represents the diminution in value of the car; and that while the duty to mitigate applies to a consequential loss, it is irrelevant to that direct loss (the diminution in the value of the car), which is suffered as soon as the car is damaged and cannot be mitigated. This may be thought controversial because one appears to be compensating the claimant for more than the loss suffered. Where it is unreasonable as between claimant and defendant for the chattel to be repaired rather than replaced, as where the article is neither unique nor irreplaceable and the cost of the repair greatly exceeds the replacement cost of the chattel itself, then the claimant cannot recover more than the replacement cost.[596] Similarly, it is submitted that the cost of repairing a ship could not be recovered if at the time the damage was caused she was on her way 27-120

587 *The Kate* [1899] P. 165; *The Racine* [1906] P. 273; *The Philadelphia* [1917] P. 101; *The Fortunity* [1961] 1 W.L.R. 351. See, generally, Knott [1993] L.M.C.L.Q. 502.

588 *Liesbosch Dredger v S.S. Edison* [1933] A.C. 449, per Lord Wright at 464.

589 *Liesbosch Dredger v S.S. Edison* [1933] A.C. 449 at 465. See also *The Arpad* [1934] P. 189, per Greer LJ at 217.

590 *The London Corp* [1935] P. 70.

591 *Dodd Properties (Kent) Ltd v Canterbury City Council* [1980] 1 W.L.R. 433.

592 *The Kingsway* [1918] P. 344. In *Ironfield v Eastern Gas Board* [1964] 1 W.L.R. 1125n. the cost of repair of a damaged motorcar was borne by the owner's insurers, but the owner was obliged to pay £10 for the excess insurance on the car and also lost his "no claims bonus". It was held that damages in respect of both these items of loss could be recovered.

593 *The York* [1929] P. 178, per Scrutton LJ at 184–185; *The London Corp* [1935] P. 70.

594 *Burdis v Livsey* [2002] EWCA Civ 510; [2003] Q.B. 36. For criticism of this decision, not least for being inconsistent with the denial of hire costs in *Dimond v Lovell* [2002] 1 A.C. 384 HL; see Burrows, *Remedies for Torts, Breach of Contract and Equitable Wrongs*, 4th edn (2019) pp.212-214.

595 [2013] EWCA Civ 1704; [2015] 1 W.L.R. 160.

596 *Darbishire v Warran* [1963] 1 W.L.R. 1067; cf. *O'Grady v Westminster Scaffolding Ltd* [1962] 2 Lloyd's Rep. 238. Similar principles apply to damage to buildings: *Moss v Christchurch Rural DC* [1925] 2 K.B. 750: *Hole & Son (Sayers Common) v Harrisons of Thurnscoe* [1973] 1 Lloyd's Rep. 345; *Taylor (Wholesale) v Hepworths* [1977] 1 W.L.R. 659; *Farmer Giles Ltd v Wessex Water Authority* [1988] 2 E.G.L.R. 189. But the reinstatement measure may nevertheless be awarded where

to the breakers' yard, but only the diminution in the value of the ship as scrap. If the claimant proves a reduction in the value of the chattel due to its having had to be repaired, damages may be recovered over and above the cost of the repair.[597]

27-121 In addition to having to pay the cost of repairing his damaged goods the owner will also be deprived of their use during the period needed for their repair, and for this loss he is entitled to recover. The question is what is the use which, but for the wrong, he would have had of his goods, and what (excluding the element of uncertain and speculative and special profits) he would otherwise have earned by their use.[598] Thus, profits which would in any event have been lost because, for example, other necessary repairs were to be carried out are not recoverable.[599]

27-122 It is generally reasonable for the owner of a damaged chattel to avoid any loss of profits by hiring a substitute for the period during which his own is under repair, in which case he is entitled to recover the cost of hiring as damages for loss of use.[600] This is, however, subject to two qualifications, namely, that the actual hiring of a substitute must be strictly pleaded and proved as special damage[601] and that the hiring must be reasonable.[602] The principle is that the claimant may recover what his chattel would have earned if it had not been damaged, not that he may recover such out-of-pocket expenses as he may actually have incurred,[603] and if, for example, the cost of hiring exceeds the profit which could have been earned, only the latter may be recovered.[604] Moreover if, as a result of hiring a substitute the owner of the damaged chattel is enabled to make a greater profit than he would have

---

the court considers that it is reasonable to have the property reinstated (e.g. because the claimant is resident there) and this is the claimant's intention: *Hollebone v Midhurst and Fernhurst Building Ltd* [1968] 1 Lloyd's Rep. 38; *Dodd Properties (Kent) Ltd v Canterbury City Council* [1980] 1 W.L.R. 433 at 456-457, per Donaldson LJ; *Ward v Cannock Chase DC* [1986] Ch. 546; cf. *Dominion Mosaics Tile Co Ltd v Trafalgar Trucking Co Ltd* [1990] 2 All E.R. 246 (cost of leasing property elsewhere awarded). See also the following contract cases: *Radford v De Froberville* [1977] 1 W.L.R. 1262; *Tito v Waddell (No.2)* [1977] Ch. 106 at 328–338; *Miniscombe Properties Ltd v Sir Alfred McAlpine* (1986) 279 E.G. 759; *Dean v Ainley* [1987] 1 W.L.R. 1729; *Ruxley Electronics Construction Ltd v Forsyth* [1996] A.C. 344 HL.

597 *Payton v Brooks* [1974] R.T.R. 169.

598 *The Argentino* (1888) 13 P. & D. 191; affirmed (1889) 14 App. Cas. 519; *The Kate* [1899] P. 165; *Admiralty Commissioners v S.S. Valeria* [1922] 2 A.C. 242; *The Fortunity* [1961] 1 W.L.R. 351; *The Naxos* [1972] 1 Lloyd's Rep. 149. cf. *The Pacific Concord* [1961] 1 W.L.R. 873. See also *Bacon v Cooper (Metals) Ltd* [1982] 1 All E.R. 397.

599 *Admiralty Commissioners v S.S. Chekiang* [1926] A.C. 637; *The York* [1929] P. 178; *Carslogie Steamship Co v Royal Norwegian Government* [1952] A.C. 292; *Edmund Handcock (1929) v The Ernesto (Owners)* [1952] 1 Lloyd's Rep. 467; *The Hassel* [1962] 2 Lloyd's Rep. 139; *The Ferdinand Retzlaff* [1972] 2 Lloyd's Rep. 120; *Elpidoforos Shipping Corp v Furness Withy (Australia) Pty Ltd* [1987] 1 Lloyd's Rep. 258.

600 *Macrae v Swindells* [1954] 1 W.L.R. 597; *The Hebridean Coast* [1961] A.C. 545; *Moore v DER Ltd* [1971] 1 W.L.R. 1476; *Martindale v Duncan* [1973] 1 W.L.R. 574; *Daily Office Cleaning Contractors Ltd v Shefford* [1977] R.T.R. 361.

601 *S.S. Strathfillan v S.S. Ikala* [1929] A.C. 196; *The Hebridean Coast* [1961] A.C. 545.

602 See *Moore v DER Ltd* [1971] 1 W.L.R. 1476; *Martindale v Duncan* [1973] 1 W.L.R. 574; *Daily Office Cleaning Contractors Ltd v Shefford* [1977] R.T.R. 361.

603 *Admiralty Commissioners v S.S. Valeria* [1922] 2 A.C. 242; *Dixons (Scholars Green) Ltd v JL Cooper Ltd* [1970] R.T.R. 222.

604 Street, *Principles of the Law of Damages*, p.207; *Hussain v EUI Ltd* [2019] EWHC 2647 (QB); [2020] R.T.R. 7 (though even where the cost of hire significantly exceeds the avoided loss of profit it remains open to a claimant to prove that she acted reasonably in incurring hire charges: [2019] EWHC 2647 (QB); [2020] R.T.R. 7 at [16.6] per Pepperall J). For a different example of unreasonable hiring, see *Watson Norie v Shaw* [1967] 1 Lloyd's Rep. 515.

done if his own chattel had not been damaged, that additional profit must be set against his loss.[605]

Even in the case of non-profit-earning chattels the claimant may be entitled to damages for loss of use. This was laid down in a series of cases concerning ships,[606] but the principle applies equally to chattels of all kinds.[607] As Earl Halsbury LC said, in a famous passage[608]: "Supposing a person took away a chair out of my room and kept it for twelve months, could anybody say you had a right to diminish the damages by shewing that I did not usually sit in that chair, or that there were plenty of other chairs in the room? The proposition so nakedly stated appears to me to be absurd." So, for example, in *The Mediana*[609] damages were awarded to a harbour board for the loss of use of one of their lightships which had been damaged by the defendant's negligence, even though the lightship was replaced immediately by a spare one which was kept by the board for just such an emergency. **27-123**

Damages for the loss of use of a non-profit-earning chattel cannot, of course, be assessed by reference to loss of profits, and even if the chattel in question is one which could be put to a commercial use, its hypothetical profit-earning capacity in other hands is immaterial.[610] If a substitute has been hired, then the cost can be recovered, provided that the chattel hired and the sum paid were both reasonable.[611] So in *Bee v Jensen*,[612] hire costs incurred by the claimant's insurer[613] were held recoverable by the claimant from the tortfeasor because they were reasonable costs for a car that had been reasonably hired. This was so even though some of those costs included payments which went beyond the strict hire costs and included a sum paid by the hiring company to an affiliated company of the insurer. In another of the "credit hire" cases, *Stevens v Equity Syndicate Management Ltd*,[614] it was held that a claimant who is not impecunious is entitled only to the basic hire rate (i.e. the locally available rate for cars in the same group as the claimant's car) and not **27-124**

---

605 *The World Beauty* [1969] P. 12 (reversed in part, without affecting this point [1970] P. 144).

606 *The Greta Holme* [1897] A.C. 596; *The Mediana* [1900] A.C. 113; *The Marpessa* [1907] A.C. 241; *Admiralty Commissioners v S.S. Chekiang* [1926] A.C. 637; *Admiralty Commissioners v S.S. Susquehanna* [1926] A.C. 655; *The Hebridean Coast* [1961] A.C. 545.

607 *Birmingham Corp v Sowsbery* (1969) 113 S.J. 877; Yell, "Damages for loss of use of a motor vehicle" (1982–83) 2 Lit. 3; *Giles v Thompson* [1994] 1 A.C. 142; *Beechwood Birmingham Ltd v Hoyer Group UK Ltd* [2010] EWCA Civ 647; [2011] Q.B. 357; *West Midlands Travel Ltd v Aviva Insurance UK Ltd* [2013] EWCA Civ 887; [2014] R.T.R. 10. cf. *Alexander v Rolls Royce Motor Cars Ltd* [1996] R.T.R. 95 CA, in which damages for loss of use of a Rolls Royce car were refused because the claimant had other cars and there was no evidence of inconvenience or loss of enjoyment while repairs to the car were being carried out (or awaited).

608 *The Mediana* [1900] A.C. 113 at 117.

609 [1900] A.C. 113.

610 *Admiralty Commissioners v S.S. Susquehanna* [1926] A.C. 655. (Admiralty oil tanker. Damage for loss of use not to be assessed by reference to what such a tanker could have earned in commercial employment.) See also *The Hebridean Coast* [1961] A.C. 545 at 562, per Devlin LJ.

611 *HL Motorworks (Willesden) Ltd v Alwahbi* [1977] R.T.R. 276 (reasonable to hire a Rolls Royce while the claimant's own Rolls Royce was being repaired); *Stone v Fulleylove* [1985] C.L.Y. 929. In *McAll v Brooks* [1984] R.T.R. 99 CA, on an analogy with the personal injury case of *Donnelly v Joyce* [1974] Q.B. 454 (para.27-26), hiring charges were awarded even where a third party and not the claimant had incurred them; see, similarly, *Giles v Thompson* [1994] 1 A.C. 142. But in the light of *Hunt v Severs* [1994] 2 A.C. 350 HL (para.27-27), *McAll v Brooks* was not followed in *Dimond v Lovell* [2002] 1 A.C. 384, HL.

612 [2007] EWCA Civ 923; [2007] 4 All E.R. 791.

613 Applying the normal approach to insurance, established in *Bradburn v Great Western Ry* (1874) L.R. 10 Ex.1, the fact that it was the insurer, rather than the claimant, who bore the hire costs was irrelevant to the assessment of the damages.

614 [2015] EWCA Civ 93; [2015] 4 All E.R. 458.

a higher rate, which confers additional benefits, charged by a credit hire company. In *Beechwood Birmingham Ltd v Hoyer Group UK Ltd*,[615] it was held that the claimant company should have mitigated its loss by replacing the damaged car from its stock, rather than hiring in a replacement, during the period while the car was being repaired. But while the cost of hire could not therefore be recovered, damages for loss of use were awarded and these were to be measured by the interest on the capital value of a car of the type damaged, plus depreciation, over the repair period. Otherwise the method of assessment will vary according to the circumstances of the case. In *The Mediana*[616] the parties had agreed to an assessment of damages based upon the cost to the harbour board of maintaining the spare lightship; in *The Marpessa*,[617] where a non-profit-making dredger belonging to a harbour board was put out of service, the House of Lords considered that the right basis was the daily cost of maintaining and operating the dredger, plus depreciation. In *West Midlands Travel Ltd v Aviva Insurance UK Ltd*,[618] where a bus company was able to replace the damaged bus, during the repair period, from its spare capacity (i.e. it operated its buses in such a way that a damaged bus could be replaced) it was held that damages for loss of use should be assessed during the repair period according to the capital tied up in the damaged bus, the wasted expenses, and depreciation. No single method of assessment can be appropriate for all cases,[619] but in the ultimate resort, if no other basis reveals itself, the claimant may be entitled at least to interest on the capital value of his chattel for the period it is out of use.[620]

(c) Betterment

27-125 The courts have sometimes been criticised for purportedly leaving the claimant overcompensated by not deducting from the full repair or replacement cost of property damaged or destroyed by the defendant's tort (or breach of contract) an amount for "betterment"; that is, for the fact that the replacement or repaired property is in a better condition than the property before it was damaged or destroyed. The classic example is *The Gazelle*[621] where the claimant's ship was damaged in a collision with the defendant's ship caused by the defendant's negligence. In the claimant's action for damages for the costs of repairing his ship and replacing items destroyed, the assessors of the damages had deducted one-third from those costs because the claimant was getting new for old. But Dr

---

615 [2010] EWCA Civ 647; [2011] Q.B. 357.

616 [1900] A.C. 113.

617 [1907] A.C. 241; *Birmingham Corp v Sowsberry* (1969) 113 S.J. 877.

618 [2013] EWCA Civ 887; [2014] R.T.R. 10.

619 *Admiralty Commissioners v S.S. Chekiang* [1926] A.C. 637, per Viscount Dunedin at 642, per Lord Sumner at 649; *Admiralty Commissioners v S.S. Susquehanna* [1926] A.C. 655, per Viscount Dunedin at 662.

620 *Admiralty Commissioners v S.S. Chekiang* [1926] A.C. 637; *The Hebridean Coast* [1961] A.C. 545 at 562. In view of the difficulty of determining the capital value of some non-profit-earning chattels (e.g. warships: see *Admiralty Commissioners v S.S. Chekiang*, above, per Lord Sumner at 647–648) this is a much less exact measure than might at first appear. There may, however, be no other possible course but to use it with all its disadvantages: *The Hebridean Coast*, above, per Lord Reid at 578.

621 (1844) 2 Wm. Rob. 279. See also *The Pactolus* (1856) Swab. 173 at 174–175, per Dr Lushington; *The Munster* (1896) 12 T.L.R. 264 at 265, per Jeune P; *Dominican Mosaics & Tile Co Ltd v Trafalgar Trucking Co Ltd* [1990] 2 All E.R. 246. See also the following contract cases: *Harbutt's Plasticine Ltd v Wayne Tank and Pump Co Ltd* [1970] 1 Q.B. 447; *Bacon v Cooper (Metals) Ltd* [1982] 1 All E.R. 397.

Lushington overruled this. He said, " … if that party derives incidentally a greater benefit than mere indemnification, it arises only from the impossibility of otherwise effecting such indemnification without exposing him to some loss or burden, which the law will not place upon him".[622] But it is strongly arguable that *The Gazelle* and other cases following it did not necessarily contradict the compensatory principle because it was not clear that the betterment represented a real benefit to the claimant. In *The Gazelle* the claimant would only realise a gain from the betterment if the ship were to be sold and there was little likelihood of that. A principled approach, which accepts that a betterment which constitutes a clear and real benefit will be deducted in assessing damages, was adopted by the Court of Appeal in *Voaden v Champion (The Baltic Surveyor)*.[623] The claimant's pontoon had been sunk and lost by reason of the defendant's negligence. At first instance Colman J had awarded £16,000 in respect of the pontoon on the basis that a replacement would have cost £60,000 and had a life of 30 years but the old pontoon only had eight years of life left in it. He therefore awarded 8/30ths of £60,000. That deduction for "betterment" was upheld by the Court of Appeal as being correct in principle (albeit that Colman J's view that his approach only applied where one was concerned with replacement rather than repair was doubted). Provided the new for old constituted a true (pecuniary) benefit to the claimant, it should be deducted.

7. Recovery of Costs of Action[624]

A successful claimant cannot bring a fresh action against the defendant in order to recover as damages his "extra costs", that is, the difference between the costs which the defendant was ordered to pay and the costs actually incurred, nor can he claim such damages in the original action.[625] In general, this is an obvious restriction.[626] But the justification is less obvious where the bringing of the previous proceedings constituted, or involved, a tort and the claimant seeks damages for that tort. This issue is of importance to malicious prosecution and kindred torts.[627] In *Quartz Hill Gold Mining Co v Eyre*[628] the Court of Appeal held that the incurring of "extra costs" was not such damage as would support an action for the malicious presentation of a winding-up petition, and in *Berry v British Transport Commission*[629] Diplock J, at first instance, held that the same was true for malicious prosecution where the claimant had been awarded costs against the prosecutor, even though the amount awarded was less than the amount reasonably expended on the defence. The Court of Appeal, however, refused to extend that rule to costs in **27-126**

622 (1844) 2 Wm. Rob. 279 at 281.

623 [2002] EWCA Civ 89; [2002] 1 Lloyd's Rep. 623.

624 For an excellent analysis of this area, see Louise Merrett, "Costs as Damages" (2009) 125 L.Q.R. 468.

625 *Cockburn v Edwards* (1881) 18 Ch. D. 449; *Quartz Hill Gold Mining v Eyre* (1883) 11 Q.B.D. 674; *Berry v British Transport Commission* [1962] 1 Q.B. 306; *Ross v Caunters (A Firm)* [1980] Ch. 297 at 323-324; *The Ocean Dynamic* [1982] 2 Lloyd's Rep. 88; *Lonrho Plc v Fayed (No.5)* [1994] 1 W.L.R. 1489 CA.

626 Edelman, *McGregor on Damages*, 20th edn (2017), para.21-003: "It would make nonsense of the rules about costs if the successful party in an action who has been awarded costs could claim in a further action by way of damages the amount by which the costs awarded him fell short of the costs actually incurred by him."

627 e.g. conspiracy as in *Lonrho v Fayed (No.5)* [1993] 1 W.L.R. 1489.

628 (1883) 11 Q.B.D. 674.

629 [1961] 1 Q.B. 149.

criminal cases.[630] Diplock J's decision on this point was, accordingly, reversed and the position is, therefore, that "extra costs" incurred by persons accused of criminal offences do constitute legal damage and so may be claimed by them in actions against persons whose wrongful acts caused them to be incurred. Another exception to the rule is where, in breach of contract, a litigant has brought proceedings in a jurisdiction where no costs are normally recoverable: the innocent party is entitled to recover, as damages for breach of contract, the costs of having the action struck out by the foreign court.[631] The main justification for the rule denying damages for the "extra costs" incurred in previous civil proceedings is that "extra costs" cannot be accepted as legal damage[632] because the costs awarded are all that were reasonably incurred for the purposes of the litigation: if a successful litigant has been awarded his costs he cannot be heard to say that the litigation itself caused him any loss.[633] In the past this has been regarded as fictitious[634] but in *Lonrho v Fayed (No.5)*[635] Evans LJ said: "That fiction has now largely disappeared[636] ... It is no longer necessary, therefore, to regret the common law rule, and in addition there are other reasons of policy which continue to support it, not least the desirability of bringing litigation to a close."

27-127 The position has traditionally been different where the claimant has in previous proceedings been held liable to a third party as a result of the defendant's wrongful act and now seeks to recover from the defendant the damages and costs which he has had to pay. In this situation he has been held entitled, inter alia, to "extra costs", i.e. to such costs as he has reasonably incurred over and above any costs awarded.[637] But this different approach in respect of costs incurred in respect of proceedings by a third party was doubted in *British Racing Drivers' Club Ltd v*

---

630 [1962] 1 Q.B. 306. See also *Savill v Roberts* (1698) 12 Mod. 208. Note Devlin LJ's suggestion that there should be one standard of costs as between litigants and another when those costs form a legitimate item of damage in a separate cause of action flowing from a different and additional wrong: [1962] 1 Q.B. 306 at 322.

631 *Union Discount Co Ltd v Zoller* [2001] EWCA Civ 1755; [2002] 1 W.L.R. 1517. In *National Westminster Bank Plc v Rabobank Nederland (No.3)* [2007] EWHC 1742 (Comm); [2008] 1 All E.R. (Comm) 243, it was held that costs compensated by a damages award, where there had been a breach of a jurisdiction or anti-suit clause by bringing proceedings in a foreign court, could include costs that in England would be assessed on an indemnity basis and not merely on a standard basis. This was because, applying the normal principle of damages, the limit to the recovery of damages for costs was provided by the duty to mitigate which was consistent with the recovery of indemnity costs (the key feature of which is that the burden of proving that the costs were reasonably incurred is on the paying party).

632 *Doe v Davis* (1795) 1 Esp. 358; *Hathaway v Barrow* (1807) 1 Camp. 151; *Sinclair v Eldred* (1811) 4 Taunt. 7; *Jenkins v Biddulph* (1827) 4 Bing. 160; *Grace v Morgan* (1836) 2 Bing. N.C. 534. Cf. *Agius v Great Western Colliery Co* [1899] 1 Q.B. 413; *The Solway Prince* (1914) 3 T.L.R. 56.

633 *Quartz Hill Gold Mining Co v Eyre* (1883) 11 Q.B.D. 674 at 682-683, per Brett MR; at 690, per Bowen LJ.

634 See *Berry v British Transport Commission* [1962] 1 Q.B. 306 at 320–323, per Devlin LJ; at 336, per Danckwerts LJ. Blackburn J spoke of the rule as "artificial" as long ago as 1869; *Wren v Weild (No.2)* (1869) L.R. 4 Q.B. 730 at 736.

635 [1993] 1 W.L.R. 1489 at 1511. See also per Stuart-Smith LJ at 1506–1507.

636 This was because, at the time of Evans LJ's judgment, the amount recoverable on taxation under RSC Ord.62, r.12 was "a reasonable amount in respect of all costs reasonably incurred" (the standard basis) or "all costs ... except insofar as they are of an unreasonable amount or have been unreasonably incurred" (the indemnity basis). But see now CPR r.44.4, which, for costs assessed on the standard basis, introduces an additional test of proportionality.

637 *Berry v British Transport Commission* [1962] 1 Q.B. 306 at 321, per Devlin LJ. Such cases usually arise out of breaches of contract. See, e.g. *Hammond Co v Bussey* (1887) 20 Q.B.D. 79; *Agius v Great Western Colliery Co* [1899] 1 Q.B. 413.

Hextall Erskine Co[638] where the claimant had settled a previous action brought by it against third parties on terms by which the claimant and the third parties were to pay their own costs. The claimant now brought an action for negligent advice against its solicitors and claimed, as damages, those costs. Carnwath J held that they were entitled only to what they would have been awarded as costs and not their full costs. He said:

> "The expenditure on the professional fees of solicitors and accountants was, as I have held, expenditure incurred by the [claimants] in reasonably mitigating their loss. Prima facie therefore, it is claimable under the ordinary rules relating to mitigation. However, litigation costs have traditionally been subject to special rules for policy reasons. Prior to the change in the taxation rules there was an established distinction between such costs incurred in proceedings between the same parties, and those incurred in proceedings against third parties. This was anomalous, given that similar policy considerations applied in each case. The most recent cases show that the position must be reconsidered in the light of the changes to the taxation rules. This enables the anomaly to be resolved … Accordingly, where costs on the standard basis have been recovered from the defendant in other proceedings, there is no basis for an additional claim by way of damages. In principle the same reasoning must in my view apply where, as in this case, the other proceedings have been settled on terms that each side pays his own costs. The present defendant should not be worse off, in respect of the basis of taxation, because no order for costs was made in the other proceedings."[639]

8. Equitable Damages

Jurisdiction to award damages[640] In any case in which a cause of action at common law has accrued the claimant is entitled to damages and if, for any reason, his claim for an injunction is rejected his claim for damages will nevertheless succeed. Such a situation is to be distinguished from that in which the court grants damages in *substitution* for an injunction. Section 2 of the Chancery Amendment Act 1858 (Lord Cairns' Act) conferred on the Court of Chancery the power to award damages in addition to or in substitution for an injunction in all cases in which it had jurisdiction to entertain an application for an injunction. The object of this provision might have been to prevent a litigant being "bandied about from one court to another",[641] for if an injunction was refused the claimant need no longer apply to a common law court for damages. On this limited view, the provisions became superfluous when, following the Judicature Act 1873,[642] both law and equity were administered in the same court. But the jurisdiction to award equitable damages in **27-128**

638 [1996] 3 All E.R. 667. See also *Lonrho v Fayed (No.5)* [1993] 1 W.L.R. 1489 at 1511, in which Evans LJ said, "[n]ow that the fiction has become largely fact … it is questionable whether the right to recover so-called extra costs is still justified, even when the claim is made against a third party to the original action".

639 [1996] 3 All E.R. 667 at 691.

640 Jolowicz [1975] C.L.J. 224; Wakefield and Ingham [1981] Conv. 286. For equitable damages for the equitable wrong of breach of confidence, see Ch.26. For the different remedy of equitable compensation awarded for, e.g. breach of fiduciary duty, see *Nocton v Lord Ashburton* [1941] A.C. 932 HL; *Target Holdings v Redfern* [1996] A.C. 421 HL; *Bristol & West Building Society v Mothew* [1998] Ch. 1 CA; *Swindle v Harrison* [1997] 4 All E.R. 705 CA; *Gwembe Valley Development Co Ltd v Koshy* [2003] EWCA Civ 1048; [2004] 1 B.C.L.C. 131.

641 *Ferguson v Wilson* (1866) 2 Ch. App.77 at 82, per Turner LJ.

642 Judicature Act 1873, re-enacted as Senior Courts Act 1981 s.49.

lieu of an injunction was preserved[643] and is now embodied in s.50 of the Senior Courts Act 1981. The significant effect is that a claimant may be awarded damages for a cause of action which has not yet accrued but is only apprehended.[644]

27-129 The scope of the jurisdiction remains, however, problematic. On one view,[645] equitable damages cannot be awarded unless the court considers that an injunction *should* be granted. But this would lead to "the *reductio ad absurdum* that the jurisdiction to award damages under the Act exists only when, by definition, it should not be exercised".[646] The correct approach therefore seems to be that suggested in *Hooper v Rogers*,[647] that the jurisdiction to award damages in lieu of an injunction exists where the court *could* have granted an injunction "however unwisely".[648] If, then, on the rules discussed in the next chapter,[649] the court may grant an injunction, but, having regard to all the circumstances, exercises its discretion not to do so, it should next consider whether to award damages under s.50 of the 1981 Act.

27-130 According to a series of judicial pronouncements,[650] the traditional approach has been that the discretion to award damages under the Act should be exercised sparingly. This is because the award of damages in substitution for an injunction restraining future injury may obviously have the result that the defendant is allowed to purchase the right to inflict an injury upon the claimant. Guidelines on the circumstances in which such damages might nevertheless be awarded emerge from several authorities. In *Shelfer v City of London Electrical Lighting Co*[651] A.L. Smith LJ stated the "good working rule that: (1) if the injury to the [claimant's] legal rights is small; (2) and is one which is capable of being estimated in money; (3) and is one which can be adequately compensated by a money payment; (4) and the case is one in which it would be oppressive to the defendant to grant an injunction: then damages in substitution for an injunction may be given". The rule has been followed in many cases[652] although it has sometimes been criticised as being too

---

[643] Supreme Court of Judicature Act 1873 s.16 and Statute Law Revision Act 1898 s.1. See *Leeds Industrial Co-operative Society Ltd v Slack* [1924] A.C. 851.

[644] *Leeds Industrial Co-operative Society Ltd v Slack* [1924] A.C. 851.

[645] This is implicit in the speech of Lord Upjohn in *Redland Bricks Ltd v Morris* [1970] A.C. 652 at 655.

[646] Jolowicz [1975] C.L.J. 224 at 240.

[647] [1975] Ch. 43.

[648] [1975] Ch. 43 at 48, per Russell LJ.

[649] See paras 28-06 to 28-22. Problems undoubtedly arise in deciding whether a defence to a claim for an injunction goes to jurisdiction or to the exercise of the discretion. The courts tend to prefer the latter, thus retaining the possibility of awarding equitable damages: *Price v Strange* [1978] Ch. 337 (lack of mutuality in a claim for specific performance). See also *Johnson v Agnew* [1978] Ch. 176, allowing such damages even though specific performance had become impossible: it had been possible when the proceedings were begun. The point did not arise for decision in the House of Lords: [1980] A.C. 367.

[650] *Shelfer v City of London Electric Lighting Co* [1895] 1 Ch. 287 at 315–316, per Lindley LJ; [1895] 1 Ch. 287 at 322, per A.L. Smith LJ; *Cowper v Laidler* [1903] 2 Ch. 337 at 341, per Buckley J; *Leeds Industrial Co-operative Society Ltd v Slack* [1924] A.C. 851 at 861, per Viscount Finlay; *Slack v Leeds Industrial Co-operative Society Ltd* [1924] 2 Ch. 475 at 485, per Pollock MR.

[651] [1895] 1 Ch. 287 at 322.

[652] e.g. *Price v Hilditch* [1930] 1 Ch. 500; *Kelsen v Imperial Tobacco Co (of Great Britain and Ireland) Ltd* [1957] 2 Q.B. 334; *Morris v Redland Bricks Ltd* [1967] 1 W.L.R. 967 (reversed on grounds not affecting the point [1970] A.C. 652); *Kennaway v Thompson* [1981] Q.B. 88; *Elliott v Islington LBC* [1991] 10 E.G. 145; *Jaggard v Sawyer* [1995] 1 W.L.R. 269 CA; *Regan v Paul Properties DPF (No.1) Ltd* [2006] EWCA Civ 1391; [2007] Ch. 135; *Watson v Croft Promosport Ltd* [2009] EWCA Civ 15; [2009] 3 All E.R. 249; *Hkruk II (CHC) Ltd v Heaney* [2010] EWHC 2245 (Ch); [2010] 3 E.G.L.R. 15.

specific or rigid.[653] It has been suggested that the conduct of the defendant may be a relevant factor in inclining the court against the award of damages: "if he has endeavoured to steal a march upon the [claimant] or to evade the jurisdiction of the court"[654]; or if he "knew he was doing wrong, and was taking his chance about being disturbed in doing it".[655] Conversely, some judges have clearly not thought it essential that all of A.L. Smith LJ's conditions be satisfied to justify awarding damages. They have been prepared to do this where the harm resulting to the defendant from the injunction would be out of all proportion to the injury inflicted on the claimant.[656] Other circumstances which have been said to justify an award under the Act are: where "the [claimant] has shown that he only wants money"[657]; where there is "really a question" as to whether the claimant's rights have been infringed and the defendant has acted "fairly and not in an unneighbourly spirit"[658]; and where the claimant has to some degree acquiesced in the wrongdoing but not so as to deprive himself of a remedy altogether.[659]

In *Coventry v Lawrence*,[660] the Supreme Court, in the context of the tort of private nuisance, looked afresh at the award of damages in lieu of an injunction. The leading judgment was given by Lord Neuberger. His Lordship indicated that, at least in relation to private nuisance, the courts should be more willing than has generally been the case in the past to award damages in lieu of an injunction; and that the *Shelfer* criteria should not be rigidly applied. Moreover, the public interest should always be a relevant factor in deciding whether to award damages rather than an injunction for private nuisance, as sometimes should be the fact that planning permission has been granted to the defendant. **27-131**

Although reversed on liability by the House of Lords,[661] there was a very interesting discussion at first instance of the power to award equitable damages in *Marcic v Thames Water Utilities Ltd (No.2)*.[662] The claimant owned property that was regularly subject to flooding. In an action against the defendant, a sewerage undertaker, the claimant sought damages and a mandatory injunction ordering the defendant to implement a scheme to stop the flooding. Judge Richard Havery QC held that the defendant was liable—it was this aspect of his decision that was held to be incorrect by the House of Lords—for the wrong of infringing the claimant's Convention rights under the Human Rights Act 1998 s.6. However, he refused a mandatory injunction on the ground that this would require supervision by the court, but held that damages should be awarded for both past and future wrongs. The claimant was therefore entitled to the difference between the value his property **27-132**

---

653 Especially in *Fishenden v Higgs and Hill Ltd* (1935) 153 L.T. 128 at 138, per Hanworth MR; at 141, per Romer LJ; at 144, per Maugham LJ. See also *Colls v Home and Colonial Stores Ltd* [1904] A.C. 179 at 212-213, per Lord Lindley, and *Woollerton and Wilson Ltd v Richard Costain Ltd* [1970] 1 W.L.R. 411 at 414, per Stamp J.

654 *Colls v Home and Colonial Stores Ltd* [1904] A.C. 179, per Lord Macnaghten at 193. See also *Pugh v Howells* (1984) 48 P. & C.R. 298 CA.

655 *Smith v Smith* (1875) L.R. 20 Eq. 500 at 505, per Sir George Jessel MR.

656 e.g. *Bowes v Law* (1870) L.R. 9 Eq. 636; *Sharp v Harrison* [1922] 1 Ch. 502.

657 *Shelfer v City of London Electric Lighting Co* [1895] 1 Ch. 287 at 317, per Lindley LJ; *Sampson v Hodson-Pressinger* [1981] 3 All E.R. 710.

658 *Colls v Home and Colonial Stores Ltd* [1904] A.C. 179 at 193, per Lord Macnaghten.

659 *Sayers v Collyer* (1884) 28 Ch. D. 103; *HP Bulmer Ltd and Showerings Ltd v J Bollinger SA* [1977] 2 C.M.L.R. 625.

660 [2014] UKSC 13; [2014] A.C. 822; see also paras 19-152, 28-11.

661 [2003] UKHL 66; [2004] 2 A.C. 42.

662 [2002] Q.B. 1003.

would have had if rendered non-susceptible to wrongful flooding less its actual value. With regard to damages for future flooding caused by the future wrongs, these were awarded in substitution for the mandatory injunction. The judge was satisfied that the defendants would commit the future wrongs because they intended not to carry out the works necessary to remedy the flooding. Pressed with the argument that he should follow the common law and refuse equitable damages for the future wrongs, Judge Havery QC said: "The common law would not afford the [claimant] just satisfaction. He would have to bring onerous proceedings from time to time to enforce his rights. Nor would he be able to recover any diminution in the value of his property caused by the prospect of future wrongs."[663] In awarding equitable damages for future wrongs, he also rejected a novel argument that this would be contrary to the jurisprudence on the European Convention on Human Rights.

27-133 **Measure of damages** It has been stated by Lord Wilberforce, with the concurrence of other members of the House of Lords, that, apart from cases "where damages could not be claimed at all at common law, there is sound authority for the proposition that the Act does not provide for the assessment of damages on any new basis".[664] The implication of this is that the common law principles of assessment[665] apply to those losses which have already been sustained,[666] while an analogous compensatory approach should be adopted with regard to future acts which the injunction, had it been granted, would have covered. As at common law, equitable damages for a tort have alternatively been assessed on a restitutionary basis.[667] However, this must now be read subject to *Morris-Garner v One Step (Support) Ltd*[668] which has rejected a restitutionary analysis of what had previously been called "Wrotham Park damages". Damages under Lord Cairns' Act "are a monetary substitute for what is lost by the withholding of" of injunctive relief:

> "One possible method of quantifying damages under this head is on the basis of the economic value of the right which the court has declined to enforce, and which it has consequently rendered worthless. Such a valuation can be arrived at by reference to the amount which the claimant might reasonably have demanded as a quid pro quo for the relaxation of the obligation in question. The rationale is that, since the withholding of specific relief has the same practical effect as requiring the claimant to permit the infringe-

---

663 [2002] Q.B. 1003 at [17].

664 *Johnson v Agnew* [1980] A.C. 367 at 400. See also *Surrey CC v Bredero Homes Ltd* [1993] 1 W.L.R. 1361; *Jaggard v Sawyer* [1995] 1 W.L.R. 269. But note the observation of Lord Reed in *Morris-Garner v One Step (Support) Ltd* [2018] UKSC 20; [2019] A.C. 649 at [47] that it was "necessary to treat with care" Lord Wiberforce's remarks on this point in *Johnson v Agnew*.

665 See paras 27-02 to 27-19.

666 e.g. *Kine v Jolly* [1905] 1 Ch. 480; *Griffith v Richard Clay & Sons Ltd* [1912] 2 Ch. 291; *Wills v May* [1923] 1 Ch. 317.

667 *Bracewell v Appleby* [1975] Ch. 408 at 419–420; *Carr-Saunders v Dick McNeil Associates Ltd* [1986] 1 W.L.R. 922 at 932, per Millett J; *Jones v Ruth* [2011] EWCA Civ 804; [2012] 1 W.L.R. 1495 at [36]–[41]; see generally paras 27-150 to 27-151. In *Coventry v Lawrence* [2014] UKSC 13; [2014] A.C. 822 the Supreme Court left open the possibility of there being an award of "gain-based damages" in lieu of an injunction for the tort of private nuisance. See also *Wrotham Park Estate Co Ltd v Parkside Houses Ltd* [1974] 1 W.L.R. 798 at 815 (equitable damages for breach of a restrictive covenant); *Att Gen v Blake* [2001] 1 A.C. 268 HL (account of profits for breach of contract). In *Tamares (Vincent Square) Ltd v Fairpoint* [2007] EWHC 212 (Ch); [2007] 1 W.L.R. 2167, damages for infringing a right to light granted in lieu of a mandatory restorative injunction were rationalised as "compensating" for the lost opportunity of obtaining an injunction.

668 [2018] UKSC 20; [2019] A.C. 649. See paras 27-150 to 27-151.

> ment of his rights, his loss can be measured by reference to the economic value of such permission."[669]

But that is not the only approach to assessing damages under Lord Cairns' Act, and the court must judge what method of quantification "will give a fair equivalent for what is lost by the refusal of the injunction."[670]

9. Exemplary Damages[671]

(a) Distinguished from aggravated damages

Where the manner of commission of the tort was such as to injure the claimant's proper feelings of dignity and pride, higher damages than would otherwise have been justified may be awarded.[672] Such aggravated damages, as they are known, have been awarded for several different types of tort,[673] but they have featured most typically in defamation cases and have already been considered in that context.[674] From the defendant's point of view the award may appear to incorporate an element of punishment imposed by the court for his bad conduct, but the intention is rather to compensate the claimant for injury to his feelings and the amount payable should reflect this. **27-134**

Aggravated damages are thus, at least in theory, quite distinct from exemplary or punitive damages[675] which are awarded to teach the defendant that "tort does not **27-135**

---

669 [2018] UKSC 20; [2019] A.C. 649 at [95](4), per Lord Reed.

670 [2018] UKSC 20; [2019] A.C. 649 at [95](5), per Lord Reed.

671 See, generally, *Aggravated, Exemplary and Restitutionary Damages*, Law Commission Report No.247 (1997).

672 *Rookes v Barnard* [1964] A.C. 1129 at 1221, per Lord Devlin; *Broome v Cassell & Co Ltd* [1972] A.C. 1027 at 1071 and 1073, per Lord Hailsham LC; [1972] A.C. 1027 at 1085–1086, per Lord Reid. The bad conduct of the claimant may have a countervailing effect on the award of aggravated damages; *O'Connor v Hewitson* [1979] Crim. L.R. 46 CA.

673 See, e.g. *Ansell v Thomas* [1974] Crim. L.R. 31, CA; *W v Meah* [1986] 1 All E.R. 935; *Appleton v Garrett* [1996] P.I.Q.R. P1; *JXL v Britton* [2014] EWHC 2571 (QB); *WCC v Steer* [2019] EWHC 1874 (QB); *Doherty v Ministry of Defence* [2020] NICA 9 (assault and battery); *Bracegirdle v Orford* (1813) 2 M. & S. 77; *McMillan v Singh* (1985) 17 H.L.R. 120 CA (trespass to land); *Archer v Brown* [1985] Q.B. 401 (deceit); *Thompson v Commissioner of Police for the Metropolis* [1998] Q.B. 498 CA (false imprisonment and malicious prosecution); *Alexander v Home Office* [1988] 1 W.L.R. 968; *Deane v Ealing LBC* [1993] I.C.R. 329; *Gbaja-Biamila v DHL International (UK) Ltd* [2000] I.C.R. 730; *Armitage, Marsden and HM Prison Service v Johnson* [1997] I.C.R. 275 (racial discrimination); *Vento v Chief Constable of West Yorkshire Police (No.2)* [2002] EWCA Civ 1871; [2003] I.R.L.R. 102; *Zaiwalla & Co v Walia* [2002] I.R.L.R. 697 (sex discrimination); *Campbell v MGN Ltd* [2004] UKHL 22; [2004] 2 A.C 457 (breach of confidence); *Mosley v News Group Newspapers Ltd* [2008] EWHC 1777 (QB); [2008] E.M.L.R. 20 (breach of privacy/confidence); *Richard v BBC* [2018] EWHC 1837 (Ch); [2019] Ch. 169 (breach of privacy). But aggravated damages were held to be irrecoverable for the tort of negligence in *Kralj v McGrath* [1986] 1 All E.R. 54 at 61. For general consideration of damages for mental distress for torts see Burrows, *Remedies for Torts, Breach of Contract and Equitable Wrongs*, 4th edn (2019), pp.281–292; Murphy, "The Nature and Domain of Aggravated Damages" [2010] C.L.J. 353.

674 See para.21-226. For malicious falsehood, see paras 22-16 to 22-17.

675 See Lord Hailsham LC's discussion of terminology in *Broome v Cassell & Co Ltd* [1972] A.C. 1027 at 1073-1074. His Lordship's preference for the word "exemplary" is followed here, although the *Law Commission in its Report No.247* (1997), para.5.39 prefers the term "punitive damages". See also *R. v Secretary of State for Transport Ex p. Factortame Ltd (No.5)* [1998] 1 C.M.L.R. 1353; [1997] Eu. L.R. 475 (QBD) ("penal damages").

pay" and to deter him and others from similar conduct in the future.[676] Nevertheless, the two kinds of damages are not always easy to keep apart from one another in practice, and in many older cases large awards have been given without its being made clear whether this was done on the compensatory or the punitive principle.[677] Now, however, that it has been made clear that exemplary damages may be awarded only in certain classes of case[678] the maintenance of the distinction is important. Despite Lord Devlin's opinion that, in general, aggravated damages can do most if not all the work that could be done by exemplary damages,[679] it has to be borne in mind that, except where exemplary damages are permissible, every award of damages, including aggravated damages where appropriate, must be justifiable on the basis of compensation. If it is not, the inference will be that an improper element of punishment of the defendant or of simple bounty for the claimant has entered into the assessment and the award will, accordingly, be struck down on appeal.[680] It is submitted that the law would be improved in terms of clarity if aggravated damages were regarded as nothing more than "mental distress damages" or "damages for injured feelings" and if the very term "aggravated damages" was replaced by either of those phrases.[681] Certainly the relationship between aggravated damages and damages that are awarded for injured feelings irrespective of aggravating conduct is not straightforward,[682] and can be arbitrary.[683] In

---

676 *Broome v Cassell & Co Ltd* at 1073, per Lord Hailsham LC. See McCardie J's discussion of the distinction (in relation to the now defunct claim for damages for adultery) in *Butterworth v Butterworth* [1920] P. 126 at 139-150; *McCarey v Associated Newspapers Ltd (No.2)* [1965] 2 Q.B. 86 at 104-105, per Pearson LJ; *John v MGN Ltd* [1997] Q.B. 586 CA; *Thompson v Commissioner of Police for the Metropolis* [1998] Q.B. 498 CA.

677 e.g. *Merest v Harvey* (1814) 5 Taunt. 442; *Elliott v Nicklin* (1818) 5 Price 641; *Emblen v Myers* (1861) 6 H. & N. 54; *Thompson v Hill* (1870) L.R. 5 C. & P. 564.

678 See paras 27-136 to 27-144.

679 *Rookes v Barnard* [1964] A.C. 1129 at 1230.

680 *McCarey v Associated Newspapers Ltd (No.2)* [1965] 2 Q.B. 86. The distinction between aggravated and exemplary damages thus incidentally furnishes appellate courts with an additional instrument for the control of juries' awards of damages.

681 This was recommended by the Law Commission in its Report, *Aggravated, Exemplary and Restitutionary Damages*, Law Commission Report No.247 (1997), para.2.42; Draft Bill, cl.13.

682 For the view that there should be no separate award of aggravated damages over and above a general award for injury to feelings, see *McConnell v Police Authority for Northern Ireland* [1997] I.R.L.R. 625 at 629; *Gbaja-Biamila v DHL International (UK) Ltd* [2000] I.C.R. 730; *R. (on the application of Diop) v Secretary of State for the Home Department* [2018] EWHC 3420 (Admin); [2019] A.C.D. 30 at [46]. See also *Richardson v Howie* [2004] EWCA Civ 1127; [2005] P.I.Q.R. Q3, where it was said, in an assault and battery case, that a court should not characterise as aggravated damages an award of damages for injury to feelings, including for any indignity, humiliation or anger caused by an attack, except possibly in a wholly exceptional case. See further *Martins v Choudhary* [2007] EWCA Civ 1379; [2008] 1 W.L.R. 617: while normally it is better to separate out damages for psychiatric harm from damages for injury to feelings, it is usually preferable, following *Richardson v Howie*, not to separate out damages for injury to feelings from aggravated damages (though note the reservations about the ruling in *Richardson v Howie* expressed by the Northern Ireland Court of Appeal in *Doherty v Ministry of Defence* [2020] NICA 9 at [27] to [29]). For an enlightened and rigorous examination of these issues in the context of an award of damages for victimisation of a "whistleblower", see *Commissioner of Police of the Metropolis v Shaw* [2012] I.C.R. 464 EAT.

683 Distinguishing between injury to feelings which is the result of the wrong itself and injury to feelings which is the result of the manner in which the wrong was committed is highly artificial, since any injury to feelings will be the product of both; it also rests on the assumption that there is a "normal" or standard way of committing the wrong and an "abnormal" or aggravated way of committing it (which correspond to awards of "basic" compensation and "aggravated" compensation) the threshold between which the court is required to identify: *R. (on the application of Diop) v*

Rowlands v Chief Constable of Merseyside Police[684] the Court of Appeal stressed that, as aggravated damages are compensatory and not punitive, a judge and/or jury must be careful to ensure that there is no double recovery between "basic" and "aggravated" damages for assault, false imprisonment and malicious prosecution by the police. So in principle where damages for distress, humiliation and injury to feelings have been fully compensated as part of the "basic" damages, they should not be the subject of further compensation in the form of an award of aggravated damages.[685] In practice it may make little difference whether awards are characterised as aggravated damages or whether the defendant's conduct has simply resulted in such injury to the claimant's feelings that would justify an award towards the higher end of the bracket for pain and suffering.[686] Aggravated damages are to compensate for a person's injured feelings and mental distress, and so they cannot be awarded to a company.[687]

(b) Scope of exemplary damages[688]

It was formerly supposed that exemplary damages could be awarded in almost any case of tort if the defendant's conduct had been particularly outrageous. In 1964, however, the House of Lords, through the speech of Lord Devlin in *Rookes v Barnard*,[689] laid down that exemplary damages, as distinct from aggravated damages, should only be awarded in two specific categories of case,[690] unless, of course, they were expressly authorised by statute.[691] These categories comprise, first, cases of "oppressive, arbitrary or unconstitutional action by the servants of the government" and, secondly, cases in which "the defendant's conduct has been calculated by him to make a profit for himself which may well exceed the compensation pay- **27-136**

Secretary of State for the Home Department [2018] EWHC 3420 (Admin); [2019] A.C.D. 30 at [44]–[45].

684 [2006] EWCA Civ 1773; [2007] 1 W.L.R. 1065.

685 On the facts of the case, it was held that an award of aggravated damages might have been appropriate so that the trial judge should have left that question to the jury.

686 See *BXB v Watch Tower and Bible Tract Society of Pennsylvannia* [2020] EWHC 156 (QB); [2020] 4 W.L.R. 42 at [207] per Chamberlain J.

687 *Collins Stewart Ltd v The Financial Times Ltd* [2005] EWHC 262 (QB); [2006] E.M.L.R. 5; *Eaton Mansions (Westminster) Ltd v Stinger Compania de Inversion SA* [2013] EWCA Civ 1308; [2014] H.L.R. 4.

688 A claim for exemplary damages must be specifically pleaded: CPR r.16.4(c).

689 [1964] A.C. 1129.

690 [1964] A.C. 1129 at 1220–1233.

691 At that time, the only statute expressly authorising the award of exemplary damages was the Reserve and Auxiliary Forces (Protection of Civil Interests) Act 1951 s.13(2), on which, however, see *Broome v Cassell & Co Ltd* [1972] A.C. 1027 at 1133, per Lord Kilbrandon. Another example now, in the context of outrageous infringement of rights by the press, is contained in the Crime and Courts Act 2013 ss.34–39. Perhaps the Copyright, Designs and Patents Act 1988 s.97(2) also does so. On this see *Williams v Settle* [1960] 1 W.L.R. 1072; *Rookes v Barnard* [1964] A.C. 1129 at 1225, per Lord Devlin; *Broome v Cassell & Co Ltd* [1972] A.C. 1027 at 1080–1081, per Lord Hailsham LC; [1972] A.C. 1027 at 1134, per Lord Kilbrandon; *Beloff v Pressdram Ltd* [1973] 1 All E.R. 241 at 265; *Nichols Advanced Vehicle Systems Inc v Rees* [1979] R.P.C. 127; [1985] R.P.C. 445. In *Redrow Homes Ltd v Bett Brothers Plc* [1999] 1 A.C. 197 HL (Sc.) it was decided that, as a matter of statutory interpretation, additional damages could not be added to an account of profits under s.97(2) of the 1988 Act. While not deciding the point, Lord Clyde said that damages under s.97(2) were, more probably, aggravated rather than exemplary. The Law Reform (Miscellaneous Provisions) Act 1934 s.1(2), makes reference to exemplary damages, but only to provide that they may not be recovered in proceedings brought for the benefit of the estate of a deceased person.

able to the [claimant]".[692] In cases falling within one or other of these categories Lord Devlin considered that exemplary damages were justified by authority and that they served a useful purpose in vindicating the strength of the law.[693] In general, however, his Lordship declared that exemplary damages were anomalous for they confuse the civil and criminal functions of the law[694] and also lay the defendant open to the possibility of punishment without the safeguard which the criminal law gives to an offender.[695]

27-137 Although the Privy Council subsequently upheld the view of the High Court of Australia that *Rookes v Barnard* does not apply in that country[696] and although Lord Devlin's judgment was heavily criticised by the Court of Appeal in *Broome v Cassell & Co Ltd*[697] the House of Lords in that case,[698] by a majority,[699] restored the authority of *Rookes v Barnard*. As several of their Lordships pointed out, however, Lord Devlin's words must not be treated as if they were contained in a statute; care must be taken to avoid treating phrases which are only illustrative or descriptive as if they were definitive and exhaustive.[700] Subject to this warning it is now settled that, so far as English law is concerned, exemplary damages (as distinct from aggravated compensatory damages) may be awarded only in cases falling within one of the categories specified by Lord Devlin:

(1) oppressive, arbitrary or unconstitutional action by the servants of the government; and
(2) where the defendant's conduct has been calculated by him to make a profit for himself which may well exceed the compensation payable.

(i) Oppressive, arbitrary or unconstitutional action by the servants of the government

27-138 The examples of this category cited by Lord Devlin include such cases as *Wilkes v Wood*[701] where large damages were awarded for the search of the claimant's house carried out under an illegal general warrant. In *Att Gen of St Christopher, Nevis and Anguilla v Reynolds*[702] the category was held by the Privy Council to cover unconstitutional detention by the Governor of the State in insanitary and humiliating conditions. The most common example of exemplary damages being awarded in this category has been in actions against the police for torts such as assault and

---

692 [1964] A.C. 1129 at 1226.

693 cf. *Broome v Cassell & Co Ltd* [1972] A.C. 1027 at 1087, per Lord Reid, and see the general observations of Lord Wilberforce, [1972] A.C. 1027 at 1113-1116.

694 [1964] A.C. 1129 at 1221.

695 [1964] A.C. 1129 at 1227.

696 *Australian Consolidated Press Ltd v Uren* [1969] 1 A.C. 590. See *Uren v John Fairfax & Sons Pty Ltd* (1968) 117 C.L.R. 118. The reception of *Rookes v Barnard* in other Commonwealth countries has been mixed. See Fridman, "Punitive Damages in Tort" (1970) 48 Can. Bar Rev. 373; Waddams, *The Law of Damages*, 3rd edn, paras 11.190–11.200; *Taylor v Beere* [1982] 1 N.Z.L.R. 81; *A v Bottrill* [2002] UKPC 44; [2003] 1 A.C. 449.

697 [1971] 2 Q.B. 354.

698 [1972] A.C. 1027.

699 Viscount Dilhorne's was, perhaps, a less than full-blooded dissent, but his Lordship had more sympathy for the views expressed in the Court of Appeal than did his brethren.

700 [1972] A.C. 1027 at 1068, 1077, per Lord Hailsham LC; [1972] A.C. 1027 at 1085, per Lord Reid. See also the observations of Lord Wilberforce ([1972] A.C. 1027 at 1113–1116) on the dangers in the practical application of Lord Devlin's analysis.

701 (1763) Lofft 1; *Huckle v Money* (1763) 2 Wils. K.B. 205; *Benson v Frederick* (1766) 3 Bur. 1845.

702 [1980] A.C. 637.

false imprisonment.[703] The restriction to "servants of the government" which was emphasised by Lord Devlin[704] has been criticised as illogical on the ground that it is conduct rather than status which should be capable of attracting punishment. It is justified by the fact that servants of the government are also servants of the people so that their use of power must always be subordinate to their duty of service.[705] On the other hand it is clear from dicta in *Broome v Cassell & Co Ltd* that "servants of the government" should be broadly, not technically, construed and that the contrast is between "the government" on the one hand and private individuals on the other.[706] So an award of exemplary damages may be made in an appropriate case against a police officer or a local government official even though neither is a servant of the Crown. But the defendant must be exercising governmental power and in *AB v South West Water Services Ltd*[707] it was felt that that constituted a different idea in this context than in relation to whether a decision can be judicially reviewed or whether a body is an emanation of the state for the purposes of European Community law. The actions of a nationalised corporation in contaminating drinking water and failing to warn the public properly of this were therefore held not to fall within the first category, even if exemplary damages could be awarded for the tort of public nuisance (which, it was held, they could not be). It has been held that the three types of action cited by Lord Devlin are distinct so that a claimant does not necessarily have to show that an unconstitutional action is either "oppressive" or "arbitrary".[708] In *R. (Lumba) v Secretary of State for the Home Department*[709] the claimants, who had been detained in breach of public law, were held entitled to damages for the tort of false imprisonment. But as they would have been detained in any event, had correct procedures been followed, the damages should be nominal only.[710] There was no justification for exemplary damages even though the conduct of the Home Office officials had been deplorable.

---

703 See, e.g. *White v Commissioner of Police of the Metropolis*, *The Times*, 24 April 1982; *George v Commissioner of Police of the Metropolis*, *The Times*, 31 March 1984; *Connor v Chief Constable of Cambridgeshire*, *The Times*, 11 April 1984; *Holden v Chief Constable of Lancashire* [1987] Q.B. 380; *Thompson v Commissioner of Police for the Metropolis* [1998] Q.B. 498 CA. In this last case, guideline figures were laid down for juries on quantum (including exemplary damages) in false imprisonment and malicious prosecution actions against the police. As regards exemplary damages it was said that, if awarded, they should not be less than £500 but not more than £50,000; and it would be unusual for exemplary damages to be more than three times the sum of (basic and aggravated) compensatory damages. See also *Muuse v Secretary of State for the Home Department* [2010] EWCA Civ 453 stressing, in a case of false imprisonment, that it was the outrageous nature of the tortious conduct that made exemplary damages appropriate within this category and there was no need to find that the defendant had acted with malice.

704 "I should not extend this category ... to oppressive actions by private corporations or individuals": [1964] A.C. 1129 at 1226.

705 [1964] A.C. 1129; *Broome v Cassell & Co Ltd* [1972] A.C. 1027 at 1134, per Lord Kilbrandon; cf. [1972] A.C. 1027 at 1088, per Lord Reid. Lord Reid admits the illogicality of the distinction between "servants of the government" and private persons, and justifies it simply on the ground that the anomaly of exemplary damages should not be carried further than authority compels.

706 [1972] A.C. 1027 at 1077–1078, per Lord Hailsham LC; [1972] A.C. 1027 at 1087–1088, per Lord Reid; [1972] A.C. 1027 at 1128, 1130, per Lord Diplock.

707 [1993] Q.B. 507. cf. *Bradford City Metropolitan Council v Arora* [1991] 2 Q.B. 507 where the public/private divide drawn for judicial review purposes was also rejected but so as to *award* exemplary damages.

708 *Holden v Chief Constable of Lancashire* [1987] Q.B. 380. The fact that a police officer is acting without authority does not by itself render the act unconstitutional for this purpose; [1987] Q.B. 380 at 387–388.

709 [2011] UKSC 12; [2012] 1 A.C. 245.

710 See also *Bostridge v Oxleas NHS Foundation Trust* [2015] EWCA Civ 79; [2015] Med. L.R. 113;

27-139 In a series of decisions of the Privy Council, "vindicatory damages" awarded for infringement of constitutional rights have been awarded in circumstances where exemplary damages might otherwise have been awarded within the first of Lord Devlin's categories. So, for example, In *Att Gen of Trinidad and Tobago v Ramanoop*,[711] there had been an unconstitutional arrest, assault and detention by a police officer. It was held that there was jurisdiction under s.14 of the Constitution of Trinidad and Tobago to award the victim, in addition to compensatory damages, damages for infringement of his constitutional rights. These additional damages were to vindicate the claimant's constitutional right, to emphasise the gravity of the breach, to reflect the sense of public outrage, and to deter further infringements. Although recognised as covering the same ground as punitive or exemplary damages, the Privy Council thought that, as punishment in the sense of retribution was not the object of this additional award, the expressions "punitive damages" or "exemplary damages" were here better avoided. In *Takitota v Att Gen*[712] it was held that a court should not award both vindicatory damages and exemplary damages because of the overlap between them. It remains to be seen whether these vindicatory damages will be used in English law for the infringement by the State of a person's rights under the Human Rights Act 1998.[713] While in *R. (Lumba) v Secretary of State for the Home Department*[714] three of the nine Supreme Court Justices (Lord Walker, Lord Hope and Baroness Hale) would have been willing to award "vindicatory damages" for the tort of false imprisonment, the majority did not think such damages were appropriate; and some of the judges, especially Lord Dyson giving the leading judgment, cast severe doubt on whether vindicatory damages are ever justified as a remedy in tort (as opposed to being given for the infringement of a constitutional right where there is a written constitution).[715]

(ii) Defendant's conduct has been calculated by him to make a profit which may well exceed the compensation payable

27-140 This category has fallen to be considered in a number of actions for defamation,[716] including *Broome v Cassell & Co Ltd* itself.[717] But the main use of this category has been in actions by tenants against landlords for wrongful harassment

and *Parker v Chief Constable of Essex* [2018] EWCA Civ 2788; [2019] 1 W.L.R. 2238 where awards of nominal, rather than substantive, damages were made where claimants had been unlawfully detained due to a procedural error, but would have been lawfully detained but for the error in procedure. Contrast *R. (on the application of Hemmati) v Secretary of State for the Home Department* [2019] UKSC 56; [2019] 3 W.L.R. 1156 where the policy under which the claimants were detained was unlawful; claimants entitled to substantive damages.

711 [2005] UKPC 15; [2006] 1 A.C. 328. See similarly *Merson v Cartwright* [2005] UKPC 38; *Inniss v Att Gen for St Christopher and Nevis* [2008] UKPC 42.

712 [2009] UKPC 11; (2009) 26 B.H.R.C. 578.

713 See the obiter dicta of Lord Scott in *Ashley v Chief Constable of Sussex Police* [2008] UKHL 25; [2008] 1 A.C. 962 at [22]. One argument against the use of such damages for infringement of convention rights under the Human Rights Act 1998 is that such damages have not been awarded by the Strasbourg Court: see generally *R. (on the application of Greenfield) v Secretary of State for the Home Department* [2005] UKHL 14; [2005] 1 W.L.R. 673.

714 [2011] UKSC 12; [2012] 1 A.C. 245.

715 See similarly Burrows, "Damages and Rights" in Nolan and Robertson (eds), *Rights and Private Law* (2012), pp.275, 303–307.

716 e.g. *McCarey v Associated Newspapers Ltd (No.2)* [1965] 2 Q.B. 86; *Broadway Approvals Ltd v Odhams Press Ltd (No.2)* [1965] 1 W.L.R. 805; *Manson v Associated Newspapers Ltd* [1965] 1 W.L.R. 1038; *Riches v News Group Newspapers Ltd* [1986] Q.B. 256; *John v MGN Ltd* [1997] Q.B. 586 CA.

or eviction founded on the torts of trespass or nuisance.[718] For example, in *Drane v Evangelou*,[719] in which a landlord had forcefully entered premises of which the claimant was the tenant and had taken various steps to evict him, an award of £1,000 exemplary damages for the trespass involved was upheld by the Court of Appeal as coming within the second category, though both Lawton and Goff LJJ considered that it could have been justified as aggravated damages. Similarly, in *Guppys (Bridport) Ltd v Brookling and James*,[720] two tenants were awarded exemplary damages for the tort of nuisance where their landlord, in an attempt to evict them, had (during building work) removed all the internal sanitary and washing facilities, discontinued the supply of water to the external toilets and cut off the electricity. Again in *Design Progression Ltd v Thurloe Properties Ltd*[721] exemplary damages were awarded to a tenant for breach by a landlord of its statutory duty under s.1(3) of the Landlord and Tenant Act 1988. Occasionally exemplary damages have also been awarded under the second category for tortious interference with the claimant's business.[722] In *Borders (UK) Ltd v Commissioner of Police of the Metropolis*[723] the Court of Appeal held that exemplary damages were appropriate in a case where "tens, possibly hundreds, of thousands of new books" had been stolen from the claimants by shoplifters and sold by the defendant from his market stalls. A recent trend has been for exemplary damages to be awarded for insurance fraud.[724] A good example was *AXA Insurance UK Plc v Financial Claims Solutions Ltd*[725] where fictitious motor accident claims, alleged to involve insured policyholders of AXA, were brought and initially succeeded but were ultimately thwarted when the sophisticated fraud was exposed. Punitive damages of £20,000 (in addition to compensatory damages) were awarded within Lord Devlin's second category for the tort of deceit and unlawful means conspiracy. Finally, in *AT v Dulghieru*[726] exemplary damages were awarded under this category for the torts of unlawful conspiracy, false imprisonment and assault by forcing several women from Moldova to work as prostitutes.

---

717 [1972] A.C. 1027.

718 See J. Goudkamp and E. Katsampouka, "An Empirical Study of Punitive Damages" (2018) 38 O.J.L.S. 90, which reported on a study of every electronically accessible judgment in England, Wales and Northern Ireland between January 2000 and December 2015 in which punitive damages were sought (146 claims). Most claims were made for "interference with property" (35.6 per cent) and punitive damages were awarded in 53.8 per cent of those claims. In contrast there were very few such claims for defamation and privacy (5.5 per cent) and there were no awards of punitive damages in respect of those claims.

719 [1978] 1 W.L.R. 455.

720 (1984) 14 H.L.R. 1. See also, e.g. *McMillan v Singh* (1985) 17 H.L.R. 120 CA; *Millington v Duffy* (1984) 17 H.L.R. 232 CA; *Asghar v Ahmed* (1985) 17 H.L.R. 25; *Ramdath v Daley* (1993) 25 H.L.R. 273 (also illustrating the point that there can be no exemplary damages under this category where the defendant is acting for another's benefit); *Ramzan v Brookwide Ltd* [2011] EWCA Civ 985; [2012] 1 All E.R. 903 (exemplary damages awarded for the tort of trespass to land).

721 [2004] EWHC 324 (Ch); [2005] 1 W.L.R. 1; para.27-144.

722 *Bell v Midland Ry Co* (1861) 10 C.B. (N.S.) 287; *Messenger Newspaper Group Ltd v National Graphical Association* [1984] I.C.R. 345.

723 [2005] EWCA Civ 197; *The Times*, 15 April 2005.

724 The study by J. Goudkamp and E. Katsampouka, "An Empirical Study of Punitive Damages" (2018) 38 O.J.L.S. 90 shows that, where sought, exemplary damages are very commonly awarded in respect of insurance fraud (for the tort of deceit). As they say, at 114: "The award of punitive damages for insurance fraud, which has been possible only since the demise of the cause-of-action test, constitutes a new trend in the case law."

725 [2018] EWCA Civ 1330; [2019] R.T.R. 1.

726 [2009] EWHC 225 (QB).

27-141 Lord Devlin's reason for including this category is broadly expressed as justifying the award of exemplary damages "whenever it is necessary to teach a wrongdoer that tort does not pay".[727] The mere fact that everything published in a newspaper or a book is published with a view to making a profit does not mean, therefore, that exemplary damages should be awarded for every defamatory statement published; something much more deliberate is required.[728] On the other hand, a broad interpretation of Lord Devlin's words should be applied: they are not restricted to money-making in the strict sense[729] and the word "calculated" does not imply that the defendant must have indulged in careful mathematical computation. "What is necessary is that the tortious act must be done with guilty knowledge for the motive that the chances of economic advantage outweigh the chances of economic, or perhaps physical, penalty."[730] As Parker LJ expressed it in *Riches v News Group Newspapers Ltd*,[731] a libel case, "there must have been evidence which would have entitled the jury, after due directions, to find (a) that the defendants knew the article complained of to be defamatory or were reckless whether it was so or not and (b) that they published because they took the view that it would, in a broad sense, pay them to publish and risk the consequences of any action the [claimants] might take". In *Broome v Cassell & Co Ltd* itself the defendant publishers had produced a book containing gravely defamatory allegations about the conduct of the claimant, a retired naval officer, when he was in command of a convoy escort during the war. There was ample evidence to show that the defendants knew, well before publication, that the book contained passages which were both defamatory of the claimant and untrue, and thus to justify the jury in inferring that they went ahead with publication "with the most cold-blooded and clear sighted appreciation of what they were doing".[732] The jury's award of £25,000 exemplary damages in addition to £15,000 compensatory damages was, therefore, upheld by a majority of the House of Lords as allowable under Lord Devlin's second category.[733]

---

727 [1964] A.C. 1129 at 1227. But an attempt to conceal the commission of a tort, with the object of limiting the amount of damages payable, does not fall within this category: *AB v South West Water Services Ltd* [1993] Q.B. 507. It may be that a modern justification for Lord Devlin's second category is that it provides for "the confiscation of profits which cannot be got at through the ordinary compensatory mechanisms" and so is more in the nature of a restitutionary remedy than a penalty: see *Borders (UK) Ltd v Commissioner of Police of the Metropolis* [2005] EWCA Civ 197; *The Times,* 15 April 2005 at [26] and [40], per Sedley LJ and Rix LJ respectively.

728 *McCarey v Associated Newspapers Ltd (No.2)* [1965] 2 Q.B. 86; *Broadway Approvals Ltd v Odhams Press Ltd (No.2)* [1965] 1 W.L.R. 805; *Manson v Associated Newspapers Ltd* [1965] 1 W.L.R. 1038.

729 *Drane v Evangelou* [1978] 1 W.L.R. 455 at 459, per Lord Denning MR, citing Lord Devlin [1964] A.C. 1129 at 1227.

730 *Broome v Cassell & Co Ltd* [1972] A.C. 1027 at 1079, per Lord Hailsham LC; [1972] A.C. 1027 at 1088, per Lord Reid; [1972] A.C. 1027 at 1094, per Lord Morris; [1972] A.C. 1027 at 1101, per Viscount Dilhorne; [1972] A.C. 1027 at 1129, per Lord Diplock; [1972] A.C. 1027 at 1133, per Lord Kilbrandon. In *Borders (UK) Ltd v Commissioner of Police of the Metropolis* [2005] EWCA Civ 197; *The Times,* 15 April 2005 at [23] Sedley LJ said that "calculated" meant "likely" to make a profit beyond what would probably be recovered in cash or in kind by legal process.

731 [1986] Q.B. 256 at 284.

732 [1972] A.C. 1027 at 1058, per Lord Hailsham LC.

733 Viscount Dilhorne and Lords Wilberforce and Diplock dissenting on the ground of inadequacy in the judge's direction to the jury.

(c) Rejection of the "cause of action test"

After some conflict in the cases, it was decided by the Court of Appeal in *AB v South West Water Services Ltd*[734] that *Cassell v Broome* required that the tort be one for which exemplary damages had been awarded prior to 1964. If this was not so, no exemplary damages could be awarded even if the case fell within one of Lord Devlin's categories. A claim for exemplary damages for the tort of public nuisance in supplying contaminated drinking water to inhabitants of Camelford, Cornwall, was therefore struck out as public nuisance was not a tort for which exemplary damages had been awarded prior to *Rookes v Barnard*. The same applied to alternative claims in the tort of negligence and for liability under the Consumer Protection Act 1987 and the Water Act 1945. It also followed from the decision that no exemplary damages could be awarded for torts, such as negligence, deceit, misfeasance in public office and unlawful discrimination, because those torts failed the "cause of action test" (i.e. they were not torts for which exemplary damages had been awarded pre-1964). **27-142**

This view was rejected, however, in *Kuddus v Chief Constable of Leicestershire*[735] where the House of Lords overruled *AB v South West Water Services Ltd* and held that the "cause of action test" should be removed. On the facts of the case this meant that, if the other requirements for the award of exemplary damages were satisfied, exemplary damages could be awarded for the tort of misfeasance in public office. It was noted that the need to search through old authorities to find a pre-1964 award of exemplary damages was unfortunate, especially since aggravated and exemplary damages have only been clearly distinguished since *Rookes v Barnard* itself, and it may well be difficult to determine the characterisation of an award of damages in an older case. The removal of the cause of action test in *Kuddus* means that, apart from infringement of a Convention right under the Human Rights Act 1998 (where the wording of the Act[736] and the jurisprudence of the European Court of Human Rights indicate that no exemplary damages can be awarded), exemplary damages can be awarded for any tort[737] provided the facts fall within the *Rookes v Barnard* categories. **27-143**

The application of *Kuddus* is well-illustrated by *Design Progression Ltd v* **27-144**

---

[734] [1993] Q.B. 507. See Reed (1993) 143 N.L.J. 929; Burrows (1993) 109 L.Q.R. 358. See also, denying exemplary damages for European Community law wrongs, *R. v Secretary of State for Transport Ex p. Factortame Ltd (No.5)* [1998] 1 C.M.L.R. 1353; [1997] Eu. L.R. 475 QBD (on appeal, there was no discussion of exemplary, as opposed to compensatory, damages: [2000] 1 A.C. 524 HL). In *Francis v Brown* (1998) 30 H.L.R. 143 CA, there was no mention of *AB v South West Water Services* as barring exemplary damages for unlawful eviction under ss.27–28 of the Housing Act 1988, although they were in any event denied because one of the joint defendants did not merit punishment (see para.27-148).

[735] [2001] UKHL 29; [2002] 2 A.C. 122.

[736] s.8(3) of the Human Rights Act 1998 refers to the award being necessary to afford "just satisfaction" to the claimant which appears to be a reference to compensation alone. See *Anufrijeva v London Borough of Southwark* [2003] EWCA Civ 1406; [2004] Q.B. 1124.

[737] In *Mosley v News Group Newspapers Ltd* [2008] EWHC 1777 (QB); [2008] E.M.L.R. 20, it was held that exemplary damages could not be given for breach of the equitable wrong of breach of confidence/privacy as this would require a development of the law that was not justified in terms of necessity and proportionality. For general consideration of the question of whether exemplary damages can be awarded for equitable wrongs, see Burrows, *Remedies for Torts, Breach of Contract and Equitable Wrongs*, 4th edn (2019), pp.536–537.

Thurloe Properties Ltd[738] in which exemplary damages were awarded against a landlord for breach of its statutory duty under s.1(3) of the Landlord and Tenant Act 1988 in failing to give a decision, within a reasonable time, on a tenant's application for a licence to assign. Peter Smith J explained that, following the removal of the cause of action test in *Kuddus v Chief Constable of Leicestershire*, it was possible for exemplary damages to be awarded for breach of statutory duty under the 1988 Act. Here the facts fell within the second category in *Rookes v Barnard* because the landlord had behaved in a cynical way designed to frustrate the tenant's legitimate expectation of being able to assign the premises. The landlord's aim had been to force the tenant out of the premises and then to be able itself to rent the premises out at a higher rent. In addition to compensatory damages (the amount of which was not fixed but appeared to be approximately £111,000), the judge awarded £25,000 exemplary damages. He made it clear that this went beyond any profit that the landlord had actually made and was designed to deter similar conduct by the landlord in the future and to mark the court's disapproval of its past conduct.

27-145 In New Zealand, it was previously decided in *A v Bottrill*[739] that, in the context of the tort of negligence, there could be outrageous conduct justifying exemplary damages, even without subjective recklessness. But that was departed from in *Couch v Attorney General (No.2)*,[740] so that subjective recklessness is a necessary minimum requirement for exemplary damages (albeit that the cause of action may be the tort of negligence).

(d) Factors to be considered

27-146 In addition to setting out the categories of case in which exemplary damages may be awarded, Lord Devlin gave expression to three considerations which must be borne in mind in any case in which an award of exemplary damages is being claimed.[741] First, the claimant must himself be the victim of the punishable behaviour; secondly, the power to award exemplary damages must be used with restraint for it may be a weapon against as well as for liberty,[742] thirdly, the means of the defendant, irrelevant in the assessment of compensatory damages, are material,[743] as is everything which aggravates or mitigates the defendant's conduct, for example provocation by the claimant.[744] Lord Devlin also said that the jury must be directed, if the case falls within one of the categories, that "if, but only if, the sum which they have in mind to award as compensation (which may, of course, be a sum aggravated by the way in which the defendant has behaved to the [claimant]) is inadequate to punish him for his outrageous conduct, ... then it can award

738 [2004] EWHC 324 (Ch); [2005] 1 W.L.R. 1. Although not mentioned by the judge, the breach of statutory duty can be classified as a statutory tort.

739 [2002] UKPC 44; [2003] 1 A.C. 449.

740 [2010] NZSC 27; [2010] N.Z.L.R. 149.

741 [1964] A.C. 1129 at 1227–1228.

742 See also *John v Mirror Group Newspapers Ltd* [1997] Q.B. 586 at 619, where Sir Thomas Bingham MR said: "... principle requires that an award of exemplary damages should never exceed the minimum sum necessary to meet the public purpose underlying such damages ...".

743 In vicarious liability cases, where exemplary damages are being awarded against an employer for the conduct of its employee, the means of the employee are irrelevant and do not limit the award against the vicariously liable employer: *Thompson v Metropolitan Police Commissioner* [1998] Q.B. 498. But see the comments of Lord Mackay in *Kuddus v Chief Constable of Leicestershire Constabulary* [2001] UKHL 29; [2002] 2 A.C. 122 at [47].

744 *O'Connor v Hewitson* [1978] Crim. L.R. 46. See also *Bishop v Commissioner of Police of the Metropolis* (1989) 133 S.J. 1626.

some larger sum".[745] It is, in other words, essential that the punitive effect of the award of compensatory damages be taken into account when the award of exemplary damages, if any, is under consideration and that no such award should be made unless the required punitive or exemplary element is insufficiently supplied by the award of compensatory damages alone.[746] In *Ramzan v Brookwide Ltd*[747] the Court of Appeal, while upholding an award of exemplary damages for the tort of trespass to land as being justified to deter similar conduct, reduced the quantum of exemplary damages that had been awarded at first instance by two-thirds to £20,000. Rather confusingly, the Court of Appeal reasoned that one had to be careful to ensure that the award of exemplary damages did not infringe the principle, in relation to the concurrent claim for breach of trust, that the claimant must elect for either compensation or an account of profits. One must also take into account the sanctions (if any) imposed on the defendant by the criminal law so that the defendant is not punished twice or excessively for the same offence.[748] It is therefore clear that exemplary damages do not have to be awarded just because the facts fall within one of Lord Devlin's categories.[749]

Insurance In *Lancashire County Council v Municipal Mutual Insurance Ltd*[750] it was held that, at least where exemplary damages are being awarded against a **27-147**

---

745 [1964] A.C. 1129 at 1227–1228; *Broome v Cassell & Co Ltd* [1972] A.C. 1027 at 1059–1060, 1081–1082, per Lord Hailsham LC. It was because, in their opinions, the judge had failed to make this point sufficiently clear that a minority of the House of Lords considered that the verdict could not be allowed to stand.

746 The opinion of Lord Wilberforce that English law contains a "heavy, indeed exorbitant, punitive element in its costs system" may be considered important: [1972] A.C. 1027 at 1114–1115. As to the separation of awards of compensatory and exemplary damages, see *Rookes v Barnard* [1964] A.C. 1129 at 1228, per Lord Devlin; *Broome v Cassell & Co Ltd* [1972] A.C. 1027 at 1094 and 1099–1100, per Lord Morris; [1972] A.C. 1027 at 1115–1116, per Lord Wilberforce; [1972] A.C. 1027 at 1126, per Lord Diplock; *Att Gen of St Christopher, Nevis and Anguilla v Reynolds* [1980] A.C. 637 at 662–663, per Lord Salmon; *John v MGN Ltd* [1997] Q.B. 586 CA; *Thompson v Commissioner of Police for the Metropolis* [1998] Q.B. 498 CA; *The Gleaner Co Ltd v Abrahams* [2003] UKPC 55; [2004] 1 A.C. 628. In *Borders (UK) Ltd v Commissioner of Police of the Metropolis* [2005] EWCA Civ 197; *The Times,* 15 April 2005 the Court of Appeal considered that an award of exemplary damages would probably still leave the claimants undercompensated for theft of their property on a massive scale. But the fact that there was an element of compensation did not prevent the award from falling within Lord Devlin's second category for exemplary damages.

747 [2011] EWCA Civ 985; [2012] 1 All E.R. 903.

748 *Devonshire and Smith v Jenkins* (1979) LAG Bull. 114, CA; *Archer v Brown* [1985] Q.B. 401; cf. *Asghar v Ahmed* (1985) 17 H.L.R. 25. See also *Loomis v Rohan* (1974) 46 D.L.R. (3d) 423; *Daniels v Thompson* [1998] 3 N.Z.L.R. 22; upheld on appeal as *W v W* [1999] 2 N.Z.L.R. 1 PC (abrogated by the Injury Prevention, Rehabilitation and Compensation Act 2001, NZ, s.319). In *Gray v Motor Accident Commission* (1999) 73 A.L.J.R. 45, it was held by the High Court of Australia that, where a defendant had been imprisoned for the conduct in question (deliberately injuring the claimant by driving a car at him), there was an automatic bar against the claimant being awarded exemplary damages in an action for negligence. In *Borders (UK) Ltd v Commissioner of Police of the Metropolis* [2005] EWCA Civ 197; *The Times,* 15 April 2005 the Court of Appeal considered that the fact that the defendant had been sentenced to 30 months' imprisonment and that his assets were likely to be subject to a confiscation order under the Criminal Justice Act 1988 did not preclude an award of exemplary damages. But on the facts the exemplary award in practice covered the claimants' loss. Sedley LJ commented, at [28] that the unusual situation in which an award of exemplary damages was, in practice, compensatory "has to make up in justice what it lacks in logic". An award of exemplary damages was made in *AT v Dulghieru* [2009] EWHC 225 (QB) even though there had been criminal proceedings and confiscation orders made against the defendants.

749 *Holden v Chief Constable of Lancashire* [1987] Q.B. 380.

750 [1997] Q.B. 897 CA.

defendant on the basis of vicarious liability for another's tort (here against a county council or police chief constable for false imprisonment and malicious prosecution by police constables), there is no public policy prohibiting insurance against a liability to pay exemplary damages. It was also held that the insurance policy in question, although phrased in terms of indemnifying against a liability to pay compensation, could be and should be construed as indemnifying against a liability to pay exemplary damages.

27-148 **Joint defendants** In *Broome v Cassell & Co Ltd*[751] the action was brought against both the author and the publisher of the offending book, and a single award of damages, including exemplary damages, was made against both. It was held by the House of Lords that this was correct, and it was emphasised by the House that, if an award of exemplary damages is made in an action brought against several defendants, then not only must there be a single judgment but the sum awarded must reflect only the lowest figure for which any of the defendants can be held liable: if even one of them does not deserve punishment, or if the compensatory damages awarded are in themselves sufficient punishment for any one defendant, then exemplary damages must not be awarded at all.[752] In *Rowlands v Chief Constable of Merseyside Police*,[753] the question of whether a chief officer of police can be vicariously liable for exemplary damages was carefully considered. It was held that for policy reasons such an award should be possible (even though this meant that the financial means of the "servant" joint tortfeasor would be irrelevant). In Moore-Bick LJ's words: "Only by this means can awards of an adequate amount be made against those who bear public responsibility for the officers concerned."[754] On the facts, exemplary damages of £7,500 were awarded in addition to compensatory (including aggravated) damages of £12,350.

27-149 **Several claimants** The question arose in *Riches v News Group Newspapers Ltd*[755] as to the approach to be taken where there are several claimants. The Court of Appeal held that, in such a case, the total amount of exemplary damages considered fair for the defendant to pay should first be decided on. Then that amount can be divided among the claimants. Parker LJ said that a jury should be instructed to proceed by the following steps: decide how much each claimant should receive by way of compensation and aggregate those sums; consider whether the case is appropriate for exemplary damages; consider whether the aggregate of compensatory damages is enough to punish the defendant; if it is not, consider what total sum the defendant ought to pay; divide the difference between the total sum which the defendant ought to pay and the aggregate for compensatory damages by the number

751 [1972] A.C. 1027. The author was not a party to the proceedings in the House of Lords but was represented in the Court of Appeal.

752 See also *Francis v Brown* (1998) 30 H.L.R. 143 CA. Apparently the rule applies to aggravated as well as to exemplary damages: [1972] A.C. 1027 at 1063, per Lord Hailsham LC In *Kuddus v Chief Constable of Leicestershire Constabulary* [2001] UKHL 29; [2002] 2 A.C. 122 at [128] this consideration led Lord Scott to doubt whether exemplary damages were ever appropriate in a case against an employer based on vicarious liability, where the conduct of the employer does not merit punishment (although Lord Scott emphasised the anomalous nature of exemplary damages; cf. the speeches Lord Nicholls and Lord Hutton).

753 [2006] EWCA Civ 1773; [2007] 1 W.L.R. 1065.

754 [2006] EWCA Civ 1773; [2007] 1 W.L.R. 1065 at [47]. For the Law Commission's detailed reasoning on this, coming to the same conclusion, see *Aggravated, Exemplary and Restitutionary Damages Report No.247* paras 5.209–5.230.

755 [1986] Q.B. 256.

of claimants and add the figure so arrived at to each of the compensatory sums; award to each claimant the total so arrived at as one undivided sum but state, if asked to do so, whether that sum exceeds what would have been awarded for compensation only and, if so, what would have been awarded for such compensation. In the case itself the Court of Appeal set aside a total award of £250,000 exemplary damages to the claimants for libel because, inter alia, there had been no direction on this point by the trial judge and there was the possibility that the jury had considered that £25,000 rather than £250,000 (£2,500 rather than £25,000 to each claimant) should be the total amount of exemplary damages. In *R. (Lumba) v Secretary of State for the Home Department*[756] one of the reasons for not awarding exemplary damages was that there were others in the same position as the claimants who were not before the court.

10. Restitutionary Damages[757]

The aim of damages may sometimes be to strip away part or all of the gains made by the tortfeasor from the tort (i.e. to reverse the defendant's wrongful enrichment), rather than to compensate the claimant for his loss, although this remains controversial. Sometimes referred to as "*Wrotham Park* damages"[758] or "hypothetical release damages" (i.e. damages assessed according to what the claimant could reasonably have charged the defendant for releasing the defendant from the duty that has been broken had the defendant approached the claimant immediately before committing the tort) it was unclear whether such awards are concerned to compensate the claimant for loss or are restitutionary as being concerned to strip the tortfeasor of some of the wrongful gains. Other restitutionary remedies for torts are well-established: for example the equitable remedy of accounting for profits, which has long been awarded for intellectual property torts[759] and has arguably been awarded for the tort of deceit[760]; and the action for money had and received which, through the misleadingly named doctrine of "waiver of tort" can be awarded in respect of the wrongful acquisition of the claimant's property through torts such as conversion or trespass to goods.[761] It would be incorrect to say, therefore, that there is no precedent for the award of restitutionary remedies for a tort. The main cases in which restitutionary *damages* have been (or appear to have been) awarded have **27-150**

---

756 [2011] UKSC 12; [2012] 1 A.C. 245 at [167].

757 See, generally, *Aggravated, Exemplary and Restitutionary Damages*, Law Commission Report No.247 (1997), Pt III; see para.27-151 fn.765.

758 Named after the breach of restrictive covenant case of *Wrotham Park Estate Co Ltd v Parkside Homes Ltd* [1974] 1 W.L.R. 798.

759 e.g. Patents Act 1977 s.61(1)(d); *Siddell v Vickers* (1892) 9 R.P.C. 152 (infringement of patent); Copyright, Designs and Patents Act 1988 s.96(2); *Potton Ltd v Yorkclose Ltd* [1990] F.S.R. 11; *Island Records Ltd v Tring International Plc* [1996] 1 W.L.R. 1256 (infringement of copyright); *Slazenger & Sons v Spalding & Bros* [1910] 1 Ch. 257 (infringement of trade mark); *Lever v Goodwin* (1887) 36 Ch. D. 1; *My Kinda Town Ltd v Soll* [1983] R.P.C. 15 (reversed on liability [1983] R.P.C. 407) (passing off). See paras 24-55, 25-20.

760 *Murad v Al Saraj* [2004] EWHC 1235 (Ch). But in the Court of Appeal [2005] EWCA Civ 959; [2005] W.T.L.R. 1573 Arden LJ at [46] rejected that interpretation and said that the amount of profits was given only for breach of fiduciary duty; contrast Clarke LJ at [164]. A restitutionary claim for the tort of deceit was denied in *Halifax Building Society v Thomas* [1996] Ch. 217 CA.

761 e.g. *Oughton v Seppings* (1830) 1 B. & Ad. 241; *United Australia v Barclays Bank Ltd* [1941] A.C. 1; *Chesworth v Farrar* [1967] 1 Q.B. 407. See para.30-02.

concerned the tort of trespass to land.[762] Of these, perhaps the most important is *Ministry of Defence v Ashman*[763] in which the Court of Appeal held that damages against a tenant who had wrongfully ignored a notice to quit Royal Air Force accommodation should be assessed according to what it would have cost her to rent alternative local authority accommodation had any been available and not according to the Royal Air Force's loss. Hoffmann LJ said:

> "A person entitled to possession of land can make a claim against a person who has been in occupation without his consent on two alternative bases. The first is for the loss which he has suffered in consequence of the defendant's trespass. This is the normal measure of damages in the law of tort. The second is the value of the benefit which the occupier has received. This is a claim for restitution. The two bases of claim are mutually exclusive and the [claimant] must elect before judgment which of them he wishes to pursue. These principles are not only fair but … also well established by authority. It is true that in earlier cases it has not been expressly stated that a claim for mesne profit for trespass can be a claim for restitution. Nowadays I do not see why we should not call a spade a spade. In this case the Ministry of Defence elected for the restitutionary remedy."[764]

27-151 Given that the principle of restitutionary damages has been accepted, the difficult question of the criteria for determining whether a tort triggers restitutionary damages remains. Three main views could be distilled from the academic literature.[765] The first, and widest, was that restitutionary damages should be available for any tort provided a gain has been acquired by (i.e. has been factually caused by) the tort. A second was that proprietary torts only should trigger restitution.[766] A third view was that any tort deliberately committed with a view to gain (i.e. cyni-

[762] See, e.g. *Penarth Dock Engineering Co Ltd v Pounds* [1963] 1 Lloyd's Rep. 359; *Bracewell v Appleby* [1975] Ch. 408; *Swordheath Properties Ltd v Tabet* [1979] 1 W.L.R. 285; *Field Common Ltd v Elmbridge BC* [2008] EWHC 2079 (Ch); [2009] 1 P. & C.R. 1; *Stadium Capital Holdings (No.2) Ltd v St Marylebone Property Co Plc* [2010] EWCA Civ 952; *Ramzan v Brookwide Ltd* [2011] EWCA Civ 985; [2012] 1 All E.R. 903; *Jones v Ruth* [2011] EWCA Civ 804; [2012] 1 W.L.R. 1495 at [36]-[41];*Eaton Mansions (Westminster) Ltd v Stinger Compania De Inversion SA* [2013] EWCA Civ 1308; [2014] H.L.R. 4 (all trespass to land cases). See also *Carr-Saunders v Dick McNeil Associates Ltd* [1986] 1 W.L.R. 922 (nuisance); *Seager v Copydex (No.2)* [1969] 1 W.L.R. 809 (breach of confidence). But the possibility of there being an award of "gain-based damages" in lieu of an injunction for the tort of private nuisance was left open by the Supreme Court in *Coventry v Lawrence* [2014] UKSC 13; [2014] A.C. 822. Also of interest is the analysis of tort cases in *Surrey CC v Bredero Homes Ltd* [1993] 1 W.L.R. 1361 (breach of contract); and *Att Gen v Blake* [2001] 1 A.C. 268 HL (breach of contract). cf. cases either refusing restitutionary damages, or clearly preferring a compensatory interpretation, such as *Stoke-on-Trent City Council v W&J Wass Ltd* [1988] 1 W.L.R. 1406; *Jaggard v Sawyer* [1995] 1 W.L.R. 269 CA; *Severn Trent Water Ltd v Barnes* [2004] EWCA Civ 570; [2004] 2 E.G.L.R. 95; *Tamares (Vincent Square) Ltd v Fairpoint* [2007] EWHC 212 (Ch); [2007] 1 W.L.R. 2167; *Forsyth-Grant v Allen* [2008] EWCA Civ 505; [2008] 27 E.G. 118; *Devenish Nutrition Ltd v Sanofi-Aventis SA* [2008] EWCA Civ 1086; [2009] Ch. 390, noted by Odudu and Virgo [2009] C.L.J. 34.

[763] (1993) 66 P. & C.R. 195. See also *Ministry of Defence v Thompson* [1993] 40 E.G. 148.

[764] (1993) 66 P. & C.R. 195 at 200–201.

[765] See, e.g. Birks, *An Introduction to the Law of Restitution*, Ch.X; Burrows, *The Law of Restitution*, 3rd edn (Oxford: OUP, 2011), Ch.24; Birks, *Civil Wrongs: A New World* (Butterworth Lectures, 1990-91); Beatson, *The Use and Abuse of Unjust Enrichment*, pp.206–243; Edelman, *McGregor on Damages*, 20th edn (2017), Chs 14 and 15; Edelman, *Gain-Based Damages* (2002); Jackman [1989] C.L.J. 302.

[766] See especially *Devenish Nutrition Ltd v Sanofi-Aventis SA* [2008] EWCA Civ 1086; [2009] Ch. 390. But a restriction to the type of tort is not easy to reconcile with the fact that an account of profits was awarded for a "non-proprietary" breach of contract in *Att Gen v Blake* [2001] 1 A.C. 268.

cally committed) should enable the courts to award restitutionary damages.[767] The issue has now been considered by the Supreme Court in *Morris-Garner v One Step (Support) Ltd*.[768] Although the case concerned a breach of contract, the Supreme Court also discussed tort cases in seeking to clarify the purpose and scope of "Wrotham Park damages" or "hypothetical release damages". Several important points emerge from the leading judgment given by Lord Reed (with whom Lady Hale, Lord Wilson and Lord Carnwath agreed): (i) the preferred terminology for these damages is "negotiating damages"; (ii) the purpose of these damages is to compensate for a loss (albeit not a loss in the ordinary sense) and not to remove gains from the defendant; (iii) such damages will be apt where one is concerned with the infringement of a proprietary right (or, it would seem, analogously, where the right infringed was designed to protect an asset of the claimant); and (iv) it is possible that such damages may be awarded more widely in equity in lieu of an injunction under the Senior Courts Act 1981 s.50.[769] The difficulty of quantifying a claimant's loss does not justify a court in abandoning the attempt to do so and making an award which cannot be regarded as compensatory; nor does the deliberate nature of the defendant's breach of duty, nor the claimant's interest in preventing the defendants' profit-making activities, justify a non-compensatory award.[770] Damages based on a hypothetical release fee cannot be awarded simply because the court considers that that is a "just response". On the facts of *Morris-Garner*, where there had been a breach of a contractual non-compete clause, "negotiating damages" were not available (although a court might use a hypothetical bargain as an evidential tool in assessing the claimant's ordinary loss). This was because there had been no infringement of a proprietary right and the damages were not being sought or awarded in lieu of an injunction.

11. Appeals on Quantum of Damages[771]

Appeals from jury The right to a jury trial in a civil case is now confined to claims for malicious prosecution or false imprisonment or where there is a charge of fraud.[772] What we are here dealing with, an appeal on quantum from a jury, is now, therefore, a rare occurrence. The traditional rule is that an appellate court will not interfere, in the absence of a misdirection,[773] unless it appears that the jury "must have acted improperly and so have brought about a palpably wrong result. If the figure of an award seems to be outrageous, or so extravagant that no other jury 27-152

767 An analogy can here be drawn with the second category of exemplary damages recognised in *Rookes v Barnard* [1964] A.C. 1129. See also *Borders (UK) Ltd v Commissioner of Police of the Metropolis* [2005] EWCA Civ 197; *The Times*, 15 April 2005 on the relationship between exemplary and restitutionary damages.

768 [2018] UKSC 20; [2019] A.C. 649.

769 See para.27-133.

770 [2018] UKSC 20; [2019] A.C. 649 at [96]–[97].

771 Generally, see Edelman, *McGregor on Damages*, 20th edn (2017), Ch.53.

772 Senior Courts Act 1981 s.69; County Courts Act 1984 s.66. The right to a jury trial in defamation cases was removed by the Defamation Act 2013 s.11. When there were juries in defamation cases, deference was shown to their awards and levels of awards for non-pecuniary loss in personal injury cases were cited to them: see, generally: *John v MGN Ltd* [1997] Q.B. 586 and *Kiam v MGN Ltd* [2002] EWCA Civ 43; [2003] Q.B. 281. But in the former case, the Court of Appeal did substitute a figure of £35,000 compensatory damages for the "excessive" £75,000 damages awarded by the jury; and substituted a figure of £50,000 exemplary damages for the "manifestly excessive" £275,000 awarded by the jury.

773 See *Warren v King* [1964] 1 W.L.R. 1.

would repeat it, then there might, in some cases, be ground for suspecting that a jury has been partial or perverse."[774] However, in *Rantzen v Mirror Group Newspapers (1986) Ltd*[775] the Court of Appeal held that the threshold for interfering with jury awards in defamation cases should be lowered from that traditionally insisted on so as properly to protect freedom of expression as required by the European Convention on Human Rights. With regard to personal injury actions, the Court of Appeal in *Ward v James*[776] earlier ruled not only that juries should only be used in exceptional cases but also that, where they are used, the Court of Appeal should no longer feel the same hesitancy as it formerly did in upsetting awards. The Court of Appeal (or the Supreme Court[777]) has power to order a new trial or can substitute a sum of damages that it considers proper in place of that awarded by the jury.[778] In *Thompson v Commissioner of Police for the Metropolis*,[779] where the claims were for malicious prosecution and false imprisonment, the Court of Appeal, inter alia, substituted £15,000 exemplary damages for the £200,000 awarded to the claimant.

27-153 **Appeals from judge sitting alone** In general the classic statement of Lord Wright in *Davies v Powell Duffryn Collieries Ltd*[780] that the appellate court should intervene only if "the judge has acted upon a wrong principle of law, or has misapprehended the facts, or has for these or other reasons made a wholly erroneous estimate of the damage suffered" remains valid.[781] But here too there have been significant developments in the field of personal injury actions. The impetus for such developments has been the practice of itemisation of the various heads of damage.[782] The Court of Appeal must consider these items separately and, as Edmund Davies LJ remarked in *Smith v Manchester Corp*,[783] "if the award under one head is clearly wrong, it should be interfered with, even though ultimately there may be no very substantial variation in the global award". The modern practice is to acknowledge that for many types of injury there is a permissible range of award and the court therefore interferes only when the trial judge's assessment lies outside that range.[784]

---

774 *Scott v Musial* [1959] 2 Q.B. 429 at 438, per Morris LJ. For examples of the innumerable statements to similar effect, see *Praed v Graham* (1889) 24 Q.B.D. 53 at 55, per Lord Esher MR; *Smith v Schilling* [1928] 1 K.B. 429 at 433, per Scrutton LJ; at 440, per Greer LJ; *Davies v Powell Duffryn Associated Collieries Ltd* [1942] A.C. 601 at 616, per Lord Wright; *Morey v Woodfield (No.2)* [1964] 1 W.L.R. 16n. at 19, per Pearce LJ; at 21, per Harman LJ; *Broome v Cassell & Co Ltd* [1972] A.C. 1027 at 1065-1066, per Lord Hailsham LC; *Blackshaw v Lord* [1984] Q.B. at 27, per Stephenson LJ; *Sutcliffe v Pressdram Ltd* [1991] 1 Q.B. 153 at 176, per Lord Donaldson MR, at 184, per Nourse LJ.

775 [1994] Q.B. 670.

776 [1966] 1 Q.B. 273.

777 *Grobbelaar v News Group Newspapers Ltd* [2002] UKHL 40; [2002] 1 W.L.R. 3024 (in which the House of Lords restored the jury's defamation verdict in favour of the claimant, which had been quashed by the Court of Appeal, but reduced damages from £85,000 to £1).

778 CPR r.52.10.

779 [1998] Q.B. 498.

780 [1942] A.C. 601 at 617.

781 See the restatements in, e.g. *H West & Son Ltd v Shephard* [1964] A.C. 326 at 352–353, per Lord Morris; *Dingle v Associated Newspapers Ltd* [1964] A.C. 371 at 393–394, per Lord Radcliffe; *Yorkshire Electricity Board v Naylor* [1968] A.C. 529 at 542–543, per Lord Morris; *Pickett v British Rail Engineering Ltd* [1980] A.C. 136 at 151, per Lord Wilberforce. See also *Wilson v Pilley* [1957] 1 W.L.R. 1138 (appeal from county court).

782 See paras 27-20 to 27-22.

783 (1974) 17 K.I.R. 1 at 6–7. See also *K v JMP Co* [1976] Q.B. 85 (a fatal accident claim); *Lai Wee Lian v Singapore Bus Service (1978) Ltd* [1984] A.C. 729 at 735.

784 *George v Pinnock* [1973] 1 W.L.R. 118 at 125, per Orr LJ; cf. *Moeliker v A Reyrolle & Co* [1977] 1 W.L.R. 132 at 144, per Stephenson LJ.

Chapter 28

INJUNCTIONS

Table of Contents

1. Introduction

Principle on which injunction granted[1] In addition to the remedy by action for damages in respect of torts which have actually been committed, there is, in certain cases, a remedy by way of injunction to prevent the commission of torts which are threatened or anticipated or, in cases of continuing injuries, to restrain their **28-01**

[1] D. Bean, *Injunctions*, 13th edn (2018); A. Burrows, *Remedies for Torts, Breach of Contract and Equitable Wrongs*, 4th edn (2019), Ch.23; R. Sharpe, *Injunctions and Specific Performance*, 4th edn (2012), Pt I; I. Spry, Equitable Remedies, 9th edn (2013), Ch.4. See generally J. Murphy, "Rethinking injunctions in Tort Law" (2007) 27 O.J.L.S. 509.

continuance. The principle upon which such injunction is granted is that the injury to be inflicted would be of such a character that the claimant could not practically be compensated in damages. In some cases the injunction takes a mandatory form, particularly where the defendant has created a permanent source of injury, such as the erection of a building to the nuisance of the claimant's lights or to the obstruction of his right of way, or has wrongfully taken a conveyance of land to defeat the claimant's rights: in such a case the court orders him to restore the claimant to his right by removing the offending building or reversing the conveyance. In all such cases, breach of the court's order is a contempt of court and may be punished as such.

28-02 **Torts of all kinds may be restrained by injunction where "just or convenient"** The power to grant an injunction is now possessed by all divisions of the High Court and also by the county court in cases falling within its jurisdiction.[2] Injunctions may be granted in all cases in which it appears to the court to be "just or convenient" to do so, but these words do not confer an arbitrary discretion on the court. Their effect is to enable the court to grant such injunctions as could formerly have been granted by a court of equity.[3] In an appropriate case, therefore, an injunction may be granted in relation to any form of tortious conduct.[4] The breach of statutory obligations which are supported by criminal sanctions does not give rise to a tortious claim unless the court considers that such was the intention of Parliament[5]; where no such inference is drawn (and no other private wrong is made out) the court may not grant an injunction to a private individual in respect of the breach.[6] In *Burris v Azadani*[7] the Court of Appeal upheld an injunction imposing an "exclusion zone" on the defendant to prevent repetition of his tortious harassment of the claimant. It was acknowledged that the effect of the order was to forbid certain lawful actions on the part of the defendant, namely his use of the highway. But it was held that an injunction can be granted restraining conduct that is not itself

---

2 Senior Courts Act 1981 s.37(1); County Courts Act 1984 s.38. By the County Court Remedies Regulations 2014 (SI 2014/982) the county court generally has no jurisdiction to grant a search (*Anton Piller*) order but does now have jurisdiction to make a freezing (*Mareva*) injunction.

3 *North London Railway v Great Northern Ry* (1883) 11 Q.B.D. 30; *South Carolina Insurance Co v Assurantie Maatschappij de Zeven Provincien NV* [1987] A.C. 24 HL; *UL v BK* [2013] EWHC 1735 (Fam); [2014] Fam. 35 at [14].

4 See, e.g. *Saxby v Easterbrook* (1878) 3 C.P.D. 339 (defamation); *Egan v Egan* [1975] Ch. 218 (assault); *Erven Warnink BV v J Townend & Sons (Hull) Ltd* [1979] A.C. 731 (passing-off); *X v Y* [1988] 2 All E.R. 648 (breach of confidence); *Coflexip SA v Scott Comex Seaway MS Ltd* [2001] 1 All E.R. 952 (Note) (patent infringement); *Secretary of State for Environment, Food and Rural Affairs v Meier* [2009] UKSC 11; [2009] 1 W.L.R. 2780; *London (Mayor) v Hall* [2010] EWCA Civ 817; [2011] 1 W.L.R. 504 (trespass to land); *Brand v Berki* [2014] EWHC 2979 (QB) (tort of harassment under the Protection from Harassment Act 1997). In *Bird v O'Neal* [1960] A.C. 907 an injunction was granted to restrain picketing which was being carried on with threats of intimidation. In *Miller v Jackson* [1977] Q.B. 966 at 980, Lord Denning MR said that he did not know of a case where an injunction had been granted to stop a negligent action.

5 Ch.8. For an example of an injunction being granted to restrain the tort of breach of statutory duty, see *Warder v Cooper* [1970] 1 Ch. 495; cf. *McCall v Abelesz* [1976] Q.B. 585.

6 *Thorne v British Broadcasting Corp* [1967] 1 W.L.R. 1104; *Gouriet v Union of Post Office Workers* [1978] A.C. 435; *Lonhro Ltd v Shell Petroleum Co Ltd* [1982] A.C. 173; *RCA Corp v Pollard* [1983] 1 Ch. 135. See too the Australian decision in *Smethurst v Commissioner of Police* [2020] HCA 14.

7 [1995] 1 W.L.R. 1372.

tortious (or otherwise unlawful), if such an order is necessary to prevent a tort.[8] This has since been extended to cover cases concerned with likely breaches by third parties. Thus holders of intellectual property rights may sue internet service providers to force blocking of websites where this is necessary to prevent infringement of their rights, not by the providers, but by the persons operating the websites.[9]

Although under the general law of tort no injunction can be granted in the absence of some tortious right of action in the claimant,[10] there are two exceptions. First, a statutory body or office-holder may obtain an injunction to prevent unjustified interference with the performance of its (or his) functions.[11] Secondly, it is now clear that the infringement of the claimant's human rights can give adequate ground for an injunction even if not otherwise wrongful.[12] Most of the decisions tend to concern art.8 of the European Convention on Human Rights (the right to privacy)[13] or art.2 (the right to life).[14] There are further rights vested in public authorities to obtain injunctions respecting crimes or matters affecting the public generally;[15] but these are a matter of public law rather than tort, and are not discussed further here. 28-03

Injunction against whom? An injunction may be granted on principle against anyone subject to the jurisdiction of the court. It is not however the practice to grant an order against a minor who has no earnings from which a fine for disobedience can be paid and who is too young to be sent to prison; nor yet generally against a person whose mental incapacity means that he is incapable of understanding the order.[16] It is not absolutely necessary to identify the defendant by name or even 28-04

---

8 See too *Cuadrilla Bowland Ltd v Persons Unknown* [2020] EWCA Civ 9; [2020] 4 W.L.R. 29 at [111]–[112].

9 *Cartier International AG v British Sky Broadcasting Ltd* [2016] EWCA Civ 658; [2017] 1 All E.R. 700. See S. Gee, "The jurisdiction to grant injunctions against innocent third parties, the internet and Cartier v British Telecommunications Plc in the Supreme Court" (2018) 40 E.I.P.R. 571.

10 See, e.g. *Day v Brownrigg* (1878) 10 Ch. D. 294 (naming suburban villa identically with grander neighbouring property, with concomitant confusion and injury to *amour propre*: no injunction, since no right infringed). See generally on this, A. Tettenborn "Injunctions Without Damages" (1987) 38 N.I.L.Q. 118.

11 See, e.g. *Broadmoor Hospital Authority v R.* [2000] Q.B. 775 CA (injunction granted to hospital authority to support performance of its statutory duty); also *Re Oriental Credit Ltd* [1988] Ch. 204 (company liquidator).

12 *Venables v News Group Newspapers Ltd* [2001] Fam. 430 put the point beyond doubt (child murderer granted new identity, with attendant injunctions, on the basis of the right to life under art.2).

13 *Re KT* [2004] EWHC 3428 (Fam) (allegations in open court of pederasty); *Re Guardian News & Media Ltd* [2010] UKSC 1; [2010] 2 A.C. 697 (non-secret allegations of terrorist involvement: would harm subject's engagement with community).

14 As in *Venables v News Group Newspapers Ltd* [2001] Fam. 430, above; also *Venables v News Group Newspapers Ltd*, unreported, 30 July 2010 QBD (same person allowed to suppress information about (new) name under which convicted in open court on child pornography charges after release). cf. *Mills v News Group Newspapers Ltd* [2001] E.M.L.R. 41 (no sufficient threat shown to prevent disclosure of Heather Mills' address).

15 These include the Attorney General's power, either on his own initiative or in a relator action, to seek an injunction to uphold the public interest (e.g. *Gouriet v Union of Post Office Workers* [1978] A.C. 435; and *Att-Gen v Harris* [1961] 1 Q.B. 74); and those of local authorities, which under s.222 of the Local Government Act can obtain injunctions for the benefit of the locality (e.g. *Stoke-on-Trent BC v B & Q (Retail) Ltd* [1984] A.C. 754; *Runnymede BC v Ball* [1986] 1 W.L.R. 353; *Birmingham City Council v Afsar* [2020] EWHC 864 (QB); [2020] E.L.R. 341). Other specific powers allow injunctive relief in favour of public authorities in such matters as breaches of trading standards, noise pollution, unlawful discrimination and anti-social behaviour. See D. Bean, *Injunctions*, 13th ed (2018), paras 4-42–4-44; 4-58 and 4-65–4-69.

16 *Wookey v Wookey* [1991] Fam. 121.

designation. An order may thus be made against representatives of an unincorporated association, or of other groups whose members have the same interest, on behalf of all members of that association or group, so that a breach of the injunction will render the representatives liable for contempt.[17] In *Bloomsbury Publishing Group Plc v News Group Newspapers Ltd*,[18] it was confirmed that the jurisdiction went further, and that an injunction could be granted against a person or persons not named but merely described as those committing the wrongful act in question; a jurisdiction now widely used in respect of unlawful protests and other activities.[19] In addition injunctions may be expressly granted *contra mundum*, certainly where human rights are engaged[20] and probably elsewhere.[21] It should also be noted that even where not a person to whom an injunction is addressed, any person who interferes with the due administration of justice by intentionally frustrating the purpose of an injunction can be liable in contempt.[22]

28-05 **Discretion of court** The grant of an injunction, being an equitable remedy, is always discretionary and this discretion belongs to the trial judge: an appellate court may not substitute its own views on the merits of the case but may intervene only "if the judge misdirected himself in law, took into account irrelevant matters or failed to take into account relevant matters".[23] The principles governing the exercise of the discretion differ according to the nature of the injunction sought. Where an injunction is sought to restrain the continuation of a wrongful act which interferes with the claimant's rights and is prohibitory in substance as well as in form, then

---

17 *Taff Vale Ry Co v Amalgamated Society of Railway Engineers* [1901] A.C. 426; *Greig v Insole* [1978] 1 W.L.R. 302; *Michaels (Furriers) Ltd v Askew* (1983) 127 S.J. 597 CA; *EMI Records v Kudhail* [1985] F.S.R. 36. See CPR r.19.6.

18 [2003] EWHC 1205; [2003] 1 W.L.R. 1633 (unknown persons threatening to publish pirated versions of Harry Potter book). The power is particularly useful against anonymous groups of trespassers.

19 e.g. *Hampshire Waste Services Ltd v Persons Intending to Trespass and/or Trespassing upon Chineham Incinerator Site* [2003] EWHC 1738 (Ch); [2004] Env. L.R. 9; *Secretary of State for Environment, Food and Rural Affairs v Meier* [2009] UKSC 11; [2009] 1 W.L.R. 2780; *Boyd v Ineos Upstream Ltd* [2019] EWCA Civ 515; [2019] 4 W.L.R. 100. More recently a more general order was made against anyone contemplating climbing the Shard in the City. See *Re King-Thompson* [2019] EWHC 2962 (QB); also *RGCM Ltd v Lockwood* [2019] EWHC 1937 (Ch). There is no injustice to anyone in making such an order provided the description is sufficiently certain to identify those included and those who are not. Note, however, the restrictions on such orders in *Canada Goose UK Retail Ltd v Persons Unknown* [2020] EWCA Civ 303; [2020] 1 W.L.R. 2802. See generally J. Seymour, "Injunctions Enjoining Non-Parties: Distinction without Difference" [2007] C.L.J. 605.

20 *X (formerly known as Mary Bell) v O'Brien* [2003] EWHC 1101 (Fam); [2003] E.M.L.R. 37; *OPQ v BJM* [2011] EWHC 1059 (QB); [2011] E.M.L.R. 23; *RXG v Ministry of Justice* [2019] EWHC 2026 (QB); [2019] E.M.L.R. 25.

21 That such orders were possible was admitted in *Ambrosiadou v Coward* [2013] EWHC 58 (QB); [2013] 2 F.C.R. 359. Such an order appears to have been made in *Re King-Thompson* [2019] EWHC 2962 (QB) (general order against climbing the Shard in the City), and was definitely made in *Vastint Leeds BV v Persons Unknown* [2018] EWHC 2456 (Ch); [2019] 4 W.L.R. 2.

22 *Z Ltd v A-Z* [1982] Q.B. 558 (freezing injunction); *Att Gen v Times Newspapers Ltd* [1992] 1 A.C. 191; *Att Gen v Punch Ltd* [2002] UKHL 50; [2003] 1 A.C. 1046. It has been held at first instance that such contempt proceedings against third parties can be brought only in respect of interim, and not final, injunctions: *Jockey Club Ltd v Buffham* [2002] EWHC 1866 (QB); [2003] Q.B. 462. But such a curious hobble on the court's power seems, with respect, doubtful: compare the comments of Lord Neuberger MR in *Hutcheson v Popdog Ltd (News Group Newspapers Ltd, third party)* [2011] EWCA Civ 1580; [2012] 1 W.L.R. 782 at [26].

23 *Duport Steels Ltd v Sirs* [1980] 1 W.L.R. 142 at 171, per Lord Scarman. See also Lord Diplock at 163–164.

an injunction is fairly readily granted.[24] The grant of a mandatory injunction, which is an injunction in positive terms[25] requiring the defendant to take some specific action involving, typically, the carrying out of certain works, on the other hand, can never be "as of course"[26] and depends upon a number of factors in addition to those which may affect the grant of prohibitory injunctions.[27]

2. PROHIBITORY INJUNCTIONS

The mere proof of a legal wrong done in the past is insufficient to entitle the claimant to an injunction. The court must be satisfied that the interference with the claimant's right[28] is continuing, as in many cases of nuisance and some of trespass, or that it is likely to be repeated unless restrained.[29] Furthermore, even if this is done, the decision whether to grant an injunction remains essentially discretionary.[30] Thus while in the case of substantial interference with the claimant's rights there should be a presumption in favour of injunctive relief, with the defendant having to advance a case why it should not be available,[31] it is no longer the case, if it ever was,[32] that an injunction can be had save in exceptional circumstances or on any **28-06**

24 *Coventry v Lawrence* [2014] UKSC 13; [2014] A.C. 822 at [100] and [121] (Lord Neuberger, with the apparent agreement of Lords Carnwath and Mance). At one time it was regularly said in the case of a prohibitory order that the claimant got his injunction "as of course" unless there were exceptional circumstances (*Morris v Redland Bricks Ltd* [1970] A.C. 652 at 664, per Lord Upjohn; *Pride of Derby etc Ltd v British Celanese Ltd* [1953] 1 Ch. 149 at 181, per Lord Evershed MR; [1953] 1 Ch. 149 at 194, per Romer LJ). But today this is too favourable to the claimant, since it lays insufficient stress on the essentially discretionary nature of the whole exercise of deciding whether to grant an injunction. It should be noted that even if an injunction is granted, its operation may be suspended for a time where appropriate (see e.g. *Morris v Redland Bricks Ltd* [1970] A.C. 652 at 664, per Lord Upjohn; *Woollerton & Wilson Ltd v Richard Costain Ltd* [1970] 1 W.L.R. 411; *Coventry v Lawrence (No 2)* [2014] UKSC 46; [2015] A.C. 106 in which the injunction prohibiting the defendant's use of a race track was suspended until such time as the claimants' home was fit for habitation after it had been damaged by fire). This was particularly true where the defendant was a public utility: see, e.g. *Price's Patent Candle Co v London CC* [1908] 2 Ch. 526; *Pride of Derby etc Ltd v British Celanese Ltd* [1953] Ch. 149; and also A. Ogus & G. Richardson, "Economics and the Environment: A Study of Private Nuisance" [1977] C.L.J. 284, 311–314.

25 *Jackson v Normandy Brick Co* [1899] 1 Ch. 438.

26 *Morris v Redland Bricks Ltd* [1970] A.C. 652 at 665, per Lord Upjohn.

27 See paras 28-14 to 28-19.

28 Actual damage is not necessary so long as an actionable interference with proprietary rights is shown: *Jones v Llanrwst Urban DC* [1911] 1 Ch. 393; *Sevenoaks DC v Pattullo & Vinson Ltd* [1984] Ch. 211.

29 *Proctor v Bayley* (1889) 42 Ch. D. 390. In *Weller v Associated Newspapers Ltd* [2015] EWCA Civ 1176; [2016] 1 W.L.R. 1541 a prohibitory injunction preventing the publication of photographs was ordered in a situation where the defendant had said that they would not publish the photographs again but refused to give an undertaking to the court to that effect.

30 "The court's power to award damages in lieu of an injunction involves a classic exercise of discretion, which should not, as a matter of principle, be fettered": Lord Neuberger in *Coventry v Lawrence* [2014] UKSC 13; [2014] A.C. 822 at [120]: see too at [170] (Lord Clarke).

31 See *Coventry v Lawrence* [2014] UKSC 13; [2014] A.C. 822 at [100] and [121] (Lord Neuberger, with whom Lords Carnwath and Mance seemingly agreed). See too the earlier *Regan v Paul Properties DPF (No.1) Ltd* [2006] EWCA Civ 1391; [2007] Ch. 135, which to that extent at least seems to remain good law.

32 As had been suggested by a line of authority prior to the Supreme Court's decision in *Coventry*: e.g. *Shelfer v City of London Electric Lighting Co* [1895] 1 Ch 287, 323 (A.L. Smith LJ); and *Regan v Paul Properties DPF (No.1) Ltd* [2006] EWCA Civ 1391; [2007] Ch. 135 at [70]–[73] (Mummery LJ).

similar basis.[33] Nor can the matter be reduced to simple rules.[34] As Millett LJ put it in *Jaggard v Sawyer*[35]:

> "Reported cases are merely illustrations of circumstances in which particular judges have exercised their discretion, in some cases by granting an injunction, and in others by awarding damages instead. Since they are all cases on the exercise of a discretion, none of them is a binding authority on how the discretion should be exercised. The most that any of them can demonstrate is that in similar circumstances it would not be wrong to exercise the discretion in the same way. But it does not follow that it would be wrong to exercise it differently."

28-07 **Claimant's conduct** The grant of an injunction being discretionary, no complete or exhaustive list of relevant factors can be drawn up. However, the claimant's own conduct is clearly a relevant factor, so that condonation of the acts complained of, at least until withdrawn, will deprive him of this remedy.[36] Thus, where the defendants had given notice to the claimants—a canal company—of their intention to lay pipes for the purposes of drawing water from the canal and the claimants' agents had superintended the laying of the pipes and were aware of the expense incurred by the defendants, it was held that no injunction to restrain the defendants from continuing to draw water would be granted, even though the defendants were unable to make out a defence of leave and licence to an action at law on the same facts.[37] In *Armstrong v Sheppard & Short Ltd*,[38] the defendants had entered upon a small strip of land owned by the claimant and had laid a sewer under its surface. The claimant subsequently claimed damages for trespass and an injunction to restrain the further discharge of effluent through or under his land, and in evidence he denied that he had ever given the defendants permission to construct the sewer. On this he was disbelieved, but it was accepted that when he gave his assent to the work he was unaware of his own proprietary interest in the land in question. It was held that the defendants had no defence to an action for damages for trespass,[39] but that no injunction would issue, partly at least because the claimant had misled the defendants and had attempted to mislead the court.

---

33 "[A]n approach which involves damages being awarded only in 'very exceptional circumstances' [is] simply wrong in principle": *Coventry v Lawrence* [2014] UKSC 13; [2014] A.C. 822 at [119] (Lord Neuberger). See too Lord Clarke at [171]; also the discussions in the earlier nuisance cases of *Colls v Home & Colonial Stores Ltd* [1904] A.C. 179, 193, 212–213 (Lords M'Naghten and Lindley); and *Fishenden v Higgs & Hill Ltd* (1935) 153 L.T. 128, 139 (Lord Hanworth MR), largely approved of in Coventry's case.

34 Compare A.L. Smith LJ's nineteenth-century suggestion, now discountenanced, that to avoid an injunction it generally had to be shown, cumulatively, that (1) the injury to the claimant's rights was small; (2) that any injury could be estimated in money; (3) that any injury could be made good by a small money payment; and (4) that it would be oppressive to grant specific relief (*Shelfer v City of London Electric Lighting Co* [1895] 1 Ch. 287, 322–323). At best this is now a working rule or starting-point.

35 [1995] 1 W.L.R. 269, 288, approved by Lord Neuberger in *Coventry v Lawrence* [2014] UKSC 13; [2014] A.C. 822 at [120].

36 *Monson v Tussauds Ltd* [1894] 1 Q.B. 671. There can be no consent or acquiescence if the claimant is unaware of the defendant's activities or even if he expressly purports to give his consent but does so in ignorance of his own proprietary rights: *Armstrong v Sheppard and Short Ltd* [1959] 2 Q.B. 384 at 396, per Lord Evershed MR.

37 *Rochdale Canal Co v King* (1851) 2 Sim. (N.S.) 78; *Wood v Sutcliffe* (1851) 2 Sim. (N.S.) 163.

38 [1959] 2 Q.B. 384.

39 Nominal damages only were awarded.

Trivial harm Another ground upon which the issue of an injunction was refused in *Armstrong v Sheppard & Short Ltd* was the triviality of the harm caused to the claimant by the passage of effluent through the sewer under the surface of his land.[40] That the triviality of the harm suffered by the claimant[41] is in itself a ground for the refusal of an injunction has been affirmed on more than one occasion.[42] However, it has also been held several times that for the claimant to be entitled to an injunction it is not necessary that the harm caused by the repetition or continuance of the wrong should be substantial[43]; and indeed some 50 years ago it was said that "the very fact that no harm is done is a reason for rather than against the granting of an injunction: for if there is no damage done the damage recovered in the action will be nominal and if the injunction is refused the result will be no more nor less than a licence to continue the tort … in return for a nominal payment".[44] It is difficult to see how the authorities on this matter can be reconciled.[45] But it is suggested, especially in the light of the decision in *Coventry v Lawrence*,[46] that today the better view is that triviality of harm is a factor tending to militate against the grant of a prohibitory injunction. On the other hand, this may depend on the conduct involved, and in particular direct invasions of property may be subject to a special principle, such that an injunction will be granted against even harmless incursions unless good reason to the contrary is shown.[47] **28-08**

Impossibility of compliance It is sometimes taken to be a reason for refusing an injunction that compliance with it by the defendant would be impossible or illegal. **28-09**

---

40 [1959] 2 Q.B. at 396–397, per Lord Evershed MR. His Lordship indicated that an award of damages under Lord Cairns' Act (paras 27-128 to 27-133) might have been appropriate, but no claim for such damages was made.

41 The court should also take account of the risks of harm which have not yet materialised: see, e.g. *Miller v Jackson* [1977] Q.B. 966 at 986, where in his dissenting judgment Geoffrey Lane LJ took account of the fact that the playing of cricket by the defendants had not only caused physical harm to the claimant's property but had also created a risk of personal injury. Lord Denning MR and Cumming-Bruce LJ, however, thought that it was not unreasonable to expect the claimant and her family to keep out of the garden while cricket was being played (respectively, at 981 and 989).

42 *Goldsmid v Tunbridge Wells Improvement Commissioners* (1866) L.R. 1 Ch. 349 at 354–355, per Turner LJ; *Llandudno Urban DC v Woods* [1899] 2 Ch. 705; *Behrens v Richards* [1905] 2 Ch. 614.

43 *John Trenberth Ltd v National Westminster Bank Ltd* (1979) 39 P. & C.R. 104; *Patel v WH Smith (Eziot) Ltd* [1987] 1 W.L.R. 853; *Anchor Brewhouse Developments Ltd v Berkley House (Docklands Developments) Ltd* (1987) 38 B.L.R. 82.

44 *Woollerton & Wilson Ltd v Richard Costain Ltd* [1970] 1 W.L.R. 411 at 413, per Stamp J cited with approval in *Patel v WH Smith* (Eziot) Ltd [1987] 1 W.L.R. 853 at 860, per Balcombe LJ. The learned judge nevertheless suspended the operation of the injunction which was to restrain the defendants from allowing the jib of their crane to enter the claimant's air space, for long enough to enable them to complete their building operations. In *Charrington v Simons & Co Ltd* [1971] 1 W.L.R. 598 the Court of Appeal expressed its reservations on this aspect of Stamp J.'s decision; and in *John Trenberth Ltd v National Westminster Bank Ltd* (1979) 39 P. & C.R. 104; and in *Jaggard v Sawyer* [1995] 1 W.L.R. 269 CA, it was treated as wrong.

45 The suggestion that the triviality of the harm caused is a reason for not granting an injunction except where the consequences of the wrongful act, however slight, will endure indefinitely (see, e.g. *Att Gen v Sheffield Gas Consumer Co* (1852) 3 De G.M. & G. 304 at 314–315, per Lord Cranworth LJ) is inconsistent with, e.g. *Armstrong v Sheppard & Short Ltd* above and *Woollerton & Wilson Ltd v Richard Costain Ltd* above.

46 [2014] UKSC 13; [2014] A.C. 822.

47 Older authority certainly said as much: see e.g. Balcombe LJ in *Patel v W.H. Smith (Eziot) Ltd* [1987] 1 W.L.R. 853, 858. This was cited and followed without criticism in at least two post-Coventry cases, *Canary Wharf Investments Ltd v Brewer* [2018] EWHC 1760 (QB); and *Fitzwilliam Land Co v Cheesman* [2018] EWHC 3139 (QB) at [42].

In the context of prohibitory injunctions, however, there is little authority to support this,[48] if only because inaction in the nature of things is rarely impossible, and it is undoubtedly the case that a prohibitory injunction will not be refused merely because compliance will put the defendant to trouble or expense. In *Pride of Derby etc Ltd v British Celanese Ltd*,[49] for example, serious river pollution was caused by the discharge into a river by the defendant local authority of insufficiently treated sewage. The Court of Appeal held that the inadequacy of the defendants' plant to treat the current level of sewage, which was the result of an increase in the local population, and the alleged impossibility of avoiding the insufficiently treated discharge were not grounds for refusing an injunction. The solution was to issue the injunction and to suspend its operation for a time so as to give the defendant the opportunity to carry out the necessary expansion of its sewerage system.[50]

28-10 **Uncertainty** It is well-established, albeit that there have been relatively few case law examples, that a prohibitory injunction (as well as a mandatory injunction)[51] must be sufficiently clear and precise so that the defendant knows which acts are prohibited and which are not. For example, in *OPO v Rhodes*,[52] the Supreme Court overturned the grant of an interim prohibitory injunction restraining the defendant from publishing a book about his life, including the sexual abuse he had suffered as a child, using "graphic" language. The Supreme Court held that there was no arguable case that publication of the book would constitute the actionable tort of intentionally inflicting physical or psychological harm (i.e. the tort applied in *Wilkinson v Downton*).[53] But the Supreme Court also decided that the form of the interim injunction granted was objectionable because what is meant by "graphic", even as amplified by the Court of Appeal, was too imprecise and uncertain. In the words of Lady Hale and Lord Toulson, giving the leading judgment, "Any injunction must be framed in terms sufficiently specific to leave no uncertainty about what the affected person is or is not allowed to do".[54]

28-11 **Relevance of the public interest**[55] It might seem to follow a fortiori that if economic consequences to the defendant do not justify the refusal of an injunction, so also the social and economic effects on third parties should be ignored, but until recently authority was unclear. Nineteenth-century cases suggested both the relevance[56] and irrelevance[57] of third party effects; and this continued into the twentieth century. The Court of Appeal in *Shelfer v City of London Electric Light-*

48 But see *Earl of Harrington v Derby Corp* [1905] 1 Ch. 205 at 220, per Buckley J; *Pride of Derby etc Ltd v British Celanese Ltd* [1953] Ch. 149 at 181, per Evershed MR.
49 [1953] Ch. 149.
50 On suspended injunctions, see para.28-05 fn.24.
51 See para.28-19.
52 [2015] UKSC 32; [2016] A.C. 219.
53 [1897] 2 Q.B. 57.
54 [2015] UKSC 32; [2016] A.C. 219 at [79]. The certainty of the defendant's duty under the injunction is also relevant in enforcement proceedings: a person should not be liable to a penalty save where it was made sufficiently precise what he was, or was not, to do in order not to incur it. See *Cuadrilla Bowland Ltd v Persons Unknown* [2020] EWCA Civ 9; [2020] 4 W.L.R. 29.
55 J. McLaren, "The Common Law Nuisance Action and the Environmental Battle" (1972) 10 Osgoode Hall L.J. 505, especially at 552–556.
56 e.g. *Wood v Sutcliffe* (1851) 2 Sim. (N.S.) 163; *Raphael v Thames Valley Ry Co* (1866) L.R. 2 Eq. 37 at 46.
57 e.g. *Att Gen v Birmingham BC* (1858) 4 K. & J. 528 at 539–540.

ing Co[58] came down firmly against letting the interests of third parties or the public override the private interests of the claimant. By contrast, in *Miller v Jackson*[59] Lord Denning MR and Cumming-Bruce LJ, relying on the pre-*Shelfer* cases, held that the courts were under a duty to consider the interests of the public[60]; but subsequently, in *Kennaway v Thompson*[61] a different division of the Court of Appeal returned to *Shelfer* and refused to follow the approach taken in *Miller v Jackson*. However, despite cases such as this it was never seriously accepted that the public interest was entirely irrelevant[62]; and today it is clear that, at least in principle, account may be taken of third party effects. In *Coventry v Lawrence*,[63] a nuisance case where the issue was discussed at length, Lord Neuberger had no doubt whatever on the point:

> "I find it hard to see how there could be any circumstances in which it arose and could not, as a matter of law, be a relevant factor. Of course, it is very easy to think of circumstances in which it might arise but did not begin to justify the court refusing, or, as the case may be, deciding, to award an injunction if it was otherwise minded to do so. But that is not the point. The fact that a defendant's business may have to shut down if an injunction is granted should, it seems to me, obviously be a relevant fact, and it is hard to see why relevance should not extend to the fact that a number of the defendant's employees would lose their livelihood, although in many cases that may well not be sufficient to justify the refusal of an injunction. Equally, I do not see why the court should not be entitled to have regard to the fact that many other neighbours in addition to the claimant are badly affected by the nuisance as a factor in favour of granting an injunction."[64]

Human rights Where a claimant seeks an injunction to prevent what would otherwise be a clear tort committed against it, it seems clear that in so far as the defendant's human rights would be engaged, that may be relevant to the decision whether to grant the injunction.[65] The point normally arises in connection with defamation and art.10 of the European Convention on Human Rights,[66] but it is **28-12**

58 [1895] 1 Ch. 287.

59 [1977] Q.B. 966 at 981 and 988.

60 "Courts of equity will not ordinarily and without special necessity interfere by injunction where the injunction will have the effect of very materially injuring the rights of third persons not before the court": [1977] Q.B. 966 at 988 (Cumming-Bruce LJ). See also *Tetley v Chitty* [1986] 1 All E.R. 663 at 674, per McNeill J, although in that case an injunction was granted.

61 [1981] Q.B. 88. The terms of the injunction granted in this case were very detailed. See similarly *Watson v Croft Promosport Ltd* [2009] EWCA Civ 15; [2009] 3 All E.R. 249 in which an injunction was granted to restrain a nuisance constituted by noise from the defendant's car racing circuit. The injunction prohibited racing for more than 40 days a year. See also *Rosling v Pinnegar* (1987) 53 P. & C.R. 124.

62 For an obvious example, see *Dennis v Ministry of Defence* [2003] EWHC 793 (QB); [2003] Env. L.R. 34 (understandably, no injunction against operations from a large and noisy Lincolnshire RAF base, given the effects of such an order on the patent public interest in effective defence).

63 [2014] UKSC 13; [2014] A.C. 822.

64 [2014] UKSC 13; [2014] A.C. 822 at [124]. See too Lord Carnwath at [240] onwards, where the arguments are analysed in detail. Earlier, see cases such as *Wheeler v JJ Saunders Ltd* [1996] Ch. 19, 35 (Peter Gibson J).

65 *London (Mayor) v Hall* [2010] EWCA Civ 817; [2011] 1 W.L.R. 504 at [42] (Neuberger MR); *London (Mayor Commonalty and Citizens) v Samede* [2012] EWCA Civ 160; [2012] 2 All E.R. 1039. For guidance on the matter, see *Bromley LBC v Persons Unknown* [2020] EWCA Civ 12; [2020] H.R.L.R. 6 (which also makes it clear that public authorities must take account of duties under the Equality Act 2010 when seeking injunctions).

66 See, e.g. *Greene v Associated Newspapers Ltd* [2004] EWCA Civ 1462; [2005] Q.B. 972. See further para.21-03.

entirely general.[67] However, the presumption is very strong that property rights and rights existing to protect the public should be enforced.[68]

28-13 **Secrecy and proceedings for injunctions** Where celebrities or others seek injunctions to prevent dissemination of private information, it is fairly commonplace, for obvious reasons, for the court to order that the claimant or the defendant or both must not be named.[69] In *PJS v News Group Newspapers*[70] the Supreme Court held that an interim injunction preventing publication of a story about the private life of the claimant, or the naming of the claimant, should continue—because the injunction still had some purpose—even though the story had been published, along with the name of the claimant, in the USA, Canada and Scotland and on social media. In some other cases, concerning so-called "super-injunctions",[71] the court very exceptionally may go further and order that the fact that the proceedings have taken place and that an injunction has been granted should themselves not be publicised.[72]

3. MANDATORY INJUNCTIONS

28-14 A mandatory injunction is never issued "as of course" and is always at the discretion of the court. While emphasising this, however, in *Morris v Redland Bricks Ltd*[73] Lord Upjohn found it possible to state certain general principles for the exercise by the court of its discretion.[74]

---

67 *London (Mayor) v Hall* [2010] EWCA Civ 817; [2011] 1 W.L.R. 504, above. See too *Tabernacle v Secretary of State for Defence* [2009] EWCA Civ 23.

68 See, e.g. *London (Mayor) v Hall* [2010] EWCA Civ 817; [2011] 1 W.L.R. 504, above (protesters); *London (Mayor Commonalty and Citizens) v Samede* [2012] EWCA Civ 160; [2012] 2 All E.R. 1039 (protesters outside St Paul's cathedral); *West Sussex CC v Persons Unknown* [2013] EWHC 4024 (QB) (protesters on highway).

69 The cases are legion. See, e.g. *JIH v News Group Newspapers Ltd* [2011] EWCA Civ 42; [2011] 1 W.L.R. 1645; *ETK v News Group Newspapers Ltd* [2011] EWCA Civ 439; [2011] 1 W.L.R. 1827; *CTB v News Group Newspapers Ltd* [2011] EWHC 1232 (QB).

70 [2016] UKSC 26; [2016] A.C. 1081. See further para.26-56.

71 See generally *Report of the Committee on Super-Injunctions: Super-Injunctions, Anonymised Injunctions and Open Justice* (chaired by Lord Neuberger MR, 2010). In that report there was awareness of only four such injunctions having been granted. This may well have been optimistic at the time (James Robinson in an article in *The Guardian* for 13 October 2009 referred to that paper alone having been served with some twelve such orders that year). But it seems numbers are now very much down: N. Wilcox, "Last gasp of the super-injunction" (2014) 25 Ent. L.R. 13 (summarising and commenting on the 2013 statistics supplied by the MoJ on the subject). See further para.26-57.

72 *Donald v Ntuli* [2010] EWCA Civ 1276; [2011] 1 W.L.R. 294 at [43]. An example is an injunction in draconian terms issued in 2010 to prevent reporting of developments where a British couple were kidnapped by Somali pirates, on the basis that any media coverage at all, even of the proceedings, might hamper negotiations and put their lives at risk. After their release the injunction was discharged and the story of the affair was widely aired on the Web: e.g. *http://www.bbc.co.uk/news/mobile/uk-11752027*. Another is *RJW v Guardian News & Media Ltd*, unreported, 11 September 2009, suppressing allegations of toxic dumping in Africa by Trafigura Beheer BV and also the existence of the injunction itself (the matter was later publicised in Parliament by Paul Farrelly MP on 12 October 2009).

73 [1970] A.C. 652 at 665–666. The other members of the House of Lords present all agreed with Lord Upjohn's speech.

74 As with prohibitory injunctions—see para.28-07—a mandatory injunction may be refused because of the claimant's own conduct; see, e.g. *Tollemache & Cobbold Breweries Ltd v Reynolds* (1983) 268 E.G. 52, where a mandatory injunction was refused on the ground, inter alia, that the party seek-

(i) Probability of serious damage A mandatory injunction can only be granted where the claimant shows a very strong probability that grave damage will accrue to him in the future if the intervention of the court is denied. The power to issue mandatory injunctions, though it should be exercised unhesitatingly in a proper case, must be used sparingly and with caution and only in cases "in which extreme, or at all events, very serious damage" will ensue if the injunction is withheld.[75] 28-15

(ii) Damages not a sufficient remedy The damage which will follow a refusal of an injunction must be such that damages awarded in respect of it would not be a sufficient remedy. This, as Lord Upjohn pointed out, is no more than the application of the general principle of equity.[76] 28-16

(iii) Compliance illegal or cost of compliance excessive Relief will be refused where compliance by the defendant would be illegal.[77] Moreover, in contrast to prohibitory injunction cases, the cost to the defendant of compliance with a mandatory injunction must be taken into account. If, for example, the defendant has erected a building which obstructs the claimant's ancient lights, then the court will take into consideration "not only the injury to the [claimant] but also the amount which has been laid down by the defendant" before it will issue an injunction requiring the building to be removed.[78] In *Morris v Redland Bricks Ltd* itself the defendant's excavations of earth and clay had led to a withdrawal of support from the claimants' lands, some of which had already fallen away when the action was brought, and further subsidence was likely. The county court judge had granted a mandatory injunction ordering the defendants to restore support to the claimants' land, and one of the grounds upon which this part of his judgment was reversed was that the work required would have cost approximately £29,000, a sum out of all proportion to the value of the land which was at risk.[79] 28-17

Such considerations have no place, however, if the defendant has acted wantonly or unreasonably in relation to the claimant's rights or has tried to steal a march on him or on the court, and in such a case the defendant may be ordered to do positive work to restore the status quo even if the expense to him is out of all proportion to the corresponding advantage which would accrue to the claimant. *Daniel v Ferguson*[80] is a clear case. Immediately upon receiving notice of a motion for an 28-18

ing it had demonstrated "an attitude in regard to this litigation of extreme pettiness", per Ackner LJ at 56.

75 *Durell v Pritchard* (1865) 1 Ch. App. 244. See also *Leakey v National Trust for Places of Historic Interest and Natural Beauty* [1978] Q.B. 849; affirmed on other grounds [1980] Q.B. 485, where a mandatory injunction in a case involving falls of land from the defendant's property was refused on the ground that the remedial action already taken by the defendant was satisfactory; cf. *Kelsen v Imperial Tobacco Co* [1957] 2 Q.B. 334.

76 See para.28-01.

77 *Harold Stephen Co v Post Office* [1977] 1 W.L.R. 1172 where an injunction was refused on the ground, inter alia, that compliance would require the defendant Post Office to discriminate unlawfully between different consumers and to aid and abet its employees in the commission by them of criminal offences.

78 *Smith v Smith* (1875) L.R. 20 Eq. 500 at 505, per Jessel MR; *Colls v Home & Colonial Stores Ltd* [1904] A.C. 179 at 212, per Lord Lindley. See also *Att Gen v Colchester Corp* [1955] 2 Q.B. 207.

79 [1970] A.C. 652 at 667.

80 [1891] 2 Ch. 27; *Krehl v Burrell* (1879) 11 Ch. D. 146; *Woodhouse v Newry Navigation Co* [1898] 1 I.R. 161; *Colls v Home and Colonial Stores Ltd* [1904] A.C. 179 at 193, per Lord MacNaghten; *Pugh v Howells* (1984) 48 P. & C.R. 298 CA; *Ottercroft Ltd v Scandia Care Ltd* [2016] EWCA Civ

injunction to restrain him from building so as to obstruct the claimant's lights the defendant engaged extra men and proceeded as rapidly as possible with the building of a wall. The Court of Appeal held that even though the claimant's right to light had not yet been established an order for the removal of the wall must issue at once; its erection had been an attempt to anticipate the order of the court.

28-19 **(iv) Order must be precise** If, in the exercise of its discretion the court decides that the case is a proper one for the issue of a mandatory injunction, then the court must be careful to see that the defendant knows exactly what he has to do, not just as a matter of law but as a matter of fact, so that in carrying out the order of the court he can give his contractors the proper instructions.[81] In *Morris v Redland Bricks Ltd*, the injunction issued by the judge had done no more than require the defendants "to take all necessary steps to restore the support" to the claimants' land within a certain period of time. It thus offended against this principle and could not be allowed to stand.

4. ACTION QUIA TIMET

28-20 As a general rule, it is premature for the claimant to come to the court for an injunction before a complete cause of action has accrued, for instance, in a case where damage is the gist of the action, before damage has actually occurred. Nevertheless, the court must in certain cases issue an injunction quia timet to restrain conduct which, if allowed to go forward, would almost certainly lead to substantial damage to the claimant. Thus, for example, where the members of a trade union had begun to picket the claimant's hotel in order to prevent the delivery to it of fuel oil, but had not yet succeeded in interfering with deliveries to such an extent that the picketing amounted to a nuisance, an injunction to restrain further picketing was issued because there was no doubt that the defendants, or some of them, did threaten or intend to interfere with the delivery of the oil, if necessary for months, by placing pickets for the purpose of sustaining the embargo.[82]

28-21 The power to grant a quia timet injunction is undoubted,[83] and extends to mandatory as well as prohibitory injunctions, but it is exercised sparingly[84] and only when

---

867. See too *Esso Petroleum Co Ltd v Kingswood Motors (Addlestone) Ltd* [1974] Q.B. 142 (defendant induced breach of contract by causing garage to be conveyed to it to defeat tie: order to reconvey land transferred).

[81] *Att Gen v Staffordshire CC* [1905] 1 Ch. 336 at 342, per Joyce J; *Kennard v Cory Bros & Co Ltd* [1922] 1 Ch. 265 at 274, per Sargant J (affirmed [1922] 2 Ch. 1); *Fishenden v Higgs & Hill Ltd* (1935) 153 L.T. 128 at 142, per Maugham LJ.

[82] *Torquay Hotel Co Ltd v Cousins* [1969] 2 Ch. 106 at 120, per Stamp J (affirmed, ibid.).

[83] See, e.g. *Earl of Ripon v Hobart* (1843) 3 M. & K. 169; *Fletcher v Bealey* (1884) 28 Ch. D. 688; *Att Gen v Manchester Corp* [1893] 2 Ch. 87; *White v Mellin* [1895] A.C. 154; *Cowper v Laidler* [1903] 2 Ch. 337; *Att Gen v Nottingham Corp* [1904] 1 Ch. 673; *British Railway Traffic & Electric Co Ltd v CRC Co Ltd* [1922] 2 K.B. 260; *Morris v Redland Bricks Ltd* [1970] A.C. 652 at 665, per Lord Upjohn.

[84] Even in *Litchfield-Speer v Queen Anne's Gate Syndicate (No.2) Ltd* [1919] 1 Ch. 407, where there was a threatened obstruction of the claimant's ancient lights and P.O. Lawrence J considered that the case for a quia timet injunction had been made out, his Lordship preferred to make a declaration to the effect that the defendants were not entitled to build so as to obstruct the claimant's light, with liberty to apply for an injunction should it become necessary. In *Bridlington Relay Ltd v Yorkshire Electricity Board* [1965] Ch. 436 at 445, Buckley J held that it would be wrong for the court to grant a quia timet injunction to compel the defendant to do something which it appeared to be willing to do without the intervention of the court.

the possibility of damage is very high.[85] It is also commonly stated that the damage must be imminent. Thus in *Lemos v Kennedy Leigh Development Co Ltd*[86] the claimants, fearing damage to their property from the roots of trees growing on adjoining land, began proceedings in 1959. The evidence showed that damage might be expected by 1962, but the Court of Appeal held that there was not sufficient imminence of damage to justify an action. In *Hooper v Rogers*,[87] on the other hand, where there was a "real possibility" that damage would result to the claimant's property "in time",[88] it was held that a quia timet mandatory injunction could have been issued; and Russell LJ said that the use of the word "imminent" indicated no more than that the injunction must not be granted prematurely.[89] It is respectfully submitted that this leaves the matter completely open as, indeed, his Lordship seems to have intended, for he also said that the degree of probability of future damage is not an absolute standard: "what is to be aimed at is justice between the parties, having regard to all the relevant circumstances".[90] This decision of the Court of Appeal may indicate that quia timet injunctions will be more readily granted than in the past, but the case is difficult to reconcile with *Lemos v Kennedy Leigh Development Co Ltd*[91] and, moreover, the decision that an injunction might have been granted was necessary only as the foundation of an award of damages under Lord Cairns' Act.[92] No injunction was actually issued.

In the cases mentioned above no complete cause of action had, so far as material, accrued to the claimant when he began his proceedings, and for this reason the actions are classed as quia timet. In *Morris v Redland Bricks Ltd*,[93] however, the defendants' excavations had already caused some subsidence of the claimants' land and, accordingly, a complete cause of action had already accrued to them. Even so, in Lord Upjohn's opinion, the claim for a mandatory injunction was quia timet because, damages having been awarded for the subsidence which had already occurred and an injunction having been issued to restrain the defendants from committing further tortious acts, the claimants' remedies for the legal wrongs which had already taken place were exhausted.[94] It is true that in a case of withdrawal of support from land a fresh cause of action accrues with each new subsidence[95] and thus—as Lord Upjohn pointed out—the claimants could take further proceedings if further subsidence were to occur. Nevertheless, if an action is to be classed as quia timet whenever the claimant has recovered redress for such damage as he has already suffered, even if only in the same proceedings as those in which the mandatory injunction is claimed, it is difficult to see that, exceptional cases apart, a claim for a mandatory injunction can ever be other than quia timet.[96] It is submitted, 28-22

85 See the cases cited in fn.75.

86 (1961) 105 S.J. 178; (1960) 175 E.G. 1199 CA. See also *Fletcher v Bealey* (1885) L.R. 28 Ch. D. 688.

87 [1975] Ch. 43.

88 [1975] Ch. 43 at 50, per Russell LJ.

89 [1975] Ch. 43 at 50, per Russell LJ.

90 [1975] Ch. 43 at 50, per Russell LJ.

91 This case was cited by counsel in *Hooper v Rogers*, but is not referred to in the judgments.

92 See paras 27-128 to 27-133.

93 [1970] A.C. 652.

94 [1970] A.C. 652 at 664 and 665.

95 *Darley Main Colliery v Mitchell* (1886) 11 App. Cas. 127.

96 Although Lord Upjohn gave an example of a claim for a mandatory injunction which would not, in his Lordship's opinion, be quia timet ([1970] A.C. at 665), it is not clear how the case put differs materially from that actually before the House. The mandatory injunction issued in *Esso Petroleum*

therefore, that while nothing of substance should turn on this issue of classification, Lord Upjohn's description of the mandatory injunction claimed as quia timet was out of line with the traditional approach and for this reason is probably best disregarded.[97]

5. INTERIM INJUNCTIONS[98]

(a) American Cyanamid

28-23 Injunctions of all kinds, including mandatory injunctions,[99] may be granted on an interlocutory application. Such an application is made when, of course, the legal validity of the claim or the factual basis for it may be uncertain and, as Lord Diplock said in the leading case of *American Cyanamid Co v Ethicon Ltd*[100]:

> "it was to mitigate the risk of injustice to the [claimant] during the period before that uncertainty could be resolved that the practice arose of granting him relief by way of interlocutory injunction ... The object of the interlocutory injunction is to protect the [claimant] against injury by violation of his right for which he could not be adequately compensated in damages recoverable in the action if the uncertainty were resolved in his favour at the trial."

The granting of such an injunction is a matter of discretion, but the courts have not been slow to lay down guidelines as to how it should be exercised. Until the *American Cyanamid* case, the general opinion, restated by the House of Lords in *JT Stratford & Son Ltd v Lindley*,[101] was that the claimant had to establish a prima facie case.[102] In the *American Cyanamid* case, Lord Diplock, with the concurrence of the other Law Lords, denied that there was any such rule and held that, provided there was a "serious question" to be tried, the matter should be decided on the balance of convenience[103] and the following principles should be applied in determining which way the balance of convenience lies.[104]

28-24 First, the court should consider the adequacy of the claimant's and defendant's respective remedies in damages either at the trial, if the injunction be refused and

Co Ltd v Kingswood Motors (Addlestone) Ltd [1974] Q.B. 142 was not quia timet but the case was of an unusual character.

97 J. Jolowicz, "Damages in Equity—A Study of Lord Cairns' Act" [1975] C.L.J. 224, 244–245.

98 Although in the past these have usually been referred to as "interlocutory injunctions", the term preferred in the Civil Procedure Rules is "interim injunctions": see CPR r.25.1(1)(a).

99 *Hervey v Smith* (1855) 1 K. & J. 389; *Hermann Loog v Bean* (1884) L.R. 26 Ch. D. 306; *Daniel v Ferguson* [1891] 2 Ch. 27; *Canadian Pacific Ry v Gaud* [1949] 2 K.B. 239 CA; *Esso Petroleum Co Ltd v Kingswood Motors (Addlestone) Ltd* [1974] Q.B. 142.

100 [1975] A.C. 396 at 406.

101 [1965] A.C. 269 at 338, per Lord Upjohn.

102 See also *Newson v Pender* (1884) L.R. 27 Ch. D. 43; *Canadian Pacific Ry v Gaud* [1949] 2 K.B. 239.

103 [1975] A.C. 396 at 407–409.

104 [1975] A.C. 396 at 408. For a clearer setting out of the principles, see *Fellowes & Son v Fisher* [1976] Q.B. 122, per Browne LJ at 137–138. Sir John Donaldson MR in *Francome v Mirror Group Newspapers Ltd* [1984] 1 W.L.R. 892 at 899 expressed preference for the term "balance of justice" as against "balance of convenience". See also *Cayne v Global Natural Resources Plc* [1984] 1 All E.R. 225 at 237, per May LJ. For an interpretation of *American Cyanamid*, according to which the courts can always take into account any clear view they have reached as to the relative strengths of the parties' cases (albeit that they should rarely attempt to resolve complex issues of disputed fact or law), see *Series 5 Software Ltd v Clarke* [1996] 1 All E.R. 853.

the claimant finally succeeds, or on the claimant's undertaking in damages[105] if it be granted and the defendant finally succeeds.[106] If these considerations leave the matter in doubt, various factors depending on the nature of the case must be taken into account to see where the balance of convenience lies. These include: the difficulty in framing the injunction in clear and fair terms[107]; the degree of injury to each party if the application is not granted but that party succeeds at the trial[108]; whether either party would enjoy an unfair advantage if matters were left open until the trial[109]; that the defendant is unarguably committing a legal wrong so that the only arguable defence is that the claimant is not the person entitled to complain of that wrong[110]; and delay by the claimant in seeking the injunction.[111] Only if the uncompensatable disadvantage to each party caused by the grant or refusal of the injunction, as the case may be, would not differ widely, is it proper to take account, in tipping the balance, of the relative strengths of each party's case as revealed by the evidence adduced at the hearing of the application. Where other factors are evenly balanced, "it is a counsel of prudence to take such measures as are calculated to preserve the status quo"[112]; and according to Lord Diplock in *Garden Cottage Foods Ltd v Milk Marketing Board*[113] the status quo means "the state of affairs existing during the period immediately preceding the issue of the writ claiming the permanent injunction or, if there be unreasonable delay between the issue of the writ and the motion for an interlocutory injunction, the period immediately preceding the motion". Where an interlocutory injunction is granted to prevent some form of unfair competition, such as the unlawful poaching of employees, the injunction should aim to neutralise any unfair advantage that would otherwise accrue to the defendant.[114]

---

105 See further para.28-34.

106 For applications see *Polaroid Corp v Eastman Kodak* [1977] F.S.R. 25; and *Garden Cottage Foods Ltd v Milk Marketing Board* [1984] A.C. 130 (damages to claimant adequate, hence no injunction); *Laws v Florinplace Ltd* [1981] 1 All E.R. 659; and *Mercury Communications Ltd v Scott-Garner* [1984] Ch. 37 (undertaking by claimant to pay damages adequate, hence injunction). In *B v D* [2014] EWCA Civ 229; [2015] 1 W.L.R. 771 the Court of Appeal held that a party could plead that damages were inadequate despite the fact that the reason they were inadequate was an agreement to limit their amount.

107 *Potters-Ballotini v Weston-Baker* [1977] R.P.C. 202 CA at 209, per Scarman LJ; *The Who Group Ltd and Polydor Ltd v Stage One* (Records) Ltd [1980] 2 C.M.L.R. 429 at 435; *Garden Cottage Foods Ltd v Milk Marketing Board* [1984] A.C. 130 at 145–147.

108 *American Cyanamid Co v Ethicon Ltd* [1975] A.C. 396 at 408, per Lord Diplock; *Home Box Office Inc v Channel 5 Home Box Office Ltd* [1982] F.S.R. 449; *Hodge Clemco Ltd v Airblast Ltd* [1995] F.S.R. 806.

109 *Dunford and Elliot Ltd v Johnson and Firth Brown Ltd* [1977] 1 Lloyd's Rep. 505 at 514, per Roskill LJ.

110 *Mail Newspapers Plc v Express Newspapers Plc* [1987] F.S.R. 90.

111 *Roussel-Uclaf v GD Searl & Co Ltd* [1978] 1 Lloyd's Rep. 225; *Express Newspapers Ltd v Liverpool Daily Post and Echo Plc* [1985] 1 W.L.R. 1089 at 1098.

112 *American Cyanamid Co v Ethicon Ltd* [1975] A.C. 396 at 409.

113 [1984] A.C. 130 at 140. For other views on the meaning of the status quo in this context see, e.g. *Fellowes & Son v Fisher* [1976] Q.B. 122 at 141; *Budget Rent A Car International Inc v Manos Slough Ltd* (1977) 121 S.J. 374 CA; *Alfred Dunhills v Sunoptic* [1979] F.S.R. 337 CA. And subsequent to the *Garden Cottage* case, see *Graham v Delderfield* [1992] F.S.R. 313 CA, where it was held to be the position at the date of the service, rather than of the issue of the writ, that fixed the status quo.

114 This is the so-called "springboard" principle. see generally *Forse v Secarma Ltd* [2019] EWCA Civ 215; [2019] I.R.L.R. 587.

(b) Exceptional situations

28-25 Lord Diplock's final principle was that "there may be many other special factors to be taken into consideration in the particular circumstances of individual cases".[115] This dictum was regarded by Lord Denning MR in *Fellowes & Son v Fisher*[116] as giving the courts licence to apply the old prima facie case rule to cases where the application of Lord Diplock's principles was inappropriate: and he thought that this was so in cases of industrial disputes, breach of confidence, covenants in restraint of trade, passing off, and in many commercial cases. However, in *Lawrence David Ltd v Ashton*[117] and *County Sound Plc v Ocean Sound Plc*[118] the Court of Appeal clarified that the *American Cyanamid* principles apply in the normal way to covenants in restraint of trade and passing off respectively. Lord Denning's judgment in *Fellows v Rother DC* was expressly disapproved.[119] In the light of this, an alternative view of Lord Diplock's dictum seems preferable, namely that in certain situations the *American Cyanamid* principles must be weighed against other considerations.[120] It is, of course, impossible to give an exhaustive list of such exceptional situations but some important categories have emerged from the cases.[121]

28-26 **Trial unlikely** The first was recognised by Lord Diplock himself in *NWL Ltd v Woods*.[122] The balance of convenience approach, adumbrated in the *American Cyanamid* case is particularly appropriate in relation to a remedy which is both "temporary and discretionary",[123] but where, as in a trade dispute, "the grant or refusal of the interlocutory injunction will have the practical effect of putting an end to the action because the harm that will have been already caused to the losing party by its grant or refusal is complete and of a kind which money cannot constitute any worthwhile recompense, the degree of likelihood that the [claimant] would have succeeded in establishing his right to an injunction if the action had gone to trial, is a factor to be brought into the balance by the judge in weighing the risks that may result from his deciding the application one way rather than the other".[124] Similarly

---

115 *American Cyanamid Co v Ethicon Ltd* [1975] A.C. 396 at 409.

116 [1976] Q.B. 122 at 133–134. Lord Denning M.R. took a similar approach in, e.g. *Hubbard v Pitt* [1976] Q.B. 142; *Dunford & Elliot Ltd v Johnson and Firth Brown Ltd* [1977] 1 Lloyd's Rep. 505; and, as agreed with by the other Court of Appeal judges, in *Office Overload Ltd v Gunn* [1977] F.S.R. 39; and *Newsweek Inc v BBC* [1979] R.P.C. 441 CA.

117 [1991] 1 All E.R. 385. cf. *Lansing Linde Ltd v Kerr* [1991] 1 W.L.R. 251.

118 [1991] F.S.R. 367.

119 Also disapproved was the approach of the Court of Appeal in *Office Overload v Gunn* [1977] F.S.R. 39 (covenant in restraint of trade); and *Newsweek Inc v BBC* [1979] R.P.C. 441 CA (passing off).

120 For an alternative interpretation of *American Cyanamid*, see *Series 5 Software Ltd v Clarke* [1996] 1 All E.R. 853, para.28-23 fn.104.

121 In addition to the categories listed in paras 28-26 to 28-32, *Group Jose Re Co SA v Walbrook Insurance Co Ltd* [1996] 1 W.L.R. 1152 CA; and *Czarnikow-Rionda Sugar Trading Inc v Standard Bank London Ltd* [1999] 2 Lloyd's Rep. 187 show that *American Cyanamid* does not apply to interim injunctions restraining a bank or beneficiary from effecting payment under a letter of credit: rather the court must be satisfied that there is a clear prima facie case that the beneficiary is acting fraudulently in drawing on the credit.

122 [1979] 1 W.L.R. 1294.

123 [1975] A.C. 396 at 405, per Lord Diplock.

124 [1979] 1 W.L.R. 1294 at 1307. In trade dispute cases the rule in *American Cyanamid* is modified, in that the court must have regard to the likelihood of a successful defence under s.219 (protection from certain tort liabilities) or s.220 (peaceful picketing) of the Trade Union and Labour Relations

in *Cayne v Global Natural Resources Plc*,[125] where an interim injunction was sought to stop a company merger, the *American Cyanamid* principles were thought inappropriate and it was held that the claimant needed to show an overwhelming case because the grant of the injunction would effectively decide the issue in the claimant's favour. Kerr LJ said that the *American Cyanamid* principles should be restricted to cases where, "a trial is in fact likely to take place in the sense that the [claimants'] case shows that they are genuinely concerned to pursue their claim to trial, and that they are seeking the injunction as a means of a holding operation pending the trial".[126]

Public interest Secondly, in some cases it is appropriate to take account of the public interest, for example, where the defendant is a local authority carrying out public duties[127]; or where there is an industrial dispute affecting the public[128]; or where the defendant is operating "at least near the boundary of the criminal law"[129]; or where the main application is for judicial review of a public authority's approval of a rival company's product and interim relief, by way of a stay of the approval, is sought pending the decision of the European Court of Justice.[130] It is also relevant here to mention *R. v Secretary of State for Transport Ex p. Factortame (No.2)*[131] in which it was held by the House of Lords that where (pending a decision by the European Court of Justice) an interim injunction is sought to restrain the enforcement by the Secretary of State of an English statute on the grounds of incompatibility with European law, the public interest in the enforcement of what, on the face of it, is the law of the land requires that no injunction should normally be granted unless the claimant establishes a strong prima facie case of invalidity. Lord Goff, giving the leading speech, saw this approach as not affecting the initial threshold to be crossed under *Cyanamid* but as going instead to the balance of convenience.[132] **28-27**

Freedom of speech Thirdly, special considerations arise in connection with freedom of speech, especially since the enactment of art.10 of the European **28-28**

(Consolidation) Act 1992. See s.221(2) of that Act; *Mercury Communications Ltd v Scott-Garner* [1984] Ch. 37; *Dimbleby & Sons v NUJ* [1984] 1 W.L.R. 427; *Thomas v National Union of Mineworkers* [1986] Ch. 20; and *Serco Ltd v National Union of Rail, Maritime & Transport Workers* [2011] EWCA Civ 226; [2011] I.C.R. 848 at [10]–[14] (Elias LJ).

125 [1984] 1 All E.R. 225 CA. See also *Bryanston Finance Ltd v De Vries (No.2)* [1976] Ch. 63; *Fulwell v Bragg* (1983) 127 S.J. 171; *Cambridge Nutrition Ltd v BBC* [1990] 3 All E.R. 523 CA.

126 [1984] 1 All E.R. 225 at 234.

127 *Smith v Inner London Education Authority* [1978] 1 All E.R. 411 CA.

128 e.g. *Beaverbrook Newspapers Ltd v Keys* [1978] I.C.R. 582; *NWL Ltd v Woods* [1979] 1 W.L.R. 1294; *Duport Steel Ltd v Sirs* [1980] 1 W.L.R. 142; *Metropolitan Borough of Solihull v National Union of Teachers* [1985] I.R.L.R. 211.

129 *Laws v Florinplace Ltd* [1981] 1 All E.R. 659 at 688, per Vinelott J.

130 *R. v Ministry of Agriculture Ex p. Monsanto* [1999] Q.B. 1161.

131 [1991] 1 A.C. 603. See also *R. v HM Treasury Ex p. British Telecommunications Plc* [1994] 1 C.M.L.R. 621 CA (where the main application was for judicial review to quash Regulations made by the Treasury and an interim injunction requiring amendment of the Regulations was sought pending a decision of the European Court of Justice). Post-Brexit cases such as these will of course be of less importance.

132 In *R. v Secretary of State for Health Ex p. Imperial Tobacco Ltd* [2001] 1 W.L.R. 127 the House of Lords left unresolved the question whether domestic law or Community law applies to determine whether an interim injunction should be granted restraining the Secretary of State from making regulations to implement an allegedly invalid directive.

Convention of Human Rights into English law. In any case where an injunction is sought, or sought to be enforced, the constraints of art.10 must be observed.[133] It has been held that the *American Cyanamid* case has not affected previous rulings[134] that interim injunctions should not be issued in a libel action where the defendant raises a defence, whether of justification, fair comment on a matter of public interest, or privilege, unless the defence would obviously fail at trial.[135] Moreover, in *Greene v Associated Newspapers Ltd*[136] the Court of Appeal held that that common law approach in defamation cases had not been altered by s.12(3) of the Human Rights Act 1998 (which lays down in all cases where freedom of speech may be in issue that no interim injunction to restrain a publication shall be granted "unless the court is satisfied that the applicant is likely to establish that publication should not be allowed").

28-29 One might expect a similar approach in cases of breach of confidence or disclosure of private information. Before 2004 there were some doubts over this.[137] In *Cream Holdings Ltd v Banerjee*,[138] however, the House of Lords settled the matter. It made it clear that because of s.12(3) of the Human Rights Act 1998 the test for interim injunctions at least in breach of confidence cases had in general to be whether the applicant was "more likely than not" to succeed at trial, although there might be exceptional cases, for instance where the potential adverse consequences of disclosure were particularly grave. It followed that in such cases the burden on the claimant was slightly less demanding than in libel: he had to show, not that the defence had to fail, but merely that his prospects of success were

---

[133] *Cuadrilla Bowland Ltd v Persons Unknown* [2020] EWCA Civ 9; [2020] 4 W.L.R. 29 at [100]–[112] (here applied to the otherwise unlawful interference with the activities of "frackers"). In the event, the injunction here was held properly granted and properly enforceable.

[134] *Coulson v Coulson* (1887) 3 T.L.R. 846; *Bonnard v Perryman* [1891] 2 Ch. 269; *Monson v Tussauds* [1899] 1 Q.B. 671 (where it was argued that the right of the jury to try the issue would otherwise be usurped); *Fraser v Evans* [1969] 1 Q.B. 349. See also on passing off: *Sim v HJ Heinz & Co Ltd* [1959] 1 W.L.R. 313.

[135] *Bestobell Paints v Bigg* [1975] F.S.R. 421; *Harakas v Baltic Mercantile and Shipping Exchange Ltd* [1982] 1 W.L.R. 958; *T Smith & Nephew Ltd v 3M United Kingdom Plc* [1983] R.P.C. 92; *Herbage v Pressdram Ltd* [1984] 1 W.L.R. 1160; *Al-Fayed v The Observer Ltd*, *The Times*, 14 July 1986 CA; *Khashoggi v IPC Magazines Ltd* [1986] 1 W.L.R. 1412; *Kaye v Robertson* [1991] F.S.R. 62; *Holley v Smyth* [1998] Q.B. 726 CA (libel and malicious falsehood). In *Femis-Bank (Anguilla) Ltd v Lazar* [1991] Ch. 391, it was held that, similarly to defamation cases, the protection of free speech is an important factor in deciding whether to grant an interim injunction to restrain an alleged conspiracy to injure so that such an injunction should only be granted where the claimant has established a strong prima facie case (as in *Gulf Oil Ltd v Page* [1987] Ch. 327). The need to protect free speech was also emphasised by the Court of Appeal in discharging an interim injunction in *Cambridge Nutrition Ltd v BBC* [1990] 3 All E.R. 523 (breach of contract). But in *Microdata Information Services Ltd v Rivendale Ltd* [1991] F.S.R. 681 CA; followed in, e.g. *Essex Electric (Pte) Ltd v IPC Computers (UK) Ltd* [1991] F.S.R. 690, the approach in defamation cases was not extended to what was in substance an action for the tort of interference with contract.

[136] [2004] EWCA Civ 1462; [2005] Q.B. 972. See too the privacy case of *LNS v Persons Unknown* [2010] EWHC 119 (QB); [2010] E.M.L.R. 16.

[137] In favour of the approach were *Woodward v Hutchins* [1977] 1 W.L.R. 760; *Lion Laboratories Ltd v Evans* [1985] Q.B. 526; *Boehringer Ingelheim Ltd v Vetplus Ltd* [2007] EWCA Civ 583; [2007] F.S.R. 29 (a malicious falsehood case), and a number of public figure privacy cases, e.g. *Ferdinand v MGN Ltd* [2011] EWHC 2454 (QB); and *McClaren v News Group Newspapers Ltd* [2012] EWHC 2466 (QB); [2012] E.M.L.R. 33. But a less free-speech-friendly approach was adopted in a number of others, such as *Schering Chemicals Ltd v Falkman Ltd* [1982] Q.B. 1; *Francome v Mirror Group Newspapers Ltd* [1984] 1 W.L.R. 892; *Att Gen v Observer Newspapers Ltd* [1989] 2 F.S.R. 3; and *Att Gen v Guardian Newspapers Ltd* [1987] 1 W.L.R. 1248.

[138] [2004] UKHL 44; [2005] 1 A.C. 253.

sufficiently favourable to justify such an order being made in the particular circumstances of the case.[139] In *Browne v Associated Newspapers Ltd*[140] the Court of Appeal, in applying the flexible approach in *Cream Holdings Ltd v Banerjee*, upheld the grant of an interim injunction restraining publication by a newspaper of some (but not all) allegedly confidential information relating to a relationship between the claimant and another man. Sir Anthony Clarke MR said that it was for the claimant to persuade the court that he would probably (more likely than not) succeed, and went on:

> "By 'succeed at trial' we understand Lord Nicholls [in *Banerjee*] to mean that the claimant is likely to succeed after the court has carried out the relevant balance between the claimant's rights under article 8 and the newspaper's rights under article 10."[141]

In *UK Oil and Gas Investments Plc v Persons Unknown*[142] it was held that in any case where freedom of speech was in issue, even one involving property rights rather than publication of material, the claimant had to show that it was more likely than not to succeed at trial.[143]

Dispute of law Fourthly, it has been held that *American Cyanamid* does not apply where there is only a dispute as to the law and not a factual dispute,[144] or where there is no arguable defence to the claim.[145] 28-30

Mandatory injunction Finally, although Lord Hoffmann in obiter dicta has stated that this is incorrect,[146] *American Cyanamid* principles have been held to be inapplicable where the interim injunction sought is mandatory and not prohibitory.[147] 28-31

---

139 Note that in *Greene v Associated Newspapers Ltd* [2004] EWCA Civ 1462; [2005] Q.B. 972, decided after *Banerjee*, the Court of Appeal made it clear that the more restrictive test continued to apply in defamation cases.

140 [2007] EWCA Civ 295; [2008] Q.B. 103. *Banerjee* was also applied to breach of confidence claims in the later decisions in *Donald v Ntuli* [2010] EWCA Civ 1276; [2011] 1 W.L.R. 294; and *ABC v Telegraph Media Group Ltd* [2018] EWCA Civ 2329; [2019] 2 All E.R. 684. It has in addition been applied to an invasion of privacy case: see *PJS v News Group Newspapers Ltd* [2016] UKSC 26; [2016] A.C. 1081 (but there it was made clear that privacy might require greater protection because, unlike confidential information, it merited protection even where the information was possibly known to some of the public).

141 [2007] EWCA Civ 295; [2008] Q.B. 103.

142 [2018] EWHC 2252 (Ch); [2019] J.P.L. 161.

143 That case concerned injunctions to prevent anti-fracking protests. In *Fitzwilliam Land Co v Cheesman* [2018] EWHC 3139 (QB) at [41], the same approach was applied by agreement to trespass by anti-hunt protestors. On the other hand, since the right of freedom of speech will hardly ever trump landowners' property rights in injunction cases, the victory for free speech is somewhat Pyrrhic.

144 *Bradford Metropolitan City Council v Brown* (1987) 19 H.L.R. 16. See also *Office Overload Ltd v Gunn* [1977] F.S.R. 39 at 44, per Bridge LJ; *Athletes Foot Marketing Associates Inc v Cobra Sports Ltd* [1980] R.P.C. 343 at 348–349; *Lawrence David Ltd v Ashton* [1991] 1 All E.R. 385 at 393 and 396.

145 *Official Custodian for Charities v Mackey* [1985] Ch. 151. See also *Athletes Foot Marketing Associates Inc v Cobra Sports Ltd* [1980] R.P.C. 343; *Att Gen v Barker* [1990] 3 All E.R. 257 at 262, per Nourse LJ.

146 *National Commercial Bank Jamaica Ltd v Olint Corp Ltd* [2009] UKPC 16; [2009] 1 W.L.R. 1405 at [19].

147 *Locabail International Finance Ltd v Agroexport* [1986] 1 W.L.R. 657 at 665; *Films Rover International v Cannon Films Sales Ltd* [1987] 1 W.L.R. 670 at 681–682; *Jakeman v South West Thames RHA* [1990] I.R.L.R. 62. See also *De Falco v Crawley BC* [1980] Q.B. 460 at 481; *R. v Kensington & Chelsea Royal LBC Ex p. Hammell* [1989] Q.B. 518.

But as to what are the relevant principles to be applied, there has been a divergence of views. In *Locabail International Finance Ltd v Agroexport*[148] the Court of Appeal, following the traditional approach,[149] held that a mandatory injunction will be issued at an interlocutory stage only in a clear case, that is where there is a high degree of assurance (higher than that appropriate for a prohibitory injunction) that at the trial it would appear that the injunction had rightly been granted. But a somewhat different approach was taken by Hoffmann J in *Films Rover International Ltd v Cannon Film Sales Ltd*[150] and was repeated by him in obiter dicta in *National Commercial Bank Jamaica Ltd v Olint Corp Ltd*.[151] For him the basic question is not so much whether the injunction sought was prohibitory or mandatory but whether the injustice to the defendant if the application were granted and the claimant subsequently failed at the trial would outweigh the injustice to the claimant if the application were refused and he subsequently succeeded at the trial; the Court of Appeal in the *Locabail* case was therefore merely laying down a guideline rather than a rule, which reflected the fact that mandatory injunctions, if granted at an interlocutory stage, *generally* create greater risks of injustice to the defendant in the manner described than prohibitory injunctions. Applying this approach in the *Films Rover* case, Hoffmann J granted an interim mandatory injunction even though the claimant could not establish a strong prima facie case. In *National Commercial Bank Jamaica Ltd v Olint Corp Ltd*[152] there was no triable issue so that no interim injunction should have been granted (whether prohibitory or mandatory).

28-32 Subsequent to the *Films Rover* case[153] in *Nottingham Building Society v Europdynamics Systems*[154] Chadwick J put forward a four point formulation that was approved by the Court of Appeal in *Zockoll Group Ltd v Mercury Communications Ltd*[155] "as being all the citation that should in future be necessary". Chadwick J's four-point formulation was as follows:

> "First the overriding consideration, as for all interim injunctions, is which course is likely to involve the least risk of injustice if it turns out to be 'wrong'. Secondly, in considering whether to grant a mandatory injunction, the court must keep in mind that an order which requires a party to take some positive step at an interlocutory stage, may well carry a greater risk of injustice if it turns out to have been wrongly made than an order which merely prohibits action, thereby preserving the status quo. Thirdly, it is legitimate, where a mandatory injunction is sought, to consider whether the court does feel a high degree of assurance that the plaintiff will be able to establish his right at trial. That is because the greater the degree of assurance the plaintiff will ultimately establish his right, the less will be the risk of injustice if the injunction is granted. But, finally, even where the court is unable to feel any high degree of assurance that the plaintiff will establish his right, there may still be circumstances in which it is appropriate to grant a mandatory injunction at

---

148 [1986] 1 W.L.R. 657. This was followed by Auld J in *Jakeman v South West Thames RHA* [1990] I.R.L.R. 62. See also *Leisure Data v Bell* [1988] F.S.R. 367 CA; *Moran v University of Salford (No.2)*, *The Times*, 23 November 1993 CA.

149 See, e.g. *Shepherd Homes Ltd v Sandham* [1971] Ch. 340 at 351.

150 [1987] 1 W.L.R. 670.

151 [2009] UKPC 16; [2009] 1 W.L.R. 1405.

152 [2009] UKPC 16; [2009] 1 W.L.R. 1405.

153 But not mentioned by Lord Hoffmann in *National Commercial Bank Jamaica Ltd v Olint Corp Ltd* [2009] UKPC 16; [2009] 1 W.L.R. 1405.

154 [1993] F.S.R. 468 at 474.

155 [1998] F.S.R. 354 at 366.

> an interlocutory stage. Those circumstances will exist where the risk of injustice if this injunction is refused sufficiently outweigh the risk of injustice if it is granted."

In the *Nottingham Building Society* case itself, the interim remedy sought, and granted, ordered the delivery up of computer software in a case where Chadwick J was satisfied, with a high degree of assurance, that the claimant would succeed at trial.[156] In the *Zockoll* case an interim mandatory injunction requiring performance of a contractual obligation was refused.

(c) Function of appellate court

The function of an appellate court in relation to a decision on the granting or refusal of an interim injunction was considered by the House of Lords in *Hadmor Productions Ltd v Hamilton*[157] and in *Garden Cottage Foods Ltd v Milk Marketing Board*.[158] In the latter Lord Diplock explained the position as follows: **28-33**

> "[An appellate court] is entitled to exercise an original discretion of its own only when it has come to the conclusion that the judge's exercise of his discretion was based on some misunderstanding of the law or of the evidence before him, or on an inference that particular facts existed or did not exist, which, although it was one that might legitimately have been drawn on the evidence that was before the judge, can be demonstrated to be wrong by further evidence that has become available by the time of the appeal, or on the ground that there has been a change of circumstances after the judge made his order that would have justified his acceding to an application to vary it. Since reasons given by judges for granting or refusing interlocutory injunctions may sometimes be sketchy, there may also be occasional cases where, even though no erroneous assumption of law or fact can be identified, the judge's decision to grant or refuse the injunction is so aberrant that it must be set aside on the ground that no reasonable judge regardful of his duty to act judicially could have reached it."[159]

(d) Undertaking as to damages

An interim injunction freezes the situation and prevents the defendant from taking some action which, at the trial, may prove to be lawful. Such an injunction may, therefore, cause the defendant to suffer substantial loss and, accordingly, will not normally be granted unless it is accompanied by an undertaking given by the claimant[160] to the court to pay to the defendant such damages as it is just that the defendant should receive if the issue of the injunction should turn out to have been unjustified.[161] Formerly, it was thought that no such undertaking could be required **28-34**

156 Although not mentioned, it would appear that the order fell within the Torts (Interference with Goods) Act 1977 s.4.

157 [1983] 1 A.C. 191.

158 [1984] A.C. 130.

159 [1984] A.C. 130 at 137.

160 The undertaking should be supported by specific evidence of the claimant's ability to meet it: *Brigid Foley Ltd v Elliott* [1982] R.P.C. 433.

161 See, generally, S. Gee, "The Undertaking in Damages" [2006] L.M.C.L.Q. 181. The practice of making an undertaking as to damages a condition of the issue of an interim injunction is said to be over 100 years old and to be almost universal: *Hoffmann-La Roche & Co AG v Secretary of State for Trade and Industry* [1975] A.C. 295 at 356, per Lord Wilberforce. See also at 360–362, per Lord Diplock. If the claimant accepts an undertaking from the defendant in lieu of an injunction, a cross-undertaking in damages by the claimant will be inserted unless the contrary is expressed: *Practice*

of the Crown as a condition of its obtaining an injunction,[162] but it appears that this was because, until the Crown Proceedings Act 1947, the Crown could not be made liable in damages in the ordinary way. Today, therefore, there is no reason why an undertaking in damages should not be required of the Crown when it sues to protect a proprietary interest of its own.[163] On the other hand, no such undertaking should be required, at least in the absence of special circumstances,[164] when the Crown brings proceedings for the purposes of enforcing the law and not for protection of its own interests. Thus, where the Crown sought an interim injunction to restrain the defendants from selling drugs at a price in excess of that fixed by a statutory regulation, and the defence was that the regulation was ultra vires and so void, it was held that the Crown was entitled to succeed and that no undertaking in damages should be required as a condition of the issue of the injunction.[165] The privilege not to give an undertaking in damages is, moreover, not limited to the Crown: on principle it extends generally to public authorities seeking interim injunctions to enforce the law for the benefit of the community.[166]

(e) Search orders

28-35 A search order is what was previously known as an *Anton Piller* order.[167] The power of the High Court to grant such an order has been placed on a firm statutory

---

Note [1904] W.N. 203. For the undertaking as to damages in the context of search (*Anton Piller*) orders and freezing (*Mareva*) injunctions, see para.28-43, para.28-45 and para.28-49. In *Blue Town Investments Ltd v Higgs & Hill Plc* [1990] 1 W.L.R. 696, where a claimant chose not to apply for an interim injunction so as to avoid having to give a cross-undertaking in damages, it was held that the claim for a permanent injunction, which was very unlikely to succeed, would be struck out unless the claimant applied for an interim injunction accompanied by a cross-undertaking in damages. But in *Oxy Electric Ltd v Zainuddin* [1991] 1 W.L.R. 115 it was doubted whether a court had such a jurisdiction to impose conditions on the rights of a litigant to prosecute his claim in the normal way. For the approach to striking out, for want of prosecution, proceedings to enforce a cross-undertaking in damages, see *Barratt Manchester Ltd v Bolton MBC* [1998] 1 W.L.R. 1003. For rejection of the argument that a defendant can recover, on a cross-undertaking in damages, not only for its own loss but also the loss of third parties, see *Smithkline Beecham Plc v Apotex Europe Ltd* [2006] EWCA Civ 658; [2007] Ch. 71.

[162] *Att Gen v Albany Hotel Co* [1896] 1 Ch. 696.

[163] *Hoffmann-La Roche & Co AG v Secretary of State for Trade and Industry* [1975] A.C. 295 at 341, per Lord Reid; at 351, per Lord Morris; at 357–358, per Lord Wilberforce; at 361–363, per Lord Diplock; at 370–371, per Lord Cross.

[164] *Hoffmann-La Roche & Co AG v Secretary of State for Trade and Industry* [1975] A.C. 295 at 363, per Lord Diplock.

[165] *Hoffmann-La Roche & Co AG v Secretary of State for Trade and Industry* [1975] A.C. 295 Lord Wilberforce dissenting; see also *Director General of Fair Trading v Tobyward Ltd* [1989] 1 W.L.R. 517.

[166] *Kirklees MBC v Wickes Building Supplies Ltd* [1993] A.C. 227 HL. This is criticised by Zuckerman, (1993) 12 C.J.Q. 268. *Kirklees* was applied in *Securities and Investment Board v Lloyd-Wright* [1993] 4 All E.R. 210 in holding that the S.I.B. need not give a cross-undertaking in damages even in respect of a worldwide freezing (*Mareva*) injunction; and more recently in *Financial Services Authority v Sinaloa Gold Plc* [2013] UKSC 11; [2013] 2 A.C. 28 (on which, see J. Varuhas & P. Turner, "Injunctions, undertakings in damages and the public-private divide" (2014) 130 L.Q.R. 33).

[167] The new terminology is that laid down in CPR r.25.1(1)(h). The old terminology was based on the leading case, *Anton Piller KG v Manufacturing Processes Ltd* [1976] Ch. 55. See generally, S. Gee, *Commercial Injunctions*, 6th edn (2016); M. Hoyle, *Freezing and Search Orders*, 4th edn (2006); M. Dockray & H. Laddie, "Piller Problems" (1990) 106 L.Q.R. 601; D. Capper, "The Duties of a Plaintiff with an Anton Piller Order" (1998) 49 N.I.L.Q. 210. Scott J pointed out in *Columbia Picture*

footing by s.7 of the Civil Procedure Act 1997. A search order is an interim mandatory injunction, which is almost invariably granted ex parte and usually orders the defendant to allow the claimant to enter his premises[168] for the purposes of searching for, inspecting, and seizing property infringing the claimant's rights or documents relevant to the claim against the defendant. It is given where speed and secrecy are vital to prevent the defendant destroying or disposing of such property or documents. While developed to deal with cases involving intellectual property, search orders have been granted in other contexts.[169] Special principles have been developed to govern search orders, and the general rule in *American Cyanamid v Ethicon*[170] does not apply.

28-36 In *Anton Piller KG v Manufacturing Processes Ltd*[171] the claimants asserted that the defendants were passing information to German manufacturers in breach of confidence and copyright. They wanted an injunction to stop this but, in the meantime, fearful that, once the defendants had notice of an action, incriminating documents would be disposed of, they sought and were granted an injunction enabling them to enter the defendants' premises, to inspect relevant documents and to seize any belonging to them. According to Ormrod LJ there were three essential pre-conditions for the making of such an order:

> "First, there must be an extremely strong prima facie case. Secondly, the damages, potential or actual, must be very serious for the applicant. Thirdly, there must be clear evidence that the defendants have in their possession incriminating documents or things, and that there is a real possibility that they may destroy such material before any application inter partes can be made."[172]

But in applying these three pre-conditions it is important to bear in mind the comments of Hoffmann J in *Lock International Plc v Beswick*,[173] he said:

> "To borrow a useful concept from the jurisdiction of the European Community, there must be proportionality between the perceived threat to the [claimant's] rights and the remedy granted. The fact that there is overwhelming evidence that the defendant has behaved wrongfully in his commercial relationships does not necessarily justify an *Anton Piller* order … The more intrusive orders allowing searches of premises or vehicles require a careful balancing of, on the one hand, the [claimant's] right to recover his property or to preserve important evidence against, on the other hand, violation of the privacy of a defendant who has had no opportunity to put his side of the case."

Industries v Robinson [1987] Ch. 38 at 71, that "*Anton Piller* orders are almost invariably accompanied by *Mareva* injunctions".

168 By s.7(3) of the Civil Procedure Act 1997, a search order can only be granted in respect of premises in England and Wales. For cases concerning foreign premises prior to the Act, see *Altertext Inc v Advanced Data* [1985] 1 W.L.R. 957; *Protector Alarms Ltd v Maxim Alarms Ltd* [1978] F.S.R. 442; *Cook Industries Inc v Galliher* [1979] Ch. 439.

169 See, e.g. *Emanuel v Emanuel* [1982] 1 W.L.R. 669 (ancillary relief after divorce): *Yousif v Salama* [1980] 1 W.L.R. 1540 (contract debt).

170 [1975] A.C. 396.

171 [1976] Ch. 55.

172 [1976] Ch. 55 at 62. In *Dunlop Holdings Ltd v Staravia Ltd* [1982] Com. L.R. 3 CA, the last part of the third requirement was relaxed slightly, Oliver LJ saying "It is seldom that one can get cogent or actual evidence of a threat to destroy material or documents, so it is necessary for it to be inferred from the evidence which is before the court". Certainly the character of the defendant is very important: for example, a search order should not be granted against a practising barrister: *Randolph M Fields v Alison Watts* (1985) 129 S.J. 67 CA.

173 [1989] 1 W.L.R. 1268 at 1281.

28-37 It was also stressed in the *Anton Piller* case that the defendant must be given the opportunity to consider the order, to consult his own solicitor and to apply to court for its discharge if improperly obtained[174]; and the claimant's solicitor must attend at the execution of the order.[175] In Ormrod LJ's words: "Great responsibility clearly rests on the solicitors for the applicant to ensure that the carrying out of such an order is meticulously carefully done with the fullest respect for the defendant's rights ...".[176] The order actually made in the *Anton Piller* case was based on Templeman J's precedent in *EMI v Pandit*[177] according to which the claimant should give the usual undertaking in damages required for interim injunctions[178] and the order should specify the maximum number of persons to accompany the solicitor, the address of the premises to be searched,[179] and the documents or property being sought.[180] It was also explained in the *Anton Piller* case that the effect of the order is not to allow the claimant to force entry and in this it differs from a search warrant; but if the defendant disobeys the order this will not merely be evidence against him but will constitute a contempt of court.[181]

28-38 In an important statement on the practice and procedure to be followed in obtaining and executing search orders, Sir Donald Nicholls VC in *Universal Thermosensors Ltd v Hibben*[182] made the following main points:

(1) In general search orders should only be executed on working days in office hours when a solicitor can be expected to be available should the defendant need to seek legal advice.
(2) If the order is to be executed at a private house, and it is at all likely that a woman may be in the house alone, the solicitor serving the order must be, or must be accompanied by, a woman.
(3) Unless seriously impracticable, a detailed list of the items being removed

174 These requirements have been strengthened by the insistence in *AB v CDE* [1982] R.P.C. 509 that the defendant must be told of his right to legal advice and that copies of the evidence in support of the search order application should be taken to show to the defendant. All these requirements are incorporated in the standard form of search order set out as an annex to the Practice Direction on Interim Injunctions, CPR Pt 25 para.25APD (hereinafter referred to as the *CPR Practice Direction*).

175 A search order should be served by a "supervising solicitor". See the *CPR Practice Direction*: para.28-38 fn.184.

176 [1976] Ch. 55 at 62. In *VDU Installations Ltd v Integrated Computer Systems* [1989] F.S.R. 378 the claimant's solicitor was held to be in contempt for improper execution of the *Anton Piller* order.

177 [1975] 1 W.L.R. 302. See the *Anton Piller case* [1976] Ch. 55 at 61.

178 The court must be satisfied that the claimant is good for such damages: *Vapormatic Co v Sparex Ltd* [1976] 1 W.L.R. 939. See also Sch.C(7) of the standard form of search order annexed to the *Practice Direction*.

179 An order allowing entry "at any other of the defendant's premises" should not be granted: *Protector Alarms Ltd v Maxim Alarms Ltd* [1978] F.S.R. 442.

180 In *Columbia Pictures Inc v Robinson* [1987] Ch. 38 at 77, Scott J stressed that orders should be drawn up as narrowly as possible and that no material should be taken unless clearly covered by the terms of the order. See also *LT Piver SARL v S & J Perfume Co Ltd* [1987] F.S.R. 159.

181 In *Bhimji v Chatwani* [1991] 1 W.L.R. 989, Scott J held that disobeying an *Anton Piller* order and applying for its discharge would not necessarily mean that the defendant would be punished for contempt but that it put the defendant "at the risk of committal". Something more was needed to justify punishment (for example, evidence to suggest that the making of the application was merely a device to postpone the search; or evidence of impropriety in respect of the documents in any of the premises to be searched that took place during the period of the delay).

182 [1992] 1 W.L.R. 840 at 859–861. This statement formed the basis for the *CPR Practice Direction*. All the points made by Sir Donald Nicholls VC are in the standard form for a search order annexed to that Practice Direction.

should be prepared at the premises before they are removed, and the defendant should be given an opportunity to check that list at the time.

(4) An order that the defendant should not inform others (except his lawyers) of the existence of the order should be valid for only a few days.

(5) Unless there is good reason for doing otherwise, the order should not be executed at business premises save in the presence of a responsible officer or representative of the company or trader in question.

(6) A means should be devised whereby the search order cannot be used by a claimant to search through the documents of a competitor.[183]

(7) The use of the claimant's solicitor as an officer of the court to see that the order is property executed has not proved satisfactory. Judges should therefore give serious consideration to the desirability of insisting that: (a) the order be served, and its execution supervised, by a solicitor other than a member of the firm of solicitors acting for the claimant in the action[184]; (b) the solicitor should be experienced and have some familiarity with search orders; (c) the solicitor should prepare a written report on the execution of the order; (d) a copy of that report should be served on the defendant; (e) in any event, the claimant should return to court within a few days and present that report at an inter partes hearing preferably to the judge who made the order.

The Vice Chancellor recognised that this procedure would add considerably to the cost of executing search orders, but thought this necessary in order to prevent search orders falling into disrepute:

> "If [claimants] wish to take advantage of this truly Draconian type of order, they must be prepared to pay for the safeguards which experience has shown are necessary if the interests of defendants are fairly to be protected."[185]

(i) Order for disclosure and interrogatories

Several additional points on search orders have emerged from decisions subsequent to the *Anton Piller* case. In *EMI v Sarwar*[186] the Court of Appeal accepted that an order for disclosure and interrogatories could be added to the search order, which meant that in that case the defendants were ordered to name their suppliers of pirate cassette tapes, and to hand over documents, such as order books, relating to the infringing tapes. For a time this extension made search orders doubly effective. But then in *Rank Film Distribution v Video Information Centre*[187] the House of Lords reluctantly held that the privilege against self-incrimination meant that discovery and interrogatories should not be ordered against the defendant where compliance would render him liable to prosecution. However, in its application to civil proceedings relating to the infringement of intellectual property rights or passing-off, this decision was immediately reversed and the privilege against self- **28-39**

[183] By the Practice Direction, the standard form of search order does not require the person served with the order to allow anyone, who in the view of the supervising solicitor could gain commercially from anything he might read or see, on the premises if the person served with the order objects.

[184] By the Practice Direction, this independent solicitor is called a "supervising solicitor".

[185] [1992] 1 W.L.R. 840 at 861.

[186] [1977] F.S.R. 146. Disclosure of the whereabouts of the listed items and the names of the suppliers of, and customers for, them is required by para.4 of the standard form of search order set out in the *CPR Practice Direction*.

[187] [1982] A.C. 380.

incrimination withdrawn by s.72 of the Senior Courts Act 1981. This basically provides that in any such proceedings[188] a person shall not be excused from answering any questions put to him, or complying with any court order made, on the ground that to do so would expose him to criminal proceedings for a related offence[189]; but that any statement or admission made in answering the questions or complying with the order shall not be admissible against him in criminal proceedings for any related offence. This is a compromise, modelled on s.31 of the Theft Act 1968,[190] and for a claimant in intellectual property cases, it restores the full effectiveness of the search order. However, in *Tate Access Floors Inc v Boswell*[191] it was held that, except where s.72 of the Senior Courts Act 1981 applies, if there is a real risk of a conspiracy to defraud charge (as there very often will be in search order cases) the privilege against self-incrimination means that no search order should be made against individual defendants except to recover property belonging to the claimants. The Rank Film order was interpreted as extending not merely to discovery and interrogatories but also to the order permitting search and seizure of documents other than the infringing copies themselves. In *C Plc v P*[192] computers were seized during a search order and placed in the custody of the supervising solicitor for "imaging" by a computer expert. The imaging uncovered highly objectionable images of children. It was held that the privilege against self-incrimination, whether in criminal or civil proceedings, did not extend to material—such as, in this case, the offending images on the computers—which was independent of the order (i.e. the offending material had not been ordered to be produced).

28-40 In *Bayer AG v Winter*[193] it was held by the Court of Appeal that where the disclosure of the whereabouts of documents or the particulars of transactions has been ordered in aid of a search order, additional injunctions restraining a defendant from leaving the jurisdiction and ordering the surrender of his passport can be ordered where these are felt necessary to render the ancillary orders effective. To render the search more effective a defendant may be ordered to display or print out

---

188 Which have been held to include proceedings for breach of commercial, but not personal, confidentiality: *Phillips v News Group Newspapers Ltd* [2012] UKSC 28; [2013] 1 A.C. 1 (victim of phone-hacking could rely on s.72, but only because eavesdropped material included commercial matters).

189 In *Universal City Studios Inc v Hubbard* [1984] Ch. 225 it was held that a "related offence" for proceedings within s.72(2)(c) of the Senior Courts Act 1981 can be one unconnected with intellectual property rights or passing off if it is an "offence revealed by the facts on which the [claimant] relies in these proceedings". See also *Phillips v News Group Newspapers Ltd* [2012] UKSC 28; [2013] 1 A.C. 1 at [41]–[46] (claim for breach of confidence by phone-hacking: conspiracy to commit that offence would be related offence).

190 But in one way wider, since under the 1968 Act the privilege against self-incrimination is withdrawn only in respect of specified offences (i.e. those under that Act), whereas under s.72 it is withdrawn in respect of all related offences. See *Phillips v News Group Newspapers Ltd* [2012] UKSC 28; [2013] 1 A.C. 1 at [41] (Lord Walker).

191 [1991] Ch. 512. cf. *Twentieth Century Fox v Tryare Ltd* [1991] F.S.R. 58. In *AT & T Istel Ltd v Tully* [1993] A.C. 45 HL, the privilege against self-incrimination, which would otherwise have provided the defendants with a defence to an order to file affidavits setting out their dealings with certain assets and exhibiting documents relating to dealing with such assets, did not apply because the Crown Prosecution Service had unequivocally agreed not to make use of the material divulged in compliance with the disclosure order. That undertaking provided adequate alternative protection for the defendants. See also *IBM United Kingdom Ltd v Prima Data International Ltd* [1994] 1 W.L.R. 719 in which a search order was not set aside because the defendant was told in everyday language of his privilege right but expressly declined to claim it.

192 [2007] EWCA Civ 493; [2008] Ch. 1.

193 [1986] 1 W.L.R. 497.

on a computer any relevant computer-readable documents[194] and to deliver up keys necessary to open locked drawers and cabinets.[195]

(ii) *Full disclosure by claimant required*

28-41 As with all ex parte orders the claimant must make full disclosure to the court of all material matters and in several cases search orders have been discharged for failure to comply with this requirement.[196] In *Columbia Pictures Inc v Robinson*[197] Scott J said: "the nature of *Anton Piller* orders requires that the affidavits in support of applications for them ought to err on the side of excessive disclosure. In the case of material falling into the grey area of possible relevance, the judge, not the [claimant's] solicitors, should be the judge of relevance". There is a continuing duty of disclosure after the grant of the search order up to the time of the execution of the order.[198]

(iii) *Custody and non-use of items seized*

28-42 An undertaking should be given that any articles obtained as a result of the order will be retained by the claimant's solicitors in safe custody.[199] Indeed in *Columbia Pictures Inc v Robinson*[200] Scott J considered that the claimant's solicitors should return anything not belonging to the claimant after copying, so that the material should be out of the defendant's hands for a relatively short period of time.[201] He also thought that if the ownership of seized material was in dispute it should not be retained by the claimant's solicitors pending trial but should rather be delivered to the defendant's solicitors.[202] A similar undertaking by the claimant that is often impliedly or expressly insisted on is not to use any documents or information obtained as a result of the search order for a collateral purpose or, as it is sometimes

---

194 *Gates v Swift* [1982] R.P.C. 339. See also para.3 of the standard form of search order laid down by the Practice Direction.

195 *Hazel Grove Music Co Ltd v Elster Enterprises* [1983] F.S.R. 379.

196 See, e.g. *Thermax v Schott Industrial Glass* [1981] F.S.R. 289; *Wardle Fabrics v Myristis* [1984] F.S.R. 263; *Jeffrey Rogers Knitwear Production Ltd v Vinola (Knitwear) Manufacturing Co* [1985] F.S.R. 184. In *Dormeuil Frères SA v Nicolian International (Textiles) Ltd* [1988] 1 W.L.R. 1362, Sir Nicolas Browne-Wilkinson V C held that the courts have a discretion whether to discharge an ex parte order for material non-disclosure (on this point following decisions on what are now called freezing orders—see para.28-54); and that it was not the correct procedure to discharge an ex parte injunction at an interlocutory hearing. But search orders have subsequently been discharged at the interlocutory stage in *Lock International Plc v Beswick* [1989] 1 W.L.R. 1268; *O'Regan v Iambic Productions Ltd* (1989) 139 N.L.J. 1378; *Swedac Ltd v Magnet & Southerns Plc* [1990] F.S.R. 89 CA; *NAF NAF SA v Dickens (London) Ltd* [1993] F.S.R. 424. And in *Tate Access Floors v Boswell* [1991] Ch. 512 Sir Nicolas Browne-Wilkinson accepted that he had been wrong in Dormeuil Frères in thinking that normally an ex parte injunction should not be discharged at the interlocutory stage.

197 [1987] Ch. 38 at 77.

198 *O'Regan v Iambic Productions Ltd* (1989) 139 N.L.J. 1378.

199 See, e.g. *Universal City Studios v Mukhtar & Sons Ltd* [1976] 1 W.L.R. 568; *Customs & Excise Commissioners v Hamlin & Co* [1984] 1 W.L.R. 509. See also Sch.D to the standard form of search order laid down by the Practice Direction.

200 [1987] Ch. 38 at 77. Scott J also regarded it as essential that a detailed record of the material to be taken should be made by the claimant's solicitors before its removal.

201 See also *LT Piver SARL v S & J Perfume Co Ltd* [1987] F.S.R. 159 at 160. See also Sch.D to the standard form of search order laid down by the Practice Direction.

202 Provided the defendant's solicitors gave an undertaking for its safe custody and production, if required, in court. See also Sch.D to the standard form of search order laid down by the Practice Direction.

stated, save for the purpose of civil proceedings in connection with the subject-matter of the action.[203] But this undertaking does not prevent the claimant using the information to bring civil proceedings against third parties implicated in the same wrongful handling of the same infringing goods.[204] Nor does it prevent documents seized being used in contempt proceedings against the defendant for failure to comply fully with the search order.[205] But according to Lord Oliver in *Crest Homes Plc v Marks*,[206] "the court will not release or modify the implied undertaking … save in special circumstances and where the release or modification will not occasion injustice to the person giving discovery".

(iv) Improperly obtained orders

28-43 Several principles have been laid down regarding improperly obtained search orders. First, the defendant is technically guilty of contempt if he disobeys a search order which is subsequently discharged although the courts may choose not to impose a penalty.[207] Secondly, evidence gained under an improperly obtained search order is admissible.[208] Thirdly, an improperly obtained search order can be discharged, if there is some practical purpose in so doing, even though the order has been fully executed[209]; but, whether discharged or not, the defendant has a claim against the claimant in accordance with the latter's undertaking as to damages.[210]

(v) Order after judgment

28-44 In *Distributori Automatici Italia SpA v Halford General Trading Co Ltd*[211] a search order was granted after judgment to aid execution of it. Leggatt J said:

"Where there is a real risk of justice being thwarted by a defendant intent on rendering

---

203 See, e.g. *Hallmark Cards v Image Arts* [1977] F.S.R. 150 CA; *Sony Corp v Time Electronics* [1981] F.S.R. 333; *General Nutrition Ltd v Pattni* [1984] F.S.R. 403; *Customs & Excise Commissioners v Hamlin & Co* [1984] 1 W.L.R. 509. See also Sch.C to the standard form of search order laid down by the Practice Direction.

204 *Sony Corp v Anand* [1981] F.S.R. 398. See also *Bayer AG v Winter (No.3)* [1986] E.C.C. 465, in which information obtained from a search order was allowed to be used to claim freezing injunctions in Austria and Switzerland. cf. *Twentieth Century Fox v Tryrare Ltd* [1991] F.S.R. 58.

205 *Crest Homes Plc v Markes* [1987] A.C. 829. Additionally the House of Lords there held that it was no bar that the documents had been seized under a later search order relating to proceedings that were technically different from those out of which the contempt issue (for contravention of an earlier search order) arose. See also *Garvin v Domus Publishing Ltd* [1989] Ch. 335 (seized documents could be used in proceedings for contempt for breach of an earlier freezing injunction). cf. *Cobra Gulf Ltd v Rata* [1998] Ch. 109.

206 *Crest Homes Plc v Marks* [1987] A.C. 829 at 860.

207 *Hallmark Cards v Image Arts* [1977] F.S.R. 150; *WEA Records v Visions Channel 4 Ltd* [1983] 1 W.L.R. 721 at 726; *Wardle Fabrics v Myristis* [1984] F.S.R. 263; *Columbia Pictures Inc v Robinson* [1987] Ch. 38 at 72. See also *Bhimji v Chatwani* [1991] 1 W.L.R. 989; para.28-37 fn.181.

208 *Helliwell v Piggot-Sims* [1980] F.S.R. 582. cf. *Universal City Studios Inc v Hubbard* [1984] Ch. 225 at 237.

209 *Booker McConnell Plc v Plascow* [1985] R.P.C. 425; *Columbia Pictures Inc v Robinson* [1987] Ch. 38 at 85–87. cf. *WEA Records Ltd v Visions Channel 4 Ltd* [1983] 1 W.L.R. 721 at 727–728.

210 *WEA Records Ltd v Visions Channel 4 Ltd* [1983] 1 W.L.R. 721 at 727–728; *Columbia Pictures Inc v Robinson* [1987] Ch. 38 at 85–87. cf. *Booker McConnell Plc v Plascow* [1985] R.P.C. 425. In *Al-Rawas v Pegasus Energy Ltd* [2008] EWHC 617 (QB); [2009] 1 All E.R. 346, which concerned the assessment of damages under the undertaking as to damages where search orders and freezing injunctions had been set aside, it was held that damages for loss of management time, "general damages" and "aggravated damages" should be awarded in accordance with normal principles of damages.

211 [1985] 1 W.L.R. 1066.

any judgment nugatory, the need for an *Anton Piller* order may be even greater in aid of execution than of judgment. In my judgment the court has jurisdiction to make an *Anton Piller* after judgment for the purpose of eliciting documents which are essential to execution and which would otherwise be unjustly denied to the judgment creditor."[212]

By granting the order after judgment two accompanying adjustments to the usual search order are being made: first, in this situation the order is being given to prevent information *essential to execution* being destroyed or disposed of; secondly, while this search order can still be regarded as interim it is interim in the sense of not being finally determinative of the rights of the parties rather than in the usual sense of being given prior to trial or other hearing in which final judgment is given.

(vi) *Abuse of search orders*

The search order is a very important weapon in the armoury of claimants wishing to protect intellectual property. The judges are well aware, however, that the remedy is a drastic one[213] which may be abused by claimants[214] and have reacted to such abuses by re-emphasising and strengthening the principles designed to safeguard the defendant as well as awarding damages in accordance with the claimant's cross-undertaking, which may include aggravated and exemplary damages.[215] **28-45**

(f) Freezing injunctions

A freezing injunction (once known as a *Mareva* injunction[216]) is an interim prohibitory injunction, almost invariably granted without notice, and usually restraining the defendant from removing assets from the jurisdiction or disposing of assets within it. In rare circumstances[217] the order may also extend to restraining the defendant from dealing with assets outside the jurisdiction (a "worldwide **28-46**

[212] [1985] 1 W.L.R. 1066 at 1073. *Mareva* injunctions have also been granted after judgment: see para.28-56.

[213] "It has to be accepted that a common, perhaps the usual, effect of the service and execution of an *Anton Piller* order is to close down the business which, on the applicant's evidence, is being carried on in violation of their rights": per Scott J in *Columbia Pictures Inc v Robinson* [1987] Ch. 38 at 73. But in *Chappell v UK* [1989] F.S.R. 617 the European Court of Human Rights held that search orders do not infringe art.8 of the European Convention which gives an individual the rights to have his private life and home respected.

[214] *Columbia Pictures Inc v Robinson* [1987] Ch. 38. See also *Systematica Ltd v London Computer Centre Ltd* [1983] F.S.R. 313 at 316–317; *Lock International Plc v Beswick* [1989] 1 W.L.R. 1268; *Universal Thermosensors Ltd v Hibben* [1992] 1 W.L.R. 840.

[215] *Digital Equipment v Darkcrest Ltd* [1984] Ch. 512; *Columbia Pictures Inc v Robinson* [1987] Ch. 38; *Al-Rawas v Pegasus Energy Ltd* [2008] EWHC 617 (QB); [2009] 1 All E.R. 346. See also, generally, *Universal Thermosensors Ltd v Hibben* [1992] 1 W.L.R. 840. The claimant may also be refused costs: *Systematica Ltd v London Computer Centre Ltd* [1983] F.S.R. 313.

[216] The new terminology is that laid down in CPR r.25.1(1)(f). See, generally S. Gee, *Commercial Injunctions*, 6th edn (2016); M. Hoyle, *Freezing and Search Orders*, 4th edn (2006); A. Zuckerman, "Interlocutory Remedies in Quest of Procedural Fairness" (1993) 56 M.L.R. 325; A. Zuckerman, "Mareva Injunctions and Security for Judgment" (1993) 109 L.Q.R. 432. See also the standard forms of freezing injunction set out as an Annex to the Practice Direction on Interim Injunctions, CPR Pt 25 para.25PD (referred to below as the *CPR Practice Direction*).

[217] With regard to what constitutes "rare circumstances", it was thought important in *Derby & Co Ltd v Weldon* [1990] Ch. 48 that on the facts an order affecting only assets in England and Wales might for practical purposes be virtually useless. Similarly in the *Republic of Haiti v Duvalier* [1990] 1 Q.B. 202. Staughton LJ said, at 216–217: "What to my mind is determinative is the plain and admit-

freezing injunction").[218] Described by Lord Denning extra-judicially as "the greatest piece of judicial law reform in my time"[219] and by Donaldson LJ as "one of the law's two nuclear weapons"[220] (the other being the search order)[221] the purpose of a freezing injunction is to prevent a defendant frustrating the satisfaction of a judgment that the claimant may get against him. Prior to *Mareva Compania Naviera SA v International Bulkcarriers SA*,[222] in which this type of injunction was developed, the basic rule was that a court could not give any form of security to a creditor until judgment had been given in the creditor's favour.[223] Initially the jurisdiction to grant a freezing injunction was seen as resting on the general statutory provision, now the Senior Courts Act 1981 s.37(1), to grant injunctions where "just and convenient to do so".[224] Since then the jurisdiction (as regards assets within England and Wales) has been put on a clear statutory footing by s.37(3) of the Senior Courts Act 1981, which has also confirmed that freezing injunctions are not restricted to being ordered against foreign defendants or to prevent the removal of assets from the jurisdiction.[225] In several cases it has been stressed that a freezing injunction operates in personam and not in rem and does not constitute full pre-trial attachment or give priority over other creditors.[226] Special principles have been developed to govern freezing injunctions and the principles laid down in *American Cyanamid Co*

---

ted intention of the defendants to move their assets out of the reach of the courts of law, coupled with the resources they have obtained and the skill they have hitherto shown in doing that, and the vast amount of money involved. This case demands international cooperation between all nations." In *Derby & Co Ltd v Weldon (No.3 & No.4)* [1990] Ch. 65 Lord Donaldson MR thought that what was meant was merely that a worldwide freezing injunction ought to be granted only when it was really necessary.

218 *Babanaft International Co SA v Bassatne* [1990] Ch. 13; *Republic of Haiti v Duvalier* [1990] 1 Q.B. 202; *Derby & Co Ltd v Weldon* [1990] Ch. 48; *Derby & Co v Weldon (No.3 & No.4)* [1990] Ch. 65; *Morris v Mahfouz* [1994] 1 W.L.R. 708; *Mobil Cerro Negro Ltd v Petroleos de Venezuela SA* [2008] EWHC 532 (Comm); [2008] 2 All E.R. (Comm) 1034. Relevant undertakings are set out in Schedule B to the standard form of worldwide freezing injunction, laid down in the Practice Direction. In *Derby & Co Ltd v Weldon (No.6)* [1990] 1 W.L.R. 1139 it was recognised that in exceptional circumstances an English court, as part of a worldwide freezing injunction, can order the transfer of assets to a jurisdiction in which English judgments and orders are recognised from a jurisdiction where they are not recognised. Apart from the very exceptional case, a freezing injunction granted by an English court in support of a foreign judgment or arbitration award should be confined to assets within, not outside, England and Wales; *Rosseel NV v Oriental Commercial and Shipping (UK) Ltd* [1990] 1 W.L.R. 1387 CA. See *Motorola Credit Corp v Uzan* [2003] EWCA Civ 752; [2004] 1 W.L.R. 113 for the considerations to be taken into account in deciding whether to make a worldwide freezing injunction under s.25 of the Civil Jurisdiction and Judgments Act 1982. For guidelines as to the exercise of the court's discretion to grant permission to enforce a worldwide freezing order abroad, see *Dadourian Group International Inc v Simms* [2006] EWCA Civ 399; [2006] 1 W.L.R. 2499; [2006] 3 All E.R. 48. A post-judgment worldwide freezing order can be granted in aid of English proceedings, as in *Masri v Consolidated Contractors International UK Ltd (No.2)* [2007] EWHC 3010 (Comm); [2008] 1 All E.R. (Comm) 305; affirmed [2008] EWCA Civ 303; [2009] Q.B. 450. See generally L. Merrett, "Worldwide freezing orders in Europe" [2008] L.M.C.L.Q. 71.

219 *The Due Process of Law* (1980), p.134.

220 *Bank Mellat v Mohammed Ebrahim Nikpour* [1985] F.S.R. 87 at 92.

221 A freezing injunction and a search order can be granted together in one order.

222 [1975] 2 Lloyd's Rep. 509.

223 *Lister v Stubbs* (1890) L.R. 45 Ch. D. 1. How far this remains the case is controversial: see now *Attorney General of Hong Kong v Reid* [1994] 1 A.C. 324; and *Sinclair Investments (UK) Ltd v Versailles Trade Finance Ltd (In Administration)* [2011] EWCA Civ 347; [2012] Ch. 453.

224 Senior Courts Act 1981 s.37(1). This remains important as the relevant source of the jurisdiction to grant worldwide freezing injunctions.

225 This had been accepted prior to the Act in *Prince Abdul Rahman v Abu-Taha* [1980] 1 W.L.R. 1268.

226 e.g. *Cretanor Maritime Co Ltd v Irish Marine Management Ltd (The Cretan Harmony)* [1978] 1 W.L.R. 966; *Iraqi Ministry of Defence v Arcepey Shipping Co* [1981] Q.B. 65; *Ninemia Maritime*

Ltd v Ethicon Ltd[227] are inapplicable.[228] A final introductory point is that, while the two have tended to be merged in some cases, a preservation order,[229] granted where the claimant is seeking a proprietary remedy (most commonly a so-called "tracing remedy"), is different from a freezing injunction and will be granted more readily.[230]

(i) A good arguable case

There are several essential prerequisites for the grant of a freezing injunction. First, the claimant must show "a good arguable case"[231] in a cause of action[232] against the defendant. This is not as stringent a standard as that required for sum- **28-47**

Corp v Trave Schiffahrtsgesellschaft GmbH (The Niedersachsen) [1983] 1 W.L.R. 1412; *K/S A/S Admiral Shipping v Portlink Ferries Ltd* [1984] 2 Lloyd's Rep. 166; cf. *Z Ltd v A-Z* [1982] Q.B. 558 at 573, per Lord Denning. For the same reason a freezing injunction covering realty is not registrable as a land charge: *Stockler v Fourways Estates Ltd* [1984] 1 W.L.R. 25. It follows that payment out to a secured creditor is not prohibited by a freezing injunction. No variation of the order is needed to effect it, though if, out of an abundance of caution, such a variation is sought, it will not be refused: *Taylor v Van Dutch Marine Holding Ltd* [2017] EWHC 636 (Ch); [2017] 1 W.L.R. 2571.

227 [1975] A.C. 396.

228 *Polly Peck International Plc v Nadir (No.2)* [1992] 4 All E.R. 769.

229 Made under CPR r.25.1(1)(c)(i), or in the exercise of the courts' inherent equitable jurisdiction.

230 The distinction is most clearly brought out in *Polly Peck International Plc v Nadir (No.2)* [1992] 4 All E.R. 769 in which it was held that the *American Cyanamid* principles apply to a preservation order. See also *Investment and Pensions Advisory Service Ltd v Gray* [1990] B.C.L.C. 38 (court may be less willing to allow a variation if the claimant is asserting a proprietary tracing claim to the assets which the defendant seeks to use for ordinary expenses). A further distinction between the principles governing a freezing injunction, on the one hand, and a proprietary injunction (designed to protect property in which the claimant alleges proprietary rights) on the other, was brought out in *Boreh v Republic of Djibouti* [2015] EWHC 769 (Comm); [2015] 3 All E.R. 577 (given that the former type of order is more draconian than the latter, it will be discharged and, on the facts, was discharged—whereas the latter may not be and, on the facts, was not discharged—because of deliberately misleading information provided to the court by the claimant's solicitor). In *Director of the Assets Recovery Agency v Creaven* [2005] EWHC 2726 (Admin); [2006] 1 W.L.R. 622 a freezing order in support of a civil claim for asset recovery under Pt 5 of the Proceeds of Crime Act 2002 was held to be governed by similar principles to those applicable to a freezing injunction in support of a proprietary claim.

231 *Rasu Maritima SA v Perusahaan Pertambangan Minyak Dan Gas Bumi Negara (The Pertamina)* [1978] Q.B. 644; *Ninemia Maritime Corp v Trave Schiffahrtsgesellschaft GmbH (The Niedersachsen)* [1983] 1 W.L.R. 1412.

232 In *Siskina v Distos Compania Naviera SA (The Siskina)* [1979] A.C. 210 it was held that an English court must have jurisdiction over the main cause of action, but this was modified by s.25(1) of the Civil Jurisdiction and Judgments Act 1982. By this, English courts were empowered to grant interim relief when the action had been or was to be brought in a court within the EC (or, under the Lugano Convention within the EEA) and the subject-matter of the action was within the scope of the Brussels Regulation (now Regulation (EU) 1215/2012) (on which, see *Crédit Suisse Fides Trust SA v Cuoghi* [1998] Q.B. 818). Section 25(2) recognised an express discretion to refuse relief on the ground that the courts would formerly have had no jurisdiction. Under a power in s.25(3), the Civil Jurisdiction and Judgments Act 1982 (Interim Relief) Order 1997 (SI 1997/302) further extended the effect of s.25 of the 1982 Act to proceedings commenced, or to be commenced, otherwise than in a Brussels or Lugano Contracting State and to proceedings outside the scope of the Brussels Regulation (on the interpretation of which, see *Royal Bank of Scotland Plc v FAL Oil Co Ltd* [2012] EWHC 3628 (Comm); [2013] 1 Lloyd's Rep. 327). For a case in which s.25(2) of the Civil Jurisdiction and Judgments Act 1982 was applied to refuse a freezing order in support of proceedings in the USA, see *United States of America v Abacha* [2014] EWCA Civ 1291; [2015] 1 W.L.R. 1917. For discussion of whether s.25(3) of the Civil Jurisdiction and Judgments Act 1982 allows freezing injunctions to be ordered in aid of a foreign arbitration, see *ETI Euro Telecom International NV v Republic of Bolivia* [2008] EWCA Civ 880; [2009] 1 W.L.R. 665.

mary judgment,[233] but is higher than under *American Cyanamid v Ethicon*.[234] The cause of action is generally for the recovery of a debt or contractual damages or for the return of money in a tracing action. But freezing injunctions have been granted in respect of tort actions.[235] It is essential, however, that the cause of action is one for which the freezing injunction can afford some protection; hence a claim for a declaration in the absence of any claim for an immediate money judgment cannot ground a freezing injunction.[236] In *Fourie v Le Roux*,[237] it was held by the House of Lords in discharging a freezing injunction that it was essential for the claimant to point to proceedings already brought, or about to be brought, so as to show where and on what basis he expects to recover judgment against the defendant. In Lord Scott's words: "I find it very difficult to visualise a case where the grant of a freezing order, made without notice, could be said to be properly made in the absence of any formulation of the case for substantive relief that the applicant for the order intended to institute."[238] It is also essential that there is a *pre-existing* cause of action so that a court cannot grant a conditional freezing injunction that will come into effect if, as and when the cause of action that the claimant fears will arise does arise.[239]

(ii) *Real risk of defendant's assets being disposed of*

28-48 Secondly, the claimant should give some ground for believing that there is a real risk of the defendant's assets[240] being disposed of so that a judgment or award in favour of the claimant would remain unsatisfied.[241] Where the defendant has assets beyond what is needed to satisfy the claim the freezing injunction should be

---

233 *Rasu Maritima SA v Perusahaan Pertambangan Minyak Dan Gas Bumi Negara (The Pertamina)* [1978] Q.B. 644; *Ninemia Maritime Corp v Trave Schiffahrtsgesellschaft GmbH (The Niedersachsen)* [1983] 1 W.L.R. 1412.

234 [1975] A.C. 396. See *Polly Peck International Plc v Nadir (No.2)* [1992] 4 All E.R. 769 at 786.

235 e.g. *Allen v Jambo Holdings* [1980] 1 W.L.R. 1252 (Fatal Accidents Act 1976 and personal injury); *Z Ltd v A-Z* [1982] Q.B. 558 (conspiracy); *Allied Arab Bank Ltd v Hajjar* [1988] Q.B. 787 (conspiracy); *VTB Capital Plc v Nutritek International Corp* [2013] UKSC 5; [2013] 2 A.C. 337 (conspiracy); *JSC BTA Bank v Ablyazov (No 5)* [2015] UKSC 64; [2015] 1 W.L.R. 4754 (fraud).

236 *Steamship Mutual Underwriting Assoc (Bermuda Ltd) v Thakur Shipping* [1986] 2 Lloyd's Rep. 439 CA; *Siporex Trade SA v Comdel Commodities Ltd* [1986] 2 Lloyd's Rep. 428.

237 [2007] UKHL 1; [2007] 1 W.L.R. 320.

238 [2007] UKHL 1; [2007] 1 W.L.R. 320 at [35].

239 *Veracruz Transportation Inc v VC Shipping Co Inc and Den Norske Bank A/S (The Veracruz I)* [1992] 1 Lloyd's Rep. 353. See also *Steamship Mutual Underwriting Assoc v Thakur* [1986] 2 Lloyd's Rep. 439 (Note). *The Veracruz I* is criticised by L. Collins, "The legacy of The Siskina" (1992) 108 L.Q.R. 175. In *Re Q's Estate* [1999] 1 Lloyd's Rep. 931 it was held that: (1) a court can grant a freezing injunction in respect of a dispute that is to be referred to arbitration; and that (2) a freezing injunction can be granted prior to the accrual of a cause of action with its operation suspended until accrual. See also *Rowland v Gulfpac Ltd* [1999] 1 Lloyd's Rep. Bank. 86; *Papamichael v National Westminster Bank Plc* [2002] 1 Lloyd's Rep. 332. A freezing injunction can be granted in support of a claim for contribution (even in favour of alleged fraudsters): *Kazakhstan Kagazy Plc v Zhunus* [2016] EWCA Civ 1036; [2017] 1 W.L.R. 1360.

240 "Assets" includes money that may be acquired after the grant of the freezing injunction, such as the proceeds of a life assurance policy: *TDK Tape Distributor (UK) Ltd v Videochoice Ltd* [1986] 1 W.L.R. 141. See also *Cretanor Maritime Co Ltd v Irish Marine Management Ltd (The Cretan Harmony)* [1978] 1 W.L.R. 966. Under the extended definition of the defendant's "assets" in the modern form of freezing order, a defendant's "assets" include the proceeds of loans paid into the bank account of the defendant (so that the bank would be in breach of the freezing order by releasing those proceeds): *JSC BTA Bank v Ablyazov (No 5)* [2015] UKSC 64; [2015] 1 W.L.R. 4754.

241 *Third Chandris Shipping Corp v Unimarine SA* [1979] Q.B. 645; *Z. Ltd v A-Z* [1982] Q.B. 558;

limited to the maximum amount needed for satisfaction.[242] A freezing injunction will not knowingly be granted or continued in respect of assets owned solely[243] by a third party[244] (though for obvious reasons a court is not bound to accept a third party's contention that the assets in question belong to it and not the defendant[245]). Where an asset of the defendant is in the hands of a third party,[246] or the third party is debtor to the defendant so as to give rise to an asset in the latter's hands potentially available to the claimant,[247] then an injunction may be granted against the third party.

Ninemia Maritime Corp v Trave Schiffahrtsgesellschaft GmbH (The Niedersachsen) [1983] 1 W.L.R. 1412; *Montecchi v Shimco (UK) Ltd* [1979] 1 W.L.R. 1180; *Establissement Esefka International Anstalt v Central Bank of Nigeria* [1979] 1 Lloyd's Rep. 445 CA. In the latter two cases there was no such risk. In *Polly Peck International Plc v Nadir (No.2)* [1992] 4 All E.R. 769 it was explained that the circumstances would have to be unusual for a freezing injunction to be granted against a bank. On the appointment of an administrative receiver, a freezing injunction against a company should normally be varied or discharged because there is no longer a risk of dissipation of the assets to frustrate a judgment; *Capital Cameras Ltd v Harold Lines Ltd* [1991] 1 W.L.R. 54. In *Mobil Cerro Negro Ltd v Petroleos de Venezuala SA* [2008] EWHC 532 (Comm); [2008] 2 All E.R. (Comm) 1034 it was held that, to be relevant, the dissipation of assets must be by conduct that is unjustifiable. The same test (that there must be a real risk of disposal) applies also to that form of freezing order that is referred to as a "notification order", i.e. an injunction that the defendant should not dispose of assets without informing the claimant: *Holyoake v Candy* [2017] EWCA Civ 92; [2018] Ch. 297.

242 *Z Ltd v A-Z* [1982] Q.B. 558. See also *Ghoth v Ghoth* [1992] 2 All E.R. 920 CA (which concerned matrimonial proceedings). While a maximum sum is usually inserted, in *JSC BTA Bank v Ablyazov (No.2)* [2009] EWHC 3267 (Comm); [2010] 1 All E.R. (Comm) 1040 the maximum sum (£175 million) was limited to assets within England and Wales (i.e. the defendant was only free to deal with assets abroad if assets within the jurisdiction remained above the maximum sum).

243 The courts are prepared to grant freezing injunctions in respect of joint property, such as bank accounts: see *Z Ltd v A-Z* [1982] Q.B. 558. Indeed, it is now standard for orders to refer to assets "whether they are solely or jointly owned": see the form appended to Mostyn J's judgment explaining the underlying principles in *UL v BK* [2013] EWHC 1735 (Fam); [2014] Fam. 35.

244 *SCF Finance Co Ltd v Masri* [1985] 1 W.L.R. 876; *Allied Arab Bank Ltd v Hajjar (No.2)* [1988] Q.B. 944. See also *Prekookeanska Plovidba v LNT Lines SRL* [1989] 1 W.L.R. 753 (money held in a solicitor's client account, for a client against whom judgment has been entered, and over which the solicitor has a lien for unpaid costs, is to be excluded from the ambit of a freezing injunction). It was once not the practice not to include assets held by the defendant as a bare trustee (*Federal Bank of the Middle East v Hadkinson* [2000] 1 W.L.R. 1695); but today the practice is to include them (*JSC BTA Bank v Solodchenko* [2010] EWCA Civ 1436; [2011] 1 W.L.R. 888).

245 See, e.g. *SCF Finance Co Ltd v Masri* [1985] 1 W.L.R. 876 (wife's contention that bank account did not contain defendant husband's assets did not necessitate discharge of the freezing injunction).

246 *TSB Private Bank International SA v Chabra* [1992] 1 W.L.R. 231 (company holding assets arguably the beneficial property of the defendant added as second defendant and made subject to a freezing injunction; despite lack of cause of action against company, injunction treated as ancillary to main proceedings). Similarly with the owner of property held on trust for the judgment debtor: *Mercantile Group (Europe) AG v Aiyela* [1994] Q.B. 366. In *Yukong Line Ltd v Rendsburg Investments Corp* [2001] 2 Lloyd's Rep. 113 CA it was held that a freezing injunction might still be granted where the defendant's assets could not be specifically identified in the hands of the third party; in such circumstances the order would cover the general assets of the third party up to the amount of the defendant's assets apparently held. But this cannot be used as a back-door way of sidelining separate corporate personality, even if the holding company may de facto control its affiliate: *Parbulk II AS v PT Humpuss Intermoda Transportasi TBK* [2011] EWHC 3143 (Comm); [2011] 2 C.L.C. 988 at [42] (Gloster J).

247 See *Parbulk II AS v PT Humpuss Intermoda Transportasi TBK* [2011] EWHC 3143 (Comm); [2011] 2 C.L.C. 988 at [62] (Gloster J); also the decision of the High Court of Australia in *Cardile v LED Builders Pty Ltd* [1999] HCA 18; (1999) 198 C.L.R. 380; and the Cayman Islands decision in *Algosaibi v Saad Investment Co Ltd* (CICA 1 of 2010). Analogous is *C Inc Plc v L* [2001] 2 Lloyd's Rep. 459 (beneficiary of trust monies held by defendant amenable to order on basis of defendant trustee's right to indemnity). In *Revenue & Customs Commissioners v Egleton* [2006] EWHC 2313

(iii) *Undertaking in damages*

28-49 Thirdly, as with all interim injunctions the claimant should give an undertaking in damages.[248] Moreover, an undertaking should be given to indemnify any third party for loss suffered as a result of complying with the freezing injunction[249] (for example, a bank's administrative costs in locating the defendant's account and issuing instructions regarding it). Normally further undertakings exacted are to issue a claim form forthwith and to serve the defendant with copies of the order and affidavit.[250]

(iv) *Defendant's business and living expenses or legal costs*

28-50 A crucial restriction is that the order made should not prevent the defendant incurring, in good faith, business or living expenses or legal costs: a freezing injunction that has been granted may be discharged or varied accordingly to enable the defendant to pay off debts or to meet reasonable living expenses.[251] In *Iraqi Ministry of Defence v Arcepey Shipping Co*[252] the test applied was whether the money was required for a purpose that did not conflict with the policy underlying the jurisdic-

---

(Ch); [2007] 1 All E.R. 606 the applicant for a freezing injunction was a creditor petitioning for the winding up of a company for the company's failure to pay VAT. It was held that a freezing injunction could be granted in respect of the assets of third parties who, although they were not holding the company's assets, were alleged to be debtors. However, in all normal circumstances, the application for the freezing injunction should be brought by a provisional liquidator (who is charged with deciding whether to pursue the company's claims against alleged debtors) and not a petitioning creditor. (The relevant cause of action, therefore, would be that of the company and not the petitioning creditor so that the "third party" objection would not arise.)

[248] *Third Chandris Shipping Corp v Unimarine SA* [1979] Q.B. 645. The court should generally be sure that the defendant is good for the undertaking and may insist on security; *Ashtiani v Kashi* [1987] Q.B. 888. See Sch.B(2) of the standard forms annexed to the *Practice Direction*. cf. *Allen v Jambo Holdings Ltd* [1980] 1 W.L.R. 1252. For consideration of whether there should be fortification of a party's undertaking in damages in support of a freezing injunction, see *Energy Venture Partners Ltd v Malabu Oil and Gas Ltd* [2014] EWCA Civ 1295; [2015] 1 W.L.R. 2309. But if security was not insisted on at the time the freezing injunction was granted it should not be ordered when the injunction has been discharged: *Commodity Ocean Transport Corp v Basford Unicorn Industries Ltd (The Mito)* [1987] 2 Lloyd's Rep. 197. For the approach to claims for damages enforcing the undertaking see *Cheltenham & Gloucester Building Society v Ricketts* [1993] 1 W.L.R. 1545; and *Fiona Trust & Holding Corporation v Privalov (No. 2)* [2016] EWHC 2163 (Comm); [2017] 2 All E.R. 570. But a cross-undertaking may not be required of a public authority that seeks a freezing injunction in exercise of its law enforcement function: *Securities & Investment Board v Lloyd-Wright* [1993] 4 All E.R. 210; *United States Securities & Exchange Commission v Manterfield* [2009] EWCA Civ 27; [2010] 1 W.L.R. 172. For the award of damages under the undertaking, see *Al-Rawas v Pegasus Energy Ltd* [2008] EWHC 617 (QB); [2009] 1 All E.R. 346 above at para.28-43.

[249] *Searose Ltd v Seatrain (UK) Ltd* [1981] 1 W.L.R. 894; *Clipper Maritime Co of Monravia v Mineralimportexport (The Marie Leonhardt)* [1981] 1 W.L.R. 1262; *Z Ltd v A-Z* [1982] Q.B. 558; *Guinness Peat Aviation (Belgium) NV v Hispania Lineas Aereas SA* [1992] 1 Lloyd's Rep. 190.

[250] *Z Ltd v A-Z* [1982] Q.B. 558. See also Sch.B(3) to the standard forms annexed to the *Practice Direction*. In *Siporex Trade SA v Comdel Commodities Ltd* [1986] 2 Lloyd's Rep. 428 a freezing injunction was discharged because, inter alia, no originating summons had been issued two months after the grant of the freezing injunction.

[251] Note a point of procedure. In *Ocean Software Ltd v Kay* [1992] Q.B. 583 CA, it was held that the Court of Appeal does not have jurisdiction to entertain an application to discharge a freezing injunction which it had granted on appeal from a judge of the High Court. The application should be made at first instance.

[252] [1981] 1 Q.B. 65. See also *Avant Petroleum Inc v Gatoil Overseas Inc* [1986] 2 Lloyd's Rep. 236; *Normid Housing Association Ltd v Ralphs & Mansell (Note)* [1989] 1 Lloyd's Rep. 274; *Camdex International Ltd v Bank of Zambia (No.2)* [1997] 1 W.L.R. 632 CA; *Customs and Excise Commis-*

tion to grant a freezing injunction: and it was held that it did not so conflict where the defendant was "seeking in good faith to make payments which he considers he should make in the ordinary course of business".[253] Similarly in *PCW (Underwriting Agencies) Ltd v Dixon*[254] the freezing injunction was varied so as to allow the defendant £1,000 per week for the expense of "living as he has always lived",[255] £27,404 for paying bills "such as he has always incurred"[256] and £50,000 for the legal costs of defending himself in the proceedings.[257] On the other hand in *A v B (X Intervening)*[258] a third party failed to gain a variation releasing £400,000 so that the defendant could honour cheques payable to the third party that had been dishonoured prior to the freezing injunction because Parker J was not satisfied that the payment was one "which would normally have been made out of such assets had there been no injunction".[259] In general a variation will not be granted unless the court is satisfied that the defendant has insufficient other assets, including foreign assets,[260] to pay his debts or expenses.[261] But where the third party creditor is itself the bank holding the defendant's assets the court will vary the freezing injunction at the instance of the bank without needing to be satisfied of the insufficiency of other assets, so as to allow the bank to exercise its usual contractual rights of set-off in respect of facilities granted prior to the injunction.[262] It should be noted that the reasoning behind the "ordinary expenditure" exception is limited

---

sioners v Anchor Foods Ltd (No.2) [1999] 1 W.L.R. 1139; *Nomihold Securities Inc v Mobile Telesystems Finance SA* [2011] EWCA Civ 1040; [2012] 1 All E.R. (Comm) 223.

253 [1981] 1 Q.B. 65 at 73.

254 [1983] 2 All E.R. 158. See also *Law Society v Shanks* [1988] 1 F.L.R. 504; *TTMI Ltd of England v ASM Shipping Ltd of India* [2005] EWHC 2666 (Comm); [2006] 1 Lloyd's Rep. 401 (freezing injunction refused because defendant needed its only asset within the jurisdiction to pay for its legal expenses).

255 [1983] 2 All E.R. 158 at 162. Lloyd J suspected that the claimant had put forward the wholly unrealistic figure of £100 for living expenses in order to bring unfair pressure on the defendant to settle.

256 [1983] 2 All E.R. 158 at 162.

257 cf. *TDK Tape Distributor (UK) Ltd v Videochoice Ltd* [1986] 1 W.L.R. 141; ordinary living expenses do not include the high legal costs of engaging a QC to defend a criminal prosecution. It was clarified in *United Mizrahi Bank Ltd v Doherty* [1998] 1 W.L.R. 435, that the expenses proviso does not give the defendant (or third parties, *e.g.* solicitors, receiving the expenses from the defendant) immunity from liability for breach of trust, or knowing receipt, by paying or receiving those expenses.

258 [1983] Lloyd's Rep. 532.

259 [1983] Lloyd's Rep. 532 at 534. In *Atlas Maritime Co SA v Avalon Maritime Ltd (The Coral Rose) (No.1)* [1991] 4 All E.R. 769 the Court of Appeal refused to vary a freezing injunction to allow the defendant company to repay a loan to its parent company.

260 *Ashtiani v Kashi* [1987] Q.B. 888 at 901; see too *Parvalorem v Oliveira* [2013] EWHC 4195 (Ch); and also the little-reported *National Bank of Greece v Constantinos Dimitriou, The Times,* 16 November 1987 CA.

261 *A v C (No.2)* [1981] Q.B. 961; *PCW (Underwriting Agencies) Ltd v Dixon* [1983] 2 All E.R. 158. cf. *Campbell Mussells v Thompson* (1984) 81 L.S. Gaz. 2140. Although the defendant has no other funds a freezing injunction will not be discharged to allow the payment of legal expenses if the court is satisfied that funds will be made available by the defendant's parent company to meet those expenses: *Atlas Maritime Co SA v Avalon Maritime Ltd (The Coral Rose) (No.3)* [1991] 1 W.L.R. 917 CA.

262 *Oceanica Castelana Armadora SA v Mineralimportexport (The Theotokos)* [1983] 1 W.L.R. 1294. Indeed Lloyd J thought that to avoid putting a bank to the trouble of applying for a variation freezing injunctions ought to be worded so as to make clear that the bank has such rights. This is so in the standard forms of freezing injunction annexed to the Practice Direction. A third party bank is entitled to an unfettered variation to realise and dispose of assets covered by the freezing order, in which it has a security interest, provided it is acting in good faith in the ordinary course of its business: *Gangway Ltd v Caledonian Park Investments (Jersey) Ltd* [2001] 2 Lloyd's Rep. 715. See also *Prekookeanska Plovidba v LNT Lines SRL* [1989] 1 W.L.R. 753; the right of set-off in an order

to cases where the liability of the defendant has not been established. Once judgment has been obtained, the claimant has a prima facie right to his money in any event: it follows that from this point the exception applies, if at all, only to a very limited extent.[263]

(v) Position of third parties

28-51 What is the effect of a freezing injunction on a third party (usually a bank) holding the defendant's assets? In *Z Ltd v A-Z*[264] it was emphasised that once a third party holding the assets has notice of the injunction it is bound on pain of contempt not to allow the defendant to remove assets contrary to the injunction. So that the third party knows exactly what its obligations are, the order should identify the assets with as much precision as possible.[265] For example, in the case of a bank account it should if possible specify at which branch the defendant's account is held and the number of the account. The order should also make clear the amount of the assets covered by the injunction and how much is to be allowed to be withdrawn for, for example, normal living expenses.[266] In some cases not involving banks the potential inconvenience and loss to a third party holding the claimant's assets has been considered to be such that the freezing injunction has been discharged, rather than forcing the third party to rely on the claimant's undertaking as to damages.[267] For worldwide freezing injunctions a special proviso is insisted on which is designed to protect third parties (who are not subject to the jurisdiction of the English court) in dealing with assets outside the jurisdiction.[268] In *Commissioners*

---

includes the right of solicitors to recover unpaid costs from a client account.

263 *Emmott v Michael Wilson & Partners Ltd* [2019] EWCA Civ 219; [2019] 4 W.L.R. 53.

264 [1982] Q.B. 558. See also the standard forms of freezing injunction annexed to the *Practice Direction*. cf. *Law Society v Shanks* [1988] 1 F.L.R. 504 where it was said that a third party holding assets to the defendant's order does not contravene the freezing injunction by handing them over to the defendant unless it is known that the assets will be dissipated. See also *Bank Mellat v Kazmi* [1989] Q.B. 541 (a debtor of the defendant with notice of the freezing injunction and of the probability that the defendant will not comply with it ought not to pay the debt directly to the defendant); *Lakatamia Shipping Co Ltd v Su* [2014] EWCA Civ 636; [2015] 1 W.L.R. 291 (dealing by a third party company may also be indirectly covered by a freezing injunction if the potential impact of the dealings of that company is to diminish the value of the share-holding of the defendant in that third party company).

265 See also the standard forms of freezing injunction annexed to the Practice Direction.

266 See also the standard forms of freezing injunction annexed to the Practice Direction.

267 *Galaxia Maritima SA v Mineralimportexport (The Eleftherios)* [1982] 1 W.L.R. 539 (defendant's coal on third party's ship); *Unicorn Shipping Ltd v Demet Navy Shipping Co Ltd* [1987] 2 F.T.L.R. 109 (defendant's bunkers on third party's ship).

268 *Derby & Co Ltd v Weldon (Nos 3 and 4)* [1990] Ch. 65; see also the standard form of worldwide freezing injunction annexed to the *Practice Direction*. cf. *Babanaft International Co SA v Bassatne* [1990] Ch. 13; *Republic of Haiti v Duvalier* [1990] 1 Q.B. 202; *Derby & Co Ltd v Weldon* [1990] Ch. 48. See also *Ghoth v Ghoth* [1992] 2 All E.R. 920 CA (which concerned matrimonial proceedings). In *Baltic Shipping Co v Translink Shipping Ltd* [1995] 1 Lloyd's Rep. 673 a further proviso (going beyond that in *Derby & Co Ltd v Weldon (No.3 & No.4)* [1990] Ch. 65, which applies only to those who are not subject to the jurisdiction of the English courts) was inserted into a freezing injunction to protect a bank from being in contempt of the English courts where it complies with what it reasonably believes to be its legal obligations in the state where the assets are situated. In *Bank of China v NBM* [2002] 1 W.L.R. 844, the Court of Appeal upheld David Steel J.'s decision that that further proviso (the *Baltic* proviso) should be included in a world-wide freezing order unless inappropriate, rather than only included if appropriate.

of Customs and Excise v Barclays Bank Plc[269] it was held that no duty of care to prevent payment out of accounts was owed by a bank to the claimants who had obtained a freezing injunction against the bank's customer. The bank was therefore not liable to the claimants in the tort of negligence for mistakenly allowing money to be paid out of the customer's account in contravention of the freezing injunction.

(vi) Order for disclosure and interrogatories

With regard to ancillary relief in aid of a freezing injunction, the court may order disclosure and interrogatories against the defendant[270] or against a third party holding the defendant's assets.[271] This will most commonly be used to enable the claimant to establish the whereabouts and amount of the defendant's assets, including foreign assets.[272] But in *Sociedade Nacional de Combustiveis de Angola UEE v Lundqvist*[273] it was held that the defendants' privilege against self-incrimination (for conspiracy to defraud) meant that the order to state the value of his assets overseas should be discharged. In contrast the order to state the nature and location of those assets was upheld. Although the claimant will often give an undertaking not to use the information obtained in any civil or criminal proceedings without the permission of the court, a court will not require exceptional circumstances before it will grant such permission in respect of contempt proceedings for a failure to make full disclosure.[274] **28-52**

269 [2006] UKHL 28; [2007] 1 A.C. 181.

270 *A v C* [1981] Q.B. 956; *Bekhor (AJ) & Co Ltd v Bilton* [1981] Q.B. 923; *Motorola Credit Corp v Uzan* [2003] EWCA Civ 752; [2004] 1 W.L.R. 113 (a disclosure order is prima facie the normal provision where a freezing injunction is granted); *JSC BTA Bank v Solodchenko* [2011] EWHC 2163 (Ch); [2013] Ch. 1. See also the standard forms of freezing injunction annexed to the Practice Direction. In *House of Spring Gardens v Waite* [1985] F.S.R. 173 it was held that the defendants could be cross-examined on their affidavits. See also *Bayer AG v Winter* [1986] 1 W.L.R. 497 at 503, per Fox LJ. But in *Bayer AG v Winter (No.2)* [1986] 1 W.L.R. 540 Scott J thought that no order for cross-examination could be made without consent. In *Bird v Hadkinson* [2000] C.P. Rep. 21, it was held that a disclosure order contained in a freezing injunction required the defendant not merely to tell the truth but also to take reasonable steps to investigate the truth or otherwise of the answer.

271 *Bankers Trust Co v Shapira* [1980] 1 W.L.R. 1274. See also *Mercantile Group (Europe) AG v Aiyela* [1994] Q.B. 366 (discovery in aid of a post-judgment freezing injunction ordered against a third party who had become mixed up in her husband's arrangements to defeat execution of the judgment against him).

272 *Babanaft International Co SA v Bassatne* [1990] Ch. 13; *Republic of Haiti v Duvalier* [1990] 1 Q.B. 202; *Derby & Co Ltd v Weldon* [1990] Ch. 48; *Derby & Co Ltd v Weldon (No.3 & No.4)* [1990] Ch. 65. But, as shown in the *Duvalier* and *Weldon* cases above, an order for the disclosure of foreign assets is normally conditional on the claimant giving an undertaking not to use the information in proceedings abroad against the defendant without the leave of the English court. In *Gidrxslme Shipping Co Ltd v Tantomar-Transportes Maritimos Lda* [1995] 1 W.L.R. 299 although the post-award freezing injunction was confined to assets within the jurisdiction a disclosure order was made in respect of worldwide assets.

273 [1991] 2 Q.B. 310 CA, noted by A. Zuckerman, "Mareva Injunction v The Privilege Against Self-Incrimination" (1990) 106 L.Q.R. 389. See also *United Norwest Co-operative Ltd v Johnstone, The Times,* 24 February 1994; *Den Norske Bank ASA v Antonatos* [1999] Q.B. 271 CA. For one limited way around the privilege, see *AT & T Istel Ltd v Tully* [1993] A.C. 45 HL; see para.28-39 fn.191.

274 *Dadourian Group International Inc v Simms (No.2)* [2006] EWCA Civ 1745; [2007] 1 W.L.R. 2967.

(vii) *Order for delivery up of goods and entry to premises*

28-53 A defendant may also be ordered to deliver up goods or to allow the claimant to enter his premises to seize goods in aid of a freezing injunction[275] and in *CBS (UK) Ltd v Lambert*[276] several guidelines were laid down in deciding whether to grant such an order. First, there should be clear evidence that the defendant is likely, unless restrained by order, to dispose of or otherwise deal with his chattels in order to deprive the claimant of the fruits of any judgment he may obtain. Moreover, the court should be slow to order the delivery up of property unless there is some evidence or inference that the property has been acquired by the defendant as a result of his alleged wrongdoing. Secondly, no order should be made for delivery up of a defendant's clothes, bedding, furnishings, materials or stock-in-trade likely to be used in a lawful business—except that furnishings of great value bought for the purposes of frustrating judgment creditors can be included in an order. Thirdly, the order should specify as clearly as possible what chattel or classes of chattels are to be delivered up. Fourthly, as with a search order, the order must not authorise the claimant to enter on the defendant's premises or to seize the defendant's property save by the defendant's permission. Fifthly, no order should be made for delivery up to anyone other than the claimant's solicitor or a receiver appointed by the High Court. Sixthly, so far as chattels held by third parties are concerned, the guidelines set out in *Z Ltd v A-Z*[277] should be followed. Finally, provision should always be made for liberty to stay, vary or discharge the order. In some cases even more extreme ancillary orders in aid of a freezing injunction have been discussed. In *Bayer AG v Winter*[278] the Court of Appeal, while primarily concerned with relief ancillary to search order, did accept that additional injunctions restraining a defendant from leaving the jurisdiction and ordering the surrender of his passport could be granted where these were felt necessary to render freezing injunctions more effective.

(viii) *Full disclosure by claimant required*

28-54 As with all ex parte injunctions the claimant must make full disclosure of all material matters[279] and in several cases freezing injunctions have been discharged

---

[275] *Johnson v L & A Philatelics Ltd* [1981] F.S.R. 286. See also *CBS (UK) Ltd v Lambert* [1983] Ch. 37; although at 42 Lawton LJ referred to Stephenson LJ's description in *Bekhor (AJ) & Co Ltd v Bilton* [1981] Q.B. 923 at 955 of "piling *Piller* on *Mareva*" this order is probably better viewed as similar to, rather than being, a true search order. The latter is designed to prevent the defendant disposing of the claimant's property or evidence relevant to his main action and is subject to particular conditions reflecting that purpose: see para.28-35 onwards.

[276] [1983] Ch. 37 at 44–45.

[277] [1982] Q.B. 558.

[278] [1986] 1 W.L.R. 497 CA; see too *B v B (Passport Surrender: Jurisdiction)* [1998] 1 W.L.R. 329. This is normally the appropriate procedure, rather than using the antique and lumbering writ *ne exeat regno* under the provisions of s.6 of the Debtors Act 1869. See *Allied Arab Bank v Hajjar* [1988] Q.B. 787; and cf. *Al Nahkel for Contracting and Trading Ltd v Lowe* [1986] Q.B. 235.

[279] *Third Chandris Shipping Corp v Unimarine SA* [1979] Q.B. 645. The test of a relevant matter for these purposes is whether objectively speaking the facts could reasonably be regarded as material, with materiality to be construed in a reasonable and not excessive manner: see the Irish decisions in *Bambrick v Cobley* [2005] IEHC 43; and *Camden Street Investments Ltd v Vanguard Property Finance Ltd* [2013] IEHC 478 at [48]. The duty of disclosure continues (i.e. the claimant must return to court if material circumstances change) after the grant of the ex parte injunction; *Commercial Bank*

for failure to comply with this requirement.[280] But the courts are not bound to discharge a freezing injunction for material non-disclosure and, even if they do, they can grant a fresh one based on the facts existing at the time of the application to discharge.[281]

(ix) Duty to continue with claim

The claimant who has been granted a freezing injunction is under a duty to press on with the main action and the injunction will be discharged if this is not complied with. In *Town and Country Building Soc v Daisystar Ltd*[282] Farquharson LJ said: **28-55**

"It is the duty of a litigant in a case where a Mareva injunction has been granted, to press on with his claim so that the other party is subject to the order for the minimum amount of time necessary and not kept in limbo. If such a litigant does not for any reason wish to proceed with his claim, even temporarily, then he ought of his own motion to seek the discharge of the injunction from the court."

(x) Order after judgment

A freezing injunction can be granted after judgment to restrain a judgment debtor from disposing of his assets pending execution.[283] While such an injunction is not interim in the usual meaning of the term, it has been regarded as interim and hence as falling within s.37(3) of the Senior Courts Act 1981 because "it is not finally determinative of the rights of the parties but is merely in aid of the court's procedure and safeguarding the rights of the parties in the proceedings".[284] **28-56**

6. Injunctions and Declarations Against the Crown

Section 21 of the Crown Proceedings Act 1947 provides that: "… where in any proceedings against the Crown any such relief is sought as might in proceedings between subjects be granted by way of injunction or specific performance, the court **28-57**

of the Near East Plc v ABC and D [1989] 2 Lloyd's Rep. 319.

280 *Negocios del Mar SA v Doric Shipping Corp SA (The Assios)* [1979] 1 Lloyd's Rep. 331; *Bank Mellat v Nikpour* [1985] F.S.R. 87; *Siporex Trade SA v Comdel Commodities Ltd* [1986] 2 Lloyd's Rep. 428; *Dubai Bank Ltd v Galadari* [1990] 1 Lloyd's Rep. 120; *Gulf Interstate Oil Corp v Ant Trade & Transport Ltd of Malta, The Giovanna* [1999] 1 Lloyd's Rep. 867; *Swift-Fortune Ltd v Magnifica Marine SA, The Capaz Duckling* [2007] EWHC 1630 (Comm); [2008] 1 Lloyd's Rep. 54.

281 *Yardley & Co Ltd v Higson* [1984] F.S.R. 304 CA; *Eastglen Int Corp v Monpare SA* (1987) 137 N.L.J. 56; *Lloyds Bowmaker Ltd v Britannia Arrow Holdings Plc* [1988] 1 W.L.R. 1337; *Brink's-MAT Ltd v Elcombe* [1988] 1 W.L.R. 1350; *Behbehani v Salem* [1989] 1 W.L.R. 723; *Ali & Fahd Shobokski Group Ltd v Moneim* [1989] 1 W.L.R. 710; *Memory Corp Plc v Sidhu (No.2)* [2001] 1 W.L.R. 1443 CA.

282 (1989) 139 N.L.J. 1563 CA. See also *Comdel Commodities Ltd v Siporex Trade SA* [1997] 1 Lloyd's Rep. 424 CA.

283 *Orwell Steel Ltd v Asphalt & Tarmac (UK) Ltd* [1984] 1 W.L.R. 1097; *Hill Samuel & Co Ltd v Littaur (No.2)* (1985) 129 S.J. 433. See also *Deutsche Schachtbau- und Tiefbohrgesellschaft MbH v Ras Al Khaimah National Oil Co* [1987] 3 W.L.R. 1023; *Law Society v Shanks* [1988] 1 F.L.R. 504; *Babanaft International Co SA v Bassatne* [1990] Ch. 13. A freezing injunction may also be granted in support of a costs order prior to taxation of costs: *Jet West Ltd v Haddican* [1992] 1 W.L.R. 487 CA. With regard to a freezing injunction to aid enforcement of an arbitration award, see *Nomihold Securities Inc v Mobile Telesystems Finance SA* [2011] EWCA Civ 1040; [2012] 1 All E.R. (Comm) 223; *Cruz City 1 Mauritius Holdings v Unitech Ltd* [2014] EWHC 3704 (Comm); [2015] 1 Lloyd's Rep. 191.

284 *Hill Samuel & Co Ltd v Littaur* (1985) 135 N.L.J. 57 at 58, per Bingham J.

shall not grant an injunction or make an order for specific performance, but may in lieu thereof make an order declaratory of the rights of the parties...". While this means that an injunction cannot be directly ordered against the Crown,[285] it was explained in the leading case of *M v Home Office*[286] that an injunction, including an interim injunction, can be granted against an officer of the Crown when sued in his personal capacity and, in judicial review proceedings (to which s.21 does not apply), when sued in his official capacity. As s.21 suggests, a claimant will commonly be equally satisfied with a declaration against the Crown and there is now power to award an interim declaration.[287]

[285] See *Harper v Home Secretary* [1955] Ch. 238; *Merricks v Heathcoat-Amory* [1955] Ch. 567; *Factortame Ltd v Secretary of State for Transport* [1990] 2 A.C. 85 HL. But an interim injunction can be granted against the Crown to protect the claimant's directly effective European Community rights: *Factortame Ltd v Secretary of State for Transport (No.2)* [1991] 1 A.C. 603 ECJ and HL. The implementation of a decision by the Crown can be stayed pending judicial review of that decision; *R. v Secretary of State for Education and Science Ex p. Avon CC (No.2)* [1991] 1 Q.B. 558: cf. *R. v Secretary of State for the Home Department Ex p. Muboyayi* [1992] Q.B. 244.

[286] [1994] 1 A.C. 377 HL.

[287] CPR r.25.1(1)(b). For the suggested use of an interim declaration under CPR r.25.1(1)(b) to resolve a bank's dilemma in not wishing to pay money out to a customer suspected of fraud, see *Bank of Scotland v A Ltd* [2001] 1 W.L.R. 751 CA; and for further clarification, *Amalgamated Metal Trading Ltd v City of London Police Financial Investigation Unit* [2003] EWHC 703 (Comm); [2003] 1 W.L.R. 2711. For the previous law, denying that the courts have power to grant interim declarations, see *International General Electric Co of New York Ltd v Commissioners of Customs and Excise* [1962] Ch. 784; *R. v IRC Ex p. Rossminster Ltd* [1980] A.C. 952.

Chapter 29

SELF-HELP

Table of Contents

1. Introduction

Right of self-help There are certain situations where the party injured is not necessarily bound to resort to the courts for his remedy, but is entitled to take the law into his own hands and redress the wrong himself. Such is the right, for example, in the case of trespasses to the person or property. **29-01**

2. Defence of the Person

Self-defence It is lawful for one person to use force towards another in the defence of his own person, but this force must not transgress the reasonable limits of the occasion, what is reasonable force being a question of fact in each case.[1] But the law does not require that a person when labouring under a natural feeling of resentment consequent on gross provocation should very nicely measure the weight of his blows.[2] A mere assault may justify a battery,[3] but there must be some proportion between the aggression and the defence. Ordinary violence must be repelled by ordinary means, and a deadly weapon should not be used except against a deadly attack. "A man cannot justify a maim for every assault; as if A strike B, B cannot justify the drawing his sword and cutting off his hand; but it must be such an as- **29-02**

---

1 Even if the defendant cannot make out a complete defence to an action for assault or battery, damages may be reduced by reason of the claimant's provocation: *Murphy v Culhane* [1977] Q.B. 94 CA; *Barnes v Nayer, The Times,* 19 December 1986 CA; but not for contributory negligence: *Co-operative Group (CWS) Ltd v Pritchard* [2011] EWCA Civ 329; [2012] Q.B. 320. See further paras 3-68 and 14-94.

2 *Cross v Kirkby*, *The Times,* 5 April 2000 CA.

3 *Titley v Foxall* (1785) 2 Ld. Ken. 308; *Dale v Wood* (1822) 7 Moore 33. Certainly a person does not himself commit an assault by putting himself in a fighting attitude to defend himself against an attack: *Moriarty v Brooks* (1834) 6 C. & P. 684 at 685, per Lord Lyndhurst CB. Several criminal cases suggested that a person being attacked was always bound to retreat as far as possible before using force in self-defence, but this notion was condemned in *R. v Bird* [1985] 1 W.L.R. 816.

sault whereby probably his life may be in danger."[4] So too, in the case of unlawful arrest, "the person arrested may use force to avoid being arrested, but he must not use more force than necessary".[5] Alongside self-defence, analogous principles apply to the defence of others so that a stranger may intervene to do what is reasonably necessary to rescue a person under attack.[6]

29-03 **Criminal Justice and Immigration Act 2008 s.76** In the context of the defence of self-defence in the criminal law, it is laid down in the Criminal Justice and Immigration Act 2008 s.76, confirming the common law, that whether the degree of force used by the defendant was reasonable is to be decided by reference to the circumstances as the defendant honestly believed them to be even if mistaken (unless the mistaken belief was attributable to voluntary intoxication). Sections 76(5A) and (6) also make clear (although this also appears to be essentially declaratory of the existing law) that force will not be reasonable if "disproportionate"; and that in what is termed "a householder case" (e.g. where the defendant (D) is violent to a burglar) "the degree of force used by D is not to be regarded as having been reasonable in the circumstances as D believed them to be if it was grossly disproportionate in those circumstances".[7] As we shall now explain, however, self-defence in the criminal law is not identical to self-defence in tort, so that one cannot apply a simple "read across" of s.76 from the defence in criminal law to the defence in tort.

29-04 In *Ashley v Chief Constable of Sussex Police*[8] the House of Lords clarified two important differences between self-defence in criminal law and self-defence to claims for the tort of trespass to the person. First, in contrast to criminal law, the burden of proof with regard to self-defence in civil law is on the defendant. Secondly, in criminal law an honest but mistaken belief—even if unreasonable—that it is necessary to defend oneself is a defence to a criminal assault.[9] In contrast, in civil law the defendant must show that, where he is being attacked or in imminent danger of attack, he honestly *and reasonably* believed that it was necessary to defend himself (as well as that the force used was reasonable in all the circumstances). Indeed, the majority of their Lordships left open whether there is

4 per curiam, *Cook v Beal* (1697) Ld. Ray 176. See *Cockroft v Smith* (1705) 11 Mod. 43; *R. v Driscoll* (1841) 1 C. & M. 214; *Dean v Taylor* (1855) 11 Ex. 68; *R. v Shannon* (1980) 71 Cr. App. R. 192, CA; *Revill v Newbery* [1996] Q.B. 567, CA; see para.29-10.

5 *R. v Wilson* [1955] 1 W.L.R. 493, per Lord Goddard CJ. In *R. v Jones* [1978] 3 All E.R. 1098 CA, it was held reasonable for a woman to sink her teeth into a policeman's arm to prevent his unlawfully taking her fingerprints without her consent. But in *R. v Jackson* [1985] R.T.R. 257 at 264 it was considered unreasonable force when a motorist, who was trying to make off after a collision, resisted a technically unlawful attempt to seize the keys of his car by violently winding up his car window, trapping the hand of the man who was trying to seize them, and then driving away dragging the man alongside.

6 *R. v Duffy* [1967] 1 Q.B. 63.

7 The precise impact of s.76(5A) was carefully analysed in the context of an attack on a burglar in the criminal law in *R. (on the application of Collins) v Secretary of State for Justice* [2016] EWHC 33 (Admin); [2016] Q.B. 862 in which it was decided that, applying the Human Rights Act 1998, that subsection was not incompatible with art.2 ("the right to life") of the European Convention of Human Rights.

8 [2008] UKHL 25; [2008] 1 A.C. 962.

9 *R. v Williams (Gladstone)* [1987] 3 All E.R. 411 CA; *Beckford v The Queen* [1988] A.C. 130 PC; *Blackburn v Bowering* [1994] 1 W.L.R. 1324 CA; Criminal Justice and Immigration Act 2008 s.76(4). But the mistaken belief must not have been induced by voluntary intoxication: *R. v O'Grady* [1987] Q.B. 995; Criminal Justice and Immigration Act 2008 s.76(5). The same approach applies where one acts to prevent a crime, para.29-05.

any defence of self-defence at all in civil law where the defendant cannot show that there was actually an attack or an imminent danger of attack. In other words, it may be irrelevant that the defendant mistakenly and reasonably believed that there was an actual or imminent attack: what may be needed is proof that there was in fact an attack or imminent attack.[10]

Criminal Law Act 1967 s.3 This provides that: **29-05**

> "(1) A person may use such force as is reasonable in the circumstances[11] in the prevention of crime, or in effecting or assisting in the lawful arrest of offenders or suspected offenders or of persons unlawfully at large.
> (2) Subsection (1) above shall replace the rules of the common law on the question when force used for a purpose mentioned in the subsection is justified by that purpose."

There is some doubt about the relationship between this section and the common law of private defence (whether as a defence to a crime or a tort).[12] Although it undoubtedly overlaps with private defence at common law where the attack warded off constitutes a criminal offence, private defence at common law is wider, conferring a right to use force against attacks that are not criminal acts—for example, by a mentally disordered person. Presumably s.3 and private defence at common law coexist.[13] A person can avail himself of both when they overlap, or either in the area not covered by the other. Section 3, like private defence at common law, requires the force used to be reasonable.[14] Presumably this means both the minimum force needed to accomplish the permitted object, and force which it is reasonable to use to prevent the offence, balancing the harmfulness of the offence against the harmfulness of the force needed to prevent it.[15] In the context of criminal law (but not tort) the Criminal Justice and Immigration Act 2008 s.76,[16] applies to a defence under s.3(1) of the Criminal Law Act 1967[17] as it does to the common law defence to a crime of self-defence.

3. DEFENCE OF PROPERTY[18]

Defence of property Reasonable force again may be used in defence of property, real or personal, so as to resist something in the nature of a trespass and in defence of actual possession (whether with a good title or not) or the right of possession.[19] **29-06**

---

[10] But see *Alleyne v Commissioner of Police of the Metropolis* [2012] EWHC 3955 (QB) at [128]–[135].

[11] See *Farrell v Secretary of State for Defence* [1980] 1 W.L.R. 172.

[12] Harlow (1974) Crim. L.R. 528; Baker, *Glanville Williams' Textbook of Criminal Law*, 4th edn (2015), paras 24-034 and 24-035.

[13] This is supported by *R. v Cousins* [1982] Q.B. 526 at 530.

[14] See *Allen v Metropolitan Police Commissioner* [1980] Crim. L.R. 441.

[15] The Criminal Law Revision Committee in drafting this provision (Cmnd.2659, s.23) pointed out that since the clause was "framed in general terms, it is not limited to arrestable or any other class of offences, though in the case of very trivial offences it would very likely be held that it would not be reasonable to use even the slightest force to prevent them".

[16] See para.29-03.

[17] Criminal Justice and Immigration Act 2008 s.76(2)(b).

[18] Although not considered below, the Criminal Law Act 1967 s.3, affords a defence where one is defending one's property against criminal conduct. For discussion in relation to defence of the person, see para.29 05.

[19] For what is meant by actual possession or the right to possession (which is the same for the defence

In *Dean v Hogg*,[20] the defendant had engaged a steamboat for the conveyance of himself and a party but the vessel remained under the management and control of the captain. The claimant having come on board was ordered to withdraw by the defendant and on refusal was forcibly expelled. It was held that the defendant had not such possession of the vessel as to justify him in expelling an intruder on his own authority. In *Holmes v Bagg*[21] the claimant and defendant were both members of a cricket club. A match was going on and the claimant interfered with the game and persisted in remaining on that part of the ground reserved to the players, of whom the defendant was one. The latter had him removed forcibly and in an action of assault pleaded as justification that he was defending the possession of the two elevens engaged in the game. It was held, however, that such a plea could not be supported.[22]

29-07 **Violent trespass** A forcible attempt to enter the land of another may be resisted by force at once, without the necessity of a request to desist.[23] "It is lawful to oppose force to force, and if one breaks down the gate or comes into my close *vi et armis*, I need not request him to be gone, but may lay my hands upon him immediately, for it is but returning violence with violence. So if one comes forcibly and takes away my goods, I may oppose him without any more ado, for there is no time to make a request."[24] On the other hand, if a person has entered peaceably a request to leave must be made to him before force can be used to effect an expulsion, unless in the meantime he has used violence.[25]

29-08 **Attempts to trespass** It is not necessary in order to justify the use of force that the person against whom it is employed should have actually at the time committed a trespass. "If the claimant has taken the key of the defendant's car and is about to enter it, the defendant is entitled to resist this potential trespass."[26]

29-09 **Limit in use of force in defending property** It has been said that it is never lawful for the purpose of resisting trespass to property to use violence likely to imperil life or limb.[27] This, however, is probably an oversimplification. The truth is thought to be rather that unreasonable force may not be used in resisting a trespass to property, and extreme violence will rarely be reasonable to such an end; but that it is a question of fact what force is reasonable, and extreme force could in rare

---

of property as it is for the right to sue for trespass) see paras 16-43 to 16-68, 18-10 to 18-27, 18-74 to 18-75.

20 (1834) 10 Bing. 345. But the captain could have properly ordered expulsion. See also *Thomas v Marsh* (1833) 5 C. & P. 596; *Roberts v Taylor* (1845) 1 C.B. 117; *Scott v Brown (Matthew) & Co Ltd* (1885) 51 L.T. 746; *Harrison v Rutland (Duke)* [1893] 1 Q.B. 142; *Revill v Newbery* [1996] Q.B. 567 CA; see para.29-10.

21 (1853) 1 El. & Bl. 782.

22 It is suggested in the judgment (1 E. & B. 786) that it would have been a good plea if the defendant had alleged that he caused the claimant to be removed on the ground that he was disturbing persons lawfully playing a lawful game.

23 *Weaver v Bush* (1798) 8 T.R. 78; *Polkinhorn v Wright* (1845) 8 Q.B. 197; *Webster v Watts* (1847) 11 Q.B. 311.

24 per curiam, *Green v Goddard* (1704) 2 Salk. 641.

25 *Polkinhorn v Wright* (1845) 8 Q.B. 197 at 206.

26 *Street on Torts*, 15th edn (2018), p.318.

27 2 Inst. 316; *Moriarty v Brooks* (1834) 6 C. & P. 684.

circumstances be reasonable force.[28] In the first instance, land or goods may be defended by assault and battery but not by wounding.[29] But a person who meets resistance when he uses such force in the protection of his property is entitled to try harder,[30] and the extent to which he may lawfully escalate the violence depends on the value of the property and the kind of harm threatened to it. Thus in *Collins v Renison*[31] the claimant sued for an assault committed by throwing him off a ladder, the foot of which he had placed in the defendant's garden in order to carry out a minor repair to the claimant's house next door. It was pleaded that the claimant was trespassing and had persisted in the trespass though requested to desist, and that thereupon the defendant "gently shook the ladder, which was a low ladder, and gently overturned it and gently threw the [claimant] from it upon the ground, thereby doing as little damage as possible to the [claimant]". It was held that this plea was bad, since it disclosed a degree of violence which could not be justified for the purpose of preventing the trespass alleged. At the other end of the spectrum, it was said in *R. v Hussey*[32] that a man may use even lethal violence to prevent trespassers unlawfully evicting him from his home—though it is questionable if that degree of force was reasonable on the facts of *Hussey's* case.[33]

In the leading modern case of *Revill v Newbery*,[34] an occupier, sleeping in a garden shed to protect it, fired a shot through a hole in the door, hitting and wounding in the arm and chest a burglar who was attempting to break in. The Court of Appeal held that while the occupier did not intend to hit the burglar, he was in breach of his common law duty of care. Damages were therefore awarded to the burglar albeit reduced by two-thirds for contributory negligence. The court considered that the defendant used greater violence than was justified in defence of property (or person). Neill LJ said: "Each case must depend on its own facts. There may well be cases where in order to frighten a burglar away a gun is discharged in the air and the burglar is injured because unexpectedly he is on the roof. That, however, is not this case."[35] In the words of Millett LJ: "For centuries the common law has permitted reasonable force to be used in defence of the person or property. Violence may be returned with necessary violence. But the force used must not exceed the limits of what is reasonable in the circumstances. Changes in society and in social perceptions have meant that what might have been considered reasonable at one time would no longer be so regarded; but the principle remains the same. The assailant or intruder may be met with reasonable force but no more; the use of excessive violence against him is an actionable wrong."[36] **29-10**

More than moderate force may be used to repel an attack on property which is combined with an attack on the person: robbery etc. And possibly such force may be used, even in the first instance, against a really violent attack on really valuable property which it is obvious that moderate force will not be able to stem—such as a group of rioters who are trying to burn down a house. This derives support from **29-11**

28 Baker, *Glanville Williams' Textbook of Criminal Law*, 4th edn (2015), para.24-059.

29 *Revill v Newbery* [1996] Q.B. 567 CA: para.29-10. cf. Lord Denning MR's obiter dicta in *Murphy v Culhane* [1977] Q.B. 94 at 98.

30 *R. v Hinchcliffe* (1823) 1 Lew. 161.

31 (1754) 1 Say. 138. See also *Gregory v Hill* (1799) 8 T.R. 299.

32 (1924) 18 Cr. App. R. 160 CCA; *R. v Meade and Belt* (1823) 1 Lew. 184.

33 *Lanham* (1966) Crim. L.R. 368 at 426.

34 [1996] Q.B. 567.

35 [1996] Q.B. 567 at 578.

36 [1996] Q.B. 567 at 580.

the criminal law decision in *Att Gen's Reference (No.2 of 1983)*,[37] where a defendant had armed himself with petrol-bombs and sulphuric acid with which to repel further attacks by rioters who had earlier smashed and looted his shop. The Court of Appeal held such a defendant entitled to an acquittal on charges of unlawfully possessing explosives and noxious substances "if he can satisfy the jury on the balance of probabilities that his object was to protect himself or his family or his property against imminent apprehended attack and to do so by means which he believed were no more than reasonably necessary to meet the force used by the attackers".[38] In the context of criminal law (but not tort) the Criminal Justice and Immigration Act 2008 s.76,[39] applies to the common law defence of defence of property[40] as it does to the common law defence to a crime of self-defence.

29-12 **Burden of proof** In the Court of Appeal in *Ashley v Chief Constable of Sussex Police*,[41] two cases on defence of property[42] were cited in support of the principle that in civil law the burden of proving defence of property, and analogously self-defence which was actually in issue in that case, is on the defendant. The majority (Sir Anthony Clarke MR and Auld LJ) also thought that those two cases required that defence of property was actually necessary for the defence to be made out in civil law. In that respect they thought that there was a difference between the civil law on defence of property (e.g. in a claim for trespass to property) and on self-defence (in a claim for trespass to the person). In contrast, Arden LJ regarded the two cases as supporting the view that the defendant's *reasonable* belief that defence to property is necessary counts. The House of Lords in this case[43] did not choose between these two different interpretations of the requirements of the "defence of property".

29-13 **Re-entry on land** He who is entitled to the immediate possession of realty may make an entry, and may justify in a civil action the use of so much force as is necessary to enable him to effect the entry and to expel an intruder therefrom, provided the degree of violence used does not exceed what is reasonably necessary to effect his purpose.[44] But by the Protection from Eviction Act 1977, landlords are forbidden to evict from a dwelling-house without a court order,[45] or to harass tenants to make them leave.[46] These provisions are penal.[47] How far they affect civil liability

---

37 [1984] Q.B. 456.

38 [1984] Q.B. 456 at 471 (emphasis added).

39 See para.29-03.

40 Criminal Justice and Immigration Act 2008 s.76(2)(aa).

41 [2006] EWCA Civ 1085; [2007] 1 W.L.R. 398; see para.29-03.

42 *Cresswell v Sirl* [1948] 1 K.B. 241; and *Cope v Sharpe (No.2)* [1912] 1 K.B. 496.

43 [2008] UKHL 25; [2008] 1 A.C. 962.

44 *Hemmings v Stoke Poges Golf Club* [1920] 1 K.B. 720; *Secretary of State for Environment Food and Rural Affairs v Meier* [2009] UKSC 11; [2009] 1 W.L.R. 2780 at [27].

45 ss.2, 3. CPR Pt 55 provides for recovery of possession by court order. The owner's right of self-help has influenced the Court of Appeal in deciding that there is no power to suspend the operation of such orders when made: *McPhail v Persons Unknown* [1973] Ch. 447, although this authority has been doubted in the light of art.8 ECHR: *Malik v Fassenfelt* [2013] EWCA Civ 798; [2013] 3 E.G.L.R. 99. The comments of Ward LJ were, however, strictly obiter and *McPhail* remains at present good law: Lees [2013] Conv 516 at 522.

46 s.1.

47 In *McCall v Abelesz* [1976] Q.B. 585, the Court of Appeal held that harassment contrary to what is now s.1 conferred no right of action for damages for breach of statutory duty; but earlier in *Warder*

by reducing a landlord's defence in a civil action for trespass is not entirely clear.[48] The Criminal Law Act 1977 Pt II enacts more general restrictions on self-help to recover land, but the effect of these provisions in civil law is also doubtful.[49]

Recaption of chattels He who is entitled to the immediate possession of a chattel may commit an assault[50] to recover it from anyone who has it in his actual possession and wrongfully detains it, provided that such possession was wrongful in its inception, as, for example, if the party assaulted has taken the chattel by a trespass[51] or even as an innocent purchaser has acquired it by an act of conversion from someone without title.[52] And in some circumstances at least, a person who has the right to wrest a chattel from the hands of someone unlawfully detaining it also has the right to enter another's property to retake it.[53] No more force must be used, however, than is necessary to effect recaption.[54] But it is submitted that if a person has a chattel bailed to him and unlawfully refuses to give it up on the termination of the bailment, the owner must bring an action and cannot use force to recover his property, since the original possession was lawful[55] and the same rule would apply where the vendor of a chattel wrongfully refuses to make delivery to the purchaser.[56] The Law Reform Committee believed that this branch of the law[57] required clarification and recommended that, provided no more force is used than is reasonable, a person should be entitled to use force to recover a chattel of which he has been wrongfully deprived. The criterion should be the reasonableness of the action in retaking, or of entering in order to retake the chattel. But with regard to entry **29-14**

---

v Cooper [1970] 1 Ch. 495, Stamp J held that unlawful eviction contrary to what is now s.3 was actionable. By ss.27–28 of the Housing Act 1988 damages are recoverable for unlawful eviction based essentially on the gain to the landlord of the eviction.

48 Quaere whether a landlord could be sued for trespass rather than for breach of statutory duty for doing acts which he would be entitled to do to gain possession at common law but which constitute offences under the Protection from Eviction Act 1977.

49 In *Hemmings v Stoke Poges Golf Club* [1920] 1 K.B. 720 CA, it was held that the Statutes of Forcible Entry, which these provisions abolish and replace, did not affect the position at common law.

50 But it is not lawful to imprison a man for the purpose of compelling a restitution of property: *Harvey v Mayne* (1872) I.R. 6 C.L. 417.

51 This passage (from the 10th edn) was declared to be a correct statement of the law in *Devoe v Long* [1951] 1 D.L.R. 203; in this case the Appeal Division of the New Brunswick Supreme Court criticised the statements in *Blades v Higgs* (1861) C.B. (N.S.) 713 at 720–721 as going beyond what was necessary for the decision, and held that there is no right of forcible recaption from a person who originally obtained lawful possession. But in favour of a right of forcible recaption not being confined to cases of wrongful taking and extending to all wrongful detention, see *Salmond and Heuston on the Law of Torts*, 21st edn (1996) p.573.

52 As to revesting of stolen goods or their value to the owner upon conviction, see Powers of Criminal Courts (Sentencing) Act 2000 s.148.

53 See para.18-36.

54 *R. v Milton* (1827) 1 M. & M. 107; *Devoe v Long* [1951] 1 D.L.R. 203.

55 *R. v Milton* (1827) 1 M. & M. 107; *Devoe v Long* [1951] 1 D.L.R. 203.

56 It is on this principle that the cases of entry upon land for the recaption of goods have been decided; see note to *Webb v Beavan* (1844) 6 M. & G. 1055 at 1056, where Littlejohn J is reported as having said: " … as if a man takes my goods and brings them upon his own land, I can enter into his land and take my goods, for the entry is lawful, for they came upon his land by his own wrong. But it is otherwise if I bail goods to a man. I cannot enter his house and take the goods for they did not come there by wrong but by the act of us both." See also *Devoe v Long* [1951] 1 D.L.R. 203. cf. *Fleming's The Law of Torts*, 10th edn (2011), para.5.130.

57 *18th Report*, Cmnd.4774 (1971), para.116 onwards.

this opinion has not gone unchallenged.[58] The criterion of reasonableness would render resort to such self-help a dangerous remedy.

29-15 In *R. v Mitchell*[59] it was held that the appellant's car had been unlawfully parked so that the issue of recaption of his car, which was being detained by a wheel-clamp, did not arise. Recaption could only arise, if at all, if the detention had been wrongful. The Court of Appeal, Criminal Division, cited the whole of the previous paragraph with apparent approval, and said that, while the law on recaption remained unclear, there was no general rule that a person is entitled to use reasonable force to recover a chattel of which he has been wrongfully deprived.

4. PROTECTION OF PROPERTY AGAINST DAMAGE BY DOMESTIC ANIMALS

29-16 **Common law** At common law a landowner could justify shooting a dog which was trespassing upon his land if it was necessary to save game or animals in actual peril at the time. The Court of Appeal laid down in *Cresswell v Sirl*[60] that the onus is on the landowner to prove: (1) that at the time of the shooting the dog was actually attacking or would renew its attack if left at large; and (2) that there was no other practicable means of protecting his animals or that in all the circumstances he acted reasonably as regarding it as necessary to shoot. A dog which was merely trespassing could be scared off, but it was not permissible to shoot at it to kill.[61]

29-17 Section 9 of the Animals Act 1971, now states the law upon killing or injuring a dog to protect livestock. It provides:

"(1) In any civil proceedings against a person (in this section referred to as the defendant) for killing or causing injury to a dog it shall be a defence to prove—

(a) that the defendant acted for the protection of any livestock and was a person entitled to act for the protection of that livestock; and

(b) that within forty-eight hours of the killing or injury notice thereof was given by the defendant to the officer in charge of a police station.

(2) For the purposes of this section a person is entitled to act for the protection of any livestock if, and only if—

(a) the livestock or the land on which it is belongs to him or to any person under whose express or implied authority he is acting; and

(b) the circumstances are not such that liability for killing or causing injury to the livestock would be excluded by section 5(4) of this Act.

(3) Subject to subsection (4) of this section, a person killing or causing injury to a dog shall be deemed for the purposes of this section to act for the protection of any livestock if, and only if, either—

---

58 Law Commission, Working Paper 54, where it is said that "a forcible entry to recover a chattel, which involved an application, display or immediate threat of force likely to dissuade a person from fear of violence to his person from offering lawful resistance to the entry, should never be regarded as reasonable" (para.39).

59 [2003] EWCA Crim 2188; [2004] R.T.R. 14.

60 [1948] 1 K.B. 241. See generally 13th edn of this work, para.562. This was one of the two cases (the other being *Cope v Sharpe (No.2)* [1912] 1 K.B. 496) relied on by the Court of Appeal in *Ashley v Chief Constable of Sussex Police* [2006] EWCA Civ 1085; [2007] 1 W.L.R. 398 for the principle that in civil law the burden of proving defence of property is on the defendant. The majority (Sir Anthony Clarke MR and Auld LJ) also thought that the two cases required that defence of property was actually necessary for the defence to be made out in civil law. See para.29-12.

61 *Barnard v Evans* [1925] 2 K.B. 794. Presumably if the dog was accidentally killed or injured in the course of a reasonable attempt to scare it off, there would be no liability; cf. *R. v Hinchcliffe* (1823) 1 Lew. 161.

(a) the dog is worrying or is about to worry the livestock and there are no other reasonable means of ending or preventing the worrying; or

(b) the dog has been worrying livestock, has not left the vicinity and is not under the control of any person and there are no practicable means of ascertaining to whom it belongs.[62]

(4) For the purposes of this section the condition stated in either of the paragraphs of the preceding subsection shall be deemed to have been satisfied if the defendant believed that it was satisfied and had reasonable ground for that belief.

(5) For the purposes of this section—

(a) an animal belongs to any person if he owns it or has it in his possession; and

(b) land belongs to any person if he is the occupier thereof."

This statutory defence is considerably wider than the former common law, in that it permits the killing of a dog which has finished "worrying" and is still at large in the vicinity, whether or not it is likely soon to renew the attack. On the other hand, it is narrower than the common law in that it only applies to dogs worrying livestock.[63] There is still plenty of work for the common law defence, which is not completely superseded.[64] Thus a defendant needs to justify at common law if he harms an animal other than a dog—for example, a cat or tame bird—which is worrying livestock; or if he harms any animal, including a dog, which is damaging something other than livestock—for example, tame pigeons which eat his crops,[65] or a tomcat which persistently enters his house and sprays.[66] The test at common law appears to come down to this: was it reasonable in the circumstances for the defendant to do what he did in order to protect his property? 29-18

5. Justifiable Advance Means of Protection

Contrast with types of force at time of invasion The justifiable means which an owner can take in advance to safeguard his property are wider than the types of force he can justifiably use at the time of the invasion. Dallas J in *Deane v Clayton*,[67] said: 29-19

"Is it illegal to place spikes or glass upon a wall, and if a party climbing over be thereby wounded or cut, can he bring an action?[68] And yet if I were to see a trespasser coming down my area, or getting over the garden wall, I could not drive the spike into his hand or cut him with the glass. The doctrine depends on a broad distinction. Presence in its very nature is more or less protection; absence is abandonment and dereliction for the time; presence may supply means and limit what it supplies; but if during absence property can only be protected by such means as may be resorted to in the case of presence, all property lying open to inroad can have no protection, at least by any act of the party himself; for to say that he can only be protected when absent by such means as he could use if present is a contradiction in the nature of things."

Therefore, the owner of a wood may lawfully set dog spears in it for the protec-

---

62 "Worrying" is not defined in the Act, but see Dogs (Protection of Livestock) Act 1953 s.1(2).

63 "Livestock" is defined by s.11; see para.20-17 fn.88.

64 The Act applies only to civil liability, and therefore the common law rules continue to apply to criminal proceedings, subject to any special defence in the statute defining an offence.

65 *Hamps v Darby* [1948] 2 K.B. 311.

66 *Prentice* (1960) 32 A.L.J. 372.

67 (1817) 7 Taunt. 489 at 521.

68 But the occupier may now be liable under the Occupiers' Liability Act 1984: paras 11-62 to 11-78.

tion of his game, and if a trespassing dog is killed by running against one of the spears, no action will lie at the suit of the owner of the dog, notwithstanding that no game may have been in peril at the time.[69]

29-20 **Setting traps intended to cause serious bodily injury** In no circumstances can a person, for the purpose of protecting his property in his absence, justify the setting of a spring-gun or man-trap or other instrument intended to cause serious bodily injury to human beings. Thus in *Bird v Holbrook*,[70] where the defendant, having had flowers stolen from his garden, set in the garden for its future protection a spring-gun, and the claimant, a boy who was in search of a fowl which had strayed into the garden, and who had no knowledge of the existence of the gun,[71] got over the garden wall and, coming into contact with the gun, was injured, the defendant was held liable. The Offences against the Person Act 1861[72] prohibits the setting of spring-guns, man-traps, and other engines[73] calculated to destroy human life or with intent to inflict grievous bodily harm, subject to the proviso that it is not a criminal offence to set such weapons at night for the protection of a dwelling-house. But the Act does not affect civil liability.

29-21 **Watch-dogs** By s.5(3) of the Animals Act 1971 it is a defence to the strict liability laid down under that Act[74] for harm caused by an animal that the claimant was a trespasser on the premises or structure where the animal was kept provided that the animal was not kept there for protection of persons or property or that, if the animal was kept there for that purpose, keeping it there was not unreasonable. In *Cummings v Grainger*[75] the Court of Appeal held that it was reasonable for the purposes of s.5(3) to leave a fierce watch-dog loose to deter trespassers, as long as due warning of its presence was given. However, the Guard Dogs Act 1975[76] forbids the use of unchained guard-dogs except to guard dwelling-houses and farms, and although this Act purports not to affect civil liability, the Court of Appeal thought that it might no longer be possible to regard the use of a guard-dog in contravention of the Act as a reasonable mode of defence. Even if the defence under s.5(3)

---

69 *Deane v Clayton* (1817) 7 Taunt. 489, per Gibbs CJ and Dallas J; *Jordin v Crump* (1841) 8 M. & W. 782. Absence of notice to the owner of the dog is immaterial, ibid. See also *Ponting v Noakes* [1894] 2 Q.B. 281 at 289.

70 (1828) 4 Bing. 628. This decision was under the common law, the cause of action having arisen prior to the passing of the Spring Guns Act 1827 (re-enacted by the Offences against the Person Act 1861 s.31). The earlier and very similar case of *Ilott v Wilkes* (1820) 3 B. & A. 304, went against the trespasser on the ground he knew of the danger, but this decision would seem of little authority today, since it is straining the facts to infer that an intruder with knowledge is willing to run the risk of being shot. Nor is it easy to sympathise with the belief, judicially expressed, that the protection of game in this way was justifiable because it encouraged landowners to reside on their estates. For a review of all the cases on spring-guns in common law jurisdictions, see (1970-71) 56 Iowa L.R. 1219.

71 The defendant had deliberately refrained from putting up warning notices "less the villain should not be detected".

72 s.31, re-enacting the Spring Guns Act 1827.

73 The wording does not include electric wire traps: *R. v Munks* [1964] 1 Q.B. 304. A purposive approach to this section may be seen in *R v Cockburn* [2008] EWCA Crim 316; [2008] Q.B. 882.

74 See paras 20-03 to 20-16.

75 [1977] Q.B. 397 CA. "True, it was a fierce dog" said Lord Denning MR "But why not? A gentle dog would be no good."

76 *Hobson v Gledhill* [1978] 1 W.L.R. 215.

is made out it is possible that a trespassing claimant, who has been injured by a watch-dog, may succeed in a claim under the Occupiers' Liability Act 1984.[77]

6. PROTECTION OF PROPERTY AGAINST THE FORCES OF NATURE

Relationship to other rights of self-help Analogous to the cases of self-protection dealt with above are those in which an act causing damage to an innocent person is sought to be justified on the ground that it was necessary for the protection of the doer of it against either the forces of nature or the wrongful act of a third party. But as the owner is not here directly resisting a wrongdoer, this protection of property is probably best regarded as an aspect of the defence of necessity.[78] 29-22

Protection of property against incursions of the sea or inland floods[79] An owner of land, situated on the sea coast, is not bound at common law to maintain on his own land a barrier against the sea for the benefit of inland owners.[80] On the other hand, he is entitled to protect his land from the incursions of the sea by building a groin or sea wall, and if the effect of his so doing is to cause the sea to flow with greater violence against the land of the adjoining owners and do damage he will not be responsible.[81] But he may not remove from his own land a deposit of shingle or other natural barrier against the sea, if its removal would cause injury to the premises of a neighbouring landowner, at least where the neighbouring landowner is the Crown with its duty to preserve the realm from the inroads of the sea; although there is nothing prima facie unlawful in an owner of the foreshore removing the shingle for purposes of sale.[82] It makes no difference that the threatened premises are themselves a wall and drainage system erected and made as protective works.[83] 29-23

A landowner may lawfully erect a barrier to prevent flood water from coming on his land, although the natural consequence of his doing so is to cause more water to flow on to his neighbour's land.[84] It makes no difference that he erects the bar- 29-24

---

77 See paras 11-62 to 11-78.

78 See paras 3-146 to 3-149, 18-59.

79 For protection of one's property against fire, see *Cope v Sharpe (No.2)* [1912] 1 K.B. 496. This was one of the two cases (the other being *Cresswell v Sirl* [1948] 1 K.B. 241) relied on by the Court of Appeal in *Ashley v Chief Constable of Sussex Police* [2006] EWCA Civ 1085; [2007] 1 W.L.R. 398 for the principle that in civil law the burden of proving defence of property is on the defendant. The majority (Sir Anthony Clarke MR and Auld LJ) also thought that the two cases required that defence of property was actually necessary for the defence to be made out in civil law. See para.29-12.

80 *Hudson v Tabor* (1877) L.R. 2 Q.B.D. 290. But in *Fellowes v Rother Urban DC* [1983] 1 All E.R. 513 it was held that a coast protection authority can owe a duty of care to neighbouring landowners not to lower the height of a groyne.

81 *R. v Pagham Sewers Commissioners* (1828) 8 B. & C. 355.

82 *Att Gen v Tomline* (1880) L.R. 14 Ch. D. 58; *Holien v Tipping* [1915] 1 Ir. R. 210.

83 *Canvey Island Commissioners v Preedy* [1922] 1 Ch. 179.

84 *Nield v L & NW Ry* (1874) L.R. 10 Ex. 4; *Maxey Drainage Board v GN Ry* (1912) 106 L.T. 429; *Gerrard v Crowe* [1921] 1 A.C. 395; *Lagan Navigation Co v Lambeg Bleaching Co* [1927] A.C. 226. The Court of Appeal found the rule to be compatible with art.8 and art.1 of Protocol 1 ECHR: *Arscott v Coal Authority* [2004] EWCA Civ 892; [2005] Env L.R. 6. The same principle is illustrated by *Greyvensteyn v Hattingh* [1911] A.C. 355. In that case the defendant drove back a swarm of locusts from his land with the result that they went on to and damaged the claimant's cultivated lands. As he acted only to protect himself he was held not liable. With regard to the protection of one's land against water naturally passing to it from higher land, see paras 19-124 to 19-131.

rier inside his boundary, leaving part of his land unprotected from the floods. If the flood waters collect on that area and subsequently discharge themselves on to his neighbour's land, he will not be liable so long as he does not actively assist their discharge nor obstruct a regular channel.[85] But he cannot interfere with a regular stream or with the course of ordinary flood water; and, therefore, if a river has a flood channel, he must not block it up or interfere with it to the detriment of the neighbouring land.[86] If, however, there is no defined course which flood water is accustomed to take, a riparian owner can keep off flood water by raising the height of the river banks.[87] If flood water has collected on land, as, for example, against a railway embankment, the landowner is not entitled to discharge it deliberately on to his neighbour's land,[88] for "there is a difference between protecting yourself from an injury which is not yet suffered by you and getting rid of the consequences of an injury which has occurred to you".[89] But if the water drains away naturally and does damage, the landowner is not liable.[90] Similarly, if the force of water collected bursts the embankment or retaining wall, the owner is not liable for the resulting damage.[91]

29-25 **Access to neighbouring land for repairs** In the absence of an easement or licence, the occupier of property which has suffered damage from natural or other causes has no right at common law to enter his neighbour's property in order to effect repairs, however difficult it may be for him to repair without doing so.[92] This is an old source of trouble between neighbours. The Law Commission recommended that the law should be changed so as to enable a person by application to court to obtain a right of access to neighbouring land for the purpose of carrying out preservation work to his own land.[93] These recommendations were made law by the Access to Neighbouring Land Act 1992.[94]

7. Abatement of Nuisances

29-26 **Private nuisances** There exists a right to self-help against a nuisance, called the right of abatement; and a very similar right of self-redress for trespass by encroachment.[95] The victim of a nuisance can lawfully put an end to it by acts done on his own property, where this is possible. Thus he can trim the overhanging

---

85 *Gerrard v Crowe* [1921] 1 A.C. 395.

86 *Menzies v Breadalbane* (1828) 3 Bli. (N.S.) 414; *R. v Trafford* (1831) 1 B. & Ad. 874; *Orr-Ewing v Colquhoun* (1877) 2 App. Cas. 839 at 857.

87 *Gerrard v Crowe* [1921] 1 A.C. 395; *Lagan Navigation Co v Lambeg Bleaching Co* [1927] A.C. 226.

88 *Whalley v Lancashire and Yorkshire Ry* (1884) L.R. 13 Q.B.D. 131; *Maung Bya v Maung Kyi Nyo* (1925) L.R. 52 Ind. App. 385 (where the authorities are reviewed by Lord Atkinson).

89 per Lindley LJ, *Whalley v Lancashire and Yorkshire Ry* (1884) L.R. 13 Q.B.D. 131 at 140.

90 *Whalley v Lancashire and Yorkshire Ry* (1884) L.R. 13 Q.B.D. 131 at 137, per Brett MR; per Baggallay LJ at 139.

91 *Tennent v Earl of Glasgow* (1864) 2 Macq. 22 HL.

92 *John Trenberth Ltd v National Westminster Bank Ltd* (1979) 39 P. & C.R. 104. It was the origin of the dispute in *Collins v Renison* (1754) 1 Say. 138.

93 Law Commission No.151, *Rights of Access to Neighbouring Land* (1985).

94 See also the Party Wall etc. Act 1996 s.8, which confers a right of entry for the purpose of executing work under the Act. It is important, however, to serve the appropriate notices and follow the procedures under the 1996 Act, otherwise the works may be regarded as a trespass: *Rashid v Sharif* [2014] EWCA Civ 377. cf. *Fattahi v Charles Grosvenor Ltd* [2019] EWHC 3497 (QB).

95 *Burton v Winters* [1993] 1 W.L.R. 1077.

branches of his neighbour's tree.[96] But more important, he can lawfully enter the wrongdoer's property and remove the trouble at source. Thus he may enter his neighbour's land and remove an accumulation of filth and offal which interferes with the use and enjoyment of his own property.[97] It is even said that he may enter and pull down a wall which has been erected so as to obstruct his easement of light.[98]

The right to abate a nuisance has fallen into a certain amount of judicial disfavour and various limitations have been put upon it.[99] It is suggested that the right of abatement is nowadays subject to the following conditions: **29-27**

(a) It must be possible to abate the nuisance peacefully. If the abatement of a nuisance involves an entry upon the offender's land, and such entry is resisted, the abator probably cannot justify a resort to force, even though abatement cannot be effected without it. Thus Blackstone said that the party aggrieved is only entitled to abate "so as he commits no riot in the doing of it".[100] Presumably reasonable force could be used in a case of great urgency—for example, a fire which is likely to spread.

(b) It must be a case in which a court has not refused a mandatory injunction[101] or would not refuse one if the claimant chose to go to court. If it were otherwise, the wrongdoer could be made to suffer loss out of all proportion to any damage which has been done: a large and valuable building could be demolished for a trivial encroachment on a right of way which a small sum of money would adequately compensate. Clearly, caution must be exercised when demolishing buildings under the purported exercise of a right of abatement.

(c) The abatement must be done so as to cause as little damage as possible, not only to the wrongdoer, but also to innocent parties and to the public.[102] If there are alternative methods of abatement, one of which will be less injurious to the wrongdoer than the other, the least injurious method must be adopted, subject to this, that "where the alternative way involves an interference either with the property of an innocent person or the wrongdoer the interference must be with the property of the wrongdoer".[103]

(d) The right of abatement is generally lost if it is not exercised promptly.[104] The explanation for this general restriction is that where there has been adequate time for legal action through the courts, there is no good reason to allow

---

[96] *Lemmon v Webb* [1895] A.C. 1.

[97] *Jones v Williams* (1843) 11 M. & W. 176; see also *Raikes v Townsend* (1804) 2 Smith 9.

[98] *R. v Rosewell* (1699) 2 Salk. 459.

[99] *Earl of Lonsdale v Nelson* (1823) 2 B. & C. 302 at 312, per Best J; *Lane v Capsey* [1891] 3 Ch. 411, per Collins LJ; *Lagan Navigation Co v Lambeg Bleaching Co* [1927] A.C. 226 at 244, per Lord Atkinson; *Burton v Winters* [1993] 1 W.L.R. 1077 CA.

[100] 3 Bl. Comm. Ch. 1, s.4; *Colchester Corp v Brooke* (1845) 7 Q.B. 339 at 377, per Lord Denman CJ. A person who used force in order to abate a nuisance would presumably find himself in trouble with the criminal law, but it does not necessarily follow that he could be sued by the author of the nuisance unless real damage were inflicted upon him. To allow him an action would in a sense be allowing him the benefit of his own wrong.

[101] *Burton v Winters* [1993] 1 W.L.R. 1077 CA.

[102] *Lagan Navigation Co v Lambeg Bleaching Co* [1927] A.C. 226 at 241, 246.

[103] *Roberts v Rose* (1865) L.R. 1 Ex. 82, per Blackburn J at 89; cf. *Greenslade v Halliday* (1830) 6 Bing. 379; *Mills v Brooker* [1919] 1 K.B. 555.

[104] *Burton v Winters* [1993] 1 W.L.R. 1077 CA; *Macnab v Richardson* [2008] EWCA Civ 1631; [2009] 3 E.G.L.R. 1.

self-redress. However, this will not apply to simple cases such as an overhanging branch or an encroaching root, which would not justify the expense of legal proceedings.

(e) Although the authorities are not entirely clear, the wrongdoer must in some cases be given notice. It has been held that no notice is necessary when a man cuts back branches of trees which overhang his land, so long as he does so without going on his neighbour's land[105]; or where a nuisance involves such immediate danger to life or health as to render it unsafe to wait.[106] It has also been repeatedly said that a man may without notice enter upon land to abate a nuisance, if the person who created the nuisance is still in occupation,[107] and despite conflicting dicta[108] this could still be the law. On the other hand, notice is necessary where abatement involves pulling down an inhabited house,[109] or where it involves entering on land in the possession of a person who is not responsible for the creation of the nuisance.[110] It has been said that, except in the case of overhanging boughs or immediate danger, notice is always necessary before abatement of a nuisance of omission,[111] but it is very doubtful whether such a rule exists.[112] In a leading modern case, *Delaware Mansions Ltd v Westminster City Council*,[113] it was laid down by the House of Lords that, as a general proposition, the owner of a tree was entitled to notice before a neighbour incurred the costs of underpinning and piling to stop continuing damage to his building by encroaching roots from the tree. In Lord Cooke's words: "[I]t cannot be right to visit the authority or owner responsible for a tree with a large bill for underpinning without giving them notice of the damage and the opportunity of avoiding further damage by removal of the tree."[114]

29-28 A person is not obliged to exercise his right of abatement so that he will not lose his right to damages nor will he be refused an injunction, if he prefers not to abate.[115] But if he does abate a nuisance, he is still entitled to damages sustained before the abatement or for the costs incurred (or to be incurred) in abating the nuisance.[116]

---

105 *Lemmon v Webb* [1895] A.C. 1 at 5, per Lord Herschell; [1894] 3 Ch. 1 CA.

106 *Lemmon v Webb* [1894] 3 Ch. 1; and see *Jones v Williams* (1843) 11 M. & W. 176, and *Earl of Lonsdale v Nelson* (1823) 2 B. & C. 302.

107 See *Jones v Williams* (1843) 11 M. & W. 176; cited with apparent approval in *Lemmon v Webb* [1894] 3 Ch. 1, in the Court of Appeal; per Scrutton LJ, *Job Edwards v Birmingham Navigations* [1924] 1 K.B. 341 at 355; *Earl of Lonsdale v Nelson* (1823) 2 B. & C. 302 at 311 and 312, per Best J.

108 *Lemmon v Webb* [1895] A.C. 1 at 5, per Lord Herschell; at 8, per Lord Davey. Their Lordships spoke in very general terms and probably did not intend to overrule the dicta in *Jones v Williams*, which had been cited in argument and with approval in the judgment in the court below.

109 *Perry v Fitzhowe* (1846) 8 Q.B. 757; *Jones v Jones* (1862) 1 H. & C. 1.

110 *Penruddock's Case* (1597) 5 Rep. 1006; *Jones v Williams* (1843) 11 M. & W. 176.

111 *Earl of Lonsdale v Nelson* (1823) 2 B. & C. 302 at 311.

112 See *Jones v Williams* (1843) 11 M. & W. 176 at 181, per Parke B; *Lemmon v Webb* [1895] A.C. 1 at 8, per Lord Davey.

113 [2001] UKHL 55; [2001] 1 A.C. 321.

114 [2001] UKHL 55; [2001] 1 A.C. 321 at [34].

115 *Lemmon v Webb* [1894] 3 Ch. 1 at 24, per Kay LJ; *Smith v Giddy* [1904] 2 K.B. 448; *Job Edwards v Birmingham Navigations* [1924] 1 K.B. 341 at 356, per Scrutton LJ; *Leakey v National Trust for Places of Historic Interest or National Beauty* [1980] Q.B. 485 at 523; *Bradburn v Lindsay* [1983] 2 All E.R. 408 at 413; *Lawlor v Johnston* [1905] V.L.R. 714; *Morgan v Khyatt* [1962] N.Z.L.R. 791 at 796; *Fleming's The Law of Torts*, 10th edn (2011), para. 21.280.

116 *Delaware Mansions Ltd v Westminster City Council* [2001] UKHL 55; [2001] 1 A.C. 321; *Abbahall Ltd v Smee* [2002] EWCA Civ 1831; [2003] 1 W.L.R. 1472 at [28]. For previous doubts as

In cases where the nuisance consists in the spreading over one's land of a neighbour's tree or the like, the right to abate exists although no action would lie in the absence of damage.[117] Nor in any case where nuisance exists need the abator wait until actual damage has happened, if in the nature of things it is certain to happen. Thus, if his neighbour's eaves improperly project over his land, he may pull them down before any rain has fallen.[118] 29-29

Nuisance to common rights In the case of nuisance to common rights, abatement by a commoner is allowed where the act causing the nuisance is prima facie unlawful.[119] Thus, where the lord of the manor put rabbits on the common or planted trees there, inasmuch as such acts are prima facie lawful and only become wrongful if a sufficiency of common is not left, the onus of proving this insufficiency lying on the commoner, however great the nuisance may be, the commoner cannot justify digging up the rabbit-burrows,[120] or cutting down the trees,[121] but is left to his remedy by action. If the lord has exceeded his right it is for the law to determine the quantum of the excess. But where the lord makes an enclosure on the common, inasmuch as an enclosure is prima facie wrongful, the onus of proving that a sufficiency of common is left being upon the lord, the commoner may justify an abatement of the nuisance by pulling down the fence, if the lord is unable to establish that he had left a sufficiency of common.[122] 29-30

The building of a house upon a common, at all events if done by a stranger or another commoner,[123] is on the face of it an unlawful act, and therefore a commoner may justify pulling down the house and he may lawfully do so, even if the occupier is living in it at the time, provided he has previously given the occupier reasonable notice to remove it.[124] But in the absence of such notice he cannot lawfully pull it down while the parties are in it[125]: 29-31

> "There is obviously a wide distinction between the case of parties suddenly coming to the dwelling-house alleged to be a nuisance, and in which the occupier and his family are actually dwelling and in the house, and without notice or demand forcibly pulling it down, and a case in which the occupier of the house has had previous notice and been requested to remove the building, but has persisted in remaining in the house with his family in defiance of the notice and request."[126]

Public nuisances In order to maintain an action for a public nuisance an individual must show some direct, particular and substantial damage to himself other and beyond that suffered by other members of the public[127]; and it would seem 29-32

---

to the law on this, see the 18th edn of this work para.31-25.

117 *Smith v Giddy* [1904] 2 K.B. 448.

118 *Penruddock's Case* (1597) 5 Rep. 1006; *Norrice v Baker* (1613) 1 R.R. 393.

119 See *R. v Dyer* (1952) 36 Cr. App. R. 155.

120 *Cooper v Marshall* (1757) 1 Bur. 259.

121 *Kirby v Sadgrove* (1795-97) 1 B. & P. 13; *Hope v Osborne* [1913] 2 Ch. 349.

122 *Arlett v Ellis* (1827) 7 B. & C. 346.

123 And semble also if the house be built by the lord, *Perry v Fitzhowe* (1846) 8 Q.B. 757.

124 *Davies v Williams* (1851) 16 Q.B. 546; *Lane v Capsey* [1891] 3 Ch. 411.

125 *Perry v Fitzhowe* (1846) 8 Q.B. 757; *Jones v Jones* (1862) 1 H. & C. 1.

126 *Davies v Williams* (1851) 16 Q.B. 546 at 555–556.

127 *Ricket v Metropolitan Ry* (1867) L.R. 2 H.L. 175; *Benjamin v Storr* (1874) L.R. 9 C. & P. 400.

that abatement too is only permissible if the public nuisance affects the abator with special damage.[128] Lord Denman, in *Colchester Corp v Brooke*,[129] said:

> "A public nuisance becomes a private one to him who is specially and in some particular way inconvenienced thereby as in the case of a gate across a highway which prevents a traveller from passing and which he may therefore throw down; but the ordinary remedy for a public nuisance is itself public, that of indictment, and such individual who is only injured as one of the public can no more proceed to abate than he can bring an action."

In the case of an obstruction to a public way, such as the placing of posts and rails across it, any member of the public may abate the nuisance and pull the obstruction down,[130] but so far only as if necessary to the exercise of his right of passage.[131] Again, where an oyster bed was wrongfully placed in the channel of a navigable river so as to cause a nuisance to the public right of passage, a private individual navigating a vessel in the river could not justify damaging the bed by wilfully running his vessel against it, if he might with reasonable convenience have exercised his right of passage by using some other portion of the channel.[132] Moreover, abatement on the public way is not lawful where the nuisance is caused by omission to maintain or repair (as opposed to nuisances caused by positive acts of obstruction) at least where the abatement consists of a substantial operation, for example, erecting a bridge, which cannot be effected by ordinary use of the way.[133]

29-33 **Obstructions etc on highways** Local authorities, successors to the former highway surveyors, can at common law remove obstructions to or encroachments on the highway without the necessity of taking legal proceedings; and the alternative procedure given them by statute[134] does not deprive them of their common law right of abatement.[135]

8. DISTRESS DAMAGE FEASANT[136]

29-34 **Right of distress damage feasant** If a man finds the chattel of another unlawfully on his land and doing damage, he may seize it and detain it impounded, in order to compel the owner of the offending chattel to make compensation for the damage done. This right is known as distress damage feasant. The manner of the exercise of this right is regulated by much the same rules of the common law as in the case of distress for rent. The various statutes giving a power of sale for distress for rent do not, however, confer a power of sale in the case of distress damage feas-

[128] *Dimes v Petley* (1850) 15 Q.B. 276; *Bateman v Bluck* (1852) 18 Q.B. 870; *Bagshaw v Buxton Local Board of Health* (1875) L.R. 1 Ch. D. 220 at 224; *Salmond and Heuston on the Law of Torts*, 21st edn (1996), p.576. But *Winterbottom v Lord Derby* (1867) L.R. 2 Ex. 316 suggests that the right of abatement is not limited to cases in which the party might bring an action.

[129] (1845) 7 Q.B. 339.

[130] *Webber v Sparkes* (1842) 10 M. & W. 485; *Huddart v Rigby* (1869) L.R. 5 Q.B. 139.

[131] *Dimes v Petley* (1850) 15 Q.B. 276 at 283.

[132] *Colchester Corp v Brooke* (1845) 7 Q.B. 339 at 377; and see *Lagan Navigation Co v Lambeg Bleaching Co* [1927] A.C. 226 at 245.

[133] *Campbell Davys v Lloyd* [1901] 2 Ch. 518.

[134] Highways Act 1980 ss.143, 149, 152, 154.

[135] *Reynolds v Presteign Urban DC* [1896] 1 Q.B. 604; *Harris v Northamptonshire CC* (1897) 61 J.P. 599.

[136] For the common law, see Williams, *Liability for Animals* (1939), pp.1–123. For the position under the Animals Act, see North, *Civil Liability for Animals* (2012), paras 3.47–3.60.

ant at common law. Where damage-causing chattels are distrained not at common law, but under s.7 of the Animals Act 1971, there is a power of sale.[137]

What may be distrained Section 7 of the Animals Act 1971, has abolished the right in relation to the seizure and detention of "animals" and substituted for the common law a statutory procedure for detention. The detention cannot last longer than 48 hours unless notice has been given to a police station and, if known, to the animal's owner. The right also ceases on sufficient tender of compensation or if no compensation is due under s.4, on claim by a person entitled to possession of the animal. There is also provision for sale after 14 days and for accounting for the proceeds of sale and, while detained, the animal must be cared for and fed. Special provisions apply in the case of horses. The Control of Horses Act 2015[138] inserted additional sections in the 1971 Act to deal with an increasing problem whereby horses, often cheaply acquired, were abandoned or left to graze on land other than that of their owner.[139] Local authorities and occupiers are given the power to sell or dispose of such horses after only four days.[140] 29-35

Though the common law right of distress damage feasant was usually exercised over straying livestock, it also applied to other chattels found encumbering a man's land, for example, railway rolling-stock.[141] This right continues both as to inanimate chattels and indeed possibly to animals not within the statutory definition of "livestock",[142] and must therefore be considered and contrasted with the statutory provisions. 29-36

There is no privilege from distress damage feasant, "it being but natural justice that whatever doth the injury should be a pledge to make compensation for it".[143] For the sake of avoiding breaches of the peace, an exception exists in the case of things in actual use.[144] 29-37

Who may distrain The distress at common law being a remedy for trespass, the right can, as a rule, be exercised only by a person who has a sufficient possession of land to entitle him to maintain an action of trespass.[145] But no action for trespass is maintainable so long as the distress is retained.[146] Detention under the Act is available only to the "occupier" but does not preclude an action for damages, since it is 29-38

[137] See para.29-43.

[138] See also the Control of Horses (Wales) Act 2014.

[139] During the second reading of the Control of Horses Bill it was estimated that 3,000 to 4,000 horses were being "fly-grazed" in England (see *Hansard* 24 October 2014).

[140] See further paras 29-40 to 29-43 below.

[141] *Ambergate etc Ry v Midland Ry* (1853) 2 E. & B. 793. One hears of its occasional use when aircraft have landed on crops and caused damage. It might be of importance in relation to motor vehicles parked, without the owner's consent, on private property, para.29-40.

[142] As defined in s.11. The Act abolishes the common law right in relation to "any animal" but since the provisions only specify "livestock", it is arguable that the repeal must be taken as coterminous with the substitution. The point is only of practical significance in relation to cats and dogs. The literal language of the Act may, however, prevail in relation to them.

[143] Gilbert, *Distress*, 4th edn (1823), p.49.

[144] *Storey v Robinson* (1795) 6 T.R. 138; *Field v Adames* (1840) 12 A. & E. 649; *Read v Burley* (1597) Cro. Eliz. 596. Quaere: taking a horse to a pound with the rider on him, Gilbert, *Distress*, 4th edn (1823), p.49. It will be remembered here that Pickwick was conducted to a pound seated in a wheelbarrow, though it is questionable that this incident affords authority for the possible exception suggested.

[145] *Burt v Moore* (1793) 5 T.R. 329; *Churchill v Evans* (1809) 1 Taunt. 529.

[146] *Boden v Roscoe* [1894] 1 Q.B. 608.

thought reasonable not to oblige the occupier to proceed to sale if he can expect to recover more than the value of the livestock in an action for damages.[147]

29-39 **No trespass, no distress** At common law there could be no distress unless there had been an entry in the nature of trespass. The statutory right of detention is confined to "straying livestock", which is not under the control of any person. The requirement of absence of control therefore corresponds with the common law exception relating to actual use.[148] But the relation between trespass and "straying" is by no means as close. Thus to drive animals deliberately on to another's land is a trespass, but they can be hardly said to have "strayed".[149] The difficulty seems to arise because at common law trespass included both direct intrusion of the sort mentioned and cattle-trespass which covered "straying". The statutory right would not seem to include the former sort of intrusion, unless the courts interpreted the Act to be as fully inclusive of the common law scope of distress damage feasant.

29-40 **Actual damage** To justify the distress at common law, there must not only be a trespass but also actual damage. In *Arthur v Anker*,[150] the wheel-clamping of a car, parked without authorisation on private land, was held not to be justified by distress damage feasant because no damage had been caused, albeit that damage would include denial, or obstruction, of the use of the land.[151] Again, if an animal strayed into a paved yard the mere fact of its presence did not make it distrainable.[152] Under the Animals Act detention is possible by virtue of straying on to the occupier's land, but the right to detain ceases after tender sufficient to satisfy any claim for damage or expenses under s.4[153] or, if he has no such claim, when the livestock is claimed by a person entitled to its possession.[154]

29-41 **Time and place** The distress at common law can only be made during the continuance of the trespass, and the distrainor must be actually in the locus in quo,[155] as the animal could not be followed off the land. It had to be seized then and there,[156] and it would seem that even if it was still on the land it was not distrainable unless

---

[147] *Law Commission Report No.13*, para.72.

[148] See para.29-37.

[149] s.7 is captioned "Detention and sale of trespassing livestock", which suggests an equivalence with cattle trespass in its statutory form under s.4 of the Act.

[150] [1997] Q.B. 564 CA.

[151] But the wheel-clamping did not constitute tortious interference with the car because there was a defence of volenti (i.e. the driver had impliedly consented to that risk). cf. *Vine v Waltham Forest LBC* [2000] 1 W.L.R. 2383 CA (wheel-clamping constituted tortious interference with the car because the defence of volenti could not be established). See para.3-105 fn.391. Note that the Protection of Freedoms Act 2012 s.54 makes wheel-clamping a criminal offence in some circumstances, and the driver's consent does not render the wheel-clamping lawful for the purposes of the offence.

[152] *Wormer v Biggs* (1845) 2 C. & K. 31; *Ambergate Ry v Midland Ry* (1853) 2 E. & B. 793 seems contrary, but the point of damage was not argued. For a full discussion, see Williams, *Liability for Animals* (1939), pp.70–76.

[153] s.4A in the case of horses.

[154] Animals Act 1971 s.7(3)(b), (c). For horses see s.7C(3) and s.7C(4).

[155] *Clement v Miller* (1800) 3 Esp. 95.

[156] *Vaspor v Edwards* (1701) 12 Mod. 658 at 661, per Holt CJ; Co Litt. 161a. It was held by Lord Eldon (*Clement v Milner* (1800) 3 Esp. 95) that if a man came into a field before the trespassing cattle got out of it he might follow them; but according to all the other authorities there is in this kind of distress no such right of taking on a fresh pursuit.

actually doing damage or likely to do damage.[157] Accordingly if an animal trespassed on two occasions and on the second was taken for a trespass, the impounding could only be to answer for the damage done at the time, and not for that done previously.[158] This is substantially the position under the Animals Act, because a claim under s.4 for damages or expenses referred to in s.7 does not include any such claim for damages or expenses incurred in respect of the livestock before the straying in connection with which it is detained.[159] A distress at common law may be taken in the night-time by the distrainor, "otherwise it may be the beasts will be gone before he can take them".[160] There is nothing in the Act to restrict the time at which straying livestock may be detained, and the Act appears to contemplate that, as at common law, the seizure by the occupier must be on the land on to which the livestock has strayed.

For what damage chattels are distrainable At common law chattels are distrainable for all damage consequent on the trespass, whether the injury is to land or other chattels. Detention under the Animals Act may be for damage to "the land or to any property on it",[161] but the Act also allows detention where there is no claim under s.4.[162] As at common law[163] it would seem that a person detaining cannot claim reward in the nature of "salvage". **29-42**

The right of sale The Animals Act introduced a right of sale, which does not exist at common law. By s.7(4) the right arises after 14 days' detention, and the sale must be in a market or by public auction. But no sale may take place if proceedings are pending for the return of the livestock or for compensation under s.4. In the case of horses the detainor can sell or destroy the horse after 96 hours from the commencement of the detention, if the horse is unclaimed or the expenses are unmet.[164] Section 7(5) deals with the case where the sale has taken place and the proceeds (less costs) exceed the amount of a claim which the vendor had under s.4, and provides that the excess shall be payable to the person who would be entitled to the possession of the livestock but for the sale.[165] The Act does not provide for the case if damage caused by the livestock exceeds the proceeds of sale, but presumably after the sale the occupier may sue under s.4 for the balance of his loss. If, having no claim under s.4, the detainor nevertheless sells, it would seem that he holds the proceeds for the owner of the livestock and must account to him. **29-43**

---

157 *Wormer v Biggs* (1845) 2 C. & K. 31.

158 *Vaspor v Edwards* (1701) 12 Mod. 658, per Holt CJ; Gilbert, *Distress*, 4th edn (1823), p.22.

159 s.7(7). The same limitation applies to claims in respect of horses: see s.7C(8).

160 Co. Litt. 142a.

161 s.4(1)(a); s.4A(2)(a) makes the same provision in respect of damage by horses.

162 s.7(3)(c). For provisions relating generally to the detention of horses see s.7C.

163 *Sorrell v Paget* [1950] K.B. 252 CA.

164 See s.7C(5). These more draconian provisions reflect the purpose of the Control of Horses Act 2015 to address the mischief known as "fly grazing": see para.29-35 above.

165 For an equivalent provision in the case of horses see s.7C(6).

CHAPTER 30

DISCHARGE OF TORTS

TABLE OF CONTENTS

1. INTRODUCTION

Forms of discharge When there is a vested right for a tort it may be discharged by the death of one of the parties (although nowadays this is very much the exception rather than the rule), by waiver, by accord and satisfaction, by release, by judgment recovered, and by limitation. Discharge by death has already been dealt with,[1] and limitation is the subject of the next chapter; it remains to consider the other methods. 30-01

2. WAIVER: ELECTION

"Waiver of tort" "Waiver of tort" is a term that has most commonly been used to refer to the situation where a claimant seeks a restitutionary remedy (reversing the defendant's wrongful enrichment) for a tort rather than the usual remedy of compensatory damages.[2] Used in this sense "waiver of tort" is a misleading and 30-02

[1] See paras 27-78 to 27-85.

[2] For the law on restitution for a tort see Birks, *An Introduction to the Law of Restitution*, Ch.X; A. Burrows, *Remedies for Torts, Breach of Contract, and Equitable Wrongs*, 4th edn (2019), Ch.19; Edelman, *Gain-Based Damages* (2002); J. Edelman, *McGregor on Damages*, 20th edn (2017) Chs

unfortunate term for it has nothing to do with the tort being extinguished. On the contrary, the tort is the foundation of the claim. As Lord Atkin said in the leading case of *United Australia Ltd v Barclays Bank Ltd*[3]: "in the ordinary case the [claimant] has never the slightest intention of waiving, excusing or in any kind of way palliating the tort. If I find that a thief has stolen my securities and is in possession of the proceeds, when I sue him for them I am not excusing him. I am protesting violently that he is a thief and because of his theft I am suing him."

30-03 **Waiver by an election inconsistent with a tort claim** By contrast a tort is discharged when the claimant chooses a right that is inconsistent with complaining about the tort. In Lord Atkin's words in *United Australia Ltd v Barclays Bank Ltd*[4]: "it is essential to bear in mind the distinction between choosing one of two alternative remedies, and choosing one of two inconsistent rights ... if a man is entitled to one of two inconsistent rights it is fitting that when with full knowledge he has done an unequivocal act showing that he has chosen the one he cannot afterwards pursue the other, which after the first choice is by reason of the inconsistency no longer his to choose". This occurs, for example, where a defrauded seller chooses to affirm the contract and sue for the price rather than reclaiming the goods and suing for damages for deceit; or where a landlord chooses to sue for rent rather than bringing ejectment proceedings by way of forfeiture for breach of covenant; or where a principal ratifies a contract his agent has made on his behalf rather than bringing an action against the agent for negligence and breach of authority.[5] Again, where the claimant's bankruptcy, with his knowledge and acquiescence, had proceeded upon the basis that a certain bill of sale given by him was valid, it was held that he could not afterwards bring an action for wrongful seizure of his goods under the bill of sale alleging that it was invalid.[6] It has been held that full knowledge in this context does not necessarily connote a full appreciation of the possible legal consequences of one's decision.[7]

30-04 **Election between alternative remedies**[8] But where on the same facts the claimant has alternative remedies for one (or more) cause(s) of action—for example, where the defendant has converted by wrongfully selling the claimant's goods so that the claimant can seek restitution to recover the proceeds of sale or compensatory damages, or where the defendant has fraudulently made a contractual promise

15–16; Beatson, *The Use and Abuse of Unjust Enrichment* (1991), pp.206–243; Winfield, *Province of the Law of Tort* (1931), pp.168-176. See also Lord Wright, "United Australia v Barclays Bank Ltd" (1941) 57 L.Q.R. 184; Fridman, "Waiver of Tort" (1955) 18 M.L.R. 1; Hedley, "The Myth of Waiver of Tort" (1984) 100 L.Q.R. 653. See also paras 27-150 to 27-151.

3 [1941] A.C. 1 at 28–29.

4 [1941] A.C. 1 at 28–30. See also *United Railways of Havana and Regla Warehouses Ltd, Re* [1961] A.C. 1007 at 1065, per Lord Denning.

5 In *Verschures Creameries v Hull and Netherlands S.S. Co* [1921] 2 K.B. 608 at 611, Scrutton LJ recognised that it was irrelevant that the agent had in no way altered his position as a consequence of the election. This decision was approved in the *United Australia* case.

6 *Roe v Mutual Loan Fund* (1887) 19 Q.B.D. 347. cf. *Smith v Baker* (1873) L.R. 8 C.P. 350 at 357, per Honeyman J.

7 *Balgobin v South West RHA* [2012] UKPC 11; [2013] 1 A.C. 582 at [31] (on analogous principles of election and merger of causes of action).

8 For criticism of the requirement to elect between compensation and restitution, see A. A. Burrows, *Understanding the Law of Obligations* (1998), pp.40–44. See generally Watterson, "Alternative and Cumulative Remedies: What is the Difference?" (2003) 11 R.L.R. 7.

to the claimant which he had no intention of keeping and has broken it so that the claimant can sue him in tort or contract—election, barring other claims, need only be made prior to judgment[9] or, vis-à-vis a different defendant,[10] prior to satisfaction of an earlier judgment. In *United Australia Ltd v Barclays Bank Ltd*[11] a cheque payable to the appellants was converted by the M company and collected for it by the respondents. The appellants brought an action against the M company for the amount of the cheque, either as money lent or as money had and received to the appellants' use. The appellants discontinued this action and afterwards brought an action against the bank for damages for conversion of the cheque. Reversing the Court of Appeal, the House of Lords held that the appellants by having merely instituted proceedings for restitution were not precluded from succeeding in the action for conversion damages. Viscount Simon LC stated that, if judgment had been obtained against the M company for restitution, this would have barred the claimant's action for damages against the company: but judgment against the company, not followed by satisfaction, would not have barred any claims against the bank.[12] Similarly it has been held that if A breaks his contract with B at the inducement of C and B is awarded and paid damages by A for the breach of contract, he will not be entitled to sue C for procuring the breach of contract.[13] Again, a claimant cannot be awarded both an account of profits and compensatory damages for an intellectual property tort.[14] But in *Mayor of Salford v Lever*,[15] the Court of Appeal held that, if a principal is defrauded by reason of a bribe being given to his agent, he has cumulative remedies: not only may he recover the amount of the bribe from the agent or sub-agent[16] but he may also recover from the briber full damages for the fraud. In *Mahesan v Malaysia Government etc Housing Society Ltd*,[17] however, the Privy Council doubted this decision and refused to apply it to enable the principal to recover from the agent both the bribe and full damages for fraud.

The clearest modern statement on alternative remedies, albeit that the case **30-05**
concerned a breach of trust rather than tort, is the Privy Council's judgment in *Tang*

---

9 In *Island Records Ltd v Tring International Plc* [1996] 1 W.L.R. 1256, it was held that a claimant is entitled to defer election, between an account of profits and damages, until after there has been an inquiry as to the amount of profits.

10 Unless a joint tortfeasor: see para.30-37.

11 [1941] A.C. 1. Bovill CJ's *obiter dicta* in *Smith v Baker* (1873) L.R. 8 C. & P. 350 at 355 was expressly disapproved. The Lords' decision is also inconsistent with the reasoning in *Simms, Re* [1934] Ch. 1 that the bringing of an action by a trustee in bankruptcy against a receiver for trespass in carrying on a business bars a claim for profits as money had and received.

12 [1941] A.C. 1 at 18–21.

13 *Bird v Randall* (1762) 3 Bur. 1345. Lord Mansfield even expressed a doubt whether the claimant could have succeeded in his action against C if he had recovered judgment against A without having been paid.

14 *Neilson v Betts* (1871) L.R. 5 H.L. 1; *DeVitre v Betts* (1873) L.R. 6 H.L. 319; *Colbeam Palmer Ltd v Stock Affiliates Pty Ltd* (1968) 122 C.L.R. 25; *Island Records Ltd v Tring International Plc* [1996] 1 W.L.R. 1256. S.61(2) of the Patents Act 1977 reads: "the court shall not, in respect of the same infringement, both award the proprietor of a patent damages and order that he shall be given an account of the profits."

15 [1891] 1 Q.B. 168. See *Bagnall v Carlton* (1877) L.R. 6 Ch. D. 371. As to judgment without satisfaction on a collateral remedy, see *Drake v Mitchell* (1803) 3 East 251.

16 *Powell and Thomas v Evan Jones & Co* [1905] 1 K.B. 11; but see *Hamlyn v Houston & Co* [1903] 1 K.B. 81.

17 [1979] A.C. 374; see A. Tettenborn, "Bribery, Corruption and Restitution: the Strange Case of Mr Mahesan" (1979) 95 L.Q.R. 68.

Man Sit (Deceased) v Capacious Investments Ltd.[18] Lord Nicholls distinguished alternative and cumulative remedies and said:

> "The law frequently affords an injured person more than one remedy for the wrong he has suffered. Sometimes the two remedies are alternative and inconsistent. The classic example, indeed, is (1) an account of the profits made by a defendant in breach of his fiduciary obligation and (2) damages for the loss suffered by the [claimant] by reason of the same breach. The former is measured by the wrongdoer's gain, the latter by the injured party's loss ... Faced with alternative and inconsistent remedies a [claimant] must choose, or elect, between them. He cannot have both. The basic principle governing when a [claimant] must make his choice is simple and clear. He is required to choose when, but not before, judgment is given in his favour and the judge is asked to make orders against the defendant."[19]

30-06 **Acceptance of proceeds of tort**[20] A mere demand of the money does not amount to an election[21]; but where the demand was assented to and a sum paid on account, it was held that the tort was discharged.[22] Where the defendant had sent to the claimants an account of the proceeds of certain goods converted by him and after deducting expenses had paid over the balance, which the claimants had retained, it was held that the claimants had waived their right to treat him as a wrongdoer.[23] It is not, however, in every case that the mere receipt of the proceeds of a conversion operates as an election not to sue in tort. Thus, where the finder of a note had cashed it and, he being afterwards arrested on a charge of larceny, some of the money was handed over to the owner, the latter sued successfully in trover for the balance.[24]

3. ACCORD AND SATISFACTION[25]

30-07 **Accord and satisfaction** Any man who has a cause of action against another may agree with him to accept in substitution for his legal remedy any consideration. The agreement is called an accord and the consideration is called satisfaction.

30-08 **Accord without performance of satisfaction** When the satisfaction agreed upon has been performed and accepted, the original right of action is discharged and the accord and satisfaction constitute a complete defence to any further proceedings upon that right of action.[26] In general, the right of action is not discharged until the satisfaction is performed and part performance is not sufficient.[27] If before

---

[18] [1996] A.C. 514. P. Birks, "Inconsistency between compensation and restitution" (1996) 112 L.Q.R. 375.

[19] [1996] A.C. 514 at 521. See also *Ramzan v Brookwide Ltd* [2011] EWCA Civ 985; [2012] 1 All E.R. 903.

[20] In contrast to paras 30-03 to 30-04, one is here concerned with where the proceeds are obtained other than through satisfaction of a judgment. But the principles are analogous.

[21] *Hurst v Gwennap* (1817) 2 Stark N.P. 306; *Valpy v Sanders* (1848) 5 C.B. 886.

[22] *Lythgoe v Vernon* (1860) 5 H. & N. 180.

[23] *Brewer v Sparrow* (1827) 7 B. & C. 310.

[24] *Burn v Morris* (1836) 4 Tyr. 485; and see *Rice v Reed* [1900] 1 Q.B. 54.

[25] On this subject, see *Chitty on Contracts*, 32nd edn (2015), Vol.1, Ch.22.

[26] *Lane v Applegate* (1815) 1 Stark. N.P. 97; *Jones v Sawkins* (1847) 5 C.B. 142; *Boosey v Wood* (1865) 3 H. & C. 484; *Bell v Galynski* [1974] 2 Lloyd's Rep. 13 CA.

[27] *Peytoe's Case* (1611) 9 Rep. 77b; *Allen v Harris* (1696) 1 Ld. Ray 122; *James v David* (1793) 5 T.R. 141; *Wray v Milestone* (1839) 5 M. & W. 21; *Carter v Wormald* (1847) 1 Ex. 81; *Gabriel v Dresser* (1855) 15 C.B. 622. It is undecided whether, when there has been part performance of an accord,

performance the claimant, in breach of the executory accord, proceeds upon the original cause of action, the accord affords no defence thereto, but the defendant may counterclaim damages for its breach.[28] It seems also that if the defendant does not fulfil the terms of the accord, the claimant may sue him upon it, even though the original right of action has not been discharged.[29] If, however, it can be shown that the agreement was for the original cause of action to be discharged by the defendant's promise, rather than by its performance, the original cause of action is discharged from the date when the promise was made.[30] It is in each case a question of construction whether it was intended that the cause of action should be discharged, not in the future on certain things being done, but forthwith upon the agreement to do certain things.[31]

Necessity for consideration An accord, like any other agreement, is not binding unless it is supported by consideration. The traditional view is that delivery of something to which the claimant is already legally entitled does not constitute a sufficient consideration,[32] nor, where a liquidated sum is indisputably due, does payment of that amount,[33] unless there is some consideration for the abandonment of the excess, such as payment at an earlier date,[34] or payment by a third party.[35] However, the courts have more recently been willing to find consideration provided there is a practical benefit to the claimant.[36] Where the demand is disputed, or the 30-09

the person who has accepted it can sue on the original cause of action without restoring or giving credit for what he has received; and, if the part performance be of such a nature that it cannot be restored or given credit for, whether the original cause of action can be sued on at all: *Morris v Baron & Co* [1918] A.C. 1.

28 *British Russian Gazette etc Ltd v Associated Newspapers Ltd* [1933] 2 K.B. 616 at 650, 654, per Greer LJ.

29 *British Russian Gazette etc Ltd v Associated Newspapers Ltd* [1933] 2 K.B. 616. It seems that the contrary views expressed by Eyre LCJ in *Lynn v Bruce* (1794) 2 H.Bl. 317 are not good law, and that case must be treated as deciding only that the accord was not enforceable without satisfaction. *Reeves v Hearne* (1836) 1 M. & W. 323, appears to have turned upon a similar point. See the comments of Greer LJ on these two cases in *British Russian Gazette etc Ltd v Associated Newspapers Ltd* [1933] 2 K.B. 616 at 651. If someone who was not a party to the original action has become a party to an accord, he may be sued thereon, even though the satisfaction has not been executed: *Henderson v Stobart* (1850) 5 Ex. 99.

30 Com. Dig. Accord (B4); *Cartwright v Cooke* (1832) 3 B. & Ad. 701; *Crowther v Farrer* (1850) 15 Q.B. 677; *Flockton v Hall* (1849) 14 Q.B. 380; affirmed (1851) 16 Q.B. 1039; *Morris v Baron & Co* [1918] A.C. 1, per Lord Atkinson at 35; *British Russian Gazette etc Ltd v Associated Newspapers Ltd* [1933] 2 K.B. 616; *Jameson v Central Electricity Generating Board* [2000] 1 A.C. 455. It should be expressly pleaded that the making of the agreement was accepted as discharging the original cause of action: *Flockton v Hall*. The early view of the law appears to have been that a right of action could never be discharged until the satisfaction had been performed, and some of the older authorities, which appear to lay down this rule without the reservation mentioned in the text, go too far. See *British Russian Gazette etc Ltd v Associated Newspapers Ltd*, where the history of the law is discussed.

31 *Elton Cop Dyeing Co Ltd v Broadbent & Son Ltd* (1919) 89 L.J.K.B. 186.

32 Vin. Ab. *Accord*, A 4, citing 9 Edw. 4, 19.

33 *McManus v Bark* (1870) L.R. 5 Ex. 65; *Foakes v Beer* (1884) 9 App. Cas. 605; *D & C Builders Ltd v Rees* [1966] 2 Q.B. 617; *Selectmove Ltd, Re* [1995] 1 W.L.R. 474; *Ferguson v Davies* [1997] 1 All E.R. 315 CA; *Collier v P & M J Wright (Holdings) Ltd* [2007] EWCA Civ 1329; [2008] 1 W.L.R. 643 at [3].

34 *Pinnel's Case* (1602) 5 Rep. 117a; *Smith v Trowsdale* (1854) 3 E. & B. 83.

35 *Bidder v Bridges* (1887) 37 Ch. D. 406; *Hirachand Punamchand v Temple* [1911] 2 K.B. 330.

36 *Williams v Roffey Bros & Nicholls (Contractors) Ltd* [1991] 1 Q.B. 1; *MWB Business Exchange Centres Ltd v Rock Advertising Ltd* [2016] EWCA Civ 553; [2017] Q.B. 604 (reversed on other grounds at [2018] UKSC 24; [2019] A.C. 119, where the point was left open: see at [18]–[20]).

amount unliquidated, payment of any sum agreed upon by the parties is a good satisfaction.[37] The abandonment of a claim made bona fide, although in fact unfounded, is a sufficient consideration.[38]

30-10 **Parol evidence** When the satisfaction has been performed, the executed accord may be proved by parol evidence, even though it be a contract of a kind required by law to be evidenced by writing.[39] It seems also that even where the agreement was for the cause of action to be discharged before performance it has that effect, even though it is unenforceable for want of writing. But the point is by no means settled.[40] It has been said that the non-enforceability of the agreement would be a material fact in deciding whether it was intended that the original cause of action be discharged without performance, but that once this has been established, the non-enforceability is immaterial.[41]

30-11 **Accord and satisfaction a question of fact** Whether there has been an accord and satisfaction is a question of fact,[42] and when the question arises correspondence between the parties is admissible in evidence even though marked "without prejudice".[43] The claimant may accept a sum in satisfaction of his rights in respect of injuries then known, on the understanding that if the mischief should turn out to be worse than it then appeared, he is to have a right to further damages, or he may accept a sum in satisfaction only of one of his claims,[44] or he may enter into a binding agreement with the defendant that the defendant shall pay a certain proportion of his damages, leaving only the total figure to be determined by the court.[45] If, however, he agrees to accept a sum of money in satisfaction of all future and consequential injuries, he cannot make any further claim, though his injuries may turn out to be much more serious than was supposed.[46] If he has signed a receipt for a sum of money in full satisfaction and discharge of all claims, it is a question of fact whether there has been an agreement to accept that sum in satisfaction of all future claims, or whether it extended only to damage which had arisen up to the date of the payment.[47] An accord and satisfaction induced by the misrepresenta-

---

37 *Wilkinson v Byers* (1834) 1 A. & E. 106; *Cooper v Parker* (1855) 15 C.B. 822.

38 *Callisher v Bischoffsheim* (1870) L.R. 5 Q.B. 449; *Miles v New Zealand Alford Estate Co* (1886) L.R. 32 Ch. D. 266; *Kingsford v Oxenden* (1891) 55 J.P. 798 CA; *Holsworthy Urban DC v Holsworthy RDC* [1907] 2 Ch. 62.

39 *Lavery v Turley* (1860) 6 H. & N. 239.

40 *Morris v Baron & Co* [1918] A.C. 1 at 13, where the old authorities to the contrary (*Case v Barber* (1672) T. Ray. 450; *Wickham v Taylor* (1672) T. Jones 168; Com. Dig. Accord (B4) 4, 6) were said (per Finlay LC at 13) not to be good law; Lord Atkinson (at 36) expressly refrained from expressing any opinion.

41 *Morris v Baron & Co* [1918] A.C. 1 at 13.

42 *Day v McLea* (1889) L.R. 22 Q.B.D. 610; *Neuchatel Asphalte Co Ltd v Barnett* [1957] 1 W.L.R. 356.

43 *Tomlin v Standard Telephones and Cables Ltd* [1969] 1 W.L.R. 1378.

44 *Roberts v Eastern Counties Ry* (1859) 1 F. & F. 460; *Lee v Lancashire and Yorkshire Ry* (1871) L.R. 6 Ch. 527.

45 *Tomlin v Standard Telephones and Cables Ltd* [1969] 1 W.L.R. 1378. See also *S v Distillers Co (Biochemicals) Ltd* [1970] 1 W.L.R. 114.

46 *Rideal v GW Ry* (1859) 1 F. & F. 706; *Dornan v Allan* (1900) 3 F. 112; *Huckle v LCC* (1910) 27 T.L.R. 112; cf. *Bank of Credit and Commerce International SA v Ali* [2001] UKHL 8; [2002] 1 A.C. 251 where a release of all claims was held, as a matter of construction, not to bar a (contractual) claim for stigma damages which had not been in the parties' contemplation.

47 *Lee v Lancashire and Yorkshire Ry* (1871) L.R. 6 Ch. 527; *Ellen v GN Ry* (1901) 17 T.L.R. 453; *Oliver v Nautilus Steam Shipping Co* [1903] 2 K.B. 639 at 648; *WW Duncan & Co, Re* [1905] 1 Ch.

tion[48] or undue influence[49] of either party is not binding, and neither party can set up as an accord and satisfaction something that has been rendered nugatory by his own act.[50]

Satisfaction by third party If satisfaction is made by a third party who is not himself liable, and is accepted by the party having the cause of action, this is a bar to an action if it was made by the third party as agent for and on account of the party liable to the action and with his prior authority or subsequent ratification.[51] **30-12**

4. RELEASE

Release Any surrender of a right of action may be spoken of as a release; but the term is usually applied where the surrender is by deed, and, therefore, requires no consideration.[52] A release by indenture is only available in favour of those who are expressed as parties thereto.[53] An absolute covenant not to sue is equivalent to a release, and may be so pleaded.[54] Where a person has been induced to execute a release by fraud, the release is not binding.[55] A release, or accord and satisfaction, is not binding on an infant.[56] **30-13**

5. JUDGMENT RECOVERED

When an action is brought before an English tribunal of competent jurisdiction[57] and proceeds to final judgment, the original right of action is destroyed;[58] the original cause of action thus terminates by merging in the judgment.[59] So, whether the claimant has succeeded (even though the judgment is unsatisfied) or failed, he **30-14**

307; *Nathan v Ogdens Ltd* (1905) 94 L.T. 126; *Bell v Galynski* [1974] 2 Lloyd's Rep. 13 CA; *Bristow v Grout*, *The Times*, 9 November 1987 CA.

48 *Stewart v GW Ry* (1865) 2 D.J. & S. 319; *Horry v Tate & Lyle Refineries Ltd* [1982] 2 Lloyd's Rep. 416.

49 *Stewart v GW Ry* (1865) 2 D.J. & S. 319; *Horry v Tate & Lyle Refineries Ltd* [1982] 2 Lloyd's Rep. 416.

50 *Turner v Browne* (1846) 3 C.B. 157.

51 *Jones v Broadhurst* (1850) 9 C.B. 173 at 193; *Belshaw v Bush* (1851) 11 C.B. 191 at 207; *James v Isaacs* (1852) 12 C.B. 791; *Simpson v Eggington* (1855) 10 Ex. 845 at 847; *Walter v James* (1871) L.R. 6 Ex. 124. The contrary views expressed in *Edgcombe v Rodd* (1804) 5 East 294 at 301; *Grymes v Blofield*, Cro. Eliz. 541; Com. Dig. Accord (A2) 5; Rolle Abr. 471 cannot be regarded as good law on this point. As to accord and satisfaction where there are joint wrongdoers or claimants, see para.30-37 onwards.

52 For an example of a release of an action in tort, see *Phillips v Clagett* (1843) 11 M. & W. 84.

53 *Storer v Gordon* (1814) 3 M. & S. 308.

54 per curiam, *Ford v Beech* (1848) 11 Q.B.D. 852 at 871. As to the effect of release to or by joint parties, see para.30-37 onwards.

55 *Hirshfield v London Brighton etc Ry* (1876) L.R. 2 Q.B.D. 1.

56 *Mattei v Vautro* (1898) 78 L.T. 682; *Stephens v Dudbridge Ironworks Co* [1904] 2 K.B. 225. It was held in the Canadian case of *Butterfield v Sibbitt* [1950] 4 D.L.R. 302 that the infant need not return money received in settlement before bringing his action, but that such money should be taken into account in assessing the damages.

57 *Eastwood & Holt v Studer* (1926) 31 Com. Cas. 251.

58 *King v Hoare* (1844) 13 M. & W. 494; *European Central Ry, Re* (1876) L.R. 4 Ch. D. 33; *Isaacs & Sons Ltd v Salbstein* [1916] 2 K.B. 139; *Republic of India v India S.S. Co Ltd* [1993] A.C. 410 HL at 417–418.

59 This principle can be regarded as simply an aspect of the res judicata doctrine: see para.30-24; cf. *Republic of India v India S.S. Co Ltd* [1993] A.C. 410 at 417–418.

cannot bring the same action against the same party. The judgment is binding and conclusive upon the parties to the action and their privies.

(a) Damages for one cause of action must be recovered once and for all

30-15 Damages resulting from one and the same cause of action must be assessed and recovered once and for all. This rule applies even though the further damage which is the subject of the second action had not yet occurred or was unknown to the claimant,[60] and whether the tort is actionable per se or only on proof of damage.[61] So, there cannot be two actions for two separate forms of personal injury arising from a single act of negligence, even where one of the injuries only comes to light after damages for the first injury have been recovered.[62] On a similar basis, it has been said that injuries to different body parts caused by different blows struck in the course of the same assault are to be treated as caused by the same wrongful act and must all be sued for together.[63] So too in fraud; thus if, as a consequence of a fraudulent misrepresentation, a person on different occasions buys different amounts of stock, he cannot have a separate action for each purchase. By similar reasoning, a single publication containing a number of defamatory statements is to be regarded as one wrongful act, so that it is not open to the aggrieved party to select certain sentences and sue upon them, and then after judgment to sue on other parts of the libel.[64] Yet again, where a trespasser causes damage to land, as where he digs a hole in it, he is liable to pay compensation only once; the owner cannot sue repeatedly for further losses caused by the continued existence of the damage.[65]

(b) Avoidance of the rule because different cause of action

30-16 The rule stated above, it should be noted, strictly speaking only bars repeated claims on the same cause of action. The test whether a previous action is a bar is not, it has been said, "whether the damages sought to be recovered are different,

---

60 *Fetter v Beale* (1701) 1 Ld. Ray 339; sub nom. *Fitter v Veal* (1706) 12 Mod. 542; *Townend v Askern Coal and Iron Co* [1934] Ch. 463. See too Lord Sumner in *Clark v Urquhart* [1930] A.C. 28, 54. ("A claimant furthermore must prove and recover damages arising from one and the same cause of action once and for all; he cannot claim principal in one proceeding and interest in another.")

61 In *Darley Main Colliery Co v Mitchell* (1886) 11 App. Cas. 127 at 145 Lord Bramwell suggested that the cause of action did not arise until the further subsidence occurred and that there were two causes of action—the removal of coal under the claimant's surface and in addition to this the removal of other coal and consequent creeping and further subsidence. Lord Bramwell suggested that the question whether successive actions would lie depended upon whether the act complained of was actionable without proof of damage or not. But this view will not fit all the cases. cf. *Maberley v Peabody & Co* [1946] 2 All E.R. 192. Salmond preferred the opposite view to that expressed in the text above: see *Salmond & Heuston on the Law of Torts*, 21st edn (1996), pp.552–553, which is supported by *Johnson v Mount Albert BC* [1979] 2 N.Z.L.R. 234 at 243. On the *Darley* case, see also para.30-18.

62 *Bristow v Grout, The Times,* 9 November 1987; the same principle was applied in a case of battery in *Fetter v Beale* (1701) 1 Ld. Ray 339; sub nom. *Fitter v Veal* (1706) 12 Mod. 542. cf. *Read v Great Eastern Ry* (1868) L.R. 3 Q.B. 555; *Russell & Sons v Waterford & Limerick Ry* (1885) 16 L.R. Ir. 314.

63 *Macdougall v Knight* (1890) 25 Q.B.D. 1 at 8, per Lord Esher.

64 *Macdougall v Knight* (1890) 25 Q.B.D. 1.

65 *Clegg v Dearden* (1848) 12 Q.B. 576; *Spoor v Green* (1874) L.R. 9 Ex. 99.

but whether the cause of action is the same."[66] If the same facts give rise to different causes of action (because, for example, they disclose more than one act) there is no automatic bar on successive actions.[67] So it has been held that if A wrongfully charges B with some crime and has him arrested and prosecuted, B may bring two separate actions, one for malicious prosecution and another for false imprisonment.[68] Again, successive actions may be brought for the publication of the same defamatory matter in different newspapers,[69] and indeed, since the sale of every copy is a separate wrong,[70] in theory there is nothing to prevent a separate action on the publication of each copy of the same issue with separately assessed damages.[71] So too where the defendant had wrongfully seized and then sold certain sheep of the claimant, the claimant was held able to sue separately in trespass for the taking and in trover for the sale.[72]

Even where there is only one wrongful act, if as a result two distinct rights are infringed, the infringement of each right will give rise to a distinct cause of action. It has thus been held that where a single act causes damage to property and personal injury, recovery by the claimant for the property damage does not bar a subsequent claim for the injury.[73] **30-17**

If the act complained of creates a continuing source of damage, then in cases in which damage is not of the essence of the action, such as trespass, a fresh cause of action arises *de die in diem*; in cases where damage is of the essence, such as nuisance, a fresh cause of action arises on each occasion when fresh damage **30-18**

---

[66] *Gibbs v Cruikshank* (1872-73) L.R. 8 C. & P. 454, 460, per Bovill J; see too *Bulmer Rayon & Co v Freshwater* [1933] A.C. 661.

[67] *Seddon v Tutop* (1796) 6 T.R. 607; *Drake v Mitchell* (1803) 3 East 251; *Thorpe v Cooper* (1828) 5 Bing. 116 at 129; *Hadley v Green* (1832) 2 C. & J. 374; *Brunsden v Humphrey* (1884) 14 Q.B.D. 141 at 147; *Wegg-Prosser v Evans* [1895] 1 Q.B. 108; cf. *Bagot (Lord) v Williams* (1824) 3 B. & C. 238, where the claimant was held to have recovered upon all his claims and therefore barred from raising any of them in a subsequent action. If all matters in difference are referred to an arbitrator, his award is a bar to all subsequent claims as to matters in difference which were in fact referred: *Dunn v Murray* (1829) 9 B. & C. 780; aliter, if they were not included in the reference: *Ravee v Farmer* (1791) 4 T.R. 146. As to infringement of copyright, see *Ash v Hutchinson* [1936] Ch. 489 (printers liable for separate tort of printing).

[68] *Guest v Warren* (1854) 9 Ex. 379. See too *Gibbs v Cruikshank* (1873) L.R. 8 C. & P. 454 (trespass and wrongful distress: successful replevin claim no bar to trespass action).

[69] See *Associated Newspapers Ltd v Dingle* [1964] A.C. 371. This is distinct from the single publication rule in s.8 of the Defamation Act 2013 which applies if a person publishes a statement to the public and subsequently publishes (whether or not to the public) that statement (or one substantially the same as the first publication).

[70] *Duke of Brunswick v Pepper* (1848) 2 C. & K. 683; but see Defamation Act 1952 s.12, para.21-244.

[71] As was almost the case in *Goldsmith v Sperrings* [1977] 1 W.L.R. 478, where the claimant sued 36 different newsagents who had distributed *Private Eye*. Where actions are unduly multiplied, a defendant can in theory have them stayed as an abuse of the process of the court: *Macdougall v Knight* (1890) 25 Q.B.D. 1. As to the damages which may be recovered in such a case, see para.21-244. See also para.30-38.

[72] *Lacon v Barnard* (1622) Cro. Car. 35.

[73] *Brunsden v Humphrey* (1884) 14 Q.B.D. 141; *Goldrei, Foucard & Son v Sinclair and Russian Chamber of Commerce in London* [1918] 1 K.B. 180; *Sandberg v Giesbrecht* (1963) 42 D.L.R. (2d) 107 B.C.S.C. (where, however, the claimant was penalised in costs for causing a multiplicity of proceedings); *O'Sullivan and McCann v Williams* [1992] 3 All E.R. 385 CA (bailee entitled to bring a separate action for her personal injury even though the bailor had recovered damages for the damage to the bailed car); *Republic of India v India S.S. Co Ltd* [1993] A.C. 410 at 420. The cause of action does not matter: the rule applies not only to negligence, but also where the claims sound in trespass: *Brunsden v Humphrey* (1884) 14 Q.B.D. 141.

accrues. So if a person wrongfully puts something on the land of another, he is under separate liabilities in trespass for placing the object and for leaving it there[74]; from which it follows that satisfaction of the former claim does not bar a claim in respect of the latter.[75] So too, in cases of ongoing nuisances, successive actions may from time to time be brought in respect of their continuance,[76] despite the fact that in nuisance prospective damages cannot otherwise be given except under Lord Cairns' Act.[77] Again, in the case of damage caused by the withdrawal of support to land, the making of the excavation on one's own land is in no sense a wrong; the wrong consists wholly in the damage which is caused, and therefore a fresh action may be brought as each fresh subsidence occurs, although the several subsidences result from the same excavation.[78]

30-19 However, it should be noted that in recent years the right to bring separate actions arising out of causes of action technically separate, but in fact intimately connected, has been considerably restricted through the use of the doctrine of abuse of process. Thus in *Talbot v Berkshire CC*,[79] the Court of Appeal was critical of the decision in *Brunsden v Humphrey*[80] (which held that a claimant could bring an action for damage to his cab and then a later action for personal injury arising out of the same accident) suggesting that the case might have been decided differently on this basis. This matter is dealt with below.[81]

(c) Award of damages once and for all: the problem of future and latent injury

30-20 The rule that damages for a single cause of action must be claimed once and for all can create serious difficulties in personal injury claims, since the judge often has to base damages on an estimate of future uncertainties or prognoses. In *Hawkins v New Mendip Engineering Ltd*,[82] for example, there was a risk that the claimant might develop epilepsy, but his future was likely to remain unknown until about five

---

74 *Thompson v Gibson* (1841) 7 M. & W. 456; *Clarke v MGW Ry* [1895] 2 Ir. R. 294; *Konskier v Goodman* [1928] 1 K.B. 421.

75 *Holmes v Wilson* (1839) 10 A. & E. 503; *Hudson v Nicholson* (1839) 5 M. & W. 437.

76 *Shadwell v Hutchinson* (1831) 2 B. & Ad. 97; *Whitehouse v Fellowes* (1861) 10 C.B. (N.S.) 765; and a reversioner may, of course, sue for the damage to his interest in the premises, although the occupier may already have recovered judgment: see para.19-65.

77 *Battishill v Reed* (1856) 18 C.B. 696; and see *West Leigh Colliery Co v Tunnicliffe* [1908] A.C. 27, 30–34. See paras 27-128 to 27-133.

78 *Darley Main Colliery Co v Mitchell* (1886) 11 App. Cas. 127 (and especially Lord Bramwell's opinion); *Crumbie v Wallsend Local Board* [1891] 1 Q.B. 503; *West Leigh Colliery Co v Tunnicliffe* [1908] A.C. 27; *Morris v Redland Bricks Ltd* [1970] A.C. 625; *Stone & Knight Ltd v City of Birmingham DC* (1989) 13 Con. L.R. 118. For clarification that the *Darley* case was unusual because the digging was not a wrongful act and gave rise to a cause of action only where there was subsidence, see *Homburg Houtimport BV v Agrosin Private Ltd, The Starsin* [2003] UKHL 12; [2004] 1 A.C. 715 at [91], per Lord Hoffmann. An owner or lessee of minerals cannot, however, be made liable for damage caused by subsidence occasioned by the working of the minerals by his predecessor in title, although the damage does not occur until after the owner or lessee comes into possession: *Greenwell v Low Beechburn Coal Co* [1897] 2 Q.B. 165; *Hall v Duke of Hall* [1900] 2 Ch. 493; and see para.30-15.

79 [1994] Q.B. 290. See also *Cahoon v Franks* (1967) 63 D.L.R. (2d) 274 Can. Sup Ct, where *Brunsden v Humphrey* was disapproved.

80 (1884) 14 Q.B.D. 141

81 See para.30-26.

82 [1966] 1 W.L.R. 1341; *Stevens v William Nash Ltd* [1966] 1 W.L.R. 1550.

years after the accident. Nevertheless damages had to be awarded on the basis of the court's then imperfect knowledge. To some extent these difficulties are mitigated by the rule that if matters change within the time allowed for an appeal, fresh evidence of these events may be admitted, since otherwise that court would be prevented from dealing with the reality of the case before it.[83] Nevertheless the rules governing the admissibility of fresh evidence on appeal are understandably restrictive in view of the need to ensure the finality of judgments; and, when the time for appealing has expired, the discretion to reopen a case on fresh evidence will normally be exercised only if the particular exigencies of justice outweigh the general undesirability of doing so. In the ordinary course of events, therefore, if the seriousness of the claimant's condition does not emerge until some time after the trial, there is no way either of securing a new assessment of his damages or of obtaining an additional award.

A number of solutions, though only partial ones, have been found to this problem. **30-21** The court has long, for instance, had the power to postpone trial of the issue of damages, or order the separate trial of liability and damages, a procedure most appropriate to cases of personal injuries where the claimant's medical prognosis has not settled.[84] This can moreover now be combined with the power to make an interim award of damages.[85] In addition, "provisional damages" can be awarded in personal injury cases,[86] a solution which addresses the problem highlighted by *Hawkins v New Mendip Engineering Ltd*.[87] A more radical solution, available since 2005, is a power given to the courts to award reviewable periodical payments in respect of damages for future pecuniary loss in cases of personal injury and death.[88]

(d) Satisfied judgments

There are cases in which, other than under the doctrine of merger or election, a **30-22** claimant is barred from bringing an action by reason of his success in a previous proceeding for the same or a different cause; but in such cases he must not only have obtained a judgment, but under that judgment must have obtained full satisfaction for his injury. This therefore rests on a ground altogether different from that of res judicata, in which it is immaterial whether the judgment is satisfied or not and indeed whether it was in favour of the claimant or against him. One example arises from trover: if the damages in an action of trover are assessed on the basis of the full value of the chattel converted and are paid, the owner, being fully compensated,

---

83 *Mulholland v Mitchell* [1971] A.C. 666. See too *Jenkins v Richard Thomas & Baldwins Ltd* [1966] 1 W.L.R. 476; *Murphy v Stone-Wallwork (Charlton) Ltd* [1969] 1 W.L.R. 1023; *McCann v Sheppard* [1973] 1 W.L.R. 540; *Lim Poh Choo v Camden and Islington AHA* [1980] A.C. 174; *Perry v Sidney Phillips & Son* [1982] 1 W.L.R. 1297. See also *Noble v Owens* [2010] EWCA Civ 224; [2010] 1 W.L.R. 2491 (Court of Appeal remitted question whether the claimant had fraudulently misled the trial judge as to his injuries to High Court judge who, if fraud was proved, would proceed to reassess the damages).

84 CPR r.3.1. See *Hawkins v New Mendip Engineering Ltd* [1966] 1 W.L.R. 1341, per Winn LJ; *Stevens v William Nash Ltd* [1966] 1 W.L.R. 1550 at 1554–1555, per Winn LJ. Note, however, *Coenen v Payne* [1974] 1 W.L.R. 984, where the court made clear its opinion that the normal practice should continue to be the trial of liability and damages together.

85 See para.27-71.

86 Senior Courts Act 1981 s.32A. See para.27-72.

87 [1966] 1 W.L.R. 1341; para.30-20.

88 See Courts Act 2003 ss.100–101, amending the Damages Act 1996, and the Damages (Variation of Periodical Payments) Order 2005 (SI 2005/841). See para.27-76.

is divested of his property and cannot afterwards maintain an action for a different conversion of the same chattel.[89]

(e) Judgment of foreign court in claimant's favour

30-23 The traditional rule is that the judgment of a foreign court does not in itself create anything more than a simple contract debt, so that there is no merger of the cause of action.[90] Formerly this meant that the claimant could sue either on the foreign judgment or on the original cause of action unless the judgment had been satisfied, in which case the cause of action was at an end.[91] But the impact of the traditional rule has been restricted by s.34 of the Civil Jurisdiction and Judgments Act 1982, which provides:

> "No proceedings may be brought by a person in England and Wales or Northern Ireland on a cause of action in respect of which a judgment has been given in his favour in proceedings between the same parties, or their privies, in a court in another part of the United Kingdom or in a court of an overseas country, unless that judgment is not enforceable or entitled to recognition in England or Wales or, as the case may be, in Northern Ireland."[92]

Where there are separate causes of action against different defendants for the same damage, a judgment obtained against one of them in a foreign court, even though satisfied, is not a bar to proceedings against the other for the same damage in courts of this country, save that the damages awarded to the claimant must be reduced by the amount by which they have been pro tanto satisfied by the foreign judgment.[93]

6. RES JUDICATA

(a) Principle of res judicata

30-24 Under the principle of res judicata, even if no judgment has been recovered in the same action against the same party,[94] a litigant in a civil action may be estopped from relitigating what has previously been finally decided against him by a competent court.[95] This is a rule of public policy based on the desirability that litiga-

---

89 Torts (Interference with Goods) Act 1977 s.5(1), affirming the common law.

90 *Higgens's Case* (1605) 6 Co. Rep. 44b; *Hall v Odber* (1809) 11 East 118; *Smith v Nicholls* (1839) 5 Bing. N.C. 208; *Republic of India v India Steamship Co Ltd* [1993] A.C. 410 HL.

91 *Bank of Australasia v Harding* (1850) 9 C.B. 661; *Barber v Lamb* (1860) 8 C.B. (N.S.) 95; *Taylor v Hollard* [1902] 1 K.B. 676.

92 On which, see *Republic of India v India S.S. Co Ltd* [1993] A.C. 410 HL; *Republic of India v India Steamship Co Ltd (No.2)* [1998] A.C. 878. Note too that no proceedings for the recovery of a sum payable under a foreign judgment to which Pt I of the Foreign Judgments (Reciprocal Enforcement) Act 1933, as modified, applies, other than proceedings by way of registration of the judgment, can be brought in any court in the UK: see s.6 of that Act.

93 *Kohnke v Karger* [1951] 2 K.B. 670.

94 See paras 30-14 to 30-23. This may be labelled "cause of action estoppel" and precludes a party from re-litigating the same cause of action unless fraud or collusion is alleged so as to justify setting aside the earlier judgment.

95 This may be labelled "issue estoppel". See generally *Henderson v Henderson* (1843) Hare 100, 115 (Wigram V-C); *Hoystead v Taxation Commissioner* [1926] A.C. 155; *New Brunswick Rail Co v British and French Trust Corp* [1939] A.C. 1; *SCF v Masri (No.3)* [1987] Q.B. 1028; *Bobolas v Economist Newspaper Ltd* [1987] 1 W.L.R. 1101. The previous court does not have to be a court of

tion should not drag on indefinitely and that a defendant should not be oppressed by successive actions when one would do.[96] A foreign decision in a non-European state, if recognised by the English courts as a decision made with jurisdiction, has the same effect;[97] as does a decision entitled to recognition under Ch.III of the Brussels I Regulation Recast or Title III of the Lugano Convention 2007.[98]

(b) Abuse of process and estoppel

Res judicata may once have been limited to previous decisions between the same parties on the same matter, but it is now regarded as an aspect of a wider doctrine of abuse of process which can be referred to as the "wider principle of *Henderson v Henderson*". Under this, the courts have an inherent jurisdiction to strike out as vexatious and abusive not only a claim or defence which not only has been already decided in previous proceedings between the same parties against the party raising it, but also more generally any allegation which might have been raised in any previous proceedings in which the facts necessary to raise it have been decided against him.[99] The law was helpfully summarised by Lord Sumption in *Virgin Atlantic Airways Ltd v Zodiac Seats UK Ltd*,[100] who noted that "res judicata" is in **30-25**

record: *Re May* (1885) 28 Ch. D. 516 at 518; indeed the principle can also apply to successive proceedings before non-statutory disciplinary or regulatory tribunals: see *R (on the application of Coke-Wallis) v Institute of Chartered Accountants in England and Wales* [2011] UKSC 1; [2011] 2 A.C. 146; and *Clark v In Focus Asset Management and Tax Solutions Ltd* [2014] EWCA Civ 118; [2014] 1 W.L.R. 2502. Consent orders can equally give rise to an estoppel by res judicata: see *Zurich Insurance Co Plc v Hayward* [2011] EWCA Civ 641; [2011] C.P. Rep. 39 (but note also *Spicer v Tuli* [2012] EWCA Civ 845; [2012] 1 W.L.R. 3088). Spencer-Bower, Turner & Handley, *The Doctrine of Res Judicata*, 5th edn (2019), Pt I; R. Munday, *Cross and Tapper on Evidence*, 13th edn (2018), pp.88–100.

[96] *Barrow v Bankside Members Agency Ltd* [1996] 1 W.L.R. 257, 260 (Sir Thomas Bingham MR). The policy that underpins this rule is relevant to successive pre-trial applications for the same relief, but should be applied less strictly than in relation to a final decision of the court: *Woodhouse v Consignia Plc* [2002] EWCA Civ 275; [2002] 1 W.L.R. 2558 at [56].

[97] Dicey, Morris & Collins on the *Conflict of Laws* (15th edn), paras.14-30–14-32.

[98] Dicey, Morris & Collins on the *Conflict of Laws* (15th edn), para.14-220; and *Hoffmann v Krieg* (Case C-156/86) [1988] E.C.R. 645. At the time of writing it is unclear what the status of EU and EEA judgments will be after the end of the transition period following Brexit.

[99] This may also be labelled "issue estoppel in the wider sense" or "the wider principle of *Henderson v Henderson*". In addition to cases such as *Henderson v Henderson* (1843) 3 Hare 100 at 115; see *Macdougall v Knight* (1890) 25 Q.B.D. 1; *Stephenson v Garnett* [1898] 1 Q.B. 677; *Mackenzie-Kennedy v Air Council* [1927] 2 K.B. 517, per Scrutton LJ at 528; *Greenhalgh v Mallard* [1947] 2 All E.R. 255; *Wright v Bennett (No.2)* [1948] W.N. 62; *Hunter v Chief Constable of the West Midlands* [1982] A.C. 529; *Yat Tung Investment Co Ltd v Dao Heng Bank Ltd* [1975] A.C. 581; *Brisbane City Council v Att Gen of Queensland* [1979] A.C. 411; *North West Water Authority v Binnie and Partners* [1990] 3 All E.R. 547; *Talbot v Berkshire CC* [1994] Q.B. 290 (wider principle of *Henderson v Henderson* applies to personal injury actions); *Barrow v Bankside Agency Ltd* [1996] 1 W.L.R. 257 CA; *C (A Minor) v Hackney LBC* [1996] 1 W.L.R. 789 CA; *Johnson v Gore Wood & Co* [2001] 2 A.C. 1 HL; *Woodhouse v Consigna Plc* [2002] EWCA Civ 275; [2002] 1 W.L.R. 2558 at [56].

[100] [2013] UKSC 46; [2014] 1 A.C 160 at [17]–[26] (with the full agreement of the Court). For further clarification, in the context of setting aside a judgment for fraud, see *Takhar v Gracefield Developments Ltd* [2019] UKSC 13; [2019] 2 W.L.R. 984. Lord Sumption made clear at [61]–[62] that setting aside a judgment for fraud involves neither cause of action estoppel nor issue estoppel but it is concerned with an abuse of process and therefore falls within the wider principle of *Henderson v Henderson* (1843) Hare 100 at 115.

fact a "portmanteau term which is used to describe a number of different legal principles with different juridical origins".[101]

30-26 Abuse of process may in addition provide a way round some of the technicalities of "cause of action estoppel." In *Talbot v Berkshire CC*,[102] the Court of Appeal was critical of the decision in *Brunsden v Humphrey*[103] (which held that a claimant could bring an action for damage to his cab and then a later action for personal injury arising out of the same accident) suggesting that the case might have been decided differently on this basis if *Henderson v Henderson*[104] had been cited. Stuart-Smith LJ commented that *Henderson* appeared to have escaped attention in the field of personal injury litigation. The principle requires the parties to bring their whole substantial case before the court so that all aspects of the case may be finally decided (subject to any appeal) once and for all. In the absence of special circumstances the parties cannot return to court to advance arguments, claims or defences which they could have put forward on the first occasion but failed to raise. In *Talbot* the Court of Appeal gave three examples of special circumstances where the rule would not apply: (a) where the claimant was unaware of the existence of the claim; (b) where an agreement was made between the parties holding the action in abeyance; and (c) where the claimant had not brought his case earlier in reliance on a representation made by the defendant. But the fact that the claimant would suffer an injustice by not being able to advance his claim was not a special circumstance, otherwise the rule would hardly ever apply, nor is the fact that the defendant or his insurers were aware of the possibility of a separate or more extensive claim.[105] *Talbot* should now be considered, however, in the light of the decision of the House of Lords in *Johnson v Gore Wood & Co (A Firm)*.[106]

30-27 In *Johnson v Gore Wood & Co (A Firm)*[107] the House of Lords held that *Henderson v Henderson* should not be rigidly applied. Lord Bingham confirmed that *Henderson* was closely connected with the principle of "abuse of process", that is the power that any court of justice must possess to prevent misuse of its procedure. The bringing of a claim or the raising of a defence in later proceedings might amount to an abuse if the court was satisfied (the onus being on the party alleging abuse) that the claim or defence should have been raised in the earlier proceedings, something which would rarely be the case, unless the later proceedings involved an element of unjust harassment. It was thus wrong to hold that merely because a matter *could* have been raised in earlier proceedings it *should* have been. The court should instead take a broad, merits-based approach. Decisions in

---

[101] [2013] UKSC 46; [2014] 1 A.C 160 at [17].

[102] [1994] Q.B. 290. See also *Cahoon v Franks* (1967) 63 D.L.R. (2d) 274 Can. Sup Ct, where *Brunsden v Humphrey* was disapproved.

[103] (1884) 14 Q.B.D. 141.

[104] (1843) 3 Hare 100. See para.30-24.

[105] The potential for the rule to produce real injustice is illustrated by *Wain v F Sherwood and Sons Transport Ltd* [1999] P.I.Q.R. P159 where the Court of Appeal held that it applied even where the claimant had not advanced an earlier claim due the negligence of his lawyer barrister, but due to the advocate's immunity from suit [which has subsequently been abolished] the claimant had no redress for that negligence. The prospect, or otherwise, of a remedy against a third party was irrelevant.

[106] [2002] 2 A.C. 1. See para.30-27.

[107] [2002] 2 A.C. 1; commented on by Handley (2002) 118 L.Q.R. 397; Watt (2001) 20 C.J.Q. 90. The principles laid down in *Johnson v Gore Wood & Co* were applied by the Court of Appeal in *Playboy Club London Ltd v Banca Nazionale Del Lavoro SpA* [2018] EWCA Civ 2025 in deciding that it was not an abuse of process for the claimant to bring a deceit claim even though it had failed in its earlier negligence claim.

earlier cases should be read in the light of the guidance from House of Lords in *Johnson v Gore Wood*.[108]

Where the parties in earlier proceedings have negotiated a settlement on the basis that there are issues which remain outstanding and are not included in the settlement, it is not necessarily an abuse for the claimant to bring subsequent proceedings, as in *Johnson* itself, where the claims of a company against a firm of solicitors were settled, but it was clear that a director of the company also had personal claims against the firm in respect of the same negligent advice.[109] **30-28**

An award of compensation by magistrates has been held to be a bar to a subsequent civil action, even though the jurisdiction of the magistrates was limited so that they could not award adequate damages.[110] But where a person had obtained an order from a magistrate under s.40 of the Metropolitan Police Act 1839 for the delivery up of goods improperly detained, it was held that in a subsequent action he might counterclaim for special damage arising out of the same detention, because the magistrate had no jurisdiction to deal with the special damage.[111] **30-29**

(c) Contribution proceedings

In *Wood v Luscombe*,[112] EW, a pillion passenger on a motorcycle ridden by his son JW, had been injured in a collision between that motorcycle and another ridden by SL. EW claimed damages from SL and SL joined JW as a third party seeking contribution under what is now the Civil Liability (Contribution) Act 1978.[113] In previous proceedings by SL against JW both riders had been found equally to blame for the collision, and Streatfeild J held that JW was bound by that finding for the purposes of the claim for contribution. On the other hand, in the almost precisely similar case of *Randolph v Tuck*,[114] Lawton J held that the result of the previous proceedings between the drivers of vehicles involved in a collision was not binding upon them for the purposes of a claim for contribution which was raised in the action brought against them both by the passenger of one of them. The defendants' duties to each other, which had been in issue in the previous proceedings, and their duties to the claimant, which were in issue in the third party proceedings for contribution, were separate and distinct duties so that no estoppel could be raised. **30-30**

The Civil Liability (Contribution) Act 1978 s.1(5) provides: **30-31**

---

108 The Supreme Court in *Virgin Atlantic Airways Ltd v Zodiac Seats UK Ltd* [2013] UKSC 46; [2014] 1 A.C 160 rejected the argument that this signified that the principle in *Henderson v Henderson* was to be re-categorised as being concerned with abuse of process, taking it out of the domain of res judicata altogether. While res judicata and abuse of process are juridically very different, they are overlapping legal principles with the common underlying purpose of limiting abusive and duplicative litigation: [2013] UKSC 46 at [25], per Lord Sumption.

109 See also *Toth v Ledger* [2002] P.I.Q.R. P1 CA, claim for bereavement damages under the Fatal Accidents Act 1976 settled; the claimant entitled to continue with his common law claim in respect of psychiatric damage.

110 *Wright v London General Omnibus Co* (1877) L.R. 2 Q.B.D. 271; *Birmingham Corp v Allsopp* (1918) 88 L.J.K.B. 549.

111 *Midland Ry v Martin* [1893] 2 Q.B. 172. See also *Webster v Armstrong* (1885) 54 L.J.Q.B. 236.

112 [1966] 1 Q.B. 169; *Marginson v Blackburn BC* [1939] 2 K.B. 426; *Bell v Holmes* [1956] 1 W.L.R. 1359.

113 See paras 4-13 to 4-28.

114 [1962] 1 Q.B. 175; *Johnson v Cartledge and Matthews* [1939] 3 All E.R. 654.

> "A judgment given in any action brought in any part of the United Kingdom by or on behalf of the person who suffered the damage in question against any person from whom contribution is sought under this section shall be conclusive in the proceedings for contribution as to any issue determined by that judgment in favour of the person from whom the contribution is sought."

This clarifies the position where the facts, adapting *Wood v Luscombe*, are thus: following the collision, driver SL sues driver JW and JW is held not liable; JW's passenger EW sues SL, and SL seeks contribution from JW. Here, SL will be bound by the finding in the earlier action in favour of JW who will therefore not be liable for contribution. However, the scope of s.1(5) is limited. It makes binding the findings in the earlier proceedings only in so far as they were *in favour of* the person from whom contribution is sought. So if, in the original action, JW had been held *liable* to SL, in the later contribution proceedings SL could not invoke s.1(5) to bind JW with the finding in the original action that JW was at fault, because this was a finding *against* the person from whom contribution is sought.[115] Whether or not JW is bound by this finding depends on the common law, which means either *Wood v Luscombe* or *Randolph v Tuck*, whichever is correct. In *Wall v Radford*[116] Popplewell J preferred *Wood v Luscombe* to *Randolph v Tuck*.[117] In an action by V (a passenger of W's) against two negligent drivers, W and R, it had been decided that W and R were equally liable to V so that the amount of contribution between W and R was 50 per cent. W's subsequent action against R (which was not one seeking contribution so s.1(5) of the Civil Liability (Contribution) Act 1978 was irrelevant) was held to be barred by issue estoppel and judgment for W of 50 per cent damages to be assessed was entered.

(d) Statutory defence to an action for assault

30-32 In certain cases previous proceedings before a magistrate founded on the same subject-matter form a statutory defence to an action of assault. Section 44 of the Offences Against the Person Act 1861 provides that: "If the justices, upon the hearing of any case of assault or battery upon the merits, where the complaint was preferred by or on behalf of the party aggrieved, shall deem the offence not to be proved, or shall find the assault or battery to have been justified, or so trifling as not to merit any punishment, and shall accordingly dismiss the complaint, they shall forthwith make out a certificate … stating the fact of such dismissal, and shall deliver such certificate to the party against whom the complaint was preferred." For a certificate to be issued, the hearing must be *upon the merits*. Thus no certificate

---

115 A problem arises as to whether a finding that the party from whom contribution is sought (D2) was liable in part only, because of C's (the original claimant's) contributory negligence, counts as a finding in favour of D2 or against him. It probably depends upon who seeks to challenge the finding in the contribution proceedings: D1 or D2. Probably D1 is precluded from saying that D2 was more to blame than he was held to be, but it is open to D2 to argue that he was less.

116 [1991] 2 All E.R. 741. See also *Talbot v Berkshire CC* [1994] Q.B. 290, where the Court of Appeal suggested that, had it been relied on, the wider principle of *Henderson v Henderson* (1843) 3 Hare 100 might have afforded a complete answer to W's claim in *Wall v Radford*.

117 Prior to *Wall v Radford* the most important support for *Wood v Luscombe* was provided by *Marginson v Blackburn BC* [1939] 2 K.B. 426, which though distinguishable, is a decision of the Court of Appeal and contains authoritative dicta to the point: *Wood v Luscombe* [1966] 1 Q.B. 169 at 173. See also the statement of principle of Lush J in *Ord v Ord* [1923] 2 K.B. 432 at 439–444. See also *Cross & Tapper on Evidence*, 13th edn (2019), pp.98–99.

is available in a case where the defendant pleaded guilty,[118] nor where the prosecution came to an end because the prosecutor gave notice that he would not further prosecute the summons.[119] By s.45 the party obtaining such a certificate shall be released from all further[120] proceedings, civil or criminal. If on conviction the defendant is fined or imprisoned instead of discharged, there is no question of a certificate: but s.45 further provides that in such a case, once the defendant has served his imprisonment or paid the fine, further proceedings are barred just as if a certificate had been issued.[121]

Dismissal of charge In the case of a dismissal of the charge, it is the granting of the certificate and not the dismissal itself which operates as a release. The certificate can only be proved by itself and therefore it must show upon the face of it that there was such dismissal as is contemplated by the Act, namely, after a hearing "on the merits", and upon one of the grounds mentioned in the Act.[122] The magistrates are bound to grant the certificate upon application, and may be compelled to do so by a mandatory order.[123] There is no time limit for making the application. The word "'forthwith' in the section does not make the immediate grant of the certificate a condition of its validity, but means 'forthwith if demanded'".[124] **30-33**

Conviction If the defence relied on is a conviction, this must be proved by one of the recognised modes of proof.[125] If the justices simply order the defendant to enter into a recognisance for the future, there is no conviction within the meaning of the Act.[126] A conviction and discharge conditionally on the defendant's giving security to be of good behaviour, under s.16(2) of the Summary Jurisdiction Act 1879, would apparently have been sufficient[127]; and so, presumably, would a conviction followed by conditional or absolute discharge under s.12 of the Powers of Criminal Courts (Sentencing) Act 2000. **30-34**

Proceedings by other parties Section 45 of the Offences Against the Person Act 1861 relieves the party from all further proceedings, whether at the suit of the party assaulted or of anyone else. So a husband could not recover under the old action for loss of consortium,[128] for his injury consequential on an assault upon his wife.[129] **30-35**

---

118 *Ellis v Burton* [1975] 1 W.L.R. 386.

119 *Reed v Nutt* (1890) 24 Q.B.D. 669.

120 *Masper v Brown* (1876) 34 L.T. 254; *Holden v King* (1876) 35 L.T. 479. A conviction after judgment for the claimant in an action for assault, but before appeal by the defendant has been heard, does not affect the claimant's right to recover, as the appeal does not constitute "further proceedings": *Magee v Storey* [1929] N.I. 134 CA. The fact that a servant possesses a certificate of dismissal does not bar proceedings against his master where it is claimed that the alleged assault was committed in the course of the servant's employment: *Corney v Minister of Labour* [1958] C.L.Y. 2656 Cty Ct.

121 A person convicted and bound over in his own recognisance cannot rely upon s.45: *Gibbons v Harris* (1956) 106 L.J. 828.

122 *Skuse v Davis* (1839) 10 A. & E. 635.

123 *Hancock v Somes* (1859) 1 E. & E. 795.

124 *Costar v Hetherington* (1859) 1 E. & E. 802.

125 At common law, by the production of the original record or an examined copy: *Hartley v Hindmarsh* (1866) L.R. 1 C. & P. 553; or, under the Police and Criminal Evidence Act 1984 s.73, by a certificate of conviction (Crown Court) or memorandum of conviction (magistrates' court), or under the Evidence Act 1851 s.13 (certified under hand of clerk of court).

126 *Hartley v Hindmarsh* (1866) L.R. 1 C. & P. 553.

127 *R. v Miles* (1890) 24 Q.B.D. 423.

128 Abolished by the Administration of Justice Act 1982 s.2.

But the conviction of a servant for an assault is no bar to an action against his master, if the assault is committed in the course of the servant's employment.[130]

30-36 **Proposed reform** In its *Report on Offences Against the Person and General Principles* in 1993[131] the Law Commission recommended the repeal of ss.44–45 of the Offences against the Person Act 1861. This has not occurred.

7. JOINT AND CONCURRENT WRONGDOERS[132]

30-37 **Joint wrongdoers: at common law** The general rule at common law is that where there is a joint cause of action against two or more persons, a discharge as against one of them operates as a discharge against all. If accord be made with one joint tortfeasor and satisfaction accepted,[133] or if he be released, all others are discharged.[134] "It is, we think, clear law that a release granted to one joint tortfeasor or to one joint debtor, operates as a discharge to the other joint tortfeasor or the other joint debtor, the reason being that the cause of action, which is one and indivisible, having been released, all persons otherwise liable thereto are consequently released."[135] The common law rule was practically most inconvenient to claimants, and was accordingly limited by the courts in various ways.[136] Thus it was held that a covenant or agreement not to sue does not get rid of the cause of action, and therefore only operates in favour of the person with whom it is made.[137] It was also held that an order of court staying an action against one joint tortfeasor, pursuant to such an agreement, does not extinguish the cause of action against the other.[138] And most important, if a party purports to release one wrongdoer with

---

129 *Masper v Brown* (1876) 1 C.P.D. 97.

130 *Dyer v Munday* [1895] 1 Q.B. 742.

131 Law Commission No.218. See similarly the *Criminal Law Revision Committee's Fourteenth Report*, Cmnd.7844, paras 163-164.

132 We are here concerned with joint tortfeasors rather than several tortfeasors causing the same damage (who are sometimes referred to as joint and several tortfeasors). For consideration of the effect of settlement with one joint and several tortfeasor on claims against another joint and several tortfeasor, see *Jameson v Central Electricity Generating Board* [2000] 1 A.C. 455, which was distinguished and explained in *Heaton v Axa Equity and Law Life Assurance Society Plc* [2002] UKHL 15; [2002] 2 A.C. 329. See generally paras 4-02 to 4-12.

133 *Thurman v Wild* (1840) 11 A. & E. 453. See *Mayor of Salford v Lever* (1890) 25 Q.B.D. 363; [1891] 1 Q.B. 168; *Cutler v McPhail* [1962] 2 Q.B. 292. cf. *Gardiner v Moore* [1969] 1 Q.B. 55 at 92, per Thesiger J. See also *Morris v Wentworth-Stanley* [1999] Q.B. 1004: accord and satisfaction with one joint debtor released other joint debtors.

134 Co. Lit 232; and see *Bulmer Rayon & Co v Freshwater* [1933] A.C. 661.

135 *Duck v Mayeu* [1892] 2 Q.B. 511 at 513, per A.L. Smith LJ.

136 Some judges have suggested that the release rule has been impliedly abrogated by s.6 of the Law Reform (Married Women and Tortfeasors) Act 1935, now s.3 of the Civil Liability (Contribution) Act 1978 (para.30-38): *Bryanston Finance Ltd v de Vries* [1975] Q.B. 703 at 723, per Lord Denning MR; *Watts v Aldington* [1999] L. & T.R. 578; *The Times,* 16 December 1993, per Steyn LJ. See also *Thompson v Australian Capital Television Pty Ltd* (1996) 186 C.L.R. 574; discussed by Hewitt (1998) 72 A.L.J. 73.

137 *Hutton v Eyre* (1815) 6 Taunt. 289; *Gardiner v Moore* [1969] 1 Q.B. 55. But see *Bryanston Finance Ltd v de Vries* [1975] Q.B. 703 at 723, per Lord Denning MR: "The right solution nowadays is for any sum paid by the one wrongdoer under the settlement to be taken into account when assessing damages against the other wrongdoer. If the [claimant] recovers more, he gets the extra. If he recovers less, he loses and has to pay the costs; and as between the joint wrongdoers themselves, there can be contribution according to what is just and equitable" under what is now the Civil Liability (Contribution) Act 1978.

138 *Apley Estates Co v De Bernales* [1947] Ch. 217 CA (per Somervell LJ quaere, whether the Law

a reservation of his right of action against another, this is to be taken as an agreement not to sue rather than as a release.[139] If a tort is waived by the election of an alternative remedy or an inconsistent right in respect of one of the tortfeasors, the election is binding as against the other.[140]

Joint wrongdoers: statute With regard to recovery of judgment against joint tortfeasors, the common law rule that a judgment obtained against one joint tortfeasor, though unsatisfied, released the others[141] was abrogated by s.6 of the Law Reform (Married Women and Tortfeasors) Act 1935. This was limited to joint tortfeasors, and did not cover, for example, joint debtors; and how far it succeeded in changing the law even in relation to joint tortfeasors was unclear because of some flaws in drafting. In 1978, this provision was replaced by the Civil Liability (Contribution) Act. This reverses the common law rule governing the effect of judgment against joint defendants in terms which are general and are not limited to joint tortfeasors, and also attempts to remedy some of the drafting problems of its predecessor.[142] Section 3 provides that: **30-38**

> "Judgment recovered against any person liable in respect of any debt or damage shall not be a bar to an action, or to the continuance of an action,[143] against any other person who is (apart from any such bar) jointly liable with him in respect of the same debt or damage."

Section 6(1)(b) of the Law Reform Act 1935 used to restrict the total amount of damages which a claimant could recover as a result of subsequent actions to the sum for which he was given judgment in the first action.[144] Section 4 of the 1978 Act abolished this restriction, but provides that the claimant shall not be entitled to costs in any later action, unless the court thinks there were reasonable grounds for suing a group of defendants in succession rather than together.[145] This abolition does not

---

Reform (Married Women and Tortfeasors) Act 1935—now the Civil Liability (Contribution) Act 1978—has any application in this situation).

[139] *Duck v Mayeu* [1892] 2 Q.B. 511; *Goldrei, Foucard & Son v Sinclair* [1918] 1 K.B. 180 at 188, 192; see *Bryanston Finance v De Vries* [1975] Q.B. 703 at 732, per Lord Diplock, and *Gladman Commercial Properties v Fisher Hargreaves Proctor* [2013] EWCA Civ 1466; [2014] C.P. Rep. 13 (no express or implied reservation of Gladman's right to sue).

[140] *Buckland v Johnson* (1854) 15 C.B. 145. The claimant having sued and obtained judgment (but not satisfaction) from one tortfeasor was not allowed to sue the other for the money had and received. The reason given by Jervis CJ, that the judgment in trover changed the property, is wrong: see *Brinsmead v Harrison* (1870-71) L.R. 6 C.P. 584 at 589; and *Ellis v Stenning* [1932] 2 Ch. 81. Maule J put the decision on the ground of the election. cf. also *Rice v Reed* [1900] 1 Q.B. 54. See paras 30-03 to 30-05.

[141] For the old rule, see *Brown v Wootton* (1604) Cro. Jac. 73; *Brinsmead v Harrison* (1871-72) L.R. 6 C. & P. 584; *Dyer v Munday* [1895] 1 Q.B. 742; *Parr v Snell* [1923] 1 K.B. 1 at 6; *Ash v Hutchinson & Co* [1936] Ch. 489.

[142] But in *Morris v Wentworth-Stanley* [1999] Q.B. 1004, it was held that s.3 of the Civil Liability (Contribution) Act 1978 did not apply to a judgment obtained by consent: that judgment embodied an accord and satisfaction and the applicable rule was that an accord and satisfaction with one joint debtor released other joint debtors. For the right to contribution between joint tortfeasors, see para.4-13 onwards.

[143] These words obviate the problem, circumnavigated in *Bryanston Finance v de Vries* [1975] Q.B. 703; and in *Wah Tat Bank Ltd v Chan* [1975] A.C. 507, that s.6(1)(a) of the 1935 Act, on the face of it, failed to cover the case where the claimant sued both defendants jointly, obtaining judgment against one before the other.

[144] See 14th edn, para.635 fn.10.

[145] This limitation would not apply in cases like *Goldrei Foucard & Son v Sinclair* [1918] 1 K.B. 180 where the remedy sought against one of the defendants is not by way of damages but for rescission

affect the general rule that a claimant can extract no more than the measure of his loss when he executes judgment, however many the defendants against whom judgment has been recovered. Where a claim against several defendants, based upon the same facts, had been framed in more than one way, and the claimant accepts a sum paid into court by one of the defendants in satisfaction of one of the causes of action then if the damages recoverable upon all the claims are in fact the same, and if the sum accepted is sufficient to cover these damages, the whole of the claim against all the defendants is at an end.[146]

30-39 **Other concurrent wrongdoers** Where one wrongdoer A is liable for a given loss jointly and severally, rather than merely jointly, with another wrongdoer B, there is no rule, even at common law, that judgment against A bars the cause of action against B.[147] However, satisfaction of the judgment against A, if that judgment was based on compensating the claimant's full loss, bars any subsequent claim against B; and the same goes for a satisfied compromise of the claim against A entered into on the basis that the claimant is being fully compensated.[148] On the other hand, if on a proper interpretation of the compromise agreement it is not intended fully to compensate the claimant (for instance because the claimant is happy to limit the amount received to A's capacity to pay, or because of some contractual limit on A's liability), it does not affect the claimant's rights against B.[149] A practically important example in this connection is where recovery against A has been reduced because of the claimant's contributory negligence, but the claim against B is unaffected: a claim against B to make up recovery of the full amount of loss remains possible.[150]

8. JOINT CLAIMANTS

30-40 **Joint claimants** Where two or more persons have a joint action of tort in respect of a joint interest, any one of them may release it, make accord and accept satisfaction, or, it is presumed, waive it by election.[151] If, however, he does so in fraud of his co-claimants and in collusion with the wrongdoer, the fraud is a good equitable ground to prevent the transaction being set up in answer to the action.[152]

30-41 **Joint claimant may recover separately to the extent of interest** If one of such persons brings an action, although the other parties jointly interested ought to be joined with him, yet if no objection is taken, he can proceed and recover to the

and repayment of money paid by the claimant.

146 *Beadon v Capital Syndicate Ltd* (1912) 28 T.L.R. 427; *Clark v Urquhart* [1930] A.C. 28. See CPR r.36.17. Questions of costs remain open and in the discretion of the court.

147 *Heaton v AXA Equity & Law Life Assurance Society Plc* [2002] UKHL 15; [2002] 2 A.C. 329 at [8]–[9] (Lord Bingham).

148 *Jameson v CEGB* [2000] 1 A.C. 455.

149 *Heaton v AXA Equity & Law Life Assurance Society Plc* [2002] UKHL 15; [2002] 2 A.C. 329 at [5] (Lord Bingham).

150 See *Appleby v Northern Devon Healthcare NHS Trust* [2012] EWHC 4356 (QB); and *Wright v Barts Health NHS Trust* [2016] EWHC 1834 (QB); [2016] Med. L.R. 545 (clinical negligence claims following claims against employers for industrial injuries partly due to the claimant's fault).

151 *Wallace v Kelsall* (1840) 7 M. & W. 264; *Phillips v Clagett* (1843) 11 M. & W. 84; *Steeds v Steeds* (1889) 22 Q.B.D. 537, is not an authority to the contrary. A compromise of an action by one of several co-claimants does not, as of course, entitle him to have his name struck off as co-claimant: *Mathews, Re* [1905] 2 Ch. 460.

152 *De Pothonier v De Mattos* (1858) El. Bl. & El. 461.

extent of his interest, and the other parties can maintain an action subsequently in respect of their interests. Thus, one of several part owners of the chattel suing by himself in trover was held entitled to damages to the value of his share.[153] But a bailee cannot recover damages in respect of the bailed chattel if the bailor has already recovered damages against the tortfeasor for that damage, albeit that the bailor may have to account to the bailee in respect of the latter's interest in the chattel.[154]

---

153 *Addison v Overend* (1796) 6 T.R. 766; *Sedgworth v Overend* (1797) 7 T.R. 279; *Bloxam v Hubbard* (1804) 5 East 407. See, however, *Broadbent v Ledward* (1839) 11 A. & E. 209 (delivery to one of several bailors). This limitation of damage applies where the part owner seeks to recover on the strength of his title. If he is in actual possession the rule is probably the same. See this subject discussed, para.16-43 onwards.

154 *O'Sullivan and McCann v Williams* [1992] 3 All E.R. 385 CA.

Chapter 31

LIMITATION

Table of Contents

1. GENERAL[1]

31-01 At common law there was no limitation period within which actions must be brought. In 1623 a Limitation Act was passed, which governed the matter until the Limitation Act 1939, which provided for a uniform period of six years for all actions founded on tort. Since 1939, limitation of actions has had the almost continu-

[1] See generally, McGee, *Limitation Periods*, 8th edn (2018); Prime and Scanlon, *The Law of Limitation*, 2nd edn (2001); Oughton, Lowry and Merkin, *Limitation of Actions* (1998); Law Commission Consultation Paper No.151, *Limitation of Actions* (1998); Law Commission Report, *Limitation of Actions*, Law Com. No.270 (2001); A.S. Burrows, "Some Recurring Issues in Relation to the Limitation of Actions" in A. Dyson, J. Goudkamp and F. Wilmot-Smith (eds), *Defences in Tort* (Oxford: Hart, 2015), pp.311–329.

ous attention of law reformers, and there have been frequent changes. The law is now almost entirely[2] contained in the Limitation Act 1980,[3] although this consolidating statute has itself been amended by, among others, the Latent Damage Act 1986,[4] the Consumer Protection Act 1987 Pt I,[5] and the Defamation Act 1996 s.5.[6] By s.2 of the Limitation Act 1980 the general limitation period for an action founded on tort is six years from the date on which the cause of action accrued,[7] with a three year period for most claims based upon personal injury.[8] Proceedings must be begun, normally by the issue of a claim form, within the period provided by the statute.[9] Once the claim form has been issued, the claimant will have a further four months within which to serve it.[10] The court has a discretion to extend the period for serving the claim form, but, after the expiry date of the time for service, including any extension, the court may extend the period for service only if the court has failed to serve the claim form, or the claimant has taken all reasonable steps to serve the claim form but has been unable to do so, and in either case, the claimant has acted promptly in making the application.[11]

---

2 For exceptions, see Carriage by Air Act 1961; Railways (Convention on International Carriage by Rail) Regulations 2005; Merchant Shipping Act 1995. See paras 31-78 to 31-81.

3 The Limitation Act 1980 binds the Crown, except in certain specified cases such as recovery of tax: s.37.

4 See paras 31-71 to 31-77.

5 See para.31-83.

6 See para.31-82.

7 A claim for damages for breach of EC law is an action for a tort within s.2 of the 1980 Act: *R. v Secretary of State for Transport Ex p. Factortame (No.6)* [2001] 1 W.L.R. 942; *Phonographic Performance Ltd v Department of Trade and Industry* [2004] EWHC 1795 (Ch); [2004] 1 W.L.R. 2893; *Re 2019 Rail Franchising Litigation* [2019] EWCA Civ 2259; [2020] 1 P. & C.R. 17. While this period contrasts with the short period available to bring a judicial review action, it was pointed out that a tort action does not directly challenge public authority decisions and the action is not an action in public law.

8 Limitation Act 1980 s.11(1).

9 Proceedings are started when the claim form is issued by the court at the request of the claimant (CPR r.7.2). However, where the claim form as issued was received by the court office on a date earlier than the date on which it was issued by the court, the claim is "brought" for the purposes of the Limitation Act 1980 on that earlier date (see CPR PD 7 PD.5): this procedural rule was applied in *Barnes v St Helens MBC* [2006] EWCA Civ 1372; [2007] 1 W.L.R. 879. See also *Page v Hewetts Solicitors* [2012] EWCA Civ 805; [2012] C.P. Rep. 40. In *Atha v Liddle* [2018] EWHC 1751 (QB); [2018] 1 W.L.R. 4953, the claim was treated as having been brought on the date it was received by the court despite the wrong fee being paid. The existence of conflicting first instance decisions on the point was noted, and it was suggested that Court of Appeal guidance was required.

10 CPR r.7.5. Where the claim form is to be served out of the jurisdiction, the period is six months.

11 CPR r.7.6. For consideration of the words "all reasonable steps to serve the claim form" see *Nanglegan v Royal Free Hampstead NHS Trust* [2001] EWCA Civ 127; [2002] 1 W.L.R. 1043. On the court's failure to serve the claim form see *Cranfield v Bridgegrove Ltd* [2003] EWCA Civ 656; [2003] 1 W.L.R. 2441. If the claimant cannot bring his case within CPR r.7.6(3) he cannot rely on the court's general discretion under CPR r.3.1(2)(a) (to extend or shorten the time for compliance with any rule), since this is excluded by the wording of r.7.6(3): *Vinos v Marks & Spencer Plc* [2001] 3 All E.R. 784 CA; nor can he rely on CPR r.6.15 (allowing the court to authorise an alternative method of service) retrospectively, because r.6.8 is prospective: *Nanglegan v Royal Free Hampstead NHS Trust* [2001] EWCA Civ 127; [2002] 1 W.L.R. 1043 at [31], per May LJ; nor by relying on CPR r.3.9 (relief from sanctions for failing to comply with any rule): *Infantino v MacLean* [2001] 3 All E.R. 802 QBD. The court does have discretion, however, under CPR r.6.16 (the power of the court to dispense with service) which can be exercised retrospectively in "an appropriate case", though this requires "exceptional circumstances": *Anderton v Clwyd CC* [2002] EWCA Civ 933; [2002] 1 W.L.R. 3174; *Wilkey v BBC* [2002] EWCA Civ 1561; [2003] 1 W.L.R. 1; *Cranfield v Bridgegrove Ltd* [2003] EWCA Civ 656; [2003] 1 W.L.R. 2441 at [32]; *Akram v Adam (No.2)* [2004] EWCA Civ

(a) Limitation is a matter of practice and procedure

31-02 Under the Limitation Act 1623, the expiry of the period of limitation did not extinguish the right of the claimant in any case, but merely barred his remedy. This was altered, so far as real property is concerned, by the Real Property Limitation Act 1833[12] and under s.3 of the Limitation Act 1980[13] the title to personalty may also be extinguished after the limitation period has expired. The ten-year long-stop period in s.11A(3) of the 1980 Act, which applies to actions under Pt I of the Consumer Protection Act 1987, also extinguishes the claimant's right of action.[14] Otherwise, however, the Limitation Act 1980 does not extinguish the claimant's cause of action. It only imposes a time-limit within which the claimant's action should be brought.[15] The Act is procedural, so that, subject to s.35 of the Act, Rules of Court may regulate its operation.[16] A defendant who wishes to rely on the defence of limitation must plead specifically that the action is out of time[17] and the Act confers no right on him other than to plead the defence if he chooses to do so.[18] If a claim form, albeit a defective one, has been issued within the time allowed, the court can, as a matter of practice, permit the claimant to amend it[19] and the defendant has no right, even after the limitation period has expired, to have it remain defective.[20] Indeed, the courts appear to have become more lenient than previously[21] to claimants who seek amendments to their claim forms or pleadings after the limitation period has expired,[22] a practice which has correspondingly reduced

---

1601; [2005] 1 W.L.R. 2762.

12 Now the Limitation Act 1980 s.17. See para.18-80 onwards.

13 See paras 31-29 to 31-32.

14 See para.31-83. See also the Carriage by Air Act 1961; para.31-80. Contrast the 15-year long-stop under the Limitation Act 1980 s.14B, which bars the remedy but does not extinguish the claimant's right of action: *Financial Services Compensation Scheme Ltd v Larnell (Insurances) Ltd* [2005] EWCA Civ 1408; [2006] Q.B. 808.

15 An important practical consequence of this distinction is that no contribution can be recovered by D1 from D2 where the claimant's action against D2 is extinguished, as opposed to being merely barred, by a limitation period.

16 *Rodriguez v RJ Parker (Male)* [1967] 1 Q.B. 116; *Mitchell v Harris Engineering Co Ltd* [1967] 2 Q.B. 703. The Civil Procedure Act 1997 s.1 provides that there are to be "rules of court ... governing the practice and procedure to be followed in (a) the civil division of the Court of Appeal, (b) the High Court, and (c) county courts". The Law Reform Committee thought that the law relating to the limitation of actions was too important a matter for the Rules Committee to have an open-ended power to unmake it, and proposed a section in the Limitation Act to restrict the rule-making power in this area (L.R.C. 21st Report, Cmnd.6923 (1977), Pt V). Accordingly, what is now the Limitation Act 1980 s.35 was enacted by the Limitation (Amendment) Act 1980. This limits the making of rules granting a judge a discretion to permit certain amendments after the expiry of the limitation period; see paras 31-19 and 31-20.

17 CPR 16 PD13.1. Wherever feasible a judge should decide the limitation point by a preliminary hearing by reference to the pleadings and written witness statements and the extent and content of disclosure: *KR v Bryn Alyn Community (Holdings) Ltd (In Liquidation)* [2003] EWCA Civ 85; [2003] Q.B. 1441 at [74].

18 *Rodriguez v RJ Parker (Male)* [1967] 1 Q.B. 116, per Nield J.

19 *Welsh Development Agency v Redpath Dorman Long Ltd* [1994] 1 W.L.R. 1409 CA, at 1417. See generally paras 31-19 and 31-20.

20 *Mitchell v Harris Engineering Co Ltd* [1967] 2 Q.B. 703 at 718, per Lord Denning MR. See also *Pontin v Wood* [1962] 1 Q.B. 594; *Presentaciones Musicales SA v Secunda* [1994] Ch. 271.

21 See, e.g. *Mabro v Eagle Star & British Dominions Insurance Co Ltd* [1932] 1 K.B. 485; *Hilton v Sutton Steam Laundry* [1946] K.B. 65; *Davies v Elsby Brothers Ltd* [1961] 1 W.L.R. 170.

22 See paras 31-19 and 31-20.

the "benefit" to defendants given by the Act.[23] The implementation of the Civil Procedure Rules does not appear to have changed this.[24]

(b) Burden of proof

As limitation is a defence, one might have expected the burden of proof to lie with the defendant.[25] But the authorities established that the burden of proving that the case falls within the limitation period is on the claimant.[26] Where, in a personal injuries action, there is an application under s.33 of the Limitation Act 1980 to disapply the primary limitation period the burden of proving that it is just and equitable to allow the action to proceed is also on the claimant.[27] **31-03**

(c) How time is computed

In computing the time of limitation, the day on which the cause of action arose is, as a rule, excluded, and the day on which the action is commenced is included.[28] Thus if C is injured on 8 November 2005, he can sue at any time up to and including the whole of 8 November 2008. The principle is that "where the act done from which the computation is made is one to which the party against whom it runs is privy, the day of the act done may reasonably be included; but where it is one to which he is a stranger it ought to be excluded".[29] If the last day of the period is a Sunday, or other day on which the court offices are closed, the claimant has until the first day following on which the offices are open in which to issue his claim form.[30] In *Matthew v Sedman*[31] the Court of Appeal held that in a case where a cause of action accrues on failure to meet a midnight deadline, the position is different. The cause of action is treated as accruing on the stroke of midnight, and not shortly thereafter, and the following day is therefore not discounted from the limitation period. **31-04**

23 See, e.g. *Rodriguez v RJ Parker (Male)* [1967] 1 Q.B. 116; *Mitchell v Harris Engineering Co Ltd* [1967] 2 Q.B. 703; *Braniff v Holland and Hannen and Cubitts (Southern) Ltd* [1969] 1 W.L.R. 1533.

24 See *International Distillers & Vintners Ltd v JF Hillebrand (UK) Ltd, The Times,* 25 January 2000.

25 See *Pullen v Gutteridge, Haskins & Davey Pty Ltd* (1992) Aust. Torts Rep. 81 Victoria S.C., noted by Mullany (1993) 109 L.Q.R. 215.

26 *Cartledge v E Jopling & Sons Ltd* [1963] A.C. 758 at 784; *London Congregational Union Inc v Harriss and Harriss* [1988] 1 All E.R. 15; *Crocker v British Coal Corp* (1995) 29 B.M.L.R. 159; *Arab Monetary Fund v Hashim* [1996] 1 Lloyd's Rep. 589 (in which a previous version of para.31-03 was cited); *Lloyds Bank Plc v Crosse & Crosse* [2001] EWCA Civ 366; [2001] P.N.L.R. 34 at [41]; *Haward v Fawcetts* [2006] UKHL 9; [2006] 1 W.L.R. 682 at [106], per Lord Mance; *Fiona Trust & Holding Corp v Privalov* [2010] EWHC 3199 (Comm) at [135], per Andrew Smith J (decision upheld without mentioning limitation sub nom. *Fiona Trust & Holding Corp v Skarga* [2013] EWCA Civ 275).

27 See para.31-54.

28 *Marren v Dawson Bentley & Co* [1961] 2 Q.B. 135. cf. per Mathew LJ in *Goldsmiths' Co v West Metropolitan Ry* [1904] 1 K.B. 1 at 5 (applied in *Stewart v Chapman* [1951] 2 K.B. 792 DC; and distinguished in *Hare v Gocher* [1962] 2 Q.B. 641).

29 *Hardy v Ryle* (1829) 9 B. & C. 603 at 608; *Freeman v Read* (1863) 4 B. & S. 174 at 184, per Cockburn CJ.

30 *Pritam Kaur v S Russell & Sons Ltd* [1973] 1 Q.B. 336; not following *Morris v Richards* (1881) 45 L.T. 210; *Gelmini v Moriggia* [1913] 2 K.B. 549; *Hartley v Birmingham City DC* [1992] 1 W.L.R. 968.

31 [2019] EWCA Civ 475; [2020] Ch. 85. An appeal is awaited.

(d) No suspension of limitation period once time has started to run

31-05 As a general rule, once the limitation period has started to run it cannot be suspended; only the issue of the claim form stops time running. It is not broken by a subsequently accruing disability, nor by the fact that for the time being there was nobody in existence who could sue.[32] If a person having a vested cause of action dies before he can commence proceedings, and no personal representative is appointed until the time has expired, the action is barred.[33] Where, however, a debtor takes out administration to his creditor, the remedy is suspended, and the statute ceases to run during the administration.[34] And where there has been fraud or deliberate concealment by the defendant after the cause of action accrued a new limitation period starts from the date when the claimant discovered, or ought reasonably to have discovered, the concealment.[35] The parties may agree, expressly or impliedly, to extend the time for the claimant to issue proceedings, but the mere fact that negotiations towards a settlement were in progress when the limitation period expired will not constitute such an agreement, unless the defendant's conduct is such that he is estopped from relying on the defence.[36]

(e) Starting the limitation period

31-06 The basic rule is that the limitation period runs from the date that the claimant's cause of action accrues.[37] There are a number of exceptions to this rule which are designed to postpone the running of the limitation period in circumstances where it is thought the basic rule can be unfair to claimants. So there are specific provisions covering claimants who were under a disability when the cause of action accrued,[38] cases of fraud or deliberate concealment by the defendant,[39] claims arising out of personal injury or death,[40] and claims in respect of latent damage as a result of negligence.[41]

(i) Accrual of the cause of action

31-07 A distinction must be drawn between torts actionable per se, and torts actionable only on the proof of damage. Where a tort is actionable per se, it accrues at the time of the defendant's wrongful act. When, therefore, there is a trespass, libel,

---

[32] *Smith v Hill* (1746) 1 Wils. 134; *Doe d. Duroure v Jones* (1791) 4 T.R. 300; *Homfray v Scroope* (1849) 13 Q.B. 509.

[33] *Rhodes v Smethurst* (1838–40) 4 M. & W. 42; 6 M. & W. 351; *Penny v Brice* (1865) 18 C.B. (N.S.) 393; *Boatwright v Boatwright* (1873) L.R. 17 Eq. 71.

[34] *Seagram v Knight* (1867) L.R. 2 Ch. 628 at 632 and 633.

[35] *Sheldon v RHM Outhwaite (Underwriting Agencies) Ltd* [1996] A.C. 102; see para.31-28.

[36] *Deerness v John Keeble & Son Ltd* [1983] 2 Lloyd's Rep. 260, where the House of Lords declined to infer such an agreement from continuing negotiations and an interim payment; *K Lokumal & Sons (London) Ltd v Lotte Shipping Co Pte Ltd* [1985] 2 Lloyd's Rep. 28.

[37] Limitation Act 1980 s.2, specifying a six-year limitation period.

[38] See para.31-21.

[39] See para.31-22 onwards.

[40] See para.31-36 onwards. This includes special rules for actions under Pt 1 of the Consumer Protection Act 1987 in respect of defective products: see para.31-83.

[41] See para.31-71 onwards.

or other act which of itself constitutes a wrong, time begins to run from the act itself, or, if there are several acts, in respect of each act from the date of its commission.[42]

Where there is a continuing wrong, such as a continuing nuisance, or a continuing trespass,[43] every fresh continuance is a fresh cause of action, and therefore a claimant who sues after the cessation of the wrong may recover for such portions of it as lie within the period limited. For example, where the claimant was discharged from a wrongful imprisonment of a month's duration on 14 December, and issued proceedings on 14 June (the period of limitation being then six months), it was held that he was entitled to sue in respect of the trespass to his person committed on 14 December.[44] But where a defendant maliciously opposed the discharge from custody of the claimant, and thereby caused a prolongation of his imprisonment under the judge's order, the time was held to run from the malicious act and not from the termination of the imprisonment; although a continuing damage, the imprisonment was not a continuing wrong, for the detention of the claimant was the act of the court.[45] In an action for libel, the defence of limitation was previously negatived by proof that a single copy of the libel had been published by the defendant within the period of limitation.[46] This was amended by s.8 of the Defamation Act 2013, which introduced a "single publication rule": where a statement that is "substantially the same" is published on a further occasion, the limitation period will continue to run from the date of the initial publication. Its application depends therefore on interpretation of whether the subsequent statement is indeed substantially the same. Equally, the single publication rule will not protect a defendant where the circumstances of the subsequent publication are "materially different".[47] 31-08

When the tort is actionable only on proof of damage, then there is no cause of action, and time does not begin to run until some damage actually occurs.[48] Thus 31-09

---

[42] See, e.g. *Sevcon Ltd v Lucas CAV Ltd* [1986] 1 W.L.R. 462 HL, where it was held that the cause of action for infringement of a patent accrued, and hence time ran, from the date of the acts of infringement (1974–1977) even though the claimants did not have the right to sue until later (1982) when the patent was sealed. On the facts the claimants were statute-barred as they did not issue proceedings until 1984.

[43] See para. 30-18.

[44] *Hardy v Ryle* (1829) 9 B. & C. 603. The case arose under s.8 of the Constable Protection Act 1750, now repealed. cf. *O'Connor v Isaacs* [1956] 2 Q.B. 288. See also *Massey v Johnson* (1809) 12 East 67; and *Bailey v Warden* (1815) 4 M. & S. 400. In contrast, in claims for malicious prosecution, the cause of action will not accrue until the proceedings forming the basis of the action for malicious prosecution have been favourably determined: *Dunlop v HM Customs & Excise*, *The Times*, 17 March 1998 CA.

[45] *Violett and Sympson* (1857) 8 E. & B. 344.

[46] *Duke of Brunswick v Harmer* (1849) 14 Q.B. 185.

[47] See further para.31-82.

[48] *Saunders v Edwards* (1662) 1 Sid. 95; *Littleboy v Wright* (1662) 1 Sid. 95; *Roberts v Read* (1812) 16 East 215; *Whitehouse v Fellowes* (1861) 10 C.B. (N.S.) 765. In *Yorkshire Electricity Board v British Telecom Plc* [1986] 1 W.L.R. 1029 HL, it was held that the cause of action created by the Public Utilities Street Works Act 1950 accrues when the owning undertakers reasonably incur the expense of making good the damage to their apparatus, not when the apparatus is damaged. In *Claimants in the Royal Mail Group Litigation v Royal Mail Group Ltd* [2020] EWHC 97 (Ch), it was cautioned that not all breaches of statutory duty require damage in order to be actionable: for example, if there had been an actionable obligation under applicable regulations to supply an invoice within 30 days of a supply taking place (which the court held there was not), a breach would take place on the 31st day if there was no invoice. It was unnecessary to go on and look for a date when damage accrued. However, if the action was directly against the state in the form of "*Francovich* damages", the time period would run from the date at which damage accrued. In *Spencer v Secretary of State for Work*

in cases of withdrawal of support, each subsidence gives an independent cause of action which may be sued for within the six years following its occurrence[49]; and when the subsidence is a continuing process each fresh damage caused by its continuance gives a fresh cause of action.[50] Similarly in cases of negligence time runs from the date of the damage, not of the negligent act or omission so that, for example, a person injured by a negligently manufactured chattel may sue the manufacturer within three years of his injury, even though more than three years have elapsed since the chattel left the factory. In *Evans v PricewaterhouseCoopers LLP*, concerning negligence claims in relation to advice as to the legality of tax avoidance schemes, it was held to be arguable that no damage was suffered until it was determined by the tax authorities that there was a taxable gain, in 2013, rather than at the time when the schemes were entered into.[51]

(ii) The problem of latent damage

31-10 The fact that the cause of action accrues *when the damage occurs*, not when it is discovered by the claimant has caused a number of problems for the courts. In *Cartledge v E Jopling & Sons Ltd*[52] the claimant had over a period of years been exposed to noxious dust as a consequence of certain breaches of duty by the defendants, his employers, and as a result had contracted pneumoconiosis. There had, however, been no breach of duty by the defendants during the six years immediately preceding the issue of proceedings (six years being the relevant period of limitation at the time) and, although the disease had not revealed itself until later, the claimant had actually suffered actionable injury to his lungs more than six years before the proceedings were begun.[53] The House of Lords felt bound to hold, therefore, that his claim was statute-barred. Again in *Pirelli General Cable Works Ltd v Oscar Faber and Partners*[54] the House of Lords held that a cause of action in tort for negligent advice given by an engineer in relation to the design of a chimney accrued (and hence the six-year limitation period began) when the damage occurred—which was regarded as when there were cracks in the chimney—rather than when the damage became reasonably discoverable.[55] As the chimney

---

and Pensions [2008] EWCA Civ 750; [2009] Q.B. 358, it was held that the cause in action in tort for "*Francovich* damages" against the state-for an alleged failure by the government, contrary to EU Law, to provide a remedy in a personal injury case-accrued at the date of the personal injury.

49 *Backhouse v Bonomi* (1861) 9 H.L.C. 503; *Darley Main Colliery Co v Mitchell* (1886) 11 App. Cas. 127. See para.30-18.

50 *Crumbie v Wallsend Local Board* [1891] 1 Q.B. 503. See also *Phonographic Performance Ltd v DTI* [2004] EWHC 1795 (Ch); [2004] 1 W.L.R. 2893: breach of statutory duty by failure to implement EC directive was not statute-barred because that tort was both continuing and required damage, and hence the claimant could recover for damage sustained in the six years before the issue of proceedings.

51 *Evans v PricewaterhouseCoopers LLP* [2019] EWHC 1505 (Ch); [2019] P.N.L.R. 28. The Court also held that it was arguable that there were continuing breaches beyond 2010 causing distinct damage, and on this basis too the claims would not be struck out.

52 [1963] A.C. 758; *Archer v Catton & Co Ltd* [1954] 1 W.L.R. 775; *Brazier v Ministry of Defence* [1965] 1 Lloyd's Rep. 26. cf. *Clarkson v Modern Foundries Ltd* [1957] 1 W.L.R. 1210.

53 See especially, per Lord Pearce [1963] A.C. 758 at 778–779.

54 [1983] 2 A.C. 1. *Pirelli* was applied in *Dove v Banham Patent Locks* [1993] 1 W.L.R. 1436 (cause of action accrued at the date of a burglary following the defendant's negligent installation of a security gate).

55 Overruling *Sparham-Souter v Town & Country Developments (Essex) Ltd* [1976] Q.B. 858 CA, which had applied a discoverability test. *Pirelli* has not been followed in other jurisdictions: *Brian*

cracked in April 1970 and proceedings were not issued until October 1978 the action was time-barred even though the claimant owner neither knew of the cracks nor could reasonably have been expected to discover them before October 1972. The House of Lords deplored the result but felt that anything else would involve conflict with *Cartledge v Jopling* which they were not prepared to overrule.

The problem that this situation created for claimants, that their causes of action had become statute-barred before they were even aware that they had suffered any damage, was remedied by amendments to the Limitation Act, with special limitation regimes applying to claims for personal injury or death[56] and to claims arising in the tort of negligence for other forms of loss where the damage is latent.[57] The three-year limitation period in cases of personal injury or death runs from either when the cause of action accrued or when the claimant had knowledge of certain material facts, whichever is the later. The court also has a discretion to override this limitation period and allow the action to proceed out of time. For other forms of latent damage (in the tort of negligence), the limitation period is either six years from when the cause of action accrued or (if this expires later) three years from when the claimant had knowledge of certain material facts. This is subject to a "long-stop" of 15 years from the date of the negligent act or omission which applies whether or not the claimant is aware of the damage, and there is no discretion to override the fixed limitation periods. 31-11

Many of the uncertainties surrounding latent damage arose from claims in respect of defectively constructed buildings, but in *Murphy v Brentwood DC*[58] the House of Lords concluded that where a building is defectively constructed or designed the resulting damage to the building is pure economic loss and accordingly is not the subject of a duty of care in negligence.[59] This largely rendered redundant in respect of defective buildings the latent damage limitation scheme introduced into the Limitation Act 1980 by the Latent Damage Act 1986. Economic loss remains actionable, however, under the principle of *Hedley Byrne & Co Ltd v Heller & Partners Ltd*[60] and this type of claim tends now to arise most frequently in the context of professional liability. The question of precisely when a client suffers damage as a result of relying on professional advice is significant for the accrual of the cause of action against the negligent professional, though the client is entitled to rely on the latent damage provisions. 31-12

In *Forster v Outred & Co*[61] solicitors had negligently failed to advise the claimant that what she thought was only temporary security for bridging finance to her son was in fact a permanent mortgage of her farm to cover all her son's present and future debts to a company. It was held that damage occurred, and hence time started 31-13

Morgan v Park Developments (1983) I.R.L.M. 156; *Kamloops v Nielson* (1984) 10 D.L.R. (4th) 641. In *Invercargill City Council v Hamlin* [1996] A.C. 624 the Privy Council held that it was open to the New Zealand courts to apply a reasonable discoverability test, it being a matter of policy to be determined according to local conditions.

56 See para.31-36 onwards.

57 See para.31-71 onwards.

58 [1991] 1 A.C. 398 HL; *Department of the Environment v Thomas Bates & Sons Ltd* [1991] 1 A.C. 499; *Bellefield Computer Services Ltd v Turner & Sons Ltd* [2000] B.L.R. 97 CA; *Payne v John Setchell Ltd* [2002] P.N.L.R. 7.

59 *Pirelli* remains valid in so far as it lays down that, if there is a cause of action in negligence, it accrues at the date of the damage and not the date of discoverability: *Abbott v Will Gannon & Smith Ltd* [2005] EWCA Civ 198; [2005] P.N.L.R. 30.

60 [1964] A.C. 465.

61 [1982] 1 W.L.R. 86.

to run, from when she executed the mortgage thereby diminishing the value of her land, even though the actual demand for her to repay her son's debts did not arise until two years later. Similarly, it has been held that a claimant suffered damage as soon as he took a lease of property in reliance on a surveyor's negligently prepared report,[62] or as soon as he executed a contract in reliance on the negligent advice of a solicitor.[63] On the other hand, *Forster v Outred & Co* has been distinguished in other cases in which the claimant was regarded as suffering damage at a date later than when he acted in reliance on negligent advice[64]; and in *Law Society v Sephton & Co*[65] the House of Lords drew a distinction between a contingent liability that may depress the value of other property, as in *Forster*, and a contingent liability that stands alone which, until the contingency occurs, is not as such damage for the purposes of the accrual of a cause of action in negligence.

31-14 Although concerning the date from which interest is payable, rather than limitation, a leading case on the date at which damage is suffered (and hence the cause of action in the tort of negligence accrues) for negligent advice is *Nykredit Mortgage Bank Plc v Edward Erdman Group Ltd (No.2)*.[66] Here the claimants had lent money on the security of a property that had been negligently overvalued.[67] Lord Nicholls, giving the leading speech, first dealt with what he regarded as a simple case:

> "A purchaser buys a house which has been negligently overvalued or which is subject to a local land charge not noticed by the purchaser's solicitor. Had he known the true posi-

---

[62] *Secretary of State for the Environment v Essex, Goodman and Suggitt* [1986] 1 W.L.R. 1432. See also *Kitney v Jones Lang Wootton* (1988) 20 E.G. 88; *Lee v Thompson* (1989) 40 E.G. 89 CA; *Iron Trades Mutual Insurance Co Ltd v JK Buckenham Ltd* [1990] 1 All E.R. 808; *Islander Trucking Ltd v Hogg Robinson Gardner Mountain (Marine) Ltd* [1990] 1 All E.R. 826; *Bell v Peter Browne & Co* [1990] 2 Q.B. 495; *Knapp v Ecclesiastical Insurance Group Plc* [1998] P.N.L.R. 172; *Byrne v Hall Pain & Foster* [1999] 1 W.L.R. 1849; *Shore v Sedgwick Financial Services Ltd* [2008] EWCA Civ 863; [2008] P.N.L.R. 37; *Pegasus Management Holdings SCA v Ernst & Young* [2010] EWCA Civ 181; [2010] 3 All E.R. 297; *Axa Insurance Ltd v Akther and Darby Solicitors* [2009] EWCA Civ 1166; [2010] 1 W.L.R. 1662; *Halsall v Champion Consulting Ltd* [2017] EWHC 1079 (QB); [2017] P.N.L.R. 35.

[63] *DW Moore & Co Ltd v Ferrier* [1988] 1 W.L.R. 267. See also *McCarroll v Statham Gill Davies* [2002] EWCA Civ 425; [2003] P.N.L.R. 25; *Nouri v Marvi* [2010] EWCA Civ 1107; [2011] P.N.L.R. 7; *Green v Eadie* [2011] EWHC B24 (Ch); [2012] Ch. 363; *Boycott v Perrins Guy Williams* [2011] EWHC 2969 (Ch); [2012] P.N.L.R. 25; *Lane v Cullens Solicitors* [2011] EWCA Civ 547; [2012] Q.B. 693 (in a claim by the administrator of an estate against his solicitor for negligent failure to advise him not to distribute the estate it was held that the claimant's loss was suffered when he distributed the estate); *Osborne v Follett Stock* [2017] EWHC 1811 (QB); [2017] P.N.L.R. 35.

[64] In *UBAF Ltd v European American Banking Corp* [1984] Q.B. 713 an allegedly negligent defendant had induced the claimant to lend money to an insolvent company outside the limitation period and inside the limitation period it had defaulted on the loan. The Court of Appeal held that time ran from the default on the loan. In *Mathew v Maughold Life Assurance Co, The Times,* 23 January, 1985, it was held that time ran against a negligent accountant from when financial loss eventually resulted from the advice and not from when the advice was originally acted upon (the decision was overturned on a different point by the Court of Appeal: [1955–95] P.N.L.R. 309, *The Times,* 19 February 1987). See also *First National Commercial Bank v Humberts* [1995] 2 All E.R. 673 CA. In *Berney v Saul* [2013] EWCA Civ 640; [2013] P.N.L.R. 26 it was held that the cause of action against the defendant solicitor accrued when the solicitor settled the claimant's action against a third party and not before.

[65] [2006] UKHL 22; [2006] 2 A.C. 543.

[66] [1997] 1 W.L.R. 1627.

[67] The measure of damages in such a case was dealt with in *South Australia Asset Management Corp v York Montague Ltd* [1997] A.C. 191 HL; see para.2-186 onwards.

> tion the purchaser would not have bought. In such a case, the purchaser's cause of action in tort accrues when he completes the purchase. He suffers actual damage by parting with his money and receiving in exchange property worth less than the price he paid."[68]

He then went on to the more difficult case where, as a result of negligent advice, property is acquired as security for a loan. In this situation it was a matter of fact when legally relevant loss was first suffered. This would not in all cases be the date when the loan transaction was completed: if the borrower did not default, the lender might not suffer any loss (even though it had entered into a bad bargain and, in that sense, suffered detriment as soon as the loan transaction was completed). It could also not be said that in all cases the cause of action accrues when the lender realises his deficient security or becomes entitled to have recourse to that security: the lender might become aware of the deficiency before those dates and wish to commence proceedings. On the facts of this particular case, there was a loss at the date of the loan transaction (March 1990), because the borrower defaulted at once and the amount lent at all times exceeded the true value of the property. Interest was held to be payable from December 1990, when the lender had sustained its full allowable loss.

In *Law Society v Sephton & Co*[69] the Law Society brought a claim in the tort of negligence against the defendant accountants who had failed to inspect properly the accounts of a corrupt solicitor. The solicitor over a six-year period had misappropriated over £750,000 from his client account. Subsequently the Law Society had made payments to former clients of the corrupt solicitor from the Solicitors Compensation Fund. It was held that the cause of action in negligence was not time-barred because it accrued only when claims were made for compensation from the Fund. Prior to then, the Law Society had only a contingent liability to pay out compensation. Such a pure contingent liability, which might or might not eventuate, did not count as damage so as to constitute the accrual of a cause of action. This situation was to be distinguished from that dealt with in almost all the prior English cases, which concerned entering into disadvantageous transactions or suffering a diminution in value of an asset. 31-15

(iii) Transfer of property which has sustained latent damage

A further problem relating to the accrual of a cause of action is, what is the consequence of damaged property, in respect of which there is a cause of action, changing hands?[70] This remains of interest even if much of its practical importance has been removed by the recognition in *Murphy v Brentwood DC*[71] that a negligently constructed or designed building gives rise to non-actionable pure economic loss rather than actionable damage to property. Normal principle would dictate that, if damage to the property had already occurred before the claimant acquired an interest in it, the claimant would have no right of action unless the previous owner had assigned that right to him.[72] But in *Pirelli* Lord Fraser did not 31-16

---

68 [1997] 1 W.L.R. 1627 at 1630.

69 [2006] UKHL 22; [2006] 2 A.C. 543.

70 Robertson (1983) 99 L.Q.R. 559; Jones (1984) 100 L.Q.R. 413.

71 [1991] 1 A.C. 398 HL.

72 *Anns v Merton LBC* [1978] A.C. 728 at 758, per Lord Wilberforce; *Perry v Tendring DC* (1984) 30 Build. L.R. 118, *Audsley v Leeds City Council*, *The Times*, 2 June 1988. See also *Sparham-Souter v Town & Country Developments (Essex) Ltd* [1976] Q.B. 858 at 868 and 873; *Trendtex Trading Corp*

say that in such a case the claimant had no claim at all, rather he said, "I think the true view is that the duty of the builder and of the local authority is owed to owners of the property as a class, and that if time runs against one owner, it also runs against all his successors in title".[73] This suggests a novel principle whereby a new owner can indeed sue but only during the remainder of the limitation period which has already started running against the previous owner. Section 3 of the Latent Damage Act 1986, which applies where the claimant acquired his interest after 18 September 1986,[74] adopts a somewhat similar approach. If a previous owner had an accrued cause of action (provided it accrued after 18 September 1980)[75] for negligent damage to property,[76] a new owner acquires a fresh cause of action for that negligence which is to be treated as having accrued at the date of accrual of the original cause of action.[77] But the new owner gains no such action if he (at the time he acquired his interest in the property) or a previous owner knew or ought to have known of the damage: that is, the damage must be latent.[78]

(iv) Concurrent liability in contract and tort[79]

31-17 A breach of contract is actionable per se, and so a cause of action for breach of contract accrues, and the limitation period starts, when the contract is broken rather than when the damage flows from the breach. This contrasts with the accrual of a cause of action in the tort of negligence which does require damage. Accordingly, in a case of concurrent liability in contract and tort,[80] (which arises in many professional-client relationships) where damage occurs at a later point in time than the breach of duty it will be to the claimant's advantage for limitation purposes to

---

v Credit Suisse [1980] Q.B. 629, especially at pp.656–657; affirmed at [1982] A.C. 679.

73 [1983] 2 A.C. 1 at 18. See also *Jones v Stroud DC* [1986] 1 W.L.R. 1141 at 1149.

74 Latent Damage Act 1986 s.4(3).

75 Latent Damage Act 1986 s.4(4), which goes on to add that this restriction does not apply where the limitation period founded on the original cause of action would have been postponed because of deliberate concealment of relevant facts under s.32(1)(b) of the 1980 Act.

76 This is confined to negligence in tort and does not include a cause of action for breach of a contractual duty of care: *Payne v John Setchell Ltd* [2002] P.N.L.R. 7.

77 Applying the time-limits laid down for latent damage in ss.14A–14B of the Limitation Act 1980, as inserted by the Latent Damage Act 1986 s.1, the limitation period is therefore six years from the date of the *original* cause of action or three years from when the claimant had knowledge, whichever is the longer, and subject to a 15-year long-stop from the date of the negligent act or omission: see para.31-71. By s.3(3) of the 1986 Act, s.28 of the 1980 Act (extension of any limitation period in case of claimant under a disability: see para.31-21) does not apply in relation to the fresh cause of action.

78 It is clear (inter alia from the side note to s.3) that s.3 was intended to cover latent damage alone; it does not include other situations where a new owner and the previous owner do not know nor could reasonably be expected to know of property damage. Hence, s.3 has not overturned *Leigh & Sillivan Ltd v Aliakmon Shipping Co Ltd* [1986] A.C. 785 (which was approved in *Homburg Houtimport BV v Agrosin Private Ltd, The Starsin* [2003] UKHL 12; [2004] 1 A.C. 715). For liability under the Consumer Protection Act 1987, the problem of successive ownership of latently damaged property has been dealt with by s.5(5), which lays down that, for the purposes of Pt I of that Act, damage "shall be regarded as having occurred at the earliest time at which a person with an interest in the property had knowledge of the material facts about the loss or damage". Sections 5(6)–(7) explain "knowledge of the material facts".

79 See paras 1-03 to 1-05, 9-06 onwards.

80 It has been established that there is no objection to concurrent liability in contract and tort: *Henderson v Merrett Syndicates Ltd* [1995] 2 A.C. 145 HL. See also, e.g. *Esso Petroleum Co Ltd v Mardon* [1976] Q.B. 801; *Midland Bank Trust Co Ltd v Hett, Stubbs and Kemp* [1979] Ch. 384.

sue for the tort of negligence rather than for breach of contract. In *Henderson v Merrett Syndicates Ltd*[81] the House of Lords accepted that a claimant is entitled to pursue whichever action will give him a practical advantage on the question of limitation.

(v) Parties in existence

There can be no cause of action if there are not in existence both a potential claimant and a potential defendant[82] and so, for example, if goods belonging to an intestate's estate are converted, time will not begin to run until letters of administration have been granted. Similarly, if the wrongdoer is entitled to diplomatic immunity at the time of the tort[83] there is at that time no defendant capable of being sued and time will not, therefore, begin to run until he ceases to be so entitled.[84] It does not matter, however, that the identity of the wrongdoer is unknown to the claimant if all the ingredients of the cause of action are in existence and so, where a car was stolen by a person or persons unknown, the claim in respect of that conversion was barred six years later, notwithstanding that the claimant never had any practical possibility of bringing proceedings against the thief.[85] The effect of a direction under Companies Act 1985 s.651(1) that the dissolution of a company was void is that the company is treated as continuing to exist, and thus accrual of a cause of action occurs at the time at which it would have happened had there been no dissolution.[86] **31-18**

2. New Claims in Pending Actions

A new claim made in the course of an existing action is deemed to be a separate action and to have been commenced, in the case of a CPR Pt 20 claim, on the date on which that claim was commenced, and in the case of any other new claim, on **31-19**

---

81 [1995] 2 A.C. 145. The more favourable accrual time was the very reason why the claimant sought to establish the tort of negligence in both *Henderson v Merrett Syndicates Ltd* and *Midland Bank Trust Co Ltd v Hett, Stubbs and Kemp* [1979] Ch. 384. Note that in *Midland Bank Trust Co Ltd v Hett Stubbs & Kemp*, Oliver J held that an omission to perform a contractual duty could constitute a "continuing breach of contract" up to the point at which it was no longer possible to perform the duty (a ruling that had the effect of extending the period for the accrual of the cause of action); cf. *Bell v Peter Browne & Co* [1990] 2 Q.B. 495 CA, where the Court of Appeal held that the defendant solicitors' failure to remedy an initial breach of contract did not give rise to a "continuing duty". The majority of the Court of Appeal in *Capita (Banstead 2011) Ltd v RFIB Group Ltd* [2015] EWCA Civ 1310; [2016] Q.B. 835, indicated that they preferred (and indeed, as a matter of precedent, were bound to apply) *Bell v Peter Browne & Co* on this point rather than *Midland Bank Trust Co Ltd v Hett, Stubbs and Kemp*. A contractual exclusion or limitation clause (including one limiting the time during which a claim can be brought) operates vis-à-vis the tort as well as the contractual claim: *William Hill Organisation v Bernard Sunley & Sons Ltd* (1983) 22 B.L.R. 1; *Southern Water Authority v Carey* [1985] 2 All E.R. 1077 at 1093–1094.

82 *Thomson v Lord Clanmorris* [1900] 1 Ch. 718 at 728, 729, per Vaughan Williams LJ.

83 See para.5-39.

84 *Musurus Bey v Gadban* [1894] 1 Q.B. 533. See also *Douglas v Forrest* (1828) 4 Bing. 686 at 704, per Best CJ. For the duration of diplomatic immunity, see para.5-40.

85 *RB Policies at Lloyd's v Butler* [1950] 1 K.B. 76; Goodman, "First Catch Your Defendant—Limitation and the Unknown Tortfeasor" (1966) 29 M.L.R. 366. See also *Clark v Forbes Stuart (Thames Street) Ltd (Intended Action)* [1964] 1 W.L.R. 836.

86 *Smith v White Knight Laundry Ltd* [2001] EWCA Civ 660; [2002] 1 W.L.R. 616. See now Companies Act 2006 ss.1024–1032.

the same date as the original claim.[87] A "new claim" is any claim by way of set-off or counter-claim,[88] any claim involving the addition or substitution of a new cause of action or a new party, and a claim made in or by way of a Pt 20 claim.[89] As a general rule, the court has no discretion to add or substitute a new party or a new cause of action in existing proceedings after the expiry of the relevant limitation period, since this would have the effect of depriving a defendant of an accrued limitation defence.[90]

31-20 Section 35 of the Limitation Act 1980, in combination with CPR rr.17.4 and 19.5, which deal with amendments to statements of case and the addition or substitution of new parties after the end of a relevant limitation period, respectively, allows for three exceptions to this rule:

- First, where the action is in respect of personal injuries or death and the court exercises its discretion under s.33 to disapply the three year limitation period specified by ss.11 or 12 in relation to the new party or the new cause of action.[91]
- Secondly, in the case of a claim involving a new party, if the relevant limitation period was current when the proceedings were started and the addition or substitution of the new party is necessary.[92] The addition or substitu-

---

87 Limitation Act 1980 s.35(1). This "relation back" theory has been criticised: see James (1987) 38 N.I.L.Q. 257. It has been rejected for some actions not governed by the Limitation Act 1980: *Ketteman v Hansel Properties* [1987] A.C. 189 HL (action commenced before operation of the 1980 Act); *Payabi v Armstel Shipping Corp* [1992] Q.B. 907 (contractual or substantive time limit, e.g. the Hague Rules time-limit).

88 At first sight, there appears to be an exception for "an original set-off or counterclaim" (defined as "a claim made by way of set-off or … by way of counterclaim by a party who has not previously made any claim in the action"): Limitation Act 1980 s.35(3). But it was controversially decided, as a matter of statutory interpretation, in *Al-Rawas v Hassan Khan and Co* [2017] EWCA Civ 42; [2017] 1 W.L.R. 2301 that this does not permit an original set-off or counterclaim to be brought where already time-barred at the time of the action. Rather an original set-off or counterclaim was regarded as being merely an exception to the restrictions on adding or substituting a new cause of action or party in s.35(5). For earlier cases, see *Lloyd's Bank v Wojcik, The Independent,* 19 January 1998 CA; and *Law Society v Wemyss* [2008] EWHC 2515 (Ch); [2009] 1 W.L.R. 2254 (in which it was held that although the counterclaim fell within s.35(3) of the Limitation Act 1980 as an original counterclaim, the amendment to the claim form needed to bring that counterclaim should be refused under CPR r.17.4(2)).

89 Limitation Act 1980 ss.35(2) and (1)(a). The Civil Procedure Rules replaced the term "third party proceedings" with "Part 20 claim". The old terminology is still used in the Limitation Act 1980; see s.35(2) for the definition.

90 Limitation Act 1980 s.35(3). If the limitation period has not expired at the date when the application to amend is heard the court has a wide discretion to allow the amendments: CPR r.19.2; *Welsh Development Agency v Redpath Dorman Long Ltd* [1994] 1 W.L.R. 1409, 1417 CA. The relevant date is when the court is considering the matter, not when the application for leave was made: *Welsh Development Agency v Redpath Dorman Long Ltd*; *Bajwa v Furini* [2004] EWCA Civ 412; [2004] 1 W.L.R. 1971. The 10-year long-stop period under the Consumer Protection Act 1987 is a "period of limitation" for the purposes of the rules: *Horne-Roberts v SmithKline Beecham Plc* [2001] EWCA Civ 2006; [2002] 1 W.L.R. 1662. For the ECJ's ruling on the need to apply s.35(3) in a way that is compatible with the 10-year long-stop dictated by the product liability directive, see *O'Byrne v Aventis Pasteur SA* C-358/08 [2010] 1 W.L.R. 1375; explained by the Supreme Court in *O'Byrne v Aventis Pasteur MSD Ltd* [2010] UKSC 23; [2010] 1 W.L.R. 1412.

91 Limitation Act 1980 s.35(3); CPR r.19.5(4). The s.33 application must be made before or at the same time as the application for leave to amend: *Welsh Development Agency v Redpath Dorman Long Ltd* [1994] 1 W.L.R. 1409 CA. See also *Howe v David Brown Tractors (Retail) Ltd (Rustons Engineering Co Ltd, Third Party)* [1991] 4 All E.R. 30.

92 Limitation Act 1980 s.35(5)(b); CPR r.19.5(2).

tion of a new party will be "necessary" only if the court is satisfied that: (a) the new party is to be substituted for a party who was named in the claim form in mistake for the new party; (b) the claim cannot properly be carried on by or against the original party unless the new party is added or substituted as claimant or defendant[93]; or (c) the original party has died or had a bankruptcy order made against him and his interest or liability has passed to the new party.[94]

- The third exception is where the claim involves the addition or substitution of a new cause of action,[95] if the new cause of action arises out of the same or substantially the same facts in respect of which the party applying for permission has already claimed a remedy in the proceedings.[96] The question of what constitutes "the same or substantially the same facts" has been said to be "substantially a matter of impression".[97] In deciding whether a

---

93 See, e.g. *Merrett v Babb* [2001] EWCA Civ 214; [2001] Q.B. 1174, where a claim was mistakenly brought by one co-owner of property against a valuer in respect of a negligent valuation for the whole of the financial loss attributable to the negligence. The other co-owner could be added as a claimant. But in *Roberts v Gill & Co* [2010] UKSC 22; [2011] 1 A.C. 240 the Supreme Court, in refusing the amendment sought, held that, although it was necessary to join the administrator for a representative action to carry on, the action that had been brought was in the claimant's personal capacity and there was no need to join the administrator for that action to carry on. See also, refusing the amendment sought, *Nemeti v Sabre Insurance Co Ltd* [2013] EWCA Civ 1555; [2014] P.I.Q.R. P12.

94 Limitation Act 1980 s.35(6); CPR r.19.5(3). CPR r.17.4(3) requires that the mistake as to the name of a party be genuine, but CPR r.19.5(3)(a) states simply that a new party may be substituted for a party who was named in the claim form by mistake. However, in *International Distillers and Vinters Ltd v JF Hillebrand (UK) Ltd, The Times,* 25 January 2000 QBD it was held that it would be unlikely for an application for substitution of a new party under CPR r.19.5(3)(a) to succeed unless the original mistake was genuine. For discussion of the meaning of a mistake as to name, see *Morgan Est (Scotland) Ltd v Hanson Concrete Products Ltd* [2005] EWCA Civ 134; [2005] 1 W.L.R. 2557. An amendment to alter the capacity in which a party claims may be permitted if the new capacity is one which that party had when the proceedings started or has since acquired: CPR r.17.4(4). Where, during the course of proceedings, the interests of the original claimant devolve upon another party this is unaffected by the limitation period. Leave can be given to amend the claim form and statement of case to substitute a party under what is now CPR r.19.2: *Yorkshire Regional HA v Fairclough Building* [1996] 1 W.L.R. 210 (substituting Bradford Hospitals National Health Service Trust for Yorkshire Regional Health Authority). A new party can be substituted after the end of the limitation period under the mistake exception even though the claimant was no longer mistaken when the limitation period expired: *O'Byrne v Aventis Pasteur MSD Ltd* [2007] EWCA Civ 966; [2008] 1 W.L.R. 1188; but reversed by the Supreme Court [2010] UKSC 23; [2010] 1 W.L.R. 1412. See also *Lockheed Martin Corp v Willis Group Ltd* [2010] EWCA Civ 927; [2010] P.N.L.R. 34; *Insight Group Ltd v Kingston Smith* [2012] EWHC 3644 (QB); [2014] 1 W.L.R. 1448.

95 A claim for a new remedy does not necessarily constitute a new cause of action: *Lloyd's Bank Plc v Rogers (No.2)* [1999] 3 E.G.L.R. 83 CA.

96 Limitation Act 1980 s.35(5)(a); CPR r.17.4(2). A statement of case can be amended after the expiry of the limitation period to add a new claim which is founded on the defendant's version of the facts rather than those in the claimant's existing claim: *Goode v Martin* [2001] EWCA Civ 1899; [2002] 1 W.L.R. 1828. See also *Charles Church Developments Ltd v Stent Foundations Ltd* [2006] EWHC 3158; [2007] 1 W.L.R. 1203 in which *Goode v Martin* was applied and extended to allow an amendment after the expiry of the limitation period to add a new claim against one defendant which was founded on a second defendant's version of the facts.

97 *Welsh Development Agency v Redpath Dorman Long Ltd* [1994] 1 W.L.R. 1409 at 1419 CA. In the case of a fatal accident, a claim on behalf of the deceased's dependants under the Fatal Accidents Act 1976 will usually arise out of the same facts or substantially the same facts as a claim on behalf of the estate under the Law Reform (Miscellaneous Provisions) Act 1934: *Booker v Associated British Ports* [1995] P.I.Q.R. P375 CA. On claims arising out "substantially the same facts" see also: *Dornan v JW Ellis & Co Ltd* [1962] 1 Q.B. 583, *Hay v London Brick Co Ltd* [1989] 2 Lloyd's Rep. 7; *Hancock Shipping Co Ltd v Kawasaki Heavy Industries Ltd (The Casper Trader)* [1992] 1 W.L.R.

proposed amendment amounts to a new cause of action, it is necessary to compare the pleading of the essential facts before and after the proposed amendment, leaving out the non-essential facts.[98]

Where the court has jurisdiction to permit an amendment after the relevant period of limitation has expired, it must still exercise a discretion as to whether to allow the amendment, taking into account the prejudice to the respective parties.[99]

3. PERSONS UNDER A DISABILITY[100]

31-21 A person is under a disability while he is an infant (i.e. he is under the age of 18) or lacks capacity (within the meaning of the Mental Capacity Act 2005) to conduct legal proceedings.[101] If a person to whom a right of action accrues is, at the date of the accrual, under a disability the action may be brought within six years[102] from when he ceases to be under the disability or dies, whichever event first occurs.[103] Thus, an infant has an indefeasible right to bring an action for personal injuries at any time before the age of 21[104]; and where a claimant is under a permanent disability there is effectively no limitation period.[105] To this rule there are, however, two provisos: (i) the rule does not apply where the right of action first accrued to some person (not under a disability) through whom the person under the disability claims[106]; (ii) where a right of action which has accrued to a person under a disability accrues to another person under a disability, no further extension of time is allowed by reason of the disability of the second person.[107] It was also said, obiter, in *Toropdar v D*[108] that a person could be granted a negative declaration that he was not liable to the injured party even though the limitation period had not, and would not, run out (because the injured party was under 18) and might never have run out (if he had suffered permanent brain damage). If the claimant had capacity when the action accrued, but subsequently lacks capacity this does not prevent time running.[109] Where a person lacked capacity when he acquired knowledge for the purposes of the latent damage limitation period laid down in s.14A(4)(b) of the

---

1025 CA; *Sion v Hampstead HA* [1994] 5 Med. L.R. 170. An allegation of fraud does not arise out of substantially the same facts as an allegation of negligence: *Paragon Finance Plc v DB Thakerar & Co* [1999] 1 All E.R. 400 CA. See also *Berezovsky v Abramovich* [2011] EWCA Civ 153; [2011] 1 W.L.R. 2290; *Bellinger v Mercer Ltd* [2014] EWCA Civ 996; [2014] 1 W.L.R. 3597.

98 *Savings and Investment Bank Ltd v Fincken* [2001] EWCA Civ 1639; *The Times,* 15 November 2001.

99 *Hancock Shipping Co Ltd v Kawasaki Heavy Industries Ltd (The Casper Trader)* [1992] 1 W.L.R. 1025 CA. The exercise of the discretion is subject to the overriding objective "to deal with cases justly and at proportionate cost": CPR r.1.1.

100 See, generally, Jones (1995) 15 C.J.Q. 258.

101 Limitation Act 1980 s.38(2) (as amended by the Mental Capacity Act 2005). For the previous law on "unsoundness of mind" see the 20th edn of this work at para.32-22.

102 For personal injury and death actions the period is three years: s.28(6); for claims for contribution the period is two years: s.28(5); for defamation actions the period is one year: s.28(4A). For actions under the Consumer Protection Act 1987 the period is three years, but the ten-year long-stop cannot be overridden: s.28(7); see para.31-83.

103 Limitation Act 1980 s.28(1).

104 *Tolley v Morris* [1979] 1 W.L.R. 592.

105 *Headford v Bristol and District HA* [1995] 6 Med. L.R. 1.

106 Limitation Act 1980 s.28(2). And see s.38(5).

107 Limitation Act 1980 s.28(3).

108 [2009] EWHC 567 (QB); [2010] Lloyd's Rep. I.R. 358. For criticism of this reasoning, see Patten, "When is a Limitation Period not a Limitation Period?" [2010] C.J.Q. 284.

109 *Purnell v Roche* [1927] 2 Ch. 142. In a personal injuries action this rule can be mitigated by the exercise of the court's discretion: Limitation Act 1980 s.33(3)(d) (see para.31-64); see also *Kirby v*

Limitation Act 1980, but did not lack capacity when the cause of action accrued, an action may be brought within three years from when he ceased to lack capacity or died (whichever first occurred).[110]

4. FRAUD, MISTAKE AND DELIBERATE CONCEALMENT

Fraud or deliberate concealment of relevant facts by the defendant has the effect of postponing the commencement of the limitation period. Section 32 of the Limitation Act 1980,[111] is a re-draft of s.26 of the Limitation Act 1939, designed not to change the existing law, but to bring the statute more obviously into line with the interpretation which the courts had put upon it.[112] Section 32(1) now provides: 31-22

"... where in the case of any action for which a period of limitation is prescribed by this Act, either—

(a) the action is based upon the fraud of the defendant; or
(b) any fact relevant to the plaintiff's right of action has been deliberately concealed from him by the defendant; or
(c) the action is for the relief from the consequences of a mistake;

the period of limitation shall not begin to run until the plaintiff has discovered the fraud, concealment or mistake (as the case may be) or could with reasonable diligence have discovered it."

There is no difficulty about the case where the action is based upon the defendant's fraud.[113] Actions for relief from the consequence of a mistake fall outside the scope of this work.[114] The words "any fact relevant to the plaintiff's right of action has been deliberately concealed from him by the defendant" require further comment.

Deliberate concealment Deliberate concealment of facts relevant to the claimant's right of action[115] is enough to bring s.32(1)(b) into operation. There is no need for any extra element of moral turpitude beyond what is inherent in deliber- 31-23

Leather [1965] 2 Q.B. 367: where the tort causes immediate lack of capacity, time does not run.

110 Limitation Act 1980 s.28A(1); but the 15-year long-stop cannot be overridden: s.28A(2). See para.31-71 onwards.

111 As amended by the Latent Damage Act 1986 s.2(2), which adds s.32(5)—see para.31-77—and by the Consumer Protection Act 1987 which adds s.32(4A)—see para.31-83. As to trustees, see s.21 of the Limitation Act 1980; *Thorne v Heard* [1895] A.C. 495. A defendant may be estopped from relying on limitation even where he is not guilty of concealed fraud: *Kaliszewska v John Clague and Partners* [1984] C.I.L.L. 131. For the old common law doctrine of concealed fraud, see 15th edn of this work, para.9-44.

112 Law Reform Committee, *Twenty-First Report: limitation of actions* (1977), Cmnd.6923, Pt II.

113 For consideration of when a claimant first has knowledge of a fraud for the purposes of s.32(1)(a), see *Barnstaple Boat Co Ltd v Jones* [2007] EWCA Civ 727; [2008] 1 All E.R. 1124.

114 See, e.g. *Kleinwort Benson Ltd v Lincoln City Council* [1999] 2 A.C. 349 HL; *Deutsche Morgan Grenfell Group Plc v IRC* [2006] UKHL 49; [2007] 1 A.C. 558. In *The Test Claimants in the Franked Investment Group Litigation v Revenue and Customs Commissioners* [2012] UKSC 19; [2012] 2 A.C. 337 it was authoritatively confirmed that s.32(1)(c) applies only where mistake is an essential element of the cause of action (as, most obviously, where the claim is for restitution for unjust enrichment based on a mistake of fact or law).

115 In *Johnson v Chief Constable of Surrey*, *The Times*, 23 November 1992 CA, it was held that to be relevant to the claimant's right of action, the fact must be a fact without which the cause of action is incomplete: s.32(1)(b) is not concerned with facts which may merely improve the substantive or evidential strength of the claim. See also *Lowsley v Forbes* [1999] 1 A.C. 329 at 343, where Lord Lloyd doubted whether the defendant's concealment of himself or his assets would be the concealment of a fact relevant to a right of action. In *Williams v Lishman Sidwell Campbell & Price Ltd*

ate concealment.[116] This is underlined by s.32(2): "For the purpose of subsection (1) above, deliberate commission of a breach of duty in circumstances in which it is unlikely to be discovered for some time amounts to deliberate concealment of the facts involved in that breach of duty." This preserves and confirms the case law on s.26 of the Limitation Act 1939, according to which the start of the limitation period is postponed whenever the defendant has committed the wrong, knowingly or recklessly,[117] in circumstances such as to prevent the claimant coming to know of his cause of action.[118] For example, in *Beaman v ARTS Ltd*[119] the claimant, in 1935, before going abroad deposited certain packages with the defendants for storage. She was prevented by the war from returning home, and in August 1940, the defendants, without informing the claimant, examined the packages and, having formed the view that the contents were worthless, gave them to the Salvation Army. During 1946 the claimant returned to England and in November 1946, having discovered what had happened, she commenced proceedings against the defendants for conversion. It was held that the defendants' conduct amounted to fraudulent concealment within s.26(b) of the 1939 Act and therefore that the period of limitation was postponed. On the other hand in *Kitchen v Royal Air Force Association*[120] the failure of solicitors to inform the claimant of her possible claim under the Fatal Accidents Act did not of itself constitute fraudulent concealment within the same provision, but their concealment of an offer by the potential defendants to pay £100 in respect of her husband's death—an offer which they hushed up lest she asked them to press for more, and so forced them to disclose their negligence in failing to issue proceedings within the limitation period—did amount to such fraudulent concealment. Accordingly, the period of limitation in respect of their own negligence was postponed.

31-24 In *Brocklesby v Armitage and Guest*[121] the Court of Appeal controversially held that, for the purposes of s.32(1)(b), it was sufficient that the defendant solicitors had acted deliberately in committing the breach of duty in circumstances in which it was unlikely to be discovered for some time, even though they did not know that, as a matter of law, they were committing a breach and so could have no intention of concealing it. But in *Cave v Robinson Jarvis & Rolf*[122] the House of Lords disap-

---

[2010] EWCA Civ 418; [2010] P.N.L.R. 25 it was suggested, obiter, that where there are subsequent causes of action for professional negligence concealment of facts relevant to the first cause of action can carry on through to constitute concealment of facts in relation to the second cause of action.

116 *Beaman v ARTS Ltd* [1949] 1 K.B. 550 at 567, per Somervell LJ.

117 Negligence is not enough: *King v Victor Parsons & Co* [1973] 1 W.L.R. 29.

118 *Kitchen v Royal Air Force Association* [1958] 1 W.L.R. 563; *Clark v Woor* [1965] 1 W.L.R. 650; *Applegate v Moss* [1971] 1 Q.B. 406; *King v Victor Parsons & Co* [1973] 1 W.L.R. 29; *Lewisham London Borough v Leslie & Co Ltd* (1978) 250 E.G. 1289; *William Hill Organisation v Bernard Sunley & Sons Ltd* (1983) 22 B.L.R. 1; *Costa v Georghiou* (1984) 134 N.L.J. 82. For cases on s.32(1)(b) itself, see *Westlake v Bracknell DC* (1987) 19 H.L.R. 375; *Gray v TP Bennett & Son* (1984) 43 Build. L.R. 63; *Skerratt v Linfax Ltd* [2003] EWCA Civ 695; [2004] P.I.Q.R. P10, per Waller LJ at [20]: "it is difficult to conceive of a case of concealment unless that concealment takes place either at the very time that the cause of action is accruing, or unless it takes place after the cause of action was accrued" (defendant requiring claimant to sign a disclaimer before permitting claimant to ride on a go-kart track did not amount to deliberate concealment); *AIC Ltd v ITS Testing Services (UK) Ltd* [2006] EWCA Civ 1601; [2007] 1 All E.R. (Comm) 667; [2007] 1 Lloyd's Rep. 555.

119 [1949] 1 K.B. 550.

120 [1958] 1 W.L.R. 563.

121 [2002] 1 W.L.R. 598 CA.

122 [2002] UKHL 18; [2003] 1 A.C. 384.

proved that interpretation and held that s.32(1)(b) and 32(2) operate only where the defendant knew he was committing, or intended to commit, a breach of duty; inadvertent want of care is insufficient. Lord Millett commented that the effect of *Brocklesby* was to deprive a professional person, charged with having given negligent advice, of any effective limitation defence. Concealment and non-disclosure, though different concepts, both require knowledge of the fact which is to be kept secret, and: "A man cannot sensibly be said either to conceal or to fail to disclose something of which he is ignorant."[123] Accordingly, his Lordship concluded that:

> "section 32 deprives a defendant of a limitation defence in two situations: (i) where he takes active steps to conceal his own breach of duty after he has become aware of it; and (ii) where he is guilty of deliberate wrongdoing and conceals or fails to disclose it in circumstances where it is unlikely to be discovered for some time. But it does not deprive a defendant of a limitation defence where he is charged with negligence if, being unaware of his error or that he has failed to take proper care, there has been nothing for him to disclose."[124]

The Court of Appeal applied *Cave v Robinson Jarvis & Rolf* in *Williams v Fanshaw Porter & Hazelhurst*.[125] A trainee legal executive, B, acting for the claimant, agreed to a consent order whereby a doctor, against whom the claimant had issued proceedings, ceased to be a party to the action. A subsequent application to rejoin the doctor was dismissed. B did not inform the claimant of either the consent order or the failed attempt to rejoin the doctor because he was embarrassed by the mistake. The Court of Appeal held that this fell within s.32(1)(b). By taking a conscious decision not to inform the claimant about the consent order, B deliberately concealed facts relevant to the claimant's right of action against the solicitors. It was irrelevant that B's motive for concealing the facts was to avoid embarrassment and not to conceal from the claimant the possibility that she might have a claim in negligence against the solicitors: "What is relevant to s.32(1)(b) is the fact of concealment, not the reason or motive for it."[126] Moreover, where a defendant has deliberately concealed a fact realising that it was relevant (or reckless as to whether or not it was relevant) to an actual or a potential claim against him, the fact that the defendant believed that any potential claim against him would, if pursued, fail, does not prevent his conduct from falling with s.32(1)(b).[127] 31-25

Fraud or deliberate concealment by defendant's agent Like its predecessor, s.32 expressly makes the defendant responsible for the fraud or concealment of his agent.[128] The term "agent" appears in this context to include an independent 31-26

---

[123] [2002] UKHL 18; [2003] 1 A.C. 384 at [21].

[124] [2002] UKHL 18; [2003] 1 A.C. 384 at [25]. *Cave* was applied in *Kimathi v Foreign and Commonwealth Office* [2018] EWHC 1169 (QB), where it was also held that where the claimant had knowledge of sufficient facts to establish their action, the concealment of additional information did not defeat the limitation defence. The claimant's argument that additional facts may increase the strength of the claims was rejected as irrelevant.

[125] [2004] EWCA Civ 157; [2004] 1 W.L.R. 3185.

[126] [2004] EWCA Civ 157; [2004] 1 W.L.R. 3185 at [16], per Park J.

[127] [2004] EWCA Civ 157; [2004] 1 W.L.R. 3185 at [38], per Mance LJ. See further, at [35]–[39], the discussion by Mance LJ of the two possible interpretations of the mental element required under s.32(1)(b).

[128] See the final paragraph of s.32(1).

contractor. Thus in *Applegate v Moss*[129] a developer engaged a builder to erect a house, which the developer then sold in the course of erection to the claimant. The developer was held to be guilty of concealed fraud through the conduct of the builder in knowingly building on inadequate foundations, whether or not he had instructed the builder to skimp his work. This section also taints the defendant with the concealed fraud or concealment of any person through whom he claims, and that person's agent. Thus in *Eddis v Chichester Constable*[130] the facts assumed for the purpose of a preliminary issue were that the tenant for life of a picture, which was an heirloom and the property of the claimant trustees, had sold the picture to the defendants,[131] through their agent, in 1951. In so doing he had acted in fraud of the claimants and the defendants' agent knew this. Subsequently the defendants sold the picture to an American art gallery and in 1963, after the death of the tenant for life, the claimants discovered the loss of the picture and sued the defendants for conversion. The Court of Appeal held that the tenant for life was a person through whom the defendants claimed, and thus that what is now s.32(1)(b) applied, that the defendants could not rely on what is now ss.32(3) and 32(4)[132] because their agent knew of the fraud and, thirdly, that what is now s.32(1)(b) operated so as not only to allow a claimant to bring his action more than six years after the accrual of the cause of action but also so as to prevent the extinction of the title of the original owner.[133] The defence of limitation therefore failed.

31-27 **Knowledge of claimant's agent** Under s.32 time runs against the claimant from when he discovered the fraud, concealment or mistake or could with reasonable diligence have discovered it. One question that this raises is whether the claimant is bound by what his agent has or should have discovered. While in some building cases it was taken for granted that the claimants were bound by what their architects should have discovered,[134] in *Peco Arts Inc v Hazlitt Gallery*[135] Webster J held that as a matter of construction the acts or omissions of an agent of a *claimant* are not

[129] [1971] 1 Q.B. 406. See also *Clark v Woor* [1965] 1 W.L.R. 650; *King v Victor Parsons & Co* [1973] 1 W.L.R. 29; *Lewisham London Borough v Leslie & Co Ltd* (1978) 250 E.G. 1289 (all contract cases).

[130] [1969] 2 Ch. 345.

[131] The first defendant, executrix of the tenant for life, was not concerned in the proceedings on the preliminary issue. The remaining defendants were art dealers.

[132] By s.32(3): "Nothing in this section shall enable any action (a) to recover, or recover the value of, any property; or (b) to enforce any charge against, or set aside any transaction affecting, any property; to be brought against the purchaser of the property or any person claiming through him in any case where the property has been purchased for valuable consideration by an innocent third party since the fraud or concealment or (as the case may be) the transaction in which the mistake was made took place". By s.32(4), "a purchaser is an innocent third party for the purposes of this section (a) in the case of fraud or concealment of any fact relevant to the [claimant's] right of action, if he was not a party to the fraud or (as the case may be) to the concealment of that fact and did not at the time of the purchase know or have reason to believe that the fraud or concealment had taken place; and (b) in the case of mistake, if he did not at the time of the purchase know or have reason to believe that the mistake had been made."

[133] Thus, s.32 appears to control the operation of s.3(2) as well as of s.3(1).

[134] *Lewisham London Borough v Leslie & Co Ltd* (1979) 250 E.G. 1289; *William Hill Organisation v Bernard Sunley & Sons Ltd* (1983) 22 B.L.R. 1 (both were essentially contract cases).

[135] [1983] 1 W.L.R. 1315. The defendant had sold the claimant a picture which was allegedly by Ingres but was really a worthless reproduction. Sometime after the purchase, the claimant had it valued by Sotheby's for insurance purposes and they failed to notice that it was a reproduction. It was held that Sotheby's negligence (if any) was not to be attributed to the claimant for the purposes of s.32.

to be attributed to the claimant for these purposes. Section 32(1) expressly says: "References in this subsection to the defendant include references to the defendant's agent ..." and *expressio unius, exclusio alterius*.

Effect of concealment after accrual of the action In *Sheldon v RHM Outhwaite (Underwriting Agencies) Ltd*[136] a majority of the House of Lords decided that s.32(1) applies to deliberate concealment even where that concealment takes place after the limitation period has started to run. That is, deliberate concealment has the effect of starting the period of limitation running again from the date on which the concealment has, or could reasonably have, been discovered. 31-28

5. Extinction of Title on Conversion and Detinue

Until 1939 the rule that the expiry of the limitation period does not extinguish the right but merely bars the remedy applied to conversion and detinue as to other torts with the result that, although the owner of a chattel who had been wrongfully deprived of it might not be able to sue for its return or for damages for its conversion, he did not thereby lose his title to it. If, therefore, he could recover possession of the chattel otherwise than by action he was entitled to do so and, moreover, any fresh wrongful act in relation to the chattel by a third person gave the owner a new cause of action against him for which time ran afresh.[137] In *Spackman v Foster*[138] certain deeds belonging to the claimants were fraudulently taken from them by a third party in 1859 and deposited by him with the defendant, who held them, bona fide and without knowledge of the fraud, as security for a loan. The claimants did not discover their loss until 1882, when they demanded the return of the deeds from the defendant, and on his refusal to give them up they brought their action. Their claim for the return of their deeds succeeded. Their title to them was unaffected by the original conversion by the third party, and, so far as their claim against the defendant was concerned, time only ran from the date of his refusal to deliver up the deeds, he having committed no wrongful act in relation to them until that date. 31-29

The law on this matter was altered in 1939 by what is now s.3 of the Limitation Act 1980, which made two main changes from the previous position: 31-30

> "(1) Where any cause of action in respect of the conversion of a chattel has accrued to any person and, before he recovers possession of the chattel, a further conversion takes place, no action shall be brought in respect of the further conversion after the expiration of six years from the accrual of the cause of action in respect of the original conversion.
>
> (2) Where any such cause of action has accrued to any person and the period prescribed for bringing that action has expired and he has not during that period recovered possession of the chattel, the title of that person to the chattel shall be extinguished."

First, therefore the rule that time runs afresh from a second or subsequent wrongful act was abrogated, and the period of limitation for all causes of action arising in relation to the chattel was made six years from the first conversion or wrongful

136 [1996] A.C. 102.

137 *Miller v Dell* [1891] 1 Q.B. 468. See also *Wilkinson v Verity* (1871) L.R. 6 C. & P. 206.

138 (1883) 11 Q.B.D. 99. cf. *M'Combie v Davies* (1805) 6 East 538.

detention unless, of course, the owner has recovered possession in the meantime.[139] Secondly, once the period of limitation in respect of the first wrongful act had expired and if the owner had not recovered possession, his title to the chattel was extinguished.[140] If, therefore, facts similar to those in *Spackman v Foster* were to arise after 1939, the decision would be different. There had been a conversion of the deeds by the third party in 1859, and six years thereafter the claimants would have lost the opportunity of bringing proceedings in respect of that or any subsequent wrongful act in relation to the deeds. Furthermore, the expiry of six years from the original conversion would have extinguished the claimants' title to the deeds with the result that the defendant's refusal to give them up would not have been wrongful.

31-31 This simple solution applied even if the original conversion amounted to theft: after six years, the thief could no longer be sued (subject to s.32 about concealed fraud[141]); and the thief also acquired title to the stolen goods. This was thought to be undesirable,[142] and what is now the Limitation Act 1980 s.4,[143] was passed to put the thief outside the benefit of s.3:

> "(1) The right of any person from whom a chattel is stolen to bring an action in respect of the theft shall not be subject to the time limits under sections 2 and 3(1) of this Act, but if his title to the chattel is extinguished under section 3(2) of this Act he may not bring an action in respect of a theft preceding the loss of his title, unless the theft in question preceded the conversion from which time began to run for the purposes of section 3(2).
>
> (2) Subsection (1) above shall apply to any conversion related to the theft of a chattel as it applies to the theft of a chattel; and, except as provided below, every conversion following the theft of a chattel before the person from whom it is stolen recovers possession of it shall be regarded for the purposes of this section as related to the theft.[144]
>
> If anyone purchases the stolen chattel in good faith neither the purchase nor any conversion following it shall be regarded as related to the theft.
>
> (3) Any cause of action accruing in respect of the theft or any conversion related to the theft of a chattel to any person from whom the chattel is stolen shall be disregarded for the purpose of applying section 3(1) or (2) of this Act to his case."

31-32 These complex provisions can probably[145] be summarised as follows:

(1) The owner of stolen property can sue the original thief, anyone who re-

---

139 s.3(1).

140 s.3(2); *Beaman v ARTS Ltd* [1949] 1 K.B. 550 at 557, per Lord Greene MR; *Eddis v Chichester Constable* [1969] 2 Ch. 345 at 360–361, per Winn LJ. It is respectfully submitted that the suggestion implicit in the judgment of Winn LJ that the original owner's title is not extinguished until after a second conversion or wrongful detention has occurred should not be followed. All that s.3(2) requires is that the time within which an action for any such second or subsequent wrongful act must be brought shall have expired and that occurs, by s.3(1), six years after the first such wrongful act, whether any further wrongful act actually occurs or not.

141 See para.31-22.

142 Law Reform Committee, *Twenty-First Report: limitation of actions* (1977), Cmnd.6923, Pt III.

143 Enacted by the Limitation (Amendment) Act 1980. By s.4(5) of the Limitation Act 1980 "theft" includes obtaining a chattel by deception or blackmail.

144 By s.4(4), where in an action for conversion it is proved that the chattel was stolen from the claimant or anyone through whom he claims, it is presumed that any subsequent conversion is related to the theft unless the contrary is shown. The definition of theft in the Theft Act 1968 is wide enough to ensure that many such conversions amount to further thefts from the original owner.

145 The difficulty and uncertainty of these provisions has attracted unfavourable comment: see the commentary to the Limitation (Amendment) Act 1980 in *Current Law Statutes*. One wonders if any

steals them, and (subject to (3) below) anyone who, following a theft, commits a further conversion of the property not amounting to a theft, although the limitation period has elapsed.

(2) The owner of stolen property does not lose his title to it after the passage of six years from the theft.

(3) However, there is an exception where a chattel once stolen is converted by someone buying it in good faith. For claims against him, the limitation period runs for six years from his purchase.[146] In such a case the owner's title becomes barred six years after the purchase. And when this has happened, the owner loses the right to sue for any theft or theft-related conversion which occurred after the purchase—although he may still sue for a theft or theft-related conversion which took place before it.

It should be noticed that s.4 appears to give considerable protection to the person from whom a chattel is originally stolen, but less to the person who loses property by a conversion not amounting to a theft, which is thereafter stolen.[147]

6. LIMITATION AND DISMISSAL FOR WANT OF PROSECUTION

Limitation periods encourage claimants to bring proceedings promptly and penalise delay prior to the commencement of the action, but they cannot address the problem of delay after proceedings have been issued. Before the introduction of the Civil Procedure Rules, the courts had limited power to deal with the problem of delay by the parties after the commencement of proceedings. One option available to the court was to strike out an action, on the application of the defendant, for want of prosecution. However, it was held by the House of Lords in *Birkett v James*[148] that, in the absence of intentional and contumelious delay, such as disobedience to a peremptory order of the court, the dismissal of an action for want of prosecution before the expiry of the limitation period applicable to the cause of action would only be justified in the most exceptional circumstances, since the claimant could simply issue fresh proceedings within the time allowed by Parliament. This rule could produce patent injustice to defendants where claimants with the benefit of long limitation periods could effectively delay proceedings for years.[149] **31-33**

The position has changed significantly since the introduction of the Civil **31-34**

---

injustice formerly arising from s.3 of the Limitation Act could ever have been worth such a complicated measure to put it right. See generally *City of Gotha v Sotheby's (No.2)*, *The Times*, 8 October 1998; Law Commission Consultation Paper No.151, paras 3.108–3.115, 13.44–13.70.

146 Proviso to s.4(2).

147 If X steals C's bicycle and keeps it, C can sue X forever; if X subsequently gives it away to Y, C can sue Y forever; and, unless and until someone buys it in good faith, C will never even begin to lose his title by prescription. However, if Z, the bursar of a college, gives away C's bicycle at the end of term to X because he thinks that C has abandoned it, it seems that ss.3(1) and 3(2) start to operate from Z's conversion. If, therefore, Y steals the bicycle from X more than six years later, C has lost his title and cannot sue Y in conversion, as well as being statute-barred in his claims against Z and X. And if Y steals the bicycle from X within six years, this will under the Theft Act be a theft from C as well as from X, and C will be able to sue Y in respect of the conversion forever (Limitation Act 1980 s.4(3)); but C will nevertheless lose his title to the bicycle after six years from Z's conversion because s.3(2) will continue to operate despite any subsequent thefts.

148 [1978] A.C. 297. See also *Department of Transport v Chris Smaller (Transport) Ltd* [1989] A.C. 1197; *James Lazenby & Co v McNicholas Construction Co Ltd* [1995] 1 W.L.R. 615.

149 As, e.g. in *Tolley v Morris* [1979] 1 W.L.R. 592 where proceedings were issued in 1967 but no further steps were taken until 1977. As an infant at the time of the accident, the claimant's limitation period

Procedure Rules. In *Biguzzi v Rank Leisure Plc*[150] (an appeal on an application to strike out a statement of case in relation to a personal injury claim for want of prosecution), the Court of Appeal considered the relevance of decisions given before the coming into force of the Civil Procedure Rules. Lord Woolf MR approved the view of the trial judge that decisions under the old procedure are not binding—or even persuasive—authority in relation to the Civil Procedure Rules: "earlier authorities are no longer generally of any relevance once the Civil Procedure Rules apply."[151] In exercising its powers under the Civil Procedure Rules the court has to ensure that a just result is achieved.[152] CPR r.3.4(2)(b) gives the court the power to strike out a statement of case if it is an abuse of the court's process or is otherwise likely to obstruct the just disposal of the proceedings and r.3.4(2)(c) confers the same power where there has been a failure to comply with a rule, practice direction or court order.[153] This confers a wide discretion on the court and does not require proof of prejudice to either of the parties.[154] Prejudice to the defendant is still relevant as part of a general inquiry as to what is just, but there is no longer any need to seek out prejudice or ascribe it to a particular period or particular periods of delay.[155] This does not mean that the issues that were previously relevant to the question of striking out a claim for want of prosecution are no longer relevant, but simply that the technicalities that surrounded the application of some the principles are no longer relevant.[156]

31-35 In *Purefuture Ltd v Simmons & Simmons*[157] Clarke LJ identified the following propositions as relevant to an application to strike out for want of prosecution: (1) whether it would be fair or just to allow the action to go to trial. In deciding this question the court must consider its alternative powers so that a decision may, but need not necessarily be, the same as would have obtained under the old rules; (2) prejudice remains relevant to the issue of what is just; (3) in many cases there will be alternatives that will allow the case to be dealt with justly without taking the draconian step of striking out; (4) in coming to its decision the court should consider: (a) the overriding objective in Pt 1 of the CPR; (b) the flexibility to deal with this type of claim given by the court's case management powers; (c) the rules which allow striking out (in an appropriate case) are to be interpreted in accordance with the overriding objective; and (d) no single one of the available range of powers is inherently more appropriate than any other, so that the court should

---

in respect of personal injuries did not expire until three years after her 18th birthday (when she ceased to be under a disability—see para.31-21), and so the action could not be struck out for mere inactivity on the claimant's part until 1982.

150 [1999] 1 W.L.R. 1926 CA; *Clark v University of Lincolnshire and Humberside* [2000] 1 W.L.R. 1988 CA.

151 [1999] 1 W.L.R. 1926 at 1934, Lord Woolf noted that before April 1999 the ability of the courts to control delay had been unduly restricted by decisions such as *Birkett v James*.

152 In line with the overriding objective, which is that the court should deal with cases justly: CPR r.1.1.

153 CPR r.3.1(2)(m) also provides that the court may take any other step or make any other order for the purpose of managing the case and furthering the overriding objective.

154 *Axa Insurance Co Ltd v Swire Fraser Ltd* [2001] C.P. Rep. 17; *The Times*, 29 January 2000 CA at [20], per Tuckey LJ.

155 *Axa Insurance Co Ltd v Swire Fraser Ltd* [2001] C.P. Rep. 17; *The Times*, 29 January 2000 CA at [19]. *Biguzzi* was not authority for treating delay or the failure to comply with the rules more leniently than under the old rules. Rather, the new rules permitted the courts to adopt a more flexible approach.

156 *Nasser v The United Bank of Kuwait* [2001] EWCA Civ 1454 at [27], per Sir Christopher Slade.

157 [2001] C.P. Rep. 30 at [54]–[57] CA.

consider all its relevant powers; (5) whether the prejudice is so serious that it would be unjust to the defendant to require the case to be tried.[158]

7. Actions for Personal Injuries and Death[159]

(a) General

In 1954 the period of limitation was reduced from six to three years "in the case of actions for damages for negligence, nuisance or breach of duty (whether the duty exists by virtue of a contract or of a provision made by or under a statute or independently of any contract or any such provision) where the damages claimed by the plaintiff for the negligence, nuisance or breach of duty consist of or include damages in respect of personal injuries to the plaintiff or any other person".[160] The provision is now contained in s.11(1) of the Limitation Act 1980. "Personal injuries" includes any disease or impairment of a person's physical or mental condition.[161] A mother's wrongful birth claim is, in relation to her pregnancy and childbirth, a claim in respect of personal injuries.[162] And, although the financial costs of bringing up a disabled child have been characterised as purely economic loss,[163] it has been held that since the mother's claim was clearly a claim for personal injuries, 31-36

158 See also *Annodeus Ltd v Gibson*, *The Times*, 3 March 2000 Ch. D., where Neuberger J identified a number of factors relevant to the determination of a strike out for want of prosecution. However, in *Audergon v La Baguette Ltd* [2002] EWCA Civ 10; [2002] C.P. Rep. 27 at [107], Jonathan Parker LJ commented that: "I do respectfully doubt the value of adopting a judicially-created checklist which does not appear in the rule itself. Inherent in such an approach ... is the danger that a body of satellite authority may be built up, rather as it was under the old rules in relation to the dismissal of an action for want of prosecution, leading in effect to the rewriting of the relevant rule through the medium of judicial decision."

159 See generally Jones, *Limitation Periods in Personal Injury Actions* (1995); Davies (1982) 98 L.Q.R. 249; Morgan (1982) 1 C.J.Q. 109; James (1998) Med. L. Rev. 62. For personal injury and death claims governed by the Merchant Shipping Act 1995, see para.31-78, by the Carriage by Air Act 1961, see para.31-80, by the Railways (Convention on International Carriage by Rail) Regulations 2005, see para.31-81, by the Consumer Protection Act 1987, see para.31-83, and by the Automated and Electric Vehicles Act 2018, see para.31-87.

160 Law Reform (Limitation of Actions etc) Act 1954 s.2(1).

161 Limitation Act 1980 s.38(1). See para.27-56 fn.286. A claim against an insurance broker is not a claim for damages in respect of personal injuries even though the claim arises out of the fact that the claimant has suffered such injuries; *Ackbar v Green & Co Ltd* [1975] Q.B. 582. Cf. *Howe v David Brown Tractors (Retail) Ltd* [1991] 4 All E.R. 30 CA; *Burns v Shuttlehurst Ltd* [1999] 1 W.L.R. 1449 CA. See also *Bennett v Greenland Houchen & Co* [1998] P.N.L.R. 458 CA (a claim for solicitors' negligence, which included a claim for damages for distress and depression, fell within s.11—and was therefore time-barred—as being a claim which included damages in respect of personal injuries); *Oates v Harte Reade & Co (A Firm)* [1999] P.I.Q.R. P120 QBD (claim for financial loss arising from solicitor's negligence in the handling of matrimonial ancillary relief proceedings which included a claim for "anxiety and stress" subject to the three-year limitation period); cf. *Pounds v Eckford Rands (A Firm)* [2003] Lloyd's Rep. P.N. 195 (QBD) (claimant entitled to amend a claim in respect of solicitors' alleged negligence in handling her ancillary relief proceedings by deleting all reference to her claim for personal injury, because the defendants had not previously raised the limitation defence and the vast bulk of the claim was for economic loss, not personal injury). See also *Norman v Aziz* [2000] P.I.Q.R. P72 CA (claim against the owner of a motor vehicle for permitting a driver to use the vehicle without insurance falls within s.11 rather than s.2).

162 *Walkin v South Manchester HA* [1995] 1 W.L.R. 1543. See also *Das v Ganju* [1999] P.I.Q.R. P260 CA. See generally on damages for wrongful birth, paras 27-60 to 27-66.

163 *Greenfield v Irwin* [2001] EWCA Civ 113; [2001] 1 W.L.R. 1279. In *McFarlane v Tayside Health Board* [2000] 2 A.C. 59 the House of Lords held that the financial cost of bringing up a healthy child following negligent advice about, or the negligent performance of, a sterilisation operation are not recoverable, but in *Parkinson v St James and Seacroft University Hospital NHS Trust* [2001] EWCA

the claim in respect of the childrearing costs constituted an action for damages "consisting of or including damages in respect of personal injuries" which was a different question from whether the claim for the cost of raising a disabled child was pure or consequential economic loss.[164] Dyslexia constitutes a "personal injury" where a claim is brought against an education authority for negligent failure to diagnose dyslexia and hence to improve a dyslexic's ability to read and write: although the defendant does not cause the dyslexia, failure to improve the ability to read and write is analogous to a failure to treat a physical injury which a defendant does not itself cause.[165]

31-37 The reduction of the period to three years increased the possibility that the claimant's cause of action would be statute-barred before he knew of its existence—particularly where he suffered an injury which appeared slight, but had progressively worsening consequences.[166] Accordingly, two attempts have been made by Parliament to avoid the claimant suffering prejudice in this way. The first was the Limitation Act 1963,[167] which introduced the possibility of the limitation period being extended. An injured person could apply for the leave of the court to bring his action outside the normal three-year limitation period if he had been ignorant of certain facts relating to his cause of action for all or most of that period. Then, if leave was granted, and the claimant also proved at the trial that a number of conditions were fulfilled, the expiry of the three-year limitation period afforded no defence to the action. Unfortunately, the provisions of the Limitation Act 1963 were over-complicated and worked extremely badly.[168] Thus they were repealed and replaced by the Limitation Act 1975,[169] the provisions of which now form part of the Limitation Act 1980. (Hereafter, references will be to the 1980 Act.)

31-38 In outline, the present scheme is as follows. In cases involving personal injuries, the limitation period is three years, but time begins to run *either* from when the cause of action accrues, *or* from the date of the claimant's "knowledge", whichever is the later. Where the three-year limitation period has expired, the court has a wide discretionary power to override a time-limit in a personal injury case, and to allow an action to proceed notwithstanding. (The Act creates the word "disapply" to describe this process.)[170] The question whether an action is time-barred can be separated out by the court, in the exercise of its general duty to manage cases, as a

Civ 530; [2002] Q.B. 266 the Court of Appeal held that this did not preclude a claim for the additional costs of raising a disabled child (the status of *Parkinson* is unclear after the ruling of the House of Lords in *Rees v Darlington Memorial Hospital* [2003] UKHL 52; [2004] 1 A.C. 309; paras 7-99, 27-60 to 27-66).

164 *Godfrey v Gloucestershire Royal Infirmary NHS Trust* [2003] EWHC 549 (QB); [2003] Lloyd's Rep. Med. 398 at [35], per Leveson J, applying *Walkin v South Manchester HA* [1995] 1 W.L.R. 1543. Thus, s.11 of the Act applied.

165 *Adams v Bracknell Forest BC* [2004] UKHL 29; [2005] 1 A.C. 76.

166 As in *Cartledge v E Jopling & Sons Ltd* [1963] A.C. 758; para.31-10.

167 For detailed examination, see 14th edn of this work, paras 622–626.

168 In *Central Asbestos Co Ltd v Dodd* [1973] A.C. 518 at 529, Lord Reid said the Limitation Act 1963 had "a strong claim to the distinction of being the worst drafted Act on the statute book".

169 Enacting recommendations of the Law Reform Committee, *Twentieth Report (Interim Report on Limitation of Actions: In Personal Injury Claims)* (1974), Cmnd.5630. Neither the 1963 nor 1975 Limitation Acts had retrospective effect prior to 1954 and hence an action that was time-barred before 1954 remains so: *Arnold v Central Electricity Generating Board* [1988] A.C. 228 HL. See also *McDonnell v Congregation of Christian Brothers Trustees* [2003] UKHL 63; [2004] 1 A.C. 1101.

170 Limitation Act 1980 s.33(2).

preliminary issue[171]; or can be raised by the defendant before the trial of the claim by making an application for an order under Pt 23 of the Civil Procedure Rules. Otherwise it will be dealt with at the trial of the claim.

In *Stubbings v Webb*[172] the House of Lords took a false step in deciding that the three-year limitation period for personal injuries—which can run from the date of the claimant's knowledge and can be disapplied at the courts' discretion under s.33—did not apply where the cause of action for the personal injury was trespass to the person. Instead s.2 was applied so that there was a six-year time bar from the date of the trespass. This decision was heavily criticised[173] and required odd distinctions to be drawn in the subsequent case law.[174] It was finally overruled in *A v Hoare*.[175] Claims for trespass to the person causing personal injury (the facts concerned sexual abuse of children) therefore fall within s.11 and s.33 of the Limitation Act 1980 and not within s.2 of that Act. The limitation period is, therefore, three years from the date of knowledge and the courts have a discretion to exercise under s.33 rather than the claim being statute-barred six years after the relevant trespass. **31-39**

(b) Claimant's knowledge

When, in a personal injuries case, time runs from the date of a person's "knowledge" then, according to s.14(1), that date is the date on which he first had knowledge, actual or constructive, of *all* the following facts: **31-40**

"(a) that the injury in question was significant; and
(b) that the injury was attributable in whole or in part to the act or omission which is alleged to constitute negligence, nuisance or breach of duty; and
(c) the identity of the defendant; and
(d) if it is alleged that the act or omission was that of a person other than the defendant, the identity of that person and the additional facts supporting the bringing of an action against the defendant."

(i) *Significant injury: s.14(1)(a)*

An injury is significant if the person whose date of knowledge is in question would reasonably have considered it sufficiently serious to justify his instituting proceedings for damages against a defendant who did not dispute liability and was **31-41**

[171] CPR r.1.4. *Buck v English Electric Co Ltd* [1977] 1 W.L.R. 806; *Firman v Ellis* [1978] Q.B. 886; *Walkley v Precision Forgings Ltd* [1979] 1 W.L.R. 606; *Chappell v Cooper* [1980] 1 W.L.R. 958; *Leadbitter v Hodge Finance Ltd* [1982] 2 All E.R. 167.

[172] [1993] A.C. 498.

[173] See, e.g. Rogers (1993) 143 N.L.J. 258; McGee (1993) 109 L.Q.R. 356; Allinson [1996] J.P.I.L. 19; Mullis (1997) 5 Med. L. Rev. 22; Law Commission Report No. 270, *Limitation of Actions* (1998).

[174] In *S v W* [1995] 1 F.L.R. 862 the claimant sued her mother for negligently failing to protect her from the sexual abuse by her father that she had suffered as a child. Since the action was not for trespass to the person (no trespass was alleged against the mother), *Stubbings v Webb* was distinguished and the claim was governed by ss.11 and 33 of the Limitation Act 1980 rather than s.2. Again in *KR v Bryn Alyn Community Holdings Ltd* [2003] EWCA Civ 85; [2003] Q.B. 1441 negligence claims against employers for psychiatric illness, caused by a failure to stop sexual abuse of children in their institutions, were held to fall within ss.11 and 33 of the Limitation Act 1980; yet the claims against the employees who carried out the abuse, and the employer's vicarious liability for those deliberate torts, fell within s.2.

[175] [2008] UKHL 6; [2008] 1 A.C. 844.

able to satisfy a judgment.[176] In *A v Hoare*[177] the House of Lords decided that the test in s.14(2) is entirely impersonal.[178] One decides whether a reasonable person would have considered the injuries sufficiently serious to justify instituting proceedings for damages taking into account the actual knowledge of the claimant or, by reason of s.14(3), the constructive knowledge of the claimant.[179] It is therefore incorrect to regard s.14(2) and s.14(3) as applying the same standard; and a number of previous cases[180] were thought incorrect in accepting that some "subjective" elements could be relevant under s.14(2).[181] In so far as the actual claimant, given his or her state of mind or intelligence, could not reasonably have been expected to institute proceedings, this would be a matter to be taken into account in exercising the discretion under s.33 where one of the factors is "the reasons for … the delay on the part of the plaintiff".[182] In the words of Lord Hoffmann:

> "[T]he test itself is an entirely impersonal standard: not whether the claimant himself would have considered the injuries sufficiently serious to justify proceedings but whether he would 'reasonably' have done so. You ask what the claimant knew about the injury he had suffered, you add any knowledge he had about the injury which may be imputed to him under s.14(3) and you then ask whether a reasonable person with that knowledge would have considered the injury sufficiently serious to justify his instituting proceedings for damages against the defendant who did not dispute liability and was able to satisfy a judgment …"[183]

And later he said:

> "[The test] is applied to what the claimant knew or was deemed to have known but the standard itself is impersonal. The effect of the claimant's injuries upon what he could reasonably have been expected to do is therefore irrelevant."[184]

Baroness Hale did not agree with her fellow Lords on this question of the correct interpretation of s.14(2). She said, "[i]t is much simpler to ask what the claimant knew or ought to have known and then apply an objective test of significance to those facts … But that is not what the subsection says at present."[185]

31-42 Once the claimant has knowledge of one injury that is significant, time begins to run in respect of another injury sustained in the same accident even though he does not then know that that injury is significant.[186] Where a claim is brought in the tort of negligence for psychiatric illness caused by sexual abuse, the relevant

---

176 Limitation Act 1980 s.14(2).

177 [2008] UKHL 6; [2008] 1 A.C. 844.

178 The interpretation of s.14(2) in *A v Hoare* was applied in *Field v British Coal Corp* [2008] EWCA Civ 912 (deafness).

179 See para.31-51.

180 e.g. *McCafferty v Metropolitan Police Commissioner* [1977] 1 W.L.R. 1073; and *KR v Bryn Alyn Community (Holdings) Ltd* [2003] EWCA Civ 85; [2003] Q.B. 1441.

181 It is plainly irrelevant therefore that the claimant may have refrained from bringing an action for fear of losing his job (correctly regarded as irrelevant in *McCafferty v Metropolitan Police Receiver* [1977] 1 W.L.R. 1073) or because he had been able to continue working and thought he would be "sponging" if he were to claim damages (correctly regarded as irrelevant in *Buck v English Electric Co Ltd* [1977] 1 W.L.R. 806).

182 See para.31-61.

183 [2008] UKHL 6; [2008] 1 A.C. 844 at [34].

184 [2008] UKHL 6; [2008] 1 A.C. 844 at [39].

185 [2008] UKHL 6; [2008] 1 A.C. 844 at [59].

186 *Bristow v Grout, The Times,* 3 November 1986; affirmed on a different point, *The Times,* 9 November 1987.

significant injury may be the later onset of the psychiatric illness rather than the immediate physical or mental injuries caused by the abuse.[187]

(ii) Injury attributable to the act or omission alleged to constitute negligence, nuisance or breach of duty: s.14(1)(b)

It is sufficient that the claimant knows in general terms that his condition is due to the acts or omissions of the defendant and knowledge of the precise details is unnecessary. So in *Wilkinson v Ancliffe (BLT) Ltd*[188] the claimant suffered asthma in 1981 which he believed to be the result of inhaling toxic fumes in the course of his work for the defendant. In November 1981 a hospital examination confirmed a probable connection between his chest condition and toxic fumes, but it was not until 1984 that he learnt from a report by an expert chemist exactly where the defendant's method of work was at fault in exposing him to excessive quantities of fumes. It was held that he had sufficient knowledge to set the limitation period running in November 1981, since he then knew in general terms that his condition resulted from a failure to provide a safe system of work. Similarly, in *Nash v Eli Lilly*[189] the Court of Appeal stressed that: "What is required is knowledge of the essence of the act or omission to which the injury is attributable". **31-43**

The meaning of "attributable" and the question of what qualifies as "actual knowledge" was considered in *Spargo v North Essex District HA*.[190] The Court of Appeal made it clear that the claimant only needed to have a low level of knowledge before time started running against her. Brooke LJ said that the following principles could be derived from the decisions on s.14(1)(b)[191]: **31-44**

"(1) The knowledge required to satisfy s.14(1)(b) is a broad knowledge of the essence of the causally relevant act or omission to which the injury is attributable;

(2) "Attributable" in this context means 'capable of being attributed to', in the sense of being a real possibility;

(3) A [claimant] has the requisite knowledge when she knows enough to make it reasonable for her to begin to investigate whether or not she has a case against the defendant. Another way of putting this is to say that she will have such knowledge if she so firmly believes that her condition is capable of being attributed to an act or omission which she can identify (in broad terms) that she goes to a solicitor to seek advice about making a claim for compensation;

(4) On the other hand she will not have the requisite knowledge if she thinks she knows the acts or omissions she should investigate but in fact is barking up the wrong tree: or if her knowledge of what the defendant did or did not do is so vague or general that she cannot fairly be expected to know what she should investigate; or if her state of mind is such that she thinks her condition is capable of being attributed to the act or omission alleged to constitute negligence, but she is not sure

---

187 *KR v Bryn Alyn Community Holdings Ltd* [2003] EWCA Civ 85; [2003] Q.B. 1441; *H v Northampton CC* [2004] EWCA Civ 526; [2005] P.I.Q.R. P7. cf. *B v Nugent Care Society* [2009] EWCA Civ 827; [2010] 1 W.L.R. 516 where the sexual abuse claim was founded on the tort of trespass to the person.

188 [1986] 1 W.L.R. 1352.

189 [1993] 1 W.L.R. 782 at 800.

190 [1997] P.I.Q.R. P235.

191 [1997] P.I.Q.R. P235 at P242. In *AB v Ministry of Defence* [2012] UKSC 9; [2013] 1 A.C. 78 at [68], Lord Walker said that summaries, such as that by Brooke LJ, "may be unhelpful if treated as if they were statutory texts".

> about this, and would need to check with an expert before she could be properly said to know that it was."[192]

It has been said that these principles were intended not simply as guidelines, but as binding rules.[193]

31-45 It is not sufficient for the claimant to know merely that the relevant damage had been caused by *an* act or omission of the defendant. It must be knowledge of "the act or omission which is alleged to constitute negligence". Thus:

> "The [claimant] does not have to know that he has a cause of action or that the defendant's acts can be characterised in law as negligent or as falling short of some standard of professional or other behaviour … He must have known the facts which can fairly be described as constituting the negligence of which he complains. It may be that knowledge of such facts will also serve to bring home to him the fact that the defendant has been negligent or at fault. But that in itself is not a reason for saying that he need not have known them."[194]

In *Smith v West Lancashire HA*[195] the claimant had been told that the initial treatment had not worked and that there was nothing further that could be done. He presumed that he had received proper treatment, but in fact the operation had been performed too late to achieve full recovery. Russell LJ said that the alleged negligence consisted of the omission to operate promptly, together with the failure properly to diagnose his condition. The reality was that the claimant did not know that there had been an omission to operate at all until he received advice to that effect from his own expert witness:

> "True, he knew that he had not had an operation on or about November 12, 1981, but that knowledge cannot, in my judgment, be knowledge of an omission 'which is alleged to constitute negligence'. One cannot know of an omission without knowing what it is that is omitted. In this case, that was an operation to reduce the fracture dislocations, as opposed to conservative treatment. Simply to tell the [claimant] that the first course of treatment had not worked, is not the same as imbuing the [claimant] with the knowledge of an omission to operate."[196]

31-46 In some cases, particularly those involving allegations of medical negligence, the

---

[192] In *O'Driscoll v Dudley HA* [1998] Lloyd's Rep. Med. 210 at 221. Stuart-Smith LJ said that the fourth *Spargo* principle "must be read as postulating a situation antithetical to that covered by the third principle; i.e. the fourth principle postulates a state of mind short of a firm belief which takes a potential claimant to a solicitor". The reference in principle (4) to "the need to check with an expert" was a reference to the need for an expert's opinion before even the claimant can be said to know that the attributability of her condition to a particular "act or omission" was a real possibility: "That is not the same investigation as is referred to in the first limb of principle three; this latter is an investigation into whether the [claimant] 'has a case against the defendant' … an investigation which must be carried out whilst the limitation clock is ticking" (at 221–222). See also *Roberts v Winbow* [1999] P.I.Q.R. P77 CA, for discussion of the distinction between Brooke LJ's principles (3) and (4).

[193] *Griffin, Lawson and Williams v Clywd HA* [2001] EWCA Civ 818; [2001] P.I.Q.R. P420; *Corbin v Penfold Metallising Co Ltd* [2000] Lloyd's Rep. Med. 247 at 249 CA.

[194] *Hallam-Eames v Merrett Syndicates Ltd* [1996] 7 Med. L.R. 122 at 126, per Hoffmann LJ. This case was concerned with the interpretation of the analogous provision in s.14A of the Limitation Act 1980 in respect of claims for economic loss.

[195] [1995] P.I.Q.R. P514 CA.

[196] [1995] P.I.Q.R. P514 CA at 517. See also *Parry v Clwyd HA* [1997] P.I.Q.R. P1; *Hind v York HA* [1998] P.I.Q.R. P235. In *James v East Dorset HA* (1999) 59 B.M.L.R. 196 the Court of Appeal held that a patient whose condition had deteriorated following an operation and who inferred that it had not been a success, nonetheless did not acquire knowledge within s.14 when there was nothing to alert him to the fact that he had suffered an injury during the operation.

claimant may develop a mistaken belief as to the cause of his injuries. In this situation, the claimant may have been "barking up the wrong tree", in which case he does not have the relevant knowledge. For the claimant to have knowledge that an injury was attributable to the act or omission which is alleged to constitute negligence it is not sufficient for the claimant to know simply that his injury was attributable to "the treatment" or "the defendant's conduct". In *Khan v Ainslie*[197] the claimant initially believed, incorrectly, that eye drops put into his eye for the purpose of a test in 1983 were the cause of the loss of sight in his left eye. He was not aware, until he received an expert's report in 1989, that the problems with his eye were attributable to an omission to refer him for immediate treatment. Despite the fact that the claimant clearly believed that his eye problems were attributable to the defendants' conduct, it was held that the relevant date was 1989 when the report was obtained, because until that stage the claimant had no knowledge of the attributability of his disability to delay, and was ignorant of the link to the act or omission on which he now relied as being negligent. Similarly, in *Rowbottom v Royal Masonic Hospital*[198] the claimant believed that complications arising from a wound infection following surgery for a hip replacement, leading eventually to amputation of his leg, were due to the failure of a drain inserted into his leg. He believed that he had been given prophylactic antibiotics. He did not acquire knowledge that he had not been given prophylactic antibiotics until he received confirmation from a medical expert that it was reasonable to assume that if there was no record of antibiotics having been given then he probably had not received any.

(iii) Defendant's identity: s.14(1)(c)

The obvious case where the claimant does not know the identity of the defendant is where he is knocked down by a hit-and-run driver, but there are less obvious cases. Thus where a manual labourer did not know the name of his employer because it was one of a number of limited companies all with similar names, and the name of the wrong one was entered on his contract of employment, time did not run against him until the name of the right one was discovered.[199] **31-47**

(iv) Vicarious liability etc: s.14(1)(d)

Section 14(1)(d) applies where it is alleged that the act or omission was that of a person other than the defendant, in which case the claimant must have knowledge of "the identity of that person and the additional facts supporting the bringing of an action against the defendant". This is designed to cover circumstances in which an employer is vicariously liable for the conduct of an employee, but the wording **31-48**

197 [1993] 4 Med. L.R. 319 QBD.

198 [2002] EWCA Civ 87; [2002] Lloyd's Rep. Med. 173; [2003] P.I.Q.R. P1; *Spargo v North Essex District HA* [1997] P.I.Q.R. P235 at P242, per Brooke LJ. In *Baig v City & Hackney HA* [1994] 5 Med. L.R. 221, 224 Rougier J commented that though a sufficiently firm conviction will suffice for the purpose of knowledge, the conviction must be right, in the sense that it accords with the way in which the case is ultimately advanced in reliance on specialist opinion: "It seems to me to be a travesty of language to hold that somebody who approaches his case in a wholly erroneous belief—however strong—as to the cause of his injury could ever have the requisite knowledge. On the contrary, he has the reverse."

199 *Simpson v Norwest Holst Southern Ltd* [1980] 1 W.L.R. 968; see similarly *Cressey v Timm & Son* [2005] EWCA Civ 763; [2005] 1 W.L.R. 3926. cf. *Walford v Richards* [1976] 1 Lloyd's Rep. 526.

is not limited to vicarious liability, as such, but would cover those situations where a defendant owes a non-delegable duty and this primary duty is broken as a result of the conduct of another person. For example, if C is run over by X, an employee of the D company, who is driving a lorry in the course of his employment, time does not begin to run against C and in favour of D until C discovers that X was D's servant and driving in the course of his employment.

(v) Ignorance of the law irrelevant

31-49 It is the claimant's knowledge of *facts* that governs the commencement date. The proviso to s.14(1) specifically states that the claimant's ignorance that, as a matter of law, the facts would give him a cause of action is irrelevant.[200] This is the case even where the claimant has received incorrect advice about the legal position, whether from a lawyer or not.[201] Although ignorance of the law is irrelevant to the question of the claimant's knowledge for the purpose of s.14, it is relevant to the court's exercise of discretion under s.33.[202]

(vi) Distinguish "knowledge" and "belief"

31-50 Knowledge is not the same as "reasonable belief" or "suspicion",[203] although there comes a point at which the claimant's belief will turn into knowledge. In *Nash v Eli Lilly*[204] the Court of Appeal thought it incorrect to draw a rigid distinction between belief and knowledge, for a firmly-held belief can constitute knowledge. "If the [claimant] held a firm belief which was of sufficient certainty to justify the taking of the preliminary steps for proceedings by obtaining advice about making a claim for compensation, then such belief is knowledge and the limitation period would begin to run."[205] On the other hand,

> " ... a firm belief held by the [claimant] that his injury was attributable to the act or omission of the defendant, but in respect of which he thought it necessary to obtain reassurance or confirmation from experts, medical, or legal, or others, would not be regarded as knowledge until the result of his enquiries was known to him, or, if he delayed in obtaining that confirmation, until the time at which it was reasonable for him to have got it. If

---

200 *Broadley v Guy Clapham & Co* [1994] 4 All E.R. 439; *Dobbie v Medway HA* [1994] 1 W.L.R. 1234 CA; *Hallam-Eames v Merrett Syndicates Ltd* [1996] 7 Med. L.R. 122; [1955-95] P.N.L.R. 672 CA; *Saxby v Morgan* [1997] P.I.Q.R. P531; *Rowe v Kingston-Upon-Hull City Council* [2003] EWCA Civ 1281; [2004] P.I.Q.R. P16 (claim for failure to diagnose and ameliorate dyslexia was time-barred because the claimant was held to have the relevant knowledge under s.14(1)(a) nearly six years before proceedings were issued even though he did not know that he had a potential cause of action against the education authorities until a later High Court decision: that was irrelevant being a matter of law not fact).

201 See *Farmer v National Coal Board, The Times,* 27 April 1985 CA, where erroneous legal advice by a union official that the claimant's action had no chance of success did not prevent time running against the claimant, since from facts ascertainable by her she could reasonably have acquired the necessary knowledge.

202 Limitation Act 1980 s.33(3)(a) and (e); *Brooks v Coates (UK) Ltd* [1984] 1 All E.R. 702 at 713; *Coad v Cornwall and Isles of Scilly HA* [1997] 1 W.L.R. 189 CA.

203 *Wilkinson v Ancliff (BLT) Ltd* [1986] 1 W.L.R. 1352.

204 [1993] 1 W.L.R. 782. See also *Halford v Brookes* [1991] 1 W.L.R. 428 at 443, per Lord Donaldson MR.

205 [1993] 1 W.L.R. 782 at 796.

negative expert advice is obtained, that fact must be considered in combination with all other relevant facts in deciding when, if ever, the [claimant] had knowledge".[206]

So in *Sniezek v Bundy (Letchworth) Ltd*[207] the Court of Appeal said that, applying the third principle from *Spargo v North Essex District HA*,[208] there was a distinction between a claimant who has a firm belief that he has a significant injury, attributable to his working conditions (especially one that takes him to a solicitor for advice about a claim), a belief that he retains whatever contrary advice he receives, and a claimant who believes that he may have, or even probably has, a significant injury which is attributable to his working conditions, but is not sure and feels it necessary to have expert advice on those questions. The former has knowledge of significant injury and attribution for the purposes of s.14, but the latter does not. In *AB v Ministry of Defence*,[209] the Supreme Court (by a majority of four to three) held that claims for injury or death, allegedly caused to ex-servicemen by radiation exposure during nuclear testing in the 1950s, were time-barred. The majority held that a claimant must be treated as having the requisite knowledge under s.14(1) once he issued proceedings. It could not be correct that the weak case of the claimants should be regarded as not time-barred because better evidence as to attributability might yet emerge. In the words of Lord Wilson JSC "it is a legal impossibility for a claimant to lack knowledge of attributability for the purpose of section 14(1) at a time after the date of the issue of his claim. By that date he must in law have had knowledge of it".[210]

(vii) *Constructive knowledge*

To a certain extent, a person's "knowledge" includes constructive as well as actual knowledge. Section 14(3) provides that: **31-51**

> "For the purposes of this section a person's knowledge includes knowledge which he might reasonably have been expected to acquire—
>
> (a) from facts observable or ascertainable by him; or
> (b) from facts ascertainable by him with the help of medical or other appropriate expert advice which it is reasonable for him to seek;
>
> but a person shall not be fixed under this subsection with knowledge of a fact ascertainable only with the help of expert advice so long as he has taken all reasonable steps to obtain (and, where appropriate, to act on) that advice."

The policy of s.14(3) is to encourage the claimant to seek expert advice as soon as possible. If he does not, time runs against him. If he does, he is not prejudiced by being deemed to know all that the expert should have discovered but did not, or discovered but failed to tell him.

---

206 [1993] 1 W.L.R. 782 at 796. The Court of Appeal also disapproved *Davis v Ministry of Defence, The Times,* 7 August, 1985, to the extent that that decision appeared to regard it as arguable that knowledge, having been acquired, could be retrospectively lost by the subsequent obtaining of expert advice for the purpose of legal proceedings. cf. *Spargo v North Essex District HA* [1997] P.I.Q.R. P235; *Ali v Courtaulds Textiles Ltd* [1999] Lloyd's Rep. Med. 301 CA.

207 [2000] P.I.Q.R. P213

208 See para.31-44.

209 [2012] UKSC 9; [2013] 1 A.C. 78.

210 [2012] UKSC 9; [2013] 1 A.C. 78 at [2].

31-52 In *Driscoll-Varley v Parkside HA*[211] it was held that the relevant question is whether it was unreasonable for this claimant not to seek advice (the burden of proof being on the defendant), taking account of both subjective and objective criteria. This approach was followed in *Nash v Eli Lilly & Co*,[212] where the Court of Appeal held that the situation, character and the intelligence of the claimant need to be taken into account. However, a far more objective approach was followed in *Forbes v Wandsworth HA*.[213] Here, the claimant alleged that a second operation on his leg had been negligently delayed, with the result that his leg had had to be amputated. He had not however realised that the amputation might have been the result of negligence on the part of the hospital until, having consulted a solicitor, he received a medical report explaining the consequences of the delay. This was 10 years after the amputation. The Court of Appeal found that a reasonable claimant would have started investigating whether there might be a claim (i.e. the claimant had constructive knowledge) within 12–18 months after the amputation. Doubt was cast on whether the claimant's intelligence and character could properly be considered under s.14(3) without undermining the objective nature of the test. A similar view was taken by Colman J in *Parry v Clwyd HA*.[214] Noting that *Nash v Eli Lilly* and *Forbes v Wandsworth HA* could not be reconciled, he preferred the exclusively objective approach in *Forbes*. It has now been established by a majority of the House of Lords in *Adams v Bracknell Forest BC*[215] that the *Forbes* view is correct and that the more subjective approach in *Nash v Eli Lilly* should not be followed. The test is whether a reasonable claimant, having suffered the injury in question, ought reasonably to have known the relevant facts. While the situation of the claimant is relevant, his character and intelligence are not. So, the claimant's personal characteristics, such as shyness or embarrassment or a reluctance to make a fuss, are irrelevant. In Lord Hoffmann's words: "[Section] 14(3) requires one to assume that a person who is aware that he has suffered a personal injury, serious enough to be something about which he would go and see a solicitor if he knew he had a claim, will be sufficiently curious about the causes of the injury to seek whatever expert advice is appropriate."[216] If the injury itself would reasonably inhibit a claimant from seeking advice, that is a factor which must be taken into account.[217]

---

211 [1991] 2 Med. L.R. 346.

212 [1993] 1 W.L.R. 782. See also *Davis v City and Hackney HA* [1991] 2 Med. L.R. 366.

213 [1997] Q.B. 402.

214 [1997] P.I.Q.R. P1.

215 [2004] UKHL 29; [2005] 1 A.C. 76.

216 [2004] UKHL 29; [2005] 1 A.C. 76 at [47]. But in *Whiston v London Strategic HA* [2010] EWCA Civ 195; [2010] 1 W.L.R. 1582 at [55] it was held that what Lord Hoffmann said at [47] was not part of the ratio of *Adams* and should not be read as a formula applicable to every case. See also *Johnson v Ministry of Defence* [2012] EWCA Civ 1505; [2013] P.I.Q.R. P7; *Platt v BRB (Residuary) Ltd* [2014] EWCA Civ 1401; [2015] P.I.Q.R. P7.

217 [2004] UKHL 29; [2005] 1 A.C. 76 at [49]. Baroness Hale speculated that there may be a difference between personal characteristics which affect the claimant's ability to acquire information and those which affect his reaction to what he did know, and therefore did not entirely rule out consideration of the claimant's personal characteristics. Lord Walker agreed that this distinction may be useful in some cases. Much depends upon what is meant by a "personal characteristic" of the claimant. If the court is required to look objectively at the reasonableness of the claimant's conduct, taking into account his personal circumstances (including the effects of the accident), there is a distinct possibility, as Lord Walker suggested, that the subjective and the objective may be elided. If, for example, as a result of the injury the claimant develops depression and is then unable to deal with

The effect of s.14(3) is shown by *Marston v British Railways Board*[218] A man was injured by a chip which broke from the head of a hammer. The hammer was submitted to experts. They reported that it was correctly tempered: they did not say that, although correctly tempered, it had been damaged by misuse before it was issued to the victim of the accident, a fact which suggested that the defendant was negligent in failing to check it and withdraw it from service. It was over 10 years later that this fact came to light. Time was held to run, not from the expert examination, but from when the fact was discovered. On the other hand, in *Henderson v Temple Pier Co Ltd*[219] the claimant was held to have knowledge of the relevant facts (in this case of the identity of the defendants) from the moment when his solicitor ought to have discovered that fact. The proviso in s.14(3) did not protect the claimant because the knowledge in question was not "ascertainable only with the help of expert advice". A claimant is also not protected where the relevant expert advice is on the law since it is knowledge of facts not law which is important.[220] **31-53**

(c) The court's discretion

By s.33(1) the court may allow an action to proceed notwithstanding the expiry of the limitation period if it considers that it is equitable to do so. The discretion is exercised by the court directing that the provisions of s.11 shall not apply to the action. The burden of showing that it would be equitable to disapply the limitation period lies on the claimant[221] but, although the contrary has sometimes been said,[222] it is incorrect to describe the burden on the claimant as a heavy one.[223] In a multi-party action, the court must consider the exercise of its discretion separately with regard to each of the claimants joining in the action.[224] **31-54**

various aspects of daily living, including summoning the energy to investigate the causes of the injury, is this lack of drive a subjective "personal characteristic" (to be ignored) or is it an objective "personal circumstance" (to be taken into account)? Would serious, pre-existing, physical disabilities which impaired the claimant's ability to investigate a claim be a personal circumstance or a personal characteristic?

218 [1976] I.C.R. 124. In *Walkley v Precision Forgings Ltd* [1979] 1 W.L.R. 606 at 610, Lord Wilberforce doubted whether the decision was right on the facts, although he did not explain why.

219 [1998] 1 W.L.R. 1540 CA. See also *Leadbitter v Hodge Finance Ltd* [1982] 2 All E.R. 167; *Nash v Eli Lilly* [1991] 2 Med. L.R. 169 at 180–182 (Hidden J) approved [1993] 1 W.L.R. 782 at 800 CA; *Khan v Ainslie* [1993] 4 Med. L.R. 319 at 325; *Copeland v Smith* [2000] 1 W.L.R. 1371 CA. cf. *Fowell v National Coal Board*, *The Times*, 28 May 1986, in which the Court of Appeal thought that a solicitor was not an expert under s.14(3)(b), although his actual knowledge (quaere constructive knowledge) could be attributed to the claimant under normal agency principles.

220 *Leadbitter v Hodge Finance Ltd* [1982] 2 All E.R. 167 at 174. See also *Farmer v National Coal Board*, *The Times*, 27 April 1985; para.31-49 fn.201.

221 *Thompson v Brown Construction (Ebbw Vale) Ltd* [1981] 1 W.L.R. 744; *Nash v Eli Lilly & Co* [1993] 1 W.L.R. 782; *Sayers v Hunters* [2012] EWCA Civ 1715; [2013] 1 W.L.R. 1695; *Carroll v Chief Constable of Greater Manchester Police* [2017] EWCA Civ 1992; [2018] 4 W.L.R. 32.

222 It is "an exceptional indulgence to a claimant, to be granted only where equity between the parties demands it": *KR v Bryn Alyn Community (Holdings) Ltd (In Liquidation)* [2003] EWCA Civ 85; [2003] Q.B. 1441 at [74]; *Buckler v Sheffield City Council* [2004] EWCA Civ 920; [2005] P.I.Q.R. P3 at [25], [27].

223 *AB v Ministry of Defence* [2010] EWCA Civ 1317; (2011) 117 B.M.L.R. 101 at [96]; *Sayers v Hunters* [2012] EWCA Civ 1715; [2013] 1 W.L.R. 1695.

224 *Nash v Eli Lilly & Co* [1993] 1 W.L.R. 782. For the approach to s.33 in relation to multi-party claims for historic sexual abuse in children's homes, see *B v Nugent Care Society* [2009] EWCA Civ 827; [2010] 1 W.L.R. 516. Despite this general principle, it was pertinent in *Hutson v Tata Steel UK Ltd* [2019] EWHC 1608 (QB) that it would not necessarily best serve the overriding objective (of deal-

31-55 The discretion under s.33 is expressed in the widest terms: "Parliament has now decided that uncertain justice is preferable to certain injustice."[225] Nevertheless, it was decided by the House of Lords in *Walkley v Precision Forgings Ltd*[226] that the discretion could not be exercised where the claimant had previously begun an action for the same damage against the same defendant within the limitation period but had failed to proceed with that action for whatever reason.[227] This decision caused difficulty over many years[228] until the House of Lords took the momentous step in *Horton v Sadler*[229] of overruling *Walkley*. This means that the s.33 discretion can be exercised so as allow a claim to proceed (and was so exercised in this case) even though the claimant has previously begun an action but has failed to proceed with it. In the words of Lord Bingham of Cornhill: "I feel bound to conclude that the reasoning of the *Walkley* decision was unsound, that it has given rise to distinctions which disfigure the law in this area and that the effect has been to restrict unduly the broad discretion which Parliament conferred."[230] Applying *Horton v Sadler*, there is no abuse of process, and the discretion in s.33 of the Limitation Act 1980 can be exercised, where a second claim form has been issued (outside the limitation period) and validly served, following the negligent failure to serve a first claim form in the time allowed for service.[231] In *Mutua v Foreign and Commonwealth Office*[232] it was held that claims should be allowed to proceed under s.33 even though they were commenced 50 years after the expiry of the limitation period.

31-56 Paragraphs 31-54 and 31-55 must now be read in the light of the summary of general principles applicable to s.33 set out by Sir Terence Etherton MR in *Chief Constable of Greater Manchester v Carroll*.[233] He set out the following 13 general principles:

"1. Section 33 is not confined to a 'residual class of cases'. It is unfettered and requires the judge to look at the matter broadly: *Donovan v Gwentoys Ltd* [1990] 1 WLR 472 at 477E; *Horton v Sadler* [2006] UKHL 27; [2007] 1 AC 307, at [9] (approving the Court of Appeal judgments in *Finch v Francis* (unreported) 21 July 1977); *A v Hoare* [2008] UKHL 6, [2008] AC 844, at [45], [49], [68] and [84]; *Sayers v Lord Chelwood* [2012] EWCA Civ 1715, [2013] 1 WLR 1695, at [55].

2. The matters specified in section 33(3) are not intended to place a fetter on the discretion given by section 33(1), as is made plain by the opening words 'the court shall have regard to all the circumstances of the case', but to focus the attention of the court on matters which past experience has shown are likely to call for evaluation in the exercise of the discretion and must be taken into a consideration by the judge: *Donovan's* case, at 477H–478A.

3. The essence of the proper exercise of the judicial discretion under section 33 is

ing with cases justly and proportionately) to determine limitation defences as a preliminary issue in individual cases where there is group litigation.

225 *Firman v Ellis* [1978] Q.B. 886 at 911, per Ormrod LJ.

226 [1979] 1 W.L.R. 606.

227 The claimant may have given notice that he was discontinuing the action, or the claim form may not have been issued in time, or the action may have struck out for failure to comply with the Civil Procedure Rules.

228 For the details, see the 19th edn of this work paras 33-54 to 33-55.

229 [2006] UKHL 27; [2007] 1 A.C. 307.

230 [2006] UKHL 27; [2007] 1 A.C. 307 at [28].

231 *Aktas v Adepta* [2010] EWCA Civ 1170; [2011] Q.B. 894. See also *Davidson v Aegis Defence Services (BVI) Ltd* [2013] EWCA Civ 1586; [2014] 2 All E.R. 216.

232 [2012] EWHC 2678 (QB).

233 [2017] EWCA Civ 1992; [2018] 4 W.L.R. 32 at [42].

that the test is a balance of prejudice and the burden is on the claimant to show that his or her prejudice would outweigh that to the defendant: *Donovan's* case, at 477E; *Adams v Bracknell Forest Borough Council* [2005] 1 AC 76, at [55], approving observations in *Robinson v St Helens Metropolitan Borough Council* [2003] PIQR P128 at [32] and [33]; *McGhie v British Telecommunications plc* [2005] EWCA Civ 48, (2005) 149 SJLB 114, at [45]. Refusing to exercise the discretion in favour of a claimant who brings the claim outside the primary limitation period will necessarily prejudice the claimant, who thereby loses the chance of establishing the claim.

4. The burden on the claimant under section 33 is not necessarily a heavy one. How heavy or easy it is for the claimant to discharge the burden will depend on the facts of the particular case: *Sayers's* case at [55].

5. Furthermore, while the ultimate burden is on a claimant to show that it would be inequitable to disapply the statute, the evidential burden of showing that the evidence adduced, or likely to be adduced, by the defendant is, or is likely to be, less cogent because of the delay is on the defendant: *Burgin v Sheffield City Council* [2005] EWCA Civ 482 at [23]. If relevant or potentially relevant documentation has been destroyed or lost by the defendant irresponsibly, that is a factor which may weigh against the defendant: *Hammond v West Lancashire Health Authority* [1998] Lloyd's Rep Med 146.

6. The prospects of a fair trial are important: *A v Hoare* at [60]. The Limitation Acts are designed to protect defendants from the injustice of having to fight stale claims, especially when any witnesses the defendant might have been able to rely on are not available or have no recollection and there are no documents to assist the court in deciding what was done or not done and why: *Donovan's* case, at 479A; *Robinson's* case at [32]; *Adams'* case at [55]. It is, therefore, particularly relevant whether, and to what extent, the defendant's ability to defend the claim has been prejudiced by the lapse of time because of the absence of relevant witnesses and documents: *Robinson's* case at [33]; *Adams'* case at [55]; and *A v Hoare* at [50].

7. Subject to considerations of proportionality (as outlined in (11) below), the defendant only deserves to have the obligation to pay due damages removed if the passage of time has significantly diminished the opportunity to defend the claim on liability or amount: *Cain v Francis* [2008] EWCA Civ 1451, [2009] QB 754 at [69].

8. It is the period after the expiry of the limitation period which is referred to in sub-subsections 33(3)(a) and (b) and carries particular weight: *Donovan's* case at 478G. The court may also, however, have regard to the period of delay from the time at which section 14(2) was satisfied until the claim was first notified: *Donovan's* case at 478H and 479H–480C; *Cain's* case at [74]. The disappearance of evidence and the loss of cogency of evidence even before the limitation clock starts to tick is also relevant, although to a lesser degree: *Collins v Secretary of State for Business Innovation and Skills* [2014] EWCA Civ 717, [2014] PIQR P19 at [65].

9. The reason for delay is relevant and may affect the balancing exercise. If it has arisen for an excusable reason, it may be fair and just that the action should proceed despite some unfairness to the defendant due to the delay. If, on the other hand, the reasons for the delay or its length are not good ones, that may tip the balance in the other direction: *Cain's* case at [73]. I consider that the latter may be better expressed by saying that, if there are no good reasons for the delay or its length, there is nothing to qualify or temper the prejudice which has been caused to the defendant by the effect of the delay on the defendant's ability to defend the claim.

10. Delay caused by the conduct of the claimant's advisers rather than by the claimant may be excusable in this context: *Corbin v Penfold Metallising Co Ltd* [2000] Lloyd's Rep Med 247.

11. In the context of reasons for delay, it is relevant to consider under subsection 33(3)(a) whether knowledge or information was reasonably suppressed by the

claimant which, if not suppressed, would have led to the proceedings being issued earlier, even though the explanation is irrelevant for meeting the objective standard or test in section 14(2) and (3) and so insufficient to prevent the commencement of the limitation period: *A v Hoare* at [44]–[45] and [70].

12. Proportionality is material to the exercise of the discretion:*Robinson's* case at [32] and [33]; *Adams's* case at [54]–[55]. In that context, it may be relevant that the claim has only a thin prospect of success (*McGhie's* case at [48]), that the claim is modest in financial terms so as to give rise to disproportionate legal costs (*Robinson's* case at [33]; *Adams's* case at [55]); *McGhie's* case at [48]), that the claimant would have a clear case against his or her solicitors (*Donovan's* case at 479F), and, in a personal injury case, the extent and degree of damage to the claimant's health, enjoyment of life and employability (*Robinson's* case at [33];*Adams's* case at [55]).

13. An appeal court will only interfere with the exercise of the judge's discretion under section 33, as in other cases of judicial discretion, where the judge has made an error of principle, such as taking into account irrelevant matters or failing to take into account relevant matters, or has made a decision which is wrong, that is to say the judge has exceeded the generous ambit within which a reasonable disagreement is possible: *KR v Bryn Alyn Community (Holdings) Ltd* [2003] EWCA Civ 783, [2003] QB 1441 at [69]; *Burgin's* case at [16]."

In *Carroll* itself, the Court of Appeal declined to interfere with the judge's decision not to apply the limitation period. Here, the delay beyond the limitation period that was attributable to the claimant himself was relatively short and was found to have been excusable. Subsequent delay was not the claimant's fault, arising instead from a misapprehension on the part of his legal advisors as to when the limitation period would begin to run.

(i) The balance of prejudice

31-57 In deciding whether it is equitable to disapply the limitation period, the court must have regard to the degree to which the provisions of s.11 (or 11A[234] or 12,[235] as the case may be) prejudice the claimant or any person he represents, and also to the degree to which the exercise of the discretion in favour of claimant would prejudice the defendant or any person whom he represents. The prejudice to the claimant comes from the loss of the opportunity to pursue his claim against the defendant. In assessing the degree of prejudice the court must take an overall view of the claimant's prospect of success in the action.[236] Where the claimant has a weak claim, or a claim for a small sum of damages,[237] he will suffer less prejudice if the court refuses to disapply the limitation period than would be the case if the claim was a strong one for substantial damages.

31-58 In *Hartley v Birmingham City DC*,[238] the Court of Appeal held that, as the prejudice to the defendant resulting from the loss of the limitation defence will

[234] See para.31-83.

[235] See para.31-70.

[236] See *Dale v British Coal Corp* [1992] P.I.Q.R. 373 at 380; *Forbes v Wandsworth HA* [1997] Q.B. 402 at 417. In *JL v Bowen* [2017] EWCA Civ 82; [2017] P.I.Q.R. P11 a trial judge's decision to disapply the limitation period in a case of alleged historic sexual abuse (continuing into adulthood) was overturned because, inter alia, the judge had artificially ignored his adverse findings against the claimant when considering the limitation question.

[237] *Robinson v St Helens MBC* [2002] EWCA Civ 1099; [2003] P.I.Q.R. P9 at [33]; *Adams v Bracknell Forest BC* [2004] UKHL 29; [2005] 1 A.C. 76 at [54]–[55].

[238] [1992] 1 W.L.R. 968.

always or almost always be balanced by the prejudice to the claimant, from the operation of the limitation period, the loss of the defence as such is of small importance. It was suggested that what is of paramount importance is the effect of the delay on the defendant's ability to defend the claim. The court held that in assessing the degree of prejudice to each party, it is also legitimate to take into account the fact that the claimant has a potential claim against his solicitors and that the defendant is insured, and has a claim against his insurers. In *Nash v Eli Lilly* the Court of Appeal thought that the guidelines applied in *Hartley v Birmingham City DC* are not of universal significance.[239] Purchas LJ noted that even where the claimant has a poor case, lacking in merit, there may be significant and lasting prejudice to the defendant if the limitation provisions are disapplied. The true prejudice to the defendant has been described not as the prejudice of meeting a liability but of having to defend or otherwise deal with a stale claim.[240] This prejudice may be just as great if the claimant's claim is unmeritorious, and especially so where the claimant is impecunious, as the defendant will not be able to recover the costs of a successful defence.[241]

However, in *Cain v Francis*,[242] the Court of Appeal controversially went one step further than Hartley by stating that, in balancing the prejudice to the defendant and claimant under s.33(1) of the Limitation Act 1980, the loss of the limitation defence in itself does not count as a prejudice to the defendant. This was thought to be because the application of a limitation defence should be seen as a windfall to a defendant who would otherwise be liable to pay damages. The relevant prejudice to the defendant was therefore confined to asking whether the delay had disadvantaged the defendant in defending the claim. In Smith LJ's words: "[T]he basic question to be asked is whether it is fair and just in all the circumstances to expect the defendant to meet his claim on the merits, notwithstanding the delay in commencement. The length of the delay will be important, not so much for itself as to the effect it has had. To what extent has the defendant been disadvantaged in his investigation of the claim and/or the assembly of evidence, in respect of the issues of both liability and quantum?"[243] **31-59**

(ii) The six listed factors

In deciding whether to exercise its discretion, s.33 requires the court to have regard to all the circumstances of the case,[244] and in particular to the six factors listed in s.33(3)(a)–(f).[245] **31-60**

239 In *Ramsden v Lee* [1992] 2 All E.R. 204, the defendant suggested that there should be a guideline that in the absence of fault on the part of the defendant leading to the claimant missing a limitation period, the limitation period should be adhered to save where the delay has been minimal. The Court of Appeal held that there was no need for such a guideline, the interpretation of which would promote its own litigation.

240 *Ward v Foss, The Times,* 29 November 1993 CA; *Robinson v St Helens Metropolitan BC* [2002] EWCA Civ 1099; [2003] P.I.Q.R. P9 at [32]; *Adams v Bracknell Forest BC* [2004] UKHL 29; [2005] 1 A.C. 76 at [54]–[55].

241 *Lye v Marks & Spencer Plc, The Times,* 15 February 1988 CA; *Forbes v Wandsworth HA* [1997] Q.B. 402.

242 [2008] EWCA Civ 1451; [2009] Q.B. 754.

243 [2008] EWCA Civ 1451; [2009] Q.B. 754 at [73]. This passage was cited with approval in *Davidson v Aegis Defence Services (BVI) Ltd* [2013] EWCA Civ 1586; [2014] 2 All E.R. 216.

244 The time that elapsed before the claimant's date of knowledge can be taken into account as part of "all the circumstances of the case" but it should be accorded less weight than, e.g. s.33(3)(b), which

(1) "s.33(3)(a) The length of, and the reasons for, the delay on the part of the plaintiff."

31-61 **Length of and reasons for the delay** Delay, for the purposes of s.33(3)(a), means the delay after the expiry of the limitation period rather than delay since the accrual of the cause of action or since the date of knowledge[246] (though the court is able to take into account any earlier delay by the claimant as part of all the "circumstances of the case").[247] A short delay (of days or weeks rather than years) is unlikely to cause the defendant any prejudice.[248] However, where there has been a delay of five or six years since the expiry of the limitation period, there will be a rebuttable presumption that the defendant will suffer prejudice.[249] The court will take into account the date on which the defendant received sufficient notification of the claim to be able to prepare a defence.[250] The inquiry into the reasons for the delay is a subjective one. Provided that the claimant genuinely held the belief to which the delay is attributed, it is not relevant that the belief was unreasonable.[251] The fact that the claimant did not appreciate his legal rights (while irrelevant for s.14) is a relevant consideration.[252] Equally, the courts have taken into account that the claimant thought he would be "sponging" if he made a claim[253]; the claimant's desire not to litigate over something which at the time he merely regarded as an "irritating nuisance"[254]; the claimant's wish not to antagonise the surgeon responsible for her continuing care[255]; and the claimant's concern that he may risk losing his job should the medical condition claimed to be caused the employer's breach (addiction) become known.[256]

(2) "s.33(3)(b) The extent to which, having regard to the delay, the evidence adduced or likely to be adduced by the plaintiff or the defendant is likely to be ess cogent than if the actions had been brought within the time allowed."

---

is a specifically listed factor and would be undermined if one placed equal weight on such an earlier lapse of time: *Collins v Secretary of State for Business Innovation and Skills* [2014] EWCA Civ 717.

245 Where the time-limit depends on the date of knowledge of a person other than the claimant—as, e.g. in a claim under the Fatal Accidents Act 1976—then by s.33(5) references in s.33(3) to "the plaintiff" are to be construed as including references to that person. For the purposes of s.33(3)(a), (e), (f) a claimant may be interrogated about any legal advice he has received and must say whether it was favourable or unfavourable to starting an action, notwithstanding the rule of professional privilege: *Jones v GD Searle & Co Ltd* [1979] 1 W.L.R. 101.

246 *Thompson v Brown* [1981] 1 W.L.R. 744 at 751; *Cairns-Jones v Christie Tyler South West Wales Division Ltd* [2010] EWCA Civ 1642.

247 *Donovan v Gwentoys Ltd* [1990] 1 W.L.R. 472; *McDonnell v Walker* [2009] EWCA Civ 1257; [2010] P.I.Q.R. P5; *Davidson v Aegis Defence Services (BVI) Ltd* [2013] EWCA Civ 1586; [2014] 2 All E.R. 216.

248 *Firman v Ellis* [1978] Q.B. 886. Cf. *Davis v Soltenpur* (1983) 133 N.L.J. 720.

249 *Buck v English Electric Co Ltd* [1977] 1 W.L.R. 806.

250 See *Ward v Foss, The Times,* 29 November 1993.

251 *Coad v Cornwall HA* [1997] 1 W.L.R. 189.

252 *Brooks v JP Coats (UK) Ltd* [1984] I.C.R. 158; *Halford v Brookes* [1991] 1 W.L.R. 428; *Coad v Cornwall HA* [1997] 1 W.L.R. 189.

253 *Buck v English Electrical Co Ltd* [1977] 1 W.L.R. 806.

254 *McCafferty v Metropolitan Police District Receiver* [1977] 1 W.L.R. 1073 at 1081.

255 *Driscoll-Varley v Parkside HA* [1991] 2 Med. L.R. 346.

256 *Carroll v Chief Constable of Greater Manchester Police* [2017] EWCA Civ 1992; [2018] 4 W.L.R. 32.

Extent to which the evidence is less cogent As the wording of this paragraph (s.33(3)(b)) makes clear, the only delay to be considered is delay since the limitation period expired. Where this date is several years after the date of the conduct of the defendant in question, a further delay of some years may not be considered to have a significant effect on the cogency of the evidence for the purposes of this paragraph.[257] The factors which the court will consider under this head include the extent to which a party is unable to present oral evidence because witnesses have died or cannot be traced, or that such evidence is less cogent because a witness' memory has faded. Similarly it will be relevant if documentary evidence has been lost or destroyed by the defendant,[258] or (in the case of an industrial injury) that the claimant's old place of work has been closed down.[259] The decisive question is whether it is still possible to have a fair trial of the claim.[260] 31-62

(3) "s.33(3)(c) The conduct of the defendant after the cause of action arose, including the extent (if any) to which he responded to requests reasonably made by the plaintiff for information or inspection for the purpose of ascertaining facts which were or might be relevant to the plaintiff's cause of action against the defendant."

Conduct of the defendant Section 33(3)(c) is concerned only with procedural matters, where the forensic tactics of the defendant may lead to a delay by the claimant in issuing proceedings.[261] The conduct of the defendant which forms the basis of the claim will not be relevant.[262] The defendant is not obliged to volunteer information, but must not be obstructive in enabling a claimant to obtain relevant information. The conduct of the defendant, for these purposes includes the conduct of his solicitors and his insurers as they will in general deal with any requests for information.[263] 31-63

257 *Colegrove v Smyth* [1994] 5 Med. L.R. 111.

258 Though the court will be unsympathetic if it is found that the destruction policy adopted by the defendant was unreasonable. In *Hammond v West Lancashire HA* [1998] Lloyd's Rep. Med. 146, the Court of Appeal held that the judge was entitled to discount any prejudice suffered by the defendant as a result of the destruction of x-rays forming part of the claimant's medical records after the defendant had been notified of the claim.

259 *Price v United Engineering Steel Ltd* [1998] P.I.Q.R. P407.

260 *Rowe v Kingston-Upon-Hull City Council* [2003] EWCA Civ 1281; [2004] P.I.Q.R. P16; *A v Trustees of the Watchtower Bible and Tract Society* [2015] EWHC 1722 (QB) at [58], per Globe J (the facts concerned historic sexual abuse). See *Catholic Child Welfare Society v CD* [2018] EWCA Civ 2342; [2019] E.L.R. 1 (limitation period in sexual abuse case not disapplied under s.33 because, in particular, the long delay meant that relevant witnesses on behalf of the defendant could not now be called). In *Brookes v J & P Coats (UK) Ltd* [1984] I.C.R. 158, s.11 was disapplied after a 12-year delay. While it was accepted that the cogency of the defendant's evidence was impaired it was thought that a clear enough picture could be presented for a fair trial. The system of work was in issue which was easier to recall than the sequence of events comprising a single incident. See also *Ashe Construction Ltd v Burke* [2003] EWCA Civ 717; [2004] P.I.Q.R. P11, which also involved an allegation of an unsafe system of work, where it was possible to have a "respectably fair trial" despite the considerable delay.

261 *Halford v Brookes* [1991] 1 W.L.R. 428. See also *Marston v British Railways Board* [1976] I.C.R. 126.

262 *Beattie v British Steel Plc* unreported 6 March 1997; *Hodgson v Imperial Tobacco Ltd (No.3)* unreported 4 February 1999.

263 *Thompson v Brown* [1981] 1 W.L.R. 744 at 751.

(4) "s.33(3)(d) The duration of any disability of the plaintiff arising after the date of the accrual of the cause of action."

31-64 **Duration of claimant's disability** "Disability", for the purposes s.33(3)(d), has the same meaning as under s.28 of the 1980 Act.[264] Since minority can never supervene, s.33(3)(d) applies only to supervening mental incapacity. It does not include purely physical disability, though such disability can be taken into account under s.33(3) as one of the circumstances of the case.[265] Time does not begin to run against a person under a disability until he ceases to be under the disability, but a supervening disability does not stop the limitation period running.[266] The court may have regard to such a disability when considering whether to exercise its discretion to allow the action to proceed notwithstanding the expiry of the limitation period.

(5) "s.33(3)(e) The extent to which the plaintiff acted promptly and reasonably once he knew whether or not the act or omission of the defendant, to which the injury was attributable, might be capable at that time of giving rise to an action for damages."

31-65 **Claimant's conduct** Under s.33(3)(e), the claimant's actions are judged from the date on which he actually knew that there might be a claim for damages. Where the claimant has acted promptly it will not be held against him under this heading that his lawyers were dilatory and allowed the limitation period to expire without issuing a claim form: that is, there is no rule of law that the faults of the claimant's solicitor are to be attributed to the claimant.[267]

(6) "s.33(3)(f) The steps, if any, taken by the plaintiff to obtain medical, legal or other expert advice and the nature of any such advice he may have received."

31-66 **Claimant's efforts to obtain expert advice** Any legal advice received by the claimant is irrelevant as far as the determination of his "date of knowledge" is concerned. However, under s.33(3)(f) the legal advice received (e.g. that, incorrectly, there is no cause of action) is to be taken into account in considering whether to exercise its discretion to disapply the limitation period.[268] Conversely, the failure of the claimant to seek legal advice, even if based on an honest subjective belief that he did not have a claim, may be culpable and count against the exercise of

[264] See para.31-21.

[265] See *Yates v Thakeham Tiles Ltd* [1995] P.I.Q.R. P135 CA; *Thomas v Plaistow* [1997] P.I.Q.R. P540 CA.

[266] See para.31-21.

[267] *Das v Ganju* [1999] P.I.Q.R. P260 CA; *Corbin v Penfold Metallising Co Ltd* [2000] Lloyd's Rep. Med. 247 CA; *Steeds v Peverel Management Services Ltd* [2001] EWCA Civ 419; *The Times*, 16 May 2001; *Ashe Construction Ltd v Burke* [2003] EWCA Civ 717; [2004] P.I.Q.R. P136. Though the fact that the claimant would have a claim against his solicitors for the damages he could have obtained from the defendant will be a highly relevant consideration in assessing the extent to which the claimant will be prejudiced by a decision not to disapply the limitation period. See *Thompson v Brown* [1981] 1 W.L.R. 744.

[268] *Halford v Brookes* [1991] 1 W.L.R. 428; *Das v Ganju* [1999] P.I.Q.R. 260 CA.

discretion in the claimant's favour.[269] The position may be different if the claimant has been misled by the defendants as to whether or not there was a cause of action.[270]

(iii) *Other factors*

31-67 Though the six factors listed in s.33(3) are mandatory, they are not exhaustive. The court must consider all the circumstances of the case.[271] Other factors which have been considered relevant to the court's exercise of its discretion include any claim the claimant may have against his solicitor for missing the limitation period.[272] The court may also take account of the insurance position of both the claimant and the defendant,[273] or that the defendant was initially impecunious but had subsequently become wealthy and was therefore worth suing[274] or the state of the litigation[275] or that some claims will proceed against the defendant in any event because they are not time-barred.[276] The honesty or otherwise of the claimant will also be taken into account.[277]

(iv) *Role of the appellate courts*

31-68 As in other cases where the court of first instance is afforded a wide discretion, the Court of Appeal will be reluctant to interfere with the exercise of the s.33 discretion by the trial judge. In *Conry v Simpson*, Stephenson LJ said that "[i]t is not for an appellate court to reverse the discretion of the judge ... unless he has gone very wrong".[278] In *Halford v Brookes* it was said that the Court of Appeal "should be slow to interfere with the exercise of the judge's discretion unless it can be shown that

---

269 *Skerratt v Linfax Ltd (t/a Go Karting for Fun)* [2003] EWCA Civ 695; [2004] P.I.Q.R. P124 at [46].

270 *Skerratt v Linfax Ltd (t/a Go Karting for Fun)* [2003] EWCA Civ 695; [2004] P.I.Q.R. P124.

271 *Taylor v Taylor, The Times,* 14 April 1984 CA; *Donovan v Gwentoys* [1990] 1 W.L.R. 472; *Nash v Eli Lilly & Co* [1993] 1 W.L.R. 782. In *RE v GE* [2015] EWCA Civ 287 it was held that the trial judge had correctly exercised his discretion under s.33 in refusing to disapply the limitation period in respect of a claim for historic sexual abuse (i.e. the tort of trespass) in a case where there had been significant delays by the claimant in proceeding with the case. In Etherton LJ's words, at [79], "what the court must do, as the judge did in this case, is to go through the specific factors listed in section 33(3) and then stand back and look at all the circumstances of the case."

272 *Firman v Ellis* [1978] Q.B. 886; *Thompson v Brown* [1981] 1 W.L.R. 744 at 750; *Ramsden v Lee* [1992] 2 All E.R. 204, CA; *Hartley v Birmingham City DC* [1992] 1 W.L.R. 968 CA.

273 *Firman v Ellis* [1978] Q.B. 886; *Liff v Peasley* [1980] 1 W.L.R. 781.

274 In *A v H* [2008] EWHC 1573 (QB) the defendant, who had attempted to rape the claimant, was initially not worth suing so that the claimant had not issued proceedings. Sixteen years later, the defendant won £7 million on the National Lottery and, on hearing of this, the claimant issued proceedings against him for the tort of trespass to the person. Exercising his discretion under s.33, Coulson J allowed the claim to proceed.

275 In *Workvale Ltd (No.2), Re* [1992] 1 W.L.R. 416, the claim was very nearly ready for trial and all the interlocutory proceedings had been completed when it was discovered by both parties that the writ issued was a nullity because the defendant company had been dissolved, making it necessary to issue further proceedings. The parties' readiness for trial was a very relevant consideration.

276 *Shepherd v Firth Brown Ltd*, unreported 17 April 1985; cf. *Hodgson v Imperial Tobacco Ltd (No.3)*, unreported 4 February 1999.

277 Where the claimant has exaggerated his injuries or otherwise failed to give a truthful account to the court, the court is unlikely to find it equitable to exercise its discretion in his favour: *Long v Tolchard & Sons Ltd* [2001] P.I.Q.R. P18 CA.

278 [1983] 3 All E.R. 369 at 374.

the judge erred in principle or that his decision was manifestly wrong".[279] The judge must, for example, have taken into account a factor which is irrelevant, or failed to consider (or give sufficient weight to) those factors listed in s.33(3) of the Limitation Act 1980.

(d) Claims on behalf of the estate

31-69 The Law Reform (Miscellaneous Provisions) Act 1934 provides that an action survives for the benefit of a deceased person's estate.[280] Where the action is, as it usually is, a claim for personal injuries, special rules concerning limitation apply, which may be summarised as follows:

(1) If the claimant died after the expiry of the limitation period in cases of personal injury, then there is no claim of his to survive for the benefit of his estate. However, it is open to his personal representatives to ask the court to override the limitation period under s.33 of the Limitation Act 1980.[281] In such a case, the criteria[282] which a court is supposed to take into account when overriding the limitation period in favour of a living claimant are modified to take account of the fact that he is now dead. Section 33(5) says, in effect, "where the criteria say 'claimant', read 'deceased'". And by s.33(4) the court shall have regard to the length of, and the reasons for the delay by the deceased in taking action against the defendant.

(2) If the claimant died before the limitation period expired, a new limitation period begins to run under s.11(5) of the Limitation Act 1980.[283] This new period is three years from either the date of the death, or from the date of the personal representative's knowledge, whichever is the later. The meaning of "personal representative" is elaborated in s.11(6).[284] If there is more than one personal representative, and their dates of knowledge are different, then it is the earliest date that counts.[285]

If, despite the fresh limitation period, the claim by the estate still manages to be statute-barred by the time proceedings are begun, then it is nevertheless open to the personal representatives to ask the court to override the new limitation period in their favour.[286]

---

279 [1991] 1 W.L.R. 428 at 436 at 566.

280 See para.27-79.

281 This is clear both from the general scope of s.33(1), and the way in which s.33(4) and (5) are drafted.

282 Set out at paras 31-60 to 31-67.

283 It might have been better to allow such actions to be governed so far as possible in the same way as those brought by injured persons themselves, with time running from the accrual of the cause of action or the date of the deceased's knowledge before his death, and a maximum period of three years from the death if the injured person died without the requisite knowledge. Cases of hardship could then have been left to the court's discretion under s.33.

284 It includes any person who is or has been a personal representative, including an executor who has not proved the will, whether or not he has renounced probate; but not anyone appointed only as a special personal representative in relation to settled land. "Knowledge" includes anything which the personal representative learnt while a personal representative, or previously.

285 s.11(7).

286 s.33. See para.31-54 onwards.

(e) Fatal Accident Act claims

An action under the Fatal Accidents Act 1976[287] can in principle be statute-barred in one of two ways: 31-70

(1) At the time of his death, the deceased must have been in a position to sue the defendant had he survived injured by the wrongful act instead of dying because of it. Therefore if the limitation period expired between the deceased's injury and his death from his wounds, no Fatal Accidents Act claim can come into existence. Thus if the deceased died of his wounds four years after being injured by the defendant, no Fatal Accidents Act claim would normally arise; though it could arise if it was not yet three years since the deceased acquired the relevant knowledge under s.14(1), e.g. the identity of the person who injured him. In deciding whether the deceased's hypothetical personal injuries action—and hence the dependant's actual Fatal Accidents Act claim—is thus statute-barred, the possibility that the deceased could have applied to the court to override the limitation period under s.33 is disregarded.[288]

Although the possibility that the deceased could have invoked the court's s.33 discretion is disregarded when determining whether his cause of action was statute-barred, the claimants in a Fatal Accidents Act claim may ask the court to exercise its discretion under s.33 of the Limitation Act 1980 and override the limitation period which would have barred the deceased's claim, and hence bars theirs. This is provided for by s.33.[289] The power of the court in this respect is qualified, however, by s.33(2). It can only "disapply" for these purposes the normal time-limit in personal injury cases. If the deceased's claim was statute-barred by, say, the time-limit in the Carriage by Air Act 1961,[290] there is no power to override. When the court exercises its discretion in such a case, the criteria[291] it has to take into account are modified in the same way as when it is dealing with a Law Reform Act claim in which it is asked to override a limitation period which ran out in the lifetime of the deceased.

(2) Where a cause of action under the Fatal Accidents Act does arise, it must be brought within three years[292] from *either* the date of the death, *or* "knowledge" of the person for whose benefit it is brought, whichever is the later.[293] Where there are several potential Fatal Accidents Act claimants, then the limitation period runs separately against each of them: if one had the required knowledge more than three years before the action, the action is statute-barred against him but not against the others.[294] The court has power to direct that such a claimant shall be excluded.[295] If the dependant's Fatal Accidents Act claim becomes statute-barred because it is not brought within

[287] See para.27-87 onwards.
[288] Limitation Act 1980 s.12(1).
[289] *Skitt v Khan* [1997] 8 Med. L.R. 105 CA.
[290] See para.31-80.
[291] See para.31-54 onwards.
[292] The three-year period was first introduced by s.3 of the Law Reform (Limitation of Actions etc) Act 1954. Previously the limitation period had been 12 months.
[293] Limitation Act 1980 s.12(2).
[294] Limitation Act 1980 s.13(1).
[295] Limitation Act 1980 s.13(2).

three years, the dependant can ask the court to exercise its discretion to disapply the primary limitation period to allow the claim to proceed.[296]

8. NEGLIGENCE ACTIONS FOR LATENT DAMAGE (OTHER THAN PERSONAL INJURY)

31-71 **The Latent Damage Act 1986 ss.1–2**[297] In *Pirelli General Cable Works Ltd v Oscar Faber and Partners*[298] the House of Lords recognised that its rejection of the discoverability test for when time starts to run could cause injustice to claimants who could lose their cause of action before they knew of its existence. Sections 1 and 2 of the Latent Damage Act 1986[299] amended the Limitation Act 1980, introducing a limitation regime for latent damage (other than personal injury) caused by negligence. The Latent Damage Act was intended principally to deal with the problem of latent damage which occurred when buildings were defectively constructed or designed. However, the decision of the House of Lords in *Murphy v Brentwood DC*[300] that where a building is defective due to negligent construction the owner can no longer maintain an action for damage to the building itself nor in respect of removing a dangerous defect which creates a risk of physical injury to persons or other property because such claims are to be treated as a form of pure economic loss means that, in this context, the Act has ceased to have any practical relevance. A dangerous latent defect in a building which caused damage to "other property" would give rise to an action,[301] but it is unlikely that the damage would be latent, and if such a defect caused personal injuries then the limitation rules for personal injuries would apply. Thus, in practice, the application of the Act is largely limited to claims in respect of financial loss against negligent professional advisers.

31-72 By the Limitation Act 1980 s.14A the limitation period applicable to any action for damages for negligence (other than one to which s.11 applies, i.e. in respect of personal injuries) is six years from the date on which the cause of action accrued or three years from the "starting date", whichever expires later.[302] The "starting date" is defined in very similar terms to the claimant's date of knowledge under s.14(1). It is the earliest date on which the claimant (or any person in whom the cause of action was vested before him) first had both a right to bring an action, and knowledge of: (a) the material facts about the damage; (b) that the damage was caused by the defendant's negligence; (c) the identity of the defendant; and (d) if the negligence was that of a person other than the defendant, the identity of that person and the facts supporting an action against the defendant.[303] Material facts are such facts about the damage as would lead a reasonable person who had suffered such damage to consider it sufficiently serious to justify his instituting proceedings for damages against a defendant who did not dispute liability and was able to

---

296 Limitation Act 1980 s.33; para.31-54. In this situation the court will have regard to the reasons for the dependant's delay, not the deceased's: s.33(5).

297 See generally, Capper, *Latent Damage Act 1986* (1987); James [1998] Conv. 466; McGee (2000) 20 C.J.Q. 39. The Latent Damage Act 1986 s.3 deals with the accrual of a cause of action to successive owners in respect of latent damage to property: para.31-16.

298 [1983] 2 A.C. 1; see para.31-10.

299 The 1986 Act followed recommendations made by the Law Reform Committee, *24th Report: Latent Damage* (1985), Cmnd.9390.

300 [1991] 1 A.C. 398 HL.

301 See, e.g. *Nitrigin Eireann Teoranta v Inco Alloys Ltd* [1992] 1 W.L.R. 498.

302 Limitation Act 1980 s.14A(1)–(4).

303 Limitation Act 1980 s.14A(5), (6) and (8).

satisfy a judgment: not all of the damage needs to be known.[304] Ignorance of the law does not prevent time running,[305] and the claimant is fixed with constructive knowledge, including the knowledge of experts.[306]

Section 14B provides that an action for damages for negligence (other than for personal injuries) shall not be brought more than 15 years from the date of the act or omission which is alleged to constitute negligence. This overrides s.14A, so it is irrelevant that the cause of action has not yet accrued (i.e. no damage has occurred) or that the starting date has not yet occurred (i.e. the damage is still latent). This 15-year "long-stop" under s.14B bars the remedy but does not extinguish the claimant's right of action.[307] There is no discretion to disapply the time-limits in ss.14A and 14B. 31-73

Scope of the latent damage provisions Sections 14A(1) and 14B apply to any "action for damages for negligence" (other than personal injuries), but there is no definition of negligence. Section 14A contrasts sharply with s.14 (and s.11) where the words "negligence, nuisance or breach of duty" are used. It would seem, therefore, that it is not intended to apply to an action in nuisance or other "breach of duty". Section 14A does not apply to a claim for damages under s.2(1) of the Misrepresentation Act 1967 because under s.2(1) there is no onus on the claimant to prove negligence.[308] Nor does it apply to the statutory cause of action under the Defective Premises Act 1972.[309] The Court of Appeal has held that s.14A does not apply to an action for breach of contract founded on an allegation of negligent or careless conduct.[310] To the extent that a claimant may be able to bring an action in the tort of negligence, based on a concurrent duty of care in tort[311] (a situation which will apply to many professional-client relationships) this problem can be avoided. If this were not the case the rather odd consequence would be that a client suing a professional person in contract would be unable to rely on the latent damage provisions, whereas a third party suing in tort would have the benefit of the Act. 31-74

Claimant's knowledge Albeit that the layout of the sections differs, the definition of "knowledge" for the purposes of the test in s.14A is similar to that in s.14 of the 1980 Act (governing personal injury and death claims)[312] and gives rise to similar issues of interpretation. In the leading case of *Haward v Fawcetts*,[313] s.14A was examined for the first time by the House of Lords. It was held that a claim 31-75

---

304 Limitation Act 1980 s.14A(7). See *Hamlin v Edwin Evans* (1996) 80 B.L.R. 85; applied in *Trainer v Cramer Pelmont* [2019] EWHC 2501 (QB); [2020] P.N.L.R. 3.

305 Limitation Act 1980 s.14A(9).

306 Limitation Act 1980 s.14A(10).

307 *Financial Services Compensation Scheme Ltd v Larnell (Insurances) Ltd* [2005] EWCA Civ 1408; [2006] Q.B. 808.

308 *Laws v The Society of Lloyd's* [2003] EWCA Civ 1887; *The Times*, 23 January 2004 at [78]–[93]; *Thomas v Taylor Wimpey Developments Ltd* [2019] EWHC 1134 (TCC); [2019] P.N.L.R. 26.

309 *Payne v John Setchell Ltd* [2002] P.N.L.R. 7.

310 *Société Commerciale de Réassurance v ERAS (International) Ltd* (Note) [1992] 2 All E.R. 82 CA; approving *Iron Trades Mutual Insurance Co Ltd v JK Buckenham Ltd* [1990] 1 All E.R. 808. The non-applicability of ss.14A and 14B to breach of a contractual duty of care is further supported by the Parliamentary debates prior to the passing of the Act and by the general tenor of the Law Reform Committee's 24th Report.

311 See *Henderson v Merrett Syndicates Ltd* [1995] 2 A.C. 145.

312 See paras 31-40 to 31-53.

313 [2006] UKHL 9; [2006] 1 W.L.R. 682. The test for "knowledge" under s.14A has been examined in a number of other cases: see, e.g. *Felton v Gaskill Osborne & Co* [1993] 43 E.G. 118; *Spencer-*

against an accountant for negligent advice (or failure to advise), leading to loss-making investments in 1994 and 1995, was statute-barred. The claimant had had the relevant knowledge more than three years before commencing proceedings in December 2001. The case principally turned on the interpretation of s.14A(8)(a): "that the damage was attributable in whole or in part to the act or omission which is alleged to constitute negligence." Their Lordships adverted to the apparent tension between s.14A(8) and s.14A(9). According to the latter, "knowledge that any acts or omissions did or did not, as a matter of law, involve negligence is irrelevant". Their Lordships recognised that knowledge that the defendant had given "flawed" advice was necessary under s.14A(8)(a); and that the courts could safely look for knowledge that, factually, "something had gone wrong" without contravening s.14A(9).[314]

31-76 **Claimant under a disability** The normal disability provisions in s.28[315] are geared towards a limitation period starting from when the cause of action accrued. But this does not cover the case where the claimant is under a disability at the time when he acquires "knowledge" for the purposes of s.14A(4)(b). Section 28A(1) makes a similar provision for that case as well, providing that where a person was under a disability at the time when he acquired knowledge for the purposes of s.14A(4)(b), but not under a disability when the cause of action accrued, an action may be brought within three years from when he ceased to be under a disability or died (whichever first occurred).[316] But by s.28A(2) there can be no postponement for disability by virtue of s.28A(1) beyond the 15-year long-stop period.

31-77 **Deliberate concealment** Neither s.14A nor s.14B apply to cases of deliberate concealment of the relevant facts which, accordingly, are governed by the terms of s.32(1)(b) and s.2.[317] Thus, in cases of latent damage that has been deliberately concealed by the defendant the limitation period is six years from when the claim-

---

Ward v Humberts [1995] 1 E.G.L.R. 123, CA; *Hallam-Eames v Merrett Syndicates Ltd* [1996] 7 Med. L.R. 122; *Abbey National Plc v Sayer Moore* [1999] E.G.C.S. 114; *Birmingham Midshires Building Society v Wrethin* [1999] P.N.L.R. 685; [1999] Lloyd's Rep. P.N. 133; *Mortgage Corp Plc v Lambert & Co* [1999] Lloyd's Rep. P.N. 947; *Webster v Cooper Burritt* [2000] Lloyd's Rep. P.N. 167; *Oakes v Hopcroft* [2000] Lloyd's Rep. Med. 394 CA; *Bowie v Southorns* [2002] EWHC 1389 (QB); [2003] P.N.L.R. 7; *McCarroll v Statham Gill Davies* [2003] EWCA Civ 425; [2003] P.N.L.R. 25; *Gravgaard v Aldridge & Brownlee* [2004] EWCA Civ 1529; [2005] P.N.L.R. 19; *Shore v Sedgwick Financial Services Ltd* [2008] EWCA Civ 863; [2008] P.N.L.R. 37. In *Graham v Entec Europe Ltd* [2003] EWCA Civ 1177; [2003] 4 All E.R. 1345, it was held that, where an insurer is bringing a subrogated action in the insured's name, the insurer's knowledge—including the knowledge of its loss adjuster—is relevant under s.14A. See (subsequent to *Haward v Fawcetts*) *Harris Springs Ltd v Howes* [2007] EWHC 3271 (TCC); [2008] B.L.R. 229; *Boycott v Perrins Guy Williams* [2011] EWHC 2969 (Ch); [2012] P.N.L.R. 25; *Integral Memory Plc v Haines Watt* [2012] EWHC 342 (Ch); [2012] S.T.I. 1385; *Roger Ward Associates Ltd v Britannia Assets (UK) Ltd* [2013] EWHC 1653 (QB); *Jacobs v Sesame Ltd* [2014] EWCA Civ 1410; [2015] P.N.L.R. 6; *Schumann v Veale Wasbrough* [2015] EWCA Civ 441; [2015] P.N.L.R. 25; *Trainer v Cramer Pelmont* [2019] EWHC 2501 (QB); [2020] P.N.L.R. 3.

[314] The approach to s.14A(8) in *Hallam-Eames v Merrett Syndicates Ltd* [1996] 7 Med. L.R. 122 was approved, while that in *HF Pension Trustees Ltd v Ellison* [1999] P.N.L.R. 894 was disapproved.

[315] See para.31-21.

[316] s.28A(1) is unlikely to be much used because most claimants who are under a disability when they acquire "knowledge" will also have been under a disability when the cause of action accrued to them and will thus be saved by s.28 irrespective of s.28A(1). It is perhaps for this reason that no analogous provision applies to personal injury or death or to actions under Pt I of the Consumer Protection Act 1987.

[317] Limitation Act 1980 s.32(5). See para.31-22 onwards.

ant discovered the concealment, or could reasonably have done so, and there is no 15-year long-stop.

9. OTHER SPECIAL PERIODS OF LIMITATION

(a) Merchant Shipping Act 1995

Section 190 of the Merchant Shipping Act 1995 (formerly s.8 of the Maritime Conventions Act 1911) provides for a general period of limitation of two years for all claims in respect of damage to or loss of a ship, her cargo or freight or property on board, and for damages for loss of life or personal injuries suffered by any person on board, caused by the fault of another ship.[318] This period may, however, be extended by the court to such extent and on such conditions as it thinks fit[319] and must be extended if the court is satisfied that there has not, during the period, been a reasonable opportunity of arresting the defendant ship within the jurisdiction of the court, or within the territorial waters of the country to which the claimant's ship belongs or in which the claimant resides or has his principal place of business.[320] Where the Act applies it is exclusive of other periods of limitation, so that the period appropriate to the case of a death on board one ship, caused by the negligence of another, is two years, and not three as provided for in the Fatal Accidents Act claims.[321] On the other hand, the Act applies only to actions brought against a ship other than the ship on which the injury, loss or damage was sustained, and so where a seaman was killed in a collision at sea caused by the negligence of the ship on which he was serving, it was held that the period of limitation for actions under the Fatal Accidents Acts and the Law Reform (Miscellaneous Provisions) Act 1934 in respect of his death was three years in each case.[322] **31-78**

The Merchant Shipping Act 1995 also gives effect to the Athens Convention applying to the international carriage of passengers and their luggage by sea.[323] Section 183 of and Sch.6 to that Act deal with claims in respect of personal injuries or damage to baggage suffered by passengers at sea. By art.16 of Sch.6 a limitation period of two years applies to any such claim.[324] In the case of a claim for personal injury to a passenger, or for loss or damage to luggage, this period starts running **31-79**

---

318 A sailing dinghy being used on a reservoir for pleasure purposes is not a vessel "used in navigation" and so falls outside s.190 of the Merchant Shipping Act 1995: *Curtis v Wild* [1991] 4 All E.R. 172. A jet-ski also falls outside s.190: *Steedman v Schofield* [1992] 2 Lloyd's Rep. 163.

319 For the principles on which the discretion is exercised, see *The Kashmir* [1923] P. 85; *The Arraiz* (1924) 132 L.T. 715; *The Vadne* [1959] 2 Lloyd's Rep. 480; *The Alnwick* [1965] P. 357; *The Gaz Fountain* [1987] 1 F.T.L.R. 423; *Asianic International Panama SA and Transocean Transport Corp v Transocean Ro-Ro Corp (The Seaspeed America)* [1990] 1 Lloyd's Rep. 150; *Gold Shipping Navigation Co SA v Lulu Maritime Ltd* [2009] EWHC 1365 (Admlty); [2010] 2 All E.R. (Comm) 64 (which also clarified that the two-year period extends to counterclaims).

320 Merchant Shipping Act 1995 s.190(5), (6).

321 See *The Caliph* [1912] P. 213; *The Alnwick* [1965] P. 357. See also Limitation Act 1980 s.39.

322 *The Niceto de Larrinaga* [1986] P. 80.

323 The 1995 Act was amended by the Merchant Shipping (Convention Relating to the Carriage of Passengers and their Luggage by Sea) Order 2014, SI 2014/1361, to put into effect the 2002 Protocol to the Athens Convention.

324 See *Norfolk v My Travel Group* [2004] 1 Lloyd's Rep. 106 (county court); *Michael v Musgrove, The Sea Eagle* [2011] EWHC 1438 (Admlty); [2012] 2 Lloyd's Rep. 37. But in *Feest v South West Strategic Health Authority* [2015] EWCA Civ 708; [2016] Q.B. 503 it was held that the two-year limitation period under the Athens Convention does not bar a claim by an alleged tortfeasor for contribution against the carrier, under the Civil Liability (Contribution) Act 1978, in respect of personal injury to a passenger. Article 16(3) of Sch.6 extends the two years, up to a long-stop of three

from the date of disembarkation. In the case of a claim for death, the period starts running from the later of the date when the passenger should have disembarked, or the date of the death (provided that the limitation period calculated from the date of death does not exceed three years from the date of disembarkation). The period may be extended by agreement between the parties,[325] but it may not be disapplied under s.33 of the Limitation Act 1980.[326]

(b) Carriage by Air Act 1961

31-80 The Carriage by Air Act 1961,[327] which gives effect to the Warsaw and Montreal Conventions scheduled to the Act, governs the right to damages for injuries and damage suffered in an accident[328] in the course of air travel.[329] It lays down a scheme of strict liability but by art.29 in Sch.1 and art.35 in Sch.1B the right to damages is extinguished if an action is not brought within two years from the date of arrival at the destination, or from the date when the aircraft ought to have arrived, or from the date on which the carriage stopped.[330] Similar provisions are contained in the Carriage by Air Act (Application of Provisions) Order 2004[331] in cases to which the 1961 Act (or EU legislation) does not apply. However, the limitation period for claims under Council Regulation (EC) 261/2004 for compensation for cancellation of, or long delays to, flights is governed by national law and in England and Wales, applying s.9 of the Limitation Act 1980, the period is therefore six years.[332]

(c) Railways (Convention on International Carriage by Rail) Regulations 2005

31-81 Claims in respect of personal injury or death caused to a passenger as a result of an accident connected with international carriage by rail (or other actions arising out of the carriage) are governed by the Railways (Convention on International Car-

---

years, where there is domestic legislation providing for "suspension" or "interruption" of the limitation period: this provision was held to include the domestic law's postponement of the limitation period for disability (by reason of age) in the Scottish case of *Warner v Scapa Flow Charters* [2018] UKSC 52; [2018] 1 W.L.R. 4974.

[325] See art.16, para.4 to Sch.6.

[326] See *Higham v Stena Sealink Ltd* [1996] 1 W.L.R. 1107.

[327] See also Carriage by Air (Supplementary Provisions) Act 1962.

[328] The onset of deep vein thrombosis, as a result of cramped seating, is not an "accident" within the meaning of art.17 of the Warsaw Convention: *Re Deep Vein Thrombosis and Air Travel Group Litigation* [2005] UKHL 72; [2006] 1 A.C. 495.

[329] The Act was amended by the Carriage by Air Acts (Implementation of Protocol No.4 of Montreal, 1975) Order 1999 (SI 1999/1312), and the Carriage by Air Acts (Implementation of the Montreal Convention 1999) Order 2002 (SI 2002/263).

[330] That this two-year period is the relevant limitation period follows from s.39 of the Limitation Act 1980, which saves other limitation enactments. Moreover, s.33(2) of the 1980 Act uses the 1961 Act to illustrate the point that there is only a discretion to disapply s.12(1) where the reason why the person injured could no longer maintain an action was because of the s.11 time-limit and not some other time-limit. See *Sidhu v British Airways* [1997] A.C. 430; *Laroche v Spirit of Adventure (UK) Ltd* [2009] EWCA Civ 12; [2009] Q.B. 778; *Hall v Heart of England Balloons Ltd* [2010] 1 Lloyd's Rep. 373 (Birmingham County Court). See generally Todd, *Limitation Periods in Personal Injury Claims* (1982), pp.8–9; Jones, *Limitation Periods in Personal Injury Actions* (1995), pp.232–233.

[331] SI 2004/1899.

[332] *Dawson v Thomson Airways Ltd* [2014] EWCA Civ 845; [2015] 1 W.L.R. 883.

riage by Rail) Regulations 2005[333] which give effect to a 1999 Protocol to the Convention concerning International Carriage by Rail 1980.[334] The limitation period is three years, running from the day after the date of the accident in the case of personal injury claims, and the day of the death for claims in relation to the death of a passenger, subject to an absolute limitation period of five years from the date of the accident, beyond which no claims may be brought.[335] But the right of action is lost, subject to certain exceptions, if the claimant does not give notice in writing of the accident to, or make a claim for damages from, the railway that is liable or the railway of his departure, destination, domicile or usual place of residence within 12 months of his becoming aware of the loss or damage.[336] Of the exceptions the most important include cases where the railway that is liable has learned of the accident and cases where the claimant proves that the accident was caused by a fault of the railway.[337] On the other hand, where a claim for damages has been made to one of the railways mentioned, the running of time for the purposes of the limitation of actions is suspended until such time as the railway rejects the claim by notification in writing and returns the supporting documents.[338] Other claims (i.e. other than for personal injury or death) are governed by a limitation period of one year.[339]

(d) Defamation

The law on limitation periods for defamation and malicious falsehood was reformed by the Defamation Act 1996, which inserted ss.4A and 32A into the Limitation Act 1980.[340] Section 4A lays down a limitation period of one year from the accrual of the cause of action, which is made subject to the court's discretion (provided for in s.32A) to disapply that limitation period. The factors that the court must take into account in exercising its discretion are: the length of, and the reasons for, the delay on the part of the claimant[341]; the date at which the claimant became aware of the facts relevant to the cause of action and the extent to which he acted promptly and reasonably once he knew whether or not the facts in question might be capable of giving rise to an action[342]; and the extent to which relevant evidence is likely to be unavailable or less cogent than would have been the case if the action had been brought within the limitation period set by s.4A.[343] These factors correspond to ss.33(3)(a), (b) and (e) of the Limitation Act 1980 in relation to personal injury claims.[344] In refusing to disapply s.32A of the Limitation Act 1980 the Court 31-82

333 SI 2005/2092.

334 Cmnd. 4873. The convention is commonly referred to as "COTIF". See also the Rail Passengers' Rights and Obligations Regulations 2010 (SI 2010/1504), giving effect to Regulation (EC) No 1371/2007 which in turn gives effect in the EU to the Convention concerning International Carriage by Rail 1980.

335 art.60(1).

336 arts 55(1), 58(1).

337 art.58(2).

338 art.60(4).

339 art.60(2)–(3): increased to two years where, e.g. there has been wilful misconduct.

340 s.28, which applies to persons under a disability, was amended correspondingly so that by s.28(4A) the limitation period is one year from the claimant ceasing to be under a disability: see para.31-21.

341 s.32A(2)(a).

342 s.32A(2)(b).

343 s.32A(2)(c).

344 The other factors in s.33(3)(c), (d) and (f) were presumably thought irrelevant or insufficiently

of Appeal in *Bewry v Reed Elsevier UK Ltd*[345] made clear that special considerations apply to libel claims which mean that disapplication of the one-year limitation period is likely to be exceptional. Sharp LJ said the following:

> "it is clear that special considerations apply to libel actions which are relevant to the exercise of this discretion. In particular, the purpose of a libel action is vindication of a claimant's reputation. A claimant who wishes to achieve this end by swift remedial action will want his action to be heard as soon as possible. Such claims ought therefore to be pursued with vigour, especially in view of the ephemeral nature of most media publications. These considerations have led to the uniquely short limitation period of one year which applies to such claims and explain why the disapplication of the limitation period in libel actions is often described as exceptional."[346]

(e) Consumer Protection Act 1987

31-83 Part I of the Consumer Protection Act 1987[347] renders producers and (in certain circumstances) suppliers strictly liable for personal injury, death or damage to "consumer" property (other than to the defective product itself)[348] caused by defective products. Section 11A of the Limitation Act 1980 created a 10-year long-stop in respect of actions for breach of the 1987 Act, which runs from the time when the defendant supplied the defective product to another.[349] After the 10-year period, the right of action is extinguished.[350] For actions for personal injury (including where the action survives for the benefit of the estate under s.1 of the Law Reform (Miscellaneous Provisions) Act 1934) the basic time-limits are otherwise the same as under s.11; that is, three years from the date when the cause of action accrued (or death) or the date of the injured person's (or personal representative's) knowledge, whichever is the later.[351] These same basic limits (i.e. three years from the accrual of the cause of action or from the date of knowledge) apply also to an action for loss of or damage to property.[352] For actions under the Fatal Accidents Act 1976 for

important to defamation as opposed to personal injury actions.

345 [2014] EWCA Civ 1411; [2015] 1 W.L.R. 2565.

346 [2014] EWCA Civ 1411; [2015] 1 W.L.R. 2565 at [5]. Nevertheless, it was thought equitable to extend the limitation period in *Boyo v Lloyds Bank plc* [2019] EWHC 2279 (QB), where there was evidence of ill health on the part of the claimant and preparedness to bring an action had been indicated.

347 Pt I of the Act came into force on 1 March 1988; Consumer Protection Act 1987 (Commencement No.1) Order 1987 (SI 1987/1680). By s.50(7) no person is to be liable in respect of a product which was supplied to any person by its producer before 1 March 1988. On the Act generally, see Ch.11.

348 Consumer Protection Act 1987 s.5(2). There is no claim for property damage if the property was not for private use and consumption (s.5(3)) or if the damages would not exceed £275 (s.5(4)).

349 Limitation Act 1980 s.11A(3). A product is supplied, or in the words of Directive 85/374 "put into circulation", when it is taken out of the manufacturing process operated by the producer and enters a marketing process in the form in which it is offered to the public in order to be used or consumed: *O'Byrne v Sanofi Pasteur MSD Ltd* [2006] 1 W.L.R. 1606; [2006] 2 C.M.L.R. 24 ECJ.

350 In *Horne-Roberts v SmithKline Beecham Plc* [2001] EWCA Civ 2006; [2002] 1 W.L.R. 1662 it was held that the Limitation Act 1980 s.35 permits the addition of a new party to the action even after the expiry of the 10-year long-stop period in s.11A(3). See para.31-20. For the ECJ's ruling on the need to apply s.35(3) in a way that is compatible with the 10-year long-stop dictated by the product liability directive, see *O'Byrne v Aventis Pasteur SA* C-358/08 [2010] 1 W.L.R. 1375; explained by the Supreme Court in *O'Byrne v Aventis Pasteur MSD Ltd* [2010] UKSC 23; [2010] 1 W.L.R. 1412.

351 ss.11A(4)–(5). The date of knowledge in s.11A is defined in the Limitation Act 1980 s.14(1A) in similar, but not identical, terms to the definition in s.14(1).

352 s.11A(4). The date of knowledge is defined in the Limitation Act 1980 s.14(1A)–(3). As a result of

death caused by a defective product[353] the basic limits remain those laid down in s.12 of the 1980 Act (subject to the ten-year long-stop).[354] The s.33 discretion to disapply the basic time-limits applies to all actions under Pt I of the 1987 Act,[355] although there is no discretion to disapply the 10-year long-stop,[356] nor where damages are confined to damages for loss of or damage to property.[357] Section 28(7) of the Limitation Act 1980, which applies to claimants under a disability, provides that the 10-year long-stop overrides the normal disability provisions in s.28,[358] which otherwise apply but with three years substituted for six years in s.28(1). Section 32(4A) provides that the postponement of the limitation period for fraud, mistake or deliberate concealment[359] does not override the 10-year long-stop.

(f) Human Rights Act 1998

By s.7(5) of the Human Rights Act 1998, proceedings for breach by a public authority of a person's Convention rights under the Human Rights Act 1998 must be brought within one year from the date on which the act complained of took place or such longer period as the court considers equitable having regard to all the circumstances. The discretion under s.7(5) is analogous to that under s.33 of the Limitation Act 1980 so that the court should have regard to all the circumstances of the claimant, including the circumstances of the group in a group action.[360] However, it has been suggested that the limitation period of one year is an indication that actions against public authorities should be brought promptly.[361] In *O'Connor v Bar Standards Board*[362] it was held that the conduct of the Bar Standards Board in bringing and pursuing disciplinary proceedings against the claimant was, for the purposes of s.7(5), a single continuing act which continued until the Visitors to the Inns of Court allowed the claimant's appeal: i.e. the limitation period of one year did not start to run until the single continuing act had ceased. The claimant's action under the Human Rights Act 1998 was therefore com- 31-84

s.5(5) of the Consumer Protection Act 1987, designed to deal with the problem of the successive ownership of latently damaged property (see para.31-16 fn.78) it will surely be very rare (a possible example being one co-owner having knowledge while the other does not) for there to be a difference between the date of the accrual of the cause of action and the claimant's date of knowledge. It is not entirely clear what is intended to be covered by the latter part of s.11A(4)(b)—"in the case of loss of or damage to property, the date of knowledge of the plaintiff *or (if earlier) of any person in whom his cause of action was previously vested*" (emphasis added)—and of s.14(1A), "in determining the date on which a person first had such knowledge, there shall be disregarded, … in a case relating to loss of or damage to property, any knowledge which that person had on a date on which he had no right of action by virtue of Pt I of [the 1987] Act in respect of the loss or damage".

353 By s.6(1) of the 1987 Act, liability under Pt 1 of the 1987 Act shall be deemed to have been caused, for the purposes of the Fatal Accidents Act 1976, by that person's wrongful act, neglect or default.

354 The date of knowledge in s.12, so far as that is concerned with death caused by a defective product, is defined in the Limitation Act 1980 ss.14(1A), 14(2) and (3).

355 Limitation Act 1980 s.33(1)(a).

356 Limitation Act 1980 s.33(1A)(a).

357 Limitation Act 1980 s.33(1A)(b).

358 See para.31-21.

359 See para.31-22 onwards.

360 *Dobson v Thames Water Utilities Ltd* [2007] EWHC 2021 (TCC); [2008] 2 All E.R. 362 (partly reversed on a different point at [2009] EWCA Civ 28; [2009] 3 All E.R. 319); *M v Ministry of Justice* [2009] EWCA Civ 419; (2009) 159 N.L.J. 860.

361 *Solaria Energy UK Ltd v Department for Business, Energy and Industrial Strategy* [2019] EWHC 2188 (TCC); [2019] B.L.R. 610.

362 [2017] UKSC 78; [2017] 1 W.L.R. 4833.

menced within a year of the date on which the act complained of took place and was not time-barred.

(g) Public authorities

31-85 Formerly public authorities and persons acting in pursuance or execution or intended execution of an Act of Parliament were protected by periods of limitation shorter than those applicable to other classes of defendants.[363] These special periods of limitation were abolished by s.1 of the Law Reform (Limitation of Actions etc) Act 1954,[364] and the periods of limitation are the same whatever the class of the defendant.

(h) Contribution between tortfeasors

31-86 Section 6 of the Law Reform (Married Women and Tortfeasors) Act 1935, which provided for claims to contribution between tortfeasors,[365] made no provision for the limitation of such claims and so, probably, they had to be brought within six years of their accrual. This was changed by s.4 of the Limitation Act 1963, which reduced that period to two years from the date when the right to contribution accrued. This date was defined as the date of the judgment or award against the tortfeasor claiming contribution, if he had been held liable, and if he had admitted liability to the person injured by his tort, the time when the amount to be paid by him in discharge of his liability had been agreed. This section was deficient because it left unclear the position where a person settled a claim against him under a *denial*[366] of liability. In 1978,[367] s.4 of the Limitation Act 1963 was recast as what is now s.10 of the Limitation Act 1980.[368] By s.10(3), where the tortfeasor seeking contribution is held liable by a judge or arbitrator, the cause of action accrues when the judgment or award is given.[369] The judgment or award referred to is a judgment or award which ascertains the quantum, and not merely the existence of the tortfeasor's liability so that, where there are separate judgments or awards in relation to liability and quantum, the two-year limitation period runs from the judgment or award on quantum.[370] By s.10(4), if the claim is settled, with or without an admission of liability, the cause of action accrues when the amount to be paid is agreed. In *Knight v Rochdale Healthcare NHS Trust*[371] it was held that time ran from

363 See 10th edn of this work, p.257.

364 For details of the Acts repealed, see 11th edn of this work, p.258. In *Arnold v Central Electricity Generating Board* [1988] A.C. 228, it was held that an action against a public authority that was time-barred before 1954 remains so.

365 See now the Civil Liability (Contribution) Act 1978. See para.4-13 onwards.

366 See *Stott v West Yorkshire Road Car Co Ltd* [1971] 2 Q.B. 651.

367 Civil Liability (Contribution) Act 1978 Sch.1 para.6.

368 By s.28(5) the disability provision—s.28(1)—applies with two years substituted for six. See para.31-21.

369 s.10(3) goes on to clarify that no account is to be taken of any judgment or award given on appeal in so far as it varies the amount of damages awarded against the tortfeasor.

370 *Aer Lingus Plc v Gildercroft Ltd* [2006] EWCA Civ 4; [2006] 1 W.L.R. 1173. Similarly, an interim payment does not start the two-year limitation period running: *Jellett v Brooke* [2016] EWHC 2828 (QB); [2017] 1 W.L.R. 1177.

371 [2003] EWHC 1831 (QB); [2004] 1 W.L.R. 371. This was approved in *Chief Constable of Hampshire v Southampton CC* [2014] EWCA Civ 1541; [2015] P.I.Q.R. P5.

the date of the agreement even though that agreement was later embodied in a consent order; that is, that s.10(4) of the Limitation Act applied, not s.10(3).

(i) Automated and Electric Vehicles Act 2018

The Automated and Electric Vehicles Act 2018 (which is not yet in force) makes a number of prospective changes to the Limitation Act 1980, with a commencement date yet to be fixed. In particular, s.11B Limitation Act 1980 provides a limitation period of three years for the liability of insurers, and of owners of uninsured vehicles in certain circumstances, set out in s.2 of the Automated and Electric Vehicles Act 2018. These liabilities apply in the case of accidents caused by automated vehicles when driving themselves on roads or other public places, so that the ordinary liability of a driver of the vehicle cannot apply. The three year limitation period in s.11B runs from the time of the accident, or (in a case where personal injury is caused), from the claimant's date of knowledge. Similarly, a new s.10A of the Limitation Act 1980 sets out a limitation period of two years for claims by insurers and owners of automated vehicles pursuant to s.5 of the Automated and Electric Vehicles Act 2018, which provides that any other person liable to the injured party is under the same liability as the insurer or owner. The two year period in s.10A commences when the right of action against other liable parties accrues, namely at the time that the insurer or owner's liability to the injured party is settled. Most other provisions of the Limitation Act in relation to personal injury (for example s.14 and s.33) do not apply to the liability of insurers and owners of automated vehicles created by the 2018 Act. **31-87**

(j) Other statutes

By s.39 of the Limitation Act 1980, the Act does not apply to any action or arbitration for which a period of limitation is prescribed by any other enactment, or to any action or arbitration to which the Crown is a party and for which, if it were between subjects, a period of limitation would be prescribed by any such enactment. **31-88**

INDEX

LEGAL TAXONOMY
FROM SWEET & MAXWELL

This index has been prepared using Sweet & Maxwell's Legal Taxonomy. Main index entries conform to keywords provided by the Legal Taxonomy except where references to specific documents or non-standard terms (denoted by quotation marks) have been included. These keywords provide a means of identifying similar concepts in other Sweet & Maxwell publications and online services to which keywords from the Legal Taxonomy have been applied. Readers may find some minor differences between terms used in the text and those which appear in the index. Suggestions to *sweetandmaxwell.taxonomy@tr.com.*

Conflicts of Interest, 6th edition
Charles Hollander QC, Simon Salzedo QC
978-0-414-07533-7
August 2020
Hardback / ProView eBook / Westlaw UK

The new edition of *Conflicts of Interest* provides authoritative guidance on the law relating to conflicts of interest in all its dimensions, from client conflict and personal conflict to commercial and judicial conflict. It explains in detail the current legal position in various professional sectors. Whilst principally focused on the law applicable to lawyers, it also considers accountants, the City, directors, estate agents and insurance brokers. It helps the user avoid potential conflicts of interest and provides practical advice and remedies for ones that arise.
Conflicts of Interest has been described by the Court of Appeal as the leading textbook on conflicts and is often cited in court. In a recent case, it was argued that a failure to refer the court to *Conflicts of Interest* on an application without notice was itself a material non-disclosure.

Contact us: Tel: +44 (0)345 600 9355
Order online: *sweetandmaxwell.co.uk*